Acronyms, Initialisms & Abbreviations Dictionary

Gale's publications in the acronyms and abbreviations field include:

Acronyms, Initialisms & Abbreviations Dictionary series:

Acronyms, Initialisms & Abbreviations Dictionary (Volume 1). A guide to acronyms, initialisms, abbreviations, and similar contractions, arranged alphabetically by abbreviation.

New Acronyms, Initialisms & Abbreviations (Volume 2). An interedition supplement in which terms are arranged alphabetically both by abbreviation and by meaning.

Reverse Acronyms, Initialisms & Abbreviations Dictionary (Volume 3). A companion to Volume 1 in which terms are arranged alphabetically by meaning of the acronym, initialism, or abbreviation.

Acronyms, Initialisms & Abbreviations Dictionary Subject Guide series:

Computer & Telecommunications Acronyms (Volume 1). A guide to acronyms, initialisms, abbreviations, and similar contractions used in the field of computers and telecommunications in which terms are arranged alphabetically both by abbreviation and by meaning.

Future Subject Guide topics will include business and trade, health and medicine, military and government, and associations and institutions.

International Acronyms, Initialisms & Abbreviations Dictionary series:

International Acronyms, Initialisms & Abbreviations Dictionary (Volume 1). A guide to foreign and international acronyms, initialisms, abbreviations, and similar contractions, arranged alphabetically by abbreviation.

New International Acronyms, Initialisms & Abbreviations (Volume 2). An interedition supplement in which terms are arranged alphabetically both by abbreviation and by meaning.

Reverse International Acronyms, Initialisms & Abbreviations Dictionary (Volume 3). A companion to Volume 1 in which terms are arranged alphabetically by meaning of the acronym, initialism, or abbreviation.

Periodical Title Abbreviations series:

Periodical Title Abbreviations: By Abbreviation (Volume 1). A guide to abbreviations commonly used for periodical titles, arranged alphabetically by abbreviation.

Periodical Title Abbreviations: By Title (Volume 2). A guide to abbreviations commonly used for periodical titles, arranged alphabetically by title.

New Periodical Title Abbreviations (Volume 3). An interedition supplement in which terms are arranged alphabetically both by abbreviation and by title.

ISSN 0270-4404

Acronyms, Initialisms & Abbreviations Dictionary

A Guide to More Than 420,000 Acronyms, Initialisms, Abbreviations, Contractions, Alphabetic Symbols, and Similar Condensed Appellations

Covering: Aerospace, Associations, Biochemistry, Business and Trade, Data Processing, Domestic and International Affairs, Education, Electronics, Genetics, Government, Information Technology, Labor, Law, Medicine, Military, Periodicals, Pharmacy, Physiology, Politics, Religion, Science, Societies, Sports, Technical Drawings and Specifications, Telecommunications, Transportation, and Other Fields

Twelfth Edition
1988

Volume 1

Part 3
P-Z

Julie E. Towell
and
Helen E. Sheppard
Editors

GALE RESEARCH COMPANY • BOOK TOWER • DETROIT, MICHIGAN 48226

Editors: Julie E. Towell, Helen E. Sheppard

Senior Assistant Editors: Prindle LaBarge, Anthony J. Scolaro
Assistant Editors: Barbara Cumming Cameron, Pamela Dear, Claire A. Selestow
Editorial Assistant: Ellen Ankenbrandt

Contributing Editors: Leland G. Alkire, Jr., Mildred Hunt, Edwin B. Steen, Miriam M. Steinert

Production Manager: Mary Beth Trimper
Production Associate: Darlene K. Maxey
Production Assistant: Linda A. Davis
Art Director: Arthur Chartow

Editorial Data Systems Director: Dennis LaBeau
Supervisor of Systems and Programming: Diane H. Belickas
Program Design: Barry M. Trute

Editorial Data Entry Supervisor: Doris D. Goulart
Editorial Data Entry Associate: Jean Hinman Portfolio
Senior Data Entry Assistants: Sue Lynch, Joyce M. Stone, Anna Marie Woolard

Chairman: Frederick G. Ruffner
President: J. Kevin Reger
Publisher: Dedria Bryfonski
Associate Editorial Director: Ellen T. Crowley
Director, Indexes and Dictionaries Division: Ann Evory
Senior Editor, Dictionaries: Donna Wood

Library of Congress Catalog Card Number 84-643188
ISBN 0-8103-2505-5
ISSN 0270-4404

Computerized photocomposition by
Computer Composition Corporation
Madison Heights, Michigan

Printed in the United States of America

Contents

Volume 1

Part 1   A-F

Volume 1

Part 2   G-O

Volume 1

Part 3   P-Z

Editorial Policies

Determining the subject areas to be covered in a book such as this is not nearly so difficult as deciding on the type of terms to be selected from each field. In other words, "Where should the line be drawn?"

The definitions of terms offered in the Preface are deliberately simplified, and some students of language may hold out for more precise or more limiting definitions. Strictly speaking, for instance, acronyms are words made from the tips of other words—but the question immediately arises, "How large a tip?" Some linguists insist on syllables and accept as acronyms only such terms as ARBOR from the virological term, *Arthropod Borne*. One of the most common uses of abbreviated terms, however, is in the shortening of designations by the use of only initial-letter "tips." AID (*Agency for International Development*), SRO (*Standing Room Only*), MP (*Military Police*), and thousands of similar terms are examples of this practice. Some refer to such terms not as acronyms (even when they are pronounceable), but as initialisms or "abecedisms."

Thus, to some, the difference among terms is based solely on structure; to others, the important consideration is pronounceability. Many use "acronym" and "initialism" almost interchangeably, and the designation "abbreviation" is sometimes used as an umbrella-term for *all* types of alphabetical short-forms.

What Is Included?

Which of these points of view is linguistically correct is not important here; and, quite possibly, there is no single correct theory. The essential point that concerned the editors was that no user of the book should be disappointed because the term for which he or she sought an explanation was omitted on a technicality. It was decided, therefore, to include in *AIAD* all terms of the types described above and defined in the Preface, as well as terms that *appear* to be of those types and may be thought to be acronyms, initialisms, or abbreviations when encountered in reading or conversation.

Thus, one will find in *AIAD* some entries that might be considered alphabetical *symbols* rather than one of the terms in the title. These include the Selective Service classifications, such as 4-F and 1-H; the symbols for chemical elements, such as K for potassium; etc. There is an entry for ACTION, an independent government agency, because it is nearly always written in uppercase and appears to be an acronym. Actually, as the entry explains, the word is not an acronym and the letters do not represent other words.

No attempt is made to list acronyms or initialisms of local businesses or associations, local units of government, or other terms in limited use.

Should Shortened Terms Be Pronounced?

On this point, the editors suggest that you let your conscience—and whatever common usage you know of—be your guide. Pronunciation is almost entirely a matter of choice. Some people pronounce alphabetical forms, whenever possible, as if they were complete words. Others prefer to rattle off the individual letters. As has been indicated, if one adheres strictly to the "acronyms are pronounceable" school of thought, the decision whether or not to pronounce as a word can be critical. The less structured viewpoint that the designations "acronym" and "initialism" are interchangeable to a great extent, is probably more manageable. It may also help to avoid ensnarement in this consideration: is COD (Cash on Delivery) rightfully an acronym because it *may* be pronounced as "cod," or correctly an initialism because it is *never* expressed except letter by letter?

Occasionally, an initialism will acquire an unofficial stray letter or sound that never appears in print, but that renders the term pronounceable. SNCC (*Student National [formerly, Nonviolent] Coordinating Committee*), for example, was widely pronounced "snick." For such cases as this, discreet and careful listening is essential.

To Capitalize or Not to Capitalize?

It is comparatively rare, and is becoming even less common, for acronyms and initialisms to be written any way other than in all-capital letters, without periods. There are occasional exceptions, especially in scientific or technical notation (names of chemical elements, for example), but it appears that the overwhelming tendency is toward the use of all capitals and the omission of all periods. The capitalization of abbreviations for common nouns, such as TV for Television, is typical.

The editors have speculated on the reasons for the tendency to use all capitals, without periods, and found no single answer. It seems significant, however, that the equipment that is widely being used today for records and/or for communication—such as Teletypes, computer printout units, punched cards, etc.—had, in its early days of development, only uppercase letters, and, except for the Teletype, a relatively limited capacity for characters, punctuation, and spacing.

The general rule of all-capital letters could not logically be applied to all entries, however. Unlike certain other types of terms that might be written in various ways, academic degrees, for example, often include both capital and lowercase letters. The degree of Bachelor of Science may be abbreviated BS, but it is also often expressed as B Sc, and it would not have been appropriate to apply the "all capital" rule to material of this type. "T" indicates "tablespoon" to a cook, and its lowercase form, "t," indicates "teaspoon"—the difference could be crucial in any recipe. Also, although conjunctions, prepositions, and articles are usually ignored in the formation of an initialism, they are occasionally found in such instances as C of C for Chamber of Commerce, which would rarely be written as COFC.

Another important exception is made with abbreviations of periodical titles. Those made up of a *series* of abbreviations are traditionally written in upper- and lowercase: Econ Comput Econ Cybern Stud Res (Economic Computation and Economic Cybernetics Studies and Research). The often extraordinary length of such "short" forms would be somewhat overwhelming if set in full capitals: ECON COMPUT ECON CYBERN STUD RES.

The form of some widely used acronyms has evolved through the years until, in current usage, these terms are written as common nouns. "RADAR" became "Radar" and is now "radar." For consistency, such items are entered in *AIAD* in their original all-capital form. When used as a part of another entry (NGL—Neodymium Glass LASER), they are also entered in uppercase, to indicate to the uninitiated that they are acronyms or initialisms and will be found as separate entries in their own alphabetical place in the dictionary. (Such acronyms-within-meanings are generally not translated within each entry because of the difficulty of correcting all such translations should the meaning for the term later change. By directing the user to the term's own listing in *AIAD,* only that main entry will have to be updated.) When this type of acronym is part of the official title of an organization or a publication, it is generally given as the source indicates.

Finally, the use of uppercase or lowercase letters in alphabetical *codes,* such as library symbols, MARC codes, and others, is frequently significant. These terms have therefore been picked up as given by the authoritative source.

Updating and Categorizing

As was indicated in the Preface, updating of entries is a continuing effort. Terms are updated as changes come to our attention, but obviously not all entries in the book can be kept constantly current.

Where possible, and if not already implied in the entry itself, a parenthetical category or identifier follows many terms. Examples are [*World War II*], [*Library of Congress*], [*Air Force*], and so forth. The purpose is to put as many entries as possible into some kind of context, since *AIAD* entries come from hundreds of different subject areas. These added identifiers may indicate that the entry is connected with or originated by the given category, or it may simply be an indication that the term is abbreviated in that particular way by the organization, group, or categorization used.

The identifier following an entry—such as [*FAA*] or [*Veterans Administration*]—is usually the one current when the term was picked up for *AIAD.* The agency or organization used as an identifier may since have been altered in structure or dissolved; and while the entry for the agency itself may indicate the change, the identifiers in other related terms will not necessarily be altered. For example, the Department of Health, Education, and Welfare (HEW) became the Department of Health and Human Services (HHS) in 1979. The entry for HEW indicates this change:

HEW......................Department of Health, Education, and Welfare . . . [*Later, HHS*]

There are, however, many other entries in the dictionary that are followed by the designation [HEW]. Some of these have been changed to indicate the term's ongoing connection with the new agency. Others retain their [HEW] category, since it cannot be presumed that all designations for departmental units, processes, etc., are currently used by the superseding agency.

Arrangement of Terms

Acronyms, initialisms, and abbreviations are arranged alphabetically in letter-by-letter sequence, regardless of spacing, punctuation, or capitalization. Neither ampersands, articles, conjunctions, nor prepositions are considered in the alphabetizing. If the same abbreviation has more than one meaning, the various *meanings* are then subarranged alphabetically, in word-by-word sequence.

After this principal arrangement of terms will follow any forms of the entry using Arabic numerals. (Roman numerals sort as alphabetics.) These numeric forms are, in turn, followed by pluralized forms (usually indicated by an apostrophe and lowercase "s" to emphasize that the "s" is not part of the initialism). Finally come entries in which a parenthetical explanatory word is an integral part of the term: A (Bomb), C (Section), D (Day), etc. For example:

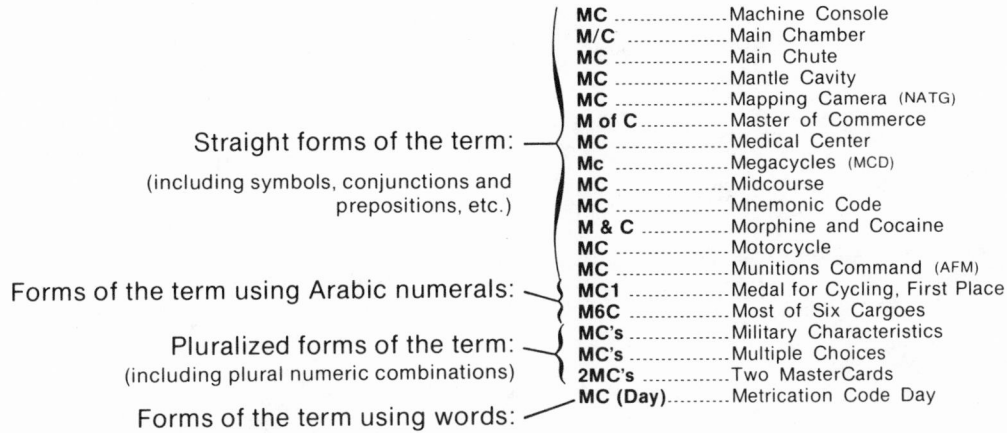

With respect to arrangement of terms and their meanings, it should be kept in mind that the point of reference for the user is the *abbreviation* rather than its meaning. Therefore, it is deliberate when there are two listings of, for example, the International Airline Stewards and Stewardesses Association under slightly different initialisms, both of which were encountered in one or another of the various sources used to compile this dictionary.

List of Selected Sources

Each of the print sources included in the following list contributed at least 50 terms. It would be impossible to cite a source for every entry in *Acronyms, Initialisms, and Abbreviations Dictionary (AIAD)* because the majority of terms are sent by outside contributors, are uncovered through independent research by the editorial staff, or surface as miscellaneous broadcast or print media references.

For sources used on an ongoing basis, only the latest edition is listed. For most of the remaining sources, the edition that was used is cited. The editors will provide further information about these sources upon request.

Unless further described in an annotation, the publications listed here contain no additional information about the acronym, initialism, or abbreviation cited in *AIAD.* For the user's convenience, a key to these symbols can also be found on the end sheets.

(AABC)   *Catalog of Abbreviations and Brevity Codes.* Washington, D.C.: Department of the Army, 1981. [Use of source began in 1969]

(AAG)   *Aerospace Abbreviations Glossary.* Report Number AG60-0014. Prep. by General Dynamics/Astronautics. San Diego, 1962.

(ADA)   *The Australian Dictionary of Acronyms and Abbreviations.* 2nd ed. Comp. by David J. Jones. Leura, NSW, Australia: Second Back Row Press Pty. Ltd., 1981.

(AFIT)   *Compendium of Authenticated Systems and Logistics.* Washington, D.C.: Air Force Institute of Technology. [Use of source began in 1984]

(AFM)   *Air Force Manual of Abbreviations.* Washington, D.C.: Department of the Air Force, 1975. [Use of source began in 1969]

(ARC)   *Agricultural Research Centres: A World Directory of Organizations and Programmes.* 2 vols. Ed. by Nigel Harvey. Harlow, Essex, England: Longman Group, 1983; distributed in US by Gale Research Co., Detroit.
> A world guide to official, educational, industrial, and independent research centers which support research in the fields of agriculture, veterinary medicine, horticulture, aquaculture, food science, forestry, zoology, and botany.

(ASF)   *Guide to Names and Acronyms of Organizations, Activities, and Projects.* Food and Agriculture Organization of the United Nations. Fishery Information, Data, and Statistics Service and US National Oceanic and Atmospheric Administration. Aquatic Sciences and Fisheries Information System Reference Series, Number 10, 1982. N.p.

(BJA)   *Biblical and Judaic Acronyms.* By Lawrence Marwick. New York: Ktav Publishing House, Inc., 1979.

(BUR)   *Computer Acronyms and Abbreviations Handbook.* Tokyo: Burroughs Co. Ltd., 1978.

(CAAL)   *CAAL COMOPTEVFOR Acronym and Abbreviation List.* (CAAL) (U) Operational Test and Evaluation Force. Norfolk, Va.: 1981.

(CED)   *Current European Directories.* 2nd ed. Ed. by G. P. Henderson. Beckenham, Kent, England: CBD Research, 1981; distributed in US by Gale Research Co., Detroit.

(CET)   *Communications-Electronics Terminology.* AFM 11-1. Vol. 3. Department of the Air Force, 1973.

(CINC) *A CINCPAC Glossary of Commonly Used Abbreviations and Short Titles.* By LTC J. R. Johnson. Washington, D.C., 1968.

(CMD)   *Complete Multilingual Dictionary of Computer Terminology.* Comp. by Georges Nania. Chicago: National Textbook Co., 1984.
         Computer-related terms in Spanish, French, Italian, Portuguese, and English. Indexes in French, Italian, Spanish, and Portuguese are also provided.

(CNC)   *Codes for the Names of Countries.* National Bureau of Standards. Washington, D.C.: US Government Printing Office, 1977, 1983.

(CSR)   *Computer Science Resources: A Guide to Professional Literature.* Ed. by Darlene Myers. White Plains, N.Y.: Knowledge Industry Publications, Inc., 1981.
         Covers several types of computer-related literature including journals, technical reports, directories, dictionaries, handbooks, and university computer center newsletters. Five appendices cover career and salary trends in the computer industry, user group acronyms, university computer libraries, and trade fairs and shows.

(DEN)   *Dictionary of Electronics and Nucleonics.* By L. E. C. Hughes, R. W. B. Stephens, and L. D. Brown. New York: Barnes & Noble, 1969.

(DIT)   *Dictionary of Informatics Terms in Russian and English.* By. G. S. Zhdanov, E. S. Kolobrodov, V. A. Polushkin, and A. I. Cherny. Moscow: Nauka, 1971.

(DLA)   *Dictionary of Legal Abbreviations Used in American Law Books.* 2nd ed. Comp. by Doris M. Bieber. Buffalo, N.Y.: William S. Hein & Co., 1985.

(DSUE) *A Dictionary of Slang and Unconventional English.* 8th ed. By Eric Partridge. Ed. by Paul Beale. New York: Macmillan Publishing Co., 1984.

(EA)   *Encyclopedia of Associations.* 22nd ed. Vol. 1, *National Organizations of the U.S.* Ed. by Karin E. Koek and Susan Boyles Martin. Detroit: Gale Research Co., 1987. [Use of source began in 1960]
         A guide to trade, professional, and other nonprofit associations that are national and international in scope and membership and that are headquartered in the United States. Entries include name and address; telephone and telex number; chief official; and a description of the purpose, activities, and structure of the organization.

(EA-IO) *Encyclopedia of Associations.* 21st ed. Vol. 4, *International Organizations.* Ed. by Karin E. Koek. Detroit: Gale Research Co., 1987. [Use of source began in 1985]
         A guide to trade, professional, and other nonprofit associations that are international in scope and membership and that are headquartered outside the United States. Entries include name and address; principal foreign language name; telephone and telex number; chief official; and a description of the purpose, activities, and structure of the organization.

(EGAO) *Encyclopedia of Governmental Advisory Organizations.* 6th ed. Ed. by Denise M. Allard and Donna Batten. Detroit: Gale Research Co., 1987. [Use of source began in 1975]
         A reference guide to approximately 5,000 permanent, continuing, and ad hoc US Presidential Advisory Committees, Interagency Committees, and other government-related boards, panels, task forces, commissions, conferences, and other similar bodies serving in a consultative, coordinating, advisory, research, or investigative capacity. Entries include name and address, telephone number, designated federal employee, history, recommendation and findings of the committee, staff size, publications, and subsidiaries. Also includes indexes to personnel, reports, federal agencies, presidential administration, and an alphabetical and keyword index.

(EISS) *Encyclopedia of Information Systems and Services.* 7th ed. Ed. by Amy Lucas and Kathleen Young Marcaccio. Detroit: Gale Research Co., 1987. [Use of source began in 1976]

> An international guide to computer-readable databases, database producers and publishers, online vendors and time-sharing companies, telecommunications networks, and many other information systems and services. Entries include name and address, telephone number, chief official, and a detailed description of the purpose and function of the system or service.

(FAAC) *Contractions Handbook.* Changes. Department of Transportation. Federal Aviation Administration, 1985. [Use of source began in 1969]

(FAAL) *Location Identifiers.* Department of Transportation. Federal Aviation Administration. Air Traffic Service. 7350.5A. Washington, D.C., 1982.

(GEA) *Government Economic Agencies of the World: An International Directory of Governmental Organisations concerned with Economic Development and Planning.* A Keesing's Reference Publication. Ed. by Alan J. Day. Harlow, Essex, England: Longman Group Ltd., 1985; distributed in US by Gale Research Co., Detroit.

> Covers over 170 countries and territories. Two introductory sections for each area cover economic data and prevailing economic and political conditions. Individual entries provide title, address, and names of chief officials of each agency. Current activities and financial structure of each agency are also detailed. An index of agency officials is provided.

(GPO) *Style Manual.* Rev. ed. Washington, D.C.: US Government Printing Office, 1984.

> Terms are included in Chapter 24, Foreign Languages.

(IBMDP) *IBM Data Processing Glossary.* 6th ed. White Plains, N.Y.: IBM Corp., 1977.

(IEEE) *IEEE Standard Dictionary of Electrical and Electronics Terms.* Ed. by Frank Jay. New York: The Institute of Electrical and Electronics Engineers, Inc., 1977, 1984.

> Includes definitions for thousands of electrical and electronics terms. Each entry includes a numeric source code.

(INF) *Infantry.* Vol. 76. Fort Benning, Ga.: U.S. Army Infantry Training School, 1986. [Use of source began in 1983]

(IRC) *International Research Centers Directory 1986-1987.* 3rd ed. Ed. by Kay Gill and Darren L. Smith. Detroit: Gale Research Co., 1986 (And supplements, ed. by Darren L. Smith, 1986).

> A world guide to government, university, independent, nonprofit, and commercial research and development centers, institutes, laboratories, bureaus, test facilities, experiment stations, and data collection and analysis centers, as well as foundations, councils, and other organizations which support research.

(KSC) *A Selective List of Acronyms and Abbreviations.* Comp. by the Documents Department, Kennedy Space Center Library, 1971, 1973.

(LCCP) *MARC Formats for Bibliographic Data.* Appendix II. Library of Congress. Washington, D.C., 1982.

(LCLS) *Symbols of American Libraries.* 13th ed. Washington, D.C.: Catalog Management and Publication Division, Library of Congress, 1985.[Use of source began in 1980]

(MCD) *Acronyms, Abbreviations, and Initialisms.* Comp. by Carl Lauer, St. Louis, Mo: McDonnell Douglas Corp., 1986. [Use of source began in 1969]

(MDG) *Microcomputer Dictionary and Guide.* By Charles J. Sippl. Champaign, Ill: Matrix Publishers, Inc., 1975.

> A listing of definitions for over 5,000 microelectronics terms. Seven appendices.

(MSA)   *Military Standard Abbreviations for Use on Drawings, and in Specifications, Standards, and Technical Documents.* MIL-STD-12D. Department of Defense, 1981. [Use of source began in 1975]

(MSC)   *Annotated Acronyms and Abbreviations of Marine Science Related Activities.* 3rd ed. Rev. by Charlotte M. Ashby and Alan R. Flesh. Washington, D.C.: US Department of Commerce. National Oceanographic and Atmospheric Administration. Environmental Data Service. National Oceanographic Data Center, 1976, 1981.

(MUGU)   *The Mugu Book of Acronyms & Abbreviations.* Management Engineering Office, Pacific Missile Range, California, 1963, 1964.

(NASA)   *Glossary, Acronyms, Abbreviations.* Space Transportation System and Associated Payloads. Prep. by A. M. Koller, Jr. National Aeronautics and Space Administration, N.p., 1977.

(NATG)   *Glossary of Abbreviations Used in NATO Documents.* AAP 15 (B)., N.p., 1979. [Use of source began in 1976]

(NG)   *NAVAIR Glossary of Unclassified Common-Use Abbreviated Titles and Phrases.* NAVAIRNOTE 5216 AIR-6031., N.p., July, 1969.

(NLC)   *Symbols of Canadian Libraries.* 11th ed. National Library of Canada. Minister of Supply and Services Canada, 1985.

(NOAA)   *NOAA Directives Manual.* 66-13 Acronyms. 1971.

(NQ)   *NASDAQ/CQS Symbol Directory.* New York: NASDAQ, Inc., 1983.

(NRCH)   *A Handbook of Acronyms and Initialisms.* Nuclear Regulatory Commission. NUREG-0544. Rev. 2. Division of Technical Information and Document Control. Washington, D.C., 1985.

(NVT)   *Naval Terminology.* NWP3 (Rev. B). Department of the Navy. Office of the Chief of Naval Operations, 1980. [Use of source began in 1974]
         Includes a section on definitions of naval terminology.

(OAG)   *Official Airline Guide Worldwide Edition.* Oak Brook, Ill.: Official Airlines Guide, Inc., 1984. [Use of source began in 1975]

(OCD)   *Oxford Classical Dictionary.* 2nd ed. Ed. by N. G. Hammond and H. H. Scullard. London: Oxford University Press, 1970.

(OCLC)   *OCLC Participating Institutions Arranged by OCLC Symbol.* Dublin, Ohio: OCLC, 1981.

(OICC)   *Abbreviations and Acronyms.* Des Moines, Iowa: Iowa State Occupational Information Coordinating Committee, 1986.

(PD)   *Political Dissent: An International Guide to Dissident, Extra-Parliamentary, Guerrilla and Illegal Political Movements.* A Keesing's Reference Publication. Comp. by Henry W. Degenhardt. Ed. by Alan J. Day. Harlow, Essex, England: Longman Group, 1983; distributed in US by Gale Research Co., Detroit.
         Includes the history and aims of approximately 1,000 organizations, with details of their leaderships.

(PPE)   *Political Parties of Europe.* 2 vols. Ed. by Vincent E. McHale. The Greenwood Historical Encyclopedia of the World's Political Parties. Westport, Conn.: Greenwood Press, 1983.
         One of a series of reference guides to the world's significant political parties. "Each guide provides concise histories of the political parties of a region and attempts to detail the evolution of ideology, changes in organization, membership, leadership, and each party's impact upon society."

(PPW)   *Political Parties of the World.* 2nd ed. A Keesing's Reference Publication. Comp. and ed. by Alan J. Day and Henry W. Degenhardt. Harlow, Essex, England: Longman Group, 1980, 1984; distributed in US by Gale Research Co., Detroit.
> Covers historical development, structure, leadership, membership, policy, publications, and international affiliations. For each country, an overview of the current political situation and constitutional structure is provided.

(RCD)   *Research Centers Directory.* 11th ed. Ed. by Mary Michelle Watkins. Detroit: Gale Research Co., 1987. [Use of source began in 1986]
> A guide to university-related and other nonprofit research organizations carrying on research in agriculture, astronomy and space sciences, behavioral and social sciences, computers and mathematics, engineering and technology, physical and earth sciences and regional and area studies.

(RDA)   *Army RD & A Magazine.* Alexandria, Va.: Development, Engineering, and Acquisition Directorate, Army Materiel Command, 1986. [Use of source began in 1979]

(ROG)   *Dictionary of Abbreviations.* By Walter T. Rogers, FRSL. London: George Allen & Co. Ltd., 1913. Reprint. Detroit: Gale Research Co., 1969.

(SEIS)   *Seismograph Station Codes and Characteristics.* Geological Survey. Circular 791. By Barbara B. Poppe, Debbi A. Naab, and John S. Derr. Washington, D.C.: U.S. Department of the Interior, 1978.

(TEL)   *Telephony's Dictionary.* 1st ed. By Graham Langley. Chicago: Telephony Publishing Corp., 1982.
> Includes definitions for over 14,000 U.S. and international terms. Ten appendices.

(TSPED)   *Trade Shows and Professional Exhibits Directory.* 2nd ed. Ed. by Robert J. Elster. Detroit: Gale Research Co., 1987. [Use of source began in 1986]
> A guide to scheduled events providing commercial display facilities, including conferences, conventions, meetings, fairs and festivals, etc. Entries include name of trade show; sponsor name, address, and telephone number; attendance figures; principal exhibits; special features; publications; and date and location of shows.

(TSSD)   *Telecommunications Systems and Services Directory.* 2nd ed. Ed. by Martin Connors. Detroit: Gale Research Co., 1985. (And supplement, 1987)
> An international descriptive guide to approximately 2,000 telecommunications organizations, systems, and services. Entries include name and address, telephone number, chief official, and a description of the purposes, technical structure, and background of the service or system.

Acronyms, Initialisms & Abbreviations Dictionary

P-Z

P

P .... Aircraft [*Wind triangle problems*]
P .... All India Reporter, Patna   (DLA)
P .... Armour Pharmaceutical Co. [*Research code symbol*]
P .... Assistant in Private Practice [*Chiropody*] [*British*]
P .... Asta Werke AG [*Germany*] [*Research code symbol*]
P .... Bristol Laboratories [*Research code symbol*]
P .... cis-Platinum [*Cisplatin*] [*Also, cis-DDP, CDDP, CPDD, CPT, DDP*] [*Antineoplastic drug*]
P .... Dainippon Pharmaceutical Co. [*Japan*] [*Research code symbol*]
p .... Density [*Heat transmission symbol*]
P .... Departure
p .... Difficulty [*Of a test item*] [*Psychology*]
P .... Farbenfabriken Bayer [*Germany*] [*Research code symbol*]
P .... Farmitalia [*Italy*] [*Research code symbol*]
P .... Faulty Punctuation [*Used in correcting manuscripts, etc.*]
P .... Force of Concentrated Load
P .... Games [*or Matches*] Played [*Sports statistics*]
P .... Hole P-Type Semiconductor Material
P .... Indian Law Reports, Patna Series   (DLA)
P .... Law Reports, Probate, Divorce, and Admiralty [*Since 1890*] [*England*]   (DLA)
P .... Lepetit [*Italy*] [*Research code symbol*]
p .... Momentum [*Symbol*] [*IUPAC*]
P .... Office of Personnel [*Coast Guard*]
p .... On Probation [*Navy*] [*British*]
P .... Orbital Period [*of a comet*] [*In years*]
p .... P-Doped Semiconductor [*Photovoltaic energy systems*]
P .... P-Register [*Data processing*]
P .... Pacer
P .... Pacific Coast Stock Exchange [*Later, PSE*]
p------........ Pacific Ocean [*MARC geographic area code*] [*Library of Congress*]   (LCCP)
P .... Pacific Reporter   (DLA)
P .... Pacific Standard Time   (FAAC)
P .... Packed Lunches [*School meals*] [*British*]
P .... Paddington Railway Station   (ROG)
P .... Paddle
P .... Page
P .... Paid This Year [*In stock listings of newspapers*]
P .... Pain [*Medicine*]
P .... Paired [*for or against*] [*Votes in Congress*]
P .... Paise [*Monetary unit in India*]
P .... Palace   (ROG)
P .... Palacio [*A publication*]
P .... Palaestra [*A publication*]
P .... Pale   (ADA)
P .... Pallet [*Spacelab*] [*NASA*]   (NASA)
P .... Pamphlet
P .... Pancuronium [*A muscle relaxant*]
P .... Papa [*Pope*] [*Latin*]
P .... Papa [*Phonetic alphabet*] [*International*]   (DSUE)
P .... Paper
P .... Papilla [*Optic*] [*Medicine*]
P .... Para [*Monetary unit in Yugoslavia*]
p .... Para [*Chemistry*]
P .... Parachutist [*Army skill qualification identifier*]   (INF)
P .... Paragraph   (ADA)
P .... Paralegal Program [*Association of Independent Colleges and Schools specialization code*]
P .... Parallax
P .... Parallel
P .... Paramecin [*A protozoan toxin*]
P .... Parashah   (BJA)
P .... Pardon   (ADA)
P .... Parental
P .... Parish   (ROG)
P .... Parity [*Atomic physics*]
P .... Park
P .... Parking Place [*Traffic sign*] [*British*]
P .... Parlophone [*Record label*] [*Great Britain, Italy, Australia, etc.*]

P .... Parson
P .... Part
P .... Partial [*Astronomy*]
P .... Participle [*Grammar*]
P .... Partim [*In Part*]
P .... Party
P .... Parve [*or Pareve*] [*In food labeling, indicates food is kosher and can be used with either meat or dairy products*]
P .... Passed [*Examination*]
P .... Passing Showers [*Meteorology*]
P .... Past
P .... Paste
P .... Pasteurella [*Genus of bacteria*]
P .... Pastor
P .... Patchy [*Decelerometer readings*] [*Aviation*]   (FAAC)
P .... Patent
P .... Pater [*Father*] [*Latin*]
P .... Patient
P .... Patrol [*Designation for all US military aircraft*]
P .... Patron
P .... Pattern
P .... Paused Program [*Data processing*]
P .... Pavilion   (ROG)
P .... Pawn [*Chess*]
P .... Pax [*Peace*] [*Latin*]
P .... Pay
P .... Paymaster [*Military*]   (ROG)
P .... Pazmaveb [*A publication*]
P .... Peak
P .... Peat   (ROG)
P .... Pebbles [*Quality of the bottom*] [*Nautical charts*]
P .... Pectoral [*Anatomy*]   (ROG)
p .... Peculiar [*Astronomy*]
P .... Pen [*Sports*]
p .... Pence [*Monetary unit in Great Britain*]
P .... Pencil Tube   (MDG)
P .... Pengo [*Monetary unit in Hungary until 1946*]
P .... Penicillin
p .... Penni(a) [*Penny or Pence*] [*Monetary unit*] [*Finland*]   (GPO)
P .... Pennsylvania   (DLA)
P .... Pennsylvania State Library, Harrisburg, PA [*Library symbol*] [*Library of Congress*]   (LCLS)
P .... Penny
P .... Pentachlorophenol [*Also, PCP*] [*Wood preservative*] [*Organic chemistry*]   (TEL)
P .... People
P .... Per
P .... Percentile
P .... Perceptual
P .... Perceptual Speed [*A factor ability*] [*Psychology*]
P .... Perch
P .... Perchloroethylene [*Also, TCE*] [*Dry cleaning*]
P .... Percussion
P .... Pere [*Father*] [*French*]
P .... Perforation
P .... Performance [*Army*]   (INF)
P .... Performer
P .... Perianth
P .... Pericardium [*Medicine*]
P .... Perimeter
P .... Period
P .... Perishable
P .... Permanent Stay [*in hospital*] [*British*]
P .... Perpetuus [*Uninterrupted*] [*Latin*]
p .... Perseverate [*Psychology*]
P .... Persian   (DLA)
P .... Persimmon
P .... Persistence [*Medicine*]
P .... Person
P .... Person to Person [*Telecommunications*]   (TEL)
P .... Personality Organization and Stability [*Eysenck*] [*Psychology*]

P .... Personnel
P .... Perspectives [*A publication*]
P .... Perstetur [*Continue*] [*Pharmacy*]   (ROG)
P .... Persuasion [*Novel by Jane Austen*]
P .... Peseta [*Monetary unit in Spain and Latin America*]
P .... Pesewa [*Monetary unit in Ghana*]
P .... Pesher   (BJA)
P .... Peshitta   (BJA)
P .... Peso [*Monetary unit in Spain and Latin America*]
P .... Peta [*A prefix meaning multiplied by 10^{15}*] [*SI symbol*]
P .... Peter [*Phonetic alphabet*] [*World War II*]   (DSUE)
P .... Peter [*New Testament book*]
P .... Peters' United States Supreme Court Reports [*26-41 United States*]   (DLA)
P .... Petrol [*British Waterways Board sign*]
P .... Peyote
P .... Pfizer, Inc. [*Research code symbol*]
P .... Pharmacopoeia
P .... Phencyclidine [*An anesthetic*]
P .... Phenolphthalein [*Chemical indicator*]
P .... Philadelphia [*Pennsylvania*] [*Mint mark, when appearing on US coins*]
P .... Phillips Petroleum Co. [*NYSE symbol*]
P .... Philologus. Zeitschrift fuer Klassische Altertum [*A publication*]
P .... Philosophy [*A publication*]
P .... Phoenician   (BJA)
P .... Phon [*Unit of loudness level*]
p .... Phosphate [*One-letter symbol*] [*Biochemistry*]
p .... Phosphoric Residue [*As substituent on nucleoside*] [*Biochemistry*]
P .... Phosphorus [*Chemical element*]
P .... Photographic Reconnaissance Capability [*When suffix to Navy aircraft designation*]
P .... Phrase Structure Rule [*Linguistics*]
P .... Physiology [*Medical Officer designation*] [*British*]
P .... Pianissimo [*Very Softly*] [*Music*]
P .... Piano [*Softly*] [*Music*]
P .... Piano [*Musical instrument*]
P .... Piaster [*Monetary unit in Spain, Republic of Vietnam, and some Middle Eastern countries*]
P .... Pica [*Typography*]   (ADA)
P .... Pickering's Massachusetts Reports [*18-41 Massachusetts*]   (DLA)
p .... Pico [*A prefix meaning divided by one trillion*] [*SI symbol*]
P .... Picot [*Crochet*]   (ROG)
P .... Pie
P .... Pied [*Foot*] [*French*]
P .... Pigs   (ROG)
P .... Pilaster [*Technical drawings*]
P .... Pillar [*Buoy*]
P .... Pilot
P .... [*Marc*] Pincherle [*When used in identifying Vivaldi's compositions, refers to cataloging of his works by musicologist Pincherle*]
P .... Pink
P .... Pinnule
P .... Pint
P .... Pip [*Phonetic alphabet*] [*Pre-World War II*]   (DSUE)
P .... Pipe
P .... Pipe Rolls [*British*]
P .... Pique; Inclusions [*Diamond clarity grade*]
P .... Pitch [*Technical drawings*]
P .... Pitch [*or Pitcher*] [*Baseball*]
P .... Pitman-Moore Co. [*Research code symbol*]
P .... Pius [*Dutiful*] [*Latin*]
P .... Placebo [*Medicine*]
P .... Planed
P .... Planning
P .... Plasma
P .... Plate [*Electron tube*] [*Technical drawings*]
P .... Platform
P .... Pleasant
P .... Plug
P .... Plus [*More*]
P .... Poco [*Somewhat*] [*Music*]
P .... Poetry [*A publication*]
P .... Poids [*Feet*] [*French*]
P .... Point [*Lacrosse position*]
P .... Point
P .... Point-to-Point Radio [*FAA designator*]   (CET)
P .... Poise [*Unit of dynamic viscosity*]
P .... Poison
P .... Polar [*Air mass*]   (FAAC)
P .... Polar Distance [*Navigation*]
P .... Polarization
P .... Pole
P .... Political Division [*Geography*]
P .... Polka [*Music*]
P .... Polonystyka [*A publication*]
P .... Polyneuropathy [*Medicine*]
P .... Pond [*Maps and charts*]

P .... Pondere [*By Weight*] [*Latin*]
P .... Ponendum [*To Be Placed*] [*Latin*]
P .... Ponte [*A publication*]
P .... Pontifex [*Bishop*] [*Latin*]
P .... Poop [*Portion of a ship*]
P .... Poor Skiing Conditions
P- .... Poorly Organized, Unstable Personality [*Eysenck*] [*Psychology*]
P .... Pope
P .... Popular Response [*Rorschach*] [*Psychology*]
P .... Population
P .... Populus [*People*] [*Latin*]
P .... Porcelain
P .... Port [*Maps and charts*]
P .... Portable   (MDG)
P .... Portion
P .... Portugal
P .... Position
p .... Positive [*Crystal*]
P .... Post [*After*] [*Latin*]
P .... Post
P .... Postage
P .... Posten [*Sentry*] [*German military*]
P .... Posterior
P .... Postpartum [*Medicine*]
P .... Pouce [*Inch*] [*French*]
P .... Pounds [*As measurement of total stress*] [*Aerospace*]   (AAG)
P .... Pour [*For*] [*French*]
P .... Power [*Symbol*] [*IUPAC*]
P .... Poynting Vector [*Electromagnetism*]   (DEN)
P .... Practical
P .... Practical Intelligence
P .... Pre-1920 [*Deltiology*]
P .... Preceding
P .... Precipitation Ceiling [*Aviation weather reports*]   (FAAC)
P .... Predicate
P .... Prednisolone [*Endocrinology*]
P .... Prednisone [*Also, PDN, Pr, Pred, Pro*] [*Antineoplastic drug*] [*Endocrinology*]
P .... Preferred
P .... Prefix [*Indicating a private radiotelegram*]
P .... Preliminary
P .... Premolar [*Dentistry*]
P .... Presbyopia [*Ophthalmology*]
P .... Presbyterian
P .... Prescribing
P .... Present
P .... Present BIT [*Binary Digit*] [*Data processing*]
P .... Preset
P .... President
P .... Press [*Publishing*]
P .... Pressure [*or p*] [*Symbol*] [*IUPAC*]
P .... Pressurized Tank [*Liquid gas carriers*]
P .... Pridie [*The Day Before*] [*Latin*]
P .... Priest
P .... Priestly Source [*Biblical scholarship*]
P .... Primary
P .... Primary [*or Push*] Wave [*Earthquakes*]
P .... Primitive
P .... Primus [*First*] [*Latin*]
P .... Prince
P .... Princeps [*First Edition*] [*French*]
P- .... Princess   (ROG)
P .... Principal
P .... Print
P .... Priority [*Telecommunications*]   (TEL)
P .... Prisoner [*Military*]
P .... Private
P .... Private Trust [*Includes testamentary, investment, life insurance, holding title, etc.*]   (DLA)
P .... Private Venture
P .... Privy   (ROG)
P .... Pro [*For*] [*Latin*]
P .... Probability [*or Probability Ratio*] [*Statistics*]
P .... Probate
P .... Probe   (MSA)
P .... Probucol [*Anticholesteremic*]
P .... Procarbazine [*Also, PC, PCB, Pr*] [*Antineoplastic drug*]
P .... Proconsul
P .... Producer [*Films, television, etc.*]
P .... Product
P .... Production [*of Energy*]
P .... Profession
P .... Professional [*Civil Service employees designation*]
P .... Proficiency
P .... Profit
P .... Progesterone [*A hormone*]
P .... Program   (KSC)
P .... Progressive
P .... Prohibited Area [*Followed by identification*]
P .... Proline [*One-letter symbol; see Pro*]

P .... Prompt [*i.e., the right side*] [*A stage direction*]
P .... Prop
P .... Propagation Distribution [*Broadcasting*]
P .... Proportion in a Specific Class
P .... Proposed Departure [*Aviation*]   (FAAC)
P .... Propulsion   (AAG)
P .... Protein
P .... Proteinuria [*Clinical chemistry*]
P .... Protestant
P .... Protet [*Protest*] [*French*]
P .... Proto [*Linguistics*]
p .... Proton [*A nuclear particle*]
P .... Protoplasmic [*Freeze etching in microscopy*]
P .... Prototroch
P .... Prototype   (AAG)
P .... Provisional
P .... Psychiatry
P .... Psychometrist [*Psychology*]
P .... Public Houses [*Public-performance tariff class*] [*British*]
P .... Publications
P .... Pudding [*Phonetic alphabet*] [*Royal Navy*] [*World War I*]   (DSUE)
P .... Pugillum [*Medicine*]   (ROG)
P .... Pugillus [*A Pinch*] [*Pharmacy*]   (ROG)
P .... Pulled Up [*Horse racing*]
P .... Pulse
P .... Pump   (AAG)
P .... Punch
P .... Punic   (BJA)
P .... Punkt [*Point*] [*German military*]
P .... Punter [*Football*]
P .... Pupil
P .... Purchased   (AAG)
P .... Purinethol [*Mercaptopurine*] [*Also, M, MP*] [*Antineoplastic drug*]
P .... Purl [*Knitting*]
P .... Purple
P .... Purpure [*Purple*] [*Heraldry*]
P .... Pursuit [*Airplane designation*]
P .... Put [*In options listings of newspapers*]
P .... Pya [*Monetary unit in Burma*]
p .... Pyranose [*One-letter symbol*] [*Biochemistry*]
P .... Pyroxene Subgroup [*Acmite, sodium metasilicate, potassium metasilicate, diopside, wollastonite, hypersthene*] [*CIPW classification*] [*Geology*]
P .... Single Paper [*Wire insulation*]   (AAG)
P .... Soft Pad [*Missile launch environment symbol*]
P .... Warner-Lambert Pharmaceutical Co. [*Research code symbol*]
P-2 .... Propaganda Due [*Secret Italian Masonic organization, allegedly tied to the Roman Catholic church*]
P₂ .... Pulmonic Second Sound [*Medicine*]
P3 .... Portable Plotting Package   (NRCH)
3P .... Three-Pole [*or Triple Pole*] [*Switch*]
4P .... Four-Pole [*Switch*]
7P .... Lesotho [*Aircraft nationality and registration mark*]   (FAAC)
8P .... Barbados [*Aircraft nationality and registration mark*]   (FAAC)
P 14 .... Pattern 14 Rifle [*Made in the US for Great Britain, beginning in 1914*]
P₅₀ .... Partial pressure of oxygen at 50% hemoglobin saturation [*Medicine*]
5P's .... Poet, Printer, Publisher, Publican, and Player [*Nickname given to William Oxberry (fl. 1784-1824)*]
P (Card) ..... Personal Card [*Containing person's name, address, age, description, job, habits, haunts, movements*] [*Used in Belfast, Northern Ireland*]
P (Day) .... Production Day [*Army*]   (AABC)
PA .... B. F. Jones Memorial Library, Aliquippa, PA [*Library symbol*] [*Library of Congress*]   (LCLS)
PA .... [*The*] Item Requested Is a Controlled Item That May Be Released Only By Written Authority of the Proponent. Please See DA Pamphlet 310-1 for Identification of and Address of Proponent [*Supply action error code*] [*Army*]
PA .... Office of Public Affairs [*DoD*]
PA .... Onze Pius-Almanak [*A publication*]
PA .... Pacific Affairs [*A publication*]
PA .... Pad Abort [*NASA*]   (KSC)
P & A .... Page and Adams' Code [*1912*]   (DLA)
PA .... Paging and Area Warning   (MCD)
Pa .... Paideia [*A publication*]
Pa .... Paine's United States Circuit Court Reports   (DLA)
PA .... Paired Associates [*Psychometrics*]
PA .... Pakistan Army
PA .... Paleopathology Association
PA .... Palestine Affairs [*New York*] [*A publication*]   (BJA)
PA .... Palladium [*Chemical element*]   (ROG)
PA .... Pan American World Airways, Inc. [*See also PAA, PAN-AM, PN*] [*ICAO designator*]   (MCD)
PA .... Panama [*Two-letter standard code*]   (CNC)
PA .... Paper Advance   (BUR)
PA .... Par Amitie [*By Favor*] [*French*]
PA .... Par Autorite [*By Authority*] [*French*]

P in A .... Parallax in Altitude [*Navigation*]
PA .... Paralysis Agitans
PA .... Parametric Amplifier
Pa .... Paranoia [*Psychology*]
PA .... Parapsychological Association, Inc.
PA .... Parents Anonymous [*Los Angeles, CA*]   (EA)
PA .... Parents' Association
PA .... Parish
PA .... Parliamentary Affairs [*A publication*]
PA .... Parti de l'Action [*Party of Action*] [*Moroccan*]   (PPW)
PA .... Parti Affectae [*To the Affected Part*] [*Pharmacy*]
PA .... Partial Application [*Military*]   (AFIT)
PA .... Participating Activity [*Responsible for standardization efforts*] [*DoD*]
PA .... Participial Adjective [*Grammar*]
PA .... Particular Average
PA .... Partners of the Americas   (EA)
Pa .... Paru [*A publication*]
Pa .... Pascal [*Symbol*] [*SI unit of pressure*]
PA .... Passenger Agent
PA .... Passenger Ship
PA .... Pastoral Music [*A publication*]
PA .... Patient
PA .... Patrol Aircraft   (NATG)
PA .... Pattern Analysis [*Test*]
P & A .... Pay and Allowances
PA .... Paying Agent   (DLA)
P/A .... Payment Authority [*Business and trade*]
PA .... Pending Availability
PA .... Pendulous Axis [*Accelerometer*]   (IEEE)
PA .... Pennsylvania [*Postal code*]
PA .... Pennsylvania Supreme Court Reports [*1845-date*]   (DLA)
PA .... People's Alliance [*Althydubandalag*] [*Icelandic*]   (PPW)
PA .... Peptide Absorption
PA .... Per Abdomen
PA .... Per Adresse [*Care Of*] [*German*]
PA .... Per Annum [*By the Year*] [*Latin*]
PA .... Per Auguri [*Used on visiting cards to express congratulations, birthday wishes, etc.*] [*Italy*]
P & A .... Percussion and Auscultation [*Medicine*]
PA .... Performance Analysis
PA .... Performance Appraisal Required [*Civil Service*]
PA .... Performing Arts [*US Copyright Office class*]
PA .... Periodic Acid [*Inorganic chemistry*]
pA .... Periplanone A [*Biochemistry*]
PA .... Permanent Address   (ROG)
PA .... Permanent Appointment
PA .... Permanently Associated [*Telecommunications*]   (TEL)
PA .... Pernicious Anemia [*Hematology*]
PA .... Personal Affairs   (AFM)
PA .... Personal Appearance
PA .... Personal Assistant [*British*]
PA .... Personal Audit [*Psychological testing*]
P & A .... Personnel and Administration [*Army*]   (AABC)
PA .... Personnel Area   (NRCH)
PA .... Petroleum Abstracts [*A publication*]
PA .... Pfizer, Inc. [*Research code symbol*]
PA .... Phentolamine [*Antiadrenergic*]
PA .... Philippine Army
PA .... Philippine Association   (EA)
PA .... Phonocardiogram Amplifier
PA .... Phosphatidic Acid [*Biochemistry*]
PA .... Phosphoarginine [*Biochemistry*]
PA .... Photoallergenic [*Response*] [*Medicine*]
PA .... Photodiode Amplifier
PA .... Phthalic Anhydride [*Organic chemistry*]
PA .... Physical Activity   (MCD)
PA .... Physician's Assistant
PA .... Physics Abstracts
PA .... Picatinny Arsenal [*New Jersey*] [*Later, Armament Development Center*] [*Army*]
pA .... Picoampere
PA .... Pierre Allain [*Lightweight rock-climbing boot named after its designer*]
PA .... Pierre Arpels [*Jewelry designer*]
PA .... Pills Anonymous [*Later, DA*] [*An association*]   (EA)
P/A .... Pilotless Aircraft
P & A .... Pioneer and Ammunition
PA .... Pirke Avot   (BJA)
PA .... Planning Assistance [*An association*]   (EA)
P & A .... Plans and Analysis
PA .... Plasma Aldosterone [*Endocrinology*]
PA .... Plasminogen Activator [*Neurobiology*]
PA .... Platelet Adhesiveness [*Hematology*]
PA .... Platform Assembly   (MCD)
PA .... Point of Aim [*Military*]
PA .... Points Against [*Football*]
P/A .... Polar to Analog   (KSC)
PA .... Polar Atlantic [*American air mass*]
PA .... Police Academy
PA .... Pollution Abstracts [*A publication*]

Pa	Polonystyka [*A publication*]
PA	Polyacetal [*Organic chemistry*]
PA	Polyacrylic [*Organic chemistry*]
PA	Polyanhydride [*Organic chemistry*]
PA	Polyarteritis [*Medicine*]
PA	Polymer Adhesive
PA	Port Agency [*Army*]
PA	Position Approximate [*Nautical charts*]
PA	Positive Addiction [*Self-improvement method developed by William Glasser, MD*]
PA	Positive Attitude
PA	Post Adjutant
PA	Post Amplifier
PA	Postal Assistant
PA	Posterior Anterior [*Medicine*]
PA	Posterior Aorta
PA	Postmortem Aging [*of meat*]
PA	Potsmokers Anonymous [*New York, NY*] (EA)
PA	Power Amplifier
PA	Power Approach [*Aerospace*]
PA	Power of Attorney
P/A	Power of Authority
PA	Practice Amendment (AAG)
PA	Prealbumin [*Biochemistry*]
PA	Preamplifier
PA	Prearm
PA	Preavailability
PA	Precision Approach (FAAC)
PA	Precomputed Altitude
P & A	Prediction and Allocation
PA	Predictive Analyzer [*Data processing*] (DIT)
PA	Prefect-Apostolic [*Roman Catholic*]
PA	Preliminary Acceptance (KSC)
PA	Preparing Activity [*Responsible for Federal document and study projects*]
PA	Presence Africaine [*A publication*]
PA	Present Again (ADA)
PA	Preservation Action (EA)
PA	Presidents Association [*New York, NY*] (EA)
PA	Press Agent
PA	Press Association Ltd. [*London, England*] (EISS)
PA	Pressure Actuated [*Switch*]
PA	Pressure Alarm (NRCH)
PA	Pressure Altitude [*Aviation*]
PA	Pressure Angle (MSA)
PA	Pressure Area [*Medicine*]
PA	Price Analyst
P & A	Price and Availability
PA	Primary Anemia [*Medicine*]
PA	Prince Albert Coat [*Slang*]
PA	Principal Axes
PA	Principle of Adding [*New math*]
PA	Prior to Admission [*Medicine*]
P & A	Priorities and Allocations (MUGU)
PA	Priority Aggregate
PA	Privacy Act
PA	Private Account [*Banking*]
PA	Private Architect [*British*]
PA	Pro Anno [*For the Year*] [*Latin*]
PA	Pro Applicatione [*To Be Applied*] [*Pharmacy*] (ROG)
PA	Pro Arte [*A publication*]
PA	Proactivator [*Medicine*]
PA	Proanthocyanidin (Assay) [*Analytical chemistry*]
PA	Probability of Acceptance (KSC)
P/A	Problem Analysis (NASA)
PA	Probleme der Agyptologie [*A publication*] (BJA)
P & A	Procedures and Analysis
PA	Process Allocator [*Telecommunications*] (TEL)
PA	Process Automation (CMD)
PA	Procurement Agency (MCD)
PA	Procurement Appropriations (AABC)
PA	Procurement, Army
P & A	Procurement and Assignment
PA	Procurement Authorization
PA	Product Analysis (IEEE)
PA	Product Assurance (NASA)
PA	Production Adjustment
PA	Production Assistant
P & A	Professional and Administrative (AAG)
PA	Profile Angle (MSA)
PA	Program Access
PA	Program Account (NG)
PA	Program Address
PA	Program Administrator (MCD)
PA	Program Agent (OICC)
PA	Program for the Aging (OICC)
PA	Program Aid [*A publication*]
PA	Program Analysis [*Data processing*]
PA	Program Application Instructions [*Telecommunications*] (TEL)
PA	Program Assessment (MCD)
PA	Program Attention Key [*Data processing*]

PA	Program Authorization (AFM)
PA	Programable Automation
PA	Progressive Alliance [*Defunct*] (EA)
PA	Project Administration (MCD)
PA	Project Authorization
PA	Proliferating Angioendotheliomatosis
PA	Prolonged-Action [*Pharmacy*]
PA	Prolotherapy Association (EA)
PA	Property Administrator [*DoD*]
PA	Prophylactic Antibiotic
PA	Proponent Agency [*Army*]
PA	Proportional Action (AAG)
PA	Proposal Authorization
PA	Proprietary Association [*Washington, DC*] (EA)
PA	Prosecuting Attorney
Pa	Protactinium [*or Protoactinium*] [*Chemical element*]
PA	Protected Area [*Nuclear energy*] (NRCH)
P & A	Protection and Advocacy [*System*] [*To protect the rights of developmentally disabled persons*]
PA	Protestant Alliance (EA)
PA	Prothonotary Apostolic
PA	Provisional Allowance
PA	Pseudo-Astronomy
PA	Pseudoaneurysm [*Medicine*]
PA	Pseudomonas aeruginosa [*Bacterium*]
PA	Psychoanalyst
PA	Psychogenic Aspermia [*Medicine*]
PA	Psychological Abstracts [*A publication*]
PA	Psychological Age
PA	Public Accountant
PA	Public Act
PA	Public Address [*Amplification equipment*] [*Communications*]
PA	Public Administration
PA	Public Administration [*A publication*]
PA	Public Advocate (EA)
PA	Public Affairs
PA	Public Archives [*of Canada*]
PA	Public Assistance
PA	Publication Announcement
PA	Publishers' Alliance [*Sun Lakes, AZ*] (EA)
PA	Publishers' Association [*London, England*] (DIT)
PA	Pull and Adjust [*Brace*] [*Medicine*]
PA	Pulmonary Angiography [*Medicine*]
PA	Pulmonary Artery [*Medicine*]
PA	Pulmonary Atresia [*Medicine*]
PA	Pulpoaxial [*Dentistry*]
PA	Pulse Amplifier
PA	Puppeteers of America
PA	Purchasing Agent
PA	Purge Alarm [*Nuclear energy*] (NRCH)
PA	Put Away [*Papers*] [*British*]
PA	Puumala [*Vole virus*]
PA	Pyro Ammonia (ROG)
PA	Pyrrolizidine Alkaloid [*Toxicology*]
PAA	Pa-An [*Burma*] [*Airport symbol*] (OAG)
PAA	Pan American Minerals Corp. [*Toronto Stock Exchange symbol*] [*Vancouver Stock Exchange symbol*]
PAA	Pan American World Airways, Inc. [*See also PA, PAN-AM, PN*]
PAA	Pancretan Association of America (EA)
PAA	Panguna [*Solomon Islands*] [*Seismograph station code, US Geological Survey*] (SEIS)
paa	Papuan-Australian [*MARC language code*] [*Library of Congress*] (LCCP)
PAA	Para-Azoxyanisole [*Organic chemistry*]
PAA	Parke, Davis & Co. [*Research code symbol*]
PAA	Parti Affectae Applicandus [*Apply to the Affected Part*] [*Pharmacy*]
PAA	Pay Adjustment Authorization
PAA	Peruvian-American Association (EA)
PAA	Petroleum Administration Act [*Canada*]
PAA	Phased Array Antenna
PAA	Phenanthrene Amino Alcohol [*Organic chemistry*]
PAA	Phenanthrylacetamide [*Organic chemistry*]
PAA	Phenylacetic Acid [*Organic chemistry*]
PAA	Phosphonoacetic Acid [*Antiviral compound*]
PAA	Photographers Association of America [*Later, Professional Photographers of America*]
PAA	Photon Activation Analysis
PAA	Planar Array Antenna
PAA	Plasminogen Activator Activity [*Neurobiology*]
PAA	Platelet Associated Activity [*Pharmacology*]
PAA	Polish Association of America [*Later, Northern Fraternal Life Insurance*] (EA)
PAA	Polyacrylamide [*Also, PAAM*] [*Organic chemistry*]
PAA	Polyacrylic Acid [*Organic chemistry*]
PAA	Polycyclic Aromatic Amine [*Organic chemistry*]
PAA	Population Association of America (EA)
PAA	Post Award Action
PAA	Potato Association of America (EA)
PAA	Power Amplifier Assembly
PAA	Primary Aircraft Authorized

PAA .... Primary Auxiliary Area (NRCH)
PAA .... Print Advertising Association [*Defunct*] (EA)
PAA .... Procurement of Ammunition, Army (AABC)
PAA .... Procurement Appropriation, Army (MCD)
PAA .... Professional Archers Association
PAA .... Programme d'Aide aux Athletes [*Athlete Assistance Program*] [*Canada*]
PAA .... Pyridineacetic Acid [*Organic chemistry*]
PAAA .... Premium Advertising Association of America [*Later, PMAA*] (EA)
PAAAS .... Proceedings. American Academy of Arts and Sciences [*A publication*]
PAAAS .... Publication. American Association for the Advancement of Science [*A publication*]
PAABS .... Pan-American Association of Biochemical Societies
PAABS Rev ... PAABS [*Pan-American Association of Biochemical Societies*] Revista [*United States*] [*A publication*]
PAABS Symp ... PAABS [*Pan-American Association of Biochemical Societies*] Symposium [*A publication*]
PAAC .... Pacific and Asian Affairs Council
PAAC .... Program Analysis Adaptable Control [*Data processing*]
PA Acad Sci Proc ... Pennsylvania Academy of Science. Proceedings [*A publication*]
PAACE ...... Precision Aircraft Armament Control Experiment (RDA)
PAACS ...... Prior Active Army Commissioned Service
PAADAR .... Passive Airborne Detection and Ranging (MSA)
PAADC ...... Principal Air Aide-de-Camp [*RAF*] [*British*]
PA Admin Bull ... Pennsylvania Bulletin (DLA)
PA Admin Code ... Pennsylvania Administrative Code (DLA)
PAAECI ...... Pan American Association of Educational Credit Institutions [*See also APICE*] (EA-IO)
PAAES ...... Prior Active Army Enlisted Service
PAAES .... Publications. American Archaeological Expedition to Syria [*A publication*] (BJA)
PAAFCS .... Prior Active Air Force Commissioned Service
PAAFES .... Prior Active Air Force Enlisted Service
PAAGE ...... Panel on Alternate Approaches to Graduate Education (EA)
PA Ag Exp ... Pennsylvania. Agricultural Experiment Station. Publications [*A publication*]
PA Agric Exp Stn Bull ... Pennsylvania. Agricultural Experiment Station. Bulletin [*A publication*]
PA Agric Exp Stn Prog Rep ... Pennsylvania. Agricultural Experiment Station. Progress Report [*A publication*]
PAAJR .... Proceedings. American Academy for Jewish Research [*A publication*]
PAAM .... Polyacrylamide [*Also, PAA*] [*Organic chemistry*]
P/AAMHRC ... Pacific/Asian American Mental Health Research Center [*University of Illinois at Chicago*] [*Research center*] (RCD)
PAAN .... Product Assurance Alert Notice (MCD)
PAANA .... Proceedings. Australian Society of Animal Production [*A publication*]
PAANS .... Association PanAfricaine des Sciences Neurologiques [*Pan African Association of Neurological Sciences*] (EA-IO)
PAANS .... Pan African Association of Neurological Sciences (EA-IO)
PAAO .... Pan-American Association of Ophthalmology [*Dallas, TX*] (EA)
PAAORLBE ... Pan-American Association of Oto-Rhino-Laryngology and Broncho-Esophagology (EA-IO)
PAAP......... Panjabi Adabi Academy Publication [*A publication*]
PAAP......... Peaceful Alternatives to the Atlantic Pact
PAAP......... Provisional Algal Assay Procedure [*Test measuring impact of chemicals on algal growth*]
PAAR......... American Academy in Rome. Papers and Monographs [*A publication*]
PA Arch...... Pennsylvania Archaeologist [*A publication*]
PA Archaeol ... Pennsylvania Archaeologist [*A publication*]
PAAS........ Phased Array Antenna System
PAAS........ Proceedings. American Antiquarian Society [*A publication*]
PAAT........ Personnel and Administrative Assistance Team [*Navy*] (NVT)
PAATA .... Praktika tes Akademias Athenon [*A publication*]
PAATI........ Phased Array Antenna Technology Investigation
PAAWWW ... Pacific Asian American Women Writers West (EA)
PAAXOP..... Pan-Dodecanesian Association of America "Xanthos O Philikos" (EA)
PAb .... Abington Free Library, Abington, PA [*Library symbol*] [*Library of Congress*] (LCLS)
PAB .... Cabrini College, Library, Radnor, PA [*OCLC symbol*] (OCLC)
PAB .... Panair do Brasil, SA
PAB .... Para-Aminobenzoic Acid [*Also, PABA*] [*Biochemistry*]
PAB .... Paramaribo [*Suriname*] [*Geomagnetic observatory code*]
PAB .... Parti des Paysans, Artisans, et Bourgeois [*Farmers', Artisans', and Burghers' Party*] [*Swiss*] (PPE)
PAB .... Patent Abstracts Bibliography [*NASA*]
PAB .... Patrick Air Force Base [*Florida*]
PAB .... Peanut Advisory Board (EA)
PAB .... Pension Appeals Board [*Canada*]
PAB .... Petroleum Administrative Board [*Terminated, 1936*]
PAB .... Plastic Assault Boat [*Navy*]
PAB .... Police Administration Building
PAB .... Preliminary As-Built [*Nuclear energy*] (NRCH)
PAB .... Price Adjustment Board
PAB .... Price Agreement Bulletin

PAB .... Primary Auxiliary Building [*Nuclear energy*] (NRCH)
PAB .... Priorities Allotment Board
PAB .... Priority Assignment Base (MCD)
PAB .... Program Advisory Board (MCD)
PAB .... Psychiatric Attitudes Battery [*Psychology*]
PAB .... Pulmonary Artery Banding [*Cardiology*]
PAB .... Pulsed Adsorption Bed [*Process*]
PAB .... Purple Agar Base [*Media*] [*Microbiology*]
PABA........ Para-Aminobenzoic Acid [*Also, PAB*] [*Biochemistry*]
PA BA .... Pennsylvania Bar Association. Reports (DLA)
PABA........ Progressive Angus Breeders Association
PA Bar Asso Q ... Pennsylvania Bar Association. Quarterly [*A publication*]
PA B Ass'n Q ... Pennsylvania Bar Association. Quarterly [*A publication*]
PA B Brief ... Pennsylvania Bar Brief (DLA)
PABD......... Precise Access Block Diagram
PABE......... Program and Budget Estimate (MCD)
PABFSA ..... Pediatric Association of Black French-Speaking Africa [*Abidjan, Ivory Coast*] (EA-IO)
PABIA........ Pathologie et Biologie [*A publication*]
PA Bk Cas ... Pennsylvania Bank Cases (DLA)
PABLA........ Problem Analysis by Logical Approach
PABLE........ Payable (ROG)
PABMI........ Performing Arts Biography Master Index [*A publication*]
PA Browne (Pa) ... Browne's Reports [*Pennsylvania*] (DLA)
PA Browne R ... Browne's Reports [*Pennsylvania*] (DLA)
PABS.......... Pan-American Biodeterioration Society (EA)
PABS.......... Para-Aminobenzensulfonamide [*Antibiotic*]
PA Bsns Survey ... Pennsylvania Business Survey [*A publication*]
PABST .... Primary Adhesively Bonded Structural Technology [*Aviation*]
PABT......... Pabst Brewing Co. [*NASDAQ symbol*] (NQ)
PA Bur Topogr Geol Surv Miner Resour Rep ... Pennsylvania. Bureau of Topographic and Geologic Survey. Mineral Resource Report [*A publication*]
PABV......... Pyroactuated Ball Valve
PABVA .... Pesquisa Agropecuaria Brasileira. Serie Veterinaria [*A publication*]
P(A)BX....... Private (Automatic) Branch Exchange [*Telecommunications*] (DEN)
PAC........... Canada. Fisheries and Marine Service. Northern Operations Branch. Pacific Region. Data Report Series [*A publication*]
PAC........... cis-Platinum [*Cisplatin*], Adriamycin, Cyclophosphamide [*Antineoplastic drug regimen*]
PAC........... Pacific (AFM)
Pac .... Pacific [*Record label*] [*France*]
PAC........... Pacific Air Command [*Air Force*]
PAC........... Pacific Ocean
Pac .... Pacific Reporter (DLA)
PAC........... Pacific Telesis Group [*NYSE symbol*]
PAC........... Package Attitude Control [*NASA*]
PAC........... Packaged Assembly Circuit
PAC........... Packard Automobile Classics (EA)
PAC........... Pak-Man Resources, Inc. [*Vancouver Stock Exchange symbol*]
PAC........... Palo Alto - Branner [*California*] [*Seismograph station code, US Geological Survey*] [*Closed*] (SEIS)
PAC........... Pan-Africanist Congress [*South Africa*]
PAC........... Pan American College [*Texas*]
PAC........... Pan-American Congress
PAC........... Panama City [*Panama*] Paitilla Airport [*Airport symbol*] (OAG)
PAC........... Papular Acrodermatitis of Childhood
PAC........... Para-Aminoclonidine [*Biochemistry*]
PAC........... Para-Aminosalicylic Acid Calcium Salt [*Pharmacology*]
PAC........... Parachute and Cable Defence [*British*]
PAC........... Parametric Amplifier Converter
P-A-C .... Parent-Adult-Child [*Transactional analysis*]
PAC........... Parker Aircraft Corporation (MCD)
PAC........... Partido Autentico Constitucional [*Authentic Constitutional Party*] [*El Salvador*]
PAC........... Parts Allocation Chart (MCD)
PAC........... Pascagoula, MS [*Location identifier*] [*FAA*] (FAAL)
PAC........... Passed the Final Examination of the Advanced Class [*Military College of Science*] [*British*]
PAC........... Passive Acoustic Classification (NVT)
PAC........... Patient Airlift Center [*Aeromedical evacuation*]
PAC........... Payment after Closing [*Insurance*]
PAC........... Peace Action Center [*Defunct*] (EA)
PAC........... Pearson Aircraft, Inc. [*Port Angeles, WA*] [*FAA designator*] (FAAC)
PAC........... Pedagogic Automatic Computer (IEEE)
PA C........... Pennsylvania Commonwealth Court Reports (DLA)
PAC........... People's Army Congress (CINC)
PAC........... Performance Analysis and Control
PAC........... Performance Assured Certification
PAC........... Personal Analog Computer
PAC........... Personnel and Administration Center [*Army*] (AABC)
PAC........... Personnel Administration Certificate (ADA)
PAC........... Perturbed Angular Correlation
PAC........... Petroleum Advisory Committee [*of Organization for Economic Cooperation and Development*] (EGAO)
PAC........... Pharmaceutical Advertising Council [*New York, NY*] (EA)

PAC............ Phenacetin [*Acetophenetidin*], Aspirin, Caffeine
            [*Pharmacology*]
PAC........... Photoacoustic [*Spectroscopy*]
PAC........... Piper Aircraft Corporation
PAC........... Planning Advisory Committee   (OICC)
PAC........... Plasma Arc Chamber
PAC........... Plasma Arc Cutting [*Welding*]
PAC........... Plowshare Advisory Committee [*AEC*]
PACC......... Pneumatic Analog Computer
PAC........... Pneumatic Auxiliary Console   (AAG)
PAC........... Pod Air Conditioner   (AAG)
PAC........... Policy Advisory Center
PAC........... Policy Advisory Committee [*of Office of Economic Opportunity
            local program*]
PAC........... Polish-American Congress   (EA)
PAC........... Political Action Caucus [*Superseded by LPAC*]   (EA)
PAC........... Political Action Committee [*Generic term*]
PAC........... Polled Access Circuit
PAC........... Pollution Abatement and Control
PAC........... Polycyclic Aromatic Compound [*Organic chemistry*]
PAC........... Population Action Council   (EA)
PAC........... Post Award Conference   (MCD)
PAC........... Powdered Activated Carbon [*Adsorbent*]
PAC........... Pre-Action Calibration [*Gunnery*]   (NVT)
PAC........... Preauthorized Check Plan [*Insurance*]
PAC........... Premature Atrial Contraction [*Medicine*]
PAC........... Pressure Alpha Center   (MCD)
PAC........... Primary Address Code   (AFM)
PAC........... Prime [*or Principal*] Associate Contractor   (MCD)
PAC........... Printing Accountants Club   (EA)
PAC........... Problem Action Center [*NASA*]   (NASA)
PAC........... Production Acceleration Capacity
PAC........... Professional Activities Survey [*Medicine*]
PAC........... Program Acquisition Cost   (MCD)
PAC........... Program Adjustment Committee
PAC........... Program Advisory Committee
PAC........... Program Allocation Checker
PAC........... Programable Automatic Comparator
PAC........... Progress Assessment Chart [*Psychology*]
PAC........... Project Advisory Committee   (EGAO)
PAC........... Promoting Achievement through Communications [*Education*]
PAC........... Protect America's Children [*An association*]   (EA)
PAC........... Protection Auxiliary Cabinet [*Nuclear energy*]   (NRCH)
PAC........... Public Access Control
PAC........... Public Accounts Committee [*British government*]
PAC........... Public Affairs Committee   (EA)
PAC........... Public Affairs Coordinator [*Nuclear energy*]   (NRCH)
PAC........... Public Archives of Canada
PAC........... Publishers' Ad Club [*Later, PPA*] [*New York, NY*]   (EA)
PAC........... Pulmonary Artery Catheter [*Medicine*]
PAC........... Pure and Applied Chemistry [*IUPAC*]
PAC........... Pursuant to Authority Contained In
PAC........... Put and Call [*Stock market*]
PAC-10 ... Pacific 10 Conference   (EA)
Pac A........ Pacific Affairs [*A publication*]
PACA .... Perishable Agricultural Commodities Act, 1930
PACA .... Picture Agency Council of America [*New York, NY*]   (EA)
PACA .... Principal Assistant County Architect [*British*]
PACA .... Proceedings. African Classical Association [*A publication*]
PACAB...... Pacific Affairs. Current Awareness Bulletin [*A publication*]
PACADV ... Pacific Fleet Advance Headquarters [*Guam*]
PACAF ...... Pacific Air Forces
PACAFBASECOM ... Pacific Air Forces Base Command
Pac Aff ...... Pacific Affairs [*A publication*]
Pac Affairs ... Pacific Affairs [*A publication*]
PACAF-OA ... Pacific Air Forces Operations Analysis
Pac Arts Newsl ... Pacific Arts Newsletter [*A publication*]
PACAS...... Patient Care System   (AABC)
PA Cas ...... Pennsylvania Supreme Court Cases [*Sadler*]   (DLA)
PACAS...... Personnel Access Control Accountability System   (MCD)
PACAS...... Psychological Abstracts Current Awareness Service   (EISS)
PACB......... Pan-American Coffee Bureau [*Defunct*]   (EA)
Pac Bird Obs ... Pacific Bird Observer [*A publication*]
Pac Builder Eng ... Pacific Builder and Engineer [*A publication*]
PA CC ...... Pennsylvania County Court Reports   (DLA)
PACC .... Portable Arm Control Console   (KSC)
PACC .... Problem Action Control Center [*NASA*]   (NASA)
PACC .... Products Administration Contract Control
PACC .... Protected Air-Cooled Condenser [*Nuclear energy*]   (NRCH)
PACC .... Provident Life & Accident [*NASDAQ symbol*]   (NQ)
PACCALL ... Pacific Fleet Calls [*Radio call signs*]
Pac Chem Eng Cong Proc ... Pacific Chemical Engineering Congress.
            Proceedings [*United States*] [*A publication*]
Pac Chem Metall Ind ... Pacific Chemical and Metallurgical Industries [*A
            publication*]
PACCIOS ... Pan American Council of International Committee of Scientific
            Management
PACCO ...... Cisplatin, Adriamycin, Cyclophosphamide, CCNU [*Lomustine*],
            Oncovin [*Vincristine*] [*Antineoplastic drug regimen*]
Pac Coast Gas Assoc Proc ... Pacific Coast Gas Association. Proceedings [*A
            publication*]

Pac Coast LJ ... Pacific Coast Law Journal   (DLA)
Pac Coast Med ... Pacific Coast Medicine [*A publication*]
Pac Com .... Pacific Community [*Tokyo*] [*A publication*]
PACCOM ... Pacific Fleet Communications Instructions
Pac Commun ... Pacific Community [*A publication*]
PA CCR ...... Pennsylvania County Court Reports   (DLA)
PA CC Reps ... Pennsylvania County Court Reports   (DLA)
PACCS...... Pan American Cancer Cytology Society [*Defunct*]   (EA)
PACCS...... Post Attack Command and Control System [*Military*]
PACCS/ADA ... Post Attack Command and Control System/Airborne Data
            Automation [*Military*]
PACCT...... PERT [*Program Evaluation and Review Technique*] and Cost
            Correlation Technique
PACD .... Pacific Division [*Military*]
Pac 2d .... Pacific Reporter, Second Series   (DLA)
PACDA...... Personnel and Administration, Combat Development Activity
            [*Army*]   (AABC)
PA C Dec WCC ... Pennsylvania Courts, Decisions in Workmen's
            Compensation Cases   (DLA)
Pac Discovery ... Pacific Discovery [*A publication*]
PACDIV...... Pacific Division [*Military*]
PACE........ PACE (Pacing and Clinical Electrophysiology) [*A publication*]
PACE........ PACE (Process and Chemical Engineering) [*A publication*]
PACE........ Pacific Agricultural Cooperative for Export [*San Francisco,
            CA*]   (EA)
PACE........ Pacific Alternate Command Element   (CINC)
PACE........ Packaged CRAM [*Card Random-Access Memory*] Executive
            [*NCR Corp.*] [*Data processing*]
PACE........ Packet of Accelerated Christian Education [*Educational
            material marketed by fundamentalist company,
            Accelerated Christian Education*]
PACE........ Passive Attitude Control Experimental [*Satellite*]
PACE........ Performance and Cost Evaluation
PACE........ Performing Arts, Culture, and Entertainment [*Proposed cable
            television system*]
PACE........ Personalized Aerobics for Cardiovascular Enhancement
PACE........ Phased Array Control Electronics
PACE........ Physics and Chemistry Experiment
PACE........ Plan for Action by Citizens in Education
PACE........ Planetary Association for Clean Energy   (EA)
PACE........ Planned Action with Constant Evaluation [*Data processing*]
PACE........ Plant Acquisition and Construction Equipment   (NRCH)
PACE........ Plant and Capital Equipment   (MCD)
PACE........ Portable Acoustic Collection Equipment   (MCD)
PACE........ Precision Analog Computing Equipment
PACE........ Preflight Acceptance Checkout Equipment
PACE........ Prelaunch Automatic Checkout Equipment
PACE........ Priority Activities in Cancer Education
PACE........ Prisoners Accelerated Creative Exposure [*An association*]
PACE........ Procedural Approach to the Composition of Essays [*In book
            title*]
PACE........ Process and Chemical Engineering [*A publication*]
PACE........ Professional Activities for Continuing Education [*AEC*]
PACE........ Professional and Administrative Career Examination [*Formerly,
            FSEE*] [*Civil Service*]
PACE........ Professional Association of Consulting Engineers
PACE........ Program for Afloat College Education [*Navy*]   (NVT)
PACE........ Programed Automatic Communications Equipment
PACE........ Programing Analysis Consulting Education   (IEEE)
PACE........ Project for the Advancement of Church Education
PACE........ Projects to Advance Creativity in Education [*HEW*]
PACE........ Providing Avenues for Continuing Encouragement [*Scholarship
            awarded by Fraternity of Recording Executives*]
PACE........ Provisioning Action Control Evaluation [*Military*]   (AFIT)
PACED ...... Program for Advanced Concepts in Electronic Design
PACE/LV ... Preflight Acceptance Checkout Equipment-Launch Vehicle
PACEMAKER ... Public Agency Career Employment Maker [*OEO project*]
PACENS ... Patient Census
PACER ...... Part and Component Evaluation Report [*NASA*]
PACER ...... Planning Automation and Control for Evaluating Requirements
PACER ...... Portable Aircraft Condition Evaluator Recorder
PACER ...... Postadoption Center for Education and Research
PACER ...... Postoperational Analysis Critique and Exercise Report
            [*Military*]   (CAAL)
PACER ...... Prescriptive Analysis for Curriculum Evaluation [*Vocational
            guidance*]
PACER ...... Priority for Allocation/Application of COMSEC Equipment
            Resources   (MCD)
PACER ...... Process Assembly Case Evaluator Routine [*Data processing*]
PACER ...... Program of Active Cooling Effects and Requirements
PACER ...... Program-Assisted Console Evaluation and Review [*Air Force*]
PACER ...... Programed Automatic Circuit Evaluator and Recorder
PACERS...... Pacing and Cardiac Electrophysiology Retrieval System
            [*Intermedics, Inc.*] [*Freeport, TX*] [*Information
            service*]   (EISS)
PACES ...... Political Action Committee for Engineers and Scientists
PACE-S/C ... Preflight Acceptance Checkout Equipment for Spacecraft
PAC-EX...... Canadian National Packaging Exposition [*Packaging
            Association of Canada*]   (TSPED)
PACEX ...... Pacific Exchange [*System*] [*Military*]   (AFM)
PACF......... Pacific

Pac Fisherman ... Pacific Fisherman [*A publication*]
PACFLAP... Pacific Fleet Augmentation Plan [*Navy*]   (NVT)
PACFLT ..... Pacific Fleet
PACFLTCOM ... Pacific Fleet Command
PACFLTMOPHOTOU ... Pacific Fleet Mobile Photographic Unit   (MUGU)
PACFORNET ... Pacific Coast Forest Research Information Network [*Later, WESTFORNET*] [*Forest Service*]   (EISS)
PACFW ...... President's Advisory Committee for Women [*Terminated, 1980*]   (EGAO)
PACGCS .... Prior Active Coast Guard Commissioned Service
PACGEEIA ... Pacific Area Ground Environment Electronic Installation Agency   (CINC)
Pac Geol .... Pacific Geology [*A publication*]
PACGES .... Prior Active Coast Guard Enlisted Service
PACGO ...... President's Advisory Committee on Government Organization [*Abolished, 1961*]
PACGSR .... Pan American Center for Geographical Studies and Research [*See also CEPEIGE*]   (EA-IO)
PacH.......... Pacific Historian [*A publication*]
PACH .... Performing Arts Center for Health [*New York University/ Bellevue Hospital, New York, NY*] [*Superseded by Center for Dance Medicine -CDM*]
PACH .... Public Administration Clearing House [*1931-1956*]
PACHACH ... Partizanim-Chayalim-Chalutzim   (BJA)
PACHEDPEARL ... Pacific Headquarters, Pearl Harbor, Hawaii [*Navy*]
Pac Hist R ... Pacific Historical Review [*A publication*]
Pac Hist Rev ... Pacific Historical Review [*A publication*]
Pac Hist Rev ... Pacific History Review [*A publication*]
Pac Hortic ... Pacific Horticulture [*A publication*]
PacHR .... Pacific Historical Review [*A publication*]
PACIA .... Particle Counting Immunoassay
PACIF........ Pacific
Pacif Aff ..... Pacific Affairs [*A publication*]
Pacific Bus ... Pacific Business [*A publication*]
Pacific CLJ ... Pacific Coast Law Journal [*San Francisco*]   (DLA)
Pacific His R ... Pacific Historical Review [*A publication*]
Pacific Islands M ... Pacific Islands Monthly [*A publication*]
Pacific Islands Yrbk ... Pacific Islands Year Book [*A publication*]
Pacific L J ... Pacific Law Journal [*A publication*]
Pacific Northw Q ... Pacific Northwest Quarterly [*A publication*]
Pacific Perspect ... Pacific Perspective [*A publication*]
Pacific Rep ... Pacific Reporter   (DLA)
Pacific Sci ... Pacific Science [*A publication*]
Pacific Sociol R ... Pacific Sociological Review [*A publication*]
Pacif Imp.... Pacific Imperialism Notebook [*A publication*]
Pacif Rep ... Pacific Reporter   (DLA)
PACIFY ...... Parents and Alumni Committee Involved for Youth [*Brown University*]
PACIMS ..... Passive Chemical Ionization Mass Spectrometry
Pac Insects ... Pacific Insects [*A publication*]
Pac Insects Mongr ... Pacific Insects Monograph [*A publication*]
Pac Insects Monogr ... Pacific Insects Monograph [*A publication*]
PACIR .... Practical Approach to Chemical Information Retrieval
PACIT........ Passive and Active Interface Test [*Electronic warfare*]
Pac J Math ... Pacific Journal of Mathematics [*A publication*]
Pack .... Packaging [*A publication*]
Packag Abstr ... Packaging Abstracts [*A publication*]
PACKAGE ... Planned Aids for Cross-Culture Knowledge, Action and Growth in Effectiveness
Package Dev ... Package Development [*A publication*]
Package Dev Syst ... Package Development and Systems [*A publication*]
Package Eng ... Package Engineering [*A publication*]
Package Engng ... Package Engineering [*A publication*]
Packag (India) ... Packaging (India) [*A publication*]
Packag Rev (S Afr) ... Packaging Review (South Africa) [*A publication*]
Packa Rev ... Packaging Review [*A publication*]
Packer Process ... Packer, Processor [*A publication*]
Pac Law Mag ... Pacific Law Magazine   (DLA)
Pac Law Reptr ... Pacific Law Reporter [*San Francisco*]   (DLA)
Pac Leg N... Pacific Legal News   (DLA)
PACM........ Passive Countermeasures   (MSA)
PACM......... Pulse Amplitude Code Modulation [*Electronics*]
Pac Mar Fish Comm Annu Rep ... Pacific Marine Fisheries Commission. Annual Report [*A publication*]
Pac Mar Fish Comm Bull ... Pacific Marine Fisheries Commission. Bulletin [*A publication*]
Pac Med Surg ... Pacific Medicine and Surgery [*A publication*]
PACMETNET ... Pacific Meteorological Network   (AAG)
PACMI........ President's Advisory Committee on Management Improvement [*Terminated, 1973*]
PACMISRAN ... Pacific Missile Range [*Later, WTR*]   (MUGU)
PACMISRANFAC ... Pacific Missile Range Facility [*Obsolete*]
PACMISTESTCEN ... Pacific Missile Test Center [*Navy*]
Pac Mo ...... Pacific Monthly [*Portland, Oregon*] [*A publication*]
PA Cmwlth ... Pennsylvania Commonwealth Court Reports   (DLA)
P Ac Nat S ... Proceedings. Academy of Natural Sciences of Philadelphia [*A publication*]
PACNAVFACENGCOM ... Pacific Division Naval Facilities Engineering Command
PACNCO.... Personnel Assistance Center Noncommissioned Officer   (INF)
Pac Neighbours ... Pacific Neighbours [*A publication*]

PACNET..... Plymouth Audioconferencing Network [*Plymouth Polytechnic*] [*Plymouth, England*] [*Telecommunications*]   (TSSD)
Pac Northwesterner ... Pacific Northwesterner [*A publication*]
Pac Northwest Sea ... Pacific Northwest Sea [*A publication*]
PacNQ........ Pacific Northwest Quarterly [*A publication*]
Pac NWQ ... Pacific Northwest Quarterly [*A publication*]
PACNY....... Pawnbrokers' Association of the City of New York [*Bronx, NY*]   (EA)
PA Co........ Pennsylvania County Courts   (DLA)
PACO .... Pivot Ambulating Crutchless Orthosis [*Medicine*]
PACO .... Polaris Accelerated Change Operation [*Missiles*]
PACO .... Primary Administrative Contracting Officer [*Military*]   (AFIT)
PACOB...... Propulsion Auxiliary Control Box   (AAG)
PA Co Ct ... Pennsylvania County Court Reports   (DLA)
PA Co Ct R ... Pennsylvania County Court Reports   (DLA)
PACOM...... Pacific Command [*Military*]
PACOMEP ... Pacific Command Emergency Procedures   (CINC)
PACOMEW ... Pacific Command Electronic Warfare   (CINC)
PACOMINTS ... Pacific Command Intelligence School   (CINC)
PA Commw ... Pennsylvania Commonwealth Court Reports   (DLA)
PA Commw Ct ... Pennsylvania Commonwealth Court Reports   (DLA)
PA Com Pl ... Pennsylvania Common Pleas Reporter   (DLA)
PA Cons Stat ... Pennsylvania Consolidated Statutes   (DLA)
PA Cons Stat Ann ... Pennsylvania Consolidated Statutes, Annotated   (DLA)
PA Cons Stat Ann (Purdon) ... Pennsylvania Consolidated Statutes, Annotated [*Purdon*]   (DLA)
PACOPS ..... Pacific Air Force Operations   (MCD)
PACOR...... Passive Correlation and Ranging
PACORE .... Parabolic Corner Reflector
PACORNALOG ... Pacific Coast Coordinator of Naval Logistics
PA Corp .... Pennsylvania Corporation Reporter   (DLA)
PA Corp R ... Pennsylvania Corporation Reporter   (DLA)
PA Corp Rep ... Pennsylvania Corporation Reporter   (DLA)
PA County Ct ... Pennsylvania County Court Reports   (DLA)
PA CP....... Pennsylvania Common Pleas Reporter   (DLA)
PACP......... Propulsion Auxiliary Control Panel [*NASA*]   (KSC)
PACPhA..... Proceedings. American Catholic Philosophical Association [*A publication*]
Pac Pharm ... Pacific Pharmacist [*A publication*]
Pac Philos Q ... Pacific Philosophical Quarterly [*A publication*]
Pac Phil Q ... Pacific Philosophical Quarterly [*A publication*]
PA C Pl ..... Pennsylvania Common Pleas   (DLA)
P Ac Poli S ... Proceedings. Academy of Political Science [*A publication*]
Pac Pulp Pap Ind ... Pacific Pulp and Paper Industry [*A publication*]
Pac Q......... Pacific Quarterly [*A publication*]
Pac R......... Pacific Reporter [*Commonly cited as P*]   (DLA)
PA CR........ Pennsylvania County Court Reports   (DLA)
PACR .... Performance and Compatibility Requirements
PACR .... Perimeter Acquisition RADAR   (MSA)
PACRAO .... Pacific Association of Collegiate Registrars and Admission Officers
Pac Rep..... Pacific Reporter [*Commonly cited as P*]   (DLA)
PACREP..... Port Activities Report [*Navy*]
Pac Repr .... Pacific Reporter   (DLA)
Pac Res ..... Pacific Research [*Formerly, Pacific Research and World Empire Telegram*] [*A publication*]
PACRESFLT ... Pacific Reserve Fleet
Pac Rockets ... Pacific Rockets [*A publication*]
Pac Rocket Soc Bull ... Pacific Rocket Society. Bulletin [*A publication*]
PACS .... Pacific Area Communications System   (MCD)
PACS .... Particle Analysis Cameras for the Shuttle [*NASA*]
PACS .... Patient Accounting, Census, and Statistics
PACS .... Peace and Common Security   (EA)
PACS .... Physics and Astronomy Classification Scheme
PACS .... Picture Archival and Communications
PACS .... Plant Automation Communication System [*IBM Corp.*]
PACS .... Pointing and Attitude Control System   (NASA)
PACS .... Post Attack Communication System
PACS .... Process Automation & Computer Systems
PACS .... Program Authorization Control System   (MCD)
PACSCAT ... Pacific Ionospheric Scatter   (CINC)
Pac Sci ..... Pacific Science [*A publication*]
Pac Sci Congr Proc ... Pacific Science Congress. Proceedings [*A publication*]
Pac Sci Congr Rec Proc ... Pacific Science Congress. Record of Proceedings [*A publication*]
Pac Search ... Pacific Search [*United States*] [*A publication*]
Pac Sociol R ... Pacific Sociological Review [*A publication*]
Pac Soc Rev ... Pacific Sociological Review [*A publication*]
PacSp .... Pacific Spectator [*A publication*]
PACT.......... Pan American Commission of Tampa   (EA)
PACT.......... Participating and Assertive Consumer Training [*Health education*]
PACT.......... Pay Actual Computer Time
PACT.......... Performing Arts Council for the Transvaal
PACT.......... Performing Arts for Crisis Training [*New York, NY*]   (EA)
PACT.......... Philco Automatic Circuit Tester
PACT.......... Plan of Action for Challenging Times [*Educational program for low-income students*]   (EA)
PACT.......... Portable Aircraft Calibration Tracker [*NASA*]

PACT.......... Powdered Activated Carbon Treatment [*For wastewater*] [*E. I. Du Pont De Nemours & Co., Inc.*]
PACT.......... Precision Aircraft Control Technology   (MCD)
PACT.......... Private Agencies Collaborating Together [*New York, NY*]   (EA)
PACT.......... Processing and Communications Terminal   (MCD)
PACT.......... Production Analysis Control Technique [*Navy*]
PACT.......... Program for Automatic Coding Techniques [*Data processing*]
PACT.......... Programable Asynchronous Clustered Teleprocessing
PACT.......... Programed Analysis Computer Transfer   (KSC)
PACT.......... Programed Automatic Circuit Tester
PACT.......... Project for the Advancement of Coding Techniques
PACT.......... Provide Addict Care Today [*Later, NADAP*]
PACT.......... Public Action Coalition on Toys [*Opposes sexist toys*]
PACTA...... Packed Tape Assembly
PACTEX..... Pacific-Texas [*Pipeline*]
PACT/NADAP ... National Association on Drug Abuse Problems   (EA)
PACTS ...... Parents, Administrators, Community, Teachers, and Students [*School-community groups*]
PACUSA .... Pacific Air Command, United States Army
PACV .... Patrol Air-Cushion Vehicle [*Also called Hovercraft*] [*Navy*]
PACV .... Personnel Air-Cushion Vehicle
PACV .... Post Accident Containment Venting [*Nuclear energy*]   (NRCH)
Pac View .... Pacific Viewpoint [*New Zealand*] [*A publication*]
Pac Wine Spirit Rev ... Pacific Wine Spirit Review [*A publication*]
PACX .... Private Automatic Computer Exchange
PAD........... Anthropology of Development Programme [*McGill University*] [*Canada*] [*Research center*]   (RCD)
PAD........... Packet Assembler/Disassembler [*Switching technique*] [*Data processing*]
PAD........... Padder [*Capacitor*] [*Electronics*]
PAD........... Paderborn [*West Germany*] [*Airport symbol*]   (OAG)
PAD........... Padova [*Italy*] [*Seismograph station code, US Geological Survey*]   (SEIS)
PAD........... Palestine Arab Delegation   (EA)
PAD........... Partido de Accion Democrata [*Democratic Action Party*] [*Spanish*]   (PPW)
PAD........... Partido Accion Democratica [*Democratic Action Party*] [*Salvadoran*]   (PPW)
PAD........... Passive Acoustic Detection [*Military*]   (CAAL)
PAD........... Passive Air Defense [*British*]
PAD........... Payable after Death [*Insurance*]   (ADA)
PAD........... Pedagogischer Austauschdienst [*Pedagogical Exchange Service*] [*German*]
PAD........... Performance Analysis and Design [*Nuclear energy*]   (NRCH)
PAD........... Performing Arts Directory [*A publication*]
PAD........... Permissible Accumulated Dose
PAD........... Personal Articulation Device [*Facetious term for pre-word-processing equipment*]
PAD........... Peters' United States District Court Reports, Admiralty Decisions   (DLA)
PAD........... Petroleum Administration for Defense [*Abolished, 1954*]
PAD........... Phenacetin [*Acetophenetidin*], Aspirin, Deoxyephedrine [*Pharmacology*]
PAD........... Pilotless Aircraft Division [*Navy*]
PAD........... Pitch Axis Definition
PAD........... Pitless Adapter Division of Water Systems Council [*Chicago, IL*]   (EA)
PAD........... Planning Action Directive [*Military*]   (AFIT)
PAD........... Polyaperture Device [*NASA*]   (KSC)
PAD........... Pontoon Assembly Depot   (NVT)
PAD........... Pontoon Assembly Detachment
PAD........... Poor Acquisition Data   (AAG)
PAD........... Port of Aerial Debarkation [*Air Force*]
PAD........... Positioning Arm Disk
PAD........... Post-Activation Diffusion   (IEEE)
PAD........... Potential Area of Danger [*Navigation*]
PAD........... Power Amplifier Device [*or Driver*]
PAD........... Preadvisory Data   (KSC)
PAD........... Precise Access Diagram
PAD........... Preferred Arrival Date   (AFM)
PAD........... Preliminary Advisory Data   (MCD)
PAD........... Presence and Amplitude Detector
PAD........... Primary Afferent Depolarization [*Electrophysiology*]
PAD........... Professional Administrative Development [*Medicine*]
PAD........... Program Action Directive   (AFM)
PAD........... Program Analysis for Documentation [*Data processing*]
PAD........... Program Approval Document [*NASA*]   (KSC)
PAD........... Project Approval Document [*NASA*]
PAD........... Propellant-Actuated Device
PAD........... Provisional Acceptance Date   (NATG)
PAD........... Public Affairs Division [*Military*]   (AABC)
PAD........... Public Assistance Director [*Federal disaster planning*]
PAD........... Pueblo Army Depot [*Colorado*]
PAD........... Pulmonary Artery Diastolic [*Pressure*] [*Cardiology*]
PAD........... Pulsatile Assist Device [*Cardiology*]
PAD........... Pulse Averaging Discriminator
PAD........... Pulsed Amperometric Detection [*Electroanalytical chemistry*]
PADA .... Payroll Automation for Department of Agriculture
PADA .... Pharmacists Against Drug Abuse [*Spring House, PA*]   (EA)
PADA .... Prespin Automatic Dynamic Alignment

PADA .... Public Address Assembly [*Ground Communications Facility, NASA*]
PADA .... (Pyridylazo)dimethylaniline [*Organic chemistry*]
PADAC...... Professional Art Dealers Association of Canada
PADAF...... Pacific Command Air Defense Analysis Facility   (CINC)
PADAL...... Pattern for Analysis, Decision, Action, and Learning
PADAR...... Passive Airborne Detection and Ranging
PADAR...... Program Approval Disposal and Redistribution [*Army*]   (AABC)
PADAT...... Psychological Abstracts Direct Access Terminal
PADC........ Pennsylvania Avenue Development Corporation [*Washington, DC*] [*Federal corporation*]
PA D & C .... Pennsylvania District and County Reports   (DLA)
PA D & C 2d ... Pennsylvania District and County Reports, Second Series   (DLA)
PA D & C 3d ... Pennsylvania District and County Reports, Third Series   (DLA)
PA D & C Rep ... Pennsylvania District and County Reports   (DLA)
PADD .... Petroleum Administration for Defense District [*Department of Energy*]
PADD .... Planned Active Duty Date [*Military*]
PADD .... Portable Acoustic Doppler Detector
PADDS...... Procurement Automated Data Document System [*Military*]   (RDA)
PADEL....... Pattern Description Language
PA Dent J... Pennsylvania Dental Journal [*A publication*]
PA Dep Environ Resour Water Resour Bull ... Pennsylvania. Department of Environmental Resources. Water Resources Bulletin [*A publication*]
PA Dep For Waters Water Resour Bull ... Pennsylvania. Department of Forests and Waters. Water Resources Bulletin [*A publication*]
PA Dep L & I Dec ... Pennsylvania Department of Labor and Industry Decisions   (DLA)
PA Dep Rep ... Pennsylvania Department Reports   (DLA)
PA Dept Int Affairs Monthly Bull ... Pennsylvania. Department of Internal Affairs. Monthly Bulletin [*A publication*]
PADESM .... Parti des Desherites de Madagascar [*Party of the Deprived of Madagascar*]
PADF........ Pan American Development Foundation [*Washington, DC*]   (EA)
PADGERC ... PACOM [*Pacific Command*] Air Defense Ground Environment Requirements Committee   (CINC)
PADGT....... Past Assistant Deputy Grand Treasurer [*Freemasonry*]
PADI.......... Parti pour l'Avancement de la Democratie en Ituri [*Party for Democratic Advancement in Ituri*]
PADI.......... Professional Association of Diving Instructors
Padiatr Pad ... Paediatrie und Paedologie [*A publication*]
Padin.......... Partido de Integracion Nacional [*National Integration Party*] [*Peruvian*]   (PPW)
PADIS .... Pan-African Documentation and Information System [*Economic Commission for Africa*] [*United Nations*] [*Addis Ababa, Ethiopia*]   (EISS)
PA Dist....... Pennsylvania District Reporter   (DLA)
PA Dist & Co ... Pennsylvania District and County   (DLA)
PA Dist & Co R ... Pennsylvania District and County Reports   (DLA)
PA Dist & Co Repts ... Pennsylvania District and County Reports   (DLA)
PA Dist & C Rep ... Pennsylvania District and County Reports   (DLA)
PA Dist R... Pennsylvania District Reporter   (DLA)
PA Dist Rep ... Pennsylvania District Reports   (DLA)
PADL........ Part and Assembly Description Language [*Data processing*]
PADL........ Pilotless Aircraft Development Laboratory [*Navy*]
PADLA ...... Programable Asynchronous Dual Line Adapter
PADLOC .... Passive Active Detection and Location   (IEEE)
PADLOC .... Passive Detection and Location of Countermeasures [*Air Force*]
PADMIS ..... Patient Administration Information System [*Military*]   (AABC)
PADO .... Proposed Advanced Development Objective [*Army*]   (AABC)
PADOC....... Pay Adjustment Document
PADP........ Physicians Against the Death Penalty   (EA)
PADP......... Proposal for Advanced Development Program
PA Dp Agr An Rp ... Pennsylvania. Department of Agriculture. Annual Report [*A publication*]
PADR......... Parts and Data Record System   (MCD)
PA DR........ Pennsylvania District Reports   (DLA)
PADR......... Preferential Arrival/Departure Route [*Aviation*]   (FAAC)
PADR......... Production Administration Deficiency Report [*DoD*]
PADRA...... Pass to Air Defense RADAR   (FAAC)
PADRE ...... Patient Automatic Data Recording Equipment   (IEEE)
PADRES.... Padres Asociados para Derechos, Religiosos, Educativos, y Sociales [*Organization of Mexican-American priests*]
PADS......... Passive-Active Data Simulation
PADS......... Passive Advanced Sonobuoy
PADS......... Performance Analysis and Design Synthesis [*Computer program*] [*NASA*]
PADS......... Personnel Automated Data System [*TIMMS*] [*Navy*]
PADS......... Plant Alarm and Display System   (NRCH)
PADS......... Position and Azimuth Determining System [*Aviation*]
PADS......... Precision Aerial Display System
PADS......... Programer Advanced Debugging System [*Data processing*]
PADS......... Publications. American Dialect Society [*A publication*]

PADSD ...... Proceedings. Analytical Division. Chemical Society [*A publication*]
PADT .... Postalloy Diffusion Transistor
PADUD ...... Program of Advanced Professional Development, University of Denver College of Law   (DLA)
PAE .... Everett, WA [*Location identifier*] [*FAA*]   (FAAL)
PAE .... Executive Air Charter [*San Jose, CA*] [*FAA designator*]   (FAAC)
PAE .... Paea [*Society Islands*] [*Seismograph station code, US Geological Survey*]   (SEIS)
P AE .... Partes Aequales [*Equal Parts*] [*Pharmacy*]
PAE .... Passed Assistant Engineer [*British*]
PAE .... Peoria & Eastern Railway [*Absorbed into Consolidated Rail Corp.*] [*AAR code*]
PAE .... Phase Angle Error
PAE .... Phthalic Acid Esters [*Organic chemistry*]
PAE .... Physical Aptitude Examination   (AFM)
PAE .... Pioneer Systems, Inc. [*American Stock Exchange symbol*]
PAE .... Port of Aerial Embarkation [*Air Force*]
PAE .... Post-Accident Environment [*Nuclear energy*]   (IEEE)
PAE .... Preliminary Airworthiness Evaluations
PAE .... Preliminary Army Evaluation   (MCD)
PAE .... Preventive Action Engineer   (NASA)
PAE .... Problem Assessment Engineering   (NASA)
PA & E .... Program Analysis and Evaluation
PAE .... Public Affairs Event   (NVT)
PAEAC ...... Parliamentary Association for Euro-Arab Cooperation   (EA)
PAEC .... Philippines Atomic Energy Commission
PAECT ...... Pollution Abatement and Environmental Control Technology   (AABC)
PAED .... Paediatric [*or Paediatrics*]
PAED .... Plans, Analysis, and Evaluation Division [*Army*]   (MCD)
Paedag Hist ... Paedagogica Historica [*A publication*]
Paedagogica Hist ... Paedagogica Historica [*A publication*]
Paedagog Run ... Paedagogische Rundschau [*A publication*]
Paediatr Fortbildungskurse Prax ... Paediatrische Fortbildungskurse fuer die Praxis [*A publication*]
Paediatr Grenzgeb ... Paediatrie und Grenzgebiete [*A publication*]
Paediatr Indones ... Paediatrica Indonesiana [*A publication*]
Paediatr Paedol ... Paediatrie und Paedologie [*A publication*]
Paediatr Paedol (Suppl) ... Paediatrie und Paedologie (Supplementum) [*A publication*]
PAEDP ...... Pulmonary Artery End-Diastolic Pressure [*Cardiology*]
PAEI .... Periscope Azimuth Error Indicator
PAEI .... Purchasing Agents of the Electronic Industry [*Rosedale, NY*]   (EA)
PAEL .... Preliminary Allowance Equipage List [*Military*]   (CAAL)
PA Elec Ass Eng Sect Transm Distrib ... Pennsylvania Electric Association. Engineering Section. Transmission and Distribution Committee. Minutes [*A publication*]
PA Electr Assoc Annu Rep ... Pennsylvania Electric Association. Annual Report [*A publication*]
PA Electr Assoc Eng Sect Minutes Meet ... Pennsylvania Electric Association. Engineering Section. Minutes of the Meeting [*A publication*]
PAEM .... Program Analysis and Evaluation Model   (IEEE)
PA Energy Ext Serv News ... Pennsylvania Energy Extension Service. News [*A publication*]
PAEP .... Preliminary Annual Engineering Plan [*Military*]   (AFIT)
P AEQ .... Partes Aequales [*Equal Parts*] [*Pharmacy*]
PAES .... Phenyl(aminoethyl)sulfide [*Biochemistry*]
PAES .... Publications. Princeton University Archaeological Expeditions to Syria [*A publication*]
PAET .... Planetary Atmosphere Experimental [*or Experiments*] Test [*NASA*]
PAF .... Pacific Air Forces
PAF .... Pacific American Airlines, Inc. [*Burbank, CA*] [*FAA designator*]   (FAAC)
PAF .... Pacific Aqua Foods Ltd. [*Toronto Stock Exchange symbol*] [*Vancouver Stock Exchange symbol*]
PAF .... Page Address Field
PAF .... Pan American Foundation [*Defunct*]   (EA)
PAF .... Payload Attachment Fitting
PAF .... Peak Annual Funding   (NASA)
PA F .... Pennsylvania Folklife [*A publication*]
PA & F .... Percussion, Auscultation, and Fremitus [*Medicine*]
PAF .... Performing Arts Foundation   (EA)
PAF .... Peripheral Address Field
PAF .... Personal Article Floater [*Air baggage insurance*]
PAF .... Philippine Air Force
PAF .... Platelet-Activating Factor [*Hematology*]
PAF .... Platelet Aggregation Factor [*Hematology*]
PAF .... Polaris Accelerated Flight [*Chamber*] [*Missiles*]
PAF .... Port-Aux-Francais [*Kerguelen Islands*] [*Seismograph station code, US Geological Survey*] [*Closed*]   (SEIS)
PAF .... Portable Arc Furnace
PAF .... Portuguese Air Force
PAF .... Preadmission Assessment Form [*Health Care Financing Administration*]
PAF .... Prearranged Fire
PAF .... Preatomized Fuel [*Trademark*] [*Petroform product*]

PAF .... Premature Anti-Fascist [*World War II designation used by Army Counterintelligence Department*]
PAF .... Price Analysis File   (AFIT)
PAF .... Printed and Fired Circuit
PAF .... Pro-American Forum   (EA)
PAF .... Production Assembly Facility
PAF .... Pseudo-Archaic Forgery
PAF .... Pseudoamniotic Fluid [*Gynecology*]
PAF .... Psychoanalytic Assistance Fund [*New York, NY*]   (EA)
PAF .... Public Agenda Foundation   (EA)
PAF .... Public Art Fund   (EA)
PAF .... Publication Authority Form   (AAG)
PAF .... Pulmonary Arteriovenous Fistula [*Medicine*]
PAFA .... Pan-American Festival Association   (EA)
PAFAM ...... Performance and Failure Assessment Monitor   (MCD)
PAFAMS ... Pan American Federation of Associations of Medical Schools [*See also FEPAFEM*]   (EA-IO)
PA Farm Econ ... Pennsylvania Farm Economics [*A publication*]
PAFATU ..... Pan-African Federation of Agricultural Trade Unions   (EA)
PAFB .... Patrick Air Force Base [*Florida*]
PAFC .... Paul Anka Fan Club   (EA)
PAFC .... Phase-Locked Automatic Frequency Control [*Telecommunications*]
PAFC .... Phosphoric Acid Fuel Cell [*Energy source*]
PAFCS ...... Prior Active Foreign Commissioned Service
PAFE .... Place Accepted for Enlistment
PAFEA .... Patologiches'kaia Fiziologiia i Eksperimental'naia Terapiia [*A publication*]
PAFES .... Pan American Federation of Engineering Societies
PA Fid .... Pennsylvania Fiduciary Reporter   (DLA)
PA Fiduc ..... Pennsylvania Fiduciary Reporter   (DLA)
PAFMECSA ... Pan African Freedom Movement for East, Central, and Southern Africa [*Superseded in 1963 by the liberation committee of the Organization of African Unity*]   (PD)
PA Folklife ... Pennsylvania Folklife [*A publication*]
PA For .... Pennsylvania Forests [*A publication*]
PA Fruit News ... Pennsylvania Fruit News [*A publication*]
PAFS .... Primary Air Force Specialty
PAFS .... Publications. American Folklore Society [*A publication*]
PAFSC ...... Primary Air Force Specialty Code
PAFT .... Polish American Folk Theatre
PAFVA .... Polish Air Force Veterans Association   (EA)
PAG .... I Pagliacci [*Opera*]   (DSUE)
PAG .... Pagadian [*Philippines*] [*Airport symbol*]   (OAG)
PAG .... Paget Resources Ltd. [*Vancouver Stock Exchange symbol*]
Pag .... Pagoda
PAG .... Panagjuriste [*Bulgaria*] [*Geomagnetic observatory code*]
PAG .... Parts Acquisition Group
PAG .... Party for the Autonomy of Gibraltar   (PPW)
PAG .... Periaqueductal Gray Matter [*Brain anatomy*]
PAG .... Polyacrylamide Gel [*Analytical chemistry*]
PAg .... Poultry-Related Antigens [*Immunology*]
PAG .... Poverty Advisory Group
PAG .... Precision Alignment Gyrocompass
PAG .... Precursor Active Galaxies
PAG .... Pregnancy-Associated alpha-Glycoprotein [*Gynecology*]
PAG .... Preliminary Analysis Group   (NATG)
PAG .... Professional Activities Group
PAG .... Professional Auto Group, Inc.
PAG .... Program Assessment Guide [*Department of Labor*]   (OICC)
PAG .... Progress Analysis Group [*Navy*]   (MCD)
PAG .... Project Advisory Group [*Army*]
PAG .... Property Advisory Group [*British*]
PAG .... Protective Action Guide [*Federal Radiation Council*]
PAG .... Protein Advisory Group [*United Nations*]
PAG .... Protein-Calorie Advisory Group [*United Nations*]
PAG .... Spring Garden College, Philadelphia, PA [*OCLC symbol*]   (OCLC)
PAGA .... Pan American Grace Airways, Inc. [*Also, PANAGRA*]
PaGa .... Printing and Graphic Arts [*A publication*]
PAGAA .... Pesquisa Agropecuaria Brasileira. Serie Agronomia [*A publication*]
PAGAN ...... Pattern Generation Language [*Data processing*]
PAGDC ...... Past Assistant Grand Director of Ceremonies [*Freemasonry*]   (ROG)
PAGE .... Page America Group [*NASDAQ symbol*]   (NQ)
Page .... Page's Three Early Assize Rolls, County of Northumberland [*Surtees Society Publications, Vol. 88*]   (DLA)
PAGE .... PERT [*Program Evaluation and Review Technique*] Automated Graphical Extension   (KSC)
PAGE .... Philatelic Association of Government Employees
PAGE .... Piston Arrestment Gas Entrapment System [*SPRINT launch cell*]   (AABC)
PAGE .... Polyacrylamide Gel Electrophoresis [*Analytical chemistry*]
PAGE .... Preliminary Automated Ground Environment
Page Contr ... Page on Contracts   (DLA)
PAGEL ...... Priced Aerospace Ground Equipment List
PA Gen As ... Pennsylvania General Assembly [*A publication*]
PA Geol ...... Pennsylvania Geology [*A publication*]
PA Geol Surv Atlas ... Pennsylvania. Geological Survey. Atlas [*A publication*]

PA Geol Surv Gen Geol Rep ... Pennsylvania. Geological Survey. General Geology Report [*A publication*]
PA Geol Surv Inf Circ ... Pennsylvania. Geological Survey. Information Circular [*A publication*]
PA Geol Surv Miner Resour Rep ... Pennsylvania. Geological Survey. Mineral Resource Report [*A publication*]
PA Geol Surv Prog Rep ... Pennsylvania. Geological Survey. Progress Report [*A publication*]
PA Geol Surv Water Resour Rep ... Pennsylvania. Geological Survey. Water Resource Report [*A publication*]
PAGEOS .... Passive Geodetic Earth-Orbiting Satellite [*NASA*]
PA-Ger .... Pennsylvania-German [*A publication*]
PAGES .... Program Affinity Grouping and Evaluation System
PAGI .... Photographic and Gelatin Industries [*Japan*]
PAGICEP ... Petroleum and Gas Industry Communications Emergency Plan [*FCC*]
PAGL .... Pulsed Argon Gas LASER
PAGMK ...... Primary African Green Monkey Kidney [*Cells*]
PAGO .... Pacific Gold & Uranium [*NASDAQ symbol*] (NQ)
PAGS .... Parti de l'Avant-Garde Socialiste [*Socialist Vanguard Party*] [*Algerian*] (PD)
PA G S .... Pennsylvania. Geological Survey [*A publication*]
PAGS .... Polish-American Guardian Society (EA)
PAGS .... Proceedings. Australian Goethe Society [*A publication*]
PAGTU ...... Pan-American Ground Training Unit
PAGVA ...... Progres Agricole et Viticole [*A publication*]
PAGYB ...... Pennsylvania Geology [*A publication*]
PAH .... Paducah [*Kentucky*] [*Airport symbol*] (OAG)
PAH .... Pahoa [*Hawaii*] [*Seismograph station code, US Geological Survey*] [*Closed*] (SEIS)
PAH .... Panorama Air Tour, Inc. [*Honolulu, HI*] [*FAA designator*] (FAAC)
PAH .... Para-Aminohippuric [*Biochemistry*]
PAH .... Parts Application Handbook
PAH .... Payload Accommodations Handbook [*NASA*] (NASA)
PAH .... Phase Adjusting Hub
PAH .... Phenylalanine Hydroxylase [*An enzyme*]
PAH .... Polycyclic [*or Polynuclear*] Aromatic Hydrocarbon [*Organic chemistry*]
PAH .... Pulmonary Artery Hypertension [*Medicine*]
PAH .... Push and Hold [*Push button*]
PAHA .... Para-Aminohippuric Acid
PAHA .... Polish American Historical Association (EA)
Pahasapa Q ... Pahasapa Quarterly [*A publication*]
PAHBAH .... Para-Hydroxybenzoic Acid Hydrazide [*Organic chemistry*]
PAHC .... Pan American Highway Congresses
PAHC .... Pontifical Association of the Holy Childhood (EA)
PAHEA ...... Pharmaceutica Acta Helvetiae [*A publication*]
PAHEF .... Pan American Health and Education Foundation [*Washington, DC*] (EA)
PAHEL .... Pay Records and Health Records
PA His ...... Pennsylvania History [*A publication*]
PA Hist ...... Pennsylvania History [*A publication*]
PAHL .... Pressure Alarm, High-Limit [*Nuclear energy*] (NRCH)
Pahlavi Med J ... Pahlavi Medical Journal [*A publication*]
PAHO .... Pan American Health Organization [*OAS*]
PAHO .... PanAmerican Health Organization [*Washington, DC*] (EA)
PAHO .... Paraho Development Corp. [*NASDAQ symbol*] (NQ)
PAHR .... Post Accident Heat Removal [*Nuclear energy*]
PAHS .... Passive Annual Heat Storage [*Housing technology*]
PAI .... Pacific Aerospace Index (DIT)
PAI .... Pacific American Income Shares, Inc. [*NYSE symbol*]
PAI .... Pacific American Institute (EA)
PAI .... Pacoima, CA [*Location identifier*] [*FAA*] (FAAL)
Pai .... Paige's New York Chancery Reports (DLA)
Pai .... Paine's United States Circuit Court Reports (DLA)
PAI .... Parti Africain de l'Independance [*African Independence Party*] [*Senegalese*] (PPW)
PAI .... Parts Application Information
PAI .... Passive-Aggressive Index [*Psychology*]
PAI .... Percent Adherence Index
PAI .... Personal Accident Insurance
PAI .... Personal Adjustment Inventory [*Psychology*]
PAI .... Personnel Accreditation Institute [*Alexandria, VA*] (EA)
PAI .... Phosphate Adsorption Index [*Analytical chemistry*]
PAI .... Photographic Administrators, Incorporated [*Glenhead, NY*] (EA)
PAI .... Piedmont Aviation, Incorporated [*Air carrier designation symbol*]
PAI .... Pirchei Agudath Israel (EA)
PA & I .... Planning, Analysis, and Integration
PAI .... Plunger Actuated Indexer
PAI .... Poale Agudath Israel of America (EA)
PAI .... Polish Assistance, Incorporated [*An association*] (EA)
PAI .... Polyamide-Imide [*Organic chemistry*]
PAI .... Prearrival Inspection
PAI .... Precise Angle Indicator
PAI .... Processed Apples Institute (EA)
PAI .... Production Adjustment Index [*Word processing*]
PAI .... Professional Athletes International (EA)
PAI .... Programer Appraisal Instrument [*Data processing*] (IEEE)

PAI .... Property Agents International
PAI .... Public Affairs Information, Inc. [*Sacramento, CA*] [*Database producer*] [*Information service*]
PAI .... Public Affairs Institute [*Defunct*] (EA)
PAI .... Public Assistance Information [*A publication*]
PAIAA .... Proceedings. National Academy of Sciences (India). Section A [*A publication*]
PAIB .... Polish-American Information Bureau [*Later, PATIB*] (EA)
PAIC .... Persia and Iraq Command [*World War II*]
PAIC .... Public Address Intercom System (NRCH)
PAICC .... Professional Association of the Interstate Commerce Commission
Pai Ch .... Paige's New York Chancery Reports (DLA)
PAID .... Pan African Institute for Development [*Douala, Cameroon*] (EA-IO)
PAID .... Personnel and Accounting Integrated Data [*System*] [*Veterans Administration*]
PAID .... Price and Item Display [*British*]
Paideia Studies in Nature of Modern Math ... Paideia Studies in the Nature of Modern Mathematics [*A publication*]
PAIDOL ...... Paidologist [*A publication*]
PAIDS .... Pediatric Acquired Immune Deficiency Syndrome [*Medicine*]
PAIF .... Persia and Iraq Force [*World War II*]
PAIg .... Platelet Associated Immunoglobulin [*Hematology*]
PAIGC .... Partido Africano da Independencia da Guine e do Cabo Verde [*African Party for the Independence of Guinea and Cape Verde*] (PPW)
Paige .... Paige's New York Chancery Reports (DLA)
Paige Ch ... Paige's New York Chancery Reports [*1828-45*] (DLA)
Paige Ch Rep ... Paige's New York Chancery Reports (DLA)
Paige's Ch ... Paige's New York Chancery Reports (DLA)
PAIgG .... Platelet-Associated Immunoglobulin G [*Hematology*]
PAIGH .... Pan American Institute of Geography and History [*OAS*]
PAIL .... Post Attack Intercontinental Link
PAILS .... Projectile Airburst and Impact Location System
PAIM .... Parti Africain pour l'Independance des Masses [*African Party for the Independence of the Masses*] [*Senegalese*] (PPW)
PAIM .... Primary Air Inlet Muffler (MCD)
PAIMEG ..... Pan American Institute of Mining, Engineering, and Geology [*Defunct*]
Paine .... Paine's United States Circuit Court Reports (DLA)
Paine CC .... Paine's United States Circuit Court Reports (DLA)
Paine CCR ... Paine's United States Circuit Court Reports (DLA)
Paine Cir Ct R ... Paine's United States Circuit Court Reports (DLA)
Paine Elect ... Paine on Elections (DLA)
Pain Fr .... Pain Francais [*A publication*]
Pain Suppl ... Pain. Supplement [*A publication*]
Paint .... Paintbrush [*A publication*]
PAINT .... Painting (ROG)
PAINT .... Post Attack Intelligence
PAINT .... Primera Asociacion Internacional de Noticieros y Television [*First International Newsreel and TV Association*]
Paint Colour Rec ... Paint and Colour Record [*A publication*]
Paint Decor ... Painting and Decorating [*A publication*]
Painters J ... Painters and Allied Trades Journal [*A publication*]
Paint Ind ..... Paint Industry [*A publication*]
Paint Ind Mag ... Paint Industry Magazine [*A publication*]
Painting Technol (Tokyo) ... Painting Technology (Tokyo) [*A publication*]
Paint J .... Paint Journal [*A publication*]
Paint J .... Paint Journal of Australia and New Zealand [*A publication*]
Paint J Aust NZ ... Paint Journal of Australia and New Zealand [*A publication*]
Paint Manuf ... Paint Manufacture [*England*] [*A publication*]
Paint Oil Colour J ... Paint Oil and Colour Journal [*A publication*]
Paints Pak ... Paints in Pakistan [*A publication*]
Paint Technol ... Paint Technology [*A publication*]
Paint Varn Prod ... Paint and Varnish Production [*A publication*]
PAIP .... Production Acceleration Insurance Program
PAIP .... Public Affairs and Information Program [*Atomic Industrial Forum*] (NRCH)
PAIR .... Performance and Improved Reliability
PAIR .... Performance and Integration Retrofit
PAIR .... Precision Approach Interferometer RADAR (MCD)
PAIR .... Procurement Automated Integrated Requirements (MCD)
PAIR .... Psychological Audit for Interpersonal Relations [*Psychology*]
PAIRC .... Polish American Immigration and Relief Committee (EA)
PAIRS .... Product Assurance Information Retrieval System [*Boeing*]
PAIRS .... Program for the Analysis of Infrared Spectra [*Computer program*] [*Analytical chemistry*]
PAIS .... Padre Island National Seashore [*National Park Service designation*]
PAIS .... Partido Autentico Institucional Salvadoreno [*Salvadoran Authentic Institutional Party*] (PPW)
PAIS .... Personnel Authentication Identification System (MCD)
PAIS .... Petroleum Abstracts Information Services [*University of Tulsa*] [*Oklahoma*] [*Information service*] (EISS)
PAIS .... Project Analysis Information System [*Agency for International Development*]
PAIS .... Prototype Advanced Indicator System (MCD)
PAIS .... Psychological Abstracts Information Services [*American Psychological Association*]

PAIS .... Public Affairs Information Service [*New York, NY*] [*Bibliographic database*] [*A publication*]

PAIT .... Program for Advancement of Industrial Technology [*Canada*]

PAIX .... Pacific Alaska Airlines [*Air carrier designation symbol*]

PA J .... American Academy of Physicians' Assistants. Journal [*A publication*]

PAJ .... Kansas City, MO [*Location identifier*] [*FAA*]   (FAAL)

PA J .... PA Journal [*Formerly, Physician's Associate*] [*A publication*]

PAJ .... Pan-African Journal [*A publication*]

PAJ .... Performing Arts Journal [*A publication*]

PAJA .... Parachute Jumping Activity   (FAAC)

PAJAR .... Parti Rakyat Jati Sarawak [*Sarawak Native People's Party*] [*Malaysian*]   (PPW)

PAJHS .... Publication. American Jewish Historical Society [*A publication*]

PAK .... Hanapepe, HI [*Location identifier*] [*FAA*]   (FAAL)

PAK .... Pacific Alaska Airlines [*Fairbanks, AK*] [*FAA designator*]   (FAAC)

PAK .... Pakistan [*Three-letter standard code*]   (CNC)

PAK .... Panzer Abwehr Kanone [*Cannon Against Armor*] [*German antitank gun*]

PAK .... Polycyclic Aromatic Ketone [*Organic chemistry*]

PAK .... Power Amplifier Klystron

PAK .... Program Attention Key [*Data processing*]   (BUR)

Pak Assoc Adv Sci Annu Rep ... Pakistan Association for the Advancement of Science. Annual Report [*A publication*]

Pak Bar J .... Pakistan Bar Journal   (DLA)

Pak Cottons ... Pakistan Cottons [*A publication*]

Pak Crim LJ ... Pakistan Criminal Law Journal   (DLA)

Pak Dent Rev ... Pakistan Dental Review [*A publication*]

Pak Dev R ... Pakistan Development Review [*A publication*]

Pak Dev Rev ... Pakistan Development Review [*A publication*]

Pak DR .... Pakistan Development Review [*A publication*]

Pak Geogr Rev ... Pakistan Geographical Review [*A publication*]

Pak Geol Surv Inf Release ... Pakistan Geological Survey. Information Release [*A publication*]

Pak Geol Surv Rec ... Pakistan Geological Survey. Records [*A publication*]

PAKISTAN ... Nation in Asia, the name of which is said to be coined from Punjab (P), Afghan border states (A), Kashmir (K), Sind (S), and Baluchistan (TAN). Name also means "land of the pure" in Hindustani.

Pakistan Develop R ... Pakistan Development Review [*A publication*]

Pakistan Econ and Social R ... Pakistan Economic and Social Review [*A publication*]

Pakistan Eng ... Pakistan Engineer [*A publication*]

Pakistan J Biol Agr Sci ... Pakistan Journal of Biological and Agricultural Sciences [*A publication*]

Pakistan J For ... Pakistan Journal of Forestry [*A publication*]

Pakistan J Med Res ... Pakistan Journal of Medical Research [*A publication*]

Pakistan J Sci ... Pakistan Journal of Science [*A publication*]

Pakistan J Sci Ind Res ... Pakistan Journal of Scientific and Industrial Research [*A publication*]

Pakistan J Sci Res ... Pakistan Journal of Scientific Research [*A publication*]

Pakistan J Soil Sci ... Pakistan Journal of Soil Sciences [*A publication*]

Pakistan Lib Bull ... Pakistan Library Bulletin [*A publication*]

Pakistan Lib R ... Pakistan Library Review [*A publication*]

Pakistan Phil J ... Pakistan Philosophical Journal [*A publication*]

Pakist J Agric Sci ... Pakistan Journal of Agricultural Sciences [*A publication*]

Pakist J Bot ... Pakistan Journal of Botany [*A publication*]

Pakist J Scient Res ... Pakistan Journal of Scientific Research [*A publication*]

Pakist J Zool ... Pakistan Journal of Zoology [*A publication*]

Pak J Agric Sci ... Pakistan Journal of Agricultural Sciences [*A publication*]

Pak J Agri Res ... Pakistan Journal of Agricultural Research [*A publication*]

Pak J Biochem ... Pakistan Journal of Biochemistry [*A publication*]

Pak J Biol Agric Sci ... Pakistan Journal of Biological and Agricultural Sciences [*A publication*]

Pak J Bot .... Pakistan Journal of Botany [*A publication*]

Pak J Fam Plann ... Pakistan Journal of Family Planning [*A publication*]

Pak J For .... Pakistan Journal of Forestry [*A publication*]

Pak J Geriatr ... Pakistan Journal of Geriatrics [*A publication*]

Pak J Health ... Pakistan Journal of Health [*A publication*]

Pak J Med Res ... Pakistan Journal of Medical Research [*A publication*]

Pak J Pharm ... Pakistan Journal of Pharmacy [*A publication*]

Pak J Sci .... Pakistan Journal of Science [*A publication*]

Pak J Sci Ind Res ... Pakistan Journal of Scientific and Industrial Research [*A publication*]

Pak J Sci Res ... Pakistan Journal of Scientific Research [*A publication*]

Pak J Zool ... Pakistan Journal of Zoology [*A publication*]

Pak Libr Ass Q J ... Pakistan Library Association. Quarterly Journal [*A publication*]

Pak Libr Rev ... Pakistan Library Review [*A publication*]

Pak LR .... Pakistan Law Reports [*India*]   (DLA)

Pak L Rev ... Pakistan Law Review   (DLA)

Pak Med Forum ... Pakistan Medical Forum [*A publication*]

Pak Med J ... Pakistan Medical Journal [*A publication*]

Pak Med Rev ... Pakistan Medical Review [*A publication*]

Pak Nurs Health Rev ... Pakistan Nursing and Health Review [*A publication*]

Pak Philos Congr Proc ... Pakistan Philosophical Congress. Proceedings [*A publication*]

PakQ .... Pakistan Quarterly [*A publication*]

PakR .... Pakistan Review [*A publication*]

PAKS .... Packaging Systems Corp. [*NASDAQ symbol*]   (NQ)

Pak Sci Conf Proc ... Pakistan Science Conference. Proceedings [*A publication*]

Pak Sup Ct Q ... Pakistan Supreme Court Law Quarterly [*Lahore, Pakistan*]   (DLA)

PAKT .... Petroleum Acreage Corp. of Texas [*NASDAQ symbol*]   (NQ)

PAL .... Allegheny County Law Library, Pittsburgh, PA [*OCLC symbol*]   (OCLC)

PAL .... Pacific Aeronautical Library

PAL .... Pacific Air Lines

pal .... Pahlavi [*MARC language code*] [*Library of Congress*]   (LCCP)

PAL .... Paired-Associates Learning [*Task*] [*Psychology*]

PAL .... Palace

Pal .... Palamedes [*of Gorgias*] [*Classical studies*]   (OCD)

PAL .... Palatine [*or Palatinate*] [*Genealogy*]

PAL .... Paleography   (ROG)

PAL .... Paleontology

PAL .... Paleozoic [*Period, era, or system*] [*Geology*]

PAL .... Palestine

PAL .... Palisades [*New York*] [*Seismograph station code, US Geological Survey*]   (SEIS)

PAL .... Pallor   (KSC)

Pal .... Palmer's Assizes at Cambridge [*England*]   (DLA)

Pal .... Palmer's English King's Bench Reports [*1619-29*]   (DLA)

Pal .... Palmer's Reports [*53-60 Vermont*]   (DLA)

PAL .... Paloma Petroleum Ltd. [*Toronto Stock Exchange symbol*]

PAL .... Paradox Application Language [*ANSA*] [*Data processing*]

PAL .... Parcel Air Lift [*US Postal Service*]

PAL .... Parser Assembly Language [*Data processing*]

PAL .... Parts Authorization List   (KSC)

PAL .... Patent Associated Literature

PAL .... Pathology Laboratory [*Test*]

PAL .... Pectin Acid Lyase [*An enzyme*]

PAL .... Pedagogic Algorithmic Language [*Data processing*]

PAL .... People Against Chlordane [*Jericho, NY*]   (EA)

PAL .... People-Animals-Love [*Washington, DC*]   (EA)

PAL .... Perceptual Alternatives Laboratory [*University of Louisville*] [*Research center*]   (RCD)

PAL .... Performance Assessment Logic

PAL .... Peripheral Access Lattices

PAL .... Permanent Artificial Lighting   (IEEE)

PAL .... Permissive Action Link [*Army*]

PAL .... Permissive Arming Line [*or Link*]

PAL .... Personnel Accounting Level [*Air Force*]   (AFM)

PAL .... Personnel Airlock [*Nuclear energy*]   (NRCH)

PAL .... Personnel Augmentation List [*Military*]

PAL .... Phase Alternation Line [*West German color television system*]

PAL .... Phenylalanine Ammonia-Lyase [*An enzyme*]

PAL .... Philippine Air Lines

PAL .... Pipe Analysis Log [*Gas well*]

PAL .... Police Athletic League

PAL .... Poly-DL-alanine Poly-L-lysine [*Biochemical analysis*]

PAL .... Portable Ambush Light [*Military*] [*Australia*]   (RDA)

PAL .... Posterior Axillary Line [*Medicine*]

PAL .... Power Assist Lathe

PAL .... Preapproved Loan [*Business and trade*]

PAL .... Precision Artwork Language [*Data processing*]

PAL .... Prescribed Action Link [*DoD*]

PAL .... Present Atmospheric Level

PAL .... Price and Availability List   (CINC)

PAL .... Princeton Accelerator Laboratory

PAL .... Prisoner-at-Large

PAL .... Pro Alesia [*A publication*]

PAL .... Problem Action Log   (AAG)

PAL .... Process Assembler Language

PAL .... Process Audit List   (MCD)

PAL .... Production and Application of Light   (MCD)

PAL .... Profile Automobile League   (EA)

PAL .... Programable Algorithm Machine Assembly Language [*Data processing*]

PAL .... Programable Array Logic [*Data processing*]   (IEEE)

PAL .... Programed Application Library [*IBM Corp.*]

PAL .... Programed Audit Library

PAL .... Programer Assistance and Liaison [*Data processing*]   (NRCH)

PAL .... Progressive Alliance of Liberia   (PPW)

PAL .... Prototype Application Loop [*Nuclear energy*]   (NRCH)

PAL .... Psycho-Acoustic Laboratory [*Harvard University*]   (MCD)

PAL .... Public Archives of Canada Library [*UTLAS symbol*]

PAL .... Publications Allowance List [*Military*]   (CAAL)

PAL .... Pulsed Argon LASER

PAL .... Push and Latch [*Push button*]

PA L .... University of Pennsylvania. Law Review [*A publication*]

PALA .... N-(Phosphoacetyl)-L-aspartate [*Biochemistry*]

Pala .... Partido Laborista [*Labor Party*] [*Panamanian*]   (PPW)

PALA .... Partition Affinity Ligand Assay [*Analytical microbiology*]

PALA .... Passenger Acceptance and Load Accumulation [*Aviation*]

PALA .... Phosphonoacetyl-L-Aspartate [*Biochemistry*]

PALA .... Polish American Librarians Association   (EA)

PALAEOB ... Palaeobotany

Palaeoecol Afr Surround Isl ... Palaeoecology of Africa and the Surrounding Islands [*A publication*]
PALAEOG ... Palaeography
Palaeogeogr Palaeoclimatol Palaeoecol ... Palaeogeography, Palaeoclimatology, Palaeoecology [*A publication*]
Palaeogeo P ... Palaeogeography, Palaeoclimatology, Palaeoecology [*A publication*]
Palaeont..... Palaeontographica [*A publication*]
PALAEONT ... Palaeontology
Palaeont Abh (Dames u Kayser) ... Palaeontologische Abhandlungen (Dames und Kayser) [*A publication*]
Palaeontogr Abt A ... Palaeontographica. Abteilung A. Palaeozoologie-Stratigraphie [*A publication*]
Palaeontogr Abt A Palaeozool-Stratigr ... Palaeontographica. Abteilung A. Palaeozoologie-Stratigraphie [*A publication*]
Palaeontogr Abt B ... Palaeontographica. Abteilung B. Palaeophytologie [*A publication*]
Palaeontogr Am ... Palaeontographica Americana [*A publication*]
Palaeontogr Ital ... Palaeontographia Italia [*A publication*]
Palaeontogr Soc Monogr ... Palaeontographical Society. Monographs [*A publication*]
Palaeontogr Soc Monogr (Lond) ... Palaeontographical Society. Monographs (London) [*A publication*]
Palaeontol Afr ... Palaeontologia Africana [*A publication*]
Palaeontol Jugosl ... Palaeontologia Jugoslavica [*A publication*]
Palaeontol Mex Inst Geol (Mex) ... Palaeontologia Mexicana. Instituto de Geologia (Mexico) [*A publication*]
Palaeontol Pap Publ Geol Surv Queensl ... Palaeontology Papers. Geological Survey of Queensland [*A publication*]
Palaeontol Pol ... Palaeontologia Polonica [*A publication*]
Palaeontol Sin Ser B ... Palaeontologia Sinica. Series B [*A publication*]
Palaeontol Sin Ser C ... Palaeontologia Sinica. Series C [*A publication*]
Palaeontol Sin Ser D ... Palaeontologia Sinica. Series D [*A publication*]
Palaeontol Soc Japan Trans Proc NS ... Palaeontological Society of Japan. Transactions and Proceedings. New Series [*A publication*]
Palaeontol Soc Jpn Spec Pap ... Palaeontological Society of Japan. Special Papers [*A publication*]
Palaeontol Z ... Palaeontologische Zeitschrift [*A publication*]
Palaeont Soc Japan Trans and Proc ... Palaeontological Society of Japan. Transactions and Proceedings [*A publication*]
Palaeont Zeitschr ... Palaeontologische Zeitschrift [*A publication*]
Palaeont Zs ... Palaeontologische Zeitschrift [*A publication*]
Palaeovertebrata. Mem Extraordinaire ... Palaeovertebrata. Memoire Extraordinaire [*A publication*]
Palaeovertebr (Montp) ... Palaeovertebrata (Montpellier) [*A publication*]
Pal Ag........ Paley on Principal and Agent [*3rd ed.*] [*1833*] (DLA)
Pa Lang & Lit ... Papers on Language and Literature [*A publication*]
PALAPA ... Indonesian satellite
PALASM .... Programable Array Logic Assembler [*Data processing*] (IEEE)
PA Law J.... Pennsylvania Law Journal (DLA)
PA Law Jour ... Pennsylvania Law Journal [*Philadelphia*] (DLA)
PA Laws..... Laws of the General Assembly of the Commonwealth of Pennsylvania (DLA)
PA Law Ser ... Pennsylvania Law Series (DLA)
PALAY ...... Palabora Mining Cl A ADR [*NASDAQ symbol*] (NQ)
Pal B........ Paleontological Bulletins [*A publication*]
PALC......... Passenger Acceptance and Load Control [*Aviation*]
PALC......... Point Arguello Launch Complex
PalCl .... Palestra del Clero [*Rovigo, Italy*] [*A publication*]
PALCO ... Pan American Liaison Committee of Women's Organizations (EA)
PALCON .... Pallet-Size Container (MCD)
Pal Conv ... Paley on Summary Convictions [*10th ed.*] [*1953*] (DLA)
PALCOR.... Palestine Correspondence [*A publication*]
PALCRU .... Pay and Allowances Accrue From [*Air Force*]
PALCS ...... Permissive Action Link Cypher System (MCD)
PAL-D ...... Phase Alternation Line Delay (IEEE)
PALE .... Pelvis and Legs Elevating [*Pilot seat*]
PalEF......... Palestine Exploration Fund [*A publication*]
PA Leg Gaz ... Legal Gazette (Pennsylvania) (DLA)
PA Leg Gaz ... Legal Gazette Reports (Campbell) [*Pennsylvania*] (DLA)
PA Legis Serv ... Pennsylvania Legislative Service [*Purdon*] (DLA)
Paleobiol Cont ... Paleobiologie Continentale [*A publication*]
PALEOECOL ... Paleoecologic
PALEOGEOG ... Paleogeographic
PALEONT... Paleontologic
Paleontol Evol-Barc Inst Prov Paleontol ... Paleontologia y Evolucion-Barcelona. Instituto Provincial de Paleontologia [*A publication*]
Paleontol J ... Paleontological Journal [*A publication*]
Paleontol Mex ... Paleontologia Mexicana [*A publication*]
Paleontol Sb ... Paleontologicheskii Sbornik [*A publication*]
Paleontol Soc Mem ... Paleontological Society. Memoir [*A publication*]
Paleontol Stratigr Litol ... Paleontologiya Stratigrafiya i Litologiya [*A publication*]
Paleontol Zh ... Paleontologicheskii Zhurnal [*A publication*]
Paleont Pap Publs Geol Suv QD ... Paleontology Papers. Publications. Geological Survey of Queensland [*A publication*]
Paleont Research Lab Special Inv Rept ... Paleontological Research Laboratories. Special Investigation. Report [*A publication*]
PalEQ .... Palestine Exploration Quarterly [*A publication*]

Palest Board Sci Ind Res Rep ... Palestine Board for Scientific and Industrial Research. Reports [*A publication*]
Palest Citrogr ... Palestine Citrograph [*A publication*]
Palestine Explor Q ... Palestine Exploration Quarterly [*A publication*]
Palestine Explor Quart ... Palestine Exploration Quarterly [*A publication*]
Palest J Bot Hortic Sci ... Palestine Journal of Botany and Horticultural Science [*A publication*]
Palest J Bot Jerusalem Ser ... Palestine Journal of Botany. Jerusalem Series [*A publication*]
Palest J Bot Jerus Ser ... Palestine Journal of Botany. Jerusalem Series [*A publication*]
Palest J Bot Rehovot Ser ... Palestine Journal of Botany. Rehovot Series [*A publication*]
Palest Trib ... Palestine Tribune [*A publication*]
Pal Ex Q ..... Palestine Exploration Quarterly [*A publication*]
Paley Ag..... Paley on Principal and Agent (DLA)
Paley Mor Ph ... [*William*] Paley's Moral Philosophy [*England*] (DLA)
Paley Princ & Ag ... Paley on Principal and Agent [*3rd ed.*] [*1833*] (DLA)
PA LG........ Legal Gazette (Pennsylvania) (DLA)
PA LG........ Legal Gazette Reports (Campbell) [*Pennsylvania*] (DLA)
Palgrave..... Palgrave's Proceedings in Chancery (DLA)
Palgrave..... Palgrave's Rise and Progress of the English Commonwealth (DLA)
Palg Rise Etc ... Palgrave's Rise and Progress of the English Commonwealth (DLA)
Palg Rise & Prog ... Palgrave's Rise and Progress of the English Commonwealth [*1832*] (DLA)
PALI .... Pacific and Asian Linguistics Institute [*University of Hawaii*]
PALI .... Prince Albert's Light Infantry [*Military unit*] [*British*]
PA Lib Assn Bull ... Pennsylvania Library Association. Bulletin [*A publication*]
PALINET .... Pennsylvania Area Library Network
PALINET/ULC ... PALINET and Union Library Catalogue of Pennsylvania [*Philadelphia, PA*] [*Library network*]
PALIS........ Property and Liability Information System
PalJ .... Palaestina-Jahrbuch [*A publication*]
PA LJ......... Pennsylvania Law Journal (DLA)
PA LJ......... Pennsylvania Law Journal Reports [*1842-52*] (DLA)
PalJb .... Palaestina-Jahrbuch [*A publication*]
PA LJR .... Clark's Pennsylvania Law Journal Reports (DLA)
PALL .... Pallet [*Freight*]
Palladio...... Palladio Rivista di Storia dell Architettura [*A publication*]
Pall Mall M ... Pall Mall Magazine [*A publication*]
Palm.......... Palmer's Assizes at Cambridge [*England*] (DLA)
Palm.......... Palmer's English King's Bench Reports [*1619-29*] (DLA)
Palm.......... Palmer's Reports [*53-60 Vermont*] (DLA)
PALM .... Palmistry (ADA)
Palm.......... Palmyrene (BJA)
PALM .... Precision Altitude and Landing Monitor [*Aircraft location*]
Palm Comp L ... Palmer's Company Law [*22nd ed.*] [*1976*] (DLA)
Palm Comp Prec ... Palmer's Company Precedents [*17th ed.*] [*1956-60*] (DLA)
Palmer .... Palmer's Assizes at Cambridge [*England*] (DLA)
Palmer .... Palmer's English King's Bench Reports (DLA)
Palmer Co Prec ... Palmer's Company Precedents [*16 eds.*] [*1877-1952*] (DLA)
Palmer Pr Comp ... Palmer's Private Companies [*41st ed.*] [*1950*] (DLA)
Palm Pr Lords ... Palmer's Practice in the House of Lords [*1830*] (DLA)
PALMS .... Provisioning Automated Logistics Material System (MCD)
Palm Sh ..... Palmer's Shareholders [*34th ed.*] [*1936*] (DLA)
Palm Wr ..... Palmer's Law of Wreck [*1843*] (DLA)
PALO......... Port Amenities Liaison Officer [*British*] (DSUE)
PALOS .... Pacific Logistic Operations - Streamline [*Army*]
PALP .... Palpable [*Medicine*]
PALP .... Pyridoxal Phosphate [*Also, PLP*] [*Biochemistry*]
PALPI .... Palpitation [*Medicine*]
palpit......... Palpitation [*Medicine*]
PALR .... Permissive Action Link Report [*Army*] (AABC)
PA L Rec ..... Pennsylvania Law Record (DLA)
PA L Rev .... University of Pennsylvania. Law Review [*A publication*]
PALS .... Patient Advocacy Legal Service [*An association*] [*Defunct*] (EA)
PA LS .... Pennsylvania Law Series (DLA)
PALS .... Permissive Action Link System [*Army*]
PALS .... Phase Alternation Line Simple [*TV decoding system*]
PALS .... Photo Area and Location System (NASA)
PALS .... Point Arguello Launch Site (AAG)
PALS .... Precision Approach and Landing System (NASA)
PALSb .... Prestaged Ammunition Loading System [*Army*] (RDA)
PalSb .... Palestinskii Sbornik [*Moscow/Leningrad*] [*A publication*]
Pal Sbor .... Palestinskii Sbornik [*A publication*]
PA L Ser ..... Pennsylvania Law Series (DLA)
PALS-G...... Passive Artillery Locating System - Ground Based (MCD)
PALSG....... Personnel and Logistics Systems Group [*Military*] (AABC)
PALSGR..... Palsgrave Dictionary [*A publication*]
PAlt .... Altoona Area Public Library, Altoona, PA [*Library symbol*] [*Library of Congress*] (LCLS)
PALT .... Present Altitude [*Aviation*] (FAAC)
PALT .... Procurement Administrative Lead Time

PALTREU... Palaestina Treuhandstelle zur Beratung Deutscher Juden [*A publication*]

PALU.......... Progressive Arbeiders- en Landbouwersunie [*Progressive Workers' and Farm Laborers' Union*] [*Surinamese*] (PPW)

Palyaval Tanacs ... Palyavalasztasi Tanacsadas [*A publication*]

Palynol Bull ... Palynological Bulletin [*A publication*]

PAM .... Palermo [*California*] [*Seismograph station code, US Geological Survey*] (SEIS)

PAM .... Palestine Archaeological Museum [*Jerusalem*] (BJA)

PAM .... Pamour, Inc. [*Toronto Stock Exchange symbol*]

Pam............ Pampa [*Record label*] [*Brazil*]

PAM .... Pamphlet (AFM)

PAM .... Panama City, FL [*Location identifier*] [*FAA*] (FAAL)

PAM .... Panoramic

PAM .... Parameter Adjusting Mechanism

PAM .... Parametric Amplifier (NATG)

PAM .... Parents Against Molesters [*Norfolk, VA*] (EA)

PAM .... Partitioned Access Method [*Data processing*]

PAM .... Payload Assist Module (MCD)

PA M........... Pennsylvania Magazine of History and Biography [*A publication*]

PAM .... People's Action Movement [*Nevisian*] (PPW)

PAM .... People's Anti-War Mobilization (EA)

PAM .... Performance Analysis Model (MCD)

PAM .... Performing Arts Medicine

PAM .... Peripheral Adapter Module

PAM .... Personal Accounting Management

PAM .... Personal Applications Manager [*Hewlett-Packard Co.*]

PAM .... Personnel Action Memorandum [*Military*]

PAM .... Phase-Amplitude Modulation

PAM .... Phased Array Module

PAM .... Philosophies, Ancient and Modern [*A publication*]

PAM .... Phoenix Airborne Missile

PAM .... Pittsburgh, Allegheny & McKees Rocks Railroad Co. [*AAR code*]

PAM .... Planning, Activation, Modification [*Army reorganization*]

PAM .... Pole Amplitude Modulation (IEEE)

PAM .... Portable Alpha Monitor

PAM .... Portable Automated Mesonet [*Meteorology*]

PAM .... Position and Altitude Monitor (MCD)

PAM .... Post-Accident Monitoring [*Nuclear energy*] (NRCH)

PAM .... Postacceptance Modification

PAM .... Potential Acuity Meter [*Instrumentation*]

PAM .... Power Assist Module [*NASA*]

PAM .... Pralidoxime Methiodide [*Biochemistry*]

PAM .... Presbyterian Association of Musicians (EA)

PAM .... Primary Access Method [*Sperry UNIVAC*]

PAM .... Primary Acquired Melanosis [*Oncology*]

PAM .... Primary Amoebic Meningitis [*or Meningoencephalitis*] [*Medicine*]

PAM .... Primary Auxiliary Memory [*Unit*] [*Data processing*] (MCD)

PAM .... Priorities and Allocations Manual [*Army*] (AABC)

PAM .... Process Automation Monitor [*Texas Instruments, Inc.*]

PAM .... Processor and Memory [*Data processing*]

PAM .... Procurement Aids Man [*Marine Corps*]

PAM .... Procurement of Aircraft and Missiles

PAM .... Program Analysis Memorandum (MCD)

PA-M .... Program Authorization - Map [*Military*] (AFIT)

PAM .... Programable Algorithm Machine [*Data processing*]

PAM .... Programme Alimentaire Mondial [*World Food Program*]

PAM .... Pulmonary Alveolar Macrophage [*Attacks inhaled particles*]

PAM .... Pulse-Address MODEM

PAM .... Pulse Amplitude Modulation [*Electronics*]

PAM .... Pyridine Aldoxime Methiodide [*Biochemistry*]

PAM .... Pyridine Aldoxime Methyl [*Pharmacology*]

PAM .... University of Pennsylvania, School of Medicine, Philadelphia, PA [*OCLC symbol*] (OCLC)

PAm .... Wissahickon Valley Public Library, Ambler, PA [*Library symbol*] [*Library of Congress*] (LCLS)

PAMA......... Pan American Medical Association [*Also known as Association Medica Pan Americana*] [*West Palm Beach, FL*] (EA)

PAMA......... Para-Dimethylaminophenylazopyridine [*An indicator*] [*Chemistry*]

PAM-A .... Payload Assist Module - Atlas Class (MCD)

PAMA......... Polish Alma Mater of America (EA)

PAMA......... Professional Aviation Maintenance Association [*St. Ann, MO*] (EA)

PAMA......... Pulse-Address Multiple Access [*Satellite communications*]

PAMAC...... Parts and Materials Accountability Control

P Am Ac Ins ... Proceedings. American Academy and Institute of Arts and Letters [*A publication*]

PA Mag Hist ... Pennsylvania Magazine of History and Biography [*A publication*]

PAMAI........ Program of Action for Mediation, Arbitration, and Inquiry [*American Library Association*]

P Am Ass Ca ... Proceedings. American Association for Cancer Research [*A publication*]

Pamatky Prir ... Pamatky a Priroda [*A publication*]

PAMC........ Pakistan Army Medical Corps

PAMC........ Provisional Acceptable Means of Compliance (MCD)

PAmC......... Temple University, Ambler Campus, Ambler, PA [*Library symbol*] [*Library of Congress*] (LCLS)

P Am Cath P ... Proceedings. American Catholic Philosophical Association [*A publication*]

PAMCCS.... Prior Active Marine Corps Commissioned Service

PAMCES.... Prior Active Marine Corps Enlisted Service

PAMCS ...... Phoenix Airborne Missile Control System

PAM-D .... Payload Assist Module - Delta Class (MCD)

PAMD........ Price and Management Data

PAMD........ Process Automation Monitor/Disk Version [*Texas Instruments, Inc.*]

Pam Div Wood Technol For Comm NSW ... Pamphlet. Division of Wood Technology. Forestry Commission. New South Wales [*A publication*]

PAMDS ...... Price and Management Data Section [*of a stock list*] [*Navy*]

PAME .... Pandemokratiki Agrotikon Metapon Ellados [*Pan-Democratic Agrarian Front of Greece*] (PPE)

PAME .... Primary Amoebic Meningoencephalitis [*Medicine*]

PA Med ..... Pennsylvania Medicine [*A publication*]

PA Med J... Pennsylvania Medical Journal [*A publication*]

PAMF .... Portable Arc Melting Furnace

PAM-FM..... Pulse Amplitude Modulation - Frequency Modulation [*Electronics*]

PAmh .... Amherst Papyri [*A publication*] (OCD)

PAMI .... Personnel Accounting Machine Installation

PAMI .... Professional Arts Management Institute (EA)

Pamiet Pulawski ... Pamietnik Pulawski [*A publication*]

Pamiet Zjazdu Otolaryngol Pol Katowicach ... Pamietnik Zjazdu Otolaryngologow Polskich w Katowicach [*A publication*]

Pam Iowa State Univ Sci Tech Coop Ext Serv ... Pamphlet. Iowa State University of Science and Technology. Cooperative Extension Service [*A publication*]

PAMIS........ Processing and Manufacturing in Space [*European Space Agency*]

PAMIS........ Psychological Operations Automated Management Information System (MCD)

PA Misc..... Pennsylvania Miscellaneous Reports (DLA)

PamL......... Pamietnik Literacki [*A publication*]

P Am Math S ... Proceedings. American Mathematical Society [*A publication*]

PAMN........ Procurement Aircraft and Missiles, Navy [*An appropriation*]

PAMO........ Port Air Materiel Office

PAMP .... Pampero [*River Plate gale*] [*Nautical term*] (DSUE)

PAMPA...... Pacific Area Movement Priority Agency [*Military*]

PamPAC .... Pamela's Political Action Committee [*Nickname of "Democrats for the '80's," a committee founded by Pamela Harriman*]

PAMPER .... Practical Application of Mid-Points for Exponential Regression

PAMPH....... Pamphlet [*Freight*]

Pamph .... Pamphleteer [*A publication*]

Pamph Amat Ent Soc ... Pamphlet Amateur Entomologists' Society [*A publication*]

Pamph Dep Agric Un S Afr ... Pamphlet. Department of Agriculture. Union of South Africa [*A publication*]

Pamph Div Sci Publs Volcani Cent Agric Res Orgn ... Pamphlet. Division of Scientific Publications. Volcani Center. Agricultural Research Organisation [*A publication*]

Pamph Div Wood Technol For Comm NSW ... Pamphlet. Division of Wood Technology. Forestry Commission. New South Wales [*A publication*]

Pamph Idaho Bur Mines Geol ... Pamphlet. Idaho Bureau of Mines and Geology [*A publication*]

P Am Phil S ... Proceedings. American Philosophical Society [*A publication*]

Pamph Laws ... Pamphlet Laws, Acts (DLA)

Pamphlet Archre ... Pamphlet Architecture [*A publication*]

Pamphl For Res Educ Proj For Dep (Sudan) ... Pamphlet. Forestry Research and Education Project. Forests Department (Khartoum, Sudan) [*A publication*]

Pamphl Laws ... Pamphlet Laws, Acts (DLA)

Pamph Volcani Inst Agric Res ... Pamphlet. Volcani Institute of Agricultural Research [*A publication*]

Pam Pulaw ... Pamietnik Pulawski [*A publication*]

Pam Pulawski ... Pamietnik Pulawski [*A publication*]

PAMPUS .... Photons for Atomic and Molecular Processes and Universal Studies [*Physics*]

PAMRF....... Palo Alto Medical Research Foundation [*Palo Alto, CA*] [*Research center*] (RCD)

PAMRS....... Parameter Adaptive Model Reference System

PAMS......... North-Holland Series in Probability and Applied Mathematics [*Elsevier Book Series*] [*A publication*]

PAMS........ Pad Abort Measuring System [*NASA*] (KSC)

PAMS........ Papers. American Musicological Society [*A publication*]

PAMS........ Portable Acoustic Monitoring System

PAMS........ Post-Accident Monitoring System [*Nuclear energy*] (NRCH)

PAMS........ Preselected Alternate Master-Slave [*Telecommunications*] (TEL)

PAMS........ Proceedings. American Mathematical Society [*A publication*]

PAMS........ Procurement Action Management System (MCD)

PAMS........ Public Access Message System

PAMSB....... Pharos of Alpha Omega Alpha Honor Medical Society [*A publication*]

P Am S Info ... Proceedings. American Society for Information Science [*A publication*]

PamSL .... Pamietnik Slowianski Czasopismo Naukowe Posiecone Slowianoznawstwu [*A publication*]

PAMTGG .... Pan Am Makes the Going Great [*Title of ballet choreographed by George Balanchine, taken from Pan American World Airways' slogan*] [*Pronounced "pam-ti-guh-guh"*]

PAMUSA .... Post Attack Mobilization of the United States Army

PAMWA ...... Pan American Medical Women's Alliance [*Jackson, MS*] (EA)

PAMX .... Pancho's Mexican Buffet [*NASDAQ symbol*] (NQ)

PAMYA ...... Proceedings. American Mathematical Society [*A publication*]

PAN .... National Action Party [*Mexico*] (PD)

PAN .... Paladin Resources Ltd. [*Vancouver Stock Exchange symbol*]

Pan .... Panache [*A publication*]

PAN .... Panama [*Three-letter standard code*] (CNC)

Pan .... Panchromatic (DEN)

Pan .... Panegyricus [*of Pliny the Younger*] [*Classical studies*] (OCD)

PAN .... Panimavida [*Chile*] [*Seismograph station code, US Geological Survey*] [*Closed*] (SEIS)

PAN .... Panis [*Bread*] [*Pharmacy*] (ROG)

pan .... Panjabi [*MARC language code*] [*Library of Congress*] (LCCP)

Pan .... Panorama [*A publication*]

PAN .... Panoramic (MSA)

Pan .... Pantheon [*Record label*] [*France, etc.*]

PAN .... Pantry (MSA)

Pan .... Pastoral Music Notebook [*A publication*]

PAN .... Pattani [*Thailand*] [*Airport symbol*] (OAG)

PAN .... Peace Action Network (EA)

PAN .... Pennsylvania Animal Network [*Coalition operated by Trans-Species Unlimited*]

PAN .... Pennsylvania Association of Notaries (EA)

PAN .... Performing Artists Network [*Electronic network*]

PAN .... Periarteritis Nodosa [*Also, PN*] [*Medicine*]

PAN .... Periodic Alternating Nystagmus [*Ophthalmology*]

PAN .... Peroxyacetyl Nitrate [*Lacrimator*]

PAN .... Pesticides Action Network (EA)

PAN .... Polled Access Network

PAN .... Polska Akademia Nauk [*Polish Academy of Sciences*] [*Warsaw*] [*A publication*]

PAN .... Polyacrylonitrile [*Organic chemistry*]

PAN .... Positional Alcohol Nystagmus [*Physiology*]

PAN .... Primary Account Number [*Business and trade*]

PAN .... Project Authorization Notice (MCD)

PAN .... Propodial Anlage [*Zoology*]

PAN .... Publications Account Number [*DoD*]

PAN .... Pyridylazonaphthol [*An indicator*] [*Chemistry*]

PAN .... Switchboard Panel [*Telecommunications*] (TEL)

PanA .... Pan-Africanist [*A publication*]

PANA .... Pan-Asia News Agency Ltd. [*Also, PANASIA*] [*Hong Kong*]

PANA .... Polish-American Numismatic Association (EA)

PANAGRA ... Pan American Grace Airways, Inc. [*Also, PAGA*]

PANAIR ..... Panama Air Lines

Panal .... Papuan National Alliance (PPW)

PANALU .... Parti National Lumumba [*Lumumba National Party*]

PAN-AM .... Pan American World Airways, Inc. [*See also PA, PAA, PN*]

Panama Admin Recursos Minerales Mapa ... Republica de Panama. Administracion de Recursos Minerales. Mapa [*A publication*]

PANAMAC ... Pan American World Airways Communications System

Panama Univ Dept Geografia Pub ... Panama Universidad. Departamento de Geografia. Publicacion [*A publication*]

Panamer Soil Conserv Congr ... Panamerican Soil Conservation Congress [*A publication*]

Pan Am Fisherman ... Pan American Fisherman [*A publication*]

Pan Am Health Organ Off Doc ... Pan American Health Organization. Official Document [*A publication*]

Pan Am Health Organ Res Prog ... Pan American Health Organization. Research in Progress [*A publication*]

Pan Am Health Organ Sci Publ ... Pan American Health Organization. Scientific Publication [*A publication*]

Pan-Am Inst Geography and History Pub ... Pan-American Institute of Geography and History. Publication [*A publication*]

Pan Am Inst Min Eng Geol US Sect Tech Pap ... Pan American Institute of Mining Engineering and Geology. United States Section. Technical Paper [*A publication*]

Pan Am M ... Pan American Magazine [*A publication*]

PanAmSat ... Pan American Satellite [*Greenwich, CT*] [*Telecommunications service*] (TSSD)

Pan-Am TS ... Pan-American Treaty Series (DLA)

Pan Am Union Bol Ciencia y Tecnologia ... Pan American Union. Boletin de Ciencia y Tecnologia [*A publication*]

Pan Am Union Bul ... Pan American Union. Bulletin [*A publication*]

PanAR .... Pan American Review [*A publication*]

PANAR .... Panoramic RADAR

PANASIA ... Organization of Pan Asian-American Women (EA)

PANASIA ... Pan-Asia News Agency Ltd. [*Also, PANA*] [*Hong Kong*]

PANB .... Panic Bolt

PANC .... Power Amplifier Neutralizing Capacitor (DEN)

PANCAN .... [*The*] Panama Canal

PANCANCO ... Panama Canal Company [*Superseded by Panama Canal Commission*]

PANCAP .... Practical Annual Capacity [*FAA*]

PANCO ...... Procurement Aids Noncommissioned Officer [*Marine Corps*]

PAND .... Pandering [*FBI standardized term*]

PAND .... Passive Air Navigation Device

PAND .... Performing Artists for Nuclear Disarmament (EA)

PANDA ...... Prestel Advanced Network Design Architecture

PANDEX ..... Name of an all-inclusive index covering fields of science, technology and medicine; composed of Greek prefix Pan meaning all and -Dex from word index

PANDLCHAR ... Pay and Allowances Chargeable

PANDORA ... Passive and Active Signal Digital Correlator Analyzer (MCD)

PANDS ...... Pay and Supply [*Coast Guard*]

PANDS ...... Print and Search Processor [*Data processing*]

PANE .... Park News [*A publication*]

Paneg .... Panegyricus [*of Isocrates*] [*Classical studies*] (OCD)

panendo ..... Panendoscopy [*Medicine*]

PANES ...... Prior Active Navy Enlisted Service

PANES ...... Program for Analysis of Nonlinear Equilibrium and Stability [*NASA*]

PANF .... Plan Account Number File [*IRS*]

PANFI .... Precision Automatic Noise Figure Indicator

PANGCS ... Prior Active National Guard Commissioned Service

PANGES ... Prior Active National Guard Enlisted Service

PANH .... Panhandling [*FBI standardized term*]

PANH .... Picolinaldehyde Nicotinoylhydrazone [*Reagent*]

Panhandle Geol Soc Strat Cross Sec ... Panhandle Geological Society. Stratigraphic Cross Section [*A publication*]

PANHONLIB ... Panama, Honduras, and Liberia [*Acronym used to refer to merchant ships operating under "flags of convenience"*]

PANI .... Patriarch Athenagoras National Institute (EA)

PANIC .... Planned Attack on Nine Inner Cities [*to build education parks*]

Pan Indian Ocean Sci Congr Proc Sect D Agr Sci ... Pan Indian Ocean Science Congress. Proceedings. Section D. Agricultural Sciences [*A publication*]

Panjab Univ (Chandigarh) Cent Adv Stu Geol Publ ... Panjab University (Chandigarh). Centre of Advanced Study in Geology. Publication [*A publication*]

PAnL .... Lebanon Valley College, Annville, PA [*Library symbol*] [*Library of Congress*] (LCLS)

PANLIBHON ... Panama, Liberia, and Honduras [*Acronym used to refer to merchant ships operating under "flags of convenience"*]

PANLIBHONCO ... Panama-Liberia-Honduras-Costa Rica

Panminerva Med ... Panminerva Medica [*A publication*]

PANNAP ..... Panavia New Aircraft Project (MCD)

PANNR .... Previous Applicants Need Not Reapply [*Civil Service*]

Panorama Democr Chr ... Panorama Democrate Chretien [*A publication*]

Panorama Econ (Mexico) ... Panorama Economico (Mexico) [*A publication*]

PA NP .... Brightly's Pennsylvania Nisi Prius Reports (DLA)

PANPA .... Pacific Area Newspaper Publishers Association [*North Sydney, NSW, Australia*] (EA-IO)

Pan-Pac Ent ... Pan-Pacific Entomologist [*A publication*]

Pan-Pac Entomol ... Pan-Pacific Entomologist [*A publication*]

Pan-Pacif Ent ... Pan-Pacific Entomologist [*A publication*]

Pan Pipes ... Pan Pipes of Sigma Alpha Iota [*A publication*]

PANPKHL .. Polska Akademia Nauk. Oddzial w Krakowie. Prace Komisji Historycznoliterackiej [*A publication*]

PANPKS ..... Polska Akademia Nauk. Oddzial w Krakowie. Prace Komisji Slowianoznawstwa [*A publication*]

Pan i Prawo ... Panstwo i Prawo [*A publication*]

PANPUB ..... Panel Publishers (DLA)

P An Rel M ... Proceedings. Annual Reliability and Maintainability Symposium [*A publication*]

PANS .... Pansophic Systems [*NASDAQ symbol*] (NQ)

PANS .... Pest Articles News Summaries [*Commonwealth Mycological Institute*] [*Kew, England*] [*A publication*]

PANS .... Positioning and Navigation System

PANS .... Procedures for Air Navigation Services [*ICAO*]

PANS .... Programable Augmented Noise Source [*Military*] (CAAL)

PANS .... Puromycin Aminonucleoside [*Biochemistry*]

PANSDOC ... Pakistan National Scientific and Documentation Center [*Later, PASTIC*]

PANSEAFRON ... Panama Sea Frontier

PANSMET ... Procedures for Air Navigation Services - Meteorology (IEEE)

Panstw Sluzba Geol Panstw Inst Geol Biul ... Panstwowa Sluzba Geologiczna. Pantswowy Instytut. Geologiczny Biuletyn [*A publication*]

PANT .... Pantograph (KSC)

Panta J Med ... Panta Journal of Medicine [*A publication*]

PAntin .... [*The*] Antinoe Papyrus of Theocritus [*Classical studies*] (OCD)

PAntinoop ... Antinoopolis Papyri [*A publication*] (OCD)

PANTO .... Pantomime

PANTS .... Pantaloons (DSUE)

PA Nurse .... Pennsylvania Nurse [*A publication*]

PANW .... Pan-Western Corp. [*NASDAQ symbol*] (NQ)

PANX .... Panex Industries [*NASDAQ symbol*] (NQ)

PANY .... Platinumsmiths Association of New York (EA)

PANY .... Port Authority of New York [*Later, PANYNJ*]

PANYNJ .... Port Authority of New York and New Jersey [*Formerly, PANY*]

Panz Ann .... Panzer Annales [*A publication*]

PAO............ Palo Alto, CA [*Location identifier*] [*FAA*]   (FAAL)

PAO............ Paotow [*Republic of China*] [*Seismograph station code, US Geological Survey*]   (SEIS)

PAO............ Paramount Resources, Inc. [*Vancouver Stock Exchange symbol*]

PaO.............. Paranoia Obvious [*Psychology*]

PAO............ Peacetime Acquisition Objective [*DoD*]   (AFIT)

PAO............ Peak Acid Output [*Physiology*]

PAO............ Penalty Appeals Officer [*IRS*]

PA/O.......... Performing Arts/Omaha [*Nebraska*]

PAO............ Pinellas Area Office [*Energy Research and Development Administration*]

PAO............ Polyalkyleneoxide [*Organic chemistry*]

PAO............ Primary Action Office [*or Officer*] [*Military*]

PAO............ Prince Albert's Own [*Military unit*] [*British*]

PAO............ Principal Administrative Officer

PAO............ Pro Athletes Outreach   (EA)

PAO............ Product Activity/Operational Code   (MCD)

PAO..... Product Assurance Operations [*Army*]

PAO............ Program Action Officer [*Navy*]   (CAAL)

PAO............ Project Action Officer [*Air Force*]   (AFIT)

PAO............ Project Administration Officer [*Military*]   (AFIT)

PAO............ Property Action Order

PAO............ Public Affairs Office [*NASA*]

PAO............ Public Affairs Officer [*Embassies*]

PAO............ Pulsed Avalanche Diode Oscillator [*Telecommunications*]   (IEEE)

PAOA........ Pan American Odontological Association   (EA)

PAOC........ Pentacostal Assemblies of Canada

PAOC........ Pollution Abatement Operations Center   (MCD)

PAOC........ Principal Administrative Officers Committee [*Chiefs of Staff*] [*World War II*]

PAOL.......... Poly-alpha-olefin [*Organic chemistry*]

PAOP........ Pulmonary Artery Occlusion Pressure [*Cardiology*]

PAORB....... Problemes Actuels d'Oto-Rhino-Laryngologie [*A publication*]

PAOS......... Proceedings. American Oriental Society [*A publication*]

PAOT......... Persons at One Time

P/AP.......... Painter/Apprentice Painter   (AAG)

PAP............ Papanicolaou [*Diagnosis, smear, stain, or test*] [*Medicine*]

PAP............ Paper   (DSUE)

PAP............ Paper Bound [*Books*]   (ROG)

pap............. Papilla [*Medicine*]

PAP............ Papyrologica [*A publication*]

Pap............. Papyrus   (BJA)

PAP............ Para-Aminophenol [*Organic chemistry*]

PAP............ Parti d'Action Paysanne [*Farmers Actions Party*] [*Upper Volta*]

PAP............ Participatory Anthropic Principle [*Term coined by authors John Barrow and Frank Tipler in their book, "The Anthropic Cosmological Principle"*]

PAP............ Partido Accion Popular [*Popular Action Party*] [*Ecuador*]

PAP............ Partido Accion Popular [*Popular Action Party*] [*Peru*]

PaP............ Past and Present [*A publication*]

PAP............ Patrol Amphibian Plane

PaP............ Patterns of Prejudice [*A publication*]

PAP............ Paulin [*H.*] & Co. Ltd. [*Toronto Stock Exchange symbol*]

PAP............ Payload Activity Planner [*NASA*]

PAP............ Peak Airway Pressure [*Physiology*]

PAP............ Pension Administration Plan [*Insurance*]

PAP............ People's Action Party [*Malaya*]

PAP............ People's Action Party [*Singapore*]   (PPW)

PAP............ People's Alliance Party [*Solomon Islands*]   (PPW)

PAP............ Peroxidase-Antiperoxidase [*Immunochemistry*]

PAP............ Personal Auto Policy [*Insurance*]

PAP............ Personnel Allocation Plan [*Navy*]

PAP............ Personnel Assistance Point   (AABC)

PAP............ Phase Advance Pulse

PAP............ Phenolphthalein in Paraffin [*Emulsion*]

PAP......... Phenyl Acid Phosphate [*Organic chemistry*]

PAP............ Phosphoadenosine Phosphate [*Biochemistry*]

PAP............ Photodiode Array Processing   (MCD)

PAP............ Photonic Array Processor [*Device for manipulating light beams in an optical computer*]

PAP............ Physics and Astronomy Programs [*NASA*]

PAP........... Pierced Aluminum Plank [*Technical drawings*]

PAP............ Pilotless Aircraft Program   (NG)

PAP............ Platelet Alkaline Phosphatase [*An enzyme*]

P a P........... Poco a Poco [*Little by Little*] [*Music*]

PAP............ Pokeweed Antiviral Protein [*Immunochemistry*]

PAP............ Political Asylum Project   (EA)

PAP............ Politiki Aneksartitos Parataksis [*Independent Political Front*] [*Greek*]   (PPE)

PAP............ Polska Agencja Prasowa [*Polish Press Agency*]

PAP............ Poly(acryloylpyrrolidine) [*Organic chemistry*]

PAP............ Port-Au-Prince [*Haiti*] [*Airport symbol*]   (OAG)

PAP............ Prearranged Payments [*Business and trade*]

PAP............ Primary Atypical Pneumonia [*Medicine*]

PAP............ Prison-Ashram Project [*Durham, NC*]   (EA)

PAP............ Procurement and Production   (AFIT)

PAP............ Product Assurance Plan [*Army*]   (AABC)

PAP............ Production Allocation Program

PAP............ Project Aerospace Plane   (AAG)

PAP............ Projected Average Progress   (NG)

PAP............ Prostatic Acid Phosphatase [*An enzyme*]

PAP............ Proton Attenuation Procedure

PAP............ Psychobiology and Psychopathology [*Elsevier Book Series*] [*A publication*]

PAP............ Public Affairs Program [*of the American Friends Service Committee*]   (EA)

PAP............ Public Assistance Program

PAP............ Pulmonary Alveolar Proteinosis [*Medicine*]

PAP............ Pulmonary Arterial [*or Artery*] Pressure [*Medicine*]

PAPA......... Probabilistic Automatic Pattern Analyzer [*Data processing*]

PAPA......... Proceedings. American Philological Association [*A publication*]

PAPA......... Programer and Probability Analyzer [*Data processing*]   (IEEE)

Pap Am Chem Soc Div Paint Plast Print Ink ... Papers. American Chemical Society. Division of Paint, Plastics, and Printing Ink [*A publication*]

Pap Amer Soc Agr Eng ... Paper. American Society of Agricultural Engineers [*A publication*]

Pap Anthro ... Papers in Anthropology [*Oklahoma*] [*A publication*]

Pap Archit Sci Unit Univ Queensl ... Paper. Architectural Science Unit. University of Queensland [*A publication*]

PAPAS .... Pin and Pellet Assay System [*Nuclear energy*]   (NRCH)

Pap ASAE ... Paper. American Society of Agricultural Engineers [*A publication*]

PAPAV .... Papaver Poppy [*Botany*]   (ROG)

Pap Avulsos Dep Zool (Sao Paulo) ... Papeis Avulsos do Departmento de Zoologia (Sao Paulo) [*A publication*]

Pap Avulsos Dep Zool Secr Agric Ind Comer (Sao Paulo) ... Papeis Avulsos do Departmento de Zoologia. Secretaria de Agricultura Industria e Comercio (Sao Paulo) [*A publication*]

Pap Avul Zool ... Papeis Avulsos de Zoologia [*A publication*]

Pap Bibliogr Soc Am ... Papers. Bibliographical Society of America [*A publication*]

Pap Bibliog Soc Am ... Papers. Bibliographical Society of America [*A publication*]

Pap Bibl Soc Am ... Papers. Bibliographical Society of America [*A publication*]

Papbrd Pkg ... Paperboard Packaging [*A publication*]

PAPC......... Philological Association of the Pacific Coast [*A publication*]

Pap Carton Cellul ... Papier. Carton et Cellulose [*A publication*]

PAPCNY..... Portuguese American Progressive Club of New York   (EA)

Pap Coal Util Symp Focus SO₂ Emiss Control ... Papers. Coal Utilization Symposium. Focus on SO_2 Emission Control [*A publication*]

Pap Commonw For Conf ... Paper. Commonwealth Forestry Conference [*A publication*]

Pap Congr Aust NZ Assoc Adv Sci ... Australian and New Zealand Association for the Advancement of Science. Congress. Papers [*A publication*]

Pap Congr Fed Int Precontrainte ... Papers. Congress of the Federation Internationale de la Precontrainte [*A publication*]

Pap Conv Am Nurs Assoc ... Papers from the Convention. American Nurses' Association [*A publication*]

Pap Converting ... Paper Converting [*A publication*]

Pap Czech Soil Sci Conf ... Papers. Czechoslovak Soil Science Conference [*A publication*]

Pap Dep Agric QD Univ ... Papers. Department of Agriculture. University of Queensland [*A publication*]

Pap Dep Geol QD Univ ... Papers. Department of Geology. University of Queensland [*A publication*]

Pap Dep Geol Queensl Univ ... Papers. Department of Geology. University of Queensland [*A publication*]

Pap Dep Geol Univ QD ... Papers. Department of Geology. University of Queensland [*A publication*]

Pap Dep Zool QD Univ ... Papers. Department of Zoology. University of Queensland [*A publication*]

PAPE......... Photoactive Pigment Electrophotography   (IEEE)

PAPEF........ Parkside Petroleum [*NASDAQ symbol*]   (NQ)

PAPER....... Prairie Association of Publishers Education Representatives [*Canada*]

Paper & Board Abs ... Paper and Board Abstracts [*A publication*]

Paperboard Packag ... Paperboard Packaging [*A publication*]

Paperboard Pkg ... Paperboard Packaging [*A publication*]

PAPERCHEM ... Paper Chemistry [*Institute of Paper Chemistry*] [*Appleton, WI*] [*Bibliographic database*]

Paper Film Foil Conv ... Paper, Film, and Foil Converter [*A publication*]

Paper Makers Merch Dir ... Paper Makers and Merchants. Directory of All Nations [*A publication*]

PAPERMAN ... Payroll and Accounting, Personnel Management, Manpower Utilization [*Air Force*]

Paper Mkr ... Paper Maker [*A publication*]

Paper Pulp Mill Catalogue ... Paper and Pulp Mill Catalogue/Engineering Handbook [*A publication*]

Papers Biblio Soc Am ... Papers. Bibliographical Society of America [*A publication*]

Papers in Ed (Anstey Coll) ... Papers in Education (Anstey College of Physical Education) [*A publication*]

Papers Far East Hist ... Papers on Far Eastern History [*A publication*]

Papers & Proc Roy Soc Tas ... Papers and Proceedings. Royal Society of Tasmania [*A publication*]

Papers Proc Roy Soc Tasmania ... Papers and Proceedings. Royal Society of Tasmania [*A publication*]

Papers and Proc Roy Soc Tasmania ... Papers and Proceedings. Royal Society of Tasmania [*A publication*]

Papers & Proc Tas Hist Res Assn ... Papers and Proceedings. Tasmanian Historical Research Association [*A publication*]

Paper Technol ... Paper Technology [*A publication*]

Paper Tr J ... Paper Trade Journal [*A publication*]

Paper Twine J ... Paper and Twine Journal [*A publication*]

Paper Yrb... Paper Year Book [*A publication*]

Papeterie Numero Spec ... Papeterie. Numero Special [*A publication*]

Pap FAO/IUFRO World Consult For Tree Breed ... Paper. FAO [*Food and Agriculture Organization of the United Nations*]/IUFRO [*International Union of Forestry Research Organization*] World Consultation on Forest Tree Breeding [*A publication*]

Pap Far Eas ... Papers on Far Eastern History [*A publication*]

Pap Far East Hist ... Papers on Far Eastern History [*Australia*] [*A publication*]

Pap Film Foil Converter ... Paper, Film, and Foil Converter [*A publication*]

Pap Geol Surv Can ... Papers. Geological Survey of Canada [*A publication*]

Pap Gifu Univ Sch Med ... Papers. Gifu University. School of Medicine [*Japan*] [*A publication*]

Pap Grt Barrier Reef Comm ... Papers. Great Barrier Reef Committee [*A publication*]

PAPH.......... (Pyridinealdehyde)pyridylhydrazone [*Organic chemistry*]

PAPhilosS .... Proceedings. American Philosophical Society [*A publication*]

PAPhS........ Proceedings. American Philosophical Society [*A publication*]

PAPI .... Precision Approach Path Indicator [*Aviation*]   (FAAC)

Papier (Darmstadt) Beil ... Papier (Darmstadt). Beilage [*A publication*]

Papierfabr Wochenbl Papierfabr ... Papierfabrikant - Wochenblatt fuer Papierfabrikation [*A publication*]

Papiergesch ... Papier Geschichte [*A publication*]

Papierverarb ... Papier- und Kunststoffverarbeiter [*A publication*]

Pap Ind....... Paper Industry [*A publication*]

Pap Ind Pap World ... Paper Industry and Paper World [*A publication*]

Pap Inst Def Anal ... Paper. Institute for Defense Analyses [*A publication*]

Pap Inst Post Off Electr Eng ... Printed Papers. Institution of Post Office Electrical Engineers [*A publication*]

Pap Inst Therm Spring Res Okayama Univ ... Papers. Institute for Thermal Spring Research. Okayama University [*A publication*]

Pap Int Conf Fluid Sealing ... Paper. International Conference on Fluid Sealing [*A publication*]

Papirip Magy Grafika ... Papiripar es Magyar Grafika [*A publication*]

Pap Is Afr ... Papers in International Studies. Africa Series. Ohio University [*A publication*]

Pap Is Se A ... Papers in International Studies. Southeast Asia Series. Ohio University [*A publication*]

Pap J .... Papir-Journalen [*A publication*]

PAPL........ Preliminary Allowance Parts List [*Military*]   (CAAL)

Pap Lab Tree-Ring Res Univ Ariz ... Papers. Laboratory of Tree-Ring Research. University of Arizona [*A publication*]

Pap Lanc Co Hist Soc ... Historical Papers. Lancaster County Historical Society [*Pennsylvania*] [*A publication*]

Pap Lang L ... Papers on Language and Literature [*A publication*]

Pap Lang Lit ... Papers on Language and Literature [*A publication*]

Pap Ling..... Papers in Linguistics [*A publication*]

PAPM........ Passed Assistant Paymaster [*British*]

Pap Maker (London) ... Paper Maker and British Paper Trade Journal (London) [*A publication*]

Pap Makers Assoc (GB Irel) Proc Tech Sect ... Paper Makers' Association (Great Britain and Ireland). Proceedings of the Technical Section [*A publication*]

Pap Makers Mon J ... Paper Makers' Monthly Journal [*A publication*]

Pap Maker (Wilmington Del) ... Paper Maker (Wilmington, Delaware) [*A publication*]

Pap Meteorol Geophys (Tokyo) ... Papers in Meteorology and Geophysics (Tokyo) [*A publication*]

Pap Met Geo ... Papers in Meteorology and Geophysics [*A publication*]

Pap Mich Acad ... Papers. Michigan Academy of Science, Arts, and Letters [*A publication*]

Pap Mich Acad Sci ... Papers. Michigan Academy of Science, Arts, and Letters [*A publication*]

Pap Mich Acad Sci Arts Lett ... Papers. Michigan Academy of Science, Arts, and Letters [*A publication*]

Pap Mill News ... Paper Mill News [*A publication*]

Pap Mill Wood Pulp News ... Paper Mill and Wood Pulp News [*A publication*]

PAPMOP .... Product Assurance Program Management Operations Plan   (MCD)

Pap N Haven Col Hist Soc ... Papers. New Haven Colony Historical Society [*A publication*]

Pap Norw State Game Res Inst ... Papers. Norwegian State Game Research Institute [*A publication*]

Pap Nyomdatech ... Papir es Nyomdatechnika [*A publication*]

Papo........... Partido de Accion Popular [*Popular Action Party*] [*Panamanian*]   (PPW)

PAPOC....... Parents' Alliance to Protect Our Children   (EA)

PAPOILA.... Pacis Amico, Persecutionis Osore, Joanne Lockio Anglo [*Pseudonym used by John Locke*]

PAPOVA..... Papilloma Virus, Polyoma Virus, Vacuolating Virus

PapOxy ...... Oxyrhynchus Papyri [*A publication*]

PAPP .... Para-Aminopropiophenone [*Pharmacology*]

PAPP .... Parametric Aircraft Performance Program   (MCD)

PAPP .... Pregnancy-Associated Plasma Protein

PAPPA .... Pulp and Paper Prepackaging Association [*Later, SSI*]   (EA)

Pap Peabody Mus Archaeol Ethnol Harv Univ ... Papers. Peabody Museum of Archaeology and Ethnology. Harvard University [*A publication*]

PAPPGM .... Preliminary Army Planning and Program Guidance Memorandum   (MCD)

Pap Phil Ling ... Papers in Philippine Linguistics. Pacific Linguistics. Series A [*Canberra*] [*A publication*]

Pap Presentations Proc Digital Equip Comput Users Soc ... Papers and Presentations-Proceedings. Digital Equipment Computer Users Society [*A publication*]

Pap Print Dig ... Paper and Printing Digest [*A publication*]

Pap Proc R Soc Tas ... Papers and Proceedings. Royal Society of Tasmania [*A publication*]

Pap Proc R Soc Tasm ... Papers and Proceedings. Royal Society of Tasmania [*A publication*]

Pap Proc R Soc Tasmania ... Papers and Proceedings. Royal Society of Tasmania [*A publication*]

Pap Proc Tas Hist Res Assoc ... Tasmanian Historical Research Association. Papers and Proceedings [*A publication*]

Pap ja Puu ... Paperi ja Puu [*A publication*]

Pap Puu...... Paperi ja Puu - Papper och Tra [*A publication*]

Pap Puu B Painos ... Paperi ja Puu. B Painos [*A publication*]

Pap Puu Painos ... Paperi ja Puu. A Painos [*A publication*]

PA Prac........ Standard Pennsylvania Practice   (DLA)

PAPRICAN ... Pulp and Paper Research Institute of Canada [*McGill University*] [*Research center*] [*Pointe Claire, PQ*]   (RCD)

Pap Roy Soc Tasm ... Royal Society of Tasmania. Papers and Proceedings [*A publication*]

Pap R Sociol ... Papers. Revista de Sociologia [*A publication*]

PAPS.......... Periodic Acid-Schiff with Phenylhydrazine Interposition [*A stain*]

PAPS.......... Periodic Armaments Planning System   (MCD)

PAPS.......... Permissive Arming and Protection System [*AEC*]

PAPS.......... Phosphoadenosine Phosphosulfate [*Also, APPS*] [*Biochemistry*]

PAPS.......... Phosphoadenylyl Sulfate [*Biochemistry*]

PAPS.......... Proceedings. American Philosophical Society [*A publication*]

PAPS.......... Procurement and Production Status System

PAPS.......... Public Assistance Processing System

PA PSC ...... Pennsylvania Public Service Commission Annual Report   (DLA)

PA PSC Dec ... Pennsylvania Public Service Commission Decisions   (DLA)

Pap Sci Ser ... Papers in Science Series [*A publication*]

Pap SE As Ling ... Papers in South East Asian Linguistics. Pacific Linguistics. Series A [*Canberra*] [*A publication*]

Pap SESA ... Paper. SESA [*Society for Experimental Stress Analysis*] [*A publication*]

Pap Ship Res Inst (Tokyo) ... Papers of Ship Research Institute (Tokyo) [*A publication*]

PAPSI........ Pregnancy-Associated Prostaglandin Synthetase Inhibitor [*Endocrinology*]

Pap S Shields Archaeol Hist Soc ... Papers. South Shields Archaeological and Historical Society [*A publication*]

P Ap St Dalho ... Applied Statistics. Proceedings of Conference at Dalhousie University [*A publication*]

Pap Sthn Afr ... Paper Southern Africa [*A publication*]

PA Psychiatr Q ... Pennsylvania Psychiatric Quarterly [*A publication*]

Pap Symp Coal Manage Tech ... Papers Presented before the Symposium on Coal Management Techniques [*A publication*]

Pap Symp Coal Mine Drainage Res ... Papers Presented before the Symposium on Coal Mine Drainage Research [*A publication*]

Pap Symp Coal Prep Util ... Papers Presented before the Symposium on Coal Preparation and Utilization [*A publication*]

Pap Symp Manage ... Papers Presented before the Symposium on Management [*A publication*]

Pap Symp Surf Min Reclam ... Papers Presented before the Symposium on Surface Mining and Reclamation [*A publication*]

Pap Symp Underground Min ... Papers Presented before the Symposium on Underground Mining [*A publication*]

Pap Synth Conf Proc ... Paper Synthetics Conference. Proceedings [*United States*] [*A publication*]

PAPTE........ President's Advisory Panel on Timber and the Environment

Pap Tech Mtg Int Union Conserv Nature ... Paper. Technical Meeting. International Union for the Conservation of Nature and Natural Resources [*A publication*]

Pap Technol ... Paper Technology [*England*] [*A publication*]

Pap Technol ... Paper Technology and Industry [*A publication*]

Pap Technol Ind ... Paper Technology and Industry [*A publication*]

Pap Trade J ... Paper Trade Journal [*A publication*]

Papua New Guin Agric J ... Papua and New Guinea Agricultural Journal [*A publication*]

Papua New Guinea Agric J ... Papua and New Guinea Agricultural Journal [*A publication*]

Papua New Guinea Agr J ... Papua and New Guinea Agricultural Journal [*A publication*]

Papua New Guinea Dep Agric Stock Fish Annu Rep ... Papua New Guinea. Department of Agriculture, Stock, and Fisheries. Annual Report [*A publication*]
Papua New Guinea Dep Agric Stock Fish Res Bull ... Papua New Guinea. Department of Agriculture, Stock, and Fisheries Research Bulletin [*A publication*]
Papua New Guinea Geol Surv Mem ... Papua New Guinea Geological Survey. Memoir [*A publication*]
Papua New Guinea Med J ... Papua New Guinea Medical Journal [*A publication*]
Papua & NG ... Papua and New Guinea Law Reports [*A publication*]
PAPUFA ..... Physiologically Active Polyunsaturated Fatty Acid [*Nutrition*]
Pap Univ MO-Columbia Dep Agric Econ ... Paper. University of Missouri-Columbia. Department of Agricultural Economics [*A publication*]
Pap US Geol Surv Wat Supply ... Paper. United States Geological Survey. Water Supply [*A publication*]
PAPVR .... Partial Anomalous Pulmonary Venous Return
Papy .... Papy's Reports [*5-8 Florida*]   (DLA)
Pap Ztg ..... Papier-Zeitung [*A publication*]
PAQ .... Palmer, AK [*Location identifier*] [*FAA*]   (FAAL)
PAQ .... Partially Allocated Quotas [*Ocean fishery management*]
PAQ .... Position Analysis Questionnaire
PAQ .... Preliminary Allowance Quantity [*Military*]   (CAAL)
PAQ .... Process Average Quality
PAQR .... Polyacenequinone Radical [*Organic chemistry*]
PAR .... Page Address Register
PAR .... Parabolic Aluminized Reflector
PAR .... Paracel Islands [*Three-letter standard code*]   (CNC)
PAR .... Parachute
PAR .... Paragon Resources [*Vancouver Stock Exchange symbol*]
Par .... Paragone [*A publication*]
PAR .... Paragraph   (AAG)
Par .... Parah   (BJA)
PAR .... Paralipomenon [*Old Testament book*] [*Douay version*]
PAR .... Parallax
PAR .... Parallel   (KSC)
PAR .... Parallelogram [*Geometry*]   (ADA)
PAR .... Parameter
PAR .... Parametric Amplifier
PAR .... Paraphrase   (ADA)
PAR .... Parcel
PAR .... Parenthesis
Par .... Parents' Magazine and Better Family Living [*Later, Parents' Magazine*] [*A publication*]
PAR .... Paris [*France*] [*Airport symbol*]   (OAG)
PAR .... Paris - Parc St. Maur [*France*] [*Seismograph station code, US Geological Survey*]   (SEIS)
PAR .... Parish
PAR .... Parity   (ADA)
Par .... Parker's English Exchequer Reports   (DLA)
Par .... Parker's New York Criminal Reports   (DLA)
PAR .... Parochial
Par .... Parsons' Reports [*65-66 New Hampshire*]   (DLA)
PAR .... Partido Accion Renovadora [*Political party in El Salvador*]
PAR .... Partido Aragones Regionalista [*Aragonese Regional Party*] [*Spanish*]   (PPW)
PAR .... Partito Anti-Reformista [*Anti-Reform Party*] [*Maltese*]   (PPE)
PAR .... Parts Approval Request   (MCD)
PAR .... Payload Adapter Ring
PAR .... Peacetime Airborne Reconnaissance   (AFM)
PAR .... Peak Accelerometer Recorder   (IEEE)
PAR .... Peak-to-Average Ratio [*Communications*]
PAR .... Pennsylvania Advanced Reactor
PAR .... People Against Racism [*Civil rights organization*]
PAR .... People Against Rape   (EA)
PAR .... Perennial Allergic Rhinitis [*Medicine*]
PAR .... Performance Analysis and Review
PAR .... Performance Analysis Routine [*Data processing*]
PAR .... Performance Appraisal Report   (NRCH)
PAR .... Performing Arts Review [*A publication*]
PAR .... Perimeter Acquisition RADAR [*Army*]
PAR .... Perimeter Array RADAR   (MCD)
PAR .... Personnel Activity Report [*Office of Management and Budget*]
PAR .... Personnel Activity Request
PAR .... Personnel Advancement Requirement [*Navy*]   (NVT)
PAR .... PERT [*Program Evaluation and Review Technique*] Analysis Report   (KSC)
PAR .... Phased Array RADAR
PAR .... Photosynthetically Active Radiation
PAR .... Physiological Aging Rate
PAR .... Planning Action Request   (MCD)
PAR .... Platelet Aggregate Ratio [*Hematology*]
PAR .... Positive Attitudinal Reinforcement [*In George Lee Walker novel "The Chronicles of Doodah"*]
PAR .... Post Adjudicative Review [*Social Security Administration*]   (OICC)
PAR .... Post Attach Requirements   (AAG)
PAR .... Postanesthesia [*or Postanesthetic*] Room [*Medicine*]
PAR .... Postanesthetic Recovery [*Medicine*]
PAR .... Potassium-Adsorption-Ratio

PAR .... Precision Aerotech [*American Stock Exchange symbol*]
PAR .... Precision Aircraft Reference
PAR .... Precision Approach RADAR [*Aviation*]
PAR .... Princeton Applied Research Corp.
PAR .... Priority Action Report   (AAG)
PAR .... Priority Action Request   (AAG)
PAR .... Probabilistic Analysis of Risk   (KSC)
PAR .... Problem Accountability Record   (NASA)
PAR .... Problem Action Record   (KSC)
PAR .... Problem Action Request   (NASA)
PAR .... Problem Analysis Report   (MCD)
PAR .... Problem Analysis and Resolution
PAR .... Process Action Request
PAR .... Product Acceptance Review   (NASA)
PAR .... Product of Antigenic Recognition [*Immunochemistry*]
PAR .... Production Action Request   (MCD)
PAR .... Production Analysis Report
PAR .... Production, Augmentation, and Reliability   (NG)
PAR .... Production Automated Riveting
PAR .... Professional Abstracts Registries [*Database Innovations, Inc.*]
PAR .... Profile of Average Reflectivity
PAR .... Program Address Register
PAR .... Program Adjustment Request [*Navy*]
PAR .... Program Administrator's [*Progress*] Report [*DoD*]
PAR .... Program-Aid Routine [*Data processing*]
PAR .... Program for Alcohol Recovery
PAR .... Program Allocation and Reimbursements   (AFIT)
PAR .... Program Analysis and Review
PAR .... Program Appraisal Report
PAR .... Program Appraisal and Review   (IEEE)
PAR .... Program Assessment Report [*or Review*]   (MCD)
PAR .... Program Audience Rating
PAR .... Progressive Aircraft Repair [*or Rework*]
PAR .... Project Audit Report
PAR .... Promotion Appraisal Report   (FAAC)
PAR .... Public Administration Review [*A publication*]
PAR .... Pulse Acquisition RADAR [*Military*]   (NG)
PAR .... Purchasing Approval Request   (NRCH)
PAR .... Push and Release [*Push button*]
PAR .... (Pyridylazo)resorcinol [*Organic chemistry*]
PARA .... Parachute
PARA .... Paragraph   (AFM)
PARA .... Paraguay
para .... Paraplegic
PARA .... Particle Aiding Replication of Adenovirus [*Virology*]
PARA .... Policy Analysis and Resource Allocation [*Department of State*]
P-88/ARA .... Project '88: Americans for the Reagan Agenda   (EA)
PARABAT ... Parachute Battalion [*Army*]
paracent ..... Paracentesis [*Medicine*]
PARACOMPT ... Parameter Analysis of Respiration Agents Considering Operations Motivation Protection and Time Model   (MCD)
PARACS .... Perimeter Acquisition RADAR Attack Characterization System   (MCD)
PARADE ..... Passive-Active Range Determination
Par Adm ..... Parsons on the Law of Shipping and Admiralty   (DLA)
PARADROP ... Airdrop by Parachute
PARAF .... Paragon Resources [*NASDAQ symbol*]   (NQ)
PAR AFF .... Pars Affecta [*The Part Affected*] [*Pharmacy*]
PARAFRAG ... Parachute Fragmentation Bomb [*Air Force*]
PARAKU .... Pasokan Rakyat Kalimantan Utara [*North Kalimantan People's Forces*] [*Malaya*]
PARAM ...... Parameter   (KSC)
Paramagn Rezon ... Paramagnitnyj Rezonans [*A publication*]
Para-Med ... Para-Medico [*A publication*]
PARAMEDIC ... [*A*] Medical Service Person Qualified to Participate in Parachute Activities [*Air Force*] [*In a nonmilitary context, may refer to one who serves as a physician's assistant*]
Paramed Int ... Paramedics International [*A publication*]
PARAMI ..... Parsons Active Ring-Around Miss Indicator
Par Am Law ... Parsons' Commentaries on American Law   (DLA)
Par Am Law Comm ... Parsons' Commentaries on American Law   (DLA)
PARAMP .... Parametric Amplifier
Par Ant .... Parochial Antiquities   (DLA)
PARAPSYCH ... Parapsychology
PARARESCUE ... Rescue by Individuals Parachuted to Distressed Persons [*Air Force*]
Par Arter .... Paroi Arterielle-Arterial Wall [*A publication*]
PARASEV ... Paraglider Research Vehicle [*NASA*]
Parasit .... Parasitica [*A publication*]
Parasitol .... Parasitology [*A publication*]
Parasitol Hung ... Parasitologia Hungarica [*A publication*]
Parasitol Schriftenr ... Parasitologische Schriftenreihe [*A publication*]
PARASYN ... Parametric Synthesis [*Data processing*]
PARATHORMONE ... Parathyroid Hormone [*Endocrinology*]
PARATROOPS ... Parachute Infantry [*Military*]
Parazitol Sb ... Parazitologicheskii Sbornik [*A publication*]
Parazity Zhivotn Rast ... Parazity Zhivotnykh i Rastenii [*A publication*]
PARB .... Perimeter Acquisition RADAR Building [*Army*]   (AABC)
Parbhani Agric Coll Mag ... Parbhani Agricultural College Magazine [*A publication*]
Par Bills & N ... Parsons on Bills and Notes   (DLA)

PARC .... Pacific Air Rescue Center [*or Command*] (CINC)
PARC .... Palo Alto Research Center [*Xerox Corp.*]
PARC .... Pan-African Resource Center (EA)
PARC .... Park Communications [*NASDAQ symbol*] (NQ)
PARC .... President's Appalachian Regional Commission
PARC .... Progressive Aircraft Reconditioning [*or Repair*] Cycle
PARCA .... Pan American Railway Congress Association
PARCH ...... Parchment (ADA)
PARCHM ..... Parchment (ROG)
PARCHT .... Parchment
PaRCL .... Parsec Research Control Language [*Pronounced "parkul"*]
              [*Parsec Research*] [*Robotics*]
Par Cont ..... Parsons on Contracts (DLA)
PARCP .... PEMARS [*Procurement of Equipment and Missiles, Army
              Management and Accounting Reporting System*]
              Accounting and Reporting Control Point [*Army*]
PARCS .... Perimeter Acquisition RADAR Attack Characterization System
              [*Army*]
PARD .... Parts Application Reliability Data (IEEE)
PARD .... Periodic and Random Deviation
PARD .... Personnel Actions and Records Directorate [*Military Personnel
              Center*] (AABC)
PARD .... Pilot Airborne Recovery Device [*A balloon-parachute*]
PARD .... Pilotless Aircraft Research Division [*Later, Applied Materials
              and Physics Division*] [*Langley Research Center*]
PARD .... Post-Accident Radioactivity Depletion [*Nuclear
              energy*] (NRCH)
PARD .... Precision Annotated Retrieval Display [*System*] [*Data
              processing*]
PARDAC .... Parallel Digital-to-Analog Converter
Par Dec ..... Parsons' Decisions [*2-7 Massachusetts*] (DLA)
PARDENTL ... Paradental
PARDON .... Pastors' Anonymous Recovery-Directed Order for Newness
              [*Rehabilitation program for troubled clergymen*] [*Defunct*]
PARDOP..... Passive Ranging Doppler
PARDP .... Perimeter Acquisition RADAR Data Processor [*Army*] (AABC)
PARE .... People Against Racism in Education
PAREA ...... Pharmacological Reviews [*A publication*]
PAREC ...... Pay Record
PA Rec .... Pennsylvania Record (DLA)
PAREN ...... Parenthesis [*or Parentheses*] (AFM)
PAREN ...... Progressive Aircraft Engine Repair
PARENT ..... Parenteral
Parent Aust ... Parent Australia [*A publication*]
Parent & Cit ... Parent and Citizen [*A publication*]
Parents ...... Parents' Magazine [*A publication*]
PARENTS... People of America Responding to Educational Needs of
              Today's Society (EA)
Parents' Mag ... Parents' Magazine and Better Family Living [*Later, Parents'
              Magazine*] [*A publication*]
PARENTSQ ... Parent Squadron Base [*Military*] (NVT)
PA Rep .... Pennsylvania Reports (DLA)
Par Eq Cas ... Parsons' Select Equity Cases [*1842-51*] [*Pennsylvania*] (DLA)
Par Eq Cases ... Parsons' Select Equity Cases [*Pennsylvania*] (DLA)
PAREX .... Programed Accounts Receivable Extra Service [*Data
              processing*]
PARF .... Paradise Fruit Co. [*NASDAQ symbol*] (NQ)
PARFAS..... Passive Radio Frequency Acquisition System
PARFOX..... [*Front*] Parapet Foxhole (MCD)
PARFR........ Program for Applied Research on Fertility Regulation
              [*Northwestern University*] [*Research center*]
Parfuem Kosmet ... Parfuemerie und Kosmetik [*West Germany*] [*A
              publication*]
Parfum Cosmet Savons ... Parfums, Cosmetiques, Savons [*A publication*]
Parfum Mod ... Parfumerie Moderne [*A publication*]
Parfums Cos ... Parfums, Cosmetiques, Aromes [*A publication*]
Parfums Cosmet Savons ... Parfums, Cosmetiques, Savons [*A publication*]
Parfums Cosmet Savons Fr ... Parfums, Cosmetiques, Savons de France [*A
              publication*]
Parfums Fr ... Parfums de France [*A publication*]
PARGS....... Parks and Recreation Girls Service
PARI .... Parent Attitude Research Instrument [*A questionnaire*]
PARIS........ Pictorial and Artifact Retrieval and Information System [*Data
              processing*]
PARIS........ Planning Aid for Retail Information System [*IBM Corp.*]
PARIS........ Pour l'Amenagement et le Renouveau Institutionel et Social
              [*French political party*]
PARIS........ Pulse Analysis-Recording Information System
Paris Med... Paris Medical [*A publication*]
ParisR .... Paris Review [*A publication*]
Paris Rev.... Paris Review [*A publication*]
Paris Univ Lab Micropaleontol Trav ... Paris. Universite. Laboratoire de
              Micropaleontologie. Travaux [*A publication*]
Paris Univ Lab Paleontol Trav ... Paris. Universite. Laboratoire de
              Paleontologie. Travaux [*A publication*]
PARK......... Parkerized [*Metallurgy*] [*Tradename*]
Park........... Parker's English Exchequer Reports [*1743-67*] (DLA)
Park........... Parker's New Hampshire Reports (DLA)
Park........... Parker's New York Criminal Cases [*1823-68*] (DLA)
PARK......... Parks. International Journal for Managers of National Parks,
              Historic Sites, and Other Protected Areas [*A publication*]

PARKA ...... Pacific Acoustic Research Kaneoche-Alaska
Park Adm... Park Administration [*A publication*]
Park Arb.... Parker on Arbitration [*1820*] (DLA)
Park CR..... Parker's New York Criminal Reports (DLA)
Park Cr Cas ... Parker's New York Criminal Cases (DLA)
Park Crim L ... Parker's New York Criminal Reports (DLA)
Park Crim (NY) ... Parker's New York Criminal Cases (DLA)
Park Crim R ... Parker's New York Criminal Reports (DLA)
Park Crim Rep ... Parker's New York Criminal Reports (DLA)
Park Cr Rep ... Parker's New York Criminal Reports (DLA)
Park Dig..... Parker's California Digest (DLA)
Park Dow ... Park. Dower [*1819*] (DLA)
Parker .... Parker on the Laws of Shipping and Insurance
              [*England*] (DLA)
Parker .... Parker's English Exchequer Reports (DLA)
Parker .... Parker's New Hampshire Reports (DLA)
Parker .... Parker's New York Criminal Reports [*6 vols.*] (DLA)
Parker's Crim R ... Parker's New York Criminal Reports (DLA)
Parker's Crim Rep (NY) ... Parker's New York Criminal Reports (DLA)
Parker's Cr R ... Parker's New York Criminal Reports (DLA)
Park Exch ... Parker's English Exchequer Reports [*1743-67*] (DLA)
Park Hist Ch ... Parkes' History of Court of Chancery [*1828*] (DLA)
Park Ins..... Parker's Insurance [*8 eds.*] [*1787-1842*] [*England*] (DLA)
Park NH..... Parker's New Hampshire Reports (DLA)
Park Rev Cas ... Parker's English Exchequer Reports [*Revenue
              Cases*] (DLA)
Parks & Rec ... Parks and Recreation [*A publication*]
Parks & Wild ... Parks and Wildlife [*A publication*]
Parks Wildl ... Parks and Wildlife [*A publication*]
PARL.......... Parallel
PARL.......... Parliament
PARL.......... Prince Albert RADAR Laboratory
Parl Aff....... Parliamentary Affairs [*A publication*]
Parlam Beil Polit Zeitgesch ... Parlament Beilage aus Politik und
              Zeitgeschichte [*A publication*]
PARLARS... Particulars
PARLB....... Parliamentary Borough
Parl Cas ..... Parliamentary Cases [*House of Lords Reports*] (DLA)
Parl Deb ..... Parliamentary Debates [*A publication*]
PAR Legis Bul ... PAR [*Public Affairs Research*] Legislative Bulletin [*A
              publication*]
Parl Eur Doc ... Parlement Europeen. Documents de Seance (DLA)
Parl Hist Eng ... Parliamentary History of England [*Pre-1803*] (DLA)
Parliam Aff ... Parliamentary Affairs [*A publication*]
Parliam Liaison Group Altern Energy Strategies Bull ... Parliamentary
              Liaison Group for Alternative Energy Strategies. Bulletin [*A
              publication*]
PARLIKDER ... Partiya Litsom k Derevne [*The Party Face to Face with the
              Countryside*] [*Given name popular in Russia after the
              Bolshevik Revolution*]
Parlim Aff... Parliamentary Affairs [*A publication*]
PARLO ...... Parlando [*Music*] (ROG)
Parl Reg ..... Parliamentary Register [*England*] (DLA)
PARLT ...... Parliament
PARLTY .... Parliamentary
PARLY....... Parliamentary
PARM........ Parallelogram [*Geometry*] (ROG)
Par M........ Parents' Magazine [*A publication*]
PARM........ Participating Manager
PARM........ Partido Autentico de la Revolucion Mexicana [*Authentic Party
              of the Mexican Revolution*] (PPW)
PARM........ Persistent Antiradiation Missile (MCD)
PARM........ Program Analysis for Resource Management
PARMA ...... Program for Analysis, Reporting, and Maintenance [*Data
              processing*]
PARMA ...... Public Agency Risk Managers Association (EA)
PARMEDL ... Paramedical
Par Nucl ..... Particles and Nuclei [*A publication*]
PAROCH .... Parochial (ROG)
Paroch Ant ... Kennett's Parochial Antiquities (DLA)
Parod Epic Gr Rel ... Parodorum Epicorum Graecorum Reliquiae [*A
              publication*] (OCD)
Parodontal Acad Rev ... Parodontologie and Academy Review [*A
              publication*]
Parole et Soc ... Parole et Societe [*A publication*]
PAROQ....... Partners Oil Co. [*NASDAQ symbol*] (NQ)
PAROS....... Passive Ranging on Submarines [*Navy*]
PAROSS..... Passive/Active Reporting Ocean Surveillance System
              [*Navy*] (NVT)
PAROX....... Paroxysmal [*Medicine*]
PARP......... PAR Pharmaceutical [*NASDAQ symbol*] (NQ)
PARP......... Production Assistance Report to Pricing [*DoD*]
Par Part..... Parsons on Partnership [*1889*] (DLA)
Par Pass..... Parola del Passato [*A publication*]
PARPRO..... Peacetime Aerial Reconnaissance Program [*Military*] (NVT)
PARR......... Pakistan Atomic Research Reactor
PARR......... Par Technology Corp. [*NASDAQ symbol*] (NQ)
ParR .... Paris Review [*A publication*]
Par R .... Parsons' Select Equity Cases [*Pennsylvania*] (DLA)
ParR .... Partisan Review [*A publication*]
PARR......... Post Accident Radioactivity Removal (NRCH)

PARR.......... Procurement Authorization and Receiving Report [*NASA*] (KSC)
PARR.......... Program Analysis and Resources Review
PARRA .... Parramatta [*Prison in New South Wales*] [*Australia*] (DSUE)
PARRS .... Postal Analysis Response and Reporting System [*Computer system designed to track mail through the US Postal Service*] [*R. R. Donnelley & Sons Co.*]
PARRS .... Psychological Abstracts Reference Retrieval System [*Syracuse University*]
PARS.......... Parachute Altitude Recognition System (MCD)
Pars........... Parsons' Select Equity Cases [*1842-51*] [*Pennsylvania*] (DLA)
PARS.......... Passenger Airlines Reservation System
PARS.......... Patrol Analysis Recording System [*British*]
PARS.......... Perimeter Acquisition RADAR [*Characterization*] System (MCD)
PARS.......... Photoacoustic Raman Spectroscopy
PARS.......... Pilotless Aircraft Research Station [*NASA*]
PARS.......... Procurement Accounting and Reporting System [*Navy*] (NVT)
Pars Ans .... Property Accountability Record System (NASA)
Pars Ans .... Parsons' Answer to the Fifth Part of Coke's Reports (DLA)
Pars Bills & N ... Parsons on Bills and Notes (DLA)
Pars Cont... Parsons on Contracts (DLA)
Pars Dec .... Parsons' Decisions [*2-7 Massachusetts*] (DLA)
PARSEC..... Parallax Second [*Unit of interstellar-space measure*]
PARSEC..... Parser and Extensible Compiler [*Programing language*] (CSR)
PARSECS ... Program for Astronomical Research and Scientific Experiments Concerning Space
Pars Eq Cas ... Parsons' Select Equity Cases [*1842-51*] [*Pennsylvania*] (DLA)
PARSET ..... Precision Askania Range System of Electronic Timing (MUGU)
PARSEV..... Paraglider Research Vehicle [*NASA*] (KSC)
PARSIM..... Perimeter Acquisition RADAR Simulation [*Missile system evaluation*] (RDA)
PARSIP ..... Point Arguello Range Safety Impact Predictor (MUGU)
Pars Mar Ins ... Parsons on Marine Insurance (DLA)
Pars Mar Law ... Parsons on Maritime Law (DLA)
Pars Merc Law ... Parsons on Mercantile Law (DLA)
Parsons'... Parsons' Select Equity Cases [*Pennsylvania*] (DLA)
PARSQ ...... Pararescue
Pars Sel Eq Cas (PA) ... Parsons' Select Equity Cases [*Pennsylvania*] (DLA)
Pars S Eq Cas ... Parsons' Select Equity Cases [*Pennsylvania*] (DLA)
Pars Shipp & Adm ... Parsons on Shipping and Admiralty (DLA)
PARSYM .... Partial Symmetry
PARSYN..... Parametric Synthesis [*Data processing*]
PART.......... Pan American Round Tables in the USA [*Defunct*] (EA)
PART.......... Partial (MSA)
PART.......... Participate (AABC)
PART.......... Participle [*Grammar*]
PART.......... Particular
PART.......... Partis [*A Part*] [*Pharmacy*]
PART.......... Partner (ADA)
PART.......... Parts Allocation Requirements Technique
PART.......... Performing Arts Repertory Theater
PARTAC..... Precision Askania Range Target Acquisition and Control (MUGU)
Part Accel ... Particle Accelerators [*A publication*]
PART AEQ ... Partes Aequales [*Equal Parts*] [*Pharmacy*]
PART AEQUAL ... Partes Aequales [*Equal Parts*] [*Pharmacy*] (ROG)
Part An....... De Partibus Animalium [*of Aristotle*] [*Classical studies*] (OCD)
PART DOLENT ... Partes Dolentes [*Painful Parts*] [*Pharmacy*]
Parth.......... Parthenius [*First century BC*] [*Classical studies*] (OCD)
Partic .... Participating (DLA)
Partic .... Participation (DLA)
PARTIC ..... Participial [*Grammar*]
PARTIC ..... Particle
PARTIC ..... Particular
PARTICO ... Parti d'Interets Congolais [*Party for Congolese Interests*]
Partidas ..... Moreau-Lislet and Carleton's Laws of Las Siete Partidas in Force in Louisiana (DLA)
Partisan R ... Partisan Review [*A publication*]
Partisan Rev ... Partisan Review [*A publication*]
PARTN .... Partnership (ADA)
PARTNER... Proof of Analog Results through a Numerical Equivalent Routine [*Data processing*]
Part and Nucl ... Particles and Nuclei [*A publication*]
Part Nucl.... Particles and Nuclei [*A publication*]
Part Or ...... Partitiones Oratoriae [*of Cicero*] [*Classical studies*] (OCD)
PARTR .... Particular (ROG)
Part R .... Partisan Review [*A publication*]
PARTS .... Precision Approach RADAR Training System (MCD)
PART VIC ... Partitis Vicibus [*In Divided Parts*] [*Pharmacy*]
Party.......... Party Newspapers [*A publication*]
PARU .... Personnel Applied Research Unit [*Canadian military*]
PARU.......... Photographic and Reproduction Unit
PARU.......... Police Aerial Reinforcement [*or Resupply*] Unit [*Thailand*] (CINC)
PARU.......... Postanesthetic Recovery Unit [*Medicine*]
PARV.......... Paravane [*Anti-moored-mine device*] (KSC)
PARV.......... Parvus [*Small*] [*Pharmacy*]
PARVSTRCRA ... Paravane and Stores Crane [*Engineering*]
Par Wills..... Parsons on Wills [*1854*] (DLA)

PaS............ Pamietnik Slowianski [*A publication*]
PAS .... Papers. American School of Classical Studies [*Athens*] [*A publication*]
PAS .... Para-Aminosalicylic [*Acid*] [*Organic chemistry*]
PAS .... Parametric Amplifier System
PaS............ Paranoia Subtle [*Psychology*]
PAS .... Paros [*Greece*] [*Airport symbol*] (OAG)
PAS .... Parti Islanse Malaysia [*Islamic Party of Malaysia*] (PPW)
PAS .... Partido de Accion Socialista [*Socialist Action Party*] [*Costa Rican*] (PPW)
PAS .... Partito de Azione de Sardegna [*Sardinian Action Party*] [*Italy*] (PPW)
PAS .... Pasadena [*California*] [*Seismograph station code, US Geological Survey*] (SEIS)
PA S .... Pascal Second
PAS .... Pascal Source File [*Data processing*]
PAS .... Passage (AABC)
PAS .... Passed to the Adjacent Sector
PAS .... Patients' Aid Society
PAS .... Payload Accommodations Studies [*NASA*] (NASA)
PA S .... Pennsylvania Superior Court Reports (DLA)
PAS .... Percussive Arts Society
PAS .... Perigee-Apogee Satellite [*Aerospace*]
PAS .... Perigee-Apogee Stage [*Aerospace*]
PAS .... Perigee-Apogee System [*Aerospace*]
PA/S .... Periodic Acid/Schiff [*A stain*]
PAS .... Peripheral Anterior Synechia [*Ophthalmology*]
PAS .... Personal Acquaintance Service
PAS .... Personnel Accounting Symbol [*Air Force*] (AFM)
PAS .... Personnel Accounting System [*Marine Corps*]
PAS .... Personnel Activity Sequence (AAG)
PAS .... Personnel Administration Section [*Library Administration Division of ALA*]
PAS .... Personnel Assignment Survey (MCD)
PAS .... Phase Address System
PAS .... Phase Array System
PAS .... Philanthropic Advisory Service
PAS .... Photoacoustic Spectrometry [*Also, OAS*]
PAS .... Physicians for Automotive Safety [*Armonk, NY*] (EA)
PAS .... Pierce Arrow Society (EA)
PAS .... Pilots Advisory Service
PAS .... Pilot's Attack Sight [*British*]
PAS .... Pioneer America Society (EA)
PAS .... Plasma Arc System
PAS .... Pneumatic Air Saw
PAS .... Polish Academy of Sciences
PAS .... Polish Astronautical Society
PAS .... Poly(alkyl Sulfone) [*Organic chemistry*]
PAS .... Polyarylsulfone [*Organic chemistry*]
PAS .... Postacoustic Spectroscopy
PAS .... Posterior Area of [*Loose*] Skin
PAS .... Postponed Accounting System [*Banking*]
PAS .... Postsecondary Agricultural Students (OICC)
PAS .... Power Apparatus and Systems (MCD)
PAS .... Preaward Survey [*To determine a contractor's capability*] [*DoD*]
PAS .... Precise Acquisition System
PAS .... Presidential Appointee Subject
PAS .... Primary Alerting System
PAS .... Principal Assistant Secretary
PAS .... Privacy Act Statement (NRCH)
PAS .... Processed Array Signal
PAS .... Procurement Action System (MCD)
PAS .... Procurement Appropriation, Secondary (MCD)
PAS .... Product Assurance Survey
PAS .... Product Availability Search (MCD)
PAS .... Professional Activity Study [*Later, CPHA*]
PAS .... Professor of Aerospace Studies [*Air Force*] (AFIT)
PAS .... Professor of Air Science [*Air Force*]
PAS .... Program Activity Structure
PAS .... Program Address Storage (IEEE)
PAS .... Program of Advanced Studies
PAS .... Progressive Accumulated Stress [*Psychiatry*]
PAS .... Propulsion and Auxiliary Systems Department [*David W. Taylor Naval Ship Research and Development Center*]
PAS .... Public Address System
PAS .... Public Administration Service (EA)
PAS .... Pulmonary Artery Stenosis [*Medicine*]
PAS .... Pump Actuator Set
PAS .... Pyrotechnics Arming Switch
Pas .... Terminus Paschae [*Easter Term*] [*Latin*] (DLA)
PASA .... Pacific American Steamship Association [*Later, AIMS*]
PASA .... Para-Aminosalicylic Acid [*Organic chemistry*]
PASA .... Personnel Administrative Services Agency [*Army*]
PASAR ...... Psychological Abstracts Search and Retrieval
PASB .... Pan American Sanitary Bureau [*Executive organ of PAHO*]
PASb.......... Predneaziatskii Sbornik Voprosy Khattologii i Khurritologii [*A publication*] (BJA)
PASBI........ Palo Alto Social Background Inventory [*Psychology*]
PASC .... Pacific Area Standards Congress [*American National Standards Institute*]

PASC .... Palestine Armed Struggle Command   (PD)
PASC .... Pan American Sanitary Conference
PASC .... Pan American Standards Commission [See also
               COPANT]   (EA-IO)
PASC .... Parkscan. Parks Canada [A publication]
Pasc .... Paschal [Easter Term]   (DLA)
Pasc .... Paschal's Reports [25, 28-31 Texas]   (DLA)
PASC .... Primitive Art Society of Chicago   (EA)
PASCAL ..... Philips Automatic Sequence Calculator
PASCAL ..... Program Applique a la Selection et a la Compilation
               Automatique de la Litterature [Centre National de la
               Recherche Scientifique-Informascience] [Bibliographic
               database]
PASCAL ..... [A] programing language [1968] [Named after French
               mathematician Blaise Pascal, 1623-62]
PASCH .... Pascha [Easter] [Church calendars]   (ROG)
Pasch .... Paschal [Easter Term]   (DLA)
Paschal ...... Paschal's Reports [28-31 Texas] [Supplement to Vol.
               25]   (DLA)
Paschal's Ann Const ... Paschal's United States Constitution,
               Annotated   (DLA)
Pasch Dig... Paschal's Texas Digest of Decisions   (DLA)
PA Sch J .... Pennsylvania School Journal [A publication]
PASCT .... Pan American Society for Chemotherapy of Tuberculosis [See
               also SAQT]   (EA-IO)
PASE .... Post-Apollo Space Electrophoresis [European Space Agency]
PASE .... Power-Assisted Storage Equipment   (IEEE)
PASED .... Proceedings. Annual Symposium. Society of Flight Test
               Engineers [A publication]
PASEP .... Passed Separately [Military]
PASF .... Photographic Art and Science Foundation   (EA)
PASG .... Patent Abstracts Section, Official Gazette [Federal
               government] [A publication]
PASG .... Pulse Amplifier/Symbol Generator
PASG .... Pulse Analyzer Signal Generator
PASGT .... Personnel Armor System for Ground Troops   (RDA)
PASI .... Pacific Silver Corp. [NASDAQ symbol]   (NQ)
PASI .... Professional Associate, Chartered Surveyors' Institution [Later,
               ARICS]
PASIC .... Percussive Arts Society International Convention [Percussive
               Arts Society]   (TSPED)
PASITAM ... Program of Advanced Studies of Institution Building and
               Technical Assistance Methodologies [MUCIA]
PASJD .... Passive Solar Journal [A publication]
PASL .... Polish Americans for the Statue of Liberty   (EA)
PASLA .... Programable Asynchronous Line Adapter
PASM .... Periodic Acid - Silver Methenamine [Biological stain]
PASM .... Preaward Survey Monitor [DoD]
PASMB .... Proceedings. Australian Society of Medical Research [A
               publication]
Pas Mus ..... Pastoral Music [A publication]
PASN .... Parisian, Inc. [NASDAQ symbol]   (NQ)
PASO .... Pan American Sanitary Organization
PASO .... Pan American Sports Organization [See also ODEPA]   (EA-IO)
PA/SO .... Port Antisubmarine Officer [Navy]
PASOC .... Partido de Accion Socialista [Party of Socialist Action]
               [Spanish]   (PPW)
PASOK .... Panellinion Sosialistikon Kinema [Pan-Hellenic Socialist
               Movement] [Greek]   (PPE)
PASOLS.... Pacific Area Senior Officer Logistics Seminar   (MCD)
PA/SP .... Positioner Antenna and Solar Panel [NASA]
PAS(PR).... Principal Assistant Secretary (Priority)
PASQA...... Pasquale Food Co. Cl A [NASDAQ symbol]   (NQ)
PASQB ...... Pasquale Food Co. Cl B [NASDAQ symbol]   (NQ)
PASRB ...... Preaward Survey Review Board [DoD]
PASS......... Panic Attack Sufferers' Support Groups [Brooklyn, NY]   (EA)
PASS......... Parents Against Subliminal Seduction   (EA)
PASS......... Parts Analysis Summary Sheet
PASS......... Passage [Maps and charts]   (KSC)
PASS......... Passenger   (KSC)
PASS......... Passim [Everywhere] [Latin]
PASS......... Passive
PASS......... Passive-Active Surveillance System   (MCD)
PASS......... Patrol Advanced Surveillance System   (MCD)
PASS......... Pay/Personnel Administrative Support System   (NVT)
PASS......... Penetration Aids/Strike System   (NG)
PASS......... Performance Analysis Subsystem [Military]   (CAAL)
PASS......... Petroleum Abstracts Search Service [Online information
               service]
PASS......... Phased Array Sector Scanner [Instrument for measuring
               ultrasound] [Trademark of General Electric Co.]
PASS......... Planning and Scheduling System   (NASA)
PASS......... Policyowner Attitude Survey Service [LIMRA]
PASS......... Precision Autocollimating Solar Sensor
PASS......... Private Alarm Signalling System
PASS......... Pro-Am Sports Systems [Cable-television network]
PASS......... Procurement Aging and Staging System [Military]   (AABC)
PASS......... Procurement Automated Source System [Small Business
               Administration] [Washington, DC] [Information
               service]   (EISS)
PASS......... Production Automated Scheduling System   (IEEE)

PASS......... Professional Airways Systems Specialists   (EA)
PASS......... Professional Association of Secretarial Services [Denver,
               CO]   (EA)
PASS......... Program Aid Software Systems [Data processing]   (IEEE)
PASS......... Program Alternative Simulation System   (KSC)
PASS......... Program Analysis of Service Systems [Procedure to evaluate
               human service programs]
PASS......... Programed Access/Security System [Card Key Systems]
PASSA ...... Pacific American Steamship Association [Later, AIMS]   (EA)
Passenger Transp ... Passenger Transport [A publication]
Passeng Transp J ... Passenger Transport Journal [England] [A publication]
PASSIM...... President's Advisory Staff on Scientific Information
               Management
PASS-IN-REVIEW ... Priority Aircraft Subsystem Suitability Intensive
               Review   (MCD)
PASSION ... Program for Algebraic Sequences Specifically of Input-Output
               Nature [Data processing]
PASSR ...... Passenger
PASSWD... Password [Data processing]
PAST........ Pasteurella [Genus of bacteria]
PAST......... Pastillus [A Lozenge, Troch, Pastil] [Pharmacy]   (ROG)
Past.......... Pastoral Epistles   (BJA)
PAST......... Pastorate
PA St .... Pennsylvania State Reports   (DLA)
PAST......... Portable Arming System Trainer   (MCD)
PAST......... Process Accessible Segment Table
PAST......... Professor of Air Science and Tactics
PAST......... Propulsion and Associated Systems Test   (MCD)
PA Stat Ann ... Pennsylvania Statutes, Annotated   (DLA)
PA Stat Ann (Purdon) ... Pennsylvania Statutes, Annotated [Purdon]   (DLA)
PA State... Pennsylvania State Reports   (DLA)
PA State Coll Miner Ind Exp Stn Circ ... Pennsylvania State College. Mineral
               Industries Experiment Station. Circular [A publication]
PA State Coll Stud ... Pennsylvania State College. Studies [A publication]
PA State R ... Pennsylvania State Reports   (DLA)
PA State Univ Coll Agric Agric Exp Stn Prog Rep ... Pennsylvania State
               University. College of Agriculture. Agricultural Experiment
               Station. Progress Report [A publication]
PA State Univ Coll Agric Ext Serv Spec Circ ... Pennsylvania State
               University. College of Agriculture. Agricultural Extension
               Service. Special Circular [A publication]
PA State Univ Coll Earth Miner Sci Exp Stn Circ ... Pennsylvania State
               University. College of Earth and Mineral Sciences.
               Experiment Station. Circular [A publication]
PA State Univ Coll Earth Miner Sci Spec Publ ... Pennsylvania State
               University. College of Earth and Mineral Sciences. Special
               Publication [A publication]
PA State Univ Coll Eng Eng Proc ... Pennsylvania State University. College
               of Engineering. Engineering Proceedings [A publication]
PA State Univ Coll Eng Eng Res Bull ... Pennsylvania State University.
               College of Engineering. Engineering Research Bulletin [A
               publication]
PA State Univ Earth Miner Sci Exp Stn Circ ... Pennsylvania State
               University. Earth and Mineral Sciences Experiment
               Station. Circular [A publication]
PA State Univ Miner Ind Exp Stn Circ ... Pennsylvania State University.
               Mineral Industries Experiment Station. Circular [A
               publication]
PA State Univ Sch For Resour Res Briefs ... Pennsylvania State University.
               School of Forest Resources. Research Briefs [A
               publication]
PA State Univ Stud ... Pennsylvania State University. Studies [A publication]
PastBl........ Pastoralblaetter [Stuttgart] [A publication]
Past Care & Couns Abstr ... Pastoral Care and Counseling Abstracts [A
               publication]
PA St Coll An Rp ... Pennsylvania State College. Annual Report [A
               publication]
Pasteur Inst South India Coonoor Annu Rep Dir Sci Rep ... Pasteur Institute
               of Southern India. Coonoor Annual Report of the Director
               and Scientific Report [A publication]
PASTIC ...... Pakistan Scientific and Technical Information Center
               [Formerly, PANSDOC] [Quaid-I-Azan University Campus]
               [Islamabad, Pakistan]
Past Mus .... Pastoral Music [A publication]
PAstO .... Our Lady of Angels College, Aston, PA [Library symbol]
               [Library of Congress]   (LCLS)
Pastoralist ... Pastoralist and Grazier [A publication]
Pastoral Rev ... Pastoral Review [A publication]
Pastoral Rev Graz Rec ... Pastoral Review and Graziers' Record [A
               publication]
Past & Pres ... Past and Present [A publication]
Past Pres.... Past and Present. Studies in the History of Civilization [A
               publication]
Past Presen ... Past and Present [A publication]
Past Psych ... Pastoral Psychology [A publication]
Past R........ Pastoral Review and Graziers' Record [A publication]
PA St R ...... Pennsylvania State Reports   (DLA)
PASTRAM ... Passenger Traffic Management
Past Rev.... Pastoral Review and Graziers' Record [A publication]
PA St Tr .... Pennsylvania State Trials [Hogan]   (DLA)
PASU......... Pan-African Socialist Union [Southern Rhodesia]

PASU......... Patrol Aircraft Service Unit
PASU......... Performing Arts Study Unit [*American Topical Association*] (EA)
PASU......... Provisional Approval for Service Use [*Navy*] (NVT)
PA Summary ... Summary of Pennsylvania Jurisprudence (DLA)
PA Super ... Pennsylvania Superior Court Reports (DLA)
PA Super Ct ... Pennsylvania Superior Court Reports (DLA)
PA Superior Ct ... Pennsylvania Superior Court Reports (DLA)
PASUS ...... Pan American Society of the United States (EA)
PASWEPS ... Passive Antisubmarine Warfare Environmental Protection System [*Navy*] (NATG)
PASYD ...... Policy Analysis and Information Systems [*A publication*]
PAt .... Allentown Public Library, Allentown, PA [*Library symbol*] [*Library of Congress*] (LCLS)
PAT .... Athenaeum of Philadelphia, Philadelphia, PA [*OCLC symbol*] (OCLC)
Pat............ Indian Law Reports, Patna Series (DLA)
Pat............ Indian Rulings, Patna Series [*1929-47*] (DLA)
PAT .... International Brotherhood of Painters and Allied Trades
PAT .... National Patents Appeal Tribunal [*England*] (DLA)
PAT .... Parametric Artificial Talker
PAT .... Paroxysmal Atrial [*or Auricular*] Tachycardia [*Medicine*]
PAT .... Parts Accountability Technique (MCD)
PAT .... Passive Acoustic Torpedo
PAT .... Passive Angle Track (NVT)
PAT .... Patent (KSC)
PAT .... Patent Rolls [*British*]
Pat............ Paterson's Scotch Appeals, House of Lords (DLA)
Pat............ Pathe [*Record label*] [*France*]
PAT .... Patient
PAT .... Patna [*India*] [*Airport symbol*] (OAG)
Pat............ Paton's Scotch Appeal Cases, House of Lords (DLA)
PAT .... Patras [*Greece*] [*Seismograph station code, US Geological Survey*] (SEIS)
PAT .... Patriarch [*Greek Church*] (ROG)
PAT .... Patrick Air Force Base [*Florida*] (KSC)
PAT .... Patrol
PAT .... Patten Corp. [*NYSE symbol*]
PAT .... Pattern
PAT .... Pattern Analysis Test
PAT .... Peninsula Air Transport Co. [*Michigan*] (FAAC)
PAT .... People's Action Team [*South Vietnam*]
PAT .... Performance Appraisal Team (NRCH)
PAT .... Peripheral Assignment Table (CMD)
PAT .... Personalized Array Translator (IEEE)
PAT .... Personnel Authorization Table [*Air Force*]
PAT .... Petroleum Air Transport, Inc. [*Lafayette, IN*] [*FAA designator*] (FAAC)
PAT .... Phenylaminotetrazole [*Psychology*]
PAT .... Physics Achievement Test
PAT .... Picric Acid Turbidity Test
PAT .... Picture Arrangement Test
PAT .... Plasma Arc Tunnel
PAT .... Plastic Apply Template (MCD)
PAT .... Plenum Air Tread [*Army amphibian vehicle*]
PAT .... Plutonium Air Transportable [*Nuclear energy*] (NRCH)
PAT .... Point after Touchdown [*Football*]
PAT .... Political Action Teams
PAT .... Polyaminotriazole [*Organic chemistry*]
PAT .... Position Adjusting Type
PAT .... Postavailability Trials
PAT .... Power Ascension Testing (IEEE)
PAT .... Pre-Apprenticeship Training Allowance (ADA)
PAT .... Preadmission Testing
PAT .... Prearranged Transfers
PAT .... Precision Aim Technique [*for helicopters*] [*Army*] (RDA)
PAT .... Prediction Analysis Techniques
PAT .... Pregnancy at Term [*Gynecology*]
PAT .... Preliminary Acceptance Trials [*Navy*]
PAT .... Prescription Athletic Turf [*Trademark for an artificial turf*]
PAT .... Pressure Assembled Thyristor
PAT .... Priority Air Travel
PAT .... Prism Adaptation Test [*Ophthalmology*]
PAT .... Problem Action Team [*NASA*] (NASA)
PAT .... Procedures Authorized Task (MCD)
PAT .... Process Analysis Team
PAT .... Production Acceptance Test (KSC)
PAT .... Production Assessment Test
PAT .... Professional, Administrative, and Technical (OICC)
PAT .... Proficiency Analytical Testing [*National Institute on Occupational Safety and Health*]
PAT .... Program Analysis Team (KSC)
PAT .... Program Attitude Test (IEEE)
PAT .... Programed Activity Transmission (MCD)
PAT .... Programer Aptitude Test
PAT .... Progressive Achievement Tests in Reading (ADA)
PAT .... Property and Accounting Technician [*Navy*]
PAT .... Pseudoadder Tree [*Data processing*]
PAT .... Psychoacoustic Testing
PAT .... Pulsed Amplifier Tube

PaT .... Purge-and-Trap [*Technique*] [*Environmental Protection Agency*]
PAtA........... Air Products & Chemicals, Inc., Allentown, PA [*Library symbol*] [*Library of Congress*] (LCLS)
PATA......... Pacific American Tankship Association [*Defunct*] (EA)
PATA......... Pacific Area Travel Association [*San Francisco, CA*]
PATA......... Pacific Asia Travel Association (EA)
PATA......... Patagonia [*Region of South America*] (ROG)
PATA......... Plenum Air Tread, Amphibious [*Army vehicle*]
PATA......... Pneumatic All-Terrain Amphibian (IEEE)
PATA......... Professional Aeromedical Transport Association (EA)
Pat Abr ...... Paterson's Abridgment of Poor Law Cases [*1857-63*] (DLA)
Pat App ...... Craigie, Stewart, and Paton's House of Lords Appeals from Scotland [*1726-1857*] (DLA)
Pat App Cas ... Paterson's Scotch Appeal Cases (DLA)
Pat App Cas ... Paton's Scotch Appeal Cases [*Craigie, Stewart, and Paton*] (DLA)
PATASWDEVGRU ... Patrol Antisubmarine Warfare Development Group
PATB......... Patriot Bancorp [*NASDAQ symbol*] (NQ)
PATBOMRON ... Patrol-Bombing Squadron
PAtC.......... Cedar Crest College, Allentown, PA [*Library symbol*] [*Library of Congress*] (LCLS)
PATC......... Paroxysmal Atrial [*or Auricular*] Tachycardia [*Medicine*]
PATC......... Pioneer Automobile Touring Club (EA)
PAT-C .... Position, Attitude, Trajectory-Control [*Aerospace*] (AAG)
PATC......... Potomac Appalachian Trail Club (EA)
PATC......... Professional, Administrative, Technical, and Clerical [*Bureau of Labor Statistics survey*]
PATCA ...... Panama Air Traffic Control Area
PATCA ...... Phase Lock Automatic Tuned Circuit Adjustment [*Telecommunications*]
PATCA ...... Professional and Technical Consultants Association [*San Jose, CA*] (EA)
Pat Cas ...... Reports of Patent, Design, and Trade Mark Cases [*England, Scotland, Ireland*] (DLA)
PATCENT ... Patching Central [*Army*] (AABC)
PA-TCH-SP ... Periodic Acid-Thiocarbohydrazide-Silver Proteinate [*Test*] [*Cytology*]
PATCO....... Professional Air Traffic Controllers Organization [*Defunct*] (EA)
PATCOM.... Patriot Communications Model (MCD)
Pat Comp... Paterson's Compendium of English and Scotch Law (DLA)
PATD......... Patented
Pat Dec ...... Decisions of the Commissioner of Patents (DLA)
Pat Des & TM Rev ... Patent, Design, and Trade Mark Review [*India*] (DLA)
Pat Dig ...... Pattison's Missouri Digest (DLA)
PATDPA.... Deutsche Patent Datenbank [*German Patent Database*] [*German Patent Office*] [*Munich, West Germany*] [*Information service*] (EISS)
PAT & E...... Product Acceptance Testing and Evaluation (MCD)
PATE......... Programed Automatic Telemetry Evaluator
PATE......... Programed Automatic Test Equipment
PATE......... Psychodynamics and Therapeutic Education
PATELL...... Psychological Abstracts Tape Edition Lease or Licensing
Patentbl ..... Patentblatt [*A publication*]
Patentbl Ausg A ... Patentblatt. Ausgabe A [*A publication*]
Patentbl Ausg B ... Patentblatt. Ausgabe B [*A publication*]
Patentjoernaal (S Afr) ... Patentjoernaal (South Africa) [*A publication*]
Patent Off Soc Jour ... Patent Office Society. Journal [*A publication*]
Pater .... Paterson's New South Wales Reports (DLA)
Pater .... Paterson's Scotch Appeal Cases (DLA)
Pater Ap Cas ... Paterson's Scotch Appeal Cases (DLA)
Pater App... Paterson's Scotch Appeal Cases (DLA)
Paters Comp ... Paterson's Compendium of English and Scotch Law (DLA)
Paterson .... Paterson on the Game Laws (DLA)
Paterson .... Paterson on the Liberty of the Subject (DLA)
Paterson .... Paterson's Compendium of English and Scotch Law (DLA)
Paterson .... Paterson's Law and Usages of the Stock Exchange (DLA)
Paterson .... Paterson's Scotch Appeal Cases (DLA)
Paterson .... Paterson's Supreme Court Reports [*New South Wales, Australia*] (DLA)
Paterson Sc App Cas ... Paterson's Scotch Appeal Cases (DLA)
PATF......... Pathfinder Petroleum [*NASDAQ symbol*] (NQ)
PATF......... Program Activation Task Force [*Military*] (AFIT)
PATF......... Property Accountability Task Force [*Army*] (MCD)
PATFOR..... Patrol Force
Pat Game L ... Paterson on the Game Laws [*1861*] (DLA)
PATH......... Pathology (AABC)
Pat & H .... Patton, Jr., and Heath's Reports [*Virginia Special Court of Appeals*] (DLA)
PATH......... Performance Analysis and Test Histories (KSC)
PATH......... Pituitary Adrenotrophic Hormone [*Endocrinology*]
PATH......... Port Authority Trans-Hudson [*New York*]
PATH......... Preserve American Patriotic Holidays Committee (EA)
PATH......... Program for Appropriate Technology in Health (EA)
PATH......... Prospectors and Treasure Hunters Guild (EA)
PATHAT..... Precision Aim-Technique Heliborne Antitank [*Gun system concept*] [*Ballistic Research Laboratory*] (RDA)
Path Biol .... Pathologie et Biologie [*Paris*] [*A publication*]
Path Europ ... Pathologia Europaea [*A publication*]
Pat HL Sc ... Paterson's Scotch Appeal Cases (DLA)

Pat HL Sc ... Paton's Scotch Appeal Cases   (DLA)
Path Microb ... Pathologia et Microbiologia [*A publication*]
Pathobiol Annu ... Pathobiology Annual [*A publication*]
PATHOL..... Pathological   (MSA)
Pathol......... Pathology [*A publication*]
Pathol Annu ... Pathology Annual [*A publication*]
Pathol Biol ... Pathologie et Biologie [*Paris*] [*A publication*]
Pathol Biol (Paris) ... Pathologie Biologie (Paris) [*A publication*]
Pathol Eur ... Pathologia Europaea [*A publication*]
Pathol Eur Suppl ... Pathologia Europaea. Supplement [*A publication*]
Pathol Gen ... Pathologie Generale [*A publication*]
Pathol Microbiol ... Pathologia et Microbiologia [*A publication*]
Pathol Microbiol Suppl ... Pathologia et Microbiologia. Supplementum [*Switzerland*] [*A publication*]
Pathol Res Pract ... Pathology. Research and Practice [*A publication*]
Pathol Vet ... Pathologia Veterinaria [*A publication*]
Path Res Pract ... Pathology. Research and Practice [*A publication*]
PATHS .... Peer Attitudes Toward the Handicapped Scale [*Educational testing*]
PATI .... Passive Airborne Time-Difference Intercept [*Navy*]
PATIA........ Pacific Area Trading and Investment Area
Patiala....... Indian Law Reports, Patiala Series   (DLA)
PATIB........ Polish-American Travel Information Bureau [*New York, NY*]   (EA)
Patient Couns Health Educ ... Patient Counselling and Health Education [*A publication*]
PATINA ...... Potomac Antique Tools and Industries Association   (EA)
Pat Ins........ Paton on Insurance [*1962*]   (DLA)
Pat J .... Patent Journal, Including Trademarks and Models [*South Africa*]   (DLA)
PATK........ Patrick Industries, Inc. [*NASDAQ symbol*]   (NQ)
PAtL .... Lehigh County Historical Society, Allentown, PA [*Library symbol*] [*Library of Congress*]   (LCLS)
Pat Law Rev ... Patent Law Review   (DLA)
Pat Licens ... Paterson's Licensing Acts Annual   (DLA)
Pat LJ........ Patna Law Journal [*India*]   (DLA)
Pat LR .... Patent Law Review   (DLA)
Pat LR .... Patna Law Reports [*India*]   (DLA)
Pat L Reptr ... Patna Law Reporter [*India*]   (DLA)
Pat L Rev.... Patent Law Review   (DLA)
Pat LT........ Patna Law Times [*India*]   (DLA)
Pat LW........ Patna Law Weekly   (DLA)
PAtM .... Muhlenberg College, Allentown, PA [*Library symbol*] [*Library of Congress*]   (LCLS)
Patma-Banasirakam Handes Ist-Filol Zh ... Patma-Banasirakam Handes. Istorkofilologicheskii Zhurnal [*A publication*]
PATMI........ Powder Actuated Tool Manufacturers' Institute [*St. Charles, MO*]   (EA)
Pat Mort ..... Patch on Mortgages [*1821*]   (DLA)
Pat & Mr ..... Paterson and Murray's Reports [*1870-71*] [*New South Wales*]   (DLA)
PATMRG .... PACOM [*Pacific Command*] Air Target Materials Review Group   (CINC)
Pat & Mur ... Paterson and Murray's Supreme Court Reports [*New South Wales, Australia*]   (DLA)
PATN......... Pattern   (MDG)
Patna J Med ... Patna Journal of Medicine [*A publication*]
PATO.......... Partial Acceptance and Takeover Date [*Telecommunications*]   (TEL)
PATO......... Pattetico [*Pathetically*] [*Music*]   (ROG)
Pat Off........ Patent Office   (DLA)
Pat Off Gaz ... Official Gazette. United States Patent Office [*A publication*]
Pat Off J ... Patent Office Journal [*India*]   (DLA)
Pat Off Rep ... Patent Office Reports   (DLA)
Pat Off Soc J ... Patent Office Society. Journal [*A publication*]
Patol Clin Ostet Ginecol ... Patologia e Clinica Ostetrica e Ginecologica [*A publication*]
Patol Fiziol Ehksp Ter ... Patologicheskaya Fiziologiya i Eksperimental'naya Terapiya [*A publication*]
Patol Fiziol Eksp Ter ... Patologicheskaya Fiziologiya i Eksperimental'naya Terapiya [*A publication*]
PATOLIS.... Patent Online Information System [*Database*] [*Japan*]
Patol-Mex ... Patologia-Mexico City [*A publication*]
Patol Pol..... Patologia Polska [*A publication*]
Patol Sper ... Patologia Sperimentale [*A publication*]
Paton.......... Craigie, Stewart, and Paton's Scotch Appeal Cases   (DLA)
Paton App Cas ... Paton's Scotch Appeal Cases   (DLA)
Paton Sc App Cas ... Paton's Scotch Appeal Cases   (DLA)
PA Top G S Com ... Pennsylvania Topographic and Geologic Survey Commission [*A publication*]
PA Topogr Geol Surv Bull A ... Pennsylvania Topographic and Geologic Survey. Bulletin A. Atlas Series [*A publication*]
PA Topogr Geol Surv Bull C ... Pennsylvania. Bureau of Topographic and Geologic Survey. Bulletin C [*County Report*] [*A publication*]
PA Topogr Geol Surv Bull G ... Pennsylvania. Bureau of Topographic and Geologic Survey. Bulletin G [*General Geology Report*] [*A publication*]
PA Topogr Geol Surv Bull M ... Pennsylvania Topographic and Geologic Survey. Bulletin M [*A publication*]

PA Topogr Geol Surv Bull W ... Pennsylvania Topographic and Geologic Survey. Bulletin W [*A publication*]
PA Topogr Geol Surv Geol Atlas PA ... Pennsylvania. Bureau of Topographic and Geologic Survey. Geologic Atlas of Pennsylvania [*A publication*]
PA Topogr Geol Surv Inform Circ ... Pennsylvania. Bureau of Topographic and Geologic Survey. Information Circular [*A publication*]
PA Topogr Geol Surv Miner Resour Rep ... Pennsylvania Topographic and Geologic Survey. Mineral Resources Report [*A publication*]
PA Topogr Geol Surv Progr Rep ... Pennsylvania. Bureau of Topographic and Geologic Survey. Progress Report [*A publication*]
PA Topogr Geol Surv Spec Bull ... Pennsylvania. Bureau of Topographic and Geologic Survey. Special Bulletin [*A publication*]
PATOS .... Patent-Online-System [*Bertelsmann Datenbankdienste GmbH*] [*Database*]
PATP......... Preliminary Authority to Proceed   (NASA)
PATP......... Production Acceptance Test Procedure   (MCD)
PATP......... (Pyridylcarbonylamino)tetrahydropyridine [*Biochemistry*]
PATPEND... Patent Pending
PAT-PTR.... US Patent Data Base - Patent Technology Reports [*Patent and Trademark Office*] [*Database*]
PATR......... Patriarch
PATR......... Patriotic   (ROG)
PATR......... Patron
PATR......... Production Acceptance Test Requirement   (MCD)
PATRA........ Printing, Packaging, and Allied Trades Research Association
Pa Trade J ... Paper Trade Journal [*A publication*]
PATRDL ..... Pan American Tung Research and Development League [*Defunct*]   (EA)
Patr Elect Cas ... Patrick's Election Cases [*1824-49*] [*Upper Canada*]   (DLA)
PATREU ..... Palaestina Treuhandstelle zur Beratung Deutscher Juden [*A publication*]
PATRIC ...... Pattern Recognition and Information Correlations [*Police crime-detection computer*]
PATRIC ...... Pattern Recognition Interpretation and Correlation   (CET)
PATRICIA... Practical Algorithm to Receive Information Coded in Alphanumeric [*Information retrieval*]
Patrick El Cas ... Patrick's Election Cases [*Canada*]   (DLA)
PATRIOT.... Phased Array Tracking to Intercept of Target [*Air defense system unit*] [*Army*]   (RDA)
Pa Tr J........ Paper Trade Journal [*A publication*]
PATROL ..... Program for Administrative Traffic Reports On-Line [*Computer program*] [*Bell System*]
PatrolGr ...... Patrologia Graeca   (BJA)
PatrolLat ..... Patrologia Latina   (BJA)
PATRON..... Patrol Squadron
Patronato Biol Anim Rev ... Patronato de Biologia Animal. Revista [*A publication*]
Patronato Invest Cient Tec "Juan De La Cierva" Mem ... Patronato de Investigacion Cientifica y Tecnica "Juan De La Cierva". Memoria [*A publication*]
Patronato Invest Cient Tec "Juan De La Cierva" Publ Tec ... Patronato de Investigacion Cientifica y Tecnica "Juan De La Cierva". Publicaciones Tecnicas [*A publication*]
PATS......... Payment and Telecommunication Services Corp. [*New York, NY*] [*Telecommunications*]   (TSSD)
PATS......... People Against Tobacco Smoke   (EA)
PATS........ Personnel Assistance Teams [*Military*]
PATS......... Personnel in an Awaiting Training Status [*Air Force*]   (AFM)
PATS........ Portable Acoustic Tracking System for Divers   (MCD)
PATS......... Preacademic Training Student [*Military*]
PATS......... Preauthorized Automatic Transfer Scheme [*Banking*]
PATS......... Precision Altimeter Techniques Study
PATS......... Predicasts Abstract Terminal System [*Data processing*]
PATS......... Program for Analysis of Time Series   (NASA)
PATS......... Propulsion Analysis Trajectory Simulation [*Computer program*] [*NASA*]
PATSEARCH ... Patent Search [*Data processing*]
Pat Ser .... Indian Law Reports, Patna Series   (DLA)
Pat St Tr...... Paton on Stoppage in Transitu [*1859*]   (DLA)
PATSU ...... Patrol Aircraft Service Unit
PATSY .... Parametric Test Synthesis [*Data processing*]
PATSY .... Picture Animal Top Star of the Year [*or Performing Animal Television Star of the Year*] [*American Humane Association award*]
PATSY ...... Programer's Automatic Testing System
PATT........ Partial Automatic Translation Technique
PATT......... Patent   (ROG)
PATT......... Pattern   (AAG)
PATT......... Patton Oil Co. [*NASDAQ symbol*]   (NQ)
PATT......... Project for the Analysis of Technology Transfer [*NASA*]
PATTERN... Planning Assistance Through Technical Evaluation of Relevance Numbers [*RAND Corp.*]
Pattern Recognition ... Journal. Pattern Recognition Society [*A publication*]
Pattern Recognition Lett ... Pattern Recognition Letters [*A publication*]
Patt & H...... Patton, Jr., and Heath's Reports [*Virginia*]   (DLA)
Patt & Heath R ... Patton, Jr., and Heath's Reports [*Virginia*]   (DLA)
Patt & H (VA) ... Patton, Jr., and Heath's Reports [*Virginia*]   (DLA)
Pat TM & Copy J ... Patent, Trademark, and Copyright Journal [*A publication*]

Pat TM & Copyr J of R & Educ ... Patent, Trademark, and Copyright Journal of Research and Education   (DLA)
Patton & H ... Patton, Jr., and Heath's Reports [*Virginia Special Court of Appeals*]   (DLA)
Patton & Heath ... Patton, Jr., and Heath's Reports [*Virginia*]   (DLA)
Patton & H (VA) ... Patton, Jr., and Heath's Reports [*Virginia Special Court of Appeals*]   (DLA)
Patt Recog ... Pattern Recognition [*A publication*]
Pat & Tr Mk Rev ... Patent and Trade Mark Review [*A publication*]
PATU......... Pan American Taekwondo Union   (EA)
PATWAS.... Pilots Automatic Telephone Weather Answering Service
PATWING... Patrol Wing [*Later, Fleet Air Wing*]
PATWINGLANTFLT ... Patrol Wing [*later, Fleet Air Wing*] Atlantic Fleet
PATWINGSCOFOR ... Patrol Wing [*later, Fleet Air Wing*] Scouting Force
PAU............ Pacific Command Frequency Allocation and Uses   (CINC)
PAU............ Pan American Union [*Central organ and permanent secretariat of the OAS*]
PAU............ Pattern Articulation Unit [*Data processing*]
PAU............ Pauk [*Burma*] [*Airport symbol*]   (OAG)
PAU............ Pauzhetka [*USSR*] [*Seismograph station code, US Geological Survey*]   (SEIS)
pau............ Pennsylvania [*MARC country of publication code*] [*Library of Congress*]   (LCCP)
PAU............ Pilotless Aircraft Unit
PAU............ Polska Akademia Umiejetnosci [*A publication*]
PAU............ Portable Annotation Unit [*Military*]   (CAAL)
PAU............ Precision Approach - UNICOM [*Aviation*]
PAU............ Present Address Unknown
PAU............ Probe Aerodynamic Upper   (MCD)
PAU............ Production Assurance Unit   (MCD)
PAU............ Programmes Analysis Unit [*British*]   (MCD)
PAU............ University of Pennsylvania, Philadelphia, PA [*OCLC symbol*]   (OCLC)
PAU-AN ..... Polska Akademia Umiejetnosci. Archivum Neophilologicum [*A publication*]
PAUBM ...... Pan American Union of Baptist Men   (EA)
PAUCA...... Proceedings. Royal Australian Chemical Institute [*A publication*]
PAUCA....... Providence Association of Ukrainian Catholics in America   (EA)
PAUDGET ... Photometer, Automated Universal Distribution Gonielectric Type
PAUG .... Professional Apple Users Group   (ADA)
PAUL.......... Paullum [*A Little*] [*Pharmacy*]
PAULS ...... Pennsylvania Union List of Serials
Paulus........ Julius Paulus. Sententiae Receptae   (DLA)
PA Univ Lab Contr ... Pennsylvania University. Laboratory Contributions [*A publication*]
PA Univ Mus Bul ... Pennsylvania University. University Museum. Bulletin [*A publication*]
PA Univ Schoolmen's Week Proc ... Pennsylvania University. Schoolmen's Week. Proceedings [*A publication*]
Paus .... Pausanias [*Second century AD*] [*Classical studies*]   (OCD)
PAUSE .... People Against Unconstitutional Sex Education
PAusL .... Papers in Australian Linguistics [*A publication*]
P Aust Bioc ... Proceedings. Australian Biochemical Society [*A publication*]
PAUT.......... Pennsylvania & Atlantic Railroad Co. [*Absorbed into Consolidated Rail Corp.*] [*AAR code*]
PAUX.......... Pauxillum [*A Little*] [*Pharmacy*]
P/AV .... Particular Average
PaV............. Pathe-Vox [*Record label*] [*France*]
PAV .... Paulo Afonso [*Brazil*] [*Airport symbol*]   (OAG)
PAV .... Pavia [*Italy*] [*Seismograph station code, US Geological Survey*]   (SEIS)
PAV .... Pavilion
Pav .... Pavo [*Constellation*]
PAV .... Pay Adjustment Voucher [*Military*]
PAV .... Personnel Allotment Voucher
PAV .... Phase Angle Voltmeter
PAV .... Position and Velocity
PAV .... Poste-Avion [*Airmail*] [*French*]
PAV .... Potential Acquisition Valuation Method [*Management*]
PAV .... Pressure-Actuated Valve   (NASA)
PAV .... Pressure Altitude Variation [*Aviation*]
PAV .... Propellant-Actuated Valve
PAV .... Public Access Videotex
PAV .... Puella Americana Vallensis [*Valley Girl*] [*Teenaged girl who follows the fads, fashions, and slang originated among teenagers in California's San Fernando Valley*]
PAVA.......... Polish Army Veterans Association of America   (EA)
PAVAS ...... Performing and Visual Arts Society   (EA)
PAVE......... Position and Velocity Extraction
PAVE......... Primary Auditory Visual Experience [*National Visitor Center*]
PAVE......... Principles and Applications of Value Engineering
PAVe.......... Procarbazine, Alanine Nitrogen Mustard [*L-Phenylanine mustard, L-PAM*], Velban [*Vinblastine*] [*Antineoplastic drug regimen*]
PAVE......... Professional Audiovisual Education Study
PAVE......... Programed Analysis for Value Engineers
PAVE PAWS ... Precision Acquisition of Vehicle Entry Phased Array Warning System

PAVF......... Pulmonary Arteriovenous Fistula [*Medicine*]
PAVFC .... Princeton Azimuthally-Varying-Field Cyclotron
Pavia Univ Ist Geol Atti ... Pavia Universita. Istituto Geologico. Atti [*A publication*]
Pav J Biol ... Pavlovian Journal of Biological Science [*A publication*]
PAVLA .... Papal Volunteers for Latin America [*Defunct*]
Pavlovian J Biol Sci ... Pavlovian Journal of Biological Science [*A publication*]
Pavlov J Biol Sci ... Pavlovian Journal of Biological Science [*A publication*]
Pavlov J Higher Nerv Act ... Pavlov Journal of Higher Nervous Activity [*A publication*]
PAVM........ Patrons of the Arts in the Vatican Museum   (EA)
PAVM........ Phase Angle Voltmeter
PAVMT...... Pavement
PAVN........ People's Army of Vietnam
PA/VR .... Public Assistance/Vocational Rehabilitation
PAVS........ Pulmonary Arterial Vasconstrictor Substance [*Medicine*]
PAVT........ Position and Velocity Tracking
PAW .... Pambwa [*Papua New Guinea*] [*Airport symbol*]   (OAG)
PAW .... Panel of American Women   (EA)
PA of W ..... Pentecostal Assemblies of the World   (EA)
PAW .... People for the American Way   (EA)
PAW .... Percussive Arc Welder
PAW .... Petroleum Administration for War [*World War II*]
PAW .... Plasma Arc Welding
PAW .... Powered All the Way
PAW .... Pulmonary Artery Wedge Pressure [*Cardiology*]
PAWA........ Pan American Women's Association   (EA)
PAWAF...... Polish American Workmen's Aid Fund [*Later, Polish National Alliance of Brooklyn, U.S.A.*]   (EA)
PAWB........ Pacific Western Bancshares [*NASDAQ symbol*]   (NQ)
PA WC Bd Dec ... Pennsylvania Workmen's Compensation Board Decisions   (DLA)
PA WC Bd Dec Dig ... Digest of Decisions, Pennsylvania Workmen's Compensation Board   (DLA)
PA WC Bd (Dep Rep Sup) ... Workmen's Compensation Supplement to Department Reports of Pennsylvania   (DLA)
PAWE........ Program for Analysis of the World Ecosystem
PAWLC ...... Pan-American Weightlifting Confederation   (EA)
PAWN........ Poole, Aberley, Worthington, and Nolen [*Four early residents of Pawn, Oregon. The city derives its name from the initial letters of their surnames*]
PAWOS ...... Portable Automatic Weather Observing Station   (MCD)
PAWP........ Pulmonary Artery Wedge Pressure [*Medicine*]
PAWS........ Parachute Altitude Wind Sensor
PAWS........ Pets Are Worth Safeguarding [*An association*]
PAWS........ Phased Array Warning System
PAWS........ Polar Automatic Weather Station   (NG)
PAWS........ Portable Automatic Weather Station   (MUGU)
PAWS........ Programed Automatic Welding System
PAX .... OPTEVFOR Detachment, Patuxent River, MD [*Navy*]   (CAAL)
PAX .... Pan Central Explorations Ltd. [*Toronto Stock Exchange symbol*]
PAX .... Passenger   (AFM)
PAX .... Patuxent River [*Maryland*]   (MCD)
PAX .... Paxson [*Alaska*] [*Seismograph station code, US Geological Survey*]   (SEIS)
Pax .... Paxton [*Record label*] [*Great Britain*]
PAX .... Physical Address Extension
PAX .... Private Automatic Exchange [*Telecommunications*]
PAXCON ... Passenger Airlift Contract [*Military*]
PAXTA ...... Paxton [*Frank*] Co. [*NASDAQ symbol*]   (NQ)
PAY .... Pamol [*Malaysia*] [*Airport symbol*]   (OAG)
PAYC .... Payco American Corp. [*NASDAQ symbol*]   (NQ)
PAYCOM.... Payload Command [*NASA*]   (MCD)
PAYDAT..... Payload Data [*NASA*]   (MCD)
PAYE.......... Pay-As-You-Earn [*Income tax*] [*British*]
PAYE.......... Pay As You Earn [*Student loan program*]
PAYE.......... Pay As You Enter
PAYERS..... Program Accomplishment Year to Date Evaluation Reviews
Pay & Iv Carr ... Payne and Ivamy's Carriage by Sea [*10th ed.*] [*1976*]   (DLA)
PAYLD .... Payload
PAYM .... Paymaster [*Military*] [*British*]   (ROG)
PAYMARCORPS ... Paymaster, Marine Corps
PAYMR...... Paymaster
PAYMT...... Payment
PAYMTR .... Paymaster [*Military*] [*British*]   (ROG)
PAYN......... Pay'n Save Corp. [*NASDAQ symbol*]   (NQ)
PAYS......... Patriotic American Youth Society
PAYSU ...... P'Eylim-American Yeshiva Student Union   (EA)
PAYT......... Payment
PAYX......... Paychex, Inc. [*NASDAQ symbol*]   (NQ)
PAZ .... Palaeozoic Axial Zone [*Geophysics*]
PAZ .... Poza Rica [*Mexico*] [*Airport symbol*]   (OAG)
PAZA......... Pan American Zebu Association [*Later, IZBA*]   (EA)
PB.............. Air Burundi [*ICAO designator*]   (FAAC)
PB.............. Bachelor of Philosophy
PB.............. Bethlehem Public Library, Bethlehem, PA [*Library symbol*] [*Library of Congress*]   (LCLS)
PB.............. Dr. Karl Thomae GmbH [*Germany*] [*Research code symbol*]
P/B............. Pad and Boom [*Refueling*] [*Aerospace*]   (MSA)

PB............. Paedagogische Blaetter [*A publication*]
PB............. Painted Base   (AAG)
PB............. Panama Basin
PB............. Pantheon Babylonicum: Nomina Deorum [*A publication*]
PB............. Paper Base   (MSA)
PB............. Paperboard Industries [*Toronto Stock Exchange symbol*]
PB............. Paraffin Bath [*Medicine*]
PB............. Parke-Bernet [*Later, SPB*] [*Manhattan art auction house*]
PB............. Parliamentary Bill [*British*]   (ROG)
PB............. Particle-Beam Weapon
PB............. Parts Breakdown
PB............. Passbook [*Banking*]
PB............. Passed Ball
PB............. Pastor Bonus [*A publication*]
PB............. Patrol Boat [*Navy symbol*]
PB............. Patrol Bomber
PB............. Pawnbroker
PB............. Pay Board
PB............. Peanut Butter [*Brand name of the Red Wing Co.*]
PB............. Pennsylvania Ballet
PB............. Pentaborane [*Rocket fuel*]
PB............. Pentobarbital [*Organic chemistry*]
PB............. Peripheral Buffer
PB............. Permanent Bunkers
PB............. Pharmacopoeia Britannica [*British Pharmacopoeia*]
PB............. Phenobarbital [*A drug*]
P & B .... Phenobarbital and Belladonna [*A drug regimen*]
PB............. Philosophiae Baccalaureus [*Bachelor of Philosophy*]
PB............. Phonetically Balanced [*With reference to word lists*]
PB............. Physikalische Berichte [*Physics Briefs*] [*Database*] [*Information retrieval*]
PB............. Picket Boat [*Navy*]
PB............. Piebald
PB............. Pilotless Bomber [*Air Force*]
PB............. Pinchbeck [*Jewelry*]   (ROG)
PB............. Pink Bollworm [*Cotton pest*]
PB............. Pipe Break [*Nuclear energy*]   (NRCH)
PB............. Piperonyl Butoxide [*Organic chemistry*]
PB............. Pit Border [*Paleobotany*]
PB............. Pitney-Bowes, Inc.
PB............. Planning Board
P & B .... Planning and Budgeting [*Military*]   (AFIT)
PB............. Plasminogen Binding [*Hematology*]
PB............. Plate Block [*Philately*]
PB............. Playback   (KSC)
Pb............. Playboy [*A publication*]
PB............. Plot Board   (KSC)
PB............. Plugboard
Pb............. Plumbum [*Lead*] [*Chemical element*]
PB............. Plymouth Brethren   (ROG)
PB............. Pocket Book
PB............. Poetry Bag [*A publication*]
PB............. Police Burgh
PB............. Policy Board   (OICC)
PB............. Polybenzene [*Organic chemistry*]
PB............. Polybutylene [*Organic chemistry*]
PB............. Polymyxin B [*An antibiotic*]
PB............. Pony Baseball [*An association*]   (EA)
PB............. Population Biology
PB............. Ports and Beaches   (NATG)
PB............. Power Boiler
PB............. Power Brakes [*Automobile ads*]
PB............. Prabuddha Bharata [*Calcutta*] [*A publication*]
PB............. Prayer Book
PB............. Preburner [*NASA*]   (NASA)
PB............. Preliminary Breakdown
Pb............. Presbyopia [*Ophthalmology*]
PB............. Presiding Bishop [*Episcopal Church*]
PB............. Pressure Breathing
P & B .... Price and Budgeting   (MCD)
PB............. Primary Buffer [*Chemistry*]
PB............. Primary Bus [*Data processing*]   (CAAL)
PB............. Primitive Baptist
PB............. Prisoners' Barracks   (ADA)
PB............. Private Business [*Slang*] [*British*]
PB............. Privately Bonded
PB............. Production Base   (MCD)
PB............. Profile Block   (MCD)
PB............. Program Board
PB............. Program Breakdown
P-as-B .... Program as Broadcast [*Radio*]   (DEN)
PB............. Property Book [*Army*]   (AABC)
PB............. Proportional Band
PB............. Provisional Battalion [*Military*] [*A publication*]   (ROG)
PB............. Przeglad Biblioteczny [*A publication*]
PB............. Ptychodiscus brevis [*An alga, the cause of the red tide*]
PB............. Public   (DSUE)
PB............. Publications Board [*Later, CFSTI, NTIS*]
PB............. Publications Bulletin
PB............. Publisher's Name [*Online database field identifier*]
P & B .... Pugsley and Burbridge's New Brunswick Reports   (DLA)

PB............. Pull Box   (AAG)
PB............. Pulse Beacon   (KSC)
PB............. Purplish Blue
PB............. Push from the Bush [*A publication*]
PB............. Push Button
PB4............ Plate Block of Four [*Philately*]
PBA .... Academy of the New Church, Bryn Athyn, PA [*OCLC symbol*]   (OCLC)
PBa........... Academy of the New Church, Bryn Athyn, PA [*Library symbol*] [*Library of Congress*]   (LCLS)
PBA .... Paid by Agent [*Business and trade*]
PBA .... Partido Barrientista Autentico [*Bolivian*]   (PPW)
PBA .... Patrol Boat, Air Cushion   (MCD)
PBA .... Patrolmen's Benevolent Association
PBA .... Pencil Beam Antenna
PBA .... Permanent Budget Account
PBA .... Physical Blowing Agent [*Plastics technology*]
PBA .... Pill Box Antenna
PBA .... Pine Bluff Arsenal [*Army*]   (AABC)
PBA .... Plant Breeding Abstracts [*A publication*]
PBA .... Plastic Bag Association [*Scarsdale, NY*]   (EA)
PBA .... Polar Bear Association   (EA)
PBA .... Polish Beneficial Association   (EA)
PBA .... Polybenzamide [*Organic chemistry*]
PBA .... Polyclonal B Cell Activator [*Hematology*]
PBA .... Port Blair [*Andaman Islands*] [*Seismograph station code, US Geological Survey*]   (SEIS)
PBA .... Poultry Breeders of America
PBA .... President of the British Academy
PBA .... Pressure Breathing Assistor [*Medicine*]
PBA .... Printing Brokerage Association [*Arlington, VA*]   (EA)
PBA .... Proceedings. British Academy [*A publication*]
PBA .... Professional Bookmen of America [*Later, Pi Beta Alpha*]   (EA)
PBA .... Professional Bowlers Association of America
PBA .... Provincetown-Boston Airlines, Inc.
PBA .... Public Buildings Administration [*Functions transferred to PBS, 1949*]
PBA .... Pulpobuccoaxial [*Dentistry*]
PBAA.......... Periodical and Book Association of America [*New York, NY*]   (EA)
PBAA.......... Poly(butadiene-acrylic Acid) [*Organic chemistry*]
PBAC .... Pacific Bantam Austin Club   (EA)
PBAC .... PBA, Inc. [*NASDAQ symbol*]   (NQ)
PBAC .... Program Budget Advisory Committee [*Army*]
PB-AESRS ... Property Book - Army Equipment Status Reporting System   (AABC)
PBAL......... Provincetown-Boston Airlines, Inc. [*NASDAQ symbol*]   (NQ)
PBAN......... Poly(butadiene-acrylonitrile) [*Organic chemistry*]
PBAN......... Popular Bancshares [*NASDAQ symbol*]   (NQ)
PBANB .... Pathobiology Annual [*A publication*]
PBAPRS ..... Program/Budget Accounting and Progress Reporting System [*Proposed*] [*Navy*]
PBAPS ...... Peach Bottom Atomic Power Station   (NRCH)
PBAPS ...... Pipe Break Air Piping System   (IEEE)
PBAPS ...... Pipe Break Automatic Protective System   (IEEE)
PBASA ...... Proceedings. Bihar Academy of Agricultural Sciences [*A publication*]
PBAT......... Pyro Battery   (KSC)
PBB .... Bloomsburg State College, Bloomsburg, PA [*OCLC symbol*]   (OCLC)
PBB .... Parallel by Bit
PBB .... Paranaiba [*Brazil*] [*Airport symbol*]   (OAG)
PBB .... Polybrominated Biphenyl [*Flame retardant, toxic chemical*]
PBB .... Posterior Basal Body [*Botany*]
PBB .... Private Boxes and Bags
PBBCAS..... Program-Based Budget Classification and Analysis System [*Pronounced "pib-kaz"*] [*Office of Management and Budget*]
PBBCD....... Promoclim B. Bulletin du Genie Climatique [*A publication*]
PBbChi ..... Columbia County Historical Society, Bloomsburg, PA [*Library symbol*] [*Library of Congress*]   (LCLS)
PBBFI........ Pearl S. Buck Birthplace Foundation, Incorporated   (EA)
PBBH........ Peter Bent Brigham Hospital [*Boston*]
PBBHA ...... Pharmacology, Biochemistry, and Behavior [*A publication*]
PBbS .... Bloomsburg State College, Bloomsburg, PA [*Library symbol*] [*Library of Congress*]   (LCLS)
PBC........... Columbia/Mt. Pleasant, TN [*Location identifier*] [*FAA*]   (FAAL)
PBC........... Pacific Bible College [*California*]
PBC........... Packed by Carrier
PBC........... Panamerican Badminton Confederation [*Calgary, AB*]   (EA-IO)
PBC........... Parallel by Character
PBC........... Pedal Branch of Columellar [*Muscle*]
PBC........... Pen and Brush Club   (EA)
PBC........... People's Bicentennial [*later, Business*] Commission
PBC........... Peripheral Blood Cells [*Medicine*]
PBC........... Peripheral Bus Computer [*Bell System*]
PBC........... Personnel/Burden Carrier Manufacturers Association [*Pittsburgh, PA*]   (EA)
PBC........... Plain Bond Copier [*Pitney Bowes*]
PBC........... Planning and the Black Community   (EA)
PBC........... Point of Basal Convergence

PBC	Practice Bomb Contained (NG)
PBC	Primary Biliary Cirrhosis [Medicine]
PBC	Program Booking Center [Telecommunications] (TEL)
PBC	Program Budget Committee [Military]
PBC	Psychometric Behavior Checklist [Psychology]
PBC	Public Buildings Commission [Functions transferred to PBA, 1939]
PBCA	Pacific Bible College of Azusa [California]
PBCA	Paperboard Butter Chip Association
PBCB	Pierce-Blank Die (Class B) (MCD)
PBCC	Pitney Bowes Credit Corporation
PBCCH	Pentabromochlorocyclohexane [Flame retardant] [Organic chemistry]
PBCE........	Pine Bluff Cotton Exchange (EA)
PBCMO	Poly(bis(chloromethyl)oxetane) [Organic chemistry]
PB/COC	Plymouth Barracuda/Cuda Owners Club (EA)
PBCS........	Persian Bicolor and Calico Society (EA)
PBCS........	Post Boost Control System [Aerospace]
PBCT........	Peoples Banking Corporation [NASDAQ symbol] (NQ)
PBCT........	Proposed Boundary Crossing Time [Aviation]
PBC-USA ...	Polar Bear Club - USA [Coney Island, NY] (EA)
PBC-WS	Polar Bear Club - Winter Swimmers [Later, PBC-USA] (EA)
PBD	Pacific Basin Development Corp. [Vancouver Stock Exchange symbol]
PBD	Paperboard (MSA)
PBD	Paul-Bunnell-Davidsohn [Test] [Immunology]
PBD	Payload Bay Door [NASA] (NASA)
PBD	Phenylbiphenylyloxadiazole [Analytical biochemistry]
PBD	Pierce-Blank Die (MCD)
PBD	Plenum Bleed Duct [Hovercraft]
PBD	Polybutadiene [Organic chemistry]
PBD	Porbandar [India] [Airport symbol] (OAG)
PBD	Power Building (NATG)
PBD	Precise Block Diagram
PBD	Pressboard (MSA)
PBD	Program Budget Decision [DoD]
PBD	Program Budget Directive (MCD)
PBD	Program Budget Document (MCD)
Pbd Abstr ...	Paper and Board Abstracts [A publication]
PBDC	Pacific Basin Development Council (EA)
PBDF........	Payload Bay Door Forward [NASA] (MCD)
PBDG	Push-Button Data Generator (IEEE)
PBDI	Position Bearing and Distance Indicator (MCD)
PBDM........	Payload Bay Door Mechanism [NASA] (NASA)
Pbd Pkg	Paperboard Packaging [A publication]
PBDU........	Pancreaticobiliary Ductal Union [Anatomy]
PBe...........	Beaver Memorial Library, Beaver, PA [Library symbol] [Library of Congress] (LCLS)
PBE	Paint, Body, and Equipment [Automotive engineering]
PBE	Paschen-Back Effect [Spectroscopy]
PBE	Pemberton Exploration [Vancouver Stock Exchange symbol]
PBE	Perlsucht Bacillary Emulsion [Medicine]
PBE	Piggyback Experiment
PBE	Present-Barrel-Equivalent
PBE	Prompt Burst Experiments [Nuclear energy] (NRCH)
PBE	Prompt-by-Example [Data processing]
PBE	Proton Balance Equation
PBE	Proton Binding Energy
PBE	Puerto Berrio [Colombia] [Airport symbol] (OAG)
PBEA........	Paint, Body, and Equipment Association [Kansas City, MO] (EA)
PBEA Newsletter ...	Pennsylvania Business Education Association. Newsletter [A publication]
PBEB	Pentabromoethylbenzene [Flame retardant] [Organic chemistry]
PBeC........	Beaver County Court House, Beaver, PA [Library symbol] [Library of Congress] (LCLS)
PBEC........	Pacific Basin Economic Council
PBEC........	Public Broadcasting Environment Center [Corporation for Public Broadcasting]
PBEIST......	Planning Board European Inland Surface Transport [Army] (AABC)
PBel...........	Centre County Library, Bellefonte, PA [Library symbol] [Library of Congress] (LCLS)
PBelC........	Centre County Court House, Bellefonte, PA [Library symbol] [Library of Congress] (LCLS)
PBEN........	Puritan-Bennett Corp. [NASDAQ symbol] (NQ)
PBER........	Program Budget Execution Review [Army]
PBerol	Berlin Papyri [A publication] (OCD)
PBf	Carnegie Free Library, Beaver Falls, PA [Library symbol] [Library of Congress] (LCLS)
PBF	Fast Patrol Boat [Ship symbol] [NATO] (NATG)
PBF	Patriotic Burmese Forces [World War II]
PBF	Pine Bluff [Arkansas] [Airport symbol] [Obsolete] (OAG)
PBF	Plastic Bottle Feeder
PBF	Plates for Beam Forming (DEN)
PBf	Portal Blood Flow [Physiology]
PBF	Power Burst Facility [Nuclear reactor]
PBf	Pulmonary Blood Flow [Medicine]
PBFA........	Particle Beam Fusion Accelerator
PBFC........	Peter Breck Fan Club [Mecklenburg, NY] (EA)

PBFD........	Pierce Bland and Form Die (MSA)
PBfG.........	Geneva College, Beaver Falls, PA [Library symbol] [Library of Congress] (LCLS)
PBFG.........	Guided Missile Fast Patrol Boat [Ship symbol] (NATG)
PBFL.........	Planning for Better Family Living [UN Food and Agriculture Organization]
PBFP.........	Provisioning Budget Forecast Procedure (MCD)
PBF/WR	Presiding Bishop's Fund for World Relief [New York, NY] (EA)
PBG.........	Phenylbiguanide [Biochemistry]
PBG.........	Plattsburgh, NY [Location identifier] [FAA] (FAAL)
PBG.........	Porphobilinogen [Clinical chemistry]
PBG.........	Program and Budget Guidance
PBGC........	Pension Benefit Guaranty Corporation [Government agency]
PBGI.........	Piedmont Bankgroup [NASDAQ symbol] (NQ)
PBH.........	Patrol Boat, Hydrofoil (MCD)
PBH.........	Phillips, WI [Location identifier] [FAA] (FAAL)
PBH.........	Post Biblical Hebrew [Language, etc.] (BJA)
PBHP........	Pounds per Brake Horsepower
PB-HTGR ...	Peach Bottom High-Temperature Gas-Cooled Reactor
PBI.........	Paper Bag Institute [Scarsdale, NY] (EA)
PBI.........	Partial Background Investigation
PBI.........	Paving Brick Institute
PBI.........	Pen and Brush, Incorporated [An association] (EA)
PBI.........	Philadelphia Bible Institute [Pennsylvania]
PBI.........	Pitch Boundary Indicator (MCD)
PBI.........	Pitney-Bowes, Incorporated [NYSE symbol]
PBI.........	Plant Biological Institute [University of Saskatchewan] [Canada]
PBI.........	Plant Biotechnology Institute [National Research Council of Canada] [Research center] (RCD)
PBI.........	Plant Breeding Institute [British]
PBI.........	Plastic Bottle Institute [New York, NY] (EA)
PBI.........	Plumbing Brass Institute [Later, PMI] (EA)
PBI.........	Polybenzimidazole [Organic chemistry] (NATG)
PBI.........	Poly(phenylenebibenzimidazole) [Organic chemistry]
PBI.........	Poor Bloody Infantry [British military slang]
PBI.........	Process Branch Indicator
PBI.........	Projected Books, Incorporated [Defunct] (EA)
PBI.........	Prophylactic Brain Irradiation [Oncology]
PBI.........	Protein-Bound Iodine [Clinical chemistry]
PBI.........	Pupil Behavior Inventory [Psychology]
PBI.........	Push-Button Indicator
PBI.........	Puzzle Buffs International (EA)
PBI.........	West Palm Beach [Florida] [Airport symbol]
PBIBA........	Pochvy Bashkirii i Puti Ratsional'nogo Ikh Ispol'zovaniya [A publication]
PBIC........	Poly(butyl Isocyanate) [Organic chemistry]
PBIC..........	Programable Buffer Interface Card [Data processing] (NASA)
PBICSGH ...	Permanent Bureau of International Congresses for the Sciences of Genealogy and Heraldry (EA)
PBIF.........	Pacific Bible Institute of Fresno [California]
PBIL	Polybenzimidazolone [Organic chemistry]
PBIM.........	Programable Buffer Interface Module (MCD)
PBIP.........	Paperbound Books in Print [A publication]
PBIP.........	Pulse Beacon Impact Predictor (AAG)
PBISTP......	Peter Burwash International Special Tennis Programs (EA)
PBIT.........	Parity BIT [Binary Digit] [Data communications]
PB/IWT	Ports and Beaches and Inland Waterways Transports [Military] (NATG)
PB and J.....	Peanut Butter and Jelly
PBJ.............	Presa Benito Juarez [Mexico] [Seismograph station code, US Geological Survey] (SEIS)
PBJC	Palm Beach Junior College [Lakeworth, FL]
PBJOD	Plant Biochemical Journal [A publication]
PBK	Pamietnik Biblioteki Kornickiej [A publication]
PBK	Paperback
PBK	Payload Bay Kit [NASA] (NASA)
PBK	Phi Beta Kappa [Honorary society]
PBL.............	Bethlehem Public Library, Bethlehem, PA [OCLC symbol] (OCLC)
PBl.............	Blairsville Public Library, Blairsville, PA [Library symbol] [Library of Congress] (LCLS)
PBL.............	Lehigh University, Bethlehem, PA [Library symbol] [Library of Congress] (LCLS)
PBL.............	Payload Bay Liner [NASA] (MCD)
PBL.............	Peripheral Blood Leukocyte [or Lymphocyte] [Hematology]
PBL.............	[The] Philadelphia Belt Line Railroad Co. [AAR code]
PBL.............	Photo Butt Line (MSA)
PBL.............	Planetary Boundary Layer [Aerospace]
PBL.............	Potential Binding Level [Of natural waters for metal ions]
PBL.............	Probable (FAAC)
PBL.............	Product Baseline (MCD)
PBL.............	Public Broadcast Laboratory
pbl.............	Publisher [MARC relator code] [Library of Congress]
PBL.............	Puerto Cabello [Venezuela] [Airport symbol] (OAG)
PBlbM	Montgomery County Community College, Blue Bell, PA [Library symbol] [Library of Congress] (LCLS)
PBLG.........	Polybenzyl-L-glutamate [Biochemistry]
PBLS.........	Production Baseline Set (MCD)
PBLSA........	Publius [A publication]

PBm .... Bryn Mawr College, Bryn Mawr, PA [*Library symbol*] [*Library of Congress*] (LCLS)
PBM............ Paramaribo [*Surinam*] [*Airport symbol*] (OAG)
PBM............ Patrol Search Plane [*Navy designation for Mariner aircraft*]
PBM............ Peripheral Blood Mononuclear [*Cells*] [*Hematology*]
PBM............ Permanent Bench Mark
PBM............ Poetry Book Magazine [*A publication*]
PBM............ Pressure Bias Modulation (MCD)
PBM............ Principal Beach Master [*RAF*] [*British*]
PBM............ Probability Based-Matched [*Database search techniques*]
PBM............ Probability-Based Matching
PBM............ Production Base Modernization (MCD)
PBM............ Program Budget Manager (MCD)
PBM............ Program Business Management (NASA)
PBmA........ American College of Life Underwriters, Bryn Mawr, PA [*Library symbol*] [*Library of Congress*] (LCLS)
PBMA .... Peanut Butter Manufacturers Association [*Later, PBNPA*] (EA)
PBMC........ Moravian College and Theological Seminary, Bethlehem, PA [*Library symbol*] [*Library of Congress*] (LCLS)
PBMC........ Peripheral Blood Mononuclear Cells [*Hematology*]
PBMCA ...... Archives of the Moravian Church, Bethlehem, PA [*Library symbol*] [*Library of Congress*] (LCLS)
PBMEA ...... Perspectives in Biology and Medicine [*A publication*]
PBmL .... Ludington Public Library, Bryn Mawr, PA [*Library symbol*] [*Library of Congress*] (LCLS)
PBML .... Prague Bulletin of Mathematical Linguistics [*A publication*]
PBMR .... Pennsylvania Bureau of Municipal Research (MCD)
PBMR .... Provisional Basic Military Requirements (NATG)
PBMW .... Moravian College, Bethlehem, PA [*Library symbol*] [*Library of Congress*] (LCLS)
PBN .... Northampton County Area Community College, Bethlehem, PA [*Library symbol*] [*Library of Congress*] (LCLS)
PBN .... Pe Ben Oilfield Services Ltd. [*Toronto Stock Exchange symbol*]
PBN .... Physical Block Number
PBN .... Porto Amboin [*Angola*] [*Airport symbol*] (OAG)
PBN .... Primary Block Number [*Data processing*]
PBN .... Pyrolytic Boron Nitride [*Inorganic chemistry*]
PBNA.......... Partial Body Neutron Activation [*Radiology*]
PBNA .... Phenyl-beta-naphthylamine [*Organic chemistry*]
PBNC .... Peoples Bancorp [*NASDAQ symbol*] (NQ)
PBNE.......... Philadelphia, Bethlehem & New England Railroad Co. [*AAR code*]
PBNM.......... Parallel Bar Noise Maker [*Antiacoustic torpedo device*]
PBNP.......... Phipps Bend Nuclear Plant (NRCH)
PBNP.......... Point Beach Nuclear Plant (NRCH)
PBNPA ...... Peanut Butter and Nut Processors Association [*Potomac, MD*] (EA)
PBO............ Packed by Owner
PBO............ Paraburdoo [*Australia*] [*Airport symbol*] (OAG)
pbo............ Placebo [*Medicine*]
PBO............ Plotting Board Operator (MUGU)
PBO............ Polski Biuletyn Orientalistyczny [*A publication*]
PBO............ Poor Bloody Observer [*British World War I military slang*] (DSUE)
PBO............ Property Book Officer [*Army*] (AABC)
PBO............ Push-Button Operation
PBOD.......... Phytoplankton Biochemical Oxygen Demand [*Oceanography*]
PBOI.......... Public Board of Inquiry
PBOIP........ Preliminary Basis of Issue Plan [*Military*] (MCD)
PBOS .... Planning Board for Ocean Shipping [*Army*] [*NATO*] (AABC)
PBP .... [*The*] Paper Bag Players (EA)
PBP .... Paperbound Books in Print [*A publication*]
PB/P............ Particleboard/Plywood
PBP .... Pay by Phone [*Business and trade*]
PBP .... Pellin-Broca Prism [*Physics*]
PBP .... Penicillin-Binding Protein [*Biochemistry*]
PBP .... Pinkas Bractwa Pogrzebowego [*A publication*]
PBP .... Plotting Board Plot (MUGU)
PBP .... Point by Point
PBP .... Power Bias Panel
PBP .... Pregnenolone Binding Protein [*Endocrinology*]
PBP .... Private Brand Proneness [*Marketing*]
PBP .... Production Base Plan (MCD)
PBP .... Program Board Panel
PBP .... Program and Budget Planning
PBP .... Push-Button Panel
PBPB........ Pyridinium Bromide Perbromide [*Inorganic chemistry*]
PBPE .... Population Biology/Physiological Ecology [*Program*] [*National Science Foundation*]
PBPITMT.... Production Base Productivity Improvement through Manufacturing Technology (MCD)
PBPM .... Poultry Byproduct Meal
PBPS........ Paulist Bible Pamphlet Series [*Glen Rock, NJ*] [*A publication*] (BJA)
PBPS........ Post Boost Propulsion System [*Aerospace*]
PBPTC ...... Palm Beach Psychotherapy Training Center (EA)
PBQ .... Poste De La Baleine [*Quebec*] [*Seismograph station code, US Geological Survey*] (SEIS)
PBQ .... Preschool Behavior Questionnaire

PBr .... Carnegie Public Library, Bradford, PA [*Library symbol*] [*Library of Congress*] (LCLS)
PBR .... Pabst Blue Ribbon [*Beer*]
PBR .... Packed Bed Reactor
PBR .... Patapsco & Back Rivers Railroad Co. [*AAR code*]
P and BR ... Patristic and Byzantine Review [*A publication*]
PBR .... Patrol Boat, River [*Navy symbol*]
PBR .... Payment by Results [*Payment system*]
PBR .... Pebble-Bed Reactor
PBR .... Pembroke, NH [*Location identifier*] [*FAA*] (FAAL)
PBR .... Pencil Beam RADAR
PBR .... Pigment-Binder Ratio [*Weight*]
PBR .... Plant Breeders' Rights
PBR .... Plum Brook Reactor
PBR .... Pole Broken [*Telecommunications*] (TEL)
PBR .... Power Breeder Reactor (AAG)
PBR .... Precision Bombing Range
PBR .... Pressurized Ballistic Range [*NASA*]
PBR .... Progress in Brain Research [*Elsevier Book Series*] [*A publication*]
PBR .... Pyridine-Butadiene Rubber
PBra .... Carnegie Free Library, Braddock, PA [*Library symbol*] [*Library of Congress*] (LCLS)
PBRA .... Polska Bibliografja Biblijna Adnotowana [*A publication*]
PBRA .... Practical Bomb Rack Adapter (NG)
PBRA.......... Professional Bicycle Racers Association [*Defunct*] (EA)
PBracAL.... Allegheny International, Inc. [*Formerly, Allegheny Ludlum Industries, Inc.*], Brackenridge, PA [*Library symbol*] [*Library of Congress*] (LCLS)
PBRCA ...... Proceedings. British Ceramic Society [*A publication*]
PBRE........... Pebble-Bed Reactor Experiment
PBRERP .... Permanent Board for Review of the Enlisted Retention Program
PBRERS .... Permanent Board for Review of the Enlisted Rating Structure
PBRESD .... Polar Branch, Research Environmental Science Division [*Army*]
PBRF .... Plum Brook Reactor Facility [*Lewis Research Center*]
PBriR .... Rohm & Haas Co., Bristol, PA [*Library symbol*] [*Library of Congress*] (LCLS)
P/BRK .... Power Brake [*Automotive engineering*]
PBroGS ...... Church of Jesus Christ of Latter-Day Saints, Genealogical Society Library, Philadelphia Branch, Broomall, PA [*Library symbol*] [*Library of Congress*] (LCLS)
PBRS.......... Pupil Behavior Rating Scale [*Psychology*]
PBRS.......... Push-Button Rotary Switch
PBS .... Bethlehem Steel Corp., Charles H. Herty, Jr., Memorial Library, Bethlehem, PA [*Library symbol*] [*Library of Congress*] (LCLS)
PBS .... Pacific Biological Station [*Department of Fisheries and Oceans*] [*Canada*] [*Research center*] (RCD)
PBS .... Palestine Broadcasting Service (BJA)
PBS .... Parenchymatous Bundle Sheath [*Botany*]
PBS .... Parimutuel Betting System
PBS .... Particulate Biogenic Silica [*Environmental science*]
PBS .... Parts Breakdown Structure
PBS .... Peninsular Base Section [*Military*]
PBS .... Periscope Bombsight Stabilizer
PBS .... Personal Bibliographic Software, Inc. [*Ann Arbor, MI*] [*Information service*] (EISS)
PBS .... Peterborough Board of Education [*UTLAS symbol*]
PBS .... Phosphate-Buffered Saline
PBS .... Pigeon Bay [*South Carolina*] [*Seismograph station code, US Geological Survey*] (SEIS)
PBS .... Pilgrim Regional Bank Shares, Inc. [*NYSE symbol*]
PBS .... Podiatry Bibliographical Society [*Defunct*] (EA)
PBS .... Polarization Beam Splitter
PBS .... Potere Battericida del Sangue [*Bactericidal Property of the Blood*] [*Medicine*]
PBS .... Power Breakfast Syndrome [*Suffered by late-risers forced to attend breakfast meetings*]
PBS .... Prefabricated Bituminous Surfacing
PBS .... Pressure Boundary Subsystem [*Nuclear energy*] (NRCH)
PBS .... Primer Binding Site [*Genetics*]
PBS .... Production Base Support [*Military*] (AABC)
PBS .... Professional Bibliographic System [*Database manager package*] [*Personal Bibliographic Software, Inc.*] [*Ann Arbor, MI*]
PBS .... Professional Bowhunters Society (EA)
PBS .... Program Board Stowage
PBS .... Program Breakdown Structure
PBS .... Program and Budgeting System (OICC)
PBS .... Project Breakdown Structure [*Nuclear energy*] (NRCH)
PBS .... Protestant Big Sisters
PBS .... Public Broadcasting System [*Sometimes facetiously translated "Petroleum Broadcasting System," because of many grants from oil companies*] [*Washington, DC*]
PBS .... Public Buildings Service [*of General Services Administration*]
PBS .... Publications. Babylonian Section. University Museum. University of Pennsylvania [*Philadelphia*] [*A publication*]
PBS .... Push-Button Switch
PBSA.......... Papers. Bibliographical Society of America [*A publication*]
PBSA.......... Phosphate-Buffered Saline Azide [*Culture medium*]

PBSA .... Publications. Bibliographical Society of America [*A publication*]
PBSB .... Prudential Bank [*NASDAQ symbol*] (NQ)
PBSC .... Papers. Bibliographical Society of Canada [*A publication*]
PBSCMA .... Peanut Butter Sandwich and Cookie Manufacturers Association [*Later, PBNPA*] (EA)
PBSE .... Philadelphia-Baltimore Stock Exchange [*Later, PBW*]
PBSED ...... Proceedings. Bioenergy R and D Seminar [*A publication*]
PBSM .... Plastic Bonded Starter Mix
PBSR .... Papers. British School at Rome [*A publication*]
PBSteel ...... Bethlehem Steel Corp., Charles M. Schwab Memorial Library, Bethlehem, PA [*Library symbol*] [*Library of Congress*] (LCLS)
PBSUV ...... Papers. Bibliographical Society. University of Virginia [*A publication*]
PBSW .... Push-Button Switch
PBT .... Pacific Ballet Theatre
PBT .... Para-Bandit Target
PBT .... Parity Bit Test
PBT .... Passband Tuning
PBT .... Peoria Board of Trade (EA)
PBT .... Permian Basin Royalty Trust [*NYSE symbol*]
PBT .... Piggyback Tape [*or Twistor*] [*Data processing*]
PBT .... Pittsburgh Ballet Theatre
PBT .... Polybay Tier
PBT .... Polybenzothiazole [*Organic chemistry*]
PBT .... Polybutylene Terephthalate [*Organic chemistry*]
PBT .... Preferred Body Temperature [*Physiology*]
PBT .... Preliminary-Breath-Test [*Device used by police to determine whether or not a driver is legally intoxicated*]
PBT .... Push-Button Telephone
PBT .... Red Bluff, CA [*Location identifier*] [*FAA*] (FAAL)
PBTE .... Performance-Based Teacher Evaluation (OICC)
PBTF .... Pump Bearing Test Facility [*Nuclear energy*]
P/BTN .... Push Button [*Automotive engineering*]
PBTP .... Polybutylene Terephthalate [*Organic chemistry*]
PBTS .... Proton Beam Transport System
PBTX .... Ptychodiscus brevis Toxin [*Florida red-tide toxin*]
PBU .... Bucknell University, Lewisburg, PA [*OCLC symbol*] (OCLC)
PBU .... Perry Basin [*Utah*] [*Seismograph station code, US Geological Survey*] (SEIS)
PBU .... Putao [*Burma*] [*Airport symbol*] (OAG)
PBUP .... Perforated Backup Plate
PBut .... Butler Public Library, Butler, PA [*Library symbol*] [*Library of Congress*] (LCLS)
PButV .... United States Veterans Administration Hospital, Butler, PA [*Library symbol*] [*Library of Congress*] (LCLS)
PBUU .... Palm Beach County Utilities Class B SV US [*Toronto Stock Exchange symbol*]
PBV .... English Prayer Book Version (BJA)
PBV .... Pedal Blood Vessel
PBV .... Post Boost Vehicle [*Missiles*] (AFM)
PBV .... Predicted Blood Volume [*Medicine*]
PBV .... Pulmonary Blood Volume [*Medicine*]
PBVM .... Presentation of the Blessed Virgin Mary [*Roman Catholic women's religious order*]
PBVR .... [*The*] Port Bienville Railroad [*AAR code*]
PBvu .... Andrew Bayne Memorial Library, Bellevue, PA [*Library symbol*] [*Library of Congress*] (LCLS)
PBW .... Particle Beam Weapon
PBW .... Parts by Weight (IEEE)
PBW .... Percussive Butt Welder
PBW .... Philadelphia Stock Exchange [*Formerly, Philadelphia-Baltimore-Washington Stock Exchange*] [*Later, PSE*]
PBW .... Pink Bollworm [*Cotton pest*]
PBW .... Posterior Bite Wing [*Dentistry*]
PBW .... Power by Wire [*Flight control*]
PBW .... Proportional Bandwidth (MCD)
PBW .... Pulse Burst Wave
PBWAA ...... Professional Basketball Writers Association of America (EA)
PBWEE ...... Pilot Boll Weevil Eradication Experiment [*Department of Agriculture*]
PBWF .... Pulse Burst Waveform
PBX .... Plastic Bonded Explosive
PBX .... Private Branch Exchange [*Telecommunications*]
PBY .... Kayenta, AZ [*Location identifier*] [*FAA*] (FAAL)
PBY .... Patrol Bomber [*Navy designation for Catalina aircraft*]
PBY .... Pep Boys - Manny, Moe & Jack [*NYSE symbol*]
PBZ .... Phenoxybenzamine [*Also, POB*] [*Adrenergic blocking agent*]
PBZ .... Phenylbutazone [*Anti-inflammatory compound*]
PBZ .... Plettenberg [*South Africa*] [*Airport symbol*] (OAG)
PBZ .... Pyribenzamine [*Antihistamine*] [*Trademark*]
PBzN .... Peroxybenzoyl Nitrate [*Lacrimator*]
PC .... All India Reporter, Privy Council [*1914-50*] (DLA)
PC .... British and Colonial Prize Cases [*1914-22*] (DLA)
PC .... Civilian Personnel Division [*Coast Guard*]
PC .... Coastal Escort [*Ship symbol*] (NATG)
PC .... Communist Party [*Peruvian*] (PD)
PC .... Indian Rulings, Privy Council [*1929-47*] (DLA)
PC .... J. Lewis Crozer [*Chester Public*] Library, Chester, PA [*Library symbol*] [*Library of Congress*] (LCLS)

PC .... Judicial Committee of the Privy Council (DLA)
PC .... Pacific Coast Railroad [*AAR code*] [*Terminated*]
PC .... Package Control [*or Controller*]
PC .... Pad Coordinator [*NASA*]
PC .... Palmitoyl Carnitine [*Biochemistry*]
PC .... Pan Malaysian Air Transport [*Malaysia*] [*ICAO designator*] (FAAC)
PC .... [*The*] Panama Canal
Pc .... Pancuronium [*A muscle relaxant*]
PC .... Panoramic Camera
PC .... Paper Chromatography
PC .... Paper or Cloth [*Freight*]
PC .... Paper Copy
PC .... Paracortical Hyperplasia [*Oncology*]
PC .... Paraula Cristiana [*A publication*]
PC .... Parent Care [*Salt Lake City, UT*] (EA)
PC .... Parent Cells
PC .... Parental Control [*Channel lockout*] [*Video technology*]
P & C .... Parge and Core [*Construction*]
PC .... Parish Church [*British*] (ROG)
PC .... Parish Council
PC .... Parliamentary Cases (DLA)
PC .... PARSEC [*Parallax Second*] [*See PARSEC*]
PC .... Parti Communiste [*Communist Party*] [*Luxembourg*] (PPW)
PC .... Participation Certificate
PC .... Partido Colorado [*Colorado Party*] [*Uruguayan*] (PPW)
PC .... Partido Conservador [*Conservative Party*] [*Ecuadorean*] (PPW)
PC .... Parts Catalog (KSC)
PC .... Passenger Certificate [*Shipping*]
PC .... Past Commander
PC .... Patent Cases (DLA)
PC .... Patent Committee (MCD)
PC .... Path Control [*Data processing*] (IBMDP)
PC .... Patres Conscripti [*Senators*] [*Latin*]
PC .... Patrol Craft
PC .... Patrol Vessel, Submarine Chaser [*Navy symbol*]
PC .... Pay Clerk
PC .... Paymaster-Captain [*Navy*] [*British*]
PC .... Paymaster-Commander [*Navy*] [*British*]
PC .... Peace Commissioner [*Ireland*]
PC .... Peace Corps
PC .... Peake's Commentary on the Bible [*A publication*]
PC .... Peg Count [*Telecommunications*] (TEL)
PC .... Penal Code (DLA)
PC .... Penetrating Cell
PC .... [*The*] Penn Central Corp. [*NYSE symbol*]
PC .... Penn Central Transportation Co. [*Subsidiary of Penn Central Co.*] [*Absorbed into Consolidated Rail Corp.*] [*AAR code*]
PC .... Penny Cyclopoedia [*British*] [*A publication*] (ROG)
PC .... Pensiero Critico [*A publication*]
PC .... People's China [*A publication*]
PC .... People's Conference [*Indian*] (PPW)
PC .... Per Centum [*By the Hundred*] [*Latin*]
PC .... Per Condoglianza [*Used on visiting cards to express condolence*] [*Italy*]
PC .... Percent
PC .... Perciconia circinata [*A toxin-producing fungus*]
PC .... Perfectae Caritatis [*Decree on the Appropriate Renewal of the Religious Life*] [*Vatican II document*]
PC .... Perfins Club (EA)
PC .... Performance Code
PC .... Performance Contract (OICC)
PC .... Pericentral
PC .... Pericynthion [*Perilune, or low point, in lunar orbit*]
PC .... Peripheral Cell
PC .... Peripheral Control (BUR)
PC .... Perpetual Curate
PC .... Personal Computer
PC .... Personal Correction
PC .... Personnel Carrier [*A vehicle*]
PC .... Petro-Canada
PC .... Petty Cash
PC .... Pharmacy Corps [*Army*]
PC .... Phase Coherent (CET)
PC .... Pheochromocytoma [*Oncology*]
PC .... Philippine Constabulary
PC .... Philosophical Classics [*A publication*]
PC .... Phobia Clinic [*White Plains Hospital Medical Center*] [*White Plains, NY*] (EA)
PC .... Phosphatidylcholine [*Lecithin*] [*Biochemistry*]
PC .... Phosphocholine [*Biochemistry*]
PC .... Phosphocreatine [*Also, PCr*] [*Creatine phosphate; see CP*] [*Biochemistry*]
PC .... Phosphorylcholine [*Biochemistry*]
PC .... Photocell
PC .... Photoconductor
PC .... Photocounting
Pc .... Phthalocyanine [*Organic chemistry*]
P & C .... Physical and Chemical (AAG)
PC .... Physocyanin [*Biochemistry*]

PC .... Pick Up Cargo   (AFM)
pC .... Picocoulomb
pC .... Picocurie [*Also, pCi*]
PC .... Picture   (MDG)
PC .... Piece   (AAG)
PC .... Pilotage Charts [*Air Force*]
pc .... Pitcairn [*MARC country of publication code*] [*Library of Congress*]   (LCCP)
PC .... Pitch Channel
PC .... Pitch Circle [*Technical drawings*]
PC .... Pitch Control   (KSC)
PC .... Pittsburgh Commerce Institute
PC .... Plaid Cymru [*Welsh national liberation party*]
P/C .... Plane Captain   (MUGU)
PC .... Plane Change   (MCD)
PC .... Plane Commander
PC .... Planetary Citizens [*An association*]   (EA)
PC .... Planning Card   (AAG)
PC .... Planning Concept   (MCD)
PC .... Plant Computer   (NRCH)
PC .... Planting Council [*Bedford, MA*]   (EA)
PC .... Plasma Cell [*Oncology*]
PC .... Plasma Chromatography
PC .... Plasmacytoma [*Medicine*]
PC .... Plastic Core
PC .... Plate Circuit   (DEN)
PC .... Platelet Concentrate [*Hematology*]
PC .... Platelet Count [*Hematology*]
PC .... Platform/Crane
PC .... Pleas of the Crown   (DLA)
PC .... Plenum Chamber
PC .... Plug Cock   (AAG)
PC .... Plug Compatible [*Data processing*]   (BUR)
PC .... Pocket Computer
PC .... Point of Curve [*Technical drawings*]
P-C .... Polar to Cartesian
PC .... Polar Continental [*American air mass*]
PC .... Polar Crane [*Nuclear energy*]   (NRCH)
P/C .... Police Car
PC .... Police-Constable [*Scotland Yard*]
PC .... Police Court [*British*]   (ROG)
P/C .... Polizza di Carico [*Bill of Lading*] [*Italy*] [*Business and trade*]
PC .... Polycarbonate [*Organic chemistry*]
PC .... Polycarbosilane [*Organic chemistry*]
PC .... Polymer-Concrete   (KSC)
PC .... Pondus Civile [*Civil (Avoirdupois) Weight*] [*Pharmacy*]   (ROG)
PC .... Poni Curavit [*Caused to Be Placed*] [*Latin*]
PC .... Poor Clares [*Roman Catholic women's religious order*]
PC .... Poor Classes [*British*]   (DSUE)
PC .... Popular Cult
PC .... Population Census
PC .... Population Communication [*Pasadena, CA*]   (EA)
PC .... Population Council [*New York, NY*]   (EA)
PC .... Port Call
PC .... Port Committee   (NATG)
PC .... Port Control [*Telecommunications*]   (TEL)
PC .... Portable Computer
PC .... Portacaval [*Medicine*]
PC .... Portion Control [*Food service*]
PC .... Portland Cement
Pc .... Positive Wave in Children [*Neurophysiology*]
PC .... Post Card   (ROG)
PC .... Post Cibum [*After Meals*] [*Pharmacy*]
PC .... Post Commander [*Military*]
PC .... Post Consulatum [*After the Consulate*] [*Latin*]
PC .... Postal Clerk [*Navy rating*]
PC .... Postcard
PC .... Postcode   (ADA)
PC .... Postcoital [*Medicine*]
PC .... Posterior Chamber [*Ophthalmology*]
PC .... Posterior Commissure [*Neuroanatomy*]
pc .... Pottery Cache   (BJA)
PC .... Pour Condoler [*To Offer Sympathy*] [*French*]
PC .... Power Contactor
PC .... Power Control [*System*]   (NG)
P-C .... Power Conversion   (CET)
PC .... Practice Cases   (DLA)
PC .... Precarrier
PC .... Precaution Category [*For clinical laboratories*]
PC .... Precedents in Chancery   (DLA)
PC .... Precordia [*Anatomy*]
PC .... Preparatory Commission
PC .... Preparatory Committee
PC .... Presence Chretienne [*A publication*]
PC .... Present Complaint [*Medicine*]
PC .... Presidents Club [*Commercial firm*] [*Houston, TX*]   (EA)
PC .... Pressure Chamber
PC .... Pressure Controller
PC .... Price Commission [*Cost of Living Council*]
PC .... Price Control Cases   (DLA)
P/C .... Price/Cost

PC .... Prices Current
P & C .... Prideaux and Cole's English Reports [*4 New Sessions Cases*]   (DLA)
P-in-C .... Priest-in-Charge [*Church of England*]
PC .... Priest Confessor
PC .... Primary Center
PC .... Primary Circuit   (MCD)
PC .... Primary Code
PC .... Primary Control   (MCD)
PC .... Prime Contractor
PC .... Prime Cost
PC .... Prince Edward Island Provincial Library, Charlottetown, Prince Edward Island [*Library symbol*] [*National Library of Canada*]   (NLC)
PC .... Principal Chaplain   (ADA)
PC .... Principal Component
PC .... Print Club   (EA)
PC .... Printed Circuit
PC .... Printer Control
P & C .... Prism and Cover (Test) [*Ophthalmology*]
PC .... Prisoner of Conscience   (BJA)
PC .... Private Concerns [*An association*] [*Defunct*]   (EA)
PC .... Private Contract [*Tea trade*]   (ROG)
PC .... Private Corporation [*Often follows office listing of an associated group, such as a group of physicians practicing together*]
PC .... Privatization Council   (EA)
PC .... Privilege Car [*on a train*] [*Theatre slang*]
PC .... Privileged Character [*A favored student*] [*Teen slang*]
PC .... Privy Council [*or Councillor*] [*British*]
PC .... Prize Court   (DLA)
PC .... Probable Cause [*Legal term*]
PC .... Probate Court [*British*]   (ROG)
PC .... Problems of Communism [*A publication*]
PC .... Procarbazine [*Also, P, PCB, Pr*] [*Antineoplastic drug*]
PC .... Procedure Civile [*Civil Procedure*]   (DLA)
PC .... Process Computer   (NRCH)
PC .... Process Control   (DEN)
PC .... Processing Center [*Telecommunications*]   (TEL)
PC .... Processor Controller [*Data processing*]   (MDG)
PC .... Procurement Command [*Army*]
P & C .... Procurement and Contracting   (AFM)
PC .... Producers' Council [*Later, CPMC*]   (EA)
PC .... Production Certificate   (MCD)
PC .... Production Company [*Films, television, etc.*]
PC .... Production Control   (MCD)
PC .... Production Costs
PC .... Professional Communication   (MCD)
PC .... Professional Corporation
PC .... Professors of Curriculum   (EA)
PC .... Program Change
PC .... Program Committee [*UN Food and Agriculture Organization*]
PC .... Program Communications [*Military*]   (AFIT)
PC .... Program Control
PC .... Program Coordination   (IEEE)
PC .... Program Counter
PC .... Programed Check   (AAG)
PC .... Progressive Conservative
PC .... Project Censored [*An association*]   (EA)
PC .... Project Children [*Greenwood Lake, NY*]   (EA)
PC .... Project Control   (NASA)
PC .... Project Coordinator   (NG)
PC .... Projector Charge
PC .... Proof Coins [*Numismatics*]
P/C .... Property/Casualty [*Insurance*]
PC .... Proposed Change
PC .... Propositional Calculus [*Logic*]
PC .... Propulsive Coefficient
PC .... Propylene Carbonate [*Organic chemistry*]
PC .... Prospectors Club [*Later, PCI*]
PC .... Prosthetics Center [*Veterans Administration*]
PC .... Protective Climate [*Solar heating*]
PC .... Protective Cover   (MCD)
PC .... Proto-Canaanite   (BJA)
PC .... Protocol Converter   (MCD)
PC .... Provincial Commissioner [*British government*]
PC .... Provisional Costs
PC .... Provocative Concentration [*Immunology*]
PC .... Pseudocode   (AAG)
PC .... Pseudoconditioning Control [*Neurophysiology*]
PC .... Public Citizen [*An association*]   (EA)
PC .... Public Contracts
PC .... Publications in Climatology   (MCD)
PC .... [*The*] Publishers' Circular [*A publication*]   (ROG)
PC .... Pubococcygeus [*Muscle*] [*Anatomy*]
PC .... Pulmonary Capillary [*Medicine*]
PC .... Pulsating Current
PC .... Pulse Cleaned [*Dust filtration*]
PC .... Pulse Comparator   (AAG)
PC .... Pulse Compression
PC .... Pulse Controller

PC .... Pulse Counter [*Data processing*] (MDG)
PC .... Pulverized Coal [*Fuel technology*]
PC .... Punched Card [*Data processing*]
PC .... Puns Corps (EA)
PC .... Purchase Card
P & C .... Purchasing and Contracting
PC .... Purchasing and Contracting
PC .... Pure Clairvoyance [*Psychical research*]
PC .... Purified Concentrate
P & C .... Put and Call [*Stock market*]
PC .... Pyrrolinecarboxylic Acid [*Biochemistry*]
PC .... Single Paper Single Cotton [*Wire insulation*] (AAG)
PC .... Submarine Chaser [*173 foot*] [*Navy symbol*] [*Obsolete*]
PC .... Sumitomo Chemical Co. [*Japan*] [*Research code symbol*]
PC .... Trust Territory of the Pacific Islands [*Two-letter standard
                  code*] (CNC)
PC1 .... Postal Clerk, First Class [*Navy rating*]
PC1 .... Power Control One [*Hydraulic*] (MCD)
PC2 .... Postal Clerk, Second Class [*Navy rating*]
PC2 .... Power Control Two [*Hydraulic*] (MCD)
PC3 .... Postal Clerk, Third Class [*Navy rating*]
PC-10 .... Personal Copier [*Canon Inc.*]
PCA .... Acts of the Privy Council [*England*] (DLA)
PCA .... Calgon Corp., Pittsburgh, PA [*OCLC symbol*] (OCLC)
PCA .... Pacific Communications Area [*Air Force*] (MCD)
PCA .... Panama Canal Authority
PCA .... Paper Converters Association [*Defunct*] (EA)
PCA .... Paperweight Collectors' Association
PCA .... Papillon Club of America (EA)
PCA .... Para-Chloroaniline [*Organic chemistry*]
PCA .... Para-Coumaric Acid [*Organic chemistry*]
PCA .... Parachute Club of America [*Later, USPA*] (EA)
PCA .... Parietal Cell Antibodies [*Immunology*]
PCA .... Parliamentary Commissioner for Administration [*British*]
PCA .... Parti Communiste Algerien [*Algerian Communist Party*]
PCA .... Partido Comunista de Argentina [*Communist Party of
                  Argentina*] (PD)
PCA .... Parts Control Area [*NASA*] (KSC)
PCA .... Passive Cutaneous Anaphylaxis [*Immunochemistry*]
PCA .... Patient-Controlled Analgesia
PCA .... Patriotic Catholic Association [*Name given to nationalized
                  Catholic Church in China*]
P & CA ...... Paying and Collecting Area (AFM)
PCA .... Peak Clipping Amplifier
PCA .... Pekingese Club of America (EA)
PCA .... Pennsylvania Commuter Airlines [*New Cumberland, PA*] [*FAA
                  designator*] (FAAC)
PCA .... Pentachloraniline [*Organic chemistry*]
PCA .... Pentachloroanisole [*Organic chemistry*]
PCA .... Percent Cortical Area [*Neurology*]
PCA .... Perchloric Acid [*Inorganic chemistry*]
PCA .... Pericruciate Association [*Cortex, of cat*]
PCA .... Peripheral Circulatory Assist [*Medicine*]
PCA .... Peritoneal Carcinomatosis [*Oncology*]
PCA .... Permanent Change of Assignment
PCA .... Permanent Court of Arbitration
PCA .... Personal Cash Allowance
PCA .... Photon Counting Array [*Instrumentation*]
PCA .... Physical Configuration Audit [*Military, NASA*]
PCA .... Pinnacle [*Alaska*] [*Seismograph station code, US Geological
                  Survey*] (SEIS)
PCA .... Pitcairn Cierva Autogiro [*Aeronautics*]
PCA .... Pitch Control Assembly (MCD)
PCA .... Plane Circular Aperture
PCA .... Plasma Catecholamine [*Biochemistry*]
PCA .... Plasma-Covered Antenna
PCA .... Plate Count Agar [*Microbiology*]
PCA .... Pneumatic Control Assembly (NASA)
PCA .... Point of Closest Approach
PCA .... Polar Cap Absorption
PCA .... Polycrystalline Alumina
PCA .... Poodle Club of America (EA)
PCA .... Pool Critical Assembly [*Nuclear reactor*]
PCA .... Popular Culture Association (EA)
PCA .... Porous-Coated Anatomical [*Prosthesis*]
PCA .... Porsche Club of America
PCA .... Port Communications Area [*Telecommunications*] (TEL)
PCA .... Portacaval Anastomosis [*Animal model of chronic liver
                  disease*]
PCA .... Portage Creek [*Alaska*] [*Airport symbol*] (OAG)
PCA .... Portland Cement Association [*Skokie, IL*] (EA)
PCA .... Ports Canada
PCA .... Positive Control Area
PCA .... Positive Controlled Airspace
PCA .... Postconstruction Availability (NVT)
PCA .... Posterior Cerebral Artery [*Brain anatomy*]
PCA .... Posterior Communicating Artery [*Anatomy*]
PCA .... Posterior Cricoarytenoid [*A muscle of the larynx*]
PCA .... Potash Company of America, Inc. [*Toronto Stock Exchange
                  symbol*]
PCA .... Power Conditioning Assembly

PCA .... Power Control Assembly (NASA)
PCA .... Precontractual Authorization
PCA .... Prescribed Concentration of Alcohol (ADA)
PCA .... President's Council on Aging [*Inactive*]
PCA .... Primary Carbon Assimilation [*Botany*]
PCA .... Primary Control Assembly [*Nuclear energy*] (NRCH)
PCA .... Primary Coolant Activity [*Nuclear energy*] (NRCH)
PCA .... Prime Candidate Alloy (MCD)
PCA .... Prime Condition Aircraft
PCA .... Principal Component Analysis
PCA .... Principal Control Authority (NATG)
PCA .... Prindle Class Association (EA)
PCA .... Print Council of America (EA)
PCA .... Printed Circuit Assembly [*Telecommunications*] (TEL)
PCA .... Printer Communications Adapter
PCA .... Printing Corporation of America
PCA .... Private Communications Association [*Later, NCA*]
PCA .... Proceedings. Classical Association [*A publication*]
PCA .... Process Control Analyzer
PCA .... Procoagulant Activity
PCA .... Procrastinators' Club of America (EA)
PCA .... Producers Commission Association (EA)
PCA .... Production Credit Association
PCA .... Professional Chess Association (EA)
PCA .... Professional Comedians' Association (EA)
PCA .... Program Change Analysis [*DoD*]
PCA .... Program Coupler Assembly (KSC)
PCA .... Progress Change Authority
PCA .... Progressive Citizens of America
PC & A ...... Project Control and Administration [*NASA*]
PCA .... Protective Clothing Arrangement [*Telecommunications*] (TEL)
PCA .... Protective Connecting Arrangement
                  [*Telecommunications*] (TEL)
PCA .... Public Archives, Charlottetown, Prince Edward Island [*Library
                  symbol*] [*National Library of Canada*] (NLC)
PCA .... Puli Club of America (EA)
PCA .... Pulp Chemicals Association [*New York, NY*] (EA)
PCA .... Pulse Counter Adapter
PCA .... Pyrotechnic Control Assembly [*NASA*]
PCA .... Pyrrolidonecarboxylic Acid [*Organic chemistry*]
PCAA .... Pancretan Association of America (EA)
PCaab .... Parietal Cell Autoantibody [*Immunology*]
PCAAS ...... Proceedings. Connecticut Academy of Arts and Sciences [*A
                  publication*]
PCAC .... Partially Conserved Axial-Vector Current
PCAC .... Private College Admissions Center [*Later, NAAPHE*]
PC Act ...... Probate Court Act (DLA)
PCAG .... Pentobarbital-Chlorpromazine-Alcohol Group [*Medicine*]
PCAG .... Research Station, Agriculture Canada [*Station de Recherches,
                  Agriculture Canada*] Charlottetown, Prince Edward Island
                  [*Library symbol*] [*National Library of Canada*] (NLC)
PCAI .... PCA International [*NASDAQ symbol*] (NQ)
PCalS .... California State College, California, PA [*Library symbol*]
                  [*Library of Congress*] (LCLS)
PCAM .... Partitioned Content Addressable Memory
PCAM .... Punched Card Accounting Machine [*Data processing*]
PCamA .... Alliance College, Cambridge Springs, PA [*Library symbol*]
                  [*Library of Congress*] (LCLS)
PCAMIC ..... People Concerned About MIC [*Methyl Isocyanate*] (EA)
PCAP .... Post Commercial Action Plan [*International Trade
                  Administration*]
PC App ...... Law Reports, Privy Council, Appeal Cases [*England*] (DLA)
PCAPS ...... Production Control and Planning System (MCD)
PCAR .... Paccar, Inc. [*NASDAQ symbol*] (NQ)
PCarl .... Bosler Free Library, Carlisle, PA [*Library symbol*] [*Library of
                  Congress*] (LCLS)
PCarlA .... United States Army War College, Carlisle Barracks, PA [*Library
                  symbol*] [*Library of Congress*] (LCLS)
PCarlD .... Dickinson College, Carlisle, PA [*Library symbol*] [*Library of
                  Congress*] (LCLS)
PCarlD-L .... Dickinson School of Law, Sheeley-Lee Law Library, Carlisle,
                  PA [*Library symbol*] [*Library of Congress*] (LCLS)
PCarlH .... Cumberland County Historical Society and Hamilton Library
                  Association, Carlisle, PA [*Library symbol*] [*Library of
                  Congress*] (LCLS)
PCarlMH .... United States Army, Military History Research Collection,
                  Carlisle Barracks, PA [*Library symbol*] [*Library of
                  Congress*] (LCLS)
PCarlPL ...... United States Army, Carlisle Barracks Post Library, Carlisle
                  Barracks, PA [*Library symbol*] [*Library of
                  Congress*] (LCLS)
PCARS ...... Point Credit Accounting and Reporting System (AFM)
PCAS .... Possible Carotid Artery System [*Medicine*]
PCAS .... Primary Central Alarm Station [*Nuclear energy*] (NRCH)
P Cas .... Prize Cases [*Trehearn and Grant*] [*England*] (DLA)
P Cas .... Prize Cases [*1914-22*] [*England*] (DLA)
PCAS .... Proceedings. Cambridge Antiquarian Society [*A publication*]
PCAS .... Proceedings. Classical Association of Scotland [*A publication*]
PCAS .... Punch Card Accounting System [*Data processing*]
PCASS ...... Parts Control Automated Support System [*Database*]
PCAU .... Parachute Course Administrative Unit [*Military*] [*British*] (INF)

PCAU .... Philippine Civil Affairs Unit [*Army unit which supplied emergency subsistence after end of Japanese dominance*] [*World War II*]
PCAV .... Principal Component Analysis with Varimax Rotation
PCB .... Central Pennsylvania District Library Center, Bellefonte, PA [*OCLC symbol*]   (OCLC)
PcB .... Near Point of Convergence [*Ophthalmology*]
PCB .... Page Control Block [*Data processing*]   (IBMDP)
PCB .... Paracervical Block [*Anesthesiology*]
PCB .... Parti Communiste de Belgique [*Communist Party of Belgium*]   (PPE)
PCB .... Partido Comunista de Bolivia [*Communist Party of Bolivia*] [*La Paz*]   (PPW)
PCB .... Partido Comunista do Brasil [*Communist Party of Brazil*] [*Pro-Albanian*]   (PPW)
PCB .... Parts Control Board
PCB .... Patent Compensation Board [*Energy Research and Development Administration*]
PCB .... Petty Cash Book [*Business and trade*]
PCB .... Planning Change Board   (AAG)
PCB .... Plenum Chamber Burning
PCB .... Poetry Chapbook [*A publication*]
PCB .... Polychlorinated Biphenyl [*Organic chemistry*]
PCB .... Polychlorobenzene
PCB .... Port Check BIT [*Binary Digit*] [*Telecommunications*]   (TEL)
PCB .... Power Circuit Breaker   (MSA)
PCB .... Power Control Box   (NASA)
PCB .... Precambrian Shield Resources Ltd. [*Toronto Stock Exchange symbol*]
PCB .... Primary Carpet Backing
PCB .... Printed Circuit Board   (MCD)
PCB .... Prix de Cession de Base [*Basic Wholesale Price*] [*French*]
PCB .... Procarbazine [*Also, P, PC, Pr*] [*Antineoplastic drug*]
PCB .... Process Control Block
PCB .... Product Configuration Baseline   (NASA)
PCB .... Program Communication Block
PCB .... Program Control Block [*Data processing*]   (BUR)
PCB .... Project Change Board   (AAG)
PCB .... Project Control Branch [*Social Security Administration*]
PCB .... Property Control Branch [*of Allied Military Government*] [*Post-World War II*]
PCB .... Proprietor of Copyright on a Work by a Corporate Body
PCB .... Propulsion [*Ground*] Control Box   (AAG)
PCB .... Public Coin Box [*Telecommunications*]   (TEL)
PCB .... Publisher's Central Bureau
PCBA .... Pepsi-Cola Bottlers Association [*Ft. Lauderdale, FL*]   (EA)
PCBA .... Printed Circuit Board Assembly   (MCD)
PCBB........ Power Conditioning Brass Board   (MCD)
PCBB........ Primary Commercial Blanket Bond [*Insurance*]
PCBC .... Partially Conserved Baryon Current [*IEEE*]
PCBC .... Polk County Biomedical Consortium [*Library network*]
PCBC .... Progressive Conservative Broadcasting Corporation [*Fictional version of the Canadian Broadcasting Corp.*]
PCBCL ...... Printed Circuit Board Configuration List   (MCD)
PCBD .... Polychlorinated Benzodioxin [*Organic chemistry*]
PCBDA...... Put and Call Brokers and Dealers Association [*Inactive*] [*New York, NY*]   (EA)
PCBG .... Primary Care Block Grant
PCB-ML ..... Partido Comunista Marxista-Leninista de Bolivia [*Marxist-Leninist Communist Party of Bolivia*]   (PPW)
PCBPB ...... Pesticide Biochemistry and Physiology [*A publication*]
PCBR........ Printed Circuit Board Repair   (MCD)
PCBR......... Progress in Clinical and Biological Research [*Elsevier Book Series*] [*A publication*]
PC/BRD ..... Printed Circuit Board [*Automotive engineering*]
PCBRD ...... Progress in Clinical and Biological Research [*A publication*]
PCBS......... Plastic Connector Backing Shell
PCBS......... Positive Control Bombardment System [*Air Force*]
PCBS......... Printed Circuit Board Socket
PCBS......... Pupil Classroom Behavior Scale
PCBTS ...... Portable Cesium Beam Time Standard
PCC........... Acts of the Privy Council, Colonial Series   (DLA)
PCC........... Chief Postal Clerk [*Navy rating*]
PCC........... Pacific Cal Air [*Oakland, CA*] [*FAA designator*]   (FAAC)
PCC........... Pacific Cruise Conference [*Formerly, TPPC*] [*Defunct*]   (EA)
PCC........... Package Carrier Committee   (EA)
PCC........... Pad Control Center [*NASA*]   (NASA)
PCC........... Paid Circulation Council [*Later, ASCMP*]
PCC........... Palestinian Ceramic Chronology [*200BC-70AD*] [*A publication*]   (BJA)
PCC........... Panama Canal Commission [*Independent government agency*]
PCC........... Panama Canal Company [*Superseded by Panama Canal Commission*]
PCC........... Panamerican Cultural Circle   (EA)
PCC........... Parent and Child Center [*Project Head Start*]
PCC........... Parochial Church Council [*Church of England*]
PCC........... Partial Crystal Control   (IEEE)
PCC........... Partido Comunista Chileno [*Communist Party of Chile*]   (PD)
PCC........... Partido Comunista Cubano [*Communist Party of Cuba*]   (PPW)
PCC........... Partido Conservador Colombiano [*Conservative Party of Colombia*]   (PPW)

PCC........... Party of Catalan Communists   (PPW)
PCC........... Pasadena City College [*California*]
PCC........... Patient Care Coordinator [*Medicine*]
PCC........... Payload Control and Checkout [*NASA*]   (NASA)
PCC........... Peak Cathode Current
PCC........... People's Caretakers' Council [*Rhodesian*]
PCC........... People's Christian Coalition [*Later, Sojourners*]   (EA)
PCC........... Pepper Community
PCC........... Per-Command Course   (MCD)
PCC........... Per Copia Conforme [*True Copy*] [*Italy*]
PCC........... Performance Certification Component [*SQT*]   (MCD)
PCC........... Performance Criteria Categories   (MCD)
PCC........... Peripheral Control Computer
PCc........... Periscopic Concave [*Ophthalmology*]
PCC........... Personal Computer Coprocessor
PCC........... Personnel Control Center [*Air Force*]   (AFM)
PCC........... Personnel Coordination Center [*Army*]
PCC........... Peters' United States Circuit Court Reports   (DLA)
PCC........... Phenylchlorocarbene [*Organic chemistry*]
PCC........... Pheochromocytoma [*Also, PHEO*] [*Medicine*]
PCC........... Phosphate Carrier Compound
PCC........... Physical Coal Cleaning [*Fuel technology*]
PCC........... Pilarcitos Creek [*California*] [*Seismograph station code, US Geological Survey*]   (SEIS)
PCC........... Pilot Control Console
PCC........... Piperidinocyclohexanecarbonitrile [*Organic chemistry*]
PCC........... Planning Coordination Conference [*NATO*]   (NATG)
PCC........... Plastics in Construction Council [*Later, CCS*]
PCC........... Plug Compatible Computers   (ADA)
PCC........... Plutonium Concentrator Concentrate [*Nuclear energy*]   (NRCH)
PCC........... Point of Compound Curve   (KSC)
PCC........... Pointe Clairde Public Library [*UTLAS symbol*]
PCC........... Poison Control Center
PCC........... Polarity Coincidence Correlator
PCC........... Political Consultative Committee [*Warsaw Pact*]
PCC........... Political Consultative Council   (CINC)
PCC........... Polycore Composite Construction [*Automotive engineering*]
PCC........... Polymer-Cement Concrete   (KSC)
PCC........... Polynesian Cultural Center   (EA)
PCC........... Poor Clares of St. Colette [*Roman Catholic women's religious order*]
PCC........... Population Crisis Committee [*Washington, DC*]   (EA)
PCC........... Portable Cable Checker
PCC........... Portland Cement Concrete
PCC........... Positive Control Communication
PCC........... Postal Concentration Center
PCC........... Postal and Courier Communications [*British*]
PCC........... Pour Copie Conforme [*Certified True Copy*] [*French*]
PCC........... Power Control Console [*Diving apparatus*]
PCC........... Pre-Command Course [*Military*]
PCC........... Precipitated Calcium Carbonate [*Inorganic chemistry*]
PCC........... Precompressor Cooling   (MCD)
PCC........... Prematurely Condensed Interphase Chromosome [*Genetics*]
PCC........... Prerogative Court of Canterbury [*English court previously having jurisdiction over wills*]
PCC........... Presbyterian Charismatic Communion [*Later, PRR*] [*An association*]   (EA)
PCC........... President of the Canteen Committee [*Military*] [*British*]
PCC........... President's Conference Committee
PCC........... Printed Circuit Conference
PCC........... Private Carrier Conference [*of ATA*] [*Alexandria, VA*]   (EA)
PCC........... Privy Council Cases [*British*]
PC(C)........ Privy Councillor (Canada)
PCC........... Problem Control and Contact Unit [*IRS*]
PCC........... Process Chemistry Cell   (NRCH)
PCC........... Process Control Computer
PCC........... Processor Control Console [*Telecommunications*]   (TEL)
PCC........... Product Control Center [*DoD*]
PCC........... Production Compression Capability
PCC........... Production Control Centers   (MCD)
PCC........... Program Control Counter
PCC........... Program Controlled Computer   (DIT)
PCC........... Progress Control Clerk [*DoD*]
PCC........... Project Control Center
PCC........... Prothrombin Complex Concentrates [*Hematology*]
PCC........... Provincial Congress Committee
PCC........... Provisioning Control Code [*Military*]   (AFIT)
PCC........... Psychometric Colorimeter Chamber   (MCD)
PCC........... Pulse Counter Chain
PCC........... Pulverized Coal Combustion [*or Combustor*]
PCC........... Purolator Courier Corporation [*NYSE symbol*]
PCC........... Pyridinium Chlorochromate [*Organic chemistry*]
PCC........... Pyroconvective Cooling
PC(C)........ Submarine Chaser (Control) [*173 foot*] [*Navy symbol*] [*Obsolete*]
PCCA .... Confederation Art Gallery and Museum, Charlottetown, Prince Edward Island [*Library symbol*] [*National Library of Canada*]   (NLC)
PCCA .... Pacific Class Catamaran Association   (EA)
PCCA .... Pattern-Contingent Chromatic Aftereffects
PCCA .... Pewter Collectors Club of America

PCCA .... Playing Card Collectors' Association (EA)
PCCA .... Police Car Collectors Association (EA)
PCCA .... Postcard Collector's Club of America [*Defunct*] (EA)
PCCA .... Power and Communication Contractors Association
　　　　　　　　[*Alexandria, VA*] (EA)
PCCAF .... Procedure Change Control Action Form (AAG)
PCCAF .... Procedure Committee Change Authorization Form (AAG)
PCCB .... Payload Configuration Control Board [*NASA*] (MCD)
PCCB .... Program Configuration Control Board [*NASA*] (NASA)
PCCB .... Project Configuration Control Board [*Army*] (AABC)
PCCC .... Participating College Correspondence Course (MUGU)
PCCCD ..... Proceedings. Annual Allerton Conference on Communication,
　　　　　　　　Control, and Computing [*A publication*]
PCCD .... Peristaltic Charge-Coupled Device (IEEE)
PCCE .... Pacific Coast Coin Exchange
PCCEI .... Permanent Charities Committee of the Entertainment
　　　　　　　　Industries [*Formed by a merger of Permanent Charities
　　　　　　　　Committee of the Motion Picture Industries and Radio-
　　　　　　　　Television-Recording-Advertising Charities*] [*Los Angeles,
　　　　　　　　CA*] (EA)
PCCEMRSP ... Permanent Commission for the Conservation and
　　　　　　　　Exploitation of the Maritime Resources of the South
　　　　　　　　Pacific
PCCES .... Planning and Coordinating Committee for Environmental
　　　　　　　　Studies [*National Research Council*]
PCCF .... Plan Case Control File [*IRS*]
PCCG .... Protestant Cinema Critics Guild [*Later, PCG*] (EA)
PCCH .... Pentachlorocyclohexene [*Organic chemistry*]
PCCI .... Paper Cup and Container Institute [*Later, SSI*] (EA)
PCCI .... President's Committee on Consumer Interests [*Terminated,
　　　　　　　　1971*]
PCCL .... People's Community Civic League (EA)
PCCL .... Precontract Cost Letter [*Navy*] (NG)
PCCM .... Master Chief Postal Clerk [*Navy rating*]
PCCM .... Price Communications [*NASDAQ symbol*] (NQ)
PCCM .... Private Circuit Control Module [*Telecommunications*] (TEL)
PCCM .... Program Change Control Management (NASA)
PCCM .... Program Control Contract Manager (MCD)
PCCN .... Part Card Change Notice (KSC)
PCCN .... Port Call Control Number (AABC)
PCCN .... Preliminary Configuration Control Number (AAG)
PCCN .... Provisioning Contract Control Number (NASA)
PCCNL ...... Pacific Coast Coordinator of Naval Logistics
PCCO .... Plant Clearance Contracting Officer [*DoD*]
PCCOA ..... Coles Associates Ltd., Charlottetown, Prince Edward Island
　　　　　　　　[*Library symbol*] [*National Library of Canada*] (NLC)
PCCP .... Preliminary Contract Change Proposal (KSC)
PCCR .... Publishing Center for Cultural Resources [*New York, NY*] (EA)
PCCS .... Parti Conservateur Chretien-Social [*Conservative Christian-
　　　　　　　　Social Party*] [*Swiss*] (PPE)
PCCS .... Photographic Camera Control System (KSC)
PCCS .... Positive Control Communications System
PCCS .... Processor Common Communications System
PCCS .... Program Change Control System (NG)
PCCS .... Program and Cost Control System [*Army*] (RDA)
PCCS .... Publications Contract Coverage Schedule (MCD)
PCCS .... Senior Chief Postal Clerk [*Navy rating*]
PCCSD ...... Proceedings. International Conference on Cybernetics and
　　　　　　　　Society [*A publication*]
PCCT .... Percept and Concept Cognition Test [*Psychology*]
P-CCU .... Post Coronary Care Unit
PCCU .... President's Commission on Campus Unrest (EA)
PCCU .... Punched Card Control Unit [*Data processing*] (AABC)
PCD .... Democratic Conservative Party [*Nicaraguan*] (PD)
PCD .... Pacific Car Demurrage Bureau, San Francisco CA [*STAC*]
PCD .... Panama Canal Department
PCD .... Partido Comunista Dominicano [*Dominican Communist Party*]
　　　　　　　　[*Dominican Republic*] (PPW)
PCD .... Phenylchlorodiazirine [*Organic chemistry*]
PCD .... Photoconductive Decay [*Semiconductor material*]
PCD .... Planned Completion Date [*Telecommunications*] (TEL)
PCD .... Plasma Cell Dyscrasia [*Medicine*]
PCD .... Plutonium Concentrator Distillate [*Nuclear energy*] (NRCH)
PCD .... Pneumatic Control Distributors (KSC)
PCD .... Polycystic Disease [*of kidneys*] [*Medicine*]
PCD .... Port Control Diagnostic [*Telecommunications*] (TEL)
PCD .... Positive Control Document (MCD)
Pcd .... Postcard (BJA)
PCD .... Pounds per Capita per Day (AAG)
PCD .... Power Control Device [*Nuclear energy*] (NRCH)
PCD .... Power Control and Distribution
PCD .... Precision Course Direction [*Aerospace*] (MCD)
PCD .... Pressure Control Distributor (KSC)
PC & D ...... Priest, Confessor, and Doctor (ROG)
PCD .... Primary Ciliary Dyskinesia [*Medicine*]
PCD .... Primary Current Distribution [*Electroplating*]
PCD .... Procedural Change Directive (KSC)
PCD .... Procurement and Contracts Division [*NASA*]
PCD .... Procurement Control Document (MCD)
PCD .... Production Common Digitizer
PCD .... Program Change Decision [*Military*]

PCD .... Program Control Display System [*NATO Air Defense Ground
　　　　　　　　Environment*] (NATG)
PCD .... Program Control Document (KSC)
PCD .... Project Control Drawing (AAG)
PCD .... Pulmonary Clearance Delay [*Medicine*]
PCDA .... Post Card Distributors Association
PCDB .... Poison Control Data Base [*Database*]
PCDC .... Diagnostic Chemicals Ltd., Charlottetown, Prince Edward
　　　　　　　　Island [*Library symbol*] [*National Library of
　　　　　　　　Canada*] (NLC)
PCDC .... Plutonium Canister Decontamination Cell [*Nuclear
　　　　　　　　energy*] (NRCH)
PCDD .... Pentachlorodioxin [*Organic chemistry*]
PCDD .... Polychlorinated Dibenzodioxin [*Organic chemistry*]
PCDDS ...... Private Circuit Digital Data Service
　　　　　　　　[*Telecommunications*] (TEL)
PCDF .... Polychlorinated Dibenzofuran [*Organic chemistry*]
PCDHi .... Delaware County Historical Society, Chester, PA [*Library
　　　　　　　　symbol*] [*Library of Congress*] (LCLS)
PCDI .... Per Capita Disposable Income
PCDI .... Pierce Die
PCDJ .... Pakistan Committee for Democracy and Justice (EA)
PCDL .... Pro-Choice Defense League [*Hempstead, NY*] (EA)
PCdoB .... Partido Comunista do Brasil [*Communist Party of
　　　　　　　　Brazil*] (PPW)
PC-DOS ..... Personal Computer Disk Operating System [*IBM's version of
　　　　　　　　Microsoft program*]
PCDP .... Pilot Control and Display Panel
PCDP .... Punched Card Data Processing
PCD-PRP .... Pueblo, Cambio, y Democracia - Partido Roldosista Popular
　　　　　　　　[*People, Change, and Democracy - Popular Roldosista
　　　　　　　　Party*] [*Ecuadorean*] (PPW)
PCDR .... Procedure (AAG)
PCDS .... Payload Command Decoder Subunit [*NASA*] (KSC)
PCDS .... Power Conversion and Distribution System
PCDS .... Procurement Congressional Descriptive Summary
　　　　　　　　[*Army*] (RDA)
PCDS .... Project Control Drawing System (AAG)
PCDU .... Payload Command Decoder Unit [*NASA*] (NASA)
PCDUS ...... Plasma Cell Dyscrasias of Unknown Significance [*Medicine*]
PCE .... Pacific East Air, Inc. [*Los Angeles, CA*] [*FAA
　　　　　　　　designator*] (FAAC)
PCE .... Page Communications Engineers, Inc. [*Canada*] (MCD)
PCE .... Painter Creek, AK [*Location identifier*] [*FAA*] (FAAL)
PCE .... Partido Comunista Ecuatoriano [*Communist Party of
　　　　　　　　Ecuador*] (PPW)
PCE .... Partido Comunista de Espana [*Communist Party of Spain*]
　　　　　　　　[*Madrid*] (PPE)
PCE .... Patrol Escort [*Patrol Craft Escort*] [*Navy symbol*]
PCE .... Pedco Energy Ltd. [*Vancouver Stock Exchange symbol*]
PCE .... Perchloroethylene [*Organic chemistry*]
PCE .... Peripheral Control Element
PCE .... Personal Consumption Expenditure
PCE .... Physical Capacities Evaluation [*Test of hand skills*]
PCE .... Piece [*Numismatics*]
PCE .... Plasma Chamber Evacuation Subsystem (MCD)
PCE .... Plug Compatible Ethernet
PCE .... Polyarthrite Chronique Evolutive [*Chronic Evolutive
　　　　　　　　Polyarthritis*] [*Medicine*] [*French*]
PCE .... Positive Continuous Engagement [*Automotive engineering*]
PCE .... Power Conditioning Equipment
PC of E ...... Presbyterian Church of England
PCE .... Pressure to Clutch Engage [*Aerospace*] (AAG)
PCE .... Prince Edward Island Department of Education, Charlottetown,
　　　　　　　　Prince Edward Island [*Library symbol*] [*National Library of
　　　　　　　　Canada*] (NLC)
PCE .... Privy Councillor, England (ROG)
PCE .... Production Check Equipment (MCD)
PCE .... Professional Care, Inc. [*American Stock Exchange symbol*]
PCE .... Program Cost Estimate (AFM)
PCE .... Pseudocholinesterase [*Same as ACAH*] [*An enzyme*]
PCE .... Pulmocutaneous Exchange
PCE .... Punch Card Equipment [*Data processing*] (AFM)
PCE .... Pyrometric Cone Equivalent [*Refractory industry*]
PCE .... Submarine Chaser Escort
PCEA .... Pacific Coast Electrical Association
PCEA .... Phosphate Chemicals Export Association (EA)
PCEAA ...... Professional Construction Estimators Association of America
　　　　　　　　[*Cornelius, NC*] (EA)
PCEA Bol Trimest Exp Agropecu ... PCEA Boletin Trimestral de
　　　　　　　　Experimentacion Agropecuaria [*A publication*]
PCE(C) ...... Patrol Vessel, Escort (Control) [*180 feet*] [*Navy symbol*]
　　　　　　　　[*Obsolete*]
PCEDURE ... Procedure (ROG)
PCEEDGS ... Proceedings (ROG)
PCEEO .... President's Committee on Equal Employment Opportunity
　　　　　　　　[*Later, OFCCP*] [*Department of Labor*]
PCEH .... President's Committee on Employment of the Handicapped
PCEI .... Prime Contract End Item (MCD)
PCEM .... Parliamentary Council of the European Movement
PCEM .... Process Chain Evaluation Model (IEEE)

PCEM........ Program Committee on Education for Mission (EA)
PCE-R .... Partido Comunista de Espana - Reconstituido [*Reconstituted Spanish Communist Party*] (PD)
PCER.......... Patrol Rescue Escort [*Patrol Craft Escort Rescue*] [*Navy symbol*]
P Cert Ed ... Professional Certificate in Education
PCET........ Personal Computer Extended Technology [*Computer bus*]
PCETF........ Power Conversion Equipment Test Facility
PCEU.......... Partido Comunista de Espana Unificado [*Unified Communist Party of Spain*] (PPW)
PCEU.......... Pulse Compression/Expansion Unit
PCF .... Pacific Air Express [*Honolulu, HI*] [*FAA designator*] (FAAC)
PCF .... Pacific Ridge Resources [*Vancouver Stock Exchange symbol*]
PCF .... Pacificulture Foundation (EA)
PCF .... Parents Choice Foundation [*Waban, MA*] (EA)
PCF .... Parti Communiste Francais [*French Communist Party*] [*Paris*] (PPW)
PCF .... Patrol Craft (Fast) [*Navy symbol*]
PCF .... Patrol Craft, Inshore [*Navy symbol*]
PCF .... Payload Control Facility [*NASA*] (MCD)
PCF .... Peace Centers Foundation [*Later, UDC*] (EA)
PCF .... Pentagon Counterintelligence Force
PCF .... Personal Card File
PCF .... Personnel Control Facility [*Military*] (AABC)
PCF .... Pharyngoconjunctival Fever [*Medicine*]
PCF .... Plan Characteristics File [*IRS*]
PCF .... Postcard Club Federation (EA)
PCF .... Potential Conflict Forecasts [*Army*]
PCF .... Potentially Critical Failures
PCF .... Pounds per Cubic Foot
PCF .... Power Cathode Follower
PCF .... Power per Cubic Foot
PCF .... Prairie Chicken Foundation (EA)
PCF .... Primary Checkpoint File
PCF .... Probability of Consequence Factor
PCF .... Processed Citation File
PCF .... Program Change Factor
PCF .... Program Checkout Facility
PCF .... Program Control Facility
PCF .... Programed Cryptographic Facility [*Data processing*]
PCF .... Prothrombin Conversion Factor [*Hematology*]
PCF .... Public Concern Foundation (EA)
PCF .... Pulse Compression Filter
PCF .... Pulse-to-Cycle Fraction
PCFA........ Pin, Clip, and Fastener Association [*Later, PCFS*] (EA)
PCFE........ Polytrifluorochloroethylene [*Organic chemistry*]
PCFE........ Prime Contractor Furnished Equipment (MCD)
PCFIA........ Particle Concentration Fluorescence Immunoassay
PCFO........ Position Classification Field Office
PCFP........ Predicted Comparative Failure Probability
PCFR.......... Programmatic Center for Fire Research [*National Bureau of Standards*]
PCFS.......... Pin, Clip, and Fastener Services [*An association*] [*Hartford, CT*] (EA)
PCG........... Guided Missile Coastal Escort [*Ship symbol*] (NATG)
PCG........... Pacific Gas & Electric Co. [*NYSE symbol*]
PCG........... Paracervical Ganglion [*Anatomy*]
PCG........... Parti Communiste de Guadeloupe [*Communist Party of Guadeloupe*] (PPW)
PCG........... PezCorona Gold Corp. [*Vancouver Stock Exchange symbol*]
PCG........... Phonocardiogram [*Cardiology*]
PCG........... Plains Cotton Growers (EA)
PCG........... Planning and Control Guide
PCG........... Power Conditioning Group (MCD)
PCG........... Printed Circuit Generator
PCG........... Programable Character Generator
PCG........... Protestant Cinema Guild [*Formerly, PCCG*] [*Defunct*]
PCG........... Pulsed Coaxial Gun
PCGD........ Pollution Control Guidance Document
PCGLA...... Physics and Chemistry of Glasses [*A publication*]
PCGM....... Pacific Coast Garment Manufacturers [*Later, AAMA*] (EA)
PCGN....... Permanent Committee of Geographical Names [*Later, BGN*]
PCGS .... Protein Crystal Growth System
PCGVB...... Pairwise Correlated Generalized Valence Bond [*Physics*]
PCH.......... Cheyney State College, Cheyney, PA [*OCLC symbol*] (OCLC)
PC & H....... Packing, Crating, and Handling (AFM)
PCH.......... Parent Compound Handbook [*Later, Ring Systems Handbook*] [*American Chemical Society*]
PCH.......... Paroxysmal Cold Hemoglobinuria [*Medicine*]
PCH.......... Partido Comunista de Honduras [*Communist Party of Honduras*] (PD)
PCH.......... Patrol Craft (Hydrofoil) [*Navy symbol*]
PCh.......... Phosphocholine [*Biochemistry*]
PCH.......... Physicochemical Hydrodynamics [*A publication*]
PCH.......... Pitch
PCH.......... Potlatch Corp. [*Formerly, PFI*] [*NYSE symbol*]
PCH.......... Prepare Chassis
Pch.......... Principal Chaplain [*Navy*] [*British*]
PCH.......... Punch (KSC)
PCH.......... Purchase
PCHAR...... Printing Character [*Data processing*]

PCHBD...... Patchboard (MSA)
PCHC........ Holland College, Charlottetown, Prince Edward Island [*Library symbol*] [*National Library of Canada*] (NLC)
PChCo ...... Conococheague District Library, Chambersburg, PA [*Library symbol*] [*Library of Congress*] (LCLS)
PCHCY...... Parents Campaign for Handicapped Children and Youth (EA)
PCHD........ Purchased (ROG)
PCHE........ Poor Clare Nuns of the Holy Eucharist [*Roman Catholic religious order*]
PCHE........ Purchase (ROG)
PCHEA...... Petro/Chem Engineer [*A publication*]
Pchel Mir.... Pchelovodnyi Mir [*A publication*]
Pchel Zhizn ... Pchelovodnaya Zhizn' [*A publication*]
PCheS........ Cheyney State College, Cheyney, PA [*Library symbol*] [*Library of Congress*] (LCLS)
PCHG........ Punching
PCHK........ Parity Check [*Data communications*] (TEL)
PCHL........ Pacific Coast Hockey League [*Later, Western Hockey League*] (EA)
PCHN........ Peerless Chain [*NASDAQ symbol*] (NQ)
PCHN........ Programed Course, Home Nursing [*Red Cross*]
PCH PhysicoChem Hydrodyn ... PCH: PhysicoChemical Hydrodynamics [*Later, Physicochemical Hydrodynamics*] [*England*] [*A publication*]
PCHR........ Panamanian Committee for Human Rights (EA)
PCHR........ Pentecostal Coalition for Human Rights (EA)
PCHR........ Purchaser (ROG)
PCHRG...... Public Citizen Health Research Group [*Washington, DC*] (EA)
PCHSR...... Purchaser
PCH & T .... Packaging, Crating, Handling, and Transportation (CINC)
PCHT........ Packaging, Crating, Handling, and Transportation (AABC)
PCHT........ Parchment (MSA)
PChW........ Wilson College, Chambersburg, PA [*Library symbol*] [*Library of Congress*] (LCLS)
PCI .... Packet Communications, Incorporated
PCI .... Panel Call Indicator
PCI .... Parti Communiste Internationaliste [*Internationalist Communist Party*] [*French*] (PPE)
PCI .... Partito Comunista Italiano [*Italian Communist Party*] [*Rome*]
PCI .... Pattern of Cockpit Indication
PCI .... Pattern Correspondence Index
PCI .... Pax Christi International (EA-IO)
PCI .... Payless Cashways, Incorporated [*NYSE symbol*]
PCI .... PCL Industries Ltd. [*Toronto Stock Exchange symbol*]
PCI .... Pellet Clad Interaction [*Nuclear energy*] (NRCH)
PCI .... Periodic Conformance Inspection (MCD)
PCI .... Peripheral Command Indicator
PCI .... Peripheral Controller Interface
PCI .... Personal Computer Interface [*Varitronics Systems, Inc.*]
PCI .... Photographic Credit Institute (EA)
PCI .... Physical Configuration Inspection (AFIT)
PCI .... Physical Configuration Item [*Military*]
pCi .... Picocurie [*Also, pC*]
PCI .... Pilot Club International (EA)
PCI .... Pilot Controller Integration (IEEE)
PCI .... Pipe Collectors International (EA)
PCI .... Planning Card Index (AAG)
PCI .... Plant Control Interface
PCI .... Pneumatic Circuit Indicator
PCI .... Political Campaign Institute [*Commercial firm*] (EA)
PCI .... Portable Cesium Irradiator
PCI .... Portable Compass Indicator
PCI .... Possible Criminal Informant
PCI .... Potato Chip Institute, International [*Later, PC/SFA*] (EA)
PCI .... Powder Coating Institute [*Alexandria, VA*] (EA)
PCI .... Pre-Counseling Inventory [*Psychology*]
PCI .... Precision Components, Incorporated [*Addison, IL*] [*Telecommunications service*] (TSSD)
PCI .... Prestressed Concrete Institute [*Chicago, IL*] (EA)
PCI .... Privy Council Decisions [*India*] (DLA)
PCI .... Privy Councillor, Ireland (ROG)
PCI .... Process Control Interface
PCI .... Product Configuration Identification (KSC)
PCI .... Product Cost Index
PCI .... Production Control Information [*Sheffield, England*] [*Software supplier*]
PCI .... Program Check Interruption [*Data processing*] (MDG)
PCI .... Program Control Input (NASA)
PCI .... Program-Controlled Interruption [*Data processing*] (IBMDP)
PCI .... Program in Correctional Institutions (OICC)
PCI .... Programable Communications Interface
PCI .... Project Concern International [*San Diego, CA*] (EA)
PCI .... Prophylactic Cranial Irradiation [*Oncology*]
PCI .... Prospectors Club International (EA)
PCI .... Trust Territory of the Pacific Islands [*Three-letter standard code*] (CNC)
PCIAOH...... Permanent Commission and International Association on Occupational Health (EA-IO)
PCIC.......... Poison Control Information Center
PC & IC ...... Polaris Control and Information Center [*Missiles*]

PCICS .... Permanent Council of the International Convention of Stresa
　　　　　　　　on Cheeses　(EA-IO)
PCIEC .... Permanent Committee for International Eucharistic
　　　　　　　　Congresses　(EA)
PCIEC .... Pontifical Committee for International Eucharistic
　　　　　　　　Congresses　(EA)
PCIFC........ Patsy Cline International Fan Club　(EA)
PCIFC........ Permanent Commission of the International Fisheries
　　　　　　　　Convention
PCII .... Protocol Computers [*NASDAQ symbol*]　(NQ)
PCIJ .... Permanent Court of International Justice Cases　(DLA)
PCIJ Ann R ... Permanent Court of International Justice Annual
　　　　　　　　Reports　(DLA)
PCIL .... Pilot-Controlled Instrument Landing [*Aviation*]　(NASA)
PCILO........ Perturbative Configuration Interaction [*Based on*] Localized
　　　　　　　　Orbitals [*Quantum mechanics*]
PCIM .... Parti du Congres de l'Independance de Madagascar [*Party of
　　　　　　　　the Congress for Malagasy Independence*]
PCIMP........ President's Commission on Income Maintenance
　　　　　　　　Programs　(EA)
PCIMR....... Centre for Information and Technical Assistance, Institute of
　　　　　　　　Man and Resources, Charlottetown, Prince Edward Island
　　　　　　　　[*Library symbol*] [*National Library of Canada*]　(NLC)
PCIN.......... Program Change Identification Number　(NASA)
PC-IOC...... Posterior Chamber - Intraocular Lens [*Ophthalmology*]
PCIOMR ..... Preconditioning Interim Operating Management
　　　　　　　　Recommendation [*Nuclear energy*]　(NRCH)
PCIOS .... Processor Common Input/Output System [*Data processing*]
PCIP .... Poseidon [*Missile*] Communication Improvement Program
　　　　　　　　[*Navy*]
PCIRO .... Preparatory Commission for International Refugee
　　　　　　　　Organization
PCIS .... Patient Care Information System [*Datacare, Inc.*]　(EISS)
PCIS .... Primary Containment Isolation System [*Nuclear
　　　　　　　　energy*]　(NRCH)
PCIS .... Production Control Information System　(NVT)
PCIS .... Professional Career Information Service [*Department of Labor*]
PCIYRA .... Pacific Coast Intercollegiate Yacht Racing Association
PCJ............. Peoples Jewellers Ltd. [*Toronto Stock Exchange symbol*]
PCJ............. Pontifical College Josephinum [*Ohio*]
PCJ............. Pontifical College Josephinum, Worthington, OH [*OCLC
　　　　　　　　symbol*]　(OCLC)
PCJ............. Sisters of the Poor Child Jesus [*Roman Catholic religious
　　　　　　　　order*]
PC Judg ..... Privy Council Judgments [*India*]　(DLA)
PCK........... Phase Control Keyboard
PCK........... Pilot Check　(FAAC)
PCK........... Porcupine Creek, AK [*Location identifier*] [*FAA*]　(FAAL)
PCK........... Primary Chicken Kidney [*Cell line*]
PCK........... Printed Circuit Keyboard
PCK........... Processor Controlled Keying [*Data processing*]
PCKB .... Printed Circuit Keyboard
PCKD .... Polycystic Kidney Disease [*Medicine*]
Pckgng Eng ... Packaging Engineering [*A publication*]
Pckgng Rev ... Packaging Review [*A publication*]
PCL .... Alberta Attorney General, Provincial Court Libraries [*UTLAS
　　　　　　　　symbol*]
PCL .... Clarion Free Library, Clarion, PA [*Library symbol*] [*Library of
　　　　　　　　Congress*]　(LCLS)
PCL .... Confederation Centre Library, Charlottetown, Prince Edward
　　　　　　　　Island [*Library symbol*] [*National Library of
　　　　　　　　Canada*]　(NLC)
PCL .... Pachaco Lake [*California*] [*Seismograph station code, US
　　　　　　　　Geological Survey*]　(SEIS)
PCL .... Pacific Coast League [*Baseball*]
PCL .... Parallel Communications Link
PCL .... Parcel
PCL .... Parti Communiste Libanais [*Lebanese Communist
　　　　　　　　Party*]　(PPW)
PCL .... Parti Communiste de Luxembourg [*Communist Party of
　　　　　　　　Luxembourg*]　(PPE)
PCL .... Pencil　(MSA)
PCL .... Permissible Contamination Limits [*Nuclear energy*]　(NRCH)
PCL .... Persistent Corpus Luteum [*Medicine*]
PCL .... Phillips Cables Limited [*Toronto Stock Exchange symbol*]
PCL .... Pilot-Controlled Lighting [*Aviation*]　(FAAC)
PCL .... Planning Configuration List
PCL .... Planning and Conservation League　(EA)
PCL .... Plasma Cell Leukemia [*Oncology*]
PCL .... Polycaprolactone [*Organic chemistry*]
PCL .... Positive Control Line
PCL .... Posterior Cruciate Ligament [*Anatomy*]
PCL .... Power Control List　(MCD)
PCL .... Preliminary Change Letter [*Navy*]　(NG)
PCL .... Premier Cruise Lines
PCL .... Primary Coolant Loop　(NASA)
PCL .... Printed Circuit Lamp
PCL .... Printer Control Language
PCL .... Procedural Control Language [*1971*] [*Data processing*]　(CSR)
PCL .... Process Capability Laboratory
PCL .... Programing Checklist　(MCD)

PCL .... Project Control Ledgers [*Navy*]　(NG)
PCL .... Pseudocleistogamous [*Botany*]
PCL .... Pucallpa [*Peru*] [*Airport symbol*]　(OAG)
PCL .... Pulse Compression Loop
PCLA .... Power Control Linkage Assembly
PCLA .... Process Control Language [*Texas Instruments, Inc.*]
PCLA .... Project Coordination and Liaison Administration　(OICC)
PCLB .... [*The*] Price Company [*NASDAQ symbol*]　(NQ)
PCLD......... Dependent Political Entity [*Board on Geographic Names*]
PCLDI........ Prototype Closed-Loop Development Installation [*Nuclear
　　　　　　　　energy*]　(NRCH)
PCLG......... Public Citizen Litigation Group　(EA)
PCLI .... Independent Political Entity [*Board on Geographic Names*]
PCLJ .... Pacific Coast Law Journal　(DLA)
PCLK......... Pay Clerk
PCLLG .... Ollennu's Principles of Customary Land Law in Ghana　(DLA)
PCLMP....... President's Advisory Committee on Labor-Management Policy
　　　　　　　　[*Abolished, 1973*]
PCLN......... Personalcomputer Literaturnachweis [*Datendienst Weiss*]
　　　　　　　　[*Database*]
PCLO......... Passenger Control Liaison Office [*or Officer*] [*Army*]　(AABC)
PCLQA ...... Physics and Chemistry of Liquids [*A publication*]
P CI R .... Parker's New York Criminal Reports　(DLA)
PCLR......... PR [*Public Relations*] Committee for Licensing and
　　　　　　　　Registration　(EA)
P CI R .... Privy Council Reports　(DLA)
PCIS .... Clarion State College, Clarion, PA [*Library symbol*] [*Library of
　　　　　　　　Congress*]　(LCLS)
PCLS .... Law Society of Prince Edward Island, Charlottetown, Prince
　　　　　　　　Edward Island [*Library symbol*] [*National Library of
　　　　　　　　Canada*]　(NLC)
PCLS .... Prototype Closed-Loop System [*Nuclear energy*]　(NRCH)
PCLT .... Portable Coded LASER Target
PCLT .... Prototype Closed-Loop Test [*Nuclear energy*]　(NRCH)
PCIvU .... Ursinus College, Collegeville, PA [*Library symbol*] [*Library of
　　　　　　　　Congress*]　(LCLS)
PCLX .... Section of Independent Political Entity [*Board on Geographic
　　　　　　　　Names*]
PCM .... Coastal Escort Medium [*200-500 tons*] [*Ship symbol*]　(NATG)
PCM .... Parabolic Collimator Mirror
PCM .... Parallel Cutter Mechanism
PCM .... Parity Check Matrix　(MCD)
PCM .... Parti des Classes Moyennes [*Middle Class Party*]
　　　　　　　　[*Luxembourg*]　(PPE)
PCM .... Parti Communiste Marocain [*Moroccan Communist Party*]
PCM .... Parti Communiste Martiniquais [*Communist Party of
　　　　　　　　Martinique*]　(PPW)
PCM .... Partido Comunista Mexicano [*Mexican Communist
　　　　　　　　Party*]　(PPW)
PCM .... Passive Countermeasure
PCM .... Penalty Cost Model
PCM .... Pending Contractual Matters　(NRCH)
PCM .... Per Calendar Month [*Business and trade*]　(ADA)
PCM .... Percent Milli　(NRCH)
PCM .... Phase Change Materials [*Solar energy*]
PCM .... Phase Conjugate Mirror
PCM .... Phase Contrast Microscopy
PCM .... Philippine Campaign Medal
PCM .... PIPES Buffer with Calcium and Magnesium
PCM .... Pitch Control Motor
PCM .... Plug Compatible Mainframe [*Data processing*]
PCM .... Plug Compatible Manufacturer [*Data processing*]
PCM .... Plug Compatible Memory
PCM .... Police Court Mission [*British*]　(ROG)
PCM .... Polyimide Composite Material
PCM .... Port Command Area [*Telecommunications*]　(TEL)
PCM .... Post Column Method [*Chromatography*]
PCM .... Postmammillary Caudal Magnocellular Nuclei [*Neuroanatomy*]
PCM .... Power-Cooling Mismatch
PCM .... Precision Condenser Microphone
PCM .... President's Certificate of Merit [*Military award*]　(AFM)
PCM .... Process Control Module [*Telecommunications*]　(TEL)
PCM .... Profiling Current Meter [*Oceanography*]　(MSC)
PCM .... Program Configuration Manager
PCM .... Program Continuity Memorandum [*Military*]
PCM .... Program Cost Management　(MCD)
PCM .... Project Cost Model [*Project Software Ltd.*] [*Software package*]
PCM .... Protein-Calorie Malnutrition [*Medicine*]
PCM .... Pulse Code Modulation [*Telecommunications*]
PCM .... Pulse-Count Modulation [*Data processing*]
PCM .... Punch Card Machine [*Data processing*]
PCMA......... Pennsylvania Coal Mining Association [*Harrisburg, PA*]　(EA)
PCMA......... Personal Computer Management Association [*Commercial
　　　　　　　　firm*] [*Orange, CA*] [*Information service*]　(EA)
PCMA......... Phenylcyclopropanemethylamine [*Organic chemistry*]
PCMA........ PostCard Manufacturers Association [*Inactive*] [*Washington,
　　　　　　　　DC*]　(EA)
PCMA......... Prince Edward Island Department of Municipal Affairs,
　　　　　　　　Charlottetown, Prince Edward Island [*Library symbol*]
　　　　　　　　[*National Library of Canada*]　(NLC)

PCMA......... Professional Convention Management Association [*Birmingham, AL*]   (EA)
PCMB........ Para-Chloromercuribenzoate [*Organic chemistry*]
PCMBS ..... Para-Chloromercuriphenylsulfonic Acid [*Organic chemistry*]
PCMC........ Para-Chloro-meta-cresol [*Organic chemistry*]
PCMC........ Provided Chief of Mission Concurs [*Army*]
PCMD........ Particle Count Monitoring Device   (KSC)
PCMD........ Passive Count Monitoring Device   (KSC)
PCMD........ Pulse Code Modulation Digital
PCME........ Pulse Code Modulation Event
PCM-FM.... Pulse Code Modulation - Frequency Modulation
PCMGS...... Pulse Code Modulated Ground Station
PCMH........ Postgraduate Center for Mental Health [*New York, NY*] [*Research center*]   (EA)
PCMI .... Photo-Chemical Machining Institute [*Lafayette Hills, PA*]   (EA)
PCMI .... Photochromic Microimage [*Microfiche*]
PCMI .... Plastic Container Manufacturers Institute [*West Long Branch, NJ*]   (EA)
PCMIA....... Pittsburgh Coal Mining Institute of America [*Formed by a merger of CMIA and Pittsburgh Coal Mining Institute*] [*Pittsburgh, PA*]   (EA)
PCMK........ Piece Mark
PC-ML....... Marxist-Leninist Communist Party [*Bolivian*]   (PPW)
PCML .... Parti Communiste Marxiste-Leniniste [*Marxist-Leninist Communist Party*] [*French*]   (PPW)
PCML .... Partito Comunista Marxista-Leninista [*Marxist-Leninist Communist Party*] [*Sanmarinese*]   (PPE)
PCML .... President's Committee on Migratory Labor [*Terminated, 1964*]
PCMLF....... Parti Communiste Marxiste-Leniniste Francais [*French Marxist-Leninist Communist Party*] [*Dissolved, 1978*]   (PPW)
PC(ML)I ..... Partito Comunista (Marxista-Leninista) de Italia [*Communist Party of Italy (Marxist-Leninist)*]   (PPE)
PCMMU..... Pulse Code Modulation Master Unit [*Electronics*]   (NASA)
PCM/NRZ ... Pulse Code Modulation/Nonreturn to Zero   (KSC)
PCMO........ Principal Clinical Medical Officer [*British*]
PCMO........ Principal Colonial Medical Officer [*British*]
PCMP........ (Phenylcyclohexyl)methylpiperidine [*Organic chemistry*]
PCMP........ Preliminary Configuration Management Plan   (MCD)
PCM-PS ..... Pulse Code Modulation - Phase-Shift
P Cmp Sc St ... Proceedings. Computer Science and Statistics [*A publication*]
PCMR........ Patient Computer Medical Record
PCMR........ Photochromic Microreproduction   (DIT)
PCMR........ President's Committee on Mental Retardation [*Washington, DC*]
PCMS........ Para-Chloromercuriphenyl Sulfonate [*or Sulfonic Acid*] [*Organic chemistry*]
PCMS........ Production Control Monitoring System   (NVT)
PCMS........ Pulse Code Modulation Shared   (MCD)
PCMS........ Punch Card Machine System [*Data processing*]
PCMTE........ Pulse Code Modulation and Timing Equipment   (KSC)
PCMTEA .... Pulse Code Modulation and Timing Electronics Assembly
PCMTS....... Pulse Code Modulation Telemetry System   (AAG)
PCMU........ Physico-Chemical Measurements Unit [*British*]
PCMU........ Propellant Calibration Measuring Unit   (KSC)
PCMX........ Para-Chloro-meta-xylenol [*Antiseptic compound*]
PCN........... Package Control Number
PCN........... Page Change Notice   (MCD)
PCN........... PanCana Minerals [*Toronto Stock Exchange symbol*]
PCN........... Part Control Number   (AAG)
PCN........... Partido Comunista de Nicaragua [*Communist Party of Nicaragua*]   (PD)
PCN........... Partido de Conciliacion Nacional [*National Reconciliation Party*] [*Salvadoran*]   (PPW)
PCN........... Partido Conservador Nicaraguense [*Nicaraguan Conservative Party*]   (PPW)
PCN........... Parts Change Notice   (MCD)
PCN........... Penicillin [*Antibiotic*]
PCN........... Permanent Control Number   (MCD)
PCN........... Piacenza [*Italy*] [*Seismograph station code, US Geological Survey*] [*Closed*]   (SEIS)
PCN........... Pitcairn Islands [*Three-letter standard code*]   (CNC)
PCN........... Planning Change Notice
PCPF......... Players Chess News [*A publication*]
PCN........... Point Comfort & Northern Railway Co. [*AAR code*]
PCN........... Polychlorinated Naphthalene [*Organic chemistry*]
PCN........... Position Control Number   (AFM)
PCN........... Post Christum Natum [*After the Birth of Christ*] [*Latin*]   (ROG)
PCN........... Primary Care Network [*Medical insurance*]
PCN........... Primary Care Nursing
PCN........... Princeton Aviation Corp. [*Princeton, NJ*] [*FAA designator*]   (FAAC)
PCN........... [*The*] Print Collector's Newsletter [*A publication*]
PCN........... Procedure Change Notice
PCN........... Processing Control Number
PCN........... Procurement Control Number   (AFM)
PCN........... Product Control Number   (AFM)
PCN........... Production Change Number   (KSC)
PCN........... Program Change Notice   (MCD)
PCN........... Program Control Number   (AFM)

PCN........... Project Control Number   (AAG)
PCN........... Proposal Control Number   (AAG)
PCN........... Public Convenience and Necessity [*Department of Transportation*]
PCN........... Publication Change Notice   (MCD)
PCN........... Pulse Compression Network
PCNA .... Porsche Cars North America, Inc.
PCNA .... Proliferating Cell Nuclear Antigen [*Cytology, immunology*]
PCNB .... Pentachloronitrobenzene [*Agricultural fungicide*]
PCNB .... Permanent Control Narcotics Board
PCNDP....... Publication. Centre National de Documentation Pedagogique [*A publication*]
PCNF........ Pacific Central NOTAM [*Notice to Airmen*] Facility [*Military*]
PCNR........ Part Control Number Request   (AAG)
PCNS........ Polar Coordinates Navigation System
PCNY .... Proofreaders Club of New York [*Flushing, NY*]   (EA)
PCO........... Conococheague District Library, Chambersburg, PA [*OCLC symbol*]   (OCLC)
PCO........... Patient Complains Of [*Medicine*]
PCO........... Pest Control Operator
PCO........... Philadelphia College of Osteopathy [*Pennsylvania*]
PCO........... Phoenix Canada Oil Co. Ltd. [*Toronto Stock Exchange symbol*]
PCO........... Photosynthetic Carbon Oxidation [*Plant metabolism*]
PCO........... [*The*] Pittston Company [*NYSE symbol*]
PCO........... Placement Contracting Officer [*Army*]   (AABC)
P & CO ...... Plans and Combat Operations
PCO........... Plant Clearance Officer [*DoD*]
PCO........... Plant Clearance Order
PCO........... Police Commissioner's Office
PCO........... Polycystic Ovary [*Gynecology*]
PCO........... Ponca City [*Oklahoma*] [*Seismograph station code, US Geological Survey*]   (SEIS)
PCO........... Post Checkout Operations
PCO........... Prince Consort's Own [*Military unit*] [*British*]
PCO........... Principal Coast Officer [*Customs*] [*British*]   (ROG)
PCO........... Principal Contracting Officer [*Air Force*]
PCO........... Printing Control Officer [*Air Force*]   (AFM)
PCO........... Privy Council Office [*British*]
PCO........... Proceedings. Congress of Orientalists [*A publication*]
PCO........... Procurement Change Order   (MCD)
PCO........... Procuring Contracting Office [*or Officer*] [*Military*]
PCO........... Procuring Contrast Offer
PCO........... Program Comparator
PCO........... Program Controlled Output   (NASA)
PCO........... Program Coordination Office   (AAG)
PCO........... Project Control Office   (MCD)
PCO........... Property Control Office [*of Allied Military Government*] [*Post-World War II*]
PCO........... Proposed Change Order   (AFIT)
PCO........... Prospective Commanding Officer [*Navy*]
PCO........... Provisioning Contracting Officer [*Military*]   (AFIT)
PCO........... Publications Control Officer [*DoD*]
PCO........... Purchase Change Order   (MCD)
PCO........... Purchasing Contracting Officer
PCOA........ Pharmacy Corporation of America [*NASDAQ symbol*]   (NQ)
PCOAD....... Powder Coatings [*A publication*]
P Coast LJ ... Pacific Coast Law Journal   (DLA)
PCOB(UN) ... Permanent Central Opium Board (United Nations)
PCOC........ Partit Comunista Obrero de Catalunya [*Communist Workers' Party of Catalonia*]   (PPW)
PCOD........ Polycystic Ovarian Disease [*Medicine*]
PCOE........ Partido Comunista Obrero de Espana [*Communist Workers' Party of Spain*]   (PPW)
PCOG .... Press Clippings of Greenland [*A publication*]
PCOGA ...... Pacific Coast Oyster Growers Association [*Seattle, WA*]   (EA)
PCOI........ Purcell Company, Incorporated [*NASDAQ symbol*]   (NQ)
PCOMB...... Physics of Condensed Matter [*A publication*]
P Comp Lit ... Proceedings. Comparative Literature Symposium [*A publication*]
PCON .... Para-Chloro-ortho-nitroaniline [*Also, PCONA*] [*Organic chemistry*]
PCONA...... Para-Chloro-ortho-nitroaniline [*Also, PCON*] [*Organic chemistry*]
PCONA...... Pest Control [*A publication*]
PCOPF....... President's Council on Physical Fitness [*Later, PCPFS*]   (KSC)
PC & OR .... Procurement, Commitment, and Obligation Record [*Navy*]
PCoR......... Robert Morris College, Coraopolis, PA [*Library symbol*] [*Library of Congress*]   (LCLS)
PCOS .... Polycystic Ovarian Syndrome [*Also, POS*] [*Gynecology*]
PCOS .... Primary Communications-Oriented System   (IEEE)
PCOS .... Process Control Operating System
P-COSWA ... Pugwash Conferences on Science and World Affairs
PCOT .... Payload Center Operations Team [*NASA*]   (MCD)
PCOTES..... Prototype Carrier Operational Test and Evaluation Site [*Military*]   (CAAL)
PCOV........ Precombustor Oxidizer Valve   (KSC)
PCOYO...... President's Council on Youth Opportunity [*Defunct*]   (EA)
PCP........... Pacific Coast Philology [*A publication*]
PCP........... Paired Cone Pigments [*Vision physiology*]
PCP........... Palestinian Communist Party   (PD)

PCP .... PanCanadian Petroleums [*Toronto Stock Exchange symbol*] [*Vancouver Stock Exchange symbol*]
PCP .... Paraguayan Communist Party
PCP .... Parallel Cascade Processor   (IEEE)
PCP .... Parallel Circular Plate   (IEEE)
PCP .... Partido Comunista Paraguayano [*Paraguayan Communist Party*]   (PD)
PCP .... Partido Comunista Peruano [*Peruvian Communist Party*]   (PPW)
PCP .... Partido Comunista Portugues [*Portuguese Communist Party*]   (PPE)
PCP .... Partido Comunista Puertorriqueno [*Puerto Rican Communist Party*]   (PPW)
PCP .... Passenger Control Point   (AABC)
PCP .... Past Chief Patriarch [*Freemasonry*]
PCP .... Patient Care Publications
PCP .... Peace Corps Physician
PCP .... Pentachlorophenol [*Wood preservative*] [*Organic chemistry*]
PCP .... Peripheral Control Program
PCP .... Peripheral Control Pulse [*Data processing*]
PCP .... (Phenylcyclohexyl)piperidine [*or Phencyclidine*] [*Anesthetic*] [*A street drug*]
PCP .... Philadelphia College of Pharmacy and Science, Philadelphia, PA [*OCLC symbol*]   (OCLC)
PCP .... Phosphor Coated Paper
PCP .... Photon-Coupled Pair   (IEEE)
PCP .... Pilot Control Panel
PCP .... Planar Combat Problem
PCP .... Platoon Command Post [*Military*]   (RDA)
PCP .... Pneumatics Control Panel   (AAG)
PCP .... Pneumocystis Carinii Pneumonia [*Microbiology*]
PCP .... Polaroid Color Pack Camera
PCP .... Polychloroprene [*Organic chemistry*]
PCP .... Poorly Characterized Phase [*Mineralogy*]
PCP .... Portable Code Processor
PCP .... Portuguese Communist Party
PCP .... Post-Construction Permit   (NRCH)
PCP .... Postgraduate Center for Psychotherapy [*Later, Postgraduate Center for Mental Health*]   (EA)
PCP .... Potential Contractor Program   (MCD)
PCP .... Power Control Panel   (AAG)
PCP .... Preassembled Cable in Pipe
PCP .... Preliminary Cost Proposal   (MCD)
PCP .... Pressurization Control Panel [*NASA*]   (KSC)
PCP .... Primary Care Physician
PCP .... Primary Command Point [*Military*]   (CAAL)
PCP .... Primary Control Program [*Data processing*]
PCP .... Primary Coolant Pump [*Nuclear energy*]   (NRCH)
PCP .... Printed Circuit Patchboard
PCP .... Process Control Processor   (IEEE)
PCP .... Process Control Program [*Nuclear energy*]   (NRCH)
PCP .... Processor Control Program
PCP .... Product Change Proposal   (MCD)
PCP .... Production Change Point
PCP .... Program Change Procedure
PCP .... Program [*or Project*] Change Proposal [*DoD*]
PCP .... Program Control Plan   (AAG)
PCP .... Program Control Procedure [*Nuclear energy*]   (NRCH)
PCP .... Programable Communication Processor
PCP .... Progressive Conservative Party [*Canadian*]   (PPW)
PCP .... Progressive Constitutionalist Party [*Maltese*]   (PPE)
PCP .... Project Control Plan   (IEEE)
PCP .... Project Cost Plan   (NASA)
PCP .... Prototype Communications Processor
PCP .... Pulse Comparator
PCP .... Pulse Cytophotometry [*Hematology*]
PCP .... Punched Card Punch [*Data processing*]   (IEEE)
PcP .... Reflected P Wave [*Earthquakes*]
PCPA .... Pacific Conservatory of the Performing Arts
PCPA .... Panel of Consultants for the Performing Arts [*of CFC*]
PCPA .... Para-Chlorophenoxyacetic Acid [*Organic chemistry*]
PCPA .... Para-Chlorophenylalanine [*Biochemistry*]
PCPA .... Poor Clares of Perpetual Adoration [*Roman Catholic women's religious order*]
PCPA .... Protestant Church-Owned Publishers Association [*Nashville, TN*]   (EA)
PCPAC ...... Parker-Coltrane Political Action Committee   (EA)
PCPBMA .... Pacific Coast Paper Box Manufacturers' Association [*Los Angeles, CA*]   (EA)
PCPC .... Power Conversion Products Council [*Later, PCPCI*]   (EA)
PCPCA ...... Pairpoint Cup Plate Collectors of America [*New Bedford, MA*]   (EA)
PCPCI .... Power Conversion Products Council International [*Libertyville, IL*]   (EA)
PCPCN ...... Part Card Procurement Change Notice   (KSC)
PCPE .... Partido Comunista de los Pueblos de Espana [*Communist Party of the Peoples of Spain*] [*Madrid*]
PCPF .... President's Council on Physical Fitness [*Later, PCPFS*]
PCPFS .... President's Council on Physical Fitness and Sports   (EGAO)
PCPG .... Primary Clock Pulse Generator
PCPHA ...... Plant and Cell Physiology [*A publication*]

PCPhS .... Proceedings. Cambridge Philological Society [*A publication*]
PCPI .... Parent Cooperative Preschools International
PCPI .... Permanent Committee on Patent Information [*World Intellectual Property Organization*] [*Geneva, Switzerland*] [*Information service*]   (EISS)
PCPI .... Personal Computer Products [*San Diego, CA*] [*NASDAQ symbol*]   (NQ)
PCPI .... President's Commission on Personnel Interchange [*Later, President's Commission on Executive Exchange*]
PCPJ .... Peoples Coalition for Peace and Justice [*Defunct*]
PCPL .... Planning Library, Charlottetown, Prince Edward Island [*Library symbol*] [*National Library of Canada*]   (NLC)
PCPL .... Production Control Priority List   (MCD)
PCPL .... Proposed Change Point Line [*NASA*]   (KSC)
PCPM .... PERT [*Program Evaluation and Review Technique*] Cost Performance Measurement
PCP M-L .... Partido Comunista de Portugal, Marxista-Leninista [*Marxist-Leninist Communist Party of Portugal*]   (PPE)
PCPN .... Precipitation   (FAAC)
PCPP .... (Para-Chlorophenoxy)propionic Acid [*Organic chemistry*]
PCPP .... Peace Corps Partnership Program   (EA)
PCPP .... Plasma Chemistry and Plasma Processing [*A publication*]
PCPPD ...... Plasma Chemistry and Plasma Processing [*A publication*]
PCPS .... Philadelphia College of Pharmacy and Science [*Pennsylvania*]
PCPS .... Pool Cooling and Purification System [*Nuclear energy*]   (NRCH)
PCPS .... Proceedings of the Cambridge Philological Society [*A publication*]   (OCD)
PCPS .... Pulse-Coded Processing System
PCPSD ...... Progress in Colloid and Polymer Science [*A publication*]
PCPT .... Para-Chlorophenylthio [*Organic chemistry*]
PCPT .... Perception
PCPT .... Perception. Canadian Magazine of Social Comment [*A publication*]
PCPT .... Physical Combat Proficiency Test [*Army*]
PCPT .... Post Conference Provisioning Tape   (MCD)
PCPV .... Prestressed Concrete Pressure Vessel
PCQ .... Production Control Quantometer
PCQ .... Productivity Criteria Quotient
PCQ .... Professional Capabilities Questionnaire [*Jet Propulsion Laboratory, NASA*]
PCQ .... Yuma, AZ [*Location identifier*] [*FAA*]   (FAAL)
PCQEH ...... Queen Elizabeth Hospital, Charlottetown, Prince Edward Island [*Library symbol*] [*National Library of Canada*]   (NLC)
PCR .... Island Pacific Air [*Maui, HI*] [*FAA designator*]   (FAAC)
PCR .... Page Control Register
PCR .... Parker's Criminal Reports [*New York*]   (DLA)
PCR .... Parti Communiste Reunionnais [*Communist Party of Reunion*]   (PPW)
PCR .... Partido Comunista Revolucionario [*Revolutionary Communist Party*] [*Peruvian*]   (PPW)
PCR .... Partidul Comunist Roman [*Romanian Communist Party*]   (PPE)
PCR .... Pass Card Reader [*Telecommunications*]   (TEL)
PCR .... Patient Charge Ratio
PCR .... Payload Changeout Room [*NASA*]   (NASA)
PCR .... PC Resource [*A publication*]
PCR .... Peninsular Chemresearch [*Calgon Corp.*]
PCR .... Pennsylvania Corporation Reporter   (DLA)
PCR .... Pennsylvania County Court Reports   (DLA)
P & CR ...... Performance and Compatibility Requirements
PCR .... Perini Corporation [*American Stock Exchange symbol*]
PCR .... Periodic Current Reversal [*Electrochemistry*]
PCR .... Peripheral Control Routine   (CMD)
PCr .... Phosphocreatine [*Also, CP, PC*] [*Biochemistry*]
PCR .... Photoconductive Relay   (IEEE)
PCR .... Photoconductive Resonance [*Physics*]
PCR .... Photosynthetic Carbon Reduction [*Plant metabolism*]
PCR .... Planned Component Replacement [*Predictive maintenance schedule*]
PCR .... Planning Change [*or Check*] Request   (AAG)
P & CR ...... Planning and Compensation Reports [*Legal*] [*British*]
PCR .... Pneumatic Checkout Rack   (KSC)
PCR .... Pneumatic Control Regulator   (KSC)
PCR .... Pollution Control Report [*Navy*]
PCR .... Polychromatic Color Removal [*Printing technology*]
PCR .... Polymerase Chain Reaction [*Genetics*]
PCR .... Population Census Report   (OICC)
PCR .... Powell Cycle Registry   (EA)
PCR .... Power Conversion Room
PCR .... Pressure Check Range
PCR .... Prestressed Ceramic RADOME
PCR .... Preventative Cyclic Retransmission [*Telecommunications*]   (TEL)
PCR .... Primary Chemotherapy-Radiotherapy [*Oncology*]
PCR .... Primary Cosmic Radiation
PCR .... Print Command Register
PCR .... Procedure Change Request [*NASA*]
PCR .... Procurement Center Representatives [*Small Business Administration*]
PCR .... Production Change Request   (MCD)
PCR .... Production Control Record [*NASA*]   (KSC)
PCR .... Program Change Request [*DoD*]

PCR............ Program Control Register
PCR............ Program Control Report
PCR............ Progress Curve Report
PCR............ Project Control Room [*NASA*]   (NASA)
PCR............ Project on Corporate Responsibility   (EA)
PCR............ Project Cost Record [*or Report*] [*NASA*]   (KSC)
P & CR........ Property and Compensation Reports   (DLA)
PCR............ Publication Change Request   (MCD)
PCR............ Publication Contract Requirements
PCR............ Puerto Carreno [*Colombia*] [*Airport symbol*]   (OAG)
PCR............ Pulse Compression RADAR
PCR............ Punched Card Reader [*Data processing*]   (BUR)
PCR............ Punched Card Requisition [*Data processing*]   (MCD)
PCRA......... Phantom Class Racing Association   (EA)
PCR & A..... Picked Cold, Rolled, and Annealed [*Metallurgy*]   (ROG)
PCRA......... Poland China Record Association   (EA)
PCRB.......... Parks Canada. Research Bulletin [*A publication*]
PCRB.......... Personnel and Control Room Building   (NRCH)
PCRB.......... Pollution Control Revenue Bond [*Environmental Protection
                  Agency*]
PCRB.......... Project Change Review Board
PCRC......... Pacific Concerns Resource Center   (EA)
PCRC......... Paraffined Carton Research Council [*Later, Paperboard
                  Packaging Council*]
PCRC......... Perinatal Clinical Research Center [*Case Western Reserve
                  University*] [*Research center*]   (RCD)
PCRCA....... Pickled, Cold-Rolled, and Close-Annealed [*Metal*]
PCRD......... Primary Control Rod Driveline [*Nuclear energy*]   (NRCH)
PCRDM...... Primary Control Rod Drive Mechanism [*Nuclear
                  energy*]   (NRCH)
PC Rep...... English Privy Council Reports   (DLA)
PCRF.......... Paralysis Cure Research Foundation   (EA)
PCRF.......... Parker Chiropractic Research Foundation [*Fort Worth,
                  TX*]   (EA)
PCRI........... Papanicolaou Cancer Research Institute [*University of Miami*]
                  [*Research center*]
PCRIF........ PCR Industries [*NASDAQ symbol*]   (NQ)
PCRM........ Primary Certified Reference Material   (NRCH)
PCRML....... Parti Communiste Revolutionnaire - Marxiste-Leniniste
                  [*Revolutionary Marxist-Leninist Communist Party*]
                  [*French*]   (PPW)
PCRPS....... Program for Collaborative Research in the Pharmaceutical
                  Sciences [*University of Illinois at Chicago*] [*Information
                  service*]   (EISS)
PCRR......... Pennsylvania Central Railroad   (ROG)
PCRS......... Poor Clergy Relief Society [*British*]
PCRS......... Precision Chiropractic Research Society [*Also known as Spinal
                  Stress Research Society*] [*Brea, CA*]   (EA)
PCRS......... Primary Control Rod System [*Nuclear energy*]   (NRCH)
PCRS......... Primary CRITICOMM [*Critical Intelligence Communications
                  System*] Relay Station   (CET)
PCRSB....... Proceedings. Canadian Rock Mechanics Symposium [*A
                  publication*]
PCRV......... Prestressed Concrete Reactor Vessel
PCS............ IEEE Professional Communication Society [*New York,
                  NY*]   (EA)
PCS............ Pace Car Society   (EA)
PCS............ Pacific Command Ship
PCS............ Palliative Care Service
PCS............ Paracas [*Peru*] [*Seismograph station code, US Geological
                  Survey*] [*Closed*]   (SEIS)
PCS............ Parents' Confidential Statement [*Education*]
PCS............ Parti Chretien-Social [*Christian Social Party*]
                  [*Luxembourg*]   (PPW)
PCS............ Parti Communiste Suisse [*Communist Party of
                  Switzerland*]   (PPE)
PCS............ Particle Counting System
PCS............ Particulates, Condensables, and Solubles [*In gases*]
PCS............ Partido Comunista Salvadoreno [*Salvadoran Communist
                  Party*]   (PPW)
PCS............ Partito Comunista Sammarinese [*Communist Party of San
                  Marino*]   (PPE)
PCS............ Parts, Components, Subassemblies
PCS............ Parts Control System [*DoD*]
PCS............ Passive Containment System [*Nuclear energy*]   (NRCH)
PCS............ Patrol Vessel, Submarine Chaser (Control) [*136 feet*] [*Navy
                  symbol*] [*Obsolete*]
PCS............ Patterns of Care Study [*Roentgenography*]
PCS............ Paul Claudel Society   (EA)
PCS............ Payload Checkout System [*NASA*]   (NASA)
PCS............ Payload Control Supervisor [*NASA*]   (MCD)
PCS............ Periodical Control System [*Libraries*]
PCS............ Permanent Change of Station [*Military*]
PCS............ Personal Computing System
PCS............ Personnel Capabilities System [*Jet Propulsion Laboratory,
                  NASA*]
PCS............ Personnel Change of Station
PCS............ Pharmaceutical Card System   (MCD)
PCS............ Phase Combining System [*Trademark*] [*A solubilizer in
                  scintillation counting*]
PCS............ Phase Compensator System

PCS............ Philippine Collectors Society   (EA)
PCS............ PhonoCardioScan [*Heart examination equipment*]
PCS............ Photon Correlation Spectroscopy
PCS............ Physical Control System
PCS............ Pictorial Cancellation Society   (EA)
PCS............ Pieces
PCS............ Pilot Control System   (MCD)
PCS............ Pitch Control System   (MCD)
PCS............ Planning Control Sheet
PCS............ Plant Computer System   (NRCH)
PCS............ Plant Control System [*Nuclear energy*]   (NRCH)
PCS............ Plastic Connector Shell
PCS............ Platoon Combat Skills [*Army*]   (INF)
PCS............ Plausible Conflict Situations [*Army*]
PCS............ Pneumatic Control System [*Gas chromatography*]
PCS............ Pointing-Control System
PCS............ Port Command Store [*Telecommunications*]   (TEL)
PCS............ Port Control Store [*Telecommunications*]   (TEL)
PCS............ Port Control System [*Telecommunications*]   (TEL)
PCS............ Portable Communications System
PCS............ Portacaval Shunt [*Medicine*]
PCS............ Position Classification Standard [*Civil Service*]
PCS............ Position, Course, and Speed
PCS............ Postal Church Service
PCS............ Postal Commemorative Society   (EA)
PCS............ Postcardiotomy Syndrome [*Medicine*]
PCS............ Postcaval [*or Portacaval*] Shunt [*Medicine*]
PCS............ Posterior Concave Side
PCS............ Posts, Camps, and Stations [*Military*]
PC & S....... Posts, Camps, and Stations [*Military*]
PCS............ Potash Corporation of Saskatchewan [*Canada*]
PCS............ Power Conditioning System
PCS............ Power Conversion System
PCS............ Powered Causeway Section [*Military*]   (CAAL)
PCS............ Precision Casting Standard   (MCD)
PCS............ Preconscious
PC & S....... Preliminary Command and Sequencing [*Viking lander mission*]
                  [*NASA*]
PCS............ Preliminary Component Specification
PCS............ Pressure Control System
PCS............ Primary Calibration System
PCS............ Primary Cancer Site [*Oncology*]
PCS............ Primary Conditioning Solution
PCS............ Primary Control Ship [*Navy*]
PCS............ Primary Coolant System   (MSA)
PCS............ Principal Clerk of Session
PCS............ Principal Coordinating Scientist [*NASA*]   (KSC)
PCS............ Print Contrast Scale   (IEEE)
PCS............ Print Contrast Signal [*Data processing*]
PCS............ Print Contrast System   (BUR)
PCS............ Probability of Correct Selection [*Statistics*]
PCS............ Probability of Crew Survival   (AAG)
PCS............ Procedure Completion Sheet   (MCD)
PCS............ Process Computer System   (NRCH)
PCS............ Process Control Sheet [*Nuclear energy*]   (NRCH)
PCS............ Process Control System
PCS............ Production Control Section
PCS............ Production Control System   (BUR)
PCS............ Professional Car Society   (EA)
PCS............ Program Cost Status [*Report*]   (MCD)
PCS............ Program Counter Store
PCS............ Programable Communications Subsystem
PCS............ Project Control Sheet [*Data processing*]
PCS............ Project Control System [*Data processing*]
PCS............ Project Coordination Staff [*NASA*]   (KSC)
PCS............ Property Control System
PCS............ Proprietary Computer Systems, Inc. [*Van Nuys, CA*]
                  [*Information service*]   (EISS)
PCS............ Provision Coordinate Schedule   (MCD)
PCS............ Public Choice Society   (EA)
PCS............ Publication Control Sheet   (MCD)
PCS............ Pump Control Sensor
PCS............ Punched Card System [*Data processing*]
PCS............ Pyrotechnics Circuit Simulator
PCS............ Submarine Chaser
PCS............ Sun Shipbuilding & Dry Dock Co., Chester, PA [*Library symbol*]
                  [*Library of Congress*]   (LCLS)
PCSA........ Power Crane and Shovel Association [*Milwaukee, WI*]   (EA)
PCSA........ Seaman Apprentice, Postal Clerk, Striker [*Navy rating*]
PCS(A)...... Submarine Chaser (Air Cushion)   (MCD)
PCsB......... Baptist Bible College of Pennsylvania, Clarks Summit, PA
                  [*Library symbol*] [*Library of Congress*]   (LCLS)
PCSC........ Control Submarine Chaser [*136 feet*] [*Navy symbol*] [*Obsolete*]
PCSC........ Power Conditioning, Switching, and Control
PCSC........ Principal Commonwealth Supply Committee [*World War II*]
PCSD........ Partido Cristao Social Democratico [*Christian Social
                  Democratic Party*] [*Portuguese*]   (PPE)
PCSD........ Polychloro(chloromethylsulfonamido)diphenyl Ether
                  [*Insectproofing agent for wool*]
PCSE......... Pacific Coast Stock Exchange [*Later, PSE*]   (EA)

PCSE......... President's Committee on Scientists and Engineers [*Expired, 1958*]
PCSE......... Printed Circuit Soldering Equipment
PC/SFA...... Potato Chip/Snack Food Association [*Formerly, NPCI, PCI*] [*Later, SFA*]
PCSFSK.... Phase Comparison Sinusoidal Frequency Shift Keying
PCSG......... Public Cryptography Study Group [*American Council on Education*] [*Defunct*]   (EA)
PCSH .... Pierce Shell
PCS(H)...... Submarine Chaser (Hydrofoil)   (MCD)
PCSI......... Paragon Communication [*NASDAQ symbol*]   (NQ)
PCSM........ Percutaneous Stone Manipulation [*Medicine*]
PCSN .... Seaman, Postal Clerk, Striker [*Navy rating*]
PCSNA....... Processing [*England*] [*A publication*]
PCSP........ Programed Communications Support Program [*Air Force*]   (AFM)
PCSPS ...... Principal Civil Service Pension Scheme [*British*]
PCSS .... Platform Check Subsystem
PCSS......... Princess   (ROG)
PCST........ Precision Castparts [*NASDAQ symbol*]   (NQ)
PCSW........ President's Commission on the Status of Women
PCT .... Pacific Coast Tariff Bureau, San Francisco CA [*STAC*]
PCT .... Pacific Crest Trail
PCT .... Paper Crepe Tape
PCT .... Para-Chlorotoluene [*Organic chemistry*]
PCT .... Parti Communiste Tunisien [*Tunisian Communist Party*] [*Tunis*]   (PD)
PCT .... Parti Congolais du Travail [*Congolese Labor Party*]   (PPW)
PCT .... Partido Conservador Tradicional [*Traditionalist Conservative Party*] [*Nicaraguan*]
PCT .... Patent Cooperation Treaty [*1978*]
PCT .... Peak Centerline Temperature   (NRCH)
PCT .... Peak Cladding Temperature   (NRCH)
PCT .... Percent [*or Percentage*]
PCT .... Percentage [*Used instead of "average"*] [*Baseball*]
PCT .... Performance Correlation Technique
PCT .... Periodic Confidence Test
PCT .... Peripheral Control Terminal
PCT .... Personality Completion Test [*Psychology*]
PCT .... Pharmacy and Chemistry Technician [*Navy*]
PCT .... Philadelphia College of Textiles and Science, Philadelphia, PA [*OCLC symbol*]   (OCLC)
PCT .... Photoinduced Charge Transfer [*Electrochemistry*]
PCT .... Photon-Coupled Transistor   (IEEE)
PCT .... Physical Correlate Theory [*Psychophysics*]
PCT .... Picture
PCT .... Planning and Control Techniques
PCT .... Plasmacrit Test [*Medicine*]
PCT .... Plasmacytoma [*Medicine*]
PCT .... Platelet Count [*Hematology*]
PCT .... Polychemotherapy [*Oncology*]
PCT .... Polychlorinated Terphenyl [*Pesticide*]
PCT .... Polychloroterphenyl [*Organic chemistry*]
PCTS .... Porphyria Cutanea Tarda [*Disease*] [*Medicine*]
PCT .... Portable Camera-Transmitter
PCT .... Portable Conference Telephone [*Bell Laboratories*]
PCT .... Positron Computed Tomography
PCT .... Potential Current Transformer
PCT .... Precinct
PCT .... Preliminary Change Transmittal   (AAG)
PCT .... Pressure Concentration Temperature
PCT .... Prime Contract Termination   (AAG)
PCT .... Princeton [*New Jersey*] [*Airport symbol*] [*Obsolete*]   (OAG)
P Ct .... Probate Court   (DLA)
PCT .... Production Confirmatory Test   (MCD)
PCT .... Program Control Table [*Data processing*]
PCT .... Programa de Cooperacion Tecnica [*Program of Technical Cooperation - PTC*] [*Organization of American States*] [*Washington, DC*]
PCT .... Project Control Tool   (BUR)
PCT .... Property Captial Trust [*American Stock Exchange symbol*]
PCT .... Proximal Convoluted Tubule [*of a nephron*]
PCT .... Pulse Compression Tube
PCT .... Pulse Count [*Telecommunications*]   (TEL)
PCT .... Wesman Personnel Classification Test
PCTA .... Pentachlorothioanisole [*Organic chemistry*]
PCTB .... Pacific Coast Tariff Bureau
PCTC .... Penn Central Transportation Company
PCTC .... Pyrotechnic Circuit Test Console   (KSC)
PCTDS .... Problem and Change Tracking Directory System
PCTE .... Portable Commercial Test Equipment   (NASA)
PCTEB .... Pennsylvania Council of Teachers of English. Bulletin [*A publication*]
PCTE Bulletin ... Pennsylvania Council of Teachers of English. Bulletin [*A publication*]
PCTF .... Plant Component Test Facility [*Nuclear energy*]
PCTFE .... Polychlorotrifluoroethylene [*Organic chemistry*]
PCTM .... PC Telemart, Inc. [*NASDAQ symbol*]   (NQ)
PC/TM ...... Performance Criteria and Test Methods Task
PCTM .... Pulse-Count Modulation   (MSA)
PCTNB .... Perception [*A publication*]

PCTO .... Payload Cost Tradeoff Optimization [*NASA*]   (NASA)
PCTP .... Partido Comunista dos Trabalhadores Portugueses [*Portuguese Workers' Communist Party*]   (PPW)
PCTP .... Pierce Template
PCTR .... Physical Constant Test Reactor
PCTR .... Program Counter
PCTR .... Pulsed Column Test Rig [*Chemical engineering*]
PCTS .... Pentagon Consolidated Telecommunications System   (MCD)
PCTS .... Portable Cesium Time Standard
PCTS .... President's Committee for Traffic Safety   (EA)
PCTV .... Private Channel Television
PCtvL .... Lukens Steel Co., Coatesville, PA [*Library symbol*] [*Library of Congress*] [*Obsolete*]   (LCLS)
PCtvVA ...... United States Veterans Administration Hospital, Medical Library, Coatesville, PA [*Library symbol*] [*Library of Congress*]   (LCLS)
PCU........... Paging Control Unit [*Telecommunications*]   (TEL)
PCU........... Pain Control Unit
PCU........... Partido Conservador Unido [*Chilean Catholic political party*]
PCU........... Passenger Control Unit   (MCD)
PCU........... Payload Checkout Unit [*NASA*]   (MCD)
PCU........... Peripheral Control Unit   (CMD)
PCU........... Picayune, MS [*Location identifier*] [*FAA*]   (FAAL)
PCU........... Pneumatic Checkout Unit   (AAG)
PCU........... Pod Cooling Unit   (AAG)
PCU........... Portable Checkout Unit
PCU........... Portuguese Continental Union of the United States of America   (EA)
PCU........... Pound Centigrade Unit
PCU........... Power Conditioning Unit
PCU........... Power Control Unit
PCU........... Power Conversion Unit   (IEEE)
PCU........... Pressure Control Unit   (MCD)
PCU........... Price [*Utah*] [*Seismograph station code, US Geological Survey*]   (SEIS)
PCU........... Print Control Unit
PCU........... Processor Control Unit
PCU........... Program Control Unit [*Data processing*]
PCU........... Progress Control Unit   (KSC)
PCU........... Progressive Care Unit [*Medicine*]
PCU........... Protective Care Unit [*Medicine*]
PCU........... Protein-Calorie Undernutrition [*Medicine*]
PCU........... Punched Card Utility [*Data processing*]
PCU........... University of Prince Edward Island, Charlottetown, Prince Edward Island [*Library symbol*] [*National Library of Canada*]   (NLC)
PCUA .... Power Controller Unit Assembly   (IEEE)
PCUA .... Profit Control Users Association   (EA)
PCUC .... Positive Continuous Ullage Control
PCU/HDR... Primary Control Unit, Hydraulics   (AAG)
PCUI.......... Partito Comunista Unificado di Italia [*Unified Communist Party of Italy*]   (PPE)
PCUR .... Pulsating Current
PCUS .... Propeller Club of the United States [*Washington, DC*]   (EA)
PC-USA ..... Pax Christi - USA [*Formerly, APA*] [*An association*]   (EA)
PCUSEQ ... Pressure Control Unit Sequencer   (AAG)
PCUUS ...... Polish Council of Unity in the United States   (EA)
PCV........... Pacific Concord Resources Corp. [*Vancouver Stock Exchange symbol*]
PCV........... Packed Cell Volume [*Hematocrit value*]
PCV........... Partido Comunista Venezolana [*Venezuelan Communist Party*]   (PPW)
PCV........... Partido Comunista de Venezuela [*Communist Party of Venezuela*]
PCV........... Peace Corps Volunteer
PCV........... Petty Cash Voucher   (MCD)
PCV........... Pneumatic Control Valve
PCV........... Pollution Control Valve   (IEEE)
PCV........... Polycythemia Vera [*Also, PV*] [*Hematology*]
PCV........... Porcine Cirovirus
PCV........... Positive Crankcase Ventilation [*For automotive antipollution systems*]
PCV........... Precheck Verification [*NASA*]   (NASA)
PCV........... Pressure Control Valve   (AAG)
PCV........... Primate Calicivirus
PCV........... Purge Control Valve   (NASA)
PCV........... Pyrocatechol Violet [*Also, PV*] [*An indicator*] [*Chemistry*]
PCV........... Veterans Affairs, Canada [*Affaires des Anciens Combattants Canada*] Charlottetown, Prince Edward Island [*Library symbol*] [*National Library of Canada*]   (NLC)
PCvA .... Allentown College of Saint Francis de Sales, Center Valley, PA [*Library symbol*] [*Library of Congress*]   (LCLS)
PCVB......... Pyro Continuity Verification Box [*NASA*]   (NASA)
PCVC .... Public Citizens Visitors Center [*An association*] [*Defunct*]   (EA)
PCVD........ Plasma Chemical Vapor Deposition
PCVL........ Pilot-Controlled Visual Landing [*Aviation*]   (NASA)
PCW.......... Personal Computer World Show [*Montbuild Ltd.*]   (TSPED)
PCW.......... Plate Control Wedge [*Printing technology*]
PCW.......... Port Clinton, OH [*Location identifier*] [*FAA*]   (FAAL)
PCW.......... Previously Complied With
PCW.......... Primary Cooling Water [*Reactor*]

PCW .... Princess Charlotte of Wales [*Military unit*] [*British*]
PCW .... Principal Conductor of the Works [*Freemasonry*]
PCW .... Program Control Word
PCW .... Proprietor of Copyright on a Composite Work
PCW .... Pulmonary Capillary Wedge [*Medicine*]
PCW .... Pulsed Continuous Wave   (IEEE)
PCW .... Widener College, Chester, PA [*Library symbol*] [*Library of Congress*]   (LCLS)
PCWBS ...... Preliminary Contract Work Breakdown Structure   (MCD)
PCWCA ...... Poured Concrete Wall Contractors Association [*Indianapolis, IN*]   (EA)
PCWO .... Production Control Work Order   (MCD)
PCWP .... Pulmonary Capillary Wedge Pressure [*Medicine*]
PCWU .... Port Commissioners Workers' Union [*Indian*]
PCX .... Pacific Express [*Chico, CA*] [*FAA designator*]   (FAAC)
PCx .... Periscopic Convex [*Ophthalmology*]
PCX .... Plasma Confinement Experiment [*Physics*]
PCY .... Pacific Cypress Minerals [*Vancouver Stock Exchange symbol*]
PCY .... Pittsburgh, Chartiers & Youghiogheny Railway Co. [*AAR code*]
PCY .... Prerogative Court of York [*English court previously having jurisdiction over wills*]
PCYF .... President's Council on Youth Fitness [*Later, PCPF, PCPFS*]   (EA)
PCYMF ...... Pacific Cypress Minerals Ltd. [*NASDAQ symbol*]   (NQ)
PCZ .... Canal Zone [*Three-letter standard code*] [*Obsolete*]   (CNC)
PCZ .... Waupaca, WI [*Location identifier*] [*FAA*]   (FAAL)
PD .... Democratic Party [*Ecuadorean*]   (PD)
PD .... Doctor of Pedagogy
PD .... Doctor of Pharmacy
PD .... Doctor of Philosophy
PD .... Dublin Pharmacopoeia
PD .... Interpupillary Distance
PD .... Ipec Aviation Pty. Ltd. [*Australia*] [*ICAO designator*]   (FAAC)
P & D .... Law Reports, Probate and Divorce [*1865-75*]   (DLA)
PD .... Law Reports, Probate, Divorce, and Admiralty Division [*1875-90*] [*England*]   (DLA)
p/d .... Packs per Day [*Cigarettes*] [*Medicine*]
PD .... Pad   (MCD)
PD .... Paget's Disease [*Medicine*]
PD .... Paid
PD .... Paix et Droit [*Paris*] [*A publication*]
PD .... Palisade Diabase [*Geology*]
Pd .... Palladium [*Chemical element*]
PD .... Pancreatic Divisum [*Medicine*]
PD .... Pancreatic Duct [*Anatomy*]
PD .... Pants Down [*At a disadvantage*] [*Slang*]   (DSUE)
PD .... Papier und Druck [*A publication*]
pd .... Papilla Diameter [*Medicine*]
PD .... Papillary Distance
PD .... Parkinsonism Dementia [*Medicine*]
PD .... Parkinson's Disease [*Medicine*]
PD .... Parliamentary Debates [*A publication*]
PD .... Pars Distalis [*Medicine*]
PD .... Part Damaged [*Tea trade*]   (ROG)
PD .... Parti Democratique [*Democratic Party*] [*Luxembourg*]   (PPE)
PD .... Partial Discharge [*High-voltage testing*]   (IEEE)
PD .... Particle-Density [*Forensic science*]
PD .... Partido Democrata [*Democratic Party*] [*Chile*]
PD .... Partido Democrata [*Democratic Party*] [*Costa Rican*]   (PPW)
PD .... Partner Air Services A/S [*Norway*] [*ICAO designator*]   (FAAC)
PD .... Passed
PD .... Passive Detection [*Electronics*]
PD .... Paste-Down [*Album*] [*Photography*]   (ROG)
PD .... Pay Department [*Army*] [*British*]   (ROG)
PD .... Peak Detector
PD .... Pediatric [*or Pediatrics*]
PD .... Pennsylvania Dutchman [*A publication*]
PD .... Pension and Bounty [*Department of the Interior*]   (DLA)
PD .... People's Democracy [*Irish political party*]
PD .... Pepper Dust [*An adulterating element*]
PD .... Per Diem
PD .... Per Diliquium [*By Deliquescence*] [*Pharmacy*]   (ROG)
PD .... Performance Demonstration   (MCD)
PD .... Period   (AABC)
PD .... Peripheral Device   (BUR)
PD .... Peritoneal Dialysis [*Medicine*]
PD .... Permanent Deactivation
P & D .... Perry and Davison's English Queen's Bench Reports [*1834-44*]   (DLA)
PD .... Personnel Department
PD .... Personnel Distribution [*Army*]
PD .... Phase Discriminator
PD .... Phelps Dodge Corp. [*NYSE symbol*]
PD .... Phenyldichlorarsine [*A war gas*]
PD .... Philosophiae Doctor [*Doctor of Philosophy*]
PD .... Phosphate Dehydrogenase
PD .... Phosphodiester [*Organic chemistry*]
PD .... Photodiode
PD .... Phyllis Dorothy James White [*In name P. D. James*] [*Author*]
PD .... Physical Damage [*Insurance*]
PD .... Physical Disabilities

PD .... Physical Distribution   (ADA)
PD .... Physics Department
P & D .... Pick Up and Delivery [*Business and trade*]
PD .... Pictorial Display   (MCD)
PD .... Pierce's Disease [*Plant pathology*]
PD .... Pilot Dogs [*An association*] [*Columbus, OH*]   (EA)
P & D .... Pioneer and Demolition Section [*Army*]
PD .... Piskei Din Shel Bet ha-Mishpat ha-'Elyon le-Yisrael   (BJA)
PD .... Pitch Diameter
PD .... Pitch Down   (MCD)
PD .... Pivoted Door   (AAG)
PD .... Plane Disagreement [*Telecommunications*]   (TEL)
PD .... Planned Derating [*Electronics*]   (IEEE)
PD .... Planning Directive   (NG)
PD .... Planning Document
PD .... Plans Division [*Military*]
PD .... Plasma Desorption [*of ions for analysis*]
PD .... Plasma Display
PD .... Plate Dissipation
PD .... Platelet Deaggregation [*Hematology*]
PD .... Poetic Drama [*A publication*]
PD .... Point Defense
PD .... Point Detonating [*Projectile*]
PD .... Polar Distance [*Navigation*]
PD .... Police Department
pd .... Pond [*Pound*] [*Monetary unit*] [*Afrikaans*]
PD .... Pontoon Dock
PD .... Poorly Differentiated [*Medicine*]
PD .... Population Density   (NRCH)
PD .... Population Distribution   (NRCH)
PD .... Population Doubling
PD .... Port of Debarkation [*Navy*]
PD .... Port Director
PD .... Port Du [*Carriage Forward*] [*French*]
PD .... Port Dues
PD .... Position Description
PD .... Position Doubtful [*Nautical charts*]
PD .... Positive Displacement
PD .... Post Diluvium [*After the Flood*] [*Latin*]   (ROG)
PD .... Postage Due
PD .... Postal District
PD .... Postdated
PD .... Posterior Deltoid [*Myology*]
PD .... Posterior Digestive [*Gland*]
PD .... Postnasal Drainage [*Medicine*]
PD .... Potential Difference [*Electricity*]
PD .... Pound   (ROG)
PD .... Power Distribution
PD .... Predeployment
P/D .... Predicted [*NASA*]   (KSC)
PD .... Predilute
PD .... Preference for Duty
PD .... Pregnanediol [*Biochemistry*]
PD .... Preliminary Design
PD .... Presidential Determination
PD .... Presidential Directive
PD .... Presidential Documents [*A publication*]
PD .... Pressor Dose [*Medicine*]
Pd .... Pressure, Diastolic [*Cardiology*]
PD .... Pressure Drop   (KSC)
PD .... Presumptive Disability [*Title XVI*] [*Social Security Administration*]   (OICC)
PD .... Prevention Detention [*Scotland Yard*]
PD .... Prime Driver
PD .... Printer Driver
PD .... Printer's Devil   (ROG)
PD .... Priority Designator
PD .... Priority Directive
PD .... Prism Diopter
PD .... Prisoner's Dilemma
PD .... Privatdozent [*Tutor*] [*German*]
PD .... Private Detective
pd .... Pro Defendente [*On Behalf of Defendant*] [*Latin*]   (DLA)
PD .... Probability of Damage   (MCD)
PD .... Probability of Detection
P & D .... Probate and Divorce [*Legal*] [*British*]
PD .... Problem Definition [*Army*]
PD .... Procurement Data
PD .... Procurement Directive
P & D .... Procurement and Distribution [*Military*]
PD .... Procurement District [*Air Force*]   (AFIT)
PD .... Procurement Division
PD .... Procurement Drawing
P/D .... Product Development
PD .... Production Department
PD .... Production and Deployment Phase   (MCD)
PD .... Program Deceleration   (KSC)
PD .... Program Decoder
PD .... Program Directive   (NG)
PD .... Program Director [*Television*]

PD	Programa Democratico [*Democratic Program*] [*Spanish*] (PPE)
PD	Progression of Disease [*Medicine*]
PD	Project Directive (NASA)
PD	Project Document
PD	Projected Decision Date (NRCH)
PD	Projected Display
PD	Promotion Director
PD	Propellant Dispersion (KSC)
PD	Property Damage
PD	Proposal Development (AAG)
PD	Protective Device (BUR)
PD	Provisioning Document
PD	Proximity Detector
PD	Prussian Dollar (ROG)
PD	Pseudohomogeneous Axial Dispersion Model [*Fluid dynamics*]
PD	Psychodynamic
Pd	Psychopathic Deviate [*Psychology*]
PD	Psychotic Depression [*Medicine*]
PD	Public Domain
PD	Publication Date [*Online database field identifier*]
PD	Publisher's Directory [*Formerly, BPD*] [*A publication*]
PD	Pulmonary Disease [*Medicine*]
PD	Pulpodistal [*Dentistry*]
PD	Pulse Detector [*Spectroscopy*]
PD	Pulse Doppler
PD	Pulse Driver
PD	Pulse Duration
P-D	Punch-Die (MSA)
PD	Punch Driver
pd	Pupillary Distance [*Medicine*]
PD	Purchase Description
PD	Pyloric Dilator [*Neuron*]
P 2d	Pacific Reporter, Second Series (DLA)
PDA	Pacific Dermatologic Association [*Evanston, IL*] (EA)
PDA	Parallel Data Adapter
PDA	Parametric Design Analysis (RDA)
PDA	Parenteral Drug Association [*Philadelphia, PA*] (EA)
PdA	Partei der Arbeit [*Labor Party*] [*Swiss*] (PPE)
PDA	Parti Democratico da Angola [*Democratic Party of Angola*]
PDA	Parti Dolonti Applicandum [*Apply to Painful Part*] [*Pharmacy*] (ROG)
PDA	Partit Democrata d'Andorra [*Andorran Democratic Party*] (PPW)
Pd'A	Partito d'Azione [*Action Party*] [*Italy*] (PPE)
PDA	Parts Disposal Area (MCD)
PDA	Pasadena Energy [*Vancouver Stock Exchange symbol*]
PDA	Patent Ductus Arteriosus [*Cardiology*]
PDA	Patient Data Automation
PDA	Payroll Deduction Authorization (MCD)
PDA	Peak Distribution Analyzer
PDA	Pediatric Allergy
PDA	Permanent Duty Assignment [*Air Force*] (AFM)
PDA	Personal Deposit Account [*Banking*]
PDA	Phenylenediamine [*Chemistry*]
PDA	Philadelphia Dance Alliance
PDA	Phorbol Diacetate [*Organic chemistry*]
PDA	Photodiode Array [*Instrumentation*]
PDA	Photon Detector Assembly (MCD)
PDA	Physical Device Address [*Data processing*] (IBMDP)
PDA	Piperidinedicarboxylic Acid [*Organic chemistry*]
PDA	Point Density Analysis [*Mathematics*]
PDA	Point Director Array
PDA	Poise Distribution Amplifier (AFM)
PDA	Polarization Diversity Array
PDA	Poly(dimethylacrylamide) [*Organic chemistry*]
PDA	Ponta Delgada [*Azores*] [*Seismograph station code, US Geological Survey*] (SEIS)
PDA	Population Drainage Area [*Civil Defense*]
PDA	Post-Deflection Accelerator (DEN)
PDA	Post-Delivery Availability [*Military*] (NVT)
PDA	Post-Design Analysis
PDA	Potato Dextrose Agar [*Culture media*]
PDA	Pour Dire Adieu [*To Say Farewell*] [*On visiting cards*] [*French*]
PDA	Power Distribution Assembly (KSC)
PDA	Precision Drive Axis (KSC)
PDA	Predelivery Acceptance Test [*NASA*]
PDA	Predicted Drift Angle [*Navigation*]
PDA	Predocketed Application (NRCH)
PDA	Preliminary Design Acceptance (NRCH)
PDA	Preliminary Design Approval [*or Authorization*] (NRCH)
PDA	Preliminary Design Assessment [*Nuclear energy*] (NRCH)
PDA	Principal Development Activity [*Navy*]
PDA	Principal Development Authority (MCD)
PDA	Private Doctors of America [*Formerly, American Association of Councils of Medicals Staffs - CMS*] [*New Orleans, LA*] (EA)
PDA	Probability Discrete Automata (IEEE)
PDA	Probability Distribution Analyzer [*Statistics*]
PDA	Probate, Divorce, and Admiralty [*England*] (DLA)
PDA	Processor and Distribution Assembly [*Viking lander analysis equipment*] [*NASA*]
PDA	Procurement Defense Agencies [*DoD*]
PDA	Product Departure Authorization
PDA	Professional Drivers Association
PDA	Program Developing Agency [*Military*] (CAAL)
PDA	Prolonged Depolarizing Afterpotential [*Neurophysiology*]
PDA	Propanediamine [*Organic chemistry*]
PDA	Propellant Drain Area (NASA)
PDA	Property Disposal Account [*Military*] (NG)
PDA	Property Disposal Agent [*Military*] (NG)
PDA	Proposed Development Approach [*Navy*]
PDA	Propylenediamine [*Organic chemistry*]
PDA	Prospectors' and Developers' Association [*Canada*]
PDA	Public Display of Affection [*Slang*]
PDA	Puerto Inirida [*Colombia*] [*Airport symbol*] (OAG)
PDA	Pulse Demodulation Analysis
PDA	Pulse Distribution Amplifier
PDA	Pump Drive Assembly
PDAB	Para-(Dimethylamino)benzaldehyde [*Organic chemistry*]
PDAB	Physical Disability Appeals Board [*Military*] (AFM)
PDAC	Professional Development Advisory Committee [*American Occupational Therapy Association*]
PDAD	Photodiode Array Detector [*Spectrophotometry*]
PDAD	Probate, Divorce, and Admiralty Division [*Legal*] [*British*] (ROG)
PDAFSC	Projected Duty Air Force Specialty Code (AFM)
PDAGA	Pediatriia, Akusherstvo, i Ginekologiia [*A publication*]
PDAID	Problem Determination Aid [*Data processing*] (MDG)
PDalCM	College Misericordia, Dallas, PA [*Library symbol*] [*Library of Congress*] (LCLS)
PDAM	Periodontal Disease-Associated Microbiotae [*Dentistry*]
PDanMHi ...	Montour County Historical Society, Danville, PA [*Library symbol*] [*Library of Congress*] (LCLS)
PDanSH	Danville State Hospital, Danville, PA [*Library symbol*] [*Library of Congress*] (LCLS)
PDAP	Programable Digital Autopilot (MCD)
PDAP	Provincial Development Assistance Program [*Agency for International Development*]
PDAR	Parts Drawing Approval Request (MCD)
PDAR	Producibility Design Analysis Report (AAG)
PDAR	Program Description and Requirements [*NASA*] (NASA)
PDARR	Production Drawing and Assembly Release Record (AAG)
PDAS	Photo Data Analysis System [*Navy*]
PDAS	Plant Data Acquisition System (NRCH)
PDAS	[*A*] Popular Dictionary of Australian Slang [*A publication*]
PDASD	Principal Deputy Assistant Secretary of Defense
PDATE	Production Date [*Data processing*]
Pd B	Bachelor of Pedagogy
PDB	Packard Data Bank (EA)
PDB	Para-Dichlorobenzene [*Insecticide for moths, etc.*]
PDB	Partei der Deutschsprachigen Belgier [*Party of German-Speaking Belgians*] (PPW)
PDB	Pedro Bay [*Alaska*] [*Airport symbol*] (OAG)
PDB	Pee Dee Belemnite
PDB	Performance Data Book (NASA)
PDB	Periodical Directories and Bibliographies [*A publication*]
PDB	Personality Data Base
PDB	Phorbol Dibutyrate [*Also, PDBu*] [*Organic chemistry*]
PDB	Phosphorus-Dissolving Bacteria [*Microbiology*]
PDB	Plasma Diagnostic Base
PDB	Positive Displacement Blower
PDB	Power Distribution Box (NASA)
PDB	President's Daily Brief
PDB	Price Decontrol Board [*Post-World War II*]
PDB	Process Descriptor Base [*Telecommunications*] (TEL)
PDB	Project Development Brochure [*Military*]
PDBA	Personnel Database Application (MCD)
PDBH	Production Broach (AAG)
PDBIA	Periodicum Biologorum [*A publication*]
PDBM	Pulse Delay Binary Modulation (MCD)
PDBP	Powered Disposal Bomb Pod (AAG)
PDBU	Pesticides Documentation Bulletin
PDBu	Phorbol Dibutyrate [*Also, PDB*] [*Organic chemistry*]
PDBz	Phorbol Dibenzoate [*Organic chemistry*]
PDC	Christian Democratic Party [*Panamanian*] (PD)
PDC	Community College of Philadelphia, Philadelphia, PA [*OCLC symbol*] (OCLC)
PDC	Mueo [*New Caledonia*] [*Airport symbol*] (OAG)
PDC	Pacific Defense College (CINC)
PDC	Package Design Council [*New York, NY*] (EA)
PDC	Pacte Democratica per Catalunya [*Democratic Pact for Catalonia*] [*Spanish*] (PPE)
PDC	Paper Distribution Council [*Great Neck, NY*] (EA)
PDC	Parallel Data Communicator (AAG)
PDC	Parallel Data Controller
PDC	Parametric Defense Coverage
PDC	Parti Democrate Chretien [*Christian Democratic Party*] [*Burundi*]
PDC	Parti Democrate-Chretien Suisse [*Christian Democratic Party of Switzerland*] (PPE)

PDC............ Partido da Democracia Cristao [*Christian Democratic Party*] [*Portuguese*] (PPW)
PDC............ Partido Democracia Cristiana [*Christian Democratic Party*] [*Guatemalan*] (PPW)
PDC............ Partido Democrata Cristiano [*Christian Democratic Party*] [*Peruvian*] (PPW)
PDC............ Partido Democrata Cristiano [*Christian Democratic Party*] [*Honduran*] (PPW)
PDC............ Partido Democrata Cristiano [*Christian Democratic Party*] [*Paraguayan*] (PPW)
PDC............ Partido Democrata Cristiano [*Christian Democratic Party*] [*Bolivian*] (PPW)
PDC............ Partido Democrata Cristiano [*Christian Democratic Party*] [*Costa Rican*] (PPW)
PDC............ Partido Democrata Cristiano [*Christian Democratic Party*] [*Panamanian*] (PPW)
PDC............ Partido Democrata Cristiano [*Christian Democratic Party*] [*Salvadoran*]
PDC............ Partido Democratico Cristao [*Christian Democratic Party*] [*Brazil*]
PDC............ Partido Democratico Cristiano [*Christian Democratic Party*] [*Argentina*] (PPW)
PDC............ Partido Democratico Cristiano [*Christian Democratic Party*] [*Chilean*] (PPW)
PDC............ Partito della Democrazia Cristiana [*Christian Democratic Party*] [*Italy*]
PDC............ Pentadecylcatechol [*An allergen*]
PDC............ People's Defence Committee [*Ghanaian*] (PD)
PDC............ Per Diem, Travel and Transportation Allowance Committee for Departments of the Army, Navy, and Air Force
PDC............ Performance Data Computer
PDC............ Personnel Data Card
PDC............ Personnel Distribution Command
PDC............ Philosophy Documentation Center [*Bowling Green State University*] [*Bowling Green, OH*]
PDC............ Photo-Data Card [*Trademark*] [*Data processing*]
PDC............ Photonuclear Data Center [*National Bureau of Standards*]
PDC............ Pieve Di Cadore [*Italy*] [*Seismograph station code, US Geological Survey*] [*Closed*] (SEIS)
PDC............ Plastic Dielectric Capacitor
PDC............ Polaris Documentation Control [*Missiles*]
PDC............ Policy Determination Committee (AAG)
PDC............ Polystyrene Dielectric Capacitor
PDC............ Population Documentation Center [*Food and Agriculture Organization*] [*United Nations*] [*Information service*] [*Rome, Italy*] (EISS)
PDC............ Position Depth Charge
PDC............ Power Distribution and Control
PDC............ Power Distribution Cubiale (NATG)
PDC............ Practice Depth Charge
PDC............ Prairie Du Chien, WI [*Location identifier*] [*FAA*] (FAAL)
PDC............ Predefined Command (MCD)
PDC............ Predocketed Construction (NRCH)
PDC............ Preliminary Diagnostic Clinic
PDC............ Premission Documentation Change [*NASA*] (KSC)
PDC............ Premium and Dispersion Credits [*Insurance*]
PDC............ Prescott Development Corp. [*Vancouver Stock Exchange symbol*]
PDC............ Prevention of Deterioration Center [*Defunct*] (EA)
PDC............ Price Decontrol Board [*Post-World War II*] (DLA)
PDC............ Private Diagnostic Clinic
PDC............ Probability of Detection and Conversion [*Military*]
PDC............ Procurement Document Change (NASA)
PDC............ Production Decision Criteria
PDC............ Professional Development Center
PDC............ Proficiency Data Card
PDC............ Program Data Cards (OICC)
PDC............ Program Data Coordinator (MCD)
PDC............ Project Data Card
PDC............ Project Data Control (MCD)
PDC............ Prosthetic Distribution Center [*Veterans Administration*]
PDC............ Public Documents Commission [*Government agency*]
PDC............ Publications Distribution Center [*Military*] (AFM)
PDC............ Publishers' Data Center, Inc.
PDC............ Pulse-Duration Commutator
PDC............ Pyrotechnic Devices Checker
PDC............ Single Paper Double Cotton [*Wire insulation*] (AAG)
PDCA......... Painting and Decorating Contractors of America [*Falls Church, VA*] (EA)
PDCA......... Pioneer Dairymen's Club of America (EA)
PDCA......... Pug Dog Club of America (EA)
PDCA......... Purebred Dairy Cattle Association (EA)
PDCAU....... Pete Duel - Clube da Amizade do Universo [*Pete Duel Universal Friendship Club - PDUFC*] [*Rio De Janeiro, Brazil*] (EA-IO)
PDCG......... Partido Democracia Cristiana Guatemalteca [*Guatemalan Christian Democratic Party*] (PPW)
PDCI........... Parti Democratique de la Cote-D'Ivoire [*Democratic Party of the Ivory Coast*] (PPW)

Pdck........... Probability of Detection Conversion and Kill [*for an interceptor system*] [*Military*]
PDCL......... Provisioning Data Check List [*NASA*] (KSC)
PDCO......... Property Disposal Contracting Officer [*Military*]
PDCP......... Pilot's Display Control Panel
PDCP......... Private Development Corporation of the Philippines
PDCR......... Project Data Compliance Report (MCD)
PDCRC...... Periodontal Disease Clinical Research Center [*State University of New York at Buffalo*] [*Research center*] (RCD)
PDCS......... Parallel Digital Computing System
PDCS......... Partito Democratico Cristiano Sammarinese [*Christian Democratic Party of San Marino*] (PPE)
PDCS......... Performance Data Computer System (MCD)
PDCS......... Power Distribution and Control System [*or Subsystem*] [*NASA*] (NASA)
PDCS......... Processing Distribution and Control System
PDCS......... Programable Data Collection System [*Military*] (CAAL)
PDCS......... Prototype Die Casting Service
PDCU......... Plotting Display Control Unit
Pd D........... Doctor of Pedagogy
PDD........... Pancreatic Dorsal Duct [*Anatomy*]
PDD........... Past Due Date
PDD........... Phorbol Didecanoate [*Organic chemistry*]
PDD........... Physical Damage Division [*Navy*]
PDD........... Physical Defense Division [*Army*]
PDD........... Plotting Data Distributor (MCD)
P & DD...... Plumbing and Deck Drain (MSA)
PDD........... Post Dialing Delay [*Telecommunications*] (TEL)
PDD........... Precision Depth Digitizer [*Oceanography*]
PDD........... Preferred Delivery Date (AFM)
PDD........... Preliminary Design and Development (MCD)
PDD........... Premodulation Processor - Deep Space - Data
PDD........... Principal Distribution Depot [*DoD*]
PDD........... Priority Delivery Date (AFM)
PDD........... Probability Density Distribution [*Statistics*]
PdD........... Probleme der Dichtung [*A publication*]
PDD........... Procurement Description Data [*DoD*]
PD & D...... Product Design & Development [*Radnor, PA*] [*A publication*]
PDD........... Professional Development Division [*American Occupational Therapy Association*]
PDD........... Program Description Document [*Military*] (CAAL)
PDD........... Program Design Data
PDD........... Program Dimension Drawing (MCD)
PDD........... Program Directive Document (RDA)
PDD........... Projected Data Display
PDD........... Projected Decision Date (NRCH)
PDD........... Prospective Decision Date (NRCH)
PDD........... Provisioning Description Data
PDD........... Public Documents Department [*Government Printing Office*]
PDD........... Pulse Delay Device
PDD........... Puy-De-Dome [*France*] [*Seismograph station code, US Geological Survey*] [*Closed*] (SEIS)
PDDA........ Power Driver Decontamination Apparatus (NATG)
PDDAIO..... Parts for Direct Discrete Analog Input/Output (MCD)
PDDB........ Phenododecinium [*or Phenoxyethyldimethyl-dodecylammonium*] Bromide [*Antiseptic*]
PDDB........ Product Definition Database (MCD)
PDDF......... Propargyl(dideaza)folic Acid [*Biochemistry*]
PDDGM...... Past District Deputy Grand Master [*Freemasonry*]
PD Div'l Ct .... Probate, Divorce, and Admiralty Divisional Court [*England*] (DLA)
PDDLS....... Post D-Day Logistic Support (AABC)
PDDM........ Disciples of the Divine Master [*Roman Catholic women's religious order*]
PDD/RDD... Priority Delivery Date/Required Delivery Date (AFM)
PDDS........ Program Definition Data Sheet
PDE........... Pandie Pandie [*Australia*] [*Airport symbol*] [*Obsolete*] (OAG)
PDE........... Parade
Pde........... Parade [*Record label*]
PDE........... Paroxysmal Dyspnea on Exertion [*Medicine*]
PDE........... Partei fuer Deutschland und Europa [*Party for Germany and Europe*] [*West Germany*] (PPW)
PDE........... Partial Differential Equation
PDE........... Pee Dee Air Express, Inc. [*Florence, SC*] [*FAA designator*] (FAAC)
PDE........... Personnel Development and Education (MCD)
PDE........... Phosphatidyl(dimethyl)ethanolamine [*Biochemistry*]
PDE........... Phosphodiesterase [*An enzyme*]
PDE........... Pilot's Discrete Encoder
PDE........... Position-Determining Equipment
PDE........... Preliminary Determination of Epicenters [*A publication*] [*National Oceanic and Atmospheric Administration*]
PDE........... Pride Resources Ltd. [*Vancouver Stock Exchange symbol*]
PDE........... Production Design Engineers
PDE........... Projectile Development Establishment [*British*]
PDE........... Propellant Disposition Effects
PDE........... Prospective Data Element [*Army*] (AABC)
PD & E....... Provisioning Documentation and Effort [*Military*] (AFIT)
PDED......... Partial Double Error Detection
PDEL......... Partial Differential Equation Language [*Data processing*]

PDELAN..... Partial Differential Equation Language [*Data processing*] (CSR)
PDEP......... Preliminary Draft Equipment Publication (MCD)
PDEQ .... Profile of DARCOM Environmental Quality (MCD)
PDES......... Preliminary Draft Environmental Statement (NRCH)
PDET........ Probability of Detection, Evaluation, and Transfer (MCD)
PDF .... Paget's Disease Foundation [*Brooklyn, NY*] (EA)
PDF .... Pair Distribution Function [*Physical chemistry*]
PDF .... Parkinson's Disease Foundation [*New York, NY*] (EA)
PDF .... Parti Democrate Francais [*French Democratic Party*] (PPW)
PDF .... Particle Distribution Function
PDF .... Passive Direction Finding
PDF .... Pavement Depth Factor (ADA)
PDF .... Peace Development Fund (EA)
PDF .... Planet Drum Foundation [*San Francisco, CA*] (EA)
PDF .... Plant Design Factor [*Nuclear energy*] (NRCH)
PDF .... Point Detonating Fuze
PDF .... Popular Democratic Front [*Jordan*]
PDF .... Post Defense Force
PDF .... Post Detection Filter [*Telecommunications*] (TEL)
PDF .... Principal Direction of Fire [*Military*]
PDF .... Probability Density Function [*Statistics*]
PDF .... Probability Distribution Function [*Statistics*]
PDF .... Processor Defined Function
PDF .... Production and Distribution of Foodstuffs [*British*]
PDF .... Program Data File
PDF .... Project Design Flood (NRCH)
PDFCS Pennsylvania Dutch Folk Culture Society (EA)
PDFD......... Predemonstration Fusion Device
PDFD......... Pulsed Doppler Frequency Diversity (NG)
PDFLP........ Popular Democratic Front for the Liberation of Palestine
PDFRR....... Program Directors Flight Readiness Review [*NASA*] (KSC)
PDFWPR .... Physical Disabilities Fieldwork Performance Report [*Occupational therapy*]
PDG........... Padang [*Indonesia*] [*Airport symbol*] (OAG)
PDG........... Parachute Drop Glider
PDG........... Parti Democratique Gabonais [*Gabonese Democratic Party*] (PPW)
PDG........... Parti Democratique de Guinee [*Democratic Party of Guinea*] (PPW)
PDG........... Passive Defense Group (MUGU)
PDG........... Patent Documentation Group (DIT)
PDG........... Personalistic Discussion Group - Eastern Division (EA)
PDG........... Precision Drop Glider [*Army*]
PDG........... Pregnanediol Glucuronide [*Endocrinology*]
PDG........... President Directeur General [*President Director General*] [*French*]
PDG........... Pretty Damn Good
PDG........... Professional Dyers Guild [*Defunct*]
PDG........... Programs Development Group (MUGU)
PDG........... Proposal Development Group [*Aerospace*] (AAG)
PDGA .... Pteroyldiglutamic Acid [*Pharmacology*]
PDGDL .... Plasma Dynamics and Gaseous Discharge Laboratory [*MIT*] (MCD)
PDGF......... Platelet Derived Growth Factor [*Genetics*]
P-DGs........ Presidents-Directeurs Generaux
PDGS .... Probe Drill Guidance System
PDGS .... Product Design Graphics System [*Prime Computer Ltd.*] [*Software package*]
PDGY .... Prodigy Systems, Inc. [*NASDAQ symbol*] (NQ)
PDH........... Packaged Disaster Hospital [*Public Health Service*]
PDH........... Passive Defense Handbook [*Navy*] (MCD)
PDH........... Past Dental History
PDH........... Planned Derated Hours [*Electronics*] (IEEE)
PDH........... Pocket Dosimeter-High (MCD)
PDH........... Pyruvate Dehydrogenase [*An enzyme*]
PDHC......... Pyruvate Dehydrogenase Complex [*Biochemistry*]
PDH & DS... Plant Data Handling and Display System [*Nuclear energy*] (NRCH)
PDHF......... Postdilution Hemofiltration [*Medicine*]
PDHMUA.... Publication. Department of History. Muslim University (Aligarh) [*A publication*]
PDHV-RDA ... Parti Democratique de la Haute Volta-Rassemblement Democratique Africain [*Democratic Party of Upper Volta-African Democratic Rally*]
PDI .... Partai Demokrasi Indonesia [*Indonesian Democratic Party*] (PPW)
PDI .... Parti Democratique de l'Independance [*Democratic Independence Party*] [*Moroccan*]
PDI .... Partito Democratica Italiana [*Italian Democratic Party*] (PPE)
PDI .... Payload Data Interleaver [*NASA*] (NASA)
PDI .... Personal Disposable Income
PDI .... Pictorial Deviation Indicator (AAG)
PDI .... Pilot Direction Indicator [*Electronic communications*]
PDI .... Plumbing and Drainage Institute [*Indianapolis, IN*] (EA)
PDI .... Porto D'Ischia [*Italy*] [*Seismograph station code, US Geological Survey*] [*Closed*] (SEIS)
PDI .... Post Detection Integration (MCD)
PDI .... Powered Descent Initiation [*Aerospace*]
PDI .... Pre-Delivery Inspection
PDI .... Predeployment Inspection [*Navy*] (NVT)

PDI .... Premdor [*Toronto Stock Exchange symbol*]
PDI .... Program Design, Incorporated [*Commercial firm*]
PDI .... Program with Developing Institutions (EA)
PDI .... Project Data Index [*Jet Propulsion Laboratory, NASA*]
PDI .... Protein Dispersibility Index [*Analytical chemistry*]
PDI .... Protein Disulfide-Isomerase [*An enzyme*]
PDI .... Psychomotor Development Index [*Bayley Scales of Infant Development*]
PDI .... Public Demographics, Incorporated [*Cincinnati, OH*] (EISS)
Pdi............ Transdiaphragmatic [*Pressure*]
PDial........ Poetry Dial [*A publication*]
PDIC......... Periodic (AFM)
PDIC......... Public Demands Implementation Convention [*Indian*] (PPW)
PDIIS........ Priority Defense Items Information System
PDIL......... Power Dependent Insertion Limits (NRCH)
PDIL......... Prueba del Desarrollo Inicial del Lenguaje [*Standardized test of Spanish language-speaking ability in children from three to seven years old*]
PDIO......... Parallel Digital Input/Output
PDIO......... Photodiode
P-DIOL ...... Pregnanediol [*Biochemistry*]
PDIP......... Preflight Data Insertion Program (NVT)
PDIP......... Program Development Increment Package [*Military*]
PDIR......... Priority Disassembly and Inspection Report
PDIS......... Parts Dissection Information System
PDIS......... Payload Data Interleaver System [*NASA*] (MCD)
PDIS......... Proceedings. National Symposia [*A publication*]
PDIS......... Product Description Information Standards [*or System*]
PDISCH...... Pump Discharge
PDISPL...... Positive Displacement [*Engineering*]
PDIUM....... Partito Democratico Italiano di Unita Monarchica [*Italian Democratic Party of Monarchical Unity*] (PPE)
P Div......... Law Reports, Probate Division [*England*] (DLA)
PDJ........... Plaine Des Jarres [*South Vietnam*]
PDJ........... Precision Drill Jig
PDJB .... Precision Drill Jig Bushing
PD/JV........ Project Definition/Joint Validation (MCD)
PDK .... Atlanta [*Georgia*] De Kalb/Peachtree Airport [*Airport symbol*] [*Obsolete*] (OAG)
PDK .... Phi Delta Kappa [*Fraternity*]
PDK .... Phileleftheron Demokratikon Kendron [*Liberal Democratic Union*] [*Greek*] (PPE)
PDK .... Phileleftheron Demokratikon Komma [*Liberal Democratic Party*] [*Greek*] (PPE)
PDL .... Page Description Language [*Computer graphics*]
PDL .... Partido Democrata Liberal [*Liberal Democratic Party*] [*Madrid, Spain*]
PDL .... Parts Deletion List (MSA)
PDL .... Parts Difference List (MCD)
PDL .... Parts Documentation List (MCD)
PDL .... Pass Down the Line [*Book*] [*Navy*] (MUGU)
PDL .... Periodontal Ligament [*Dentistry*]
PDL .... Permanent Duty Location
PDL .... Photodissociation Dye LASER
PDL .... Placer Development Limited [*Toronto Stock Exchange symbol*] [*Vancouver Stock Exchange symbol*]
PDL .... Pocket Dosimeter-Low (MCD)
PDL .... Ponta Delgada [*Portugal*] [*Airport symbol*] (OAG)
PDL .... Poorly Differentiated Lymphocytic [*Lymphoma classification*]
PDL .... Population Doubling Level [*Cytology*]
pdl............ Poundal [*Unit of force*]
PDL .... Poverty Datum Line
PDL .... Precision Delay Line
PDL .... Presidential Realty Corp. [*American Stock Exchange symbol*]
PDL .... Procedure Definition Language [*Data processing*] (BUR)
PDL .... Procedure Distribution List (MCD)
PDL .... Procurement Data List
PDL .... Product Disaster Loans [*Small Business Administration*]
PDL .... Professional Development League (EA)
PDL .... Program Description Language (MCD)
PDL .... Program Design Language (NASA)
PDL .... Programed Digital Logic
PDL .... Project Document List
PdL .... Provincia di Lucca [*A publication*]
PDL .... Publishers' Databases Limited [*Publishing consortium*] [*British*]
PDL .... Pulsed Dye LASER
PDLC........ Partido Liberal de Cataluna [*Liberal Democratic Party of Catalonia*] (PPW)
PDL/FT² Poundals per Square Foot
PDLL .... Poorly Differentiated Lymphatic [*or Lymphocytic*] Lymphoma [*Oncology*]
PDLM .... Periodic Depot Level Maintenance
PDL S/FT² ... Poundal Seconds per Square Foot
PDLT......... P-Channel Depletion-Load Triode Inverter
Pd M .... Master of Pedagogy
PDM .... Parti Democratique Malgache [*Malagasy Democratic Party*]
PDM .... Partial Descriptive Method
PDM .... Patient Data Management
PDM .... Pendant Drop Method

PDM .... People's Democratic Movement [*Turks and Caicos Islands*] (PPW)
PDM .... Percent Deviation from the Median
PDM .... Physical Distribution Management
PDM .... Physicians Drug Manual [*A publication*]
PDM .... Physiological Data Monitor
PDM .... Pittsburgh - Des Moines, Inc. [*American Stock Exchange symbol*]
PDM .... Poetry and Drama Magazine [*A publication*]
PDM .... Portable Differential Magnetometer
PDM .... Power Density Meter
PDM .... Practical Data Manager [*Hitachi Ltd.*] [*Japan*]
PDM .... Precedence Diagraming Method (MCD)
PDM .... Presidential Decision Memorandum [*Jimmy Carter Administration*]
PDM .... Print Down Module
PDM .... Processor Data Monitor (NASA)
PDM .... Production Decision Criteria Matrix
PDM .... Program Data Manager (MCD)
PDM .... Program Decision Memo [*Navy*]
PDM .... Programed Depot Maintenance (MCD)
PDM .... Progres et Democratie Moderne [*Progress and Modern Democracy*] [*French*] (PPE)
PDM .... Project Design Memo
PDM .... Publications Distribution Manager [*Military*] (AFM)
PDM .... Pulse Delta Modulation (IEEE)
PDM .... Pulse-Duration Modulation [*Data transmission*]
PDM .... Push Down Memory [*Data processing*]
PDMA .... Peninsula Drafting Management Association
PDMA .... Product Development and Management Association [*Indianapolis, IN*] (EA)
PDME .... Pendant-Drop Melt Extraction [*Metal fiber technology*]
PDM-FM ...... Pulse-Duration Modulation - Frequency Modulation (CET)
PDMLA .... PDM. Physicians' Drug Manual [*A publication*]
PDMLR .... Post-Development Maintainability Logistics Review (MCD)
PDMM .... Push Down Memory MODEM [*Data processing*]
PDMO .... Production Mold (AAG)
PDMP .... Positive Displacement Mechanical [*or Metering*] Pump
PDMR .... Provisioning Data Master Record (MCD)
PDMS .... Physiological Data Monitoring System
PDMS .... Plant Design and Management System [*Computer Aided Design Centre*] [*Software package*]
PDMS .... Plasma Desorption Mass Spectroscopy
PDMS .... Point Defense Missile System [*NATO*] (NATG)
PDMS .... Polydimethylsiloxane [*Organic chemistry*]
PDMS .... Power-Plant and Process Design Management System [*Data processing*]
PDMS .... Program Definition and Management System (MCD)
PDMT .... Predominate (FAAC)
PDMU .... Passive Data Memory Unit
PDMU .... Production Mock-Up (AAG)
PDN .... Paradyne Corp. [*NYSE symbol*]
PDN .... Partido Democratico Nacional [*National Democratic Party*] [*Chile*]
PDN .... Partido Democratico Nacional [*National Democratic Party*] [*Venezuela*]
PDN .... Partito Democratico Nazionalista [*Democratic Nationalist Party (1921-1926)*] [*Maltese*] (PPE)
PDN .... Partnerships Data Net [*Washington, DC*] (EA)
PDN .... Petition Denied
PDN .... Port Heiden, AK [*Location identifier*] [*FAA*] (FAAL)
PDN .... Prednisone [*Also, P, Pr, Pred, Pro*] [*Antineoplastic drug*] [*Endocrinology*]
PDN .... Problem Documentation Number (AAG)
PDN .... Production (AFM)
PDN .... Properly Driven Net
PDN .... Public Data Network [*Packet-switching network*] [*British Telecommunications PLC*] [*London*]
PDNC .... Presidents' Day National Committee (EA)
PDNPD .... Physica D. Nonlinear Phenomena [*A publication*]
PD/NSC ..... Presidential Directives/National Security Council
PDO .... Philips & Du Pont Optical Co. [*Wilmington, DE*]
PDO .... Postman's Delivery Office
PDO .... Printer Direction Optimizer (BUR)
PD-O .... Program Directive - Operations (KSC)
PDO .... Property Disposal Officer [*Military*]
PdO .... Psychopathic Deviate Obvious [*Psychology*]
PDO .... Publications Distribution Officer [*Military*]
PDoB .... Bucks County Free Library, Doylestown, PA [*Library symbol*] [*Library of Congress*] (LCLS)
PDoBHi ...... Bucks County Historical Society, Doylestown, PA [*Library symbol*] [*Library of Congress*] (LCLS)
PDOC .... Particulate and/or Dissolved Organic Carbon [*Chemistry*]
PDOC .... Proceed Directly on Course [*Aviation*] (FAAC)
PDOD .... Phytoplankton Dissolved Oxygen Deficit [*Oceanography*]
PDOL .... Publishers Discount Option List
PDoN .... Delaware Valley College of Science and Agriculture, Doylestown, PA [*Library symbol*] [*Library of Congress*] (LCLS)
PDowN ...... Newcomen Society in North America, Downingtown, PA [*Library symbol*] [*Library of Congress*] (LCLS)

PDP .... Packaging Development Plan
PDP .... Pakistan Democratic Party (PD)
PDP .... Parallel Distributed Processing [*A simulation of mental processes*]
PDP .... Parliamentary Democratic Party [*Burmese*]
PdP .... Parola del Popolo [*A publication*]
PDP .... Parti Democrate Populaire [*Popular Democratic Party*] [*French*] (PPE)
PDP .... Partido Democrata Popular [*Popular Democratic Party*] [*Spanish*] (PPW)
PDP .... Partido Democrata Popular [*People's Democratic Party*] [*Dominican Republic*] (PPW)
PDP .... Partido da Direita Portuguesa [*Party of the Portuguese Right*] (PPE)
PDP .... Partito Democratico Populare [*Popular Democratic Party*] [*Sanmarinese*] (PPE)
PDP .... Payload Distribution Panel [*NASA*] (MCD)
PDP .... Pentadecylphenol [*Organic chemistry*]
PDP .... People's Democratic Party [*Sudanese*]
PDP .... Personal Development Program (MCD)
PDP .... Philadelphia, PA [*Location identifier*] [*FAA*] (FAAL)
PDP .... Philippine Democratic Party [*Pilipino Lakas Ng Bayan*] (PPW)
PDP .... Pilot District Project [*Office of Economic Opportunity*] [*Defunct*] (EA)
PDP .... Pitch-Depitch (AAG)
PDP .... Planning Development Program (OICC)
PDP .... Plasma Diagnostics Package [*NASA*]
PDP .... Plasma Display Panel [*Data processing*]
PDP .... Popular Democratic Party [*Puerto Rican*]
PDP .... Positive Displace Pump (NRCH)
PDP .... Post Detection Processor [*Military*] (CAAL)
PDP .... Post-Drug Potentiation
PDP .... Post-Insertion Deorbit Preparation (MCD)
PDP .... Power Distribution Panel
PDP .... Preliminary Definition Plan (NASA)
PDP .... Preliminary Design Phase
PDP .... Preliminary Design Proposal (MCD)
PDP .... Present-Day Primers [*A publication*]
PDP .... Pressure Distribution Panel (AAG)
PDP .... Principal Display Panel [*Packaging*]
PDP .... Procedure Definition Processor [*Data processing*]
PDP .... Process Development Pile [*Nuclear reactor*]
PDP .... Procurement Data Package (AABC)
PDP .... Production Data Package (MCD)
PDP .... Professional Development Document (AFM)
PDP .... Professional Development Program [*Military*]
PDP .... Program Decision Package [*Military*]
PDP .... Program Definition Phase
PDP .... Program Development Paper (MCD)
PDP .... Program Development Plan [*NASA*]
PDP .... Programed Data Processor
PDP .... Programed Digital Processor
PDP .... Progressive Democratic Party [*Montserrat*] (PPW)
PDP .... Progressive Democratic Party [*St. Vincentian*] (PPW)
PDP .... Project Definition Phase [*Nuclear energy*] (NRCH)
PDP .... Project Development Plan
PDP .... Punta Del Este [*Uruguay*] [*Airport symbol*] (OAG)
PDPA .... People's Democratic Party of Afghanistan [*Kabul*] (PPW)
PDPA .... Production Pattern (AAG)
PDPC .... Position Display Parallax Corrected
PDPC .... Post Detection Pulse Compression [*Military*] (CAAL)
PDPF .... Packet Data Processing Facility (MCD)
PDPGM ...... Past Deputy Provincial Grand Master [*Freemasonry*]
PDPM .... Preliminary Draft Presidential Memo
PDPOA ...... Proposal Directive Plan of Action (MCD)
PDPR .... Pandick Press [*NASDAQ symbol*] (NQ)
PDPR .... Present-Day Preachers [*A publication*]
PDPRA ...... Plastics Design and Processing [*A publication*]
PDPS .... Parts Data Processing System [*Bell Telephone*]
PDPS .... Program Data Processing Section (AAG)
PDPS .... Program Definition Phase Studies [*Navy*]
PDPT .... Parti Democratique des Populations Togolaises [*Togolese Democratic People's Party*]
PDQ .... Packages Delivered Quick [*Allegheny Airlines service*]
PDQ .... Parodies Done Quirkily [*Humorous translation of Peter Schickele's PDQ Bach*]
PDQ .... PDQ Air Charter, Inc. [*Pontiac, MI*] [*FAA designator*] (FAAC)
PDQ .... [*Javier*] Perez De Cuellar [*Peruvian diplomat*] [*Initialism is derived from the pronunciation of his last name*]
PDQ .... Permanent Durable Quality [*Paper*]
PDQ .... Pertinent Data Quest (MCD)
PDQ .... Photo Data Quantizer
PDQ .... Physician's Data Query [*National Cancer Institute*]
PDQ .... Please Draw Quickly [*Initialism used as title of TV series*]
PDQ .... Point, Digital, Qualifier [*In automobile name Opel PDQ*]
PDQ .... Pretty Damn Quick
PDQ .... Price and Delivery Quotations
PDQ .... Prime Motor Inns, Inc. [*NYSE symbol*]
PDQ .... Programed Data Quantizer
PDQ .... Protocol Data Query [*Database*] [*National Institutes of Health*]

PDQC	Physicians Data Query: Cancer Information File [*Database*]
PDQD	Physicians Data Query: Directory File [*Database*]
PDQP	Physicians Data Query: Protocol File [*Database*]
PDR	Page Data Register
PDR	Pakistan Development Review [*A publication*]
PDR	Peak Dose Rate [*Radiation*] (AAG)
PDR	Periscope Depth Range [*SONAR*]
PDR	Periscope Detection RADAR (NG)
PDR	Pharma-Dokumentationsring [*Pharma Documentation Ring*] [*Oss, Netherlands*] [*Information service*] (EISS)
PDR	Phase Data Recorder (KSC)
PDR	Phase Delay Rectifier
PDR	Philippine Defense Ribbon
PDR	Physicians' Desk Reference [*A publication*]
PDR	Pilot's Display Recorder
PDR	Piskei Din Shel Batei ha-Din ha-Rabaniyim be-Yisrael (BJA)
PDR	Plant Disease Reporter [*A publication*]
PD & R	Policy Development and Research
PDR	Position Distribution Report [*DoD*]
PDR	Pounder (MSA)
PDR	Powder
PDR	Power Directional Relay
PDR	Predetection Recording
PDR	Predetermined Demand Rate
PDR	Preferential Departure Route [*Aviation*] (FAAC)
PDR	Preliminary Data Report
PDR	Preliminary Data Requirements (NASA)
PDR	Preliminary Design Report (NRCH)
PDR	Pressurized Deuterium Reactor
P & DR	Price and Delivery Request
PDR	Price Description Record [*Data processing*] (IBMDP)
PDR	Priority Data Reduction
PDR	Process Dynamics Recorder
PDR	Processed Data Recorder
PDR	Processing Data Rate (IEEE)
PDR	Procurement Data Reference
PDR	Program Design Review (MCD)
PDR	Program Director's Review [*NASA*] (NASA)
PDR	Program Discrepancy Report (IEEE)
PDR	Program Document Requirement (BUR)
PDR	Program Drum Recording
PDR	Proliferative Diabetic Retinopathy [*Ophthalmology*]
PDR	Public Document Room (NRCH)
PDR	Publications Data Request
PDR	Pulse Doppler RADAR
PDR	Pulse Duty Ratio
PDRA	Professional Drag Racing Association (EA)
PDRC	Clinical Research Center for Periodontal Disease [*University of Florida*] [*Research center*] (RCD)
PDRC	Poultry Disease Research Center [*University of Georgia*] [*Research center*] (RCD)
PDRC	Preliminary Design Review Commercial (MCD)
PDRC	Pressure Difference Recording Controller
PDRC	Professional Development and Recruitment Career Program [*Military*]
PDRC	Program Development Review Committee [*Navy*] (CAAL)
PDRD	Procurement Data Requirements Document (NASA)
PDRF	Passive Defense Recovery Force (MUGU)
PDRH	Partido Democratico Revolucionario Hondureno [*Revolutionary Democratic Party of Honduras*]
PDRI	Publications. Diaspora Research Institute [*A publication*]
PdRK	Pesikta de-Rav Kahana (BJA)
PDRL	Permanent Disability Retired List
PDRL	Procurement Data Requirements List (NASA)
PDRM	Payload Deployment and Retrieval Mechanism [*NASA*]
PDRM	Postdetrital Remanent Magnetization [*Geophysics*]
PDRMA	Portable Drilling Rig Manufacturers Association [*Chicago, IL*] (EA)
PDRP	Program Data Requirement Plan (NRCH)
PD & RS	Payload Deployment and Retrieval Subsystem [*NASA*] (NASA)
PDRY	Peoples' Democratic Republic of Yemen
PDS	Auburn/Lewiston, ME [*Location identifier*] [*FAA*] (FAAL)
PDS	Package Data System (NASA)
PDS	Paid-During-Service [*Magazine subscriptions*]
PDS	Parameter Driven Software, Inc. [*Birmingham, MI*] [*Software manufacturer*]
PDS	Paroxysmal Depolarizing Shift [*Physiology*]
PDS	Parti Democratique Senegalais [*Senegalese Democratic Party*] (PPW)
PDS	Partido Democrata Socialista [*Socialist Democratic Party*] [*Panamanian*] (PPW)
PDS	Partitioned Data Set [*Data processing*] (NASA)
PDS	Partito di Democrazia Socialista [*Socialist Democracy Party*] [*Sanmarinese*] (PPW)
PDS	Passive Detection System (NVT)
PDS	Penultimate Digit Storage [*Telecommunications*] (TEL)
PDS	Performer Design Sheet
PDS	Perimeter Defense System (MCD)
PDS	Permanent Duty Station [*Air Force*] (AFM)
PDS	Perry Drug Stores, Inc. [*NYSE symbol*]
PDS	Personal Development Study [*Psychology*]
PDS	Personnel Daily Summary [*Army*] (AABC)
PDS	Personnel Data Summary (FAAC)
PDS	Personnel Data System [*Air Force*]
PDS	Personnel Decontamination Station (MCD)
PDS	Personnel Delivery System
PDS	Petroleum Data System [*University of Oklahoma*] [*Databank*] (EISS)
PDS	Petroleum Data System [*Petroleum Information Corp.*] [*Houston, TX*] [*Information service*] (EISS)
PDS	Pharma-Dokumentations-Service [*Pharma Documentation Service*] [*Information service*] [*Frankfurt, West Germany*] (EISS)
PDS	Phased Development Shuttle [*NASA*] (KSC)
PDS	Photo-Digital Store
PDS	Photodischarge Spectroscopy (MCD)
PDS	Planning Data Sheet (KSC)
PDS	Plant Data System [*Nuclear energy*] (NRCH)
PDS	Plasma-Derived Serum
PDS	Plasma Display (MCD)
PDS	Pneumatic Distribution System
PDS	Polydimethylsiloxane [*Organic chemistry*]
PDS	Polydioxanone [*Organic chemistry*]
PDS	Portable Data System (MCD)
PDS	Portable Duress Sensor (MCD)
PDS	Post Design Services [*British*] (RDA)
PDS	Power Density Spectra (IEEE)
PDS	Power Distribution System [*or Subsystem*]
PDS	Power Drive System
PDS	Preadsorb-Dilute-Shake [*Phage growth method*]
PDS	Predocketed Special Project (NRCH)
PDS	Priority Distribution System [*Military*] (AFM)
PDS	Prisoner Detention System
PDS	Probability Distribution Subprogram [*Data processing*] (BUR)
PDS	Problem Data System (MCD)
PD/S	Problem Definition/Solution
PDS	Problem Descriptor System
PDS	Procedures Development Simulator (KSC)
PDS	Procurement Data Sheet
PDS	Product Design Standard
PDS	Production Data Sheet (MCD)
PDS	Program Data Sheets (AABC)
PDS	Program Data Source (BUR)
PDS	Program Design Specification (CAAL)
PDS	Program Development Specialist
PDS	Program Development System [*Data processing*]
PDS	Program Distribution System
PDS	Programable Data Station [*or System*]
PDS	Propellant Dispersion System (MCD)
PdS	Psychopathic Deviate Subtle [*Psychology*]
PDS	Pulse Doppler Seeker
PDS	Punch Driver Selectric
PDS	Purchasing Department Specification (MSA)
PDS-A	Personnel Data System - Airmen [*Air Force*]
PDSA	Predesign and Systems Analysis [*NASA*] (KSC)
PDS-A(I)	Personnel Data System - Airmen (Interim) [*Air Force*] (AFM)
PDS-C	Personnel Data System - Civilian [*Air Force*] (AFM)
PDSC	Publishers Data Service Corporation [*Monterey, CA*]
PDSD	Point Detonating Self-Destroying [*Projectile*]
PDSDD	Plotting Display Subchannel Data Distributor (MCD)
PDSE	Production Sample (AAG)
P & DSEC ...	Pioneer and Demolition Section [*Army*]
PDSI	Palmer Drought Severity Index [*Meteorology*]
PDSI	Performance Data Services, Incorporated [*Falls Church, VA*] [*Software manufacturer*]
PDSI	Portable Digital Strain Indicator
PDSK	Petroleum Distribution System - Korea [*Army*] (MCD)
PDSM	Powder Diffraction Search-Match System [*International Data Center*]
PDS/MAGEN ...	Problem Descriptor System/Matrix Generation [*Programing language*] [*1965*] (CSR)
PDSMS	Point Defense Surface Missile System
PDS-O	Personnel Data System - Officers [*Air Force*] (AFM)
PDSOF	Public Domain Software on File [*Facts on File, Inc.*] [*New York, NY*] [*Information service*] (EISS)
PDSP	Personnel Data System - Planning [*Air Force*] (AFM)
PDSPI	Polyurethane Division, Society of the Plastics Industry [*New York, NY*] (EA)
PDSQ	Point Detonating Super-Quick Fuze (NATG)
PDSS	Physical Disabilities Special Interest Section [*American Occupational Therapy Association*]
PDSS	Post-Deployment Software System (MCD)
PDST	Pacific Daylight Saving Time (KSC)
PDSTT	Pulse Doppler Single Target Track [*Military*] (CAAL)
PDT	Pacific Daylight Time
PDT	Panoramic Design Technique
PDT	Parallel Data Transmission
PdT	Parti du Travail [*Labor Party*] [*Swiss*] (PPE)
PDT	Pendleton [*Oregon*] [*Airport symbol*] (OAG)
PDT	Performance Demonstration Test
PDT	Personal Data Transmitter [*From the movie "Aliens"*]
PDT	Planned Data to Transportation [*DoD*]

PDT .... Plasma Display Terminal [*Data processing*]
PDT .... Pollable Data Terminal [*Bell System*]
PDT .... Population Doubling Time [*Cytology*]
PDT .... Posting Data Transfer [*Air Force*]   (AFM)
PDT .... Power Distribution Trailer   (NATG)
PDT .... Predelivery Test   (MCD)
PDT .... Predictor Display Technique
PDT .... President Mines [*Vancouver Stock Exchange symbol*]
PDT .... Proceedings. European Society of Drug Toxicity [*Elsevier Book Series*] [*A publication*]
PDT .... Processed Directional Transmission [*Military*]   (NVT)
PDT .... Programable Data Terminal [*Digital Equipment Corp.*]   (IEEE)
PDT .... Pulse Delay Time
PDT .... (Pyridyl)diphenyltriazine [*Analytical chemistry*]
PDT-1 .... Picatinny Arsenal Detonation Trap Number 1   (AABC)
3PDT .... Triple-Pole, Double-Throw [*Switch*]   (MUGU)
4PDT .... Four-Pole, Double-Throw [*Switch*]
PDTA........ Production Tape   (AAG)
PDTA........ Professional Dance Teachers Association   (EA)
PDTA........ Propylenediaminetetraacetic Acid [*Organic chemistry*]
PDTC........ Philadelphia Depository Trust Company
PDTF .... Program Development and Test Facility [*Social Security Administration*]
PDTMR....... Phalloidin Tetramethylrhodamine [*Biochemistry*]
PDTS........ Program Development Tracking System [*Data processing*]
PDTS........ Programable Data Terminal Set [*Military*]   (CAAL)
PDT & T..... Post-Delivery Test and Trials [*Military*]   (CAAL)
PDTTT....... Post-Delivery Test and Trial Team   (MCD)
PDU........... Pacific Democrat Union [*Canberra, ACT, Australia*]   (EA-IO)
PDU........... Parti Dahomeen de l'Unite [*Dahomean Unity Party*]
PDU........... Parti Democrate Unifie [*Unified Democratic Party*] [*Name replaced by Section Voltaique de Rassemblement*]
PDU........... Paysandu [*Uruguay*] [*Airport symbol*]   (OAG)
PDU........... Phase Demodulation Unit
PDU........... Photomultiplier Detector Unit   (KSC)
PDU........... Pilot's Display Unit   (MCD)
PDU........... Power Distribution Unit   (AAG)
PDU........... Power Drive Unit   (MCD)
PDU........... Pressure Distribution Unit
PDU........... Process Development Unit [*Chemical engineering*]
PDU........... Production Distribution Unit   (AAG)
PDU........... Programable Delay Unit
PDU........... Programable Diagnostic Unit [*TACOM*] [*Army*]   (RDA)
PDU........... Project Development Unit [*Chemical engineering*]
PDU........... Projection Display Unit
PDU........... Protocol Data Unit
PDU........... Pulse Detection Unit   (NASA)
PDUFC .... Pete Duel Universal Friendship Club [*Rio De Janeiro, Brazil*]   (EA-IO)
PdUP .... Partito di Unita Proletaria per il Comunismo [*Democratic Party of Proletarian Unity for Communism*] [*Italy*]   (PPE)
PDur .... Papyri Durani   (BJA)
PDUR........ Predischarge Utilization Review [*Medicine*]
PDV .... Ponderosa Ventures, Inc. [*Vancouver Stock Exchange symbol*]
PDV .... Premodulation Processor - Deep Space - Voice
PDV .... Pressure Disconnect Valve   (MCD)
PDV .... Probability of Detection and Verification [*Military*]   (CAAL)
PDVN........ Power-Driven
PDW .... Evansville, IN [*Location identifier*] [*FAA*]   (FAAL)
PDW .... Personal Defense Weapon [*Army*]   (INF)
PDW .... Priority Delayed Weather [*Aviation*]   (FAAC)
PDX .... Passive Dosimeter Experiment   (KSC)
PDX .... Place Decrement in Index
PDX .... Poloidal Divertor Experiment [*Princeton University*]
PDX .... Portland [*Oregon*] [*Airport symbol*]   (OAG)
PDX .... Prado Explorations Ltd. [*Toronto Stock Exchange symbol*]
PDX .... Private Digital Exchange
PDY .... Piccadilly Resources Ltd. [*Vancouver Stock Exchange symbol*]
PDY .... Principal Duty [*Military*]
PDZ .... Ontario, CA [*Location identifier*] [*FAA*]   (FAAL)
PDZ-1 .... Pedernales [*Venezuela*] [*Airport symbol*]   (OAG)
PDZI .... Przeglad Zachodni [*A publication*]
PDZRA ...... Prace Dzialu Zywenia Roslin i Nawozenia [*A publication*]
PE.............. Easton Area Public Library, Easton, PA [*Library symbol*] [*Library of Congress*]   (LCLS)
PE.............. Ice Pellets [*Meteorology*]
PE.............. Pacific Electric Railway [*AAR code*]
PE.............. Parity Error
PE.............. Patrol Vessel, Eagle [*Eagle boat*] [*Navy symbol*] [*Obsolete*]
PE.............. Peacetime Establishment [*Military*]   (NATG)
Pe .... Peclet Number [*IUPAC*]
PE.............. Pectinesterase [*Also, PME*] [*An enzyme*]
Pe .... Pentyl [*Biochemistry*]
PE.............. Percussionist [*A publication*]
PE.............. Period Ending
PE.............. Periodic   (AAG)
PE.............. Peripheral Equipment   (AAG)
PE.............. Periscope
PE.............. Permanent Echo [*RADAR*]
PE.............. Permissible Error   (ADA)
PE.............. Persistent Estrus [*Endocrinology*]

PE.............. Personal Effects
PE.............. Personnel, Enlisted [*or Enlisted Personnel Division*] [*Coast Guard*]
PE.............. Personnel Equipment [*Air Force*]   (AFM)
PE.............. Personnel Equivalent [*DoD*]
PE.............. Personnel Executive [*A publication*]
pe .... Peru [*MARC country of publication code*] [*Library of Congress*]   (LCCC)
PE.............. Peru [*Two-letter standard code*]   (CNC)
PE.............. Petroleum Economist [*London*] [*A publication*]   (BJA)
PE.............. Petroleum Engineer
PE.............. Pharmacopaeia Edinensis [*Edinburgh Pharmacopoeia*] [*A publication*]   (ROG)
PE.............. Pharyngoesophageal [*Medicine*]
PE.............. Phase Encoding [*Magnetic tape recording*] [*Data processing*]   (MDG)
PE.............. Phenylephrine
PE.............. Philadelphia Electric Co. [*NYSE symbol*]
PE.............. Philippine Educator [*A publication*]
PE.............. Phoenix Air Service GmbH, Munchen [*West Germany*] [*ICAO designator*]   (FAAC)
PE.............. Phosphatidylethanolamine [*Biochemistry*]
PE.............. Photoelectric
PE.............. Photoemission [*Physics*]
PE.............. Phycoerythrin [*Biochemistry*]
PE.............. Physical Education
PE.............. Physical Examination
PE.............. Physiological Ecology
PE.............. Pictorial Eleven [*Later, PES*] [*An association*]   (EA)
PE.............. Pigment Epithelium [*of the retina*]
P & E .... Pike and Eel [*A pub at Cambridge University*] [*British*]   (DSUE)
PE.............. Pilot Error
PE.............. Pinion End
PE.............. Pistol Expert
PE.............. Planetary Explorer [*NASA*]
PE.............. Planification de l'Emploi [*Canadian Jobs Strategy - CJS*]
P/E .... Planning Economics Group, Boston [*Information service*]   (EISS)
PE.............. Planning Estimate
P & E .... Planning and Estimating   (AAG)
PE.............. Plant Engineering   (AAG)
PE.............. Plant Equipment   (MCD)
PE.............. Plasma Emission [*Spectrophotometry*]
PE.............. Plasma Exchange [*Medicine*]
PE.............. Plastic Explosive   (NATG)
PE.............. Pleural Effusion [*Medicine*]
PE.............. Poesia Espanola [*A publication*]
PE.............. Politique Etrangere [*A publication*]
PE.............. Pollen Equivalent [*Immunology*]
PE.............. Polyelectrolyte [*Organic chemistry*]
PE.............. Polyethylene [*Organic chemistry*]
PE.............. Port of Embarkation [*Military*]
P of E .... Port of Embarkation [*Military*]
P of E .... Portal of Entry [*Bacteriology*]
PE.............. Position Effect [*Parapsychology*]
PE.............. Position Error
PE.............. Post Engineer [*Army*]   (AABC)
PE.............. Post Exchange [*Marine Corps*]
PE.............. Potato Eaters   (EA)
PE.............. Potential Energy
PE.............. Potential Excess [*of stock*] [*DoD*]
PE.............. Powdered Extract [*Pharmacy*]
PE.............. Practical Exercise
PE.............. Pre-Eclampsia [*Medicine*]
PE.............. Pre-Emption [*Telecommunications*]   (TEL)
P-E .... Precipitation-Evaporation
PE.............. Preliminary Evaluation
PE.............. Preliminary Exploitation   (MCD)
PE.............. Presiding Elder
PE.............. Pressure Enclosure   (MCD)
Pe .... Pressure on Expiration [*Medicine*]
P/E .... Price/Earnings Ratio [*Relation between price of a company's stock and its annual net income*]
PE.............. Priced Exhibit   (MCD)
PE.............. Primary Electricity
PE.............. Prime Equipment
PE.............. Primitive Endoderm [*Cytology*]
PE.............. Primitive Equation
PE.............. Prince Edward Island [*Canadian province*] [*Postal code*]
PE.............. Principal Engineer   (AAG)
PE.............. Printer's Error
P & E .... Privileges and Elections Subcommittee [*US Senate*]
PE.............. Probable Error [*Statistics*]
PE.............. Problems of Economics [*A publication*]
PE.............. Procedures Evaluation [*DoD*]
PE.............. Processing Element [*of central processing unit*]
PE.............. Procurement Executive [*British*]
P & E .... Procurement and Expedition
PE.............. Production Engineering
PE.............. Production Executive [*British*]
PE.............. Professional Education   (AFM)

PE.............. Professional Engineer
P/E............. Professional and Executive [*Employment register*] [*British*]
PE.............. Program Element (AFM)
PE.............. Program Evaluation (OICC)
PE.............. Programed Exciter
PE.............. Project Engineer
PE.............. Project Equality (EA)
P & E......... Propellants and Explosives [*Military*] (AABC)
PE.............. Proponent Evaluation (MCD)
PE.............. Protected Environment
PE.............. Protestant Episcopal
PE.............. Proteus Engine [*Hovercraft*]
PE.............. Pulley End
PE.............. Pulmonary Edema [*Medicine*]
PE.............. Pulmonary Effusion [*Medicine*]
PE.............. Pulmonary Embolism [*Medicine*]
PE.............. Pulse Echo [*Materials research*]
PE.............. Pulse Encoding [*Data processing*]
PE.............. Purchased Equipment
PE.............. Pyroelectric
P & E......... Pyrotechnical and Explosive [*NASA*] (KSC)
Pe .... Warner-Lambert Pharmaceutical Co. [*Research code symbol*]
PEA .... Papillary Eccrine Adenoma [*Oncology*]
PEA .... Pattern Error Analysis
PEA .... Patterson Experimental Array (MCD)
PEA .... Payload Enclosure Assembly (MCD)
Pea .... Peake's English Nisi Prius Reports [*1790-1812*] (DLA)
PEA .... Pella, IA [*Location identifier*] [*FAA*] (FAAL)
PEA .... Penneshaw [*Australia*] [*Airport symbol*] (OAG)
PEA .... Phenethyl Alcohol [*Organic chemistry*]
PEA .... Phenylethylamine [*Biochemistry*]
PEA .... Phosphoethanolamine [*Organic chemistry*]
PEA .... Pilot's Employment Agency
PEA .... Pitch Error Amplifier
PEA .... Plant Engineering Agency
PEA .... Plastics Engineers Association [*Defunct*] (EA)
PEA .... Platform Electronics Assembly (KSC)
PEA .... Poly(ethyl Acrylate) [*Organic chemistry*]
PEA .... Portuguese East Africa [*Mozambique*]
PEA .... Potash Export Association (EA)
PEA .... Primary Expense Account
PEA .... Private Employment Agency (OICC)
PEA .... Process Environmental Analysis
PEA .... Process Equipment Accessory (MCD)
PEA .... Program Element Administrator [*Navy*] (NG)
PEA .... Progressive Education Association [*Defunct*]
PEA .... Public Education Association
PEA .... Push-Effective Address [*Data processing*] (IEEE)
PEA .... Pyridylethylamine [*Organic chemistry*]
Pea (2)....... Peake's Additional Cases Nisi Prius [*170 English Reprint*] [*1795-1812*] (DLA)
PEAA......... Program Elements Activity Accounts (MCD)
Pea Add Cas ... Peake's English Nisi Prius Reports [*Vol. 2*] (DLA)
PEABA ...... Petroleum Abstracts [*A publication*]
Peab L Rev ... Peabody Law Review (DLA)
Peabody J E ... Peabody Journal of Education [*A publication*]
Peabody J Ed ... Peabody Journal of Education [*A publication*]
Peabody J Educ ... Peabody Journal of Education [*A publication*]
Peabody Mus Nat Hist Yale Univ Bull ... Peabody Museum of Natural History. Yale University. Bulletin [*A publication*]
PEAC......... Photoelectric Auto Collimator
PEAC......... Photoelectroanalytical Chemistry
Peace .... Peace Newsletter [*A publication*]
Peace .... Peace/Non-Violence [*A publication*]
PEACE ...... People Emerging Against Corrupt Establishments [*Underground military newspaper*]
PEACE ...... Project Evaluation and Assistance, Civil Engineering [*Air Force*]
Peacemak ... Peacemaker [*A publication*]
Peace Nws ... Peace News [*A publication*]
PeaceResAb ... Peace Research Abstracts [*A publication*]
Peace Res Ja ... Peace Research in Japan [*A publication*]
Peace Res Rev ... Peace Research Reviews [*A publication*]
PEACESAT ... Pan-Pacific Education and Communications Experiments Using Satellites [*NASA*]
Peace and Sci ... Peace and the Sciences [*A publication*]
PEACU ...... Plastic Energy Absorption in Compression Unit (IEEE)
PEAD........ Presidential Emergency Action Document
PEADS ...... Presidential Emergency Action Direction System (MCD)
Peake .... Peake's Cases [*1790-1812*] (DLA)
Peake Add Cas ... Peake's Additional Cases Nisi Prius [*1795-1812*] (DLA)
Peake Ev ... Peake on the Law of Evidence (DLA)
Peake NP ... Peake's English Nisi Prius Cases [*170 English Reprint*] (DLA)
Peake NP Add Cas ... Peake's Additional Cases Nisi Prius [*170 English Reprint*] [*England*] (DLA)
Peake NP Add Cas (Eng) ... Peake's Additional Cases Nisi Prius [*170 English Reprint*] [*England*] (DLA)
Peake NP Cas ... Peake's English Nisi Prius Cases [*170 English Reprint*] [*1790-1812*] (DLA)
Peake NP Cas (Eng) ... Peake's English Nisi Prius Cases [*170 English Reprint*] (DLA)

PEALQ .... Publishing, Entertainment, Advertising, and Allied Fields Law Quarterly [*A publication*]
Pea MS...... Peachey on Marriage Settlements [*1860*] (DLA)
PEAMUSE ... Peabody Museum of Archaeology and Ethnology [*Harvard University*] [*Research center*] (RCD)
Peanut J Nut World ... Peanut Journal and Nut World [*A publication*]
Peanut Sci ... Peanut Science [*A publication*]
PEAP........ Pad Emergency Air Pack [*NASA*] (KSC)
PEAP........ Principal Error Axis for Position
PEAP........ Program Evaluation Analysis Plan (MCD)
PeAR .... Die Provinzeinteilung des Assyrischen Reiches [*A publication*] (BJA)
Pearce CC ... Pearce's Reports in Dearsley's English Crown Cases (DLA)
Pearce-Sellards Ser Tex Mem Mus ... Pearce-Sellards Series. Texas Memorial Museum [*A publication*]
PEARL....... Committee for Public Education and Religious Liberty
PEARL....... Performance Evaluation of Amplifiers from a Remote Location
PEARL....... Periodicals Automation, Rand Library
PEARL....... Personal Equipment and Rescue/Survivable Lowdown (MCD)
PEARL....... Process and Experiment Automation Real-Time Language [*Data processing*]
PEARL....... Program for EPS [*Electrical Power System*] Analysis and Rapid Look-Ahead [*NASA computer program*]
PEARL....... Programed Editor and Automated Resources for Learning
PEARLA ..... Pupils Equal and React to Light and Accomodation [*Medicine*]
Pears .... Pearson's Reports [*1850-80*] [*Pennsylvania*] (DLA)
Pearson..... Pearson's Common Pleas [*Pennsylvania*] (DLA)
Pears (PA) ... Pearson's Reports [*1850-80*] [*Pennsylvania*] (DLA)
PEART....... Passive Electronic Advanced Receiver (MCD)
PEAS........ Physical Estimation and Attraction Scales
PEAS........ Presbyterian Educational Association of the South [*Defunct*] (EA)
Peasant Stud Newsl ... Peasant Studies Newsletter [*A publication*]
PEAT........ Pricing Evaluation for Audit Technique [*Finance*]
PEAT........ Programer Exercised Autopilot Test (AAG)
PEAT........ Programme Elargi d'Assistance Technique [*Expanded Program of Technical Assistance*] [*United Nations*]
Peat Plant Yearb ... Peat and Plant Yearbook [*A publication*]
PEAV........ Principal Error Axis for Velocity
PE B .... Bachelor of Pedagogy (ROG)
Pe B.......... Bachelor of Pediatrics
PEB .... Parametric Empirical Bayes [*Statistics*]
PEB .... Pebble [*Jewelry*] (ROG)
Peb............ Pebble [*A publication*]
PEB .... Performance Evaluation Board (MCD)
PEB .... Philippine Economy Bulletin [*A publication*]
PEB .... Phycoerythrobilin [*Biochemistry*]
PEB .... Physical Evaluation Board [*Military*]
PEB .... Population-Environment Balance [*Washington, DC*] (EA)
PEB .... Porcelain Enamel Bath [*Classified advertising*] (ADA)
PEB .... Positive Expulsion Bladder
PEB .... Production Efficiency Board [*British*] [*World War II*]
PEB .... Propulsion Examining Board [*Navy*] (NVT)
PEB .... Prototype Environmental Buoy [*Marine science*] (MSC)
PEB .... Pulmonary Ectopic Beat [*Cardiology*]
PEB .... Pulsed Electron Beam (IEEE)
PEBA........ Polyether Block Amide [*Plastics technology*]
PEBA........ Pulsed Electron Beam Annealer [*Photovoltaic energy systems*]
PEBA........ Purified Extract of Brucella abortus
PEBAB ...... Para-(Ethoxybenzylidene)aminobenzonitrile [*Also, EBCA*] [*Organic chemistry*]
PEB & B...... Porcelain Enamel Bath and Basin [*Classified advertising*] (ADA)
PEBB........ Public Employees Blanket Bond
PEBCO...... Port Elizabeth Black Civic Organization [*South African*] (PD)
PEBCO...... Program Evaluation and Budget Committee [*American Library Association*]
PEBD........ Pay Entry Base Date
PEBG........ Phenethylbiguanide [*Same as PEDG*] [*Antidiabetic compound*]
PEBH........ Physical Evaluation Board Hospital [*Military*]
PEBL .... Port Everglades Belt Line Railway [*AAR code*] [*Obsolete*]
PEBLO....... Physical Evaluation Board Liaison Officer [*Air Force*] (AFM)
PEBS........ Pulsed Electron Beam Source (MCD)
PEC .... Aero Sport [*Vancouver, WA*] [*FAA designator*] (FAAC)
PEC .... American Irish Political Education Committee [*Stony Point, NY*] (EA)
PEc............ Ellwood City Area Public Library, Ellwood City, PA [*Library symbol*] [*Library of Congress*] (LCLS)
PEC .... IEEE Power Electronics Council [*New York, NY*] (EA)
PEC .... Pacific Command Electronic Intelligence Center (MCD)
PEC .... Palestine Economic Commission
PEC .... Panasoni Energy Corporation [*Vancouver Stock Exchange symbol*]
PEC .... Passive Equipment Cabinet [*Military*] (CAAL)
PEC .... Peak Electrode Current
PEC .... Pectoral [*Lungs and Chest*] [*Medicine*] (ROG)
PEC .... Pedal Excretory Cell
PEC .... Pelican [*Alaska*] [*Airport symbol*] (OAG)
PEC .... Pennsylvania Engineering Corporation [*American Stock Exchange symbol*]

PEC .... Perfil de Evaluacion del Comportamiento [*Standardized test of elementary through high school students' behavior at school, at home, and with peers*]
PEC .... Peritoneal Exudate Cells [*Hematology*]
PEC .... Perkin-Elmer Corporation   (MCD)
PEC .... Perris [*California*] [*Seismograph station code, US Geological Survey*]   (SEIS)
PEC .... Persistent Early Curvature
PEC .... Petro-Canada
PEC .... Phenylene Ether Copolymer [*Organic chemistry*]
PEC .... Photoelectric Cell
PEC .... Physics, Engineering, and Chemistry   (AAG)
PEC .... Planetary Entry Capsule [*Aerospace*]
PEC .... Plant Equipment Codes [*DoD*]
PeC .... Poesia e Critica [*A publication*]
PEC .... Positive Engagement Clutch
PEC .... Potasse et Engrais Chimiques
PEC .... Predicted Environmental Concentration
PEC .... Presbyterian Evangelical Coalition   (EA)
PEC .... Previous Element Coding
PEC .... Production Equipment Code
PEC .... Production Executive Committee
PEC .... Program Element Code   (AFM)
PEC .... Program Environment Control
PEC .... Program Evaluation Center [*Navy*]   (AFIT)
PEC .... Propulsion Environmental Chamber
PEC .... Prova Elementi Combustibili [*An Italian fast reactor*]
PEC .... Pyridylethylcysteine [*Biochemistry*]
PEC .... Pyrogenic Exotoxin C [*Medicine*]
PECA .... Petroleum Equipment Contractors Association   (EA)
PECAN .... Pulse Envelop Correlation Air Navigation
PE CARD .... Production Estimate Card   (MSA)
PECBI .... Professional Engineers Conference Board for Industry   (EA)
PECC .... Panel of Experts on Climatic Change [*Marine science*]   (MSC)
PECC .... Precanceled Envelope Collectors Club   (EA)
PECC .... Product Engineering Control Center [*Telecommunications*]   (TEL)
PECDS .... Professional Engineering Career Development Series [*Book series*]
PECE .... Proposed Engineering Change Estimate
PECF .... Pseudoextracellular Fluid [*for biocompatibility testing*]
PECFA .... Presidential Election Campaign Fund Act of 1966
PECHA .... Petroleum Chemistry USSR [*English Translation*] [*A publication*]
Peche Marit ... Peche Maritime [*A publication*]
PECI .... Preliminary Equipment Component Index [*or Inventory*]
PECI .... Productivity Enhancing Capital Investment [*DoD*]
PECIP .... Productivity Enhancing Capital Investment Program   (MCD)
Peck .... Peck's Reports [*7 Tennessee*] [*1921-24*]   (DLA)
Peck .... Peck's Reports [*24-30 Illinois*]   (DLA)
Peck .... Peckwell's English Election Cases [*1802-06*]   (DLA)
Peck El Cas ... Peckwell's English Election Cases   (DLA)
Peck Elec Cas ... Peckwell's English Election Cases [*1802-06*]   (DLA)
Peck (III) .... Peck's Reports, Illinois Supreme Court Reports [*11-22, 24-30*]   (DLA)
Peck (Tenn) ... Peck's Reports [*7 Tennessee*]   (DLA)
Peck Tr ...... Peck's Trial [*Impeachment*]   (DLA)
Peckw .... Peckwell's English Election Cases   (DLA)
PECM .... Passive Electronics Countermeasures [*Military*]   (NG)
PECM .... Preliminary Engineering Change Memorandum [*Air Force*]   (CET)
PECN .... Publishers Equipment [*NASDAQ symbol*]   (NQ)
PECO .... Peace Country [*Grande Prairie, Alberta*] [*A publication*]
PECO .... Pecos National Monument
PECO .... Premier Energy Corporation [*NASDAQ symbol*]   (NQ)
PECOS .... Program Environment Checkout System
PECOS .... Project Evaluation and Control System   (MCD)
PECP .... Preliminary Engineering Change Proposal
PECR .... Program Error Correction Report
PECS .... Plant Engineering Check Sheet   (AAG)
PECS .... Portable Environmental Control System [*NASA*]
PECS .... Princeton Encyclopedia of Classical Sites [*A publication*]
Pecsi Muesz Sz ... Pecsi Mueszaki Szemle [*Hungary*] [*A publication*]
PECT .... Pectori [*To the Chest*] [*Pharmacy*]
PECUL .... Peculiar   (ROG)
PECUS .... Personal Engineering Computer User's Society [*Boston, MA*]   (EA)
PECUY .... Pecuniary   (ROG)
PECWG ...... Piaster Expenditure Control Working Group [*Military*]
Ped .... Pedagogia [*A publication*]
PED .... Pedagogue
PED .... Pedal
PED .... Peddler [*or Peddling*] [*FBI standardized term*]
PED .... Pedestal   (AAG)
PED .... Pedestrian
PED .... Pediatrics   (AABC)
PED .... Pedlary   (ROG)
PED .... Pedro Aguirre Cerda [*Antarctica*] [*Seismograph station code, US Geological Survey*] [*Closed*]   (SEIS)
PED .... Period End Date   (MCD)
PED .... Personnel Equipment Data

PED .... Photoemission Diode
PEd .... Physical Education
PED .... Positive Expulsion Device
PED .... Production Eligibility Date   (MUGU)
PED .... Production Engineering Division [*University of Wisconsin - Madison*] [*Research center*]   (RCD)
PED .... Program Element Description
PED .... Program Element Directive
PED .... Program Execution Directive   (AAG)
PED .... Promotion Eligibility Date [*Military*]
PED .... Proton-Enhanced Diffusion
PED .... Public Employee Department [*Supersedes GEC*] [*AFL-CIO*]   (EA)
PEd .... Pulmonary Edema [*Medicine*]
PED .... Pure Edge Dislocation
PED .... Pyramid Element Designator
PED .... Springfield, TN [*Location identifier*] [*FAA*]   (FAAL)
PEDA .... Pedal Artery
PEDA .... Personnel Equipment Data Analysis
Pedagog Fak Plzni Sb Ser Chem ... Pedagogicka Fakulta v Plzni. Sbornik. Serie Chemie [*A publication*]
Pedagog Sem ... Pedagogical Seminary [*A publication*]
Pedag i Psihol ... Pedagogika i Psihologija [*A publication*]
Pedag Szle ... Pedagogiai Szemle [*A publication*]
Pedag Tidskr ... Pedagogisk Tidskrift [*A publication*]
Ped B......... Bachelor of Pedagogy
PEDC .... Personal Effects Distribution Center
Ped Clin NA ... Pediatric Clinics of North America [*A publication*]
PEDCUG ... Planning Engineers Desktop Computer Users Group   (EA)
Ped D .... Doctor of Pedagogy
PEDD........ Program Element Descriptive Data   (CAAL)
PEddyB ..... Baldwin Locomotive Works, Eddystone, PA [*Library symbol*] [*Library of Congress*] [*Obsolete*]   (LCLS)
PEDET....... Pedetemptim [*Gradually*] [*Pharmacy*]
PEDG .... Phenethyldiguanide [*Same as PEBG*] [*Antidiabetic compound*]
Pedia........ Pediatrics [*A publication*]
Pediat Nurs ... Pediatric Nursing [*A publication*]
Pediatr Adolesc Endocrinol ... Pediatric and Adolescent Endocrinology [*A publication*]
Pediatr Akush Ginekol ... Pediatriia, Akusherstvo, i Ginekologiia [*A publication*]
Pediatr Ann ... Pediatric Annals [*A publication*]
Pediatr Clin N Am ... Pediatric Clinics of North America [*A publication*]
Pediatr Clin North Am ... Pediatric Clinics of North America [*A publication*]
Pediatr Dent ... Pediatric Dentistry [*A publication*]
Pediat Res ... Pediatric Research [*A publication*]
Pediatr Esp ... Pediatria Espanola [*A publication*]
Pediatria Arch ... Pediatria. Archivio di Patologia e Clinica Pediatrica [*A publication*]
Pediatrics Suppl ... Pediatrics Supplement [*A publication*]
Pediatr Int ... Pediatria Internazionale [*A publication*]
Pediatr Listy ... Pediatricke Listy [*A publication*]
Pediatr Med Chir ... Pediatria Medica e Chirurgica [*A publication*]
Pediatr Mod ... Pediatria Moderna [*A publication*]
Pediatr Nephrol ... Pediatric Nephrology [*A publication*]
Pediatr News ... Pediatric News [*A publication*]
Pediatr Nurs ... Pediatric Nursing [*A publication*]
Pediatr Nurse Pract ... Pediatric Nurse Practitioner [*A publication*]
Pediatr Pharmacol ... Pediatric Pharmacology [*A publication*]
Pediatr Pol ... Pediatria Polska [*A publication*]
Pediatr Prat ... Pediatria Pratica [*A publication*]
Pediatr Radiol ... Pediatric Radiology [*A publication*]
Pediatr Res ... Pediatric Research [*A publication*]
PEDIN........ Peapod Dinghy
P Edin Math ... Proceedings. Edinburgh Mathematical Society [*A publication*]
PE Dir .... Physical Education Director
PEdiS .... Edinboro State College, Edinboro, PA [*Library symbol*] [*Library of Congress*]   (LCLS)
Ped M........ Master of Pedagogy
PEDMAN .... PACFLT [*Pacific Fleet*] Enlisted Personnel Distribution Manual   (CINC)
PEDN........ Planned Event Discrepancy Notification [*NASA*]   (KSC)
Pedobiolog ... Pedobiologia [*A publication*]
Pedod Fr .... Pedodontie Francaise [*A publication*]
Pedology (Leningr) ... Pedology (Leningrad) [*A publication*]
PEDRO ...... Pneumatic Energy Detector with Remote Optics
PEDRTC..... Pediatric
PEDS........ Packaging Engineering Data System   (AFM)
PEDS........ Pediatrics
PEDS........ Peltier Effect Diffusion Separation [*Physical chemistry*]
PEDS........ Program Element Descriptive Summary   (CAAL)
PEDS........ Protective Equipment Decontamination Section [*Nuclear energy*]   (NRCH)
Ped Sem .... Pedagogical Seminary [*A publication*]
PEDSTL ..... Pedestal[*s*] [*Freight*]
PEDT......... Pendant [*Jewelry*]   (ROG)
PEDT......... Peridot [*Jewelry*]   (ROG)
PEDUC...... Professeurs d'Economie Domestique des Universites Canadiennes [*Canadian University Teachers of Home Economics - CUTHE*]

PEE	Photoelectron Emission
PEE	Photoemission Effect
PEE	Pressure Environmental Equipment (NVT)
PEE	Program Estimating Equation
P & EE	Proof and Experimental Establishments (RDA)
PEE	Talkeetna, AK [Location identifier] [FAA] (FAAL)
PEEAD	Promoclim E [A publication]
PEEC........	Personnel Emergency Estimator Capability
PEEC........	Programable Electronic Engine Control [Automotive engineering]
PEEC........	Project for an Energy-Enriched Curriculum [Department of Energy]
PEECD	Petroleum Economist [A publication]
PEEID.......	Petroleum Engineer International [A publication]
PEEK	People for the Enjoyment of Eyeballing Knees [Group opposing below-the-knee fashions introduced in 1970]
PEEK	Periodically Elevated Electronic Kibitzer
PEEK	Polyetherketone [Organic chemistry]
Peel Valley Hist Soc J ...	Peel Valley Historical Society. Journal [A publication]
PEEP	Panel of Experts on Environmental Pollution [Marine science] (MSC)
PEEP	Pilot's Electronic Eyelevel Presentation [British]
PEEP	Porous Electrode Electrostatic Precipitation
PEEP	Positive End Expiratory Pressure [Medicine]
PEEP	Production Electronic Equipment Procurement Status Report
Peeples & Stevens ...	Peeples and Stevens' Reports [80-97 Georgia] (DLA)
Peer...........	Peerless [Record label] [USA, Mexico]
PEER	Planned Experience for Effective Relating
PEER	Price Escalation Estimated Rates
PEER	Program of Equal Employment Opportunity Evaluation Reports
PEER	Project on Equal Education Rights [National Organization for Women]
PEERC	Production Engineering Education and Research Center
Peere Wms ...	Peere-Williams' English Chancery and King's Bench Cases [1695-1736] (DLA)
PEF...........	Packaging Education Foundation (EA)
PEF...........	Palestine Endowment Funds [Later, PEF Israel Endowment Funds] (EA)
PEF...........	Palestine Exploration Fund
PEF...........	Peak Expiratory Flow [Pulmonary function]
PEF...........	Performance Efficiency Factor (AFIT)
PEF...........	Personal Effects Floater [Insurance]
PEF...........	Personality Evaluation Form [Psychology]
PEF...........	Phil Esposito Foundation (EA)
PEF...........	Physical Electronics Facility (MCD)
PEF...........	Plastics Education Foundation (EA)
PEF...........	Polyethylene Foam
PEF...........	Prediction Error Filter [Wave frequency and phase modifier]
PEF...........	Presbyterian Evangelistic Fellowship [Decatur, GA] (EA)
PEF...........	Pro Ecclesia Foundation (EA)
PEF...........	Program Estimating Factor (AFM)
PEF...........	Proposal Evaluation Form (AAG)
PEF...........	Psychiatric Evaluation Form [Psychology]
PEFA	Palestine Exploration Fund. Annual [A publication]
PEFCO	Private Export Funding Corporation
PEFO	Payload Effects Follow-On Study [NASA] (NASA)
PEFO	Petrified Forest National Park
PEFQ	Palestine Exploration Fund. Quarterly Statement [A publication]
PEFQS	Palestine Exploration Fund. Quarterly Statement [London] [A publication] (BJA)
PEFQST	Palestine Exploration Fund. Quarterly Statement [London] [A publication] (BJA)
PEFR	Peak Expiratory Flow Rate
PEFT	Peripheral Equipment Functional Test (CAAL)
PEFTOK	Philippine Expeditionary Force to Korea [United Nations]
PEFU	Panel of Experts on Fish Utilization [FAO] (ASF)
PEFV	Partial Expiratory Flow-Volume [Physiology]
PEG	General Analine & Film Co., General Research Laboratory, Easton, PA [Library symbol] [Library of Congress] [Obsolete] (LCLS)
PEG	Pacific Environmental Group [Marine science] (MSC)
Peg...........	Pegaso [A publication]
Peg...........	Pegasus [Constellation]
PEG	Performance Evaluation Group (CINC)
PEG	Petrochemical Energy Group [Washington, DC] (EA)
PEG	Pneumatic Explosion Generator
PEG	Pneumoencephalogram [Medicine]
PEG	Polyethylene Glycol [Organic chemistry]
PEG	Previous Endorsement(s) Guaranteed [Banking]
PEG	Principle of the Equivalent Generator
PEG	Priorities for ELINT Guidance (MCD)
PEG	Process Evaluation Guide [Graphic Communications Association]
PEG	Program Evaluation Group [Air Force]
PEG	Project Engineering Guide (MCD)
PEG	Protection Engineers Group [United States Telephone Association] [Telecommunications]
PEG	Public Service Enterprise Group, Inc. [NYSE symbol]
PEGA	Polyethylene Glycol Adipate [Organic chemistry]
PEGDE	Pentaethylene Glycol Dodecyl Ether [Organic chemistry]
PEGE	Program for Evaluation of Ground Environment
PEGR........	Press Extracts on Greenland [A publication]
PEGR........	Proportional Exhaust Gas Recirculation [Engines]
Pegs	Pegasus [Constellation]
PEGS........	Polyethylene Glycol Succinate [Organic chemistry]
PEGS........	Project Engineering Graphics System [Computer Aided Design Centre] [Software package]
PEGS........	Publications. English Goethe Society [A publication]
PEH	Pehpei [Republic of China] [Seismograph station code, US Geological Survey] (SEIS)
PEH	Pehuajo [Argentina] [Airport symbol] (OAG)
PEH	Periods of European History [A publication]
PEH	Planning Estimate Handbook
PEH	Plus Each Hour [Aviation] (FAAC)
PEHA	Pentaethylenehexamine [Organic chemistry]
PEHi	Northampton County Historical and Genealogical Society, Mary Illick Memorial Library, Easton, PA [Library symbol] [Library of Congress] (LCLS)
Pei	Parole e le Idee [A publication]
PEI.............	Patriotic Education, Incorporated (EA)
PEI.............	Peine [Chile] [Seismograph station code, US Geological Survey] [Closed] (SEIS)
PEI.............	Pennsylvania Real Estate Investments Trust SBI [American Stock Exchange symbol]
PEI.............	Pereira [Colombia] [Airport symbol] (OAG)
PEI.............	Petrocel Industries Incorporated [Vancouver Stock Exchange symbol]
PEI.............	Petroleum Equipment Institute [Tulsa, OK] (EA)
PEI.............	Planning Executives Institute
PEI.............	Plant Engineering Inspection (AAG)
PEI.............	Polyethylenimine [Organic chemistry]
PEI.............	Porcelain Enamel Institute [Arlington, VA] (EA)
PEI.............	Postejaculatory Interval [Physiology]
PEI.............	Precipitation-Efficiency Index
PEI.............	Preliminary Engineering Inspection [NASA] (KSC)
PEI.............	Prince Edward Island [Canadian province]
PEI.............	Prince Edward Island Provincial Library [UTLAS symbol]
PEI.............	Prince Edward Island Reports [Haviland's] (DLA)
PEI.............	Professional Engineers in Industry
PEIA	Poultry and Egg Institute of America (EA)
PEIC	Periodic Error Integrating Controller
PEID	Program Element Identifier [Military] (AFIT)
PEILS	PACOM [Pacific Command] Executive Intelligence Summary (MCD)
PEIN	PEI, Inc. [NASDAQ symbol] (NQ)
Peine Salzgitter Ber ...	Peine und Salzgitter Berichte [A publication]
Peint Pigm Vernis ...	Peintures, Pigments, Vernis [A publication]
PEIP	Presidential Executive Interchange Program [Federal government]
PEIR	Problem Equipment Indicator Reports (MCD)
PEIR	Project Equipment Inspection Record [NASA] (KSC)
PEI Rep	Prince Edward Island Reports [Haviland's] [1850-1914] (DLA)
PEI Rev Stat ...	Prince Edward Island Revised Statutes [Canada] (DLA)
PEIS	Programatic Environmental Impact Statement (NRCH)
PEI Stat	Prince Edward Island Statutes [Canada] (DLA)
PEITA	Professional Equestrian Instructors and Trainers Association (EA)
PEITV	Preliminary Encapsulated Inert Test Vehicle (MCD)
PEJ.............	Pakistan Economic Journal [A publication]
PEJ.............	Premolded Expansion Joint [Technical drawings]
PEJO	Plant Engineering Job Order (AAG)
PEJOA.......	Personnel Journal [A publication]
PEK	Beijing [China] [Airport symbol] (OAG)
PEK	Jacksonville, FL [Location identifier] [FAA] (FAAL)
PEK	Peking [Republic of China] [Geomagnetic observatory code]
PEK	Peking [Chiufeng] [Republic of China] [Seismograph station code, US Geological Survey] (SEIS)
PEK	Pekoe [Tea trade] (ROG)
PEK	Perkiomen Airways Ltd. [Reading, PA] [FAA designator] (FAAC)
PEK	Phase-Exchange Keying [Data processing] (IEEE)
PEK	Phi Epsilon Kappa [Fraternity]
Peking R	Peking Review [A publication]
PEL.............	Lafayette College, Easton, PA [Library symbol] [Library of Congress] (LCLS)
PEL.............	Paid Educational Leave (ADA)
PEL.............	Panhandle Eastern Pipe Line Co. [NYSE symbol]
PEL.............	Pelaneng [Lesotho] [Airport symbol] (OAG)
PEL.............	Peldehue [Chile] [Seismograph station code, US Geological Survey] (SEIS)
Pel	Pelopidas [of Plutarch] [Classical studies] (OCD)
PEL.............	Penguin English Library [A publication]
PEL.............	Peritoneal Exudate Lymphocytes [Hematology]
PEL.............	Permissible Exposure Limit
PEL.............	Philatelic Esperanto League [See also ELF] (EA-IO)
PEL.............	Photoelectron Layer
PEL.............	Picture Element [Single element of resolution in image processing] (IBMDP)
PEL.............	Precision Elastic Limit
PEL.............	Priests Eucharistic League (EA)

PEL............ Professional Education Libraries [*UTLAS symbol*]
PEL............ Proportional Elastic Limit
PEIC.......... Elizabethtown College, Elizabethtown, PA [*Library symbol*] [*Library of Congress*] (LCLS)
PELC .... Professional Engineers' Legislative Committee
PELEC...... Photoelectric (MSA)
PEleph .... Elephantine Papyri [*A publication*] (OCD)
PELG........ Poly(ethyl L-Glutamate) [*Organic chemistry*]
Pelham....... Pelham's Reports [*A publication*]
Pelham....... Pelham's South Australia Reports [*1865-66*] (DLA)
PELL.......... Papers on English Language and Literature [*A publication*]
PELL........ Publications in English Language and Literature [*A publication*]
PELR........ Peeler
PELRY....... Pelsart Resources ADR [*NASDAQ symbol*] (NQ)
PELS .... Precision Emitter Location System [*Air Force*] (MCD)
PELS .... Propionyl Erythromycin Lauryl Sulfate [*Antimicrobial agent*]
PELSS .... Precision Emitter Location Strike System [*Air Force*]
Pelt............ Peltier's Orleans Appeals [*1917-23*] (DLA)
PELT .... Princeton Electronic [*NASDAQ symbol*] (NQ)
PEM............ Parametric Earth Model [*Geodynamics*]
PEM............ Parasitic Encephalitis Meningitis [*Medicine*]
PeM............ Parole e Metodi [*A publication*]
PEM............ Payload Ejection Mechanism
PEM............ Pem Air Ltd. [*Pembroke, ON*] [*FAA designator*] (FAAC)
PEM............ Pembrokeshire [*County in Wales*] (ROG)
PEM............ Perrot Memorial Library, Old Greenwich, CT [*OCLC symbol*] (OCLC)
PEM............ Personal Exposure Monitor [*Environmental chemistry*]
PEM............ Petrox Energy & Minerals [*Toronto Stock Exchange symbol*] [*Vancouver Stock Exchange symbol*]
PEM............ Phased Equipment Modernization (AABC)
PEM............ Philco Electronic Module
PEM............ Photoelastic Modulator [*Instrumentation*]
PEM............ Photoelectromagnetic
PEM............ Photoelectron Microscopy
PEM............ Photoemission Microscope
PEM............ Photographic Equipment and Materials (NATG)
PEM............ Plant Engineer Mechanical (AAG)
PE & M ...... Plant Engineering and Maintenance (MCD)
PEM............ Plant Engineering and Maintenance (NASA)
PEM............ Polaris Evaluation Missile
PEM............ Position Encoding Module (CAAL)
PEM............ Prescription-Event Monitoring
PEM............ Primary Enrichment Medium [*Microbiology*]
PEM............ Probable Error of Measurement
PEM............ Processing Element Memory [*Data processing*]
PEM............ Product Effectiveness Manual
PEM............ Production Engineering Measures [*Army*] (MCD)
PEM............ Production Evaluation Missile [*Military*] (CAAL)
PEM............ Program Element Monitor (AFM)
PEM............ Project Engineering Memorandum
PEM............ Protein Energy Malnutrition [*Medicine*]
PEM............ Puerto Maldonado [*Peru*] [*Airport symbol*] (OAG)
PEMA .... Process Equipment Manufacturers Association [*Falls Church, VA*] (EA)
PEMA .... Procurement Equipment Maintenance, Army (MCD)
PEMA .... Procurement, Equipment, Missiles, Army
PEMA .... Procurement of Equipment and Munition Appropriations [*Military*] (AABC)
PEMA .... Production-Equipment-Missile Agency [*Army*]
PEMAP....... President's Environmental Merit Award Program [*Environmental Protection Agency*]
PEMARS .... Procurement of Equipment and Missiles, Army Management and Accounting Reporting System (AABC)
PEMB .... Pembroke College [*Oxford and Cambridge Universities*] (ROG)
PEMB .... Pembrokeshire [*County in Wales*]
Pemb Judg ... Pemberton's Judgments and Orders (DLA)
PEMBS...... Pembrokeshire [*County in Wales*]
PEMC........ Pele Medical Corporation [*NASDAQ symbol*] (NQ)
PEMCONS ... Photographic Equipment Management Control System
PEMD........ Program for Export Market Development [*Canada*]
PEMF .... Pulsating Electromagnetic Field
PEMJ.......... Pemmican Journal [*A publication*]
PEMJA .... Pesticides Monitoring Journal [*A publication*]
P & EML ...... Personnel and Equipment Modification List [*Air Force*]
PEMO........ Plant Engineering Maintenance Order
PEMO........ Production Engineering and Manufacturing Organization (AAG)
PEM Process Eng Mag ... PEM Process Engineering Magazine [*A publication*]
PEMS .... Physical, Emotional, Mental, Safety [*Model for charting procedure*] [*Medicine*]
PEMS .... Portable Environmental Measuring System
PEMS .... Professional Education of the Media Specialist
PEMS .... Propulsion Energy Management Study (MCD)
PEMT .... Phosphatidylethanolamine Methyltransferase [*An enzyme*]
PEN............ Astoria, OR [*Location identifier*] [*FAA*] (FAAL)
PEN............ Federation Internationale des PEN Clubs [*International PEN*] (EA-IO)

PEN .... International PEN [*Official name; PEN, never spelled out in use, is said to stand for poets, playwrights, editors, essayists, novelists*] (EA-IO)
PEN .... Penang [*Malaysia*] [*Airport symbol*] (OAG)
PEN .... Pendeli [*Greece*] [*Geomagnetic observatory code*]
PEN .... Penetration (AFM)
PEN .... Penicillin [*Antibiotic*]
PEN .... Peninsula [*Maps and charts*]
PEN .... Penitent
Pen .... Pennewill's Delaware Reports (DLA)
Pen .... Pennington's New Jersey Reports [*2, 3 New Jersey*] (DLA)
PEN .... Pensacola [*Florida*] [*Seismograph station code, US Geological Survey*] [*Closed*] (SEIS)
Pen .... Pensamiento [*Madrid*] [*A publication*]
PEN .... Pentazocine [*An analgesic*]
PEN .... Pentobarbital [*Sedative*]
PEN .... Pentode (DEN)
PEN .... Pentron Industries, Inc. [*American Stock Exchange symbol*]
PEN .... Physicians Education Network [*St. Petersburg, FL*] (EA)
PEN .... Professional Enrichment News [*Portuguese*] (BJA)
PEN .... Program Element Number [*Data processing*] (KSC)
PEN .... Program Error Note [*Data processing*]
PENA .... Primary Emission Neuron Activation (IEEE)
PENAID ...... Penetration Aid [*Weaponry*]
PENB .... Poultry and Egg National Board [*Later, AEB*] (EA)
PENBASE ... Peninsular Base Section [*Military*]
Pen C .... Penal Code (DLA)
PENCIL ...... Pictorial Encoding Language [*Data processing*] (IEEE)
PENCIL ...... Portable Encoder/Illustrator [*Facetious term for pre-word-processing equipment*]
Pend.......... Pendant (ROG)
PEND......... Pendens [*Weighing*] [*Pharmacy*]
PEND......... Pending
PENDA .... Polish Endocrinology [*A publication*]
Pen Dec ..... Pension Decisions [*Department of the Interior*] (DLA)
PENDORF ... Penetrate Dorfman [*FBI investigation of Teamster leader Allen Dorfman*]
Penelitian Indones ... Penelitian Laut di Indonesia [*A publication*]
Penelitian Laut Indones (Mar Res Indones) ... Penelitian Laut in Indonesia (Marine Research in Indonesia) [*A publication*]
P/E NEWS ... Petroleum/Energy Business News Index [*American Petroleum Institute*] [*New York, NY*] [*Bibliographic database*]
PenG .... Penicillin G [*Antibacterial agent*]
PENG .... Photo-Electro-Nystagmography [*Medicine*]
PENG .... Prima Energy Corp. [*NASDAQ symbol*] (NQ)
PEng .... Professional Engineer
PENGEM .... Penetrate Gray Electronics Markets [*FBI "sting" operation, 1982, in which employees of Japanese computer firms were caught attempting to obtain proprietary information illegally from IBM Corp.*]
Pengum Lemb Penelit Kehutanan ... Pengumuman. Lembaga Penelitian Kehutanan [*A publication*]
PENIC .... Penicillin
Penic Cam ... Penicillum Camelinum [*A Camel's-Hair Brush*] [*Pharmacy*]
PENIT .... Penitentiary
Penjelidikan Indones ... Penjelidikan Laut di Indonesia [*A publication*]
PENJERDEL ... Pennsylvania, New Jersey, Delaware
Penn .... Pennewill's Delaware Reports (DLA)
Penn .... Pennington's New Jersey Reports (DLA)
PENN........ Pennsylvania
Penn .... Pennsylvania State Reports (DLA)
PENN........ Pennsylvanian [*Period, era, or system*] [*Geology*]
Penn .... Pennypacker's Unreported Pennsylvania Cases (DLA)
PENNA .... Pennsylvania
Penna Law Journal ... Pennsylvania Law Journal (DLA)
Penna LJ.... Pennsylvania Law Journal (DLA)
Penna R...... Pennsylvania State Reports (DLA)
Penna SR .... Pennsylvania State Reports (DLA)
Penna St ... Pennsylvania State Reports (DLA)
Penna State Rep ... Pennsylvania State Reports (DLA)
Penn Ba Q ... Pennsylvania Bar Association. Quarterly [*A publication*]
Penn Beekpr ... Pennsylvania Beekeeper [*A publication*]
Penn Co Ct Rep ... Pennsylvania County Court Reports (DLA)
Penn Corp Rep ... Pennsylvania Corporation Reporter (DLA)
Penn Del .... Pennewill's Delaware Reports (DLA)
Penn Dent J ... Penn Dental Journal [*A publication*]
Penn Dist & Co Rep ... Pennsylvania District and County Reports (DLA)
Penn Dist Rep ... Pennsylvania District Reports (DLA)
Penne........ Pennewill's Delaware Reports [*17-23 Delaware*] [*1897-1909*] (DLA)
Pennew...... Pennewill's Delaware Reports (DLA)
Pennewill ... Pennewill's Delaware Supreme Court Reports [*1897-1909*] (DLA)
Penn Geol Surv Atlas ... Pennsylvania. Geological Survey. Atlas [*A publication*]
Penn Geol Surv Bull ... Pennsylvania. Geological Survey. Bulletin [*A publication*]
Penn Geol Surv Gen Geol Rep ... Pennsylvania. Geological Survey. General Geology Report [*A publication*]
Penn Geol Surv Ground Water Rep ... Pennsylvania. Geological Survey. Ground Water Report [*A publication*]

Penn Geol Surv Inform Circ ... Pennsylvania. Geological Survey. Information Circular [*A publication*]
Penn Geol Surv Progr Rep ... Pennsylvania. Geological Survey. Progress Report [*A publication*]
Penn German Soc Proc ... Pennsylvania German Society. Proceedings [*A publication*]
Penn Hist ... Pennsylvania History [*A publication*]
Penning ..... Pennington's New Jersey Reports [*2, 3 New Jersey*]   (DLA)
Pen NJ .... Pennington's New Jersey Reports [*2, 3 New Jersey*]   (DLA)
Penn Law Jour ... Pennsylvania Law Journal   (DLA)
Penn LG ..... Pennsylvania Legal Gazette   (DLA)
Penn LG ..... Pennsylvania Legal Gazette Reports [*Campbell*]   (DLA)
Penn Lib Assn Bull ... Pennsylvania Library Association. Bulletin [*A publication*]
Penn LJ ..... Pennsylvania Law Journal   (DLA)
Penn LJR .... Pennsylvania Law Journal Reports, Edited by Clark [*1842-52*]   (DLA)
Penn L Rec ... Pennsylvania Law Record [*Philadelphia*]   (DLA)
Penn L Rev ... Pennsylvania Law Review   (DLA)
Penn Mag H ... Pennsylvania Magazine of History and Biography [*A publication*]
Penn Mag Hist Biog ... Pennsylvania Magazine of History and Biography [*A publication*]
Penn Mo ..... Penn Monthly [*A publication*]
Penn Nurse ... Pennsylvania Nurse [*A publication*]
PENNORTH ... Pennyworth [*British*]   (ROG)
Penn R .... Pennsylvania State Reports   (DLA)
Penn Rep ... Pennsylvania State Reports   (DLA)
Penn Rep ... Penrose and Watts' Pennsylvania Reports   (DLA)
PennsF .... Pennsylvania Folklife [*A publication*]
Penn St .... Pennsylvania State Reports   (DLA)
PENNSTAC ... Penn State University Automatic Digital Computer
Penn Stat ... Pennsylvania State Reports   (DLA)
Penn State F ... Penn State Farmer [*A publication*]
Penn State Rep ... Pennsylvania State Reports   (DLA)
Penn State Univ Exp Sta Bull ... Pennsylvania State University. Experiment Station. Bulletin [*A publication*]
Penn State Univ Exp Sta Circ ... Pennsylvania State University. Experiment Station. Circular [*A publication*]
Penn St M Q ... Penn State Mining Quarterly [*A publication*]
Penn Stock & F ... Pennsylvania Stockman and Farmer [*A publication*]
Penn St Rep ... Pennsylvania State Reports   (DLA)
Penn Super ... Pennsylvania Superior Court Reports   (DLA)
Pennsyl M ... Pennsylvania Magazine of History and Biography [*A publication*]
Pennsylvania Acad Sci Newsletter ... Pennsylvania Academy of Science. Newsletter [*A publication*]
Pennsylvania Acad Sci Proc ... Pennsylvania Academy of Science. Proceedings [*A publication*]
Pennsylvania Bus Survey ... Pennsylvania Business Survey [*A publication*]
Pennsylvania Geol Survey Bull ... Pennsylvania. Geological Survey. Bulletin [*A publication*]
Pennsylvania Geol Survey Inf Circ ... Pennsylvania. Geological Survey. Information Circular [*A publication*]
Pennsylvania Geol Survey Prog Rept ... Pennsylvania. Geological Survey. Progress Report [*A publication*]
PENNTAP ... Pennsylvania Technical Assistance Program [*Pennsylvania State University*] [*University Park, PA*]
Penn Univ Mus Bul ... Pennsylvania University. University Museum. Bulletin [*A publication*]
Penny .... Pennypacker's Pennsylvania Colonial Cases   (DLA)
Penny .... Pennypacker's Unreported Pennsylvania Cases   (DLA)
Penny Col Cas ... Pennypacker's Pennsyulvania Colonial Cases   (DLA)
Penny M ..... Penny Magazine [*A publication*]
Penny Mech Chem ... Penny Mechanic and the Chemist [*A publication*]
Pennyp ...... Pennypacker's Unreported Pennsylvania Cases   (DLA)
Pennyp Col Cas ... Pennypacker's Pennsylvania Colonial Cases   (DLA)
Pennyp (PA) ... Pennypacker's Unreported Pennsylvania Cases   (DLA)
PENOL ...... Penology
Pen P .... Penault's Prerosti de Quebec   (DLA)
PENRAD ..... Penetration RADAR
Penr Anal ... Penruddocke's Short Analysis of Criminal Law [*2nd ed.*] [*1842*]   (DLA)
Pen Ref ...... Penal Reformer [*1934-39*]   (DLA)
Pen Ref League M Rec ... Penal Reform League Monthly Record [*1909-12*]   (DLA)
Pen Ref League Q Rec ... Penal Reform League Quarterly Record [*1912-20*]   (DLA)
PENREP ..... Penetration Report [*National Security Agency*]
PENRF .... Pennant Resources [*NASDAQ symbol*]   (NQ)
Penrose Ann ... Penrose Annual [*A publication*]
Penr & W ..... Penrose and Watts' Pennsylvania Reports [*1829-32*]   (DLA)
PENS .... Magic Marker Industries [*NASDAQ symbol*]   (NQ)
PENS .... Partido Espanol Nacional Sindicalista [*Political party*] [*Spain*]
PENS .... Polymer Ejection for Noise Suppression
PENSAM .... Penetration Survivability Assessment Model   (MCD)
Pensamiento Polit ... Pensamiento Politico [*A publication*]
PensCr .... Pensamiento Cristiano. Tribuna de Exposicion del Pensamiento Evangelico [*Cordoba, Argentina*] [*A publication*]   (BJA)
Pensee Nat ... Pensee Nationale [*A publication*]

Pensez Plast ... Pensez Plastiques [*A publication*]
Pensiero Med ... Pensiero Medico [*A publication*]
Pensiero Polit ... Pensiero Politico [*A publication*]
Pension FA ... Pension Fund Sponsors Ranked by Assets [*A publication*]
Pensions .... Pensions and Investments [*Later, Pension & Investment Age*] [*A publication*]
Pension Wld ... Pension World [*A publication*]
Pens & Profit Sharing (P-H) ... Pension and Profit Sharing [*Prentice-Hall, Inc.*]   (DLA)
Pens Rep (BNA) ... Pension Reporter [*Bureau of National Affairs*]   (DLA)
PenST .... Penicillin Skin Test [*Immunology*]
Pen St R ..... Pennsylvania State Reports   (DLA)
PENT .... Penetrate   (AABC)
PENT .... Pennsylvania Enterprises [*NASDAQ symbol*]   (NQ)
PENT .... Pentagon
PENT .... Pentameter
Pent .... Pentateuch   (BJA)
PENT .... Pentecost
PENT .... Pentode   (AAG)
PENTAC ..... Penetration for Tactical Aircraft [*Air Force*]
PENTENG ... Pentagon English [*Pseudotechnical language*]
P Ent S Ont ... Proceedings. Entomological Society of Ontario [*A publication*]
P Ent S Was ... Proceedings. Entomological Society of Washington [*A publication*]
PENVAL ..... Penetration Evaluation [*Military*]   (NVT)
PENW .... Penetrating Wound
Pen & W ...... Penrose and Watts' Pennsylvania Reports [*1829-32*]   (DLA)
Pen Wld ...... Pension World [*A publication*]
PENZ .... Penzance [*City in England*]   (ROG)
Penz Ped Inst Ucen Zap ... Penzenskii Pedagogiceskii Institut Imeni V. G. Belinskogo. Ucenye Zapiski [*A publication*]
Penz Politehn Inst Ucen Zap Mat Meh ... Penzenskii Politehniceskii Institut. Matematika i Mehanika. Ucenye Zapiski [*A publication*]
Penzuegyi Szemle ... Penzuegyi Szemle [*A publication*]
Penzugyi Szle ... Penzugyi Szemle [*A publication*]
PEO .... Pankypria Ergatiki Omospondia [*Pancyprian Federation of Labour*] [*The "Old Trade Unions"*] [*Cyprus*]
PEO .... Patrol Emergency Officer   (NRCH)
PEO .... People
peo .... Persian, Old [*MARC language code*] [*Library of Congress*]   (LCCP)
PEO .... Petroleum & Resources Corp. [*NYSE symbol*]
PEO .... Philanthropic and Educational Organization [*Sometimes facetiously translated as "Pop Eats Out"*]
PEO .... Planners for Equal Opportunity [*Defunct*]   (EA)
PEO .... Plant Engineering Order
PEO .... Plant Equipment Operator [*Nuclear energy*]   (NRCH)
PEO .... Poly(ethylene oxide) [*Acronym is trade name owned by Seitetsu Kagaku Co.*]
PEO .... Principal Executive Officer [*Civil Service*] [*British*]
PEO .... Process Engineering Order
PEO .... Product Engineering Office
PEO .... Production Engineering Order
PEO .... Program Evaluation Office
PEO .... Progressive External Ophthalmoplegia
PEO .... Propulsion Engineering Office   (MCD)
PEO .... Prospective Engineer Officer
PEO .... Public Employment Office [*State Employee Security Agency*]   (OICC)
PEOC .... Publishing Employees Organizing Committee [*AFL-CIO*]
PEOED .... Proceedings. European Offshore Petroleum Conference and Exhibition [*A publication*]
Peo L Adv ... People's Legal Advisor [*Utica, NY*]   (DLA)
PEOP .... Peoples Ban Corp. [*NASDAQ symbol*]   (NQ)
Peop J .... People's Journal [*A publication*]
Peoples ...... Peoples' Reports [*77-97 Georgia*]   (DLA)
Peopl Tax ..... People and Taxes [*A publication*]
Peoria Med Month ... Peoria Medical Monthly [*A publication*]
PEOS .... Propulsion and Electrical Operating System   (IEEE)
PEOUD .... Petroleum Outlook [*A publication*]
Peo World ... People's World [*A publication*]
PEP .... Charlotte, NC [*Location identifier*] [*FAA*]   (FAAL)
PEP .... Paperless Electronic Payment [*Business and trade*]
PEP .... Paperless Entry Processing User Group [*Defunct*]   (CSR)
PEP .... Parenting, Education, and Political Involvement [*Jack and Jill of America*]
PEP .... Parti Evangelique Populaire [*Popular Protestant Party*] [*Swiss*]   (PPE)
PEP .... Partitioned Emulation Program [*Data processing*]   (BUR)
PEP .... Pauli Exclusion Principle [*Physics*]
PEP .... Peak Energy Product
PEP .... Peak Envelope Power [*Telecommunications*]
PEP .... Peer Evaluation Program [*College of American Pathologists*]
PEP .... People for Energy Progress   (EA)
PEP .... Pepitilla [*Race of maize*]
PEP .... Peppermint   (DSUE)
PEP .... PepsiCo Inc. [*NYSE symbol*]
PEP .... Performance Effectiveness [*or Evaluation*] Program [*Navy*]
PEP .... Peripheral Event Processor [*Data processing*]
PEP .... Perkin-Elmer Processor [*Computer*]
PEP .... Personal Equity Plan [*Finance*]

PEP .... Personal Exercise Programer
PEP .... Personality-Profile Exam
PEP .... Personnel Exchange Program [*Navy*]   (NVT)
PEP .... Pfizer, Inc., Research Center Library, Easton, PA [*Library symbol*] [*Library of Congress*]   (LCLS)
PEP .... Phenethyl Propionate [*Insect attractant*] [*Organic chemistry*]
PEP .... Phosphoenolpyruvate [*Biochemistry*]
PEPIA .... Photoelectric Potential
PEP .... Photoelectrophoresis
PEP .... Photographic Exploitation Products   (MCD)
PEP .... Physical Education Program
PEP .... Physiological Evaluation of Primates
PEP .... Pipeline Expanding Polymer
PEP .... Piping Efficiency Program
PEP .... Planar Epitaxial Passivated
PEP .... Planetary Ephemeris Program   (IEEE)
PEP .... Planetary Exploration Plan [*NASA*]
PEP .... Plant Equipment Package [*DoD*]
PEP .... Platform Electronic Package
PEP .... Platform Evaluation Program
PEP .... Plessey Electronic Payroll   (DEN)
PEP .... Plume Exposure Pathway [*Nuclear emergency planning*]
PEP .... Political and Economic Planning [*A British organization*] [*Later, Policy Studies Institute*]
PEP .... Polyestradiol Phosphate [*Endocrinology*]
PEP .... Polyethylene Powder
PEP .... Polynominal Error Protection   (MCD)
PEP .... Positron-Electron Project [*High-energy accelerator*]
PEP .... Positron Electron Proton [*Physics*]
PEP .... Power Evaluation Program
PEP .... Power Extension Package   (MCD)
PEP .... Power Extension Plant   (MCD)
PEP .... Practical Engineering Paperwork
PEP .... Pratt & Whitney Engine Program [*Aviation*]   (NG)
PEP .... Pre-Ejection Period [*Cardiology*]
PEP .... Preamplifier Extension Plug
PEP .... President's Economy Program
PEPSI .... Preventive Enforcement Patrol [*New York City police*]
PEP .... Primate Equilibrium Platform
PEP .... Princeton Experiment Package [*NASA*]
PoP .... Principal of Pedagogy [*Academic degree*]
PEP .... Printer-Emulation Package [*Software*]
PEP .... Priority Energy Policy [*Environmental Protection Agency*]
PEP .... Procurement Evaluation Panel [*Air Force*]   (MCD)
PEP .... Producibility Engineering and Planning   (AABC)
PEP .... Product Engineering and Production   (MCD)
PEP .... Production Engineering Planning
PEP .... [*The*] Productivity Effectiveness Program [*Title of a pamphlet by Robert Gedaliah that describes sedentary exercises for desk-bound workers*]
PEP .... Professional Enhancement Project [*American Occupational Therapy Association*]
PEP .... Proficiency Examination Program   (MCD)
PEP .... Program Element Plan   (AFIT)
PEP .... Program Evaluation Procedure [*Air Force*]
PEP .... Progressive Exercise Program
PEP .... Projects and Exports Policy [*Board of Trade*] [*British*]
PEP .... Promoting Enduring Peace   (EA)
PEP .... Promotion Evaluation Pattern
PEP .... Proposal Equipment Packages   (MCD)
PEP .... Proposal Evaluation Panel   (MCD)
PEP .... Proposal Evaluation Plan [*or Program*]   (MCD)
PEP .... Protection in Evaluation Procedures
PEP .... Proton-Electron-Proton [*Nuclear physics*]
PEP .... Public Employment Program
PEP .... Pulse Echo Pattern
PEPA .... Peptidase A [*An enzyme*]
PEPA .... Petroleum Electric Power Association [*Abilene, TX*]   (EA)
PEPA .... Protected Environment plus Prophylactic Antibiotics [*Oncology*]
PEPA .... Pulse Echo Pattern Analyzer
PEPAG .... Physical Electronics and Physical Acoustics Group [*MIT*]   (MCD)
PEPAOP ..... (Phenylethyl)phenylacetoxypiperidine [*Organic chemistry*]
PEPAS .... WHO Centre Regional du Pacifique Occidental pour la Promotion de la Planification et des Etudes Appliquees en Matiere d'Environnement [*WHO Western Pacific Regional Centre for the Promotion of Environmental Planning and Applied Studies*]   (EA-IO)
PEPAS .... WHO Western Pacific Regional Centre for the Promotion of Environmental Planning and Applied Studies   (EA-IO)
PEPC .... Peptidase C [*An enzyme*]
PEPC .... Phosphoenolpyruvate Carboxylase [*An enzyme*]
PEPC .... Polynomial Error Protection Code [*Data processing*]
PEPC .... Potomac Electric Power Company
PEPCK .... Phosphoenolopyruvate Carboxykinase [*An enzyme*]
PEPCO .... Potomac Electric Power Company
PEPD .... Peptidase D [*An enzyme*]
PEPE .... Parallel Element Processing Ensemble [*Burroughs Corp.*]   (BUR)

PEPE .... Prolonged Elevated-Pollution Episode [*Environmental Protection Agency*]
PEPG .... Piezoelectric Power Generation
PEPG .... Port Emergency Planning Group [*NATO*]   (NATG)
PEPI .... Physical Education Public Information [*Film*]
PEPI .... Piezo Electric Products [*NASDAQ symbol*]   (NQ)
PEPI .... Pre-Ejection Period Index [*Cardiology*]
PEPIA .... Physics of the Earth and Planetary Interiors [*A publication*]
Pepinier Hortic Maraichers ... Pepinieristes, Horticulteurs, Maraichers [*France*] [*A publication*]
PEPL .... Peoples Restaurants [*NASDAQ symbol*]   (NQ)
PEPL .... Preliminary Engineering Parts List
PEPLAN .... Polaris Executive Plan [*British*]
PEPMC...... Printing Estimators and Production Men's Club [*New York, NY*]   (EA)
PEPMIS ..... Plant Equipment Packages Management Information System   (MCD)
PEPP .... Planetary Entry Parachute Program [*NASA*]
PEPP .... Professional Engineers in Private Practice
PEPPA....... Preparedness for Emergency Plant Pest Action [*In Animal and Plant Health Inspection Service publication PEPPA Pot*]
Pepperdine LR ... Pepperdine Law Review [*A publication*]
Pepperdine L Rev ... Pepperdine Law Review [*A publication*]
Pepper & L Dig ... Pepper and Lewis' Digest of Laws [*Pennsylvania*]   (DLA)
PEPR .... Precision Encoding and Pattern Recognition Device [*Data processing*]
PEPS .... National Committee on Public Employee Pension Systems   (EA)
PEPS .... Peperomia and Exotic Plant Society [*Formerly, PS*]   (EA)
PEPS .... Peptidase S [*An enzyme*]
PEPS .... Pesticide Enforcement Policy Statement [*Environmental Protection Agency*]
PEPS .... Priced Exhibit Preliminary System   (MCD)
PEPS .... Production Engineering Productivity System [*Camtek Ltd.*] [*Software package*]
PEPS .... Program Element Plan Supplement
PEPSB....... Perception and Psychophysics [*A publication*]
PEPSI .... Plasma Electron Profiles, Symmetric Integrals   (MCD)
PEPSS ...... Programable Equipment for Personnel Subsystem Simulation
PEPSU ...... All India Reporter, Patiala and East Punjab States Union [*1950-57*]   (DLA)
PEPSU ...... Patiala and East Punjab States Union
PEPSY....... Precision Earth-Pointing System   (MCD)
PEP/USA ... Parkinson's Educational Program - USA [*Newport Beach, CA*]   (EA)
PEPUSL .... Pepperdine University School of Law   (DLA)
PEpW .... Westinghouse Electric Corp., East Pittsburgh, PA [*Library symbol*] [*Library of Congress*]   (LCLS)
PEQ .... Palestine Exploration Quarterly [*A publication*]
PEQ .... Pecos City, TX [*Location identifier*] [*FAA*]   (FAAL)
PEQ .... Personal Experience Questionnaire [*Psychology*]
PEQ .... Petroquin Resources Ltd. [*Vancouver Stock Exchange symbol*]
PEQUA ...... Production Equipment Agency
PEQUOD .... Pacific Equatorial Ocean Dynamics
PEr .... Erie Public Library, Erie, PA [*Library symbol*] [*Library of Congress*]   (LCLS)
PER .... Parity Error Rate
PER .... Partido Estadista Republicano [*Political party*] [*Puerto Rican*]
PER .... Peak Expiration Rate [*Medicine*]
Pe R.......... Pennewill's Delaware Reports   (DLA)
Per........... Perera's Select Decisions [*Ceylon*]   (DLA)
PER.......... Performance Evaluation Report [*DoD*]
PER .... Perhaps   (ROG)
Per........... Pericles [*of Plutarch*] [*Classical studies*]   (OCD)
Per........... Pericles [*Shakespearean work*]
PER .... Perigee   (KSC)
Per........... Periochae [*of Livy*] [*Classical studies*]   (OCD)
PER .... Period
Per........... Period [*Record label*]
PER .... Periodical   (ROG)
PER .... Permian Airways, Inc. [*Midland, TX*] [*FAA designator*]   (FAAC)
PER .... Permission   (AABC)
Per........... Perseus [*Constellation*]
PER .... Persia [*Obsolete*]
per........... Persian, Modern [*MARC language code*] [*Library of Congress*]   (LCCP)
PER .... Person
PER .... Personnel   (KSC)
Per........... Perspective [*A publication*]
Per........... Perspectives [*A publication*]
PER .... PERT [*Program Evaluation and Review Technique*] Event Report
PER .... Perth [*Australia*] [*Seismograph station code, US Geological Survey*] [*Closed*]   (SEIS)
PER .... Perth [*Australia*] [*Airport symbol*]   (OAG)
PER .... Peru [*Three-letter standard code*]   (CNC)
PER .... Phase Engineering Report
PER .... Physical Examination Rate [*Military*]   (AFM)
PER .... Planning, Evaluation, and Reporting [*Education-improvement system*]
PER .... Pominex Ltd. [*Toronto Stock Exchange symbol*]

PER .... Ponca City, OK [*Location identifier*] [*FAA*]   (FAAL)
PER .... Pope, Evans & Robbins, Inc. [*American Stock Exchange
                symbol*]
PER .... Port Everglades Railway [*AAR code*]
PER .... Post Engineer Request
PER .... Preliminary Engineering Report   (KSC)
PER .... Price Earnings Ratio [*Finance*]
PER .... Product Engineering Recommendation [*Automotive
                engineering*]
PER .... Production Engine Remanufacturers Program [*Automotive
                engineering*]
PER .... Professional and Executive Recruitment Service [*British*]
PER .... Proficiency Evaluation Review
PER .... Program Event Recording [*Data processing*]   (MDG)
PER .... Program Execution Request
PER .... Proposal Evaluation Report   (MCD)
PER .... Protein Efficiency Ratio [*Nutrition*]
PER .... Public Employees Roundtable   (EA)
PER .... Pyrotechnical Evaluation Range [*Army*]   (RDA)
PERA .... Planning and Engineering for Repair and Alteration [*Navy*]
PERA .... Production Engine Remanufacturers Association [*Glendale,
                CA*]   (EA)
PERA .... Production Engineering Research Association [*Research
                center*] [*British*]   (IRC)
PERA .... Production Engineering Research Association of Great Britain
                [*Melton Mowbray, Leies., England*]   (EISS)
PERAM .... Personnel Action Memorandum [*Military*]
PER AN ...... Per Annum [*By the Year*] [*Latin*]
PER ANN .... Per Annum [*By the Year*] [*Latin*]
Per A R ...... Performing Arts Review [*A publication*]
PERB .... Public Employment Relations Board
Per Biol ...... Periodicum Biologorum [*A publication*]
PERC .... Peace on Earth Research Center
PERC .... Perceptronics, Inc. [*NASDAQ symbol*]   (NQ)
PERC .... Percolator   (DSUE)
PERC .... Percussion   (AAG)
PERC .... Pittsburgh Energy Research Center [*Later, PETC*] [*Energy
                Research and Development Administration*]
PERC .... Processor Emergency Recovery Circuit [*Bell System*]
PERC .... Professional Engineering and Research Consultants
PERC .... Public Employment Relations Commission
PERCAM ..... Performance and Cost Analysis Model   (MCD)
PERCAP ..... Persian Gulf Requirements and Capabilities [*Military*]
PERCASREPT ... Personnel Casualty Report [*Military*]   (NVT)
PERCENT... Per Centum [*By the Hundred*] [*Latin*]
Percept Cognit Devel ... Perceptual Cognitive Development [*A publication*]
Percept & Motor Skills ... Perceptual and Motor Skills [*A publication*]
Percept Mot Skills ... Perceptual and Motor Skills [*A publication*]
Percept Psychophys ... Perception and Psychophysics [*A publication*]
PERCHLOR ... Perchloride [*Chemistry*]   (ROG)
PERCI........ Personnel Contamination Instrumentation
Perc Mot Sk ... Perceptual and Motor Skills [*A publication*]
Perc Notes ... Percussive Notes [*A publication*]
PERCOM.... Peripheral Communications   (FAAC)
PERCOM.... Personnel Command   (MCD)
PERCOMPASIA ... South East Asian Personal Computer Hardware and
                Software Show   (TSPED)
Per con....... Per Contra [*On the Other Side*] [*Latin*]
PERCOS..... Performance Coding System
Perc Psych ... Perception and Psychophysics [*A publication*]
Per CS...... Perrault's Conseil Superieur [*Canada*]   (DLA)
PERD......... Perdendo [*or Perdendosi*] [*Softer and Slower*] [*Music*]
PERD......... Perdendosi [*Softer and Slower*] [*Music*]
PERD......... Periodic   (MSA)
PERD......... Perused   (ROG)
PERDA .... Per Diem   (NOAA)
Per & Dav ... Perry and Davison's English King's Bench Reports [*1838-
                41*]   (DLA)
PERDDiMS ... Personnel Deployment and Distribution Management System
                [*Military*]   (AABC)
PERDEN..... Perdendo [*or Perdendosi*] [*Softer and Slower*] [*Music*]
PERDEN..... Perdendosi [*Softer and Slower*] [*Music*]
PERDEX..... Permuted Formula Index [*Molecular formula indexing*]
Peredovoi Opyt Stroit Eksp Shakht ... Peredovoi Opyt v Stroitel'stve i
                Ekspluatatsii Shakht [*USSR*] [*A publication*]
PEREF....... Personal Effects
PEREF........ Propellant Engine Research Environmental Facility
Pererab Gaza Gazov Kondens Nauchno-Tekh Obz ... Pererabotka Gaza i
                Gazovogo Kondensata. Nauchno-Tekhnicheskii Obzor [*A
                publication*]
Pererab Tverd Topl ... Pererabotka Tverdogo Topliva [*USSR*] [*A publication*]
PERF .... Perfect
PERF .... PerfectData, Inc. [*NASDAQ symbol*]   (NQ)
PERF .... Perforate   (KSC)
PERF .... Perforation   (DSUE)
PERF .... Performance   (KSC)
PERF .... Police Executive Research Forum   (EA)
Perf Art C ... Performing Arts in Canada [*A publication*]
Perf Art J.... Performing Arts Journal [*A publication*]
Perf Art R.... Performing Arts Review [*A publication*]
Perf Arts .... Performing Arts in Canada [*A publication*]

Perf Arts Can ... Performing Arts in Canada [*A publication*]
Perf Arts R ... Performing Arts Review [*A publication*]
PERFCE ..... Performance
PERFD........ Performed   (ROG)
Perf Eval Rev ... Performance Evaluation Review [*A publication*]
PERFINS .... Perforated Insignia [*Philately*]
PERFM .... Perform   (ROG)
Performance Eval ... Performance Evaluation [*A publication*]
Performance Eval Rev ... Performance Evaluation Review [*A publication*]
Perf Right... Performing Right [*A publication*]
Perfumer.... Perfumer and Flavorist [*A publication*]
Perfum Essent Oil Rec ... Perfumery and Essential Oil Record [*A publication*]
Perfum Flavorist ... Perfumer and Flavorist [*A publication*]
Perfum Flavour ... Perfumery and Flavouring [*Japan*] [*A publication*]
Perfum J .... Perfumers' Journal [*A publication*]
Perfum Kosmet ... Perfumerie und Kosmetik [*A publication*]
PERFW .... Perforating Wound
PErG........... Gannon University, Erie, PA [*Library symbol*] [*Library of
                Congress*]   (LCLS)
PERG........ Pergola [*Classified advertising*]   (ADA)
PERG........ Production Emergency Redistribution Group
PERG......... Production Equipment Redistribution Group
Pergamon Ser Monogr Lab Tech ... Pergamon Series of Monographs in
                Laboratory Techniques [*A publication*]
Pergamon Texts Inorg Chem ... Pergamon Texts in Inorganic Chemistry [*A
                publication*]
Perg I S Da ... Pergamon International Series on Dance and Related
                Disciplines [*A publication*]
PERGO .... Project Evaluation and Review with Graphic Output   (IEEE)
PERGRA..... Permission Granted [*Military*]
PERH......... Perhaps
PerHi .... Erie County Historical Society, Erie, PA [*Library symbol*]
                [*Library of Congress*]   (LCLS)
PERI .... Pea Ridge National Military Park
PERI .... Perigee
PERI .... Perimeter   (AABC)
PERI .... Periscope
PERI .... Platemakers Educational and Research Institute [*Later, IAP*]
PERI .... Production Equipment Redistribution Inventory [*Army*]
PERI .... Production Equipment Reserve Inventory [*Navy*]   (NG)
PERI .... Protein Engineering Research Institute [*Japanese
                governmental and industrial consortium*]
PERIAP ...... Periapical [*Dentistry*]
PERIM .... Perimeter   (KSC)
Perinat Med ... Perinatal Medicine [*A publication*]
Perinat Neonat ... Perinatology/Neonatology [*A publication*]
PERINTREP ... Periodic Intelligence Report   (NATG)
PERINTREPT ... Periodic Intelligence Report
PERINTSUM ... Periodic Intelligence Summary [*Army*]   (AABC)
Period Biol ... Periodicum Biologorum [*A publication*]
Period Mat ... Periodico di Matematiche [*A publication*]
Period Mat 5 ... Periodico di Matematiche. Serie V [*A publication*]
Period Math Hung ... Periodica Mathematica Hungarica [*A publication*]
Period Mineral ... Periodico di Mineralogia [*Italy*] [*A publication*]
Periodont Abstr ... Periodontal Abstracts. Journal of the Western Society of
                Periodontology [*A publication*]
Period Polytech ... Periodica Polytechnica [*A publication*]
Period Polytech Chem Eng ... Periodica Polytechnica. Chemical Engineering
                [*A publication*]
Period Polytech Civ Eng ... Periodica Polytechnica. Civil Engineering
                [*Hungary*] [*A publication*]
Period Polytech Civ Engng ... Periodica Polytechnica. Civil Engineering [*A
                publication*]
Period Polytech Electr Eng ... Periodica Polytechnica. Electrical Engineering
                [*A publication*]
Period Polytech Eng ... Periodica Polytechnica. Engineering [*A publication*]
Period Polytech Mech Eng ... Periodica Polytechnica. Mechanical
                Engineering [*Hungary*] [*A publication*]
Period Polytech Mech Engng ... Periodica Polytechnica. Mechanical
                Engineering [*A publication*]
Period Polytech Trans Engng ... Periodica Polytechnica. Transportation
                Engineering [*A publication*]
Period Speaking ... Periodically Speaking [*A publication*]
PERIPH....... Periphery   (KSC)
Peripl M Eux ... Periplus Maris Euxini [*of Arrian*] [*Classical studies*]   (OCD)
PERIS .... Periscope   (KSC)
PERJ .... Perjury [*FBI standardized term*]
PERJY .... Perjury   (ROG)
PERK .... Payroll Earnings Record Keeping
Perk........... Perkins on Conveyancing   (DLA)
Perk........... Perkins on Pleading   (DLA)
Perk........... Perkins' Profitable Book [*Conveyancing*] [*1523*]   (DLA)
PERK .... Perquisite
PERK .... Prospective Evaluation of Radial Keratotomy [*for eye surgery*]
Perkins J.... Perkins School of Theology. Journal [*A publication*]
Per & Kn.... Perry and Knapp's English Election Reports [*1838*]   (DLA)
Perk Pr Bk ... Perkins' Profitable Book [*Conveyancing*]   (DLA)
PERL .... Perkins-Elmer Robot Language
PERL .... Perusal   (ROG)
PERL .... Pictorial Engineering and Research Laboratory
PERL .... Prepositioned Equipment Requirements List [*Navy*]   (MCD)

PERL .... Public Employee Relations Library [*of Public Personnel Association*]
PERLA .... Pupils Equal, React to Light and Accommodation [*Medicine*]
PERM .... Permanent Employee   (DSUE)
PERM .... Permeability
PERM .... Permian [*Period, era, or system*] [*Geology*]
PERM .... Permission   (MSA)
PERM .... Permutation   (DSUE)
PERM .... Program Evaluation for Repetitive Manufacture   (IEEE)
PERMACAP ... Personnel Management and Accounting Card Processor
PERMACAPS ... Personnel Management and Accounting Card Processing System   (MCD)
PERMAFROST ... Permanent Frost
PerManAb ... Personal Management Abstracts [*A publication*]
PERMAS .... Personnel Management Assistance System [*Military*]   (AABC)
PERMAS .... Personnel Management Assistance Team [*Military*]
PERMB ...... Permeability
Permbledhje Stud Inst Kerkimeve Gjeol Miner ... Permbledhje Studimesh. Instituti i Kerkimeve Gjeologijke dhe Minerale [*A publication*]
Permbledhje Stud Inst Stud Kerkimeve Ind Miner ... Permbledhje Studimesh. Instituti i Studimeve dhe Kerkimeve Industirale e Minerale [*A publication*]
PErMC .... Mercyhurst College, Erie, PA [*Library symbol*] [*Library of Congress*]   (LCLS)
PERME .... Propellants, Explosives, and Rocket Motors Establishment [*British*]   (RDA)
Perm Found Med Bull ... Permanente Foundation Medical Bulletin [*A publication*]
Perm Gos Ped Inst Ucen Zap ... Permskii Gosudarstvennyi Pedagogiceskii Institut. Ucenye Zapiski [*A publication*]
Perm Gos Univ Ucen Zap ... Permskii Gosudarstvennyi Universitet Imeni A. M. Gor'kogo. Ucenye Zapiski [*A publication*]
PERMIC ...... Personnel Management Information Center [*Navy*]   (NVT)
PERMINVAR ... Permeability Invariant
PERMIXT .... Permixtus [*Mixed*] [*Pharmacy*]   (ROG)
PERMLY ..... Permanently
Perm Politehn Inst Sb Naucn Trudov ... Permskii Politehniceskii Institut. Sbornik Naucnyh Trudov [*A publication*]
PERMR .... Permanent Residence
PERMREP ... Permanent Representation to North Atlantic Council [*NATO*]   (NATG)
PERMS .... Process and Effluent Radiological Monitoring System [*Nuclear energy*]   (NRCH)
PERMSS .... Process and Effluent Radiological Monitoring and Sampling System [*Nuclear energy*]   (NRCH)
PERMT .... Permanent   (ROG)
PERMU .... Permanent Magnet Users Association [*Defunct*]   (EA)
Perm Way ... Permanent Way [*A publication*]
PERNOGRA ... Permission Not Granted [*Military*]
PER OP EMET ... Peracta Operatione Emetici [*When the Operation of the Emetic is Finished*] [*Pharmacy*]   (ROG)
Per Or Cas ... Perry's Oriental Cases [*Bombay*]   (DLA)
PEROX .... Peroxide
PERP .... Perpendicular   (AAG)
PERP .... Perpetual   (ADA)
Per P .... Perrault's Prevoste de Quebec   (DLA)
PERP .... Personnel Processing   (MUGU)
Perpet .... Perpetual   (DLA)
Per Poly CE ... Periodica Polytechnica. Chemical Engineering [*A publication*]
Per Poly EE ... Periodica Polytechnica. Electrical Engineering [*A publication*]
Per Poly ME ... Periodica Polytechnica. Mechanical Engineering [*A publication*]
Per Pract B ... Personnel Practice Bulletin [*A publication*]
Per Pro .... Per Procurationem [*By Proxy, By the Action Of*] [*Legal term*] [*Latin*]
PER PROC ... Per Procurationem [*By Proxy, By the Action Of*] [*Legal term*] [*Latin*]
Per Psy ...... Personnel Psychology [*A publication*]
PERR .... Premature Engine Removal Rate   (AAG)
Perrault ...... Perrault's Conseil Superieur [*Canada*]   (DLA)
Perrault ...... Perrault's Prevoste de Quebec   (DLA)
Perrault ...... Perrault's Quebec Reports   (DLA)
PERRLA ..... Pupils Equal, Round, React to Light and Accommodation [*Medicine*]
Perry .... Perry's Oriental Cases [*Bombay*]   (DLA)
Perry .... [*Sir Erskine*] Perry's Reports in Morley's East Indian Digest   (DLA)
Perry & D .... Perry and Davison's English King's Bench Reports   (DLA)
Perry & D (Eng) ... Perry and Davison's English King's Bench Reports   (DLA)
Perry Ins .... Perry's English Insolvency Cases [*1831*]   (DLA)
Perry & K .... Perry and Knapp's English Election Cases   (DLA)
Perry & Kn ... Perry and Knapp's English Election Cases   (DLA)
Perry OC .... Perry's Oriental Cases [*Bombay*]   (DLA)
PERS .... Performance Evaluation Reporting System [*DoD*]
Pers .... Persae [*of Aeschylus*] [*Classical studies*]   (OCD)
Pers .... Perseus [*Constellation*]
PERS .... Persia [*Obsolete*]
Pers .... Persius [*34-62AD*] [*Classical studies*]   (OCD)
PERS .... Person

PERS .... Personal
PERS .... Personal Diagnostics [*NASDAQ symbol*]   (NQ)
Pers .... Personalist [*A publication*]
PERS .... Personnel   (AFM)
Pers .... Personnel [*A publication*]
Pers .... Perspektiv [*A publication*]
PERS .... Preliminary Engineering Reports   (MUGU)
PERSACLIT ... Peritus in Sacred Liturgy [*Roman Catholic*]
PERSACS ... Personnel Structure and Composition System [*Military*]
Pers Adm ... Personnel Administrator [*A publication*]
Pers Am Hist ... Perspectives in American History [*A publication*]
PERSC .... Public Education Religion Studies Center   (EA)
PERSCEN ... Personnel Center
PERSCON ..... Personnel Support of Contingency Operations [*Military*]
Pers Comput World ... Personal Computer World [*A publication*]
PERSCON ... Personnel Control [*Military*]
PERSD ...... Personnel Department [*Marine Corps*]
PERSDEP ... Personnel Deployment Report [*Military*]
PERSEP ..... Pershing Survivability Evaluation Program [*Military*]   (MCD)
PERSEVCE ... Perseverance   (ROG)
PERSEXP ... Personal Expense Money
Pers Finance LQ ... Personal Finance Law Quarterly Report [*A publication*]
Pers Guid J ... Personnel and Guidance Journal [*A publication*]
Pershad ... Privy Council Judgments [*1829-69*] [*India*]   (DLA)
Pers Inj Comment'r ... Personal Injury Commentator   (DLA)
Pers Inj LJ ... Personal Injury Law Journal   (DLA)
PERSINS ..... Personnel Information System [*Army*]
PERSINSCOM ... Personnel Information Systems Command [*Army*]   (AABC)
PERSINSD ... Personnel Information Systems Directorate [*Military Personnel Center*]   (AABC)
PERSIR .... Personnel Inventory Report   (AABC)
Pers J .... Personnel Journal [*A publication*]
PERSL .... Personal
Pers Manage ... Personnel Management [*A publication*]
Pers Manage Abstr ... Personnel Management Abstracts [*A publication*]
Pers Mgt ...... Personnel Management [*A publication*]
Pers New Mus ... Perspectives of New Music [*A publication*]
PERSOF ..... Personnel Officer [*Navy*]
Person .... Personalist [*A publication*]
PERSON ..... Personnel Simulation On-Line [*Department of State*] [*Computer program*]
Personal & Soc Psychol Bull ... Personality and Social Psychology Bulletin [*A publication*]
Personnel Exec ... Personnel Executive [*A publication*]
Personnel Guidance J ... Personnel and Guidance Journal [*A publication*]
Personnel & Guid J ... Personnel and Guidance Journal [*A publication*]
Personnel J ... Personnel Journal [*A publication*]
Personnel Manag (London) ... Personnel Management (London) [*A publication*]
Personnel Mgmt ... Personnel Management [*A publication*]
Personnel Mgt Abstracts ... Personnel Management Abstracts [*A publication*]
Personnel Practice B ... Personnel Practice Bulletin [*A publication*]
Personnel Practice Bul ... Personnel Practice Bulletin [*A publication*]
Personnel Psych ... Personnel Psychology [*A publication*]
Personnel Psychol ... Personnel Psychology [*A publication*]
Personn Pract Bull ... Personnel Practice Bulletin [*A publication*]
PERSP .... Perspective   (MSA)
Persp .... Perspective [*Record label*]
PERSPAY ... Personnel and Pay [*Project*] [*Navy*]
Persp Biol ... Perspectives in Biology and Medicine [*A publication*]
Perspec ...... Perspective [*A publication*]
Perspec Biol & Med ... Perspectives in Biology and Medicine [*A publication*]
Perspec Ed ... Perspectives on Education [*A publication*]
Perspect Accredit ... Perspectives on Accreditation [*A publication*]
Perspect Am Hist ... Perspectives in American History [*A publication*]
Perspect Biol Med ... Perspectives in Biology and Medicine [*A publication*]
Perspect Brain Sci ... Perspectives in the Brain Sciences [*A publication*]
Perspect Cardiovasc Res ... Perspectives in Cardiovascular Research [*A publication*]
Perspect Hum Reprod ... Perspectives in Human Reproduction [*A publication*]
Perspect Int ... Perspectives Internationales [*A publication*]
Perspective K ... Perspective (Karachi) [*A publication*]
Perspectives Latino-Am ... Perspectives Latino-Americaines [*A publication*]
Perspect Med ... Perspectives in Medicine [*A publication*]
Perspect Medicaid Medicare Manage ... Perspectives on Medicaid and Medicare Management [*A publication*]
Perspect Nephrol Hypertens ... Perspectives in Nephrology and Hypertension [*A publication*]
Perspect Pediatr Pathol ... Perspectives in Pediatric Pathology [*A publication*]
Perspect Polon ... Perspectives Polonaises [*A publication*]
Perspect Powder Metall ... Perspectives in Powder Metallurgy [*A publication*]
Perspect Psychiatr ... Perspectives Psychiatriques [*A publication*]
Perspect Psychiatr Care ... Perspectives in Psychiatric Care [*A publication*]
Perspect Virol ... Perspectives in Virology [*A publication*]
Perspekt Phil ... Perspektiven der Philosophie [*A publication*]
Persp N Mus ... Perspectives of New Music [*A publication*]
Pers Prac Bul ... Personnel Practice Bulletin [*A publication*]

Pers Pract Bull ... Personnel Practice Bulletin [*A publication*]
PERSPROC ... Personnel Processing
Pers Psych ... Personnel Psychology [*A publication*]
Pers Psych C ... Perspectives in Psychiatric Care [*A publication*]
Pers Psychol ... Personnel Psychology [*A publication*]
Pers Rep Exec ... Personal Report for the Executive [*A publication*]
PERSSEPCENT ... Personnel Separation Center
PERSTAT... Personnel Status Report [*Military*]
PERSTATREP ... Personnel Status Report [*Military*]
PERS & TRACOMD ... Personnel and Training Command
PERSTRAN ... Personal Transportation [*Navy*]
PERSYST... Personal Systems Technology, Inc. [*Irvine, CA*] [*Hardware manufacturer*]
PERT .... Patients Experience of the Relationship with the Therapist Method
PERT .... Pertain (AABC)
PERT .... Pertussis [*Whooping cough*]
PERT .... Program Evaluation Research Task (IEEE)
PERT .... Program Evaluation and Review Technique [*Data processing*] [*Computer performance management*]
PERTCO..... Program Evaluation and Review Technique with Cost
PERTHS .... Perthshire [*County in Scotland*]
PERTO .... Pertaining To (NVT)
Per Tr .... Perry on Trusts (DLA)
PERTRAN... Perturbation Transport [*NASA*]
PERTSIM.... Program Evaluation and Review Technique Simulation [*Game*]
PERT-TAM ... Program Evaluation and Review Technique Task, Action, and Milestone Items
PERT/TIME ... Program Evaluation and Review Technique/Time Analyzer [*Sperry UNIVAC*]
PERU .... Production Equipment Records Unit (IEEE)
Peru Dir Gen Mineria Bol ... Peru Ministerio de Fomento y Obras Publicas. Direccion General de Mineria. Boletin [*A publication*]
PERUG .... Perusing (ROG)
Peru Minist Agric Dir Gen Invest Agropecu Bol Tec ... Peru. Ministerio de Agricultura. Direccion General de Investigaciones Agropecuarias. Boletin Tecnico [*A publication*]
Peru Minist Agric Serv Invest Promoc Agrar Bol Tec ... Peru. Ministerio de Agricultura. Servicio de Investigacion y Promocion Agraria. Boletin Tecnico [*A publication*]
PERUSA..... Perspectives - United States of America [*History course*]
Peru Serv Geol Min Bol ... Peru. Servicio de Geologia y Mineria. Boletin [*A publication*]
Peru Serv Geol Min Estud Espec ... Peru. Servicio de Geologia y Mineria. Estudios Especiales [*A publication*]
Peru Serv Geol Min Geodinamica Ing Geol ... Peru. Servicio de Geologia y Mineria. Geodinamica e Ingenieria Geologica [*A publication*]
PERUV .... Peruvian
PERV .... Pervert [*or Perverted*] [*FBI standardized term*]
PErV .... United States Veterans Administration Hospital, Erie, PA [*Library symbol*] [*Library of Congress*] (LCLS)
PErVM....... Villa Maria College, Erie, PA [*Library symbol*] [*Library of Congress*] (LCLS)
PERYLENE ... Peri-Dinaphthalene [*A fluorophore*] [*Organic chemistry*]
PES .... IEEE Power Engineering Society [*New York, NY*] (EA)
PES .... Pan European Survey [*A publication*]
PES .... Paraendocrine Syndrome [*Endocrinology*]
PES .... Parent Egg Seed
PES .... Partido Ecuatoriano Socialista [*Ecuadorean Socialist Party*]
PES .... Parts Engineering Support
PES .... Patent Examining System
PES .... Pecos Resources [*Vancouver Stock Exchange symbol*]
Pes .... Pesahim (BJA)
PES .... Peshawar [*Pakistan*] [*Seismograph station code, US Geological Survey*] [*Closed*] (SEIS)
PES .... Philosophy of Education Society (EA)
PES .... Photoelectric Scanner
PES .... Photoelectron Spectroscopy
PES .... Photojet Edge Sensor
PES .... Physicians Equity Services
PES .... Pictorial Eleven Society [*Formerly, PE*] [*Absorbed by PCS*] (EA)
PES .... Pointing Error Sensor (MCD)
PES .... Polyethersulfone [*Organic chemistry*]
PES .... Polyethylene Sodium Sulfonate [*Anticoagulant*]
PES .... Post-Enumeration Survey [*Statistics*]
PES .... Postextrasystolic Potentiation [*Cardiology*]
PES .... Poultry and Egg Situation
PES .... Power Engineering Society
PES .... Preexcitation Syndrome [*Cardiology*]
Pes .... Pressure, End-Systole [*Cardiology*]
PES .... Problem-Etiology-Signs [*or Symptoms*] [*Nursing*]
PES .... Production Engineering Service
PES .... Production Engineering Specification (NG)
PES .... Professional Examination Service
PES .... Program Emphasis Statement [*US Employment Service*] [*Department of Labor*]
PES .... Program Execution System
PES .... Programed Electrical Stimulation [*Neurophysiology*]
PES .... Projected Engagement Scheduler [*Military*] (CAAL)

PESA.......... Petroleum Electric Supply Association [*Defunct*] (EA)
PESA.......... Petroleum Equipment Suppliers Association [*Houston, TX*] (EA)
PESA.......... Proton Elastic-Scattering Analysis
Pesca Mar ... Pesca y Marina [*A publication*]
Pesca Pesqui ... Pesca y Pesquisa [*A publication*]
PESC Rec IEEE Power Electron Spec Conf ... PESC Record. IEEE [*Institute of Electrical and Electronics Engineers*] Power Electronics Specialists Conference [*A publication*]
PESD.......... Program Element Summary Data [*DoD*]
PESD.......... Program Execution Subdirective (AABC)
PESDC........ Properties of Electrolyte Solutions Data Center [*National Bureau of Standards*]
PESDS .... Program Element Summary Data Sheet [*DoD*]
Pesh .... Peshitta [*Syriac translation of the Bible*] (BJA)
Peshawar.... All India Reporter, Peshawar [*1933-50*] (DLA)
Peshawar.... Indian Rulings, Peshawar Series [*1933-47*] (DLA)
P & ESI .... Physical and Engineering Sciences Division [*Army Research Office*]
PESIA........ Postal Employees Salary Increase Act of 1960
PESIC........ Parti du Progres Economique et Social des Independants Congolais Luluabourg [*Party for Economic and Social Progress of the Congolese Independents in Luluabourg*]
Pesik .... Pesikta de-Rav Kahana (BJA)
Pesikt .... Pesikta de-Rav Kahana (BJA)
PesiktR ...... Pesikta Rabbati (BJA)
PESM .... Photoelectron Spectromicroscope
PESO.......... Participation Enriches Science, Music, and Art Organizations [*Orlando, Florida*]
PESO.......... Plant Engineering Shop Order (AAG)
PESO.......... Product Engineering Services Office [*DoD*]
PESOD .... Proceedings. Electrochemical Society [*A publication*]
PESOS .... Prepare, Explain, Show, Observe, Supervise [*Formula*] [*LIMRA*]
PESPD .... Periodically Speaking [*A publication*]
Pesqui Agropecuar Brasil Ser Agron ... Pesquisa Agropecuaria Brasileira. Serie Agronomia [*A publication*]
Pesqui Agropecuar Brasil Ser Vet ... Pesquisa Agropecuaria Brasileira. Serie Veterinaria [*A publication*]
Pesqui Agropecu Bras ... Pesquisa Agropecuaria Brasileira [*A publication*]
Pesqui Agropecu Bras Ser Agron ... Pesquisa Agropecuaria Brasileira. Serie Agronomia [*A publication*]
Pesqui Agropecu Bras Ser Vet ... Pesquisa Agropecuaria Brasileira. Serie Veterinaria [*A publication*]
Pesqui Agropecu Bras Ser Zootec ... Pesquisa Agropecuaria Brasileira. Serie Zootecnia [*A publication*]
Pesqui Agropecu Nordeste Recife ... Pesquisas Agropecuarias do Nordeste Recife [*A publication*]
Pesqui Bot (Porto Alegre) ... Pesquisas Botanica (Porto Alegre) [*A publication*]
Pesqui Commun (Porto Alegre) ... Pesquisas Communications (Porto Alegre) [*A publication*]
Pesqui Med ... Pesquisa Medica [*A publication*]
Pesquisas Antropol ... Pesquisas Antropologia [*A publication*]
Pesqui Secc B Cienc Nat (Porto Alegre) ... Pesquisas. Seccao B. Ciencias Naturais (Porto Alegre) [*A publication*]
Pesqui Zool (Porto Alegre) ... Pesquisas Zoologia (Porto Alegre) [*A publication*]
PesR........... Pesikta Rabbati (BJA)
PESR.......... Planning Element System Report (NATG)
PESR......... Precision Echo Sounder Recorder
PESR......... Pseudoequivalent Service Rounds [*Military*] (NVT)
PEsS .... East Stroudsburg State College, East Stroudsburg, PA [*Library symbol*] [*Library of Congress*] (LCLS)
PESS .... Pessus [*Pessary*] [*Pharmacy*]
PEST .... Parameter Entity Symbol Translator [*Elstree Computing Ltd.*] [*Software package*]
PEST .... Parameter Estimation by Sequential Testing [*Computer*]
PEST .... Pesticide Evaluation Summary Tabulation
PEST .... Production Evaluation Surveillance Test
Pest Bioch ... Pesticide Biochemistry and Physiology [*A publication*]
Pest Contr ... Pest Control [*A publication*]
Pest Contro ... Pest Control [*A publication*]
Pest Control Circ ... Pest Control Circular [*A publication*]
PESTD .... Proceedings. European Society of Toxicology [*A publication*]
PESTDOC ... Pest Control Literature Documentation [*Derwent Publications Ltd.*] [*Bibliographic database*] [*Information service*] [*London, England*] (EISS)
PESTF........ Proton Event Start Forecast [*Solar weather information*]
Pestic Abstr ... Pesticides Abstracts and News Summary [*A publication*]
Pestic Abstr News Sum Sect C Herbic ... Pesticides Abstracts and News Summary. Section C. Herbicides [*A publication*]
Pestic Biochem Physiol ... Pesticide Biochemistry and Physiology [*A publication*]
Pestic Monit J ... Pesticides Monitoring Journal [*A publication*]
Pestic Progr ... Pesticide Progress [*A publication*]
Pestic Res Rep Agric Can ... Pesticide Research Report. Agriculture Canada [*A publication*]
Pestic Sci... Pesticide Science [*A publication*]
Pestic Tech ... Pesticide and Technique [*A publication*]

Pest Infest Control Lab Rep (Lond) ... Pest Infestation Control. Laboratory Report (London) [*A publication*]
Pest Infest Control (Lond) ... Pest Infestation Control. Laboratory Report (London) [*A publication*]
Pest Infest Res Rep Pest Infest Lab Agric Res Counc ... Pest Infestation Research Report. Pest Infestation Laboratory. Agricultural Research Council [*A publication*]
Pest Mon J ... Pesticides Monitoring Journal [*A publication*]
Pest Sci..... Pesticide Science [*A publication*]
PESY .... People Say. Bimonthly Newsletter [*Canada*] [*A publication*]
PET .... Panel on Education and Training [*COSATI*]
PET .... Panel on Educational Terminology [*Office of Education*]
PET .... Parent Effectiveness Training [*A course of study*]
PET .... Particle Electrostatic Thruster
PET .... Patterned Epitaxial Technology   (IEEE)
PET .... Pelotas [*Brazil*] [*Airport symbol*]   (OAG)
PET .... Pentaerythritol [*Organic chemistry*]
PET .... Pentaerythritol Tetranitrate [*Also, PETN*] [*Explosive, vasodilator*]
PET .... Performance Evaluation Team   (NRCH)
PET .... Performance Evaluation Test
PET .... Periodic Environmental Test
PET .... Periodic Evaluation Test
PET .... Peripheral Equipment Tester [*Data processing*]   (BUR)
PET .... Personal Effectiveness Training   (MCD)
PET .... Personal Electronic Transactor [*Computer*] [*Commodore Business Machines*]
PET .... Pet, Inc., Corporate Information Center, St. Louis, MO [*OCLC symbol*]   (OCLC)
Pet............. Peter [*New Testament book*]
Pet............. Peters   (DLA)
Pet............. Peters' Prince Edward Island Reports [*1850-72*] [*Canada*]   (DLA)
Pet............. Peters' United States Circuit Court Reports   (DLA)
Pet............. Peters' United States District Court Reports, Admiralty Decisions   (DLA)
Pet............. Peters' United States Supreme Court Reports [*26-41 United States*]   (DLA)
Pet............. Petihta   (BJA)
PET .... Petition
PET .... Petrine [*Of, or relating to, Peter the Apostle or Peter the Great*]
PET .... Petroleum
PET .... Petropavlovsk [*USSR*] [*Geomagnetic observatory code*]
PET .... Petropavlovsk [*USSR*] [*Seismograph station code, US Geological Survey*]   (SEIS)
PET .... Petrotech, Inc. [*Toronto Stock Exchange symbol*]
PET .... Photoemission Tube
PET .... Phototropic Energy Transfer
PET .... Physical Equipment Table
PET .... Pierre Elliott Trudeau [*Canadian prime minister*] [*Acronymic designation considered derogatory*]
PET .... Point of Equal Time [*Aviation*]
PET .... Polyester
PET .... Poly(ethylene Terephthalate) [*Organic chemistry*]
PET .... Portable Earth Terminal [*NASA*]
PET .... Portable Electronic Telephone
PET .... Position-Event-Time
PET .... Positron-Emission Tomography
PET .... Potential Evapotranspiration
PET .... Pre-Eclamptic Toxemia [*Medicine*]
PET .... Pre-Employment Training   (OICC)
PET .... Preliminary Evaluation Team
PET .... Preliminary Examination Team [*NASA*]
PET .... Preprimary Evaluation and Training
PET .... Pressurization Events Trainer
PET .... Probe Ephemeris Tape
PET .... Process Evaluation Tester
PET .... Production Environmental Tests
PET .... Production Evaluation Test
PET .... Program Evaluator and Tester [*Data processing*]
PET .... Prototype Evaluation Test
PET .... Psychiatric Emergency Team
PET .... Pupil Evaluation Team [*Education*]
PETA......... Pentaerythritol Triacrylate [*Organic chemistry*]
PETA......... People for the Ethical Treatment of Animals [*Washington, DC*]   (EA)
PETA......... Performance Evaluation and Trend Analysis   (NASA)
PETA......... Plutonium Equipment Transfer Area [*Nuclear energy*]   (NRCH)
PETA......... Portable Electronic Traffic Analyzer [*British*]
Pet Ab....... Petersdorff's Abridgment   (DLA)
Pet Abr....... Petersdorff's Abridgment [*1660-1823*]   (DLA)
Pet Ad .... Peters' United States District Court Reports, Admiralty Decisions   (DLA)
Pet Ad Dec ... Peters' United States District Court Reports, Admiralty Decisions   (DLA)
Pet Adm ...... Peters' United States District Court Reports, Admiralty Decisions   (DLA)
Pet Adm App ... Peters' United States District Court Reports, Admiralty Decisions [*Appendix*]   (DLA)
Pet Ad R..... Peters' United States District Court Reports, Admiralty Decisions   (DLA)

Pet Age ...... Petroleum Age [*A publication*]
PETAT....... Periodic Inspection Turn-Around Time [*Military*]   (AFIT)
Pet Bail...... Petersdorff on Bail [*1824*]   (DLA)
Pet Br .... Bellewe's Cases Tempore Henry VIII [*England*]   (DLA)
Pet Br .... Brooke's New Cases [*Petit Brooke*] [*1515-58*]   (DLA)
PETC.......... Pittsburgh Energy Technology Center [*Formerly, PERC*] [*Department of Energy*]
PETC.......... Portable Equipment Test Chamber   (MCD)
Pet CC....... Peters' United States Circuit Court Reports   (DLA)
Pet Chem Ind Conf Rec Conf Pap ... Petroleum and Chemical Industry Conference. Record of Conference Papers [*United States*] [*A publication*]
Pet Chem Ind Dev ... Petroleum and Chemical Industry Developments [*India*] [*A publication*]
Pet Chem (USSR) ... Petroleum Chemistry (USSR) [*A publication*]
Pet Cir CR ... Peters' Condensed United States Circuit Court Reports   (DLA)
Pet Cond.... Peters' Condensed Reports, United States Supreme Court   (DLA)
Pet Cond Rep ... Peters' Condensed United States Circuit Court Reports   (DLA)
PETD......... Petroleum Development [*NASDAQ symbol*]   (NQ)
Pet Dig ...... Peters' United States Digest   (DLA)
Pet Dig ...... Peticolas' Texas Digest   (DLA)
PETE......... Petersburg National Battlefield
PETE......... Pneumatic End to End
PETE......... Product Engineering Tribute to Excellence
PETE......... Proof and Experimental Test Establishment [*Canada*]   (MCD)
Pet Econ ..... Petroleum Economist [*A publication*]
Pet Eng ...... Petroleum Engineer [*A publication*]
Pet Eng Int ... Petroleum Engineer International [*A publication*]
Pet Equip ... Petroleum Equipment [*A publication*]
Pet Equip Serv ... Petroleum Equipment and Services [*A publication*]
Peter .... Analysis and Digest of the Decisions of Sir George Jessel, by A. P. Peter [*England*]   (DLA)
Petermanns Geog Mitt ... Petermanns Geographische Mitteilungen [*A publication*]
Petermanns Geogr Mitt ... Petermanns Geographische Mitteilungen [*A publication*]
Petermanns Mitt ... Petermanns. A. Mitteilungen aus J. Perthes Geographischer Anstalt [*A publication*]
Petermanns Mitt Erg ... Petermanns Mitteilungen. Ergaenzungsheft [*Gotha*] [*A publication*]
Peterm Geog ... Petermanns Geographische Mitteilungen [*A publication*]
Peter Phot Mag ... Petersen's Photographic Magazine [*A publication*]
Peters .... Haviland's Prince Edward Island Chancery Reports, by Peters [*1850-72*] [*Canada*]   (DLA)
Peters .... Peters' United States Supreme Court Reports [*26-41 United States*]   (DLA)
Peters' Ad ... Peters' United States District Court Reports, Admiralty Decisions   (DLA)
Peters Adm ... Peters' United States District Courts Reports, Admiralty Decisions   (DLA)
Peters' Adm Dec ... Peters' United States District Court Reports, Admiralty Decisions   (DLA)
Peters' Admiralty Dec ... Peters' United States District Court Reports, Admiralty Decisions   (DLA)
Peters' Adm R ... Peters' United States District Court Reports, Admiralty Decisions   (DLA)
Peters Adm Rep ... Peters' United States District Court Reports, Admiralty Decisions   (DLA)
Peters CC ... Peters' United States Circuit Court Reports   (DLA)
Petersd Ab ... Petersdorff's Abridgment   (DLA)
Pet Gaz ...... Petroleum Gazette [*A publication*]
Pet & Gaze ... Petrol si Gaze [*Romania*] [*A publication*]
Pet Gaze Supl ... Petrol si Gaze. Supliment [*Romania*] [*A publication*]
Pet Geol ...... Petroleum Geology [*A publication*]
Pet Geol Taiwan ... Petroleum Geology of Taiwan [*A publication*]
Petg Pr & Ag ... Petgrave's Principal and Agent [*1857*]   (DLA)
Peth Dis ...... Petheram's Discovery by Interrogations [*1864*]   (DLA)
Pet Hydrocarbons ... Petroleum and Hydrocarbons [*India*] [*A publication*]
PETI .... Percent of Travel Involved   (FAAC)
PETI .... Portable Electronic Typewriter Interface [*Applied Creative Technology, Inc.*]
Pet Indep ... Petroleum Independent [*A publication*]
Pet Inf........ Petrole Informations [*A publication*]
Pet Int .... Petroleo Internacional [*A publication*]
Pet Interam ... Petroleo Interamericano [*A publication*]
Pet Int (London) ... Petroleum International (London) [*A publication*]
Petit Br....... Petit Brooke, or Brooke's New Cases, English King's Bench [*1515-58*]   (DLA)
Petit J Brass ... Petit Journal du Brasseur [*A publication*]
PETITN....... Petition
Pet L Nat .... Petersdorff's Law of Nations   (DLA)
Pet Manage ... Petroleum Management [*A publication*]
Pet Mitt ...... Petermanns Mitteilungen [*A publication*]
Pet M & S ... Petersdorff's Master and Servant [*1876*]   (DLA)
PETN......... Pentaerythritol Tetranitrate [*Also, PET*] [*Explosive, vasodilator*]
PETN......... Petition
Pet News.... Petroleum News [*Taiwan*] [*A publication*]
Pet Newsl... Petroleum Newsletter [*A publication*]

PETNR....... Petitioner
PETOA ...... Petrotecnica [*A publication*]
Pet Outlook ... Petroleum Outlook [*A publication*]
PETP .... (Phenylethyl)phenyltetrahydropyridine [*Organic chemistry*]
PETP .... Poly(ethylene Terephthalate) [*Organic chemistry*]
PETP .... Preliminary Engineering Technical Proposal
Pet Petrochem ... Petroleum and Petrochemicals [*Japan*] [*A publication*]
Pet Petrochem Int ... Petroleum and Petrochemical International [*England*] [*A publication*]
Pet P M....... Petersen's Photographic Magazine [*A publication*]
Pet Press Serv ... Petroleum Press Service [*England*] [*A publication*]
Pet Process....... Petroleum Processing [*A publication*]
PETQ .... Petro Quest, Inc. [*NASDAQ symbol*]   (NQ)
PETR .... Petitioner
PETR .... Petra Resources, Inc. [*NASDAQ symbol*]   (NQ)
PETRA........ Positron-Electron Tandem Ring Accelerator [*Nuclear*]
PETRASAFE ... Petroleum Transport Scheme for Assistance in Freight Emergencies [*A publication*]
PETRB....... Petroleum Review [*A publication*]
PETRD........ Petrologie [*A publication*]
Pet Refiner ... Petroleum Refiner [*A publication*]
PETRES ..... Petroleum Reserves [*Navy*]
PETRESO... Petroleum Reserves Office [*or Officer*]
Pet Rev........ Petrocorp Review [*A publication*]
Pet Rev....... Petroleum Review [*A publication*]
PETRIBURG ... Petriburgensis [*Signature of the Bishops of Peterborough*] [*Latin*]   (ROG)
Petr Inde .... Petroleum Independent [*A publication*]
PETRL....... Petroleum   (AABC)
PETRO .... Petroleum
Petro/Chem Eng ... Petro/Chem Engineer [*A publication*]
PETRODEG ... Petroleum Degrading [*Agent*]
PETROFERTIL ... PETROBRAS Fertilizantes, SA [*State enterprise*] [*Rio De Janeiro, Brazil*]
PETROG.... Petrographic
PETROGR ... Petrography
PETROL ..... Petroleum
PETROL ..... Petrology
Petrol Abstr ... Petroleum Abstracts [*A publication*]
Petrol Eng ... Petroleum Engineer [*A publication*]
Petrol Eng Int ... Petroleum Engineer International [*A publication*]
Petroleos Mexicanos Servicio Inf ... Petroleos Mexicanos Servicio de Informacion [*A publication*]
Petroleum ... Petroleum Economist [*A publication*]
Petroleum Gaz ... Petroleum Gazette [*A publication*]
Petrol Gaz ... Petroleum Gazette [*A publication*]
Petrol Geol ... Petroleum Geology [*A publication*]
Petrol Independ ... Petroleum Independent [*A publication*]
Petrol Inform ... Petrole Informations [*A publication*]
Petrol News ... Petroleum News [*A publication*]
Petrol Rev ... Petroleum Review [*A publication*]
Petrol Tecnol ... Petroleo y Tecnologia [*A publication*]
PETROMIN ... General Petroleum & Mineral Organization [*Saudi Arabia state-owned oil company*]
PETROMISA ... PETROBRAS Mineracao Sociedade Anonima [*State enterprise*] [*Rio De Janeiro, Brazil*]
Petron........ Petronius [*First century AD*] [*Classical studies*]   (OCD)
PETRONET ... Petroleum Network [*Distribution and interdiction model*]   (MCD)
Petron Satyric ... Petronius' [*Titus*] Arbiter, Satyricon, Etc.   (DLA)
PETROPHIL ... Petroleum Philatelic Society International   (EA)
PETROPOL ... Petropolis [*St. Petersburg*] [*Imprint*] [*Latin*]   (ROG)
Petrozavodsk Gos Univ Ucen Zap ... Petrozavodskii Gosudarstvennyi Universitet. Ucenye Zapiski [*A publication*]
Petr Sit....... Petroleum Situation [*A publication*]
PETS .... Pacific Electronics Trade Show
PETS .... Peripheral Equipment Test Set
PETS .... Polaris Engineering Technical Service [*Missiles*]
PETS .... Positions Equipment Task Summary   (AAG)
PETS .... Prior to Expiration of Term of Service [*Reenlistments*] [*Military*]
PETS .... Programed Extended Time Sharing [*Data processing*]
Pet SC....... Peters' United States Supreme Court Reports [*26-41 United States*]   (DLA)
PETSEC ..... Petroleum Section [*Allied Force Headquarters*]
Pet Substitutes ... Petroleum Substitutes [*A publication*]
Pet Suppl... Supplement to Petersdorff's Abridgment   (DLA)
PETT .... Pettibone Corp. [*NASDAQ symbol*]   (NQ)
PETT .... Phototropic Energy Transfer Technique
PETT .... Positron Emission Transaxial [*or Transverse*] Tomography [*Roentgenography*]
PETTA....... Petroleum Times [*A publication*]
Pet Tech.... Petrole et Techniques [*A publication*]
Pet Technol ... Petroleum Technology [*A publication*]
Pet Tech Rev ... Petroleum Technical Review [*A publication*]
Pet Times... Petroleum Times [*A publication*]
Pet Today ... Petroleum Today [*A publication*]
Petty SR ... Petty Sessions Review [*A publication*]
PETV .... Planar Epitaxial Tuning Varactor
PETV .... Process Evaluation Test Vehicle
Pet W........ Petroleum Week [*A publication*]
Pet World ... Petroleum World [*London*] [*A publication*]

Pet World (London) ... Petroleum World (London) [*A publication*]
Pet World (Los Angeles) ... Petroleum World (Los Angeles) [*A publication*]
Pet World Oil ... Petroleum World and Oil [*A publication*]
Pet World Oil Age ... Petroleum World and Oil Age [*A publication*]
PETX .... PETX Petroleum [*NASDAQ symbol*]   (NQ)
PEU .... Paneuropa-Union [*Paneuropean Union*] [*Munich, West Germany*]   (EA-IO)
PEU .... Paneuropean Union [*Munich, West Germany*]   (EA-IO)
PEU .... Port Expander Unit
PEU .... Protected Environment Unit [*Medicine*]
PEUA......... Pelvic Exam under Anesthesia [*Medicine*]
PEUBA ...... Publikacije Elektrotehnickog Fakulteta Univerziteta u Beogradu. Serija Matematika i Fizika [*A publication*]
PEUU......... Polyether Polyurethane Urea [*Organic chemistry*]
peV............ Peak Electron Volts
PEV .... Peak Envelope Voltage [*Telecommunications*]   (TEL)
PEV .... Pleasant Valley [*California*] [*Seismograph station code, US Geological Survey*]   (SEIS)
P Evang..... Pentecostal Evangel [*A publication*]
PEVE......... Prensa Venezolana [*Press agency*] [*Venezuela*]
PEVI .... Perry's Victory and International Peace Memorial National Monument
PEVL .... Polyethylene Expanded Video Longitudinal Cable   (MCD)
PEVM .... Personal'naia Elektronnaia Vychislitel'naia Mashina [*Personal Computer*] [*Russian*]
PEVM .... Professional'naia Elektronnaia Vychislitel'naia Mashina [*Professional Computer*] [*Russian*]
PEW .... Passive Electronics Warfare   (NG)
PEW .... Percussion Welding
PEW .... Peshawar [*Pakistan*] [*Airport symbol*]   (OAG)
PEW .... Philosophy East and West [*A publication*]
PE & W ..... Philosophy East and West [*A publication*]
PEWO........ Plant Engineering Work Order   (MCD)
PEWR .... Plant Engineering Work Release   (AAG)
PEWS .... Platoon Early Warning System   (RDA)
PEWS .... Plutonium Equipment Warm Shop [*Nuclear energy*]   (NRCH)
PEWV .... Pulmonary Extravascular Water Volume [*Physiology*]
PEX .... People Express [*Newark, NJ*] [*FAA designator*]   (FAAC)
PEX .... Per Example
PEX .... Phenazine Ethosulfate [*Biochemistry*]
PEX .... Pronto Explorations Ltd. [*Vancouver Stock Exchange symbol*]
PEXP .... People Express Airlines, Inc. [*NASDAQ symbol*]   (NQ)
PEXRAD.... Programed Electronic X-Ray Automatic Diffractometer
PEY .... Pengelly Mines Ltd. [*Vancouver Stock Exchange symbol*]
PEY .... Photoelectric Yield
PEZ .... Pleasanton, TX [*Location identifier*] [*FAA*]   (FAAL)
PEZAF....... Pezamerica Resources Corp. [*NASDAQ symbol*]   (NQ)
PF .... Frankford Public Library, Frankford, PA [*Library symbol*] [*Library of Congress*]   (LCLS)
PF .... French Polynesia [*Two-letter standard code*]   (CNC)
PF .... Pacifica Foundation   (EA)
PF .... Paderewski Foundation [*Defunct*]   (EA)
PF .... Page Footing   (BUR)
PF .... Page Formatter   (MDG)
PF .... Panchromatic Film   (ADA)
PF .... Paper and Foil [*Capacitor*]   (DEN)
pf .... Paracel Islands [*MARC country of publication code*] [*Library of Congress*]   (LCCP)
PF .... Parachute Facility   (NASA)
PF .... Parachute Flare   (NVT)
PF .... Parafascicular Nucleus [*Neuroanatomy*]
PF .... Parallel Fold
PF .... Parapsychology Foundation   (EA)
PF .... Partition Free   (NRCH)
PF .... Passage Free   (ROG)
PF .... Pathfinder Fund [*An association*] [*Chestnut Hill, MA*]   (EA)
PF .... Patriotic Front [*Zimbabwean*]   (PPW)
PF .... Patrol Vessel, Frigate [*Navy symbol*]
P/F .... Pattern Flight [*Also, P/FLT*]   (MUGU)
PF .... Payload Forward Bus [*NASA*]   (MCD)
PF .... Payload Function [*NASA*]   (MCD)
PF .... Peace and Freedom Party   (DLA)
PF .... Peak Flow [*Medicine*]
PF .... Peak Frequency
PF .... Peanut Flour
PF .... Pedal Furrow
PF .... Pen Friends   (EA)
PF .... Pennsylvania Folklife [*A publication*]
PF .... Pensee Francaise [*A publication*]
PF .... Pension Fund
PF .... Peregrine Fund   (EA)
PF .... Perfect
PF .... Performance Factor
PF .... Perfusion Fixation [*Histology*]
PF .... Permanent Force [*Canadian Militia before 1940*]
PF .... Permeability Factor
pf .... Perofskite [*CIPW classification*] [*Geology*]
PF .... Personal Fouls [*Basketball*]
PF .... Personal Security File [*Number*] [*British Secret Service*]
PF .... Personality Factor
P & F.......... Petroleum and Fuel

Pf	Pfeifferella [*Genus of bacteria*]
PF	Pfennig [*Monetary unit in Germany*]
PF	Pfleuger Flug-Betriehs GmbH [*Germany*] [*ICAO designator*] (FAAC)
PF	Phenol-Formaldehyde [*Organic chemistry*]
PF	Philatelic Foundation (EA)
PF	Philosophy Forum [*A publication*]
PF	Photogrammetric Facility [*Army*]
P & F	Photography and Focus [*A publication*]
PF	Physicians Forum [*Chicago, IL*] (EA)
PF	Pianoforte [*Soft, then Loud*] [*Music*]
pF	Picofarad
P & F	Pike and Fischer's Administrative Law (DLA)
P & F	Pike and Fischer's Federal Rules Service (DLA)
P & F	Pike and Fischer's OPA Price Service (DLA)
PF	Pilgrim Fellowship [*Supports foreign missionaries*] (EA)
PF	[*The*] Pioneer & Fayette Railroad Co. [*AAR code*]
PF	Piu Forte [*A Little Louder*] [*Music*]
PF	Plain Face [*Construction*]
PF	Plane Frame [*Camutek*] [*Software package*]
P & F	Planning and Forecasting (MCD)
PF	Planning Forum [*Formed by a merger of NASCP and Planning Executives Institute - PEI*] [*Oxford, OH*] (EA)
P & F	Plant and Facilities
PF	Plantar Fasciaitis [*Medicine*]
PF	Plantar Flexion [*Medicine*]
PF	Platelet Factor [*Hematology*]
PF	Plentiful Foods [*A publication*] [*Department of Agriculture*]
PF	Plot Function [*Data processing*]
PF	Pneumatic Float
PF	Poco Forte [*Rather Loud*] [*Music*]
PF	Poe Foundation (EA)
PF	Poesie Francaise [*A publication*]
PF	Point Foundation (EA)
PF	Point of Frog [*Electronics*] (MSA)
PF	Points For [*Football*]
PF	Pole Fittings [*JETDS nomenclature*] [*Military*] (CET)
PF	Police Forces [*British*]
PF	Police Foundation (EA)
PF	Polisario Front [*Popular Front for the Liberation of Saguia El Hamra and Rio De Oro*] [*Moroccan*] (PD)
PF	Polish Folklore [*A publication*]
PF	Poloidal Field (MCD)
PF	Popular Foodservice [*A publication*]
PF	Popular Forces [*ARVN*]
PF	Por Favor [*Please*] [*Portuguese*]
PF	Portal Fibrosis [*Medicine*]
PF	Position Failure
P/F	Post Flight (AFIT)
PF	Postage Free (ROG)
PF	Posture Foundation [*Initialism is used in brand of sneaker shoe, PF Flyers*]
PF	Power Factor [*Radio*]
PF	Power Frame [*Telecommunications*] (TEL)
PF	Powered Flight (NASA)
PF	Prace Filologiczne [*A publication*]
P/F	Practical Factors
PF	Preference
PF	Preferred
PF	Preflight
PF	Pressure Fan (AAG)
PF	Prime Function (NASA)
PF	Probability of Failure (NASA)
PF	Procurator Fiscal
PF	Profile (KSC)
PF	Program Function [*Data processing*] (IBMDP)
PF	Programable Format [*Perforating keyboard*]
PF	Progressive Foundation (EA)
PF	Project Friend (EA)
PF	Projectile Fragment
PF	Proof
PF	Prop Forward
PF	Proposed Finding [*Nuclear energy*] (NRCH)
PF	Protection Factor
PF	Protoplasmic Fracture [*Freeze etching in microscopy*]
PF	Proximity Fuze [*Bomb, rocket, or shell*]
PF	PsychoHistory Forum [*Ridgewood, NJ*] (EA)
PF	Psynetics Foundation (EA)
P/F	Pteropod/Foraminifera [*Ratio in coastal waters*]
PF	Public Finance [*A publication*]
PF	Pulmonary Factor [*Medicine*]
PF	Pulse Frequency
PF	Pulverized Fuel
P F	Pump-Out Facilities [*Nautical charts*]
PF	Punch Off [*Data processing*] (BUR)
PF	Purge Fans [*Nuclear energy*] (NRCH)
PF	Pygmy Fund (EA)
PFA	Panarcadian Federation of America (EA)
PFA	Papermakers Felt Association (EA)
PFA	Para-Fluorophenylalanine [*Biochemistry*]
PFA	Parti de la Federation Africaine [*African Federation Party*]

PFA	Participating Field Activity [*DoD*]
PFA	Perfluoroalkoxy [*Organic chemistry*]
PFA	Phosphonoformic Acid [*Antiviral compound*]
PFA	Pianists Foundation of America (EA)
PFA	Pierce Ferry [*Arizona*] [*Seismograph station code, US Geological Survey*] [*Closed*] (SEIS)
PFA	Pierre Fauchard Academy [*Summit, IL*] (EA)
PFA	Pioneer Fraternal Association (EA)
PFA	Pitch Follow-Up Amplifier
PFA	Plan for Action (MCD)
PFA	Polish Falcons of America (EA)
PFA	Polyfurfuryl Alcohol [*Organic chemistry*]
PFA	Polyurethane Foam Association [*Southfield, MI*] (EA)
PFA	Popular Flying Association [*British*]
PFA	Post Flight Analysis
PFA	Prescription Footwear Association [*New York, NY*] (EA)
PFA	Prison Families Anonymous [*Hempstead, NY*] (EA)
PFA	Professional Farmers of America (EA)
PFA	Professional Fraternity Association (EA)
PFA	Program and File Analysis
PFA	Proportional Fluid Amplifier
PFA	Pulverized Fuel Ash (IEEE)
PFA	Pure Fluid Amplification
PFAB	Prairie Farm Assistance Act
8PFAB	Eight-Parallel-Form Anxiety Battery [*Psychology*]
PFAC	Panepirotic Federation of America and Canada (EA)
P/FACCTL	Pad Facility Controls [*Aerospace*] (AAG)
PFAD	Palm Fatty Acid Distillate [*Organic chemistry*]
Pfaelzer H	Pfaelzer Heimat [*A publication*]
PFAM	Programed Frequency Amplitude Modulation
PFAP	Poly(fluoroalkoxyphosphazene) [*Organic chemistry*]
PFAR	Popular Front for Armed Resistance [*Pakistan*]
PFAR	Power Fail Automatic Restart [*Data processing*]
PFAR	Preliminary Failure Analysis Report [*NASA*] (KSC)
PFAT	Preliminary Flight Appraisal Test (MCD)
PFAW	People for the American Way (EA)
PFAX	Primefax, Inc. [*NASDAQ symbol*] (NQ)
PFB	Partei Freier Buerger [*Free Citizens' Party*] [*West Germany*] (PPW)
PFB	Passo Fundo [*Brazil*] [*Airport symbol*] (OAG)
PFB	Payload Feedback [*NASA*] (MCD)
PFB	Payload Forward Bus [*NASA*] (MCD)
PFB	Photo Flash Battery
PFB	Pneumatic Float Bridge
PFB	Position Feedback (MCD)
PFB	Preformed Beams [*SONAR*]
PFB	Pressure Fed Booster (NASA)
PFB	Pressurized Fluid-Bed [*Chemical engineering*]
PFB	Provisional Frequency Board [*ITU*]
PFBA	Poly(perfluorobutyl Acrylate) [*Organic chemistry*]
PFBC	Pressurized Fluidized Bed Combustion
PFBFA	Power Farming and Better Farming Digest (Australia) [*A publication*]
PFBHA	Pentafluorobenzylhydroxylamine Hydrochloride [*Analytical biochemistry*]
PFBRG	Pneumatic Float Bridge
PFC	Pacific City, OR [*Location identifier*] [*FAA*] (FAAL)
PFC	Passed Flying College [*British*]
PFC	Pathfinder Industries Ltd. [*Formerly, Pathfinder Financial Corporation*] [*Toronto Stock Exchange symbol*]
PFC	Peak Follower Circuit
PFC	Peculiar Facility Change (AAG)
PFC	Pen Fancier's Club (EA)
PFC	Pennsylvania Public Library Film Center, University Park, PA [*OCLC symbol*] (OCLC)
PFC	Perfluorocarbon [*Organic chemistry*]
PFC	Perfluorochemical [*Organic chemistry*]
PFC	Performance Flight Certification [*NASA*] (NASA)
PFC	Permanent Families for Children [*An association*] [*New York, NY*] (EA)
PFC	Persistent Fetal Circulation [*Medicine*]
PFC	Physicians for Choice (EA)
PFC	Plan Filing Cabinet
PFC	Plaque-Forming Cell [*Immunochemistry*]
PFC	Pneumatic Function Controller
PFC	Police Forces [*British*]
PFC	Positive Feedback Circuit
PFC	Postflight Checklist (MCD)
PFC	Power Factor Corrector (MCD)
PFC	Prairie Fiction Collection, Alberta Culture [*UTLAS symbol*]
PFC	Praying for Corporal [*Private First Class desirous of promotion, or female in wartime desirous of a boyfriend*]
PFC	Preflight Console (MCD)
PFC	Preliminary Flight Certification [*NASA*]
PFC	Presley-ites Fan Club (EA)
PFC	Pressure Function Controller
PFC	Primary Flight Control
PFC	Private, First Class [*Army*]
PFC	Progressive Fish-Culturist [*A publication*]
PFC	Pulse-Flow Coulometry
PFC	Pulsed Flame Combustor

PFCA......... Performance Ford Club of America   (EA)
PFCA......... Plastic Food Container Association [*Defunct*]
PFCD......... Primary Flight Control Display
PFCE......... Preface   (ROG)
PFCE......... Preference   (AAG)
PFCF......... Payload Flight Control Facility [*NASA*]   (MCD)
PFCM........ Pittsburgh Festival of Contemporary Music [*Record label*]
PFCO........ Position Field Classification Officer
PFCO........ Preferred Financial [*NASDAQ symbol*]   (NQ)
PFCS........ Primary Flight Control System   (MCD)
PFCS........ Primary Flow Control System [*Nuclear energy*]   (NRCH)
PFCS........ Program and Funds Control System   (MCD)
PFD .... Particle [*or Proton*] Flux Density
PFD .... Perfluorodecalin [*Organic chemistry*]
PFD .... Personal Flotation Device [*Life jacket*]
PFD .... Planning Factors Development   (MCD)
PFD .... Position Fixing Device   (ADA)
PFD .... Power Flux Density [*Telecommunications*]   (TEL)
PFD .... Preferred [*Stock*]   (AAG)
PFD .... Preliminary Functional Description   (CINC)
PFD .... Present for Duty
PFD .... Primary Flash Distillate [*Chemical technology*]
PFD .... Primary Flight Display
PFD .... Process Flow Diagram   (NRCH)
PFD .... Puffed [*Freight*]
PFD .... Pulse-Frequency Diversity [*Electronics*]   (NG)
PFDA........ Perfluorodecanoic Acid [*Organic chemistry*]
PFDA........ Post Flight Data Analysis
PFDA........ Precision Frequency Distribution Amplifier
PFDA........ Pulse-Frequency Distortion Analyzer
PFDCCA .... Prodemca: Friends of the Democratic Center in Central America [*Washington, DC*]   (EA)
PFDR........ Pathfinder [*Aircraft*]
PFDR........ Preferred Risk Life [*NASDAQ symbol*]   (NQ)
PfdrBad...... Pathfinder Badge [*Military decoration*]   (AABC)
PFE........... Pacific Fruit Express Co. [*AAR code*]
PFE........... Partido Feminista de Espana [*Feminist Party of Spain*]   (PPW)
PFE........... Pfizer, Inc. [*NYSE symbol*]
PFE........... Physics of Failure in Electronics [*A publication*]   (MCD)
PFE........... Plenum Fill Experiment [*Nuclear energy*]   (NRCH)
PFE........... Post Fire Evaluation [*Military*]   (CAAL)
PFE........... Post Flight Evaluation
PFE........... Priests for Equality   (EA)
PFE........... Program for Executives
PFE........... Purchaser Furnished Equipment   (NATG)
PFEFES...... Pacific and Far East Federation of Engineering Societies
PFEL......... Pacific Far East Line
PFEP .... Programable Front-End Processor [*Data processing*]
PFES .... Pan American Federation of Engineering Societies
PFES .... Proposed Final Environmental Statement [*Department of Energy*]
PFES .... Pure Fluid Encoder System
PFF........... Pathfinder Force [*British RADAR designation which became overall synonym for RADAR*] [*Military*]
PFF........... Permanent Family File [*Navy*]   (NG)
PFF........... Planning Factors File   (MCD)
PFF........... Police Field Force   (CINC)
PFF........... Porcine Follicular Fluid [*Endocrinology*]
PFF........... Primary Focus Feed [*Satellite communications*]
PFF........... Proposed Fabric Flammability Standard [*Consumer Product Safety Commission*]
PFF........... Protein Fat-Free [*Food technology*]
PFFC .... Parallel-Flow Film Cooling
PFF Convrt ... Paper, Film, and Foil Converter [*A publication*]
PFF Convt ... Paper, Film, and Foil Converter [*A publication*]
PFF Inc....... Police-FBI Fencing, Incognito [*Phony fencing ring operated by Washington, DC, law enforcement agents during 1976 to identify and arrest area thieves*]
PFFS .... Pacific First Federal Savings Bank [*NASDAQ symbol*]   (NQ)
PFFX .... Profiling Fixture
PFG........... Paeoniflorigenone [*Biochemistry*]
PFG........... Pfennig [*Penny*] [*Monetary unit in Germany*]
PFG........... Piping and Filter Gallery   (NRCH)
PFG........... Primary Frequency Generator
PFG........... Pulsed Field Gradient [*Electroanalytical chemistry*]
PFGGA ...... Professional Geographer [*A publication*]
PFGM........ Guided Missile Patrol Escort [*Ship symbol*]   (NATG)
PFGX........ Pacific Fruit Growers Express
PFH .... Hudson, NY [*Location identifier*] [*FAA*]   (FAAL)
PFH .... Pafco Financial Holdings [*Toronto Stock Exchange symbol*]
PfH .... Pfaelzische Heimatblaetter [*A publication*]
PFHA........ Paso Fino Horse Association [*Bowling Green, FL*]   (EA)
PFI........... Pacific Forest Industries   (EA)
PFI........... People First International [*Salem, OR*]   (EA)
PFI........... Pet Food Institute [*Washington, DC*]   (EA)
PFI........... Photo Finishing Institute [*Defunct*]   (EA)
PFI........... Physical Fitness Index
PFI........... Picture and Frame Institute [*Defunct*]   (EA)
PFI........... Pie Filling Institute [*Defunct*]   (EA)
PFI........... Pipe Fabrication Institute [*Springdale, PA*]   (EA)
PFI........... Port Fuel Injector [*Automotive engines*]

PFI .... Power Failure Indicator [*NASA*]   (KSC)
PFI .... Prison Fellowship International [*Washington, DC*]   (EA)
PFI .... Profile Index. Micromedia Limited [*A publication*]
PFIA .... Police and Firemen's Insurance Association   (EA)
PFIA .... Prudential Fixed Income Advisors [*Business and trade*]
PFIAB .... President's Foreign Intelligence Advisory Board [*Abolished, 1977*]   (AFM)
PFIB .... Pentafluoroiodosylbenzene [*Organic chemistry*]
PFil .... Prace Filologiczne [*A publication*]
PFil .... Przeglad Filozoficzny [*A publication*]
PFIM.......... Pure Fluid Impact Modulator
PFIN.......... P & F Industries, Inc. [*NASDAQ symbol*]   (NQ)
PFI & R ...... Part Fill In and Ram [*Construction*]
Pfitzner ..... Hans Pfitzner-Gesellschaft. Mitteilungen [*A publication*]
PFIU .... Plot File Import Utility [*IBM Corp.*]
Pfizer Med Monogr ... Pfizer Medical Monographs [*A publication*]
PFJ .... Patreksfjordur [*Iceland*] [*Airport symbol*]   (OAG)
PFJ .... Polar Front Jet Stream   (ADA)
PFJR.......... Patellafemoral Joint Reaction [*Physiology*]
PFK .... Payload Function Key [*NASA*]   (MCD)
PFK .... Perfluorokerosene [*Heat transfer agent*]
PFK .... Phosphofructokinase [*An enzyme*]
PFK .... Programed Function Keyboard [*Data processing*]
PFL............ Fort Sill, OK [*Location identifier*] [*FAA*]   (FAAL)
PFL............ Pacific Cassiar [*Formerly, Pacific Cassiar Limited*] [*Toronto Stock Exchange symbol*] [*Vancouver Stock Exchange symbol*]
PFL............ Pennsylvania Folklife [*A publication*]
PFL............ Primary Freon Loop   (NASA)
PFL............ Propulsion Field Laboratory
PFL............ Public Facility Loans
PFLA .... Popular Front for the Liberation of Ahvaz [*Iran*]
PFLAB........ Pfluegers Archiv [*A publication*]
PFLAB........ Pfluegers Archiv. European Journal of Physiology [*A publication*]
P-FLAG ...... Federation of Parents and Friends of Lesbians and Gays   (EA)
Pflanzenschutzber ... Pflanzenschutzberichte [*A publication*]
Pflanzenschutz-Nachr ... Pflanzenschutz-Nachrichten [*A publication*]
Pflanzenschutz-Nachr (Am Ed) ... Pflanzenschutz-Nachrichten (American Edition) [*A publication*]
PflBau PflSchutz PflZucht ... Pflanzenbau, Pflanzenschutz, Pflanzenzucht [*A publication*]
PFLDA........ Physics of Fluids [*A publication*]
PFLF.......... People, Food, and Land Foundation   (EA)
PFLFT .... Pubblicazioni. Facolta di Lettere e Filosofia. Universita di Torino [*A publication*]
PFLO .... Popular Front for the Liberation of Oman   (PD)
PFLOAG..... Popular Front for the Liberation of Oman and the Arabian Gulf   (PD)
PFLOLS...... Portable Fresnel-Lens Optical-Landing System   (NG)
PFLP.......... Popular Front for the Liberation of Palestine   (PD)
PFLP-GC.... Popular Front for the Liberation of Palestine - General Command   (PD)
PFLSA........ Physics of Fluids. Supplement [*A publication*]
P/FLT......... Pattern Flight [*Also, P/F*]   (MUGU)
Pflueg Arch ... Pfluegers Archiv. European Journal of Physiology [*A publication*]
Pfluegers Arch Eur J Physiol ... Pfluegers Archiv. European Journal of Physiology [*A publication*]
Pfluegers Arch Ges Physiol ... Pfluegers Archiv fuer die Gesamte Physiologie [*A publication*]
Pfluegers Archiv Gesamte Physiol Menschen Tiere ... Pfluegers Archiv fuer die Gesamte Physiologie des Menschen und der Tiere [*A publication*]
PFLUS........ Publications. Faculte des Lettres. Universite de Strasbourg [*A publication*]
PFLV .... Pressure Fed Launch Vehicle [*NASA*]   (KSC)
PFM........... Little Franciscan Sisters of Mary [*Roman Catholic religious order*]
PFM........... Pacific Minesearch Ltd. [*Vancouver Stock Exchange symbol*]
PFM........... Patriots of Fort McHenry   (EA)
PFM........... Physiological Flow Model [*For simulating medical conditions*]
PFM........... Pitch Follow-Up Motor
PFM........... Plan for Maintenance [*Navy*]
PFM........... Planning Factors Management   (MCD)
PFM........... Platform   (NASA)
PFM........... Porcelain Fused to Metal [*Dentistry*]
PFM........... Power Factor Meter
PFM........... Precision Frequency Multivider   (KSC)
PFM........... Predictor Frame Memory
PFM........... Pressure Flow Meter
P & FM....... Programs and Financial Management [*Navy*]
PFM........... Pulse-Forming Machine
PFM........... Pulse-Frequency Modulation [*RADAR*]
P/FM......... Pylon/Fin Movement
PFM........... University of Pittsburgh, Falk Library - Health Professions, Pittsburgh, PA [*OCLC symbol*]   (OCLC)
PFMA .... Pipe Fittings Manufacturers Association [*Later, APFA*]   (EA)
PFMA .... Plumbing Fixture Manufacturers Association [*Defunct*]   (EA)
PFMC .... Pacific Fishery Management Council   (EA)
PFMR .... Pasadena Foundation for Medical Research [*California*]

PFMR .... Project Funds Management Record (MCD)
PFN .... Panama City [*Florida*] [*Airport symbol*] (OAG)
PFN .... Pantyffynnon [*British depot code*]
PFN .... Parti des Forces Nouvelles [*New Forces Party*] [*French*] (PPW)
PFN .... Passamaquoddy Ferry & Navigation Co. [*AAR code*]
PFN .... Permanent File Name
PFN .... Plasma Fibronectin [*Biochemistry*]
PFN .... Pulse-Forming Network
PFNA .... Pentecostal Fellowship of North America (EA)
PFNS .... Position Fixing Navigation System (AABC)
PFNTU .... Pathfinder Navigation Training Unit [*Military*]
PFO .... Paphos [*Cyprus*] [*Airport symbol*] (OAG)
PFO .... Partly Filled Out [*Questionnaire*]
PFO .... Patent Foramen Ovale [*Cardiology*]
PFO .... Pitch Follow-Up Operation
PFO .... Pomona Public Library, Pomona, CA [*OCLC symbol*] (OCLC)
PFO .... Postal Finance Officer
PFO .... Procurement Field Office
PFO .... Pyrolysis Fuel Oil [*Petroleum refining*]
PFO .... Spofford, TX [*Location identifier*] [*FAA*] (FAAL)
PFOBA .... Paso Fino Owners and Breeders Association [*Later, PFHA*] (EA)
PFOD .... Presumed Finding of Death [*DoD*]
PFol .... Ridley Township Public Library, Folsom, PA [*Library symbol*] [*Library of Congress*] (LCLS)
PFouad .... Les Papyrus Fouad I [*A publication*] (OCD)
PFP .... Partnership for Productivity International (EA)
PFP .... Peace and Freedom Party (EA)
PFP .... Pensions for Professionals, Inc.
PFP .... Pentafluoropropionate [*or Pentafluoropropionyl*] [*Organic chemistry*]
PFP .... Pet-Facilitated Psychotherapy [*Psychiatry*]
PFP .... Platelet-Free Plasma [*Hematology*]
PFP .... Popular Front Party [*Ghanaian*] (PPW)
PFP .... Pore Forming Protein [*Biochemistry*]
PFP .... Post Flight Processor
PFP .... Postage Forward Parcels
PFP .... Products for Power [*Automotive components manufacturer*]
PFP .... Program File Processor
PFP .... Program Financial Plan (NASA)
PFP .... Program Forecast Period [*Military*] (AFIT)
PFP .... Programable Function Panel (NASA)
PFP .... Progressiewe Federale Party [*Progressive Federal Party*] [*South African*] (PPW)
PFP .... Proving for Production (MCD)
PFP .... Publishers for Peace [*An association*]
PFPA .... Pentafluoropropionic Anhydride [*Organic chemistry*]
PFPA .... Pro-Family Press Association [*Manassas, VA*] (EA)
PFPI .... Partnership for Productivity International [*Washington, DC*] (EA)
PFPI .... Pentafluoropropionyl Imidazole [*Organic chemistry*]
PFPM .... Production Flight Procedures Manual (MCD)
PFQ .... Preflight Qualification
PFr .... Franklin Public Library, Franklin, PA [*Library symbol*] [*Library of Congress*] (LCLS)
PFR .... Part Failure Rate
PFR .... Peak Flow Rate [*or Reading*] [*Medicine*]
PFR .... Perforator (DEN)
PFR .... Perkins Family Restaurant [*NYSE symbol*]
PFR .... Permanent Factory Repairable (MCD)
PFR .... Personal Financial Record (AABC)
PFR .... Pfarrer [*Pastor*] [*German*]
PFR .... Photoflash Relay
PFR .... Pike Fry Rhabdovirus
PFR .... Plug-Flow Reactor [*Engineering*]
PFR .... Polarized Frequency Relay
PFR .... Power Fail Recovery System [*Data processing*] (MDG)
PFR .... Power Fail/Restart
PFR .... Power Failure Release
PFR .... Precision Fathometer Recorder [*Raytheon Co.*]
PFR .... Preferred Resources, Inc. [*Vancouver Stock Exchange symbol*]
PFR .... Preflight Review [*NASA*] (KSC)
PFR .... Preheating, Falling-Film, Rising-Film [*Sections of a concentrator*] [*Chemical engineering*]
PFR .... Preliminary Flight Rating [*Air Force*]
PFr .... Presence Francophone [*A publication*]
PFR .... Problem/Failure Report
PFR .... Programed Film Reader [*System*]
pfr. .... Proofreader [*MARC relator code*] [*Library of Congress*]
PFR .... Prototype Fast Reactor
PFR .... Pulmonary Blood Flow Redistribution [*Medicine*]
PFR .... Pulse Frequency (MDG)
PFR .... Punch Feed Read (CMD)
PFRA .... Prairie Farm Rehabilitation Administration [*Canada*]
PFRA .... Problem-Focused Research Applications [*of ASRA*] [*National Science Foundation*]
PFRA .... Professional Football Referees Association (EA)
PFRA .... Professional Football Researchers Association (EA)
P & F Radio Reg ... Pike and Fischer's Radio Regulation Reporter (DLA)
PFRC .... Pacific Forest Research Centre [*Canada*] (ARC)
PFRD .... Preferred [*Stock*]

PFredY .... Joseph A. Yablonski Memorial Clinic, Fredericktown, PA [*Library symbol*] [*Library of Congress*] (LCLS)
PFRMG .... Performing (ROG)
PFRS .... Portable Field Recording System [*NASA*] (KSC)
PFRT .... Preliminary Flight Rating Test [*Air Force*]
PFRT .... Preliminary Flight Readiness Test [*NASA*] (KSC)
PFS .... P. F. Smith's Pennsylvania State Reports [*51-81 1/2 Pennsylvania*] (DLA)
PFS .... Parallel Filter System
P & FS .... Particles and Fields Subsatellite (KSC)
PFS .... Particles and Fields Subsatellite
PFS .... Percent Full Scale (KSC)
PFS .... Peripheral Fixed Shim [*Nuclear energy*] (NRCH)
PFS .... Personal and Family Survival [*Civil Defense*]
PFS .... Personal Filing System [*Data-base program*] [*Software Publishing Corp.*]
PFS .... Photofragment Spectroscopy
PFS .... Pitch Follow-Up System
PFS .... Pittsburgh, PA [*Location identifier*] [*FAA*] (FAAL)
PFS .... Porous Friction Surface [*Airfield pavement*]
PFS .... Precision Frequency Source
PFS .... Preflight School [*Military*]
PFS .... Press Fit Socket
PFS .... Primary Frequency Supply [*Telecommunications*] (TEL)
PFS .... Programable Frequency Standard
PFS .... Progress in Filtration and Separation [*Elsevier Book Series*] [*A publication*]
PFS .... Propellant Feed System
PFS .... Pulmonary Function Score [*Physiology*]
PFS .... Pure Fluid System
PFSA .... Pour Faire Ses Adieux [*To Say Good-Bye*] [*French*]
PFSh .... Partia Fashismit e Shqiperise [*Fascist Party of Albania*] (PPE)
PFSH .... Porcine Follicle Stimulating Hormone [*Endocrinology*]
PFSI .... Pittock Financial Service [*NASDAQ symbol*] (NQ)
PFSL .... Prudential Financial Services [*NASDAQ symbol*] (NQ)
P F Smith ... P. F. Smith's Pennsylvania State Reports [*51-81 1/2 Pennsylvania*] (DLA)
PFSO .... Postal Finance and Supply Office (AFM)
PFSR .... Program Financial Status Report (AAG)
PFSV .... Pilot-to-Forecaster Service (FAAC)
PFT .... Page Frame Table (BUR)
PFT .... Pancreatic Function Test [*Medicine*]
PFT .... Paper, Flat Tape
PFT .... Parafascicular Thalamotomy [*Medicine*]
PFT .... Parallel Fourier Transform
PFT .... Pet-Facilitated Therapy [*Psychiatry*]
PFT .... Physical Fitness Test
PFT .... Plastic Fuel Tank
PFT .... Portable Flame Thrower
PFT .... Positive Flight Termination (MUGU)
PFT .... Preflight Team [*Air Force*] (AFM)
PFT .... Preflight Tool (MCD)
PFT .... Professional Football Trainers (EA)
PFT .... Program Flying Training [*Air Force*] (AFM)
PFT .... Projective Field Theory
PFT .... Pulmonary Function Test [*Medicine*]
PFT .... Pulse Fourier Transform
PFTA .... Payload Flight Test Article [*NASA*] (MCD)
PFTB .... Preflight Test Bus (MCD)
PFTC .... Pestalozzi-Froebel Teachers College [*Illinois*]
PFTE .... Pianoforte [*Soft, then Loud*] [*Music*]
PFTE .... Portable Field Trainer/Evaluator (MCD)
PFTM .... Preliminary Flight Test Memo
PFTR .... Preliminary Flight Test Report
PFU .... Passive Filtration Unit
PFU .... Plaque-Forming Unit [*Immunochemistry*]
PFU .... Please Follow Up
PFU .... Pock-Forming Unit
PFU .... Preparation for Use
PFUA .... Pitch Follow-Up Amplifier
PFUEI .... Prime Focus Universal Extragalactic Instrument [*Astronomy*]
PFUM .... Pitch Follow-Up Motor
PFUO .... Pitch Follow-Up Operation
PFUS .... Pitch Follow-Up System
PFV .... Pestalozzi-Froebel-Verband [*Pestalozzi-Froebel Association*]
PFV .... Philippine Forces, Vietnam
PFV .... Physiological Full Value
PFV .... Pour Faire Visite [*To Make a Call*] [*French*]
PFVEA .... Professional Film and Video Equipment Association [*Irving, TX*] (EA)
PFW .... Power, Fulcrum, Weight
PFW .... Progressive Free Wave
PFWA .... Professional Football Writers of America (EA)
PFwB .... Budd Co., Fort Washington, PA [*Library symbol*] [*Library of Congress*] (LCLS)
PFWOAD ... Place from Which Ordered to Active Duty [*Military*]
PFwR .... William H. Rorer, Inc., Fort Washington, PA [*Library symbol*] [*Library of Congress*] (LCLS)
PFX .... Prefix (ROG)
PFX .... Proflex Ltd. [*Vancouver Stock Exchange symbol*]
PFY .... Prior Fiscal Year (AFIT)

PFYA..........	Predicted First-Year Average [*Law school*]
PFZ..........	Polar Front Zone [*Marine science*]　(MSC)
PF-ZAPU	Patriotic Front - Zimbabwe African People's Union　(PD)
PG	Air Gabon Cargo [*ICAO designator*]　(FAAC)
PG	Page [*or Pagination*] [*Online database field identifier*]
PG	Palestine Gazette [*A publication*]
PG	Papua New Guinea [*Two-letter standard code*]　(CNC)
PG	Paralysie Generale [*General Paralysis*] [*Medicine*] [*French*]
PG	Paregoric [*Slang*]
PG	Parental Guidance Suggested [*Formerly, GP*] [*Some material may not be suitable for preteenagers*] [*Movie rating*]
PG	Paris Granite
PG	Partial Gum [*Philately*]
PG	Past Grand [*Freemasonry*]
PG	Paste Grain [*Bookbinding*]
PG	Patrol Combatant [*Gunboat*] [*Navy symbol*]
PG	Patrologia Graeca [*A publication*]
PG	Patrologiae Cursus. Series Graeca [*A publication*]　(OCD)
PG	Pay Grade
PG	Pay Group
PG	Paying Guest
PG	PEACE [*Program for Emergency Assistance, Cooperation, and Education*] for Guatemala　(EA)
PG	Pedal Ganglion
PG	Pedal Groove
PG	Pelham Grenville Wodehouse [*British humorist, 1881-1975*]
Pg	Pentagram [*One billion metric tons*]
PG	Peptidoglycan [*Biochemistry*]
PG	Permanent Glow [*Telecommunications*]　(TEL)
PG	Permanent Grade
PG	Persian Gulf　(MCD)
PG	Pharmacopoeia Germanica [*German Pharmacopoeia*]
PG	Phosphatidylglycerol
PG	Phosphogluconate [*Biochemistry*]
PG	Photogrammetry
PG	Picogram
PG	Pipers Guild　(EA)
PG	Planning Group [*DoD*]
PG	Planning Guide [*HUD*]
PG	Plasma Glucose [*Hematology*]
PG	Plate Glass
PG	Plate-Glazed [*Paper*]
PG	Pollen Grain [*Botany*]
PG	Polyethylene Glycol [*Organic chemistry*]
PG	Polygalacturonase [*An enzyme*]
PG	Polyglycine [*Biochemistry*]
PG	Port Group [*Telecommunications*]　(TEL)
PG	Portugal
PG	Portuguese [*Language, etc.*]
pg	Portuguese Guinea [*Guinea-Bissau*] [*MARC country of publication code*] [*Library of Congress*]　(LCCP)
PG	Position Guide　(MCD)
PG	Postgraduate [*Refers to courses or students*] [*Slang*]
PG	Power Gain
PG	Power Generation　(MCD)
PG	Preacher General
PG	Predicted Grade [*IRS*]
PG	Pregnanediol Glucuronide [*Endocrinology*]
PG	Pregnant
PG	Press Gallery [*US Senate*]
PG	Pressure Gauge　(KSC)
PG	Prisonnier de Guerre [*Prisoner of War - POW*] [*French*]
PG	Pro-German [*Prisoner of war term*] [*World War I*]　(DSUE)
P & G	Procter & Gamble Co.
PG	Procter & Gamble Co. [*NYSE symbol*]
PG	Producers Group　(EA)
PG	Professional Group　(MCD)
PG	Program Generic [*Data processing*]　(TEL)
PG	Program Guidance
PG	Programer　(AAG)
PG	Project Group
PG	Proof Gallon [*Wines and spirits*]
PG	Propyl Gallate [*Antioxidant*] [*Organic chemistry*]
PG	Prostaglandin [*Also, Pg*] [*Biochemistry*]
PG	Protein Granule
PG	Proteoglycan [*Biochemistry*]
PG	Prothoracic Gland [*Insect anatomy*]
PG	Province Guard [*Cambodia*]　(CINC)
PG	Proving Ground
PG	Przeglad Geograficzny [*A publication*]
PG	Public Gaol [*British*]
PG	Pulse Gate
PG	Pulse Generator
PG	Pure Gum [*of envelopes*]
PG	Pyoderma Gangrenosum [*Medicine*]
PG	Pyrolytic Graphite　(MCD)
PG	Pyrotechnic Gyro　(AAG)
PG-13	Parental Guidance Suggested [*Now: Parents Strongly Cautioned. Some material may be inappropriate for children under 13*] [*Movie rating*]
PGA	Page [*Arizona*] [*Airport symbol*]　(OAG)

PGA	Paragould [*Arkansas*] [*Seismograph station code, US Geological Survey*]　(SEIS)
PGA	Pega Capital Resources [*Toronto Stock Exchange symbol*]
PGA	Pendulous Gyro Accelerometer
PGA	Phosphoglyceric Acid [*Biochemistry*]
PGA	Pin-Grid-Array [*Motorola, Inc.*]
PGA	Polyglycolic Acid [*Organic chemistry*]　(RDA)
PGA	Poly(L-glutamic Acid) [*Organic chemistry*]
PGA	Power Gain Antenna
PGA	Power Generating Assembly　(KSC)
PGA	Pressure Garment Assembly
PGA	Printing and Graphic Arts [*A publication*]
PGA	Producers Guild of America [*Beverly Hills, CA*]　(EA)
PGA	Professional Golfers' Association of America　(EA)
PGA	Professional Graphics Adaptor [*IBM Corp.*]
PGA	Professional Group Audio
PGA	Programable Gain Amplifier　(MCD)
PGA	Programable Gate Array
PGA	Prostaglandin A [*Biochemistry*]
PGA	Prostaglandin Analog [*Biochemistry*]
PGA	Pteroylmonoglutamic Acid [*Folic acid*] [*Also, FA, PteGlu*] [*Biochemistry*]
PGA	Punta Gorda Isles, Inc. [*American Stock Exchange symbol*]
PGA	Purchased Gas Adjustment
PGA	Pyrolysis Gas Analysis
PGAA	Upjohn Co. [*Research code symbol*]
PGAA	Prompt Gamma-Ray Activation Analysis
P-GABA	Phenyl-gamma-aminobutyric Acid [*Organic chemistry*]
PGAC	Professional Group - Automatic Control
PGAH	Pineapple Growers Association of Hawaii　(EA)
PGAM	Pacific Gamble Robinson Co. [*NASDAQ symbol*]　(NQ)
PGAM	Phosphoglyceromutase [*An enzyme*]
PGANE	Professional Group on Aeronautical and Navigational Electronics
PGA-NOC ...	Permanent General Assembly of National Olympic Committees
PGAP	Professional Group - Antennas and Propagation
PGAPL	Preliminary Group Assembly Parts List
PGAR	Provisional Government of the Algerian Republic
PGase	Polygalacturonase [*An enzyme*]
PGAZA	Petrol si Gaze [*A publication*]
Pg B	Bachelor of Pedagogy
PGB	Patrol Gunboat [*Navy symbol*]　(NATG)
PGB	Prostaglandin B [*Biochemistry*]
PGB	Protestant Guild for the Blind [*Belmont, MA*]　(EA)
PGB	Pyrographalloy Boron
PGBA	Piece Goods Buyers Association [*Defunct*]　(EA)
PGBA	Possum Growers and Breeders Association　(EA)
PGBD	Pegboard [*Freight*]
PGBM	Pulse Gate Binary Modulation　(MCD)
PGbSH	Seton Hill College, Greensburg, PA [*Library symbol*] [*Library of Congress*]　(LCLS)
PGBTR	Professional Group - Broadcast and Television Receivers
PGBTS	Professional Group - Broadcast Transmission Systems
PGbU	University of Pittsburgh at Greensburg, Greensburg, PA [*Library symbol*] [*Library of Congress*]　(LCLS)
PGC	Geneva College, Beaver Falls, PA [*OCLC symbol*]　(OCLC)
PGC	Gettysburg College, Gettysburg, PA [*Library symbol*] [*Library of Congress*]　(LCLS)
PGC	Pacific Geoscience Centre [*Canadian Department of Energy, Mines, and Resources*] [*Research center*]　(RCD)
PGC	Pagurian Corporation Ltd. [*Toronto Stock Exchange symbol*]
PGC	Past Grand Commander [*Freemasonry*]　(ROG)
PGC	Pelican Gospel Commentaries [*Harmondsworth*] [*A publication*]
PGC	Per Gyro Compass [*Navigation*]
PGC	Persian Gulf Command [*World War II*]
PGC	Pontine Gaze Center [*Eye anatomy*]
PGC	Port Group Control [*Telecommunications*]　(TEL)
PGC	Potassium Gold Cyanide [*Inorganic chemistry*]
PGC	Potential Gas Committee
PGC	Primordial Germ Cell
PGC	Process Gas Chromatography
PGC	Process Gas Consumers Group　(EA)
PGC	Professional Graphics Controller [*IBM Corp.*]
PGC	Program Generation Center [*Military*]　(CAAL)
PGC	Programed Gain Control
PGC	Proving Ground Command [*Air Force*]
PGC	Pulsed Gas Crymotography
PGC	Pyrolysis Gas Chromatography
PGcC	Grove City College, Grove City, PA [*Library symbol*] [*Library of Congress*]　(LCLS)
PGCC	Power Generation Control Complex [*Nuclear energy*]　(NRCH)
PGCE	Post Graduate Certificate of Education
PGCh	Past Grand Chaplain [*Freemasonry*]
PGCOA	Pennsylvania Grade Crude Oil Association [*Bradford, PA*]　(EA)
PGCP	Professional Group - Component Parts
PGCRA	Professional Golf Club Repairmen's Association [*Dunedin, FL*]　(EA)
PGCS	Professional Group - Communications Systems
PGCT	Professional Group - Circuit Theory

PGCU .... International Printing and Graphic Communications Union
PGD .... Pango Gold Mines Ltd. [*Toronto Stock Exchange symbol*]
PGD .... Past Grand Deacon [*Freemasonry*]
PGD .... Phosphogluconate Dehydrogenase [*Also, PGDH*] [*An enzyme*]
PGD .... Pinion Gear Drive
PGD .... Planar Gas Discharge   (MCD)
PGD .... Prostaglandin D [*Biochemistry*]
PGD .... Pulse Generator Display
PGD .... Punta Gorda [*Florida*] [*Airport symbol*]   (OAG)
PGDB .... Propylene Glycol Dibenzoate [*Organic chemistry*]
PGDC .... Provincial Grand Director of Ceremonies [*Freemasonry*]
PGDCS ...... Power Generation, Distribution, and Control
                     Subsystem (MCD)
PGDF .... Pilot Guide Dog Foundation [*Columbus, OH*]   (EA)
PGDH .... 15-Hydroxyprostaglandin Dehydrogenase [*An enzyme*]
PGDH .... Phosphogluconate Dehydrogenase [*Also, PGD*] [*An enzyme*]
PGDN .... Propylene Glycol Dinitrate [*Organic chemistry*]
PGDS .... Pioneer Ground Data System
PGDS .... Pulse Generator Display System
PG & E ...... Pacific Gas and Electric [*Rock music group*]
PG & E ...... Pacific Gas & Electric Co.
PGE .... Pacific Great Eastern Railway Co. [*Nicknames: Prince George
                     Eventually, Please Go Easy*] [*Later, British Columbia
                     Railway*] [*AAR code*]
PGE .... Page Petroleum Ltd. [*Toronto Stock Exchange symbol*]
PGE .... Phenyl Glycidyl Ether [*Organic chemistry*]
PGE .... Platinum Group Element [*Chemistry*]
PGE .... Population Growth Estimation
PGE .... Pore Gradient Electrophoresis
PGE .... Portland General Electric Co., Library, Portland, OR [*OCLC
                     symbol*]   (OCLC)
PGE .... Portland Grain Exchange   (EA)
PGE .... Precision Gimbal Experiment
PGE .... Prime Group Engineer   (AAG)
PGE .... Professional Group - Education
PGE .... Prostaglandin E [*Biochemistry*]
PGE .... Purge   (NASA)
PGED .... Professional Group - Electronic Devices
PGEM .... Professional Group - Engineering Management
PGEWS ...... Professional Group on Engineering Writing and Speech
                     [*Institute of Radio Engineers; now IEEE*]
PGF .... Pacific Gamefish Foundation [*Honolulu, HI*]   (EA)
PGF .... Perpignan [*France*] [*Airport symbol*]   (OAG)
PGF .... Plerocercoid Growth Factor [*Endocrinology*]
PGF .... Presentation Graphic Feature [*Data processing*]
PGF .... Prostaglandin F [*Biochemistry*]
PGFC .... Periodical Guide for Computerists [*Applegate Computer
                     Enterprises*] [*Grants Pass, OR*] [*Information
                     service*]   (EISS)
PGFS .... Pennsylvania German Folklore Society. Bulletin [*A publication*]
PGG .... Petrogold Financial Corp. [*Vancouver Stock Exchange symbol*]
PGG .... Pneumatic Ground Group
PGG .... Power Generation Group   (NRCH)
PGG .... Prostaglandin G [*A prostaglandin endoperoxide*]
                     [*Biochemistry*]
PGGJ-A ...... Philippine Geographical Journal [*A publication*]
PGH .... Patrol Gunboat (Hydrofoil) [*Navy symbol*]
PGH .... Pituitary Growth Hormone [*Endocrinology*]
PGH .... Port Group Highway [*Telecommunications*]   (TEL)
PGH .... Prostaglandin H [*A prostaglandin endoperoxide*]
                     [*Biochemistry*]
PGHA .... Park Gallatin Hereford Association   (EA)
PGHFE ...... Professional Group - Human Factors in Electronics
Pgh Leg Journal ... Pittsburgh Legal Journal [*Pennsylvania*]   (DLA)
PGHM .... Payload Ground Handling Mechanism [*NASA*]   (MCD)
PGHMPR .... People's Great Hural of the Mongolian People's Republic
PGHS .... Public-General Hospital Section [*American Hospital
                     Association*]   (EA)
PGHTA ...... Progress in Hemostasis and Thrombosis [*A publication*]
PGHTS ...... Port Group Highway Timeslot [*Telecommunications*]   (TEL)
PGI .... Chitato [*Angola*] [*Airport symbol*]   (OAG)
PGI .... Paris Gestion Informatique [*Paris Informatics Administration*]
                     [*France*] [*Information service*]   (EISS)
PGI .... Peripheral Graphics, Incorporated
PGI .... Phosphoglucoisomerase [*An enzyme*]
PGI .... Ply-Gem Industries, Inc. [*American Stock Exchange symbol*]
PGI .... Port Group Interface [*Telecommunications*]   (TEL)
PGI .... Professional Group - Instrumentation
PGI .... Project Group, Incorporated [*Advertising agency*] [*Acronym
                     now used as official name of agency*]
PGI .... Prostaglandin I [*Biochemistry*]
PGI .... Provigo, Incorporated [*Toronto Stock Exchange symbol*]
PGI .... Pyrotechnics Guild International [*White Marsh, MD*]   (EA)
PGIE .... Professional Group - Industrial Electronics
PGiess .... Griechische Papyri im Museum des Oberhessischen
                     Geschichtsvereins zu Giessen [*A publication*]   (OCD)
PGIM .... Professional Group on Instrumentation and Measurement
                     [*National Bureau of Standards*]
PGIS .... Project Grant Information System
PGIT .... Professional Group - Information Theory
PGJ .... Personnel and Guidance Journal [*A publication*]

PGJ .... Pipeline Girth Joint
PGJD .... Past Grand Junior Deacon [*Freemasonry*]
PGJN .... Pomegranate Guild of Judaic Needlework   (EA)
P & G Jour ... Pipeline and Gas Journal [*A publication*]
PGJW .... Past Grand Junior Warden [*Freemasonry*]   (ROG)
PGK .... Pangkalpinang [*Indonesia*] [*Airport symbol*]   (OAG)
PGK .... Phosphoglycerate Kinase [*An enzyme*]
PGI .... Glenside Free Library, Glenside, PA [*Library symbol*] [*Library
                     of Congress*]   (LCLS)
PGL .... Lutheran Theological Seminary, Gettysburg, PA [*Library
                     symbol*] [*Library of Congress*]   (LCLS)
PGL .... Pascagoula, MS [*Location identifier*] [*FAA*]   (FAAL)
PGL .... Peoples Energy Corp. [*NYSE symbol*]
PGL .... Persistent Generalized Lymphadenopathy [*Medicine*]
PGL .... Phosphoglycolipid
PGL .... Polyglutaraldehyde [*Organic chemistry*]
PGL .... Portable Gas LASER
PGL .... Provincial Grand Lodge [*Freemasonry*]
PGL .... Pulsed Gas LASER
PGladM ...... Mary J. Drexel Home, Gladwyne, PA [*Library symbol*] [*Library
                     of Congress*] [*Obsolete*]   (LCLS)
PGIB .... Beaver College, Glenside, PA [*Library symbol*] [*Library of
                     Congress*]   (LCLS)
PGLC .... Pyrolysis Gas Liquid Chromatography
PGL-Hi ...... Lutheran Historical Society, Gettysburg, PA [*Library symbol*]
                     [*Library of Congress*]   (LCLS)
PGLOY ...... Philips Gloeilampen New York Shares [*NASDAQ symbol*]   (NQ)
PGM .... Messiah College Learning Center, Grantham, PA [*OCLC
                     symbol*]   (OCLC)
PGM .... Papyri Graecae Magicae [*A publication*]   (OCD)
PGM .... Past Grand Master [*Freemasonry*]
PGM .... Patrol Vessel, Motor Gunboat [*Navy symbol*] [*Obsolete*]
PGM .... Perron Gold Mines [*Vancouver Stock Exchange symbol*]
PGM .... Petermanns Geographische Mitteilungen [*A publication*]
PGM .... Phosphoglucomutase [*An enzyme*]
PGM .... Planetary Gearhead Motor [*Aerospace*]
PGM .... Platinum Group Metal [*In meteorites*]
PGM .... Port Graham, AK [*Location identifier*] [*FAA*]   (FAAL)
PGM .... Postgraduate Medicine [*A publication*]
PGM .... Precision Guided Munition   (MCD)
PGM .... Program
PGM .... Program Guidance Memorandum
PGMA .... Poly(glyceryl Methacrylate) [*Organic chemistry*]
PGMA .... Pulsed Gas Metal Arc   (KSC)
PGME .... Professional Group - Medical Electronics
PGMIL .... Professional Group - Military Electronics   (MUGU)
PGMILE ..... Professional Group - Military Electronics   (AAG)
PGMS .... Professional Grounds Management Society [*Formerly, NAPG*]
PGMSJ ...... Professional Group of Mathematical Symbol Jugglers   (MUGU)
PGMT .... Pigment   (MSA)
PGMTT ...... Professional Group - Microwave Theory and Techniques
PGN .... Phi Gamma Nu [*Fraternity*]
PGN .... Pigeon   (ADA)
PGN .... Platinum Group Nugget [*In meteorites*]
PGN .... Portland General Corp. [*NYSE symbol*]
PGN .... Proliferative Glomerulonephritis [*Medicine*]
PGNAA ...... Prompt Gamma Neutron Activation Analysis [*Analytical
                     chemistry*]
PGNCS ...... Primary Guidance, Navigation, and Control System [*or
                     Subsystem*] [*Apollo*] [*NASA*]   (MCD)
PGND .... Propaganda   (AABC)
PGNGD ...... Prace Instytutu Gornictwa Naftowego i Gazownictwa [*A
                     publication*]
PGNS .... Polar Gas News [*A publication*]
PGNS .... Primary Guidance and Navigation System [*Apollo*] [*NASA*]
PGNS .... Professional Group - Nuclear Science
PGO .... Page, OK [*Location identifier*] [*FAA*]   (FAAL)
PGO .... Past Grand Orient [*Freemasonry*]   (ROG)
PGO .... Peroxidase-Glucose Oxidase [*Also, GOD-POD*] [*Enzyme
                     mixture*]
PGO .... Ponto-Geniculate-Occipital [*Electroencephalography*]
PGO .... Positive Grid Oscillator
PGOA .... Pagecorp Class A [*Toronto Stock Exchange symbol*]
PGOR .... Payload Ground Operation Requirements [*NASA*]   (NASA)
PGORS ...... Payload Ground Operation Requirements Study
                     [*NASA*]   (MCD)
PGP .... Phosphoglycolate Phosphatase [*An enzyme*]
PGP .... Pico Glass Pellet
PGP .... Planning Grant Program
PGP .... Precision Gas Products [*Commercial firm*]
PGP .... Prepaid Group Practice [*Health care*]
PGP .... Programable Graphics Processor
PGP .... Prostaglandin Production
PGP .... Puerta Galera [*Philippines*] [*Seismograph station code, US
                     Geological Survey*]   (SEIS)
PGP .... University of Southern Maine at Portland, Portland, ME [*OCLC
                     symbol*]   (OCLC)
PGPEP ...... Professional Group - Product Engineering and Production
PGPI .... Protein Grain Products International [*McLean, VA*]   (EA)
PGPR .... Plant-Growth-Promoting Rhizobacteria
PGPS .... Packaged Gas Pressure System

PGPT.........	Professional Group - Production Techniques
PGR...........	Pakistan Geographical Review [*A publication*]
PGR...........	Paragould, AR [*Location identifier*] [*FAA*] (FAAL)
PGR...........	Parental Guidance Recommended [*Movie classification*] (ADA)
PGR...........	Peregrine Petroleum [*Vancouver Stock Exchange symbol*]
PGR...........	PGR. Press Gallery Report [*A publication*] (ADA)
PGR...........	Plant Growth Regulation [*A publication*]
PGR...........	Polymerized Grass Extract [*Immunology*]
PGR...........	Precision Graphic Recorder
PgR...........	Progesterone Receptor [*Endocrinology*]
PGR...........	Psychogalvanic Reflex [*or Response*] [*Psychology*]
PGR...........	Pyrogallol Red [*Also, PR*] [*An indicator*] [*Chemistry*]
PGraM.......	Messiah College, Grantham, PA [*Library symbol*] [*Library of Congress*] (LCLS)
PGRC.........	Program Guidance and Review Committee (AABC)
PGrev........	Greenville Area Public Library, Greenville, PA [*Library symbol*] [*Library of Congress*] (LCLS)
PGrevT......	Thiel College, Greenville, PA [*Library symbol*] [*Library of Congress*] (LCLS)
PGRF.........	Pulse Group Repetition Frequency
PGRFI........	Professional Group - Radio Frequency Interference
PGRM.........	Parti Gerakan Rakyat Malaysia [*People's Action Party of Malaysia*] (PPW)
PGRQC......	Professional Group - Reliability and Quality Control
PGRS.........	Pergerakan Guerilja Rakyat Sarawak [*Sarawak People's Guerrilla Forces*] [*Malaya*]
PGRSA......	Plant Growth Regulator Society of America (EA)
PGRT.........	Petroleum Gas and Revenue Tax [*Canada*]
PGS...........	Naval Postgraduate School [*Monterey, CA*]
PGS...........	Pagosa Springs [*Colorado*] [*Seismograph station code, US Geological Survey*] [*Closed*] (SEIS)
PGS...........	Papergram System [*Military*] (CAAL)
PGS...........	Parallel Gap Soldering
PGS...........	Passive Geodetic Satellite [*NASA*]
PGS...........	Passive Gravity Stabilization
PGS...........	Peach Springs, AZ [*Location identifier*] [*FAA*] (FAAL)
PGS...........	Pegasus Club [*St. Louis, MO*] [*FAA designator*] (FAAC)
PGS...........	Pennsylvania German Society
PGS...........	Pennsylvania German Society. Proceedings and Addresses [*A publication*]
PGS...........	Plane Grating Spectrograph
PGS...........	Plant Growth Substance
PGS...........	Plasma Generator System
PGS...........	Polish Genealogical Society (EA)
PGS...........	Polymer Glass Sealant
PGS...........	Portable Ground Station
PGS...........	Power Generation System [*or Subsystem*]
PGS...........	Power Generator Section (KSC)
PGS...........	Precision Gunnery System [*Army training device*] (INF)
PGS...........	Predicted Ground Speed [*Navigation*]
PGS...........	President of the Geographical Society [*British*] (ROG)
PGS...........	President of the Geological Society [*British*]
PGS...........	Pressure-Gradient Single-Ended [*Microphone*] (DEN)
PGS...........	Pretty Good Stuff [*Liquor*]
PGS...........	Professional Guidance Systems, Inc. [*Lansing, MI*] [*Information service*] (EISS)
PGS...........	Program Generation System [*Data processing*] (MDG)
PGS...........	Propellant Gauging System
PGS...........	Prostaglandin Synthase [*An enzyme*]
PGS...........	Provincial Grand Secretary [*Freemasonry*]
PGSB........	Past Grand Sword Bearer [*Freemasonry*] (ROG)
PGSB........	Provincial Grand Sword-Bearer [*Freemasonry*]
PGSC........	Persian Gulf Service Command
PGSCOL....	Naval Postgraduate School
PGSD........	Past Grand Senior Deacon [*Freemasonry*]
PGSE........	Payload Ground Support Equipment [*NASA*] (MCD)
PGSE........	Peculiar Ground Support Equipment [*DoD*]
PGSEL......	Priced Ground Support Equipment List (AAG)
PGSET......	Professional Group on Space Electronics and Telemetry (AAG)
PGSP.........	Pennsylvania German Society. Proceedings and Addresses [*A publication*]
PGSR........	Psychogalvanic Skin Resistance [*Otolaryngology*]
PGSTAP.....	Pressure, Gas, Start, Turbine, Auxiliary Pump-Drive Assembly [*Pronounced "pigstap"*]
PGSU........	Propellant [*or Propulsion*] Gas Supply Unit
PGSW........	Past Grand Senior Warden [*Freemasonry*]
PGT...........	Page Table [*Data processing*] (IBMDP)
PGT...........	Partido Guatemalteco del Trabajo [*Guatemalan Labor Party*] (PD)
PGT...........	Past Grand Treasurer [*Freemasonry*]
PGT...........	Per Gross Ton [*Shipping*]
PGT...........	Photo Glow Tube
PGT...........	Pigtail (MSA)
PGT...........	Pollen Grain Trajectory [*Botany*]
PGT...........	Potato Extract-Glucose-Thiamine Hydrochloride [*Growth medium*]
PGT...........	Power Grid Tube
PGTAA......	Prager Tieraerztliches Archiv [*A publication*]
PGTO........	Portuguese Government Trade Office (EA)

PGTS.........	Precision Gunnery Training System [*Army*] (INF)
PGTSND.....	Puget Sound [*FAA*] (FAAC)
PGTTT.......	Precision Gear Train Tools and Test
PGU...........	Gannon University, Nash Library, Erie, PA [*OCLC symbol*] (OCLC)
PGU...........	Pegasus Gold, Inc. [*Toronto Stock Exchange symbol*]
PGU...........	Plant Growth Unit (MCD)
PGU...........	Postgonococcal Urethritis [*Medicine*]
PGU...........	Pressure Gas Umbilical (KSC)
PGU...........	Propulsion Gas Umbilical
PGUE........	Professional Group - Ultrasonic Engineering
PGULF.......	Pegasus Gold Ltd. [*NASDAQ symbol*] (NQ)
PGUT........	Phosphogalactose Uridyltransferase [*An enzyme*] [*Known as Galactose-1-phosphate Uridylyltransferase*]
PGV...........	Greenville [*North Carolina*] [*Airport symbol*] (OAG)
PGV...........	Proximal Gastric Vagotomy [*Medicine*]
PGVC.........	Professional Group - Vehicular Communications
PGW..........	Parallel Gap Welding
PGW..........	Past Grand Warden [*Freemasonry*]
PGW..........	Pressure Gas Welding
PGW..........	United Plant Guard Workers of America
PGWG........	Parliamentary Group for World Government
PGWS........	P. G. Wodehouse Society (EA)
PGwvG.......	Gwynedd-Mercy College, Gwynedd Valley, PA [*Library symbol*] [*Library of Congress*] (LCLS)
PGX...........	Prostaglandin X [*or Prostacyclin*] [*Biochemistry*]
PGY...........	Global Yield Fund, Inc. [*NYSE symbol*]
PGY...........	Postgraduate Year
PGY...........	San Diego, CA [*Location identifier*] [*FAA*] (FAAL)
PGZ...........	Ponta Grossa [*Brazil*] [*Airport symbol*] (OAG)
PH..............	Czechoslovakia [*License plate code assigned to foreign diplomats in the US*]
PH..............	Netherlands [*Aircraft nationality and registration mark*] (FAAC)
Ph..............	[*The*] New Testament in Modern English [*1958*] [*J. B. Phillips*] [*A publication*] (BJA)
PH..............	Paedigogica Historica [*A publication*]
PH..............	Page Heading (BUR)
PH..............	Pakistan Horizon [*A publication*]
PH..............	Parker-Hannifin Corp. [*NYSE symbol*]
PH..............	Past History [*Medicine*]
P of H........	Patron of Husbandry
P & H........	Patton, Jr., and Heath's Reports [*Virginia Special Court of Appeals*] (DLA)
PH..............	Pearl Harbor, Hawaii
PH..............	Pennsylvania History [*A publication*]
PH..............	Performance History
PH..............	Persistent Hepatitis [*Medicine*]
PH..............	Personal Hygiene (MCD)
Ph..............	Phallacidin [*Biochemistry*]
PH..............	Phantom Circuit [*Telecommunications*] (TEL)
Ph..............	Pharmacia AB [*Sweden*] [*Research code symbol*]
Ph..............	Pharmacopoeia
PH..............	Phase (KSC)
Ph..............	Phenyl [*Organic chemistry*]
PH..............	Phiala [*Bottle*] [*Pharmacy*]
Ph'.............	Philadelphia [*Chromosome*]
Ph..............	Philippians [*New Testament book*] (BJA)
ph..............	Philippines [*MARC country of publication code*] [*Library of Congress*] (LCCP)
PH..............	Philippines [*Two-letter standard code*] (CNC)
Ph..............	Phillimore's English Ecclesiastical Reports (DLA)
Ph..............	Phillips' English Chancery Reports [*1841-49*] (DLA)
Ph..............	Phillips' English Election Cases [*1780-81*] (DLA)
Ph..............	Philologus. Zeitschrift fuer Klassische Altertum [*A publication*]
Ph..............	Philosophisches Jahrbuch [*A publication*]
Ph..............	Philosophy [*A publication*]
Ph..............	Phoenix [*A publication*]
PH..............	Phone (MDG)
Ph..............	Phosphate
PH..............	Phot [*Electronics*] (DEN)
PH..............	Photographer's Mate [*Navy rating*]
PH..............	Photography Program [*Association of Independent Colleges and Schools specialization code*]
Ph..............	Photostat (BJA)
PH..............	Phrase (ADA)
Ph..............	Physica [*of Aristotle*] [*Classical studies*] (OCD)
PH..............	Physically Handicapped (OICC)
PH..............	Picohenry
P/H.............	Pier to House [*Classified advertising*] (ADA)
Ph..............	Pilot-Helicopter [*Navy*] [*British*]
PH..............	Pilot House
PH..............	Pinch Hitter [*Baseball*]
PH..............	Plane Handler [*Navy*]
PH..............	Polynesian Airlines Ltd. [*ICAO designator*] (FAAC)
PH..............	Porta Hepatis [*Anatomy*]
PH..............	Porter House [*Initials often used as a pattern on clothing designed by this firm*]
P/H.............	Postage and Handling
pH..............	Pouvoir Hydrogene [*Hydrogen Power*] [*Negative logarithm of effective H ion concentration*] [*Chemistry*]

PH............. Powerhouse
PH............. Practitioner's Handbooks [*A publication*]
PH............. Precipitation Hardening
P-H...... Prentice-Hall, Inc. [*Publishers*]
PH............. Presidential Medal of Honour [*Botswana*]
PH............. Previous History [*Medicine*]
PH............. Primary Hyperparathyroidism
PH............. Probability of Hit [*Military*] (MCD)
PH............. Project Handclasp [*Navy*] [*Community relations program*]
        [*Arlington, VA*] (EA)
PH............. Prospect Hill [*Vole virus*]
PH............. Provence Historique [*A publication*]
PH............. Przeglad Historyczny [*A publication*]
PH............. Public Health
PH............. Public House [*A drinking establishment*] [*British*]
PH............. Purple Heart [*Decoration given to personnel wounded in
        military service*]
PH1............ Photographer's Mate, First Class [*Navy rating*]
1PH........... Single-Phase
PH2............ Photographer's Mate, Second Class [*Navy rating*]
2PH........... Two-Phase
PH3............ Photographer's Mate, Third Class [*Navy rating*]
3PH........... Three-Phase
PHA........... Chicago, IL [*Location identifier*] [*FAA*] (FAAL)
PHa........... Hazelton Public Library, Hazelton, PA [*Library symbol*] [*Library
        of Congress*] (LCLS)
PHA........... Pachena Industries Ltd. [*Vancouver Stock Exchange symbol*]
PHA........... Palomino Horse Association (EA)
PHA........... Passive Hemagglutination [*Immunology*]
PHA........... Peripheral Hyperalimentation (Solution) [*Medicine*]
PHA........... Peruvian Heart Association [*Wadsworth, IL*] (EA)
Pha........... Philologica [*A publication*]
PHA........... Philosophia Antiqua [*A publication*]
PHA........... Phytohemagglutinin [*Immunology*]
PHA........... Poly(hydroxystearic Acid) [*Organic chemistry*]
PHA........... Port Heiden [*Alaska*] [*Seismograph station code, US
        Geological Survey*] [*Closed*] (SEIS)
PHA........... Poultry Husbandry Adviser [*Ministry of Agriculture, Fisheries,
        and Food*] [*British*]
PHA........... Preferred Hotels Association [*Also known as Preferred Hotel
        Worldwide*] [*Lombard, IL*] (EA)
PHA........... Prelaunch Hazard Area (MUGU)
PHA........... Preliminary Hazard Analyses (NASA)
PHA........... Professional Handlers Association (EA)
PHA........... Professional Horsemen's Association (EA)
PHA........... Public Housing Administration [*or HHFA; disbanded 1965*]
PHA........... Pulse Height Analysis [*Spectroscopy*]
PHA........... State Library of Pennsylvania, Harrisburg, PA [*OCLC
        symbol*] (OCLC)
PHA's........ Public Housing Agencies
PHAA........ Airman Apprentice, Photographer's Mate, Striker [*Navy rating*]
PHAA........ Percheron Horse Association of America (EA)
PHAA........ Positive High-Angle of Attack
PHAA........ Professional Horsemen's Association of America (EA)
PhAb........ Photographic Abstracts [*A publication*]
PHABY...... Pharmacia AB ADR [*NASDAQ symbol*] (NQ)
PHADA...... Public Housing Authorities Directors Association (EA)
PHAGA...... Philippine Agriculturist [*A publication*]
Phal CC..... Phalen's Criminal Cases (DLA)
PHALSE..... Phreakers, Hackers, and Laundry Service Employees [*East
        Coast group of computer trespassers raided by the FBI*]
P-H Am Lab Arb Awards ... American Labor Arbitration Awards [*Prentice-
        Hall, Inc.*] (DLA)
P-H Am Lab Cas ... American Labor Cases [*Prentice-Hall, Inc.*] (DLA)
PHAMOS.... Promote Hemodynamics and Metabolism in an Orbiting
        Satellite (KSC)
PHAN...... Airman, Photographer's Mate, Striker [*Navy rating*]
PHANT...... Phantom-Glass [*Theater term*] (DSUE)
PHAP........ Provincial Health Assistance Program [*Vietnam*]
PHAR........ Pharmacology
PHAR........ Pharmacontrol Corp. [*NASDAQ symbol*] (NQ)
PHAR........ Pharmacopoeia (ROG)
PHAR........ Pharmacy (MSA)
PHarA........ AMP, Inc., Harrisburg, PA [*Library symbol*] [*Library of
        Congress*] (LCLS)
PHARA...... Pharmazie [*A publication*]
Phar B........ Bachelor of Pharmacy
PHarC........ Harrisburg Area Community College, Harrisburg, PA [*Library
        symbol*] [*Library of Congress*] (LCLS)
PharC........ Pharmaceutical Chemist [*British*]
PHarD........ Dauphin County Library System, Harrisburg, PA [*Library
        symbol*] [*Library of Congress*] (LCLS)
Phar D .... Doctor of Pharmacy
PHarH....... Pennsylvania Historical and Museum Commission, Harrisburg,
        PA [*Library symbol*] [*Library of Congress*] (LCLS)
Phar M....... Master of Pharmacy
PHARM..... Pharmaceutical
PHARM...... Pharmacist [*or Pharmacy*]
PHARM...... Pharmacology
Pharm Abstr ... Pharmaceutical Abstracts [*A publication*]
PHARMAC ... Pharmacology

Pharmaceutical J ... Pharmaceutical Journal and Transactions [*A
        publication*]
Pharmacog Tit ... Pharmacognosy Titles [*A publication*]
PHARMACOL ... Pharmacological (MSA)
Pharmacol ... Pharmacology [*A publication*]
Pharmacol Biochem Behav ... Pharmacology, Biochemistry, and Behavior [*A
        publication*]
Pharmacol Clin ... Pharmacologia Clinica [*A publication*]
Pharmacolog ... Pharmacologist [*A publication*]
Pharmacol Physicians ... Pharmacology for Physicians [*A publication*]
Pharmacol R ... Pharmacological Research Communications [*A publication*]
Pharmacol Res Commun ... Pharmacological Research Communications [*A
        publication*]
Pharmacol Rev ... Pharmacological Reviews [*A publication*]
Pharmacol Sleep ... Pharmacology of Sleep [*A publication*]
Pharmacol Ther ... Pharmacology and Therapeutics [*A publication*]
Pharmacol Ther (B) ... Pharmacology and Therapeutics. Part B. General and
        Systematic Pharmacology [*A publication*]
Pharmacol Ther Dent ... Pharmacology and Therapeutics in Dentistry [*A
        publication*]
Pharmacol Ther Part A Chemother Toxicol Metab Inhibitors ...
        Pharmacology and Therapeutics. Part A. Chemotherapy,
        Toxicology, and Metabolic Inhibitors [*A publication*]
Pharmacol Ther Part B Gen Syst Pharmacol ... Pharmacology and
        Therapeutics. Part B. General and Systematic
        Pharmacology [*A publication*]
Pharmacol Ther Part C ... Pharmacology and Therapeutics. Part C. Clinical
        Pharmacology and Therapeutics [*A publication*]
Pharmacol Toxicol (Engl Transl) ... Pharmacology and Toxicology (English
        Translation of Farmakologiya Toksikologiya) [*Moscow*] [*A
        publication*]
Pharmacol Toxicol (USSR) ... Pharmacology and Toxicology (USSR) [*A
        publication*]
Pharm Acta Helv ... Pharmaceutica Acta Helvetiae [*A publication*]
Pharm Act H ... Pharmaceutica Acta Helvetiae [*A publication*]
Pharma Int Engl Ed ... Pharma International (English Edition) [*A publication*]
Pharmakeutickon Delt Epistem Ekodosis ... Pharmakeutikon Deltion.
        Epistemonike Ekodosis [*A publication*]
Pharmakopsy ... Pharmakopsychiatrie Neuro-Psychopharmakologie [*A
        publication*]
Pharmakopsychiatr Neuro-Psychopharmakol ... Pharmakopsychiatrie
        Neuro-Psychopharmakologie [*A publication*]
Pharm Aquitaine ... Pharmacien d'Aquitaine [*A publication*]
Pharm Arch ... Pharmaceutical Archives [*A publication*]
Pharm Bio B ... Pharmacology, Biochemistry, and Behavior [*A publication*]
Pharm Biol ... Pharmacien Biologiste [*A publication*]
Pharm Bull Nihon Univ ... Pharmaceutical Bulletin. Nihon University [*A
        publication*]
Pharm Chem J ... Pharmaceutical Chemistry Journal [*A publication*]
PHARMCL ... Pharmaceutical
Pharm Cosmet ... Pharmaceuticals and Cosmetics [*A publication*]
Pharm Cosmet Rev ... Pharmaceutical and Cosmetics Review [*South Africa*]
        [*A publication*]
Pharm D..... Doctor of Pharmacy
Pharm Delt Epistem Ekdosis ... Pharmkeutikon Deltion Epistemonike
        Ekdosis [*A publication*]
Pharm Era ... Pharmaceutical Era [*A publication*]
Pharm Hist ... Pharmacy in History [*A publication*]
Pharm Ind ... Pharmazeutische Industrie [*A publication*]
Pharm Ind Yugosl ... Pharmaceutical Industry of Yugoslavia [*A publication*]
Pharm Int ... Pharmacy International [*Netherlands*] [*A publication*]
Pharm J...... Pharmaceutical Journal [*A publication*]
Pharm J NZ ... Pharmaceutical Journal of New Zealand [*A publication*]
Pharm J Pharm ... Pharmaceutical Journal and Pharmacist [*A publication*]
Pharm M .... Master of Pharmacy
Pharm Manage ... Pharmacy Management [*A publication*]
Pharm Monogr ... Pharmaceutical Monographs [*A publication*]
Pharm Post ... Pharmazeutische Post [*A publication*]
Pharm Prax ... Pharmazeutische Praxis [*A publication*]
Pharm Presse ... Pharmazeutische Presse [*A publication*]
Pharm Rev ... Pharmaceutical Review [*A publication*]
Pharm Rev ... Pharmacological Reviews [*A publication*]
Pharm Rundsch ... Pharmazeutische Rundschau [*A publication*]
Pharm Rural ... Pharmacien Rural [*A publication*]
Pharm Soc Jpn J ... Pharmaceutical Society of Japan. Journal [*A
        publication*]
Pharm Tijdschr Belg ... Pharmaceutische Tijdschrift voor Belgie [*A
        publication*]
Pharm Times ... Pharmacy Times [*A publication*]
Pharm Unserer Zeit ... Pharmazie in Unserer Zeit [*A publication*]
Pharm Weekbl ... Pharmaceutisch Weekblad [*A publication*]
Pharm Weekbl Sci ... Pharmaceutisch Weekblad. Scientific Edition [*A
        publication*]
Pharm Zentralhalle ... Pharmazeutische Zentralhalle [*A publication*]
Pharm Z Russl ... Pharmaceutische Zeitschrift fuer Russland [*A publication*]
Pharm Ztg ... Pharmazeutische Zeitung [*A publication*]
Pharm Ztg (Berl) ... Pharmazeutische Zeitung (Berlin) [*A publication*]
Pharm Ztg Ver Apotheker-Ztg ... Pharmazeutische Zeitung. Vereinigt mit
        Apotheker-Zeitung [*West Germany*] [*A publication*]
Pharos........ Pharos of Alpha Omega Alpha Honor Medical Society [*A
        publication*]

PHAROS .... Phased Array RADAR Operational Simulation [*Army*]   (AABC)
PHarP .... Harrisburg Polyclinic Hospital, Harrisburg, PA [*Library symbol*] [*Library of Congress*]   (LCLS)
PHAS .... Phaser Systems, Inc. [*NASDAQ symbol*]   (NQ)
PHAS .... Pulse Height Analyzer System
PHASR ...... Personnel Hazards Associated with Space Radiation [*Satellite*]
PHatfB .... Biblical School of Theology, Hatfield, PA [*Library symbol*] [*Library of Congress*]   (LCLS)
PHatU .... Union Library Co., Hatboro, PA [*Library symbol*] [*Library of Congress*] [*Obsolete*]   (LCLS)
PHav .... Haverford Township Free Library, Havertown, PA [*Library symbol*] [*Library of Congress*]   (LCLS)
P Hawaii En ... Proceedings. Hawaiian Entomological Society [*A publication*]
Ph B .... Bachelor of Pharmacy
Ph B .... Bachelor of Philosophy
Ph B .... Bachelor of Physical Culture
PHB .... Para-Hexadecylaminobenzoate [*Clinical chemistry*]
PHB .... Parliament House Book [*Scotland*]   (DLA)
PHB .... Parnaiba [*Brazil*] [*Airport symbol*]   (OAG)
PHB .... Pensioner Health Benefit Card   (ADA)
Ph B .... Philobiblon [*A publication*]
Ph B .... Philosophiae Baccalaureus [*Bachelor of Philosophy*]
PHB .... Philosophische Bibliothek [*Meiner*] [*A publication*]
PHB .... Photographic Bulletin   (MCD)
PHB .... Poly(hydroxybenzoate) [*Organic chemistry*]
PHB .... Polyhydroxybutyrate [*Organic chemistry*]
PHB .... Public Health Bibliography
PHB .... Public Health Service Building
PHBA .... Palomino Horse Breeders of America   (EA)
Ph B in Arch ... Bachelor of Philosophy in Architecture
PHBCD .... Physica B + C [*A publication*]
Ph B in Com ... Bachelor of Philosophy in Commerce
Ph BD .... Doctor of Bible Philosophy
Ph B in Ed ... Bachelor of Philosophy in Education
PHBHA .... Physiology and Behavior [*A publication*]
PHBLA .... Physikalische Blaetter [*A publication*]
PHBOA ...... Physiologia Bohemoslovenica [*Later, Physiologia Bohemoslovaca*] [*A publication*]
PHBRZ .... Phosphor Bronze
PHC .... Chief Photographer's Mate [*Navy rating*]
PHC .... Children's Hospital of Pittsburgh, Pittsburgh, PA [*OCLC symbol*]   (OCLC)
PHC .... Haverford College, Haverford, PA [*Library symbol*] [*Library of Congress*]   (LCLS)
PHC .... Pacific Hurricane Centers [*National Weather Service*]
PHC .... Palmitoyl Homocysteine [*Biochemistry*]
PHC .... Personal Holding Company [*Generic term*]
PHC .... Perturbed-Hardness Chain [*Molecular thermodynamics*]
Ph C .... Pharmaceutical Chemist
Ph C .... Philosopher of Chiropractic
PHC .... Photographic Change   (MCD)
PHC .... Population Housing Census   (OICC)
PHC .... Port Harcourt [*Nigeria*] [*Airport symbol*]   (OAG)
PHC .... Port Hardy [*British Columbia*] [*Seismograph station code, US Geological Survey*]   (SEIS)
PHC .... Posthospital Care [*Medicine*]
PHC .... [*A*] Prairie Home Companion [*National Public Radio program*]
PHC .... Primary Health Care
PHC .... Primary Hepatic Carcinoma [*Medicine*]
PHC .... Proliferative Helper Cells [*Immunology*]
Ph'c .... Philadelphia Chromosome
PHCA .... Pathonic Network Class A [*Toronto Stock Exchange symbol*]
PHCA .... Pleasure Horse Club of America   (EA)
PHCAA .... Physics in Canada [*A publication*]
PHCAA .... Public Health Cancer Association of America [*Defunct*]   (EA)
P-H Cas ..... American Federal Tax Reports [*Prentice-Hall, Inc.*]   (DLA)
PHCBA ...... Photochemistry and Photobiology [*A publication*]
PHCC .... Preferred Health Care [*NASDAQ symbol*]   (NQ)
PHCC .... Punjab High Court Cases [*India*]   (DLA)
Ph Ch .... Phillips' English Chancery Reports   (DLA)
PHCI .... Peak Health Care, Incorporated [*NASDAQ symbol*]   (NQ)
PHCIB .... Plumbing-Heating-Cooling Information Bureau   (EA)
PhCL .... Pharmacochemistry Library [*Elsevier Book Series*] [*A publication*]
PHCLIS ...... Protected Home Circle Life Insurance Society   (EA)
PHCM .... Master Chief Photographer's Mate [*Navy rating*]
P-H Corp .... Corporation [*Prentice-Hall, Inc.*]   (DLA)
PHCS .... Senior Chief Photographer's Mate [*Navy rating*]
PHCV-SD ... Phase Conversion and Step-Down   (MSA)
PHD .... Dixmont State Hospital, Sewickley, PA [*OCLC symbol*]   (OCLC)
Ph D .... Doctor of Pharmacy
Ph D .... Doctor of Philosophy [*Philosophae Doctor*]
PHD .... Duncan Aviation, Inc. [*Lincoln, NE*] [*FAA designator*]   (FAAC)
PHD .... New Philadelphia, OH [*Location identifier*] [*FAA*]   (FAAL)
PHD .... Parallel Head Disk
PhD .... Perfect Hard Disk [*Century Data Systems*] [*Data processing*]
Phd .... Phaedo [*of Plato*] [*Classical studies*]   (OCD)
PHD .... Phase-Shift Driver   (CET)

Ph D .... Philosophiae Doctor [*Doctor of Philosophy*]
PHD .... Photoelectron Diffraction [*Spectroscopy*]
PH D .... Piled Higher and Deeper [*Humorous interpretation of the Ph D degree*]
PHD .... Pilot's Horizontal Display [*Aviation*]   (CAAL)
PHD .... Port Huron & Detroit Railroad Co. [*AAR code*]
PH D .... Pre-Pearl Harbor Dad [*A humorous wartime degree*]
PHD .... Precision High Dose
PHD .... Pride, Hustle, and Drive
PHD .... Public Health Department
PHD .... Public Health Director
PHD .... Pulse Height Discrimination
PHDDS ...... PSRO Hospital Discharge Data Set
PhDEd .... Doctor of Philosophy in Education [*British*]   (ADA)
PhD(Med) ... Doctor of Philosophy (Medicine)   (ADA)
PhDMH ...... Doctor of Philosophy in Mechanics and Hydraulics
PHDr .... Doctor of Philosophy
Phdr .... Phaedrus [*of Plato*] [*Classical studies*]   (OCD)
PHDR .... Preliminary Hardware Design Review
PHDS .... Post-Harvest Documentation Service [*Kansas State University*] [*Manhattan, KS*]   (EISS)
PHE .... Aviation POL [*Petroleum, Oil, and Lubrication*] Handling Equipment   (NATG)
PHE .... Eastern State School and Hospital, Trevose, PA [*OCLC symbol*]   (OCLC)
PHE .... Periodic Health Examination
PHE .... Petroleum Handling Equipment   (MCD)
Phe .... Phenylalanine [*Also, F*] [*An amino acid*]
Phe .... Phoenix [*Constellation*]
PHE .... Photo Engravers & Electrotypers Ltd. [*Toronto Stock Exchange symbol*]
PHE .... Port Hedland [*Australia*] [*Airport symbol*]   (OAG)
PHE .... Preflight Heat Exchanger [*NASA*]   (KSC)
PHEA .... Public Health Engineering Abstracts [*A publication*]
Phear Wat ... Phear's Rights of Water [*1859*]   (DLA)
PHEDA ...... Physics Education [*A publication*]
PHEI .... Penetrator, High-Explosive, Incendiary   (MCD)
PhEJ .... Philippine Economic Journal [*A publication*]
PHEL .... Petroleum Helicopter [*NASDAQ symbol*]   (NQ)
P Helm Soc ... Proceedings. Helminthological Society of Washington [*A publication*]
PHeM .... Hershey Medical Center, Hershey, PA [*Library symbol*] [*Library of Congress*]   (LCLS)
PHEMA ...... Poly(hydroxyethyl Methacrylate) [*Organic chemistry*]
phen .... o-Phenanthroline [*Organic chemistry*]
PHEN .... Phenolic   (AAG)
Pheney Rep ... Pheney's New Term Reports [*England*]   (DLA)
PH Eng ...... Public Health Engineer
PHENO ...... Phenobarbital [*A drug*]
pheno .... Phenotype
PHENO ...... Precise Hybrid Elements for Nonlinear Operation   (IEEE)
PHEO .... Pheochromocytoma [*Also, PCC*] [*Medicine*]
PHERMEX ... Pulsed High-Energy Radiographic Machine Emitting X-Rays
P-H Est Plan ... Estate Planning [*Prentice-Hall, Inc.*] [*A publication*]
Ph Ev .... Phillips on Evidence [*10th ed.*] [*1852*]   (DLA)
Ph E W ...... Philosophy East and West [*A publication*]
PHEWA ...... Presbyterian Health, Education, and Welfare Association [*Formerly, NPHWA, UPHEWA*] [*New York, NY*]   (EA)
PHF .... Fairview State Hospital, Waymart, PA [*OCLC symbol*]   (OCLC)
PHF .... Newport News [*Virginia*] [*Airport symbol*]   (OAG)
PHF .... Paired Helical Filaments [*Neuroanatomy*] [*Term coined by Dr. Robert Terry to describe the components of neurofibrillary tangles in the brains of Alzheimer's Disease patients*]
PHF .... Patrick Henry Foundation   (EA)
PHF .... Peak Hour Factor [*Transportation*]
PHF .... Peanut Hull Flour
PHF .... Pergamon Holding Foundation [*Liechtenstein*]
PHF .... Personal Hygiene Facility [*NASA*]   (NASA)
PHF .... Phoenix House Foundation [*New York, NY*]   (EA)
PHF .... Plug Handling Fixture   (NRCH)
PHF .... Process Holding Fixture   (MCD)
PHF .... Procurement History File [*DoD*]
PHFA .... Potomac Horse Fever Agent
PHFEA ...... Physica Fennica [*A publication*]
P-H Fed Taxes ... Federal Taxes [*Prentice-Hall, Inc.*]   (DLA)
PHFG .... Primary Human Fetal Glial [*Cytology*]
Ph G .... Graduate in Pharmacy
PHG .... Phenate-Hexamine Goggle [*British World War I anti-poison-gas helmet*]
PHG .... Phillipsburg, KS [*Location identifier*] [*FAA*]   (FAAL)
PHG .... Prototype Hydrofoil Gunboat
PHG .... Scranton State General Hospital, Scranton, PA [*OCLC symbol*]   (OCLC)
PHGA .... Pteroylhexaglutamylglutamic [*or Pteroylheptaglutamic*] Acid [*Biochemistry*]
PhGABA .... Phenyl-gamma-aminobutyric Acid [*Tranquilizer*]
Phgly .... Phenylglycine [*An amino acid*]
Phgn .... Physiognomonica [*of Aristotle*] [*Classical studies*]   (OCD)
P HGT .... Package Height [*Freight*]
PHH .... Andrews, SC [*Location identifier*] [*FAA*]   (FAAL)

PHH .... Haverford State Hospital, Haverford, PA [*OCLC symbol*] (OCLC)
PHH .... PHH Group Canadian Funds [*Toronto Stock Exchange symbol*]
PHH .... PHH Group, Inc. [*NYSE symbol*]
PHH .... Phillips Head [*Screw*]
PHH .... Puu Huluhulu [*Hawaii*] [*Seismograph station code, US Geological Survey*] [*Closed*] (SEIS)
PHHC .... Programable Hand-Held Calculator (RDA)
PHi .... Historical Society of Pennsylvania, Philadelphia, PA [*Library symbol*] [*Library of Congress*] (LCLS)
PhI .... International Pharmacopoeia
PHI .... Petroleum Helicopters, Incorporated (MCD)
PHI .... Philadelphia [*Pennsylvania*] [*Seismograph station code, US Geological Survey*] [*Closed*] (SEIS)
PHI .... Philippine Long Distance Telephone Co. [*American Stock Exchange symbol*]
Phi .... Philips [*Holland & International*] [*Record label*]
PHI .... Philipsburg State General Hospital, Philipsburg, PA [*OCLC symbol*] [*Inactive*] (OCLC)
PHI .... Philosophie Informationsdienst [*Philosophy Information Service*] [*University of Dusseldorf*] [*Dusseldorf, West Germany*] [*Information service*] (EISS)
Phi .... Philosophy [*A publication*]
PHI .... Phosphohexose Isomerase [*An enzyme*]
Phi .... Physeptone [*A narcotic substitute*]
PHI .... Physiological Hyaluronidase Inhibitor [*Biochemistry*]
PHI .... Polarity Health Institute (EA)
PHI .... Position and Homing Indicator
PHI .... Programme Hydrologique International [*International Hydrological Program - IHP*] (MSC)
PHI .... Public Health Inspector [*British*]
PHIAL .... Phiala [*Bottle*] [*Pharmacy*]
PHIB .... Amphibious
PHib .... Hibeh Papyri [*A publication*] (OCD)
PHIBB .... Project for Historical Biobibliography [*A publication*]
PHIBCB ...... Amphibious Construction Battalion [*Also, ACB*] (NVT)
PHIBCORPAC ... Amphibious Corps, Pacific Fleet [*Marine Corps*]
PHIBCORPS ... Amphibious Corps [*Marine Corps*]
PHIBDET .... Amphibious Detachment
PHIBDETIND ... Amphibious Detachment, India
PHIBEU ...... Amphibious Forces, Europe
PHIBEX ...... Amphibious Exercise [*NATO*]
PHIBFOR .... Amphibious Forces
PHIBGROUP ... Amphibious Group
PHIBGRU ... Amphibious Group
PHIBLANT ... Amphibious Forces, Atlantic Fleet
PHIBLEX .... Amphibious Landing Exercise [*Navy*] (NVT)
PHIBNAW ... Amphibious Forces, Northwest African Waters
PHIBOPS ... Amphibious Operations [*Navy*] (NVT)
PHIBPAC .... Amphibious Forces, Pacific Fleet
PHIBRAIDEX ... Amphibious Raid Exercise [*Navy*] (NVT)
PHIBRECONEX ... Amphibious Reconnaissance Exercise [*Navy*] (NVT)
PHIBREFTRA ... Amphibious Refresher Training [*Navy*] (CAAL)
PHIBRFT .... Amphibious Refresher Training [*Navy*] (NVT)
PHIBRON ... Amphibious Squadron
PHIBSEU ... Amphibious Forces, Europe
PHIBSFORPAC ... Amphibious Forces, Pacific Fleet
PHIBSKDN ... Amphibious Ship Shakedown Cruise [*Navy*] (NVT)
PHIBSLANT ... Amphibious Forces, Atlantic Fleet
PHIBSPAC ... Amphibious Forces, Pacific Fleet
PHIBSS ...... Amphibious Schoolship [*Navy*] (NVT)
PHIBSTRAPAC ... Training Command Amphibious Forces, US Pacific Fleet
PHIBSUKAY ... Amphibious Bases, United Kingdom
PHIBTF .... Amphibious Task Force [*Navy*] (NVT)
PHIBTRA .... Training Command Amphibious Forces
PHIBTRABASE ... Amphibious Training Base [*Navy*]
PHIBTRAEX ... Amphibious Training Exercise [*Navy*] (NVT)
PHIBTRAINLANT ... Training Command Amphibious Forces, US Atlantic Fleet
PHIBTRAINPAC ... Training Command Amphibious Forces, US Pacific Fleet
PHIBTRALANT ... Training Command Amphibious Forces, US Atlantic Fleet
PHIBTRANS ... Amphibious Transport [*Navy*]
PHIBTRAPAC ... Training Command Amphibious Forces, US Pacific Fleet
PHIBTRBASE ... Amphibious Training Base [*Navy*]
PHIBWARTRACEN ... Amphibious Warfare Training Center [*Navy*]
PHIC .... Poly(hexyl Isocyanate) [*Organic chemistry*]
Phi D .... Doctor of Philanthropy
Phi Del Kap ... Phi Delta Kappan [*A publication*]
Phi D K ... Phi Delta Kappan [*A publication*]
PHIGS .... Programers Hierarchical Interactive Graphics Standard
PHIGS .... Programers Hierarchical Interactive Graphics System [*IBM Corp.*]
Phil .... Orationes Philippicae [*of Cicero*] [*Classical studies*] (OCD)
PHIL .... Philadelphia [*Pennsylvania*]
Phil .... Philadelphia Reports (DLA)
Phil .... Philemon [*New Testament book*]
Phil .... Philharmonia [*Record label*]
PHIL .... Philharmonic
Phil .... Philippians [*New Testament book*]
Phil .... Philippine Island Reports [*1901-46*] (DLA)
PHIL .... Philippines (AFM)

Phil .... Phillimore's English Ecclesiastical Reports (DLA)
Phil .... Phillips' English Chancery Reports [*1841-49*] (DLA)
Phil .... Phillips' English Election Cases [*1780-81*] (DLA)
Phil .... Phillips' Illinois Reports (DLA)
Phil .... Phillips' North Carolina Law Reports (DLA)
Phil .... Phillips' Treatise on Insurance (DLA)
Phil .... Philoctetes [*of Sophocles*] [*Classical studies*] (OCD)
Phil .... Philologus. Zeitschrift fuer Klassische Altertum [*A publication*]
PHIL .... Philology
Phil .... Philopoemen [*of Plutarch*] [*Classical studies*] (OCD)
PHIL .... Philosophy
PHIL .... Programable Algorithm Machine High-Level Language [*Data processing*]
PHILA .... Philadelphia [*Pennsylvania*]
Phila .... Philadelphia Reports [*1850-91*] [*Pennsylvania*] (DLA)
Philad .... Philadelphia Reports [*Pennsylvania*] (DLA)
PHILADA .... Philadelphia (ROG)
Philada R ... Philadelphia Reports [*Pennsylvania*] (DLA)
Philada Rep ... Philadelphia Reports [*Pennsylvania*] (DLA)
PHILADEL ... Philadelphia (ROG)
Philadelphia Leg Int ... Philadelphia Legal Intelligencer [*Pennsylvania*] (DLA)
Philadelphia Med ... Philadelphia Medicine [*A publication*]
Philadelphia Rep ... Philadelphia Reports [*Pennsylvania*] (DLA)
Phil Ag .... Philippine Agriculturist [*A publication*]
Phila Geog Soc Bull ... Philadelphia Geographical Society. Bulletin [*A publication*]
Phil Ag R .... Philippine Agricultural Review [*A publication*]
Phila Law Lib ... Philadelphia Law Library (DLA)
Phila Leg Int ... Philadelphia Legal Intelligencer [*Pennsylvania*] (DLA)
Phila LJ ...... Philadelphia Law Journal (DLA)
Phila Med ... Philadelphia Medicine [*A publication*]
Phila Med J ... Philadelphia Medical Journal [*A publication*]
Phila Med Phys J ... Philadelphia Medical and Physical Journal [*A publication*]
Phila Mus Bull ... Philadelphia Museum of Art. Bulletin [*A publication*]
philan .... Philanthropical (BJA)
PHILANTHR ... Philanthropic (ROG)
Phila Orch ... Philadelphia Orchestra. Program Notes [*A publication*]
Phila (PA) ... Philadelphia Reports [*1850-91*] [*Pennsylvania*] (DLA)
Phila Reports ... Philadelphia Reports [*Pennsylvania*] (DLA)
Philat Aust ... Philately from Australia [*A publication*]
Philat Bul ... Philatelic Bulletin [*A publication*]
Philately from Aust ... Philately from Australia
Philat Pregl ... Philatelen Pregled [*A publication*]
Phil Books ... Philosophical Books [*A publication*]
Phil Bull ..... Philatelic Bulletin [*A publication*]
Phil Bus R ... Philippine Business Review [*A publication*]
Phil C .... Philosophy in Chiropractic
Phil Civ & Can Law ... Phillimore's Civil and Canon Law (DLA)
PHILCOM ... Philippine Global Communications, Inc. [*Manila*] [*Telecommunications*] (TSSD)
PHILCON ... Philippine Contingent [*Military*]
Phil Context ... Philosophy in Context [*A publication*]
Phil Cop ..... Phillips' Law of Copyright Designs (DLA)
Phil D .... Philosophiae Doctor [*Doctor of Philosophy*]
PHILDANCO ... Philadelphia Dance Company
Phil Dom .... Phillimore's Law of Domicil (DLA)
Phil East West ... Philosophy East and West [*A publication*]
Phil Ecc ...... Phillimore's Ecclesiastical Judgments (DLA)
Phil Ecc ...... Phillimore's English Ecclesiastical Law [*2 eds.*] [*1873, 1895*] (DLA)
Phil Ecc ...... Phillimore's English Ecclesiastical Reports [*1809-21*] (DLA)
Phil Ecc Judg ... Phillimore's Ecclesiastical Judgments [*1867-75*] (DLA)
Phil Ecc Law ... Phillimore's English Ecclesiastical Law [*2 eds.*] [*1873, 1895*] (DLA)
Phil Ecc R .. Phillimore's English Ecclesiastical Reports [*161 English Reprint*] [*1809-21*] (DLA)
Phil Educ Proc ... Proceedings. Far Western Philosophy of Education Society [*A publication*]
Phil El Cas ... Phillips' English Election Cases (DLA)
Philem .... Philemon [*New Testament book*]
Phil Eq .... Phillips' North Carolina Equity Reports [*1866-68*] (DLA)
Phil Ev .... Phillips on Evidence (DLA)
Phil Ev Cow & H & Edw Notes ... Phillips on Evidence, Notes by Cowen, Hill, and Edwards (DLA)
PHILEX .... Philadelphia Stock Exchange [*Also, PSE, PHLX*]
Phil Exch .... Philosophic Exchange [*A publication*]
Phil Fam Cas ... Phillipps' Famous Cases in Circumstantial Evidence (DLA)
Phil Forum (Boston) ... Philosophical Forum (Boston) [*A publication*]
Phil Forum (De Kalb) ... Philosophy Forum (De Kalb) [*A publication*]
Phil Geog J ... Philippine Geographical Journal [*A publication*]
Philhar .... Philharmonic [*A publication*]
Phil ILJ .... Philippine International Law Journal (DLA)
Phil Ind .... Philosopher's Index [*A publication*]
Phil Inq .... Philosophical Inquiry [*A publication*]
Phil Ins .... Phillips on Insurance (DLA)
Phil Insan ... Phillips on Lunatics [*1858*] (DLA)
Phil Int Law ... Phillimore's International Law (DLA)
Phil Int LJ ... Philippine International Law Journal (DLA)
Phil Int Rom Law ... Phillimore's Introduction to the Roman Law (DLA)

Phil Invest ... Philosophical Investigators [*A publication*]
Philip Abstr ... Philippine Abstracts [*A publication*]
Philipp AEC ... Philippine Atomic Energy Commission. Publications [*A publication*]
Philipp AEC Annu Rep ... Philippine Atomic Energy Commission. Annual Report [*A publication*]
Philipp AEC Rep ... Philippine Atomic Energy Commission. Reports [*A publication*]
Philipp Agric ... Philippine Agriculturist [*A publication*]
Philipp Agric Eng J ... Philippine Agricultural Engineering Journal [*A publication*]
Philipp Agric Rev ... Philippine Agricultural Review [*A publication*]
Philipp At Bull ... Philippine Atomic Bulletin [*A publication*]
Philipp Bur Mines Inf Circ ... Philippines. Bureau of Mines. Information Circular [*A publication*]
Philipp Bur Mines Rep Invest ... Philippines. Bureau of Mines. Report of Investigations [*A publication*]
Philipp Bur Mines Spec Proj Ser Publ ... Philippines. Bureau of Mines. Special Projects Series. Publication [*A publication*]
Philipp Entomol ... Philippine Entomologist [*A publication*]
Philipp For ... Philippine Forests [*A publication*]
Philipp Geogr J ... Philippine Geographical Journal [*A publication*]
Philipp Geol ... Philippine Geologist [*A publication*]
Philippine ... Philippine Reports (DLA)
Philippine Ag R ... Philippine Agricultural Review [*A publication*]
Philippine Agr ... Philippine Agriculturist [*A publication*]
Philippine Agr Situation ... Philippine Agricultural Situation [*A publication*]
Philippine Co ... Philippine Code (DLA)
Philippine Econ J ... Philippine Economic Journal [*A publication*]
Philippine Farm Gard ... Philippine Farms and Gardens [*A publication*]
Philippine Internat LJ ... Philippine International Law Journal [*Manila, Philippines*] (DLA)
Philippine Int'l LJ ... Philippine International Law Journal (DLA)
Philippine J Nutr ... Philippine Journal of Nutrition [*A publication*]
Philippine J Plant Ind ... Philippine Journal of Plant Industry [*A publication*]
Philippine J Pub Adm ... Philippine Journal of Public Administration [*A publication*]
Philippine J Pub Admin ... Philippine Journal of Public Administration [*A publication*]
Philippine J Sci ... Philippine Journal of Science [*A publication*]
Philippine LJ ... Philippine Law Journal (DLA)
Philippine L Rev ... Philippine Law Review (DLA)
Philippine Planning J ... Philippine Planning Journal [*A publication*]
Philippine Rice Corn Progr ... Philippines Rice and Corn Progress [*A publication*]
Philippine Sociol R ... Philippine Sociological Review [*A publication*]
Philippine Stud ... Philippine Studies [*A publication*]
Philipp J Agric ... Philippine Journal of Agriculture [*A publication*]
Philipp J Anim Ind ... Philippine Journal of Animal Industry [*A publication*]
Philipp J Cardiol ... Philippine Journal of Cardiology [*A publication*]
Philipp J Coconut Stud ... Philippine Journal of Coconut Studies [*A publication*]
Philipp J Crop Sci ... Philippine Journal of Crop Science [*A publication*]
Philipp J For ... Philippine Journal of Forestry [*A publication*]
Philipp J Intern Med ... Philippine Journal of Internal Medicine [*A publication*]
Philipp J Nurs ... Philippine Journal of Nursing [*A publication*]
Philipp J Nutr ... Philippine Journal of Nutrition [*A publication*]
Philipp J Ophthal ... Philippine Journal of Ophthalmology [*A publication*]
Philipp J Pediatr ... Philippine Journal of Pediatrics [*A publication*]
Philipp J Plant Ind ... Philippine Journal of Plant Industry [*A publication*]
Philipp J Pub Admin ... Philippine Journal of Public Administration [*A publication*]
Philipp J Sci ... Philippine Journal of Science [*A publication*]
Philipp J Sci Sect B ... Philippine Journal of Science. Section B. Medical Sciences [*A publication*]
Philipp J Sci Sect C ... Philippine Journal of Science. Section C. Botany [*A publication*]
Philipp J Surg Obstet Gynecol ... Philippine Journal of Surgery, Obstetrics, and Gynecology [*A publication*]
Philipp J Surg Surg Spec ... Philippine Journal of Surgery and Surgical Specialties [*A publication*]
Philipp J Vet Med ... Philippine Journal of Veterinary Medicine [*A publication*]
Philipp Lumberm ... Philippine Lumberman [*A publication*]
Philipp Med World (1946-1951) ... Philippine Medical World (1946-1951) [*A publication*]
Philipp Med World (1952-1962) ... Philippine Medical World (1952-1962) [*A publication*]
Philipp Min J ... Philippine Mining Journal [*A publication*]
Philipp Nucl J ... Philippines Nuclear Journal [*A publication*]
Philipp Quart Cult Soc ... Philippine Quarterly of Culture and Society [*A publication*]
Philipp Sci ... Philippine Scientist [*A publication*]
Philipp Sugar Inst Q ... Philippine Sugar Institute. Quarterly [*A publication*]
Philips ... Philips Music Herald [*A publication*]
PhilipSa ... Philippiana Sacra [*Manila*] [*A publication*]
Philips Ind Eng Bul ... Philips Industrial Engineering Bulletin [*A publication*]
Philips J Res ... Philips Journal of Research [*A publication*]
Philips Res Rep ... Philips Research Reports [*A publication*]

Philips Res Rep Suppl ... Philips Research Reports. Supplements [*A publication*]
Philips Serv Sci Ind ... Philips Serving Science and Industry [*A publication*]
PhilipSt ... Philippine Studies [*Manila*] [*A publication*]
Philips Tech Rev ... Philips Technical Review [*A publication*]
Philips Tech Rundsch ... Philips Technische Rundschau [*A publication*]
Philips Tech Rundschau ... Philips Technische Rundschau [*Netherlands*] [*A publication*]
Philips Telecommun Rev ... Philips Telecommunication Review [*A publication*]
Philips Weld Rep ... Philips Welding Reporter [*A publication*]
Phili S Rev ... Philippine Sociological Review [*A publication*]
Phil J Ag ..... Philippine Journal of Agriculture [*A publication*]
Phil Jahr ..... Philosophisches Jahrbuch [*A publication*]
Phil J Ling ... Philippine Journal of Linguistics [*A publication*]
Phil J Pub Admin ... Philippine Journal of Public Administration [*A publication*]
Phil Jrl .... Business Journal (Philippines) [*A publication*]
Phil J Sci ..... Philippine Journal of Science [*A publication*]
Phil Jud ...... Phillimore's Ecclesiastical Judgments [*1867-75*] [*England*] (DLA)
Phil Judg .... Phillimore's Ecclesiastical Judgments [*1867-75*] (DLA)
Phill .... Phillips' English Chancery Reports [*41 English Reprint*] (DLA)
Phill .... Phillips' English Election Cases [*1780-81*] (DLA)
Phill .... Phillips' Illinois Reports [*152-245 Illinois*] (DLA)
Phill .... Phillips' North Carolina Equity Reports (DLA)
Phill .... Phillips' North Carolina Law Reports [*61 North Carolina*] [*1866-68*] (DLA)
Phil Lab R ... Philippine Labor Review [*A publication*]
Phil Lab Rel J ... Philippine Labour Relations Journal (DLA)
Phil Law ...... Phillips' North Carolina Law Reports (DLA)
Phill Ch ...... Phillips' English Chancery Reports [*41 English Reprint*] [*1841-49*] (DLA)
Phill Ch (Eng) ... Phillips' English Chancery Reports [*41 English Reprint*] (DLA)
Phil LD .... Doctor of Lithuanian Philology
Phill Ecc Judg ... Phillimore's Ecclesiastical Judgments [*1867-75*] (DLA)
Phill Ecc R ... Phillimore's English Ecclesiastical Reports [*1809-21*] (DLA)
Phill Eq (NC) ... Phillips' North Carolina Equity Reports (DLA)
Phil Lic ...... Licentiate of Philosophy [*British*]
Phillim .... Phillimore's English Ecclesiastical Reports (DLA)
Phillim Dom ... Phillimore's Law of Domicil (DLA)
Phillim Eccl ... Phillimore's Ecclesiastical Judgments [*1867-75*] (DLA)
Phillim Eccl ... Phillimore's English Ecclesiastical Reports [*161 English Reprint*] [*1809-21*] (DLA)
Phillim Ecc Law ... Phillimore's English Ecclesiastical Law (DLA)
Phillim Eccl (Eng) ... [*J.*] Phillimore's English Ecclesiastical Reports [*161 English Reprint*] (DLA)
Phillim Int Law ... Phillimore's International Law (DLA)
Phil Ling ..... Philosophical Linguistics [*A publication*]
Phill Ins ...... Phillips on Insurance (DLA)
Phillip J Sci ... Phillippine Journal of Science [*A publication*]
Phillips .... Phillips' English Chancery Reports (DLA)
Phillips .... Phillips' English Election Cases [*1780-81*] (DLA)
Phillips .... Phillips' Illinois Reports [*152-245 Illinois*] (DLA)
Phillips .... Phillips' North Carolina Equity Reports (DLA)
Phillips .... Phillips' North Carolina Law Reports (DLA)
Phil Lit .... Philosophy and Literature [*A publication*]
Phil LJ .... Philippine Law Journal [*Manila*] (DLA)
Phill L (NC) ... Phillips' North Carolina Law Reports (DLA)
Phil Log ...... Philosophie et Logique [*A publication*]
Phil L Rev ... Philippine Law Review (DLA)
Philly .... Philadelphia
Phil & M ...... Philip and Mary (DLA)
Phil Mag ..... Philosophical Magazine [*A publication*]
Phil & Mar ... Philip and Mary (DLA)
Phil Math ..... Philosophia Mathematica [*A publication*]
Phil Mech Liens ... Phillips on Mechanics' Liens (DLA)
Phil Natur ... Philosophia Naturalis [*A publication*]
Phil NC ...... Phillips' North Carolina Law Reports (DLA)
Philo .... Philo Judaeus [*First century AD*] [*Classical studies*] (OCD)
Philol .... Philologus [*A publication*] (OCD)
PHILOL ...... Philology
Philologus ZKA ... Philologus. Zeitschrift fuer Klassische Altertum [*A publication*]
Philol Q ...... Philological Quarterly [*A publication*]
Philol Suppl ... Philologus, Supplement [*A publication*] (OCD)
PHILOM .... Philomathes [*Lover of Learning*] (ROG)
PHILOMATH ... Philomathematicus [*Lover of Mathematics*] (ROG)
PHILOS ...... Philosophy
Philos .... Philosophy [*A publication*]
Philos Book ... Philosophical Books [*A publication*]
Philos Collect R Soc London ... Philosophical Collections. Royal Society of London [*A publication*]
Philos East & West ... Philosophy East and West [*A publication*]
Philos EW ... Philosophy East and West [*A publication*]
Philos Foru ... Philosophy Forum [*A publication*]
Philos Forum ... Philosophical Forum [*A publication*]
Philos Forum ... Philosophy Forum [*A publication*]
Philos His ... Philosophy and History [*A publication*]

Philos Hist ... Philosophy and History. German Studies Section I [*A publication*]
Philosl .... Philosopher's Index [*A publication*]
Philos J ...... Philosophical Journal [*A publication*]
Philos Jahr ... Philosophisches Jahrbuch [*A publication*]
Philos Lit .... Philosophy and Literature [*A publication*]
Philos M ..... Philosophical Magazine [*A publication*]
Philos Mag ... Philosophical Magazine [*A publication*]
Philos Mag A ... Philosophical Magazine A. Physics of Condensed Matter, Defects, and Mechanical Properties [*A publication*]
Philos Mag B ... Philosophical Magazine B. Physics of Condensed Matter, Electronic, Optical, and Magnetic Properties [*A publication*]
Philos Math ... Philosophia Mathematica [*A publication*]
Philos Nat ... Philosophia Naturalis [*A publication*]
Philos Natur ... Philosophia Naturalis [*A publication*]
Philosophy of Ed Soc Proc ... Philosophy of Education Society of Great Britain. Proceedings [*A publication*]
Philos Phen ... Philosophy and Phenomenological Research [*A publication*]
Philos & Phenom Res ... Philosophy and Phenomenological Research [*A publication*]
Philos Pub ... Philosophy and Public Affairs [*A publication*]
Philos & Pub Affairs ... Philosophy and Public Affairs [*A publication*]
Philos Publ Aff ... Philosophy and Public Affairs [*A publication*]
PhilosQ ...... Philosophical Quarterly [*A publication*]
Philos Quart ... Philosophical Quarterly [*A publication*]
Philos R ...... Philosophical Review [*A publication*]
PhilosRdschau ... Philosophische Rundschau [*A publication*]
Philos Rev ... Philosophical Review [*A publication*]
Philos Rhet ... Philosophy and Rhetoric [*A publication*]
PhilosRund ... Philosophische Rundschau [*A publication*]
Philos Sci ... Philosophy of Science [*A publication*]
Philos Soc Sci ... Philosophy of the Social Sciences [*A publication*]
Philos S Sc ... Philosophy of the Social Sciences [*A publication*]
Philos Stud ... Philosophical Studies [*A publication*]
Philos Studies ... Philosophical Studies [*Dordrecht*] [*A publication*]
Philos Stud Ser Philos ... Philosophical Studies Series in Philosophy [*A publication*]
Philo Stds ... Philosophical Studies [*A publication*]
Philos Tod ... Philosophy Today [*A publication*]
Philostr ...... Philostratus [*Second century AD*] [*Classical studies*] (OCD)
Philos Trans R Soc A ... Philosophical Transactions. Royal Society of London. Series A [*A publication*]
Philos Trans R Soc Lond A Math Phys Sci ... Philosophical Transactions. Royal Society of London. Series A. Mathematical and Physical Sciences [*A publication*]
Philos Trans R Soc Lond Biol ... Philosophical Transactions. Royal Society of London. Series B. Biological Sciences [*A publication*]
Philos Trans R Soc London ... Philosophical Transactions. Royal Society of London [*A publication*]
Philos Trans R Soc London A ... Philosophical Transactions. Royal Society of London. Series A. Mathematical and Physical Sciences [*A publication*]
Philos Trans R Soc London Ser A ... Philosophical Transactions. Royal Society of London. Series A [*A publication*]
Phil (PA) .... Philadelphia Reports [*Pennsylvania*] (DLA)
Phil Papers ... Philosophical Papers [*A publication*]
Phil Pat ...... Phillips on Patents (DLA)
Phil Perspekt ... Philosophische Perspektiven [*A publication*]
Phil Phenomenol Res ... Philosophy and Phenomenological Research [*A publication*]
Phil Plan J ... Philippine Planning Journal [*A publication*]
Phil Pol Sci J ... Philippine Political Science Journal [*A publication*]
Phil Post ...... Philharmonic Post [*A publication*]
Phil Pub Affairs ... Philosophy and Public Affairs [*A publication*]
PHILPUC .... Philippine Presidential Unit Citation Badge [*Military decoration*]
Phil Q .... Philippines Quarterly [*A publication*]
Phil Q .... Philosophical Quarterly [*A publication*]
Phil Q Cult Soc ... Philippine Quarterly of Culture and Society [*A publication*]
Phil Qy ...... Philological Quarterly [*A publication*]
Phil R .... Philadelphia Reports [*Pennsylvania*] (DLA)
Phil R .... Philosophical Review [*A publication*]
PhilR .... Philosophy and Rhetoric [*A publication*]
Phil R Bus Econ ... Philippine Review of Business and Economics [*A publication*]
Phil Reform ... Philosophia Reformata [*A publication*]
Phil Rep ...... Philadelphia Reports [*Pennsylvania*] (DLA)
Phil Res Arch ... Philosophy Research Archives [*A publication*]
Phil Res R ... Philips Research Reports [*A publication*]
Phil Rev ...... Philosophical Review [*A publication*]
Phil Rev (Taiwan) ... Philosophical Review (Taiwan) [*A publication*]
Phil Rhet ...... Philosophy and Rhetoric [*A publication*]
Phil Rom Law ... Phillimore's Private Law among the Romans (DLA)
Phil Rundsch ... Philosophische Rundschau [*A publication*]
PhilS .... Philosophical Studies [*A publication*]
Phil Sacra ... Philippine Sacra [*A publication*]
Phil Sci ...... Philosophy of Science [*A publication*]
PHILSEAFRON ... Philippine Sea Frontier
Phil Soc ...... Philological Society. Transactions [*A publication*]
Phil Soc Cr ... Philosophy and Social Criticism [*A publication*]

Phil Soc Crit ... Philosophy and Social Criticism [*A publication*]
Phil Sociol R ... Philippine Sociological Review [*A publication*]
Phil Soc Sci ... Philosophy of the Social Sciences [*A publication*]
Phil Soc Sci Hum R ... Philippine Social Sciences and Humanities Review [*A publication*]
PHILSOM ... Periodical Holdings in the Library of the School of Medicine [*Washington University School of Medicine*] [*Library network*]
Phil St Tr .... Phillipps' State Trials [*Prior to 1688*] (DLA)
Phil Stud .... Philippine Studies [*A publication*]
Phil Stud .... Philosophical Studies [*A publication*]
Phil Stud (Ireland) ... Philosophical Studies (Ireland) [*A publication*]
PhilT .... Philosophy Today [*A publication*]
Phil Tech R ... Philips Technical Review [*A publication*]
Phil Today ... Philosophy Today [*A publication*]
Phil Trans Roy Soc Lond ... Philosophical Transactions. Royal Society of London [*A publication*]
Phil Trans Roy Soc Lond B ... Philosophical Transactions. Royal Society of London. Series B. Biological Sciences [*A publication*]
Phil Trans Roy Soc London Ser A Math Phys Sci ... Philosophical Transactions. Royal Society of London. Series A. Mathematical and Physical Sciences [*A publication*]
Phil Trans R Soc ... Philosophical Transactions. Royal Society [*A publication*]
Phil Unters ... Philologische Untersuchungen [*A publication*] (OCD)
Phil Woch ... Philologische Wochenschrift [*A publication*]
Phil Wochenschr ... Philologische Wochenschrift [*A publication*] (OCD)
Phil Yb Int'l L ... Philippine Yearbook of International Law [*Manila, Philippines*] (DLA)
PHIN .... Position and Homing Inertial Navigator
PHINA .... Pharmazeutische Industrie [*A publication*]
PHIND .... Pharmaceutical and Healthcare Industries News Database [*V & O Publications Ltd.*] [*Richmond, Surrey, England*] [*Information service*] (EISS)
PHIND .... Pharmacy International [*A publication*]
P-H Ind Rel Lab Arb ... Industrial Relations, American Labor Arbitration [*Prentice-Hall, Inc.*] (DLA)
P-H Ind Rel Union Conts ... Industrial Relations, Union Contracts, and Collective Bargaining [*Prentice-Hall, Inc.*] (DLA)
PHINet .... Prentice-Hall Information Network [*Prentice-Hall Information Services*] [*New York, NY*] [*Information service*] (EISS)
Phip .... Phipson's Digest, Natal Reports [*South Africa*] (DLA)
Phip .... Phipson's Reports, Natal Supreme Court [*South Africa*] (DLA)
Phip Ev .... Phipson on Evidence [*12th ed.*] [*1976*] (DLA)
Phipson ...... Reports of Cases in the Supreme Court of Natal (DLA)
PHIS .... Program Hardware Interface Specification (CAAL)
PHITAP ...... Predesigned [*or Priority*] High-Interest Tactical Air [*Acoustic forecast*] Prediction (MCD)
PHITAR ...... Predesignated High-Interest Tactical Area [*Navy*] (NVT)
Phi T Roy A ... Philosophical Transactions. Royal Society of London. Series A. Mathematical and Physical Sciences [*A publication*]
Phi T Roy B ... Philosophical Transactions. Royal Society of London. Series B. Biological Sciences [*A publication*]
PHJ .... Danville State Hospital, Danville, PA [*OCLC symbol*] (OCLC)
PhJ .... Philosophisches Jahrbuch [*A publication*]
Ph Jb .... Philosophisches Jahrbuch [*A publication*]
PHJC .... Penn Hall Junior College [*Pennsylvania*] [*Closed, 1973*]
PHJC .... Poor Handmaids of Jesus Christ [*Ancilla Domini Sisters*] [*Roman Catholic religious order*]
PHJC .... Port Huron Junior College [*Michigan*]
PHJRD .... Philips Journal of Research [*A publication*]
PHK .... Pahokee, FL [*Location identifier*] [*FAA*] (FAAL)
PHK .... Personal Hygiene Kit (MCD)
PhK .... Phosphorylase Kinase [*An enzyme*]
PHK .... Porter [*H. K.*] Co., Inc. [*NYSE symbol*]
PHK .... Postmortem Human Kidney [*Cells*]
PHKOA .... Photographische Korrespondenz (Austria) [*A publication*]
PHL .... Allentown State Hospital, Allentown, PA [*OCLC symbol*] (OCLC)
Ph L .... Licentiate of Pharmacy
Ph L .... Licentiate in Philosophy
PHL .... Periodical Holdings List [*Libraries*]
PHL .... Philadelphia [*Pennsylvania*] [*Airport symbol*]
PHL .... Philippines [*Three-letter standard code*] (CNC)
PHL .... Philips Industries, Inc. [*NYSE symbol*]
PHL .... Phillips Michigan City Flying Service [*Michigan City, IN*] [*FAA designator*] (FAAC)
PHL .... Pressure to Horizontal Locks [*Missiles*] (AAG)
PHL .... Public Health Law
PHLA .... Plasma Postheparin Lipolytic Activity [*Clinical chemistry*]
PHLAG .... Phillips Petroleum Load and Go [*System*]
Phlb .... Philebus [*of Plato*] [*Classical studies*] (OCD)
PHLBA .... Phlebologie [*A publication*]
Phld .... Philodemus [*First century BC*] [*Classical studies*] (OCD)
Phl Freep ... Philadelphia Free Press [*A publication*]
PHLH .... Phillips Head [*Screw*]
Phlm .... Philemon [*New Testament book*]
PHLODOT ... Phase Lock Doppler Tracking [*System*] (MUGU)
PHLS .... Public Health Laboratory Service [*British*]
PHLSB .... Public Health Laboratory Service Board [*British*]
PHLTA .... Physics Letters [*A publication*]

PHLX .... Philadelphia Stock Exchange [*Also, PHILEX, PSE*]
Ph M........... Master in Pharmacy
Ph M........... Master of Philosophy
PHM .... Mayview State Hospital, Bridgeville, PA [*OCLC symbol*] (OCLC)
PHM .... Patrol Combatant Missile (Hydrofoil) [*Navy symbol*]
PHM .... Patterson-Harker Method [*Physics*]
PHM .... Petroleum Helicopters, Inc. [*Lafayette, LA*] [*FAA designator*] (FAAC)
PHM .... Phantom (MSA)
PHM .... Pharmacist's Mate [*Navy rating*]
PHM .... Phase Meter
PHM .... Phase Modulation [*Radio data transmission*] (DEN)
Phm .... Philemon [*New Testament book*] (BJA)
Ph & M........ Philip and Mary (DLA)
PhM .... Philips Minigroove [*Record label*]
PHM .... Posterior Hyaloid Membrane [*Eye anatomy*]
PHM .... Power Hybrid Microcircuit
PHM .... Pulte Home Corp. [*NYSE symbol*]
PHMA......... Plastic Houseware Manufacturers Association
PHMAA........ Philosophical Magazine [*A publication*]
Ph Mag....... Philosophical Magazine [*A publication*]
Phm B .... Bachelor of Pharmacy
PHMB......... Para-Hydroxymercuribenzoate [*Biochemistry*]
PHMBA........ Physics in Medicine and Biology [*A publication*]
PHMC......... Probe Heater Motor Controller (MCD)
PHMDP........ Pharmacist's Mate, Dental Prosthetic Technician [*Navy rating*]
Phm G .... Graduate in Pharmacy
PHMGB ...... Pharmacology [*A publication*]
PHMMA...... Physics of Metals and Metallography [*English Translation*] [*A publication*]
PHMS .... Para-Hydroxymercuriphenylsulfonate [*Organic chemistry*]
PHMS .... Patrol Hydrofoil Missile Ship [*Navy/NATO*]
PHMS .... Polish Historical Military Society (EA)
PHMTD....... Previews of Heat and Mass Transfer [*A publication*]
PHMWO ..... Prospect Hill Millimeter Wave Observatory [*Waltham, MA*] [*Air Force*]
PHN........... Norristown State Hospital, Norristown, PA [*OCLC symbol*] (OCLC)
PHN........... Phone (KSC)
PHN........... Port Huron, MI [*Location identifier*] [*FAA*] (FAAL)
PHN........... Public Health Nurse
PHNOA....... Physica Norvegica [*A publication*]
PHNTA .... Phonetica [*A publication*]
PHNY......... Pearl Harbor Navy Yard [*Later, Pearl Harbor Naval Shipyard*]
P-H NYETR ... Prentice-Hall New York Estate Tax Reports (DLA)
PHO .... Phenolic Heavy Oil
PhO .... Philologia Orientalis [*A publication*]
PHO .... Point Hope [*Alaska*] [*Airport symbol*] (OAG)
PHO .... Polk State School and Hospital, Polk, PA [*OCLC symbol*] (OCLC)
PHO .... Port Health Officer
PHO .... Puu Honuaula [*Hawaii*] [*Seismograph station code, US Geological Survey*] (SEIS)
PHOAC....... Photographer's Mate, Combat Aircrewman [*Navy rating*] [*Obsolete*]
Phob.......... Previous Highroller, on a Budget [*Lifestyle classification*]
PHOC .... Photo-Control [*NASDAQ symbol*] (NQ)
PHOC .... Photocopy (MSA)
PHOD .... Philadelphia Ordnance Depot [*Military*] (AAG)
PHODEC .... Photometric Determination of Equilibrium Constants [*Data processing*]
Phoe.......... Phoenix [*Constellation*]
Phoen......... Phoenician (BJA)
Phoen......... Phoenissae [*of Euripides*] [*Classical studies*] (OCD)
PHOENIX.... Plasma Heating Obtained by Energetic Neutral Injection Experiment (IEEE)
PhoenixC ... Phoenix: The Classical Association of Canada [*A publication*]
PhoenixK ... Phoenix (Korea) [*A publication*]
Phoenix Q ... Phoenix Quarterly [*A publication*]
PHOFL........ Photoflash (AAG)
PHOG .... Phone-A-Gram Systems [*NASDAQ symbol*] (NQ)
PHOM .... Photographer's Mate [*Navy rating*] [*Obsolete*]
PHON .... Phoenician
PHON .... Phone-Mate [*NASDAQ symbol*] (NQ)
Phon.......... Phonetica [*A publication*]
PHON .... Phonetics
PHON .... Phonogram (ROG)
PHON .... Phonograph (AAG)
PHONCON ... Telephone Conversation [*or Conference*]
PHONET..... Phonetics (ROG)
P HONG..... Ponchong [*Tea trade*] (ROG)
PHONO....... Phonograph (MSA)
PHONOG..... Phonography
PHONOL .... Phonology
PhonPr....... Phonetica Pragensia [*A publication*]
PHOPD ...... Photobiochemistry and Photobiophysics [*A publication*]
PHOPT .... Pseudohypoparathyroidism [*Endocrinology*]
Phorm .... Phormio [*of Terence*] [*Classical studies*] (OCD)
PHOS .... Phosphate (KSC)
PHOS .... Phosphorescent (KSC)

PHOS .... Phosphorus [*Chemical symbol is P*]
PHOSCHEM ... Phosphate Chemicals Export Association [*Chicago, IL*] (EA)
PHOSI .... Preliminary Handbook of Operations and Service Instructions
PHOSIAC ... Photographically Stored Information Analog Comparator
Phospho Potas ... Phosphorus and Potassium [*A publication*]
Phosphore Agric ... Phosphore et Agriculture [*France*] [*A publication*]
Phosphor Sulfur Relat Elem ... Phosphorus and Sulfur and the Related Elements [*A publication*]
Phosphorus ... Phosphorus and Potassium [*A publication*]
Phosphorus Agric ... Phosphorus in Agriculture [*A publication*]
Phot........... Photius [*Ninth century AD*] [*Classical studies*] (OCD)
PHOT......... Photograph
PHOT......... Photographer [*Navy rating*] [*British*]
Phot.......... Photon [*A publication*]
PHOT......... Photronics Corp. [*NASDAQ symbol*] (NQ)
PHOTABS ... Photographic Abstracts [*Pergamon*] [*Database*]
PHOTAC .... Phototypesetting and Composing [*AT & T*]
Phot Appln Sci ... Photographic Applications in Science, Technology, and Medicine [*A publication*]
PHOTEX..... [*Day*] Photographic Exercise [*Military*] (NVT)
PHOTINT.... Photographic Intelligence [*Military*]
PHOTO....... Photograph (AAG)
Photo Abstr ... Photographic Abstracts [*A publication*]
Photobiochem Photobiophys ... Photobiochemistry and Photobiophysics [*A publication*]
Photobiochem and Photobiophys ... Photobiochemistry and Photobiophysics [*A publication*]
Photo Can ... Photo Canada [*A publication*]
Photochem P ... Photochemistry and Photobiology [*A publication*]
Photochem Photobiol ... Photochemistry and Photobiology [*A publication*]
Photochem Photobiol Rev ... Photochemical and Photobiological Reviews [*A publication*]
Photoelastic Soil Mech J ... Photoelastic and Soil Mechanics Journal [*A publication*]
Photoelectr Spectrom Group Bull ... Photoelectric Spectrometry Group Bulletin [*A publication*]
PHOTOG .... Photographic
Photog Abstr ... Photographic Abstracts [*A publication*]
PHOTOGR ... Photography
Photogr Alle ... Photographie fuer Alle [*A publication*]
Photogramma ... Photogrammetria [*A publication*]
Photogramm Eng ... Photogrammetric Engineering [*Later, Photogrammetric Engineering and Remote Sensing*] [*A publication*]
Photogramm Eng Remote Sensing ... Photogrammetric Engineering and Remote Sensing [*A publication*]
Photogramm Rec ... Photogrammetric Record [*A publication*]
Photographie Forsch ... Photographie und Forschung [*A publication*]
Photogr Appl Sci Technol and Med ... Photographic Applications in Science, Technology, and Medicine [*A publication*]
Photogr Appl Sci Technol Med ... Photographic Applications in Science, Technology, and Medicine [*A publication*]
Photogr Eng ... Photographic Engineering [*A publication*]
Photogr E R ... Photogrammetric Engineering and Remote Sensing [*A publication*]
Photogr Forsch ... Photographie und Forschung [*A publication*]
Photogr Ind ... Photographische Industrie [*A publication*]
Photogr J ... Photographic Journal [*A publication*]
Photogr J Sect A ... Photographic Journal. Section A. Pictorial and General Photography [*A publication*]
Photogr J Sect B ... Photographic Journal. Section B. Scientific and Technical Photography [*A publication*]
Photogr Korresp ... Photographische Korrespondenz [*A publication*]
Photogr Sci Eng ... Photographic Science and Engineering [*A publication*]
Photogr Sci Tech ... Photographic Science and Technique [*A publication*]
Photogr Sensitivity ... Photographic Sensitivity [*A publication*]
Photogr Welt ... Photographische Welt [*A publication*]
Photogr Wiss ... Photographie und Wissenschaft [*A publication*]
PHOTOLITH ... Photolithographic
Photo-M ..... Photo-Miniature [*A publication*]
PHOTOM.... Photometry
Photo-Mag ... Photo-Magazin [*A publication*]
Photo Mkt ... Photo Marketing [*A publication*]
Photophysiol Curr Top ... Photophysiology. Current Topics [*A publication*]
Photoplay ... Photoplay, Movies, and Video [*A publication*]
Photosynthe ... Photosynthetica [*A publication*]
Photo Tech ... Photo Technique [*A publication*]
PHOTRIPART ... Photo Triangulation Party [*Military*]
PHOTRON ... Photographic Squadron [*Navy*]
Phot Sci En ... Photographic Science and Engineering [*A publication*]
PHOTUB.... Phototube (KSC)
PHO/TY...... Photo Type [*Deltiology*]
PHP .... Pacific Hawaiian Products Co. [*Later, PHP Co.*]
PHP .... Packing-House Products [*Food industry*]
PHP .... Parts, Hybrids, and Packaging (MCD)
PHP .... Passive Hyperpolarizing Potential [*Neurochemistry*]
PHP .... Payload Handling Panel (MCD)
PHP .... Peace, Happiness, Prosperity for All [*A publication*]
PH and P .... Peace, Health, and Prosperity
PHP .... Pennhurst State School and Hospital, Spring City, PA [*OCLC symbol*] (OCLC)

PHP .... Petroleum Heat & Power Co. [*American Stock Exchange symbol*]
PHP .... Philip, SD [*Location identifier*] [*FAA*]   (FAAL)
PHP .... Phillip Resources, Inc. [*Vancouver Stock Exchange symbol*]
PhP .... Philologica Pragensia [*A publication*]
PhP .... Philologike Protochronia [*A publication*]
PHP .... Philosophia Patrum   (BJA)
PHP .... Physician's Health Plan
PHP .... Pinane Hydroperoxide [*Organic chemistry*]
PHP .... Planetary Horizon Platform [*Aerospace*]
PHP .... Post-Hostilities Planning Subcommittee of the Chiefs of Staff Committee [*World War II*]
PHP .... Pounds per Horsepower
PHP .... Prentice Hall Press [*Publisher*]
PHP .... Prepaid Health Plan
PHP .... Presbyterian Hunger Program [*Atlanta, GA*]   (EA)
PHP .... Propeller Horsepower
PHP .... Pseudohypoparathyroidism [*Endocrinology*]
PHP .... Pump Horsepower
PHPA .... Pacific Herring Packers Association   (EA)
PHPC .... Post-Hostilities Planning Committee [*Navy*] [*World War II*]
PHPHB .... P-heptyl-p-hydroxy Benzoate [*A preservative used in the making of American and British beer*]
Ph & Phen R ... Philosophy and Phenomenological Research [*A publication*]
PHPL .... Parallel Hardware Processing Language [*1977*] [*Data processing*]   (CSR)
PHPLA .... Physiologia Plantarum [*A publication*]
PHPS .... Post-Hostilities Planning Staff [*World War II*]
PHPT .... Portable High-Potential Tester
PHPT .... Primary Hyperparathyroidism
PHPV .... Persistent Hyperplastic Primary Vitreous [*Ophthalmology*]
PHPXA .... Pharmazeutische Praxis [*A publication*]
PhQ .... Philosophical Quarterly [*A publication*]
PHQ .... Postal Headquarters [*British*]
PHR .... Pacific Harbour [*Fiji*] [*Airport symbol*]   (OAG)
PHR .... Pacific Historical Review [*A publication*]
PHR .... Parts per Hundred of Rubber
PHR .... Peak Heart Rate [*Cardiology*]
PHR .... Peak Height Ratio
PHR .... Philippine Historical Review [*A publication*]
PhR .... Philosophical Review [*A publication*]
PHR .... Phorbol [*Organic chemistry*]
PHR .... Photographic Reconnaissance
PHR .... Phrase
PHR .... Pounds per Hour   (AAG)
PHR .... Preheater   (KSC)
PHR .... Process Heat Reactor [*Program*]
PHR .... Public Health Reports [*A publication*]
PHR .... Pulse-Height Resolution [*By photomultiplier tubes*]
PHR .... Retreat State Hospital, Hunlock Creek, PA [*OCLC symbol*]   (OCLC)
PHRA .... Poverty and Human Resources Abstracts [*A publication*]
PHRC .... Palestine Human Rights Campaign   (EA)
Ph Rdschau ... Philosophische Rundschau [*A publication*]
PHRE .... Public Health Reports [*A publication*]
PHREA .... Physiological Reviews [*A publication*]
PHREN .... Phrenology
Ph Rep .... Philadelphia Reports [*Pennsylvania*]   (DLA)
Ph Res .... Philosophy and Phenomenological Research [*A publication*]
Ph Rev .... Philosophical Phenomenological Review [*A publication*]
PHRF .... Performance Handicap Racing Fleet
Ph & Rh ...... Philosophy and Rhetoric [*A publication*]
PHRHD .... Pump, Hydraulic Ram, Hand-Driven   (MSA)
PHRI .... Public Health Research Institute of the City of New York, Inc. [*New York, NY*] [*Research center*]   (RCD)
PHRK .... Power and Heat Rejection Kit [*NASA*]
PHRR .... Parenchymal Hepatic Resection Rate [*Medicine*]
PHRS .... Paul Harris Stores [*NASDAQ symbol*]   (NQ)
PHRS .... Portable Heat Rejection System
PHRV .... Public Health Reviews [*A publication*]
PHRVA .... Physical Review [*A publication*]
PHS .... Packaging, Handling, and Storage   (MCD)
PHS .... Pallottine House of Studies
PHS .... Pathological Human Serum [*Serology*]
PHS .... Payload Handling Station [*NASA*]   (MCD)
PHS .... Personal Health Survey [*Psychology*]
PHS .... Personal Hygiene Subsystem [*NASA*]   (KSC)
PhS .... Philologische Studien [*A publication*]
PhS .... Philosophical Studies [*A publication*]
PHS .... Phitsanuloke [*Thailand*] [*Airport symbol*]   (OAG)
PHS .... Photographic Historical Society   (EA)
PHS .... Postal History Society   (EA)
PHS .... Postcard History Society   (EA)
PHS .... Posthypnotic Suggestion [*Psychology*]
PHS .... Prepared Hessian Surfacing [*Air Force*]
PHS .... Presbyterian Historical Society   (EA)
PHS .... Price History System   (MCD)
PHS .... Printing Historical Society [*British*]
PHS .... Public Health Service [*HEW*]
PHS .... Public Health Service. Publications [*A publication*]
PHS .... Pumped Hydro Storage [*Power source*]

PHS .... Somerset State Hospital, Somerset, PA [*OCLC symbol*]   (OCLC)
PHSA .... Pearl Harbor Survivors Association
PHSA .... Polymerized Human Serum Albumin [*Biochemistry*]
PHS of A ..... Postal History Society of the Americas   (EA)
PHSBB .... Physics Bulletin [*A publication*]
PHSC .... Pluripotent Hematopoietic Stem Cells [*Cytology*]
PHSC .... Postal History Society of Canada   (EA)
PHSC .... Private Hospital Supplementary Charges   (ADA)
PHSCA .... Philippine Journal of Science [*A publication*]
PHSG .... Postal History Study Group [*Crete, NE*]   (EA)
PHSI .... Pearle Health Service [*NASDAQ symbol*]   (NQ)
PHSI .... Plant Health and Seeds Inspectorate [*Ministry of Agriculture, Fisheries, and Food*] [*British*]
PHSIA .... Physiotherapy [*A publication*]
PHSIG .... Pan Hellenic Society Inventors of Greece in USA   (EA)
PHSNA .... Philosophia Naturalis [*A publication*]
PHSNB .... Physics of Sintering [*A publication*]
PHSNZ .... Postal History Society of New Zealand   (EA)
PHSO .... Partially Hydrogenated Soybean Oil [*Cooking fat*]
PHSO .... Postal History Society of Ontario [*Later, PHSC*]   (EA)
Ph Soc .... Philosophy/Social Theory/Sociology [*A publication*]
Ph Soc Glasgow Pr ... Philosophical Society of Glasgow. Proceedings [*A publication*]
P-H Soc Sec Taxes ... Social Security Taxes [*Prentice-Hall, Inc.*]   (DLA)
Ph Soc Wash B ... Philosophical Society of Washington. Bulletin [*A publication*]
PHSP .... Phase-Splitter   (MSA)
PHSP .... Public Health Service Publications
PHSPS ...... Preservation, Handling, Storage, Packaging, and Shipping   (NRCH)
PhSR .... Philippine Sociological Review [*A publication*]
PHSSA ...... Physica Status Solidi [*A publication*]
PHST .... Packaging, Handling, Storage, and Transportation
PhSt .... Philosophical Studies [*A publication*]
PHSTB .... Physica Scripta [*A publication*]
Ph St Tr ..... Phillipps' State Trials   (DLA)
PHSYB .... Photosynthetica [*A publication*]
PHT .... Paris, TN [*Location identifier*] [*FAA*]   (FAAL)
PHT .... Passive Hemagglutination Technique [*Immunology*]
PHT .... Personhistorisk Tidskrift [*A publication*]
PhT .... [*The*] Phoenix and the Turtle [*Shakespearean work*]
pht .... Photographer [*MARC relator code*] [*Library of Congress*]
PHT .... Phototube
Pht .... Phthaloyl [*Also, Phth*] [*Biochemistry*]
PHT .... Physical Therapy Technician [*Navy*]
PHT .... Pitch, Hit, and Throw [*Youth competition sponsored by professional baseball*]
PHT .... Portal Hypertension [*Medicine*]
PHT .... Preheat
PHT .... Progressive Household Technicians [*An association*]   (EA)
PHT .... Putting Hubby Through [*College "degree" earned by some wives*]
PHT .... Torrance State Hospital, Torrance, PA [*OCLC symbol*]   (OCLC)
PHTab .... President's Hundred Tab [*Military decoration*]   (AABC)
PHTAT .... Para-Hydroxytriamterene [*Biochemistry*]
PHTATS ...... Para-Hydroxytriamterene Sulfate [*Biochemistry*]
P-H Tax ...... Federal Taxes [*Prentice-Hall, Inc.*]   (DLA)
P-H Tax Ct Mem ... Tax Court Memorandum Decisions [*Prentice-Hall, Inc.*]   (DLA)
P-H Tax Ct Rep & Mem Dec ... Tax Court Reported and Memorandum Decisions [*Prentice-Hall, Inc.*]   (DLA)
PHTC .... Pharmatec, Inc. [*NASDAQ symbol*]   (NQ)
PHTC .... Pneumatic Hydraulic Test Console   (KSC)
PhTD .... Physical Therapy Doctor
PHTEA ...... Physics Teacher [*A publication*]
PHTED .... Physiology Teacher [*A publication*]
PHTF .... Pearl Harbor Training Facility [*Navy*]
Phth .... Phthaloyl [*Also, Pht*] [*Organic chemistry*]
PHTN .... Photon Sources, Inc. [*NASDAQ symbol*]   (NQ)
PHTOA .... Physics Today [*A publication*]
PHTS .... Primary Heat Transport System [*Nuclear energy*]   (NRCH)
PHTTA .... Philips Technische Tijdschrift [*A publication*]
PHU .... Pressure, Hydraulic Unit
PHuJ .... Juniata College, Huntingdon, PA [*Library symbol*] [*Library of Congress*]   (LCLS)
PHum .... Przeglad Humanistyczny [*A publication*]
P-H Unrep Tr Cas ... Prentice-Hall Unreported Trust Cases   (DLA)
PHUZA .... Physik in Unserer Zeit [*A publication*]
PHV .... Paramount Home Video
PHV .... Phase Velocity
PHV .... Pro Haec Vice [*For This Turn*] [*Latin*]   (ROG)
PHV .... Wernersville State Hospital, Wernersville, PA [*OCLC symbol*]   (OCLC)
PHVA .... Plasma Homovanillic Acid [*Biochemistry*]
PHVPS .... Primary High-Voltage Power Supply
PHW .... Pemberton Houston Willoughby Investment Corp. [*Toronto Stock Exchange symbol*] [*Vancouver Stock Exchange symbol*]
PHW .... Phalaborwa [*South Africa*] [*Airport symbol*]   (OAG)
PHW .... Philatelic Hobbies for the Wounded   (EA)

PhW............ Philologische Wochenschrift [*A publication*]
PHW .... Warren State Hospital, Warren, PA [*OCLC symbol*] (OCLC)
PHWA .... Professional Hockey Writers' Association   (EA)
PHWA .... Protestant Health and Welfare Assembly [*Schaumburg, IL*] (EA)
PHWEA ...... Pharmaceutisch Weekblad [*A publication*]
PHWR .... Pressurized Heavy Water Reactor
PHX .... Partial Hepectomy [*Medicine*]
PHX .... PHL Corp. [*NYSE symbol*]
PHX .... Phoenix [*Arizona*] [*Airport symbol*] (OAG)
PHX .... Woodville State Hospital, Carnegie, PA [*OCLC symbol*] (OCLC)
PHXA .... Phoenix American, Inc. [*NASDAQ symbol*] (NQ)
PHXQA ...... Phoenix Quarterly [*A publication*]
PHY .... C. Howard Marcy State Hospital, Pittsburgh, PA [*OCLC symbol*] (OCLC)
PHY .... Norman, OK [*Location identifier*] [*FAA*] (FAAL)
PHY .... Pharyngitis
Phy .... Phylon [*A publication*]
Phy .... Physalaemin [*Biochemistry*]
PHY .... Physical
PHY .... Physician
PHYB .... Pioneer Hi-Bred International [*NASDAQ symbol*] (NQ)
PHYBA .... Phyton (Buenos Aires) [*A publication*]
PHYCOM .... Physicians Communication Service [*Database*]
Phyl .... Phylon [*A publication*]
PHYL .... Physiological
PHYMA ...... Phytomorphology [*A publication*]
PHYS .... Physical   (AFM)
PHYS .... Physician
PHYS .... Physicist   (ADA)
PHYS .... Physics
PHYS .... Physiology
Phys A .... Physica A. Europhysics Journal [*A publication*]
PHYSA .... Physica (Amsterdam) [*A publication*]
Phys Abstr ... Physics Abstracts [*A publication*]
Phys Acoust ... Physical Acoustics. Principles and Methods [*A publication*]
Phys Act Rep ... Physical Activities Report [*A publication*]
Phys Appl ... Physics and Applications [*A publication*]
Phys Atoms and Molecules ... Physics of Atoms and Molecules [*A publication*]
Phys B .... Physica B. Europhysics Journal. Low Temperature and Solid State Physics [*A publication*]
PHYSBE ..... Physiological Simulation Benchmark Experiment
Phys Ber .... Physikalische Berichte [*A publication*]
Phys Bl .... Physikalische Blaetter [*A publication*]
Phys Briefs ... Physics Briefs [*West Germany*] [*A publication*]
Phys Bull .... Physics Bulletin [*A publication*]
Phys Bull (Peking) ... Physics Bulletin (Peking) [*A publication*]
Phys C .... Physica C. Europhysics Journal. Atomic, Molecular, and Plasma Physics Optics [*A publication*]
Phys Can .... Physics in Canada [*A publication*]
Phys C Glas ... Physics and Chemistry of Glasses [*A publication*]
Phys Chem ... Physical Chemistry [*A publication*]
Phys & Chem ... Physics and Chemistry [*A publication*]
Phys-Chem Biol (Chiba) ... Physico-Chemical Biology (Chiba) [*A publication*]
Phys Chem Earth ... Physics and Chemistry of the Earth [*A publication*]
Phys and Chem Earth ... Physics and Chemistry of the Earth [*A publication*]
Phys Chem Fast React ... Physical Chemistry of Fast Reactions [*A publication*]
Phys Chem Glasses ... Physics and Chemistry of Glasses [*A publication*]
Phys and Chem Glasses ... Physics and Chemistry of Glasses. Section B. Journal. Society of Glass Technology [*A publication*]
Phys Chem Liq ... Physics and Chemistry of Liquids [*A publication*]
Phys Chem Mater Layered Struct ... Physics and Chemistry of Materials with Layered Structures [*A publication*]
Phys Chem Miner ... Physics and Chemistry of Minerals [*A publication*]
Phys Chem (NY) ... Physical Chemistry (New York) [*A publication*]
Phys Chem Ser Monogr ... Physical Chemistry. Series of Monographs [*A publication*]
Phys Chem Space ... Physics and Chemistry in Space [*A publication*]
Phys Condens Matter ... Physics of Condensed Matter [*A publication*]
Phys Con Matt ... Physics of Condensed Matter [*A publication*]
Phys D .... Physica D [*A publication*]
Phys Daten ... Physik Daten [*Physics Data*]
Phys-Diaet Ther ... Physikalisch-Diaetetische Therapie [*West Germany*] [*A publication*]
Phys Didakt ... Physik und Didaktik [*A publication*]
Phys Earth Planetary Interiors ... Physics of the Earth and Planetary Interiors [*A publication*]
Phys Earth Planet Inter ... Physics of the Earth and Planetary Interiors [*A publication*]
PHYSEC ..... Physical Security   (MCD)
Phys Ed ...... Physical Educator [*A publication*]
Phys Ed Bul ... Physical Education Bulletin for Teachers in Secondary Schools [*A publication*]
Phys Ed J ... Physical Education Journal [*A publication*]
Phys Educ ... Physical Education [*A publication*]
Phys Educ ... Physical Educator [*A publication*]
Phys Educ Newsl ... Physical Education Newsletter [*A publication*]

Phys Energ Fortis Phys Nucl ... Physica Energiae Fortis et Physica Nuclearis [*People's Republic of China*] [*A publication*]
Phys Energi Fort Phys Nuclear ... Physica Energiae Fortis et Physica Nuclearis [*People's Republic of China*] [*A publication*]
Phys Eng .... Physical Engineer
Phys Environ Rep Dep Archit Sci Syd Univ ... Physical Environment Report. Department of Architectural Science. University of Sydney [*A publication*]
Phys E Plan ... Physics of the Earth and Planetary Interiors [*A publication*]
PHYSEXAM ... Physical Examination
Phys Failure Electron ... Physics of Failure in Electronics [*A publication*]
Phys Fenn ... Physica Fennica [*A publication*]
Phys Fit Newsl ... Physical Fitness Newsletter [*A publication*]
Phys Fit Res Dig ... Physical Fitness Research Digest [*A publication*]
Phys Fluids ... Physics of Fluids [*A publication*]
Phys Fluids Suppl ... Physics of Fluids. Supplement [*A publication*]
Phys Grundlagen Med Abh Biophys ... Physikalische Grundlagen der Medizin. Abhandlungen aus der Biophysik [*A publication*]
Physica A ... Physica A. Theoretical and Statistical Physics [*A publication*]
Physica B ... Physica B. Europhysics Journal. Low Temperature and Solid State Physics [*A publication*]
Physica C ... Physica C. Europhysics Journal. Atomic, Molecular, and Plasma Physics Optics [*A publication*]
Physical Educ J ... Physical Education Journal [*A publication*]
Physica Status Solidi A ... Physica Status Solidi. Sectio A [*A publication*]
Physica Status Solidi B ... Physica Status Solidi. Sectio B [*A publication*]
Physician Assist ... Physician Assistant [*Later, Physician Assistant/Health Practitioner*] [*A publication*]
Physician Assist Health Pract ... Physician Assistant/Health Practitioner [*A publication*]
Physician Comput Monthly ... Physician Computer Monthly [*A publication*]
Physicians Manage ... Physicians Management [*A publication*]
Physician Sportsmed ... Physician and Sports Medicine [*A publication*]
Physician and Surg ... Physician and Surgeon [*A publication*]
Physicochem Hydrodyn ... Physicochemical Hydrodynamics [*England*] [*A publication*]
Physics & Chem ... Physics and Chemistry [*A publication*]
Physics Ed ... Physics Education [*A publication*]
Physics Teach ... Physics Teacher [*A publication*]
Physikunterr ... Physikunterricht [*A publication*]
PHYSIO ...... Physiotherapy [*Medicine*]
PHYSIOG ... Physiognomy [*Slang*]   (DSUE)
PHYSIOG ... Physiographic
PHYSIOL .... Physiological   (MSA)
PHYSIOL .... Physiology   (ROG)
Physiol Behav ... Physiology and Behavior [*A publication*]
Physiol Biochem Cultiv Plants ... Physiology and Biochemistry of Cultivated Plants [*A publication*]
Physiol Biochem Cult Plants (USSR) ... Physiology and Biochemistry of Cultivated Plants (USSR) [*A publication*]
Physiol Bohemoslov ... Physiologia Bohemoslovaca [*A publication*]
Physiol Can ... Physiology Canada [*A publication*]
Physiol Chem Phys ... Physiological Chemistry and Physics [*Later, Physiological Chemistry and Physics and Medical NMR*] [*A publication*]
Physiol Ecol ... Physiology and Ecology [*A publication*]
Physiol Ent ... Physiological Entomology [*A publication*]
Physiol Menschen ... Physiologie des Menschen [*A publication*]
Physiologia Comp Oecol ... Physiologia Comparata et Oecologia [*A publication*]
Physiol Pathophysiol Skin ... Physiology and Pathophysiology of the Skin [*A publication*]
Physiol Pharmacol Physicians ... Physiology and Pharmacology for Physicians [*A publication*]
Physiol Physicians ... Physiology for Physicians [*A publication*]
Physiol Plant ... Physiologia Plantarum [*A publication*]
Physiol Plant Pathol ... Physiological Plant Pathology [*A publication*]
Physiol Plant Suppl ... Physiologia Plantarum. Supplementum [*A publication*]
Physiol Psychol ... Physiological Psychology [*A publication*]
Physiol Rev ... Physiological Reviews [*A publication*]
Physiol Soc Philadelphia Monogr ... Physiological Society of Philadelphia. Monographs [*A publication*]
Physiol Teach ... Physiology Teacher [*A publication*]
Physiol Veg ... Physiologie Vegetale [*A publication*]
Physiol Zool ... Physiological Zoology [*A publication*]
Physiother Can ... Physiotherapy Canada [*A publication*]
Physis - Riv Internaz Storia Sci ... Physis. Rivista Internazionale di Storia della Scienza [*A publication*]
Physis Secc A Oceanos Org ... Physis. Seccion A: Oceanos y Sus Organismos [*A publication*]
Physis Secc A Oceanos Sus Org ... Physis. Seccion A: Oceanos y Sus Organismos [*A publication*]
Physis Secc B Aguas Cont Org ... Physis. Seccion B: Aguas Continentales y Sus Organismos [*A publication*]
Physis Secc B Aguas Cont Sus Org ... Physis. Seccion B: Aguas Continentales y Sus Organismos [*A publication*]
Physis Secc C Cont Org Terr ... Physis. Seccion C: Continentes y Organismos Terrestres [*A publication*]
Phys Kondens Mater ... Physik der Kondensierten Materie [*A publication*]
PHYSL .... Physiological   (AFM)

Physl Behav ... Physiology and Behavior [*A publication*]
Physl Bohem ... Physiologia Bohemoslovaca [*A publication*]
Physl Chem ... Physiological Chemistry and Physics [*Later, Physiological Chemistry and Physics and Medical NMR*] [*A publication*]
Phys Lett.... Physics Letters [*Netherlands*] [*A publication*]
Phys Lett A ... Physics Letters. A [*A publication*]
Phys Lett B ... Physics Letters. B [*A publication*]
Phys Lett C ... Physics Letters. Section C [*Netherlands*] [*A publication*]
Phys Letters ... Physics Letters [*A publication*]
Physl Plant ... Physiologia Plantarum [*A publication*]
Physl Pl P ... Physiological Plant Pathology [*A publication*]
Physl Psych ... Physiological Psychology [*A publication*]
Physl Veget ... Physiologie Vegetale [*A publication*]
Physl Zool ... Physiological Zoology [*A publication*]
Phys Med Bi ... Physics in Medicine and Biology [*A publication*]
Phys Med Biol ... Physics in Medicine and Biology [*A publication*]
Phys Med and Biol ... Physics in Medicine and Biology [*A publication*]
Phys Met.... Physics of Metals [*A publication*]
Phys Methods Chem Anal ... Physical Methods in Chemical Analysis [*A publication*]
Phys Met Metallogr ... Physics of Metals and Metallography [*A publication*]
PHYSN .... Physician
Phys News ... Physics News Bulletin. Indian Physics Association [*A publication*]
Phys Norv ... Physica Norvegica [*A publication*]
Phys Norveg ... Physica Norvegica [*A publication*]
PHYSOG .... Physiognomy [*Slang*] (DSUE)
Phys Pap.... Physics Papers [*A publication*]
Phys Pap Silesian Univ Katowice ... Physics Papers. Silesian University in Katowice [*Poland*] [*A publication*]
Phys Quantum Electron ... Physics of Quantum Electronics [*A publication*]
Phys R........ Physical Review [*A publication*]
Phys Rep.... Physics Reports. Review Section of Physics Letters. Section C [*Netherlands*] [*A publication*]
Phys Rep Kumamoto Univ ... Physics Reports Kumamoto University [*A publication*]
Phys Rep Phys Lett Sect C ... Physics Reports. Physics Letters. Section C [*A publication*]
Phys Rev .... Physical Review [*A publication*]
Phys Rev A ... Physical Review. A. General Physics [*A publication*]
Phys Rev A 3 ... Physical Review. A. General Physics. Third Series [*A publication*]
Phys Rev A Gen Phys ... Physical Review. A. General Physics [*A publication*]
Phys Rev B 3 ... Physical Review. B. Condensed Matter. Third Series [*A publication*]
Phys Rev B Conden Matt ... Physical Review. B. Condensed Matter [*A publication*]
Phys Rev B Condens Matter ... Physical Review. B. Condensed Matter [*A publication*]
Phys Rev C ... Physical Review. C. Nuclear Physics [*A publication*]
Phys Rev C 3 ... Physical Review. C. Nuclear Physics. Third Series [*A publication*]
Phys Rev D ... Physical Review. D. Particles and Fields [*A publication*]
Phys Rev D 3 ... Physical Review. D. Particles and Fields. Third Series [*A publication*]
Phys Rev L ... Physical Review. Letters [*A publication*]
Phys Rev Lett ... Physical Review. Letters [*A publication*]
Phys Rev Sect A ... Physical Review. Section A [*A publication*]
Phys Rev Sect B ... Physical Review. Section B [*A publication*]
Phys Rev Suppl ... Physical Review. Supplement [*A publication*]
Phys Scr .... Physica Scripta [*A publication*]
Phys Sintering ... Physics of Sintering [*Yugoslavia*] [*A publication*]
Phys Soc Lond Proc ... Physical Society of London. Proceedings [*A publication*]
Phys Solariterr ... Physica Solariterrestris [*A publication*]
Phys Solid Earth (Engl Ed) ... Physics of the Solid Earth (English Edition) [*A publication*]
Phys Stat Sol A ... Physica Status Solidi. A [*A publication*]
Phys Stat Sol B ... Physica Status Solidi. B [*A publication*]
Phys Status Solidi ... Physica Status Solidi [*A publication*]
Phys Status Solidi A ... Physica Status Solidi. A [*A publication*]
Phys Status Solidi B ... Physica Status Solidi. B. Basic Research [*A publication*]
Phys St S-A ... Physica Status Solidi. A. Applied Research [*A publication*]
Phys St S-B ... Physica Status Solidi. B. Basic Research [*A publication*]
Phys Teach ... Physics Teacher [*A publication*]
Phys Tech Biol Res ... Physical Techniques in Biological Research [*A publication*]
Phys Technol ... Physics in Technology [*A publication*]
PHYSTER... Physical Therapy (AABC)
Phys Ther... Physical Therapy [*A publication*]
Phys Thin Films ... Physics of Thin Films. Advances in Research and Development [*A publication*]
Phys Today ... Physics Today [*A publication*]
Phys Unserer Zeit ... Physik in Unserer Zeit [*A publication*]
Phys Verh ... Physikalische Verhandlungen [*A publication*]
PHYSY ...... Physiology
Phys Z........ Physikalische Zeitschrift [*East Germany*] [*A publication*]
PHYT.......... Physio Technology [*NASDAQ symbol*] (NQ)
Phyt............ Phytopathology [*A publication*]
PHYTA .... Phytopathology [*A publication*]

PHYTB .... Physics in Technology [*A publication*]
Phytiat Phytopharm ... Phytiatrie-Phytopharmacie [*A publication*]
Phytiatr-Phytopharm Rev Fr Med Pharm Veg ... Phytiatrie-Phytopharmacie. Revue Francaise de Medicine et de Pharmacie des Vegetaux [*A publication*]
Phytochem ... Phytochemistry [*Oxford*] [*A publication*]
Phytochemistr (Oxf) ... Phytochemistry (Oxford) [*A publication*]
Phytoma Def Cult ... Phytoma. Defense des Cultures [*France*] [*A publication*]
Phytomorph ... Phytomorphology [*A publication*]
Phytomorphol ... Phytomorphology [*A publication*]
Phyton Aust ... Phyton. Annales Rei Botanicae Austria [*A publication*]
Phyton Int J Exp Bot ... Phyton. International Journal of Experimental Botany [*A publication*]
Phyton Rev Int Bot Exp ... Phyton. Revista Internacional de Botanica Experimental [*A publication*]
PHYTOPATH ... Phytopathology
Phytopathol ... Phytopathology [*A publication*]
Phytopathol Mediterr ... Phytopathologie Mediterranea [*A publication*]
Phytopathol News ... Phytopathology News [*A publication*]
Phytopathol Z ... Phytopathologische Zeitschrift [*A publication*]
Phytopathol ZJ Phytopathol ... Phytopathologische Zeitschrift/Journal of Phytopathology [*A publication*]
Phytopath Z ... Phytopathologische Zeitschrift [*A publication*]
Phytoprot... Phytoprotection [*A publication*]
PHYVA .... Physiologie Vegetale [*A publication*]
PHYZA ...... Phytopathologische Zeitschrift [*A publication*]
PHZ .... Ashland State General Hospital, Ashland, PA [*OCLC symbol*] (OCLC)
PHZAA ...... Pharmazeutische Zeitung. Vereinigt mit Apotheker-Zeitung [*A publication*]
PHZIA........ Pharamazeutische Zeitung [*A publication*]
PHZOA ...... Physiological Zoology [*A publication*]
PI .... Packaging Institute [*Later, PI/USA*] (EA)
PI .... Paducah & Illinois Railroad [*AAR code*]
PI .... Pagine Istriane [*A publication*]
PI .... Pancreatic Insufficiency [*Gastroenterology*]
PI .... Pansophic Institute (EA)
PI .... Pantera International (EA)
PI .... Paper Insulated
PI .... Paracel Islands [*Two-letter standard code*] (CNC)
PI .... Parallel Input [*Data processing*] (BUR)
PI .... Parity Index [*EEO*]
P & I .... Parole e le Idee [*A publication*]
PI .... Parti Independantiste [*Quebec*]
PI .... Particle Integration (CAAL)
PI .... Partido Independente [*Independent Party*] [*Costa Rica*]
PI .... Partido Intransigente [*Intransigent Party*] [*Argentina*] (PD)
PI .... Patient's Interests [*Medicine*]
PI .... Patrol Inspector [*Immigration and Naturalization Service*]
PI .... Payload Interrogator (MCD)
PI .... Per Inquiry [*Advertising*]
PI .... Perceptions, Incorporated [*An association*] [*Millburn, NJ*] (EA)
PI .... Perceptual Isolation
PI .... Performance Improvement
PI .... Performance Index
PI .... Performance Indicator (MCD)
P & I .... Performance and Interface [*Specification*] [*NASA*] (NASA)
PI .... Periodic Inspection [*Military*] (AFM)
PI .... Periodicals Institute [*West Caldwell, NJ*] (EA)
PI .... Peripheral Iridectomy [*Medicine*]
PI .... Perlite Institute [*Commack, NY*] (EA)
PI .... Permeability Index [*Clinical chemistry*]
PI .... Personal Identification
PI .... Personal Income
PI .... Personal Injury [*Insurance*]
PI .... Personal Injury Accident [*British police term*]
PI .... Personal Investment [*A publication*] (ADA)
PI .... Personality Inventory [*Psychology*]
PI .... Peru Indigena [*A publication*]
PI .... Petroleum Information Corp. (EISS)
PI .... Pharmacopoeia Internationalis [*International Pharmacopoeia*]
PI .... Phenanthroimidazole [*Organic chemistry*]
PI .... Phenyl Isocyanate [*Organic chemistry*]
PI .... Philippine Islands
PI .... Philippines [*Aircraft nationality and registration mark*] (FAAC)
Pi .... Phosphate, Inorganic [*Chemistry*]
PI .... Phosphatidylinositol [*Biochemistry*]
PI .... Photo International (EA-IO)
P-I .... Photogrammetric Instrumentation (AAG)
PI .... Photointerpretation [*or Photointerpreter*]
PI .... Photoionization [*Physical chemistry*]
PI .... Physical Inventory (NRCH)
PI .... Physically Impaired
PI .... Piedmont Aviation, Incorporated [*ICAO designator*] (OAG)
PI .... Pig Iron
PI .... Pigeon Trainer [*Navy*]
PI .... Pilot. Fort Smith and Simpson [*Northwest Territory, Canada*] [*A publication*]
PI .... Pilot International [*Macon, GA*] (EA)
PI ,.............. Pilot Item (MCD)
PI .... Pilotless Intercepter [*Air Force*]

PI .... Pink (ROG)
PI .... Pipe [*Freight*]
P & I .... Piping and Instrumentation [*Nuclear energy*]   (NRCH)
PI .... Plaque Index [*Dentistry*]
PI .... Plasma Iron [*Hematology*]
PI .... Plastochron Index [*Botany*]
PI .... Pneumatosis Intestinalis [*Medicine*]
PI .... Point of Impact   (AFM)
PI .... Point Initiating
PI .... Point Insulating
PI .... Point of Interception [*Navigation*]
PI .... Point of Intersection
PI .... Poison Ivy [*Campers' slang*]
PI .... Polyimide [*Organic chemistry*]
PI .... Polyisoprene [*Organic chemistry*]
PI .... Pompeiiana, Incorporated [*An association*]   (EA)
PI .... Poni Iussit [*Ordered to Be Placed*] [*Latin*]
PI .... Popcorn Institute [*An association*] [*Chicago, IL*]   (EA)
PI .... Population Institute [*An association*] [*Washington, DC*]   (EA)
PI .... Portfolio Insurance [*Finance*]
PI .... Positive Interlace [*Television*]
P & I .... Postage and Insurance [*Doll collecting*]
PI .... Postimpressionist [*School of painting*]
PI .... Postinoculation [*Medicine*]
PI .... Postischemic [*Medicine*]
PI .... Potash Institute [*Later, PPI*]   (EA)
PI .... Potomac Institute [*An association*] [*Washington, DC*]   (EA)
PI .... Power Injection
PI .... Power Input
PI .... Precision Instrument   (NVT)
PI .... Predicted Impact   (MCD)
PI .... Pregnancy Induced [*Gynecology*]
PI .... Preinduction [*Medicine*]
PI .... Preliminary Inspection   (MCD)
PI .... Preliminary Investigation   (NASA)
PI .... Preliminary Issue
PI .... Preparatory Interval [*Psychometrics*]
PI .... Prepositioned Instruction [*DoD*]
PI .... Present Illness [*Medicine*]
PI .... Pressure Indicator
Pi .... Pressure of Inspiration [*Medicine*]
PI .... Primacord Interstage
PI .... Primary Infarction [*Medicine*]
P & I .... Principal and Interest   (ADA)
PI .... Principal Investigator   (MCD)
PI .... Printer [*Navy*]
PI .... Printers' Ink [*A publication*]
PI .... Priority Interrupt   (IEEE)
PI .... Private Institution [*British*]
PI .... Private Investigator
PI .... Proactive Inhibition [*Psychology*]
PI .... Process Instrumentation [*Nuclear energy*]   (NRCH)
PI .... Processor Interface
PI .... Procurement Inspection   (MCD)
PI .... Procurement Item   (NASA)
PI .... Product Improvement   (MCD)
P/I .... Production Illustration   (MSA)
PI .... Production Interval
PI .... Productivity Index   (IEEE)
PI .... Program Indicator   (IEEE)
PI .... Program Indicator Code   (CMD)
PI .... Program Instruction [*Data processing*]   (BUR)
PI .... Program of Instrumentation   (MUGU)
PI .... Program Interrupt
PI .... Program Introduction
PI .... Program Issuances [*Assistance Payments Administration, HEW*]
PI .... Programed Information [*Data processing*]
PI .... Programed Instruction
PI .... Programed Introduction   (MCD)
PI .... Project Intrex [*Massachusetts Institute of Technology*]   (EA)
PI .... Prolactin Inhibitor [*Endocrinology*]
P & I .... Properties and Installations
PI .... Property Index [*British police term*]
PI .... Propidium Iodide [*Fluorescent dye*]
PI .... Proportional-Plus Integral [*Digital control*]
PI .... Protamine Insulin
Pi .... Protease Inhibitor
P & I .... Protection and Indemnity [*Business and trade*]
PI .... Protocol Internationale
PI .... Psychiatric Institute
PI .... Psychosynthesis Institute   (EA)
PI .... Public Information
PI .... Publication Instructions
PI .... Pulmonary Incompetence [*Medicine*]
PI .... Pulmonary Indices [*Medicine*]
PI .... Pulmonary Infarction [*Medicine*]
PI .... Pulmonary Intervertebral Disc [*Medicine*]
PI .... Pulse Induction   (ADA)
PI .... Purge Isolation [*Nuclear energy*]   (NRCH)
PI .... Pyritization Index [*Geoscience*]

PI .... Trademark for an ophthalmic drug
PI1 .... Pinedale [*Wyoming*] [*Seismograph station code, US Geological Survey*] [*Closed*]   (SEIS)
PI1 .... State Correctional Institute at Camp Hill, Camp Hill, PA [*OCLC symbol*]   (OCLC)
PI2 .... Pinedale [*Wyoming*] [*Seismograph station code, US Geological Survey*] [*Closed*]   (SEIS)
PI2 .... State Correctional Institute at Dallas, Dallas, PA [*OCLC symbol*]   (OCLC)
PI3 .... Pinedale [*Wyoming*] [*Seismograph station code, US Geological Survey*] [*Closed*]   (SEIS)
P³I .... Preplanned Product Improvement [*DoD*]
PI3 .... State Correctional Institute at Grateford, Grateford, PA [*OCLC symbol*]   (OCLC)
PI4 .... Pinedale [*Wyoming*] [*Seismograph station code, US Geological Survey*] [*Closed*]   (SEIS)
PI4 .... State Correctional Institute at Huntingdon, Huntingdon, PA [*OCLC symbol*]   (OCLC)
PI5 .... Pinedale [*Wyoming*] [*Seismograph station code, US Geological Survey*] [*Closed*]   (SEIS)
PI5 .... State Correctional Institute at Muncy, Muncy, PA [*OCLC symbol*]   (OCLC)
PI6 .... Pinedale [*Wyoming*] [*Seismograph station code, US Geological Survey*] [*Closed*]   (SEIS)
PI6 .... State Correctional Institute at Pittsburgh, Pittsburgh, PA [*OCLC symbol*]   (OCLC)
PI7 .... Pinedale [*Wyoming*] [*Seismograph station code, US Geological Survey*] [*Closed*]   (SEIS)
PI7 .... State Regional Correctional Facility, Greensburg, PA [*OCLC symbol*]   (OCLC)
PIA .... Pacific Islands Association [*Long Beach, NY*]   (EA)
PIA .... Packaged Ice Association [*Formerly, NAII, NIA*] [*Chicago, IL*]   (EA)
PIA .... Pakistan International Airlines Corp.
PIA .... Parapsychology Institute of America   (EA)
PIA .... Passive Immunological Agglutination
PIA .... Peoria [*Illinois*] [*Airport symbol*]   (OAG)
PIA .... Perfumery Importers Association [*Defunct*]   (EA)
PIA .... Peripheral Interface Adapter [*Data processing*]
PIA .... Personnel Inventory Analysis [*Army*]
PIA .... Petroleum Incentives Administration [*Canada*]
PIA .... Phenylisopropyladenosine [*Biochemistry*]
PIA .... Piano [*Softly*] [*Music*]
PIA .... Pilots International Association [*Minneapolis, MN*]   (EA)
PIA .... Pitten [*Austria*] [*Seismograph station code, US Geological Survey*]   (SEIS)
PIA .... Plasma Insulin Activity [*Clinical chemistry*]
PIA .... Plastics Institute of America
PIA .... Plug-In Amplifier
PIA .... Polycultural Institution of America
PIA .... Positive Ion Accelerator
PIA .... Positron Intensity Accumulator   (MCD)
PIA .... Preinstallation Acceptance
PIA .... Primary Insurance Account [*Social Security Administration*]   (OICC)
PIA .... Primary Insurance Amount
PIA .... Principal Industry Activity [*IRS*]
PIA .... Printing Industries of America [*Arlington, VA*]   (EA)
PIA .... Proceedings. Irish Academy [*A publication*]
PIA .... Production Inventory Analysis   (AAG)
PIA .... Professional Insurance Agents [*Formerly, NAMIA*] [*An association*] [*Alexandria, VA*]   (EA)
PIA .... Psychiatric Institute of America [*For-profit network of private psychiatric hospitals*]   (EA)
PIA .... Public Information Act
PIA .... Public Information Adviser [*NATO*]   (NATG)
PIA .... Pumice Institute of America   (EA)
PIA .... White Haven Center, White Haven, PA [*OCLC symbol*]   (OCLC)
505 PIA ...... 505th Parachute Infantry Association   (EA)
PIAA .... Pre-Arrangement Interment Association of America [*Washington, DC*]   (EA)
PIAAD .... Proceedings. Indian Academy of Sciences. Series. Chemical Sciences [*A publication*]
PIAC .... Permanent International Altaistic Conference   (EA)
PIAC .... Petroleum Industry Advisory Committee [*British*]
PIAC .... Problem Identification and Correction [*DoD*]   (AFIT)
PIACS .... Pacific Integrated Automatic Communications Systems [*Military*]
PIACT .... Program for the Introduction and Adaptation of Contraceptive Technology [*Seattle, WA*]   (EA)
PIADC ...... Plum Island Animal Disease Center [*Formerly, PIADL*]
PIADL .... Plum Island Animal Disease Laboratory [*of ARS, Department of Agriculture*] [*Later, PIADC*]
Piaget Theor Help Prof ... Piagetian Theory and the Helping Professions [*A publication*]
PIAMA .... Professional Institute for the American Management Association   (OICC)
PIAMD .... Proceedings. Indian Academy of Sciences. Series. Mathematical Sciences [*A publication*]
PIANC .... Permanent International Association of Navigation Congresses [*Brussels, Belgium*]   (EA-IO)

Pland......... Papyri Iandanae [*A publication*]   (OCD)
PIAND....... Proceedings. Indian Academy of Sciences. Series. Animal Sciences [*A publication*]
PIANG....... Piangendo [*Plaintive*] [*Music*]
PIANISS..... Pianissimo [*Very Softly*] [*Music*]
Piano Q...... Piano Quarterly [*A publication*]
Piano Quart... Piano Quarterly [*A publication*]
Piano Tech... Piano Technician [*A publication*]
PIAP......... Psychologists Interested in the Advancement of Psychotherapy [*Later, APA*]   (EA)
PIAPACS.... Psychophysiological Information Acquisition, Processing, and Control System
PIAR......... Problem Identification and Analysis Report [*Military*]   (CAAL)
PIAR......... Project Impact Analysis Report   (MCD)
PIARC....... Permanent International Association of Road Congresses [*See also AIPCR*]   (EA-IO)
PIAS......... Photographic Inventory and Accountancy System
PIAS......... Piaster [*Monetary unit in Spain, Republic of Vietnam, and some Middle Eastern countries*]
PIAS......... Program Impact Analysis Scenario
PIASA....... Polish Institute of Arts and Sciences in America   (EA)
P I A Sci A... Proceedings. Indian Academy of Sciences. Section A [*A publication*]
P I A Sci B... Proceedings. Indian Academy of Sciences. Section B [*A publication*]
PIASH........ Proceedings. Israel Academy of Sciences and Humanities [*Jerusalem*] [*A publication*]
PIASS........ Paris International Aviation and Space Salon   (MCD)
PIAT......... Peabody Individual Achievement Test [*Education*]
PIAT......... Projector Infantry, Antitank [*British shoulder-controlled weapon*]
PIB............ George Junior Republic, Grove City, PA [*OCLC symbol*]   (OCLC)
PIB............ Laurel/Hattiesburg [*Mississippi*] [*Airport symbol*]   (OAG)
PIB............ Pacific Inland Tariff Bureau, Portland OR [*STAC*]
PIB............ Papuan Infantry Battalion
PIB............ Parachute Infantry Battalion [*Army*]
PIB............ Partial Ileal Bypass [*Medicine*]
PIB............ Partido Indio de Bolivia
PIB............ Payload Integration Bay [*NASA*]   (KSC)
PIB............ Pender Island [*British Columbia*] [*Seismograph station code, US Geological Survey*]   (SEIS)
PIB............ Periodic Information Briefing   (MCD)
PIB............ Personal Information Briefing [*of returning POW's*] [*Air Force*]
PIB............ Petroleum Information Bureau
PIB............ Photo Intelligence Brief   (AFM)
PIB............ Photo Interpretation Brief   (MCD)
PIB............ Plug-In Blank
PIB............ Polar Ionospheric Beacon
PIB............ Polyisobutylene [*Organic chemistry*]
PIB............ Polytechnic Institute of Brooklyn [*Later, PINY*]   (MCD)
PIB............ Preliminary Instruction Book
PIB............ Prices and Incomes Board [*British*]
PIB............ Processor Interface Buffer [*Telecommunications*]   (TEL)
PIB............ Product Improvement Bulletin
PIB............ Programable Input Buffer
PIB............ Propellant Inspection Building [*NASA*]   (KSC)
PIB............ Public Information Bulletin [*Australian Taxation Office*] [*A publication*]
PIB............ Publishers Information Bureau [*New York, NY*]   (EA)
PIB............ Publishing Information Bulletin [*A publication*]
PIB............ Pulse Interference Blanker
PIB............ Pyrotechnic Installation Building [*NASA*]   (KSC)
PIBA......... Pacific Indonesian Business Association
PIBA......... Primary Industry Bank of Australia Ltd.   (ADA)
PIBAC....... Permanent International Bureau of Analytical Chemistry of Human and Animal Food
PIBAL........ Pilot Balloon Observation
PIBAL........ Polytechnic Institute of Brooklyn Aeronautical Laboratory   (MCD)
PIBALS....... Pilot Balloon Soundings
PIBC.......... Pacific Institute of Bio-Organic Chemistry
PIBD.......... Point Initiating, Base Detonating [*Projectile*]
PIBL.......... PEMA [*Procurement of Equipment and Missiles, Army*] Item Baseline List   (AABC)
PIBMM....... Permanent International Bureau of Motorcycle Manufacturers
PIBMRI....... Polytechnic Institute of Brooklyn, Microwave Research Institute   (IEEE)
PIBOL........ Pilot Back Up Control
PIBS.......... Polar Ionospheric Beacon Satellite [*NASA*]
PIC............ Calverton, NY [*Location identifier*] [*FAA*]   (FAAL)
PIC............ Craig House Technoma Workshop, Pittsburgh, PA [*OCLC symbol*]   (OCLC)
PIC............ Pacific Insurance Conference
PIC............ Pacific Intelligence Center   (MCD)
PIC............ Paired-Ion Chromatography
PIC............ Particle in Cell [*Gas solid*]
PIC............ Payload Integration Center [*NASA*]   (MCD)
PIC............ Payload Integration Contractor   (MCD)
PIC............ Peak Identification Computer

PIC............ Pershing Instant Comment [*Donaldson, Lufkin & Jenrette*] [*Database*]
PIC............ Personal Identification Code [*Banking*]
PIC............ Pesticides Information Center [*National Agricultural Library*] [*Terminated, 1969*]
PIC............ Petrochemical Investing Corporation
PIC............ Photographic Industry Council [*Rochester, NY*]   (EA)
PIC............ Photographic Interpretation Center   (MCD)
PIC............ Physical Inorganic Chemistry [*Elsevier Book Series*] [*A publication*]
PIC............ Piccadilly Saloon [*London*]   (DSUE)
PIC............ Piccolo [*Music*]   (ROG)
PIC............ [*The*] Pickens Railroad Co. [*Later, PICK*] [*AAR code*]
Pic............. Picrotoxin [*Biochemistry*]
Pic............. Pictor [*Constellation*]
PIC............ Picture   (AABC)
PIC............ Pilot in Command [*Aviation*]   (FAAC)
PIC............ Pilot-Integrated Cockpit   (AAG)
PIC............ Pine Cay [*British West Indies*] [*Airport symbol*] [*Obsolete*]   (OAG)
PIC............ Planned Insurance Coverage
PIC............ Plasma Insulin Concentration [*Clinical chemistry*]
PIC............ Plastic Insulated Conductor
PIC............ Polyethylene Insulated Conductor [*Telecommunications*]
PIC............ Polymer-Impregnated Concrete   (KSC)
PIC............ Position Independent Code [*Telecommunications*]   (TEL)
PIC............ Positive Ion Chamber
PIC............ Postinflammatory Corticoid [*Medicine*]
PIC............ Power Information Center [*Interagency Advanced Power Group*] [*Washington, DC*]
PIC............ Power Integrated Circuit [*Data processing*]
PIC............ Preinstallation Calibration   (KSC)
PIC............ Preinstallation Checkout   (NASA)
PIC............ Premium Industry Club [*Schiller Park, IL*]   (EA)
PIC............ Presbyterian Interracial Council   (EA)
PIC............ Pressure Indicator Controller [*Aerospace*]
PIC............ Primate Information Center [*University of Washington*] [*Seattle, WA*]
pic............. Prince Edward Island [*Canada*] [*MARC country of publication code*] [*Library of Congress*]   (LCCP)
PIC............ Printer Interface Cartridge [*Epson America, Inc.*]
PIC............ Priority Interrupt Controller
PIC............ Private Industry Council [*Generic term for group that helps provide job training*]
PIC............ Procedures for Instrument Calibration
PIC............ Process Interface Control
PIC............ Processor Input Channel   (NVT)
PIC............ Procurement Information Center
PIC............ Procurement Information for Contracts [*AFSC*]
PIC............ Product of Incomplete Combustion
PIC............ Professional Instrument Course [*Aeronautics*]
PIC............ Professional Interfraternity Conference [*Later, PFA*]   (EA)
PIC............ Program Identification Code   (MUGU)
PIC............ Program for Improved Contract Management [*Military*]   (AFIT)
PIC............ Program Information Center
PIC............ Program Initiations and Commitments   (AAG)
PIC............ Program Instruction, Calibration [*Marine Corps*]
PIC............ Program Interrupt Control [*Data processing*]
PIC............ Programable Interval Clock   (NASA)
PIC............ Programmable Interrupt Controller [*Data processing*]
PIC............ Project Information Center
PIC............ Pseudo-Isocytidine [*Antineoplastic compound*]
PIC............ Public Information Center [*Nuclear energy*]   (NRCH)
PIC............ Public Information Committee [*of the NATO Military Committee*]   (NATG)
PIC............ Pulsed Ionization Chamber
PIC............ Purpose Identification Code
PIC............ Pursuant to Instructions Contained In   (MUGU)
PIC............ Pyro Initiator Capacitors   (NASA)
PIC............ Pyro Initiator Controller   (NASA)
PICA........... Palestine Israelite Colonisation Association
PICA........... Police Insignia Collector's Association   (EA)
PICA........... Porch Index of Communicative Ability [*Psychology*]
PICA........... Posterior Inferior Cerebellar Artery [*Anatomy*]
PICA........... Power Industry Computer Applications   (MCD)
PICA........... Primary Inventory Control Activity   (MCD)
PICA........... Printing Industry Computer Associates, Inc.
PICA........... Private Investment Company for Asia, SA
PICA........... Procedures for Inventory Control Afloat [*Navy*]
PICA........... Professional Insurance Communicators of America [*Formerly, MICE*] [*Indianapolis, IN*]   (EA)
PICA........... Programing Interpersonal Curricula for Adolescents [*Learning model*] [*Education*]
PICA........... Project for Integrated Catalogue Automation [*Royal Netherlands Library*] [*Cataloging cooperative*]   (EISS)
PICA........... Property Services Agency Information on Construction and Architecture [*Property Service Agency Library Service*] [*Database*]
PICA........... Public Interest Computer Association [*Washington, DC*]   (EA)
PICAC........ Porch Index of Communicative Ability in Children [*Psychology*]

PICAC .... Power Industry Computer Applications Conference   (MCD)
PICADAD ... Place Identification/Characteristics and Area/Distance and Direction [*Bureau of Census*]
PICAM .... Proceedings. International Congress of Americanists [*A publication*]
PICAO .... Provisional International Civil Aviation Organization [*Later, ICAO*]
Picardie Inform ... Picardie Information [*A publication*]
PICB .... Peabody Institute of the City of Baltimore [*Maryland*]
PICC .... Parts for Import Cars Coalition [*Cleveland, OH*]   (EA)
PICC .... Piccadilly Cafeterias [*NASDAQ symbol*]   (NQ)
PICC .... Piccolo
PICC .... Plastics in Construction Council [*Later, CCS*]   (EA)
PICC .... Provisional International Computation Center
PICCO .... Pennsylvania Industrial Chemical Corporation [*Trademark*]
PICE .... Product Improved Compatibility Electronics   (MCD)
PICE .... Programable Integrated Control Equipment
PICED .... Proceedings. International Conference on Noise Control Engineering [*A publication*]
PICEE .... President's Interagency Committee on Export Expansion [*Absorbed by President's Export Council in 1979*]   (EGAO)
PICE/PIA ... Printing Industry Credit Exchange/PIA [*of the Printing Industries of America*] [*Arlington, VA*]   (EA)
PICG .... Programme International de Correlation Geologique [*International Geological Correlation Programme - IGCP*]   (EA-IO)
PICGC .... Permanent International Committee for Genetic Congresses
PicGPA ...... Picrylated Guinea Pig Albumin [*Immunochemistry*]
PICI .... Publications. Institut de Civilisation Indienne [*A publication*]
P I Civ E 1 ... Proceedings. Institution of Civil Engineers. Part 1. Design and Construction [*A publication*]
P I Civ E 2 ... Proceedings. Institution of Civil Engineers. Part 2. Research and Theory [*A publication*]
PICK .... Part Information Correlation Key
PICK .... [*The*] Pickens Railroad Co. [*Formerly, PIC*] [*AAR code*]
Pick .... Pickering's Massachusetts Supreme Judicial Court Reports [*1822-39*]   (DLA)
PICK .... Pickwick [*Refers to an inferior quality cigar*]   (DSUE)
Picker Clin Scintil ... Picker Clinical Scintillator [*A publication*]
PICKFAIR ... [*Mary*] Pickford and [*Douglas*] Fairbanks [*Acronym is name of estate once owned by these early film stars*]
Pickle .... Pickle's Reports [*85-108 Tennessee*]   (DLA)
PICKLE ...... President's Intelligence Checklist [*Daily report prepared by CIA*]
Pickle Pak Sci ... Pickle Pak Science [*A publication*]
Pick (Mass) ... Pickering's Massachusetts Reports [*18-41 Massachusetts*]   (DLA)
PICL .... Proceedings. International Congress of Linguists [*A publication*]
PICM .... Master Chief Precision Instrumentman [*Navy rating*]
PICM .... Party of the Independence Congress of Madagascar
PICM .... Permanent International Committee of Mothers
PICMME ..... Provisional Intergovernmental Committee for Movement of Migrants in Europe   (NATG)
PICN .... Pic 'N' Save Corp. [*NASDAQ symbol*]   (NQ)
PIC-NF .... Picroindigocarmine-Nuclear Fast Red [*A biological stain*]
PICO .... International Congress of Orientalists. Proceedings [*A publication*]
PICO .... Person in Column One [*1980 census*]
PICO .... Polar Ice Core Drilling Office [*National Science Foundation*]   (MSC)
PICO .... Proceedings. International Congress of Orientalists [*A publication*]
PICO .... Product Improvement Control Office   (AFM)
PICO .... Purchasing Internal Change Order   (MCD)
PICOA .... Physicians Insurance of Ohio [*NASDAQ symbol*]   (NQ)
PICOE .... Programed Initiations, Commitments, Obligations, and Expenditures [*AFSC*]
PICOMM .... Potter Instrument Coordinated Measuring Machine
PICON .... Process Intelligent Control [*A data processing system from LISP Machine, Inc.*]
PICORNAVIRUS ... Pico Ribonucleic Acid Virus
PICOST ...... Probability of Incurring Estimated Costs [*Military*]   (MCD)
PICP .... Proceedings. International Congress of Philosophy [*A publication*]
PICP .... Program Interface Control Plan   (NASA)
PICPAB ...... Phenomena Induced by Charged Particle Beams
PICPS .... Proceedings. International Congress of Phonetic Sciences [*A publication*]
PICPSA ...... Permanent International Commission for the Proof of Small-Arms [*Liege, Belgium*]   (EA-IO)
PICRC .... Pesticide and Industrial Chemicals Research Center [*Public Health Service*]
PICRS .... Program Information Control and Retrieval System   (NASA)
PICRS .... Program Information Coordination and Review Service   (NASA)
PICS .... Permit Imprint Collectors Society   (EA)
PICS .... Perpetual Inventory Control System
PICS .... Personnel Information Communication [*or Control*] System [*Data processing*]

PICS .... Pharmaceutical Information Control System   (DIT)
PICS .... Photo Index and Cataloging System   (NASA)
PICS .... Photography in Community Self-Development [*Program of Master Photo Dealers and Finishers Association*]
PICS .... Pioneer Image Converter System [*NASA*]
PICS .... Plug-In Inventory Control System [*Bell System*]
PICS .... Predefined Input Control Sequence   (MCD)
PICS .... Procurement Information Control System [*NASA*]
PICS .... Production Information and Control System [*IBM Corp.*] [*Software package*]
PICS .... Production Inventory Control System
PICS .... Productivity Improvement and Control System   (BUR)
PICS .... Program Information and Control System   (MCD)
PICS/DCPR ... Plug-In Inventory Control System/Detailed Continuing Property Record [*Telecommunications*]   (TEL)
PICT .... Perceived Instrumentality of the College Test
Pict .... Pictor [*Constellation*]
PICT .... Pictorial   (ROG)
PICT .... Project on the Improvement of College Teaching
Pict Dict Rome ... Pictorial Dictionary of Ancient Rome [*A publication*]   (OCD)
PICTOMAP ... Photographic Image Conversion by Tonal Masking Procedures   (MCD)
PictR .... Pictorial Review [*A publication*]
PICTUREBALM ... [*A*] programing language [*1979*]   (CSR)
PICU .... Parallel Instruction Control Unit
PICU .... Pediatric Intensive Care Unit [*Medicine*]
PICU .... Priority Interrupt Control Unit [*Data processing*]   (MDG)
PICU .... Pulmonary Intensive Care Unit [*Medicine*]
PICUTPC .... Permanent and International Committee of Underground Town Planning and Construction
PID .... D. T. Watson Home for Crippled Children, Leetsdale, PA [*OCLC symbol*]   (OCLC)
PID .... Pain Intensity Differences [*Medicine*]
PId .... Parole e le Idee [*A publication*]
PID .... Partial Initial Decision [*Nuclear energy*]   (NRCH)
PID .... Partido de Integracion Democrata [*Democratic Integration Party*] [*Argentina*]   (PPW)
PID .... Passenger Information Display
PID .... Patrol Input Device   (MCD)
PID .... Pelvic Inflammatory Disease [*Medicine*]
PID .... Phenindione [*or Phenylindandione*] [*Anticoagulant*]
PID .... Photointerpretation Department [*Military*]
PID .... Photoionization Detector
PID .... Photon-Induced Dissociation [*For spectral studies*]
PID .... Pictorial Information Digitizer [*Data processing*]   (DIT)
PID .... Pilot-Induced Deceleration
P & ID .... Piping and Instrumentation Diagram [*Nuclear energy*]   (NRCH)
P & ID .... Piping & Instrumentation Diagrams [*Calcomp Ltd.*] [*Software package*]
PID .... Political Intelligence Department [*British*] [*World War II*]
PID .... Port Identification [*Telecommunications*]   (TEL)
PID .... Primary Immunodeficiency Disease [*Medicine*]
PID .... Prime Item Development   (MCD)
P & ID .... Process and Instrumentation Diagram [*Nuclear energy*]   (NRCH)
PID .... Procurement Information Digest   (AFM)
PID .... Procurement Item/Identification Description [*DoD*]
PID .... Program Information Document   (MCD)
PID .... Program Introduction Document   (NASA)
PID .... Project Implementation Directive [*Air Force*]
PID .... Prolapsed Intervertebral Disc [*Medicine*]
PID .... Proportional-Integral-Differentiated [*Digital control algorithm*]
PID .... Proportional-Plus Integral-Plus Derivative [*Digital control algorithm*]
PID .... Protruded Intervertebral Disc [*Medicine*]
PID .... Pseudo Interrupt Device
PID .... Public Information Division [*Military*]
PIDA .... Payload Installation and Deployment Aid [*NASA*]   (NASA)
PIDA .... Pet Industry Distributors Association [*Baltimore, MD*]   (EA)
PIDC .... Philadelphia Industrial Development Corporation
PIDCOM ..... Process Instruments Digital Communication System [*Beckman Industries*]
PIDD .... Passive Identification/Detection and Direction   (MCD)
PI/DE .... Passive Identification/Direction Finding Equipment   (MCD)
PIDE .... Policia Internacional e de Defesa do Estado [*Police for the Control of Foreigners and Defense of the State*] [*Portugal and Portuguese Africa*]
PIDEP .... Preinterservice Data Exchange Program
PIDL .... Position Involves Intermittent Duty at Isolated Locations   (FAAC)
PIDP .... Pilot Information Display Panel
PIDP .... Programable Indicator Data Processor [*Military*]   (CAAL)
PIDR .... Product Inspection Discrepancy Report   (MCD)
PIDRA .... Portable Insulin Dosage-Regulating Apparatus [*Medicine*]
PIDRS .... Photographic Instrumentation Data Recording System   (MCD)
PIDS .... Portable Image Display System   (NASA)
PIDS .... Prime Item Development Specification
PIDSA .... Population Information Documentation System for Africa
PIE .... Elwyn Institute, Elwyn, PA [*OCLC symbol*]   (OCLC)

PIE............. Pacific Islands Ecosystems [*Springfield, VA*] [*Department of the Interior*] [*Bibliographic database*]
PIE............. Pacing Item Evaluation (MCD)
PIE............. Parallel Instruction Execution [*Data processing*] (BUR)
PIE............. Parallel Interface Element
PIE............. Patent Information Exploitation [*Canadian Patent Office*]
PIE............. Payload Integration Equipment [*NASA*] (MCD)
PIE............. Payroll Audit, Indexing, and Expiration
PIE............. Photo-Induced Electrochromism
PIE............. Piedmont Aviation, Inc. [*NYSE symbol*]
PIE............. Pietermaritzburg [*South Africa*] [*Seismograph station code, US Geological Survey*] [*Closed*] (SEIS)
PIE............. Pipestone Petroleums [*Toronto Stock Exchange symbol*] [*Vancouver Stock Exchange symbol*]
PIE............. Plug-In Electronics
PIE............. Plume Interaction Experiment [*Army*] (RDA)
PIE............. Poly(iminoethylene) [*Organic chemistry*]
PIE............. Portable Information Evaluation
PIE............. Post-Irradiation Examination [*Nuclear energy*] (NRCH)
PIE............. Post-Irradiation Experiment [*Nuclear energy*] (NRCH)
PIE............. Preimplantation Embryo
PIE............. Program for Increased Education [*Military*]
PIE............. Program Interrupt Entry [*Data processing*]
PIE............. Public Interest Economics Foundation [*Defunct*] (EA)
PIE............. Publications Indexed for Engineering [*A publication*]
PIE............. Pulmonary Infiltration with Eosinophilia [*Medicine*]
PIE............. Pulse Interference Eliminator [*RADAR*]
PIE............. Pulse Interference Emitting (MCD)
PIE............. St. Petersburg [*Florida*] [*Airport symbol*] (OAG)
PIEA.......... Pencil Industry Export Association [*Defunct*] (EA)
PIEA.......... Petroleum Industry Electrical Association [*Later, ENTELEC*] (EA)
PIEA.......... Pre-Arrangement Interment Exchange of America [*Later, PIAA*]
PIE-C........ Public Interest Economics Center (EA)
PIECOST.... Probability of Incurring Estimated Costs [*Military*]
PIECP........ Preliminary Impact Engineering Change Proposal (MCD)
PIEEA......... Proceedings. Institution of Electrical Engineers [*A publication*]
P IEEE........ Proceedings. Institute of Electrical and Electronics Engineers [*A publication*]
P IEE (Lond) ... Proceedings. Institution of Electrical Engineers (London) [*A publication*]
PIE-F.......... Public Interest Economics Foundation [*Defunct*] (EA)
Pieleg Polozna ... Pielegniarka i Polozna [*A publication*]
Pienpuu Toimikun Julk ... Pienpuualan Toimikunnan Julkaisu [*A publication*]
PIEP............ Primary Irritation Evaluation Program
Pierce RR..... Pierce on Railroad Law (DLA)
PIERS........ Port Import Export Reporting Services [*Journal of Commerce, Inc.*] [*Database*]
PIES.......... Packaged Interchangeable Electronic System
PIES.......... Penning Ionization Electron Spectroscopy
PIES.......... Project Independence Evaluation System [*Energy policy*]
PIESD........ Proceedings. Indian Academy of Sciences. Series. Earth and Planetary Sciences [*A publication*]
PIEWD....... Prace Naukowe Instytutu Energoelektryki Politechniki Wroclawskiej [*A publication*]
PIF............. Paris et Ile-De-France. Memoires [*A publication*]
P & IF......... Paris et Ile-De-France. Memoires [*A publication*]
PIF............. Payload Integration Facility [*NASA*] (KSC)
PIF............. Personnel Identification Feature [*Navy*] (NVT)
PIF............. Pilot Information File
PIF............. Place in Inactive File
PIF............. Point Initiating Fuze
PIF............. Positive Identification Feature (MCD)
PIF............. Predictive Influence Function [*Statistics*]
PIF............. Preparer Inventory File [*IRS*]
PIF............. Productivity Investment Fund [*Program*] [*Air Force*]
PIF............. Program Information File
PIF............. Prolactin-Release Inhibiting Factor [*Also, PRIH*] [*Endocrinology*]
PIF............. Proliferation Inhibitory Factor [*Immunochemistry*]
PIF............. Provision of Industrial Facilities (AABC)
PIF............. Pseudo-Identification Feature (MCD)
PIFAO........ Publications. Institut Francais d'Archeologie Orientale du Caire [*A publication*]
PIFAO BEC ... Publications. Institut Francais d'Archeologie Orientale. Bibliotheque d'Etudes Coptes [*A publication*]
PIFAS........ Publicaciones. Instituto de Filologia. Anejo de Sphinx [*A publication*]
PIFI............ Pressure-Induced Intracranial Focal Ischemia [*Medicine*]
PIFLD........ Problemy Yadernoi Fiziki i Kosmicheskikh Luchei [*A publication*]
PIFMLL....... Proceedings. International Federation for Modern Languages and Literatures [*A publication*]
PIFOV........ Planet in Field of View [*NASA*]
PIFR.......... Peak Inspiratory Flow Rate [*Medicine*]
PIFS.......... Plume-Induced Flow Separation
PIFS.......... Prime Item Fabrication Specification
PIFT........... Platelet Immunofluorescence Test [*Analytical biochemistry*]
PIFUA........ Powerplant and Industrial Fuel Use Act of 1978

PIFWD........ Prace Naukowe Instytutu Fizyki Politechniki Wroclawskiej [*A publication*]
PIG............. Glenn Mills School, Glenn Mills, PA [*OCLC symbol*] (OCLC)
PIG............. Pacific Institute of Geography
PIG............. Pendulous Integrating Gyro
PIG............. Phillips Ionization Gauge
PIG............. Photo-Island Grid
Pig............. Pig Iron [*A publication*]
Pig............. Pigott's Common Recoveries [*3 eds.*] [*1739-92*] (DLA)
PIG............. Pride, Integrity, Guts [*Police alternative for the appellation applied to police by radical groups*]
PIG............. Process Ink Gamut [*Printing technology*]
PIG............. Production Image Generator (MCD)
PIG............. Production Installation Group [*Military*] (CAAL)
PIG............. Pulse Inert Gas
PIGA.......... Pendulous Integrating Gyro Accelerometer
PIGBA........ Proceedings. Royal Institution of Great Britain [*A publication*]
Pig Judg.... Pigott's Foreign Judgments [*3rd ed.*] [*1908-09*] (DLA)
PIGLET...... Purchase Information, Gifts, Loans, Exchanges Tracking [*Suggested name for the Library of Congress computer system*]
PIGM......... Pigmentum [*Paint*] [*Pharmacy*]
PIGMA........ Pressurized Inert Gas Metal Arc (KSC)
Pigm Cell ... Pigment Cell [*A publication*]
Pigment Resin Tech ... Pigment and Resin Technology [*A publication*]
Pigment Resin Technol ... Pigment and Resin Technology [*A publication*]
PIGMI......... Pion Generator for Medical Irradiation [*Radiology*]
PIGMI......... Position Indicating General Measuring Instrument
Pig News Inf ... Pig News and Information [*A publication*]
Pig & R....... Pigott and Rodwell's English Registration Appeal Cases [*1843-45*] (DLA)
Pig Rec....... Pigott's Recoveries [*England*] (DLA)
PIGS.......... PAFEC Interactive Graphics System [*PAFEC Ltd.*] [*Software package*]
PIGS.......... Poles, Italians, Greeks, and Slavs
PIGS.......... Portable Inertial Guidance System
PIGU......... Pendulous Integrating Gyro Unit
PIH............. Phenylisopropylhydrazine [*Pharmacology*]
PIH............. Pocatello [*Idaho*] [*Airport symbol*] (OAG)
PIH............. Pork Industry Handbook [*A publication*]
PIH............. Pregnancy-Induced Hypertension [*Gynecology*]
PIH............. Prolactin-Release Inhibiting Hormone [*Endocrinology*]
PIH............. Public and Indian Housing [*HUD*]
PIH............. St. Gabriel's Hall, Phoenixville, PA [*OCLC symbol*] (OCLC)
PIHANS...... Publications de l'Institut Historique et Archeologique Neerlandais de Stamboul [*Leiden*] [*A publication*]
PIHM......... Polish Institute of Hydrology and Meteorology
PII............. Fairbanks, AK [*Location identifier*] [*FAA*] (FAAL)
PII............. Positive Immittance Inverter (IEEE)
PII............. Primary Irritation Indices [*for skin*]
PII............. Printing Industry Institute [*A graphic arts training school*]
PII............. Procurement Instrument Identification [*Navy*] (NG)
PII............. Pueblo International, Incorporated [*NYSE symbol*]
PII............. Sleighton School, Darling, PA [*OCLC symbol*] (OCLC)
PIIAA......... Proceedings. National Institute of Sciences of India. Part A. Physical Sciences [*A publication*]
PIIC............ Pergamon International Information Corporation [*Information service*] (EISS)
PIIC............ Pilgrim Intergroup Investment Corporation [*NASDAQ symbol*] (NQ)
PIIF............ Proteinase Inhibitor Inducing Factor [*Biochemistry*]
PIIM........... Planned Interdependency Incentive Method
PIIN............ Procurement Instruction Identification Number [*Army*] (AABC)
PIIN............ Procurement Instrument Identification Numbering [*System*] [*Navy*]
PI/INT'L...... Packaging Institute International [*Stamford, CT*] (EA)
PIJ............. Pickled-in-Jar [*Food technology*]
PIJAC........ Pet Industry Joint Advisory Council [*Washington, DC*] (EA)
PIJR........... Product Improvement Joint Review [*Military*]
PIK............ Glasgow [*Scotland*] Prestwick Airport [*Airport symbol*] (OAG)
PIK............ Payment in Kind
PIK............ Portable Injection Kit
Pike........... Pike's Reports [*1-5 Arkansas*] (DLA)
Pike & F Adm Law ... Pike and Fischer's Administrative Law (DLA)
Pike & F Fed Rules Service ... Pike and Fischer's Federal Rules Service (DLA)
Pike & Fischer Admin Law ... Pike and Fischer's Administrative Law (DLA)
Pike H of L ... Pike's History of the House of Lords (DLA)
PIKM.......... PIK. Northern Magazine for Children [*Northwest Territory, Canada*] [*A publication*]
PIKS.......... American Sports Advisors [*NASDAQ symbol*] (NQ)
PIL............. Brazos Santiago, TX [*Location identifier*] [*FAA*] (FAAL)
PIL............. Papers in Linguistics [*A publication*]
PIL............. Parti de l'Independance et de la Liberte [*Party for Independence and Liberty*] [*Congo - Leopoldville*]
PIL............. Payment in Lieu
PIL............. Percentage Increase in Loss [*Statistics*]
PIL............. Petroleum Investments Limited [*NYSE symbol*]
PIL............. Pilar [*Argentina*] [*Geomagnetic observatory code*]
PIL............. Pilar [*Cordoba*] [*Seismograph station code, US Geological Survey*] (SEIS)

PIL............. Pilula [*Pill*] [*Pharmacy*]
PIL............. Pistol Petroleum [*Vancouver Stock Exchange symbol*]
PIL............. Pitt Interpretive Language [*Data processing*]   (DIT)
PIL............. Plastic Impregnated Laminate
PIL............. Practice Instrument Landing   (ADA)
PIL............. Preferred Item List   (RDA)
PIL............. Processing Information List [*Data processing*]
PIL............. Procurement Information Letter   (MCD)
PIL............. Publications International Limited
PIL............. Purple Indicating Light   (MSA)
PILA .... Power Industry Laboratory Association   (EA)
PILAC....... Pulsed Ion Linear Accelerator
PILC .... Paper-Insulated, Lead-Covered Cable [*Telecommunications*]
PILCF........ Pilgrim Coal Corp. [*NASDAQ symbol*]   (NQ)
PILL........... Newport Dock [*British depot code*]
PILL........... Programed Instruction Language Learning [*Data processing*]
PILO .... Public Information Liaison Officer [*Military*]
PILOA....... Prace Instytutu Lotnictwa [*A publication*]
PILOT....... Paton Lyall Tosh [*Rock music group*]
PILOT....... Payment in Lieu of Taxes
PILOT....... Permutation Indexed Literature of Technology   (IEEE)
PILOT....... Piloted Low-Speed Test [*Aerospace*]
PILOT....... Printing Industry Language for Operations of Typesetting
PILP......... Parametric Integer Linear Program [*Data processing*]
PILP........... Program of Industry/Laboratory Projects [*National Research Council of Canada*]
PILP........... Pseudoinfinite, Logarithmically Periodic
PILS .... Pilsener Lager   (DSUE)
PILS .... Precision Instrument Landing System
PIL STA.... Pilot Station [*Nautical charts*]
PILTA....... Payment in Lieu of Taxes Act
PIm............ Immaculata College, Immaculata, PA [*Library symbol*] [*Library of Congress*]   (LCLS)
PIM........... Pacem in Maribus [*Secondary name for the International Ocean Institute*]   (MSC)
PIM........... Pacific Islands Monthly [*A publication*]
PIM........... Pacific Rim Energy [*Vancouver Stock Exchange symbol*]
PIM........... Parallel Inference Machine [*Data processing*]
PIM........... Penalties in Minutes [*Hockey*]
PIM........... Peripheral Interface Module
PIM........... Pine Mountain, GA [*Location identifier*] [*FAA*]   (FAAL)
PIM........... Plan of Intended Movement   (MUGU)
PIM........... Plated Interconnecting Matrix
PIM........... Plug-In Module   (MCD)
PIM........... Point of Intended Movement [*Military*]
PIM........... Politica Internacional (Madrid) [*A publication*]
PIM........... Polyphase Induction Motor
PIM........... Position and Intended Movement   (NATG)
PIM........... Position in Miles   (MCD)
PIM........... Precision Indicator of the Meridian
PIM........... Precision Instrument Mount
PIM........... Presa Del Infiernillo [*Mexico*] [*Seismograph station code, US Geological Survey*] [*Closed*]   (SEIS)
PIM........... Pricing Instructions Memorandum   (MCD)
PIM........... Processor Interface Module
PIM........... Product Information Memoranda
PIM........... Program Integration Manual
PIM........... Program Interface Module
PIM........... Progress in Industrial Microbiology [*Elsevier Book Series*] [*A publication*]
PIM........... Provincial Institute of Mining
PIM........... Pulse Intensity Modulation
PIM........... Pulse Interval Modulation
PIM........... South Mountain Restoration Center, South Mountain, PA [*OCLC symbol*]   (OCLC)
PiMA .... Ateneo de Manila University, Manila, Philippines [*Library symbol*] [*Library of Congress*]   (LCLS)
PIMA .... Paper Industry Management Association [*Arlington Heights, IL*]   (EA)
PIMA .... Plug-In Module Assembly   (MCD)
PIMA .... Prime Intermediate Maintenance Activity
PIMA .... Professional Insurance Mass-Marketing Association [*Bethesda, MD*]   (EA)
PIMA Mag ... PIMA [*Paper Industry Management Association*] Magazine [*United States*] [*A publication*]
PIMA Yrb ... PIMA [*Paper Industry Management Association*] Yearbook [*A publication*]
PIMBel .... Pracy Instytuta Movaznaustva Akademii Nauk Belaruskaj SSR [*A publication*]
PIMCC....... Packards International Motor Car Club   (EA)
PIMCO....... Poultry Industry Manufacturers Council [*Defunct*]   (EA)
PIME.......... Petrofi Irodalmi Muzeum Evkonyve [*A publication*]
PIME.......... Pontifical Institute for Mission Extension [*Roman Catholic men's religious order*]
PIMI........... Preinactivation Material Inspection [*Military*]   (NVT)
PIMIA .... Potentiometric Ionophore Modulated Immunoassay [*Electrochemistry*]
PIMK .... Portable Injection Molding Kit
PIMMA ...... Professional Insurance Mass-Marketing Association   (EA)
PIMNY....... Printing Industries of Metropolitan New York

PIMO .... Presentation of Information for Maintenance and Operation [*DoD*]
PIMS .... Personnel Inventory Management System [*AT & T*]
PIMS .... Photoionization Mass Spectrometry
PIMS .... Profit Impact of Marketing Strategy
PIMS .... Programable Implantable Medication System
PIMSA .... Prensa Independiente Mexicana, Sociedad Anonima [*Press agency*] [*Mexico*]
PIMSST...... Pontifical Institute of Mediaeval Studies. Studies and Texts [*A publication*]
PIMST .... Pontifical Institute of Mediaeval Studies. Studies and Texts [*A publication*]
PIMTB .... Proceedings. Annual Technical Meeting. International Metallographic Society, Inc. [*A publication*]
Pi Mu Epsilon J ... Pi Mu Epsilon Journal [*A publication*]
PIN .... Jasper, TX [*Location identifier*] [*FAA*]   (FAAL)
PIN .... P-Type Intrinsic N-Type [*or Positive-Intrinsic-Negative*]
PIN .... Page and Item Number
PIN .... Parallel Input
PIN .... Pennsylvania School for the Deaf, Philadelphia, PA [*OCLC symbol*]   (OCLC)
PIN .... People in Need [*Food program sponsored by family of kidnapped heiress, Patricia Hearst, 1974*]
PIN .... Personal Identification Number [*Banking*]
PIN .... Personal Injury Notice   (AAG)
PIN .... Piece Identification Number
PIN .... Pinedale [*Wyoming*] [*Seismograph station code, US Geological Survey*] [*Closed*]   (SEIS)
PIN .... Pinion   (MSA)
Pin .... Pinney's Wisconsin Supreme Court Reports [*1839-52*]   (DLA)
PIN .... Plan Identification Number   (AFM)
PIN .... Plant Information Network [*Fish and Wildlife Service*] [*Ceased operation*]   (EISS)
PIN .... Plastics Industry Notes [*Later, CIN*]
PIN .... Police Information Network [*San Francisco Bay area, California*]
PIN .... Position Indicator
PIN .... Positive-Intrinsic-Negative [*or P-Type Intrinsic N-Type*]
PIN .... Preliminary Imagery Nomination File   (MCD)
PIN .... Product Information Network [*McGraw-Hill Information Systems Co.*] [*New York, NY*] [*Information service*]   (EISS)
PIN .... Program Identification Number   (MUGU)
PIN .... Proposal Identification Number   (AAG)
PIN .... Public Service Co. of Indiana, Inc. [*NYSE symbol*]
PINA .... Parallax in Altitude [*Navigation*]
PINA .... Potash Institute of North America [*Later, PPI*]   (EA)
PINCCA...... Price Index Numbers for Current Cost Accounting [*Service in Information and Analysis*] [*Databank*] [*British*]   (EISS)
PIND.......... Particle Impact Noise Detection
Pind........... Pindar [*518-438BC*] [*Classical studies*]   (OCD)
PINE .... Passive Infrared Night Equipment   (MCD)
Pineapple Q ... Pineapple Quarterly [*A publication*]
Pine Inst Am Abstr Chem Sect ... Pine Institute of America. Abstracts. Chemical Section [*A publication*]
Pine Inst Am Tech Bull ... Pine Institute of America. Technical Bulletin [*A publication*]
PINES........ Public Information on Nuclear Energy Service [*American Nuclear Society*]
Ping Chat Mortg ... Pingrey's Treatise of Chattel Mortgages   (DLA)
PINGP .... Prairie Island Nuclear Generating Plant   (NRCH)
PINH .... Pyridoxal Isonicotinoylhydrazone [*Biochemistry*]
PINN........... Pinnacles National Monument
Pinn............ Pinney's Wisconsin Reports   (DLA)
PINN........... Proposed International Nonproprietary Name [*Drug research*]
Pinney........ Pinney's Wisconsin Reports   (DLA)
Pinney (sv) ... Pinney's Wisconsin Reports   (DLA)
PINO........... Positive Input - Negative Output [*Data processing*]
PINS .... Personnel Information System [*Army*]   (AABC)
PINS .... Persons in Need of Supervision [*Classification for delinquent children*]
PINS .... Point-in-Space   (MCD)
PINS .... Political Information System [*Databank of political strategist Richard Wirthlin*]
PINS .... Portable Inertial Navigation System
PINSAC..... PINS [*Portable Inertial Navigation System*] Alignment Console
PINSTD ...... Preinserted
PINT .... Pioneer International Corp. [*NASDAQ symbol*]   (NQ)
PINT .... Purdue Interpretive Program
PINT .... Purdue Interpretive Programming and Operating System   (MCD)
Pint Acabados Ind ... Pinturas y Acabados Industriales [*A publication*]
PInU .... Indiana University of Pennsylvania, Indiana, PA [*Library symbol*] [*Library of Congress*]   (LCLS)
Pin (Wis) .... Pinney's Wisconsin Reports   (DLA)
Pin Wis R.... Pinney's Wisconsin Reports   (DLA)
PINX .... Pinxit [*He, or She, Painted It*] [*Latin*]
PINXT........ Pinxit [*He, or She, Painted It*] [*Latin*]   (ROG)
PINY .... Polytechnic Institute of New York [*Formerly, PIB*]
PIO .... Palestine Information Office   (EA)
PIO .... Parallel Input/Output
PIO .... Pheniminooxazolidinone [*Pharmacology*]

PIO .... Pi Omicron National Sorority   (EA)
PIO .... Pielago [*Ship's rigging*]   (ROG)
PIO .... Pilot-Induced Oscillation
PIO .... Pilot Information Office
PIO .... Pinon, NM [*Location identifier*] [*FAA*]   (FAAL)
PIO .... Pioneer Airlines, Inc. [*Denver, CO*] [*FAA designator*]   (FAAC)
PIO .... Pioneer Electronic Corp. [*NYSE symbol*]
PIO .... Poets International Organisation   (EA-IO)
PIO .... Position Iterative Operation
PIO .... Precision Interactive Operation [*Data processing*]
PIO .... Private Input/Output [*Telecommunications*]   (TEL)
PIO .... Processor Input-Output [*Data processing*]   (MDG)
PIO .... Programed Input/Output
PIO .... Provisioned Item Order   (MCD)
PIO .... Public Information Office [*or Officer*]
PIO .... Western Pennsylvania School for the Deaf, Pittsburgh, PA [*OCLC symbol*]   (OCLC)
PIOCS .... Physical Input-Output Control System [*Data processing*]   (BUR)
PIOG .... [*The*] Pioneer Group [*NASDAQ symbol*]   (NQ)
PION .... Pioneer   (AABC)
Pioneering Concepts Mod Sci ... Pioneering Concepts in Modern Science [*A publication*]
Pioneers' Assoc of SA Pubs ... Pioneers' Association of South Australia. Publications [*A publication*]
PIOS .... Pioneer-Standard Electronics, Inc. [*NASDAQ symbol*]   (NQ)
PIOTA........ Post Irradiation Open Test Assembly [*Nuclear energy*]   (NRCH)
PIOTA........ Proximity Instrumented Open Test Assembly [*Nuclear energy*]   (NRCH)
PIOU .... Parallel Input-Output Unit [*Data processing*]   (IEEE)
PIP............. Pan-Iranist Party   (PPW)
PIP............. Para-Isothiocyanatephenethylamine [*Biochemistry*]
PIP............. Partido Independentista Puertorriqueno [*Puerto Rican Independence Party*]   (PPW)
PIP............. Partners in Progress [*Government*] [*Civil rights*]
PIP............. Pasuquin [*Philippines*] [*Seismograph station code, US Geological Survey*]   (SEIS)
PIP............. Path Independent Protocol
PIP............. Payload Interface Plan [*NASA*]   (NASA)
PIP............. Payment in Part [*Business and trade*]
PIP............. Penny Illustrated Paper [*A publication*]
PIP............. Periodic Interim Payments
PIP............. Peripheral Interchange Program [*Data processing*]
PIPER......... Peripheral Interface Programer [*Circuit*] [*Data processing*]
PIP............. Persistent Internal Polarization
PIP............. Personal Identification Project [*Data processing*]
PIP............. Personal Injury Protection [*Insurance*]
PIPIDA....... Personal Innovation Program
PIP............. Personnel Interface Processor   (MCD)
PIP............. Petroleum Incentives Program [*Canada*]
PIP............. Phosphatidylionositol Phosphate [*Biochemistry*]
PIPJ........... Photo Image Processor   (MCD)
PIP............. Photo Interpretive Program   (BUR)
PIP............. Picture-in-a-Picture [*Multi-Vision Products*] [*Video technology*]
PIP............. Pilot Point [*Alaska*] [*Airport symbol*]   (OAG)
PIP............. Piperacillin [*An antibiotic*]
PIP............. Plant Instrumentation Program
PIP............. Plant-in-Place
PIP............. Policy Improvement Program
PIP............. Policy Integration Program
PIP............. Population Information Program [*Johns Hopkins University*] [*Baltimore, MD*] [*Information service*]   (EA)
PIP............. Portable Instrumentation Package [*Military*]   (CAAL)
PIP............. Position Indicating Probe   (IEEE)
PIP............. Postal Instant Press [*American Stock Exchange symbol*]
PIP............. Power Input Panel
PIP............. Prearrival Inspection Procedure
PIP............. Precise Installation Position
PIP............. Predicted Impact Point [*Aerospace*]   (AAG)
PIP............. Predicted Intercept Point
PIP............. Preliminary Information Pamphlet
PIP............. Preparatory Investment Protection [*For the consortia which invested in deep sea mining*]
PIP............. Preparedness and Industrial Planning
PIP............. Pretty Important Person
PIP............. Primary Indicating Position Data Logger   (IEEE)
PIP............. Prior Immobilization and Positioning [*Roentgenology*]
PIP............. Probabilistic Information Processing
PIP............. Problem Identification Program   (MCD)
PIP............. Problem Input Preparation [*Data processing*]   (BUR)
PIP............. Procedural Information Pamphlet
PIP............. Proceedings in Print [*A bibliographic publication*]
PIP............. Product Improvement   (MCD)
PIP............. Product Improvement Plan
PIP............. Product Improvement Program [*Air Force*]
PIP............. Product Improvement Proposal   (MCD)
PIP............. Product Introductory Presentation
PIP............. Production Implementation Program   (AAG)
PIP............. Production Improvement Program [*Navy*]   (NG)
PIP............. Production Instrumentation Package   (NASA)
PIP............. Productivity Improvement Program [*Department of Labor*]

PIP............. Profit Improvement Program
PIP............. Program Implementation Plan   (MCD)
PIP............. Program Integration Plan
PIP............. Program in Process [*Data processing*]   (BUR)
PIP............. Programable Integrated Processor   (IEEE)
PIP............. Progressive Inspection Plan [*Navy*]   (NG)
PIP............. Project Implementation Plan
PIP............. Project on Information Processing   (IEEE)
PIP............. Project Initiation Period
PIP............. Projected Impact Point [*Aviation*]
PIP............. Proof in Print
PIP............. Proposal Instruction Package   (MCD)
PIP............. Proprietary Information Protection
PIP............. Prototypic Inlet Piping [*Nuclear energy*]   (NRCH)
PIP............. Prove in Plan   (MCD)
PIP............. Proximal Interphalangeal [*Joint*]
PIP............. Psychotic Inpatient Profile [*Psychology*]
PIP............. Public and Institutional Property [*Insurance*]
PIP............. Puerto Rican Independence Party   (PD)
PIP............. Puerto Rican Independent Party
PIP............. Pulse Input Proportional [*Electro-optical system*]
PIP............. Pulsed Integrating Pendulum
PIP............. Western Psychiatric Institute and Clinic, University of Pittsburgh, Pittsburgh, PA [*OCLC symbol*]   (OCLC)
PIPA .... Pacific Industrial Property Association
PIPA .... Pulse Integrating Pendulum Accelerometers
PIPA .... Pulse Integrating Pendulum Assembly   (NASA)
PIPACE ...... Peacetime Intelligence Plan, Allied Central Europe [*NATO*]   (NATG)
Pip & C Mil L ... Pipon and Collier's Military Law [*3rd ed.*] [*1865*]   (DLA)
PIPE .... Pipeline. Report of the Northern Pipeline Agency [*A publication*]
PIPE .... Pipestone National Monument
PIPE .... Plumbing Industry Progress and Education Fund
PIPECO ...... Photoion-Photoelectron Coincidence [*Spectroscopy*]
Pipeline Eng ... Pipeline Engineer [*A publication*]
Pipeline Gas J ... Pipeline and Gas Journal [*A publication*]
Pipeline & Gas J ... Pipeline and Gas Journal [*A publication*]
Pipe Line Ind ... Pipe Line Industry [*A publication*]
Pipeline Manage Oper Eng Gas Distrib News ... Pipeline Management, Operations, Engineering, and Gas Distribution News [*A publication*]
Pipeln Ind ... International Pipe Line Industry [*A publication*]
PIPER........ Pulsed Intense Plasma for Exploratory Research
PIPES .... Piperazinediethanesulfonic Acid [*A buffer*]
Pipes Pipelines Int ... Pipes and Pipelines International [*A publication*]
Pipes & Pipelines Int ... Pipes and Pipelines International [*A publication*]
PIPIDA....... Para-Isopropylphenyl(iminodiacetic Acid)
Piping Eng ... Piping Engineering [*A publication*]
Piping Process Mach (Tokyo) ... Piping and Process Machinery (Tokyo) [*A publication*]
PIPJ........... Proximal Interphalangeal Joint [*Anatomy*]
PIPLD .... Proceedings. Indian Academy of Sciences. Series. Plant Sciences [*A publication*]
PIPO .... Parallel-In Parallel-Out [*Telecommunications*]   (TEL)
PIPO .... Phase-In, Phase-Out   (MCD)
PIPPAP...... Pile for Producing Power and Plutonium [*Nuclear energy*]   (NRCH)
PIPR .... Plant-in-Place Records
PIPR .... Polytechnic Institute of Puerto Rico
PIPR .... Public Interest Public Relations   (EA)
PIPS .... Pattern Information Processing System
PIPS .... Peabody Intellectual Performance Scale [*Education*]
PIPS .... Postinjection Propulsion Subsystem [*NASA*]
PIPS .... Professional Institute of the Public Service of Canada [*See also IPFP*]
PIPS .... Properties of Irregular Parts System   (MCD)
PIPSCR ...... Philippine Islands Public Service Commission Reports   (DLA)
PIPSD........ Preprint. Institut Prikladnoi Matematiki Akademii Nauk SSSR [*A publication*]
PIPUCR...... Philippine Islands Public Utility Commission Reports   (DLA)
PIPWA....... Paper Industry and Paper World [*A publication*]
PIQ .... Parallel Instruction Queue
PIQ .... Program Idea Quotient [*Study to determine audience receptivity to new TV program*]
PIQ .... Property in Question
PIQ .... State Regional Correctional Facility at Mercer, Mercer, PA [*OCLC symbol*]   (OCLC)
PIQA.......... Proofing, Inspection, and Quality Assurance [*Military*]
PIQSY .... Probes for the International Quiet Solar Year [*OSS*]
PIQUA .... Pit and Quarry [*A publication*]
PIR............. Pacific Islands Regiments [*Australia*]
PIR............. Packaging Information Record   (MCD)
PIR............. Parachute Infantry Regiment [*Military*]
PIR............. Paragnostic Information Retrieval [*Parapsychology*]
PIR............. Partido de la Izquierda Revolucionaria [*Party of the Revolutionary Left*] [*Bolivian*]   (PPW)
PIR............. Peak Intensity Ratio [*Spectroscopy*]
PiR............. Pecat' i Revoljucija [*A publication*]
PIR............. Pennsylvania Rehabilitation Center, Johnstown, PA [*OCLC symbol*]   (OCLC)

PIR............. Periodic Incremental Release [*Physiology*]
PIR............. Periodic Intelligence Report
PIR............. Periodic Intelligence Review [*Supreme Allied Commander, Atlantic*]   (NATG)
PIR............. Personnel Information Report [*or Roster*]
PIR............. Petrolite Irradiation Reactor
PIR............. Philippine Independence Ribbon
PIR............. Phoenix International Raceway
PIR............. Photo Interpretation Report [*Air Force*]   (AFM)
PIR............. Photographic Intelligence Report [*Military*]
PIR............. Pier I Imports [*NYSE symbol*]
PIR............. Pierre [*South Dakota*] [*Airport symbol*]   (OAG)
PIR............. Pirmasens [*Federal Republic of Germany*] [*Seismograph station code, US Geological Survey*]   (SEIS)
PIR............. Plug-In Relay
PIR............. Postinhibitory Rebound [*Physiology*]
PIR............. Precision Instrument Runway [*Aviation*]   (FAAC)
PIR............. Precision Instrumentation RADAR
PIR............. Predicted Intercept Range [*Military*]   (CAAL)
PIR............. Pressure Ignition Rocket   (NATG)
PIR............. Priority Information Requirement [*Military intelligence*]   (INF)
PIR............. Process and Indoctrinate Recruits
PIR............. Procurement Initiation Request   (MCD)
PIR............. Product Improvement Review
PIR............. Product Information Release
PIR............. Production Inspection Record
PIR............. Program Incident Report
PIR............. Project Independence Report
PIR............. Prosopographia Imperii Romani [*A publication*]
PIR............. Protein Identification Resource [*National Biomedical Research Foundation*] [*Georgetown University Medical Center*] [*Washington, DC*] [*Information service*]   (EISS)
PIR............. Pure India Rubber [*Cables*]
PIRA........... Printing Industry Research Association
PIRA........... Prison Industries Reorganization Administration [*Terminated, 1940*]
PIRA........... Provisional Irish Republican Army
PIRAD........ Proximity Information, Range, and Disposition
PIRAZ........ Positive Identification RADAR Advisory Zone   (NVT)
PIRB.......... Position Indicating Radio Beacon
PIRC.......... Portable Inflatable Recompression Chamber   (MCD)
PIRC.......... Preventive Intervention Research Center for Child Health [*Yeshiva University*] [*Research center*]   (RCD)
PIRCS........ Passive Infrared Confirming Sensor   (MCD)
PIRD.......... Program Instrumentation Requirements Document [*NASA*]
PIRED........ Power Industry Research [*A publication*]
PI Rep........ Philippine Island Reports   (DLA)
PIREP........ Pilot Report [*Pertaining to meteorological conditions*] [*FAA*]
PIRFC........ Pilot Requests Forecast   (FAAC)
PIRG.......... Public Interest Research Group [*Formed by consumer-advocate Ralph Nader*]
PIRGIM...... Public Interest Research Group in Michigan [*Pronounced "purge-em"*]
PIRI........... Psychologists Interested in Religious Issues [*Later, APA*]   (EA)
PIRID......... Passive Infrared Intrusion Detector   (NVT)
PIRINC...... Petroleum Industry Research Foundation, Incorporated
PIRN.......... Preliminary Interface Revision Notice [*NASA*]   (KSC)
PIRO.......... Pictured Rocks National Lakeshore [*National Park Service designation*]
PIRP.......... Provisional International Reference Preparation
PIRR.......... Parts Installation and Removal Record [*NASA*]   (KSC)
PIRR.......... Problem Investigation and Repair Record [*NASA*]   (KSC)
PIRR.......... PWRS [*Prepositioned War Reserve Stock*] Interrogation and Readiness Reporting System [*Navy*]
PIRRB........ Photo Intelligence Requirements Review Board [*Military*]
PIRS.......... Personal Information Retrieval System
PIRS.......... Philosopher's Information Retrieval System [*Bowling Green State University*]
PIRS.......... Pollution Incident Reporting System [*Coast Guard*] [*Washington, DC*]
PIRS.......... Poseidon Information Retrieval System [*Missiles*]
PIRS.......... Project Information Retrieval System [*HEW*]
PIRT.......... Precision Infrared Tracking
PIRT.......... Precision Infrared Triangulation
Pis............. In Pisonem [*of Cicero*] [*Classical studies*]   (OCD)
PIS............. Parts Identification Service
PIS............. Passenger Information System
PIS............. Passive Infrared System
PIS............. Photographic Interpretation Section
PIS............. Pisa [*Italy*] [*Seismograph station code, US Geological Survey*] [*Closed*]   (SEIS)
PIS............. Poitiers [*France*] [*Airport symbol*]   (OAG)
PIS............. Position Indicator System
PIS............. Positive Ion Source
PIS............. Postal Inspection Service
PIS............. Pressure Indicating Switch   (NRCH)
PIS............. Process Instrument Sheet
PIS............. Process Instrumentation System [*Nuclear energy*]   (NRCH)
PIS............. Product Information Specialist
PIS............. Provisional International Standard
PIS............. Pulse Integration System

PIS............. Pulsed Illumination Source
PiS............. Puskin i Ego Sovremenniki [*A publication*]
PIS............. Stevens Trade School, Lancaster, PA [*OCLC symbol*]   (OCLC)
PISA.......... Persistent Information Space Architecture [*Data processing*]
PISA.......... Polish Independent Student Association [*EA*]
PISA.......... Public Interest Satellite Association [*Defunct*]   (EA)
PISAB........ Pulse Interference Separation and Blanking [*RADAR*]
PISAD .... Proceedings. International Symposium on Automotive Technology and Automation [*A publication*]
PISC.......... Parris Island, South Carolina [*Marine Corps*]
PISC.......... Petroleum Industry Security Council [*Austin, TX*]   (EA)
Pisc.......... Pisces [*Constellation*]
PISCU .... Pacific International Service Uts [*NASDAQ symbol*]   (NQ)
PISE .... No Pilot Balloon Observation Due to Unfavorable Sea Conditions [*National Weather Service*]   (FAAC)
PISG .... Pitcairn Islands Study Group [*American Philatelic Society*]   (EA)
PISH .... Program Instrumentation Summary Handbook [*NASA*]   (KSC)
Pishch Promst Kaz Mezhved Resp Nauchno Tekh Sb ... Pishchevaya Promyshlennost Kazakhstana Mezhvedomstvennyi Respublikanskii Nauchno Tekhnicheskii Sbornik [*A publication*]
Pishch Prom-st (Kiev 1965) ... Pishchevaya Promyshlennost (Kiev, 1965) [*A publication*]
Pishch Promst (Moscow) ... Pishchevaya Promyshlennost (Moscow) [*A publication*]
Pishch Prom-st' Nauchno-Proizvod Sb ... Pishchevaya Promyshlennost' Nauchno-Proizvodstvennyi Sbornik [*A publication*]
Pishch Promst SSSR ... Pishchevaya Promyshlennost SSSR [*A publication*]
Pis'ma Astron Zh ... Pis'ma v Astronomicheskii Zhurnal [*A publication*]
Pis'ma Zh Ehksp Teor Fiz ... Pis'ma v Zhurnal Ehksperimental'noj i Teoretическeskoj Fiziki [*A publication*]
Pis'ma Zh Tekh Fiz ... Pis'ma v Zhurnal Tekhnicheskoi Fiziki [*A publication*]
Pis'ma v Zh Tekh Fiz ... Pis'ma v Zhurnal Tekhnicheskoi Fiziki [*A publication*]
Pism Pam Vostoka ... Pis'mennye Pamiatniki Vostoka [*A publication*]
PISO.......... Parallel-In Serial-Out [*Telecommunications*]   (TEL)
PISP .... Pipe Springs National Monument
PIST .... Piston [*Automotive engineering*]
Pist.......... Piston's Mauritius Reports   (DLA)
Piston........ Piston's Mauritius Reports [*1861-62*]   (DLA)
PISW .... Process Interrupt Status Word
PI/T .... Parallel Interface/Timer [*Motorola, Inc.*]
PIT............. Part-Time, Intermittent, Temporary [*Nuclear energy*]
PIT............. Parti de l'Independance et du Travail [*Party of Independence and Labor*] [*Senegalese*]   (PPW)
PIT............. Performance Improvement Tests
PIT............. Peripheral Input Tape [*Data processing*]
PIT............. Peripheral Interface Tests   (MCD)
PIT............. Permanent Income Theory [*Econometrics*]
PIT............. Personal Income Tax
PIT............. Phase Inversion Temperature [*of emulsions*]
PIT............. Photographic Interpretation Technique
PIT............. Picture Identification Test [*Psychology*]
PIT............. Picture Impressions Test [*Psychology*]
PIT............. Pilot Instructor Training [*Aviation*]   (FAAC)
PIT............. Pirates Gold Corp. [*Vancouver Stock Exchange symbol*]
PIT............. Pittsburgh [*Pennsylvania*] [*Airport symbol*]
PIT............. Pittsburgh [*Pennsylvania*] [*Seismograph station code, US Geological Survey*] [*Closed*]   (SEIS)
PIT............. Plasma Iron Transport [*Hematology*]
PIT............. Polar Ionospheric Trough
PIT............. Polaris Industrial Team [*Missiles*]
PIT............. Pre-Induction Training
PIT............. Preinstallation Test [*NASA*]   (KSC)
PIT............. Prevailing-In Torque [*Automotive engineering*]
PIT............. Print Illegal and Trace
PIT............. Processing of Indexing Terms
PIT............. Product Improvement Test
PIT............. Program Instruction Tape [*Data processing*]   (IEEE)
PIT............. Programable Interval Timer
PIT............. Programed Instruction Text
PIT............. Projected Inactive Time [*Data processing*]
PIT............. Provincial Institute of Textiles
PIT............. Psychological Insight Test [*Psychometrics*]
PIT............. University of Pittsburgh, Pittsburgh, PA [*OCLC symbol*]   (OCLC)
PITA .... Pacific International Trapshooting Association   (EA)
PITA .... Provincial Institute of Technology and Art
Pitanie Udobr Rast ... Pitanie i Udobrenie Rastenii [*A publication*]
PITB .... Pacific Inland Tariff Bureau
PITBB .... Piano Teachers Journal [*A publication*]
Pitblado Lect ... Isaac Pitblado's Lectures on Continuing Legal Education   (DLA)
PITC .... Phenylisothiocyanate [*Organic chemistry*]
PITC .... Photoinduced Tunnel Current
Pitc.......... Pitcairn's Criminal Trials [*1488-1624*] [*Scotland*]   (DLA)
Pitc Crim Tr ... Pitcairn's Ancient Criminal Trials [*Scotland*]   (DLA)
PITCOM ..... Parliamentary Information Technology Committee [*Political communications*] [*British*]
Pitc Tr .... Pitcairn's Criminal Trials [*3 Scotland*]   (DLA)

PITE .... Project on Information Technology and Education [*Carnegie Corp. of New York*] (EA)
PITG .... Payload Integration Task Group [*NASA*] (NASA)
PITI .... Principal, Interest, Taxes, Insurance [*Real estate*]
Pitisc Lex ... Pitisci's Lexicon (DLA)
PITKA .... Proceedings. Institut Teknologi Bandung. Supplement [*A publication*]
Pit L .... University of Pittsburgh. Law Review [*A publication*]
Pitm Prin & Sur ... Pitman on Principal and Surety (DLA)
PITN .... Polyisothianaphthene [*Organic chemistry*]
Pit & Quar ... Pit and Quarry [*A publication*]
Pit Quarry ... Pit and Quarry [*A publication*]
PITR .... Plasma Iron Transport [*or Turnover*] Rate [*Hematology*]
PITS .... Passive Intercept Tracking System
PITS .... Payload Integration Test Set [*NASA*] (MCD)
PITS .... Photoinduced Transient Spectroscopy
PITS .... Propulsion Integration Test Stand
Pit Sur .... Pitman on Principal and Surety [*1840*] (DLA)
Pitt .... Pittsburgh, PA (DLA)
PITT .... Polaris Integrated Test Team [*Missiles*]
Pitt LJ .... Pittsburgh Legal Journal (DLA)
Pitt Rivers Mus Univ Oxford Occas Pap Technol ... Pitt Rivers Museum. University of Oxford. Occasional Papers on Technology [*A publication*]
Pitts .... Pittsburgh, PA (DLA)
Pitts .... Pittsburgh Reports (DLA)
Pittsb .... Pittsburgh, PA (DLA)
Pittsb .... Pittsburgh Reports (DLA)
Pittsbg Bs ... Pittsburgh Business Review [*A publication*]
Pittsb Leg J ... Pittsburgh Legal Journal [*Pennsylvania*] (DLA)
Pittsb Leg J NS ... Pittsburgh Legal Journal, New Series [*Pennsylvania*] (DLA)
Pittsb Leg J (OS) ... Pittsburgh Legal Journal, Old Series (DLA)
Pittsb Leg J (PA) ... Pittsburgh Legal Journal [*Pennsylvania*] (DLA)
Pittsb LJ ..... Pittsburgh Legal Journal [*Pennsylvania*] (DLA)
Pittsb L Rev ... Pittsburgh Law Review (DLA)
Pittsb R (PA) ... Pittsburgh Reporter [*Pennsylvania*] (DLA)
Pittsburgh Bus R ... Pittsburgh Business Review [*A publication*]
Pittsburgh Leg J ... Pittsburgh Legal Journal [*Pennsylvania*] (DLA)
Pittsburgh Leg Journal ... Pittsburgh Legal Journal [*Pennsylvania*] (DLA)
Pittsburgh Sch ... Pittsburgh Schools [*A publication*]
Pittsburgh Univ Bull ... Pittsburgh University. Bulletin [*A publication*]
Pittsburgh Univ Sch Ed J ... Pittsburgh University. School of Education Journal [*A publication*]
Pitts Leg J ... Pittsburgh Legal Journal [*Pennsylvania*] (DLA)
Pitts Leg J (NS) ... Pittsburgh Legal Journal, New Series [*Pennsylvania*] (DLA)
Pitts Leg Jour ... Pittsburgh Legal Journal [*Pennsylvania*] (DLA)
Pitts LJ .... Pittsburgh Legal Journal (DLA)
Pitts LJ (NS) ... Pittsburgh Legal Journal, New Series (DLA)
Pitts L Rev ... University of Pittsburgh. Law Review [*A publication*]
Pitts R .... Pittsburgh Reports [*Pennsylvania*] (DLA)
Pitts Rep ..... Pittsburgh Reports (DLA)
Pitts Rep (PA) ... Pittsburgh Reports [*Pennsylvania*] (DLA)
Pitt Sym ..... Pittsburgh Symphony Orchestra. Program Notes [*A publication*]
Pitture Vern ... Pitture e Vernici [*A publication*]
PITU .... Pipe or Tubing [*Freight*]
PITY-EM..... Principal-Interest, Taxes, Energy, and Maintenance [*Real estate*]
PIU .... East Pennsylvania Psychiatric Institute, Philadelphia, PA [*OCLC symbol*] (OCLC)
PIU .... Path Information Unit [*Data processing*]
PIU .... Photographic Interpretation Unit [*Marine Corps*]
PIU .... Pilot Information Utilization
PIU .... Piura [*Peru*] [*Airport symbol*] (OAG)
PIU .... Plug-In Unit
PIU .... Polymerase-Inducing Unit
PIU .... Power Intercept Unit [*Military*] (CAAL)
PIU .... Power Interface Unit (MCD)
PIU .... Private Islands Unlimited (EA)
PIU .... Process Input Unit [*Data processing*] (BUR)
PIU .... Process Interface Unit
PIU .... Programer Interface Unit (MCD)
PIU .... Pyrotechnic Initiator Unit (MCD)
PiU .... University of the Philippines, Quezon City, Philippines [*Library symbol*] [*Library of Congress*] (LCLS)
PIUG .... Parti Independantiste de l'Unite Guyanaise [*Pro-Independence Party of Guyanese Unity*] [*French*] (PPW)
PIUMP .... Plug-In Unit Mounting Panel
PIUS .... Process Inherent Ultimately Safe [*Nuclear reactor*]
PI/USA .... Packaging Institute, United States of America [*Later, PI/INT'L*] (EA)
PIUT .... Paiute Oil & Mining [*NASDAQ symbol*] (NQ)
PIV .... Parainfluenza Virus
PIV .... Peak Inverse Voltage [*RADAR*]
PIV .... Piva [*Solomon Islands*] [*Seismograph station code, US Geological Survey*] [*Closed*] (SEIS)
PIV .... Pivot [*Automotive engineering*]
PIV .... Planet in View [*NASA*]
PIV .... Plug-In Valve

PIV............ Positive Infinitely Variable
PIV............. Post Indicator Valve
PIV............. Product Inspection Verification
PIV............. Propellant Isolation Valve
PIV............. Scotland School for Veterans' Children, Scotland, PA [*OCLC symbol*] (OCLC)
PIVADS ...... Product Improved Vulcan Air Defense System (MCD)
PIVD.......... Protruded Intervertebral Disc [*Medicine*]
PIVED......... Plasma-Injection Vacuum Energy Diverter
PIVN.......... Public Interest Video Network/New Voices Radio (EA)
PIVS .... Particle-Induced Visual Sensations
PivS .... Pivnicne Sjajvo [*A publication*]
PIVT .... Production Improvement Verification Test
PIW .... Petroleum Intelligence Weekly [*A publication*]
PIW .... Plastic Insulated Wire
PIW .... Polski Instytut Wydawniczy [*A publication*]
PIW .... Ports and Inland Waterways
PIW .... Program Interrupt Word
PIW .... Woodhaven Center, Philadelphia, PA [*OCLC symbol*] (OCLC)
PIWC .... Petroleum Industry War Council
PIWG .... Product Improvement Working Group [*Military*] (AFIT)
PIWI........... No Pilot Balloon Observation Due to High, or Gusty, Surface Wind [*National Weather Service*] (FAAC)
PIWWC..... Planetary Initiative for the World We Choose (EA)
PIX .... Pico Island [*Azores*] [*Airport symbol*] (OAG)
PIX............. Picture
PIX............. Picture Rocks, PA [*Location identifier*] [*FAA*] (FAAL)
PIX............. Pinxit [*He, or She, Painted It*] [*Latin*] (ROG)
PIX............. Proton-Induced X-Ray Analysis
PIX............. School Pictures, Inc. [*American Stock Exchange symbol*]
PIX............. Youth Development Center, Loysville, Loysville, PA [*OCLC symbol*] (OCLC)
Pix Aud ..... Pixley on Auditors [*8th ed.*] [*1901*] (DLA)
PIXE .... Proton-Induced X-Ray Emission
PIXEL .... Picture Element [*Single element of resolution in image processing*]
PIY............. Youth Development Center, New Castle, New Castle, PA [*OCLC symbol*] (OCLC)
PIZ............. Point Lay [*Alaska*] [*Airport symbol*] (OAG)
PIZ............. Point Lay, AK [*Location identifier*] [*FAA*] (FAAL)
PIZ............. Youth Development Center, Waynesburg, Waynesburg, PA [*OCLC symbol*] (OCLC)
PIZZ........... Pizzicato [*Plucked*] [*Music*]
PJ .... Bombay High Court Printed Judgments (DLA)
PJ .... ICC [*Interstate Commerce Commission*] Practitioners' Journal [*A publication*]
PJ .... Netherlands Antilles [*Aircraft nationality and registration mark*] (FAAC)
PJ .... Pajamas
PJ .... Palastinajahrbuch des Deutschen Evangelischen Instituts fuer Altertumswissenschaft des Heiligen Landes zu Jerusalem [*Berlin*] [*A publication*]
PJ .... Panel Jack
PJ .... Parteijargon [*Party Language*] [*German*]
PJ .... Peregrine Air Services Ltd. [*Great Britain*] [*ICAO designator*] (FAAC)
PJ .... Peripheral Jet (AAG)
PJ .... Personnel Journal [*A publication*]
PJ .... Petajoule (ADA)
PJ .... Pharmaceutical Journal [*A publication*]
PJ .... Philosophisches Jahrbuch [*A publication*]
PJ .... Picojoule [*Logic gate efficiency measure*] (MDG)
PJ .... Piece Jointe [*Enclosure*] [*French*] (NATG)
PJ .... Plasma Jet (AAG)
PJ .... Plastic Jacket
P & J........... Plaza y Janes [*Publisher*] [*Spain*]
PJ .... Police Justice
PJ .... Poradnik Jezykowy [*A publication*]
PJ .... Presiding Judge
PJ .... Presiding Probate Judge [*British*] (ROG)
PJ .... Preussische Jahrbuecher [*A publication*]
PJ .... Prince of Jerusalem [*Freemasonry*]
PJ .... Privacy Journal [*A publication*]
PJ .... Probate Judge
PJ .... Procurement Justification [*Navy*]
PJ .... Project Jonah (EA)
PJ .... Prudhoe Bay Journal [*A publication*]
PJ .... Pulsejet
PJ's .... Pajamas [*Slang*]
PJ's .... Physical Jerks [*Exercise*] [*Slang*] [*British*] (DSUE)
PJA............ Abington Library Society, Jenkintown, PA [*Library symbol*] [*Library of Congress*] [*Obsolete*] (LCLS)
PJa .... Papers on Japan [*A publication*]
PJACA ...... Proceedings. Japan Academy [*A publication*]
PJAIA .... Philippine Journal of Animal Industry [*A publication*]
PJAIG........ Alverthorpe Gallery, Rosenwald Collection, Jenkintown, PA [*Library symbol*] [*Library of Congress*] (LCLS)
P Jap Acad ... Proceedings. Japan Academy [*A publication*]
PJB............. Pad Journal Bearing

PJB............ Palastinajahrbuch des Deutschen Evangelischen Instituts fuer Altertumswissenschaft des Heiligen Landes zu Jerusalem [*Berlin*] [*A publication*]
PJB............ Premature Junctional Beat [*Cardiology*]
PJb............ Preussische Jahrbuecher [*A publication*]
PJBD......... Permanent Joint Board on Defense [*US, Canada*]
PJC............ Paducah Junior College [*Kentucky*]
PJC............ Paris Junior College [*Texas*]
PJC............ Pensacola Junior College [*Florida*]
PJC............ Perkinston Junior College [*Mississippi*]
PJC............ Post Junior College [*Connecticut*]
PJC............ Poteau Junior College [*Oklahoma*]
PJC............ Pratt Junior College [*Kansas*]
PJC............ University of Pittsburgh, Johnstown, Johnstown, PA [*OCLC symbol*] (OCLC)
PJCA......... Jean Coutu Group (PJC) Class A SV [*Toronto Stock Exchange symbol*]
PJCTL....... Projectile (MSA)
PJD............ Pedro Dome [*Alaska*] [*Seismograph station code, US Geological Survey*] [*Closed*] (SEIS)
PJE............ Parachute Jumping Exercise
PJE............ Peabody Journal of Education [*A publication*]
PJE............ Project Engineer
PJE............ Pulse Jet Engine
PJES.......... Photojet Edge Sensor
PJez.......... Prace Jezykoznawcze Polskiej Akademii Nauk [*A publication*]
PJF............ Peripheral Jet (Flat-Bottom)
PJF............ Pharmaceutical Journal Formulary (ROG)
PJF............ Pin Jointed Framework
PJFS.......... Philip Jose Farmer Society (EA)
PJG.......... Panjgur [*Pakistan*] [*Airport symbol*] (OAG)
PJG.......... Potts Junction [*Guam*] [*Seismograph station code, US Geological Survey*] (SEIS)
PJGG......... Philosophisches Jahrbuch der Gorres-Gesellschaft [*A publication*]
PJH............ Piper, Jr., H. E., Philadelphia PA [*STAC*]
PJI............. Parachute Jump Instructor [*Military*] [*British*] (INF)
PJI............. Point Judith, RI [*Location identifier*] [*FAA*] (FAAL)
PJILMCC.... Philip C. Jessup International Law Moot Court Competition (EA)
PJJ............ Provincial Judges Journal [*A publication*]
P JI............ Pharmaceutical Journal [*A publication*] (ROG)
PJL............ Philippine Journal of Linguistics [*A publication*]
PJLB.......... Lower Burma Printed Judgments (DLA)
PJLT.......... Philippine Journal of Language Teaching [*A publication*]
PJM............ Pennsylvania-Jersey-Maryland [*Electric power pool*]
PJM............ Polymer Jell Material
PJM............ Postjunctional Membrane
PJM............ Power Jets Memorandum
PJN............ Fort Lauderdale, FL [*Location identifier*] [*FAA*] (FAAL)
PJN............ Philippine Journal of Nursing [*A publication*]
PJNu.......... Philippine Journal of Nutrition [*A publication*]
PJo............ Cambria County Library System, Johnstown, PA [*Library symbol*] [*Library of Congress*] (LCLS)
PJO........... Pioneer Jupiter Orbit [*NASA*]
PJOP........ Preliminary Joint Operation Procedure (KSC)
PJOPA....... Pakistan Journal of Psychology [*A publication*]
PJoU.......... University of Pittsburgh at Johnstown, Johnstown, PA [*Library symbol*] [*Library of Congress*] (LCLS)
PJP............ Philippine Journal of Pediatrics [*A publication*]
PJPA.......... Philippine Journal of Public Administration [*A publication*]
PJPC........ Plug/Jack Patch Cord
PJPI........... Philippine Journal of Plant Industry [*A publication*]
PJR............ Peoria, IL [*Location identifier*] [*FAA*] (FAAL)
PJR............ Peterson, J. Robert, New York NY [*STAC*]
PJR............ Philadelphia Journalism Review [*A publication*]
PJR............ Port Jersey [*AAR code*]
PJR............ Power Jets Report
PJRCM....... Philippine Junior Red Cross Magazine [*A publication*]
P Jr & H...... Patton, Jr., and Heath's Reports [*Virginia Special Court of Appeals*] (DLA)
PJS............ Newport News, VA [*Location identifier*] [*FAA*] (FAAL)
PJS............ Peripheral Jet (Skegs)
PJS........... Peutz-Jeghers Syndrome [*Oncology*]
PJS............ Philippine Journal of Science [*A publication*]
PJs............ Physical Jerks [*Exercise*] [*Slang*] [*British*] (DSUE)
PJS............ Piezojunction Sensor
PJSS.......... Plug and Jack Set
PJSS.......... PACAF [*Pacific Air Forces*] Jungle Survival School (AFM)
PJSS.......... Philippine Journal of Surgical Specialties [*A publication*]
PJT............ Paroxysmal Junctional Tachycardia [*Cardiology*]
PJT............ Practical Job Training (MCD)
PJT............ Pulse Jitter Tester
PJTN.......... Projection (MSA)
PJTR.......... Projector (MSA)
PJU............ Juniata College, Huntingdon, PA [*OCLC symbol*] (OCLC)
PJV............ Pump Jet Vehicle
PK .... Indonesia [*Aircraft nationality and registration mark*] (FAAC)
pK'............. Negative Log of the Dissociation Constant [*Medicine*]
PK .... Pack (AAG)
PK .... Package (MCD)

pk .... Pakistan [*MARC country of publication code*] [*Library of Congress*] (LCCP)
PK .... Pakistan [*Two-letter standard code*] (CNC)
PK .... Pakistan International Airlines Corp. [*ICAO designator*] (FAAC)
PK .... Park
PK .... Peak [*Maps and charts*]
PK .... Peck (AAG)
P & K .... Perry and Knapp's English Election Cases [*1833*] (DLA)
PK .... Phileleftheron Komma [*Liberal Party*] [*Greek*] (PPE)
PK .... Philologike Kypros [*A publication*]
PK .... Pike
PK .... Pink (FAAC)
PK .... Pinkas ha-Kehilot [*Encyclopedia of Jewish Communities*] [*A publication*]
PK .... Pole Cat [*Slang*]
PK .... Position Keeper
PK .... Postbox [*Turkish*]
PK .... Prausnitz-Kuestner [*Reaction*] [*Immunology*]
PK .... Prawo Kanoniczne [*A publication*]
PK .... Preacher's Kid [*Slang*]
PK .... Pridie Kalendas [*The Day before the Calends*] [*Latin*]
PK .... Principal Keeper [*Slang for a warden*]
PK .... Probability of Kill (MCD)
PK .... Problemy Kibernetiki [*A publication*]
PK .... Prophets and Kings (BJA)
PK .... Protein Kinase [*Also, PKase*] [*An enzyme*]
PK .... Przeglad Klasyczny [*A publication*]
PK .... Przeglad Koscielny [*A publication*]
PK .... Psychokinesis
PK .... Pyruvate Kinase [*An enzyme*]
P-K4 .... Pawn to King Four [*Standard opening to a game of chess. Pawn is moved to the fourth square in front of the king*]
PKA .... Napaskiak [*Alaska*] [*Airport symbol*] (OAG)
PKA .... Napaskiak, AK [*Location identifier*] [*FAA*] (FAAL)
PKA .... Paul Kagan Associates, Inc. [*Carmel, CA*] [*Information service*] [*Telecommunications*] (EISS)
PKA .... Pi Kappa Alpha [*Fraternity*]
PKA .... Primary Knock-on-Atom (MCD)
PKA .... Professional Karate Association
PkAF .... Pakistani Air Force
PKAFA ...... PKA [*Professional Karate Association*] Fighters Association (EA)
PKase........ Protein Kinase [*Also, PK*] [*An enzyme*]
PKB .... Parkersburg [*West Virginia*] [*Airport symbol*] (OAG)
PKB .... Parkersburg, WV [*Location identifier*] [*FAA*] (FAAL)
PKB .... Photoelectric Keyboard
PKB .... Portable Keyboard
PKC .... Cocoa, FL [*Location identifier*] [*FAA*] (FAAL)
PKC .... Pannill Knitting Company, Inc. [*NYSE symbol*]
PKC .... Peckham Road [*California*] [*Seismograph station code, US Geological Survey*] (SEIS)
PKC .... Position Keeping Computer
PKC .... Protein Kinase C [*An enzyme*]
PKD .... Pac Ed Systems Corp. [*Vancouver Stock Exchange symbol*]
PKD .... Park Rapids, MN [*Location identifier*] [*FAA*] (FAAL)
PKD .... Parker Drilling Co. [*NYSE symbol*]
PKD .... Partially Knocked Down [*Consignment*] [*Shipping*]
PKD .... Philip K. Dick [*Science fiction writer*]
PKD .... Pi Kappa Delta [*Society*]
PKD .... Programable Keyboard and Display [*Data processing*] (NASA)
PKDOM ..... Pack for Domestic Use
PKDR-B..... Pakistan Development Review [*A publication*]
PKDS .... Philip K. Dick Society (EA)
PKE .... Park Electrochemical Corp. [*NYSE symbol*]
PKE .... Parker, CA [*Location identifier*] [*FAA*] (FAAL)
PKE .... Parkes [*Australia*] [*Airport symbol*] (OAG)
PKE .... Public-Key Encryption [*Microcomputer technology*]
PKF .... Park Falls, WI [*Location identifier*] [*FAA*] (FAAL)
PKF .... Parkfield Array [*California*] [*Seismograph station code, US Geological Survey*] (SEIS)
PKF .... Primary Kidney Fold
PKG.......... Package (AFM)
PKG.......... Parking (KSC)
PKG.......... Phonocardiogram
Pkg Abstr... Packaging Abstracts [*A publication*]
PKGE .... Package
Pkg Eng .... Package Engineering [*A publication*]
Pkg (India) ... Packaging (India) [*A publication*]
P-K GL .... [*A.*] Philippson and [*E.*] Kirsten, Die Griechischen Landschaften [*A publication*] (OCD)
Pkg (London) ... Packaging (London) [*A publication*]
Pkg News... Packaging News [*A publication*]
Pkg Technol ... Packaging Technology and Management [*A publication*]
PKH .... Park Hill [*California*] [*Seismograph station code, US Geological Survey*] (SEIS)
PKHO .... Protivo-Khimicheskaia Oborona [*A Chemical Defense*] [*USSR*]
PKHOW..... Pack Howitzer [*Marine Corps*]
PKI .... Parkland Industries Ltd. [*Toronto Stock Exchange symbol*]
PKI .... Partai Katolik Indonesia [*Catholic Party of Indonesia*]
PKI .... Partai Komunis Indonesia [*Communist Party of Indonesia*]

PKI .... Partai Kristen Indonesia [*Christian Party of Indonesia*]
P & KI .... Promisel & Korn, Inc. [*Bethesda, MD*] [*Information service*] (EISS)
PKIKA .... Praxis der Kinderpsychologie und Kinderpsychiatrie [*A publication*]
PKJ .... Pitanja Knjizevnosti a Jezika [*A publication*]
PKK .... Kurdish Workers' Party [*Turkey*] (PD)
PKK .... Pakokku [*Burma*] [*Airport symbol*] (OAG)
PKK .... Porkkala [*Finland*] [*Seismograph station code, US Geological Survey*] (SEIS)
PkKP .... Pakistan National Scientific and Documentation Center, Karachi, Pakistan [*Library symbol*] [*Library of Congress*] (LCLS)
PKL .... Parklane Technologies, Inc. [*Vancouver Stock Exchange symbol*]
PKL .... Pi Kappa Lambda [*Society*]
PKLB .... Pharmakinetics Laboratories [*NASDAQ symbol*] (NQ)
PK-LT .... Psychokinesis on Living Targets
PKM .... Perigee Kick Motor (MCD)
PK-MB .... Psychokinetic Metal-Bending [*Parapsychology*]
PKMKCMD ... Perhaps ...Kids Meeting Kids Can Make a Difference (EA)
PKN .... Aspen, CO [*Location identifier*] [*FAA*] (FAAL)
PKN .... Pangkalanbuun [*Indonesia*] [*Airport symbol*] (OAG)
PKN .... Pauken [*Kettledrums*]
PKN .... Perkin-Elmer Corp. [*NYSE symbol*]
PKNG HSE ... Packing House [*Freight*]
PKO .... Parakou [*Benin*] [*Airport symbol*] (OAG)
PKO .... Peace-Keeping Operation (MCD)
PKO .... Perdant par Knockout [*Losing by a Knockout*] [*French*]
PKOH .... Park-Ohio Industries [*NASDAQ symbol*] (NQ)
PKOM .... Publicationen der Kaiserlich Osmanischen Museen [*Constantinople*] [*A publication*]
PKOMA ...... Physik der Kondensierten Materie [*A publication*]
P Kon Ned A ... Proceedings. Koninklijke Nederlandse Akademie van Wetenschappen. Series A. Mathematical Sciences [*A publication*]
P Kon Ned B ... Proceedings. Koninklijke Nederlandse Akademie van Wetenschappen. Series B. Physical Sciences [*A publication*]
P Kon Ned C ... Proceedings. Koninklijke Nederlandse Akademie van Wetenschappen. Series C. Biological and Medical Sciences [*A publication*]
PKP .... Palestiner Komunistische Partei [*Palestine Communist Party*] (BJA)
PKP .... Partido Komunista ng Pilipinas [*Communist Party of the Philippines*] (PPW)
PKP .... Penetrating Keratoplasty [*Ophthalmology*]
PKP .... Perustuslaillinen Kansanpuolue [*Constitutional People's Party*] [*Finland*] (PPE)
PKP .... Polskie Koleje Panstwowe [*Polish State Railways*]
PKP .... Preknock Pulse
PKP .... Pukapuka [*French Polynesia*] [*Airport symbol*] (OAG)
PKP .... Purple-K-Powder
PK/PK .... Peak-to-Peak (MCD)
PKpP .... Pennwalt Corp., King Of Prussia, PA [*Library symbol*] [*Library of Congress*] (LCLS)
PKQ .... Dallas-Fort Worth, TX [*Location identifier*] [*FAA*] (FAAL)
PKR .... P. K. Le Roux Dam [*South Africa*] [*Seismograph station code, US Geological Survey*] (SEIS)
PKR .... Picker
PKR .... Pokhara [*Nepal*] [*Airport symbol*] (OAG)
PKRDD .... Pravitel'stvennaya Komissiya po Raketam Dalnego Deistviya [*State Commission for the Study of the Problems of Long-Range Rockets*] [*USSR*]
PKs .... Bayard Taylor Memorial Library, Kennett Square, PA [*Library symbol*] [*Library of Congress*] (LCLS)
PKS .... Packs of Cigarettes Smoked
PKS .... Phi Kappa Sigma [*Fraternity*]
PKSCAT ..... Parkes Catalogue of Radio Sources [*Australian National Radio Astronomy Observatory*] [*Information service*] [*Parkes, NSW*] (EISS)
PKSCU .... PKS/Communications Uts [*NASDAQ symbol*] (NQ)
PKSEA .... Pack for Overseas
PKSh .... Partia Komuniste e Shqiperise [*Communist Party of Albania*] [*Later, PPSh*] (PPE)
PKsL .... Longwood Gardens Library, Kennett Square, PA [*Library symbol*] [*Library of Congress*] (LCLS)
Pks & Rec ... Parks and Recreation [*A publication*]
PKSS .... Probability of Kill Single Shot (MCD)
PKT .... Packet
PKT .... Phase Keying Technique
PKT .... Phi Kappa Tau [*Fraternity*]
PKT .... Pittsburgh Theological Seminary, Pittsburgh, PA [*OCLC symbol*] (OCLC)
PKT .... Pocket (MSA)
PKTDA .... Prace Komisji Technologii Drewna. Poznanskie Towarzystwo Przyjaciol Nauk [*A publication*]
PKU .... Pekanbaru [*Indonesia*] [*Airport symbol*] (OAG)
PKU .... Phenylketonuria [*Congenital metabolism disorder*] [*Medicine*]
PKU-P .... PKU [*Phenylketonuria*] Parents [*San Anselmo, CA*] (EA)

PKuS .... Kutztown State College, Kutztown, PA [*Library symbol*] [*Library of Congress*] (LCLS)
PkV .... Peak Kilovolts
PKV .... Port Lavaka, TX [*Location identifier*] [*FAA*] (FAAL)
PKVJA .... PKV [*Punjabrao Krishi Vidyapeeth*] Research Journal [*A publication*]
PKV Res J ... PKV [*Punjabrao Krishi Vidyapeeth*] Research Journal [*A publication*]
PKW .... Kenosha, WI [*Location identifier*] [*FAA*] (FAAL)
PKW .... Personenkraftwagen [*Automobile*] [*German*]
PKW .... Selebi-Phikwe [*Botswana*] [*Airport symbol*] (OAG)
PKWAY ...... Parkway (MSA)
PKWY .... Parkway (KSC)
PKWY .... Parkway Co. [*NASDAQ symbol*] (NQ)
PKY .... Palangkaraya [*Indonesia*] [*Airport symbol*] (OAG)
PKY .... Parkway (MCD)
PKy .... Pneumatike Kypros [*A publication*]
PKY .... Tri-City Air Taxi [*San Bernardino, CA*] [*FAA designator*] (FAAC)
PKZ .... Pensacola, FL [*Location identifier*] [*FAA*] (FAAL)
PKZZD .... Problemy Kontrolya i Zashchita Atmosfery ot Zagryazneniya [*A publication*]
PL .... Empresade Transporte Aere de Peru [*ICAO designator*] (FAAC)
PL .... Front Line [*Revolutionary group*] [*Italy*]
PL .... Lancaster County Library, Lancaster, PA [*Library symbol*] [*Library of Congress*] (LCLS)
PL .... Packing List
PL/ .... Padlock (AAG)
PL .... Pail
PL .... Palaeographia Latina [*A publication*]
PL .... Palm Leaf [*Reaction*] [*Medicine*]
PL .... Pamietnik Literacki [*A publication*]
PL .... Pamphlet Laws (DLA)
PL .... Panel Left [*Nuclear energy*] (NRCH)
PL .... Paperleg [*A favored student*] [*Teen slang*]
PL .... Papers in Linguistics [*A publication*]
PL .... Parish Line R. R. [*AAR code*]
PL .... Parti Liberal [*Liberal Party (1974-1979)*] [*Belgium*] (PPE)
PL .... Partial Loss [*Insurance*]
PL .... Partido Liberal [*Liberal Party*] [*Portuguese*] (PPE)
PL .... Partido Liberal [*Liberal Party*] [*Spanish*] (PPE)
PL .... Partido Liberal [*Liberal Party*] [*Panamanian*] (PPW)
PL .... Partido Liberal [*Liberal Party*] [*Paraguayan*] (PPW)
PL .... Partido Liberal [*Liberal Party*] [*Honduran*]
PL .... Partido Libertador [*Brazil*]
PL .... Parting Line [*Castings*] (AAG)
PL .... Parts List
PL .... Path Loss [*Communications*]
PL .... Patrol Land [*Aviation*]
PL .... Patrologia Latina [*A publication*]
PL .... Patrologiae Cursus. Series Latina [*A publication*] (OCD)
Pl .... Paul (BJA)
P & L .... Paul and Lisa [*An association*] [*Old Saybrook, CT*] (EA)
PL .... Paulist League (EA)
PL .... Payload [*NASA*] (KSC)
PL .... Paymaster-Lieutenant [*Navy*] [*British*]
PL .... Pectate Lyase [*An enzyme*]
PL .... People for Life [*An association*] (EA)
PL .... People's Lobby (EA)
PL .... Perceived Level [*Noise*]
PL .... Perception of Light
P/L .... Personal Lines
PL .... Personnel Laboratory [*Air Research and Development Command*] [*Air Force*] (AAG)
PL .... Petty Larceny
PL .... Phase Line
PL .... Philosophical Library [*A publication*]
PL .... Phospholipid [*Biochemistry*]
PL .... Photolocator (MCD)
PL .... Photoluminescence
PL .... Pile
PL .... Pipeline
PL .... Piping Loads [*Nuclear energy*] (NRCH)
PL .... Pitch Line (MSA)
PL .... Placebo [*Medicine*]
PL .... Placental Lactogen [*Endocrinology*]
PL .... Plain (MSA)
PL .... Plain Language [*As opposed to coded message*] [*Military*]
PL .... Plans
PL .... Plantagenet [*Genealogy*] (ROG)
pl .... Plasma
PL .... Plastic Laboratory [*Princeton University*] (MCD)
PL .... Plastic Limit (IEEE)
PL .... Plastic Surgery [*Medicine*]
pl .... Plastid [*Botany*]
PL .... Plate (KSC)
PL .... Plateau Length
PL .... Platinum [*Chemistry*] (ROG)
Pl .... Plato [*Fourth century BC*] [*Classical studies*] (OCD)
PL .... Platoon (NATG)

PL............. Platz [Square] [German]
PL............. Players League [Major league in baseball, 1890]
PL............. Pleasure (ROG)
PL............. Ploshchad [Square] [Russian]
Pl............. Plowden's English King's Bench Commentaries [or Reports] [1550-80] (DLA)
PL............. Plug (AAG)
PL............. Plume [Numismatics]
PL............. Plural
PL............. Poet Laureate
PL............. Poet Lore [A publication]
PL............. Poetry London [A publication] [British]
P & L........ Points and Lines [Military] (CAAL)
Pl............. Poiseuille [Unit of dynamic viscosity]
pl............. Poland [MARC country of publication code] [Library of Congress] (LCCP)
PL............. Poland [Two-letter standard code] (CNC)
PL............. Policy Loan
P & L........ Politics and Letters [A publication]
PL............. Poly-L-lysine [Also, PLL] [Biochemical analysis]
PL............. Poor Law (DLA)
P of L........ Port of London (ROG)
PL............. Portable Low-Power [Reactor] (NRCH)
PL............. Position Line [Navigation]
PL............. Position Location [DoD]
PL............. Post Landing [NASA] (KSC)
PL............. Post Laundry [Army]
P & L........ Power and Lighting (MSA)
P & L........ Pratt & Lambert, Inc.
PL............. Prayers for Life [An association] (EA)
PL............. Prelaunch (NASA)
PL............. Preliminary Leaf [Bibliography]
PL............. Pressurizer Level (IEEE)
PL............. Price Level [Economics]
PL............. Price List
PL............. Princess Louise's Sutherland and Argyll Highlanders [Military] [British] (ROG)
PL............. Private Line
PL............. Procedure Library
PL............. Product Liability
PL............. Product License
PL............. Production Language
PL............. Production List (AAG)
P/L............ Profit and Loss [Accounting]
P and L...... Profit and Loss [Accounting]
PL............. Program Logic [Data processing] (TEL)
PL............. Programing Language [Data processing]
PL............. Programming Languages Series [Elsevier Book Series] [A publication]
PL............. Progressive Labor [A faction of Students for a Democratic Society]
PL............. Project Leader
PL............. Project Lighthawk (EA)
PL............. Project Local [Defunct] (EA)
PL............. Prolymphocytic Leukemia [Also, PLL] [Oncology]
PL............. Propagation Loss
PL............. Propellant Loading [NASA] (KSC)
PL............. Property Line (MSA)
PL............. Proportional Limit
P/L............ Proprietary Limited (ADA)
PL............. Propulsion Laboratory [Army]
PL............. Prospective Loss
PL............. Provisioning List (MCD)
PL............. Pseudolumina [Anatomy]
PL............. Psychological Laboratory (MCD)
PL............. Public Law [An act of Congress]
PL............. Public Liability [Business and trade]
PL............. Public Library
PL............. Pulpolingual [Dentistry]
PL............. Pulse Length (NVT)
PL............. Pyridoxal [Also, Pxl] [Biochemistry]
PL............. Radio Positioning Land Station [ITU designation] (CET)
PL/1 .... Programing Language, Version One [Data processing] (MCD)
PLA........... Pakistan Liberation Army (PD)
PLA........... Palau [Palau Islands] [Seismograph station code, US Geological Survey] [Closed] (SEIS)
PLA........... Palestine Liberation Army
PLA........... Parachute Location Aid (MCD)
PLA........... Parlar Resources Ltd. [Vancouver Stock Exchange symbol]
PLA........... Party of Labor of Albania (PPW)
PLA........... Passengers' Luggage in Advance [Railway] (ROG)
PLA........... Patriotic Liberation Army [Burmese] (PD)
PLA........... Pedro Leon Abroleda Brigade [Colombia] (PD)
PLA........... People's Liberation Army [Communist China]
PLA........... People's Liberation Army [Indian] (PD)
PLA........... Phase Locked Arrays [Physics]
PLA........... Philatelic Literature Association [Later, APRL] (EA)
PLA........... Physiological Learning Aptitude (KSC)
PLA........... Pitch Lock Actuator (MCD)
PLA........... Place (ADA)

PLA........... Placebo [Medicine]
PLA........... Plain Language Address [Telecommunications] (TEL)
PLA........... Plan of Launch Azimuth [Aerospace] (AAG)
PLA........... Planned Labor Application [Military] (AFIT)
PLA........... Planned Landing Area [NASA]
PLA........... Playboy Enterprises, Inc. [NYSE symbol]
PLA........... Plaza (ADA)
PLA........... Poetry League of America (EA)
PLA........... Poly-L-arginine [Biochemistry]
PLA........... Polylactic Acid [Organic chemistry] (RDA)
PLA........... Polynesian Airways [Honolulu, HI] [FAA designator] (FAAC)
PLA........... Popular Library of Art [A publication]
PLA........... Port of London Authority [British]
PLA........... Potential Leaf Area [Botany]
PLA........... Power Lever Angle
PLA........... Practice Landing Approach [Aviation]
PLA........... Practice Low Approach [Aviation] (FAAC)
PLA........... Price Level Adjusted Accounting (ADA)
PLA........... Print Load Analyzer
PLA........... Private Libraries Association
PLA........... Programable Line Adapter
PLA........... Programable Logic Array [Data processing]
PLA........... Proton Linear Accelerator
PLA........... Psycholinguistic Age [Education]
PLA........... Psychological Learning Aptitude (MCD)
PLA........... Public Library Association [Chicago, IL] (EA)
PLa........... Pulpolabial [Dentistry]
PLA........... Pulpolinguoaxial [Dentistry]
PLA........... Pulsed LASER Annealing [Semiconductor technology]
PLA........... Pulverized Limestone Association [Hunt Valley, MD] (EA)
PLA........... University of Pittsburgh, Law School, Pittsburgh, PA [OCLC symbol] (OCLC)
PLA$_2$....... Phospholipase A$_2$ [An enzyme]
PLAA......... Positive Low Angle of Attack
PLA AEPS ... PLA [Public Library Association] Alternative Education Programs Section
PLA AFLS ... PLA [Public Library Association] Armed Forces Library Section
PLAAR....... Packaged Liquid Air-Augmented Rocket (MCD)
PLAAS....... Plasma Atomic Absorption System [Spectrometry]
PLAB......... Philadelphia Library Association. Bulletin [A publication]
PLAB......... Philippine Library Association. Bulletin [A publication]
PLA Bull..... PLA [Pennsylvania Library Association] Bulletin [A publication]
PLAC......... Placebo [Medicine]
PLAC......... Post-Launch Analysis of Compliance [NASA]
Plac Abbrev ... Placitorum Abbreviatio [Latin] (DLA)
Plac Angl Nor ... Placita Anglo-Normannica Cases [1065-1195] (DLA)
Plac Ang Nor ... Bigelow's Placita Anglo-Normanica (DLA)
PLACE ...... Position Location and Aircraft Communication Equipment
PLACE ...... Position Location and Communications Experiment [NASA]
PLACE ...... Positioner Layout and Cell Evaluator [Robotics]
PLACE ...... Post-LANDSAT Advanced Concept Evaluation (MCD)
PLACE ...... Programa Latinoamericano de Cooperacion Energetica [Latin American Energy Cooperation Program] [Quito, Ecuador] (EA-IO)
PLACE ...... Programing Language for Automatic Checkout Equipment
Plac Gen .... Placita Generalia [Latin] (DLA)
PLACID...... Payload Aboard, Caution in Descent [NASA]
PLA CIS ..... PLA [Public Library Association] Community Information Section
PLACO .... Planning Committee [International Organization for Standardization] (IEEE)
PLAD......... Parachute Low-Altitude Delivery [Air Force]
PLAD......... Price-Level-Adjusted Deposit
PLADS....... Parachute Low-Altitude Delivery System [Air Force]
PLADS ...... Pulsed LASER Airborne Depth Sounding System [Naval Oceanographic Office]
PLAFB....... Plattsburgh Air Force Base [New York] (AAG)
PLAFSEP ... Processing Libraries - Anecdotes, Facetia, Satire, Etc., Periodicals [A publication]
PLAGM...... Placid, Louisiana Land and Exploration, Amerada Hess, Getty, and Marathon [Oil-and gas-holding bloc in Alaska]
PLAIC........ Purdue Laboratory for Applied Industrial Control [Purdue University] [Research center] (RCD)
PLAID........ Programed Learning Aid
Plain Ra...... Plain Rapper [A publication]
Plains Anthropol ... Plains Anthropologist [A publication]
PLAKA ...... Planovoe Khozyaistvo [A publication]
PLAL......... Pro-Life Action League
PLAM........ Practice Limpet Assembly Modular [Navy] (CAAL)
PLAM........ Price-Level Adjusted Mortgage
PLA MLS.... PLA [Public Library Association] Metropolitan Libraries Section
PLAN........ People's Liberation Army of Namibia (PPW)
Plan........... Planning (DLA)
PLAN........ Polska Ludowa Akcja Niepodleglosci [A publication]
PLAN........ Positive Locator Aid to Navigation
PLAN........ Problem Language Analyzer [Data processing]
PLAN........ Program Language Analyzer [Data processing] (IEEE)
PLAN........ Program for Learning in Accordance with Needs [Westinghouse Learning Corp.]
PLAN........ Programing Language Nineteen-Hundred [Data processing]

PLAN.......... Protect Life in All Nations (EA)
PLAN.......... Public Libraries Automation Network [*California State Library*] [*Sacramento, CA*]
PLANA .... Planta [*A publication*]
PLANAT ..... North Atlantic Treaty Regional Planning Group
Planc.......... Pro Plancio [*of Cicero*] [*Classical studies*] (OCD)
Plan Can .... Plan Canada [*A publication*]
PLANCODE ... Planning, Control, and Decision Evaluation System [*IBM Corp.*]
Plan & Comp ... Planning and Compensation Reports [*England*] (DLA)
Planen Pruef Investieren PPI ... Planen-Pruefen-Investieren. PPI [*West Germany*] [*A publication*]
PLANES ..... Programed Language-Based Enquiry System
PLANET ..... Planned Logistics Analysis and Evaluation Technique [*Air Force*]
Planet Assoc Clean Energy Newsl ... Planetary Association for Clean Energy. Newsletter [*Canada*] [*A publication*]
Planet Spac ... Planetary and Space Science [*A publication*]
Planet Space Sci ... Planetary and Space Science [*A publication*]
PLANEX ..... [*The*] Planning Exchange Database [*Pergamon InfoLine*] [*Database*] [*Information service*] [*Glasgow, Scotland*] (EISS)
PLANEX ..... Planning Exercise [*Military*] (NVT)
Pl Ang-Norm ... Placita Anglo-Normannica Cases [*Bigelow*] (DLA)
Plan Higher Educ ... Planning for Higher Education [*A publication*]
Plan Hospod ... Planovane Hospodarstvi [*A publication*]
Plan Hoz... Planovoe Hozjajstvo [*A publication*]
Planif Habitat Inform ... Planification, Habitat, Information [*A publication*]
Plan Inovtn ... Planned Innovation [*A publication*]
PLANIT....... Programing Language for Interaction and Teaching [*1966*] [*Data processing*]
Plan Khoz ... Planovoe Khozyaistvo [*A publication*]
PLANMAN ... Planned Maintenance [*Contract Data Research*] [*Software package*]
PLANN .... Plant Location Assistance Nationwide Network
Plann Admin ... Planning and Administration [*A publication*]
Plann Build Dev ... Planning and Building Developments [*A publication*]
Planned Innov ... Planned Innovation [*England*] [*A publication*]
PLANNER... [A] programing language (CSR)
PLANNET... Planning Network
Planning and Adm ... Planning and Administration [*A publication*]
Planning Bul ... Planning Bulletin [*A publication*]
Planning Develop Netherl ... Planning and Development in the Netherlands [*A publication*]
Planning History Bull ... Planning History Bulletin [*A publication*]
Plann News ... Planning News [*A publication*]
Plann Pam Nat Plann Ass ... Planning Pamphlets. National Planning Association [*A publication*]
Plan Rev..... Planning Review [*A publication*]
PLANS .... Position Location and Navigation System
PLANS .... Program Logistics and Network Scheduling System (IEEE)
PLANS .... Programing Language for Allocation and Network Scheduling [*1975*] [*Data processing*] (CSR)
Planseeber Pulvermet ... Planseeberichte fuer Pulvermetallurgie [*A publication*]
Plant.......... De Plantatione [*Philo*] (BJA)
Plant.......... Plant Maintenance and Engineering [*A publication*]
PLANT........ Program for Linguistic Analysis of Natural Plants (IEEE)
Planta Med ... Planta Medica [*A publication*]
Plant Bibliogr ... Plant Bibliography [*A publication*]
Plant Biochem J ... Plant Biochemical Journal [*A publication*]
Plant Breed Abstr ... Plant Breeding Abstracts [*A publication*]
Plant Bull Rubber Res Inst Malays ... Planters' Bulletin. Rubber Research Institute of Malaysia [*A publication*]
Plant Cell Physiol ... Plant and Cell Physiology [*A publication*]
Plant Cell Physiol (Kyoto) ... Plant and Cell Physiology (Kyoto) [*A publication*]
Plant Cell Physiol (Tokyo) ... Plant and Cell Physiology (Tokyo) [*A publication*]
Plant Cel P ... Plant and Cell Physiology [*A publication*]
Plant Cultiv Repub Argent Inst Bot Agric (B Aires) ... Plantas Cultivadas en la Republica Argentina. Instituto de Botanica Agricola (Buenos Aires) [*A publication*]
Plant Dis Leafl Dept Agr Biol Br (NSW) ... Plant Disease Leaflet. Department of Agriculture. Biological Branch (New South Wales) [*A publication*]
Plant Dis R ... Plant Disease Reporter [*A publication*]
Plant Dis Rep ... Plant Disease Reporter [*A publication*]
Plant Dis Rep Suppl ... Plant Disease Reporter. Supplement [*A publication*]
Plant Energy Manage ... Plant Energy Management [*A publication*]
Plant Eng ... Plant Engineer [*A publication*]
Plant Eng ... Plant Engineering [*A publication*]
Plant & Eng Applications ... Plant and Engineering Applications [*A publication*]
Plant Eng (Lond) ... Plant Engineer (London) [*A publication*]
Plant Engng ... Plant Engineering [*A publication*]
Plant Engng & Maint ... Plant Engineering and Maintenance [*A publication*]
Plant Eng (Tokyo) ... Plant Engineer (Tokyo) [*A publication*]
Planter .... Planter and Sugar Manufacturer [*A publication*]

PLANTFACTS ... Steel Plants Information System [*German Iron and Steel Engineers Association*] [*Dusseldorf*] [*Information service*] (EISS)
Plant Field Lab Mimeo Rep Fla Univ ... Plantation Field Laboratory Mimeo Report. Florida University [*A publication*]
Plant Food Rev ... Plant Food Review [*A publication*]
Plant Foods Hum Nutr ... Plant Foods for Human Nutrition [*A publication*]
Plant Gard ... Plants and Gardens [*A publication*]
Pl Anth .... Plains Anthropologist [*A publication*]
Plant Ind Dig (Manila) ... Plant Industry Digest (Manila) [*A publication*]
Plant Ind Ser Chin-Amer Joint Comm Rural Reconstr ... Plant Industry Series. Chinese-American Joint Commission on Rural Reconstruction [*A publication*]
Plant Maint ... Plant Maintenance [*A publication*]
Plant Maint Import Substitution ... Plant Maintenance and Import Substitution [*A publication*]
Plant Manage Eng ... Plant Management and Engineering [*A publication*]
Plant Med Phytother ... Plantes Medicinales et Phytotherapie [*A publication*]
Plant Operations Prog ... Plant/Operations Progress [*A publication*]
Plant Oper Manage ... Plant Operating Management [*A publication*]
Plant Path ... Plant Pathology [*London*] [*A publication*]
Plant Pathol ... Plant Pathology [*A publication*]
Plant Pathol (Lond) ... Plant Pathology (London) [*A publication*]
Plant Physiol ... Plant Physiology [*A publication*]
Plant Physiol (Bethesda) ... Plant Physiology (Bethesda) [*A publication*]
Plant Physiol Suppl ... Plant Physiology. Supplement [*A publication*]
Plant Physl ... Plant Physiology [*A publication*]
Plant & Power Services Eng ... Plant and Power Services Engineer [*A publication*]
Plant Propagat ... Plant Propagator [*A publication*]
Plant Prot... Plant Protection [*A publication*]
Plant Prot Bull ... Plant Protection Bulletin [*A publication*]
Plant Prot Bull (Ankara) ... Plant Protection Bulletin (Ankara) [*A publication*]
Plant Prot Bull (New Delhi) ... Plant Protection Bulletin (New Delhi) [*A publication*]
Plant Sci Bull ... Plant Science Bulletin [*A publication*]
Plant Sci L ... Plant Science Letters [*A publication*]
Plant Sci Lett ... Plant Science Letters [*A publication*]
Plant Sci (Lucknow) ... Plant Science (Lucknow) [*A publication*]
Plant Sci (Lucknow India) ... Plant Science (Lucknow, India) [*A publication*]
Plant Sci (Sofia) ... Plant Science (Sofia) [*A publication*]
Plants Gard ... Plants and Gardens [*A publication*]
Plant Sys E ... Plant Systematics and Evolution [*A publication*]
Plant Syst Evol ... Plant Systematics and Evolution [*A publication*]
PLANY .... Protestant Lawyers Association of New York (EA)
PLAO........ Parts List Assembly Order (MCD)
PLAP .... Placental Alkaline Phosphatase [*An enzyme*]
PLAP .... Power Lever Angle Position (MCD)
Pla Par....... Placita Parliamentaria [*Latin*] [*England*] (DLA)
PLapK .... Keystone Junior College, La Plume, PA [*Library symbol*] [*Library of Congress*] (LCLS)
PLA PLSS ... PLA [*Public Library Association*] Public Library Systems Section
PLARA .... Plastverarbeiter [*A publication*]
PLARS........ Position Location and Reporting System [*Military*] (INF)
PLAS......... Plaster (AAG)
PLAS......... Private Line Assured Service [*Telecommunications*] (TEL)
PLAS......... Program Logical Address Space
PLAS......... Programable Link Adaptation System (MCD)
Plas Desgn ... Plastics Design Forum [*A publication*]
Plas Eng..... Plastics Engineering [*A publication*]
Plas Ind Eur ... Plastics Industry Europe [*A publication*]
PLASMA ... Parents League of Americans Studying Medicine Abroad (EA)
Plasma Phys ... Plasma Physics [*A publication*]
Plasma Phys Contr Nucl Fusion Res Conf Proc ... Plasma Physics and Controlled Nuclear Fusion Research. Conference Proceedings [*A publication*]
Plasma Phys Index ... Plasma Physics Index [*West Germany*] [*A publication*]
Plas Massy ... Plasticheskie Massy [*A publication*]
PLASMEX ... International Plastics Exhibition (TSPED)
PLA SMLS ... PLA [*Public Library Association*] Small and Medium-Sized Libraries Section
Plas R Surg ... Plastic and Reconstructive Surgery [*A publication*]
Plas Rubbers Text ... Plastics, Rubbers, Textiles [*A publication*]
Plas Rub Int ... Plastics and Rubber International [*A publication*]
Plas Rubr ... Plastics and Rubber Weekly [*A publication*]
PLAST....... Propellant Loading and All Systems Test [*NASA*] (KSC)
Plast Abstr ... Plastic Abstracts [*A publication*]
Plast Age ... Plastics Age [*A publication*]
Plast Aust ... Plastics in Australia [*A publication*]
Plast Bldg Constr ... Plastics in Building Construction [*A publication*]
Plast Build Constr ... Plastics in Building Construction [*A publication*]
Plast Bull (London) ... Plastics Bulletin (London) [*A publication*]
Plast Busin ... Plastics Business [*A publication*]
Plast Compd ... Plastics Compounding [*A publication*]
Plast Compounding ... Plastics Compounding [*A publication*]
Plast Des Process ... Plastics Design and Processing [*A publication*]
Plast Dig .... Plastics Digest [*A publication*]
PLASTEC... Plastics Technical Evaluation Center [*Army*] [*Vicksburg, MS*]
PLASTEC Note ... PLASTEC [*Plastics Technical Evaluation Center*] Note [*A publication*]

PLASTEC Rep ... PLASTEC [*Plastics Technical Evaluation Center*] Report [*A publication*]
Plaste Kaut ... Plaste und Kautschuk [*A publication*]
Plaste u Kaut ... Plaste und Kautschuk [*A publication*]
Plast Eng ... Plastics Engineering [*A publication*]
Plast Engng ... Plastics Engineering [*A publication*]
PLASTEUROTEC ... Groupement Europeen des Fabricants de Pieces Techniques Plastiques [*European Group of Fabricators of Technical Plastics Parts*] (EA-IO)
Plast Flash ... Plastiques Flash [*A publication*]
Plast Hmoty Kauc ... Plasticke Hmoty a Kaucuk [*A publication*]
Plastico ... Noticiero del Plastico [*A publication*]
Plastic Prod ... Plastic Products [*A publication*]
Plastics in Aust ... Plastics in Australia [*A publication*]
Plast Ind ... Plastic Industry [*India*] [*A publication*]
Plast Ind News ... Plastics Industry News [*A publication*]
Plast Ind News (Jap) ... Plastics Industry News (Japan) [*A publication*]
Plast Ind (Paris) ... Plastiques et Industrie (Paris) [*A publication*]
Plast Inst Trans ... Plastics Institute. Transactions [*A publication*]
Plast Inst Trans J ... Plastics Institute. Transactions and Journal [*A publication*]
Plast Inst Trans J Conf Suppl ... Plastics Institute. Transactions and Journal. Conference Supplement [*A publication*]
Plast Kauc ... Plasty a Kaucuk [*A publication*]
Plast Massen Wiss Tech ... Plastische Massen in Wissenschaft und Technik [*A publication*]
Plast Massy ... Plasticheskie Massy [*A publication*]
Plast Mater (Tokyo) ... Plastics Materials (Tokyo) [*A publication*]
Plast M & E ... Plastics Machinery and Equipment [*A publication*]
Plast Mod ... Plasticos Modernos [*A publication*]
Plast Mod Elast ... Plastiques Modernes et Elastomeres [*A publication*]
Plast Mod Elastomeres ... Plastiques Modernes et Elastomeres [*A publication*]
Plast News ... Plastics News [*A publication*]
Plast Paint Rubber ... Plastics, Paint, and Rubber [*A publication*]
Plast Panorama ... Plast Panorama Scandinavia [*A publication*]
Plast and Polym ... Plastics and Polymers [*A publication*]
Plast Polym ... Plastics and Polymers [*A publication*]
Plast Polym Conf Suppl ... Plastics and Polymers. Conference Supplement [*A publication*]
Plast Prod ... Plastic Products [*A publication*]
Plast Prog India ... Plastics Progress in India [*A publication*]
Plast Reconstr Surg ... Plastic and Reconstructive Surgery [*A publication*]
Plast Reconstr Surg Transplant Bull ... Plastic and Reconstructive Surgery and the Transplantation Bulletin [*A publication*]
Plast Renf Fibres Verre Text ... Plastiques Renforces Fibres de Verre Textile [*A publication*]
Plast Resinas ... Plasticos y Resinas [*Mexico*] [*A publication*]
Plast em Rev ... Plasticos em Revista [*A publication*]
Plast Rubber ... Plastics and Rubber [*Later, Plastics and Rubber International*] [*A publication*]
Plast and Rubber ... Plastics and Rubber [*Later, Plastics and Rubber International*] [*A publication*]
Plast Rubber Int ... Plastics and Rubber International [*A publication*]
Plast and Rubber Int ... Plastics and Rubber International [*A publication*]
Plast Rubber Mater Appl ... Plastics and Rubber. Material and Applications [*A publication*]
Plast Rubber News ... Plastics and Rubber News [*South Africa*] [*A publication*]
Plast Rubber Proc Appl ... Plastics and Rubber Processing and Applications [*A publication*]
Plast Rubber Process ... Plastics and Rubber Processing and Applications [*A publication*]
Plast & Rubber Process & Appl ... Plastics and Rubber Processing and Applications [*A publication*]
Plast Rubber Wkly ... Plastics and Rubber Weekly [*England*] [*A publication*]
Plast Rubb News ... Plastics and Rubber News [*South Africa*] [*A publication*]
Plast Rubb Process Appln ... Plastics and Rubber Processing and Applications [*A publication*]
Plast Rub Wkly ... Plastics and Rubber Weekly [*A publication*]
Plast (S Afr) ... Plastics (Southern Africa) [*A publication*]
Plast (S Africa) ... Plastics (Southern Africa) [*A publication*]
Plast Technol ... Plastics Technology [*A publication*]
Plast Today ... Plastics Today [*A publication*]
Plast Trends ... Plastics Trends [*A publication*]
Plast Univers ... Plasticos Universales [*A publication*]
Plast World ... Plastics World [*A publication*]
PLAT ... Pilot-LOS [*Line of Sight*] Landing Aid Television (NG)
PLAT ... Plateau [*Board on Geographic Names*]
PLAT ... Platelet [*Hematology*]
PLAT ... Platform (KSC)
PLAT ... Platinum [*Chemical symbol is Pt*] (AAG)
PLAT ... Platonic
PLAT ... Platoon
PLAT ... Platt National Park
PLAT ... Present Latitude [*Aviation*] (FAAC)
PLATA ... Plating [*A publication*]
Plateau Q Mus North Ariz ... Plateau. Quarterly of the Museum of Northern Arizona [*A publication*]
PLATF ... Platform (AAG)
Plating & Surface Finish ... Plating and Surface Finishing [*A publication*]

Platinum Met Rev ... Platinum Metals Review [*A publication*]
PLATN ... Platinum [*Chemistry*] (ROG)
PLATO ... Pennzoil Louisiana and Texas Offshore [*Oil industry group*]
PLATO ... Platform Observables Subassembly
PLATO ... Programed Logic for Automatic Teaching [*or Training*] Operations [*University of Illinois*] [*Programing language*]
Platoon Sch ... Platoon School [*A publication*]
PLATR ... Pawling Lattice Test Rig [*United Nuclear Co.*]
PLatS ... Saint Vincent College, Latrobe, PA [*Library symbol*] [*Library of Congress*] (LCLS)
Plat Surf Finish ... Plating and Surface Finishing [*A publication*]
Platt ... Platt on the Law of Covenants [*1829*] (DLA)
Platt ... Platt on Leases (DLA)
Platt Cov ... Platt on the Law of Covenants (DLA)
Platt Leas ... Platt on Leases [*1847*] (DLA)
Plaut ... Plautus [*Third century BC*] [*Classical studies*] (OCD)
PLAV ... Polish Legion of American Veterans (EA)
PLAVLA ... Polish Legion of American Veterans USA Ladies Auxiliary (EA)
PLAWA ... Plastics World [*A publication*]
Plaxton ... Plaxton's Canadian Constitutional Decisions (DLA)
PLAY ... [*The*] Playgoer [*A publication*]
Playb ... Playboy [*A publication*]
Players Mag ... Players Magazine [*A publication*]
Playmate ... Children's Playmate Magazine [*A publication*]
PLAZ ... Plaza Communications [*NASDAQ symbol*] (NQ)
PLB ... Papyrologica Lugduno-Batava [*A publication*]
PLB ... Payload Bay [*NASA*] (MCD)
PLB ... Per Pound [*Freight*]
PLB ... Personal Locator Beacon [*Military*] (AFM)
PLB ... Plattsburgh [*New York*] [*Airport symbol*] (OAG)
PLB ... Plattsburgh, NY [*Location identifier*] [*FAA*] (FAAL)
PLB ... Plumbing Mart [*Vancouver Stock Exchange symbol*]
PLB ... Poor Law Board
PLB ... Proctolin-Like Bioactivity [*Neurobiology*]
PLB ... Public Light Bus [*British*]
PLB ... Pullbutton (AAG)
PLBD ... Payload Bay Door [*NASA*] (MCD)
PLBD ... Plugboard (MSA)
Pl Biochem J ... Plant Biochemical Journal [*A publication*]
PLBK ... Playback (NASA)
PLBLK ... Pillow Block
PLBR ... Prototype Large Breeder Reactor [*Also, NCBR*]
Pl Breed Abstr ... Plant Breeding Abstracts [*A publication*]
PLBYD ... Plan og Bygg [*A publication*]
PLC ... Pacific Logging Congress [*Portland, OR*] (EA)
PLC ... Palomares Road [*California*] [*Seismograph station code, US Geological Survey*] (SEIS)
PLC ... Partido Liberal Constitucionalista [*Constitutionalist Liberal Party*] [*Nicaraguan*] (PPW)
PLC ... Patrice Lumumba Coalition [*New York, NY*] (EA)
PLC ... Paymaster-Lieutenant-Commander [*Navy*] [*British*]
PLC ... Periventricular Leukomalacia Complex [*Medicine*]
PLC ... Perry-Link Cubmarine [*A submersible vehicle*]
PLC ... Phospholipase C [*An enzyme*]
PLC ... Pilot Laboratories Corporation [*Vancouver Stock Exchange symbol*]
PLC ... Placer Development Ltd. [*American Stock Exchange symbol*]
Pl C ... Placita Coronae [*Pleas of the Crown*] [*Latin*] (DLA)
PLC ... Platform Control
PLC ... Platoon Leader's Class
PLC ... Pneumatic Lead Cutter
PLC ... Poet Laureatus Caesareus [*Imperial Poet Laureate*] [*Latin*] (ROG)
PLC ... Point Loma College [*California*]
PLC ... Poor Law Commissioners [*British*]
PLC ... Power Lever Control (MCD)
PLC ... Power Line Carrier
PLC ... Power Line Communications
PLC ... Predictive Linguistic Constraint
PLC ... Presbyterian Lay Committee (EA)
PLC ... Primary Leadership Course [*Army*]
PLC ... Primary Location Code [*Data processing*]
PLC ... Prime Level Code
PLC ... Princeton University Library Chronicle [*A publication*]
PLC ... Process Liquid Chromatography
PLC ... Production Line Configured [*Military*] (CAAL)
PLC ... Products List Circular [*Patents*]
PLC ... Program Level Change Tape [*Data processing*] (IBMDP)
PLC ... Programable Logic Control [*Data processing*]
PLC ... Programing Language Committee [*CODASYL*]
PLC ... Proinsulin-Like Compound [*Endocrinology*]
PLC ... Pseudophase Liquid Chromatography
PLC ... Public Lands Council (EA)
PLC ... Public Lighting Commission
PLC ... Public Limited Company [*British*]
PLCA ... Pipe Line Contractors Association [*Dallas, TX*] (EA)
PLCAA ... Professional Lawn Care Association of America [*Marietta, GA*] (EA)
PLCAI ... Pipe Line Contractors Association, International (EA)
PLCB ... Pseudoline Control Block [*Data processing*]
PLCC ... Primary Liver Cell Cancer [*Oncology*]

PLCD.......... Product Liability Common Defense [*An association*] [*Falls Church, VA*] (EA)
PLCEA .... Part-Length Control Element Assembly [*Nuclear energy*] (NRCH)
PLCEDM .... Part-Length Control Element Drive Mechanism [*Nuclear energy*] (NRCH)
PLCHB .... Physiological Chemistry and Physics [*Later, Physiological Chemistry and Physics and Medical NMR*] [*A publication*]
PLCLAS ..... Propagation Loss Classification System [*Navy*] (NVT)
PLCM .... Propellant Loading Control Monitor [*NASA*] (KSC)
PLCM & ND ... Proceedings. Linguistic Circle of Manitoba and North Dakota [*A publication*]
PLCN.......... Parts List Change Notice (MCD)
PLCN-A...... Plan Canada [*A publication*]
PLCNY .... Publications. Linguistic Circle of New York [*A publication*]
Pl Com .... Plowden's English King's Bench Commentaries [*or Reports*] [*1550-80*] [*England*] (DLA)
PL Com ..... Poor Law Commissioner (DLA)
PLCOP .... Prelaunch Checkout Plan [*NASA*] (KSC)
PLCPB .... Plant and Cell Physiology [*A publication*]
PLCS........ Proceedings. London Classical Society [*A publication*]
PLCS........ Propellant Loading Control System [*NASA*] (AAG)
PLCU......... Propellant Level Control Unit [*NASA*] (KSC)
PLCY .... Policy (AFM)
PLD .... Partial Lipodystrophy [*Medicine*]
PLD .... Partido de la Liberacion Dominicana [*Dominican Liberation Party*] [*Dominican Republic*] (PPW)
PL)d .... Path Loss, Downlink [*Communications*]
PLD .... Payload [*NASA*]
PLD .... Personnel Letdown Device
PLD .... Phase Lock Demodulator
PLD .... Phospholipase D [*An enzyme*]
PLD .... Plaid (ADA)
PLD .... Plated (MSA)
PLD .... Played Matches [*Cricket*] (ROG)
PLD .... Portland, IN [*Location identifier*] [*FAA*] (FAAL)
PLD .... Posterior Latissimus Dorsi [*Anatomy*]
PLD .... Posterolateral Dendrite [*Neurology*]
PLD .... Potentially Lethal Damage [*Medicine*]
PLD .... Precision LASER Designator (RDA)
PLD .... Primary Layer Depth [*Military*] (CAAL)
PLd .... Principle of Limit Design
PLD .... Probable Line of Deployment [*Army*] (AABC)
PLD .... Procurement Legal Division [*Later, Office of General Counsel*] [*Navy*]
PLD .... Product Line Development
PLD .... Program Listing Document (MCD)
PLD .... Programable Logic Device
PLD .... Protective LASER Devices (MCD)
PLD .... Public Libraries Division. Reporter [*A publication*]
PLD .... Pulse-Length Discriminator (IEEE)
PLD .... Pulse Level Detector (MCD)
PLdaC .... Calvary Baptist School of Theology, Lansdale, PA [*Library symbol*] [*Library of Congress*] (LCLS)
PLDC........ Preliminary List of Design Changes
PLDC........ Primary Leadership Development Course [*Army*] (INF)
PLDC........ Primary Long-Distance Carrier [*Telephone service*]
PLDI .... Payload Data Interleaver [*NASA*] (MCD)
PLDI .... Plastic Die [*Tool*] (AAG)
P & L Dig Laws ... Pepper and Lewis' Digest of Laws [*Pennsylvania*] (DLA)
PLDK .... Peabody Language Development Kits [*Education*]
PLDM .... Payload Management [*NASA*] (MCD)
PLDMI .... Precise LASER Distance Measuring Instrument
PLDP .... Parti Liberal Democrate et Pluraliste [*Belgium*] (PPW)
PLD-PACOM ... Petroleum Logistical Data - Pacific Command (CINC)
PLDR......... Potentially Lethal Damage Repair [*Medicine*]
PLDRA ...... Plant Disease Reporter [*A publication*]
PLDS .... Payload Support [*NASA*] (MCD)
PLDT .... Philippine Long Distance Telephone
PLDTS....... Propellant Loading Data Transmission System [*NASA*] (KSC)
PLE........... Encyclopedia of Pennsylvania Law (DLA)
PLE........... Phased Loading Entry [*Data processing*]
PLE........... [*The*] Pittsburgh & Lake Erie Railroad Co. [*AAR code*]
PLE........... Planned Life Extension [*Pershing*] (MCD)
Ple .... Pleiade [*Record label*] [*France*]
PLE........... Plesetsk [*Satellite launch complex*] [*USSR*]
PLE........... Preliminary Logistics Evaluation
PLE........... Primary Loss Expectancy [*Insurance*]
PLE........... Prudent Limit of Endurance (NVT)
PLE........... Pulse Length Error (MCD)
PLE........... Pulsed LASER Experiment
PLEA .... Pacific Lumber Exporters Association [*Portland, OR*] (EA)
PLEA .... Poverty Lawyers for Effective Advocacy
PLEA .... Prototype Language for Economic Analysis [*Data processing*] (EISS)
PLEADGS ... Pleadings [*Legal term*] (ROG)
PLEASE ..... Parolees, Law-Enforcement Assist Student Education [*Project to reduce drug abuse among junior and senior high school students in California*]
PLeB.......... Bucknell University, Lewisburg, PA [*Library symbol*] [*Library of Congress*] (LCLS)

PLebHi .... Lebanon County Historical Society, Lebanon, PA [*Library symbol*] [*Library of Congress*] (LCLS)
PLebV .... United States Veterans Administration Hospital, Lebanon, PA [*Library symbol*] [*Library of Congress*] (LCLS)
PLEGA ...... Plant Engineering [*A publication*]
P Leg J ...... Pittsburgh Legal Journal [*Pennsylvania*] (DLA)
P Leg Jour ... Pittsburgh Legal Journal [*Pennsylvania*] (DLA)
PLEI........... Public Law Education Institute
PLEN .... Plenipotentiary
PLEN .... Plenum Publishing Corp. [*NASDAQ symbol*] (NQ)
PLENA....... Plant Engineering [*A publication*]
PLENAPS... Plans for the Employment of Naval and Air Forces of the Associated Powers in the Eastern Theatre in the Event of War with Japan
PLENCH.... Pliers and Wrench [*Combination tool*]
PLEND....... Plumbing Engineer [*A publication*]
P & LERR... [*The*] Pittsburgh & Lake Erie Railroad Co.
PLESA....... Programs for Persons with Limited English-Speaking Ability [*Department of Labor*]
PLEURO..... Pleuropneumonia [*Veterinary medicine*] (DSUE)
PLEY .... Pauley Petroleum [*NASDAQ symbol*] (NQ)
PLF............ Franklin and Marshall College, Lancaster, PA [*Library symbol*] [*Library of Congress*] (LCLS)
PLF............ Free Library of Philadelphia, Philadelphia, PA [*OCLC symbol*] (OCLC)
PLF............ Pacific Legal Foundation (EA)
PLF............ Page Length Field
PLF............ Palestine Liberation Front (PD)
PLF............ Parachute Landing Fall [*Military*]
PLF............ Patient Load Factor (AFM)
PLF............ People's Liberation Forces [*Ethiopian*]
PLF............ Perilymph Fistula [*Medicine*]
PLF............ Phase Lock Frequency
PLF............ Phone Line Formatter
PLF............ Plaintiff
PLF............ Polar Lipid Fraction [*Biochemistry*]
PLF............ Positive Lock Fastener
PLF............ Power for Level Flight [*Aeronautics*]
PLF............ Private Line Telephone
PLF............ Proposition Letter Formula
PLFA .... Primary Level Field Activity [*Defense Supply Agency*]
Plf Adv ...... Plaintiff's Advocate [*A publication*]
PLFC......... Pulaski Furniture [*NASDAQ symbol*] (NQ)
PLFCA....... Peggy Lee Fan Club and Archives (EA)
PLFE......... Presidential Life Corp. [*NASDAQ symbol*] (NQ)
PLFF......... Plaintiff
PLFS......... Polarforschung [*A publication*]
PLFTR .... Please Furnish Transportation Requests (NOAA)
PLFUR .... Please Furnish (NOAA)
PLG .... Piling (MSA)
PLG .... Place Oil & Gas Ltd. [*Toronto Stock Exchange symbol*]
PLG .... Plane Guard (NVT)
PLG .... Pleural Ganglion [*Medicine*]
PLG .... Plug (AAG)
PLG .... Poetae Lyrici Graeci [*A publication*] (OCD)
PLG .... Polygyros [*Greece*] [*Seismograph station code, US Geological Survey*] (SEIS)
PLG .... Poor Law Guardian [*British*]
PLG .... Probleme de Lingvistica Genarala [*A publication*]
PLG .... Prolyl(leucyl)glycinamide [*Biochemistry*]
PLG .... Pulsed Light Generator
PLGAA ...... Plants and Gardens [*A publication*]
PLGC......... Presbyterians for Lesbian/Gay Concerns (EA)
PLGFA....... Poligrafiya [*A publication*]
PLGJA .... Pipeline and Gas Journal [*A publication*]
PLGL .... Plate Glass
PLGM .... NYC Parents of Lesbians and Gay Men (EA)
PLGR......... Plunger (MSA)
PLGS .... Partita Liberale Giovani Somali [*Somali Liberal Youth Party*]
PLGT .... Prototype Lunar Geologist Tool
P-LGV .... Psittacosis-Lymphogranuloma Venereum [*Medicine*]
PLH .... Hamilton Watch Co., Lancaster, PA [*Library symbol*] [*Library of Congress*] [*Obsolete*] (LCLS)
PLH .... Palaemontes-Lightening Hormone
PLH .... Partido Liberal de Honduras [*Liberal Party of Honduras*] (PPW)
PLH .... Payload Handling [*NASA*] (NASA)
PLH .... Plymouth [*England*] [*Airport symbol*] (OAG)
PLHi .... Lancaster County Historical Society, Lancaster, PA [*Library symbol*] [*Library of Congress*] (LCLS)
PLHID....... Plant Hire [*A publication*]
PLHJA .... Plumbing and Heating Journal [*A publication*]
PLhS .... Lock Haven State College, Lock Haven, PA [*Library symbol*] [*Library of Congress*] (LCLS)
pli .... Pali [*MARC language code*] [*Library of Congress*] (LCCP)
PLI............ Panarea [*Lipari Islands*] [*Seismograph station code, US Geological Survey*] (SEIS)
PLI............ Partido Liberal Independiente [*Independent Liberal Party*] [*Nicaraguan*] (PPW)
PLI............ Partito Liberale Italiano [*Italian Liberal Party*] [*Rome*] (PPW)
PLI............ Passenger and Immigration Lists Index [*A publication*]

PLI............. Payload Interrogator [*NASA*]   (MCD)
PLI............. Pilot Location Indicator
PLI............. Power Level Indicator
PLI............. Practising Law Institute   (EA)
PLI............. Preload Indicating
PLI............. Private Line Interface
PLI............. Proctolin-Like Immunoactivity [*Neurobiology*]
PLI............. Public Lands Institute   (EA)
PLI............. Pulsed LASER Interferometry
PLIA .... Pollution Liability Insurance Association [*Chicago, IL*]   (EA)
PLIANT....... Procedural Language Implementing Analog Techniques [*Data processing*]   (IEEE)
PLIB .... Pacific Lumber Inspection Bureau [*Bellevue, WA*]   (EA)
PLIM......... Post Launch Information Message [*NASA*]   (KSC)
PLIMC....... Pipe Line Insurance Managers Conference [*Defunct*]   (EA)
PLimT....... Tyler Arboretum, Lima, PA [*Library symbol*] [*Library of Congress*]   (LCLS)
PLIN .... Power Line Impedance Network
PLINA....... Pipe Line Industry [*A publication*]
PLing......... Papers in Linguistics [*A publication*]
PLINK........ American People/Link [*American Design and Communication*] [*Arlington Heights, IL*] [*Information service*]   (EISS)
PLIS .... Preclinical Literature Information System [*Data processing*]
PLISN....... Parts List Item Sequence Number   (MCD)
PLISN....... Provisioning List Item Sequence Number   (NASA)
PLISP........ [*A*] programing language   (CSR)
PLISSIT..... Permission, Limited Information, Specific Suggestions, and Intensive Therapy [*Occupational therapy*]
PLIT.......... Petrolite Corp. [*NASDAQ symbol*]   (NQ)
PLITTY ...... Private Line Teletypewriter Service [*Telecommunications*]   (TEL)
PLIW......... Preload Indicating Washer
PLJ............ Pennsylvania Law Journal   (DLA)
PLJ............ Philippine Library Journal [*A publication*]
PLJ............ Pittsburgh Legal Journal [*Pennsylvania*]   (DLA)
PLJ............ Punjab Law Reporter [*India*]   (DLA)
PLJ............ Pure Lemon Juice
PLJ NS....... Pittsburgh Legal Journal, New Series [*Pennsylvania*]   (DLA)
PLK .... Branson, MO [*Location identifier*] [*FAA*]   (FAAL)
PLK .... Phi Lambda Kappa [*Fraternity*]
PLK .... Plank   (AAG)
PLK .... Plucky Little King [*Used by Western diplomats in Amman in reference to King Hussein of Jordan*]
PLK .... Poincare-Lighthill-Kuo [*Method*]
PLKAA ...... Plaste und Kautschuk [*A publication*]
PLKR......... Peacoat Locker
PLL........... Pall Corp. [*American Stock Exchange symbol*]
PLL........... Pallet [*Building construction*]
PLL........... Papers on Language and Literature [*A publication*]
PLL........... Parts Load List   (MCD)
PLL........... Peripheral Light Loss
PLL........... Phase-Locked Loop [*NASA*]
PLL........... Polo, IL [*Location identifier*] [*FAA*]   (FAAL)
PLL........... Poly-L-lysine [*Also, PL*] [*Biochemistry*]
PLL........... Positive Logic Level
PLL........... Prescribed Load List [*Vehicle maintenance operation*] [*Army*]
PLL........... Prolymphocytic Leukemia [*Also, PL*] [*Oncology*]
PLLAA....... Royal Society. Proceedings. Series A. Mathematical and Physical Sciences [*A publication*]
P & L Laws ... Private and Local Laws   (DLA)
PLLE.......... Prueba de Lectura y Lenguaje Escrito [*Standardized test of reading and writing in Spanish for students in grades 3 through 10*]
PLLL.......... Parallel Petroleum Corp. [*NASDAQ symbol*]   (NQ)
PLLL.......... Posterior Lateral Line Lobe [*Of electric fishes*]
PLLP.......... Polish Literature/Litterature Polonaise [*A publication*]
PLLR .... Phase Lock Loop Receiver
PLLRC....... Public Land Law Review Commission [*Terminated, 1970*]
PLLT......... Pallet   (NATG)
PLLTN........ Pollution
PLLVM .... Pennsylvania Farm Museum of Landis Valley, Lancaster, PA [*Library symbol*] [*Library of Congress*]   (LCLS)
PLM........... Pacific Law Magazine   (DLA)
PLM........... Packaged Liquid Missile
PLM........... Pakistan Liberation Movement   (PD)
PLM........... Palembang [*Indonesia*] [*Airport symbol*]   (OAG)
PLM........... Palomar [*California*] [*Seismograph station code, US Geological Survey*]   (SEIS)
PLM........... Papers in Linguistics of Melanesia [*A publication*]
PLM........... Passive Line Monitor [*Datapoint*]
PLM........... Passive Lunar Marker
PLM........... Payload Management [*NASA*]   (NASA)
PLM........... Payload Monitoring [*NASA*]   (NASA)
PLM........... People's Liberation Movement [*Montserrat*]   (PPW)
PLM........... Percent Labeled Mitosis [*Cytology*]
PLM........... Phleomycin [*Biochemistry*]
PLM........... Plastic Laminating Mold   (MCD)
PLM........... PLM Companies, Inc. [*American Stock Exchange symbol*]
PLM........... Plymouth Financial [*Vancouver Stock Exchange symbol*]
PLM........... Poetae Latini Minores [*A publication*]   (OCD)
PLM........... Polarized Light Microscopy

PLM........... Poor Law Magazine   (DLA)
PLM........... Power Line Modulation   (AABC)
PLM........... Prelaunch Monitor [*NASA*]   (KSC)
PLM........... Preliminary   (KSC)
PLM........... Product Line Manager
PLM........... Production Line Maintenance [*Air Force*]
PLM........... Production Line Manufacturing
PL/M .... Programing Language/Microcomputers [*Intel Corp.*] [*1973*] [*Data processing*]   (CSR)
PLM........... Programing Logic Manual
PLM........... Pulse-Length Modulation
PLMA........ Private Label Manufacturers Association [*New York, NY*]   (EA)
PLMA........ Producers Livestock Marketing Association [*Later, IPLA*]   (EA)
PL Mag...... Poor Law Magazine [*1858-1930*] [*Scotland*] [*A publication*]   (DLA)
PLMB .... Plumbing   (AAG)
PLMD .... Payload Mating Dolly
PLME........ Peak Local Mean Error   (MCD)
PLMEA ...... Planta Medica [*A publication*]
PLMG........ Publishers' Library Marketing Group [*Formerly, PLPG*] [*New York, NY*]   (EA)
PLMHi .... Lancaster Mennonite Conference Historical Society, Lancaster, PA [*Library symbol*] [*Library of Congress*]   (LCLS)
PLMN........ Plasmine Corp. [*NASDAQ symbol*]   (NQ)
PLMP........ Program Logistic Management Plan   (MCD)
PLMR .... Paris, Lyons, and Mediterranean Railway   (ROG)
PLMR .... Post Launch Memorandum Report
PLMS .... Palms
PLMS .... Plastic Master [*Tool*]   (AAG)
PLMS .... Preservation of Library Materials Section [*Resources and Technical Services Division*] [*American Library Association*]
PLMS .... Program Logistics Master Schedule [*NASA*]   (NASA)
PLMX .... PL/M Extended [*Programing language*]   (CSR)
PLMX .... PLM Financial Services [*NASDAQ symbol*]   (NQ)
PLN .... Flight Plan [*Aviation code*]
PLN .... Partido Liberacion Nacional [*National Liberation Party*] [*Costa Rican*]   (PPW)
PLN .... Partido Liberal Nacionalista [*Nationalist Liberal Party*] [*Nicaragua*]
PLN .... Pellston [*Michigan*] [*Airport symbol*]   (OAG)
PLN .... Pellston, MI [*Location identifier*] [*FAA*]   (FAAL)
PLN .... Plain
PLN .... Plane   (MSA)
PLN .... Plauen [*German Democratic Republic*] [*Seismograph station code, US Geological Survey*]   (SEIS)
PLN .... Program Line Number [*DoD*]
PLN .... Program Logic Network   (NASA)
PLNAP....... Pro-Life Nonviolent Action Project   (EA)
Pln Dealr .... Cleveland Plain Dealer [*A publication*]
PLNG......... Planning
PLNN......... Planning   (MCD)
PLNN-A...... Plan [*A publication*]
PLNO......... Plano Petroleum Corp. [*NASDAQ symbol*]   (NQ)
PLNR .... Planar   (MSA)
PLNS .... Plains   (MCD)
PLNS .... Plains Resources [*NASDAQ symbol*]   (NQ)
PLNSTD ..... Planned Standard Equipment [*Navy*]   (AFIT)
PLNSW Staff News ... Public Library of New South Wales. Staff News [*A publication*]
PLNT .... Planet   (MSA)
PLNTY....... Planetary   (MSA)
PLO .... Pacific Launch Operations [*NASA*]
PLO .... Palestine Liberation Organization   (PD)
PLO .... Parts List Only   (MCD)
PLO .... Passenger Liaison Office [*Military*]   (AABC)
PLO .... Payload Officer [*NASA*]   (MCD)
PLO .... Pensiero e Linguaggio in Operazioni/Thought and Language in Operations [*A publication*]
PLO .... Pentagon Liaison Office   (MCD)
PLO .... Phase-Locked Oscillator
PLO .... Plans Officer
PLO .... Poor Law Office   (ROG)
PLO .... Port Liaison Officer
PLO .... Port Lincoln [*Australia*] [*Airport symbol*]   (OAG)
PLO .... Program Line Organization
PLO .... Programed Local Oscillator
PLO .... Project Line Organization
PLO .... Public Land Order [*Interior*]
PLO .... Pulsed LASER Oscillator
PLO .... Pulsed Locked Oscillator
PLOA .... Proposed Letter of Agreement   (MCD)
PLOB......... Patrol Log Observations [*Aviation*]   (DSUE)
PLOB......... Place of Birth
PLOCAP..... Post Loss-of-Coolant Accident Protection [*Nuclear energy*]   (NRCH)
PLOCSA..... Personal Liaison Officer, Chief of Staff, Army   (AABC)
PLOD........ Periodic List of Data [*Data processing*]
PLOD......... Planetary Orbit Determination   (IEEE)

Plodorodie Pochv Karelii Akad Nauk SSSR Karel'sk Filial ... Plodorodie Pochv Karelii. Akademiya Nauk SSSR. Karel'skii Filial [*A publication*]
PLOM .... Prescribed Loan Optimization Model   (AABC)
P Lond Math ... Proceedings. London Mathematical Society [*A publication*]
PLondon .... Greek Papyri in the British Museum [*A publication*]   (OCD)
PLONEF ..... Plates on Elastic Foundations [*Structures & Computers Ltd.*] [*Software package*]
PLONG .... Present Longitude [*Aviation*]   (FAAC)
PLOO .... Pacific Launch Operations Office [*NASA*]
PLOP .... Planetary Landing Observation Package [*Aerospace*]
PLOP .... Policy Options/Options Politiques [*A publication*]
PLOP .... Pressure Line of Position [*Air Force*]
PLor .... Saint Francis College, Loretto, PA [*Library symbol*] [*Library of Congress*]   (LCLS)
PLOS .... Primary Line of Sight [*Sextants*]
PLOT .... Plotting
PLOT .... Porous Layer, Open Tubular Column [*Gas chromatography*]
PLOT .... Probability of Launch on Time   (MCD)
Plot .... Vita Plotini [*of Porphyry*] [*Classical studies*]   (OCD)
Ploughs ..... Ploughshares [*A publication*]
Plovdiv Univ Naucn Trud ... Plovdivski Universitet. Naucni Trudove [*A publication*]
PLOW .... Petunia Lovers of the World
Plow .... Plowden's English King's Bench Commentaries [*or Reports*]   (DLA)
Plowd .... Plowden's English King's Bench Commentaries [*or Reports*]   (DLA)
PLOYREP ... Unit Deployment Report   (CINC)
PLP .... La Palma [*Panama*] [*Airport symbol*]   (OAG)
PLP .... Palo [*Philippines*] [*Seismograph station code, US Geological Survey*]   (SEIS)
PLP .... Parliamentary Labour Party [*British*]
PLP .... Parti Liberal Progressiste [*Liberal Progressive Party*] [*Moroccan*]   (PPW)
PLP .... Parti pour la Liberation du Peuple [*People's Liberation Party*] [*Senegalese*]   (PPW)
PLP .... Parti de la Liberte et du Progres [*Party of Liberty and Progress*] [*Belgium*]   (PPE)
PLP .... Partido de los Pobres [*Poor People's Party*] [*Mexico*]   (PD)
PLP .... Partners for Livable Places [*Washington, DC*]   (EA)
PLP .... Parts List Page   (KSC)
PLP .... Pattern Learning Parser
PLP .... Periodate Lysine-Paraformaldehyde
PLP .... Phillips Petroleum Co. [*Toronto Stock Exchange symbol*]
PLP .... Plains Petroleum Co. [*NYSE symbol*]
PLP .... Polyoma-Like Particle [*Genetics*]
PLP .... Post Launch Phase
PLP .... Presentation Level Protocol [*AT & T Videotex System*]
PLP .... Principal Locating Point [*Automotive engineering*]
PLP .... Procedural Language Processor
PLP .... Process Layup Procedure
PLP .... Product Liability Prevention [*Conference*]
PLP .... Progressive Labor Party   (EA)
PLP .... Progressive Liberal Party [*Bahamian*]   (PPW)
PLP .... Proteolipid [*Biochemistry*]
PLP .... Proteolipid Protein [*Biochemistry*]
PLP .... Pyridoxal Phosphate [*Also, PALP*] [*Biochemistry*]
PLPA .... Pageable Link-Pack Area
PLPA .... Permissive Low-Pressure Alarm   (IEEE)
Pl Par .... Placita Parliamentaria [*Latin*]   (DLA)
PLPB .... Petroleum Labor Policy Board [*Abolished, 1936*]
PLPBD .... Pulpboard
PL & PD ..... Public Liability and Property Damage [*Insurance*]
PLPG .... Publishers' Library Promotion Group [*Later, PLMG*]   (EA)
PLP GRNDG ... Pulp Grinding [*Freight*]
PLPHA .... Plant Physiology [*A publication*]
PLPHB .... Plasma Physics [*A publication*]
Pl Physics ... Plasma Physics [*A publication*]
Pl Physiol (Lancaster) ... Plant Physiology (Lancaster) [*A publication*]
Pl Physiol (Wash) ... Plant Physiology (Washington) [*A publication*]
PLPLS-LHS ... Proceedings. Leeds Philosophical and Literary Society. Literary and Historical Section [*A publication*]
PLPLS-SS ... Proceedings. Leeds Philosophical and Literary Society. Scientific Section [*A publication*]
PLPP .... Position Location Post Processor   (MCD)
Pl & Pr Cas ... Pleading and Practice Cases [*1837-38*] [*England*]   (DLA)
Pl Prot (Tokyo) ... Plant Protection (Tokyo) [*A publication*]
PLPS .... Packaged Liquid Propellant System
PLPS .... Propellant Loading and Pressurization System [*NASA*]
PLPSA .... Physiological Psychology [*A publication*]
PLPUA .... Planseeberichte fuer Pulvermetallurgie (Austria) [*A publication*]
PLQ .... Plaque   (MSA)
PLQ .... Tallahassee, FL [*Location identifier*] [*FAA*]   (FAAL)
PLR .... LaRoche College, Pittsburgh, PA [*OCLC symbol*]   (OCLC)
PLR .... Pacific Law Reporter   (DLA)
PLR .... Pakistan Law Reports   (DLA)
PLR .... Pakistan Law Review   (DLA)
PLR .... Palestine Law Reports [*A publication*]
PLR .... Parlake Resources Ltd. [*Toronto Stock Exchange symbol*]

PLR .... Partido Liberal Radical [*Radical Liberal Party*] [*Ecuadorean*]   (PPW)
PLR .... Partido Liberal Radical [*Radical Liberal Party*] [*Paraguayan*]   (PPW)
PLR .... Patent Law Review   (DLA)
PLR .... Patent Log Reading [*Navigation*]
PLR .... Patna Law Reporter [*India*]   (DLA)
PLR .... Pell City, AL [*Location identifier*] [*FAA*]   (FAAL)
PLR .... Pennsylvania Law Record [*Philadelphia*]   (DLA)
P-LR .... Pennsylvania Legislative Reference Bureau, Harrisburg, PA [*Library symbol*] [*Library of Congress*]   (LCLS)
PLR .... Periodic Logistical Report
PLR .... Philippine Liberation Ribbon
PLR .... Pillar   (MSA)
PLR .... Pliers   (MSA)
PLR .... Plymouth Rubber Co., Inc. [*American Stock Exchange symbol*]
PLR .... Portable LASER Range-Finder
PL & R .... Postal Laws and Regulations [*Later, Postal Manual*]
PLR .... Power Line Radiation [*Radioscience*]
PLR .... Presentation Loss Rate   (MCD)
PLR .... Pressure Level Recorder
PLR .... Primary Loss Retention [*Insurance*]
PLR .... Private Legislation Reports [*Scotland*]   (DLA)
PLR .... Program Life Requirement   (NG)
PLR .... Psychological Laboratories   (KSC)
PLR .... Public Lending Right [*Royalty for books borrowed from public libraries*] [*British*]
PLR .... Puller   (MSA)
PLR .... Pulse Link Relay [*Telecommunications*]   (TEL)
PLR .... Pulse Link Repeater [*Telecommunications*]   (TEL)
PLR .... Punjab Law Reporter [*India*]   (DLA)
PLR .... University of Pittsburgh. Law Review [*A publication*]
PLRA .... Partido Liberal Radical Autentico [*Authentic Liberal Radical Party*] [*Paraguayan*]   (PD)
PLRACTA ... Position Location, Reporting, and Control of Tactical Aircraft [*Military*]
PLRB .... Property Loss Research Bureau [*Schaumburg, IL*]   (EA)
PLRC .... Pulsed LASER Remote Crosswind Sensor   (MCD)
PLRCA .... Pharmacological Research Communication [*A publication*]
PLRCAE ..... Radio Corp. of America, Electron Tube Division, Engineering Section, Lancaster, PA [*Library symbol*] [*Library of Congress*] [*Obsolete*]   (LCLS)
PLRD .... Pull Rod
PLR Dacca ... Pakistan Law Reports, Dacca Series   (DLA)
PLRF .... Pediatric Liver Research Foundation [*Inactive*] [*Cherry Hill, NJ*]   (EA)
pLRF .... Placental Luteinizing Hormone-Releasing Factor [*Endocrinology*]
PLRI .... Posterolateral Rotation Instability [*Sports medicine*]
PLRJ & K .... Punjab Law Reporter, Jammu and Kashmir Section [*India*]   (DLA)
PLR Kar ...... Pakistan Law Reports, Karachi Series [*1947-53*]   (DLA)
PLR Lah ...... Pakistan Law Reports, Lahore Series [*1947-55*]   (DLA)
PLRPF .... Personnel Loss Rate Planning Factors   (MCD)
PLRS .... Pelorus
PLRS .... Phase Lock Receiving System
PLRS .... Position Location Reporting System [*Military*]
PLRSA .... Plasticos y Resinas [*A publication*]
Plrs' Bull Rubb Res Inst Malaya ... Planters' Bulletin. Rubber Research Institute of Malaya [*A publication*]
PLRS/TIDS ... Position Location Reporting System/Tactical Information Distribution Systems [*Military*]   (RDA)
PLRSTN ..... Pelorus Stand
PLRT .... Polarity   (MCD)
PLRV .... Payload Launch Readiness Verification [*NASA*]   (MCD)
PLRV .... Potato Leafroll Virus
PLRWP .... Pakistan Law Reports, West Pakistan Series   (DLA)
PLS .... Palomar-Leiden Survey
PLS .... Parcels   (MSA)
PLS .... Parsons Language Sample
PLS .... Parti Liberal Suisse [*Liberal Party of Switzerland*]   (PPE)
PLS .... Partial Least Squares
PLS .... Patrol Locator System [*Army*]
PLS .... Payload Systems   (MCD)
PLS .... Peerless Tube Co. [*American Stock Exchange symbol*]
PLS .... Peninsula Library System [*Belmont, CA*] [*Library network*]
PLS .... People's Law School [*An association*]   (EA)
PLS .... Peralto Resources Corp. [*Vancouver Stock Exchange symbol*]
PLS .... Periodic Log System
PLS .... Pitch Limit Switch
PLS .... Plaisance [*Mauritius*] [*Geomagnetic observatory code*]
PLS .... Plasma Light Source
PLS .... Plates [*Classical studies*]   (OCD)
PLS .... Please   (AFM)
PLS .... Plugging Switch   (IEEE)
PLS .... Pneumatic Limit Switch
PLS .... Polson, MT [*Location identifier*] [*FAA*]   (FAAL)
PLS .... Portable Laboratory Salinometer
PLS .... Post Landing and Safing [*NASA*]   (NASA)
PLS .... Precautions, Limitations, and Setpoints [*Nuclear energy*]   (NRCH)

PLS.............	President of the Linnaean Society [British]
PLS.............	Primary Landing Site (MCD)
PLS.............	Private Line Service
PLS.............	Product Line Simulator
PLS.............	Professional Legal Secretary [Designation awarded by National Association of Legal Secretaries]
PLS.............	Programable Logic Sequencer [Data processing]
PLS.............	Propellant Loading Sequencer (AAG)
PLS.............	Propellant Loading System
PLS.............	Providenciales [British West Indies] [Airport symbol] (OAG)
PLS.............	Pulse (MSA)
PLS.............	Pulsed LASER System
PLS.............	Pulsed Light Source
PLS.............	Purnell Library Service [Commercial firm]
PLSCB.......	Policy Sciences [A publication]
PLSD.........	Promotion List Service Date [Air Force]
PLSFC.......	Part Load Specific Fuel Consumption [Gas turbine]
PLSGT........	Platoon Sergeant [Marine Corps]
PLSHD......	Polished [Freight]
PLSL.........	Propellants and Life Support Laboratory [NASA] (NASA)
PLSN.........	Pulsation (MSA)
PLSO.........	Propellant Life Support and Ordnance [NASA] (KSC)
PLSOA......	Plant and Soil [A publication]
PLSP.........	Payload Signal Processor [NASA] (MCD)
PLSP.........	Prelaunch Survival Probability (CINC)
PLSR.........	Pulsar Oil & Gas [NASDAQ symbol] (NQ)
PLSR.........	Pulsator (MSA)
PLSS.........	Portable Life Support System [or Subsystem] [NASA]
PLSS.........	Post-Landing Survival System [NASA]
PLSS.........	Precision Location Strike System [Air Force]
PLSS.........	Prelaunch Status Simulator
PLSSA.......	Planetary and Space Science [A publication]
PLSSRS.....	Plant and Soil Science Research Station [Southern Illinois University at Carbondale] [Research center] (RCD)
PLSSU........	Portable Life Support Stretcher Unit [Military] (CAAL)
PLSTC.......	Plastic (AAG)
PLSTR.......	Plasterer (ADA)
PLSV.........	Propellant Latching Solenoid Valve
PLT.............	Columbus, NE [Location identifier] [FAA] (FAAL)
PLT.............	Lancaster Theological Seminary of the United Church of Christ, Lancaster, PA [Library symbol] [Library of Congress] (LCLS)
PLT.............	Lutheran Theological Seminary, Philadelphia, PA [OCLC symbol] (OCLC)
PLT.............	Pacific Lighting Corp. [NYSE symbol]
PLT.............	Pallet (AABC)
PLT.............	Partido Liberal Teete [Teete Liberal Party] [Paraguayan] (PPW)
PLT.............	Patna Law Times [India] (DLA)
Plt..............	Peltier's Orleans Appeals Decisions [Louisiana] (DLA)
PLT.............	Photoluminescent Thermometer
PLT.............	Pilot (AFM)
PLT.............	Pilot Knob [California] [Seismograph station code, US Geological Survey] (SEIS)
PLT.............	Pipeline Time
PLT.............	Plaint [Legal term] (ROG)
PLT.............	Planar Tube
PLT.............	Plant
PLT.............	Plate
PLT.............	Platelet [Hematology]
PLT.............	Platoon (AABC)
PLT.............	Port Light
PLT.............	Post Loading Test (NG)
PLT.............	Power Line Transient (IEEE)
PLT.............	Primed Lymphocyte Typing [Hematology]
PLT.............	Princeton Large Torus [Nuclear reactor]
PLT.............	Private Line Telephone
PLT.............	Private Line Teletypewriter
PLT.............	Procurement Lead Time
PLT.............	Production Lead Time
PLT.............	Program Library Tape [Data processing] (IEEE)
PLT.............	Programed Learning Textbook
PLT.............	Progress in Low Temperature Physics [Elsevier Book Series] [A publication]
PLT.............	Psittacosis-Lymphogranuloma Venereum Trachoma [Microbiology]
PLT.............	Pulsed Light Theodolite
PLT.............	Punjab Law Times [India] (DLA)
PLT.............	South Carolina Aeronautics Commission [Columbia, SC] [FAA designator] (FAAC)
PLTC.........	Propellant Loading Terminal Cabinet (AAG)
PLTD.........	Plated
PLTEA.......	Plastics Technology [A publication]
PLTF.........	Par Leadership Training Foundation [Defunct] (EA)
PLTF.........	Plaintiff [Legal term] (ROG)
PLTF.........	Purple Loosestrife Task Force (EA)
PLTFF.......	Plaintiff
PLTFM......	Platform
PLTG.........	Plating
PLT GL......	Plate Glass [Freight]
PLTHS.......	Pilothouse

PLT LT	Pilot Light (MSA)
PLTR	Plan for Long-Range Technical Requirements
PLTR	Plotter (MSA)
PLTRY	Poultry [Freight]
PLTS	Precision LASER Tracking System (NASA)
PLTVA	Plastvaerlden [A publication]
PLU	Partido Liberal Unificado [Unified Liberal Party] [Paraguayan] (PPW)
PL)u	Path Loss, Uplink [Communications]
PLU	Phi Lambda Upsilon [Fraternity]
PLU	Platoon Leaders Unit [Marine Corps]
PLU	Plural
PLU	Plutonium [Chemical symbol is Pu] (AAG)
PLU	Preservation of Location Uncertainty [Strategy for protecting missiles] [Military]
PLU	Pressure Lubrication Unit
PLU	Propellant Loading and Utilization (AAG)
Plucne Bolesti Tuberk ...	Plucne Bolesti i Tuberkuloza [A publication]
PLUCON	Plutonium Decontamination Emergency Teams
PLUDA	Plutonium-Dokumentation [A publication]
PLUG.........	Propellant Loading and Utilization Group (AAG)
PLUGE	Picture Line-Up Generator [Television]
PLuL.........	Lincoln University, Lincoln University, PA [Library symbol] [Library of Congress] (LCLS)
PLUM	Payload Launch Module
PLUM	Priority Low-Use Minimal
PLUMB	Plumbum [Lead] [Pharmacy]
Plumb Heat J ...	Plumbing and Heating Journal [A publication]
Plumbing Eng ...	Plumbing Engineer [A publication]
Plumbing Heat Equip News ...	Plumbing and Heating Equipment News [A publication]
Plum Contr ...	Plumptre on Contracts [2nd ed.] [1897] (DLA)
PLUNA	Primeras Lineas Uruguayas de Navegacion Aerea [Uruguayan National Airlines]
PLund	Papyri Lundenses [A publication] (OCD)
PLUP	Pluperfect [Grammar]
PLUPF.......	Pluperfect [Grammar]
PLUR	Photo Lab Usage Reporting (MCD)
PLUR	Plural
Plural Soc ...	Plural Societies [The Hague] [A publication]
PLUS	Parent Loans to Undergraduate Students [Later, ALAS]
PLUS	PERT [Program Evaluation and Review Technique] Lifecycle Unified System
PLUS	Portable Lightweight Upper Air Sounding System (MCD)
PLUS	Potential Long Supply Utilization Screening (NATG)
PLUS	Precision Loading and Utilization System (AAG)
PLUS	Prima Leben und Sparen [Quality Living and Saving] [Brand name and discount store chain in West Germany and US]
PLUS	Procedures for Long Supply Assets Utilization Screening [DoD]
PLUS	Program Library Update System
PLUS	Programed Learning under Supervision
PLUS	Programing Language for UNIVAC [Universal Automatic Computer] Systems [Data processing] (CSR)
PLUS	Project Literacy US [Joint project of American Broadcasting Company and Public Broadcasting Service]
PLUSF.......	Plexus Corp. [NASDAQ symbol] (NQ)
Plut..........	Plutarch [First century AD] [Classical studies] (OCD)
Plut..........	Plutus [of Aristophanes] [Classical studies] (OCD)
PLUTA........	Pollution [A publication]
PLUTHARCO ...	Plutonium, Uranium, Thorium Assembly Reactivity Code
PLUTO	Pipeline under the Ocean [British project] [World War II]
PLUTO	Plutonium [Loop-Testing] Reactor [British] (DEN)
Plutonium-Dok ...	Plutonium-Dokumentation [West Germany] [A publication]
PLV.............	Peak Left Ventricular [Pressure] [Cardiology]
PLV.............	Phu-Lien [Kien-An] [Vietnam] [Seismograph station code, US Geological Survey] (SEIS)
PLV.............	Postlanding Vent [or Ventilation] [Apollo] [NASA]
PLV.............	Power Limiting Valve
PLV.............	Sterling Air Service, Inc. [Sterling, CO] [FAA designator] (FAAC)
PLVC.........	Post-Landing Vent Control [NASA] (KSC)
PLVRZD	Pulverized (MSA)
PLW...........	Palu [Indonesia] [Airport symbol] (OAG)
PLW...........	Patna Law Weekly [India] (DLA)
PLW...........	Plow (FAAC)
PLW...........	Preload Washer
PL/WA	Plain Washer [Automotive engineering]
PLWG.........	Photographic Labs Working Group [Range Commanders Council] [NASA]
PLX.............	Plantronics, Inc. [NYSE symbol]
PLX.............	Plexus [Medicine]
PLX.............	Position Launch [Search mode wherein X signifies the launch mode number] (MCD)
PLX.............	Propellant Loading Exercise (MCD)
PLX.............	Robinson, IL [Location identifier] [FAA] (FAAL)
PLY.............	[The] Plessey Co. Ltd. [NYSE symbol]
Ply	Plymouth [Record label]
PLY.............	Polaris Energy [Vancouver Stock Exchange symbol]
PLYGA	Psychologia: An International Journal of Psychology in the Orient [A publication]

PLYHD .... Polyhedron [*A publication*]
PLYINST .... Command Comply Current Instructions
PLYM .... Plymouth [*England*]
PLYMCHAN ... Plymouth Subarea Channel [*NATO*]   (NATG)
Plyn Voda Zdra Tech ... Plyn Voda a Zdravotni Technika [*A publication*]
PLYPASSPORT ... Application for Passport for Self and/or Dependents Accordance BUPERS Manual [*Navy*]
PLYWD....... Plywood   (AAG)
Plyw and Plyw Prod ... Plywood and Plywood Products [*A publication*]
Plyw Plyw Prod ... Plywood and Plywood Products [*A publication*]
PLZ............ Plaza   (MCD)
PLZ............ Please
PLZ............ Polarize   (MSA)
PLZ............ Port Elizabeth [*South Africa*] [*Airport symbol*]   (OAG)
PLZ............ Programing Languages for the Zilog [*Data processing*]   (CSR)
PLZA .... Plaza Commerce Bancorp [*NASDAQ symbol*]   (NQ)
Plzen Lek Sb ... Plzensky Lekarsky Sbornik [*A publication*]
Plzen Lek Sb Suppl ... Plzensky Lekarsky Sbornik. Supplementum [*A publication*]
PLZN .... Polarization   (MSA)
PLZT .... Pb-based Lanthanum-doped Zirconate Titanates
PM .... Brymon Airways [*Great Britain*] [*ICAO designator*]   (FAAC)
PM............ [*The*] Chesapeake & Ohio Railway Co. (Pere Marquette District) [*AAR code*]
PM............ Ha-Po'el ha-Mizrahi   (BJA)
PM............ International Journal of Psychiatry in Medicine [*A publication*]
P & M........ Law Reports, Probate and Matrimonial Cases [*England*]   (DLA)
PM............ Pacific Mail   (ROG)
PM............ Pad Mechanic [*Aerospace*]
PM............ Painting Machine
PM............ Palace of Minos [*A publication*]
PM............ Paleographie Musicale [*A publication*]
PM............ Pamphlet
PM............ Panel Meter   (IEEE)
PM............ Paper Maker [*A publication*]
PM............ Paper Money [*A publication*]
PM............ Parameter [*Data processing*]
P M........... Paris Match [*A publication*]
PM............ Parlor Maid
PM............ Parole et Mission [*A publication*]
PM............ Partito Monarchico [*Monarchist Party*] [*Italy*]   (PPE)
P/M .... Parts per Million   (IEEE)
PM............ Passed Midshipman
PM............ Passed Motion
PM............ Past Master [*Freemasonry*]
PM............ Patriotikon Metopon [*Patriotic Front*] [*Greek Cypriot*]   (PPE)
PM............ Patternmaker [*Navy rating*]
PM............ Payload Midbody [*NASA*]   (MCD)
PM............ Paymaster
PM............ Peace Museum   (EA)
PM............ Pectoralis Major [*Anatomy*]
PM............ Peculiar Meter
PM............ Penalty Minutes [*Hockey*]
PM............ Per Month
PM............ Pere Marquette Railroad
PM............ Perfect Master [*Freemasonry*]
PM............ Performance Monitor [*NASA*]   (NASA)
PM............ Periodic Maintenance   (AFM)
PM............ Permanent Magnet [*Loudspeaker*]
PM............ Petermanns Geographische Mitteilungen [*A publication*]
PM............ Petit Mal [*Epilepsy*]
PM............ Phase Modulation [*Radio data transmission*]
PM............ Phased Maintenance   (MCD)
PM............ Philippine Manager [*A publication*]
PM............ Phorbol Monomyristate [*Organic chemistry*]
PM............ Phosphoramide Mustard [*Antineoplastic drug*]
PM............ Photo Master   (MCD)
PM............ Photomultiplier
PM............ Phyllosticta maydis [*A toxin-producing fungus*]
P/M .... Physical Medicine [*Medical Officer designation*] [*British*]
PM............ Physical Medicine
PM............ Piae Memoriae [*Of Pious Memory*] [*Latin*]
pm............ Picometer
PM............ Pilot Motor   (MSA)
PM............ Pioneer Ministries   (EA)
PM............ Pit Membrane [*Paleobotany*]
PM............ Planetary Mission [*NASA*]   (NASA)
PM............ Plasma Membrane [*Cytology*]
PM............ Plasmalemma [*Cytology*]
PM............ Plaster Master   (MSA)
PM............ Plastic Mold   (MCD)
P/M .... Player/Missile [*Atari computers*]
PM............ Plus Minus [*More or less*]
P or M........ Plus or Minus   (MSA)
PM............ PM. Pharmacy Management [*A publication*]
PM............ Polar Medal   (ADA)
PM............ Polarization Modulation   (MCD)
PM............ Police Magistrate
PM............ Policy Memorandum [*Military*]
PM............ Poliomyelitis [*Medicine*]
PM............ Pollen Mass [*Botany*]

P & M........ Pollock and Maitland's History of English Common Law   (DLA)
PM............ Polymethacrylic [*Organic chemistry*]
PM............ Polymorph [*Hematology*]
PM............ Polymyositis [*Medicine*]
PM............ Pondus Medicinale [*Medicinal Weight*] [*Pharmacy*]   (ROG)
PM............ Pontifex Maximus
PM............ Poor Metabolism [*Medicine*]
PM............ Pope and Martyr [*Church calendars*]
PM............ Popular Mechanics [*A publication*]
PM............ Portable Magnetometer [*NASA*]
PM............ Portable Medium-Power [*Reactor*]   (NRCH)
PM............ Post Magazine and Insurance Monitor [*A publication*]
PM............ Post Meridiem [*After Noon*] [*Latin*]
PM............ Post Mortem [*After Death*] [*Examination*] [*Latin*]
PM............ Postal Manual
PM............ Postmark [*Deltiology*]
PM............ Postmaster
PM............ Postmodernist [*Architecture*]
PM............ Potentiometer   (DEN)
PM............ Potting Mold   (MCD)
PM............ Pounds per Minute
PM............ Powder Metallurgy
PM............ Power Module   (MCD)
PM............ Powlesland & Mason [*Railway*] [*Wales*]
PM............ Pratt & Lambert, Inc. [*American Stock Exchange symbol*]
PM............ Precious Metal
PM............ Preincubation Mixture
PM............ Premium
PM............ Premolar [*Dentistry*]
PM............ Preparation Meetings [*Quakers*]
PM............ Prepared Message
PM............ Presidential Memo
PM............ Presse Medicale [*A publication*]
PM............ Pressure Multiplier [*Nuclear energy*]   (NRCH)
PM............ Presystolic Murmur [*Cardiology*]
PM............ Preventive Maintenance
PM............ Preventive Medicine [*Also, PVNTMED*]   (AFM)
PM............ Priest and Martyr [*Church calendars*]
PM............ Prime Minister
PM............ Prime Mover   (MCD)
PM............ Primitive Methodists   (ROG)
PM............ Principal Matron [*Navy*] [*British*]
PM............ Principle of Multiplying [*New math*]
PM............ Prize Money
PM............ Pro Memoria [*In Remembrance*] [*Latin*]
PM............ Pro Mense [*Per Month*] [*Latin*]
PM............ Pro Mille [*Per Thousand*] [*Latin*]
P & M........ Probate and Matrimonial [*Legal*] [*British*]
PM............ Procedures Manual   (IEEE)
PM............ Process Manual
PM............ Process Metallurgy [*Elsevier Book Series*] [*A publication*]
P & M........ Processes and Materials   (NASA)
PM............ Processing Module [*Data processing*]
PM............ Procurement and Material
PM............ Production Manager
PM............ Production Mode
PM............ Profit Motivated [*Housing*]
PM............ Program   (NG)
PM............ Program Manager   (MCD)
PM............ Program Memorandum   (MCD)
PM............ Program Milestone [*NASA*]   (NASA)
PM............ Program Monitoring   (MUGU)
PM............ Project Magic [*Inglewood, CA*]   (EA)
PM............ Project Manager [*Military*]
Pm............ Promethium [*Chemical symbol*]
PM............ Propellant Management   (KSC)
PM............ Property Management   (OICC)
PM............ Propulsion Memorandum
PM............ Propulsion Module [*NASA*]   (KSC)
PM............ Prostatic Massage [*Medicine*]
PM............ Province du Maine [*A publication*]
PM............ Provost Marshal
PM............ Public Management [*A publication*]
PM............ Publicity Man [*Slang*]
PM............ Pulmonary Macrophages [*Medicine*]
PM............ Pulpomesial [*Dentistry*]
PM............ Pulse Modulation
Pm............ Pumice [*Quality of the bottom*] [*Nautical charts*]
PM............ Punjabi Muslim [*Pakistan*]
PM............ Purchase Memo   (MCD)
PM............ Purchase Money
PM............ Purchase Money Mortgage [*Business and trade*]
PM............ Purchasing Manager
PM............ Purpose-Made [*Construction*]
P/M .... Put of More [*Stock exchange*]
PM............ Pyridoxamine [*Also, Pxm*] [*Biochemistry*]
PM............ St. Pierre and Miquelon [*Two-letter standard code*]   (CNC)
PM............ Sisters of the Presentation of Mary [*Roman Catholic religious order*]
PM1........... Patternmaker, First Class [*Navy rating*]
PM2........... Patternmaker, Second Class [*Navy rating*]

PM3 .... Patternmaker, Third Class [*Navy rating*]
PMA .... Allegheny College, Meadville, PA [*Library symbol*] [*Library of Congress*] (LCLS)
PMA .... Combined International Corp. [*NYSE symbol*]
PMA .... Pacific Maritime Association [*San Francisco, CA*] (EA)
PMA .... Pan-Macedonian Association
PMA .... Panorama Petroleums [*Vancouver Stock Exchange symbol*]
PMA .... Papillary, Marginal, Attached [*With reference to gingivae*] [*Dentistry*]
PMA .... Paramethoxyamphetamine
PMA .... Parts Manufacturer Approval (MCD)
PMA .... Peat Moss Association (EA)
PMA .... Pemba Island [*Tanzania*] [*Airport symbol*] (OAG)
PMA .... Pencil Makers Association [*Moorestown, NJ*] (EA)
PMA .... Performance Monitor Annunciator [*NASA*] (MCD)
PMA .... Permanent Mailing Address
PMA .... Personal Money Allowance
PMA .... Personnel Management Assistance
PMA .... Petroleum Monitoring Agency [*Ministry of Energy, Mines, and Resources*] [*Canada*]
PMA .... Pharmaceutical Manufacturers Association [*Formed by a merger of ADMA and American Pharmaceutical Manufacturers Association*] [*Washington, DC*] (EA)
PMA .... Phenylmercuric Acetate [*Also, PMAC*] [*Herbicide and fungicide*]
PMA .... Philadelphia Musical Academy
PMA .... Philippine Mahogany Association [*Defunct*] (EA)
PMA .... Phonograph Manufacturers Association (EA)
PMA .... Phorbol Myristate Acetate [*Also, PTA, TPA*] [*Organic chemistry*]
PMA .... Phosphomolybdic Acid [*Organic chemistry*]
PMA .... Photo Marketing Association International [*Formed by a merger of MPDFA and National Photographic Dealers Association*] [*Jackson, MI*] (EA)
PMA .... Physical Memory Address
PMA .... Pine Manor College, Chestnut Hill, MA [*OCLC symbol*] (OCLC)
PMA .... Planetary Microbiological Assay [*Aerospace*]
PMA .... Plastic Mock-Up Assembly
PMA .... Pole-Mounted Amplifier
PMA .... Police Management Association (EA)
PMA .... Police Marksman Association (EA)
PMA .... Polish Museum of America (EA)
PMA .... Poly(methyl Acrylate) [*Organic chemistry*]
PMA .... Polyurethane Manufacturers Association [*Glen Ellyn, IL*] (EA)
PMA .... Port Moller [*Alaska*] [*Seismograph station code, US Geological Survey*] (SEIS)
PMA .... Positive Mental Attitude
PMA .... Power Marketing Administration [*Department of Energy*]
PMA .... Preamplifier Module Assembly
PMA .... Precious Metal Adder (Cost) (MCD)
PMA .... Precious Metal Anode
PMA .... Precision Measurements Association
PMA .... Precision Metalforming Association [*Richmond Heights, OH*] (EA)
PMA .... Primary Mental Abilities [*Test*] [*Education*]
PMA .... Priority Memory Access
PMA .... Prison Mission Association (EA)
P M A .... Proceedings. Musical Association [*A publication*]
PMA .... Procurement and Management Assistance [*Small Business Administration*]
PMA .... Procurement Methods Analyst (AFM)
PMA .... Produce Marketing Association (EA)
PMA .... Production and Marketing Administration [*Department of Agriculture*] [*Functions dispersed, 1953*]
PMA .... Professional Managers Association (EA)
PMA .... Professional Manufacturers' Agents (EA)
PMA .... Professional Mariners Alliance [*New York, NY*] (EA)
PMA .... Programa Mundial de Alimentos [*World Food Program*]
PMA .... Progressive Muscular Atrophy [*Medicine*]
PMA .... Project Manager, Air Systems Command [*Navy*]
PMA .... Project Military Adviser (NATG)
PMA .... Protected Memory Address
PMA .... Publications. Mediaeval Academy [*A publication*]
PMA .... Pulpomesioaxial [*Dentistry*]
PMA .... Pump-Motor Assembly
PMA .... Purchase Methods Analyst
PMA .... Pyridylmercuric Acetate [*Fungicide*] [*Organic chemistry*]
PMA .... Pyromellitic Acid [*Organic chemistry*]
PMAA .... Paper Makers Advertising Association (EA)
PMAA .... Petroleum Marketers Association of America [*Washington, DC*] (EA)
PMAA .... Promotion Marketing Association of America [*Formerly, PAAA*] [*New York, NY*] (EA)
PMAA .... Property Management Association of America [*Silver Spring, MD*] (EA)
PM-AAH .... Project Manager, Advanced Attack Helicopter [*Military*]
PMAC .... Parallel Memory Address Counter [*Data processing*]
PMAC .... Phenylmercuric Acetate [*Also, PMA*] [*Herbicide and fungicide*]
PMAC .... Preliminary Maintenance Allocation Chart (MCD)
PMAC .... Provisional Military Administrative Council [*Political party*] [*Ethiopian*] (PD)

PMACODS ... Project Manager, Army Container Oriented Distribution System (MCD)
PM & ACS ... Procurement Management and Acquisition Control System [*Social Security Administration*]
PMAD .... Performance Monitor Annunciation Driver [*NASA*] (MCD)
PMadW ...... Westinghouse Electric Corp., Waltz Mill Site Library, Madison, PA [*Library symbol*] [*Library of Congress*] (LCLS)
PMAESA .... Port Management Association of Eastern and Southern Africa (EA)
PMAF .... Polaris Missile Assembly Facility
PMAFS .... Public Members Association of the Foreign Service (EA)
PMAG .... Program Manager Assistance Group [*Military*] (MCD)
PMAG .... Provisional Military Advisory Group
PMAI .... Piano Manufacturers Association International [*Dallas, TX*] (EA)
PMaine .... Province du Maine [*A publication*]
PMAI News Lett ... PMAI [*Powder Metallurgy Association of India*] News Letter [*A publication*]
PMALS .... Prototype Miniature Air-Launched System
PMAN .... Piedmont Management [*NASDAQ symbol*] (NQ)
PMA News ... PMA [*Pharmaceutical Manufacturers Association*] Newsletter [*A publication*]
PManM ...... Mansfield State College, Mansfield, PA [*Library symbol*] [*Library of Congress*] (LCLS)
PMANY ..... Pattern Makers Association of New York (EA)
PMAP .... Performance Monitor Annunciation Panel [*NASA*] (MCD)
PMAPP ...... Combined International Corp. Conv Pfd [*NASDAQ symbol*] (NQ)
PMAR .... Page Map Address Register
PMAR .... Precious Metals Area Representative [*DoD*] (AFIT)
PMAR .... Preliminary Maintenance Analysis Report [*Aerospace*] (AAG)
PMarhSO ... Sun Oil Co., Marcus Hook, PA [*Library symbol*] [*Library of Congress*] (LCLS)
PMARP ...... Peacetime Manpower Allocation Requirements Plan (CINC)
PMAS .... Purdue Master Attitude Scales [*Psychology*]
PMASAL .... Publications. Michigan Academy of Science, Arts, and Letters [*A publication*]
PM-ASE ..... Project Manager, Aircraft Survivability Equipment [*Military*]
PM-ASH ..... Project Manager, Advanced Scout Helicopter [*Military*]
PMAT .... Page Map Address Table [*NASA*] (NASA)
PMAT .... Primary Mental Abilities Test [*Education*]
PMAT .... Purdue Mechanical Adaptability Test
PMAX .... Petromax Energy Corp. [*NASDAQ symbol*] (NQ)
PMB .... Pacific Motor Tariff Bureau, Inc., Oakland CA [*STAC*]
PMB .... Paranormal Metal Bending
PMB .... Pembina, ND [*Location identifier*] [*FAA*] (FAAL)
PMB .... Performance Measurement Baseline (MCD)
PMB .... Physical Metallurgy Branch
PMB .... Pilot Make Busy (IEEE)
PMB .... Polychrome Methylene Blue
PMB .... Polymethylbenzene [*Organic chemistry*]
PMB .... Polymorphonuclear Basophilic [*Leucocytes*] [*Hematology*]
PMB .... Postmenopausal Bleeding [*Medicine*]
PMB .... Potato Marketing Board [*British*]
PMB .... Practice Multiple Bomb (MCD)
PMB .... Print Measurement Bureau [*Founded in 1971*] [*Canada*] [*Also the name of a database*]
PMB .... Program Management Board (AFM)
PMB .... PROM [*Programable Read-Only Memory*] Memory Board
PMBAA ...... Publications. Institut Royal Meteorologique de Belgique. Serie A [*A publication*] ue
PMBC .... Phuket Marine Biological Center [*Marine science*] (MSC)
PMBIAS ..... Percentage Median Bias [*Statistics*]
PMBR .... Practice Multiple Bomb Rack (NG)
PMBU .... Personal Member of the Baptist Union [*British*]
PMBX .... Private Manual Branch Exchange [*Communications*]
PMC .... Carnegie-Mellon University, Pittsburgh, PA [*OCLC symbol*] (OCLC)
PMC .... Chief Patternmaker [*Navy rating*]
PMC .... Little Missionary Sisters of Charity [*Roman Catholic religious order*]
PMC .... Pacific Marine Center [*National Ocean Survey*]
PMC .... Pacific Missile Center [*Marine science*] (MSC)
PMC .... Pan Metal [*formerly, Patton Morgan*] Corporation [*Ammunition manufacturer*]
PMC .... Parents of Murdered Children [*Later, POMC*] (EA)
PMC .... Partially Mission Capable [*Maintenance and supply*] (MCD)
PMC .... Payload Monitoring and Control [*NASA*] (NASA)
PMC .... Penguin Modern Classics [*Book publishing*]
PMC .... Pennsylvania Military College
PMC .... People's Mandate Committee (EA)
PMC .... Peripheral Mononuclear Cell [*Cytology*]
PMC .... Peritoneal Mast Cell
PMC .... Phased Maintenance Checklist (MCD)
PMC .... Phenolic Molding Compound
PMC .... Phenylmercuric Chloride [*Antiseptic*]
PMC .... Philatelic Music Circle
PM & C ...... Plant Monitoring and Control [*IBM Corp.*]
PMC .... Plaster-Molded Cornice [*Construction*]
PMC .... Pollen Mother Cell [*Botany*]
PMC .... Post Maintenance Check (MCD)

PMC .... Post Manufacturing Checkout (KSC)
PMC .... Posterior Medial Corner of Knee [*Sports medicine*]
PMC .... Powdered Metal Cathode
PMC .... Precision Machining Commercialization (MCD)
PMC .... Predictive Multisensor Correlation
PMC .... Premium Merchandising Club of New York [*Union, NJ*] (EA)
PMC .... Premotor Cortex [*Neuroanatomy*]
PMC .... President of the Mess Committee [*Military*] [*British*]
PMC .... Pressurized Membrane Container
PMC .... Prime Mover Control [*Valve*]
PMC .... Princeton Microfilm Corporation
PmC .... Princeton Microfilm Corporation, Princeton, NJ [*Library symbol*] [*Library of Congress*] (LCLS)
PMC .... Private Mailing Card [*Deltiology*]
PMC .... Private Medical Communication
PMC .... Private Meter Check [*Telecommunications*] (TEL)
PMC .... Pro Maria Committee (EA)
PMC .... Procurement Committee (MCD)
PMC .... Procurement Management Code [*Military*] (AFIT)
PMC .... Procurement, Marine Corps [*An appropriation*]
PMC .... Procurement Method Coding [*DoD*]
PMC .... Program Management Control
PMC .... Program Management Course [*Army*] (RDA)
PMC .... Program Marginal Checking
PMC .... Programable Machine Controller (NRCH)
PMC .... Progress in Medicinal Chemistry [*Elsevier Book Series*] [*A publication*]
PMC .... Project Manufacturing Controller (MCD)
PMC .... Propellant Monitor and Control (AFM)
PMC .... Pseudo Machine Code [*Data processing*] (BUR)
PMC .... Pseudomembranous Colitis [*Medicine*]
PMC .... Public Media Center (EA)
PMC .... Puerto Montt [*Chile*] [*Airport symbol*] (OAG)
PMC .... Pumice (MSA)
PM-CAWS ... Project Manager for Cannon Artillery Weapon Systems (RDA)
PMCB .... Partially Mission Capable Both [*Maintenance and supply*] (MCD)
P/MCB ...... Project/Miscellaneous Change Board (MCD)
PMCC .... Peerless Motor Car Club (EA)
PMCC .... Post Mark Collectors' Club
PMCD .... Post Mortem Core Dump [*Data processing*]
PMCF .... Post Maintenance Check Flight (MCD)
PMCHi .... Crawford County Historical Society, Meadville, PA [*Library symbol*] [*Library of Congress*] (LCLS)
PM & C-HI ... Plant Monitoring and Control - Host Interface [*IBM Corp.*]
PMCI .... Phosphate Mining Company of Christmas Island Ltd.
PMck .... Carnegie Free Library of McKeesport, McKeesport, PA [*Library symbol*] [*Library of Congress*] (LCLS)
PMCL .... Periodica de Re Morali Canonica Liturgica [*A publication*]
PMCL .... Posterior Medial Collateral Ligament [*Anatomy*]
PMCM .... Master Chief Patternmaker [*Navy rating*]
PMCM .... Partially Mission Capable Maintenance [*Maintenance and supply*] (MCD)
PMCM .... Permanent Mold Casting Mold (MCD)
PMCP .... Photo-Marker Corporation [*NASDAQ symbol*] (NQ)
PMCS .... Partially Mission Capable Supply [*Maintenance and supply*] (MCD)
PMCS .... Phoenix Materials [*NASDAQ symbol*] (NQ)
PMCS .... Preventive Maintenance Checks and Services [*for Army vehicles*] (INF)
PMCS .... Program Management and Control System [*Army*] (RDA)
PMCS .... Pulse-Modulated Communications System
PMCS .... Senior Chief Patternmaker [*Navy rating*]
PMCT .... PAL [*Permissive Action Link*] Management Control Team [*Army*] (AABC)
PMCU .... Personal Member of the Congregational Union [*British*]
PMCV .... Programed Multichannel Valve [*Chromatography*]
PMD .... Palmdale, CA [*Location identifier*] [*FAA*] (FAAL)
PMD .... Palmdale/Lancaster [*California*] [*Airport symbol*] (OAG)
PMD .... Palmer Industries Ltd. [*Vancouver Stock Exchange symbol*]
PMD .... Panel-Mounted Display (MCD)
PMD .... Part Manufacturing Design
PMD .... Payload Mating Dolly [*NASA*]
PMD .... Payload Module Decoder [*NASA*]
PMD .... Pharmaco-Medical Documentation, Inc. [*Chatham, NJ*] [*Information service*] (EISS)
PMD .... Post Mortem Dump [*Data processing*]
PMD .... Preventive Maintenance, Daily (MCD)
PMD .... Preventive Maintenance Division [*Air Force*]
PMD .... Primary Myocardial Disease [*Medicine*]
PMd .... Private Physician
PMD .... Processing, Marketing, and Distribution
PMD .... Program Management Directive [*Air Force*]
PMD .... Program Module Dictionary
PMD .... Program Monitoring and Diagnosis
PMD .... Programed Multiple Development [*Analytical chemistry*]
PMD .... Progressive Muscular Dystrophy [*Medicine*]
PMD .... Project Manager Development (MCD)
PMD .... Projected Map Display
PMD .... Psychiatric Military Duty

PMDA .... Peace Messenger. Diocese of Athabasca. Peace River [*A publication*]
PMDA .... Photographic Manufacturers and Distributors Association [*New York, NY*] (EA)
PMDA .... Pyromellitic Dianhydride [*Organic chemistry*]
PMDAMT ... Pacific Mobile Depot Activity Maintenance Team (CINC)
PMDC .... Project for Mathematical Development of Children [*National Science Foundation*]
PMDD .... Personnel Management Development Directorate [*Military Personnel Center*] (AABC)
PMDF .... Project Master Data File [*For spacecraft*]
PMDG .... Pentamethylene Diguanidine [*Organic chemistry*]
PMDL .... Post M-Day Deployment List [*Military*] (AABC)
PMDL .... Provisional Military Demarcation Line (CINC)
PMDM .... Polyhedra Molecular Demonstration Model
PMDM .... Poly(mellitic Dianhydride Methacrylate) [*Organic chemistry*]
PMDO .... Phased Maintenance During Overhaul
PMDP .... Pavement Marking Demonstration Program [*Federal Highway Administration*]
PMDP .... Project Manager Development Program [*Army*] (RDA)
PMDR .... Parametric Monotone Decreasing Ratio [*Statistics*]
PMDR .... Phosphorescence-Microwave Double Resonance
PMDR .... Provisioning Master Data Record
PMDS .... (Phenylmercury)dodecenyl Succinate [*Antimicrobial agent*]
PMDS .... Pilot Map Display System
PMDS .... Projected Map Display System
PMDS .... Property Management and Disposal Service [*Abolished, 1973*] [*General Services Administration*]
PMDT .... Pentamethyldiethylenetriamine [*Organic chemistry*]
PME .... Caltech Political Military Exercise [*International relations simulation game*]
PME .... Passive Microelectronic Element
PME .... Peace Movement of Ethiopia (EA)
PME .... Pectin Methylesterase [*Also, PE*] [*An enzyme*]
PME .... Pedal Mode Ergometer
PME .... Performance Monitoring Equipment (NVT)
PME .... Phosphatidylmonomethylethanolamine [*Biochemistry*]
PME .... Phosphomonoester [*Biochemistry*]
PME .... Phosphorylated Monester [*Organic chemistry*]
PME .... Photomagnetoelectric
PME .... Pinosylvin Methyl Ether [*Organic chemistry*]
PME .... Polymorphonuclear Eosinophile [*Hematology*]
PME .... Prace i Materialy Etnograficzne [*A publication*]
PME .... Precision Measuring Equipment (AFM)
PME .... Primary Mission Equipment
PME .... Prime Ministers of England [*A publication*]
PME .... Process and Manufacturing Engineering (NRCH)
PME .... Processor Memory Enhancement
PME .... Professional Military Education (AFM)
PME .... Professional Military Ethic (MCD)
PME .... Project Manager, Electronics System Command [*Navy*]
PME .... Protective Multiple Earthing [*Electricity*]
PMEA .... Powder Metallurgy Equipment Association (EA)
PMEA .... Production and Maintenance Engineering Agent (MCD)
PMEA .... Publishing Manufacturers Executive Association [*Sea Girt, NJ*] (EA)
PMEAR .... Preliminary Maintenance Engineering Analysis Requirement (MCD)
PMED .... Proto-Med, Inc. [*NASDAQ symbol*] (NQ)
PMedS .... Delaware County Institute of Science, Media, PA [*Library symbol*] [*Library of Congress*] (LCLS)
PMEE .... Prime Mission Electronic Equipment [*NASA*] (KSC)
PMEF .... Petroleum Marketing Education Foundation [*Alexandria, VA*] (EA)
PMEL .... Pacific Marine Environmental Laboratory [*National Oceanic and Atmospheric Administration*]
PMEL .... Precision Measuring Equipment Laboratory
PMELA .... Plastiques Modernes et Elastomeres [*A publication*]
PM-ENDOR ... Polarization Modulated Electron Nuclear Double Resonance [*Spectroscopy*]
PMer .... Mercer Free Library, Mercer, PA [*Library symbol*] [*Library of Congress*] (LCLS)
PMES .... Personnel Management Evaluation System [*Department of Labor*]
PMES .... Productivity Measurement and Evaluation System (MCD)
PMES .... Proposed Material Erection Schedule (MCD)
PMEST .... Personality, Matter, Energy, Space, Time [*Colon classification, S. R. Ranganathan*] [*Library science*]
PMET .... Painter Metal (AAG)
PMEV .... Panel-Mounted Electronic Voltmeter
PMEXPO .... Property Management Exposition [*Bachner Communications*] (TSPED)
PMF .... Pakistan Mazdoor Federation
PMF .... Parts Master File (MCD)
PMF .... Performance Monitor Function [*NASA*] (NASA)
PMF .... Perigee Motor Firing (MCD)
PMF .... Permanent Magnetic Field
PMF .... Permanent Military Force (ADA)
PMF .... Personnel Master File [*Army*] (AABC)
PMF .... Pilot Mortar Fire
PM of F .... Presidential Medal of Freedom (AABC)

PMF............	Price Master File (MCD)
PMF............	Principle Management Facility (MCD)
PMF............	Pro Media Foundation (EA)
PMF............	Probable Maximum Flood (NRCH)
PMF............	Processed Message File (MCD)
PMF............	Professional Medical Film (AABC)
PMF............	Program Management Facility (MCD)
PMF............	Progressive Massive Fibrosis
PMF............	Proton Motive Force [Physics]
PMFA.........	Fireman Apprentice, Patternmaker, Striker [Navy rating]
PMFAA.......	Pokroky Matematiky, Fyziky, a Astronomie [A publication]
PM-FAC	Prednisone, Methotrexate, Fluorouracil, Adriamycin, Cyclophosphamide [Antineoplastic drug regimen]
PMFC........	Pacific Marine Fisheries Commission [Portland, OR] (EA)
PMFC........	Patsy Montana Fan Club (EA)
PMFG........	Peerless Manufacturing [NASDAQ symbol] (NQ)
PM/FL........	Performance Monitor/Fault Locator [Military] (CAAL)
PMFLT	Pamphlet (MSA)
PMFN........	Fireman, Patternmaker, Striker [Navy rating]
PMFPAC	Polaris Missile Facility, Pacific Fleet
PMFS	Pulsed Magnetic Field System
PMFWCMA ...	Paper Mill Fourdrinier Wire Cloth Manufacturers Association [Later, FWC] (EA)
PMG	Pall Mall Gazette [A publication]
PMG	Paymaster General [Navy]
PMG	Permanent Magnet Generator
PMG	Phase Modulation Generator
PMG	Physiological Measurement Group
PMG	Pinto Malartic [Vancouver Stock Exchange symbol]
PMG	Polymethylgalacturonase [An enzyme]
PMG	Ponta Pora [Brazil] [Airport symbol] (OAG)
PMG	Port Moresby [Papua New Guinea] [Geomagnetic observatory code]
PMG	Port Moresby [Papua New Guinea] [Seismograph station code, US Geological Survey] (SEIS)
PMG	Postmaster General
PMG	Poultry Marketing Guide
PMG	Prediction Marker Generator
PMG	Propodial Mucus Gland [Zoology]
PMG	Provisional Military Government [Ethiopia]
PMG	Provost Marshal General [Army]
P1MG	P1 [Code] for Multigroup [Method] [Nuclear energy] (NRCH)
PMGDINYC ...	Production Men's Guild of the Dress Industry of New York City (EA)
PMGO........	Office of the Provost Marshal General [Army]
PMGS	Provost Marshal General's School, United States Army
PMGW	Primary Mission Gross Weight
PMH	Past Medical History
PMH	Portsmouth, OH [Location identifier] [FAA] (FAAL)
PMH	Probable Maximum Hurricane (NRCH)
PMH	Production per Man-Hour
PMHB	Pennsylvania Magazine of History and Biography [A publication]
PMHBA	Polish Medical Science and History Bulletin [A publication]
PMHC........	Pyridinylmethylethylene(hydrazinecarbothioamide) [Organic chemistry]
P & MHEL ...	Pollock and Maitland's History of English Common Law (DLA)
PMHL........	Preferred Measurement Hardware List [NASA] (NASA)
PMH/M.......	Productive Man-Hours per Month [Navy] (NG)
PMHP	Para-Menthane Hydroperoxide [Organic chemistry]
PMHS	Polymethylhydrosiloxane [Organic chemistry]
PMHS	Proceedings. Massachusetts Historical Society [A publication]
PMi............	Milton Public Library, Milton, PA [Library symbol] [Library of Congress] (LCLS)
PMI	Palma [Mallorca Island] [Airport symbol] (OAG)
PMI............	Parmac Mines [Vancouver Stock Exchange symbol]
PMI............	Past [or Previous] Medical Illness
PMI............	Patient Medication Instruction
PMI............	Pearlitic Malleable Iron (MCD)
PMI............	Pennsylvania Muscle Institute [University of Pennsylvania] [Research center] (RCD)
PMI............	Peripheral Maintenance, Incorporated [Fairfield, NJ] [Hardware manufacturer]
PMI............	Permanent Manufacturing Information (MSA)
PMI............	Plant Manager Instructions (NRCH)
PMI............	Plasma-Materials Interactions (MCD)
PMI............	Plumbing Manufacturers Institute [Glen Ellyn, IL] (EA)
PMI............	Point of Maximal Impulse [Medicine]
PMI............	Point of Maximum Intensity
PMI............	Postmyocardial Infarction [Syndrome] [Medicine]
PMI............	Precision Methods, Incorporated [Lorton, VA] [Hardware manufacturer]
PMI............	Preliminary Maintenance Inspection (MCD)
PMI............	Premark International, Inc. [NYSE symbol]
PMI............	Prescriptive Math Inventory
PMI............	Present Medical Illness
PMI............	Presidential Management Incentives [Office of Management and Budget]
PMI............	Pressed Metal Institute [Later, AMSA]
PMI............	Preventive Maintenance Inspection (AFM)
PMI............	Primary Measurement Instrument

PMI	Principal Maintenance Inspector (NASA)
PMI	Private Mortgage Insurance [Insurance of mortgages by private insurers]
PMI	Processor Monitoring Instrument [Data processing] (ADA)
PMI	Program Management Instruction
PMI	Programable Machine Interface (MCD)
PMI	Project Management Institute [Drexel Hill, PA] (EA)
PMI	Proposed Military Improvement (CAAL)
PMI	Pseudomatrix Isolation
PMI	Purchased Materials Inspection
PMIA	Parallel Multiplexer Interface Adapter (MCD)
PMIA	Presidential Management Improvement Award
PMIC.........	Parallel Multiple Incremental Computer
PMIC.........	Payload Mission Integration Contract (MCD)
PMIC.........	Periodic Maintenance Information Cards (MCD)
PMIC.........	Personnel Management Information Center [Air Force] (AFM)
PMIG.........	Programers Minimal Interface to Graphics (MCD)
PMIJ	Pulse-Modulated Infrared Jammer
PMilan........	Papiri Milanesi [A publication] (OCD)
PMilS.........	Millersville State College, Millersville, PA [Library symbol] [Library of Congress] (LCLS)
PMIP	Pan Malayan Islamic Party
PMIP	Postmaintenance Inspection Pilot
PMIR..........	Program Manager's Integration Review [NASA] (NASA)
PMIR..........	Psi-Mediated Instrumental Response [Parapsychology]
PMIRD	Passive Microwave Intercept Receiver Display
PMIS	Passive Microwave Imaging System [NASA]
PMIS	Personnel Management Information System [NASA]
PMIS	Plant Monitoring and Information System [Nuclear energy] (NRCH)
PMIS	Precision Mechanisms in Sodium (NRCH)
PMIS	Printing Management Information Systems
PMITS	Post Mobilization Individual Training and Support (MCD)
PMIZ..........	PM Industries, Inc. [NASDAQ symbol] (NQ)
PMJ	Pulse-Modulated Jammer
PMK	Panel Marking Kit
PMK	Pitch Mark (AAG)
PMK	Pointe Molloy [Kerguelen Islands] [Seismograph station code, US Geological Survey] (SEIS)
PMK	Portable Molding Kit
PMK	Postmark
PMK	Primark Corp. [NYSE symbol]
PMKM	Past Master, Knights of Malta [Freemasonry] (ROG)
PMKY	Pittsburgh, McKeesport & Youghiogheny [AAR code]
PML	Pakistan Muslim League [Political party]
PML	Parts Material List
PML	Pattern Makers' League of North America
PML	Physical Memory Level
PML	[The] Pierpont Morgan Library (BJA)
PML	Polymer Microdevice Laboratory [Case Western Reserve University] [Research center] (RCD)
PML	Polymorphonuclear Leukocyte [Hematology]
PML	Port Moller [Alaska] [Airport symbol] (OAG)
PML	Port Moller, AK [Location identifier] [FAA] (FAAL)
PML	Posterior Mitral Leaflet [Cardiology]
PML	Preliminary Materials List [NASA]
PML	Probable Maximum Loss [Insurance]
PML	Progressive Multifocal Leukoencephalopathy [Oncology]
PML	Promotion Management List [Pronounced "pemell"] [Air Force]
PML..........	University of Windsor, Paul Martin Law Library [UTLAS symbol]
PMLA	Proceedings of the Modern Language Association [A publication]
PMLA	Production Music Libraries Association [New York, NY] (EA)
PMLA	Publications. Modern Language Association of America [Database] [A publication]
PMLAAm....	Publications. Modern Language Association of America [A publication]
PMLC	Programed Multiline Controller
PMLE.........	Polymorphous Light Eruption [Medicine]
PMLG	Poly(methyl L-Glutamate) [Organic chemistry]
PMLM........	Photosensitive Membrane Light Modulator
PMLO	Principal Military Landing Offices [British]
PMLPC.......	Permanent Mass Layoffs and Plant Closing Program [Bureau of Labor Statistics] (OICC)
PMLV	Permanent Magnet Latch Valve
PMM..........	Military Morale Division [Coast Guard]
PMM..........	Pall Mall Magazine [A publication]
PMM..........	Peace Mission Movement (EA)
PMM..........	Pedestal-Mounted Manipulator [Nuclear energy] (NRCH)
PMM..........	Penobscot Marine Museum (EA)
PMM..........	Personnel Management Manual (ADA)
PMM..........	Poly(methyl Methacrylate) [Also, PMMA] [Organic chemistry]
PMM..........	Pool Maintenance Module [Telecommunications] (TEL)
PMM..........	Portavideo [Vancouver Stock Exchange symbol]
PMM..........	Presa Malpaso [Mexico] [Seismograph station code, US Geological Survey] (SEIS)
PMM..........	Professional Music Men, Inc. (EA)
PMM..........	Profile Milling Machine
PMM..........	Programable Microcomputer Module

PMM.........	Property Management Manual (MCD)
PMM.........	Pullman, MI [*Location identifier*] [*FAA*] (FAAL)
PMM.........	Pulse Mode Multiplex
PMM.........	Purchase-Money Mortgage
PMMA.......	Pere Marquette Memorial Association (EA)
PMMA.......	Poly(methyl Methacrylate) [*Also, PMM*] [*Organic chemistry*]
PMMA.......	Publications. Metropolitan Museum of Art. Egyptian Expedition [*New York*] [*A publication*]
PMMB.......	Parallel Memory-to-Memory Bus
PMMC.......	Permanent Magnetic Movable Coil
PM-MEP....	Project Manager - Mobile Electric Power [*DoD*]
PMMF........	Precious Metals Master File [*DoD*] (AFIT)
PMMF........	Presbyterian Medical Mission Fund [*A publication*]
PMMI.........	Packaging Machinery Manufacturers Institute [*Washington, DC*] (EA)
PMMLA.....	Papers. Midwest Modern Language Association [*A publication*]
PMMP........	Preventive Maintenance Management Program
PMMR.......	Panel-Mounted Microfilm Reader
PMMR.......	Passive Multichannel Microwave Radiometer [*NASA*]
PMMS.......	Phrenicon Metabolic Monitoring System
PMMS.......	Plainsong and Mediaeval Music Society (EA)
PMMS.......	Program Master Milestone Schedule (MCD)
PMN..........	Pacific Mountain Network [*Television*]
PMN..........	Pahute Mesa [*Nevada*] [*Seismograph station code, US Geological Survey*] [*Closed*] (SEIS)
PMN..........	Panglima Mangku Negara [*Malaysian Honour*]
PMN..........	Permian Resources Ltd. [*Vancouver Stock Exchange symbol*]
PMN..........	Phenylmercuric Nitrate [*Antiseptic*]
PMN..........	Polymorphonuclear [*Hematology*]
PMN..........	Polymorphonuclear Neutrophilic [*Hematology*]
PMN..........	Postman
PMN..........	Premanufacture Notification [*Environmental Protection Agency*]
PMN..........	Premarket Notification [*Requirement for introducing new chemicals into the EEC*]
PMN..........	Program Management Network (MCD)
PMN..........	Proposed Material Need (MCD)
PMN..........	Pullman Co. [*NYSE symbol*]
PMN..........	Pumani [*Papua New Guinea*] [*Airport symbol*] (OAG)
PM-NAVCON ...	Project Manager, Navigation and Control [*Military*]
PMNL.........	Polymorphonuclear Leucocyte [*Hematology*]
PMNP........	Platform-Mounted Nuclear Plant (NRCH)
PMNR........	Periadenitis Mucosa Necrotica Recurrens [*Medicine*]
PMN/SFS...	People's Music Network for Songs of Freedom and Struggle (EA)
PM-NUC.....	Project Manager for Nuclear Munitions [*Army*] (RDA)
PMNV........	Project Manager, Night Vision (RDA)
PMNWA......	Pressemitteilung Nordrhein-Westfalen [*A publication*]
PMo...........	Monessen Public Library, Monessen, PA [*Library symbol*] [*Library of Congress*] (LCLS)
PMO..........	Palermo [*Italy*] [*Airport symbol*] (OAG)
PMO..........	Palermo Resources, Inc. [*Vancouver Stock Exchange symbol*]
PMO..........	Perroni, Martin, O'Reilly [*Commercial firm*]
PMO..........	Personnel Management Officer (INF)
PMO..........	Perturbation Molecular Orbital [*Theory*]
PMO..........	Pianissimo [*Very Softly*] [*Music*] (ROG)
PMO..........	Pine Mountain Observatory
PMO..........	Polaris Material Office [*Missiles*]
PMO..........	Polaris Missile Office
PMO..........	Pomariorio [*Tuamotu Archipelago*] [*Seismograph station code, US Geological Survey*] (SEIS)
PMO..........	Port Meteorological Office [*National Weather Service*]
PMO..........	Postal Money Order [*Military*]
PMO..........	Postmenopausal Osteoporosis [*Medicine*]
PMO..........	Prime Minister's Office [*Canada*]
PMO..........	Principal Medical Officer
PMO..........	Product Manager's Office (RDA)
PMO..........	Product Manufacturing Organization
PMO..........	Profit Making Organization
PMO..........	Program Management Office [*NASA*] (KSC)
PMO..........	Project Management Office [*Army*] (AABC)
PMO..........	Property Movement Order
PMO..........	Provost Marshal's Office
PMO..........	Psychiatric Military Officer
PMOA........	Prospectors and Mine Owners Association (EA)
PMOC........	Pioneer Mission Operations Center [*NASA*]
PMODA......	Phenyl(mercapto)oxadiazole [*Reagent*]
PMOG........	Plutonium Maintenance and Operating Gallery [*Nuclear energy*] (NRCH)
PMOG.......	Proposed Material Ordering Guide (MCD)
PMOJ........	Pesticides Monitoring Journal [*A publication*]
PMOLANT ...	Polaris Material Office, Atlantic Fleet [*Missiles*]
PMOM........	Performance Management Operations Manual [*NASA*] (NASA)
PMON........	Performance Management Operations Network [*NASA*] (NASA)
PMOPAC....	Polaris Material Office, Pacific Fleet [*Missiles*]
PMOS........	Permanent Manned Orbital Station (AAG)
PMOS........	Positive-Channel Metal-Oxide Semiconductor [*Telecommunications*] (TEL)
PMOS.........	Primary Military Occupational Specialty [*Army*]

PMOSA......	Perceptual and Motor Skills [*A publication*]
PMOSC......	Primary Military Occupational Specialty Code [*Army*] (AABC)
PMP...........	Packed Main Parachute
PMP...........	Parallel Microprogramed Processor [*Data processing*]
PMP...........	Parent Mass Peak
PMP...........	Parents' Magazine Press
PMP...........	Parti du Mouvement Populaire de la Cote Francaise des Somalis [*Popular Movement Party of French Somaliland*]
PMP...........	Partito Monarchico Popolare [*Popular Monarchist Party*] [*Italy*] (PPE)
PMP...........	Parts, Materials, and Packaging (MCD)
PMP...........	Parts, Materials, and Processes (MCD)
PMP...........	Passive Measurement Program
PMP...........	Past Menstrual Period [*Medicine*]
PMP...........	Performance Management Package [*NASA*] (NASA)
PmP...........	Pergamon Press, Inc., Fairview Park, Elmsford, NY [*Library symbol*] [*Library of Congress*] (LCLS)
PMP...........	Persistent Mentoposterior [*A fetal position*] [*Obstetrics*]
PMP...........	Peter Miller Apparel Group [*Toronto Stock Exchange symbol*]
PMP...........	Phenyl(methyl)pyrazolone [*An organic pigment*]
PMP...........	Pimaga [*Papua New Guinea*] [*Airport symbol*] (OAG)
PMP...........	Planned Maintenance Plan (MCD)
PMP...........	Poly(metal Phosphinate) [*Organic chemistry*]
PMP...........	Poly(methylpentene) [*Organic chemistry*]
PMP...........	Pompano Beach, FL [*Location identifier*] [*FAA*] (FAAL)
PMP...........	Pompeii [*Italy*] [*Seismograph station code, US Geological Survey*] [*Closed*] (SEIS)
PMP...........	Pontifical Mission for Palestine [*New York, NY*] (EA)
PMP...........	Position Management Program
PMP...........	Powdered Metal Part
PMP...........	Preliminary Mission Profile (MCD)
PMP...........	Premodulation Processor
PMP...........	Preoperational Monitoring Program [*Nuclear energy*] (NRCH)
PMP...........	Pressure Measurement Package
PMP...........	Preventive Maintenance Plan (KSC)
PMP...........	Preventive Maintenance Procedure [*Nuclear energy*] (NRCH)
PMP...........	Previous Menstrual Period [*Medicine*]
PMP...........	Prime Motor Inns, Inc. [*NYSE symbol*]
PMP...........	Prism-Mirror-Prism [*For electron microscopy*]
PMP...........	Probable Maximum Precipitation (NRCH)
PMP...........	Professor of Moral Philosophy
PMP...........	Program Management Plan
PMP...........	Program Monitor Panel
PMP...........	Progressive Merger Procedure [*Econometrics*]
PMP...........	Project Master Plans [*Military*]
PMP...........	Project on Military Procurement (EA)
PMP...........	Protective Mobilization Plan
PMP...........	Pulsed Microwave Power
PMP...........	Pump (KSC)
PMP...........	Pyridoxamine Phosphate [*Biochemistry*]
PMPA........	Permanent Magnet Producers Association [*Later, MMPA*] (EA)
PMPA........	Petroleum Marketing Practices Act
PMPA........	Proximal Main Pulmonary Artery [*Anatomy*]
PMPA........	Publications. Missouri Philological Association [*A publication*]
PMPEA......	Professional Motion Picture Equipment Association [*Later, PFVEA*] (EA)
PMPFR......	Program Manager's Preflight Review [*NASA*] (KSC)
PMPL.........	Preferred Mechanical Parts List [*NASA*] (NASA)
PMPM........	Perpetual Motion Poetry Machine
PMPM........	Phase Margin Performance Measure [*Manual control system*]
PMPM........	Programable Multiple Position Machine (MCD)
PMPM........	Pulse Mode Performance Model (KSC)
PMPMA......	Plastic and Metal Products Manufacturers Association [*New York, NY*] (EA)
PMPP........	Program Management Phase-Out Plan [*Military*] (AFIT)
PMPPI........	Polymethylenepolyphenyl Polyisocyanate [*Organic chemistry*]
PMQ..........	Perito Moreno [*Argentina*] [*Airport symbol*] (OAG)
PMQ..........	Permanent Married Quarters [*Canadian Forces*]
PMQ..........	Phytylmenaquinone [*Vitamin K*] [*Also, K*] [*Biochemistry*]
PMQ..........	Primitive Methodist Quarterly Review [*A publication*] (ROG)
PMR..........	Micron Products [*American Stock Exchange symbol*]
PMR..........	Pacific Missile Range [*Later, WTR*]
PMR..........	Palmer [*Alaska*] [*Seismograph station code, US Geological Survey*] (SEIS)
PMR..........	Palmerston North [*New Zealand*] [*Airport symbol*] (OAG)
PMR..........	Parabolic Microwave Reflector
PMR..........	Partidul Muncitoresc Roman [*Romanian Workers' Party*]
PMR..........	Parts Material Requirements File
PMR..........	Payload Mass Ratio
PMR..........	Paymaster
PMR..........	Performance Measurement Report [*NASA*] (NASA)
PMR..........	Performance Monitoring Receiver
PMR..........	Perinatal Mortality Rate [*Medicine*]
PMR..........	Philippine Mining Record [*A publication*]
PM & R......	Physical Medicine and Rehabilitation
PMR..........	Planned Maintenance Requirements
PMR..........	Polymerization of Monomer Reactants [*Organic chemistry*]
PMR..........	Polymyalgia Rheumatica [*Medicine*]
PMR..........	Portable Microfiche Reader [*DASA Corp.*]
PMR..........	Postmaster

PMR............	Potential Military Relevance
PMR............	Power Monitor Relay
PMR............	Preliminary Materials Review
PMR............	Pressure Modulation Radiometer
PMR............	Preventive Maintenance and Repair [Aviation] (MCD)
PMR............	Primary Mission Readiness
PMR............	Proceedings. Patristic, Mediaeval, and Renaissance Conference [A publication]
PMR............	Procurement Management Review [DoD]
PMR............	Profoundly Mentally Retarded
PMR............	Program Management Responsibility (MCD)
PMR............	Program Manager's Review [NASA] (NASA)
PMR............	Programed Mixture Ratio (KSC)
PMR............	Progress in Mutation Research [Elsevier Book Series] [A publication]
PMR............	Project Management Report
PMR............	Property Movement Request (MCD)
PMR............	Proportionate Mortality Rate [or Ratio]
PMR............	Proton Magnetic Resonance
PMR............	Provisioning Master Record (MCD)
PMRA........	Projected Manpower Requirements Account [Navy]
PMRAFNS ...	Princess Mary's Royal Air Force Nursing Service [British]
PMRB	Preliminary Materials Review Board
PMRC........	Parents' Music Resource Center (EA)
PMRC........	Prepositioned Material Receipt Card [DoD]
PMRC........	Proctor Maple Research Center [University of Vermont] [Research center] (RCD)
PMRD........	Prepositioned Material Receipt Documents (MCD)
PMRDET	Pacific Missile Range Detachment [Obsolete] (MUGU)
PMRF	Pacific Missile Range Facility [Obsolete] (MSC)
PMRFAC	Pacific Missile Range Facility [Obsolete] (MUGU)
PMRG........	Preliminary Materials Review Group [NASA] (KSC)
PMRGA	Prace Morski Instytut Rybacki w Gdyni [A publication]
PMRI...........	Posteromedial Rotation Instability [Sports medicine]
PMRL	Pulp Manufacturers' Research League
PMRM	Periodic Maintenance Requirements Manual [Navy]
PMRMO.....	Protectable Mobilization Reserve Materiel Objective [Army] (AABC)
PMRMR	Protectable Mobilization Reserve Materiel Requirements [Army]
PMRN........	Parents' Music Resource Network (EA)
PMRO........	Popular Magazine Review Online [Data Base Communications Corp.] [Topsfield, MA] [Information service] (EISS)
PMRP	Petroleum Material Requirements Plan (MCD)
PMRP	Precious Metals Recovery Program [DoD] (AFIT)
PM-RPV	Project Manager, Remotely Piloted Vehicle [Military]
PMRR	Pacific Missile Range Representative [Obsolete] (MUGU)
PMRR	Pre-Mate Readiness Review [NASA] (KSC)
PMRS	Parachute Medical Rescue Service [Boulder, CO] (EA)
PMRS	Physical Medicine and Rehabilitation Service
PMRS	Progress of Medieval and Renaissance Studies in the United States and Canada [A publication]
PMRSG	Pacific Missile Range Study Group [Obsolete]
PMRT	Program Management Responsibility Transfer (MCD)
PMRTD......	Program Management Responsibility Transfer Date (AFIT)
PMRTF	Pacific Missile Range Tracking Facility [Obsolete] (MUGU)
PMRTP	Program Management Responsibility Transfer Plan (AFIT)
PMRY	Presidio of Monterey [Military] (AABC)
PMS...........	Palmer - Arctic Valley [Alaska] [Seismograph station code, US Geological Survey] (SEIS)
PMS...........	Pantone Matching System [Printing]
PMS...........	Para-Methylstyrene [Organic chemistry]
PMS...........	Parallel Mass Spectrometer
PMS...........	Particle Measuring Systems [Aerosol measurement device]
PMS...........	People's Medical Society (EA)
PMS...........	People's Message System [For Apple II computers] [Electronic bulletin board]
PMS...........	Perceptual and Motor Skills [A publication]
PMS...........	Performance Management System [NASA]
PMS...........	Performance Measurement System (MCD)
PMS...........	Performance Monitoring System [Army] [Fort Belvoir, VA] (NASA)
PMS...........	Permanent Magnet Speaker
PMS...........	Personnel Management Series [Civil Service Commission]
PMS...........	Personnel Management System [Air Force] (AFM)
PMS...........	Phenazine Methosulfate [Biochemistry]
PMS...........	Phoenix Missile System
PMS...........	Phytophthora megasperma var. sojae [A fungus]
PMS...........	Picturephone Meeting Service [AT & T]
PMS...........	Pitch Microwave System
PMS...........	Planned Maintenance System [SNMMS]
PMS...........	Planned Maintenance Systems [Falls Church, VA] [Software manufacturer]
PMS...........	Planned Missile System
PMS...........	Plant Monitoring System [Nuclear energy] (NRCH)
PMS...........	Plastic to Metal Seal
PMS...........	PM Industries, Inc. [Vancouver Stock Exchange symbol]
PMS...........	Polaris Missile System
PMS...........	Policy Management Systems, Inc.
PMS...........	Pollution Monitoring Satellite
PMS...........	Poor Miserable Soul [Medical slang]

PMS...........	Popular Music and Society [A publication]
PMS...........	Portable Monitoring Set (MCD)
PMS...........	Post-Marketing Surveillance
PMS...........	Post-Merger Syndrome [Business and trade]
PMS...........	Post-Mortem Survival [Parapsychology]
PMS...........	Postmenopausal Syndrome [Medicine]
PMS...........	Power Management System
PMS...........	Prang-Mark Society (EA)
PMS...........	Pre-Midshipmen School
PMS...........	Predicted Manning System [Military]
PMS...........	Pregnant Mare's Serum [Endocrinology]
PMS...........	Premenstrual [Stress] Syndrome [Medicine]
PMS...........	President of the Meteorological Society [British]
PmS	Preston Microfilming Services Ltd., Toronto, ON, Canada [Library symbol] [Library of Congress] (LCLS)
PMS...........	Preventive Maintenance System
PMS...........	Probability of Mission Success [Aerospace] (AAG)
PMS...........	Probable Maximum Surge [Nuclear energy] (NRCH)
PMS...........	Processors, Memories, and Switches [Programing language] (CSR)
PMS...........	Production Management System [Safe Computing Ltd.] [Software package]
PMS...........	Professor of Military Science
PMS...........	Program Management Support
PMS...........	Program Management System [Data processing]
PMS...........	Program Master Schedule (MCD)
PMS...........	Project Management System [IBM Corp.] [Data processing]
PMS...........	Project Manager, Ships
PMS...........	Public Management Sources [A publication]
PMS...........	Public Message Service [Western Union Corp.]
PMSA........	Office of the Project Manager Selected Ammunition [DoD]
PMSA........	PM [Product Management] Materiel Systems Assessment (RDA)
PMSA........	Posterior Middle Suprasylvian Area [Anatomy]
PMSA........	Primary Metropolitan Statistical Area [Census Bureau]
P/MSA	Project/Major Subcontractor Affected (MCD)
PMSC........	Policy Management Systems [NASDAQ symbol] (NQ)
PMSCD......	Proceedings. Microscopical Society of Canada [A publication]
PMSD........	Parti Mauricien Social-Democrate [Mauritian Social Democratic Party] (PPW)
PMS/DOD ...	Performance Measurement System/Department of Defense
PMSE	Percentage Mean Squared Error [Statistics]
PMSE	Program Management Simulation Exercise [Aerospace]
PMSF	Phenylmethylsulfonyl Fluoride [Analytical chemistry]
PMSFN	Planetary Manned Space Flight Network [Aerospace] (MCD)
PMSG........	Peace Movement Study Group [Colgate University] [Hamilton, NY] (EA)
PMSG........	Pregnant Mare's Serum Gonadotrophin [Endocrinology]
PMSGT.......	Paymaster Sergeant [Marine Corps]
PMSN........	Permission (FAAC)
PMSO........	Project Management Staff Officer [Military] (AFIT)
PMSO........	Project Management Support Office [Army] (RDA)
PMSP........	Photon-Counting Microspectrophotometer
PMSP........	Preliminary Maintainability and Spare Parts
PMSPS.......	Project Management Staffing Practices Study [Navy] (NG)
PMSR........	Patternmaker, Ship Repair [Navy rating]
PMSR........	Physical, Mental, Social, Religious ["Fourfold Life" symbol of American Youth Foundation]
PMSRC	Pittsburgh Mining and Safety Research Center [Bureau of Mines]
PMSRP.......	Physical and Mathematical Sciences Research Paper (IEEE)
PMSS	Personnel Mobility Support System [Military]
PMSS	Precision Measuring Subsystem (KSC)
PMSS	Progress in Mathematical Social Sciences [Elsevier Book Series] [A publication]
PMS/SMS ...	Planned Maintenance System for Surface Missile Ships
PMS & T	Professor of Military Science and Tactics
PMST	Professor of Military Science and Tactics (MUGU)
PMSX	Processor Memory Switch Matrix
PMT............	Medical Photography Technician [Navy]
PMT............	Para-Methoxytoluene [Organic chemistry]
PMT............	Partido Mexicano de los Trabajadores [Mexican Workers' Party] (PPW)
PMT............	Payment (AFM)
PMT............	Pennsylvania Motor Truck Association, Inc., Harrisburg PA [STAC]
PMT............	Perceptual Maze Test [Psychology]
PMT............	Permanent Magnet Twistor [Memory] [Bell Laboratories]
PMT............	Permit (FAAC)
PMT............	Phase-Modulated Transmission
PMT............	Philip Michael Thomas [Co-star in TV series "Miami Vice"]
PMT............	Photomechanical Transfer [Negative paper] [Eastman Kodak]
PMT............	Photomultiplier Tube
PMT............	Pilgrim Airlines [New London, CT] [FAA designator] (FAAC)
PMT............	Pine Mountain [Oregon] [Seismograph station code, US Geological Survey] (SEIS)
PMT............	Planning/Management Team (MCD)
PMT............	PMC Technologies Ltd. [Vancouver Stock Exchange symbol]
PMT............	Polaromicrotribometry [Analytical chemistry]
PMT............	Portable Magnetic Tape
PMT............	Power Microwave Tube

PMT........... Premenstrual Tension [Medicine]
PMT........... Prepare Master Tape
PMT........... Preventive Maintenance Time (MCD)
PMT........... Production Monitoring Test (NG)
PMT........... Program Master Tape
PMT........... Programed Math Tutorial [National Science Foundation]
PMT........... Pulse-Modulator Tube
PMTC .... Pacific Missile Test Center [Navy]
PMTC .... Pittsburgh Mining Technology Center [Department of Energy]
PMTD .... Post Mortem Tape Dump [Data processing]
PMTF Zh Prikl Mekh Tekh Fiz ... PMTF. Zhurnal Prikladnoi Mekhaniki Tekhnickeskio Fiziki [A publication]
PMTHP....... Project Mercury Technical History Program [NASA]
PMTO .... Project Manager Test Offices [Military]
PMTP .... Production Missile Test Program
P/MTR....... Potentiometer [Automotive engineering]
PM TRADE ... Office of the Project Manager for Training Devices [Military] (RDA)
PMTS .... Predetermined Motion Time Systems [Management]
PMTS .... Premenstrual Tension Syndrome [Medicine]
PMTT .... Phase-Modulated Telemetry Transmission
PMU .... Paimiut, AK [Location identifier] [FAA] (FAAL)
PMU .... Performance Monitor Unit [Communications]
PMU .... Physical Mock-Up
PMU .... Plant Makeup [Nuclear energy] (NRCH)
PMU .... Pontifical Missionary Union [Formerly, MUCUSA] [Later, PMUPR] (EA)
PMU .... Portable Memory Unit [Data processing]
PMU .... Pressure Measuring Unit (KSC)
PMU .... Preventive Medicine Unit [Navy] (NVT)
PMU .... Progress in Medical Ultrasound [Elsevier Book Series] [A publication]
PMUPR....... Pontifical Missionary Union of Priests and Religious [Formerly, MUCUSA, PMU] (EA)
PMUS........ Permanently Mounted User Set [Data processing] (ADA)
PM-UTTAS ... Project Manager, Utility Tactical Transport Aircraft System [Military]
PMUX .... Programable Multiplex [Data processing] (TEL)
PMv .... Monroeville Public Library, Monroeville, PA [Library symbol] [Library of Congress] (LCLS)
PMV........... Parcel Mail Vans [British railroad term]
PMV........... Plasma Membrane Vesicle [Cytology]
PMV........... Plattsmouth, NE [Location identifier] [FAA] (FAAL)
PMV........... Politically Motivated Violence (ADA)
PMV........... Porlamar [Venezuela] [Airport symbol] (OAG)
PMV........... Prime Mission Vehicle (MCD)
PMV........... Pro Mundi Vita [An association] (EA-IO)
PMV........... Prolapsing Mitral Valve [Cardiology]
PMvAC .... Community College of Allegheny County, Boyce Campus, Monroeville, PA [Library symbol] [Library of Congress] (LCLS)
PMvK .... Koppers Co., Inc., Research Department, Monroeville, PA [Library symbol] [Library of Congress] (LCLS)
PMVR .... Prime Mover [Technical drawings]
PMvS.......... United States Steel Corp., Research Center Library, Monroeville, PA [Library symbol] [Library of Congress] (LCLS)
PMW.......... Parts Manufacturing Workmanship
PMW.......... Pole Mountain [Wyoming] [Seismograph station code, US Geological Survey] [Closed] (SEIS)
PMW.......... Private Microwave [System]
PMW.......... Progressive Mine Workers of America
PMW.......... Project Magic Wand [Military] (MCD)
PMW.......... Prompt Mobilization Designation Withdrawn
PMWP .... Probable Maximum Winter Precipitation (NRCH)
PMX........... Packet Multiplexer
PMX........... Palmer, MA [Location identifier] [FAA] (FAAL)
PMX........... Private Manual Exchange
PMX........... Protected Message Exchange
PMyE.......... Evangelical Congregational School of Theology, Myerstown, PA [Library symbol] [Library of Congress] (LCLS)
PMYOB ...... Please Mind Your Own Business
PMZ........... Plymouth, NC [Location identifier] [FAA] (FAAL)
pn----- .... North Pacific [MARC geographic area code] [Library of Congress] (LCCP)
PN .... North Pole
PN .... Pacific Communications Net [Air Force]
PN .... Pakistan Navy
PN .... Palus Nebularum [Lunar area]
PN .... Pan Am Corp. [NYSE symbol]
PN .... Pan American World Airways, Inc. [NYSE symbol] [See also PA, PAA, PAN-AM]
pn .... Panama [MARC country of publication code] [Library of Congress] (LCCP)
PN .... Papillary or Nodular Hyperplasia [Medicine]
PN .... Parenteral Nutrition [Medicine]
PN .... Part Number
PN .... Partido Nacional [Blanco Party] [Uruguayan] (PPW)
PN .... Partido Nacional [National Party] [Honduran] (PPW)
PN .... Partido Nacional [National Party] [Dominican Republic]
PN .... Perceived Noise

PN .... Percussion Note [Physiology]
PN .... Percussive Notes [A publication]
PN .... Performance Number
PN .... Periarteritis [or Polyarteritis] Nodosa [Also, PAN] [Medicine]
PN .... Perigean Range
PN .... Peripheral Nerve [Anatomy]
PN .... Peripheral Neuropathy [Medicine]
PN .... Personal Name (BJA)
PN .... Personal Names from Cuneiform Inscriptions of the Cassite Period [A publication] (BJA)
PN .... Personnelman [Navy rating]
PN .... Phenolic Nylon
PN .... Philippine Aero Transport, Inc. [Philippines] [ICAO designator] (FAAC)
PN .... Philippine Navy (CINC)
PN .... Piedmont & Northern Railway Co. [AAR code]
P/N........... Pin Number (AAG)
PN .... Pitcairn Islands [Two-letter standard code] (CNC)
PN .... Place-Name
PN .... Planners Network (EA)
PN .... Plant Normal [Nuclear energy] (NRCH)
PN .... Plasticity Number (AAG)
PN .... Please Note
PN .... Pneumatic
PN .... Pneumonia [Medicine]
PN .... Poe Newsletter [A publication]
PN .... Poesia Nuova [A publication]
PN .... Poetry Northwest [A publication]
PN .... Position Pennant [Navy] [British]
P/N........... Positive/Negative
PN .... Postal Note (ADA)
PN .... Postnatal [Medicine]
Pn .... Poznan [A publication]
PN .... Practical Nurse
PN .... Preliminary Notification (NRCH)
PN .... Prior Notice Required (FAAC)
PN .... Pro Nervia [A publication]
PN .... Production Notice (KSC)
PN .... Program Notice (KSC)
PN .... Program Number [Horse racing]
PN .... Programable Network
PN .... Project Note
PN .... Project Number [Data processing] [Online database field identifier]
PN .... Promissory Note [Business and trade]
PN .... Pronuclei [Embryology]
PN .... Pseudonoise
PN .... Pseudorandom Number
PN .... Psychiatric Nurse
P & N .... Psychiatry and Neurology
PN .... Psychoneurologist
PN .... Psychoneurotic [Cases, patients, etc.]
PN .... Public Network [Telecommunications]
PN .... Publisher's Name [Online database field identifier]
PN .... Pulse Network (KSC)
PN .... Punch On
PN .... Putative Neurotransmitter [Biochemistry]
PN .... Pyridoxine [or Pyridoxol] [Also, Pxn] [Biochemistry]
PN .... Pyrrolnitrin [Antifungal antibiotic]
PN .... Regular Pending Transaction [IRS]
PN1............ Personnelman, First Class [Navy rating]
PN2............ Personnelman, Second Class [Navy rating]
PN3............ Personnelman, Third Class [Navy rating]
PNA .... Pakistan National Alliance (PD)
PNA .... Pamplona [Spain] [Airport symbol] (OAG)
PNA .... Paper Napkin Association
PNA .... Para-Nitroaniline [Organic chemistry]
PNA .... Parenting in a Nuclear Age [An association] (EA)
PNA .... Parisiensis Nomina Anatomica [Paris Anatomical Nomenclature] [Medicine]
PNA .... Partacoona [Australia] [Seismograph station code, US Geological Survey] (SEIS)
PNA .... Parti Nationale Africain [African National Party] [Chad]
PNA .... Passed, but Not Advanced
PNA .... Peanut Agglutinin [Immunology]
PNA .... Pentosenucleic Acid [Biochemistry]
PNA .... Pinedale, WY [Location identifier] [FAA] (FAAL)
PNA........... Pioneer Corp. [Formerly, Pioneer Natural Gas Co.] [NYSE symbol]
PNA .... Polish National Alliance of the United States of North America (EA)
PNA .... Polish Nobility Association (EA)
PNA .... Polynuclear Aromatic [Organic chemistry]
PNA .... Processing Terminal Network Architecture [Data processing] (BUR)
PNA .... Project Network Analysis
PNAB........ Percutaneous Needle Aspiration Biopsy [Medicine]
PNAF........ Plan Name and Address File [IRS]
PNAF........ Potential Network Access Facility
PNAH .... Polynuclear Aromatic Hydrocarbon [Environmental chemistry]
PNAS.......... Palletized Night Attack System

PNAS......... Proceedings. National Academy of Sciences [*A publication*]
P NAS Ind A ... Proceedings. National Academy of Sciences. India. Section A. Physical Sciences [*A publication*]
P NAS Ind B ... Proceedings. National Academy of Sciences. India. Section B. Biological Sciences [*A publication*]
P NAS US... Proceedings. National Academy of Sciences. United States of America [*A publication*]
PNAvQ....... Positive-Negative Ambivalent Quotient [*Psychology*]
PNazMHi.... Moravian Historical Society, Nazareth, PA [*Library symbol*] [*Library of Congress*]　(LCLS)
PNB............ North Platte, NE [*Location identifier*] [*FAA*]　(FAAL)
PNB............ Pacific Northwest Ballet
PNB............ Particle/Neutral Beam　(MCD)
PNB............ Pomio [*New Britain*] [*Seismograph station code, US Geological Survey*] [*Closed*]　(SEIS)
PNBA......... Pennbancorp [*NASDAQ symbol*]　(NQ)
PNBAS...... ((Para-Nitrophenyl)azo)salicylic Acid [*A dye*] [*Organic chemistry*]
PNBC......... Pacific Northwest Bibliographic Center [*Library network*]
P²NBC²....... Physiological and Psychological Effects of NBC [*Nuclear, Biological, and Chemical Warfare*] and Extended Operations [*Army study project*]　(INF)
PNBF......... Peak Nucleate Boiling Flux
PNBMS...... Pacific Northwest Bird and Mammal Society　(EA)
PNBS......... Pyridinium(nitro)benzenesulfonate [*Organic chemistry*]
PNBT......... Para-Nitroblue Tetrazolium
PNBT......... Planters Corp. [*NASDAQ symbol*]　(NQ)
PNC............ Chief Personnelman [*Navy rating*]
PNc............ New Castle Free Public Library, New Castle, PA [*Library symbol*] [*Library of Congress*]　(LCLS)
PNC............ Northampton County Area Community College, Bethlehem, PA [*OCLC symbol*]　(OCLC)
PNC............ Palestine National Council　(PD)
PNC............ Parti National Caledonien [*Caledonian National Party*]　(PPW)
PNC............ Partido Nacional Ceuti [*Ceuta National Party*]　(PPW)
PNC............ Partidual Nationale Crestine [*National Christian Party*] [*Romanian*]　(PPE)
PNC............ Passenger Name Check-In　(MCD)
PNC............ Pencrude Resources, Inc. [*Vancouver Stock Exchange symbol*]
PNC............ Penicillin
PNC............ People's National Congress [*Guyanese*]　(PD)
PNC............ Personal Names from Cuneiform Inscriptions of Cappadocia [*A publication*]
PNC............ Philatelic-Numismatic Combination [*or Commemorative*]
PNC............ Phosphonitrilic Chloride [*Inorganic chemistry*]
PNC............ Physitest Normalise Canadien [*Canadian Standardized Test of Fitness - CSTF*]
PNC............ Pine Canyon [*California*] [*Seismograph station code, US Geological Survey*]　(SEIS)
PNC............ Ponca City [*Oklahoma*] [*Airport symbol*]　(OAG)
PNC............ Ponca City, OK [*Location identifier*] [*FAA*]　(FAAL)
PNC............ Postnatal Clinic
PNC............ Premature Nodal Contraction [*Cardiology*]
PNC............ Programed Numerical Control
PNC............ Prohibition National Committee　(EA)
PNC............ Pseudonurse Cells [*Cytology*]
PNCB......... Para-Nitrochlorobenzene [*Organic chemistry*]
PNCC........ Partial Network Control Center
PNCF........ PNC Financial Corp. [*NASDAQ symbol*]　(NQ)
PNCH........ Partido Nacional Conservador de Honduras [*National Conservative Party of Honduras*]
PNCH........ Proceedings. National Conference on Health Education Goals [*A publication*]
PNCH........ Punch
PNCM........ Master Chief Personnelman [*Navy rating*]
PNCOC...... Primary Noncommissioned Officer Course [*Army*]　(INF)
PNCR........ Pancretec, Inc. [*NASDAQ symbol*]　(NQ)
PNCS........ Private Network Communication Systems　(MCD)
PNCS........ Senior Chief Personnelman [*Navy rating*]
PNCTD...... Proceedings. National Conference on Power Transmission [*A publication*]
PND............ Paroxysmal Nocturnal Dyspnea [*Medicine*]
PND............ Parti des Nationalistes du Dahomey [*Dahomean Nationalists Party*]
PND............ Partido Nacional Democratico [*National Democratic Party*] [*Dominican Republic*]
PND............ Partido Nacional Democratico [*National Democratic Party*] [*Costa Rican*]　(PPW)
PND............ Partidul National-Democratic [*National Democratic Party*] [*Romanian*]　(PPE)
PND............ Passive Navigation Device
PND............ Pending
PND............ Postnasal Drip [*Medicine*]
PND............ Premodulation Processor - Near Earth Data　(KSC)
PND............ Present Next Digit
PND............ Program Network Diagram [*Telecommunications*]　(TEL)
PND............ Pseudonyms and Nicknames Dictionary [*A publication*]
PND............ Punta Gorda [*Belize*] [*Airport symbol*]　(OAG)
PNdB........ Perceived Noise Decibels
PNDC........ Parallel Network Digital Computer　(IEEE)
PNDC........ Progressive Neuronal Degeneration of Childhood [*Medicine*]

PNDC......... Provisional National Defence Council [*Ghanaian*]　(PD)
PNDG......... Pending　(AFM)
PNDI........... Pennsylvania Natural Diversity Inventory [*Bureau of Forestry*] [*Harrisburg*] [*Information service*]　(EISS)
PNDLR...... Pendular
PNDM........ Project Nondesign Memo
PNDO........ Partial Neglect of Differential Overlap [*Physics*]
PNE............ Pacific National Exhibition Home Show [*Southex Exhibitions*]　(TSPED)
PNE............ Paine College, Warren A. Candler Library, Augusta, GA [*OCLC symbol*]　(OCLC)
PNE............ Panhandle Eastern Corp. [*Toronto Stock Exchange symbol*]
PNE............ Peaceful Nuclear Explosion
PNE............ Philadelphia [*Pennsylvania*] North Philadelphia [*Airport symbol*]　(OAG)
PNE............ Philadelphia, PA [*Location identifier*] [*FAA*]　(FAAL)
PNE............ Practical Nurse's Education
PNEC........ Primary Navy Enlisted Classification [*Code*]
PNEC........ Proceedings. National Electronics Conference [*A publication*]
PNed........ Pharmacopeia Nederlandsche [*Netherlands Pharmacopoeia*]
PNERL...... Pacific Northwest Environmental Research Laboratory [*Marine science*]　(MSC)
PNES........ Pines
PNET........ Peaceful Nuclear Explosions Treaty [*Officially, Treaty on Underground Nuclear Explosions for Peaceful Purposes*]
PNET........ Primitive Neuroectodermal Tumor [*Oncology*]
PNEU........ Parents' National Educational Union [*British*]
PNEU........ Pneumatic　(AAG)
PNEUG...... Pneumatic Pressure Generator　(MCD)
PNEUM...... Pneumatic
Pneum Dig & Druckluft Prax ... Pneumatic Digest and Druckluft Praxis [*A publication*]
PNEUMO.... Pneumothorax [*Medicine*]
Pneumolog Hung ... Pneumologia Hungarica [*Hungary*] [*A publication*]
Pneumol/Pneumol ... Pneumonologie/Pneumonology [*A publication*]
Pneumonol-P ... Pneumonologie/Pneumonology [*A publication*]
Pneumonol Pol ... Pneumonologia Polska [*A publication*]
PNEUROP ... European Committee of Manufacturers of Compressors, Vacuum Pumps, and Pneumatic Tools　(EA)
PNF............ Pacific National Financial Corp. [*Toronto Stock Exchange symbol*] [*Vancouver Stock Exchange symbol*]
PNF............ Palestine National Front　(PD)
PNF............ Palestine National Fund [*Palestine Liberation Organization*]
PNF............ Partito Nazionale Fascista [*National Fascist Party*] [*Italy*]　(PPE)
PNF............ Peierls-Nabarro Force [*Physics*]
PNF............ Penn Traffic Co. [*American Stock Exchange symbol*]
PNF............ Phosphonitrilic Fluoroelastomer [*Synthetic rubber*]
PNF............ Postnuclear Fraction [*Biochemical tissue analysis*]
PNF............ Prenex Normal Form [*Logic*]
PNF............ Proprioceptive Neuromuscular Facilitation [*Neurology*]
PNFD......... Present Not for Duty [*Military*]
PNFI.......... Petawawa National Forestry Institute [*Canadian Forestry Service*] [*Research center*]　(RCD)
PNG............ Pacific Northern Gas Ltd. [*Toronto Stock Exchange symbol*] [*Vancouver Stock Exchange symbol*]
PNG............ Papua New Guinea　(ADA)
PNG............ Papua New Guinea [*Three-letter standard code*]　(CNC)
PNG............ Paranagua [*Brazil*] [*Airport symbol*]　(OAG)
PNG............ Partido Nacional Guevarista [*Ecuadorean*]　(PPW)
PNG............ Penghu [*Hokoto*] [*Republic of China*] [*Seismograph station code, US Geological Survey*]　(SEIS)
PNG............ Persona Non Grata [*Unacceptable Person*] [*Latin*]
PNG............ Plant Nitrogen in Grain [*Harvest nitrogen index*]
PNG............ Professional Numismatists Guild　(EA)
PNG............ Pseudonoise Generator
PNGCS...... Primary Navigation, Guidance and Control System　(KSC)
PNGFA....... Pacific Northwest Grain and Feed Association　(EA)
PNGL......... Papers in New Guinea Linguistics [*A publication*]
P & NGLR ... Papua and New Guinea Law Reports [*A publication*]
PNGS......... Primary Navigation System
PNH............ North Hills School District Instructional Materials Center, Pittsburgh, PA [*OCLC symbol*]　(OCLC)
PNH............ Pan Head [*Design engineering*]
PNH............ Paroxysmal Nocturnal Hemoglobinuria [*Medicine*]
PNH............ Parti National d'Haiti [*National Party of Haiti*]
PNH............ Partido Nacional de Honduras [*National Party of Honduras*]
PNH............ Partido Nacional Hondureno [*Honduran National Party*]
PNH............ Phnom Penh [*Cambodia*] [*Airport symbol*]　(OAG)
PNH............ Pitcher Mountain [*New Hampshire*] [*Seismograph station code, US Geological Survey*]　(SEIS)
PNH............ Public Service Co. of New Hampshire [*NYSE symbol*]
PNHA......... Physicians National Housestaff Association [*Defunct*]
PNHDL....... Panhandle [*FAA*]　(FAAC)
PNHS......... Pacific Northwest Heather Society [*Later, NAHS*]　(EA)
PNI............. Part Number Index　(MCD)
PNI............. Partai Nasionalis Indonesia [*Nationalist Party of Indonesia*]
PNI............. Partido Nacional Independiente [*National Independent Party*] [*Costa Rican*]　(PPW)
PNI............. Peripheral Nerve Injury [*Medicine*]

PNI .... Pharmaceutical News Index [*Data Courier, Inc.*] [*Louisville, KY*] [*Bibliographic database*] [*Information service*] [*A publication*]
PNI .... Pinerola [*Italy*] [*Seismograph station code, US Geological Survey*]   (SEIS)
PNI .... Ponape [*Caroline Islands*] [*Airport symbol*]   (OAG)
PNI .... Positive Noninterfering [*Alarm system*]
PNI .... Postnatal Infection [*Medicine*]
PNI .... Principal Neo-Tech, Incorporated [*Toronto Stock Exchange symbol*]
PNI .... Publications. Netherlands Institute of Archaeology and Arabic Studies [*Cairo*] [*A publication*]
PNI .... Punjab Native Infantry [*India*]
PNIC .... Pleasure Navigation International Joint Committee [*See also CINP*]   (EA-IO)
P-NID .... Precedence Network In-Dialing [*Telecommunications*]   (TEL)
PNII .... Prentiss Normal and Industrial Institute [*Mississippi*]
PNIIA .... Prace Naukowe Instytutu Inzynierii Ochrony Srodowiska Politechniki Wroclawskiej [*A publication*]
PNIO .... Priority National Intelligence Objectives   (MCD)
PNIP .... Positive-Negative-Intrinsic-Positive [*Electron device*]   (MSA)
PNJ .... Paterson [*New Jersey*] [*Seismograph station code, US Geological Survey*]   (SEIS)
PNJ .... Paterson, NJ [*Location identifier*] [*FAA*]   (FAAL)
PNJ .... Polar Night Jet Stream   (ADA)
PNJHS .... Proceedings. New Jersey Historical Society [*A publication*]
PNK .... Pinkham Creek [*Montana*] [*Seismograph station code, US Geological Survey*] [*Closed*]   (SEIS)
PNK .... Polynucleotide Kinase [*An enzyme*]
PNK .... Pontianak [*Indonesia*] [*Airport symbol*]   (OAG)
PNkA .... Aluminum Co. of America, Alcoa Research Laboratories Library, New Kensington, PA [*Library symbol*] [*Library of Congress*]   (LCLS)
PNL .... Pacific Naval Laboratory [*British*]   (MCD)
PNL .... Pacific Northwest Laboratory [*Department of Energy*]
PNL .... Panel   (KSC)
PNL .... Pantelleria [*Italy*] [*Airport symbol*]   (OAG)
PNL .... Parti National Liberal [*National Liberal Party*] [*Lebanese*]   (PPW)
PNL .... Partidul National Liberal [*National Liberal Party*] [*Romanian*]   (PPE)
PNL .... Peanut Lectin [*Immunochemistry*]
PNL .... Peninsula [*Alaska*] [*Seismograph station code, US Geological Survey*]   (SEIS)
PNL .... Penril Corp. [*American Stock Exchange symbol*]
PNL .... Perceived Noise Level
PNL .... Pine Bell Mines [*Vancouver Stock Exchange symbol*]
PNL .... Polytechnic of North London, School of Librarianship, London, England [*OCLC symbol*]   (OCLC)
PNL .... Prescribed Nuclear Load [*Military*]   (AABC)
PNL .... Przewodnik Naukowy i Literacki [*A publication*]
PNL .... Pulsed Neodymium LASER
PNLA .... Pacific Northwest Library Association
PNLA .... Pacific Northwest Loggers Association   (EA)
PNLA Q ...... Pacific Northwest Library Association. Quarterly [*A publication*]
pnlbd .... Panelboard [*National Electrical Code*]   (IEEE)
PNLBRG ..... Panel Bridge   (MUGU)
PNLM .... Palestine National Liberation Movement   (BJA)
PNLO .... Principal Naval Liaison Officer [*British*]
PNLT .... Perceived Noise Level, Tone Corrected
PNM .... Pan-Somali Nationalist Movement
PNM .... Partido Nacionalista de Mexicano [*Nationalist Party of Mexico*]
PNM .... Partito Nazionale Monarchico [*National Monarchist Party*] [*Italy*]   (PPE)
PNM .... People's National Movement [*Trinidadian and Tobagan*]   (PD)
PNM .... Perspectives of New Music [*A publication*]
Pnm .... Phantom [*A publication*]
PNM .... Phenolic Nylon with Microballoon
PNM .... Price Negotiation Memorandum   (MCD)
PNM .... Public Service Co. of New Mexico [*NYSE symbol*]
PNM .... Pulse Number Modulation
PNMC .... Phenyl Methylcarbamate [*Organic chemistry*]
PNMO .... Provided No Military Objection Exists [*Army*]
PNMPA ...... Psychiatrie, Neurologie, und Medizinische Psychologie [*A publication*]
PNMT .... Phenylethanolamine N-Methyltransferase [*An enzyme*]
PNMUB ..... Perspectives of New Music [*A publication*]
PNMUD ..... PNM Update [*A publication*]
PNN .... Penn Engineering & Manufacturing Corp. [*American Stock Exchange symbol*]
PNN .... Pinnacle Mountain [*Alaska*] [*Seismograph station code, US Geological Survey*]   (SEIS)
PNN .... Princeton, ME [*Location identifier*] [*FAA*]   (FAAL)
PNNCF ...... Pacific Northern Naval Coastal Frontier
PNNT .... Pennant   (MSA)
PNo .... Montgomery County-Norristown Public Library, Norristown, PA [*Library symbol*] [*Library of Congress*]   (LCLS)
PNO .... Nashville, TN [*Location identifier*] [*FAA*]   (FAAL)
PNO .... Parti Nationaliste Occitan [*Occitanian Nationalist Party*] [*French*]   (PPE)

PNO .... Pendleton [*Oregon*] [*Seismograph station code, US Geological Survey*]   (SEIS)
PNO .... Preliminary Notification [*Nuclear energy*]   (NRCH)
PNO .... Premium Notice Ordinary [*Insurance*]
PNO .... Principal Naval Overseer [*British*]
PNO .... Principal Nursing Officer
PNOA .... Para-Nitro-ortho-anisidine [*Organic chemistry*]
PNOC .... Proposed Notice of Change
PNO-CI ...... Pair Natural Orbital Configuration Interaction [*Atomic physics*]
PNoH .... Norristown State Hospital, Norristown, PA [*Library symbol*] [*Library of Congress*]   (LCLS)
PNohM ...... Mary Immaculate Seminary, Northampton, PA [*Library symbol*] [*Library of Congress*]   (LCLS)
PNOK .... Primary Next of Kin [*Army*]   (AABC)
PNOM .... Procedural Nomenclature   (MCD)
PNOPO .... Parliament National Organisations and Public Offices [*British*]
PNortHi ..... Historical Society of Montgomery County, Norristown, PA [*Library symbol*] [*Library of Congress*] [*Obsolete*]   (LCLS)
PNOT .... Para-Nitro-ortho-toluidine [*Organic chemistry*]
PNOU-A ...... Planning Outlook [*A publication*]
PNP .... Pakistan National Party   (PD)
PNP .... Para-Nitrophenol [*or Nitrophenyl*] [*Organic chemistry*]
PNP .... Parti National Populaire [*National Popular Party*] [*Canadian*]   (PPW)
PNP .... Parti National du Progres [*National Progress Party*] [*Congo - Leopoldville*]
PNP .... Partido Nacionalista Popular [*Popular Nationalist Party*] [*Panamanian*]   (PPW)
PNP .... Partido Nacionalista del Pueblo [*Bolivian*]   (PPW)
PNP .... Partido Nuevo Progresista [*New Progressive Party*] [*Puerto Rican*]   (PPW)
PNP .... Partidul National Poporului [*National People's Party*] [*Romanian*]   (PPE)
PNP .... Pay'n Pak Stores, Inc. [*NYSE symbol*]
PNP .... Peake's English Nisi Prius Cases [*1790-1812*]   (DLA)
PNP .... Pediatric Nurse Practitioner
PNP .... Penuelas [*Puerto Rico*] [*Seismograph station code, US Geological Survey*]   (SEIS)
PNP .... People's National Party [*Jamaican*]   (PPW)
PNP .... People's National Party [*Ghanaian*]   (PPW)
PNP .... Peripheral Neuropathy [*Medicine*]
PNP .... Popondetta [*Papua New Guinea*] [*Airport symbol*]   (OAG)
PNP .... Popular Nationalist Party [*Panamanian*]   (PD)
PNP .... Positive-Negative-Positive [*Transistor*]
PNP .... Precision Navigation Project
PNP .... Prenegotiation Position   (MCD)
PNP .... Progressive National Party [*Turks and Caicos Islands*]   (PPW)
PNP .... Psychogenic Nocturnal Polydipsia [*Medicine*]
PNP .... Purine-Nucleoside Phosphorylase [*An enzyme*]
PNP .... Pyridoxine Phosphate [*Biochemistry*]
PNPA .... Para-Nitrophenyl Acetate [*Organic chemistry*]
PNPF .... Piqua Nuclear Power Facility [*Energy Research and Development Administration*]
PNPG .... Para-Nitrophenylglycerine [*Biochemistry*]
PNPH .... Parti National Progressiste d'Haiti [*National Progressive Party of Haiti*]
PNPL .... Para-Nitrophenyl Laurate [*Organic chemistry*]
PNPN .... Positive-Negative-Positive-Negative [*Transistor*]   (MUGU)
PNPP .... Para-Nitrophenyl Phosphate [*Organic chemistry*]
PNPP .... Perry Nuclear Power Plant   (NRCH)
PNPR .... Positive-Negative Pressure Respiration
PNPS .... Palisades Nuclear Power Station   (NRCH)
PNPS .... Plant Nitrogen Purge System   (IEEE)
PNPSD .... Prace Naukowe Politechniki Szczecinskiej [*A publication*]
PNQ .... Pacific Northwest Quarterly [*A publication*]
PNQ .... Poona [*India*] [*Airport symbol*]   (OAG)
PNR .... Partido Nacional Republicano [*National Republican Party*] [*Paraguayan*]
PNR .... Partido Nacional Republicano [*National Republican Party*] [*Portuguese*]   (PPE)
PNR .... Partido Nacional Revolucionario [*National Revolutionary Party*] [*Venezuela*]
PNR .... Partido Nacionalista Renovador [*Nationalist Renewal Party*] [*Guatemalan*]   (PPW)
PNR .... Partido Nacionalista Revolucionario [*Revolutionary Nationalist Party*] [*Ecuadorean*]   (PPW)
PNR .... Partij Nationalistische Republiek [*Nationalist Republic Party*] [*Surinamese*]   (PPW)
PNR .... Passenger Name Record [*Airlines*]
PNR .... Peninsula Airlines, Inc. [*Port Angeles, WA*] [*FAA designator*]   (FAAC)
PNR .... Pennant Resources Ltd. [*Toronto Stock Exchange symbol*]
PNR .... Penrod [*Nevada*] [*Seismograph station code, US Geological Survey*] [*Closed*]   (SEIS)
PNR .... Pioneer
PNR .... Pittsburgh Naval Reactors Office [*Energy Research and Development Administration*]
PNR .... Point of No Return [*Aviation*]
PNR .... Pointe Noire [*Congo*] [*Airport symbol*]   (OAG)
PNR .... Popular News and Review [*A publication*]
PNR .... Preliminary Negotiation Reports

PNR .... Primary Navigation Reference   (AAG)
PNR .... Prior Notice Required   (AFM)
PNR .... Prisoner
PNR .... Proximal Negative Response
PNR .... Pulse Nuclear Radiation   (AAG)
PNRBC .... Pacific Northwest River Basin Commission
PNRC .... Pacific Northwest Regional Commission [*Department of Commerce*]
PNRHSL ..... Pacific Northwest Regional Health Science Library [*Library network*]
PNRLW .... Penril Corp. Wts [*NASDAQ symbol*]   (NQ)
PNRS .... Project Notification and Review System [*Department of Labor*]
PNS .... Pansophic Systems, Inc. [*NYSE symbol*]
PNS .... Parasympathetic Nervous System
PNS .... Part Number Specification   (MCD)
PNS .... Peculiar and Nonstandard Items   (AAG)
PNS .... Penas [*Bolivia*] [*Seismograph station code, US Geological Survey*]   (SEIS)
PNS .... Pennington's Stores Ltd. [*Toronto Stock Exchange symbol*]
PNS .... Pensacola [*Florida*] [*Airport symbol*]   (OAG)
PNS .... Peripheral Nervous System [*Medicine*]
PNS .... Perkins Nuclear Station   (NRCH)
PNS .... Philadelphia & Norfolk Steamship [*AAR code*]
PNS .... Philippines News Service
PNS .... Plate Number Society [*Defunct*]   (EA)
PNS .... Portsmouth Naval Shipyard [*New Hampshire*]
PNS .... Prescribed Nuclear Stockage [*Military*]   (AABC)
PNS .... Professor of Naval Science
PNS .... Publishers Newspaper Syndicate
PNSA.......... Pacific Northwestern Ski Association   (EA)
PNSA.......... Peanut and Nut Salters Association [*Later, PBNPA*]   (EA)
PNSA.......... Seaman Apprentice, Personnelman, Striker [*Navy rating*]
PNSCP ...... Plan for Navy Satellite Communications Plan
PNSI.......... Polhemus Navigational Sciences, Incorporated   (MCD)
PNSL .... Peninsula Federal Savings & Loan [*NASDAQ symbol*]   (NQ)
PNSN .... Seaman, Personnelman, Striker [*Navy rating*]
PNS & T..... Professor of Naval Science and Tactics [*Naval ROTC*]
PNSUS ...... Place Name Survey of the United States   (EA)
PNSY.......... Portsmouth Naval Shipyard [*New Hampshire*]
PNt .... Newtown Library Co., Newtown, PA [*Library symbol*] [*Library of Congress*] [*Obsolete*]   (LCLS)
PNT .... Paint   (MSA)
Pnt............. Panart [*Record label*] [*Cuba, USA*]
PNT .... Pantasote, Inc. [*American Stock Exchange symbol*]
PNT .... Para-Nitrotoluene [*Organic chemistry*]
PNT .... Paroxysmal Nodal Tachycardia [*Cardiology*]
PNT .... Patient   (AABC)
PNT .... Pentagon
PNT .... Penticton [*British Columbia*] [*Seismograph station code, US Geological Survey*]   (SEIS)
PNT .... Petromet Resources Ltd. [*Toronto Stock Exchange symbol*] [*Vancouver Stock Exchange symbol*]
PNT .... Point
PNT .... Pontiac, IL [*Location identifier*] [*FAA*]   (FAAL)
PNTA .... Pacific Northwest Trade Association
PNTA......... Pentair, Inc. [*NASDAQ symbol*]   (NQ)
PNtB .... Bucks County Community College, Newton, PA [*Library symbol*] [*Library of Congress*]   (LCLS)
PNtC .... Council Rock High School, Newtown, PA [*Library symbol*] [*Library of Congress*]   (LCLS)
PNTC .... Panatech Research & Development [*NASDAQ symbol*]   (NQ)
PNTC .... Parti National Travailliste Camerounais [*Cameroonese National Workers' Party*]
PNTCENS ... Patient Census Report
PNTD......... Painted
PNTD......... Personnel Neutron Threshold Detector   (IEEE)
PN/TDMA .. Pseudo Noise/Time Division Multiple Access   (MCD)
PNtE......... Ellis College, Newtown, PA [*Library symbol*] [*Library of Congress*] [*Obsolete*]   (LCLS)
PNTG......... Printing   (ROG)
PNTGN...... Pentagon   (MSA)
PNTO......... Portuguese National Tourist Office [*Casa de Portugal*]   (EA)
PNTOS ...... Para-Nitrotoluene-ortho-sulfonic Acid [*Organic chemistry*]
PNTR........ Painter   (FAAC)
PNTR........ Pinetree Computer Systems [*NASDAQ symbol*]   (NQ)
PNTR........ Pointer   (MCD)
PNts .... Newtown Public Library, Newtown Square, PA [*Library symbol*] [*Library of Congress*]   (LCLS)
PNU........... Palestine National Union   (BJA)
PNU........... Panguitch [*Utah*] [*Airport symbol*]   (OAG)
PNU........... Personennamen der Texte aus Ugarit [*A publication*]   (BJA)
PNU........... Pneumatic Scale Corp. [*American Stock Exchange symbol*]
PNU........... Protein Nitrogen Units [*Clinical chemistry*]
PNUA .... Partito Nazionale Unito Africa [*National Party of United Africans*] [*Somalia*]
PNUA .... Polish National Union of America   (EA)
PNUD .... Programa de las Naciones Unidas para el Desarrollo [*United Nations Development Program - UNDP*] [*Spanish*]   (MSC)
PNUD .... Programme des Nations Unies pour le Developpement [*United Nations Development Program*]

PNUE.......... Programme des Nations Unies pour l'Environnement [*United Nations Environment Programme - UNEP*] [*Nairobi, Kenya*]   (EA-IO)
PNUED .... Preprint. Akademiya Nauk Ukrainskoi SSR. Institut Elektrodinamiki [*A publication*]
PNUMA ...... Programa de las Naciones Unidas para el Medio Ambiente [*United Nations Environmental Programme Regional Office for Latin America*] [*Mexico City, Mexico*]   (EA-IO)
PNUS......... Prace Naukowe Uniwersytetu Slaskiego [*A publication*]
PNUT......... Portable Nursing Unit Terminal
PNUT......... Possible Nuclear Underground Test
P Nutr Soc ... Proceedings. Nutrition Society [*A publication*]
PNUTS .... Possible Nuclear Test Site [*Pronounced "peanuts"*] [*Air Force intelligence*]
PNV .... National Velasquista Party [*Ecuadorean*]   (PPW)
PNV .... Parti National Voltaique [*Voltaic National Party*]
PNV .... Partido Nacional Velasquista [*National Velasquista Party*] [*Ecuadorean*]   (PPW)
PNV .... Partido Nacionalista Vasco [*Basque Nationalist Party*] [*Spanish*]   (PPE)
PNV .... Patino N. V. [*Toronto Stock Exchange symbol*]
PNV .... Perini Investment Properties, Inc. [*American Stock Exchange symbol*]
PNVAL .... Previously Not Available [*Army*]   (AABC)
PNVD .... Passive Night Vision Devices [*Army*]   (AABC)
PNVS......... Pilot Night Vision System [*Army*]   (MCD)
PNVTS ...... Pyrotechnics No-Voltage Test Set
PNW .... Pacific Northwest
PNW .... [*The*] Prescott & Northwestern Railroad Co. [*AAR code*]
PNWC........ Pacific Northwest Writers' Conference
PNwC .... Westminster College, New Wilmington, PA [*Library symbol*] [*Library of Congress*]   (LCLS)
PNWL .... Pacific Northwest Laboratory [*AEC*]
PNX .... Imperial Airways, Inc. [*St. Paul, MN*] [*FAA designator*]   (FAAC)
PNX .... Pneumothorax [*Medicine*]
PNXT .... Pinxit [*He, or She, Painted It*] [*Latin*]
PNY .... Camp Parks, CA [*Location identifier*] [*FAA*]   (FAAL)
PNY .... Piedmont Natural Gas Co., Inc. [*NYSE symbol*]
PNY .... Plattsburg [*New York*] [*Seismograph station code, US Geological Survey*]   (SEIS)
PNY .... Poetry New York [*A publication*]
PNY .... Portuguese Navy
PNYA .... Port of New York Authority [*Later, PANYNJ*]
PNYMD ...... Polytechnic Institute of New York. Department of Mechanical and Aerospace Engineering. Report POLY M/AE [*A publication*]
PNZ .... Pennzoil Co., Exploration Library, Houston, TX [*OCLC symbol*]   (OCLC)
PNZ .... Petrolina [*Brazil*] [*Airport symbol*]   (OAG)
PO .... Dust Devils [*Aviation code*]   (FAAC)
po----- .... Oceanica [*MARC geographic area code*] [*Library of Congress*]   (LCCP)
PO .... Officer Personnel Division [*Coast Guard*]
PO .... Oil City Library, Oil City, PA [*Library symbol*] [*Library of Congress*]   (LCLS)
PO .... Pacific Ocean
P & O .... Paints and Oil
PO .... Parallel Output [*Data processing*]   (BUR)
PO .... Parity Odd
PO .... Parking Orbit [*NASA*]
PO .... Parole Officer
P/O .... Part Of   (KSC)
PO .... Passport Office [*Department of State*]
PO .... Patent Office [*Later, PTO*] [*Department of Commerce*]
PO .... Patrologia Orientalis [*A publication*]
P & O .... Peninsular & Oriental Steam Navigation Co. [*Steamship line*]
PO .... Per Os [*By Mouth*] [*Pharmacy*]
PO .... Performance Objectives   (OICC)
P & O .... Performance and Operational [*Test or reports*]
PO .... Period of Onset [*Medicine*]
PO .... Permit Office [*British*]   (ROG)
PO .... Peroxidase [*Also, POD*] [*An enzyme*]
PO .... Personnel Officer
PO .... Pesticides Office [*Environmental Protection Agency*]
PO .... Petty Officer [*Navy*]
PO .... Philharmonic Orchestra [*Music*]
P/O .... Phone Order [*Medicine*]
P & O .... Pickled and Oiled
PO .... Pilot Officer
PO .... Planetary Orbit
PO .... Planning Objectives
P & O .... Planning and Operations
P & O .... Plans and Operations Division [*War Department*] [*World War II*]
PO .... Poco [*Somewhat*] [*Music*]
Po............. Poesie [*A publication*]
PO .... Polarity   (AAG)
PO .... Pole [*Unit of measurement*]
Po............. Polet [*A publication*]
PO .... Police Officer
PO .... Political Officer [*NATO*]   (NATG)

P/O	Pollen/Ovule Ratio [*Botany*]
Po	Polonium [*Chemical element*]
PO	Polyolefin [*Organic chemistry*]
Po	Polyzoa [*Quality of the bottom*] [*Nautical charts*]
PO	Poona Orientalist [*A publication*]
PO	Por Orden [*By Order*] [*Spanish*]
PO	Port Flag [*Navy*] [*British*]
PO	Port Officer
P & O	Portland & Ogdensburgh Railroad
PO	Portugal [*NATO*] (AFM)
po	Portugal [*MARC country of publication code*] [*Library of Congress*] (LCCP)
Po	Portuguese (DLA)
PO	Position Offered
P & O	Positioning and Orientation
PO	Post Office
PO	Post Office Department [*Canada*]
PO	Post Orbit [*NASA*]
PO	Postal Officer
PO	Postal Order
PO	Postoperative [*Medicine*]
PO	Postpay Coin Telephone [*Telecommunications*] (TEL)
PO	Power-Operated
PO	Power Oscillator [*Electronics*]
PO	Power Output
PO	Prairie Overcomer [*A publication*]
PO	Pre-Authorization Order
PO	Preoperational (MCD)
PO	Preoptic [*Area of the brain*]
PO	Presbyteri Oratorii [*Oratorians*] [*Roman Catholic religious order*]
PO	Presbyterorum Ordinis [*Decree on the Ministry and Life of Priests*] [*Vatican II document*]
PO	Preventive Officer [*British*] (ROG)
PO	Previous Orders
POO	Principal Officer [*Foreign Service*]
PO	Printout
PO	Private Office [*Documents issued by the Secretary General, NATO*] (NATG)
PO	Privately Owned (AFM)
PO	Probation Officer
PO	Procurement Objective (NVT)
PO	Production Offset (AABC)
PO	Production Order (KSC)
PO	Professor Ordinarius [*Ordinary Professor*] [*Latin*] (ROG)
PO	Program Objective
PO	Program Office [*Air Force*] (CET)
PO	Program Originator (AFM)
PO	Programed Oscillator
PO	Project Office [*or Officer*] [*Military*]
PO	Project ORBIS [*New York, NY*] (EA)
PO	Project Order [*DoD*]
PO	Project Overcome [*Minneapolis, MN*] (EA)
PO	Proposals Outstanding
PO	Proposition One [*An association*] (EA)
PO	Propylene Oxide [*Organic chemistry*]
P/O	Protea Lugdiens [*South Africa*] [*ICAO designator*] (FAAC)
PO	Province of Ontario [*Canada*]
PO	Provisioning Order (AFM)
PO	Przeglad Orientalistyczny [*A publication*]
PO	Psychological Operation [*Military*] (CINC)
PO	Public Office [*British*] (ROG)
PO	Public Official
PO	Pulse Output
PO	Pulsed Carrier without Any Modulation Intended to Carry Information (IEEE)
PO	Punted Over [*Boating*] [*British*] (ROG)
PO	Purchase Order
PO	Purchasing Office [*DoD*] (AFIT)
PO	Putout [*Baseball*]
PO	Radio Positioning Mobile Station [*ITU designation*] [*Telecommunications*] (CET)
PO1	Petty Officer, First Class [*Navy*]
PO2	Petty Officer, Second Class [*Navy*]
PO3	Petty Officer, Third Class [*Navy*]
PO'd	Put Out [*i.e., angry*] [*Bowdlerized version*]
PO'ed	Put Out [*i.e., angry*] [*Bowdlerized version*]
POA	Pacific Ocean Area [*World War II*]
POA	Pahoa, HI [*Location identifier*] [*FAA*] (FAAL)
POA	Pancreatic Oncofetal Antigen [*Immunochemistry*]
POA	Panel of Americans [*Defunct*] (EA)
POA	Peacetime Operating Assets [*DoD*] (AFIT)
POA	Petroleum Operating Agreement (CINC)
POA	Phalangeal Osteoarthritis [*Medicine*]
POA	Phenoxyacetic Acid [*Organic chemistry*]
POA	Place of Acceptance [*Business and trade*]
POA	Plan of Action (NASA)
POA	Pontifica Opera di Assistenza [*Pontifical Relief Organization*]
POA	Port of Arrival
POA	Porto Alegre [*Brazil*] [*Airport symbol*] (OAG)
POA	Power of Attorney
POA	Preoptic Area [*of the brain*]
POA	Price on Application [*Business and trade*] (ADA)
POA	Primary Optic Afferents
POA	Primary Optic Atrophy
POA	Prison Officers' Association [*A union*] [*British*]
POA	Privately Owned Aircraft (FAAC)
POA	Privately Owned Automobile
POA	Proof of Accounts
POA	Provisional Operating Authorization [*for nuclear power plant*]
POA	Public Order Act
POA	Purchased on Assembly (KSC)
POAA	Planetary Operations Analysis Area [*NASA*]
POAA	Problems of the Arctic and the Antarctic [*A publication*]
POAA	Property Owners Association of America [*Defunct*] (EA)
POAC	Pony of the Americas Club (EA)
POA Chronicle	Professional Officers' Association Chronicle [*A publication*]
POACS	Prior Other Active Commissioned Service [*Military*]
POAE	Port of Aerial Embarkation [*Air Force*]
POAE	Principal Officer of Aircraft Equipment [*Ministry of Aircraft Production*] [*British*] [*World War II*]
POAES	Prior Other Active Enlisted Service [*Military*]
POAG	Primary Open-Angle Glaucoma [*Ophthalmology*]
POAHEDPEARL	Pacific Ocean Areas Headquarters Pearl Harbor
POALS	Petty Officers Advanced Leadership School [*Navy*] (MUGU)
POA & M	Plan of Action and Milestones (NVT)
POAN	Procurement of Ordnance and Ammunition - Navy
POAR	Problem-Objective-Approach-Response [*System of planning patient care*] [*Medicine*]
POAR	Project Order Action Request [*Navy*] (NG)
poas---	American Samoa [*MARC geographic area code*] [*Library of Congress*] (LCCP)
POAS	Pankypria Omospondia Anexartiton Syntechnion [*Pancyprian Federation of Independent Trade Unions*] [*Cyprus*]
POASP	Plans and Operations Automated Storage Program [*Military*]
POATSC	Pacific Overseas Air Technical Service Command
POAU	Protestants and Other Americans United [*for Separation of Church and State*]
POB	Fayetteville, NC [*Location identifier*] [*FAA*] (FAAL)
POB	Parti Ouvrier Belge [*Belgian Workers' Party*] [*Later, Belgian Socialist Party*] (PPE)
POB	Penicillin, Oil, Beeswax [*Medicine*]
POB	Perfluorooctyl Bromide [*Organic chemistry*]
POB	Persons on Board [*Aviation*]
POB	Phenoxybenzamine [*Later, PBZ*] [*Organic chemistry*]
POB	Place of Birth
POB	Point of Beginning
POB	Point of Business
POB	Polarboken [*A publication*]
POB	Post Office Box
POB	Postal Bulletin [*A publication*]
POB	Power Outlet Box
POB²	Prepped Out Beyond Belief [*Book title*]
POBAL	Powered Balloon [*System*]
POBATO	Propellant on Board at Takeoff
POBCOST	Probabilistic Budgeting and Forward Costing (MCD)
POBI	Polar Biology [*A publication*]
pobp---	British Solomon Islands [*MARC geographic area code*] [*Library of Congress*] (LCCP)
POBR	Problem-Oriented Basic Research [*National Science Foundation*]
POBUD	Polymer Bulletin [*A publication*]
POBY	Prior Operating Budget Year [*Military*] (AFIT)
POC	Clarion State College, Oil City, PA [*Library symbol*] [*Library of Congress*] (LCLS)
POC	La Pocatiere [*Quebec*] [*Seismograph station code, US Geological Survey*] (SEIS)
POC	La Verne, CA [*Location identifier*] [*FAA*] (FAAL)
POC	Parallel Optical Computer
POC	Parti d'Opposition Congolais [*Congolese Opposition Party*]
POC	Particulate Organic Carbon
POC	Particulate Organic Concentration [*Environmental science*]
POC	Payload Operations Center [*NASA*] (NASA)
P & OC	Peninsular & Oriental (Steam Navigation) Company Ltd. (ROG)
POC	Peugeot Owners' Club (EA)
POC	Pick Off, Circuit
POC	Planning Objective Coordinator
POC	Poco Petroleums Ltd. [*Toronto Stock Exchange symbol*]
POC	Pocono Air Lines, Inc. [*East Stroudsburg, PA*] [*FAA designator*] (FAAC)
POC	Poculum [*Cup*] [*Pharmacy*]
POC	Point of Contact (AABC)
POC	Porsche Owners Club (EA)
POC	Port of Call
POc	Porte-Oceane [*Record label*] [*France*]
POC	Post of the Corps
POC	Postoperative Care [*Medicine*]
POC	Postoral Ciliary [*Gland*]
POC	Power Control
POC	Precision Oscillator Crystal
POC	Preliminary Operational Capability [*Military*] (AFIT)

POC........... Principal Operating Component
POC........... Prisoners of Conscience [*File of persons imprisoned for political or religious beliefs kept by Amnesty International*]
POC........... Privately Owned Conveyance [*Army*]
PoC .... Problems of Communism [*A publication*]
POC........... Proceed [*or Proceeding*] on Course [*Aviation*] (FAAC)
POC........... Process Operator Console
POC........... Proche-Orient Chretien [*A publication*]
POC........... Production Operational Capability
POC........... Production Order Change (KSC)
POC........... Professional Officer Course [*AFROTC*] (AFM)
POC........... Programs of Cooperation (MCD)
POC........... Proopiocortin [*Biochemistry*]
POC........... Purchase Order Closeout [*NASA*]
POC........... Purchase Order Contract
POC........... Purgeable Organic Carbon [*Chemistry*]
POCA .... Association of Psychiatric Outpatient Centers of America [*Glen Ridge, NJ*] [*Association retains acronym of its former name*] (EA)
POCA .... Public Offender Counselors Association [*Alexandria, VA*] (EA)
PO Cas ...... Perry's Oriental Cases [*1843-52*] [*Bombay*] (DLA)
POCASEA ... Protection of Children Against Sexual Exploitation Act of 1977
POCB .... Plain Ol' Country Boy
POCC .... Payload Operations Control Center [*NASA*] (NASA)
POCC .... Program Operation Control Center [*Space science*]
Poc Costs ... Pocock on Costs [*1881*] (DLA)
POCE .... Proof-of-Concept Experiment [*Solar thermal conversion*]
POCH .... Progressiven Organisationen der Schweiz [*Progressive Organizations of Switzerland*] (PPE)
P-O Chr...... Proche-Orient Chretien [*A publication*]
Poch Urozhai Latv Nauch-Issled Inst Zemled ... Pochva i Urozhai. Latviiskii Nauchno-Issledovatel'skii Institut Zemledeliya [*A publication*]
Pochv Issled Primen Udobr ... Pochvennye Issledovaniya i Primenenie Udobrenii [*A publication*]
Pochvoved ... Pochvovedenie [*A publication*]
Pochvozn Agrokhim ... Pochvoznanie i Agrokhimiya [*A publication*]
Pochv Usloviya Eff Udobr ... Pochvennye Usloviya i Effektivnost Udobrenii [*A publication*]
Pochvy Baskh Puti Ratsion Ikh Ispol'z ... Pochvy Bashkirii i Puti Ratsional'nogo Ikh Ispol'zovaniya [*USSR*] [*A publication*]
Pochvy Yuzhn Urala Povolzhya ... Pochvy Yuzhnogo Urala i Povolzh'ya [*A publication*]
poci---........ Caroline Islands [*MARC geographic area code*] [*Library of Congress*] (LCCP)
POCI.......... Pontiac-Oakland Club International (EA)
POCIBO ..... Polar Circling Balloon Observatory
POCIL .... Pocillum [*Little Cup*] [*Pharmacy*] (ROG)
Pocill .... Pocillum [*Little Cup*] [*Pharmacy*]
POCL .... Project Office Change Letter
POCM........ Partido Obrero y Campesino de Mexico [*Mexican political party*]
POCM........ Postal Contracting Manual [*Postal Service*]
POCN .... Purchase Order Change Notice
POCO .... Physiology of Chimpanzees in Orbit [*NASA*]
POCO .... Power On - Clock On [*Aerospace*]
POCO .... Purchase Order Change Order (AAG)
POCO .... Purchase Order Closeout (AAG)
pocp---........ Canton and Enderbury Islands [*MARC geographic area code*] [*Library of Congress*] (LCCP)
POCP .... Program Objectives Change Proposal
POCR .... Program Objectives Change Request [*DoD*]
POCS .... Patent Office [*later, PTO*] Classification System
PO & CS ..... Post Office and Civil Service Committee [*Obsolete*] [*US Senate*]
Po Ct .... Police Court (DLA)
POCTA ...... Prevention of Cruelty to Animals Society Member (DSUE)
POCUL ...... Poculum [*Cup*] [*Pharmacy*] (ROG)
pocw---...... Cook Island [*MARC geographic area code*] [*Library of Congress*] (LCCP)
POD........... Pacific Ocean Division [*Army Corps of Engineers*]
POD........... Parent Organization Designator (MCD)
POD........... Parents of Diabetics
POD........... Pay on Delivery [*Business and trade*]
POD........... Payable on Death
POD........... Payload Operations Division [*NASA*] (MCD)
POD........... Permissible Operating Distance [*Army*] (AFIT)
POD........... Peroxidase [*Also, PO*] [*An enzyme*]
POD........... Place of Discharge
POD........... Plan of the Day
POD........... Pneumatically Operated Disconnect (KSC)
POD........... Pocket Oxford Dictionary [*A publication*]
POD........... Podkamennaya [*USSR*] [*Geomagnetic observatory code*]
POD........... Podor [*Senegal*] [*Airport symbol*] (OAG)
POD........... Point-of-Origin Device (IEEE)
POD........... Port of Debarkation [*Military*]
POD........... Port of Delivery [*Shipping*]
POD........... Port of Discharge [*Navy*]
POD........... Post of Duty
POD........... Post Office Department [*Later, United States Postal Service*]
POD........... Post Office Directory

POD........... Postoperative Day [*Medicine*]
POD........... Precision Orbit Determination (MCD)
POD........... Professional and Organizational Development [*In association name Professional and Organizational Development Network in Higher Education*] (EA)
POD........... Program Operation Description
POD........... Programed Operational Date (AFIT)
POD........... Proof of Debt [*Business and trade*]
POD........... Proof of Design (MCD)
POD........... Pulse Omission Detector (MCD)
POD........... Purchase Order Deviation (KSC)
PODA .... Priority-Oriented Demand Assignment
PODAF ...... Post Operation Data Analysis Facility
PODAF ...... Power Density Exceeding a Specified Level over an Area with an Assigned Frequency Band (IEEE)
PODAPS.... Portable Data Processing System
PODAS ...... Portable Data Acquisition System
PODBCA ... Post Office Department Board of Contract Appeals (AFIT)
PODCC ...... Plan, Organize, Direct, Coordinate, Control [*Principles of management*]
Pod D .... Doctor of Podiatry
PODE .... Pacific Ocean Division Engineers (CINC)
PODEX ...... [*Night*] Photographic Exercise [*Military*] (NVT)
PODF......... Post of Duty File
Podgot Koksovanie Uglei ... Podgotovka i Koksovanie Uglei [*A publication*]
Podgot Vosstanov Rud ... Podgotovka i Vosstanovlenie Rud [*A publication*]
PODIM........ Poseidon Design Information Memo [*Missiles*]
P & O Div.... Planning and Operations Division [*Military*]
PODM......... Preliminary Orbit Determination Method [*Computer*] [*NASA*]
PODO .... Profit on Day One [*Classification for new newspaper*]
PODRS....... Patent Office [*later, PTO*] Data Retrieval System
PODS .... Parents of Down's Syndrome (EA)
PODS .... Postoperative Destruct System (MCD)
PODSC...... Parents of Down's Syndrome Children [*Rockville, MD*] (EA)
Podstawowe Probl Wspolczesnej Tech ... Podstawowe Problemy Wspolczesnej Techniki [*A publication*]
Podst Sterow ... Podstawy Sterowania [*A publication*]
PODU .... Praci Odes'koho Derzavnoho Universytetu [*A publication*]
PODUC...... Provided [*Following Named*] Officers Have Not Departed Your Command [*Amend Assignment Instructions as Indicated*] [*Army*] (AABC)
PODx......... Postoperative Diagnosis [*Medicine*]
PODx......... Preoperative Diagnosis [*Medicine*]
Podzemn Gazif Uglei ... Podzemnaya Gazifikatsiya Uglei [*USSR*] [*A publication*]
Podzemn Gazif Uglei (1934-35) ... Podzemnaya Gazifikatsiya Uglei (1934-35) [*A publication*]
Podzemn Gazif Uglei (1957-59) ... Podzemnaya Gazifikatsiya Uglei (1957-59) [*A publication*]
Podzemn Vody SSSR ... Podzemnye Vody SSSR [*A publication*]
POE .... Fort Polk [*Louisiana*] [*Airport symbol*] (OAG)
POE .... Fort Polk, LA [*Location identifier*] [*FAA*] (FAAL)
POE .... Panel on the Environment [*of President's Science Advisory Committee*]
POE .... Payment Option Election (MCD)
POE .... People of the Earth (EA)
POE .... Pilot Operational Equipment (MCD)
POE .... Plank-on-Edge
POE .... Pneumatically Operated Equipment (AAG)
Poe .... Poetik [*A publication*]
POE .... Polyoxyethylene [*Organic chemistry*]
POE .... Port of Embarkation
POE .... Port of Entry
POE .... Post-Operations Evaluation (MCD)
POE .... Postoperative Endophthalmitis [*Ophthalmology*]
POE .... Predicted Operational Environment [*Military*] (CAAL)
POE .... Pretesting Orientation Exercises [*US Employment Service*] [*Department of Labor*]
POE .... Print Out Effect
POE .... Projected Operational Environment (NVT)
POE .... Pulsar Energy/Resources [*Vancouver Stock Exchange symbol*]
poea---........ Easter Island [*MARC geographic area code*] [*Library of Congress*] (LCCP)
POEA .... Poe & Associates [*NASDAQ symbol*] (NQ)
POEA .... Protection of Offshore Energy Assets [*Navy*] (NVT)
POEAS ...... Planetary Orbiter Error Analysis Study Program
Poe Chpbk ... Poetry Chapbook [*A publication*]
POED .... Program Organization for Evaluation and Decision
POEIT........ Provisional Organization for European Inland Transportation [*World War II*]
P O Elect Engrs J ... Post Office Electrical Engineers. Journal [*A publication*]
P O Electr Eng J ... Post Office Electrical Engineers. Journal [*A publication*]
POEMS ...... Polyneuropathy Associated with Organomegaly Endocrine Disorders, Myeloma, and Skin Modifications
POEMS ...... Polyoxyethylene Monostearate [*Organic chemistry*]
POENIT ..... Poenitentia [*Penance*] [*Latin*] (ADA)
POEOP ...... Polyoxyethyleneoxypropylene [*Organic chemistry*]
Poe Pal ...... Poetry Palisade [*A publication*]
Poe Pl........ Poe on Pleading and Practice (DLA)
POERD ...... Power Engineer [*A publication*]
PoeS........... Poe Studies [*A publication*]

POESID ...... Position of Earth Satellite in Digital Display (MCD)
Poe Stud .... Poe Studies [*A publication*]
Poet .... De Poetis [*of Suetonius*] [*Classical studies*] (OCD)
POET .... Petty Officer Enroute Training [*Navy*] (NVT)
Poet .... Poetica [*of Aristotle*] [*Classical studies*] (OCD)
Poet .... Poetica [*A publication*]
Poet .... Poetry [*A publication*]
POET .... Primed Oscillator Expendable Transponder [*Military*] (CAAL)
POET .... Psychological Operations Exploitation Team [*Vietnam*]
PoetC .... Poet and Critic [*A publication*]
Poet L .... Poet Lore [*A publication*]
Poet Mel Gr ... Poetae Melici Graeci [*A publication*] (OCD)
POETRI ...... Programme on Exchange and Transfer of Information on Community Water Supply and Sanitation [*International Reference Center for Community Water Supply and Sanitation*] [*Information service*] [*Rijswick, Netherlands*] (EISS)
Poet Rom Vet ... Poetarum Romanorum Veterum Reliquiae [*A publication*] (OCD)
Poetry Mag ... Poetry Magazine [*A publication*]
Poetry NW ... Poetry Northwest [*A publication*]
Poetry R ..... Poetry Review [*London*] [*A publication*]
Poetry Wale ... Poetry Wales [*A publication*]
POETS .... Phooey on Everything, Tomorrow's Saturday [*Bowdlerized version*]
Poets .... Poets in the South [*A publication*]
POETS .... Push Off Early, Tomorrow's Saturday [*Bowdlerized version*]
POEU .... Post Office Engineering Union [*British*]
Poeyana Inst Biol La Habana Ser A ... Poeyana Instituto de Biologia. La Habana. Serie A [*A publication*]
Poeyana Inst Biol La Habana Ser B ... Poeyana Instituto de Biologia. La Habana. Serie B [*A publication*]
Poeyana Inst Zool Acad Cienc Cuba ... Poeyana Instituto de Zoologia. Academia de Ciencias de Cuba [*A publication*]
POF .... Planned Outage Factor [*Electronics*] (IEEE)
POF .... Point-of-Failure [*Data processing*] (IBMDP)
POF .... Police Officer, Female
POF .... Poplar Bluff [*Missouri*] [*Airport symbol*] (OAG)
POF .... Poplar Bluff, MO [*Location identifier*] [*FAA*] (FAAL)
POF .... Positive Opening Fin (MCD)
POF .... Postovulatory Follicle [*Endocrinology*]
POF .... Prilozi za Orijentalnu Filologiju [*A publication*]
POF .... Privately Owned Firearm (MCD)
POF .... Prolific Petroleum [*Vancouver Stock Exchange symbol*]
POF .... Pyruvate Oxidation Factor [*Biochemistry*]
POFA .... Programed Operational Functional Appraisal [*Navy*]
POFA/IPOFA ... Programed Operational Functional Appraisal/Integrated Programed Operational Functional Appraisal [*Navy*] (NVT)
pofj--- .... Fiji [*MARC geographic area code*] [*Library of Congress*] (LCCP)
POFO .... Po Folks, Inc. [*NASDAQ symbol*] (NQ)
POFOOGUSA ... Protection of Foreign Officials and Official Guests of the United States Act
pofp .... French Polynesia [*MARC geographic area code*] [*Library of Congress*] (LCCP)
POG .... Official Gazette. United States Patent Office [*A publication*]
POG .... Parents of Gays (EA)
POG .... Petty Officer's Guide [*A publication*] [*Navy*]
POG .... Piping Instrumentation and Operating Gallery [*Nuclear energy*] (NRCH)
Pog .... Pogledi [*A publication*]
POG. .... Port Gentil [*Gabon*] [*Airport symbol*] (OAG)
POG .... Position of Germany [*British*] [*World War II*]
POG .... Post Office Guide [*Book of regulations*] [*British*]
POG .... Provisional Ordnance Group [*Military*]
POGASIS ... Planetary Observation Geometry and Science Instrument Sequence Program [*Aerospace*]
POGaz .... Post Office Gazette [*British*] [*A publication*]
POGE .... Planning Operational Gaming Experiment [*Game*]
POGE .... Polar Geography and Geology [*A publication*]
pogg--- .... Galapagos Islands [*MARC geographic area code*] [*Library of Congress*] (LCCP)
Poggendorffs Ann ... Poggendorffs Annalen [*A publication*]
pogn--- .... Gilbert and Ellice Islands [*Tuvalu*] [*MARC geographic area code*] [*Library of Congress*] (LCCP)
POGO .... Pennzoil Offshore Gas Operators [*Oil industry group*]
POGO .... Personal Objectives and Goals (MCD)
Pogo .... Pogonomyrinex Occidentalis [*A genus of ants*]
POGO .... Polar Orbiting Geophysical Observatory [*NASA*]
POGO .... Programer-Oriented Graphics Operation (IEEE)
POGR .... Poplar Grove National Cemetery
POGS .... National Association of Post Office and General Service Maintenance Employees [*Later, APWU*] [*AFL-CIO*]
POGSI .... Policy Group on Scientific Information [*Marine science*] (MSC)
POGT .... Power-Operated Gun Turret
pogu--- .... Guam [*MARC geographic area code*] [*Library of Congress*] (LCCP)
POH .... Placed off Hire
POH .... Planned Outage Hours [*Electronics*] (IEEE)
POH .... Pocahontas, IA [*Location identifier*] [*FAA*] (FAAL)

POH .... Pull-Out Harness
POHC .... Principal Organic Hazardous Constituent [*Environmental chemistry*]
POHI .... Physically or Otherwise Health Impaired
POHMA ...... Project for the Oral History of Music in America
POHS .... Presumed Ocular Histoplasmosis Syndrome [*Ophthalmology*]
POHWARO ... Pulsated, Overheated, Water Rocket [*Swiss space rocket*]
POI .... Parking Orbit Injection [*NASA*]
POI .... Parti Oubanguien de l'Independance [*Ubangi Independence Party*]
POI .... Period of Interest (MCD)
POI .... Personal Orientation Inventory [*Psychology*]
POI .... Plan of Instruction
POI .... Point of Impact
POI .... Poison
POI .... Pre-Overhaul Inspection (MCD)
POI .... Pressure-Operated Initiator (MCD)
POI .... Product of Inertia (MCD)
POI .... Program of Instruction
POI .... Public Office of Information (MCD)
POI .... Purchase Order Item (KSC)
POIC .... Petty Officer in Charge [*Navy*] (NVT)
POIC .... Poly(octyl Isocyanate) [*Organic chemistry*]
POIF .... Plan Organization Index File [*IRS*]
Poimennye Pochvy Russ Ravniny ... Poimennye Pochvy Russkoi Ravniny [*A publication*]
POINTER .... Particle Orientation Interferometer [*ASD*]
POINTERM ... Appointment Will Be Regarded as Having Terminated upon This Date
POINTMAIL ... Letter Appointment in Mail
Point Point Commun ... Point-to-Point Communication [*A publication*]
Point Point Telecommun ... Point-to-Point Telecommunications [*A publication*]
Points Appui Econ Rhone-Alpes ... Points d'Appui pour l'Economie Rhone-Alpes [*A publication*]
POIP .... Potential Offender Identification Program
POIPCD ...... Patent Office and Industrial Property and Copyright Department [*British*]
POIQT .... Performance-Oriented Infantry Qualification Test (INF)
POIR .... Project Officers Interim Report [*Air Force*] (MCD)
POIS .... Poisoning [*FBI standardized term*]
POIS .... Procurement Operations Information System (MCD)
POIS .... Prototype On-Line Instrument Systems [*Data processing*] (NRCH)
POIS .... Purchase Order Information System (MCD)
POISE .... Panel on Inflight Scientific Experiments [*NASA*]
POISE .... Photosynthetic Oxygenation Illuminated by Solar Energy
POISE .... Pointing and Stabilization Platform Element [*Army*] (MCD)
POIT .... Power of Influence Test [*Psychology*]
POJ .... Patent Office Journal [*India*] (DLA)
POJ .... Selma, AL [*Location identifier*] [*FAA*] (FAAL)
poji--- .... Johnston Atoll [*MARC geographic area code*] [*Library of Congress*] (LCCP)
POK .... Sacramento, CA [*Location identifier*] [*FAA*] (FAAL)
poki--- .... Kermadec Islands [*MARC geographic area code*] [*Library of Congress*] (LCCP)
Pokroky Mat Fyz Astron ... Pokroky Matematiky, Fyziky, a Astronomie [*A publication*]
Pokroky Praskove Metal ... Pokroky Praskove Metalurgie [*A publication*]
Pokroky Praskove Metal VUPM ... Pokroky Praskove Metalurgie VUPM [*Vyzkumny Ustav pro Praskovou Metalurgii*] [*A publication*]
Pokroky Vinohrad Vina- Vysk ... Pokroky vo Vinohradnickom a Vinarskom Vyskume [*A publication*]
POL .... Pacific Oceanographic Laboratories [*Later, Pacific Marine Environmental Laboratory*]
POL .... Pair Orthogonalized Lowdin [*Physics*]
POL .... Parents of Large Families
POL .... Paul Otchakovsky-Laurens [*Publishing imprint, named for imprint editor*]
POL .... Pemba [*Mozambique*] [*Airport symbol*] (OAG)
POL .... Petroleum, Oil, and Lubricants [*Military*]
POL .... Pola [*Yugoslavia*] [*Seismograph station code, US Geological Survey*] [*Closed*] (SEIS)
POL .... Polacca [*Ship's rigging*] (ROG)
POL .... Poland [*Three-letter standard code*] (CNC)
POL .... Polar Airways, Inc. [*Anchorage, AK*] [*FAA designator*] (FAAC)
POL .... Polarity [*or Polarize*] (KSC)
POL .... Police
POL .... Policy
pol .... Polish [*MARC language code*] [*Library of Congress*] (LCCP)
POL .... Polish (AAG)
Pol .... Politica [*of Aristotle*] [*Classical studies*] (OCD)
POL .... Political
Pol .... Politics [*A publication*]
Pol .... Pollexfen's English King's Bench Reports [*1669-85*] (DLA)
POL .... Polonium [*Chemical symbol is Po*] (AAG)
Pol .... Polonystyka [*Warsaw*] [*A publication*]
Pol .... [*Epistle of*] Polycarp (BJA)
Pol .... Polydor & Deutsche Grammophon [*Record label*] [*Germany, Europe, etc.*]

POL .... Polymerase [*An enzyme*]
Pol .... Polyphon [*Record label*] [*Denmark, etc.*]
POL .... Port of Loading
POL .... Problem-Oriented Language [*Data processing*]
POL .... Procedure-Oriented Language [*Data processing*]
POL .... Process-Oriented Language [*Data processing*]   (IEEE)
POL .... Provisional Operating License [*for nuclear power plant*]
POL .... Public Opinion Laboratory [*Northern Illinois University*]
     [*Research center*]   (RCD)
POLA .... Polaris Resources [*NASDAQ symbol*]   (NQ)
POLA .... Project on Linguistic Analysis
PolAb .... Pollution Abstracts [*A publication*]
Pol Acad Sci Inst Ecol Rep Sci Act ... Polish Academy of Sciences. Institute
     of Ecology. Report on Scientific Activities [*A publication*]
Pol Acad Sci Inst Fundam Tech Res Nonlinear Vib Probl ... Polish Academy
     of Sciences. Institute of Fundamental Technical Research.
     Nonlinear Vibration Problems [*A publication*]
Pol Acad Sci Inst Fundam Tech Res Proc Vib Probl ... Polish Academy of
     Sciences. Institute of Fundamental Technical Research.
     Proceedings of Vibration Problems [*A publication*]
Pol Acad Sci Inst Geophys Publ Ser D ... Polish Academy of Sciences.
     Institute of Geophysics. Publications. Series D.
     Atmosphere Physics [*A publication*]
Pol Acad Sci Med Sect Ann ... Polish Academy of Sciences. Medical
     Section. Annals [*A publication*]
POLAD .... Political Adviser
Pol Akad Nauk Inst Geofiz Mater Pr ... Polska Akademia Nauk. Instytut
     Geofizyki. Materialy i Prace [*A publication*]
Pol Akad Nauk Kom Ceram Pr Ser Ceram ... Polska Akademia Nauk.
     Komisja Ceramiczna. Prace. Serja Ceramika [*A
     publication*]
Pol Akad Nauk Kom Krystalogr Biul Inf ... Polska Akademia Nauk. Komisja
     Krystalografii. Biuletyn Informacyjny [*A publication*]
Pol Akad Nauk Oddzial Krakowie Kom Nauk Mineral Pr Mineral ... Polska
     Akademia Nauk. Oddzial w Krakowie. Komisja Nauk
     Mineralogicznych. Prace Mineralogiczne [*A publication*]
Pol Akad Nauk Oddzial Krakowie Nauk Mineral Pr Mineral ... Polska
     Akademia Nauk. Oddzial w Krakowie. Komisja Nauk
     Mineralogicznych. Prace Mineralogiczne [*A publication*]
Pol Akad Nauk Oddzial Krakowie Pr Kom Ceram Ceram ... Polska
     Akademia Nauk. Oddzial w Krakowie. Prace Komisji
     Ceramicznej. Ceramika [*A publication*]
Pol Akad Nauk Oddzial Krakowie Pr Kom Ceram Ser Ceram ... Polska
     Akademia Nauk. Oddzial w Krakowie. Prace Komisji
     Ceramicznej. Serja Ceramika [*A publication*]
Pol Akad Nauk Oddzial Krakowie Pr Kom Metal-Odlew Metalurg ... Polska
     Akademia Nauk. Oddzial w Krakowie. Prace Komisji
     Metalurgiczno-Odlewniczej. Metalurgia [*A publication*]
Pol Akad Nauk Oddzial Krakowie Pr Kom Nauk Tech Ser Ceram ... Polska
     Akademia Nauk. Oddzial w Krakowie. Prace Komisji Nauk
     Technicznych. Serja. Ceramika [*A publication*]
Pol Akad Nauk Pr Inst Masz Przeplyw ... Polska Akademia Nauk. Prace
     Instytutu Maszyn Przeplywowych [*A publication*]
Pol Akad Nauk Pr Kom Nauk Tech Metal Fiz Met Stopow ... Polska
     Akademia Nauk. Prace Komisji Nauk Technicznych
     Metalurgia Fizyka Metali i Stopow [*A publication*]
Pol Akad Nauk Pr Kom Nauk Tech Ser Ceram ... Polska Akademia Nauk.
     Prace Komisji Nauk Technicznych. Serja Ceramika [*A
     publication*]
Pol Akad Umiejet Pr Roln Lesne ... Polska Akademia Umiejetnosci. Prace
     Rolniczo-Lesne [*A publication*]
Polam LJ .... Polamerican Law Journal   (DLA)
Pol Am Stds ... Polish American Studies [*A publication*]
Poland China ... Poland China World [*A publication*]
Poland Inst Geol Biul ... Poland. Instytut Geologiczny. Biuletyn [*A
     publication*]
POLANG .... Polarization Angle [*Telecommunications*]
POLAR .... Production Order Location and Reporting [*NASA*]   (NASA)
POLAR .... Projected Operational Logistics Analysis Requirements
Pol Arch Hydrobiol ... Polskie Archiwum Hydrobiologii/Polish Archives of
     Hydrobiology [*A publication*]
Pol Arch Med Wewn ... Polskie Archiwum Medycyny Wewnetrznej [*A
     publication*]
Pol Arch Wet ... Polskie Archiwum Weterynaryjne [*A publication*]
Pol Arch Weter ... Polskie Archiwum Weterynaryjne [*A publication*]
POLARIS .... Polar-Motion Analysis by Radio Interferometric Surveying
     [*Geodetic measuring facilities*]
Polarogr Ber ... Polarographische Berichte [*A publication*]
Polar Rec ... Polar Record [*A publication*]
Pol Bildung ... Politische Bildung [*A publication*]
Pol C .... Political Code   (DLA)
POLCAP..... Petroleum, Oils, and Lubricants Capabilities   (MCD)
POLCOD .... Police Code [*INTERPOL*]
Pol Code .... Political Code   (DLA)
Pol Communication and Persuasion ... Political Communication and
     Persuasion [*A publication*]
Pol Cont ..... Pollock on Contracts   (DLA)
POLDAM .... POL [*Petroleum, Oil, and Lubricants*] Installations Damage
     Report   (NATG)
Pol Dig Part ... Pollock's Digest of the Laws of Partnership   (DLA)
POLDPS ..... Pioneer Off-Line Data-Processing System [*NASA*]

POLE .... Point-of-Last-Environment [*Data processing*]   (IBMDP)
POLEA .... Polski Tygodnik Lekarski [*A publication*]
Pol Ecol Bibliogr ... Polish Ecological Bibliography [*A publication*]
Pol Ecol Stud ... Polish Ecological Studies [*A publication*]
Pol Endocrinol ... Polish Endocrinology [*A publication*]
Pol Eng .... Polish Engineering [*A publication*]
Pol Eng Rev ... Polish Engineering Review [*A publication*]
Pol Etrang ... Politique Etrangere [*Paris*] [*A publication*]
POLEX .... Polar Experiment
POLEX........ Political Exercise [*International relations game*]
POLEX-NORTH ... Polar Experiment in the Northern Hemisphere   (MSC)
POLEX-SOUTH ... Polar Experiment in the Southern Hemisphere   (MSC)
POLFA .... Polarforschung [*A publication*]
Pol Fedn Newsl ... Police Federation Newsletter   (DLA)
POLGEN..... Problem-Oriented Language Generator [*Data
     processing*]   (BUR)
POLI .... Postal Life [*A publication*]
POLIA......... Polimery [*A publication*]
POLIC........ Petroleum Intersectional Command   (AABC)
Police J ...... Police Journal [*A publication*]
Police Mag ... Police Magazine [*A publication*]
Police Mag (Syria) ... Police Magazine (Syria) [*A publication*]
Police Res Bull ... Police Research Bulletin [*A publication*]
Police Rev ... Police Review [*A publication*]
Police Sc Abs ... Police Science Abstracts [*A publication*]
Policlinico Sez Chir ... Policlinico. Sezione Chirurgica [*A publication*]
Policlinico Sez Med ... Policlinico. Sezione Medica [*A publication*]
Policlinico Sez Prat ... Policlinico. Sezione Practica [*A publication*]
Policy Anal ... Policy Analysis [*Later, Journal of Policy Analysis and
     Management*] [*A publication*]
Policy Pol ... Policy and Politics [*A publication*]
Policy Publ Rev ... Policy Publication Review [*England*] [*A publication*]
Policy Rev ... Policy Review [*A publication*]
Policy Sci ... Policy Sciences [*A publication*]
Policy Stud ... Policy Studies [*A publication*]
Policy Stud J ... Policy Studies Journal [*A publication*]
Policy Stud Rev ... Policy Studies Review [*A publication*]
POLID........ Power Line [*A publication*]
Poligr Promst Obz Inf ... Poligraficheskaya Promyshlennost. Obzornaya
     Informatsiya [*A publication*]
Polim Mashinostr ... Polimery v Mashinostroenii [*Ukrainian SSR*] [*A
     publication*]
Polim Mater Ikh Issled ... Polimernye Materialy i Ikh Issledovanie [*A
     publication*]
Polim Med ... Polimery w Medycynie [*A publication*]
Polim Medziagos Ju Tyrimas ... Polimerines Medziagos ir Ju Tyrimas [*A
     publication*]
Polim Medziagu Panaudojimas Liaudies Ukyje ... Polimeriniu Medziagu
     Panaudojimas Liaudies Ukyje [*A publication*]
Polim Sb Tr Nauchnoizsled Inst Kauch Plastmasova Promst ... Polimeri.
     Sbornik ot Trudove na Nauchnoizsledovatelskiya Institut
     po Kauchukova i Plastmasova Promishlenost [*A
     publication*]
Polim Sb Tr Nauchnoizsled Inst Prerabotka Plastmasi ... Polimeri. Sbornik
     ot Trudove na Nauchnoizsledovatelskiya Institut po
     Prerabotka na Plastmasi [*A publication*]
Polim Tworzwa ... Polimery Tworzywa [*Poland*] [*A publication*]
Polim Tworz Wielk ... Polimery Tworzywa Wielkoczasteczkowe [*Poland*] [*A
     publication*]
Polim Tworz Wielkoczast ... Polimery-Tworzywa Wielkoczasteczkowe [*A
     publication*]
Pol Inst Geol Bibliogr Geol Pol ... Poland. Instytut Geologiczny. Bibliografia
     Geologiczna Polski [*A publication*]
Pol Inst Meteorol Gospod Wodnej Pr ... Poland. Instytut Meteorologii i
     Gospodarki Wodnej. Prace [*A publication*]
POLIO .... Poliomyelitis [*Medicine*]
Poliplasti Mater Rinf ... Poliplasti e Materiali Rinforzati [*A publication*]
Poliplasti Plast Rinf ... Poliplasti e Plastici Rinforzati [*A publication*]
Poli Q .... Political Quarterly [*A publication*]
POLIS......... Parliamentary On-Line Information System [*House of
     Commons Library*] [*Bibliographic database*] [*Information
     service*] [*British*]   (EISS)
POLIS........ Petroleum Intersectional Service
POLIS........ Political Institutions Simulation [*Game*]
POLISARIO ... [*Frente*] Popular para la Liberacion de Saguia El Hamra y Rio
     De Oro [*Popular Front for the Liberation of Saguia El
     Hamra and Rio De Oro*] [*Western Sahara*]
Poli Sci....... Political Science [*A publication*]
Poli Sci Q ... Political Science Quarterly [*A publication*]
Polish Acad Sci Fluid Flow ... Polish Academy of Sciences. Transactions.
     Institute of Fluid Flow Machinery [*Warsaw*] [*A publication*]
Polish Am Stud ... Polish American Studies [*A publication*]
Polish F ...... Polish Film [*A publication*]
Polish J Chem ... Polish Journal of Chemistry [*A publication*]
Polish J Pharmacol Pharmacy ... Polish Journal of Pharmacology and
     Pharmacy [*A publication*]
Polish Mus ... Polish Music [*A publication*]
Polish Perspect ... Polish Perspectives [*A publication*]
Polish R...... Polish Review [*A publication*]
Polish Sociol B ... Polish Sociological Bulletin [*A publication*]

Polish Tech & Econ Abstr ... Polish Technical and Economic Abstracts [*A publication*]
Poli Societ ... Politics and Society [*A publication*]
POLIT .... Political
Polit Aff ...... Political Affairs [*A publication*]
Polit Aujourd ... Politique d'Aujourd'hui [*A publication*]
Polit Belge ... Politique Belge [*A publication*]
POLITBUREAU .... Political Bureau [*of USSR*]
POLITBURO ... Politicheskoe Byuro [*Political Bureau of USSR*]
Polit Dir ...... Politica del Diritto [*A publication*]
Politech Warsz Pr Inst Podstaw Konstr Masz ... Politechnika Warszawska. Prace Instytutu Podstaw Konstrukcji Maszyn [*A publication*]
Politech Warsz Pr Nauk Mech ... Politechnika Warszawska. Prace Naukowe. Mechanika [*A publication*]
Polit Eco .... Review of Radical Political Economics [*A publication*]
Polit Econ ... Politica ed Economia [*A publication*]
Polit ed Econ ... Politica ed Economia [*A publication*]
Polit Ekon ... Politicka Ekonomie [*A publication*]
Polit Etr ...... Politique Etrangere [*A publication*]
Polit Foisk Kozlem ... Politikai Foiskola Kozlemenyei [*A publication*]
Polit Gazdasag Tanulmany ... Politikai Gazdasagtan Tanulmanyok [*A publication*]
Politic St .... Political Studies - London [*A publication*]
Polit Int (Roma) ... Politica Internazionale (Roma) [*A publication*]
Polit Meinung ... Politische Meinung [*A publication*]
Polit Methodol ... Political Methodology [*A publication*]
Polit Perspect ... Politiek Perspectief [*A publication*]
Polit Q .... Political Quarterly [*A publication*]
Polit Quart ... Political Quarterly [*A publication*]
Polit Rdsch ... Politische Rundschau [*A publication*]
Polit Sci ..... Political Science [*A publication*]
Polit Sci Ann ... Political Science Annual [*A publication*]
Polit Scientist ... Political Scientist [*A publication*]
Polit Sci Q ... Political Science Quarterly [*A publication*]
Polit Sci R ... Political Science Review [*A publication*]
Polit Sci R-er ... Political Science Reviewer [*A publication*]
Polit Sci (Wellington) ... Political Science (Wellington) [*A publication*]
Polit and Soc ... Politics and Society [*A publication*]
Polit Soc Econ Rev ... Political, Social, Economic Review [*A publication*]
Polit Spolecz ... Polityka Spoleczna [*A publication*]
Polit Stud ... Politische Studien [*Muenchen*] [*A publication*]
Polit Theor ... Political Theory [*A publication*]
Polit Today ... Politics Today [*A publication*]
Polit Vjschr ... Politische Vierteljahresschrift [*A publication*]
Polit Vjschr Sonderh ... Politische Vierteljahresschrift. Sonderheft [*A publication*]
Polit u Zeitgesch ... Politik und Zeitgeschichte [*A publication*]
Pol J Chem ... Polish Journal of Chemistry [*A publication*]
Pol J Ecol ... Polish Journal of Ecology [*A publication*]
Poljopriv Pregl ... Poljoprivredni Pregled [*A publication*]
Poljopriv Sumar ... Poljoprivredna i Sumarstvo [*A publication*]
Poljopriv Znan Smotra ... Poljoprivredna Znanstvena Smotra [*A publication*]
Poljopr Sumar ... Poljoprivredna i Sumarstvo [*A publication*]
Poljopr Znan Smotra ... Poljoprivredna Znanstvena Smotra [*A publication*]
Poljopr Znanst Smotra ... Poljoprivredna Znanstvena Smotra [*A publication*]
Pol J Phar ... Polish Journal of Pharmacology and Pharmacy [*A publication*]
Pol J Pharmacol Pharm ... Polish Journal of Pharmacology and Pharmacy [*A publication*]
Pol J Soil Sci ... Polish Journal of Soil Science [*A publication*]
POLL .... Pollex [*An Inch*] [*Pharmacy*]
Poll .... Polonista (Lublin) [*A publication*]
Poll Abstr ... Pollution Abstracts [*A publication*]
Pollack Mihaly Muesz Foeisk Tud Koezl ... Pollack Mihaly Mueszaki Foeiskola Tudomanyos Koezlemenyei [*A publication*]
POLLD .... Pollimo [*A publication*]
Pollen Grain US For Serv Southeast Area ... Pollen Grain. United States Forest Service. Southeastern Area [*A publication*]
Pollock & Maitl ... Pollock and Maitland's History of English Common Law (DLA)
Pol LQ .... Police Law Quarterly (DLA)
POLLS .... Parliamentary On-Line Library Study [*Atomic Energy Authority*] [*British*]
Pollut Abstr ... Pollution Abstracts [*A publication*]
Pollut Atmos ... Pollution Atmospherique [*A publication*]
Pollut Control ... Pollution Control [*Japan*] [*A publication*]
Pollut Eng ... Pollution Engineering [*A publication*]
Pollut Eng Technol ... Pollution Engineering and Technology [*A publication*]
Pollution .... Pollution Equipment News [*A publication*]
Pollut Monitor ... Pollution Monitor [*A publication*]
Pollut Tech ... Pollution Technology [*A publication*]
POLLY .... [*A*] programing language [*1973*] (CSR)
Pol Mach Ind ... Polish Machine Industry [*A publication*]
Pol Med J ... Polish Medical Journal [*A publication*]
Pol Med Sci Hist Bull ... Polish Medical Science and History Bulletin [*A publication*]
Pol Methodol ... Political Methodology [*A publication*]
poln--- .... Central and Southern Line Islands [*MARC geographic area code*] [*Library of Congress*] (LCCP)
Polnohospod ... Polnohospodarstvo [*A publication*]
POLO .... Pacific Command Operations Liaison Office (AABC)

POLO .... Plant and Office Layout (MCD)
POLO .... Polar Orbiting Lunar Observatory [*Satellite*]
POLO .... Polaris Oil & Gas [*NASDAQ symbol*] (NQ)
Pologne Aff Occid ... Pologne et les Affaires Occidentales [*A publication*]
Pologne Contemp ... Pologne Contemporaine [*A publication*]
POLOPS .... Polynomial Operations [*Air Force*]
Pol'ovnicky Zb ... Pol'ovnicky Zbornik [*A publication*]
PolP .... Polish Perspectives [*A publication*]
Pol Perspect ... Polish Perspectives [*A publication*]
Pol Pismo Entomol ... Polskie Pismo Entomologiczne [*A publication*]
Pol Pismo Entomol Ser B Entomol Stosow ... Polskie Pismo Entomologiczne. Seria B. Entomologia Stosowana [*A publication*]
Pol and Polit ... Policy and Politics [*A publication*]
Pol Przegl Chir ... Polski Przeglad Chirurgiczny [*A publication*]
Pol Przegl Radiol ... Polski Przeglad Radiologii i Medycyny Nuklearnej [*A publication*]
Pol Przegl Radiol Med Nukl ... Polski Przeglad Radiologii i Medycyny Nuklearnej [*A publication*]
Pol Psych B ... Polish Psychological Bulletin [*A publication*]
Pol Q .... Political Quarterly [*A publication*]
Pol Quar ..... Political Quarterly [*A publication*]
Pol R .... Policy Review [*A publication*]
PolR .... Polish Review [*New York*] [*A publication*]
POLR .... Polymeric Resources [*NASDAQ symbol*] (NQ)
POLRA .... Polar Record [*A publication*]
Pol Rev Radiol Nucl Med ... Polish Review of Radiology and Nuclear Medicine [*A publication*]
Pol Sci .... Policy Sciences [*A publication*]
Pol Sci .... Political Science [*A publication*]
Pol Science Q ... Political Science Quarterly [*A publication*]
Pol Sci Q ... Political Science Quarterly [*A publication*]
Pol Sci R .... Political Science Review [*Jaipur*] [*A publication*]
Polska Akad Nauk Met ... Polska Akademia Nauk. Metalurgia [*A publication*]
Polska Akad Nauk Oddzial Krakowie Pr Kom Nauk Tech Ceram ... Polska Akademia Nauk. Oddzial w Krakowie. Prace Komisji Nauk Technicznych. Ceramika [*A publication*]
Polska Biblio Analit Mech ... Polska Bibliografia Analityczna. Mechanika [*A publication*]
Polska Gaz Lekar ... Polska Gazeta Lekarska [*A publication*]
Polskie Arch Med Wewnetrznej ... Polskie Archiwum Medycyny Wewnetrznej [*A publication*]
Polskie Archwm Wet ... Polskie Archiwum Weterynaryjne [*A publication*]
Polskie Pismo Entomol ... Polskie Pismo Entomologiczne [*A publication*]
Polskie Pismo Entomol Ser B Entomol Stosow ... Polskie Pismo Entomologiczne. Seria B. Entomologia Stosowana [*A publication*]
Pols Nat ..... Polson's Law of Nations [*1848*] (DLA)
Pol & Soc ... Politics and Society [*A publication*]
Pol Soc B ... Polish Sociological Bulletin [*A publication*]
Pol Stud ..... Political Studies [*A publication*]
Pol Studien ... Politische Studien [*Muenchen*] [*A publication*]
Pol Studies ... Political Studies [*A publication*]
Pol Stud J ... Policy Studies Journal [*A publication*]
Pol Szt Lud ... Polska Sztuka Ludowa [*A publication*]
Pol Tech Abstr ... Polish Technical Abstracts [*A publication*]
Pol Tech Econ Abstr ... Polish Technical and Economic Abstracts [*A publication*]
Pol Technol News ... Polish Technological News [*A publication*]
Pol Tech Rev ... Polish Technical Review [*A publication*]
Pol Theory ... Political Theory [*A publication*]
POLTHN ..... Polyethylene [*Organic chemistry*]
POLTL .... Political (AFM)
Pol Today ... Politics Today [*A publication*]
Pol Tow Entomol Klucze Oznaczania Owadow Pol ... Polskie Towarzystwo Entomologiczne. Klucze do Oznaczania Owadow Polski [*A publication*]
Pol Tow Geol Rocz ... Polskie Towarzystwo Geologiczne. Rocznik [*A publication*]
Pol Tyg Lek ... Polski Tygodnik Lekarski [*A publication*]
Pol Tyg Lek Wiad Lek ... Polski Tygodnik Lekarski i Wiadomosci Lekarskie [*A publication*]
Poluch Strukt Svoistva Sorbentov ... Poluchenie, Struktura, i Svoistva Sorbentov [*A publication*]
Poluch Svoistva Tonkikh Plenok ... Poluchenie i Svoistva Tonkikh Plenok [*Ukrainian SSR*] [*A publication*]
Poluprovdn Prib Tekh Elektrosvyazi ... Poluprovodnikovye Pribory v Tekhnike Elektrosvyazi [*A publication*]
Poluprovodn Ikh Primen Elektrotekh ... Poluprovodniki i Ikh Primenenie v Elektrotekhnike [*A publication*]
Poluprovodn Prib Ikh Primen ... Poluprovodnikovye Pribory i Ikh Primenenie [*A publication*]
Poluprovodn Prib Primen ... Poluprovodnikovye Pribory i Ikh Primenenie [*A publication*]
Poluprovodn Tekh Mikroehlektron ... Poluprovodnikovaya Tekhnika i Mikroehlektronika [*A publication*]
Poluprov Prib Ikh Primen Sb Statei ... Poluprovodnikovye Pribory i Ikh Primenenie. Sbornik Statei [*USSR*] [*A publication*]
Poluprov Tekh Mikroelektron ... Poluprovodnikovaya Tekhnika i Mikroehlektronika [*Ukrainian SSR*] [*A publication*]
POLUT .... Pollution

POLWAR .... Political Warfare
POLWARADDIR ... Political Warfare Advisory Directorate
POLXZ....... Polydex Chemicals [*NASDAQ symbol*]   (NQ)
Pol'y .... Policy   (DLA)
POLY .... Polyester
POLY .... Polyethylene   (DEN)
POLY .... Polygamy [*FBI standardized term*]
POLY .... Polymorphonuclear Leukocyte [*Medicine*]
POLY .... Polytechnic
POLY-AE/AM Rep (Polytech Inst NY Dep Aerosp Eng Appl Mech) ...
              POLY-AE/AM Report (Polytechnic Institute of New York.
              Department of Aerospace Engineering and Applied
              Mechanics) [*A publication*]
Polyarn Siyaniya Svechenie Nochnogo Neba ... Polyarnye Siyaniya i
              Svechenie Nochnogo Neba [*A publication*]
Polyar Siyaniya ... Polyarnye Siyaniya [*USSR*] [*A publication*]
Polyb......... Polybius [*Second century BC*] [*Classical studies*]   (OCD)
Pol Yb of Internat L ... Polish Yearbook of International Law [*Warsaw*]   (DLA)
Polyc .... [*Epistle of*] Polycarp   (BJA)
POLYEST... Polyester
Polym......... Polymusic [*Record label*]
Polym Age ... Polymer Age [*A publication*]
Polym Appl ... Polymer Application [*Japan*] [*A publication*]
Polym Bull ... Polymer Bulletin [*A publication*]
Polym Bull (Berlin) ... Polymer Bulletin (Berlin) [*A publication*]
Polym Commun ... Polymer Communications [*A publication*]
Polym Compos ... Polymer Composites [*A publication*]
Polym Engng Rev ... Polymer Engineering Reviews [*A publication*]
Polym Engng Sci ... Polymer Engineering and Science [*A publication*]
Polym Eng S ... Polymer Engineering and Science [*A publication*]
Polym Eng Sci ... Polymer Engineering and Science [*A publication*]
Polym Eng and Sci ... Polymer Engineering and Science [*A publication*]
Polymer J... Polymer Journal [*A publication*]
Polym J ...... Polymer Journal [*A publication*]
Polym Mech ... Polymer Mechanics [*A publication*]
Polym Monogr ... Polymer Monographs [*A publication*]
Polym News ... Polymer News [*A publication*]
POLYMODE ... Polygon-MODE [*Mid-Ocean Dynamics Experiment*] [*Soviet-
              US cooperative undersea weather exploration*]
Polym Paint Colour J ... Polymers, Paint, and Colour Journal [*A publication*]
Polym-Plast ... Polymer-Plastics Technology and Engineering [*A publication*]
Polym-Plast Technol Eng ... Polymer-Plastics Technology and Engineering
              [*A publication*]
Polym Prepr Am Chem Soc Div Polym Chem ... Polymer Preprints.
              American Chemical Society. Division of Polymer Chemistry
              [*A publication*]
Polym Preprints ... Polymer Preprints [*A publication*]
Polym Rep ... Polymer Report [*A publication*]
Polym Sci Technol ... Polymer Science and Technology [*A publication*]
Polym Sci USSR ... Polymer Science. USSR [*English Translation of
              Vysokomolekulyarnye Soyedineniya. Series A*] [*A
              publication*]
POLYN .... Polynesia
Polyn Soc J ... Polynesian Society Journal [*A publication*]
POLYOX..... Poly(ethylene Oxide) [*Trademark*]
Polysaccharides Biol Trans Conf ... Polysaccharides in Biology.
              Transactions of the Conference [*A publication*]
Polysar Prog ... Polysar Progress [*A publication*]
Polyscope Comput and Elektron ... Polyscope. Computer and Elektronik [*A
              publication*]
Polytech Inst Brooklyn Microwave Res Inst Symp Ser ... Polytechnic
              Institute of Brooklyn. Microwave Research Institute.
              Symposia Series [*A publication*]
Polytech Tijdschr Bouwk Wegen- & Waterbouw ... Polytechnisch Tijdschrift
              Bouwkune Wegen- en Waterbouw [*A publication*]
Polytech Tijdschr Ed A ... Polytechnisch Tijdschrift. Editie A.
              Werktuigbouwkunde en Elektrotechniek [*A publication*]
Polytech Tijdschr Ed B ... Polytechnisch Tijdschrift. Editie B [*A publication*]
Polytech Tijdschr Elektrotech Elektron ... Polytechnisch Tijdschrift.
              Elektrotechniek. Elektronica [*A publication*]
Polytech Tijdschr Procestech ... Polytechnisch Tijdschrift. Procestechniek
              [*A publication*]
Polytech Tijdschr Werktuigbouw ... Polytechnisch Tijdschrift.
              Werktuigbouw [*A publication*]
Polytech Weekbl ... Polytechnisch Weekblad [*A publication*]
Polytek Revy ... Polyteknisk Revy [*Norway*] [*A publication*]
POLYTRAN ... Polytranslation Analysis and Programing   (IEEE)
Polyt Rv...... Polytechnic Review [*A publication*]
POLYU .... PolyComputers, Inc. Uts [*NASDAQ symbol*]   (NQ)
POM .... Operation: Peace of Mind [*Later, Runaway Hotline*] [*An
              association*]   (EA)
POM .... Pallet-Only Mode [*NASA*]   (NASA)
POM .... Particulate Organic Matter [*Environmental chemistry*]
POM .... Personnel, Operations, Maintenance   (MCD)
POM .... Phenomenon of Man [*Project*]   (EA)
POM .... Police Officer, Male
POM .... Polycyclic Organic Matter
POM .... Poly(oxymethylene) [*Organic chemistry*]
POM .... Pomeranian Dog   (DSUE)
POM .... Pomona [*California*] [*Seismograph station code, US Geological
              Survey*] [*Closed*]   (SEIS)

POM .... Pomona, CA [*Location identifier*] [*FAA*]   (FAAL)
POM .... Pool Operational Module [*Telecommunications*]   (TEL)
POM .... Port Moresby [*Papua New Guinea*] [*Airport symbol*]   (OAG)
POM .... Position Modulator   (NRCH)
POM .... Potomac Electric Power Co. [*NYSE symbol*]
POM .... Preparation for Overseas Movement [*Military*]
POM .... Prescription Only Medicine [*British*]
POM .... Printer Output Microfilm
POM .... Priority of Movements [*Military*] [*British*]
POM .... Program Objectives Memorandum [*Military*]
POM .... Program Operation Mode
POM .... Project Office Memo
POMA .... Petty Officer's Military Academy [*Navy*]
POMAR ..... Position Operational, Meteorological Aircraft Report
POMAR ..... Preventive Operational Maintenance and Repair
              [*Military*]   (NVT)
POMAS ..... Procurement Office for Military Automotive Supplies
POM/BES ... Program Objective Memorandum/Budget Estimate
              Submission   (MCD)
POMC........ Parents of Murdered Children [*Formerly, PMC*] [*Cincinnati,
              OH*]   (EA)
POMC........ Pro-Opiomelanocortin [*Endocrinology*]
Pom Code Rem ... Pomeroy on Code Remedies   (DLA)
Pom Const Law ... Pomeroy's Constitutional Law of the United States   (DLA)
POMCUS.... Prepositioned Overseas Materiel Configured in Unit Sets
              [*Army*]   (AABC)
POMDA ..... Postgraduate Medicine [*A publication*]
POMDD ..... Poznanskie Roczniki Medyczne [*A publication*]
pome---..... Melanesia [*MARC geographic area code*] [*Library of
              Congress*]   (LCCP)
POME........ Prisoner of Mother England [*Nineteenth-century convict in
              penal colony of Australia; term is said to have been
              shortened eventually to "pom" or "pommie" as a
              nickname for any Australian. A second theory maintains
              that the nickname is short for "pomegranate," a red fruit,
              and refers to the sunburn that fair-skinned Englishmen
              quickly acquire upon arrival in Australia.*]
POME........ Problems-Objectives-Methods-Evaluation [*Planning method*]
Pom Eq Jur ... Pomeroy's Equity Jurisprudence   (DLA)
Pom Eq Juris ... Pomeroy's Equity Jurisprudence   (DLA)
POMERID ... Pomeridianus [*In the Afternoon*] [*Pharmacy*]
Pomeroy .... Pomeroy's Reports [*73-128 California*]   (DLA)
POMF .... Polaris Missile Facility
POMFLANT ... Polaris Missile Facility, Atlantic Fleet
POMFPAC ... Polaris Missile Facility, Pacific Fleet
POMGEN.... Program Objective Memorandum Generator [*Military*]
POMH........ National Association of Post Office Mail Handlers, Watchmen,
              Messengers, and Group Leaders [*Later, NPOMHWMGL*]
POMI .... Preliminary Operating and Maintenance Instructions
              [*Aerospace*]   (AAG)
Pomiary Autom Kontrola ... Pomiary Automatyka Kontrola [*A publication*]
POMINS ..... Portable Mine Neutralization System   (MCD)
POMJA....... Polish Medical Journal [*A publication*]
POMM .... Preliminary Operating and Maintenance Manual
              [*Military*]   (AABC)
Pomme Terre Fr ... Pomme de Terre Francaise [*A publication*]
POMO........ Production-Oriented Maintenance Organization   (MCD)
POMOL ...... POMCUS Objective Levels [*Military*]
POMOL ...... Pomology
POMOLA .... Poor Man's Optical Landing System
Pomol Fr .... Pomologie Francaise [*A publication*]
Pomol Fruit Grow Soc Annu Rep ... Pomological and Fruit Growing Society.
              Annual Report [*A publication*]
Pomp.......... Epistula ad Pompeium [*of Dionysius Halicarnassensis*]
              [*Classical studies*]   (OCD)
Pomp.......... Pompeius [*of Plutarch*] [*Classical studies*]   (OCD)
POMP......... Pomposo [*Grandly*] [*Music*]   (ROG)
POMP......... Prednisone, Oncovin [*Vincristine*], Methotrexate, Purinethol
              [*Mercaptopurine*] [*Antineoplastic drug regimen*]
POMP........ Principal Outer Membrane Protein
Pompebl .... Pompebledon [*A publication*]
POMR........ Problem-Oriented Medical Record
Pom Rem ... Pomeroy on Civil Remedies   (DLA)
Pom Rem & Rem Rights ... Pomeroy on Civil Remedies and Remedial
              Rights   (DLA)
POMR/PST ... Partido Obrero Marxista Revolucionario/Partido Socialista de
              los Trabajadores [*Marxist Revolutionary Workers' Party/
              Socialist Workers' Party*] [*Peruvian*]   (PPW)
POMS........ Panel on Operational Meteorological Satellites
POMS........ Profile of Mood States [*A questionnaire*]
POMSA ..... Post Office Management Staffs Association [*A union*] [*British*]
POMS-BI.... Profile of Mood States-Bipolar Form
POMSEE .... Performance, Operating and Maintenance Standards for
              Electronic Equipment   (NG)
POMSIP ..... Post Office Management and Service Improvement Program
              [*Obsolete*]
Pom Spec Perf ... Pomeroy on Specific Performance of Contracts   (DLA)
POMT........ Planning and Operations Management Team   (MCD)
POMV........ National Federation Post Office Motor Vehicle Employees
              [*Later, APWU*]   (EA)
POMV........ Privately Owned Motor Vehicle   (NATG)

PON........... Paraoxonase [*An enzyme*]
PON........... Particulate Organic Nitrogen
PON........... Ponce [*Puerto Rico*] [*Seismograph station code, US Geological Survey*]   (SEIS)
PON........... Ponder Oils Ltd. [*Toronto Stock Exchange symbol*]
Pon............ Ponte [*A publication*]
PON........... Pontoon   (AAG)
PON........... Pride of Newark [*Feigenspan beer*]
PON........... Program Opportunity Notice [*Energy Research and Development Administration*]
PONA........ Paraffins, Olefins, Naphthenes, Aromatics
PONBRG.... Pontoon Bridge   (MUGU)
POND........ Pondere [*By Weight*] [*Latin*]
POND........ Ponderosus [*Heavy*] [*Pharmacy*]
PONE........ Polar News. Japan Polar Research Association [*A publication*]
ponl---........ New Caledonia [*MARC geographic area code*] [*Library of Congress*]   (LCCP)
ponn---........ New Hebrides [*MARC geographic area code*] [*Library of Congress*]   (LCCP)
Po Now....... Poetry Now [*A publication*]
PONS........ Platt's Oilgram News Service
PONS........ Polar Notes [*A publication*]
PONS........ Profile of Nonverbal Sensitivity [*Psychology*]
PONSA....... Platt's Oilgram News Service [*A publication*]
PONSE....... Personnel of the Naval Shore Establishment [*Report*]   (NG)
PONSI....... Program of Noncollegiate Sponsored Instruction   (OICC)
Pont........... Epistulae ex Ponto [*of Ovid*] [*Classical studies*]   (OCD)
PONT......... Pontiac [*Automotive engineering*]
PONTA...... Popular New Titles from Abroad [*Book acquisition program for libraries*]
Ponte Riv M ... Ponte. Rivista Mensile di Politica e Letteratura [*A publication*]
Pontif Acad Sci Acta ... Pontificia Academia Scientiarum. Acta [*A publication*]
Pontif Acad Sci Comment ... Pontificia Academia Scientiarum. Commentarii [*A publication*]
Pontif Acad Sci Scr Varia ... Pontificia Academia Scientiarum. Scripta Varia [*A publication*]
ponu---........ Nauru [*MARC geographic area code*] [*Library of Congress*]   (LCCP)
PONUC...... Post Office National Users' Council [*British*]
PONY........ Prostitutes of New York
PONY........ Protect Our Nation's Youth [*Baseball league*] [*Name usually written Pony*]
PONY........ Purpose of Neighborhood Youth [*Foundation*]
PONYA...... Port of New York Authority [*Later, PANYNJ*]
POO........... Panel on Oceanography
POO........... Platforms of Opportunity [*Marine science*]   (MSC)
POO........... Pocos De Caldas [*Brazil*] [*Airport symbol*]   (OAG)
POO........... Poona [*India*] [*Seismograph station code, US Geological Survey*]   (SEIS)
POO........... Post Office Order
POO........... Priority Operational Objective [*Military*]
POO........... Program Operations Officer [*Social Security Administration*]
POOD........ Permanent Officer of the Day [*or Deck*] [*Navy*]
POOD........ Provisioning Order Obligating Document
POOFF...... Preservation of Our Femininity and Finances [*Women's group opposing below-the-knee fashions introduced in 1970*]
POOFF...... Professional Oglers of Female Figures [*Men's group opposing below-the-knee fashions introduced in 1970*]
Poona Agr Col Mag ... Poona Agricultural College Magazine [*A publication*]
Poona Agric Coll Mag ... Poona Agricultural College Magazine [*A publication*]
POOP........ Process Oriented Observation Program [*NORPAX*]   (MSC)
POOR........ Prevention of Over-Radiation [*Military*]
POOS........ Priority Order Output System [*Japan*]   (DIT)
POOW....... Petty Officer of the Watch [*Navy*]   (NVT)
POP........... Panoramic Office Planning
POP........... Parallel Output Platform
POP........... Parents of Punkers [*Long Beach, CA*]   (EA)
POP........... Paroxypropione [*or Paraoxypropiophenone*] [*Endocrinology*]
POP........... Partido de Orientacion Popular [*Popular Orientation Party*] [*Salvadoran*]   (PPW)
POP........... Pay One Price
POP........... Payload Optimized Program [*NASA*]   (KSC)
POP........... Peak Overpressure [*Nuclear energy*]   (NRCH)
POP........... Period of Performance   (MCD)
POP........... Perpendicular Ocean Platform [*Oceanography*]
POP........... Perpendicular to Orbit Plane [*NASA*]   (KSC)
POP........... Persistent Occipit Posterior [*A fetal position*] [*Obstetrics*]
POP........... Pharmacists in Ophthalmic Practice [*Philadelphia, PA*]   (EA)
POP........... Pipeline Outfit, Petroleum   (MCD)
POP........... Plasma Osmotic Pressure [*Medicine*]
POP........... Plaster of Paris
POP........... Point of Purchase [*Advertising*]
POP........... Pollution and Overpopulation
POP........... Pope & Talbot, Inc. [*NYSE symbol*]
Pop........... Popham's English King's Bench Reports [*1592-1627*]   (DLA)
POP........... Popondetta [*Papua New Guinea*] [*Seismograph station code, US Geological Survey*] [*Closed*]   (SEIS)
POP........... Popping [*Mining engineering*]
POP........... Popular

Pop........... Populare [*Record label*] [*Romania*]
POP........... Population   (AAG)
POP........... Population Division [*Census*]   (OICC)
POP........... Post Office Plan
POP........... Post Office Preferred
POP........... Post Office Preferred [*British*]
POP........... Posterior Odds Processing [*Weather forecasting*] [*National Science Foundation*]
POP........... Postoperative [*Medicine*]
POP........... Power On/Off Protection
POP........... Preburner Oxidizer Pump   (MCD)
POP........... Preflight Operations Procedure   (MCD)
POP........... Prelaunch Operations Plan [*NASA*]   (NASA)
POP........... Premanagement Orientation Program [*LIMRA*]
POP........... Pressurizer-over-Pressure Protection System   (IEEE)
POP........... Primary Operation
pop........... Printer of Plates [*MARC relator code*] [*Library of Congress*]
POP........... Printing-Out Paper
POP........... Profit Option Plan [*Retailing*]
POP........... Program Obligation Plan   (KSC)
POP........... Program Operating Plan
POP........... Programed Operators and Primitives [*Data processing*]
POP........... Project Objective Plan   (NG)
POP........... Prompt Ordering Plan
POP........... Proof-Of Principle [*Test*]
POP........... Proof of Purchase
POP........... Puerto Plata [*Dominican Republic*] [*Airport symbol*]   (OAG)
POP........... Pump Optimizing Program
POPA........ Patent Office [*later, PTO*] Professional Association
POPA........ Pet Owners' Protective Association
POPA........ Property Owners' Protection Association
POPAE....... Protons on Protons and Electrons [*Physics*]
POPAI....... Point-of-Purchase Advertising Institute [*Fort Lee, NJ*]   (EA)
Pop Astron ... Popular Astronomy [*A publication*]
Pop B .... Population Bulletin [*A publication*]
POP & B .... Proposed Operating Program and Budget [*Army*]
Pop Bul ...... Population Bulletin [*A publication*]
Pop Bull Colo State Univ Agr Exp Sta ... Popular Bulletin. Colorado State University. Agricultural Experiment Station [*A publication*]
popc---....... Pitcairn [*MARC geographic area code*] [*Library of Congress*]   (LCCP)
Pop Comput ... Popular Computing [*A publication*]
POP-CON... Populist Conservative [*Wing of the Republican Party represented by Congressmen Gingrich, Kemp, and Lott*]
POPD .... Power-Operated
POPDA....... Polish Psychological Bulletin [*A publication*]
POPDA....... Polyoxypropylenediamine [*Organic chemistry*]
Pop Dev R ... Population and Development Review [*New York*] [*A publication*]
POPE......... Parents for Orthodoxy in Parochial Education [*Group opposing sex education in schools*]
Pope Cust ... Pope on Customs and Excise [*11th ed.*] [*1828*]   (DLA)
Pop Educ ... Popular Educator [*A publication*]
Pop Electr ... Popular Electronics [*A publication*]
Pope Lun.... Pope on Lunacy   (DLA)
Pop Gard.... Popular Gardening [*A publication*]
Pop Govt.... Popular Government [*A publication*]
POPGUN .... Policy and Procedure Governing the Use of Nicknames [*Army*]   (AABC)
Poph.......... Popham's English King's Bench Reports [*1592-1627*]   (DLA)
Poph (2)..... Cases at the End of Popham's Reports   (DLA)
Popham ..... Popham's English King's Bench Reports [*79 English Reprint*] [*1592-1626*]   (DLA)
POPI.......... Fast Food Operators [*NASDAQ symbol*]   (NQ)
POPI.......... Post Office Position Indicator [*A form of long-range position indicator*] [*British*]
Pop Index... Population Index [*A publication*]
POPINFORM ... Population Information Network [*UNESCO*]
POPINS ...... Population Information System [*UNESCO*]
POPLAB..... International Program of Laboratories for Population Statistics
POPLER ..... [*A*] programing language   (CSR)
POPLINE.... Population Information On-Line [*Population Information Program, Johns Hopkins University*] [*Bibliographic database*]   (EISS)
POPLIT....... Popliteal [*Anatomy*]
Pop Mech... Popular Mechanics [*A publication*]
Pop Mech... Popular Mechanics Magazine [*A publication*]
Pop Med (Tokyo) ... Popular Medicine (Tokyo) [*A publication*]
POPMIP...... Portable Ocean Platform Motion Instrumentation Package [*Marine science*]   (MSC)
Pop Mo L Tr ... Popular Monthly Law Tracts [*1877-78*]   (DLA)
Pop Mus Per Ind ... Popular Music Periodicals Index [*A publication*]
Pop Mus & Soc ... Popular Music and Society [*A publication*]
POPO .... Polar Post. Polar Postal History Society of Great Britain [*A publication*]
POPO .... Push-On, Pull-Off [*Data processing*]
POPOA....... Phosphorus and Potassium [*A publication*]
POPPD....... Plant/Operations Progress [*A publication*]
Pop Per Ind ... Popular Periodical Index [*A publication*]
Pop Phot .... Popular Photography [*A publication*]
Pop Photog ... Popular Photography [*A publication*]

Pop Plast.... Popular Plastics [*A publication*]
Pop Plast Annu ... Popular Plastics Annual [*A publication*]
POPR........ Pilot Overhaul Provisioning Review
POPR........ Prototype Organic Power Reactor
POPS......... Free-Fall Pop-Up Ocean Bottom Seismometer [*Marine science*]   (MSC)
POPS........ Pantograph Optical Projection System   (IEEE)
POPS........ Parachute Opening Proximity Sensor   (MCD)
POPS......... People Opposed to Pornography in Schools [*Group opposing sex education in schools*]
POPS......... Platt's Oilgram Price Service
pops---...... Polynesia [*MARC geographic area code*] [*Library of Congress*]   (LCCP)
POPS......... Preserve Our Presidential Sites   (EA)
POPS......... Pressurizer Overpressure Protection System [*Nuclear energy*]   (NRCH)
POPS......... Process Operating System [*Toshiba Corp.*] [*Japan*]
POPS......... Procurers of Painted-Label Sodas   (EA)
POPS......... Program for Operator Scheduling [*Bell System computer program*]
POPS......... Project Operations [*Navy*]   (NVT)
POPS......... Pyrotechnic Optical Plume Simulator   (MCD)
Pop Sci .... Popular Science Monthly [*A publication*]
POP SCI MO ... Popular Science Monthly [*A publication*]   (ROG)
Pop Sci (Peking) ... Popular Science (Peking) [*A publication*]
Pop Sci R ... Popular Science Review [*A publication*]
POPSE .... Project Office for Physical Security Equipment [*Army*]   (RDA)
POPSER..... Polaris Operational Performance Surveillance Engineering Report [*Missiles*]
POPSI........ Precipitation and Off-Path Scattered Interference [*Report*] [*FCC*]
POPSIPT .... Project Operations in Port [*Navy*]   (NVT)
Pop Stud.... Population Studies [*London*] [*A publication*]
Pop Stud (Lo) ... Population Studies (London) [*A publication*]
Pop Stud (NY) ... Population Studies (New York) [*A publication*]
POPT........ Pretesting Orientation or Purpose of Testing [*US Employment Service*] [*Department of Labor*]
Population R ... Population Review [*A publication*]
Popul et Avenir ... Population et Avenir [*A publication*]
Popul Bull ... Population Bulletin [*A publication*]
Popul Bull UN Econ Comm West Asia ... Population Bulletin. United Nations Economic Commission for Western Asia [*A publication*]
Popul B UN Econ Com West Asia ... Population Bulletin. United Nations Economic Commission for Western Asia [*A publication*]
Popul Counc Annu Rep ... Population Council. Annual Report [*A publication*]
Popul et Famille ... Population et Famille [*A publication*]
Popul et Famille/Bevolk en Gezin ... Population et Famille/Bevolking en Gezin [*A publication*]
Popul Forum ... Population Forum [*A publication*]
Popul Ind ... Population Index [*A publication*]
Popul Newsl ... Population Newsletter [*A publication*]
Popul Rep (A) ... Population Reports. Series A. Oral Contraceptives [*A publication*]
Popul Rep (B) ... Population Reports. Series B. Intrauterine Devices [*A publication*]
Popul Rep (D) ... Population Reports. Series D. Sterilization (Male) [*A publication*]
Popul Rep (G) ... Population Reports. Series G. Prostaglandins [*A publication*]
Popul Rep (H) ... Population Reports. Series H. Barrier Methods [*A publication*]
Popul Rep (I) ... Population Reports. Series I. Periodic Abstinence [*A publication*]
Popul Rep (J) ... Population Reports. Series J. Family Planning Programs [*A publication*]
Popul Rep (K) ... Population Reports. Series K. Injectables and Implants [*A publication*]
Popul Rep (L) ... Population Reports. Series L. Issues in World Health [*A publication*]
Popul Rep (M) ... Population Reports. Series M. Special Topics [*A publication*]
Popul Rep Spec Top Monogr ... Population Reports. Special Topics. Monographs [*A publication*]
Popul Rev... Population Review [*A publication*]
Popul et Societes ... Population et Societes [*A publication*]
Popul Stud ... Population Studies [*A publication*]
POPUS .... Post Office Processing Utility Subsystem [*Telecommunications*]   (TEL)
POPYA ...... Portugaliae Physica [*A publication*]
POQ........... Production Offset Quantity [*Military*]
POQ........... Provided Otherwise Qualified [*Military*]   (AABC)
POQ........... Public Opinion Quarterly [*A publication*]
POQ........... Push Off Quickly [*i.e., Be quick about it*] [*British*]
POR........... Parking Orbit Rendezvous [*NASA*]   (MCD)
POR........... Partido Obrero Revolucionario [*Revolutionary Workers Party*] [*Peruvian*]
POR........... Partido Obrero Revolucionario [*Revolutionary Workers Party*] [*Bolivian*]   (PPW)
POR........... Partido Obrero Revolucionario [*Revolutionary Workers Party*] [*Argentina*]
POR........... Patent Office Reports   (DLA)

POR............ Patrol Operations Report
POR............ Pay on Return [*Business and trade*]
POR............ Payable on Receipt [*Business and trade*]
POR............ Periodic Operation Report
POR............ Personnel Occurrence Report [*RAF*] [*British*]
POR............ Pilot Opinion Rating
POR............ Plutonium Organic Recycle [*Nuclear energy*]   (NRCH)
PoR............ Poetry Review [*London*] [*A publication*]
POR............ Pola Resources Ltd. [*Vancouver Stock Exchange symbol*]
POR............ Pori [*Finland*] [*Airport symbol*]   (OAG)
POR............ Port of Refuge [*Shipping*]
POr............ Porta Orientale [*A publication*]
POR............ Portec, Inc. [*NYSE symbol*]
POR............ Portion
POR............ Portland [*Maine*] [*Seismograph station code, US Geological Survey*] [*Closed*]   (SEIS)
POR............ Portrait
Por............. Portugale [*A publication*]
por............. Portuguese [*MARC language code*] [*Library of Congress*]   (LCCP)
POR............ Portuguese
POR............ Post Office Rifles [*Military*] [*British*]   (ROG)
POR............ Preparation of Overseas Replacement [*Military*]   (RDA)
POR............ Press on Regardless [*Automotive marathon*]
POR............ Price on Request
POR............ Problem-Oriented Records [*Medicine*]
POR............ Problem-Oriented Routine [*IEEE*]
POR............ Project Officers Report   (MCD)
POR............ Psychotherapy Outcome Research
POR............ Purchase Order Request
PORAC........ Peace Officers Research Association of California
PORACC ... Principles of Radiation and Contamination Control
PORB......... Production Operations Review Board [*NASA*]   (NASA)
PORC .... Partido Obrero Revolucionario-Combate [*Revolutionary Struggle Workers' Party*] [*Bolivian*]   (PPW)
PORC .... Plant Operations Review Committee [*Nuclear energy*]   (NRCH)
PORC .... Porcelain   (AAG)
PORCD........ Population Reports. Series C [*United States*] [*A publication*]
PORCN........ Production Order Records Change Notice   (KSC)
PORCO...... Port Control Office
PORD .... Performance and Operations Requirements Document [*NASA*]   (NASA)
PORDA...... Personnel Officers of Research and Development Agencies
PORDB....... Ports and Dredging [*A publication*]
PORDIR...... Port Director
PORE.......... Point Reyes National Seashore [*National Park Service designation*]
PORE.......... Polar Record [*A publication*]
POREA .... Post Office Regional Employees' Association [*Defunct*]   (EA)
POREP .... Position Report [*Air Force*]
PORES .... Purchase Order Receiving System   (MCD)
Porg .... Person of Restricted Growth [*Lifestyle classification*] [*Slang term used to describe a person of limited cultural awareness*]
PORGIE...... Paperback Original [*Award for best original paperback books of the year*]
PORI........... Polaris Operational Readiness Instrumentation [*Missiles*]
PORK .... Sooner State Farms [*NASDAQ symbol*]   (NQ)
PORLA ...... Practica Oto-Rhino-Laryngologica [*A publication*]
PORM......... Plus or Minus
PORN .... Pornography   (DSUE)
PORN .... Protect Our Responsibilities Now [*Book title*]
PORNO...... Pornography   (DSUE)
Poroshk Metall ... Poroshkovaya Metallurgiya [*A publication*]
Poroshk Metall (Kiev) ... Poroshkovaya Metallurgiya (Kiev) [*A publication*]
Poroshk Metall (Kuibyshev) ... Poroshkovaya Metallurgiya (Kuibyshev) [*A publication*]
Porosh Met ... Poroshkovaya Metallurgiya [*A publication*]
PORP......... Partial Ossicular Replacement Prosthesis
Porph .... Porphyry [*Third century AD*] [*Classical studies*]   (OCD)
PORR......... Preliminary Operations Requirements Review [*NASA*]   (NASA)
PORR......... Purchase Order Revision Request
PORS.......... Polar Research [*A publication*]
PORS.......... Product Output Reporting System
PORS.......... Publications in Operations Research Series [*Elsevier Book Series*] [*A publication*]
PORSE .... Post Overhaul Reaction Safeguard Examination [*Navy*]   (NVT)
PORT......... Photo-Optical Recorder Tracker
PORT......... Portable   (KSC)
PORT......... Porter   (DSUE)
Port .... Porter's Alabama Supreme Court Reports [*1834-39*]   (DLA)
Port .... Porter's Indiana Reports [*3-7 Indiana*]   (DLA)
PORT........ Portland Railroad
PORT......... Portmanteau   (DSUE)
PORT......... Portrait
PORT......... Portugal
Port .... Portugale [*A publication*]
PORT......... Prescriptive Objective Reference Testing [*Vocational guidance*]
Port Acta Biol A ... Portugaliae Acta Biologica. A. Morfologia, Fisiologia, Genetica, e Biologia Geral [*A publication*]

Port Acta Biol Ser A ... Portugaliae Acta Biologica. Serie A [*A publication*]
Port Acta Biol Ser B ... Portugaliae Acta Biologica. Serie B [*A publication*]
PORTAL ..... Process-Oriented Real-Time Algorithmic Language [*1978*] [*Data processing*] (CSR)
Port (Ala) ... Porter's Alabama Reports (DLA)
Port Ala R ... Porter's Alabama Reports (DLA)
PORTAPAK ... Portable, Self-Contained, Instrument Package
Porter .... Porter's Alabama Reports (DLA)
Porter .... Porter's Indiana Reports [*3-7 Indiana*] (DLA)
Porter (Ala) ... Porter's Alabama Reports (DLA)
Porter R ...... Porter's Alabama Reports (DLA)
Porter's Ala R ... Porter's Alabama Reports (DLA)
Porter's R ... Porter's Alabama Reports (DLA)
Porter's Repts ... Porter's Alabama Reports (DLA)
Portfo .... Portfolio [*A publication*]
Portfo (Den) ... Portfolio (Dennie's) [*A publication*]
Port Gazette ... Melbourne Harbour Trust Port Gazette [*A publication*]
Portia L J ... Portia Law Journal [*A publication*]
Port Ins ..... Porter's Laws of Insurance (DLA)
Port Lab Nac Eng Civ Mem ... Portugal. Laboratorio Nacional de Engenharia Civil. Memoria [*A publication*]
Portland Cem Ass Advanced Eng Bull ... Portland Cement Association. Advanced Engineering Bulletin [*A publication*]
Portland Cem Ass J PCA Res Develop Lab ... Portland Cement Association. Journal of the PCA Research and Development Laboratories [*A publication*]
Portland Soc N H Pr ... Portland Society of Natural History. Proceedings [*A publication*]
Portland UL Rev ... Portland University. Law Review (DLA)
Port Melb ... Port of Melbourne [*A publication*]
Port Melbourne Quart ... Port of Melbourne Quarterly [*A publication*]
Port of Melbourne Quart ... Port of Melbourne Quarterly [*A publication*]
Port Melb Q ... Port of Melbourne Quarterly [*A publication*]
Port of Melb Q ... Port of Melbourne Quarterly [*A publication*]
Port of Melb Quart ... Port of Melbourne Quarterly [*A publication*]
Port Minist Ultramar Junta Invest Ultramar Mem Ser Antropol ... Portugal. Ministerio do Ultramar. Junta de Investigacoes do Ultramar. Memorias. Serie Antropologica e Etnologica [*A publication*]
Port Minist Ultramar Junta Invest Ultramar Mem Ser Botanica ... Portugal. Ministerio do Ultramar. Junta de Investigacoes do Ultramar. Memorias. Serie Botanica [*A publication*]
Port Minist Ultramar Junta Invest Ultramar Mem Ser Geol ... Portugal. Ministerio do Ultramar. Junta de Investigacoes do Ultramar. Memorias. Serie Geologica [*A publication*]
PORTN .... Portion (ROG)
PORTP .... Partido Obrero Revolucionaria Trotskista Posadista [*Bolivian*] (PPW)
Port P .... Portuguese Pharmacopoeia [*A publication*]
Port Phillip Gaz ... Port Phillip Gazette [*A publication*]
Port Phy ..... Portugaliae Physica [*A publication*]
Port Phys ... Portugaliae Physica [*A publication*]
Port R .... Portland Review [*A publication*]
PORTREP ... Port [*or Anchorage*] Capacity Report [*Navy*] (NVT)
PORTS ...... Portsmouth [*City in England*]
Ports Dredging Oil Rep ... Ports and Dredging and Oil Report [*A publication*]
Port Serv Fom Min Estud Notas Trab ... Portugal. Servico de Fomento Mineiro. Estudos, Notas, e Trabalhos [*A publication*]
Port Serv Geol Mem ... Portugal. Servicos Geologicos. Memoria [*A publication*]
PORTSREP ... Ports Report File (MCD)
PORTSUM ... Port [*or Anchorage*] Summary Report [*Navy*] (NVT)
Port of Syd ... Port of Sydney [*A publication*]
Port Syd ..... Port of Sydney [*A publication*]
Port of Sydney J ... Port of Sydney Journal [*A publication*]
Portug Acta Biol ... Portugaliae Acta Biologica [*A publication*]
Portugal Math ... Portugaliae Mathematica [*A publication*]
Portugal Phys ... Portugaliae Physica [*A publication*]
Port UL Rev ... Portland University. Law Review (DLA)
PORV .... Pilot-Operated Relief Valve [*Nuclear energy*] (NRCH)
PORV .... Power-Operated Relief Valve [*Nuclear energy*] (NRCH)
PORX .... Porex Technologies [*NASDAQ symbol*] (NQ)
POS .... Pacific Ocean Ship (NASA)
POS .... Pacific Orchid Society of Hawaii (EA)
POS .... Parent Operating Service (MCD)
POS .... Patent Office Society (EA)
POS .... Peacetime Operating Stock [*Military*] (CINC)
POS .... Period of Service
POS .... Photo Optic System
POS .... Pico Resources [*Vancouver Stock Exchange symbol*]
POS .... Plan of Service (OICC)
POS .... Plant Operating System [*Nuclear energy*] (NRCH)
P-O-S .... Point-of-Sale
POS .... Point-of-Sale Terminal [*Data transmission*] (TSSD)
POS .... Polycystic Ovarian Syndrome [*Also, PCOS*] [*Gynecology*]
POS .... Port Of Spain [*Trinidad and Tobago*] [*Airport symbol*] (OAG)
POS .... Portable Oxygen System (MCD)
POS .... Position (KSC)
POS .... Positive (AFM)
Pos .... Possible
POS .... Post Office Scheme [*Regulations*] [*British*]

POS .... Preferred Overseas Shore Duty
POS .... Pretoria Oriental Series [*A publication*]
POS .... Primary Operating System (IEEE)
POS .... Primary Oxygen System
POS .... Problem Oriented System
POS .... Program Order Sequence
POS .... Protein, Oil, and Starch [*Pilot manufacturing plant established by the Canadian government*]
POS .... Pupil Observation Survey [*Education*]
POS .... Purchase Order Supplement
POSA .... Patriotic Order Sons of America
POSA .... Payment Outstanding Suspense Accounts (NATG)
POSA .... Preliminary Operating Safety Analysis [*Nuclear energy*] (NRCH)
POSARS ..... Plan of Service Automated Reporting System [*Employment and Training Administration*] [*Department of Labor*]
POSB .... Polish Sociological Bulletin [*A publication*]
POSB .... Post Office Savings Bank
posc--- ...... Santa Cruz Islands [*MARC geographic area code*] [*Library of Congress*] (LCCP)
P & OSCC ... Plans and Operations for the Safeguard Communications Command [*Army*] (RDA)
POSCH ...... Program of Surgical Control of Hyperlipidemia
POSCOR .... Position Correct (CAAL)
POSD .... Personnel on Station Date [*Army*] (AABC)
POSD .... Program for Optical System Design
POSD .... Project Operation Support Division [*NASA*]
POSDCORB ... Planning, Organizing, Staffing, Directing, Coordinating, Reporting, and Budgeting [*Principles of management*]
POSDSPLT ... Positive Displacement
POSE .... Parents Opposed to Sex Education
POSE .... Photogrammetric Ocean Survey Equipment
POSE .... Power Operational Support Equipment
Posebna Izdan ... Posebna Izdanja [*A publication*]
Posebna Izd Biol Inst N R Srb Beograd ... Posebna Izdanja Bioloski Institut N R Srbije Beograd [*A publication*]
Posebna Izd Geol Glas (Sarajevo) ... Posebna Izdanja Geoloskog Glasnika (Sarajevo) [*A publication*]
Posey UC ... Texas Unreported Cases (DLA)
Posey Unrep Cas ... Posey's Unreported Cases [*Texas*] (DLA)
POSH .... Permuted on Subject Headings [*Indexing technique*]
POSH .... Personal & Organizational Security Handbook [*A publication*]
POSH .... Port Outwardbound, Starboard Homewardbound [*Some claim that this acronym describes the location of shaded cabins on ships carrying British officers to the Far East and back. Many etymologists, however, believe that the origin of the word "posh" is unknown*]
posh .... Samoa Islands [*MARC geographic area code*] [*Library of Congress*] (LCCP)
POSI .... Positech Corp. [*NASDAQ symbol*] (NQ)
POSID .... Polyarnye Siyaniya [*A publication*]
POSIP .... Portable Ship's Instrumentation Package
POSIT .... Position (NVT)
POSIT .... Positive
POSIT .... Positivism (ROG)
POSITREPS ... Position Reports
POSITRON ... Positive Electron
POSKP .... Polski Osrodek Spoleczno-Kulturalny Posk [*Polish Social and Cultural Association - PSCA*] [*London, England*] (EA-IO)
POsi .... Papyri Osloenses [*A publication*] (OCD)
POSL .... Posi-Seal International [*NASDAQ symbol*] (NQ)
PosLuth ..... Positions Lutheriennes [*Paris*] [*A publication*]
POSM .... National Association of Post Office and General Service Maintenance Employees [*Later, APWU*] [*AFL-CIO*]
POSM .... Patient-Operated Selector Mechanism [*Pronounced "possum"*]
POSMA ...... Postal Service Manual [*A publication*]
POSN .... Position (AFM)
posn--- .... Solomon Islands [*MARC geographic area code*] [*Library of Congress*] (LCCP)
POSNA .... Pediatric Orthopaedic Society of North America [*Formed by a merger of Pediatric Orthopaedic Society and Pediatric Orhtopaedic Study Group*] [*Richmond, VA*] (EA)
POS/NAV ... Position/Navigation [*System*] [*Military*] (INF)
P & OSNCo ... Peninsular & Oriental Steam Navigation Company [*Steamship line*]
POSR .... Peacetime Operating Stock Requirement [*Military*] (AFIT)
POS R .... Positive Review [*A publication*] (ROG)
POSRIP ...... People Organized to Stop Rape of Imprisoned Persons [*Napa, CA*] (EA)
POSS .... Palomar Observatory Sky Survey [*NASA*]
POSS .... Passive Optical Satellite Surveillance [*System*] (NATG)
POSS .... Photo-Optical Surveillance Subsystem
POSS .... Portable Oceanographic Survey System (MCD)
POSS .... Possession (AFM)
POSS .... Possessive (ROG)
POSS .... Possible
POSS .... Possis Corp. [*NASDAQ symbol*] (NQ)
POSS .... Prototype Optical Surveillance System
POSS .... Proximal Over-Shoulder Strap [*Medicine*]

POSSE .... Parents Opposed to Sex and Sensitivity Education [*An association*]
POSSE .... Police Operations Systems Support System Elementary
POSSE .... Progressive Onslaught to Stamp out Stock Errors [*Navy*]   (NG)
POSSED..... Possessed   (ROG)
Posselt's Text J ... Posselt's Textile Journal [*A publication*]
POSSLQ..... Persons of Opposite Sex Sharing Living Quarters
POSSON..... Possession
POSSUB..... Possible Submarine [*Navy*]   (NVT)
POSSUM.... Polar Orbiting Satellite System - University of Michigan [*Designed by engineering students*]
Post........... De Posteritate Caini [*of Philo*]   (BJA)
POST......... Passive Optical Scan Tracker   (MCD)
POST......... Passive Optical Seeker Technique
POST......... Payload Operations Support Team [*NASA*]   (MCD)
POST......... Peace Officer Standards and Training
POST......... Piezoelectric-Oscillator Self-Tuned [*Electric system*]
POST......... Point-of-Sale Transaction
POST......... Polaris Operation Support Task Group [*Missiles*]
POST......... Polymer Science and Technology [*A publication*]
POST......... Positive   (AAG)
POST......... [*The*] Poster [*A publication*]   (ROG)
post........... Posterior
Post........... Post's Reports [*42-64 Missouri*]   (DLA)
Post........... Post's Reports [*23-26 Michigan*]   (DLA)
POST......... Power-On Self Test [*IBM-PC feature*]
POST......... Production-Oriented Scheduling Techniques   (MCD)
POST......... Program to Optimize Shuttle [*or Simulated*] Trajectories [*NASA*]   (KSC)
POST......... Programer Operating Standards Technique
POST-A...... Population Studies [*A publication*]
Postal Bull ... Postal Bulletin. Weekly [*A publication*]
Postal Bull US Postal Serv ... Postal Bulletin. United States Postal Service [*A publication*]
Postal Spvr ... Postal Supervisor [*A publication*]
POST AUR ... Post Aurem [*Behind the Ear*] [*Pharmacy*]
PostB .... Postilla Bohemica [*A publication*]
Post Bioch ... Postepy Biochemii [*A publication*]
Postdiplom Sem Fiz ... Postdiplomski Seminar iz Fizike [*A publication*]
Postdiplom Sem Mat ... Postdiplomski Seminar iz Matematike [*A publication*]
Post Dir ...... Post's Paper Mill Directory [*A publication*]
POSTE .... Postage   (ROG)
Postepy Astron ... Postepy Astronomii [*A publication*]
Postepy Astronaut ... Postepy Astronautyki [*A publication*]
Postepy Biochem ... Postepy Biochemii [*A publication*]
Postepy Biol Komorki ... Postepy Biologii Komorki [*A publication*]
Postepy Fiz ... Postepy Fizyki [*A publication*]
Postepy Fizjol ... Postepy Fizjologii [*A publication*]
Postepy Fiz Med ... Postepy Fizyki Medycznej [*A publication*]
Postepy Hig Med Dosw ... Postepy Higieny i Medycyny Doswiadczalnej [*A publication*]
Postepy Mikrobiol ... Postepy Mikrobiologii [*A publication*]
Postepy Nauk Roln ... Postepy Nauk Rolniczych [*A publication*]
Postepy Tech Jad ... Postepy Techniki Jadroweki [*A publication*]
Postepy Technol Masz Urzadz ... Postepy Technologii Maszyn i Urzadzen [*A publication*]
POSTER..... Post Strike Emergency Reporting
Poste's Gaius Inst ... Poste's Translation of Gaius   (DLA)
Poste Telecommun ... Poste e Telecommunicazioni [*A publication*]
POSTFAT... Postfinal Acceptance Trials [*Navy*]   (NVT)
Postg Med J ... Postgraduate Medical Journal [*A publication*]
Postgrad Courses Pediatr ... Postgraduate Courses in Pediatrics [*A publication*]
Postgrad Med ... Postgraduate Medicine [*A publication*]
Postgrad Med J ... Postgraduate Medical Journal [*A publication*]
Postgrad Med J Suppl ... Postgraduate Medical Journal. Supplement [*A publication*]
Postgrad Med Ser ... Postgraduate Medicine Series [*A publication*]
Postgr Med ... Postgraduate Medicine [*A publication*]
POSTH .... Posthumous
Post Harvest Technol Cassava ... Post Harvest Technology of Cassava [*A publication*]
POST-J ...... Polymer Science and Technology - Journals [*A publication*]
Postmasters Adv ... Postmasters Advocate [*A publication*]
Post-Medieval Arch ... Post-Medieval Archaeology [*A publication*]
Post-Medieval Archaeol ... Post-Medieval Archaeology [*A publication*]
Post O E E J ... Post Office Electrical Engineers. Journal [*A publication*]
Post Office Hist Soc Trans ... Post Office Historical Society. Transactions [*Queensland*] [*A publication*]
POSTOP..... Postoperative [*Medicine*]
POST-P...... Polymer Science and Technology - Patents [*A publication*]
POSTP ...... Posterior Probability [*Computations*]
POSTPRO ... Postprocessor [*Computer*] [*Coast Guard*]
Post & Reg ... Postage and Registration   (DLA)
Post Scr ..... Post Script [*A publication*]
POST SING SED LIQ ... Post Singulas Sedes Liquidas [*After Every Loose Stool*] [*Pharmacy*]
POSWa....... Pozprawy Komisji Orientalistycznej Towarzystwa Naukowego Warszawskiego [*A publication*]
POSWG ...... Poseidon Software Working Group [*Missiles*]

POT .... Parallel Output
POT .... Pennsylvania-Ontario Transportation Co. [*AAR code*]
POT .... Piston Operated Transducer
POT .... Pitch-Orthogonal Thrust
POT .... Plain Old Telephone [*Bell System's basic model*]
Po T .... Poetics Today [*A publication*]
POT .... Port Antonio [*Jamaica*] [*Airport symbol*]   (OAG)
POT .... Portable Outside Toilet [*A unit of mobility equipment*] [*Military*]
POT .... Potable
POT .... Potassium [*Chemical symbol is K*]
POT .... Potato   (ROG)
POT .... Potentate
POT .... Potential   (AFM)
POT .... Potentiometer
Pot............ Potion
POT .... Potsdam [*German Democratic Republic*] [*Seismograph station code, US Geological Survey*]   (SEIS)
POT .... Potsdam [*German Democratic Republic*] [*Later, NGK*] [*Geomagnetic observatory code*]
POT .... Pottle [*Unit of measure*]   (ROG)
POT .... Pottsville Free Public Library, Pottsville, PA [*OCLC symbol*]   (OCLC)
POT .... Potus [*A Drink*] [*Pharmacy*]
POT .... Prevailing-Out Torque [*Automotive engineering*]
POT .... Princess of Tasmania [*Ferry between the Mainland Australia and Tasmania*]   (DSUE)
PotAGT ...... Potential Abnormality of Glucose Tolerance [*Medicine*]
POTANN ..... Potomac Annex [*Navy*]
Potash J ..... Potash Journal [*A publication*]
Potash Rev ... Potash Review [*A publication*]
Potash Trop Agric ... Potash and Tropical Agriculture [*A publication*]
Potassium Potasio Kalium Symp ... Potassium Potasio Kalium Symposium [*A publication*]
POTASWG ... Poseidon Test Analysis Software Working Group [*Missiles*]
Potato Handb ... Potato Handbook [*A publication*]
Potato M ..... Potato Magazine [*A publication*]
Potato Res ... Potato Research [*A publication*]
Pot Aust ..... Pottery in Australia [*A publication*]
POTC .... PERT [*Program Evaluation and Review Technique*] Orientation and Training Center
POTCP .... Partially Oxidized Tetracyanoplatinate Compound [*Inorganic, one-dimensional conductor*]
POTD......... Player of the Decade [*Sports*]
Pot Dwar .... Potter's Edition of Dwarris on Statutes   (DLA)
P O Telecommun J ... Post Office Telecommunications Journal [*A publication*]
Potfuzetek Termeszettud Kozl ... Potfuzetek a Termeszettudomanyi Kozlonyhoz [*A publication*]
Poth Bail a Rente ... Pothier's Traite du Contrat de Bail a Rente   (DLA)
Poth Cont..... Pothier's Contracts   (DLA)
Poth Cont de Change ... Pothier's Traite du Contrat de Change   (DLA)
Poth Contr Sale ... Pothier's Treatise on the Contract of Sale   (DLA)
Poth Cont Sale ... Pothier's Treatise on the Contract of Sale   (DLA)
Pothier Pand ... Pothier on Pandectae Justinianeae, Etc.   (DLA)
Poth Ob..... Pothier on the Law of Obligations   (DLA)
Poth Obl..... Pothier on the Law of Obligations   (DLA)
Poth Oblig ... Pothier on the Law of Obligations   (DLA)
Poth Pand ... Pothier's Pandects   (DLA)
Poth Part.... Pothier on Partnership   (DLA)
POT & I....... Preoverhaul Tests and Inspections [*Navy*]   (NVT)
POTIB........ Polaris Technical Information Bulletin [*Missiles*]
potl---......... Tokelau Islands [*MARC geographic area code*] [*Library of Congress*]   (LCCP)
POTMC ...... Protective Outfit Toxicological Microclimate Controlled   (RDA)
POTMLD ..... Potential Mixed Layer Depth
POTN......... Problems of the North [*A publication*]
poto---........ Tonga [*MARC geographic area code*] [*Library of Congress*]   (LCCP)
POTOMAC ... Patent Office Techniques of Mechanized Access and Classification [*Automation project, shut down in 1972*]
Potomac Appalachian Trail Club Bull ... Potomac Appalachian Trail Club. Bulletin [*A publication*]
Potosi Univ Autonoma Inst Geologia y Metalurgia Fol Tec ... Universidad Autonoma Potosina Folletos Tecnicos Publicados por el Instituto de Geologia y Metalurgia [*A publication*]
Potravin Chladici Tech ... Potravinarska a Chladici Technika [*A publication*]
POTS......... Petty Officer Telegraphist Special [*DSUE*]
POTS......... Photo-Optical Terrain Simulator   (MUGU)
POTS......... Plain Old Telephone Service [*Humorous term for Long Lines Department of AT & T*]
POTS......... PORI [*Polaris Operational Readiness Instrumentation*] Operational Test System [*Missiles*]
POTS......... Precision Optical Tracking System   (KSC)
POTS......... Preoverhaul Tests [*Navy*]   (NVT)
POTS......... Purchase of Telephone Services Contracts
pott--- .... Trust Territory of the Pacific Islands [*MARC geographic area code*] [*Library of Congress*]   (LCCP)
Pott Corp ... Potter on Corporations   (DLA)
Pott Dwarris ... Potter's Edition of Dwarris on Statutes   (DLA)
Potter......... Potter's Reports [*4-7 Wyoming*]   (DLA)
Potter Am Mo ... Potter's American Monthly [*A publication*]

Pottery .... Pottery in Australia [*A publication*]
Pottery in Aust ... Pottery in Australia [*A publication*]
Pottery Aust ... Pottery in Australia [*A publication*]
Pottery Gaz Glass Trade Rev ... Pottery Gazette and Glass Trade Review [*A publication*]
Pottery Glass Rec ... Pottery and Glass Record [*A publication*]
Potts LD ..... Potts' Law Dictionary [*3rd ed.*] [*1815*] (DLA)
POTUS .... President of the United States
Potvrda Valjanosti Broj Inst Meh Poljopr ... Potvrda o Valjanosti Broj-Institut za Mehanizaciju Poljoprivrede [*A publication*]
POTW .... Potable Water (KSC)
POTWA ...... Polimery Tworzywa [*A publication*]
POTWS ...... Publicly Owned Treatment Works [*Environmental Protection Agency*]
POU .... Paramount Resources Ltd. [*Toronto Stock Exchange symbol*]
POU .... Placenta, Ovary, Uterus [*Medicine*]
POU .... Poughkeepsie [*New York*] [*Airport symbol*] (OAG)
POU .... Poughkeepsie, NY [*Location identifier*] [*FAA*] (FAAL)
POU .... Pouilloux [*France*] [*Seismograph station code, US Geological Survey*] (SEIS)
POUF .... Projects of Optimum Urgency and Feasibility
Poughkeepsie Soc N Sc Pr ... Poughkeepsie Society of Natural Science. Proceedings [*A publication*]
Poult .... Poultry Forum [*A publication*]
Poult Advis ... Poultry Adviser [*A publication*]
Poult Bull ... Poultry Bulletin [*A publication*]
Poultry Dig ... Poultry Digest [*A publication*]
Poultry Livestock Comment ... Poultry and Livestock Comment [*A publication*]
Poultry Process ... Poultry Processing and Marketing [*A publication*]
Poultry Sci ... Poultry Science [*A publication*]
Poult Sci .... Poultry Science [*A publication*]
Poult World ... Poultry World [*A publication*]
POUP .... Post Overhaul Upkeep Period
poup--- .... United States Miscellaneous Pacific Islands [*MARC geographic area code*] [*Library of Congress*] (LCCP)
Pour Sci (Paris) ... Pour la Science (Paris) (Edition Francaise de Scientific American) [*A publication*]
POUS .... Partido Operario de Unidade Socialista [*Workers' Party for Socialist Unity*] [*Portuguese*] (PPW)
POUS .... Partido Operario Unificado Socialista [*Unified Socialist Workers Party*] [*Portuguese*] (PPE)
POV .... Peak Operated Valve (MCD)
POV .... Peak Operating Voltage
POV .... Personally Owned Vehicle
POV .... Pinch-Off Voltage
POV .... Pittsburgh & Ohio Valley Railway Co. [*AAR code*]
POV .... Plane of Vibration
POV .... Pneumatically Operated Valve
POV .... Point of View
POV .... Pressure-Operated Valve (MCD)
POV .... Privately Owned Vehicle (NVT)
POV .... Purchase, Outside Vendors
POV .... Putting-On Voltage [*Doppler navigation*] (DEN)
Poverkhn Yavleniya Polim ... Poverkhnostnye Yavleniya v Polimerakh [*A publication*]
Poverkhn Yavleniya Zhidk Zhidk Rastvorakh ... Poverkhnostnye Yavleniya v Zhidkostyakh i Zhidkikh Rastvorakh [*A publication*]
POVEU .... Program Operations Vocational Education Unit (OICC)
Pov & Human Resour Abstr ... Poverty and Human Resources Abstracts [*A publication*]
Pov L Rep... Poverty Law Reporter [*Commerce Clearing House*] (DLA)
POVORTAD ... Positive Vorticity Advection [*Meteorology*] (FAAC)
Povysh Plodorodiya Pochv Nechernozemn Polosy ... Povyshenie Plodorodiya Pochv Nechernozemnoi Polosy [*A publication*]
POW .... Pay Order of Withdrawal
POW .... Paying Their Own Way
POW .... Perception of Ward [*Scales*] [*Psychology*]
POW .... Petty Officer of the Watch [*Navy*]
POW .... Powasson Encephalitis [*Medicine*]
POW .... Power
POW .... Power Corp. of Canada [*Toronto Stock Exchange symbol*] [*Vancouver Stock Exchange symbol*]
POW .... Powhatan [*Arkansas*] [*Seismograph station code, US Geological Survey*] (SEIS)
POW .... Prince of Wales
POW .... Prisoner of War [*Also, PW*]
POW .... Progressive Order of the West [*Defunct*] (EA)
POW .... PSE, Inc. [*American Stock Exchange symbol*]
POWACO ... Portable Water Coolant Circulator
Pow App Proc ... Powell's Law of Appellate Proceedings (DLA)
PoWBN .... Biblioteka Narodowa [*National Library*], Warsaw, Poland [*Library symbol*] [*Library of Congress*] (LCLS)
PoWC .... Instytut Informacji Naukowej, Technicznej, i Ekonomicznej, Warsaw, Poland [*Library symbol*] [*Library of Congress*] (LCLS)
Pow Car ..... Powell's Inland Carriers [*2nd ed.*] [*1861*] (DLA)
Pow Cont ... Powell on Contracts (DLA)
POWD .... Powdered
Powder Coat ... Powder Coatings [*A publication*]

Powder Eng ... Powder Engineering [*USSR*] [*A publication*]
Powder Ind Res ... Powder Industry Research [*A publication*]
Powder Met ... Powder Metallurgy [*A publication*]
Powder Metall ... Powder Metallurgy [*A publication*]
Powder Metall Def Technol ... Powder Metallurgy in Defense Technology [*A publication*]
Powder Metall Int ... Powder Metallurgy International [*A publication*]
Powder Technol ... Powder Technology [*A publication*]
Powder Technol (Lausanne) ... Powder Technology (Lausanne) [*A publication*]
Powder Technol (Tokyo) ... Powder Technology (Tokyo) [*A publication*]
Pow Dev ..... Powell's Essay upon the Learning of Devises, Etc. (DLA)
Powd Metall ... Powder Metallurgy [*A publication*]
POWDR ...... Protect Our Wetlands and Duck Resources [*Department of the Interior*]
Powd Tech ... Powder Technology [*A publication*]
POWER ...... People Organized and Working for Economic Rebirth [*Program for black economic development*]
POWER ...... Professionals Organized for Women's Equal Rights [*Feminist group*]
POWER ...... Programed Operational Warshot Evaluation and Review
POWER ...... Promote Our Wonderful Energy Resources [*in organization name, "American POWER Committee"*] (EA)
PowerConvers Int ... PowerConversion International [*A publication*]
Power Eng ... Power Engineering [*A publication*]
Power Eng (India) ... Power Engineer (India) [*A publication*]
Power Eng J Acad Sci (USSR) ... Power Engineering Journal. Academy of Sciences [*USSR*] [*A publication*]
Power Eng (NY Eng Transl) ... Power Engineering (New York, English Translation) [*A publication*]
Power F ...... Power Farming [*A publication*]
Power Farming Aust ... Power Farming in Australia [*A publication*]
Power Farming Better Farming Dig Aust NZ ... Power Farming and Better Farming Digest in Australia and New Zealand [*Later, Power Farming*] [*A publication*]
Power Farming Mag ... Power Farming Magazine [*A publication*]
Power Fuel Bull ... Power and Fuel Bulletin [*A publication*]
Power Gener ... Power Generation [*A publication*]
Power Ind... Power Industry, Including Industrial Power and Industry Power [*A publication*]
Power Ind Res ... Power Industry Research [*England*] [*A publication*]
Power Plant S Afr ... Power and Plant in Southern Africa [*A publication*]
Power Plant South Afr ... Power and Plant in Southern Africa [*A publication*]
Power Pl Eng ... Power Plant Engineering [*A publication*]
Power Reactor Technol ... Power Reactor Technology [*Japan*] [*A publication*]
Power Reactor Technol Reactor Fuel Process ... Power Reactor Technology and Reactor Fuel Processing [*United States*] [*A publication*]
Power Reactor Technol (Tokyo) ... Power Reactor Technology (Tokyo) [*A publication*]
Power React Technol ... Power Reactor Technology [*A publication*]
Powers .... Powers' Reports, New York Surrogate Court (DLA)
Power Sources Symp Proc ... Power Sources Symposium. Proceedings [*United States*] [*A publication*]
Power's Sur ... Powers' Reports, New York Surrogate Court (DLA)
Power Trans Des ... Power Transmission Design [*A publication*]
Power Transm Des ... Power Transmission Design [*A publication*]
Power Works Eng ... Power and Works Engineering [*A publication*]
Power & Works Engng ... Power and Works Engineering [*A publication*]
Pow Ev .... Powell on Evidence [*10th ed.*] [*1921*] (DLA)
powf--- .... Wallis and Futuna [*MARC geographic area code*] [*Library of Congress*] (LCCP)
powk--- ...... Wake Island [*MARC geographic area code*] [*Library of Congress*] (LCCP)
POWL .... Powell Industries, Inc. [*NASDAQ symbol*] (NQ)
Powloki Ochr ... Powloki Ochronne [*A publication*]
Pow Mort ... Powell on Mortgages [*6th ed.*] [*1826*] (DLA)
Pow Mortg ... Powell on Mortgages (DLA)
PoWP .... Biblioteka Golowna Politechniki Warszawsjiej (Warsaw Technical University Central Library), Warsaw, Poland [*Library symbol*] [*Library of Congress*] (LCLS)
POWR .... Power Resources Corp. [*NASDAQ symbol*] (NQ)
Pow R & D ... Power, Rodwell, and Drew's English Election Cases [*1847-56*] (DLA)
POWS .... Project Operating Work Statement [*NASA*] (NASA)
POWS .... Pyrotechnic Outside Warning System (IEEE)
pows--- ...... Western Samoa [*MARC geographic area code*] [*Library of Congress*] (LCCP)
POW-SIG ... Pagan/Occult/Witchcraft Special Interest Group (EA)
Pow Surr ... Powers' Reports, New York Surrogate Court (DLA)
POWTECH ... International Powder and Bulk Solids Technology Exhibition and Conference (TSPED)
POWU .... Post Office Work Unit [*Computer performance measure*] [*British Telecom*]
PoWU .... Uniwersytet Warszawski [*University of Warsaw*], Warsaw, Poland [*Library symbol*] [*Library of Congress*] (LCLS)
POWWER ... Power of World Wide Energy Resources [*In organization name "Natural POWWER"*] (EA)
Powys N ..... Powys Newsletter [*A publication*]
Powys Rev ... Powys Review [*A publication*]

POX............ Partial Oxidation [*Organic chemistry*]

POX............ Point of Exit

poxd---....... Mariana Islands [*MARC geographic area code*] [*Library of Congress*]   (LCCP)

poxe---....... Marshall Islands [*MARC geographic area code*] [*Library of Congress*]   (LCCP)

poxf---........ Midway Islands [*MARC geographic area code*] [*Library of Congress*]   (LCCP)

poxh---....... Niue [*MARC geographic area code*] [*Library of Congress*]   (LCCP)

POxy........... Oxyrhynchus Papyri [*A publication*]

POY........... Partially Oriented Yarns

POY........... Powell, WY [*Location identifier*] [*FAA*]   (FAAL)

POY........... Prairie Oil Royalties Co. Ltd. [*American Stock Exchange symbol*] [*Toronto Stock Exchange symbol*]

Poynt M & D ... Poynter on Marriage and Divorce [*2nd ed.*] [*1824*]   (DLA)

POZ........... Poznan [*Poland*] [*Airport symbol*]   (OAG)

Pozharnaya Okhr ... Pozharnaya Okhrana [*A publication*]

Poznan Rocz Med ... Poznanskie Roczniki Medyczne [*Poland*] [*A publication*]

Poznan Stud ... Poznan Studies [*A publication*]

Poznan Tow Przyj Nauk Pr Kom Mat Przyr ... Poznanskie Towarzystwo Przyjaciol Nauk. Prace Komisji Matematyczno-Przyrodnicze j [*A publication*]

Poznan Tow Przyj Nauk Pr Kom Mat Przyr Pr Chem ... Poznanskie Towarzystwo Przyjaciol Nauk. Prace Komisji Matematyczno-Przyrodniczej. Prace Chemiezne [*A publication*]

Poznan Tow Przyj Nauk Pr Kom Med Dosw ... Poznanskie Towarzystwo Przyjaciol Nauk. Prace Komisji Medycyny Doswiadezalnej [*A publication*]

Poznan Tow Przyj Nauk Pr Kom Nauk Podstawowych Stosow ... Poznanskie Towarzystwo Przyjaciol Nauk. Prace Komisji Nauk Podstawowych Stosowanych [*A publication*]

Poznan Tow Przyj Nauk Pr Kom Nauk Roln Kom Nauk Lesn ... Poznanskie Towarzystwo Przyjaciol Nauk. Prace Komisji Nauk Rolniczych i Komisji Nauk Lesnych [*A publication*]

Poznan Tow Przyj Nauk Wydz Lek Pr Kom Farm ... Poznanskie Towarzystwo Przyjaciol Nauk. Wydzial Lekarski. Prace Komisji Farmaceutycznej [*A publication*]

Poznan Tow Przyj Nauk Wydz Lek Pr Kom Med Doswi ... Poznanskie Towarzystwo Przyjaciol Nauk. Wydzial Lekarski. Prace Komisji Medycyny Doswiadczalnej [*Poland*] [*A publication*]

Poznan Tow Przyj Nauk Wydz Mat-Przyr Kom Biol Pr ... Poznanskie Towarzystwo Przyjaciol Nauk. Wydzial Matematyczno-Przyrodniczy. Komisja Biologiczna Prace [*Poland*] [*A publication*]

PP.............. Brazil [*Aircraft nationality and registration mark*]   (FAAC)

PP.............. Descent through Cloud [*Procedure*] [*Aviation code*]   (FAAC)

PP.............. Die Palmyrenischen Personennamen [*A publication*]

PP.............. Eisai Co. Ltd. [*Japan*] [*Research code symbol*]

PP.............. Free Library of Philadelphia, Philadelphia, PA [*Library symbol*] [*Library of Congress*]   (LCLS)

P & P......... Packing and Preservation

PP.............. Page Printer   (NVT)

PP.............. Pages

PP.............. Palestine Post [*A publication*]

PP.............. Palisades Plant [*Nuclear energy*]   (NRCH)

PP.............. Palus Putretudinis [*Lunar area*]

PP.............. Pan Pipes [*A publication*]

PP.............. Pancreatic Polypeptide [*Biochemistry*]

PP.............. Panel Point [*Technical drawings*]

PP.............. Pangu Pati [*Political party*] [*Papua New Guinean*]   (PPW)

PP.............. Papa [*Pope*]

pp.............. Papua New Guinea [*MARC country of publication code*] [*Library of Congress*]   (LCCP)

PP.............. Papyrusfunde und Papyrusforschung [*A publication*]

PP.............. Parallel Processor

PP.............. Parcel Post

PP.............. Paris Publications, Inc.

PP.............. Parish Priest

PP.............. Parliamentary Paper [*A publication*]

PP.............. Parliamentary Papers [*British*]

PP.............. Parola del Passato [*A publication*]

PP.............. Part Paid [*Business and trade*]

PP.............. Parti du Peuple [*People's Party*] [*Burundi*]

PP.............. Partia Popullore [*Popular Party*] [*Albanian*]   (PPE)

P/P............ Partial Pay [*Air Force*]

PP.............. Partial Pressure

PP.............. Partial Program

PP.............. Particular [*Named*] Port [*British*]   (ROG)

PP.............. Partido Panamenista [*Panamanian Party*]   (PPW)

PP.............. Partido Popular [*Popular Party*] [*Spanish*]   (PPE)

PP.............. Partido Populista [*Populist Party*] [*Argentina*]

PP.............. Parts Per

PP.............. [*The*] Passionate Pilgrim [*Shakespearean work*]

PP.............. Passive Participle

PP.............. Past Participle

PP.............. Past Patriarch [*Freemasonry*]   (ROG)

P & P......... Past and Present [*A publication*]

PP.............. Past President

PP.............. Pastor Pastorum [*Shepherd of the Shepherds*] [*Latin*]   (ROG)

P/P............ Patch Panel   (NASA)

PP.............. Pater Patriae [*The Father of His Country*] [*Latin*]

PP.............. Patres [*Fathers*] [*Latin*]

PP.............. Patriarchs and Prophets

PP.............. Patriotic Party [*British*]

PP.............. Patrol Vessels [*Navy symbol*]   (MUGU)

PP.............. Pauley Petroleum [*American Stock Exchange symbol*]

PP.............. Pay Period   (FAAC)

P and P...... Payments and Progress Committee [*NATO*]   (NATG)

PP.............. Peace PAC   (EA)

PP.............. Peak-to-Peak

PP.............. Peak Pressure

PP.............. Peanut Pals [*An association*]   (EA)

PP.............. Pedal Pulse

PP.............. Pellagra Preventive [*Factor*] [*See also PPF*] [*Biochemistry*]

PP.............. Pension Plan

PP.............. People's Party [*Halkci Partisi*] [*Turkey*]   (PPW)

PP.............. Pep Pill [*Slang*]

PP.............. Per Procurationem [*By Proxy, By the Action Of*] [*Legal term*] [*Latin*]

PP.............. Periodical Publications [*British Library shelf designation*]

PP.............. Peripheral Processor [*Data processing*]

PP.............. Periportal [*Anatomy*]

PP.............. Periproct [*Invertebrate anatomy*]

PP.............. Permanent Party

PP.............. Permanent Press   (ADA)

PP.............. [*Length between*] Perpendiculars [*Shipbuilding*]

P-P............ Person to Person [*Word processing*]

PP.............. Personal Property

PP.............. Pet Pride [*An association*] [*Pacific Palisades, CA*]   (EA)

PP.............. Petroleum Point

PP.............. Petticoat Peeping [*From one girl to another, in reference to dress disarrangement*]

PP.............. Philo-Phobe [*Psychological testing*]

PP.............. Philologica Pragensia [*A publication*]

PP.............. Philosophia Patrum [*A publication*]

PP.............. Physical Profile

PP.............. Physical Properties

PP.............. Pianissimo [*Very Softly*] [*Music*]

PP.............. Picked Ports

PP.............. Pickpocket

P/P............ Pier to Pier   (ADA)

PP.............. Piers Plowman [*Middle English poem*]

PP.............. Piissimus [*Most Holy*] [*Latin*]

PP.............. Pilot Parents [*Omaha, NE*]   (EA)

PP.............. Pilot Punch

PP.............. Pilotless Plane

PP.............. Pinepointer [*A publication*]

PP.............. Piping

PP.............. Piscataqua Pioneers   (EA)

PP.............. Piu Piano [*More Softly*] [*Music*]

PP.............. PIXEL-Processing [*Data processing*]

PP.............. Placental Protein [*Gynecology*]

PP.............. Plan Profile

PP.............. Plane Parallel

PP.............. Plane Polarized [*Telecommunications*]   (TEL)

PP.............. Planetary Programs [*NASA*]

PP.............. Planned Parenthood

PP.............. Planning Package [*NASA*]   (NASA)

PP.............. Planning Purpose

P & P......... Plans and Policies

P & P......... Plans and Programs

PP.............. Plant Protection

PP.............. Plasma Protein

PP.............. Plasmapheresis [*Hematology*]

PP.............. Plaster of Paris

P to P......... Plate to Plate   (DEN)

PP.............. Play or Pay   (ROG)

PP.............. Please Pay   (ROG)

PP.............. Pleural Pressure [*Medicine*]

PP.............. Plot Points [*Data processing*]

PP.............. Pluvius Policy [*Insurance against rain*]

PP.............. Poetry Project   (EA)

P/P............ Point-to-Point [*Air Force*]

PP.............. Polar Pacific [*American air mass*]

PP.............. Pole Piece   (DEN)

PP.............. Polizei Pistole [*Police Pistol*] [*Walther Waffenfabrik, German arms manufacturer*]

PP.............. Polypeptide [*Biochemistry*]

PP.............. Polypropylene [*Organic chemistry*]

PP.............. Polypyrrole [*Photovoltaic energy systems*]

PP.............. Pom-Pom [*Gun*]

PP.............. Pontificum [*Of the Popes*] [*Latin*]

PP.............. Population (Paris) [*A publication*]

PP.............. Port Pipe   (ADA)

PP.............. Posa Piano [*Handle with Care*] [*Italy*]

PP.............. Position Paper   (MCD)

PP.............. Post Pagado [*Postage Paid*] [*Spanish*]

PP.............. Post Partum [*After Birth*] [*Latin*]   (ADA)

PP.............. Post Position [*Racing*]

P & P............. Postage and Packing
PP.............. Postage Paid
PP.............. Posterior Pituitary [*Medicine*]
PP.............. Postpartum [*Medicine*]
PP.............. Postpass
PP.............. Postponed
PP.............. Postprandial [*After Meals*] [*Pharmacy*]
PP.............. Pounds Pressure
PP.............. Pour Presenter [*To Present*] [*French*]
PP.............. Power Package
PP.............. Power Plant
PP.............. Power Play [*Hockey*]
PP.............. Power Supplies [*JETDS nomenclature*] [*Military*] (CET)
PP.............. Prace Polonistyczne [*Warsaw*] [*A publication*]
PP.............. Praemissis Praemittendis [*Omitting Preliminaries*] [*Latin*]
PP.............. Praepter Propter [*Approximately*] [*Pharmacy*]
PP.............. Prepaid
PP.............. Preparative Flag [*Navy*] [*British*]
PP.............. Preparing, Providing [*Pharmacy*] (ROG)
PP.............. Prepregnancy [*Medicine*]
PP.............. Preprinted
PP.............. Preprocessor
PP.............. Preproduction (KSC)
PP.............. Prescribed Period [*Social Security Administration*] (OICC)
PP.............. Present Participle [*Grammar*]
PP.............. Present Position [*Military*]
PP.............. Press Packed
PP.............. Pressure Pattern (MCD)
PP.............. Pressure-Proof [*Technical drawings*]
PP.............. Pretty Poor [*Slang*] [*Bowdlerized version*]
P & P.......... Pride and Prejudice [*Novel by Jane Austen*]
PP.............. Primary Pressure (NRCH)
PP.............. Primary Producers (ADA)
PP.............. Princess Pat's [*Princess Patricia of Connaught's Light Infantry*]
              [*Military unit*] [*Canada*]
PP.............. Principal
PP.............. Principal Point
PP.............. Print Positions
PP.............. Print-Punch [*Data processing*] (BUR)
PP.............. Printer Page [*Data processing*]
PP.............. Prior Permission
P/P............. Private Passenger
PP.............. Private Patient [*Medicine*]
PP.............. Private Practice [*Chiropody*] [*British*]
PP.............. Private Property [*Military*]
PP.............. Privately Printed
PP.............. Procurement Plan (MCD)
P & P.......... Procurement and Production
PP.............. Producer Price
PP.............. Production Processes
P & P.......... Production and Procurement [*Military*]
PP.............. Professional Paper
PP.............. Professor Publicus [*Public Professor*] [*Latin*] (ROG)
PP.............. Program Package (MCD)
PP.............. Program Paper
PP.............. Program Product [*Data processing*]
PP.............. Programing Plan (AFM)
PP.............. Progress Payments [*Military procurement*]
PP.............. Project Priesthood (EA)
PP.............. Project Proposal (KSC)
PP.............. Proletarian Party
PP.............. Proodeftiki Parataxis [*Progressive Front*] [*Greek
              Cypriot*] (PPE)
PP.............. Propeller Pitch
PP.............. Proportional Part
PP.............. Propulsion Power (KSC)
PP.............. Prothrombin-Proconvertin [*Hematology*]
PP.............. Proton-Proton [*Nuclear physics*]
PP.............. Protoporphyria [*Medicine*]
PP.............. Protoporphyrin [*Biochemistry*]
PP.............. Provisioning Procedures [*Corps of Engineers*]
PP.............. Proximal Phalanx [*Anatomy*]
PP.............. Przeglad Powszechny [*Revue Universelle*] [*A publication*]
PP.............. Psychic Phenomena
PP.............. Psychological Profile
PP.............. Psychologists and Psychiatrists [*in service*] [*British*]
P/P............. Pterocephaliid-Ptychaspid [*Paleogeologic boundary*]
PP.............. Public Property
PP.............. Publie Par [*Published By*] [*French*]
P or P.......... Publish or Perish [*Said of scholars, scientists, etc.*]
PP.............. Pulse Polarography [*Analytical chemistry*]
PP.............. Pulse Pressure [*Medicine*]
PP.............. Pulvis Patrum [*The Fathers' Powder (or Jesuits' Powder)*]
              [*Pharmacy*] (ROG)
PP.............. Punctum Proximum [*Near Point*] [*Latin*]
PP.............. Punctum Proximum (Of Convergence) [*Ophthalmology*]
PP.............. Purchase Power [*Commercial firm*] (EA)
PP.............. Purchased Parts
PP.............. Push-Pull [*Technical drawings*]
PP.............. Pusher Plane
PP.............. Pyrophosphate [*Chemistry*]

PPA............. Athenaeum of Philadelphia, Philadelphia, PA [*Library symbol*]
              [*Library of Congress*] (LCLS)
PPA............. National Plant Protection Association
PP & A........ Palpation, Percussion, and Auscultation [*Medicine*]
PPA............. Palpitation, Percussion, Auscultation [*Medicine*]
PPA............. Pampa, TX [*Location identifier*] [*FAA*] (FAAL)
PPA............. Panamerican/Panafrican Association (EA)
PPA............. Paper Pail Association [*Defunct*] (EA)
PPA............. Paper Plate Association [*Later, SSI*] (EA)
PPA............. Parcel Post Association [*Later, PSA*] (EA)
PPA............. Parents for Private Adoption [*Pawlet, VT*] (EA)
PPa............. Parola del Passato [*A publication*]
PPA............. Partido Patriotico Arubano [*Aruban Patriotic Party*]
              [*Netherlands Antillean*] (PPW)
PPA............. Partido Peronista Autentico [*Authentic Peronist Party*]
              [*Argentina*]
PPA............. Pathology Practice Association [*Washington, DC*] (EA)
PPA............. Peppa Resources [*Vancouver Stock Exchange symbol*]
PPA............. Per Power of Attorney [*Business and trade*]
PPA............. Perennial Plant Association (EA)
PPA............. Periodical Publishers Association [*Later, MCA*] (EA)
PPA............. Pesticide Producers Association [*Washington, DC*] (EA)
PPA............. Pet Producers of America (EA)
PPA............. Phenylpropanolamine [*Organic chemistry*]
PPA............. Phenylpropanolamine(hydrochloride) [*Also, PPH, PPM*]
              [*Decongestant*]
PPA............. Phenylpyruvic Acid [*Organic chemistry*]
PPA............. Phiala Prius Agitata [*Having First Shaken the Bottle*]
              [*Pharmacy*]
PPA............. Photo Peak Analysis (IEEE)
PPA............. Pictorial Photographers of America (EA)
PPA............. Pie De Palo [*Argentina*] [*Seismograph station code, US
              Geological Survey*] (SEIS)
PPA............. Pilots and Passengers Association [*Glen Burnie, MD*] (EA)
PPA............. Pitch Precession Amplifier
PPA............. Pittsburgh Pneumonia Agent [*Microbiology*]
PPA............. Plant Patent Act [*1930*]
PPA............. Policyholders Protective Association of America (EA)
PPA............. Polymer Permeation Analyzer
PPA............. Poly(phosphoric Acid) [*Inorganic chemistry*]
PPA............. Popcorn Processors Association [*Later, PI*]
PPA............. Postpartum Amenorrhea [*Medicine*]
PPA............. Poultry Publishers Association (EA)
PPA............. Power Plant Automation
PPA............. Powerplant Performance Analysis
PPA............. Presidents' Professional Association [*Later, Presidents
              Association*] (EA)
PPA............. Princeton-Pennsylvania Accelerator [*Closed, 1972*] [*AEC*]
PPA............. Principal Port Authority [*British*] (ROG)
PPA............. Printing Platemakers Association
PPA............. Priority Problem Areas (MCD)
PPA............. Produce Packaging Association [*Later, PMA*] (EA)
PPA............. Professional Panhellenic Association [*Later, PFA*] (EA)
PPA............. Professional Photographers of America [*Des Plaines, IL*] (EA)
PPA............. Professional Programmers Association (EA)
PPA............. Professional Putters Association (EA)
PPA............. Program Problem Area
PPA............. Progress Presse Agentur GmbH [*Press agency*] [*West
              Germany*]
PPA............. Progressive Party of America [*Third party in 1948 Presidential
              race*]
PPA............. Protestant Press Agency [*British*]
PPA............. Prudent Purchaser Arrangement [*Medical insurance*]
PPA............. Prudent Purchasing Agreement
PPA............. Pseudopassive Array
PPA............. Public Personnel Association [*Later, IPMA*] (EA)
PPA............. Publishers' Publicity Association [*New York, NY*] (EA)
PPa............. Pulmonary Artery Pressure [*Cardiology*]
PPA............. Pulse Plasma Accelerator
PPA............. Pulsed Power Amplifier
PPA............. Purple Plum Association [*Defunct*] (EA)
PPAA........... Patres Amplissimi [*Cardinals*] [*Latin*]
PPAA........... Personal Protective Armor Association [*Nashville, TN*] (EA)
PPAB.......... Program and Policy Advisory Board [*UN Food and Agriculture
              Organization*]
PPABP........ American Baptist Publication Society, Philadelphia, PA [*Library
              symbol*] [*Library of Congress*] [*Obsolete*] (LCLS)
PPAC.......... Pennsylvania Pacific [*NASDAQ symbol*] (NQ)
PPAC.......... Pesticide Policy Advisory Committee [*Environmental
              Protection Agency*]
PPAC.......... Primary Progress Assessment Chart [*Psychology*]
PPAC.......... Product Performance Agreement Center [*Military*]
PPACE........ United States Army, Corps of Engineers, Philadelphia District
              Library, Custom House, Philadelphia, PA [*Library symbol*]
              [*Library of Congress*] (LCLS)
PPACHi....... American Catholic Historical Society, Philadelphia, PA [*Library
              symbol*] [*Library of Congress*] (LCLS)
PPADS........ Parawing Precision Aerial Delivery System (MCD)
PPAEM....... Albert Einstein Medical Center, Northern Division,
              Philadelphia, PA [*Library symbol*] [*Library of
              Congress*] (LCLS)

PPAFA....... Pennsylvania Academy of the Fine Arts, Philadelphia, PA [*Library symbol*] [*Library of Congress*] [*Obsolete*] (LCLS)
PPAG......... Personnel Profile - Age by Grade [*Army*]
PPAK......... Atwater Kent Museum, Philadelphia, PA [*Library symbol*] [*Library of Congress*] (LCLS)
PPAL......... Principal (ROG)
PPalZ......... New Jersey Zinc Co. [*of Pennsylvania*], Technical Library, Palmerton, PA [*Library symbol*] [*Library of Congress*] (LCLS)
PPAmP....... American Philosophical Society, Philadelphia, PA [*Library symbol*] [*Library of Congress*] (LCLS)
PPAmS....... American Sunday School Union, Philadelphia, PA [*Library symbol*] [*Library of Congress*] [*Obsolete*] (LCLS)
PPAmSR .... American Sugar Refining Co., Philadelphia, PA [*Library symbol*] [*Library of Congress*] [*Obsolete*] (LCLS)
PPAmSwM ... American Swedish Historical Foundation, Philadelphia, PA [*Library symbol*] [*Library of Congress*] (LCLS)
PPAN......... Academy of Natural Sciences of Philadelphia, Philadelphia, PA [*Library symbol*] [*Library of Congress*] (LCLS)
PPAp.......... Apprentices' Free Library, Philadelphia, PA [*Library symbol*] [*Library of Congress*] [*Obsolete*] (LCLS)
PPAP......... People's Party of Arunachal Pradesh [*Indian*] (PPW)
PPAR......... Project Performance Audit Report
PPArmA..... Armstrong Association of Philadelphia, Philadelphia, PA [*Library symbol*] [*Library of Congress*] [*Obsolete*] (LCLS)
PPAS......... Patti Page Appreciation Society (EA)
PPAS......... Portable Public Address System (MCD)
PPAS......... Potassium Picrate Active Substances [*Measure of detergent content of water*]
PPAS......... Probability Proportional to Aggregate Size [*Statistics*]
PPAtR........ Atlantic Refining Co., Philadelphia, PA [*Library symbol*] [*Library of Congress*] (LCLS)
PPATY....... Preparatory (ROG)
PPAuC........ Automobile Club of Philadelphia, Philadelphia, PA [*Library symbol*] [*Library of Congress*] [*Obsolete*] (LCLS)
PPAUS ...... Peat Producers Association of the United States (EA)
PPAW........ Public Policy Affecting Women Task Force (EA)
PP & B ...... Paper, Printing, and Binding [*Publishing*]
PPB .... Parachute Paraglider Building [*NASA*] (KSC)
PPB .... Parts per Billion
PPB .... Petro-Canada Products, Inc. [*Toronto Stock Exchange symbol*] [*Vancouver Stock Exchange symbol*]
PPB .... Philadelphia Bar Association, Philadelphia, PA [*Library symbol*] [*Library of Congress*] (LCLS)
P-P-B......... Planning-Programing-Budgeting [*System*] [*Army*]
PPB .... Political Party Broadcast [*Television*] [*British*]
PPB .... Polybiblion. Partie Litteraire [*A publication*]
PPB .... Poly(para-benzamide) [*Organic chemistry*]
PPB .... Positive Pressure Breathing [*Aerospace*]
PPB .... Power Plant Bulletin (MCD)
PPB .... Precision Pressure Balance
PPB .... Pres Prudente [*Brazil*] [*Airport symbol*] (OAG)
PPB .... Primary Propulsion Branch [*Manned Spacecraft Center*]
PPB .... Private Posting Box
PPB .... Production Parts Breakdown (MCD)
PPB .... Program Performance Baseline (NASA)
PPB .... PROM [*Programable Read-Only Memory*] Programer Board
PPB .... Provisioning Parts Breakdown
PPB .... Push-Pull Bearing
PPBB......... Partai Pesaka Bumiputra Bersatu [*United Traditional Bumiputra Party*] [*Malaysian*] (PPW)
PPBB......... Prime Power Brass Board (MCD)
PPBC......... Plant Pathogenic Bacteria Committee (EA)
P PBD........ Paper or Paperboard [*Freight*]
PPBD......... Port of Palm Beach District [*AAR code*]
PPBES....... Planning, Programing, Budgeting, and Execution System [*Army*] (RDA)
PPBES....... Program Planning-Budgeting-Evaluation System Project (EA)
PPBESP .... Program Planning-Budgeting-Evaluation System Project (EA)
PPBF......... Pan-American Pharmaceutical and Biochemical Federation
PPBG......... Preliminary Program and Budget Guidance
PPBI .... Balch Institute, Philadelphia, PA [*Library symbol*] [*Library of Congress*] (LCLS)
PPBM .... Pulse Polarization Binary Modulation (MCD)
PPBMIS..... Planning, Programing, and Budgeting Management Information System [*Army*]
PPBR......... Program Plan and Budget Request (OICC)
PPBS......... Planning, Programing, and Budgeting System [*Army*]
PPBS......... Positive Pressure Breathing System [*Aerospace*]
PPBS......... Postprandial Blood Sugar [*Clinical chemistry*]
PPBUA ...... Personnel Practice Bulletin [*A publication*]
PPC .... College of Physicians of Philadelphia, Philadelphia, PA [*Library symbol*] [*Library of Congress*] [*OCLC symbol*] (LCLS)
PP-C........... Free Library of Philadelphia, Carson Collection, Philadelphia, PA [*Library symbol*] [*Library of Congress*] (LCLS)
PPC .... Pan Pacific Centers (EA)
PPC .... Paperboard Packaging Council [*Formed by a merger of FPBAA and Institute for Better Packaging - IBP*] [*Washington, DC*] (EA)
PPC .... Partial Pay Card

PPC .... Partido Popular Cristiano [*Christian Popular Party*] [*Peruvian*] (PPW)
PPC .... Parting Post Calls (MCD)
PPC .... Partitu Populare Corsu [*Corsican*] (PD)
PPC .... Parts Preference Code [*Military*] (AFIT)
PPC .... Patres Conscripti [*Senators*] [*Latin*] (ROG)
PPC .... Patrick Petroleum Company [*NYSE symbol*]
PPC .... Patrol Plane Commander
PPC .... Peak Power Control [*Telecommunications*] (TEL)
PPC .... Per Pupil Cost (AFM)
PPC .... Permission to Photocopy (MCD)
PPC .... Personal Portable Computer
PPC .... Personal Productivity Center
PPC .... Petroleum Planning Committee [*Obsolete*] [*NATO*] (NATG)
PPC .... Phased Provisioning Code (NASA)
PPC .... Philatelic Press Club [*Later, IPPC*]
PPC .... Photographic Processing Cells (AFM)
PpC .... Pick Publishing Corporation, New York, NY [*Library symbol*] [*Library of Congress*] (LCLS)
PP & C ...... Pickpocket and Confidence [*Police term*]
PPC .... Picture Postcard
PPC .... Pierce's Perpetual Code [*1943*] (DLA)
PPC .... Pine Pass [*British Columbia*] [*Seismograph station code, US Geological Survey*] [*Closed*] (SEIS)
PPC .... Plain Paper Copier [*Electrophotography*]
PPC .... Plain Plaster Cornice [*Construction*]
PPC .... Plant Pest Control Division [*of ARS, Department of Agriculture*]
PPC .... Platform Position Computer
PPC .... Plug Patch Cord
PPC .... Plutonium Process Cell [*Nuclear energy*] (NRCH)
PPC .... Plutonium Product Cell [*Nuclear energy*] (NRCH)
PPC .... Point of Possible Collision [*Navigation*]
PPC .... Polyphthalate-Polycarbonate
PPC .... Positive Peer Control
PPC .... Posterior Parietal Cortex [*Brain anatomy*]
PPC .... Postpulmonary Complications
PPC .... Pour Prendre Conge [*To Take Leave*] [*French*]
PPC .... Power Pack Charger
PPC .... Power Plant Change (NVT)
PPC .... Pre-Proposal Conference (MCD)
PPC .... Precision Photomechanical Corporation
PPC .... Preprocessing Center [*NASA*] (NASA)
PPC .... President of the Privy Council [*Canada*]
PPC .... Primary Power Control (MCD)
PPC .... Print Position Counter
PPC .... Priority Placement Certificate [*Military*] (AFM)
PP & C .... Production Planning and Control [*Military*] (AABC)
PPC .... Production Planning and Control
PPC .... Professional Personal Computer
PPC .... Program Planning and Control (AAG)
PPC .... Program Planning Coordination Office [*United Nations*]
PPC .... Progressive Patient Care
PPC .... Project Physics Course [*National Science Foundation*]
PPC .... Project Planning Centre for Developing Countries [*Research center*] [*British*] (IRC)
PP & C .... Project Planning and Control (NG)
PPC .... Prospect Creek, AK [*Location identifier*] [*FAA*] (FAAL)
PPC .... Proximal Palmar Crease [*Anatomy*]
PPC .... Psychorotrophic Plate Count [*Bacteriology*]
PPC .... Publishers Publicity Circle
PPC .... Pulsed Power Circuit (IEEE)
PPCA........ Plasma [*or Proserum*] Prothrombin Conversion Accelerator [*Factor VII*] [*Also, SPCA*] [*Hematology*]
PPCAA ...... Parole and Probation Compact Administrators Association [*Defunct*] (EA)
PPCAP ...... People to People Citizen Ambassador Program (EA)
PPCB........ Page Printer Control Block [*Data processing*]
PPCC .... Carpenters' Company, Philadelphia, PA [*Library symbol*] [*Library of Congress*] (LCLS)
PPCC .... Particles per Cubic Centimeter
PPCCH....... Chestnut Hill College, Philadelphia, PA [*Library symbol*] [*Library of Congress*] (LCLS)
PPCE........ Portable Pneumatic Checkout Equipment (KSC)
PPCF......... Plasmin Prothrombin Conversion Factor [*Factor V*] [*Hematology*]
PPCH......... People-to-People Committee for the Handicapped [*Washington, DC*] (EA)
PPCH........ Pilot Pouch [*Aviation*] (FAAC)
PPCI .... Curtis Institute of Music, Philadelphia, PA [*Library symbol*] [*Library of Congress*] (LCLS)
PPCiC .... Civic Club of Philadelphia, Philadelphia, PA [*Library symbol*] [*Library of Congress*] [*Obsolete*] (LCLS)
PPCIG........ Personal Property Consignment Instruction Guide (MCD)
PPC Jrl...... Polymers, Paint, and Colour Journal [*A publication*]
PPCLI......... Princess Patricia of Connaught's Light Infantry [*Military unit*] [*Canada*]
PPCM........ Philadelphia County Medical Society, Philadelphia, PA [*Library symbol*] [*Library of Congress*] [*Obsolete*] (LCLS)
PPCO .... Philadelphia College of Osteopathic Medicine, Philadelphia, PA [*Library symbol*] [*Library of Congress*] (LCLS)

PPCoC .... Community College of Philadelphia, Philadelphia, PA [*Library symbol*] [*Library of Congress*] (LCLS)
PPCoIP .... Colonial Penn Group, Inc., Marketing Research Library, Philadelphia, PA [*Library symbol*] [*Library of Congress*] (LCLS)
PPComm .... Commercial Museum, Philadelphia, PA [*Library symbol*] [*Library of Congress*] [*Obsolete*] (LCLS)
PPCP .... Propellant Pneumatic Control Panel (KSC)
PPCPC .... Philadelphia City Planning Commission, Philadelphia, PA [*Library symbol*] [*Library of Congress*] (LCLS)
PPCPSG ..... Polish POW Camps Philatelic Study Group (EA)
PPCS .... National Carl Schurz Memorial Foundation, Philadelphia, PA [*Library symbol*] [*Library of Congress*] [*Obsolete*] (LCLS)
PPCS .... Person to Person: Collect and Special Instruction [*Telecommunications*] (TEL)
PPCS .... Precision Pointing Control System [*Engineering*]
PPCS .... Production Planning and Control System
PPCS .... Project Planning and Control System [*Social Security Administration*]
PPCuP .... Curtis Publishing Co., Research Library, Philadelphia, PA [*Library symbol*] [*Library of Congress*] [*Obsolete*] (LCLS)
PPD .... Drexel University, Philadelphia, PA [*Library symbol*] [*Library of Congress*] (LCLS)
PPD .... Humacao-Palmas [*Puerto Rico*] [*Airport symbol*] (OAG)
PPD .... Papered (ROG)
PPD .... Parti Populaire Djiboutien [*Djibouti People's Party*] (PPW)
PPD .... Parti Progressiste Dahomeen [*Dahomey Progressive Party*]
PPD .... Partido Popular Democratico [*Popular Democratic Party*] [*Puerto Rican*] (PPW)
PPD .... Parts Provisioning Document
PPD .... Payload Position Data
PPD .... Pepsin Pancreatin Digest [*Food protein digestibility assay*]
P & PD .... Percussion and Postural Drainage
PPD .... Personnel Planning Data [*Navy*]
PPD .... Personnel Priority Designator [*Military*] (AFM)
PPD .... Pitch Phase Detector
PPD .... Plains Petroleum [*Vancouver Stock Exchange symbol*]
PPD .... Point Position Data
PPD .... Portuguese Popular Democrats
PPD .... Postpaid
PPD .... Pre-Paid Legal Services, Inc. [*American Stock Exchange symbol*]
PPD .... Prepaid
PPD .... Presidential Protective Division [*US Secret Service*]
PPD .... Proficiency Pay Designator [*Military*] (AABC)
PPD .... Prognostic Prediction Devices
PPD .... Program Planning Directives [*NASA*] (KSC)
PPD .... Program Planning Document (NG)
PPD .... Progressive Perceptive Deafness [*Medicine*]
PPD .... Project Planning Directive (NG)
PPD .... Propria Pecunia Dedicavit [*With His Own Money He Offered It*] [*Latin*] (ROG)
PPD .... Propulsion and Power Division [*Manned Spacecraft Center*] [*NASA*]
PPD .... Provisioning Procurement Data
PPD .... Pulse-Type Phase Detector
PPD .... Purified Protein Derivative [*Tuberculin*]
PPDA .... Para-Phenylenediamine [*Organic chemistry*]
PPDA .... Phenyl Phosphorodiamidate [*Fertilizer technology*]
PPDB .... Personnel Planning Data Book [*Navy*]
PPDB .... Point-Positioning Data Base [*Cartography*] (RDA)
PPDC .... Dental Cosmos Library, Philadelphia, PA [*Library symbol*] [*Library of Congress*] [*Obsolete*] (LCLS)
PPDC .... Paraguayan People's Documentation Center (EA-IO)
PPDC .... Partido Popular Democratica Cristiana [*Popular Christian Democratic Party*] [*Spanish*] (PPE)
PPDC .... Programing Panels and Decoding Circuits
PPDD .... Plan Position Data Display
PPDD .... Preliminary Project Design Description (NRCH)
PPDDS ...... Private Practice Dental Delivery System
PPDef-M .... Defense Personnel Support Center, Directorate of Medical Material Library, Philadelphia, PA [*Library symbol*] [*Library of Congress*] (LCLS)
PPDF .... Poisson Probability Distribution Function [*Mathematics*]
PPDGF .... Porcine Platelet-Derived Growth Factor [*Biochemistry*]
PPDIL .... Prepower Dependent Insertion Limits [*Nuclear energy*] (NRCH)
PPDio .... Diocesan Library, Philadelphia, PA [*Library symbol*] [*Library of Congress*] [*Obsolete*] (LCLS)
PPDM .... E. I. DuPont de Nemours & Co., Marshall Laboratory, Philadelphia, PA [*Library symbol*] [*Library of Congress*] (LCLS)
PPDMG ...... Popular Priced Dress Manufacturers Group [*Later, Apparel Manufacturers Association*] (EA)
PPDO .... Personal Paid Days Off
PPDP .... Preliminary Project Development Plan [*NASA*]
PPDP .... Preprogram Definition Phase
PP-DPH ...... Free Library of Philadelphia, Library for the Blind and Physically Handicapped, Philadelphia, PA [*Library symbol*] [*Library of Congress*] (LCLS)

PPDR .... Pilot Performance Description Record
PPDR .... Population and Development Review [*A publication*]
PP/DR .... Preliminary Performance Design Requirements
PPDR .... Production Packing Depth Range (NG)
PPDrop ...... Dropsie University, Philadelphia, PA [*Library symbol*] [*Library of Congress*] (LCLS)
PPDS .... Physical Property Data Service [*Institution of Chemical Engineers*] [*Rugby, England*] [*Databank*] [*Information service*] (EISS)
PPD-S .... Purified Protein Derivative-Standard [*Tuberculin*]
PPDSE .... International Plate Printers, Die Stampers, and Engravers' Union of North America
PPDT .... (Phenylpyridyl)diphenyltriazine [*Analytical chemistry*]
PPDT .... Poly(phenyleneterephthalamide) [*Organic chemistry*]
PPE .... Independent Union of Plant Protection Employees in the Electrical and Machine Industry
PPE .... Parti Populaire Europeen [*European Peoples' Party - EPP*] [*Brussels, Belgium*] (EA-IO)
PPE .... Personal Protective Equipment [*General Motors Corp.*]
PPE .... Philosophy, Politics, Economics [*Oxford University*]
PPE .... Pipette [*Chemistry*]
PPE .... Platform Position Equipment
PPE .... Polyphenylether (IEEE)
PPE .... Polyphosphate Ether [*Inorganic chemistry*]
PPE .... Porcine Pancreatic Elastase [*An enzyme*]
PPE .... Portable Purge Equipment [*NASA*]
PPE .... Potomac Pacific Engineering, Inc.
PPE .... Predicted Period-of-Effect [*Meteorology*]
PPE .... Premodulation Processing Equipment
PPE .... Preproduction Evaluation (NG)
PPE .... Problem Program Efficiency (IEEE)
PPE .... Problem Program Evaluator
PPE .... Program Planning and Evaluation
PPE .... Prototype Production Evaluation (NG)
PPE .... Purchasing Power Equivalent
PPEB .... Eastern Baptist Theological Seminary, Philadelphia, PA [*Library symbol*] [*Library of Congress*] (LCLS)
PPEB .... [*The*] Pottery of Palestine from the Earliest Times to the End of the Early Bronze Age [*A publication*] (BJA)
PPeda .... Problemi di Pedagogia [*A publication*]
PPEF .... Public Policy Education Fund (EA)
PPEFH .... E. F. Hutton & Co., Philadelphia, PA [*Library symbol*] [*Library of Congress*] [*Obsolete*] (LCLS)
PPEMA ...... Portable Power Equipment Manufacturers Association [*Formerly, CSMA*] [*Bethesda, MD*] (EA)
PPENA .... Plant and Power Services Engineer [*A publication*]
PPEng .... Engineers' Club, Philadelphia, PA [*Library symbol*] [*Library of Congress*] [*Obsolete*] (LCLS)
PPEP .... Eastern Pennsylvania Psychiatric Institute, Philadelphia, PA [*Library symbol*] [*Library of Congress*] (LCLS)
P/PEP .... Progress Performance Evaluation Panel [*Job Corps*]
PPES .... Pilot Performance Evaluation System [*Air Force*]
PPeSchw ... Schwenkfelder Historical Library, Pennsburg, PA [*Library symbol*] [*Library of Congress*] (LCLS)
PPET .... Pollock Petroleum, Inc. [*NASDAQ symbol*] (NQ)
PPF .... Franklin Institute, Philadelphia, PA [*Library symbol*] [*Library of Congress*] [*OCLC symbol*] (LCLS)
PPF .... Pacific Peace Fund (EA)
PPF .... Palestine Pioneer Foundation (EA)
PPF .... Parsons [*Kansas*] [*Airport symbol*] (OAG)
PPF .... Parsons, KS [*Location identifier*] [*FAA*] (FAAL)
PPF .... Parti Populaire Francais [*French Popular Party*] (PPE)
PPF .... Patriotic People's Front [*Hungary*]
PPF .... Payload Processing Facility [*Air Force*] (NASA)
PPF .... Peacetime Planning Factors
PPF .... Peak Power Frequency
PPF .... Pellagra Preventive Factor [*See also PP*] [*Biochemistry*]
PPF .... People's Police Force (CINC)
PPF .... Personal Property Floater [*Insurance*]
PPF .... Phase Pushing Factor
PPF .... Photophoretic Force [*Pressure exerted by light*]
PPF .... Plasma Protein Fraction [*Hematology*]
PPF .... Poetarum Philosophorum Graecorum Fragmenta [*A publication*] (OCD)
PPF .... Poly(phenolformaldehyde) [*Organic chemistry*]
PPF .... Porous Polyurethane Foam [*Also, PUF*] [*Plastics technology*]
PPF .... Presbyterian Peace Fellowships (EA)
PPF .... Privatefoeretagarnas Partioganisation i Finland [*Finnish Private Entrepreneurs' Party*] (PPE)
PPF .... Provision of Production Facilities [*Military*] (AABC)
PPF .... United Association of Journeymen and Apprentices of the Plumbing and Pipe Fitting Industry of the United States and Canada
PPFA .... Planned Parenthood Federation of America [*New York, NY*] (EA)
PPFA .... Plastic Pipe and Fittings Association [*Glen Ellyn, IL*] (EA)
PPFA .... Professional Picture Framers Association (EA)
PPFA .... United States Army, Frankford Arsenal Library, Philadelphia, PA [*Library symbol*] [*Library of Congress*] (LCLS)

PPFAR....... Federal Archives and Records Center, General Services Administration, Philadelphia, PA [*Library symbol*] [*Library of Congress*] (LCLS)
PPFC.......... People's Pearl and Fishery Corporation [*Government corporation*] [*Rangoon, Burma*]
PPFC.......... Philadelphia Fellowship Commission, Philadelphia, PA [*Library symbol*] [*Library of Congress*] [*Obsolete*] (LCLS)
PPFD.......... Photosynthetically Active Photon Flux Density [*Botany*]
PPFF .... Poisson Probability Frequency Function [*Mathematics*]
PPF-G....... Germantown Laboratories, Inc., Philadelphia, PA [*Library symbol*] [*Library of Congress*] (LCLS)
PPFHi .... Historical Society of Frankford, Philadelphia, PA [*Library symbol*] [*Library of Congress*] [*Obsolete*] (LCLS)
PPFJC .... Federation of Jewish Charities, Philadelphia, PA [*Library symbol*] [*Library of Congress*] [*Obsolete*] (LCLS)
PPFML ...... Fidelity Mutual Life Insurance Co., Philadelphia, PA [*Library symbol*] [*Library of Congress*] (LCLS)
PPFO.......... Paris Procurement Field Office
PPFPR....... F. P. Ristine & Co., Philadelphia, PA [*Library symbol*] [*Library of Congress*] [*Obsolete*] (LCLS)
PPFr .... Friends' Free Library of Germantown, Philadelphia, PA [*Library symbol*] [*Library of Congress*] (LCLS)
PPFR .... Plutonium Product Filter Room [*Nuclear energy*] (NRCH)
PPFRB....... Federal Reserve Bank of Philadelphia, Philadelphia, PA [*Library symbol*] [*Library of Congress*] (LCLS)
PPFRT....... Prototype Preliminary Flight Rating Test
PPG .... German Society of Pennsylvania, Philadelphia, PA [*Library symbol*] [*Library of Congress*] (LCLS)
PPG .... Pacific Proving Ground [*AEC*]
PPG .... Pago Pago [*Samoa*] [*Airport symbol*] (OAG)
PPG .... Pago Pago, AQ [*Location identifier*] [*FAA*] (FAAL)
PPG .... PEMA [*Procurement of Equipment and Missiles, Army*] Policy and Guidance (AABC)
PPG .... Periodical Press Gallery [*US Senate*]
PPG .... Personnel Processing Group
PPG .... Phoenizisch-Punische Grammatik [*A publication*]
PPG .... Photoplethysmography [*Medicine*]
PPG .... Picopicogram
PPG .... Piezoelectric Power Generation
PPG .... Pipe Plug
PPG .... Planned Procurement Guide
PPG .... Planning and Policy Guidance (MCD)
PPG .... Planning and Programing Guidance (AABC)
PPG .... Plasma Power Generator
PPG .... Player Piano Group (EA-IO)
PPG .... Poly(propylene Glycol) [*Organic chemistry*]
PPG .... Power-Play Goal [*Hockey*]
PPG .... PPG Industries, Inc. [*Formerly, Pittsburgh Plate Glass Co.*] [*NYSE symbol*]
PPG .... PPG Industries, Inc., Coatings and Resins Division, Allison Park, PA [*OCLC symbol*] (OCLC)
PPG .... Primary Pattern Generator [*Bell Laboratories*]
PPG .... Program Planning Guide (OICC)
PPG .... Program Policy Guidelines
PPG .... Program Pulse Generator (IEEE)
PPG .... Propulsion and Power Generation
PPGA......... Personal Producing General Agent [*Insurance*]
PPGA......... Post Pill Galactorrhea-Amenorrhea [*Medicine*]
PPGE......... General Electric Co., Philadelphia, PA [*Library symbol*] [*Library of Congress*] (LCLS)
PPGE-M ..... General Electric Co., Missile and Space Vehicle Department, Aerosciences Laboratory, Philadelphia, PA [*Library symbol*] [*Library of Congress*] (LCLS)
PPGen .... Genealogical Society of Pennsylvania, Philadelphia, PA [*Library symbol*] [*Library of Congress*] (LCLS)
PPGenH ..... Philadelphia General Hospital Laboratories, Philadelphia, PA [*Library symbol*] [*Library of Congress*] [*Obsolete*] (LCLS)
PPGeo .... Geographical Society of Philadelphia, Philadelphia, PA [*Library symbol*] [*Library of Congress*] [*Obsolete*] (LCLS)
PPGH......... Philadelphia General Hospital, Philadelphia, PA [*Library symbol*] [*Library of Congress*] (LCLS)
PPGi .... Girard College, Philadelphia, PA [*Library symbol*] [*Library of Congress*] [*Obsolete*] (LCLS)
PPGJW ..... Past Pro-Grand Junior Warden [*Freemasonry*] (ROG)
PPGM........ Past Provincial Grand Master [*Freemasonry*]
PPGM........ Planning-Programing Guidance Memo [*Navy*]
PPGO .... Past Pro-Grand Organist [*Freemasonry*] (ROG)
PPGO .... Past Pro-Grand Orient [*Freemasonry*] (ROG)
PPGP .... Past Pro-Grand Pursuivant [*Freemasonry*] (ROG)
PPGraph .... Graphic Sketch Club, Philadelphia, PA [*Library symbol*] [*Library of Congress*] [*Obsolete*] (LCLS)
PPGratz...... Gratz College, Philadelphia, PA [*Library symbol*] [*Library of Congress*] [*Obsolete*] (LCLS)
PPGRC ...... Public Policy and Government Relations Council
PPGS......... Publications. Pennsylvania German Society [*A publication*]
PPGSB....... Past Pro-Grand Sword Bearer [*Freemasonry*] (ROG)
PPGSN ...... Past Provincial Grand Senior [*Freemasonry*] (ROG)
PPGSW ..... Past Provincial Grand Senior Warden [*Freemasonry*]
PP Guide.... Prescription Proprietaries Guide [*A publication*]
PPGW........ Past Pro-Grand Warden [*Freemasonry*] (ROG)
PPH .... Paid Personal Holiday

PPH .... Pamphlet
PPH .... Parts per Hundred
PPH .... Persistent Pulmonary Hypertension [*Medicine*]
PPH .... Petroleum Pipehead
PPH .... Phenylpropanolamine(hydrochloride) [*Also, PPA, PPM*] [*Decongestant*]
PPH .... Phosphopyruvate Hydratase [*An enzyme*]
PPH .... Postpartum Hemorrhage [*Medicine*]
PPH .... Pounds per Hour (NG)
PPH .... Primary Pulmonary Hypertension [*Medicine*]
PPH .... Prophet Resources Ltd. [*Vancouver Stock Exchange symbol*]
PPH .... Pulses per Hour
PPHa .... Hahnemann Medical College and Hospital, Philadelphia, PA [*Library symbol*] [*Library of Congress*] (LCLS)
PPHA .... Peak Pulse Height Analysis
PPHA .... Private Proprietary Homes for Adults
PPHBA .... Peruvian Paso Half-Blood Association [*Later, PPPBR*] (EA)
PPHFC .... Holy Family College, Philadelphia, PA [*Library symbol*] [*Library of Congress*] (LCLS)
P Ph L .... Papers in Philippine Linguistics [*A publication*]
PPHM .... Parts per Hundred Million
P-PH-M ..... Pulse Phase Modulation (DEN)
PPHN......... Persistent Pulmonary Hypertension of the Newborn [*Medicine*]
PPHOPT .... Pseudo-Pseudohypoparathyroidism [*Also, PPHP*] [*Endocrinology*]
PPHor......... Pennsylvania Horticultural Society, Philadelphia, PA [*Library symbol*] [*Library of Congress*] (LCLS)
PPHP .... Pseudo-Pseudohypoparathyroidism [*Also, PPHOPT*] [*Endocrinology*]
PPHPB....... Problemy Projektowe Hutnictwa i Przemyslu Maszynowego [*A publication*]
PPHPI........ Henry Phipps Institute, Philadelphia, PA [*Library symbol*] [*Library of Congress*] [*Obsolete*] (LCLS)
PPHR .... Planned Parenthood Review [*A publication*]
PPHRA ...... Philosophy and Phenomenological Research [*A publication*]
PPHRD ...... Photochemical and Photobiological Reviews [*A publication*]
PPHRII....... Parents of Premature and High Risk Infants International (EA)
PPHRNA .... Peruvian Paso Horse Registry of North America (EA)
PPHS .... Partisan Prohibition Historical Society (EA)
PPHSL....... Periodical Publication in Harvard Science Libraries
PPHT .... (Phenylethyl-propylamino)hydroxytetralin [*Biochemistry*]
PPHYA ...... Plant Physiology [*English Translation*] [*A publication*]
PPi .... Carnegie Library of Pittsburgh, Pittsburgh, PA [*Library symbol*] [*Library of Congress*] (LCLS)
PPI............. Institute for Psychosomatic and Psychiatric Research and Training [*Michael Reese Hospital and Medical Center, University of Chicago*] [*Research center*] (RCD)
PPI............. Packing, Postage, and Insurance
PPI............. Padangpandjang [*Sumatra*] [*Seismograph station code, US Geological Survey*] (SEIS)
PPI............. Pakistan Press International
PPI............. Parcel Post, Insured
PPI............. Patient Package Insert [*Instructional leaflet distributed with certain prescription drugs*]
PPI............. Pensioners for Peace International [*Great Malvern, England*] (EA-IO)
PPI............. Pergamon Press, Incorporated
PPI............. Personality and Personal Illness Questionnaires [*Psychology*]
PPI............. Personnel Planning Information
PPI............. Phoenix Precision Instrument Co.
PPI............. Pickle Packers International [*St. Charles, IL*] (EA)
PPI............. Pico Products, Incorporated [*American Stock Exchange symbol*]
PPI............. Pictorial Position Indicator
PPI............. Pilgrim Coal Corp. [*Vancouver Stock Exchange symbol*]
PPI............. Pilgrim Holdings Ltd. [*Vancouver Stock Exchange symbol*]
PPI............. PIPA [*Pulsed Integrating Pendulous Accelerometer*] Pulse Integrator
PPI............. Piston Position Indicator
PPI............. Plan Position Indicator Mode [*Data processing*] (ADA)
PPI............. Plane Position Indicator [*RADAR*]
PPI............. Planen-Pruefen-Investieren [*A publication*]
PPI............. Plasma Protein Isolate [*Food technology*]
PPI............. Plastics Pipe Institute [*New York, NY*] (EA)
PPI............. Plot Position Indicator
PPI............. Policy Proof of Interest
PPI............. Polyphthalimide [*Organic chemistry*]
PPI............. POM [*Program Objective Memorandum*] Preparation Instructions [*Military*]
PPI............. Port Pirie [*Australia*] [*Airport symbol*] (OAG)
PPI............. Postage Paid Impression
PPI............. Potash and Phosphate Institute [*Formerly, API, PI, PINA*] (EA)
PPI............. Preceding Preparatory Interval [*Psychometrics*]
PPI............. Preferred Parts Index
PPI............. Preplant Incorporated [*Herbicides*] [*Agriculture*]
PPI............. Prepleading Investigation [*Law*]
PPI............. Present Pain Intensity
PPI............. Present Position Indicator [*Aviation*]
PPI............. Primary Personal Interest [*Personnel study*]
PPI............. Producer Price Index [*Department of Labor*]
PPI............. Program Position Indicator

PPI............. Programable Peripheral Interface   (MCD)
PPI............. Project Procurement Instructions [*Jet Propulsion Laboratory, NASA*]
PPI............. Property Protection Insurance
PPI............. Public-Private Interface
PPI............. Pulse Position Indicator   (MCD)
PPI............. Pulses per Inch   (CMD)
PPi............. Pyrophosphate, Inorganic [*Chemistry*]
PPi-A.......... Carnegie Library of Pittsburgh, Allegheny Regional Branch, Monroeville, PA [*Library symbol*] [*Library of Congress*]   (LCLS)
PPiAC........ Community College of Allegheny County, Pittsburgh, PA [*Library symbol*] [*Library of Congress*]   (LCLS)
PPiAL........ Allegheny County Law Library, Pittsburgh, PA [*Library symbol*] [*Library of Congress*]   (LCLS)
PPiAM........ Pittsburgh Academy of Medicine, Pittsburgh, PA [*Library symbol*] [*Library of Congress*]   (LCLS)
PPIB.......... Programable Protocol Interface Board
PPiC.......... Carnegie-Mellon University, Pittsburgh, PA [*Library symbol*] [*Library of Congress*]   (LCLS)
PPiCa......... Carlow College, Pittsburgh, PA [*Library symbol*] [*Library of Congress*]   (LCLS)
PPiCa-O..... Carlow College, Our Lady of Mercy Academy, Pittsburgh, PA [*Library symbol*] [*Library of Congress*]   (LCLS)
PPiCC........ Chatham College, Pittsburgh, PA [*Library symbol*] [*Library of Congress*]   (LCLS)
PPICR........ Institute for Cancer Research, Philadelphia, PA [*Library symbol*] [*Library of Congress*]   (LCLS)
PPiD.......... Duquesne University, Pittsburgh, PA [*Library symbol*] [*Library of Congress*]   (LCLS)
PPID.......... Polaris-Poseidon Intelligence Digest   (MCD)
PPiD-L........ Duquesne University, School of Law, Pittsburgh, PA [*Library symbol*] [*Library of Congress*]   (LCLS)
PPiE.......... E. D'Appolonia Consulting Engineers, Pittsburgh, PA [*Library symbol*] [*Library of Congress*]   (LCLS)
PPIF.......... Photo Processing Interpretation Facility
PPIFC........ Pauline Pinkney International Fan Club   (EA)
PPiGulf....... Gulf Research & Development Co., Pittsburgh, PA [*Library symbol*] [*Library of Congress*]   (LCLS)
PPiHB........ Carnegie-Mellon University, Hunt Institute for Botanical Documentation, Pittsburgh, PA [*Library symbol*] [*Library of Congress*]   (LCLS)
PPiHi......... Historical Society of Western Pennsylvania, Pittsburgh, PA [*Library symbol*] [*Library of Congress*]   (LCLS)
PPiIl.......... International Poetry Forum, Pittsburgh, PA [*Library symbol*] [*Library of Congress*]   (LCLS)
PPiK.......... Ketchum, McLeod & Grove, Inc., Pittsburgh, PA [*Library symbol*] [*Library of Congress*]   (LCLS)
PPiL.......... LaRoche College, Pittsburgh, PA [*Library symbol*] [*Library of Congress*]   (LCLS)
PPIL.......... Priced Provisioned Item List   (MCD)
PPiM......... Carnegie-Mellon University, Mellon Institute, Pittsburgh, PA [*Library symbol*] [*Library of Congress*]   (LCLS)
PPiMS....... Mine Safety Appliances Co., Pittsburgh, PA [*Library symbol*] [*Library of Congress*]   (LCLS)
PPIn.......... Independence National Historical Park, Philadelphia, PA [*Library symbol*] [*Library of Congress*]   (LCLS)
PPINA........ Insurance Co., of North America, Corporate Archives, Philadelphia, PA [*Library symbol*] [*Library of Congress*]   (LCLS)
PPINICI...... Pulsed Positive Ion-Negative Ion Chemical Ionization [*Instrumentation*]
PPiPP........ Point Park College, Pittsburgh, PA [*Library symbol*] [*Library of Congress*]   (LCLS)
PPiPPG...... PPG Industries, Inc., Glass Research Center, Information Services Library, Pittsburgh, PA [*Library symbol*] [*Library of Congress*]   (LCLS)
PPiPT........ Pittsburgh Theological Seminary, Pittsburgh, PA [*Library symbol*] [*Library of Congress*]   (LCLS)
PPIR.......... Personnel Planning Information Report   (MCD)
PPiR.......... Rockwell International Corp., Pittsburgh, PA [*Library symbol*] [*Library of Congress*]   (LCLS)
PPIRO........ Planned Position Indicator Readout   (NVT)
PPIS.......... Product Profile Information System [*Shell Oil Co.*]
PPIU.......... Programable Peripheral Interface Unit
PPiU.......... University of Pittsburgh, Pittsburgh, PA [*Library symbol*] [*Library of Congress*]   (LCLS)
PPiU-A....... University of Pittsburgh, Henry Clay Frick Fine Arts Center, Pittsburgh, PA [*Library symbol*] [*Library of Congress*]   (LCLS)
PPiU-BL..... University of Pittsburgh, Blair-Lippincott Library, Eye and Ear Hospital of Pittsburgh, Pittsburgh, PA [*Library symbol*] [*Library of Congress*]   (LCLS)
PPiU-H....... University of Pittsburgh, Maurice and Laura Falk Library of the Health Professions, Pittsburgh, PA [*Library symbol*] [*Library of Congress*]   (LCLS)
PPiU-L........ University of Pittsburgh, Law School, Pittsburgh, PA [*Library symbol*] [*Library of Congress*]   (LCLS)
PPiU-LS..... University of Pittsburgh, Graduate School of Library and Information Sciences, Pittsburgh, PA [*Library symbol*] [*Library of Congress*]   (LCLS)

PPiU-NS..... University of Pittsburgh, Natural Sciences Library, Pittsburgh, PA [*Library symbol*] [*Library of Congress*]   (LCLS)
PPiU-PH..... University of Pittsburgh, Graduate School of Public Health, Pittsburgh, PA [*Library symbol*] [*Library of Congress*]   (LCLS)
PPiU-PIA.... University of Pittsburgh, Graduate School of Public and International Affairs, Pittsburgh, PA [*Library symbol*] [*Library of Congress*]   (LCLS)
PPiUS........ United States Steel Corp., Pittsburgh, PA [*Library symbol*] [*Library of Congress*]   (LCLS)
PPiU-SF..... University of Pittsburgh, Stephen Collins Foster Memorial [*Music*] Library, Pittsburgh, PA [*Library symbol*] [*Library of Congress*]   (LCLS)
PPiUSM...... United States Department of the Interior, Bureau of Mines, Pittsburgh Research Center, Pittsburgh, PA [*Library symbol*] [*Library of Congress*]   (LCLS)
PPiW........ Westinghouse Electric Corp., Research and Development Center, Pittsburgh, PA [*Library symbol*] [*Library of Congress*]   (LCLS)
PPiW-N....... Westinghouse Electric Corp., Nuclear Center Library, Pittsburgh, PA [*Library symbol*] [*Library of Congress*]   (LCLS)
PPiWP........ Western Psychiatric Institute and Clinic, University of Pittsburgh, Pittsburgh, PA [*Library symbol*] [*Library of Congress*]   (LCLS)
PPJ............ Pressure Plane Joint
PPJ............ Prilozi Proucavanju Jezika [*A publication*]
PPJ............ Pure Pancreatic Juice
PPJ............ Thomas Jefferson University, Philadelphia, PA [*Library symbol*] [*Library of Congress*]   (LCLS)
PPJea......... Jeanes Hospital, Philadelphia, PA [*Library symbol*] [*Library of Congress*] [*Obsolete*]   (LCLS)
PPJO......... Pli Premier Jour Officiel [*Official First Day Cover - OFDC*] [*Canada Post Corp.*]
PPJ-S......... Thomas Jefferson University, Scott Memorial Library, Philadelphia, PA [*Library symbol*] [*Library of Congress*]   (LCLS)
PPJW......... Past Pro-Junior Warden [*Freemasonry*]   (ROG)
PPK.......... Paired Perpendicular Keratotomy [*Procedure to correct astigmatism*]
PPK .... Paramp Pump Klystron
PPK .... Parti Progressiste Katangais [*Political party*]
PPK .... Personal Preference Kit [*Small bag in which astronauts are allowed to take personal mementos*]
PPK .... Polizei Pistole Kriminal [*Pistol suitable for undercover police or detective use*] [*Walther Waffenfabrik, German arms manufacturer*]
PPK .... Punt, Pass, and Kick [*Youth competition sponsored by professional football*]
PPKCB....... Prace Komisji Ceramicznej. Polskiej Akademii Nauk. Ceramica [*A publication*]
PPKG .... Power Package   (MSA)
PPKGA...... Ponpu Kogaku [*A publication*]
PPL............ Library Co. of Philadelphia, Philadelphia, PA [*Library symbol*] [*Library of Congress*]   (LCLS)
PPL............ Palmer Physical Laboratory [*Princeton University*]   (MCD)
PPL............ Pembina Resources Limited [*Toronto Stock Exchange symbol*]
PPL............ Penicilloyl Polylysine [*Pharmacology*]
PPL............ Pennsylvania Power & Light Co. [*NYSE symbol*]
PPL............ Per Pupil Limitation   (AFM)
PPL............ Peter Peregrinus Limited [*Publisher*]
PPL............ Phenylpropanolamine [*Biochemistry*]
PPL............ Physical Properties Laboratory [*Oklahoma State University*] [*Research center*]   (RCD)
PPL............ Plan Position Landing   (DEN)
PPL............ Plasma Physics Laboratory [*Also known as PPPL*]
PPL............ Plasma Propulsion Laboratory   (MCD)
PPL............ Plutonium Product Loadout [*Nuclear energy*]   (NRCH)
PPL............ Polybiblion. Partie Litteraire [*A publication*]
PPL............ Polymorphic Programing Language [*1971*] [*Data processing*]   (CSR)
PPL............ Populated Place [*Board on Geographic Names*]
PPL............ Power Plant Laboratory   (MUGU)
PPL............ Prace Polonistyczne (Lodz) [*A publication*]
PPL............ Predictive Period LASER   (KSC)
PPL............ Preferential Planning List
PPL............ Preferred Parts List
PPL............ Preliminary Parts List
PPL............ Priced Parts List   (NASA)
P/PL.......... Primary Payload [*NASA*]   (NASA)
PPL............ Princeton Polymer Laboratories
PPL............ Private Pilot Licence [*British*]
PPL............ Program Production Library [*Data processing*]
PPL............ Project Priority List [*Environmental Protection Agency*]
PPL............ Provisioning Parts List   (AAG)
PPL............ Purchased Parts List
PPL............ Puu Pili [*Hawaii*] [*Seismograph station code, US Geological Survey*]   (SEIS)
PpL............ W. & F. Pascoe Proprietory Ltd., Milsons Point, Australia [*Library symbol*] [*Library of Congress*]   (LCLS)
PPLA......... Practice Precautionary Landing Approach [*Aviation*]

PPLas......... La Salle College, Philadelphia, PA [*Library symbol*] [*Library of Congress*] (LCLS)
PPLD .... Pikes Peak Library District [*Internationally recognized computerized library system*]
PPLDF....... Professional Protector and Legal Defense Fund
PPLE .... Partial Preliminary Logistic Evaluation
PPLE .... Participle [*Grammar*]
PPLE .... Principle (ROG)
PPLI........... Provisioning Parts List Index (MCD)
PPLL........... Military Order of the Loyal Legion of the United States, [*Civil*] War Library and Museum, Philadelphia, PA [*Library symbol*] [*Library of Congress*] (LCLS)
PPLN .... Pipeline
PPLO .... Pleuropneumonia-Like Organisms [*Bacteriology*]
PPLP .... Photopolymers Lithograph Plate
P PLPBD..... Paper or Pulpboard [*Freight*]
PPLS .... Precision Position Locator System [*Army*]
PPLS .... Preferred Parts List System (MCD)
PPLS .... Propellant and Pressurant Loading System [*NASA*] (KSC)
PPLT .... Lutheran Theological Seminary, Philadelphia, PA [*Library symbol*] [*Library of Congress*] (LCLS)
PPLX .... Section of Populated Place [*Board on Geographic Names*]
PPM.......... Aberdeen, MD [*Location identifier*] [*FAA*] (FAAL)
PPM.......... Mercantile Library, Philadelphia, PA [*Library symbol*] [*Library of Congress*] [*Obsolete*] (LCLS)
P & PM...... Packing and Packaging Manual (MCD)
ppm.......... Papermaker [*MARC relator code*] [*Library of Congress*]
PPM.......... Parti Pekerja-Pekerja Malaysia [*Workers' Party of Malaysia*] (PPW)
PPM.......... Parti du Peuple Mauritanien [*Mauritanian political party*]
PPM.......... Parti Progressiste Martiniquais [*Progressive Party of Martinique*] (PPW)
PPM.......... Partido del Pueblo Mexicano [*Mexican People's Party*] (PPW)
PPM.......... Parts per Million
PPM.......... Parts per Minute (MCD)
PPM.......... Peak Power Meter
PPM.......... Peak Program Meter [*Television*]
PPM.......... Periodic Permanent Magnet
PPM.......... Periodic Pulse Metering [*Telecommunications*] (TEL)
PPM.......... Personnel Priority Model (MCD)
PPM.......... Personnel Program Manager [*Navy*]
PPM.......... Phenylpropanolamine(hydrochloride) [*Also, PPA, PPH*] [*Decongestant*]
PPM.......... Phosphopentomutase [*An enzyme*]
PPM.......... Pilot Production Model [*Military*] (CAAL)
PPM.......... Planned Preventive Maintenance (IEEE)
PPM.......... Popocatepetl [*Mexico*] [*Seismograph station code, US Geological Survey*] (SEIS)
PPM.......... Position and Pay Management [*Army*] (AABC)
PPM....... Postage Prepaid in Money
PPM....... Postpass Message
PPM....... Pounds per Minute
PPM....... Prairie Print Makers [*Defunct*] (EA)
PPM....... Previous Processor Mode
PPM....... Production Planning Memorandum
PPM....... Project Profile Manual
PPM....... Public Personnel Management [*A publication*]
PPM.......... Pulp and Paper Magazine of Canada [*A publication*]
PPM.......... Pulse Position Modulation [*Radio data transmission*]
PPM.......... Pulses per Minute
PPMA .... Plastic Products Manufacturers Association [*Later, Plastic and Metal Products Manufacturers Association*] (EA)
PPMA .... Political Products Manufacturers Association [*Ferndale, NY*] (EA)
PPMA .... Post-Poliomyelitis Muscular Atrophy [*Medicine*]
PPMA .... Precision Potentiometer Manufacturers Association [*Later, Variable Resistive Components Institute*] (EA)
PPMA .... Pulp and Paper Manufacturers Association [*Later, PPMMA*] (EA)
PPMC .... People to People Music Committee (EA)
PPME .... Pacific Plate Motion Experiment (NASA)
PPMFC....... Preprints on Precision Measurement and Fundamental Constants [*National Bureau of Standards*]
PPMG........ Professional Publishers Marketing Group [*New York, NY*] (EA)
PPMI........... Pilot Plant Meat Irradiator
PPMI........... Printed Paper Mat Institute (EA)
PPMIN....... Pulses per Minute (MSA)
PPMis........ Misericordia Hospital, Philadelphia, PA [*Library symbol*] [*Library of Congress*] [*Obsolete*] (LCLS)
PPML........... Preferred Parts and Materials List [*NASA*]
PPMMA...... Pulp and Paper Machinery Manufacturers Association [*Washington, DC*] (EA)
PPMMB ..... Periodica Polytechnica. Mechanical Engineering [*A publication*]
PPMNA...... Polski Przeglad Radiologii i Medycyny Nuklearnaj [*A publication*]
PPMO .... Pershing Project Manager's Office (RDA)
PPMol....... Moore College of Art, Philadelphia, PA [*Library symbol*] [*Library of Congress*] (LCLS)
PPMR .... Purchased Parts Material Requirements
PPMS .... Pitt Press Mathematical Series [*A publication*]

PPMS .... Poly(para-Methylstyrene) [*Organic chemistry*]
PPMS .... Program Performance Measurement Systems (IEEE)
PPMS .... Purdue Perceptual-Motor Survey [*Kephart Scale*]
PPMV .... Parts per Million by Volume
PPN .... Numismatic and Antiquarian Society, Philadelphia, PA [*Library symbol*] [*Library of Congress*] [*Obsolete*] (LCLS)
PPN .... Papenoo [*Society Islands*] [*Seismograph station code, US Geological Survey*] (SEIS)
PPN .... Parameterized Post-Newtonian [*Gravity*]
PPN .... Parti Progressiste Nigerien [*Nigerian Progressive Party*]
PPN .... Partido Progreso Nacional [*National Progress Party*] [*Costa Rican*] (PPW)
PPN .... Peak-to-Peak Noise [*Instrumentation*]
PPN .... Peroxypropionyl Nitrate [*Organic chemistry*]
PPN .... Polyphosphonate [*Organic chemistry*]
PPN .... Popayan [*Colombia*] [*Airport symbol*] (OAG)
PPN .... Portland Public Library, Portland, ME [*OCLC symbol*] (OCLC)
PPN .... Procurement Program Number [*Military*]
PPN .... Project, Programer Number
PPN .... Proportion (ROG)
PPNA........ Peak Phrenic Nerve Activity [*Medicine*]
PP & NA .... Private Plants and Naval Activities
PPNCFL .... Proceedings. Pacific Northwest Conference on Foreign Languages [*A publication*]
PPNDG...... Petition Pending
PPNF........ Price-Pottenger Nutrition Foundation [*LaMesa, CA*] (EA)
PPNG........ Penicillinase-Producing Neisseria gonorrhoeae
PPNICI ...... Pulsed Positive/Negative Ion Chemical Ionization
P/PNL .... Pocket Panel [*Automotive engineering*]
PPNMC ..... United States Navy, Naval Regional Medical Center, Philadelphia, PA [*Library symbol*] [*Library of Congress*] (LCLS)
PPNSC .... Preferred Procurement Number Selector Code [*Military*] (AFIT)
PPNSCA.... Policy Plans and National Security Council Affairs
PPNWA ...... N. W. Ayer & Son, Philadelphia, PA [*Library symbol*] [*Library of Congress*] [*Obsolete*] (LCLS)
PPO .... Photographic Program Office [*NASA*] (KSC)
PPO .... Platelet Peroxidase [*An enzyme*]
PPO .... Pleuropneumonia Organisms [*Bacteriology*]
PPO .... Polyphenol Oxidase [*An enzyme*]
PPO .... Polyphenylene Oxide [*Organic chemistry*]
PPO .... Poly(propylene Oxide) [*Organic chemistry*]
PPO .... Port Postal Office (AFM)
PPO .... Power Plant Operating
PPO .... Preferred-Provider Organization [*Medicine*]
PPO .... Pressed Plutonium Oxide
PPO .... Principal Priority Officer
PPO .... Prior Permission Only (AFM)
PPO .... Procurement Planning Officer
PPO .... Program Printout (MCD)
PPO .... Projected Program Objective (NG)
PPO .... Publications and Printing Office [*Military*]
PPO .... Pure Plutonium Oxide
PPO .... Push-Pull Output (DEN)
PPO$_2$...... Partial Pressure of Oxygen (CAAL)
PPol........... Pensiero Politico [*A publication*]
PPol........... Przeglad Polski [*A publication*]
PPOS......... Saint George United Methodist Church, Philadelphia, PA [*Library symbol*] [*Library of Congress*] (LCLS)
PPOSN ...... Proposition (ROG)
PPow........ Przeglad Powszechny [*A publication*]
PPP .... Pacific Peacemaker Project (EA)
PPP .... Pakistan People's Party (PD)
PPP .... Paper, Printing, Publishing [*Department of Employment*] [*British*]
PPP .... Parallel Pattern Processor
PPP .... Partai Persatuan Pembangunan [*United Development Party*] [*Indonesian*] (PPW)
PPP .... Partido del Pueblo de Panama [*Panamanian People's Party*] (PPW)
PPP .... Peak Pulse Power
PPP .... Pentose-phosphate Pathway [*Metabolism*]
PPP .... People's Patriotic Party [*Burmese*] (PD)
PPP .... People's Political Party [*St. Vincentian*] (PPW)
PPP .... People's Progress Party [*Papua New Guinean*] (PPW)
PPP .... People's Progressive Party [*Solomon Islander*] (PPW)
PPP .... People's Progressive Party [*Anguillan*] (PPW)
PPP .... People's Progressive Party [*Gambian*] (PPW)
PPP .... People's Progressive Party [*Guyanese*] (PD)
PPP .... Permanent Party Personnel (MCD)
PPP .... Perpex Peristaltic Pump
PPP .... Personal Property Policy [*Insurance*]
PPP .... Phased Project Planning [*NASA*] (KSC)
PPP .... Pianississimo [*As Softly As Possible*] [*Music*]
PPP .... Pickford Projective Pictures [*Psychology*]
PPP .... Pipelines, Politics, and People. Capital Communications Limited [*A publication*]
PPP .... Plan Position Presentation
PPP .... Planning Purpose Proposal
PPP .... Platelet-Poor Plasma [*Hematology*]

PPP .... Pluripotent Progenitor [*Cytology*]
PPP .... Pogo Producing Co. [*NYSE symbol*]
PPP .... Polluter Pays Principle
PPP .... Portable Plotting Package [*Nuclear energy*]   (NRCH)
PPP .... Positive Pressure Paradox
PPP .... Prescriptive Parent Programing [*Education*]
PPP .... Prescriptive Program Plan [*Education*]
PPP .... Pretty Poor Planning
PPP .... Prison Pen Pals   (EA)
PPP .... Production Part Pattern   (MCD)
PPP .... Profit and Performance Planning
PPP .... Progressive People's Party [*Liberian*]   (PPW)
PPP .... Propria Pecunia Posuit [*Erected at His Own Expense*] [*Latin*]
PPP .... Proserpine [*Australia*] [*Airport symbol*]   (OAG)
PPP .... Province Pacification Plan   (CINC)
PPP .... Provisioning Program Plan   (MCD)
P & PP .... Pull and Push Plate
PPP .... Purchasing Power Parity [*Economics*]
PPPA .... Poison Prevention Packaging Act
PPPA .... Professional Pool Players Association   (EA)
PPPA .... Pulp and Paper Prepackaging Association [*Later, SSI*]
PPPBR .... Peruvian Paso Part-Blood Registry [*Formerly, PPHBA*]   (EA)
PPPC .... Petroleum Pool Pacific Coast
PPPC .... Pipe Plug Producers Council   (EA)
PPPCA .... Philadelphia College of Art Library, Philadelphia, PA [*Library symbol*] [*Library of Congress*]   (LCLS)
PPPCity...... Philadelphia City Institute Branch Free Library, Philadelphia, PA [*Library symbol*] [*Library of Congress*] [*Obsolete*]   (LCLS)
PPPCO .... Pennsylvania College of Optometry, Philadelphia, PA [*Library symbol*] [*Library of Congress*]   (LCLS)
PPPCPh ..... Philadelphia College of Pharmacy and Science, Philadelphia, PA [*Library symbol*] [*Library of Congress*]   (LCLS)
PPPE .... Pennsylvania Economy League, Inc., Eastern Division, Philadelphia, PA [*Library symbol*] [*Library of Congress*]   (LCLS)
PPPE .... People, Plans, and the Peace. Peace River Planning Commission [*A publication*]
PPPEA .... Pulp, Paper, and Paperboard Export Association of the United States [*Bethlehem, PA*]   (EA)
PPPEC ...... Philadelphia Electric Co., Philadelphia, PA [*Library symbol*] [*Library of Congress*]   (LCLS)
PPPEE....... Pulsed Pinch Plasma Electromagnetic Engine   (AAG)
PPPFM .... Free and Accepted Masons of Pennsylvania, Grand Lodge Library, Philadelphia, PA [*Library symbol*] [*Library of Congress*]   (LCLS)
PPPG......... People's Progressive Party of Guyana
PPPH......... Pennsylvania Hospital, Philadelphia, PA [*Library symbol*] [*Library of Congress*]   (LCLS)
PPPHA ...... Philadelphia Housing Association, Philadelphia, PA [*Library symbol*] [*Library of Congress*] [*Obsolete*]   (LCLS)
PPPHC ...... Philadelphia Tuberculosis and Health Association, Philadelphia, PA [*Library symbol*] [*Library of Congress*] [*Obsolete*]   (LCLS)
PPPH-I........ Institute of the Pennsylvania Hospital, Philadelphia, PA [*Library symbol*] [*Library of Congress*]   (LCLS)
PPPI .... Insurance Society of Philadelphia, Philadelphia, PA [*Library symbol*] [*Library of Congress*] [*Obsolete*]   (LCLS)
PPPI .... Precision Plan Position Indicator
PPPI .... Projection Plan Position Indicator
PPPI .... Pulp, Paper, and Paperboard Institute USA [*Later, API*]
PPPL .... Philadelphia Board of Public Education, Pedagogical Library, Philadelphia, PA [*Library symbol*] [*Library of Congress*]   (LCLS)
PPPL .... Princeton Plasma Physics Laboratory [*Also known as PPL - Plasma Physics Laboratory*]
PPPL .... Printed Planning Parts List
PPPL .... Program Preferred Parts List
PPPlanP ..... Planned Parenthood of Southeast Pennsylvania, Philadelphia, PA [*Library symbol*] [*Library of Congress*]   (LCLS)
PPPlay....... Plays and Players Club, Philadelphia, PA [*Library symbol*] [*Library of Congress*] [*Obsolete*]   (LCLS)
PPPM .... Philadelphia Museum of Art, Philadelphia, PA [*Library symbol*] [*Library of Congress*]   (LCLS)
PPP & M .... Preservation, Packaging, Packing, and Marking
PPPMD...... Pishchevaya Promyshlennost. Seriya 12. Spirtavya i Likero-Vodochnaya Promyshlennost [*A publication*]
PPPM-I....... Philadelphia Museum of Art, College of Art, Philadelphia, PA [*Library symbol*] [*Library of Congress*] [*Obsolete*]   (LCLS)
PPPP .... Past Performance and Present Posture   (AAG)
PPPP .... People's Peace and Prosperity Party [*Defunct*]   (EA)
PPPP .... Proposed Partial Package Program   (MUGU)
PPPPI .... Photographic Projection Plan Position Indicator   (DEN)
PPPR .... Philadelphia Transportation Co., Philadelphia, PA [*Library symbol*] [*Library of Congress*] [*Obsolete*]   (LCLS)
PPPRC ...... Poor Richard Club, Philadelphia, PA [*Library symbol*] [*Library of Congress*] [*Obsolete*]   (LCLS)
PPPres ...... Presbyterian University of Pennsylvania, Scheie Eye Institute Library, Philadelphia, PA [*Library symbol*] [*Library of Congress*]   (LCLS)
PPPRF........ Pan Pacific Public Relations Federation

PPPrHi........ Presbyterian Historical Society, Philadelphia, PA [*Library symbol*] [*Library of Congress*]   (LCLS)
PPPrI.......... Printing Institute, Philadelphia, PA [*Library symbol*] [*Library of Congress*] [*Obsolete*]   (LCLS)
PPProM...... Provident Mutual Life Insurance Co., Philadelphia, PA [*Library symbol*] [*Library of Congress*] [*Obsolete*]   (LCLS)
PPPSB....... Philadelphia College of the Bible, Philadelphia, PA [*Library symbol*] [*Library of Congress*]   (LCLS)
PPPTe .... Philadelphia College of Textiles and Science, Philadelphia, PA [*Library symbol*] [*Library of Congress*]   (LCLS)
PPQ .... Abandoned Police Post [*Board on Geographic Names*]
PPQ .... Parts per Quadrillion
PPQ .... Pittsfield, IL [*Location identifier*] [*FAA*]   (FAAL)
PPQ .... Planning Purpose Quote
PPQ .... Polyphenylquinoxaline [*Resin*]
PPQA......... Pageable Partition Queue Area [*Data processing*]
P & P Qtly ... Pulp and Paper Quarterly Statistics [*A publication*]
PPr .... Paedagogische Provinz [*A publication*]
PPR .... Palomino Pony Registry
PPR .... Paper
PPR .... Partido Proletariano Revolucionario [*Proletarian Revolutionary Party*] [*Portuguese*]   (PPW)
PPR .... Payload Preparation Room [*VAFB*] [*NASA*]   (MCD)
PPR .... Peak Production Rate
PPR .... Periodic Personnel Report
PPR .... Permanent Pay Record
PPR .... Philosophy and Phenomenological Research [*A publication*]
PPR .... Photo-Plastic-Recording
PPR .... Photographic Press Review [*A publication*] [*British*]
PPR .... Pilot, Pressure Regulator   (MCD)
PPR .... Polish People's Republic
PPR .... Politieke Partij Radikalen [*Radical Political Party*] [*The Netherlands*]   (PPE)
PPR .... Polska Partia Robotnicza [*Polish Workers' Party*]
PPR .... Portable Propagation Recorder [*Bell System*]
PPR .... Potential Problem Report [*Navy*]   (CAAL)
PPR .... Present Participle [*Grammar*]
PPR .... Price. Procedural Regulation [*United States*]   (DLA)
PPR .... Price's Precipitation Reaction [*Medicine*]
PPR .... Principal Probate Registry   (DLA)
PPR .... Prior Permission Required   (FAAC)
PPR .... Production Parts Release   (KSC)
PPR .... Production Progress Report   (MCD)
PPR .... Program Progress Review
PPR .... Program Proposal Request
PPR .... Project Progress Report   (OICC)
PPR .... Proper [*Heraldry*]
PPR .... Proprietary Procurement Request   (NG)
PPR .... Provisioning Preparedness Review [*Navy*]   (CAAL)
P & PR .... Psychoanalysis and the Psychoanalytic Review [*A publication*]
PPR .... Purchase Parts Request   (KSC)
PPRA......... Past President of the Royal Academy [*British*]
PPRA......... Preliminary Personnel Requirements Analysis [*Navy*]
PPRAA ...... Polski Przeglad Radiologiczny [*A publication*]
PPRBD ...... Paperboard [*Freight*]
PPRC........ Personnel Program Review Committee [*Military*]
PPRC........ Prepositioned Receipt Card   (AABC)
PPRCl........ Rittenhouse Club, Philadelphia, PA [*Library symbol*] [*Library of Congress*] [*Obsolete*]   (LCLS)
PPRD........ Pontypool Road [*Welsh depot code*]
PPRDS ...... Products and Process Research and Development Support
P Prehist S ... Proceedings. Prehistoric Society [*A publication*]
PPREP....... Periodic Personnel Reports   (MCD)
PPREPT..... Periodic Personnel Report   (AABC)
PPRETS ..... Reformed Episcopal Seminary, Philadelphia, PA [*Library symbol*] [*Library of Congress*] [*Obsolete*]   (LCLS)
PPRF .... Paramedian Pontine Reticular Formation [*Neuroanatomy*]
PPRF .... Pulse Pair Repetition Frequency   (MCD)
PPRF .... Rosenbach Foundation, Philadelphia, PA [*Library symbol*] [*Library of Congress*]   (LCLS)
PPRFA....... Poliplasti e Plastici Rinforzati [*A publication*]
PPRG......... Precambrian Paleobiology Research Group
PPRGF....... Richard Gimbel Foundation for Literary Research, Philadelphia, PA [*Library symbol*] [*Library of Congress*] [*Obsolete*]   (LCLS)
PPRI .... PACOM [*Pacific Command*] Priority Number   (CINC)
PPRIBA ..... Past President of the Royal Institute of British Architects
PPRibP....... Phosphoribose Diphosphate [*Biochemistry*]
PPRIC....... Pulp and Paper Research Institute of Canada
PPRL .... Poisonous Plant Research Laboratory [*Agricultural Research Service*] [*Research center*]   (RCD)
PPRM .... Population Protection and Resources Management [*Military*] [*British*]
PPRN......... Preliminary Publication Revision Notice
PPRN......... Purchased Parts Requirement Notice   (KSC)
PPRO......... Per Procuration [*Business and trade*]
P Proc Hampshire Field Club ... Papers and Proceedings. Hampshire Field Club and Archaeological Society [*A publication*]
PProv .... Padova e la Sua Provincia [*A publication*]
PPRPF........ Regional Planning Federation, Philadelphia, PA [*Library symbol*] [*Library of Congress*] [*Obsolete*]   (LCLS)

PPRS......... Promotions and Placements Referral System   (MCD)

PPrStBrt .... Perspectives in Probability and Statistics: in Honor of M. S. Bartlett [*A publication*]

PPRWP....... Poor Precordial R-Wave Progression [*Cardiology*]

PPS .... Paco Pharmaceutical Services, Inc. [*NYSE symbol*]

PPS .... Page Printing System [*Honeywell, Inc.*] [*Data processing*]

PPS .... Paper Publications Society [*Amsterdam, The Netherlands*]   (EA)

PPS .... Parallel Processing System [*Data processing*]   (MDG)

PPS .... Parameter Processing System   (CAAL)

PPS .... Parliamentary Private Secretary [*British*]

PPS .... Parti Populaire Senegalais [*Senegalese People's Party*]   (PPW)

PPS .... Parti Populaire Syrien [*Syrian People's Party*]   (BJA)

PPS .... Parti du Progres et du Socialisme [*Party of Progress and Socialism*] [*Moroccan*]   (PPW)

PPS .... Parti Progressiste Soudanais [*Sudanese Progressive Party*]

PPS .... Partia e Punes e Shqiperise [*Party of Labor of Albania - PLA*]   (PPW)

PPS .... Partial Pressure Sensor

PPS .... Partido Popular Salvadoreno [*Salvadoran Popular Party*]   (PPW)

PPS .... Partido Popular Socialista [*Popular Socialist Party*] [*Argentina*]   (PPW)

PPS .... Partido Popular Socialista [*Popular Socialist Party*] [*Mexico*]   (PPW)

PPS .... Partito Populare Somalo [*Somali People's Party*]

PPS .... Parts Provisioning System   (KSC)

PPS .... Patchboard Programing System

PPS .... Payload Power Switch

PPS .... Pension and Profit-Sharing Tax Journal [*A publication*]

PPS .... Peoples Oil Ltd. [*Vancouver Stock Exchange symbol*]

PPS .... Personal Preference Scale [*Psychology*]

PPS .... Personal Protection Squad [*of the London Metropolitan Police*]

PPS .... Personnel/Payroll System

PPS .... Petroleum Press Service

PPS .... Petroleum Production Survey [*Bureau of Mines*]

PPS .... Phantom Phanatics Society   (EA)

PPS .... Phosphorous Propellant System   (KSC)

PPS .... Photophoretic Spectroscopy

PPS .... Photopolarimeter Spectrometer

PPS .... Photovoltaic Power Supply

PPS .... Piece Part Specification   (MCD)

PPS .... Pierpont [*South Carolina*] [*Seismograph station code, US Geological Survey*]   (SEIS)

PPS .... Pitt Press Series [*A publication*]

PPS .... Plant Parasitic Systems

PPS .... Plant Protection System [*Nuclear energy*]   (NRCH)

PPS .... Plasma Power Supply

PPS .... Plutonium Product Storage [*Nuclear energy*]   (NRCH)

PPS .... Pneumatic Power Subsystem   (NASA)

PPS .... Policy Processing Sheet [*Insurance*]

PPS .... Polonus Philatelic Society

PPS .... Polska Partia Socjalistyczna [*Polish Socialist Party*]

PPS .... Poly(para-phenylene Sulfide) [*Organic chemistry*]

PPS .... Post-Polio Sequelae [*Medicine*]

PPS .... Post-Postscriptum [*Further Postscript*] [*Latin*]

PPS .... Post Production Service   (AAG)

PPS .... Post Production Support   (MCD)

PPS .... Postpartum Sterilization [*Medicine*]

PPS .... Postperfusion Syndrome [*Medicine*]

PPS .... Pounds per Second   (AAG)

PPS .... Precision Power Supply

PPS .... Prepositioned Stock   (NG)

PPS .... Prescribed Payments System   (ADA)

PPS .... Primary Paraffin Sulfonate [*Organic chemistry*]

PPS .... Primary Power Standard

PPS .... Primary Power System   (NRCH)

PPS .... Primary Pressure Standard

PPS .... Primary Propulsion System [*Spacecraft*]

PPS .... Printer/Plotter System   (MCD)

PPS .... Prior Preferred Stock

PPS .... Private Practice Section [*American Physical Therapy Association*] [*Washington, DC*]   (EA)

PPS .... Probability Proportional to Size [*Statistics*]

PPS .... Proceedings. Prehistoric Society [*A publication*]

PPS .... Production Planning System [*TDS Business Systems Ltd.*] [*Software package*]

PPS .... Program Performance Specification   (CAAL)

PPS .... Program Planning Summary   (OICC)

PPS .... Program Planning System [*DoD*]

PPS .... Program Policy Staff [*UN Food and Agriculture Organization*]

PPS .... Programable Patch System

PPS .... Programable Power Supply

PPS .... Programed Processor System

PPS .... Programing Program Strela [*Data processing*]

PPS .... Progressive Pneumonia of Sheep

PPS .... Project for Public Spaces   (EA)

PPS .... Propose   (FAAC)

PPS .... Prospective Payment System [*For hospital care*]

PPS .... Provisioning Performance Schedule   (AFM)

PPS .... Provisioning Policy Statement   (MCD)

PPS .... Public and Private [*Nongovernment*] Schools [*Public-performance tariff class*] [*British*]

PPS .... Publications. Philological Society [*A publication*]

PPS .... Puerto Princesa [*Philippines*] [*Airport symbol*]   (OAG)

PPS .... Pulses per Second [*Data transmission*]

PPSA .... Pan-Pacific Surgical Association [*Honolulu, HI*]   (EA)

PPSAS .... Program Planning and Status Assessment System [*Nuclear energy*]   (NRCH)

PPSB .... Prothrombin, Proconvertin, Stuart Factor, Antihemophilic B Factor [*Blood coagulation factors*] [*Hematology*]

PPSC......... Physical Profile Serial Code

PPSC......... Privacy Protection Study Commission [*Government commission*]

PPSCI........ Seamen's Church Institute, Philadelphia, PA [*Library symbol*] [*Library of Congress*] [*Obsolete*]   (LCLS)

PPSD .... Polska Partia Socialno-Demokratyczna [*Polish Social-Democrat Party*]

PPSD .... Proposed

PPSE .... Petroleum Economist [*A publication*]

PPSE .... Purpose

PPSEAWA ... Pan-Pacific and South-East Asia Women's Association [*Tokyo, Japan*]   (EA-IO)

PPSEI........ Progres Politique, Social, et Economique de l'Itasy [*Political, Social, and Economic Progress of the Itasy*]

PPSF .... Palestinian Popular Struggle Front   (BJA)

PPS-FR ...... Polska Partia Socjalistyczna - Frakcja Rewolucyjna [*Polish Socialist Party - Revolutionary Faction*]   (PPE)

PPSG......... Piston and Pin Standardization Group [*Later, NEPMA*]   (EA)

PPSG......... Spring Garden College, Philadelphia, PA [*Library symbol*] [*Library of Congress*]   (LCLS)

PPSh .... Partia e Punes e Shqiperise [*Labor Party of Albania*] [*Formerly, PKSh*]   (PPE)

PPSH......... Pseudovaginal Perineoscrotal Hypospadias [*Medicine*]

PPSI......... Paco Pharmaceutical Services [*NASDAQ symbol*]   (NQ)

PPSIA........ "Personal Property Shipping Information" [*Pamphlet*] Is Applicable [*Military*]   (AABC)

PPSJ .... Pressure Plane Swivel Joint

PPSJ .... Saint Joseph's College, Philadelphia, PA [*Library symbol*] [*Library of Congress*]   (LCLS)

PPSJ-AF .... Saint Joseph's College, Academy of Food Marketing, Philadelphia, PA [*Library symbol*] [*Library of Congress*]   (LCLS)

PPSKED..... Provisioning Performance Schedule   (MCD)

PPSKF........ SmithKline Corp., Philadelphia, PA [*Library symbol*] [*Library of Congress*]   (LCLS)

PPSL .... Program Parts Selection List

PPSL .... Provisioning Parts Selection List   (MCD)

PPSMEC .... Procurement, Precedence of Supplies, Material and Equipment Committee [*Joint Communications Board*]

PPSN......... Present Position [*Aviation*]   (FAAC)

PPSN......... Public Packet Switched Network [*Telecommunications*]

PPSN......... Purchased Part Shortage Notice

PPSOPR..... Sun Oil Co., General Office Library, Philadelphia, PA [*Library symbol*] [*Library of Congress*] [*Obsolete*]   (LCLS)

PPSP .... Page Printer Spooling System [*Data processing*]

PPSP .... Ponderosa Pine or Sugar Pine [*Lumber*]

PPSPS........ Plutonium Product Shipping Preparation Station [*Nuclear energy*]   (NRCH)

PPSR......... Periodic Personnel Strength Report [*Army*]   (AABC)

PPSS......... Foundation for the President's Private Sector Survey on Cost Control   (EA)

PPSSCC..... President's Private Sector Survey on Cost Control [*Task force*]

PPStarr ...... Starr Center Association, Philadelphia, PA [*Library symbol*] [*Library of Congress*] [*Obsolete*]   (LCLS)

PPStCh ...... Saint Charles Borromeo Seminary, Philadelphia, PA [*Library symbol*] [*Library of Congress*]   (LCLS)

PPSteph..... William B. Stephens Memorial Library, Philadelphia, PA [*Library symbol*] [*Library of Congress*] [*Obsolete*]   (LCLS)

PPSV .... Plutonium Product Storage Vault [*Nuclear energy*]   (NRCH)

PPS-WRN... Polska Partia Socjalistyczna - Wolnosc, Rownosc, Niepodleglosc [*Polish Socialist Party - Freedom, Equality, Independence*]   (PPE)

PPSYA .... Personnel Psychology [*A publication*]

PPT............ Pamatai [*French Polynesia*] [*Geomagnetic observatory code*]

PPT............ Papeete [*French Polynesia*] [*Airport symbol*]   (OAG)

PPT............ Papeete [*Society Islands*] [*Seismograph station code, US Geological Survey*]   (SEIS)

PPT............ Parti Progressiste Tchadien [*Progressive Party of Chad*]

PPT............ Parts per Trillion

PPT............ Period Pulse Train

PPT............ Periodic Programs Termination [*Data processing*]

PPT............ Peripheral Performance Test   (CAAL)

PPT............ Pine Point Mines [*Toronto Stock Exchange symbol*] [*Vancouver Stock Exchange symbol*]

PPT............ Pitch Precession Torquer

PPT............ Polypurine Tract [*Genetics*]

PPT............ Poppet [*Engineering*]

PPT............ Post Production Test

PPT............ Practical Policy Test [*Psychology*]

PPT............ Praecipitatus [*Precipitated*] [*Pharmacy*]

PPT............ Praeparata [*Prepared*] [*Pharmacy*]   (ROG)

PPT............ Precipitate (MSA)
PPT............ Preproduction Tests [*Army*]
PPT............ Preprotachykinin [*Biochemistry*]
PPT............ Process Page Table [*Telecommunications*] (TEL)
PPT............ Product Positioning Time (AFM)
PPT............ Production Prototype
PPT............ Project Planning Technique (MCD)
PPT............ Prompt (ROG)
PPT............ Propyl(thio)uracil [*Biochemistry*]
PPT............ Public and Private Transport
PPT............ Pulse Plasma Thruster
PPT............ Punched Paper Tape [*Data processing*]
PPT............ Temple University, Philadelphia, PA [*Library symbol*] [*Library of Congress*] (LCLS)
PPT............ Theosophical Society, Philadelphia, PA [*Library symbol*] [*Library of Congress*] [*Obsolete*] (LCLS)
PPTA J .... PPTA [*Post-Primary Teachers Association*] Journal [*A publication*]
PPTB .... Pin-Pack Test Board
PPTC......... People-to-People Tennis Committee (EA)
PPTC .... Purchased Part Tab Card
PPTD......... Precipitated
PPT-D........ Temple University, Dental-Pharmacy School, Philadelphia, PA [*Library symbol*] [*Library of Congress*] (LCLS)
PPTEC....... Polymer-Plastics Technology and Engineering [*A publication*]
PPTF .... Public Policy Task Force [*Defunct*] (EA)
pPTH .... Porcine Parathyroid Hormone [*Endocrinology*]
PPTI .... Passport Travel [*NASDAQ symbol*] (NQ)
PPTJ.......... Theodore F. Jenkins Memorial Law Library, Philadelphia, PA [*Library symbol*] [*Library of Congress*] (LCLS)
PPTL .... Postpartum Tubal Ligation [*Medicine*]
PPTL .... Pulp and Paper Traffic League [*Defunct*] (EA)
PPT-L........ Temple University, Law School, Philadelphia, PA [*Library symbol*] [*Library of Congress*] (LCLS)
PPT-M....... Temple University, Medical School, Philadelphia, PA [*Library symbol*] [*Library of Congress*] (LCLS)
PPTMR ...... Personal Property Traffic Management Regulation
PPTN......... Precipitation
PPTO......... Personal Property Transportation Officer
PPTO......... Principal Professional and Technology Officer [*British*]
PPTR .... Punched Paper Tape Reader [*Data processing*]
PPTri .... Tri-Institutional Library, Philadelphia, PA [*Library symbol*] [*Library of Congress*] (LCLS)
PPT-T........ Temple University, School of Theology, Philadelphia, PA [*Library symbol*] [*Library of Congress*] (LCLS)
PPTY .... Property (AFM)
PPU .... Cocoa, FL [*Location identifier*] [*FAA*] (FAAL)
PPU .... Papun [*Burma*] [*Airport symbol*] (OAG)
PPU .... Parti Populaire des Ueles [*Ueles People's Party*]
PPU .... Payment for Public Use [*Canada*]
PPU .... Peace Pledge Union [*British*]
PPU .... Peninsula Petroleum Corp. [*Vancouver Stock Exchange symbol*]
PPU .... Peoria & Pekin Union Railway Co. [*AAR code*]
PPU .... Peripheral Processing Unit [*Data processing*]
PPU .... Platform Position Unit
PPU .... Preproduction Unit (MCD)
PPU .... Prime Power Unit
PPU .... Professional Psychics United (EA)
PPU .... Promontory Point [*Utah*] [*Seismograph station code, US Geological Survey*] [*Closed*] (SEIS)
PPUAES..... Publications. Princeton University Archaeological Expedition to Syria in 1904-5 and 1909 [*A publication*]
PPUG........ United Gas Improvement Corp., Philadelphia, PA [*Library symbol*] [*Library of Congress*] [*Obsolete*] (LCLS)
PPULC ...... Union Library Catalogue of Pennsylvania, Philadelphia, PA [*Library symbol*] [*Library of Congress*] (LCLS)
PPUNA ...... United States Naval Aircraft Factory, Philadelphia, PA [*Library symbol*] [*Library of Congress*] [*Obsolete*] (LCLS)
PPUnC ...... University Club, Philadelphia, PA [*Library symbol*] [*Library of Congress*] [*Obsolete*] (LCLS)
PPUNH ...... United States Naval Home, Philadelphia, PA [*Library symbol*] [*Library of Congress*] [*Obsolete*] (LCLS)
PPUSDA..... United States Department of Agriculture, Agricultural Research Service, Eastern Utilization Research and Development Division, Philadelphia, PA [*Library symbol*] [*Library of Congress*] (LCLS)
PPV .... Pay-per-View [*Pay-television service*]
PPV .... People-Powered Vehicle [*Recreational vehicle powered by pedaling*]
PPV .... Plum Pox Virus [*Plant pathology*]
PPV .... Positive Pressure Ventilation [*Medicine*]
PPV .... Preprogramed Vehicles (MCD)
P/PV.......... Public/Private Ventures [*Philadelphia, PA*] [*Formerly, Corporation for Public/Private Ventures, Inc.*] [*Research center*] (RCD)
PPV .... United States Veterans Administration Hospital, Philadelphia, PA [*Library symbol*] [*Library of Congress*] (LCLS)
PPVT......... Peabody Picture Vocabulary Test
PPVT-R ...... Peabody Picture Vocabulary Test - Revised [*Education*]

PP-W .... Free Library of Philadelphia, H. Josephine Widener Memorial Branch, Philadelphia, PA [*Library symbol*] [*Library of Congress*] [*Obsolete*] (LCLS)
PPW .... PacifiCorp [*NYSE symbol*]
PPW .... Papa Westray [*Scotland*] [*Airport symbol*] (OAG)
PPW .... Parts per Weight
PPW .... Petitions for Patent Waiver
PPW .... Plane-Polarized Wave
PPW .... Ponderosa Pine Woodwork Association [*Absorbed by NWWDA*] (EA)
PPW .... Potato Processing Waste
PPW .... Prace Polonistyczne (Wroclaw) [*A publication*]
P & PW ..... Publicity and Psychological Warfare
PPWA .... Ponderosa Pine Woodwork Association [*Absorbed by NWWDA*]
PPWa........ Wagner Free Institute of Science, Philadelphia, PA [*Library symbol*] [*Library of Congress*] (LCLS)
PPWC........ Pulp, Paper, and Woodworkers of Canada
PPWD........ S. S. White Co., Philadelphia, PA [*Library symbol*] [*Library of Congress*] [*Obsolete*] (LCLS)
PPWe .... Westminster Theological Seminary, Philadelphia, PA [*Library symbol*] [*Library of Congress*] (LCLS)
PPWF .... Pakistan Petroleum Workers' Federation
PPWI .... Wistar Institute of Anatomy and Biology, Philadelphia, PA [*Library symbol*] [*Library of Congress*] (LCLS)
PPWiH........ Wills Eye Hospital, Philadelphia, PA [*Library symbol*] [*Library of Congress*] (LCLS)
PPWM........ Medical College of Pennsylvania, Philadelphia, PA [*Library symbol*] [*Library of Congress*] (LCLS)
PPWP .... Planned Parenthood - World Population [*Later, PPFA*] (EA)
PPWR .... Prepositioned War Reserves [*Army*]
PPX .... Packet Protocol Extension
PPX .... Port Moller, AK [*Location identifier*] [*FAA*] (FAAL)
PPX .... Private Packet Exchange
PPY .... Pages per Year [*Facetious criterion for determining insignificance of Supreme Court Justices*] [*Proposed by University of Chicago professor David P. Currie*]
PPY .... Prophesy Development [*Vancouver Stock Exchange symbol*]
PPYH......... Young Men's and Young Women's Hebrew Association, Philadelphia, PA [*Library symbol*] [*Library of Congress*] [*Obsolete*] (LCLS)
PPYSA ...... Plant Physiology. Supplement [*A publication*]
PPYU .... Party of Popular Yemenite Unity (PD)
PPZ............ Proton Polar Zone
PPZ............ Zoological Society of Philadelphia, PA [*Library symbol*] [*Library of Congress*] [*Obsolete*] (LCLS)
PPZI .... Przeglad Pismiennictwa Zagadnien Informacji [*A publication*]
PQ .... Pack Quickly [*Humorous interpretation for Parti Quebecois*] [*Canada*]
PQ .... Pakistan Quarterly [*A publication*]
PQ .... Panic in Quebec [*Humorous interpretation for Parti Quebecois*] [*Canada*]
PQ .... Parliamentary Question [*British*]
PQ .... Parti Quebecois [*Quebec separatist political party*]
P & Q .... Peace and Quiet
PQ .... Performer Quotient [*TV-performer rating*]
PQ .... Permeability Quotient
PQ .... Personality Quotient [*Psychology*]
PQ .... Philological Quarterly [*A publication*]
PQ .... Philosophical Quarterly [*A publication*]
PQ .... Physically Qualified
PQ .... Piano Quarterly [*A publication*]
PQ .... Planetary Quarantine [*NASA*]
PQ .... Plant Quarantine Division [*of ARS, Department of Agriculture*]
PQ .... Plastoquinone [*Biochemistry*]
PQ .... Pollution Quotient
PQ .... Polyquinoxaline [*Organic chemistry*]
P-Q........... Porphyrin-Quinone [*Photochemistry*]
PQ .... PQ Corp. [*Formerly, Philadelphia Quartz Co.*]
PQ .... Premium Quality (MUGU)
PQ .... Previous Question [*Parliamentary law*]
P and Q .... Prime Quality [*Slang*]
pq............. Pro Querente [*For, or On Behalf Of, Plaintiff*] [*Latin*] (DLA)
PQ............. Province Quebec [*Quebec*] [*Canadian province*] [*Postal code*]
PQ .... Psi Quotient [*Parapsychology*]
PQ .... Psychiatric Quarterly [*A publication*]
PQ .... Public Quarters
PQ .... Puerto Rico International Airlines, Inc. [*Prinair*] [*ICAO designator*] (OAG)
PQ .... United States Patent Quarterly (DLA)
P's & Q's.... Of expression "Mind your P's and Q's." Exact origin unclear, but theories include: admonishment of pub-owners that British drinkers be aware of number of "Pints and Quarts" being marked on their accounts; warning to apprentice typesetters that "p" and "q" fonts be carefully restored to correct case, since each could so easily be mistaken for the other; cautioning of French dancing masters that pupils be aware of position of their "Pieds" [*feet*] and "Queues" [*wigs*] in executing the deep bow of a formal curtsey.
PQA........... Parts Quality Assurance

PQA............ Petroleum Quality Assurance
PQA............ Plant Quality Assurance
PQA............ Procurement Quality Assurance [*Program*] [*DoD*]
PQA............ Production Quality Assurance
PQA............ Project Quality Assurance
PQA............ Protected Queue Area [*Data processing*]   (BUR)
PQAD......... Plant Quality Assurance Director [*Nuclear energy*]   (NRCH)
PQAI......... Procurement Quality Assurance Instruction
PQAM........ Project Quality Assurance Manager [*Nuclear energy*]   (NRCH)
PQAP......... Planned Quality Assurance Program [*Navy*]
PQAP......... Procurement Quality Assurance Program [*DoD*]
PQB........... Quebecor, Inc. [*American Stock Exchange symbol*]
PQC........... Paul Quinn College [*Texas*]
PQC........... Paul Quinn College, Waco, TX [*OCLC symbol*]   (OCLC)
PQC........... Precision Quartz Crystal
PQC-C........ Production Quality Control
PQCS........ Philippine Quarterly of Culture and Society [*A publication*]
PQD........... Partido Quisqueyano Democrata [*Quisqueyan Democratic Party*] [*Dominican Republic*]   (PPW)
PQD........... Percentage Quartile Deviation [*Statistics*]
PQD........... Predicted Quarterly Demand
PQD........... Pyroelectric Quad Detector
PQDMB..... Percentage Quartile Deviation Median Bias [*Statistics*]
PQE........... Parents for Quality Education [*Pasadena, CA*]   (EA)
PQE........... Principal Quality Engineers [*British*]   (RDA)
PQE........... Project Quality Engineering
PQEP......... Product Quality Evaluation Plan [*Military*]   (AABC)
PQGS........ Propellant Quantity Gauge [*or Gauging*] System [*Apollo*] [*NASA*]
PQI............ Presque Isle [*Maine*] [*Airport symbol*]   (OAG)
PQI............ Presque Isle, ME [*Location identifier*] [*FAA*]   (FAAL)
PQI............ Professional Qualification Index   (AFM)
PQL........... Prior Quarter Liability [*IRS*]
PQLI......... Physical Quality of Life Index [*Overseas Development Council*]
PQM.......... Pacific Quarterly (Moana): An International Review of Arts and Ideas [*A publication*]
PQM.......... Pilot Qualified in Model   (NVT)
PQM.......... Post Quartermaster [*Marine Corps*]
PQM.......... Pulse Quaternary Modulation
PQMC....... Philadelphia Quartermaster Center [*Merged with Defense Clothing and Textile Supply Center*] [*Military*]
PQMD....... Philadelphia Quartermaster Depot [*Military*]
PQMD....... Propellant Quantity Measuring Device
PQMDO..... Proposed Quality Material Development Objective   (NATG)
PQMR....... Preliminary Quantitative Material Requirements   (MCD)
PQN.......... Pahaquarry [*New Jersey*] [*Seismograph station code, US Geological Survey*]   (SEIS)
PQN.......... Pipestone, MN [*Location identifier*] [*FAA*]   (FAAL)
PQN.......... Principal Quantum Number [*Atomic physics*]
PQO.......... Phoenix, AZ [*Location identifier*] [*FAA*]   (FAAL)
PQP........... Planetary Quarantine Plan [*NASA*]
PQP........... Prequalification Prototype   (KSC)
PQQ........... Port Macquarie [*Australia*] [*Airport symbol*]   (OAG)
PQQPRI...... Provisional Qualitative and Quantitative Personnel Requirements Information [*Army*]   (AABC)
PQR........... Performance Qualification Requirement
PQR........... Personnel Qualification Roster [*Military*]   (AABC)
PQR........... Procedure Qualification Record [*Nuclear energy*]   (NRCH)
PQS........... Palestine Exploration Fund. Quarterly Statement [*A publication*]
PQS........... Personnel Qualification Standards [*Military*]   (NVT)
PQS........... Pilot Station [*Alaska*] [*Airport symbol*]   (OAG)
PQS........... Production Quotation Support
PQS........... Promotion Qualification Score [*Military*]
PQT........... Parquet Resources, Inc. [*Toronto Stock Exchange symbol*]
PQT........... Polyquinazolotriazole [*Organic chemistry*]
PQT........... Preliminary Qualification Test   (MCD)
PQT........... Production Qualification and Testing
PQT........... Professional Qualification Test [*of the National Security Agency*]
PQT........... Prototype Qualification Testing   (RDA)
PQT-C....... Prototype Qualification Test - Contractor   (MCD)
PQT-G....... Prototype Qualification Test - Government   (MCD)
PQT-SE...... Prototype Qualification Test - Service Evaluation   (MCD)
P Qu .... Philippines Quarterly [*A publication*]
PQU.......... Salisbury, MD [*Location identifier*] [*FAA*]   (FAAL)
PQUE........ Print Queue Processor [*Data processing*]
PQW.......... Placita de Quo Warranto, Record Commission [*England*]   (DLA)
PQZ........... Premium Quality Zinc
PR............. Abbott Laboratories [*Research code symbol*]
PR............. Aircrew Survival Equipmentman [*Navy rating*]
PR............. Pacific Reporter   (DLA)
PR............. Painter   (ADA)
PR............. Pair   (KSC)
PR............. Pakistan Railways
PR............. Panama Red [*Variety of marijuana*]
PR............. Panel Receptacle
PR............. Parachute Rigger [*Navy*]   (KSC)
PR............. Parallax and Refraction
PR............. Parcel Receipt [*Business and trade*]

PR............. Parents Rights   (EA)
PR............. Paris Review [*A publication*]
PR............. Parish Register
P & R .... Parks and Recreation [*A publication*]
PR............. Parliamentary Report [*British*]
PR............. Parliamentary Reports [*England*]   (DLA)
PR............. Parrott Rifle
PR............. Parti Republicain [*Republican Party*] [*Martiniquais*]   (PPW)
PR............. Parti Republicain [*Republican Party*] [*French*]   (PPW)
PR............. Partial Remission [*Medicine*]
PR............. Partial Response [*Oncology*]
PR............. Partido Radical [*Radical Party*] [*Chile*]
PR............. Partido Radical [*Radical Party*] [*Spanish*]   (PPE)
PR............. Partido Reformista [*Reformist Party*] [*Dominican Republic*]   (PPW)
PR............. Partido Revolucionario [*Revolutionary Party*] [*Guatemalan*]   (PPW)
PR............. Partisan Review [*A publication*]
PR............. Partito Radicale [*Radical Party*] [*Founded, 1955*] [*Italy*]   (PPE)
PR............. Party Raayat [*Leftist organization in Singapore*]   (CINC)
PR............. Passengers' Risk   (ROG)
PR............. Pastor
PR............. Patient Relations [*Medicine*]
PR............. Patria Roja [*Red Fatherland*] [*Peruvian*]   (PD)
PR............. Patrol Vessel, River Gunboat [*Navy symbol*]
PR............. Pattern Recognition   (BUR)
PR............. Payroll
PR............. Peer Review
PR............. Peking Review [*A publication*]
P & R .... Pelvic and Rectal [*Medicine*]
PR............. Penicillium roqueforti [*Toxin*] [*Oncology*]
PR............. Pennsylvania Reports [*Penrose and Watts*]   (DLA)
PR............. Penny Resistance [*An association*]   (EA)
PR............. Per
PR............. Per Price [*Business and trade*]
PR............. Per Rectum [*Medicine*]
PR............. Percentage Rates
PR............. Percentile Rank
PR............. Performance Rating   (OICC)
PR............. Performance Ratio   (AAG)
PR............. Performance Report   (AFM)
PR............. Performance Requirement
P & R .... Performance and Resources   (NASA)
PR............. Peripheral Resistance [*Medicine*]
PR............. Perirenal [*Nephrology*]
PR............. Permanens Rector [*Permanent Rector*]
PR............. Permissive Reassignment [*Air Force*]   (AFM)
PR............. Pershing Rifles [*Honorary military organization*]
PR............. Persistency Rater [*LIMRA*]
PR............. Personality Record [*Psychological testing*]
PR............. Personnel Resources [*An association*] [*Philadelphia, PA*]   (EA)
PR............. Pesikta Rabbati   (BJA)
PR............. Petroleum Review [*A publication*]
PR............. Pharmaceutical Record [*New York*] [*A publication*]
PR............. Phenol Red
P & R .... Philadelphia & Reading Railway
PR............. Philadelphia Reports [*Pennsylvania*]   (DLA)
PR............. Philippine Airlines, Inc. [*PAL*] [*ICAO designator*]   (FAAC)
PR............. Philippine Island Reports   (DLA)
PR............. Philosophical Review [*A publication*]
P & R .... Philosophy and Rhetoric [*A publication*]
PR............. Phosphorylase-Rupturing [*Biochemistry*]
PR............. Photographic Reconnaissance [*Military*]   (MCD)
PR............. Photoreacting [*or Photoreactivation*] [*Biochemistry*]
PR............. Photorecorder
PR............. Photoresist
P/R............ Photosynthesis/Respiration [*Biochemistry*]
P & R .... Picture and Resume [*Theatre slang*]
P & R .... Pigott and Rodwell's Reports in Common Pleas [*1843-45*]   (DLA)
PR............. Pilot Rating
PR............. Pinch Runner [*Baseball*]
PR............. Pineal Recess [*Neuroanatomy*]
PR............. Pipe Rail   (AAG)
PR............. Pitch Ratio
P/R............ Pitch/Roll   (MCD)
PR............. Pittsburgh Reports [*1853-73*] [*Pennsylvania*]   (DLA)
PR............. Pityriasis [*Dermatology*]
PR............. Planetary RADAR [*Equipment box*]
PR............. Planning Reference
P & R .... Planning and Review   (MCD)
PR............. Plant Recovery [*Nuclear energy*]   (NRCH)
PR............. Plant Report
PR............. Please Return
PR............. Plotting and RADAR
PR............. Ply Rating [*Tires*]   (NATG)
PR............. Podravska Revija [*A publication*]
PR............. Poetry Review [*A publication*]
PR............. Policy Review   (MCD)
PR............. Polish Register [*Polish ship classification society*]
PR............. Ponceau Red [*Biological stain*]

PR.............. Poor Rate [British]   (ROG)
PR.............. Populus Romanus [The Roman People] [Latin]
PR.............. Position Record   (NASA)
PR.............. Position Report [Air Force]
PR.............. Post Request
PR.............. Post-Resuscitation
PR.............. Postal Regulations   (DLA)
PR.............. Poste Recommandee [Registered Post]
PR.............. Posterior Ridge
PR.............. Pounder [Gun]
PR.............. Pour Remercier [To Express Thanks] [French]
PR.............. Power Range [Nuclear energy]   (NRCH)
PR.............. Power Return
Pr.............. Practice Reports [Various jurisdictions]   (DLA)
Pr.............. Practitioner [A publication]
PR.............. Prairie   (MCD)
Pr.............. Prandtl Number [IUPAC]
Pr.............. Praseodymium [Chemical element]
PR.............. Prayer
PR.............. Pre-Raphaelite
PR.............. Preacher
PR.............. Precedence Rating [Military]   (AFIT)
Pr.............. Prednisone [Also, P, PDN, Pred, Pro] [Antineoplastic drug]
         [Endocrinology]
PR.............. Preferred [Stock exchange term]
PR.............. Prefix [Indicating a private radiotelegram]   (BUR)
PR.............. Pregnancy Rate [Medicine]
PR.............. Preliminary Report
PR.............. Premature Release [Telecommunications]   (TEL)
PR.............. Prepare Reply
PR.............. Preposition
PR.............. Presbyopia [Ophthalmology]
PR.............. Presbyterian   (ROG)
PR.............. Present
Pr.............. Presentation [Gynecology]
PR.............. Presidency   (ROG)
Pr.............. Press [Christchurch, New Zealand] [A publication]
PR.............. Press Release
PR.............. Pressure
PR.............. Pressure Ratio
PR.............. Pressure Recorder   (NRCH)
PR.............. Pressure Regulator   (KSC)
Pr.............. Prevention [A publication]
PR.............. Price [Online database field identifier]
PR.............. Price Communications Corp. [American Stock Exchange
         symbol]
PR.............. Price Redetermination
Pr.............. Price's English Exchequer Reports [1814-24]   (DLA)
PR.............. Priest
PR.............. Primitive
PR.............. Prince
PR.............. Prince Regent   (ROG)
PR.............. Princess Royal's [Military unit] [British]
PR3.............. Principal Register [Data processing]
PR.............. Printed [or Printer]
PR.............. Printing Request   (MCD)
PR.............. Prior
PR.............. Priority Regulation
PR.............. Priory
PR.............. Prism
pr.............. Prismatic Tank [Liquid gas carriers]
pr.............. Private   (DLA)
PR.............. Private Road [Maps and charts] [British]   (ROG)
PR.............. Prize Ring [Boxing]
PR.............. Pro Rata
PR.............. Probate Reports   (DLA)
Pr.............. Probe [A publication]
PR.............. Problem Report   (MCD)
Pr.............. Problemata [of Aristotle] [Classical studies]   (OCD)
Pr.............. Procarbazine [Also, P, PC, PCB] [Antineoplastic drug]
PR.............. Procedural Regulations [Civil Aeronautics Board]
PR.............. Procedures Review [DoD]
PR.............. Proceedings. American Society of University Composers [A
         publication]
PR.............. Process-Reactive [Scale] [Psychometrics]
PR.............. Proctologist
PR.............. Procurement Regulations
PR.............. Procurement Request
PR.............. Production Rate
PR.............. Production Requirements [Military]   (AFIT)
P/R.............. Productivity/Respiration [Physiology]
PR.............. Profile Reliability   (MCD)
P-R.............. Progesterone Receptor [Endocrinology]
P-as-R.............. Program as Recorded [Radio]   (DEN)
PR.............. Program Register [Data processing]   (BUR)
PR.............. Program Requirements   (KSC)
PR.............. Progress Report
PR.............. Progressive Resistance
Pr.............. Prohemio [A publication]
PR.............. Project Release [An association]   (EA)
PR.............. Project Report

PR.............. Prolactin [Also, LTH, PRL] [Endocrinology]
PR.............. Prolonged-Release [Pharmacy]
Pr.............. Prometheus [A publication]
PR.............. Pronominal [Grammar]   (ROG)
PR.............. Pronoun
PR.............. Pronounced
PR.............. Proper
PR.............. Proportional Representation [in legislatures, etc.]
PR.............. Proposed Regulation
PR.............. Proposed Request
Pr.............. Propyl [Organic chemistry]
Pr.............. Prostor [Moscow] [A publication]
PR.............. Protective Reaction [Bombing raid] [Vietnam]
PR.............. Protestant   (ADA)
PR.............. Prototype
PR.............. Proved
PR.............. Provencal [Language, etc.]
Pr.............. Proverbs [Old Testament book]   (BJA)
Pr.............. Proximal
PR.............. Pseudorandom
PR.............. Pseudoresidual
PR.............. Psychedelic Review [A publication]
PR.............. Psychoanalytic Review [A publication]
PR.............. Psychological Review [A publication]
PR.............. Public Relations
PR.............. Public Responsibility
PR.............. Public Roads [A publication]
PR.............. Puerto Rican [Derogatory term]
pr.............. Puerto Rico [MARC country of publication code] [Library of
         Congress]   (LCCP)
PR.............. Puerto Rico [Postal code]
PR.............. Puerto Rico [Two-letter standard code]   (CNC)
PR.............. Puerto Rico Supreme Court Reports   (DLA)
PR.............. Pulse Rate
PR.............. Pulse Ratio   (IEEE)
PR.............. Pulse Regenerator
P & R.............. Pulse and Respiration [Medicine]
PR.............. Punctum Remotum [Far Point] [Latin]
PR.............. Punjab Record [India]   (DLA)
PR.............. Purchase Request
PR.............. Purple   (AAG)
PR.............. Purplish Red
PR.............. Pyke's Reports [Canada]   (DLA)
pr.............. Pyrite [CIPW classification] [Geology]
PR.............. Pyrogallol Red [Also, PGR] [An indicator] [Chemistry]
PR.............. Pyrolytic Release
PR+.............. Reactor Pressure Plus   (NRCH)
PR.............. Reading Public Library, Reading, PA [Library symbol] [Library
         of Congress]   (LCLS)
PR.............. River Gunboat [Navy symbol]
PR.............. Upper Canada Practice Reports [1850-1900] [Ontario]   (DLA)
PR1.............. Parachute Rigger, First Class [Navy]
PR2.............. Parachute Rigger, Second Class [Navy]
PR3.............. Parachute Rigger, Third Class [Navy]
PR's.............. Partial Responders [to medication]
PR's.............. Planning References   (AAG)
PRA.............. Albright College, Reading, PA [Library symbol] [Library of
         Congress]   (LCLS)
PRA.............. Division of Policy Research and Analysis [National Science
         Foundation]
PRA.............. Parabolic Reflector Antenna
PRA.............. Parana [Argentina] [Airport symbol]   (OAG)
PRA.............. Parti du Regroupement Africain [African Regroupment Party]
         [Banned, 1974] [Upper Volta]
PRA.............. Parti du Regroupement Africain [African Regroupment Party]
         [Niger]   (PD)
PRA.............. Partido Revolucionario Autentico [Authentic Revolutionary
         Party] [Bolivian]   (PPW)
PRA.............. Pay Readjustment Act [1942]
PRA.............. Pay Record Access
PRA.............. Paymaster-Rear-Admiral [Navy] [British]
PRA.............. Payroll Auditor [Insurance]
PRA.............. Peak Recording Accelerograph [Accelerometer]   (IEEE)
PRA.............. Pendulous Reference Axis [Accelerometer]   (IEEE)
PRA.............. People's Revolutionary Army [Grenada]
PRA.............. Permanent Restricted Area [USSR]   (NATG)
PRA.............. Personnel Research Activity [Later, NPTRL] [Navy]
PRA.............. Pilots Rights Association [Washington, DC]   (EA)
PRA.............. Planetary Radio Astronomy
PRA.............. Planned Restricted Availability [Military]   (NVT)
PRA.............. Plasma Renin Activity [Hematology]
PRA.............. Plutonium Recycle Acid [Nuclear energy]   (NRCH)
PRA.............. Policy Research and Analysis
PRA.............. Popular Rotorcraft Association
PRA.............. Praha [Prague] [Czechoslovakia] [Seismograph station code,
         US Geological Survey]   (SEIS)
PRA.............. Prairiefire Rural Action [Des Moines, IA]   (EA)
pra.............. Prakrit [MARC language code] [Library of Congress]   (LCCP)
PRA.............. Precision Axis   (KSC)
PRA.............. Premium Audit
PRA.............. Prerefund Audit [IRS]

PRA .... President of the Royal Academy [*British*]
PRA .... Primary Reviewing Authority
PrA .... Primer Acto [*Madrid*] [*A publication*]
PRA .... Print Alphanumerically [*Data processing*]　(MDG)
PRA .... Probabilistic Risk Assessment [*Computer-based technique for accident prediction*]
PRA .... Probation and Rehabilitation of Airmen [*Air Force*]　(AFM)
PRA .... Production Reader Assembly　(KSC)
PRA .... Progesterone Receptor Assay [*Clinical chemistry*]
PRA .... Program Reader Assembly [*Data processing*]
PRA .... Projected Requisition Authority [*Army*]　(AABC)
PRA .... Proust Research Association　(EA)
PRA .... Psoriasis Research Association [*San Carlos, CA*]　(EA)
PRA .... Psychological Research Associates
PRA .... Public Resources Association [*Defunct*]　(EA)
PRA .... Public Roads Administration
PRA .... Puerto Rico Area Office [*AEC*]
PRA .... US 1869 Pictorial Research Associates　(EA)
PRAA .... Airman Apprentice, Parachute Rigger, Striker [*Navy rating*]
PRAB .... Prab Robots, Inc. [*NASDAQ symbol*]　(NQ)
Pra Bhar ..... Prabuddha Bharata [*Calcutta*] [*A publication*]
Prac .... Practical　(DLA)
PRAC .... Practice　(AABC)
PRAC .... Pressure Ratio Acceleration Control [*Gas turbine engine*]
PRAC .... Program Resource Advisory Committee [*TRADOC*]　(MCD)
PRAC .... Public Relations Advisory Committee
PRACA .... Practitioner [*A publication*]
PRACA .... Problem Reporting and Corrective Action　(MCD)
PRACA .... Puerto Rican Association for Community Affairs [*New York, NY*]　(EA)
Prac Accnt ... Practical Accountant [*A publication*]
Prac Act .... Practice Act　(DLA)
Prac Anth... Practical Anthropology [*A publication*]
Pra Cas ...... Prater's Cases on Conflict of Laws　(DLA)
Praca Zabezp Spolecz ... Praca i Zabezpieczenie Spoleczne [*A publication*]
Prace Brnenske Zakl Ceskoslov Akad Ved ... Prace Brnenske Zakladny Ceskoslovenske Akademie Ved [*A publication*]
Prace Inst Bad Lesn ... Prace Instytut Badawezy Lesnictwa [*A publication*]
Prace Inst Tech Drewna ... Prace Instytut Technologii Drewna [*A publication*]
Prace Inst Technol Drewna ... Prace Instytut Technologii Drewna [*A publication*]
Prace Nauk Akad Ekon Poznan ... Prace Naukowe Akademii Ekonomicznej w Poznaniu [*A publication*]
Prace Nauk Akad Ekon Wroclaw ... Prace Naukowe Akademii Ekonomicznej we Wroclawiv [*A publication*]
Prace Nauk Inst Cybernet Techn Politech Wroclaw Ser Konfer ... Wroclaw. Politechnika. Instytut Cybernetyki Technicznej. Prace Naukowe. Seria Konferencje [*A publication*]
Prace Nauk Inst Cybernet Techn Politech Wroclaw Ser Monograf ... Wroclaw. Politechnika. Instytut Cybernetyki Technicznej. Prace Naukowe. Seria Monografie [*A publication*]
Prace Nauk Inst Cybernet Techn Wroclaw Ser Stud i Materialy ... Wroclaw. Politechnika. Instytut Cybernetyki Technicznej. Prace Naukowe. Seria Studia i Materialy [*A publication*]
Prace Nauk Inst Mat Politech Wroclaw Ser Konfer ... Wroclaw Politechnika Wroclawska. Instytutu Matematyki. Prace Naukowe. Seria Konferencje [*A publication*]
Prace Nauk Inst Mat Politech Wroclaw Ser Monograf ... Prace Naukowe Instytutu Matematyki Politechniki Wroclawskiej. Seria Monografie [*A publication*]
Prace Nauk Inst Mat Politech Wroclaw Ser Stud Materialy ... Politechniki Wroclawskiej. Instytutu Matematyki. Prace Naukowe. Seria Studia i Materialy [*A publication*]
Prace Nauk Inst Mat Politech Wroclaw Ser Stud i Materialy ... Politechniki Wroclawskiej. Instytutu Matematyki. Prace Naukowe. Seria Studia i Materialy [*A publication*]
Prace Nauk Inst Ochr Rosl ... Prace Naukowe Instytutu Ochrony Roslin [*A publication*]
Prace Nauk Uniw Slask Katowic ... Prace Naukowe Uniwersytetu Slaskiego w Katowicach [*A publication*]
Prace Stud Vysokej Skolej Doprav Spojov Ziline Ser Mat-Fyz ... Prace a Studie Vysokej Skoly Dopravy a Spojov v Ziline. Seria Matematicko-Fyzikalna [*A publication*]
Prace Stud Vysokej Skolej Doprav Ziline Ser Mat-Fyz ... Prace a Studie Vysokej Skoly Dopravnej v Ziline. Seria Matematicko-Fyzikalna [*A publication*]
Prace Vyzkum Ust Lesn Hosp Mysl ... Prace Vyzkumneho Ustavu Lesneho Hospodarstvi a Myslivosti [*A publication*]
Prace Wroclaw Towarz Nauk Ser A ... Prace Wroclawskiego Towarzytstwa Naukowego. Series A [*A publication*]
Prace Zakr Nauk Roln Lesn (Poznan) ... Prace z Zakresu Nauk Rolniczych i Lesnych (Poznan) [*A publication*]
Prac F .... Practical Farmer [*A publication*]
Prac Forecast ... Practical Forecast for Home Economics [*A publication*]
Prac Home Econ ... Practical Home Economics [*A publication*]
PRACL .... Page-Replacement Algorithm and Control Logic [*Data processing*]
Prac Law .... Practical Lawyer [*A publication*]
Prac Lawyer ... Practical Lawyer [*A publication*]
Prac Lek..... Pracovni Lekarstvi [*A publication*]

PRACSATS ... Practical Satellites
PRACT ...... Practical　(ROG)
PRACT ...... Practitioner
Pract Account ... Practical Accountant [*A publication*]
Pract Adm ... Practising Administrator [*A publication*]
Pract Colloid Chem ... Practical Colloid Chemistry [*A publication*]
Pract Comput ... Practical Computing [*A publication*]
Pract Dig.... Practice Digest [*A publication*]
Pract Electron ... Practical Electronics [*A publication*]
Pract Electronics ... Practical Electronics [*A publication*]
Pract Energy ... Practical Energy [*A publication*]
Pract Eng (Chicago) ... Practical Engineer (Chicago) [*A publication*]
Pract Eng (London) ... Practical Engineering (London) [*A publication*]
Pract House ... Practical Householder [*England*] [*A publication*]
Practition... Practitioner [*A publication*]
Pract M ...... Practical Magazine [*A publication*]
Pract Metallogr Spec Issues ... Practical Metallography. Special Issues [*A publication*]
Pract Methods Electron Microsc ... Practical Methods in Electron Microscopy [*A publication*]
Pract Otol (Kyoto) ... Practica Otologica (Kyoto) [*A publication*]
Pract Oto-Rhino-Laryngol ... Practica Oto-Rhino-Laryngologica [*A publication*]
Pract Power Farming ... Practical Power Farming [*A publication*]
Pract Reg... Practical Register in the Common Pleas [*England*]　(DLA)
Pract Spectrosc ... Practical Spectroscopy [*A publication*]
Pract Spectrosc Ser ... Practical Spectroscopy Series [*A publication*]
Pract Surf Technol ... Practical Surface Technology [*Japan*] [*A publication*]
Pract Welder ... Practical Welder [*A publication*]
Pract Wireless ... Practical Wireless [*A publication*]
Pract Woodworking ... Practical Woodworking [*England*] [*A publication*]
Prac Wel..... Practical Welder [*A publication*]
PRAD.......... Pitch Ratio Adjust Device　(MCD)
PRADA .... Partido Revolucionario Dominicano Autentico [*Dominican Republic*]
Pr Adm Dig ... Pritchard's Admiralty Digest [*3rd ed.*] [*1887*]　(DLA)
PRADOR .... PRF [*Pulse Repetition Frequency*] Ranging Doppler RADAR
PRAED .... Practical Energy [*A publication*]
praef......... Praefatio [*Latin*]　(OCD)
PrAeg......... Probleme der Aegyptologie [*Leiden*] [*A publication*]
Praehist Z ... Praehistorische Zeitschrift [*A publication*]
Praem .... De Praemiis et Poenis [*of Philo*]　(BJA)
Praep Evang ... Praeparatio Evangelica [*of Eusebius*] [*Classical studies*]　(OCD)
Praep Pharmazie ... Praeparative Pharmazie [*A publication*]
PRAF.......... Passenger-Reserved Air Freight
Prager Med Wochenschr ... Prager Medizinische Wochenschrift [*A publication*]
Prag Micro ... Pragmatics Microficke [*A publication*]
PR Agric Exp Stn Bull ... Puerto Rico Agricultural Experiment Station. Bulletin [*A publication*]
PR Agric Exp Stn Tech Pap ... Puerto Rico Agricultural Experiment Station. Technical Paper [*A publication*]
Prague Bull Math Linguist ... Prague Bulletin of Mathematical Linguistics [*A publication*]
Prague St... Studies in English by Members of the English Seminar of the Charles University, Prague [*A publication*]
Prague Stud Math Linguist ... Prague Studies in Mathematical Linguistics [*A publication*]
Pra H & W... Prater on Husband and Wife [*2nd ed.*] [*1836*]　(DLA)
Prairie Gard ... Prairie Garden [*A publication*]
Prairie Nat ... Prairie Naturalist [*A publication*]
Prairie Sch ... Prairie Schooner [*A publication*]
Prairie Schoon ... Prairie Schooner [*A publication*]
Prairie Sch R ... Prairie School Review [*A publication*]
PRAIS........ Passive Ranging Interferometer Sensor
PRAIS........ Pesticide Residue Analysis Information Service [*British*]
PRAJ......... Peace Research Abstracts Journal [*A publication*]
Prakla-Seismos Rep ... Prakla-Seismos Report [*West Germany*] [*A publication*]
Prakruti Utkal Univ J Sci ... Prakruti Utkal University Journal of Science [*A publication*]
Prakt Akad Athenon ... Praktika tes Akademias Athenon [*A publication*]
Prakt Ak Ath ... Praktika tes Akademias Athenon [*A publication*]
Prakt Anaesth ... Praktische Anaesthesie, Wiederbelebung, und Intensivtherapie [*A publication*]
Prakt Arzt ... Praktische Arzt [*A publication*]
Prakt Bl Pflanzenbau Pflanzenschutz ... Praktische Blaetter fuer Pflanzenbau und Pflanzenschutz [*A publication*]
Prakt Chem ... Praktische Chemie [*A publication*]
Prakt Desinfekt ... Praktische Desinfektor [*A publication*]
Prakt Energiek ... Praktische Energiekunde [*A publication*]
Prakt Hell Hydrobiol Inst ... Praktika. Hellenic Hydrobiological Institute [*A publication*]
Praktika ..... Praktika tes en Athenais Arkhaiologikes Hetairias [*A publication*]
Prakt Landtech ... Praktische Landtechnik [*A publication*]
Prakt Lek ... Prakticky Lekar [*A publication*]
Prakt Metallogr ... Praktische Metallographie [*A publication*]
Prakt Metallogr Sonderb ... Praktische Metallographie. Sonderbaende [*A publication*]

Prakt Schadlingsbekampf ... Praktische Schadlingsbekampfer [*A publication*]
Prakt Tierarzt ... Praktische Tieraerzt [*German Federal Republic*] [*A publication*]
Prakt Vet (Moskva) ... Praticheskaia Veterinariia (Moskva) [*A publication*]
Prakt Wegw Bienenz ... Praktischer Wegweiser fuer Bienenzuechter [*A publication*]
Prakt Yad Fiz ... Praktikum po Yadernoi Fizike [*A publication*]
PRAM .... Perambulator [*British*]
PRAM .... Poseidon Random Access Memory [*Missiles*]
PRAM .... Productivity, Reliability, Availability, and Maintainability Office [*Air Force*]
PRAM .... Program Requirements Analysis Method
PRAM .... Propelled Ascent Mine
PRAMC ...... Pramana [*A publication*]
PRAN .... Airman, Parachute Rigger, Striker [*Navy*]
PRAN .... Proust Research Association. Newsletter [*A publication*]
PRAND .... Prandium [*Dinner*] [*Pharmacy*]
PRANG .... Puerto Rico Air National Guard
PRAP .... Provisions of Following Reference Apply [*Army*] (AABC)
PraPol .... Prace Polonistyczne [*Warsaw*] [*A publication*]
PRAR .... Partido Revolucionario Autentico Rios [*Bolivian*] (PPW)
PRARS ...... Pitch, Roll, Azimuth Reference System (NG)
PRAS .... Pension and Retirement Annuity System
Pra S .... Prairie Schooner [*A publication*]
PRAS .... Prereduced, Anaerobically Sterilized [*Microbiology*]
PRASD .... Personnel Research Activity, San Diego [*California*] [*Navy*]
PRAT .... Predicted Range Against Target [*Military*] (NVT)
PRAT .... Pressure-Retaining Amphipod Trap [*Deep-sea biology*]
PRAT .... Production Reliability Acceptance Test
P RAT AET ... Pro Ratione Aetatis [*According to Age*] [*Pharmacy*] (ROG)
P Rat Aetat ... Pro Rata Aetatis [*According to Age*] [*Pharmacy*]
Pratica Med ... Pratica del Medico [*A publication*]
Prat Ind Mec ... Pratique des Industries Mecanique [*A publication*]
Prat Soudage ... Pratique du Soudage [*A publication*]
Pratt .... Pratt's Contraband-of-War Cases (DLA)
Pratt .... Pratt's Supplement to Bott's Poor Laws [*1833*] (DLA)
Pratt Fr Soc ... Pratt on Friendly Societies [*15th ed.*] [*1931*] (DLA)
Pratt High ... Pratt and Mackenzie on Highways [*21st ed.*] [*1967*] (DLA)
Pratt Sav B ... Pratt on Savings Banks [*6th ed.*] [*1845*] (DLA)
Pratt SL ...... Pratt on Sea Lights [*2nd ed.*] [*1858*] (DLA)
Prat Vet Equine ... Pratique Veterinaire Equine [*A publication*]
PRAUS .... Programme de Recherche sur l'Amiante de l'Universite de Sherbrooke [*Asbestos Research Program*] [*University of Sherbrooke*] [*Quebec*] [*Information service*] (EISS)
PRAVA ...... Pravda [*A publication*]
PRAW .... Personnel Research Activity, Washington, DC [*Obsolete*] [*Navy*]
PRaW .... Wyeth Laboratories, Radnor, PA [*Library symbol*] [*Library of Congress*] (LCLS)
PRAWL ...... Puerto Rican American Women's League
Prax .... Brown's Practice [*Praxis*] [*or Precedents*] in Chancery (DLA)
PRAXA ...... Praxis [*A publication*]
Prax Can ... Praxis Almae Curiae Cancellariae [*Brown*] (DLA)
Prax Forsch ... Praxis und Forschung [*A publication*]
Praxis .... Praxis des Neusprachlichen Unterrichts [*A publication*]
Praxis Int ..... Praxis International [*A publication*]
Praxis Math ... Praxis der Mathematik [*A publication*]
Prax Kinder ... Praxis der Kinderpsychologie und Kinderpsychiatrie [*A publication*]
Prax Kinderpsychol Kinderpsychiatr ... Praxis der Kinderpsychologie und Kinderpsychiatrie [*A publication*]
Prax Klin Pneumol ... Praxis und Klinik der Pneumologie [*A publication*]
Prax Naturw ... Praxis der Naturwissenschaften [*A publication*]
Prax Naturwiss Phy ... Praxis der Naturwissenschaften. Physik [*A publication*]
Prax Naturwiss Phys Unterr Sch ... Praxis der Naturwissenschaften. Physik im Unterricht der Schulen [*A publication*]
Prax Naturwiss Teil 3 ... Praxis der Naturwissenschaften. Teil 3. Chemie [*West Germany*] [*A publication*]
Prax Pneumol ... Praxis der Pneumologie [*A publication*]
Prax Psychother ... Praxis der Psychotherapie [*A publication*]
Prax Schriftenr Phys ... Praxis Schriftenreihe Physik [*A publication*]
Prax Vet ..... Praxis Veterinaria [*A publication*]
PRAZ .... Prazosin [*Antihypertension compound*]
Prazsky Sbor Hist ... Prazsky Sbornik Historicky [*A publication*]
PRB .... Panel Review Board (KSC)
PRB .... Parabola [*Mathematics*]
PRB .... Parachute Refurbishment Building [*NASA*] (NASA)
PRB .... Paso Robles, CA [*Location identifier*] [*FAA*] (FAAL)
PRB S .... Pension Review Board [*Canada*]
PRB .... Personnel Reaction Blank [*Psychology*]
PRB .... Personnel Records Branch [*Army*] (AABC)
PRB .... Personnel Requirements Branch (MUGU)
PRB .... Personnel Research Branch [*Army*] (MCD)
PRB .... Planned Requirements - Bureau Directed
PRB .... Plant Review Board (NRCH)
PRB .... Polar Research Board [*National Academy of Sciences*]
PRB .... Population Reference Bureau, Inc. [*An association*] [*Washington, DC*] (EA)
PRB .... Pre-Raphaelite Brotherhood

PRB .... Procedure Review Board [*Nuclear energy*] (NRCH)
PRB .... Procurement Review Board (MCD)
PRB .... Program Review Board
PRB .... Prosthetics Research Board
PRB .... Public Roads Bureau
PRBA .... Puerto Rican Bar Association (EA)
PRBA(AG) ... Personnel Research Board of the Army, Adjutant General
PrBayA ...... American Junior College of Puerto Rico, Bayamon, PR [*Library symbol*] [*Library of Congress*] (LCLS)
PrBayC ...... Bayamon Central University (Universidad Central de Bayamon), Bayamon, Puerto Rico [*Library symbol*] [*Library of Congress*] (LCLS)
PRBC .... Packed Red Blood Cells [*Medicine*]
PRBD .... Paraboloid
PRBG .... Puerto Rican Board of Guardians [*Defunct*] (EA)
PRBK .... Provident Bancorp [*NASDAQ symbol*] (NQ)
PRBL .... Probable (FAAC)
PRBLC .... Parabolic
PRBLTY ..... Probability (FAAC)
PRBMD ...... Physical Review Section B. Condensed Matter [*A publication*]
PRBNT .... Prebent
Pr Bot Sadu Kiiv Derzh Univ ... Pratsi Botanichnogo Sadu. Kiivs'kii Derzhavnii Universitet [*A publication*]
PRBS .... Pseudorandom Binary Sequence [*Data processing*]
PRBSG .... Pseudorandom Binary Sequence Generator [*Data processing*] (NRCH)
PRBT .... Precision Remote Bathythermograph
PRC .... Chief Aircrew Survival Equipmentman [*Formerly, Chief Parachute Rigger*] [*Navy rating*]
PRC .... Part Requirement Card
PRC .... Partial Response Coding (IEEE)
PRC .... Partido Republicano Calderonista [*Calderonista Republican Party*] [*Costa Rican*] (PPW)
PRC .... Parts Release Card (KSC)
PRC .... Passaic River Coalition (EA)
PRC .... Passenger Reservation Center
PRC .... Penrose Resources Corporation [*Vancouver Stock Exchange symbol*]
PRC .... Pension Research Council [*Philadelphia, PA*] (EA)
PRC .... Pension Rights Center [*Washington, DC*] (EA)
PRC .... People's Redemption Council [*Liberian*] (PD)
PRC .... People's Republic of China [*Mainland China*]
PRC .... People's Republic of the Congo
PRC .... Permanent Regular Commissions [*Army*] [*British*]
PRC .... Personality Research Center [*University of Texas at Austin*] [*Research center*] (RCD)
PRC .... Personnel Readiness Center [*Air Force*]
PRC .... Personnel Recovery Center [*Military*]
PRC .... Personnel Reporting Code [*Army*] (AABC)
PRC .... Phase-Response Curve
PRC .... Physical Review Council [*DoD*]
PRC .... Pierce (MSA)
PRC .... Planned Requirements, Conversion (NG)
PRC .... Planning Research Corp. [*In company name, PRC Realty Systems*] [*McLean, VA*] [*Software manufacturer*]
PRC .... Plant Records Center [*of the American Horticultural Society*] (EISS)
PRC .... Plasma Renin Concentration [*Hematology*]
PRC .... Plastic Roller Conveyor
PRC .... Plutonium Rework Cell [*Nuclear energy*] (NRCH)
PRC .... Point of Reverse Curve (MSA)
PRC .... Point Reyes [*California*] [*Seismograph station code, US Geological Survey*] [*Closed*] (SEIS)
PRC .... Population Research Center [*University of Chicago*] [*Research center*] (RCD)
PRC .... Population Resource Center [*New York, NY*] (EA)
PRC .... Post Roman Conditam [*After the Founding of Rome*] [*Latin*]
PRC .... Postal Rate Commission
PRC .... Poultry Research Center
PRC .... Poultry Research Centre [*of the Agricultural Research Council*] [*British*] (ARC)
PRC .... Power Reflection Coefficient [*of RADAR signals*]
PRC .... Prattsburgh Railway Corporation [*AAR code*]
PRC .... Preoral Ciliary [*Gland*]
PRC .... Prescott [*Arizona*] [*Airport symbol*] (OAG)
PRC .... Prescott, AZ [*Location identifier*] [*FAA*] (FAAL)
PRC .... Pressure Recorder Controller (NRCH)
PRC .... Primary Routing Center [*Telecommunications*] (TEL)
PRC .... Primate Research Center
PRC .... Printer Control
PRC .... Priory Cell
Pr C .... Prize Cases (DLA)
PRC .... Problem Resolution Coordinator [*IRS*]
PRC .... Procaterol [*Pharmacology*]
PRC .... Procedure Review Committee (AAG)
PRC .... Procession Register Clock
PRC .... Proconsul
PRC .... Procurement Request Code [*Military*] (AFIT)
PRC .... Production Readjustments Committee [*WPB*]
PRC .... Products Research & Chemical Corp. [*NYSE symbol*]

PRC .... Professional Reference Center [*Los Angeles County Office of Education*] [*Downey, CA*] [*Library network*]
PRC .... Professional Relations Council [*American Chemical Society*]
PRC .... Program Review Committee   (AFM)
PrC .... Proster in Cas [*A publication*]
PRC .... Providence College, Phillips Memorial Library, Providence, RI [*OCLC symbol*]   (OCLC)
PRC .... Pyrotechnic Rocket Container
PRC .... Revolutionary Socialist Party [*Peruvian*]   (PD)
Pr Ca .... Great War Prize Cases by Evans [*England*]   (DLA)
PRCA .... Palamino Rabbit Co-Breeders Association   (EA)
PRCA .... Parks, Recreation and Cultural Affairs Administration [*New York City*]
PRCA .... People's Republic of China Army   (MCD)
PRCA .... Pitch and Roll Channel Assembly   (MCD)
PRCA .... President of the Royal Canadian Academy
PRCA .... Problem Reporting and Corrective Action   (NASA)
PRCA .... Professional Rodeo Cowboys Association   (EA)
PRCA .... Puerto Rico Communications Authority
PRCA .... Pure Red Cell Aplasia [*Hematology*]
PrCaC .... Colegio Universitario de Cayey, Cayey, PR [*Library symbol*] [*Library of Congress*]   (LCLS)
PRCAD ...... Primary Care [*A publication*]
PRCAFL .... Publications. Research Center in Anthropology, Folklore, and Linguistics [*A publication*]
PRCB .... Program Requirements Control Board [*NASA*]
PRCBD ...... Program Requirements Control Board Directive [*NASA*]   (NASA)
PRCC .... Peoria Record Club [*Record label*]
PRCC .... Puerto Rico Cancer Center [*University of Puerto Rico*] [*Research center*]   (RCD)
PRCCh ...... Principal Roman Catholic Chaplain [*Navy*] [*British*]
PRCE .... Pierce [*S. S.*] Co., Inc. [*NASDAQ symbol*]   (NQ)
Pr Cent Inst Ochr Pr ... Prace Centralnege Instytutu Ochrony Pracy [*A publication*]
Pr Cesk Vyzk Slevarenskeho ... Prace Ceskoslovenskeho Vyzkumu Slevarenskeho [*A publication*]
PRCESSN ... Processing
PRCF .... Petroleum Resources Communications Foundation [*Canada*]
PRCF .... Plutonium Recycle Critical Facility [*Nuclear energy*]
PR Ch .... Practical Register in Chancery [*England*]   (DLA)
Pr Ch .... Precedents in Chancery, Edited by Finch [*1689-1722*] [*England*]   (DLA)
PRCH .... Precharge
PRCH .... Proprietary Chapel [*Church of England*]
Pr Chem .... Prace Chemiczne [*A publication*]
Pr Chem Pr Nauk Uniw Slask Katowic ... Prace Chemiczne. Prace Naukowe Uniwersytetu Slaskiego w Katowicach [*A publication*]
PRCHT ...... Parachute   (AFM)
Prcht Bad... Parachutist Badge [*Army*]
Pr CKB ...... Practice Cases, in the King's Bench [*England*]   (DLA)
PRCLS ...... Property Investors of Colorado [*NASDAQ symbol*]   (NQ)
PRCM .... Master Chief Aircrew Survival Equipmentman [*Navy rating*] [*Formerly, Master Chief Parachute Rigger*]
PRCM .... Passive Radiation Countermeasure
PRCMC ...... Percussionist [*A publication*]
PRCMT ...... Procurement   (MSA)
PRCN .... Precision   (MSA)
PR-CNTL .... Product Control Register
PRC & NW ... Pierre, Rapid City & Northwestern Railroad [*Nickname: Plenty Rough Country and No Women*]
PRCO .... Pacific Requisition Control Office [*Navy*]
Pr Co .... Prerogative Court   (DLA)
Pr Cont...... Pratt's Contraband-of-War Cases [*1861*]   (DLA)
PRCP .... Power Remote Control Panel   (AAG)
PRCP .... Practical Register in the Common Pleas   (DLA)
PRCP .... President of the Royal College of Physicians [*British*]
PRCP .... President of the Royal College of Preceptors [*British*]   (ROG)
PRCP .... Puerto Rican Communist Party
PRCPTN .... Precipitin [*Test*] [*Immunology*]
PRCR .... Protective Cover   (AAG)
PRCS .... Passive and Remote Crosswind Sensor   (MCD)
PRCS .... Personal Radio Communications System [*General Electric Co.*]
PRCS .... Personal Report of Confidence as a Speaker [*Psychology*]
PRCS .... Polish Red Cross Society
PRCS .... President of the Royal College of Surgeons [*British*]
PRCS .... Process   (AFM)
P/RCS .... Propulsion and Reaction Control Subsystem [*NASA*]   (KSC)
PRCS .... Psychological Response Classification System
PRCS .... Purchase Requisition Change Supplement
PRCS .... Senior Chief Aircrew Survival Equipmentman [*Navy rating*] [*Formerly, Senior Chief Parachute Rigger*]
PRCSG ...... Processing   (MSA)
PRCST .... Precast   (AAG)
PRCT .... Pool Repair Cycle Time   (MCD)
PRCTN ...... Precaution   (FAAC)
PRCU .... Power Regulating and Control Unit   (CET)
PRCUA ...... Polish Roman Catholic Union of America   (EA)
P and RD .... Decisions of the Department of the Interior, Pension and Retirement Claims [*United States*]   (DLA)
PRD .... Part Reference Designator

PRD .... Parti Democratique Dahomeen [*Dahomey Democratic Party*]
PRD .... Parti Radical-Democratique Suisse [*Radical Democratic Party of Switzerland*]   (PPE)
PRD .... Partial Reaction of Degeneration
PRD .... Partido Reformista Democratico [*Democratic Reformist Party*] [*Spanish*]   (PPW)
PRD .... Partido de Renovacion Democratica [*Democratic Renewal Party*] [*Costa Rican*]   (PPW)
PRD .... Partido Revolucionario Democratico [*Democratic Revolutionary Party*] [*Panamanian*]   (PPW)
PRD .... Partido Revolucionario Dominicano [*Dominican Revolutionary Party*] [*Dominican Republic*]   (PPW)
PRD .... Period
PRD .... Periodontics and Restorative Dentistry
PRD .... Personal Radiation Dosimeter   (KSC)
PR & D .... Personal Rest and Delay [*Air Force*]   (AFM)
PRD .... Personnel Readiness Date [*Army*]   (AABC)
PRD .... Personnel Records Division [*Army*]   (AABC)
PRD .... Personnel Requirements Data   (AAG)
PRD .... Personnel Research Division [*Navy*]   (MCD)
PRD .... Personnel Resources Data
PRD .... Piezoelectric Resonating Device
PRD .... Planned Residential Development
PRD .... Polaroid Corp. [*NYSE symbol*]
PRD .... Polytechnic Research & Development Co.   (AAG)
PRD .... Postal Regulating Detachment [*Military*]
PRD .... Postradiation Dysplasia [*Medicine*]
PRD .... Potentially Reportable Deficiency [*Nuclear energy*]   (NRCH)
PRD .... Power Range Detector   (IEEE)
PRD .... Power Requirement Data
PR & D .... Power, Rodwell, and Drew's English Election Cases [*1847-56*]   (DLA)
PRD .... Predicted Range of the Day [*Military*]   (NVT)
PRD .... Preretro Update Display
PRD .... Princeton Reference Design   (MCD)
PRD .... Printer Driver
PRD .... Printer Dump
PRD .... Pro Rate Distribution [*Clause*] [*Insurance*]
PRD .... Process Requirements Drawing   (MCD)
PRD .... Procurement Regulation Directive [*NASA*]   (NASA)
PRD .... Procurement Requirements Document [*NASA*]   (NASA)
PRD .... Production Responsibilities Document   (MCD)
PRD .... Productivity Research Division [*Office of Personnel Management*]
PRD .... Proficiency Rating Designator [*Military*]
PRD .... Program [*or Project*] Requirement Data [*NASA*]   (KSC)
PRD .... Program Requirement Document [*Air Force*]
PRD .... Projected Rotation Date   (NG)
PR & D .... Public Research and Development
PRD .... Puerto Rico, Decisiones   (DLA)
PRD .... Push Rod [*Mechanical engineering*]
PRDA .... Program Research and Development Announcement [*Energy Research and Development Administration*]
PRDC .... Personnel Research and Development Center [*Office of Personnel Management*]
PRDC .... Polar Research and Development Center [*Army*]
PRDDO ...... Partial Retention of Diatomic Differential Overlap [*Physics*]
PRDE .... Preliminary Determination of Epicenters [*A publication*] [*National Oceanic and Atmospheric Administration*]
PR & D El Cas ... Power, Rodwell, and Drew's English Election Cases   (DLA)
PRDF .... Political Rights Defense Fund   (EA)
PRDG .... Princess Royal's Dragoon Guards [*Military unit*] [*British*]   (ROG)
Pr & Div ..... Law Reports, Probate and Divorce [*England*]   (DLA)
PRDL .... Personnel Research and Development Laboratory [*Navy*]   (MCD)
PRDN .... Partido de Reconciliacion Democratica Nacional [*Party of National Democratic Reconciliation*] [*Guatemala*]
PRDP .... Power Reactor Demonstration Program
PRDR .... Preproduction Reliability Design Review [*Navy*]   (CAAL)
PRDR .... Production Request Design Review
PRDV .... Peak Reading Digital Voltmeter
PRDX .... Prediction Program [*NASA*]
Pr Dzialu Zywenia Rosl Nawoz ... Prace Dzialu Zywenia Roslin i Nawozenia [*Poland*] [*A publication*]
PRE .... Bureau for Private Enterprise
PRE .... Partido Republicano Evolucionista [*Republican Evolutionist Party*] [*Portuguese*]   (PPE)
PRE .... Partner-Resisted Exercise [*Army*]   (INF)
PRE .... Personal Rescue Enclosure   (NASA)
PRE .... Petroleum Refining Engineer
PRE .... Photoreactivating
PRE .... Portable RADAR Equipment
PRE .... Precinct
PRE .... Precision Airlines [*North Springfield, VT*] [*FAA designator*]   (FAAC)
PRE .... Predecessor   (KSC)
PRE .... Prefect
PRE .... Prefix
PRE .... Preliminary
PRE .... Premier Industrial Corp. [*NYSE symbol*]

PRE .... Prepayment Coin Telephone [*Telecommunications*]   (TEL)
PRE .... Presbyterian Historical Society, Philadelphia, PA [*OCLC symbol*]   (OCLC)
PRE .... President of the Royal Society of Painter-Etchers and Engravers [*British*]
PRE .... Pretoria [*South Africa*]   (KSC)
PRE .... Pretoria [*South Africa*] [*Seismograph station code, US Geological Survey*]   (SEIS)
PRE .... Processing Refabrication Experiment   (NRCH)
PRE .... Progressive Resistive Exercise [*Medicine*]
PRE .... Public Relations Exchange [*Minneapolis, MN*]   (EA)
PRE .... Pulse Radiation Effect
PRE .... Realencyclopaedie fuer Protestantische Theologie und Kirche [*A publication*]
PRE .... Spanish Catalonian Battalion   (PD)
PREA .... Pension Real Estate Association [*Washington, DC*]   (EA)
PREAG ...... Photographic Reconnaissance Equipment Advisory Group [*Military*]
PREAMP .... Preamplifier   (AAG)
PREAP .... Prison Research Education Action Project [*Orwell, VT*]   (EA)
PRE-ARM ... People's Rights Enforced Against Riots and Murder [*Vigilante group in New Jersey*]
PREB .... Prebendary
Preb Dig.... Preble Digest, Patent Cases   (DLA)
PREC......... Precambrian [*Period, era, or system*] [*Geology*]
PREC......... Precedence   (AABC)
PREC......... Preceding
PREC......... Precentor   (ROG)
PREC......... Precious   (ROG)
PREC......... Precision   (AABC)
PREC......... Propulsion Research Environmental Chamber
PREC......... Public Revenue Education Council   (EA)
PRECA ...... Pauly-Wissowas Realencyclopaedie der Classichen Altertumswissenschaft [*A publication*]
Precamb Res ... Precambrian Research [*A publication*]
Precambrian Res ... Precambrian Research [*A publication*]
Precast Concr ... Precast Concrete [*A publication*]
Prec in Ch ... Precedents in Chancery, Edited by Finch [*24 English Reprint*] [*1689-1722*]   (DLA)
Prec Ch ... Precedents in Chancery, Edited by Finch [*24 English Reprint*]   (DLA)
Prec in Ch (Eng) ... Precedents in Chancery, Edited by Finch [*24 English Reprint*]   (DLA)
PRECD ...... Precede   (FAAC)
Pre Ch........ Precedents in Chancery, Edited by Finch   (DLA)
PRECIP ...... Precipitated
PRECIS ...... Pre-Coordinate Indexing System
PRECIS ...... Preserved Context Index System [*British Library*] [*Information service*] [*London, England*]
Precis Eng ... Precision Engineering [*A publication*]
Precis Engng ... Precision Engineering [*A publication*]
Precis Met ... Precision Metal [*A publication*]
Precis Met Molding ... Precision Metal Molding [*A publication*]
PRECO ...... Preparatory Commission of the United Nations Organization
PRECOM .... Precommissioning [*Military*]
PRECOM .... Preliminary Communications Search [*Military*]   (NVT)
PRECOMDET ... Precommissioning Detail [*Navy*]   (NVT)
PRECOMG ... Precommissioning [*Military*]   (NVT)
PRECOMM ... Preliminary Communications [*Military*]   (NVT)
PRECOMMDET ... Precommissioning Detail [*Navy*]
PRECOMMSCOL ... Precommissioning School [*Navy*]
PRECOMP ... Prediction of Contingency Maintenance and Parts Requirements   (MCD)
PRED......... Predicate
PREMOD .... Predicted
PRED......... Prediction   (AFM)
Pred .... Prednisone [*Also, P, PDN, Pr, Pro*] [*Antineoplastic drug*] [*Endocrinology*]
PREDECE ... Predecease   (ROG)
Predel no Dopustimye Konts Atmos Zagryaz ... Predel no Dopustimye Kontsentratsii Atmosfernykh Zagryaznenii [*A publication*]
Predi 161.... Predicasts. Recreational Vehicles Industry Study 161 [*A publication*]
Predi 162.... Predicasts. World Rubber and Tire Markets Industry Study 162 [*A publication*]
Predi 163.... Predicasts. Glass and Advanced Fibers Industry Study 163 [*A publication*]
Predi 165.... Predicasts. Water Treatment Chemicals Industry Study 165 [*A publication*]
Predi 168.... Predicasts. World Housing Industry Study 168 [*A publication*]
PredicadorEv ... El Predicador Evangelico [*Buenos Aires*] [*A publication*]
PREDICT.... Prediction of Radiation Effects by Digital Computer Techniques
Predi P55.... Predicasts. Industrial Packaging Paper Trends P-55 [*A publication*]
Pr Edw I...... Prince Edward Island   (DLA)
Pr Edw I...... Prince Edward Island Reports [*Canada*]   (DLA)
Pr Edw Isl... Prince Edward Island   (DLA)
Pr Edw Isl... Prince Edward Island Reports [*Canada*]   (DLA)
PRE-EMPTN ... Pre-Emption   (ROG)
PREF .... Preface
PREF .... Prefecture

PREF .... Preference   (AFM)
PREF .... Preferred   (KSC)
PREF .... Prefix   (AAG)
PREF .... Prefocused
PREF .... Propulsion Research Environmental Facility
PREFAB .... Prefabricated   (KSC)
PREFACE... Pre-Freshman and Cooperative Education for Minorities in Engineering
PREF-AP .... Prefect-Apostolic [*Roman Catholic*]
PREFAT ..... Prepare Final Acceptance Trials [*Navy*]   (NVT)
PREFCE ..... Preface   (ROG)
PREFLT..... Preflight   (KSC)
PREFLTSCOL ... Preflight School [*Military*]
PREFMD..... Preformed
PREFRAM ... Prepare Fleet Rehabilitation and Modernization Overhaul [*Navy*]   (NVT)
PREG......... Pregnancy
preg........... Pregnant
PREG......... Pregnenolone [*Endocrinology*]
pregang ..... Preganglionic [*Anatomy*]
Pregled Naucnoteh Rad Inform Zavod Tehn Drveta ... Pregled Naucnotehnickih Radova i Informacija. Zavod za Tehnologiiu Drveta [*A publication*]
Pregl Probl Ment Retard Osoba ... Pregled Problema Mentalno Retardiranih Osoba [*A publication*]
Preh .... Prehistoire [*A publication*]
Prehist Arieg ... Prehistoire Ariegeoise [*A publication*]
Prehlad Lesnickej Lit ... Prehl'ad Lesnickej. Drevarskej. Celulozovej a Papierenskej Literatury [*A publication*]
Prehl Lesn Mysliv Lit ... Prehled Lesnicke a Myslivecke Literatury [*A publication*]
Prehl Zahr Zemed Lit ... Prehled Zahranicni Zemedelske Literatury [*A publication*]
Prehl Zemed Lit ... Prehled Zemedelske Literatury [*A publication*]
Prehl Zemed Lit Zahr Domaci ... Prehled Zemedelske Literatury Zahranicni i Domaci [*A publication*]
Prehrambeno Tehnol Rev ... Prehrambeno Tehnoloska Revija [*A publication*]
PREINACT ... Prepare Inactivation [*Navy*]   (NVT)
PREINSURV ... Prepare for Board of Inspection and Survey [*Navy*]   (NVT)
PREJ .... Prejudice   (AABC)
PREL .... Preliminary
PREL .... Preliminary Evaluation [*Orbit identification*]
PREL .... Prelude [*Music*]   (ROG)
PREL .... Priority Reconnaissance Exploitation List   (CINC)
PRELA....... Prensa Latina, Angencia Informativa Latinoamericana [*Press agency*] [*Cuba*]
PRELIM ..... Preliminary   (AFM)
Prelim Rep Dir Gen Mines (Queb) ... Preliminary Report. Direction Generale des Mines (Quebec) [*A publication*]
Prelim Rep Rehovot Nat Univ Inst Agr ... Preliminary Report. Rehovot. National and University Institute of Agriculture [*A publication*]
PRELIMY.... Preliminary   (ROG)
PRELOG..... People's Revolutionary League of Ghana   (PPW)
PRELORT... Precision Long-Range Tracking RADAR
PREM .... Premature [*Medicine*]
PREM .... Premier   (ROG)
PREM .... Premium   (AFM)
PREMA...... Pulp Refining Equipment Manufacturers Association   (EA)
PRE-MED ... Previous to Appearance in MEDLINE [*Latham, NY*] [*Bibliographic database*]
PREMEDU ... Preventive Medicine Unit
PREMES .... Premises   (ROG)
PREMOD .... Premodeling Data Output [*Environmental Protection Agency*]
PREMODE ... Preliminary Mid-Ocean Dynamics Experiment [*Marine science*]   (MSC)
PREMS...... Premises   (DSUE)
Pren Act..... Prentice's Proceedings in an Action [*2nd ed.*] [*1880*]   (DLA)
prenat .... Prenatal
PR Enferm ... Puerto Rico y Su Enferma [*A publication*]
PrEng......... Professional Engineer
Prensa Med Argent ... Prensa Medica Argentina [*A publication*]
Prensa Med Mex ... Prensa Medica Mexicana [*A publication*]
preocc....... Preoccupied [*Biology, taxonomy*]
PREOP ...... Preoperative [*Medicine*]
PREOS ...... Predicted Range for Electrooptical Systems [*Military*]   (CAAL)
PREOVHL... Prepare for Shipyard Overhaul [*Navy*]   (NVT)
PREP .... Pacific Range Electromagnetic Platform   (AAG)
PREP .... Peace Research and Education Project
PREP .... Peacetime Requirements and Procedures [*Strategic Air Command*]   (MUGU)
PREP .... Persons Responsive to Educational Problems   (EA)
PREP .... Plan, Rehearse, Edit, and Psych [*Public speaking preparation technique*]
PREP .... Plasma Rotating Electrode Process [*Metallurgy*]
PREP .... Predischarge Education Program [*DoD*]
PREP .... Preparation [*or Preparatory*]
PREP .... Prepare   (AFM)
PREP .... Preposition

PREP .... Productivity Research and Extension Program [*North Carolina State University*] [*Research center*]   (RCD)
PREP .... Programed Educational Package
PREP .... Purchasing, Receiving, and Payable System
PREP .... Putting Research into Educational Practice [*Information service of ERIC*]
Prepak .... People's Revolutionary Party of Kungleipak [*Indian*]   (PD)
PREPARE... Project for Retraining of Employable Persons as Relates to EDP
Prep Bioch ... Preparative Biochemistry [*A publication*]
Prep Biochem ... Preparative Biochemistry [*A publication*]
PREPD .... Prepared
PREPE........ Prepare   (ROG)
PREPG .... Preparing
Prep Inorg React ... Preparative Inorganic Reactions [*A publication*]
PREPN ...... Preparation
PREPOS ...... Preposition   (AABC)
PREPOSTOR ... Prepositioned Storage [*Army*]   (AABC)
PREPPSA... Prepare Postshakedown Availability [*Navy*]   (NVT)
Preppy .... Preparatory School Alumnus [*Lifestyle classification*]
Prepr Am Chem Soc Div Fuel Chem ... Preprints. American Chemical Society. Division of Fuel Chemistry [*A publication*]
Prepr Amer Wood Pres Ass ... Preprint. American Wood Preservers' Association [*A publication*]
Prepr Am Soc Lubr Eng ... Preprints. American Society of Lubrication Engineers [*A publication*]
Prepr Daresbury Lab ... Preprint. Daresbury Laboratory [*A publication*]
Prepr Div Pet Chem Am Chem Soc ... Preprints. American Chemical Society. Division of Petroleum Chemistry [*A publication*]
PREPREG... Pre-Impregnated Glass Fibers [*Fiberglass production*]
Preprint Inst Eng Aust Conf ... Preprint. Institution of Engineers of Australia. Conference [*A publication*]
PREPRO..... Preprocessor [*Computer*] [*Coast Guard*]
PREPROD ... Preproduction Model [*Military*]   (AFIT)
Prepr Pap Annu Conf Australas Corros Assoc ... Australasian Corrosion Association. Preprinted Papers of the Annual Conference [*A publication*]
Prepr Pap Natl Meet Div Environ Chem Am Chem Soc ... Preprints of Papers Presented at National Meeting. Division of Environmental Chemistry. American Chemical Society [*A publication*]
Prepr Pap Natl Meet Div Water Air Waste Chem Am Chem Soc ... Preprints of Papers Presented at National Meeting. Division of Water, Air, and Waste Chemistry. American Chemical Society [*A publication*]
Prepr Pap Oilseed Process Clin ... Preprints of Papers. Oilseed Processing Clinic [*A publication*]
Prepr Ser ... Preprint Series. University of Oslo. Institute of Mathematics [*A publication*]
Prepr Ser Inst Math Univ Oslo ... Preprint Series. Institute of Mathematics. University of Oslo [*Norway*] [*A publication*]
PREPS........ Predischarge Remedial Education Program [*For servicemen*]
PREPS........ Preparations   (ROG)
PREPSCOL ... Preparatory School
PREQUAL ... Prequalified [*NASA*]   (KSC)
Prer .... Prerogative Court   (DLA)
PRER .... Prevention Resources [*A publication*]
PRERECPAC ... Preplanned Reconnaissance Pacific   (CINC)
Prerog Ct ... Prerogative Court, New Jersey   (DLA)
PRES......... Premises   (ROG)
Pres............ Presbyterian [*A publication*]
PRES......... Presbyterian
PRES......... Presence
PRES......... Present   (AAG)
PRES......... Preserved
PRE-S........ Preshaving   (MSA)
PRES......... President
PRES......... President of the Royal Entomological Society [*British*]
PRES......... Pressure   (FAAC)
PRES......... Preston R. R. [*AAR code*]
PRES......... Presumptive [*Grammar*]
Pres Abs .... Preston's Abstracts of Title [*2nd ed.*] [*1823-24*]   (DLA)
PRESAC ..... Photographic Reconnaissance System Analysis by Computer
PresAfr....... Presence Africaine [*A publication*]
PRESAILEDREP ... Forecast Sailing Report [*Navy*]   (NVT)
PRESB .... Presbyterian
PRESB .... Prescribe   (AABC)
Presb Q ...... Presbyterian Quarterly Review [*A publication*]
Presb R ...... Presbyterian Review [*A publication*]
Presb & Ref R ... Presbyterian and Reformed Review [*A publication*]
PRESBY ..... Presbytery
Presbyt-St. Luke's Hosp Med Bull ... Presbyterian-St. Luke's Hospital. Medical Bulletin [*A publication*]
Presbyt-St. Luke's Hosp Res Rep ... Presbyterian-St. Luke's Hospital. Research Report [*A publication*]
Pres C of E Ch ... Presbyterian Church of England Chaplain [*Navy*] [*British*]
Pre-Sch Years ... Pre-School Years [*A publication*]
Pres Coll Physiol Inst J ... Presidency College. Physiological Institute Journal [*A publication*]
Pres Conv ... Preston on Conveyancing [*5th ed.*] [*1819-29*]   (DLA)

PRESCORE ... Program for the Rapid Estimation of Construction Requirements
PRESCR..... Prescription   (MSA)
Presence Afr ... Presence Africaine [*A publication*]
Preserv Madeiras ... Preservacao de Madeiras [*A publication*]
Preserv Madeiras Bol Tec ... Preservacao de Madeiras. Boletim Tecnico [*A publication*]
Pres Est ..... Preston on Estates [*3rd ed.*] [*1829*]   (DLA)
PRESET ...... Preset Spin Echo Technique
Pres Fal...... Falconer's Decisions, Scotch Court of Session [*1744-51*]   (DLA)
Pres Fal...... Gilmour and Falconer's Reports, Scotch Court of Session   (DLA)
Pres Falc.... President Falconer's Scotch Session Cases [*Gilmour and Falconer*] [*1681-86*]   (DLA)
PRESFR...... Pressure Falling Rapidly [*Meteorology*]   (FAAC)
Pres His S ... Presbyterian Historical Society. Journal [*A publication*]
Pres His SJ ... Presbyterian Historical Society. Journal [*A publication*]
PRESIG ...... Pressurizing   (KSC)
PRESIGN.... Procedure Sign
PRESINSURV ... Inspection and Survey Board [*Navy*]
Pres J .... Presbyterian Journal [*A publication*]
Pres Leg...... Preston on Legacies [*1824*]   (DLA)
Pres Life..... Presbyterian Life [*A publication*]
PRESNAVWARCOL ... Naval War College
PRESPROC ... Presidential Proclamation
PRESRR...... Pressure Rising Rapidly [*Meteorology*]   (FAAC)
PRESS .... Pacific Range Electromagnetic Signature Studies [*or System*] [*Military*]   (NG)
PRESS .... Parti Republicain Social du Senegal [*Social Republican Party of Senegal*]
PRESS .... Pressure   (MCD)
PRESS .... Property Record for Equipment Servicing and Sharing   (MCD)
PRESSAR... Presentation Equipment for Slow Scan RADAR
Presse Actual ... Presse Actualite [*A publication*]
Pressedienst Bundesminist Bild Wiss ... Pressedienst. Bundesministerium fuer Bildung und Wissenschaft [*A publication*]
Presse Med ... Presse Medicale [*A publication*]
Presse Med Belge ... Presse Medicale Belge [*A publication*]
Pressemitt Nordrh-Westfalen ... Pressemitteilung Nordrhein-Westfalen [*A publication*]
Presse Therm Clim ... Presse Thermale et Climatique [*A publication*]
Presse-Umsch ... Presse-Umschau [*A publication*]
PRESSO..... Program for Elective Surgical Second Opinion [*Blue Cross/Blue Shield*]
Pres Stud Q ... Presidential Studies Quarterly [*A publication*]
Pressure Eng ... Pressure Engineering [*Japan*] [*A publication*]
PRESSURS ... Pre-Strike Surveillance/Reconnaissance System   (MCD)
PREST........ Present   (ROG)
PRES'T...... President
PRE-ST ...... Prestart   (AAG)
Prest Conv ... Preston on Conveyancing   (DLA)
Prest Est ... Preston on Estates   (DLA)
Prest Merg ... Preston on Merger   (DLA)
PRESTMO ... Prestissimo [*Very Fast*] [*Music*]   (ROG)
PRESTO ..... Personnel Response and Evaluation System for Target Obscuration [*Military*]   (RDA)
PRESTO ..... Prestissimo [*Very Fast*] [*Music*]   (ROG)
PRESTO..... Program for Rapid Earth-to-Space Trajectory Optimization [*NASA*]
PRESTO ..... Program Reporting and Evaluation System for Total Operations [*AFSC*]
PRESY........ President Brand Gold Mining ADR [*NASDAQ symbol*]   (NQ)
PRET .... Preterit [*Past tense*] [*Grammar*]   (ROG)
PRET .... Pretoria [*South Africa*]   (ROG)
Pre-tap...... Pret-a-Porter [*Ready-to-Wear*] [*French*]
PRETCHREP ... Preliminary Technical Report   (MCD)
PRETECHREP ... Preliminary Technical Report [*Army*]   (AABC)
PRETTYBLUEBATCH ... Philadelphia, Regular, Exchange, Tea, Total, Young, Belles, Lettres, Universal, Experimental, Bibliographical, Association, To, Civilize, Humanity [*From Edgar Allan Poe story "How to Write a Blackwood Article"*]
Preuss Jahrb ... Preussische Jahrbuecher [*A publication*]
Preuss Sitzb ... Preussische Akademie der Wissenschaften. Sitzungsbericht [*A publication*]
PREV .... Prevention
PREV .... Previous   (AFM)
PREV .... Revere [*Paul*] Investors, Inc. [*NASDAQ symbol*]   (NQ)
PrevAGT ..... Previous Abnormality of Glucose Tolerance
PREVENT .... Precertification to Verify Necessary Treatment
Prev Fract Conf Aust Fract Group ... Prevention of Fracture. Conference of the Australian Fracture Group [*A publication*]
Previd Soc ... Previdenza Sociale [*A publication*]
PREVLV ..... Prevalve
Prev Med.... Preventive Medicine [*A publication*]
PREVMEDU ... Preventive Medicine Unit
Prev Stomatol ... Prevenzione Stomatologica [*A publication*]
PREVT....... Preventative
PREW .... Preway, Inc. [*NASDAQ symbol*]   (NQ)

PREWI........ Press Wireless [*A radio service for the transmission of news*]
PREXA ...... Personal Report for the Executive [*A publication*]
Pr Exch ...... Price's English Exchequer Reports [*1814-24*]   (DLA)
PRF............ Palestine Rejection Front   (BJA)
PRF............ Partial Reinforcement [*Training*]
PRF............ Partido Revolucionario Febrerista [*Febrerista Revolutionary Party*] [*Paraguayan*]   (PPW)
PRF............ Penetration Room Filtration [*Nuclear energy*]   (NRCH)
prf............. Performer [*MARC relator code*] [*Library of Congress*]
PRF............ Personality Research Form [*Psychology*]
PRF............ Personnel Readiness File [*Army*]   (AABC)
PRF............ Petroleum Research Fund
PRF............ Phenol/Resorcinol/Formaldehyde [*Plastics technology*]
PRF............ Plastics Recycling Foundation [*Washington, DC*]   (EA)
PRF............ Plutonium Reclamation Facility [*Nuclear energy*]
PRF............ Plymouth Rock Foundation   (EA)
PRF............ Plywood Research Foundation [*Tacoma, WA*]   (EA)
PRF............ Point Response Function [*Of a telescope*]
PRF............ Pontine Reticular Formation [*Neurophysiology*]
PRF............ Porpoise Rescue Foundation   (EA)
PRF............ Primary Reference Fuel
PRF............ Pro-Air [*Mountain View, CA*] [*FAA designator*]   (FAAC)
PRF............ Processor Request Flag [*Telecommunications*]   (TEL)
PRF............ Prolactin-Releasing Factor [*Endocrinology*]
PRF............ Proliferation Regulatory Factor [*Biochemistry*]
PRF............ Proof   (KSC)
PRF............ Protein Rich Fraction [*Food analysis*]
PRF............ Psychiatric Research Foundation
PRF............ Psychical Research Foundation
PRF............ Psychosynthesis Research Foundation   (EA)
PRF............ Public Relations Foundation
PRF............ Public Residential Facility
PRF............ Publications Reference File [*Government Printing Office*] [*Washington, DC*] [*Database*]   (MCD)
PRF............ Publications Romanes et Francaises [*A publication*]
PRF............ Puerto Rico Federal Reports   (DLA)
PRF............ Pulse Rate Frequency   (MUGU)
PRF............ Pulse Recurrence Frequency
PRF............ Pulse Repetition Frequency [*Data processing*]
PRF............ Purchase Rate Factor
PRF............ Purdue Research Foundation [*Purdue University*] [*Research center*]   (MCD)
Pr Falc....... President Falconer's Scotch Session Cases [*1744-51*]   (DLA)
PRFAW...... Personnel Research Field Activity, Washington [*Navy*]   (MUGU)
PRFC.......... Plymouth Rock Fanciers Club   (EA)
PRFCN........ Purification
PRFCS .... Prefocus
PRFD.......... Pulse Recurrence Frequency Discrimination [*Telecommunications*]   (TEL)
PRFE .... Polar Reflection Faraday Effect
PR Fed .... Puerto Rico Federal Reports   (DLA)
PRFG.......... Proofing [*Freight*]
PRFI .... Portable Range-Finder/Illuminator
PRFI .... Puerto Rican Family Institute [*An association*] [*New York, NY*]   (EA)
PRFIA........ Phase-Resolved Fluoroimmunoassay
Pr Fiz Pr Nauk Uniw Slaskiego Katowic ... Prace Fizyczne. Prace Naukowe Uniwersytetu Slaskiego w Katowicach [*Poland*] [*A publication*]
Pr Fiz Pr Nauk Uniw Slask Katowic ... Prace Fizyczne. Prace Naukowe Uniwersytetu Slaskiego w Katowicach [*A publication*]
PRFL .... Pressure Fed Liquid   (KSC)
PRFM .... Performance   (MSA)
PRFM .... Pseudorandom Frequency Modulated [*Data processing*]
PRFO .... Prairie Forum. Journal. Canadian Plains Research Centre [*A publication*]
PRFR .... Proofer [*Freight*]
PRFRD .... Proofread   (MSA)
PRFS .... Phase-Resolved Fluorescence Spectroscopy
PRFT .... Press Fit
PRFT .... Presser Foot
PRFU .... Processor Ready for Use [*Telecommunications*]   (TEL)
PRG............ Gilbert Associates, Inc., Reading, PA [*Library symbol*] [*Library of Congress*]   (LCLS)
PRG............ Parabolic Radius Gage   (MCD)
PRG............ Paris, IL [*Location identifier*] [*FAA*]   (FAAL)
PRG............ Peerless Carpet Corp. [*Toronto Stock Exchange symbol*]
PRG............ People's Revolutionary Government [*Grenadian*]   (PD)
PRG............ Perennial Rye Grass [*Immunology*]
PRG............ Perugia [*Italy*] [*Seismograph station code, US Geological Survey*]   (SEIS)
PRG............ Pick Resources Guide [*ALLM Books*] [*England*] [*Information service*]   (EISS)
PRG............ Plastic Radial Grating
PRG............ Prague [*Czechoslovakia*] [*Airport symbol*]   (OAG)
PRG............ Procedure Review Group [*Nuclear energy*]   (NRCH)
PRG............ Program Regulation Guide
PRG............ Program Review Group [*Military*]
PRG............ Provisional Revolutionary Government [*Vietcong*]
PRG............ Purge   (AAG)
PRGC .... Past Royal Grand Cross [*Freemasonry*]   (ROG)

Pr Geol-Mineral Acta Univ Wratislav ... Prace Geologiczno-Mineralogiczne. Acta Universitatis Wratislaviensis [*A publication*]
Pr Gl Inst Gorn ... Prace Glownego Instytutu Gornictwa [*Poland*] [*A publication*]
Pr Gl Inst Gorn Komun ... Prace Glownego Instytutu Gornictwa. Komunikat [*A publication*]
Pr Gl Inst Przem Rolnego Spozyw ... Prace Glownego Instytutu Przemyslu Rolnego i Spozywczego [*A publication*]
PRGM........ Program   (AFM)
PRGMG ..... Programing   (MSA)
PRGMR ...... Programer   (AFM)
Pr Gory Goretskaga Navuk Tav ... Pratsy Gory Goretskaga Navukov aga Tavarystva [*A publication*]
PRGR.......... Progroup, Inc. [*NASDAQ symbol*]   (NQ)
PRGS.......... President of the Royal Geographical Society [*British*]
PRGS.......... Prognosis   (AABC)
PRH .... Partido Revolucionario Hondureno [*Honduras Revolutionary Party*]   (PPW)
PRH .... Petrol Railhead
PRH .... Phrae [*Thailand*] [*Airport symbol*]   (OAG)
PRH .... Program Requirements Handbook   (MUGU)
PRHA .... Prolactin-Releasing Hormone [*Endocrinology*]
PRHA .... President of the Royal Hibernian Academy [*British*]
PR Health Bull ... Puerto Rico Health Bulletin [*A publication*]
PRHi .... Historical Society of Berks County, Reading, PA [*Library symbol*] [*Library of Congress*]   (LCLS)
PrHlit........ Prace Historycznoliterackie [*A publication*]
PRI............. Farmington, MO [*Location identifier*] [*FAA*]   (FAAL)
PRI............. Pacific Resources, Incorporated [*NYSE symbol*]
PRI............. Pain Rating Index
PRI............. Paint Research Institute   (EA)
PRI............. Paleontological Research Institution   (EA)
PRI............. Partido Revolucionario Institucional [*Mexican political party*]
PRI............. Partito Repubblicano Italiano [*Italian Republican Party*]   (PPW)
PRI............. Peace Research Institute [*Later, Institute for Policy Studies*]   (EA)
PRI............. Performance Registry International
PRI............. Personnel Research, Incorporated [*Durham, NC*] [*Information service*]   (EISS)
PRI............. Petroleum Recovery Institute [*Calgary, AB*] [*Research center*]   (RCD)
PRI............. Phosphate Rock Institute [*Defunct*]   (EA)
PRI............. Photo RADAR Intelligence
PRI............. Photographic Reconnaissance and Interpretation   (NATG)
PRI............. Pineapple Research Institute of Hawaii   (EA)
PRI............. Plastics and Rubber Institute [*London, England*]   (EA-IO)
PRI............. Polymer Research Institute [*University of Massachusetts*] [*Research center*]   (RCD)
PRI............. Polymer Research Institute [*Polytechnic Institute of New York*] [*Research center*]   (RCD)
PRI............. Praslin Island [*Seychelles Islands*] [*Airport symbol*]   (OAG)
PRI............. Preliminary Rifle Instruction
PRI............. Prescriptive Reading Inventory
PRI............. President Regimental Institutes [*British*]
PRI............. President of the Royal Institute (of Painters in Water Colours) [*British*]   (ROG)
PRI............. President of the Royal Institution (London)   (ROG)
PRI............. Prevention Routiere Internationale [*International Prevention of Road Accidents*]   (EA-IO)
Pri............. Price's English Exchequer Reports [*1814-24*]   (DLA)
Pri............. Price's English Mining Commissioners' Cases   (DLA)
PRI............. Priest [*California*] [*Seismograph station code, US Geological Survey*]   (SEIS)
PRI............. Primary   (KSC)
PRI............. Prime Computer Inc., Corporation Library, Framingham, MA [*OCLC symbol*]   (OCLC)
PRI............. Princeville Airways, Inc. [*Honolulu, HI*] [*FAA designator*]   (FAAC)
PRI............. Priority   (AFM)
PRI............. Priority Repair Induction [*Code*]
PRI............. Priority Requirement for Information   (AFM)
PRI............. Prison
PRI............. Private
PRI............. Prize [*or Prizeman*] [*British*]   (ROG)
PRI............. Processing Research Institute [*Carnegie Mellon University*]
PRI............. Program Revision Intent
PRI............. Proteus Resources, Incorporated [*Vancouver Stock Exchange symbol*]
PRI............. Psoriasis Research Institute [*Stanford, CA*]   (EA)
PRI............. Puerto Rican Independence [*Later, GPRG*] [*An association*]   (EA)
PRI............. Puerto Rico [*Three-letter standard code*]   (CNC)
PRI............. Pulse Rate Increases [*Medicine*]
PRI............. Pulse Rate Indicator
PRI............. Pulse Recurrence [*or Repetition*] Interval   (NATG)
PRI............. Pure Research Institute [*Later, BRINC*]   (EA)
PRIA .... Peer Review Improvement Act of 1982
PRIA .... President of the Royal Irish Academy
PRIA .... Priam Corp. [*NASDAQ symbol*]   (NQ)
PRIA .... Proceedings. Royal Irish Academy [*A publication*]

PRIA .... Public Rangelands Improvement Act of 1978
PRIAA .... Proceedings. Royal Irish Academy. Section A. Mathematical and Physical Sciences [*A publication*]
PRIAM .... Precision Range Information Analysis for Missiles   (MCD)
PrIAU-SJ .... Inter-American University of Puerto Rico, San Juan Campus, San Juan, PR [*Library symbol*] [*Library of Congress*]   (LCLS)
PRIBA .... President of the Royal Institute of British Architects
PRIBA .... Proceedings. Royal Irish Academy. Section B. Biological, Geological, and Chemical Science [*A publication*]
Pribliz Metod Resen Differencial Uravnen ... Priblizennye Metody Resenija Differencial nyh Uravnenii [*A publication*]
Prib Metody Anal Izluch ... Pribory i Metody Analiza Izluchenii [*A publication*]
Pribory i Sistemy Avtomat ... Pribory i Sistemy Avtomatiki [*A publication*]
Prib Sist Avtom ... Pribory i Sistemy Avtomatiki [*A publication*]
Prib Sist Upr ... Pribory i Sistemy Upravleniya [*A publication*]
Prib i Tekh Eksp ... Pribory i Tekhnika Eksperimenta [*A publication*]
Prib Tekhn ... Pribory i Tekhnika Eksperimenta [*A publication*]
Prib Ustroistva Sredstv Avtom Telemekh ... Pribory i Ustroistva Sredstv Avtomatiki i Telemekhaniki [*A publication*]
PRIC Dec .... Puerto Rico Industrial Commission Decisions   (DLA)
Price .... Price's English Exchequer Reports   (DLA)
Price .... Price's English Mining Commissioners' Cases   (DLA)
PRICE .... Pricing Review to Intensify Competitive Environment [*Data processing*]
PRICE .... Programed Review of Information for Costing and Evaluation   (MCD)
Price Liens ... Price on Maritime Liens [*1940*]   (DLA)
Price Min Cas ... Price's Mining Cases   (DLA)
Price Notes PC ... Price's Notes of Practice Cases in Exchequer [*1830-31*] [*England*]   (DLA)
Price Notes PP ... Price's Notes of Points of Practice, English Exchequer Cases   (DLA)
Price PC ..... Price's English Practice Cases [*1830-31*]   (DLA)
Price Pr Cas ... Price's English Practice Cases   (DLA)
Price & St ... Price and Stewart's Trade Mark Cases   (DLA)
Price Waterhouse R ... Price Waterhouse Review [*A publication*]
Price Waterhouse Rev ... Price Waterhouse Review [*A publication*]
Prickett ...... Prickett's Reports [*1 Idaho*]   (DLA)
PRICOM ..... Prison Commission [*British*]
PRID .... Pridie [*The Day Before*] [*Latin*]
PriD .... Princeton Datafilm, Inc., Princeton, NJ [*Library symbol*] [*Library of Congress*]   (LCLS)
Prid & C ...... Prideaux and Cole's English Reports [*4 New Sessions Cases*] [*1850-51*]   (DLA)
Prid Ch W ... Prideaux's Directions to Churchwardens [*10th ed.*] [*1835*]   (DLA)
Prid & Co ... Prideaux and Cole's English Reports [*4 New Sessions Cases*] [*1850-51*]   (DLA)
PRIDCO ...... Puerto Rico Industrial Development Company
Prid Conv ... Prideaux's Forms and Precedents in Conveyancing [*24th ed.*] [*1952*]   (DLA)
PRIDE .... People for Rehabilitating and Integrating the Disabled through Education [*New York City*]
PRIDE .... Perfection Requires Individual Defect Elimination
PRIDE .... Personal Responsibility in Daily Effort [*Military Airlift Command's acronym for the Zero Defects Program*]
PRIDE .... Priority Receiving with Inter-Departmental Efficiency [*Data processing*]
PRIDE .... Production of Reliable Items Demands Excellence [*Navy*]   (NG)
PRIDE .... Professional Results in Daily Effort [*Strategic Air Command's acronym for the Zero Defects Program*]
PRIDE .... Programed Reliability in Design Engineering
PRIDE .... Promote Real Independence for the Disabled and Elderly [*In organization name, P.R.I.D.E. Foundation*]   (EA)
PRIDE .... Prompt Response Insurance Delivery Express
PRIDE .... Protection of Reefs and Islands from Degradation and Exploitation
Prid Judg ... Prideaux's Judgments and Crown Debts [*4th ed.*] [*1854*]   (DLA)
PRIF .... Prior Year Refund Information File [*IRS*]
PRI-FLY ..... Primary Flight Control [*on an aircraft carrier*] [*Navy*]
PRIGA .... Prace Instytutu Geologii [*A publication*]
PRIH .... Prolactin-Release Inhibiting Factor [*Also, PIF*] [*Endocrinology*]
Prikladnaya Geofiz ... Prikladnaya Geofizika [*A publication*]
Prikl Biokhim Mikrobiol ... Prikladnaya Biokhimiya i Mikrobiologiya [*A publication*]
Prikl Geofiz ... Prikladnaya Geofizika [*A publication*]
Prikl Geom i Inzener Grafika ... Prikladnaja Geometrija i Inzenernaja Grafika [*A publication*]
Prikl Mat .... Prikladnaya Matematika i Mekhanika [*A publication*]
Prikl Mat Mekh ... Prikladnaya Matematika i Mekhanika [*A publication*]
Prikl Mat i Mekh ... Prikladnaya Matematika i Mekhanika [*A publication*]
Prikl Mat i Programmirovanie ... Prikladnaja Matematika i Programmirovanie [*A publication*]
Prikl Meh ... Akademija Nauk Ukrainskoi SSR. Otdelenie Matematiki. Mehaniki i Kibernetiki. Prikladnaja Mehanika [*A publication*]

Prikl Mekh ... Akademiya Nauk Ukrainskoi SSR. Otdelenie Matematiki. Mekhaniki i Kibernetiki. Prikladnaya Mekhanika [*A publication*]
Prikl Mekh ... Prikladnaya Mekhanika [*A publication*]
Prikl Problemy Proc i Plast ... Gor'kovskii Gosudarstvennyi Universitet Imeni N. I. Lobacevskogo. Prikladnye Problemy Procnosti i Plasticnosti [*A publication*]
Prikl Yad Fiz ... Prikladnaya Yadernaya Fizika [*A publication*]
Prikl Yad Spektrosk ... Prikladnaya Yadernaya Spektroskopiya [*A publication*]
PrilKJIF ...... Prilozi za Knjizevnost, Jezik, Istoriju, i Folklor [*A publication*]
Prilozi .... Prilozi za Knjizevnost, Jezik, Istoriju, i Folklor [*A publication*]
PrilPJ .... Prilozi Proucavanju Jezika [*A publication*]
PRIM .... Plans and Reports Improvement Memorandum [*Military*]   (CAAL)
PRIM .... Plume Radiation Intensity Measurement   (MUGU)
PRIM .... Primages, Inc. [*NASDAQ symbol*]   (NQ)
PRIM .... Primary   (AFM)
PRIM .... Primate
PRIM .... Primitive
PRIM .... Program for Information Managers [*Later, AIM*] [*An association*]
PRIMA .... Pollutant Response in Marine Animals [*Marine science*]   (MSC)
PRIMA .... Public Risk Insurance Management Association   (EA)
PRIMAR ..... Program to Improve Management of Army Resources   (AABC)
Primary Educ ... Primary Education [*A publication*]
Primary J ... Primary Journal [*A publication*]
Primary Maths ... Primary Mathematics [*A publication*]
Primary Sci Bull ... Primary Science Bulletin [*A publication*]
PRIMATE ... Personal Retrieval of Information by Microcomputer and Terminal Ensemble
Primates Med ... Primates in Medicine [*A publication*]
Primatolog ... Primatologia [*A publication*]
PRIME .... Planning through Retrieval of Information for Management Extrapolation
PRIME .... Precision Integrator for Meteorological Echoes   (IEEE)
PRIME .... Precision Recovery Including Maneuvering Entry [*Air Force*]
PRIME .... Prescribed Right to Income and Maximum Equity
PRIME .... Priority Improved Management Effort   (KSC)
PRIME .... Priority Improvement Effort [*DoD*]
PRIME .... Priority Management Efforts [*Army*]
PRIME .... Priority Management Evaluation [*Navy*]
PRIME .... Processing, Research, Inspection, and Marine Extension [*Marine science*]   (MSC)
PRIME .... Program Independence, Modularity, Economy
PRIME .... Program Research in Integrated Multiethnic Education [*Defunct*]   (EA)
PRIME .... Programed Instruction for Management Education [*American Management Association*]
Prim Ed-Pop Ed ... Primary Education - Popular Educator [*A publication*]
Prim Educ ... Primary Education [*A publication*]
Primenen Mat Ekonom ... Primenenie Matematiki v Ekonomike [*A publication*]
PRIMENET ... Prime Network Software Package [*Prime Computer, Inc.*]
Primen Mat Metodov Biol ... Primenenie Matematicheskikh Metodov v Biologii [*A publication*]
Primen Mikroelem Sel-khoz Akad Nauk UkrSSR ... Primenenie Mikroelementov Sel'skom Khozyaistve. Akademiya Nauk Ukrainskoi SSR [*A publication*]
Primen Polim Mater Nar Khoz ... Primenenie Polimernykh Materialov v Narodnom Khozyaistve [*A publication*]
Primen Tsifrovykh Analogovykh Vychisl Mash Yad Fiz Tekh ... Primenenie Tsifrovykh i Analogovykh Vychislitel'nykh Mashin v Yadernoi Fizike i Tekhnike [*A publication*]
Primen Ul'traakust Issled Veshchestva ... Primenenie Ul'traakustiki k Issledovaniyu Veshchestva [*A publication*]
PRIMER ...... Patient Record Information for Education Requirements [*Data processing*]
PRIMES ..... Productivity Integrated Measurement System [*Army*]
PRIMIR .... Product Improvement Management Information Report
PRIM LUC ... Prima Luce [*Early in the Morning*] [*Pharmacy*]
PRIM M .... Primo Mane [*Early in the Morning*] [*Pharmacy*]
PRIM METH ... Primitive Methodist [*A publication*]
PRIMOS ..... Prime Operating System [*Prime Computer, Inc.*]
PRIM & R ... Public Responsibility in Medicine and Research   (EA)
PRIMS .... Product Requirement Information Management System   (MCD)
PRIMTRA ... Air Primary Training
PRIN .... Partido Revolucionario de la Izquierda Nacionalista [*National Leftist Revolutionary Party*] [*Bolivian*]   (PPW)
PRIN .... Performance Risk Index Number   (NG)
PRIN .... Princeton [*New Jersey*] [*Seismograph station code, US Geological Survey*]   (SEIS)
PRIN .... Principal
PRIN .... Principality   (ROG)
PRIN .... Principally   (ROG)
PRIN .... Principia [*Elements*] [*Latin*]   (ROG)
PRIN .... Principle   (ROG)
PRINAIR .... Puerto Rico National Airlines
Princ .... Princeton Review [*A publication*]
PRINC .... Principal

PRINC .... Principle
PRINCE ...... Parts Reliability Information Center [*NASA*]
PRINCE ...... Programed International Computer Environment [*International relations simulation game*]
PRINCE ...... Programed Reinforced Instruction Necessary to Continuing Education
PRINCE/APIC ... Parts Reliability Information Center/Apollo Parts Information Center [*NASA*]
Prince S B ... Princeton Seminary Bulletin [*A publication*]
Princeton Coll B ... Princeton College. Bulletin [*A publication*]
Princeton Conf Cerebrovasc Dis ... Princeton Conference on Cerebrovascular Diseases [*A publication*]
Princeton Conf Cereb Vasc Dis ... Princeton Conference on Cerebral Vascular Diseases [*Later, Princeton Conference on Cerebrovascular Diseases*] [*A publication*]
Princeton Math Ser ... Princeton Mathematical Series [*A publication*]
Princeton Mus Rec ... Princeton University. Museum of Historic Art. Record [*A publication*]
Princeton Stud Math Econom ... Princeton Studies in Mathematical Economics [*A publication*]
Princeton Univ Lib Chron ... Princeton University Library Chronicle [*A publication*]
Princ Food Rice ... Principal Food. Rice [*A publication*]
Principia Cardiol ... Principia Cardiologica [*A publication*]
Princ ns ..... Princeton Review (New Series) [*A publication*]
PrincSB ...... Princeton Seminary Bulletin [*A publication*]
PrincSemB ... Princeton Seminary Bulletin [*Princeton, NJ*] [*A publication*]
Princ Theol R ... Princeton Theological Review [*A publication*]
Princ Univ Bull ... Princeton University Bulletin [*A publication*]
PRIND .... Present Indications Are [*Aviation*] (FAAC)
PRINDUS ... Prison Industries [*Industries conducted in English prisons*]
PRING .... Partido Revolucionario de Izquierda Nacional Gueiler [*Revolutionary Party of the National Left - Gueiler Wing*] [*Bolivian*] (PPW)
PRIN-L .... Partido Revolucionario de la Izquierda Nacional Laboral (PPW)
PRINM .... Partido Revolucionario de la Izquierda Nacional Moller [*Bolivian*] (PPW)
PRINMUS ... Principal Musician [*Marine Corps*]
PRINOBC/NEC ... Primary Navy Officer Billet Classification and Navy Enlisted Classification
PRINP .... Pacific Resources Pfd [*NASDAQ symbol*] (NQ)
Pr Inst Badaw Lesn ... Prace Instytutu Badawczego Lesnictwa [*A publication*]
Pr Inst Celul Papier ... Prace Instytutu Celulozowo-Papierniczego [*A publication*]
Pr Inst Elektrotech ... Prace Instytutu Elektrotechniki [*A publication*]
Pr Inst Elektrotech (Warsaw) ... Prace Instytutu Elektrotechniki (Warsaw) [*A publication*]
Pr Inst Geol Korisnikh Kopalin Akad Nauk Ukr ... Pratsi. Institut Geologii Korisnikh Kopalin. Akademiya Nauk Ukrains'koi [*A publication*]
Pr Inst Gidrobiol Akad Nauk Ukr RSR ... Pratsi Instytutu Gidrobiologii. Akademiya Nauk Ukrains'koi RSR [*A publication*]
Pr Inst Gospod Wodnej ... Prace Instytutu Gospodarki Wodnej [*A publication*]
Pr Inst Hutn ... Prace Instytutow Hutniczych [*A publication*]
Pr Inst Inz Chem Politech Warsz ... Prace Instytutu Inzynierii Chemicznej Politechniki Warszawskiej [*A publication*]
Pr Inst Jedwabiu Nat ... Prace Instytutu Jedwabiu Naturalnego [*A publication*]
Pr Inst Lab Badaw Przem Spozyw ... Prace Instytutow i Laboratoriow Badawczych Przemyslu Spozywczego [*A publication*]
Pr Inst Lacznosci ... Prace Instytutu Lacznosci [*A publication*]
Pr Inst Masz Mat ... Prace Instytutu Maszyn Matematycznych [*A publication*]
Pr Inst Masz Przeplyw ... Prace Instytutu Maszyn Przeplywowych [*A publication*]
Pr Inst Masz Przeplyw Pol Akad Nauk ... Prace Instytutu Maszyn Przeplywowych. Polska Akademia Nauk [*Poland*] [*A publication*]
Pr Inst Mech Precyz ... Prace Instytutu Mechaniki Precyzyjnej [*Poland*] [*A publication*]
Pr Inst Met ... Prace Instytutu Metalurgue [*A publication*]
Pr Inst Metal Gliwice (Pol) ... Prace Instytutu Metalurgii. Gliwice (Poland) [*A publication*]
Pr Inst Metal Zelaza ... Prace Instytutu Metalurgii Zelaza [*A publication*]
Pr Inst Meteorol Gospod Wodnej ... Prace Instytutu Meteorologii i Gospodarki Wodnej [*A publication*]
Pr Inst Met Niezelaz ... Prace Instytutu Metali Niezelaznych [*A publication*]
Pr Inst Minist Hutn (Pol) ... Prace Instytutu Ministerstwa Hutnictwa (Poland) [*A publication*]
Pr Inst Naft (Krakow) ... Prace Instytutu Naftowego (Krakow) [*Poland*] [*A publication*]
Pr Inst Odlew Zesz Spec ... Prace Instytutu Odlewnictwa. Zeszyty Specjalne [*A publication*]
Pr Inst Odlew Zesz Specjalne ... Prace Instytutu Odlewnictwa. Zeszyty Specjalne [*Poland*] [*A publication*]
Pr Inst Przem Cukrow ... Prace Instytutu Przemyslu Cukrowniczego [*A publication*]
Pr Inst Przem Miecz ... Prace Instytutu Przemyslu Mieczarskiego [*A publication*]

Pr Inst Przem Org ... Prace Instytutu Przemyslu Organicznego [*A publication*]
Pr Inst Przem Skorzanego ... Prace Instytutu Przemyslu Skorzanego [*A publication*]
Pr Inst Przem Szkla Ceram ... Prace Instytutu Przemyslu Szkla i Ceramiki [*A publication*]
Pr Inst Przem Wlok Lykowych ... Prace Instytutu Przemyslu Wlokien Lykowych [*A publication*]
Pr Inst Sadow Ser E Mater Zjazdow Konf ... Prace Instytutu Sadownictwa. Seria E. Materialy Zjazdow i Konferencji [*A publication*]
Pr Inst Sadow Skierniew ... Prace Instytutu Sadownictwa w Skierniewicach [*A publication*]
Pr Inst Sadow Skierniewicach ... Prace Instytutu Sadownictwa w Skierniewicach [*A publication*]
Pr Inst Tech Budow Ser 1 ... Prace Instytutu Techniki Budowlanej. Seria 1. Materialy Budowlane i Ich Zastosowanie [*A publication*]
Pr Inst Tech Budow Ser 2 ... Prace Instytutu Techniki Budowlanej. Seria 2. Konstrukeje Budowlane i Inzynierskie [*A publication*]
Pr Inst Tech Ciepl ... Prace Instytutu Techniki Cieplnej [*Poland*] [*A publication*]
Pr Inst Tele- & Radiotech ... Prace Instytutu Tele- i Radiotechnicznego [*A publication*]
Pr Inst Wlok ... Prace Instytutu Wlokiennictwa [*A publication*]
PRINT .... Pre-Edited Interpretive System [*Data processing*]
PRINT .... Public Release of Information and Transcripts [*Student legal action organization*]
Print Art ..... Printing Art [*Massachusetts*] [*A publication*]
Print Art Q ... Printing Art Quarterly [*A publication*]
Print Bookbind Trade Rev ... Printing and Bookbinding Trade Review [*A publication*]
Print Coll Q ... Print Collector's Quarterly [*A publication*]
Print Equip Eng ... Printing Equipment Engineer [*A publication*]
Print Graph Arts ... Printing and Graphic Arts [*A publication*]
Printing ...... Printing Impressions [*A publication*]
Printing Abs ... Printing Abstracts [*A publication*]
Printing Abstr ... Printing Abstracts [*A publication*]
Printing Impr ... Printing Impressions [*A publication*]
Printing and Pub ... Printing and Publishing [*A publication*]
Printing Trades J ... Printing Trades Journal [*A publication*]
Print Mag ... Printing Magazine [*A publication*]
Print Manag ... Printing Management [*A publication*]
Print & Pub ... Printing and Publishing [*A publication*]
Print Sales ... Printed Salesmanship [*A publication*]
Print Technol ... Printing Technology [*A publication*]
Print Trades J ... Printing Trades Journal [*A publication*]
PRINUL ...... Puerto Rico International Undersea Laboratory
PRIO .... International Peace Research Institution, Oslo [*Norway*]
PRIOR .... Program for In-Orbital Rendezvous [*Antisatellite system*] [*Air Force*]
PRIP .... Park Restoration and Improvement Program [*National Park Service*]
PRIP .... Parts Reliability Improvement Program
PRIP .... Planned Retirement Income Program [*Institute of Financial Management*]
PRIPACSEVOCAM ... Primary Pacific Secure Voice Communications [*Navy*] (CAAL)
Pr IPO .... Prace IPO [*Instytutu Przemyslu Organicznego*] [*A publication*]
PRIPP .... Pacific Research Institute for Public Policy [*San Francisco, CA*] (EA)
P R Ir Ac A ... Proceedings. Royal Irish Academy. Section A. Mathematical, Astronomical, and Physical Science [*A publication*]
P R Ir Ac B ... Proceedings. Royal Irish Academy. Section B. Biological, Geological, and Chemical Science [*A publication*]
P R Ir Ac C ... Proceedings. Royal Irish Academy. Section C. Archaeology, Celtic Studies, History, Linguistics, Literature [*A publication*]
Prir Gaz Sib ... Prirodnyi Gaz Sibiri [*A publication*]
Prir-Mat Fak Univ Kiril Metodij-Skopje God Zb Biol ... Prirodno-Matematicka Fakultet na Univerzitetot Kiril i Metodij-Skopje. Godisen Zbornik. Biologija [*A publication*]
Prir Mat Fak Univ Kiril Metodij-Skopje God Zb Sek A ... Prirodno-Matematicka Fakultet na Universitetot Kiril i Metodij-Skopje. Godisen Zbornik. Sekcja A. Matematika, Fizika, i Hemija [*A publication*]
Prir (Moscow) ... Priroda (Moscow) [*A publication*]
Prirod-Mat Fak Univ Kiril i Metodij Skopje Godisen Zb ... Prirodno-Matematicka Fakultet na Univerzitetot Kiril i Metodij Skopje. Godisen Zbornik [*A publication*]
Prirod-Mat Fak Univ Kiril Metodij Skopje Godisen Zb ... Prirodno-Matematicka Fakultet na Univerzitetot Kiril i Metodij Skopje. Godisen Zbornik [*A publication*]
Prirodonauc Muz Skopje Posebno Izd ... Prirodonaucen Muzej Skopje Posebno Izdanie [*A publication*]
Prirodosl Istraz Acta Biol ... Prirodoslovna Istrazivanja Acta Biologica [*A publication*]
Prirodosl Istraz Acta Geol ... Prirodoslovna Istrazivanja Acta Geologica [*A publication*]
Prirodoved Cas Slezsky ... Prirodovedny Casopis Slezsky [*A publication*]
Prirodoved Pr Ustavu Cesk Akad Ved Brne ... Prirodovedne Prace Ustavu Ceskoslovenske Akademie Ved v Brne [*A publication*]
Prir (Sofia) ... Priroda (Sofia) [*A publication*]

Prir Tr Resur Levoberezhnoi Ukr Ikh Ispolz ... Prirodnye i Trudot ye Resursy Levoberezhnoi Ukrainy i Ikh Ispolzovanie [*A publication*]

Prir Usloviya Zapadn Sib ... Prirodnye Usloviya Zapadnoi Sibiri [*A publication*]

PRIS .... Pacific Range Instrumentation Satellite　(MUGU)

PRIS .... Pesticide Research Information System [*Agriculture Canada*] [*Ottawa, ON*] [*Information service*]　(EISS)

PRIS .... Prison　(ROG)

PRIS .... Prisoner　(AFM)

PRIS .... Program Resource Information System [*Department of Agriculture*]

PRIS .... Propeller Revolution Indicator System　(MSA)

Prisadki Smaz Maslam ... Prisadki i Smazochnym Maslam [*A publication*]

PRISCO ...... Price Stabilization Corporation

PRISD .... Proceedings. Indian Academy of Sciences. Series. Engineering Sciences [*A publication*]

PRISE .... Page Reader Input System with Editing　(NVT)

PRISE .... Pennsylvania Resources and Information Center for Special Education [*Montgomery County Intermediate Unit*] [*King of Prussia*] [*Information service*]　(EISS)

PRISE .... Pennsylvania's Regional Instruction System for Education [*Network of colleges and universities*]

PRISE .... Program for Integrated Shipboard Electronics

PRISIC .... Photographic Reconnaissance Interpretation Section [*Squadron*] Intelligence Center [*JICPOA*]

Pris Jrnl ..... Prisoners Journal [*A publication*]

PRISM .... Parameter Related Internal Standard Method [*Statistical procedure*]

PRISM .... Pattern Recognition Information Synthesis Modeling [*Market analysis*]

PRISM .... Personnel Record Information Systems for Management

PRISM .... Personnel Requirements Information System Methodology　(NVT)

PRISM .... Power Reactor Inherently Safe Module [*Nuclear energy*]

PRISM .... Profile of Real/Ideal Scholastic Motivation　(ADA)

PRISM .... Program Reliability Information System for Management [*Polaris*]

PRISM .... Programed Integrated System Maintenance　(NG)

PRISM .... Progressive Refinement of Integrated Supply Management　(AFM)

PRISNET .... Private Switching Network [*Telecoms*] [*Singapore*]

PRISNET .... Private Switching Network Service [*Telecommunications*]

Prison L Rptr ... Prison Law Reporter　(DLA)

Prison Serv J ... Prison Service Journal　(DLA)

PrisrAcSci&Hum ... Proceedings. Israel Academy of Sciences and Humanities [*Jerusalem*] [*A publication*]

PRISS .... Plaza Realty Investors SBI [*NASDAQ symbol*]　(NQ)

PRIST .... Paper Radioimmunosorbent Test [*Analytical biochemistry*]

Pritch M & D ... Pritchard's Divorce and Matrimonial Causes [*3rd ed.*] [*1874*]　(DLA)

Pritch Quar Sess ... Pritchard's Quarter Sessions　(DLA)

PRIV .... Private

PRIV .... Privative

PRIV .... Privilege

Privacy Rept ... Privacy Report [*A publication*]

Private Pract ... Private Practice [*A publication*]

PRIVAUTH ... Travel Authorized via Privately-Owned Vehicle with Understanding No Additional Cost to Government Involved

Priv C App ... Privy Council Appeals [*England*]　(DLA)

Priv CDI ...... Indian Privy Council Decisions　(DLA)

Priv Counc App ... Privy Council Appeals [*England*]　(DLA)

Priv Counc DI ... Privy Council Decisions [*India*]　(DLA)

PRIVE .... Private　(ROG)

Priv Hous Fin ... Private Housing Finance　(DLA)

Priv Lib .... Private Library [*A publication*]

Priv Libr ..... Private Library [*A publication*]

Priv maintd ... Privately Maintained [*Nautical charts*]

PRIZE .... Program for Research in Information Systems Engineering [*University of Michigan*] [*Research center*]　(RCD)

Prize CR ..... Prize Court Reports [*South Africa*]　(DLA)

PRIZM .... Potential Rating Index by ZIP [*Zone Improvement Plan*] Market [*Advertising*]

PRJ .... American Junior College of Puerto Rico, Bayamon, PR [*OCLC symbol*]　(OCLC)

PRJ .... Port Royal [*Jamaica*] [*Seismograph station code, US Geological Survey*]　(SEIS)

PrJ .... Preussische Jahrbuecher [*A publication*]

PRJ .... Public Relations Journal [*A publication*]

PRJC .... Pearl River Junior College [*Mississippi*]

PRJC .... Puerto Rico Junior College

PRJMP .... Pressure Jump　(FAAC)

PR J Public Health Trop Med ... Puerto Rico Journal of Public Health and Tropical Medicine [*A publication*]

PRK .... Democratic People's Republic of Korea [*Three-letter standard code*]　(CNC)

PRK .... Paraskevi [*Lesbos*] [*Greece*] [*Seismograph station code, US Geological Survey*]　(SEIS)

PRK .... Park

PRK .... Parkside Petroleum [*Toronto Stock Exchange symbol*] [*Vancouver Stock Exchange symbol*]

PRK .... People's Republic of Kampuchea [*Formerly, Cambodia*]　(PD)

PRK .... Pridie Kalendas [*The Day before the Calends*] [*Latin*]

PRK .... Primary Rat Kidney [*Cells*]

PRKG .... Parking

Pr Kom Biol (Poznan) ... Prace Komisji Biologicznej (Poznan) [*A publication*]

Pr Kom Biol Poznan Tow Przyj Nauk ... Prace Komisji Biologicznej. Poznanskie Towarzystwo Przyjaciol Nauk [*Poland*] [*A publication*]

Pr Kom Krystalogr Pol Akad Nauk Inst Nisk Temp Badan Strukt ... Prace Komitetu Krystalografii. Polska Akademia Nauk. Instytut Niskich Temperatur i Badan Strukturalnych [*A publication*]

Pr Kom Mat-Przyr Poznan Tow Przyj Nauk ... Prace Komisji Matematyczno-Przyrodniczej. Poznanskie Towarzystwo Przyjaciol Nauk [*Poland*] [*A publication*]

Pr Kom Nauk Roln Kom Nauk Lesn Poznan Tow Przyj Nauk ... Prace Komisji Nauk Rolniczych i Komisji Nauk Lesnych. Poznanskiej Towarzystwo Przyjaciol [*A publication*]

Pr Kom Nauk Roln Lesn (Poznan) ... Prace Komisji Nauk Rolniczych i Lesnych. Poznanskie Towarzystwo Przyjaciol Nauk (Poznan) [*A publication*]

Pr Kom Nauk Tech Pol Akad Nauk Ser Ceram ... Prace Komisji Nauk Technicznych. Polska Akademia Nauk. Serja Ceramika [*A publication*]

Pr Kom Technol Drewna Poznan Tow Przyj Nauk ... Prace Komisji Technologii Drewna. Poznanskie Towarzystwo Przyjaciol Nauk [*Poland*] [*A publication*]

PRKPA .... Probleme der Kosmichen Physik [*A publication*]

PRKRA .... Parks and Recreation [*A publication*]

PRL .... Pacht, Ross et Al, Los Angeles, CA [*OCLC symbol*]　(OCLC)

PRL .... Page Revision Log　(NASA)

PRL .... Parallel　(MSA)

PRL .... Parti Reformateur Liberal [*Liberal Reform Party*] [*Belgium*]　(PPW)

PRL .... Parti Republicain de la Liberte [*Republican Party for Liberty*] [*French*]　(PPE)

PRL .... Parti Republicain de la Liberte [*Republican Party for Liberty*] [*Upper Volta*]

PRL .... Partido Radical Liberal [*Radical Liberal Party*] [*Ecuadorean*]

PRL .... Parts Requirement List　(KSC)

PRL .... Peace Research Laboratory [*Later, LPRL*] [*An association*]　(EA)

PRL .... Personnel Research Laboratory [*DoD*]

PRL .... Pesticide Research Laboratory and Graduate Study Center [*Pennsylvania State University*] [*Research center*]　(RCD)

PRL .... Petroleum Refining Laboratory [*Pennsylvania State University*]　(MCD)

PRL .... Philco Resources [*Vancouver Stock Exchange symbol*]

PRL .... Photoreactivating Light

PRL .... Physiological Research Laboratories [*University of California at San Diego*] [*Research center*]

PRL .... Pioneering Research Laboratory [*Massachusetts*] [*Army*]

PRL .... Planning Requirements List　(MCD)

PRL .... Plastics Research Laboratory [*MIT*]　(MCD)

PRL .... Preamble

PRL .... Precision Reduction Laboratory　(AFM)

PRL .... Predicted Repair Level　(MCD)

PRL .... Pressure Ratio Limiter　(MCD)

PRL .... Priority Rate Limiting　(MCD)

PRL .... Progressive Republican League

PRL .... Project Research Laboratory

PRL .... Prolactin [*Also, LTH, PR*] [*Endocrinology*]

PRL .... Propulsion Research Laboratory

PRL .... Publications Requirements List　(NG)

PRLASR ..... Population Research Laboratory. University of Alberta. Department of Sociology. Alberta Series Report [*A publication*]

PR Laws Ann ... Laws of Puerto Rico, Annotated　(DLA)

PRLC .... Pittsburgh Regional Library Center [*Chatham College*] [*Pittsburgh, PA*] [*Library network*]

PRLEA .... Pracovni Lekarstvi [*A publication*]

PRLI .... Purchase Request Line Item [*DoD*]

PRLINK ...... Public Relations Society of America Online Information Service　(EISS)

PrLit .... Prace Literackie [*A publication*]

PRLKA .... Przeglad Lekarski [*A publication*]

PRLP .... Planetary Rocket Launcher Platform　(AAG)

PRLP .... Puerto Rico Legal Project [*of the National Lawyers Guild*]　(EA)

PRLS .... Pima Regional Library Service [*Library network*]

PRLS .... Pulsed Ruby LASER System

PRLST .... Price List

PRLTA .... Physical Review. Letters [*A publication*]

PRLTRL & M ... Printer, Lithographer, and Multilith Operator [*Navy*]

PRLW .... Parti des Reformes et de la Liberte de Wallonie [*Belgium*]　(PPW)

PRLWCSR ... Population Research Laboratory. University of Alberta. Department of Sociology. Western Canada Series Report [*A publication*]

PRLX .... Parallax　(AAG)

PRLX .... Parlex Corp. [*NASDAQ symbol*]　(NQ)

Prm .... Parmenides [*of Plato*] [*Classical studies*]　(OCD)

PRM............ Parsons Mountain [*South Carolina*] [*Seismograph station code, US Geological Survey*] (SEIS)
PRM............ Parti de Regroupement Mauritanien [*Mauritanian Regroupment Party*]
PRM............ Partial Response Method
PRM............ Partially Reflecting Mirror
PRM............ Partially Regulated Module
PRM............ Payload Retention Mechanism [*NASA*] (NASA)
PRM............ Personal Radiation Monitor [*Military*]
PRM............ Petition [*or Proposal*] for Rule Making (NRCH)
PRM............ Photoreceptor Membrane [*Of the eye*]
PRM............ Pilots Radio Manual
PRM............ Pit Rib Meristem [*Botany*]
PRM............ Polski Rocznik Muzykologiczny [*A publication*]
PRM............ Power Range Monitor (IEEE)
PRM............ Preformed Road Markings [*Road markings embedded in the pavement rather than painted on street's surface*]
PRM............ Preliminary Requirements Model [*NASA*]
PRM............ Premium
PRM............ Presidential Review Memorandum [*Jimmy Carter Administration*]
PRM............ Pressure Remanent Magnetization
PRM............ Prime (AAG)
PRM............ Prime Computer, Inc. [*NYSE symbol*]
PRM............ Process Radiation Monitor (NRCH)
PRM............ Programer Reference Manual [*Data processing*]
PRM............ Programing and Resources Management [*NASA*] (MCD)
PRM............ Promote (AABC)
PrM............ Protestantische Monatshefte [*A publication*]
PRM............ Publications Requirements Manager [*DoD*]
PRM............ Pulse Rate Modulation
PRMA........ Permeator Corp. [*NASDAQ symbol*] (NQ)
PRMA........ Proceedings. Royal Musical Association [*A publication*]
PrMan........ Prayer of Manasses [*Apocrypha*] (BJA)
PR of MAN ... [*The*] Prayer of Manasses, King of Judah [*Apocrypha*]
PRMAR....... Primary Mission Area [*Military*] (CAAL)
Pr Mater Nauk Inst Matki Dziecka ... Prace i Materialy Naukowe. Instytut Matki i Dziecka [*A publication*]
Pr Mater Pershogo Khark Derzh Med Inst ... Pratsi i Materiali Pershogo Kharkivs'kogo Derzhavnogo Medichnogo Institutu [*A publication*]
Pr Mater Zootech ... Prace i Materialy Zootechniczne [*A publication*]
PRMC........ Puerto Rican Migration Consortium (EA)
PRMCL....... Periodica de Re Morali Canonica Liturgica [*A publication*]
PRMD......... Pro-Med Capital, Inc. [*NASDAQ symbol*] (NQ)
PRMEA....... Presse Medicale [*A publication*]
Pr Med Opolskie Tow Przyj Nauk Wyd Nauk Med ... Prace Medyczne. Opolskie Towarzystwo Przyjaciol Nauk. Wydzial 5. Nauk Medycznych [*A publication*]
PRMG........ Piston Ring Manufacturers Group [*Later, NEPMA*] (EA)
Pr Min........ Printed Minutes of Evidence (DLA)
PR/MIPR .... Purchase Request/Military Interdepartmental Purchase Request (AFIT)
PRMLD....... Premolded [*Technical drawings*] (MSA)
Pr Moravskoslezske Akad Ved Prir ... Prace Moravskoslezske Akademie Ved Prirodnich [*A publication*]
Pr Morsk Inst Rybacki Gdyni ... Prace Morski Instytut Rybacki w Gdyni [*Poland*] [*A publication*]
PRMR......... Primer (MSA)
PRMSB....... Proceedings. Royal Microscopical Society [*A publication*]
PRMSC ...... Proceedings. Annual Reliability and Maintainability Symposium [*A publication*]
PRMSD....... Problemy Mashinostroeniya [*A publication*]
PRMTR....... Parameter (AAG)
Pr Muz Ziemi ... Prace Muzeum Ziemi [*A publication*]
PRN .... Greenville, AL [*Location identifier*] [*FAA*] (FAAL)
PRN .... Pahrock Range [*Nevada*] [*Seismograph station code, US Geological Survey*] (SEIS)
PRN .... Partido Republicano Nacional [*National Republican Party*] [*Costa Rican*]
PRN .... Partido de la Revolucion Nacional [*Party of the National Revolution*] [*Bolivian*] (PPW)
PRN .... Parts Requirement Notice (KSC)
PRN .... Peace Research Network [*of Consortium on Peace Research, Education, and Development*] (EA)
PRN .... Physicians Radio Network
PRN .... Playfulness, Revelry, Nonsense [*Quarterly Newsletter of Nurses for Laughter*] [*Title is derived from the pharmaceutical term PRN (Pro Re Nata)*] [*A publication*]
PRN .... PR Newswire [*New York, NY*] [*Information service*] (EISS)
PRN .... Pridie Nonas [*The Day before the Nones*] [*Latin*]
PRN .... Print Numerically (DEN)
PRN .... Pristina [*Yugoslavia*] [*Airport symbol*] (OAG)
PRN .... Pro Re Nata [*Whenever Necessary*] [*Pharmacy*]
PRN .... Procurement Reallocation Notice
PRN .... Program Release Notice [*NASA*] (NASA)
PRN .... Prominent Resources Corp. [*Vancouver Stock Exchange symbol*]
PRN .... Pronasale [*Anatomy*]

PRN .... Pseudorandom Noise
PRN .... Pseudorandom Number
PRN .... Puerto Rican Cement Co., Inc. [*NYSE symbol*]
PRN .... Pulse Ranging Navigation
PRN .... Pulse Ranging Network (KSC)
pRNA......... Ribonucleic Acid, Polysomal [*Biochemistry, genetics*]
Pr Naturwiss Teil 3 ... Praxis der Naturwissenschaften. Teil 3. Chemie [*A publication*]
Pr Nauk Inst Chem Org Fiz Politech Wroclaw ... Prace Naukowe Instytutu Chemii Organicznej i Fizycznej Politechniki Wroclawskiej [*A publication*]
Pr Nauk Inst Chem Org Fiz Politech Wroclaw Ser K ... Prace Naukowe Instytutu Chemii Organicznej i Fizycznej Politechniki Wroclawskiej. Seria. Konferencje [*A publication*]
Pr Nauk Inst Chem Org Fiz Politech Wroclaw Ser Konf ... Prace Naukowe Instytutu Chemii Organicznej i Fizycznej Politechniki Wroclawskiej. Seria Konferencje [*A publication*]
Pr Nauk Inst Chem Org Fiz Politech Wroclaw Ser S ... Prace Naukowe Instytutu Chemii Organicznej i Fizycznej Politechniki Wroclawskiej. Seria Studia i Materialy [*A publication*]
Pr Nauk Inst Chem Technol Nafty Wegla Politech Wroclaw ... Prace Naukowe Instytutu Chemii i Technologii Nafty i Wegla Politechniki Wroclawskiej [*Poland*] [*A publication*]
Pr Nauk Inst Cybern Tech Politech Wroclaw Ser K ... Prace Naukowe Instytutu Cybernetyki Technicznej Politechniki Wroclawskiej. Seria Konferencje [*A publication*]
Pr Nauk Inst Cybern Tech Politech Wroclaw Ser M ... Prace Naukowe Instytutu Cybernetyki Technicznej Politechniki Wroclawskiej. Seria Monografie [*A publication*]
Pr Nauk Inst Cybern Tech Politech Wroclaw Ser S ... Prace Naukowe Instytutu Cybernetyki Technicznej Politechniki Wroclawskiej. Seria Studia i Materialy [*A publication*]
Pr Nauk Inst Fiz Politech Wroclaw ... Prace Naukowe Instytutu Fizyki Politechniki Wroclawskiej [*A publication*]
Pr Nauk Inst Fiz Politech Wroclaw Ser M ... Prace Naukowe Instytutu Fizyki Politechniki Wroclawskiej. Seria Monografie [*A publication*]
Pr Nauk Inst Fiz Politech Wroclaw Ser Monogr ... Prace Naukowe Instytutu Fizyki Politechniki Wroclawskiej. Seria Monografie [*A publication*]
Pr Nauk Inst Fiz Politech Wroclaw Ser S ... Prace Naukowe Instytutu Fizyki Politechniki Wroclawskiej. Seria Studia i Materialy [*A publication*]
Pr Nauk Inst Fiz Tech Politech Wroclaw ... Prace Naukowe Instytutu Fizyki Technicznej Politechniki Wroclawskiej [*A publication*]
Pr Nauk Inst Geotech Politech Wroclaw ... Prace Naukowe Instytutu Geotechniki Politechniki Wroclawskiej [*Poland*] [*A publication*]
Pr Nauk Inst Gorn Politech Wroclaw ... Prace Naukowe Instytutu Gornictwa Politechniki Wroclawskiej [*Poland*] [*A publication*]
Pr Nauk Inst Inz Chem Urzadz Ciepl Politech Wroclaw Ser M ... Prace Naukowe Instytutu Inzynierii Chemicznej i Urzadzen Cieplnych Politechniki Wroclawskiej. Seria. Monografie [*A publication*]
Pr Nauk Inst Inz Chem Urzadzen Cieplnych Politech Wroclaw ... Prace Naukowe Instytutu Inzynierii Chemicznej i Urzadzen Cieplnych Politechniki Wroclawskiej [*Poland*] [*A publication*]
Pr Nauk Inst Inz Ochr Srodowiska Politech Wroclaw ... Prace Naukowe Instytutu Inzynierii Ochrony Srodowiska Politechniki Wroclawskiej [*Poland*] [*A publication*]
Pr Nauk Inst Materialozn Mech Tech Politech Wroclaw ... Prace Naukowe Instytutu Materialoznawstwa i Technicznej Politechniki Wroclawskiej [*A publication*]
Pr Nauk Inst Materialozn Mech Tech Politech Wroclaw Ser M ... Prace Naukowe Instytutu Materialoznawstwa i Mechaniki Technicznej Politechniki Wroclawskiej. Seria. Monografie [*A publication*]
Pr Nauk Inst Materialozn Mech Tech Politech Wroclaw Ser S ... Prace Naukowe Instytutu Materialoznawstwa i Mechaniki Technicznej Politechniki Wroclawskiej. Seria. Studia i Materialy [*A publication*]
Pr Nauk Inst Mat Politech Wroclaw Ser M ... Prace Naukowe Instytutu Matematyki Politechniki Wroclawskiej. Seria Monografie [*A publication*]
Pr Nauk Inst Mat Politech Wroclaw Ser S ... Prace Naukowe Instytutu Matematyki Politechniki Wroclawskiej. Seria Studia i Materialy [*A publication*]
Pr Nauk Inst Metrol Elektr Politech Wroclaw Ser K ... Prace Naukowe Instytutu Metrologii Elektrycznej Politechniki Wroclawskiej. Seria. Konferencje [*A publication*]
Pr Nauk Inst Metrol Elektr Politech Wroclaw Ser Konf ... Prace Naukowe Instytutu Metrologii Elektrycznej Politechniki Wroclawskiej Seria. Konferencje [*A publication*]
Pr Nauk Inst Metrol Elektr Politech Wroclaw Ser M ... Prace Naukowe Instytutu Metrologii Elektrycznej Politechniki Wroclawskiej. Seria. Monografie [*A publication*]
Pr Nauk Inst Metrol Elektr Politech Wroclaw Ser S ... Prace Naukowe Instytutu Metrologii Elektrycznej Politechniki Wroclawskiej. Seria. Studia i Materialy [*A publication*]

Pr Nauk Inst Ochr Rosl ... Prace Naukowe Instytutu Ochrony Roslin [*A publication*]

Pr Nauk Inst Ochr Rosl (Warsz) ... Prace Naukowe Instytutu Ochrony Roslin (Warszawa) [*A publication*]

Pr Nauk Inst Przem Org (Warsaw) ... Prace Naukowe Instytutu Przemyslu Organicznego (Warsaw) [*A publication*]

Pr Nauk Inst Tech Ciepl Mech Plynow Politech Wroclaw ... Prace Naukowe Instytutu Techniki Cieplnej i Mechaniki Plynow Politechniki Wroclawskiej [*A publication*]

Pr Nauk Inst Tech Ciepl Mech Plynow Politech Wroclaw Ser M ... Prace Naukowe Instytutu Techniki Cieplnej i Mechaniki Plynow Politechniki Wroclawskiej. Seria. Monografie [*A publication*]

Pr Nauk Inst Tech Ciepl Mech Plynow Politech Wroclaw Ser S ... Prace Naukowe Instytutu Techniki Cieplnej i Mechaniki Plynow Politechniki Wroclawskiej. Seria. Studia i Materialy [*A publication*]

Pr Nauk Inst Technol Elektron Politech Wroclaw ... Prace Naukowe Instytutu Technologii Elektronowej Politechniki Wroclawskiej [*A publication*]

Pr Nauk Inst Technol Elektron Politech Wroclaw Ser Monogr ... Prace Naukowe Instytutu Technologii Elektronowej Politechniki Wroclawskiej. Seria Monografie [*A publication*]

Pr Nauk Inst Technol Elektron Politech Wroclaw Ser S ... Prace Naukowe Instytutu Technologii Elektronowej Politechniki Wroclawskiej. Seria. Studia i Materialy [*A publication*]

Pr Nauk Inst Technol Nieorg Nawozow Miner Politech Wroclaw ... Prace Naukowe Instytutu Technologii Nieorganicznej i Nawozow Mineralnych Politechniki Wroclawskiej [*A publication*]

Pr Nauk Inst Technol Org Tworz Sztucz Politech Wroclaw Ser S ... Prace Naukowe Instytutu Technologii Organicznej i Tworzyw Sztucznych Politechniki Wroclawskiej. Seria. Studia i Materialy [*A publication*]

Pr Nauk Inst Technol Org Tworzyw Sztucznych Politech Wroclaw ... Prace Naukowe Instytutu Technologii Organicznej i Tworzyw Sztucznych Politechniki Wroclawskiej [*A publication*]

Pr Nauk Inst Telekomun Akust Politech Wroclaw Ser K ... Prace Naukowe Instytutu Telekomunikacji i Akustyki Politechniki Wroclawskiej. Seria. Konferencje [*A publication*]

Pr Nauk Inst Telekomun Akust Politech Wroclaw Ser M ... Prace Naukowe Instytutu Telekomunikacji i Akustyki Politechniki Wroclawskiej. Seria. Monografie [*A publication*]

Pr Nauk Inst Telekomun Akust Politech Wroclaw Ser S ... Prace Naukowe Instytutu Telekomunikacji i Akustyki Politechniki Wroclawskiej. Seria. Studia i Materialy [*A publication*]

Pr Nauk Inst Ukladow Elektromasz Politech Wroclaw Ser S ... Prace Naukowe Instytutu Ukladow Elektromaszynowych Politechniki Wroclawskiej. Seria. Studia i Materialy [*A publication*]

Pr Nauk Politech Szczecin ... Prace Naukowe Politechniki Szczecinskiej [*Poland*] [*A publication*]

Pr Nauk Politech Wroclaw Ser Konf ... Prace Naukowe Politechniki Wroclawskiej. Seria Konferencje [*A publication*]

Pr Nauk Uniw Slask Katowicach ... Prace Naukowe Uniwersytetu Slaskiego w Katowicach [*A publication*]

Pr Nauk Uniw Slask Katowic Pr Fiz ... Prace Naukowe Uniwersytetu Slaskiego w Katowicach. Prace Fizyczne [*A publication*]

Pr Nauk Wyzsz Szk Ekon Wroclawiu ... Prace Naukowe Wyzszej Szkoly Ekonomicznej we Wroclawiu [*A publication*]

PRNBA ...... Proceedings. Research Institute for Nuclear Medicine and Biology [*A publication*]

PRNC .... Potomac River Naval Command [*Washington, DC*]

PRNC .... Puerto Rico Nuclear Center

PRNDL ...... Park, Reverse, Neutral, Drive, Low [*Automotive term for automatic gearshift indicator in cars; pronounced "prindle"*]

PRNET .... Packet Radio Network

PRNG .... Purging   (MSA)

PRNHA .... Professional Nursing Home [*A publication*]

PRNN .... Project North Newsletter [*A publication*]

PRNT .... Plaque Reduction Neutralization Test [*Immunochemistry*]

PRNTG .... Printing   (MSA)

PRNTR ...... Printer

PRNTV ...... Preventive

PRO .... International Proteins Corp. [*American Stock Exchange symbol*]

PRO .... Pacific Research Office   (CINC)

PRO .... Parallel Rod Oscillator

PRO .... Particle Reduction Oven

PRO .... Parts Release Order

PRO .... Patients' Rights Organization   (EA)

PRO .... Peer Review Organization [*Medicare*]

PRO .... Performing Rights Organization [*Formerly, BMI-Canada Ltd.*] [*Canada*]

PRO .... Perry, IA [*Location identifier*] [*FAA*]   (FAAL)

PRO .... Personnel Relations Officer [*for Shore Stations*] [*Navy*]

PRO .... Pitch Response Operator

PRO .... Planned Requirements, Outfitting [*Navy*]   (NG)

PRO .... Planning Resident Order   (KSC)

PRO .... Plant Representative Officer   (MCD)

PRO .... Population Renewal Office [*An association*] [*Kansas City, MO*]   (EA)

Pro .... Prednisone [*Also, P, PDN, PR, Pred*] [*Antineoplastic drug, Endocrinology*]

PRO .... Principal Public Library [*Library network*]

PRO .... Print Octal   (DEN)

PRO .... Pro Musica [*A publication*]

PRO .... Probate

PRO .... Probation

PRO .... Probationer   (DSUE)

PRO .... Problem Resolution Office [*IRS*]

PRO .... Procedure   (AABC)

PRO .... Procurement Research Office [*Army*]

PRO .... Production Repair Order

PRO .... Professional

PRO .... Professional Racing Organization of America [*Later, USCF*]   (EA)

PRO .... Professional Resellers Organization   (EA)

PRO .... Professional Review Organization [*Medicare*]

PRO .... Proficiency

PRO .... Proflavine [*An antiseptic*]

PRO .... Programable Remote Operation [*Computer Devices, Inc.*]

PRO .... Progressive

Pro .... Proline [*Also, P*] [*An amino acid*]

Pro .... Prolyl [*Biochemistry*]

PRO .... Pronation [*Medicine*]

PRO .... Pronto Exploration [*Toronto Stock Exchange symbol*]

PRO .... Propeller Order

PRO .... Prophylactic   (AABC)

PRO .... Prostitute   (ADA)

Pro .... Protein

PRO .... Protest

Pro .... Prothrombin [*Factor II*] [*Hematology*]

PRO .... Proved

pro .... Provencal [*MARC language code*] [*Library of Congress*]   (LCCP)

Pro .... Proverbs [*Old Testament book*]   (BJA)

PRO .... Province   (ROG)

PRO .... Provost

PRO .... Public Record Office [*British*]

PRO .... Public Relations Office [*or Officer*] [*Usually military*]

PROA .... Polymer Research Corp. of America [*NASDAQ symbol*]   (NQ)

PROA .... Puerto Rico Operations Area

ProAOS ..... Proceedings. American Oriental Society [*Baltimore, MD*] [*A publication*]

Prob .... English Probate and Admiralty Reports for Year Cited   (DLA)

Prob .... Law Reports, Probate Division   (DLA)

PROB .... Probability   (KSC)

PROB .... Probably

Prob .... Probate   (DLA)

PROB .... Probation [*FBI standardized term*]

PROB .... Problem

Prob .... Quod Omnis Probus Liber Sit [*of Philo*]   (BJA)

PROB .... TII Computer Systems [*NASDAQ symbol*]   (NQ)

Prob (1891) ... Law Reports, Probate Division [*1891*]   (DLA)

Probab Math Stat ... Probability and Mathematical Statistics [*A publication*]

Probab Math Statist ... Probability and Mathematical Statistics [*A publication*]

Prob Actuels ORL ... Problemes Actuels d'Oto-Rhino-Laryngologie [*A publication*]

Prob & Adm Div ... Probate and Admiralty Division Law Reports   (DLA)

Prob Agric Ind Mex ... Problemas Agricolas e Industriales de Mexico [*A publication*]

Probat .... Probation   (DLA)

Prob C .... Probate Code   (DLA)

Prob Com .. Problems of Communism [*A publication*]

Prob Commun ... Problems of Communism [*A publication*]

PROBCOST ... Probabilistic Budgeting and Forward Costing

Prob Ct Rep ... Probate Court Reporter [*Ohio*]   (DLA)

PROBDET ... Probability of Detection [*Navy*]   (NVT)

Prob Div ..... Probate Division, English Law Reports   (DLA)

Prob & Div ... Probate and Divorce, English Law Reports   (DLA)

PROBE .... Performance Review of Base Supply Effectiveness [*Air Force*]   (AFM)

PROBE .... Program Optimization and Budget Evaluation [*Military*]

PROBE .... Program for Research on Objectives-Based Evaluation [*UCLA*]

Prob Econ ... Problems of Economics [*A publication*]

PROBES ..... Processes and Resources of the Bering Sea Shelf [*University of Alaska*]

PROBFOR ... Probability Forecasting [*Computer program*] [*Bell System*]

PROBIT ...... Probability Unit [*Statistics*]

Prob J .... Probation Journal   (DLA)

Prob Khig ... Problemi na Khigienata [*A publication*]

Probl Actuels Biochim Appl ... Problemes Actuels de Biochimie Appliquee [*A publication*]

Probl Actuels Endocrinol Nutr ... Problemes Actuels d'Endocrinologie et de Nutrition [*A publication*]

Probl Actuels Ophthal ... Problemes Actuels d'Ophthalmologie [*A publication*]

Probl Actuels Otorhinolaryngol ... Problems Actuels d'Otorhinolaryngologie [*A publication*]

Probl Actuels Paediatr ... Problemes Actuels de Paediatrie [*A publication*]
Probl Actuels Phoniatr Logop ... Problemes Actuels de Phoniatrie et Logopedie [*A publication*]
Probl Actuels Psychotherap ... Problemes Actuels de Psychotherapie [*A publication*]
Probl Agr (Bucharest) ... Probleme Agricole (Bucharest) [*A publication*]
Probl Agric ... Probleme Agricole [*A publication*]
Probl Agrofiz ... Problemy Agrofizyki [*A publication*]
Probl Arkt Antarkt ... Problemy Arktiki i Antarktiki [*A publication*]
Probl Arktiki Antarkt ... Problemy Arktiki i Antarktiki [*A publication*]
Probl Arktiki Antarktiki ... Problemy Arktiki i Antarktiki [*USSR*] [*A publication*]
Probl Attuali Sci Cult ... Problemi Attuali di Scienza e di Cultura [*A publication*]
Probl Biol ... Problems in Biology [*A publication*]
Probl Biol Krajiny ... Problemy Biologie Krajiny [*A publication*]
Probl Bioniki ... Problemy Bioniki [*A publication*]
Probl Bioniki Resp Mezhved Nauchno-Tekh Sb ... Problemy Bioniki Respublikanskii Mezhvedomstvennyi Nauchno-Tekhnicheskii Sbornik [*A publication*]
Probl Bor'by Protiv Burz Ideol ... Problemy Bor'by Protiv Burzuaznoj Ideologii [*A publication*]
Probl Commu ... Problems of Communism [*A publication*]
Probl Control Inf Theor ... Problems of Control and Information Theory [*A publication*]
Probl Control and Inf Theory ... Problems of Control and Information Theory [*A publication*]
Probl Control and Inf Theory (Engl Transl Pap Rus) ... Problems of Control and Information Theory (English Translation of the Papers in Russian) [*A publication*]
Probl Cybern ... Problems of Cybernetics [*A publication*]
Probl Cybern (USSR) ... Problems of Cybernetics (USSR) [*A publication*]
Probl Dal'nego Vost ... Problemy Dal'nego Vostok [*A publication*]
Probl Desarr ... Problemas del Desarrollo [*A publication*]
Probl Dialektiki ... Problemy Dialektiki [*A publication*]
Probl Drug Depend ... Problems of Drug Dependence [*A publication*]
Probl Econ ... Problems of Economics [*A publication*]
Probl Econ (Bucharest) ... Probleme Economice (Bucharest) [*A publication*]
Probl Ekol ... Problemy Ekologii [*A publication*]
Probl Ekon Morja ... Problemy Ekonomiki Morja [*A publication*]
Probl Ekon (Warszawa) ... Problemy Ekonomiczne (Warszawa) [*A publication*]
Probleme de Automat ... Probleme de Automatizare [*A publication*]
Probleme Prot Plantelor ... Probleme de Protectia Plantelor [*A publication*]
Problemi Tehn Kibernet ... Problemi na Tehniceskata Kibernetika [*Problems of Engineering Cybernetics*] [*A publication*]
Problems Control Inform Theory/Problemy Upravlen Teor Inform ... Problems of Control and Information Theory. Problemy Upravlenija i Teorii Informacii [*Budapest*] [*A publication*]
Problems Inform Transmission ... Problems of Information Transmission [*A publication*]
Problemy Jadern Fiz i Kosm Lucei ... Problemy Jadernoi Fiziki i Kosmiceskih Lucei [*A publication*]
Problemy Kibernet ... Problemy Kibernetiki [*A publication*]
Problemy Kosmich Biol Akad Nauk SSSR ... Problemy Kosmicheskoi Biologii. Akademiya Nauk SSSR [*A publication*]
Problemy Mat ... Bydgoszcz. Whzsza Szkola Pedagogiczna. Zeszyty Naukowe. Problemy Matematyczne [*A publication*]
Problemy Mat Anal Sloz Sistem ... Problemy Matematiceskogo Analiza Sloznyh Sistem [*A publication*]
Problemy Matematiceskogo Analiza ... Problemy Matematiceskogo Analiza [*Leningrad*] [*A publication*]
Problemy Slucain Poiska ... Akademija Nauk Latviiskoi SSR. Institut Elektroniki i Vyceslitel'noi Tehniki. Problemy Slucainogo Poiska [*A publication*]
Problemy Teor Gravitacii i Element Castic ... Problemy Teorii Gravitacii i Elementarnyh Castic [*A publication*]
Probl Endokrinol ... Problemy Endokrinologii [*A publication*]
Probl Endokrinol Gormonoter ... Problemy Endokrinologii i Gormonoterapii [*Later, Problemy Endokrinologii*] [*A publication*]
Probl Endokrinol (Mosk) ... Problemy Endokrinologii (Moskva) [*A publication*]
Probl Entrep Agric ... Problemes de l'Enterprise Agricole [*A publication*]
Probl Evol ... Problemy Evolyutsii [*A publication*]
Probl Farine ... Problemes de Farine [*A publication*]
Probl Farm ... Problemy na Farmatsiyata [*A publication*]
Probl Festkoerperelektron ... Probleme der Festkoerperelektronik [*A publication*]
Probl Filos Nauc Kommunizma ... Problemy Filosofii i Naucnogo Kommunizma [*A publication*]
Probl Fiz Atmos ... Problemy Fiziki Atmosfery [*A publication*]
Probl Fiz Elem Chastits At Yadra ... Problemy Fiziki Elementarnykh Chastits i Atomnogo Yadra [*A publication*]
Probl Fiziol Gipotal ... Problemy Fiziologii Gipotalamusa [*A publication*]
Probl Fiziol Opt ... Problemy Fiziologicheskoj Optiki [*A publication*]
Probl Fiziol Patol Vyssh Nervn Deyat ... Problemy Fiziologii i Patologii Vysshei Nervnoi Deyatel'nosti [*A publication*]
Probl Fiz Khim ... Problemy Fizicheskoi Khimii [*A publication*]
Probl Funkts Morfol ... Problemy Funktsional'noi Morfologii [*A publication*]
Probl Gastroenterol ... Problemy Gastroenterologii [*A publication*]

Probl Gematol Pereliv Krovi ... Problemy Gematologii i Perelivaniya Krovi [*A publication*]
Probl Geol Nefti ... Problemy Geologii Nefti [*USSR*] [*A publication*]
Probl Gestione ... Problemi di Gestione [*A publication*]
Probl Gos Prava ... Problemy Gosudarstva i Prava [*A publication*]
Probl Hematol Blood Transfus ... Problems of Hematology and Blood Transfusion [*A publication*]
Probl Hematol Blood Transfus (USSR) ... Problems of Hematology and Blood Transfusion (USSR) [*A publication*]
Probl Inf & Doc ... Probleme de Informare si Documentare [*A publication*]
Probl Inf Docum ... Probleme de Informare si Documentare [*A publication*]
Probl Inf Transm ... Problems of Information Transmission [*A publication*]
Probl Inf Transm (USSR) ... Problems of Information Transmission (USSR) [*A publication*]
Probl Inzh Geol Sev Kavk ... Problemy Inzhenernoi Geologii Severnogo Kavkaza [*A publication*]
Probl Kamen Litya ... Problemy Kamennogo Lit'ya [*A publication*]
Probl Khig ... Problemi na Khigienata [*A publication*]
Probl Kibern ... Problemy Kibernetiki [*A publication*]
Probl Kinet Katal ... Problemy Kinetiki i Kataliza [*A publication*]
Probl Kontrolya Zashch Atmos Zagryaz ... Problemy Kontrolya i Zashchita Atmosfery ot Zagryazneniya [*A publication*]
Probl Kosm Biol ... Problemy Kosmicheskoi Biologii [*A publication*]
Probl Kosm Fiz ... Problemy Kosmicheskoi Fiziki [*A publication*]
Probl Kosm Phys ... Probleme der Kosmichen Physik [*West Germany*] [*A publication*]
Probl Kriolitologii ... Problemy Kriolitologii [*A publication*]
Probl Low Temp Phys Thermodyn ... Problems of Low Temperature Physics and Thermodynamics [*A publication*]
Probl Mashinostr ... Problemy Mashinostroeniya [*Ukrainian SSR*] [*A publication*]
Probl Mat Fiz ... Problemy Matematiceskoj Fiziki [*A publication*]
Probl Med Wieku Rozwoj ... Problemy Medycyny Wieku Rozwojowego [*A publication*]
Probl Metalloved Fiz Met ... Problemy Metallovedeniya i Fiziki Metallov [*USSR*] [*A publication*]
Probl Metalloved Term Obrab ... Problemy Metallovedeniya i Termicheskoi Obrabotki [*A publication*]
Probl Metodol Ist-Filos Issled ... Problemy Metodologii Istoriko-Filosofskogo Issledovanija [*A publication*]
Probl Morfopatol ... Probleme de Morfopatologie [*A publication*]
Probl Narodonas Trud Resursov ... Problemy Narodonaselenija i Trudovyh Resursov [*A publication*]
Probl Nauc Kommunizma (Leningrad) ... Problemy Naucnogo Kommunizma (Leningrad) [*A publication*]
Probl Nauc Kommunizma (Moskva) ... Problemy Naucnogo Kommunizma (Moskva) [*A publication*]
Probl Nauc Uprav Soc Processami ... Problemy Naucnogo Upravlenija Social'nymi Processami [*A publication*]
Probl Neftegazonosn Tadzh ... Problemy Neftegazonosnosti Tadzhikistana [*A publication*]
Probl Nefti Gaza Tyumeni ... Problemy Nefti i Gaza Tyumeni [*A publication*]
Probl Neirokhim ... Problemy Neirokhimii [*A publication*]
Probl Neirokhir ... Problemy Neirokhirurgii [*A publication*]
Probl Neirokhir (1955-1963) ... Problemy Neirokhirurgii (1955-1963) [*A publication*]
Probl Neirokhir Resp Mezhved Sb ... Problemy Neirokhirurgii Respublikanskii Mezhvedomstvenhyi Sbornik [*A publication*]
Probl North ... Problems of the North [*A publication*]
Probl Oncol (Engl Transl Vopr Onkol) ... Problems of Oncology (English Translation of Voprosy Onkologii) [*A publication*]
Probl Onkol (Sofia) ... Problemi na Onkologiyata (Sofia) [*A publication*]
Probl Organ ... Problemy Organizacji [*A publication*]
Probl Osad Geol Dokembr ... Problemy Osadochnoy Geologii Dokembriya [*A publication*]
Probl Osobo Opasnykh Infekts ... Problemy Osobo Opasnykh Infektsii [*A publication*]
Probl Osvoeniya Pustyn ... Problemy Osvoeniya Pustyn [*A publication*]
Probl Osvo Pustyn ... Problemy Osvoeniya Pustyn [*A publication*]
Probl Parazitol ... Problemy Parazitologii [*A publication*]
Probl Patol Comp ... Probleme de Patologie Comparata [*A publication*]
Probl Peredachi Inf ... Problemy Peredachi Informatsii [*A publication*]
Probl Pereda Inf ... Problemy Peredachi Informatsii [*A publication*]
Probl Pnevmol Ftiziatr ... Problemi na Pnevmologiyata i Ftiziatriyata [*A publication*]
Probl Polesya ... Problemy Poles'ya [*A publication*]
Probl Polit Soc ... Problemes Politiques et Sociaux [*A publication*]
Probl Proch Mashinostr ... Problemy Prochnosti v Mashinostroenii [*USSR*] [*A publication*]
Probl Prochn ... Problemy Prochnosti [*A publication*]
Probl Prochn Mashinostr ... Problemy Prochnosti v Mashinostroenii [*A publication*]
Probl Proj ... Problemy Projectowa [*A publication*]
Probl Prot Plant ... Probleme de Protectia Plantelor [*A publication*]
Probl Psychol (Engl Transl Vopr Psikhol) ... Problems of Psychology (English Translation of Voprosy Psikhologii) [*A publication*]
Probl Razrab Polezn Iskop ... Problemy Razrabotki Poleznykh Iskopaemykh [*A publication*]
Probl Rentgenol Radiobiol ... Problemi na Rentgenologiyata i Radiobiologiyata [*A publication*]

Probl Ser.... Problemy Severa [*A publication*]
Probl Sicur Soc ... Problemi della Sicurezza Sociale [*A publication*]
Probl Soc Aktivnosti ... Problemy Social'noj Aktivnosti [*A publication*]
Probl Social (Milano) ... Problemi del Socialismo (Milano) [*A publication*]
Probl Soc Prognoz ... Problemy Social'nogo Prognozirovanija [*A publication*]
Probl Soc Zair ... Problemes Sociaux Zairois [*A publication*]
Probl Soc Zairois ... Problemes Sociaux Zairois [*A publication*]
Probl Sov Geol ... Problemy Sovetskoi Geologii [*USSR*] [*A publication*]
Probl Sovrem Khim Koord Soedin ... Problemy Sovremennoi Khimii Koordinatsionnykh Soedinenii [*USSR*] [*A publication*]
Probl Sovrem Khim Koord Soedin Leningr Gos Univ ... Problemy Sovremennoj Khimii Koordinatsionnykh Soedinenij. Leningradskij Gosudarstvennyj Universitet [*A publication*]
Probl Sovrem Teor Elem Chastits ... Problemy Sovremennmoi Teorii Elementarnykh Chastits [*A publication*]
Prob LT ...... Probyn on Land Tenure [*4th ed.*] [*1881*]   (DLA)
Probl Tech Med ... Problemy Techniki w Medycynie [*A publication*]
Probl Tekh Elektrodin ... Problemy Tekhnicheskoi Elektrodinamiki [*A publication*]
Probl Tekh Kibern ... Problemy na Tekhnicheskata Kibernetika [*A publication*]
Probl Tekh Kibern na Robotikata ... Problemy na Tekhnicheskata Kibernetika i Robotikata [*A publication*]
Probl Teor Gravitatsii Elem Chastits ... Problemy Teorii Gravitatsii i Elementarnykh Chastits [*USSR*] [*A publication*]
Probl Teploenerg Prikl Teplofiz ... Problemy Teploenergetiki i Prikladnoi Teplofiziki [*USSR*] [*A publication*]
Probl Ter.... Probleme de Terapeutica [*A publication*]
Probl Ter Stomatol ... Problemy Terapeuticheskoi Stomatologii [*A publication*]
Probl Treniya Iznashivaniya ... Problemy Treniya i Iznashivaniya [*A publication*]
Probl Tuberk ... Problemy Tuberkuleza [*A publication*]
Probl Virol (Engl Transl Vopr Virusol) ... Problems of Virology (English Translation of Voprosy Virusologii) [*A publication*]
Probl Yad Fiz Kosm Luchej ... Problemy Yadernoj Fiziki i Kosmicheskikh Luchej [*A publication*]
Probl Zaraznite Parazit Bolesti ... Problemi na Zaraznite i Parazitnite Bolesti [*A publication*]
Probl Zhivotnovod ... Problemy Zhivotnovodstva [*A publication*]
Probl Zooteh Vet ... Probleme Zootehnice si Veterinare [*A publication*]
Prob & Mat ... Probate and Matrimonial Cases   (DLA)
PROBOUT ... Proceed On or About   (MUGU)
Prob Pr Act ... Probate Practice Act   (DLA)
Prob R .... Probate Reports   (DLA)
Prob Rep....... Probate Reports   (DLA)
Prob Rep Ann ... Probate Reports, Annotated   (DLA)
PROBSUB ... Probable Submarine   (NVT)
PROBUS..... Program Budget System [*Military*]
Prob Vostok ... Problemy Vostokovedeniia [*A publication*]
PROC .... Performing Rights Organization of Canada [*See also SDE*]
PROC .... Pro-Cel International, Inc. [*NASDAQ symbol*]   (NQ)
PROC .... Problems of Communism [*A publication*]
PROC .... Procedure   (AAG)
PROC .... Proceedings
Proc........... Procellaria [*A publication*]
PROC .... Process   (AABC)
PROC .... Procession   (ROG)
PROC .... Processor [*or Processing*]
Proc........... Proclamation   (DLA)
PROC .... Proctor
PROC .... Procure   (AABC)
PROC .... Procurement   (MSA)
PROC .... Programing Computer [*Data processing*]
PROC .... Proposed Required Operational Capability   (AABC)
ProcAAAS ... Proceedings. American Association for the Advancement of Science [*A publication*]
Proc A Biol Colloq ... Proceedings. Annual Biology Colloquium [*A publication*]
Proc Abstr Soc Biol Chem (Bangalore) ... Proceedings and Abstracts. Society of Biological Chemists (Bangalore) [*A publication*]
Proc Acad Nat Sci Phila ... Proceedings. Academy of Natural Sciences of Philadelphia [*A publication*]
Proc Acad Pol Sci ... Proceedings. Academy of Political Science [*A publication*]
Proc Acad Sci Armenian SSR ... Proceedings. Academy of Sciences of the Armenian SSR [*A publication*]
Proc Acad Sci United Prov Agra Oudh India ... Proceedings. Academy of Sciences. United Provinces of Agra and Oudh India [*A publication*]
Proc Acad Sci USSR Geochem Sect ... Proceedings. Academy of Sciences of the USSR. Geochemistry Section [*A publication*]
Proc Agric Soc (Trinidad Tobago) ... Proceedings. Agricultural Society (Trinidad and Tobago) [*A publication*]
Proc Agron Soc NZ ... Proceedings. Agronomy Society of New Zealand [*A publication*]
Proc Agr Outlook Conf ... Proceedings. Agricultural Outlook Conference [*A publication*]
Proc Agr Pestic Tech Soc ... Proceedings. Agricultural Pesticide Technical Society [*A publication*]

Proc Air Pollut Contr Ass ... Proceedings. Air Pollution Control Association [*A publication*]
Proc Alaska Sci Conf ... Proceedings. Alaska Science Conference [*A publication*]
Proc Alfred Benzon Symp ... Proceedings. Alfred Benzon Symposium [*A publication*]
Proc Alumni Assoc (Malaya) ... Proceedings. Alumni Association (Malaya) [*A publication*]
Proc Am Acad Arts Sci ... Proceedings. American Academy of Arts and Sciences [*A publication*]
ProcAmAcAS ... Proceedings. American Academy of Arts and Sciences [*A publication*]
Proc Am Ant Soc ... Proceedings. American Antiquarian Society [*A publication*]
Proc Am Assoc Cancer Res ... Proceedings. American Association for Cancer Research [*A publication*]
Proc Am Assoc State Highw Off ... Proceedings. American Association of State Highway Officials [*A publication*]
Proc Am Concr Inst ... Proceedings. American Concrete Institute [*A publication*]
Proc Am Congr Surv Mapp ... Proceedings. American Congress on Surveying and Mapping [*A publication*]
Proc Am Cranberry Grow Assoc ... Proceedings. American Cranberry Growers' Association [*A publication*]
Proc Am Cranberry Growers' Ass ... Proceedings. American Cranberry Growers' Association [*A publication*]
Proc Am Diabetes Assoc ... Proceedings. American Diabetes Association [*A publication*]
Proc Am Doc Inst ... Proceedings. American Documentation Institute [*A publication*]
Proc A Meet Coun Fertil Applic ... Proceedings. Annual Meeting. Council on Fertilizer Application [*A publication*]
Proc A Meet Pl Physiol Univ MD ... Proceedings. Annual Meeting. American Society of Plant Physiologists at the University of Maryland [*A publication*]
Proc Amer Acad Arts Sci ... Proceedings. American Academy of Arts and Sciences [*A publication*]
Proc Amer Ass State Highw Offic ... Proceedings. American Association of State Highway Officials [*A publication*]
Proc Amer Phil Ass ... Proceedings and Addresses. American Philosophical Association [*A publication*]
Proc Amer Philos Soc ... Proceedings. American Philosophical Society [*A publication*]
Proc Amer Phil Soc ... Proceedings. American Philosophical Society [*A publication*]
Proc Amer Power Conf ... Proceedings. American Power Conference [*A publication*]
Proc Amer Soc Anim Pro W Sect ... Proceedings. American Society of Animal Production. Western Section [*A publication*]
Proc Amer Soc Anim Sci W Sect ... Proceedings. American Society of Animal Science. Western Section [*A publication*]
Proc Amer Soc Bakery Eng ... Proceedings. American Society of Bakery Engineers [*A publication*]
Proc Amer Soc Brew Chem ... Proceedings. American Society of Brewing Chemists [*A publication*]
Proc Amer Soc Hort Sci ... Proceedings. American Society for Horticultural Science [*A publication*]
Proc Amer Soc of Internat L ... Proceedings. American Society of International Law   (DLA)
Proc Amer Wood-Preserv Ass ... Proceedings. American Wood-Preservers' Association [*A publication*]
Proc Am Math Soc ... Proceedings. American Mathematical Society [*A publication*]
Proc Am Pet Inst Div Refining ... Proceedings. American Petroleum Institute. Division of Refining [*A publication*]
Proc Am Pet Inst Refin Dep ... Proceedings. American Petroleum Institute. Refining Department [*A publication*]
Proc Am Pet Inst Sect 1 ... Proceedings. American Petroleum Institute. Section 1 [*A publication*]
Proc Am Pet Inst Sect 2 ... Proceedings. American Petroleum Institute. Section 2. Marketing [*A publication*]
Proc Am Pet Inst Sect 3 ... Proceedings. American Petroleum Institute. Section 3. Refining [*A publication*]
Proc Am Pet Inst Sect 4 ... Proceedings. American Petroleum Institute. Section 4. Production [*A publication*]
Proc Am Pet Inst Sect 5 ... Proceedings. American Petroleum Institute. Section 5. Transportation [*A publication*]
Proc Am Pet Inst Sect 6 ... Proceedings. American Petroleum Institute. Section 6. Interdivisional [*A publication*]
Proc Am Pet Inst Sect 8 ... Proceedings. American Petroleum Institute. Section 8. Science and Technology [*A publication*]
Proc Am Pet Inst Sect III Refining ... Proceedings. American Petroleum Institute. Section III. Refining [*A publication*]
Proc Am Pharm Manuf Assoc Annu Meet ... Proceedings. American Pharmaceutical Manufacturers' Association. Annual Meeting [*A publication*]
Proc Am Pharm Manuf Assoc Midyear East Sect Meet ... Proceedings. American Pharmaceutical Manufacturers' Association. Midyear Eastern Section Meeting [*A publication*]
Proc Am Philos Soc ... Proceedings. American Philosophical Society [*A publication*]

Proc Am Phil Soc ... Proceedings. American Philosophical Society [*A publication*]

Proc Am Phytopathol Soc ... Proceedings. American Phytopathological Society [*A publication*]

Proc Am Power Conf ... Proceedings. American Power Conference [*A publication*]

Proc Am Soc Civ Eng ... Proceedings. American Society of Civil Engineers [*A publication*]

Proc Am Soc Civ Eng Transp Eng J ... Proceedings. American Society of Civil Engineers. Transportation Engineering Journal [*A publication*]

Proc Am Soc Enol ... Proceedings. American Society of Enologists [*A publication*]

Proc Am Soc Hortic Sci ... Proceedings. American Society for Horticultural Science [*A publication*]

Proc Am Soc Hort Sci ... Proceedings. American Society for Horticultural Science [*A publication*]

Proc Am Soc Inf Sci ... Proceedings. American Society for Information Science [*A publication*]

Proc Am Soc Test & Mater ... Proceedings. American Society for Testing and Materials [*A publication*]

Proc Am Vet Med Assoc ... Proceedings. American Veterinary Medical Association [*A publication*]

Proc Am Water Works Assoc ... Proceedings. American Water Works Association [*A publication*]

Proc Am Wood-Preserv Assoc ... Proceedings. American Wood-Preservers' Association [*A publication*]

Proc Anal Div Chem Soc ... Proceedings. Analytical Division of the Chemical Society [*A publication*]

Proc Anim Care Panel ... Proceedings. Animal Care Panel [*A publication*]

Proc Annu AIChE Southwest Ohio Conf Energy Environ ... Proceedings. Annual AIChE [*American Institute of Chemical Engineers*] Southwestern Ohio Conference on Energy and the Environment [*A publication*]

Proc Annu Allerton Conf Circuit Syst Theory ... Proceedings. Annual Allerton Conference on Circuit and System Theory [*Later, Proceedings. Annual Allerton Conference on Communication, Control, and Computing*] [*A publication*]

Proc Annu Allerton Conf Commun Control Comput ... Proceedings. Annual Allerton Conference on Communication, Control, and Computing [*Formerly, Annual Allerton Conference on Circuit and System Theory*] [*United States*] [*A publication*]

Proc Annu Battery Res Dev Conf ... Proceedings. Annual Battery Research and Development Conference [*A publication*]

Proc Annu Biochem Eng Symp ... Proceedings. Annual Biochemical Engineering Symposium [*United States*] [*A publication*]

Proc Annu Biol Colloq (Oreg State Univ) ... Proceedings. Annual Biology Colloquium (Oregon State University) [*A publication*]

Proc Annu Biomed Sci Instrum Symp ... Proceedings. Annual Biomedical Sciences Instrumentation Symposium [*A publication*]

Proc Annu Blueberry Open House ... Proceedings. Annual Blueberry Open House [*A publication*]

Proc Annu Calif Weed Conf ... Proceedings. Annual California Weed Conference [*A publication*]

Proc Annu Conf Agron Soc NZ ... Proceedings. Annual Conference. Agronomy Society of New Zealand [*A publication*]

Proc Annu Conf Autom Control Pet Chem Ind ... Proceedings. Annual Conference on Automatic Control in the Petroleum and Chemical Industries [*A publication*]

Proc Annu Conf Biol Sonar Diving Mammals ... Proceedings. Annual Conference on Biological Sonar and Diving Mammals [*A publication*]

Proc Annu Conf Environ Chem Hum Anim Health ... Proceedings. Annual Conference on Environmental Chemicals. Human and Animal Health [*A publication*]

Proc Annu Conf Manitoba Agron ... Proceedings. Annual Conference of Manitoba Agronomists [*A publication*]

Proc Annu Conf MD Del Water Sewage Assoc ... Proceedings. Annual Conference. Maryland-Delaware Water and Sewage Association [*A publication*]

Proc Annu Conf Microbeam Anal Soc ... Proceedings. Annual Conference. Microbeam Analysis Society [*A publication*]

Proc Annu Conf Reinf Plast Compos Inst Soc Plast Ind ... Proceedings. Annual Conference. Reinforced Plastics/Composites Institute. Society of the Plastics Industry [*A publication*]

Proc Annu Conf Southeast Assoc Game Fish Comm ... Proceedings. Annual Conference. Southeastern Association of Game and Fish Commissioners [*A publication*]

Proc Annu Congr S Afr Sugar Technol Assoc ... Proceedings. Annual Congress. South African Sugar Technologists Association [*A publication*]

Proc Annu Connector Symp ... Proceedings. Annual Connector Symposium [*A publication*]

Proc Annu Conv Assoc Am Pestic Control Off ... Proceedings. Annual Convention Association. American Pesticide Control Officials [*A publication*]

Proc Annu Conv Gas Process Assoc Meet Pap ... Proceedings. Annual Convention. Gas Processors Association. Meeting Papers [*A publication*]

Proc Annu Conv Gas Process Assoc Tech Pap ... Proceedings. Annual Convention. Gas Processors Association. Technical Papers [*A publication*]

Proc Annu Conv Nat Gas Process Assoc Tech Pap ... Proceedings. Annual Convention. Natural Gas Processors Association. Technical Papers [*United States*] [*A publication*]

Proc Annu Conv Natur Gas Process Ass Tech Pap ... Proceedings. Annual Convention. Natural Gas Processors Association. Technical Papers [*A publication*]

Proc Annu Conv Oil Technol Assoc ... Proceedings. Annual Convention. Oil Technologists Association [*A publication*]

Proc Annu Conv Philipp Sugar Assoc ... Proceedings. Annual Convention. Philippine Sugar Association [*A publication*]

Proc Annu Conv Sugar Technol Assoc India ... Proceedings. Annual Convention. Sugar Technologists' Association of India [*A publication*]

Proc Annu East Theor Phys Conf ... Proceedings. Annual Eastern Theoretical Physics Conference [*A publication*]

Proc Annu Eng Geol Soils Eng Symp ... Proceedings. Annual Engineering Geology and Soils Engineering Symposium [*A publication*]

Proc Annu Eng Geol Symp ... Proceedings. Annual Engineering Geology Symposium [*A publication*]

Proc Annu Environ Water Resour Eng Conf ... Proceedings. Annual Environmental and Water Resources Engineering Conference [*A publication*]

Proc Annu Fall Meet Calif Nat Gasoline Assoc ... Proceedings. Annual Fall Meeting. California Natural Gasoline Association [*A publication*]

Proc Annu Fall Meet West Gas Process Oil Refiners Assoc ... Proceedings. Annual Fall Meeting. Western Gas Processors and Oil Refiners Association [*A publication*]

Proc Annu Freq Control Symp ... Proceedings. Annual Frequency Control Symposium [*A publication*]

Proc Annu Holm Semin Electr Contacts ... Proceedings. Annual Holm Seminar on Electrical Contacts [*A publication*]

Proc Annu Ind Pollut Conf ... Proceedings. Annual Industrial Pollution Conference [*United States*] [*A publication*]

Proc Annu Instrum Conf ... Proceedings. Annual Instrumentation Conference [*A publication*]

Proc Annu Int Conf Fault Tolerant Comput ... Proceedings. Annual International Conference on Fault-Tolerant Computing [*A publication*]

Proc Annu Int Game Fish Res Conf ... Proceedings. Annual International Game Fish Research Conference [*A publication*]

Proc Annu Meat Sci Inst ... Proceedings. Annual Meat Science Institute [*A publication*]

Proc Annu Meet Agric Res Inst ... Proceedings. Annual Meeting. Agricultural Research Institute [*A publication*]

Proc Annu Meet Am Assoc Vet Lab Diagn ... Proceedings. Annual Meeting. American Association of Veterinary Laboratory Diagnosticians [*A publication*]

Proc Annu Meet Amer Soc Hort Sci Caribbean Reg ... Proceedings. Annual Meeting. American Society for Horticultural Science. Caribbean Region [*A publication*]

Proc Annu Meet Am Pet Inst ... Proceedings. Annual Meeting. American Petroleum Institute [*A publication*]

Proc Annu Meet Am Psychopathol Assoc ... Proceedings. Annual Meeting. American Psychopathological Association [*A publication*]

Proc Annu Meet Am Sect Int Sol Energy Soc ... Proceedings. Annual Meeting. American Section. International Solar Energy Society [*A publication*]

Proc Annu Meet Am Soc Anim Sci West Sect ... Proceedings. Annual Meeting. American Society of Animal Science. Western Section [*A publication*]

Proc Annu Meet Am Soc Bak Eng ... Proceedings. Annual Meeting. American Society of Bakery Engineers [*A publication*]

Proc Annu Meet Am Soc Inf Sci ... Proceedings. Annual Meeting. American Society for Information Science [*A publication*]

Proc Annu Meet Am Soybean Assoc ... Proceedings. Annual Meeting. American Soybean Association [*A publication*]

Proc Annu Meet Biochem (Hung) ... Proceedings. Annual Meeting of Biochemistry (Hungary) [*A publication*]

Proc Annu Meet Can Soc Agron ... Proceedings. Annual Meeting. Canadian Society of Agronomy [*A publication*]

Proc Annu Meet Chem Spec Manuf Assoc ... Proceedings. Annual Meeting. Chemical Specialties Manufacturers Association [*A publication*]

Proc Annu Meet Electron Microsc Soc Am ... Proceedings. Annual Meeting. Electron Microscopy Society of America [*A publication*]

Proc Annu Meet Fert Ind Round Table ... Proceedings. Annual Meeting. Fertilizer Industry Round Table [*A publication*]

Proc Annu Meeting Amer Soc Int Law ... Proceedings. Annual Meeting. American Society of International Law [*A publication*]

Proc Annu Meet Int Magnesium Assoc ... Proceedings. Annual Meeting. International Magnesium Association [*A publication*]

Proc Annu Meet Jpn Endocrinol Soc ... Proceedings. Annual Meeting. Japan Endocrinological Society [*A publication*]

Proc Annu Meet Med Sect Am Counc Life Insur ... Proceedings. Annual Meeting. Medical Section. American Council of Life Insurance [*A publication*]

Proc Annu Meet Met Powder Assoc ... Proceedings. Annual Meeting. Metal Powder Association [*A publication*]

Proc Annu Meet Nat Assoc Corros Eng ... Proceedings. Annual Meeting. National Association of Corrosion Engineers [*A publication*]

Proc Annu Meet Nat Ass Wheat Growers ... Proceedings. Annual Meeting. National Association of Wheat Growers [*A publication*]

Proc Annu Meet Natl Jt Comm Fert Appl ... Proceedings. Annual Meeting. National Joint Committee on Fertilizer Application [*A publication*]

Proc Annu Meet Nat Res Counc Agr Res Inst ... Proceedings. Annual Meeting. National Research Council. Agricultural Research Institute [*A publication*]

Proc Annu Meet N Cent Weed Contr Conf ... Proceedings. Annual Meeting. North Central Weed Control Conference [*A publication*]

Proc Annu Meet NJ ... Proceedings. Annual Meeting. New Jersey Mosquito Extermination Association [*A publication*]

Proc Annu Meet Northeast Weed Sci Soc ... Proceedings. Annual Meeting. Northeastern Weed Science Society [*A publication*]

Proc Annu Meet NY State Hort Soc ... Proceedings. Annual Meeting. New York State Horticultural Society [*A publication*]

Proc Annu Meet Pac Coast Fertil Soc ... Proceedings. Annual Meeting. Pacific Coast Fertility Society [*A publication*]

Proc Annu Meet Soc Promot Agric Sci ... Proceedings. Annual Meeting. Society for the Promotion of Agricultural Science [*A publication*]

Proc Annu Meet US Anim Health Assoc ... Proceedings. Annual Meeting. United States Animal Health Association [*A publication*]

Proc Annu Meet Utah Mosq Abatement Assoc ... Proceedings. Annual Meeting. Utah Mosquito Abatement Association [*A publication*]

Proc Annu Meet West Div Am Dairy Sci Assoc ... Proceedings. Annual Meeting. Western Division. American Dairy Science Association [*A publication*]

Proc Annu Meet W Farm Econ Ass ... Proceedings. Annual Meeting. Western Farm Economics Association [*A publication*]

Proc Annu Mid-Am Spectrosc Symp ... Proceedings. Annual Mid-America Spectroscopy Symposium [*A publication*]

Proc Annu Midwest Fert Conf ... Proceedings. Annual Midwest Fertilizer Conference [*A publication*]

Proc Annu Nat Dairy Eng Conf ... Proceedings. Annual National Dairy Engineering Conference [*A publication*]

Proc Annu Nat Dairy Food Eng Conf ... Proceedings. Annual National Dairy and Food Engineering Conference [*A publication*]

Proc Annu Power Sources Conf ... Proceedings. Annual Power Sources Conference [*A publication*]

Proc Annu Purdue Air Qual Conf ... Proceedings. Annual Purdue Air Quality Conference [*A publication*]

Proc Annu Reliab Maintainability Symp ... Proceedings. Annual Reliability and Maintainability Symposium [*A publication*]

Proc Annu Reliab Maintain Symp ... Proceedings. Annual Reliability and Maintainability Symposium [*A publication*]

Proc Annu Rochester Conf High Energy Nucl Phys ... Proceedings. Annual Rochester Conference on High Energy Nuclear Physics [*A publication*]

Proc Annu Rocky Mount Bioeng Symp ... Proceedings. Annual Rocky Mountain Bioengineering Symposium [*A publication*]

Proc Annu Rocky Mt Bioeng Symp ... Proceedings. Annual Rocky Mountain Bioengineering Symposium [*A publication*]

Proc Annu San Franc Cancer Symp ... Proceedings. Annual San Francisco Cancer Symposium [*A publication*]

Proc Annu Sci Meet Comm Probl Drug Depend US Nat Res Counc ... Proceedings. Annual Scientific Meeting. Committee on Problems of Drug Dependence. US National Research Council [*A publication*]

Proc Annu Sess Ceylon Assoc Adv Sci ... Proceedings. Annual Session. Ceylon Association for the Advancement of Science [*A publication*]

Proc Annu Southwest Pet Short Course ... Proceedings. Annual Southwestern Petroleum Short Course [*United States*] [*A publication*]

Proc Annu Symp Eng Geol Soils Eng ... Proceedings. Annual Symposium on Engineering Geology and Soils Engineering [*A publication*]

Proc Annu Symp Eugen Soc ... Proceedings. Annual Symposium of the Eugenics Society [*A publication*]

Proc Annu Symp Freq Control ... Proceedings. Annual Symposium on Frequency Control [*A publication*]

Proc Annu Symp Incremental Motion Control Syst Devices ... Proceedings. Annual Symposium. Incremental Motion Control Systems and Devices [*A publication*]

Proc Annu Tall Timbers Fire Ecol Conf ... Proceedings. Annual Tall Timbers Fire Ecology Conference [*A publication*]

Proc Annu Tech Conf Soc Vac Coaters ... Proceedings. Annual Technical Conference. Society of Vacuum Coaters [*A publication*]

Proc Annu Tech Meet Inst Environ Sci ... Proceedings. Annual Technical Meeting. Institute of Environmental Sciences [*A publication*]

Proc Annu Tech Meet Int Metallogr Soc Inc ... Proceedings. Annual Technical Meeting. International Metallographic Society, Inc. [*A publication*]

Proc Annu Tech Meet Tech Assoc Graphic Arts ... Proceedings. Annual Technical Meeting. Technical Association. Graphic Arts [*A publication*]

Proc Annu Tung Ind Conv ... Proceedings. Annual Tung Industry Convention [*A publication*]

Proc Annu UMR-MEC Conf Energy ... Proceedings. Annual UMR-MEC [*University of Missouri at Rolla - Missouri Energy Council*] Conference on Energy [*A publication*]

Proc Annu West Tex Oil Lifting Short Course ... Proceedings. Annual West Texas Oil Lifting Short Course [*A publication*]

Proc Annu WWEMA Ind Pollut Conf ... Proceedings. Annual WWEMA [*Water and Wastewater Equipment Manufacturers Association*] Industrial Pollution Conference [*United States*] [*A publication*]

PRO CAPILL ... Pro Capillis [*For the Hair*] [*Pharmacy*]

Proc APREA ... Proceedings. APREA [*American Peanut Research and Education Association*] [*A publication*]

Proc Aris Soc ... Proceedings. Aristotelian Society [*A publication*]

Proc Ark Acad Sci ... Proceedings. Arkansas Academy of Science [*A publication*]

Proc Arkansas Acad Sci ... Proceedings. Arkansas Academy of Science [*A publication*]

Proc Asian-Pac Congr Cardiol ... Proceedings. Asian-Pacific Congress of Cardiology [*A publication*]

Proc ASIS Annu Meet ... Proceedings. ASIS [*American Society for Information Science*] Annual Meeting [*A publication*]

Proc Ass Asphalt Paving Technol ... Proceedings. Association of Asphalt Paving Technologists [*A publication*]

Proc Ass Econ Biol ... Proceedings. Association of Economic Biologists [*A publication*]

Proc Assoc Asphalt Paving Technol ... Proceedings. Association of Asphalt Paving Technologists [*A publication*]

Proc Assoc Off Seed Anal ... Proceedings. Association of Official Seed Analysts [*A publication*]

Proc Assoc Off Seed Anal (North Am) ... Proceedings. Association of Official Seed Analysts (North America) [*A publication*]

Proc Assoc Plant Prot Kyushu ... Proceedings. Association for Plant Protection of Kyushu [*A publication*]

Proc Ass Offic Seed Anal ... Proceedings. Association of Official Seed Analysts [*A publication*]

Proc Ass Plant Prot Hokuriku ... Proceedings. Association of Plant Protection of Hokuriku [*A publication*]

Proc Ass Plant Prot Kyushu ... Proceedings. Association for Plant Protection of Kyushu [*A publication*]

Proc Ass S Agr Workers ... Proceedings. Association of Southern Agricultural Workers [*A publication*]

Proc Astron Soc Aust ... Proceedings. Astronomical Society of Australia [*A publication*]

Proc Astr Soc Aust ... Proceedings. Astronomical Society of Australia [*A publication*]

Proc Aust Ass Clin Biochem ... Proceedings. Australian Association of Clinical Biochemists [*A publication*]

Proc Aust Assoc Neurol ... Proceedings. Australian Association of Neurologists [*A publication*]

Proc Aust Biochem Soc ... Proceedings. Australian Biochemical Society [*A publication*]

Proc Aust Bldg Res Congr ... Australian Building Research Congress. Proceedings [*A publication*]

Proc Aust Build Res Congr ... Australian Building Research Congress. Proceedings [*A publication*]

Proc Aust Ceram Conf ... Australian Ceramic Conference. Proceedings [*A publication*]

Proc Aust Ceramic Conf ... Australian Ceramic Conference. Proceedings [*A publication*]

Proc Aust Clay Miner Conf ... Australian Clay Minerals Conference. Proceedings [*A publication*]

Proc Aust Comput Conf ... Proceedings. Australian Computer Conference [*A publication*]

Proc Aust Conf Nucl Tech Anal ... Australian Conference on Nuclear Techniques of Analysis. Proceedings [*A publication*]

Proc Aust Grasslds Conf ... Proceedings. Australian Grasslands Conference [*A publication*]

Proc Aust Inst Min and Metall ... Australasian Institute of Mining and Metallurgy. Proceedings [*A publication*]

Proc Aust Inst Min Metall ... Proceedings. Australasian Institute of Mining and Metallurgy [*A publication*]

Proc Aust Physiol Pharmacol Soc ... Proceedings. Australian Physiological and Pharmacological Society [*A publication*]

Proc Aust Pulp Pap Ind Tech Assoc ... Proceedings. Australian Pulp and Paper Industry Technical Association [*A publication*]

Proc Australasian Poultry Sci Conv ... Proceedings. Australasian Poultry Science Convention [*A publication*]

Proc Australas Inst Min and Metall ... Australasian Institute of Mining and Metallurgy. Proceedings [*A publication*]

Proc Australas Inst Min Metall ... Proceedings. Australasian Institute of Mining and Metallurgy [*A publication*]

Proc Aust Road Res Bd ... Australian Road Research Board. Proceedings [*A publication*]

Proc Aust Road Research Board ... Australian Road Research Board. Proceedings [*A publication*]

Proc Aust Soc Anim Prod ... Proceedings. Australian Society of Animal Production [*A publication*]

Proc Aust Soc Med Res ... Proceedings. Australian Society for Medical Research [*A publication*]

Proc Aust Weed Conf ... Proceedings. Australian Weed Conference [*A publication*]

Proc Auto Div Instn Mech Engrs ... Proceedings. Institution of Mechanical Engineers. Auto Division [*A publication*]

Proc Berkeley Symp Math Stat Probab ... Proceedings. Berkeley Symposium on Mathematical Statistics and Probability [*A publication*]

Proc Bienn Conf Inst Briquet Agglom ... Proceedings. Biennial Conference. Institute for Briquetting and Agglomeration [*A publication*]

Proc Bienn Conf Int Briquet Assoc ... Proceedings. Biennial Conference. International Briqueting Association [*A publication*]

Proc Bienn Gas Dyn Symp ... Proceedings. Biennial Gas Dynamics Symposium [*A publication*]

Proc Bihar Acad Agric Sci ... Proceedings. Bihar Academy of Agricultural Sciences [*A publication*]

Proc Bihar Acad Agr Sci ... Proceedings. Bihar Academy of Agricultural Sciences [*A publication*]

Proc Biol Soc Wash ... Proceedings. Biological Society of Washington [*A publication*]

Proc Bird Control Semin ... Proceedings. Bird Control Seminar [*A publication*]

Proc Bos Soc ... Proceedings. Bostonian Society [*A publication*]

Proc Bot Soc Br Isles ... Proceedings. Botanical Society of the British Isles [*A publication*]

Proc Br Acad ... Proceedings. British Academy [*A publication*]

Proc Br Acoust Soc ... Proceedings. British Acoustical Society [*A publication*]

Proc Br Ceram Soc ... Proceedings. British Ceramic Society [*A publication*]

Proc Brit Ac ... Proceedings. British Academy [*A publication*]

Proc Brit Acad ... Proceedings. British Academy [*A publication*]   (OCD)

Proc Brit Ceram Soc ... Proceedings. British Ceramic Society [*A publication*]

Proc Brit Weed Contr Conf ... Proceedings. British Weed Control Conference [*A publication*]

Proc Brown Univ Symp Biol Skin ... Proceedings. Brown University Symposium on the Biology of Skin [*A publication*]

Proc Br Soc Anim Prod ... Proceedings. British Society of Animal Production [*A publication*]

Proc Calif Acad Sci ... Proceedings. California Academy of Sciences [*A publication*]

Proc Calif Ann Weed Conf ... Proceedings. California Annual Weed Conference [*A publication*]

Proc Camb Philos Soc ... Proceedings. Cambridge Philosophical Society [*A publication*]

Proc Camb Phil Soc Math Phys Sci ... Proceedings. Cambridge Philosophical Society. Mathematical and Physical Sciences [*A publication*]

Proc Cambridge Antiq Soc ... Proceedings. Cambridge Antiquarian Society [*A publication*]

Proc Cambridge Ant Soc ... Proceedings. Cambridge Antiquarian Society [*A publication*]

Proc Cambridge Philos Soc ... Proceedings. Cambridge Philosophical Society [*A publication*]

Proc Cambridge Phil Soc ... Proceedings. Cambridge Philological Society [*A publication*]

Proc Can Cancer Res Conf ... Proceedings. Canadian Cancer Research Conference [*A publication*]

Proc Can Centen Wheat Symp ... Proceedings. Canadian Centennial Wheat Symposium [*A publication*]

Proc Can Fed Biol Soc ... Proceedings. Canadian Federation of Biological Societies [*A publication*]

Proc Can Nat Weed Comm E Sect ... Proceedings. Canadian National Weed Committee. Eastern Section [*A publication*]

Proc Can Nat Weed Comm W Sect ... Proceedings. Canadian National Weed Committee. Western Section [*A publication*]

Proc Can Phytopathol Soc ... Proceedings. Canadian Phytopathological Society [*A publication*]

Proc Can Rock Mech Symp ... Proceedings. Canadian Rock Mechanics Symposium [*A publication*]

Proc Can Soc Forensic Sci ... Proceedings. Canadian Society of Forensic Science [*A publication*]

Proc Caribb Reg Am Soc Hort Sci ... Proceedings. Caribbean Region. American Society for Horticultural Science [*A publication*]

Proc Cath... Proceedings. Catholic Theological Society of America [*A publication*]

Proc Cath Phil Ass ... Proceedings. American Catholic Philosophical Association [*A publication*]

Proc Cellul Conf ... Proceedings. Cellulose Conference [*A publication*]

Proc Chem Soc ... Proceedings. Chemical Society [*A publication*]

Proc Chem Soc (London) ... Proceedings. Chemical Society (London) [*A publication*]

Proc Chin Physiol Soc Chengtu Branch ... Proceedings. Chinese Physiological Society. Chengtu Branch [*A publication*]

PROCCIR ... Procurement Circular [*Air Force*]   (AFIT)

Proc Clin Dial Transplant Forum ... Proceedings. Clinical Dialysis and Transplant Forum [*A publication*]

Proc Coal Mining Inst Amer ... Proceedings. Coal Mining Institute of America [*A publication*]

Proc Coll Med Univ Philipp ... Proceedings. College of Medicine. University of the Philippines [*A publication*]

Proc Coll Nat Sci Sect 2 Seoul Nat Univ ... Proceedings. College of Natural Sciences. Section 2. Physics, Astronomy. Seoul National University [*A publication*]

Proc Coll Nat Sci Sect 3 Seoul Nat Univ ... Proceedings. College of Natural Sciences. Section 3. Chemistry. Seoul National University [*A publication*]

Proc Coll Nat Sci Sect 4 Seoul Nat Univ ... Proceedings. College of Natural Sciences. Section 4. Life Sciences. Seoul National University [*A publication*]

Proc Coll Nat Sci Sect 5 Seoul Nat Univ ... Proceedings. College of Natural Sciences. Section 5. Geology, Meteorology, and Oceanography. Seoul National University [*A publication*]

Proc Coll Nat Sci Seoul Natl Univ ... Proceedings. College of Natural Sciences. Seoul National University [*A publication*]

Proc Colloq Int Potash Inst ... Proceedings. Colloquium of the International Potash Institute [*A publication*]

Proc Conf Aust Road Res Board ... Proceedings. Conference of the Australian Road Research Board [*A publication*]

Proc Conf Aust Soc Sugar Cane Technol ... Australian Society of Sugar Cane Technologists. Proceedings of the Conference [*A publication*]

Proc Conf Eng Med Biol ... Proceedings. Conference of Engineering in Medicine and Biology [*A publication*]

Proc Conf Great Lakes Res ... Proceedings. Conference on Great Lakes Research [*A publication*]

Proc Conf Hot Lab Equip ... Proceedings. Conference on Hot Laboratories and Equipment [*A publication*]

Proc Conf Remote Syst Technol ... Proceedings. Conference on Remote Systems Technology [*A publication*]

Proc Conf Silic Ind ... Proceedings. Conference on the Silicate Industry [*A publication*]

Proc Conf Solid State Devices ... Proceedings. Conference on Solid State Devices [*A publication*]

Proc Congenital Anomalies Res Assoc Annu Rep ... Proceedings. Congenital Anomalies. Research Association. Annual Report [*A publication*]

Proc Cong Mediterr Phytopathol Union ... Proceedings. Congress. Mediterranean Phytopathological Union [*A publication*]

Proc Congr Ann Corp Ingen For (Quebec) ... Proceedings. Congres Annuel. Corporation des Ingenieurs Forestiers (Quebec) [*A publication*]

Proc Congr Eur Soc Haematol ... Proceedings. Congress of the European Society of Haematology [*A publication*]

Proc Congr Hung Assoc Microbiol ... Proceedings. Congress of the Hungarian Association of Microbiologists [*A publication*]

Proc Congr Int Assoc Sci Study Ment Defic ... Proceedings. Congress. International Association for the Scientific Study of Mental Deficiency [*A publication*]

Proc Congr Int Potash Inst ... Proceedings. Congress of the International Potash Institute [*A publication*]

Proc Congr Int Soc Blood Transfus ... Proceedings. Congress of the International Society of Blood Transfusion [*A publication*]

Proc Congr Int Soc Sugar Cane Technol ... Proceedings. Congress. International Society of Sugar Cane Technologists [*A publication*]

Proc Congr Int Union For Res Organ ... Proceedings. Congress. International Union of Forest Research Organizations [*A publication*]

Proc Congr Jpn Soc Cancer Ther ... Proceedings. Congress. Japan Society for Cancer Therapy [*A publication*]

Proc Congr S Afr Genet Soc ... Proceedings. Congress. South African Genetic Society [*A publication*]

Proc Congr S Afr Sug Technol Ass ... Proceedings. Congress. South African Sugar Technologists' Association [*A publication*]

Proc Conv Int Assoc Fish Wildl Agencies ... Proceedings. Convention. International Association of Fish and Wildlife Agencies [*A publication*]

Proc Cornell Nutr Conf Feed Mfr ... Proceedings. Cornell Nutrition Conference for Feed Manufacturers [*A publication*]

Proc Cosmic-Ray Res Lab Nagoya Univ ... Proceedings. Cosmic-Ray Research Laboratory. Nagoya University [*A publication*]

Proc Crop Sci Chugoku Br Crop Sci Soc ... Proceedings. Crop Science. Chugoku Branch of the Crop Science Society [*A publication*]

Proc Crop Sci Soc Jap ... Proceedings. Crop Science Society of Japan [*A publication*]

Proc Crop Sci Soc Jpn ... Proceedings. Crop Science Society of Japan [*A publication*]

ProcCTSA ... Proceedings. Catholic Theological Society of America [*A publication*]

PROCD ...... Procedure   (AFM)

PROCD ...... Proceed   (AFM)

PROCD ...... Processing [*Johannesburg*] [*A publication*]

Proc Devon Archaeol Soc ... Proceedings. Devon Archaeological Society [*A publication*]

Proc Devon Arch Soc ... Proceedings. Devon Archaeological Society [*A publication*]

Proc Distill Feed Conf ... Proceedings. Distillers Feed Conference [*A publication*]

Proc Distill Feed Res Counc Conf ... Proceedings. Distillers Feed Research Council Conference [*A publication*]

Proc Div Refin Am Pet Inst ... Proceedings. Division of Refining. American Petroleum Institute [*A publication*]

Proc Dorset Natur Hist Archaeol Soc ... Proceedings. Dorset Natural History and Archaeological Society [*A publication*]

Proc Dorset Natur Hist Arch Soc ... Proceedings. Dorset Natural History and Archaeological Society [*A publication*]

PROCDRE ... Procedure (ROG)

Proc Easter Sch Agric Sci Univ Nottingham ... Proceedings. Easter School in Agricultural Science. University of Nottingham [*England*] [*A publication*]

Proc Ecol Soc Aust ... Proceedings. Ecological Society of Australia [*A publication*]

PROCED .... Procedure

Proc Edinburgh Math Soc ... Proceedings. Edinburgh Mathematical Society [*A publication*]

Proc Edinburgh Math Soc 2 ... Proceedings. Edinburgh Mathematical Society. Series 2 [*A publication*]

Proc Edinburgh Math Soc Edinburgh Math Notes ... Proceedings. Edinburgh Mathematical Society. Edinburgh Mathematical Notes [*A publication*]

Proceedings of the IEEE ... Proceedings. Institute of Electrical and Electronics Engineers [*A publication*]

Proc Egypt Acad Sci ... Proceedings. Egyptian Academy of Sciences [*A publication*]

Proc Eighth Br Weed Control Conf ... Proceedings. Eighth British Weed Control Conference [*A publication*]

Proc Electron Components Conf ... Proceedings. Electronic Components Conference [*A publication*]

Proc Electron Microsc Soc Am ... Proceedings. Electron Microscopy Society of America [*A publication*]

Proc Electron Microsc Soc South Afr ... Proceedings. Electron Microscopy Society of Southern Africa [*A publication*]

Proc Endoc Soc Aust ... Proceedings. Endocrine Society of Australia [*A publication*]

Proc Eng Soc Hong Kong ... Proceedings. Engineering Society of Hong Kong [*A publication*]

Proc Eng Soc West PA ... Proceedings. Engineers' Society of Western Pennsylvania [*A publication*]

Proc Entomol Soc Amer N Cent Br ... Proceedings. Entomological Society of America. North Central Branch [*A publication*]

Proc Entomol Soc BC ... Proceedings. Entomological Society of British Columbia [*A publication*]

Proc Entomol Soc Brit Columbia ... Proceedings. Entomological Society of British Columbia [*A publication*]

Proc Entomol Soc Manit ... Proceedings. Entomological Society of Manitoba [*A publication*]

Proc Entomol Soc Manitoba ... Proceedings. Entomological Society of Manitoba [*A publication*]

Proc Entomol Soc Ont ... Proceedings. Entomological Society of Ontario [*A publication*]

Proc Entomol Soc Ontario ... Proceedings. Entomological Society of Ontario [*A publication*]

Proc Entomol Soc Wash ... Proceedings. Entomological Society of Washington [*A publication*]

Proc Entomol Soc Wash DC ... Proceedings. Entomological Society of Washington, DC [*A publication*]

Proc Ent Soc Br Columb ... Proceedings. Entomological Society of British Columbia [*A publication*]

Proc Ent Soc Manitoba ... Proceedings. Entomological Society of Manitoba [*A publication*]

Proc Ent Soc Ont ... Proceedings. Entomological Society of Ontario [*A publication*]

Proc Ent Soc Wash ... Proceedings. Entomological Society of Washington [*A publication*]

Proc Environ Eng Sci Conf ... Proceedings. Environmental Engineering and Science Conference [*A publication*]

Process Autom ... Process Automation [*A publication*]

Process Bio ... Process Biochemistry [*A publication*]

Process Biochem ... Process Biochemistry [*A publication*]

Process Chem Eng ... Process and Chemical Engineering [*A publication*]

Process Control Autom ... Process Control and Automation [*A publication*]

Process Des Dev ... Process Design and Development [*A publication*]

Process Econ Int ... Process Economics International [*A publication*]

Process Eng ... Process Engineering [*A publication*]

Process Eng Mag ... Process Engineering Magazine [*A publication*]

Process Engng ... Process Engineering [*A publication*]

Process Eng Plant and Control ... Process Engineering. Plant and Control [*A publication*]

Process Instrum ... Process Instrumentation [*A publication*]

Process Ser Okla State Univ Agr Exp Sta ... Processed Series. Oklahoma State University. Agricultural Experimental Station [*A publication*]

Process Stud ... Process Studies [*A publication*]

Process Technol Int ... Process Technology International [*A publication*]

Proces-Verb Seances Soc Sci Phys Nat Bordeaux ... Proces-Verbaux des Seances. Societe des Sciences Physiques et Naturelles de Bordeaux [*France*] [*A publication*]

Proc Eur Dial Transplant Assoc ... Proceedings. European Dialysis and Transplant Association [*A publication*]

Proc Eur Soc Toxicol ... Proceedings. European Society of Toxicology [*A publication*]

Proc Fac Eng Tokai Univ ... Proceedings. Faculty of Engineering. Tokai University [*Japan*] [*A publication*]

Proc Fac Sci Tokai Univ ... Proceedings. Faculty of Science. Tokai University [*Japan*] [*A publication*]

Proc Farm Seed Conf ... Proceedings. Farm Seed Conference [*A publication*]

Proc FEBS Meet ... Proceedings. FEBS [*Federation of European Biochemical Societies*] Meeting [*A publication*]

Proc Fertil Soc ... Proceedings. Fertilizer Society [*A publication*]

Proc Finn Dent Soc ... Proceedings. Finnish Dental Society of Washington [*A publication*]

Proc Fla Lychee Grow Ass ... Proceedings. Florida Lychee Growers Association [*A publication*]

Proc Fla State Hortic Soc ... Proceedings. Florida State Horticultural Society [*A publication*]

Proc Fla State Hort Soc ... Proceedings. Florida State Horticultural Society [*A publication*]

Proc Fla St Hort Soc ... Proceedings. Florida State Horticultural Society [*A publication*]

Proc Florida State Hortic Soc ... Florida. State Horticultural Society. Proceedings [*A publication*]

Proc Food ... Processed Prepared Food [*A publication*]

Proc For Microclim Symp Can Dep Fish For ... Proceedings. Forest Microclimate Symposium. Canada Department of Fisheries and Forestry [*A publication*]

Proc For Prod Res Soc ... Proceedings. Forest Products Research Society [*A publication*]

Proc For Symp LA Sch For ... Proceedings. Annual Forestry Symposium. Louisiana State University. School of Forestry and Wildlife Management [*A publication*]

Proc Forum Fundam Surg Probl Clin Congr Am Coll Surg ... Proceedings. Forum on Fundamental Surgical Problems. Clinical Congress of the American College of Surgeons [*A publication*]

Proc (Fourth) NZ Geogr Conf ... Proceedings. (Fourth) New Zealand Geographical Conference [*A publication*]

Proc FRI Symp For Res Inst NZ For Serv ... Proceedings. FRI Symposium. Forest Research Institute. New Zealand Forest Service [*A publication*]

Proc Front Educ Conf ... Proceedings. Frontiers in Education Conference [*A publication*]

Proc Fujihara Mem Fac Eng Keio Univ (Tokyo) ... Proceedings. Fujihara Memorial Faculty of Engineering. Keio University (Tokyo) [*A publication*]

Proc Gas Cond Conf ... Proceedings. Gas Conditioning Conference [*United States*] [*A publication*]

Proc Genet Soc Can ... Proceedings. Genetics Society of Canada [*A publication*]

Proc Gen Meet Soc Ind Microbiol ... Proceedings. General Meeting of the Society for Industrial Microbiology [*A publication*]

Proc Geol Ass Can ... Proceedings. Geological Association of Canada [*A publication*]

Proc Geol Assoc ... Proceedings. Geologists' Association [*A publication*]

Proc Geol Soc China ... Proceedings. Geological Society of China [*Taipei*] [*A publication*]

Proc Geol Soc Lond ... Proceedings. Geological Society of London [*A publication*]

Proc Geol Soc S Afr ... Proceedings. Geological Society of South Africa [*A publication*]

Proc Geophys Soc Tulsa ... Proceedings. Geophysical Society of Tulsa [*A publication*]

Proc Ghana Acad Arts Sci ... Proceedings. Ghana Academy of Arts and Sciences [*A publication*]

Proc Grassl Soc South Afr ... Proceedings. Grassland Society of Southern Africa [*A publication*]

Proc Great Plains Agr Conf ... Proceedings. Great Plains Agriculture Conference [*A publication*]

Proc Gulf Caribb Fish Inst ... Proceedings. Gulf and Caribbean Fisheries Institute [*A publication*]

Proc Hampshire Field Club ... Proceedings. Hampshire Field Club and Archaeological Society [*A publication*]

Proc Hampshire Fld Club Archaeol Soc ... Proceedings. Hampshire Field Club and Archaeological Society [*A publication*]

Proc Hawaii Acad Sci ... Proceedings. Hawaiian Academy of Science [*A publication*]

Proc Hawaii Entomol Soc ... Proceedings. Hawaiian Entomological Society [*A publication*]

Proc Hawaii Ent Soc ... Proceedings. Hawaiian Entomological Society [*A publication*]

Proc Hawaii Int Conf Syst Sci ... Proceedings. Hawaii International Conference on System Science [*A publication*]

Proc Hawaii Top Conf Part Phys ... Proceedings. Hawaii Topical Conference in Particle Physics [*A publication*]

Proc Heat Transfer Fluid Mech Inst ... Proceedings. Heat Transfer and Fluid Mechanics Institute [*A publication*]

Proc Helminthol Soc Wash ... Proceedings. Helminthological Society of Washington [*A publication*]

Proc Helminthol Soc (Wash DC) ... Proceedings. Helminthological Society (Washington, DC) [*A publication*]

Proc Helminth Soc Wash ... Proceedings. Helminthological Society of Washington [*A publication*]

Proc High Lysine Corn Conf ... Proceedings. High Lysine Corn Conference [*A publication*]

Prochnost Din Aviats Dvigatelei ... Prochnost i Dinamika Aviatsionnykh Dvigatelei [*USSR*] [*A publication*]

Proc Hokkaido Symp Plant Breed Crop Sci Soc ... Proceedings. Hokkaido Symposium of Plant Breeding and Crop Science Society [*A publication*]

Proc Hokuriku Br Crop Sci Soc (Jap) ... Proceedings. Hokuriku Branch of Crop Science Society (Japan) [*A publication*]

Proc Hung Annu Meet Biochem ... Proceedings. Hungarian Annual Meeting for Biochemistry [*A publication*]

Proc Hydrol Symp ... Proceedings. Hydrology Symposium [*A publication*]

Proc IEE-A ... Institution of Electrical Engineers. Proceedings. A [*A publication*]

Proc IEE-B ... Institution of Electrical Engineers. Proceedings. B [*A publication*]

Proc IEE-C ... Institution of Electrical Engineers. Proceedings. C [*A publication*]

Proc IEEE ... Proceedings. IEEE [*A publication*]

Proc IEEE Conf Decis Control ... Proceedings. IEEE Conference on Decision and Control [*A publication*]

Proc IEEE Conf Decis Control Incl Symp Adapt Processes ... Proceedings. IEEE Conference on Decision and Control Including the Symposium on Adaptive Processes [*A publication*]

Proc IEEE Int Symp Circuits Syst ... Proceedings. IEEE International Symposium on Circuits and Systems [*A publication*]

Proc IEE H ... Proceedings. Institution of Electrical Engineers. H [*A publication*]

Proc IEE I ... Proceedings. Institution of Electrical Engineers. I [*A publication*]

Proc Ill Mining Inst ... Proceedings. Illinois Mining Institute [*A publication*]

Proc Imp Acad Japan ... Proceedings. Imperial Academy of Japan [*A publication*]

Proc Imp Acad (Tokyo) ... Proceedings. Imperial Academy (Tokyo) [*A publication*]

Proc Indiana Acad Sci ... Proceedings. Indiana Academy of Science [*A publication*]

Proc Indian Acad Sci ... Proceedings. Indian Academy of Sciences [*A publication*]

Proc Indian Acad Sci A ... Proceedings. Indian Academy of Sciences. Section A [*A publication*]

Proc Indian Acad Sci Anim Sci ... Proceedings. Indian Academy of Sciences. Animal Sciences [*A publication*]

Proc Indian Acad Sci Chem Sci ... Proceedings. Indian Academy of Sciences. Chemical Sciences [*A publication*]

Proc Indian Acad Sci Earth Planetary Sci ... Proceedings. Indian Academy of Sciences. Earth and Planetary Sciences [*A publication*]

Proc Indian Acad Sci Earth and Planet Sci ... Proceedings. Indian Academy of Sciences. Earth and Planetary Sciences [*A publication*]

Proc Indian Acad Sci Earth Planet Sci ... Proceedings. Indian Academy of Sciences. Earth and Planetary Sciences [*A publication*]

Proc Indian Acad Sci Eng Sci ... Proceedings. Indian Academy of Sciences. Engineering Sciences [*A publication*]

Proc Indian Acad Sci Math Sci ... Proceedings. Indian Academy of Sciences. Mathematical Sciences [*A publication*]

Proc Indian Acad Sci Plant Sci ... Proceedings. Indian Academy of Sciences. Plant Sciences [*A publication*]

Proc Indian Acad Sci Sect A ... Proceedings. Indian Academy of Sciences. Section A [*A publication*]

Proc Indian Acad Sci Sect A Chem Sci ... Proceedings. Indian Academy of Sciences. Section A. Chemical Sciences [*A publication*]

Proc Indian Acad Sci Sect B ... Proceedings. Indian Academy of Sciences. Section B [*A publication*]

Proc Indian Acad Sci Sect C ... Proceedings. Indian Academy of Sciences. Section C. Engineering Sciences [*India*] [*A publication*]

Proc Indian Assoc Cultiv Sci ... Proceedings. Indian Association for Cultivation of Sciences [*A publication*]

Proc Indian Natl Sci Acad A ... Proceedings. Indian National Science Academy. Part A. Physical Sciences [*A publication*]

Proc Indian Natl Sci Acad Part A ... Proceedings. Indian National Science Academy. Part A [*A publication*]

Proc Indian Natl Sci Acad Part A Phys Sci ... Proceedings. Indian National Science Academy. Part A. Physical Sciences [*A publication*]

Proc Indian Natl Sci Acad Part B ... Proceedings. Indian National Science Academy. Part B. Biological Sciences [*A publication*]

Proc Indian Natl Sci Acad Part B Biol Sci ... Proceedings. Indian National Science Academy. Part B. Biological Sciences [*A publication*]

Proc Indian Sci Congr ... Proceedings. Indian Science Congress [*A publication*]

Proc Ind Waste Conf ... Proceedings. Industrial Waste Conference [*A publication*]

Proc Ind Waste Conf Purdue Univ ... Proceedings. Industrial Waste Conference. Purdue University [*A publication*]

Proc Ind Waste Util Conf ... Proceedings. Industrial Waste Utilization Conference [*A publication*]

Proc Inst Chem (Calcutta) ... Proceedings. Institution of Chemists (Calcutta) [*A publication*]

Proc Inst Civ Eng ... Proceedings. Institution of Civil Engineers [*London*] [*A publication*]

Proc Inst Civ Eng ... Proceedings. Institution of Civil Engineers. Part 2. Research and Theory [*United Kingdom*] [*A publication*]

Proc Inst Civ Eng (London) Suppl ... Proceedings. Institution of Civil Engineers (London). Supplement [*A publication*]

Proc Inst Civ Eng Part 1 ... Proceedings. Institution of Civil Engineers. Part 1. Design and Construction [*A publication*]

Proc Inst Civ Eng Part 2 ... Proceedings. Institution of Civil Engineers. Part 2. Research and Theory [*United Kingdom*] [*A publication*]

Proc Inst Elec Eng (London) ... Proceedings. Institution of Electrical Engineers (London) [*A publication*]

Proc Inst Elec Eng Pt B Elec Power Appl ... Proceedings. Institution of Electrical Engineers. Part B. Electric Power Applications [*A publication*]

Proc Inst Elec Eng Pt E Computers Digital Tech ... Proceedings. Institution of Electrical Engineers. Part E. Computers and Digital Techniques [*A publication*]

Proc Inst Elec Eng Pt F Commun Radar Signal Process ... Proceedings. Institution of Electrical Engineers. Part F. Communications, Radar, and Signal Processing [*A publication*]

Proc Inst Elec Eng Pt G Electron Circuits Syst ... Proceedings. Institution of Electrical Engineers. Part G. Electronics Circuits and Systems [*A publication*]

Proc Inst Elec Eng Pt H Microwaves Opt Antennas ... Proceedings. Institution of Electrical Engineers. Part H. Microwaves, Optics, and Antennas [*A publication*]

Proc Inst Elec Engrs ... Proceedings. Institution of Electrical Engineers [*A publication*]

Proc Inst Elect ... Proceedings. Institution of Electrical Engineers [*A publication*]

Proc Inst Electr Eng ... Proceedings. Institution of Electrical Engineers [*A publication*]

Proc Inst Electr Eng (London) ... Proceedings. Institution of Electrical Engineers (London) [*A publication*]

Proc Inst Electr Eng Part 4 ... Proceedings. Institution of Electrical Engineers. Part 4. Monographs [*A publication*]

Proc Inst Electr Eng Part A ... Proceedings. Institution of Electrical Engineers. Part A. Power Engineering [*A publication*]

Proc Inst Electr Eng Part A Suppl ... Proceedings. Institution of Electrical Engineers. Part A. Supplement [*A publication*]

Proc Inst Electr Eng Part B ... Proceedings. Institution of Electrical Engineers. Part B. Electronic and Communication Engineering Including Radio Engineering [*A publication*]

Proc Inst Environ Sci ... Proceedings. Institute of Environmental Sciences [*A publication*]

Proc Inst Fd Sci Technol ... Proceedings. Institute of Food Science and Technology [*A publication*]

Proc Inst Mech Eng ... Proceedings. Institution of Mechanical Engineers [*A publication*]

Proc Inst Mech Eng (London) ... Proceedings. Institution of Mechanical Engineers (London) [*A publication*]

Proc Inst Mech Eng Part A ... Proceedings. Institution of Mechanical Engineers. Part A. Power and Process Engineering [*A publication*]

Proc Inst Mech Eng Part B ... Proceedings. Institution of Mechanical Engineers. Part B. Management and Engineering Manufacture [*A publication*]

Proc Inst Mech Eng Part C ... Proceedings. Institution of Mechanical Engineers. Part C. Mechanical Engineering Science [*A publication*]

Proc Inst Mech Engrs ... Proceedings. Institution of Mechanical Engineers [*A publication*]

Proc Inst Med Chic ... Proceedings. Institute of Medicine of Chicago [*A publication*]

Proc Inst Nat Sci Nihon Univ ... Proceedings. Institute of Natural Sciences. Nihon University [*A publication*]

Proc Instn Civ Engrs ... Proceedings. Institution of Civil Engineers [*A publication*]

Proc Instn Civ Engrs I II ... Proceedings. Institution of Civil Engineers. Parts I and II [*A publication*]

Proc Instn Elect Engrs ... Proceedings. Institution of Electrical Engineers [*A publication*]

Proc Instn Mech Engrs ... Proceedings. Institution of Mechanical Engineers [*A publication*]

Proc Instn Radio Electron Engrs Aust ... Proceedings. Institution of Radio and Electronics Engineers of Australia [*A publication*]

Proc Instn Radio Engrs Aust ... Proceedings. Institution of Radio Engineers of Australia [*A publication*]

Proc Inst Oceanogr Fish Bulg Acad Sci ... Proceedings. Institute of Oceanography and Fisheries. Bulgarian Academy of Sciences [*A publication*]

Proc Inst Pomol (Skierniewice Pol) Ser E Conf Symp ... Proceedings. Research Institute of Pomology (Skierniewice, Poland). Series E. Conferences and Symposia [*A publication*]

Proc Inst Radio Electron Eng Aust ... Proceedings. Institution of Radio and Electronics Engineers of Australia [*A publication*]

Proc Inst Railw Signal Eng ... Proceedings. Institution of Railway Signal Engineers [*A publication*]

Proc Inst Refrig ... Proceedings. Institute of Refrigeration [*A publication*]

Proc Instrum Soc Am ... Proceedings. Instrument Society of America [*A publication*]

Proc Inst Statist Math ... Proceedings. Institute of Statistical Mathematics [*A publication*]

Proc Inst Teknol Bandung ... Proceedings. Institut Teknologi Bandung [*Indonesia*] [*A publication*]

Proc Inst Teknol Bandung Suppl ... Proceedings. Institut Teknologi Bandung. Supplement [*Indonesia*] [*A publication*]

Proc Int Acad Oral Pathol ... Proceedings. International Academy of Oral Pathology [*A publication*]

Proc Int Assoc Milk Dealers ... Proceedings. International Association of Milk Dealers [*A publication*]

Proc Int Assoc Test Mater ... Proceedings. International Association for Testing Materials [*A publication*]

Proc Int Assoc Theor Appl Limnol ... Proceedings. International Association of Theoretical and Applied Limnology [*A publication*]

Proc Int Assoc Vet Food Hyg ... Proceedings. International Association of Veterinary Food Hygienists [*A publication*]

Proc Int Astronaut Congr ... Proceedings. International Astronautical Congress [*A publication*]

Proc Int Barley Genet Symp ... Proceedings. International Barley Genetics Symposium [*A publication*]

Proc Int Bot Congr ... Proceedings. International Botanical Congress [*A publication*]

Proc Int Colloq Plant Anal Fert Probl ... Proceedings. International Colloquium on Plant Analysis and Fertilizer Problems [*A publication*]

Proc Int Comm Glass ... Proceedings. International Commission on Glass [*A publication*]

Proc Int Conf Biochem Probl Lipids ... Proceedings. International Conference on Biochemical Problems of Lipids [*A publication*]

Proc Int Conf Cent High Energy Form ... Proceedings. International Conference. Center for High Energy Forming [*A publication*]

Proc Int Conf Cybern Soc ... Proceedings. International Conference on Cybernetics and Society [*A publication*]

Proc Int Conf Fire Saf ... Proceedings. International Conference on Fire Safety [*A publication*]

Proc Int Conf Fluid Sealing ... Proceedings. International Conference on Fluid Sealing [*A publication*]

Proc Int Conf High Energy Rate Fabr ... Proceedings. International Conference on High Energy Rate Fabrication [*A publication*]

Proc Int Conf Int Assoc Water Pollut Res ... Proceedings. International Conference of the International Association on Water Pollution Research [*A publication*]

Proc Int Conf Lasers ... Proceedings. International Conference on Lasers [*A publication*]

Proc Int Conf Noise Control Eng ... Proceedings. International Conference on Noise Control Engineering [*A publication*]

Proc Int Conf Peaceful Uses Atomic Energy ... Proceedings. International Conference on the Peaceful Uses of Atomic Energy [*A publication*]

Proc Int Conf Plant Growth Regulat ... Proceedings. International Conference on Plant Growth Regulation [*A publication*]

Proc Int Conf Plant Pathog Bact ... Proceedings. International Conference on Plant Pathogenic Bacteria [*A publication*]

Proc Int Conf Sci Aspects Mushroom Grow ... Proceedings. International Conference on Scientific Aspects of Mushroom Growing [*A publication*]

Proc Int Conf Wildl Dis ... Proceedings. International Conference on Wildlife Disease [*A publication*]

Proc Int Congr Anim Reprod Artif Insemin ... Proceedings. International Congress on Animal Reproduction and Artificial Insemination [*A publication*]

Proc Int Congr Biochem ... Proceedings. International Congress of Biochemistry [*A publication*]

Proc Int Congr Crop Prot ... Proceedings. International Congress on Crop Protection [*A publication*]

Proc Int Congr Ent ... Proceedings. International Congress of Entomology [*A publication*]

Proc Int Congr Entomol ... Proceedings. International Congress of Entomology [*A publication*]

Proc Int Congr Food Sci Technol ... Proceedings. International Congress of Food Science and Technology [*A publication*]

Proc Int Congr Genet ... Proceedings. International Congress of Genetics [*A publication*]

Proc Int Congr Geront ... Proceedings. International Congress on Gerontology [*A publication*]

Proc Int Congr Gerontol ... Proceedings. International Congress of Gerontology [*A publication*]

Proc Int Congr Hist Sci ... Proceedings. International Congress of the History of Science [*A publication*]

Proc Int Congr Hum Genet ... Proceedings. International Congress of Human Genetics [*A publication*]

Proc Int Congr Ment Retard ... Proceedings. International Congress on Mental Retardation [*A publication*]

Proc Int Congr Microbiol Stand ... Proceedings. Intrnational Congress for Microbiological Standardization [*A publication*]

Proc Int Congr Mushroom Sci ... Proceedings. International Congress on Mushroom Science [*A publication*]

Proc Int Congr Nephrol ... Proceedings. International Congress of Nephrology [*A publication*]

Proc Int Congr Nutr (Hamburg) ... Proceedings. International Congress of Nutrition (Hamburg) [*A publication*]

Proc Int Congr Pharmacol ... Proceedings. International Congress on Pharmacology [*A publication*]

Proc Int Congr Photosynth Res ... Proceedings. International Congress on Photosynthesis Research [*A publication*]

Proc Int Congr Primatol ... Proceedings. International Congress of Primatology [*A publication*]

Proc Int Congr Protozool ... Proceedings. International Congress on Protozoology [*A publication*]

Proc Int Congr Psychother ... Proceedings. International Congress of Psychotherapy [*A publication*]

Proc Int Congr Pure Appl Chem ... Proceedings. International Congress of Pure and Applied Chemistry [*A publication*]

Proc Int Congr Radiat Prot ... Proceedings. International Congress of Radiation Protection [*A publication*]

Proc Int Congr Refrig ... Proceedings. International Congress of Refrigeration [*A publication*]

Proc Int Congr Zool ... Proceedings. International Congress of Zoology [*A publication*]

Proc Int Dist Heat Assoc ... Proceedings. International District Heating Association [*A publication*]

Proc Internat School of Phys Enrico Fermi ... Proceedings. International School of Physics "Enrico Fermi" [*A publication*]

Proc Intersoc Energy Conver Eng Conf ... Proceedings. Intersociety Energy Conversion Engineering Conference [*A publication*]

Proc Interuniv Fac Work Conf ... Proceedings. Interuniversity Faculty Work Conference [*A publication*]

Proc Int Grassland Congr ... Proceedings. International Grassland Congress [*A publication*]

Proc Int Hort Congr ... Proceedings. International Horticultural Congress [*A publication*]

Proc Int Hortic Congr ... Proceedings. International Horticultural Congress [*A publication*]

Proc Int ISA Biomed Sci Instrum Symp ... Proceedings. International ISA [*Instrument Society of America*] Biomedical Sciences Instrumentation Symposium [*A publication*]

Proc Int Meet Biol Stand ... Proceedings. International Meeting of Biological Standardization [*A publication*]

Proc Int Microelectron Symp ... Proceedings. International Microelectronics Symposium [*A publication*]

Proc Int Ornithol Congr ... Proceedings. International Ornithological Congress [*A publication*]

Proc Int Pharmacol Meet ... Proceedings. International Pharmacological Meeting [*A publication*]

Proc Int Pl Propag Soc ... Proceedings. International Plant Propagators' Society [*A publication*]

Proc Int Sch Phys Enrico Fermi ... Proceedings. International School of Physics "Enrico Fermi" [*A publication*]

Proc Int Sci Congr Cultiv Edible Fungi ... Proceedings. International Scientific Congress on the Cultivation of Edible Fungi [*A publication*]

Proc Int Seaweed Symp ... Proceedings. International Seaweed Symposium [*A publication*]

Proc Int Seed Test Ass ... Proceedings. International Seed Testing Association [*A publication*]

Proc Int Seed Test Assoc ... Proceedings. International Seed Testing Association [*A publication*]

Proc Int Shade Tree Conf ... Proceedings. Annual Meetings. International Shade Tree Conference [*A publication*]

Proc Int Soc Soil Sci ... Proceedings. International Society of Soil Science [*A publication*]

Proc Int Soc Sugar Cane Technol ... Proceedings. International Society of Sugar Cane Technologists [*A publication*]

Proc Int Symp Enzyme Chem ... Proceedings. International Symposium on Enzyme Chemistry [*A publication*]

Proc Int Symp Food Irradiation ... Proceedings. International Symposium on Food Irradiation [*A publication*]

Proc Int Symp Fresh Water Sea ... Proceedings. International Symposium on Fresh Water from the Sea [*A publication*]

Proc Int Symp Mult Valued Logic ... Proceedings. International Symposium on Multiple-Valued Logic [*A publication*]

Proc Int Symp Poll ... Proceedings. International Symposium on Pollination [*A publication*]

Proc Int Symp Princess Takamatsu Cancer Res Fund ... Proceedings. International Symposium of the Princess Takamatsu Cancer Research Fund [*A publication*]

Proc Int Symp Remote Sens Environ ... Proceedings. International Symposium on Remote Sensing of Environment [*A publication*]

Proc Int Symp Remote Sensing Environ ... Proceedings. International Symposium on Remote Sensing of Environment [*A publication*]

Proc Int Tech Conf APICS ... Proceedings. International Technical Conference. American Production and Inventory Control Society [*A publication*]

Proc Int Union Biol Sci Ser B ... Proceedings. International Union of Biological Sciences. Series B [*A publication*]

Proc Int Union Forest Res Organ ... Proceedings. International Union of Forest Research Organizations [*A publication*]

Proc Int Vet Congr ... Proceedings. International Veterinary Congress [*A publication*]

Proc Int Water Qual Symp ... Proceedings. International Water Quality Symposium [*A publication*]

Proc Int Wheat Genet Symp ... Proceedings. International Wheat Genetics Symposium [*A publication*]

Proc Int Wheat Surplus Util Conf ... Proceedings. International Wheat Surplus Utilization Conference [*A publication*]

Proc Int Wire Cable Symp ... Proceedings. International Wire and Cable Symposium [*A publication*]

Proc Iowa Acad Sci ... Proceedings. Iowa Academy of Science [*A publication*]

Proc Iraqi Sci Soc ... Proceedings. Iraqi Scientific Societies [*A publication*]

Proc IRE ..... Proceedings. IRE [*Institute of Radio Engineers*] [*United States*] [*A publication*]

Proc ISA ..... Proceedings. Instrument Society of America [*A publication*]

Proc Jap Acad ... Proceedings. Japan Academy [*A publication*]

Proc Japan Acad Ser B Phys Biol Sci ... Proceedings. Japan Academy. Series B. Physical and Biological Sciences [*A publication*]

Proc Jap Soc Civ Eng ... Proceedings. Japan Society of Civil Engineers [*A publication*]

ProcJPES ... Proceedings. Jewish Palestine Exploration Society [*A publication*]

Proc Jpn Acad ... Proceedings. Japan Academy [*A publication*]

Proc Jpn Acad Ser A ... Proceedings. Japan Academy. Series A. Mathematical Sciences [*A publication*]

Proc Jpn Acad Ser B ... Proceedings. Japan Academy. Series B. Physical and Biological Sciences [*A publication*]

Proc Jpn At Ind Forum Inc ... Proceedings. Japan Atomic Industrial Forum, Incorporated [*A publication*]

Proc Jpn Cem Eng Assoc ... Proceedings. Japan Cement Engineering Association [*A publication*]

Proc Jpn Conf Radioisot ... Proceedings. Japan Conference on Radioisotopes [*A publication*]

Proc Jpn Congr Mater Res ... Proceedings. Japan Congress on Materials Research [*A publication*]

Proc Jpn Pharmacol Soc ... Proceedings. Japanese Pharmacology Society [*A publication*]

Proc Jpn Soc Civ Eng ... Proceedings. Japan Society of Civil Engineers [*A publication*]

Proc Jpn Soc Clin Biochem Metab ... Proceedings. Japan Society of Clinical Biochemistry and Metabolism [*A publication*]

Proc Jpn Soc Reticuloendothel Syst ... Proceedings. Japan Society of the Reticuloendothelial System [*A publication*]

Proc Kansai Plant Prot Soc ... Proceedings. Kansai Plant Protection Society [*A publication*]

Proc Kanto-Tosan Plant Prot Soc ... Proceedings. Kanto-Tosan Plant Protection Society [*A publication*]

Proc Kinki Symp Crop Sci Plant Breed Soc ... Proceedings. Kinki Symposium of Crop Science and Plant Breeding Society [*A publication*]

Proc K Ned Akad Wet ... Proceedings. Koninklijke Nederlandse Akademie van Wetenschappen [*A publication*]

Proc K Ned Akad Wet B ... Proceedings. Koninklijke Nederlandse Akademie van Wetenschappen. Series B. Physical Sciences [*A publication*]

Proc K Ned Akad Wet Ser A ... Proceedings. Koninklijke Nederlandse Akademie van Wetenschappen. Series A. Mathematical Sciences [*A publication*]

Proc K Ned Akad Wet Ser B ... Proceedings. Koninklijke Nederlandse Akademie van Wetenschappen. Series B. Physical Sciences [*A publication*]

Proc K Ned Akad Wet Ser B Palaeontol Geol Phys Chem ... Proceedings. Koninklijke Nederlandse Akademie van Wetenschappen. Series B. Palaeontology, Geology, Physics, and Chemistry [*Later, Proceedings. Koninklijke Nederlandse Akademie van Wetenschappen. Series B. Palaeontology, Geology, Physics, Chemistry, Anthropology*] [*A publication*]

Proc K Ned Akad Wet Ser B Phys Sci ... Proceedings. Koninklijke Nederlandse Akademie van Wetenschappen. Series B. Physical Sciences [*A publication*]

Proc K Ned Akad Wet Ser C ... Proceedings. Koninklijke Nederlandse Akademie van Wetenschappen. Series C. Biological and Medical Sciences [*A publication*]

Proc K Ned Akad Wet Ser C Biol Med Sci ... Proceedings. Koninklijke Nederlandse Akademie van Wetenschappen. Series C. Biological and Medical Sciences [*A publication*]

Proc LA Acad Sci ... Proceedings. Louisiana Academy of Sciences [*A publication*]

Proc LA Ass Agron ... Proceedings. Louisiana Association of Agronomists [*A publication*]

Proc Leatherhead Dist Local Hist Soc ... Proceedings. Leatherhead and District Local History Society [*A publication*]

Proc Lebedev Phys Inst ... Proceedings (Trudy). P. N. Lebedev Physics Institute [*A publication*]

Proc Leeds Phil Lit Soc Sci Sect ... Proceedings. Leeds Philosophical and Literary Society. Scientific Section [*A publication*]

Proc Leeds Philos & Lit Soc ... Proceedings. Leeds Philosophical and Literary Society [*A publication*]

Proc Leeds Philos Lit Soc Lit Hist Sect ... Proceedings. Leeds Philosophical and Literary Society. Literary and Historical Section [*A publication*]

Proc Leucocyte Cult Conf ... Proceedings. Leucocyte Culture Conference [*A publication*]

Proc Lincoln Coll Farmers Conf ... Proceedings. Lincoln College. Farmer's Conference [*A publication*]

Proc Linnean Soc NSW ... Proceedings. Linnean Society of New South Wales [*A publication*]

Proc Linn Soc Lond ... Proceedings. Linnean Society of London [*A publication*]

Proc Linn Soc London ... Proceedings. Linnean Society of London [*A publication*]

Proc Linn Soc NSW ... Proceedings. Linnean Society of New South Wales [*A publication*]

Proc Linn Soc NY ... Proceedings. Linnean Society of New York [*A publication*]

Proc Liverpool Geol Soc ... Proceedings. Liverpool Geological Society [*A publication*]

Proc London Math Soc ... Proceedings. London Mathematical Society [*A publication*]

Proc London Math Soc 3 ... Proceedings. London Mathematical Society. Third Series [*A publication*]

Proc Lunar Sci Conf ... Proceedings. Lunar Science Conference [*United States*] [*A publication*]

Proc Malacol Soc Lond ... Proceedings. Malacological Society of London [*A publication*]

Proc Mark Milk Conf ... Proceedings. Market Milk Conference [*A publication*]

Proc Mar Safety Council USCG ... Proceedings. Marine Safety Council. United States Coast Guard [*A publication*]

Proc Mass Hist Soc ... Proceedings. Massachusetts Historical Society [*A publication*]

Proc Math Phys Soc (Egypt) ... Proceedings. Mathematical and Physical Society (Egypt) [*A publication*]

Proc Mayo Clin ... Proceedings. Staff Meetings of the Mayo Clinic [*A publication*]

Proc Mayo Clin Staff Meet ... Proceedings. Mayo Clinic Staff Meeting [*A publication*]

Proc MD Nutr Conf Feed Manuf ... Proceedings. Maryland Nutrition Conference for Feed Manufacturers [*A publication*]

Proc Medico-Legal Soc Vict ... Proceedings. Medico-Legal Society of Victoria [*A publication*]

Proc Microbiol Res Group Hung Acad Sci ... Proceedings. Microbiological Research Group. Hungarian Academy of Science [*A publication*]

Proc Microsc Soc Can ... Proceedings. Microscopical Society of Canada [*A publication*]

Proc Mid-Atl Ind Waste Conf ... Proceedings. Mid-Atlantic Industrial Waste Conference [*United States*] [*A publication*]

Proc Midwest Fert Conf ... Proceedings. Midwestern Fertilizer Conference [*A publication*]

Proc Mine Med Off Assoc ... Proceedings. Mine Medical Officers Association [*A publication*]

Proc Minn Acad Sci ... Proceedings. Minnesota Academy of Sciences [*A publication*]

Proc Minutes Ann Meet Agric Res Inst ... Proceedings and Minutes. Annual Meeting of the Agricultural Research Institute [*A publication*]

Proc Mont Acad Sci ... Proceedings. Montana Academy of Sciences [*A publication*]

Proc Mont Nutr Conf ... Proceedings. Montana Nutrition Conference [*A publication*]

Proc Montpellier Symp ... Proceedings. Montpellier Symposium [*A publication*]

Proc Mtg Comm For Tree Breeding Can ... Proceedings. Meeting Committee on Forest Tree Breeding in Canada [*A publication*]

Proc Mtg Sect Int Union For Res Organ ... Proceedings. Meeting of Section. International Union of Forest Research Organizations [*A publication*]

Proc Nagano Pref Agr Exp Sta ... Proceedings. Nagano Prefectural Agricultural Experiment Station [*A publication*]

Proc NA Sci ... Proceedings. National Academy of Sciences [*A publication*]

Proc Nat Acad Sci ... Proceedings. National Academy of Sciences. United States of America [*A publication*]

Proc Nat Acad Sci (India) Sect A ... Proceedings. National Academy of Sciences (India). Section A [*A publication*]

Proc Nat Acad Sci USA ... Proceedings. National Academy of Sciences. United States of America [*A publication*]

Proc Nat Acad Sci USA Biol Sci ... Proceedings. National Academy of Sciences. United States of America. Biological Sciences [*A publication*]

Proc Nat Acad Sci USA Phys Sci ... Proceedings. National Academy of Sciences. United States of America. Physical Sciences [*A publication*]

Proc Nat Ass Wheat Growers ... Proceedings. National Association of Wheat Growers [*A publication*]

Proc Nat Conf AIAS ... Proceedings. National Conference. Australian Institute of Agricultural Science [*A publication*]

Proc Nat Conf Fluid Power Annu Meet ... Proceedings. National Conference on Fluid Power. Annual Meeting [*A publication*]

Proc Nat Electron Conf ... Proceedings. National Electronics Conference [*A publication*]

Proc Nat Food Eng Conf ... Proceedings. National Food Engineering Conference [*A publication*]

Proc Nat Gas Process Assoc Tech Pap ... Proceedings. Natural Gas Processors Association. Technical Papers [*A publication*]

Proc Nat Gas Processors Assoc Annu Conv ... Proceedings. Natural Gas Processors Association. Annual Convention [*A publication*]

Proc Natl Acad Sci (India) ... Proceedings. National Academy of Sciences (India) [*A publication*]

Proc Natl Acad Sci (India) Sect A ... Proceedings. National Academy of Sciences (India). Section A. Physical Sciences [*A publication*]

Proc Natl Acad Sci (India) Sect A (Phys Sci) ... Proceedings. National Academy of Sciences (India). Section A (Physical Sciences) [*A publication*]

Proc Natl Acad Sci (India) Sect B ... Proceedings. National Academy of Sciences (India). Section B. Biological Sciences [*A publication*]

Proc Natl Acad Sci (India) Sect B (Biol Sci) ... Proceedings. National Academy of Sciences (India). Section B (Biological Sciences) [*A publication*]

Proc Natl Acad Sci USA ... Proceedings. National Academy of Sciences. United States of America [*A publication*]

Proc Natl Biomed Sci Instrum Symp ... Proceedings. National Biomedical Sciences Instrumentation Symposium [*A publication*]

Proc Natl Cancer Conf ... Proceedings. National Cancer Conference [*A publication*]

Proc Natl Conf Adm Res ... Proceedings. National Conference on the Administration of Research [*A publication*]

Proc Natl Conf Fluid Power ... Proceedings. National Conference on Fluid Power [*United States*] [*A publication*]

Proc Natl Conf Fluid Power Annu Meet ... Proceedings. National Conference on Fluid Power. Annual Meeting [*A publication*]

Proc Natl Conf Methadone Treat ... Proceedings. National Conference on Methadone Treatment [*A publication*]

Proc Natl Conv Study Inf Doc ... Proceedings. National Convention for the Study of Information and Documentation [*Japan*] [*A publication*]

Proc Natl Counc Sci Dev (Repub China) ... Proceedings. National Council on Science Development (Republic of China) [*A publication*]

Proc Natl Electron Conf ... Proceedings. National Electronics Conference [*A publication*]

Proc Natl Food Eng Conf ... Proceedings. National Food Engineering Conference [*A publication*]

Proc Natl Incinerator Conf ... Proceedings. National Incinerator Conference [*A publication*]

Proc Natl Inst Sci (India) ... Proceedings. National Institute of Sciences (India) [*A publication*]

Proc Natl Inst Sci (India) Part A ... Proceedings. National Institute of Sciences (India). Part A. Physical Sciences [*A publication*]

Proc Natl Inst Sci (India) Part A Phys Sci ... Proceedings. National Institute of Sciences (India). Part A. Physical Sciences [*A publication*]

Proc Natl Inst Sci (India) Part A Suppl ... Proceedings. National Institute of Sciences (India). Part A. Supplement [*A publication*]

Proc Natl Inst Sci (India) Part B ... Proceedings. National Institute of Sciences (India). Part B. Biological Sciences [*A publication*]

Proc Natl Inst Sci (India) Part B Biol Sci ... Proceedings. National Institute of Sciences (India). Part B. Biological Sciences [*A publication*]

Proc Natl Meet Biophys Biotechnol Finl ... Proceedings. National Meeting on Biophysics and Biotechnology in Finland [*A publication*]

Proc Natl Open Hearth Basic Oxygen Steel Conf ... Proceedings. National Open Hearth and Basic Oxygen Steel Conference [*A publication*]

Proc Natl Sci Counc (Repub China) ... Proceedings. National Science Council (Republic of China) [*A publication*]

Proc Natl Shellfish Assoc ... Proceedings. National Shellfisheries Association [*A publication*]

Proc Natl Symp Radioecol ... Proceedings. National Symposium on Radioecology [*A publication*]

Proc Natl Telecommun Conf ... Proceedings. National Telecommunications Conference [*A publication*]

Proc Natn Acad Sci (India) ... Proceedings. National Academy of Sciences (India) [*A publication*]

Proc Natn Acad Sci (USA) ... Proceedings. National Academy of Sciences (United States of America) [*A publication*]

Proc Natn Ent Soc (USA) ... Proceedings. National Entomological Society (United States of America) [*A publication*]

Proc Natn Inst Sci India ... Proceedings. National Institute of Sciences of India [*A publication*]

Proc Nat Silo Ass ... Proceedings. National Silo Association [*A publication*]

Proc Nat Telemetering Conf ... Proceedings. National Telemetering Conference [*A publication*]

Proc ND Acad Sci ... Proceedings. North Dakota Academy of Sciences [*A publication*]

Proc Near E S Afr Irrig Pract Semin ... Proceedings. Near East South Africa Irrigation Practices Seminar [*A publication*]

Proc Nebr Acad Sci Affil Soc ... Proceedings. Nebraska Academy of Sciences and Affiliated Societies [*A publication*]

Proc Ned Akad Wet ... Proceedings. Koninklijke Nederlandse Akademie van Wetenschappen [*A publication*]

Proc News Aust Oil Colour Chem Assoc ... Proceedings and News. Australian Oil and Colour Chemists Association [*A publication*]

Proc News Aust Oil Colour Chemists Assoc ... Proceedings and News. Australian Oil and Colour Chemists Association [*A publication*]

Proc NH Acad Sci ... Proceedings. New Hampshire Academy of Science [*A publication*]

Proc Ninth Int Grassld Congr ... Proceedings. Ninth International Grassland Congress [*A publication*]

Proc NJ Mosq Control Assoc ... Proceedings. New Jersey Mosquito Control Association [*A publication*]

Proc N Mex W Tex Phil Soc ... Proceedings. New Mexico-West Texas Philosophical Society [*A publication*]

Proc North Cent Branch Entomol Soc Am ... Proceedings. North Central Branch. Entomological Society of America [*A publication*]

Proc North Cent Weed Control Conf ... Proceedings. North Central Weed Control Conference [*A publication*]

Proc Northeast Weed Contr Conf ... Proceedings. Northeastern Weed Control Conference [*A publication*]

Proc Northeast Weed Sci Soc ... Proceedings. Northeastern Weed Science Society [*A publication*]

Proc Northwest Conf Struct Eng ... Proceedings. Northwest Conference of Structural Engineers [*A publication*]

Proc Northwest Wood Prod Clin ... Proceedings. Northwest Wood Products Clinic [*A publication*]

Proc NS Inst Sci ... Proceedings. Nova Scotian Institute of Science [*A publication*]

Proc Ntheast For Tree Impr Conf ... Proceedings. Northeastern Forest Tree Improvement Conference [*A publication*]

Proc Nucl Phys Solid State Phys Symp ... Proceedings. Nuclear Physics and Solid State Physics Symposium [*India*] [*A publication*]

Proc Nutr Soc ... Proceedings. Nutrition Society [*A publication*]

Proc Nutr Soc Aust ... Proceedings. Nutrition Society of Australia [*A publication*]

Proc Nutr Soc South Afr ... Proceedings. Nutrition Society of Southern Africa [*A publication*]

Proc NY St Hist Assn ... Proceedings. New York State Historical Association [*A publication*]

Proc NY St Hort Soc ... Proceedings. New York State Horticultural Society [*A publication*]

Proc NZ Ecol Soc ... Proceedings. New Zealand Ecological Society [*A publication*]

Proc NZ Grassl Assoc ... Proceedings. New Zealand Grassland Association [*A publication*]

Proc NZ Grassl Assoc Conf ... Proceedings. New Zealand Grassland Association. Conference [*A publication*]

Proc NZ Grassld Ass ... Proceedings. New Zealand Grassland Association [*A publication*]

Proc NZ Inst Agr Sci ... Proceedings. New Zealand Institute of Agricultural Science [*A publication*]

Proc NZ Soc Anim Proc ... Proceedings. New Zealand Society of Animal Production [*A publication*]

Proc NZ Weed Conf ... Proceedings. New Zealand Weed and Pest Control Conference [*A publication*]

Proc NZ Weed Control Conf ... Proceedings. New Zealand Weed Control Conference [*A publication*]

Proc NZ Weed Pest Contr Conf ... Proceedings. New Zealand Weed and Pest Control Conference [*A publication*]

Proc NZ Weed & Pest Control Conf ... Proceedings. New Zealand Weed and Pest Control Conference [*A publication*]

PROCO....... Programed Combustion [*Ford Motor Co.*]

PROCO....... Projects for Continental Operations [*World War II*]

Proc Ohio State Hortic Soc ... Proceedings. Ohio State Horticultural Society [*A publication*]

Proc Ohio State Hort Soc ... Proceedings. Ohio State Horticultural Society [*A publication*]

Proc Oil Recovery Conf Tex Petrol Res Comm ... Proceedings. Oil Recovery Conference. Texas Petroleum Research Committee [*A publication*]

Proc Okla Acad Sci ... Proceedings. Oklahoma Academy of Science [*A publication*]

PROCOM ... Procedures Committee [*Institute of Electrical and Electronics Engineers*] (IEEE)

PROCOM ... Procurement Committee

PROCOMEXCHI ... Mexican-Chicano Cooperative Programs on Mexican-US-Chicano Futures (EA)

PROCOMP ... Process Computer [*Data processing*]

PROCOMP ... Program Compiler [*Data processing*] (IEEE)

PROCON.... Request Diagnosis, Prognosis, Present Condition, Probable Date and Mode of Disposition of Following Patient Reported in Your Hospital [*Military*]

Proc Ont Ind Waste Conf ... Proceedings. Ontario Industrial Waste Conference [*A publication*]

Procop .... Procopius [*Sixth century AD*] [*Classical studies*]   (OCD)

Proc Oreg Acad Sci ... Proceedings. Oregon Academy of Science [*A publication*]

Proc Oreg Weed Conf ... Proceedings. Oregon Weed Conference [*A publication*]

Proc Osaka Prefect Inst Public Health Ed Ind Health ... Proceedings. Osaka Prefectural Institute of Public Health. Edition of Industrial Health [*A publication*]

Proc Osaka Public Health Inst ... Proceedings. Osaka Public Health Institute [*Japan*] [*A publication*]

PROCOTIP ... Promotion Cooperative du Transport Individuel Publique [*Public cars for private use to reduce traffic congestion*] [*Also known as TIP*] [*France*]

Proc PA Acad Sci ... Proceedings. Pennsylvania Academy of Science [*A publication*]

Proc Pac Coast Gas Ass ... Proceedings. Pacific Coast Gas Association, Inc. [*California*] [*A publication*]

Proc Pac Northwest Fert Conf ... Proceedings. Pacific Northwest Fertilizer Conference [*A publication*]

Proc Pac Northwest Ind Waste Conf ... Proceedings. Pacific Northwest Industrial Waste Conference [*A publication*]

Proc Pac Sci Congr ... Proceedings. Pacific Science Congress [*A publication*]

Proc Pak Acad Sci ... Proceedings. Pakistan Academy of Sciences [*A publication*]

Proc Pakistan Statist Assoc ... Proceedings. Pakistan Statistical Association [*A publication*]

Proc Pak Sci Conf ... Proceedings. Pakistan Science Conference [*A publication*]

Proc Pap Annu Conf Calif Mosq Control Assoc ... Proceedings and Papers. Annual Conference. California Mosquito Control Association [*A publication*]

Proc Pap Annu Conf Calif Mosq Vector Control Assoc ... Proceedings and Papers. Annual Conference. California Mosquito and Vector Control Association [*A publication*]

Proc Pap Int Union Conserv Nature Nat Resour ... Proceedings and Papers. International Union for the Conservation of Nature and Natural Resources [*A publication*]

Proc Path Soc Phila ... Proceedings. Pathological Society of Philadelphia [*A publication*]

Proc Paving Conf ... Proceedings. Paving Conference [*A publication*]

Proc Peoria Acad Sci ... Proceedings. Peoria Academy of Science [*A publication*]

Proc Pharm Soc Egypt ... Proceedings. Pharmaceutical Society of Egypt [*A publication*]

Proc Phil As ... Proceedings. American Philological Association [*A publication*]

Proc Phil Educ Soc Austl ... Proceedings. Philosophy of Education Society of Australasia [*A publication*]

Proc Phil Educ Soc GB ... Proceedings. Philosophy of Education Society of Great Britain [*A publication*]

Proc Phil Soc ... Proceedings. American Philosophical Society [*A publication*]

Proc Phys Math Soc Jpn ... Proceedings. Physico-Mathematical Society of Japan [*A publication*]

Proc Phys Semin Trondheim ... Proceedings. Physics Seminar in Trondheim [*Norway*] [*A publication*]

Proc Phys Soc Jpn ... Proceedings. Physical Society of Japan [*A publication*]

Proc Phys Soc (London) ... Proceedings. Physical Society (London) [*A publication*]

Proc Phytochem Soc ... Proceedings. Phytochemical Society [*A publication*]

Proc Plant Propagators' Soc ... Proceedings. Plant Propagators' Society [*United States*] [*A publication*]

Proc PN Lebedev Phys Inst ... Proceedings. P. N. Lebedev Physics Institute [*A publication*]

Proc PN Lebedev Phys Inst Acad Sci USSR ... Proceedings. P. N. Lebedev Physics Institute. Academy of Sciences of the USSR [*A publication*]

Proc Porcelain Enamel Inst Tech Forum ... Proceedings. Porcelain Enamel Institute. Technical Forum [*A publication*]

Proc Power Plant Dyn Control Test Symp ... Proceedings. Power Plant Dynamics. Control and Testing Symposium [*A publication*]

Proc Prac ... Proctor's Practice   (DLA)

Proc Prehist Soc ... Proceedings. Prehistoric Society [*A publication*]

Proc Prod Liability Prev Conf ... Proceedings. Product Liability Prevention Conference [*A publication*]

Proc PS ...... Proceedings. Prehistoric Society [*A publication*]

Proc Public Health Eng Conf ... Proceedings. Public Health Engineering Conference [*Loughborough University of Technology*] [*A publication*]

Proc QD Soc Sug Cane Tech ... Queensland Society of Sugar Cane Technologists. Proceedings [*A publication*]

Proc QD Soc Sug Cane Technol ... Proceedings. Queensland Society of Sugar Cane Technologists [*A publication*]

Proc Queensl Soc Sugar Cane Technol ... Proceedings. Queensland Society of Sugar Cane Technologists [*A publication*]

Proc Queensl Soc Sug Cane Technol ... Queensland Society of Sugar Cane Technologists. Proceedings [*A publication*]

Proc Queens Soc Sugar Cane Technol ... Queensland Society of Sugar Cane Technologists. Proceedings [*A publication*]

Proc Radio Club Am ... Proceedings. Radio Club of America [*A publication*]

Proc Radioisot Soc Philipp ... Proceedings. Radioisotope Society of the Philippines [*A publication*]

Proc R Agric Hort Soc S Aust ... Royal Agricultural and Horticultural Society of South Australia. Proceedings [*A publication*]

Proc Rajasthan Acad Sci ... Proceedings. Rajasthan Academy of Sciences [*A publication*]

Proc R Aust Chem Inst ... Proceedings. Royal Australian Chemical Institute [*A publication*]

Proc R Can Inst ... Proceedings. Royal Canadian Institute [*A publication*]

Proc Reg Conf Int Potash Inst ... Proceedings. Regional Conference. International Potash Institute [*A publication*]

Proc Relay Conf ... Proceedings. Relay Conference [*A publication*]

Proc Reliab Maint Conf ... Proceedings. Reliability and Maintainability Conference [*A publication*]

Proc Remote Syst Technol Div ANS ... Proceedings. Remote Systems Technology Division of the American Nuclear Society [*A publication*]

Proc Rencontre Moriond ... Proceedings. Rencontre de Moriond [*A publication*]

Proc R Entomol Soc Lond Ser A Gen Entomol ... Proceedings. Royal Entomological Society of London. Series A. General Entomology [*A publication*]

Proc R Entomol Soc Lond Ser B Taxon ... Proceedings. Royal Entomological Society of London. Series B. Taxonomy [*A publication*]

Proc Rep Belfast Nat Hist Philos Soc ... Proceedings and Reports. Belfast Natural History and Philosophical Society [*A publication*]

Proc Rep S Seedmen's Ass ... Proceedings and Reports. Southern Seedmen's Association [*A publication*]

Proc Res Conf Res Counc Am Meat Inst Found Univ Chicago ... Proceedings. Research Conference Sponsored by the Research Council of the American Meat Institute Foundation. University of Chicago [*A publication*]

Proc Res Inst Atmos Nagoya Univ ... Proceedings. Research Institute of Atmospherics. Nagoya University [*A publication*]

Proc Res Inst Nucl Med Biol ... Proceedings. Research Institute for Nuclear Medicine and Biology [*A publication*]

Proc Res Inst Nucl Med Biol Hiroshima Univ ... Proceedings. Research Institute for Nuclear Medicine and Biology. Hiroshima University [*Japan*] [*A publication*]

Proc Res Inst Oceanogr Fish (Varna) ... Proceedings. Research Institute of Oceanography and Fisheries (Varna) [*A publication*]

Proc Res Soc Jpn Sugar Refineries' Technol ... Proceedings. Research Society of Japan. Sugar Refineries' Technologists [*A publication*]

Proc R Geogr Soc Australas S Aust Br ... Proceedings. Royal Geographical Society of Australasia. South Australian Branch [*A publication*]

Proc R Geogr Soc Australas South Aust Branch ... Proceedings. Royal Geographical Society of Australasia. South Australian Branch [*A publication*]

Proc R Geog Soc Aust S Aust Br ... Proceedings. Royal Geographical Society of Australasia. South Australian Branch [*A publication*]

Proc R Inst GB ... Proceedings. Royal Institution of Great Britain [*A publication*]

Proc R Instn Gt Br ... Proceedings. Royal Institution of Great Britain [*A publication*]

Proc R Ir Acad ... Proceedings. Royal Irish Academy [*A publication*]

Proc R Ir Acad A ... Proceedings. Royal Irish Academy. Section A. Mathematical, Astronomical, and Physical Science [*A publication*]

Proc R Ir Acad Sect B ... Proceedings. Royal Irish Academy. Section B. Biological, Geological, and Chemical Science [*A publication*]

Proc R Irish Acad Sect A ... Proceedings. Royal Irish Academy. Section A. Mathematical, Astronomical, and Physical Science [*A publication*]

Proc R Irish Acad Sect B ... Proceedings. Royal Irish Academy. Section B. Biological, Geological, and Chemical Science [*A publication*]

Proc R Microsc Soc ... Proceedings. Royal Microscopical Society [*England*] [*A publication*]

Proc RNS ... Proceedings. Royal Numismatic Society [*A publication*]

Proc Robert A Welch Found Conf Chem Res ... Proceedings. Robert A. Welch Foundation. Conferences on Chemical Research [*A publication*]

Proc Rochester Acad Sci ... Proceedings. Rochester Academy of Science [*A publication*]

Proc Rocky Mt Coal Min Inst ... Proceedings. Rocky Mountain Coal Mining Institute [*A publication*]

Proc Royal Aust Chem Inst ... Proceedings. Royal Australian Chemical Institute [*A publication*]

Proc Royal Irish Acad ... Proceedings. Royal Irish Academy [*A publication*]
Proc Royal Soc Canad ... Proceedings. Royal Society of Canada [*A publication*]
Proc Royal Soc London Ser A ... Proceedings. Royal Society of London. Series A. Mathematical and Physical Sciences [*A publication*]
Proc Roy Anthropol Inst ... Proceedings. Royal Anthropological Institute [*A publication*]
Proc Roy Anthropol Inst Gr Brit Ir ... Proceedings. Royal Anthropological Institute of Great Britain and Ireland [*A publication*]
Proc Roy Aust Chem Inst ... Proceedings. Royal Australian Chemical Institute [*A publication*]
Proc Roy Entomol Soc Lond ... Proceedings. Royal Entomological Society of London [*A publication*]
Proc Roy Entomol Soc Lond C ... Proceedings. Royal Entomological Society of London. Series C. Journal of Meetings [*A publication*]
Proc Roy Entomol Soc London Ser A ... Proceedings. Royal Entomological Society of London. Series A [*A publication*]
Proc Roy Geog Soc Austral ... Proceedings. Royal Geographical Society of Australia. South Australian Branch [*A publication*]
Proc Roy Inst Gr Brit ... Proceedings. Royal Institution of Great Britain [*A publication*]
Proc Roy Ir Acad B C ... Proceedings. Royal Irish Academy. Series B and C [*A publication*]
Proc Roy Irish Acad ... Proceedings. Royal Irish Academy [*A publication*]
Proc Roy Irish Acad Sect A ... Proceedings. Royal Irish Academy. Section A. Mathematical, Astronomical, and Physical Science [*A publication*]
Proc Roy Phys Soc Edinb ... Proceedings. Royal Physical Society of Edinburgh [*A publication*]
Proc Roy Soc B ... Proceedings. Royal Society of London. Series B. Biological Sciences [*A publication*]
Proc Roy Soc Can ... Proceedings. Royal Society of Canada [*A publication*]
Proc Roy Soc Canada ... Proceedings. Royal Society of Canada [*A publication*]
Proc Roy Soc Edinb ... Proceedings. Royal Society of Edinburgh [*A publication*]
Proc Roy Soc Edinb B ... Proceedings. Royal Society of Edinburgh. Section B. Biological Sciences [*A publication*]
Proc Roy Soc London ... Proceedings. Royal Society of London [*A publication*]
Proc Roy Soc Med ... Proceedings. Royal Society of Medicine [*A publication*]
Proc Roy Soc QD ... Royal Society of Queensland. Proceedings [*A publication*]
Proc Roy Soc Ser A ... Proceedings. Royal Society. Series A [*A publication*]
Proc Roy Soc Vict ... Royal Society of Victoria. Proceedings [*A publication*]
Proc Roy Zool Soc NSW ... Royal Zoological Society of New South Wales. Proceedings [*A publication*]
Proc R Philos Soc Glasgow ... Proceedings. Royal Philosophical Society of Glasgow [*A publication*]
Proc R Physiogr Soc Lund ... Proceedings. Royal Physiograph Society at Lund [*A publication*]
Proc R Phys Soc Edinb ... Proceedings. Royal Physical Society of Edinburgh [*A publication*]
Proc R Soc A ... Proceedings. Royal Society of London. Series A [*A publication*]
Proc R Soc Can ... Proceedings. Royal Society of Canada [*A publication*]
Proc R Soc Edinb Nat Environ ... Proceedings. Royal Society of Edinburgh. Section B. Natural Environment [*A publication*]
Proc R Soc Edinb Sect A ... Proceedings. Royal Society of Edinburgh. Section A. Mathematical and Physical Sciences [*Later, Proceedings. Royal Society of Edinburgh. Mathematics*] [*A publication*]
Proc R Soc Edinb Sect A Math Phys Sci ... Proceedings. Royal Society of Edinburgh. Section A. Mathematical and Physical Sciences [*Later, Proceedings. Royal Society of Edinburgh. Mathematics*] [*A publication*]
Proc R Soc Edinb Sect B ... Proceedings. Royal Society of Edinburgh. Section B. Biological Sciences [*A publication*]
Proc R Soc Edinb Sect B Nat Environ ... Proceedings. Royal Society of Edinburgh. Section B. Natural Environment [*A publication*]
Proc R Soc Edinburgh Biol Sci ... Proceedings. Royal Society of Edinburgh. Section B. Biological Sciences [*A publication*]
Proc R Soc Edinburgh Sect A ... Proceedings. Royal Society of Edinburgh. Section A. Mathematical and Physical Sciences [*A publication*]
Proc R Soc Edinburgh Sect A ... Proceedings. Royal Society of Edinburgh. Section A. Mathematics [*A publication*]
Proc R Soc Lond ... Proceedings. Royal Society of London. B. Biological Sciences [*A publication*]
Proc R Soc Lond B Biol Sci ... Proceedings. Royal Society of London. Series B. Biological Sciences [*A publication*]
Proc R Soc Lond Biol ... Proceedings. Royal Society of London. Series B. Biological Sciences [*A publication*]
Proc R Soc London A ... Proceedings. Royal Society of London. Series A. Mathematical and Physical Sciences [*A publication*]
Proc R Soc London Ser A ... Proceedings. Royal Society of London. Series A. Mathematical and Physical Sciences [*A publication*]
Proc R Soc Med ... Proceedings. Royal Society of Medicine [*A publication*]
Proc R Soc Med Suppl ... Proceedings. Royal Society of Medicine. Supplement [*England*] [*A publication*]

Proc R Soc NZ ... Proceedings. Royal Society of New Zealand [*A publication*]
Proc R Soc QD ... Proceedings. Royal Society of Queensland [*A publication*]
Proc R Soc Queensl ... Proceedings. Royal Society of Queensland [*A publication*]
Proc R Soc VIC ... Royal Society of Victoria. Proceedings [*A publication*]
Proc R Soc Vict ... Proceedings. Royal Society of Victoria [*A publication*]
Proc R Soc Victoria ... Proceedings. Royal Society of Victoria [*A publication*]
Proc Ruakura Farmers Conf ... Proceedings. Ruakura Farmers' Conference [*A publication*]
Proc Ruakura Farmers Conf Week ... Proceedings. Ruakura Farmers' Conference Week [*A publication*]
Proc Rudolf Virchow Med Soc City NY ... Proceedings. Rudolf Virchow Medical Society in the City of New York [*A publication*]
Proc R Zool Soc NSW ... Proceedings. Royal Zoological Society of New South Wales [*A publication*]
PROCS .... Proceedings
Proc S Afr Soc Anim Prod ... Proceedings. South African Society of Animal Production [*A publication*]
Proc S Afr Sugar Technol Assoc Annu Congr ... Proceedings. South African Sugar Technologists Association. Annual Congress [*A publication*]
Proc San Diego Biomed Symp ... Proceedings. San Diego Biomedical Symposium [*A publication*]
Proc SA Scot ... Proceedings. Society of Antiquaries of Scotland [*A publication*]
Proc S Aust Brch R Geogr Soc Australas ... Royal Geographical Society of Australasia. South Australian Branch. Proceedings [*A publication*]
Proc SC Hist Assn ... Proceedings. South Carolina Historical Association [*A publication*]
Proc Sci Assoc Nigeria ... Proceedings. Science Association of Nigeria [*A publication*]
Proc Sci Inst Kinki Univ ... Proceedings. Science Institution. Kinki University [*A publication*]
Proc Sci Sect Toilet Goods Assoc ... Proceedings. Scientific Section of the Toilet Goods Association [*A publication*]
PROCSD .... Processed
Proc SD Acad Sci ... Proceedings. South Dakota Academy of Science [*A publication*]
Proc S Dak Acad Sci ... Proceedings. South Dakota Academy of Science [*A publication*]
Proc Sea Grant Conf ... Proceedings. Sea Grant Conference [*A publication*]
Proc (Second) Malays Soil Conf (Kuala Lumpur) ... Proceedings. (Second) Malaysian Soil Conference (Kuala Lumpur) [*A publication*]
Proc Sect Sci Is Acad Sci Humanit ... Proceedings. Section of Sciences. Israel Academy of Sciences and Humanities [*A publication*]
Proc Sect Sci K Ned Akad Wet ... Proceedings. Section of Sciences K. Nederlandse Akademie van Wetenschappen [*A publication*]
Proc Seed Protein Conf ... Proceedings. Seed Protein Conference [*A publication*]
Proc Serono Symp ... Proceedings. Serono Symposia [*A publication*]
Proc SESA ... Proceedings. Society for Experimental Stress Analysis [*A publication*]
Proc Shikoku Br Crop Sci Soc (Jap) ... Proceedings. Shikoku Branch of Crop Science Society (Japan) [*A publication*]
Proc Silvic Conf ... Proceedings. Silviculture Conference [*A publication*]
Proc Soc Agric Bacteriol ... Proceedings. Society of Agricultural Bacteriologists [*A publication*]
Proc Soc Am For ... Proceedings. Society of American Foresters [*A publication*]
Proc Soc Anal Chem ... Proceedings. Society for Analytical Chemistry [*A publication*]
Proc Soc Antiq Scot ... Proceedings. Society of Antiquaries of Scotland [*A publication*]
Proc Soc Antiq Scotland ... Proceedings. Society of Antiquaries of Scotland [*A publication*]
Proc Soc Appl Bact ... Proceedings. Society for Applied Bacteriology [*A publication*]
Proc Soc Appl Bacteriol ... Proceedings. Society for Applied Bacteriology [*A publication*]
Proc Soc Biol Chem India ... Proceedings. Society of Biological Chemists of India [*A publication*]
Proc Soc Exp Biol Med ... Proceedings. Society for Experimental Biology and Medicine [*A publication*]
Proc Soc Exp Biol (NY) ... Proceedings. Society for Experimental Biology and Medicine (New York) [*A publication*]
Proc Soc Exp Stress Anal ... Proceedings. Society for Experimental Stress Analysis [*A publication*]
Proc Soc Ind Microbiol ... Proceedings. Society for Industrial Microbiology [*A publication*]
Proc Soc Inf Disp ... Proceedings. Society for Information Display [*A publication*]
Proc Soc Protozool ... Proceedings. Society of Protozoologists [*A publication*]
Proc Soc Relay Eng ... Proceedings. Society of Relay Engineers [*A publication*]
Proc Soc Study Fertil ... Proceedings. Society for the Study of Fertility [*A publication*]

Proc Soc Water Treat Exam ... Proceedings. Society for Water Treatment and Examination [*A publication*]

Proc Soil Crop Sci Soc Fla ... Proceedings. Soil and Crop Science Society of Florida [*A publication*]

Proc Soil Sci Soc Am ... Proceedings. Soil Science Society of America [*A publication*]

Proc Soil Sci Soc Amer ... Proceedings. Soil Science Society of America [*A publication*]

Proc Somerset Arch Natur Hist Soc ... Proceedings. Somerset Archaeology and Natural History Society [*A publication*]

Proc South Afr Electron Microsc Soc Verrigtings ... Proceedings. Southern African Electron Microscopy Society-Verrigtings [*A publication*]

Proc Southeast Asian Reg Semin Trop Med Public Health ... Proceedings. Southeast Asian Regional Seminar on Tropical Medicine and Public Health [*A publication*]

Proc Southeastcon Reg 3 (Three) Conf ... Proceedings. Southeastcon Region 3 (Three) Conference [*United States*] [*A publication*]

Proc South For Tree Improv Conf ... Proceedings. Southern Forest Tree Improvement Conference [*A publication*]

Proc South Lond Entom and Nat Hist Soc ... Proceedings. South London Entomological and Natural History Society [*A publication*]

Proc South Wales Inst Eng ... Proceedings. South Wales Institute of Engineers [*A publication*]

Proc South Weed Conf ... Proceedings. Southern Weed Conference [*A publication*]

Proc South Weed Sci Soc ... Proceedings. Southern Weed Science Society [*A publication*]

Proc Southwest Agr Trade Farm Policy Conf ... Proceedings. Southwestern Agricultural Trade Farm Policy Conference [*A publication*]

Proc SPE Symp Form Damage Control ... Proceedings. Society of Petroleum Engineers. American Institute of Mining, Metallurgical, and Petroleum Engineers. Symposium on Formation Damage Control [*A publication*]

Proc SPE Symp Improv Oil Recovery ... Proceedings. Society of Petroleum Engineers. American Institute of Mining, Metallurgical, and Petroleum Engineers. Symposium on Improved Oil Recovery [*A publication*]

Proc Sprinkler Irrig Assoc Tech Conf ... Proceedings. Sprinkler Irrigation Association. Technical Conference [*A publication*]

Proc Staff Meetings Mayo Clin ... Proceedings. Staff Meetings of the Mayo Clinic [*A publication*]

Proc Staffs Iron Steel Inst ... Proceedings. Staffordshire Iron and Steel Institute [*A publication*]

Proc State Coll Wash Inst Dairy ... Proceedings. State College of Washington. Institute of Dairying [*A publication*]

Proc State Horti Assoc PA ... Proceedings. State Horticultural Association of Pennsylvania [*A publication*]

Proc Steel Treat Res Soc ... Proceedings. Steel Treating Research Society [*A publication*]

Proc Steklov Inst Math ... Proceedings. Steklov Institute of Mathematics [*A publication*]

Proc Sth Conf For Tree Impr ... Proceedings. Southern Conference on Forest Tree Improvement [*A publication*]

Proc Sth Weed Control Conf ... Proceedings. Southern Weed Control Conference [*A publication*]

Proc Sth Weed Sci Soc ... Proceedings. Southern Weed Science Society [*A publication*]

Proc 1st Vic Weed Conf ... Proceedings. First Victorian Weed Conference [*A publication*]

Proc Suffolk Inst Arch ... Proceedings. Suffolk Institute of Archaeology [*A publication*]

Proc Suffolk Inst Archaeol Hist ... Proceedings. Suffolk Institute of Archaeology and History [*A publication*]

Proc Sugar Beet Res Assoc ... Proceedings. Sugar Beet Research Association [*A publication*]

Proc Summer Comput Simul Conf ... Proceedings. Summer Computer Simulation Conference [*A publication*]

Proc Summer Conf Spectrosc Its Appl ... Proceedings. Summer Conference on Spectroscopy and Its Application [*A publication*]

Proc Summer Inst Part Phys ... Proceedings. Summer Institute on Particle Physics [*A publication*]

Proc S Wales Inst Eng ... Proceedings. South Wales Institute of Engineers [*A publication*]

Proc Symp Appl Math ... Proceedings. Symposia in Applied Mathematics [*A publication*]

Proc Symp Biol Skin ... Proceedings. Symposium on the Biology of Skin [*A publication*]

Proc Symp Chem Data Append R Aust Chem Inst ... Proceedings. Symposium on Chemical Data. Royal Australian Chemical Institute [*A publication*]

Proc Symp Chem Physiol Pathol ... Proceedings. Symposium on Chemical Physiology and Pathology [*A publication*]

Proc Symp Effects Ionizing Radiat Seed Signific Crop Impr ... Proceedings. Symposium on the Effects of Ionizing Radiation on Seeds and Their Significance for Crop Improvement [*A publication*]

Proc Symp Eng Probl Fusion Res ... Proceedings. Symposium on Engineering Problems of Fusion Research [*A publication*]

Proc Symp Explos Pyrotech ... Proceedings. Symposium on Explosives and Pyrotechnics [*A publication*]

Proc Symp Fertil Indian Soils ... Proceedings. Symposium on Fertility of Indian Soils [*A publication*]

Proc Symp Isotop Plant Nutr Physiol (Vienna Austria) ... Proceedings. Symposium on Isotopes in Plant Nutrition and Physiology (Vienna, Austria) [*A publication*]

Proc Symp Particleboard ... Proceedings. Symposium on Particleboard [*A publication*]

Proc Symp Rock Mech ... Proceedings. Symposium on Rock Mechanics [*A publication*]

Proc Symp Turbul Liq ... Proceedings. Symposium on Turbulence in Liquids [*A publication*]

Proc Symp Use Isotop Weed Res ... Proceedings. Symposium on the Use of Isotopes in Weed Research [*Vienna, Austria*] [*A publication*]

Proc Symp Use Radioisotop Soil Plant Nutr Stud ... Proceedings. Symposium on the Use of Radioisotopes in Soil-Plant Nutrition Studies [*A publication*]

Proc Symp Waste Manage ... Proceedings. Symposium on Waste Management [*A publication*]

Proc Synth Pipeline Gas Symp ... Proceedings. Synthetic Pipeline Gas Symposium [*A publication*]

PROCT .... Proctology

Proc Tall Timbers Conf Ecol Anim Control Habitat Manage ... Proceedings. Tall Timbers Conference on Ecological Animal Control by Habitat Management [*A publication*]

Proc Tall Timbers Fire Ecol Conf ... Proceedings. Tall Timbers Fire Ecology Conference [*A publication*]

Proc Tech Conf Soc Vac Coaters ... Proceedings. Technical Conference. Society of Vacuum Coaters [*A publication*]

Proc Tech Mtg Int Union Conserv Nature ... Proceedings. Technical Meeting. International Union for Conservation of Nature and Natural Resources [*A publication*]

Proc Tech Program Natl Electron Packag Prod Conf ... Proceedings. Technical Program. National Electronic Packaging and Production Conference [*A publication*]

Proc Tex Water Sewage Works Short Sch ... Proceedings. Texas Water and Sewage Works Short School [*A publication*]

Proc Tex Water Util Short Sch ... Proceedings. Texas Water Utilities Short School [*A publication*]

Proc Therm Power Conf ... Proceedings. Thermal Power Conference [*A publication*]

PROCTO .... Proctoscopy [*Medicine*]

PROCTOR ... Priority Routine Organizer for Computer Transfers and Operations of Registers

PROCTOT ... Priority Routine Organizer for Computer Transfers and Operations and Transfers

Proc Trans Br Entomol Nat Hist Soc ... Proceedings and Transactions. British Entomological and Natural History Society [*A publication*]

Proc Trans Croydon Natur Hist Sci Soc ... Proceedings and Transactions. Croydon Natural History and Scientific Society [*A publication*]

Proc and Trans Rhod Sci Assoc ... Proceedings and Transactions. Rhodesia Scientific Association [*A publication*]

Proc Trans Rhod Sci Assoc ... Proceedings and Transactions. Rhodesia Scientific Association [*A publication*]

Proc Trans R Soc Can ... Proceedings and Transactions. Royal Society of Canada [*A publication*]

Proc Tree Wardens Arborists Util Conf ... Proceedings. Tree Wardens, Arborists, and Utilities Conference [*A publication*]

Proc and Tr Liverpool Biol Soc ... Proceedings and Transactions. Liverpool Biological Society [*A publication*]

Proc Tr PN Lebedev Phys Inst ... Proceedings (Trudy). P. N. Lebedev Physics Institute [*A publication*]

Proc (Trudy) P N Lebedev Phys Inst ... Proceedings (Trudy). P. N. Lebedev Physics Institute [*A publication*]

ProCTS ...... Proceedings. College Theology Society [*A publication*]

Proc Turbomachinery Symp ... Proceedings. Turbomachinery Symposium [*A publication*]

Proc Turfgrass Sprinkler Irrig Conf ... Proceedings. Turfgrass Sprinkler Irrigation Conference [*A publication*]

PROCU .... Processing Unit

Proc UNESCO Conf Radioisot Sci Res ... Proceedings. UNESCO Conference on Radioisotopes in Scientific Research [*A publication*]

Proc Univ MD Nutr Conf Feed Mfr ... Proceedings. University of Maryland. Nutrition Conference for Feed Manufacturers [*A publication*]

Proc Univ MO Annu Conf Trace Subst Environ Health ... Proceedings. University of Missouri. Annual Conference on Trace Substances in Environmental Health [*A publication*]

Proc Univ Otago Med Sch ... Proceedings. University of Otago Medical School [*A publication*]

Proc USAID Ghana Agr Conf ... Proceedings. USAID [*United States Agency for International Development*]. Ghana Agriculture Conference [*A publication*]

Proc US Natl Mus ... Proceedings. United States National Museum [*A publication*]

Proc Ussher Soc ... Proceedings. Ussher Society [*A publication*]

Proc Utah Acad Sci ... Proceedings. Utah Academy of Sciences, Arts, and Letters [*A publication*]

Proc Utah Acad Sci Arts Lett ... Proceedings. Utah Academy of Sciences, Arts, and Letters [*A publication*]

PROCVAL ... Validation Procedures Library [*Social Security Administration*]

Proc Vertebr Pest Conf ... Proceedings. Vertebrate Pest Conference [*A publication*]

Proc Veterans Adm Spinal Cord Inj Conf ... Proceedings. Veterans Administration Spinal Cord Injury Conference [*A publication*]

Proc Vib Probl ... Proceedings of Vibration Problems [*A publication*]

Proc VIC Weeds Conf ... Proceedings. Victorian Weeds Science Society [*A publication*]

Proc Virchow-Pirquet Med Soc ... Proceedings. Virchow-Pirquet Medical Society [*A publication*]

Proc Wash Anim Nutr Conf ... Proceedings. Washington Animal Nutrition Conference [*A publication*]

Proc Wash State Univ Symp Particleboard ... Proceedings. Washington State University Symposium on Particleboard [*A publication*]

Proc Weed Soc NSW ... Proceedings. Weed Society of New South Wales [*A publication*]

Proc West Can Weed Control Conf ... Proceedings. Western Canadian Weed Control Conference [*A publication*]

Proc West Chapter Int Shade Tree Conf ... Proceedings. Western Chapter. International Shade Tree Conference [*A publication*]

Proc West Eur Conf Photosyn ... Proceedings. Western Europe Conference on Photosynthesis [*A publication*]

Proc West For Conserv Ass ... Proceedings. Western Forestry Conference. Western Forestry and Conservation Association [*A publication*]

Proc West Found Vertebr Zool ... Proceedings. Western Foundation of Vertebrate Zoology [*A publication*]

Proc West Pharmacol Soc ... Proceedings. Western Pharmacology Society [*A publication*]

Proc West Snow Conf ... Proceedings. Western Snow Conference [*A publication*]

Proc West Soc Weed Sci ... Proceedings. Western Society of Weed Science [*A publication*]

Proc West Virginia Acad Sci ... Proceedings. West Virginia. Academy of Science [*A publication*]

Proc Wis Hist Soc ... Proceedings. Wisconsin State Historical Society [*A publication*]

Proc Wld For Congr ... Proceedings. World Forestry Congress [*A publication*]

Proc World Congr Agr Res ... Proceedings. World Congress of Agricultural Research [*A publication*]

Proc World Congr Fertil Steril ... Proceedings. World Congress on Fertility and Sterility [*A publication*]

Proc World Congr Gastroenterol ... Proceedings. World Congress of Gastroenterology [*A publication*]

Proc World For Congr ... Proceedings. World Forestry Congress [*A publication*]

Proc World Pet Congr ... Proceedings. World Petroleum Congress [*A publication*]

Proc World Poultry Congr ... Proceedings. World Poultry Congress [*A publication*]

Proc W Va Acad Sci ... Proceedings. West Virginia Academy of Science [*A publication*]

Proc Yorks Geol Soc ... Proceedings. Yorkshire Geological Society [*England*] [*A publication*]

Proc Zool Soc (Calcutta) ... Proceedings. Zoological Society (Calcutta) [*A publication*]

Proc Zool Soc Lond ... Proceedings. Zoological Society of London [*A publication*]

PROD .... Office of Production [*National Security Agency*]

PROD .... Prisoner Rehabilitation on Discharge [*A publication*]

PROD .... Produce

PROD .... Product [*or Production*] (AABC)

PROD .... Professional Drivers Council for Safety and Health

PROD .... Professional Over-the-Road Drivers [*Part of Teamsters Union*]

PRODAC .... Programed Digital Automatic Control [*Data processing*]

PRODAN .... Propionyl(dimethylamino)naphthalene [*Organic chemistry*]

Prod Anim ... Produzione Animale [*A publication*]

PRODASE ...... Protein Database

PRODC ...... Production Command [*Army*]

Proden .... Proyecto de Desarrollo Nacional [*Project for National Development*] [*Chilean*] (PPW)

Prod Eng .... Product Engineering [*A publication*]

Prod Eng (Cleveland) ... Production Engineering (Cleveland) [*A publication*]

Prod Eng (Lond) ... Production Engineer (London) [*A publication*]

Prod Engng ... Production Engineering [*A publication*]

Prod Engr ... Production Engineer [*London*] [*A publication*]

Prod Finish ... Product Finishing [*Cincinnati*] [*A publication*]

Prod Finish (Cinci) ... Product Finishing (Cincinnati) [*A publication*]

Prod Finish (Cincinnati) ... Products Finishing (Cincinnati) [*A publication*]

Prod Finish (Lond) ... Product Finishing (London) [*A publication*]

Prod G Am J ... Producers Guild of America. Journal [*A publication*]

Prod Invent Manage ... Production and Inventory Management [*A publication*]

Prod and Inventory Manage ... Production and Inventory Management [*A publication*]

Prod Lait Mod ... Production Laitiere Moderne [*A publication*]

Prod Liability Int ... Product Liability International [*A publication*]

Prod Liab Int ... Product Liability International [*A publication*]

Prod Liab Rep ... Product Liability Reporter [*Commerce Clearing House*] (DLA)

Prod Manage ... Production Management [*A publication*]

Prod Marketing ... Produce Marketing [*A publication*]

Prod Miner Serv Fom Prod Miner Avulso ... Producao Mineral Servico de Fomento da Producao Mineral. Avulso [*A publication*]

Prod Miner Serv Fom Prod Miner Bol ... Producao Mineral Servico de Fomento da Producao Mineral. Boletim [*A publication*]

Prod Mkt .... Product Marketing [*A publication*]

Prod Mktg ... Product Marketing [*A publication*]

Prod Mon ... Producers Monthly [*United States*] [*A publication*]

Prodn J ...... Production Journal [*A publication*]

PRODON .... Production

PRO DOS ... Pro Dose [*For a Dose*] [*Pharmacy*]

Prod Pharm ... Produits Pharmaceutiques [*France*] [*A publication*]

Prod Probl Pharm ... Produits et Problemes Pharmaceutiques [*A publication*]

Prod Proj Trends Bldg ... Products, Projects, and Trends in Building [*A publication*]

Prod Publ Int Crop Impr Ass ... Production Publication. International Crop Improvement Association [*A publication*]

Prod Rev ... Producers' Review [*A publication*]

Prod with Safety ... Production with Safety [*A publication*]

Prod Tech (Osaka) ... Production and Technique (Osaka) [*Japan*] [*A publication*]

Prod Tech (Suita) ... Production and Technique (Suita) [*Japan*] [*A publication*]

Producers R ... Producers' Review [*A publication*]

Producers' Rev ... Producers' Review [*A publication*]

Product Eng ... Product Engineering [*A publication*]

Product et Gestion ... Production et Gestion [*A publication*]

Production ... Production Engineering [*A publication*]

Produits Pharm ... Produits et Problemes Pharmaceutiques [*A publication*]

PRODUTAS ... Proceed on Duty Assigned [*Military*]

PRODVAL ... Product Validation (MCD)

Prod Veg Cereale Plante Teh ... Productia Vegetala Cereale si Plante Tehnice [*A publication*]

Prod Veg Mec Agric ... Productia Vegetala. Mecanizarea Agriculturii [*A publication*]

Prod Yb FAO ... Production Yearbook FAO [*Food and Agriculture Organization*] [*A publication*]

Proefstn Akkerbouw Lelystad Versl Interprov Proeven ... Proefstation voor de Akkerbouw Lelystad. Verslagen van Interprovinciale Proeven [*A publication*]

Proefstn Akkerbouw (Wageningen) Versl Interprov Proeven ... Proefstation voor de Akkerbouw (Wageningen). Verslagen van Interprovinciale Proeven [*A publication*]

Proektn Nauchno-Issled Inst Ural Promstroiniiproekt Tr ... Proektnyi i Nauchno-Issledovatel'skii Institut "Ural'skii Promstroiniiproekt." Trudy [*A publication*]

Pro Engr ..... Professional Engineer [*A publication*]

Pro Ex .... Protein Exchange [*Dietetics*]

PROEXPA ... Promotora Espanola de Exportadores Alimentarios [*Trade association*] [*Barcelona, Spain*]

PROF .... Peace Research Organization Fund

PROF .... Profanity [*FBI standardized term*]

PROF .... Profession [*or Professional*]

PROF .... Professional Investors [*NASDAQ symbol*] (NQ)

PROF .... Professional Office System

PROF .... Professor

PROF .... Pupil Registering and Operational Filing [*Data processing*]

PROFAC ..... Propulsive Fluid Accumulator

Prof Admin ... Professional Administration [*A publication*]

PROFAGTRANS ... Proceed by First Available Government Transportation [*Military*]

Prof Builder & Apt Bus ... Professional Builder and Apartment Business [*A publication*]

Prof Builder/Apt Bus ... Professional Builder and Apartment Business [*A publication*]

Prof Burd ... Commemoratio Professorum Burdigalensium [*of Ausonius*] [*Classical studies*] (OCD)

Prof Corp Guide (P-H) ... Professional Corporation Guide [*Prentice-Hall, Inc.*] (DLA)

PROFCY ..... Proficiency

Prof Eng ..... Professional Engineer

Prof Eng (Pretoria) ... Professional Engineer (Pretoria) [*A publication*]

Prof Eng (Wash DC) ... Professional Engineer (Washington, DC) [*A publication*]

Professional Eng ... Professional Engineer [*A publication*]

Professions et Entr ... Professions et Entreprises [*A publication*]

PROFESSL ... Professional

Prof Geog ... Professional Geographer [*A publication*]

Prof Geologist ... Professional Geologist [*A publication*]

PROFILE .... Programed Functional Indices for Laboratory Evaluation [*RAND Corp.*]

PROFILE .... [*A*] programing language (CSR)

Profils Econ Nord-Pas-De-Calais ... Profils de l'Economie Nord-Pas-De-Calais [*A publication*]
Prof Inferm ... Professioni Infermieristiche [*A publication*]
PROFIT...... Program for Financed Insurance Techniques
PROFIT...... Programed Reviewing, Ordering, and Forecasting Inventory Technique
PROFIT...... Propulsion Flight Control Integration Technology (MCD)
PROFL...... Professional
Prof Med Assist ... Professional Medical Assistant [*A publication*]
Prof Nutr .... Professional Nutritionist [*A publication*]
PROFP........ Proficiency Pay [*Military*]
Prof Pap Geol Surv ... Professional Paper. [*US*] Geological Survey [*A publication*]
Prof Pap Ser Fla Dep Nat Resour Mar Res Lab ... Professional Papers Series. Florida Department of Natural Resources. Marine Research Laboratory [*A publication*]
Prof Pap US Geol Surv ... Professional Papers. United States Geological Survey [*A publication*]
Prof Print ... Professional Printer [*A publication*]
Prof Psycho ... Professional Psychology [*A publication*]
Prof Regulation N ... Professional Regulation News [*A publication*]
Prof Rpt...... Professional Report [*A publication*]
PROFS .... Professional Office System [*IBM Corp.*]
PROFS .... Prototype Regional Observation and Forecasting Service [*National Oceanic and Atmospheric Administration*]
Prof Saf ...... Professional Safety [*A publication*]
Prof Safety ... Professional Safety [*A publication*]
Prof Sanit Manage ... Professional Sanitation Management [*A publication*]
PROG .... Prognosis [*or Prognostication*] (AAG)
PROG .... Program (KSC)
PROG .... Programer [*or Programing*]
PROG .... Progress (AABC)
Prog .... Progressive [*A publication*]
PROG .... Progressive Corp. [*NASDAQ symbol*] (NQ)
Prog Aeronaut Sci ... Progress in Aeronautical Science [*A publication*]
Prog Aerosp Sci ... Progress in Aerospace Sciences [*A publication*]
Prog Agric ... Progresso Agricolo [*A publication*]
Prog Agric Ariz ... Progressive Agriculture in Arizona [*A publication*]
Prog Agric Vitic ... Progres Agricole et Viticole [*France*] [*A publication*]
Prog Agri Fr ... Progres Agricole de France [*A publication*]
Prog Allerg ... Progress in Allergy [*A publication*]
Prog Allergy ... Progress in Allergy [*A publication*]
Prog Anal At Spectrosc ... Progress in Analytical Atomic Spectroscopy [*A publication*]
Prog Anal Chem ... Progress in Analytical Chemistry [*A publication*]
Prog Androl ... Progres en Andrologie [*A publication*]
Prog Appl Mater Res ... Progress in Applied Materials Research [*A publication*]
Prog Arch ... Progressive Architecture [*A publication*]
Prog Astronaut Aeronaut ... Progress in Astronautics and Aeronautics [*A publication*]
Prog Astronaut Rocketry ... Progress in Astronautics and Rocketry [*A publication*]
Prog At Med ... Progress in Atomic Medicine [*A publication*]
Prog Batteries Sol Cell ... Progress in Batteries and Solar Cells [*A publication*]
Prog Biochem Biophys ... Progress in Biochemistry and Biophysics [*People's Republic of China*] [*A publication*]
Prog Biochem Pharmacol ... Progress in Biochemical Pharmacology [*A publication*]
Prog Biol Sci Relat Dermatol ... Progress in the Biological Sciences in Relation to Dermatology [*A publication*]
Prog Biomass Convers ... Progress in Biomass Conversion [*A publication*]
Prog Biometeorol ... Progress in Biometeorology [*A publication*]
Prog Biometeorol Div A ... Progress in Biometeorology. Division A. Progress in Human Biometeorology [*Netherlands*] [*A publication*]
Prog Bioorg Chem ... Progress in Bioorganic Chemistry [*A publication*]
Prog Biophys Biophys Chem ... Progress in Biophysics and Biophysical Chemistry [*A publication*]
Prog Biophys Mol Biol ... Progress in Biophysics and Molecular Biology [*A publication*]
Prog Biophys and Mol Biol ... Progress in Biophysics and Molecular Biology [*A publication*]
Prog Boron Chem ... Progress in Boron Chemistry [*A publication*]
Prog Bot..... Progress in Botany [*A publication*]
Prog Bot Fortschr Bot ... Progress in Botany-Fortschritt der Botanik [*A publication*]
Prog Brain Res ... Progress in Brain Research [*A publication*]
Prog Cancer Res Ther ... Progress in Cancer Research and Therapy [*A publication*]
Prog Cardiol ... Progress in Cardiology [*A publication*]
Prog Cardiovasc Dis ... Progress in Cardiovascular Diseases [*A publication*]
Prog Ceram Sci ... Progress in Ceramic Science [*A publication*]
Prog Chem Fats ... Progress in the Chemistry of Fats and Other Lipids [*A publication*]
Prog Chem Fats Other Lipids ... Progress in the Chemistry of Fats and Other Lipids [*A publication*]
Prog Chem Fibrinolysis Thrombolysis ... Progress in Chemical Fibrinolysis and Thrombolysis [*A publication*]
Prog Chem Toxicol ... Progress in Chemical Toxicology [*A publication*]

Prog Clin Biol Res ... Progress in Clinical and Biological Research [*A publication*]
Prog Clin Cancer ... Progress in Clinical Cancer [*A publication*]
Prog Clin Immunol ... Progress in Clinical Immunology [*A publication*]
Prog Clin Neurophysiol ... Progress in Clinical Neurophysiology [*A publication*]
Prog Clin Pathol ... Progress in Clinical Pathology [*A publication*]
Prog Colloid Polym Sci ... Progress in Colloid and Polymer Science [*A publication*]
Prog Cryog ... Progress in Cryogenics [*A publication*]
Prog Cryst Growth Charact ... Progress in Crystal Growth and Characterization [*A publication*]
Prog Cryst Phys ... Progress in Crystal Physics [*A publication*]
PROGDEV ... Program Device (KSC)
Prog Dielectr ... Progress in Dielectrics [*A publication*]
Prog Drug Metab ... Progress in Drug Metabolism [*A publication*]
Prog Drug Res ... Progress in Drug Research [*A publication*]
Prog Educ ... Progress in Education [*A publication*]
Prog Educ ... Progressive Education [*A publication*]
Prog Educ (Poona) ... Progress of Education (Poona) [*India*] [*A publication*]
Prog Elem Part Cosmic Ray Phys ... Progress in Elementary Particle and Cosmic Ray Physics [*A publication*]
Prog Energy Combust Sci ... Progress in Energy and Combustion Science [*A publication*]
Prog Explor Tuberc ... Progres de l'Exploration de la Tuberculose [*A publication*]
Prog Exp Pers Res ... Progress in Experimental Personality Research [*A publication*]
Prog Exp Tumor Res ... Progress in Experimental Tumor Research [*A publication*]
Prog Ex Tum ... Progress in Experimental Tumor Research [*A publication*]
Prog F .... Progressive Farmer and Farm Woman [*A publication*]
Prog Farmer West ... Progressive Farmer for the West [*A publication*]
Prog Farming ... Progressive Farming [*A publication*]
Prog Farming/Farmer ... Progressive Farming/Farmer [*A publication*]
Prog Fish-C ... Progressive Fish-Culturist [*A publication*]
Prog Fish-Cult ... Progressive Fish-Culturist [*A publication*]
Prog Food Nutr Sci ... Progress in Food and Nutrition Science [*A publication*]
Prog Fotogr (Barcelona) ... Progresso Fotografico (Barcelona) [*A publication*]
Prog Fotogr (Milan) ... Progresso Fotografico (Milan) [*A publication*]
Prog Gastroenterol ... Progress in Gastroenterology [*A publication*]
Prog Geogr ... Progress in Geography [*A publication*]
Prog Grocer ... Progressive Grocer [*A publication*]
Prog Gynecol ... Progress in Gynecology [*A publication*]
Prog Heat Mass Transf ... Progress in Heat and Mass Transfer [*A publication*]
Prog Heat Mass Transfer ... Progress in Heat and Mass Transfer [*A publication*]
Prog Hematol ... Progress in Hematology [*A publication*]
Prog Hemostasis Thromb ... Progress in Hemostasis and Thrombosis [*A publication*]
Prog Hemost Thromb ... Progress in Hemostasis and Thrombosis [*A publication*]
Prog High Polym ... Progress in High Polymers [*A publication*]
Prog High Temp Phys Chem ... Progress in High Temperature Physics and Chemistry [*A publication*]
Prog Histochem Cytochem ... Progress in Histochemistry and Cytochemistry [*A publication*]
Prog Hort ... Progressive Horticulture [*India*] [*A publication*]
Prog Hortic ... Progressive Horticulture [*A publication*]
Prog Immunobiol Stand ... Progress in Immunobiological Standardization [*A publication*]
Prog Ind Microbiol ... Progress in Industrial Microbiology [*A publication*]
Prog Infrared Spectrosc ... Progress in Infrared Spectroscopy [*A publication*]
Prog Inorg Chem ... Progress in Inorganic Chemistry [*A publication*]
Prog Instr Bul ... Programmed Instruction Bulletin [*A publication*]
Prog Instr & Ed Tech ... Programmed Instruction and Educational Technology [*A publication*]
Prog Learn ... Programmed Learning and Educational Technology [*A publication*]
Prog Learn Disabil ... Progress in Learning Disabilities [*A publication*]
PROGLIB... Production Program Library [*Social Security Administration*]
Prog Lipid Res ... Progress in Lipid Research [*A publication*]
Prog Liver Dis ... Progress in Liver Diseases [*A publication*]
Prog Low Temp Phys ... Progress in Low Temperature Physics [*A publication*]
PRO GM ..... Pro Grand Master [*Freemasonry*]
Prog Mater Sci ... Progress in Materials Science [*A publication*]
Prog Mat Sc ... Progress in Materials Science [*A publication*]
Prog Med ... Progres Medical [*A publication*]
Prog Med Chem ... Progress in Medicinal Chemistry [*A publication*]
Prog Med Ge ... Progress in Medical Genetics [*A publication*]
Prog Med Genet ... Progress in Medical Genetics [*A publication*]
Prog Med (Istanbul) ... Progressus Medicinae (Istanbul) [*A publication*]
Prog Med Parasitol Jpn ... Progress in Medical Parasitology in Japan [*A publication*]
Prog Med Psychosom ... Progres en Medecine Psychosomatique [*A publication*]

Prog Med (Rome) ... Progresso Medico (Rome) [*A publication*]
Prog Med (Tokyo) ... Progress in Medicine (Tokyo) [*A publication*]
Prog Med Vi ... Progress in Medical Virology [*A publication*]
Prog Med Virol ... Progress in Medical Virology [*A publication*]
PROGMG ... Programing
Prog Mol Subcell Biol ... Progress in Molecular and Subcellular Biology [*A publication*]
Prog Neurobiol ... Progress in Neurobiology [*A publication*]
Prog Neurol Psychiatry ... Progress in Neurology and Psychiatry [*A publication*]
Prog Neurol Surg ... Progress in Neurological Surgery [*A publication*]
Prog Neuropathol ... Progress in Neuropathology [*A publication*]
Prog Neuro-Psychopharmacol ... Progress in Neuro-Psychopharmacology [*A publication*]
PROGNO .... Prognosen-Trends-Entwicklungen [*Forecasts-Trends-Developments*] [*Society for Business Information*] [*Munich, West Germany*] [*Information service*]   (EISS)
Prog Nucleic Acid Res ... Progress in Nucleic Acid Research [*A publication*]
Prog Nucleic Acid Res Mol Biol ... Progress in Nucleic Acid Research and Molecular Biology [*A publication*]
Prog Nucl Energy ... Progress in Nuclear Energy [*England*] [*A publication*]
Prog Nucl Energy Anal Chem ... Progress in Nuclear Energy. Analytical Chemistry [*A publication*]
Prog Nucl Energy Ser 1 ... Progress in Nuclear Energy. Series 1. Physics and Mathematics [*A publication*]
Prog Nucl Energy Ser 2 ... Progress in Nuclear Energy. Series 2. Reactors [*A publication*]
Prog Nucl Energy Ser 3 ... Progress in Nuclear Energy. Series 3. Process Chemistry [*A publication*]
Prog Nucl Energy Ser 4 ... Progress in Nuclear Energy. Series 4. Technology, Engineering, and Safety [*A publication*]
Prog Nucl Energy Ser 5 ... Progress in Nuclear Energy. Series 5. Metallurgy and Fuels [*A publication*]
Prog Nucl Energy Ser 6 ... Progress in Nuclear Energy. Series 6 [*England*] [*A publication*]
Prog Nucl Energy Ser 8 ... Progress in Nuclear Energy. Series 8. The Economics of Nuclear Power Including Administration and Law [*A publication*]
Prog Nucl Energy Ser 9 ... Progress in Nuclear Energy. Series 9 [*England*] [*A publication*]
Prog Nucl Energy Ser 10 ... Progress in Nuclear Energy. Series 10. Law and Administration [*A publication*]
Prog Nucl Energy Ser 11 ... Progress in Nuclear Energy. Series 11. Plasma Physics and Thermonuclear Research [*A publication*]
Prog Nucl Energy Ser 12 ... Progress in Nuclear Energy. Series 12. Health Physics [*A publication*]
Prog Nucl Energy Ser VII Med Sci ... Progress in Nuclear Energy. Series VII. Medical Sciences [*A publication*]
Prog Nucl Magn Reson Spectrosc ... Progress in Nuclear Magnetic Resonance Spectroscopy [*A publication*]
Prog Nucl Med ... Progress in Nuclear Medicine [*A publication*]
Prog Nucl Phys ... Progress in Nuclear Physics [*A publication*]
Prog Nucl Tech Instrum ... Progress in Nuclear Techniques and Instrumentation [*Netherlands*] [*A publication*]
Prog Obstet Gynecol ... Progres en Obstetrique et Gynecologie [*A publication*]
Prog Oceanogr ... Progress in Oceanography [*A publication*]
PROGOFOP ... Program of Operation [*Data processing*]
Prog Ophtalmol ... Progres en Ophtalmologie [*A publication*]
Prog Opt .... Progress in Optics [*A publication*]
Prog Org Chem ... Progress in Organic Chemistry [*A publication*]
Prog Org Coat ... Progress in Organic Coatings [*A publication*]
Prog Org Coatings ... Progress in Organic Coatings [*A publication*]
Prog Oto-Rhino-Laryngol ... Progres en Oto-Rhino-Laryngologie [*A publication*]
Prog Part Nucl Phys ... Progress in Particle and Nuclear Physics [*England*] [*A publication*]
Prog Pediatr Hematol/Oncol ... Progress in Pediatric Hematology/Oncology [*A publication*]
Prog Pediatr Pueric ... Progresos de Pediatria y Puericultura [*A publication*]
Prog Pediatr Radiol ... Progress in Pediatric Radiology [*Switzerland*] [*A publication*]
Prog Pediatr Surg ... Progress in Pediatric Surgery [*A publication*]
Prog Perfum Cosmet ... Progressive Perfumery and Cosmetics [*A publication*]
Prog Photogr ... Progress in Photography [*A publication*]
Prog Phys ... Progress of Physics [*East Germany*] [*A publication*]
Prog Physiol Psychol ... Progress in Physiological Psychology [*A publication*]
Prog Physiol Sci (Engl Transl Usp Fiziol Nauk) ... Progress in Physiological Sciences (English Translation of Uspekhi Fiziologicheskikh Nauk) [*A publication*]
Prog Phytochem ... Progress in Phytochemistry [*A publication*]
Prog Plast ... Progressive Plastics [*A publication*]
Prog Polym Sci ... Progress in Polymer Science [*A publication*]
Prog Powder Metall ... Progress in Powder Metallurgy [*A publication*]
Prog Protozool Proc Int Congr Protozool ... Progress in Protozoology. Proceedings. International Congress on Protozoology [*A publication*]
Prog Psychiatr Drug Treat ... Progress in Psychiatric Drug Treatment [*A publication*]

Prog Psychobiol Physiol Psychol ... Progress in Psychobiology and Physiological Psychology [*A publication*]
Prog Quantum Electron ... Progress in Quantum Electronics [*A publication*]
Prog Radiat Ther ... Progress in Radiation Therapy [*A publication*]
Progr Agr ... Progresso Agricolo [*A publication*]
Progr Agr Ariz ... Progressive Agriculture in Arizona [*A publication*]
Progr Agr Vitic ... Progres Agricole et Viticole [*A publication*]
Program Autom Libr Inf Syst ... Program. Automated Library and Information Systems [*England*] [*A publication*]
Program and Comput Software ... Programming and Computer Software [*A publication*]
Program Learn and Educ Technol ... Programmed Learning and Educational Technology [*A publication*]
Programmed Learning ... Programmed Learning and Educational Technology [*A publication*]
Programming and Comput Software ... Programming and Computer Software [*A publication*]
Program News Comput Libr ... Program. News of Computers in Libraries [*A publication*]
Program Notes Assoc Univ Programs Health Adm ... Program Notes. Association of University Programs in Health Administration [*A publication*]
Progr Bull Alberta Univ Ext Dept ... Progress Bulletin. Alberta University Extension Department [*A publication*]
Progr Card ... Progress in Cardiovascular Diseases [*A publication*]
Progr Contr Eng ... Progress in Control Engineering [*A publication*]
Progr Coop Centroamer Mejor Maiz ... Programa Cooperativo Centroamericano para el Mejoramiento del Maiz [*A publication*]
Prog React Kinet ... Progress in Reaction Kinetics [*A publication*]
Prog Rech Cancer ... Progres dans les Recherches sur le Cancer [*A publication*]
Prog Rech Exp Tumeurs ... Progres de la Recherche Experimentale des Tumeurs [*A publication*]
Prog Rech Pharm ... Progres des Recherches Pharmaceutiques [*A publication*]
Prog Rep Ariz Exp Stn ... Progress Report. Arizona Experiment Station [*A publication*]
Prog Rep Clovers Spec Purpose Legumes Res ... Progress Report. Clovers and Special Legumes Research [*A publication*]
Prog Rep Colo Exp Stn ... Progress Report. Colorado Experiment Station [*A publication*]
Prog Rep Exp Stns (Tanzania) ... Progress Reports. Experiment Stations (Tanzania) [*A publication*]
Prog Rep Minist Agric Fish Fd Exp Husb Fms Exp Hort Stns ... Progress Report. Ministry of Agriculture, Fisheries, and Food. Experimental Husbandry Farms and Experimental Horticulture Stations [*A publication*]
Prog Rep Nucl Energy Res Jpn ... Progress Report. Nuclear Energy Research in Japan [*A publication*]
Prog Reprod Biol ... Progress in Reproductive Biology [*A publication*]
Prog Rep Texas Agric Exp Stn ... Progress Report. Texas Agricultural Experiment Station [*A publication*]
Prog Res .... Progress thru Research [*A publication*]
Progres Arch ... Progressive Architecture [*A publication*]
Progres Ed ... Progressive Education [*A publication*]
Prog Res Emphysema Chronic Bronchitis ... Progress in Research in Emphysema and Chronic Bronchitis [*A publication*]
Progres Med (Paris) ... Progres Medical (Paris) [*A publication*]
Progreso Med (Habana) ... Progreso Medico (Habana) [*A publication*]
Prog Respir Res ... Progress in Respiration Research [*A publication*]
Progres Scientif ... Progres Scientifique [*A publication*]
Progressive Archit ... Progressive Architecture [*A publication*]
Progress in Math ... Progress in Mathematics [*A publication*]
Progress Organic Coatings ... Progress in Organic Coatings [*A publication*]
Progress Phytochem ... Progress in Phytochemistry [*A publication*]
Progressv ... Progressive [*A publication*]
Progres Techn ... Progres Technique [*A publication*]
Progres Vet ... Progres Veterinaire [*A publication*]
Progr Hum Geogr ... Progress in Human Geography. International Review of Current Research [*A publication*]
Progr Mater Sci ... Progress in Materials Science [*A publication*]
Progr Math (Allahabad) ... Progress of Mathematics (Allahabad) [*A publication*]
Progr Nucl Energy Ser III Process Chem ... Progress in Nuclear Energy. Series III. Process Chemistry [*A publication*]
Progr Nucl Energy Ser II Reactors ... Progress in Nuclear Energy. Series II. Reactors [*A publication*]
Progr Nucl Energy Ser I Phys Math ... Progress in Nuclear Energy. Series I. Physics and Mathematics [*A publication*]
Progr Nucl Energy Ser IV Technol Eng ... Progress in Nuclear Energy. Series IV. Technology and Engineering [*A publication*]
Progr Nucl Energy Ser VI ... Progress in Nuclear Energy. Series VI. Biological Sciences [*A publication*]
Progr Nucl Energy Ser VIII Econ ... Progress in Nuclear Energy. Series VIII. Economics [*A publication*]
Progr Nucl Energy Ser V Met Fuels ... Progress in Nuclear Energy. Series V. Metallurgy and Fuels [*A publication*]
Progr Nucl Energy Ser XI Plasma Phys Thermonucl Res ... Progress in Nuclear Energy. Series XI. Plasma Physics and Thermonuclear Research [*A publication*]

Progr Nucl Energy Ser X Law Admin ... Progress in Nuclear Energy. Series X. Law and Administration [*A publication*]
Progr Offic Journee Interreg Recolte Mec Mais-Grain ... Programme Officiel. Journee Interregionale de Recolte Mechanique du Mais-Grain [*A publication*]
Progr Plast ... Progressive Plastics [*A publication*]
Progr Polymer Sci ... Progress in Polymer Science [*A publication*]
Progr Powder Met ... Progress in Powder Metallurgy [*A publication*]
Progr Rep Cereal Breed Lab ... Progress Report. Cereal Breeding Laboratory [*A publication*]
Progr Rep Colo State Univ Agr Exp Sta ... Progress Report. Colorado State University. Agricultural Experiment Station [*A publication*]
Progr Rep Conn Agr Exp Sta ... Progress Report. Connecticut Agricultural Experiment Station [*A publication*]
Progr Rep Idaho Agr Res ... Progress Report. Idaho Agricultural Research [*A publication*]
Progr Rep KY Agr Exp Sta ... Progress Report. Kentucky Agricultural Experiment Station [*A publication*]
Progr Rep PA Agric Exp Sta ... Progress Report. Pennsylvania State University. Agricultural Experiment Station [*A publication*]
Progr Rep PA State Univ Agr Exp Sta ... Progress Report. Pennsylvania State University. Agricultural Experiment Station [*A publication*]
Progr Rep Ser Ala Agr Exp Sta ... Progress Report Series. Alabama Agricultural Experiment Station [*A publication*]
Progr Rep Tex Agr Exp Sta ... Progress Report. Texas Agricultural Experiment Station [*A publication*]
Progr Rep Tohoku Agr Exp Sta ... Progress Report. Tohoku Agricultural Experiment Station [*A publication*]
Progr Rep Univ Nebr Coll Agr Dept Agr Econ ... Progress Report. University of Nebraska. College of Agriculture. Department of Agricultural Economics [*A publication*]
Progr Rev For Prod Lab (Ottawa) ... Program Review. Forest Products Laboratory (Ottawa) [*A publication*]
Progr Rev For Prod Lab (Vancouver) ... Program Review. Forest Products Laboratory (Vancouver) [*British Columbia, Canada*] [*A publication*]
Progr Rubber Technol ... Progress of Rubber Technology [*A publication*]
Progr Stiintei ... Progresele Stiintei [*A publication*]
Prog Sci ... Progres Scientifique [*France*] [*A publication*]
Prog Sci Technol Rare Earths ... Progress in the Science and Technology of the Rare Earths [*A publication*]
Prog Semicond ... Progress in Semiconductors [*A publication*]
Prog Sep Purif ... Progress in Separation and Purification [*A publication*]
Prog Solid State Chem ... Progress in Solid State Chemistry [*England*] [*A publication*]
Prog Stereochem ... Progress in Stereochemistry [*A publication*]
Prog Surf Membr Sci ... Progress in Surface and Membrane Science [*A publication*]
Prog Surf Sci ... Progress in Surface Science [*A publication*]
Prog Surg ... Progress in Surgery [*A publication*]
Prog Tech ... Progres Technique [*A publication*]
Prog Technol ... Progress in Technology [*United States*] [*A publication*]
Prog Tekhnol Mashinostr ... Progressivnaya Tekhnologiya Mashinostroeniya [*A publication*]
Prog Ter ... Progresso Terapeutico [*A publication*]
Prog Theor Biol ... Progress in Theoretical Biology [*A publication*]
Prog Theor Org Chem ... Progress in Theoretical Organic Chemistry [*A publication*]
Prog Theor Phys ... Progress of Theoretical Physics [*A publication*]
Prog Theor Phys Suppl ... Progress of Theoretical Physics. Supplement [*A publication*]
Prog Thin-Layer Chromatogr Relat Methods ... Progress in Thin-Layer Chromatography and Related Methods [*A publication*]
Prog T Phys ... Progress of Theoretical Physics [*A publication*]
PROGVAL ... Validation Program Library [*Social Security Administration*]
Progve Fmg ... Progressive Farming [*A publication*]
Prog Vet ... Progresso Veterinario [*A publication*]
Prog Virol Med ... Progres en Virologie Medicale [*A publication*]
Prog Water Technol ... Progress in Water Technology [*A publication*]
PROH ... Prohibit
PROH ... Prohibition [*FBI standardized term*]
PROH ... Promoting Health [*A publication*]
Prohib ... Prohibited
PROI ... President of the Royal Institute of Oil Painters [*British*]
PRO-IF ... Personal Radio Operators International Federation [*Formerly, ARC*] (EA)
PROIMREP ... Proceed Immediately - Report for Purpose Indicated [*Military*]
Pro Indian Soc of Internat L ... Proceedings of the Conference. Indian Society of International Law [*New Delhi, India*] (DLA)
Proizvod Elektrostali ... Proizvodstvo Elektrostali [*A publication*]
Proizvod Issled Stalei Splavov ... Proizvodstvo i Issledovanie Stalei i Splavov [*A publication*]
Proizvod Koksa ... Proizvodstvo Koksa [*A publication*]
Proizvod Krupnykh Mash ... Proizvodstvo Krupnykh Mashin [*A publication*]
Proizvod Nauchno-Issled Inst Inzh Izyskaniyam Stroit Tr ... Proizvodstvennyi i Nauchno-Issledovatel'skii Institut po Inzhenernym Izyskaniyam v Stroitel'stve. Trudy [*A publication*]
Proizvod Smaz Mater ... Proizvodstvo Smazochnykh Materialov [*A publication*]

Proizvod Stochnye Vody ... Proizvodstvennye Stochnye Vody [*A publication*]
Proizvod Svarnykh Besshovnykh Trub ... Proizvodstvo Svarnykh i Besshovnykh Trub [*A publication*]
Proizvod Trub ... Proizvodstvo Trub [*A publication*]
Proizv Shin RTI i ATI ... Proizvodstvo Shin Rezinotekhnicheskikh i Asbestotekhnicheskikh Izdelii [*A publication*]
PROJ ... Project (AFM)
PROJ ... Projectile (AFM)
PROJ ... Projector
Proj Civ Trav Econ ... Projet. Civilisation, Travail, Economie [*France*] [*A publication*]
PROJECT ... Project Engineering Control
Project Hist Biobibliog ... Project for Historical Biobibliography [*A publication*]
Project IUCN/Wld Wildl Fund ... Project. International Union for Conservation of Nature. World Wildlife Fund. Joint Project Operations [*A publication*]
PROJID ... Project Identification [*Data processing*]
PROJMGR ... Project Manager
PROJMGRASWS ... Project Manager, Antisubmarine Warfare Systems
PROJMGRFBM ... Project Manager, Fleet Ballistic Missile [*Navy*]
PROJMGRSMS ... Project Manager, Surface Missile Systems [*Navy*]
Proj Rep Victoria Minist Conserv Environ Stud Program ... Victoria. Ministry for Conservation. Environmental Studies Program. Project Report [*A publication*]
PROL ... Priority Requirement Objective List (AFM)
PROL ... Prologue
PROLAMAT ... Programing Languages for Machine Tools [*Conference*]
PROLAN ... Processed Language [*Data processing*]
Prolif ... Proliferative [*or Proliferation*]
PROLLAP ... Professional Library Literature Acquisition Program
PRO LOC et TEM ... Pro Loco et Tempore [*For the Place and Time*] [*Latin*] (ROG)
PRO LOC et TEM ... Pro Loco et Tempore [*For the Place and Time*] [*Latin*] (ROG)
PROLOG ... Program Logistics (NG)
PROLOG ... Programing in Logic [*Programing language*] [*1970*]
PROLT ... Procurement Lead Time
P Rom ... Papers in Romance [*A publication*]
PROM ... Passive Range of Motion [*Medicine*]
PROM ... Pockels Readout Optical Modulator
PROM ... Premature [*or Prolonged*] Rupture of Membranes [*Gynecology*]
PROM ... Program, Resources, Objectives, Management [*Air Force Systems Command technique*]
PROM ... Programable Read-Only Memory [*Data processing*]
PROM ... Progressive Range of Motion [*Medicine*]
PROM ... Promenade [*Maps and charts*]
PROM ... Prominent
Prom ... Promissory (DLA)
PROM ... Promontory
PROM ... Promote [*or Promotion*] (AFM)
PROM ... Promulgate (AABC)
Pro-MACE ... Prednisone, Methotrexate with Leucovorin, Adriamycin, Cyclophosphamide, Epipodophyllin [*Etoposide, VP-16*] [*Antineoplastic drug regimen*]
Prom Aerod ... Promyshlennaya Aerodinamika [*USSR*] [*A publication*]
PROMAP ... Program for the Refinement of the Materiel Acquisition Process [*Army*] (AABC)
Prom Energ ... Promyshlennaya Energetika [*A publication*]
Pro Met ... Pro Metal [*A publication*]
Promet-Meteorol Fortbild ... Promet-Meteorologische Fortbildung [*West Germany*] [*A publication*]
PROMEX ... Productivity Measurement Experiment [*National Bureau of Standards*]
PROMIM ... Programable Multiple Ion Monitor
PROMIS ... Problem-Oriented Medical Information System [*Computerized patient-management system*]
PROMIS ... [*A*] Process Management and Information System [*I. P. Sharp Associates Ltd.*] [*Software package*]
PROMIS ... Project-Oriented Management Information System
PROMIS ... Prosecutor's Management Information System [*Law Enforcement Assistance Administration*]
PROML ... Promulgate
PROMO ... Promotion [*Slang*] (DSUE)
Promoclim A Actual Equip Tech ... Promoclim A. Actualites, Equipement, Technique [*France*] [*A publication*]
Promoclim E ... Promoclim E. Etudes Thermiques et Aerauliques [*A publication*]
Promoclim Ind Therm Aerauliques ... Promoclim. Industries Thermiques et Aerauliques [*A publication*]
Promot Dent ... Promotion Dentaire [*A publication*]
PROMPT ... Production, Reviewing, Organizing, and Monitoring of Performance Techniques (BUR)
PROMPT ... Program Monitoring and Planning Techniques (IEEE)
PROMPT ... Program to Record Official Mail Point-to-Point Times [*Postal Service program*]
PROMPT ... Project Management and Production Team Technique [*Data processing*]

PROMPT .... Project Reporting Organization and Management Planning Technique
PROMS ...... Procurement Management System (MCD)
PROMS ...... Program Monitoring System (MCD)
PROMS ...... Projectile Measurement System [*Data processing*] [*Army*]
Promst Arm ... Promyshlennost Armenii [*A publication*]
Prom-st Arm Sov Nar Khoz Arm SSR Tekh-Ekon Byull ... Promyshlennost Armenii. Sovet Narodnogo Khozyajstva Armyanskoj SSR. Tekhniko-Ekonomicheskij Byulleten [*A publication*]
Promst Beloruss ... Promyshlennost Belorussii [*A publication*]
Prom-st Khim Reaktivov Osobo Chist Veshchestv ... Promyshlennost Khimicheskikh Reaktivov i Osobo Chistykh Veshchestv [*USSR*] [*A publication*]
Promst Khim Reakt Osobo Chist Veshchestv ... Promyshlennost Khimicheskikh Reaktivov i Osobo Chistykh Veshchestv [*A publication*]
Prom-st Org Khim ... Promyshlennost Organicheskoi Khimii [*USSR*] [*A publication*]
PROMT....... Precision Optimized Measurement Time [*Spectroscopy*]
PROMT....... Predicasts Overviews of Marketing and Technology [*Business database*]
PROMT....... Programable Miniature Message Terminal (MCD)
Prom Teplotekh ... Promyshlennaya Teplotekhnika [*Ukrainian SSR*] [*A publication*]
PROMUS .... Provincial-Municipal Simulator [*Computer-based urban management system*]
PROMY ...... Promissory (ROG)
Prom Zagryaz Vodoemov ... Promyshlennye Zagryazneniya Vodoemov [*A publication*]
PRON .... Patriotyczny Ruch Odrodzenia Narodowego [*Patriotic Movement for National Rebirth*] [*Warsaw, Poland*]
PRON .... Procurement Request Order Number [*Army*] (AABC)
PRON .... Pronation
PRON .... Pronominal (ADA)
PRON .... Pronoun
PRON .... Pronounced
PRON .... Pronunciation (ROG)
Pro Nat ...... Pro Natura [*A publication*]
Pro-Nica.... Professionals - Nicaragua (EA)
PRONTO .... Program for Numeric Tool Operation [*Data processing*]
PRONTO .... Programable Network Telecommunications Operating System
prooem ...... Prooemium (BJA)
PROOF .... Precision Recording (Optical) of Fingerprints
PROOF .... Projected Return on Open Office Facilities [*Computer program*]
proOLMC ... Pro-Opiolipomelanocortin [*Endocrinology*]
PROP.......... Performance Review for Operating Programs (BUR)
PROP.......... Pilot Repair Overhaul and Provisioning (MUGU)
PROP.......... Planetary Rocket Ocean Platform
PROP.......... Prerelease Orientation Program [*Reformatory program*]
PROP.......... Preservation of the Rights of Prisoners [*An association*] [*British*]
PROP.......... Production Operators [*NASDAQ symbol*] (NQ)
PROP.......... Profit Rating of Projects
PROP.......... Propaganda (AFM)
PROP.......... Propellant (KSC)
PROP.......... Propeller
PROP.......... Proper
PROP.......... Propertius [*Roman poet, c. 29BC*] [*Classical studies*] (ROG)
PROP.......... Property
Prop .... Property [*A publication*]
PROP.......... Property Release Option Program [*HUD*]
PROP.......... Proportional (KSC)
PROP.......... Proposal (AAG)
PROP.......... Proposed (AFM)
PROP.......... Proposition
PROP.......... Proprietor
PROP.......... Propulsion (AAG)
PROP.......... Propylthiouracil [*Also, PT, PTU*] [*Thyroid inhibitor*]
PROPA ...... Propagation (FAAC)
PROPAC .... Progressive Political Action Committee (EA)
PROPAC .... Prospective Payment Assessment Commission [*Washington, DC*] (EGAO)
PROPAKASIA ... International Food Processing and Packaging Technology Exhibition and Conference for South East Asia (TSPED)
PROPAL..... Proportional
PRO-PAY ... Proficiency Pay [*Military*]
Prop & Comp ... Property and Compensation Reports (DLA)
Prop & Comp R ... Property and Compensation Reports (DLA)
Propellants Explos ... Propellants and Explosives [*A publication*]
PROPH ...... Prophylactic
PROPL....... Proportional
Prop Law.... Property Lawyer [*1826-30*] (DLA)
Prop Law Bull ... Property Law Bulletin (DLA)
Prop Law NS ... Property Lawyer, New Series [*England*] (DLA)
PROPLING ... Propelling
PROPLOSS... Propagation Loss (NVT)
PROPN ...... Proportion (MSA)
PROPON .... Proportion (ROG)
PROPR .... Proprietary (ROG)

PROPR .... Proprietor
Propr Agric ... Propriete Agricole [*A publication*]
PROPRE..... Property Press (DLA)
PROPRSS ... Proprietress (ROG)
PROPS .... Properties
PROPS .... Proprietors
PROPTRY... Proprietary [*Freight*]
PROPUL ..... Propulsion
PROR.......... Predicted Orbit
PRORA .... Programs for Research on Romance Authors
PRO RAT AET ... Pro Ratione Aetatis [*According to Age*] [*Pharmacy*]
PrOrChr ...... Proche-Orient Chretien [*Jerusalem*] [*A publication*]
PRO RECT ... Pro Recto [*Rectal*] [*Pharmacy*]
PROREP..... Proceed Ship, Command Station Reporting Duty or Purpose Indicated [*Military*]
Pr O S......... Princeton Oriental Series [*A publication*]
PROS.......... Professional Reactor Operator Society (EA)
PROS.......... Proscenium [*Theater term*] (DSUE)
PROS...... Prosecution (ROG)
PROS.......... Prosody
Pros............ Prospetti [*A publication*]
PROS.......... Prosthetic (AABC)
PROS.......... Prostitute (DSUE)
PROS.......... Prostrate
PROSAM ... Programed Single-Axis Mount [*Military camera*]
Pros Atty .... Prosecuting Attorney (DLA)
PRosC .... Rosemont College, Rosemont, PA [*Library symbol*] [*Library of Congress*] (LCLS)
PROSE .... Problem Solution Engineering [*Programing language*] [*Data processing*] (CSR)
PROSECON ... Prosecution (ROG)
PROSI .... Procedure Sign [*Aviation*] (FAAC)
PROSI .... Public Relations Office of the Sugar Industry
PROSIG...... Procedure Signal [*Navy*]
PROSIGN ... Procedure Sign [*Military*] (AABC)
PROSIM .... Production System Simulator [*Data processing*]
PROSINE.... Procedure Sign [*Military*]
Pro Soc Water Treat Exam ... Proceedings. Society for Water Treatment and Examination [*A publication*]
Prosop Att ... Prosopographia Attica [*A publication*] (OCD)
prosp.......... Prospectively (DLA)
PROSPECT ... Proponent Sponsored Engineer Corps Training [*Army Corps of Engineers*]
Prosp R ...... Prospective Review [*A publication*]
PROSPRO ... Process Systems Program
Pr Osr Badaw-Rozwoj Elektron Prozniowej ... Prace Osrodka Badawczo-Rozwojowego Elektroniki Prozniowej [*A publication*]
Pr Osrodka Badawczo-Rozwojowego Przetwornikow Obrazu ... Prace Osrodka Badawczo-Rozwojowego Przetwornikow Obrazu [*A publication*]
Pr Osrodka Badaw Rozwojowego Elektron Prozniowej ... Prace Osrodka Badawczo-Rozwojowego Elektroniki Prozniowej [*A publication*]
PROST .... Prostitute [*or Prostitution*] [*FBI standardized term*]
Prostagland ... Prostaglandins [*A publication*]
Prostaglandins Med ... Prostaglandins and Medicine [*A publication*]
PROSTH...... Prosthesis
Prosthet and Orthotics Int ... Prosthetics and Orthotics International [*A publication*]
Prosthet Orthot Int ... Prosthetics and Orthotics International [*A publication*]
PROSY .... People's Republic of South Yemen (BJA)
PROT.......... Protect [*or Protection*] (MSA)
PROT.......... Protective Corp. [*NASDAQ symbol*] (NQ)
PROT.......... Protein
PROT.......... Protest (ROG)
PROT.......... Protestant
Prot .... Protestantismo [*Rome*] [*A publication*]
PROT.......... Protinus [*Speedily*] [*Pharmacy*]
Prot .... Protocol (DLA)
PROT.......... Prototype
PROT.......... Protractor (AAG)
Prot Aer ...... Protection Aerienne [*A publication*]
PROTAP..... Professional Opportunities through Academic Partnership [*National War College*]
PROTAP..... Protonotary Apostolic [*Roman Catholic*]
Prot Civ Secur Ind ... Protection Civile et Securite Industrielle [*A publication*]
Prot CJ....... Protocol on the Statute of the European Communities Court of Justice (DLA)
Prot Coat Met ... Protective Coatings on Metals [*A publication*]
PROTCT..... Protective (AAG)
PROTECON ... Process and Test Control [*Pendar Technical Association Ltd.*] [*Software package*]
PROTECT ... Probabilities Recall Optimizing the Employment of Calibration Time (KSC)
Protein Nucl Acid Enzyme ... Protein Nucleic Acid Enzyme [*A publication*]
Protein Synth Ser Adv ... Protein Syntheses: A Series of Advances [*A publication*]
PRO TEM ... Pro Tempore [*For the Time Being*] [*Latin*]
PRO TEM et LOC ... Pro Tempore et Loco [*For the Time and Place*] [*Latin*] (ROG)

PRO TEM et LOC ... Pro Tempore et Loco [*For the Time and Place*] [*Latin*] (ROG)
Prot Epis His M ... Protestant Episcopal Church. Historical Magazine [*A publication*]
Protes Dent ... Protesista Dental [*A publication*]
Protet Stomatol ... Protetyka Stomatologiczna [*A publication*]
PROTEUS ... [*A*] programing language (CSR)
PROTEUS ... Propulsion Research and Open Water Testing of Experimental Underwater Systems (MCD)
PROTHROM ... Prothrombin [*Hematology*]
Protides Biol Fluids Proc Colloq ... Protides of the Biological Fluids. Proceedings of the Colloquium [*Belgium*] [*A publication*]
Protides Biol Fluids Proc Colloq (Bruges) ... Protides of the Biological Fluids. Proceedings of the Colloquium (Bruges) [*A publication*]
PROTIMEREP ... Proceed in Time Report Not Later Than [*Hour and/or date indicated*] [*Military*]
Prot Met ..... Protection of Metals [*A publication*]
Prot Metals ... Protection of Metals [*A publication*]
Prot Met (USSR) ... Protection of Metals (Union of Soviet Socialist Republics) [*A publication*]
PROTN .... Procedure Turn [*Aviation*] (FAAC)
PROTO .... Protoporphyrin [*Hematology*]
PROTO .... Prototype (KSC)
Protok Fischereitech ... Protokolle zur Fischereitechnik [*A publication*]
Prot PI .... Protocol on Privileges and Immunities of the European Economic Community (DLA)
PROTR .... Protractor (MSA)
Protr .... Protrepticus [*of Clemens Alexandrinus*] [*Classical studies*] (OCD)
Prot Vitae ... Protectio Vitae [*A publication*]
Proudf Land Dec ... United States Land Decisions [*Proudfit*] (DLA)
PROUS .... Proceed to a Port in Continental United States [*Military*]
PRO US EXT ... Pro Usu Externo [*For External Use*] [*Pharmacy*]
Prouty .... Prouty's Reports [*61-68 Vermont*] (DLA)
Prov. .... De Providentia [*of Seneca the Younger*] [*Classical studies*] (OCD)
PROV .... Provencal [*Language, etc.*]
PROV .... Provence [*France*] (ROG)
PROV .... Proverb
Prov .... Proverbs [*Old Testament book*]
PROV .... Provide (KSC)
PROV .... Provident Institute for Savings of Boston [*NASDAQ symbol*] (NQ)
PROV .... Province
Prov .... Provincia [*A publication*]
PROV .... Provincial
Prov .... Provincial [*A publication*]
PROV .... Provinciale [*Provincial*] [*The Netherlands*]
PROV .... Provision [*or Provisional*] (AFM)
Prov .... Provisional Light [*Navigation signal*]
PROV .... Provost
Prov Buenos Aires Com Invest Cient Inf ... Provincia de Buenos Aires. Comision de Investigaciones Cientificas. Informes [*A publication*]
Prov Can Stat ... Statutes of the Province of Canada (DLA)
Prov Cons ... De Provinciis Consularibus [*of Cicero*] [*Classical studies*] (OCD)
PROVCORPV ... Provisional Corps, Vietnam
PROVD .... Provided
Provence Hist ... Provence Historique [*A publication*]
Provence Univ Ann Geol Mediterr ... Provence Universite. Annales. Geologie Mediterraneenne [*A publication*]
Provence Univ Lab Paleontol Hum Prehist Etud Quat Mem ... Provence Universite. Laboratoire de Paleontologie Humaine et de Prehistoire. Etudes Quaternaires. Memoire [*A publication*]
PROVER ..... Procurement for Minimum Total Cost through Value Engineering and Reliability
PROVER ..... Procurement, Value, Economy, Reliability
ProvGM ...... Provincial Grand Master [*Freemasonry*]
PROVGR ...... Proving Grounds
Provid .... De Providentia [*of Philo*] (BJA)
Providence Hosp Detroit Med Bull ... Providence Hospital of Detroit. Medical Bulletin [*A publication*]
PROVIS ...... Provision
PROVMAAG ... Provisional Military Assistance Advisory Group (CINC)
PROVMAAG-K ... Provisional Military Assistance Advisory Group, Korea (CINC)
PROVMAIN ... Other Provisions Basic Orders Remain in Effect
provns .... Provisions (DLA)
PROVO ...... Proviso (ROG)
PROVO ...... Provocateur (DSUE)
PROVO ...... Provost Marshal [*Australian*] [*World War II*] (DSUE)
PROVONS ... Provisions
PROVOST ... Priority Research Objectives for Vietnam Operations Support
Prov St .... Statutes, Laws, of the Province of Massachusetts (DLA)
PROWDELREP ... Proceed Without Delay Report Duty or Purpose Indicated [*Military*]
PROWLER ... Programmable Robot Observer with Logical Enemy Response [*Developed by Robot Defense Systems of Thornton, CO*]
PROWORD ... Procedure Word

PROX .... Proximity (AABC)
PROX .... Proximo [*In Next Month*] [*Latin*]
PROX ACC ... Proxime Accessit [*Next in Order of Merit*] [*Latin*]
PRO-XAN ... Protein-Xanthophyll [*Alfalfa protein concentrate process*]
PROXI .... Projection by Reflection Optics of Xerographic Images (IEEE)
Proyecto Desarrollo Pesq Publ ... Proyecto de Desarrollo Pesquero. Publicacion [*A publication*]
P Roy S Med ... Proceedings. Royal Society of Medicine [*A publication*]
P Roy Soc A ... Proceedings. Royal Society of London. Series A. Mathematical and Physical Sciences [*A publication*]
P Roy Soc B ... Proceedings. Royal Society of London. Series B. Biological Sciences [*A publication*]
PRP .... Panretinal Photocoagulation [*Ophthalmology*]
PRP .... Parent Rule Point (MCD)
PRP .... Parti Republicain du Progres [*Republican Progress Party*] [*Central African*] (PD)
PRP .... Parti de la Revolution Populaire [*People's Revolutionary Party*] [*Zairian*] (PD)
PRP .... Partido de Representacao Popular [*Brazil*]
PRP .... Partido Republicano Portugues [*Portuguese Republican Party*] (PPE)
PRP .... Partido Revolucionario Popular [*Popular Revolutionary Party*] [*Portuguese*] (PPE)
PRP .... Peace Resource Project (EA)
PRP .... Peak Radiated Power (CET)
PRP .... People's Redemption Party [*Nigerian*] (PPW)
PRP .... People's Revolutionary Party [*Benin*]
PRP .... People's Revolutionary Party [*North Vietnam*]
PRP .... Personnel Reliability Program [*Air Force*]
PRP .... Phantom Range Pod (MCD)
PRP .... Phase Review Package (MCD)
PRP .... Pickup-Zone Release Point
PRP .... Platelet-Rich Plasma [*Hematology*]
PRP .... Position Report Printout
PRP .... Postbuckled Rectangular Plate
PRP .... Potentially Responsible Party [*Environmental Protection Agency*]
PRP .... Power-Deployed Reserve Parachute (MCD)
PRP .... Premature-Removal Period (MCD)
PRP .... Prepare (FAAC)
PRP .... Prerigor Pressurization [*Meat processing*]
PRP .... Pressure Rate Product [*In treadmill test*]
PrP .... Prion Protein [*Biochemistry*]
PRP .... Problem Resolution Program [*IRS*]
PRP .... Procurement Requirements Package (MCD)
PRP .... Production Requirements Plan
PRP .... Production Reserve Policy
PRP .... Program Requirements Package [*Data processing*]
PRP .... Program Review Panel [*Army*] (AABC)
PRP .... Progress in Radiopharmacology [*Elsevier Book Series*] [*A publication*]
PRP .... Progressive Rework Plan
PRP .... Progressive Rubella Panencephalitis [*Medicine*]
PRP .... Proliferative Retinopathy Photocoagulation
PRP .... Proline-Rich Protein [*Biochemistry*]
PRP .... Proper Return Port [*Shipping*]
PRP .... Prospective Reimbursement Plan [*Medicaid*]
PrP .... Protein Phosphatase [*An enzyme*]
PRP .... Pseudorandom Pulse
PRP .... Psychotic Reaction Profile [*Psychology*]
PRP .... Public Relations Personnel [*Navy*]
PRP .... Pulse Recurrence [*or Repetition*] Period (CET)
PRP .... Purchase Request Package (MCD)
PRP .... Purple (MSA)
PRP .... Purpose (MSA)
PRP .... Reformed Presbyterian Theological Seminary, Pittsburgh, PA [*OCLC symbol*] (OCLC)
PRPA .... Professional Race Pilots Association [*Later, USARA*] (EA)
PRPB .... Parti de la Revolution Populaire du Benin [*Benin People's Revolutionary Party*] (PD)
PRPC .... Public Relations Policy Committee [*NATO*] (NATG)
PRPEF .... Prairie Pacific Energy [*NASDAQ symbol*] (NQ)
PRPF .... Planar Radial Peaking Factor [*Network analysis*] (IEEE)
PRPG .... Proportioning
PRPHL .... Peripheral
PRPL .... PACOM [*Pacific Command*] Reconnaissance Priority List (CINC)
PRPL .... People's Democratic Republic of Laos
PRPL .... Procurement Repair Parts List (AAG)
PRPLN .... Propulsion (MSA)
PRPLNT ..... Propellant (KSC)
PRPLT .... Propellant (MSA)
PRPNE .... Propane [*Organic chemistry*]
PrPol .... Prace Polonistyczne [*Warsaw*] [*A publication*]
PRPOOS ..... Plankton Rate Processes in Oligotrophic Oceans [*Cooperative research project*]
PRPP .... Phosphoribosylpyrophosphate [*Biochemistry*]
PRPP .... Phosphorylribose Pyrophosphate [*Biochemistry*]
PRPP .... Pseudoresidual Plot Program
PRPQ .... Programing Request for Price Quotation [*Data processing*]
PR PR .... Praeter Propter [*About, Nearly*] [*Latin*] (ROG)

Pr Primer ... Prairie Primer [*A publication*]
Pr Przem Inst Elektron ... Prace Przemyslowego Instytutu Elektroniki [*A publication*]
Pr Przem Inst Elektron (Warsaw) ... Prace Przemyslowego Instytutu Elektroniki (Warsaw) [*A publication*]
Pr Przem Inst Telekomun ... Prace Przemyslowego Instytutu Telekomunikacji [*A publication*]
PRPS .... Pressure Rise per Stage   (MCD)
PRPS .... Program Requirement Process Specification   (KSC)
PRPSA .... Petroleum Press Service [*A publication*]
PRPSD .... Proposed   (MSA)
PRPSL .... Proposal   (MSA)
PRPT .... Parti Revolutionnaire du Peuple Tunisien [*Revolutionary Party of the Tunisian People*]   (PD)
PRPT .... Probe Post [*A publication*]
PRPTA .... Proceedings. Association of Asphalt Paving Technologists [*A publication*]
PRPUC .... Philippine Republic Presidential Unit Citation [*Military award*]   (AFM)
PRPUCE ..... Philippine Republic Presidential Unit Citation Emblem [*Military decoration*]
PRPYA .... Praxis der Psychotherapie [*A publication*]
PRQ .... Houston, TX [*Location identifier*] [*FAA*]   (FAAL)
PRQA .... Passenger Ride Quality Apparatus [*Public transportation*]
PRR .... Parts Replacement Request   (KSC)
PRR .... Passenger Reservation Request   (NVT)
PRR .... Passive Ranging RADAR
PRR .... Pawling Research Reactor
PRR .... Pennsylvania Railroad Co. [*AAR code*] [*Obsolete*]
PRR .... Perrine, FL [*Location identifier*] [*FAA*]   (FAAL)
PRR .... Perris [*California*] [*Seismograph station code, US Geological Survey*] [*Closed*]   (SEIS)
PRR .... Placement Revision Request
PRR .... Planning Release Record   (AAG)
Pr R .... Practice Reports [*Various jurisdictions*]   (DLA)
Pr R .... Practice Reports [*Quebec*]   (DLA)
Pr R .... Practice Reports [*Ontario*]   (DLA)
PRR .... Pre-Raphaelite Review [*A publication*]
PRR .... Preliminary Requirements Review   (KSC)
PRR .... Premature Removal Rate
PRR .... Presbyterian and Reformed Renewal Ministries International [*Formerly, PCC*]   (EA)
PRR .... Presbyterian and Reformed Review [*A publication*]
PRR .... Pressure Rise Rate [*Nuclear energy*]   (NRCH)
PRR .... Prism Resources Ltd. [*Vancouver Stock Exchange symbol*]
PRR .... Producer's Reliability Risk
PRR .... Production Readiness Review
PRR .... Production Research Reports
PR & R .... Professional Rights and Responsibilities
PRR .... Program Requirements Review [*NASA*]   (NASA)
PRR .... Program Revision Report   (KSC)
PRR .... Proline-Rich Protein [*Biochemistry*]
PRR .... Proton Relaxation Rate
PRR .... Public Relations Review [*A publication*]
PRR .... Publication Revision Request   (AAG)
PRR .... Puerto Rico Reactor   (NRCH)
PRR .... Puerto Rico Supreme Court Reports   (DLA)
PRR .... Pulse Recurrence [*or Repetition*] Rate   (MUGU)
PrRA .... Academia Maria Reina, Rio Piedras, PR [*Library symbol*] [*Library of Congress*]   (LCLS)
PRRA .... Puerto Rico Reconstruction Administration [*Terminated, 1955*]
Pr Rady Nauk-Tech Huty Lenina ... Prace Rady Naukowo-Technicznej Huty Imienia Lenina [*A publication*]
PRRB .... Physics Reports. Reprints Book Series [*Elsevier Book Series*] [*A publication*]
PRRB .... Provider Reimbursement Review Board [*Medicare*]
PRRC .... New Mexico Petroleum Recovery Research Center [*New Mexico Institute of Mining and Technology*] [*Research center*]   (RCD)
PRRC .... Pitch/Roll Rate Changer Assembly   (MCD)
PrRe .... Evangelical Seminary, Rio Piedras, PR [*Library symbol*] [*Library of Congress*]   (LCLS)
PRREA .... Philips Research Reports [*A publication*]
Pr Reg BC ... Practical Register in the Bail Court   (DLA)
Pr Reg Ch ... Practical Register in Chancery [*1 vol.*]   (DLA)
Pr Reg CP ... Practical Register in the Common Pleas [*1705-42*]   (DLA)
Pr Rep .... Practice Reports [*Ontario*]   (DLA)
Pr Rep .... Practice Reports [*England*]   (DLA)
Pr Rep BC ... Lowndes, Maxwell, and Pollock's English Bail Court Practice Reports   (DLA)
PRRFC .... Planar Randomly Reinforced Fiber Composite
PRRI .... Puerto Rico Rum Institute [*Later, PRRPA*]
PRRM .... Program Review and Resources Management [*NASA*]
PRRM .... Pulse Repetition Rate Modulation [*Data transmission*] [*Data processing*]   (TEL)
PRRPA .... Puerto Rico Rum Producers Association [*Old San Juan, PR*]
PRR & Regs ... Commonwealth of Puerto Rico Rules and Regulations   (DLA)
PRRS .... Positioning Reporting Recording System   (RDA)
PRRS .... Problem Reporting and Resolution System [*Military*]   (CAAL)
PR-RSV ..... Rous Sarcoma Virus, Prague Strain

PRS .... Pacific Rocket Society   (EA)
PRS .... Padre Resources [*Vancouver Stock Exchange symbol*]
PRS .... Pairs
PRS .... Paraiso [*California*] [*Seismograph station code, US Geological Survey*]   (SEIS)
PRS .... Parametric Ruled Surface   (MCD)
PRS .... Parasi [*Solomon Islands*] [*Airport symbol*]   (OAG)
PRS .... Partei fuer Renten-, Steuer-, und Soziale Gerechtigkeit [*Party for Equitable Pensions, Taxation, and Social Services*] [*West Germany*]   (PPW)
PRS .... Parti de la Revolution Socialiste [*Party of Socialist Revolution*] [*Senegal*]
PRS .... Parti de la Revolution Socialiste [*Party of Socialist Revolution*] [*Benin*]
PRS .... Partido de la Revolucion Socialista [*Party of the Socialist Revolution*] [*Cuba*]
PRS .... Passive RADAR Surveillance [*Military*]   (CAAL)
PRS .... Pattern Recognition Society [*Georgetown University Medical Center*] [*Washington, DC*]   (EA)
PRS .... Pattern Recognition System
PRS .... Payload Retention Subsystem [*NASA*]   (NASA)
PRS .... Pennsylvania-Reading Seashore Lines [*Absorbed into Consolidated Rail Corp.*]
PRS .... Performance Rating System   (OICC)
PRS .... Performing Right Society [*British*]
PRS .... Personal Recording System
PRS .... Personality Rating Scale [*Psychology*]
PRS .... Personnel Readiness System [*Air Force*]
PRS .... Personnel Rescue System   (MCD)
PRS .... Personnel Research Section [*Army*]
PRS .... Personnel Research Staff [*Department of Agriculture*]
PRS .... Perspectives in Religious Studies [*A publication*]
PRS .... Philatelic Research Society
PRS .... Philosophical Research Society   (EA)
PRS .... Photo Resist Spinner
PRS .... Photographic Reconnaissance System
PRS .... Physically Restricted Status [*Military*]
PRS .... Pipe Roll Society   (EA)
PRS .... Planar Rider System
PRS .... Planning Record Sheet
PRS .... Plasma Renin Substrate [*Hematology*]
PRS .... Pneumatic Reading System
PRS .... Pointing Reference System   (KSC)
PRS .... Population Research Service [*Austin, TX*] [*Information service*]   (EISS)
PRS .... Power Reactant Subsystem [*NASA*]   (NASA)
PRS .... Power Relay Satellite
PrS .... Prairie Schooner [*A publication*]
PRS .... Prayers   (ROG)
PRS .... Precision Ranging System
PRS .... Precision Rotary Stripper
PRS .... President of the Royal Society [*British*]
PRS .... Presidential Airways [*Philadelphia, PA*] [*FAA designator*]   (FAAC)
PRS .... Presidio Oil Co. [*American Stock Exchange symbol*]
PRS .... Presidio, TX [*Location identifier*] [*FAA*]   (FAAL)
PRS .... Press   (MSA)
PRS .... Pressure Reducing Station
PRS .... Pressure Response Spectrum [*Nuclear energy*]   (NRCH)
PRS .... Primary Recovery Ship [*NASA*]
PRS .... Primary Recovery Site [*NASA*]   (KSC)
PRS .... Procedure Review Section [*Social Security Administration*]
PRS .... Process Radiation Sampler   (NRCH)
PRS .... Product Requirement Schedule   (MCD)
PRS .... Production Recording System
PRS .... Production Release System   (MCD)
PRS .... Program Requirements Summary   (MUGU)
PRS .... Property Recovery Section
PRS .... Propodial Sinus [*Zoology*]
PRS .... Protestant Reformation Society   (EA)
PRS .... Provide Repair Service [*Navy*]   (NVT)
PRS .... Provisioning Requirements Statement [*Navy*]
PRS .... Pseudorandom Sequence
PRSA .... Pan-Rhodian Society of America   (EA)
PRSA .... Power Reactant Storage Assembly [*NASA*]   (MCD)
PRSA .... President of the Royal Scottish Academy
PRSA .... Public Relations Society of America [*Formed by a merger of American Council on Public Relations and National Association of Public Relations Counsel*] [*New York, NY*]   (EA)
PRSA .... Puerto Rico Statehood Commission   (EA)
PrSaC .... Colegio Universitario del Sagrado Corazon [*College of the Sacred Heart*], Santurce, PR [*Library symbol*] [*Library of Congress*]   (LCLS)
Prsb Q .... Presbyterian Quarterly Review [*A publication*]
PRSC .... Plutonium Rework Sample Cell [*Nuclear energy*]   (NRCH)
PRSC .... Puerto Rican Solidarity Committee   (EA)
PRSCR .... Puerto Rico Supreme Court Reports   (DLA)
PRSD .... Portable Rectilinear Scanning Device
PRSD .... Power Reactant Storage [*or Supply*] and Distribution [*NASA*]   (NASA)

PRSD......... Pressed (AAG)
PRSDS ...... Power Reactant Storage and Distribution System (MCD)
PrSE........... El Mundo Publishing Co., San Juan, PR [Library symbol]
　　　　　　[Library of Congress] (LCLS)
PRSE......... President of the Royal Society of Edinburgh
PRSE......... Proceedings. Royal Society of Edinburgh [A publication]
PRSEC ...... Payroll Section
P RS Edin A ... Proceedings. Royal Society of Edinburgh. Section A.
　　　　　　Mathematics [A publication]
P RS Edin B ... Proceedings. Royal Society of Edinburgh. Section B. Natural
　　　　　　Environment [A publication]
PRSG......... Personal Radio Steering Group [Ann Arbor, MI]
　　　　　　[Telecommunications service] (TSSD)
PRSG......... Pulse-Rebalanced Strapdown Gyro (MCD)
PRSH......... President of the Royal Society for the Promotion of Health
　　　　　　[British]
PRSL .... Pennsylvania-Reading Seashore Lines [Absorbed into
　　　　　　Consolidated Rail Corp.] [AAR code]
PRSL .... Progressive Savings & Loan [NASDAQ symbol] (NQ)
PRSM......... Proceedings. Royal Society of Medicine [A publication]
PRSMA...... Proceedings. Royal Society of Medicine [A publication]
PRSMN...... Pressman (AABC)
PRSN......... Provisional Relative Sunspot Number [NASA]
PRSNG...... Pressing
Prsnrs........ Prisoners [A publication]
PRSNT ...... Present (FAAC)
PRSR......... Presser (MSA)
PRSRV ...... Preservative (AAG)
PRSRZ....... Pressurize (MSA)
PRSS......... Pennsylvania-Reading Seashore Lines [Absorbed into
　　　　　　Consolidated Rail Corp.]
PRSS......... Problem Report Squawk Sheet [NASA] (NASA)
PRSSA ...... Public Relations Student Society of America (EA)
PRSSA ...... Puerto Rico Mainland US Statehood Students
　　　　　　Association (EA)
PRSSD ...... Pressed
PRST......... Persist (FAAC)
PRST......... Probability Reliability Sequential Tests (MCD)
Pr Stat....... Private Statutes (DLA)
Pr Statneho Geol Ustavu (Bratisl) ... Prace Statneho Geologickeho Ustavu
　　　　　　(Bratislava) [A publication]
Pr Statneho Geol Ustavu (Bratislava) ... Prace Statneho Geologickeho
　　　　　　Ustavu (Bratislava) [A publication]
PRSTC ...... Prosthetic
Pr Stud Vyzk Ustav Vodohospod ... Prace a Studie. Vyzkumny Ustav
　　　　　　Vodohospodarsky [A publication]
Pr Stud Zakl Badan Nauk Gorn Okregu Przem Pol Akad Nauk ... Prace i
　　　　　　Studia Zakladu Badan Naukowych Gornoslaskiego Okregu
　　　　　　Przemyslowego Polskiej Akademii Nauk [Poland] [A
　　　　　　publication]
PRSUA ...... Plastic and Reconstructive Surgery [A publication]
PRSVN ...... Preservation (AABC)
PRSW........ President of the Royal Scottish Water Colour Society
PrSW......... World University, San Juan, PR [Library symbol] [Library of
　　　　　　Congress] (LCLS)
PrSW-I ...... World University, International Institute of the Americas,
　　　　　　Barbosa Esq. Guayama, San Juan, PR [Library symbol]
　　　　　　[Library of Congress] (LCLS)
PRT .... Parr Terminal Railroad [AAR code]
PRT .... Part (AAG)
PRT .... Participating Research Teams [Department of Energy]
PRT .... Partido Revolucionario de los Trabajadores [Workers'
　　　　　　Revolutionary Party] [Uruguayan] (PD)
PRT .... Partido Revolucionario de los Trabajadores [Workers'
　　　　　　Revolutionary Party] [Argentina] (PD)
PRT .... Partido Revolucionario de los Trabajadores [Workers'
　　　　　　Revolutionary Party] [Peruvian] (PPW)
PRT .... Pattern Recognition Technique
PRT .... Periodic Reevaluation Tests
PRT .... Personal Rapid Transit [Computer-guided transit system]
PRT .... Personnel Research Test
PRT .... Petroleum Revenue Tax [British]
PRT .... Pharmaceutical Research and Testing [Public Health Service]
PRT .... Philadelphia Reading Test [Education]
PRT .... Phosphoribosyltransferase [Also, PRTase] [An enzyme]
PRT .... Photoradiation Therapy [Oncology]
PRT .... Physical Readiness Training [Army] (INF)
P & RT .... Physical and Recreational Training [Navy] [British]
PRT .... Platinum Resistance Thermometer
PRT .... Point Retreat, AK [Location identifier] [FAA] (FAAL)
PRT .... Port
PRT .... Portable Radiation Thermometer
PRT .... Portable Radio Telephone
PRT .... Portable Remote Terminal
PRT .... Portable Router Template (MCD)
PRT .... Portugal [Three-letter standard code] (CNC)
PRT .... Power Recovery Turbine
PRT .... Prato [Italy] [Seismograph station code, US Geological
　　　　　　Survey] (SEIS)
PRT .... Precision Radiation Thermometer
PRT .... Preliminary Reference Trajectory [NASA] (KSC)

PRT .... Pressurized Relief Tank (NRCH)
prt .... Printer [MARC relator code] [Library of Congress]
PRT .... Printer [Data processing] (MDG)
PRT .... Problem Resolution Tasking System [Army] (INF)
PRT .... Procurement Review Team
PRT .... Procurement Round Table (EA)
PRT .... Product Range Testing [Business and trade]
PRT .... Production Reliability Test
PRT .... Production Run Tape
PRT .... Program Reference Table
PRT .... Prompt Relief Trip (NRCH)
Prt .... Protagoras [of Plato] [Classical studies] (OCD)
PRT .... Prova di Restituzione Termica [Italy] [Medicine]
PRT .... Provost
PRT .... Prudential Realty Trust [NYSE symbol]
PRT .... Publications Requirements Tables (AAG)
PRT .... Pulse Recurrence [or Repetition] Time (CET)
PRT .... Pulsed RADAR Transmitter
PRTB .... Partido Revolucionario de Trabajadores Bolivianos [Bolivian
　　　　　　Workers' Revolutionary Party] (PD)
PRTBR........ Partido Revolucionario de los Trabajadores de Bolivia Romero
　　　　　　[Bolivian] (PPW)
PRTC......... Partido Revolucionario de los Trabajadores Centroamericanos
　　　　　　[Revolutionary Party of Central American Workers]
　　　　　　[Salvadoran] (PD)
PRTC......... Partido Revolucionario de los Trabajadores Centroamericanos
　　　　　　[Revolutionary Party of Central American Workers]
　　　　　　[Guatemalan] (PPW)
PRTC......... Ports Canada
PRTC......... Precision Technologies [NASDAQ symbol] (NQ)
PRTCD....... Progres Technique [A publication]
PRTCD....... Puerto Rico Tax Court Decisions (DLA)
PRTD......... Portland Traction Co. [AAR code]
PRTG......... Printing (AFM)
PrThR........ Princeton Theological Review [A publication]
PRTKT....... Parts Kit
PRTLS........ Powered Return to Launch Site [NASA] (MCD)
PRTLY....... Partially
PRTM......... Printing Response-Time Monitor
PRTN......... Partition
PRTO......... Preservation Research and Testing Office [Library of
　　　　　　Congress] (EA)
PRTOT ...... Prototype Real-Time Optical Tracker [Data processing]
PRT Polym Age ... PRT Polymer Age [A publication]
PRTR......... Plutonium Recycle Test Reactor
PRTR......... Printer
Prt Rep....... Practice Reports (DLA)
PRTRL....... Printer, Lithographer [Navy]
PRTRM....... Printer, Offset Process [Navy]
PRTRNS..... Programable Transformer Converter (MCD)
PRTS......... Personal Rapid Transit System [Computer-guided transit
　　　　　　system]
PRTS......... Politisch-Religioese Texte aus der Sargonidenzeit [A
　　　　　　publication]
PRTS......... Pretoria Theological Series [A publication] (BJA)
PrtSc......... Print Screen [Computer keyboard]
PRTY......... Priority
PRU........... Packet Radio Unit
PRu............ Paedagogische Rundschau [A publication]
PRU........... Peripheral Resistance Unit [Medicine]
PRU........... Photographic Reconnaissance Unit [Aircraft] [Marine Corps]
PRU........... Pneumatic Regulation Unit (AAG)
PRU........... Polarity Reversal Unit [Electrochemistry]
PRU........... Primary Replacement Unit
PRU........... Programs Research Unit (KSC)
PRU........... Prome [Burma] [Airport symbol] (OAG)
PRU........... Provincial Reconnaissance Unit [Military]
PRU........... Prudential Property & Casualty Insurance Co., Holmdel, NJ
　　　　　　[OCLC symbol] (OCLC)
PRU........... Pruhonice [Czechoslovakia] [Seismograph station code, US
　　　　　　Geological Survey] (SEIS)
PrU........... University of Puerto Rico, Rio Piedras, PR [Library symbol]
　　　　　　[Library of Congress] (LCLS)
PRUAA...... President of the Royal Ulster Academy of Arts
PRUC .... Partido Revolucionario de Union Civico [Revolutionary Party
　　　　　　for Civic Union] [Costa Rica]
PRUC .... Practice Reports [1848-1900] [Upper Canada] (DLA)
PRUD........ Partido Revolucionario de Unificacion Democratica
　　　　　　[Revolutionary Party of Democratic Unification] [El
　　　　　　Salvador]
PrU-H .... University of Puerto Rico, Humacao Regional College,
　　　　　　Humacao, PR [Library symbol] [Library of
　　　　　　Congress] (LCLS)
PRUL......... Programs Unlimited [NASDAQ symbol] (NQ)
PrU-L......... University of Puerto Rico, Law Library, San Juan, PR [Library
　　　　　　symbol] [Library of Congress] (LCLS)
PrU-M........ University of Puerto Rico, School of Medicine, San Juan, PR
　　　　　　[Library symbol] [Library of Congress] (LCLS)
PrU-MA ..... University of Puerto Rico, Mayaguez Campus, Mayaguez,
　　　　　　Puerto Rico [Library symbol] [Library of
　　　　　　Congress] (LCLS)

Prum Potravin ... Prumysl Potravin [*A publication*]
PrU-MS ...... University of Puerto Rico, Department of Marine Sciences, Mayaguez, PR [*Library symbol*] [*Library of Congress*]　(LCLS)
PRUND .... Plastics and Rubber News [*A publication*]
PrU-NS .... University of Puerto Rico, Natural Science Library, Rio Piedras, PR [*Library symbol*] [*Library of Congress*]　(LCLS)
PRUS .... Prussia [*Obsolete*]
PRUSAF ..... Puerto Rico, USA Foundation　(EA)
Pr Ustavu Naft Vyzk ... Prace Ustavu pro Naftovy Vyzkum [*A publication*]
Pr Ustavu Vyzk Paliv ... Prace Ustavu pro Vyzkum Paliv [*Czechoslovakia*] [*A publication*]
Pr Ustavu Vyzk Vyuziti Paliv ... Prace Ustavu pro Vyzkum a Vyuziti Paliv [*A publication*]
PRV .... Peak Reverse Voltage
PRV .... Pearl River Valley Railroad Co. [*AAR code*]
PRv .... Philosophical Review [*A publication*]
PRV .... Polycythemia Rubra Vera [*Medicine*]
PRV .... Porvoo [*Finland*] [*Seismograph station code, US Geological Survey*] [*Closed*]　(SEIS)
PRV .... Pour Rendre Visite [*To Make a Call*] [*French*]
PRV .... Pressure Reducing [*or Regulation*] Valve
PRV .... Pressure Relief Valve
PRV .... Princess Ventures [*Vancouver Stock Exchange symbol*]
PRV .... Prior Record Variable [*Criminal sentencing*]
PRV .... Propeller Revolution
Prv .... Proverbs [*Old Testament book*]
PRV .... Provisional Reconnaissance Unit
PRV .... Pseudorabies Virus
PRV .... Pseudorelative Velocity
Prv .... Pyruvenol [*Biochemistry*]
PRVD .... Procurement [*or Purchase*] Request for Vendor Data　(AAG)
PRVD .... Provide　(FAAC)
PRVEP .... Pattern Reversal Visual Evoked Potential
PRVNTV ..... Preventive
PRVOA ...... Pravda Vostoka [*A publication*]
PRVS .... Penetration Room Ventilation System　(IEEE)
PRVT .... Product Reliability Validation Test　(MCD)
PRVT .... Production Readiness Verification Testing　(MCD)
PRVW .... Preview　(MSA)
PRVYD .... Polyteknisk Revy [*A publication*]
Pr Vyzk Ustavu CS Naft Dolu ... Prace Vyzkumneho Ustavu CS Naftovych Dolu [*A publication*]
Pr Vyzk Ustavu Lesn Hospod Myslivosti (Strnady) ... Prace Vyzkumneho Ustavu Lesneho Hospodarstvi a Myslivosti (Strnady) [*A publication*]
PRW .... Paired Wire [*Telecommunications*]　(TEL)
PRW .... Percent Rated Wattage
PRW .... Polymerized Ragweed [*Immunology*]
PRW .... Press Relations Wire [*Commercial firm*]　(EA)
PRW .... Prosser [*Washington*] [*Seismograph station code, US Geological Survey*]　(SEIS)
PRW .... World University, San Juan, PR [*OCLC symbol*]　(OCLC)
PRWAD ...... Professional Rehabilitation Workers with the Adult Deaf [*Later, American Deafness and Rehabilitation Association*]　(EA)
PrWCJewSt ... Proceedings. World Congress of Jewish Studies [*Jerusalem*] [*A publication*]
PRWD .... Priority Regular World Day
PRWI .... Prince William Forest Park [*National Park Service designation*]
Pr Winter .... Probability Winter School. Proceedings of the Fourth Winter School on Probability [*A publication*]
PRWO .... Puerto Rican Revolutionary Workers Organization
PRWRA ...... Puerto Rican Water Resources Authority
PRWS .... President of the Royal Society of Painters in Water Colours [*British*]
PRWV .... Peak Reserve Working Voltage
Pr Wydz Nauk Tech Bydgoskie Tow Nauk Ser A ... Prace Wydzialu Nauk Technicznych. Bydgoskie Towarzystwo Naukowe. Seria A. Technologia Chemiczna [*A publication*]
Pr Wydz Nauk Tech Bydgoskie Tow Nauk Ser C ... Prace Wydzialu Nauk Technicznych. Bydgoskie Towarzystwo Naukowe. Seria C. Elektronika, Elektrotechnika [*A publication*]
PRX .... Paris [*Texas*] [*Airport symbol*]　(OAG)
PRX .... Paris, TX [*Location identifier*] [*FAA*]　(FAAL)
PRX .... Pressure Regulation Exhaust
PRY .... Paraguay [*Three-letter standard code*]　(CNC)
PRY .... Parys [*South Africa*] [*Seismograph station code, US Geological Survey*]　(SEIS)
PRY .... Pittway Corp. [*American Stock Exchange symbol*]
P Ryl .... Catalogue of the Greek Papyri in the John Rylands Library at Manchester [*A publication*]　(OCD)
PRZ .... Portales, NM [*Location identifier*] [*FAA*]　(FAAL)
PrZ .... Praehistorische Zeitschrift [*A publication*]
PRZ .... Prism Entertainment Corp. [*American Stock Exchange symbol*]
PRZ .... Przhevalsk [*USSR*] [*Seismograph station code, US Geological Survey*]　(SEIS)
Pr Zakresu Lesn ... Prace z Zakresu Lesnictwa [*Poland*] [*A publication*]
Pr Zakresu Nauk Roln ... Prace z Zakresu Nauk Rolniczych [*A publication*]
Prz Arch ..... Przeglad Archeologiczny [*A publication*]
Przegd St ..... Przeglad Statystyczny [*A publication*]
Przeglad Bibliot ... Przeglad Biblioteczny [*A publication*]

Przeglad Geog ... Przeglad Geograficzny [*A publication*]
Przeglad Hist ... Przeglad Historyczny [*A publication*]
Przeglad Mech ... Przeglad Mechaniczny [*A publication*]
Przeglad Papier ... Przeglad Papierniczy [*A publication*]
Przeglad Statyst ... Przeglad Statystyczny [*A publication*]
Przeglad Statyst ... Przeglad Statystyczny. Polska Akademia Nauk. Komitet Statystyki i Ekonometrii [*A publication*]
Przeglad Wlok ... Przeglad Wlokienniczy [*A publication*]
Przegl Antropol ... Przeglad Antropologiczny [*A publication*]
Przegl Bibl ... Przeglad Biblioteczny [*A publication*]
Przegl Budow ... Przeglad Budowlany [*A publication*]
Przegl Dermatol ... Przeglad Dermatologiczny [*A publication*]
Przegl Dermatol Wenerol ... Przeglad Dermatologii i Wenerologii [*A publication*]
Przegl Elektr ... Przeglad Elektroniki [*A publication*]
Przegl Elektron ... Przeglad Elektroniki [*A publication*]
Przegl Elektrotech ... Przeglad Elektrotechniczny [*A publication*]
Przegl Epidemiol ... Przeglad Epidemiologiczny [*A publication*]
Przegl Geofiz ... Przeglad Geofizyczny [*A publication*]
Przegl Geogr ... Przeglad Geograficzny [*A publication*]
Przegl Geogr Pol Geogr Rev ... Przeglad Geograficzny-Polish Geographical Review [*A publication*]
Przegl Geol ... Przeglad Geologiczny [*A publication*]
Przegl Gorn ... Przeglad Gorniczy [*A publication*]
Przegl Gorn Hutn ... Przeglad Gorniczo Hutniczy [*A publication*]
Przegl Hist ... Przeglad Historycyzny [*A publication*]
Przegl Hodowlany ... Przeglad Hodowlany [*A publication*]
Przegl Komunik ... Przeglad Komunikacyjny [*A publication*]
Przegl Lek ... Przeglad Lekarski [*A publication*]
Przegl Mech ... Przeglad Mechaniczny [*A publication*]
Przegl Morski ... Przeglad Morski [*A publication*]
Przegl Nauk Tech Akad Gorn Hutn Krakowie Ser H ... Przeglad Naukowo Techniczny. Akademia Gorniczo Hutnicza w Krakowie Seria H. Hutnictwo [*A publication*]
Przegl Odlew ... Przeglad Odlewnictwa [*A publication*]
Przegl Organ ... Przeglad Organizacji [*A publication*]
Przegl Przem Olejowego ... Przeglad Przemyslu Olejowego [*A publication*]
Przegl Papiern ... Przeglad Papierniczy [*A publication*]
Przegl Skorzany ... Przeglad Skorzany [*A publication*]
Przegl Socjol ... Przeglad Socjologiczny [*A publication*]
Przegl Spawalnictwa ... Przeglad Spawalnictwa [*A publication*]
Przegl Telekomun ... Przeglad Telekomunikacyjny [*A publication*]
Przegl Wlok ... Przeglad Wlokienniczy [*A publication*]
Przegl Wojsk Ladowych ... Przeglad Wojsk Ladowych [*Poland*] [*A publication*]
Przegl Zachod ... Przeglad Zachodni [*A publication*]
Przegl Zboz Mlyn ... Przeglad Zbozowo Mlynarski [*A publication*]
Przegl Zbozowo Mlyn ... Przeglad Zbozowo Mlynarski [*A publication*]
Przegl Zool ... Przeglad Zologiczny [*A publication*]
Przekazy .... Przekazy/Opinie [*A publication*]
Przem Chem ... Przemysl Chemiczny [*A publication*]
Przem Drzew ... Przemysl Drzewny [*A publication*]
Przem Drzewny ... Przemysl Drzewny [*A publication*]
Przem Ferment ... Przemysl Fermentacyjny [*A publication*]
Przem Ferment Rolny ... Przemysl Fermentacyjny i Rolny [*A publication*]
Przem Naft ... Przemysl Naftowy [*A publication*]
Przem Roln Spozyw ... Przemysl Rolny i Spozywczy [*A publication*]
Przem Spozyw ... Przemysl Spozywczy [*A publication*]
Przem Spozywczy ... Przemysl Spozywczy [*A publication*]
Przem Wlok ... Przemysl Wlokienniczy [*A publication*]
Przemy Chem ... Przemysl Chemiczny [*A publication*]
PrzH .... Przeglad Humanistyczny [*A publication*]
PrzK .... Przeglad Kulturalny [*A publication*]
PrzKl .... Przeglad Klasyczny [*A publication*]
PrzOr .... Przeglad Orientalistyczny [*Cracow/Warsaw*] [*A publication*]
PRZPB .... Przeglad Psychologiczny [*A publication*]
PrzZ .... Przeglad Zachodni [*A publication*]
PS .... Abbott Laboratories [*Research code symbol*]
PS .... American Political Science Association. Quarterly [*A publication*]
PS .... Chloropicrin [*Poison gas*] [*Army symbol*]
PS .... Pacific Southwest Airlines [*ICAO designator*]　(OAG)
PS .... Pacific Spectator [*A publication*]
P & S .... Packers and Stockyards
PS .... Packing Sheet　(MCD)
PS .... Paddle Steamer　(ADA)
PS .... Paediatric Surgery
PS .... Painting System
PS .... Paleontological Society　(EA)
PS .... Palestinskii Sbornik [*A publication*]
PS .... Palm Society [*Later, IPS*]　(EA)
PS .... Pamietnik Slowianski [*A publication*]
P & S .... Paracentesis and Suction [*Medicine*]
PS .... Parachute Subsystem [*NASA*]　(NASA)
PS .... Paradoxical Sleep
P/S .... Parallel to Serial Converters　(MCD)
PS .... Parents of Suicides [*Hackensack, NJ*]　(EA)
PS .... Parity Switch
PS .... Parliamentary Secretary [*British*]
PS .... Parlor Snake [*Slang for "to escort visitors around post"*]
PS .... Parochial School

PS.............. Parrot Society (EA)
ps .... PARSEC [*Parallax Second*] [*See PARSEC*]
PS.............. Parti Socialiste [*Socialist Party*] [*Belgium*] (PPW)
PS.............. Parti Socialiste - Federation de la Reunion [*Reunion Federation of the Socialist Party*] (PPW)
PS.............. Partially Synergistic [*Pharmacology*]
PS.............. Partido Socialista [*Socialist Party*] [*Chile*]
PS.............. Partido Socialista [*Socialist Party*] [*Uruguayan*]
PS.............. Partido Socialista Portuguesa [*Portuguese Socialist Party*] (PPE)
PS.............. Partido Socialista - Uno [*Socialist Party - One*] [*Also, PS-1*] [*Bolivian*] (PPW)
PS.............. Parts Shipper
PS.............. Pascal Software, Inc. [*Moorhead, MN*] [*Hardware manufacturer*]
PS.............. Passed School of Instruction [*of Officers*] [*British*]
PS.............. Passenger Service
PS.............. Passenger Steamer
PS.............. Passing Scuttle
PS.............. Pathologic Stage
PS.............. Pathological (Surgical) Staging [*For Hodgkin's Disease*]
PS.............. Patient's Serum [*Medicine*]
PS.............. Patrol Ship (CINC)
PS.............. Patrologia Syriaca (BJA)
PS.............. Patton Society (EA)
PS.............. Pavel Stepanek [*Czech ESP performer*]
P & S .... Pay and Supply [*Coast Guard*]
PS.............. Payload Shroud (MCD)
PS.............. Payload Specialist [*NASA*] (MCD)
PS.............. Payload Station [*NASA*] (MCD)
PS.............. Payload Support [*NASA*] (NASA)
PS.............. Paymaster Sergeant
PS.............. Pedagogical Seminary and Journal of Genetic Psychology [*A publication*]
PS.............. Pedal Sinus
PS.............. Penal Servitude
PS.............. Pensiero e Scuola [*A publication*]
PS.............. Peperomia Society [*Later, PEPS*] (EA)
PS.............. Per Ship
PS.............. Per Speculum [*Medicine*]
PS.............. Perception Schedule
PS.............. Perceptual Speed (Test) [*Psychology*]
PS.............. Performance Score
PS.............. Performance Standard
PS.............. Periodic Syndrome [*Medicine*]
PS.............. Peripheral Shock [*Psychology*]
PS.............. Permanent Secretary
PS.............. Permanent Signal [*Telecommunications*] (TEL)
PS.............. Personal Secretary
PS.............. Personal Skills
PS.............. Personal Survival
PS.............. Personal System [*IBM computer introduced in 1987*]
PS.............. Personnel Subsystem
PS.............. Peru Solidarity [*An association*] (EA)
PS.............. Pet Switchboard [*Aids individuals whose pets have been lost or stolen*] [*Shingle Springs, CA*] (EA)
PS.............. Petty Sessions (DLA)
PS.............. Phase Separation
PS.............. Phase-Shift
PS.............. Phenomenally Speedy Ordinary [*Photographic plates*] (ROG)
PS.............. Philalethes Society (EA)
PS.............. Philippine Scouts
PS.............. Philippine Studies [*A publication*]
PS.............. Phillnathean Society (EA)
PS.............. Phosphate-Saline [*A buffer*] [*Cell culture*]
PS.............. Phosphatidylserine [*Biochemistry*]
PS.............. Photochemical System
PS.............. Photoemission Scintillation (MCD)
PS.............. Photographic Service
PS.............. Photometer System (KSC)
PS.............. Photosystems
PS.............. Phylaxis Society (EA)
PS.............. Physical Sciences
PS.............. Physical Status [*Medicine*]
PS.............. Picket Ships [*Navy*]
ps .... Picosecond
PS.............. Pilgrim Power Station (NRCH)
PS.............. Pilgrim Society (EA)
PS.............. Pineal Stalk [*Neuroanatomy*]
PS.............. Pirandello Society (EA)
PS.............. Pistol Sharpshooter [*Army*]
PS.............. [*The*] Pittsburg & Shawmut Railroad Co. [*AAR code*]
P & S .... [*The*] Pittsburg & Shawmut Railroad Co.
PS.............. Pituitary Stalk [*Neuroanatomy*]
PS.............. Planet Stories [*A publication*]
PS.............. Planetary Society (EA)
P & S .... Planking and Strutting [*Construction*]
PS.............. Planning and Scheduling
PS.............. Planning Study (AAG)
PS.............. Plant Stress [*Horticulture*]
P & S .... Plant and Structures [*Aviation*] (FAAC)

PS.............. Plastic Surgery [*Medicine*]
PS.............. Platform (Sided)
PS.............. Plea Side (ROG)
PS.............. Plotting System
PS.............. Plus
PS.............. Pneumatic System
P/S.............. Point of Shipment
PS.............. Point of Switch
PS.............. Point of Symmetry
PS.............. Polaris Standard [*Missiles*]
PS.............. Polarity Scale [*Psychology*]
PS.............. Police Sergeant [*Scotland Yard*]
PS.............. Policy Statement
PS.............. Political Studies [*A publication*]
Ps .... Polyporus sulphureus [*A fungus*]
PS.............. Polystyrene [*Organic chemistry*]
PS.............. Polysulfone [*Also, PSO*] [*Organic chemistry*]
P/S.............. Polyunsaturated/Saturated [*Fatty acid ratio*]
PS.............. Porlock Society (EA)
PS.............. Port Security
P & S ...... Port and Starboard
P/S.............. Port or Starboard
PS.............. Port Store [*Telecommunications*] (TEL)
PS.............. Port Strobe [*Telecommunications*] (TEL)
PS.............. Pos-Escrito [*Postscript*] [*Portuguese*]
PS.............. Post Script [*A publication*]
PS.............. Post Scriptum [*Written Afterwards, Postscript*] [*Latin*]
PS.............. Postal Satsang [*An association*] (EA)
PS.............. Postal Service [*US*]
PS.............. Poster Society (EA)
PS.............. Potassium Sorbate [*Food additive*]
PS.............. Potentiometer Synchro
P/S.............. Power Section (NG)
PS.............. Power Source
PS.............. Power Station (MCD)
PS.............. Power Steering [*Automobile ads*]
PS.............. Power Supply
PS.............. Powys Society [*Sale, Cheshire, England*] (EA)
PS.............. Prairie Schooner [*A publication*]
PS.............. Prairies Service [*Record series prefix*] [*Canada*]
PS.............. Pravoslavnyi Sobesiednik [*A publication*]
PS.............. Predictive Saccades [*Ophthalmology*]
PS.............. Prehistoric Society (EA)
PS.............. Preliminary Study
PS.............. Presentation Services [*Data processing*] (IBMDP)
PS.............. Press to Start (KSC)
P-S .... Pressure-Sensitive
PS.............. Pressure Sensor
PS.............. Pressure Switch
Ps .... Pressure, Systolic [*Cardiology*]
PS.............. Prime Select (MCD)
PS.............. Prime Sponsor
PS.............. Principal Sojourner [*Freemasonry*] (ROG)
PS.............. Principal Subject [*In a sonata or rondo*] [*Music*] (ROG)
PS.............. Prior Service [*Military*]
PS.............. Private Screenings [*Cable TV programing service*]
PS.............. Private Secretary
PS.............. Private Security Program [*Association of Independent Colleges and Schools specialization code*]
PS.............. Private Siding [*Rail*] [*Shipping*]
PS.............. Privy Seal [*British*]
PS.............. Probability of Survival (MCD)
PS.............. Problem Specification
PS.............. Process Solution (MCD)
PS.............. Process Specification
PS.............. Process Studies [*A publication*]
PS.............. Process Subsystem [*Telecommunications*] (TEL)
PS.............. Processor Status
PS.............. Procurement Specification (MCD)
PS.............. Product Standards (MCD)
PS.............. Product Support
PS.............. Program Simulation (OICC)
PS.............. Program Specification (MCD)
PS.............. Program Start (KSC)
PS.............. Program Store [*Data processing*] (IEEE)
PS.............. Program Summary (NG)
PS.............. Programing System
PS.............. Project Slip
PS.............. Project Stock (AABC)
PS.............. Proler International Corp. [*NYSE symbol*]
PS.............. Prolifers for Survival (EA)
PS.............. Prometheus Society (EA)
PS.............. Prompt Side [*of a stage*] [*i.e., the right side*] [*A stage direction*]
PS.............. Proof Shot [*Ammunition*]
PS.............. Proof Stress
PS.............. Propellant Supply (KSC)
PS.............. Propellant System
PS.............. Prostaglandin Synthetase [*An enzyme*]
PS.............. Protective Service
PS.............. Protein Synthesis
PS.............. Proto-Semitic (BJA)

PS .... Proton Synchrotron [Nuclear energy]
PS .... Protoplasmic Surface [Freeze etching in microscopy]
PS .... Provost-Sergeant
PS .... Psalm
Ps .... Psalms [Old Testament book]
PS .... Pseudo [Classical studies]   (OCD)
PS .... Psychology Society [Formerly, EMSO]   (EA)
PS .... Psychometric Society   (EA)
PS .... Psychonomic Society
PS .... Psychotic
PS .... Public Sale
PS .... Public School
PS .... Public Services
PS .... Public Statutes   (DLA)
PS .... Public Stenographer
PS .... Publication Standard
PS .... Publishing Services [American Library Association]
PS .... Puget Sound [Also, Puget Sound Naval Shipyard]
                 [Washington]
PS .... Pull Switch
PS .... Pulmonary Stenosis [Medicine]
PS .... Pulse Sensor   (KSC)
PS .... Pulse Shaper
PS .... Pulse Stretcher
PS .... Pulses per Second [Data transmission]   (DEN)
PS .... Pumping Station   (NATG)
P & S .... Purchase and Sale [Business and trade]
PS .... Purdon's Pennsylvania Statutes   (DLA)
PS .... Purity-Supreme [Supermarkets]
PS .... Pyloric Stenosis [Medicine]
ps---- .... South Pacific [MARC geographic area code] [Library of
                 Congress]   (LCCP)
PS .... South Pole [Also, SP]
PS .... Static Pressure
PS .... Swarthmore Public Library, Swarthmore, PA [Library symbol]
                 [Library of Congress]   (LCLS)
PS .... Transport [Russian aircraft symbol]
PS-1 .... Partido Socialista - Uno [Socialist Party - One] [Also, PS]
                 [Bolivian]   (PD)
PS3 .... PROBE [Program Optimization and Budget Evaluation] Staff
                 Support System [Military]
PSA .... Pacific Science Association [Honolulu, HI]
PSA .... Pacific Southwest Airlines
P & SA .... Packers and Stockyards Administration [Department of
                 Agriculture]
PSA .... Papeles de Son Armadans [A publication]
PSA .... Parametric Semiconductor Amplifier
PSA .... Parcel Shippers Association [Formerly, PPA] [Washington,
                 DC]   (EA)
PSA .... Parti Socialiste Autonome [Autonomous Socialist Party]
                 [French]   (PPE)
PSA .... Parti Solidaire Africain [African Solidarity Party] [Congo -
                 Leopoldville]
PSA .... Particle Size Analyzer
PSA .... Partido Socialista Aponte [Bolivian]   (PPW)
PSA .... Partido Socialista Argentino [Socialist Party of Argentina]
PSA .... Partito Socialista Autonomo [Autonomous Socialist Party]
                 [Swiss]   (PPW)
PSA .... Past Shakedown Availability [Military]
PSA .... Pastel Society of America   (EA)
PSA .... Path Selection Algorithm [Telecommunications]   (TEL)
PSA .... Path of Steepest Ascent [Statistical design of experiments]
PSA .... Payload Service Area [NASA]   (NASA)
PSA .... People's Supreme Assembly [Yemeni]   (PPW)
PSA .... Personal Service Agreements   (MCD)
PSA .... Personnel and Service Area   (NRCH)
PSA .... Petersburg [Alaska] [Seismograph station code, US Geological
                 Survey]   (SEIS)
PSA .... Peugeot Societe Anonyme [French]
PSA .... Philippine Sugar Association [Later, PSC]   (EA)
PSa .... Philippiniana Sacra [A publication]
PSA .... Philosophy of Science Association   (EA)
PSA .... Phobia Society of America [Rockville, MD]   (EA)
PSA .... Photographic Society of America [Philadelphia, PA]   (EA)
PSA .... Phycological Society of America
PSA .... Pisa [Italy] [Airport symbol]   (OAG)
PsA .... Pisces Austrinus [Constellation]
PSA .... Pisces Society of America
PSA .... Play Schools Association [New York, NY]   (EA)
PSA .... Pleasant Sunday Afternoons
PSA .... Plumeria Society of America   (EA)
PSA .... Pneumatic Sensor Assembly
PSA .... Poe Studies Association   (EA)
PSA .... Poetry Society of America   (EA)
PSA .... Police Science Abstracts [A publication]
PSA .... Polysilicic Acid [Organic chemistry]
PSA .... Port Storage Area [Telecommunications]   (TEL)
PSA .... Portable Sanitation Association [Bloomington, MN]   (EA)
PSA .... Portable Sound Analyzer
PSA .... Post Shakedown Availability
PSA .... Potential Surface Analysis   (ADA)

PSA .... Poultry Science Association   (EA)
PSA .... Power Servo Amplifier   (KSC)
PSA .... Power Servo Assembly   (MCD)
PSA .... Power Supply Assembly
PSA .... Power Switching Assembly
PSA .... Prefabricated Surfacing Aluminum
PSA .... Preferred Storage Area   (MCD)
PSA .... President of the Society of Antiquaries [British]
PSA .... Pressure Sensitive Adhesive [Trademark]
PSA .... Pressure Suit Assembly
PSA .... Pressure-Swing Adsorption [Chemical engineering]
PSA .... Pressure Switch Assembly   (NASA)
PSA .... Presunrise Authority
PSA .... Probabilistic Safety Analysis   (NRCH)
PSA .... Procurement Seminar for Auditors [Army]
PSA .... Product Safety Association   (EA)
PSA .... Product Support Administration   (MCD)
PSA .... Professional Salespersons of America [Albuquerque,
                 NM]   (EA)
PSA .... Professional Skills Alliance   (EA)
PSA .... Professional Stringers Association [Omaha, NE]   (EA)
PSA .... Program Study Authorization   (KSC)
PSA .... Prolonged Sleep Apnea
PSA .... Property Services Agency [Department of the Environment]
                 [British]
PSA .... Prostate-Specific Antigen [Immunochemistry]
PSA .... Provisional Site Acceptance   (NATG)
PSA .... Psalm
Psa .... Psalms [Old Testament book]
PSA .... Pseudomonic Acid [Biochemistry]
PSA .... Psychological Operations Support Activity [Military]   (MCD)
PSA .... Psychologists for Social Action [Defunct]   (EA)
PSA .... Psychopharmacology Abstracts [A publication]
PSA .... Public Securities Association [New York, NY]   (EA)
PSA .... Public Service Announcement
PSA .... Publication Services Associates, Inc. [Schenectady, NY]
                 [Information service]   (EISS)
PSA .... Publication Systems Associates, Inc. [Schenectady, NY]
                 [Information service]   (EISS)
PSA .... Push Down Stack Automaton [Data processing]
PSAA .... Pakistan Students' Association of America
PSAA .... Polish Singers Alliance of America   (EA)
PSAA .... Poststimulatory Auditory Adaptation
PSAB .... Production Systems Acceptance Branch [Social Security
                 Administration]
PSAC .... Passive Satellite Attitude Control
PSAC .... Personnel Service Company [Army]   (AABC)
PSAC .... President's Science Advisory Committee [Terminated, 1973]
                 [Executive Office of the President]
PSAC .... Private Security Advisory Council [Terminated, 1977]
                 [Department of Justice]   (EGAO)
PSAC .... Product Safety Advisory Council [Consumer Product Safety
                 Commission]
PSAC .... Public Service Alliance of Canada [Labor union of federal
                 government employees]
PSAcPh ...... Prostate-Specific Acid Phosphatase [An enzyme]
PSACPOO ... Presidents Scientific Advisory Committee Panel on
                 Oceanography [Marine science]   (MSC)
PSAC TD .... Publications. Societe d'Archeologie Copte. Textes et
                 Documents [A publication]
PSAD .... Predicted Site Acquisition Data [NASA]
PSAD .... Prediction, Simulation, Adaptation, Decision [Data processing]
Ps Af .... Psychopathologie Africaine [A publication]
PSAGN .... Poststreptococcal Acute Glomerulonephritis [Medicine]
PSAIR .... Priority Specific Air Information Request [Defense Mapping
                 Agency]   (MCD)
PSAL .... Programing System Activity Log [Data processing]
PSAL .... Public Schools Athletic League
PSALI .... Permanent Supplementary Artificial Lighting of
                 Interiors   (IEEE)
PSAM .... Partitioned Sequence Access Method
PSAM .... Publications. Service des Antiquites du Maroc [A publication]
PSANDT .... Pay, Subsistence, and Transportation [Military]
PSANP .... Phenol-Soluble Acidic Nuclear Protein[s] [Biochemistry]
PSAP .... Plane Stress Analysis and Plot [Data processing]
PSAP .... Public Safety Answering Point [Telecommunications]   (TEL)
PSAP .... Pulmonary Surfactant Apoprotein [Biochemistry]
PsaQ .... Psychoanalytic Quarterly [A publication]
PSAR .... Platform Shock Attenuation and Realignment System   (MCD)
PSAR .... Pneumatic [or Pressure] System Automatic Regulator   (AAG)
PSAR .... Preliminary Safety Analysis Report [NASA]
PSAR .... Programable Synchronous/Asynchronous Receiver   (IEEE)
PsaR .... Psychoanalytic Review [A publication]
PSarg .... Pre-Sargonic   (BJA)
PSAS .... Papers in International Studies. Africa Series. Ohio University
                 [A publication]
PSAS .... Proceedings. Society of Antiquaries of Scotland [A publication]
PSAS .... Production Systems Acceptance Section [Social Security
                 Administration]
PSASS .... Perishable Subsistence Automated Supply System [DoD]
PSASV .... Phase-Sensitive Anodic Stripping Voltammetry

PSAT......... Predicted Site Acquisition Table [*NASA*]
PSAT......... Preliminary Scholastic Aptitude Test
PSAT......... Programable Synchronous/Asynchronous Transmitter (IEEE)
PSAUSA.... Polish Socialist Alliance of the United States of America (EA)
PSAVA...... Pribory i Sistemy Avtomatiki [*A publication*]
PSAX......... Pacific Southwest Airlines [*Air carrier designation symbol*]
PSB........... Pacific Science Board [*National Academy of Sciences*]
PSb........... Palestinskij Sbornik [*A publication*]
PSB........... Parti Socialiste Belge [*Belgian Socialist Party*]
PSB........... Philatelic Sales Branch [*Later, PSD*] [*US Postal Service*]
PSB........... Philipsburg, PA [*Location identifier*] [*FAA*] (FAAL)
PSB........... Phosphorus-Solubilizing Bacteria [*Microbiology*]
PSB........... Plant Safety Bureau
PSB........... Plant Service Building [*Nuclear energy*] (NRCH)
PSB........... Premium Savings Bond [*British*]
PSB........... Program Specification Block [*IBM Corp.*]
PSB........... Protected Specimen Brush [*Medicine*]
PsB........... Psychological Bulletin [*A publication*]
PSBA......... Proceedings. Society of Biblical Archaeology [*A publication*]
PSBF......... Pearl S. Buck Foundation [*Perkasie, PA*] (EA)
PSBG........ Pregnancy-Specific beta-Glycoprotein [*Gynecology*]
PSBH......... Pad Safety in Blockhouse
PSBL......... Possible (FAAC)
PSBLS....... Permanent Space Based Logistics System
PSBMA...... Professional Services Business Management Association
           [*Later, PSMA*] (EA)
PSBR......... Pennsylvania State University Breazeale Nuclear Reactor
           [*Research center*] (RCD)
PSBR......... Public Sector Borrowing Requirement
PSBS......... Policy Sciences Book Series [*Elsevier Book Series*] [*A*
           publication]
PSBT......... Pilot Self-Briefing Terminal (FAAC)
PSBU......... Psychopharmacology Bulletin [*A publication*]
PSBUA...... Psychological Bulletin [*A publication*]
PSC........... Congolese Socialist Party [*Zairian*] (PD)
PSC........... Isla De Pascua [*Easter Island*] [*Seismograph station code, US
           Geological Survey*] [*Closed*] (SEIS)
PSC........... Pacific Science Center
PSC........... Pacific Science Council
PSC........... Pacific South Coast Freight Bureau, San Francisco CA [*STAC*]
PSC........... Pacific Studies Center [*Mountain View, CA*] [*Research
           center*] (EA)
PSC........... Palestine Solidarity Committee [*Defunct*] (EA)
PSC........... Palmer Skin Conductance
PSC........... Parallel to Serial Converter
PSC........... Parallel Switch Control (MCD)
PSC........... Parents Sharing Custody [*Marina Del Rey, CA*] (EA)
PSC........... Parti Socialiste Camerounais [*Cameroonese Socialist Party*]
PSC........... Parti Socialiste Centrafricain [*Central African Socialist
           Party*] (PD)
PSC........... Partido Social Cristiano [*Social Christian Party*]
           [*Ecuadorean*] (PPW)
PSC........... Partido Social Cristiano [*Social Christian Party*]
           [*Guatemalan*] (PPW)
PSC........... Partido Social Cristiano [*Social Christian Party*] [*Bolivia*]
PSC........... Partido Socialcristiano Nicaraguense [*Nicaraguan Social
           Christian Party*] (PPW)
PSC........... Partido Socialista de Catalunya [*Catalan Socialist Party*]
           [*Spanish*] (PPE)
PSC........... Pasco [*Washington*] [*Airport symbol*] (OAG)
PSC........... Pasco, WA [*Location identifier*] [*FAA*] (FAAL)
PSC........... Passed Staff College [*British*]
PSC........... Paul Smiths College [*New York*]
PSCH......... Peacetime Subcontract
PSC........... Pembroke State College [*North Carolina*]
PSC........... Per Standard Compass [*Navigation*]
PSC........... Percentage of Successful Collisions [*Obstetrics*]
PSC........... Personal Supercomputer [*Culler Scientific Systems Corp.*]
PSC........... Personnel Status Change (KSC)
PSC........... Personnel Subsystem Cost
PSC........... Petty Sessional Court [*British*] (ROG)
PSC........... Phase-Sensitive Converter
PSC........... Philadelphia Service Center [*IRS*]
PSC........... Philadelphia Suburban Corporation [*NYSE symbol*]
PSC........... Philander Smith College [*Little Rock, AR*]
PSC........... Philippine Sugar Commission (EA)
PSC........... Phonemic Spelling Council
PSC........... Photosensitive Cell (IEEE)
PSC........... Physical Sciences Center
PSC........... Physical Sciences Committee [*Terminated, 1977*]
           [*NASA*] (EGAO)
PSC........... Physical Security/Pilferage Code (MCD)
Psc........... Pisces [*Constellation*]
pSC........... Plasmid Stanley Cohen [*Molecular biology*]
PSC........... Pluripotent Stem Cell [*Cytology*]
PSC........... Plutonium Stripping Concentrate [*Nuclear energy*] (NRCH)
PSC........... Polar Science Center [*University of Washington*] [*Research
           center*] (RCD)
PSC........... Polar Stratospheric Clouds
PSC........... Polaroid Stereoscopic Chroncyclegraph

PSC........... Population Studies Center [*University of Michigan*] [*Research
           center*] (RCD)
PSC........... Porcelain on Steel Council [*Defunct*] (EA)
PSC........... Post-Storage Checkout [*NASA*] (KSC)
PSC........... Postal Service Center
PSC........... Posterior Subcapsular Cataracts [*Ophthalmology*]
PSC........... Potentiometer Strip Chart
PSC........... Potomac State College [*of West Virginia University*]
PSC........... Power Supply Calibrator
PSC........... Pressure Suit Circuit (KSC)
PSC........... Pressure System Control (AAG)
PSC........... Prestressed Concrete (ADA)
PSC........... Presumptive Hematopoietic Stem Cell
PSC........... Price Signal Code (AABC)
PSC........... Primary Sclerosing Cholangitis [*Medicine*]
PSC........... Principal Subordinate Command (NATG)
PSC........... Printer Systems Corporation [*Gaithersburg, MD*] [*Hardware
           manufacturer*]
PSC........... Private Sector Council (EA)
PS & C....... Private Siding and Collected One End
PSC........... PROBE [*Program Optimization and Budget Evaluation*]
           Steering Committee [*Military*]
PSC........... Processing Service Centers [*Social Security Administration*]
PSC........... Processing and Spectral Control
PSC........... Procurement Source Code (AFM)
PSC........... Product Support Confidential (AAG)
PSC........... Professional Services Council [*Formerly, NCPSF*] (EA)
PSC........... Program Schedule Chart (NASA)
PSC........... Program Service Center [*Social Security
           Administration*] (OICC)
PSC........... Program Standards Checker [*Data processing*]
PSC........... Program Status Chart [*Data processing*]
PSC........... Program Structure Code (AFM)
PSC........... Programable Sample Changer [*Spectroscopy*]
PSC........... Project Systems Control (MCD)
PSC........... Prototype System Characteristics
PSC........... Public Service Careers [*Program*] [*Department of Labor*]
PSC........... Public Service Commission [*Usually, of a specific state*]
PSC........... Public Service Company
PSC........... Pulse Synchronized Contraction [*In the vascular system*]
           [*Medicine*]
PSC........... Sandoz AG [*Switzerland*] [*Research code symbol*]
PSc........... Scranton Public Library, Scranton, PA [*Library symbol*]
           [*Library of Congress*] (LCLS)
PSC........... Swarthmore College, Swarthmore, PA [*Library symbol*]
           [*Library of Congress*] [*OCLC symbol*] (LCLS)
PscA......... Pisces Austrinus [*Constellation*]
PSCA........ Polish Social and Cultural Association [*London, England*] (EA-
           IO)
PSCA........ Pressure Suit Conditioning Assembly (MCD)
PSCA........ Profit Sharing Council of America [*Chicago, IL*] (EA)
PSCB........ Padded Sample Collection Bag [*NASA*]
PSCBG...... Paper Shipping-Containers Buyers Group
PS & CC.... Packaging, Storage, and Containerization Center
           [*DARCOM*] (MCD)
PSCC........ Photo Systems Controller Console (KSC)
PSCD........ Plutonium Stripping Concentration Distillate [*Nuclear
           energy*] (NRCH)
PSCD........ Program for the Study of Crime and Delinquency [*Ohio State
           University*] [*Research center*] (RCD)
PSCF......... Processor Storage Control Function
PSCFB....... Pacific South Coast Freight Bureau
PSCG........ Power Supply Control Group [*Military*] (CAAL)
PSCH........ Postoperative Suprachoroidal Hemorrhage [*Medicine*]
P Sch........ Prairie Schooner [*A publication*]
PSC-Hi...... Friends Historical Library of Swarthmore College, Swarthmore,
           PA [*Library symbol*] [*Library of Congress*] (LCLS)
PSCHO...... Psychopharmacology [*A publication*]
PSCI......... Plastic Shipping Container Institute [*Chicago, IL*] (EA)
PSCL........ Papers and Studies in Contrastive Linguistics [*A publication*]
PSCL........ Programed Sequential Control Language
PSCL........ Propellants System Components Laboratory [*Kennedy Space
           Center*] [*NASA*]
PScLL....... Lackawanna Bar Association Law Library, Scranton, PA
           [*Library symbol*] [*Library of Congress*] (LCLS)
PScM......... Marywood College, Scranton, PA [*Library symbol*] [*Library of
           Congress*] (LCLS)
PSCM........ Process Steering and Control Module
           [*Telecommunications*] (TEL)
PSCN........ Partido Socialcristiano Nicaraguense [*Nicaraguan Social
           Christian Party*] (PPW)
PSCN........ Permanent System Control Number (MCD)
PSCN........ Preliminary Specification Change Notice [*NASA*] (NASA)
PSCO........ Pennsylvania State College of Optometry
PSCO........ Personnel Survey Control Officer (AABC)
PSCOB...... Psychiatric Communications [*A publication*]
P S Conf Co... Proceedings. Southern Conference on Corrections [*A
           publication*]
PSCP........ Palestine Symphonic Choir Project (EA)
PSCP........ Polar Continental Shelf Project [*Canada*]
PSCP........ Public Service Careers Program [*Department of Labor*]

PSC-P .... Swarthmore College Peace Collection, Swarthmore, PA [*Library symbol*] [*Library of Congress*] (LCLS)
PSCPD .... Philadelphia Signal Corps Procurement District [*Army*]
PSC-PSOE ... Partit dels Socialistes de Catalunya [*Party of Socialists of Catalonia*] (PPW)
PSCPT ...... Preschool Self-Concept Picture Test [*Psychology*]
PScQ .... Political Science Quarterly [*A publication*]
PSCR .... Permanent Scratch File [*Data processing*]
PSCR .... Photo-Selective Copper Reduction [*For circuit board manufacture*]
PSCR .... Priority System Change Request
PSCR .... Production Schedule Completion Report [*DoD*]
PSCR .... Public Service Commission Reports (DLA)
P Scribe ..... Portland Scribe [*A publication*]
PSCS .... Pacific Scatter Communications System [*Air Force*] (CET)
PSCS .... Program Support Control System
PSCU .... Power Supply Control Unit (CET)
PScU .... University of Scranton, Scranton, PA [*Library symbol*] [*Library of Congress*] (LCLS)
PSCUS ...... Peters' United States Surpeme Court Reports [*26-41 United States*] (DLA)
PSCXC ...... Photographic Sciences [*NASDAQ symbol*] (NQ)
PSD .... Destour Socialist Party [*Tunisian*] (PD)
PSD .... Doctor of Political Science
Ps D .... Doctor of Psychology
Ps D .... Doctor of Psychology in Metaphysics
PSD .... Doctor of Public Service
PSD .... Packed Switched Data
PSD .... Parti Social-Democrate [*Social Democratic Party*] [*French*] (PPW)
PSD .... Parti Social Democrate de Madagascar et des Comores [*Social Democratic Party of Madagascar and Comores*]
PSD .... Particle Size Distribution
PSD .... Partido Social-Democrata [*Social-Democrat Party*] [*Spanish*] (PPE)
PSD .... Partido Social Democrata [*Social Democratic Party*] [*Bolivian*] (PPW)
PSD .... Partido Social Democrata [*Social Democratic Party*] [*Mexico*] (PPW)
PSD .... Partido Social Democratico [*Social Democratic Party*] [*Nicaraguan*] (PPW)
PSD .... Partido Social Democratico [*Social Democratic Party*] [*Brazil, El Salvador*]
PSD .... Partido Socialista Democratico [*Democratic Socialist Party*] [*Guatemalan*] (PD)
PSD .... Partido Socialista Democratico [*Democratic Socialist Party*] [*Argentina*] (PPW)
PSD .... Passed (ROG)
PSD .... Passing Scene Display
PSD .... Past Start Date
PSD .... Patient Symptom Diary
PSD .... Permanent Signal Detection [*Telecommunications*] (TEL)
PSD .... Personal Services Department [*Navy*] [*British*]
PSD .... Personnel Services Division [*Army*]
PSD .... Personnel System [*or Subsystem*] Development (AAG)
PSD .... Pescadero [*California*] [*Seismograph station code, US Geological Survey*] (SEIS)
PSD .... Petroleum Safety Data [*American Petroleum Institute*]
PSD .... Petty Session Division (DLA)
PSD .... Phase-Sensitive Demodulator
PSD .... Phase Shifter Driver
PSD .... Philatelic Sales Division [*Formerly, PSB*] [*US Postal Service*]
PSD .... Photoconductive, Semiconductive Device
PSD .... Photon Stimulated Desorption [*For analysis of surfaces*]
PSD .... Physical Sciences Data [*Elsevier Book Series*] [*A publication*]
PSD .... Pitch Servo Drive
PSD .... Polystyrene, Deuterated [*Organic chemistry*]
PSD .... Post Sending Delay
PSD .... Postsynaptic Density [*Neurophysiology*]
PSD .... Power Spectral [*or Spectrum*] Density
PSD .... Preferred Sea Duty
PSD .... Pressure-Sensitive Devices (MCD)
PSD .... Prevention of Significant Deterioration [*Environmental Protection Agency*]
PS & D .... Private Siding and Delivered One End
PSD .... Procedural Support Data
PSD .... Processing Status Display [*NASA*]
PSD .... Procurement Surveys Division [*NASA*] (MCD)
PSD .... Professional Service Dates [*Formerly, ADBD*]
PSD .... Professional Systems Division [*American Institute of Architects Service Corp.*] [*Washington, DC*] [*Information service*] (EISS)
PSD .... Program Status Documents [*Data processing*]
PSD .... Program Status Doubleword
PSD .... Program Support Document (MUGU)
PSD .... Promotion Service Date
PSD .... Propellant Slosh Dynamics
PSD .... Propellant Storage Depot [*NASA*]
PSD .... Protective Serum Dilution
PSD .... Protective Structures Division [*Office of Civil Defense*]

PSD .... Pseudosingle Domain [*Behavior of grains in rocks*] [*Geophysics*]
PSD .... Puget Sound Power & Light Co. [*NYSE symbol*]
PSD .... Pulse Shape Discriminator
PSD .... Pure Screw Dislocation
PSD .... Social Democratic Party [*Mexico*] (PD)
PSDA .... Partial Source Data Automation (NVT)
PSDA .... Particle Size Distribution Analysis [*Statistics*]
PSDC .... Pennsylvania State Data Center [*Pennsylvania State University, Institute of State and Regional Affairs*] [*Middletown*] [*Information service*] (EISS)
PSDC .... Plant Sciences Data Center [*Formerly, Plant Records Center*] [*American Horticultural Society*] [*Mt. Vernon, VA*]
PSDC .... Power Sprayer and Duster Council (EA)
PSDC .... Protective Structures Development Center [*Military*]
PSDD .... Preliminary System Design Description (NRCH)
PSDDS ...... Pilot [*or Public*] Switched Digital Data Service [*Telecommunications*] (TEL)
Psdepgr .... Pseudepigrapha (BJA)
PSDF .... Popular Self-Defense Force [*Local armed units protecting Vietnamese hamlets*]
PSDF .... Propulsion Systems Development Facility (KSC)
PSDI .... Partido Social Democratico Independente [*Independent Social Democratic Party*] [*Portuguese*] (PPE)
PSDI .... Partito Socialista Democratico Italiano [*Italian Social Democratic Party*]
PSDI .... Project Software & Development, Incorporated [*Cambridge, MA*] [*Software manufacturer*]
PSDIAD ...... Photostimulated Desorption Ion Angular Distribution [*Surface analysis*]
PSDIS .... Partito Socialista Democratico Indipendente Sammarinese [*Independent Social Democratic Party of San Marino*] (PPE)
PSdM .... Mennonite Publishing House, Scottsdale, PA [*Library symbol*] [*Library of Congress*] (LCLS)
PSDP .... Payload Station Distribution Panel [*NASA*] (MCD)
PSDP .... Personnel Subsystem Development Plan
PSDP .... Phrase Structure and Dependency Parser (DIT)
PSDP .... Programable Signal Data Processor (MCD)
PSDR .... Planning and Scheduling Document Record [*NASA*] (NASA)
PSDS .... Packet Switched Data Service [*Telecommunications*] (TEL)
PSDS .... Partito Socialista Democratico Sammarinese [*Social Democratic Party of San Marino*] (PPE)
PSDS .... Passing Scene Display System
PSDS .... Permanently Separated from Duty Station [*Military*]
PS & DS ..... Program Statistics and Data Systems
PSDT .... President (ROG)
PSDTC ...... Pacific Securities Depository Trust Company
PSDU .... Power Switching Distribution Unit
PSDVB ...... Poly(styrene-Divinylbenzene) [*Organic chemistry*]
PSE .... Pacific Stock Exchange [*San Francisco, CA*] (EA)
PSE .... Packet-Switching Exchange
PSE .... Partido Socialista Ecuatoriano [*Ecuadorean Socialist Party*] (PPW)
PSE .... Partido Socialista de Euskadi [*Basque Socialist Party*] [*Spanish*]
PSE .... Passive Seismic Experiment [*NASA*]
PSE .... Payload Service Equipment [*NASA*] (MCD)
PSE .... Payload Support Equipment [*NASA*] (MCD)
PSE .... Peculiar Support Equipment [*NASA*] (NASA)
PSE .... Personnel Subsystem Elements [*Army*] (AABC)
PSE .... Phase-Shifter, Electronic
PSE .... Philadelphia Stock Exchange, Inc. [*Also, PHILEX, PHLX*] [*Formerly, PBW*]
PSE .... Physical Security Equipment [*Army*] (RDA)
PSE .... Phytochemical Society of Europe (EA)
PSE .... Pitch Steering Error
PSE .... Pleasant Saturday Evenings
PSE .... Pleasant Sunday Evenings (ROG)
PSE .... Please (MDG)
PSE .... Point of Subjective Equality [*Psychology*]
PSE .... Polestar Exploration, Inc. [*Vancouver Stock Exchange symbol*]
PSE .... Ponce [*Puerto Rico*] [*Airport symbol*] (OAG)
PSE .... Portal Systemic Encephalopathy [*Medicine*]
PSE .... Power System Engineering (MCD)
PSE .... Prague Studies in English [*A publication*]
PSE .... Pressurized Subcritical Experiment
PSE .... Prevention of Stripping Equipment (NATG)
PSE .... Princeton Studies in English [*A publication*]
PSE .... Principal Staff Element [*Defense Supply Agency*]
PSE .... Priority Standardization Effort [*Army*] (AABC)
PSE .... Probability of Successful Engagement [*Military*] (CAAL)
PSE .... Product Support Engineering (MCD)
PSE .... Programed System Evolution (MCD)
PSE .... Protein Separation Efficiency [*Food technology*]
PSE .... Psychological Stress Evaluator [*Lie detector*]
PSE .... Public Service Electric & Gas Co., Newark, NJ [*OCLC symbol*] (OCLC)
PSE .... Public Service Employment
PSE .... Pulse Sense
PSEA .... Physical Security Equipment Agency [*Army*]

PSEA......... Pleaters, Stitchers, and Embroiderers Association [*New York, NY*]   (EA)
PSEAL....... Papers in South East Asian Linguistics [*A publication*]
PSEBM...... Proceedings of the Society for Experimental Biology and Medicine [*A publication*]
P/SEC....... Personal Secretary
PSEC......... Picosecond
PSE & C ..... Power Supply Engineering and Construction [*Nuclear energy*]   (NRCH)
PSEF .... Pennsylvania Science and Engineering Foundation
PSEF .... Plastic Surgery Educational Foundation [*Chicago, IL*]   (EA)
PSE & G ..... Public Service Electric & Gas Co.
PSEKUT ..... Paar Sammukest Eesti Kirjanduse Uurimise Teed [*A publication*]
PSEL .... Publications. Societe Egyptologique a l'Universite d'Etat de Leningrad [*A publication*]
PSelS .... Susquehanna University, Selinsgrove, PA [*Library symbol*] [*Library of Congress*]   (LCLS)
PSEMA...... Parti Social d'Education des Masses Africaines [*African Party for Social Education of the Masses*] [*Upper Volta*]
PSENA ...... Photographic Science and Engineering [*A publication*]
PSEP .... Passive Seismic Experiments Package [*NASA*]
PSEQ......... Pupil Services Expectation Questionnaire
PS & ER...... Production Support and Equipment Replacement   (AABC)
PSES .... Pretreatment Standards for Existing Sources [*Environmental Protection Agency*]
Pseud........ Pseudepigrapha   (BJA)
PSEUD ...... Pseudonym
Pseudep...... Pseudepigrapha   (BJA)
PSEW .... Project on the Status and Education of Women   (EA)
PSewD .... Dixmont State Hospital, Sewickley, PA [*Library symbol*] [*Library of Congress*]   (LCLS)
PSF .... Pakistan Science Foundation
PSF .... Panama Sea Frontier
PSF .... Panhandle & Santa Fe Railway Co. [*AAR code*]
P & SF .... Panhandle & Santa Fe Railway Co.
PSF .... Parti Social Francais [*French Social Party*]   (PPE)
PSF .... Passive Solar Foundation   (EA)
PSF .... Payload Structure Fuel [*Ratio*]
PSF .... Per Square Foot   (ADA)
PSF .... Permanent Signal Finder
PSF .... Philippine Sea Frontier
PSF .... Pittsfield, MA [*Location identifier*] [*FAA*]   (FAAL)
PSF .... Plutonium Stripper Feed [*Nuclear energy*]   (NRCH)
PSF .... Point Spread Function
PSF .... Popular Struggle Front [*Palestinian*]   (PD)
PSF .... Port Stanley [*Falkland Islands*] [*Seismograph station code, US Geological Survey*] [*Closed*]   (SEIS)
PSF .... Pounds per Square Foot
PSF .... Presidio of San Francisco [*Military*]   (AABC)
PSF .... Prime Subframe   (MCD)
PSF .... Probability of Spurious Fire [*Military*]   (CAAL)
PSF .... Processing and Storage Facility [*NASA*]   (NASA)
PSF .... Program for the Study of the Future   (EA)
PSF .... Progres Social Francais [*French Social Progress*]   (PPE)
PSF .... Progressive Space Forum   (EA)
PSF .... Provisional Sinn Fein [*Northern Ireland*]
PSF .... Provisional System Feature [*Telecommunications*]   (TEL)
PSF .... Pseudosarcomatous Fasciitis [*Medicine*]
PSF .... Saint Francis College, Loretto, PA [*OCLC symbol*]   (OCLC)
PSFAM...... Parameter Sensitive Frequency Assignment Method   (MCD)
PS/FC .... Power Supply/Fuel Cell   (MCD)
PSFC......... Process Supercritical Fluid Chromatography
PSFC......... Provisional Special Forces Company   (CINC)
PSFC/HIMH ... Pete Shelley Fan Club/Harmony in My Head   (EA)
PSFD......... Public-Sector Financial Deficit
PSFL .... Puget Sound Freight Lines [*AAR code*]
PSFQ........ Pupil Services Fulfillment Questionnaire
PSFS .... Philadelphia Savings Fund Society [*NASDAQ symbol*]   (NQ)
PSG.......... Pacific Seabird Group   (EA)
PSG.......... Palestine Study Group [*New Brunswick, NJ*]   (EA)
PSG.......... Parachute Study Group   (EA)
PSG.......... Parti Socialiste Guyanais [*Guiana Socialist Party*]   (PPW)
PSG.......... Passage   (FAAC)
PSG.......... Passing   (FAAC)
PSG.......... Pechiney-Saint-Gobain [*Commercial firm*] [*France*]
PSG.......... Petersburg [*Alaska*] [*Airport symbol*]   (OAG)
PSG.......... Petersburg, AK [*Location identifier*] [*FAA*]   (FAAL)
PSG.......... Phosphate-Saline-Glucose [*A buffer*] [*Cell culture*]
PSG.......... Phosphosilicate Glass   (IEEE)
PSG.......... Planning Systems Generator
PSG.......... Platoon Sergeant [*Army*]   (AABC)
PSG.......... Post Stall Gyration   (MCD)
PSG.......... Power Subsystem Group   (MCD)
PSG.......... Presystolic Gallop [*Cardiology*]
PSG.......... Production System Generator
PSG.......... Professional Specialty Group
PSG.......... Programable Sound Generator [*Chip*] [*Atari, Inc.*]
PSG.......... PS Group, Inc. [*NYSE symbol*]
PSG.......... Psychogalvanometer
PSG.......... Publishing Systems Group [*Trenton, NJ*]   (EA)

PSG........... Pulse Sequence Generation [*Instrumentation*]
PSGA .... Parkinson Support Groups of America [*Beltsville, MD*]   (EA)
PSGA .... Pedal Steel Guitar Association   (EA)
PSGA .... Professional Skaters Guild of America   (EA)
PSGM........ Past Supreme Grand Master [*Freemasonry*]
PSGN .... Post-Streptococcal Glomerulonephritis [*Medicine*]
PSGR......... Passenger   (AFM)
PSGT......... Platoon Sergeant [*Military*]
PSGTCAEI ... Permanent Secretariat of the General Treaty on Central American Economic Integration [*Guatemala City, Guatemala*]   (EA-IO)
PSGW........ Past Senior Grand Warden [*Freemasonry*]
PSH .... Friends Historical Library of Swarthmore College, Swarthmore, PA [*OCLC symbol*]   (OCLC)
PSH .... Parshall, ND [*Location identifier*] [*FAA*]   (FAAL)
PSH .... Permanent Shift of Hearing
PSH .... Peshawar [*Pakistan*] [*Seismograph station code, US Geological Survey*]   (SEIS)
PSH .... Phase Shift   (MSA)
PSH .... Polystyrene, Hydrogenous [*Organic chemistry*]
PSH .... Post-Stimulus Histogram [*Psychometrics*]
PSH .... Preselect Heading   (NG)
PSH .... Pressure Switch, High [*Nuclear energy*]   (NRCH)
PSH .... Program Support Handbook
PSH .... Proximity Sensing Head
PSH .... Publications Statistiques Hongroises [*Hungary*]
PSHADL...... Publications. Societe Historique et Archeologique dans le Duche de Limbourg [*A publication*]
PSHAL ...... Publications. Societe Historique et Archeologique dans le Duche de Limbourg [*A publication*]
P Shaw ..... Patrick Shaw's Justiciary Cases [*1819-31*] [*Scotland*]   (DLA)
PSHC .... Permanent Secretariat of the Hemispheric Congress   (EA)
PSHC .... Public Speaking and Humor Club [*Brooklyn, NY*]   (EA)
PSHD......... Phase-Shift Driver   (MSA)
PSHED .... Psychologie Heute [*A publication*]
PSHF .... Polysulfone Hollow Fiber [*Filtration membrane*]
PSHIGDL.... Publications. Section Historique. Institut Grand-Ducal de Luxembourg [*A publication*]
PSHIL .... Publications. Section Historique. Institut Grand-Ducal de Luxembourg [*A publication*]
PSHL.......... Publications. Societe Historique et Archeologique dans le Duche de Limbourg [*A publication*]
PSHR......... Pusher [*Freight*]
PShS .... Shippensburg State College, Shippensburg, PA [*Library symbol*] [*Library of Congress*]   (LCLS)
PSI............. Pacer Software, Incorporated [*La Jolla, CA*] [*Software manufacturer*]
PSI............. Paid Service Indication [*Telecommunications*]   (TEL)
PSI............. Paper Stock Institute of America [*New York, NY*]   (EA)
PSI............. Parapat [*Sumatra*] [*Seismograph station code, US Geological Survey*]   (SEIS)
PSI............. Partai Socialis Indonesia [*Socialist Party of Indonesia*]
PSI............. Participation Systems, Incorporated [*Electronics Communications Co.*] [*Winchester, MA*] [*Telecommunications*]   (TSSD)
PSI............. Partito Socialista Italiano [*Italian Socialist Party*]   (PPE)
PSI............. Pasni [*Pakistan*] [*Airport symbol*]   (OAG)
PSI............. Passive Solar Institute   (EA)
P & SI .... Pay and Supply Instruction [*Coast Guard*]
PSI............. Per Square Inch   (ADA)
PSI............. Peripherally Synapsing Interneuron [*Neurology*]
PSI............. Permanent Staff Instructor [*Military*] [*British*]
PSI............. Permuterm Subject Index [*Institute for Scientific Information*] [*A publication*]   (EISS)
Psl............. Perpetual Storage, Inc., Salt Lake City, UT [*Library symbol*] [*Library of Congress*]   (LCLS)
PSI............. Personal Service Income
PSI............. Personalized System of Instruction
PSI............. Personnel Security Investigation
PSI............. Phenomenological Systems, Incorporated
PSI............. Photometric Sunspot Index
PSI............. Physical, Sensitivity, Intellectual [*Biorhythms*]
PSI............. Piccole Storie Illustrate [*A publication*]
PSI............. Plan Speed Indicator
PSI............. Planned Start Installation [*Telecommunications*]   (TEL)
PSI............. Play Skills Inventory
PSI............. Policy Studies Institute [*Research center*] [*British*]   (IRC)
PSI............. Pollutant Standards Index
p-Si............ Polycrystalline Silicon [*Photovoltaic energy systems*]
PSI............. Porta Systems Corp. [*American Stock Exchange symbol*]
PSI............. Positive Self-Image [*Psychology*]
PSI............. Pounds per Square Inch
PSI............. Power per Square Inch
PSI............. Praed Street Irregulars [*An association*]   (EA)
PSI............. Pre-Sentence Investigation   (OICC)
PSI............. Preprogramed Self-Instruction [*Data processing*]   (IEEE)
PSI............. Present Serviceability Index   (IEEE)
PSI............. Preservice Inspection [*Nuclear energy*]   (NRCH)
PSI............. Pressure Sensitive Identification
PSI............. Problem-Solving Information [*Apparatus*]
PSI............. Problem Solving Interpreter [*Computer language*]

PSI............. Process System Index
PSI............. Process Systems, Incorporated
PSI............. Proctorial System of Instruction   (IEEE)
PSI............. Product Support Instructions   (AAG)
PSI............. Production Stock Item   (MCD)
PSI............. Professional Secretaries International [*Formerly, NSA*] [*Kansas City, MO*]   (EA)
PSI............. Program Status Information [*Data processing*]   (MCD)
PSI............. Program Supply Interest   (MCD)
PSI............. Programed School Input   (NVT)
PSI............. Project Starlight International   (EA)
PSI............. Protosynthex Index
PSI............. Psychosomatic Inventory [*Psychology*]
PSI............. Pubblicazioni. Societa Italiana per la Ricerca dei Papiri Greci e Latini in Egitto [*Florence*] [*A publication*]
PSI........... Public Service International [*See also ISP*] [*Feltham, England*]   (EA-IO)
PSI............. Publications Standing Instruction   (AAG)
PSIA .... Paper Stock Institute of America   (EA)
PSIA .... Pounds per Square Inch Absolute
PSIA .... President of the Society of Industrial Artists [*British*]
PSIA .... Production System Integration Area
PSIA .... Professional Ski Instructors of America   (EA)
PSIA .... Public Security Investigation Agency [*Japan*]   (CINC)
PSIC .... Passenger Service Improvement Corporation
PSIC .... Passive Solar Industries Council   (EA)
PSIC .... Process Signal Interface Controller
PSIC .... Production Scheduling and Inventory Control
PSICD .... Proceedings. IEEE Computer Society's International Computer Software and Applications Conference [*A publication*]
PSICP........ Program Support Inventory Control Point
PSID .... Partial Seismic Intrusion Device   (MCD)
PSID .... Patrol Seismic Intrusion Detector [*DoD*]
PSID .... Pounds per Square Inch Differential   (MCD)
PSID .... Preliminary Safety Information Document [*Nuclear energy*]   (NRCH)
PS/IDS ...... Physical Security/Intrusion Detection System   (MCD)
PSIEP .... Project on Scientific Information Exchange in Psychology [*Superseded by Office of Communication*]
PSIG .... Pounds per Square Inch Gauge
PSIL .... Potential Selected Item List   (MCD)
PSIL .... Preferred Speech Interference Level
PSI-LOGO ... Listing of Oil and Gas Opportunities [*Online Resource Exchange, Inc.*] [*Database*]
PSIM .... Power System Instrumentation and Measurement   (MCD)
PSIM .... Problem–Solving Instructional Material [*National Science Foundation project*]
PSIP .... Private Sector Initiative Program [*Department of Labor*]
PSIR Bull Monogr ... PSIR [*Pakistan Council of Scientific and Industrial Research*] Bulletin Monograph [*A publication*]
PSIS .... Pounds per Square Inch Sealed   (NASA)
PSISIG .... Psychic Science International Special Interest Group   (EA)
PSIUP........ Partito Socialista Italiano di Unita Proletaria [*Italian Socialist Party of Proletarian Unity (1945-1947)*]   (PPE)
PSIV .... Passive
PSJ............. Parallel Swivel Joint
PSJ............. Philosophical Studies of Japan [*A publication*]
PSJ............. Plane Swivel Joint
PSJ............. Poso [*Indonesia*] [*Airport symbol*]   (OAG)
PSJ............. Pressure Switch Joint
PSJ............. Public Service Job   (OICC)
PSJS .... Pier and Span Junction Set   (MCD)
PSK .... Dublin, VA [*Location identifier*] [*FAA*]   (FAAL)
PSK .... Phase-Shift Keying [*Data processing*]
PSK .... Power Supply Kit
PSK .... Private Secretary to the King [*British*]
PSK .... Program Selection Key [*Data processing*]   (BUR)
PSK .... Protection Survey Kit
PSK .... Pulse Shift Keying   (CAAL)
PSKI.......... Pikes Peak Ski Corp. [*NASDAQ symbol*]   (NQ)
PSKJ.......... Pitanja Savremenog Knjizevnog Jezika [*A publication*]
PSKM .... Phase-Shift Keying MODEM
Pskov Ped Inst Fiz-Mat Fak Ucen Zap ... Pskovskii Pedagogiceskii Institut. Fiziko-Matematiceskii Fakul'tet. Ucenye Zapiski [*A publication*]
PSK-PCM... Phase-Shift Keying - Pulse Code Modulation
PSL............. Paymaster-Sub-Lieutenant [*Navy*] [*British*]
PSL............. Peabody Short Line R. R. [*Army*]
PSL............. Personnel Skill Levels   (AAG)
PSL............. Photographic Science Laboratory [*Navy*]
PSL............. Physical Sciences Laboratory [*University of Wisconsin - Madison, New Mexico State University*] [*Research center*]
PSL............. Pipe Sleeve
PSL............. Pocket Select Language [*Burroughs Corp.*]
PSL............. Polskie Stronnictwo Ludowe [*Polish Peasant Party (1945-1947)*]   (PPE)
PSL............. Polskie Stronnictwo Ludowe [*Polish Peasant Party (1903-1913)*]   (PPE)
PSL............. Polymer Science Library [*Elsevier Book Series*] [*A publication*]
PSL............. Potential Source List   (MCD)
PSL............. Power and Signal List [*Telecommunications*]   (TEL)

PSL............. Power Source Logic
PS & L .... Power Switching and Logic
PSL............. Practical Storage Life
PSL............. Pressure Seal   (NASA)
PSL............. Pressure-Sensitive Label
PSL............. Primary Standards Laboratory
PSL............. Private Sector Liquidity
PSL............. Problem Specification Language
PSL............. Process Simulation Language [*Data processing*]   (TEL)
PSL............. Program Support Library   (MCD)
PSL............. Project Support Laboratory [*Military*]   (CAAL)
PSL............. Propulsion Systems Laboratory [*USATACOM*]   (RDA)
PSL............. Public School League [*Sports*]
PSL............. South Hills Library Association, Pittsburgh, PA [*OCLC symbol*]   (OCLC)
PSLA .... Polish Sea League of America   (EA)
Psl Admr .... Personnel Administrator [*A publication*]
PSLC .... Pawathy Stare Literatury Ceske [*A publication*]
PSLC .... Private Security Liaison Council [*Jackson, MS*]   (EA)
Psl Exec .... Personnel Executive [*A publication*]
Psl & Guid J ... Personnel and Guidance Journal [*A publication*]
PSLI .... Packet Switch Level Interface
PSLI .... Partito Socialista dei Lavoratori Italiani [*Socialist Party of Italian Workers*]   (PPE)
PSLI .... Penta Systems International [*NASDAQ symbol*]   (NQ)
PSLI .... Physalaemin-Like Immunoreactivity [*Medicine*]
PSL-Lewica ... Polskie Stronnictwo-Lewica [*Polish Peasant Party-Left (1947-1949)*]   (PPE)
PSL-Lewica ... Polskie Stronnictwo Ludowe-Lewica [*Polish Peasant Party-Left (1913-1920)*]   (PPE)
PSLLS .... Pulsed Solid-State LASER Light Source
PSL-NW ..... Polskie Stronnictwo Ludowe-Nowe Wyzwolenie [*Polish Peasant Party-New Liberation*]   (PPE)
PSL-Piast... Polskie Stronnictwo Ludowe-Piast [*Polish Peasant Party-Piast*]   (PPE)
PSL/PSA... Problem Statement Language/Problem Specification Analyzer [*Data processing*]
PSLS .... Pan Stock Line Station   (MCD)
PSLT .... Picture Story Language Test
PSLT .... Pressurized Sonobuoy Launch Tube [*Navy*]   (CAAL)
PSL-Wyzwolenie ... Polskie Stronnictwo Ludowe-Wyzwolenie [*Polish Peasant Party-Liberation*]   (PPE)
PSM............ Mauritian Socialist Party   (PD)
PSM............ Pagine di Storia della Medicina [*A publication*]
PSM............ Parc Saint-Maur [*France*] [*Later, CLF*] [*Geomagnetic observatory code*]
PSM............ Parcel Sorting Machine
PSM............ Parti Socialiste Monegasque [*Monaco Socialist Party*]   (PPW)
PSM............ Past Savio Movement   (EA)
PSM............ Peak Selector Memory [*Data processing*]
PSM............ Pennwalt Corp. [*Formerly, Pennsalt Chemicals Corp.*] [*NYSE symbol*]
PSM............ Personnel Subsystem Manager [*Army*]   (AABC)
PS & M ...... Personnel Supervision and Management Division of ASTSECNAV's Office [*Absorbed into SECP, 1944*]
PSM............ Personnel Systems Management [*Air Force*]   (AFM)
PSM............ Phase-Sensitive Modulator   (MCD)
PSM............ Phase-Shifter Module
PSM............ Philippine Studies (Manila) [*A publication*]
PSM............ Pia Societas Missionum [*Fathers of the Pious Society of Missions, Pallottini*] [*Roman Catholic religious order*]
PSM............ Pioneer Metals Corp. [*Formerly, Maverick Mountain Resources Ltd.*] [*Vancouver Stock Exchange symbol*]
PSM............ Please See Me
PSM............ Plymouth State College of the University of New Hampshere, Plymouth, NH [*OCLC symbol*]   (OCLC)
PSM............ Portsmouth, NH [*Location identifier*] [*FAA*]   (FAAL)
PSM............ Postal Service Manual [*A publication*]   (AFM)
PSM............ Postsynaptic Membrane [*Neurology*]
PSM............ Power Strapping Machine
PSM............ Power System Module
PSM............ Presystolic Murmur [*Cardiology*]
PSM............ Prism   (MSA)
PSM............ Pro Sanctity Movement   (EA)
P & SM ...... Procurement and Subcontract Management [*NASA*]   (NASA)
PSM............ Product Support Manual   (AAG)
PSM............ Program-Sensitive Malfunction
PSM............ Program Support Management [*NASA*]   (KSC)
PSM............ Programing Support Monitor [*Texas Instruments, Inc.*]
PSM............ Propellant Storage Module [*NASA*]
PSM............ Public School Magazine [*A publication*]
PSM............ Pyro Substitute Monitor [*NASA*]   (NASA)
PSM............ Pytannja Slov'jans'koho Movoznavstva [*A publication*]
PSm .... Thesaurus Syriacus [*R. Paine Smith*] [*A publication*]   (BJA)
PSMA .... Power Saw Manufacturers Association [*Later, CSMA*]   (EA)
PSMA .... President of the Society of Marine Artists [*British*]
PSMA........ Professional Services Management Association [*Formerly, PSBMA*] [*Alexandria, VA*]   (EA)
PSMA........ Progressive Spinal Muscular Atrophy [*Medicine*]
PSMA........ Pyrotechnic Signal Manufacturers Association [*Stamford, CT*]   (EA)

PSMD .... Photo Selective Metal Deposition
PSMDC ...... Psychological Medicine [*A publication*]
PSMEA .... Psychosomatic Medicine [*A publication*]
PSMF .... Protein Sparing Modified Fast
PSMFC .... Pacific States Marine Fisheries Commission
PSMI .... Phase-Shift Modal Interference
PSMI .... Precise Ship Motion Instrument
PSMIT .... Programing Services for Multimedia Industry Terminals [*IBM Corp.*]
PSML .... Prague Studies in Mathematical Linguistics [*A publication*]
PSML .... Processor System Modeling Language [*1976*] [*Data processing*] (CSR)
PSMM .... Multimission Patrol Ship [*Symbol*]
PSMMA ...... Plastic Soft Materials Manufacturers Association [*New York, NY*] (EA)
PSMR .... Parts Specification Management for Reliability
PSMR .... Pneumatic [*or Pressure*] System Manifold [*or Manual*] Regulator (AAG)
PSMS .... Permanent Section of Microbiological Standardization (MCD)
PSMSC ...... Psychotherapie und Medizinische Psychologie [*A publication*]
PSMSL .... Permanent Service for Mean Sea Level (EA-IO)
PSMT .... Perishable Sheet Metal Tool (MCD)
PSMUD ...... Psychology of Music [*A publication*]
PSN .... Package Sequence Number
PSN .... Packet Switching Node
PSN .... Palestine, TX [*Location identifier*] [*FAA*] (FAAL)
PSN .... Parti de la Solidarite Nationale [*Party of National Solidarity*] [*Luxembourg*] (PPE)
PSN .... Partial Shipment Number [*DoD*]
PSN .... Partido Socialista Nicaraguense [*Nicaraguan Socialist Party*] (PPW)
PSN .... Permanent Sort Number [*Data processing*]
PSN .... Position
PSN .... Private Satellite Network, Inc. [*New York, NY*] [*Telecommunications*] (TSSD)
PSN .... Processing Serial Number (MCD)
PSN .... Program Summary Network (MCD)
PSN .... Progressive Student Network (EA)
PSN .... Provisioning Sequence Number (MCD)
PSN .... Public Switched Network (BUR)
PSNA .... Phytochemical Society of North America (EA)
PSNA .... Powys Society of North America [*Chappaqua, NY*] (EA)
PSNB .... Puget Sound Bancorp [*NASDAQ symbol*] (NQ)
PSNC .... Parti Socialiste de la Nouvelle Caledonie [*Socialist Party of New Caledonia*] (PPW)
PSNC .... Public Service Co. of North Carolina [*NASDAQ symbol*] (NQ)
PSNCF .... Pacific Southern Naval Coastal Frontier
PSNCO .... Personnel Staff Noncommissioned Officer [*Military*]
PSNEB .... Psychiatric Annals [*A publication*]
PSNL .... Personnel (FAAC)
P & SNP ...... Pay and Subsistence of Naval Personnel [*Budget appropriation title*]
PSNP .... Pebble Springs Nuclear Plant (NRCH)
PSNR .... Positioner
PSNR .... Power Signal-to-Noise Ratio
PSNRP .... Position Report [*Aviation*] (FAAC)
PSNS .... Physical Science for Nonscience Students
PSNS .... Pretreatment Standards for New Indirect Sources [*Environmental Protection Agency*]
PSNS .... Programable Sampling Network Switch
PSNS .... Puget Sound Naval Shipyard [*Bremerton, WA*] (MCD)
PSNSR ...... Position Sensor (MCD)
PSNSY ...... Puget Sound Naval Shipyard [*Bremerton, WA*]
PSNT .... Pismo Swiete Nowego Testamentu [*Posen*] [*A publication*]
PSNT .... Present [*Legal term*] (ROG)
PSO .... Pad Safety Officer [*Aerospace*] (MCD)
PSO .... Paint Spray Outfit
PSO .... Pasto [*Colombia*] [*Seismograph station code, US Geological Survey*] (SEIS)
PSO .... Pasto [*Colombia*] [*Airport symbol*] (OAG)
PSO .... Pauli Spin Operator [*Physics*]
PSO .... Peacetime Stockage Objective [*DoD*] (AFIT)
PSO .... Penobscot Shoe Co. [*American Stock Exchange symbol*]
PSO .... Personnel Security Officer [*Military*]
PSO .... Piano-Shaped Object
PSO .... Pilot Systems Operator
PSO .... Planet Sensor Output
PSO .... Policy Studies Organization (EA)
PSO .... Political Survey Officers [*Navy*]
PSO .... Polysulfone [*Also, PS*] [*Organic chemistry*]
PSO .... Presidential Security Office [*Republic of Vietnam*] (CINC)
PSO .... Primary Standardization Office (AABC)
PSO .... Principal Scientific Officer [*British*]
PSO .... Procurement Services Office
PSO .... Product Support Organization
PSO .... Profco Resources Ltd. [*Vancouver Stock Exchange symbol*]
PSO .... Program Staff Officer
PSO .... Provisions Supply Office
PSO .... Public Safety Officer
PSO .... Publications Supply Officer [*Military*]
PSO .... Publicity Security Officer [*Navy*]

PSOA .... Pro Stock Owners Association (EA)
PSOB .... Paper Society for the Overseas Blind [*Defunct*] (EA)
PSoc. .... Przeglad Socjologiczny [*A publication*]
P Soc Exp M ... Proceedings. Society for Experimental Biology and Medicine [*A publication*]
PSOE .... Partido Socialista Obrero Espanol [*Spanish Socialist Workers' Party*] (PPE)
PSOLMHT ... Pious Society of Our Lady of the Most Holy Trinity (EA)
PSom .... Mary S. Biesecker Public Library, Somerset, PA [*Library symbol*] [*Library of Congress*] (LCLS)
PSomHi ...... Somerset County Historical and Genealogical Society, Somerset, PA [*Library symbol*] [*Library of Congress*] (LCLS)
PSON .... Person (ROG)
PSONAL ..... Personal (ROG)
PSOP .... Parti Socialiste des Ouvriers et Paysans [*Socialist Party of Workers and Peasants*] [*France*]
PSOP .... Power System Optimization Program [*Data processing*]
PSP .... Pace-Setting Potential [*Physiology*]
PSp .... Pacific Spectator [*A publication*]
PSP .... Package Size Proneness [*Marketing*]
PSP .... Packaging Shipping Procedures
PSP .... Packet Switching Processor
PSP .... Pad Safety Plan
PSP .... Palm Springs [*California*] [*Airport symbol*] (OAG)
PSP .... Palm Springs, CA [*Location identifier*] [*FAA*] (FAAL)
PSP .... Pancreatic Spasmolytic Peptide [*Biochemistry*]
PSP .... Paralytic Shellfish Poisoning [*Marine biology*]
PSP .... Parathyroid Secretory Protein [*Biochemistry*]
PSP .... Parti Socialiste Polynesien [*Polynesian Socialist Party*] (PPW)
PSP .... Parti Soudanais Progressiste [*Sudanese Progressive Party*] [*Malian*]
PSP .... Partido Social Progresista [*Social Progressive Party*] [*Brazil*]
PSP .... Partido Socialista del Peru [*Socialist Party of Peru*] (PPW)
PSP .... Partido Socialista Popular [*Popular Socialist Party*] [*Peruvian*] (PPW)
PSP .... Partido Socialista Popular [*Popular Socialist Party*] [*Spanish*] (PPE)
PSP .... Partido Socialista Portuguesa [*Portuguese Socialist Party*] (PPW)
PSP .... Parts Screening Program
PSP .... Patrol Seaplane
PSP .... Payload Signal Processor [*NASA*] (NASA)
PSP .... Payload Support Plan [*NASA*] (MCD)
PSP .... Peak Sideband Power (DEN)
PSP .... Performance Shaping Parameters (IEEE)
PSP .... Performance Standards Program
PSP .... Personal Success Program
PSP .... Personnel Subsystem Process [*Army*] (AABC)
PSP .... Phenolsulfonephthalein [*Chemical indicator*]
PSP .... Pierced Steel Planking [*Military*]
PSP .... Plane Strain Plastometer
PSP .... Planet Scan Platform [*NASA*] (KSC)
PSP .... Planned Standard Programing [*Data processing*]
PSP .... Plasma Spraying [*Welding*]
PSP .... Platform Sensor Package
PSP .... Polyfactorial Study of Personality [*Psychology*]
PSP .... Poly(styrene peroxide) [*Organic chemistry*]
PSP .... Portable Service Processor (IEEE)
PSP .... Post-Shoring-Polyethylene [*Method of constructing underground homes*]
PSP .... Postsynaptic Potential [*Neurophysiology*]
PSP .... Power System Planning
PSP .... Praja Socialist Party [*Indian*] (PPW)
PSP .... Predictive Smooth Pursuit [*Ophthalmology*]
PSP .... Prestart Panel [*Aerospace*] (AAG)
PSP .... Priced Spare Parts [*Military*] (AFIT)
PSP .... Primary Sodium Pump [*Nuclear energy*] (NRCH)
PSP .... Primary Supply Point [*Military*] (AFM)
PSP .... Primary Support Point [*Military*] (AFM)
PSP .... Product Service Publication [*General Motors Corp.*]
PSP .... Product Support Program (NG)
PSP .... Program Segment Prefix [*Data processing*]
PSP .... Program Support Plan
PSP .... Programable Signal Processor (MCD)
PSP .... Progressive Socialist Party [*Lebanon*] (BJA)
PSP .... Progressive Supranuclear Palsy [*Neurology*]
PSP .... Protective Shielding Program
PSP .... Protocol for Specific Purpose
PSP .... Provincia de Sao Pedro [*Brazil*] [*A publication*]
PSP .... Pseudopregnancy [*Gynecology*]
PSP .... Public Storage Canadian Prop. [*Limited Partnership Units*] [*Toronto Stock Exchange symbol*]
PSP .... Puerto Rican Socialist Party (PD)
PSP .... Swarthmore College Peace Collection, Swarthmore, PA [*OCLC symbol*] (OCLC)
PSPA .... Pacific Seafood Processors Association [*Formerly, APF*] [*Seattle, WA*] (EA)
PSPA .... Passive Solar Products Association (EA)
PSPA .... Pressure Static Probe Assembly (MCD)

PSPA.......... Professional School Photographers of America [*Jackson, MI*] (EA)
PSPC.......... President's Soviet Protocol Committee [*World War II*]
PSPCD...... Proceedings. Annual Southwestern Petroleum Short Course [*A publication*]
PSPD.......... Position-Sensitive Proportional Detector [*For X-ray diffraction*]
PSP & E..... Product Support Planning and Estimating (AAG)
PSPEN...... Primary/Secondary Peace Education Network (EA)
PSPF.......... Potential Single Point Failures [*NASA*] (KSC)
PSPF.......... Prostacyclin Stimulating Plasma Factor [*Endocrinology*]
PSPFLI...... Pulsed Single Photon Fluorescence Lifetime Instrumentation
PSPGV...... Primary Sodium Pump Guard Vesel [*Nuclear energy*] (NRCH)
PSPHA...... Psychophysiology [*A publication*]
PSphR........ Rohm & Haas Co., Research Library Services, Spring House, PA [*Library symbol*] [*Library of Congress*] (LCLS)
PSPL.......... Priced Spare Parts List
PSPL.......... Progressive Socialist Party of Lebanon
PSPLR...... Priced Spare Parts List Revision
PSPM........ Procurement Seminar for Project Management [*Army*]
PSPMW...... International Brotherhood of Pulp, Sulphite, and Paper Mill Workers [*Later, UPIU*]
PSPOB...... Psychiatria Polska [*A publication*]
PSPOS...... Philological Society. Publications. Occasional Studies [*A publication*]
PSPP.......... Preliminary System Package Plan
PSPP.......... Program System Package Plan
PSPP.......... Proposed System Package Plan
PSPR.......... Personnel Subsystem Products [*Army*] (AABC)
PSPS.......... Paddle Steamer Preservation Society
PSPS.......... Pesticides Safety Precautions Scheme [*British*]
PSPS.......... Planar Silicon Photoswitch (IEEE)
PS to PS..... Private Siding to Private Siding
PSPS.......... Product Support Procurement Summary (MCD)
PSPS.......... Program Support Plan Summary
PSPSB...... Psychotherapy and Psychosomatics [*A publication*]
PSPT.......... Passport (AABC)
PSPT.......... Planar Silicon Power Transistor
PSQ............ Personnel Security Questionnaire
PSQ............ Philologische Studien und Quellen [*A publication*]
PSQ............ Political Science Quarterly [*A publication*]
PSQA........ Pageable System Queue Area [*Data processing*] (MCD)
PSQAA...... Psychoanalytic Quarterly [*A publication*]
PSQSA...... Psychiatric Quarterly. Supplement [*A publication*]
PSQUA...... Psychiatric Quarterly [*A publication*]
PSR............ Pacific Security Region
PSR............ Pacific Sociological Review [*A publication*]
PSR............ Packed Snow on Runway [*Aviation*] (FAAC)
PSR............ Pad Safety Report [*NASA*]
PSR............ Pain Sensitivity Range [*Biometrics*]
PSR............ Panoramic Stereo Rectification
PSR............ Parachute Status Report [*Army*] (AABC)
PSR............ Partido Socialista Revolucionario [*Revolutionary Socialist Party*] [*Peruvian*] (PPW)
PSR............ Partido Socialista Revolucionario [*Revolutionary Socialist Party*] [*Portuguese*] (PPE)
PSR............ Partido Socialista Revolucionario [*Revolutionary Socialist Party*] [*Mexico*] (PPW)
PSR............ Party Socialiste Revolutionnaire [*Socialist Revolutionary Party*] [*Lebanese*] (PPW)
PSR............ Paul's Scarlet Rose [*Plant cell line*]
PSR............ Pennsylvania State Reports (DLA)
PSR............ Pennsylvania State University Reactor (NRCH)
PSR............ Perfectly Stirred Reactor
PSR............ Performance Summary Report (NG)
PSR............ Peripheral Shim Rods [*Nuclear energy*] (NRCH)
PSR............ Pescara [*Italy*] [*Airport symbol*] (OAG)
PSR............ Petaluma & Santa Rosa Railroad Co. [*AAR code*]
PSR............ Petrostates Resource Corp. [*Vancouver Stock Exchange symbol*]
PSR............ Petty Sessions Review [*A publication*]
PSR............ Phase Sequence Relay
PSR............ Philatelic Societies' Record [*A publication*] [*British*]
PSR............ Philippine Sociological Review [*A publication*]
PSR............ Physical Sciences Research Program [*North Carolina State University*] [*Research center*] (RCD)
PSR............ Physicians for Social Responsibility (EA)
PSR............ Plow-Steel Rope
PSR............ Point of Safe Return (MCD)
PSR............ Policy Status Report [*Insurance*]
PSR............ Political Science Review [*A publication*]
PSR............ Political and Social Reform Movement [*British*]
PSR............ Portable Seismic Recorder
PSR............ Post-Sinusoidal Resistance
PSR............ Postal Service Representative [*British*]
PSR............ Power System Relaying (MCD)
PSR............ Predicted SONAR Range [*Military*] (NVT)
PSR............ Price-Sales Ratio
PSR............ Problem Status Report (MCD)
PSR............ Processor State Register
PSR............ Procurement Status Report (IEEE)
PSR............ Program Status Register

PSR............ Program Status Report
PSR............ Program Study Request (AAG)
PSR............ Program Summary Record [*Military*] (AFIT)
PSR............ Program Support Requirements (KSC)
PSR............ Programing Status Report [*Data processing*]
PSR............ Programing Support Representative [*IBM Corp.*]
PSR............ Progress Summary Report
PSR............ Project Scan Record
PSR............ Project Summary Report (MCD)
PSR............ Propeller Shaft Rate [*Navy*] (CAAL)
PSR............ Proton Storage Ring [*Nuclear physics*]
PSR............ Prototype Systems Review
PSR............ Provisioning Support Request [*Military*] (CAAL)
PsR............ Psychoanalytic Review [*A publication*]
PsR............ Psychological Review [*A publication*]
PSR............ Public Service Co. of Colorado [*NYSE symbol*]
PSR............ Pulmonary Stretch Receptors [*Medicine*]
PSRA........ Professional Soccer Reporter's Association [*Glen Rock, NJ*] (EA)
PSRAAALAA ... President's Special Representative and Adviser on African, Asian, and Latin American Affairs [*Department of State*]
PSRC........ Plastic Surgery Research Council [*Springfield, IL*] (EA)
PSRC........ Public Service Research Council (EA)
PSRD........ Personnel Shipment Ready Date [*Army*] (AABC)
PSRD........ Program Support Requirements Document (KSC)
PSRE........ Partido Socialista Revolucionario Ecuatoriano [*Socialist Revolutionary Party of Ecuador*] (PPW)
PSREA...... Psychoanalytic Review [*A publication*]
PSRED...... Psychological Research [*A publication*]
PSRF.......... Product Support Reports and Functions
PSRF.......... Profit Sharing Research Foundation [*Evanston, IL*] (EA)
PSRI.......... Particulate Solid Research Institute
PSRI.......... Position Subject Return of Incumbent (FAAC)
PSRIA........ Papers. Ship Research Institute [*A publication*]
PSRL.......... Post Strike Reconnaissance List [*Military*] (CINC)
PSRM........ Parti Sosialis Rakyat Malaysia [*Malaysian People's Socialist Party*] (PPW)
PSRM........ Post-Scram Reactivity Monitor [*Nuclear energy*] (NRCH)
PSRM........ Pressurization Systems Regulator Manifold (AAG)
PSRM........ Processor State Register Main [*Data processing*]
PSRMA...... Pacific Southwest Railway Museum Association (EA)
PSR-ML/MIR-el Militante ... Partido Socialista Revolucionario (Marxista-Leninista)/Movimiento de Izquierda Revolucionaria-El Militante [*Revolutionary Socialist Party (Marxist-Leninist)/ Militant Movement of the Revolutionary Left*] [*Peruvian*] (PPW)
PSRMLS.... Pacific Southwest Regional Medical Library [*Library network*]
PSRMT...... Piecewise-Sinusoidal Reaction Matching Technique [*Antenna*] [*Navy*]
PSRO........ Passenger Standing Route Order [*Army*] (AABC)
PSRO........ Professional Standards Review Organization [*Generic term for groups of physicians who may review the policies and decisions of their colleagues*]
PSRP.......... Physical Sciences Research Papers [*Air Force*] (MCD)
PSRPD...... Prakla-Seismos Report [*A publication*]
PSRR.......... Product and Support Requirements Request [*Data processing*] (IBMDP)
PSRS.......... Portable Seismic Recording System
PSRS.......... Position Subject to Rotating Shifts (FAAC)
PSrS.......... Slippery Rock State College, Slippery Rock, PA [*Library symbol*] [*Library of Congress*] (LCLS)
PSRT.......... Passive Satellite Research Terminal
PSRU........ Processor State Register Utility [*Data processing*]
PSRVA...... Psychological Review [*A publication*]
PSRWD...... Policy Studies Review [*A publication*]
PSS............ Hastings, NE [*Location identifier*] [*FAA*] (FAAL)
PSS............ International Production, Service, and Sales Union
PSS............ Packet Switch Stream [*British Telecommunications Plc*] [*London*] [*Information service*] (EISS)
PSS............ Packet Switching Service [*Telecommunications*] [*Information service*] [*British*] (EISS)
PSS............ Pad Safety Supervision [*Aerospace*] (AAG)
PSS............ Palomar Sky Survey [*NASA*]
PSS............ Parti Socialiste Suisse [*Social Democratic Party of Switzerland*] (PPE)
PSS............ Parti de Solidarite Senegalaise [*Senegalese Solidarity Party*]
PSS............ Partito Socialista Sammarinese [*Socialist Party of San Marino*] (PPE)
PSS............ Partito Socialista Somalo [*Somali Socialist Party*]
PSS............ Passenger Service Systems [*Airlines*]
PSS............ Patent Search System [*Pergamon*] [*Database*] [*Data processing*] [*British*]
PSS............ Pauli Spin Susceptibility [*Physics*]
PSS............ Payload Specialist Station [*NASA*] (NASA)
PSS............ Payload Support System [*NASA*] (MCD)
PSS............ Peace Science Society (EA)
PSS............ Performance Standard Sheet
PSS............ Personal Signaling System
PSS............ Personnel Subsystem [*Air Force*] (AFM)
PSS............ Personnel Support System [*Army*] (AABC)
PSS............ Physiological Saline Solution [*Physiology*]

PSS .... Planetary Scan System [*or Subsystem*]
PSS .... Planned Systems Schedule (AAG)
PSS .... Planning Summary Sheets (AAG)
PSS .... Plant Science Seminar [*Later, ASP*]
PS/S .... Plumbing Supervisor/Specialist (AAG)
PSS .... Plunger Snap Switch
PSS .... Pneumatic Supply Subsystem (AAG)
PSS .... Poly(styrenesulfonate) [*Organic chemistry*]
PSS .... Porcine Stress Syndrome [*Veterinary medicine*]
PSS .... Portable Simulation System (MCD)
PSS .... Posadas [*Argentina*] [*Airport symbol*] (OAG)
PSS .... Postal Savings System [*Terminated, 1966*]
PSS .... Postscripts
PSS .... Power Supply Section
PSS .... Power System Synthesizer
PSS .... Precancel Stamp Society
PSS .... Presbyteri Sancti Sulpicii [*Sulpicians*] [*Roman Catholic men's religious order*]
P/S/S .... Price/Stern/Sloan [*Publishers*]
PSS .... Primary Sampling System (NRCH)
PSS .... Princess (ROG)
PS to S .... Private Siding to Station
PSS .... Probabilistic Safety Study [*Nuclear energy*] (NRCH)
PSS .... Process Sampling System (NRCH)
PSS .... Professor of Sacred Scripture
PSS .... Progressive Science Series [*A publication*]
PSS .... Progressive Systemic Sclerosis [*Medicine*]
PSS .... Propellant Supply System [*or Subsystem*]
PSS .... Proprietary Software Systems [*Data processing*] (IEEE)
PSS .... Propulsion Subsystem Structure
PSS .... Propulsion Support System (KSC)
PSS .... Protective Security Service
PSS .... Psalms [*Old Testament book*]
PSS .... Pseudo Spread Spectrum (MCD)
PSS .... Psychiatric Services Section [*of the American Hospital Association*] [*Later, SCSMHPS*] (EA)
PSS .... Psychiatric Status Schedules [*Psychology*]
PSS .... Pubblicazioni del Seminario de Semitistica. Instituto Orientale de Napoli [*A publication*]
PSS .... Public Services Satellite
PSS .... Public Storage Canadian Prop. II [*Limited Partnership Units*] [*Toronto Stock Exchange symbol*]
PSS .... Push-Button Selection Station
PSSA .... Pitch Starting Synchro Assembly
PSSAANDPS ... Permanent Secretariat of the South American Agreement on Narcotic Drugs and Psychotropic Substances [*Buenos Aires, Argentina*] (EA-IO)
PSSAB .... Physica Status Solidi. Sectio A. Applied Research [*A publication*]
PSSB .... Passing Stopped School Bus [*Traffic offense charge*]
PSSBB ...... Public School System Blanket Bond [*Insurance*]
PSSC .... Petroleum Security Subcommittee [*of Foreign Petroleum Supply Committee*] [*Terminated, 1976*] (EGAO)
PSSC .... Physical Science Study Committee [*National Science Foundation*]
PSSC .... Pious Society of Missionaries of St. Charles [*Later, CS*] [*Roman Catholic men's religious order*]
PSSC .... Public Service Satellite Consortium [*Washington, DC*] [*Telecommunications*] [*Information service*] (EA)
PSSEAS .... Papers in International Studies. Southeast Asia Series. Ohio University [*A publication*]
PSSEP .... Preliminary System Safety Engineering Plan
PSSF .... Little Sisters of the Holy Family [*Roman Catholic religious order*]
PSSG .... Physical Science Study Group
PSSGL .... Penn State Series in German Literature [*A publication*]
PSSHR ...... Philippine Social Sciences and Humanities Review [*A publication*]
PSSI .... Primary Specialty Skill Identifier [*Military*] (AABC)
PSSIIS .... Partito Socialista: Sezione Italiana del Internazionale Socialista [*Socialist Party: Italian Section of International Socialism*] (PPE)
PSSK .... Probability of Single Shot Kill [*Of a guided missile*]
PSSM .... Preliminary Science Meeting [*NASA*]
PSSMA ...... Paper Shipping Sack Manufacturers' Association [*Scarsdale, NY*] (EA)
PSSO .... Pass Slip Stitch Over [*Knitting*]
PsSol .... Psalms of Solomon [*Pseudepigrapha*] (BJA)
PSSP .... Payload Specialist Station Panel [*NASA*] (MCD)
PSSP .... Phone Center Staffing and Sizing Program [*Telecommunications*] (TEL)
PSSR .... Parallel-Shaft Speed Reducer
PSSR .... Philippine Social Science Review [*A publication*]
PSSR .... Problem Status and Summary Report [*NASA*] (KSC)
PSSR .... Provisioning Supply Support Requests [*DoD*]
PSSRA ...... Public Service Staff Relations Act [*Canada*]
PSSRB ...... Public Service Staff Relations Board [*Canada*]
PSSS .... Philosophic Society for the Study of Sport (EA)
PSSS .... Proceedings. Shevchenko Scientific Society. Philological Section [*A publication*]

PSSSP .... Proceedings. Shevchenko Scientific Society. Philological Section [*A publication*]
PSST .... Periodic Significant Scheduled Tasks [*NASA*] (NASA)
PSSTA ...... Port Security Station [*Coast Guard*]
PSSU .... Patch Survey and Switching Unit (MCD)
PST .... Pacific Standard Time
PST .... Pacific Summer Time
PST .... Pair Selected Ternary [*Data processing*]
PST .... Partido Socialista de los Trabajadores [*Socialist Workers' Party*] [*Mexico*] (PPW)
PST .... Partido Socialista de los Trabajadores [*Socialist Workers' Party*] [*Colombia*] (PPW)
PST .... Paste
PST .... Pastry (MSA)
PST .... Pasture Canyon [*Utah*] [*Seismograph station code, US Geological Survey*] [*Closed*] (SEIS)
PS & T ...... Pay, Subsistence, and Transportation [*Military*]
PSt .... Pennsylvania State University, University Park, PA [*Library symbol*] [*Library of Congress*] (LCLS)
PST .... Performance Specification Tree
PST .... Periodic Self-Test [*Data processing*]
PST .... Peristimulus Time [*Neurophysiology*]
PST .... Personnel Subsystem Team [*Military*] (AFIT)
PST .... Peseta [*Monetary unit in Spain and Latin America*]
PST .... Petrie Stores Corp. [*NYSE symbol*]
PST .... Philadelphia Suburban Transportation [*AAR code*]
PST .... Philological Society. Transactions [*A publication*]
PST .... Piston Shock Tunnel
PST .... Point of Spiral Tangent (KSC)
PST .... Polaris Star Tracker [*Missiles*]
PST .... Polished Surface Technique (IEEE)
PST .... Pontifical Institute of Mediaeval Studies. Studies and Texts [*A publication*]
PST .... Post-Stimulus Time
PST .... Pressure-Sensitive Tape
PST .... Primary Surge Tank [*Nuclear energy*] (NRCH)
PST .... Prior Service Training [*US Army Reserve*] (INF)
PST .... Priority Selection Table [*Data processing*] (IBMDP)
PST .... Product Support Technician
PST .... Professional, Scientific, and Technical
PST .... Profit Sharing Trustee (DLA)
PST .... Program Synchronization Table (CMD)
PST .... Project ST [*Later, NSTA*] (EA)
PST .... Propeller STOL [*Short Takeoff and Landing*] Transport
3PST .... Triple-Pole, Single-Throw [*Switch*] (MUGU)
4PST .... Four-Pole, Single-Throw [*Switch*]
PSTA .... Packaging Science and Technology Abstracts [*International Food Information Service*] [*Database*] [*Frankfurt, West Germany*]
PSTA .... Partido Socialista Tito Atahuichi [*Bolivian*] (PPW)
PSt-A .... Pennsylvania State University, Agricultural Library, University Park, PA [*Library symbol*] [*Library of Congress*] (LCLS)
PSta .... Philippine Statistician [*A publication*]
PSTA .... Pre-Sea Trial Audit (MCD)
PSt-All ...... Pennsylvania State University, Allentown Campus, Allentown, PA [*Library symbol*] [*Library of Congress*] (LCLS)
PSt-Alt ...... Pennsylvania State University, Altoona Campus, Altoona, PA [*Library symbol*] [*Library of Congress*] (LCLS)
PSTAU ...... Pastabilities Food Uts [*NASDAQ symbol*] (NQ)
PSt-B .... Pennsylvania State University, Berks Campus, Wyomissing, PA [*Library symbol*] [*Library of Congress*] (LCLS)
PSTB .... Picture Story Test Blank [*Psychology*]
PSTB .... Propulsion System Test Bed [*for ABC helicopters*] (RDA)
PSTB .... Puget Sound Tug & Barge [*AAR code*]
PSt-Be ...... Pennsylvania State University, Beaver Campus, Monaca, PA [*Library symbol*] [*Library of Congress*] (LCLS)
PS & TC ..... Population Studies and Training Center [*Brown University*] [*Research center*] (RCD)
PSTC .... Pressure Sensitive Tape Council [*Glenview, IL*] (EA)
PSTC .... Product Support Task Control (AAG)
PSTC .... Public Switched Telephone Circuits [*Telecommunications*] (TEL)
PStcA .... American Philatelic Research Library, State College, PA [*Library symbol*] [*Library of Congress*] (LCLS)
PSt-Ca ...... Pennsylvania State University, Capitol Campus, Middletown, PA [*Library symbol*] [*Library of Congress*] (LCLS)
PStcH .... HRB-Singer, Inc., Science Park, State College, PA [*Library symbol*] [*Library of Congress*] (LCLS)
PSt-D .... Pennsylvania State University, DuBois Campus, DuBois, PA [*Library symbol*] [*Library of Congress*] (LCLS)
PSTD .... Potato Spindle Tuber Disease
PstdE .... Eastern College, St. Davids, PA [*Library symbol*] [*Library of Congress*] (LCLS)
PSt-De ...... Pennsylvania State University, Delaware Campus, Chester, PA [*Library symbol*] [*Library of Congress*] (LCLS)
PSt-E .... Pennsylvania State University, Behrend Campus, Erie, PA [*Library symbol*] [*Library of Congress*] (LCLS)
PSTE .... Personnel Subsystem Test and Evaluation
PST-E .... Priority Selection Table Extension [*Data processing*] (IBMDP)
PSTEP .... Pre-Service Teacher Education Program [*National Science Foundation*]

PSt-F.......... Pennsylvania State University, Fayette Campus, Uniontown, PA [*Library symbol*] [*Library of Congress*]   (LCLS)
PSTF .... Pioneer Station Training Facility [*NASA*]
PSTF .... Pressure Suppression Test Facility [*Nuclear energy*]   (IEEE)
PSTF .... Profit Sharing Trust Fund
PSTF .... Proximity Sensor Test Facility [*Nuclear energy*]   (NRCH)
PSTF .... Pump Seal Test Facility [*Nuclear energy*]   (NRCH)
PSTGC ...... Per Steering Compass [*Navigation*]
PSt-H .... Pennsylvania State University, Hazelton Campus, Hazelton, PA [*Library symbol*] [*Library of Congress*]   (LCLS)
PSTH.......... Peristimulus Time Histogram
PSTH.......... Poststimulus Time Histiogram [*Medical statistics*]
PSTI .... Pancreatic Secretory Trypsin Inhibitor [*Biochemistry*]
PSTIAC ...... Pavements and Soil Trafficability Information Analysis Center [*Army Corps of Engineers*] [*Vicksburg, MS*]   (EISS)
PSTIQ........ Plastiline, Inc. [*NASDAQ symbol*]   (NQ)
PSt-KP .... Pennsylvania State University, King of Prussia Graduate Center, King of Prussia, PA [*Library symbol*] [*Library of Congress*]   (LCLS)
PSTL .... Pastoral
PSTL .... Pistol   (MSA)
PSTL .... Postal   (AFM)
PSTM .... Persistent Standoff Target Marker   (MCD)
PSTMA .... Paper Stationery and Tablet Manufacturers Association [*Later, PCA*]   (EA)
PSt-MA ...... Pennsylvania State University, Mont Alto Campus, Mont Alto, PA [*Library symbol*] [*Library of Congress*]   (LCLS)
PSt-McK .... Pennsylvania State University, McKeesport Campus, McKeesport, PA [*Library symbol*] [*Library of Congress*]   (LCLS)
PS & TN...... Pay, Subsistence, and Transportation, Navy
PSTN.......... Piston   (MSA)
PSTN.......... Public Switched Telephone Network
PSt-NK....... Pennsylvania State University, New Kensington Campus, New Kensington, PA [*Library symbol*] [*Library of Congress*]   (LCLS)
PSt-O .... Pennsylvania State University, Ogontz Campus, Abington, PA [*Library symbol*] [*Library of Congress*]   (LCLS)
PSTO.......... Principal Sea Transport Officer
PSTOA .... Psychology Today [*A publication*]
PSt-PiN ...... Pennsylvania State University, School of Nursing, Allegheny General Hospital, Pittsburgh, PA [*Library symbol*] [*Library of Congress*]   (LCLS)
PSTR.......... Pacesetter Corp. [*NASDAQ symbol*]   (NQ)
PSTR.......... Penn State TRIGA [*Training Reactor, Isotopes General Atomic*] Reactor
P/STRG...... Power Steering [*Automotive engineering*]
PSTS.......... Passive SONAR Tracking System
PSt-S.......... Pennsylvania State University, Scranton Campus, Scranton, PA [*Library symbol*] [*Library of Congress*]   (LCLS)
PSt-Sk .... Pennsylvania State University, Schuylkill Campus, Schuylkill Haven, PA [*Library symbol*] [*Library of Congress*]   (LCLS)
PSt-SV .... Pennsylvania State University, Shenango Valley Campus, Sharon, PA [*Library symbol*] [*Library of Congress*]   (LCLS)
PStu .... Philippine Studies [*A publication*]
PSTV........... Potato Spindle Tuber Virus
PSTV........... Private Screening, Inc. [*NASDAQ symbol*]   (NQ)
PSt-WB ...... Pennsylvania State University, Wilkes-Barre Campus, Wilkes-Barre, PA [*Library symbol*] [*Library of Congress*]   (LCLS)
PSt-WS ...... Pennsylvania State University, Worthington Scranton Campus, Dunmore, PA [*Library symbol*] [*Library of Congress*]   (LCLS)
PSt-Y......... Pennsylvania State University, York Campus, York, PA [*Library symbol*] [*Library of Congress*]   (LCLS)
PSTYY....... President Steyn Gold Mining ADR [*NASDAQ symbol*]   (NQ)
PSTZG .... Pasteurizing [*Freight*]
PSu............ John R. Kaufman, Jr., [*Sunbury*] Public Library, Sunbury, PA [*Library symbol*] [*Library of Congress*]   (LCLS)
PSU .... Package Size Unspecified
PSU .... Packet Switching Unit
PSU .... Parti Socialiste Unifie [*Unified Socialist Party*] [*French*]   (PPW)
PSU .... Partially Sighted Unit   (ADA)
PSU .... Partido Socialista Unificado [*Socialist Unification Party*] [*Argentina*]   (PPW)
PSU .... Partido Socialista Uruguayo [*Uruguayan Socialist Party*]   (PD)
PSU .... Partidul Socialist Unitar [*Unitary Socialist Party*] [*Romanian*]   (PPE)
PSU .... Partito Socialista Unificato [*Unified Socialist Party*] [*Italy*]   (PPE)
PSU .... Partito Socialista Unitario [*Socialist Unity Party*] [*Sanmarinese*]   (PPW)
PSU .... Partito Socialista Unitario [*Unitary Socialist Party*] [*Italy*]   (PPE)
PSU .... Path Setup [*Telecommunications*]   (TEL)
PSU .... Pennsylvania State University
PSU .... Pet Services, Unlimited [*Commercial firm*] [*Brooklyn, NY*]   (EA)
PSU .... Philatelic Sales Unit
PSU .... Photosynthetic Unit
PSU .... Plasma Spray Unit
PSU .... Port Storage Utility [*Telecommunications*]   (TEL)

PSU .... Portland State University
PSU .... Power Supply Unit   (MSA)
PSU .... Power Switching Unit   (MCD)
PSU .... Pressure Status Unit   (AAG)
PSU .... Primary Sampling Unit [*Statistics*]
PSU .... Processor Speed Up [*Computer memory core*]
PSU .... Program Storage Unit [*Data processing*]   (MDG)
PSU-ADA .... Pennsylvania State University-Abstracts of Doctoral Dissertations [*A publication*]
PSUB .... Piston-Supported Upper Bearing
PSUC .... Partit Socialista Unificat de Catalunya [*Unified Socialist Party of Catalonia*] [*Spanish*]   (PPE)
PSULI......... Partito Socialista Unitario de Lavoratori Italiani [*Unitary Socialist Party of Italian Workers*]   (PPE)
PSUN.......... Piper Hydro, Inc. [*NASDAQ symbol*]   (NQ)
PSuQ.......... Philologische Studien und Quellen [*A publication*]
PSUR.......... Pennsylvania State University Reactor
PSURAO .... Pennsylvania State University Radio Astronomy Observatory
PSurg .... Plastic Surgery [*Medicine*]
PSV .... Pictorial Study of Values [*Psychology*]
PSV .... Planetary Space Vehicle [*NASA*]   (NASA)
PSV .... Portable Sensor Verifier   (AAG)
PSV .... Positive Start Voltage
PSV .... Preserve   (MSA)
PSV .... Probability State Variable [*Statistics*]
PSV .... Progressieve Surinaamse Volkspartij [*Progressive Suriname People's Party*]   (PPW)
PSV .... Psychological, Social, and Vocational [*Adjustment factors*]
PSV .... Public Service Vehicle
PSV .... Saint Vincent College, Latrobe, PA [*OCLC symbol*]   (OCLC)
PSvcBad .... Presidential Service Badge [*Military decoration*]   (AABC)
PSVD......... Polystyrene-Divinylbenzene Copolymer [*Organic chemistry*]
PSVM .... Phase-Sensitive Voltmeter
PSVOA ...... Purse Seine Vessel Owners Association [*Seattle, WA*]   (EA)
PSVOMA.... Purse Seine Vessel Owners Marketing Association [*Later, PSVOA*]   (EA)
PSVP......... Pilot Secure Voice Project [*NATO Integrated Communications System*]   (NATG)
PSVT......... Paroxysmal Supraventricular Tachycardia [*Cardiology*]
PSVT......... Passivate [*Metallurgy*]
PSVTN ...... Preservation   (MSA)
PSVTV....... Preservative   (MSA)
PS & W ...... Pacific, Southern & Western Railroad [*Nickname: Play Safe and Walk*]
PSW .... Pacific Southwest Forest and Range Experiment Station [*Department of Agriculture*] [*Research center*]
PSW .... Pinetree Software Canada Ltd. [*Vancouver Stock Exchange symbol*]
PSW .... Plasma Spray Welder
PSW .... Politically Simulated World [*Computer-assisted political science game*]
PSW .... Potential Switch
PSW .... Potentiometer Slidewire
PSW .... Powerplant Specific Weight
PSW .... Processor Status Word
PSW .... Program Status Word [*Data processing*]
PSW .... Psychiatric Social Worker [*British*]
4PSW .... Four-Pole Switch
PSWAD ...... Perspective Study of World Agricultural Development [*FAO*] [*United Nations*]   (MSC)
PSWB........ Public School Word-Book [*A publication*]
PSWBD .... Power Switchboard
PSWEA ...... Proceedings. South Wales Institute of Engineers [*A publication*]
PSWG........ Pressure Sine Wave Generator
PSWMOW ... Psychiatric Social Work in Mental Observation Wards [*British*]
PSWO........ Picture and Sound World Organization
PSWO........ Princess of Wales' Own [*Military*] [*British*]   (ROG)
PSWO........ Product Support Work Order
PSWOPC... Psychiatric Social Work in Out-Patient Clinics [*British*]
PSWP........ Plant Service Water Pump   (IEEE)
PSWR........ Powell Sport Wagon Registry   (EA)
PSWR........ Power Standing Wave Ratio
PSWS........ Potable and Sanitary Water System [*Nuclear energy*]   (NRCH)
PSwS .... Smith, Kline & French Co. [*Later, SmithKline Corp.*], Swedeland, PA [*Library symbol*] [*Library of Congress*]   (LCLS)
PSWT .... Polysonic Wind Tunnel   (MCD)
PSWT .... Psychiatric Social Work Training [*British*]
PSWTUF .... Public Service Workers' Trade Union Federation [*Ceylon*]
PSWYA ...... Psychologia Wychowawcza [*A publication*]
PSX .... Pacific Scientific Co. [*NYSE symbol*]
PSX .... Palacios, TX [*Location identifier*] [*FAA*]   (FAAL)
PSY .... Persky Air Service [*Valdosta, GA*] [*FAA designator*]   (FAAC)
PSY .... Pillsbury Co. [*NYSE symbol*]
PSY .... Port Stanley [*Falkland Islands*] [*Airport symbol*]
PSY .... PSM Technologies, Inc. [*Vancouver Stock Exchange symbol*]
PSY .... Psychiatry
PSY .... Psychological   (CINC)
PsyAb........ Psychological Abstracts [*A publication*]
Psy B .... Psychological Bulletin [*A publication*]

PSYBB .... Psychopharmacology Bulletin [*A publication*]
PSYC .... Psych Systems, Inc. [*NASDAQ symbol*] (NQ)
PSYC .... Psychology
PSYCA .... Psychiatry [*A publication*]
PSYCD .... Psychendocrinology [*A publication*]
PSYCH ...... Psychiatrist (DSUE)
PSYCH ...... Psychiatry
PSYCH ...... Psychic (ROG)
PSYCH ...... Psychology (AFM)
Psych Bull ... Psychological Bulletin [*A publication*]
PSYCHEM ... Psychiatric Chemistry
Psychiat ..... Psychiatry [*A publication*]
Psychiat Cl ... Psychiatria Clinica [*A publication*]
Psychiat Digest ... Psychiatry Digest [*A publication*]
Psychiat Fo ... Psychiatric Forum [*A publication*]
Psychiat Me ... Psychiatry in Medicine [*A publication*]
Psychiat Opin ... Psychiatric Opinion [*A publication*]
Psychiat Q ... Psychiatric Quarterly [*A publication*]
Psychiatr Ann ... Psychiatric Annals [*A publication*]
Psychiatr Annals ... Psychiatric Annals [*A publication*]
Psychiatr Clin ... Psychiatria Clinica [*A publication*]
Psychiatr Clin (Basel) ... Psychiatria Clinica (Basel) [*A publication*]
Psychiatr Enfant ... Psychiatrie de l'Enfant [*A publication*]
Psychiatr Fenn ... Psychiatria Fennica [*A publication*]
Psychiatr Hosp ... Psychiatric Hospital [*A publication*]
Psychiatr J Univ Ottawa ... Psychiatric Journal. University of Ottawa [*A publication*]
Psychiatr Neurol ... Psychiatria et Neurologia [*A publication*]
Psychiatr Neurol Jpn ... Psychiatria et Neurologia Japonica [*A publication*]
Psychiatr Neurol Med Psychol ... Psychiatrie, Neurologie, und Medizinische Psychologie [*A publication*]
Psychiatr Neurol Med Psychol (Leipz) ... Psychiatrie, Neurologie, und Medizinische Psychologie (Leipzig) [*A publication*]
Psychiatr Neurol Neurochir ... Psychiatria, Neurologia, Neurochirurgia [*A publication*]
Psychiatr Neurol Wochenschr ... Psychiatrisch Neurologische Wochenschrift [*A publication*]
Psychiatr News ... Psychiatric News [*A publication*]
Psychiatr Pol ... Psychiatria Polska [*A publication*]
Psychiatr Prax ... Psychiatrische Praxis [*A publication*]
Psychiatr Q ... Psychiatric Quarterly [*A publication*]
Psychiatr Res Rep ... Psychiatric Research Reports [*A publication*]
Psychiatr Soc ... Psychiatrie Sociale [*A publication*]
Psychiatry Med ... Psychiatry in Medicine [*A publication*]
Psychiatry Res ... Psychiatry Research [*A publication*]
Psychic R ... Psychical Review [*A publication*]
PSYCHL ..... Psychological (AFM)
Psych & MLJ ... Psychological and Medico-Legal Journal (DLA)
Psych of Music ... Psychology of Music [*A publication*]
PSYCHO ..... Psychoanalysis (DSUE)
Psychoanal Q ... Psychoanalytic Quarterly [*A publication*]
Psychoanal R ... Psychoanalytic Review [*A publication*]
Psychoanal Rev ... Psychoanalytic Review [*A publication*]
Psychoanal Stud Child ... Psychoanalytic Study of the Child [*A publication*]
Psychoanal Study Child ... Psychoanalytic Study of the Child [*A publication*]
Psychoanal Study Child Monogr Ser ... Psychoanalytic Study of the Child. Monograph Series [*A publication*]
Psychoan Q ... Psychoanalytic Quarterly [*A publication*]
Psychoan Re ... Psychoanalytic Review [*A publication*]
Psychocultural R ... Psychocultural Review [*A publication*]
PSYCHOL ... Psychology
Psychol Absts ... Psychological Abstracts [*A publication*]
Psychol Afr ... Psychologia Africana [*A publication*]
Psychol Africana ... Psychologia Africana [*A publication*]
Psychol Afr Monogr Suppl ... Psychologie Africana. Monograph and Supplement [*A publication*]
Psychol B ... Psychological Bulletin [*A publication*]
Psychol Be ... Psychologische Beitraege [*A publication*]
Psychol Beitr ... Psychologische Beitraege [*A publication*]
Psychol Bel ... Psychologica Belgica [*A publication*]
Psychol Belg ... Psychologica Belgica [*A publication*]
Psychol Bul ... Psychological Bulletin [*A publication*]
Psychol Bull ... Psychological Bulletin [*A publication*]
Psychol Can ... Psychologie Canadienne [*A publication*]
Psychol Clinic ... Psychological Clinic [*A publication*]
Psychol Erz ... Psychologie in Erziehung und Unterricht [*A publication*]
Psychol Forsch ... Psychologische Forschung [*A publication*]
Psychol Fr ... Psychologie Francaise [*A publication*]
Psychol Iss ... Psychological Issues [*A publication*]
Psychol Issues ... Psychological Issues [*A publication*]
Psychol Issues Monogr ... Psychological Issues. Monographs [*A publication*]
Psychol Learn & Motiv ... Psychology of Learning and Motivation [*A publication*]
Psychol Med ... Psychological Medicine [*A publication*]
Psychol Med ... Psychologie Medicale [*A publication*]
Psychol Monogr (Gen Appl) ... Psychological Monographs (General and Applied) [*A publication*]
Psychol Prax ... Psychologische Praxis [*A publication*]
Psychol R ... Psychological Review [*A publication*]
Psychol Rec ... Psychological Record [*A publication*]
Psychol Rep ... Psychological Reports [*A publication*]

Psychol Res ... Psychological Research [*A publication*]
Psychol Rev ... Psychological Review [*A publication*]
Psychol Rundsch ... Psychologische Rundschau [*A publication*]
Psychol Sch ... Psychology in the Schools [*A publication*]
Psychol in the Schs ... Psychology in the Schools [*A publication*]
Psychol Stu ... Psychological Studies [*A publication*]
Psychol Tod ... Psychology Today [*A publication*]
Psychol Today ... Psychology Today [*A publication*]
Psychol Women Q ... Psychology of Women Quarterly [*A publication*]
Psychometri ... Psychometrika [*A publication*]
Psychon Sci ... Psychonomic Science [*A publication*]
Psychon Sci Sect Anim Physiol Psychol ... Psychonomic Science. Section on Animal and Physiological Psychology [*A publication*]
Psychon Sci Sect Hum Exp Psychol ... Psychonomic Science. Section on Human Experimental Psychology [*A publication*]
Psychop Afr ... Psychopathologie Africaine [*A publication*]
Psychopathol Afr ... Psychopathologie Africaine [*A publication*]
Psychopathol Expression Suppl Encephale ... Psychopathologie de l'Expression. Supplement de l'Encephale [*A publication*]
Psychopathol Pict Expression ... Psychopathology and Pictorial Expression [*A publication*]
Psychopharm ... Psychopharmacologia [*A publication*]
Psychopharmacol Abstr ... Psychopharmacology Abstracts [*A publication*]
Psychopharmacol Bull ... Psychopharmacology Bulletin [*A publication*]
Psychopharmacol Commun ... Psychopharmacology Communications [*A publication*]
Psychopharmacol Suppl Encephale ... Psychopharmacologie. Supplement de l'Encephale [*A publication*]
Psychoph C ... Psychopharmacology Communications [*A publication*]
Psychophysl ... Psychophysiology [*A publication*]
Psychos Med ... Psychosomatic Medicine [*A publication*]
Psychosocial Rehabil J ... Psychosocial Rehabilitation Journal [*A publication*]
Psychosoc Proc Iss Child Ment Health ... Psychosocial Process. Issues in Child Mental Health [*A publication*]
Psychosoc Rehabil J ... Psychosocial Rehabilitation Journal [*A publication*]
Psychosomat ... Psychosomatics [*A publication*]
Psychosom Med ... Psychosomatic Medicine [*A publication*]
Psychother Psychosom ... Psychotherapy and Psychosomatics [*A publication*]
Psychother Psychosom Med Psychol ... Psychotherapie, Psychosomatik, Medizinische Psychologie [*A publication*]
Psychother Theory Res Pract ... Psychotherapy: Theory, Research, and Practice [*A publication*]
Psychoth MP ... Psychotherapie und Medizinische Psychologie [*A publication*]
Psychoth Ps ... Psychotherapy and Psychosomatics [*A publication*]
Psychoth/TR ... Psychotherapy: Theory, Research, and Practice [*A publication*]
Psych Prax ... Psychologische Praxis [*A publication*]
Psych Stud ... Psychological Studies [*Mysore*] [*A publication*]
Psych Teaching ... Psychology Teaching [*A publication*]
PsycINFO ... Psychological Abstracts Information Services [*American Psychological Association*] [*Arlington, VA*] (EISS)
PSYCTRC ... Psychiatric
PSYCTRY ... Psychiatry
Psycul R ..... Psychocultural Review [*A publication*]
PsyD .... Doctor of Psychology
PsyETA ...... Psychologists for the Ethical Treatment of Animals [*Lewiston, ME*] (EA)
PSYOP .... Psychological Operation [*Military*]
Psy R .... Proceedings of the Society for Psychical Research [*A publication*]
PsyR .... Psychoanalytic Review [*A publication*]
Psy Rund ... Psychologische Rundschau [*A publication*]
PSYS .... Programming & Systems, Inc. [*NASDAQ symbol*] (NQ)
PsyS .... Psychonomic Science [*A publication*]
PSYSA .... Psyche [*A publication*]
PsySR .... Psychologists for Social Responsibility (EA)
P Sy St Carletn ... Proceedings. Symposium on Statistics and Related Topics. Carleton University [*A publication*]
Psy T .... Psychology Today [*A publication*]
PSYU .... Public Sustained Yield Unit [*Forestry*]
PSYWAR .... Psychological Warfare
PSYWPN .... Psychological Weapon [*Military*] (AFM)
PSZ .... Partially-Stabilized Zirconia [*Ceramics*]
PSZ .... Piszkesteto [*Hungary*] [*Seismograph station code, US Geological Survey*] (SEIS)
PSZ .... Pressure Sealing Zipper
PSZ .... Pro Air Services [*Miami, FL*] [*FAA designator*] (FAAC)
PSZ .... Puerto Suarez [*Bolivia*] [*Airport symbol*] (OAG)
PSZBA ...... Prace i Studia Zakladu Badan Naukowych Gornoslaskiego Okregu Przemyslowego Polskiej Akademii Nauk [*A publication*]
Pszczelnicze Zesz Nauk ... Pszczelnicze Zeszyty Naukowe [*A publication*]
Pszczel Zesz Nauk ... Pszczelnicze Zeszyty Naukowe [*A publication*]
PSzL .... Polska Sztuka Ludowa [*A publication*]
PSZN .... Pubblicazioni. Stazione Zoologica di Napoli [*A publication*]
PT .... Brazil [*Aircraft nationality and registration mark*] (FAAC)
PT .... Duffryn Yard [*Welsh depot code*]
PT .... Motor Torpedo Boat [*Navy symbol*] [*Obsolete*]

PT	Pacific Time
PT	Pain Threshold
PT	Pallet Truck
P-T	Palomero Toluqueno [*Race of maize*]
PT	Pamietnik Teatralny [*A publication*]
PT	Paper Tape
PT	Paper Trooper [*One who salvaged paper for war effort*] [*World War II*]
PT	Para-Terphenyl [*Organic chemistry*]
PT	Parathyroid [*Medicine*]
PT	Parcel Ticket [*Business and trade*]
PT	Paroxysmal Tachycardia [*Cardiology*]
PT	Part [*Online database field identifier*]
P-T	Part-Time [*Employment*]
PT	Part Total [*Earnings less than weekly benefit amount*] [*Unemployment insurance*] (OICC)
PT	Participative Teams (MCD)
PT	Paschale Tempore [*Easter Time*] [*Latin*]
PT	Passenger Transport
PT	Passive Track [*Military*] (CAAL)
PT	Past Tense
PT	Pataca [*Monetary unit in Macau*]
PT	Patellar Tendon [*Anatomy*]
PT	Patient
PT	Patrol Torpedo Boat [*Later, PTF*] [*Navy symbol*]
PT	Pay Tone [*Telecommunications*] (TEL)
PT	Paying Teller [*Business and trade*]
PT	Payment
PT	Pencil Tube
PT	Penetrant Test (NRCH)
PT	Penetration Test (NATG)
PT	Peninsula Terminal Co. [*AAR code*]
PT	Pennant [*British naval signaling*]
PT	Pension Trustee (DLA)
PT	Per Truck
PT	Performance Test
PT	Periodic Test (NRCH)
P & T	Permanent and Total [*Disability*] [*Medicine*]
PT	Persepolis Texts (BJA)
PT	Persistent Tease [*Slang*] [*Bowdlerized version*]
P/T	Personal Time
PT	Personal Trade [*In some retail establishments, customers are assigned to salesmen in rotation. A customer who is the "PT" or personal client of a salesman is not counted as part of the salesman's share of customers*]
PT	Personal Transporter
P & T	Personnel and Training [*Military*] (MUGU)
PT	Perstetur [*Let It Be Continued*] [*Pharmacy*]
Pt	Peter [*New Testament book*]
PT	Petrol Tractor [*British*]
PT	Petroleum Times [*A publication*]
PT	Petty Theft
P & T	Pharmacy and Therapeutics
PT	Pheasant Trust (EA)
PT	Phoenix Theatre [*of Theatre, Incorporated*] [*Defunct*] (EA)
PT	Photographic Intelligenceman [*Navy rating*]
PT	Phototherapy [*Medicine*]
PT	Phototoxity [*Medicine*]
PT	Phototransistor (NRCH)
PT	Physical Teardown (MCD)
PT	Physical Therapy [*or Therapist*]
PT	Physical Training
PT	Physiotherapy [*Medicine*]
PT	Pint
PT	Pipe Tap (MSA)
PT	Pitch Trim (MCD)
PT	Placebo Treated [*Medicine*]
PT	Plain Talk [*An association*] (EA)
PT	Plain Test (MCD)
P-T	Planning and Timing [*of Investments*] [*British*]
PT	Planum Temporale [*Brain anatomy*]
P-T	Plasma Thermocouple Reactor [*Nuclear energy*] (NRCH)
PT	Plastic Tube
PT	Plastics Technology [*A publication*]
Pt	Platinum [*Chemical element*]
PT	Platoon Truck [*British*]
PT	Pleno Titulo [*With Full Title*] [*Latin*]
PT	Plenty Tough [*Slang*]
PT	Plenty Trouble [*Slang*]
PT	Plonia Technica
PT	Plotting Equipment [*JETDS nomenclature*] [*Military*] (CET)
PT	Pneumatic Tube [*Technical drawings*]
PT	Pneumothorax [*Medicine*]
PT	Point
PT	Point [*Maps and charts*]
PT	Point of Tangency
PT	Point of Turn [*Navigation*]
P/T	Pointer/Tracker (MCD)
PT	Polar Times [*A publication*]
PT	Poll-Tax Rolls [*British*]
PT	Pollen Tube [*Botany*]
PT	Polythiophene [*Organic chemistry*]
PT	Pool Temperature [*Nuclear energy*] (NRCH)
PT	Popliteal Tendon [*Anatomy*]
PT	Port
PT	Port Number [*Telecommunications*] (TEL)
PT	Port Talbot Railway [*Wales*]
PT	Portal Tract [*Anatomy*]
PT	Portugal [*Two-letter standard code*] (CNC)
pt	Portuguese Timor [*io (Indonesia) used in records cataloged after January 1978*] [*MARC country of publication code*] [*Library of Congress*] (LCCP)
PT	Positional Tolerancing
PT	Post Town
PT	Postal Telegraph Co. [*Terminated*]
PT	Poste e Telegrafi [*Post and Telegraph Service*] [*Italy*]
PT	Posterior Tibial [*Anatomy*]
P et T	Postes et Telecommunications
P & T	Posts and Timbers [*Technical drawings*]
PT	Potential Transformer
PT	Power Transfer (KSC)
PT	Precision Teaching
PT	Preferential Treatment (OICC)
PT	Preoperational Test [*Nuclear energy*] (NRCH)
PT	Press Test [*Psychology*]
P/T	Pressure/Temperature (KSC)
PT	Pressure Test (AAG)
PT	Pressure Time Fuel System [*Cummins Engine Co., Inc.*]
PT	Pressure Transducer (KSC)
PT	Pressure Transmitter (NRCH)
PT	Pressure Tubing
pt	Preterit [*Past tense*] [*Grammar*]
PT	Previous Operating Time (AFIT)
PT	Primal Therapy
PT	Primary Target [*Army*]
PT	Primary Trainer [*Aircraft*]
PT	Print (MSA)
PT	Printed Text
PT	Printer Terminal
PT	Prior Treatment [*Medicine*]
PT	Priority Telegram
PT	Private Terms
PT	Pro Tempore [*For the Time Being*] [*Latin*]
PT	Procedure Turn [*Aviation*] (FAAC)
PT	Processing Tax Division [*United States Internal Revenue Bureau*] (DLA)
PT	Processing Time
PT	Production Techniques (MCD)
PT	Production Test
P & T	Professional and Technology [*Category*] [*British*]
PT	Proficiency Testing
PT	Profile Template
PT	Program (Exercise) on Treadmill
PT	Programer and Timer
PT	Prohibited Telegrams
PT	Project Tibet (EA)
PT	Project Transition [*DoD*] (OICC)
PT	Prolong Tablets [*Pharmacy*]
PT	Proof Test (AAG)
PT	Propellant Transfer
PT	Propeller Torpedo [*Boat*]
PT	Property Transfer (KSC)
PT	Prophet
PT	Propylthiouracil [*Also, PROP, PTU*] [*Thyroid inhibitor*]
PT	Prothrombin Time [*Hematology*]
PT	Provascular Tissue [*Botany*]
PT	Provincetown-Boston Airlines, Inc. and Naples Airlines, Inc. [*ICAO designator*] (FAAC)
PT	Provisioning Team (AAG)
PT	Przeglad Teologiczny [*A publication*]
Pt	Pseudoword Target [*Psychology*]
PT	Psychology Today [*A publication*]
Pt	Pteropods [*Quality of the bottom*] [*Nautical charts*]
PT	PTP Resource Corp. [*Formerly, Petrologic Pet Ltd.*] [*Vancouver Stock Exchange symbol*]
PT	Public Trustee
PT	Publication Type [*Online database field identifier*]
P & T	Pugsley and Trueman's New Brunswick Reports (DLA)
PT	Pull-Through [*Gun cleaning*]
PT	Pulmonary Tuberculosis [*Medicine*]
PT	Pulse Timer
PT	Pulse Train
PT	Punched Tape [*Data processing*]
PT	Pupil Teacher
PT	Purchase Tax [*British*]
PT	Pure Telepathy [*Psychical research*]
PT	Pyramid Texts (BJA)
PT	Pyramidal Tract [*Anatomy*]
PT	Pytanija Tekstolohiji [*A publication*]
PT	Total Pressure
PT1	Photographic Intelligenceman, First Class [*Navy rating*]
PT2	Photographic Intelligenceman, Second Class [*Navy rating*]

PT3............ Photographic Intelligenceman, Third Class [*Navy rating*]
PTA .... National Postal Transport Association [*Later, APWU*]
PTA .... Pantorama Industries [*Toronto Stock Exchange symbol*]
PTA .... Paper and Twine Association   (EA)
PTA .... Parallel Tubular Array [*Cytology*]
PTA .... Parent-Teacher Association
PTA .... Passenger Transport Authorities [*British*]
PTA .... People Taking Action
PTA .... Percent Time Active   (CAAL)
PTA .... Percutaneous Transluminal Angioplasty [*Medicine*]
PTA .... Periodical Title Abbreviations [*A publication*]
PTA .... Personnel and Training Abstracts [*A publication*]
PTA .... Peseta [*Monetary unit in Spain and Latin America*]
PTA .... Petaluma Aero, Inc. [*Petaluma, CA*] [*FAA designator*]   (FAAC)
PTA .... Phenyltrimethylammonium [*Also, PTM, PTMA*] [*Organic chemistry*]
PTA .... Phorbol Tetradecanoyl Acetate [*Also, PMA, TPA*] [*Organic chemistry*]
PTA .... Phosphotransacetylase [*An enzyme*]
PTA .... Phosphotungstic Acid [*Inorganic chemistry*]
PTA .... Photographers' Telegraph Association
PTA .... Phototransistor Amplifier
PTA .... Physical Therapy Assistant
PTA .... Picatinny Arsenal [*New Jersey*] [*Later, Armament Development Center*] [*Army*]
PTA .... Pitch Trim Adjustment
PTA .... Pitch Trim Angle
PTA .... Planar Turbulence Amplifier   (IEEE)
PTA .... Plasma Thromboplastin Antecedent [*Factor XI*] [*Hematology*]
PTA .... Plasma Transferred Arc [*Metallurgy*]
PTA .... Platinized Titanium Anode
PTA .... Point of Total Assumption   (MCD)
PTA .... Port Alsworth [*Alaska*] [*Airport symbol*]   (OAG)
PTA .... Post Test Analysis [*NASA*]   (NASA)
PTA .... Post-Traumatic Amnesia [*Medicine*]
PTA .... Premium Transportation Authorization   (AAG)
PTA .... Pressure Transducer Assembly
PTA .... Price-Tag Awareness [*See also PTS*]
PTA .... Primary Target Area [*Military*]
PTA .... Primary Tungsten Association   (EA-IO)
PTA .... Prior to Admission [*Medicine*]
PTA .... Program Time Analyzer
PTA .... Programable Translation Array
PTA .... Proposed Technical Approach
PTA .... Propulsion Test Article [*NASA*]   (NASA)
PTA .... Prothrombin Activity [*Hematology*]
PTA .... Proton Target Area
PTA .... Pulse Torquing Assembly   (KSC)
PTA .... Punta Arenas [*Chile*] [*Seismograph station code, US Geological Survey*] [*Closed*]   (SEIS)
PTA .... Purchase Transaction Analysis
PTA .... Purified Terephthalic Acid [*Organic chemistry*]
PTAA......... Airman Apprentice, Photographic Intelligenceman, Striker [*Navy rating*]
PTAB......... Photographic Technical Advisory Board [*American National Standards Institute*]
PTAC......... Plant Transportation Advisory Committee
PTAC......... Professional and Technical Advisory Committee [*JCAH*]
PTACV ...... Prototype Tracked Air-Cushion Vehicle
PTAD......... Productivity and Technical Assistance Division [*Mutual Security Agency*] [*Abolished, 1953*]
PT AEQ ...... Partes Aequales [*Equal Parts*] [*Pharmacy*]
PTAG......... Professional Tattoo Artists Guild   (EA)
PTAH......... Phosphotungstic Acid-Hematoxylin [*A stain*]
PTAIOC ..... Proceedings and Transactions. All-India Oriental Conferences [*A publication*]
PTAL .... Para-Tolualdehyde [*Organic chemistry*]
PTA Mag ... PTA [*Parent-Teacher Association*] Magazine [*A publication*]
PTAN......... Airman, Photographic Intelligenceman, Striker [*Navy rating*]
PTANYC .... Protestant Teachers Association of New York City   (EA)
PTAR......... Prime Time Access Rule [*Television*]
PTASB .... Photographic Applications in Science, Technology, and Medicine [*A publication*]
PTAVE....... Parents and Teachers Against Violence in Education   (EA)
PTB .... Partido Trabalhista Brasileiro [*Brazilian Labor Party*]   (PPW)
PTB .... Patellar Tendon Bearing [*Medicine*]
PTB .... Perishables Tariff Bureau, Atlanta GA [*STAC*]
PTB .... Petersburg, VA [*Location identifier*] [*FAA*]   (FAAL)
PTB .... Physical Transaction Block
PTB .... Point Barrow [*Alaska*] [*Later, BRW*] [*Geomagnetic observatory code*]
PTB .... Point Barrow [*Alaska*] [*Seismograph station code, US Geological Survey*] [*Closed*]   (SEIS)
PTB .... Pressure Test Barrel
PTB .... Prior to Birth [*Medicine*]
PTB .... Process Technical Bulletin   (MCD)
PTB .... Program Time Base [*Military*]   (AFIT)
PTB .... PT Boats, Inc. [*An association*]   (EA)
PTBB......... Para-tertiary-butylbenzaldehyde [*Organic chemistry*]
PTBBA ..... Para-tertiary-butylbenzoic Acid [*Organic chemistry*]
PTBC......... Pittsburgh Brewing Company [*NASDAQ symbol*]   (NQ)

PTBD......... Percutaneous Transhepatic Biliary Drainage [*Medicine*]
PTBF......... Portal Tributary Blood Flow [*Physiology*]
PTBK......... Partbook [*Music*]
PTBL......... Portable   (AABC)
PTB Mitt..... PTB [*Physikalisch-Technische Bundesanstalt*] Mitteilungen. Amts- und Mitteilungsblatt der Physikalisch- Technische Bundesanstalt [*Braunschweig-Berlin*] [*A publication*]
PTBR......... Processing Tax Board of Review Decisions [*United States Internal Revenue Bureau*]   (DLA)
PTBR......... Punched Tape Block Reader [*Data processing*]
PTBT......... Para-tertiary-butyltoluene [*Organic chemistry*]
PTC .... Chief Photographic Intelligenceman [*Navy rating*]
PTC .... Motor Boat Subchaser [*Navy symbol*] [*Obsolete*]
PTC .... Pacific Telecommunications Council   (EA)
PTC .... Pacific Tuna Conference
PTC .... Part Through Crack [*Alloy tension*]
PTC .... Parti Travailliste Congolais [*Congolese Labor Party*]
Ptc............ Participating [*Business and trade*]
PTC .... Passive Thermal Control
PTC .... Patent, Trademark, and Copyright Institute [*Franklin Pierce College*]   (EISS)
PTC .... Patrol Vessel, Motor Torpedo Boat, Submarine Chaser [*Navy symbol*]
PTC .... Pentagon Telecommunications Center   (MCD)
PTC .... Peoria Terminal Company [*AAR code*]
PTC .... Percutaneous Cholangiography [*Medicine*]
PTC .... Percutaneous Transhepatic Cholangiogram [*Medicine*]
PTC .... Performance Test Chamber   (MCD)
PTC .... Performance Test Code
PTC .... Personnel Transfer Capsule [*Undersea technology*]
PTCS .... Personnel Transport Carrier
PTC .... Phase Transfer Catalysis [*Physical chemistry*]
PTC .... Phenylisothiocyanate [*Organic chemistry*]
PTC .... Phenylthiocarbamide [*or Phenylthiocarbamyl*] [*Organic chemistry*]
PTC .... Photographic Type Composition   (ADA)
PTC .... Pipe and Tobacco Council of America [*Defunct*]   (EA)
PTC .... Pitch Trim Compensator
PTC .... Pitch Trim Controller   (MCD)
PTC .... Plan to Clear [*Aviation*]   (FAAC)
PTC .... Plasma Thromboplastin Component [*Factor IX*] [*Also, CF*] [*Hematology*]
PTC .... Plastic Training Cartridge [*Army*]   (INF)
PTC .... Pneumatic Temperature Control
PTC .... Pneumatic Test Console
PTC .... Portable Temperature Control   (KSC)
PTC .... Porto Cannone [*Italy*] [*Seismograph station code, US Geological Survey*]   (SEIS)
PTC .... Positive Target Control   (FAAC)
PTC .... Positive Temperature Coefficient
PTC .... Positive Transmitter Control
PTC .... Post-Turnover Change [*Nuclear energy*]   (NRCH)
PTC .... Postal Telegraph Cable
PTC .... Posterior Trabeculae Carneae [*Heart anatomy*]
PTC .... Power Testing Code   (MCD)
PTC .... Power Transfer Coefficient
PTC .... Power Transmission Council
PTC .... Preoperative Testing Center
PTC .... Pressure and Temperature Control   (KSC)
PTC .... Pressure Transducer Calibrator
PTC .... Primary Technical Course [*Military*]
PTC .... Princeton Resources Corporation [*Vancouver Stock Exchange symbol*]
PTC .... Programable Test Console
PTC .... Programed Transmission Control   (BUR)
PTC .... Programer Training Center
PTC .... Promotional Telephone Call [*State Employee Security Agency*]   (OICC)
PTC .... Proof Test Capsule [*NASA*]
PTC .... Propellant Tanking Console   (AAG)
PTC .... Propulsion Test Complex   (KSC)
PTC .... Prothrombin Complex [*Hematology*]
PTC .... Psychophysical Timing Curve
PTC .... Publishing Technology Corporation [*Needham Heights, MA*] [*Information service*]   (EISS)
PTC .... Pulse Time Code
PTCA......... Patience T'ai Chi Association   (EA)
PTCA......... Percutaneous Transluminal Coronary Angioplasty [*Medicine*]
PTCA......... Plains Tribal Council of Assam [*Indian*]   (PPW)
PTCA......... Pressure Technology Corporation of America
PTCA......... Private Truck Council of America [*Washington, DC*]   (EA)
PTCAA ...... Professional Turkey Calling Association of America   (EA)
PTCAD ...... Provisional Troop Carrier Airborne Division
PTCC......... Pacific Division Transport Control Center
PTCC .... Polycast Technology [*NASDAQ symbol*]   (NQ)
PT/CC........ Problem Tracking and Change Control [*Data processing*]
PTCCS .... Polaris Target Card Computing System [*Missiles*]
PTCH......... Patch   (FAAC)
PTCI.......... Programable Terminal Communications Interface   (MCD)
PTCI.......... Pullman Transportation [*NASDAQ symbol*]   (NQ)
PTC J .... Patent, Trademark, and Copyright Journal [*A publication*]

PTCJB....... Postepy Techniki Jadrowej [*A publication*]
PTCL......... Peripheral T-Cell Lymphoma [*Oncology*]
PTCLD....... Part Called [*Stock exchange term*]
PTCM........ Master Chief Photographic Intelligenceman [*Navy rating*]
PTCM........ Pacific Telecommunications [*NASDAQ symbol*] (NQ)
PTCO........ Petroleum Equipment Tools [*NASDAQ symbol*] (NQ)
Pt Copyright & TM Cas ... Patent, Copyright, and Trade Mark Cases [*United States*] (DLA)
PTCP......... Participate (FAAC)
PTCP......... Positive Turnaround Control Point (MCD)
PTCR......... Pad Terminal Connection Room
PTCR......... Payload Terminal Connector Room [*NASA*] (MCD)
PTCRM....... Partial Thermochemical Remanent Magnetization
PTCS......... Passive Thermal Control Section [*NASA*] (NASA)
PTCS......... Pax Tibi cum Sanctis [*Peace to Thee with the Saints*] [*Latin*]
PTCS......... Planning, Training, and Checkout System (MCD)
PTCS......... Pressure Transducer Calibration System
PTCS......... Propellant Tanking Computer System (KSC)
PTCS......... Senior Chief Photographic Intelligenceman [*Navy rating*]
PTCT......... Protect (MSA)
PTCV......... Pilot-Operated Temperature Control Valve
PTD.......... Painted (AAG)
PTD.......... Particle Transfer Device
PTD.......... Permanent Total Disability [*Medicine*]
PTD.......... Phenyltriazolinedione [*Organic chemistry*]
Ptd............ Phosphatidyl
PTD.......... Photodiode Detector [*Instrumentation*]
PTD.......... Photothermal Deflection
PTD.......... Physical Teardown (MCD)
PTD.......... Pilot to Dispatcher
PTD.......... Plant Test Date [*Telecommunications*] (TEL)
PTD.......... Portland [*Oregon*] [*Seismograph station code, US Geological Survey*] (SEIS)
PTD.......... Posttuning Drift
PTD.......... Potsdam, NY [*Location identifier*] [*FAA*] (FAAL)
PTD.......... Potter Distilleries Ltd. [*Toronto Stock Exchange symbol*] [*Vancouver Stock Exchange symbol*]
PTD.......... Printed
PTD.......... Programable Threshold Detector (MCD)
PTD.......... Programed Thermal Desorber
PTD.......... Provisioning Technical Documentation
PTD.......... Provisioning Transcript Documentation (MCD)
PTDA......... Power Transmission Distributors Association [*Park Ridge, IL*] (EA)
PTDDSS..... Provisioning Technical Documentation Data Selection Sheet [*NASA*] (NASA)
PTDF......... Pacific Tuna Development Foundation (EA)
PTDF......... Procurement Technical Data File [*DoD*]
PTDIA........ Professional Truck Driver Institute of America [*Lawrence, KS*] (EA)
P & T Div .... Plans and Training Division [*Military*]
PTDOS....... Processor Technology Disk Operating System
PTDP......... Preliminary Technical Development Plan (AFM)
PTDP......... Proposed Technical Development Plan
PTDQ......... Polymerized Trimethyldihydroquinoline [*Organic chemistry*]
PTDS......... Photo Target Detection System
Ptd Salesmanship ... Printed Salesmanship [*A publication*]
PTDTL........ Pumped Tunnel Diode Transistor Logic
PTDU......... Pointing and Tracking Demonstration Unit (MCD)
PTe............ Indian Valley Public Library, Telford, PA [*Library symbol*] [*Library of Congress*] (LCLS)
PTE .... International Federation of Professional and Technical Engineers
PTE .... Page Table Entry
PTE .... Parathyroid Extract [*Medicine*]
PTE .... Partido de Trabajadores Espanoles [*Spanish Workers' Party*] (PPE)
PTE .... Passenger Transport Executive [*British*]
PTE .... Pectin transeliminase [*or Pectate Lyase*] [*An enzyme*]
PTE .... Peculiar Test Equipment
PTE .... Photographic Tasks and Equipment [*NASA*]
PT & E ...... Physical Teardown and Evaluation (MCD)
PTE .... Plate (ROG)
PTE .... Port Stephens [*Australia*] [*Airport symbol*] (OAG)
PTE .... Portable Test Equipment (AAG)
PTE .... Portage [*Alaska*] [*Seismograph station code, US Geological Survey*] (SEIS)
PTE .... Pressure Test Equipment (MCD)
PTE .... Pressure-Tolerant Electronics (IEEE)
PTE .... Primrose Tech Corp. [*Vancouver Stock Exchange symbol*]
PTE .... Private [*British*]
PTE .... Private Trade Entity
PTE .... Problem Trend Evaluation (MCD)
PTE .... Production Test Equipment (MCD)
PT & E .... Progress Tests and Examinations
Pte............ Pteroyl [*Biochemistry*]
PTEAR........ Physical Teardown and Maintenance Allocation Review (MCD)
PTeb.......... Tebtunis Papyri [*A publication*] (OCD)
PTEC......... Petrotech, Inc. [*NASDAQ symbol*] (NQ)
PTEC......... Plastics Technical Evaluation Center [*Military*]
PTED......... Pulmonary Thromboembolic Disease [*Medicine*]

PteGlu........ Pteroylmonoglutamic Acid [*Folic acid*] [*Also, FA, PGA*] [*Biochemistry*]
PT & ER..... Physical Teardown and Evaluation Review (MCD)
PTER......... Physical Teardown and Evaluation Review (MCD)
Ptero......... Pterodactyl [*A publication*]
PTES......... Productivity Trend Evaluation System (MCD)
PTETD........ Production Test Engineering Task Description (MCD)
PTETS........ Pioneer Television and Electronic Technicians Society [*Defunct*] (EA)
PTF............ Malololailai [*Fiji*] [*Airport symbol*] (OAG)
PTF............ Paralemniscal Tegmental Field [*Neuroanatomy*]
PTF............ Patch and Test Facility
PTF............ Patrol Torpedo Boat, Fast [*Formerly, PT*] [*Navy symbol*]
PTF............ Payload Test Facility [*VAFB*] [*NASA*] (MCD)
PTF............ Petersfield Oil & Minerals [*Vancouver Stock Exchange symbol*]
PTF............ Phase Transfer Function (MCD)
PTF............ Plaintiff [*Legal term*] (ROG)
PTF............ Plasma Thromboplastin Factor [*Factor VIII*] [*Also, AHF, AHG, TPC*] [*Hematology*]
PTF............ Police Training Foundation
PTF............ Polymer Thick Film
PTF............ Port Task Force
PTF............ Power Test Fail
PTF............ Production Tabulating Form (AAG)
PTF............ Program Temporary Fix [*Data processing*]
PTf............ Proof Test Facility [*Nuclear energy*]
PTF............ Propellant Tank Flow
PTFA......... Preliminary Tool and Facility Analysis (MCD)
PTFDA....... Professional Travel Film Directors Association [*Later, Professional Travelogue Sponsors - PTS*] (EA)
PTFE......... Polytetrafluoroethylene [*Organic chemistry*]
PTFHA....... Physician Task Force on Hunger in America [*Boston, MA*] (EA)
PTFM......... Platform (AAG)
PTFMA...... Peacetime Force Material Assets [*Navy*] (AFIT)
PTFMO...... Peacetime Force Materiel Objective [*Army*]
PTFMPO..... Peacetime Force Materiel Procurement Objective [*Army*]
PTFMR...... Peacetime Force Materiel Requirements [*Army*]
PTFMR-A ... Peacetime Force Materiel Requirements - Acquisition [*Army*] (AABC)
PTFMR-R ... Peacetime Force Materiel Requirements - Retention [*Army*] (AABC)
PTFP .... Public Telecommunications Facilities Program [*Department of Commerce*]
PTFS .... Publications. Texas Folklore Society [*A publication*]
PTFUR......: President's Task Force on Urban Renewal (EA)
PTFX .... Plating Fixture (AAG)
PTG .... Parent-Teacher Group
PTG .... Pennington Gap, VA [*Location identifier*] [*FAA*] (FAAL)
PTG .... Piano Technicians Guild [*Formed by a merger of American Society of Piano Technicians and National Association of Piano Tuners*] [*Kansas City, MO*] (EA)
PTG .... Pietersburg [*South Africa*] [*Airport symbol*] (OAG)
PTG .... Polaris Task Group [*Missiles*]
PTG .... Portageville [*Missouri*] [*Seismograph station code, US Geological Survey*] [*Closed*] (SEIS)
PTG .... Portuguese (ROG)
PTG .... Precise Tone Generator [*Telecommunications*] (TEL)
PTG .... Pressure Test Gauge
PTG .... Pressure Transfer Gauge
PTG .... Printing
PTG .... Professional Technical Group
PTG .... Prothoracic Gland [*Insect anatomy*]
PTG .... Pulse Target Generator
PTGA......... Pteroyltriglutamic Acid [*Pharmacology*]
PTGAP .... Professional Technical Group on Antennas and Propagation [*of the IEEE*]
Ptg Art....... Printing Art [*A publication*]
PTGBD....... Percutaneous Transhepatic Gallbladder Drainage [*Medicine*]
PTGC......... Programed Temperature Gas Chromatography
PTGEC .... Professional Technical Group on Electronic Computers [*Later, IEEE Computer Society*]
PTGEWS .... Professional Technical Group on Engineering Writing and Speech [*of the IEEE*]
PTGMA ...... Photogrammetria [*A publication*]
PTGS......... Portable Telemetry Ground Station
PTGT......... Primary Target
PTH .... Hydrofoil Motor Torpedo Boat [*Ship symbol*] (NATG)
PTH .... Pallet Torque Hook
PTH .... Panther Mines Ltd. [*Vancouver Stock Exchange symbol*]
PTH .... Paper Tape Half-Duplex
PTH .... Parathyroid Hormone [*Endocrinology*]
PTH .... Peak Tanning Hours [*Supposedly occurring between 10am and 2pm*] [*See also BROTS, SROTS*]
PTH .... Phenylthiohydantoin [*Organic chemistry*]
PTH .... Plated through Hole
PTH .... Port Heiden [*Alaska*] [*Airport symbol*] (OAG)
PTH .... Port Heiden, AK [*Location identifier*] [*FAA*] (FAAL)
PTH .... Post-Transfusion Hepatitis [*Medicine*]
PTH .... Project Top Hat (EA)
PTHA......... Pinto Horse Association of America (EA)
P Th B........ Bachelor of Practical Theology

PTHEA .... Physical Therapy [*A publication*]
PTHF .... Polytetrahydrofuran [*Organic chemistry*]
PThR .... Princeton Theological Review [*A publication*]
PTI .... Package Turn In   (MCD)
PTI .... Pancreatic Trypsin Inhibitor [*Biochemistry*]
PTI .... Party Identity [*Telecommunications*]   (TEL)
PTI .... Pathways to Independence [*An association*]   (EA)
PTI .... Patient Technology, Incorporated [*American Stock Exchange symbol*]
PTI .... Pennsylvania Transportation Institute [*Pennsylvania State University*] [*Research center*]   (RCD)
PTI .... Persistent Tolerant Infection
PTI .... Personnel Transaction Identifier [*Air Force*]   (AFM)
PTI .... Philadelphia Textile Institute
PTI .... Physical-Technical Institute [*USSR*]
PTI .... Physical Training Instructor [*British*]
PTI .... Pictorial Test of Intelligence [*Education*]
PTI .... Pipe Test Insert [*Liquid Metal Engineering Center*] [*Energy Research and Development Administration*]   (IEEE)
PTI .... Plugging Temperature Indicator [*Nuclear energy*]   (NRCH)
PTI .... Poetry Therapy Institute [*Los Angeles, CA*]   (EA)
PTI .... Porous Tungsten Ionizer
PTI .... Post Tensioning Institute [*Phoenix, AZ*]   (EA)
PTI .... Power Tool Institute [*Arlington Heights, IL*]   (EA)
PTI .... Precision Technology, Incorporated   (AAG)
PTI .... Preliminary Test Information   (KSC)
PTI .... [*The*] Press Trust of India
PTI .... Production Training Indicator [*Data processing*]
PTI .... Program Transfer Interface
PTI .... Programed Test Input   (MCD)
PTI .... Promethean Technologies, Inc. [*Vancouver Stock Exchange symbol*]
PTI .... Public Technology, Inc. [*Washington, DC*] [*Research center*]   (RCD)
PTI .... Publicacoes Tecnicas Internacionais Ltda. [*International Technical Publications Ltd.*] [*Sao Paulo, Brazil*] [*Information service*]   (EISS)
PTI .... Puntilla Lake, AK [*Location identifier*] [*FAA*]   (FAAL)
PTIC .... Patent and Trade Mark Institute of Canada
PTIL .... Parts Test Information List   (KSC)
PTIND........ Paper Technology and Industry [*A publication*]
PTIS .... Pacific Triangle Information Services [*Irvine, CA*] [*Information service*]   (EISS)
PTIS .... Plasma-Therm, Incorporated [*NASDAQ symbol*]   (NQ)
PTIS .... Programed Test Input System   (MCD)
PTIS .... Propulsion Test Instrumentation System   (KSC)
PTIWU .... Posts and Telegraphs Industrial Workers' Union [*India*]
PTIX .... Patient Technology [*NASDAQ symbol*]   (NQ)
PTJ .... Piano Technician's Journal [*A publication*]
PTJ .... Portland [*Australia*] [*Airport symbol*]   (OAG)
PTJA .... Plan to Join Airways   (FAAC)
PTK .... Polishing Tool Kit
PTK .... Pontiac, MI [*Location identifier*] [*FAA*]   (FAAL)
PTK .... Potentiometer Tapping Kit
PTL............ Part Time Legislature
PTL............ Partial Total Loss
PTL............ Pass the Loot [*Facetious translation referring to the PTL ministry*]
PTL............ Patrol [*or Patrolman*]   (AABC)
PTL............ Pay the Lady [*Facetious translation referring to the PTL ministry*]
PTL............ Peacetime Losses [*Military*]
PTL............ Penteli [*Greece*] [*Seismograph station code, US Geological Survey*]   (SEIS)
PTL............ People That Love [*Of television's "PTL Club"*]
PTL............ Perinatal Telencephalic Leukoencephalopathy [*Medicine*]
PTL............ Peripheral T-Cell Lymphoma [*Oncology*]
PTL............ Petroleum Testing Laboratory
PTL............ Phase Tracking Loop   (MCD)
PTL............ Photograph Those Ladies [*Facetious translation referring to the PTL ministry*]
PTL............ Photographic Technology Laboratory   (KSC)
PTL............ Pintle [*Design engineering*]
PTL............ Planning Test List
PTL............ Pocket Testament League   (EA)
PTL............ Praise the Lord [*Of television's "PTL Club"*]
PTL............ Pressure, Torque, and Load
PTL............ Primary Target Line [*Military*]
PTL............ Process and Test Language
PTL............ Providence Airline [*Coventry, RI*] [*FAA designator*]   (FAAC)
PTL............ Public Television Library
PTLA .... Praise the Lord Anyway
PTLA .... Publishers' Trade List Annual
PTLC .... Piedmont Triad Library Council [*Library network*]
PT-LD........ Physical Teardown - Logistics Demonstration   (MCD)
PTLD .... Post-Transfusion Liver Disease [*Medicine*]
PTLD .... Prescribed Tumor Lethal Dose [*Oncology*]
PTLEF .... Peace Through Law Education Fund   (EA)
PTLRS....... Publications and Technical Literature Research Section [*Environmental Protection Agency*]   (EISS)
PTLV .... Primate T-Lymphotropic Viruses

PTLX .... Patlex Corp. [*NASDAQ symbol*]   (NQ)
PTLY .... Partly   (FAAC)
PTM........... Palmarito [*Venezuela*] [*Airport symbol*]   (OAG)
PTM........... Passenger Traffic Manager
PTM........... Pattern Transformation Memory
PTM........... Petromac Energy, Inc. [*Vancouver Stock Exchange symbol*]
PTM........... Phase Time Modulation
PTM........... Phenyltrimethylammonium [*Also, PTA, PTMA*] [*Organic chemistry*]
PTM........... Physical Teardown and Maintenance   (MCD)
PTM........... Pietermaritzburg [*South Africa*] [*Seismograph station code, US Geological Survey*]   (SEIS)
PTM........... Pneumatic Telescope Mast
PTM........... Polaris Tactical Missile
PTM........... Portable Traffic Monitor [*Telecommunications*]   (TEL)
PTM........... Portland Terminal Co. [*AAR code*]
PTM........... Posttransfusion Mononucleosis [*Medicine*]
PTM........... Preterm Milk [*Medicine*]
PTM........... Primary Thickening Meristem [*Botany*]
PTM........... Program Timing and Miscellaneous [*Electronics*]
PTM........... Programable Terminal Multiplexer [*Texas Instruments, Inc.*]
PTM........... Programable Timer Module
PTM........... Proof Test Model [*NASA*]
PTM........... Pulse Time Modulation [*Radio*]
PTM........... Pulse Time Multiplex
PTM........... Pulse Transmission Mode   (MCD)
PTM........... Southeastern Airways Corp. [*Double Springs, AL*] [*FAA designator*]   (FAAC)
PTMA .... Phenyltrimethylammonium [*Also, PTA, PTM*] [*Organic chemistry*]
PTMA .... Phosphotungstomolybdic Acid [*Inorganic chemistry*]
PTMC .... Polaris Tender Management Computer [*Missiles*]
PTMD .... Propellant Toxicity Monitoring Devices   (KSC)
PTMDF ...... Pupils, Tension, Media, Disc, Fundus [*Medicine*]
PT & ME ... Physical Teardown and Maintenance Evaluation [*Army*]
PTMEG....... Polytetramethylene Ether Glycol [*Organic chemistry*]
PTML......... PNP [*Positive-Negative-Positive*] Transistor Magnetic Logic   (IEEE)
PTMRA ...... Platinum Metals Review [*A publication*]
PTMS .... Para-Toluidine-meta-sulfonic Acid [*Also, PTMSA*] [*Organic chemistry*]
PTMS .... Pattern Transformation Memory System
PTMS .... Publication Text Management System   (MCD)
PTMSA ...... Para-Toluidine-meta-sulfonic Acid [*Also, PTMS*] [*Organic chemistry*]
PTMT .... Poly(tetramethylene Terephthalate) [*Organic chemistry*]
PTMTLG..... Pitometer-Log [*Engineering*]
PTMU .... Power and Temperature Monitor Unit   (KSC)
PTMUD...... Postepy Technologii Maszyn i Urzadzen [*A publication*]
PTMUX...... Pulse-Time Multiplex   (MSA)
PTN .... Morgan City/Patterson [*Louisiana*] [*Airport symbol*]   (OAG)
PTN .... Partido Trabalhista Nacional [*National Workers' Party*] [*Brazil*]
PTN .... Partition   (KSC)
PTN .... Patterson, LA [*Location identifier*] [*FAA*]   (FAAL)
PTN .... Phenotemperature Normogram [*Phenology*]
PTN .... Phenytoin [*Anticonvulsant*]
PTN .... Plant Test Number [*Telecommunications*]   (TEL)
PTN .... Pluton Industries Ltd. [*Vancouver Stock Exchange symbol*]
PTN .... Portion   (FAAC)
PTN .... Potsdam [*New York*] [*Seismograph station code, US Geological Survey*]   (SEIS)
PTN .... Procedure Turn [*Aviation*]   (FAAC)
Ptn.............. Pterin [*Biochemistry*]
PTNM .... Putnam Trust Co. [*NASDAQ symbol*]   (NQ)
PTNR .... Partner   (ROG)
PTNRSHIP ... Partnership   (ROG)
PTNX......... Printronix, Inc. [*NASDAQ symbol*]   (NQ)
PTO .... Pacific Theater of Operations [*World War II*]
PTO .... Packard Truck Organization   (EA)
PTO .... Participating Test Organization [*Air Force*]
PTO .... Patent and Trademark Office [*Formerly, PO*] [*Department of Commerce*]
PTO .... Pato Branco [*Brazil*] [*Airport symbol*]   (OAG)
PTO .... People, Topics, Opinions [*A publication*] [*British*]
PTO .... Please Turn Over [*the page*]
PTO .... Port Transportation Officer
PTO .... Porto [*Serro Do Pilar*] [*Portugal*] [*Seismograph station code, US Geological Survey*]   (SEIS)
PTO .... Power Takeoff
PTO .... Power Test Operations   (MCD)
PTO .... Professional and Technology Officer [*British*]
PTO .... Project Type Organization   (AAG)
PTO .... Proof Test Orbiter [*NASA*]
PTO .... Propellant Transfer Operation   (AFM)
PTO .... Protivo-Tankovaia Oborona [*Antitank Defense*] [*USSR*]
PTO .... Public Trustee Office   (DLA)
PTO .... Pyridinethiol Oxide [*Pharmacology*]
PTOA........ Projective Tests of Attitudes
PTobA........ United States Army, Tobyhanna Army Depot Library, Tobyhanna, PA [*Library symbol*] [*Library of Congress*]   (LCLS)

PTOC .... Progress in Theoretical Organic Chemistry [*Elsevier Book Series*] [*A publication*]
PToG .... General Telephone & Electronics, GTE Sylvania, Inc., Towanda, PA [*Library symbol*] [*Library of Congress*]　(LCLS)
PTOL .... Peacetime Operating Level　(AFM)
Ptol .... Ptolemaeus Mathematicus [*Second century AD*] [*Classical studies*]　(OCD)
Ptol .... Ptolemaic　(BJA)
PTOP .... Program Test and Operations Plan
PTOS .... Paper Tape Oriented Operating System
PTOS .... Peacetime Operating Stock [*Military*]
PTOUT ...... Printout　(MSA)
PTP .... Paper Tape Perforator
PTP .... Paper Tape Punch
PTP .... Parti Togolais du Progres [*Party for Togolese Progress*]
PTP .... Peak-to-Peak
PTP .... Pensions for Technical Professionals [*An association*]
PTP .... People-to-People International　(EA)
PTP .... Percutaneous Transhepatic Selective Portography [*Roentgenography*]
PTP .... Petrologic Petroleum [*Vancouver Stock Exchange symbol*]
PTP .... Phase Transition Phenomena [*Elsevier Book Series*] [*A publication*]
PTP .... Phenyltetrahydropyridine [*Biochemistry*]
PTP .... Platinum Temperature Probe
PTP .... Point Park College, Pittsburgh, PA [*OCLC symbol*] [*Inactive*]　(OCLC)
PTP .... Point-to-Point [*Air Force*]
PTP .... Pointe-A-Pitre [*Guadeloupe*] [*Airport symbol*]　(OAG)
PTP .... Pollution Transfer Program [*Marine science*]　(MSC)
PTP .... Porous Tungsten Plug
PTP .... Post-Transfusion Purpura [*Medicine*]
PTP .... Posto Telefonico Pubblico [*Public Telephone*] [*Italy*]
PTP .... Posttetanic Potentiation [*Neurophysiology*]
PTP .... Potato Tuber Peroxidase [*An enzyme*]
PTP .... Preferred Target Point　(KSC)
PTP .... Preliminary Task Plan　(MCD)
PTP .... Pretransmission Precautionary Answer to Nature's Call [*Especially before a long program*] [*Television*]
PTP .... Primary Target Point [*NASA*]
PTP .... Production Test Plan　(MCD)
PTP .... Production Test Procedure　(NATG)
PTP .... Professional Tax Planner
PTP .... Program Task Planning　(MCD)
PTP .... Programable Text Processor [*Programing language*]　(CSR)
PTP .... Programed Turn Phase
PTP .... Proximity Test Plug [*Nuclear energy*]　(NRCH)
PTP .... Pueblo to People　(EA)
PTPC .... Professional Teaching Practices Commission　(OICC)
PTPD .... Part Paid [*Business and trade*]
PTPF .... Payee TIN [*Taxpayer Identification Number*] Perfection File [*IRS*]
PTPFA .... Poznanskie Towarzystwo Przyjaciol Nauk. Wydzial Lekarski. Prace Komisji Farmaceutycznej [*A publication*]
Pt Phil Gaz ... Port Phillip Gazette [*A publication*]
PTPI .... Professional and Technical Programs, Incorporated
PTPLF .... Petrologic Petroleum Limited [*NASDAQ symbol*]　(NQ)
PTPMA ...... Poznanskie Towarzystwo Przyjaciol Nauk. Wydzial Lekarski. Prace Komisji Medycyny Doswiadczalnej [*A publication*]
PTPN .... Poznanskie Towarzystwo Przyjaciol Nauk [*A publication*]
PTPS .... Package Test Power Supply
PTPS .... Propellant Transfer Pressurization System　(KSC)
PTPSC ...... People-to-People Sports Committee　(EA)
PTPU .... Program Tape Preparation Unit
PTQ .... Poly(tolyquinoxaline) [*Organic chemistry*]
PTR .... Pacific Test Range　(MUGU)
PTR .... Painter
PTR .... Paper Tape Reader
PTR .... Partner
PTR .... Parts Tool Requirements File
PTR .... Patuxent River [*Navy*]　(MCD)
PTR .... Perforated Tape Reader
P/Tr .... Permian/Triassic [*A geological period boundary*]
PTR .... Personality Tests and Reviews [*A publication*]
PTR .... Peterson [*Alabama*] [*Seismograph station code, US Geological Survey*]　(SEIS)
Ptr .... Petrine [*Of, or relating to, Peter the Apostle or Peter the Great*]　(BJA)
PTR .... Photoelectric Tape Reader
PTR .... Physikalisch-Technische Reichsanstalt
PTR .... Pilot Training Rate [*Navy*]
PTR .... Pleasant Harbor [*Alaska*] [*Airport symbol*]　(OAG)
PTR .... Plug-Type Receptacle
PTR .... Pool Test Reactor
PTR .... Pool Training Reactor
PTR .... Poor Transmission [*Telecommunications*]　(TEL)
PTR .... Portable Tape Recorder
PTR .... Position Track RADAR
PTR .... Positive Termination Rate [*Job Training and Partnership Act*]　(OICC)
PTR .... Power Transformers　(MCD)

PTR .... Pre-Trial Release　(OICC)
PTR .... Precision Transmitter Receiver
PTR .... Preliminary Technical Report
PTR .... Preliminary Test Report [*NASA*]　(KSC)
PTR .... Pressure-Tube Reactor
PTR .... Pretransmit Receiving
PTR .... Princeton Theological Review [*A publication*]
PTR .... Printer　(MSA)
P Tr .... Private Trust [*Includes testamentary, investment, life insurance, holding title, etc.*]　(DLA)
PTR .... Processor Tape Read
PTR .... Production Test Record
PTR .... Production Test Requirements　(KSC)
PTR .... Professional Tennis Registry, USA　(EA)
PTR .... Proficiency Testing Research　(EA)
PTR .... Program Technical Review　(MCD)
PTR .... Program Trouble Report　(KSC)
PTR .... Proof Test Reactor
PTR .... Punched Tape Reader [*Data processing*]
PTRA .... Port Terminal Railroad Association
PTRA .... Power Transmission Representatives Association [*Shawnee Mission, KS*]　(EA)
P/TRAC..... Positraction [*Automotive engineering*]
PTRAS ...... Property Trust of America [*NASDAQ symbol*]　(NQ)
PTrB .... Betz Laboratories, Inc., Trevose, PA [*Library symbol*] [*Library of Congress*]　(LCLS)
PTRC .... Personnel and Training Research Center [*Air Force*]
PTRD .... Part Redeemed [*Stock exchange term*]
PTRE .... Petrie Corp. [*NASDAQ symbol*]　(NQ)
PTREA ...... Philips Technical Review [*A publication*]
PTRF .... Peacetime Rate Factor　(AABC)
PTRF .... Peacetime Replacement Factor [*Military*]
PTRI .... Pacer Technology & Resources, Incorporated [*NASDAQ symbol*]　(NQ)
PTRI .... Pharmaceutical and Toxicological Research Institute [*Ohio State University*] [*Research center*]　(RCD)
Ptr Ink .... Printers' Ink [*A publication*]
Ptr Ink Mo ... Printers' Ink Monthly [*A publication*]
PTRJ......... Powered Thermocouple Reference Junction
PTRK......... Preston Corp. [*NASDAQ symbol*]　(NQ)
PTRL......... Petrol Industries [*NASDAQ symbol*]　(NQ)
PTRM......... Partial Thermoremanent Magnetization [*Geophysics*]
PTRO......... Personnel Transaction Register by Originator　(AABC)
PTRO......... Preoverhaul Test Requirement Outline
PTRR......... Port Townsend Railroad, Inc. [*Formerly, PTS*] [*AAR code*]
PTRSC ...... Proceedings and Transactions. Royal Society of Canada [*A publication*]
PTRY .... Pottery [*Freight*]
PTS .... Pali Text Society　(EA)
PTS .... Paper Tape-to-Magnetic Tape Conversion System　(DIT)
PTS .... Paper Tape Sender
PTS .... Papiertechnische Stiftung [*Database producer*]
PTS .... Para-Toluenesulfonic Acid
PTS .... Parameter Test Setup
PTS .... Parts
PTS .... Patellar-Tendon Supracondylar [*Anatomy*]
PTS .... Payload Test Set [*NASA*]　(NASA)
PTS .... Payload Transportation System [*NASA*]　(MCD)
PTS .... People's Translation Service [*An association*] [*Oakland, CA*]　(EA)
PTS .... Permanent Threshold Shift [*Hearing evaluation*]
PTS .... Petro-Sun International, Inc. [*Toronto Stock Exchange symbol*]
PTS .... Photogrammetric Target System [*Air Force*]
PTS .... Photothermal Spectroscopy
PTS .... Pi Tau Sigma [*Society*]
PTS .... Pittsburg, KS [*Location identifier*] [*FAA*]　(FAAL)
PTS .... Pneumatic Test Sequencer　(AFM)
PTS .... Pneumatic Test Set　(KSC)
PTS .... Pod Tail Section
PTS .... Pointing and Tracking Scope
PTS .... Port Townsend Railroad, Inc. [*Later, PTRR*] [*AAR code*]
PTS .... Power Transfer Switch
PTS .... Power Transient Suppressor　(IEEE)
PTS .... Precision Timing System
PTS .... Predicasts Terminal Systems [*Predicasts, Inc.*] [*Cleveland, OH*] [*Database*]
PTS .... Predicasts Time Series [*Series of databases*] [*Predicasts, Inc.*] [*Cleveland, OH*]
PTS .... Pressurized Thermal Shock [*Nuclear power plants*]
PTS .... Price-Tag Shock [*See also PTA*]
PTS .... Prime Time Sunday [*TV program*]
PTS .... Princeton Theological Seminary, Princeton, NJ [*OCLC symbol*]　(OCLC)
PTS .... Private Telecommunications Systems [*Radio-Suisse Ltd.*] [*Berne, Switzerland*] [*Telecommunications*]　(TSSD)
PTS .... Proactive TMDE Support　(RDA)
PTS .... Proceed to Select [*Telecommunications*]　(TEL)
PTS .... Proceed to Send [*Telecommunications*]　(TEL)
PTS .... Production Test Specification
PTS .... Professional Travelogue Sponsors [*Atlanta, GA*]　(EA)
PTS .... Program of Technology and Society [*Later, DTS*]　(EA)

PTS .... Program Test System [*Data processing*]   (IEEE)
PTS .... Program Triple Store
PTS .... Programer Test Station
PTS .... Propellant Transfer System
PTS .... Public Telephone Service [*or System*]
                 [*Telecommunications*]   (TEL)
PTS .... Pure Time Sharing [*Data processing*]   (IEEE)
PTSA........ Para-Toluenesulfonic Acid [*Organic chemistry*]
PTSA........ Parent-Teacher-Student Association [*Nickname: "Pizza"*]
PTSA........ Professional Trucking Services Association [*North Little Rock,
                 AR*]   (EA)
PT-S/C...... Proof Test Spacecraft [*NASA*]
PTSD.......... Post-Traumatic Stress Disorder [*Psychiatry*]
PTSE .... Paper Tape Splicing Equipment
PTSI .... Para-Toluene Sulfonylisocyanate [*Organic chemistry*]
PTSIC .... Petrosystems International [*NASDAQ symbol*]   (NQ)
PTSLA .... Plant Science Letters [*A publication*]
PTSO .... Personnel Transaction Summary by Originator   (AABC)
PTSP .... Peacetime Support Period [*DoD*]
PT/SP .... Pressure Tube to Spool Piece [*Nuclear energy*]   (NRCH)
PTS PROMT ... Predicasts Overview of Markets and Technology [*Predicasts,
                 Inc.*] [*Cleveland, OH*] [*Bibliographic database*]
PTSR........ Preliminary Technical Survey Report [*Military*]   (AFIT)
PTSR........ Pressure-Tube Superheat Reactor
PTSS .... Photon Target Scoring System   (AAG)
PTSS .... Princeton Time Sharing Services, Inc.
PTST .... Personnel Transaction Summary by Type Transaction   (AABC)
PTST .... Pretransfusion Serologic Testing
PTST .... Prime Time School Television [*An association*]   (EA)
PTT .... Pacific Telephone & Telegraph Co.   (FAAC)
PTT .... Part Task Trainer   (MCD)
PTT... Partial Thromboplastin Time [*Hematology*]
PTT .... Party Test [*Telecommunications*]   (TEL)
PTT .... Peak Twitch Tension [*Physiology*]
PTT .... Petrotex Resources [*Vancouver Stock Exchange symbol*]
PTT .... Physical Therapist Technician
PTT............ Post und Telegraphenverwaltung [*Postal and Telegraph
                 Administration*] [*Vienna, Austria*]
                 [*Telecommunications*] (TSSD)
PTT............ Post, Telephon und Telegraphenbetriebe [*Berne, Switzerland*]
                 [*Telecommunications*] (TSSD)
PTT............ Post Ten Tumblers [*Pseudonym used by William Maginn*]
PTT............ Postal, Telegraph, and Telephone Administration   (NATG)
PTT............ Postes, Telegraphes, et Telediffusion [*Post, Telegraph, and
                 Telephone*] [*General Post Office*] [*France*]
PTT............ Pratt, KS [*Location identifier*] [*FAA*]   (FAAL)
PTT............ Press to Transmit
PTT............ Private Tombs at Thebes [*Oxford*] [*A publication*]   (BJA)
PTT............ Production Type Test
PTT............ Program Technical Training   (AFM)
PTT............ Program Test Tape [*Data processing*]   (IEEE)
PTT............ Public Telecommunications Trust [*Proposed replacement for
                 Corporation for Public Broadcasting*]
PTT............ Pulmonary Transit Time [*Physiology*]
PTT............ Push to Talk
PTTC .... Pacific Transportation Terminal Command [*Army*]
PTTC .... Paper Tape and Transmission Code
PTTDA ...... Petroleum Today [*A publication*]
PTTDAR ..... Personnel Training and Training Devices Analysis
                 Report   (MCD)
PTTH .... Prothoracicotropic Hormone
PTTI........... Postal, Telegraph, and Telephone International [*See also IPTT*]
                 [*Brussels, Belgium*]
PTTI........... Postal, Telegraph, and Telephone International [*See also IPTT*]
                 [*Geneva, Switzerland*]   (EA-IO)
PTTI........... Precise Time and Time Interval   (AFM)
PTTI Stud... PTTI [*Postal, Telegraph, and Telephone International*] Studies
                 [*A publication*]
PTTK .... Partial Thromboplastin Time with Kaolin [*Hematology*]
PTTL .... Press-to-Test Light
PTTMC ...... PACOM [*Pacific Command*] Tactical Target Materials
                 Catalog   (CINC)
PTU .... Package Transfer Unit
PTU .... Pallet Transporter Unit [*Military*]   (CAAL)
PTU .... Parallel Transmission Unit   (AAG)
PTU .... Phenylthiourea [*Organic chemistry*]
PTU .... Pilot Test Unit [*Air Force*]
PTU .... Planning Tracking Unit   (MCD)
PTU .... Platinum [*Alaska*] [*Airport symbol*]   (OAG)
PTU .... Platinum, AK [*Location identifier*] [*FAA*]   (FAAL)
PTU .... Portable Test Unit
PTU .... Power Transfer Unit
PTU .... Propylthiouracil [*Also, PROP, PT*] [*Thyroid inhibitor*]
PTV .... Parachute Test Vehicle
PTV .... Passenger Transfer Vehicle [*Airport transportation*]
PTV .... Passenger Transport Vehicle
PTV .... Pathfinder Test Vehicle   (MCD)
PTV .... Pay Television
PTV .... Peach Tree Valley [*California*] [*Seismograph station code, US
                 Geological Survey*]   (SEIS)
PTV .... Peak-to-Valley

PTV .... Penetration Test Vehicle [*Aerospace*]
PTV .... Pietas Tutissima Virtus [*Piety Is the Safest Virtue*] [*Latin*]
                 [*Motto of Ernst, Margrave of Brandenburg (1583-1613)*]
PTV .... Pitch Thrust Vector   (KSC)
PTV .... Porous Tungsten Vaporizer
PTV .... Porterville, CA [*Location identifier*] [*FAA*]   (FAAL)
PTV .... Predetermined Time Value   (IEEE)
PTV .... Propulsion Technology Validation   (MCD)
PTV .... Propulsion Test Vehicle
PTV .... Prototype Test Vehicle   (MCD)
PTV .... Public Television
PTV .... Punched Tape Verifier [*Data processing*]
PTVA .... Propulsion Test Vehicle Assembly [*NASA*]
PTVC .... Pitch Thrust Vector Control   (KSC)
PTVD........ Portable Toxic Vapor Detector
PTVE .... Propulsion Test Vehicle Engineering [*NASA*]   (MCD)
PTVST .... Port Visit [*Navy*]   (NVT)
PTVV .... Peak-to-Valley Variation   (MCD)
PTW........... Physikalisch-Technische-Werkstatten [*Roentgenology*]
PTW........... Playing to Win   (EA)
PTW........... Point Target Weapon
PTW........... Pottstown, PA [*Location identifier*] [*FAA*]   (FAAL)
PTW........... Pressure-Type Window
PTWC........ Pacific Tsunami Warning Center [*National Weather
                 Service*]   (MSC)
PTWC........ Project on Technology, Work, and Character   (EA)
PTWF .... Pakistan Transport Workers' Federation
P-TWP....... Post-Township
PTWT .... Photo-Type Traveling Wave Tube   (NG)
PTX .... Pacific Trans-Ocean Resources Ltd. [*Toronto Stock Exchange
                 symbol*]
PTX .... Palytoxin [*Organic chemistry*]
PTx............. Parathyroidectomy [*Medicine*]
PTX .... Pertussis Toxin [*Pharmacology*]
PTX .... Picrotoxinin [*Biochemistry*]
PTX .... Polythiazide [*Organic chemistry*]
PTX .... Pressure-Temperature Composition
PTXB......... Pumiliotoxin B [*Organic chemistry*]
PTY .... Panama City [*Panama*] [*Airport symbol*]   (OAG)
PTY .... Party   (AAG)
PTY .... Proprietary
PTZ........... Pentylenetetrazole [*CNS stimulant*]
PU.............. Paid Up
PU.............. Parents United [*San Jose, CA*]   (EA)
PU.............. Participating Unit   (NVT)
PU.............. Parts Used [*Medicine*]
PU.............. Passed Urine [*Medicine*]
PU.............. Paste Up   (ADA)
PU.............. Peptic Ulcer [*Medicine*]
PU.............. Per Urethra [*Medicine*]
PU.............. Perbonate Unit [*Analytical biochemistry*]
PU.............. Percent Utilization [*Anesthesiology*]
PU.............. Peripheral Unit [*Computers*]   (MSA)
PU.............. Physical Unit [*Data processing*]   (IBMDP)
PU.............. Pick Up [*Business and trade*]
PU.............. Plant Unit
Pu.............. Plutonium [*Chemical element*]
PU.............. Polyurethane [*Also, PUR*] [*Organic chemistry*]
PU.............. Power Equipment [*JETDS nomenclature*] [*Military*]   (CET)
PU.............. Power Unit
PU.............. Pregnancy Urine [*Medicine*]
PU.............. Primeras Lineas Uruguayas [*ICAO designator*]   (FAAC)
PU.............. Prisoner's Union [*An association*] [*San Francisco, CA*]   (EA)
PU.............. Problemi di Ulisse [*A publication*]
PU.............. Processing Unit [*Data processing*]
PU.............. Processor Utility [*Telecommunications*]   (TEL)
PU.............. Production Unit   (CAAL)
PU.............. Propellant Utilization [*Air Force*]
PU.............. Propulsion Unit   (KSC)
PU.............. Proutist Universal   (EA)
PU.............. Publications   (MCD)
PU.............. Publisher [*Online database field identifier*]
PU.............. Pump Unit   (AAG)
Pu.............. Punic   (BJA)
Pu.............. Purine [*Biochemistry*]
PU.............. Purple   (ROG)
PU.............. United States Miscellaneous Pacific Islands [*Two-letter
                 standard code*]   (CNC)
PU.............. University of Pennsylvania, Philadelphia, PA [*Library symbol*]
                 [*Library of Congress*]   (LCLS)
PUA........... Partido de Unificacion Anticomunista [*Anti-Communist
                 Unification Party*] [*Guatemalan*]   (PPW)
PUA........... Plant Unique Analysis   (NRCH)
PUA........... Polish Union of America   (EA)
PUA........... Pride Users' Association [*Defunct*]   (EA)
PU-A.......... University of Pennsylvania, Morris Arboretum, Philadelphia, PA
                 [*Library symbol*] [*Library of Congress*]   (LCLS)
PUAA .... Public Utilities Advertising Association [*Later, PUCA*]   (EA)
PUAC .... Propellant Utilization Acoustical Checkout   (AAG)

PU-AC .... University of Pennsylvania, Annenberg School of Communications, Philadelphia, PA [*Library symbol*] [*Library of Congress*] (LCLS)
PUAD .... Pueblo Army Depot [*Colorado*] (AABC)
PUADA .... Pueblo Army Depot Activity (AABC)
PUAHC ...... Proceedings. Union of American Hebrew Congregations [*A publication*]
PUAR .... Pulse Acquisition RADAR [*Military*] (MSA)
PUAS .... Postal Union of the Americas and Spain [*See also UPAE*] (EA-IO)
PUASAL .... Proceedings. Utah Academy of Sciences, Arts, and Letters [*A publication*]
PUB .... Pacific University Bulletin [*A publication*]
PUB .... Partido Union Boliviana [*Bolivian Unity Party*] (PPW)
PUB .... Phycourobilin [*Biochemistry*]
PUB .... Physical Unit Block [*Data processing*]
PUB .... Puale Bay [*Alaska*] [*Seismograph station code, US Geological Survey*] (SEIS)
PUB .... Public
PUB .... Public House [*A drinking establishment*] [*British*]
PUB .... Publication (AFM)
PUB .... Publicity
PUB .... Published (AABC)
PUB .... Publisher
Pub .... Publisher [*A publication*]
PUB .... Pueblo [*Colorado*] [*Airport symbol*] (OAG)
PUB .... Pueblo, CO [*Location identifier*] [*FAA*] (FAAL)
Pub Adm .... Public Administration [*A publication*]
Pub Admin ... Public Administration [*A publication*]
Pub Admin Abstr ... Public Administration Abstracts and Index of Articles [*A publication*]
Pub Admin Survey ... Public Administration Survey [*A publication*]
Pub Adm R ... Public Administration Review [*A publication*]
Pub Adm Rev ... Public Administration Review [*A publication*]
Pub Am Stat Assn ... Publications. American Statistical Association [*A publication*]
Pub Archives Can Report ... Public Archives of Canada. Report [*A publication*]
Pub Ast S J ... Publications. Astronomical Society of Japan [*A publication*]
Pub Ast S P ... Publications. Astronomical Society of the Pacific [*A publication*]
Pub Auth .... Public Authorities (DLA)
Pub Bargaining Cas (CCH) ... Public Bargaining Cases [*Commerce Clearing House*] (DLA)
Pubbl (Bergamo) Sta Sper Maiscoltura ... Pubblicazioni (Bergamo) Stazione Sperimentale di Maiscoltura [*A publication*]
Pubbl Centro Sper Agr Forest ENCC ... Pubblicazioni. Centro di Sperimentazione Agricola e Forestale. Ente Nazionale per la Cellulosa e per la Carta [*A publication*]
Pubbl Cent Sper Agric For ... Pubblicazioni. Centro di Sperimentalzione Agricola e Forestale [*A publication*]
Pubbl Cent Sper Agric For ... Pubblicazioni. Centro di Sperimentazione Agricola e Forestale [*A publication*]
Pubbl Ente Naz Cellulosa Carta ... Pubblicazioni. Ente Nazionale per la Cellulosa e per la Carta [*A publication*]
Pubbl Fac Sci Ing Univ Trieste Ser B ... Pubblicazioni. Facolta di Scienze e d'Ingegneria. Universita di Trieste. Serie B [*A publication*]
Pubbl IAC ... Pubblicazioni. Istituto per le Applicazioni del Calcolo. Consiglio Nazionale delle Ricerche [*A publication*]
Pubbl Ist Geol Mineral Univ Ferrara ... Pubblicazioni. Istituto di Geologia e Mineralogia. Universita di Ferrara [*A publication*]
Pubbl Ist Mat Appl Fac Ingegneria Univ Stud Roma ... Pubblicazioni. Istituto di Matematica Applicata. Facolta di Ingegneria. Universita degli Studi di Roma [*A publication*]
Pubbl Oss Geofis Trieste ... Pubblicazioni. Osservatorio Geofisico di Trieste [*A publication*]
Pubbl Stn Zool Napoli ... Pubblicazioni. Stazione Zoologica di Napoli [*A publication*]
PUBC .... Presbyterians United for Biblical Concern (EA)
PUBC .... Pubcoa, Inc. [*NASDAQ symbol*] (NQ)
Pub Circ ..... Publishers' Circular and Booksellers' Record [*A publication*]
Pub Col Soc Mass ... Publications. Colonial Society of Massachusetts [*A publication*]
Pub Contract L J ... Public Contract Law Journal [*A publication*]
PUBD .... Published (ROG)
PUB DOC ... Public Documents (ROG)
Pub Dom Ast ... Publications. Dominion Astrophysical Observatory [*A publication*]
Pub Emp .... Public Employee [*A publication*]
Pub Employee Bargaining Rep (CCH) ... Public Employee Bargaining Reports [*Commerce Clearing House*] (DLA)
Pub Employee Rel Rep ... Public Employee Relations Reports (DLA)
Pub Ent Adv LQ ... Publishing, Entertainment, Advertising, and Allied Fields Law Quarterly [*A publication*]
Pub Gen Acts S Austl ... Public General Acts of South Australia (DLA)
Pub Gen Laws ... Public General Laws (DLA)
PUB HA ...... Public Hall [*Freemasonry*] (ROG)
Pub Health ... United States Public Health Service, Court Decisions (DLA)
Pub Health Nurs ... Public Health Nursing [*A publication*]
Pub Health Rep ... Public Health Reports [*A publication*]
Pub Health Rept ... Public Health Reports [*A publication*]

Pub Health Rep US Pub Health and Mar Hosp Serv ... Public Health Reports. United States Surgeon-General. Public Health and Marine Hospital Service [*A publication*]
Pub Health Rep US Pub Health Serv ... Public Health Reports. United States Public Health Service [*A publication*]
Pub Health Soc B ... Public Health Society. Bulletin [*Kuala Lumpur*] [*A publication*]
Pub Hist Inst Luxembourg ... Publications. Section Historique. Institut Grand-Ducal de Luxembourg [*A publication*]
Pub Hous ... Public Housing (DLA)
PUBINFO .... Office of Public Information [*Formerly, OPR*] [*Navy*]
Pub Interest ... Public Interest [*A publication*]
Pub L .... Public Law [*A publication*]
PUBL .... Publication
Publ Adm ... Public Administration [*A publication*]
Publ Adm R ... Public Administration Review [*A publication*]
Publ Adm Re ... Public Administration Review [*A publication*]
Publ Aff B ... Public Affairs Bulletin [*A publication*]
Publ Agric (Can) ... Publication. Agriculture (Canada) [*A publication*]
Publ Alberta Dept Agr ... Publication. Alberta Department of Agriculture [*A publication*]
Publ Amakusa Mar Biol Lab Kyushu Univ ... Publications. Amakusa Marine Biological Laboratory. Kyushu University [*A publication*]
Publ Am Assoc Adv Sci ... Publication. American Association for the Advancement of Science [*A publication*]
Publ Amer Ass Advan Sci ... Publication. American Association for the Advancement of Science [*A publication*]
Publ Amer Univ Beirut Fac Agr Sci ... Publication. American University of Beirut. Faculty of Agricultural Sciences [*A publication*]
Publ Am Inst Biol Sci ... Publication. American Institute of Biological Sciences [*A publication*]
Publ Am Univ Beirut Fac Agric Sci ... Publication. American University of Beirut. Faculty of Agricultural Sciences [*A publication*]
Publ ANARE Data Rep Ser ... Publications. ANARE [*Australian National Antarctic Research Expedition*] Data Reports Series [*A publication*]
Pub Land & Res L Dig ... Public Land and Resources Law Digest [*A publication*]
Pub Lands Dec ... Department of the Interior, Decisions Relating to Public Lands (DLA)
Publ Ass For-Cell ... Publication. Association Foret-Cellulose [*A publication*]
Publ Assoc Etude Paleontol Stratigr Houilleres ... Publication. Association pour l'Etude de la Paleontologie et de la Stratigraphie Houilleres [*A publication*]
Publ Assoc Ing Fac Polytech Mons ... Publications. Association des Ingenieurs. Faculte Polytechnique de Mons [*A publication*]
Publ Astron Soc Jpn ... Publications. Astronomical Society of Japan [*A publication*]
Publ Astron Soc Pac ... Publications. Astronomical Society of the Pacific [*A publication*]
Publ Aust Natl Univ Res Sch Phys Sci Dep Eng Phys ... Australian National University. Research School of Physical Sciences. Department of Engineering Physics. Publication [*A publication*]
Publ Avulsas Cent Pesqui Aggeu Magalhaes (Recife Braz) ... Publicacoes Avulsas do Centro de Pesquisas Aggeu Magalhaes (Recife, Brazil) [*A publication*]
Publ Avulsas Mus Nac (Rio De J) ... Publicacoes Avulsas. Museu Nacional (Rio De Janeiro) [*A publication*]
Publ Biol Dir Gen Invest Cient UANL (Univ Auton Nuevo Leon) ... Publicaciones Biologicas. Direccion General de la Investigacion Cientifica UANL (Universidad Autonoma de Nuevo Leon) [*A publication*]
Publ Brit Columbia Dept Agr ... Publication. British Columbia Department of Agriculture [*A publication*]
Publ Bur Etud Geol Minieres Colon (Paris) ... Publications. Bureau d'Etudes Geologiques et Minieres Coloniales (Paris) [*A publication*]
Publ Bur Rech Geol Geophys Minieres (Fr) ... Publications. Bureau de Rechereches Geologiques, Geophysiques, et Minieres (France) [*A publication*]
Publ Calif Dep Agric ... Publication. California Department of Agriculture [*A publication*]
Publ Canada Dep Agric ... Publication. Canada Department of Agriculture [*A publication*]
Publ Canada Dep For ... Publication. Canada Department of Forestry [*A publication*]
Publ Can Dep Agric ... Publication. Canada Department of Agriculture [*A publication*]
Publ Can Dept Agr ... Publication. Canada Department of Agriculture [*A publication*]
Publ Center Medieval Ren Stud UCLA ... Publications. Center for Medieval and Renaissance Studies. UCLA [*University of California at Los Angeles*] [*A publication*]
Publ Cent Estud Entomol Univ Chile ... Publicaciones. Centro de Estudios Entomologicos. Universidad de Chile [*A publication*]
Publ Cent Estud Leprol ... Publicacoes. Centro de Estudos Leprologicos [*A publication*]
Publ Cent Etude Util Sciures de Bois ... Publication. Centre d'Etude pour l'Utilisation des Sciures de Bois [*A publication*]

Publ Cent Natl Exploit Oceans Ser Rapp Sci Tech (Fr) ... Publications. Centre National pour l'Exploitation des Oceans. Serie. Rapport Scientifique et Technique (France) [*A publication*]

Publ Cent Natl Geol Houillere ... Publication. Centre National de Geologie Houillere [*A publication*]

Publ Cent Quim Ind (Buenos Aires) ... Publicacion. Centro de Quimicos Industriales (Buenos Aires) [*A publication*]

Publ Cent Rech Zootech Univ Louvain ... Publication. Centre de Recherches Zootechniques. Universite de Louvain [*A publication*]

Publ Centre Recherches Math Pures Ser 3 ... Publications. Centre de Recherches en Mathematiques Pures. Serie 3 [*A publication*]

Publ Centre Rech Math Pures ... Publications. Centre de Recherches en Mathematiques Pures [*A publication*]

Publ Centre Rech Math Pures 1 ... Publications. Centre de Recherches en Mathematiques Pures. Serie 1 [*A publication*]

Publ Centre Rech Math Pures Ser 3 ... Publications. Centre de Recherches en Mathematiques Pures. Serie 3 [*A publication*]

Publ Centre Tech For Trop ... Publication. Centre Technique Forestier Tropical [*A publication*]

Publ Cent Stud Citogenet Veg CNR ... Pubblicazioni. Centro di Studi per la Citogenetica Vegetale. Consiglio Nazionale delle Richerche [*A publication*]

Publ Chile Univ Cent Estud Entomol ... Publicaciones. Chile Universidad. Centro de Estudios Entomologicos [*A publication*]

Publ Choice ... Public Choice [*A publication*]

Publ Cient Univ Austral Chile (Fac Ingen For) ... Publicaciones Cientificas. Universidad Austral de Chile (Facultad de Ingenieria Forestal) [*A publication*]

Publ Clark ... Publications. Clark Library Professorship. University of California at Los Angeles [*A publication*]

Publ Cleans ... Public Cleansing [*A publication*]

Publcoes Avuls Mus Parana ... Publicacoes Avulsas. Museu Paranaense [*A publication*]

Publcoes Cult Co Diam Angola ... Publicacoes Culturais. Companhia de Diamantes de Angola [*A publication*]

Publcoes Dir Ger Servs Flor Aquic ... Publicacoes. Direccao Geral dos Servicos Florestais e Aqueicolas [*A publication*]

Publ Com Nac Energ At (Argent) Misc ... Publicaciones. Comision Nacional de Energia Atomica (Argentina). Miscelanea [*A publication*]

Publ Com Nac Energ At (Argent) Ser Fis ... Publicaciones. Comision Nacional de Energia Atomica (Argentina). Serie Fisica [*A publication*]

Publ Co-Op Ext Univ Calif ... Publication. Cooperative Extension. University of California [*A publication*]

Publ Cult Cia Diamantes Angola ... Publicacoes Culturais. Companhia de Diamantes de Angola [*A publication*]

PUBLD .... Published (ROG)

Publ Dep Agric (Can) ... Publication. Department of Agriculture (Ottawa, Canada) [*A publication*]

Publ Dep Cristalogr Miner CSIC (Spain) ... Publicaciones. Departamento de Cristalografia y Mineralogia. Consejo Superior de Investigaciones Cientificas (Spain) [*A publication*]

Publ Dep Math Lyon ... Publications. Departement de Mathematiques. Faculte des Sciences de Lyon [*A publication*]

Publ Dept Agr (Can) ... Publications. Department of Agriculture (Canada) [*A publication*]

Publ Dept Agr Conserv (Manitoba) ... Publications. Department of Agriculture and Conservation (Manitoba) [*A publication*]

Publ Dir Gen Invent Nac For (Mex) ... Publicacion. Direccion General del Inventario Nacional Forestal (Coyoacan, Mexico) [*A publication*]

Publ Diverses Mus Natl Hist Nat ... Publications Diverses. Museum National d'Histoire Naturelle [*A publication*]

Publ Dom Obs (Ottawa) ... Publications. Dominion Observatory (Ottawa) [*A publication*]

Publ Dushanb Inst Epidemiol Gig ... Publikatsiya Dushanbinskogo Instituta Epidemiologii i Gigieny [*A publication*]

Publ Earth Phys Branch (Can) ... Publication. Earth Physics Branch (Canada) [*A publication*]

Publ Earth Phys Branch Dep Energy Mines & Resour ... Publications. Earth Physics Branch. Department of Energy, Mines, and Resources [*A publication*]

Publ Econometriques ... Publications Econometriques [*A publication*]

Publ Elektroteh Fak Ser Elektroenerg ... Publikacije Elektrotehnickog Fakulteta. Serija Elektroenergetika [*A publication*]

Publ Elektroteh Fak Ser Elektron Telekommun Autom ... Publikacije Elektrotehnickog Fakulteta. Serija Elektronika Telekommunikacije. Automatika [*A publication*]

Publ Elektroteh Fak Ser Mat & Fiz ... Publikacije Elektrotehnickog Fakulteta. Serija Matematika i Fizika [*A publication*]

Publ Elektroteh Fak Univ Beogr Ser Mat Fiz ... Publikacije Elektrotehnickog Fakulteta. Univerziteta u Beogradu. Serija Matematika i Fizika [*A publication*]

Publ Energ ... Publicacion sobre Energia [*A publication*]

Publ Espec Inst Nac Invest Forest (Mex) ... Publicacion Especial. Instituto Nacional de Investigaciones Forestal (Mexico) [*A publication*]

Publ Espec Inst Oceanogr (San Paulo) ... Publicacao Especial. Instituto Oceanografico (San Paulo) [*A publication*]

Publ Espec Serv Nac Trigo Min Agr (Madrid) ... Publicaciones Especiales. Servicio Nacional del Trigo. Ministerio de Agricultura (Madrid) [*A publication*]

Publ Ethnol ... Publications in Ethnology [*A publication*]

Pub LF........ Public Law Forum (DLA)

Publ Fac Agron Univ Teheran ... Publications. Faculte d'Agronomie. Universite de Teheran [*A publication*]

Publ Fac Agr Sci Amer Univ (Beirut) ... Publications. Faculty of Agricultural Sciences. American University (Beirut) [*A publication*]

Publ Fac Cienc Fisicomat Univ Nac La Plata Ser 2 ... Publicaciones. Facultad de Ciencias Fisicomatematicas. Universidad Nacional de La Plata. Serie 2. Revista [*A publication*]

Publ Fac Dr Econ Amiens ... Publications. Faculte de Droit et d'Economie d'Amiens [*A publication*]

Publ Fac Dr Sci Polit Soc Amiens ... Publications. Faculte de Droit et des Sciences Politiques et Sociales d'Amiens [*A publication*]

Publ FAO/ECE Jt Comm Working Tech ... Publication. FAO [*Food and Agriculture Organization of the United Nations*]/ECE [*Economic Commission for Europe*] Joint Committee on Forest Working Techniques and Training Forest Workers [*A publication*]

Publ Farm (Sao Paulo) ... Publicacoes Farmaceuticas (Sao Paulo) [*A publication*]

Publ Finan ... Public Finance [*A publication*]

Publ Finance ... Public Finance [*A publication*]

Publ Fin Q ... Public Finance Quarterly [*A publication*]

Publ Fond Agathon de Potter ... Publications. Foundation Agathon de Potter [*A publication*]

Publ For Commn NSW ... Publication. Forestry Commission of New South Wales [*A publication*]

Publ Forest Res Brch Canada Dep For ... Publication. Forest Research Branch. Canada Department of Forestry [*A publication*]

Publ For Serv (Can) ... Publication. Forestry Service. Department of Fisheries and Forestry (Ottawa, Canada) [*A publication*]

Publ Found Sci Res Surinam Neth Antilles ... Publications. Foundation for Scientific Research in Surinam and the Netherlands Antilles [*A publication*]

Publ Geol Surv Queensl ... Publication. Geological Survey of Queensland [*A publication*]

Publ Group Adv Psychiatry ... Publication. Groups for the Advancement of Psychiatry [*A publication*]

Publ Gulf Coast Res Lab Mus ... Publications. Gulf Coast Research Laboratory Museum [*A publication*]

Publ Haewundae Mar Lab Pusan Fish Coll ... Publications. Haewundae Marine Laboratory. Pusan Fisheries College [*A publication*]

Publ Heal ... Public Health: The Journal of the Society of Community Medicine [*A publication*]

Publ Heal R ... Public Health Reviews [*A publication*]

Publ Health Lab ... Public Health Laboratory [*A publication*]

Publ Hea Re ... Public Health Reports [*A publication*]

Publ Hlth Rep (Wash) ... Public Health Reports (Washington, DC) [*A publication*]

Publ Hung Min Res Inst ... Publications. Hungarian Mining Research Institute [*A publication*]

Publ Hung Res Inst Mining ... Publications. Hungarian Research Institute for Mining [*A publication*]

Pub Lib....... Public Libraries [*A publication*]

Pub Lib Op ... Public Library Opinion [*A publication*]

Pub Lib Trustee ... Public Library Trustee [*A publication*]

Publicaciones Dept Agric Costa Rica ... Publicaciones. Departamento de Agricultura de Costa Rica [*A publication*]

Public Adm ... Public Administration [*A publication*]

Public Adm Bull ... Public Administration Bulletin [*A publication*]

Public Admin ... Public Administration [*A publication*]

Public Admin R ... Public Administration Review [*A publication*]

Public Admin Survey ... Public Administration Survey [*A publication*]

Public Adm R ... Public Administration Review [*A publication*]

Public Adm Rev ... Public Administration Review [*A publication*]

Public Aff Rep ... Public Affairs Report [*A publication*]

Public Anal Assoc J ... Public Analysts Association. Journal [*England*] [*A publication*]

Public Fin (Berlin) ... Public Finance (Berlin) [*A publication*]

Public Fin Q ... Public Finance Quarterly [*A publication*]

Public Health Eng ... Public Health Engineer [*England*] [*A publication*]

Public Health Eng Abstr ... Public Health Engineering Abstracts [*A publication*]

Public Health J ... Public Health Journal [*A publication*]

Public Health Lab ... Public Health Laboratory [*United States*] [*A publication*]

Public Health Monogr ... Public Health Monograph [*A publication*]

Public Health Pap ... Public Health Papers [*A publication*]

Public Health Rep ... Public Health Reports [*A publication*]

Public Health Rev ... Public Health Reviews [*A publication*]

Public Health Revs ... Public Health Reviews [*A publication*]

Public Land Resour Law Dig ... Public Land and Resources Law Digest [*United States*] [*A publication*]

Public Lib ... Public Libraries [*A publication*]

Public Opin ... Public Opinion [*A publication*]

Public Opinion Q ... Public Opinion Quarterly [*A publication*]

Public Opin Q ... Public Opinion Quarterly [*A publication*]

Public Pers Manage ... Public Personnel Management [*A publication*]
Public Rel .. Public Relations Journal [*A publication*]
Public Relations R ... Public Relations Review [*A publication*]
Public Relat J ... Public Relations Journal [*A publication*]
Public Relat Q ... Public Relations Quarterly [*A publication*]
Public Relat Rev ... Public Relations Review [*A publication*]
Public Sect ... Public Sector. New Zealand Institute of Public Administration [*A publication*]
Public Serv Action ... Public Service Action [*A publication*]
Public TC Review ... Public Telecommunications Review [*A publication*]
Public Util Fortn ... Public Utilities Fortnightly [*A publication*]
Public Works Local Gov Eng ... Public Works and Local Government Engineering [*A publication*]
Public Works Rev ... Public Works Review [*Japan*] [*A publication*]
Public Works Roads Transp ... Public Works, Roads, and Transport [*A publication*]
Public Works Ser ... Public Works and Services [*A publication*]
Public Work (Syd) ... Public Works and Services (Sydney) [*A publication*]
Publ Inst Antart Argent (B Aires) ... Publicacion. Instituto Antartico Argentino (Buenos Aires) [*A publication*]
Publ Inst Biol Apl (Barc) ... Publicaciones. Instituto de Biologia Aplicada (Barcelona) [*A publication*]
Publ Inst Biol Apl (Barcelona) ... Publicaciones. Instituto de Biologia Aplicada (Barcelona) [*A publication*]
Publ Inst Bot "Dr Goncalo Sampaio" Fac Cienc Univ Porto ... Publicacoes. Instituto de Botanica "Dr. Goncalo Sampaio." Faculdade de Ciencias. Universidade do Porto [*A publication*]
Publ Inst Edafol Hidrol Univ Nac Sur (Bahia Blanca) ... Publicaciones. Instituto de Edafologia e Hidrologia. Universidad Nacional del Sur (Bahia Blanca) [*A publication*]
Publ Inst Florestal ... Publicacao. Instituto Florestal [*A publication*]
Publ Inst Found Engng Soil Mech Rock Mech Waterways Constr ... Publications. Institute of Foundation Engineering, Soil Mechanics, Rock Mechanics, and Waterways Construction [*A publication*]
Publ Inst Fr Pet Collect Colloq Semin ... Publications. Institut Francais du Petrole. Collection Colloques et Seminaires [*France*] [*A publication*]
Publ Inst Geogr (Bogota) ... Publication. Instituto Geografico Agustin Codazzi (Bogota) [*A publication*]
Publ Inst Geophys Pol Acad Sci ... Publication. Institute of Geophysics. Polish Academy of Sciences [*A publication*]
Publ Inst Geophys Pol Acad Sci Ser A ... Publications. Institute of Geophysics. Polish Academy of Sciences. Series A. Physics of the Earth Interior [*A publication*]
Publ Inst Geophys Pol Acad Sci Ser C ... Publications. Institute of Geophysics. Polish Academy of Sciences. Series C. Earth Magnetism [*A publication*]
Publ Inst Geophys Pol Acad Sci Ser F ... Publications. Institute of Geophysics. Polish Academy of Sciences. Series F. Planetary Geodesy [*A publication*]
Publ Inst Geophys Ser D Pol Acad Sci ... Publications. Institute of Geophysics. Polish Academy of Sciences. Series D. Atmosphere Physics [*A publication*]
Publ Inst Invest Geol Diputacion Prov Barcelona ... Publicaciones. Instituto de Investigaciones Geologicas. Diputacion Provincial de Barcelona [*A publication*]
Publ Inst Mar Sci Nat Fish Univ Busan ... Publications. Institute of Marine Sciences. National Fisheries. University of Busan [*A publication*]
Publ Inst Mar Sci Univ Tex ... Publications. Institute of Marine Science. University of Texas [*A publication*]
Publ Inst Mar Sci Univ Texas ... Publications. Institute of Marine Science. University of Texas [*A publication*]
Publ Inst Math (Belgrade) ... Publications. Institut Mathematique. Nouvelle Serie (Belgrade) [*A publication*]
Publ Inst Mex Recursos Nat Renov ... Publicacion. Instituto Mexicano de Recursos Naturales Renovables [*A publication*]
Publ Inst Mineral Paleontol Quat Geol Univ Lund ... Publications. Institutes of Mineralogy, Paleontology, and Quaternary Geology. University of Lund [*A publication*]
Publ Inst Nac Nutr (Argent) Publ Cient ... Publicaciones. Instituto Nacional de la Nutricion (Argentina). Publicaciones Cientificas [*A publication*]
Publ Inst Nat Etude Agron Congo ... Publications. Institut National pour l'Etude Agronomique du Congo [*A publication*]
Publ Inst Nat Etude Agron Congo (INEAC) Serie Scientifique ... Publications. Institut National pour l'Etude Agronomique du Congo (INEAC). Serie Scientifique [*A publication*]
Publ Inst Natl Etude Agron Congo Belge Ser Sci ... Publications. Institut National pour l'Etude Agronomique du Congo Belge. Serie Scientifique [*A publication*]
Publ Inst Natl Etude Agron Congo Ser Sci ... Publications. Institut National pour l'Etude Agronomique du Congo. Serie Scientifique [*A publication*]
Publ Inst Natl Etude Agron Congo Ser Tech ... Publications. Institut National pour l'Etude Agronomique du Congo. Serie Technique [*A publication*]
Publ Inst Opt Madrid ... Publicaciones. Instituto de Optica Daza de Valdes de Madrid [*A publication*]

Publ Inst Pesqui Mar ... Publicacao. Instituto de Pesquisas da Marinha [*A publication*]
Publ Inst Quim Fis Rocasolano ... Publicaciones. Instituto de Quimica Fisica "Rocasolano" [*A publication*]
Publ Inst Rech Siderurg Ser A ... Publications. Institut de Recherches de la Siderurgie [*Saint-Germain-En-Laye*]. Serie A [*A publication*]
Publ Inst R Meteorol Belg A ... Publications. Institut Royal Meteorologique de Belgique. Serie A. Format in-4 [*A publication*]
Publ Inst R Meteorol Belg B ... Publications. Institut Royal Meteorologique de Belgique. Serie B. Format in-8 [*A publication*]
Publ Inst R Meteorol Belg Ser A ... Publications. Institut Royal Meteorologique de Belgique. Serie A. Format in-4 [*A publication*]
Publ Inst R Meteorol Belg Ser B ... Publications. Institut Royal Meteorologique de Belgique. Serie B [*A publication*]
Publ Inst Statist Univ Paris ... Publications. Institut de Statistique. Universite de Paris [*A publication*]
Publ Inst Suflos Agrotec (B Aires) ... Publicacion. Instituto de Suflos y Agrotecnia (Buenos Aires) [*A publication*]
Publ Inst Tecnol Estud Super Monterrey Ser Cienc Biol ... Publicaciones. Instituto Tecnologico y de Estudios Superiores de Monterrey. Serie Ciencias Biologicas [*A publication*]
Publ Inst Zool "Dr Augusto Nobre" Fac Cienc Porto ... Publicacoes. Instituto de Zoologia "Dr. Augusto Nobreda." Faculdade de Ciencias. Universidade do Porto [*A publication*]
Publ Inst Zootec (Rio De J) ... Publicacao. Instituto de Zootecnia (Rio De Janeiro) [*A publication*]
Publ Int Ass Scient Hydrol Symp (Budapest) ... Publication. International Association of Scientific Hydrology. Symposium (Budapest) [*A publication*]
Publ Inter ... Public Interest [*A publication*]
PUBLINX .... Public Links [*Amateur golf*]
Publius J F ... Publius. Journal of Federalism [*A publication*]
Publ Junta Nac Prod Pecu Ser A Ser Cient Invest ... Publicacoes. Junta Nacional dos Produtos Pecuarios. Serie A. Serie Cientifica e de Investigacao [*A publication*]
Publ Korean Natl Astron Obs ... Publications. Korean National Astronomical Observatory [*Republic of Korea*] [*A publication*]
Publ Lab Biochim Nutr Univ Cathol Louvain Fac Sci Agron ... Publication. Laboratoire de Biochimie de la Nutrition. Universite Catholique de Louvain. Faculte des Sciences Agronomiques [*A publication*]
Publ Lab Cent Ensayo Mater Constr (Madrid) ... Publication. Laboratorio Central de Ensayo de Materiales de Construccion (Madrid) [*A publication*]
Publ Lab Photoelasticite Ecole Polytech Fed (Zurich) ... Publications du Laboratoire de Photoelasticite. Ecole Polytechnique Federale (Zurich) [*A publication*]
Publ Law (London) ... Public Law (London) [*A publication*]
Publ Ld Capability Surv Trinidad & Tobago ... Publication. Land Capability Survey of Trinidad and Tobago [*A publication*]
Publ Ltg ..... Public Lighting [*A publication*]
Publ Mar Biol Stn Al Ghardaqa ... Publications. Marine Biological Station. Al Ghardaqa [*A publication*]
Publ Mar Lab Pusan Fish Coll ... Publications. Marine Laboratory. Pusan Fisheries College [*South Korea*] [*A publication*]
Publ Math Debrecen ... Publicationes Mathematicae. Universitatis Debreceniensis [*A publication*]
Publ Math Orsay 81 ... Publications Mathematiques d'Orsay 81 [*A publication*]
Publ Math Orsay 82 ... Publications Mathematiques d'Orsay 82 [*A publication*]
Publ Math Res Center Univ Wisconsin ... Publications. Mathematics Research Center. University of Wisconsin [*A publication*]
Publ Math Res Cent Univ Wis ... Publication. Mathematics Research Center. University of Wisconsin [*A publication*]
Publ Math Res Inst (Istanbul) ... Publications. Mathematical Research Institute (Istanbul) [*A publication*]
Publ Math Univ Bordeaux ... Publications Mathematiques. Universite de Bordeaux [*A publication*]
Publ Min Agr Ser Premios Nac Invest Agr ... Publicaciones. Ministerio de Agricultura. Serie. Premios Nacionales de Investigacion Agraria [*A publication*]
Publ Minist Agric (Can) ... Publication. Ministry of Agriculture (Canada) [*A publication*]
Publ Misc Agric Univ Chile Fac Agron ... Publicaciones Miscelaneas Agricolas. Universidad de Chile. Facultad de Agronomia [*A publication*]
Publ Misc Estac Exp Agr Tucuman ... Publicaciones Miscelaneas. Estacion Experimental Agricola de Tucuman [*A publication*]
Publ Miss State Univ Agr Ext Serv ... Publication. Mississippi State University. Agricultural Extension Service [*A publication*]
Publ Mus Hist Nat "Javier Prado" Ser A Zool ... Publicaciones. Museo de Historia Natural "Javier Prado." Series A. Zoologia [*A publication*]
Publ Mus Hist Nat "Javier Prado" Ser B Bot ... Publicaciones. Museo de Historia Natural "Javier Prado." Series B. Botanica [*A publication*]

Publ Mus Hist Nat Javier Prado Ser C Geol ... Publicaciones. Museo de Historia Natural "Javier Prado." Series C. Geologia [*A publication*]

Publ Mus Lab Mineral Geol Fac Cienc Porto ... Publicacoes. Museu e Laboratorio Mineralogico e Geologico. Faculdade de Ciencias do Porto [*A publication*]

Publ Mus Mich State Univ Biol Ser ... Publications. Museum. Michigan State University. Biological Series [*A publication*]

Publ Nat Acad Sci Nat Res Counc ... Publication. National Academy of Sciences. National Research Council [*A publication*]

Publ Natn Acad Sci Natn Res Coun (Wash) ... Publication. National Academy of Sciences. National Research Council (Washington) [*A publication*]

Publ Natuurhist Genoot Limburg ... Publicaties. Natuurhistorisch Genootschap in Limburg [*A publication*]

Publn Inst Nac Tec Agropec (B Aires) ... Publicacion. Instituto Nacional de Tecnologia Agropecuaria (Buenos Aires) [*A publication*]

Publ Obs Univ Mich ... Publications. Observatory. University of Michigan [*A publication*]

Publ Ocas Mus Cienc Nat (Caracas) Zool ... Publicaciones Ocasionales. Museo de Ciencias Naturales (Caracas). Zoologia [*A publication*]

Publ OECD (Paris) ... Publication. OECD [*Organization for Economic Cooperation and Development*] (Paris) [*A publication*]

Publ Ont Dep Agric ... Publication. Ontario Department of Agriculture and Food [*A publication*]

Publ Opin Q ... Public Opinion Quarterly [*A publication*]

Publ Pacif Nth-West Co-Op Ext Serv ... Publication. Pacific Northwest Cooperative Extension Service [*A publication*]

Publ Palaeontol Inst Univ Upps Spec Vol ... Publications. Palaeontological Institution. University of Uppsala. Special Volume [*A publication*]

Publ Pers M ... Public Personnel Management [*A publication*]

Publ Personnel Manag ... Public Personnel Management [*A publication*]

Publ Pol ...... Public Policy [*A publication*]

Publ Policy ... Public Policy [*A publication*]

PUBLR ...... Publisher

Publ Ramanujan Inst ... Publications. Ramanujan Institute [*A publication*]

Publ R Coll Physicians Edinburgh ... Publication. Royal College of Physicians of Edinburgh [*A publication*]

Publ Res Inst Math Sci ... Publications. Kyoto University. Research Institute for Mathematical Sciences [*A publication*]

Publ Res Inst Math Sci Ser A ... Publications. Research Institute for Mathematical Sciences. Series A [*Japan*] [*A publication*]

Publ Res Inst Math Sci Ser B ... Publications. Research Institute for Mathematical Sciences. Series B [*Japan*] [*A publication*]

Publ Roads ... Public Roads [*A publication*]

PUBLS .... Publications

Publ S Afr Inst Med Res ... Publications. South African Institute for Medical Research [*A publication*]

Publs ANARE Data Rep Ser ... Publications. ANARE [*Australian National Antarctic Research Expeditions*] Data Reports Series [*A publication*]

Publs ANARE Interim Rep Ser ... Publications. ANARE [*Australian National Antarctic Research Expeditions*] Interim Reports Series [*A publication*]

Publs ANARE Sci Rep Ser ... Publications. ANARE [*Australian National Antarctic Research Expeditions*] Scientific Reports Series [*A publication*]

Publs Aust Soc Soil Sci ... Publications. Australian Society of Soil Science [*A publication*]

Publs Aust Soc Soil Science ... Publications. Australian Society of Soil Science [*A publication*]

Publ Scient Univ Alger Ser B ... Publications Scientifiques. Universite d'Alger. Serie B. Sciences Physiques [*A publication*]

Publ Sci Tech Min Air ... Publications Scientifiques et Techniques. Ministere de l'Air [*France*] [*A publication*]

Publ Sci Tech Min Air Bull Serv Tech ... Publications Scientifiques et Techniques. Ministere de l'Air. Bulletins des Services Techniques [*France*] [*A publication*]

Publ Sci Tech Min Air Notes Tech ... Publications Scientifiques et Techniques. Ministere de l'Air [*France*]. Notes Techniques [*A publication*]

Publ Sci Tech Minist Air (Fr) ... Publications Scientifiques et Techniques. Ministere de l'Air (France) [*A publication*]

Publ Sci Tech Minist Air (Fr) Bull Serv Tech ... Publications Scientifiques et Techniques du Ministere de l'Air (France). Bulletin des Services Techniques [*A publication*]

Publs Co-Op Ext Univ Mass Coll Agric ... Publications. Co-Operative Extension Service. University of Massachusetts. College of Agriculture [*A publication*]

Publs Dep Agric (Alberta) ... Publications. Department of Agriculture (Alberta) [*A publication*]

Publs Dep Agric (Can) ... Publications. Department of Agriculture (Canada) [*A publication*]

Publ Sem Geom Univ Neuchatel Ser 2 ... Publications. Seminaire de Geometrie. Universite de Neuchatel. Serie 2 [*A publication*]

Publ Serv Flor Aqueic (Portugal) ... Publicacoes. Direccao Geral dos Servicos Florestais e Aqueicolas (Lisbon, Portugal) [*A publication*]

Publ Serv Geol Luxemb ... Publications. Service Geologique de Luxembourg [*A publication*]

Publ Serv Piscic Ser I-C ... Publicacao. Servico de Piscicultura. Serie I-C [*A publication*]

Publ Serv Plagas For (Madrid) ... Publicacion. Servicio de Plagas Forestales (Madrid) [*A publication*]

Publ Seto Mar Biol Lab ... Publications. Seto Marine Biological Laboratory [*A publication*]

Publs Geol Surv QD ... Publications. Geological Survey of Queensland [*A publication*]

Publs Geol Surv QD Palaeont Pap ... Publications. Geological Survey of Queensland. Palaeontological Papers [*A publication*]

PUBLSHG ... Publishing

Publ S III Univ Sch Agr ... Publication. Southern Illinois University. School of Agriculture [*A publication*]

Publs Indiana Dep Conserv ... Publications. Indiana Department of Conservation [*A publication*]

Publs Inst Natn Etude Agron Congo Ser Sci ... Publications. Institut National pour l'Etude Agronomique du Congo. Serie Scientifique [*A publication*]

Publs Manitoba Dep Agric ... Publications. Manitoba Department of Agriculture [*A publication*]

Publs Maria Moors Cabot Fdn Bot Res ... Publications. Maria Moors Cabot Foundation for Botanical Research [*A publication*]

Publs Met Dep Melb Univ ... Publications. Meteorology Department. University of Melbourne [*A publication*]

Publ Smithson Inst ... Publications. Smithsonian Institution [*A publication*]

Publ Soc Savante Alsace Reg Est ... Publications. Societe Savante d'Alsace et des Regions de l'Est [*A publication*]

Publ Soil Bur (NZ) ... Publication. Soil Bureau. Department of Scientific and Industrial Research (New Zealand) [*A publication*]

Publs Osaka Mus Nat Hist ... Publications. Osaka Museum of Natural History [*A publication*]

Publ SP Am Concr Inst ... Publication SP. American Concrete Institute [*A publication*]

Publs Petrol Search Subsidy Acts ... Publications. Petroleum Search Subsidy Acts. Bureau of Mineral Resources, Geology, and Geophysics [*Australia*] [*A publication*]

Publ Sta Fed Essais Agr (Lausanne) ... Publications. Stations Federales d'Essais Agricoles (Lausanne) [*A publication*]

Publ State Inst Agric Chem (Finl) ... Publications. State Institute of Agricultural Chemistry (Finland) [*A publication*]

Publ State Inst Tech Res ... Publications. State Institute for Technical Research [*A publication*]

Publ Systematics Ass ... Publication. Systematics Association [*A publication*]

Publ Tartu Astrofiz Obs ... Publikatsii Tartuskoi Astrofizicheskoi Observatorii [*Estonian SSR*] [*A publication*]

Publ Tec Estac Exp Agropecuar INTA (Pergamino) ... Publicaciones Tecnicas. Estacion Experimental Agropecuaria. INTA [*Instituto Nacional de Tecnologia Agropecuaria*] (Pergamino) [*A publication*]

Publ Tec Estac Exp Agropecuar Manfredi (Argentina) ... Publicaciones Tecnicas. Estacion Experimental Agropecuaria de Manfredi (Argentina) [*A publication*]

Publ Tech Charbon Fr Inf Tech ... Publications Techniques des Charbonnages de France. Informations Techniques [*A publication*]

Publ Tech Res Cen Finl Mater Process Technol ... Publication. Technical Research Centre of Finland. Materials and Processing Technology [*A publication*]

Publ Tec Inst Patol Veg (B Aires) ... Publicacion Tecnica. Instituto de Patologia Vegetal (Buenos Aires) [*A publication*]

Publ Tec Patronato Invest Cient Tec "Juan De La Cierva" ... Publicaciones Tecnicas. Patronato de Investigacion Cientifica y Tecnica "Juan De La Cierva" [*A publication*]

Publ Tehn Fak u Sarajevu ... Publikacije Tehnickog Fakulteta u Sarajevu [*A publication*]

Publ Thoresby Soc ... Publications. Thoresby Society [*A publication*]

Publ UER Math Pures Appl IRMA ... Publications. Unites d'Enseignement et de Recherche de Mathematiques Pures et Appliquees. Institut de Recherche de Mathematiques Avancees [*A publication*]

Publ Univ Auton St Domingo ... Publicaciones. Universidad Autonoma de Santo Domingo [*A publication*]

Publ Univ Calif Agric Ext Serv ... Publication. University of California. Agricultural Extension Service [*A publication*]

Publ Univ Costa Rica Ser Cienc Nat ... Publicaciones. Universidad de Costa Rica. Serie Ciencias Naturales [*A publication*]

Publ Univ Joensuu Ser B ... Publications. University of Joensuu. Series B [*Finland*] [*A publication*]

Publ Univ Joensuu Ser B-II ... Publications. University of Joensuu. Series B-II [*A publication*]

Publ Univ Kuopio Community Health Ser Orig Rep ... Publications. University of Kuopio. Community Health Series. Original Reports [*A publication*]

Publ Univ Pretoria ... Publikasies. Universiteit van Pretoria [*A publication*]

Publ Univ Sevilla Ser Med ... Publicaciones. Universidad de Sevilla. Serie Medicina [*A publication*]

Publ Univ Toronto Dep Civ Eng ... Publication. University of Toronto. Department of Civil Engineering [*A publication*]

Publ Univ Toulouse-Le Mirail Ser A ... Publications. Universite de Toulouse-Le Mirail. Serie A. [*A publication*]

Publ Univ Wis Ext ... Publication. University of Wisconsin Extension [*A publication*]

Publ US Agric Res Serv ... Publication. United States Agricultural Research Service [*A publication*]

Publ Utah Geol Assoc ... Publication. Utah Geological Association [*A publication*]

Publ W .... Publishers' Weekly [*A publication*]

Publ Welfar ... Public Welfare [*A publication*]

Publ Wiss Filmen Sekt Tech Wiss Naturwiss ... Publikationen zu Wissenschaftlichen Filmen. Sektion Technische Wissenschaften. Naturwissenschaften [*A publication*]

Publ Wks .... Public Works [*A publication*]

Publ Wks Local Govt Engng ... Public Works and Local Government Engineering [*A publication*]

Pub Manag ... Public Management [*A publication*]

Pub Mgt ..... Public Management [*A publication*]

PUBN .... Publication (MSA)

PUBNET ..... American Association of Publishers' electronic ordering system

PUBO .... Pubco Corp. [*NASDAQ symbol*] (NQ)

Pub Off ...... Public Officers (DLA)

Pub Opin .... Public Opinion [*A publication*]

Pub Opinion Q ... Public Opinion Quarterly [*A publication*]

Pub Op Q ... Public Opinion Quarterly [*A publication*]

Pub Papers ... Public Papers of the President (DLA)

Pub Pers Mgt ... Public Personnel Management [*A publication*]

Pub Pol ...... Public Policy [*A publication*]

Pub Rel Bull ... Public Relations Bulletin [*American Bar Association*] (DLA)

Pub Rel J .... Public Relations Journal [*A publication*]

Pub Rel Q ... Public Relations Quarterly [*A publication*]

Pub Res ...... Public Resources (DLA)

Pub Roads ... Public Roads [*A publication*]

Pub Roch Hist Soc ... Publication Fund Series. Rochester Historical Society [*A publication*]

PUBS .... Pop-Up Bottom Seismograph [*Marine science*] (MSC)

PUBS .... Publication Series

PUBS .... Publications (MCD)

PUBSAT .... Publication Ships Assistance Team (MCD)

PUBSAT .... Publications Special Assistance Team

Pubs Ceramicas ... Publicaciones Ceramicas [*A publication*]

Pub Ser Comm ... Public Service Commission [*Usually, of a specific state*] (DLA)

Pub Serv .... Public Service (DLA)

Pub Service J Vic ... Public Service Journal of Victoria [*A publication*]

Pub Serv Management ... Public Service Management [*A publication*]

Pub Soc Bras Nematol ... Publicacao. Sociedade Brasileira de Nematologia [*A publication*]

Pubs Petrol Search Subsidy Acts ... Publications. Petroleum Search Subsidy Acts. Bureau of Mineral Resources, Geology, and Geophysics [*Australia*] [*A publication*]

Pub St .... Public Statutes (DLA)

Pub U Rep ... Public Utilities Reports [*Also, PUR*] (DLA)

Pub Util ...... Public Utilities Fortnightly [*A publication*]

Pub Util C ... Public Utilities Code (DLA)

Pub Util Comm ... Public Utilities Commission (DLA)

Pub Util L Anthol ... Public Utilities Law Anthology (DLA)

Pub W .... Publishers' Weekly [*A publication*]

Pub Wel ...... Public Welfare [*A publication*]

PU-BZ .... University of Pennsylvania, Biology Library, Philadelphia, PA [*Library symbol*] [*Library of Congress*] (LCLS)

PUC .... Pacific Union College [*Angwin, CA*]

PUC .... Papers under Consideration

PUC .... Parti de l'Unite Congolaise [*Congolese Unity Party*]

PUC .... Pediatric Urine Collector [*Medicine*]

PUC .... Permanent Unit Code (NG)

PUC .... Pick-Up Car

PUC .... Planification d'Urgence Canada [*Emergency Planning Canada - EPC*]

PUC .... Player Unit Component (MCD)

PUC .... Pontificia Universidade Catolica [*Rio de Janeiro*]

PUC .... Popular Unity of Chile [*Political party*]

PUC .... Port Utilization Committee

PUC .... Post Urbem Conditam [*After the Building of the City of Rome*] [*Latin*]

PUC .... Presidential Unit Citation [*Military decoration*]

PUC .... Price [*Utah*] [*Airport symbol*] (OAG)

PUC .... Price, UT [*Location identifier*] [*FAA*] (FAAL)

PUC .... Processing Unit Cabinet [*Data processing*]

PUC .... Production Urgency Committee [*WPB*]

PUC .... Program Unit Code [*Military*] (AFIT)

PUC .... Provided You Concur [*Army*]

PUC .... Public Utilities Commission [*Data traffic regulator*]

PU-C .... University of Pennsylvania, Chemistry Library, Philadelphia, PA [*Library symbol*] [*Library of Congress*] (LCLS)

PUCA .... Public Utilities Communicators Association [*Formerly, PUAA*] [*New Castle, PA*] (EA)

PUCalLL ..... Publications. University of California. Languages and Literature [*A publication*]

PUCC .... Port Utilities [*AAR code*]

PUCK .... Propellant Utilization Checkout Kit (KSC)

PUCS .... Propellant Utilization Control System (KSC)

PUCU .... Propellant Utilization Control Unit

PUD .... Partido Union Democratica [*Political party in Guatemala*]

PUD .... Peptic Ulcer Disease

PUD .... Pick Up and Delivery [*Business and trade*]

PU & D .... Pick Up and Delivery [*Business and trade*]

PUD .... Planned Unit Development [*Housing*]

PUD .... Planned Urban Development

PUD .... Preretro Update Display

PUD .... Prisoner under Detention (ADA)

PUD .... Public Utility District

PUD .... Puerto Deseado [*Argentina*] [*Airport symbol*] (OAG)

PUD .... Pulmonary Disease [*Medicine*]

PU-D .... University of Pennsylvania, Evans Dental Library, Philadelphia, PA [*Library symbol*] [*Library of Congress*] (LCLS)

PUDCPAHM ... Poona University and Deccan College Publications in Archaeology and History of Maharashtra [*A publication*]

PUDN .... Perpetuation of Unit Documentation Number (MCD)

PUDOC .... Centrum voor Landbouwpublikaties en Landbouwdocumentatie [*Center for Agricultural Publishing and Documentation*] [*Ministry of Agriculture and Fisheries*] [*Wageningen, Netherlands*] [*Information service*] (EISS)

PUDOC Annu Rep ... PUDOC [*Centre for Agricultural Publishing and Documentation*] Annual Report [*A publication*]

PUDOC (Cent Landbouwpubl Landbouwdoc) Literatuuroverz ... PUDOC (Centrum voor Landbouwpublikaties en Landbouwdocumentatie) Literatuuroverzicht [*A publication*]

PUDT .... Propellant Utilization Data Translator (AAG)

PUDVM ...... Pulsed Ultrasound Doppler Velocity Meter

PUE .... Pre-Stock Unit Equipment [*Military*] [*British*]

PUE .... Presidential Unit Emblem [*Military decoration*] (AABC)

PUE .... Propellant Utilization Exerciser

PUE .... Puebla [*Mexico*] [*Seismograph station code, US Geological Survey*] [*Closed*] (SEIS)

PUE .... Puerto Obaldia [*Panama*] [*Airport symbol*] (OAG)

PUE .... Pyrexia of Unknown Etiology [*Medicine*]

PUEE .... Publications. Universite de l'Etat a Elisabethville [*A publication*]

PU-EI .... University of Pennsylvania, Moore School of Electrical Engineering, Philadelphia, PA [*Library symbol*] [*Library of Congress*] (LCLS)

Puer Rico ... Puerto Rico Libre [*A publication*]

Puerto Rico ... Puerto Rico Reports (DLA)

Puerto Rico Dept Indus Research Bull ... Puerto Rico Department of Industrial Research. Bulletin [*A publication*]

Puerto Rico F ... Puerto Rico Federal Reports (DLA)

Puerto Rico Fed ... Puerto Rico Federal Reports (DLA)

Puerto Rico Rep ... Puerto Rico Supreme Court Reports (DLA)

Puerto Rico Univ Agr Expt Sta Tech Paper ... Puerto Rico University. Agricultural Experiment Station. Technical Paper [*A publication*]

Puerto Rico Water Resources Authority Water Resources Bull ... Puerto Rico. Water Resources Authority. Water Resources Bulletin [*A publication*]

PUF .... Partido Union Federal [*Federal Union Party*] [*Argentina*]

PUF .... Pau [*France*] [*Airport symbol*] (OAG)

PUF .... People's United Front [*Bangladesh*]

PUF .... People's United Front [*Papua New Guinean*] (PPW)

PUF .... Percent Unaccounted For

PUF .... Polyurethane Film [*Plastics technology*]

PUF .... Porous Polyurethane Foam [*Also, PPF*] [*Plastics technology*]

PUF .... Presses Universitaires de France [*Publisher*]

PU-F .... University of Pennsylvania, H. H. Furness Memorial Library, Philadelphia, PA [*Library symbol*] [*Library of Congress*] (LCLS)

PUFA .... Polyunsaturated Fatty Acid [*Nutrition*]

PU-FA .... University of Pennsylvania, School of Fine Arts, Philadelphia, PA [*Library symbol*] [*Library of Congress*] (LCLS)

PUFF .... People United to Fight Frustrations [*Lubbock, TX*] (EA)

PUFF .... Picofarad (MDG)

PUFF .... Proposed Uses of Federal Funds [*Health Planning and Resource Development Act of 1974*]

Puffendorf ... Puffendorf's Law of Nature and Nations (DLA)

PUFFS .... Passive Underwater Fire Control Feasibility Study

PUFFT .... Purdue University Fast FORTRAN [*Formula Translation*] Translator [*Data processing*]

PUFI .... Packed under Federal Inspection

PUFL .... Pump Fed Liquid (KSC)

PUFO .... Pack Up and Fade Out [*End of military exercise*] [*British*] (DSUE)

PU Fort ...... Public Utilities Fortnightly (DLA)

PUFS .... Programer's Utility Filing System (DIT)

PUG .... Partially Underground [*Military*]

PUG .... PASCAL Users' Group [*Cleveland, OH*] (EA)

PUG .... Penta Users Group [*Glen Burnie, MD*] (EA)

PUG .... Port Augusta [*Australia*] [*Airport symbol*] (OAG)

PUG .... Prime Users Group [*Natick, MA*] (EA)

PUG .... Propellant Utilization and Gauging [*Apollo*] [*NASA*]

PUG............ Pugilist
PUG............ Pugillus [*A Pinch*] [*Pharmacy*]   (ROG)
Pug............ Pugsley's New Brunswick Reports [*14-16 New Brunswick*]   (DLA)
PUG............ Pulsed Universal Grid
PUG............ Pure Gold Resources [*Toronto Stock Exchange symbol*]
Puglia Chir ... Puglia Chirurgica [*A publication*]
PUGS .... Propellant Utilization and Gauging System [*Apollo*] [*NASA*]   (KSC)
Pugs........... Pugsley's New Brunswick Reports [*14-16 New Brunswick*]   (DLA)
Pugs & Bur ... Pugsley and Burbridge's New Brunswick Reports [*17-20 New Brunswick*]   (DLA)
Pugs & Burg ... Pugsley and Burbridge's New Brunswick Reports [*17-20 New Brunswick*]   (DLA)
Pugs & Tru ... Pugsley and Trueman's New Brunswick Reports [*1882-83*]   (DLA)
PUH............ Pauahi [*Hawaii*] [*Seismograph station code, US Geological Survey*]   (SEIS)
PUH............ Pregnancy Urine Hormone [*Endocrinology*]
PUHCA....... Public Utility Holding Company Act of 1935
PUHS......... Proceedings. Unitarian Historical Society [*A publication*]
PUI .... Pilot-under-Instruction [*Navy*]
PUI .... Platelet Uptake Index [*Clinical chemistry*]
PU-Ind....... University of Pennsylvania, Industrial Research Department, Philadelphia, PA [*Library symbol*] [*Library of Congress*] [*Obsolete*]   (LCLS)
PUIWP....... People for a United India and World Peace   (EA)
PUJ............. Punta Cana [*Dominican Republic*] [*Airport symbol*]   (OAG)
PUK .... Parti d'Unite Katangaise [*Katanga Unity Party*]
PUK .... Patriotic Union of Kurdistan [*Iraqi*]   (PD)
PUK .... Pechiney-Ugine-Kuhlmann [*Commercial firm*] [*France*]
PUK .... Pukarua [*French Polynesia*] [*Airport symbol*]   (OAG)
PUKOD....... Puresutoresuto Konkurito [*A publication*]
PUKS......... Pivotal Unknowables
PUL .... Percutaneous Ultrasonic Lithotripsy [*Medicine*]
PUL .... Princeton University, Princeton, NJ [*OCLC symbol*] [*Inactive*]   (OCLC)
PUL .... Program Update Library
PUL .... Propellant Utilization and Loading
PUL .... Publicker Industries, Inc. [*NYSE symbol*]
PUL .... Pulkovo [*USSR*] [*Seismograph station code, US Geological Survey*]   (SEIS)
PUL .... Pulley   (AAG)
PUL .... Pulmonary
PU-L .... University of Pennsylvania, Biddle Law Library, Philadelphia, PA [*Library symbol*] [*Library of Congress*]   (LCLS)
PULA......... Public Laws
PULC......... Princeton University Library Chronicle [*A publication*]
PULL .... Power for Underwater Logistics and Living
Pull Acc...... Pulling on Mercantile Accounts [*1846*]   (DLA)
Pull Accts ... Pulling's Law of Mercantile Accounts   (DLA)
Pull Att ...... Pulling on Attorneys and Solicitors [*3rd ed.*] [*1862*]   (DLA)
Pull Laws & Cust Lond ... Pulling's Treatise on the Laws, Customs, and Regulations of the City and Port of London   (DLA)
Pull Port of London ... Pulling's Treatise on the Laws, Customs, and Regulations of the City and Port of London   (DLA)
PULM .... Pulmonary
PULO......... Pattani United Liberation Organization [*Thai*]   (PD)
Pulp & Pa ... Pulp and Paper [*A publication*]
Pulp & Pa Can ... Pulp and Paper Magazine of Canada [*Later, Pulp and Paper (Canada)*] [*A publication*]
Pulp Pap & Board ... Pulp, Paper, and Board [*A publication*]
Pulp Pap (Can) ... Pulp and Paper (Canada) [*A publication*]
Pulp & Pap Eng ... Pulp and Paper Engineering [*A publication*]
Pulp Paper Mag Can ... Pulp and Paper Magazine of Canada [*Later, Pulp and Paper (Canada)*] [*A publication*]
Pulp Paper Manual Can ... Pulp and Paper Manual of Canada [*A publication*]
Pulp Pap Int ... Pulp and Paper International [*A publication*]
Pulpwood Annu ... Pulpwood Annual [*United States*] [*A publication*]
Pulpwood Prodn ... Pulpwood Production and Sawmill Logging [*A publication*]
PULS .... Propellant Utilization Loading System   (AAG)
PULSAR ..... Pulsating Star
PULSAR ..... Pulsed Uniform LASER-Stimulated Artificial Radiation [*Proposed acronymic designation for pulsars, in the event they are found to be artificially caused by intelligent life from outer space*]
PULSE....... Public Urban Locator Service
PULSES ..... Physical Condition, Upper Extremity Function, Lower Extremity Function, Sensory and Communication Abilities, Excretory Control, Social Support [*A neurological disability profile*]
Pulsifer (ME) ... Pulsifer's Reports [*35-68 Maine*]   (DLA)
PULSTAR... Pulse Training Assembled Reactor   (NRCH)
PULV .... Pulverized
PULV .... Pulvis [*Powder*] [*Pharmacy*]
PULV CONSPER ... Pulvis Conspersus [*Dusting Powder*] [*Pharmacy*]
PUM .... Pennsylvania University Museum
PUM .... Pomalaa [*Indonesia*] [*Airport symbol*]   (OAG)
PUM .... President of the United Mineworkers

PUM .... Processor Utility Monitor [*Telecommunications*]   (TEL)
PUM .... Pytannja Ukrajins'koho Movoznavstva [*A publication*]
PUMA........ Powered Ultralight Manufacturers Association [*Duncanville, TX*]   (EA)
PUMA........ Programable Universal Manipulator for Assembly [*General Motors Corp. assembly robot*]
PUMA........ Prostitutes' Union of Massachusetts
PU-Math..... University of Pennsylvania, Mathematics-Physics Library, Philadelphia, PA [*Library symbol*] [*Library of Congress*]   (LCLS)
PUMCODOXPURSACOMLOPAR ... Pulse-Modulated Coherent Doppler-Effect X-Band Pulse-Repetition Synthetic-Array Pulse Compression Side Lobe Planar Array
PU-Med...... University of Pennsylvania, Medical School, Philadelphia, PA [*Library symbol*] [*Library of Congress*]   (LCLS)
PU-Med-TS ... University of Pennsylvania, Medical School, Hospital Nurses Library, Philadelphia, PA [*Library symbol*] [*Library of Congress*]   (LCLS)
PUMF .... Peaceful Uses of Military Forces
PUMP .... Protesting Unfair Marketing Practices [*Student legal action organization*]
Pump Ct..... Pump Court [*London*]   (DLA)
Pump Eng (Tokyo) ... Pump Engineering (Tokyo) [*A publication*]
Pumpen & Verdichter Inf ... Pumpen und Verdichter Information [*A publication*]
Pumps....... Pumps-Pompes-Pumpen [*England*] [*A publication*]
Pumps Their Appl ... Pumps and Their Applications [*England*] [*A publication*]
PUMS........ Permanently Unfit for Military Service [*British*]
PUMST...... Polish Underground Movement (1939-1945) Study Trust   (EA)
PUMTA...... Trace Substances in Environmental Health [*A publication*]
PU-Mu .... University of Pennsylvania, University Museum, Philadelphia, PA [*Library symbol*] [*Library of Congress*]   (LCLS)
PU-Music ... University of Pennsylvania, School of Music, Philadelphia, PA [*Library symbol*] [*Library of Congress*]   (LCLS)
Pun............ All India Reporter, Punjab   (DLA)
Pun............ Indian Law Reports, Punjab Series   (DLA)
PUN........... Parti de l'Unite Nationale [*Party of National Unity*] [*Haitian*]   (PPW)
PUN........... Partido Union Nacional [*National Union Party*] [*Costa Rica*]
PUN........... Plutonyl Nitrate [*Inorganic chemistry*]
PUN........... Precision Underwater Navigation
PUN........... Prepare a New Perforated Tape for Message [*Communications*]   (FAAC)
PUN........... Puncheon [*Unit of measurement*]
Pun............ Punica [*of Silius Italicus*] [*Classical studies*]   (OCD)
PUN........... Punishment   (DSUE)
PUN........... Puno [*Peru*] [*Seismograph station code, US Geological Survey*]   (SEIS)
PUN........... Punta [*Flamenco dance term*]
PUNA .... Parti de l'Unite Nationale [*National Unity Party*] [*Congo*]
PUNC .... Practical, Unpretentious, Nomographic Computer
PUNC .... Probable Ultimate Net Cost
PUNC .... Program Unit Counter
PUNC .... Punctuation
PUNCT....... Punctuation   (ROG)
PUNGA...... Parti de l'Unite Nationale Gabonaise [*Party for Gabonese National Unity*]
Punjab Med J ... Punjab Medical Journal [*A publication*]
Punjabrao Krishi Vidyapeeth Coll Agric (Nagpur) Mag ... Punjabrao Krishi Vidyapeeth. College of Agriculture (Nagpur). Magazine [*A publication*]
Punjabrao Krishi Vidyapeeth Res J ... Punjabrao Krishi Vidyapeeth Research Journal [*A publication*]
Punjab Univ J Math (Lahore) ... Punjab University. Journal of Mathematics (Lahore) [*A publication*]
Punj Ind..... Punjab, India   (DLA)
Punj Pak..... Punjab, Pakistan   (DLA)
Punj Rec.... Punjab Record [*India*]   (DLA)
PUNS......... Partido de Liberacion Nacional del Sahara [*Political party*] [*Western Sahara*]
PUNS......... Partido de Union Nacional del Sahara [*Political party*] [*Western Sahara*]
PUNS......... Permanently Unfit for Naval Service [*British*]
PUNT......... Partido Unico Nacional de los Trabajadores [*Political party*] [*Equatorial Guinea*]
PUO........... Placed under Observation [*Medicine*]
PUO........... Prudhoe Bay [*Arkansas*] [*Airport symbol*]   (OAG)
PUO........... Prudhoe Bay, AK [*Location identifier*] [*FAA*]   (FAAL)
Puo............ [*A*] Purine Nucleoside [*Also, R*]
PUO........... Pyrexia [*fever*] of Unknown Origin [*Commonly called Trench Fever*]
P U Otago M ... Proceedings. University of Otago Medical School [*A publication*]
PUP .... Paid-Up Policy [*Insurance*]   (DSUE)
PUP .... Partido Union Patriotica [*Patriotic Union Party*] [*Dominican Republic*]   (PPW)
PUP .... Peak Underpressure [*Nuclear energy*]   (NRCH)
PUP .... People's United Party [*Belizean*]   (PPW)
PUP .... Peripheral Unit Processor [*Data processing*]
PUP .... Pickup   (FAAC)

PUP .... Pious Union of Prayer   (EA)
PUP .... Plutonium Utilization Program   (NRCH)
PUP .... Popular Unity Party [*Bangladesh*]   (PPW)
PUP .... Power Upgrade Program
Pup .... Pre-Urban Professional [*Lifestyle classification*] [*Acronym coined by TeenAge magazine to describe its typical reader*]
PUP .... Progressive Unionist Party [*Northern Ireland*]   (PPW)
PUP .... Public Utilities Panel [*EECE*]
PUP .... Pull Up Point
PUP .... Pupakea [*Hawaii*] [*Seismograph station code, US Geological Survey*] [*Closed*]   (SEIS)
PUP .... Pupil   (DSUE)
Pup .... Puppis [*Constellation*]
PUPA .... Polish Union Printers Association [*Chicago*]
PU-Penn ..... University of Pennsylvania, Penniman Library of Education, Philadelphia, PA [*Library symbol*] [*Library of Congress*] [*Obsolete*]   (LCLS)
PUPG .... Production Unit Price Goals   (MCD)
PUPID .... Pulp and Paper Industry Division [*Instrument Society of America*]
Pupp .... Puppis [*Constellation*]
PUPPI .... Pop-Up Pore Pressure Instrument [*Oceanography*]
Puppie .... Pregnant Urban Professional [*Lifestyle classification*] [*Terminology used in "The Yuppie Handbook"*]
PUPPP .... Pruritic Urticarial Papules and Plaques of Pregnancy [*Medicine*]
PU-PSW ..... University of Pennsylvania, Pennsylvania School of Social Work, Philadelphia, PA [*Library symbol*] [*Library of Congress*]   (LCLS)
PUQ .... Punta Arenas [*Chile*] [*Airport symbol*]   (OAG)
PUR .... Partido de Unificacion Revolucionaria [*Party of Revolutionary Unification*] [*Guatemala*]
PUR .... Partido Union Revolucionaria [*Cuba*]
PUR .... Patch Unit Radio [*Bell System*]
PUR .... Polyurethane [*Also, PU*] [*Organic chemistry; plastics*]
PUR .... Program of University Research
PUR .... Program Utility Routines [*Data processing*]
PUR .... Public Utilities Reports, Inc.
PUR .... Purari [*Papua New Guinea*] [*Seismograph station code, US Geological Survey*]   (SEIS)
PUR .... Purchase   (AFM)
PUR .... Purchasing Receipt [*Business and trade*]
PUR .... Purdue University Reactor
PUR .... Purdue University Research   (MCD)
PUR .... Purgative [*Medicine*]   (ROG)
PUR .... Purichlor Technology Ltd. [*Vancouver Stock Exchange symbol*]
PUR .... Purifier   (AAG)
Pur .... [*A*] Purine [*Biochemistry*]
PUR .... Purity [*of the Drug*] [*Pharmacy*]   (ROG)
PUR .... Puromycin [*Trypanocide*] [*Antineoplastic drug*]
PUR .... Purpure [*Purple*] [*Heraldry*]
PUR .... Purse   (FAAC)
PUR .... Pursuant   (AABC)
PUR .... Pursuit   (AABC)
PURA .... PACOM [*Pacific Command*] Utilization and Redistribution Agency
PURA .... Public Utilities Review Act [*1934*]
Pur A Chem ... Pure and Applied Chemistry [*A publication*]
Pur A Geoph ... Pure and Applied Geophysics [*A publication*]
PURBA .... Panjab University Research Bulletin (Arts) [*A publication*]
PURC .... Pacific Utilization Research Center [*Marine science*]   (MSC)
PURC .... Princeton University Research Center [*Marine science*]   (MSC)
PURC .... Public Utility Research Center [*University of Florida*] [*Research center*]   (RCD)
PURC .... Purchasing
PURCH .... Purchase
Purch Adm ... Purchasing Administration [*A publication*]
Purchasing ... Purchasing World [*A publication*]
PURCHG ..... Purchasing   (ROG)
Purch (S Afr) ... Purchasing (South Africa) [*A publication*]
PUR 3d .... Public Utilities Reports, Third Series   (DLA)
Purd Dig ..... Purdon's Digest of Laws [*Pennsylvania*]   (DLA)
Purd Dig Laws ... Purdon's Digest of Laws [*Pennsylvania*]   (DLA)
Purdue Ag ... Purdue Agriculturist [*A publication*]
Purdue Air Qual Conf Proc ... Purdue Air Quality Conference. Proceedings [*A publication*]
Purdue Univ Agric Exp Stn Res Bull ... Purdue University. Agricultural Experiment Station. Research Bulletin [*A publication*]
Purdue Univ Agric Exp Stn Stn Bull ... Purdue University. Agricultural Experiment Station. Station Bulletin [*A publication*]
Purdue Univ Dept Agr Ext Mimeo AY ... Purdue University. Department of Agricultural Extension. Mimeo AY [*A publication*]
Purdue Univ Eng Bull Eng Ext Ser ... Purdue University. Engineering Bulletin. Engineering Extension Series [*A publication*]
Purdue Univ Eng Exp Sta Res Bull ... Purdue University. Engineering Experiment Station. Research Bulletin [*A publication*]
Purdue Univ Ext Publ ... Purdue University. Extension Publications [*A publication*]

Purdue Univ Sch Aeronaut Astronaut Eng Sci Res Proj ... Purdue University. School of Aeronautics, Astronautics, and Engineering Sciences. Research Project [*A publication*]
Purdue Univ Water Resources Research Center Tech Rept ... Purdue University. Water Resources Research Center. Technical Report [*A publication*]
Purdue Univ Water Resour Res Cent Tech Rep ... Purdue University. Water Resources Research Center. Technical Report [*A publication*]
PURE .... People United for Rural Education   (EA)
PURE .... Present University Research Efforts [*Database*] [*Harperson Data Services*]
Pure and Appl Chem ... Pure and Applied Chemistry [*A publication*]
Pure Appl Chem ... Pure and Applied Chemistry [*A publication*]
Pure Appl Cryog ... Pure and Applied Cryogenics [*A publication*]
Pure Appl Geophys ... Pure and Applied Geophysics [*A publication*]
Pure and Appl Math ... Pure and Applied Mathematics [*A publication*]
Pure Appl Math ... Pure and Applied Mathematics [*A publication*]
Pure Appl Math Sci ... Pure and Applied Mathematika Sciences [*A publication*]
Pure Appl Phys ... Pure and Applied Physics [*A publication*]
Pure Prod... Pure Products [*A publication*]
PUREQ ...... Purchase Requisition   (NOAA)
PUREX .... Plutonium Uranium Extraction [*Nuclear energy*]
PURGE .... Pearson Universal Random Generator
PURIF .... Purification
PURM .... Project for Utilization and Redistribution of Materiel [*Air Force*]
PURMA .... Purasuchikku Materiaru [*A publication*]
PUR (NS) ... Public Utilities Reports, New Series   (DLA)
PURO .... Puroflow, Inc. [*NASDAQ symbol*]   (NQ)
PURP .... Purpose   (AFM)
PURP .... Purpure [*Purple*] [*Heraldry*]   (ROG)
PURPA .... Public Utilities Regulatory Policy Act
Purple's St ... Purple's Statutes, Scates' Compilation   (DLA)
PURS .... Partido de la Union Republicana Socialista [*Socialist Republican Union Party*] [*Bolivia*]
PURS .... Program Usage Replenishment System
PURS .... Pursuit
PURSCE ..... Pursuance   (ROG)
PURST .... Pursuant
PURV .... Powered Underwater Research Vehicle [*Navy*]
PUS .... Parliamentary Under Secretary [*British*]
PUS .... Permanent Under Secretary [*British*]   (RDA)
PUS .... Permanently Unfit for Service   (ADA)
PUS .... Personnel Utilization Sheet
PUS .... Pharmacopeia of the United States
PUS .... President of the United States
PUS .... Processor Utility Subsystem [*Telecommunications*]   (TEL)
PUS .... Propellant Utilization System
PUS .... Pusan [*South Korea*] [*Seismograph station code, US Geological Survey*] [*Closed*]   (SEIS)
PUS .... Pusan [*South Korea*] [*Airport symbol*]   (OAG)
pus .... Pushto [*MARC language code*] [*Library of Congress*]   (LCCP)
PUS .... United States Miscellaneous Pacific Islands [*Three-letter standard code*]   (CNC)
PU-S .... University of Pennsylvania, Edgar Fah Smith Memorial Library, Philadelphia, PA [*Library symbol*] [*Library of Congress*]   (LCLS)
PUSA .... Perspectives USA [*A publication*]
PUSAS .... Proposed United States of America Standard
PUSC .... Pubblicazioni. Universita Cattolica del Sacro Cuore [*A publication*]
PU-Sc .... University of Pennsylvania, Towne Scientific School, Philadelphia, PA [*Library symbol*] [*Library of Congress*]   (LCLS)
PUSE .... Propellant Utilization System Exerciser
PUSH .... People United to Save Humanity [*In organization name "Operation PUSH"*]
PUSJD .... Pious Union of St. Joseph for the Dying [*Formerly, PUSJDS*]   (EA)
PUSJDS ..... Pious Union of St. Joseph for Dying Sinners [*Later, Pious Union of St. Joseph for the Dying*]   (EA)
PUSMM ...... Parti d'Union Socialiste des Musulmans Mauritaniens [*Party for Socialist Unity of Moslems of Mauritania*]
PUSO .... Principal Unit Security Officer   (AAG)
PU-SRS ...... University of Pennsylvania, South Asia Regional Studies Library, Philadelphia, PA [*Library symbol*] [*Library of Congress*]   (LCLS)
PUSS .... Pallet Utility Support Structure   (MCD)
PUSS .... Pilots Universal Sighting System
PUT .... Persons Using Television [*Television ratings*]
PUT .... Program Update Tape
PUT .... Programable Unijunction Transistor
PUT .... Punta De Talca [*Chile*] [*Seismograph station code, US Geological Survey*]   (SEIS)
PUT .... Putnam, CT [*Location identifier*] [*FAA*]   (FAAL)
PUT .... Putrescine [*Organic chemistry*]
Puti Povysh Intensivn Prod Fotosint ... Puti Povysheniya Intensivnosti i Produktivnosti Fotosinteza [*A publication*]

Puti Povysh Intensivn Prod Fotosint Resp Mezhved Sb ... Puti Povysheniya Intensivnosti Produktivnosti Fotosinteza Respublikanskii Mezhvedomstvennyi Sbornik [*A publication*]
Puti Sint Izyskaniya Protivoopukholevykh Prep ... Puti Sinteza i Izyskaniya Protivoopukholevykh Preparatov [*A publication*]
Putnam ...... Putnam's Monthly Magazine [*A publication*]
Putnam ...... Putnam's Proceedings before the Justice of the Peace   (DLA)
PUTT .... Portable Underwater Tracking Transducer
PUTT .... Propellant Utilization Time Trace
PUU .... Piute Reservoir [*Utah*] [*Seismograph station code, US Geological Survey*]   (SEIS)
PUU .... Puerto Asis [*Colombia*] [*Airport symbol*]   (OAG)
PU-UH .... University of Pennsylvania, University Hospital, Philadelphia, PA [*Library symbol*] [*Library of Congress*]   (LCLS)
PU-UH-DeS ... University of Pennsylvania, University Hospital, De Schweinitz Collection of Ophthalmology, Philadelphia, PA [*Library symbol*] [*Library of Congress*]   (LCLS)
PUUSNA .... Polish Union of the United States of North America   (EA)
PUV .... Propellant Utilization Valve [*NASA*]   (NASA)
PUV .... Pulaski [*Virginia*] [*Seismograph station code, US Geological Survey*] [*Closed*]   (SEIS)
PU-V .... University of Pennsylvania, School of Veterinary Medicine, Philadelphia, PA [*Library symbol*] [*Library of Congress*]   (LCLS)
PUVA .... Photochemotherapy with Ultraviolet A [*Oncology*]
PUVA .... Psoralens and Ultraviolet A [*Therapy*] [*Medicine*]
PUVLV .... Propellant Utilization Valve [*NASA*]   (AAG)
PuW .... Poesie und Wissenschaft [*A publication*]
PUW .... Pullman [*Washington*] [*Airport symbol*]   (OAG)
PUW .... Pullman, WA [*Location identifier*] [*FAA*]   (FAAL)
PU-W .... University of Pennsylvania, Wharton School of Finance and Commerce, Philadelphia, PA [*Library symbol*] [*Library of Congress*]   (LCLS)
PUWP .... Polish United Workers' Party [*See also PZPR*]   (PD)
PUY .... Pula [*Yugoslavia*] [*Airport symbol*]   (OAG)
PV .... Eastern Provincial Airways [*Labrador*] [*ICAO designator*]   (OAG)
PV .... Pacific Viewpoint [*A publication*]
PV .... Papillomavirus
PV .... Par Value [*Finance*]
PV .... Paravane [*Anti-moored-mine device*] [*Obsolete*]
PV .... Parole Violator
PV .... Paromomycin-Vancomycin [*Blood agar*] [*Microbiology*]
PV .... Path Verification
PV .... Patrol Vessel
P/V .... Peak-to-Valley
PV .... [*The*] People's Voice [*Pre-World War II publication of Adam Clayton Powell, Jr., and Charlie Buchanan*]
PV .... Per Vaginam [*Medicine*]
PV .... Peripheral Vascular [*Medicine*]
PV .... Peripheral Vein [*Anatomy*]
PV .... Peroxide Value [*Food analysis*]
PV .... Petite Vitesse [*Goods train*] [*French*]
PV .... Photographic Vision [*Filter*]
PV .... Photovoltaic
PV .... Physical Vulnerability [*Number*]   (NATG)
PV .... Pigment Volume
PV .... Pilot Vessel
PV .... Pioneer Venus [*Spacecraft*]
PV .... Pipe Ventilated
PV .... Plan View   (MSA)
PV .... Planetary Vehicle [*NASA*]
PV .... Planuebergang [*Grade Crossing*] [*German military - World War II*]
PV .... Plasma Volume [*Medicine*]
PV .... Playback Verifier   (MCD)
PV .... Poesia e Verita [*A publication*]
PV .... Pole Vault
PV .... Polycythemia Vera [*Also, PCV*] [*Hematology*]
PV .... Polydor/Deutsche-Grammophon Variable Microgroove [*Record label*] [*Germany*]
PV .... Polyoma Virus
PV .... Pornovision [*Television*]
PV .... Portal Vein [*Anatomy*]
PV .... Position Vacant   (ADA)
PV .... Position Value
PV .... Positive Volume   (IEEE)
PV .... Post Village
PV .... Post-Virgil
PV .... Present Value
P/V .... Pressure/Vacuum [*or Valve*]
PV .... Pressure Vessel   (MSA)
P-V .... Pressure-Volume
PV .... Pressurization Valve
PV .... Prevailing Visibility
P/V .... Preview
PV .... Priest Vicar
PV .... Primary Valve
PV .... Prime Vertical
PV .... Princess Victoria's Royal Irish Fusiliers [*Military*] [*British*]   (ROG)

PV .... Principe de Viana [*A publication*]
PV .... Private Varnish [*Privately owned railroad cars*]
PV .... Problemy Vostokovedenija [*A publication*]
PV .... Production Validation   (AABC)
PV .... Professional Virgin   (DSUE)
PV .... Professional Volunteer
P/V .... Profit/Volume [*Ratio*]
PV .... Project Volunteer [*Oakland, CA*]   (EA)
PV .... Prometheus Vinctus [*of Aeschylus*] [*Classical studies*]   (OCD)
PV .... Public Volunteer
PV .... Public Voucher
PV .... Pull and Void   (MCD)
PV .... Pulmonary Valvotomy [*Cardiology*]
PV .... Pulmonary Vascularity [*Medicine*]
PV .... Pulmonary Vein [*Medicine*]
PV .... Pulse Voltammetry [*Analytical chemistry*]
P & V .... Pyloroplasty and Vagotomy [*Medicine*]
PV .... Pyrocatechol Violet [*Also, PCV*] [*An indicator*] [*Chemistry*]
PV .... Villanova University, Villanova, PA [*Library symbol*] [*Library of Congress*]   (LCLS)
PV1 .... Private E-1 [*Army*]
PV2 .... Private E-2 [*Army*]
PV 4 .... Pickup Trucks, Vans, and Four-Wheel-Drive Vehicles [*Initialism used as title of a publication*]
PVA .... Paralyzed Veterans of America   (EA)
PVA .... Personal Values Abstract [*Scale*]
PVA .... Poly(vinyl Alcohol) [*Also, PVAL*] [*Organic chemistry*]
PVA .... Positive Vorticity Advection [*Meteorology*]   (FAAC)
PVA .... Preburner Valve Actuator [*NASA*]   (NASA)
PVA .... Privacy Act   (MCD)
PVA .... Propellant Valve Actuator   (MCD)
PVA .... Providencia [*Colombia*] [*Airport symbol*]   (OAG)
PVAC .... Peak Volts Alternating Current   (KSC)
PVAC .... Poly(vinyl Acetate) [*Organic chemistry*]
PVAC .... Present Value of Annual Charges
PVAE .... Poly(vinyl Acetate) [*Organic chemistry*]
PVAHI .... Augustinian Historical Institute, Villanova University, Villanova, PA [*Library symbol*] [*Library of Congress*]   (LCLS)
PVAL .... Poly(vinyl Alcohol) [*Also, PVA*] [*Organic chemistry*]
PVAR .... Percentage Variance [*Statistics*]
PVAS .... Primary Voice Alert System [*NORAD*]   (MCD)
PVat II .... Il Papiro Vaticano Greco II [*A publication*]   (OCD)
PVB .... Platteville, WI [*Location identifier*] [*FAA*]   (FAAL)
PVB .... Poly(vinyl Butyral) [*Safety glass laminating material*] [*Organic chemistry*]
PVB .... Portametric Voltmeter Bridge
PVB .... Premature Ventricular Beat [*Cardiology*]
PV-B .... Villanova University, Business and Finance Library, Villanova, PA [*Library symbol*] [*Library of Congress*]   (LCLS)
PVC .... Partido de Veteranos Civiles [*Civilian Veterans' Party*] [*Dominican Republic*]   (PPW)
PVC .... Peripheral Vasoconstriction [*Medicine*]
PVC .... Periscope Viewer/Controller   (MCD)
PVC .... Permanent Virtual Circuit
PVC .... Pigment Volume Concentration
PVC .... Point of Vertical Curve
PVC .... Poly(vinyl Chloride) [*Organic chemistry*]
PVC .... Port Vila [*New Hebrides*] [*Seismograph station code, US Geological Survey*]   (SEIS)
PVC .... Position and Velocity Computer
PVC .... Potential Volume Change
PVC .... Premature Ventricular Contraction [*Cardiology*]
PVC .... Pressure Vacuum Chamber
PVC .... Pressure Volume Compensator   (KSC)
PVC .... Primary Visual Cortex [*Anatomy*]
PVC .... Prosthetic Valve (Disk) Closing [*Cardiology*]
PVC .... Provincetown [*Massachusetts*] [*Airport symbol*]   (OAG)
PVC .... Provincetown, MA [*Location identifier*] [*FAA*]   (FAAL)
PVC .... Pulmonary Venous Congestion [*Medicine*]
PVCBMA .... PVC [*Polyvinylchloride*] Belting Manufacturers Association [*Washington, DC*]   (EA)
PVCF .... Present Value Cash Flow
PVCI .... Peripheral Vision Command Indicator
PVCN .... Poly(vinyl Cinnamate) [*Organic chemistry*]
PVCS .... Portable Voice Communications System
PVD .... Pancreatic Ventral Duct [*Anatomy*]
PVD .... Paravisual Director [*British*]
PVD .... Peripheral Vascular Disease [*Medicine*]
PVD .... Physical Vapor Deposition [*Coating technology*]
PVD .... Physical Vulnerability Division [*Air Force*]
PVD .... Plan [*or Planned*] View Display [*RADAR*]   (AFM)
PVD .... Planned Variations Demonstration [*HUD*]
PVD .... Portable Vapor Detector
PVD .... Posterior Vitreous Detachment [*Ophthalmology*]
PVD .... Product Verification Demonstration   (MCD)
PVD .... Protective Vehicle Division [*US Secret Service*]
PVD .... Providence [*Rhode Island*] [*Airport symbol*]   (OAG)
PVD .... Pulmonary Vascular Disease [*Medicine*]
PV & D .... Purge, Vent, and Drain   (NASA)
PVD .... Purge, Vent, Drain System   (MCD)
PvdA .... Partij van de Arbeid [*Labor Party*] [*The Netherlands*]   (PPE)

PvdA/PTA ... Partij van de Arbeid van Belgiee/Parti du Travail de Belgique [*Belgian Labor Party*] (PPW)
PVDC .... Poly(vinylidene Chloride) [*Organic chemistry*]
PVDF .... Poly(vinylidene Fluoride) [*Organic chemistry*]
PVDL .... Precision Variable Delay Line
PVDS .... Physical Vulnerability Data Sheets (MCD)
PvdV .... Partij van de Vrijheid [*Party of Freedom*] [*The Netherlands*] (PPE)
PVE .... Pine Valley Explorers [*Vancouver Stock Exchange symbol*]
PVE .... Polyvinyl Ether [*Organic chemistry*]
PVE .... Porvenir [*Panama*] [*Airport symbol*] (OAG)
PVE .... Prolonged Vacuum Exposure
P & VE .... Propulsion and Vehicle Engineering [*A Marshall Space Flight Center laboratory*] (MCD)
PVE .... Prosthetic Valve Echogram [*Cardiology*]
PVE .... Prosthetic Valve Endocarditis [*Medicine*]
PVE .... Provisioning Engineer
PVE .... Pulmonary Vascular Effect [*Physiology*]
PVED .... Parity Violating Energy Difference [*Physical chemistry*]
PVEPP .... Preliminary Value Engineering Program Plan (MCD)
PVF .... Peak Visibility Factor
PVF .... Peripheral Visual Field [*Optics*]
PVF .... Placerville, CA [*Location identifier*] [*FAA*] (FAAL)
PVF .... Political Victory Fund [*National Rifle Association*]
PVF .... Poly(vinyl Fluoride) [*Organic chemistry*]
PVF .... Portal Venous Flow [*Medicine*]
PVF₂ .... Poly(vinylidene Fluoride) [*Organic chemistry*]
PVFD .... Pipe Ventilated, Forced Draught
PVfHi .... Valley Forge Historical Society, Valley Forge, PA [*Library symbol*] [*Library of Congress*] (LCLS)
PVFHP .... Public Voice for Food and Health Policy (EA)
PVfP .... Philadelphia Quartz Co., Valley Forge, PA [*Library symbol*] [*Library of Congress*] (LCLS)
PVG .... Periventricular Gray [*Neurobiology*]
PVG .... Portsmouth, VA [*Location identifier*] [*FAA*] (FAAL)
PVG .... Project on the Vietnam Generation (EA)
PVGC .... Pioneer Venus Gas Chromatograph [*NASA*]
PVH .... Periventricular Hemorrhage [*Medicine*]
PVH .... Phillips-Van Heusen Corp. [*NYSE symbol*]
PVH .... Porto Velho [*Brazil*] [*Airport symbol*] (OAG)
PVH .... Pulmonary Venous Hypertension [*Medicine*]
PVI .... Pacific Vocational Institute Library [*UTLAS symbol*]
PVI .... Peripheral Vascular Insufficiency [*Medicine*]
PVI .... Personal Values Inventory [*Psychology*]
PVI .... Point of Vertical Intersection
PVI .... Poly(vinyl Isobutyl Ether)
PVI .... Prevulcanization Inhibitor
PVI .... Primary Vocational Interest [*Personnel study*]
PVI .... Product Verification Inspection [*DoD*]
PVI .... Programable Video Interface
PVID .... Pipe Ventilated, Induced Draught
PVIR .... Penn Virginia Corp. [*NASDAQ symbol*] (NQ)
P & VIR ..... Pure and Vulcanized Rubber Insulation
PVJ .... Pauls Valley, OK [*Location identifier*] [*FAA*] (FAAL)
PVJC .... Palo Verde Junior College [*California*]
PVK .... Packaged Ventilation Kit [*Civil Defense*]
PVK .... Polyvinylcarbazol [*Organic chemistry*] (IEEE)
PVK .... Preveza/Lefkas [*Greece*] [*Airport symbol*] (OAG)
PVL .... Pavlikeny [*Bulgaria*] [*Seismograph station code, US Geological Survey*] (SEIS)
PVL .... Pressure to Vertical Locks
PVL .... Prevail (FAAC)
PV-L .... Villanova University, Law School, Villanova, PA [*Library symbol*] [*Library of Congress*] (LCLS)
PVLT .... Prevalent (FAAC)
PVM .... Pneumonia Virus of Mice
PVM .... Poly(vinyl Methyl Ether)
PVM .... Posterior Ventral Microtubule [*Anatomy*]
PVM .... Potentiometric Voltmeter
PVM .... Pressure Vessel Material
PVM .... Projection Video Monitor
PVM .... Protein, Vitamins, Minerals [*J. B. Williams Co. brand of liquid protein*]
PVMA .... Pressure Vessel Manufacturers Association [*Chicago, IL*] (EA)
PVMB .... Potential Variation Mixed Basis [*Photovoltaic energy systems*]
PVME .... Poly(vinyl Methyl Ether) [*Organic chemistry*]
PVMI .... Parish Visitors of Mary Immaculate [*Roman Catholic women's religious order*]
PVMTD ...... Preservation Method
PVN .... Paraventricular Nucleus [*Brain anatomy*]
PVN .... Peters Valley [*New Jersey*] [*Seismograph station code, US Geological Survey*] [*Closed*] (SEIS)
PVN .... Proven Resources Ltd. [*Vancouver Stock Exchange symbol*]
PVNGS .... Palo Verde Nuclear Generating Station (NRCH)
PVNO .... Polyvinylpyridine-N-Oxide [*Organic chemistry*]
PVNPS .... Post-Vietnam Psychiatric Syndrome
PVNS .... Pigmented Villonodular Synovitis [*Also, PVS*] [*Medicine*]
PVNT .... Prevent (AAG)
PVNTMED ... Preventive Medicine [*Also, PM*]
PVO .... Atlantic City, NJ [*Location identifier*] [*FAA*] (FAAL)
PVO .... Pioneer Venus Orbiter [*NASA*]

PVO .... Portoviejo [*Ecuador*] [*Airport symbol*] (OAG)
PVO .... Principal Veterinary Officer (ROG)
PVO .... Private Voluntary Organization
PVO .... Prosthetic Valve (Disk) Opening [*Cardiology*]
PVO .... Protivo-Voxdushnaia Oborona [*Antiaircraft Defense*] [*USSR*]
PVOD .... Peripheral Vascular Occlusive Disease [*Medicine*]
PVOR .... Precision VHF Omnirange
PV-P .... Past Vice-President
PVP .... Peripheral Venous Pressure [*Cardiology*]
PVP .... Plasma Vaporization Process
PVP .... Poly(vinylpyrrolidone) [*Organic chemistry*]
PVP .... Portal Venous Pressure [*Physiology*]
PVP .... President's Veterans Program [*Employment*]
PVP .... Pueblo Viejo [*Peru*] [*Seismograph station code, US Geological Survey*] [*Closed*] (SEIS)
PVPA .... Plant Variety Protection Act [*1970*]
PVP-I .... Poly(vinylpyrrolidone) Iodine Complex
PVPMPC .... Perpetual Vice-President-Member Pickwick Club [*From "The Pickwick Papers" by Charles Dickens*]
PVPO .... Plant Variety Protection Office [*Department of Agriculture*]
P & V Prod ... Paint and Varnish Production [*A publication*]
PVPS .... Plasma Varactor Phase Shifter
PVQ .... Deadhorse, AK [*Location identifier*] [*FAA*] (FAAL)
PVQ .... Personal Value Questionnaire [*Navy*]
PVR .... Palos Verdes [*California*] [*Seismograph station code, US Geological Survey*] [*Closed*] (SEIS)
PVR .... Peripheral Vascular Resistance [*Cardiology*]
PVR .... Platte Valley Review [*A publication*]
PVR .... Postvoiding Residual [*Medicine*]
PVR .... Precision Voltage Reference (MDG)
PVR .... Procedure Validation Report (AAG)
PVR .... Process Variable Record
PVR .... Profit/Volume Ratio
PVR .... Proliferative Vitreoretinopathy [*Ophthalmology*]
PVR .... Puerto Vallarta [*Mexico*] [*Airport symbol*] (OAG)
PVR .... Pulmonary Vascular Resistance [*Physiology*]
PVR .... Pulse Volume Rate [*Physiology*]
PVR .... Pulse Volume Recording [*Medicine*]
PVRC .... Pressure Vessel Research Committee [*National Bureau of Standards*]
PVRD .... Purge, Vent, Repressurize, and Drain (NASA)
PVRO .... Plant Variety Rights Office [*Ministry of Agriculture, Fisheries, and Food*] [*British*]
PVS .... [*The*] Pecos Valley Southern Railway Co. [*AAR code*]
PVS .... Performance Verification System
PVS .... Peritoneovenous Shunt [*Medicine*]
PVS .... Persistent Vegetative State [*Medicine*]
PVS .... Personal Videoconferencing Station [*Widcom, Inc.*] [*Los Gatos, CA*] [*Telecommunications service*] (TSSD)
PVS .... Photovoltaic System
PVS .... Pigmented Villonodular Synovitis [*Also, PVNS*] [*Medicine*]
PVS .... Plant Vent Stack [*Nuclear energy*] (NRCH)
PVS .... Plexus Visibility Score [*Medicine*]
PVS .... Polyvinylsulfonate [*Organic chemistry*]
PVS .... Post-Vietnam Syndrome
PVS .... Present Value Service [*LIMRA*]
PVS .... Pressure Vacuum System
PVS .... Principal Veterinary Surgeon [*British*]
PVS .... Proceedings. Virgil Society [*A publication*]
PVS .... Program Validation Services [*Data processing*]
PVS .... Propellant Venting System
PVS .... Pulmonary Valve Stenosis [*Cardiology*]
PVSC .... Professional Video Services Corporation [*Washington, DC*] [*Telecommunications*] (TSSD)
P-V Seances Com Int Poids Mes ... Proces-Verbaux des Seances. Comite International des Poids et Mesures [*A publication*]
P-V Seances Soc Sci Phys Nat Bord ... Proces-Verbaux des Seances. Societe des Sciences Physiques et Naturelles de Bordeaux [*A publication*]
P-V Seances Soc Sci Phys Nat Bordeaux ... Proces-Verbaux des Seances. Societe des Sciences Physiques et Naturelles de Bordeaux [*A publication*]
PV SIg .... Polyvalent Surface Immunoglobulin [*Immunology*]
P V Soc Linn Bordeaux ... Proces Verbaux. Societe Linneenne de Bordeaux [*A publication*]
PV/ST .... Premate Verification/System Test [*NASA*] (KSC)
PVT .... Pacific Vending Technology Ltd. [*Vancouver Stock Exchange symbol*]
PVT .... Page View Terminal [*Typography*] [*Videotex terminal*]
PVT .... Par Voie Telegraphique [*By Telegraph*] [*French*]
PVT .... Paroxysmal Ventricular Tachycardia [*Medicine*]
PVT .... Performance Verification Test
PV/T .... Photovoltaic/Thermal
PVT .... Physical Vapor Transport [*Materials processing*]
PVT .... Pivot (MSA)
PVT .... Point of Vertical Tangent
PVT .... Polyvalent Tolerance [*Immunology*]
PVT .... Poly(vinyltoluene) [*Organic chemistry*]
PVT .... Position Velocity-Time
PVT .... Precision Verification Test (MCD)
PVT .... Pressure, Volume, Temperature

PVT .... Private (AFM)
PVT .... Probe Velocity Transducer (KSC)
PVT .... Product Verification Test (MCD)
PVT .... Prototype Validation Test (MCD)
PVT .... Provisioning Technician
PVT .... Pulse Video Thermography [Nondestructive testing technique]
PVT .... Pyrotechnic Verification Test [NASA] (NASA)
PVTAP......... Photovoltaic Transient Analysis Computer Program
PVT-C .... Product Verification Test - Contractor (MCD)
PVT-C .... Production Validation Test - Contractor (MCD)
PVT-C .... Prototype Validation Test - Contractor (MCD)
PVTE .... Private
PVT-G .... Production Validation Testing - Government
PVTI .... Piping and Valve Test Insert [Nuclear energy] (NRCH)
PVTM .... Physical Vulnerability Technical Memorandum (MCD)
PVTOS .... Physical Vapor Transport of Organic Solutions [Materials processing]
PVTR.......... Portable Video Tape Recorder
PVU .... Perimeter Ventures Ltd. [Vancouver Stock Exchange symbol]
PVU .... Provo [Utah] [Airport symbol] (OAG)
PVU .... Provo, UT [Location identifier] [FAA] (FAAL)
PVU .... Villanova University, Villanova, PA [OCLC symbol] (OCLC)
PVV .... Fondation Europeenne "Pro Venetia Viva" [European Foundation "Pro Venetia Viva" - PVV] (EA-IO)
PVV .... Partij voor Vrijheid en Vooruitgang [Freedom and Progress Party] [Belgium] (PPW)
PVV .... Portal Venous Velocity [Physiology]
PVV .... Pressure, Vent, and Vacuum
PVW .... Plainview, TX [Location identifier] [FAA] (FAAL)
PVW .... Wilson College, Chambersburg, PA [OCLC symbol] (OCLC)
PVWA .... Planned Value of Work Accomplished
PVWS .... Planned Value of Work Scheduled (MCD)
PVY .... Pope Vanoy [Alaska] [Airport symbol] (OAG)
PVY .... Providence Energy Corp. [American Stock Exchange symbol]
PVZ .... Painesville, OH [Location identifier] [FAA] (FAAL)
PVZTA .... Plyn [A publication]
PW.............. Citizens Library, Washington, PA [Library symbol] [Library of Congress] (LCLS)
PW.............. Pacific Western Airlines Ltd. [Canada] [ICAO designator] (OAG)
PW.............. Packed Weight
PW.............. Paper Wrapper (ADA)
PW.............. Paraguay Watch [Reports on human rights violations] (EA)
PW.............. Passing Window (MSA)
PW.............. [A.] Pauly, [G.] Wissowa, and [W.] Kroll, Real-Encyclopaedie der Klassischen Altertumswissenschaft [A publication] (OCD)
PW.............. Peere-Williams' English Chancery Reports [1695-1736] (DLA)
P & W......... Penrose and Watts' Pennsylvania Reports [1829-32] (DLA)
PW.............. Pension World [A publication]
PW.............. Pension for Wounds [Navy] [British] (ROG)
PW.............. Per Week
PW.............. Pericardium Wall [Medicine]
PW.............. Petroleum Week [A publication]
PW.............. Philadelphia & Western Railroad [AAR code] [Terminated]
PW.............. Philologische Wochenschrift [A publication]
pW.............. Picowatt
PW.............. Pilot Wire (MSA)
PW.............. Pittsburgh & West Virginia Railroad [American Stock Exchange symbol]
PW.............. Pivoted Window (AAG)
PW.............. Plain Washer (MSA)
PW.............. Poetry Wales [A publication]
PW.............. Poets and Writers (EA)
PW.............. Ports and Waterways
PW.............. Position Wanted
P & W......... Post and Wire (ADA)
PW.............. Posterior Wall [Medicine]
PW.............. Postwar
PW.............. Potable Water [Nuclear energy] (NRCH)
PW.............. Power
PW.............. Power Windows [Automobile ads]
P & W......... Pratt & Whitney [Aircraft]
PW.............. Pressurized Water
PW.............. Prime Western [Zinc]
PW.............. Prince of Wales [Military unit] [British]
PW.............. Printed Wiring (MSA)
PW.............. Prisoner of War [Also, POW]
PW.............. Private Wire (NATG)
PW.............. Progesterone Withdrawal [Endocrinology]
PW.............. Projected Window (MSA)
PW.............. Projection Welding
PW.............. Protestant World [A publication]
PW.............. Providence & Worcester Co. [AAR code]
PW.............. Psychological Warfare
PW.............. Public Welfare
PW.............. Public Works
PW.............. Publishers' Weekly [A publication]
PW.............. Pulpwash [Byproduct of citrus processing]
PW.............. Pulse Width [RADAR]
PW.............. Purlwise [Knitting]

PWA .... Oklahoma City, OK [Location identifier] [FAA] (FAAL)
PWA .... Pacific Western Airlines Ltd. [Toronto Stock Exchange symbol] [Vancouver Stock Exchange symbol]
PWA .... Palmer-Houston [Alaska] [Seismograph station code, US Geological Survey] (SEIS)
PWA .... People with AIDS Coalition [New York, NY] (EA)
PWA .... Performance Warehouse Association [Hermosa Beach, CA] (EA)
PWA .... Person with AIDS
PWA .... Pharmaceutical Wholesalers Association [Later, DWA]
PWA .... Please Wait Awhile [Humorous interpretation for Pacific Western Airlines Corp.]
PWA .... Portuguese West Africa [Angola]
P & WA .... Pratt & Whitney Aircraft (KSC)
PWA .... Pratt & Whitney Aircraft (MCD)
PWA .... Pray while Aloft [Humorous interpretation for Pacific Western Airlines Corp.]
PWA .... Printed Wire Assembly [Data processing]
PWA .... Private Write Area [NASA] (NASA)
PWA .... Probably Won't Arrive [Humorous interpretation for Pacific Western Airlines Corp.]
PWA .... Product Work Authorization (NASA)
PWA .... Public Works Administration [All functions transferred to office of Federal Works Agency, 1943]
PWA .... Publishers' Weekly Announcements [Title changed to Forthcoming Books] [A publication]
PWa .... Warren Library Association and County Division, Warren, PA [Library symbol] [Library of Congress] (LCLS)
PWA .... Waynesburg College, Waynesburg, PA [OCLC symbol] (OCLC)
PWAA........ Paint and Wallpaper Association of America [Later, National Decorators Products Association] (EA)
PWAA........ Polish Western Association of America (EA)
PWAA........ Polish Women's Alliance of America (EA)
PWAA........ Professional Women's Appraisal Association [Scottsdale, AZ] (EA)
PWAC........ Periodical Writers Association of Canada
PWAC........ Pratt & Whitney Aircraft (AAG)
PWAC........ Present Worth of Annual Charges [Pronounced "p-wack"] [Bell System]
PWacD .... David Library of the American Revolution, Washington Crossing, PA [Library symbol] [Library of Congress] (LCLS)
PWAF........ Polish Workers' Aid Fund (EA)
PWAFRR .... Present Worth of All Future Revenue Requirements
PWal........... Helen Kate Furness Free Library, Wallingford, PA [Library symbol] [Library of Congress] (LCLS)
PWalPH ...... Pendle Hill Library, Wallingford, PA [Library symbol] [Library of Congress] (LCLS)
PWayC .... Waynesburg College, Waynesburg, PA [Library symbol] [Library of Congress] (LCLS)
PWb........... Osterhout Free Library, Wilkes-Barre, PA [Library symbol] [Library of Congress] (LCLS)
PWB .... Partial Weight Bearing [Medicine]
PWB .... Pencil Writing on Back [Deltiology]
PW & B ...... Philadelphia, Wilmington & Baltimore Railroad
PWB .... Pilot Weather Briefing (FAAC)
PWB .... Printed Wiring Board
PWB .... Psychological Warfare Branch [Allied Forces] [World War II]
PWB .... Pulling Whaleboat
PWBA........ Plane-Wave Born Approximation
PWBA........ Printed Wiring Board Assembly (MCD)
PWBA........ Professional Women Bowlers Association [Later, LPBT] (EA)
PWBC........ Peripheral White Blood Cells [Medicine]
PWbH........ Wyoming Historical and Geological Society, Wilkes-Barre, PA [Library symbol] [Library of Congress] (LCLS)
PWBI .... Posterior Wall of Bronchus Intermedius [Anatomy]
PWbK .... King's College, Wilkes-Barre, PA [Library symbol] [Library of Congress] (LCLS)
PWBP .... Pension and Welfare Benefit Programs [Labor-Management Services Administration]
PWBS........ Program Work Breakdown Structure (NASA)
PWbW .... Wilkes College, Wilkes-Barre, PA [Library symbol] [Library of Congress] (LCLS)
PWC .... Chester County District Library Center, Exton, PA [OCLC symbol] (OCLC)
PWC .... Pacific War Council [World War II]
PWC .... Peak Work Capacity
PWC .... Pentecostal World Conference (EA)
PWC .... Physical Work Capacity
PWC .... Poland Watch Center (EA)
PWC .... Pratt & Whitney Canada, Inc. [Montreal, PQ, Canada] [FAA designator] (FAAC)
PWC .... Printed Wiring Cards [Telecommunications]
PWC .... Prisoner of War Cage
PWC .... Prisoner of War Camp
PWC .... Prisoner of War Command
PWC .... Prisoner of War Compound
PWC .... Process Water Cooler (MSA)
PWC .... Professional Women in Construction [White Plains, NY] (EA)
PWC .... Professional Women's Caucus (EA)

PWC .... Provincial Warning Center [*NATO*]   (NATG)
PWC .... Public Works Canada [*See also TPC*]
PWC .... Public Works Center [*Navy*]
PWC .... Pulse-Width Coded
PWcC .... Chester County District Library Center, West Chester, PA [*Library symbol*] [*Library of Congress*]   (LCLS)
PWCC .... Political Warfare Coordination Committee [*London*] [*World War II*]
PWCCA ...... Pembroke Welsh Corgi Club of America   (EA)
PWCEN ...... Public Works Center [*Navy*]
PWcHi .... Chester County Historical Society, West Chester, PA [*Library symbol*] [*Library of Congress*]   (LCLS)
PW/CI/DET ... Prisoner of War/Civilian Internees/Detainees   (MCD)
PWCJS ...... Proceedings. Fifth World Congress of Jewish Studies [*1969*] [*A publication*]
PWCLANT ... Public Works Center, Atlantic [*Navy*]
PWCMS ...... Public Works Center Management System [*Navy*]
PWCPAC.... Public Works Center, Pacific [*Navy*]
PWcS .... West Chester State College, West Chester, PA [*Library symbol*] [*Library of Congress*]   (LCLS)
PWD .... Pan World Ventures, Inc. [*Vancouver Stock Exchange symbol*]
PWD .... Petroleum Warfare Department [*Ministry of Fuel and Power*] [*British*] [*World War II*]
PWD .... Plentywood, MT [*Location identifier*] [*FAA*]   (FAAL)
PWD .... Powder   (KSC)
PWD .... Power Distributor   (KSC)
PWD .... Procurement Work Directive [*Army*]   (AABC)
PWD .... Proximity Warning Device   (MCD)
PWD .... Psychological Warfare Division [*SHAEF*] [*World War II*]
PWD .... Public Works Department [*Navy*]
PWD .... Pulse-Width Detector [*or Discriminator*] [*RADAR*]
PWDC .... Philippine War Damage Commission [*Post-World War II*]
PWDCA ..... Portuguese Water Dog Club of America   (EA)
PWDEPT ... Public Works Department [*Navy*]
PWDG .... Prince of Wales' Dragoon Guards [*Military*] [*British*]   (ROG)
PWDI .... Program with Developing Institutions   (EA)
PWDMS ..... Public Works Developmental Management System [*Navy*]
PWDP......... Powder Passing
PWDR .... Partial Wave Dispersing Relation
PWDRD .... Powdered [*Freight*]
PWDS......... Protected Wireline Distribution System   (CET)
PWE .... Pauli-Weisskopf Equation [*Physics*]
PWE .... Pawnee City, NE [*Location identifier*] [*FAA*]   (FAAL)
PWE .... Political Warfare Executive [*World War II*]
PWE .... Present Worth Expenditures [*Telecommunications*]   (TEL)
PWE .... Prisoner of War Enclosure
PWE .... Pulse-Width Encoder
PWEA........ Printed Wiring and Electronic Assemblies [*NASA*]
PWEDA ...... Public Works and Economic Development Act
PWEDA ...... Public Works and Economic Development Association   (EA)
PWesAC..... Community College of Allegheny County, South Campus, West Mifflin, PA [*Library symbol*] [*Library of Congress*]   (LCLS)
PWesD .... Dresser Industries, Inc., Harbison-Walker Refractories Co., West Mifflin, PA [*Library symbol*] [*Library of Congress*]   (LCLS)
P West Ph S ... Proceedings. Western Pharmacology Society [*A publication*]
PWF............ Pacific Whale Foundation   (EA)
PWF............ Package Will Follow [*Birthday-card notation*]
PWF............ Pax World Foundation [*Bethesda, MD*]   (EA)
PWF............ Photoelectric Work Function
PWF............ Pop Warner Football [*An association*]   (EA)
PWF............ Power Financial Corp. [*Toronto Stock Exchange symbol*]
PWF............ Present Worth Factor [*Real estate*]
PWF............ Propellant Weight Fraction   (NATG)
PWF............ Pulse Wave Form
PWFG........ Primary Waveform Generator [*Telecommunications*]   (TEL)
PWFN .... Projection Weld Flange Nut
PWFR .... Plantwide Failure Reporting   (MCD)
PWG .... Panzerwagen [*Tank*] [*German military - World War II*]
PWG .... Permanent Working Group   (NATG)
PWG .... Photoelectric Web Guide
PWG .... Plastic Wire Guide
PWG .... Powergem Resources Corp. [*Vancouver Stock Exchange symbol*]
PWH .... Pellet Warhead
PWH .... Poliokeawe [*Pali*] [*Hawaii*] [*Seismograph station code, US Geological Survey*]   (SEIS)
PWH .... Precision Welding-Head
PWH .... Proprietor of Copyright on a Work Made for Hire
PWH .... Prototype Wave Height
PWHA........ Plutonium Waste Handling Area [*Nuclear energy*]   (NRCH)
PWhi........... Whitehall Township Public Library, Whitehall, PA [*Library symbol*] [*Library of Congress*]   (LCLS)
PWHQ........ Peace War Headquarters   (NATG)
PWHS........ Public Works Historical Society   (EA)
PWHT........ Post-Weld Heat Treatment [*Nuclear energy*]   (NRCH)
PWI .... Permanent Ware Institute [*Defunct*]   (EA)
PWI .... Permanent Way Institution   (EA-IO)
PWI .... Physiological Workload Index [*Aviation*]
PWI .... Pilot Warning Indicator [*or Instrument*] [*Aviation*]
PWI............ Potable Water Intake

PWI............ Prince of Wales' Island   (ROG)
PWI............ Prisoner of War Interrogation
PWI............ Projects with Industry [*Department of Education program*]
PWI............ Proximity Warning Indicator [*or Instrument*] [*Aviation*]
PWIB .... Prisoner of War Information Bureau [*Post-World War II*]
PWIF .... Plantation Workers' International Federation [*Later, IFPAAW*]
PWIN .... Prototype WWMCCS Intercomputer Network   (MCD)
PWJ........... Paine Webber Group, Inc. [*NYSE symbol*]
PWJ........... Pulsating Water-Jet Lavager [*Medicine*]   (RDA)
PWJC .... Paine, Webber, Jackson & Curtis [*Later, Paine Webber, Inc.*]
PWK .... Chicago/Wheeling, IL [*Location identifier*] [*FAA*]   (FAAL)
PWL........... Piecewise-Linear
PWL........... Port Wells [*Alaska*] [*Seismograph station code, US Geological Survey*]   (SEIS)
PWL........... Poughkeepsie, NY [*Location identifier*] [*FAA*]   (FAAL)
PWL........... Power Level
PWL........... Printed Wiring Laboratory   (MCD)
PWLB .... Public Works Loan Board [*British*]
PWM.......... PaineWebber Residential Realty, Inc. [*American Stock Exchange symbol*]
PWM.......... Planar Wing Module   (MCD)
PWM.......... Pokeweed Mitogen [*Genetics*]
PWM.......... Portable Welding Machine
PWM.......... Portland [*Maine*] [*Airport symbol*]   (OAG)
PWM.......... Portland, ME [*Location identifier*] [*FAA*]   (FAAL)
PWM.......... Printed Wiring Master
PWM.......... Pulse-Width Modulation [*Electronic instrumentation*]
PWM.......... Pulse-Width Multiplier   (IEEE)
PWMD .... Printed Wiring Master Drawing   (NASA)
PWM-FM ... Pulse-Width Modulation - Frequency Modulation [*RADAR*]
PWMIB ...... Powder Metallurgy International [*A publication*]
PWmL .... Lycoming College, Williamsport, PA [*Library symbol*] [*Library of Congress*]   (LCLS)
PWML........ Patchy White Matter Lesion [*Medicine*]
PWmP .... James V. Brown Library of Williamsport and Lycoming County, Williamsport, PA [*Library symbol*] [*Library of Congress*]   (LCLS)
P Wms....... Peere-Williams' English Chancery Reports [*1695-1736*]   (DLA)
PWMS .... Public Works Management System [*Navy*]
PWMSCM ... Pokeweed Mitogen-Stimulated Spleen-Cell-Conditioned Medium [*For growing cells*]
P Wms (Eng) ... Peere-Williams' English Chancery Reports [*1695-1736*]   (DLA)
PWN .... Polskie Wydawnictwo Naukowe [*A publication*]
PWN .... West Plains, MO [*Location identifier*] [*FAA*]   (FAAL)
PW-NWLZOA ... Pioneer Women/Na'amat, the Women's Labor Zionist Organization of America [*Formerly, PW-WLZOA*]   (EA)
PWO .... Parliamentarians for World Order   (EA)
PWO .... Prince of Wales' Own [*Military unit*] [*British*]
PWO .... Principal Welfare Officer [*Navy*] [*British*]
PWO .... Principle Warfare Officer [*British*]
PWO .... Production Work Order   (MCD)
PWO .... Public Works Officer [*Navy*]
PWOC .... Protestant Women of the Chapel
PWOP........ Pregnant without Permission [*Military*] [*World War II*]
PWOQD..... Psychology of Women Quarterly [*A publication*]
PWOR .... Prince of Wales' Own Royal [*Military unit*] [*British*]
PWP .... Barrio Florida [*Puerto Rico*] [*Seismograph station code, US Geological Survey*]   (SEIS)
PWP .... Parents without Partners [*An association*] [*Bethesda, MD*]   (EA)
PWP .... Past Worthy Patriarch
PWP .... Peasants' and Workers' Party [*Indian*]   (PPW)
PWP .... Picowatt Power   (CET)
pWp .... Picowatts, Psophometrically Weighted
PWP .... Planning Work Package   (MCD)
PWP .... Plasticized White Phosphorus
PWP .... Polish Workers' Party
PWP .... Postwar Planning [*World War II*]
PWP .... Professional Women Photographers [*New York, NY*]   (EA)
PWP .... Public Watering Place   (ADA)
PWP .... Pulmonary Wedge Pressure [*Medicine*]
PWP .... Purchase-with-Purchase [*Sales promotion*]
pW0p......... Picowatts, Psophometrically Weighted at a Point of Zero Reference Level
PWpM .... Merck, Sharp & Dohme [*Later, Merck & Co., Inc.*] Research Laboratories, Library Services, West Point, PA [*Library symbol*] [*Library of Congress*]   (LCLS)
PWPMA..... Politechnika Warszawska, Prace Naukowe. Mechanika [*A publication*]
PWPP .... Professionwide Pension Plan [*American Chemical Society*]
PWQ .... Petersburg, WV [*Location identifier*] [*FAA*]   (FAAL)
PWQ .... Preferred and Well Qualified [*Candidate designation*]
PWQM .... Protection Water Quality Management
PWR .... International Power Machines Corp. [*American Stock Exchange symbol*]
PWR .... Pilot Wire Regulator
PWR .... Port Walter, AK [*Location identifier*] [*FAA*]   (FAAL)
PWR .... Power   (KSC)
PWR .... Power Explorations [*Toronto Stock Exchange symbol*]
PWR .... Power Wirewound Resistor

PWR .... Pressurized Water Reactor
PWR .... Prevailing Wage Rate [*US Employment Service*] [*Department of Labor*]
PWR .... Prince of Wales' Royal [*Military unit*] [*British*]
PWR .... Program Work Requirement (MCD)
PWR .... Project Work Review [*Army*] (AFIT)
PWR .... Public Worship Regulation Act [*1874*] [*British*] (ROG)
PWR .... Publication Work Request (MCD)
PWRC........ Power Conversion [*NASDAQ symbol*] (NQ)
PWRCB ..... President's War Relief Control Board [*World War II*]
PWRE........ Prepositioned War Reserve Equipment [*Army*]
PWREMR.... Prepositioned War Reserve Material Requirements [*Navy*] (MCD)
PWREMS.... Prepositioned War Reserve Material Stocks [*Navy*] (MCD)
P W Rev..... Price Waterhouse Review [*A publication*]
Pwr Fmg .... Power Farming [*A publication*]
Pwr Fmg Aust NZ ... Power Farming in Australia and New Zealand and Better Farming Digest [*A publication*]
Pwr Fmg Mag ... Power Farming Magazine [*A publication*]
Pwr Frmg ... Power Farming in Australia and New Zealand [*A publication*]
Pwr Frmg Aust NZ ... Power Farming in Australia and New Zealand [*A publication*]
PWRH........ Powerhouse (MSA)
PWRM........ Prepositioned War Reserve Material (MCD)
PWRMR...... Prepositioned War Reserve Material Requirement (NVT)
PWRMRB ... Prepositioned War Reserve Materiel Requirement Balance (AFIT)
PWRMS..... Prepositioned War Reserve Material Stock (NVT)
PWRNO...... Power Failure (FAAC)
PWRO........ Pending Work Release Order (MCD)
PWROK...... Power Restored (FAAC)
PWRR........ Prepositioned War Reserve Requirements [*Army*] (NG)
PWRR-MF ... Prepositioned War Reserve Requirements for Medical Facilities [*Army*] (AABC)
PWRS........ Prepositioned War Reserve Stocks [*Army*]
PWRS........ Programable Weapons Release System (IEEE)
PWRS-MF ... Prepositioned War Reserve Stocks for Medical Facilities [*Army*] (AABC)
Pwr Wks Engng ... Power and Works Engineering [*A publication*]
PWS .... Paddle-Wheel Steamer [*Shipping*] (ROG)
PWS .... Parallel Working System
PWS .... Pattern Weavers' Society [*A union*] [*British*]
PWS .... Performance Work Statement [*DoD*]
PWS .... Peter Warlock Society (EA)
PWS .... Petrified Wood Society (EA)
PWS .... Petroleum and Water Systems [*Army*] (RDA)
PWS .... Phoenix Weapons System
PWS .... Plane-Wave Spectrum
PWS .... Plasma Wave Source [*Physics*]
PWS .... Port-Wine Stain
PWS .... Potable Water System (KSC)
PWS .... Prader-Willi Syndrome Association [*Edina, MN*] (EA)
PWS .... Predicted Wave Signaling
PWS .... Preliminary Work Statement (MCD)
PWS .... Pricing Work Statement (MCD)
PWS .... Private Wire Service
PWS .... Private Wire System (AAG)
PWS .... Program Work Statement (MCD)
PWS .... Programer Work Station
PWS .... Project Work Schedule [*Data processing*]
PWS .... Psychological Warfare Service [*Allied Forces*] [*World War II*]
PWS .... Psychological Warfare Society (EA)
PWS .... Pulau-Weh [*Sumatra*] [*Seismograph station code, US Geological Survey*] [*Closed*] (SEIS)
PWSC........ Post-War Scientific Collaboration [*British*]
PWSCC...... Prince William Sound Community College [*Alaska*]
PWsp........ Przeglad Wspotczesny [*A publication*]
PWSPP ...... Payne Whitney Suicide Prevention Program [*New York Hospital*] (EA)
PWST .... Pacwest Bancorp [*NASDAQ symbol*] (NQ)
PWST .... Protected Water Storage Tank [*Nuclear energy*] (NRCH)
PWT........... Bremerton, WA [*Location identifier*] [*FAA*] (FAAL)
PWT........... Panstwowe Wydawnictwo Techniczne [*A publication*]
PWT........... Penn West Petroleum Ltd. [*Toronto Stock Exchange symbol*]
PWT........... Pennyweight
PWT........... Picture World Test [*Psychology*]
PWT........... Progressive Wave Tube
PWT........... Propulsion Wind Tunnel [*Air Force*]
PWTC........ Powertec, Inc. [*NASDAQ symbol*] (NQ)
PWTC........ Public Works Training Center [*Navy*]
PWTC........ Public Works Transportation Center (MCD)
PWTCA ...... Powder Technology [*A publication*]
PWTCVA .... Procurement of Weapons and Tracked Combat Vehicles, Army (AABC)
PWTF .... Polish Workers Task Force (EA)
PWTN........ Power Train (AABC)
PWTN-A ..... Prace Wroclawskiego Towarzystwa Naukowego. A [*A publication*]
PWTR .... Pewter (MSA)
PWTR .... Philadelphia War Tax Resistance (EA)
PWTVA....... Procurement of Weapons and Tracked Vehicles, Army (AABC)

PWU .... Political World Union (EA)
PWV .... Pittsburgh & West Virginia Railroad [*AAR code*]
P & WV ...... Pittsburgh & West Virginia Railroad
PWV .... Precipitable Water Vapor
PWV .... Prince of Wales' Volunteers [*Military unit*] [*British*]
PWV .... Pulse Wave Velocity
PWVA........ Pacific War Veterans of America [*Defunct*]
PWVS........ Prince of Wales' Volunteer Service [*British*]
PWW .... Plannar Wing Weapon (MCD)
PWW .... Project West Wing (MCD)
PWW .... Washington and Jefferson College, Washington, PA [*Library symbol*] [*Library of Congress*] (LCLS)
PWWC........ Post War World Council [*Defunct*] (EA)
PW-WLZOA ... Pioneer Women, the Women's Labor Zionist Organization of America [*Later, PW-MWLZOA*] (EA)
PWWR........ Power Wirewound Resistor
PWX .... Permanent Working Staff [*NATO*] (NATG)
PWX .... Prisoners of War Executive [*Branch of SHAEF*] [*World War II*]
PX.............. Air Niugini [*New Guinea*] [*ICAO designator*] (FAAC)
PX.............. Pancreatectomized [*Medicine*]
PX.............. Pedro Ximenez [*A blending sherry*]
PX.............. Peroxidase [*Also, PO, POD*] [*An enzyme*]
PX.............. Physical Examination
PX.............. Please Exchange
PX.............. Pneumothorax [*Medicine*]
PX.............. Post Exchange [*Military*]
PX.............. Private Exchange
PX.............. Production Executive of the War Cabinet [*World War II*]
PX.............. Pyroxene [*Also, PYX*] [*A mineral*]
PXA .... Pulsed Xenon Arc
PXD .... Place Index in Decrement
PXD .... Post-Exercise Discussion [*NATO*] (NATG)
PXD .... Price Ex-Dividend [*Stock market*]
PXE .... Provinces X Explorations [*Vancouver Stock Exchange symbol*]
PXE .... Pseudoxanthoma Elasticum [*Medicine*]
PXF .... Primex Forest Industries Ltd. [*Vancouver Stock Exchange symbol*]
PXI .... Pax Christi International (EA)
PXI .... Pulsed Xenon Illuminator
PX In.......... Arrival Time [*Aviation*]
PXL............. Poney Explorations Limited [*Vancouver Stock Exchange symbol*]
PXL............. Pulsed Xenon LASER
PxI .... Pyridoxal [*Also, PL*] [*Biochemistry*]
PXLS .... Pulsed Xenon Light Source
PXLSS .... Pulsed Xenon Light Source System
PXM .... Projection X-Ray Microscope
Pxm .... Pyridoxamine [*Also, PM*] [*Biochemistry*]
PX Me .... Report My Arrival or Departure [*Aviation slang*]
PXN .... Panoche, CA [*Location identifier*] [*FAA*] (FAAL)
Pxn .... Pyridoxine [*Also, PN*] [*Biochemistry*]
PXO .... Porto Santo [*Portugal*] [*Airport symbol*] (OAG)
PXO .... Prospective Executive Officer
PX Out .... Takeoff Time [*Aviation*]
PXPPL........ Pull and Push Plate
PXR .... Plus-X-Reversal
PXR .... Praxis Resources Ltd. [*Vancouver Stock Exchange symbol*]
PXS .... Plexus Resources Corp. [*Toronto Stock Exchange symbol*]
PXS .... Pulsed Xenon System
PXSS .... Pulsed Xenon Solar Simulator
PXSTR........ Phototransistor (IEEE)
PXT .... Patuxent River, MD [*Location identifier*] [*FAA*] (FAAL)
PXT .... Pinxit [*He, or She, Painted It*] [*Latin*]
PXT .... Praxis Technologies [*Toronto Stock Exchange symbol*]
PXU .... Portable X-Ray Unit
PXV .... Evansville, IN [*Location identifier*] [*FAA*] (FAAL)
PXV .... Pedro Ximenez Viejo [*A blending sherry*]
PXXP.......... Pacific Express Holding [*NASDAQ symbol*] (NQ)
PXY .... Milwaukee, WI [*Location identifier*] [*FAA*] (FAAL)
Pxy .... Pyridoxyl [*Biochemistry*]
PY.............. Martin Memorial [*York City and County*] Library, York, PA [*Library symbol*] [*Library of Congress*] (LCLS)
py .... Paraguay [*MARC country of publication code*] [*Library of Congress*] (LCCP)
PY.............. Paraguay [*Two-letter standard code*] (CNC)
PY.............. Patrol Vessel, Yacht [*Navy symbol*]
PY.............. Person Years [*After radiation exposure*]
P/Y............. Pitch or Yaw
PY.............. Polysar Ltd. [*Toronto Stock Exchange symbol*] [*Vancouver Stock Exchange symbol*]
PY.............. Prior Year (AABC)
PY.............. Program Year (AFM)
PY.............. Project Yedid [*Project Friend*] (EA)
PY.............. Proto Yiddish (BJA)
PY.............. Publication Year [*Online database field identifier*]
Py .... Pyridine [*Organic chemistry*]
Py .... Pyrogen [*Medicine*]
PY.............. Pyrometer (IEEE)
PY.............. Pyronin Y [*A biological dye*]
PY.............. Surinaamse Luchtvaart Maatschappij NV [*Surinam*] [*ICAO designator*] (FAAC)

PYA .... Penn Yan, NY [Location identifier] [FAA] (FAAL)
PYA .... Pioneer Youth of America (EA)
PYA .... Plan, Year, and Age [Insurance designations]
PYA .... Psychoanalysis [Medicine]
PYA .... Pyatigorsk [USSR] [Seismograph station code, US Geological Survey] (SEIS)
PYACA .... Psychoanalytic Study of the Child [A publication]
PYAFB .... Psychologia Africana [A publication]
PYAIA .... Postepy Astronomii [A publication]
PYarE .... Electric Storage Battery Co., Yardley, PA [Library symbol] [Library of Congress] (LCLS)
Py B .... Bachelor of Pedagogy
PYB .... Borg-Warner Corp., York Division, York, PA [Library symbol] [Library of Congress] (LCLS)
PYB .... [The] Palestine Year Book [New York] [A publication] (BJA)
PYC .... Kuparuk, AK [Location identifier] [FAA] (FAAL)
PYC .... Pale Yellow Candle [Baltic coffee-house] [London] (DSUE)
PYC .... Patrol Vessel, Yacht, Coastal [Navy symbol] [Obsolete]
PYC .... Pay Your Cash [Australian slang]
PYC .... Perishability Code [Military] (AFIT)
PYC .... Playon Chico [Panama] [Airport symbol] (OAG)
PYC .... Pope and Young Club (EA)
PYC .... York College of Pennsylvania, York, PA [Library symbol] [Library of Congress] (LCLS)
PYCHB .... Psychology [A publication]
PYCOA .... Phycologia [A publication]
Pyd .... [A] Pyrimidine Nucleoside [Also, Y]
PYE .... Point Reyes, CA [Location identifier] [FAA] (FAAL)
PYE .... Protect Your Environment [Groups]
PYE .... Pryme Energy Resources [Vancouver Stock Exchange symbol]
PYF .... French Polynesia [Three-letter standard code] (CNC)
PYF .... Pay-Fone Systems, Inc. [American Stock Exchange symbol]
PYF .... Pyrenees [France] [Seismograph station code, US Geological Survey] (SEIS)
Py-FD-MS ... Pyrolysis Field Desorption Mass Spectrometry
PYG .... Peptone-Yeast-Glucose [Medium] [Microbiology]
PYGN .... Pyrogen Unit [Biochemistry]
PYGS .... Church of Jesus Christ of Latter-Day Saints, Genealogical Society Library, Gettysburg Branch, York, PA [Library symbol] [Library of Congress] (LCLS)
PYH .... Puerto Ayacucho [Venezuela] [Airport symbol] (OAG)
PYH .... York Hospital, York, PA [Library symbol] [Library of Congress] (LCLS)
PYHi .... Historical Society of York County, York, PA [Library symbol] [Library of Congress] (LCLS)
Py-HRMS ... Pyrolysis High-Resolution Mass Spectrometry
PYJ .... Louisville, KY [Location identifier] [FAA] (FAAL)
PYL .... Perry Island, AK [Location identifier] [FAA] (FAAL)
PYM .... Martin Memorial [York City and County] Library, York, PA [OCLC symbol] (OCLC)
PYM .... Pan-African Youth Movement (EA)
PYM .... Plymouth, MA [Location identifier] [FAA] (FAAL)
PYM .... Psychosomatic Medicine
PYMOA ...... Psychological Monographs [General and Applied] [A publication]
Py-MS .... Pyrolysis Mass Spectrometry
PYN .... Chicago, IL [Location identifier] [FAA] (FAAL)
PYN .... Poneloya [Nicaragua] [Seismograph station code, US Geological Survey] (SEIS)
PYNC .... Prior Year Notice [IRS]
PYNNA ...... Psychiatria, Neurologia, Neurochirurgia [A publication]
PYO .... Pick Your Own [Fruits and vegetables] (DSUE)
PYO .... Pyongyang [Heizo] [North Korea] [Seismograph station code, US Geological Survey] [Closed] (SEIS)
PYOL .... Pyramid Oil Co. [NASDAQ symbol] (NQ)
PYoW .... Westmoreland County Community College, Youngwood, PA [Library symbol] [Library of Congress] (LCLS)
PYP .... Pyrophosphate [Scintiscanning]
PYPH .... Polyphase
PYPYB .... Psychophysiology (Baltimore) [A publication]
P-Y-R .... Pitch-Yaw-Roll (AAG)
PYR .... Player Resources, Inc. [Vancouver Stock Exchange symbol]
PYR .... Prior Year Report
PYR .... Prior Year's Return [IRS]
PYR .... Pyramid [California] [Seismograph station code, US Geological Survey] (SEIS)
PYR .... Pyramid (MSA)
Pyr .... [A] Pyrimidine [Biochemistry]
PYR .... Pyrometer (AAG)
PYR .... Pyruvate [Biochemistry]
PYRCA .... Psychological Record [A publication]
PYRETH ..... Pyrethrum [Pellitory] [Pharmacology] (ROG)
PYRMD ...... Pyramid[s] [Freight]
PYRO .... Pyrogallic Acid (ROG)
PYRO .... Pyrotechnic
PYROM ...... Pyrometer [Engineering]
PYROTECH .. Pyrotechnical (ROG)
PYRREC ...... Pyrrolidinoethyl Chloride [Organic chemistry]
Pyrrh .... Pyrrhus [of Plutarch] [Classical studies] (OCD)
PYRS .... Pyramids [Board on Geographic Names]
PYRTA .... Psychological Reports [A publication]

PYS .... Primitive Yolk Sac [Embryology]
PYSCB .... Psychology in the Schools [A publication]
PYSOA .... Physiologist [A publication]
PYSSB .... Psychoanalytic Study of Society [A publication]
PYT .... Payment
PYT .... Playitas [Nicaragua] [Seismograph station code, US Geological Survey] (SEIS)
PYT .... Prentiss, MS [Location identifier] [FAA] (FAAL)
PYT .... Pretty Young Thing [In song title from the Michael Jackson album "Thriller"]
PYTCA .... Phytochemistry [A publication]
Pyth .... Pythian [of Pindar] [Classical studies] (OCD)
Py-TRMS .... Pyrolysis Time-Resolved Mass Spectrometry
PyV .... Polyoma Virus
PYV .... Yaviza [Panama] [Airport symbol] (OAG)
PYX .... Perryton, TX [Location identifier] [FAA] (FAAL)
PYX .... Pyroxene [Also, PX] [A mineral]
Pyx .... Pyxis [Constellation]
Pyxi .... Pyxis [Constellation]
PZ .... Canal Zone [Two-letter standard code] [Obsolete] (CNC)
PZ .... Lineas Aereas Paraguayas [ICAO designator] (FAAC)
PZ .... Pancreozymin [Also, CCK] [Endocrinology]
PZ .... Panzerbrechend [Armor-Piercing] [German military - World War II]
PZ .... Past Z
PZ .... Penzance [British depot code]
PZ .... Peripheral Zone [in inflorescence] [Botany]
PZ .... Phase Zero
Pz .... Phenylazobenzyloxycarbonyl [Biochemistry]
PZ .... Pick Up Zone
PZ .... Pie Zeses [May You Live Piously] [Italy]
pz .... Pieze [Unit of pressure]
PZ .... Poale Zion [Labor federation] [Later, Labor Zionist Alliance]
PZ .... Praehistorische Zeitschrift [A publication]
PZ .... Prazosin [A vasodilator]
PZ .... Prisoner of Zion (BJA)
PZ .... Protective Zone
PZ .... Prozone Phenomenon [Immunology]
PZ .... Przeglad Zachodni [A publication]
PZ .... Psychic Zodiac
PZA .... Patrol Zone Area (MCD)
PZA .... Paz De Ariporo [Colombia] [Airport symbol] (OAG)
PZA .... Piasa Commuter Airlines, Inc. [St. Louis, MO] [FAA designator] (FAAC)
PZA .... Pizza Inn, Inc. [American Stock Exchange symbol]
PZA .... Pyrazinamide [Antibacterial compound]
PZAA .... Polarized Zeeman Atomic Absorption
PZB .... Pietermaritzburg [South Africa] [Airport symbol] (OAG)
PZC .... Pezamerica Resources [Vancouver Stock Exchange symbol]
PZC .... Point of Zero Charge [Electrochemistry]
PZC .... Progressive Zionist Caucus (EA)
PZD .... Phase Zero Defense
PZDV .... Panzer-Division [Armored Division] [German military]
PZE .... Penzance [England] [Airport symbol] (OAG)
PZE .... Piezoelectric
PZFC .... Pia Zadora Fan Club [New York, NY] (EA)
PZH .... Zhob [Pakistan] [Airport symbol] (OAG)
PZI .... Indiana University of Pennsylvania, Indiana, PA [OCLC symbol] (OCLC)
PZI .... Protamine Zinc Insulin
PZKA .... Philologus. Zeitschrift fuer Klassische Altertum [A publication]
PZKiOR ...... Polish Union of Agricultural Circles and Organizations (PD)
PZKPFW ..... Panzerkampfwagen [German tank] [World War II]
PZKW .... Panzerkampfwagen [German tank] [World War II]
PZL .... Pennzoil Co. [NYSE symbol] [Toronto Stock Exchange symbol]
PZL .... Progressive Zionist League-Hashomer Hatzair (EA)
PZLSA .... Prace z Zakresu Lesnictwa [A publication]
PZM .... Pod Znamenem Marksizma [A publication]
PZO .... Peebles, OH [Location identifier] [FAA] (FAAL)
PZO .... Puerto Ordaz [Venezuela] [Airport symbol] (OAG)
PZP .... Phase Zero Program
PZP .... Pregnancy Zone Protein
PZPR .... Polska Zjednoczona Partia Robotnicza [Polish United Workers' Party - PUWP] (PPW)
PZQ .... Rogers City, MI [Location identifier] [FAA] (FAAL)
PZ(R) .... Penetration Zone (Radius) (MCD)
PZR .... Pressurizer (NRCH)
PZS .... President of the Zoological Society [British]
PZT .... Lead [Plumbum] Zirconate-Titanate [Piezoelectric transducer]
PZT .... Photographic Zenith Tube
PZT .... Piezoelectric Translator
PZT .... Piezoelectric Zirconate Titanate
PZT .... Polycrystalline Lead Zirconate Titanate [Piezoelectricity]
PZTFD .... Pis'ma v Zhurnal Tekhnicheskoi Fiziki [A publication]
PZU .... Port Sudan [Sudan] [Airport symbol] (OAG)
PZV .... New York, NY [Location identifier] [FAA] (FAAL)
PZWS .... Panstwowe Zaklady Wydawnictwo Szkolnych [A publication]
PZX .... Paragould, AR [Location identifier] [FAA] (FAAL)
PZY .... Piestany [Czechoslovakia] [Airport symbol] (OAG)
PZZ .... Pizza Patio Ltd. [Vancouver Stock Exchange symbol]

Q

Q .... Chicago, Burlington & Quincy Railroad [*Slang*]
Q .... Codex Marchalianus (BJA)
Q .... Coefficient of Association [*Statistics*]
Q .... Coenzyme Q [*Ubiquinone*] [*Also, CoQ, U, UQ*] [*Biochemistry*]
Q .... Coulomb [*Unit of quality*] (ROG)
Q .... Drone [*Designation for all US military aircraft*]
Q .... Dynamic Pressure [*NASA*]
Q .... Glutamine [*One-letter symbol; see Gln*]
Q .... Heat [*or q*] [*Symbol*] [*IUPAC*]
Q .... Merit of a Coil or Capacitor [*Electronics*]
q .... Partition Function, Particle [*Symbol*] [*IUPAC*]
Q .... Partition Function, System [*Symbol*] [*IUPAC*]
Q .... Polaris Correction [*Missiles*]
Q .... Proportion Not in a Specific Class
Q .... Q-Factor (DEN)
Q .... Qere (BJA)
Q .... Quadrans [*A Farthing*] [*Monetary unit*] [*British*]
Q .... Quadriceps [*Anatomy*]
Q .... Quadrillion BTU's [*Also known as "quads"*]
Q .... Quadrivium [*A publication*]
Q .... Quadruple
Q .... Quadruple Expansion Engine
Q .... Quaere [*Inquire*] [*Latin*]
Q .... Qualifier [*Linguistics*]
Q .... Quality Factor
Q .... Quantity
Q .... Quantity of Electricity [*Symbol*] [*IUPAC*]
Q .... Quaque [*Every*] [*Latin*]
Q .... Quart
Q .... Quarter
Q .... Quarter Word Designator [*Data processing*]
Q .... Quarterback [*Football*]
Q .... Quartering [*Military*] [*British*]
Q .... Quarterly
Q .... Quartermaster [*Military*]
Q .... Quarternary [*Geology*]
Q .... Quartile
Q .... Quartile [*Psychology*]
Q .... Quarto [*Book from 25 to 30 centimeters in height*]
Q .... Quarto Edition [*Shakespearean work*]
Q .... Quartz [*CIPW classification*] [*Geology*]
Q .... Quasi [*Almost, As It Were*] [*Latin*]
Q .... Quebec [*Phonetic alphabet*] [*International*] (DSUE)
Q .... Queen [*Phonetic alphabet*] [*Pre-World War II*] [*World War II*] (DSUE)
Q .... Queen
Q .... Queen [*Chess*]
Q .... Queenie [*Phonetic alphabet*] [*Royal Navy*] [*World War I*] (DSUE)
Q .... Queen's Quarterly [*A publication*]
Q .... Queensland [*Australia*]
Q .... Queensland Fever [*Disease first noted in farmers of Queensland, Australia*]
Q .... Queer [*Homosexual*] [*Slang*] (DSUE)
Q .... Query
Q .... Query Language [*1975*] (CSR)
Q .... Question
q .... Questioned [*Soundness of decision or reasoning in cited case questioned*] [*Used in Shepard's Citations*] (DLA)
Q .... Quetzal [*Monetary unit in Guatemala*]
Q .... Queue
Q .... Quick
Q .... Quick [*Flashing*] Light [*Navigation signal*]
Q .... Quiescit [*He Rests*] [*Latin*]
Q .... Quiller-Couch [*Sir Arthur, 1863-1944, English man of letters*] [*Letter used as pen name*]
Q .... Quinacrine [*Fluorescent method*] [*Chromosome stain*]
Q .... Quintal [*Unit of weight*]
Q .... Quintar [*Monetary unit in Albania*]
Q .... Quintus
Q .... Quinzaine [*A publication*]

Q .... Quire [*Measure of paper*]
Q .... Quisque [*Each, Every*] [*Pharmacy*]
Q .... Qumran (BJA)
Q .... Quorum (DLA)
Q .... Quotient (ADA)
Q .... Radiant Energy [*Symbol*] [*IUPAC*]
Q .... Receivership [*or Bankruptcy*] [*Designation used with NYSE symbols*]
Q .... Respiratory Quotient [*Also, RQ*] [*Physiology*]
Q .... San Quentin [*Prison*]
Q .... Semi-Interquartile Range or Quartile Deviation [*Statistics*]
Q .... Squall [*Meteorology*] (FAAC)
Q .... Volume Rate [*Heat transmission symbol*]
9Q .... Congo (Leopoldville) [*Aircraft nationality and registration mark*] (FAAC)
Q (Car) ...... Chrysler car made by Maserati
QA .... Inter City Airlines [*Great Britain*] [*ICAO designator*] (FAAC)
QA .... NRA [*National Restaurant Association*] Quality Assurance Study Group [*Chicago, IL*] (EA)
qa .... Qatar [*MARC country of publication code*] [*Library of Congress*] (LCCP)
QA .... Qatar [*Two-letter standard code*] (CNC)
QA .... Quadrans [*A Farthing*] [*Monetary unit*] [*British*] (ROG)
QA .... Quadripartite Agreement
QA .... Quality Assurance [*Data processing*]
QA .... Quarternary Ammonium [*Chemistry*]
QA .... Quarters Allowance
QA .... Query Analyzer (IEEE)
QA .... Query Author [*Proofreader's notation*]
Q & A .... Question and Answer (MSA)
QA .... Quick-Acting
QA .... Quick Assembly [*Furniture*]
QA .... Quiescent Aerial [*or Antenna*]
QA .... Quinic Acid [*Organic chemistry*]
QA .... Quisqualic Acid [*Biochemistry*]
QAA .... Alcan International Ltee. [*Alcan International Ltd.*] Jonquiere, Quebec [*Library symbol*] [*National Library of Canada*] (NLC)
QAA .... Quality Assurance Assistant [*DoD*]
QAA .... Quality Assurance Audit (MCD)
QAA .... Quinoline Amino Alcohol [*Organic chemistry*]
QAAS .... Quality Assurance Ammunition Specialist [*or Speciality*] (MCD)
QAB .... Queen Anne's Bounty
QAB .... Quick Action Button [*Military*] (CAAL)
QABA .... Biblitheque et Audiovisuel, Alma, Quebec [*Library symbol*] [*National Library of Canada*] (NLC)
QAC .... Quadrant Aimable Charge Warhead (MCD)
QAC .... Quadripartite Agreements Committee [*Military*]
QAC .... Quality Assurance Chart (MCD)
QAC .... Quality Assurance Checklist (NRCH)
QAC .... Quality Assurance Code
QAC .... Quality Assurance Criterion [*Nuclear energy*] (NRCH)
QAC .... Quarternary Ammonium Compound [*Chemistry*]
QACAD ...... Quality Assurance Corrective Action Document (NASA)
QACC Mot Trader ... QACC [*Queensland Automobile Chamber of Commerce*] Motor Trader [*A publication*]
Qad .... Qadmoniot [*Jerusalem*] (BJA)
QAD .... Quality Assurance Data
QAD .... Quality Assurance Directive
QAD .... Quality Assurance Directorate [*Materials*] [*British*]
QAD .... Quick Attach-Detach [*Engine*]
QADC .... Queen's Aide-de-Camp [*Military*] [*British*]
QADK .... Quick Attach-Detach Kit
QADS .... Quality Assurance Data System
QAE .... Quality Assurance Engineering
QAE .... Quality Assurance Evaluator [*Military*]
QAE .... Queen's Awards for Export [*British*]
QAET .... Quality Assurance Environment Testing [*Military*] (CAAL)
QAET .... Quality Assurance Evaluation Test (NG)
QAF .... Quality Assurance Function

QAFO .... Quality Assurance Field Operations
QAFS .... Amfesco Industries, Inc. [*NYSE symbol*]
Q Ag J .... Queensland Agricultural Journal [*A publication*]
QAI .... Quality Assurance Inspection
QAI .... Quality Assurance Instruction (NRCH)
QAIMNS ..... Queen Alexandra's Imperial Military Nursing Service [*British*]
QAIP .... Quality Assurance Inspection Procedure
QAIRG .... Quality Assurance Installation Review Group [*Nuclear energy*] (NRCH)
QAK .... Quick Attach Kit
QAL .... Quaderni di Archeologia della Libia [*A publication*]
QAL .... Quality Assurance Laboratory
QAL .... Quarterly Acceptance List (AFIT)
QAL .... Quarterly Accession List
QAL .... Quartz Aircraft Lamp
QAL .... Quebec Airways Limited (MCD)
QAL .... Quebec Aviation Ltd. [*Quebec City, PQ, Canada*] [*FAA designator*] (FAAC)
QALAS ...... Qualified Associate of the Land Agents' Society [*British*]
QALC .... College d'Alma, Lac St-Jean, Quebec [*Library symbol*] [*National Library of Canada*] (NLC)
QALL .... Quartz Aircraft Landing Lamp
QALTR .... Quality Assurance Laboratory Test Request (MCD)
QALY's .... Quality Adjusted Life Years
QAM .... Quadrature Amplitude Modulation
QAM .... Quality Assurance Manager
QAM .... Quality Assurance Manual
QAM .... Quaque Aente Meridiem [*Every Morning*] [*Pharmacy*]
QAM .... Queued Access Method [*Data processing*]
QAMDO ...... Quadripartite Agreed Materiel Development Objective [*Military*]
QAMIS .... Quality Assurance Monitoring Information System [*Environmental Protection Agency*]
QAML .... Centre de Documentation, Musee Laurier, Arthabaska, Quebec [*Library symbol*] [*National Library of Canada*] (NLC)
QAMR .... Quadripartite Agreed Materiel Requirement [*Military*]
QAMR .... Quality Assurance Management Review [*DoD*]
QAN .... Queensland Air Navigation Co. Ltd. [*Australia*] (ADA)
QANT .... Quantech Electronics [*NASDAQ symbol*] (NQ)
Qantas ...... Quantas Empire Airways [*A publication*]
QANTAS .... Queensland & Northern Territory Aerial Service [*Later, QANTAS Airways Ltd.*] [*Australian airline*]
Qantas E Air ... Qantas Empire Airways [*A publication*]
QAO .... Quality Assurance Office [*Navy*]
QAO .... Quality Assurance Operation
QAO .... Quality Assurance Outline
QAOP .... Quality Assurance Operating Plan
QAP .... Department of Antiquities in Palestine. Quarterly [*A publication*]
QAP .... Qualifications Appraisal Panel (OICC)
QAP .... Quality Assurance Plan
QAP .... Quality Assurance Procedures
QAP .... Quality Assurance Program
QAP .... Quality Assurance Provisions
QAP .... Quanah, Acme & Pacific Railway Co. [*AAR code*]
QAP .... Quinine, Atabrine, Plasmoquine [*Treatment for malaria*]
QAPED .... Quadripartite Agreed Plans of Engineering Design [*Military*]
QAPET .... Quadripartite Agreed Plans of Engineering Tests [*Military*]
QAPI .... Quality Assurance Program Index (NRCH)
QAPL .... Queensland Airlines Party Limited
Q Ap Math ... Quarterly of Applied Mathematics [*A publication*]
1QApoc ...... [*The*] Genesis Apocryphon from Qumran. Cave One (BJA)
QAPP .... Quality Assurance Program Plan (NRCH)
Q Appl Math ... Quarterly of Applied Mathematics [*A publication*]
Q App Math ... Quarterly of Applied Mathematics [*A publication*]
QAPST ...... Quadripartite Agreed Plans of Service Tests [*Military*]
QAR .... Quaderni di Archeologia Reggiana [*A publication*]
QAR .... Quality Assurance Record
QA & R ...... Quality Assurance and Reliability
QAR .... Quality Assurance Representative [*DoD*]
QAR .... Quality Assurance Requirements (NRCH)
QAR .... Quality Assurance Responsible/Witness (MCD)
QAR .... Quantitative Autoradiography [*Medicine*]
QAR .... Quasi-Adiabatic Representation
QAR .... Questionable Activity Report [*Employment and Training Administration*] [*Department of Labor*]
QAR .... Quick Access Recording
QARANC .... Queen Alexandra's Royal Army Nursing Corps [*British*]
QARC .... Quality Assurance Record Center (MCD)
QARC .... Quality Assurance Review Center [*National Cancer Institute*]
QARM .... Bibliotheque Municipale, Arthabaska, Quebec [*Library symbol*] [*National Library of Canada*] (NLC)
QARNNS .... Queen Alexandra's Royal Navy Nursing Service [*British*]
QAS .... Quality Assurance Service [*Medicine*]
QAS .... Quality Assurance Specialist [*DoD*]
QAS .... Question-Answering System
QAS .... Quick Action Shuttle
QASAC ...... Quality Assurance Spacecraft Acceptance Center (MCD)
QASAG ...... Experimental Farm, Agriculture Canada [*Ferme Experimentale, Agriculture Canada*] L'Assomption, Quebec [*Library symbol*] [*National Library of Canada*] (NLC)

QASAR ...... Quality Assurance Systems Analysis Review (FAAC)
QASAS ...... Quality Assurance Specialist, Ammunition Surveillance (MCD)
QASB .... Bibliotheque Municipale, Asbestos, Quebec [*Library symbol*] [*National Library of Canada*] (NLC)
QASC .... Quadripartite Armaments Standardization Committee [*Military*] (AABC)
QASK .... Quadrature Amplitude Shift Keying
QASL .... Quality Assurance Systems List (IEEE)
QASP .... Quality Assurance Standard Practice (MCD)
QAST .... Quality Assurance Service Test [*Nuclear energy*] (NG)
Qat .... Qatabanian (BJA)
QAT .... Qatar [*Three-letter standard code*] (CNC)
QAT .... Quaker Oats Co. [*Toronto Stock Exchange symbol*]
QAT .... Qualification Approval Test (NATG)
QAT .... Quality Assurance Team (MCD)
QATIP .... Quality Assurance Test and Inspection Procedures (MCD)
QATP .... Quality Assurance Technical Publications (AAG)
QAU .... Quality Assurance Unit
QAVC .... Quiet Automatic Volume Control
QAVT .... Qualification Acceptance Vibration Test [*NASA*] (NASA)
QB .... Qualified Bidders (FAAC)
QB .... Qualified Buyers
QB .... Quarterback [*Football*]
QB .... Quebecair, Inc. [*Airlines*] [*ICAO designator*] (OAG)
QB .... Queen's Bays [*Later, QDG*] [*Military unit*] [*British*]
QB .... Queen's Bench [*Legal*] [*British*]
QB .... Queen's Bench Reports, by Adolphus and Ellis, New Series (DLA)
QB .... Queen's Bishop [*Chess*]
QB .... Quick Break (MSA)
QB .... Quiet Birdmen [*An association*] (EA)
QBA .... Quality Bakers of America Cooperative [*Greenwich, CT*] (EA)
QBA .... Quality Brands Associates of America [*Defunct*] (EA)
QBA .... Quantitative Budget Analysis (MCD)
QBA .... Quebecair, Inc. [*Airlines*]
QBAC .... Quality Bakers of America Cooperative (EA)
QBACI .... Quality Bakers of America Cooperative, Incorporated
QBAN .... Qui Bixit Annos [*Who Lived _____ Years*] [*Latin*]
Q Bar News ... Queensland Bar News [*A publication*]
QBB .... Queen's Bad Bargain [*Undesirable serviceman*] [*Slang*] [*British*] (DSUE)
QBC .... Bella Coola [*Canada*] [*Airport symbol*] (OAG)
QBCB .... Quarterly Bulletin of Chinese Bibliography [*A publication*]
QBCDP ...... Quarterly Bibliography of Computers and Data Processing [*A publication*]
QBD .... Quasi Birth and Death [*Statistics*]
QBD .... Queen's Bench Division [*Military unit*] [*British*]
QB Div'l Ct ... Queen's Bench Divisional Court [*England*] (DLA)
QBDL .... Flanigan's Enterprises, Inc. [*Formerly, Big Daddy's Lounges, Inc.*] [*American Stock Exchange symbol*]
QBE .... Beaconsfield Public Library, Quebec [*Library symbol*] [*National Library of Canada*] (NLC)
QBE .... Query by Example [*Data processing search method*]
QBEC .... Bibliothequ Municipale, Becancour, Quebec [*Library symbol*] [*National Library of Canada*] (NLC)
QBEHBI ...... H. Bergstrom International Ltd., Beaconsfield, Quebec [*Library symbol*] [*National Library of Canada*] (NLC)
QBFJOTF ... [*The*] Quick Brown Fox Jumped over the Fence [*Typing exercise*]
QBFJOTLD ... [*The*] Quick Brown Fox Jumped over the Lazy Dogs [*Typing exercise*]
QBI .... Quite Bloody Impossible [*British slang, applied particularly to flying conditions*]
QBib .... Quarterly Bibliography of Computers and Data Processing [*A publication*]
QBJ .... Juniorat des Freres du Sacre-Coeur, Bramptonville, Quebec [*Library symbol*] [*National Library of Canada*] (NLC)
QBKI .... Beker Industries Corp. [*NYSE symbol*]
QBL .... Qualified Bidders List
QBLC .... Queen's Bench Reports, Lower Canada (DLA)
QBMS .... Mitel Semiconductor, Bromont, Quebec [*Library symbol*] [*National Library of Canada*] (NLC)
QBO .... Bibliotheque Municipale, Boucherville, Quebec [*Library symbol*] [*National Library of Canada*] (NLC)
QBO .... Quasi-Biennial Oscillation [*Earth science*]
Q-BOP .... Quick Basic Oxygen Process [*Steelmaking*]
QBR .... Quebecor, Inc. [*Toronto Stock Exchange symbol*]
QBR .... Queen's Bench Reports [*Legal*] [*British*]
QBR .... Queen's Bench Reports, by Adolphus and Ellis, New Series (DLA)
QBRG .... Centre Hospitalier Robert Giffard, Beauport, Quebec [*Library symbol*] [*National Library of Canada*] (NLC)
QBSM .... Que Besa Sus Manos [*Kissing Your Hands*] [*Spanish*]
QBSP .... Que Besa Sus Pies [*Kissing Your Feet*] [*Spanish*]
QBUC .... Queen's Bench Reports, Upper Canada (DLA)
Q Building Yrbk ... Queensland Building Yearbook [*A publication*]
Q Bull Am Rhodod Soc ... Quarterly Bulletin. American Rhododendron Society [*A publication*]
Q Bull Assoc Food Drug Off ... Quarterly Bulletin. Association of Food and Drug Officials [*A publication*]

Q Bull Assoc Food Drug Off US ... Quarterly Bulletin. Association of Food and Drug Officials of the United States [*Later, Quarterly Bulletin. Association of Food and Drug Officials*] [*A publication*]

Q Bull Fac Sci Tehran Univ ... Quarterly Bulletin. Faculty of Science. Tehran University [*A publication*]

Q Bull Geo-Heat Util Cent ... Quarterly Bulletin. Geo-Heat Utilization Center [*United States*] [*A publication*]

Q Bull Health Organ League Nations ... Quarterly Bulletin. Health Organisation. League of Nations [*A publication*]

Q Bull IAALD ... Quarterly Bulletin. International Association of Agricultural Librarians and Documentalists [*A publication*]

Q Bull Int Ass Agric Libr ... Quarterly Bulletin. International Association of Agricultural Librarians and Documentalists [*A publication*]

Q Bull Int Assoc Agric Libr & Doc ... Quarterly Bulletin. International Association of Agricultural Librarians and Documentalists [*A publication*]

Q Bull Mich St Univ Agric Exp Stn ... Quarterly Bulletin. Michigan State University. Agricultural Experiment Station [*A publication*]

Q Bull Natl Res Counc Can Div Mech Eng ... Quarterly Bulletin. National Research Council of Canada. Division of Mechanical Engineering [*A publication*]

Q Bull Northwest Univ Med Sch ... Quarterly Bulletin. Northwestern University Medical School [*A publication*]

Q Bull S Afr Libr ... Quarterly Bulletin. South African Library [*A publication*]

Q Bull S Afr Natl Gall ... Quarterly Bulletin. South African National Gallery [*A publication*]

QC .... QC Explorations [*Vancouver Stock Exchange symbol*]

QC .... Quad Center [*Typography*]

QC .... Quaderni della Critica [*A publication*]

QC .... Qualification Course

QC .... Quality Circle [*Labor-management team organized to increase industrial productivity*]

QC .... Quality Control [*or Controller*]

QC .... Quantek Corporation [*Trademark*]

QC .... Quantitative Command

QC .... Quantum Counter

QC .... Quarter of Coverage [*Social Security Administration*]   (OICC)

QC .... Quarterly Credit

QC .... Quartz Crystal

QC .... Quaternary Carrier [*Biochemistry*]

QC .... Quebec Central Railway Co. [*AAR code*]

QC .... Queen Consort [*British*]   (ROG)

QC .... Queen's College [*Oxford and Cambridge Universities*]   (ROG)

QC .... Queen's Counsel [*British*]

QC .... Quench Correction

QC .... Quick Cleaning   (MSA)

QC .... Quick Connect

QC .... Quick Curl [*Refers to Barbie doll hair*] [*Doll collecting*]

QC .... Quiesce-Completed [*Data processing*]   (IBMDP)

QC .... Quiescent Center [*Plant root growth*]

QC .... Quixote Center   (EA)

QC .... Societe Air-Zaire [*ICAO designator*]   (FAAC)

QCA .... Quarterly Compilation of Abstracts [*A publication*]

QCA .... Queen Charlotte Airlines Ltd.

QCAG .... Ministere de l'Agriculture, des Pecheries et de l'Alimentation, Chateauguay, Quebec [*Library symbol*] [*National Library of Canada*]   (NLC)

QCAI .... Quality Conformance Acceptance Inspection   (MCD)

Q Can Studies ... Quarterly of Canadian Studies [*A publication*]

Q Case Note ... Queensland Law Reporter Case Note [*A publication*]

QCB .... Bibliotheque Municipale, Coaticook, Quebec [*Library symbol*] [*National Library of Canada*]   (NLC)

QCB .... Quality Control Board   (MCD)

QCB .... Queue Control Block [*Data processing*]

QCC .... Bibliotheque Gaspesienne, Cap-Chat, Quebec [*Library symbol*] [*National Library of Canada*]   (NLC)

QCC .... Quaderni di Cultura Contemporanea [*A publication*]

QCC .... Qualification Correlation Certification

QCC .... Quality Communications Circle   (MCD)

QCC .... Quality Control Committee   (MCD)

QCC .... Queen Charlotte [*British Columbia*] [*Seismograph station code, US Geological Survey*]   (SEIS)

QCC .... Quenched Carbonaceous Composite [*Plasma technology*]

QCC .... Quick Connect Coupling

QCC .... Quinsigamond Community College [*Worchester, MA*]

QCCARS .... Quality Control Collection Analysis and Reporting System

QCCRS ...... Conseil Regional de la Sante et des Services Sociaux, Chicoutimi, Quebec [*Library symbol*] [*National Library of Canada*]   (NLC)

QCD .... Quality Control Data

QCD .... Quantum Chromodynamics [*Nuclear physics*]

QCDPA .... Quality Chekd Dairy Products Association [*Hinsdale, IL*]   (EA)

QCDR .... Quality Control Deficiency Report   (AFM)

QCE .... Quality Control Engineers

QCE .... Quality Control and Evaluation   (MCD)

QCEA .... Quaker Council for European Affairs   (EA)

Q Census & Statistics Bul ... Australia. Commonwealth Bureau of Census and Statistics. Queensland Office. Bulletin [*A publication*]

QCF .... Quality Control [*Tabulating*] Form   (AAG)

QCF .... Quarterly Control Contract Factor   (MCD)

QCF .... Quartz Crystal Filter

QCF .... Quench Compensation Factor

QCFO .... Quartz Crystal Frequency Oscillator

QCG .... Quartz Creek Gold Mines (BC), Inc. [*Vancouver Stock Exchange symbol*]

QCGAT ...... Quiet, Clean, General Aviation Turbofan [*NASA*]

QCH .... Hopital de Chicoutimi, Inc., Quebec [*Library symbol*] [*National Library of Canada*]   (NLC)

QCH .... Quick Connect Handle

QCHJC .... Health Sciences Information Centre, Jewish Rehabilitation Hospital [*Centre d'Information sur les Sciences de la Sante, Hopital Juif de Readaptation*] Chomedey, Quebec [*Library symbol*] [*National Library of Canada*]   (NLC)

QCHM .... Quaker Chemical [*NASDAQ symbol*]   (NQ)

QCHR .... Quality Control History Record

QCI .... Quality Conformance Inspection   (MSA)

QCI .... Quality Control Information   (AABC)

QCI .... Quarto Castello [*Italy*] [*Seismograph station code, US Geological Survey*] [*Closed*]   (SEIS)

QCI .... Queen's College, Ireland   (ROG)

QCI .... Quota Club International [*Later, QI*]

QCI's .... Queen Charlotte Islands

QCIE .... Quality Control Inspection Element   (AFIT)

QCIM .... Quarterly Cumulative Index Medicus [*A publication*]

QCIP .... Quality Control Inspection Procedure [*Nuclear energy*]   (NRCH)

QCIR .... Queen's University at Kingston Centre for International Relations [*Canada*] [*Research center*]   (RCD)

QCK .... Quick Connect Kit

Qckslv .... Quicksilver Times [*A publication*]

QCL .... Logilab, Inc., Charlebois, Quebec [*Library symbol*] [*National Library of Canada*]   (NLC)

QCL .... Quality Characteristics List   (MSA)

QCL .... Quality Checklist

QCL .... Quality Control Level

QCL .... Queensland Conveyancing Library [*A publication*]

QCLBS ...... Quarterly Check-List of Biblical Studies [*A publication*]

QCLC .... CLC of America, Inc. [*Formerly, Consolidated Leasing Corporation of America*] [*NYSE symbol*]

QCLLR .... Crown Lands Law Reports Queensland [*A publication*]

QCLLR .... Queensland Crown Lands Law Reports [*A publication*]

QCLPC ...... National Historic Park, Parks Canada [*Parc Historique National, Parcs Canada*] Coteau-du-Lac, Quebec [*Library symbol*] [*National Library of Canada*]   (NLC)

QCM .... Quality Control Manager

QCM .... Quality Control Manual

QCM .... Quality Courts Motels [*Later, QM*]

QCM .... Quantitative Computer Management   (IEEE)

QCM .... Quantum Conformal Fluctuation [*Theoretical physics*]

QCM .... Quartz Crystal Microbalance

QCM .... Quartz Crystal Monitor

QCMB .... Centre de Documentation, Musee Beaulne, Coaticook, Quebec [*Library symbol*] [*National Library of Canada*]   (NLC)

QCMM .... Bibliotheque Municipale, Cap-De-La-Madeleine, Quebec [*Library symbol*] [*National Library of Canada*]   (NLC)

QCO .... Quality Control Officer   (AAG)

QCO .... Quality Control Organization

QCO .... Quartz Crystal Oscillator

QCOA .... QCOA: Journal of the Queensland Council on the Ageing [*A publication*]

Q Colo Sch Mines ... Quarterly. Colorado School of Mines [*A publication*]

Q Coop ...... Queensland Co-Operator [*A publication*]

QCOP .... Quality Control Operating Procedure

Q Countrywoman ... Queensland Countrywoman [*A publication*]

QCP .... Quality Check Program [*DoD*]

QCP .... Quality Continuation Plan [*BMW manufacturer's warranty*]

QCP .... Quality Control Procedure

QCP .... Quezon City [*Philippines*] [*Seismograph station code, US Geological Survey*]   (SEIS)

QCPE .... Quantum Chemistry Program Exchange

QCPI .... Queen's College of Physicians, Ireland   (ROG)

QCPMS ...... Quality Control and Performance Monitoring System   (MCD)

QCPSA .... Quaker Center for Prisoner Support Activities   (EA)

QCPSK ...... Quaternary Coherent Phase-Shift Keying

QCQ .... Quebec [*Quebec*] [*Seismograph station code, US Geological Survey*]   (SEIS)

QCR .... Qualitative Construction Requirement [*Army*]

QCR .... Quality Control/Reliability

QCR .... Quality Control Report

QCR .... Quality Control Representative   (AABC)

QCR .... Quality Control Review

QCR .... Quality Control Room

QCR .... Queensland Criminal Reports [*A publication*]

QCR .... Quick Change Response [*System*]

QCR .... Quick Connect Relay

QCRCN ...... Campus Notre-Dame-De-Foy, Cap-Rouge, Quebec [*Library symbol*] [*National Library of Canada*]   (NLC)

QCRS .... Seminaire St-Augustin, Cap-Rouge, Quebec [*Library symbol*] [*National Library of Canada*]   (NLC)

QCS .... Quad-Cities Station [*Nuclear energy*]   (NRCH)

QCS .... Quality Control Standard   (AAG)

QCS .... Quality Control System

QCS............ Quality Cost System
QCS............ Query Control Station (MCD)
QCSC........ Quadripartite Chemical, Biological, Radiological
        Standardization Committee [*Military*] (AABC)
QCSEE....... Quiet, Clean, Short-Haul Experimental Engine [*NASA*]
QCSEL...... Quality Control Select Vendor (MCD)
QCSH........ Societe Historique du Saguenay, Chicoutimi, Quebec [*Library
        symbol*] [*National Library of Canada*] (NLC)
QCSM .... Quiescent Command/Service Module (MCD)
QCSS .... Quaderni di Cultura e Storia Sociale [*A publication*]
QCSSP...... Quality Control Single Source Procurement (MCD)
QCT........... Questionable Corrective Task
QCTR .... Quality Control Test Report
QCU .... Quality Courts United [*Later, QM*] (EA)
QCU .... Quartz Crystal Unit
QCU .... Quick Change Unit (MCD)
QCU .... Universite du Quebec, Chicoutimi, Quebec [*Library symbol*]
        [*National Library of Canada*] (NLC)
QCUG........ Departement de Geographie, Universite du Quebec,
        Chicoutimi, Quebec [*Library symbol*] [*National Library of
        Canada*] (NLC)
QCUGC...... Cartotheque, Universite du Quebec, Chicoutimi, Quebec
        [*Library symbol*] [*National Library of Canada*] (NLC)
Q Cum Index Med ... Quarterly Cumulative Index Medicus [*A publication*]
QCUS .... Quartz Crystal Unit Set
QCVC........ Quick Connect Valve Coupler
QCW.......... Quadrant Continuous Wave
QCWA .... Quarter Century Wireless Association
QD .... QData Systems, Inc. [*Vancouver Stock Exchange symbol*]
QD .... Quaderni Dannunziani [*A publication*]
QD .... Quaestiones Disputatae (BJA)
QD .... Quantity Distance [*Explosives*]
QD .... Quaque Die [*Every Day*] [*Pharmacy*]
QD .... Quarter Distribution [*Parapsychology*]
QD .... Quarterdeck
QD .... Quartile Deviation [*Statistics*]
QD .... Quasi Dicat [*As If One Should Say, or As Though One Should
        Say*] [*Latin*]
QD .... Quasi Dictum [*As If Said, or As Though It Had Been Said*]
        [*Latin*]
QD .... Quasi Dixisset [*As If One Had Said*] [*Latin*]
QD .... Quater in Die [*Four Times a Day*] [*Pharmacy*]
QD .... Questioned Document [*Criminology*]
Q & D .... Quick and Dirty [*Data processing*]
QD .... Quick Disconnect
QD .... Quicksilver Data [*Concord, MA*] [*Information service*] (EISS)
6QD .... Damascus Document [*or Sefer Berit Damesek*] from Qumran.
        Cave Six (BJA)
QDA.......... Quantitative Descriptive Analysis
QDA.......... Quantity Discount Agreement
QDA.......... Quarterly. Department of Antiquities in Palestine [*Jerusalem*]
        [*A publication*]
Qd Ag J ...... Queensland Agricultural Journal [*A publication*]
Qd Agric J ... Queensland Agricultural Journal [*A publication*]
QDAP .... Quarterly. Department of Antiquities in Palestine [*Jerusalem*]
        [*A publication*]
Qd Bur Invest Tech Bull ... Queensland. Department of Public Lands.
        Bureau of Investigation. Technical Bulletin [*A publication*]
Qd Bur Sug Exp Stat Tech Commun ... Queensland. Bureau of Sugar
        Experiment Stations. Technical Communication [*A
        publication*]
Qd Bur Sug Exp Stn Tech Commun ... Queensland. Bureau of Sugar
        Experiment Stations. Technical Communication [*A
        publication*]
QDC .... Quick Dependable Communications
QDC .... Quick Disconnect Cap
QDC .... Quick Disconnect Connector
QDCC........ Quick Disconnect Circular Connector
QDCE........ College Bourgchemin (CEGEP), Drummondville, Quebec
        [*Library symbol*] [*National Library of Canada*] (NLC)
Qd Chamber Manufacturers Yb ... Queensland Chamber of Manufacturers.
        Yearbook [*A publication*]
QDD .... Qualified for Deep Diving Duties [*Navy*] [*British*]
QDD .... Quantized Decision Detection
Qd Dent J ... Queensland Dental Journal [*A publication*]
Qd Dent Mag ... Queensland Dental Magazine [*A publication*]
QDE........... Qualified Designated Entities [*Independent counseling groups
        and churches involved with aiding aliens*] [*Immigration
        and Naturalization Service term*]
Q Dent Rev ... Quarterly Dental Review [*A publication*]
4QDeut32 ... Manuscript of Deuteronomy 32 from Qumran. Cave 4 (BJA)
QDF........... Quantum Distribution Function
Qd For Dep Adv Leafl ... Queensland. Department of Forestry. Advisory
        Leaflet [*A publication*]
Qd For Dep Pamph ... Queensland. Department of Forestry. Pamphlet [*A
        publication*]
Qd Forest Bull ... Queensland Forest Bulletin [*A publication*]
QDG .... Queen's Dragoon Guards [*Formerly, KDG, QB*] [*Military unit*]
        [*British*]
Qd Geogr J ... Queensland Geographical Journal [*A publication*]

Qd Geol Surv 1:250 000 Geol Ser ... Queensland. Geological Survey.
        1:250,000 Geological Series [*A publication*]
Qd Geol Surv Rep ... Queensland. Geological Survey. Report [*A publication*]
Qd Govt Min J ... Queensland Government Mining Journal [*A publication*]
QDH........... Quick Disconnect Handle
Qd Heritage ... Queensland Heritage [*A publication*]
QDHSC ...... Hopital Sainte-Croix, Drummondville, Quebec [*Library symbol*]
        [*National Library of Canada*] (NLC)
Q Digger .... Queensland Digger [*A publication*]
QDISC....... Quick Disconnect
Qd J Agric Anim Sci ... Queensland Journal of Agricultural and Animal
        Sciences [*A publication*]
Qd J Agric Sci ... Queensland Journal of Agricultural Science [*Later,
        Queensland Journal of Agricultural and Animal Sciences*]
        [*A publication*]
QDK .... Quick Disconnect Kit
QDL .... Quick Disconnect, Large
QDM.......... Bibliotheque Municipale, Drummondville, Quebec [*Library
        symbol*] [*National Library of Canada*] (NLC)
QDM .... Centre d'Information Documentaire Come-Saint-Germain,
        Drummondville, Quebec [*Library symbol*] [*National
        Library of Canada*] (NLC)
QDM .... Magnetic Heading (Zero Wind) [*to steer to reach me*] [*Aviation
        code*] (FAAC)
QDM .... Quick Disconnect, Miniature
1QDM .... [*The*] Words of Moses from Qumran. Cave One (BJA)
QDMBPT .... Quasi-Degenerate Many-Body Perturbation Theory [*Physics*]
QDN .... Quick Disconnect Nipple
Qd Nat....... Queensland Naturalist [*A publication*]
QDO .... Quadripartite Development Objective [*Military*] (AABC)
QDOPH....... Office des Personnes Handicapees du Quebec,
        Drummondville, Quebec [*Library symbol*] [*National
        Library of Canada*] (NLC)
QDP........... Quick Disconnect Pivot
Qd Prod ...... Queensland Producer [*A publication*]
QDPSK....... Quaternary Differential Phase-Shift Keying (TEL)
QDR........... Dubai Riyal [*Monetary unit in Dubai*]
QDR........... Magnetic Bearing [*from me*] [*Aviation code*] (FAAC)
QDR........... Qualification Design Review (MCD)
QDR........... Quality Data and Reporting (MCD)
QDR........... Quality Deficiency Record [*DoD*]
QDR........... Quality Deficiency Report [*DoD*]
Qd R .... Queensland Reports [*A publication*]
QDRI.......... Qualitative Development Requirement Information
QDRNT...... Quadrant (MSA)
QDRT .... Qadrant Corp. [*NASDAQ symbol*] (NQ)
QDRT........ Quadrant
QDRTR...... Quadrature
QDS........... Quality Data System (NASA)
QDS........... Quarantine Document System [*Information retrieval*] [*NASA*]
QDS........... Quick Disconnect Series
QDS........... Quick Disconnect, Small
QDS........... Quick Disconnect Swivel
Qd Surv ...... Queensland Surveyor [*A publication*]
QDT........... Quintessence of Dental Technology
QDTA .... Quantitative Differential Thermal Analysis
QDU........... Dusseldorf-Main RR [*West Germany*] [*Airport symbol*] (OAG)
Qd Univ Agric Dep Pap ... University of Queensland. Agriculture
        Department. Papers [*A publication*]
Qd Univ Bot Dep Pap ... University of Queensland. Botany Department.
        Papers [*A publication*]
Qd Univ Civ Engng Dep Bull ... University of Queensland. Department of
        Civil Engineering. Bulletin [*A publication*]
Qd Univ Comput Centre Pap ... University of Queensland. Computer Centre.
        Papers [*A publication*]
Qd Univ Ent Dep Pap ... University of Queensland. Entomology Department.
        Papers [*A publication*]
Qd Univ Fac Vet Sci Pap ... University of Queensland. Faculty of Veterinary
        Science. Papers [*A publication*]
Qd Univ Geol Dep Pap ... University of Queensland. Geology Department.
        Papers [*A publication*]
Qd Univ Pap Zool Dep ... University of Queensland. Zoology Department.
        Papers [*A publication*]
Qd Univ Zool Dep Pap ... University of Queensland. Zoology Department.
        Papers [*A publication*]
QDV........... Quick Disconnect Valve
Qd Vet Proc ... Queensland Veterinary Proceedings [*A publication*]
QDXR .... Quadriplexer
QE .... Air Tahiti [*ICAO designator*] (FAAC)
QE .... Journal of Quantum Electronics [*A publication*] (MCD)
QE .... Quadrant Elevation
QE .... Quaestiones et Salutationes in Exodum [*Philo*] (BJA)
QE .... Quality Engineering
QE .... Quality Evaluation (NG)
QE .... Queue Entry
QE .... Quod Est [*Which Is*] [*Latin*]
QE .... Quotation Estimate (MCD)
QE 2........... Queen Elizabeth 2 [*Luxury liner*]
QEA........... QANTAS Empire Airways Ltd. [*Later, QANTAS Airways Ltd.*]
QeA .... Questo e Alto [*A publication*]
QEAE .... Quarternary Ethylaminoethyl [*Organic chemistry*]

QEAM........ Quick Erecting Antenna Mast [Army] (RDA)
QEAS........ Quantum Electronics and Applications Society (MCD)
QEAV........ Quick Exhaust Air Valve
QEB........... Quality Engineering Bulletin [NASA]
QEBG........ Quellen und Eroerterungen zur Bayerischen Geschichte [A publication]
QEC........... Quantum Electronics Council
QEC........... Quantum Energy [Vancouver Stock Exchange symbol]
QEC........... Queen Elizabeth College [London]
QEC........... Quick Engine Change
QEC........... Quiesce-at-End-of-Chain [Data processing] (IBMDP)
QECA........ Quick Engine Change Assembly (NG)
QECCH...... Compton County Historical and Museum Society [Societe d'Histoire et du Musee du Comte de Compton] Eaton Corner, Quebec [Library symbol] [National Library of Canada] (NLC)
QECK........ Quick Engine Change Kit (NG)
Q Econ Comment ... Quarterly Economic Commentary [A publication]
Q Econ R .... Quarterly Economic Review [Seoul] [A publication]
QECS........ Quick Engine Change Stand (NG)
QECU........ Quick Engine Change Unit
QED........... Quantum Electrodynamics
QED........... Quentin E. Deverill [Protagonist in TV series; initialism also used as title of the series]
QED........... Quick Erection Dome
QED........... Quick Text Editor
QED........... Quod Erat Demonstrandum [Which Was the Thing to Be Proved] [Latin]
Q Ed Off Gaz ... Education Office Gazette (Queensland Department of Education) [A publication]
QEDX........ QED Exploration [NASDAQ symbol] (NQ)
QEEL........ Quality Evaluation and Engineering Laboratory [Navy]
QEEL/CO... Quality Evaluation and Engineering Laboratory, Concord [California] [Navy]
QEF........... Quod Erat Faciendum [Which Was to Be Made, or Done] [Latin]
QEH........... Queen Elizabeth Hall [London, England]
QEH........... Queen Elizabeth's Hospital School [England]
QEI........... Quod Erat Inveniendum [Which Was to Be Found Out] [Latin]
QEL........... Quality Evaluation Laboratory
QEL........... Quiet Extended Life
Q Elec Contractor ... Queensland Electrical Contractor [A publication]
QElecSC .... Quadripartite Electronic Standardization Committee [Military] (AABC)
QELS........ Quantitative Evaluation of Library Searching [Spectra matching technique]
QELS........ Quasi-Elastic Light Scattering [Also, QLS] [Particle size analysis]
QEM........... Quadrant Electrometer
QEM........... Qualified Export Manager [Designation given by American Society of International Executives]
QEN........... Quare Executionem Non [Wherefore Execution Should Not Be Issued] [Latin] (DLA)
QEngrSC ... Quadripartite Engineer Standardization Committee [Military] (AABC)
QEO........... Quality Engineering Operations
QEOP........ Quartermaster Emergency Operation Plan [Army]
QEP........... Quality Evaluation Program [College of American Pathologists]
QEP........... Quality Examination Program (AFM)
QEPL........ Quality Engineering Planning List (MCD)
QER........... Qualitative Equipment Requirements [Army] (AABC)
QER........... Quarterly Economic Review [A publication]
QES........... Quadrant Eleventh-Gram Second
QES........... Quaker Esperanto Society (EA)
QESCP....... Quality Engineering Significant Control Points (MCD)
QEST........ Quality Evaluation System Tests (NG)
QEST........ Query, Update Entry, Search, Time-Sharing System (NVT)
QET........... Quasi-Equilibrium Theory [Physical chemistry]
QEV........... Quick Exhaust Valve
QEVY........ Evans Products Co. [NYSE symbol]
QEW........... Queen Elizabeth Way [Canada]
QF............. Qabel Foundation (EA)
QF............. QANTAS Airways Ltd. [Australia] [ICAO designator] (OAG)
QF............. Qualifying Facility [Electric power]
QF............. Quality Factor
QF............. Quality Form (NRCH)
QF............. Quellen und Forschungen aus Italienischen Archiven und Bibliotheken [A publication]
QF............. Quellen und Forschungen zur Sprach- und Kulturgeschichte der Germanischen Voelker [A publication]
QF............. Quench Frequency (DEN)
QF............. Queue Full
QF............. Quick-Firing [Gun]
QF............. Quick Fix (MCD)
QF............. Quick Freeze
QFAB........ Quellen und Forschungen aus Italienischen Archiven und Bibliotheken [A publication]
QFB........... Quiet Fast Boat [Navy symbol]
QFC........... Quantitative Flight Characteristics
QFCC........ Quantitative Flight Characteristics Criteria
QFD........... Quantum Flavor Dynamics

QFD........... Quarterly Forecast Demand
QFE........... Atmospheric Pressure at Aerodrome Elevation [or Runway Threshold] [Aviation code] (FAAC)
QFE........... Columbus [Georgia] Fort Benning [Airport symbol] (OAG)
QFE........... Query Formulation and Encoding
QFF........... Quadrupole Flip-Flop [Data processing]
QFI........... Qualified Flight Instructor
QFI........... Quellen und Forschungen aus Italienischen Archiven und Bibliotheken [A publication]
QFIAB .... Quellen und Forschungen aus Italienischen Archiven und Bibliotheken [A publication]
Q Film Radio TV ... Quarterly of Film, Radio, and Television [A publication]
QFIRC .... Quick Fix Interference Reduction Capability (AFM)
QFL........... Quasi-Fermi Level
4QFlor .... Florilegium. A Miscellany from Qumran. Cave Four (BJA)
QFLOW ..... Quota Flow Control Procedures (FAAC)
QFM........... Quantized Frequency Modulation
QFM........... Quartz-Fayalite-Magnetite [Geology]
QFMR....... Quantized Frequency Modulation Repeater
QFO........... Quartz Frequency Oscillator
QFP........... Quartz Fiber Product
QFP........... Quick Fix Program
QFr .... Epistulae ad Quintum Fratrem [of Cicero] [Classical studies] (OCD)
QFR........... Quarterly Financial Report for Manufacturing Corporations [A publication]
QFR........... Quarterly Force Revision [Military] (NVT)
QFRT........ Quarterly of Film, Radio, and Television [A publication]
Q Fruit & Veg News ... Queensland Fruit and Vegetable News [A publication]
QFSK .... Quellen und Forschungen zur Sprach- und Kulturgeschichte der Germanischen Voelker [A publication]
QFSM .... Queen's Fire Service Medal for Distinguished Service [British]
QFT .... Quantized Field Theory
QFU........... Magnetic Orientation of Runway [Aviation code] (FAAC)
Q Fuel Energy Summ ... Quarterly Fuel and Energy Summary [United States] [A publication]
QG............. Bibliotheque Municipale, Gatineau, Quebec [Library symbol] [National Library of Canada] (NLC)
QG............. Quadrature Grid
QG............. Quaestiones et Salutationes in Genesin [Philo] (BJA)
QG............. Quartermaster General [Military]
QG............. Quartier General [Headquarters] [French]
QG............. Seychelles-Kilimanjaro Air Transport Ltd. [Kenya] [ICAO designator] (FAAC)
QGAP .... Centre de Documentation en Peches Maritimes, Ministere de l'Agriculture, des Pecheries et de l'Alimentation, Gaspe, Quebec [Library symbol] [National Library of Canada] (NLC)
QGBF .... Quasi-Grain Boundary Free [Photovoltaic energy systems]
QGC .... College de la Gaspesie, Gaspe, Quebec [Library symbol] [National Library of Canada] (NLC)
QGCH........ Centre Hospitalier de Gatineau, Quebec [Library symbol] [National Library of Canada] (NLC)
1QGen........ [The] Genesis Apocryphon from Qumran. Cave One (BJA)
Q Geog J .... Queensland Geographical Journal [A publication]
Q Geol Notes Geol Surv South Aust ... South Australia. Geological Survey. Quarterly Geological Notes [A publication]
QGG........... Queensland Government Gazette [A publication]
QGHR........ Quellen zur Geschichte des Humanismus und der Reformation in Facsimile-Ausgaben [A publication]
QGIG .... Queensland Government Industrial Gazette [A publication]
QGJD .... Quellen zur Geschichte der Juden in Deutschland [A publication]
QGL........... Granby Leader Mail Office, Quebec [Library symbol] [National Library of Canada] (NLC)
QGLM........ Global Marine, Inc. [NYSE symbol]
QGM........... Bibliotheque Municipale, Granby, Quebec [Library symbol] [National Library of Canada] (NLC)
QGM........... Queen's Gallantry Medal [British]
QGM........... Quellen und Studien zur Geschichte der Mathematik [A publication]
QGMath ..... Quellen und Studien zur Geschichte der Mathematik [A publication]
QGMM....... Bibliotheque Municipale, Grand'Mere, Quebec [Library symbol] [National Library of Canada] (NLC)
QGO .... Queen's Gurkha Officer [Military] [British]
Q Gov Indus Gaz ... Queensland Government Industrial Gazette [A publication]
Q Govt Min J ... Queensland Government Mining Journal [A publication]
Q Govt PRB News Bul ... Queensland Government Public Relations Bureau. News Bulletin [A publication]
QGP........... Queensland Government Publications [A publication]
Q Graingrower ... Queensland Graingrower [A publication]
QGS........... Quantity Gauging System (NASA)
QGSH........ Societe Historique du Comte de Shefford, Granby, Quebec [Library symbol] [National Library of Canada] (NLC)
QGV........... Quantized Gate Video [RADAR]
QH............. Air Florida, Inc. [ICAO designator] (FAAC)
QH............. Bibliotheque Municipale, Hull, Quebec [Library symbol] [National Library of Canada] (NLC)
QH............. Quaker History [A publication]

QH .... Quaque Hora [*Every Hour*] [*Pharmacy*]
QH .... Quartz Helix
QH .... Queensland Heritage [*A publication*]
QH .... Quorn Hounds
1QH .... Hodayot. Hymns of Thanksgiving from Qumran. Cave One (BJA)
Q2H .... Quaque Secunda Hora [*Every Second Hour*] [*Pharmacy*]
Q3H .... Quaque Tertia Hora [*Every Third Hour*] [*Pharmacy*]
Q4H .... Quaque Quarta Hora [*Every Fourth Hour*] [*Pharmacy*]
QHAC .... CEGEP de Hauterive, Baie Comeau, Quebec [*Library symbol*] [*National Library of Canada*] (NLC)
QHACR ...... Conseil Regional de la Sante et des Services Sociaux de la Region Cote-Nord, Hauterive, Quebec [*Library symbol*] [*National Library of Canada*] (NLC)
QHB .... Bell Canada Documentation Resource Center, Hull, Quebec [*Library symbol*] [*National Library of Canada*] (NLC)
QHB .... Queen's Hard Bargain [*Undesirable serviceman*] [*Slang*] [*British*] (DSUE)
QHBE .... Headquarters Economics Library, Bell Canada, Hull, Quebec [*Library symbol*] [*National Library of Canada*] (NLC)
QHBEER ..... Headquarters Engineering Economics Reference Centre, Bell Canada, Hull, Quebec [*Library symbol*] [*National Library of Canada*] (NLC)
QHC .... CEGEP de l'Outaouais, Hull, Quebec [*Library symbol*] [*National Library of Canada*] (NLC)
QHC .... Queen's Honorary Chaplain [*British*]
QHCH .... Heritage Campus, CEGEP de l'Outaouais, Hull, Quebec [*Library symbol*] [*National Library of Canada*] (NLC)
QHCL .... Centre de Documentation, CLSC de Hull, Quebec [*Library symbol*] [*National Library of Canada*] (NLC)
QHCRS ...... Conseil Regional de la Sante et des Services Sociaux de la Region Outaouais-Hull, Hull, Quebec [*Library symbol*] [*National Library of Canada*] (NLC)
QHDS .... Queen's Honorary Dental Surgeon [*British*]
QHE .... E. B. Eddy Co., Hull, Quebec [*Library symbol*] [*National Library of Canada*] (NLC)
Q Health ..... Queensland's Health [*A publication*]
QHEX .... Heck's, Inc. [*NYSE symbol*]
QHM .... Queen's Harbour Master [*British*]
QHNS .... Queen's Honorary Nursing Sister [*British*]
QHO .... Queen's Hall Orchestra
QHP .... Queen's Honorary Physician [*British*]
QHP .... Quiet Helicopter Program (RDA)
QHPJ .... Centre Hospitalier Pierre Janet, Hull, Quebec [*Library symbol*] [*National Library of Canada*] (NLC)
QHR .... Quality History Records (NRCH)
QHR .... Queensland Historical Review [*A publication*]
QHS .... Qinghaosu [*Antimalarial drug*]
QHS .... Queen's Honorary Surgeon [*British*]
QHSA .... Societe d'Amenagement de l'Outaouais, Hull, Quebec [*Library symbol*] [*National Library of Canada*] (NLC)
QHSC .... Centre Hospitalier Regional de l'Outaouais, Hull, Quebec [*Library symbol*] [*National Library of Canada*] (NLC)
QHTA Bull ... QHTA [*Queensland History Teachers Association*] Bulletin [*A publication*]
QHU .... Universite du Quebec, Hull, Quebec [*Library symbol*] [*National Library of Canada*] (NLC)
QI .... Cimber Air [*Denmark*] [*ICAO designator*] (FAAC)
QI .... Quaderni Ibero-Americani [*A publication*]
QI .... Quality Increase (AABC)
QI .... Quality Index
QI .... Quantity Indicator (KSC)
QI .... Quarterly Index [*A publication*]
QI .... Quasi-Inertial
QI .... Quota International [*Formerly, QCI*] [*Washington, DC*] (EA)
QIA .... Quaderni Ibero-Americani [*A publication*]
QIA .... Quantitative Infrared Analysis
1QIaIQIsa ... Complete Isaiah Scroll from Qumran. Cave One (BJA)
QIBA .... Quaderni Italiani di Buenos Aires [*A publication*]
QIC .... Quality Information Center
QIC .... Quality Inspection Criteria
QIC .... Quarter Inch Cartridge [*Data processing*]
QIC .... Quartz Iodine Crystal
QID .... Quater in Die [*Four Times a Day*] [*Pharmacy*]
QIDN .... Queen's Institute of District Nursing [*British*]
QIE .... Quantitative Immunoelectrophoresis Methods [*Analytical biochemistry*]
QIE-AF ...... Qualified International Executive - Air Forwarding [*Designation awarded by American Society of International Executives, Inc.*]
QIE-EM ...... Qualified International Executive - Export Management [*Designation awarded by American Society of International Executives, Inc.*]
QIE-F .... Qualified International Executive - Forwarding [*Designation awarded by American Society of International Executives, Inc.*]
QIER J .... QIER [*Queensland Institute for Educational Research*] Journal [*A publication*]
QIE-TM ...... Qualified International Executive - Traffic Management [*Designation awarded by American Society of International Executives, Inc.*]

QIFL .... Quaderni. Istituto di Filologia Latina. Universita di Padova [*A publication*]
QIG .... Quaderni. Istituto di Glottologia [*Bologna*] [*A publication*]
QIGB .... Quaderni. Istituto di Glottologia (Bologna) [*A publication*]
QIK .... Quick (MSA)
QIL .... Quad In-Line
QIL .... Quartz Incandescent Lamp
QIL .... Quartz Iodine Lamp
Q Illust ...... Quarterly Illustrator [*A publication*]
QIMA .... QIMA. Institute of Municipal Administration, Queensland Division [*A publication*]
Q Ind .... Queensland Industry [*A publication*]
Q Industry ... Queensland Industry [*A publication*]
3QInv .... [*The*] Copper Treasure Inventory Scroll from Qumran. Cave Three (BJA)
QIO .... Queue Input/Output
QIP .... PALINET [*Pennsylvania Area Library Network*] Central, Philadelphia, PA [*OCLC symbol*] (OCLC)
QIP .... Quality Inspection Point (KSC)
QIP .... Quarterly Intercession Paper [*A publication*] (ROG)
QIP .... Quarters Improvement Program (MCD)
QIP .... Quartz Insulation Part
QIP .... Quiescat in Pace [*May He, or She, Rest in Peace*] [*Latin*]
QIP Rep Natl Asphalt Pavement Assoc ... QIP Report. National Asphalt Pavement Association [*A publication*]
QISAM .... Queued Indexed Sequential Access Method [*IBM Corp.*] [*Data processing*]
QIT .... Quality Information and Test [*System*]
QJ .... Jordanian World Airways [*ICAO designator*] (FAAC)
QJ .... Quarterly Journal. University of North Dakota [*A publication*]
QJ .... Quick Junction [*Electronics*]
QJ Agric Econ ... Quarterly Journal of Agricultural Economy [*A publication*]
Q Japan Com'l Arb Ass'n ... Quarterly. Japan Commercial Arbitration Association (DLA)
QJC .... College de Joliette, Quebec [*Library symbol*] [*National Library of Canada*] (NLC)
QJCA .... Quarterly Journal of Current Acquisitions [*A publication*]
Q J Crude Drug Res ... Quarterly Journal of Crude Drug Research [*A publication*]
QJCSVA ..... Archives Provinciales des Clercs de Saint-Viateur, Joliette, Quebec [*Library symbol*] [*National Library of Canada*] (NLC)
QJE .... Quarterly Journal of Economics [*A publication*]
Q J Econ ..... Quarterly Journal of Economics [*A publication*]
QJ Eng Geol ... Quarterly Journal of Engineering Geology [*A publication*]
QJEPs .... Quarterly Journal of Experimental Psychology [*A publication*]
Q/JET .... Quadrajet Carburetor [*Automotive engineering*]
QJewR .... Quarterly Jewish Review [*A publication*]
QJewSt ...... Quarterly of Jewish Studies. Jewish Chronicle [*A publication*]
Q J Exp Physiol ... Quarterly Journal of Experimental Physiology and Cognate Medical Sciences [*A publication*]
Q J Exp Physiol Cogn Med Sci ... Quarterly Journal of Experimental Physiology and Cognate Medical Sciences [*A publication*]
Q J Exp Psy ... Quarterly Journal of Experimental Psychology [*A publication*]
Q J Exp Psychol ... Quarterly Journal of Experimental Psychology [*A publication*]
Q J Exp Psychol B ... Quarterly Journal of Experimental Psychology. B. Comparative and Physiological Psychology [*A publication*]
Q J Fla Acad Sci ... Quarterly Journal. Florida Academy of Sciences [*A publication*]
Q J For .... Quarterly Journal of Forestry [*A publication*]
Q J Forestry ... Quarterly Journal of Forestry [*A publication*]
Q J Geol Min Metall Soc (India) ... Quarterly Journal. Geological, Mining, and Metallurgical Society (India) [*A publication*]
Q J Geol Soc Lond ... Quarterly Journal. Geological Society of London [*A publication*]
Q J Geol Soc London ... Quarterly Journal. Geological Society of London [*A publication*]
QJH .... Centre Hospitalier Regional de Lanaudiere, Joliette, Quebec [*Library symbol*] [*National Library of Canada*] (NLC)
Q J Indian Chem Soc ... Quarterly Journal. Indian Chemical Society [*A publication*]
Q J Indian Inst Sci ... Quarterly Journal. Indian Institute of Science [*A publication*]
QJJ .... Seminaire de Joliette, Quebec [*Library symbol*] [*National Library of Canada*] (NLC)
QJL .... Querner, J. L., San Antonio TX [*STAC*]
QJLC .... Quarterly Journal. Library of Congress [*A publication*]
Q J Lib Con ... Quarterly Journal. Library of Congress [*A publication*]
Q J Liverpool Univer Inst Commer Res Trop ... Quarterly Journal. Liverpool University Institute of Commercial Research in the Tropics [*A publication*]
Q Jl Microsc Sci ... Quarterly Journal of Microscopical Science [*A publication*]
Q J Local Self Govt Inst ... Quarterly Journal. Local Self-Government Institute [*Bombay*] [*A publication*]
Q Jl Rubb Res Inst Ceylon ... Quarterly Journal. Rubber Research Institute of Ceylon [*later, Sri Lanka*] [*A publication*]
QJLSGI ...... Quarterly Journal. Local Self-Government Institute [*Bombay*] [*A publication*]

QJLSI .... Quarterly Journal. Local Self-Government Institute [Bombay] [A publication]
QJMA .... Musee d'Art de Joliette, Quebec [Library symbol] [National Library of Canada] (NLC)
Q J Math..... Quarterly Journal of Mathematics [A publication]
Q J Mech Ap ... Quarterly Journal of Mechanics and Applied Mathematics [A publication]
QJ Mech Appl Math ... Quarterly Journal of Mechanics and Applied Mathematics [A publication]
QJ Mech and Appl Math ... Quarterly Journal of Mechanics and Applied Mathematics [A publication]
Q J Med...... Quarterly Journal of Medicine [A publication]
Q J Micro Sc ... Quarterly Journal of Microscopical Science [A publication]
Q J Microsc Sci ... Quarterly Journal of Microscopical Science [A publication]
QJMP .... Queue Jump Command
QJMS .... Quarterly Journal. Mythic Society [A publication]
Q Jnl Speech ... Quarterly Journal of Speech [A publication]
QJOC .... College de Jonquiere, Quebec [Library symbol] [National Library of Canada] (NLC)
QJP .... Queensland Justice of the Peace [A publication]
Q J Pakistan Lib Assn ... Quarterly Journal. Pakistan Library Association [Karachi] [A publication]
Q J Pharm Pharmacol ... Quarterly Journal of Pharmacy and Pharmacology [A publication]
QJP (Mag Cas) ... Queensland Justice of the Peace (Magisterial Cases) [A publication]
QJPR .... Queensland Justice of the Peace. Reports [A publication]
Q J Pub Speak ... Quarterly Journal of Public Speaking [A publication]
QJRAA .... Quarterly Journal. Royal Astronomical Society [A publication]
Q J R Astro ... Quarterly Journal. Royal Astronomical Society [A publication]
QJR Astron Soc ... Quarterly Journal. Royal Astronomical Society [A publication]
QJRMA .... Quarterly Journal. Royal Meteorological Society [A publication]
Q J R Meteo ... Quarterly Journal. Royal Meteorological Society [A publication]
Q J R Meteorol Soc ... Quarterly Journal. Royal Meteorological Society [A publication]
Q J Rubber Res Inst Sri Lanka ... Quarterly Journal. Rubber Research Institute of Sri Lanka [formerly, Ceylon] [A publication]
QJS .... Quarterly Journal of Speech [A publication]
Q J Sc........ Quarterly Journal of Science [A publication]
Q J Sc........ Quarterly Journal of Science, Literature, and the Arts [A publication]
QJ Seismol ... Quarterly Journal of Seismology [A publication]
QJSp .... Quarterly Journal of Speech [A publication]
QJSPA....... Quarterly Journal of Speech [A publication]
Q J Speech ... Quarterly Journal of Speech [A publication]
Q J Stud Al ... Quarterly Journal of Studies on Alcohol [A publication]
Q J Stud Alcohol ... Quarterly Journal of Studies on Alcohol [A publication]
Q J Stud Alcohol Part A ... Quarterly Journal of Studies on Alcohol. Part A [A publication]
QJ Surg Sci ... Quarterly Journal of Surgical Sciences [A publication]
Q J Taiwan Mus (Taipei) ... Quarterly Journal. Taiwan Museum (Taipei) [A publication]
QJXPA....... Quarterly Journal of Experimental Psychology [A publication]
QK .... Compagnie Aeromaritime [France] [ICAO designator] (FAAC)
QK .... Kirkland Municipal Library [Bibliotheque Municipale de Kirkland] Quebec [Library symbol] [National Library of Canada] (NLC)
QK .... Queen's Knight [Chess]
QK .... Quick (FAAC)
QKB............ Brome County Historical Society, Knowlton, Quebec [Library symbol] [National Library of Canada] (NLC)
QKC .... Aero Taxi Aviation, Inc. [Lester, PA] [FAA designator] (FAAC)
QKFL......... Quick Flashing Light [Navigation signal]
Qk Froz Fd ... Quick Frozen Foods [A publication]
QKITA .... Institut de Technologie Agricole, Kamouraska, Quebec [Library symbol] [National Library of Canada] (NLC)
QKL........... Cologne/Bonn-Main RR [West Germany] [Airport symbol] (OAG)
QKPC .... Medical Library, Pfizer Canada, Inc., Kirkland, Quebec [Library symbol] [National Library of Canada] (NLC)
QKT........... Queen's Knight [Chess]
QL............. Ethyl 2-(Diisopropylamino)ethylmethylphosphonite [See EDMP] [Army symbol]
QL............. Lesotho Airways [ICAO designator] (FAAC)
QL............. Quad Left [Typography]
QL............. Quaderni Linguistici [A publication]
QL............. Quality of Living
QL............. Quantum Libet [As Much as Is Desired] [Pharmacy]
QL............. Quarrel (ROG)
QL............. Quartz-Locked
QL............. Quebec Law (DLA)
QL............. Queen's Lancers [Military unit] [British]
QL............. Queensland Lawyer [A publication]
QL............. Query Language [Data processing] (DIT)
QL............. Queue Length [Telecommunications] (TEL)
Q/L............ Quick Look (KSC)
QL............. Quintal [Unit of weight]
QL............. Quinzaine Litteraire [A publication]

QL............. Qumran Literature (BJA)
QLA........... Bibliotheque Municipale, Laval, Quebec [Library symbol] [National Library of Canada] (NLC)
QLA........... Lasham [England] [Airport symbol]
QLA/ABO... Quebec Library Association/Association des Bibliothecaires du Quebec [Canada]
QLAB......... Quick Like a Bunny
QLAC .... CEGEP Montmorency, Laval, Quebec [Library symbol] [National Library of Canada] (NLC)
QLACS...... Cite de la Sante de Laval, Quebec [Library symbol] [National Library of Canada] (NLC)
QLACW...... Canadian Workplace Automation Research Centre [Centre Canadien de Recherche sur l'Informatisation du Travail] Laval, Quebec [Library symbol] [National Library of Canada] (NLC)
QLAG .... Research Station, Agriculture Canada [Station de Recherches, Agriculture Canada] Lennoxville, Quebec [Library symbol] [National Library of Canada] (NLC)
QLAH .... Lennoxville-Ascot Historical Society Museum, Lennoxville, Quebec [Library symbol] [National Library of Canada] (NLC)
QLAP......... Quick Look Analysis Program
QLASC....... College de l'Assomption, Quebec [Library symbol] [National Library of Canada] (NLC)
QLASGPT ... Federal Training Centre, Penitentiary, Ministry of the Solicitor General [Centre Federal de Formation, Penitencier, Ministere du Solliciteur General] Laval, Quebec [Library symbol] [National Library of Canada] (NLC)
Q Law Soc J ... Queensland Law Society. Journal [A publication]
QLB .... Bishop's University, Lennoxville, Quebec [Library symbol] [National Library of Canada] (NLC)
QL Beor...... Beor's Queensland Law Reports [A publication]
QLBG .... Department of Geography, Bishop's University, Lennoxville, Quebec [Library symbol] [National Library of Canada] (NLC)
QLC........... College de Levis, Quebec [Library symbol] [National Library of Canada] (NLC)
QLC........... Quasi-Liquid Crystal [Organic chemistry]
QLCCP....... Service de Documentation et de Reference, Confederation des Caisses Populaires et d'Economie Desjardins du Quebec, Levis, Quebec [Library symbol] [National Library of Canada] (NLC)
QLCR .... Queensland Land Court Reports [A publication]
QLCRS....... Conseil Regional de la Sante et des Services Sociaux, Longueuil, Quebec [Library symbol] [National Library of Canada] (NLC)
QLCS .... Quick Look and Checkout System
QLD........... Queensland [Australia]
QLDC .... Delmar Chemicals, La Salle, Quebec [Library symbol] [National Library of Canada] (NLC)
Qld Geog J ... Queensland Geographical Journal [A publication]
Qld Govt Indust Gaz ... Queensland Government Industrial Gazette [A publication]
Qld Health ... Queensland's Health [A publication]
Qld Heritage ... Queensland Heritage [A publication]
Qld Mus Mem ... Queensland Museum. Memoirs [A publication]
Qld Nat ...... Queensland Naturalist [A publication]
Qld Parl Deb ... Queensland Parliamentary Debates [A publication]
QLDS......... Quick Look Data Station [NASA] (KSC)
Qld Sci Teach ... Queensland Science Teacher [A publication]
Qld Teach J ... Queensland Teachers Journal [A publication]
Qld Univ Law J ... University of Queensland. Law Journal [A publication]
QLE .... Bibliotheque Municipale, Levis, Quebec [Library symbol] [National Library of Canada] (NLC)
QLFD......... Qualified (KSC)
QLFY......... Qualify (FAAC)
QLG........... Quick-Look Guide
QLI .... Quality of Life Index
Q Lib .... Quantum Libet [As Much as You Please] [Pharmacy]
Q Liberal .... Queensland Liberal [A publication]
QLISP........ [A] programing language (CSR)
QLit .... Quebec Litteraire [A publication]
QLIT .... Quick Look Intermediate Tape
QLJ........... Queensland Law Journal [A publication]
QLJ (NC).... Queensland Law Journal (Notes of Cases) [A publication]
QLL .... Quartz Landing Lamp [Aviation]
QLM .... Bibliotheque Municipale de Lachine, Quebec [Library symbol] [National Library of Canada] (NLC)
QLM .... Quasi-Linear Machine
QLNLB ...... Institut Nazareth et Louis-Braille, Longueuil, Quebec [Library symbol] [National Library of Canada] (NLC)
QLO........... Bibliotheque Municipale, Longueuil, Quebec [Library symbol] [National Library of Canada] (NLC)
QLO........... Quillo Resources, Inc. [Vancouver Stock Exchange symbol]
QLOCE...... College Edouard Montpetit, Longueuil, Quebec [Library symbol] [National Library of Canada] (NLC)
QLOU .... Pratt & Whitney Aircraft Ltd., Longueuil, Quebec [Library symbol] [National Library of Canada] (NLC)
QLP .... Quality Low-Priced [Art series]
QLP .... Query Language Processor [Data processing]
QLP .... Questions Liturgiques et Paroissiales [A publication]

QLP .... Quinoxaline Ladder Polymer [*Organic chemistry*]
QLPS .... Petro-Sun International, Inc., Longueuil, Quebec [*Library symbol*] [*National Library of Canada*]   (NLC)
QLR .... Quebec Law Reports
QLR .... Queen's Lancashire Regiment [*Military unit*] [*British*]
QLR .... Queensland Law Reporter [*A publication*]
QLR .... Queensland Law Reports [*A publication*]
QL(R) .... Quick Look (Report)
QLR (Beor) ... Queensland Law Reports (Beor) [*A publication*]
QLS .... Bibliotheque Municipale, La Salle, Quebec [*Library symbol*] [*National Library of Canada*]   (NLC)
QLS .... Quasi-Elastic Light Scattering [*Also, QELS*] [*Particle size analysis*]
QLS .... Quick Look Station   (MCD)
QLSA .... Queue Line Sharing Adapter [*Data processing*]
QLSAA .... Archives des Soeurs de Sainte-Anne, Lachine, Quebec [*Library symbol*] [*National Library of Canada*]   (NLC)
QLSJ .... Queensland Law Society. Journal [*A publication*]
QLSM .... Quasi-Linear Sequential Machine
QLSS .... Research Department, J. E. Seagram & Sons Ltd., La Salle, Quebec [*Library symbol*] [*National Library of Canada*]   (NLC)
QLT .... Bibliotheque Municipale, La Tuque, Quebec [*Library symbol*] [*National Library of Canada*]   (NLC)
QLT .... Quadra Logic Technologies, Inc. [*Vancouver Stock Exchange symbol*]
QLT .... Quantitative Leak Test
QLT .... Quasi-Linear Theory
QLTV .... LTV Corp. [*Formerly, Ling-Temco-Vought, Inc.*] [*NYSE symbol*]
QLTY .... Quality   (AFM)
Qly Land R ... Fitzgibbon's Irish Land Reports [*1895-1920*]   (DLA)
QM............. Air Malawi [*ICAO designator*]   (FAAC)
QM............. Bulgaria [*License plate code assigned to foreign diplomats in the US*]
QM............. Quadrature Modulation
QM............. Qualification Motor   (MCD)
QM............. Quality Manual [*A publication*]   (MCD)
QM............. Quality Memorandum
QM............. Quality of Merit
QM............. Quality Motels [*Formerly, QCU, QCM*]   (EA)
QM............. Quantitative Methods
QM............. Quantum Mechanics
QM............. Quaque Matin [*Every Morning*] [*Pharmacy*]
QM............. Quarterly Meetings [*Quakers*]
QM............. Quarterly Memorandum
QM............. Quartermaster [*Navy rating*]   (AFM)
QM............. Queen's Messenger [*British*]
QM............. Query Module   (MCD)
QM............. Queue Manager [*Data processing*]   (CMD)
QM............. Quinacrine Mustard [*Chromosome stain*]
QM............. Quinonemethide [*Organic chemistry*]
QM............. Qumran Manuscripts   (BJA)
QM............. Quo Modo [*In What Manner*] [*Latin*]
1QM............. Milchemet, the War of the Sons of Light and the Sons of Darkness from Qumran. Cave One   (BJA)
QM1............ Quartermaster, First Class [*Navy rating*]
QM2............ Quartermaster, Second Class [*Navy rating*]
QM3............ Quartermaster, Third Class [*Navy rating*]
QMA .... Group Information Centre, Alcan Aluminum Ltd. [*Centre d'Information du Groupe, Alcan Aluminium Ltee*] Montreal, Quebec [*Library symbol*] [*National Library of Canada*]   (NLC)
QMA .... Qualified Military Available
QMA .... Qualitative Materiel Approach [*Army*]   (AABC)
QMA .... Quartermasters Association [*Later, ALA*]
QMAA .... Archives de la Chancellerie, L'Archeveche de Montreal, Quebec [*Library symbol*] [*National Library of Canada*]   (NLC)
QMAAC...... Queen Mary's Army Auxiliary Corps [*The WAAC*] [*British*]
QMAB......... Montreal Association for the Blind, Quebec [*Library symbol*] [*National Library of Canada*]   (NLC)
QMABB ...... Asselin, Benoit, Boucher, Ducharme & Lapointe, Inc., Montreal, Quebec [*Library symbol*] [*National Library of Canada*]   (NLC)
QMABB ...... TECSULT, Montreal, Quebec [*Library symbol*] [*National Library of Canada*]   (NLC)
QMAC .... Macdonald College Library, Ste-Anne-De-Bellevue, Quebec [*Library symbol*] [*National Library of Canada*]   (NLC)
QMAC .... Quadripartite Materiel and Agreements Committee [*Military*]   (AABC)
QMACL ...... Quebec Association for Children with Learning Disabilities [*Association Quebecoise pour les Enfants Souffrant de Troubles d'Apprentissage*] Montreal, Quebec [*Library symbol*] [*National Library of Canada*]   (NLC)
QMACN...... Archives de la Congregation de Notre-Dame, Montreal, Quebec [*Library symbol*] [*National Library of Canada*]   (NLC)
QMADMA... Archives, Diocese of Montreal, Anglican Church of Canada, Quebec [*Library symbol*] [*National Library of Canada*]   (NLC)

QMAE........ Aviation Electric Ltd., Montreal, Quebec [*Library symbol*] [*National Library of Canada*]   (NLC)
QMAEC...... Atomic Energy of Canada [*L'Energie Atomique du Canada*] Montreal, Quebec [*Library symbol*] [*National Library of Canada*]   (NLC)
QMAGB...... Bibliotheque Municipale, Magog, Quebec [*Library symbol*] [*National Library of Canada*]   (NLC)
Q(Maint) .... Quartermaster Maintenance [*World War II*]
QMAL........ Air Liquide Canada Ltee., Montreal, Quebec [*Library symbol*] [*National Library of Canada*]   (NLC)
QMALL...... Abbott Laboratories Ltd., Montreal, Quebec [*Library symbol*] [*National Library of Canada*]   (NLC)
QMAM....... Allan Memorial Institute, Montreal, Quebec [*Library symbol*] [*National Library of Canada*]   (NLC)
QMAMA .... Andre Marsan & Associes, Inc., Montreal, Quebec [*Library symbol*] [*National Library of Canada*]   (NLC)
QMAN .... Manville Corp. [*NYSE symbol*]
Q Manuf Yrbk ... Queensland Chamber of Manufactures. Year Book [*A publication*]
QMAO .... Qualified for Mobilization Ashore Only [*Navy*]
QMAPS ...... Quebec Aid for the Partially-Sighted [*Aide aux Insuffisants Visuels du Quebec*] Montreal, Quebec [*Library symbol*] [*National Library of Canada*]   (NLC)
QMARC ...... Archives Provinciales des Capucins, Montreal, Quebec [*Library symbol*] [*National Library of Canada*]   (NLC)
QMAS........ Archives du Seminaire de Saint-Sulpice, Montreal, Quebec [*Library symbol*] [*National Library of Canada*]   (NLC)
QMASRC ... Space Research Corp., Mansonville, Quebec [*Library symbol*] [*National Library of Canada*]   (NLC)
QMASSAS ... Centre de Documentation, Secteur Affaires Sociales, Association pour la Sante et la Securite du Travail, Montreal, Quebec [*Library symbol*] [*National Library of Canada*]   (NLC)
Q Master Plumber ... Queensland Master Plumber [*A publication*]
QMAV........ Bibliotheque des Avocats, Barreau de Montreal, Quebec [*Library symbol*] [*National Library of Canada*]   (NLC)
QMAY........ Ayerst Laboratories, Montreal, Quebec [*Library symbol*] [*National Library of Canada*]   (NLC)
QMB .... Bell Canada, Montreal, Quebec [*Library symbol*] [*National Library of Canada*]   (NLC)
QMB .... Queensbury [*England*] [*Seismograph station code, US Geological Survey*]   (SEIS)
QMB .... Quick Make-and-Break [*Contact*]   (DEN)
QMBA........ Ecole des Beaux-Arts, Montreal, Quebec [*Library symbol*] [*National Library of Canada*]   (NLC)
QMBAE...... Bristol Aero Engines Ltd., Montreal, Quebec [*Library symbol*] [*National Library of Canada*]   (NLC)
QMBAN...... Centre de Documentation, Banque Nationale du Canada, Montreal, Quebec [*Library symbol*] [*National Library of Canada*]   (NLC)
QMBB........ College Bois-De-Boulogne, Montreal, Quebec [*Library symbol*] [*National Library of Canada*]   (NLC)
QMBBL....... Beauchemin, Beaton, Lapointe, Inc., Montreal, Quebec [*Library symbol*] [*National Library of Canada*]   (NLC)
QMBD........ Translation Bureau, Canada Department of the Secretary of State [*Bureau des Traductions, Secretariat d'Etat*] Montreal, Quebec [*Library symbol*] [*National Library of Canada*]   (NLC)
QMBE........ Bureau des Economies d'Energie, Montreal, Quebec [*Library symbol*] [*National Library of Canada*]   (NLC)
QMBGC...... Bibliotheque d'Ingenierie, BG Checo International Ltee., Montreal, Quebec [*Library symbol*] [*National Library of Canada*]   (NLC)
QMBIM...... Bio-Mega, Inc., Montreal, Quebec [*Library symbol*] [*National Library of Canada*]   (NLC)
QMBL........ Law Library, Bell Canada, Montreal, Quebec [*Library symbol*] [*National Library of Canada*]   (NLC)
QMBM....... Bibliotheque de la Ville de Montreal, Quebec [*Library symbol*] [*National Library of Canada*]   (NLC)
QMBMO ..... Bank of Montreal [*Banque de Montreal*] Quebec [*Library symbol*] [*National Library of Canada*]   (NLC)
QMBMS...... Management Sciences Library, Bell Canada, Montreal, Quebec [*Library symbol*] [*National Library of Canada*]   (NLC)
QMBN........ Bibliotheque Nationale du Quebec, Montreal, Quebec [*Library symbol*] [*National Library of Canada*]   (NLC)
QMBNR...... Bell Northern Research, Montreal, Quebec [*Library symbol*] [*National Library of Canada*]   (NLC)
QMBP........ Building Products Ltd., Montreal, Quebec [*Library symbol*] [*National Library of Canada*]   (NLC)
QMBR........ Bio-Research Laboratories Ltd., Pointe-Claire, Quebec [*Library symbol*] [*National Library of Canada*]   (NLC)
QMBT........ Montreal Board of Trade [*Chambre de Commerce du District de Montreal*] Quebec [*Library symbol*] [*National Library of Canada*]   (NLC)
QMC.......... Chief Quartermaster [*Navy rating*]
QMC.......... College de Montreal, Quebec [*Library symbol*] [*National Library of Canada*]   (NLC)
QMC.......... James Carson Breckinridge Library, Quantico, VA [*OCLC symbol*]   (OCLC)
QMC.......... Quadripartite Materiel Committee [*Military*]
QMC.......... Quartermaster Clerk [*Marine Corps*]

QMC .... Quartermaster Corps [*Army*]

QMC .... Queen Mary College [*London*]

QMC .... Quick Modification Concept   (MCD)

QMCA .... Engineering Library, Canadair Ltd., Montreal, Quebec [*Library symbol*] [*National Library of Canada*]   (NLC)

QMCAD ...... Centre d'Animation, de Developpement et de Recherche en Education, Montreal, Quebec [*Library symbol*] [*National Library of Canada*]   (NLC)

QMCADQ ... Conservatoire d'Art Dramatique de Montreal, Quebec [*Library symbol*] [*National Library of Canada*]   (NLC)

QMCAE ...... CAE Electronics Ltd., Montreal, Quebec [*Library symbol*] [*National Library of Canada*]   (NLC)

QMCAG ...... College Andre Grasset, Montreal, Quebec [*Library symbol*] [*National Library of Canada*]   (NLC)

QMCAI .... Canadian Asbestos Information Centre [*Centre Canadien d'Information sur l'Amiante*] Montreal, Quebec [*Library symbol*] [*National Library of Canada*]   (NLC)

QMCAM ..... Missiles and Systems Library, Canadair Ltd., Montreal [*Library symbol*] [*National Library of Canada*]   (NLC)

QMCAR ...... Carmel de Montreal, Quebec [*Library symbol*] [*National Library of Canada*]   (NLC)

QMCAT ...... Commission de la Sante et de la Securite du Travail du Quebec, Montreal [*Library symbol*] [*National Library of Canada*]   (NLC)

QMCAV ...... Direction Generale du Cinema et de l'Audio-Visuel, Ministere des Communications du Quebec, Montreal, Quebec [*Library symbol*] [*National Library of Canada*]   (NLC)

QMCB .... Canadian Broadcasting Corp. [*Societe Radio-Canada*] Montreal, Quebec [*Library symbol*] [*National Library of Canada*]   (NLC)

QMCBE ...... Engineering Headquarters, Canadian Broadcasting Corp. [*Service de l'Ingenierie, Societe Radio-Canada*] Montreal, Quebec [*Library symbol*] [*National Library of Canada*]   (NLC)

QMCC .... Canada Cement Co., Montreal, Quebec [*Library symbol*] [*National Library of Canada*]   (NLC)

QMCCA ...... Centre Canadien d'Architecture [*Canadian Centre for Architecture*] Montreal, Quebec [*Library symbol*] [*National Library of Canada*]   (NLC)

QMCCL ...... Currie, Coopers & Lybrand Ltd., Montreal, Quebec [*Library symbol*] [*National Library of Canada*]   (NLC)

QMCCR ...... Canadian Council of Resource Ministers [*Conseil Canadien des Ministres des Ressources*] Montreal, Quebec [*Library symbol*] [*National Library of Canada*]   (NLC)

QMCCS ...... Centraide, Montreal, Quebec [*Library symbol*] [*National Library of Canada*]   (NLC)

QMCD .... Centre Documentaire, Centrale des Bibliotheques, Montreal, Quebec [*Library symbol*] [*National Library of Canada*]   (NLC)

QMCDM ..... College de Maisonneuve, Montreal, Quebec [*Library symbol*] [*National Library of Canada*]   (NLC)

QMCDP ...... Caisse de Depot et Placement du Quebec, Montreal, Quebec [*Library symbol*] [*National Library of Canada*]   (NLC)

QMCE .... Celanese Canada Ltd., Montreal, Quebec [*Library symbol*] [*National Library of Canada*]   (NLC)

QMCEA ...... Canadian Export Association [*Association Canadienne d'Exportation*] Montreal, Quebec [*Library symbol*] [*National Library of Canada*]   (NLC)

QMCEC ...... Catholic School Commission [*Commission des Ecoles Catholiques*] Montreal, Quebec [*Library symbol*] [*National Library of Canada*]   (NLC)

QMCECI ..... Centre Canadien d'Etudes et de Cooperation Internationale, Montreal, Quebec [*Library symbol*] [*National Library of Canada*]   (NLC)

QMCF .... Merck Frosst Laboratories [*Laboratoires Merck Frosst*] Montreal, Quebec [*Library symbol*] [*National Library of Canada*]   (NLC)

QMCFH ...... Centre de Documentation, Charette, Fortier, Hawey, Touche, Ross, Montreal, Quebec [*Library symbol*] [*National Library of Canada*]   (NLC)

QMCG .... Ciba-Geigy Canada Ltd., Dorval, Quebec [*Library symbol*] [*National Library of Canada*]   (NLC)

QMCGW ..... Clarkson, Gordon, Woods, Gordon, Montreal, Quebec [*Library symbol*] [*National Library of Canada*]   (NLC)

QMCHC ...... Montreal Chest Hospital Centre [*Centre Hospitalier Thoracique de Montreal*] Quebec [*Library symbol*] [*National Library of Canada*]   (NLC)

QMCHL ...... Centre Hospitalier de Lachine, Quebec [*Library symbol*] [*National Library of Canada*]   (NLC)

QMCI .... CIBA Co. Ltd., Montreal, Quebec [*Library symbol*] [*National Library of Canada*]   (NLC)

QMCICM .... Centre Interculturel Monchanin, Montreal, Quebec [*Library symbol*] [*National Library of Canada*]   (NLC)

QMCIH .... Bibliotheque de Documentation des Archives, Ville de Montreal, Quebec [*Library symbol*] [*National Library of Canada*]   (NLC)

QMCILL ...... Legal Department, C-I-L, Inc., Montreal, Quebec [*Library symbol*] [*National Library of Canada*]   (NLC)

QMCILR ..... Central Research Laboratory, Canadian Industries Ltd., McMasterville, Quebec [*Library symbol*] [*National Library of Canada*]   (NLC)

QMCIM ...... Canadian Institute of Mining and Metallurgy [*Institut Canadien des Mines et de la Metallurgie*] Montreal, Quebec [*Library symbol*] [*National Library of Canada*]   (NLC)

QMCJ .... Canadian Jewish Congress [*Congres Juif Canadien*] Montreal, Quebec [*Library symbol*] [*National Library of Canada*]   (NLC)

QMCL .... CanAtom Ltd., Montreal, Quebec [*Library symbol*] [*National Library of Canada*]   (NLC)

QMCLG ...... College Lionel Groulx, Ste-Therese, Quebec [*Library symbol*] [*National Library of Canada*]   (NLC)

QMCLK ...... Quartermaster Clerk [*Navy rating*]

QMCM .... Canadian Marconi Co., Montreal, Quebec [*Library symbol*] [*National Library of Canada*]   (NLC)

QMCM .... Master Chief Quartermaster [*Navy rating*]

QMCN .... Canadian National Railways [*Chemins de fer Nationaux du Canada*] Montreal, Quebec [*Library symbol*] [*National Library of Canada*]   (NLC)

QMCNC ...... Chemical Library, Canadian National Railways [*Bibliotheque Chimique, Chemins de fer Nationaux du Canada*] Montreal, Quebec [*Library symbol*] [*National Library of Canada*]   (NLC)

QMCOM ..... Conservatoire de Musique de Montreal, Quebec [*Library symbol*] [*National Library of Canada*]   (NLC)

QMCP .... Canadian Pacific [*Le Canadien Pacifique*] Montreal, Quebec [*Library symbol*] [*National Library of Canada*]   (NLC)

QMCR .... Canadian Copper Refiners Ltd., Montreal, Quebec [*Library symbol*] [*National Library of Canada*]   (NLC)

QMCR .... Quartermaster Corps Regulations [*Army*]

QMCRI .... Centre de Recherche Industrielle du Quebec, Montreal, Quebec [*Library symbol*] [*National Library of Canada*]   (NLC)

QMCRP ...... Conference des Recteurs et des Principaux des Universites du Quebec, Montreal, Quebec [*Library symbol*] [*National Library of Canada*]   (NLC)

QMCS .... Christian Science Reading Room, Montreal, Quebec [*Library symbol*] [*National Library of Canada*]   (NLC)

QMCS .... Quality Monitoring Control System [*Military*]   (CAAL)

QMCS .... Senior Chief Quartermaster [*Navy rating*]

QMC & SO ... Quartermaster Cataloging and Standardization Office [*Army*]

QMCSSS .... Service de Reference, Conseil de la Sante et des Services Sociaux de la Region de Montreal Metropolitain, Montreal, Quebec [*Library symbol*] [*National Library of Canada*]   (NLC)

QMCT .... Commission de Transport de la Communaute Urbaine de Montreal, Quebec [*Library symbol*] [*National Library of Canada*]   (NLC)

QMCTC ...... Quartermaster Corps Technical Committee [*Army*]

QMCTM ..... Canadian Tobacco Manufacturers' Council [*Conseil Canadien des Fabricants des Produits du Tabac*] Montreal, Quebec [*Library symbol*] [*National Library of Canada*]   (NLC)

QMCVM ..... Commission des Valeurs Mobilieres du Quebec, Montreal, Quebec [*Library symbol*] [*National Library of Canada*]   (NLC)

QMCW .... Canada Wire & Cable Ltd. Montreal, Quebec [*Library symbol*] [*National Library of Canada*]   (NLC)

QMD .... Institut Genealogique Drouin, Montreal, Quebec [*Library symbol*] [*National Library of Canada*]   (NLC)

QMDB .... College Jean-De-Brebeuf, Montreal, Quebec [*Library symbol*] [*National Library of Canada*]   (NLC)

QMDE .... Dominion Engineering Works Ltd., Montreal, Quebec [*Library symbol*] [*National Library of Canada*]   (NLC)

QMDEP ...... Quartermaster Depot [*Army*]

QMDH .... Douglas Hospital Centre [*Centre Hospitalier Douglas*] Montreal, Quebec [*Library symbol*] [*National Library of Canada*]   (NLC)

QMDK .... Quick Mechanical Disconnect Kit

QMDL .... Domtar Ltd., Montreal, Quebec [*Library symbol*] [*National Library of Canada*]   (NLC)

QMDM .... Montreal Association for the Mentally Retarded [*Association de Montreal pour les Deficients Mentaux*] Quebec [*Library symbol*] [*National Library of Canada*]   (NLC)

QMDO .... Qualitative Materiel Development Objective [*Army*]

QMDOM ..... Dominion Bridge Co. Ltd., Montreal, Quebec [*Library symbol*] [*National Library of Canada*]   (NLC)

QMDPC ...... Quartermaster Data Processing Center [*Army*]

QMDT .... Dominion Textile Co., Montreal, Quebec [*Library symbol*] [*National Library of Canada*]   (NLC)

QME .... Quarber Merkur [*A publication*]

QMEA .... Atmospheric Environment Service, Environment Canada [*Service de l'Environnement Atmospherique, Environnement Canada*] Dorval, Quebec [*Library symbol*] [*National Library of Canada*]   (NLC)

QMEC .... Monenco Consultants Ltd., Montreal, Quebec [*Library symbol*] [*National Library of Canada*]   (NLC)

QMEC .... Montreal Engineering Co. Ltd., Quebec [*Library symbol*] [*National Library of Canada*]   (NLC)

QMECB ...... Centrale des Bibliotheques, Ministere de l'Education du Quebec, Montreal, Quebec [*Library symbol*] [*National Library of Canada*]   (NLC)

QMECS ...... Experts-Conseils Shawinigan, Montreal, Quebec [*Library symbol*] [*National Library of Canada*]   (NLC)

QMED......... Quest Medical, Inc. [*NASDAQ symbol*]　(NQ)
Q Med Rev ... Quarterly Medical Review [*A publication*]
QMEE......... Environmental Protection Service, Environment Canada
　　　　　[*Service de la Protection de l'Environnement,
　　　　　Environnement Canada*] Montreal, Quebec [*Library
　　　　　symbol*] [*National Library of Canada*]　(NLC)
QMEN......... Ministere de l'Environnement, Montreal, Quebec [*Library
　　　　　symbol*] [*National Library of Canada*]　(NLC)
QMENT ...... National Theatre School [*Ecole Nationale de Theatre*]
　　　　　Montreal, Quebec [*Library symbol*] [*National Library of
　　　　　Canada*]　(NLC)
QMEP......... Ecole Polytechnique, Montreal, Quebec [*Library symbol*]
　　　　　[*National Library of Canada*]　(NLC)
QMEPCC.... Quartermaster Equipment and Parts Commodity Center
　　　　　[*Army*]
QMERS ...... E. R. Squibb & Sons Ltd., Montreal, Quebec [*Library symbol*]
　　　　　[*National Library of Canada*]　(NLC)
QMES......... Ecole Secondaire Saint-Stanislas, Montreal, Quebec [*Library
　　　　　symbol*] [*National Library of Canada*]　(NLC)
QMF .... Fraser-Hickson Institute, Montreal, Quebec [*Library symbol*]
　　　　　[*National Library of Canada*]　(NLC)
QMFA......... Montreal Museum of Fine Arts [*Musee des Beaux-Arts de
　　　　　Montreal*] Quebec [*Library symbol*] [*National Library of
　　　　　Canada*]　(NLC)
QMFAC ...... Farinon Canada, Dorval, Quebec [*Library symbol*] [*National
　　　　　Library of Canada*]　(NLC)
QMFBD ..... Federal Business Development Bank [*Banque Federale de
　　　　　Developpement*] Montreal, Quebec [*Library symbol*]
　　　　　[*National Library of Canada*]　(NLC)
QMFC......... First Church of Christ, Scientist, Montreal, Quebec [*Library
　　　　　symbol*] [*National Library of Canada*]　(NLC)
QMFCIAF ... Quartermaster Food and Container Institute for the Armed
　　　　　Forces
QMFER...... Forest Engineering Research Institute of Canada [*Institut
　　　　　Canadien de Recherches en Genie Forestier*] Pointe-
　　　　　Claire, Quebec [*Library symbol*] [*National Library of
　　　　　Canada*]　(NLC)
QMFH......... Frank W. Horner Ltd., Montreal, Quebec [*Library symbol*]
　　　　　[*National Library of Canada*]　(NLC)
QMFMO...... Federation des Medecins Omnipraticiens du Quebec,
　　　　　Montreal, Quebec [*Library symbol*] [*National Library of
　　　　　Canada*]　(NLC)
QMFMS...... Federation des Medecins Specialistes du Quebec, Montreal,
　　　　　Quebec [*Library symbol*] [*National Library of
　　　　　Canada*]　(NLC)
QMFR......... Arctic Biological Station, Fisheries and Oceans Canada
　　　　　[*Station Biologique de l'Arctique, Peches et Oceans
　　　　　Canada*] Ste-Anne-De-Bellevue, Quebec [*Library symbol*]
　　　　　[*National Library of Canada*]　(NLC)
QMFRAN.... Studium Franciscain de Theologie, Montreal, Quebec [*Library
　　　　　symbol*] [*National Library of Canada*]　(NLC)
QMG.......... QMG Holdings, Inc. [*Toronto Stock Exchange symbol*]
QMG.......... Quartermaster General [*Army*]
QMG.......... Sir George Williams Campus, Concordia University, Montreal,
　　　　　Quebec [*Library symbol*] [*National Library of
　　　　　Canada*]　(NLC)
QMGA .... Montreal Gazette, Quebec [*Library symbol*] [*National Library of
　　　　　Canada*]　(NLC)
QMGB .... Grands Ballets Canadiens, Montreal, Quebec [*Library symbol*]
　　　　　[*National Library of Canada*]　(NLC)
QMGF......... Quartermaster-General to the Forces [*Military*] [*British*]
QMGG .... Department of Geography, Sir George Williams Campus,
　　　　　Concordia University, Montreal, Quebec [*Library symbol*]
　　　　　[*National Library of Canada*]　(NLC)
QMGGM ..... University Map Collection, Department of Geography, Sir
　　　　　George Williams Campus, Concordia University,
　　　　　Montreal, Quebec [*Library symbol*] [*National Library of
　　　　　Canada*]　(NLC)
QMGH .... Montreal General Hospital [*Hopital General de Montreal*]
　　　　　Quebec [*Library symbol*] [*National Library of
　　　　　Canada*]　(NLC)
QMGL......... Genstar Ltd., Montreal, Quebec [*Library symbol*] [*National
　　　　　Library of Canada*]　(NLC)
QMGLS ..... Library Studies Program, Concordia University, Montreal,
　　　　　Quebec [*Library symbol*] [*National Library of
　　　　　Canada*]　(NLC)
QMGMC ..... Quartermaster-General of the Marine Corps
QMGO .... Quartermaster-General's Office [*Military*] [*British*]　(ROG)
QMGP......... Gerard Parizeau Ltee, Montreal, Quebec [*Library symbol*]
　　　　　[*National Library of Canada*]　(NLC)
QMGPA ...... Quarry Management and Products [*Later, Quarry
　　　　　Management*] [*A publication*]
QMGS .... Grand Seminaire, Montreal, Quebec [*Library symbol*] [*National
　　　　　Library of Canada*]　(NLC)
QMH........... Hydro-Quebec, Montreal, Quebec [*Library symbol*] [*National
　　　　　Library of Canada*]　(NLC)
QMH........... MHI Group [*NYSE symbol*]
QMHD .... Hotel-Dieu de Montreal, Quebec [*Library symbol*] [*National
　　　　　Library of Canada*]　(NLC)

QMHDE ...... Direction de l'Environnement, Hydro-Quebec, Montreal,
　　　　　Quebec [*Library symbol*] [*National Library of
　　　　　Canada*]　(NLC)
QMHE .... Ecole des Hautes Etudes Commerciales, Montreal, Quebec
　　　　　[*Library symbol*] [*National Library of Canada*]　(NLC)
QMHGC ...... Centre Hospitalier de Verdun, Quebec [*Library symbol*]
　　　　　[*National Library of Canada*]　(NLC)
QMHGF ...... Hopital General Fleury, Montreal, Quebec [*Library symbol*]
　　　　　[*National Library of Canada*]　(NLC)
QMHJT .... Hopital Jean Talon, Montreal, Quebec [*Library symbol*]
　　　　　[*National Library of Canada*]　(NLC)
QMHM........ Centre Hospitalier Jacques Viger, Montreal, Quebec [*Library
　　　　　symbol*] [*National Library of Canada*]　(NLC)
QMHME...... Hopital Marie-Enfant, Montreal, Quebec [*Library symbol*]
　　　　　[*National Library of Canada*]　(NLC)
QMHMR...... Hopital Maisonneuve-Rosemont, Montreal, Quebec [*Library
　　　　　symbol*] [*National Library of Canada*]　(NLC)
QMHND...... Hopital Notre-Dame, Montreal, Quebec [*Library symbol*]
　　　　　[*National Library of Canada*]　(NLC)
QMHNDI.... Bibliotheque des Services Infirmiers, Hopital Notre-Dame,
　　　　　Montreal, Quebec [*Library symbol*] [*National Library of
　　　　　Canada*]　(NLC)
QMHP........ Qualified Mental Health Professional
QMHQE...... Centre de Documentation, Direction de l'Environnement,
　　　　　Hydro-Quebec, Montreal, Quebec [*Library symbol*]
　　　　　[*National Library of Canada*]　(NLC)
QMHRP ...... Hopital Riviere-Des-Prairies, Montreal, Quebec [*Library
　　　　　symbol*] [*National Library of Canada*]　(NLC)
QMHSC ...... Hopital du Sacre-Coeur, Montreal, Quebec [*Library symbol*]
　　　　　[*National Library of Canada*]　(NLC)
QMHSCA ... Hopital Santa Cabrini, Montreal, Quebec [*Library symbol*]
　　　　　[*National Library of Canada*]　(NLC)
QMHSJ....... Hopital Louis H. Lafonataine, Montreal, Quebec [*Library
　　　　　symbol*] [*National Library of Canada*]　(NLC)
QMHSJA .... Hopital Ste-Jeanne-D'Arc, Montreal, Quebec [*Library symbol*]
　　　　　[*National Library of Canada*]　(NLC)
QMHSL ...... Hopital Saint-Luc, Montreal, Quebec [*Library symbol*]
　　　　　[*National Library of Canada*]　(NLC)
QMI .... Insurance Institute of the Province of Quebec [*Insitut
　　　　　d'Assurance du Quebec*] Montreal, Quebec [*Library
　　　　　symbol*] [*National Library of Canada*]　(NLC)
QMI .... Qualification Maintainability Inspection
QMIA.......... International Air Transport Association [*Association du
　　　　　Transport Aerien International*] Montreal, Quebec [*Library
　　　　　symbol*] [*National Library of Canada*]　(NLC)
QMIA.......... Quartermaster Intelligence Agency [*Merged with Defense
　　　　　Intelligence Agency*]
QMIAA .... Institut des Arts Appliques, Montreal, Quebec [*Library symbol*]
　　　　　[*National Library of Canada*]　(NLC)
QMIAG .... Institut des Arts Graphiques, Montreal, Quebec [*Library
　　　　　symbol*] [*National Library of Canada*]　(NLC)
QMIAP....... Pavillon Albert Prevost, Montreal, Quebec [*Library symbol*]
　　　　　[*National Library of Canada*]　(NLC)
QMIC.......... International Civil Aviation Organization [*Organisation de
　　　　　l'Aviation Civile Internationale*] Montreal, Quebec [*Library
　　　　　symbol*] [*National Library of Canada*]　(NLC)
QMICA .... Institute of Chartered Accountants of Quebec [*Institut
　　　　　Canadien des Comptables Agrees du Quebec*] Montreal,
　　　　　Quebec [*Library symbol*] [*National Library of
　　　　　Canada*]　(NLC)
QMICE .... Canadian Institute of Adult Education [*Institut Canadien
　　　　　d'Education des Adultes*] Montreal, Quebec [*Library
　　　　　symbol*] [*National Library of Canada*]　(NLC)
QMICM...... Institut de Cardiologie de Montreal, Quebec [*Library symbol*]
　　　　　[*National Library of Canada*]　(NLC)
QMIF .... Imasco Foods Ltd., Montreal, Quebec [*Library symbol*]
　　　　　[*National Library of Canada*]　(NLC)
QMIFQ....... Informatech France-Quebec, Montreal, Quebec [*Library
　　　　　symbol*] [*National Library of Canada*]　(NLC)
QMIG.......... Industrial Grain Products Ltd., Montreal, Quebec [*Library
　　　　　symbol*] [*National Library of Canada*]　(NLC)
QMII .... Istituto Italiano di Cultura, Montreal, Quebec [*Library symbol*]
　　　　　[*National Library of Canada*]　(NLC)
QMIIS .... Islamic Studies Library, McGill University, Montreal, Quebec
　　　　　[*Library symbol*] [*National Library of Canada*]　(NLC)
QMIIST....... International Institute of Stress [*Institut International du
　　　　　Stress*] Montreal, Quebec [*Library symbol*] [*National
　　　　　Library of Canada*]　(NLC)
QMILO........ International Labour Office [*Bureau International du Travail*]
　　　　　Montreal, Quebec [*Library symbol*] [*National Library of
　　　　　Canada*]　(NLC)
QMIM .... Institut Armand Frappier, Universite du Quebc, Laval, Quebec
　　　　　[*Library symbol*] [*National Library of Canada*]　(NLC)
QMIMM ...... Ministere des Communautes Culturelles et de l'Immigration,
　　　　　Montreal, Quebec [*Library symbol*] [*National Library of
　　　　　Canada*]　(NLC)
QMIMSO .... Quartermaster Industrial Mobilization Services Offices [*Army*]
QMINC .... Institut du Cancer de Montreal, Quebec [*Library symbol*]
　　　　　[*National Library of Canada*]　(NLC)

QMINCA..... Institut National Canadien pour les Aveugles, Montreal, Quebec [*Library symbol*] [*National Library of Canada*] (NLC)

QMINP........ Institut National de Productivite, Montreal, Quebec [*Library symbol*] [*National Library of Canada*] (NLC)

QMIP .... Institute of Parasitoloy, Macdonald College, Ste-Anne-De-Bellevue, Quebec [*Library symbol*] [*National Library of Canada*] (NLC)

QMIPP........ Institut Philippe Pinel de Montreal, Quebec [*Library symbol*] [*National Library of Canada*] (NLC)

QMIRC .... Institut de Recherches Cliniques, Montreal, Quebec [*Library symbol*] [*National Library of Canada*] (NLC)

QMIRP........ Institute for Research on Public Policy [*Institut de Recherches Politiques*] Montreal, Quebec [*Library symbol*] [*National Library of Canada*] (NLC)

QMIRS........ Informatheque IRSST [*Institut de Recherche en Sante et Securite au Travail*] Montreal, Quebec [*Library symbol*] [*National Library of Canada*] (NLC)

QMIS .... Quality Review Management Information System [*IRS*]

QMISM....... Centre de Documentation, Institut Raymond-Dewar, Montreal, Quebec [*Library symbol*] [*National Library of Canada*] (NLC)

QMISM....... Centre de Ressources Multimedia, Institution des Sourds de Montreal, Quebec [*Library symbol*] [*National Library of Canada*] (NLC)

QMIT .... Imperial Tobacco Co. of Canada Ltd., Montreal, Quebec [*Library symbol*] [*National Library of Canada*] (NLC)

QMITR........ Research Library, Imperial Tobacco Co. of Canada Ltd., Montreal, Quebec [*Library symbol*] [*National Library of Canada*] (NLC)

QMJ............ Jewish Public Library [*Bibliotheque Juive Publique, Montreal*] Quebec [*Library symbol*] [*National Library of Canada*] (NLC)

QMJB .... Jardin Botanique, Montreal, Quebec [*Library symbol*] [*National Library of Canada*] (NLC)

QMJES....... Technical Services, Joseph E. Seagram & Sons Ltd., La Salle, Quebec [*Library symbol*] [*National Library of Canada*] (NLC)

QMJG......... Jewish General Hospital, Montreal, Quebec [*Library symbol*] [*National Library of Canada*] (NLC)

QMJGI........ Institute of Community and Family Psychiatry, Jewish General Hospital, Montreal, Quebec [*Library symbol*] [*National Library of Canada*] (NLC)

QMJGL....... Lady Davis Institute for Medical Research, Jewish General Hospital, Montreal, Quebec [*Library symbol*] [*National Library of Canada*] (NLC)

QMJH .... Hopital de Mont-Joli, Inc., Quebec [*Library symbol*] [*National Library of Canada*] (NLC)

QMJHW...... Johnson & Higgins, Willis, Faber Ltd., Montreal, Quebec [*Library symbol*] [*National Library of Canada*] (NLC)

QMJJ.......... Johnson & Johnson Ltd., Montreal, Quebec [*Library symbol*] [*National Library of Canada*] (NLC)

QMJL.......... John Lovell & Son City Directories Ltd., Montreal, Quebec [*Library symbol*] [*National Library of Canada*] (NLC)

QMJLP .... Laboratoire de Police Scientifique et de Medecine Legale, Ministere de la Justice du Quebec, Montreal, Quebec [*Library symbol*] [*National Library of Canada*] (NLC)

QMJM........ Canada Department of Justice [*Ministere de la Justice*] Montreal, Quebec [*Library symbol*] [*National Library of Canada*] (NLC)

QMJSJ .... Commission des Services Juridiques, Ministere de la Justice, Montreal, Quebec [*Library symbol*] [*National Library of Canada*] (NLC)

QML .... Loyola Campus, Concordia University, Montreal, Quebec [*Library symbol*] [*National Library of Canada*] (NLC)

QML .... Qayyum Moslem League [*Pakistani*] (PD)

QML .... Qualified Manufacturers List [*DoD*]

QMLA .... Laboratoires Abbott Ltee, Montreal, Quebec [*Library symbol*] [*National Library of Canada*] (NLC)

QMLCA ...... Lower Canada Arms Collectors Association, Montreal, Quebec [*Library symbol*] [*National Library of Canada*] (NLC)

QMLCC ...... Lower Canada College Montreal, Quebec [*Library symbol*] [*National Library of Canada*] (NLC)

QMLCPF .... Bibliotheque de la Faune, Ministere du Loisir, de la Chasse et de la Peche, Montreal, Quebec [*Library symbol*] [*National Library of Canada*] (NLC)

QMLG........ Lakeshore General Hospital [*Hopital General du Lakeshore*] Pointe-Claire, Quebec [*Library symbol*] [*National Library of Canada*] (NLC)

QMLP .... Centre de Documentation, La Presse Ltee, Montreal, Quebec [*Library symbol*] [*National Library of Canada*] (NLC)

QMLQ........ Centre d Documentation, Loto-Quebec, Montreal, Quebec [*Library symbol*] [*National Library of Canada*] (NLC)

QMLR........ Constance-Lethbridge Rehabilitation Centre [*Centre de Readaptation Constance-Lethbridge*] Montreal, Quebec [*Library symbol*] [*National Library of Canada*] (NLC)

QMM .... McLennan Library, McGill University, Montreal, Quebec [*Library symbol*] [*National Library of Canada*] (NLC)

QMMAC ..... Musee d'Art Contemporain, Montreal, Quebec [*Library symbol*] [*National Library of Canada*] (NLC)

QMMAQ ..... La Magnetotheque, Montreal, Quebec [*Library symbol*] [*National Library of Canada*] (NLC)

QMMB........ Blackader/Lauterman Library of Architecture and Art, McGill University, Montreal, Quebec [*Library symbol*] [*National Library of Canada*] (NLC)

QMMBC ..... Molson Breweries of Canada Ltd., Montreal, Quebec [*Library symbol*] [*National Library of Canada*] (NLC)

QMMBZ...... Blacker-Wood Library of Zoology and Ornithology, McGill University, Montreal, Quebec [*Library symbol*] [*National Library of Canada*] (NLC)

QMMC........ Miron Co. Ltd., Montreal, Quebec [*Library symbol*] [*National Library of Canada*] (NLC)

QMMCH ..... Montreal Children's Hospital, Quebec [*Library symbol*] [*National Library of Canada*] (NLC)

QMMCR ..... Musee du Chateau de Ramezay, Montreal, Quebec [*Library symbol*] [*National Library of Canada*] (NLC)

QMMD........ Religious Studies Library, McGill University, Montreal, Quebec [*Library symbol*] [*National Library of Canada*] (NLC)

QMMDC ..... Dawson College, Montreal, Quebec [*Library symbol*] [*National Library of Canada*] (NLC)

QMME........ Engineering Library, McGill University, Montreal, Quebec [*Library symbol*] [*National Library of Canada*] (NLC)

QMME .... Physical Sciences and Engineering Library, McGill University, Montreal, Quebec [*Library symbol*] [*National Library of Canada*] (NLC)

QMMFD...... Dentistry Library, McGill University, Montreal, Quebec [*Library symbol*] [*National Library of Canada*] (NLC)

QMMG........ Map and Air Photo Library, McGill University, Montreal, Quebec [*Library symbol*] [*National Library of Canada*] (NLC)

QMMGS ..... Department of Geological Sciences, McGill University, Montreal, Quebec [*Library symbol*] [*National Library of Canada*] (NLC)

QMMH........ Mental Hygiene Istitute [*Institut de l'Hygiene Mentale*] Montreal, Quebec [*Library symbol*] [*National Library of Canada*] (NLC)

QMMHH ..... Maimonides Hospital and Home for the Aged, Montreal, Quebec [*Library symbol*] [*National Library of Canada*] (NLC)

QMMI .... Atwater Library [*Formerly, Mechanics Institute Library*] Montreal, Quebec [*Library symbol*] [*National Library of Canada*] (NLC)

QMMIQ....... Quebec Regional Office, Employment and Immigration Canada [*Bureau Regional du Quebec, Emploi et Immigration Canada*] Montreal, Quebec [*Library symbol*] [*National Library of Canada*] (NLC)

QMML........ Law Library, McGill University, Montreal, Quebec [*Library symbol*] [*National Library of Canada*] (NLC)

QMMLS ...... Library Science Library, McGill University, Montreal, Quebec [*Library symbol*] [*National Library of Canada*] (NLC)

QMMM .... Medical Library, McGill University, Montreal, Quebec [*Library symbol*] [*National Library of Canada*] (NLC)

QMMMCM ... McCord Museum, McGill University, Montreal, Quebec [*Library symbol*] [*National Library of Canada*] (NLC)

QMMMDM ... Marvin Duchow Music Library, McGill University, Montreal, Quebec [*Library symbol*] [*National Library of Canada*] (NLC)

QMMMM .... Montreal Military and Maritime Museum, Quebec [*Library symbol*] [*National Library of Canada*] (NLC)

QMMN........ Nursing/Social Work Library, McGill University, Montreal, Quebec [*Library symbol*] [*National Library of Canada*] (NLC)

QMMNS ..... Northern Studies Library, McGill University, Montreal, Quebec [*Library symbol*] [*National Library of Canada*] (NLC)

QMMO........ Osler Library, McGill University, Montreal, Quebec [*Library symbol*] [*National Library of Canada*] (NLC)

QMMOC ..... Monsanto Canada Ltd., Montreal, Quebec [*Library symbol*] [*National Library of Canada*] (NLC)

QMMOS ..... Montreal Star, Quebec [*Library symbol*] [*National Library of Canada*] (NLC)

QMMPB...... MPB Technologies, Dorval, Quebec [*Library symbol*] [*National Library of Canada*] (NLC)

QMMPS...... Physical Sciences Library, McGill University, Montreal, Quebec [*Library symbol*] [*National Library of Canada*] (NLC)

QMMRB...... Department of Rare Books and Special Collections, McGill University, Montreal, Quebec [*Library symbol*] [*National Library of Canada*] (NLC)

QMMSC ..... Howard Ross Library of Management, McGill University, Montreal, Quebec [*Library symbol*] [*National Library of Canada*] (NLC)

QMMSR...... Centre de documentation, Ministere de la Main-d'Oeuvre et de la Securite du Revenu du Quebec, Montreal, Quebec [*Library symbol*] [*National Library of Canada*] (NLC)

QMN.......... Bibliotheaue Municipale, Montreal Nord, Quebec [*Library symbol*] [*National Library of Canada*] (NLC)

QMNA .... Canadian Pulp and Paper Asssociation [*Association Canadienne des Producteurs dePates et Papiers*] Montreal, Quebec [*Library symbol*] [*National Library of Canada*] (NLC)

QMNDE ...... Hopital Notre-Dame-De-L'Esperance-De-St-Laurent, Montreal, Quebec [*Library symbol*] [*National Library of Canada*] (NLC)

QMNE......... Northern Electric Co. Ltd., Montreal, Quebec [*Library symbol*] [*National Library of Canada*] (NLC)

QMNF......... National Film Board, Montreal [*Formerly, Ottawa*] [*Office National du Film, Montreal (Anciennement Ottawa)*] Quebec [*Library symbol*] [*National Library of Canada*] (NLC)

QMNFNI ..... National Information/Distribution System, National Film Board [*Systeme d'Information et de Distribution pour les Produits Audio-Visuels Canadiens, Office National du film*] Montreal, Quebec [*Library symbol*] [*National Library of Canada*] (NLC)

QMNHH .... Health Protection Branch, Canada Department of National Health and Welfare [*Direction Generale de la Protection de la Sante, Ministere de la Sante Nationale et du Bien-Etre Social*] Montreal, Quebec [*Library symbol*] [*National Library of Canada*] (NLC)

QMNIH .... Montreal Neurological Institute and Hospital [*Institut et Hopital Neurologiques de Montreal*] Quebec [*Library symbol*] [*National Library of Canada*] (NLC)

QMNOT ...... Northern Telecom Canada Ltd., Montreal, Quebec [*Library symbol*] [*National Library of Canada*] (NLC)

QMNR......... Noranda Research Centre, Pointe-Claire, Quebec [*Library symbol*] [*National Library of Canada*] (NLC)

QMNT......... Nesbitt, Thomson & Co. Ltd., Montreal, Quebec [*Library symbol*] [*National Library of Canada*] (NLC)

QMO........... Oratoire Saint-Joseph, Montreal, Quebec [*Library symbol*] [*National Library of Canada*] (NLC)

QMO........... Qualitative Materiel Objective [*Army*] (AABC)

QMO........... Quartz Mountain State Park [*Oklahoma*] [*Seismograph station code, US Geological Survey*] (SEIS)

QMOB .... Office de Biologie, Ministere du Loisir, de la Chasse et de la Peche, Montreal, Quebec [*Library symbol*] [*National Library of Canada*] (NLC)

QMobSC .... Quadripartite Mobility Standardization Committee [*Military*] (AABC)

QMOCP ...... Canadian Livestock Feed Board [*Office Canadien des Provendes*] Montreal, Quebec [*Library symbol*] [*National Library of Canada*] (NLC)

QMOCQ ..... Office de la Construction du Quebec, Montreal, Quebec [*Library symbol*] [*National Library of Canada*] (NLC)

QMOF......... Ogilvie Flour Mills Co. Ltd., Montreal, Quebec [*Library symbol*] [*National Library of Canada*] (NLC)

QMOFJ....... Office Franco-Quebecois pour la Jeunesse, Montreal, Quebec [*Library symbol*] [*National Library of Canada*] (NLC)

QMOI......... Ordre des Infirmieres et Infirmiers du Quebec, Montreal, Quebec [*Library symbol*] [*National Library of Canada*] (NLC)

QMOLF...... Office de la Langue Francaise, Montreal, Quebec [*Library symbol*] [*National Library of Canada*] (NLC)

QMORC ..... Quartermaster Officers' Reserve Corps [*Military*]

Q(Mov)...... Quartermaster Movements [*World War II*]

QMP .... Qualitative Management Program [*Army*] (INF)

QMP .... Quarry, Mine, and Pit [*A publication*]

QMPA......... Centre de Documentation, Projet Archipel de Montreal, Quebec [*Library symbol*] [*National Library of Canada*] (NLC)

QMPA......... Quartermaster Purchasing Agency [*Army*]

QMPC......... Presbyterian College, Montreal, Quebec [*Library symbol*] [*National Library of Canada*] (NLC)

QMPC......... Quartermaster Petroleum Center [*Army*] (MUGU)

QMPCA ...... Agriculture Canada, Montreal, Quebec [*Library symbol*] [*National Library of Canada*] (NLC)

QMPCUSA ... Quartermaster Petroleum Center, United States Army

QMPE......... Pezaris Electronics Co., Montreal, Quebec [*Library symbol*] [*National Library of Canada*] (NLC)

QMPI.......... Polish Institute of Arts and Sciences in Canada [*Institut Polonais des Arts et des Sciences au Canada*] Montreal, Quebec [*Library symbol*] [*National Library of Canada*] (NLC)

QMPM .... Peat, Marwick, Mitchell et Cie., Montreal, Quebec [*Library symbol*] [*National Library of Canada*] (NLC)

QMPM .... Quantitative Methods for Public Management [*Course*]

QMPP......... Pulp and Paper Research Institute of Canada [*Institut Canadien de Recherches sur les Pates et Papiers*] Pointe-Claire, Quebec [*Library symbol*] [*National Library of Canada*] (NLC)

QMPSB ...... Protestant School Board of Greater Montreal, Quebec [*Library symbol*] [*National Library of Canada*] (NLC)

QMPSR ...... P. S. Ross & Partners, Montreal, Quebec (NLC)

QMPTI........ Potton Technical Industries, Mansonville, Quebec [*Library symbol*] [*National Library of Canada*] (NLC)

QMPW........ Price, Waterhouse & Co., Montreal, Quebec [*Library symbol*]

QMPWQ ..... Quebec Region Library, Public Works Canada [*Bibliotheque de la Region du Quebec, Travaux Publics Canada*] Montreal, Quebec [*Library symbol*] [*National Library of Canada*] (NLC)

QMQ........... Queen Mary Veterans Hospital [*Hopital Reine-Marie (Anciens combattants)*] Montreal, Quebec [*Library symbol*] [*National Library of Canada*] (NLC)

QMQAR...... Quebec Archives, Montreal, Quebec [*Library symbol*] [*National Library of Canada*] (NLC)

QMQB .... Quick-Make, Quick-Break

QMQDP...... Commission des Droits de la Personne du Quebec, Montreal, Quebec [*Library symbol*] [*National Library of Canada*] (NLC)

QMQE .... Queen Elizabeth Hospital, Montreal, Quebec [*Library symbol*] [*National Library of Canada*] (NLC)

QMR .... Qualitative Material Report

QMR .... Qualitative Materiel Requirement [*Army*]

QMR .... Qualitative Military Requirements [*NATO*] (NATG)

QMR .... Quartermaster

QMR .... Royal Bank of Canada [*Banque Royale du Canada*] Montreal, Quebec [*Library symbol*] [*National Library of Canada*] (NLC)

QMRA........ Railway Association of Canada, Montreal, Quebec [*Library symbol*] [*National Library of Canada*] (NLC)

QMRAD...... Centre de Documentation, Institut de Recherche Appliquee sur le Travail, Monreal, Quebec [*Library symbol*] [*National Library of Canada*] (NLC)

QMRAQ ..... Recherches Amerindiennes au Quebec, Montreal, Quebec [*Library symbol*] [*National Library of Canada*] (NLC)

QMRC .... Quartermaster Reserve Corps [*Military*]

QMRC .... Royal Canadian Air Force [*Corps d'Aviation Royale du Canada*] Montreal, Quebec [*Library symbol*] [*National Library of Canada*] (NLC)

QMRCH ...... Richmond County Historical Society [*Societe d'Histoire du Comte de Richmond*] Melbourne, Quebec (NLC)

QMRCM ..... Raymond, Chabot, Martin, Pare, Montreal, Quebec [*Library symbol*] [*National Library of Canada*] (NLC)

QMRD........ Reader's Digest of Canada Ltd., Montreal, Quebec [*Library symbol*] [*National Library of Canada*] (NLC)

QMRE........ Revenue Canada [*Revenu Canada*] Montreal, Quebec [*Library symbol*] [*National Library of Canada*] (NLC)

QMREC ...... Quartermaster Research and Engineering Command [*Army*]

QMREFEA ... Quartermaster Research and Engineering Field Evaluation Agency [*Merged with Troop Evaluation Test*]

QMREG ...... Regie de l'Electricite et du Gaz, Montreal, Quebec [*Library symbol*] [*National Library of Canada*] (NLC)

QMREX ...... Canada Department of Regional Industrial Expansion [*Ministere de l'Expansion Industrielle Regionale*] Montreal, Quebec [*Library symbol*] [*National Library of Canada*] (NLC)

QMRH........ Centre de Recherches en Relations Humaines, Montreal, Quebec [*Library symbol*] [*National Library of Canada*] (NLC)

QMRI .... Rehabilitation Institute of Montreal [*Institut de Rehabilitation de Montreal*] Quebec [*Library symbol*] [*National Library of Canada*] (NLC)

QMRL .... Quartermaster Radiation Laboratory [*Army*]

QMRL .... Regie du Logement, Montreal, Quebec [*Library symbol*] [*National Library of Canada*] (NLC)

QMRM .... Reddy Memorial Hospital, Montreal, Quebec [*Library symbol*] [*National Library of Canada*] (NLC)

QMRP........ Qualified Mental Retardation Professional

QMRP......... Rhone-Poulenc Pharma, Inc., Montreal, Quebec [*Library symbol*] [*National Library of Canada*] (NLC)

QMRPA ...... Quartermaster Radiation Planning Agency [*Army*]

QMRQ .... Societe de Radio-Television du Quebec, Montreal, Quebec [*Library symbol*] [*National Library of Canada*] (NLC)

QMRR........ Rolls-Royce of Canada Ltd., Montreal, Quebec [*Library symbol*] [*National Library of Canada*] (NLC)

QMRRD ..... Reginald P. Dawson Library, Town of Mount Royal, Quebec [*Library symbol*] [*National Library of Canada*] (NLC)

QMRSJA .... Archives des Religieuses Hospitalieres de Saint-Joseph, Montreal, Quebec [*Library symbol*] [*National Library of Canada*] (NLC)

QMRV .... Royal Victoria Hospital, Montreal, Quebec [*Library symbol*] [*National Library of Canada*] (NLC)

QMRVW ..... Women's Pavilion, Royal Victoria Hospital, Montreal, Quebec [*Library symbol*] [*National Library of Canada*] (NLC)

QMS .... Quadrupole Mass Spectrometer

QMS .... Quality Micro Systems [*Trademark*]

QMS .... Quality Monitoring System (MCD)

QMS .... Quarterly Journal. Mythic Society [*Bangalore*] [*A publication*]

QMS .... Quartermaster School [*Army*]

QMS .... Quartermaster Sergeant [*Military*]

QMS .... Quartermaster Stores [*Military*]

QMS .... Quicksilver Messenger Service [*Pop music group*]

QMS .... Sun Life of Canada [*Sun Life du Canada*] Montreal, Quebec [*Library symbol*] [*National Library of Canada*] (NLC)

QMSA........ Informatheque-Montreal, Ministere des Affaires Sociales du Quebec, Montreal, Quebec [*Library symbol*] [*National Library of Canada*] (NLC)

QMSA........ Seaman Apprentice, Quartermaster, Striker [*Navy rating*]

QMSA........ Service de Documentation, Ministere de la Sante et des Services Sociaux, Montreal, Quebec [*Library symbol*] [*National Library of Canada*] (NLC)

QMSAC ...... Sandoz Canada, Inc., Dorval, Quebec [*Library symbol*]
    [*National Library of Canada*]   (NLC)
QMSAP ...... Societe des Artistes Professionnels du Quebec, Montreal,
    Quebec [*Library symbol*] [*National Library of
    Canada*]   (NLC)
QMSC .... Southern Canada Power Co., Montreal, Quebec [*Library
    symbol*] [*National Library of Canada*]   (NLC)
QMSCA ...... Statistics Canada [*Statistique Canada*] Montreal, Quebec
    [*Library symbol*] [*National Library of Canada*]   (NLC)
QMSCM ..... Canadian Microfilming Co. Ltd. [*Societe Canadienne du
    Microfilm, Inc.*] Montreal, Quebec [*Library symbol*]
    [*National Library of Canada*]   (NLC)
QMSDB ...... Societe de Developpement de la Baie James, Montreal,
    Quebec [*Library symbol*] [*National Library of
    Canada*]   (NLC)
QMSDL ...... Sidbec-Dosco Ltd./Ltee., Montreal, Quebec [*Library symbol*]
    [*National Library of Canada*]   (NLC)
QMSGA ...... Archives Generales des Soeurs Grises, Montreal, Quebec
    [*Library symbol*] [*National Library of Canada*]   (NLC)
QMSGE ...... Office des Services de Garde a l'Enfance, Montreal, Quebec
    [*Library symbol*] [*National Library of Canada*]   (NLC)
QMSGME... Service General des Moyens d'Enseignement, Ministere de
    l'Education du Quebec, Montreal, Quebec [*Library
    symbol*] [*National Library of Canada*]   (NLC)
QMSGT ...... Quartermaster Sergeant [*Marine Corps*]
QMSH........ Societe Historique de Montreal, Quebec [*Library symbol*]
    [*National Library of Canada*]   (NLC)
QMSHE ...... Stadler Hurter, Montreal, Quebec [*Library symbol*] [*National
    Library of Canada*]   (NLC)
QMSI .... Quality Micro Systems [*NASDAQ symbol*]   (NQ)
QMSI .... Scolasticat de l'Immaculee-Conception, Montreal, Quebec
    [*Library symbol*] [*National Library of Canada*]   (NLC)
QMSJ .... St. Joseph's Teachers' College, Montreal, Quebec [*Library
    symbol*] [*National Library of Canada*]   (NLC)
QMSMA ..... St. Mary's Hospital, Montreal, Quebec [*Library symbol*]
    [*National Library of Canada*]   (NLC)
QMSN........ Seaman, Quartermaster, Striker [*Navy rating*]
QMSNC ...... SNC, Inc., Montreal, Quebec [*Library symbol*] [*National Library
    of Canada*]   (NLC)
QMSO .... Quartermaster Supply Officer [*Army*]
QMSO .... Shell Oil Co. of Canada, Montreal, Quebec [*Library symbol*]
    [*National Library of Canada*]   (NLC)
QMSOB ...... Le Groupe SOBECO, Montreal, Quebec [*Library symbol*]
    [*National Library of Canada*]   (NLC)
QMSTJ .... Centre d'Information sur la Sante de l'Enfant, Hopital Sainte-
    Justine, Montreal, Quebec [*Library symbol*] [*National
    Library of Canada*]   (NLC)
QMSU........ Surete du Quebec, Montreal, Quebec [*Library symbol*]
    [*National Library of Canada*]   (NLC)
QMSVM...... Centre de Service Social Ville-Marie [*Ville-Marie Social Service
    Centre*] Montreal, Quebec [*Library symbol*] [*National
    Library of Canada*]   (NLC)
QMSW........ Quartz Metal Sealed Window
QMSW........ Sherwin-Williams Co. of Canada Ltd., Montreal, Quebec
    [*Library symbol*] [*National Library of Canada*]   (NLC)
QMSWP...... Shawinigan Engineering Ltd. Co., Montreal, Quebec [*Library
    symbol*] [*National Library of Canada*]   (NLC)
QMT .... Montreal Trust Co., Quebec [*Library symbol*] [*National Library
    of Canada*]   (NLC)
QMTA......... Tomenson Alexander Ltd., Montreal, Quebec [*Library symbol*]
    [*National Library of Canada*]   (NLC)
QMTC......... Air Canada, Montreal, Quebec [*Library symbol*] [*National
    Library of Canada*]   (NLC)
QMTD......... Transportation Development Centre, Transport Canada
    [*Centre de Developpement des Transports, Transports
    Canada*] Montreal, Quebec [*Library symbol*] [*National
    Library of Canada*]   (NLC)
QMTGC...... Teleglobe Canada, Montreal, Quebec [*Library symbol*]
    [*National Library of Canada*]   (NLC)
QMTH......... Institut de Tourisme et d'Hotellerie du Quebec, Montreal,
    Quebec [*Library symbol*] [*National Library of
    Canada*]   (NLC)
QMTMO ..... Centre de Documentation, Ministere du Travail du Quebec,
    Montreal, Quebec [*Library symbol*] [*National Library of
    Canada*]   (NLC)
QMTOE ...... Quartermaster Table of Organization and Equipment [*Units*]
    [*Military*]
QMTR......... Waterways Development, Transport Canada [*Developpement
    des vois Navigables, Transports Canada*] Montreal,
    Quebec [*Library symbol*] [*National Library of
    Canada*]   (NLC)
QMU .... Universite de Montreal, Quebec [*Library symbol*] [*National
    Library of Canada*]   (NLC)
QMUA .... Service des Archives de l'Universite de Montreal, Quebec
    [*Library symbol*] [*National Library of Canada*]   (NLC)
QMUC .... Union Carbide Canada Ltd., Pointe-Aux-Trembles, Quebec
    [*Library symbol*] [*National Library of Canada*]   (NLC)
QMUDD...... Departement de Demographie, Universite de Montreal,
    Quebec [*Library symbol*] [*National Library of
    Canada*]   (NLC)

QMUE .... Bibliotheque de l'Institut d'Etudes Medievales, Universite de
    Montreal, Quebec [*Library symbol*] [*National Library of
    Canada*]   (NLC)
QMUEB ...... Ecole de Bibliotheconomie, Universite de Montreal, Quebec
    [*Library symbol*] [*National Library of Canada*]   (NLC)
QMUEC ...... L'Ecole de Criminologie, Universite de Montreal, Quebec
    [*Library symbol*] [*National Library of Canada*]   (NLC)
QMUGC...... Cartotheque, Department de Geographie, Universite de
    Montreal, Quebec [*Library symbol*] [*National Library of
    Canada*]   (NLC)
QMUGL ...... Cartotheque, Institut de Geologie, Universite de Montreal,
    Quebec [*Library symbol*] [*National Library of
    Canada*]   (NLC)
QMUQ .... Universite de Quebec, Montreal, Quebec [*Library symbol*]
    [*National Library of Canada*]   (NLC)
QMUQC...... Cartotheque, Universite du Quebec, Montreal, Quebec [*Library
    symbol*] [*National Library of Canada*]   (NLC)
QMUQEN ... Ecole Nationale d'Administration Publique, Universite du
    Quebec, Montreal, Quebec [*Library symbol*] [*National
    Library of Canada*]   (NLC)
QMUQET.... Ecole de Technolgie Superieure, Universite de Quebec,
    Montreal, Quebec [*Library symbol*] [*National Library of
    Canada*]   (NLC)
QMUQIC..... Cartotheque, INRS-Urbanisation, Montreal, Quebec [*Library
    symbol*] [*National Library of Canada*]   (NLC)
QMUQIS..... Centre de Documentation, INRS-Sante, Montreal, Quebec
    [*Library symbol*] [*National Library of Canada*]   (NLC)
QMUQIU..... Centre de Documentation INRS-Urbanisation, Montreal,
    Quebec [*Library symbol*] [*National Library of
    Canada*]   (NLC)
QMUQPA ... Pavillon des Arts, Universite du Quebec, Montreal, Quebec
    [*Library symbol*] [*National Library of Canada*]   (NLC)
QMUQTM... Tele-Universite, Universite du Quebec, Montreal, Quebec
    [*Library symbol*] [*National Library of Canada*]   (NLC)
Q Museum Memoirs ... Memoirs. Queensland Museum [*A publication*]
QMV .... RCA Victor Co. Ltd., Montreal, Quebec [*Library symbol*]
    [*National Library of Canada*]   (NLC)
QMVC .... Media Resource Centre, Vanier College, Montreal, Quebec
    [*Library symbol*] [*National Library of Canada*]   (NLC)
QMVR........ Documentation Centre, VIA Rail Canada, Inc. [*Centre de
    Documentation, VIA Rail Canada Inc.*] Montreal, Quebec
    [*Library symbol*] [*National Library of Canada*]   (NLC)
QMW .... Quartz Metal Window
QMW .... Warnock Hersey Co. Ltd., Montreal, Quebec [*Library symbol*]
    [*National Library of Canada*]   (NLC)
QMWM ...... William M. Mercer, Montreal, Quebec [*Library symbol*]
    [*National Library of Canada*]   (NLC)
QMY .... YWCA, Montreal, Quebec [*Library symbol*] [*National Library of
    Canada*]   (NLC)
QMYH........ YM - YWHA, Montreal, Quebec [*Library symbol*] [*National
    Library of Canada*]   (NLC)
QN .... Kabo Air Travels [*Nigeria*] [*ICAO designator*]   (FAAC)
QN .... Quantifier Negation [*Principle of logic*]
QN .... Quantum Number
QN .... Quaque Nocte [*Every Night*] [*Pharmacy*]
QN .... Quarterly Newsletter. American Bar Association   (DLA)
QN .... Queen [*ADA*]
QN .... Query Normalization
QN .... Question   (FAAC)
QN .... Quetzalcoatlus Northropi [*Pterosaur, a model constructed for
    the Smithsonian Institution and referred to by these
    initials*]
QN .... Quotation [*Business and trade*]
QNA........... Qatar News Agency [*BJA*]
QNat.......... Quaestiones Naturales [*of Seneca the Younger*] [*Classical
    studies*]   (OCD)
Q Natl Fire Prot Assoc ... Quarterly. National Fire Protection Association [*A
    publication*]
QNB........... Quinuclidinyl Benzilate [*Also, BZ*] [*Hallucinogen*]
QNC .... New Castle Free Public Library, New Castle, PA [*OCLC
    symbol*]   (OCLC)
QNCCR ...... Quarterly Notes on Christianity and Chinese Religion [*A
    publication*]
QNCH........ Quenched   (MSA)
QNCHRN.... Centre Hospitalier Rouyn-Noranda, Noranda, Quebec [*Library
    symbol*] [*National Library of Canada*]   (NLC)
QNCRS....... Conseil Regional de la Sante et des Services Sociaux Rouyn-
    Noranda, Noranda, Quebec [*Library symbol*] [*National
    Library of Canada*]   (NLC)
QND .... Quantum Nondemolition [*Method of measurement*]
QNH........... Altimeter Subscale Setting to Obtain Elevation When on the
    Ground [*Aviation code*]   (FAAC)
QNI .... Queen's Nursing Institute [*British*]
QNICA........ Soeurs de L'Assomption, Nocolet, Quebec [*Library symbol*]
    [*National Library of Canada*]   (NLC)
QNICS........ Seminaire de Nicolet, Quebec [*Library symbol*] [*National
    Library of Canada*]   (NLC)
QNIP.......... Institut de Police du Quebec, Nicolet, Quebec [*Library symbol*]
    [*National Library of Canada*]   (NLC)
QNL .... Quarterly News Letter [*Book Club of California*] [*A publication*]
QNMC .... Quadripartite Nonmateriel Committee [*Military*]   (AABC)

QNOAG ...... Experimental Farm, Agriculture Canada [*Ferme Experimentale, Agriculture Canada*] Normandin, Quebec [*Library symbol*] [*National Library of Canada*] (NLC)
QNS........... Quantity Not Sufficient [*Pharmacy*]
QNSC .... Qui Nhon Support Command [*Vietnam*]
QNST .... Quick Neurological Screening Test
QNT .... Quantizer (MDG)
QNT .... Quintet [*Music*]
QNTM........ Quantum Corp. [*NASDAQ symbol*] (NQ)
QNTY .... Quantity (AFM)
QO .... Otrag Range Air Service [*Zaire*] [*ICAO designator*] (FAAC)
QO .... Quaker Oats [*Trade name*]
QO .... Qualified in Ordnance [*Obsolete*] [*Navy*]
QO .... Quartermaster Operation [*Military*]
QO .... Queen's Own [*Military unit*] [*British*]
QO .... Quick Opening [*Nuclear energy*] (NRCH)
QOBV .... Quick-Opening Blowdown Valve [*Nuclear energy*] (NRCH)
QOC .... Quality of Conformance
QOC .... Quasi-Optical Circuit
QOCH........ Queen's Own Cameron Highlanders [*Military unit*] [*British*]
QOD .... Quality of Design
QOD .... Quantitative Oceanographic Data
QOD .... Quaque Otra Die [*Every Other Day*] [*Pharmacy*]
QOD .... Quick-Opening Device
QOH .... Quantity on Hand
QOH .... Quaque Otra Hora [*Every Other Hour*] [*Pharmacy*]
QOH .... Queen's Own Hussars [*Military unit*] [*British*]
QOI .... Quality Operating Instruction
Q Oil Stat ... Quarterly Oil Statistics [*France*] [*A publication*]
QOL .... Quality of Life [*Program*] [*Army*]
QOLCPF .... Bibliotheque de la Faune, Ministere du Loisir, de la Chasse et de la Pech, Orsainville, Quebec [*Library symbol*] [*National Library of Canada*] (NLC)
QOLUG...... Queensland Online Users' Group [*Australian*] (ADA)
QOMAC..... Quarter Orbit Magnetic Attitude Control
QOMY .... Queen's Own Mercian Yeomanry [*Military unit*] [*British*]
QON .... Quaque Otra Nocte [*Every Other Night*] [*Pharmacy*]
QON .... Quarter Ocean Net
Q(Ops) ...... Quartermaster Operations [*World War II*]
QOR........... Qualitative Operational Requirement [*Military*]
QOR........... Quarterly Operating Report
QOR........... Quebec Official Reports (DLA)
QOR........... Queen's Own Rifles [*Military unit*] [*British*]
QOR........... Queen's Own Royal [*Military unit*] [*British*]
QORC........ Queen's Own Rifles, Canada [*Military*] (ROG)
QORGS ..... Quasi-Optimal Rendezvous Guidance System
QORWKR ... Queen's Own Royal West Kent Regiment [*Military unit*] [*British*]
QOS .... Quality of Service [*Telecommunications*] (TEL)
QOT........... Quasi-Optical Technique
QOT........... Quote (FAAC)
QOT & E ..... Qualification, Operational Test, and Evaluation
QOWVR...... Queen's Own Westminster Volunteer Rifles [*Military*] [*British*] (ROG)
QP .... Caspair Ltd. [*Kenya*] [*ICAO designator*] (FAAC)
QP .... Quaderni Portoghesi [*A publication*]
QP .... Quadratic Programing [*Data processing*] (BUR)
QP .... Quadruple Play (DEN)
QP .... Qualification Proposal
QP .... Quantum Placet [*As Much as You Please*] [*Pharmacy*]
QP .... Quartered Partition
QP .... Quasi-Peak
QP .... Queen Post
QP .... Queen's Pawn [*Chess*] (ADA)
QP .... Queen's Pleasure [*British*]
QP .... Query Processing (MCD)
QP .... Quick Processing [*Chemicals*]
QPA........... Bibliotheque Municipale, Port-Alfred, Quebec [*Library symbol*] [*National Library of Canada*] (NLC)
QPA........... Quality Product Assurance
QPA........... Quantity per Assembly (MCD)
QPAA .... Quality Planning and Administration (MCD)
QPAG .... Experimental Farm, Agriculture Canada [*Ferme Experimentale, Agriculture Canada*] La Pocatiere, Quebec [*Library symbol*] [*National Library of Canada*] (NLC)
QPAM........ Quantized Pulsed Amplitude Modulation
QPB........... Quality Paperback Book Club [*Trademark of Book-of-the-Month Club, Inc.*]
QPC........... College de Ste-Anne, La Pocatiere, Quebec [*Library symbol*] [*National Library of Canada*] (NLC)
QPC........... Quantity per Equipment/Component
QPD........... Queensland Parliamentary Debates [*A publication*]
QPDOLL..... Quarterly Payment Demand on Legal Loan
Q Pediatr Bull ... Quarterly Pediatric Bulletin [*A publication*]
QPEI .... Quantity per End Item (MCD)
QPES......... Institut de Technologie Agricole, La Pocatiere, Quebec [*Library symbol*] [*National Library of Canada*] (NLC)
QPF........... Quantitative Precipitation Forecast (NOAA)
QPH........... Queen's Park Harriers [*British*] (ROG)
1QpHab ..... Commentary [*or Pesher on Habakkuk*] from Qumran. Cave One (BJA)
1QpHos ...... Commentary on Hosea from Qumran. Cave One (BJA)

1QPhyl .... Phylacteries [*or Tefillin*] from Qumran. Cave One (BJA)
QPI .... Quadratic Performance Index
QPI .... Quality Productivity Improvement (MCD)
QPIS .... Quality Planning Instruction Sheet (MCD)
QPL .... Qualified Parts List (AAG)
QPL .... Qualified Products List [*Military*]
Q PL .... Quantum Placet [*As Much as You Please*] [*Pharmacy*]
QPLM .... Bibliotheque Municipale, Plessisville, [*Library symbol*] [*National Library of Canada*] (NLC)
QPLR .... Queensland Planning Law Reports [*A publication*]
QPL & S..... Qualified Products Lists and Sources
QPLT .... Quiet Propulsion Lift Technology [*NASA*]
QPM .... Quality Practice Manual [*A publication*]
QPM .... Quality Program Manager (NRCH)
QPM .... Quantized Pulse Modulation
QPM .... Queen's Police Medal [*British*]
QPM .... Queen's [*Victoria*] Prime Ministers [*A publication*]
1QpMi .... Pesher [*or Commentary on Micah*] from Qumran. Cave One (BJA)
1QpNah ..... Pesher [*or Commentary on Nahum*] from Qumran. Cave One (BJA)
4QpNah ..... Pesher [*or Commentary on Nahum*] from Qumran. Cave Four (BJA)
Q/PNL .... Quarter Panel [*Automotive engineering*]
QPO........... Quasi-Periodic Oscillation [*Astronomy*]
QPOC........ Pointe-Claire Public Library [*Bibliotheque Publique de Pointe-Claire*] Quebec [*Library symbol*] [*National Library of Canada*] (NLC)
Q Police J... Queensland Police Journal [*A publication*]
QPON .... Seven Oaks International [*NASDAQ symbol*] (NQ)
Q Poul Bull ... Quarterly Poultry Bulletin [*A publication*]
QPP .... Quality Program Plan (MCD)
QPP .... Quality Program Provision
QPP .... Quantized Pulse Position
QPP .... Quebec Pension Plan [*Canada*]
QPP .... Queensland Parliamentary Papers [*A publication*]
QPP .... Quiescent Push-Pull [*Electronics*] (DEN)
QPPC .... Quarterly Production Progress Conference [*Navy*] (NG)
4QpPs37..... Pesher [*or Commentary on Psalm 37*] from Qumran. Cave Four (BJA)
QPR........... Pittsburgh Regional Library Center - Union List, Pittsburgh, PA [*OCLC symbol*] (OCLC)
QPR........... Qualitative Personnel Requirements [*NASA*] (KSC)
QPR........... Quality Progress Review (MCD)
QPR........... Quarterly Progress Report
QPR........... Quebec Practice Reports (DLA)
QPR........... Queensland Practice Reports [*A publication*]
1QPrayers ... Liturgical Fragments from Qumran. Cave One (BJA)
QPRD......... Quality Planning Requirements Document [*NASA*] (NASA)
QPRI......... Qualitative Personnel Requirements Information [*NASA*] (MCD)
QPRI......... Qualitative Personnel Requirements Inventory (MCD)
QPRM........ Bibliotheque Municipale, Princeville, Quebec [*Library symbol*] [*National Library of Canada*] (NLC)
4QPrNab .... [*The*] Prayer of Nabonidus from Qumran. Cave Four (BJA)
QPRS......... Quadrature Partial-Response System [*Telecommunications*] (TEL)
QPRS......... Quarterly Project Reliability Summary [*Navy*] (NG)
QPS........... Qualified Process Supplies (MCD)
QPS........... Qualified Processing Source
QPS........... Quality Planning Specification [*NASA*] (NASA)
QPS........... Quantitative Physical Science
QPS........... Quiescent Power Supply
QPSC .... Quiescent Power Supply Current
QPSK .... Quad-Phase Shift Key
QPSL .... Qualified Parts and Suppliers List (MCD)
QPT........... Quadrant Power Tilt (IEEE)
QQ .... Aerovias Quisqueyana [*Airlines*] [*Dominican Republic*] [*ICAO designator*] (OAG)
QQ .... Bibliotheque de Quebec, Quebec [*Library symbol*] [*National Library of Canada*] (NLC)
QQ .... Potential Hijacker [*Airline notation*]
QQ .... Qualitate Qua [*In the Capacity Of*] [*Latin*]
Q-Q............ Quantile-Quantile [*Data processing*]
QQ .... Quaque [*Each or Every*] [*Pharmacy*]
QQ .... Queen's Quarterly [*A publication*]
QQ .... Questionable Questionnaires
QQ .... Questions
Q and Q ..... Quill and Quire [*A publication*]
QQ .... Quisque [*Each, Every*] [*Pharmacy*]
QQ .... Quoque [*Also*] [*Pharmacy*]
QQA .... Archives Nationales du Quebec, Quebec, Quebec [*Library symbol*] [*National Library of Canada*] (NLC)
QQAA........ Archives de l'Archeveche de Quebec, Quebec [*Library symbol*] [*National Library of Canada*] (NLC)
QQAC........ Ministere des Affaires Culturelles du Quebec, Quebec, Quebec [*Library symbol*] [*National Library of Canada*] (NLC)
QQACJ....... Archives de la Compagnie de Jesus, Province du Canada - Francais, Saint-Jerome, Quebec, Quebec [*Library symbol*] [*National Library of Canada*] (NLC)

QQAG......... Centre de Documentation du 200, Ministere de l'Agriculture, des Pecheries et de l'Alimentation, Quebec, Quebec [*Library symbol*] [*National Library of Canada*] (NLC)

QQAI .... Bibliotheque Administrative, Ministere des Affaires Inter-Gouvernementales du Quebec, Quebec, Quebec [*Library symbol*] [*National Library of Canada*] (NLC)

QQAM .... Centre de Documentation, Ministere des Affaires Municipales du Quebec, Quebec, Quebec [*Library symbol*] [*National Library of Canada*] (NLC)

QQAND ...... Archives du Monastere Notre-Dame-Des-Agnes, Quebec, Quebec [*Library symbol*] [*National Library of Canada*] (NLC)

QQAPC ...... Cerebral Palsy Association of Quebec, Inc. [*L'Association de Paralysie Cerebrale du Quebec Inc.*] Quebec, Quebec [*Library symbol*] [*National Library of Canada*] (NLC)

QQAQS ...... Synod Office, Diocese of Quebec, Anglican Church of Canada, Quebec, Quebec [*Library symbol*] [*National Library of Canada*] (NLC)

QQAS......... Archives du Seminaire de Quebec, Quebec, Quebec [*Library symbol*] [*National Library of Canada*] (NLC)

QQASF...... Conseil des Affaires Sociales et de la Famille, Quebec, Quebec [*Library symbol*] [*National Library of Canada*] (NLC)

QQBJNQ ... Bureau de la Baie James et du Nord Quebecois, Ste-Foy, Quebec [*Library symbol*] [*National Library of Canada*] (NLC)

QQBL .... Bibliotheque Lasallienne, Quebec, Quebec [*Library symbol*] [*National Library of Canada*] (NLC)

QQBS .... Bureau de la Statistique du Quebec, Quebec, Quebec [*Library symbol*] [*National Library of Canada*] (NLC)

QQBST...... Bureau de la Science et de la Technologie, Quebec, Quebec [*Library symbol*] [*National Library of Canada*] (NLC)

QQC .... Defence Research Establishment Valcartier, Canada Department of National Defence [*Centre de Recherches pour la Defense Valcartier, Ministere de la Defense Nationale*] Courcelette, Quebec [*Library symbol*] [*National Library of Canada*] (NLC)

QQC .... Quantitative Quality Characteristics

QQCAD ...... Conservatoire d'Art Dramatique de Quebec, Quebec, Quebec [*Library symbol*] [*National Library of Canada*] (NLC)

QQCAI....... Centre de Documentation, Commission de l'Acces a l'Information, Quebec, Quebec [*Library symbol*] [*National Library of Canada*] (NLC)

QQCAT ...... Commission de la Sante et de la Securite du Travail du Quebec, Quebec, Quebec [*Library symbol*] [*National Library of Canada*] (NLC)

QQCDP ...... Commission des Droits de la Personne du Quebec, Quebec, Quebec [*Library symbol*] [*National Library of Canada*] (NLC)

QQCE .... CEGEP de Limoilou, Quebec, Quebec [*Library symbol*] [*National Library of Canada*] (NLC)

QQCH........ Departement des Archives et Statistiques de la Ville de Quebec, Quebec, Quebec [*Library symbol*] [*National Library of Canada*] (NLC)

QQCLF...... Conseil de la Langue Francaise, Quebec, Quebec [*Library symbol*] [*National Library of Canada*] (NLC)

QQCM .... College Merici, Quebec, Quebec [*Library symbol*] [*National Library of Canada*] (NLC)

QQCMQ ..... Conservatoire de Musique de Quebec, Quebec, Quebec [*Library symbol*] [*National Library of Canada*] (NLC)

QQCPS...... Conseil de la Politique Scientifique du Quebec, Quebec, Quebec [*Library symbol*] [*National Library of Canada*] (NLC)

QQCRS ...... Conseil Regional de la Sante et des Services Sociaux, Quebec, Quebec [*Library symbol*] [*National Library of Canada*] (NLC)

QQCS........ Service de Docmentation et de Bibliotheque du Complexe Scientifique, Quebec, Quebec [*Library symbol*] [*National Library of Canada*] (NLC)

QQCSF...... Conseil du Statut de la Femme, Quebec, Quebec [*Library symbol*] [*National Library of Canada*] (NLC)

QQCT........ Commission de Toponymie du Quebec, Quebec, Quebec [*Library symbol*] [*National Library of Canada*] (NLC)

QQCU........ Conseil des Universites du Quebec, Ste-Foy, Quebec [*Library symbol*] [*National Library of Canada*] (NLC)

QQE........... Wildlife and Inland Waters Library, Environment Canada [*Bibliotheque de la Faune et des Eaux Interieures, Environnement Canada*] Ste-Foy, Quebec [*Library symbol*] [*National Library of Canada*] (NLC)

QQEDOP .... Office des Professions du Quebec, Ministere de l'Education, Quebec, Quebec [*Library symbol*] [*National Library of Canada*] (NLC)

QQEN .... Ministere de l'Environnement, Ste-Foy, Quebec [*Library symbol*] [*National Library of Canada*] (NLC)

QQER .... Ministere de l'Energie et des Ressources du Quebec, Quebec, Quebec [*Library symbol*] [*National Library of Canada*] (NLC)

QQERE....... Centre de Documentation-Energie, Ministere de l'Energie et des Ressources du Quebec, Quebec, Quebec [*Library symbol*] [*National Library of Canada*] (NLC)

QQERE...... Secteur Energie, Ministere de l'Energie et des Ressources du Quebec, Quebec, Quebec [*Library symbol*] [*National Library of Canada*] (NLC)

QQERM ..... Centre de Documentation-Mines, Ministere de l'Energie et des Ressources du Quebec, Quebec, Quebec [*Library symbol*] [*National Library of Canada*] (NLC)

QQERM ..... Secteur Mines, Ministere de l'Energie et des Ressources du Quebec, Quebec, Quebec [*Library symbol*] [*National Library of Canada*] (NLC)

QQERT....... Centre de Documentation-Terres et Forets, Ministere de l'Energie et des Ressources du Quebec, Quebec, Quebec [*Library symbol*] [*National Library of Canada*] (NLC)

QQF........... Bibliotheque Franciscaine, Quebec, Quebec [*Library symbol*] [*National Library of Canada*] (NLC)

QQFPCE .... Direction de la Classification et de l'Evaluation des Emplois, Ministere de la Fonction Publique, Quebec, Quebec [*Library symbol*] [*National Library of Canada*] (NLC)

QQFTI .... Service du Traitement de l'Information, Ministere des Finances, Duberger, Quebec [*Library symbol*] [*National Library of Canada*] (NLC)

QQH .... Quaque Hora [*Every Hour*] [*Pharmacy*]

QQH .... Quaque Quarta Hora [*Every Fourth Hour*] [*Pharmacy*]

QQHD........ Hotel-Dieu de Quebec, Quebec [*Library symbol*] [*National Library of Canada*] (NLC)

QQHDM..... Musee des Augustines de l'Hotel-Dieu de Quebec, Quebec [*Library symbol*] [*National Library of Canada*] (NLC)

QQHDS...... Hotel-Dieu du Sacre-Coeur, Quebec, Quebec [*Library symbol*] [*National Library of Canada*] (NLC)

QQHEJ .... Hopital de l'Enfant-Jesus, Quebec, Quebec [*Library symbol*] [*National Library of Canada*] (NLC)

QQHFA....... Hopital St-Francois d'Assise, Quebec, Quebec [*Library symbol*] [*National Library of Canada*] (NLC)

QQ HOR ..... Quaque Hora [*Every Hour*] [*Pharmacy*]

QQHSS....... Hopital du Saint-Sacrement, Quebec, Quebec [*Library symbol*] [*National Library of Canada*] (NLC)

QQIAS........ Informatheque, Ministere des Affaires Sociales du Quebec, Quebec, Quebec [*Library symbol*] [*National Library of Canada*] (NLC)

QQIAS........ Service de Documentation, Ministere de la Sante et des Services Sociaux, Quebec, Quebec [*Library symbol*] [*National Library of Canada*] (NLC)

QQIC .... Ministere de l'Industrie, du Commerce et du Tourisme, Quebec, Quebec [*Library symbol*] [*National Library of Canada*] (NLC)

QQIF.......... Ministere des Institutions Financieres et Cooperatives, Quebec, Quebec [*Library symbol*] [*National Library of Canada*] (NLC)

QQIQRC ..... Institut Quebecois de Recherche sur la Culture, Quebec, Quebec [*Library symbol*] [*National Library of Canada*] (NLC)

QQJ .... Ministere de la Justice du Quebec, Ste-Foy, Quebec [*Library symbol*] [*National Library of Canada*] (NLC)

QQL........... Bibliotheque de l'Assemblee Nationale, Quebec, Quebec [*Library symbol*] [*National Library of Canada*] (NLC)

QQLA .... Universite Laval, Quebec, Quebec [*Library symbol*] [*National Library of Canada*] (NLC)

QQLAAA .... Secteur Art et Architecture, Universite Laval, Quebec, Quebec [*Library symbol*] [*National Library of Canada*] (NLC)

QQLAAV .... Ecole des Arts Visuels, Universite Laval, Quebec, Quebec [*Library symbol*] [*National Library of Canada*] (NLC)

QQLACA .... Cartotheque, Universite Laval, Quebec, Quebec [*Library symbol*] [*National Library of Canada*] (NLC)

QQLACH .... Centre Hospitalier, Universite Laval, Quebec, Quebec [*Library symbol*] [*National Library of Canada*] (NLC)

QQLACI..... Centre International de Recherches sur le Bilinguisme, Universite Laval, Quebec, Quebec [*Library symbol*] [*National Library of Canada*] (NLC)

QQLAD...... Faculte de Droit, Universite Laval, Quebec, Quebec [*Library symbol*] [*National Library of Canada*] (NLC)

QQLAG...... Institut de Geographie, Universite Laval, Quebec, Quebec [*Library symbol*] [*National Library of Canada*] (NLC)

QQLAGM ... Departement de Geologie et de Mineralogie, Universite Laval, Quebec, Quebec [*Library symbol*] [*National Library of Canada*] (NLC)

QQLAI .... Societa Dante Alighieri, Universite Laval, Quebec, Quebec [*Library symbol*] [*National Library of Canada*] (NLC)

QQLAS....... Bibliotheque Scientifique, Universite Laval, Quebec, Quebec [*Library symbol*] [*National Library of Canada*] (NLC)

QQLCP...... Ministere du Loisir, de la Chasse et de la Peche, Quebec, Quebec [*Library symbol*] [*National Library of Canada*] (NLC)

QQLH .... Literary and Historical Society of Quebec [*Societe Litteraire et Historique de Quebec*] Quebec [*Library symbol*] [*National Library of Canada*] (NLC)

QQMAA...... Archives du Monastere des Augustines, Quebec, Quebec [*Library symbol*] [*National Library of Canada*] (NLC)

QQMAB..... Bibliotheque du Monastere des Augustines, Quebec, Quebec [*Library symbol*] [*National Library of Canada*] (NLC)

QQMC .... Bibliotheque Administrative, Ministere des Communications du Quebec, Quebec, Quebec [*Library symbol*] [*National Library of Canada*] (NLC)

QQMF......... Laurentian Forest Research Centre, Environment Canada [*Centre de Recherches Foreestieres des Laurentides, Environement Canada*] Ste-Foy, Quebec [*Library symbol*] [*National Library of Canada*] (NLC)

QQMQ........ Musee du Quebec, Quebec [*Library symbol*] [*National Library of Canada*] (NLC)

QQMR .... Le Mussee du Royal 22e Regiment et la Regie du Royal 22e Regiment, Quebec, Quebec [*Library symbol*] [*National Library of Canada*] (NLC)

QQM & R .... Quantitative, Qualitative, Maintainability, and Reliability

QQMSRD ... Centre de Documentation, Direction du Developpement du Systeme, Ministere de la Main d'Oeuvre et la Securite du Revenu, Quebec, Quebec [*Library symbol*] [*National Library of Canada*] (NLC)

QQOLF....... Office de la Langue Francaise, Quebec, Quebec [*Library symbol*] [*National Library of Canada*] (NLC)

QQOP......... Office de Planification et de Developpement du Quebec, Quebec, Quebec [*Library symbol*] [*National Library of Canada*] (NLC)

QQOPC ...... Office de la Protection du Consommateur, Quebec, Quebec [*Library symbol*] [*National Library of Canada*] (NLC)

QQOPD ...... Direction de la Documentation, Office des Promotions du Quebec, Quebec, Quebec [*Library symbol*] [*National Library of Canada*] (NLC)

QQP........... Quick Query Program

QQPCQ ...... Parks Canada [*Parcs Canada*] Quebec, Quebec [*Library symbol*] [*National Library of Canada*] (NLC)

QQPR .... Quantitative and Qualitative Personnel Requirements

QQPRI .... Quantitative and Qualitative Personnel Requirements Information

QQPSM ...... Fisheries and Oceans Canada [*Peches et Oceans Canada*] Quebec, Quebec [*Library symbol*] [*National Library of Canada*] (NLC)

QQQE......... Centre Quebecois des Sciences de l'Eau, Universite du Quebec, Quebec, Quebec [*Library symbol*] [*National Library of Canada*] (NLC)

QQR........... Technical Information Centre, Reed Ltd., Quebec, Quebec [*Library symbol*] [*National Library of Canada*] (NLC)

QQRA .... Roche Associes Ltee., Group-Conseil, Ste-Foy, Quebec [*Library symbol*] [*National Library of Canada*] (NLC)

QQRAA ...... Regie de l'Assurance Automobile du Quebec, Sillery, Quebec [*Library symbol*] [*National Library of Canada*] (NLC)

QQRAMQ ... Regie de l'Assurance-Maladie du Quebec, Sillery, Quebec [*Library symbol*] [*National Library of Canada*] (NLC)

QQRE .... Ministere du Revenu, Ste-Foy, Quebec [*Library symbol*] [*National Library of Canada*] (NLC)

QQRRQ ...... Regie des Rentes du Quebec, Ste-Foy, Quebec [*Library symbol*] [*National Library of Canada*] (NLC)

QQRSP....... Regie des Services Publics, Ste-Foy, Quebec [*Library symbol*] [*National Library of Canada*] (NLC)

QQS........... Seminaire de Quebec, Quebec [*Library symbol*] [*National Library of Canada*] (NLC)

QQSAJ .... Secretariat a la Jeunesse, Conseil Executif, Quebec, Quebec [*Library symbol*] [*National Library of Canada*] (NLC)

QQSC........ Quadripartite Quartermaster Standardization Committee [*Military*] (AABC)

QQSCA ...... Archives des Soeurs de la Charite de Quebec, Quebec, Quebec [*Library symbol*] [*National Library of Canada*] (NLC)

QQSIP .... Societe Quebecoise d'Initiatives Petrolieres, Ste-Foy, Quebec [*Library symbol*] [*National Library of Canada*] (NLC)

QQTCG ...... Canadian Coast Guard [*Garde Cotiere Canadienne*] Quebec, Quebec [*Library symbol*] [*National Library of Canada*] (NLC)

QQTR .... Ministere des Transports, Quebec, Quebec [*Library symbol*] [*National Library of Canada*] (NLC)

QQU .... Couvent des Ursulines, Quebec, Quebec [*Library symbol*] [*National Library of Canada*] (NLC)

QQUA........ Archives du Monastere des Ursulines de Merici, Quebec, Quebec [*Library symbol*] [*National Library of Canada*] (NLC)

QQUED ...... Centre de Documentation, INRS-Education, Quebec, Quebec [*Library symbol*] [*National Library of Canada*] (NLC)

QQUIE .... Centre de Documentation, INRS-Eau, Quebec, Quebec [*Library symbol*] [*National Library of Canada*] (NLC)

QQUQ........ Universite du Quebec, Quebec, Quebec [*Library symbol*] [*National Library of Canada*] (NLC)

QQUQEN... Ecole Nationale d'Administration Publique, Universite du Quebec, Quebec, Quebec [*Library symbol*] [*National Library of Canada*] (NLC)

QQUQT ...... Tele-Universite, Universite du Quebec, Quebec, Quebec [*Library symbol*] [*National Library of Canada*] (NLC)

QQ V.......... Quae Vide [*Which See*] [*Plural form*] [*Latin*]

QQV........... Quantum Vis [*As Much as You Wish*] [*Pharmacy*] (ADA)

Q-QY......... Question or Query (AAG)

QQZ........... Jardin Zoologique de Quebec, Charlesbourg, Quebec [*Library symbol*] [*National Library of Canada*] (NLC)

QR .... Inter RCA [*Central African Republic*] [*ICAO designator*] (FAAC)

QR .... Qatar Riyal [*Monetary unit*] (BJA)

Qr .... Qere (BJA)

QR .... Quad Right [*Typography*]

QR .... Quadrans [*A Farthing*] [*Monetary unit*] [*British*] (ROG)

Q & R .... Quality and Reliability

QR .... Quality Review

QR .... Quantitative Restrictions [*International trade*]

QR .... Quantity Requested

QR .... Quantity Required

QR .... Quantum Rectum [*The Quantity Is Correct*] [*Pharmacy*]

QR .... Quarantine Report [*HEW*]

QR .... Quarter

QR .... Quarterly (ROG)

QR .... Quarterly Replenishment

QR .... Quarterly Report (OICC)

QR .... Quarterly Review

QR .... Quaternary Research [*A publication*]

QR .... Quebec Official Reports (DLA)

QR .... Queen's Regulation [*Military*] [*British*]

QR .... Queen's Rook [*Chess*] (ADA)

QR .... Queen's Royal [*Military unit*] [*British*]

Q/R............. Query/Response (MCD)

QR .... Quick Reaction

QR .... Quire [*Measure of paper*]

QR .... Quotation Request

QR .... Sources Public Library [*Bibliotheque Municipale des Sources*] Roxboro, Quebec [*Library symbol*] [*National Library of Canada*] (NLC)

QRA........... Archeveche de Rimouski, Quebec [*Library symbol*] [*National Library of Canada*] (NLC)

QRA........... Quality and Reliability Assurance (NG)

Q & RA ...... Quality and Reliability Assurance

QRA........... Quick Reaction Acquisition (MCD)

QRA........... Quick Reaction Aircraft (MCD)

QRA........... Quick Reaction Alert (AFM)

QRA........... Quick Reaction Area (MCD)

QRA........... Quick Replaceable Assembly

QRAC......... Quality and Reliability Assessment Council

QRADA....... Quaderni di Radiologia [*A publication*]

QR Ag Econ ... Quarterly Review of Agricultural Economics [*A publication*]

Q R Agric Econ ... Quarterly Review of Agricultural Economics [*A publication*]

QRAH .... Robins [*A. H.*] Co., Inc. [*NYSE symbol*]

QR & AI ...... Queen's Regulations and Admiralty Instructions [*Obsolete*] [*Navy*] [*British*]

QR Air .... Queen's Regulations and Orders for the Royal Canadian Air Force

QRAL.......... Quality and Reliability Assurance Laboratory [*NASA*] (KSC)

Q Rass Mus ... Quaderni della Rassegna Musicale [*A publication*]

QR Aust Educ ... Quarterly Review of Australian Education [*A publication*]

QRB .... Quality Review Bulletin [*A publication*]

QRB .... Quarterly Review of Biology [*A publication*]

Q R Biol ...... Quarterly Review of Biology [*A publication*]

Q R Biophys ... Quarterly Review of Biophysics [*A publication*]

QRBM........ Quasi-Random Band Model

QRC........... Quaker Resources Canada Ltd. [*Vancouver Stock Exchange symbol*]

QRC........... Quick Reaction Capability [*Electronics*]

QRC........... Quick Reaction Change (MCD)

QRC........... Quick Response Capability [*Military*]

QRCA......... Qualitative Research Consultants Association (EA)

QRCB .... College Bourget, Rigaud, Quebec [*Library symbol*] [*National Library of Canada*] (NLC)

QRCC .... Quadripartite Research Coordination Committee [*Military*] (AABC)

QRCC .... Query Response Communications Console

QRCG......... Quasi-Random Code Generator (CET)

QRCN........ College de l'Abitibi-Temiscamingue, Rouyn, Quebec [*Library symbol*] [*National Library of Canada*] (NLC)

QRCN........ Queen's Regulations and Orders for the Royal Canadian Navy

QRCR......... Quality Reliability Consumption Reports

QRCRS....... Conseil Regional de la Sante et des Services Sociaux, Rimouski, Quebec [*Library symbol*] [*National Library of Canada*] (NLC)

QRD........... Quick Reaction Development

QRDC .... Quartermaster Research and Development Command [*Army*]

QRDEA...... Quartermaster Research and Development Evaluation Agency [*Army*]

QRDS .... Quarterly Review of Drilling Statistics [*American Petroleum Institute*]

QRE........... Bibliotheque Municpale, Repentigny, Quebec [*Library symbol*] [*National Library of Canada*] (NLC)

QRE........... Quick Reaction [*or Response*] Estimate

QREB .... Quarterly Review of Economics and Business [*A publication*]

QREC .... Quartermaster Research and Engineering Command [*Army*]

Q R Econ Bu ... Quarterly Review of Economics and Business [*A publication*]

Q R Econ & Bus ... Quarterly Review of Economics and Business [*A publication*]

Q Rep Railw Tech Res Inst (Tokyo) ... Quarterly Report. Railway Technical Research Institute (Tokyo) [*A publication*]

Q Rep Univ W Indies Sch Agric ... Quarterly Report. University of the West Indies. School of Agriculture [*A publication*]

Q Rev Ag Economics ... Quarterly Review of Agricultural Economics [*A publication*]

Q Rev Agric Econ ... Quarterly Review of Agricultural Economics [*A publication*]
Q Rev Am Electroplat Soc ... Quarterly Review. American Electroplaters' Society [*A publication*]
Q Rev Aust Ed ... Quarterly Review of Australian Education [*A publication*]
Q Rev Biol ... Quarterly Review of Biology [*A publication*]
Q Rev Bioph ... Quarterly Reviews of Biophysics [*A publication*]
Q Rev Biophys ... Quarterly Reviews of Biophysics [*A publication*]
Q Rev Chem Soc (Lond) ... Quarterly Reviews. Chemical Society (London) [*A publication*]
Q Rev Drill Stat US ... Quarterly Review. Drilling Statistics for the United States [*A publication*]
Q Rev Econ Bus ... Quarterly Review of Economics and Business [*A publication*]
Q Rev Environ ... Quarterly Review on Environment [*Japan*] [*A publication*]
Q Rev Evan Luth Ch ... Quarterly Review. Evangelical Lutheran Church [*A publication*]
Q Rev F Studies ... Quarterly Review of Film Studies [*A publication*]
Q Rev Harefuah ... Quarterly Review of the Harefuah [*A publication*]
Q Rev Hist S ... Quarterly Review of Historical Studies [*A publication*]
Q Rev Juris ... Quarterly Review of Jurisprudence [*1887-88*]   (DLA)
Q Rev Lit .... Quarterly Review of Literature [*A publication*]
Q Rev Obstet Gynecol ... Quarterly Review of Obstetrics and Gynecology [*A publication*]
Q Rev Pediatr ... Quarterly Review of Pediatrics [*A publication*]
Q Rev Surg ... Quarterly Review of Surgery [*A publication*]
Q Rev Surg Surg Spec ... Quarterly Review of Surgery and Surgical Specialities [*A publication*]
Q Rev Urol ... Quarterly Review of Urology [*A publication*]
QRF .... Quadrature Rejection Frequency
QRF .... Quality Review File [*IRS*]
QRF .... Quick Reaction Force [*Military*]   (CINC)
Q R Film S ... Quarterly Review of Film Studies [*A publication*]
QRG........... Quadrupole Residual Gas
QRG........... Quick Reaction Grooming
QRG........... Quick Response Graphic
QRGA .... Quadrupole Residual Gas Analyzer
QRGAS...... Quadrupole Residual Gas Analyzer System
QRGS .... Grand Seminaire de Rimouski, Quebec [*Library symbol*] [*National Library of Canada*]   (NLC)
QRHD .... Bibliotheque Medicale, Hotel-Dieu de Roberval, Quebec [*Library symbol*] [*National Library of Canada*]   (NLC)
Q R Higher Ed Among Negroes ... Quarterly Review of Higher Education among Negroes [*A publication*]
QR Higher Ed Negroes ... Quarterly Review of Higher Education among Negroes [*A publication*]
Q R Hist Stud ... Quarterly Review of Historical Studies [*A publication*]
QRI .... Qualitative Requirements Information [*Army*]
QRI .... Quick Reaction Integration   (NASA)
QRIA.......... Quick Reaction Integration Activity   (NASA)
QRIB.......... Bibliotheque Municipale, Rock Island, Quebec [*Library symbol*] [*National Library of Canada*]   (NLC)
QRIB.......... Haskell Free Library, Rock Island, Quebec [*Library symbol*] [*National Library of Canada*]   (NLC)
QRIC.......... CEGEP de Rimouski, Quebec [*Library symbol*] [*National Library of Canada*]   (NLC)
QRIC.......... Quick Reaction Installation Capability   (CET)
QRICC .... Quick Reaction Inventory Control Center [*Army*]   (MCD)
QRIH.......... Queen's Royal Irish Hussars [*Military unit*] [*British*]
QRIM .... Institut Maritime, CEGEP de Rimouski, Quebec [*Library symbol*] [*National Library of Canada*]   (NLC)
QR J........... QR Journal. Indian Association for Quality and Reliability [*A publication*]
QRJOD....... QR [*Quality and Reliability*] Journal [*A publication*]
QRKB .... Quebec King's Bench Reports   (DLA)
QRKB .... Rapports Judiciaires de Quebec, Cour du Banc du Roi [*Quebec Law Reports, King's Bench*]   (DLA)
QRL .... Q-Switch Ruby LASER
QRL .... Quadripartite Research List [*Military*]   (AABC)
QRL .... Quarterly Review of Literature [*A publication*]
QRL .... Quaternary Research Laboratory [*University of Michigan*] [*Research center*]   (RCD)
QRL .... Quick Relocate and Link
QR of Lit..... Quarterly Review of Literature [*A publication*]
QRLY........ Quarterly
QRM .... Artificial Interference to Transmission or Reception [*Broadcasting*]
QRM .... Bibliotheque Municipale, Rimouski, Quebec [*Library symbol*] [*National Library of Canada*]   (NLC)
QRM .... Quorum Resource Corp. [*Vancouver Stock Exchange symbol*]
QRMC .... Quadrennial Review of Military Compensation [*DoD*]
QRMC .... Quick Response Multicolor Copier   (MCD)
QRMF .... Quick Reacting, Mobile Force [*Military*] [*NATO*]   (NATG)
QRMP .... Quick-Response Multicolor Printer   (RDA)
QRN........... Soeurs de Notre-Dame du Saint-Rosaire, Rimouski, Quebec [*Library symbol*] [*National Library of Canada*]   (NLC)
QROA .... Quarter Racing Owners of America   (EA)
QR & O (Can) ... Queen's Regulations and Orders for the Canadian Army
QRosc .... Pro Roscio Comoedo [*of Cicero*] [*Classical studies*]   (OCD)
QRP .... Query and Reporting Processor
QRP .... Quick Reaction Program [*Army*]

QRPAO...... Qualified Radium Plaque Adaptometer Operator [*Navy*]
QRPS......... Quick Reaction Procurement System [*Army*]   (AABC)
QRQB .... Quebec Queen's Bench Reports [*Canada*]   (DLA)
QRR........... Quadrature Rejection Ratio
QRR........... Quadrupole Resonance Response
QRR........... Qualitative Research Requirement for Nuclear Weapons Effects Information   (AABC)
QRR........... Quality Readiness Review   (MCD)
QRR........... Quarterly Research Review
QRR........... Queen's Royal Regiment [*Military unit*] [*British*]
QRR........... Quincy Railroad Co. [*AAR code*]
QRRF......... Master Quality Review Report File [*IRS*]
QRRI......... Qualitative Research Requirements Information [*Army*]
QRRR .... Distress call for emergency use only by amateur radio stations in an emergency situation
Q R Rural Economy ... Quarterly Review of the Rural Economy [*A publication*]
QRS........... Natural Interference to Transmission or Reception [*Broadcasting*]
QRS........... Qualification Review Sheet   (KSC)
QRS........... Qualified Repair Source   (AFIT)
QRS........... Quantum Readout System [*Method of measurement*]
QRS........... Quarters
QRS........... Queen's Row Spare
QRS........... Quick Reaction Sortie   (NASA)
QRSC .... Quebec Superior Court Reports   (DLA)
QRSC .... Rapports Judiciaires de Quebec, Cour Superieure [*Quebec Law Reports, Superior Court*]   (DLA)
QRSL........ Qualified Repair Source List   (AFIT)
QRSL........ Quick Reaction Space Laboratory [*NASA*]   (NASA)
QRT........... Queue Run-Time [*Data processing*]
QRT........... Quick Reaction Task   (MCD)
QRT........... Quick Reaction Team [*Military*]
QRTLY ...... Quarterly   (ROG)
QRTP......... Quick Response Targeting Program [*Lunar*]
QRTZ......... Quartz Engineering [*NASDAQ symbol*]   (NQ)
QRU........... Queen's Row Unit
QRU........... Universite du Quebec, Rimouski, Quebec [*Library symbol*] [*National Library of Canada*]   (NLC)
QRUC .... Cartotheque, Universite du Quebec, Rimouski, Quebec [*Library symbol*] [*National Library of Canada*]   (NLC)
QRUQR....... Universite du Quebec en Abitibi-Temiscamingue, Rouyn, Quebec [*Library symbol*] [*National Library of Canada*]   (NLC)
QRUS .... Queen's Row Unit Spare
QRV .... Qualified Valuer of the Real Estate Institute of New South Wales
QRV........... Quick Release Valve
QRV........... Quinn River Valley [*Nevada*] [*Seismograph station code, US Geological Survey*] [*Closed*]   (SEIS)
QRXI.......... Quarex Industries [*NASDAQ symbol*]   (NQ)
QRY........... Quality and Reliability Year
QRY........... Quarry   (KSC)
QS .... African Safari Airways [*ICAO designator*]   (FAAC)
QS .... Les Quatre Saisons [*Record label*] [*France*]
QS .... Quaderni di Semitistica [*Florence*] [*A publication*]
QS .... Quaderni di Storia [*A publication*]
QS .... Quantity Surveying
QS .... Quantum Suffecit [*A Sufficient Quantity*] [*Pharmacy*]   (ADA)
QS .... Quarter Section
QS .... Quarter Sessions
QS .... Quartermaster Sergeant [*Military*]
QS .... Queen's Scarf   (ADA)
QS .... Queen's Scholar [*British*]
QS .... Queen's Serjeant [*Military*] [*British*]   (ROG)
Q-S........... Queneau-Schuhmann [*Lead process*]
QS .... Query System [*Data processing*]
QS .... Question Standard   (NATG)
QS .... Queue Select [*Data processing*]
QS .... Quick Sweep [*Construction*]
QS .... Quiet Sleep [*Physiology*]
QS .... Quota Source   (AABC)
1QS .... Community Rule, Rule of the Congregation [*or Manual of Discipline, Serekh ha-Yahad*] from Qumran. Cave One [*BJA*]
1QS .... Divrei Berakhot [*or Blessings*] from Qumran. Cave One   (BJA)
QSA........... Quad Synchronous Adapter [*Perkin-Elmer*]
QSA........... Qualification Site Approval [*NASA*]   (NASA)
QSA........... Quick Service Assistant   (MCD)
QSABS...... Laboratoire de Sante Publique du Quebec, Ste-Anne-De-Bellevue, Quebec [*Library symbol*] [*National Library of Canada*]   (NLC)
QS AD .... Quantum Sufficiat Ad [*To a Sufficient Quantity*] [*Pharmacy*]
QSAL......... Quadripartite Standardization Agreements List [*Military*]
QSAM........ Quadrature Sideband Amplitude Modulation
QSAM........ Queued Sequential Access Method [*IBM Corp.*] [*Data processing*]
(Q)SAR ...... Quantitative Structure-Activity Relationship [*Pharmacochemistry*]
QSATS....... Quiet Short-Haul Air Transportation System
1QSb......... Divrei Berakhot [*or Blessings*] from Qumran. Cave One   (BJA)

QSBR .... Bio-Research Laboratory, Senneville, Quebec [*Library symbol*] [*National Library of Canada*] (NLC)
QSC .... Quality, Service, Cleanliness [*McDonald's Hamburger stands motto*]
QSC .... Quasi-Sensory Communication [*Parapsychology*]
QSC .... Questionnaire Service Company [*East Lansing, MI*] [*Information service*] (EISS)
QSC .... Quick Set Compound
QSCR .... Queensland. Supreme Court. Reports [*A publication*]
QSCR .... Supreme Court Reports (Queensland) [*A publication*]
QSCV .... Quality, Service, Cleanliness, and Value [*Formula for successful fast-food restaurants as taught by McDonald's Corp. at its Hamburger University*]
QSD .... Quality Surveillance Division [*Navy*]
QSDC .... Quantitative Structural Design Criteria [*NASA*]
QSE .... Qualified Scientists and Engineers
QSED .... Research Centre, Domtar Ltd., Senneville, Quebec [*Library symbol*] [*National Library of Canada*] (NLC)
QSEMH ...... Missisquoi Historical Society [*Societe d'Histoire de Missisquoi*] Stanbridge-East, Quebec [*Library symbol*] [*National Library of Canada*] (NLC)
QSF .... Bibliotheque Municipale, Ste-Foy, Quebec [*Library symbol*] [*National Library of Canada*] (NLC)
QSF .... Quasi-Static Field
QSF .... Quasi-Stationary Front
QSFAG .... Research Station, Agriculture Canada [*Station de Recherches, Agriculture Canada*] Ste-Foy, Quebec [*Library symbol*] [*National Library of Canada*] (NLC)
QSFBP .... Maison Generalice des Soeurs du Bon Pasteur, Ste-Foy, Quebec [*Library symbol*] [*National Library of Canada*] (NLC)
QSFC .... College d'Enseignement, Ste-Foy, Quebec [*Library symbol*] [*National Library of Canada*] (NLC)
QSFCAE ..... Clinique d'Aide a l'Enfance, Ste-Foy, Quebec [*Library symbol*] [*National Library of Canada*] (NLC)
QSFCM ...... College Marguerite d'Youville, Ste-Foy, Quebec [*Library symbol*] [*National Library of Canada*] (NLC)
QSFCP .... Commission de Police du Quebec, Ste-Foy, Quebec [*Library symbol*] [*National Library of Canada*] (NLC)
QSFCR .... Centre de Recherche Industrielle du Quebec, Ste-Foy, Quebec [*Library symbol*] [*National Library of Canada*] (NLC)
QSFHL .... Hopital Laval, Ste-Foy, Quebec [*Library symbol*] [*National Library of Canada*] (NLC)
QSFIG .... Centre de Documentation, INRS-Georessources, Ste-Foy, Quebec [*Library symbol*] [*National Library of Canada*] (NLC)
QSFS .... SOQUEM, Ste-Foy, Quebec [*Library symbol*] [*National Library of Canada*] (NLC)
QSG .... Quasi-Steady Glide [*NASA*]
QSG .... Quasi-Stellar Galaxy
QSGLL .... Queensland Studies in German Language and Literature [*A publication*]
QSGVT .... Quarter Scale Ground Vibration Test (MCD)
QSH .... Stanstead Historial Society, Quebec [*Library symbol*] [*National Library of Canada*] (NLC)
QSHAG ...... Saint-Hyacinthe Food Research Centre, Agriculture Canada [*Centre de Recherches Alimentaires de Saint-Hyacinthe, Agriculture Canada*] Quebec [*Library symbol*] [*National Library of Canada*] (NLC)
QSHC .... CEGEP de Shawinigan, Quebec [*Library symbol*] [*National Library of Canada*] (NLC)
QSHERA .... Archeveche de Sherbrooke, Quebec [*Library symbol*] [*National Library of Canada*] (NLC)
QSHERAN ... Centre Regional de l'Estrie, Archives Nationales du Quebec, Sherbooke, Quebec [*Library symbol*] [*National Library of Canada*] (NLC)
QSHERC .... Bibliotheque des Sciences de la Sante, CHUS-Universite de Sherbrooke, Quebec [*Library symbol*] [*National Library of Canada*] (NLC)
QSHERCR ... Conseil Regional de la Sante et des Services Sociaux des Cantons de l'Est, Sherbrooke, Quebec [*Library symbol*] [*National Library of Canada*] (NLC)
QSHERD .... Sherbrooke Daily Record, Quebec [*Library symbol*] [*National Library of Canada*] (NLC)
QSHERE ..... College de Sherbrooke (CEGEP), Quebec [*Library symbol*] [*National Library of Canada*] (NLC)
QSHERG .... Bibliotheque du Grand Seminaire, Sherbrooke, Quebec [*Library symbol*] [*National Library of Canada*] (NLC)
QSHERG .... Grand Seminaire des Saints-Apotres, Sherbrooke, Quebec [*Library symbol*] [*National Library of Canada*] (NLC)
QSHERH .... Huntingdon Gleaner, Quebec [*Library symbol*] [*National Library of Canada*] (NLC)
QSHERHD ... Centre Hospitalier Hotel-Dieu, Sherbrooke, Quebec [*Library symbol*] [*National Library of Canada*] (NLC)
QSHERL ..... Sherbrooke Library, Quebec [*Library symbol*] [*National Library of Canada*] (NLC)
QSHERM .... Monastere des Peres Redemptoristes, Sherbrooke, Quebec [*Library symbol*] [*National Library of Canada*] (NLC)
QSHERN ... Bibliotheque Municipale, Sherbrooke, Quebec [*Library symbol*] [*National Library of Canada*] (NLC)

QSHERS ..... Seminaire de Sherbrooke, Quebec [*Library symbol*] [*National Library of Canada*] (NLC)
QSHERSC ... College du Sacre-Coeur, Sherbrooke, Quebec [*Library symbol*] [*National Library of Canada*] (NLC)
QSHERSF ... Ecole Secondaire St-Francois, Sherbrooke, Quebec [*Library symbol*] [*National Library of Canada*] (NLC)
QSHERSG ... Societe de Genealogie des Cantons de l'Est, Sherbrooke, Quebec [*Library symbol*] [*National Library of Canada*] (NLC)
QSHERSH ... Societe Historique des Cantons de l'Est, Sherbrooke, Quebec [*Library symbol*] [*National Library of Canada*] (NLC)
QSHERSV ... Centre Hospitalier St-Vincent-De-Paul, Sherbrooke, Quebec [*Library symbol*] [*National Library of Canada*] (NLC)
QSHERU .... Universite de Sherbrooke, Quebec [*Library symbol*] [*National Library of Canada*] (NLC)
QSHERUA ... Galerie d'Art et Centre Culturel, Universite de Sherbrooke, Quebec [*Library symbol*] [*National Library of Canada*] (NLC)
QSHERUD ... Faculte de Droit, Universite de Sherbrooke, Quebec [*Library symbol*] [*National Library of Canada*] (NLC)
QSHERUG ... Departement de Georgraphie, Universite de Sherbrooke, Quebec [*Library symbol*] [*National Library of Canada*] (NLC)
QSHERUGC ... Cartotheque, Departement de Geographie, Universite de Sherbrooke, Quebec [*Library symbol*] [*National Library of Canada*] (NLC)
QSHERURA ... Centre de Documentation, Programme de Recherche sur l'Amiante, Universite de Sherbrooke, Quebec [*Library symbol*] [*National Library of Canada*] (NLC)
QSHERUS ... Faculte des Sciences, Universite de Sherbrooke, Quebec [*Library symbol*] [*National Library of Canada*] (NLC)
QSHM .... Municipal Library [*Bibliotheque Municipale*] Shawinigan, Quebec [*Library symbol*] [*National Library of Canada*] (NLC)
QSHS .... Seminaire Ste-Marie, Shawinigan, Quebec [*Library symbol*] [*National Library of Canada*] (NLC)
QSI .... Bibliotheque Municipale, Sept-Iles, Quebec [*Library symbol*] [*National Library of Canada*] (NLC)
QSI .... Quality Salary Increase (AFM)
QSI .... Quality Service Indicator
QSI .... Quantum Scalar Irradiance [*Instrumentation*]
QSI .... Quarterly Survey of Intentions [*Became Consumer Buying Expectations Survey*] [*Bureau of the Census*]
QSIBCP ...... Bibliotheque Centrale de Pret de la Cote-Nord, Sept-Iles, Quebec [*Library symbol*] [*National Library of Canada*] (NLC)
QSIC .... Quality Standard Inspection Criteria
QSII .... Quality Systems, Incorporated [*NASDAQ symbol*] (NQ)
QSIIOM ...... Mineralogy Laboratory, Iron Ore Co., Sept-Iles, Quebec [*Library symbol*] [*National Library of Canada*] (NLC)
QSILC .... College Jesus-Marie de Sillery, Quebec [*Library symbol*] [*National Library of Canada*] (NLC)
QSJ .... Stanstead Journal, Quebec [*Library symbol*] [*National Library of Canada*] (NLC)
QSJHD .... Hotel-Dieu de Saint-Jerome, Quebec [*Library symbol*] [*National Library of Canada*] (NLC)
QSK .... Quadriphase Shift Keying (MCD)
QSL .... Q-Switch LASER
QSL .... Qualification Status List (KSC)
QSL .... Qualified Source List [*NASA*] (NASA)
QSL .... Quarterly Stock List
QS & L .... Quarters, Subsistence, and Laundry [*Military*]
QSL .... Queue Search Limit [*Data processing*]
QSLCR .... Campus 1, Champlain Regional College, St-Lambert, Quebec [*Library symbol*] [*National Library of Canada*] (NLC)
QSLE .... Bibliotheque Municipale, Saint-Leonard, Quebec [*Library symbol*] [*National Library of Canada*] (NLC)
QSLT .... Salant Corp. [*NYSE symbol*]
QSM .... Quality Systems Management [*DoD*]
QSM .... Quarter Scale Model (MCD)
QSM .... Quarter Square Multiplier
QSM .... Quasi-Linear Sequential Machine
QSNT .... (Quinolinesulfonyl)nitrotriazole [*Organic chemistry*]
QSO .... Bibliotheque Municipale, Sorel, Quebec [*Library symbol*] [*National Library of Canada*] (NLC)
QSO .... Quasi-Biennial Stratospheric Oscillation
QSO .... Quasi-Stellar [*or QUASAR*] Object
QSOCS ...... C. Stroemgren, Sorel, Quebec [*Library symbol*] [*National Library of Canada*] (NLC)
QSOIT .... Quebec Iron and Titanium Corp. [*Fer et Titane du Quebec, Inc.*] Sorel, Quebec [*Library symbol*] [*National Library of Canada*] (NLC)
QSOP .... Quadripartite Standing Operating Procedures [*Military*]
QSP .... Quench Spray Pump (IEEE)
QSP .... Quick Search Procedure
QSPS .... Qualification Standards for Postal Field Service
QSR .... Quality Status Review (MCD)
QSR .... Quarterly Statistical Report (NRCH)
QSR .... Quarterly Status Report
QSR .... Quarterly Summary Report
QSR .... Quasi-Stellar Radio Source

QSR............ Quebec Sturgeon River Mines Ltd. [*Toronto Stock Exchange symbol*]

QSR............ Queensland State Reports [*Australia*] (DLA)

QSR............ Quick-Start Recording [*Video technology*]

QSR............ Quick Strike Reconnaissance (MCD)

QSR............ Quien Sabe Ranch [*California*] [*Seismograph station code, US Geological Survey*] (SEIS)

QSR............ Quinoline Still Residue [*Coal tar technology*]

QSR............ State Reports (Queensland) [*A publication*]

QSRA .... Quiet Short-Haul Research Aircraft [*NASA*]

QSRS .... Quasi-Stellar Radio Source

QSRTF ...... Quebec Sturgeon River Mines [*NASDAQ symbol*] (NQ)

QSS........... Quadratic Score Statistic [*Test*]

QSS........... Quadrupole Screw Ship

QSS........... Quasi-Steady State

QSS........... Quasi-Stellar Source

QSS........... Quench Spray Subsystem (IEEE)

QSS........... Quick Service Supervisor (MCD)

QSS........... Quick Supply Store (AABC)

QSS........... Quill and Scroll Society (EA)

QSSA .... Quasi-Stationary State Approximation

QSSP .... Quasi-Solid State Panel

QSSR .... Quarterly Stock Status Report

QST .... Quarterly Statements of the Palestine Exploration Fund [*A publication*]

QST .... Questmont Mines [*Vancouver Stock Exchange symbol*]

QSTAG....... Quadripartite Standardization Agreement [*Military*]

QSTAG....... Quality Standardization Agreements (MCD)

QSTAH...... Ste-Anne's Hospital, Ste-Anne-De-Bellevue, Quebec [*Library symbol*] [*National Library of Canada*] (NLC)

QSTAIAS ... Ministere des Affaires Sociales du Quebec, Ste-Anne-De-Bellevue, Quebec [*Library symbol*] [*National Library of Canada*] (NLC)

QSTAJ....... John Abbott College, Ste-Anne-De-Bellevue, Quebec [*Library symbol*] [*National Library of Canada*] (NLC)

QSTAMP.... Quality Stamp

QSTAS ...... Spar Technology Ltd., Ste-Anne-De-Bellevue, Quebec [*Library symbol*] [*National Library of Canada*] (NLC)

QSTBL ...... Abbaye De Saint-Benoit-Du-Lac, Comte De Brome, Quebec [*Library symbol*] [*National Library of Canada*] (NLC)

QSTC .... Tioxide Canada, Inc., Sorel, Quebec [*Library symbol*] [*National Library of Canada*] (NLC)

QSTFAG.... Centre de Documentation, Ministere de l'Agriculture, des Pecheries et de l'Alimentation, Ste-Foy, Quebec [*Library symbol*] [*National Library of Canada*] (NLC)

QSTFIAS ... Ministere des Affaires Sociales du Quebec, Ste-Foy, Quebec [*Library symbol*] [*National Library of Canada*] (NLC)

QSTFRA .... Centre de Documentation, Roche Associes Ltee., Ste-Foy, Quebec [*Library symbol*] [*National Library of Canada*] (NLC)

QSTHAG.... Centre de la Documentation, Ministere de l'Agriculture, des Pecheries et de l'Alimentation, St-Hyacinthe, Quebec [*Library symbol*] [*National Library of Canada*] (NLC)

QSTHHR..... Societe d'Histoire Regionale de St-Hyacinthe, Quebec [*Library symbol*] [*National Library of Canada*] (NLC)

QSTHS ...... Seminaire de St-Hyacinthe, Quebec [*Library symbol*] [*National Library of Canada*] (NLC)

QSTHTA..... Institut de Technologie Agricole et Alimentaire de St-Hyacinthe, Quebec [*Library symbol*] [*National Library of Canada*] (NLC)

QSTHUM.... Headquarters Mobile Command, Canada Department of National Defence [*Quartier-General du Commandement de la Defense Nationale*] St-Hubert, Quebec [*Library symbol*] [*National Library of Canada*] (NLC)

QSTHV ...... Faulte de Medecine Veterinaire de l'Universite de Montreal, Saint-Hyacinthe, Quebec [*Library symbol*] [*National Library of Canada*] (NLC)

QSTJ .... College Militaire Royal de Saint-Jean, Quebec [*Library symbol*] [*National Library of Canada*] (NLC)

QSTJAG..... Research Station, Agriculture Canada [*Station de Recherches, Agriculture Canada*] Saint-Jean, Quebec [*Library symbol*] [*National Library of Canada*] (NLC)

QSTJB........ Bibliotheque Municipale, Saint-Jean, Quebec [*Library symbol*] [*National Library of Canada*] (NLC)

QSTJC .... College Saint-Jean-Sur-Richelieu, Saint-Jean, Quebec [*Library symbol*] [*National Library of Canada*] (NLC)

QSTJE........ Bibliotheque Municipale, Saint-Jerome, Quebec [*Library symbol*] [*National Library of Canada*] (NLC)

QSTJECR... Conseil Regional de la Sante et des Services Sociaux Laurentides-Lanaudiere, Saint-Jerome, Quebec [*Library symbol*] [*National Library of Canada*] (NLC)

QSTJEJ...... Jesuites/Bibliotheque, Saint-Jerome, Quebec [*Library symbol*] [*National Library of Canada*] (NLC)

QSTK .... Storage Technology Corp. [*NYSE symbol*]

QSTL.......... Bibliotheque Municipale, Saint-Laurent, Quebec [*Library symbol*] [*National Library of Canada*] (NLC)

QSTNRY..... Quasi-Stationary (FAAC)

QSTOL .... Quiet-Short-Takeoff-and-Landing [*Airplane*] [*Japan*]

QSTR.......... Bibliotheque Municipale de Saint-Raphael-De-L'Ile-Bizard, Quebec [*Library symbol*] [*National Library of Canada*] (NLC)

QSTTH .... Les Industries Harnois, St-Thomas-De-Joliette, Quebec [*Library symbol*] [*National Library of Canada*] (NLC)

QSTX......... Questronics, Inc. [*NASDAQ symbol*] (NQ)

QS Wkly .... Quantity Surveyor Weekly [*A publication*]

QSY .... Quiet Sun Year

QT .... Aer Turas Teoranta [*Ireland*] [*ICAO designator*] (FAAC)

QT .... Bibliotheque Municipale, Trois-Rivieres, Quebec [*Library symbol*] [*National Library of Canada*] (NLC)

QT .... Qualification Test

QT .... Quantity

QT .... Quart (AFM)

QT .... Quarters

Qt .... Quartet [*A publication*]

QT .... Quartet [*Music*]

QT .... Quebec-Telephone [*Toronto Stock Exchange symbol*]

QT .... Questioned Trade [*on a stock exchange*]

QT .... Queuing Theory [*Telecommunications*]

QT .... Queuing Time [*Telecommunications*] (TEL)

QT .... Quick Tan [*Trademark of Plough, Inc.*]

QT .... Quick Test

QT .... Quiet [*or sub rosa, as, "On the QT"*]

QTA........... Archives Nationales du Quebec, Trois-Rivieres, Quebec [*Library symbol*] [*National Library of Canada*] (NLC)

QTA........... Le Boreal Express, Montreal [*Formerly, Trois-Rivieres*] Quebec [*Library symbol*] [*National Library of Canada*] (NLC)

QTA........... Quadrant Transformer Assembly

QTAM........ Quadrature Amplitude Modulation (MCD)

QTAM........ Queued Telecommunications Access Method [*IBM Corp.*] [*Data processing*]

QTAM........ Queued Terminal Access Method [*Data processing*]

QTB .... Quarry-Tile Base [*Technical drawings*]

QTBC .... Bibliotheque Centrale de Pret de la Mauricie, Trois-Rivieres, Quebec [*Library symbol*] [*National Library of Canada*] (NLC)

QTBO .... Tacoma Boatbuilding Co. [*NYSE symbol*]

QTC........... Quick Transmission Change (MCD)

QTCE .... CEGEP, Trois-Rivieres, Quebec [*Library symbol*] [*National Library of Canada*] (NLC)

QTCL......... College Lafleche, Trois-Rivieres, Quebec [*Library symbol*] [*National Library of Canada*] (NLC)

QTCO........ Communication-Quebec, Trois-Rivieres, Quebec [*Library symbol*] [*National Library of Canada*] (NLC)

QTCPB....... Corporation Pierre Boucher, Trois-Rivieres, Quebec [*Library symbol*] [*National Library of Canada*] (NLC)

QTCRD....... Conseil Regional de Developpement, Trois-Rivieres, Quebec [*Library symbol*] [*National Library of Canada*] (NLC)

QTCRS....... Conseil Regional de la Sante et des Services Sociaux, Trois-Rivieres, Quebec [*Library symbol*] [*National Library of Canada*] (NLC)

QTCSRV .... Commission Scolaire Regionale des Vieilles Forges, Trois-Rivieres, Quebec [*Library symbol*] [*National Library of Canada*] (NLC)

QTCSS....... Centre de Services Sociaux, Trois-Rivieres, Quebec [*Library symbol*] [*National Library of Canada*] (NLC)

QTD........... Quadruple Terminal Digits (AABC)

QTD........... Quartered

QTD........... Quasi-Two-Dimensional

QTDG .... Quaker Theological Discussion Group (EA)

QTDM........ Qazaq Tili Tarychi Men Dyalektology Jasinin Moseleleri [*A publication*]

QT DX........ Quantitas Duplex [*Double Quantity*] [*Pharmacy*]

QTE .... Ecole Normale M. L. Duplessis, Trois-Rivieres, Quebec [*Library symbol*] [*National Library of Canada*] (NLC)

QT & E ...... Qualification Test and Evaluation [*Military*]

QTE .... Qualite [*Quality*] [*French*] (ROG)

QTE .... Quote

QTE .... True Bearing [*from me*] [*Aviation code*] (FAAC)

Q Teachers J ... Queensland Teachers' Journal [*A publication*]

Q-TECH ..... Quality-Technology

4QTest ...... [*The*] Testimonia from Qumran. Cave Four (BJA)

QTEV......... Quadruple Turbo-Electric Vessel

QTF .... Quarry-Tile Floor [*Technical drawings*]

QTH........... Queued Transaction Handling [*Data processing*]

QTHSJ....... Hopital Saint-Joseph, Trois-Rivieres, Quebec [*Library symbol*] [*National Library of Canada*] (NLC)

QTHSM ...... Hopital Sainte-Marie, Trois-Rivieres, Quebec [*Library symbol*] [*National Library of Canada*] (NLC)

QTI .... Institut Albert Tessier, Trois-Rivieres, Quebec [*Library symbol*] [*National Library of Canada*] (NLC)

Q Tic Num Ant Clas ... Quaderni Ticinesi. Numismatica e Antichita Classiche [*A publication*]

Q-TIP......... Qualified Terminable Interest Property [*Plan*] [*Tax law*]

QTL .... Quantum Theory of LASERS

QTL .... Quarterly Title List

QTL .... Quintel Industries Limited [*Vancouver Stock Exchange symbol*]

4QTLevi....... Testament of Levi from Qumran. Cave Four (BJA)

QTM.......... Qualification Test Model

QTMC........ College de la Region de l'Amiante (CEGEP), Thetford-Mines, Quebec [*Library symbol*] [*National Library of Canada*] (NLC)

QTO........... Quarto [*Book from 25 to 30 centimeters in height*]

QTOL......... Quiet Takeoff and Landing [Aviation]
QTOPDQ .... Office de Planification et de Developpement du Quebec, Trois-Rivieres, Quebec [Library symbol] [National Library of Canada] (NLC)
QTOW .... Towle Manufacturing Co. [NYSE symbol]
QTP........... Qualification Test Plan [NASA] (NASA)
QTP........... Qualification Test Procedure
QTP........... Qualification Test Program
QTP........... Quality Test Plan (NRCH)
QTP........... Quantum Theory of Paramagnetism
QTP........... Quantum Theory Project [University of Florida] [Research center] (RCD)
QTPC......... Quadripartite Technical Procedures Committee [Military] (AABC)
QTPR......... Quarterly Technical Progress Report
QTR........... Qualification Test Report
QTR........... Quarry-Tile Roof [Technical drawings]
QTR........... Quarter (AFM)
QTR........... Quarterly (AFM)
QTR........... Quarterly Technical Report
QTR........... Quarterly Technical Review [Jet Propulsion Laboratory publication]
QTR........... Queenstake Resources Ltd. [Toronto Stock Exchange symbol] [Vancouver Stock Exchange symbol]
QTRLY .... Quarterly
QTRS......... Quarters
QTS........... Qualification Test Specification
QTS........... Quartz Thermometer Sensor
QTS........... Seminaire de Trois-Rivieres, Quebec [Library symbol] [National Library of Canada] (NLC)
QTT........... Quartet [Music]
QTT........... Trois-Rivieres High School, Quebec [Library symbol] [National Library of Canada] (NLC)
QTTA......... Quaderni Triestini sul Teatro Antico [A publication]
QTTE......... Quartette [Music]
QTTF......... Temifibre, Inc., Temiscaming, Quebec [Library symbol] [National Library of Canada] (NLC)
QTTP......... Q-Tags Test of Personality [Psychology]
QTU........... Qualification Test Unit
QTU........... Universite du Quebec, Trois-Rivieres, Quebec [Library symbol] [National Library of Canada] (NLC)
QTUAH....... Archives Historiques, Universite du Quebec, Trois-Rivieres, Quebec [Library symbol] [National Library of Canada] (NLC)
QTUGC ...... Cartotheque, Department de Geographie, Universite du Quebec, Trois-Rivieres, Quebec [Library symbol] [National Library of Canada] (NLC)
QTUIH .... Imprimes Historiques, Universite du Quebec, Trois-Rivieres, Quebec [Library symbol] [National Library of Canada] (NLC)
QTURA ...... Archives des Ursulines, Trois-Rivieres, Quebec [Library symbol] [National Library of Canada] (NLC)
QTUTH .... Centre de Documentation en Theatre Quebecois, Trois-Rivieres, Quebec [Library symbol] [National Library of Canada] (NLC)
Qty .... Quality
QTY........... Quantity (KSC)
QTYDESREQ ... Quantity Desired as Requested
QTZ........... Quartz (AAG)
QTZ........... Quartzite [Lithology]
QU .... Nicaragua [License plate code assigned to foreign diplomats in the US]
QU .... Quaderni dell'Umanesimo [A publication]
QU .... Quadrantectomy [Medicine]
QU .... Quail Unlimited [An association] (EA)
QU .... Quarter (ADA)
QU .... Quartermaster (ROG)
QU .... Quartern (ROG)
QU .... Quasi [Almost, As It Were] [Latin]
QU .... Quay (ROG)
QU .... Queen
QU .... Queen's University [Canada]
QU .... Query
QU .... Question
QU .... Quina [Quinine] [Pharmacy] (ROG)
QU .... Quinto Mining [Vancouver Stock Exchange symbol]
QU .... Quotation (ROG)
QU .... Uganda Airlines Corp. [ICAO designator] (FAAC)
QUA........... Quabbin [Massachusetts] [Seismograph station code, US Geological Survey] (SEIS)
QUA........... Quinterra Resources, Inc. [Toronto Stock Exchange symbol] [Vancouver Stock Exchange symbol]
QUAC........ Quadriatic Arc Computer
QUAD........ Quadrajet Carburetor [Automotive engineering]
QUAD........ Quadrangle (AAG)
QUAD........ Quadrant (KSC)
QUAD........ Quadraphonic
QUAD........ Quadrature (NASA)
QUAD........ Quadrex Corp. [NASDAQ symbol] (NQ)
QUAD........ Quadrillion
Quad .... Quadriplegic

Quad .... Quadrivium [A publication]
QUAD........ Quadruple
Quad Anat Prat ... Quaderni di Anatomia Pratica [A publication]
Quad Azione Soc ... Quaderni di Azione Sociale [A publication]
Quad Clin Ostet ... Quaderni di Clinica Ostetrica e Ginecologica [A publication]
Quad Criminol Clin ... Quaderni di Criminologia Clinica [A publication]
Quad Econ (Sarda) ... Quaderni dell'Economia (Sarda) [A publication]
Quad Ente Naz Semen Elette ... Quaderno. Ente Nazionale Sementi Elette [A publication]
Quaderni della Ra M ... Quaderni della Rassegna Musicale [A publication]
Quad Formaz ... Quaderni di Formazione [A publication]
Quad Geofis Appl ... Quaderni di Geofisica Applicata [A publication]
Quad G Fis ... Quaderni del Giornale di Fisica [Italy] [A publication]
Quad Ist Bot Univ Lab Crittogam (Pavia) ... Quaderni. Istituto Botanico. Universita Laboratorio Crittogamico (Pavia) [A publication]
Quad Merceol Ist Merceol Univ Bari ... Quaderni di Merceologia. Istituto di Merceologia. Universita Bari [A publication]
Quad Nutr ... Quaderni della Nutrizione [A publication]
Quad Nutr (Bologna) ... Quaderni della Nutrizione (Bologna) [A publication]
Quad Pignone ... Quaderni Pignone [A publication]
Quadr......... Quadragesms [Third volume of the year books of Edward III, beginning with the fortieth year of his reign] (DLA)
QUADR....... Quadruple
QUADRADAR ... Four-Way RADAR Surveillance
Quad Radiol ... Quaderni di Radiologia [A publication]
Quad Ric Progettazione ... Quaderni di Ricerca e Progettazione [A publication]
Quad Ric Sci ... Quaderni de la Ricerca Scientifica [A publication]
Quadrupl.... Quadruplicato [Four Times as Much] [Pharmacy]
QUADS....... Quality Achievement Data System (NASA)
Quad Sardi Econ ... Quaderni Sardi di Economia [A publication]
Quad Sclavo Diagn ... Quaderni Sclavo di Diagnostica Clinica e di Triestino [A publication]
Quad Sclavo Diagn Clin Lab ... Quaderni Sclavo di Diagnostica Clinica e di Laboratorio [A publication]
Quad Sociol ... Quaderni di Sociologia [A publication]
Quad Stor ... Quaderni Storici [A publication]
Quad Storia Sci Med Univ Studi Ferrara ... Quaderni di Storia della Scienza e della Medicina. Universita degli Studi di Ferrara [A publication]
Quad Urb C ... Quaderni Urbinati di Cultura Classica [A publication]
Quaest Conv ... Quaestiones Convivales [of Plutarch] [Classical studies] (OCD)
Quaest Entomol ... Quaestiones Entomologicae [A publication]
Quaest Geobiol ... Quaestiones Geobiologicae [A publication]
Quaest Graec ... Quaestiones Graecae [of Plutarch] [Classical studies] (OCD)
Quaest Inf ... Quaestiones Informaticae [A publication]
Quaestiones Math ... Quaestiones Mathematicae [A publication]
Quaest Plat ... Quaestiones Platonicae [of Plutarch] [Classical studies] (OCD)
Quaest Rom ... Quaestiones Romanae [of Plutarch] [Classical studies] (OCD)
QuakerH..... Quaker History [A publication]
QUAL .... Qualification (NG)
QUAL .... Qualitative
Qual........... Qualiton & MHV [Record label] [Hungary]
QUAL .... Quality (KSC)
Qual Assur ... Quality Assurance [A publication]
Qual Contr Appl Stat ... Quality Control and Applied Statistics [A publication]
Qual Eng .... Quality Engineer [A publication]
Qual Eval.... Quality Evaluation [A publication]
Qualite Rev Prat Controle Ind ... Qualite. Revue Pratique de Controle Industriel [A publication]
Quality .... Quality of Sheffield and South Yorkshire [A publication]
Quality Prog ... Quality Progress [A publication]
QUALN....... Qualification (ROG)
Qual Plant ... Qualitas Plantarum/Plant Foods for Human Nutrition [A publication]
Qual Plant Mater Veg ... Qualitas Plantarum et Materiae Vegetabiles [Later, Qualitas Plantarum/Plant Foods for Human Nutrition] [A publication]
Qual Plant Plant Foods Hum Nutr ... Qualitas Plantarum/Plant Foods for Human Nutrition [A publication]
Qual Prog... Quality Progress [A publication]
Qual Quant ... Quality and Quantity [A publication]
Qual Reliab J ... Quality and Reliability Journal [India] [A publication]
Qual Rev Prat Controle Ind ... Qualite. Revue Pratique de Controle Industriel [A publication]
QUALTIS.... Quality Technology Information Service [Atomic Energy Authority] [British] (EISS)
Qual Zuverlaessigk ... Qualitaet und Zuverlaessigkeit [A publication]
Qual & Zuverlaessigkeit ... Qualitaet und Zuverlaessigkeit [A publication]
Qual und Zuverlassigkeit ... Qualitat und Zuverlassigkeit [A publication]
QUAM .... Quadrature Amplitude Modulation (IEEE)
QUAN........ Quantity (KSC)
QUAN........ Quantronix Corp. [NASDAQ symbol] (NQ)
QUANGO.... Quasi-Autonomous Non-Governmental [or National Governmental] Organization [British]

QUANGO.... Quasiautonomous Nongovernmental [*or National Governmental*] Organization [*British*]
Quan Sociol ... Quantitative Sociology [*A publication*]
QUANT...... Quantitative
Quant Chem Symp ... Quantum Chemistry Symposia [*A publication*]
Quantitative Meth Unternehmungsplanung ... Quantitative Methoden der Unternehmungsplanung [*A publication*]
QUANTRAS ... Question Analysis Transformation and Search [*Data processing*]
QUANT SUFF ... Quantum Sufficiat [*A Sufficient Quantity*] [*Pharmacy*]
Quant Suff ... Quantum Sufficit [*A Sufficient Quantity*] [*Pharmacy*]
Quantum Electron (New York) ... Quantum Electronics (New York) [*A publication*]
QUAOPS .... Quarantine Operations [*Military*] (NVT)
QUAPP....... Qu'Appelle [*Canadian river*] (ROG)
QUAPS....... Quality Assurance Publications [*Navy*]
QUAR........ Quarantine (AABC)
QUAR......... Quarter [*Business and trade*]
QUAR......... Quarterly
Quar .... Quarterly Review [*A publication*]
QUARAM.... Quality and Reliability Management [*DoD*]
Quar Jour Econ ... Quarterly Journal of Economics [*A publication*]
QUARK....... Quantizer, Analyzer, and Record Keeper [*Telecommunications*] (TEL)
QUARLY..... Quarterly (ROG)
QUARPEL ... Quartermaster Water-Repellent Clothing [*Military*]
Quar R Biol ... Quarterly Review of Biology [*A publication*]
Quar Rev .... Quarterly Review [*A publication*]
Quarry Manage Prod ... Quarry Management and Products [*Later, Quarry Management*] [*A publication*]
Quarry Mgmt Products ... Quarry Management and Products [*Later, Quarry Management*] [*A publication*]
QUART....... Quadrantectomy, Axillary Dissection, Radiotherapy [*Oncology*]
QUART....... Quality Assurance and Reliability Team
QUART....... Quarterly
QUART....... Quartetto [*Quartet*] [*Music*] (ROG)
QUART....... Quartus [*Fourth*] [*Pharmacy*]
Quart Appl Math ... Quarterly of Applied Mathematics [*A publication*]
Quart Bul Ass Food Drug Offic US ... Quarterly Bulletin. Association of Food and Drug Officials of the United States [*Later, Quarterly Bulletin. Association of Food and Drug Officials*] [*A publication*]
Quart Bull Int Ass Agric Libr Docum ... Quarterly Bulletin. International Association of Agricultural Librarians and Documentalists [*A publication*]
Quart Bull Mich Agric Exp Sta ... Quarterly Bulletin. Michigan State University. Agricultural Experiment Station [*A publication*]
Quart Bull Mich State Univ Agr Exp Sta ... Quarterly Bulletin. Michigan State University. Agricultural Experiment Station [*A publication*]
Quart Colo Sch Mines ... Quarterly. Colorado School of Mines [*A publication*]
Quarterly of F R TV ... Quarterly of Film, Radio, and Television [*A publication*]
Quartermaster Food Container Inst Armed Forces Act Rep ... Quartermaster Food and Container Institute for the Armed Forces. Activities Report [*A publication*]
Quart J Adm ... Quarterly Journal of Administration [*A publication*]
Quart J Agr Econ ... Quarterly Journal of Agricultural Economy [*A publication*]
Quart J Chin For (Taipei) ... Quarterly Journal of Chinese Forestry (Taipei) [*A publication*]
Quart J Crude Drug Res ... Quarterly Journal of Crude Drug Research [*A publication*]
Quart J Econ ... Quarterly Journal of Economics [*A publication*]
Quart J Econom ... Quarterly Journal of Economics [*A publication*]
Quart J Exp Physiol ... Quarterly Journal of Experimental Physiology [*A publication*]
Quart J Exp Psychol ... Quarterly Journal of Experimental Psychology [*A publication*]
Quart J For ... Quarterly Journal of Forestry [*A publication*]
Quart J Indian Inst Sci ... Quarterly Journal. Indian Institute of Science [*A publication*]
Quart J Libr Congress ... Quarterly Journal. Library of Congress [*A publication*]
Quart J Mech Appl Math ... Quarterly Journal of Mechanics and Applied Mathematics [*A publication*]
Quart J Microsc Sci ... Quarterly Journal of Microscopical Science [*A publication*]
Quart J Micr Sc ... Quarterly Journal of Microscopical Science [*A publication*]
Quart J Roy Meteorol Soc ... Quarterly Journal. Royal Meteorological Society [*A publication*]
Quart J Taiwan Mus ... Quarterly Journal. Taiwan Museum [*A publication*]
Quart J Vet Sc India ... Quarterly Journal of Veterinary Science in India and Army Animal Management [*A publication*]
Quart LJ (VA) ... Quarterly Law Journal [*Virginia*] (DLA)
Quart L Rev (VA) ... Quarterly Law Review [*Virginia*] (DLA)
QUARTM.... Quartermaster (ROG)
Quart Nebr Agr Exp Sta ... Quarterly. Nebraska Agricultural Experiment Station [*A publication*]

Quart Newsl (Dehra Dun) ... Quarterly News Letter. Forest Research Institute and Colleges (Dehra Dun) [*A publication*]
Quart Philippine Sugar Inst ... Quarterly. Philippine Sugar Institute [*A publication*]
Quart R Agric ... Quarterly Review of Agricultural Economics [*A publication*]
Quart R Agric Econ ... Quarterly Review of Agricultural Economics [*A publication*]
Quart R Centr Bank Ireland ... Quarterly Review. Central Bank of Ireland [*A publication*]
Quart R Econ Busin ... Quarterly Review of Economics and Business [*A publication*]
Quart Rep Ry Tech Res Inst ... Quarterly Report. Railway Technical Research Institute [*Tokyo*] [*A publication*]
Quart Rev Agr Econ ... Quarterly Review of Agricultural Economics [*A publication*]
Quart Rev Agric Econ ... Quarterly Review of Agricultural Economics [*A publication*]
Quart Rev Biol ... Quarterly Review of Biology [*A publication*]
Quart Rev Guernsey Soc ... Quarterly Review. Guernsey Society [*A publication*]
Quart Univ Nebr Coll Agr Home Econ Agr Exp Sta ... Quarterly. University of Nebraska. College of Agriculture and Home Economics. Agricultural Experiment Station [*A publication*]
QUASAR .... Quasi-Stellar Radio Source
QUASAT .... Quasar Satellite [*Proposed observatory in space*]
QUASD...... Quality Assurance [*A publication*]
QUASER ..... Quantum Amplification by Stimulated Emission of Radiation
QUASS ..... Quassia [*Pharmacology*] (ROG)
QUAT .... Quater [*Four Times*] [*Pharmacy*]
QUAT .... Quaternary [*Period, era, or system*] [*Geology*]
QUAT .... Quaternary Ammonium Compound [*Class of antimicrobial agents*]
QUAT .... Quatrefoil [*Numismatics*]
Quatern Res ... Quaternary Research [*A publication*]
QUATIP...... Quality Assurance Test and Inspection Plan [*Military*] (CAAL)
Quat Res (Jap Assoc Quat Res) ... Quaternary Research (Japan Association of Quaternary Research) [*A publication*]
Quat Res (NY) ... Quaternary Research (New York) [*A publication*]
Quat Res (Tokyo) ... Quaternary Research (Tokyo) [*A publication*]
QUB........... Queen's University, Belfast [*Ireland*]
QUBMIS ..... Quantitatively Based Management Information System
quc .... Quebec [*MARC country of publication code*] [*Library of Congress*] (LCCP)
QUCA........ Quality Care, Inc. [*NASDAQ symbol*] (NQ)
QUCC......... Quaderni Urbinati di Cultura Classica [*A publication*]
QUE........... Albuquerque Public Library, Albuquerque, NM [*OCLC symbol*] (OCLC)
QUE........... Quebec [*Canadian province*]
que .... Quechua [*MARC language code*] [*Library of Congress*] (LCCP)
QUE........... Queenston Gold Mines Ltd. [*Toronto Stock Exchange symbol*]
QUE........... Quetta [*Pakistan*] [*Geomagnetic observatory code*]
QUE........... Quetta [*Pakistan*] [*Seismograph station code, US Geological Survey*] (SEIS)
Quebec Dept Nat Resources Prelim Rept ... Quebec Department of Natural Resources. Preliminary Report [*A publication*]
Quebec Dept Nat Resources Spec Paper ... Quebec Department of Natural Resources. Special Paper [*A publication*]
Quebec Dept Trade and Commerce Geog Service Pub ... Quebec Department of Trade and Commerce. Geographical Service. Publication [*A publication*]
Quebec L (Can) ... Quebec Law Reports [*Canada*] (DLA)
Quebec Pr (Can) ... Quebec Practice [*Canada*] (DLA)
Queb KB ...... Quebec Official Reports, King's Bench [*Canada*] (DLA)
Queb Pr...... Quebec Practice Reports [*1897-1943*] (DLA)
Que CA ...... Rapports Judiciaires Officiels, Cour d'Appel [*1892-date*] [*Official Law Reports, Court of Appeal*] [*Quebec*] (DLA)
Que CBR .... Rapports Judiciaires Officiels, Cour du Banc du Roi [*ou de la Reine*] [*Official Law Reports, Court of King's, or Queen's, Bench*] [*Quebec*] (DLA)
Que Cons Rech Dev For Rapp ... Quebec Conseil de la Recherche et du Developpement Forestiers. Rapport [*A publication*]
Que Cons Rech Dev For Rapp Annu ... Quebec Conseil de la Recherche et du Developpement Forestiers. Rapport Annuel [*A publication*]
Que CS....... Rapports Judiciaires Officiels, Cour Superieure [*Official Law Reports, Superior Court*] [*Quebec*] (DLA)
Que Dep Ind Commer Annu Rep ... Quebec Department of Industry and Commerce. Annual Report [*A publication*]
Que Dep Lands For Res Serv Res Pap ... Quebec Department of Lands and Forest Research Service. Research Paper [*A publication*]
Que Dep Natur Resour Geol Rep ... Quebec Department of Natural Resources. Geological Report [*A publication*]
Que Dep Natur Resour Prelim Rep ... Quebec Department of Natural Resources. Preliminary Report [*A publication*]
Que Dir Geol Trav Terrain ... Quebec Direction de la Geologie. Travaux sur le Terrain [*A publication*]
Que Dp Col Mines Br Rp ... Quebec Department of Colonization, Mines, and Fisheries. Mines Branch. Report on Mining Operations [*A publication*]
Queen Q ..... Queen's Quarterly [*A publication*]
Queens....... Queensway Studios [*Record label*] [*Great Britain*]

Queens B Bull ... Queens Bar Bulletin [*United States*] (DLA)
Queens CBA Bull ... Queens County Bar Association. Bulletin [*United States*] (DLA)
Queens Intra LJ ... Queen's Intramural Law Journal [*1968-70*] [*Canada*] (DLA)
Queen's Intramural LJ ... Queen's Intramural Law Journal (DLA)
Queens JP & Loc Auth Jo ... Queensland Justice of the Peace and Local Authorities' Journal (DLA)
QUEENSL ... Queensland [*Australia*] (ROG)
Queensl...... Queensland Reports [*A publication*]
Queensl Agric J ... Queensland Agricultural Journal [*A publication*]
Queensland Ag J ... Queensland Agricultural Journal [*A publication*]
Queensland Agr J ... Queensland Agricultural Journal [*A publication*]
Queensland Dent Mag ... Queensland Dental Magazine [*A publication*]
Queensland Gov Min J ... Queensland Government Mining Journal [*A publication*]
Queensland Govt Min Jour ... Queensland Government Mining Journal [*A publication*]
Queensland Hist R ... Queensland Historical Review [*A publication*]
Queensland J Agr Anim Sci ... Queensland Journal of Agricultural and Animal Sciences [*A publication*]
Queensland J Ag Sci ... Queensland Journal of Agricultural Science [*Later, Queensland Journal of Agricultural and Animal Sciences*] [*A publication*]
Queensland Land Court Rep ... Queensland Land Court Reports [*A publication*]
Queensland L Soc'y J ... Queensland Law Society. Journal [*A publication*]
Queensland Pap in Econ Policy ... Queensland Papers in Economic Policy [*A publication*]
Queensl Dent J ... Queensland Dental Journal [*A publication*]
Queensl Dep Agric Stock ... Queensland. Department of Agriculture and Stock. Annual Report [*A publication*]
Queensl Dep Mines Geol Surv Queensl Publ ... Queensland. Department of Mines. Geological Survey of Queensland. Publication [*A publication*]
Queensl Dep Mines Geol Surv Queensl Rep ... Queensland. Department of Mines. Geological Survey of Queensland. Report [*A publication*]
Queensl Dep Primary Ind Div Anim Ind Bull ... Queensland. Department of Primary Industries. Division of Animal Industry. Bulletin [*A publication*]
Queensl Dep Primary Ind Div Dairy Bull ... Queensland. Department of Primary Industries. Division of Dairying. Bulletin [*A publication*]
Queensl Dep Primary Ind Div Plant Ind Bull ... Queensland. Department of Primary Industries. Division of Plant Industry. Bulletin [*A publication*]
Queensl Geogr J ... Queensland Geographical Journal [*A publication*]
Queensl Geol Surv 1:250000 Geol Ser ... Queensland. Geological Survey. 1:250,000 Geological Series [*A publication*]
Queensl Geol Surv Publ ... Queensland Geological Survey. Publication [*A publication*]
Queensl Geol Surv Rep ... Queensland. Geological Survey. Report [*A publication*]
Queensl Gov Min J ... Queensland Government Mining Journal [*A publication*]
Queensl Herit ... Queensland Heritage [*A publication*]
Queen's L J ... Queen's Law Journal [*A publication*]
Queens LJ ... Queensland Law Journal and Reports [*A publication*]
Queensl J Agric & Anim Sci ... Queensland Journal of Agricultural and Animal Sciences [*A publication*]
Queensl J Agric Anim Sci ... Queensland Journal of Agricultural and Animal Sciences [*A publication*]
Queensl J Agric Sci ... Queensland Journal of Agricultural Science [*Later, Queensland Journal of Agricultural and Animal Sciences*] [*A publication*]
Queensl JP (Austr) ... Queensland Justice of the Peace Australia (DLA)
Queensl L... Queensland Law (DLA)
Queensl LJ (Austr) ... Queensland Law Journal Australia [*A publication*]
Queensl LJ & R ... Queensland Law Journal and Reports [*A publication*]
Queensl LJ & St R ... Queensland Law Journal and State Reports [*Australia*] (DLA)
Queensl LR ... Queensland Law Reports [*A publication*]
Queensl LSJ ... Queensland Law Society. Journal (DLA)
Queensl L Soc'y J ... Queensland Law Society. Journal [*A publication*]
Queensl Nat ... Queensland Naturalist [*A publication*]
Queensl Nurses J ... Queensland Nurses Journal [*A publication*]
Queens LR ... Queensland Law Reports (Beor) [*A publication*]
Queensl SC (Austr) ... Queensland. Supreme Court. Reports [*Australia*] [*A publication*]
Queensl S Ct R ... Queensland. Supreme Court. Reports [*A publication*]
Queensl Soc Sugar Cane Technol Proc ... Queensland Society of Sugar Cane Technologists. Proceedings [*A publication*]
Queensl Stat ... Queensland Statutes [*Australia*] (DLA)
Queensl St (Austr) ... Queensland State Reports [*Australia*] (DLA)
Queensl Univ Dep Civ Eng Bull ... Queensland University. Department of Civil Engineering. Bulletin [*A publication*]
Queensl Univ Dep Civ Eng Bull ... University of Queensland. Department of Civil Engineering. Bulletin [*A publication*]
Queensl Univ Dep Geol Pap ... Queensland University. Department of Geology. Papers [*A publication*]

Queensl Vet Proc ... Queensland Veterinary Proceedings (Australian Veterinary Association, Queensland Division) [*A publication*]
Queensl WN (Aus) ... Queensland Law Reporter and Weekly Notes [*Australia*] (DLA)
Queensl WN (Austr) ... Queensland Weekly Notes [*Australia*] (DLA)
Queen's Nurs J ... Queen's Nursing Journal [*A publication*]
Queen's Papers in Pure and Appl Math ... Queen's Papers in Pure and Applied Mathematics [*A publication*]
Queen's Q ... Queen's Quarterly [*A publication*]
Queen's Quart ... Queen's Quarterly [*A publication*]
Queens St R ... Queensland State Reports (DLA)
Queens Univ Therm Fluid Sci Group Rep ... Queen's University. Thermal and Fluid Science Group. Report [*A publication*]
Que KB...... Quebec Official Reports, King's Bench (DLA)
Que L......... Quebec Law (DLA)
Quellen Stud Philos ... Quellen und Studien zur Philosophie [*A publication*]
Que LR .... Quebec Law Reports [*Canada*] (DLA)
Que Minist Chasse Pech Contrib ... Quebec Ministere de la Chasse et des Pecheries. Contributions [*A publication*]
Que Minist Ind Commer Dir Rech Cah Inf ... Quebec Ministere de l'Industrie et du Commerce. Direction de la Recherche. Cahiers d'Information [*A publication*]
Que Minist Ind Commer Rapp Pech ... Quebec Ministere de l'Industrie et du Commerce. Rapport sur les Pecheries [*A publication*]
Que Minist Ind Commer Serv Biol Rapp Annu ... Quebec Ministere de l'Industrie et du Commerce. Service de Biologie. Rapport Annuel [*A publication*]
Que Minist Richesses Nat Etude Spec ... Quebec. Ministere des Richesses Naturelles. Etude Speciale [*A publication*]
Que Pr .... Quebec Practice (DLA)
Que PR .... Quebec Practice Reports (DLA)
Que (Prov) Minist Richesses Nat Rapp Prelim ... Quebec (Province). Ministere des Richesses Naturelles. Rapport Preliminaire [*A publication*]
Que QB...... Quebec Official Reports, Queen's Bench (DLA)
QUERC....... Quercus [*Oak*] [*Pharmacology*] (ROG)
Que Rev Jud ... Quebec Revised Judicial (DLA)
Que Rev Stat ... Quebec Revised Statutes [*Canada*] (DLA)
Query File Commonw Bur Hortic Plant Crops ... Query File. Commonwealth Bureau of Horticulture and Plantation Crops [*A publication*]
QUES .... Question (AAG)
QUES .... Question Mark (AABC)
Que SC...... Quebec Official Reports, Superior Court (DLA)
Que Sci ...... Quebec Science [*A publication*]
Que Soc Prot Plants Rep ... Quebec Society for the Protection of Plants. Report [*A publication*]
QUEST ...... Quality Electrical Systems Test [*Interpreter*]
QUEST ...... Quality Utilization Effectiveness Statistically Qualified
QUEST ...... Quantitative Understanding of Explosive Stimulus Transfer
QUEST ...... Quantitative Utility Estimates for Science and Technology [*RAND Corp.*]
QUEST ...... Query Evaluation and Search Technique
QUEST ...... Question
Quest Act Socialisme ... Questions Actuelles du Socialisme [*A publication*]
Que Stat...... Quebec Statutes [*Canada*] (DLA)
QUESTER ... Quick and Effective System to Enhance Retrieval [*Data processing*]
QUESTN.... Question
Questn .... Questionnaire (ADA)
QUESTOL ... Quiet Experimental Short Takeoff and Landing [*Program*] [*NASA*]
Que Super ... Quebec Official Reports, Superior Court (DLA)
Quetico-Super Wilderness Res Cent Annu Rep ... Quetico-Superior Wilderness Research Center. Annual Report [*A publication*]
Quetico-Super Wilderness Res Cent Tech Note ... Quetico-Superior Wilderness Research Center. Technical Note [*A publication*]
QU Gazette ... Queensland University. Gazette [*A publication*]
QUI .... Queen's University, Ireland
QUI .... Quincy Railroad Co. [*Later, QRR*] [*AAR code*]
QUI .... Quito [*Ecuador*] [*Seismograph station code, US Geological Survey*] [*Closed*] (SEIS)
QUI .... Quito, Ecuador, Tracking Station [*NASA*] (NASA)
QUI .... Thomas Crane Public Library, Quincy, MA [*OCLC symbol*] (OCLC)
QUIC .... Quality Data Information and Control (NASA)
QUICK........ Quotation Information Center KK [*Nihon Keizai Shimbun, Inc.*] [*Tokyo, Japan*] [*Information service*] (EISS)
QUICKTRAN ... Quick FORTRAN [*Programing language*] [*1979*]
QUID .... Quantified Intrapersonal Decision-Making [*In book title*]
QUIES .... Quiescent
QUIKQ...... Quickprint of America [*NASDAQ symbol*] (NQ)
QUIL .... Quad in Line [*Electronics*] [*Telecommunications*] (TEL)
QUILL........ Queen's University Interrogation of Legal Literature [*Queen's University of Belfast*] [*Northern Ireland*] [*Information service*] (EISS)
Quill........... Quill: Queensland Inter-Library Liaison [*A publication*]
Quill & Q ..... Quill and Quire [*A publication*]

Quim Anal ... Quimica Analitica [*A publication*]
Quim Farm ... Quimica y Farmica [*A publication*]
Quim Ind (Barcelona) ... Quimica e Industria (Barcelona) [*A publication*]
Quim Ind (Madrid) ... Quimica e Industria (Madrid) [*A publication*]
Quim Ind (Montevideo) ... Quimica Industrial (Montevideo) [*A publication*]
Quim Nova ... Quimica Nova [*A publication*]
QUIN .... Quina [*Quinine*] [*Pharmacy*] (ROG)
Quin .... Quincy's Massachusetts Reports (DLA)
QUIN .... Quintuple
Quin Bank ... Quin on Banking [*1833*] (DLA)
Quinct .... Pro Quinctio [*of Cicero*] [*Classical studies*] (OCD)
Quincy .... Quincy's Massachusetts Reports (DLA)
QUINT .... Quintetto [*Quintet*] [*Music*] (ROG)
Quint .... Quintilian [*First century AD*] [*Classical studies*] (OCD)
QUINT .... Quintuple
Quintessence Dent Technol ... Quintessence of Dental Technology [*A publication*]
Quintessence Int ... Quintessence International [*A publication*]
Quintessencia Protese Lab ... Quintessencia de Protese de Laboratorio [*A publication*]
Quintessenz J ... Quintessenz Journal [*A publication*]
Quintessenz Zahntech ... Quintessenz der Zahntechnik [*A publication*]
Quinti Quinto ... Year Book 5 Henry V [*England*] (DLA)
Quint Smyrn ... Quintus Smyrnaeus [*Classical studies*] (OCD)
Quinz Lit .... Quinzaine Litteraire [*A publication*]
QUIP .... Quad In-Line Package
QUIP .... Query Interactive Processor (IEEE)
QUIP .... QUOTA [*Query Online Terminal Assistance*] Input Processor [*Data processing*]
QUIV .... Quiver (ROG)
Quix .... Quixote [*A publication*]
QUIX .... Quixote Corp. [*NASDAQ symbol*] (NQ)
Qu Jour Int-Amer Rel ... Quarterly Journal of Inter-American Relations (DLA)
QUK .... Quaker Resources, Inc. [*Vancouver Stock Exchange symbol*]
QUL .... Quillagua [*Chile*] [*Seismograph station code, US Geological Survey*] (SEIS)
QU Law J .... University of Queensland. Law Journal [*A publication*]
Qu LJ .... Quarterly Law Journal (DLA)
QULJ .... Queensland University Law Journal [*A publication*]
Qu L Rev .... Quarterly Law Review (DLA)
QUM .... Queen's University, Medical Library [*UTLAS symbol*]
QUM .... Quillmana [*Peru*] [*Seismograph station code, US Geological Survey*] [*Closed*] (SEIS)
QUMDO ...... Qualitative Materiel Development Objective [*Army*] (AFIT)
Qu Minist Ind Commer Serv Rech Cah Inf ... Quebec. Ministere de l'Industrie et du Commerce. Service de la Recherche. Cahiers d'Information [*A publication*]
Qu Minist Terres For Serv Rech Note ... Quebec. Ministere des Terres et Forets. Service de la Recherche. Note. [*A publication*]
QUMR .... Quality Unsatisfactory Material Report (MCD)
QUMS .... Quasar Microsystems [*NASDAQ symbol*] (NQ)
Q Univ Gaz ... University of Queensland. Gazette [*A publication*]
QUNO .... Quaker United Nations Office (EA-IO)
QUODD ...... Quodlibet [*Newsletter of the Southeastern Region*] [*A publication*]
Quomodo Adul ... Quomodo Adulescens Poetas Audire Debeat [*of Plutarch*] [*Classical studies*] (OCD)
QUON .... Question (ROG)
Quon Attach ... Quoniam Attachiamenta (DLA)
QUONBLE ... Questionable (ROG)
QUOR .... Quorum [*Of Which*] [*Pharmacy*]
QUOT .... Quotation
quot .... Quoted In [*or Quoting*] (DLA)
QUOT .... Quotient (MSA)
QUOT .... Quoties [*As Often as Needed*] [*Pharmacy*]
QUOT .... Quotron Systems [*NASDAQ symbol*] (NQ)
QUOTA ...... Query Online Terminal Assistance [*Data processing*]
QUOTID ...... Quotidie [*Daily*] [*Pharmacy*]
QUOT OP SIT ... Quoties Opus Sit [*As Often as Necessary*] [*Pharmacy*]
QUP .... Quality Unit Pack
QUP .... Quonset Point [*Navy*]
Qu (Prov) Dep Mines Prelim Rep ... Quebec (Province). Department of Mines. Preliminary Report [*A publication*]
QUR .... Quinstar Resources [*Vancouver Stock Exchange symbol*]
QuSAR .... Quantitative Structure Activity Relationships [*National Institute on Drug Abuse*]
Qu Serv Faune Bull ... Quebec. Service de la Faune Bulletin [*A publication*]
QUX .... Quinella Exploration Ltd. [*Vancouver Stock Exchange symbol*]
QUY .... Quest Energy Corp. [*Vancouver Stock Exchange symbol*]
QV .... Bibliotheque Municipale, Victoriaville, Quebec [*Library symbol*] [*National Library of Canada*] (NLC)
QV .... Quality Verification [*Nuclear energy*] (NRCH)
QV .... Quantum Vis [*or Voleris*] [*As Much as You Wish*] [*Pharmacy*]
QV .... Quatro Ventos [*A publication*]
QV .... Qui Vixit [*Who Lived*] [*Latin*]
QV .... Quo Vadis [*A publication*]
QV .... Quod Vide [*or Videte*] [*Which See*] [*Latin*]
Q4V .... Quicker for Victory [*World War II*]
QVAH .... Institut de Recherche de l'Hydro-Quebec, Varennes, Quebec [*Library symbol*] [*National Library of Canada*] (NLC)

QVAI .... Centre de Documentation, INRS-Energie, Varennes, Quebec [*Library symbol*] [*National Library of Canada*] (NLC)
QVAUH .... Hoffman-La Roche Ltd., Vaudreuil, Quebec [*Library symbol*] [*National Library of Canada*] (NLC)
QVC .... College de Victoriaville, Quebec [*Library symbol*] [*National Library of Canada*] (NLC)
QVC .... Quality Value Convenience Network, Inc. [*Television*]
QVCEMBO ... Ecole Quebecoise du Meuble et du Bois Ouvre, College de Victoriaville, Quebec [*Library symbol*] [*National Library of Canada*] (NLC)
QVCSF .... Queen Victoria's Clergy Sustentation Fund [*British*]
QVEC .... Cultural Centre [*Centre Culturel*] Verdun, Quebec [*Library symbol*] [*National Library of Canada*] (NLC)
QVEC .... Qualified Voluntary Employee Contribution
QVGCCQ ... Cree Regional Authority, Grand Council of the Crees (of Quebec) [*Administration Regionale Crie, Grand Conseil des Cris (du Quebec)*] Val D'Or, Quebec [*Library symbol*] [*National Library of Canada*] (NLC)
Q Vic .... Statutes of Quebec in the Reign of Victoria (DLA)
Q Vit .... Quaderni del Vittoriale [*A publication*]
QVLBI .... Quasi-Very-Long-Baseline Interferometry
QVP .... Quality Verification Plan
QVR .... Quality Verification Report
QVR .... Queen Victoria's Rifles [*Military unit*] [*British*]
QVSLEA ..... Atmospheric Environment Service, Environment Canada [*Service de l'Environnement Atmospherique, Environnement Canada*] Ville St-Laurent, Quebec [*Library symbol*] [*National Library of Canada*] (NLC)
QVT .... Qualified Verification Testing [*NASA*]
QVVT .... Qualified Verification Vibration Testing [*NASA*] (NASA)
QW .... Inter-Island Air Services Ltd. [*Grenada*] [*ICAO designator*] (FAAC)
QW .... Poland [*License plate code assigned to foreign diplomats in the US*]
QW .... Quantum Well [*Physics*]
QW .... Quarter Wave
Q W .... Quarterly West [*A publication*]
QW .... Waterloo Public Library, Quebec [*Library symbol*] [*National Library of Canada*] (NLC)
QWA .... Quarter-Wave Antenna
QWASP ..... Quebec White Anglo-Saxon Protestant
QWBI .... Quality of Well Being Index
QWBP .... Qualification Standards for Wage Board Positions
QWC .... West Chester State College, West Chester, PA [*OCLC symbol*] (OCLC)
QWD .... Quarterly World Day
Q/WDO ...... Quarter Window [*Automotive engineering*]
QWERTY .... First six keys in the upper row of letters of a standard typewriter's keyboard [*Sometimes used as an informal name for a standard keyboard typewriter*]
QWG .... Quadripartite Working Group [*Military*]
QWG/CD .... Quadripartite Working Group on Combat Developments (MCD)
QWG/ENG ... Quadripartite Working Group on Engineering (MCD)
QWG/EW ... Quadripartite Working Group on Electronic Warfare (MCD)
QWG/LOG ... Quadripartite Working Group on Logistics [*Military*] (RDA)
QWG/PIQA ... Quadripartite Working Group on Proofing Inspection Quality Assurance (MCD)
QWG/STANO ... Quadripartite Working Group on Surveillance and Target Acquisition/Night Observation (MCD)
QWHX .... Wheeling Pittsburgh Steel Corp. [*NYSE symbol*]
QWIKTRAN ... Quick FORTRAN [*Programing language*] [*1979*] (CSR)
QWL .... Quality of Work Life [*Anti-recession program of Ford Motor Co.*]
QWL .... Quality of Working Life [*Labour Canada program*]
QWL .... Quick Weight Loss
QWLD .... Quality of Worklife Database [*Management Directions*] [*Austin, TX*] [*Information service*] (EISS)
QWMP .... Quadruped Walking Machine Program [*Army*]
QWN .... Queensland Weekly Notes (DLA)
QWN .... Weekly Notes. Queensland [*A publication*]
QWP .... Quarter-Wave Plate
QWR .... Que West Resources [*Toronto Stock Exchange symbol*] [*Vancouver Stock Exchange symbol*]
QWSH .... Congregation Shaar Hashomayim Library-Museum, Westmount, Quebec [*Library symbol*] [*National Library of Canada*] (NLC)
QWSMM .... Westmount Public Library, Quebec [*Library symbol*] [*National Library of Canada*] (NLC)
QX .... State of Qatar [*Airline*] [*ICAO designator*] (FAAC)
QXE .... Horizon Airlines, Inc. [*Seattle, WA*] [*FAA designator*] (FAAC)
QY .... Air Limousin T.A. [*France*] [*ICAO designator*] (FAAC)
QY .... Quantum Yield
QY .... Quay (ROG)
QY .... Query
7QY .... Malawi [*Aircraft nationality and registration mark*] (FAAC)
QYM .... SOLINET [*Southeastern Library Network*] Center, Atlanta, GA [*OCLC symbol*] (OCLC)
QZ .... Quartz [*Quality of the bottom*] [*Nautical charts*]
QZ .... Zambia Airways [*ICAO designator*] (FAAC)

QZM .... Quartz Mountain Gold Corp. [*Vancouver Stock Exchange
　　　　　symbol]
QZN .... Quan Zhou [*Republic of China*] [*Seismograph station code, US
　　　　　Geological Survey*]　(SEIS)

R

R	Abstracted Reappraisement Decisions (DLA)
R	Acknowledgment of Receipt [*Message handling*]
R	All India Reporter, Rajasthan (DLA)
r	Angular Yaw Velocity (AAG)
R	Antenna with Reflector
r------	Arctic Ocean and Region [*MARC geographic area code*] [*Library of Congress*] (LCCP)
R	Arginine [*One-letter symbol; see Arg*]
R	Army [*Military aircraft identification prefix*] (FAAC)
R	Cilag-Chemie AG [*Switzerland*] [*Research code symbol*]
R	Denver Laboratories [*Great Britain*] [*Research code symbol*]
R	Janssen [*Belgium*] [*Research code symbol*]
R	Kentucky Law Reporter [*1880-1908*] (DLA)
R	Molar Gas Constant [*Symbol*] [*IUPAC*] (NASA)
R	Product Moment Coefficient of Correlation [*Statistics*]
R	[*A*] Purine Nucleoside [*One-letter symbol; see Puo*]
R	R-Register [*Data processing*]
R	Rabba (BJA)
R	Rabbanite (BJA)
R	Rabbi
R	Race
r	Racemic [*Also, dl, rac*] [*Chemistry*]
R	RACON [*RADAR Beacon*]
R	RADAR Contact [*A diagonal line through R indicates RADAR service terminated; a cross through R indicates RADAR contact lost*] [*Aviation*] (FAAC)
R	Radfahrabteilung [*Bicycle Battalion*] [*German military - World War II*]
R-	Radial [*Followed by three digits; for use on instrument approach charts*] [*Aviation*]
R	Radial (FAAC)
R	Radian
R	Radiancy
R	Radiation
R	Radical
R	Radio
R	Radiology [*or Radiologist*] (ADA)
R	Radiotelegram
R	Radium [*Chemical symbol is Ra*] (KSC)
r	Radius [*Symbol*] [*IUPAC*]
R	Radius
r	Radius of Gyration (AAG)
R	Rail (MSA)
R	Railroad [*or Railway*]
R	Rain [*Meteorology*]
R	Ram
R	Rand [*Monetary unit*]
R	Range
R	Rank
R	Rankine [*Temperature scale*]
R	Rare [*Numismatics*]
R	Rare [*When applied to species*]
R	Rate
R	Ratio
R	Rational Number (MDG)
R	Rationing [*British*]
R	Rawle's Pennsylvania Reports [*1828-35*] (DLA)
R	Rayleigh Wave [*Seismology*]
R	Rays
R	Reaction (AAG)
R	Read (AAG)
R	Real
R	Realites [*A publication*]
R	Ream (ADA)
R	Rear
R	Reasoning Factor [*or Ability*] [*Psychology*]
R	Reaumur [*Temperature scale*] (MUGU)
R	Rebounds [*Basketball, hockey*]
R	Receipt (ROG)
R	Received (FAAC)
R	Received Solid [*Amateur radio*]
R	Receiver
R	Receptor [*Biochemistry*]
R	Recht [*Law*] [*German*]
R	Recipe [*Take*] [*Pharmacy*]
R	Reciprocating
R	Recite [*Swell Organ*] [*Music*]
R	Recluse
R	Reconditioned
R	Reconnaissance [*Designation for all US military aircraft*]
R	Reconstruction Committee [*British*] [*World War II*]
R	Recreations
R	Recruit (ROG)
r	Rectangular Tank [*Liquid gas carriers*]
R	Recto [*Also, RO*]
R	Rector [*or Rectory*]
R	Rectum [*Medicine*]
(R)	Rectus [*Clockwise configuration*] [*Biochemistry*] [*See RS*]
R	Red
R	Redetermination
R	Redundancy [*Used in correcting manuscripts, etc.*]
R	Referee [*Football*]
r	Referred (OICC)
R	Reflection [*Angle of*]
R	Reflexive
R	Reform [*Judaism*]
R	Refraction
R	Refrigerated Tank [*Liquid gas carriers*]
R	Refrigerator
R-	Refuse Disposal [*British Waterways Board sign*]
R	Refused [*Horse racing*]
R	Regiment
R	Regina [*Queen*] [*Latin*]
R	Registered
R	Registrar (ROG)
R	Regna [*Queen*] [*Latin*] (DLA)
R	Regular (ADA)
R	Regulating
R	Reigned
R	Reiz [*Stimulus*] [*German*] [*Psychology*]
R	Relative Humidity
R	Relaxed
R	Reliability (MCD)
R	Reluctance
R	Remote [*Telecommunications*] (TEL)
R	Repeal (DLA)
R	Repetitive [*Electronics*]
R	Replaceability (AAG)
R	Replaced [*Dentistry*]
R	Reply (ADA)
R	Reports
R	[*The*] Reports, Coke's English King's Bench (DLA)
R	Reprint
R	Republic
R	Republican
R	Republika [*Zagreb*] [*A publication*]
R	Requiescat [*He Rests*] [*Latin*]
R	Rerun [*of a television show*]
R	Rescinded (DLA)
R	Research
R	Resentment [*Psychology*]
R	Reserve
R	Reset (MDG)
R	Reside [*or Resident*]
R	Resistance [*Symbol*] [*IUPAC*]
R	Resistor
R	Resolved (DLA)
R	Respectfully [*Letter closing*]
R	Respiration
R	Respond [*or Response*]
R	Responder [*Strain of mice*]
R	Responsorium [*Responsory*]

R	Respublica [*Commonwealth*] [*Latin*]
R	Restricted [*Persons under eighteen (sixteen in some localities) not admitted unless accompanied by parent or adult guardian*] [*Movie rating*]
R	Restricted [*Immunology*]
R	Restricted [*Military document classification*]
R	Restricted Area [*Followed by identification*]
R	Retarder [*Slow*] [*On clock-regulators*] [*French*]
R	Retired [*or Retiree*]
R	Rettie's Scotch Court of Session Reports, Fourth Series (DLA)
R	Returning
R	Reverse [*Giemsa method*] [*Chromosome stain*]
R	Reverse
R	Reversed [*in Pluronic R surfactants*]
R	Revised (MCD)
R2	Revision
R	Revoked (DLA)
R	Reward
R	Rex [*King*] [*Latin*]
R	Reynolds Number [*Also, Re, RN*] [*Viscosity*]
R	Rhinitis [*Medicine*]
R	Rhode Island State Library, Providence, RI [*Library symbol*] [*Library of Congress*] (LCLS)
R	Rhodesia [*Later, Zimbabwe*] (ROG)
R	Rhodium [*Chemical element*] [*Symbol is Rh*] (ROG)
R	Rhodopsin [*Visual purple*]
R	Rhythm
R	Rial [*Monetary unit in Iran, Saudi Arabia, etc.*]
r	Ribose [*One-letter symbol; see Rib*]
R	Richard (King of England) (DLA)
R	Richtkreis [*Aiming Circle*] [*Gunnery term*] [*German military - World War II*]
R	Rickettsia
R	Rifle
R	Right [*Direction*]
R	Right [*Politics*]
R	Right [*side of a stage*] [*A stage direction*]
R	Right Edge [*Skating*]
R	Riker Laboratories, Inc. [*Research code symbol*]
R	Rimus (BJA)
R	Ring [*Technical drawings*]
R	Ring Lead [*Telecommunications*] (TEL)
R	Ring Road [*Traffic sign*] [*British*]
-R	Rinne's Test Negative [*Hearing test*]
+R	Rinne's Test Positive [*Hearing test*]
R	Rio [*River*] [*Spanish*] (ROG)
R	Rio De Janeiro [*A publication*]
R	Rise [*Electronics*]
R	Riser [*Technical drawings*]
R	Rises
R	Risk
R	River [*Maps and charts*]
R	Riveted
R	Road
R	Roan (Leather) [*Bookbinding*] (ROG)
R	Robert [*Phonetic alphabet*] [*Royal Navy*] [*World War I*] [*Pre-World War II*] (DSUE)
R	Rocket [*Missile vehicle type symbol*]
R	Rod [*Measurement*]
r	Roentgen [*Also, RU*] [*Unit measuring X and gamma radiations*]
R	Roger [*All right or OK*] [*Communications slang*]
R	Roger [*Phonetic alphabet*] [*World War II*] (DSUE)
R	Roll
R	Roller-Skating Rinks [*Public-performance tariff class*] [*British*]
R	Rollout (KSC)
R	Roman
R	Romania
R	Romania [*A publication*]
R	Romans [*New Testament book*] (BJA)
R	Romeo [*Phonetic alphabet*] [*International*] (DSUE)
R	Rood [*Unit of measurement*]
R	Rook [*Chess*]
R	Rosary
R	Roscoe's Cape Of Good Hope (DLA)
R	Rosin [*Standard material for soldering*]
R	Rotary Wing [*Aircraft designation*]
R	Rothschild [*L. F.*], Unterberg, Towbin Holdings, Inc. [*NYSE symbol*]
R	Rotor
R	Rough [*Appearance of bacterial colony*]
R	Rough Sea [*Navigation*]
R	Roussel [*France*] [*Research code symbol*]
R	Route
R	Routine (KSC)
R	Royal
R	Rubber
R	Rubidomycin [*See also D, Daunorubicin*] [*Antineoplastic drug*]
R	Ruble [*Monetary unit in the USSR*]
R	Rue [*Street*] [*French*]
R	Rule
R	Ruled [*Followed by the dates of a monarch's reign*]

R	Rum (ROG)
R	Run [*Deserted*] [*Nautical*] [*British*] (ROG)
R	Run [*Distance sailed from noon to noon*] [*Navy*] [*British*] (ROG)
R	Runic
R	Runs [*scored*] [*Baseball or cricket*]
R	Rupee [*Monetary unit in Ceylon, India, and Pakistan*]
R	Rural (MCD)
R	Russian (DLA)
R	Rydberg Constant [*Spectroscopy*] [*Symbol*] (DEN)
R	Rydge's [*A publication*]
R	Ship [*Missile launch environment symbol*]
R	Stauffer Chemical Co. [*Research code symbol*]
R	Transport [*Naval aircraft designation*]
R	Yaw Control Axis [*Symbol*]
R2	Richard II [*Shakespearean work*]
R³	Relay, Reporter, Responder [*Military*] (CAAL)
3R	Request, Retrieve, and Report [*Data processing*]
3R	Resurfacing, Restoration, and Rehabilitation [*Also, RRR*] [*Later, 4R*] [*Federal Highway Administration*]
3R	Rheingold-Rotary-Reciprocating [*Motor*]
R3	Richard III [*Shakespearean work*]
4R	Ceylon [*Sri Lanka*] [*Aircraft nationality and registration mark*] (FAAC)
4R	Resurfacing, Restoration, Rehabilitation, and Reconstruction [*Formerly, 3R, RRR*] [*Federal Highway Administration*]
5R	Madagascar [*Aircraft nationality and registration mark*] (FAAC)
8R	Guyana [*Aircraft nationality and registration mark*] (FAAC)
3R's	Readin', Ritin', and Rithmetic [*Also, RRR*]
3R's	Reference and Research Library Resources Systems [*New York State Library*] [*Albany*] [*Information service*] (EISS)
3R's	Relief, Recovery, Reform [*Elements of the New Deal*]
6R's	Remedial Readin', Remedial Ritin', and Remedial Rithmetic [*Also, RRRRRR*] [*Humorous interpretation of the three R's*]
R (Count)	Readiness Count (MCD)
R (Day)	Redeployment Day [*Military*]
RA	Coast RADAR Station [*Maps and charts*]
RA	High-Powered Radio Range (Adcock)
RA	Rabbinical Assembly (EA)
RA	RADAR Altimeter [*Aviation*] (KSC)
Ra	RADAR Station
RA	Radio Antenna
RA	Radioactive
RA	Radionic Association (EA)
Ra	Radium [*Chemical element*]
RA	Radius of Action (AAG)
Ra	Raduga [*Moscow*] [*A publication*]
RA	Ragweed Antigen [*Immunology*]
RA	Rain [*Meteorology*] (FAAC)
RA	Raise (AAG)
RA	Ramp Actuator
RA	Random Access [*Data processing*] (AAG)
RA	Range [*Aviation*]
RA	Rape [*Division in the county of Sussex*] [*British*]
RA	Rapid-American Corp.
RA	Rapid Anastigmatic (Lens) [*Photography*] (ROG)
RA	Raritan Arsenal (AAG)
Ra	Rassegna [*A publication*]
RA	Rate Action (AAG)
RA	Rate of Application
RA	Ratio Actuator (MCD)
RA	Ration
Ra	Rayleigh Number [*IUPAC*]
RA	Raynaud's Phenomenon [*Medicine*]
RA	Rayon (AAG)
RA	Read Amplifier
RA	Ready-Access [*Telecommunications*] (TEL)
RA	Ready Alert [*Navy*] (NVT)
RA	Rear Admiral [*Also, RADM, RADML*]
RA	Rear Artillery
R/A	Rear Axle [*Automotive engineering*]
RA	Receiver Attenuation
RA	Recipient Rights Adviser
R/A	Recorded Announcement [*Telecommunications*] (TEL)
RA	Records Administration (MCD)
RA	Recreation Aide [*Red Cross*]
RA	Redevelopment Act (OICC)
RA	Redstone Arsenal [*Huntsville, AL*] [*Army*]
RA	Reduced Aperture (MCD)
RA	Reduction of Area
RA	Refer to Accepter [*as, a check or draft*] [*Banking*]
RA	Refugee Agency [*NATO*] (NATG)
RA	Regional Administrator
RA	Regional Associations [*Marine science*] (MSC)
RA	Registration Act
RA	Registration Appeals (DLA)
RA	Regular Army
RA	Regulation Appeals (DLA)
RA	Rehabilitation Act (OICC)

RA	Reimbursement Authorization (AFM)
RA	Reinforced Alert (NATG)
RA	Relative Address
RA	Release Authorization
RA	Released-Action [*Pharmacy*]
RA	Reliability Analysis (AAG)
RA	Reliability Assessment (KSC)
RA	Reliability Assurance (MCD)
RA	Religious of the Apostolate of the Sacred Heart [*Roman Catholic women's religious order*]
RA	Religious of the Assumption [*Roman Catholic women's religious order*]
RA	Relocation Address
RA	Relocation Assistance [*HUD*]
RA	Remittance Advice (MCD)
RA	Renal Artery [*Anatomy*]
RA	Rental Agreement
RA	Repair Assignment (AAG)
RA	Repeat Action [*Medicine*]
R/A	Repeat Attempt [*Telecommunications*] (TEL)
Ra	Repertorio Americano [*A publication*]
RA	Replacement Algorithm
RA	Reporting Activity (MCD)
R & A	Reports and Analysis
RA	Representative Assembly
RA	Republicans Abroad (EA)
RA	Requesting Agency (MUGU)
RA	Research Abstracts [*University Microfilms International*] [*A publication*]
R & A	Research and Analysis
RA	Resident Agent (AFM)
RA	Resident Alien
RA	Resident Assistant [*College housing*]
RA	Resident Auditor
RA	Residual Air
RA	Resistor Assembly
RA	Resource Allocation (MCD)
RA	Respiratory Allergy [*Immunology*]
R-A	Response Errors [*Statistics*]
R & A	Responsibility and Action
RA	Restaurant Associates Industries, Inc. [*American Stock Exchange symbol*]
RA	Retinal Anlage [*Ophthalmology*]
RA	Retinoic Acid [*Biochemistry*]
RA	Retrograde Amnesia [*Medicine*]
RA	Return Address
R/A	Return to Author [*Bookselling*]
RA	Revenue Agent [*IRS*]
RA	Reverendus Admodum [*Very Reverend*] [*Latin*]
R & A	Review and Analysis
R & A	Review and Approval
RA	Reviewing Activity (MCD)
RA	Reviewing Authority
RA	Reviews in Anthropology [*A publication*]
RA	Revue Anglo-Americaine [*A publication*]
RA	Revue Archeologique [*A publication*]
RA	Revue des Arts [*A publication*]
RA	Revue d'Assyriologie [*A publication*]
RA	Revue d'Assyriologie et d'Archeologie Orientale [*Paris*] [*A publication*]
RA	Rheinisches Archiv [*A publication*]
RA	Rheumatoid Agglutinins [*Clinical chemistry*]
RA	Rheumatoid Arthritis [*Medicine*]
RA	Riders Association [*Commercial firm*] (EA)
RA	Right Aft (MCD)
RA	Right Angle (DEN)
RA	Right Arch [*Freemasonry*]
RA	Right Arm [*Medicine*]
RA	Right Ascension [*Navigation*]
RA	Right Atrium [*Cardiology*]
RA	Right Axilla (KSC)
RA	Ripple Adder
RA	Risk Analysis (MCD)
RA	Robbery Armed
RA	Robustrus Archistriatalis [*Bird brain anatomy*]
RA	Rocket Assist (RDA)
RA	Rokitansky-Aschoff [*Sinus*] [*Gastroenterology*]
RA	Romanistische Arbeitshefte [*A publication*]
RA	Roquefort Association (EA)
RA	Rosin Acid [*Organic chemistry*]
RA	Rosin Activated [*Standard material for soldering*]
RA	Rotary Assembly
RA	Rotogravure Association
RA	Royal Academician [*or Academy*] [*British*]
RA	Royal Academy of Arts in London [*British*]
R and A	Royal and Ancient [*Golf Club*] [*St. Andrews, Scotland*]
R & A	Royal and Ancient Golf Club of St. Andrews [*Recognized as the game's legislative authority in all countries except the US*] [*British*]
RA	Royal Arch [*Freemasonry*]
RA	Royal Art

RA	Royal Artillery [*British*]
RA	Royal Artist
RA	Royal Nepal Airlines Corp. [*ICAO designator*] (FAAC)
RA	Royal Regiment of Artillery [*Military*] [*British*]
RA	Rueckwaertiges Armeegebiet [*Rear area of an army*] [*German military*]
R & A	Rules and Administration Committee [*US Senate*]
RA	Rules on Appeal (DLA)
RA	Russian American
RA	Thermal Resistance of Unit Area [*Heat transmission symbol*]
RAA	Rabbinical Alliance of America (EA)
RA(A)	Rear-Admiral of Aircraft Carriers [*Obsolete*] [*British*]
RAA	Reeve Aleutian Airways, Inc. [*Air carrier designation symbol*]
RAA	Regenerative Agriculture Association (EA)
RAA	Regional Administrative Assistant (ADA)
RAA	Regional Airline Association [*Formerly, CAAA*] [*Washington, DC*] (EA)
RAA	Reinsurance Association of America [*Washington, DC*] (EA)
RAA	Rendiconti. Accademia di Archeologia, Lettere, e Belle Arti [*Napoli*] [*A publication*]
RAA	Renewal Assistance Administration [*HUD*]
RAA	Renin-Angiotensin-Aldosterone [*Clinical nephrology*]
RAA	Research Animal Alliance (EA)
RAA	Respiratory Aid Apparatus
RAA	Revue de l'Academie Arabe [*A publication*]
RAA	Revue Anglo-Americaine [*A publication*]
RAA	Revue de l'Art Ancien et Moderne [*A publication*]
RAA	Revue des Arts Asiatiques [*A publication*]
RAA	Right Angle Adapter
RAA	Right Ascension Angle
RAA	Right Atrial Appendage [*Medicine*]
RAA	Rockette Alumnae Association (EA)
RAA	Royal Academy of Arts [*British*] (ROG)
RAA	Rynes Aviation, Inc. [*Melrose Park, IL*] [*FAA designator*] (FAAC)
RAAA	Red Angus Association of America
RAAA	Relocation Assistance Association of America [*Englewood, CO*] (EA)
RAAAS	Remote Antiarmor Assault System (MCD)
RAAB	Remote Application and Advisory Box (MCD)
RAAC	Rome Allied Area Command [*World War II*]
RAACC	Robotics and Automation Applications Consulting Center [*Ford Motor Co.*]
RAACEF	Rear Admiral Aircraft Carriers, Eastern Fleet [*British*]
RAACT	Radioactive
RAAD	Revue. Academie Arabe de Damas [*A publication*]
RAADES	Relative Antiair Defense Effectiveness Simulation [*Military*] (CAAL)
RAAEC Nletter ...	Royal Australian Army. Educational Corps. Newsletter [*A publication*]
RA(A)EF	Rear Admiral (Administration) Eastern Fleet [*British*]
RAAF	Redstone Army Airfield [*Huntsville, AL*]
RAAF	Royal Australian Air Force
RAAF Reserve ...	Royal Australian Air Force Reserve. Magazine [*A publication*]
RAAG	Regional Aviation Assistance Group [*FAA*]
RAAG Res Notes ...	Research Notes and Memoranda of Applied Geometry for Prevenient Natural Philosophy [*Tokyo*] [*A publication*]
RAAM	Race Across America [*Annual cycling event*]
RAAM	Remote Antiarmor Mine (RDA)
RAAM	Residual-Area-Analysis Method [*Spectrometry*]
RAAM	Revue de l'Art Ancien et Moderne [*A publication*]
RAAMC	Royal Australian Army Medical Corps
RAAMS	Remote Antiarmor Mine System (AABC)
RAAN	Rendiconti. Accademia di Archeologia, Lettere, e Belle Arti (Napoli) [*A publication*]
RAAN	Repair Activity Accounting Number [*Navy*]
RAAO	Revue d'Assyriologie et d'Archeologie Orientale [*A publication*]
RAAP	Radford Army Ammunition Plant (AABC)
RAAQ	Recherches Amerindiennes au Quebec. Bulletin d'Information [*A publication*]
RAAR	RAM Address Register
RAAS	Royal Amateur Art Society [*British*]
RAAWS	RADAR Altimeter and Altitude Warning System [*Military*] (CAAL)
RAB	Rabaul [*Papua New Guinea*] [*Airport symbol*] (OAG)
RAB	Rabaul [*New Britain*] [*Seismograph station code, US Geological Survey*] (SEIS)
RAB	Rabbet (MSA)
RAB	Rabbinical
RAB	Rabbit Oil & Gas [*Vancouver Stock Exchange symbol*]
RAB	Rabelais [*French author, 1494-1553*] (ROG)
RAB	Radio Advertising Bureau [*New York, NY*] (EA)
RAB	Reactor Auxiliary Building (NRCH)
RAB	Regional Advisory Board [*American Hospital Association*]
RAB	Rent Advisory Board [*Cost of Living Council*]
RAB	Rotating Arm Basin
RABAC	Real Americans Buy American Cars [*An association*] [*Defunct*]
RABAL	Radiosonde Balloon
RABAR	Radiosonde Balloon Release (FAAC)
RABAR	Raytheon Advanced Battery Acquisition RADAR

RABB......... Rabbinical
Rabels Z..... Rabels Zeitschrift fuer Auslaendisches und Internationales Privatrecht [*Tubingen, West Germany*] (DLA)
RABET .... RADAR Beacon Transponder
RABFAC.... RADAR Beacon for Forward Air Controller
Rab Fiz Tverd Tela ... Raboty po Fizike Tverdogo Tela [*A publication*]
Rab Issled Inst Meteorol Gidrol Chast 2 ... Raboty i Issledovaniya. Institut Meteorologii i Gidrologii. Chast 2. Gidrologiya [*A publication*]
Rab Khim Rastvorov Kompleksn Soedin ... Raboty po Khimii Rastvorov i Kompleksnykh Soedinenii [*A publication*]
RABLB .... Real Academia de Buenas Letras de Barcelona [*A publication*]
RABM .... Revista de Archivos, Bibliotecas, y Museos [*A publication*]
RABMA ...... Radiobiologia si Biologia Moleculara [*A publication*]
RABNVS..... Reactor Auxiliary Building Normal Ventilation System [*Nuclear energy*]
Rabocij Klass Sovrem Mir ... Rabocij Klass i Sovremennyj Mir [*A publication*]
RABol......... Rendiconto. Sessioni della Accademia delle Scienze. Istituto di Bologna [*A publication*]
R Abolit ...... Revue Abolitionniste [*A publication*]
RABP.......... Renal Artery Bypass [*Medicine*]
Rab Post .... Pro Rabirio Postumo [*of Cicero*] [*Classical studies*] (OCD)
RABR.......... Rainbow Bridge National Monument
RABR.......... Right Angle Bulkhead Receptacle
RAbr........... Rivista Abruzzese [*A publication*]
RABS.......... Remote Air Battle Station
Rab Tyan-Shan Fiz-Geogr Sta ... Raboty Tyan-Shan'Skoi Fiziko-Geograficheskoi Stantsii. Akademiya Nauk Kirgizskoi SSR [*A publication*]
Rab Tyan Shan'skoi Fiz Geogr Stn Akad Nauk Kirg SSR ... Raboty Tyan-Shan'skoi Fiziko-Geograficheskoi Stantsii. Akademiya Nauk Kirgizskoi SSR [*A publication*]
RABV.......... Reflood Assist Bypass Valve [*Nuclear energy*] (NRCH)
RABVAL..... RADAR Bomb Evaluation (MCD)
RAC............ IEEE Robotics and Automation Council [*New York, NY*] (EA)
rac............. Racemic [*Also, dl, r*] [*Chemistry*]
RAC............ Racer Resources Ltd. [*Vancouver Stock Exchange symbol*]
RAC............ Raciborz [*Poland*] [*Seismograph station code, US Geological Survey*] (SEIS)
RAC............ Racine, WI [*Location identifier*] [*FAA*] (FAAL)
RAC............ RADAR Address Counter
R & AC........ RADAR and Air Communications
RAC............ RADAR Area Correlator
RAC............ RADAR Azimuth Converter
RAC............ Radio Adaptive Communications
RAC............ Radiological Assessment Coordinator [*Nuclear energy*] (NRCH)
RAC............ Radiometric Area Correlator (MCD)
RAC............ RAI Research Corporation [*American Stock Exchange symbol*]
RAC............ Raisin Administrative Committee (EA)
RAC............ Ram Air Charters Ltd. [*Inuvik, NT, Canada*] [*FAA designator*] (FAAC)
RAC............ Ram Air Cushion [*Aerospace*] (AAG)
RAC............ Ramsay's Appeal Cases [*Canada*] (DLA)
RAC............ Rangefinder with Automatic Compensator [*Firearms*]
RAC............ Rapid Action Change [*DoD*]
RAC............ Ration Accessory Convenience [*World War II*]
RAC............ Rational Activity Coefficient
RAC............ Reactor Accident Calculation
RAC............ Read Address Counter
RAC............ Reallexikon fuer Antike und Christentum [*A publication*] (OCD)
RAC............ Rear Admiral Commanding [*British*]
RAC............ Recessed Annular Connector
RAC............ Recombinant DNA Advisory Committee [*National Institutes of Health*]
RAC............ Recreation Advisory Council [*Bureau of Outdoor Recreation*]
RAC............ Rectified Alternating Current [*Radio*]
RAC............ Reflect Array Pulse Compressor (RDA)
RAC............ Release and Approval Center (MCD)
RAC............ Reliability Action Center [*NASA*] (NASA)
RAC............ Reliability Analysis Center [*Air Force*] [*Illinois Institute of Technology*] [*Griffiss Air Force Base, NY*] (MCD)
RAC............ Reliability Assessment of Components (KSC)
RAC............ Renal Arterial Constriction [*Medicine*]
RAC............ Repair, Alignment, and Calibration (NVT)
RAC............ Reparable Assets Control (AFM)
RAC............ Request Altitude Change [*Aviation*] (FAAC)
RAC............ Request for Authority to Contract [*Military*]
RAC............ Requisition Advice Care
RAC............ Research Advisory Committee
RAC............ Research Advisory Council
RAC............ Research Analysis Corporation [*Nonprofit contract agency*] [*Army*]
RAC............ Retail Advertising Conference [*Chicago, IL*] (EA)
RAC............ Revue de l'Art Chretien [*A publication*]
RAC............ Rivista di Archeologia Cristiana [*A publication*]
RAC............ Royal Academician (of Canada) (ROG)
RAC............ Royal Aero Club [*British*]
RAC............ Royal Agricultural College [*British*]

RAC............ Royal Air Cambodge [*Cambodian airlines*]
RAC............ Royal Arch Chapter [*Freemasonry*]
RAC............ Royal Armoured Corps [*British*]
RAC............ Royal Automobile Club [*Controlling body of motor racing in Britain*]
RAC............ Rubber Allocation Committee
RAC............ Rules of the Air and Air Traffic Control [*ICAO Air Navigation Commission*]
Ra Ca .... English Railway and Canal Cases (DLA)
RACA .... Recovered Alcoholic Clergy Association (EA)
RACA .... Regroupement d'Artistes des Centres Alternatifs [*Association of National Non-Profit Artists' Centres - ANNPAC*] [*Canada*]
RACA .... Rural Arts and Crafts Association (EA)
R Acad Cienc y Artes Barcelona Mem ... Real Academia de Ciencias y Artes de Barcelona. Memorias [*A publication*]
R Acad Farm Barcelona Discursos Recepcion ... Real Academia de Farmacia de Barcelona. Discursos de Recepcion [*A publication*]
R Acad Farm Barcelona Ses Inaug ... Real Academia de Farmacia de Barcelona. Sesion Inaugural [*A publication*]
RACathHS ... Records. American Catholic Historical Society of Philadelphia [*A publication*]
RACC .... Radiation and Contamination Control
RACC .... Regional Agricultural Credit Corporation
RACC .... Remote ARIA [*Apollo Range Instrumentation Aircraft*] Control Center [*NASA*]
RACC .... Remotely Activated Command and Control [*Military*] (CAAL)
RACC .... Reporting Activity Control Card [*Army*] (AABC)
RACC .... Research Aviation Coordinating Committee
RACC .... Rituels Accadiens [*A publication*] (BJA)
RACC .... Royal Armoured Corps Centre [*British*] (MCD)
RACCA...... Refrigeration and Air Conditioning Contractors Association - National [*Later, National Environmental Systems Contractors Association*] (EA)
Racc Fis-Chim Ital ... Raccolta Fisico-Chimica Italiana [*A publication*]
R Ac Cienc Habana An ... Real Academia de Ciencias Medicas, Fisicas, y Naturales de la Habana. Anales [*A publication*]
Raccoglitore Med Forli ... Raccoglitore Medico Fano Forli [*A publication*]
Raccolta Mem Turin Univ Fac Sci Agr ... Raccolta di Memorie. Turin. Universita. Facolta di Scienze Agrarie [*A publication*]
Racc Opuscoli Sci Filol ... Raccolta d'Opuscoli Scientifici e Filologici [*A publication*]
RACD .... Royal Army Chaplains' Department [*British*]
RACD .... Royal Army Clothing Department [*British*]
Race .... Race and Class [*A publication*]
RACE .... Radiation Adaptive Compression Equipment
RACE .... Random Access Computer Equipment
RACE .... Random Access Control Equipment (IEEE)
RACE .... Rapid Automatic Checkout Equipment
RACE .... Request Altitude Changes En Route [*Aviation*]
RACE .... Research in Advanced Communications in Europe [*European Commission*]
RACE .... Research on Automatic Computation Electronics
RACE .... Restoration of Aircraft to Combat Effectivity [*Army*]
Race Clas ... Race and Class [*A publication*]
Race Hyg.... Race Hygiene [*Japan*] [*A publication*]
RACEL .... Record of Access/Eligibility [*DoD*]
RACEP .... Random Access and Correlation for Extended Performance
Race Rela L R ... Race Relations Law Reporter [*A publication*]
Race Rela L Sur ... Race Relations Law Survey [*A publication*]
RACES .... Radio Amateur Civil Emergency Service [*Civil defense*]
RACES .... Remote Arming Common Element System
RACF.......... Resource Access Control Facility [*IBM Corp.*]
RACF.......... Revue Archeologique du Centre de la France [*A publication*]
RACFI........ Radio and Communication Facilities Inoperative
RACFOE..... Research Analysis Corporation Field Office, Europe [*Army*] (AABC)
RACG........ Radiometric Area Correlation Guidance
RACGP....... Royal Australian College of General Practitioners
RAChD....... Royal Army Chaplain's Department [*British*]
RACHS .... Records. American Catholic Historical Society of Philadelphia [*A publication*]
RACHSP..... Records. American Catholic Historical Society of Philadelphia [*A publication*]
RACIC........ Remote Area Conflict Information Center [*Battelle Memorial Institute*]
RACIS........ RADAR Computer Interaction Simulator
RACM......... Raycomm Industries [*NASDAQ symbol*] (NQ)
RACNE....... Regional Advisory Committee on Nuclear Energy
RACO .... Real America Company [*NASDAQ symbol*] (NQ)
RACO .... Rear Area Combat Operations (INF)
RACOB(WA) ... Rear Admiral Commanding Combined Operational Bases (Western Approaches) [*Britain*]
RACOMS ... Rapid Combat Mapping System [*Military*]
RACON ...... RADAR Responder Beacon
Ra (Conspic) ... RADAR Conspicuous Object
RACOON.... Radiation Controlled Balloon [*Meteorology*]
RACP .... Royal Australasian College of Physicians
RACPAS .... RADAR Coverage Penetration Analysis
RACR .... Resources Allocation Change Request

RACrist ..... Rivista di Archeologia Cristiana [*A publication*]
RAC/RJ ...... Religious Action Center of Reform Judaism [*Washington, DC*]   (EA)
RACS .... Random Access Communications System
RACS .... Recruit Allocation Control System [*Navy*]   (NVT)
RACS .... Regenerable Affinity Chromatography Support
RACS .... Remote Access Computing System [*Data processing*]
RACS .... Remote Automatic Calibration System   (NASA)
RACS .... Remote Automatic Control System   (KSC)
RACS .... Request for Approval of Contractual Support
RACS .... Rotation Axis Coordinate System   (MCD)
RACS .... Royal Australasian College of Surgeons
RACT .... Reasonable Available Control Technology [*Environmental Protection Agency*]
RACT .... Remote Access Computer Technique [*Data processing*]   (IEEE)
RACT .... Reverse-Acting
R Action Soc ... Revue d'Action Sociale [*A publication*]
RACUAHC ... Religious Action Center of the Union of American Hebrew Congregations [*Later, RAC/RJ*]   (EA)
RACYA ...... Reviews in Analytical Chemistry [*A publication*]
RACZA ...... Revista. Academia de Ciencias Exactas, Fisico-Quimicas, y Naturales de Zaragoza [*A publication*]
Rad .... Rad Jugoslavenske Academije Znanosti i Umjetnosti [*A publication*]
RAD .... RADAR
RAD .... RADAR Augmentation Device
RAD .... Radford Arsenal [*Army*]   (AAG)
RAD .... RADIAC [*Radiation Detection, Indication, and Computation*] Equipment   (NATG)
RAD .... Radial
RAD .... Radian   (MCD)
rad .... Radian [*Symbol*] [*SI unit of plane angle*]
RAD .... Radiation   (KSC)
RAD .... Radiation Absorbed Dose [*Unit of measurement of radiation energy*]
RAD .... Radiator   (AAG)
RAD .... Radical
Rad .... Radical Teacher [*A publication*]
RAD .... Radio   (AAG)
RAD .... Radiogram
Rad .... Radiola [*Record label*] [*Australia*]
RAD .... Radiology [*or Radiologist*]   (ADA)
RAD .... Radium [*Chemical symbol is Ra*]
RAD .... Radius   (AAG)
RAD .... Radix [*Root*] [*Latin*]
RAD .... Radnorshire [*County in Wales*]   (ROG)
RAD .... Raised Afterdeck
RAD .... Random Access Data   (BUR)
RAD .... Random Access Device
RAD .... Random Access Disc   (MCD)
RAD .... Rapid Access Data [*Xerox Corp.*]
RAD .... Rapid Access Data   (NRCH)
RAD .... Rapid Access Device
RAD .... Rapid Access Disk
RAD .... Rapid Access Drive   (BUR)
RAD .... Rapid Automatic Drill
RAD .... Ratio Adjust Device   (MCD)
RAD .... Ratio Analysis Diagram [*Metallurgy*]
RA(D) .... Rear-Admiral (Destroyers) [*Obsolete*] [*Navy*] [*British*]
RAD .... Recommendation Approval Document   (MCD)
RAD .... Records Arrival Date [*Bell System*]   (TEL)
RAD .... Recruiting Aids Department [*Navy*]
RAD .... Reference Attitude Display
RAD .... Regional Accountable Depot [*Military*]
RAD .... Regional Administrative Directors
RAD .... Released from Active Duty [*Navy*]
RAD .... Repair at Depot   (MCD)
RAD .... Reported for Active Duty [*Navy*]
RAD .... Request for Apollo Documents [*NASA*]   (KSC)
RAD .... Required Availability Date [*Military*]
RAD .... Requirements Action Directive   (AFM)
RAD .... Research and Advanced Development   (MCD)
R & AD ...... Research and Advanced Development
RAD .... Reservists on Active Duty [*Navy*]
RAD .... Resource Allocation Display [*Navy*]
RAD .... Resource Availability Determination   (MCD)
RAD .... Restricted Shipyard Availability Requiring Drydocking [*Navy*]   (NVT)
RAD .... Return to Active Duty [*Military*]
RAD .... Review and Approval Document   (MCD)
RAD .... Right Anterior Digestive [*Gland*]
RAD .... Right Axis Deviation [*Medicine*]
RAD .... Rite Aid Corp. [*NYSE symbol*]
RAD .... Roentgen Administered Dose
RAD .... Royal Academy of Dancing [*British*]
RAD .... Royal Albert Dock [*British*]
RAD .... Rural Areas Development
RAD .... Warroad, MN [*Location identifier*] [*FAA*]   (FAAL)
RadA .... Radical Alliance [*British*]
RADA .... Radioactive

RADA .... Random Access Discrete Address [*Army division-level battlefield radio communications system*]
RADA .... Realignment of Airdrop Activities   (MCD)
RADA .... Right Acromio-Dorsoanterior [*A fetal position*] [*Obstetrics*]
RADA .... Royal Academy of Dramatic Art [*British*]
RADAC ...... RADAR Analog Digital Data and Control   (KSC)
RADAC ...... Rapid Digital Automatic Computing
RADAC ...... Raytheon Automatic Drafting Artwork Compiler
RADACS .... Random Access Discrete Address Communications System [*Army*]
RaDaK .... Rabbi David Kimhi [*Biblical scholar, 1160-1235*]   (BJA)
RADAL .... Radio Detection and Location
Rad Am ...... Radical America [*A publication*]
Rad Amer .... Radical America [*A publication*]
RADAN ...... RADAR Analysis System   (MCD)
RADAN ...... RADAR Doppler Automatic Navigator
RADAN ...... RADAR Navigation
RADANT .... RADOME [*RADAR Dome*] Antenna   (NVT)
Radar .... Radar's Reports [*138-163 Missouri*]   (DLA)
RADAR ...... Radio Association Defending Airwave Rights   (EA)
RADAR ...... Radio Detection and Ranging
RADAR ...... Rassemblement des Democrates pour l'Avenir de la Reunion [*Rally of Democrats for the Future of Reunion*]   (PPW)
RADAR ...... Repertoire Analytique d'Articles de Revues de Quebec [*Database*] [*A publication*]
RADAR ...... Reseau d'Approvisionnement et de Debouches d'Affaires [*Business Opportunities Sourcing System - BOSS*] [*Canada*]
RADAR ...... Royal Association for Disability and Rehabilitation [*British*]
RADARC .... Radially Distributed Annular Rocket Chamber
RADAS ...... Random Access Discrete Address System
RADAT ...... RADAR Alignment Designation Accuracy Test   (MCD)
RADAT ...... RADAR Data Transmission
RADAT ...... Radio Direction and Track
RADAT ...... Radiosonde Observation Data
RADATA .... RADAR Data Transmission and Assembly   (IEEE)
RADATAC ... Radiation Data Acquisition Chart
RADAUS .... Radio-Austria AG   (TSSD)
RADAY ...... Radio Day   (CET)
RADB .... Radiometric Age Data Bank [*Geological Survey*] [*Denver, CO*]   (EISS)
RADBA ...... Radiobiology [*English Translation*] [*A publication*]
RADBIOL ... Radiobiology
RADBN ...... Radio Battalion [*Marine Corps*]
RAD(BPF) ... Rear Admiral Commanding Destroyers (British Pacific Fleet)
RADC .... RADAR Countermeasures and Deception [*Military*]   (MCD)
RADC .... Radice Corporation [*NASDAQ symbol*]   (NQ)
RADC .... Regiment Air Defense Center   (NATG)
RADC .... Rome Air Development Center [*ESD*]
RADC .... Royal Army Dental Corps [*British*]
RADCAP .... Research and Development Contributions to Aviation Progress [*Air Force*]
RADCAS .... Radiation Casualty [*Criteria for battlefield targets*]   (MCD)
RADCC ...... Radiological Control Center [*Army*]   (KSC)
RADCC ...... Rear Area Damage Control Center   (AABC)
RADC/ETR ... Rome Air Development Center Deputy for Electronic Technology [*ESD*]
RADCHM ... Radiochemistry
Rad Clinica ... Radiologia Clinica [*A publication*]
Rad Clin NA ... Radiologic Clinics of North America [*A publication*]
RADCM ...... RADAR Countermeasures and Deception [*Military*]
RADCOL .... RADC [*Rome Air Development Center*] Automatic Document Classification On-Line [*Air Force*] [*Information service*]   (EISS)
RADCOM ... Radiometric Contrast Matching   (MCD)
RADCOM ... Research and Development Command   (MCD)
RADCON ... RADAR Control
RADCON .... RADAR Data Converter   (AFM)
RADCON .... Radiological Control   (AABC)
RADCOT .... Radial Optical Tracking Theodolite   (MUGU)
RADDEF .... Radiological Defense [*To minimize the effect of nuclear radiation on people and resources*]
Rad Diagn ... Radiologia Diagnostica [*A publication*]
RADDOL .... Raddolcendo [*Gradually Softer*] [*Music*]
RADE .... Research and Development Division [*Obsolete*] [*National Security Agency*]
RADEF .... Radiological Defense [*To minimize the effect of nuclear radiation on people and resources*]
RADEM ...... Random Access Delta Modulation
Rad Eng (London) ... Radio Engineering (London) [*A publication*]
RADEP .... RADAR Departure   (FAAC)
RADER .... Rassemblement Democratique du Ruanda [*Democratic Rally of Rwanda*]
RADES .... Realistic Air Defense Engagement System [*Army*]   (RDA)
RADEX .... RADAR Exercise   (NVT)
RADEX .... Radiation Exclusion Plot [*Chart of actual or predicted fallout*]
Radex Rundsch ... Radex Rundschau [*A publication*]
Radex Runsch ... Radex Rundschau [*A publication*]
RADFAC .... Radiating Facility
RADFAL ..... Radiological Prediction Fallout Plot
RADFET ..... Radiation-Sensing Field Effect Transistor [*Instrumentation*]

RADFO .... Radiological Fallout [*Army*]
RADHAZ ..... Radiation Hazards
Rad Hist ..... Radical History Review [*A publication*]
Rad Humanist ... Radical Humanist [*A publication*]
RADI .... Radiographic Inspection [*NASA*] (AAG)
Radi .... Radium [*Record label*] [*France*]
RADIAC ...... Radiation Detection, Indication, and Computation [*Radiological measuring instruments*]
Radiata Pine Tech Bull ... Radiata Pine Technical Bulletin (Radiata Pine Association of Australia) [*A publication*]
Radiat Biol ... Radiation Biology [*England*] [*A publication*]
Radiat Bot ... Radiation Botany [*A publication*]
Radiat Data Rep ... Radiation Data and Reports [*A publication*]
Radiat Eff ... Radiation Effects [*A publication*]
Radiat Effects ... Radiation Effects [*A publication*]
Radiat Eff Lett ... Radiation Effects. Letters Section [*A publication*]
Radiat Eff Lett Sect ... Radiation Effects. Letters Section [*A publication*]
Radiat Env ... Radiation and Environmental Biophysics [*A publication*]
Radiat Environ Biophys ... Radiation and Environmental Biophysics [*A publication*]
Radiat Phys Chem ... Radiation Physics and Chemistry [*A publication*]
Radiat Prot ... Radiation Protection [*Republic of Korea*] [*A publication*]
Radiat Prot Aust ... Radiation Protection in Australia [*A publication*]
Radiat Prot Dosim ... Radiation Protection Dosimetry [*A publication*]
Radiat Prot ICRP Publ ... Radiation Protection. ICRP [*International Commission on Radiological Protection*] Publication [*A publication*]
Radiat Res ... Radiation Research [*A publication*]
Radiat Res Polym ... Radiation Research on Polymer [*Japan*] [*A publication*]
Radiat Res Rev ... Radiation Research Reviews [*A publication*]
Radiat Res Suppl ... Radiation Research. Supplement [*A publication*]
Radiats Bezop Zashch AEhS ... Radiatsionnaya Bezopasnost' i Zashchita AEhS. Sbornik Statej [*A publication*]
Radiats Fiz ... Radiatsionnaya Fizika [*A publication*]
Radiats Fiz Akad Nauk Latv SSR Inst Fiz ... Radiatsionnaya Fizika. Akademiya Nauk Latviiskoi SSR. Institut Fiziki [*Latvian SSR*] [*A publication*]
Radiats Fiz Nemet Krist ... Radiatsionnaya Fizika Nemetallicheskikh Kristallov [*A publication*]
Radiats Fiz Tverd Tela Radiats Materialoved ... Radiatsionnaya Fizika Tverdogo Tela i Radiatsionnoe Materialovedenie [*A publication*]
Radiats Gig ... Radiatsionnaya Gigiena [*USSR*] [*A publication*]
Radiat Shielding Inf Cent Rep ... Radiation Shielding Information Center. Report [*A publication*]
Radiats Tekh ... Radiatsionnaya Tekhnika [*A publication*]
Radiaz Alta Energ ... Radiazioni di Alta Energia [*A publication*]
Radiaz Radioisot ... Radiazioni e Radioisotopi [*A publication*]
RADIC .... Radical (ROG)
RADIC .... Radio Interior Communications
RADIC .... Redifon Analog-Digital Computer [*British*]
RADIC .... Research and Development Information Center (AFM)
Radical Commun Med ... Radical Community Medicine [*A publication*]
Radical Educ Dossier ... Radical Education Dossier [*A publication*]
Radical His ... Radical History Review [*A publication*]
Radical Scot ... Radical Scotland [*A publication*]
RADIC-LIB .... Radical Liberal
RADIL .... Research Animal Diagnostic and Investigative Laboratory [*University of Missouri-Columbia*] [*Research center*] (RCD)
Rad Imunol Zavoda (Zagreb) ... Radovi Imunoloskog Zavoda (Zagreb) [*A publication*]
Rad Inst Geol-Rud Istraz Ispit Nukl Drugih Miner Sirovina ... Radovi Instituta za Geolosko-Rudarska Istrazivanja i Ispitivanja Nuklearnih i Drugih Mineralnih Sirovina [*Yugoslavia*] [*A publication*]
Rad Inst Proucavanje Suzbijanje Alkohol Drugih Narkomanija ... Radovi Instituta za Proucavanje i Suzbijanje Alkoholizma i Drugih Narkomanija u Zagrebu [*A publication*]
Rad Inst Sum Istraz ... Radovi Institut za Sumarska Istrazivanja. Sumarskog Fakulteta. Sveucilista u Zagrebu [*A publication*]
RADINT ...... RADAR Intelligence
RADIO .... Radiotherapy
Radioact Sea ... Radioactivity in the Sea [*Austria*] [*A publication*]
Radioact Surv Data Jap ... Radioactivity Survey Data in Japan [*A publication*]
Radioact Waste Manage ... Radioactive Waste Management [*A publication*]
Radioact Waste Manage Nucl Fuel Cycle ... Radioactive Waste Management and the Nuclear Fuel Cycle [*A publication*]
Radioact Waste Manage and Nucl Fuel Cycle ... Radioactive Waste Management and the Nuclear Fuel Cycle [*A publication*]
Radioact Waste Manage (Oak Ridge Tenn) ... Radioactive Waste Management (Oak Ridge, Tennessee) [*A publication*]
Radioact Waste Technol ... Radioactive Waste Technology [*A publication*]
Radioaktiv Zivotn Prostr ... Radioaktivita a Zivotne Prostredie [*A publication*]
Radiobiol ... Radiobiologiya [*A publication*]
Radiobiol Biol Mol ... Radiobiologia si Biologia Moleculara [*Romania*] [*A publication*]
Radiobiol Inf Byull ... Radiobiologiya Informatsionnyi Byulleten' [*A publication*]

Radiobiol Lat ... Radiobiologica Latina [*Italy*] [*A publication*]
Radiobiol Radioter Fis Med ... Radiobiologia, Radioterapia, e Fisica Medica [*A publication*]
Radiobiol-Radiother ... Radiobiologia-Radioterapia [*A publication*]
Radiobiol-Radiother (Berl) ... Radiobiologia-Radioterapia (Berlin) [*A publication*]
Radiobiol-Radiother (Berlin) ... Radiobiologia-Radiotherapia (Berlin) [*A publication*]
Radioch Act ... Radiochimica Acta [*A publication*]
Radiochem Radioanal Lett ... Radiochemical and Radioanalytical Letters [*A publication*]
Radiochim Acta ... Radiochimica Acta [*A publication*]
Radioch Rad ... Radiochemical and Radioanalytical Letters [*A publication*]
Radio Commun ... Radio Communication [*A publication*]
Radio-Electr ... Radio-Electronics [*A publication*]
Radio Electron ... Radio Electronica [*Netherlands*] [*A publication*]
Radio-Electron ... Radio-Electronics [*A publication*]
Radio Electron Commun Syst ... Radio Electronics and Communications Systems [*A publication*]
Radio & Electron Constructor ... Radio and Electronics Constructor [*A publication*]
Radio and Electron Eng ... Radio and Electronic Engineer [*A publication*]
Radio Electron Eng ... Radio and Electronic Engineer [*A publication*]
Radio Electron Eng (London) ... Radio and Electronic Engineer (London) [*A publication*]
Radio & Electronic Eng ... Radio and Electronic Engineer [*A publication*]
Radio and Electron World ... Radio and Electronics World [*A publication*]
Radio Elec W ... Radio Electrical Weekly [*A publication*]
Radio Elektron ... Radio Elektronica [*A publication*]
Radio Elektron Schau ... Radio Elektronik Schau [*A publication*]
Radio El En ... Radio and Electronic Engineer [*A publication*]
Radio Eng Electron Phys ... Radio Engineering and Electronic Physics [*A publication*]
Radio Eng Electron (USSR) ... Radio Engineering and Electronic Physics (USSR) [*A publication*]
Radio Engrg Electron Phys ... Radio Engineering and Electronic Physics [*A publication*]
Radio Eng (USSR) ... Radio Engineering (USSR) [*A publication*]
Radio Fernsehen Elektron ... Radio Fernsehen Elektronik [*A publication*]
Radiogr ...... Radiographer [*A publication*]
Radio Ind ... Radio Industria [*A publication*]
Radioisot (Praha) ... Radioisotopy (Praha) [*A publication*]
Radioisot (Tokyo) ... Radioisotopes (Tokyo) [*A publication*]
Radiol .... Radiology
Radiol Austriaca ... Radiologia Austriaca [*A publication*]
Radiol Bras ... Radiologia Brasileira [*A publication*]
Radiol Clin ... Radiologia Clinica [*A publication*]
Radiol Clin (Basel) ... Radiologia Clinica (Basel) [*A publication*]
Radiol Clin Biol ... Radiologia Clinica et Biologica [*A publication*]
Radiol Clin N Am ... Radiologic Clinics of North America [*A publication*]
Radiol Clin North Am ... Radiologic Clinics of North America [*A publication*]
Radiol Diagn ... Radiologia Diagnostica [*A publication*]
Radiol Diagn (Berlin) ... Radiologia Diagnostica (Berlin) [*A publication*]
Radiol Health Data ... Radiological Health Data [*A publication*]
Radiol Health Data Rep ... Radiological Health Data and Reports [*A publication*]
Radiol Iugosl (Ljubljana) ... Radiologia Iugoslavica (Ljubljana) [*A publication*]
Radiol Kozl ... Radiologiai Kozlemenyek [*A publication*]
Radiol Manage ... Radiology Management [*A publication*]
Radiol Med ... Radiologia Medica [*A publication*]
Radiol Med (Torino) ... Radiologia Medica (Torino) [*A publication*]
Radiol Prat ... Radiologia Pratica [*Italy*] [*A publication*]
Radiol Prot Bull ... Radiological Protection Bulletin [*A publication*]
Radiol Rev Miss Val Med J ... Radiological Review and Mississippi Valley Medical Journal [*A publication*]
Radiol Technol ... Radiologic Technology [*A publication*]
Radio Mentor Electron ... Radio Mentor Electronic [*A publication*]
Radio Mntr ... Radio Mentor Electronic [*A publication*]
Radiom Polarogr ... Radiometer Polarographics [*A publication*]
Radio N ...... Radio News [*A publication*]
Radiophys Quantum Electron ... Radiophysics and Quantum Electronics [*A publication*]
Radiophys & Quantum Electron ... Radiophysics and Quantum Electronics [*A publication*]
Radio Sci ... Radio Science [*A publication*]
Radio Serv Bul ... Radio Service Bulletin [*A publication*]
Radiotehn i Elektron ... Akademija Nauk SSSR. Radiotehnika i Elektronika [*A publication*]
Radiotehn (Kharkov) ... Radiotehnika (Kharkov) [*A publication*]
Radiotek El ... Radiotekhnika i Elektronika [*A publication*]
Radiotekh ... Radiotekhnika [*A publication*]
Radiotekh i Elektron ... Radiotekhnika i Elektronika [*A publication*]
Radiotekh Elektron ... Radiotekhnika i Elektronika [*A publication*]
Radiotekhn ... Khar'kovski Ordena Trudovogo Krasnogo Znameni Gosudarstvennyi Universitet Imeni A.M. Gor'kogo Radiotekhnika [*A publication*]
Radiotekhn i Elektron ... Radiotekhnika i Elektronika. Akademiya Nauk SSSR [*A publication*]
Radio Telev ... Radio Television [*A publication*]
Radio Tel & Hobbies ... Radio, Television, and Hobbies [*A publication*]

Radio-TV-Electron ... Radio-TV-Electronic [*Later, RTE. Radio-TV-Electronic*] [*A publication*]

Radio-TV-Electron Serv ... Radio-TV-Electronic Service [*Later, RTE. Radio-TV-Electronic*] [*Switzerland*] [*A publication*]

Radio TVH ... Radio, Television, and Hobbies [*A publication*]

Radio & TV N ... Radio and Television News [*A publication*]

Radio es TV Szle ... Radio es TV Szemle [*A publication*]

RADIQUAD ... Radio Quadrangle [*Military*]

RADIR .... Random Access Document Indexing and Retrieval

RADIST ...... RADAR Distance Indicator

RADIT .... Radio Teletype   (IEEE)

RadJA .... Radovi Jugoslavenske Akademije Znanosti i Umjetnosti [*A publication*]

Rad Jugosl Akad Znan Umjet ... Radovi Jugoslavenske Akademije Znanosti i Umjetnosti [*A publication*]

Rad Jugoslav Akad Znan Umjet ... Radovi Jugoslavenske Akademije Znanosti i Umjetnosti [*A publication*]

Rad Jugoslav Akad Znan Umjet Odjel Prir Nauke ... Radovi Jugoslavenska Akademija Znanosti i Umjetnosti. Odjel za Prirodne Nauke [*A publication*]

RADL.......... Radial   (AAG)

RADL.......... Radiological [*or Radiology*]   (AAG)

RadL.......... Radyans'ke Literaturoznavstvo [*Kiev*] [*A publication*]

RADLAB.... Radiation Laboratory   (AAG)

RADLAC.... Radial Pulse Line Accelerators   (MCD)

RADLCEN ... Radiological Center

RADLDEF.. Radiological Defense [*To minimize the effect of nuclear radiation on people and resources*]

RADLDEFLAB ... Radiological Defense Laboratory [*NASA*]

RADLFO..... Radiological Fallout [*Army*]   (AABC)

RADLGC .... Radiologic

RADLGCL ... Radiological

RADLGY..... Radiology

RADLMON ... Radiological Monitor [*or Monitoring*]

RADLO .... Radiological Officer

RADLO .... Regional Air Defense Liaison Officer   (FAAC)

RADLOP..... Radiological Operations   (AABC)

RADLSAFE ... Radiological Safety [*Military*]

RADLSO..... Radiological Survey Officer

RADLSV ..... Radiological Survey

RadLV .... Radiation Leukemia Virus

RADLWAR ... Radiological Warfare

RADM.......... Rear Admiral [*Also, RA, RADML*]   (AAG)

R Adm .... Revue Administrative [*A publication*]

Rad Med Fak Rijeka ... Radovi Medicinskogo Fakulteta. Rijeka [*A publication*]

Rad Med Fak Zagrebu ... Radovi Medicinskogo Fakulteta u Zagrebu [*A publication*]

R Adm Empresas ... Revista. Administracao de Empresas [*A publication*]

R Admin Empresas ... Revista de Administracao de Empresas [*A publication*]

R Admin (Paris) ... Revue Administrative (Paris) [*A publication*]

R Admin Publica ... Revista. Administracion Publica [*A publication*]

RADMIS ..... Research Activities Designators Management Information System

RADML....... Rear Admiral [*Also, RA, RADM*]   (FAAC)

R Adm Municip (Rio De Janeiro) ... Revista. Administracao Municipal (Rio De Janeiro) [*A publication*]

RADMON ... Radiological Monitoring   (AFM)

R Adm Publ (Madrid) ... Revista. Administracion Publica (Madrid) [*A publication*]

R Adm Publ (Rio De Janeiro) ... Revista. Administracao Publica (Rio De Janeiro) [*A publication*]

RADN .... Radiation   (AAG)

RADN .... Radnorshire [*County in Wales*]

RADN .... Radyne Corp. [*NASDAQ symbol*]   (NQ)

RADNORS ... Radnorshire [*County in Wales*]   (ROG)

RADNOS .... No Radio [*Military*]

RADNOTE ... Radio Note [*Military*]

RADOC ..... Regional Air Defense Operations Center   (NATG)

RADOC ...... Remote Automatic Detection Contingencies

RADOD....... Research and Development Objectives Document   (MCD)

RADOME.... RADAR Dome [*NASA*]

RADON...... RADAR Beacon

RADON...... Research and Development Operational Needs   (MCD)

RADOP....... RADAR Doppler [*Missile-tracking system*]   (AAG)

RADOP....... RADAR Operator   (CET)

RADOP....... RADAR/Optical Weapons [*Military*]

RADOP....... Radio Operator [*Navy*]

RADOPR .... Radio Operator   (AAG)

RADOPWEAP ... RADAR Optical Weapons   (IEEE)

RADOSE .... Radiation Dosimeter Satellite [*NASA*]

RADOT....... Real-Time Automatic Digital Optical Tracker [*NASA*]

RADP.......... Right Acromio-Dorsoposterior [*A fetal position*] [*Obstetrics*]

Rad Phil News ... Radical Philosopher's Newsjournal [*A publication*]

RADPLANBD ... Radio Planning Board [*Navy*]

Rad Poljopriv Fak Univ Saraj ... Radovi Poljoprivrednog Fakulteta Univerziteta u Sarajevu [*A publication*]

Rad Poljopriv Fak Univ Sarajevu ... Radovi Poljoprivrednog Fakulteta Univerziteta u Sarajevu [*A publication*]

RADPROPCAST ... Radio Propagation Forecast

RADREF .... RADAR Refraction   (MCD)

RADREL ..... Radio Relay

Rad Relig ... Radical Religion [*A publication*]

RADRON .... RADAR Squadron [*Air Force*]

RAD/S....... Radians per Second

RADS .... Radiation and Dosimetry Services   (NRCH)

RADS .... Radiation Systems [*NASDAQ symbol*]   (NQ)

RADS .... Radius   (AAG)

RADS .... Rapid Area Distribution Support [*Air Force*]

RADS .... Raw Data System

RADS .... Ryukyu Air Defense System

RAD/S² ...... Radians per Second Squared

RADSAFE ... Radiological Safety [*Military*]

RADSCAT ... Radiometer/Scatterometer [*Sensor*] [*Meteorology*]

Rad Scien ... Radical Science Journal [*A publication*]

RADSO .... Radiological Survey Officer   (IEEE)

RADSOC ..... Request for Authority to Develop a System or Change [*Military*]   (AFIT)

RADSTA..... Radio Station

Rad Sum Fak i Inst Sum ... Radovi Sumarski Fakultet i Institut za Sumarstvo [*A publication*]

RadT.......... Radiola-Telefunken [*Record label*] [*Australia*]

Rad Teach ... Radical Teacher [*A publication*]

Rad Thera ... Issues in Radical Therapy [*A publication*]

RADTT .... Radio Teletypewriter   (CET)

RADU .... RADAR Analysis and Development Unit [*National Severe Storms Forecast Center*]   (NOAA)

RADU .... Ram Air-Driven Unit

RAD-UDRT ... Respect voor Arbeid en Democratie/Union Democratique pour le Respect du Travail [*Respect for Labor and Democracy/Democratic Union for the Respect of Labor*] [*Belgium*]   (PPE)

RADVS .... RADAR Altimeter and Doppler Velocity Sensor

RADWAR.... Radiological Warfare

RADWASTE ... Radioactive Waste

RADX .... Radionics, Inc. [*NASDAQ symbol*]   (NQ)

Rad Zavoda Fiz ... Radovi Zavoda za Fiziku [*A publication*]

RadZSF ...... Radovi Zavoda za Slavensku Filologiju [*A publication*]

RAE .... Arar [*Saudi Arabia*] [*Airport symbol*]   (OAG)

RAE .... RADAR Altimeter Equipment

RAE .... Radio Astronomy Explorer [*Satellite*]

RAE .... Radiodifusion Argentina al Exterior [*Broadcasting organization*] [*Argentina*]

RAE .... Range, Azimuth, and Elevation   (MCD)

RAE .... Real Academia Espanola. Boletin [*A publication*]

RAE .... Revista Augustiniana de Espiritualidad [*A publication*]

RAE .... Revue Archeologique de l'Est et du Centre-Est [*A publication*]

RAE .... Revue d'Art et d'Esthetique [*A publication*]

RAE .... Right Arithmetic Element

RAE .... Right Ascension Encoder

RAE .... Right Atrial Enlargement [*Cardiology*]

RAE .... Royal Aircraft Establishment [*British*]

RAE .... Royal Australian Engineers

RAEB .... Refractory Anemia with Excess of Blasts [*Hematology*]

RAEC .... Royal Army Educational Corps [*British*]

RAECO...... Rare-Earth Cobalt

RAEDOT..... Range, Azimuth, and Elevation Detection of Optical Targets

RAEN......... Radio Amateur Emergency Network   (IEEE)

RaeRG....... Reallexikon der Aegyptischen Religionsgeschichte [*Berlin*] [*A publication*]   (BJA)

RAES......... Radio Astronomy Experiment Selection Panel

RAES......... Ratios for Automotive Executives [*Computer software*]

RAES......... Remote Access Editing System [*Data processing*]   (IEEE)

RAeS......... Royal Aeronautical Society [*British*]   (MCD)

RAET......... Range, Azimuth, Elevation, and Time

RAETDS..... Reciprocating Aircraft Engine Type Designation System

RAF .... Racial Awareness Facilitator [*School*] [*Navy*]   (NVT)

RAF .... Red Army Faction [*Terrorist group*] [*West Germany*]

RAF .... Regular Air Force

RAF .... Requirements Allocation Form

RAF .... Requirements Analysis Form [*NASA*]   (NASA)

RAF .... Research Aviation Facility [*National Center for Atmospheric Research*]

RAF .... Reserved Air Freight

RAF .... Resource Allocation Formula

RAf .... Revue Africaine [*A publication*]

RAF .... Reynolds Analogy Factor [*Physics*]

RAF .... Royal Air Force [*British*]

RAF .... Royal Aircraft Factory [*World War I*] [*British*]

RAF .... Sacramento, CA [*Location identifier*] [*FAA*]   (FAAL)

RAFA......... Rank Annihilation Factor Analysis [*Data processing*]

RAFA......... Royal Air Forces Association [*London, England*]   (EA-IO)

Rafair........ Royal Air Force [*Airline call sign*] [*British*]

RAFAR....... Radio Automated Facsimile and Reproduction

RAFAX....... RADAR Facsimile Transmission

RAFB......... Randolph Air Force Base [*Texas*]

RAFB.......... Rickenbacker Air Force Base [*Formerly, Lockbourne Air Force Base*] [*Ohio*]

RAFB......... Royal Air Force Base [*British*]

RAFC......... Richmond Area Film Cooperative [*Library network*]

RAFC......... Royal Air Force Club [*British*]

RAFC.......... Royal Air Force College [*British*]
RAFCC...... Royal Air Force Coastal Command [*British*]
RAFD......... Rome Air Force Depot
RAFFC...... Royal Air Force Fighter Command [*British*]
RAFIA........ Radiatsionnaya Fizika. Akademiya Nauk Latviiskoi SSR.
                  Institut Fiziki [*A publication*]
RAFL .... Rainfall   (FAAC)
RAFMS....... Royal Air Force Medical Service [*British*]
RAFO......... Reserve Air Force Officers [*Later, RAFRO*] [*British*]
RAfr........... Revue Africaine [*A publication*]
RAFR......... Royal Air Force Regiment [*British*]
RAFRC....... Revolutionary Armed Forces of the Republic of Cuba
R Afr Manag ... Revue Africaine de Management [*A publication*]
RAFRO....... Royal Air Force Reserve of Officers [*Formerly, RAFO*] [*British*]
RAFRZ........ Radiosonde Observation - Freezing Levels   (FAAC)
RAFS......... R. Austin Freeman Society   (EA)
RAFS......... Regional Analysis and Forecast System [*National
                  Meteorological Center*]
RAFS......... Royal Air Force Station [*British*]   (MCD)
RAFSC....... Royal Air Force Staff College [*British*]
RAFT......... Racial Awareness Facilitator Training [*Navy program*]
RAFT......... Radially Adjustable Facility Tube   (IEEE)
RAFT......... Rear Admiral Fleet Train [*British Pacific Fleet*]
RAFT......... Recomp Algebraic Formula Translator [*Data processing*]
RAFT......... Regional Accounting and Finance Test [*Military*]   (AFM)
RAFTC....... Royal Air Forces Transport Command [*British*]
RAFVR....... Royal Air Force Volunteer Reserve [*British*]
RAG.......... Ragged   (FAAC)
Rag............ Ragland's California Superior Court Decisions   (DLA)
RAG.......... Raina un Aspazijas Gadagramata [*A publication*]
RAG.......... Readiness Analysis Group
RAG.......... Regimental Artillery Group [*USSR*]
RAg .... Related Antigen [*Immunology*]
RAG.......... Religious Arts Guild [*Defunct*]   (EA)
RAG.......... Replacement Air Group
RAG.......... Requirements Advisory Group [*Air Force*]   (MCD)
RAG.......... Resource Appraisal Group [*US Geological Survey*]
RAG.......... Retail Associates Group, Inc. [*Homesewing industry trade
                  group*]
RAG.......... Returned Ammunition Group   (NATG)
RAG.......... Reusable Agena [*NASA*]   (NASA)
RAG.......... Ring Airfoil Grenade [*Army*]
RAG.......... River Assault Group [*Military*]
RAG.......... ROM [*Read-Only Memory*] Address Gate [*Data processing*]
RAG.......... Runway Arresting Gear [*Aviation*]
RAG-1........ Rosenberg, Avraham, and Gutnick [*Strain of bacteria named
                  for its researchers: Eugene Rosenberg, Avraham
                  Reisfield, and David Gutnick*]
RAGBRAI ... [*Des Moines*] Register Annual Great Bicycle Race Across Iowa
                  [*Pronounced "ragbray"*]
RAGC........ Rainbows for All God's Children   (EA)
RAGC........ Relief General Communications Vessel
RAGC........ Royal and Ancient Golf Club [*St. Andrews, Scotland*]
R de Ag (Cuba) ... Revista de Agricultura (Cuba) [*A publication*]
R Ag (Cuba) ... Revista de Agricultura (Cuba) [*A publication*]
RAGE .... Radio Amplification of Gamma Emissions [*Antiguerrilla
                  weapon*]
RAGEA....... Razvedochnaya Geofizika [*A publication*]
RAGF......... Remote Air-Ground Facility [*Aviation*]
R Ag France ... Revue des Agriculteurs de France [*A publication*]
Ragg........... Rheumatoid Agglutinator [*Immunology*]
RagL........... Raguaglio Librario [*A publication*]
RAGN .... Ragen Corp. [*NASDAQ symbol*]   (NQ)
R Agr Econ Mal ... Review of Agricultural Economics of Malaysia [*A
                  publication*]
R Agric....... Revue de l'Agriculture [*A publication*]
R Agric Soc (Cairo) Bull Tech Sect ... Royal Agricultural Society (Cairo)
                  Bulletin. Technical Section [*A publication*]
R Agric Soc Kenya QJ ... Royal Agricultural Society of Kenya. Quarterly
                  Journal [*A publication*]
Rag Super Ct Dec (Calif) ... Ragland's California Superior Court
                  Decisions   (DLA)
RAH........... Rabbit Anti-Human [*Immunology*]
RAH........... Radiation-Anneal Hardening [*Alloy*]
RAH........... Rafha [*Saudi Arabia*] [*Airport symbol*]   (OAG)
RAH........... Receipt, Excess, Adjustment, Due-In History File [*Army*]
RAH........... Receiving Array Hydrophone
RAH........... Regressing Atypical Histiocytosis [*Medicine*]
RAH........... Reviews in American History [*A publication*]
RAH........... Right Atrial Hypertrophy [*Cardiology*]
RAH........... Royal Albert Hall [*London, England*]
RAHBol....... Real Academia de la Historia. Boletin [*A publication*]
RAHE......... Review of Allied Health Education [*A publication*]
RaHGBM .... Rabbit Anti-Human Glomerular Basement Membrane
                  [*Immunology*]
RAHO......... Rabbits Against Human Ovary [*Immunology*]
RAHO......... Royal Albert Hall Orchestra
RAHS .... Royal Australian Historical Society. Journal [*A publication*]
RAHSJ........ Royal Australian Historical Society. Journal and Proceedings
                  [*A publication*]
RAI .... Praia [*Cape Verde Islands*] [*Airport symbol*]   (OAG)

RAI .... RADAR Altimeter Indicator   (MCD)
RAI .... Radiation Applications, Incorporated
RAI .... Radioactive Interference [*NASA*]
RAI .... Radioactive Iodine [*Medicine*]
RAI .... Radioactive Isotope [*Roentgenology*]
RAI .... Random Access and Inquiry [*Data processing*]
RAI .... Range Azimuth Indicator
RAI .... Raspberry Island [*Alaska*] [*Seismograph station code, US
                  Geological Survey*]   (SEIS)
RAI .... Reliability Assurance Instructions   (KSC)
RAI .... Rencontre Assyriologique Internationale [*A publication*]
RAI .... Rendiconti. Classe di Scienze Morali e Storiche. Accademia
                  d'Italia [*A publication*]
RAI .... Repair at Intermediate   (MCD)
RAI .... Request for Additional Information   (NRCH)
RAI .... Roll Attitude Indicator [*NASA*]
RAI .... Royal Anthropological Institute [*British*]
RAI .... Royal Anthropological Institute of Great Britain and Ireland
RAI .... Royal Archaeological Institute [*British*]
RAI .... Runway Alignment Indicator [*Aviation*]
RAI .... Rural America, Incorporated [*Formerly, RHA*] [*An association*]
                  [*Washington, DC*]   (EA)
RAIA.......... Royal Australian Institute of Architects
RAIAD .... Reverse Acronyms, Initialisms, and Abbreviations Dictionary
                  [*Formerly, RAID*] [*A publication*]
RAIAM....... Random Access Indestructive Advanced Memory [*Data
                  processing*]   (MSA)
RAIB.......... Rendiconti. Accademia delle Scienze. Istituto di Bologna [*A
                  publication*]
RAIC.......... Radiological Accident and Incident Control
RAIC.......... Redstone Arsenal Information Center [*Army*]
RAIC.......... Royal Architectural Institute of Canada
RAICG....... Radiosonde Observation Icing at _____   (FAAC)
RAID.......... RADAR Identification and Direction System   (NG)
RAID.......... Ram Air-Inflated Drogue [*Military*]   (CAAL)
RAID.......... Recallable Airborne Infrared Display
RAID.......... Remote Access Interactive Debugger [*Data processing*]   (IEEE)
RAID.......... Reverse Acronyms and Initialisms Dictionary [*Later, RAIAD*] [*A
                  publication*]
RAID.......... River Assault Interdiction Division [*Navy*]   (NVT)
RAIDEX ..... Antisurface Raiders Exercise [*NATO*]   (NATG)
RAIDS .... Rapid Availability of Information and Data for Safety
                  [*NASA*]   (KSC)
RAIF .... Reseau d'Action et d'Information pour les Femmes [*Canada*]
Raiffeisen-Rundsch ... Raiffeisen-Rundschau [*A publication*]
RAIL .... Railroad Advancement through Information and Law
                  Foundation
RAIL .... Railway   (ROG)
RAIL .... Runway Alignment Indicator Light [*or Lighting*] [*Aviation*]
Rail Ca ...... Railway and Canal Cases [*1835-54*]   (DLA)
Rail & Can Cas ... English Railway and Canal Cases   (DLA)
Rail & Can Cas ... Railway and Canal Traffic Cases   (DLA)
Rail Eng...... Railway Engineer [*Later, Railway Engineer International*] [*A
                  publication*]
Rail Eng Int ... Rail Engineering International [*A publication*]
Rail Int....... Rail International [*A publication*]
Rail M......... Railway Magazine [*A publication*]
RAILS......... Remote Area Instrument Landing System [*Army*]
RAILS......... Runway Alignment Indicator Light [*or Lighting*] System
                  [*Aviation*]   (MCD)
Rail Syst Contr ... Railway Systems Control [*A publication*]
Railw Age... Railway Age [*A publication*]
Railway & Corp Law J ... Railway and Corporation Law Journal   (DLA)
Railway R ... Railway Review [*A publication*]
Railways in Aust ... Railways in Australia [*A publication*]
Railways Union Gaz ... Railways Union Gazette [*A publication*]
Railway Trans ... Railway Transportation [*A publication*]
Railw Cas... Railway Cases   (DLA)
Railw Dev News ... Railway Development News [*A publication*]
Railw Eng... Railway Engineer [*Later, Railway Engineer International*] [*A
                  publication*]
Railw Eng Int ... Railway Engineer International [*A publication*]
Railw Eng J ... Railway Engineering Journal [*Incorporated in Railway
                  Engineer International*] [*A publication*]
Railw Eng Maint ... Railway Engineering and Maintenance [*A publication*]
Railw Engr ... Railway Engineer [*Later, Railway Engineer International*] [*A
                  publication*]
Railw Gaz... Railway Gazette [*England*] [*Later, Railway Gazette
                  International*] [*A publication*]
Railw Gaz Int ... Railway Gazette International [*A publication*]
Railw Locomot Cars ... Railway Locomotives and Cars [*A publication*]
Railw Manage Rev ... Railway Management Review [*A publication*]
Railw Mech Eng ... Railway Mechanical Engineer [*United States*] [*A
                  publication*]
Railw Rev ... Railway Review [*A publication*]
Railw Signal Commun ... Railway Signalling and Communications [*United
                  States*] [*A publication*]
Railw Syst Control ... Railway Systems Control [*A publication*]
Railw Track Struct ... Railway Track and Structures [*A publication*]
RAIN.......... Relational Algebraic Interpreter
RAIN.......... Relief for Africans in Need   (EA)

RAIN.......... Royal Anthropological Institute News [*Later, Anthropology Today*] [*A publication*]

RAIN.......... Royal Anthropological Institute. Newsletter [*A publication*]

RAINBO...... Research and Instrumentation for National Bio-Science Operations   (MUGU)

RAINPAL.... Recursive Aided Inertial Navigation for Precision Approach and Landing [*NASA*]

RAIP.......... Rapport d'Activites. Institut de Phonetique [*A publication*]

RAIP.......... Requester's Approval in Principle   (NRCH)

RAIR.......... Random Access Information Retrieval [*Data processing*]   (IEEE)

RAIR.......... Rapid Advancement in Reading [*Education*]

RAIR.......... Recordak Automated Information Retrieval [*System*]

RAIR.......... Reflection Absorption Infrared Spectroscopy [*Also, IRAS, RAIRS, RAIS*]

RAIR.......... Regent Air Corp. [*NASDAQ symbol*]   (NQ)

RAIR.......... Remote Access Immediate Response [*Data processing*]

R Aircr Establ List Reports ... Royal Aircraft Establishment. List of Reports [*A publication*]

RAIRO Anal Numer ... RAIRO [*Revue Francaise d'Automatique, d'Informatique, et de Recherche Operationnelle*] Analyse Numerique [*A publication*]

RAIRO Anal Numer Numer Anal ... RAIRO [*Revue Francaise d'Automatique, d'Informatique, et de Recherche Operationnelle*]. Analyse Numerique/Numerical Analysis [*A publication*]

RAIRO Automat ... RAIRO [*Revue Francaise d'Automatique, d'Informatique, et de Recherche Operationnelle*] Automatique [*A publication*]

RAIRO Autom Syst Anal Control ... RAIRO [*Revue Francaise d'Automatique, d'Informatique, et de Recherche Operationnelle*]. Automatique/Systems Analysis and Control [*A publication*]

RAIRO Autom/Syst Anal and Control ... RAIRO [*Revue Francaise d'Automatique, d'Informatique, et de Recherche Operationnelle*] Automatique/Systems Analysis and Control [*A publication*]

RAIRO Inf/Comput Sci ... RAIRO [*Revue Francaise d'Automatique, d'Informatique, et de Recherche Operationnelle*] Informatique/Computer Science [*A publication*]

RAIRO Informat ... RAIRO [*Revue Francaise d'Automatique, d'Informatique, et de Recherche Operationnelle*] Informatique [*A publication*]

RAIRO Informat Theor ... RAIRO [*Revue Francaise d'Automatique, d'Informatique, et de Recherche Operationnelle*] Informatique Theorique [*A publication*]

RAIRO Rech Oper Oper Res ... RAIRO [*Revue Francaise d'Automatique, d'Informatique, et de Recherche Operationnelle*]. Recherche Operationnelle/Operations Research [*A publication*]

RAIRS........ Railroad Accident/Incident Reporting System [*Department of Transportation*]

RAIRS........ Reflection Absorption Infrared Spectroscopy [*Also, IRAS, RAIR, RAIS*]

RAIS.......... Range Automated Information System   (KSC)

RAIS.......... Reflection Absorption Infrared Spectroscopy [*Also, IRAS, RAIR, RAIRS*]

RAISE........ Reliability Accelerated In-Service Echelon   (MCD)

RAIT.......... Rendiconti. Reale Accademia d'Italia [*A publication*]

RAI-TV....... Radio Audizioni Italiana-Televisione [*Italian Radio Broadcasting and Television Company*]

RAIU.......... Radioiodide Uptake [*Endocrinology*]

RAIU.......... Revista de la Alliance Israelite Universelle [*A publication*]

RAIX.......... Rosenbalm Aviation [*Air carrier designation symbol*]

Raj............. All India Reporter, Rajasthan   (DLA)

Raj............. Rajaratam Revised Reports [*Ceylon*]   (DLA)

raj............. Rajasthani [*MARC language code*] [*Library of Congress*]   (LCCP)

RAJ............ Rajkot [*India*] [*Airport symbol*]   (OAG)

RAJAM....... RADAR Jamming   (FAAC)

Rajasthan... Indian Law Reports, Rajasthan Series   (DLA)

Rajasthan Agric ... Rajasthan Agriculturist [*A publication*]

Rajasthan J Agric Sci ... Rajasthan Journal of Agricultural Sciences [*A publication*]

Rajasthan Med J ... Rajasthan Medical Journal [*A publication*]

Rajasthan Univ Studies Statist ... Rajasthan University. Studies in Statistics. Science Series [*A publication*]

Rajasthan Univ Stud Statist ... Rajasthan University. Studies in Statistics. Science Series [*A publication*]

Raj Ind........ Rajasthan [*India*]   (DLA)

RAJ Tech Bull ... RAJ [*Rhodesia Agricultural Journal*] Technical Bulletin [*A publication*]

RAK............ Marrakech [*Morocco*] [*Airport symbol*]   (OAG)

RAK............ Rakhov [*USSR*] [*Seismograph station code, US Geological Survey*] [*Closed*]   (SEIS)

RAK............ Read Access Key

RAK............ Remote Access Key

RaKet.......... Rahnema-Ye Ketab [*A publication*]

Raketentech Raumfahrtforsch ... Raketentechnik und Raumfahrtforschung [*A publication*]

Rakstu Krajums Daugavpils Pedagog Inst ... Rakstu Krajums. Daugavpils Pedagogiskais Instituts [*A publication*]

RAKTP .... Royal Arch Knight Templar Priest [*Freemasonry*]

RAL .... Rabalanakaia [*New Britain*] [*Seismograph station code, US Geological Survey*]   (SEIS)

RAL .... Radio Astronomy Laboratory [*University of California, Berkeley*] [*Research center*]   (RCD)

RAL .... Ralston Purina Co. [*NYSE symbol*]

RAL .... Rapid Access Loop

RAL .... Rear Admiral Alexandria [*British*]

RAL .... Reenlistment Allowance [*Military*]

RAL .... Register of Additional Locations [*Library of Congress*]

RAL .... Remote Area Landing   (NG)

RAL .... Rendiconti. Classe di Scienze Morali e Storiche. Accademia dei Lincei [*A publication*]

RAL .... Reports and Analysis Letter   (OICC)

RAL .... Research in African Literatures [*A publication*]

RAL .... Resorcylic Acid Lactone [*Veterinary pharmacology*]

RAL .... Responsibility Assignment List [*NASA*]   (NASA)

RAL .... Revista. Academias de Letras [*A publication*]

RAL .... Reynold's Aluminum Co. of Canada Ltd. [*Toronto Stock Exchange symbol*]

RAL .... Riverband Acoustical Laboratory   (KSC)

RAL .... Riverside [*California*] [*Airport symbol*]   (OAG)

RAL .... Riverside, CA [*Location identifier*] [*FAA*]   (FAAL)

RAL .... Robotics & Automation Research Laboratory [*University of Toronto*] [*Research center*]   (RCD)

RAL .... Roswell Airlines [*Roswell, NM*] [*FAA designator*]   (FAAC)

RAL .... Rubber-Air-Lead [*Tile*]

RAL .... Rutherford and Appleton Laboratory [*British*]

RALAB .... Revue de l'Aluminum et de Ses Applications [*A publication*]

RALAC ...... RADAR Altimeter Low-Altitude Control [*Military*]   (CAAL)

RALACS.... RADAR Altimeter Low-Altitude Control System [*Military*]   (NG)

RALA-EHF ... Roycrofters-at-Large Association - Elbert Hubbard Foundation   (EA)

RAlb .... Rivista d'Albania [*A publication*]

RALD......... Richmond Area Library Directors [*Library network*]

RALF .... Relocatable Assembly Language Floating Point

RALF .... Repertoire Analytique de Litterature Francaise [*Bordeaux*] [*A publication*]

RALF .... Robotic Assistant Labor Facilitator [*In the movie "Flight of the Navigator" (1986)*]

RALFH........ Random Access Logical File Handler   (MCD)

R Alger Trav ... Revue Algerienne du Travail [*A publication*]

RALI .... Remarried Association of Long Island [*Valley Stream, NY*]   (EA)

RALI .... Resource and Land Investigation [*Program*] [*Department of the Interior*]

RALinc .... Rendiconti. Classe di Scienze Morali e Storiche. Accademia dei Lincei [*A publication*]

RALincei .... Rendiconti. Classe di Scienze Morali e Storiche. Accademia dei Lincei [*A publication*]

RALL .... Rallentando [*Gradually Slower*] [*Music*]

RALLA........ Regional Allied Long-Lines Agency [*Formerly, RELLA*]   (NATG)

R Allem ...... Revue d'Allemagne [*A publication*]

R Allemagne ... Revue d'Allemagne [*A publication*]

RALLEN .... Rallentando [*Gradually Slower*] [*Music*]   (ROG)

RALLO .... Rallentando [*Gradually Slower*] [*Music*]   (ROG)

RALPH........ Reduction and Acquisition of Lunar Pulse Heights [*NASA*]   (NASA)

RALPH........ Royal Association for the Longevity and Preservation of the Honeymooners   (EA)

RALRend.... Rendiconti. Classe di Scienze Morali e Storiche. Accademia dei Lincei [*A publication*]

RALS.......... Remote Augmented Lift System   (MCD)

RALS.......... Resources for American Literary Study [*A publication*]

RAls........... Revue d'Alsace [*A publication*]

RALS.......... Right Add, Left Subtract [*Army field artillery technique*]   (INF)

RALSA .... Restraint and Life Support Assembly   (MCD)

RAL Scav .... Reale Accademia dei Lincei. Atti. Notizie degli Scavi [*A publication*]

RALSH .... Revue Algerienne des Lettres et des Sciences Humaines [*A publication*]

RALT .... RADAR Altimeter [*Aviation*]   (NASA)

RALT .... Range Light   (AAG)

RALT .... Ranging Airborne LASER Tracker   (MCD)

RALT .... Regardless of Altitude [*Aviation*]   (FAAC)

RALT .... Routine Admission Laboratory Tests [*Medicine*]

RALU.......... Register and Arithmetic/Logic Unit [*Data processing*]

RALU.......... Rotary Analog Logic Unit   (MCD)

RALV.......... Random Access Light Valve

RaLV .... Rasheed (Rat) Leukemia Virus

RALW........ Radioactive Liquid Waste   (IEEE)

Ralw & Corp LJ ... Railway and Corporation Law Journal   (DLA)

RAM .... Rabbit Alveolar Macrophage [*Clinical chemistry*]

RAM .... Rabbit Antimouse [*Hematology*]

RAM .... RADAR Absorbing Material

RAM .... Radiation Attenuation Measurement   (CET)

RAM .... Radio-Active Magazine [*A publication*]

RAM .... Radio Attenuation Measurement [*Spacecraft for testing communications*]

RAM .... Radioactive Material

RAM .... Ramada, Inc. [*NYSE symbol*]

RAM .... Raman [*Turkey*] [*Seismograph station code, US Geological Survey*] (SEIS)
Ram .... Ramanathan's Reports [*Ceylon*] (DLA)
RAM .... Ramcor Resources, Inc. [*Vancouver Stock Exchange symbol*]
RAM .... Ramingining [*Australia*] [*Airport symbol*] (OAG)
Ram .... Ramsey's Quebec Appeal Cases (DLA)
RAM .... Random Access Measurement [*System*] [*Data processing*]
RAM .... Random Access Memory [*Data processing*]
RAM .... Random Angle Modulation
RAM .... Range-Altitude Monitor
RAM .... Rapid Alternating Movement
RAM .... Rapid Amortization Mortgage
RAM .... Rapid Area Maintenance [*Air Force*]
Ra M .... Rassegna Musicale [*A publication*]
RAM .... Raytheon Airborne Microwave (MCD)
RAM .... Recovery Aids Material (MUGU)
RAM .... Red Artillery Model [*Military*]
RAM .... Redeye Air Missile [*System*] (RDA)
RAM .... Reentry Antimissile
RAM .... Reentry Attenuation Measurement [*NASA*]
RAM .... Reform the Armed Forces Movement [*Philippines*]
RAM .... Regional Audit Manager
RAM .... Registered Apartment Manager [*Designation awarded by National Association of Home Builders*]
RAM .... Regular Army and Militia [*British*]
RAM .... Releasable Asset Program [*Military*] (AFIT)
RAM .... Reliability Assessment for Management
RAM .... Reliability, Availability, and Maintainability [*Army*]
RAM .... Religions, Ancient and Modern [*A publication*]
RAM .... Remote Access Monitor (MCD)
RAM .... Remote Area Monitoring (KSC)
RAM .... Repeater Amplitude Modulation (MCD)
RAM .... Repeating Antipersonnel Mine
RAM .... Research and Applications Module [*NASA*]
RAM .... Research Aviation Medicine [*Navy program of research into aerospace medical techniques*]
RAM .... Resident Access Methods (MCD)
RAM .... Resident Aerospace Medicine [*Physician in specialty training*] [*Military*]
RAM .... Resources Analysis and Management
RAM .... Responsibility Assignment Matrix [*NASA*] (NASA)
RAM .... Restricted Access Memory [*Data processing*] (MCD)
RAM .... Returned Account Mechanical [*Aviation*] (FAAC)
RAM .... Reverse Annuity Mortgage
RAM .... Revolutionary Action Movement
RAM .... Revue d'Ascetique et de Mystique [*A publication*]
RAM .... Right Ascension of the Meridian [*Navigation*]
RAM .... Rock Australia Magazine [*A publication*]
RAM .... Rolling Airframe Missile
RAM .... Royal Academy of Music [*British*]
RAM .... Royal Air Maroc [*Morocco*]
RAM .... Royal Arch Mason [*Freemasonry*]
RAM .... Royal Ark Mariners
RAMA .... Railway Automotive Management Association [*Newark, NJ*] (EA)
RAMA .... Recap and Movement Authorization [*NASA*] (NASA)
RAMA .... Region of Assured Mission Abort [*Military*] (CAAL)
RAMA .... Rome Air Materiel Area [*Deactivated*] [*Air Force*]
RAMAB ...... Ready Afloat Marine Amphibious Brigade (CINC)
RAMAC ...... Random Access Method of Accounting and Control [*Data processing*]
Ramachandrier A ... Ramachandrier's Cases on Adoption [*1892*] [*India*] (DLA)
Ramachandrier DG ... Ramachandrier's Cases on Dancing Girls [*1892*] [*India*] (DLA)
Ramachandrier HML ... Ramachandrier's Cases on Hindu Marriage Law [*1891*] [*India*] (DLA)
RAMARK .... RADAR Marker [*Military*]
Ram Ass ..... Ram on Assets, Debts, and Incumbrances [*2nd ed.*] [*1837*] (DLA)
RAMAZ .... Rabbi Moses Zacuto (BJA)
RAMB .... Random Access Memory Buffer [*Data processing*]
RaM-BaM ... Rabbi Moses ben Maimon [*Maimonides*] [*Jewish philosopher, 1135-1204*]
RAMBAN .... Rabbi Moses ben Nahman [*Spanish Talmudist, 1195-1270*] (BJA)
RAMBO ...... Real-Time Acquisitions Management and Bibliographic Order System [*Suggested name for the Library of Congress computer system*]
RAMC .... Rassegna di Asetica e Mistica S. Caterina da Siena [*A publication*]
RAMC .... Royal Army Medical Corps [*Initialism also facetiously translated during World War I as "Rats after Moldy Cheese," "Rob All My Comrades," or "Run Away, Matron's Coming!"*] [*British*]
Ram Cas P & E ... Ram's Cases of Pleading and Evidence (DLA)
RA/MCC .... Restricted Area/Military Climb Corridor [*Aviation*] (FAAC)
RAMCT ...... Royal Army Medical Corps, Territorials [*British*] (ROG)
RAMD .... Random Access Memory Device [*Data processing*]
RAMD .... Receiving Agency Materiel Division [*Military*]

RAM-D .... Reliability, Availability, Maintainability, and Durability [*Army*] (AABC)
RAMEC ...... Rapid Action Maintenance Engineering Change [*Navy*] (MCD)
Ram F .... Ram on Facts (DLA)
RAMFAS ... Reliability Analysis of Microcircuit Failure in Avionic Systems (MCD)
RAMIG .... Rabbit Antimouse Immunoglobulin G [*Immunology*]
RAMIS .... Rapid Access Management Information System [*Data processing*]
RAMIS .... Rapid Automatic Malfunction Isolation System
RAMIS .... Receiving, Assembly Maintenance, Inspection, Storage [*Military*]
RAMIS .... Repair, Assemble, Maintain, Issue, and Supply (MUGU)
RaMIsr .... Rassegna Mensile di Israel [*Rome*] [*A publication*]
RAMIT .... Rate-Aided Manually Implemented Tracking (NATG)
Ram Leg J ... Ram's Science of Legal Judgment [*2nd ed.*] [*1834*] (DLA)
Ram Leg Judgm (Towns Ed) ... Ram's Science of Legal Judgment, Notes by Townshend (DLA)
RAM/LOG ... Reliability, Availability, Maintainability, and Logistics (MCD)
RAMM .... Random Access Memory Module [*Data processing*]
RAMM .... Recording Ammeter (MSA)
RAMMIT ..... Reliability and Maintainability Management Improvement Techniques [*Army*]
Ram & Mor ... Ramsey and Morin's Montreal Law Reporter (DLA)
RAMMS ..... Responsive Automated Materiel Management System [*Army*] (AABC)
RAMNAC .... Radio Aids to Marine Navigation Committee [*British*]
RAMOGE .... Regional Pollution Studies in the Ligurian Sea [*Marine science*] (MSC)
RAMONT .... Radiological Monitoring
RAMOS ...... Remote Automatic Meteorological Observing Station
RAMP .... RADAR Mapping of Panama
RAMP .... RADAR Modification Program (NG)
RAMP .... Radiation Airborne Measurement Program
RAMP .... Radio Attenuation Measurement Project
Ramp. .... Ramparts Magazine [*A publication*]
RAMP .... Random Access Mechanization of Phosphorus
RAMP .... Raytheon Airborne Microwave Platform [*Sky station*]
RAMP .... Records and Archives Management Programme [*UNESCO*]
RAMP .... Recovered Allied Military Personnel
RAMP .... Regional Administrative Management Plan [*Department of Labor*]
RAMP .... Reliability and Maintainability Program
RAMP .... Research Association of Minority Professors (EA)
RAMP .... Review of Army Mobilization Planning (MCD)
R/AMP .... Rifampin [*Also, RIF, RMP*] [*Bactericide*]
RAMP .... Ring Airfoil Munition Projectile [*Army*]
RAMP .... Rural Abandoned Mine Program [*Department of Agriculture*]
RAMPART ... RADAR Advanced Measurements Program for Analysis of Reentry Techniques [*ARPA - Raytheon*]
RAMPART ... Route to Airlift Mobility through Partnership (MCD)
Ramp Mag ... Ramparts Magazine [*A publication*]
RAMPS ...... Rapid Message Preparation System (NATG)
RAMPS ...... Repatriated American Military Personnel [*World War II*]
RAMPS ...... Resources Allocation and Multiproject Scheduling
RAMS .... RADAR Target Scattering Advanced Measurement System
RAMS .... Random Access Measurement System [*Data processing*]
RAMS .... Random Access Memory Store [*Data processing*] (TEL)
RAMS .... Rascal Avionics Management System (MCD)
RAMS .... Recovery and Modification Services (MCD)
RAMS .... Reduced-Size Antenna Monopulse System
RAMS .... Regional Air Monitoring Station [*Environmental Protection Agency*]
RAMS .... Regulatory Activities Manpower System [*Nuclear energy*] (NRCH)
RAM-S .... Reliability, Availability, Maintainability - Supportability (MCD)
RAMS .... Reliability and Maintainability Studies [*Army*] (RDA)
RAMS .... Remote Area Mobility Study (MCD)
RAMS .... Remote Automatic Multipurpose Station
RAMS .... Remotely Accessible Management Systems [*Data processing*]
RAMS .... Repairables Asset Management System [*Military*] (CAAL)
RAMS .... Requirements Analysis Material Sheet [*or Study*] (MCD)
RAMS .... Right Ascension Mean Sun [*Navigation*]
RAMSA ...... Radio Aeronautica Mexicana, Sociedad Anonima
Rams App ... Ramsey's Quebec Appeal Cases [*1873-86*] (DLA)
Ramsay App Cas ... Ramsay's Appeal Cases [*Canada*] (DLA)
Ramsay App Cas (Can) ... Ramsay's Appeal Cases [*Canada*] (DLA)
Ram SC ...... Ramanathan's Supreme Court Reports [*Ceylon*] (DLA)
RAMSES .... Reprogramable Advanced Multimode Shipborne ECM System [*Canadian Navy*]
RAMSH ...... Reliability, Availability, Maintainability, Safety, and Human Factors [*Telecommunications*] (TEL)
RAMSP ...... Revista do Arquivo Municipal (Sao Paulo) [*A publication*]
RAMSS ...... Royal Alfred Merchant Seamen's Society [*British*]
RAMT .... Rudder Angle Master Transmitter
RAMTAC .... Reentry Analysis and Modeling of Target Characteristics
RAMTB .... Revue ATB [*Assistance Technique Belge*] Metallurgie [*Belgium*] [*A publication*]
RAMVAN .... Reconnaissance Aircraft Maintenance Van
Ram W .... Ram on Exposition of Wills of Landed Property [*1827*] (DLA)
Ran .... Ranae [*Frogs*] [*of Aristophanes*] [*Classical studies*] (OCD)

RAN............ Rangifer. Nordisk Organ foer Reinforskning [*A publication*]
RAN............ Rangoon [*Burma*] [*Seismograph station code, US Geological Survey*] [*Closed*] (SEIS)
RAN............ Ranitidine [*An antiulcer drug*]
RAN............ Ransome Air, Inc. [*Philadelphia, PA*] [*FAA designator*] (FAAC)
RAN............ Read around Number
RAN............ Reconnaissance/Attack Navigator
RAN............ Regional Air Navigation [*ICAO*]
RAN............ Rendiconti. Accademia di Archeologia, Lettere, e Belle Arti (Napoli) [*A publication*]
RAN............ Repair Activity Accounting Number [*Navy*]
RAN............ Reporting Accounting Number [*NG*]
RAN............ Request for Authority to Negotiate
RAN............ Resource-Adjacent Nation [*Ocean fishery management*]
RAN............ Revenue Anticipation Note
RAN............ Royal Australian Navy [*ADA*]
RANA........ Rheumatoid Arthritis Nuclear Antigen [*Immunology*]
RANA .... Rhodesia & Nyasaland Airways
RANAM...... Recherches Anglaises et Americaines [*A publication*]
RANC .... RADAR Absorption Noise and Clutter [*NASA*] (NASA)
RANCA...... Retired Army Nurse Corps Association [*San Antonio, TX*] (EA)
Ranchi Univ J Agric Res ... Ranchi University. Journal of Agricultural Research [*A publication*]
Ranchi Univ Math J ... Ranchi University. Mathematical Journal [*A publication*]
Ranch Mag ... Ranch Magazine [*A publication*]
RANCID...... Real and Not Corrected Input Data [*Data processing*]
RANCOM .. Random Communication Satellite
RAND .... Rand Capital Corp. [*NASDAQ symbol*] (NQ)
Rand............ Randall's Reports [*62-71 Ohio State*] (DLA)
Rand............ Randolph's Reports [*22-27 Virginia*] [*1821-28*] (DLA)
Rand............ Randolph's Reports [*7-11 Louisiana*] (DLA)
Rand............ Randolph's Reports [*21-56 Kansas*] (DLA)
RAND .... Research and Development [*Origin of name of RAND Corporation, a nonprofit national defense research organization*]
Rand............ Selected Rand Abstracts [*A publication*]
RANDAM.... Random Access Nondestructive Advanced Memory [*Data processing*]
Rand Com Paper ... Randolph on Commercial Paper (DLA)
Rand Corp Pap ... Rand Corporation. Papers [*A publication*]
Rand Corp Rep ... Rand Corporation. Report [*A publication*]
Rand Em Dom ... Randolph on Eminent Domain (DLA)
R ANDI .... Revista ANDI [*Asociacion Nacional de Industriales*] [*A publication*]
RANDID...... Rapid Alphanumeric Digital Indicating Device
RANDO....... Radiotherapy Analog Dosimetry
Rand Perp ... Randall on Perpetuities (DLA)
RANEL ...... Royal Australian Navy Experimental Laboratory (MCD)
Raney .... Raney's Reports [*16-20 Florida*] (DLA)
RANF Rev... RANF [*Royal Australian Nursing Federation*] Review [*A publication*]
RANG .... Rangaire Corp. [*NASDAQ symbol*] (NQ)
RANG .... Rangoon [*City in Burma*] (ROG)
Rang Cr LJ ... Rangoon Criminal Law Journal (DLA)
Rang Dec ... Sparks' Rangoon Decisions [*British Burma*] (DLA)
Range Impr Stud Calif Div For ... Range Improvement Studies. California Division of Forestry [*A publication*]
Rang LR ..... Rangoon Law Reports [*India*] (DLA)
Rank P........ Rankin on Patents [*1824*] (DLA)
Rank & S Comp L ... Ranking and Spicer's Company Law [*11th ed.*] [*1970*] (DLA)
Rank S & P Exec ... Ranking, Spicer, and Pegler on Executorship [*21st ed.*] [*1971*] (DLA)
RANKY ...... Rank Organisation ADR [*NASDAQ symbol*] (NQ)
RANL......... Rendiconti. Reale Accademia Nazionale dei Lincei [*A publication*]
RANN .... Research Applied to National Needs [*Formerly, IRRPOS*] [*National Science Foundation*] [*Obsolete*]
Rannsoknastofnun Fiskidnadarins Arsskyrs ... Rannsoknastofnun Fiskidnadarins Arsskyrsla [*A publication*]
rANP.......... Rat Atrial Natriuretic Peptide [*Biochemistry*]
RANS .... Report. Australian Numismatic Society [*A publication*]
RANS .... Revenue Anticipation Notes
RANSA...... Rutas Aereas Nacionales, Sociedad Anonima [*Venezuelan cargo airline*]
RANT......... Reentry Antenna Test
R Anthrop ... Reviews in Anthropology [*A publication*]
R Antropol (Sao Paulo) ... Revista de Antropologia (Sao Paulo) [*A publication*]
RAN(V)R .... Royal Australian Naval (Volunteer) Reserve
RANXPE.... Resident Army Nike-X Project Engineer (AABC)
RAO............ National Radio Astronomy Observatory, Charlottesville, VA [*OCLC symbol*] (OCLC)
RAO............ RADAR Operator
RAO............ Radio Astronomy Observatory [*University of Michigan*] [*Research center*]
RAO............ Rado Reef Resources [*Vancouver Stock Exchange symbol*]
RAO............ Raoul [*Raoul Island*] [*Seismograph station code, US Geological Survey*] (SEIS)
RAO............ Recueil d'Archeologie Orientale [*A publication*]

RAO............ Regional Accounting Office [*Telecommunications*] (TEL)
RAO............ Regional Administrative Office
RAO............ Regional Agricultural Officer [*Ministry of Agriculture, Fisheries, and Food*] [*British*]
RAO............ Ribeirao Preto [*Brazil*] [*Airport symbol*] (OAG)
RAO............ Right Anterior Oblique [*Medicine*]
RAO............ Rudder Angle Order (MSA)
RAOA......... Railway Accounting Officers Association
RAOB......... Radiosonde Observation
RAOB......... Royal Antediluvian Order of Buffaloes
RAOC .... Rear Area Operations Center (MCD)
RAOC .... Regional Air Operations Center (NATG)
RAOC .... Royal Army Ordnance Corps [*Formerly, AOC*] [*British*]
Rao DHL ..... Rao's Decisions on Hindu Law [*1893*] [*India*] (DLA)
RAOMP ..... Report of Accrued Obligations, Military Pay (AFM)
RAOP .... Regional Air Operations Plan (NATG)
RAOU Newsl ... RAOU [*Royal Australasian Ornithologists Union*] Newsletter [*A publication*]
RAP............ RADAR Aim Point
RAP............ Radical Alternatives to Prison [*British*]
RAP............ Radio Access Point (MCD)
RAP............ Radio Air Play
RAP............ Radiological Assistance Plan [*AEC*]
RAP............ Random Access Program [*Data processing*]
RAP............ Random Access Projector
RAP............ Rapid (AAG)
RAP............ Rapid City [*South Dakota*] [*Airport symbol*] (OAG)
RAP............ Rapid City, SD [*Location identifier*] [*FAA*] (FAAL)
RAP............ Rapindik [*New Britain*] [*Seismograph station code, US Geological Survey*] [*Closed*] (SEIS)
RAP............ Reactive Atmosphere Process
RAP............ Readiness Action Proposal (MCD)
RAP............ Readiness Assessment Program [*Navy*]
RAP............ Rear Area Protection (AABC)
RAP............ Reduced Acreage Program [*Agriculture*]
RAP............ Redundancy Adjustment of Probability (IEEE)
RAP............ Regimental Aid Post [*British*]
RAP............ Regional Acceleratory Phenomenon [*Physiology*]
RAP............ Regression Analysis Program [*Military*]
RAP............ Regression-Associated Protein [*Biochemistry*]
RAP............ Regulatory Analysis Program [*Federal government*]
RAP............ Relational Associative Processor (IEEE)
RAP............ Relationship Anecdotes Paradigm Method [*Psychology*]
RAP............ Relative Accident Probability
RAP............ Releasable Assets Program
RAP............ Reliability Assessment Prediction
RAP............ Reliability Assessment Program
RAP............ Reliable Acoustic Path
RAP............ Remedial Action Projects (MCD)
RAP............ Renal Artery Pressure [*Medicine*]
RAP............ Rental Assistance Payment Program [*HUD*]
RAP............ Requirements Analysis Package [*Data processing*]
RAP............ Resident Assembler Program
RAP............ Resident Associate Program [*Smithsonian Institution*]
RAP............ Residual Analysis Program [*Space Flight Operations Facility, NASA*]
RAP............ Resource Allocation Processor (CMD)
RAP............ Response Analysis Program [*Data processing*] (IBMDP)
RAP............ Results Analysis Plan (MCD)
RAP............ Review and Analysis Process
RAP............ Revised Accounting Procedures
RAP............ Revolutionary Action Power [*A publication*]
RAP............ Revue de l'Action Populaire [*Later, Projet*] [*A publication*]
RAp............ Revue Apologetique [*A publication*]
RAP............ Revue d'Archeologie Polonaise [*A publication*]
RAP............ Rhodesian Action Party
RAP............ Right Angle Plug
RAP............ Right Atrial Pressure [*Cardiology*]
RAP............ Ring-Around Programing (CAAL)
RAP............ Rocket-Assisted Projectile (RDA)
RAP............ "Round Up" Administration Planning Staff [*for the invasion of France*] [*World War II*]
RAP............ Rubidium Acid Phthalate [*Organic chemistry*]
RAP............ Rules for Admission to Practice (DLA)
RA-P........... Rumex Acetosa Polysaccharide [*Antineoplastic drug*]
RAP............ Rupees, Annas, Pies [*Monetary units in India*]
RAP............ Smithsonian Resident Associate Program (EA)
RAPAC...... Research Applications Policy Advisory Committee [*National Science Foundation*] (EGAO)
RAPAD...... Research Association for Petroleum Alternative Development
Rapalje & L ... Rapalje and Lawrence's Law Dictionary (DLA)
Rapal & L ... Rapalje and Lawrence's American and English Cases (DLA)
Rap Bur Nutr Anim Elev ... Rapport. Bureau de la Nutrition Animale et de l'Elevage [*A publication*]
RAPC .... Radio Administration Plenipotentiary Conference
RAPC .... Right Angle Pressure Cartridge
RAPC .... Royal Army Pay Corps [*Formerly, APC*] [*British*]
RAPCAP.... RADAR Picket Combat Air Patrol (NVT)
RAPCC...... RADAR Approach Control Center (MCD)
RAPCO...... Regional Air Priorities Control Office [*Army*] (AABC)
RAPCOE .... Random Access Programing and Checkout Equipment

RAPCON .... RADAR Approach Control [*Air Force*]
Rap Contempt ... Rapalje on Contempt (DLA)
RAPD .... Relatively Afferent Pupillary Defect [*Ophthalmology*]
RAPD .... Response Amplitude Probability Data
RAPE .... RADAR Arithmetic Processing Element [*Navy*]
RAPEC ...... Rocket-Assisted Personnel Ejection Catapult
RAPECA ..... Rassemblement du Peuple Camerounais [*Camerounese People's Rally*]
RAP-EX ...... Rear Area Protection Operations Extended (MCD)
Rap Fed Ref Dig ... Rapalje's Federal Reference Digest (DLA)
RAPH .... Recherches d'Archeologie de Philologie et d'Histoire [*Cairo*] [*A publication*]
RAPIC .... Remedial Action Program Information Center [*Department of Energy*] [*Oak Ridge, TN*] [*Information service*] (EISS)
RAPID .... Random Access Personnel Information Dissemination
RAPID .... Reactor and Plant Integrated Dynamics [*Data processing*] (KSC)
RAPID .... Reader-to-Advertiser Phone Inquiry Delivery System [*Chilton Corp.*]
RAPID .... Real-Time Acquisition and Processing of Inflight Data
RAPID .... Relative Address Programing Implementation Device [*Data processing*]
RAPID .... Remote Access Planning for Institutional Development [*Data processing*]
RAPID .... Remote Access Procedure for Interactive Design [*General Motors Corp.*]
RAPID .... Research in Automatic Photocomposition and Information Dissemination
RAPID .... Retrieval through Automated Publication and Information Digest [*Data processing*] (DIT)
RAPID .... Retrieval and Processing Information for Display
RAPID .... Retrorocket-Assisted Parachute in Flight Delivery
RAPID .... Rocketdyne Automatic Processing of Integrated Data [*Data processing*]
RAPID .... Ryan Automatic Plot Indicator Device
RAPIDS ...... Random Access Personnel Information Dissemination System [*Army*] (AABC)
RAPIDS ...... Rapid Automated Problem Identification System [*DoD*]
RAPIDS ...... Real-Time Automated Personnel Identification System
Rap Inst Fiz Tech Jad AGH ... Raport. Instytut Fizyki i Techniki Jadrowej AGH [*A publication*]
Rap Inst Nat Etude Agron Congo (INEAC) ... Rapport. Institut National pour l'Etude Agronomique du Congo (INEAC)
Rap Inst Tech Jad AGH ... Raport. Instytut Techniki Jadrowej AGH [*A publication*]
Rap Jud QBR ... Rapports Judiciaires de Quebec, Cour du Banc de la Reine [*Quebec Law Reports, Queen's Bench*] (DLA)
Rap Jud QCS ... Rapports Judiciaires de Quebec. Cour Superieure [*Quebec Law Reports, Superior Court*] (DLA)
Rap Jud Quebec CS (Can) ... Rapports Judiciaires de Quebec [*Quebec Law Reports*] [*Canada*] (DLA)
Rap Jud Quebec KB (Can) ... Rapports Judiciaires de Quebec [*Quebec Law Reports*] [*Canada*] (DLA)
Rap Jud Quebec QB (Can) ... Rapports Judiciaires de Quebec [*Quebec Law Reports*] [*Canada*] (DLA)
Rap & L ...... Rapalje and Lawrence's American and English Cases (DLA)
Rap Lar ...... Rapalje on Larceny (DLA)
Rap & Law ... Rapalje and Lawrence's American and English Cases (DLA)
Rap & L Law Dict ... Rapalje and Lawrence's Law Dictionary (DLA)
RAPLOC ...... Rapid Passive Localization (MCD)
RAPLOC-LSI ... Rapid Passive Localization - Low-Ship Impact [*Navy*] (CAAL)
RAPLOC-WAA ... Rapid Passive Localization - Wide Aperture Array [*Military*] (CAAL)
RAPM .... Reliability Assessment Prediction Model
Rap NY Dig ... Rapalje's New York Digest (DLA)
RAPO .... Rabbit Antibodies to Pig Ovary [*Immunology*]
RAPO .... Resident Apollo Project Office [*NASA*] (KSC)
Rapp .... Rapport [*A publication*]
RAPP .... Reconciliation and Purification Program [*Air Force*]
RAPP .... Registered Air Parcel Post
RAPP's .... Radiologists, Anesthesiologists, Pathologists, and Physiatrists
Rapp Act Stn Amelior Plant Maraicheres ... Rapport d'Activite. Station d'Amelioration des Plants Maraicheres [*A publication*]
Rapp Anal Phys Chim Eau Rhin ... Rapport sur les Analyses Physico-Chimiques de l'Eau du Rhin [*A publication*]
Rapp Assoc Int Chim Cerealiere ... Rapports. Association Internationale de Chimie Cerealiere [*A publication*]
Rapp BIPM ... Rapport. BIPM [*Bureau International des Poids et Mesures*] [*A publication*]
Rapp Comm Int Mer Mediter ... Rapport. Commission Internationale pour la Mer Mediterranee [*France*] [*A publication*]
Rapp Commissar Energie Atom ... Rapport. Commissariat a l'Energie Atomique [*France*] [*A publication*]
Rapp Cons Exp Rech Agron Insp Gen Agric (Algeria) ... Rapport. Conseil de l'Experimentation et des Recherches Agronomiques. Inspection Generale de l'Agriculture (Algeria) [*A publication*]
Rapp Final Conf Tech OCEAC ... Rapport Final. Conference Technique. OCEAC [*Organisation de Coordination pour la Lutte Contre les Endemies en Afrique Centrale*] [*A publication*]

Rapp Fonct Tech Inst Pasteur Dakar ... Rapport sur le Fonctionnement Technique. Institut Pasteur de Dakar [*A publication*]
RAPPI .... Random Access Plan-Position Indicator [*Air Force*]
Rapp Instn Virkeslara Skogshogsk ... Rapporter. Institutionen for Virkeslara. Skogshogskolan [*A publication*]
Rapp Inter Etude Lab J Dedek Raffinerie Tirlemontoise ... Rapport Interieur d'une Etude Effectuee au Laboratoire J. Dedek Raffinerie Tirlemontoise [*A publication*]
Rapp Korrosionsinst ... Rapport. Korrosionsinstitutet [*A publication*]
Rapp Lab Prod For Est (Can) ... Rapport. Laboratoire des Produits Forestiers de l'Est (Canada) [*A publication*]
Rapp Off Int Epizoot ... Rapport. Office International des Epizooties [*A publication*]
Rapport Conjonct ... Rapport de Conjoncture [*A publication*]
Rapp Prelim Minist Richesses Nat (Que) ... Rapport Preliminaire. Ministere des Richesses Naturelles (Quebec) [*A publication*]
Rapp Proefstn Groenteteelt Vollegrond Ned ... Rapport. Proefstation voor de Groenteteelt in de Vollegrond in Nederland [*A publication*]
Rapp P-V Reun Cons Int Explor Mer ... Rapports et Proces-Verbaux des Reunions. Conseil International pour l'Exploration de la Mer [*A publication*]
Rapp Rech Lab Cent Ponts Chaussees ... Rapport de Recherche. Laboratoire Central des Ponts et Chaussees [*A publication*]
Rapp Sci Tech CNEXO (Fr) ... Rapports Scientifiques et Techniques. CNEXO [*Centre National pour l'Exploitation des Oceans*] (France) [*A publication*]
Rapp Sven Livsmedel-Sinstitutet ... Rapport. Svenska Livsmedelsinstitutet [*A publication*]
Rapp Uppsats Avd Skogsekol Skogshogsk ... Rapporter och Uppsatser. Avdelningen foer Skogsekologi. Skogshogskolan [*A publication*]
Rapp Uppsats Instn Skoglig Mat Statist Skogshogsk ... Rapporter och Uppsatser. Institutionen foer Skoglig Matematisk Statistik. Skogshogskolan [*A publication*]
Rapp Uppsats Instn Skogsforyngr Skogshogsk ... Rapporter och Uppsatser. Institutionen foer Skogsforyngring. Skogshogskolan [*A publication*]
Rapp Uppsats Instn Skogsgenet Skogshogsk ... Rapporter och Uppsatser. Institutionen foer Skogsgenetik. Skogshogskolan [*A publication*]
Rapp Uppsats Instn Skogsprod Skogshogsk ... Rapporter och Uppsatser. Institutionen foer Skogsproduktion. Skogshogskolan [*A publication*]
Rapp Uppsats Instn Skogstax Skogshogsk ... Rapporter och Uppsatser. Institutionen foer Skogstaxering. Skogshogskolan [*A publication*]
Rapp Uppsats Instn Skogstek Skogshogsk ... Rapporter och Uppsatser. Institutionen foer Skogsteknik. Skogshogskolan [*A publication*]
RAPR .... RADAR Processor (CET)
RAPR .... Right Angle Panel Receptacle
RAPRA ...... RAPRA Technology [*Formerly, Rubber and Plastics Research Association*] (EA)
RAPRA Abst ... RAPRA [*Rubber and Plastics Research Association*] Abstract [*A publication*]
RAPRA Members J ... RAPRA [*Rubber and Plastics Research Association*] Members Journal [*England*] [*A publication*]
RAPRENOx .... Rapid Reduction of Nitrogen Oxides [*Automotive engineering*]
RAPS .... RADAR Absorbing Primary Structure (MCD)
RAPS .... RADAR Prediction System (MCD)
RAPS .... Radioactive Argon Processing System (NRCH)
RAPS .... Regional Air Pollution Study [*Environmental Protection Agency*]
RAPS .... Regulated Air Pressure System (MCD)
RAPS .... Regulatory Affairs Professionals Society [*Washington, DC*] (EA)
RAPS .... Reliable Acoustic Path SONAR (MCD)
RAPS .... Retired Army Personnel System
RAPS .... Retrieval Analysis and Presentation System [*Data processing*]
RAPS .... Risk Appraisal of Programs System
RAPS .... Role Activity Performance Scale [*Mental health*]
RAPSAG .... Rapid Sealift Acquisition Group [*Navy*]
RAPT .... Reusable Aerospace Passenger Transport (MCD)
RAPTAP ...... Random Access Parallel Tape
RAP-TAP .... Releasable Assets Program - Transferable Assets Program [*Navy*] (NG)
RAPTN .... RAPRA Trade Names [*RAPRA Technology Ltd.*] [*Information service*] [*Shrewsbury, Shrops., England*] (EISS)
Raptor Res ... Raptor Research [*A publication*]
RAPTUS ...... Rapid Thorium-Uranium System [*Nuclear reactor*]
RAPUD .... Revenue Analysis from Parametric Usage Descriptions [*Telecommunications*] (TEL)
RAPWI .... Organization for the Recovery of Allied Prisoners of War and Internees [*Initially in Headquarters of Allied Land Forces, Southeast Asia*] [*World War II*]
Rap Wit ...... Rapalje's Treatise on Witnesses (DLA)
RAQ .... Raha [*Indonesia*] [*Airport symbol*] (OAG)
RAR .... RADAR Augmentation Reliability (MCD)
RAR .... Radio Acoustic Ranging

RAR	Random Age Replacement
RAR	Rapid Access Recording (IEEE)
Rar	Rare Records [*Record label*]
RAR	Rarotonga [*Cook Islands*] [*Airport symbol*] (OAG)
RAR	Rarotonga [*Cook Islands*] [*Seismograph station code, US Geological Survey*] (SEIS)
RAR	Read around Ratio
RAR	Real Aperture RADAR
RAR	Reallexikon der Aegyptischen Religionsgeschichte [*Berlin*] [*A publication*] (BJA)
RAR	Record and Report
RAR	Redevelopment Area Resident
RAR	Reduced Aspect Ratio
RAR	Regular Army Reserve
RAR	Reliability Action Report [*or Request*]
RAR	Remote Arm Reset (MCD)
RAR	Remove Audible Ring
RAR	Renaissance and Reformation [*A publication*]
RAR	Repair as Required (AAG)
RAR	Report Authorization Record [*or Request*] (AAG)
RAR	Request RADAR Blip Identification Message [*Communications*] (FAAC)
RAR	Resource Allocation Recommendations [*Military*]
RAR	Return Address Register
RAR	Revenue Agent's Report [*IRS*]
R Ar	Revise as Required (MCD)
R Ar	Revue Archeologique [*A publication*]
R-Ar	Rhode Island State Archives, Providence, RI [*Library symbol*] [*Library of Congress*] (LCLS)
RAR	Rhodesian African Rifles [*Military unit*]
RAR	ROM [*Read-Only Memory*] Address Register
RAR	Royal Army Reserve [*British*]
RAR	Royal Australian Regiment
RAR	Rural Area Redevelopment
RARAD	RADAR Advisory (FAAC)
R Arb	Recht der Arbeit [*Right to Work*] [*German*] (DLA)
RARC	Revoked Appointment and Returned to Civilian Status [*Navy*]
RArchCr	Rivista di Archeologia Cristiana [*Rome*] [*A publication*]
R Archeol	Revue Archeologique [*A publication*]
R Arch Hist Art Louvain	Revue des Archeologues et Historiens d'Art de Louvain [*A publication*]
RARDE	Royal Armament Research and Development Establishment [*British*]
RARE	Ram Air Rocket Engine
RARE	Rare Animal Relief Effort
RARE	Rehabilitation of Addicts by Relatives and Employers
RARE	Reinforcement and Resupply of Europe (MCD)
RARE	Roadless Area Resource Evaluation
RARE	Ronne Antarctic Research Expedition [*1947-48*]
Ra Ref	RADAR Reflector
RAREF	Radiation and Repair Engineering Facility (NRCH)
RAREP	RADAR Report [*FAA*]
RARF	RADOME [*RADAR Dome*], Antenna, and Radio Frequency [*Array*] [*Electronics*]
RARG	Regulatory Analysis Review Group [*Comprising several federal agencies*]
RARI	Reporting and Routing Instructions [*Navy*]
RARMB	Razrabotka Rudnykh Mestorozhdenii [*A publication*]
RARO	Regular Army Reserve of Officers [*British*]
RAR OCC	Raro Occurrit [*Rarely Occurs*] [*Latin*] (ROG)
RARP	Radio Affiliate Replacement Plan [*Canadian Broadcasting Corporation*]
RARPC	Roczniki Akademii Rolniczej w Poznaniu [*A publication*]
RArq	Revista di Arqueologia [*A publication*]
RArqueol	Revista de Arqueologia [*A publication*]
RARR	Reinstallation and Removal Record (KSC)
RARSA	Radiation Research. Supplement [*A publication*]
RArt	Revue d'Art [*A publication*]
RArt	Royal Artillery [*British*]
RArte	Rivista d'Arte [*A publication*]
R des Arts	Revue des Arts [*A publication*]
R Arts	Revue des Arts [*A publication*]
RARU	Rackham Arthritis Research Unit [*University of Michigan*] [*Research center*] (RCD)
RARU	Radio Range Station Reported Unreliable [*Message abbreviation*]
RAS	Rabbonim Aid Society
RAS	RADAR Advisory Service
RAS	RADAR Assembly Spares (NG)
RAS	RADAR Augmentation System (MCD)
RAS	Radio Science [*A publication*]
RAS	RADOME [*RADAR Dome*] Antenna Structure
RAS	Radula Sinus
RAS	Rasht [*Iran*] [*Airport symbol*] (OAG)
RAS	Rassegna. Archivi di Stato [*A publication*]
RAS	Rassegna della Letteratura Italiana [*A publication*]
RAS	Reaction Augmentation System
RAS	Reactor Alarm System (IEEE)
RAS	Reactor Analysis and Safety (NRCH)
RAS	Readers Advisory Service [*A publication*]
RAS	Rear Area Security [*Army*] (AABC)

RAS	Recirculation Actuation Signal [*Nuclear energy*] (NRCH)
RAS	Record Assigned System (MCD)
RAS	Records and Analysis Subsystem (TEL)
RAS	Recruiting Analysis Service [*LIMRA*]
RAS	Rectified Air Speed [*Navigation*]
RAS	Recurrent Aphthous Stomatitis [*Medicine*]
RAS	Reflector Antenna System
RAS	Regional Automated Systems
RAS	Relay Antenna Subsystem [*NASA*]
RAS	Reliability, Availability, and Serviceability [*IBM Corp. slogan*] (MCD)
RAS	Remote Acquisition Station (NRCH)
RAS	Remote Area Support (MCD)
RAS	Remote Arm Set (MCD)
RAS	Renin-Angiotensin System [*Endocrinology*]
RAS	Replenishment at Sea [*Navy*]
RAS	Report Audit Summary (AAG)
RAS	Reproduction Assembly Sheet (MCD)
RAS	Requirements Allocation Sheet
RAS	Requirements Analysis Sheet [*NASA*] (KSC)
RAS	Requirements Audit System
RAS	Reticular Activating System [*Diffuse network of neurons in the brain*]
RAS	Revue Archeologique Syrienne [*A publication*]
RAS	Rheumatoid Arthritis Serum [*Factor*] [*Medicine*]
RAS	River Assault Squadron [*Navy*] (NVT)
RAS	Riverside Air Service [*Riverside, CA*] [*FAA designator*] (FAAC)
RAS	Route Accounting Subsystem [*Telecommunications*] (TEL)
RAS	Row-Address Strobe (IEEE)
RAS	Royal Accounting System [*United States Geological Survey*]
RAS	Royal Aeronautical Society [*British*]
RAS	Royal Asiatic Society [*British*]
RAS	Royal Astronomical Society [*British*]
RASA	Railway and Airline Supervisors Association [*AFL-CIO*]
RASA	Rassegna Abruzzese di Storia ed Arte [*A publication*]
RASA	Realignment of Supply Activities (MCD)
RASA	Redstone Arsenal Support Activity (MCD)
RASA	Regional Aeronautical Support Activity (AFIT)
RASC	Rear Area Security Controller
RASC	Religious Altered State of Consciousness [*Psychology*]
RASC	Rome Air Service Command [*Air Force*]
RASC	Royal Army Service Corps [*Formerly, ASC; later, RCT*] [*British*]
RASC	Royal Astronomical Society of Canada
RASCA	Radio Science [*A publication*]
RASCAL	Random Access Secure Communications Antijam Link
RASCAL	Royal Aircraft Establishment Sequence Calculator [*British*] (DEN)
RASCAP	Replenishment at Sea Corrective Action Program (MCD)
RASCC	Rear Area Security Control Center
RASC/DC	Rear Area Security and Area Damage Control [*Military*]
R Ascetique & Mystique	Revue d'Ascetique et de Mystique [*A publication*]
Raschet Konstr Neftezvod Oborudovaniya	Raschet i Konstruirovanie Neftezavodskogo Oborudovaniya [*A publication*]
Raschety Prochn	Raschety na Prochnost [*A publication*]
RASCORE	RADAR Scorer (MCD)
RASC/RCT	Royal Army Service Corps/Royal Corps of Transport [*British*]
RASD	Reference and Adult Services Division [*Formerly, RSD*] [*American Library Association*] [*Chicago, IL*]
RASD HS	RASD [*Reference and Adult Services Division*] History Section
RASD MARS	RASD [*Reference and Adult Services Division*] Machine-Assisted Reference Section
RASE	Rapid Automatic Sweep Equipment [*Air Force*]
RASE	Royal Agricultural Society of England
RASER	Radio Amplification by Stimulated Emission of Radiation
RASER	Random-to-Serial Converter
RASER	Range and Sensitivity Extending Resonator [*Electronics*]
RasF	Rassegna di Filosofia [*A publication*]
RASGN	Reassignment
RASH	Rain Showers [*Meteorology*]
RaSHI	Rabbi Solomon Bar Isaac (BJA)
RasI	Rassegna Italiana [*A publication*]
RASIB	Rendiconto. Accademia delle Scienze. Istituto di Bologna [*A publication*]
RASIDS	Range Safety Impact Display System
RASL	Royal Apex Silver [*NASDAQ symbol*] (NQ)
RASM	Remote Analog Submultiplexer (MCD)
RASMA	Revue Agricole et Sucriere de l'Ile Maurice [*A publication*]
rASMC	Rat Aortic Smooth Muscle Cells
RAsMyst	Revue d'Ascetique et de Mystique [*Paris*] [*A publication*]
RASN	Rain and Snow [*Sleet*] [*Meteorology*]
RASO	Radiological Affairs Support Office [*Obsolete*] [*Navy*]
RASO	Rear Airfield Supply Organization
RASO	Regional Aviation Supply Officer [*Navy*] (AFIT)
RASP	Receiver Active Signal Processor [*Military*] (CAAL)
RASP	Refined Aeronautical Support Program (NG)
RASP	Reliability and Aging Surveillance Program [*Air Force*]
RASP	Remote Access Switching and Patching
RASP	Retrieval and Sort Processor [*Data processing*]
RASPE	Resident Army SENSCOM [*Sentinel Systems Command*] Project Engineer (AABC)
RASPO	Resident Apollo Spacecraft Program Office [*NASA*] (KSC)

RASR.......... Regular Army Special Reserve   (ADA)
RASS.......... RADAR Acoustic Sounding System [*National Oceanic and Atmospheric Administration*]
RASS.......... RADAR Attitude Sensing System   (MCD)
RASS.......... Radio Acoustic Sounding System
RASS.......... Rapid Area Supply Support [*Military*]   (AFM)
RAss........... Revue d'Assyriologie et d'Archeologie Orientale [*A publication*]
RASS.......... Rock Analysis Storage System [*United States Geological Survey*] [*Denver, CO*]   (EISS)
RASS.......... Ruggedized Airborne Seeker Simulator   (MCD)
Rass Agr Ital ... Rassegna dell'Agricoltura Italiana [*A publication*]
RASSAN ... RADAR Sea State Analyzer [*Marine science*]   (MSC)
Rass Arch Chir ... Rassegna ed Archivio di Chirurgia [*A publication*]
Rass Chim ... Rassegna Chimica [*A publication*]
Rass Clin Ter Sci Affini ... Rassegna di Clinica Terapia e Scienze Affini [*A publication*]
RassCult .... Rassegna di Cultura [*A publication*]
Rass Econ Afr Ital ... Rassegna Economica dell'Africa Italiana [*A publication*]
Rass Econ Cam Commer Ind Agr Alessandria ... Rassegna Economica. Camera di Commercio, Industria, e Agricoltura di Alessandria [*A publication*]
Rass Econ Colon ... Rassegna Economica delle Colonie [*A publication*]
Rass Econ (Napoli) ... Rassegna Economica (Napoli) [*A publication*]
Rassegna Ital Sociol ... Rassegna Italiana di Sociologia [*A publication*]
RassFilos ... Rassegna di Filosofia [*A publication*]
Rass Fisiopatol Clin Ter ... Rassegna di Fisiopatologia Clinica e Terapeutica [*A publication*]
Rass Giuliana Med ... Rassegna Giuliana di Medicina [*A publication*]
RASSH....... Radiosondes Shipped From   (NOAA)
Rass IGI...... Rassegna Indo-Greco-Italica [*A publication*]
Rass Int Stomatol Prat ... Rassegna Internazionale di Stomatologia Pratica [*A publication*]
Rass d'It ..... Rassegna d'Italia [*A publication*]
Rass Ital Gastro-Enterol ... Rassegna Italiana di Gastro-Enterologia [*A publication*]
Rass Ital Ottalmol ... Rassegna Italiana d'Ottalmologia [*A publication*]
Rass Ital Sociol ... Rassegna Italiana di Sociologia [*A publication*]
Rass Let It ... Rassegna della Letteratura Italiana [*A publication*]
Rass Med ... Rassegna Medica [*A publication*]
Rass Med Appl Lav Ind ... Rassegna di Medicina Applicata al Lavoro Industriale [*A publication*]
Rass Med Convivium Sanit ... Rassegna Medica - Convivium Sanitatis [*A publication*]
Rass Med Cult ... Rassegna Medica e Culturale [*A publication*]
Rass Med Ind ... Rassegna di Medicina Industriale [*A publication*]
Rass Med Ind Ig Lav ... Rassegna di Medicina Industriale e di Igiene del Lavoro [*A publication*]
Rass Med Sarda ... Rassegna Medica Sarda [*A publication*]
Rass Med Sarda Suppl ... Rassegna Medica Sarda. Supplemento [*A publication*]
Rass Med Sper ... Rassegna di Medicina. Sperimentale [*A publication*]
Rass Med Sper Suppl ... Rassegna di Medicina Sperimentale. Supplemento [*A publication*]
Rass Mens Clin Patol Ter Vita Prof Med Condotto Med Prat ... Rassegna Mensile di Clinica, di Patologia, di Terapia, e di Vita Professionale del Medico Condotto e del Medico Pratico [*A publication*]
Rass Min Metall Ital ... Rassegna Mineraria e Metallurgica Italiana [*A publication*]
Rass Mus ... Rassegna Musicale [*A publication*]
Rass Mus Curci ... Rassegna Musicale Curci [*A publication*]
Rass Neuropsichiatr Sci Affini ... Rassegna di Neuropsichiatria e Scienze Affini [*A publication*]
R Assoc Canad Educ Langue Franc ... Revue. Association Canadienne d'Education de Langue Francaise [*A publication*]
Rass Odontotec ... Rassegna Odontotecnica [*A publication*]
Rass Patol Appar Respir ... Rassegna di Patologia dell'Apparato Respiratorio [*A publication*]
Rass Psicol Gen Clin ... Rassegna di Psicologia Generale e Clinica [*A publication*]
RASSR .... Reliable Advanced Solid-State RADAR
Rass Serv Soc ... Rassegna di Servizio Sociale [*A publication*]
Rass Sind Quad ... Rassegna Sindacale. Quaderni [*A publication*]
RAS-STADES ... Records Association System - Standard Data Elements System   (MCD)
Rass Trimest Odontoiatr ... Rassegna Trimestrale di Odontoiatria [*A publication*]
RASSW ...... Radical Alliance of Social Service Workers   (EA)
RAssyr .... Revue d'Assyriologie [*A publication*]
RAST .... Radioallergosorbent Test [*Immunochemistry*]
Rast........... Rastell's Entries and Statutes [*England*]   (DLA)
RAST......... Recovery, Assist, Secure, and Traverse System [*Navy*]
RAST .... Reliability and System Test
RASTA .... Radiant Augmented Special Test Apparatus   (MCD)
RASTA .... Radio Station [*Coast Guard*]
RASTAC...... Random Access Storage and Control [*Data processing*]
RASTAD..... Random Access Storage and Display [*Data processing*]
RASTAS..... Radiating Site Target Acquisition System   (MCD)
Rasteniev'd Nauki ... Rasteniev'dni Nauki [*A publication*]
Rastenievod Nauk ... Rastenievudni Nauki [*A publication*]
Rastenievud Nauki ... Rastenievudni Nauki [*A publication*]

Rast Ent .... Rastell's Entries and Statutes   (DLA)
RaStEt....... Rassegna di Studi Etiopici [*Rome*] [*A publication*]
RASTI........ Rapid Speech Transition Index [*Acoustics*]
Rastit Belki ... Rastitel'nye Belki [*A publication*]
Rastit Krainego Sev Ee Osvoenie ... Rastitel'nost Krainego Severa i Ee Osvoenie [*A publication*]
Rastit Latv SSR ... Rastitel'nost Latviiskoi SSR [*A publication*]
Rastit Resur ... Rastitel'nye Resursy [*A publication*]
Rastit Zasht ... Rastitelna Zashtita [*A publication*]
Rastit Zasht Plant Prot ... Rastitelna Zashtita/Plant Protection [*A publication*]
Rast Nauki ... Rastenievadni Nauki [*A publication*]
RASTR ...... Recorded Acoustic Signal Target Repeater
Rast Resursy ... Rastitel'nye Resursy [*A publication*]
R Astron Soc Can Pr ... Royal Astronomical Society of Canada. Selected Papers and Proceedings [*A publication*]
Rast Zashch ... Rastitelna Zashchita [*A publication*]
RaSV .... Rasheed (Rat) Sarcoma Virus
RASyr........ Revue Archeologique Syrienne [*A publication*]
RAT .... Radiological Assessment Team [*Nuclear energy*]   (NRCH)
RAT .... Ram Air Temperature
RAT .... Ram Air Turbine   (MCD)
RAT .... Ranges, Ammunition, and Targets   (MCD)
RAT .... Rat Island [*Alaska*] [*Seismograph station code, US Geological Survey*] [*Closed*]   (SEIS)
RAT .... Rated
RAT .... Rating   (AABC)
RAT .... Ratio   (AAG)
RAT .... Rations [*Military*]   (AABC)
RAT .... Raynaud's Association Trust   (EA)
RAT .... Regular Associated Troupers   (EA)
RAT .... Reliability Assurance Test
RAT .... Remote Area Terminal
RAT .... Remote Associates Test [*Psychology*]
RAT .... Repeat Action Tablet [*Pharmacology*]
R & AT ...... Research and Advanced Technology
RAT .... Reseau des Amis de la Terre [*Network of Friends of the Earth*] [*French*]   (PPE)
RAT .... Reserve Auxiliary Transformer   (IEEE)
RAT .... Resistance Armee Tunisienne [*Tunisian Armed Resistance*]   (PD)
RAT .... Restricted Articles Tariff
RAT .... Right Anterior Thigh [*Anatomy*]
RAT .... Rocket-Assisted Torpedo [*Antisubmarine warfare*]
RATA......... Rankine Cycle Air Turboaccelerator
RA/TA....... Restricted Availability/Technical Availability   (NVT)
RATAC...... RADAR Analog Target Acquisition Computer
RATAC...... Raytheon Acoustic Telemetry and Control
RATAC...... Remote Airborne Television Display of Ground RADAR Coverage via TACAN   (CET)
RATAN...... RADAR and Television Aid to Navigation
RATAV...... RADAR Terrain Avoidance
RATBP...... Revised Appendix to Be Published   (MCD)
RATC....... Rate-Aided Tracking Computer
RATCC...... RADAR Air Traffic Control Center [*Later, RATCF*] [*Navy*]
RATCC...... Regional Air Traffic Control Center   (NATG)
RATCF ...... RADAR Air Traffic Control Facility [*Formerly, RATCC*] [*Navy*]   (FAAC)
RATCON .... RADAR Terminal Control
RATD......... RADAR Automatic Target Detection [*Military*]   (CAAL)
RATE......... Rate Analysis and Transportation Evaluation [*Student legal action organization*]
RATE......... Record and Tape Exchange   (EA)
RATE......... Remote Automatic Telemetry Equipment
RATEL....... Radiotelephone
RATEL....... Raytheon Automatic Test Equipment Language [*Data processing*]   (CSR)
RATELO .... Radiotelephone Operator   (AABC)
RATER ...... Response Analysis Tester [*NASA*]
RATES ...... Rapid Access Tariff Expediting Service [*Journal of Commerce, Inc.*] [*Database*]
RATEX..... Rational Expectations [*Economics*]
RATFOR.... Rational FORTRAN [*Data processing*]
RA-TFR.... RADAR Altimeter - Terrain Following RADAR   (MCD)
RATG .... Rabbit Antithymocyte Globulin [*Immunochemistry*]
RATG .... Radiotelegraph
RATHQ...... Rath Packing [*NASDAQ symbol*]   (NQ)
RATIG .... Robert A. Taft Institute of Government   (EA)
RATIO .... Radio Telescope in Orbit   (IEEE)
Ration Drug Ther ... Rational Drug Therapy [*A publication*]
Rat News Lett ... Rat News Letter [*A publication*]
RATO .... Rocket-Assisted Takeoff [*Aviation*]
RATOG...... Rocket-Assisted Takeoff Gear [*Aviation*]   (IEEE)
RATP......... Regie Autonome des Transports Parisiens [*Paris Transport Authority*]
RATR .... Reliability Abstracts and Technical Reviews [*NASA*]
RATS......... RADAR Acquisition and Tracking System   (MCD)
RATS......... RADAR Altimeter Target Simulator   (MCD)
RATS......... Ram Air Turbine System
RATS......... Rapid Area Transportation Support [*Air Force*]   (MCD)
RATS......... Rate and Track Subsystem

RATS......... Reconnaissance and Tactical Security [Teams] [Military]
RATS......... Remote Alarm Transmission System
RATS......... Remote Area Tactical [Location and Landing] System
RATS......... Remote Area Television Service   (ADA)
RATS......... Remote Area Terminal System
RATS......... Resolver Alignment Test Set
RATSC...... Rome Air Technical Service Command [Air Force]
RATSCAT .. RADAR Target Scatter [RADAR program]
RATSEC.... Robert A. Taft Sanitary Engineering Center   (AABC)
Rat Sel Cas ... Rattigan's Select Hindu Law Cases   (DLA)
RATT......... Radio Airborne Teletype   (MCD)
RATT......... Radioteletype
RATTC...... Radio and Teletype Control Center
Rattigan ..... Rattigan's Select Hindu Law Cases [India]   (DLA)
Ratt LC...... Rattigan's Leading Cases on Hindu Law   (DLA)
Rat Unrep Cr ... Ratanlal's Unreported Criminal Cases [India]   (DLA)
RAU......... Railway African Union
RAU......... Recurrent Aphthous Ulceration [Medicine]
RAU......... Regional Acquisition Unit [NASA]   (NASA)
RAU......... Remote Acquisition Unit [NASA]   (NASA)
RAU......... River Assault Unit [Navy]
RAug .... Revue Augustinienne [A publication]
RAUIC .... Repair Activity Unit Identification Code   (MCD)
RAUIS .... Remote Acquisition Unit Interconnecting Station
            [NASA]   (NASA)
RAUK .... Rear-Admiral of the United Kingdom [Navy] [British]   (ROG)
Raumforsch u-Ordnung ... Raumforschung und Raumordnung [A
            publication]
R Aust Chem Inst J Proc ... Royal Australian Chemical Institute. Journal and
            Proceedings [A publication]
R Aust Chem Inst J Proc Suppl ... Royal Australian Chemical Institute.
            Journal and Proceedings. Supplement [A publication]
R Aust Chem Inst Proc ... Royal Australian Chemical Institute. Proceedings
            [A publication]
R Aust Plann Inst J ... RAPIJ: Royal Australian Planning Institute. Journal [A
            publication]
RAUT......... Republic Automotive Parts [NASDAQ symbol]   (NQ)
RAut & L..... Revue des Auteurs et des Livres [A publication]
RAuv .... Revue d'Auvergne [A publication]
R Aux AF .... Royal Auxiliary Air Force [Formerly, AAF] [British]
RAV .... Cravo Norte [Colombia] [Airport symbol]   (OAG)
RAV .... Ramm Venture [Vancouver Stock Exchange symbol]
RAV .... Random Access Viewer
RAV .... Raven Industries, Inc. [American Stock Exchange symbol]
RAV .... Ravensburg [Federal Republic of Germany] [Seismograph
            station code, US Geological Survey]   (SEIS)
RAV .... Ravine, PA [Location identifier] [FAA]   (FAAL)
RAV .... Reduced Availability   (MCD)
RAV .... Remotely Augmented Vehicle [Aircraft]
RAV .... Restricted Availability   (NG)
RAVC .... Royal Army Veterinary Corps [Formerly, AVC] [British]
RAVE........ RADAR Acquisition Visual-Tracking Equipment
RAVE........ Random Access Video Editing [Computerized film editing]
RAVE........ Random Access Viewing Equipment
RAVE........ Readjustment Assistance Act 74 for Vietnam Era
            Veterans   (OICC)
RAVE........ Research Aircraft for the Visual Environment [Helicopters]
            [Army]
RAVEC...... RADAR Vector
RAVEN...... Ranging and Velocity Navigation
RAVES...... Rapid Aerospace Vehicle Evaluation System [Grumman Corp.]
RAVIR........ RADAR Video Recorder   (NVT)
RAVU .... Radiosonde Analysis and Verification Unit
RAW .... Airway Resistance [Medicine]
RAW .... Arawa [Papua New Guinea] [Airport symbol]   (OAG)
RAW .... Rapid American Withdrawal [Antiwar march sponsored by
            Vietnam Veterans Against the War]   (EA)
Raw .... Rawle's Pennsylvania Reports [5 vols.]   (DLA)
RAW .... Read Alter Wire
RAW .... Read after Write
RAW .... Ready and Waiting [or Willing] [Slang]
RAW .... Reconnaissance Attack Wing [Navy]   (NVT)
RAW .... Record of the Arab World [Beirut] [A publication]
RAW .... Redmond, OR [Location identifier] [FAA]   (FAAL)
RAW .... Reliability Assurance Warranty   (MCD)
RAW .... Rent-a-Wreck Industries Corp. [Vancouver Stock Exchange
            symbol]
RAW .... Return America to Work [Also translated as "Reaganomics
            Ain't Working"] [UAW bumper sticker slogan]
RAW .... Rifleman's Assault Weapon   (MCD)
RAW .... Right Attack Wing [Women's lacrosse position]
RAW .... Rural American Women [An association]   (EA)
RAWA........ Rail-Water [Shipping]
RAWA........ Renaissance Artists and Writers Association   (EA)
RAWARA.... Rail-Water-Rail [Shipping]
RAWARC.... RADAR and Warning Coordination [Teletypewriter circuit]
RAWB........ Railroad and Airline Wage Board [Terminated, 1953]
Raw Eq...... Rawle's Equity in Pennsylvania   (DLA)
RAWIE....... Radio Weather Intercept Element
RAWIN....... RADAR Wind [Upper air observation]
RAWIND..... RADAR Wind [Upper air observation]

RAWINDS... RADAR Wind Sounding [Upper air observation]   (MSA)
RAWINS ..... RADAR Winds [Upper air observation]
RAWINSONDE ... RADAR Wind Sounding and Radiosonde [Upper air
            observation]
Rawle .... Rawle's Pennsylvania Supreme Court Reports [1828-
            35]   (DLA)
Rawle Const US ... Rawle on the Constitution of the United States   (DLA)
Rawle Cov ... Rawle on Covenants for Title   (DLA)
Rawle Pen & W ... Rawle, Penrose, and Watts' Pennsylvania Reports [1828-
            40]   (DLA)
Rawl Mun Corp ... Rawlinson's Municipal Corporations [10th ed.]
            [1910]   (DLA)
Raw Materials Survey Res Rept ... Raw Materials Survey. Resource Report
            [A publication]
Raw Mater Rep ... Raw Materials Report [Sweden] [A publication]
RAWO .... Reliability Assurance Work Order   (MCD)
RAWP........ Resource Allocation Working Party [British]
RAWS....... RADAR Altimeter Warning Set   (MCD)
RAWS....... Remote Area Weather Station
RAWS....... Remote Automatic Weather Station
RAWX........ Returned Account Weather [Aviation]   (FAAC)
RAX .... Remote Access [Data processing] [Telecommunications]
RAX .... Rio Alto Exploration Ltd. [Toronto Stock Exchange symbol]
RAX .... Rosenbalm Aviation, Inc. [Ypsilanti, MI] [FAA
            designator]   (FAAC)
RAX .... Rural Automatic Exchange   (DEN)
RAXR......... Rax Restaurants, Inc. [NASDAQ symbol]   (NQ)
RAXRA....... Radex Rundschau (Austria) [A publication]
RAY .... Rayrock Yellowknife Resources [Toronto Stock Exchange
            symbol]
RAY .... Raytech Corp. [NYSE symbol]
RAY .... Rothesay [Scotland] [Airport symbol]   (OAG)
RAY .... Royale Airlines, Inc. [Shreveport, LA] [FAA designator]   (FAAC)
RAYCI .... Raytheon Controlled Inventory [Data processing]
RAY-COM ... Raytheon Communications Equipment [Citizens band radio]
RAYDAC .... Raytheon Digital Automatic Computer   (MUGU)
Rayden .... Rayden on Divorce   (DLA)
RAYDIST .... Ray-Path Distance   (MUGU)
RAYM........ Raymond Corp. [NASDAQ symbol]   (NQ)
Raym.......... [Sir T.] Raymond's King's Bench Reports [83 English Reprint]
            [1660-84]   (DLA)
Ray Med Jur ... Ray's Medical Jurisprudence of Insanity   (DLA)
Raym Ent ... [Lord] Raymond's Entries   (DLA)
Raym Ld..... Lord Raymond's English King's Bench Reports [3 vols.]   (DLA)
Raymond ... Raymond's Reports [81-89 Iowa]   (DLA)
Raymond W Brink Selected Math Papers ... Raymond W Brink Selected
            Mathematical Papers [A publication]
Raym Sir T ... [Sir Thomas] Raymond's English King's Bench Reports   (DLA)
Raym T....... Sir Thomas Raymond's English King's Bench Reports   (DLA)
Rayn .... Rayner's English Tithe Cases [3 vols.]   (DLA)
Rayn Ti Cas ... Rayner's English Tithe Cases [1575-1782]   (DLA)
RAYOF .... Raymac Oil Corp. [NASDAQ symbol]   (NQ)
Rayon........ Rayon and Synthetic Textiles [A publication]
Rayon J ...... Rayon Journal [A publication]
Rayon J Cellul Fibers ... Rayon Journal and Cellulose Fibers [A publication]
Rayonnem Ionis ... Rayonnements Ionisants [A publication]
Rayonnem Ionis Tech Mes Prot ... Rayonnements Ionisants. Techniques de
            Mesures et de Protection [A publication]
Rayon Rev ... Rayon Revue [A publication]
Rayon Synth Yarn J ... Rayon and Synthetic Yarn Journal [A publication]
Rayon Text Mon ... Rayon Textile Monthly [A publication]
Ray Sir T .... [Sir T.] Raymond's English King's Bench Reports [83 English
            Reprint] [1660-84]   (DLA)
RAYSISTOR ... Raytheon Resistor [Electro-optical control device]
RAYSPAN ... Raytheon Spectrum Analyzer
RAY-TEL.... Raytheon Telephone [Citizens band radio]
Ray Ti Cas ... Rayner's English Tithe Cases [1575-1782]   (DLA)
RAZ .... Rolled Alloyed Zinc
RAZEL........ Range, Azimuth, and Elevation
RazFe......... Razon y Fe [Madrid] [A publication]
Raziskave Stud Kmetijski Inst Slov ... Raziskave in Studije-Kmetijski Institut
            Slovenije [A publication]
RAZON....... Range and Azimuth Only
RAZPE....... Resident ARGMA [Army Rocket and Guided Missile Agency]
            Zeus Project Engineer   (AAG)
Razpr Slov Akad Znan Umet IV ... Razprave. Slovenska Akademija Znanosti
            in Umetnosti. IV [A publication]
Razrab Ehkspl Gazov Gazokondens Mestorozhd ... Razrabotka i
            Ehksplutatsiya Gazovykh i Gazokondensatnykh
            Mestorozhdenij [A publication]
Razrab Mestorozhd Polezn Iskop (Kiev) ... Razrabotka Mestorozhdenii
            Poleznykh Iskopaemykh (Kiev) [A publication]
Razrab Mestorozhd Polezn Iskop (Tiflis) ... Razrabotka Mestorozhdenii
            Poleznykh Iskopaemykh (Tiflis) [A publication]
Razrab Neft Gazov Mestorozhd ... Razrabotka Neftyanykh i Gazovykh
            Mestorozhdenii [A publication]
Razrab Rudn Mestorozhd ... Razrabotka Rudnykh Mestorozhdenii
            [Ukrainian SSR] [A publication]
Razred Mat Fiz Teh Vede Dela ... Razred za Matematicne. Fizikalne in
            Tehnicne Vede Dela [Ljubljana]
RAZS......... Rolled Alloyed Zinc Sheet

Raz SAZU... Razprave Razreda za Filoloske in Literarne vede Slovenske Akademije Znanoste in Umetnosti [*A publication*]
Razved Geofiz ... Razvedochnaya Geofizika [*A publication*]
Razved Nedr ... Razvedka Nedr [*USSR*] [*A publication*]
Razved i Okhr Nedr ... Razvedka i Okhrana Nedr [*A publication*]
Razved Okhr Nedr ... Razvedka i Okhrana Nedr [*A publication*]
Razved Razrab Neft Gazov Mestorozhd ... Razvedka i Razrabotka Neftyanykh i Gazovykh Mestorozhdenii [*A publication*]
RB............. RADAR Beacon
R/B............ Radio Beacon
RB............. Radio Bearing   (DEN)
RB............. Radio Brenner [*Radio network*] [*West Germany*]
RB............. Rate Beacon   (AAG)
RB............. Rated Boost
RB............. Ration Book
RB............. Reactor Building   (NRCH)
RB............. Read Back [*Communications*]   (FAAC)
RB............. Read Backward
RB............. Read Buffer
RB............. Reading & Bates Corp. [*NYSE symbol*]
RB............. Recherches Bibliques [*A publication*]
RB............. Reconnaissance Bomber
RB............. Recovery Beacon
R & B .... Red and Blue   (KSC)
RB............. Red Book [*Full name is "Drug Topics Red Book," a pharmacist's guide*] [*A publication*]
RB............. Red Brigades [*Revolutionary group*] [*Italy*]
RB............. Reentry Body
RB............. Regular Budget [*United Nations*]
RB............. Relative Bearing [*Navigation*]
RB............. Relay Block   (MSA)
RB............. Religious Broadcasting [*A publication*]
R & B .... Remington and Ballinger's Code [*1910*]   (DLA)
RB............. Renaut's Bodies [*Neurology*]
RB............. Renegotiation Board [*Terminated, 1979*] [*Federal government*]
RB............. Repeated Back [*Communications*]   (FAAC)
RB............. Report Bibliography
RB............. Request Block
RB............. Rescue Boat   (FAAC)
RB............. Research Bulletin
RB............. Reserve Bank   (ADA)
RB............. Resistance Brazing
RB............. Restricted Bulletin
Rb............. Retinoblastoma [*Oncology*]
RB............. Retractable Boom
RB............. Retraining Benefits   (OICC)
RB............. Return to Bias
RB............. Reverse Blocked
RBT............. Revision Block   (MSA)
RB............. Revista Bibliotecilor [*Bucharest*] [*A publication*]
RB............. Revue Benedictine [*A publication*]
RB............. Revue Biblique [*A publication*]
RB............. Revue Bossuet [*A publication*]
R & B .... Rhythm and Blues [*Music*]
RB............. Rich Bitch [*Slang*]
RB............. Rifle Brigade
RB............. Right Buttock [*Anatomy*]
RB............. Right Fullback [*Soccer*]
RB............. Rigid Boat
RB............. Rigid Body
RB............. Ritzaus Bureau [*Press agency*] [*Denmark*]
RB............. Rivista Biblica [*Rome*] [*A publication*]
RB............. Road Bend
RB............. Roast Beef [*Restaurant slang*]
RB............. Rocket Branch   (AAG)
RB............. Rohon-Beard (Cells) [*Neurology*]
RB............. Rollback [*Telecommunications*]   (TEL)
RB............. Rollback Disability Claims [*Social Security Administration*]   (OICC)
RB............. Roller Bearing
RB............. Roman-British
R & B .... Room and Board
RB............. Rose Bengal [*A dye*]
RB............. Royal Burgh
RB............. Rubber Band   (ADA)
RB............. Rubber Base [*Technical drawings*]
Rb............. Rubidium [*Chemical element*]
RB............. Run Back [*Typography*]
RB............. Running Back [*Football*]
RB............. Rural Bank   (ADA)
RB............. Russell Bodies [*Medicine*]
RB............. Syrian Arab Airlines [*Syrian Arab Republic*] [*ICAO designator*]   (FAAC)
RBa............. Barrington Public Library, Barrington, RI [*Library symbol*] [*Library of Congress*]   (LCLS)
RBA............. Rabat [*Morocco*] [*Seismograph station code, US Geological Survey*]   (SEIS)
RBA............. Rabat [*Morocco*] [*Airport symbol*]   (OAG)
RBA............. RADAR Beacon Antenna
RBA............. Radial Blanket Assembly [*Nuclear energy*]   (NRCH)
RBA............. Radio Beacon Array

RBA............. Raisin Bargaining Association   (EA)
RBA............. Ranger Battalions Association   (EA)
RBA............. Recovery Beacon Antenna [*NASA*]   (KSC)
RBA............. Reentry Body Assembly
RBA............. Rehoboth Baster Association [*Namibian*]   (PPW)
RBA............. Relative Binding Affinity [*Chemistry*]
RBA............. Relative Byte Address [*Data processing*]   (MCD)
RBA............. Religious Booksellers Association [*Oak Park, IL*]   (EA)
RBA............. Rescue Breathing Apparatus
RBA............. Retail Bakers of America [*Hyattsville, MD*]   (EA)
RBA............. Retired Bankers Association   (EA)
RBA............. Revista de Bellas Artes [*A publication*]
RBA............. Revue Belge d'Archeologie et d'Histoire de l'Art [*A publication*]
RBA............. Roadside Business Association   (EA)
RBA............. Rotary Beam Antenna
RBA............. Rotor Blade Antenna
RBA............. Royal Society of British Architects
RBAA......... Royal Society of British Artists
RBAA......... Revue Belge d'Art et d'Archeologie [*A publication*]
RBAAP....... Riverbank Army Ammunition Plant   (AABC)
RBaB......... Barrington College, Barrington, RI [*Library symbol*] [*Library of Congress*]   (LCLS)
RBAB......... Revue des Bibliotheques et des Archives de la Belgique [*A publication*]
RBACB....... Revista Brasileira de Analises Clinicas [*A publication*]
RBAF......... Royal Belgian Air Force
RBAHA....... Revue Belge d'Archeologie et d'Histoire de l'Art [*A publication*]
RBAL......... Reprocessing Building Analytical Laboratory   (NRCH)
RBAM........ Revista. Biblioteca, Archivo, y Museo del Ayuntamiento de Madrid [*A publication*]
RBAMM...... Revista. Biblioteca, Archivo, y Museo del Ayuntamiento de Madrid [*A publication*]
RBAN .... Rainier Bancorp [*NASDAQ symbol*]   (NQ)
R Banco Republ ... Revista. Banco de la Republica [*A publication*]
RBAP......... Repetitive Bursts of Action Potential [*Electrophysiology*]
RBAPA....... Revue du Bois et de Ses Applications [*A publication*]
RBArch ..... Revue Belge d'Archeologie et d'Histoire de l'Art [*A publication*]
RBArg .... Revista Biblica con Seccion Liturgica [*Buenos Aires*] [*A publication*]
RBAUS ...... Romanian Baptist Association of United States   (EA)
RBA WWII .. Ranger Battalions Association World War II   (EA)
RBB .... Reference Books Bulletin [*A publication*]
RBB .... Revue Bibliographique Belge [*A publication*]
RBBB......... Right Bundle-Branch Block [*Cardiology*]
RBBRD ...... Revista de Biblioteconomia de Brasilia [*A publication*]
RBBS......... Remote Bulletin Board System [*For IBM computers*] [*Telecommunications*]
RBBSB ...... Right Bundle-Branch System Block [*Cardiology*]
RBBT......... Rebabbit
RBC........... Radio Beam Communications
RBC........... Rail-Borne Crane [*British*]
RBC........... Reactive Bias Circuit   (MCD)
RBC........... Red Badge of Courage [*An association*]   (EA)
RBC........... Red Blood Cell [*or Corpuscle*] [*Medicine*]
RBC........... Red Blood Count [*Medicine*]
RBC........... Redundant Battery Charger   (KSC)
RBC........... Regal-Beloit Corporation [*American Stock Exchange symbol*]
RBC........... Regional Blood Center [*Red Cross*]
RBC........... Remote Balance Control
RBC........... Retortable Barrier Container [*For food*]
RBC........... Return Beam Camera
RBC........... Revista Bimestre Cubana [*A publication*]
RBC........... Rhodesia Broadcasting Corporation
RBC........... Rio Blanco [*Colorado*] [*Seismograph station code, US Geological Survey*] [*Closed*]   (SEIS)
RBC........... Roller Bearing Corporation   (MCD)
RBC........... Rotating Beam Ceilometer [*Aviation*]
RBC........... Rotating Biological Contractors [*Processing equipment*]
RBC........... Royal Bank of Canada [*UTLAS symbol*]
RBCA......... Royal British Colonial Society of Artists
RBCA......... Rhodes Bantam Class Association   (EA)
RBCalb...... Revista Biblica. Villa Calbada [*Argentina*] [*A publication*]
R du B Can ... Revue. Barreau Canadien   (DLA)
RBCC......... Reentry Body Coordination Committee
RBCCW...... Reactor Building Closed Cooling Water   (NRCH)
RBCM........ Red Blood Cell Mass [*in circulation*]
RBCNO....... Rotating Beam Ceilometer Inoperative [*Aviation*]   (FAAC)
RBCR........ Reprocessing Building Control Room [*Nuclear energy*]   (NRCH)
RBCS .... Radio Beam Communications Set
RBCS .... Reactor Building Cooling System [*Nuclear energy*]   (NRCH)
RBCU .... Reactor Building Cooling Unit [*Nuclear energy*]   (NRCH)
RBCV .... Red Blood Cell Volume [*Hematology*]
RBCWS ...... Reactor Building Cooling Water System   (IEEE)
RBD........... Dallas, TX [*Location identifier*] [*FAA*]   (FAAL)
RBD........... Refined, Bleached, and Deodorized [*Vegetable oil technology*]
RBD........... Reliable Block Diagram   (MCD)
RBD........... Revista Bibliografica y Documental [*Madrid*] [*A publication*]
RBD........... Rice Blast Disease [*Fungal disease of crop plants*]
RBD........... Right Border of Dullness [*Cardiology*]
RBD........... Rubbermaid, Inc. [*NYSE symbol*]
RBDE......... RADAR Bright Display Equipment [*FAA*]

RBdeF .... Revista Brasileira de Filosofia [*A publication*]
RBDNRQ .... Received but Did Not Return Questionnaire   (AABC)
RBDP.......... Rocket Booster Development Program [*Aerospace*]   (AAG)
RBDS.......... RADAR Bomb Directing Systems
RBE .... Bassett, NE [*Location identifier*] [*FAA*]   (FAAL)
RBE .... Radiation Biological Equivalent
RBE .... Red Ball Express [*Military*]
RBE .... Relative Biological Effectiveness [*or Efficiency*] [*of stated types of radiation*]
RBE .... Remote Batch Entry   (CMD)
RBE .... Renabie Mines (1981) Ltd. [*Toronto Stock Exchange symbol*]
RBE .... Replacement Battery Equipment
RBEB.......... Ribbon Bridge Erection Boat   (MCD)
RBEC.......... Roller Bearing Engineers Committee   (EA)
RBEDT .... Reactor Building Equipment Drain Tank   (NRCH)
R Belge Archeol ... Revue Belge d'Archeologie et d'Histoire de l'Art [*A publication*]
R Belge Dr Int ... Revue Belge de Droit International [*A publication*]
R Belge Mus ... Revue Belge de Musicologie [*A publication*]
R Belge Philol & Hist ... Revue Belge de Philologie et d'Histoire [*A publication*]
R Belge Securite Soc ... Revue Belge de Securite Sociale [*A publication*]
R Belge Secur Soc ... Revue Belge de Securite Sociale [*A publication*]
RBelPhH..... Revue Belge de Philogogie et d'Histoire [*Brussels*] [*A publication*]
RBen .... Revue Benedictine [*A publication*]
RB/ER .... Reduced Blast/Enhanced Radiation
RBESI......... Reactor Building Exhaust System Isolation   (NRCH)
RBF .... Regional Blood Flow [*Physiology*]
RBF .... Remote Batch Facility
RBF .... Renal Blood Flow [*Medicine*]
RBF .... Retarded Bomb Fuze
RBF .... Revista Brasileira de Filosofia [*A publication*]
RBF .... Revista Brasileira de Folclore [*A publication*]
RBF .... Roberson, Fred, Louisville KY [*STAC*]
RBFC.......... Razzy Bailey Fan Club   (EA)
RBFC.......... Retract Before Firing Contractor   (NG)
RBFI .... Revista Brasileira de Filologia [*A publication*]
RBFilol .... Revista Brasileira de Filologia [*A publication*]
RBFPP....... Rocket Booster Fuel Pod Pickup   (MUGU)
RBFSA .... Revista Brasileira de Fisica [*A publication*]
RBG........... British Guiana Reports of Opinions   (DLA)
RBG........... Ransburg Corp. [*American Stock Exchange symbol*]
RBG........... Right Buccal Ganglion [*Dentistry*]
RBG........... Roseburg, OR [*Location identifier*] [*FAA*]   (FAAL)
RBGCA....... Revista Brasileira de Geociencias [*A publication*]
RBGd.......... Rocznik Biblioteki Gdanskiej Pan [*A publication*]
RBGS .... Radio Beacon Guidance System   (AAG)
RBH .... Regimental Beachhead [*Army*]
RBHA .... Rotor Blade Homing Antenna
RBHB.......... Red and Black Horizontal Bands [*Navigation markers*]
RBHGPV.... Rheinische Beitraege und Hilfsbuecher zur Germanischen Philologie und Volkskunde [*A publication*]
RBHPC ...... Rutherford B. Hayes Presidential Center   (EA)
RBHPF....... Reactor Building Hydrogen Purge Fan   (IEEE)
RBHS......... Reactor Building Heating System [*Nuclear energy*]   (NRCH)
RBI .... Rabi [*Fiji*] [*Airport symbol*]   (OAG)
RBI .... RADAR Blip Identification Message
RBI .... Radio Berlin International
RBI .... Railway Benevolent Institution [*British*]
RBI .... Range Bearing Indicator   (MCD)
RBI .... RB Industries, Inc. [*NYSE symbol*]
RBI .... Recherches Bibliques [*A publication*]
RBi............. Revue Biblique [*A publication*]
RBI .... Revue Biblique Internationale [*A publication*]
RBI .... Ripple-Blanking Input   (IEEE)
RBI .... Rivista Biblica Italiana [*Rome*] [*A publication*]
RBI .... Root Beer Institute [*Defunct*]
RBI .... Runs Batted In [*Baseball*]
RBIB .... Reserve Bank of India. Bulletin [*Bombay*] [*A publication*]
RBib........... Revue Biblique [*A publication*]
RBibIT .... Rivista Biblica Italiana [*Rome*] [*A publication*]
RBibl .... Revue des Bibliotheques [*A publication*]
R Bible ...... Revue Biblique [*A publication*]
R Biblio Brasilia ... Revista de Biblioteconomia de Brasilia [*A publication*]
R Bibl Nac (Cuba) ... Revista. Biblioteca Nacional de Cuba [*A publication*]
RBiCalz...... Revista Biblica. Rafael Calzada [*Argentina*] [*A publication*]   (BJA)
RBIF .... Red Basic Intelligence File   (MCD)
RBiIt .... Rivista Biblica Italiana [*Rome*] [*A publication*]
R Bimestr Inform Banque Maroc Com Ext ... Revue Bimestrielle d'Informations. Banque Marocaine du Commerce Exterieur [*A publication*]
RBJ............ Rebun [*Japan*] [*Airport symbol*] [*Obsolete*]   (OAG)
RBJ............ Tucson, AZ [*Location identifier*] [*FAA*]   (FAAL)
RBK........... Reebok International Ltd. [*NYSE symbol*]
RBK .... Right Bank
RBK & C .... Royal Borough of Kensington and Chelsea [*England*]
RBKr.......... Rocznik Biblioteki Pan w Krakowie [*A publication*]
RBL .... Radiation Biology Laboratory [*Smithsonian Institution*]
RBL .... Range and Bearing Launch [*Navy*]   (CAAL)

RBL .... Rebroadcast Link [*Aerial*]
RBL .... Red Bluff, CA [*Location identifier*] [*FAA*]   (FAAL)
RBL .... Reid's Base Line [*Neuroanatomy*]
RBL .... Revue Bleue [*A publication*]
RBL .... Rifled Breech-Loading [*Gun*]
RBL .... Right Buttock Line   (MCD)
RBL .... Rio Blanco Resources Limited [*Vancouver Stock Exchange symbol*]
RBL .... Ruble [*Monetary unit in the USSR*]
RBL .... Ruch Biblijny i Liturgiczny   (BJA)
R Black Pol Econ ... Review of Black Political Economy [*A publication*]
R Black Pol Economy ... Review of Black Political Economy [*A publication*]
RBLI .... Rassegna Bibliografica della Letteratura Italiana [*A publication*]
RBLS .... River Bend Library System [*Library network*]
RBM .... Range Betting Method
RBM .... Real-Time Batch Monitor [*Xerox Corp.*]
RBM .... Regional Bone Mass
R-B-M .... Reinforced Brick Masonry
RBM .... Remote Batch Module
RBM .... Resistance to Bending Moment [*Automotive engineering*]
RBM .... Retractor Bulb Motoneuron [*Neurology*]
RBM .... Revue Belge de Musicologie [*A publication*]
RBM .... Rod-Block Monitor [*Nuclear energy*]   (NRCH)
RBMA .... Radiologists Business Managers Association [*Kansas City, KS*]   (EA)
RBME .... Richard [*Cragun*], Birgit [*Keil*], Marcia [*Haydee*], Egon [*Madsen*] [*In ballet title, "Initials RBME." Refers to the four starring dancers.*]
RBML .... Repertorium fuer Biblische und Morgenlaendische Litteratur [*Leipzig*] [*A publication*]
RBM (Rev Eur Biotechnol Med) ... RBM (Revue Europeenne de Biotechnologie Medicale) [*A publication*]
RBMT .... Retrospective Bibliographies on Magnetic Tape   (NASA)
RBMU........ Regions Beyond Missionary Union [*Later, Regions Beyond Missionary Union International*]   (EA)
RBMus ...... Revue Belge de Musicologie [*A publication*]
RBN .... Brown University, Providence, RI [*OCLC symbol*]   (OCLC)
RBN .... PTS [*Predicasts*] Regional Business News [*Cleveland, OH*] [*Database*] [*Information service*]   (EISS)
RBN .... Radiobeacon [*Maps and charts*]
RBN .... Random Block Number [*Data processing*]
R Bn.......... Red Beacon [*Nautical charts*]
RBN .... Regional Business News [*Predicasts, Inc.*] [*Database*]
RBN .... Retrobulbar Neuritis [*Medicine*]
RBN .... Revista de Bibliografia Nacional [*Madrid*] [*A publication*]
RBN .... Revue Belge de Numismatique [*A publication*]
RBN .... Ribbon   (MSA)
RBN .... Rybnik [*Poland*] [*Seismograph station code, US Geological Survey*]   (SEIS)
RBNC .... Revista. Biblioteca Nacional de Cuba [*A publication*]
RBNH .... Revista. Biblioteca Nacional de Cuba [*A publication*]
RBNS......... Revue Belge de Numismatique et de Sigillographie [*A publication*]
RBO........... Ripple-Blanking Output   (IEEE)
RBO........... Russian Brotherhood Organization of the United States of America
RBOA .... Richardson Boat Owners Association   (EA)
RBOC .... Rapid Bloom Offboard Chaff [*Navy ship system*]
RBOC .... Regional Bell Operating Company
RBOF......... Receiving Basins for Off-Site Fuels [*AEC*]
R Bolsa Comer Rosario ... Revista. Bolsa de Comercio de Rosario [*A publication*]
RBOT......... Robotics Information [*Cincinnati Milacron Industries, Inc.*] [*Cincinnati, OH*] [*Database*] [*No longer offered*]
RBOT......... Robotics Information [*EIC/Intelligence, Inc.*] [*New York, NY*] [*Information service*]   (EISS)
R Bot Garden Edinb Notes ... Royal Botanical Garden of Edinburgh. Notes [*A publication*]
RBOUSA .... Russian Brotherhood Organization of the United States of America   (EA)
RBP .... Raba Raba [*Papua New Guinea*] [*Airport symbol*]   (OAG)
RBP .... Ratio Balance Panel
RBP .... Ration Breakdown Point   (AABC)
RBP .... Reactor Building Protection   (NRCH)
RBP .... Registered Business Programer [*Offered earlier by Data Processing Management Association, now discontinued*]   (IEEE)
RBP .... Retinol-Binding Protein [*Biochemistry*]
RBP .... Retractable Bow Propeller
RBP .... Return Battery Pack   (KSC)
RBP .... Riboflavin-Binding Protein [*Biochemistry*]
RBP .... Rocket Branch Panel   (AAG)
RBPCA .... Rare Breeds Poultry Club of America   (EA)
RBPCase.... Ribulose-Biphosphate Carboxylase [*Also, RUBISCO*] [*An enzyme*]
RBPD......... Religious Book Publishing Division [*of Association of American Publishers*] [*Superseded by RPG*]
RBPh .... Revue Belge de Philologie et d'Histoire [*A publication*]
RBPhil .... Revue Belge de Philologie et d'Histoire [*A publication*]

RBPMA......	Revue Belge de Pathologie et de Medecine Experimentale [*A publication*]
RBPP.........	Rotor Burst Protection Program [*NASA*]
RBQ...........	Rurrenabaque [*Bolivia*] [*Airport symbol*] (OAG)
RBQSA.......	Revista Brasileira de Quimica (Sao Paulo) [*A publication*]
RBques	Revue des Bibliotheques [*A publication*]
RBR	RADAR Boresight Range (KSC)
RBR	Rambler Exploration [*Vancouver Stock Exchange symbol*]
RBR	Refracted Bottom-Reflected Ray
RBR	Renegotiation Board Regulation [*or Ruling*]
RBr	Revista Brasiliense [*A publication*]
RBR	Rio Branco [*Brazil*] [*Airport symbol*] (OAG)
RBr	Rogers Free Library, Bristol, RI [*Library symbol*] [*Library of Congress*] (LCLS)
RBR	Rotor Blade RADAR
RBR	Rubber
rbr	Rubricator [*MARC relator code*] [*Library of Congress*]
R Bras Econ ...	Revista Brasileira de Economia [*A publication*]
R Bras Estatistica ...	Revista Brasileira de Estatistica [*A publication*]
R Brasil Econ ...	Revista Brasileira de Economia [*A publication*]
R Brasil Estatist ...	Revista Brasileira de Estatistica [*A publication*]
R Brasil Estud Polit ...	Revista Brasileira de Estudos Politicos [*A publication*]
R Brasil Geogr ...	Revista Brasileira de Geografia [*A publication*]
R Brasil Polit Int ...	Revista Brasileira de Politica Internacional [*A publication*]
RBRC	RB Robot Corporation [*NASDAQ symbol*] (NQ)
RBrHi........	Bristol Historical and Preservation Society, Bristol, RI [*Library symbol*] [*Library of Congress*] (LCLS)
RBRI	Reference Book Review Index
RBRIZED....	Rubberized
RBRJ	Revista Brasileira (Rio De Janeiro) [*A publication*]
RBRLA	Revue Bryologique et Lichenologique [*A publication*]
RBROTAL...	Resource Based, Research Oriented Teaching and Learning (ADA)
RBRRS	Rhythm and Blues Rock and Roll Society (EA)
RBrRW	Roger Williams College, Bristol, RI [*Library symbol*] [*Library of Congress*] (LCLS)
R Bryol & Lichenol ...	Revue Bryologique et Lichenologique [*A publication*]
RBS	RADAR Beacon Sequencer
RBS	RADAR Beacon System
RBS	RADAR Beam Sharpening
RBS	RADAR Bomb Scoring
RBS	RADAR Bombardment System (NATG)
RBS	RADAR Bombsight
RBS	Random Barrage System
RBS	Rare Books Section [*Association of College and Research Libraries*]
RBS	Reactor Building Spray [*Nuclear energy*] (NRCH)
RBS	Recoverable Booster System
RBS	Reformer's Book Shelf [*A publication*]
RBS	Regulae Benedicti Studia [*A publication*]
RBS	Remote Batch System
RBS	Remote Battle System
RBS	Research for Better Schools
RBS	River Bend Station [*Nuclear energy*] (NRCH)
RBS	Roberts, IL [*Location identifier*] [*FAA*] (FAAL)
RBS	Royal Society of British Sculptors
RBS	Rutherford Backscattering [*For study of surfaces*]
RBSA........	[*Member of the*] Royal Birmingham Society of Artists [*British*]
RBSC	RADAR Bomb Scoring Central (NG)
RBSc	Royal Society of British Sculptors
RBSCD......	Rare Book and Special Collections Division [*Library of Congress*]
RBSE........	RADAR Beam Sharpening Element
RBSF........	Retail Branch Stores Forum [*Alexandria, VA*] (EA)
RBSL	Regensburger Beitrage zur Deutschen Sprach- und Literaturwissenschaft [*A publication*]
RBSN........	Robeson Industries Corp. [*NASDAQ symbol*] (NQ)
RBSR.........	Reprocessing Building (Cable) Spreading Room [*Nuclear energy*] (NRCH)
RBSRA	Red Berkshire Swine Record Association (EA)
RBSS........	Recoverable Booster Support System
RBST........	Remedial and Basic Skills Training (OICC)
R & B Supp ...	Remington and Ballinger's Code, Supplement [*1913*] (DLA)
RBT	Radial Beam Tube [*Electronics*]
RBT	Rainbow Trout
RBT	Random Breath Testing (ADA)
RBT	Rational Behavior Therapy
RBT	Remote Batch Terminal
RBT	Resistance Bulb Thermometer
RBT	Reviews in Biochemical Toxicology [*Elsevier Book Series*] [*A publication*]
RBT	Ribbon Bridge Transporter (MCD)
RBT	Ringback Tone [*Telecommunications*] (TEL)
RBT	Rough Blanking Template (MCD)
RBT	Rutland Biotech Ltd. [*Vancouver Stock Exchange symbol*]
RBTA........	Road Builders Training Association (EA)
RBTE........	Replacement Battery Terminal Equipment
RBTL	RADAR Beacon Tracking Level [*FAA*]
RBTNA	Revista Brasileira de Tecnologia [*A publication*]
RBTS.........	Rider Block Tagline System [*Military*] (CAAL)
RBTWT......	Radial Beam Traveling Wave Tube [*Electronics*]
RBU...........	Red Butte Canyon [*Utah*] [*Seismograph station code, US Geological Survey*] (SEIS)
Rbu............	Ribulose [*Biochemistry*]
RBUPC	Research in British Universities, Polytechnics, and Colleges [*Formerly, SRBUC*] [*British Library*]
R Bus & Econ Res ...	Review of Business and Economic Research [*A publication*]
RBV	Reactor Building Vent (IEEE)
RBV	Relative Biological Value [*Food science*]
RBV	Return Beam Vidicon [*Satellite camera*]
RBV	Robbinsville, NJ [*Location identifier*] [*FAA*] (FAAL)
RBVC	Return Beam Vidicon Camera
RBVI	Reactor Building Ventilation Isolation (NRCH)
RBVPRM	Reactor Building Vent Process Radiation Monitor (NRCH)
RBW	RB & W Corp. [*Formerly, Russell, Burdsaw & Ward Corp.*] [*American Stock Exchange symbol*]
RBW	Walterboro, SC [*Location identifier*] [*FAA*] (FAAL)
RBX	Manteo, NC [*Location identifier*] [*FAA*] (FAAL)
Rby............	Ribitol [*or Ribityl*] [*Biochemistry*]
RBY	Ruby [*Alaska*] [*Airport symbol*] (OAG)
RBY	Ruby Resources Ltd. [*Vancouver Stock Exchange symbol*]
RBYC	Royal Berkshire Yeomanry Cavalry [*British*] (ROG)
RBYOA......	Rinsho Byori [*A publication*]
RBZ	Rabat Zaers [*Morocco*] [*Seismograph station code, US Geological Survey*] (SEIS)
RBZ	Rubidazone [*An antibiotic*]
RC	Circular Radio Beacon
RC	Congregation of Our Lady of the Retreat in the Cenacle [*Roman Catholic women's religious order*]
RC	[*The*] Item Requested Has Been Rescinded. All Stock Has Been Destroyed. Copies Are Not Available [*Advice of supply action code*] [*Army*]
RC	La Revue du Caire [*Cairo*] [*A publication*]
RC	Missouri Revised Statutes [*1855*] (DLA)
RC	Nicholl, Hare, and Carrow's Railway Cases [*1835-55*] (DLA)
RC	Nondirectional Radio Beacon [*ITU designation*] (CET)
RC	RADAR Computer (MCD)
RC	RADAR Control (DEN)
RC	Radio Car [*British*]
RC	Radio Code Aptitude Area
R/C............	Radio Command [*or Control*] (KSC)
RC	Radio Compass
R & C	Rail and Canal
RC	Railway Cases (DLA)
RC	Rainbow Coalition [*Named for the 1984 political campaign of Rev. Jesse Jackson*] [*Later, NRCI*] (EA)
RC	Rainform Compressed (MCD)
R/C............	Range Clearance [*NASA*] (KSC)
RC	Range Command [*NASA*] (NASA)
RC	Range Contractor [*NASA*] (KSC)
RC	Range Control [*NASA*] (KSC)
RC	Range Correction
RC	Rapid Change (MCD)
RC	Rapid Curing [*Asphalt grade*]
RC	Rassemblement Congolais [*Congolese Rally*] [*Buakvu*]
RC	Rate Center [*Telecommunications*] (TEL)
RC	Rate of Change
R/C............	Rate of Climb [*Aviation*]
RC	Rate Command
R/C............	Ratio Command (MCD)
RC	Ray Control
RC	Rayon and Cotton [*Freight*]
R/C............	Re-Credited
RC	Reaction Center
RC	Reaction Control
RC	Reactor Cavity (NRCH)
RC	Reactor Compartment (MSA)
RC	Reactor Coolant (NRCH)
RC	Read and Compute
RC	Reader Code
RC	Ready Calendar
RC	Real Circuit
RC	Rear Commodore [*Navy*] (NVT)
RC	Rear Connection (MSA)
R & C	Reasonable and Customary [*Refers to medical charges*] [*Insurance*]
RC	Receipt
RC	Receiver Card
RC	Reception Center [*Army*]
RC	Receptor-Chemoeffector [*Biochemistry*]
RC	Recirculatory Air (AAG)
RC	Reconnaissance Car [*British*]
R/C............	Reconsign
RC	Reconstruction Committee [*British*] [*World War II*]
RC	Record Change [*or Changer*] (AAG)
RC	Record Commissioners [*British*] (DLA)
RC	Record Count [*Data processing*]
RC	Recording Completing [*Trunk*] [*Telecommunications*] (TEL)
RC	Recording Controller (NRCH)
RC	Records Check (AFM)
R & C	Records and Control

R/C	Recovered
RC	Recovery Controller (MCD)
RC	Recruiting Center
RC	Recurring Cost (NASA)
RC	Red Cell [*or Corpuscle*] [*Hematology*]
RC	Red China
RC	Red Cross
RC	Reduced Capability (MCD)
RC	Reduced Cuing
RC	Reels [*JETDS nomenclature*] [*Military*] (CET)
RC	Reference Cavity
RC	Reference Clock [*Telecommunications*] (TEL)
RC	Referred Care [*Medicine*]
RC	Reformed Church
RC	Refrigerated Centrifuge
RC	Regional Center
RC	Regional Commandant [*Air Force*] [*British*]
RC	Regional Commissioner [*Social Security Administration*]
RC	Regional Council
RC	Register of Copyrights [*US*]
RC	Registered Criminologist
RC	Registration Cases (DLA)
RC	Regulatory Council [*FAA*] (MCD)
RC	Rehabilitation Center
RC	Rehabilitation Counselor
RC	Reinforced Concrete [*Technical drawings*]
RC	Rekishi Chiri [*A publication*]
RC	Relative [*Force*] Cost (MCD)
RC	Relay Computer (BUR)
RC	Release Card
RC	Release Clause
RC	Relief Claim
R & C	Religion y Cultura [*A publication*]
R & C	Religioni e Civitia [*A publication*]
RC	Remington's Code (DLA)
RC	Remote Computer
RC	Remote Concentrator
RC	Remote Control
RC	Rent Charge
RC	Reopened Claim [*Unemployment insurance*] (OICC)
RC	Reorder Cycle
RC	Replacement Cost [*Insurance*]
RC	Reply Coupon
RC	Report of Contact [*Social Security Administration*] (OICC)
RC	Republic Airlines, Inc. [*ICAO designator*] (FAAC)
R/C	Request for Checkage [*Navy*]
RC	Requirements Contract
RC	Rescriptum [*Counterpart*] [*Latin*]
RC	Research Center (IEEE)
RC	Research-Cottrell, Inc. [*NYSE symbol*]
RC	Reserve Components [*Military*]
RC	Reserve Corps
RC	Resin Coated (MCD)
RC	Resistance Capacitance
R-C	Resistance Coupled
R-C	Resistor-Capacitor
RC	Resolver Control
RC	Resource Capital International [*Toronto Stock Exchange symbol*]
RC	Resources Council [*New York, NY*] (EA)
RC	Respiration Ceased [*Medicine*]
RC	Respiratory Care [*A publication*]
RC	Respiratory Care [*Medicine*]
RC	Respiratory Center [*Medicine*]
RC	Responsibility Center [*Air Force*] (AFM)
RC	Rest Camp
R & C	Rest and Convalescence (ADA)
RC	Rest Cure
RC	Restrictive Cardiomyopathy [*Cardiology*]
RC	Retention Catheter [*Medicine*]
RC	Revenue Canada
RC	Revenue Cutter [*Coast Guard*]
RC	Reverse Course [*Aviation*]
RC	Reverse Current
RC	Review of the Churches [*A publication*]
R & C	Review and Comment [*Aerospace*]
RC	Review Cycle [*Military*] (AFIT)
RC	Revised Code
RC	Revista Contemporanea [*A publication*]
RC	Revista Cubana [*A publication*]
RC	Revue Celtique [*A publication*]
RC	Revue Charlemagne [*A publication*]
RC	Revue Critique [*A publication*]
RC	Revue Critique de Legislation et de Jurisprudence de Canada (DLA)
RC	Rib Cage [*Anatomy*]
RC	Ribbon-Frame Camera (MUGU)
RC	Richard of Cashel [*Pseudonym used by Richard Laurence*]
RC	Right Center [*A stage direction*]
RC	Right Center [*Position in soccer, hockey*]
RC	Right Chest [*Medicine*]
RC	Ring Counter
RC	Rivista delle Colonie [*A publication*]
RC	Road Reconnaissance (FAAC)
RC	Robert & Carriere [*France*] [*Research code symbol*]
RC	Roll Channel
RC	Roller Coating
RC	Rolls Court [*Legal*] [*British*]
RC	Roman Catholic
RC	Root Canal [*Dentistry*]
RC	Rosin Core [*Foundry technology*]
RC	Rosslyn Connecting Railroad Co. [*AAR code*]
RC	Rotary Combustion [*Automobile*]
RC	Rotation Control (NASA)
RC	Rough Cast (ADA)
RC	Rough Cutting [*Construction*]
RC	Round Corners [*Bookselling*]
R/C	Routing and Clipping (MCD)
RC	Royal Commission [*British*]
RC	Royal Crest [*British*]
RC	Royal Crown [*Soft drink brand*]
R/C	Rubber-Capped
RC	Rudder Club [*Bayside, NY*] (EA)
RC	Rules Committee [*House of Representatives*] (OICC)
RC	Ruling Cases (DLA)
RC	Ruperto-Carola [*A publication*]
RC	Rural Coalition (EA)
RC	Rural Construction
RC	Rushlight Club (EA)
R & C	Russell and Chesley's Nova Scotia Reports (DLA)
RCA	Rabbinical Council of America (EA)
RCA	RADAR Controlled Approach (NVT)
RCA	Radiative-Convective-Atmospheric [*Meteorology*]
RCA	Radio Club of America (EA)
RCA	Radio Collectors of America (EA)
RCA	Radiological Control Area (MCD)
RCA	Rapid City, SD [*Location identifier*] [*FAA*] (FAAL)
RCA	Rate Change Authorization (NVT)
RCA	Reach Cruising Altitude [*Aviation*] (FAAC)
RCA	Reaction Control Assembly
RCA	Red Cell Aggregate [*or Aggregation*] [*Hematology*]
RCA	Red Cross Act
RCA	Reformed Chruch, America (ROG)
RCA	Remote Control Amplifier (MCD)
RCA	Renault Club of America (EA)
RCA	REO [*Rawson E. Olds*] Club of America (EA)
RCA	Replacement Cost Accounting (ADA)
RCA	Republican Communications Association [*Washington, DC*] (EA)
RCA	Request for Corrective Action (AAG)
RCA	Resident Care Aide
RCA	Residential Care Alternatives
RCA	Review and Concurrence Authority
RCA	Revista Colombiana de Antropologia [*A publication*]
RCA	Ricinus communis Agglutinin [*Immunology*]
RCA	Right Coronary Artery [*Anatomy*]
RCA	Riot Control Agent (NVT)
RCA	Rocket Cruising Association (EA)
RCA	Rodeo Cowboys Association [*Later, PRCA*] (EA)
RCA	Root Cause Analysis (MCD)
RCA	Royal Cambrian Academy [*British*]
RCA	Royal Cambrian Academy of Art [*British*]
RCA	Royal Canadian Academy
RCA	Royal Canadian Academy of Arts
RCA	Royal Canadian Army (MCD)
RCA	Royal Canadian Artillery
RCA	Royal College of Art [*British*]
RCA	Soil and Water Resources Conservation Act [*1977*]
RCAA	Rocket City Astronomical Association [*Later, VBAS*] (EA)
RCAB	Review and Concurrence Advisory Board
RCAC	Radio Corporation of America Communications (MCD)
RCAC	Remote Computer Access Communications Service
RCAC	Reserve Component Assistance Coordinator (MCD)
RCAC	Royal Canadian Armoured Corps
RCACS	USREDCOM [*United States Readiness Command*] Command and Control System (AABC)
RCADV	Reverse Course and Advise [*Aviation*] (FAAC)
RCAE	Royal Correspondence of the Assyrian Empire [*A publication*] (BJA)
RCAEB	RCA [*Radio Corporation of America*] Engineer [*A publication*]
RCA Eng	RCA [*Radio Corporation of America*] Engineer [*A publication*]
RCAF	Royal Canadian Air Force
RCAFA	Revista Cafetalera [*Spain*] [*A publication*]
RCAFA	Royal Canadian Air Force Association
RCAF(WD)	Royal Canadian Air Force, Women's Division
RCAG	Remote Center Air/Ground Facility
RCAG	Remote-Controlled Air-Ground Communication Site (MCD)
RCAG	Replacement Carrier Air Group [*Military*] (AFIT)
RCAI	Railroadiana Collectors Association Incorporated (EA)
RCAJ	Royal Central Asian Society. Journal [*A publication*]
R/CAL	Resistance Calibration (MCD)
RCal	Revista Calasancia [*A publication*]

RCAls .... Revue Catholique d'Alsace [*A publication*]
RCALT ...... Reach Cruising Altitude [*Aviation*] (FAAC)
RCam .... Revista Camoniana [*Sao Paulo*] [*A publication*]
RCamA ...... [*Member of the*] Royal Cambrian Academy [*Formerly, RCA*] [*British*]
RCAMC ...... Royal Canadian Army Medical Corps
RCAN .... Recorded Announcement [*Telecommunications*] (TEL)
RCan .... Revue Canonique [*A publication*]
R Canad-Amer Et Slaves ... Revue Canadienne-Americaine d'Etudes Slaves [*A publication*]
R Canad Et Afr ... Revue Canadienne des Etudes Africaines [*A publication*]
R & Can Cas ... Railway and Canal Cases [*England*] (DLA)
R Can Etud Nationalisme ... Revue Canadienne des Etudes sur le Nationalisme [*A publication*]
R Can Sciences Info ... Revue Canadienne des Sciences de l'Information [*A publication*]
R & Can Tr Cas ... Railway and Canal Traffic Cases [*England*] (DLA)
RCAPA ...... Revista de Ciencia Aplicada [*A publication*]
RCAPC ...... Royal Canadian Army Pay Corps
RCAPDR .... Revolutionary Council of the Algerian People's Democratic Republic
RCAPS ...... Roosevelt Center for American Policy Studies (EA)
RCA R .... RCA [*Radio Corporation of America*] Review [*A publication*]
RCAR .... Religious Coalition for Abortion Rights (EA)
RCA Rev .... RCA [*Radio Corporation of America*] Review [*A publication*]
RCAS .... Requirements for Close Air Support [*Army*] (MCD)
RCAS .... Research Center for Advanced Study [*University of Texas at Arlington*] [*Research center*] (RCD)
RCAS .... Royal Central Asian Society [*British*]
RCASC ...... Royal Canadian Army Service Corps
RCAT .... Radio Code Aptitude Test
RCAT .... Radio-Controlled Aerial Target
RCAT .... Remote-Controlled Aerial Target (NATG)
RCat .... Revista de Catalunya [*A publication*]
RCAT .... Ridgetown College of Agricultural Technology [*Canada*] (ARC)
RCA Tech Not ... RCA [*Radio Corporation of America*] Technical Notes [*A publication*]
RCA Tech Notes ... RCA [*Radio Corporation of America*] Technical Notes [*A publication*]
Rc Atti Accad Naz Lincei ... Rendiconti e Atti. Accademia Nazionale dei Lincei [*A publication*]
RCAV .... Rozpravy Ceskoslovenske Akademie Ved [*A publication*]
RCB .... Radiation Control Board (AAG)
RCB .... Randomized Complete Block [*Statistical design*]
RCB .... Reactor Containment Building (NRCH)
RCB .... Ready Crew Building (NATG)
RCB .... Reflection Coefficient Bridge
RCB .... Region Control Block [*Data processing*] (BUR)
RCB .... Regulations of the Civil Aeronautics Board
RCB .... Reinforced Concrete Design [*Camutek*] [*Software package*]
RCB .... Remote Circuit Breaker (MCD)
RCB .... Remote Control Bandwidth
RCB .... Representative Church Body [*Ireland*] [*Church of England*]
RCB .... Requirements Control Board (MCD)
RCB .... Resource Control Block [*Data processing*] (IBMDP)
RCB .... Revista de Cultura Biblica [*Rio De Janeiro/Sao Paulo, Brazil*] [*A publication*]
RCB .... Revista de Cultura Brasilena [*A publication*]
RCB .... Richards Bay [*South Africa*] [*Airport symbol*] (OAG)
RCB .... Right Cornerback [*Football*]
RCB .... Rubber Control Board
RCBA .... Ratio Changers and Boosters Assembly (MCD)
RCBA .... Royal Crown Bottlers Association [*Louisville, KY*] (EA)
RCBC .... Red Cross Blood Center
rCBF .... Regional Cerebral Blood Flow [*Medicine*]
RCBHT ...... Reactor Coolant Bleed Holdup Tank (NRCH)
RCBI .... Brown [*Robert C.*] & Co. [*NASDAQ symbol*] (NQ)
RCBIA .... Revue Canadienne de Biologie [*A publication*]
RCBOA ...... Radiologica Clinica et Biologica [*A publication*]
RCBT .... Reactor Coolant Bleed Tank [*Nuclear energy*] (NRCH)
RCBW .... Radiological-Chemical-Biological Warfare
RCC .... Belleville, IL [*Location identifier*] [*FAA*] (FAAL)
RCC .... International Society of Reply Coupon Collectors (EA)
RCC .... Rachel Carson Council (EA)
RCC .... Rack Clearance Center [*Association of American Publishers*]
RCC .... RADAR Control Clouds
RCC .... RADAR Control Computer (MCD)
RCC .... RADAR Control Console [*Military*] (CAAL)
RCC .... Radio Common Carrier
RCC .... Radio Common Channels
RCC .... Radio Communications Center
RCC .... Radiochemical Centre [*United Kingdom*] (NRCH)
RCC .... Radiological Control Center [*Army*]
RCC .... Rag Chewers' Club [*Amateur radio*]
R & CC .... Railway and Canal Cases [*1835-54*] (DLA)
RCC .... Range Commanders Council [*White Sands Missile Range*] (KSC)
RCC .... Range Communications Component (MCD)
RCC .... Range Control Center
RCC .... Rape Crisis Center (EA)
RCC .... Ratio of Charges to Costs

RCC .... RCA Corporation Communications
RCC .... Re Capital Corporation [*American Stock Exchange symbol*]
RCC .... Reaction Control Center (KSC)
RCC .... Reactor Closed Cooling [*Nuclear energy*] (NRCH)
RCC .... Read Channel Continue
RCC .... Reader Common Contact
RCC .... Real-Time Computer Complex
RCC .... Receptor-Chemoeffector Complex [*Biochemistry*]
RCC .... Record Collectors' Club (EA)
R & CC .... Recorder and Communications Control (NASA)
RCC .... Recovery Control Center
RCC .... Rectangular Concrete Columns [*Jacys Computing Services*] [*Software package*]
RCC .... Red Carpet Clubs [*United Airlines' club for frequent flyers*] (EA)
RCC .... Red Cross of Constantine (EA)
RCC .... Regional Control Center [*North American Air Defense*] (FAAC)
RCC .... Regional Coordination Committee [*Work Incentive Program*]
RCC .... Reinforced Carbon-Carbon (MCD)
RCC .... Relative Casein Content [*Food analysis*]
RCC .... Remote Communications Central
RCC .... Remote Communications Complex
RCC .... Remote Communications Concentrator
RCC .... Remote Communications Console
RCC .... Remote Computer Center (MCD)
RCC .... Renal Cell Carcinoma [*Medicine*]
RCC .... Representative Church Council [*Episcopalian*]
RCC .... Rescue Control Center
RCC .... Rescue Coordination Center [*Coast Guard*]
RCC .... Rescue Crew Commander (AFM)
RCC .... Research Computing Center [*University of New Hampshire*] [*Research center*] (RCD)
RCC .... Reset Control Circuit
RCC .... Resistor Color Code (DEN)
RCC .... Resource Category Code [*Military*] (CAAL)
RCC .... Resource Control Center [*Military*] (AFIT)
RCC .... Resources for Community Change [*An association*] [*Defunct*] (EA)
RCC .... Reusable Carbon-Carbon (MCD)
RCC .... Revolutionary Command Council [*Iraqi*] (PD)
RCC .... Revue des Cours et Conferences [*A publication*]
RCC .... Rio Carpintero [*Cuba*] [*Seismograph station code, US Geological Survey*] (SEIS)
R & CC .... Riot and Civil Commotion
RCC .... Riverside City College [*California*]
RCC .... Rochester Community College, Rochester, MN [*OCLC symbol*] (OCLC)
RCC .... Rockefeller Center Cable
RCC .... Rod Cluster Control [*Nuclear energy*] (NRCH)
RCC .... Roman Catholic Church
RCC .... Roman Catholic Church Curate (ROG)
RCC .... Rough Combustion Cutoff [*NASA*]
RCC .... Rubber Covered Cable (MSA)
RCC .... Rural Construction Cadre [*Military*]
RCC .... Russian Corps Combatants (EA)
R & C Ca .... Railway and Canal Cases [*England*] (DLA)
RCCA .... Record Carrier Competition Act [*1981*]
RCCA .... Rickenbacker Car Club of America (EA)
RCCA .... Rod Cluster Control Assemblies [*Nuclear energy*] (NRCH)
RCCA .... Rough Combustion Cutoff Assembly [*NASA*] (KSC)
R & C Cas ... Railway and Canal Cases [*England*] (DLA)
RCCB .... Remote Control Circuit Breaker (NASA)
RCCC .... Range Communications Control Center [*Military*] (MCD)
RCCC .... Regional Communications Control Center [*FAA*] (FAAC)
RCCC .... Regular Common Carrier Conference [*Alexandria, VA*] (EA)
RCCC .... Reserve Component Career Counselor [*Military*] (AABC)
RCCC .... Reserve Component Coordination Council (MCD)
RC/CC .... Responsibility Center/Cost Center [*Military*] (AFIT)
RCCC .... Royal Caledonia Curling Club
RCCC .... Royal Commission on Corporate Concentration [*Canada*]
RCCC .... Royal Curling Club of Canada
RCCE .... Regional Congress of Construction Employers (EA)
RC-CE .... Revenue Canada, Customs and Excise
RCCE .... Rotating Cylinder-Collector Electrode [*Electrochemistry*]
RCCES ...... Research Centre for Canadian Ethnic Studies [*University of Calgary*] [*Research center*] (RCD)
RCCF .... Reserve Components Contingency Force
RCCFB ...... Revista CENIC [*Centro Nacional de Investigaciones Cientificas*]. Ciencias Fisicas [*Cuba*] [*A publication*]
RCCh .... Roman Catholic Chaplain [*Navy*] [*British*]
RCCH .... Roman Catholic Church
RCCL .... Royal Caribbean Cruise Line
RCCLS ...... Resource Center for Consumers of Legal Services [*Later, NRCCLS*] (EA)
RCCM .... Rivista di Cultura Classica e Medievale [*A publication*]
RCCMA ...... Rivista Critica di Clinica Medica [*A publication*]
RCC/MG ..... Range Commanders Council Meteorological Group [*White Sands Missile Range*]
RCCO .... RADAR Control Console Operator [*Military*] (CAAL)
RCCOL ...... Reinforced Concrete Column [*Camutek*] [*Software package*]
RCCOW ...... Return Channel Control Orderwire [*Military*] (CAAL)

RCCP .... Recorder and Communications Control Panel (NASA)
RCCP .... Reinforced Concrete Culvert Pipe [Technical drawings]
RCCPLD.... Resistance-Capacitance Coupled
RC & CR ..... Revenue, Civil, and Criminal Reporter [Calcutta] (DLA)
RCCRA....... Rough Combustion Cutoff Replaceable Assembly [NASA] (KSC)
RCCS .... Rate Command Control System (AAG)
RCCS .... Revista Catolica de las Cuestiones Sociales [A publication]
RCC & S ..... Riots, Civil Commotions, and Strikes [Insurance]
RCCS .... Royal Canadian Corps of Signals
RCCUS...... Republican Citizens Committee of the United States (EA)
RCD........... RADAR Cloud Detection Report [Meteorology] (FAAC)
RCD........... Rapid City [South Dakota] [Seismograph station code, US Geological Survey] (SEIS)
RCD........... Received
RCD........... Receiver-Carrier Detector
RCD........... Reconnaissance Cockpit Display
RCD........... Record
RCD........... Redox Chemiluminescence Detector [Instrumentation]
RCD........... Reduced Crude Desulfurization [Petroleum refining]
RCD........... Regent's Canal Dock [British]
RCD........... Reinforcement Control Depot [Air Force]
RCD........... Relative Cardiac Dullness [Medicine]
RCD........... Research Centers Directory [A publication]
RC & D ...... Resource Conservation and Development
RCD........... Retrofit Configuration Drawing (MCD)
RCD........... Reverse Circulation Drilling [Mining technology]
RCD........... Reverse Current Device [Electronics] (MSA)
RCD........... Rock Coring Device
RCD........... Rocket Cushioning Device (NG)
RCD........... Route Control Digit [Telecommunications] (TEL)
RCD........... Royal Canadian Dragoons [Military]
RCD........... Rural Civil Defense
RCD........... Sisters of Our Lady of Christian Doctrine [Roman Catholic religious order]
RCDA .... Religion in Communist Dominated Areas [A publication]
RCDA .... Research Career Development Awards
RCDC .... RADAR Course-Directing Center
RCDC .... RADAR Course-Directing Control (MUGU)
RCDC .... RADAR Course Directory Central [Military]
RCDC .... Radiation Chemistry Data Center [University of Notre Dame] [Notre Dame, IN] [Research center]
RCDC .... Royal Canadian Dental Corps
RCDCB...... Regional Civil Defense Coordination Boards (AABC)
RCDEP ...... Rural Civil Defense Education Program
RCDG........ Recording (MSA)
RCDHS...... Rehabilitation and Chronic Disease Hospital Section [American Hospital Association] (EA)
RCDIP .... Revue Critique de Droit International Prive [A publication]
RCDIW ...... Royal Commission on the Distribution of Income and Wealth [British]
RCDMB ..... Regional Civil and Defense Mobilization Boards
RCDMS ..... Reliability Central Data Management System [Air Force] (DIT)
RCDNA....... RADAR Cloud Detection Report Not Available [Meteorology] (FAAC)
RCDNE....... RADAR Cloud Detection Report No Echoes Observed [Meteorology] (FAAC)
RCDNO ...... RADAR Cloud Detector Inoperative Due to Breakdown Until [Followed by time] [Meteorology] (FAAC)
RCDOM...... RADAR Cloud Detector Inoperative Due to Maintenance Until [Followed by time] [Meteorology] (FAAC)
RCDP .... Record Parallel (MCD)
RCDR .... Recorder (KSC)
RCDS .... Records
RCDS .... Royal College of Defence Studies [British]
RCDS .... Rural Community Development Service [Abolished, 1970] [Department of Agriculture]
RCDT .... Reactor Coolant Drain Tank (NRCH)
RCE........... Radio Communications Equipment
RCE........... Rapid Changing Environment (AAG)
RCE........... Rapid Circuit Etch
RC de l'E .... Rapports de la Cour de l'Echiquier [Exchequer Court Reports] [Canada] (DLA)
RCE........... Reaction Control Engine
RCE........... Reactor Compatibility Experiment (NRCH)
rce........... Recording Engineer [MARC relator code] [Library of Congress]
RCE........... Reece Corp. [NYSE symbol]
RCE........... Reentry Control Electronics
RCE........... Reliability Control Engineering (AAG)
RCE........... Religious of Christian Education [Roman Catholic women's religious order]
RCE........... Remote Control Equipment (DIT)
RCE........... Repertoire Canadien sur l'Education [See also CEI] [A publication]
RCE........... Reviews in Cancer Epidemiology [Elsevier Book Series] [A publication]
RCE........... Revue Catholique des Eglises [A publication]
RCE........... Rice University, Fondren Library, Houston, TX [OCLC symbol] (OCLC)
RCE........... Roche Harbor [Washington] [Airport symbol] (OAG)
RCE........... Royal Canadian Engineers

RCE........... Union Restaurants Collectifs Europeens [European Communal Catering Association] [Berlin, West Germany] (EA-IO)
RCEA .... Recreational Coach and Equipment Association [Later, MHI]
RCEA .... Research Council Employees' Association [Canada]
RCEAC....... Regional Civil Emergency Advisory Committee [Formerly, JRCC] [Civil defense]
RCEE......... Revista. Centro de Estudios Extemoenos [A publication]
RCEEA .... Radio Communications and Electronic Engineers Association
RCEH......... Revista Canadiense de Estudios Hispanicos [A publication]
RCEI.......... Range Communications Electronics Instructions [NASA] (KSC)
RCei .... Revue Celtique [A publication]
RCEME....... Royal Canadian Electrical and Mechanical Engineers
R Centroam Econ ... Revista Centroamericana de Economia [A publication]
RCEP......... Royal Commission on Environmental Pollution [British]
RCEP......... Rural Concentrated Employment Program [Department of Labor]
RCERA....... Religious Committee for the ERA [Equal Rights Amendment] (EA)
RCERB....... Ricerche di Termotecnica [A publication]
RCERIP ...... Reserve Component Equipment Readiness Improvement Program [Military] (AABC)
RCEUSA .... Romanian Catholic Exarchy in the United States of America (EA)
RCF .... Radcliffe Resources Ltd. [Vancouver Stock Exchange symbol]
RCF .... Radiocommunication Failure Message [Aviation]
RCF .... Ratio Correction Factor
RCF .... Reader's Comment Form (IBMDP)
RCF .... Recall Finder
RCF .... Relative Centrifugal Force
RCF .... Relative Cumulative Frequency
RCF .... Remain on Company Frequency [Aviation] (FAAC)
RCF .... Remote Call Forwarding [Bell System]
RCF .... Repair Cost Factor [Navy]
RCF .... Repair Cycle Float (AABC)
RCF .... Retail Computer Facilities
RCF .... Revista Colombiana de Folclor [A publication]
RCF .... Revue du Clerge Francais [A publication]
RCF .... River Conservation Fund [Later, ARCC] (EA)
RCF .... Rotating Cylinder Flap
RCFA .... Religious Communities for the Arts (EA)
RCFA .... Royal Canadian Field Artillery [Military]
RCFC .... Ray Coble Fan Club (EA)
RCFC .... Reactor Containment Fan Cooler [Nuclear energy] (NRCH)
RCFC(U) .... Reactor Core Fan Cooling (Unit) (IEEE)
RCFF .... Repair Cycle Float Factor (MCD)
RCFP......... Reporters Committee for Freedom of the Press (EA)
RCFR......... Red Cross Field Representative
RCFR......... Royal Canadian Fleet Reserve
RCFT .... Randomized Controlled Field Trial [Statistics]
RCFU......... Rotary Carton Feed Unit
RCG.......... Radiation Concentration Guide [Formerly, MPC]
RCG.......... Radio Command Guidance (AAG)
RCG.......... Radioactivity Concentration Guide (KSC)
rCG........... Rat Chorionic Gonadotropin
RCG.......... Reaction Cured Glass [Ceramic technology]
RCG.......... Receiving (AAG)
RCG.......... Recommended Concentration Guide [Nuclear energy] (NRCH)
RCG.......... Restricted Categorical Grammar
RCG.......... Reverberation Control of Gain
RCG.......... Revue du Chant Gregorien [A publication]
RCG.......... Right Cerebral Ganglion [Anatomy]
RCGA .... Royal Canadian Garrison Artillery [Military]
RCGD .... Research Center for Group Dynamics [University of Michigan] [Research center] (RCD)
RCGJA...... Royal College of General Practitioners. Journal [A publication]
RCGM....... Reactor Cover Gas Monitor (NRCH)
RCGP....... Royal College of General Practitioners [British]
rCGRP...... Rat Calcitonin Gene-Related Peptide [Biochemistry]
RCGS .... RADAR Correlation Guidance Study
RCH.......... Reach (FAAC)
RCH.......... Revue Charlemagne [A publication]
RCH.......... Rich Resources Ltd. [Vancouver Stock Exchange symbol]
RCH.......... Riohacha [Colombia] [Airport symbol] (OAG)
RCH.......... Rotary Clothes Hoist (ADA)
RCH.......... Rural Cooperative Housing
RCHA .... Rachel Carson Homestead Association (EA)
RCHA .... Royal Canadian Horse Artillery
R Ch Com Franc Canada ... Revue. Chambre de Commerce Francaise au Canada [A publication]
RCHE .... Recherche [A publication]
RCHG........ Reduced Charge (AAG)
RCHG........ Revista Chilena de Historia y Geografia [A publication]
RCHI.......... Rauch Industries [NASDAQ symbol] (NQ)
R Ch J....... Rencontre. Chretiens et Juifs [A publication]
RChL......... Revista Chilena de Literatura [A publication]
RCHL......... Revue Critique d'Histoire et de Litterature [A publication]
RCHM........ Royal Commission on Historical Monuments [British]
RChr.......... Revue Chretienne [A publication]
RCHRA....... Regional Council on Human Rights in Asia [Manila, Philippines] (EA-IO)

RCHRA....... Revue de Chimie. Academie de la Republique Populaire Roumaine [*A publication*]
RchScR...... Recherches de Science Religieuse [*A publication*]
RCHT......... Ratchet [*Design engineering*]
RCH/TCH... Receive Channel/Transmit Channel [*Telecommunications*] (MCD)
RCI .... RADAR Coverage Indication [*or Indicator*]
RCI .... Radio Canada International
RCI .... Radio Communications Instruction (MUGU)
RCI .... Range Communications Instructions [*NASA*] (KSC)
RCI .... Read Channel Initialize
RCI .... Recommended Course Indicator
RCI .... Reggio Calabria [*Italy*] [*Seismograph station code, US Geological Survey*] (SEIS)
RCI .... Reichhold Chemicals, Incorporated [*NYSE symbol*]
RCI .... Religious of Christian Instruction [*Roman Catholic religious order*]
RCI .... Remote Control Indicator (CAAL)
RCI .... Remote Control Interface
RCI .... Request for Contract Investigation (MCD)
RCI .... Resident Cost Inspector
RCI .... Resort Condominiums International [*Indianapolis, IN*] (EA)
RCI .... Respiratory Control Index [*Biochemistry*]
RCI .... Retail Confectioners International [*Glenview, IL*] (EA)
RCI .... Revista delle Colonie Italiane [*A publication*]
RCI .... Rochester Commercial and Industrial [*Database*]
RCI .... Rogers Communications [*Toronto Stock Exchange symbol*] [*Vancouver Stock Exchange symbol*]
RCI .... Roof Consultants Institute [*Raleigh, NC*] (EA)
RCI .... Routing Control Indicator [*Telecommunications*] (TEL)
RCI .... Royal Colonial Institute [*British*]
RCIA.......... Retail Clerks International Association [*Later, UFCWIU*] (EA)
RCIA.......... Retail Credit Institute of America [*Later, NFCC*]
RCIC.......... Reactor Core Isolation Cooling (NRCH)
RCIC.......... Red Cross International Committee
RCIC.......... Regional Coastal Information Center [*National Marine Advisory Service*] (MSC)
RCIC.......... Reserve Component Issues Conference [*Military*] (MCD)
RCIC.......... Royal Canadian Infantry Corps
RCICS .... Reactor Core Isolation Cooling System (NRCH)
RCID.......... Recruiter Code Identification [*Army*] (AABC)
RCID.......... Revue Catholique des Institutions et de Droit [*A publication*]
RCIE .... Regional Council for International Education [*University of Pittsburgh*]
R Ciencias Socs (Puerto Rico) ... Revista de Ciencias Sociales (Puerto Rico) [*A publication*]
R Cienc Polit ... Revista de Ciencia Politica [*A publication*]
R Cienc Soc (Ceara) ... Revista de Ciencias Sociales (Ceara) [*A publication*]
R Cienc Soc (Puerto Rico) ... Revista de Ciencias Sociales (Puerto Rico) [*A publication*]
RCIL .... Reliability Critical Item List (AAG)
R Cin .... Revue du Cinema [*A publication*]
R Cin .... Revue du Cinema/Image et Son [*A publication*]
RCINA .... Revista Chilena de Ingenieria [*A publication*]
R Cinematografo ... Rivista del Cinematografo [*A publication*]
RCINZ .... Rogers Cablesystems CI B [*NASDAQ symbol*] (NQ)
RCIRR .... Reserve Components, Individual Ready Reserve [*Military*]
RCIS .... Research Conference on Instrumentation Science
Rc Ist Lomb Sci Lett ... Rendiconti. Istituto Lombardo di Scienze e Lettere [*A publication*]
Rc Ist Sup Sanita ... Rendiconti. Istituto Superiore di Sanita [*A publication*]
RCIU.......... Remote Computer Interface Unit
RCivB......... Revista Civilizacao Brasileira [*Rio De Janeiro*] [*A publication*]
RCIVS .... Conference Regionale du Service Volontaire International [*Regional Conference on International Voluntary Service - RCIVS*] [*Bonn, West Germany*] (EA-IO)
RCIVS .... Regional Conference on International Voluntary Service [*Bonn, West Germany*] (EA-IO)
RCJ .... RCJ Resources Ltd. [*Vancouver Stock Exchange symbol*]
RCJ .... Reaction Control Jet
RCJ .... Reinforced Composite Joint
RCJ .... Reports of Certain Judgments of the Supreme Court, Vice-Admiralty Court, and Full Court of Appeal, Lagos [*1884-92*] [*Nigeria*] (DLA)
RC(J).......... Rettie, Crawford, and Melville's Session Cases, Fourth Series [*1873-98*] [*Scotland*] (DLA)
RCJ .... Royal Courts of Justice [*British*]
RCJS .... Revista de Ciencias Juridicas y Sociales [*A publication*]
RCK........... Radio Check [*Aviation*] (FAAC)
RCK........... Ramp Check [*Aviation*] (FAAC)
RCKT .... Rockdale, TX [*Location identifier*] [*FAA*] (FAAL)
RCKT .... Rocket (FAAC)
RCKY .... Rockies [*FAA*] (FAAC)
RCKY .... Rocky Mountain Exploration [*NASDAQ symbol*] (NQ)
RCL .... Radial Collateral Ligament [*Anatomy*]
RCL .... Radiation Counter Laboratories, Inc.
RCL .... Radio Command Linkage (AAG)
RC & L .... Rail, Canal, and Lake [*Transportation*]
RCL .... Ramped Cargo Lighter
RCL .... Ramsey County Public Library, St. Paul, MN [*OCLC symbol*] (OCLC)

RCL .... Reactor Coolant Loops (NRCH)
RCL .... Recall (MSA)
RCL .... Recleared [*Aviation*] (FAAC)
RCL .... Recoil (MSA)
RCL .... Redcliff [*Vanuatu*] [*Airport symbol*] (OAG)
RCL .... Reichhold Ltd. [*Toronto Stock Exchange symbol*]
RCL .... Reliability Component List (MCD)
RCL .... Reliability Control Level (KSC)
RCL .... Remote Control Location
RCL .... Research Computation Laboratory [*University of Houston*] [*Research center*] (RCD)
RCL .... Reserved Commodity List [*World War II*]
RCL .... Review of Contemporary Law [*A publication*]
RCL .... Rivista Clasica [*A publication*]
RCL .... Royal Canadian Legion
RCL .... Ruby Crystal LASER
RCL .... Ruling Case Law
RCL .... Runway Centerline [*Aviation*]
RCLA......... Regis College Lay Apostolate (EA)
RCLAD ...... Ricerca in Clinica e in Laboratorio [*A publication*]
RCLB .... Revolutionary Communist League of Britain (PPW)
RCLC .... Reactor Coolant Leakage Calculation (IEEE)
RCLC .... Reactor Coolant Letdown Cooler [*Nuclear energy*] (NRCH)
RCLC .... Republican Congressional Leadership Council (EA)
RCLD .... Reclined (MSA)
RCIFr......... Revue du Clerge Francais [*A publication*]
RCLG .... Recoilless Gun (AABC)
RCLGGL..... Royal Commission on Local Government in Greater London [*British*]
RCLI .... Rassegna Critica della Letteratura Italiana [*A publication*]
RCLJ .... Revue Critique de Legislation et de Jurisprudence (DLA)
RCLM .... Reclaim (AABC)
RCLM .... Runway Centerline Marking [*Aviation*]
RCLMG ...... Reclaiming
RCLO .... Reports Control Liaison Officer [*Army*] (AABC)
RCLR .... Radio Communications Link Repeater (FAAC)
RCLR .... Recoilless Rifle (AABC)
RCLS .... Ramapo Catskill Library System [*Library network*]
RCLS .... Recoilless
RCLS .... Runway Centerline Lights System [*Aviation*] (FAAC)
RCLT .... Radio Communications Link Terminal (FAAC)
RCLWUNE ... Regional Commission on Land and Water Use in the Near East (EA)
RCM .... Aviation Radio and RADAR Countermeasures Technician [*Navy*]
RCM .... La Republique des Citoyens du Monde [*Commonwealth of World Citizens*]
RCM .... RADAR [*or Radio*] Countermeasures (AAG)
RCM .... Radial Compression Model [*Chromatography*]
RCM .... Radiative-Convective Model [*Meteorology*]
RCM .... Radio-Controlled Mine [*Military*]
RCM .... Radiocontrast Media [*Clinical chemistry*]
RCM .... Random Coincidence Monitor [*Beckman Instruments, Inc.*] [*Instrumentation*]
RCM .... Range Change Method [*Aircraft*]
RCM .... Rassemblement Chretien de Madagascar [*Christian Rally of Madagascar*]
RCM .... Reactor Materials [*A publication*]
RCM .... Receipt of Classified Material (AAG)
RCM .... Red Cell Mass [*Hematology*]
RCM .... Reduced Casualties and Mishaps
RCM .... Refurbished Command Module [*NASA*] (KSC)
RCM .... Regimental Corporal-Major [*British*]
RCM .... Regimental Court-Martial
RCM .... Reinforced Clostridial Medium [*Microbiology*]
RCM .... Reliability-Centered Maintenance [*DoD*]
RCM .... Reliability Corporate Memory (IEEE)
RCM .... Religious Conceptionist Missionaries [*Roman Catholic women's religious order*]
RCM .... Replacement Culture Medium [*Microbiology*]
RCM .... Rhode Island College, Providence, RI [*OCLC symbol*] (OCLC)
RCM .... Richmond [*Australia*] [*Airport symbol*] (OAG)
RCM .... Right Costal Margin [*Medicine*]
RCM .... Rosmac Resources Ltd. [*Vancouver Stock Exchange symbol*]
RCM .... Rotor Current Meter
RCM .... Rous Conditioned Medium
RCM .... Royal Canadian Mint
RCM .... Royal College of Midwives [*British*]
RCM .... Royal College of Music [*British*]
RCM .... Royal College of Music. Magazine [*A publication*]
RCM .... Royal Conservatory of Music [*Leipzig*]
RCMA......... Radio Communications Monitoring Association (EA)
RCMA......... Railroad Construction and Maintenance Association [*Later, NRC/MAI*] (EA)
RCMA......... Religious Conference Management Association [*Indianapolis, IN*] (EA)
RCMA......... Reservist Clothing Maintenance Allowance [*Military*]
RCMA......... Roof Coatings Manufacturers Association [*Northbrook, IL*] (EA)
RCMASA.... Russian Consolidated Mutual Aid Society of America (EA)
RCMAT .... Radio-Controlled Miniature Aerial Target [*Military*] (MCD)

RCMD........	Recommend (FAAC)
RCMD........	Rice Council for Market Development (EA)
RCMF........	Royal Commonwealth Military Forces (ADA)
RCMIS......	Reserve Components Management Information System [Army]
RCMM......	Registered Competitive Market Maker [Stock exchange term]
RCMP........	RCMP [Royal Canadian Mounted Police] Quarterly [A publication]
RCMP........	Royal Canadian Mounted Police [Formerly, RNWMP]
RCMPQ......	Royal Canadian Mounted Police Quarterly (DLA)
RCMPRS	Recompression
rCMR........	Regional Cerebral Metabolic Rate [Brain research]
RCMS.......	Reliability Centered Maintenance Strategy (MCD)
RCMT.......	RCM Technologies, Inc. [NASDAQ symbol] (NQ)
RCMUH	Ruperto-Carola. Mitteilungen der Vereinigung der Freunde der Studentenschaft der Universitaet Heidelberg [A publication]
RCN...........	Receipt of Change Notice
RCN...........	Reconnaissance
RCN...........	Record Control Number (AFM)
RCN...........	Record Number [Online database field identifier]
RCN...........	Recovery Communications Network
RCN...........	Recreation (MSA)
RCN...........	Report Change Notice (MCD)
RCN...........	Report Control Number (MCD)
RCN...........	Requirements Change Notice [NASA] (NASA)
RCN...........	Resource Center for Nonviolence (EA)
RCN...........	Rimacan Resources Ltd. [Vancouver Stock Exchange symbol]
RCN...........	Royal Canadian Navy [Obsolete]
RCN...........	Royal College of Nursing [British]
RCNAS......	Royal Canadian Naval Air Station
RCN Bull	RCN [Reactor Centrum Nederland] Bulletin [A publication]
RCNC	Royal Canadian Naval College [1943-1948]
RCNC	Royal Corps of Naval Constructors [British]
RCNDT......	Recondition
RCNLR	Reconnaissance Long Range [Army]
RCN Meded ...	Reactor Centrum Nederland. Mededeling [A publication]
RCNMR	Royal Canadian Navy Monthly Review [A publication]
RCNR	Royal Canadian Naval Reserve
RCN Rep	Reactor Centrum Nederland. Report [A publication]
R & C N Sc ...	Russell and Chesley's Nova Scotia Reports (DLA)
RCNSS.......	Reserve Component National Security Seminar (MCD)
RCNTR	Ring Counter (MSA)
RCNVR	Royal Canadian Naval Volunteer Reserve [1923-1945]
RCO...........	RADAR Control Officer
RCO...........	Radio Control Operator
RCO...........	Range Control Office [or Officer] [NASA] (KSC)
RCO...........	Range Cutoff (MCD)
RCO...........	Reactor Core (IEEE)
RCO...........	Receiver Cuts Out [Telecommunications] (TEL)
RCO...........	Reclamation Control Officer [Military] (AFIT)
RCO...........	Regional Catering Officer [British]
RCO...........	Remote Communication Outlet [ATCS]
RCO...........	Remote Control Office
RCO...........	Remote Control Oscillator
RCO...........	Rendezvous Compatible Orbit [Aerospace]
RCO...........	Reports Control Officer [Army] (AABC)
RCO...........	Representative Calculating Operation
RCO...........	Research Contracting Officer
RCO...........	Resistance-Controlled Oscillator
RCO...........	Rococco Resources Ltd. [Vancouver Stock Exchange symbol]
RCO...........	Royal College of Organists [British]
RCOA	Radio Club of America
RCOA	Record Club of America [Defunct]
RCOBA	Revista Chilena de Obstetricia y Ginecologia [A publication]
RCOC	Regional Communications Operations Center [Military] (MCD)
RC/OC	Reverse Current/Overcurrent (KSC)
RCOC	Royal Canadian Ordnance Corps
RCOCB	Research Communications in Chemical Pathology and Pharmacology [A publication]
RCOG	Royal College of Obstetricians and Gynaecologists [British]
RCOGB	Revista Cubana de Obstetricia y Ginecologia [A publication]
RCol	Rassegna di Coltura [A publication]
R Collect Loc ...	Revue des Collectivites Locales [A publication]
R Coll For Dep Refor Res Notes ...	Royal College of Forestry. Department of Reforestation. Research Notes [A publication]
R Coll Sci Technol Glasg Res Rep ...	Royal College of Science and Technology. Glasgow Research Report [A publication]
RColt	Rassegna di Coltura [A publication]
R Comitato G Italia B ...	Reale Comitato Geologico d'Italia. Bolletino [A publication]
R Commer ...	Revue Commerce [A publication]
RCON	Reconfiguration (FAAC)
RCOND	Resources and Conservation [A publication]
RCong	Revue Congolaise [A publication]
RConsAlim ...	Revue Conserve Alimentation [A publication]
R/CONT	Remote Control [Automotive engineering]
RCONT	Rod Control
R Contemp Sociol ...	Review of Contemporary Sociology [A publication]
R Coop Int ...	Revue de la Cooperation Internationale [A publication]
R Coree	Revue de Coree [A publication]
RCOT	Recoton Corp. [NASDAQ symbol] (NQ)

RCP	RADAR Control Panel (MCD)
RCP	RADAR Conversion Program
RCP	Radiation Constraints Panel (MCD)
RCP	Radiative-Convective-Photochemical [Meteorology]
RCP	Radical Caucus in Psychiatry [Brooklyn, NY] (EA)
RCP	Radiological Control Program (NRCH)
RCP	Rapid City Public Library, Rapid City, SD [OCLC symbol] (OCLC)
RCP	Reactor Characterization Program [Nuclear energy] (NRCH)
RCP	Reactor Coolant Pump (NRCH)
RCP	Receive Clock Pulse
rcp	Recipient [MARC relator code] [Library of Congress]
RCP	Recognition and Control Processor [Data processing] (IBMDP)
RCP	Recording Control Panel
RCP	Recovery Command Post
RCP	Rectangular Coordinate Plotter
RCP	Regimental Command Post
RCP	Regional Conservation Program
RCP	Register Clock Pulse
RCP	Registry of Comparative Pathology [Washington, DC] (EA)
RCP	Reinforced Concrete Pavement
RCP	Reinforced Concrete Pipe [Technical drawings]
RCP	Relative Competitive Preference [Marketing]
RCP	Reliability Critical Problem (AAG)
RCP	Remote Control Panel
RCP	Request for Contractual Procurement
RCP	Requirements Change Proposal
RCP	Restartable Cryogenic Propellant
RCP	Restoration Control Point [Telecommunications] (TEL)
RCP	Returns Compliance Program [Internal Revenue Service]
RCP	Revolutionary Communist Party of India (PPW)
RCP	Riboflavin Carrier Protein [Immunology]
RCP	Right Circular Polarization
RCP	Rockefeller Center Properties, Inc. [NYSE symbol]
RCP	Roman Catholic Priest (ROG)
RCP	Romanian Communist Party
RCP	Rotation Combat Personnel
RCP	Royal College of Pathologists [British]
RCP	Royal College of Physicians [British]
RCP	Royal College of Physicians of London [British]
RCP	Royal College of Preceptors [British] (ROG)
RCP	Royal Commission on the Press [British]
RCPA	Reserve Components Program of the Army (AABC)
RCPA	Rural Cooperative Power Association
RCPAC	Reserve Components Personnel and Administration Center [Army] (AABC)
RCPath.......	Royal College of Pathologists [British]
RCPB	Reactor Coolant Pressure Boundary (NRCH)
RCP(b)	Russian Communist Party (Bolsheviks)
RCPBO	Research Communications in Psychology, Psychiatry, and Behavior [A publication]
RCPC	Regional Check Processing Centers
RCPC	Royal Canadian Postal Corps [Formerly, CPC]
RCPD	Reserve Components Personnel Directorate [Office of Personnel Operations] [Army]
RCPE	Radiological Control Practices Evaluation (MCD)
RCPE	Royal College of Physicians, Edinburgh
RCPEA	Revista Chilena de Pediatria [A publication]
RCPEd	Royal College of Physicians, Edinburgh
RCPGlas	Royal College of Physicians and Surgeons, Glasgow
RCPI	Revolutionary Communist Party of India (PPW)
RCPI	Royal College of Physicians, Ireland
RCPJA.......	Royal College of Physicians of London. Journal [A publication]
RCPL	Right Circularly Polarized Light
RCPL	Royal College of Physicians, London (ROG)
RCPO	Regional Contract Property Officer
RCPP	Reinforced Concrete Pressure Pipe
RCPS	Royal College of Physicians and Surgeons of Glasgow [Later, RFPS]
RCPS(C)	Royal College of Physicians and Surgeons of Canada
RCPT.........	Receipt (AFM)
RCPT.........	Receptacle (MSA)
RCPT.........	Reception (AABC)
RCPTN	Reception (MSA)
RCPV	Riot Control Patrol Vehicle
RCQ	Reconquista [Argentina] [Airport symbol] (OAG)
RCQUD	Revista de Ciencias Quimicas [A publication]
RCR	Rabbinical Council Record [New York] [A publication]
RCR	RADAR Control Room
RCR	Rated Capacity Report [Army]
RCR	Reactor Control Room
RCR	Reader Control Relay
RCR	Reciprocating Cryogenic Refrigerator
RCR	Regenerative Cyclic Reactor [Chemical engineering]
RCR	Relative Consumption Rate [Entomology]
RCR	Respiratory Control Ratio [Medicine]
RCR	Restitution of Conjugal Rights [Legal] [British] (ROG)
RCR	Retrofit Configuration Record [NASA] (NASA)
RC-R	Revista Chicano-Riquena [A publication]
RCr	Revue Critique [A publication]
RCr	Revue Critique d'Histoire et de Litterature [A publication]

RCR........... Rochester, IN [*Location identifier*] [*FAA*]   (FAAL)
RCR........... Royal Canadian Regiment [*Military*]
RCR........... Royal Canadian Rifles [*Military unit*]
RCR........... Royal College of Radiologists [*British*]
RCR........... Runway Condition Reading [*or Report*] [*Aviation*]   (FAAC)
RCRA .... Refrigeration Compressor Rebuilders Association [*Kansas City, MO*]   (EA)
RCRA .... Resource Conservation and Recovery Act [*Pronounced "rickra"*] [*1976*]
RCRA .... Rural Cooperative and Recovery Act   (OICC)
RCRBSJ ..... Research Council on Riveted and Bolted Structural Joints [*Later, RCSC*]   (EA)
RCRC .... Rabbinic Center for Research and Counseling [*Westfield, NJ*]   (EA)
RCRC .... Reinforced Concrete Research Council   (EA)
RCRC .... Revoked Commission, Returned to Civilian Status [*Navy*]
RCRD .... Record   (AFM)
RCRF........... Rei Cretariae Romanae Fautorum Acta [*A publication*]
RCRHRCS ... Research Center for Religion and Human Rights in Closed Societies
R Crit Dr Int Prive ... Revue Critique de Droit International Prive [*A publication*]
RCRL........... Reliability Critical Ranking List   (AAG)
R1 Cro .... Croke's English King's Bench Reports Tempore Elizabeth [*1582-1603*]   (DLA)
R2 Cro .... Croke's English King's Bench Reports Tempore James I [*1603-25*]   (DLA)
R3 Cro .... Croke's English King's Bench Reports Tempore Charles I [*1625-41*]   (DLA)
RCRP........... Regional Centers for Radiological Physics [*National Cancer Institute*]
RCRR .... Roster Chaplain - Ready Reserve [*Army*]
RCRS .... Regenerative Carbon-Dioxide Removal System   (MCD)
RcRt .... Romantic Reassessment [*A publication*]
RCRUA .... Revista. Consejo de Rectores. Universidades Chilenas [*A publication*]
RCRVA .... Russian Chemical Reviews [*English Translation*] [*A publication*]
RCS........... Rabbit Aorta Contracting Substance [*TA$_2$ - see TA, Thromboxane*] [*Biochemistry*]
RCS........... RADAR Calibration Sphere
RCS........... RADAR Collimator System
RCS........... RADAR Control Ship
RCS........... RADAR Cross Section
RCS........... Radio Command System
RCS........... Radio Communications Set
RCS........... Radio Communications System [*Military*]   (CAAL)
R & CS........ Radiological and Chemical Support [*Nuclear energy*]   (NRCH)
RCS........... Rate Command System   (AAG)
RCS........... Reaction Control System [*or Subsystem*] [*Apollo*] [*NASA*]
RCS........... Reactive Current Sensing   (MCD)
RCS........... Reactor Coolant System   (NRCH)
RCS........... Rearward Communications System   (MDG)
RCS........... Reentry Control System [*Aerospace*]   (AFM)
RCS........... Refurbishment Cost Study   (KSC)
RCS........... Regional Control Station [*Military*]   (MCD)
RCS........... Reliability Control Specification
RCS........... Reliable Corrective Action Summary   (AAG)
RCS........... Reloadable Control Storage [*Data processing*]
RCS........... Remington's Compiled Statutes [*1922*]   (DLA)
RCS........... Remote Computing Service
RCS........... Remote Computing Supplies [*Downers Grove, IL*] [*Hardware manufacturer*]
RCS........... Remote Control Set
RC(S)........ Remote Control (System)   (DEN)
RCS........... Reports Control Symbol [*Military*]
RCS........... Representative Conflict Situations [*Army*]
RCS........... Request for Consultation Service   (MCD)
RCS........... Requirement Clearance Symbol [*Military*]   (AFM)
RCS........... Requirements Control Symbol [*Military*]   (MCD)
RCS........... Residential Conservation Service [*Offered by major electric and gas utilities*]
RCS........... Reticulum Cell Sarcoma [*Medicine*]
RCS........... Retrofit Configuration System   (MCD)
RCS........... Revenue Cutter Service [*Coast Guard*]
RCS........... Rich Coast Sulphur Ltd. [*Vancouver Stock Exchange symbol*]
RCS........... Ride-Control Segment [*or System*] [*Aviation*]
RCS........... Right Coronary Sinus [*Cardiology*]
RCS........... Rizzoli Corriere della Sera [*Publisher*]
RCS........... Royal Choral Society
RCS........... Royal College of Science [*British*]
RCS........... Royal College of Surgeons [*British*]
RCS........... Royal Commonwealth Society [*British*]
RCS........... Royal Corps of Signals [*British*]
RCSAV .... Rozpravy Ceskoslovenske Akademie Ved [*A publication*]
RCSC .... Radio Component Standardization Committee [*British*]
RCSC .... Reaction Control System [*or Subsystem*] Controller [*Apollo*] [*NASA*]
RCSC .... Research Council on Structural Connections [*Formerly, RCRBSJ*]   (EA)
RCSCC ...... Royal Canadian Sea Cadets Corps
RCSDE....... Reactor Coolant System Dose Equivalent   (IEEE)

RCSDP....... League of Red Cross Societies Development Program
RCSE........... Remote Control and Status Equipment   (MCD)
RCSE........... Royal College of Surgeons, Edinburgh
RCSEd .... Royal College of Surgeons, Edinburgh
RCSEng ..... Royal College of Surgeons, England
RCSF........... Rivista Critica di Storia della Filosofia [*A publication*]
RCSH .... Revue Congolaise des Sciences Humaines [*A publication*]
RCSHSB .... Red Cedar Shingle and Handsplit Shake Bureau [*Formed by a merger of Red Cedar Shingle Bureau and Handsplit Red Cedar Shake Association*] [*Bellevue, WA*]   (EA)
RCSI........... Receipt for [*or of*] Classified Security Information   (AAG)
RCSI........... Royal College of Surgeons, Ireland
RCSIS .... Radio/Cable Switching Integration System   (MCD)
RCSMC ...... Recent Advances in Studies on Cardiac Structure and Metabolism [*A publication*]
RCSS .... Radial Compression Separation System [*Chromatography*]
RCSS .... Random Communication Satellite System
RCSSA .... Regional Centre for Seismology for South America [*Lima, Peru*]   (EA-IO)
RCS Supp ... Remington's Compiled Statutes, Supplement   (DLA)
RCSX .... North American Car Corp. [*AAR code*]
RCT........... RADAR Control Trailer   (AABC)
RCT........... Radiation/Chemical Technician   (IEEE)
RCT........... Radiobeacon Calibration Transmitter
RCT........... Randomized Clinical Trial [*Medicine*]
RCT........... Randomized Control Trial [*Statistics*]
RCT........... Receipts [*Stock exchange term*]
RCT........... Received Copy of Temporary Pay Record
RCT........... Recruit
RCT........... Reed City, MI [*Location identifier*] [*FAA*]   (FAAL)
RCT........... Regimental Combat Team
RCT........... Region Control Task [*Data processing*]   (BUR)
RCT........... Remote Control [*Systems*]   (MCD)
RCT........... Remote Control Terminal   (MCD)
RCT........... Repair Cycle Time   (MCD)
RCT........... Repeat Cycle Timer
RCT........... Resolver Control Transformer
RCT........... Resource Consulting Teacher
RCT........... Response Coordination Team [*Nuclear energy*]   (NRCH)
RC-T........... Revenue Canada, Taxation
RCT........... Reversible Counter
RCT........... Rework/Completion Tag   (NRCH)
RCT........... Ridgecrest Resources [*Vancouver Stock Exchange symbol*]
RCT........... Roll Call Training
RCT........... Rorschach Content Test [*Psychology*]
RCT........... Royal Clinical Teacher [*British*]
RCT........... Royal Corps of Transport [*Army*] [*British*]
RCT........... Royal Cosmic Theology [*British*]
RCTB......... Reserve Components Troop Basis [*Army*]   (AABC)
RCTC......... Regeneratively-Cooled Thrust Chamber
RCTC......... Reserve Components Training Center [*Military*]
RCTC .... Union of Rail Canada Traffic Controllers [*See also CCFC*]
RCTCA...... Recherche Technique [*A publication*]
RCTDPOVALCAN ... Request Concurrent Travel of Dependents by Privately Owned Vehicle [*ALCAN Highway or Via Route Required*] [*Army*]   (AABC)
RCTEA .... Rubber Chemistry and Technology [*A publication*]
RCTG .... Recruiting   (AABC)
RCTL......... Resistance-Coupled Transistor Logic
RCTL......... Resistor-Capacitor Transistor Logic
RCTM......... Regional Center for Tropical Meteorology [*National Hurricane Center*]
RCTN .... Reaction   (MSA)
RCTP......... Reserve Component Troop Program
RCTPA .... Russian Castings Production [*English Translation*] [*A publication*]
RCTPS .... Revue Canadienne de Theorie Politique et Sociale [*A publication*]
R & C Tr Cas ... Railway and Canal Traffic Cases [*Neville*] [*England*]   (DLA)
RCTS......... Reactor Coolant Treatment System   (NRCH)
R (Ct of Sess) ... Rettie, Crawford, and Melville's Session Cases, Fourth Series [*1873-98*] [*Scotland*]   (DLA)
RCTSR .... Radio Code Test, Speed of Response
RCTV......... RCA Cable and Rockefeller Center Cable Pay-TV Program Service
RCTV......... Remote Controlled Target Vehicle [*Military*]   (INF)
RCU........... RADAR Calibration Unit
RCU........... RADAR Control Unit [*Military*]   (CAAL)
RCU........... Rate Construction Unit [*Hypothetical basic currency unit*]
RCU........... Reference Control Unit   (MCD)
RCU........... Relay Control Unit   (AAG)
RCU........... Remote Control Unit
RCU........... Requisition Control Unit
RCU........... Research into Chronic Unemployment [*British*]
RCU........... Research Coordinating Unit [*Oklahoma State Department of Vocational and Technical Education*] [*Stillwater, OK*]
R/CU........... Research and Curriculum Unit [*Mississippi State University*] [*Research center*]   (RCD)
RCU........... Reserve Component Unit   (AABC)
RCU........... Respiratory Care Unit [*Medicine*]
RCU........... Rio Cuarto [*Argentina*] [*Airport symbol*]   (OAG)

RCU............ Rocket Countermeasure Unit
RCUA......... Remote Checkout Umbilical Array
RCuBib....... Revista de Cultura Biblica [*Rio De Janeiro/Sao Paulo, Brazil*] [*A publication*]
RCUEP....... Research Center for Urban and Environmental Planning [*Princeton University*]
RCUL.......... Reference Control Unit Launch   (MCD)
RCUR......... Recurrent   (MSA)
R Current Activities Tech Ed ... Review of Current Activities in Technical Education [*A publication*]
RCuTeol..... Revista de Cultura Teologica [*Sao Paulo, Brazil*] [*A publication*]
RCV............ RADAR Control Van   (NATG)
RCV............ Radiation Control Valve   (NRCH)
RCV............ Receive   (AFM)
RCV............ Receiver/Exciter Subsystem [*Deep Space Instrumentation Facility, NASA*]
RCV............ Red Cell Volume [*Hematology*]
RCV............ Relative Conductor Volume
RCV............ Remote-Controlled Vehicle   (MCD)
RCV............ Replacement Cost Valuation [*Insurance*]
RCV............ Restartable Cryogenic Vehicle
RCV............ Reversed Circular Vection [*Optics*]
RCV............ Revised Claim Valuation [*Insurance*]
RCV............ Rich Cut Virginia [*Tobacco*]   (ROG)
RCV............ Riot Control Vehicle
RCVD......... Received   (MSA)
RCVG......... Receiving   (MSA)
RCVG......... Replacement Carrier Fighter Group [*V is Navy code for Fighter*]
RCVR......... Receiver   (AAG)
RCVRB....... Royal Military College of Canada. Civil Engineering Research Report [*A publication*]
RCVS......... Rassegna di Cultura e Vita Scolastica [*A publication*]
RCVS......... Remote Control Video Switch   (MCD)
RCVS......... Royal College of Veterinary Surgeons [*British*]
RCVSG....... Readiness Antisubmarine Warfare Carrier Air Wing [*Navy*]   (NVT)
RCVTB....... Recherches Veterinaires [*A publication*]
RCVV......... Rear Compressor Variable Vane
RCVW........ Readiness Attack Carrier Air Wing [*Navy*]   (NVT)
RCVY......... Recovery   (MSA)
RCW........... Raw Cooling Water [*Nuclear energy*]   (NRCH)
RCW........... Reactor Cooling Water   (NRCH)
RCW........... Record Control Word [*Data processing*]
RCW........... Register Containing Word
RCW........... Research Center on Women   (EA)
RCW........... Resident Careworker
RCW........... Return Control Word
RCWA......... Revised Code of Washington, Annotated   (DLA)
RCWI.......... Right Ventricular Cardiac Work Index [*Cardiology*]
RCWP......... Rural Clean Water Program [*Department of Agriculture*]
RCWS......... Remote Control Water Sampler
RCWS......... Russian Children's Welfare Society   (EA)
RCX............ Ladysmith, WI [*Location identifier*] [*FAA*]   (FAAL)
RCY............ Red Cross and Red Crescent Youth
RCY............ Remaining Cycles   (MCD)
RCY............ Rotating Coil Yoke
RCYRA........ Rooster Class Yacht Racing Association   (EA)
RCZ............ Radiation Control Zone
RCZ............ Rear Combat Zone   (NATG)
RCZ............ Rockingham, NC [*Location identifier*] [*FAA*]   (FAAL)
RD.............. Airlift International, Inc. [*ICAO designator*]
Rd............... Albert Rolland [*France*] [*Research code symbol*]
RD.............. Boots Pure Drug Co. [*Great Britain*] [*Research code symbol*]
RD.............. Directional Radio Beacon [*ITU designation*]   (CET)
RD.............. Distribution Is Restricted to Government Agencies Only [*Advice of supply action code*] [*Army*]
RD.............. Indian Revenue Decisions   (DLA)
rd................ Rad [*Non-SI unit; preferred unit is Gy, Gray*]
RD.............. RADAR   (DEN)
RD.............. RADAR Data
RD.............. RADAR Display
RD.............. RADARman [*Also, RDM*] [*Navy rating*]
RD.............. Radiation Detection
Rd............... Radiolaria [*Quality of the bottom*] [*Nautical charts*]
RD.............. Radiological Defense [*To minimize the effect of nuclear radiation on people and resources*]
RD.............. Random Drift
RD.............. Random Driver [*Nuclear energy*]   (NRCH)
RD.............. Range Development   (MUGU)
R/D............. Rate of Descent [*Aviation*]   (MCD)
RD.............. Raynaud's Disease [*Medicine*]
RD.............. Reaction of Degeneration [*Physiology*]
RD.............. Read   (AAG)
RD.............. Read Data
R & D......... Read and Destroy
RD.............. Read Direct
RD.............. Readiness Data
RD.............. Readiness Date
RD.............. Reappraisement Decisions   (DLA)
RD.............. Rear Door
RD.............. Receipt Day   (NRCH)

RD.............. Received Data   (IEEE)
RD.............. Recemment Degorgee [*Recently Disgorged*] [*Refers to aging of wine*] [*French*]
RD.............. Recognition Differential
RD.............. Record Description [*Data processing*]
RD.............. Recorders-Reproducers [*JETDS nomenclature*] [*Military*]   (CET)
RD.............. Recording Demand   (DEN)
RD.............. Red
RD.............. Red Pennant [*Navy*] [*British*]
RD.............. Refer to Drawer [*Banking*]
RD.............. Reference Designator   (NASA)
RD.............. Reference Document
RD.............. Reference Drawing   (NATG)
RD.............. Regio Decreto [*Royal Decree*] [*Latin*]   (DLA)
RD.............. Regional Director
RD.............. Register Drive   (MSA)
RD.............. Registered   (ROG)
RD.............. Registered Dietitian
RD.............. Reinforcement Designee [*Air Force*]   (AFM)
RD.............. Relative Density
RD.............. Relaxation Delay
RD.............. Relay Drawer
RD.............. Relay Driver
RD.............. Remove Directory [*Data processing*]
RD.............. Renaissance Drama [*A publication*]
RD.............. Renal Disease [*Medicine*]
RD.............. Rendered   (ROG)
RD.............. Replenishable Demand
RD.............. Reply Delay   (MUGU)
R of D........ Reporter of Debate [*US Senate*]
RD.............. Required Date
R & D........ Requirements and Distribution   (AFM)
RD.............. Requirements Document [*NASA*]   (KSC)
R & D........ Research and Demonstration [*Labor training*]
RD.............. Research and Development
R & D........ Research and Development
RD.............. Reserve Decoration [*Navy*] [*British*]
RD.............. Resource Development
RD.............. Respiratory Disease
RD.............. Restricted Data [*Security classification*]
RD.............. Retention and Disposal
RD.............. Retinal Detachment [*Ophthalmology*]
RD.............. Revision Directive [*Drawings*]
RD.............. Revista de Dialectologia y Tradiciones Populares [*A publication*]
RD.............. Revolutionary Development [*South Vietnam*]
R du D....... Revue du Droit   (DLA)
R de D....... Revue de Droit. Universite de Sherbrooke [*A publication*]
RD.............. Revue Historique de Droit Francais et Etranger [*A publication*]
RD.............. Reye's Disease [*Medicine*]
RD.............. Right Defense
RD.............. Right Deltoid [*Medicine*]
RD.............. Right Door [*Theater*]
RD.............. Rights in Data   (OICC)
RD.............. Ringdown [*Telecommunications*]   (TEL)
RD.............. Rive Droite [*Right Bank*] [*French*]
RD.............. Rivista Dalmatica [*A publication*]
RD.............. Rix Dollar
RD.............. Road [*Maps and charts*]   (AAG)
RD.............. Rod
RD.............. Romanovsky Dye [*Biological stain*]
RD.............. Rood [*Unit of measurement*]
RD.............. Roof Drain   (AAG)
RD.............. Root Diameter   (MSA)
R/D............. Rotary to Digital   (MCD)
RD.............. Rotodrome
RD.............. Round   (AAG)
RD.............. Royal Dragoons [*British*]
RD.............. Royal Dutch Petroleum Co. [*NYSE symbol*]
RD.............. Royal Naval Reserve Decoration [*British*]
RD.............. Ruling Date [*IRS*]
RD.............. Run Down [*Typography*]
RD.............. Running Days
RD.............. Rupture Disk   (KSC)
RD.............. Rural Deacon [*or Deaconry*] [*Church of England*]
RD.............. Rural Dean
RD.............. Rural Delivery
RD.............. Rural Development
RD.............. Rural District
rd................ Rutherford [*Unit of strength of a radioactive source*]
RD1............ RADARman, First Class [*Navy rating*]
RD2............ RADARman, Second Class [*Navy rating*]
RD3............ RADARman, Third Class [*Navy rating*]
RDA............ Radioactive Dentin Abrasion [*Dentistry*]
RDA............ Ranging Demodulator Assembly [*Deep Space Instrumentation Facility, NASA*]
RDA............ Rassemblement Democratique Africain [*Niger*]   (PD)
RDA............ Rassemblement Democratique Africain [*Ivorian*]   (PPW)
RDA............ Read Data Available

RDA............ Readers Digest Association [*Commercial firm*] [*Pleasantville, NY*] (EA)
RDA............ Real-Time Debugging Aid
RDA............ Recirculation Duct Assembly
RDA............ Recommended Daily Allowance [*Dietary*]
RDA............ Recommended Duty Assignment (AFM)
RDA............ Regional Data Associates [*Bala Cynwyd, PA*] [*Information service*] (EISS)
RDA............ Regional Dental Activity (AABC)
RDA............ Register Display Assembly
RDA............ Reliability Design Analysis (MCD)
RDA............ Remote Data Access (NASA)
RDA............ Request for Deviation Approval (MCD)
RDA............ Research and Development Abstracts [*A publication*]
RD & A........ Research, Development, and Acquisition [*A publication*]
RD & A........ Research, Development, and Acquisition [*DoD*]
RDA............ Research and Development, Army
R & DA........ Research and Development Associates for Military Food and Packaging Systems [*San Antonio, TX*] (EA)
RDA............ Resent, Demand, Appreciate [*In Sidney Simon, Leland Howe, and Howard Kirschenbaum's book "Values Clarification"*]
RDA............ Resident Data Area (NASA)
RDA............ Right Dorso Anterior [*Medicine*] (ROG)
RDA............ Rod Drop Accident (IEEE)
RDA............ Rome Daily American [*An English-language newspaper in Italy*]
RDA............ Royal Danish Army (NATG)
RDA............ Royal Defence Academy [*British*]
RDA............ Rules for the Discipline of Attorneys (DLA)
RDA............ Rural Development Act [*1972*] (OICC)
RDAC......... Report. Department of Antiquities of Cyprus [*A publication*]
RDAC......... Research and Development Acquisition Committee [*Military*]
RDAF.......... Revue de Droit Administratif et de Droit Fiscal [*Lausanne, Switzerland*] (DLA)
RDAF.......... Royal Danish Air Force
RDAFCI...... Research and Development Associates, Food and Container Institute (EA)
RDAISA...... Research, Development, and Acquisition Information Systems Agency [*Army*] (AABC)
RDAL.......... Representation Dependent Accessing Language
RDAR......... Reliability Design Analysis Report (AAG)
RDARA....... Regional and Domestic Air Route Area
RDAS......... Reflectivity Data Acquisition System
RDAT......... RADAR Data (FAAC)
RDAT......... Registered Designs Appeal Tribunal (DLA)
RDAT......... Remote Data Acquisition Terminal (NRCH)
RDAT......... Research and Development Acceptance Test
RDAT......... Rotary Digital Audio Tape
RDAU........ Remote Data Acquisition Unit
RDB........... RADAR Decoy Balloon [*Air Force*]
RDB........... Ramped Dump Barge
RDB........... Rapidly Deployable Barge [*Military*] (MCD)
RDB........... Rare Disease Database [*National Organization for Rare Disorders*] [*New Fairfield, CT*] [*Information service*] (EISS)
RDB........... Relational Database
RDB........... Research and Development Board [*Abolished, 1953, functions transferred to Department of Defense*]
RDB........... Resistance Decade Box
RDB........... Round Die Bushing
RDB........... Royal Danish Ballet
RDB........... Rural Development Board [*British*]
RDBA........ Roll Drive and Brake Assembly
RDBL........ Readable
RDBMD...... Review on the Deformation Behavior of Materials [*A publication*]
RDC........... Chief RADARman [*Navy rating*]
RDC........... RADAR Data Converter (MCD)
RDC........... RADAR Design Corporation
RDC........... RADAR Display Console
RDC........... Radiac [*Nucleonics*]
RDC........... Radiation Density Constant
RDC........... Radioactivity Decay Constant
RDC........... Rail Diesel Car
RDC........... Rapaport Diamond Corporation [*New York, NY*] [*Information service*] (EISS)
RDC........... Rapid Development Capability [*Military*] (NG)
RDC........... Rassemblement Democratique Caledonien [*Caledonian Democratic Rally*] (PPW)
RDC........... Rate Damping Control
RDC........... Read Data Check (CMD)
RDC........... Real Decisions Corporation [*Darien, CT*] [*Information service*] (EISS)
RDC........... Reduce (MSA)
RDC........... Reference Designator Code (NASA)
RDC........... Reflex Digital Control
RDC........... Refugee Documentation Centre [*Geneva, Switzerland*] [*Information service*] (EISS)
RDC........... Regional Data Center [*Marine science*] (MSC)
RDC........... Regional Dissemination Center [*NASA*]
RDC........... Reliability Data Center (KSC)
RDC........... Remote Data Collection (MCD)

RDC........... Remote Data Concentrator
RDC........... Remote Detonation Capability
RDC........... Reply Delay Compensation (MUGU)
RDC........... Request for Document Change (NASA)
RDC........... Research and Development Command [*Military*]
RDC........... Research Diagnostic Criteria [*Medicine, psychiatry*]
RdC........... Resto del Carlino [*A publication*]
RDC........... Revolutionary Development Cadre [*South Vietnam*]
RDC........... Revue de Droit Canonique [*A publication*]
RDC........... Revue de Droit Compare. Association Quebecoise pour l'Etude Comparative du Droit [*A publication*]
RDC........... Rochester Diocesan Chronicle [*A publication*]
RDC........... Rotary Dispersion Colorimeter
RDC........... Rotating Disk Contractor [*Chemical engineering*]
RDC........... Rowan Companies, Inc. [*NYSE symbol*]
RDC........... Royal Defence Corps [*British*]
RDC........... Rubber Development Corporation [*Expired, 1947*]
RDC........... Running-Down Clause [*Business and trade*]
RDC........... Rural Development and Conservation [*Department of Agriculture*]
RDC........... Rural District Council [*British*]
RDC........... Sisters of Divine Compassion [*Roman Catholic religious order*]
RDCA......... Rural District Councils Association [*British*]
RDCC........ Regional and Distribution Carriers Conference [*Alexandria, VA*] (EA)
RDCEHCY ... Research and Demonstration Center for the Education of Handicapped Children and Youth (EA)
RDCF........ Restricted Data Cover Folder (AAG)
RDCHE...... Rene Dubos Center for Human Environments (EA)
RDCM....... Master Chief RADARman [*Navy rating*]
RDCM....... Reduced Delta Code Modulation [*Digital memory*]
RDCN....... Reduction (MSA)
RDCO........ Reliability Data Control Office (AAG)
RDCP........ Remote Display Control Panel (MCD)
RDCR........ Reducer (MSA)
RDCS........ Reconfiguration Data Collection Subsystem (MCD)
RDCS........ Senior Chief RADARman [*Navy rating*]
R & DCTE ... Research and Development Center for Teacher Education [*Department of Education*]
RDCU........ Receipt Delivery Control Unit [*Social Security Administration*]
RDD........... Random Digit Dialing [*Telecommunications*]
RDD........... Rapid Demolition Device
RDD........... Rassemblement Democratique Dahomeen [*Dahomean Democratic Rally*]
RDD........... Reactor Development Division [*of AEC*]
RDD........... Redding [*California*] [*Airport symbol*] (OAG)
RDD........... Reference Design Document (KSC)
RDD........... Required Delivery Date (AABC)
RDD........... Requirements Definition Document [*NASA*] (NASA)
RDD........... Requisition Due Date (TEL)
RD & D...... Research, Development, and Demonstration
RDD........... Research and Development Directorate [*Army*]
RDD........... Return Due Date [*IRS*]
RDD........... Routine Dynamic Display (MCD)
RDDA........ Recommended Daily Dietary Allowance
RDDCS...... Range Drone Data Control System [*Military*] (CAAL)
RDD & E.... Research, Development, Diffusion [*or Dissemination*], and Evaluation
RDDM....... Reactor Deck Development Mock Up (NRCH)
RdDM....... Revue des Deux Mondes [*A publication*]
RDDMI....... Radio Digital Distance Magnetic Indicator (MCD)
RDDP........ RNA-Directed DNA Polymerase [*Formerly, RIDP*] [*An enzyme*]
RDDR........ Rod Drive
RDDS........ RADAR Data Distribution Switchboard [*Military*] (CAAL)
RDDS........ Retail Dental Delivery System [*Dentistry*]
RdDxM....... Revue des Deux Mondes [*A publication*]
RDE........... RADAR Display Equipment
RDE........... Radial Defect Examination (IEEE)
RDE........... Receptor-Destroying Enzyme [*A neuraminidase*] [*Immunochemistry*]
RDE........... Recommended Distribution of Effort [*Civil defense*]
RDE........... Reliability Data Extractor (MCD)
RD & E...... Research, Development, and Engineering
RDE........... Research and Development Establishment [*British*]
RDE........... Research Development Exchange (OICC)
RdE........... Revista de las Espanas [*A publication*]
Rd'E........... Revue d'Egyptologie [*Publiee par la Societe Francaise d'Egyptologie*] [*Cairo*] [*A publication*]
RDE........... Revue d'Esthetique [*A publication*]
RdE........... Rivista di Estetica [*A publication*]
RdE........... Rotating Disc Electrode
RDE & A.... Research, Development, Engineering, and Acquisition (RDA)
RDEB........ Recessive Dystrophic Epidermolysis Bullosa [*Also, EBDR*] [*Dermatology*]
RdelE........ Revista de Ideas Esteticas [*A publication*]
RdeInd....... Revista de las Indias [*A publication*]
R & DELSEC ... Research and Development Electronic Security (AABC)
RDEP......... Recruit Depot [*Navy*]
R Der Cienc Polit ... Revista de Derecho y Ciencias Politicas. Universidad de San Marcos [*A publication*]
R Der (Concepcion) ... Revista de Derecho (Concepcion) [*A publication*]

R Derechos Humanos ... Revista de Derechos Humanos [*A publication*]
R Der Int Cienc Diplom ... Revista de Derecho Internacional y Ciencias Diplomaticas [*A publication*]
RD & ES ..... Requirements Determination and Exercise System [*Military*] (MCD)
RdEt .... Revista de Etnografia [*A publication*]
R Deux Mondes ... Revue des Deux Mondes [*A publication*]
RDF .... RADAR Direction Finder [*or Finding*] (CET)
RDF .... Radial Distribution Function [*X-ray diffraction*]
RDF .... Radio Direction Finder [*or Finding*] (AABC)
RDF .... Rapid Deployment Force [*Military*]
RDF .... Record Definition Field [*Data processing*] (BUR)
RDF .... Redford Resources, Inc. [*Vancouver Stock Exchange symbol*]
RDF .... Reflection Direction Finding
RDF .... Refuse-Derived Fuel
RDF .... Repeater Distribution Frame (NATG)
RDF .... Reserve Defense Fleet [*Navy*]
RDF .... Resource Data File (MCD)
RDF .... Revue de France [*A publication*]
RDF .... Rheumatoid Disease Foundation [*Washington, DC*] (EA)
RDF .... Rivista di Filosofia [*A publication*]
RDF .... Royal Dublin Fusiliers [*British*]
RDFDF....... Redford Resources [*NASDAQ symbol*] (NQ)
RDFL .... Reflection Direction Finding, Low Angle (MCD)
RDF/LT ..... Rapid Deployment Force/Light Tank [*Military*] (MCD)
RDFSTA..... Radio Direction Finder Station
RDFU......... Research and Development Field Unit [*Military*]
RDFU-V ..... Research and Development Field Unit - Vietnam [*Military*] (MCD)
RDG........... Reading [*British depot code*]
RDG........... Reading [*Pennsylvania*] [*Airport symbol*] (OAG)
RDG........... Reference Drawing Group [*NATO*] (NATG)
RDG........... Regional Development Grant [*British*]
RDG........... Regis Development Corp. [*Vancouver Stock Exchange symbol*]
RDG........... Registrar Data Group [*Owings, MD*] [*Information service*] (EISS)
RDG........... Research Discussion Group [*An association*] [*Morgantown, WV*] (EA)
RDG........... Resolver Differential Generator
RDG........... Ridge (MSA)
RDG........... Right Digestive Gland
RDG........... Rounding
RDGC .... Reading Company [*NASDAQ symbol*] (NQ)
RDGE .... Resorcinol Diglycidyl Ether [*Organic chemistry*]
RDGF........ Retina-Derived Growth Factor [*Biochemistry*]
RDGTA....... Rational Drug Therapy [*A publication*]
RDH .... Radioactive Drain Header [*Nuclear energy*] (NRCH)
RDH .... Red Hill Marketing Group Ltd. [*Vancouver Stock Exchange symbol*]
RDH .... Registered Dental Hygienist
RDH .... Resource Dispersion Hypothesis [*Animal ecology*]
RdH .... Revista de Historia [*A publication*]
RDH .... Round Head
RDHER .... Revolutionary Development Hamlet Evaluation Report [*South Vietnam*]
RDI .... Radio Doppler Inertial
RDI .... Rassemblement Democratique pour l'Independance [*Quebec*]
RDI .... Reference Designation Index (MCD)
RDI .... Rejection and Disposition Item
RDI .... Released Data Index
RDI .... Relief and Development Institute [*Formerly, International Disaster Institute*] (EA)
RDI .... Remote Data Input
RDI .... Research and Development Institute, Inc. [*Montana State University*] [*Research center*] (RCD)
RDI .... Research and Development of Instrumentation [*Program*] [*Army*]
RDI .... Riley's Datashare International Ltd. [*Toronto Stock Exchange symbol*]
RDI .... Route Digit Indicator [*Telecommunications*] (TEL)
RDI .... Royal Designer for Industry [*British*]
RDI .... Rupture Delivery Interval [*Obstetrics*]
RDIA.......... Regional Development Incentives Act
R Dialect & Tradic Popul ... Revista de Dialectologia y Tradiciones Populares [*A publication*]
RdiE .... Rivista di Estetica [*A publication*]
RdiF........... Rivista di Filosofia [*A publication*]
RDIPP........ Rivista di Diritto Internazionale Privato e Processuale (DLA)
R Dir Adm ... Revista de Direito Administrativo [*A publication*]
RDIS .... Replenishment Demand Inventory System
RDIS .... Research and Development Information System [*Later, EPD/RDIS*] [*Electric Power Research Institute*] [*Information service*] (EISS)
RDIU.......... Remote Device Interface Unit
RDJ............ Readjustment
RDJ............ Rio De Janeiro [*Brazil*] [*Later, VSS*] [*Geomagnetic observatory code*]
RDJ............ Rio De Janeiro [*Brazil*] [*Seismograph station code, US Geological Survey*] (SEIS)
RdJB .... Recht der Jugend und des Bildungswesens [*Neuwied, West Germany*] (DLA)

RDJCT....... Register, Department of Justice and the Courts of the United States [*A publication*]
RDJTF .... Rapid Deployment Joint Task Force [*Military*] (RDA)
RDK........... Red Oak, IA [*Location identifier*] [*FAA*] (FAAL)
RDK........... Research and Development Kit
RDK........... Ruddick Corp. [*American Stock Exchange symbol*]
RDKN .... Redken Laboratories [*NASDAQ symbol*] (NQ)
RDL........... Radial (MSA)
RDL........... Radioactive Decay Law
RDL........... Radiological Defense Laboratory [*NASA*] (KSC)
RDL........... Rail Dynamics Laboratory
RDL........... Random Dynamic Load
RDL........... [*The*] Reactor Development Laboratory [*UKAEA*] [*British*]
RDL........... Reciprocal Detection Latency
RDL........... Recurring Document Listing (MCD)
RDL........... Redlaw Industries, Inc. [*American Stock Exchange symbol*] [*Toronto Stock Exchange symbol*]
RDL........... Regional Development Laboratory [*Philadelphia, PA*]
RDL........... Remote Display Link
RDL........... Replaceable Display Light
RDL........... Resistor Diode Logic
RdL........... Revista de Letras [*A publication*]
RdL........... Revista do Livro [*A publication*]
RDL........... Rim of Dorsal Lip
RDL........... Rocket Development Laboratory [*Air Force*]
RDLGE .... Democratic Movement for the Liberation of Equatorial Guinea (PD)
RDLN .... Retrodorsolateral Nucleus [*Neuroanatomy*]
RDLP .... Research and Development Limited Partnership [*Tax-shelter investment*]
RDLX .... Airlift International, Inc. [*Air carrier designation symbol*]
RdM........... Die Religionen der Menschheit [*A publication*] (BJA)
RDM .... RADARman [*Also, RD*]
RDM .... Radial Distribution Method
RDM .... Real-Time Data Manager (MCD)
RDM .... Recording Demand Meter
RDM .... Redmond [*Oregon*] [*Airport symbol*] (OAG)
RDM .... Relay Driver Module
RDM .... Remote Digital Multiplexer (MCD)
RDM .... Revue des Deux Mondes [*A publication*]
RdM .... Revue de la Mediterranee [*A publication*]
RdM .... Revue de Musicologie [*Paris*] [*A publication*]
RDMC........ Research and Development Management Course [*Army*]
R de D McGill ... Revue de Droit de McGill (DLA)
RDME .... Range and Distance Measuring Equipment
RDMF .... Rapidly Deployable Medical Facilities
RDMI .... Roof Drainage Manufacturers Institute [*Defunct*] (EA)
RDMS....... Range Data Measurement Subsystem (MCD)
RDMS....... Registered Diagnostic Medical Sonologist
RDMU....... Range-Drift Measuring Unit
RDN........... Rejection Disposition Notice
RDN........... Revue du Nord [*A publication*]
RDN........... Royal Danish Navy (NATG)
rDNA .... Deoxyribonucleic Acid, Recombinant [*Biochemistry; genetics*]
rDNA .... Deoxyribonucleic Acid, Ribosomal [*Biochemistry; genetics*]
RDNamur ... Revue Diocesaine de Namur [*A publication*]
R & DNET ... Research and Development Network [*Formerly, ARPANET*]
RDNG .... Reading (MSA)
RDNGB....... Ryukyu Daigaku Nogakubu Gakujutsu Hokoku [*A publication*]
RDNP......... Rassemblement Democratique Nationaliste et Progressiste [*Progressive Nationalist and Democratic Assembly*] [*Haitian*] (PD)
RDNS .... Readiness (MSA)
RDO........... Radio (AABC)
RDO........... Radio Readout
RDO........... Radiological Defense Officer [*Civil defense*]
RDO........... Range Development Officer (MUGU)
RDO........... Reconnaissance Duty Officer
RDO........... Redistribution Order [*Military*] (AFM)
RDO........... Regional Disbursing Office
RDO........... Research and Development Objectives [*Military*] (AFM)
RDO........... Research, Development, and Operation [*Military appropriation*]
R & DO ...... Research and Development Operations [*Marshall Space Flight Center*] [*NASA*] (NASA)
RDO........... River District Office [*National Weather Service*]
RDO........... Rodeo Resources Ltd. [*Vancouver Stock Exchange symbol*]
RDO........... Runway Duty Officer [*Aviation*] (MCD)
RDOC........ Reference Designation Overflow Code (NASA)
RDOM........ Restructured Division Operations Manual (MCD)
RDON .... Road Octane Number [*Fuel technology*]
RDOS........ Real-Time Disk-Operating System [*Data processing*]
RDOUT....... Readout
RDP .... RADAR Data Processing
RDP .... RADAR Digital Probe
RDP .... Radiation Degradation Product
RDP .... Range Data Processor (MCD)
RDP .... Range Deflection Protractor [*Weaponry*] (INF)
RDP .... Ration Distributing Point [*Military*]
RDP .... Reactor Development Program [*Nuclear Regulatory Commission*] (NRCH)

RDP .... Receiver and Data Processor (MCD)
RDP .... Rectifying-Demodulating Phonopneumograph [*Medicine*]
RDP .... Remote Data Processor
RDP .... Requirements Development Plan [*NASA*] (NASA)
RDP .... Research Data Publication [*Center*]
RDP .... Research and Development Plan
RD & P ...... Research, Development, and Production [*NATO*] (NATG)
RDP .... Revolutionary Development Program [*South Vietnam*]
RdP .... Revue de Paris [*A publication*]
RDP .... Ribulosediphosphate [*Also, RuBP*] [*Biochemistry*]
RDP .... Right Dorso Posterior [*Medicine*] (ROG)
RDP .... Rocca Di Papa [*Italy*] [*Seismograph station code, US Geological Survey*] (SEIS)
RdPac .... Revista del Pacifico [*A publication*]
RDPB .... RADAR Data Plotting Board
RDPB .... Research and Development Planning and Budgeting (AFIT)
RDPC .... RADAR Data Processing Center
RDPE .... RADAR Data Processing Equipment (AABC)
RDPJ .... Rail Discharge Point Jet (NATG)
RDPM .... Rail Discharge Point Mogas (NATG)
RDPM .... Revised Draft Presidential Memorandum
RDPM .... Rotary Drive Piston Motor
RDPR .... Refer to Drawer Please Represent [*Business and trade*]
RDPS .... RADAR Data Processing System
RDPS .... Remote Docking Procedures Simulator (MCD)
RDPS .... Research and Development Planning Summary
RdQ .... Reading Quotient
RDR .... Grand Forks, ND [*Location identifier*] [*FAA*] (FAAL)
RDR .... RADAR (AAG)
RDR .... Raider
RDR .... Rapid Canadian Resource Corp. [*Vancouver Stock Exchange symbol*]
RDR .... Raw Data Recorder (NASA)
RDR .... Reader (MSA)
R/DR .... Rear Door [*Automotive engineering*]
RDR .... Receive Data Register [*Data processing*] (MDG)
RDR .... Rejection Disposition Report [*NASA*] (KSC)
RDR .... Relative Digestion Rate [*Nutrition*]
RDR .... Reliability Design Review
RDR .... Reliability Diagnostic Report (AAG)
RDR .... Remote Digital Readout
RDR .... Research and Development Report
RDR .... Research Division Report
RDR .... Risk Data Report [*Insurance*]
RDR .... Ryder System, Inc. [*NYSE symbol*]
RDR .... Ryukoku Daigaku Ronshu [*A publication*]
RDRBCN .... RADAR Beacon (KSC)
RDRD .... Remote Digital Readout
R/D Res/Develop ... R/D. Research/Development [*A publication*]
R Dr Homme ... Revue des Droits de l'Homme [*A publication*]
RDRIA .... Radiazioni e Radioisotopi [*A publication*]
RDRINT ...... RADAR Intermittent (IEEE)
R Dr Int Dr Comp ... Revue de Droit International et de Droit Compare [*A publication*]
RDRKB .... Ritsumeikan Daigaku Rikogaku Kenkyusho Kiyo [*A publication*]
R Droit Int Sci Dipl Pol ... Revue de Droit International de Sciences Diplomatiques et Politiques [*A publication*]
R Droits Homme ... Revue des Droits de l'Homme [*A publication*]
R Droit Soc ... Revue de Droit Social [*A publication*]
R Dr Publ Sci Polit ... Revue du Droit Public et de la Science Politique en France et a l'Etranger [*A publication*]
R Dr Rur ..... Revue de Droit Rural [*A publication*]
RDRSMTR ... RADAR Transmitter (AAG)
RDRV .... Rhesus Diploid-Cell-Strain Rabies Vaccine
RDS .... RADAR Distribution Switchboard
RDS .... RADAUS [*Radio-Austria AG*] Data-Service [*Vienna*] [*Telecommunications*] (TSSD)
RDS .... Radio Digital System [*Telecommunications*] (TEL)
RDS .... Radius (FAAC)
RDS .... Random Dot Stereogram
RDS .... Range Destruct System
RDS .... Raytheon Data Systems Co.
RDS .... Read Strobe
RDS .... Reeds [*Music*]
RDS .... Relative Detector Sensitivity [*Robotics technology*]
RDS .... Rendezvous Docking Simulator [*Aerospace*]
RDS .... Reperimento Documentazione Siderurgica [*Iron and Steel Documentation Service*] [*Rome, Italy*] [*Information service*] (EISS)
RDS .... Request for Data Services
RDS .... Required Number of Days of Stock
RDS .... Research Defence Society [*British*]
RDS .... Research and Development Service [*Army-Ordnance*]
RDS .... Research, Development, and Standardization [*Groups*] [*Army*] (RDA)
RD & S ...... Research, Development, and Studies [*Marine Corps*]
RDS .... Research and Development Survey
RDS .... Resistive Divider Standard
RDS .... Resource Development Services [*Philadelphia, PA*] (EA)
RDS .... Respiratory Distress Syndrome [*Formerly, HMD*] [*Medicine*]

RdS .... Responsabilita del Sapere [*A publication*]
RDS .... Retail Distribution Station [*Military*] (AFM)
RDS .... Revolutionary Development Support [*South Vietnam*]
RDS .... Revolving Discussion Sequence
RDS .... Rhode Island Department of State Library Services, Providence, RI [*OCLC symbol*] (OCLC)
RDS .... Richard D. Siegrest [*Alaska*] [*Seismograph station code, US Geological Survey*] (SEIS)
RDS .... Robotic Deriveter System
RDS .... Rocketdyne Digital Simulator [*NASA*] (NASA)
RDS .... Rokeach Dogmatism Scale
RDS .... Rounds [*of ammunition*] [*Military*]
RDS .... Royal Drawing Society [*British*]
RDS .... Royal Dublin Society
RDS .... Rural Development Service [*Department of Agriculture*]
RDSA .... Seaman Apprentice, RADARman Striker [*Navy rating*]
RD/SB .... Rudder Speed Brake (MCD)
RDSD .... Reliability Design Support Document (NRCH)
RDSD .... Revolutionary Development Support Division [*South Vietnam*]
RDSM .... Remote Digital Submultiplexer (KSC)
RDS/M .... Rounds per Minute
RDSN .... RADARman, Seaman [*Navy rating*]
RDSN .... Seaman, RADARman, Striker [*Navy rating*]
RdSO .... Rivista degli Studi Orientali [*A publication*]
RDSP .... Revolutionary Development Support Plan [*or Program*] [*South Vietnam*]
Rds Rd Constn ... Roads and Road Construction [*A publication*]
RDSS .... Rapid Deployable Surveillance Systems [*Military*] (NVT)
RD Sup ...... Revenue Decisions, Supplement [*India*] (DLA)
RDT .... Radio Digital Terminal [*Bell System*]
RDT .... Rapid Decompression Test
RDT .... Reactor Development and Technology (MCD)
RDT .... Reactor Drain Tank (NRCH)
RDT .... Redoubt [*Alaska*] [*Seismograph station code, US Geological Survey*] (SEIS)
RDT .... Regular Dialysis Treatment [*Medicine*]
RDT .... Reliability Demonstration Test
RDT .... Reliability Design Test
RDT .... Reliability Development Testing (CAAL)
RDT .... Remote Data Transmitter
RDT .... Renal Dialysis Treatment [*Nephrology*]
RDT .... Repertory Dance Theatre [*Salt Lake City, UT*]
RDT .... Reserve Duty Training [*Military*]
RDT .... Resource Definition Table [*Data processing*] (IBMDP)
RDT .... Retinal Damage Threshold [*Ophthalmology*]
RdT .... Revista de Teatro [*A publication*]
RDT .... Revue de Droit du Travail (DLA)
RDT .... Richard-Toll [*Senegal*] [*Airport symbol*] (OAG)
RDT .... Rotational Direction Transmission
RDT & E ..... Research, Development, Test, and Engineering
RDT & E ..... Research, Development, Test, and Evaluation [*DoD*]
RDTE .... Research, Development, Test, and Evaluation [*DoD*]
RDTEA ...... Research, Development, Test, and Evaluation, Army
RDT & EN ... Research, Development, Test, and Evaluation, Navy
RDTF .... Revolutionary Development Task Force [*South Vietnam*]
RDTL .... Resistor Diode Transistor Logic (IEEE)
RDTLC ...... Rotating Disc Thin-Layer Chromatography
RDTournai ... Revue Diocesane de Tournai [*A publication*]
RDTP .... Revista de Dialectologia y Tradiciones Populares [*A publication*]
RDTR .... Radiator (MSA)
RDTR .... Research Division Technical Report
RDTSR .... Rapid Data Transmission System for Requisitioning [*Navy*]
RDU .... RADAR Display Unit
RDU .... Raleigh/Durham [*North Carolina*] [*Airport symbol*]
RDU .... Receipt and Despatch Unit [*Aircraft*]
RDU .... Remote Display Unit [*American Solenoid Co.*] [*Somerset, NJ*]
RDU .... Rideau Resources Corp. [*Vancouver Stock Exchange symbol*]
R Dublin Soc J Sc Pr ... Royal Dublin Society. Journal. Scientific Proceedings [*A publication*]
R Dublin Soc Rep ... Royal Dublin Society. Report [*A publication*]
RDUC .... Receiver Data from Unit Control (MCD)
R D U S....... Revue de Droit. Universite de Sherbrooke [*A publication*]
RDV .... Recoverable Drop Vehicle (MCD)
RDV .... Red Devil [*Alaska*] [*Airport symbol*] (OAG)
RDVT .... Reliability Design Verification Test
RDVU .... Rendezvous (AABC)
RDW .... Red Cell Size Distribution Width [*Hematology*]
RDW .... Response Data Word (MCD)
RDW .... Return Data Word (MCD)
RDW .... Right Defense Wing [*Women's lacrosse position*]
RDWND ..... RADAR Dome Wind [*Meteorology*] (FAAC)
RDWS .... Radiological Defense Warning System
RDWW .... United Slate Tile and Composition Roofers, Damp and Waterproof Workers Association [*Later, UURWAW*]
RDX .... Cocoa, FL [*Location identifier*] [*FAA*] (FAAL)
RDX .... Research Department Explosive [*Cyclonite*]
RDY .... Aspen, CO [*Location identifier*] [*FAA*] (FAAL)
RDY .... Ready (AAG)
RDY .... Roadway
RDY .... Royal Dockyard [*British*]

RDyTP .... Revista de Dialectologia y Tradiciones Populares [*A publication*]
RDZ .... Ringier Dokumentationszentrum [*Ringier Documentation Center*] [*Switzerland*] [*Information service*]   (EISS)
RDZ .... Rodez [*France*] [*Airport symbol*]   (OAG)
Re .... Earth or Geocentric Radius   (AAG)
RE .... Fellow of the Royal Society of Painter-Etchers and Engravers [*British*]
RE .... Nordeste Linhas Aereas Regionais SA [*Brazil*] [*ICAO designator*]   (FAAC)
Re .... Ohio Decisions Reprint   (DLA)
RE .... Radiated Emission   (IEEE)
RE .... Radiation Effects   (AAG)
RE .... Radiation Equipment   (NRCH)
RE .... Radio-Eireann [*Eire*] [*Record label*]
RE .... Radio Electrician
RE .... Radio Exposure   (AAG)
RE .... Radium Emanation
RE .... Railway Executive [*British*]
RE .... Rainform Expanded   (MCD)
RE .... Rare Earth
RE .... Rate Effect   (IEEE)
R of E .... Rate of Exchange
RE .... Rate of Exchange
RE .... Rattus Exulans [*The Polynesian rat*]
RE .... Reading-Ease [*Score*] [*Advertising*]
Re .... Real [*Mathematics*]
RE .... Real-Encyclopaedie der Klassischen Altertumswissenschaft [*A publication*]
RE .... Real Estate
RE .... Real Estate Program [*Association of Independent Colleges and Schools specialization code*]
RE .... Real Number   (DEN)
Re .... Realidad [*A publication*]
RE .... Receiver/Exciter
RE .... Recent [*Used to qualify weather phenomena*]
RE .... Rectal Examination [*Medicine*]
RE .... Red Edges
RE .... Redman Industries, Inc. [*NYSE symbol*]
RE .... Reel   (MSA)
R/E .... Reentry   (KSC)
RE .... Reference [*Online database field identifier*]
RE .... Reference Equivalent [*Telecommunications*]   (TEL)
RE .... Reformed Episcopal [*Church*]
RE .... Refrigeration Effect
RE .... Regarding
RE .... Regional Enteritis [*Medicine*]
RE .... Rehearsal Engineer   (MCD)
Re .... Reinsurance [*A publication*]
RE .... Relative Effectiveness   (MCD)
RE .... Relay Assemblies [*JETDS nomenclature*] [*Military*]   (CET)
RE .... Religious Education [*A publication*]
RE .... Religious of the Eucharist [*Roman Catholic women's religious order*]
RE .... Renewal Registration [*US Copyright Office class*]
RE .... Renovacion Espanola [*Spanish Renovation*]   (PPE)
RE .... Repair Equipment for F-15 and Subsequent Programs [*Military*]   (MCD)
RE .... Repayable to Either
RE .... Repetitive Extrasystole [*Cardiology*]
Re .... Republic [*Quezon City*] [*A publication*]
RE .... Research and Engineering
RE .... Research and Experiments Department [*Ministry of Home Security*] [*British*] [*World War II*]
RE .... Reset   (MDG)
Re .... Response [*A publication*]
RE .... Responsible Engineer   (NASA)
RE .... Rest [*or Resting*] Energy [*Medicine*]
RE .... Reticuloendothelial [*or Reticuloendothelium*] [*Medicine*]
RE .... Retinal Equivalent [*For Vitamin A*]
RE .... Retinyl Ester [*Organic chemistry*]
RE .... Reunion [*Two-letter standard code*]   (CNC)
re .... Reunion [*MARC country of publication code*] [*Library of Congress*]   (LCCP)
RE .... Reversal of Prior Entry [*Banking*]
RE .... Review and Expositor [*A publication*]
RE .... Revised Edition [*Publishing*]
RE .... Revista Eclesiastica [*A publication*]
RE .... Revue Egyptologique [*A publication*]
RE .... Revue d'Esthetique [*A publication*]
Re .... Reynolds Number [*Also, R, RN*] [*Viscosity*] [*IUPAC*]
Re .... Rhenium [*Chemical element*]
RE .... Rifle Expert
RE .... Right Eminent [*Freemasonry*]
RE .... Right End
RE .... Right Excellent
RE .... Right Eye
RE .... Risk Evaluation [*Insurance*]
RE .... Risk Exercise
RE .... Rotary Engine [*Automotive engineering*]
RE .... Royal Engineers [*Military*] [*British*]

RE .... Royal Exchange [*British*]
RE .... Royal Society of Painter-Etchers and Engravers [*British*]
RE .... Rupee [*Monetary unit in Ceylon, India, and Pakistan*]
RE .... Rural Electrification
R2E .... Realisations et Etudes Electronique [*French computer manufacturer*]
REA .... RADAR Echoing Area
REA .... Radiation Emergency Area
REA .... Railroad Evangelistic Association   (EA)
REA .... Railway Express Agency [*Later, REA Express*] [*Defunct*]
REA .... Range Error Average   (MUGU)
REA .... Rare-Earth Alloy
R & EA .... Readiness and Emergency Action [*Red Cross Disaster Services*]
REA .... Realcap Holdings Ltd. [*Toronto Stock Exchange symbol*]
REA .... Reao [*French Polynesia*] [*Airport symbol*]   (OAG)
REA .... Recycle Acid [*Nuclear energy*]   (NRCH)
REA .... Reentry Angle
REA .... Religious Education Association   (EA)
REA .... Renaissance Educational Associates   (EA)
REA .... Renal Anastomosis [*Medicine*]
REA .... Request for Engineering Authorization
REA .... Request for Equitable Adjustment [*Navy*]
REA .... Research and Education Association
REA .... Research Engineering Authorization   (AAG)
REA .... Reserve Enlisted Association [*Formerly, RFBA*]   (EA)
REA .... Responsible Engineering Activity
REA .... Revue de l'Egypte Ancienne [*Paris*] [*A publication*]
REA .... Revue des Etudes Anciennes [*A publication*]
REA .... Revue des Etudes Armeniennes [*A publication*]
REA .... Revue des Etudes Augustiniennes [*A publication*]
REA .... Rice Export Association
REA .... Ridihalgh, Eggers & Associates, Columbus, OH [*OCLC symbol*]   (OCLC)
REA .... Rocket Engine Assembly
REA .... Rubber Export Association [*Defunct*]   (EA)
REA .... Rural Education Association [*Later, NREA*]   (EA)
REA .... Rural Electrification Administration [*Department of Agriculture*]
REAC .... Reaction   (AAG)
REAC .... Reactive
REAC .... Reactor   (AAG)
REAC .... Real Estate Aviation Chapter [*Berkeley, IL*]   (EA)
REAC .... Reeves Electronic Analog Computer
REACCS ...... Reaction Access System [*Computer program*]
REACDU ...... Recalled to Active Duty
REACH ...... Reassurance to Each [*To help families of the mentally ill*]
REACH ...... Research, Education, and Assistance for Canadians with Herpes
REACH ...... Responsible Educated Adolescents Can Help   (EA)
REACH ...... Rural Employment Action and Counseling Help [*Project*]
REACK ...... Receipt Acknowledged
REACQ ...... Reacquire
REACT ...... RADAR Electrooptical Area Correlation Tracker [*Military*]   (CAAL)
REACT ...... Radio Emergency Associated Citizens Teams [*Acronym alone is now used as official association name*]   (EA)
RE ACT ...... Reconnaissance/Reaction   (MCD)
REACT ...... Register Enforced Automated Control Technique [*Cash register-computing system*]
REACT ...... Reliability Evaluation and Control Technique
REACT ...... Rese Engineering Automatic Core Tester
REACT ...... Resource Allocation and Control Technique [*Management*]
React Cent Ned Rep ... Reactor Centrum Nederland. Report [*A publication*]
React Fuel Process ... Reactor Fuel Processing [*A publication*]
React Fuel-Process Technol ... Reactor and Fuel-Processing Technology [*A publication*]
React Kin C ... Reaction Kinetics and Catalysis Letters [*A publication*]
React Kinet ... Reaction Kinetics [*Later, Gas Kinetics and Energy Transfer*] [*A publication*]
React Kinet Catal Lett ... Reaction Kinetics and Catalysis Letters [*A publication*]
Reactor Fuel Process ... Reactor Fuel Processing [*A publication*]
Reactor Mater ... Reactor Materials [*A publication*]
REAC/TS ... Radiation Emergency Assistance Center/Training Site [*Department of Energy*]
REACTS ..... Reader Action Service [*ZIP code computer*]
REACTS ..... Regional Educators Annual Chemistry Teaching Symposium
React Technol ... Reactor Technology [*A publication*]
REACTVT ... Reactivate
READ .... RADAR Echo Augmentation Device
READ .... Readability Ease Assessment Device   (MCD)
READ .... Reading Efficiency and Delinquency [*Program*]
READ .... Real-Time Electronic Access and Display [*System*] [*Data processing*]
READ .... Remedial Education for Adults
READ .... Remote Electronic Alphanumeric Display [*Data processing*]   (IEEE)
READ .... Research and Economic Analysis Division [*Office of Transportation*]
READ .... Reserve on Extended Active Duty [*Military*]

Read Dig .... Reader's Digest [*A publication*]
Read Digest ... Reader's Digest [*A publication*]
Read Educ ... Reading Education [*A publication*]
Reader .... Reader Magazine [*A publication*]
Readers D ... Readers Digest [*A publication*]
Readex .... Readex Microprint Corp., New York, NY [*Library symbol*] [*Library of Congress*] (LCLS)
Read Glass Hist ... Readings in Glass History [*A publication*]
READI .... Rocket Engine Analyzer and Decision Instrumentation
READIMP ... Readiness Improvement (MCD)
Read Improv ... Reading Improvement [*A publication*]
Reading Univ Geol Rep ... Reading University. Geological Reports [*A publication*]
READJ .... Readjusted
READJP ..... Readjustment Pay
READR .... Remain in Effect after Discharge and Reenlistment [*Refers to orders*] [*Army*]
Read Res Q ... Reading Research Quarterly [*A publication*]
READS .... Reno Air Defense Sector [*ADC*]
Read Teach ... Reading Teacher [*A publication*]
Read Time ... Reading Time [*A publication*]
READU .... Ready Duty (NVT)
READU .... Ready Unit (NVT)
Read World ... Reading World [*A publication*]
READYREP ... Ready-to-Sail Report [*Navy*] (NVT)
REA et A ..... Rite Ecossais Ancien et Accepte [*Ancient and Accepted Scottish Rite*] [*French*] [*Freemasonry*]
REAF .... Revised Engineer Active Force (MCD)
R E Ag .... Revue des Etudes Augustiniennes [*A publication*]
REAIU .... Revue des Ecoles de l'Alliance Israelite Universelle [*A publication*]
Reakt Bull ... Reaktor Bulletin [*A publication*]
Reaktortag (Fachvortr) ... Reaktortagung (Fachvortraege) [*West Germany*] [*A publication*]
Reakts Metody Issled Org Soedin ... Reaktsii i Metody Issledovaniya Organicheskikh Soedinenii [*USSR*] [*A publication*]
Reakts Sposobn Koord Soedin ... Reaktsionnaya Sposobnost' Koordinatsionnykh Soedinenii [*A publication*]
Reakts Sposobn Org Soedin ... Reaktsionnaya Sposobnost' Organicheskikh Soedinenii [*A publication*]
Reakts Sposobnost' Org Soedin Tartu Gos Univ ... Reaktsionnaya Sposobnost' Organicheskikh Soedinenij. Tartuskij Gosudarstvennyj Universitet [*A publication*]
REAL .... Re: Arts and Letters [*A publication*]
REAL .... Reliability, Inc. [*NASDAQ symbol*] (NQ)
REAL .... Routine Economic Air Lift [*Army*]
Real Anal Exchange ... Real Analysis Exchange [*A publication*]
REALCOM ... Real-Time Communications [*RCA*]
Real Estate Appraiser & Anal ... Real Estate Appraiser and Analyst [*A publication*]
Real Estate J ... Real Estate Journal [*A publication*]
Real Estate L J ... Real Estate Law Journal [*A publication*]
Real Estate R ... Real Estate Review [*A publication*]
Real Estate & Stock J ... Real Estate and Stock Journal [*A publication*]
Real Est L ... Real Estate Law Journal [*A publication*]
Real Est L Rep ... Real Estate Law Report (DLA)
Real Est Re ... Real Estate Review [*A publication*]
Real Est Rec ... Real Estate Record [*New York*] (DLA)
Real Est Rev ... Real Estate Review [*A publication*]
REAL FAMMIS ... Real-Time Finance and Manpower Management Information System [*Marine Corps*] (MCD)
Realidad Econ ... Realidad Economica [*A publication*]
Real Ist Veneto Mem ... Reale Istituto Veneto di Scienze, Lettere, ed Arti. Memorie [*A publication*]
REALIZN .... Realization (ROG)
Real M .... Realta del Mezzogiorno. Mensile di Politica Economia Cultura [*A publication*]
RealN .... Realta Nuova [*A publication*]
Real Pr Cas ... Real Property Cases [*England*] (DLA)
Real Prop Acts ... Real Property Actions and Proceedings (DLA)
Real Prop Cas ... Real Property Cases [*1843-47*] (DLA)
Real Prop P ... Real Property, Probate, and Trust Journal [*A publication*]
Real Prop Probate & Trust J ... Real Property, Probate, and Trust Journal [*A publication*]
Realta Econ ... Realta Economica [*A publication*]
Realta Mezzogiorno ... Realta del Mezzogiorno [*A publication*]
Real Wr ...... Realist Writer [*A publication*]
REAM .... Rapid Excavation and Mining [*Project*] [*Bureau of Mines*]
REAMS .... Resources Evaluation and Management System [*Army*]
REAnc .... Revue des Etudes Anciennes [*A publication*]
Reanim Med Urgence ... Reanimation et Medecine d'Urgence [*A publication*]
Reanim Organes Artif ... Reanimation et Organes Artificiels [*A publication*]
REAP .... Remote Entry Acquisition Package
REAP .... Reutilization Expedite Assets Program [*DoD*]
REAP .... Rural Environmental Assistance Program [*Department of Agriculture*]
Reap Dec ... United States Customs Court Reports, Reappraisement Decision (DLA)
REAPOR ..... Real Estate Accounts Payable and Operating Reports

Reapp Dec ... United States Customs Court Reports, Reappraisement Decision (DLA)
REAPS .... Rotary Engine Antipollution System
REAPT .... Reappoint (AFM)
REAR .... Reliability Engineering Analysis Report (IEEE)
REARM .... Renovation of Armament Manufacturing (MCD)
REArm ...... Revue des Etudes Armeniennes [*A publication*]
REARM ...... Underway Rearming [*Navy*] (NVT)
REArmen ... Revue des Etudes Armeniennes [*A publication*]
REArmNS ... Revue des Etudes Armeniennes. Nouvelle Serie [*A publication*]
REA (Rural Electr Adm) Bull (US) ... REA (Rural Electrification Administration) Bulletin (United States) [*A publication*]
REAS .... Real Estate Appraisal School [*Federal Home Loan Bank Board*]
REAS .... Reasonable (ROG)
REAS .... Register of Environment Assessments and Statements (MCD)
REAS .... Reid-Ashman, Inc. [*NASDAQ symbol*] (NQ)
REAS .... Resources, Entities Accounting Subsystem (MCD)
REASM ...... Reassemble (AAG)
REASN ...... Reason (ROG)
REASSCE ... Reassurance (ROG)
REASSEM ... Reassemble (MSA)
REASSN ..... Reassign (ROG)
REASSND ... Reassigned (ROG)
REASST ..... Reassignment (ROG)
REASSY .... Reassembly (MSA)
REASTAN ... Renton Electrical Analog for Solution of Thermal Analogous Networks
REAT .... Radiological Emergency Assistance Team [*AEC*]
REAT .... Realty Industries [*NASDAQ symbol*] (NQ)
REAug .... Revue des Etudes Augustiniennes [*A publication*]
REAUM ...... Reaumur (ROG)
REB .... R. E. Blake [*Record label*]
REB .... RADAR Evaluation Branch [*ADC*]
REB .... Reba Resources Ltd. [*Vancouver Stock Exchange symbol*]
REB .... Rebel
REB .... Rebounds [*Basketball, hockey*]
REB .... Rebuilt
REB .... Reentry Body
REB .... Relativistic Electron Beam (MCD)
REB .... Research Earth Borer
ReB .... Revista Biblica [*A publication*]
REB .... Revista Eclesiastica Brasileira [*A publication*]
ReB .... Revue Biblique [*A publication*]
REB .... Revue des Etudes Byzantines [*A publication*]
REB .... Revue Internationale des Etudes Balkaniques [*A publication*]
REB .... Rocket Engine Band
REB .... Rod End Bearing [*Army helicopter*]
REB .... Roentgen-Equivalent-Biological [*Irradiation unit*]
REBA .... Relativistic Electron Beam Accelerator
REBAR ...... Reinforcing Bar (AAG)
REBAT .... Restricted Bandwidth Techniques (NG)
REBC .... Real Estate Brokerage Council [*Chicago, IL*] (EA)
R-EBD-HS ... Recessive Epidermolysis Bullosa Dystrophia-Hallopeaun Siemens [*Dermatology*]
REBE .... Recovery Beacon Evaluation
REBECCA ... RADAR Responder Beacon [*System*] (MUGU)
REBIA .... Regional Educational Building Institute for Africa
REBK .... Repertoire des Banques de Donnees en Conversationnel [*Database*]
REBras ...... Revista Eclesiastica Brasileira [*A publication*]
REBUD .... Rehabilitation Budgeting Program [*Telecommunications*] (TEL)
REBUD .... Renewable Energy Bulletin [*A publication*]
REBUS .... Reseau des Bibliotheques Utilisant SIBIL [*Library Network of SIBIL Users*] [*University of Lausanne*] [*Switzerland*] [*Information service*] (EISS)
REBUS .... Routine for Executing Biological Unit Simulations [*Computer program*]
REByz .... Revue des Etudes Byzantines [*A publication*]
REC .... Clarion State College, Clarion, PA [*OCLC symbol*] (OCLC)
REC .... Radiant Energy Conversion
REC .... Radio Electronic Combat [*Communications*]
REC .... Railway Executive Committee [*British*]
REC .... Rain Erosion Coating
REC .... Real Estate Council
REC .... Receipt
REC .... Receiver (AAG)
REC .... Recens [*Fresh*] [*Pharmacy*]
REC .... Recent (ROG)
REC .... Reception
REC .... Recess (MSA)
REC .... Recherches sur l'Origine de l'Ecriture Cuneiforme [*A publication*] (BJA)
REC .... Recife [*Brazil*] [*Airport symbol*] (OAG)
REC .... Recipe
REC .... Recognition Equipment, Inc. [*NYSE symbol*]
REC .... Recommendation (AFM)
REC .... Record (AAG)
Rec .... Recordati [*Italy*] [*Research code symbol*]
REC .... Recorder

REC .... Recover [*or Recovery*]
REC .... Recreation
REC .... Recreo [*Guatemala*] [*Seismograph station code, US Geological Survey*]   (SEIS)
REC .... Rectifier   (IEEE)
Rec .... Recueil   (BJA)
Rec .... Recurrence [*A publication*]
REC .... Recurring   (MCD)
REC .... Regional Evaluation Center   (NVT)
REC .... Regroupement des Etudiants Camerounais [*Regrouping of Cameroonese Students*]
REC .... Rehabilitation Engineering Center for the Hearing Impaired [*Gallaudet College*] [*Research center*]   (RCD)
REC .... Rehabilitation Engineering Centers [*Department of Health and Human Services*]
REC .... REM [*Roentgen-Equivalent-Man*] Equivalent Chemical [*Irradiation unit*]
REC .... Request for Engineering Change   (MCD)
REC .... Reserve Equalization Committee [*Military*]
REC .... Residual Evaluation Center   (MCD)
REC .... Revista de Estudios Clasicos [*A publication*]
REC .... Revloc, PA [*Location identifier*] [*FAA*]   (FAAL)
REC .... Ripling Electrochemical
REC .... Rudge Enthusiasts Club   (EA)
RECA .... Residual Capabilities Assessment   (MCD)
RECA .... Revenue and Expenditure Control Act of 1968
Rec Agric Res (Belfast) ... Record of Agricultural Research (Belfast) [*A publication*]
Rec Agric Res Minist Agric (Nth Ire) ... Record of Agricultural Research. Ministry of Agriculture (Northern Ireland) [*A publication*]
Rec Agr Res (N Ireland) ... Record of Agricultural Research (Northern Ireland) [*A publication*]
Rec Ak Inst Mus ... Records. Auckland Institute and Museum [*New Zealand*] [*A publication*]
RECALC ..... Recalculated
RECAP ...... Real Estate Cost Analysis Program
RECAP ...... Recapitulation   (AABC)
RECAP ...... Reliability Engineering and Corrective Action Program
RECAP ...... Reliability Evaluation Continuous Analysis Program
RECAP ...... Resource and Capabilities Model   (KSC)
RECAP ...... Review and Command Assessment of Project [*Military*]
RECAPS ...... Regionalized Civilian Automated Pay System [*Air Force*]
Rec Asilomar Conf Circuits Syst Comput ... Record. Asilomar Conference on Circuits, Systems, and Computers [*A publication*]
Rec Ass'n Bar City of NY ... Record. Association of the Bar of the City of New York [*A publication*]
RECAT .... Ad Hoc Committee on the Cumulative Regulatory Effects on the Cost of Automotive Transportation [*Terminated, 1972*]   (EGAO)
RECAU .... Receipt Acknowledged and Understood
Rec Auckland Inst ... Records. Auckland Institute and Museum [*A publication*]
Rec Auckl Inst Mus ... Records. Auckland Institute and Museum [*A publication*]
RecAug ..... Recherches Augustiniennes [*A publication*]
Rec Aust Acad Sci ... Records. Australian Academy of Science [*A publication*]
Rec Aust Mus ... Records. Australian Museum [*A publication*]
Rec Aust Museum ... Records. Australian Museum [*A publication*]
RECBKS...... Receiving Barracks
Rec Bot Surv India ... Records. Botanical Survey of India [*A publication*]
Rec Buckinghamshire ... Records of Buckinghamshire [*A publication*]
RECC .... Rhine Evacuation and Control Command [*NATO*]   (NATG)
Rec Canterbury Mus ... Records. Canterbury Museum [*Christchurch, New Zealand*] [*A publication*]
RECCB ...... Regional Education Council of the Christian Brothers [*Formerly, CBEA, NECCB*]   (EA)
RECCE .... Reconnaissance   (CINC)
RECCEXREP ... Reconnaisance Exploitation Report   (MCD)
Rec Changer ... Record Changer [*A publication*]
Rec Chem Prog ... Record of Chemical Progress [*A publication*]
RECCO...... Reconnaissance   (NVT)
Rec Coll ..... Record Collector [*A publication*]
Rec Comm ... Record Commission [*England*]   (DLA)
Rec Conv Brit Wood Pres Ass ... Record. Annual Convention. British Wood Preserving Association [*A publication*]
RECD .... Received   (AAG)
Rec Dec..... Vaux's Recorder's Decisions [*1841-45*] [*Pennsylvania*]   (DLA)
Rec Dom Mus (Wellington) ... Records. Dominion Museum (Wellington, New Zealand) [*A publication*]
Recd Res Fac Agr Univ Tokyo ... Records of Researches. Faculty of Agriculture. University of Tokyo [*A publication*]
RECDUINS ... Received for Duty under Instruction
RECDUT..... Received for Duty
RECE.......... Relativistic Electron Coil Experiment   (MCD)
Rec Electr Commun Eng Conversat Tohoku Univ ... Record of Electrical and Communication Engineering Conversation. Tohoku University [*Japan*] [*A publication*]
Rec Eng N ... Recovery Engineering News [*A publication*]
RECENT..... Recentis [*Fresh*] [*Pharmacy*]   (ROG)

Recent Adv Aerosp Med ... Recent Advances in Aerospace Medicine [*A publication*]
Recent Advanc Bot ... Recent Advances in Botany [*A publication*]
Recent Adv Biol Psychiatry ... Recent Advances in Biological Psychiatry [*A publication*]
Recent Adv Clin Nucl Med ... Recent Advances in Clinical Nuclear Medicine [*A publication*]
Recent Adv Food Sci ... Recent Advances in Food Science [*A publication*]
Recent Adv Gastroenterol ... Recent Advances in Gastroenterology [*A publication*]
Recent Adv Phytochem ... Recent Advances in Phytochemistry [*A publication*]
Recent Adv RES Res ... Recent Advances in RES [*Reticuloendothelial System*] Research [*A publication*]
Recent Adv Stud Card Struct Metab ... Recent Advances in Studies on Cardiac Structure and Metabolism [*A publication*]
Recent Dev Chem Nat Carbon Compd ... Recent Developments in the Chemistry of Natural Carbon Compounds [*A publication*]
Recent Dev Neurobiol Hung ... Recent Developments of Neurobiology in Hungary [*A publication*]
Recenti Prog Med ... Recenti Progressi in Medicina [*A publication*]
Recent Lit Hazard Environ Ind ... Recent Literature on Hazardous Environments in Industry [*A publication*]
Recent Prog Horm Res ... Recent Progress in Hormone Research [*A publication*]
Recent Prog Med (Roma) ... Recenti Progressi in Medicina (Roma) [*A publication*]
Recent Prog Microbiol ... Recent Progress in Microbiology [*A publication*]
Recent Prog Surf Sci ... Recent Progress in Surface Science [*A publication*]
Recent Publ Gov Probl ... Recent Publications on Governmental Problems [*United States*] [*A publication*]
Recent Pubns Governmental Problems ... Recent Publications on Governmental Problems [*A publication*]
Recent Results Cancer Res ... Recent Results in Cancer Research [*A publication*]
RECEP .... Reception   (ADA)
RECETED .. Receipted   (ROG)
RECFD .... Revista Cubana de Fisica [*A publication*]
RECG .... Radioelectrocardiograph
RECG .... Reciting
RECGA...... Research and Engineering Council of the Graphic Arts Industry
RECGAI...... Research and Engineering Council of the Graphic Arts Industry [*Chadds Ford, PA*]   (EA)
Rec Geol Surv Dep North Rhod ... Records. Geological Survey Department. Northern Rhodesia [*A publication*]
Rec Geol Surv Guyana ... Records. Geological Survey of Guyana [*A publication*]
Rec Geol Surv India ... Records. Geological Survey of India [*A publication*]
Rec Geol Surv Malawi ... Records. Geological Survey of Malawi [*A publication*]
Rec Geol Surv New South Wales ... Records. Geological Survey of New South Wales [*A publication*]
Rec Geol Surv Niger ... Records. Geological Survey of Nigeria [*A publication*]
Rec Geol Surv NSW ... New South Wales. Geological Survey. Records [*A publication*]
Rec Geol Surv NSW ... Records. Geological Survey of New South Wales [*A publication*]
Rec Geol Surv Pak ... Records. Geological Survey of Pakistan [*A publication*]
Rec Geol Surv Tanganyika ... Records. Geological Survey of Tanganyika [*A publication*]
Rec Geol Surv Tasm ... Tasmania. Geological Survey. Record [*A publication*]
RECGP .... Recovery Group [*Air Force*]
Rech........... Recherche [*A publication*]
RecH .... Recusant History [*A publication*]
RECH .... Reformed Episcopal Church
RechA .... Recherches Augustiniennes [*A publication*]
Rech Aerosp ... Recherche Aerospatiale [*A publication*]
Rech Aerospat English ... La Recherche Aerospatiale. English Edition [*A publication*]
Rech Agron ... Recherches Agronomiques [*A publication*]
Rech Agron (Quebec) ... Recherches Agronomiques (Quebec) [*A publication*]
Rech Amerind ... Recherches Amerindiennes [*A publication*]
RECHAR..... Recombiner Charcoal Adsorber [*Nuclear energy*]   (NRCH)
RechBib ..... Recherches Bibliques (Journees de Colloque Biblique de Louvain) [*A publication*]
RechBibl .... Recherches Bibliques (Journees du Colloque Biblique de Louvain) [*A publication*]
Rech Chir Eur ... Recherches Chirurgicales Europeennes [*A publication*]
Rech Clin Lab ... Recherche dans la Clinique et le Laboratoire [*A publication*]
Rech Econ Louvain ... Recherches Economiques de Louvain [*A publication*]
Rechentech Datenverarb ... Rechentechnik Datenverarbeitung [*A publication*]
Recherche Aerospat ... La Recherche Aerospatiale [*A publication*]
Recherche Soc (Paris) ... Recherche Sociale (Paris) [*A publication*]
Rech Geol Afr ... Recherches Geologiques en Afrique [*A publication*]
Rech Graphique ... Recherche Graphique [*A publication*]
Rech Graphique Commun ... Recherche Graphique. Communications [*A publication*]

Rech Hydrobiol Cont ... Recherches d'Hydrobiologie Continentale [*A publication*]
Rech Int ..... Recherches Internationales a la Lumiere du Marxism [*A publication*]
Rech Invent ... Recherches et Inventions [*A publication*]
Rech Prod Foret ... Recherches sur les Produits de la Foret [*A publication*]
RECHRG .... Recharger
Rech Sci Rel ... Recherches de Science Religieuse [*A publication*]
Rech Sci Relig ... Recherches de Science Religieuse [*A publication*]
RechScR ...... Recherches de Science Religieuse [*A publication*]
Rech Soc Anonyme Etabl Roure Bertrand Fils Justin Dupont ... Recherches. Societe Anonyme des Etablissments Roure Bertrand Fils et Justin Dupont [*A publication*]
Rech Sociogr ... Recherches Sociographiques [*A publication*]
Rech Sociographiques ... Recherches Sociographiques [*A publication*]
Rech Sociol ... Recherches Sociologiques [*A publication*]
Rech Soc (Paris) ... Recherche Sociale (Paris) [*A publication*]
Rech Spat ... Recherche Spatiale [*A publication*]
RechSR ...... Recherches de Science Religieuse [*A publication*]
Rech Tech ... Recherche Technique [*A publication*]
Recht Elektrizitaetswirtsch ... Recht der Elektrizitaetswirtschaft [*West Germany*] [*A publication*]
RechTh ...... Recherches de Theologie Ancienne et Medievale [*A publication*]
Recht Landwirtsch ... Recht der Landwirtschaft [*A publication*]
Recht u Polit ... Recht und Politik. Vierteljahreshefte fuer Rechts- und Verwaltungspolitik [*Berlin, West Germany*] (DLA)
Recht Steuern Gas-Wasserfach ... Recht und Steuern im Gas- und Wasserfach [*West Germany*] [*A publication*]
Rechtstheor ... Rechtstheorie. Zeitschrift fuer Logik, Methodenlehre, Kybernetik, und Soziologie des Rechts [*Berlin, West Germany*] (DLA)
Rec Hung Agric Exp Stn A ... Records. Hungarian Agricultural Experiment Stations. A. Plant Production [*A publication*]
Rec Hung Agric Exp Stn C ... Records. Hungarian Agricultural Experiment Stations. C. Horticulture [*A publication*]
Rec Huntingdonshire ... Records of Huntingdonshire [*A publication*]
Rech Vet ...... Recherches Veterinaires [*A publication*]
Rech Vet (Paris) ... Recherches Veterinaires (Paris) [*A publication*]
Rec Indian Mus ... Records. Indian Museum [*A publication*]
Rec Indian Mus (Calcutta) ... Records. Indian Museum (Calcutta) [*A publication*]
RECIP .... Recipient
RECIP .... Reciprocate (AAG)
RECIPE ...... Recomp Computer Interpretive Program Expediter [*Data processing*]
RECIR .... Recirculating [*Automotive engineering*]
RECIRC ...... Recirculate (AAG)
RECIT .... Recitation
RECIT .... Recitative [*Music*]
RECL .... Recital (ROG)
RECL .... Reclose
Rec L .... Recovering Literature [*A publication*]
REcL .... Revue Ecclesiastique de Liege [*A publication*]
Reclam Era ... Reclamation Era [*A publication*]
Reclam Rev ... Reclamation Review [*A publication*]
Rec Laws ... Recent Laws in Canada (DLA)
Recl Med Vet Ec Alfort ... Recueil de Medecine Veterinaire. Ecole d'Alfort [*A publication*]
Recl Trav Bot Neerl ... Recueil des Travaux Botaniques Neerlandais [*A publication*]
Recl Trav Chim Pays-Bas Belg ... Recueil des Travaux Chimiques des Pays-Bas et de la Belgique [*A publication*]
Recl Trav Inst Biol (Beogr) ... Recueil des Travaux. Institut Biologique (Beograd) [*A publication*]
Recl Trav Inst Ecol Biogeogr Acad Serbe Sci ... Recueil des Travaux. Institut d'Ecologie et de Biogeographie. Academie Serbe des Sciences [*A publication*]
Recl Trav Inst Rech Struct Matiere (Belgrade) ... Recueil de Travaux. Institut de Recherches sur la Structure de la Matiere (Belgrade) [*A publication*]
Recl Trav Stn Mar Endoume Fac Sci Mars ... Recueil des Travaux. Station Marine d'Endoume. Faculte des Sciences de Marseille [*A publication*]
Recl Trav Stn Mar Endoume Marseille Fasc Hors Ser Suppl ... Recueil des Travaux. Station Marine d'Endoume-Marseille. Fascicule Hors Serie. Supplement [*A publication*]
Recl Trav Stn Mar Endoume-Mars Fasc Hors Ser Suppl ... Recueil des Travaux. Station Marine d'Endoume-Marseille. Fascicule Hors Serie. Supplement [*A publication*]
RECM .... Recommend (KSC)
RECMD ...... Recommend (AAG)
RECMECH ... Recoil Mechanism (AAG)
Rec Med Vet ... Recueil de Medecine Veterinaire [*A publication*]
Rec Med Vet Ecole Alfort ... Recueil de Medecine Veterinaire. Ecole d'Alfort [*A publication*]
Rec Med Vet Exot ... Recueil de Medecine Veterinaire Exotique [*A publication*]
Rec Mem Med Mil ... Recueil des Memoires de Medecine de Chirurgie et de Pharmacie Militaires [*A publication*]

Rec Mem et Obs Hyg et Med Vet Mil ... Recueil des Memoires et Observations sur l'Hygiene et la Medecine Veterinaires Militaires [*A publication*]
RECMF .... Radio and Electronic Component Manufacturers' Federation
RECMN ...... Recommendation
RECN .... Reconnaissance
RECNCLN ... Reconciliation (AABC)
RECNO ...... This Office Has No Record Of [*Army*] (AABC)
RECO .... Remote Command and Control (MCD)
Rec Obs Med Hop Mil ... Recueil des Observations de Medecine des Hopitaux Militaires [*A publication*]
Rec Obs Scripps Inst Oceanogr ... Records of Observations. Scripps Institution of Oceanography [*A publication*]
Rec Oceanogr Works Jpn ... Records of Oceanographic Works in Japan [*A publication*]
Rec Oceanogr Works Jpn Sp Number ... Records of Oceanographic Works in Japan. Special Number [*A publication*]
RECODEX ... Report Collection Index [*Studsvik Energiteknik AB*] [*Database*] [*Nykoping, Sweden*]
RECOG ...... Recognition [*or Recognize*] (AAG)
RECOGE .... Recognisance (ROG)
RECOGN ... Recognizance
RECOGS ...... Recognisances (ROG)
RECOL .... Retrieval Command Language [*Computer search language*]
Recomb DNA Tech Bull ... Recombinant DNA Technical Bulletin [*A publication*]
Recomb DNA Tech Bull Suppl ... Recombinant DNA Technical Bulletin. Supplement [*A publication*]
RECOMMTRANSO ... Upon Receipt of These Orders Communicate with Transportation Officer for Priority Designator via Government Air If Available to _____
RECOMP .... Recommended Completion
RECOMP .... Recomplement
RECOMP .... Redstone Computer
RECOMP .... Repairs Completed [*Military*] (NVT)
RECOMP .... Retrieval and Composition (DIT)
RECON ...... Readiness Condition [*Military*]
RECON ...... Reconnaissance (NATG)
RECON ...... Reference Conversation (FAAC)
RECON ...... Reliability and Configuration Accountability System
RECON ...... Remote Console [*NASA computer*]
RECON ...... Remote Control (KSC)
RECON ...... Resources Conservation (MCD)
RECON ...... Retrospective Conversion of Bibliographic Records [*Library of Congress*]
R Econ Banque Nat Paris ... Revue Economique. Banque Nationale de Paris [*A publication*]
RECONCE ... Reconveyance (ROG)
R Econ Centre-Est ... Revue de l'Economie du Centre-Est [*A publication*]
Reconciliation Quart ... Reconciliation Quarterly [*A publication*]
RECONCO ... Reconnaissance Company [*Military*]
R Econ Condit Italy ... Review of the Economic Conditions in Italy [*A publication*]
R Econ (Cordoba) ... Revista de Economia (Cordoba) [*A publication*]
RECOND .... Recondition (AABC)
RECONDO ... Reconnaissance Commando Doughboy (AABC)
R Econ Dr Immob ... Revue d'Economie et de Droit Immobilier [*A publication*]
R Econ Estadist ... Revista de Economia y Estadistica [*A publication*]
R Econ y Estadistica ... Revista de Economia y Estadistica [*A publication*]
RECONEX ... Raid/Reconnaissance Exercise [*Military*] (NVT)
R Econ et Fin ... Revue Economique et Financiere Ivoirienne [*A publication*]
R Econ Fr ... Revue Economique Francaise [*A publication*]
R Econ Franc ... Revue Economique Francaise [*A publication*]
R Econ Franc-Comtoise ... Revue de l'Economie Franc-Comtoise [*A publication*]
R Econ Fr-Suisse ... Revue Economique Franco-Suisse [*A publication*]
R Econ Gestion ... Revue d'Economie et de Gestion [*A publication*]
R Econ Latinoamer ... Revista de Economia Latinoamericana [*A publication*]
R Econ Merid ... Revue de l'Economie Meridionale [*A publication*]
RECONN .... Reconnaissance (AAG)
R Econ (Paris) ... Revue Economique (Paris) [*A publication*]
R Econ e Pol Ind ... Rivista di Economia e Politica Industriale [*A publication*]
R Econ Polit (Madrid) ... Revista de Economia Politica (Madrid) [*A publication*]
R Econ Polit (Paris) ... Revue d'Economie Politique (Paris) [*A publication*]
R Econ Pol (Madrid) ... Revista de Economia Politica (Madrid) [*A publication*]
R Econ Pol (Paris) ... Revue d'Economie Politique (Paris) [*A publication*]
R Econ S .... Royal Economic Society [*British*]
R Econ Soc ... Revue Economique et Sociale [*A publication*]
Recons Surg ... Reconstruction Surgery and Traumatology [*A publication*]
RECONST ... Reconstruct (AABC)
R Econ & Stat ... Review of Economics and Statistics [*A publication*]
R Econ Statist ... Review of Economics and Statistics [*A publication*]
R Econ Statistics ... Review of Economics and Statistics [*A publication*]
Reconstr Surg Traumatol ... Reconstruction Surgery and Traumatology [*A publication*]
R Econ Stud ... Review of Economic Studies [*A publication*]
R Econ Sud-Ouest ... Revue Economique du Sud-Ouest [*A publication*]

Recontr Surg Traumatol ... Reconstruction Surgery and Traumatology [*A publication*]
RECONVCE ... Reconveyance (ROG)
Record .... Record. Association of the Bar of the City of New York [*A publication*]
Record Broward County Med Assoc ... Record. Broward County Medical Association [*Florida*] [*A publication*]
Recorder Columbia Med Soc ... Recorder. Columbia Medical Society of Richland County [*South Carolina*] [*A publication*]
Recorder and Mus ... Recorder and Music [*A publication*]
Recorder & Mus Mag ... Recorder and Music Magazine [*A publication*]
Records Queen Museum ... Records. Queen Victoria Museum [*A publication*]
Records SA Museum ... Records. South Australian Museum [*A publication*]
RECorses... Revue des Etudes Corses [*A publication*]
RECOV...... Recovery (KSC)
RECOVER ... Remote Continual Verification [*Telephonic monitoring system*]
RECOVER ... Remote Control Verification [*Nuclear safeguards*]
Recovery Eng News ... Recovery Engineering News [*A publication*]
RECOVY .... Recovery
RECP......... International College of Real Estate Consulting Professionals [*Minneapolis, MN*] (EA)
RECP......... Real Estate Consulting Professional [*Designation awarded by International College of Real Estate Consulting Professionals*]
RECP......... Receptacle
RECP......... Reciprocal (AAG)
RECP......... Release Engineering Change Proposal (MCD)
RECP......... Request for Engineering Change Proposal [*NASA*]
RECP......... Rural Environmental Conservation Program
RecPap ...... Recherches de Papyrologie [*A publication*]
Rec Papua New Guinea Mus ... Records. Papua New Guinea Museum [*A publication*]
Rec Past..... Records of the Past [*A publication*]
RecPh......... Recherches Philosophiques [*A publication*]
RecPhL ...... Recherches de Philologie et de Linguistique [*Louvain*] [*A publication*]
RECPOM.... Resource Constrained Procurement Objectives for Munitions Model [*Army*]
RECPT ...... Receipt
RECPT ...... Receptacle (AAG)
RECPT ...... Reception (AAG)
Rec Queen Vic Mus ... Records. Queen Victoria Museum [*A publication*]
Rec Queen Vict Mus ... Records. Queen Victoria Museum [*A publication*]
Rec Queen Victoria Mus ... Records. Queen Victoria Museum [*A publication*]
Rec Queen Victoria Mus Launceston ... Records. Queen Victoria Museum of Launceston [*A publication*]
Rec Q Vict Mus ... Records. Queen Victoria Museum [*A publication*]
RECR......... Receiver
RECR......... Reclamation Review [*A publication*]
Rec R......... Record Review [*A publication*]
RECR......... Recreation (AABC)
RECRAS..... Retrieval System for Current Research in Agricultural Sciences [*Tokyo, Japan*]
RECRE ...... Recreation
Rec Res..... Record Research [*A publication*]
Recr Sci ..... Recreative Science [*A publication*]
RECRT ...... Recruit (AFM)
RECRYST .. Recrystallized
RECS......... Radiological Emergency Communications System [*Nuclear energy*] (NRCH)
RecS......... Recorded Sound [*A publication*]
RECS......... Representative Shuttle Environmental Control System (MCD)
RECSAM.... Southeast Asian Regional Center for Education in Science and Mathematics [*Malaysia*]
RECSAT..... Reconnaissance Satellite (NVT)
Rec S Aust Mus ... Records. South Australian Museum [*A publication*]
Rec S Aust Mus (Adelaide) ... Records. South Australian Museum (Adelaide) [*A publication*]
Rec Sci Rel ... Recherches de Science Religieuse [*A publication*]
Rec Scott Church Hist Soc ... Records of the Scottish Church History Society [*A publication*]
RECSG....... Renewable Energy Congressional Staff Group (EA)
RECSHIP.... Receiving Ship
Rec Sound ... Recorded Sound [*A publication*]
Rec South Aust Mus ... Records. South Australian Museum [*A publication*]
Rec South Aust Mus (Adelaide) ... Records of the South Australian Museum (Adelaide) [*A publication*]
RECSQUAD ... Reconnaissance Squadron [*Military*]
RecSR .... Recherches de Science Religieuse [*A publication*]
RECSTA..... Receiving Station
RECSYS..... Recreation Systems Analysis [*Data processing*]
RECT......... Receipt
RECT......... Rectangle (AAG)
RECT......... Rectificatus [*Rectified*] [*Pharmacy*]
RECT......... Rectify (AAG)
RECT......... Rectisel Corp. [*NASDAQ symbol*] (NQ)
RECT......... Rector
RECT......... Rectus [*Muscle*] [*Anatomy*]
RECTAD..... Received for Temporary Additional Duty
RECTADINS ... Received for Temporary Additional Duty under Instruction

RECTAS..... Regional Centre for Training in Aerial Surveys [*Ile-Ife, Nigeria*] (EA-IO)
RECTD .... Received for Temporary Duty
RECTD .... Recited (ROG)
RECTEMDUINS ... Received for Temporary Duty under Instruction
RECTG .... Reciting (ROG)
RecTh......... Recherches de Theologie Ancienne et Medievale [*A publication*]
RECTIFON ... Rectification (ROG)
RECTIL...... Rectilineal [*Geometry*] (ROG)
RECTON .... Reduction (ROG)
RECTR ...... Recommend Transfer Of (NOAA)
RECTR ...... Rectifier
RECTR ...... Restoration and Eighteenth Century Theatre Research [*A publication*]
Rec Trav..... Recueil des Travaux Relatifs a la Philologie et a l'Archeologie Egyptiennes et Assyriennes [*A publication*]
Rec Trav Bot Neerl ... Recueil des Travaux Botaniques Neerlandais [*Netherlands*] [*A publication*]
Rec Trav Chim ... Recueil des Travaux Chimiques des Pays-Bas [*A publication*]
Rec Trav Chim Pays-Bas ... Recueil des Travaux Chimiques des Pays-Bas [*A publication*]
Rec Trav Lab Physiol Veg Fac Sci Bordeaux ... Recueil des Travaux. Laboratoire de Physiologie Vegetale. Faculte des Sciences de Bordeaux [*A publication*]
Rec Tr Chim ... Recueil des Travaux Chimiques des Pays-Bas [*A publication*]
RECTREAT ... Received for Treatment
Recu de l'Acad de Legis ... Recueil. Academie de Legislation [*Toulouse, France*] (DLA)
Recu des Cours ... Recueil des Cours. Academie de Droit International [*Collected Courses of the Hague Academy of International Law*] [*Leiden, Netherlands*] (DLA)
Recu de Jurispr du Droit Admin ... Recueil de Jurisprudence du Droit Administratif et du Conseil d'Etat [*Brussels, Belgium*] (DLA)
RECUR .... Recurrence [*or Recurrent*] [*Medicine*]
Recur Hidraul ... Recursos Hidraulicos [*A publication*]
Recursos Hidraul ... Recursos Hidraulicos [*Mexico*] [*A publication*]
Recursos Min ... Recursos Minerales [*A publication*]
Rec US Dep State ... Record. United States Department of State [*A publication*]
Recu de la Soc Internat de Droit Penal Mil ... Recueil. Societe Internationale de Droit Penal Militaire et de Droit de la Guerre [*Strasbourg, France*] (DLA)
RECVD .... Received
RECVG....... Receiving
RECY......... Recovery (AAG)
Recycling Waste Disposal ... Recycling and Waste Disposal [*A publication*]
Rec Zool Surv India ... Records. Zoological Survey of India [*A publication*]
Rec Zool Surv Pak ... Records. Zoological Survey of Pakistan [*A publication*]
RED .... A'Beckett's Reserved Judgements (New South Wales) [*A publication*]
RED .... New South Wales Reserved Equity Decisions (DLA)
RED .... Radiation Experience Data [*Food and Drug Administration*] [*Database*]
RED .... Radical Education Dossier [*A publication*] (ADA)
RED .... Railroad Employees' Department [*of AFL-CIO*]
RED .... Range Error Detector
RED .... Rapid Excess Disposal (AABC)
RED .... Rare-Earth Device
RED .... Red Lodge, MT [*Location identifier*] [*FAA*] (FAAL)
RED .... Redeemed
Red............. Redfield's New York Surrogate Reports (DLA)
Red............. Redington's Reports [*31-35 Maine*] (DLA)
RED .... Redoubt Volcano [*Alaska*] [*Seismograph station code, US Geological Survey*] (SEIS)
RED .... Reduce [*or Reduction*] (AAG)
RED .... Redundant (KSC)
Red............ Redwar's Comments on Ordinances of the Gold Coast Colony [*1889-1909*] [*Ghana*] (DLA)
RED .... Reflection Electron Diffraction [*For surface structure analysis*]
R Ed............ Religious Education [*A publication*]
RED .... Restructured Expanded Data (MCD)
RED .... Resume Entry Device
RED .... Review, Evaluation, Disposition Board (AAG)
RED .... Ritchie's Equity Decisions [*Russell*] [*Canada*] (DLA)
REDAC...... Real-Time Data Acquisition
Red Am R Cas ... Redfield's American Railway Cases (DLA)
Red Am RR Cas ... Redfield's Leading American Railway Cases (DLA)
REDAP .... Reentrant Data Processing
REDAS .... Reduced to Apprentice Seaman [*Navy*]
Red & Big Cas B & N ... Redfield and Bigelow's Leading Cases on Bills and Notes (DLA)
REDC .... Regional Economic Development Center [*Memphis State University*] [*Research center*] (RCD)
REDC .... Revista Espanola de Derecho Canonico [*A publication*]
REDCAPE ... Readiness Capability [*Military*]
Red Cas RR ... Redfield's Leading American Railway Cases (DLA)
Red Cas Wills ... Redfield's Leading Cases on Wills (DLA)
REDCAT..... Racial and Ethnic Category [*Army*] (INF)

REDCAT..... Readiness Category [*Military*]
REDCN....... Reducing (ROG)
REDCOM.... Readiness Command [*Army*]
REDCON .... Readiness Condition [*Military*]
Red Cross M ... Red Cross Magazine [*A publication*]
REDD .... Reduced (ROG)
Redem .... Redemption (DLA)
Redf........... Redfield's New York Surrogate Reports (DLA)
Redf Am Railw Cas ... Redfield's American Railway Cases (DLA)
Redf & B ... Redfield and Bigelow's Leading Cases [*England*] (DLA)
Redf Carr ... Redfield on Carriers and Bailments (DLA)
Redf (NY)... Redfield's New York Surrogate Reports (DLA)
Redf Railways ... Redfield on Railways (DLA)
Redf R Cas ... Redfield's Railway Cases [*England*] (DLA)
Redf Sur (NY) ... Redfield's New York Surrogate Court Reports (DLA)
Redf Surr ... Redfield's New York Surrogate Reports (DLA)
Redf Surr (NY) ... Redfield's New York Surrogate Court Reports [*5 vols.*] (DLA)
Redf Wills... Redfield's Leading Cases on Wills (DLA)
RED HORSE ... Rapid Engineer Development, Heavy Operational Repair Squadron, Engineering [*Air Force*] (AFM)
REDI .... Real Estate Data, Incorporated [*Miami, FL*] [*Information service*] (EISS)
REDI .... Remote Electronic Delivery of Information [*Library science*]
REDI .... Revue Egyptienne du Droit International [*A publication*]
REDICORT ... Readiness Improvement through Correspondence Training (MCD)
REDIG IN PULV ... Redigatur In Pulverent [*Let It Be Reduced to Powder*] [*Pharmacy*] (ROG)
Redington ... Redington's Reports [*31-35 Maine*] (DLA)
Red Int L .... Reddie's Inquiries in International Law [*2nd ed.*] [*1851*] (DLA)
REDIS......... Reference Dispatch (NOAA)
REDISC...... Rediscount [*Business and trade*]
REDIST ...... Redistilled
REDISTR...... Redistribution (AFM)
REDLOG..... Logistic Readiness Report [*Navy*] (CINC)
Redman ..... Redman on Landlord and Tenant (DLA)
Red Mar Com ... Reddie's Law of Maritime Commerce [*1841*] (DLA)
Red Mar Int L ... Reddie's Researches in Maritime International Law [*1844-45*] (DLA)
Red Menac ... Red Menace [*A publication*]
REDN .... Reduction
REDNON .... Operational Readiness Report (Nonatomic) (CINC)
REDNT .... Redundant (AAG)
REDO .... RADAR Engineering Design Objectives (NG)
Redog ForsknStift Skogsarb ... Redogorelse. Forskningsstiftelsen Skogsarbeten [*A publication*]
REDOM ...... Redemption (ROG)
REDOPS..... Ready for Operations [*Reporting system*] [*DoD*]
REDOX....... Reduction and Oxidation
REDP......... Redondo Peak [*New Mexico*] [*Seismograph station code, US Geological Survey*] (SEIS)
Red Pop ..... Post Reditum ad Populum [*of Cicero*] [*Classical studies*] (OCD)
RED in PULV ... Redactus in Pulverem [*Reduce to a Powder*] [*Pharmacy*]
REDREP ..... Redeployment Report [*Military*]
R Ed Res ... Review of Educational Research [*A publication*]
Red RR Cas ... Redfield's Leading American Railway Cases (DLA)
Red Sc L ... Reddie's Science of Law [*2nd ed.*] (DLA)
Red Sen .... Post Reditum in Senatu [*of Cicero*] [*Classical studies*] (OCD)
REDSG....... Redesignate (AFM)
REDSO....... Regional Economic Development Services Office [*Foreign Service*]
REDSOD .... Repetitive Explosive Device for Soil Displacement
REDTOP..... Reactor Design from Thermal-Hydraulic Operating Parameters [*NASA*]
REDTRAIN ... Readiness Training (MCD)
REDUC....... Reducing (KSC)
R Educ .... Review of Education [*A publication*]
REDUCE..... Reduction of Electrical Demand Using Computer Equipment [*Energy management system designed by John Helwig of Jance Associates, Inc.*]
R Educ (Madrid) ... Revista de Educacion (Madrid) [*A publication*]
R Educ Res ... Review of Educational Research [*A publication*]
REDUPL ..... Reduplication
REDV......... Resource Development. Incorporating Northern Development and Oceanic Industries [*A publication*]
REDW........ Redwood National Park
Redwar....... Redwar's Comments on Ordinances of the Gold Coast Colony [*1889-1909*] [*Ghana*] (DLA)
Red Wills.... Redfield on the Law of Wills (DLA)
REDWN ..... Redrawn
REDY......... Recirculating Dialyzate [*Artificial kidney dialysis system*]
REDYP ...... Reentry Dynamics Program
REE .... Lubbock, TX [*Location identifier*] [*FAA*] (FAAL)
REE .... Rapid Extinction Effect [*Electrophysiology*]
REE .... Rare-Earth Element [*Chemistry*]
REE .... Red Earth Energy Ltd. [*Vancouver Stock Exchange symbol*]
REE .... [*Department of*] Regional Economic Expansion [*Canada*]
REE .... Respiratory Energy Expenditure [*Physiology*]
REE .... Resting Energy Expenditure

REE .... Revista de Estudios Extremenos [*A publication*]
REEA......... Real Estate Educators Association [*Chicago, IL*] (EA)
REEC......... Regional Export Expansion Council [*Department of Commerce*]
REECO ...... Reynolds Electrical & Engineering Company
Reed.......... Reed on Bills of Sale (DLA)
REED........ Resources on Educational Equity for the Disabled
Reed Fraud ... Reed's Leading Cases on Statute of Frauds (DLA)
REEDN ...... Records of Early English Drama. Newsletter [*A publication*]
Reed's Mar Equip News Mar Dig ... Reed's Marine and Equipment News and Marine Digest [*A publication*]
Reeduc Orthophon ... Reeducation Orthophonique [*A publication*]
REEFER ..... Refrigerator, Refrigerated, or Cold Storage [*Airplane, railway car, truck*]
REEG......... Radioelectroencephalograph
REEI .... Russian and East European Institute [*Indiana University*] [*Research center*] (RCD)
REEL .... Recessive-Expressive Emergent Language Scores [*For the hearing-impaired*]
REELB....... Revista Electricidade [*A publication*]
REEM .... Reserves Embarked [*Navy*] (NVT)
RE-EN .... Re-Enacted (ROG)
REEN .... Regional Energy Education Network [*National Science Teachers Association*]
REENA ...... Refrigerating Engineering [*A publication*]
REENL....... Reenlist [*Military*] (AFM)
REENLA ..... Reenlistment Allowance [*Military*]
REENLB ..... Reenlistment Bonus [*Military*]
REEP .... Range Estimating and Evaluation Procedure [*Data processing*]
REEP .... Regression Estimation of Event Probabilities (IEEE)
REEP .... Revista. Escuela de Estudios Penitenciarios [*A publication*]
REES .... Reactive Electronic Equipment Simulator (RDA)
REES .... Russian and East European Studies Area Program [*University of Pittsburgh*] [*Research center*] (RCD)
Rees' Cyclopaedia ... [*Abraham*] Rees' English Cyclopaedia (DLA)
Reese .... Reporter of Vols. 5 and 11, Heiskell's Tennessee Reports (DLA)
REETS....... Radiological Effluent and Environmental Technical Specifications (NRCH)
Reeve Eng L ... Reeve's History of the English Law (DLA)
Reeve Eng Law ... Reeve's History of the English Law (DLA)
Reeve Hist Eng Law ... Reeve's History of the English Law (DLA)
Reeves HEL ... Reeve's History of the English Law (DLA)
Reeves Hist Eng Law ... Reeve's History of the English Law (DLA)
Reeves J ... Reeves Journal [*A publication*]
RE-EXAMD ... Re-Examined (ROG)
RE-EXED .... Re-Executed (ROG)
REF .... Range Error Function [*Aerospace*] (AAG)
REF .... Rat Embryo Fibroblast [*Cells*]
REF .... Refectory (DSUE)
REF .... Refer
REF .... Referee
REF .... Reference [*Online database field identifier*] (NATG)
REF .... Referendum
REF .... Refinery [*or Refining*]
REF .... Reflection Resources [*Vancouver Stock Exchange symbol*]
REF .... Reflector
Ref........... Reformatio [*A publication*]
REF .... Reformation
REF .... Reformed
REF .... Refresher (AABC)
REF .... Refrigerant [*Cooling*] [*Medicine*] [*British*] (ROG)
REF .... Refund [*or Refunding*]
REF .... Refurbishment (NASA)
REF .... Refused (ADA)
REF .... Release of Excess Funds
REF .... Renal Erythropoietic Factor [*Medicine*]
REF .... Revista de Etnografie si Folclor [*A publication*]
REF .... Unclear Pronoun Reference [*Used in correcting manuscripts, etc.*]
REFA......... Real Estate Fund of America
REFA Nachr ... REFA [*Reichsausschuss fuer Arbeitsstudien*] Nachrichten [*A publication*]
REFC......... Refac Technology Development Corp. [*NASDAQ symbol*] (NQ)
REFC......... Reference (ROG)
REFC......... Reflections of Elvis Fan Club (EA)
REFCD .... Research and Education Foundation for Chest Disease [*Park Ridge, IL*] (EA)
Ref Ch R...... Reformed Church Review [*A publication*]
REFD........ Referred
REFD........ Refined
REFD........ Refund (AFM)
REFD CON ... Reinforced Concrete [*Freight*]
Ref Dec ...... Referee's Decision (DLA)
REF/DES.... Reference Designator Number (MCD)
REFD MTL ... Reinforced Metal [*Freight*]
Ref Dok Mosk Skh Akad ... Referaty Dokladov. Moskovskaya Sel'skokhozyaistvennaya Akademiya Imeni K. A. Timiryazeva [*A publication*]
REFD PLYWD ... Reinforced Plywood [*Freight*]

REFEC ...... Refectory (DSUE)
RefEgyhaz ... Reformatus Egyhaz [Budapest] [A publication]
Referatebl zur Raumentwicklung ... Referateblatt zur Raumentwicklung [A publication]
Referat Z .... Referativnyi Zhurnal [A publication]
Referat Zh Biol ... Referativnyi Zhurnal. Biologiya [A publication]
REFG .... Refrigerating [or Refrigeration]
REFGR .... Refrigerator
Refin Eng ... Refining Engineer [A publication]
Refiner Nat Gasoline Manuf ... Refiner and Natural Gasoline Manufacturer [A publication]
Ref J .... National Association of Referees in Bankruptcy. Journal [A publication]
REFL .... Reference Line (AAG)
REFL .... Reflectance [or Reflector] (AAG)
REFL .... Reflex
REFL .... Reflexive
REFLD .... Reflected
REFLES ...... Reference Librarian Enhancement System [University of California] [Online microcomputer system]
Reflets Econ Franc-Comtoise ... Reflets de l'Economie Franc-Comtoise [A publication]
Reflets et Perspectives ... Reflets et Perspectives de la Vie Economique [A publication]
Reflets Perspect Vie Econ ... Reflets et Perspectives de la Vie Economique [A publication]
REFLEX ...... Reserve Flexibility [Military] (MCD)
Ref Libr ...... Reference Librarian [A publication]
REFM .... Revista de Estudios Franceses (Madrid) [A publication]
REFMCHY ... Refrigerating Machinery
REFMS .... Recreation and Education for Multiple Sclerosis
REFMT .... Reinforcement
REFNO .... Reference Number (CINC)
Ref NRE ..... Refused, Not Reversible Error (DLA)
REFONE ..... Reference Our Telephone Conversation (FAAC)
REFORGER ... Return of Forces to Germany [Military]
REFORM .... Reference Form (FAAC)
REFORM .... Reformatory (ROG)
REFORMA ... National Association to Promote Library Services to the Spanish-Speaking
Refor Mon ... Reforestation Monthly [A publication]
REFP .... Reference Papers [Army] (AABC)
Ref Pres W ... Reformed and Presbyterian World [A publication]
Ref Q .... Reformed Quarterly Review [A publication]
Ref R. .... Reformed Review [A publication]
REFR .... Refractory (AAG)
REFR .... Refrigerate (KSC)
REFRACDUTRA ... Release from Active Duty for Training [Army] (AABC)
Refract J .... Refractories Journal [A publication]
Refract Mater ... Refractory Materials [A publication]
Refractor J ... Refractories Journal [A publication]
REFRAD ...... Release from Active Duty [Army]
REFRADT. ... Release from Active Duty for Training [Army] (AABC)
REFRANACDUTRA ... Release from Annual Active Duty for Training [Army] (AABC)
REFRAT ..... Release from Annual Training [Army] (AABC)
REFRD .... Refrigerated (AAG)
REFRG ...... Refrigerate (AAG)
REFRIG ..... Refrigerated Service [Shipping] [British]
Refrig .... Refrigeration [A publication]
REFRIG ..... Refrigerator
Refrig A .... Refrigeration Annual [A publication]
Refrig Air ... Refrigeration and Air Conditioning [A publication]
Refrig Air Cond & Heat ... Refrigeration Journal, Incorporating Air Conditioning and Heating [A publication]
Refrig Ann ... Refrigeration Annual [A publication]
Refrig Annual ... Refrigeration Annual [A publication]
Refrig Cold Stor ... Refrigeration, Cold Storage, and Air-Conditioning [A publication]
Refrig Cold Storage Air Cond ... Refrigeration, Cold Storage, and Air-Conditioning [A publication]
Refrig Eng ... Refrigerating Engineering [A publication]
Refrigeration J ... Refrigeration Journal [A publication]
Refrig J ...... Refrigeration Journal [A publication]
REFRIGN. ... Refrigeration
Refrig Sci Technol ... Refrigeration Science and Technology [A publication]
Refrig W ..... Refrigerating World [A publication]
Ref Serv R ... Reference Services Review [A publication]
Ref Shelf .... Reference Shelf [A publication]
REFSMMAT ... Reference to Stable Member Matrix Radiological Health (KSC)
REFSRV ..... [The] Reference Service [Mead Data Central, Inc.] [Dayton, OH] [Information service] (EISS)
REFT .... Release for Experimental Flight Test (NG)
REFTEL ...... Reference Telegram (NATG)
Ref Th R ..... Reformed Theological Review [A publication]
REFTO .... Reference Travel Order (NOAA)
RefTR .... Reformed Theological Review [Australia] [A publication]
REFTRA ...... Refresher Training (NVT)
Ref Trib ...... Referee Tribunal (DLA)
REFTS .... Resonant Frequency Tracking System

REFUL .... Refueling
REFURB ..... Refurbished
REFURDIS ... Reference Your Dispatch
REFURLTR ... Reference Your Letter
Refu Vet ..... Refuah Veterinarith [A publication]
Ref W .... Reformed World [A publication]
RefWID ...... Refugee Women in Development (EA)
Ref WM ...... Refused, Want of Merit (DLA)
REFY .... Refinery
Ref Zh .... Referativnyi Zhurnal [A publication]
Ref Zh Astron ... Referativnyi Zhurnal. Astronomiya [A publication]
Ref Zh Astron Geod ... Referativnyi Zhurnal. Astronomiya. Geodeziya [A publication]
Ref Zh Biol ... Referativnyi Zhurnal. Biologiya [A publication]
Ref Zh Biol Khim ... Referativnyi Zhurnal. Biologicheskaya Khimiya [A publication]
Ref Zh Faramakol Khimioter Sredstva Toksikol ... Referativnyi Zhurnal. Farmakologiya. Khimioterapeuticheskie Sredstva. Toksikologiya [A publication]
Ref Zh Fiz. ... Referativnyi Zhurnal. Fizika [A publication]
Ref Zh Fotokinotekh ... Referativnyi Zhurnal. Fotokinotekhnika [A publication]
Ref Zh Geod ... Referativnyi Zhurnal. Geodeziya [A publication]
Ref Zh Geod Aerosemka ... Referativnyi Zhurnal. Geodeziya i Aeros'emka [A publication]
Ref Zh Geof ... Referativnyi Zhurnal. Geofizika [A publication]
Ref Zh Geol ... Referativnyi Zhurnal. Geologiya [A publication]
Ref Zh Inf ... Referativnyi Zhurnal. Informatika [A publication]
Ref Zh Khim ... Referativnyi Zhurnal. Khimiya [A publication]
Ref Zh Khim Biol Khim ... Referativnyi Zhurnal. Khimiya. Biologicheskaya Khimiya [A publication]
Ref Zh Korroz ... Referativnyi Zhurnal. Korroziya [A publication]
Ref Zh Legk Promst ... Referativnyi Zhurnal. Legkaya Promyshlennost [A publication]
Ref Zh Mekh ... Referativnyi Zhurnal. Mekhanika [A publication]
Ref Zh Metall ... Referativnyi Zhurnal. Metallurgiya [USSR] [A publication]
Ref Zh Okhr Prir Vosproizvod Prir Resur ... Referativnyi Zhurnal. Okhrana Prirody i Vosproizvodstvo Prirodnykh Resursov [USSR] [A publication]
Ref Zh Radiats Biol ... Referativnyi Zhurnal. Radiatsionnaya Biologiya [USSR] [A publication]
Ref Zh Rastenievod ... Referativnyi Zhurnal. Rastenievodstvo [A publication]
Ref Zh Teploenerg ... Referativnyi Zhurnal. Teploenergetika [A publication]
RefZtg .... Reform Zeitung [Berlin] [A publication]
Reg .... Daily Register [New York City] (DLA)
REG .... Radiation Exposure Guide
REG .... Radioencephalogram
REG .... Random Event Generator [Psychology]
REG .... Range Extender with Gain [Bell System]
Reg .... Regal, Branch of EMI [Record label] [Spain]
REG .... Regarding
REG .... Regency Resources [Vancouver Stock Exchange symbol]
REG .... Regent
REG .... Reggio Calabria [Italy] [Airport symbol] (OAG)
REG .... Regiment
REG .... Regina [Queen] [Latin]
REG .... Region (AAG)
REG .... Regis College, Weston, MA [OCLC symbol] (OCLC)
REG .... Register (AAG)
REG .... Registered [Stock exchange term]
REG .... Registrar (ROG)
Reg .... Registration Cases (DLA)
REG .... Registry
REG .... Regular (AAG)
REG .... Regulate (AAG)
REG .... Regulating [Duties] [Navy] [British]
REG .... Regulation
REG .... Regulator (DEN)
REg .... Revue Egyptologique [A publication]
REG .... Revue des Etudes Grecques [A publication]
REG .... Rheoencephalography [Medicine]
REG .... Rock Eagle [Georgia] [Seismograph station code, US Geological Survey] (SEIS)
REgA .... Revue de l'Egypte Ancienne [A publication]
REGAF ...... Regular Air Force
REGAL .... Range and Elevation Guidance for Approach and Landing [Aviation] (FAAC)
REGAL .... Remotely Guided Autonomous Lightweight Torpedo (MCD)
Regan Rep Nurs Law ... Regan Report on Nursing Law [A publication]
Reg App ..... Registration Appeals [England] (DLA)
Reg Arch .... Registered Architect
REGARD ..... Ruby, Emerald, Garnet, Amethyst, Ruby, Diamond [Jewelry]
Reg Brev .... Registrum Omnium Brevium [Register of Writs] (DLA)
REGC .... Right Eminent Grand Commander [Freemasonry]
REG/CAN .. Registry Number/Chemical Abstracts Number [American Chemical Society information file]
Reg Cas ..... Registration Cases [England] (DLA)
Reg Cat Earthquakes ... Regional Catalogue of Earthquakes [A publication]
Reg Conf Ser Appl Math ... Regional Conference Series in Applied Mathematics [A publication]
REGD .... Registered

Reg Deb ..... Gales and Seaton's Register of Debates in Congress [*1824-37*] (DLA)

Reg Deb (Gales) ... Register of Debates in Congress [*Gales*] [*1789-91*] (DLA)

Reg Deb (G & S) ... Gales and Seaton's Register of Debates in Congress [*1824-37*] (DLA)

Regelungstech ... Regelungstechnik [*A publication*]

Regelungstech Prax ... Regelungstechnische Praxis [*A publication*]

Regelungstech Prax Prozess-Rechentech ... Regelungstechnische Praxis und Prozess-Rechentechnik [*A publication*]

Regelungstech Prax und Prozess-Rechentech ... Regelungstechnische Praxis und Prozess-Rechentechnik [*A publication*]

Regelungstech Prozess-Datenverarb ... Regelungstechnik und Prozess-Datenverarbeitung [*A publication*]

Regelungstech und Prozess-Datenverarb ... Regelungstechnik und Prozess-Datenverarbeitung [*A publication*]

Regelungstech Prozess-Datenverarbeitung ... Regelungstechnik und Prozess-Datenverarbeitung [*A publication*]

Regelungstech RT ... Regelungstechnik. RT [*West Germany*] [*A publication*]

REGEN .... Regeneration (AAG)

Regensb Univ-Ztg ... Regensburger Universitaets-Zeitung [*A publication*]

Reger .... Mitteilungen. Max Reger Instituts [*Bonn*] [*A publication*]

Reg Geol Ser NC Miner Resour Sect ... Regional Geology Series. North Carolina Mineral Resources Section [*A publication*]

Regia Soc Sci Upsal Nova Acta ... Regia Societas Scientiarum Upsaliensis. Nova Acta [*A publication*]

Regia Stn Sper Seta Boll Uffic (Italy) ... Regia Stazione Sperimentale per la Seta. Bollettino Ufficiale (Italy) [*A publication*]

REGIM .... Regimental (ROG)

REGING ...... Registering (ROG)

Regional Development J ... Regional Development Journal [*A publication*]

Regional Rail Reorg Ct ... Special Court Regional Railroad Reorganization Act (DLA)

Regional Stud ... Regional Studies [*Oxford*] [*A publication*]

Region Develop J ... Regional Development Journal [*A publication*]

Region Urb Econ ... Regional and Urban Economics Operational Methods [*A publication*]

REGIS .... Regency Investors [*NASDAQ symbol*] (NQ)

REGIS .... Register (AABC)

REGIS .... Relational General Information System

Register of Kentucky Hist Soc ... Register. Kentucky Historical Society [*A publication*]

Reg J Energy Heat Mass Transfer ... Regional Journal of Energy, Heat, and Mass Transfer [*India*] [*A publication*]

REGL .... Regimental

Reg Lib ...... Register Book (DLA)

Reg Lib ...... Registrar's Book, Chancery (DLA)

REGLN ...... Regulation (AAG)

REGLON ..... Regulation (ROG)

REGLOS .... Reserve and Guard Logistic Operations-Streamline (AABC)

Reg Maj ...... Books of Regiam Majestatem [*Scotland*] (DLA)

REGN .... Registry Number

Regnum Veg ... Regnum Vegetabile [*A publication*]

REGO .... Registration [*Of a motor vehicle*] [*Australia*] (DSUE)

Reg Om Brev ... Registrum Omnium Brevium [*Register of Writs*] [*Latin*] (DLA)

Reg Orig ..... Registrum Originale (DLA)

Reg Plac ..... Regula Placitandi (DLA)

RegProf ...... Regius Professor [*The King's Professor*] [*British*]

REGR .... Register (ROG)

REGR .... Registrar

REGR .... Regulator (AAG)

REGr .... Resources Group Review. Suncor Incorporated [*A publication*]

REGr .... Revue des Etudes Greques [*A publication*]

Reg Rep New Hebrides Geol Surv ... Regional Report. New Hebrides Geological Survey [*A publication*]

REGS .... Regulations

REGS-A ...... Regional Studies [*A publication*]

Reg Soc Sci Upsal Nova Acta ... Regia Societas Scientiarum Upsaliensis. Nova Acta [*A publication*]

REGSTD ..... Registered

REGSTR ..... Registrar

REGSTRTN ... Registration

Reg Stud .... Regional Studies [*A publication*]

Reg Stud Assoc Newsl ... Regional Studies Association Newsletter [*A publication*]

REGT .... Regent

REGT .... Regiment (AABC)

REGT .... Regulator

Reg Tech Meet Am Iron Steel Inst ... Regional Technical Meetings. American Iron and Steel Institute [*A publication*]

REGTL .... Regimental

Reg TM .... Registered Trade Mark (DLA)

REGUL ...... Regular (ROG)

Regul Bull KY Agr Exp Sta ... Regulatory Bulletin. Kentucky Agricultural Experiment Station [*A publication*]

Regul Pept ... Regulatory Peptides [*A publication*]

Reg Umb .... Regio Umbilici [*Region of the Umbilicus*] [*Pharmacy*]

Reg Urban Econ ... Regional and Urban Economics [*Netherlands*] [*A publication*]

Reg Urb Econ ... Regional Science and Urban Economics [*A publication*]

Reg Veg ..... Regnum Vegetabile [*A publication*]

Reg Writ ..... Register of Writs (DLA)

REGY .... Registry (ROG)

R Egypt Dr Int ... Revue Egyptienne de Droit International [*A publication*]

REH .... Random Evolutionary Hits

REH .... Rehoboth Beach, DE [*Location identifier*] [*FAA*] (FAAL)

REH .... Revista de Estudios Hispanicos [*A publication*]

REH .... Revue des Etudes Historiques [*A publication*]

REH .... Revue des Etudes Hongroises [*A publication*]

REHAB ...... Rehabilitate (AFM)

Rehab .... Rehabilitation [*A publication*]

Rehab Couns ... Rehabilitation Counseling Bulletin [*A publication*]

Rehabil Aust ... Rehabilitation in Australia [*A publication*]

Rehabil Lit ... Rehabilitation Literature [*A publication*]

Rehabil Nurs ... Rehabilitation Nursing [*A publication*]

Rehabil SA ... Rehabilitation in South Africa [*A publication*]

Rehabil S Afr ... Rehabilitation in South Africa [*A publication*]

Rehabil Suppl (Bratisl) ... Rehabilitacia Supplementum (Bratislava) [*A publication*]

Rehab Lit ... Rehabilitation Literature [*A publication*]

Reh Allowed ... Rehearing Allowed [*Used in Shepard's Citations*] (DLA)

REHC .... Random Evolutionary Hits per Codon

Reh Den ..... Rehearing Denied [*Used in Shepard's Citations*] (DLA)

Reh Dis ...... Rehearing Dismissed [*Used in Shepard's Citations*] (DLA)

Reh'g .... Rehearing (DLA)

REHID .... Recursos Hidraulicos [*A publication*]

Re Hist De ... Revue d'Histoire de la Deuxieme Guerre Mondiale [*A publication*]

REHNRAP ... Recreational, Entertainment, and Health Naturally Radioactive Products (NRCH)

REHom .... Revue des Etudes Homeriques [*A publication*]

REH-PR ...... Revista de Estudios Hispanicos (Rio Piedras, Puerto Rico) [*A publication*]

REHT .... Reheat (KSC)

REHVA .... Representatives of European Heating and Ventilating Associations

REI .... Rat der Europaeischen Industrieverbaende [*Council of European Industrial Federations*]

REI .... Reidovoe [*USSR*] [*Seismograph station code, US Geological Survey*] (SEIS)

REI .... Religion and Ethics Institute (EA)

REI .... Request for Engineering Information (NG)

REI .... Request for Engineering Investigation [*Nuclear energy*] (NRCH)

REI .... Research-Engineering Interaction (IEEE)

REI .... Reusable External Insulation [*of space shuttle*] [*NASA*]

REI .... Revue des Etudes Indo-Europeennes [*A publication*]

REI .... Revue des Etudes Islamiques [*A publication*]

REI .... Revue des Etudes Italiennes [*A publication*]

REI .... Runway-End Identification [*Aviation*] (NASA)

REI .... Rural Economics Institute (OICC)

REIC .... Radiation Effects Information Center [*Defunct*] [*Battelle Memorial Institute*]

REIC .... Research Industries [*NASDAQ symbol*] (NQ)

Reichhold-Albert-Nachr ... Reichhold-Albert-Nachrichten [*A publication*]

Reichsber Phys ... Reichsberichte fuer Physik [*A publication*]

Reichstoff Ind Kosmet ... Reichstoff Industrie und Kosmetik [*A publication*]

REIC (Radiat Eff Inf Cent) Rep ... REIC (Radiation Effects Information Center) Report [*A publication*]

REID .... Reid-Provident Laboratories [*NASDAQ symbol*] (NQ)

REIE .... Revue des Etudes Indo-Europeennes [*A publication*]

Reihe Informat ... Reihe Informatik [*A publication*]

REIL .... Runway-End Identification Lights [*Aviation*]

Reilly .... Reilly's English Arbitration Cases (DLA)

Reilly EA .... Reilly's European Arbitration. Lord Westbury's Decisions (DLA)

REIM .... Reimburse (AABC)

REIMB .... Reimburse (MSA)

REIMD .... Revista da Imagem [*A publication*]

REIN .... Raymond Engineering [*NASDAQ symbol*] (NQ)

REIN .... Real Estate Information Network [*Database*]

REIN .... Reinforce

Rein .... Reinstated [*Regulation or order reinstated*] [*Used in Shepard's Citations*] (DLA)

Reine Angew Metallkd Einzeldarst ... Reine und Angewandte Metallkunde in Einzeldarstellungen [*A publication*]

REINET ...... Real Estate Information Network [*National Association of Realtors*] [*Chicago, IL*] [*Information service*] (EISS)

REINF .... Refund Information File [*IRS*]

REINF .... Reinforce (AAG)

REINFD .... Reinforced (AAG)

REINFG ...... Reinforcing (AAG)

REINFM ...... Reinforcement (AAG)

Rein Foie Mal Nutr ... Rein et Foie. Maladies de la Nutrition [*France*] [*A publication*]

Reinf Plast ... Reinforced Plastics [*A publication*]

Reinf Plast (London) ... Reinforced Plastics (London) [*A publication*]

REINIT .... Reinitialize (MCD)

REINS .... RADAR-Equipped Inertial Navigation System

REINS .... Requirements Electronic Input System [*NASA*] (KSC)

REINSR ...... Reinsurance

REINV........ Reference Invoice (FAAC)
REIPS........ Real Estate Investment Properties [*NASDAQ symbol*] (NQ)
REIS .... Readiness Information System [*Army*]
REIS .... Reconstitutable and Enduring Intelligence System
REIS .... Regional Economic Information System [*Department of Commerce*] [*Washington, DC*] [*Information service*] (EISS)
REIS .... Regional Energy Information System [*Minnesota State Department of Energy and Economic Development*] [*St. Paul*] [*Information service*] (EISS)
REIS .... Research and Engineering Information Services [*Exxon Research & Engineering Co.*] [*Florham Park, NJ*] (EISS)
REIsI.......... Revue des Etudes Islamiques [*A publication*]
Reiss-Davis Clin Bull ... Reiss-Davis Clinic. Bulletin [*A publication*]
REIT .... Real Estate Investment Trust [*Generic term*]
REIT .... Reiteration [*Printing*] (ROG)
REIV .... Rocket Engine Injector Valve
REJ............ Redig, SD [*Location identifier*] [*FAA*] (FAAL)
REJ............ Reject (MSA)
REJ............ Revue des Etudes Juives [*A publication*]
Re de J ...... Revue de Jurisprudence [*Montreal*] (DLA)
REJASE ..... Reusing Junk as Something Else [*Conversion of junk into reusable items*]
REJIS .... Regional Justice Information Service [*St. Louis, MO*]
REJN .... Rejoin (AABC)
REJOD .... Reeves Journal [*A publication*]
REJU .... Reject Unit [*IRS*]
REJuiv........ Revue des Etudes Juives [*A publication*]
REJuivHJud ... Revue des Etudes Juives et Historia Judaica [*Paris*] [*A publication*]
REK .... Reykjavik [*Iceland*] [*Airport symbol*] (OAG)
REKY......... Royal East Kent Yeomanry [*Military unit*] [*British*]
REL .... Radiation Evaluation Loops (NRCH)
REL .... Radio Electrician [*Navy*] [*British*]
REL .... Radio Engineering Laboratories
REL .... Rapidly Extensible Language System [*Data processing*] (CSR)
REL .... Rare-Earth LASER
REL............ Rassemblement Europeen de la Liberte [*European Liberty Rally*] [*French*] (PPE)
REL .... Rate of Energy Loss
REL .... Reactor Equipment Limited (NRCH)
REL .... Regional Education Laboratory
REL............ Related
REL............ Relations
REL............ Relative
REL............ Relativity
REL............ Relay (AAG)
REL............ Release (AAG)
REL............ Reliability
REL............ Reliance Group Holdings, Inc. [*Formerly, Leasco Corp.*] [*NYSE symbol*]
REL............ Relic
REL............ Relie [*Bound*] [*Publishing*] [*French*]
REL............ Relief (AAG)
Rel............ Religion [*A publication*]
REL............ Religion
REL............ Reliquary and Illustrated Archaeologist [*A publication*] (ROG)
Rel............ Reliquiae [*of Suetonius*] [*Classical studies*] (OCD)
REL............ Reliquiae [*Remains*] [*Latin*]
REL............ Relizane [*Algeria*] [*Seismograph station code, US Geological Survey*] [*Closed*] (SEIS)
REL............ Relocatable [*Data processing*]
REL............ Reluctance (DEN)
REL............ Rescue Equipment Locker (AAG)
REL............ Restricted Energy Loss
REL............ Review of English Literature [*A publication*]
REL............ Revue Ecclesiastique de Liege [*A publication*]
REL............ Revue des Etudes Latines [*A publication*]
Re de L ..... Revue de Jurisprudence et Legislation [*Montreal*] (DLA)
REL............ Trelew [*Argentina*] [*Airport symbol*] (OAG)
RELA .... Real Estate Leaders of America [*Montgomery, AL*] (EA)
RELAA .... Recht der Landwirtschaft [*A publication*]
RelAb .... Religious and Theological Abstracts [*A publication*]
Relac Int.... Relaciones Internacionales [*A publication*]
RELACS ..... RADAR Emission Location Attack Control System
Relais .... Relais Statistiques de l'Economie Picarde [*A publication*]
Relais Econ Picarde ... Relais Statistiques de l'Economie Picarde [*A publication*]
RELat .... Revue des Etudes Latines [*A publication*]
Relat Annu Inst Geol Publ Hung ... Relationes Annuae. Instituti Geologici Publicii Hungarici [*A publication*]
Relata Tech Chim Biol Appl ... Relata Technica di Chimica e Biologia Applicata [*A publication*]
Relat Cient Esc Super Agric Luiz Queiroz Dep Inst Genet ... Relatorio Cientifico. Escola Superior de Agricultura Luiz de Queiroz. Departamento e Instituto de Genetica [*A publication*]
Relat DNOCS ... Relatoria. DNOCS [*Departamento Nacional de Obras Contra as Secas*] [*A publication*]
Relat Ind .... Relations Industrielles/Industrial Relations [*A publication*]
Relat Industr ... Relations Industrielles [*A publication*]
Relat Int ..... Relations Internationales [*A publication*]

Relat Int (Geneve) ... Relations Internationales (Geneve) [*A publication*]
RELATN ..... Relation (ROG)
Relazione Comm Dirett Ist Zootec Laziale (Roma) ... Relazione. Commissione Direttiva. Istituto Zootecnico Laziale (Roma) [*A publication*]
Relaz Soc... Relazioni Sociali [*A publication*]
RelB........... Religion och Bibel [*Uppsala*] [*A publication*]
RelBib .... Religion och Bibel [*Uppsala*] [*A publication*]
RELBL .... Reliability
RELBY .... When Relieved By [*Army*]
RELC .... RELC [*Regional English Language Centre*] Journal [*Singapore*] [*A publication*]
RELC .... Reliability Committee [*NASA*]
RELC .... Southeast Asian Regional English Language Center [*Singapore*]
Rel Cab ...... Religious Cabinet [*A publication*]
RELCT .... Relocate (FAAC)
RELCTD ..... Relocated
RELCV .... Regional Educational Laboratory for the Carolinas and Virginia
RELD.......... Rare-Earth LASER Device
RELDET ..... When Relieved Detached [*Duty Indicated*]
RELDIRDET ... When Relieved and When Directed Detached [*Duty Indicated*]
RELE .... Radio Electrician
RELE .... Release (ROG)
Rel Ed........ Religious Education [*A publication*]
RELET........ Reference Letter (FAAC)
Relevance Logic Newslett ... Relevance Logic Newsletter [*A publication*]
Relev Log News ... Relevance Logic Newsletter [*A publication*]
Rel d Griech ... Die Religion der Griechen [*A publication*] (OCD)
RELHA .... Revista Espanola de Literatura, Historia, y Arte [*A publication*]
RELI .... Religion Index [*American Theological Library Association*] [*Chicago, IL*] [*Bibliographic database*]
RELIA........ Rehabilitation Literature [*A publication*]
Reliab Eng ... Reliability Engineering [*A publication*]
Reliability Eng ... Reliability Engineering [*A publication*]
Reliable P J ... Reliable Poultry Journal [*A publication*]
RELiege ..... Revue Ecclesiastique de Liege [*Belgium*] [*A publication*]
RELIG........ Religion [*or Religious*]
Relig Corp ... Religious Corporations (DLA)
Relig Ed ..... Religious Education [*A publication*]
Relig Educ ... Religious Education [*A publication*]
Relig Hum ... Religious Humanism [*A publication*]
Relig in Life ... Religion in Life [*A publication*]
Relig Soc ... Religion and Society [*A publication*]
Relig Stud ... Religious Studies [*A publication*]
Relig T J ..... Religion Teacher's Journal [*A publication*]
Rel Ind....... Relations Industrielles/Industrial Relations [*A publication*]
Rel Ind One ... Religion Index One [*A publication*]
RELing ...... Revista Espanola de Linguistica [*A publication*]
RELIQ........ Reliquiae [*Remains*] [*Latin*]
RELIQ........ Reliquum [*The Remainder*] [*Pharmacy*]
RELL .... Reinforced Education Learning Laboratory [*of Youth Pride, Inc.*] (EA)
RELL .... Richardson Electron [*NASDAQ symbol*] (NQ)
RELLA........ Regional European Long-Lines Agency [*Later, RALLA*] (NATG)
Rel Life...... Religion in Life [*A publication*]
RELMA...... Robert E. Lee Memorial Association (EA)
RELMAT.... Relative Matrix (MCD)
RELMS ...... Relational Memory Systems [*San Jose, CA*] [*Hardware manufacturer*]
RELO.......... Revue. Organisation Internationale pour l'Etude des Langues Anciennes par Ordinateur [*A publication*]
RELOC .... Relocate (AAG)
RELP .... Real Estate Limited Partnerships
RELPAS ..... Restricted Express Lists/Physiological Activity Section [*National Science Foundation*]
RelPerI .... Religious Periodicals Index [*A publication*]
Rel & Pub Order ... Religion and the Public Order (DLA)
RELQ.......... Release-Quiesce [*Data processing*]
REL-R........ Reliability Report (AAG)
RELR.......... Revised and Expurgated Law Reports [*India*] (DLA)
RELS .... Redeye Launch Simulator (MCD)
RELS .... Relations
RELSA........ Radio Elektronik Schau [*A publication*]
Rel Soc...... Religion and Society [*A publication*]
Rel St .... Religious Studies [*A publication*]
Rel St Rev ... Religious Studies Review [*A publication*]
Rel Stud .... Religious Studies [*London*] [*A publication*]
RELT .... Reltron Corp. [*NASDAQ symbol*] (NQ)
RelTAbstr ... Religious and Theological Abstracts [*Myerstown, PA*] [*A publication*]
RELTD....... Related
Rel & Theol Abstr ... Religious and Theological Abstracts [*A publication*]
RELV .... Revue de l'Enseignement des Langues Vivantes [*A publication*]
RELX .... Realex Corp. [*NASDAQ symbol*] (NQ)
REM.......... C & M Aviation, Inc. [*Inyokern, CA*] [*FAA designator*] (FAAC)
REM.......... Random Entry Memory (ADA)
REM.......... Range Evaluation Missile
REM.......... Rapid Eye Movement

REM............ Raumbildentfernungsmesser [*Stereoscopic range-finder*] [*German military - World War II*]
REM............ Reaction Engine Module [*NASA*]   (KSC)
REM............ Recognition Memory [*Semionics Associates*] [*Data processing*]
REM............ Recovery Exercise Module   (MCD)
REM............ Reentry Module
REM............ Reflection Electron Microscopy
REM............ Registered Equipment Management [*Air Force*]   (AFM)
REM............ Release Engine Module   (MCD)
REM............ Release Escape Mechanism   (MCD)
REM............ Reliability Engineering Model   (KSC)
REM............ Remainder   (MSA)
REM............ Remark
Rem............ Remington [*Record label*] [*USA, Europe, etc.*]
REM............ Remit   (AABC)
Rem............ Remittance   (DLA)
REM............ Remote [*Alaska*] [*Seismograph station code, US Geological Survey*]   (SEIS)
REM............ Remove   (AAG)
REM............ Repertoire d'Epigraphie Meroitique [*A publication*]
REM............ Reserves Embarked [*Navy*]   (NVT)
REM............ Revue Ecclesiastique de Metz [*A publication*]
Re M............ Revue Musicale [*A publication*]
REM............ Rocket Engine Module   (MCD)
REM............ Roentgen-Equivalent-Man [*Later, Sv*] [*Irradiation unit*]
REMA......... Refrigeration Equipment Manufacturers Association [*Later, ARI*]   (MCD)
REMAB...... Radiation Equivalent Manikin Absorption
REMAB...... Remote Marshalling Base   (MCD)
REMAD...... Remote Magnetic Anomaly Detection
Rem Am...... Remedia Amoris [*of Ovid*] [*Classical studies*]   (OCD)
REMAP...... Record Extraction, Manipulation, and Print
REMARC.... Retrospective Machine Readable Catalog [*Carrollton Press, Inc.*] [*Arlington, VA*] [*Bibliographic database*] [*Online version of the US Library of Congress Shelflist*]
Remarques Afr ... Remarques Africaines [*A publication*]
REMAS...... Radiation Effects Machine Analysis System   (AAG)
REMBASS ... Remotely Monitored Battlefield Area Sensor System   (MCD)
REMBJTR.. Reimbursement in Accordance with Joint Travel Regulations
REMC........ Radio and Electronics Measurements Committee [*London, England*]   (DEN)
REMC........ Resin-Encapsulated Mica Capacitor
REMC........ Revista de Estudios Musicales. Departamento de Musicologia. Universidad Nacional de Cuyo [*A publication*]
REMCA ..... Reliability, Maintainability, Cost Analysis   (MCD)
REMCAL ... Radiation Equivalent Manikin Calibration
REMCE...... Remittance   (ROG)
REMCO ..... Rear Echelon Maintenance Combined Operation [*Military*]
Rem Cr Tr ... Remarkable Criminal Trials   (DLA)
REMD........ Rapid Eye Movement Deprivation
Rem'd........ Remanded   (DLA)
REME .... Royal Electrical and Mechanical Engineers [*Acronym is also humorously interpreted as "Rarely Electrically or Mechanically Efficient"*] [*Military*] [*British*]
REMED...... Remedium [*Remedy*] [*Pharmacy*]   (ROG)
Remedial Ed ... Remedial Education [*A publication*]
Remedial Educ ... Remedial Education [*A publication*]
REMES...... Reference Message   (FAAC)
REMG........ Radioelectromyograph
Rem'g........ Remanding   (DLA)
REMI .... Reliability Engineering and Management Institute   (EA)
REMI .... Remington Gold Corp. [*NASDAQ symbol*]   (NQ)
REMIC....... Real Estate Mortgage Investment Conduit [*Federal National Mortgage Association*]
REMIDS ..... Remote Minefield Identification and Deployment [*or Display*] System   (MCD)
REMILOC... Required Inservice Manyears in Lieu of Controls [*Military*]
REMIS....... Real Estate Management Information System   (BUR)
REMIT .... Remittance   (DSUE)
REMIT .... Research Effort Management Information Tabulation
Remitt .... Remittance   (DLA)
REML .... Radiation Effects Mobile Laboratory
REML .... Removal   (ROG)
REML .... Restricted Maximum Likelihood [*Statistics*]
REM-M...... Rapid Eye Movement-Movement Period
REMMPS... Reserve Manpower Management and Pay System [*Marine Corps*]
REMN........ Remain   (ROG)
REMOA ..... Revista. Escola de Minas [*Brazil*] [*A publication*]
REMOBE .... Readiness for Mobilization Evaluation   (MCD)
REMOS ..... Real-Time Event Monitor [*Data processing*]   (IEEE)
Remote Sens Environ ... Remote Sensing of Environment [*A publication*]
Remote Sensing Earth Resour ... Remote Sensing of Earth Resources [*A publication*]
Remote Sensing Environ ... Remote Sensing of Environment [*A publication*]
REMP .... Radiological Environmental Monitoring Program [*Nuclear energy*]   (NRCH)
REMP .... Research, Engineering, Mathematics, and Physics Division [*Obsolete*] [*National Security Agency*]
REMP .... Research and Evaluation Methods Program [*University of Massachusetts*] [*Research center*]   (RCD)

REMP .... Research Group for European Migration Problems
REMPAC .... Reflectivity Measurements Pacific
REMPI .... Resonant Enhanced Multiphoton Ionization [*Spectroscopy*]
REM-Q ...... Rapid Eye Movement - Quiescent Period
REMR .... Remainder
REMR .... Remington Rand Corp. [*NASDAQ symbol*]   (NQ)
Rem R .... Remington Review [*A publication*]
REMR .... Repair, Evaluation, Maintenance, Rehabilitation
REM-RAND ... Remington Rand Corp. [*Later, a division of Sperry-Rand*]
REMRO ...... Remote RADAR Operator   (MCD)
REMS .... Rapid Eye Movement State
REMS .... Reentry Measurement System
REMS .... Registered Equipment Management System [*Air Force*]
REMS .... Remote Sensors   (RDA)
ReMS .... Renaissance and Modern Studies [*A publication*]
REMSA...... Railway Engineering Maintenance Suppliers Association
REMSTA .... Remote Electronic Microfilm Storage Transmission and Retrieval
REMT .... Radiological Emergency Medical Teams   (AABC)
REMT .... Relief Electronic Maintenance Technician
REMTDS ... Rocket Engine and Motor Type Designation System
Rem Tr .... Cummins and Dunphy's Remarkable Trials   (DLA)
Rem Tr No Ch ... Benson's Remarkable Trials and Notorious Characters   (DLA)
Remy.......... Remy's Reports [*145-162 Indiana*] [*15-33 Indiana Appellate*]   (DLA)
REN .... Religion and Ethics Network [*of Consortium on Peace Research, Education, and Development*]   (EA)
REN .... Remote Enable   (IEEE)
Ren............. Renaissance [*A publication*]
REN .... Renaissance
Ren............. Renaissance [*Record label*]
REN .... Rename File [*Data processing*]
Ren............. Renascence [*A publication*]
REN .... Rencon Mining Co. [*Vancouver Stock Exchange symbol*]
REN .... Renewable
REN .... Renewal
Ren............. Renner's Gold Coast Colony Reports   (DLA)
REN .... Reno [*Nevada*] [*Seismograph station code, US Geological Survey*] [*Closed*]   (SEIS)
REN .... Revue des Etudes Napoleoniennes [*A publication*]
REN .... Ringer Equivalence Number [*Telephones*]
REN .... Rollins Environmental Services, Inc. [*NYSE symbol*]
REN .... Rural Equipment News [*A publication*]
Renais News ... Renaissance News [*A publication*]
Renaissance Q ... Renaissance Quarterly [*A publication*]
Renaiss Dr ... Renaissance Drama [*A publication*]
Renaiss Q... Renaissance Quarterly [*A publication*]
Renaiss Ref ... Renaissance and Reformation [*A publication*]
Renal Physiol ... Renal Physiology [*A publication*]
RENAT .... Revolutsiya, Nauka, Trud [*Revolution, Science, Labor*] [*Given name popular in Russia after the Bolshevik Revolution*]
Ren B.......... Renaissance Bulletin [*A publication*]
RenBib .... Rencontres Biblique [*A publication*]
RencAssyrInt ... Rencontre Assyriologique Internationale. Compte Rendu [*A publication*]
RENCB....... Revue d'Electroencephalographie et de Neurophysiologie Clinique [*A publication*]
Rencontre Biol ... Rencontre Biologique [*A publication*]
RenD .... Renaissance Drama [*A publication*]
REND .... Rendered   (ADA)
Rend........... Rendezvous [*A publication*]
Rend........... Rendiconti [*Bologna*] [*A publication*]
Rend Accad Naz XL ... Rendiconti. Accademia Nazionale dei XL [*A publication*]
Rend Accad Naz XL 4 ... Accademia Nazionale dei XL. Rendiconti. Serie 4 [*A publication*]
Rend Accad Naz XL 5 ... Accademia Nazionale dei XL. Rendiconti. Serie 5 [*A publication*]
Rend Accad Sci Fis Mat (Napoli) ... Rendiconto. Accademia delle Scienze Fisiche e Matematiche (Napoli) [*A publication*]
Rend Accad Sci Fis Mat Napoli 4 ... Societa Nazionale di Scienze, Lettere, ed Arti in Napoli. Rendiconto dell'Accademia Fisiche e Matematiche. Serie 4 [*A publication*]
Rend Acc It ... Atti. Reale Accademia d'Italia. Rendiconti. Classe di Scienze Morali [*A publication*]
Rend Atti Accad Sci Med Chir ... Rendiconti e Atti. Accademia di Scienze Mediche e Chirurgiche [*A publication*]
Rend Circ Mat Palermo ... Rendiconti. Circolo Matematico di Palermo [*A publication*]
Rend Circ Mat Palermo 2 ... Rendiconti. Circolo Matematico di Palermo. Serie II [*A publication*]
RENDD...... Rendered   (ROG)
Rend Gastro ... Rendiconti di Gastro-Enterologia [*A publication*]
Rendic Accad Sc Fis e Mat (Napoli) ... Rendiconto. Accademia delle Scienze Fisiche e Matematiche (Napoli) [*A publication*]
Rendic R Accad Sc Ist Bologna ... Rendiconto. Sessioni della Reale Accademia delle Scienze. Istituto di Bologna [*A publication*]
Rend Istit Mat Univ Trieste ... Rendiconti. Istituto di Matematica. Universita di Trieste [*A publication*]

Rend Ist Lomb ... Reale Istituto Lombardo di Scienze e Lettere. Rendiconti [*A publication*]

Rend Ist Lomb Accad Sci Lett A ... Rendiconti. Istituto Lombardo. Accademia di Scienze e Lettere. Sezione A. Scienze Matematiche, Fisiche, e Geologiche [*Italy*] [*A publication*]

Rend Ist Lomb Accad Sci Lett B ... Rendiconti. Istituto Lombardo. Accademia di Scienze e Lettere. Sezione B. Scienze Biologiche e Mediche [*Italy*] [*A publication*]

Rend Ist Lomb Sci Lett A ... Rendiconti. Istituto Lombardo di Scienze e Lettere. A. Scienze Matematiche, Fisiche, Chimiche, e Geologiche [*A publication*]

Rend Ist Mat Univ Trieste ... Rendiconti. Istituto di Matematica. Universita di Trieste [*A publication*]

Rend Ist Sci Univ Camerino ... Rendiconti. Istituti Scientifici. Universita di Camerino [*A publication*]

Rend Ist Super Sanita ... Rendiconti. Istituto Superiore di Sanita [*A publication*]

Rend Linc .. Rendiconti. Reale Accademia dei Lincei [*A publication*]

Rend Mat ... Rendiconti di Matematica [*A publication*]

Rend Mat 6 ... Rendiconti di Matematica. Serie VI [*A publication*]

Rend Mat 7 ... Rendiconti di Matematica. Serie VII [*A publication*]

Rend (Nap) ... Rendiconti. Reale Accademia di Archeologia, Lettere, ed Arti (Naples) [*A publication*]

RENDOCK ... Rendezvous and Docking [*Aerospace*]   (MCD)

Rend Pont ... Rendiconti. Pontificia Accademia Romana di Archeologia [*A publication*]

Rend Pont Acc ... Rendiconti. Pontificia Accademia Romana di Archeologia [*A publication*]

Rend R Ist Lomb Sci Lett ... Rendiconti. Reale Istituto Lombardo di Scienze e Lettere [*A publication*]

Rend Riun Annu Assoc Elettrotec Ital ... Rendiconti. Riunione Annuale. Associazione Elettrotecnica Italiana [*Italy*] [*A publication*]

Rend Riunione Assoc Elettrotec Ital ... Rendiconti. Riunione Annuale. Associazione Elettrotecnica Italiana [*A publication*]

Rend Rom Gastroenterol ... Rendiconti Romani di Gastroenterologia [*Italy*] [*A publication*]

Rend Sc Int Fis Enrico Fermi ... Rendiconti. Scuola Internazionale di Fisica "Enrico Fermi" [*A publication*]

Rend Sc Int Fis Fermi ... Rendiconti. Scuola Internazionale di Fisica "Enrico Fermi" [*A publication*]

Rend Scu Int Fis Enrico Fermi ... Rendiconti. Scuola Internazionale di Fisica "Enrico Fermi" [*Italy*] [*A publication*]

Rend Semin Fac Sci Univ Cagliari ... Rendiconti del Seminario. Facolta di Scienze. Universita di Cagliari [*A publication*]

Rend Semin Mat Fis Milano ... Rendiconti. Seminario Matematico e Fisico di Milano [*A publication*]

Rend Sem Mat Brescia ... Rendiconti. Seminario Matematico di Brescia [*A publication*]

Rend Sem Mat Fis Milano ... Rendiconti. Seminario Matematico e Fisico di Milano [*A publication*]

Rend Sem Mat Univ Padova ... Rendiconti. Seminario Matematico. Universita di Padova [*A publication*]

Rend Sem Mat Univ Politec Torino ... Rendiconti. Seminario Matematico gia Conferenze di Fisica e di Matematica. Universita e Politecnico di Torino [*A publication*]

Rend Sem Mat Univ e Politec Torino ... Rendiconti. Seminario Matematico. Universita e Politecnico di Torino [*A publication*]

Rend Soc Chim Ital ... Rendiconti. Societa Chimica Italiana [*A publication*]

Rend Soc Ital Mineral Petrol ... Rendiconti. Societa Italiana di Mineralogia e Petrologia [*A publication*]

RENDZ .... Rendezvous   (KSC)

RenE .... Reinare en Espana [*A publication*]

RENE .... Rocket Engine/Nozzle Ejector

RENEC .... Regroupement National des Etudiants Camerounais [*National Regrouping of Cameroonese Students*]

R Energie ... Revue de l'Energie [*A publication*]

Renew .... Renewal [*A publication*]

Renew Energy Bull ... Renewable Energy Bulletin [*England*] [*A publication*]

RENFE .... Red Nacional de los Ferrocariles Espanoles [*Spanish National Railways*]

R ENG .... Royal Engineers [*Military*] [*British*]   (ROG)

R Eng J ...... Royal Engineers Journal [*A publication*]

R Engl Lit ... Review of English Literature [*A publication*]

R Engl Stud ... Review of English Studies [*A publication*]

REngS .... Review of English Studies [*A publication*]

R Eng Stud ... Review of English Studies [*A publication*]

R Eng Stud ns ... Review of English Studies. New Series [*A publication*]

RENH .... Revue des Etudes Neo-Helleniques [*A publication*]

RENJA .... Russian Engineering Journal [*A publication*]

RENL .... Renal System, Inc. [*NASDAQ symbol*]   (NQ)

RENLO .... Revue. Ecole Nationale des Langues Orientales [*A publication*]

RENM .... Request for Next Message

RENMR ...... Reconnaissance Medium Range [*Army*]

RenN .... Renaissance News [*A publication*]

Renn .... Renner's Reports, Notes of Cases, Gold Coast Colony and Colony of Nigeria [*1861-1914*]   (DLA)

Ren News ... Renaissance News [*A publication*]

RENO .... Research on Norway [*A publication*]

RENOT ...... Regional Notice [*FAA*]

RENOVAND ... Renovandus [*To Be Renewed*] [*Pharmacy*]   (ROG)

RenP .... Renaissance Papers [*A publication*]

RENPE .... Rare and Endangered Native Plant Exchange   (EA)

RenQ .... Renaissance Quarterly [*A publication*]

Ren & R ..... Renaissance and Reformation [*A publication*]

RENRA .... Rentgenologiya i Radiologiya [*A publication*]

Ren & Ref ... Renaissance and Reformation [*A publication*]

RENS .... Radiation Effects on Network Systems

RENS .... Reconnaissance, Electronic Warfare, and Naval Intelligence System

REN SEM ... Renovetur Semel [*Renew Once*] [*Pharmacy*]

RENSONIP ... Reconnaissance Electronic Warfare, Special Operations, and Naval Intelligence Processing   (MCD)

RENT .... Reentry Nose Tip [*Air Force*]

RENT .... Rent-A-Center, Inc. [*NASDAQ symbol*]   (NQ)

Rent Equip ... Rental Equipment Register [*A publication*]

Rentgenogr Miner Syr'ya ... Rentgenografiya Mineral'nogo Syr'ya [*A publication*]

Rentgenol Radiol ... Rentgenologiya i Radiologiya [*A publication*]

RENU .... Reconstruction Education for National Understanding [*An association*]   (EA)

RENUNCN ... Renunciation   (ROG)

RENV .... Renovate   (AABC)

REO .... Ransom Eli Olds [*Acronym used as name of automobile manufactured by Ransom E. Olds Co.*]

REO .... Rare-Earth Oxide

REO .... Rea Gold Corp. [*Toronto Stock Exchange symbol*] [*Vancouver Stock Exchange symbol*]

REO .... Real Estate Owned [*Banking*]

REO .... Regenerated Electrical Output

REO .... Regional Executive Officer [*British*]

REO .... Reinforcements   (DSUE)

REO .... Responsible Engineering Office [*Military*]   (AFIT)

REO .... Rio Airways [*Killeen, TX*] [*FAA designator*]   (FAAC)

REO .... Rome, OR [*Location identifier*] [*FAA*]   (FAAL)

Reo .... Te Reo. Linguistic Society of New Zealand [*A publication*]

REOC .... Report When Established on Course [*Aviation*]   (FAAC)

REOC .... Royal Enfield Owners Club   (EA)

REON .... Rocket Engine Operations - Nuclear   (IEEE)

REOPT .... Reorder Point [*Army*]

Reorg .... Reorganizations   (DLA)

REORG .... Reorganize

REOS .... Rare-Earth Oxysulfide

REOS .... Reflective Electron Optical System

REOT .... Right-End-of-Tape

REOU .... Radio and Electronic Officers' Union [*British*]

Rep .... Coke's English King's Bench Reports   (DLA)

Rep .... De Republica [*of Cicero*] [*Classical studies*]   (OCD)

REP .... Die Republikaner [*Republican Party*] [*West Germany*]   (PPW)

Rep .... Knapp's Privy Council Reports [*England*]   (DLA)

REP .... RADAR Effects Processor   (MCD)

REP .... RADAR Evaluation Pod [*Spacecraft*]

REP .... Radical Education Project [*Students for a Democratic Society*]

REP .... Radiological Emergency Plan   (NRCH)

REP .... Railway Equipment and Publication Company, The, New York NY [*STAC*]

REP .... Range Error Probable [*Military*]

REP .... Range Estimation Program   (MCD)

REP .... Re-Entrant Processor

REP .... Recovery and Evacuation Program [*Marine Corps*]

REP .... Reentry Physics Program

REP .... Regional Employment Premium [*British*]

REP .... Relativistic Electron Precipitation [*Meteorology*]

REP .... Rendezvous Evaluation Pad [*NASA*]   (KSC)

REP .... Repair   (AAG)

REP .... Repeal   (ROG)

REP .... Repeat   (AAG)

Rep .... Repertoire   (DLA)

REP .... Repertory   (ADA)

REP .... Repertory Theater   (DSUE)

REP .... Repetatur [*Let It Be Repeated*] [*Pharmacy*]

REP .... Repetition   (DSUE)

REP .... Replace   (NVT)

REP .... Replication [*Telecommunications*]   (TEL)

REP .... Report   (AAG)

REP .... Reporter

REP .... Reporting Point [*Aviation*]

REP .... Representative   (AAG)

Rep .... Representing   (DLA)

REP .... Reprimand   (DSUE)

Rep .... Reprint   (DLA)

REP .... Reproductive Endocrinology Program [*University of Michigan*] [*Research center*]   (RCD)

REP .... Republic

REP .... Republican

Rep .... Republika [*Zagreb*] [*A publication*]

REP .... Repulsion

REP .... Reputation   (DSUE)

REP .... Request for Proposal   (MUGU)

REP .... Research and Economic Programs [*Department of the Treasury*]

REP .... Research Expenditure Proposal

REP .... Research Project   (FAAC)

REP .... Reserve Enlisted Program [*Military*]
REP .... Resonance Escape Probability [*Nuclear energy*]   (NRCH)
REP .... Retrograde Pyelogram [*Medicine*]
REP .... Revista de Estudios Politicos [*A publication*]
REP .... Richardson Emergency Psychodiagnostic Summary
 [*Psychology*]
REP .... Rocket Engine Processor
REP .... Roentgen-Equivalent-Physical [*Irradiation unit*]
REP .... Unnecessary Repetition [*Used in correcting manuscripts, etc.*]
Rep............. Wallace's "The Reporters"   (DLA)
REP 63........ Reserve Enlistment Program 1963   (MCD)
Rep AAS (Austral) ... Report. Meeting. Association for the Advancement of
 Science (Australia) [*A publication*]
Rep Acad Sci Ukr SSR ... Reports. Academy of Sciences of the Ukrainian
 SSR [*A publication*]
Rep Activ Dan Atom Energy Commn ... Report. Activities of the Danish
 Atomic Energy Commission [*A publication*]
Rep Aeromed Lab ... Reports. Aeromedical Laboratory [*A publication*]
Rep Aeronaut Res Inst Univ Tokyo ... Report. Aeronautical Research
 Institute. University of Tokyo [*A publication*]
Rep AFL Univ Cincinnati Dep Aerosp Eng ... Report AFL. University of
 Cincinnati. Department of Aerospace Engineering [*A
 publication*]
Rep Agric Coll Swed Ser A ... Reports. Agricultural College of Sweden.
 Series A [*A publication*]
Rep Agric Hort Res Stn Univ Bristol ... Report. Agricultural and Horticultural
 Research Station. University of Bristol [*A publication*]
Rep Agric Res Coun Radiobiol Lab ... Report. Agricultural Research
 Council. Radiobiological Laboratory [*A publication*]
Rep Agron Branch Dep Agric South Aust ... Report. Agronomy Branch.
 Department of Agriculture and Fisheries. South Australia
 [*A publication*]
Rep Aichi Inst Public Health ... Report. Aichi Institute of Public Health
 [*Japan*] [*A publication*]
REPAIRS .... Readiness Evaluation Program for Avionics Intermediate
 Repair Simulation   (MCD)
Rep Akita Prefect Inst Public Health ... Report. Akita Prefecture. Institute of
 Public Health [*Japan*] [*A publication*]
Rep Alfalfa Improv Conf ... Report. Alfalfa Improvement Conference [*A
 publication*]
REPAML..... Reply by Airmail   (FAAC)
Rep Am Univ Field Staff ... Reports. American Universities Field Staff [*A
 publication*]
Rep Anim Breed Res Organ ... Report. Animal Breeding Research
 Organisation [*A publication*]
Rep Anim Res Div (NZ) ... Report. Animal Research Division. Department of
 Agriculture (New Zealand) [*A publication*]
Rep Annu Conf Hawaii Sugar Technol ... Reports. Annual Conference.
 Hawaiian Sugar Technologists [*A publication*]
Rep Annu Conf Ontario Dept Agr Ext Br ... Report. Annual Conference.
 Ontario Department of Agriculture. Extension Branch [*A
 publication*]
Rep Annu Date Grow Inst ... Report. Annual Date Growers Institute [*A
 publication*]
Rep Annu Gen Meet Scott Soc Res Plant Breed ... Report. Annual General
 Meeting. Scottish Society for Research in Plant Breeding
 [*A publication*]
Rep Archit Sci Unit Univ Queensl ... Report. Architectural Science Unit.
 University of Queensland [*A publication*]
Rep Ariz Agr Exp Sta ... Report. Arizona Agricultural Experiment Station [*A
 publication*]
Rep Ark Agric Exp Stn ... Report. Arkansas Agricultural Experiment Station
 [*A publication*]
Rep Army Res Test Lab ... Report. Army Research and Testing Laboratory
 [*South Korea*] [*A publication*]
REPAS .... Research, Evaluation, and Planning Assistance Staff [*AID*]
Rep Assoc Hawaii Sugar Technol ... Reports. Association of Hawaiian Sugar
 Technologists [*A publication*]
Rep Ass Y ... Clayton's English Reports, York Assizes   (DLA)
REPAT........ Repatriate   (AABC)
Rep Aust Acad Sci ... Report. Australian Academy of Science [*A publication*]
Rep Aust Acad Sci ... Reports. Australian Academy of Science [*A
 publication*]
Rep Aust At Energy Comm ... Report. Australian Atomic Energy
 Commission [*A publication*]
Rep Aust CSIRO Div Text Ind ... Australia. Commonwealth Scientific and
 Industrial Research Organisation. Division of Textile
 Industry. Report [*A publication*]
Rep Aust Def Stand Lab ... Australia. Defence Standards Laboratories.
 Report [*A publication*]
Rep Aust Def Stand Lab ... Report. Australia Defence Standards
 Laboratories [*A publication*]
REPB.......... Republic   (MSA)
REPB.......... Republic Resources Corp. [*NASDAQ symbol*]   (NQ)
Rep BC-X Can For Serv Pac For Res Cent ... Report BC-X. Canadian
 Forestry Service. Pacific Forest Research Centre [*A
 publication*]
Rep Bd Health Calif ... Reports. State Board of Health of California [*A
 publication*]
Rep Bd Health Ohio ... Reports. State Board of Health of Ohio [*A
 publication*]

RepBibPhil ... Repertoire Bibliographique de la Philosophie [*A publication*]
Rep Biochem Res Found Franklin Inst ... Reports. Biochemical Research
 Foundation. Franklin Institute [*A publication*]
Rep Biomed ... Repertoire Biomed [*A publication*]
Rep Bot Surv India ... Report. Botanical Survey of India [*A publication*]
Rep Br Beekprs Ass ... Report. British Beekeepers Association [*A
 publication*]
Rep Brit Ass Adv Sc ... Report. British Association for the Advancement of
 Science [*A publication*]
Rep Brit Assoc Adv Sci ... Report. British Association for the Advancement
 of Science [*A publication*]
Rep Brit Mus Natur Hist ... Report. British Museum. Natural History [*A
 publication*]
Rep Bull Agr Exp Sta S Manchuria Ry Co ... Research Bulletin. Agricultural
 Experiment Station. South Manchuria Railway Company
 [*A publication*]
Rep Bur Miner Resour Geol Geophys ... Report. (Australia) Bureau of
 Mineral Resources. Geology and Geophysics [*A
 publication*]
Rep Bur Miner Resour Geol Geophys (Aust) ... Report. Bureau of Mineral
 Resources, Geology, and Geophysics (Australia) [*A
 publication*]
REPC......... Representation Commissioner [*Canada*]
REPC......... Research and Educational Planning Center [*University of
 Nevada - Reno*] [*Research center*]   (RCD)
REPC......... Research and Engineering Policy Council [*DoD*]
Rep in CA... Court of Appeal Reports [*New Zealand*]   (DLA)
Rep in C of A ... Reports in Courts of Appeal [*New Zealand*]   (DLA)
Rep Cacao Res Reg Cent Br Caribb ... Report on Cacao Research. Regional
 Research Centre of the British Caribbean [*A publication*]
Rep Cas Eq ... Gilbert's English Chancery Reports   (DLA)
Rep Cas Inc Tax ... Reports of Cases Relating to Income Tax [*1875*]   (DLA)
Rep Cas Madr ... Reports of Cases, Diwani Adalat, Madras   (DLA)
Rep Cas Pr ... Cooke's Practice Cases [*1706-47*]   (DLA)
Rep Cast Res Lab ... Report. Castings Research Laboratory [*A publication*]
Rep Cast Res Lab Waseda Univ ... Report. Castings Research Laboratory.
 Waseda University [*A publication*]
REPCAT ..... Report Corrective Action Taken
Rep Cent Res Inst Electr Power Ind Agric Lab ... Report. Central Research
 Institute. Electric Power Industry Agricultural Laboratory
 [*A publication*]
Rep Cent Res Inst Electr Power Ind Tech Lab ... Report. Central Research
 Institute. Electric Power Industry Technical Laboratory [*A
 publication*]
Rep Cent Res Lab Nippon Suisan Co ... Reports. Central Research
 Laboratory. Nippon Suisan Company [*A publication*]
Rep Ch .... Reports in Chancery [*1615-1710*] [*England*]   (DLA)
Rep in Ch ... Reports in Chancery [*21 English Reprint*]   (DLA)
Rep in Cha ... Bittleston's Chamber Cases [*1883-84*]   (DLA)
Rep Chem Lab Am Med Assoc ... Reports. Chemical Laboratory. American
 Medical Association [*A publication*]
Rep in Ch (Eng) ... Reports in Chancery [*21 English Reprint*]   (DLA)
Rep Chiba Inst Technol ... Report. Chiba Institute of Technology [*A
 publication*]
Rep Chief US Forest Serv ... Report of the Chief. United States Forest
 Service [*A publication*]
Rep Ch Pr .. Reports on Chancery Practice [*England*]   (DLA)
Rep Com Cas ... Commercial Cases, Small Cause Court [*1851-60*] [*Bengal,
 India*]   (DLA)
Rep Com Cas ... Report of Commercial Cases [*1895-1941*]   (DLA)
REPCOMDESPAC ... Representative of Commander Destroyers, Pacific
 Fleet
Rep Comm Accredit Rehabil Facil ... Report. Commission on Accreditation
 of Rehabilitation Facilities [*A publication*]
Rep Commonw Conf Plant Pathol ... Report. Commonwealth Conference on
 Plant Pathology [*A publication*]
Rep Commonwealth Entomol Conf ... Report. Commonwealth
 Entomological Conference [*A publication*]
Rep Commonwealth Mycol Conf ... Report. Commonwealth Mycological
 Conference [*A publication*]
Rep Comput Centre Univ Tokyo ... Report. Computer Centre. University of
 Tokyo [*A publication*]
Rep Conf Role Wheat World Food Supply ... Report. Conference on the Role
 of Wheat in the World's Food Supply [*A publication*]
Rep Congr Eur Ass Res Plant Breed ... Report. Congress of the European
 Association for Research on Plant Breeding [*A
 publication*]
Rep Const Ct ... South Carolina Constitutional Court Reports   (DLA)
Rep Constr Eng Res Inst Found (Kobe) ... Reports. Construction
 Engineering Research Institute Foundation (Kobe) [*Japan*]
 [*A publication*]
Rep Coop Res Chugoku Reg ... Report of the Cooperative Research in
 Chugoku Region [*A publication*]
Rep Cr L Com ... Reports of Criminal Law Commissioners [*England*]   (DLA)
Rep Crop Res Lesotho ... Report on Crop Research in Lesotho [*A
 publication*]
Rep CSIRO Div Fish Oceanogr ... Australia. Commonwealth Scientific and
 Industrial Research Organisation. Division of Fisheries and
 Oceanography. Report [*A publication*]

Rep CSIRO Div Text Ind Aust ... Australia. Commonwealth Scientific and Industrial Research Organisation. Division of Textile Industry. Report [*A publication*]

Rep CSIRO Sol Energy Stud ... Report. Commonwealth Scientific and Industrial Research Organisation. Solar Energy Studies [*A publication*]

REPCY .... Repair Cycle

Rep Def Stand Lab Aust ... Australia. Defence Standards Laboratories. Report [*A publication*]

Rep Deir-Alla Res Sta ... Report. Deir-Alla Research Station [*Jordan*] [*A publication*]

Rep Dep Fish Fauna West Aust ... Report. Department of Fisheries and Fauna. Western Australia [*A publication*]

Rep Dep Fish Wildl West Aust ... Report. Department of Fisheries and Wildlife. Western Australia [*A publication*]

Rep Dep Phys Univ Oulu ... Report. Department of Physics. University of Oulu [*A publication*]

Rep Dept Agric (Brit East Africa) ... Report. Department of Agriculture (British East Africa) [*A publication*]

Rep Dept Antiquities Cyprus ... Report. Department of Antiquities of Cyprus [*A publication*]

Rep Director Vet Serv Dept Agric (Union South Africa) ... Report. Director of Veterinary Services and Animal Industry. Department of Agriculture (Union of South Africa) [*A publication*]

Rep Div Bldg Res CSIRO ... Report. Division of Building Research. Commonwealth Scientific and Industrial Research Organisation [*A publication*]

Rep Div Build Res CSIRO ... Report. Division of Building Research. Commonwealth Scientific and Industrial Research Organisation [*A publication*]

Rep Div Chem Eng CSIRO ... Report. Division of Chemical Engineering. Commonwealth Scientific and Industrial Research Organisation [*A publication*]

Rep Div Chem Engng CSIRO ... Report. Division of Chemical Engineering. Commonwealth Scientific and Industrial Research Organisation [*A publication*]

Rep Div Fish Oceanogr CSIRO ... Report. Division of Fisheries and Oceanography. Commonwealth Scientific and Industrial Research Organisation [*A publication*]

Rep Div Hort Res CSIRO ... Report. Division of Horticultural Research. Commonwealth Scientific and Industrial Research Organisation [*A publication*]

Rep Div Mech Engng CSIRO ... Report. Division of Mechanical Engineering. Commonwealth Scientific and Industrial Research Organisation [*A publication*]

Rep Div Miner CSIRO ... Report. Division of Mineralogy. Commonwealth Scientific and Industrial Research Organisation [*A publication*]

Rep Div Text Ind CSIRO ... Report. Division of Textile Industry. Commonwealth Scientific and Industrial Research Organisation [*A publication*]

REPDN .... Reproduction   (AFM)

REPDU .... Report for Duty [*Military*]

REPEA .... Research and Engineers Professional Employees Association

Rep East For Prod Lab (Can) ... Report. Eastern Forest Products Laboratory (Canada) [*A publication*]

Rep ED Eng Sect CSIRO ... Report ED. Engineering Section. Commonwealth Scientific and Industrial Research Organisation [*A publication*]

Rep E Malling Res Stn ... Annual Report. East Malling Research Station [*A publication*]

Rep Eng Inst Fac Eng Tokyo Univ ... Report. Engineering Institute. Faculty of Engineering. Tokyo University [*Japan*] [*A publication*]

Rep Eng Res Lab Obayashi-Gumi Ltd ... Report. Engineering Research Laboratory. Obayashi-Gumi Limited [*Japan*] [*A publication*]

Rep Ent Soc Ont ... Report. Entomological Society of Ontario [*A publication*]

Rep Environ Sci Inst Hyogo Prefect ... Report. Environmental Science Institute of Hyogo Prefecture [*A publication*]

Rep Environ Sci Mie Univ ... Report of Environmental Science. Mie University [*A publication*]

Rep Environ Sci Res Cent Shiga Prefect ... Report. Environmental Science Research Center of Shiga Prefecture [*A publication*]

Rep Eq .... Gilbert's Reports in Equity [*England*]   (DLA)

Reperes-Econ Languedoc-Roussillon ... Reperes-Economie du Languedoc-Roussillon [*A publication*]

REPERF ..... Reperforator [*Telecommunications*]   (TEL)

REPERMSG ... Report in Person or by Message to Command or Person Indicated

Repertoire Anal Litt Francaise ... Repertoire Analytique de Litterature Francaise [*Bordeaux*] [*A publication*]

Repert Pharm ... Repertoire de Pharmacie [*A publication*]

Repert Plant Succulentarum ... Repertorium Plantarum Succulentarum [*A publication*]

REPET .... Repetatur [*Let It Be Repeated*] [*Pharmacy*]

Rep Europe ... Report from Europe [*A publication*]

Rep Evol Comm Roy Soc Lond ... Report to the Evolution Committee. Royal Society of London [*A publication*]

Rep Exp Res Stn (Cheshunt) ... Report. Experimental and Research Station. Nursery and Market Garden Industries Development Society, Ltd. (Cheshunt) [*A publication*]

Rep Fac Agr Shizuoka Univ ... Reports. Faculty of Agriculture. Shizuoka University [*A publication*]

Rep Fac Eng Nagasaki Univ ... Reports. Faculty of Engineering. Nagasaki University [*A publication*]

Rep Fac Eng Shizuoka Univ ... Reports. Faculty of Engineering. Shizuoka University [*A publication*]

Rep Fac Fish Prefect Univ Mie ... Report. Faculty of Fisheries. Prefectural University of Mie [*A publication*]

Rep Fac Sci Engrg Saga Univ Math ... Reports. Faculty of Science and Engineering. Saga University. Mathematics [*A publication*]

Rep Fac Sci Kagoshima Univ ... Reports. Faculty of Science. Kagoshima University [*A publication*]

Rep Fac Sci Kagoshima Univ (Earth Sci Biol) ... Reports. Faculty of Science. Kagoshima University. Earth Sciences and Biology [*A publication*]

Rep Fac Sci Shizuoka Univ ... Reports. Faculty of Science. Shizuoka University [*A publication*]

Rep Fac Sci Technol Meijyo Univ ... Reports. Faculty of Science and Technology. Meijyo University [*A publication*]

Rep Fam L ... Reports of Family Law [*A publication*]

Rep FAO/IAEA Tech Meet (Brunswick-Volkenrode) ... Report. FAO [*Food and Agriculture Organization of the United Nations*]/IAEA [*International Atomic Energy Agency*] Technical Meeting (Brunswick-Volkenrode) [*A publication*]

Rep Fd Res Inst (Tokyo) ... Report. Food Research Institute (Tokyo) [*A publication*]

Rep Fed Railroad Adm ... Report. Federal Railroad Administration [*United States*] [*A publication*]

Rep Ferment Ind ... Report on the Fermentation Industries [*A publication*]

Rep Ferment Res Inst ... Report. Fermentation Research Institute [*A publication*]

Rep Ferment Res Inst (Chiba) ... Report. Fermentation Research Institute (Chiba) [*A publication*]

Rep Fire Res Inst Jpn ... Report. Fire Research Institute of Japan [*A publication*]

Rep Fish Res Lab Kyushu Univ ... Report. Fishery Research Laboratory. Kyushu University [*A publication*]

Rep Food Ind Exp Stn Hiroshima Prefect ... Report. Food Industrial Experiment Station. Hiroshima Prefecture [*A publication*]

Rep Food Res Inst (Tokyo) ... Report. Food Research Institute (Tokyo) [*A publication*]

Rep Forest Dep (Tanganyika) ... Report. Forest Department (Tanganyika Territory) [*A publication*]

Rep Forest Exp Stn Hokkaido ... Annual Report. Hokkaido Branch. Government Forest Experiment Station [*A publication*]

Rep For Game Manage Res Inst ... Reports. Forestry and Game Management Research Institute [*A publication*]

REPFORMAINT ... Representative of Maintenance Force

Rep For Prod Res Inst (Hokkaido) ... Report. Hokkaido Forest Products Research Institute (Asahikawa, Hokkaido) [*A publication*]

Rep For Res ... Report on Forest Research [*A publication*]

Rep For Resour Reconn Surv Malaya ... Report. Forest Resources Reconnaissance Survey of Malaya [*A publication*]

Rep Forsknstift Skogsarb ... Report. Redogorelse. Forskningsstiftelsen Skogsarbeten [*A publication*]

Rep Freedom Hunger Campaign ... Report. Freedom from Hunger Campaign. FAO [*Food and Agriculture Organization of the United Nations*] [*A publication*]

Rep Fukushima Prefect Public Health Inst ... Report. Fukushima Prefectural Public Health Institute [*Japan*] [*A publication*]

Rep Fys Lab I Tek Hoejsk (Lyngby) ... Report. Fysisk Laboratorium I. Danmarks Tekniske Hoejskole (Lyngby) [*A publication*]

Rep GA For Res Coun ... Report. Georgia Forest Research Council [*A publication*]

Rep Gen Fish Counc Mediterr ... Report. General Fisheries Council for the Mediterranean [*A publication*]

Rep Geol Min Explor ... Report of Geological and Mineral Exploration [*South Korea*] [*A publication*]

Rep Geol Surv Dep (Zambia) ... Report. Geological Survey Department (Zambia) [*A publication*]

Rep Geol Surv Hokkaido ... Report. Geological Survey of Hokkaido [*Japan*] [*A publication*]

Rep Geol Surv Jpn ... Report. Geological Survey of Japan [*A publication*]

Rep Geol Surv (Malays) ... Report. Geological Survey (Malaysia) [*A publication*]

Rep Geol Surv Mines Dep (Uganda) ... Report. Geological Survey and Mines Department (Uganda) [*A publication*]

Rep Geol Surv NSW ... Report. Geological Survey of New South Wales [*A publication*]

Rep Geol Surv Qd ... Report. Geological Survey of Queensland [*A publication*]

Rep Geol Surv Queens ... Report. Geological Survey of Queensland [*A publication*]

Rep Geol Surv Tasm ... Report. Geological Survey. Tasmania [*A publication*]

Rep Geol Surv Vic ... Report. Geological Survey of Victoria [*A publication*]

Rep Geol Surv Vict ... Report. Geological Survey of Victoria [*A publication*]

Rep Geol Surv West Aust ... Western Australia. Geological Survey. Report [*A publication*]

Rep Geophys Geochem Explor Geol Surv Korea ... Report of Geophysical and Geochemical Exploration. Geological Survey of Korea [*A publication*]

Rep Geophys Res Stn Kyoto Univ ... Reports. Geophysical Research Station. Kyoto University [*A publication*]
Rep Geosci Miner Resour ... Report on Geoscience and Mineral Resources [*Republic of Korea*] [*A publication*]
Rep Glasshouse Crops Res Inst ... Report. Glasshouse Crops Research Institute [*A publication*]
Rep Gov Chem Ind Res Inst (Tokyo) ... Reports. Government Chemical Industrial Research Institute (Tokyo) [*A publication*]
Rep Gov Ind Res Inst (Kyushu) ... Reports. Government Industrial Research Institute (Kyushu) [*Japan*] [*A publication*]
Rep Gov Ind Res Inst (Nagoya) ... Reports. Government Industrial Research Institute (Nagoya) [*A publication*]
Rep Gov Ind Res Inst (Osaka) ... Reports. Government Industrial Research Institute (Osaka) [*A publication*]
Rep Gov Ind Res Inst (Tohoku) ... Reports. Government Industrial Research Institute (Tohoku) [*A publication*]
Rep Govt Inst Vet Research (Fusan Chosen) ... Report. Government Institute for Veterinary Research (Fusan, Chosen) [*A publication*]
Rep Govt Mech Lab (Tokyo) ... Report. Government Mechanical Laboratory (Tokyo) [*A publication*]
Rep Gr Brit Agr Res Counc ... Report. Great Britain Agricultural Research Council [*A publication*]
Rep Gr Brit Colon Pestic Res Unit CPRU/Porton ... Report. Great Britain Colonial Pesticides Research Unit. CPRU/Porton [*A publication*]
Rep Gt Brit Trop Pestic Res Unit TPRU/Porton ... Report. Great Britain Tropical Pesticides Research Unit. TPRU/Porton [*A publication*]
REPH .... Republic Health Corp. [*NASDAQ symbol*] (NQ)
REPh .... Revue de l'Enseignement Philosophique [*A publication*]
Rep Hawaii Att'y Gen ... Hawaii Attorney General Report (DLA)
Rep Health Soc Subj (Lond) ... Reports. Health and Social Subjects (London) [*A publication*]
Rep Himeji Inst Technol ... Reports. Himeji Institute of Technology [*A publication*]
REPHO .... Reference Telephone Conversation (NOAA)
Rep Hokkaido For Prod Res Inst ... Report. Hokkaido Forest Products Research Institute [*Japan*] [*A publication*]
Rep Hokkaido Inst Public Health ... Report. Hokkaido Institute of Public Health [*A publication*]
Rep Hokkaido Nat Agr Exp Sta ... Report. Hokkaido National Agricultural Experiment Station [*A publication*]
Rep Hokkaido Natn Agric Exp Stn ... Report. Hokkaido National Agricultural Experiment Station [*A publication*]
Rep Hokkaido Pref Agr Exp Sta ... Report. Hokkaido Prefectural Agricultural Experiment Station [*A publication*]
Rep Horace Lamb Inst Oceanogr ... Report. Horace Lamb Institute of Oceanography [*A publication*]
Rep Hort Exp Sta (Ontario) ... Report. Horticultural Experiment Station (Ontario) [*A publication*]
Rep Hort Exp Stn Prod Lab (Vineland) ... Report. Horticultural Experiment Station and Products Laboratory (Vineland Station) [*Ontario*] [*A publication*]
Rep Hung Acad Sci Cent Res Inst Phys ... Report. Hungarian Academy of Sciences. Central Research Institute for Physics. Koezponti Fizikai Kutato Intezet [*A publication*]
Rep Hybrid Corn Ind Res Conf ... Report. Hybrid Corn Industry. Research Conference [*A publication*]
Rep Hyogo Prefect For Exp Stn ... Report. Hyogo Prefectural Forest Experiment Station [*A publication*]
Rep IA St Apiar ... Report of Iowa State Apiarist [*A publication*]
REPIDISCA ... Pan American Information & Documentation Network on Sanitary Engineering & Environmental Sciences [*Pan American Health Organization*] [*Lima, Peru*] [*Information service*] (EISS)
REpigr .... Revue Epigraphique [*A publication*]
Rep Ill Beekeep Ass ... Report. Illinois Beekeeping Association [*A publication*]
REPIN .... Reply If Negative
Rep Ind Educ Res Cent Chungnam Natl Univ ... Report. Industrial Education Research Center. Chungnam National University [*Republic of Korea*] [*A publication*]
Rep Ind Res Inst Hyogo Prefect ... Reports. Industrial Research Institute. Hyogo Prefecture [*A publication*]
Rep Ind Res Inst Osaka Prefect ... Reports. Industrial Research Institute. Osaka Prefecture [*Japan*] [*A publication*]
Rep Inf Cent Jt Inst Lab Astrophys ... Report. Information Center. Joint Institute for Laboratory Astrophysics [*A publication*]
Rep Inst Agric Res Tohoku Univ ... Reports. Institute for Agricultural Research. Tohoku University [*A publication*]
Rep Inst Agr Res (Korea) ... Report. Institute of Agricultural Research (Korea) [*A publication*]
Rep Inst Appl Microbiol Univ Tokyo ... Reports. Institute of Applied Microbiology. University of Tokyo [*A publication*]
Rep Inst Chem Res Kyoto Univ ... Reports. Institute for Chemical Research. Kyoto University [*A publication*]
Rep Inst Fish Biol Minist Econ Aff Natl Taiwan Univ ... Report. Institute of Fishery Biology. Ministry of Economic Affairs. National Taiwan University [*A publication*]
Rep Inst Geol Sci ... Report. Institute of Geological Sciences [*A publication*]

Rep Inst High Speed Mech Tohoku Univ ... Report. Institute of High Speed Mechanics. Tohoku University [*A publication*]
Rep Inst Ind Sci Univ Tokyo ... Report. Institute of Industrial Science. University of Tokyo [*A publication*]
Rep Inst Ld Wat Mgmt Res ... Report. Institute for Land and Water Management Research [*A publication*]
Rep Inst Min Res Univ Rhod ... Report. Institute of Mining Research. University of Rhodesia [*A publication*]
Rep Inst Phys Chem Res ... Reports. Institute of Physical and Chemical Research [*A publication*]
Rep Inst Sci Technol ... Report. Institute of Science and Technology [*Republic of Korea*] [*A publication*]
Rep Inst Syst Des Optim Kans State Univ ... Report. Institute for Systems Design and Optimization. Kansas State University [*A publication*]
Rep Int Assoc Cereal Chem ... Reports. International Association of Cereal Chemistry [*A publication*]
Rep Int Pac Halibut Comm ... Report. International Pacific Halibut Commission [*A publication*]
Rep Invest Aust Gov Anal Lab ... Australian Government Analytical Laboratories. Report of Investigations [*A publication*]
Rep Invest Bur Mines Philipp ... Report of Investigations. Bureau of Mines of the Philippines [*A publication*]
Rep Invest Div Miner Resour (VA) ... Report of Investigations. Division of Mineral Resources (Virginia) [*A publication*]
Rep Invest Geol Surv MO ... Report of Investigations. Geological Survey of Missouri [*A publication*]
Rep Invest Geol Surv S Aust ... Report of Investigations. Geological Survey of South Australia [*A publication*]
Rep Invest Geol Surv South Aust ... Report of Investigations. Geological Survey of South Australia [*A publication*]
Rep Invest Gov Chem Labs West Aust ... Report of Investigations. Government Chemical Laboratories. Western Australia [*A publication*]
Rep Invest Ill State Geol Surv ... Report of Investigations. Illinois State Geological Survey [*A publication*]
Rep Invest ND Geol Surv ... Report of Investigation. North Dakota Geological Survey [*A publication*]
Rep Invest US Bur Mines ... Reports of Investigations. United States Bureau of Mines [*A publication*]
Rep Invest WA Govt Chem Labs ... Report of Investigations. Government Chemical Laboratories. Western Australia [*A publication*]
Rep Ionos Res Jpn ... Report of Ionosphere Research in Japan [*Later, Report of Ionosphere and Space Research in Japan*] [*A publication*]
Rep Ionos & Space Res Jap ... Report of Ionosphere and Space Research in Japan [*A publication*]
Rep Ionos and Space Res Jpn ... Report of Ionosphere and Space Research in Japan [*A publication*]
Rep Ion Spa ... Report of Ionosphere and Space Research in Japan [*A publication*]
Rep Iowa St Hort Soc ... Report. Iowa State Horticultural Society [*A publication*]
REPISIC ..... Report Immediate Superior in Command [*Navy*]
Rep Jur ...... Repertorium Juridicum [*England*] (DLA)
Rep Kansas Agric Exper Station ... Report. Kansas Agricultural Experiment Station [*A publication*]
Rep Kans State Board Agr ... Report. Kansas State Board of Agriculture [*A publication*]
Rep Kevo Subarct Res Stn ... Reports. Kevo Subarctic Research Station [*A publication*]
Rep Kihara Inst Biol Res ... Reports. Kihara Institute for Biological Research [*Japan*] [*A publication*]
Rep Kunst W ... Repertorium fuer Kunstwissenschaft [*A publication*]
Rep Kyushu Br Crop Sci Soc Jap ... Report. Kyushu Branch. Crop Science Society of Japan [*A publication*]
Rep Kyushu Univ For ... Reports. Kyushu University Forests [*A publication*]
REPL .... Replace (AAG)
repl .... Replacement (DLA)
REPLAB ..... Responsive Environment Programed Laboratory (IEEE)
Rep Lab Soils Fert Fac Agric Okayama Univ ... Reports. Laboratory of Soils and Fertilizers. Faculty of Agriculture. Okayama University [*A publication*]
Rep Lawrence Livermore Lab ... Report. Lawrence Livermore Laboratory. University of California [*Livermore*] [*A publication*]
Rep Lib Arts Sci Fac Shizuoka Univ ... Report. Liberal Arts of Science Faculty. Shizuoka University [*A publication*]
Rep Liberal Arts Sci Fac Shizuoka Univ Nat Sci ... Reports. Liberal Arts and Science Faculty. Shizuoka University. Natural Science [*Japan*] [*A publication*]
REPLN .... Replenish (AABC)
Rep Local Govt Bd (London) ... Reports. Local Government Board (London) [*A publication*]
REPLTR ...... Report by Letter (NVT)
REPM .... Rare Earth Permanent Magnet
REPM .... Repairman (NATG)
REPM .... Representatives of Electronic Products Manufacturers [*Later, ERA*]
Rep Mass Att'y Gen ... Report of the Attorney General, of the State of Massachusetts (DLA)

Rep Mater Res Lab Aust ... Australia. Materials Research Laboratories. Report [*A publication*]

Rep Mathematical Phys ... Reports on Mathematical Physics [*A publication*]

Rep Math Log ... Reports on Mathematical Logic [*A publication*]

Rep Math Logic ... Reports on Mathematical Logic [*Warsaw/Krakow*] [*A publication*]

Rep Math Phys ... Reports on Mathematical Physics [*A publication*]

Rep Maurit Sug Ind Res Inst ... Report. Mauritius Sugar Industry Research Institute [*A publication*]

Rep MC ...... Reports of Municipal Corporations (DLA)

REPMC ...... Representative to the Military Committee [*NATO*]

Rep MD Agr Soc ... Report. Maryland Agricultural Society [*A publication*]

Rep MD Beekprs Ass ... Report. Maryland Beekeepers' Association [*A publication*]

Rep Mech Developm Comm For Comm (Lond) ... Report. Mechanical Development Committee. Forestry Commission (London) [*A publication*]

Rep Med and Health Dept (Mauritius) ... Report. Medical and Health Department (Mauritius) [*A publication*]

Rep Med and Health Work Sudan ... Report on Medical and Health Work in the Sudan [*A publication*]

Rep Med Res Probl Jpn Anti-Tuberc Assoc ... Reports on Medical Research Problems of the Japan Anti-Tuberculosis Association [*A publication*]

Rep Meet Aust NZ Assoc Adv Sci ... Report. Meeting. Australian and New Zealand Association for the Advancement of Science [*A publication*]

Rep Melb Metrop Board Works ... Report. Melbourne and Metropolitan Board of Works [*A publication*]

REPMES .... Reply by Message (FAAC)

Rep Mich Dept Conserv Game Div ... Report. Michigan Department of Conservation. Game Division [*A publication*]

Rep Miner Bur (S Afr) ... Report. Minerals Bureau. Department of Mines (South Africa) [*A publication*]

Rep Miner Dev Div (Newfoundland) ... Report. Mineral Development Division. Department of Mines (Newfoundland) [*A publication*]

Rep Miner Res Lab CSIRO ... Report. Division of Mineralogy. Minerals Research Laboratory. Commonwealth Scientific and Industrial Research Organisation [*A publication*]

REPMIS ...... Reserve Personnel Management Information System [*Military*]

Rep Miss Agr Exp Sta ... Report. Mississippi Agricultural Experiment Station [*A publication*]

REPML .... Reply by Mail (FAAC)

Rep MRL NC State Univ Miner Res Lab ... Report MRL. North Carolina State University. Minerals Research Laboratory [*A publication*]

Rep Nat Inst Nutr ... Report. National Institute of Nutrition [*A publication*]

Rep Natl Food Res Inst (Tokyo) ... Report. National Food Research Institute (Tokyo) [*A publication*]

Rep Natl Inst Metall ... Report. National Institute for Metallurgy [*A publication*]

Rep Natl Radiol Prot Board ... Report. National Radiological Protection Board [*A publication*]

Rep Natl Res Inst Met ... Report. National Research Institute for Metals [*Tokyo*] [*A publication*]

Rep Natl Res Inst Police Sci (Jpn) Res Forensic Sci ... Reports. National Research Institute of Police Science (Japan). Research on Forensic Science [*A publication*]

Rep Natl Res Inst Pollut Resour (Kawaguchi Jpn) ... Report. National Research Institute for Pollution and Resources (Kawaguchi, Japan) [*A publication*]

Rep Natl Res Lab Metrol ... Report. National Research Laboratory of Metrology [*A publication*]

Rep Natl Water Resour Counc Repub Philipp ... Report. National Water Resources Council. Republic of the Philippines [*A publication*]

Rep Natn Fd Res Inst (Jap) ... Report. National Food Research Institute (Japan) [*A publication*]

Rep Natn Inst Genet (Misima) ... Report. National Institute of Genetics (Misima) [*A publication*]

Rep Natn Inst Metall (S Afr) ... Report. National Institute of Metallurgy (South Africa) [*A publication*]

Rep Nat Res Inst Police Sci ... Reports. National Research Institute of Police Science [*A publication*]

Rep NC Att'y Gen ... North Carolina Attorney General Reports (DLA)

Rep Neb Att'y Gen ... Report of the Attorney General of the State of Nebraska (DLA)

Rep N Engl Assoc Chem Teach ... Report. New England Association of Chemistry Teachers [*A publication*]

Rep New Hebrides Geol Surv ... Report. New Hebrides Geological Survey [*A publication*]

Rep Northeast Corn Impr Conf ... Report. Northeastern Corn Improvement Conference [*A publication*]

Rep Norw Fish Mar Invest Rep Technol Res ... Reports on Norwegian Fishery and Marine Investigation. Reports on Technological Research [*A publication*]

Rep Norw For Res Inst ... Reports. Norwegian Forest Research Institute [*A publication*]

Rep Nottingham Univ Sch Agr ... Report. Nottingham University. School of Agriculture [*A publication*]

Rep NRL Prog ... Report of NRL [*Naval Research Laboratory*] Progress [*A publication*]

Rep NZ Sci Cong ... Report. New Zealand Science Congress [*A publication*]

REPO .... Reporting Officer [*Navy*]

REPO .... Repossess

Rep Ohara Inst Agr Biol ... Report. Ohara Institute of Agricultural Biology [*A publication*]

Rep Ohara Inst Agric Biol ... Report. Ohara Institute of Agricultural Biology [*A publication*]

Rep Ont Vet Coll ... Report. Ontario Veterinary College [*A publication*]

REP-OP ...... Repetitive Operation [*Data processing*] (MDG)

Rep & Ops Atty Gen Ind ... Indiana Attorney General Reports (DLA)

Rep Ore For Res Lab ... Report. Oregon State University. Forest Research Laboratory [*A publication*]

Rep Oreg Wheat Comm ... Report. Oregon Wheat Commission [*A publication*]

Reporter Aust Inst of Crim Qrtly ... Reporter. Australian Institute of Criminology. Quarterly [*A publication*]

Reports ...... Coke's English King's Bench Reports [*76-77 ER*] [*1572-1616*] (DLA)

Reports Inst High Speed Mech Tohoku Univ ... Reports. Institute of High Speed Mechanics. Tohoku University [*A publication*]

Reports Res Inst Appl Mech Kyushu Univ ... Reports. Research Institute for Applied Mechanics. Kyushu University [*A publication*]

Rep Osaka Prefect Ind Res Inst ... Reports. Osaka Prefectural Industrial Research Institute [*Japan*] [*A publication*]

REPPAC ..... Repetitively Pulsed Plasma Accelerator

Rep Pat Cas ... Reports of Patent, Design, and Trade Mark Cases [*England*] (DLA)

Rep Pat Des & Tr Cas ... Reports of Patent, Design, and Trade Mark Cases (DLA)

Rep Phil ..... Reports on Philosophy [*A publication*]

Rep Plann Conf Strategy Virus Manage Potato II ... Report. Planning Conference on the Strategy for Virus Management in Potatoes. II [*A publication*]

Rep Popul-Fam Plann ... Reports on Population-Family Planning [*A publication*]

Rep Prefect Ind Res Inst (Shizuoka) ... Reports. Prefectural Industrial Research Institute (Shizuoka) [*Japan*] [*A publication*]

Rep Proc Int Assoc Ice Cream Manuf ... Report of Proceedings. International Association of Ice Cream Manufacturers [*A publication*]

Rep Prog Phys ... Reports on Progress in Physics [*A publication*]

Rep Prog Polym Phys (Jpn) ... Reports on Progress in Polymer Physics (Japan) [*A publication*]

Rep Progr Appl Chem ... Reports on the Progress of Applied Chemistry [*A publication*]

Rep Progr Kans Agr Exp Sta ... Report of Progress. Kansas Agricultural Experiment Station [*A publication*]

Rep Progr Kansas Agric Exp Stn ... Report of Progress. Kansas Agricultural Experiment Station [*A publication*]

Rep Progr Phys ... Reports on Progress in Physics [*A publication*]

Rep Proj LA Agr Exp Sta Dept Agron ... Report of Projects. Louisiana Agricultural Experiment Station. Department of Agronomy [*A publication*]

Rep Pr Phys ... Reports on Progress in Physics [*A publication*]

Rep QA .... Reports Tempore Queen Anne [*11 Modern*] (DLA)

Rep Quebec Soc Prot Plant ... Report. Quebec Society for the Protection of Plants [*A publication*]

REPR .... Real Estate Planning Report [*Military*] (AABC)

REPR .... Repair (ROG)

REPR .... Reports on Polar Research. Berichte zur Polarforschung [*A publication*]

REPR .... Representative

REPR .... Repressurization (MCD)

REPR .... Reprinted

Repr Acts W Austl ... Reprinted Acts of Western Australia (DLA)

Repr Bull Bk R ... Reprint Bulletin. Book Reviews [*A publication*]

Rep Rd Res Lab Minist Transp ... Report. Road Research Laboratory. Ministry of Transport [*A publication*]

Rep React Cent (Ned) ... Report. Reactor Centrum (Nederlandse) [*A publication*]

Rep Reelfoot Lake Biol Stn Tenn Acad Sci ... Report. Reelfoot Lake Biological Station. Tennessee Academy of Science [*A publication*]

Rep Reg Res Cent ICTA (Trinidad) ... Report. Regional Research Centre of the British Caribbean. Imperial College of Tropical Agriculture (Trinidad) [*A publication*]

Rep Res Dept Kyushu Electr Power Co Inc ... Report. Research Department. Kyushu Electric Power Company, Incorporated [*Japan*] [*A publication*]

Rep Res Grantees Minist Educ (Jpn) ... Reports on Researches by Grantees. Ministry of Education (Japan) [*A publication*]

Rep Res Inst Appl Mech Kyushu Univ ... Reports. Research Institute for Applied Mechanics. Kyushu University [*A publication*]

Rep Res Inst Brew ... Report. Research Institute of Brewing [*A publication*]

Rep Res Inst Electr Commun Tohoku Univ ... Reports. Research Institute of Electrical Communication. Tohoku University [*A publication*]

Rep Res Inst Ind Saf ... Reports. Research Institute of Industrial Safety [*Japan*] [*A publication*]

Rep Res Inst Ind Sci Kyushu Univ ... Reports. Research Institute of Industrial Science. Kyushu University [*A publication*]
Rep Res Inst Nat Sci ... Report. Research Institute of Natural Sciences [*Republic of Korea*] [*A publication*]
Rep Res Inst Sci Ind Kyushu Univ ... Reports. Research Institute of Science and Industry. Kyushu University [*Japan*] [*A publication*]
Rep Res Inst Sci Technol Nihon Univ ... Report. Research Institute of Science and Technology. Nihon University [*A publication*]
Rep Res Inst Strength and Fract Mater ... Reports. Research Institute for Strength and Fracture of Materials [*A publication*]
Rep Res Inst Strength Fract Mater Tohoku Univ ... Reports. Research Institute for Strength and Fracture of Materials. Tohoku University [*A publication*]
Rep Res Inst Strength Fracture Mater Tohoku Univ (Sendai) ... Reports. Research Institute for Strength and Fracture of Materials. Tohoku University (Sendai) [*Japan*] [*A publication*]
Rep Res Inst Underground Resour Min Coll Akita Univ ... Report. Research Institute of Underground Resources. Mining College. Akita University [*Japan*] [*A publication*]
Rep Res Lab Asahi Glass Co Ltd ... Report. Research Laboratory. Asahi Glass Company Limited [*A publication*]
Rep Res Lab Eng Mater Tokyo Inst Technol ... Report. Research Laboratory of Engineering Materials. Tokyo Institute of Technology [*A publication*]
Rep Res Lab Kirin Brew Co ... Report. Research Laboratories of Kirin Brewery Company [*A publication*]
Rep Res Lab Kirin Brewery Co Ltd ... Report. Research Laboratories of Kirin Brewery Company Limited [*Japan*] [*A publication*]
Rep Res Lab Shimizu Constr Co Ltd ... Reports. Research Laboratory of Shimizu Construction Company Limited [*Japan*] [*A publication*]
Rep Res Lab Surf Sci Okayama Univ ... Reports. Research Laboratory for Surface Science. Okayama University [*A publication*]
Rep Res Lab Tohoku Electr Power Co Ltd ... Report. Research Laboratory. Tohoku Electric Power Company Limited [*Japan*] [*A publication*]
Rep Res Nippon Inst Technol ... Report of Researches. Nippon Institute of Technology [*A publication*]
Rep Resour Res Inst (Kawaguchi) ... Report. Resource Research Institute (Kawaguchi) [*Japan*] [*A publication*]
Rep Res Progr Ill Agr Exp Sta ... Report. Research Progress at the Illinois Agricultural Experiment Station [*A publication*]
Rep Res Proj Dis Ornam Pl ... Report. Research Project for Diseases of Ornamental Plants (Victorian Plant Research Institute) [*A publication*]
Repr For Prod (Aust) ... Reprint. Division of Forest Products (Melbourne, Australia) [*A publication*]
Rep Rheum Dis ... Reports on Rheumatic Diseases [*A publication*]
Reprint .... English Reports, Full Reprint (DLA)
Reprint Bull Bk R ... Reprint Bulletin. Book Reviews [*A publication*]
Repr NZ For Serv ... Reprint. New Zealand Forest Service [*A publication*]
REPRO .... Reproduce (KSC)
REPROC ..... Reprocess (MCD)
Reprocess Newsl ... Reprocessing Newsletter [*A publication*]
REPROD ..... Receiver Protective Device (DEN)
Reprodn Paper News Bull ... Reproduction Paper News. Bulletin [*A publication*]
Reprodn Rev ... Reproductions Review and Methods [*A publication*]
Reprod Nutr Dev ... Reproduction, Nutrition, Developpement [*A publication*]
Reproduccio ... Reproduccion [*A publication*]
Reprographics Q ... Reprographics Quarterly [*A publication*]
Reprography Newsl ... Reprography Newsletter [*A publication*]
Reprogr Q ... Reprographics Quarterly [*A publication*]
REPROM .... Reprogramable Programable Read-Only Memory [*Data processing*] (TEL)
REPROM .... Reprogramable Read-Only Memory [*Data processing*] (KSC)
REPRON ..... Representation (ROG)
Rep Ross Conf Pediatr Res ... Report. Ross Conference on Pediatric Research [*A publication*]
Rep Rothamsted Exp Sta ... Report. Rothamsted Experimental Station [*A publication*]
Rep Rothamsted Exp Stn ... Report. Rothamsted Experimental Station [*A publication*]
REPROTOX ... Reproductive Toxicology Center [*Database*] [*Washington, DC*]
Rep Rowett Inst ... Report. Rowett Institute [*A publication*]
Repr Res SP ... Representative Research in Social Psychology [*A publication*]
Repr Stat NZ ... Reprint of the Statutes of New Zealand (DLA)
REPS .... Regional Emissions Projection System [*Environmental Protection Agency*]
REPS .... Repetitive Electromagnetic Pulse Simulator [*Army*] (RDA)
REPS .... Representative
REPSA .... Revista de Psicoanalisis [*A publication*]
Rep S Afr Assoc Adv Sci ... Report. South African Association for the Advancement of Science [*A publication*]
Rep Sch Agric Univ Nottingham ... Report. School of Agriculture. University of Nottingham [*A publication*]
Rep Sci Ind Forum ... Report. Science and Industry Forum. Australian Academy of Science [*A publication*]

Rep Sci Indust Forum ... Report. Science and Industry Forum. Australian Academy of Science [*A publication*]
Rep Sci Indust Forum Aust Acad Sci ... Report. Science and Industry Forum. Australian Academy of Science [*A publication*]
Rep Sci Living ... Reports of the Science of Living [*A publication*]
Rep Scott Beekprs Ass ... Report. Scottish Beekeepers Association [*A publication*]
Rep Sel Cas Ch ... [*W.*] Kelynge's English Chancery Reports (DLA)
Rep of Sel Cas in Ch ... [*W.*] Kelynge's Select Cases in Chancery [*1730-32*] (DLA)
Rep Ser Ark Agr Exp Sta ... Report Series. Arkansas Agricultural Experiment Station [*A publication*]
Rep Ser Ark Agric Exp Stn ... Report Series. Arkansas Agricultural Experiment Station [*A publication*]
Rep Ser Phys Univ Helsinki ... Report Series in Physics. University of Helsinki [*A publication*]
REPSHIP .... Report of Shipment [*DoD*]
REPSHIPS ... Reports of Shipments
Rep Silk Sci Res Inst ... Reports. Silk Science Research Institute [*Japan*] [*A publication*]
Rep (Sixth) Conf Int Ass Quatern Res ... Report. Sixth Conference of the International Association on Quaternary Research [*A publication*]
Rep Smithson Instn ... Report. Smithsonian Institution [*A publication*]
REPSNO ..... Report through Senior Naval Officer
Rep Soc Res City Futu ... Report of the Social Research on the City of Futu [*A publication*]
Rep Sol Energy Stud CSIRO ... Report. Solar Energy Studies. Commonwealth Scientific and Industrial Research Organisation [*A publication*]
Rep South Corn Impr Conf ... Report. Southern Corn Improvement Conference [*A publication*]
Rep Stanford Univ John A Blume Earthquake Eng Cent ... Report. Stanford University. John A. Blume Earthquake Engineering Center [*A publication*]
Rep Stat Appl Res UJSE ... Reports of Statistical Application Research. Union of Japanese Scientists and Engineers [*A publication*]
Rep State Bd Health Iowa ... Report. State Board of Health of Iowa [*A publication*]
Rep State Energy Comm WA ... Report. State Energy Commission of Western Australia [*A publication*]
Rep Statist Appl Res Un Japan Sci Engrs ... Reports of Statistical Application Research. Union of Japanese Scientists and Engineers [*A publication*]
Rep Stud Upland Farming Kawatabi Farm Tohoku Univ ... Report of the Studies on Upland Farming in Kawatabi Farm. Tohoku University [*A publication*]
Rep Sugar Exp Sta (Taiwan) ... Report. Sugar Experimental Station (Taiwan) [*A publication*]
Rep Surg Gen US Navy ... Report. Surgeon General. United States Navy [*A publication*]
Rep Surv Thirty-Two NSW River Valleys ... Report. Survey of Thirty-Two New South Wales River Valleys [*A publication*]
Rep Swed Univ Agric Sci Dep Agric Eng ... Report. Swedish University of Agricultural Sciences. Department of Agricultural Engineering [*A publication*]
Rep Swed Univ Agric Sci Dep Farm Build ... Report. Swedish University of Agricultural Sciences. Department of Farm Buildings [*A publication*]
Rep Swed Univ Agric Sci Dep For Prod ... Report. Swedish University of Agricultural Sciences. Department of Forest Products [*A publication*]
REPT .... Receipt
REPT .... Repeat (ADA)
REPT .... Repetatur [*Let It Be Repeated*] [*Pharmacy*]
REPT .... Report
REPT .... Represent (ROG)
rept .... Reprint (BJA)
Rep Taiwan Sugar Exp Stn ... Report. Taiwan Sugar Experiment Station [*A publication*]
Rep Taiwan Sugar Res Inst ... Report. Taiwan Sugar Research Institute [*A publication*]
Rep Tech Coll Hosei Univ (Tokyo) ... Report. Technical College. Hosei University (Tokyo) [*A publication*]
Rep Technol Iwate Univ ... Report on Technology. Iwate University [*Japan*] [*A publication*]
Rep Technol Res Norw Fish Ind ... Reports on Technological Research Concerning Norwegian Fish Industry [*A publication*]
Rep Tech Res Inst Taisei Corp ... Reports. Technical Research Institute. Taisei Corporation [*A publication*]
Rep Teleph Eng ... Reports on Telephone Engineering [*A publication*]
Rep Tex Water Dev Board ... Report. Texas Water Development Board [*A publication*]
Rep T F .... Reports, Court of Chancery Tempore Finch [*1673-81*] (DLA)
Rep T Finch ... Reports, Court of Chancery Tempore Finch [*1673-81*] (DLA)
Rep T Finch (Eng) ... Reports, Court of Chancery Tempore Finch [*1673-81*] [*England*] (DLA)
Rep T Hard ... Lee's English King's Bench Reports Tempore Hardwicke [*1733-38*] (DLA)

Rep T Hardw ... Lee's English King's Bench Reports Tempore Hardwicke [*1733-38*]   (DLA)

Rep T Holt ... Reports Tempore Holt, English Cases of Settlement   (DLA)

Rep T O Br ... Carter's English Common Pleas Reports Tempore Orlando Bridgman   (DLA)

Rep Tob Res Inst (Taiwan) ... Annual Report. Tobacco Research Institute (Taiwan) [*A publication*]

REPTOF ..... Reporting Officer   (NATG)

Rep Tohoku Br Crop Sci Soc Jap ... Report. Tohoku Branch. Crop Science Society of Japan [*A publication*]

Rep Tokai Br Crop Sci Soc Jap ... Report. Tokai Branch. Crop Science Society of Japan [*A publication*]

Rep Tokushima Agr Exp Sta ... Report. Tokushima Agricultural Experiment Station [*A publication*]

Rep Tokyo-to-Lab Med Sci ... Report. Tokyo-to-Lab for Medical Sciences [*A publication*]

Rep Tokyo Metrop Ind Res Inst ... Reports. Tokyo Metropolitan Industrial Research Institute [*A publication*]

Rep Tokyo Metrop Ind Tech Inst ... Report. Tokyo Metropolitan Industrial Technic Institute [*A publication*]

Rep Tokyo Univ Fish ... Report. Tokyo University. Fisheries [*A publication*]

Rep Tottori Mycol Inst ... Reports. Tottori Mycological Institute [*A publication*]

Rept Progr Appl ... Reports on the Progress of Applied Chemistry [*A publication*]

Rept Progr Polymer Phys (Japan) ... Reports on Progress in Polymer Physics (Japan) [*A publication*]

Rep T QA .... Reports Tempore Queen Anne [*11 Modern*]   (DLA)

Reptr .... [*The*] Reporter [*Boston, Los Angeles, New York, Washington*]   (DLA)

Rep Train Inst Eng Teach Kyoto Univ ... Report. Training Institute for Engineering Teachers. Kyoto University [*Japan*] [*A publication*]

REPTRANS ... Report for Transportation

Rep Trans (Devonshire) ... Report and Transactions (Devonshire) [*A publication*]

Rep Transp Tech Res Inst (Tokyo) ... Report. Transportation Technical Research Institute (Tokyo) [*A publication*]

Rep T Talb ... Reports Tempore Talbot, English Chancery   (DLA)

Rept T Finch ... Cases Tempore Finch, English Chancery   (DLA)

Rept T Holt ... Cases Tempore Holt, English King's Bench   (DLA)

Rep T Wood ... Manitoba Reports Tempore Wood   (DLA)

REPTWX .... Reply by TWX [*Teletypewriter communications*]   (FAAC)

REPUB .... Republican

Repubb Ital Minist Agri For Collana Verde ... Repubblica Italiana Ministero dell'Agricoltura e delle Foreste Collana Verde [*A publication*]

Repub Malgache Doc Bur Geol ... Republique Malgache. Documentation du Bureau Geologique [*A publication*]

Repub Rwandaise Bull Serv Geol ... Republique Rwandaise. Bulletin du Service Geologique [*A publication*]

Repub S Afr Dep Agric Tech Serv Tech Commun ... Republic of South Africa. Department of Agricultural Technical Services. Technical Communication [*A publication*]

Repub S Afr Geol Opname Bull ... Republiek van Suid-Afrika. Geologiese Opname. Bulletin [*A publication*]

Repub S Afr Geol Opname Handb ... Republiek van Suid-Afrika. Geologiese Opname. Handboek [*A publication*]

Repub Venezuela Bol Acad Cienc Fis Mat Natur ... Republica de Venezuela. Boletin. Academia de Ciencias Fisicas, Matematicas, y Naturales [*A publication*]

Repub Venezuela Bol Acad Ci Fis Mat Natur ... Republica de Venezuela. Boletin. Academia de Ciencias Fisicas, Matematicas, y Naturales [*A publication*]

REPUD .... Repudiate

Rep Univ Alaska Inst Mar Sci ... Report. University of Alaska. Institute of Marine Science [*A publication*]

Rep Univ Calif Davis Calif Water Resour Cent ... Report. University of California, Davis. California Water Resources Center [*A publication*]

Rep Univ Electro-Comm ... Reports. University of Electro-Communications [*A publication*]

Rep Univ Electro-Commun ... Reports. University of Electro-Communications [*A publication*]

Rep USA Mar Biol Stn ... Reports. USA Marine Biological Station [*A publication*]

Rep US Dep Agric For Serv North Reg State Priv For ... Report. United States Department of Agriculture Forest Service. Northern Region. State and Private Forestry [*A publication*]

REPVE .... Representative   (ROG)

Rep VT Wood Prod Conf ... Report. Vermont Wood Products Conference [*A publication*]

Rep Waite Agric Res Inst ... Report. Waite Agricultural Research Institute [*A publication*]

Rep Water Res Found Aust ... Report. Water Research Foundation of Australia [*A publication*]

Rep Water Res Found Aust Ltd ... Report. Water Research Foundation of Australia [*A publication*]

Rep Water Res Lab NSW Univ ... Report. Water Research Laboratory. University of New South Wales [*A publication*]

Rep Water Resour Res Inst Univ NC ... Report. Water Resources Research Institute. University of North Carolina [*A publication*]

Rep Water Resour Surv ... Report. Water Resources Survey. Tasmania [*A publication*]

Rep Wat Res Fdn ... Report. Water Research Foundation of Australia [*A publication*]

Rep Wat Res Fdn Aust ... Report. Water Research Foundation of Australia [*A publication*]

Rep Wat Res Lab NSW Univ ... Report. Water Research Laboratory. University of New South Wales [*A publication*]

Rep Wellcome Research Lab ... Report. Wellcome Research Laboratories [*A publication*]

Rep Welsh Pl Breed Stn ... Report. Welsh Plant Breeding Station [*A publication*]

Rep Welsh Soils Discuss Grp ... Report. Welsh Soils Discussion Group [*A publication*]

Rep Wheat Qual Conf ... Report. Wheat Quality Conference [*A publication*]

Rep World Aff ... Report on World Affairs [*A publication*]

Rep World Congr Agr Res ... Report. World Congress on Agricultural Research [*A publication*]

Rep W Scot Agr Coll Econ Dept ... Report. West of Scotland Agricultural College. Economics Department [*A publication*]

Rep Wye Agric Coll ... Report. Wye Agricultural College [*A publication*]

Rep Wye Coll Dep Hop Res ... Report. Wye College. Department of Hop Research [*A publication*]

REPYB .... Research Policy [*Netherlands*] [*A publication*]

Rep Yeungnam Univ Inst Ind Technol ... Report. Yeungnam University. Institute of Industrial Technology [*A publication*]

Rep Yeungnam Univ Inst Nat Prod ... Report. Yeungnam University. Institute of Natural Products [*A publication*]

Rep York Ass ... Clayton's English Reports, York Assizes [*England*]   (DLA)

Rep Yr Dublin Univ Coll Agr Dept ... Report of the Year. Dublin University College. Agricultural Department [*A publication*]

REQ .... Request   (AAG)

REQ .... Require   (AAG)

REQ .... Requisition

REQAFA .... Request Advise as to Further Action [*Army*]   (AABC)

REQANS ... Request Answer By [*Date*]

REQAURQN ... Request Authority to Requisition [*Army*]   (AFIT)

REQCAPS ... Requirements and Capabilities Automated Planning System   (MCD)

REQD .... Required   (AAG)

REQDI .... Request Disposition Instructions [*Army*]   (AABC)

REQFOLINFO ... Request Following Information Be Forwarded This Office [*Army*]   (AABC)

REQIBO ..... Request Item Be Placed on Back Order [*Army*]

REQID .... Request If Desired   (FAAC)

REQINT ..... Request Interim Reply By [*Date*] [*Military*]   (AABC)

REQMAD ... Request Mailing Address   (FAAC)

REQMNT ... Requirement   (NVT)

REQMT ...... Requirement

REQN .... Requisition   (AAG)

REQNOM ... Request Nomination

REQPER .... Request Permission [*Navy*]   (NVT)

REQRCM ... Request Recommendation   (FAAC)

REQRE .... Require   (ROG)

REQREC .... Request Recommendation   (NVT)

REQS .... Requires

REQSI .... Request Shipping Instructions

REQSSD .... Request Supply Status and Expected Delivery Date [*Army*]   (AABC)

REQSTD ..... Requested   (FAAC)

REQSUPSTAFOL ... Request Supply Status of Following [*Army*]   (AABC)

REQT .... Request   (ROG)

REQT .... Requirement   (AAG)

REQTAT ..... [*It Is*] Requested That   (AABC)

REQTRAC ... Request Tracer Be Initiated

REQUAL ..... Requalify

REQUCHRD ... Request Unit of Issue Be Changed to Read [*Army*]   (AABC)

REQUONS ... Requisitions

REQVER .... Requirements Verification   (IEEE)

RER .... RADAR Effects Reactor

RER .... Radiation Effects Reactor [*Air Force*]

RER .... Railway Equipment Register

RER .... Receiver/Exciter Ranging [*NASA*]

ReR .... Remington Rand Corp., Blue Bell, PA [*Library symbol*] [*Library of Congress*]   (LCLS)

RER .... Representatives for Experiment Review   (NRCH)

RER .... Rerun   (AAG)

RER .... Reseau Express Regional [*Paris subway*]

RER .... Residual Error Rate

RER .... Resource Evaluation Report   (MCD)

RER .... Respiratory Exchange Rate

RER .... Retlaw Resources, Inc. [*Vancouver Stock Exchange symbol*]

RER .... Reusable-Expendable-Reusable

RER .... Review of Educational Research [*A publication*]

RER .... Revue des Etudes Rabelaisiennes [*A publication*]

RER .... Revue des Etudes Roumaines [*A publication*]

RER .... Rough [*Surfaced*] Endoplasmic Reticulum [*Cytology*]

RER .... Rubberized Equipment Repair

RERA .... Reclamation Era [*A publication*]

RERA.......... RERA: Official Monthly Journal. Radio and Electrical Retailers' Association of New South Wales [*A publication*]
RERAD .... Reference Radio
RERC.......... Radiological Emergency Response Coordination [*Nuclear energy*]   (NRCH)
RERC.......... Rare Earth Research Conference   (EA)
RERC.......... Real Estate Research Corporation
RER & D ..... Rehabilitative Engineering Research and Development Service [*Veterans Administration*]
REREPS ..... Repair and Rehabilitation of Paved Surfaces   (MCD)
REREQ ...... Reference Requisition   (NOAA)
REREX....... Remote Readout Experiment
RERF .... Radiation Effects Research Foundation [*Formerly, ABCC*]
RERIC........ Renewable Energy Resources Information Center [*Asian Institute of Technology*] [*Bangkok, Thailand*] [*Information service*]   (EISS)
RERIF .... Rainier Energy Resources [*NASDAQ symbol*]   (NQ)
RERL .... Residual Equivalent Return Loss
Rer Nat Scr Graec Min ... Rerum Naturalium Scriptores Graeci Minores [*A publication*]   (OCD)
RERO.......... Radiological Emergency Response Operation [*Nuclear energy*]   (NRCH)
RERo .... Revue des Etudes Roumaines [*A publication*]
RERO.......... Royal Engineers Reserve of Officers [*British*]
RERP.......... Radiological Emergency Response Plan [*Nuclear emergency planning*]
RERP.......... Radiological Emergency Response Planning   (NRCH)
RERTD ...... Regelungstechnik. RT [*A publication*]
RES .... Eastman School of Music, Rochester, NY [*OCLC symbol*]   (OCLC)
RES .... Hawaiian Air Tour Service [*Honolulu, HI*] [*FAA designator*]   (FAAC)
RES .... Office of Nuclear Regulatory Research [*Nuclear Regulatory Commission*]
RES .... On Reserved List [*Army*] [*British*]   (ROG)
RES .... RADAR Environment Simulation   (NATG)
RES .... RADAR Evaluation Squadron [*Military*]
RES .... Radiation Exposure State   (NATG)
RES .... Radio-Echo Sounding [*Geophysics*]
RES .... Record Element Specification [*Data processing*]
RES .... Record Evaluation System
RES .... Rehabilitation Evolution System [*Medicine*]
ReS .... Reinare en Espana [*A publication*]
RES .... Relief Electronics Specialist
ReS............ Religion et Societes [*A publication*]
RES .... Remote Entry Services   (MCD)
RES .... Renaissance Energy Ltd. [*Toronto Stock Exchange symbol*]
RES .... Repertoire d'Epigraphie Semitique [*Paris*] [*A publication*]
RES .... Reprint Expediting Service
RES .... Research   (AAG)
Res .... Researcher [*Samar*] [*A publication*]
RES .... Reserve
RES .... Reservoir   (AAG)
RES .... Residence
RES .... Resident
RES .... Residual   (KSC)
RES .... Residue
RES .... Resigned
RES .... Resistance [*or Resistor*]   (AAG)
RES .... Resistencia [*Argentina*] [*Airport symbol*]   (OAG)
RES .... Resistor
RES .... Resolute [*Northwest Territories*] [*Seismograph station code, US Geological Survey*]   (SEIS)
RES .... Resolute Bay [*Northwest Territories*] [*Geomagnetic observatory code*]
RES .... Resolution
Res .... Resolved   (DLA)
RES .... Resonator [*Automotive engineering*]
RES .... Resources
RES .... Restaurant   (DSUE)
RES .... Restore
Res .... Resurrection   (BJA)
RES .... Reticuloendothelial Society [*Augusta, GA*]   (EA)
RES .... Reticuloendothelial System [*Medicine*]
RES .... Review of English Studies [*A publication*]
RES .... Revue de l'Enseignement Superieur [*A publication*]
RES .... Revue des Etudes Semitiques [*A publication*]
RES .... Revue des Etudes Slaves [*A publication*]
RES .... Romance of Empire Series [*A publication*]
RES .... Royal Empire Society [*British*]
RES .... Royal Entomological Society [*British*]
RES .... RPC Energy Services, Inc. [*NYSE symbol*]
ResA.......... R & E Research Associates, Palo Alto, CA [*Library symbol*] [*Library of Congress*]   (LCLS)
RESA.......... Regional Education Service Agency
RESA........ Ring-Infected Erythrocyte Surface Antigen [*Immunochemistry*]
RESA........ Scientific Research Society of America [*Later, Sigma XI, The Scientific Research Society of America*]   (EA)
Res/Accel ... Research/Accelerators [*A publication*]

Res Act Fac Sci Engrg Tokyo Denki Univ ... Research Activities. Faculty of Science and Engineering of Tokyo Denki University [*A publication*]
Res Act For Comm (Victoria Aust) ... Research Activity. Forests Commission (Victoria, Australia) [*A publication*]
RESAD .... Revista Saude [*A publication*]
Res Adv Alcohol Drug Probl ... Research Advances in Alcohol and Drug Problems [*A publication*]
RESAF....... Reserve of the Air Force
Res African Lit ... Research in African Literatures [*A publication*]
Res Afric Lit ... Research in African Literatures [*A publication*]
Res Afr Lit ... Research in African Literatures [*A publication*]
RESALIFT... Reserve Airlift   (NVT)
Res Annu Nihon Nosan Kogyo ... Research Annual. Nihon Nosan Kogyo [*A publication*]
Res Appl Ind ... Research Applied in Industry [*A publication*]
Res Appl Natl Needs Rep NSF/RA (US) ... Research Applied to National Needs. Report. NSF/RA [*National Science Foundation/ Research Applied*] (United States) [*A publication*]
Res Appl Technol Symp Mined-Land Reclam Pap ... Research and Applied Technology Symposium on Mined-Land Reclamation. Papers [*A publication*]
RESAR .... Reference Safety Analysis Report [*Nuclear energy*]   (NRCH)
Res Assoc Br Paint Colour Varn Manuf Bull ... Research Association of British Paint, Colour, and Varnish Manufacturers. Bulletin [*A publication*]
Res Bib....... Research Service Bibliographies [*A publication*]
Res Briefs ... Research Briefs [*A publication*]
Res Briefs Sch For Resour PA St Univ ... Research Briefs. School of Forest Resources. Pennsylvania State University [*A publication*]
Res Bull Agr Home Econ Exp Sta Iowa State Coll ... Research Bulletin. Agricultural and Home Economics Experiment Station. Iowa State College [*A publication*]
Res Bull Agric Exp Stn Univ Idaho ... Research Bulletin. Agricultural Experiment Station. University of Idaho [*A publication*]
Res Bull Agric Exp Stn Univ Nebr ... Research Bulletin. Agricultural Experiment Station. University of Nebraska [*A publication*]
Res Bull Agric Exp Stn Univ Wis ... Research Bulletin. Agricultural Experiment Station. College of Agriculture. University of Wisconsin [*A publication*]
Res Bull Aichi-Ken Agric Res Cent Ser B Hortic ... Research Bulletin. Aichi-Ken Agricultural Research Center. Series B. Horticulture [*Japan*] [*A publication*]
Res Bull CIMMYT ... Research Bulletin. Centro Internacional de Mejoramiento de Maiz y Trigo [*A publication*]
Res Bull Coll Exp For Hokkaido Univ ... Research Bulletins. College Experiment Forests. Hokkaido University [*A publication*]
Res Bull Coll Expt Forest Hokkaido Univ ... Research Bulletins. College Experiment Forests. Hokkaido University [*A publication*]
Res Bull Coll Gen Educ Nagoya Univ Nat Sci Psychol ... Research Bulletin. College of General Education. Nagoya University. Natural Sciences and Psychology [*A publication*]
Res Bull Electr Power Dev Co Ltd ... Research Bulletin. Electric Power Development Company Limited [*Japan*] [*A publication*]
Res Bull Exp For Hokkaido Univ ... Research Bulletin. College Experiment Forests. Hokkaido University [*A publication*]
Res Bull Fac Agr Gifu Univ ... Research Bulletin. Faculty of Agriculture. Gifu University [*A publication*]
Res Bull Fac Agric Gifu Univ ... Research Bulletin. Faculty of Agriculture. Gifu University [*A publication*]
Res Bull Fac Ed Oita Univ ... Research Bulletin. Faculty of Education. Oita University [*A publication*]
Res Bull Fac Educ Oita Univ Nat Sci ... Research Bulletin. Faculty of Education. Oita University. Natural Science [*A publication*]
Res Bull Fac Lib Arts Oita Univ ... Research Bulletin. Faculty of Liberal Arts. Oita University [*A publication*]
Res Bull Gifu Imp Coll Agr ... Research Bulletin. Gifu Imperial College of Agriculture [*A publication*]
Res Bull Hiroshima Inst Technol ... Research Bulletin. Hiroshima Institute of Technology [*A publication*]
Res Bull Hokkaido Nat Agr Exp Sta ... Research Bulletin. Hokkaido National Agricultural Experiment Station [*A publication*]
Res Bull Hokkaido Natl Agric Exp Stn ... Research Bulletin. Hokkaido National Agricultural Experiment Station [*A publication*]
Res Bull Hokkaido Natn Agric Exp Stn ... Research Bulletin. Hokkaido National Agricultural Experiment Station [*A publication*]
Res Bull Indiana Agr Exp Sta ... Research Bulletin. Indiana Agricultural Experiment Station [*A publication*]
Res Bull Int Cent Impr Maize Wheat ... Research Bulletin. International Center for the Improvement of Maize and Wheat [*A publication*]
Res Bull Iowa Agric Exp Stn ... Research Bulletin. Iowa Agricultural Experiment Station [*A publication*]
Res Bull Iowa Agric Home Econ Exp Stn ... Research Bulletin. Iowa Agricultural and Home Economics Experiment Station [*A publication*]
Res Bull Iowa St Univ Agric Home Econ Exp Stn ... Research Bulletin. Iowa State University Agricultural and Home Economics Experiment Station [*A publication*]
Res Bull Kangweon Natl Univ ... Research Bulletin. Kangweon National University [*Republic of Korea*] [*A publication*]

Res Bull Mass Agric Exp Stn ... Research Bulletin. Massachusetts Agricultural Experiment Station [*A publication*]

Res Bull Meguro Parasitol Mus ... Research Bulletin. Meguro Parasitological Museum [*A publication*]

Res Bull Meisei Univ ... Research Bulletin. Meisei University [*A publication*]

Res Bull Meisei Univ Phys Sci Eng ... Research Bulletin. Meisei University. Physical Sciences and Engineering [*A publication*]

Res Bull Missouri Agric Exp Stn ... Research Bulletin. Missouri Agricultural Experiment Station [*A publication*]

Res Bull MO Agric Exp Sta ... Research Bulletin. Missouri Agricultural Experiment Station [*A publication*]

Res Bull Nat Hist Parks Site Branch ... Research Bulletin. National Historic Parks and Site Branch [*A publication*]

Res Bull Neb Agric Exp Stn ... Research Bulletin. Nebraska Agricultural Experiment Station [*A publication*]

Res Bull Obihiro Univ Ser I ... Research Bulletin. Obihiro University. Series I [*A publication*]

Res Bull Obihiro Zootech Univ ... Research Bulletin. Obihiro Zootechnical University. Series I [*A publication*]

Res Bull Obihiro Zootech Univ Ser I ... Research Bulletin. Obihiro Zootechnical University. Series I [*A publication*]

Res Bull Ohio Agric Res Dev Center ... Research Bulletin. Ohio Agricultural Research and Development Center [*A publication*]

Res Bull Ohio Agric Res Developm Cent ... Research Bulletin. Ohio Agricultural Research and Development Center [*A publication*]

Res Bull Ore For Res Lab ... Research Bulletin. Oregon State University. Forest Research Laboratory [*A publication*]

Res Bull Panjab Univ ... Research Bulletin. Panjab University [*A publication*]

Res Bull Panjab Univ Sci ... Research Bulletin. Panjab University. Science [*A publication*]

Res Bull PCSIR Lab ... Research Bulletin. PCSIR [*Pakistan Council of Scientific and Industrial Research*] Laboratories [*A publication*]

Res Bull Plant Prot Serv (Jap) ... Research Bulletin. Plant Protection Service (Japan) [*A publication*]

Res Bull Plant Prot Serv (Jpn) ... Research Bulletin. Plant Protection Service (Japan) [*A publication*]

Res Bull Printing Bur (Tokyo) ... Research Bulletin. Printing Bureau. Ministry of Finance (Tokyo) [*A publication*]

Res Bull Purdue Univ Agr Exp Sta ... Research Bulletin. Purdue University. Agricultural Experiment Station [*A publication*]

Res Bull Reg Eng Coll (Warangal) ... Research Bulletin. Regional Engineering College (Warangal) [*A publication*]

Res Bull Saitama Agr Exp Sta ... Research Bulletin. Saitama Agricultural Experiment Station [*A publication*]

Res Bull Univ Calcutta ... Research Bulletin. University of Calcutta [*A publication*]

Res Bull Univ Farm Hokkaido Univ ... Research Bulletin. University Farm. Hokkaido University [*A publication*]

Res Bull Univ MO Coll Agr Exp Sta ... Research Bulletin. University of Missouri. College of Agriculture. Experiment Station [*A publication*]

Res Bull Univ Nebr Coll Agr Home Econ Agr Exp Sta ... Research Bulletin. University of Nebraska. College of Agriculture and Home Economics. Agricultural Experiment Station [*A publication*]

Res Bull Wis Agr Exp Sta ... Research Bulletin. Wisconsin Agricultural Experiment Station [*A publication*]

Res Bull W Scotl Coll Agric ... Research Bulletin. West of Scotland College of Agriculture [*A publication*]

RESC .... Regional Educational Service Center

RESC .... Rescind (AAG)

RESC .... Rescue (AFM)

RESC .... Roanoke Electric Steel Corporation [*NASDAQ symbol*] (NQ)

RESCAN .... Reflecting Satellite Communication Antenna

RESCAP ..... Rescue Combat Air Patrol

Res Cas ...... Reserved Cases [*Ireland*] (DLA)

Res Circ Ohio Agric Exp Stn ... Research Circular. Ohio Agricultural Experiment Station [*A publication*]

Res Circ Ohio Agr Res Develop Cent ... Research Circular. Ohio Agricultural Research and Development Center [*A publication*]

Res Clin Lab ... Research in Clinic and Laboratory [*A publication*]

Res Clin Stud Headache ... Research and Clinical Studies in Headache [*A publication*]

Res Comm C P ... Research Communications in Chemical Pathology and Pharmacology [*A publication*]

Res Commun Chem Pathol Pharmacol ... Research Communications in Chemical Pathology and Pharmacology [*A publication*]

Res Commun Psychol Psychiatry Behav ... Research Communications in Psychology, Psychiatry, and Behavior [*A publication*]

Res Communs Chem Path Pharmac ... Research Communications in Chemical Pathology and Pharmacology [*A publication*]

Res Constructs Peaceful Uses Nucl Energy ... Research Constructs on Peaceful Uses of Nuclear Energy [*Japan*] [*A publication*]

Res Corresp ... Research Correspondence [*A publication*]

Res Counc Alberta Bull ... Research Council of Alberta. Bulletin [*A publication*]

Res Counc Alberta (Can) Inform Ser ... Research Council of Alberta (Canada) Information Series [*A publication*]

Res Counc Alberta Econ Geol Rep ... Research Council of Alberta. Economic Geology Report [*A publication*]

Res Counc Alberta Geol Div Bull ... Research Council of Alberta. Geological Division. Bulletin [*A publication*]

Res Counc Alberta Geol Div Mem ... Research Council of Alberta. Geological Division. Memoir [*A publication*]

Res Counc Alberta Mimeogr Circ ... Research Council of Alberta. Mimeographed Circular [*A publication*]

Res Counc Alberta Rep ... Research Council of Alberta. Report [*A publication*]

Res Counc Isr Annu Rep ... Research Council of Israel. Annual Report [*A publication*]

RESCRU ..... Reserve Cruise [*Navy*] (NVT)

RESCU .... Radio Emergency Search Communications Unit

RESCU .... Rocket-Ejection Seat Catapult Upward [*Aviation*]

RESCUE ..... Recovery Employing Storage Chute Used in Emergencies [*Inflatable aircraft wing*]

RESCUE ..... Referring Emergency Service for Consumers' Ultimate Enjoyment [*Service plan of Recreational Vehicle Dealers of America*] (EA)

RESCUE ..... Remote Emergency Salvage and Clean Up Equipment

R Escuela Def Nac ... Revista. Escuela de Defensa Nacional [*A publication*]

RESD .... Reentry Environmental Systems Division [*General Electric Co.*] (MCD)

RESD .... Resolved (ROG)

RESDAT ..... Restricted Data [*Atomic Energy Act of 1954*]

Res Des ...... Research and Design [*A publication*]

Res Dev ...... Research/Development [*A publication*]

Res/Develop ... Research/Development [*A publication*]

Res Developm Pap For Comm (Lond) ... Research and Development Paper. Forestry Commission (London) [*A publication*]

Res Disclosure ... Research Disclosure [*A publication*]

RESDIST .... Reserve District

Research Bul ... Liberal Party of Australia. New South Wales Division. Research Bulletin [*A publication*]

Research Council Alberta Bull ... Research Council of Alberta. Bulletin [*A publication*]

Research Council Alberta Rept ... Research Council of Alberta. Report [*A publication*]

Research in Ed ... Research in Education [*A publication*]

Researches Popul Ecol Kyoto Univ ... Researches on Population Ecology. Kyoto University [*A publication*]

Research F ... Research Film [*A publication*]

Research Mgt ... Research Management [*A publication*]

RESEB .... Resources in Education [*A publication*]

Res Econ Hist ... Research in Economic History [*A publication*]

Res Educ ..... Research in Education [*England*] [*A publication*]

ResEduc .... Resources in Education [*A publication*]

RESEE .... Revue des Etudes Sud-Est Europeennes [*A publication*]

Res Electrotech Lab (Tokyo) ... Researches. Electrotechnical Laboratory (Tokyo) [*A publication*]

RESem .... Revue des Etudes Semitiques [*A publication*]

Res Eng Jeonbug Natl Univ ... Research of Engineering. Jeonbug National University [*Republic of Korea*] [*A publication*]

Res Eng Res Inst Ind Technol Jeonbug Natl Univ ... Research of Engineering. Research Institute of Industrial Technology. Jeonbug National University [*Republic of Korea*] [*A publication*]

Res Environ Disruption Interdiscip Coop ... Research on Environmental Disruption toward Interdisciplinary Cooperation [*Japan*] [*A publication*]

RESEP .... Reentry System Environmental Protection

Res & Eq J ... A'Beckett's Reserved Judgments, New South Wales [*1845*] [*Australia*] [*A publication*]

Res & Eq J ... Reserved and Equity Judgements [*New South Wales*] [*A publication*]

Res & Eq Jud ... Reserved and Equity Judgments, New South Wales [*1845*] [*A publication*]

Res & Eq Judg ... A'Beckett's Reserved Judgments, New South Wales [*1845*] [*Australia*] [*A publication*]

Res & Eq Judgm ... Reserved and Equity Judgments [*New South Wales*] [*A publication*]

RESER .... Reentry Systems Evaluation RADAR [*Aerospace*]

Reserv Cas ... Reserved Cases [*1860-64*] (DLA)

Reserve Bank India B ... Reserve Bank of India. Bulletin [*A publication*]

Reserve Bank NZ Bul ... Reserve Bank of New Zealand. Bulletin [*A publication*]

RESERVON ... Reservation (ROG)

Res Establ Risoe Rep Risoe-M (Den) ... Research Establishment Risoe. Report. Risoe-M (Denmark) [*A publication*]

Res Establ Risoe Risoe Rep (Den) ... Research Establishment Risoe. Risoe Report (Denmark) [*A publication*]

RESET .... Regression Specification Error Test [*Statistics*]

Res Exp Econ ... Research in Experimental Economics [*A publication*]

Res Exp Med ... Research in Experimental Medicine [*A publication*]

Res Exp Med (Berlin) ... Research in Experimental Medicine (Berlin) [*A publication*]

Res Exp Rec Minist Agric (Nth Ire) ... Research and Experimental Record. Ministry of Agriculture (Northern Ireland) [*A publication*]

RESF .... Research and Engineering Support Facility (MCD)

Res & Farm ... Research and Farming [*North Carolina Agricultural Experiment Station*] [*A publication*]
Res Farmers ... Research for Farmers [*A publication*]
Res Farming ... Research and Farming [*North Carolina Agricultural Experiment Station*] [*A publication*]
Res Farming (NC Agric Exp Stn) ... Research and Farming (North Carolina Agricultural Experiment Station) [*A publication*]
Res Film..... Research Film [*A publication*]
Res Fish Annu Rep Coll Fish Univ Wash ... Research in Fisheries. Annual Report of the College of Fisheries. University of Washington [*A publication*]
RESFLD ..... Residual Field   (AAG)
RESFLY....... Respectfully   (ROG)
RESFOR..... AUTODIN CRT for Secure Reserve Force   (MCD)
Res Futures ... Research Futures [*A publication*]
RESFV....... Renaissance Editions. San Fernando Valley State College [*A publication*]
RESG .... Research Engineering Standing Group [*DoD*]
Res Gamma Eta Gamma ... Rescript of Gamma Eta Gamma   (DLA)
RESGD....... Resigned
RESGND .... Resigned
RESHAPE... Resource Self-Help/Affordability Planning Effort [*Program*] [*Federal government*]   (RDA)
Res High Educ Abstr ... Research into Higher Education. Abstracts [*A publication*]
Res Higher Educ ... Research in Higher Education [*A publication*]
RESHUS..... Reseau Documentaire en Sciences Humaines de la Sante [*Network for Documentation in the Human Sciences of Health*] [*National Center for Scientific Research*] [*Paris, France*] [*Information service*]   (EISS)
RES I .... Research EMP [*Electromagnetic Pulse*] Simulator I [*Air Force*]
RESIC .... Redstone Scientific Information Center [*Army*]
RES/IC....... Reserve - In Commission [*Vessel status*]
RESID........ Residual   (AAG)
Resid Staff Physician ... Resident and Staff Physician [*A publication*]
Residue Rev ... Residue Reviews [*A publication*]
RESIG .... Resignation   (AFM)
RESIL .... Resilient
Res Immunochem Immunobiol ... Research in Immunochemistry and Immunobiology [*A publication*]
RESIN........ Resina [*Resin*] [*Pharmacy*]   (ROG)
Res Ind...... Research and Industry [*A publication*]
Res Indicat Petrol ... Resumos Indicativos do Petroleo [*A publication*]
Res Ind (New Delhi) ... Research and Industry (New Delhi) [*A publication*]
Resin Rev... Resin Review [*A publication*]
Res Inst Appl Mech Kyushu Univ Report ... Research Institute for Applied Mechanics. Kyushu University. Reports [*A publication*]
Res Inst Fund Information Sci Res Rep ... Research Institute of Fundamental Information Science. Research Report [*A publication*]
Res Inst Fund Inform Sci Res Rep ... Kyushu University. Research Institute of Fundamental Information Science. Research Report [*A publication*]
Res Inst Nedri As (Hveragerdi Icel) Rep ... Research Institute Nedri As (Hveragerdi, Iceland). Report [*A publication*]
Res Int....... Residential Interiors [*A publication*]
Res Intell News ... Research and Intelligence News [*A publication*]
Res & Invt... Research and Invention [*A publication*]
Res Ipsa ..... Res Ipsa Loquitur [*The Thing Speaks for Itself*] [*Latin*]   (DLA)
RES/IS .... Reserve - In Service [*Vessel status*]
RESIS........ Resistance
RESIST ...... Replace Essential Supplies in Sufficient Time [*Navy*]   (NVT)
RESIST ...... Reusable Surface Insulation Stresses [*NASA computer program*]
Resistencia (Ser Econ e Gestao) ... Resistencia (Serie de Economia e Gestao) [*A publication*]
Res J Dir Higher Educ (Indones) ... Research Journal. Directorate of Higher Education (Indonesia) [*A publication*]
Res J Kanpur Agr Coll ... Research Journal. Kanpur Agricultural College [*A publication*]
Res J Mahatma Phule Agric Univ ... Research Journal. Mahatma Phule Agricultural University [*A publication*]
Res J Philo Soc Sci ... Research Journal of Philosophy and Social Sciences [*Meerut Cantt, India*] [*A publication*]
RES J Reticuloendothel Soc ... RES. Journal of the Reticuloendothelial Society [*A publication*]
Res Jud ...... Res Judicatae [*A publication*]
Res J Univ Wyo Agric Exp Stn ... Research Journal. University of Wyoming. Agricultural Experiment Station [*A publication*]
RESL .... Radiological and Environmental Sciences Laboratory [*Nuclear energy*]   (NRCH)
RESL .... Revue des Etudes Slaves [*A publication*]
RESLAB ...... Research Laboratory
Res Lab Commun Sci Univ Electro-Commun Annu Rep ... Research Laboratory of Communication Science. University of Electro-Communications. Annual Report [*A publication*]
Res Lab Precis Mach Electron ... Research Laboratory Precision Machinery and Electronics [*A publication*]
Res Lab Rec ... Research Laboratory Record [*A publication*]
RESlaves ... Revue des Etudes Slaves [*A publication*]

Res L Deviance & Soc Control ... Research in Law, Deviance, and Social Control   (DLA)
Res Leafl For Res Inst NZ For Serv ... Research Leaflet. Forest Research Institute. New Zealand Forest Service [*A publication*]
Res Leafl Sav For Res Sta ... Research Leaflet. Savanna Forestry Research Station [*A publication*]
Res L & Econ ... Research in Law and Economics [*A publication*]
Res Libnship ... Research in Librarianship [*A publication*]
Res Librarianship ... Research in Librarianship [*A publication*]
Res Life Sci ... Research in Life Sciences [*A publication*]
Res Lit........ Respublica Literaria [*A publication*]
Res L & Soc ... Research in Law and Sociology   (DLA)
RESLV....... Resolve   (KSC)
RESMA....... Railway Electric Supply Manufacturers Association
Res Manag ... Research Management [*A publication*]
Res Mech... Res Mechanica [*A publication*]
Res Mech Lett ... Res Mechanica Letters [*A publication*]
Res Memo Int Inst Appl Syst Anal ... Research Memorandum. International Institute for Applied Systems Analysis [*A publication*]
Res Meth Neurochem ... Research Methods in Neurochemistry [*A publication*]
Res Mgt...... Research Management [*A publication*]
Res Mol Biol ... Research in Molecular Biology [*A publication*]
Res Monogr Cell Tissue Physiol ... Research Monographs in Cell and Tissue Physiology [*A publication*]
Res Monogr Ser Natl Inst Drug Abuse (US) ... Research Monograph Series. National Institute on Drug Abuse (United States) [*A publication*]
RESN......... Resonant
RESNA .... RESNA [*Rehabilitation Engineering Society of North America*]: Association for the Advancement of Rehabilitation Technology [*Association retains acronym from former name*] [*Washington, DC*]   (EA)
Res Natl Mus (Bloemfontein) ... Researches. National Museum (Bloemfontein) [*A publication*]
RESND .... Resources and Energy [*A publication*]
Res News Off Res Adm Univ Mich (Ann Arbor) ... Research News. Office of Research Administration. University of Michigan (Ann Arbor) [*A publication*]
Res Norw Agric ... Research in Norwegian Agriculture [*A publication*]
Res Note BC For Serv ... Research Notes. British Columbia Forest Service [*A publication*]
Res Note Bur For (Philippines) ... Research Note. Bureau of Forestry (Philippines) [*A publication*]
Res Note Colo Coll For Nat Resour ... Research Note. Colorado State University. College of Forestry and Natural Resources [*A publication*]
Res Note Div For Res (Zambia) ... Research Note. Division of Forest Research (Zambia) [*A publication*]
Res Note Fac For Univ BC ... Research Note. Faculty of Forestry. University of British Columbia [*A publication*]
Res Note For Comm NSW ... Research Note. Forestry Commission of New South Wales [*A publication*]
Res Note For Mgmt Res Ore For Res Lab ... Research Note. Forest Management Research. Oregon State University. Forest Research Laboratory [*A publication*]
Res Note FPL For Prod Lab ... Research Note FPL. Forest Products Laboratory [*United States*] [*A publication*]
Res Note N Cent Forest Exp Stn US Dep Agric ... Research Note. North Central Forest Experiment Station. US Department of Agriculture [*A publication*]
Res Note Pacif SW For Exp Stn ... Research Note. Pacific Southwest Forest and Range Experiment Station. US Department of Agriculture [*A publication*]
Res Note Prov BC Minist For ... Research Note. Province of British Columbia. Ministry of Forests [*A publication*]
Res Note QD For Serv ... Research Notes. Queensland Forest Service [*A publication*]
Res Note Res Prod Counc (NB) ... Research Note. Research and Productivity Council (New Brunswick) [*A publication*]
Res Notes in Math ... Research Notes in Mathematics [*A publication*]
Res Notes Memoranda Appl Geom Post-RAAG ... Research Notes and Memoranda of Applied Geometry in Post-RAAG [*Research Association of Applied Geometry*] [*A publication*]
Res Notes NSW For Comm ... New South Wales. Forestry Commission. Research Notes [*A publication*]
Res Notes QD Dep For ... Research Notes. Queensland Department of Forestry [*A publication*]
Res Note Tex For Serv ... Research Note. Texas Forest Service [*A publication*]
Res Note UBC For Club ... Research Notes. University of British Columbia. Forest Club [*A publication*]
Res Note Univ Tex Austin Bur Econ Geol ... Research Note. University of Texas at Austin. Bureau of Economic Geology [*A publication*]
Res Not Ford For Cent ... Research Note. Ford Forestry Center [*A publication*]
RESNS .... Review of English Studies. New Series [*A publication*]
Res Nurs Health ... Research in Nursing and Health [*A publication*]
Res Nurs Hlth ... Research in Nursing and Health [*A publication*]
RESO .... Resoluta [*Music*]   (ROG)

RESO .... Resources Bulletin. Man and Resources Conference Program [*A publication*]

RESOC .... Research Sonobuoy Configuration   (NG)

RES/OC ..... Reserve - Out of Commission [*Vessel status*]

Resoconti Assoc Min Sarda ... Resoconti. Associazione Mineraria Sarda [*A publication*]

RESOJET ... Resonant Pulse Jet

RESOLN ..... Resolution   (MSA)

RESORS ..... Remote Sensing On-Line Retrieval System [*Canada Centre for Remote Sensing*] [*Department of Energy, Mines, and Resources*] [*Database*] [*Information service*] [*Ottawa, ON*]   (EISS)

RES/OS ..... Reserve - Out of Service [*Vessel status*]

Resour Am L ... Resources for American Literary Study [*A publication*]

Resour Biosphere (USSR) ... Resources of the Biosphere (USSR) [*A publication*]

Resour Book Publ ... Resources for Book Publishers [*United States*] [*A publication*]

Resources Conserv ... Resources and Conservation [*Netherlands*] [*A publication*]

Resources Pol ... Resources Policy [*A publication*]

Resour Energy ... Resources and Energy [*Netherlands*] [*A publication*]

Resour and Energy ... Resources and Energy [*A publication*]

Resour Manage Optim ... Resource Management and Optimization [*United States*] [*A publication*]

Resour Policy ... Resources Policy [*A publication*]

Resour Recovery Conserv ... Resource Recovery and Conservation [*Netherlands*] [*A publication*]

Resour Recovery Energy Rev ... Resource Recovery and Energy Review [*A publication*]

Res Outlook ... Research Outlook [*A publication*]

Resp .... De Respiratione [*of Aristotle*] [*Classical studies*]   (OCD)

RESP .... Registered Education Savings Plan [*Canada*]

RESP .... Regulated Electrical Supply Package

ResP .... Research and Progress [*A publication*]

ResP .... Research Publications, Inc., New Haven, CT [*Library symbol*] [*Library of Congress*]   (LCLS)

RESP .... Respectively

RESP .... Respiration   (KSC)

RESP .... Respirator

RESP .... Respondent

RESP .... Response   (AAG)

RESP .... Responsible   (AFM)

Resp .... Respublica [*of Plato*] [*Classical studies*]   (OCD)

RESPA .... Real Estate Settlement Procedures Act of 1974

Res Pam (Div For Res Zambia) ... Research Pamphlet (Division of Forest Research, Zambia) [*A publication*]

Res Pam For Res Inst (Kepong) ... Research Pamphlet. Forest Research Institute (Kepong) [*A publication*]

Res Pamphl For Res Inst (Malaya) ... Research Pamphlet. Forest Research Institute (Malaya) [*A publication*]

Res Pap Dep For (QD) ... Research Paper. Department of Forestry (Queensland) [*A publication*]

Res Pap Dep For (Queensl) ... Research Paper. Department of Forestry (Queensland) [*A publication*]

Res Paper Horace Lamb Centre Oceanogr Res ... Research Paper. Horace Lamb Centre for Oceanographical Research. Flinders University [*South Australia*] [*A publication*]

Res Pap Fac For Univ BC ... Research Paper. Faculty of Forestry. University of British Columbia [*A publication*]

Res Pap For Dep West Aust ... Research Paper. Forests Department. Western Australia [*A publication*]

Res Pap Forests Dep West Aust ... Research Paper. Forests Department. Western Australia [*A publication*]

Res Pap (Forest Ser) Fed Dep Forest Res (Niger) ... Research Paper (Forest Series). Federal Department of Forest Research (Nigeria) [*A publication*]

Res Pap GA For Res Coun ... Research Paper. Georgia Forest Research Council [*A publication*]

Res Pap Geogr Univ Newcastle ... Research Papers in Geography. University of Newcastle [*A publication*]

Res Pap Horace Lamb Centre Oceanogrl Res ... Research Paper. Horace Lamb Centre for Oceanographical Research. Flinders University [*South Australia*] [*A publication*]

Res Pap Ore For Res Lab ... Research Paper. Oregon State University. Forest Research Laboratory [*A publication*]

Res Pap Phys Educ ... Research Papers in Physical Education [*A publication*]

Res Pap Sav For Res Sta ... Research Paper. Savanna Forestry Research Station [*A publication*]

Res Pap Sch For Resour PA St Univ ... Research Paper. School of Forest Resources. Pennsylvania State University [*A publication*]

Res Pap Ser Int Rice Res Inst ... Research Paper Series. International Rice Research Institute [*A publication*]

Res Pap US Forest Serv Lake St Forest Exp Stn ... Research Paper. United States Forest Service. Lake States Forest Experiment Station [*A publication*]

Res Pap (West Aust) For Dep ... Research Paper (Western Australia). Forests Dept [*A publication*]

Resp C .... Respiratory Care [*A publication*]

Resp Care ... Respiratory Care [*A publication*]

RESPD .... Revue d'Epidemiologie et de Sante Publique [*A publication*]

R Esp Der Int ... Revista Espanola de Derecho Internacional [*A publication*]

Res Phenomenol ... Research in Phenomenology [*A publication*]

REspir .... Revista de Espiritualidad [*A publication*]

Respiration Suppl ... Respiration. Supplement [*Switzerland*] [*A publication*]

Respir Circ ... Respiration and Circulation [*A publication*]

Respir Physiol ... Respiration Physiology [*A publication*]

Respir Technol ... Respiratory Technology [*A publication*]

Respir Ther ... Respiratory Therapy [*A publication*]

REspL .... Revista Espanola de Linguistica [*A publication*]

RESPLY ..... Respectively

Resp Merid ... Responsa Meridiana [*South Africa*]   (DLA)

RESPO .... Responsible Property Officer [*Army*]   (AABC)

Res Pol .... Research Policy [*A publication*]

RESPOND ... Respondere [*To Answer*] [*Pharmacy*]   (ROG)

RESPONSA ... Retrieval of Special Portions from Nuclear Science Abstracts   (DIT)

R Esp Opin Publ ... Revista Espanola de la Opinion Publica [*A publication*]

Res Popul Ecol ... Researches on Population Ecology [*A publication*]

Res Popul Ecol (Kyoto) ... Researches on Population Ecology (Kyoto) [*A publication*]

Resp Physl ... Respiration Physiology [*A publication*]

Res Preview ... Research Previews [*A publication*]

Res Prog Org-Biol Med Chem ... Research Progress in Organic-Biological and Medicinal Chemistry [*A publication*]

Res Prog Rep Purdue Univ Agric Exp Stn ... Research Progress Report. Purdue University. Agricultural Experiment Station [*Indiana*] [*A publication*]

Res Prog Rep Tokai-Kinki Natn Agric Exp Stn ... Research Progress Report. Tokai-Kinki National Agricultural Experiment Station [*A publication*]

Res Progr Rep Indiana Agr Exp Sta ... Research Progress Report. Indiana Agricultural Experiment Station [*A publication*]

Res Progr Rep Purdue Agric Exp Sta ... Research Progress Report. Purdue University. Agricultural Experiment Station [*Indiana*] [*A publication*]

Res Progr Rep Purdue Univ Agr Exp Sta ... Research Progress Report. Purdue University. Agricultural Experiment Station [*Indiana*] [*A publication*]

Res Progr Rep Tokai-Kinki Nat Agr Exp Sta ... Research Progress Report. Tokai-Kinki National Agricultural Experiment Station [*A publication*]

Res Progr Rep West Weed Control Conf ... Research Progress Report. Western Weed Control Conference [*A publication*]

Res Proj Ser Victoria Dep Agric ... Victoria. Department of Agriculture. Research Project Series [*A publication*]

RESPT .... Respondent

REspT .... Revista Espanola de Teologia [*Madrid*] [*A publication*]

Resp Technol ... Respiratory Technology [*A publication*]

Resp Ther ... Respiratory Therapy [*A publication*]

Res Publ ..... Res Publica [*A publication*]

Res Publ Assoc Res Nerv Ment Dis ... Research Publications Association for Research in Nervous and Mental Disease [*A publication*]

Res Publ Gen Mot Corp Res Lab ... Research Publication. General Motors Corporation. Research Laboratories [*A publication*]

RESPY .... Respectfully   (ROG)

Res Q .... Research Quarterly [*A publication*]

Res Q (AAHPER) ... Research Quarterly. American Association for Health, Physical Education, and Recreation [*A publication*]

Res Q Am Alliance Health Phys Educ Recreat ... Research Quarterly. American Alliance for Health, Physical Education, and Recreation [*A publication*]

Res Q Am Assoc Health Phys Educ Recreation ... Research Quarterly. American Association for Health, Physical Education, and Recreation [*A publication*]

Res Q Exerc Sport ... Research Quarterly for Exercise and Sport [*A publication*]

Res Q Ont Hydro ... Research Quarterly. Ontario Hydro [*A publication*]

Res Quart ... Research Quarterly [*A publication*]

ReSR .... Recherches de Science Religieuse [*A publication*]

RESR .... Research, Inc. [*NASDAQ symbol*]   (NQ)

Res R .... Research in Review [*A publication*]

RESR .... Resources   (AABC)

RESRC .... Resources

Resrce Recv ... Resource Recovery Update [*A publication*]

Res Rec Malawi For Res Inst ... Research Record. Malawi Forest Research Institute [*A publication*]

Res Relat Child .... Research Relating to Children [*A publication*]

RESREP .... Resident Representative   (MUGU)

Res Rep Agric Exp Stn Mich St Univ ... Research Report. Agricultural Experiment Station. Michigan State University [*A publication*]

Res Rep Agric Exp Stn Univ Wisc ... Research Report. Agricultural Experiment Station. University of Wisconsin [*A publication*]

Res Rep Agric Exp Stn Utah St Univ ... Research Report. Agricultural Experiment Station. Utah State University [*A publication*]

Res Rep Anan Tech College ... Research Reports. Anan Technical College [*A publication*]

Res Rep Autom Control Lab Fac Eng Nagoya Univ ... Research Reports. Automatic Control Laboratory. Faculty of Engineering. Nagoya University [*A publication*]

Res Rep Biotech Fac Univ Ljublj Agric Issue ... Research Reports. Biotechnical Faculty. University of Ljubljana. Agricultural Issue [*A publication*]

Res Rep Can Dept Agr Nat Weed Comm West Sect ... Research Report. Canada Department of Agriculture. National Weed Committee. Western Section [*A publication*]

Res Rep Cent Highw Res Univ Tex Austin ... Research Report. Center for Highway Research. University of Texas at Austin [*A publication*]

Res Rep Coll Agric Univ Wis ... Research Report. Experiment Station. College of Agriculture. University of Wisconsin [*A publication*]

Res Rep Coll Agric Vet Med Nihon Univ ... Research Reports. College of Agriculture and Veterinary Medicine. Nihon University [*Japan*] [*A publication*]

Res Rep Coll Eng Busan Natl Univ ... Research Report. College of Engineering. Busan National University [*A publication*]

Res Rep DAE LA St Univ Agric Exp Stn ... Research Report. Department of Agricultural Economics and Agri-Business. Louisiana State University and Agricultural Experiment Station [*A publication*]

Res Rep Dep Electl Engng Melb Univ ... Research Report. Department of Electrical Engineering. University of Melbourne [*A publication*]

Res Rep Dep Electr Eng Melb Univ ... Research Report. Department of Electrical Engineering. University of Melbourne [*A publication*]

Res Rep Div Appl Org Chem CSIRO ... Research Report. Division of Applied Organic Chemistry. Commonwealth Scientific and Industrial Research Organisation [*A publication*]

Res Rep East Sect Nat Weed Comm Can ... Research Report. Eastern Section. National Weed Committee of Canada [*A publication*]

Res Rep Electron Gen Res Inst ... Research Report. Electronics General Research Institute [*Japan*] [*A publication*]

Res Rep Fac Biotech Univ Ljublj Vet Issue ... Research Reports. Faculty of Biotechnics. University of Ljubljana. Veterinary Issue [*A publication*]

Res Rep Fac Eng Kagoshima Univ ... Research Reports. Faculty of Engineering. Kagoshima University [*Japan*] [*A publication*]

Res Rep Fac Eng Meiji Univ ... Research Reports. Faculty of Engineering. Meiji University [*A publication*]

Res Rep Fac Eng Nagoya Univ ... Research Reports. Faculty of Engineering. Nagoya University [*A publication*]

Res Rep Fac Eng Niigata Univ ... Research Report. Faculty of Engineering. Niigata University [*A publication*]

Res Rep Fac Engrg Tokyo Denki Univ ... Research Reports. Faculty of Engineering. Tokyo Denki University [*A publication*]

Res Rep Fac Eng Tokyo Denki Univ ... Research Reports. Faculty of Engineering. Tokyo Denki University [*A publication*]

Res Rep Fac Eng Toyo Univ ... Research Reports. Faculty of Engineering. Toyo University [*A publication*]

Res Rep Fac Sci and Technol Meijyo Univ ... Research Reports. Faculty of Science and Technology. Meijyo University [*A publication*]

Res Rep Fac Text Seric Shinshu Univ ... Research Reports. Faculty of Textiles and Sericulture. Shinshu University [*A publication*]

Res Rep Fish Comm Oreg ... Research Reports. Fish Commission of Oregon [*A publication*]

Res Rep Fish Wildl Serv (US) ... Research Report. Fish and Wildlife Service (United States) [*A publication*]

Res Rep Fla Agric Exp Stn ... Research Report. Florida Agricultural Experiment Station [*A publication*]

Res Rep Fla Sch For ... Research Report. University of Florida. School of Forestry [*A publication*]

Res Rep Flinders Inst Atmos Mar Sci ... Research Report. Flinders Institute of Atmospheric and Marine Sciences. Flinders University [*A publication*]

Res Rep For Prod Util Lab Miss St Univ ... Research Report. Forest Products Utilization Laboratory. Mississippi State University [*A publication*]

Res Rep For Res Inst ... Research Reports. Forest Research Institute [*A publication*]

Res Rep Fukui Tech Coll Nat Sci Eng ... Research Reports. Fukui Technical College. Natural Science and Engineering [*Japan*] [*A publication*]

Res Rep Fukuoka Agr Exp Sta ... Research Report. Fukuoka Agricultural Experiment Station [*A publication*]

Res Rep GA Agr Exp Sta ... Research Report. Georgia Agricultural Experiment Station [*A publication*]

Res Rep Hokkaido Natl Agric Exp Stn ... Research Report. Hokkaido National Agricultural Experiment Station [*A publication*]

Res Rep Hunter Valley Res Fdn ... Research Report. Hunter Valley Research Foundation [*A publication*]

Res Rep Hunter Valley Res Found ... Research Report. Hunter Valley Research Foundation [*A publication*]

Res Rep Inst For Genet ... Research Report. Institute of Forest Genetics [*A publication*]

Res Rep Inst For Genet (Korea) ... Research Report. Institute of Forest Genetics (Suwon, Korea) [*A publication*]

Res Rep Inst Industr Res (Nigeria) ... Research Report. Federal Institute of Industrial Research (Lagos, Nigeria) [*A publication*]

Res Rep Inst Inform Sci Tech Tokyo Denki Univ ... Tokyo Denki University. Institute of Information Science and Technology. Research Reports [*A publication*]

Res Rep Inst Inf Sci and Technol Tokyo Denki Univ ... Research Reports. Institute of Information Science and Technology. Tokyo Denki University [*A publication*]

Res Rep Inst Plasma Phys Nagoya Univ ... Research Report. Institute of Plasma Physics. Nagoya University [*A publication*]

Res Rep Kasetsart Univ ... Research Reports. Kasetsart University [*A publication*]

Res Rep Kitakyushu Tech Coll ... Research Report. Kitakyushu Technical College [*A publication*]

Res Rep Kochi Univ Agric Sci ... Research Reports. Kochi University. Agricultural Science [*A publication*]

Res Rep Kogakuin Univ ... Research Reports. Kogakuin University [*Japan*] [*A publication*]

Res Rep Kurume Tech Coll ... Research Reports. Kurume Technical College [*A publication*]

Res Rep Kushiro Tech College ... Research Reports. Kushiro Technical College [*A publication*]

Res Rep Lab Nucl Sci Tohoku Univ ... Research Report. Laboratory of Nuclear Science. Tohoku University [*A publication*]

Res Rep Lab Nucl Sci Tohoku Univ Suppl ... Research Report. Laboratory of Nuclear Science. Tohoku University. Supplement [*Japan*] [*A publication*]

Res Rep MAFES ... Research Report. MAFES [*Mississippi Agricultural and Forestry Experiment Station*] [*A publication*]

Res Rep Mich State Univ Agric Exp Stn ... Research Report. Michigan State University. Agricultural Experiment Station [*A publication*]

Res Rep Miss Agric For Exp Stn ... Research Report. Mississippi Agricultural and Forestry Experiment Station [*A publication*]

Res Rep Miyagi Tech College ... Research Reports. Miyagi Technical College [*A publication*]

Res Rep Mont Agric Exp Stn ... Research Report. Montana Agricultural Experiment Station [*A publication*]

Res Rep Nagano Tech Coll ... Research Report. Nagano Technical College [*Japan*] [*A publication*]

Res Rep Nagaoka Tech Coll ... Research Reports. Nagaoka Technical College [*A publication*]

Res Rep Nagoya Ind Sci Res Inst ... Research Reports. Nagoya Industrial Science Research Institute [*Japan*] [*A publication*]

Res Rep Nara Tech Coll ... Research Reports. Nara Technical College [*Japan*] [*A publication*]

Res Rep Natl Inst Nutr ... Research Report. National Institute of Nutrition [*Japan*] [*A publication*]

Res Rep Nat Sci Council Math Res Center ... Research Reports. National Science Council. Mathematics Research Center [*A publication*]

Res Rep NC Agr Exp Sta Dept Field Crops ... Research Report. North Carolina Agricultural Experiment Station. Department of Field Crops [*A publication*]

Res Rep N Cent Weed Contr Conf ... Research Report. North Central Weed Control Conference [*A publication*]

Res Rep N Dak Agr Exp Sta ... Research Report. North Dakota Agricultural Experiment Station [*A publication*]

Res Rep N Mex Agr Exp Sta ... Research Report. New Mexico Agricultural Experiment Station [*A publication*]

Res Rep Norfolk Agr Exp Sta ... Research Report. Norfolk Agricultural Experiment Station [*A publication*]

Res Rep North Cent Weed Control Conf ... Research Report. North Central Weed Control Conference [*A publication*]

Res Rep Nth Cent Weed Control Conf ... Research Report. North Central Weed Control Conference [*A publication*]

Res Rep Office Rur Dev Minist Agric For (Korea) ... Research Reports. Office of Rural Development. Ministry of Agriculture and Forestry (Suwon, South Korea) [*A publication*]

Res Rep Off Rural Dev Agri-Engine-Seric (Suwon) ... Research Reports. Office of Rural Development. Agri-Engine-Sericulture (Suwon, South Korea) [*A publication*]

Res Rep Off Rural Dev Agri-Engine (Suwon) ... Research Reports. Office of Rural Development. Agri-Engine (Suwon, South Korea) [*A publication*]

Res Rep Off Rural Dev (Crop) (Suwon) ... Research Reports. Office of Rural Development (Crop) (Suwon, South Korea) [*A publication*]

Res Rep Off Rural Dev (Hortic) (Suwon) ... Research Reports. Office of Rural Development (Horticulture) (Suwon, South Korea) [*A publication*]

Res Rep Off Rural Dev Livest (Korea Republic) ... Research Reports. Office of Rural Development. Livestock (Korea Republic) [*A publication*]

Res Rep Off Rural Dev Livest Seric (Suwon) ... Research Reports. Office of Rural Development. Livestock Sericulture (Suwon, South Korea) [*A publication*]

Res Rep Off Rural Dev (Livest) (Suwon) ... Research Reports. Office of Rural Development (Livestock) (Suwon, South Korea) [*A publication*]

Res Rep Off Rural Dev (Plant Environ) (Suwon) ... Research Reports. Office of Rural Development (Plant Environment) (Suwon, South Korea) [*A publication*]

Res Rep Off Rural Dev Seric-Vet (Suwon) ... Research Reports. Office of Rural Development. Sericulture-Veterinary (Suwon, South Korea) [*A publication*]

Res Rep Off Rural Dev (Suwon) ... Research Reports. Office of Rural Development (Suwon, South Korea) [*A publication*]

Res Rep Off Rural Dev (Suwon) Livestock ... Research Reports. Office of Rural Development (Suwon). Livestock [*South Korea*] [*A publication*]

Res Rep Off Rural Dev Vet Seric (Korea Republic) ... Research Reports. Office of Rural Development. Veterinary and Sericulture (Korea Republic) [*A publication*]

Res Rep Off Rural Dev (Vet) (Suwon) ... Research Reports. Office of Rural Development (Veterinary) (Suwon, South Korea) [*A publication*]

Res Rep Oklahoma Agric Exp St ... Oklahoma. Agricultural Experiment Station. Research Report [*A publication*]

Res Rep Ore St Univ Forest Res Lab ... Research Report. Oregon State University. Forest Research Laboratory [*A publication*]

Res Reports Fac Engng Meiji Univ ... Research Reports. Faculty of Engineering. Meiji University [*A publication*]

Res Reprod ... Research in Reproduction [*A publication*]

Res Rep Sch Civ Engng Syd Univ ... Research Report. School of Civil Engineering. University of Sydney [*A publication*]

Res Rep Shibaura Inst Technol ... Research Reports. Shibaura Institute of Technology [*Japan*] [*A publication*]

Res Rep Taiwan Sugar Exp Stn ... Research Report. Taiwan Sugar Experiment Station [*A publication*]

Res Rep Timb Res Developm Ass ... Research Report. Timber Research and Development Association [*A publication*]

Res Rep Tokyo Electrical Engrg College ... Research Reports. Tokyo Electrical Engineering College [*A publication*]

Res Rep Tokyo Natl Tech Coll ... Research Reports. Tokyo National Technical College [*A publication*]

Res Rep Univ Arkansas Eng Exp Stn ... Research Report. University of Arkansas. Engineering Experiment Station [*A publication*]

Res Rep Univ Tex Austin Cent Highw Res ... Research Report. University of Texas at Austin. Center for Highway Research [*A publication*]

Res Rep US Army Mater Command Cold Reg Res Engng Lab ... Research Report. United States Army Material Command. Cold Regions Research and Engineering Laboratory [*A publication*]

Res Rep US Fish Wildl Serv ... Research Report. United States Fish and Wildlife Service [*A publication*]

Res Rep VA Agr Exp Sta ... Research Report. Virginia Agricultural Experiment Station [*A publication*]

Res Rep West Sect Nat Weed Comm Can ... Research Report. Western Section. National Weed Committee of Canada [*A publication*]

Res Rep Wis Agr Exp Sta ... Research Report. Wisconsin Agricultural Experiment Station [*A publication*]

Res Results Dig ... Research Results Digest [*A publication*]

ResRev ... Research Review [*A publication*]

Res Rev Can Res Stn (Agassiz BC) ... Research Review. Canada Research Station. (Agassiz, British Columbia) [*A publication*]

Res Rev CSIRO Div Chem Technol ... Australia. Commonwealth Scientific and Industrial Research Organisation. Division of Chemical Technology. Research Review [*A publication*]

Res Rev Div Chem Technol CSIRO ... Research Review. Division of Chemical Technology. Commonwealth Scientific and Industrial Research Organisation [*A publication*]

Res Rev Florida State Univ Bull ... Research in Review. Florida State University. Bulletin [*A publication*]

Res Rev (Off Aerosp Res) ... Research Review (Office of Aerospace Research) [*A publication*]

RESRT ... Resort

RESS ... RADAR Echo Simulation Study [*or Subsystem*]

Res Ser Appl Geogr New Engl Univ ... Research Series in Applied Geography. University of New England [*A publication*]

Res Ser Fowlers Gap Arid Zone Res Stn ... Research Series. Fowlers Gap Arid Zone Research Station. University of New England [*A publication*]

Res Ser ICAR ... Research Series ICAR. Indian Council of Agricultural Research [*A publication*]

RESSI ... Real Estate Securities and Syndication Institute [*Chicago, IL*] (EA)

Res Stat Note ... Research and Statistics Note. Social Security Administration. Office of Research and Statistics [*A publication*]

Res Stat Note Health Care Financ Adm Off Policy Plann Res ... Research and Statistics Note. Health Care Financing Administration. Office of Policy, Planning, and Research [*A publication*]

Res Steroids ... Research on Steroids [*A publication*]

Res Stud Udaipur Univ Coll Agr ... Research Studies. Udaipur University. College of Agriculture [*A publication*]

Res Stud Wash State Univ ... Research Studies. Washington State University [*Pullman*] [*A publication*]

Res Sum Ohio Agr Res Develop Cent ... Research Summary. Ohio Agricultural Research and Development Center [*A publication*]

REST ... RADAR Electronic Scan Technique

REST ... Rain Erosion Seed Test

REST ... Range Endurance Speed and Time [*Computer*]

REST ... Reentry Environment and Systems Technology

REST ... Reentry System Test Program

REST ... Reporting System for Training [*Navy*] (NG)

REST ... Restaurant (ROG)

REST ... Restored

REST ... Restrict (AAG)

REST ... Restricted Environmental Stimulation Technique

RESt ... Review of English Studies [*A publication*]

R Est ... Revue de l'Est [*A publication*]

RESTA ... Reconnaissance, Surveillance, and Target Acquisition (AABC)

RESTA ... Revue de Stomatologie [*Later, Revue de Stomatologie et de Chirurgie Maxillo-Faciale*] [*A publication*]

RESTAS ... Reception Station System [*Army*]

RESTAT ... Reserve Components Status Reporting [*Army*] (AABC)

RESTAT ... Review of Economics and Statistics [*A publication*]

Restau Bus ... Restaurant Business [*A publication*]

Restau & Inst ... Restaurants and Institutions [*A publication*]

RESTD ... Restricted [*Security classification*] [*Military*]

Res Teach Engl ... Research in the Teaching of English [*A publication*]

R Esthet ... Revue d'Esthetique [*A publication*]

R d'Esthetique ... Revue d'Esthetique [*A publication*]

Restor Eigh ... Restoration and Eighteenth Century Theatre Research [*A publication*]

RESTR ... Restorer

RESTR ... Restrict (AABC)

RESTRACEN ... Reserve Training Center

RESTRAFAC ... Reserve Training Facility

Res Trends ... Research Trends [*A publication*]

Restric Prac ... Reports of Restrictive Practices Cases (DLA)

Restr Mgt ... Restaurant Management [*A publication*]

RESTS ... Restoration Survey

R E Stud ... Review of Economic Studies [*A publication*]

R Estud Agro-Soc ... Revista de Estudios Agro-Sociales [*A publication*]

R Estud Penitenciarios ... Revista de Estudios Penitenciarios [*A publication*]

R Estud Pol ... Revista de Estudios Politicos [*A publication*]

R Estud Sindic ... Revista de Estudios Sindicales [*A publication*]

R Estud Soc ... Revista de Estudios Sociales [*A publication*]

R Estud Vida Loc ... Revista de Estudios de la Vida Local [*A publication*]

R Estud Vida Local ... Revista de Estudios de la Vida Local [*A publication*]

RESUB ... Resources [*A publication*]

RESUB ... Resublimed

Resultats ... Resultats Statistiques du Poitou-Charentes [*A publication*]

Result Exped Cient Buque Oceanogr "Cornide de Saavedra" ... Resultados Expediciones Cientificas del Buque Oceanografico "Cornide de Saavedra" [*A publication*]

Results Probl Cell Differ ... Results and Problems in Cell Differentiation [*A publication*]

Results Res Annu Rep Univ KY Agr Exp Sta ... Results of Research. Annual Report. University of Kentucky. Agricultural Experiment Station [*A publication*]

Resumenes Invest INP-CIP ... Resumenes de Investigacion. INP-CIP [*Instituto Nacional de la Pesca-Centro de Investigaciones Pesqueras*] [*A publication*]

RESUP ... Resupply (AABC)

Resur Biosfery ... Resursy Biosfery [*A publication*]

RESURR ... Resurrection

RESUS ... Resuscitation

RESV ... Reserve Fleet [*Navy*]

RESVD ... Reserved (ROG)

Res Vet Sci ... Research in Veterinary Science [*United Kingdom*] [*A publication*]

RESVON ... Reservation (ROG)

RESVR ... Reservoir (AAG)

Res Works Grad Sch Dong A Univ ... Research Works of the Graduate School. Dong-A University [*A publication*]

RESY ... Residuary (ROG)

RET ... Rad-Equivalent Therapy [*Radiology*]

RET ... RADAR Equipment Trailer (MCD)

R-ET ... Rational-Emotive Psychotherapy [*Also known as R-EP, RT*]

RET ... Reiteration [*Printers' term*] (DSUE)

RET ... Reitman's (Canada) Ltd. [*Toronto Stock Exchange symbol*]

RET ... Relay Extractor Tool

RET ... Reliability Evaluation Test

RET ... Repetitive Extrasystole Threshold [*Cardiology*]

RE & T ... Research Engineering and Test (NASA)

RET ... Retain (AAG)

RET ... Retard (AAG)

Ret ... Reticulum [*Constellation*]

RET ... Retired (AFM)

RET ... Retract

RET ... Return [*or Returnable*] (AAG)

RET ... Revista Espanola de Teologia [*Madrid*] [*A publication*]

RET ... Right Esotropia [*Ophthalmology*]

RET ... Ring Emitter Transistor

RET ... Rost [*Norway*] [*Airport symbol*] (OAG)

RET .... Roster of Employees Transferred [*Army*]
RETA .... Refrigerating Engineers and Technicians Association
RETA .... Retrieval of Enriched Textual Abstracts [*Information retrieval program*]
RETAC ...... Regional Educational Television Advisory Council
RETAI .... Real Estate Trainers Association, International   (EA)
Retail Dist Mgmt ... Retail and Distribution Management [*A publication*]
Retailer of Q ... Retailer of Queensland [*A publication*]
RETAIN ...... Remote Technical Assistance and Information Network [*Data processing*]
RETAT........ [*It Is*] Requested That   (NVT)
RETC.......... Railroad Equipment Trust Certificate
RETC.......... Rat Embryo Tissue Culture
RETC.......... Regional Emergency Transportation Center
RETCO....... Regional Emergency Transportation Coordinator
R Et Comp Est-Ouest ... Revue d'Etudes Comparatives Est-Ouest [*A publication*]
R Et Coop... Revue des Etudes Cooperatives [*A publication*]
RETD.......... Recueil d'Etudes Theologiques et Dogmatiques [*A publication*]
RETD.......... Red Especial de Transmision de Datos [*Spanish telephone co.*]   (TEL)
RETD.......... Retained
RETD.......... Retired
RETD.......... Returned
RETEN ...... Retension   (MCD)
RETF .... Retired Document File [*IRS*]
RETG.......... Retaining
R Ethnol .... Review of Ethnology [*A publication*]
R et I.......... Regina et Imperatrix [*Queen and Empress*] [*Latin*]
Reti............ Reticulum [*Constellation*]
R et I.......... Rex et Imperator [*King and Emperor*] [*Latin*]
RETIC........ Reticulocyte [*Hematology*]
RETICS ...... Reticulocytes [*Hematology*]
RETIMP..... Raleigh-Edwards Tensile Impact Machine Pendulum
Retina Found Inst Biol Med Sci Monogr Conf ... Retina Foundation. Institute of Biological and Medical Sciences. Monographs and Conferences [*A publication*]
RETL .... Retail
RETL .... Rocket Engine Test Laboratory [*Air Force*]
Ret Liv....... Retirement Living [*A publication*]
RETMA...... Radio-Electronics-Television Manufacturers Association [*Later, Electronic Industries Association*]
RETN.......... Return   (ROG)
RETNG ...... Retraining
RETNN ...... Retension
RETNR ...... Retainer   (ADA)
RETO .... Review of Education and Training for Officers [*Military*]   (RDA)
RETORC..... Research Torpedo Configuration   (NG)
RETP .... Reliability Evaluation Test Procedure
RETP .... Reserve Entry Training Plan [*Canada*]
RETP .... Retape
RETR.......... Retainer   (ROG)
RETR.......... Retention Register [*Data processing*]
RETR.......... Retraced
RETR.......... Retract   (AAG)
RETR.......... Retrieve   (KSC)
Retract....... Retractationes [*of Augustine*] [*Classical studies*]   (OCD)
RETRAN..... Refined Trajectory Analysis
RETRANS ... [*For*] Return Transportation [*To*]
RETRD........ Retarded
RETREAD... Retiree Training for Extended Active Duty [*Military*]   (MCD)
RETREP ..... Regional Emergency Transportation Representative
RETRF........ Rural Electrification and Telephone Revolving Fund [*Department of Agriculture*]
RETRO .... Regional Environmental Training and Research Organization [*Retraining program for unemployed space-industry workers*]
RETRO ...... Retro-Rocket   (AAG)
RETRO ...... Retroactive   (AAG)
RETRO ...... Retrofire   (KSC)
RETRO ...... Retrofire Officer
RETRO ...... Retrofit
RETRO ...... Retrograde
RETROG..... Retrogressive
Retros .... Retrospective Review [*A publication*]
Retrosp ...... Retrospectively   (DLA)
RETRV....... Retrieve   (MCD)
RETS.......... Radiological Environmental Technical Specifications   (NRCH)
RETS.......... Reconfigurable Electrical Test Stand   (NASA)
RETS.......... Remoted Targets System   (MCD)
RETS.......... Renaissance English Text Society   (EA)
RETSCP...... Rocket Engine Thermal Strains with Cyclic Plasticity [*Propellant*]
RETSIE....... Renewable Energy Technologies Symposium and International Exposition [*Renewable Energy Institute*]   (TSPED)
RETSPL...... Reference Equivalent Threshold Sound Pain [*or Pressure*] Level
R Et Sud-Est Europ ... Revue des Etudes Sud-Est Europeennes [*A publication*]
RETT .... Relatively Easy to Test [*Audiology*]
Rett .... Rettie's Scotch Court of Session Cases, Fourth Series   (DLA)

Rettie .... Rettie's Scotch Court of Session Cases, Fourth Series   (DLA)
RETUA .... Revue de Tuberculose [*A publication*]
R Etud Byzantines ... Revue des Etudes Byzantines [*A publication*]
R Etud Grecques ... Revue des Etudes Grecques [*A publication*]
R Etud Islamiques ... Revue des Etudes Islamiques [*A publication*]
R Etud Juives ... Revue des Etudes Juives [*A publication*]
RETULSIGN ... Retain on Board until Ultimate Assignment Received
REU .... Rectifier Enclosure Unit [*Power supply*] [*Telecommunications*]   (TEL)
REU .... Reunion [*Three-letter standard code*]   (CNC)
REU .... Reunion Island [*Reunion Island*] [*Seismograph station code, US Geological Survey*]   (SEIS)
REU .... Reus [*Spain*] [*Airport symbol*]   (OAG)
REUMA ...... Reumatismo [*A publication*]
Reun Annu Sci Terre (Programme Resumes) ... Reunion Annuelle des Sciences de la Terre (Programme et Resumes) [*A publication*]
Reunion Latinoam Prod Anim ... Reunion Latinoamericana de Produccion Animal [*A publication*]
Reun Latinoamer Fitotec Actas ... Reunion Latinoamericana de Fitotecnia. Actas [*A publication*]
REUR.......... Reference Your
REURAD..... Reference Your Radio
REURD........ Reuse/Recycle [*A publication*]
R Europ Sci Soc ... Revue Europeenne des Sciences Sociales. Cahiers Vilfredo Pareto [*A publication*]
REURTWX ... Reference Your TWX [*Teletypewriter communications*]   (AAG)
REUSE .... Revitalize Effective Utilization of Supply Excess [*Navy*]   (NG)
REUT.......... Reuter, Inc. [*NASDAQ symbol*]   (NQ)
Rev .... Cour de Revision [*Monaco*]   (DLA)
REV .... Ratio of Earth-to-Vehicle Radii
REV .... Reentry Vehicle [*Aerospace*]
Rev .... Revelation [*New Testament book*]
REV .... Revelstoke Companies Ltd. [*Toronto Stock Exchange symbol*]
REV .... Reventador [*Race of maize*]
REV .... Revenue
REV .... Reverend
REV .... Reverse   (AAG)
REV .... Review   (AFM)
REV .... Revise [*or Revision*]   (AAG)
REV .... Revlon Group, Inc. [*NYSE symbol*]
REV .... Revocable [*Business and trade*]
REV .... Revolution   (AAG)
REV .... Rotor Entry Vehicle [*Aerospace*]
REVA.......... Recommended Vehicle Adjustment   (AABC)
Rev A .... Revue A [*Revue Trimestrielle d'Automatique*] [*Belgium*] [*A publication*]
RevA........... Revue d'Allemagne [*A publication*]
REVAB .... Relief Valve Augmented Bypass [*Nuclear energy*]   (NRCH)
Rev ABIA/SAPRO ... Revista. ABIA/SAPRO [*Associacao Brasileira das Industrias da Alimentacao/Setor de Alimentos Calorico-Proteicos*] [*A publication*]
RevAC........ Revue de l'Art Chretien [*A publication*]
Rev Acad Cienc Exactas Fis-Quim Nat Zaragoza ... Revista. Academia de Ciencias Exactas, Fisico-Quimicas, y Naturales de Zaragoza [*A publication*]
Rev Acad Cienc (Zaragoza) ... Revista. Academia de Ciencias (Zaragoza) [*A publication*]
Rev Acad Cienc Zaragoza 2 ... Revista. Academia de Ciencias Exactas, Fisico-Quimicas, y Naturales de Zaragoza. Serie 2 [*A publication*]
Rev Acad Ci Zaragoza ... Revista. Academia de Ciencias Exactas, Fisico-Quimicas, y Naturales de Zaragoza [*A publication*]
Rev Acad Colomb Cienc Exactas Fis Nat ... Revista. Academia Colombiana de Ciencias Exactas Fisicas y Naturales [*A publication*]
Rev Acoust ... Revue d'Acoustique [*A publication*]
Rev d'Acoustique ... Revue d'Acoustique [*A publication*]
Rev Act-Metallges AG ... Review of Activities - Metallgesellschaft AG [*A publication*]
Rev Adm Nac Agua (Argent) ... Revista. Administracion Nacional del Agua (Argentina) [*A publication*]
Rev Aeronaut ... Revista de Aeronautica [*A publication*]
Rev Agr ...... Revue de l'Agriculture [*A publication*]
Rev Agr France ... Revue Agricole de France [*A publication*]
Rev Agri ..... Revista de Agricultura [*Brazil*] [*A publication*]
Rev Agric (Bogota) ... Revista Agricola (Bogota) [*A publication*]
Rev Agric (Bruss) ... Revue de l'Agriculture (Brussels) [*A publication*]
Rev Agric Econ Hokkaido Univ ... Review of Agricultural Economics. Hokkaido University [*A publication*]
Rev Agric Fr ... Revue des Agriculteurs de France [*A publication*]
Rev Agric Ile Maurice ... Revue Agricole de l'Ile Maurice [*A publication*]
Rev Agricola (Chicago) ... Revista Agricola (Chicago) [*A publication*]
Rev Agric (Piracicaba) ... Revista de Agricultura (Piracicaba) [*A publication*]
Rev Agric (Piracicaba) S Paulo ... Revista de Agricultura (Piracicaba). Estado de Sao Paulo [*A publication*]
Rev Agric PR ... Revista de Agricultura de Puerto Rico [*A publication*]
Rev Agric (Recife) ... Revista de Agricultura (Recife) [*A publication*]
Rev Agric Sucr Ile Maurice ... Revue Agricole et Sucriere de l'Ile Maurice [*A publication*]
Rev Agricultura ... Revista de Agricultura [*A publication*]
Rev Agr (Mocambique) ... Revista Agricola (Mocambique) [*A publication*]

Rev Agron ... Revista Agronomica [*A publication*]
Rev Agron (Lisb) ... Revista Agronomica (Lisbon) [*A publication*]
Rev Agron Noroeste Argent ... Revista Agronomica del Noroeste Argentino [*A publication*]
Rev Agroquim Tecnol Aliment ... Revista de Agroquimica y Tecnologia de Alimentos [*A publication*]
Rev Agr (Piracicaba) ... Revista de Agricultura (Piracicaba) [*A publication*]
Rev Alcool ... Revue de l'Alcoolisme [*A publication*]
Rev Algol ... Revue Algologique [*A publication*]
Rev Alteneo Paraguayo ... Revista del Alteneo Paraguayo [*A publication*]
Rev Alum ... Revue de l'Aluminum [*A publication*]
Rev Alum Ses Appl ... Revue d'Aluminium et de Ses Applications [*France*] [*A publication*]
Rev Am Hist ... Reviews in American History [*A publication*]
Rev AMRIGS ... Revista. AMRIGS [*Associacao Medica do Rio Grande Do Sul*] [*A publication*]
Rev Anal Chem ... Reviews in Analytical Chemistry [*A publication*]
Rev Anal Numer Teoria Aproximatiei ... Revista de Analiza Numerica si Teoria Aproximatiei [*A publication*]
Rev Anal Numer Theor Approx ... Revue d'Analyse Numerique et de la Theorie de l'Approximation [*A publication*]
Rev Anal Numer Theorie Approximation ... Revue d'Analyse Numerique et de la Theorie de l'Approximation [*A publication*]
Rev Anat Morphol Exp ... Revues d'Anatomie et de Morphologie Experimentale [*A publication*]
Rev Ang-Am ... Revue Anglo-Americaine [*A publication*]
Rev Annu Chimiother Physiatr Cancer ... Revue Annuelle de Chimiotherapie et de Physiatrie du Cancer [*A publication*]
Rev Annu Chimiother Prophyl Cancer ... Revue Annuelle de Chimiotherapie et de Prophylaxie du Cancer [*A publication*]
Rev Annu Physiatr Prophyl Cancer ... Revue Annuelle de Physiatrie et de Prophylaxie du Cancer [*A publication*]
Rev Anthropol (Paris) ... Revue Anthropologique (Paris) [*A publication*]
Rev Antropol (Sao Paulo) ... Revista de Antropologia (Sao Paulo) [*A publication*]
Rev Appl Elect ... Revue des Applications de l'Electricite [*A publication*]
Rev Appl Ent ... Review of Applied Entomology [*A publication*]
Rev Appl Mycol ... Review of Applied Mycology [*A publication*]
REVAR .... Authorized Revisit Above-Mentioned Places and Vary Itinerary as Necessary
Rev Arch .... Revue Archeologique [*A publication*]
Rev Arch ECE ... Revue Archeologique de l'Est et du Centre-Est [*A publication*]
Rev Archeol ... Revue Archeologique [*A publication*]
Rev Archit Sci Unit Univ Queensl ... Review. Architectural Science Unit. University of Queensland [*A publication*]
Rev Arch Narbonn ... Revue Archeologique de Narbonnaise [*A publication*]
Rev Argent Agron ... Revista Argentina de Agronomia [*A publication*]
Rev Argent Angiol ... Revista Argentina de Angiologia [*A publication*]
Rev Argent Cancerol ... Revista Argentina de Cancerologia [*A publication*]
Rev Argent Cardiol ... Revista Argentina de Cardiologia [*A publication*]
Rev Argent Endocrinol Metab ... Revista Argentina de Endocrinologia y Metabolismo [*A publication*]
Rev Argent Implantol Estomatol ... Revista Argentina de Implantologia Estomatologica [*A publication*]
Rev Argent Microbiol ... Revista Argentina de Microbiologia [*A publication*]
Rev Argent Neurol Psiquiat y Med Leg ... Revista Argentina de Neurologia, Psiquiatria, y Medicina Legal [*A publication*]
Rev Argent Pueric Neonatol ... Revista Argentina de Puericultura y Neonatologia [*A publication*]
Rev Argent Radiol ... Revista Argentina de Radiologia [*A publication*]
Rev Argent Reumatol ... Revista Argentina de Reumatologia [*A publication*]
Rev Argent Tuberc Enferm Pulm ... Revista Argentina de Tuberculosis y Enfermedades Pulmonares [*A publication*]
Rev Argent Urol Nefrol ... Revista Argentina de Urologia y Nefrologia [*A publication*]
Rev Arhiv ... Revista Arhivelor [*A publication*]
Rev Art .... Revue de l'Art [*A publication*]
Rev Art Anc ... Revue de l'Art Ancien et Moderne [*A publication*]
Rev Asoc Argent Dietol ... Revista. Asociacion Argentina de Dietologia [*A publication*]
Rev Asoc Argent Microbiol ... Revista. Asociacion Argentina de Microbiologia [*A publication*]
Rev Asoc Bioquim Argent ... Revista. Asociacion Bioquimica Argentina [*A publication*]
Rev Asoc Cienc Nat Litoral ... Revista. Asociacion de Ciencias Naturales del Litoral [*A publication*]
Rev Asoc Geol Argent ... Revista. Asociacion Geologica Argentina [*A publication*]
Rev Asoc Med Argent ... Revista. Asociacion Medica Argentina [*A publication*]
Rev Asoc Odontol Argent ... Revista. Asociacion Odontologica Argentina [*A publication*]
Rev Asoc Prof Hosp Nac Odontol ... Revista. Asociacion de Profesionales. Hospital Nacional de Odontologia [*A publication*]
Rev Assoc Fr Tech Pet ... Revue. Association Francaise des Techniciens du Petrole [*A publication*]
Rev Assoc Med Bras ... Revista. Associacao Medica Brasileira [*A publication*]
Rev Assoc Med Minas Gerais ... Revista. Associacao Medica de Minas Gerais [*A publication*]

Rev Assoc Med Rio Grande Do Sul ... Revista. Associacao Medica do Rio Grande Do Sul [*A publication*]
Rev Assoc Paul Cir Dent ... Revista. Associacao Paulista de Cirurgioes Dentistas [*A publication*]
Rev Assyriol ... Revue d'Assyriologie et d'Archeologie Orientale [*A publication*]
Rev Astron ... Revista Astronomica [*A publication*]
Rev Asturiana Cien Med ... Revista Asturiana de Ciencias Medicas [*A publication*]
Rev Ateneo Catedra Tec Oper Dent ... Revista. Ateneo de la Catedra de Tecnica de Operatoria Dental [*A publication*]
Rev Atheroscler ... Revue de l'Atherosclerose [*France*] [*A publication*]
Rev Atheroscler Arteriopathies Peripheriques ... Revue de l'Atherosclerose et des Arteriopathies Peripheriques [*A publication*]
Rev At Ind ... Review of Atomic Industries [*Japan*] [*A publication*]
Rev Autom ... Revista de Automatica [*A publication*]
Rev Auvergne ... Revue d'Auvergne [*A publication*]
RevB .... Revista (Barcelona) [*A publication*]
Rev du B ..... Revue. Barreau de la Province de Quebec [*A publication*]
RevBAM ..... Revista. Biblioteca, Archivo, y Museo del Ayuntamiento de Madrid [*A publication*]
Rev Bank NSW ... Review. Bank of New South Wales [*A publication*]
Rev Banque ... Revue de la Banque [*A publication*]
Rev Bar ... Revue du Barreau [*A publication*]
Rev Belge ... Revue Belge de Philologie et d'Histoire [*A publication*]
Rev Belge du C ... Revue Belge du Cinema [*A publication*]
Rev Belge Dr Int'l ... Revue Belge de Droit International [*A publication*]
Rev Belge de Droit Internat ... Revue Belge de Droit International [*A publication*]
Rev Belge Hist Mil ... Revue Belge d'Histoire Militaire [*A publication*]
Rev Belge Hist Milit ... Revue Belge d'Histoire Militaire [*A publication*]
Rev Belge Homoeopath ... Revue Belge d'Homoeopathie [*A publication*]
Rev Belge Matieres Plast ... Revue Belge des Matieres Plastiques [*A publication*]
Rev Belge Med Dent ... Revue Belge de Medecine Dentaire [*A publication*]
Rev Belge Phil Hist ... Revue Belge de Philologie et d'Histoire [*A publication*]
Rev Belge Philol Hist ... Revue Belge de Philologie et d'Histoire [*A publication*]
Rev Belge Transp ... Revue Belge des Transports [*Belgium*] [*A publication*]
Rev Belg Pathol Med Exp ... Revue Belge de Pathologie et de Medecine Experimentale [*A publication*]
Rev Bel Ph ... Revue Belge de Philologie et d'Histoire [*A publication*]
Rev Bened ... Revue Benedictine [*A publication*]
Rev Bib .... Revista Bibliotecilor [*Bucharest*] [*A publication*]
Rev Bibl ...... Revue Biblique [*A publication*]
Rev Biol Acad Rep Pop Roumaine ... Revue de Biologie. Academie de la Republique Populaire Roumaine [*A publication*]
Rev Biol (Buchar) ... Revue de Biologie (Bucharest) [*A publication*]
Rev Biol (Lisb) ... Revista de Biologia (Lisbon) [*A publication*]
Rev Biol Mar ... Revista de Biologia Marina [*A publication*]
Rev Biol Med Nucl ... Revista de Biologia y Medicina Nuclear [*A publication*]
Rev Biol Oral ... Revista de Biologia Oral [*A publication*]
Rev Biol Trop ... Revista de Biologia Tropical [*A publication*]
Rev Biol Urug ... Revista de Biologia del Uruguay [*A publication*]
Rev Bio-Math ... Revue de Bio-Mathematique [*A publication*]
Rev Bl Pol ... Review of Black Political Economy [*A publication*]
RevBN .... Revista de Bibliografia Nacional [*Madrid*] [*A publication*]
Rev Bois Appl ... Revue du Bois et de Ses Applications [*A publication*]
Rev Bolsa Cereal ... Revista. Bolsa de Cereales [*A publication*]
Rev Bolsa Comer Rosario ... Revista. Bolsa de Comercio de Rosario [*A publication*]
Rev Bot Appl Agric Trop ... Revue de Botanique Appliquee et d'Agriculture Tropicale [*A publication*]
Rev Bra Ec ... Revista Brasileira de Economia [*A publication*]
Rev Bras Anestesiol ... Revista Brasileira de Anestesiologia [*A publication*]
Rev Bras Biol ... Revista Brasileira de Biologia [*A publication*]
Rev Bras Cardiovasc ... Revista Brasileira Cardiovascular [*A publication*]
Rev Bras Cir ... Revista Brasileira de Cirurgia [*A publication*]
Rev Bras Clin Ter ... Revista Brasileira de Clinica e Terapeutica [*A publication*]
Rev Bras Defic Ment ... Revista Brasileira de Deficiencia Mental [*A publication*]
Rev Bras Enferm ... Revista Brasileira de Enfermagem [*A publication*]
Rev Bras Entomol ... Revista Brasileira de Entomologia [*A publication*]
Rev Bras Fis ... Revista Brasileira de Fisica [*A publication*]
Rev Bras Gastroenterol ... Revista Brasileira de Gastroenterologia [*A publication*]
Rev Bras Geocienc ... Revista Brasileira de Geociencias [*A publication*]
Rev Bras Geogr ... Revista Brasileira de Geografia [*A publication*]
Rev Brasil Geogr ... Revista Brasileira de Geografia [*A publication*]
Rev Brasil Quim ... Revista Brasileira de Quimica [*A publication*]
Rev Bras Leprol ... Revista Brasileira de Leprologia [*A publication*]
Rev Bras Malariol Doencas Trop ... Revista Brasileira de Malariologia e Doencas Tropicais [*A publication*]
Rev Bras Malariol Doencas Trop Publ Avulsas ... Revista Brasileira de Malariologia e Doencas Tropicais. Publicacoes Avulsas [*A publication*]
Rev Bras Med ... Revista Brasileira de Medicina [*A publication*]
Rev Bras Odontol ... Revista Brasileira de Odontologia [*A publication*]
Rev Bras Oftalmol ... Revista Brasileira de Oftalmologia [*A publication*]
Rev Bras Patol Clin ... Revista Brasileira de Patologia Clinica [*A publication*]

Rev Bras Pesqui Med Biol ... Revista Brasileira de Pesquisas Medicas e Biologicas [*A publication*]
Rev Bras Psiquiatr ... Revista Brasileira de Psiquiatria [*A publication*]
Rev Bras Quim (Sao Paulo) ... Revista Brasileira de Quimica (Sao Paulo) [*A publication*]
Rev Bras Tecnol ... Revista Brasileira de Tecnologia [*A publication*]
Rev Bras Tuberc Doencas Torac ... Revista Brasileira de Tuberculose e Doencas Toracicas [*A publication*]
Rev Bryol Lichenol ... Revue Bryologique et Lichenologique [*A publication*]
Rev Bulg Geol Soc ... Review. Bulgarian Geological Society [*A publication*]
RevC .... Revista Camoniana [*Sao Paulo*] [*A publication*]
Rev C Abo PR ... Revista. Colegio de Abogados de Puerto Rico [*A publication*]
Rev C Abo PR ... Revista de Derecho. Colegio de Abogados de Puerto Rico (DLA)
Rev Cafetalera (Guatem) ... Revista Cafetalera (Guatemala) [*A publication*]
Rev Cafetera Colomb ... Revista Cafetera de Colombia [*A publication*]
Rev Can ..... Revue Canadienne [*Quebec*] (DLA)
Rev Canadienne Geographie ... Revue Canadienne de Geographie [*A publication*]
Rev Can Bio ... Revue Canadienne de Biologie [*A publication*]
Rev Can Biol ... Revue Canadienne de Biologie [*A publication*]
Rev Can D Fam ... Revue Canadienne de Droit Familial (DLA)
Rev Can Dr Com ... Revue Canadienne de Droit Communautaire (DLA)
Rev Can Econ Publique Coop Can J Public Coop Econ ... Revue Canadienne d'Economie Publique et Cooperative. Canadian Journal of Public and Cooperative Economy [*A publication*]
Rev Can Gen Electr ... Revue Canadienne de Genie Electrique [*Canada*] [*A publication*]
Rev Can Med Comp ... Revue Canadienne de Medecine Comparee [*A publication*]
Rev Can Psychol ... Revue Canadienne de Psychologie [*A publication*]
Rev Can Sante Publique ... Revue Canadienne de Sante Publique [*A publication*]
Rev Can Sci Comportement ... Revue Canadienne des Sciences du Comportement [*A publication*]
Rev Cas ...... Revenue Cases (DLA)
Rev Cas (Ind) ... Revised Cases [*India*] (DLA)
Rev Catarinense Odontol ... Revista Catarinense de Odontologie [*A publication*]
Rev d Caucho ... Revista del Caucho [*A publication*]
Rev C & C Rep ... Revenue, Civil, and Criminal Reporter [*Calcutta*] (DLA)
Rev CENIC Cienc Biol ... Revista CENIC [*Centro Nacional de Investigaciones Cientificas*]. Ciencias Biologicas [*A publication*]
Rev CENIC Cienc Fis ... Revista CENIC [*Centro Nacional de Investigaciones Cientificas*]. Ciencias Fisicas [*Cuba*] [*A publication*]
Rev Cent Cienc Biomed Univ Fed Santa Maria ... Revista. Centro de Ciencias Biomedicas. Universidade Federal de Santa Maria [*A publication*]
Rev Cent Cienc Rurais ... Revista. Centro de Ciencias Rurais [*A publication*]
Rev Cent Ed ... Revista. Centro de Estudios Educativos [*A publication*]
Rev Cent Estud Cabo Verde Ser Cienc Biol ... Revista. Centro de Estudos de Cabo Verde. Serie de Ciencias Biologicas [*A publication*]
Rev Cent Nac Patol Anim ... Revista. Centro Nacional de Patologia Animal [*A publication*]
Rev Centroam Nutr Cienc Aliment ... Revista Centroamericana de Nutricion y Ciencias de Alimentos [*A publication*]
Rev Centro Estud Agronom y Vet Univ Buenos Aires ... Revista. Centro de Estudiantes de Agronomia y Veterinaria. Universidad de Buenos Aires [*A publication*]
Rev Ceres ... Revista Ceres [*A publication*]
Rev CETHEDEC ... Revue. Centre d'Etudes Theoriques de la Detection et des Communications [*A publication*]
Rev C Genie Civil Constr ... Revue C. Genie Civil. Construction [*A publication*]
Rev Chilena Ing ... Revista Chilena de Ingenieria [*A publication*]
Rev Chil Entomol ... Revista Chilena de Entomologia [*A publication*]
Rev Chil Hist Nat ... Revista Chilena de Historia Natural [*A publication*]
Rev Chil Pediatr ... Revista Chilena de Pediatria [*A publication*]
Rev Chim ... Revista de Chimie [*A publication*]
Rev Chim Acad Repub Pop Roum ... Revue de Chimie. Academie de la Republique Populaire Roumaine [*Romania*] [*A publication*]
Rev Chim (Bucharest) ... Revista de Chimie (Bucharest) [*A publication*]
Rev Chim Mi ... Revue de Chimie Minerale [*A publication*]
Rev Chim Miner ... Revue de Chimie Minerale [*France*] [*A publication*]
Rev Chir ..... Revista de Chirurgie. Stomatologie [*A publication*]
Rev Chir Oncol Radiol ORL Oftalmol Stomatol ... Revista de Chirurgie Oncologie Radiologie ORL Oftalmologie Stomatologie [*A publication*]
Rev Chir Or ... Revue de Chirurgie Orthopedique et Reparatrice de l'Appareil Moteur [*A publication*]
Rev Cie Gen Electr ... Review of Compagnie Generale d'Electricite [*France*] [*A publication*]
Rev Cienc ... Revista de Ciencias [*Lima*] [*A publication*]
Rev Cienc Agron ... Revista de Ciencias Agronomicas [*A publication*]
Rev Cienc Agron Ser A ... Revista de Ciencias Agronomicas. Serie A [*A publication*]
Rev Cienc Agron Ser B ... Revista de Ciencias Agronomicas. Serie B [*A publication*]

Rev Cienc Apl ... Revista de Ciencia Aplicada [*A publication*]
Rev Cienc Apl (Madrid) ... Revista de Ciencias Aplicadas (Madrid) [*A publication*]
Rev Cienc Biol (Belem) ... Revista de Ciencias Biologicas (Belem) [*A publication*]
Rev Cienc Biol Ser A (Lourenco Marques) ... Revista de Ciencias Biologicas. Serie A (Lourenco Marques) [*A publication*]
Rev Cienc Biol Ser B (Lourenco Marques) ... Revista de Ciencias Biologicas. Serie B (Lourenco Marques) [*A publication*]
Rev Cience Mat Univ Lourenco Marques ... Revista de Ciencias Matematicas. Universidade de Lourenco Marques [*A publication*]
Rev Cienc Med (Lourenco Marques) ... Revista de Ciencias Medicas. Serie A (Lourenco Marques) [*A publication*]
Rev Cienc Med Ser A (Lourenco Marques) ... Revista de Ciencias Medicas. Serie A (Lourenco Marques) [*A publication*]
Rev Cienc Med Ser B (Lourenco Marques) ... Revista de Ciencias Medicas. Serie B (Lourenco Marques) [*A publication*]
Rev Cienc Psicol Neurol (Lima) ... Revista de Ciencias Psicologicas y Neurologicas (Lima) [*A publication*]
Rev Cienc Quim ... Revista de Ciencias Quimicas [*A publication*]
Rev Cienc Univ Nac Mayor San Marcos ... Revista de Ciencias. Universidad Nacional Mayor de San Marcos [*A publication*]
Rev Cienc Vet ... Revista de Ciencias Veterinarias [*A publication*]
Rev Cien Econ ... Revista de Ciencias Economicas [*A publication*]
Rev Cient CASL ... Revista Cientifica. CASL [*Centro Academico Sarmento Leite*] [*A publication*]
Rev Cient Invest Mus Hist Nat San Rafael (Mendoza) ... Revista Cientifica de Investigaciones del Museo de Historia Natural de San Rafael (Mendoza) [*A publication*]
Rev Cien Vet ... Revista de Ciencias Veterinarias [*A publication*]
Rev Circ Argent Odontol ... Revista. Circulo Argentino de Odontologia [*A publication*]
Rev Circ Odontol Sur ... Revista. Circulo Odontologico del Sur [*A publication*]
Rev Cir (Mex) ... Revista de Cirugia (Mexico) [*A publication*]
Rev Civ Code ... Revised Civil Code (DLA)
Rev Civ St ... Revised Civil Statutes (DLA)
Rev Clin Esp ... Revista Clinica Espanola [*Spain*] [*A publication*]
Rev Clin Esp Eur Med ... Revista Clinica Espanola. Europa Medica [*A publication*]
Rev Clin Med ... Revista de Clinica Medica [*A publication*]
Rev Clin Sao Paulo ... Revista Clinica de Sao Paulo [*A publication*]
Rev Coat Corros ... Reviews on Coating and Corrosion [*A publication*]
Rev Code Civ Proc ... Revised Code of Civil Procedure (DLA)
Rev Code Cr Proc ... Revised Code of Criminal Procedure (DLA)
Rev Col Med Guatem ... Revista. Colegio Medico de Guatemala [*A publication*]
Rev Col Nac Enferm ... Revista. Colegio Nacional de Enfermeras [*A publication*]
Rev Colomb Fis ... Revista Colombiana de Fisica [*A publication*]
Rev Colombiana Mat ... Revista Colombiana de Matematicas [*A publication*]
Rev Colomb Obstet Ginecol ... Revista Colombiana de Obstetricia y Ginecologia [*A publication*]
Rev Col Quim Ing Quim Costa Rica ... Revista. Colegio de Quimicos e Ingenieros Quimicos de Costa Rica [*A publication*]
REVCOM.... Revolutionary Committee [*People's Republic of China*]
Rev Commer ... Revue Commerce [*A publication*]
REVCON .... Review Conference
Rev Confed Med Panam ... Revista. Confederacion Medica Panamericana [*A publication*]
Rev Conserve ... Revue de la Conserve [*France*] [*A publication*]
Rev Conserve Aliment Mod ... Revue de la Conserve. Alimentation Moderne [*A publication*]
Rev Conserve Fr Outre-Mer ... Revue de la Conserve de France et d'Outre-Mer [*A publication*]
Rev Conserve Fr Union Fr ... Revue de la Conserve de France et de l'Union Francaise [*A publication*]
Rev Consor Cent Agr Manabi ... Revista. Consorcio de Centros Agricolas de Manabi [*A publication*]
Rev Cons Rectores Univ Chilenas ... Revista. Consejo de Rectores. Universidades Chilenas [*A publication*]
Rev Cont L ... Review of Contemporary Law [*A publication*]
Rev Coroz ... Revista de Coroziune [*Romania*] [*A publication*]
Rev Corps Sante Armees ... Revue des Corps de Sante des Armees [*A publication*]
Rev Cr Code ... Revised Criminal Code (DLA)
Rev Cresterea Anim ... Revista de Cresterea Animalelor [*A publication*]
Rev Criadores ... Revista Criadores [*A publication*]
Rev Crit ...... Revue Critique de Legislation et de Jurisprudence de Canada (DLA)
Rev Crit de Droit Internat Prive ... Revue Critique de Droit International Prive [*A publication*]
Rev Crit de Jurispr Belge ... Revue Critique de Jurisprudence Belge [*A publication*]
Rev Crit de Legis et Jur ... Revue Critique de Legislation et de Jurisprudence [*Montreal*] (DLA)
Rev C Tijdschr Civ Tech Genie Civ ... Revue C. Tijdschrift Civiele Techniek. Genie Civil [*A publication*]
Rev Cubana Cardiol ... Revista Cubana de Cardiologia [*A publication*]

Rev Cubana Cienc Agric ... Revista Cubana de Ciencia Agricola [*A publication*]
Rev Cubana Cienc Vet ... Revista Cubana de Ciencias Veterinarias [*A publication*]
Rev Cubana Cir ... Revista Cubana de Cirugia [*A publication*]
Rev Cubana de Derecho ... Revista Cubana de Derecho [*Havana, Cuba*] (DLA)
Rev Cubana Estomatol ... Revista Cubana de Estomatologia [*A publication*]
Rev Cubana Fis ... Revista Cubana de Fisica [*A publication*]
Rev Cubana Hig Epidemiol ... Revista Cubana de Higiene y Epidemiologia [*A publication*]
Rev Cubana Lab Clin ... Revista Cubana de Laboratorio Clinico [*A publication*]
Rev Cubana Med ... Revista Cubana de Medicina [*A publication*]
Rev Cubana Med Trop ... Revista Cubana de Medicina Tropical [*A publication*]
Rev Cubana Oftal ... Revista Cubana de Oftalmologia [*A publication*]
Rev Cubana Pediatr ... Revista Cubana de Pediatria [*A publication*]
Rev Cub Cienc Vet ... Revista Cubana de Ciencias Veterinarias [*A publication*]
REVCUR..... Reverse Current (AAG)
Rev Current Activities Tech Ed ... Review of Current Activities in Technical Education [*A publication*]
Rev Cytol Biol Veg ... Revue de Cytologie et de Biologie Vegetales [*France*] [*A publication*]
Rev Czech Med ... Review of Czechoslovak Medicine [*A publication*]
REVD.......... Reverend (ROG)
Rev'd.......... Reversed (DLA)
Rev Data Sci Resour ... Reviews of Data on Science Resources [*United States*] [*A publication*]
Rev Data Sci Resour Natl Sci Found ... Reviews of Data on Science Resources. National Sciences Foundation [*A publication*]
Rev Def Natl ... Revue de Defense Nationale [*France*] [*A publication*]
Rev Deform Behav Mater ... Reviews on the Deformation Behavior of Materials [*A publication*]
Rev Dent Liban ... Revue Dentaire Libanaise [*A publication*]
Rev Dent (St Domingo) ... Revista Dental (Santo Domingo) [*A publication*]
Rev de Derecho y Cienc Polit ... Revista de Derecho y Ciencias Politicas. Organo de la Facultad de Derecho. Universidad Nacional Mayor de San Marcos [*A publication*]
Rev de Derecho Esp y Amer ... Revista de Derecho Espanol y Americano [*Madrid, Spain*] (DLA)
Rev de Derecho Internac y Cienc Diplom ... Revista de Derecho Internacional y Ciencias Diplomaticas [*A publication*]
Rev de Derecho Jurispr y Admin ... La Revista de Derecho, Jurisprudencia, y Administracion (DLA)
Rev de Derecho Jurispr y Cienc Soc ... Revista de Derecho, Jurisprudencia, y Ciencias Sociales y Gaceta de los Tribunales (DLA)
Rev de Derecho Publ ... Revista de Derecho Publico. Universidad de Chile. Escuela de Derecho [*A publication*]
REV DEV .... Revolutionary Development [*South Vietnam*]
Rev Diagn Biol ... Revista de Diagnostico Biologico [*A publication*]
Rev de Direito Adm (Coimbra) ... Revista de Direito Administrativo Coimbra [*A publication*]
Rev de Direito Adm (Rio De Janeiro) ... Revista de Direito Administrativo Rio De Janeiro [*A publication*]
Rev Dir Gen Geol Minas (Ecuador) ... Revista. Direccion General de Geologia y Minas (Ecuador) [*A publication*]
Rev Doc...... Revue de la Documentation [*A publication*]
Rev D P ...... Revista de Derecho Puertorriqueno [*A publication*]
Rev DPR..... Revista de Derecho Puertorriqueno [*A publication*]
Rev du Dr ... Revue du Droit [*Quebec*] (DLA)
Rev de Dr Int'l de Sci Dip et Pol ... Revue de Droit International de Sciences Diplomatiques et Politiques [*A publication*]
Rev de Droit ... Revue de Droit. Universite de Sherbrooke [*A publication*]
Rev de Droit Canonique ... Revue de Droit Canonique [*A publication*]
Rev de Droit Compare ... Revue de Droit International et de Droit Compare [*A publication*]
Rev de Droit Contemp ... Revue de Droit Contemporain [*Brussels, Belgium*] (DLA)
Rev de Droit Hong ... Revue de Droit Hongrois (DLA)
Rev de Droit Internat et de Droit Compare ... Revue de Droit International et de Droit Compare [*A publication*]
Rev de Droit Internat de Sci Diplom ... Revue de Droit International de Sciences Diplomatiques et Politiques [*A publication*]
Rev Droit Int'l Moyen-Orient ... Revue de Droit International pour le Moyen-Orient (DLA)
Rev de Droit Penal et de Criminologie ... Revue de Droit Penal et de Criminologie [*A publication*]
Rev de Droit Penal Mil et de Droit de la Guerre ... Revue de Droit Penal Militaire et de Droit de la Guerre (DLA)
Rev Droit Penal Militaire et Dr de la Guerre ... Revue de Droit Penal Militaire et de Droit de la Guerre (DLA)
Rev Droit Public Sci Polit ... Revue du Droit Public et de la Science Politique en France et a l'Etranger [*A publication*]
Rev du Droit Publ et de la Sci Polit en France ... Revue du Droit Public et de la Science Politique en France et a l'Etranger [*A publication*]
Rev des Droits de l'Homme ... Revue des Droits de l'Homme. Droit International et Droit Compare [*A publication*]
Rev de Droit Unif ... Revue de Droit Uniforme (DLA)

Rev de Droit Uniforme ... Revue de Droit Uniforme (DLA)
Rev E.......... Revue E. Electricite, Electrotechnique Generale, Courants Forts, et Applications [*Belgium*] [*A publication*]
Rev Ecol Biol Sol ... Revue d'Ecologie et de Biologie du Sol [*A publication*]
Rev Ecol BS ... Revue d'Ecologie et de Biologie du Sol [*A publication*]
Rev Econ..... Revue Economique [*A publication*]
Rev Econ Co ... Review of the Economic Conditions in Italy [*A publication*]
Rev Econ Polit ... Revue d'Economie Politique [*A publication*]
Rev Econ S ... Review of Economic Studies [*A publication*]
Rev Econ St ... Review of Economics and Statistics [*A publication*]
Rev Econ Stat ... Review of Economic Statistics [*A publication*]
Rev Econ Stat ... Review of Economics and Statistics [*A publication*]
Rev Econ Stud ... Review of Economic Studies [*A publication*]
Rev Ecuat Entomol Parasitol ... Revista Ecuatoriana de Entomologia y Parasitologia [*A publication*]
Rev Ecuat Hig Med ... Revista Ecuatoriana de Higiene y Medicina Tropical [*A publication*]
Rev Ecuat Hig Med Trop ... Revista Ecuatoriana de Higiene y Medicina Tropical [*A publication*]
Rev Ecuat Med Cienc Biol ... Revista Ecuatoriana de Medicina y Ciencias Biologicas [*A publication*]
Rev Ecuat Pediatr ... Revista Ecuatoriana de Pediatria [*A publication*]
Rev Educ Re ... Review of Educational Research [*A publication*]
Rev E Elec Electrotech Gen ... Revue E. Electricite, Electrotechnique Generale, Courants Forts, et Applications [*A publication*]
Rev Eg........ Revue d'Egyptologie [*A publication*]
Rev Egypt de Droit Internat ... Revue Egyptienne de Droit International [*A publication*]
Rev Egyptol ... Revue Egyptologique [*A publication*]
REVEL........ Reverberation Elimination
Rev El Comm ... Review. Electrical Communication Laboratory [*Tokyo*] [*A publication*]
Rev Elec Commun Lab (Tokyo) ... Review. Electrical Communication Laboratory (Tokyo) [*A publication*]
Rev Electr ... Revista Electricidade [*Portugal*] [*A publication*]
Rev Electr Commun Lab ... Review. Electrical Communication Laboratory [*A publication*]
Rev Electr Commun Lab (Tokyo) ... Review. Electrical Communication Laboratory (Tokyo) [*A publication*]
Rev Electr & Mec ... Revue d'Electricite et de Mecanique [*A publication*]
Rev Electr Mecan ... Revue d'Electricite et de Mecanique [*France*] [*A publication*]
Rev Electroencephalogr Neurophysiol Clin ... Revue d'Electroencephalographie et de Neurophysiologie Clinique [*A publication*]
Rev Electrotec ... Revista Electrotecnica [*A publication*]
Rev Electrotec (Buenos Aires) ... Revista Electrotecnica (Buenos Aires) [*A publication*]
Rev Electrotech Energ Acad Repub Pop Roum ... Revue Electrotechnique et Energetique. Academie de la Republique Populaire Roumaine [*Romania*] [*A publication*]
Rev Elevage ... Revue de l'Elevage. Betail et Basse Cour [*A publication*]
Rev Elev Med Vet Pays Trop ... Revue d'Elevage et de Medecine Veterinaire des Pays Tropicaux [*A publication*]
Rev Empresas Publicas Medellin ... Revista Empresas Publicas de Medellin [*Columbia*] [*A publication*]
Rev Energ ... Revue de l'Energie [*A publication*]
Rev Energ Primaire ... Revue de l'Energie Primaire [*Belgium*] [*A publication*]
Rev Enferm (Lisboa) ... Revista de Enfermagem (Lisboa) [*A publication*]
Rev Enferm Nov Dimens ... Revista Enfermagem em Novas Dimensoes [*A publication*]
Rev Eng Geol ... Reviews in Engineering Geology [*United States*] [*A publication*]
Rev Engl Stu ... Review of English Studies [*A publication*]
Rev Entomol Mocambique ... Revista de Entomologia de Mocambique [*A publication*]
Rev Entomol Mocambique Supl ... Revista de Entomologia de Mocambique. Suplemento [*A publication*]
Rev Entomol (Rio De J) ... Revista de Entomologia (Rio De Janeiro) [*A publication*]
Rev Environ Health ... Reviews on Environmental Health [*A publication*]
Rev Epidem ... Revue d'Epidemiologie, Medecine Sociale, et Sante Publique [*Later, Revue d'Epidemiologie et de Sante Publique*] [*A publication*]
Rev Epidemiol Med Soc Sante Publique ... Revue d'Epidemiologie, Medecine Sociale, et Sante Publique [*Later, Revue d'Epidemiologie et de Sante Publique*] [*A publication*]
Rev Epidemiol Sante Publique ... Revue d'Epidemiologie et de Sante Publique [*A publication*]
RevEpigr.... Revue Epigraphique [*A publication*]
RevER .... Revue des Etudes Roumaines [*A publication*]
REVERB..... Reverberator [*Automotive engineering*]
REVERSY... Reversionary (ROG)
Rev Esc Agron Vet Univ Rio Grande Do Sul (Porto Alegre) ... Revista. Escola de Agronomia e Veterinaria da Universidade do Rio Grande Do Sul (Porto Alegre) [*A publication*]
Rev Esc Enferm USP ... Revista. Escola de Enfermagem. Universidade de Sao Paulo [*A publication*]
Rev Esc Odontol Tucuman ... Revista. Escuela de Odontologia. Universidad Nacional de Tucuman. Facultad de Medicina [*A publication*]

Rev Esp Anestesiol Reanim ... Revista Espanola de Anestesiologia y Reanimacion [*A publication*]

Rev Espan Fisiol ... Revista Espanola de Fisiologia [*A publication*]

Rev Esp Antropol Amer ... Revista Espanola de Antropologia Americana [*A publication*]

Rev Esp Cardiol ... Revista Espanola de Cardiologia [*A publication*]

Rev Esp de Derecho Canonico ... Revista Espanola de Derecho Canonico [*A publication*]

Rev Esp de Derecho Internac ... Revista Espanola de Derecho Internacional [*A publication*]

Rev Esp de Derecho Mil ... Revista Espanola de Derecho Militar [*A publication*]

Rev Espec ... Revista de Especialidades [*A publication*]

Rev Esp Enferm Apar Dig ... Revista Espanola de las Enfermedades del Aparato Digestivo [*A publication*]

Rev Esp Enferm Apar Dig Nutr ... Revista Espanola de las Enfermedades del Aparato Digestivo y de la Nutricion [*A publication*]

Rev Esp Estomatol ... Revista Espanola de Estomatologia [*A publication*]

Rev Esp Fis ... Revista Espanola de Fisiologia [*A publication*]

Rev Esp Fisiol ... Revista Espanola de Fisiologia [*A publication*]

Rev Esp Obstet Ginecol ... Revista Espanola de Obstetricia y Ginecologia [*A publication*]

Rev Esp Obstet Ginecol Supl ... Revista Espanola de Obstetricia y Ginecologia. Suplemento [*A publication*]

Rev Esp Oncol ... Revista Espanola de Oncologia [*A publication*]

Rev Esp Oto-Neuro-Oftalmol Neurocir ... Revista Espanola de Oto-Neuro-Oftalmologia y Neurocirugia [*A publication*]

Rev Esp Pediatr ... Revista Espanola de Pediatria [*A publication*]

Rev Esp Reum Enferm Osteoartic ... Revista Espanola de Reumatismo y Enfermedades Osteoarticulares [*A publication*]

Rev Est....... Revue de l'Est [*A publication*]

Rev Esth..... Revue d'Esthetique [*A publication*]

Rev Est His ... Revista de Estudios Hispanicos [*A publication*]

Rev Estud Extremenos ... Revista de Estudios Extremenos [*A publication*]

Rev Estud Gerais Univ Mocambique Ser 3 Cienc Med ... Revista. Estudos Gerais Universitarios de Mocambique. Serie 3. Ciencias Medicas [*A publication*]

Rev Et Anc ... Revue des Etudes Anciennes [*A publication*]   (OCD)

Rev Et Armen ... Revue des Etudes Armeniennes [*A publication*]

Rev Et Grec ... Revue des Etudes Grecques [*A publication*]   (OCD)

Rev Et Lat ... Revue des Etudes Latines [*A publication*]   (OCD)

Rev Et SE Eur ... Revue des Etudes Sud-Est Europeennes [*A publication*]

Rev Etud Augustin ... Revue des Etudes Augustiniennes [*A publication*]

Rev Etud Byz ... Revue des Etudes Byzantines [*A publication*]

Rev Etud Sud Est Eur ... Revue des Etudes Sud-Est Europeennes [*A publication*]

Rev Eur Endocrinol ... Revue Europeenne d'Endocrinologie [*A publication*]

Rev Eur Etud Clin Biol ... Revue Europeenne d'Etudes Cliniques et Biologiques [*France*] [*A publication*]

Rev Europ Papiers Cartons Complexes ... Revue Europeenne des Papiers Cartons-Complexes [*A publication*]

Rev Eur Pomme Terre ... Revue Europeenne de la Pomme de Terre [*A publication*]

Rev Exist Psychol Psychiat ... Review of Existential Psychology and Psychiatry [*A publication*]

Rev Exist Psych Psychiat ... Review of Existential Psychology and Psychiatry [*A publication*]

RevExp....... Review and Expositor [*A publication*]

Rev Exp Agrar ... Revista de Extension Agraria [*A publication*]

Rev and Expositor ... Review and Expositor [*A publication*]

Rev Fac Agrar Minist Educ Univ Nac Cuyo (Mendoza) ... Revista. Facultad de Ciencias Agrarias. Ministerio de Educacion. Universidad Nacional de Cuyo (Mendoza) [*Argentina*] [*A publication*]

Rev Fac Agron Alcance (Maracay) ... Revista. Facultad de Agronomia Alcance (Maracay) [*A publication*]

Rev Fac Agron (Maracay) ... Revista. Facultad de Agronomia (Maracay) [*A publication*]

Rev Fac Agron Univ Cent Venezuela ... Revista. Facultad de Agronomia. Universidad Central de Venezuela [*A publication*]

Rev Fac Agron Univ Fed Rio Grande Sul ... Revista. Faculdade de Agronomia. Universidade Federal do Rio Grande Do Sul [*A publication*]

Rev Fac Agron Univ Nac La Plata ... Revista. Facultad de Agronomia. Universidad Nacional de La Plata [*A publication*]

Rev Fac Agron Univ Repub Montevideo ... Revista. Facultad de Agronomia. Universidad de la Republica Montevideo [*A publication*]

Rev Fac Agron Vet (Buenos Aires) ... Revista. Facultad de Agronomia y Veterinaria (Buenos Aires) [*A publication*]

Rev Fac Agron Vet Univ B Aires ... Revista. Facultad de Agronomia y Veterinaria. Universidad de Buenos Aires [*A publication*]

Rev Fac Agron Vet Univ Rio Grande Do Sul ... Revista. Faculdade de Agronomia e Veterinaria. Universidade do Rio Grande Do Sul [*A publication*]

Rev Fac Agron Vet Univ Rio Grande Sul ... Revista. Faculdade de Agronomia e Veterinaria. Universidade do Rio Grande Do Sul [*A publication*]

Rev Fac Cienc Agrar Minist Educ Univ Nac Cuyo (Mendoza) ... Revista. Facultad de Ciencias Agrarias. Ininisterio de Educacion. Universidad Nacional de Cuyo (Mendoza) [*A publication*]

Rev Fac Cienc Agrar Univ Nac Cuyo ... Revista. Facultad de Ciencias Agrarias. Universidad Nacional de Cuyo [*A publication*]

Rev Fac Cienc Agr Univ Nac Cuyo ... Revista. Facultad de Ciencias Agrarias. Universidad Nacional de Cuyo [*A publication*]

Rev Fac Cienc 2a Ser A Cienc Mat ... Revista. Faculdade de Ciencias. Universidade de Lisboa. 2a Serie A. Ciencias Matematicas [*Portugal*] [*A publication*]

Rev Fac Cienc Med Cordoba ... Revista. Facultad de Ciencias Medicas de Cordoba [*A publication*]

Rev Fac Cienc Med Univ Catol Parana ... Revista. Faculdade de Ciencias Medicas. Universidad Catolica do Parana [*A publication*]

Rev Fac Cienc Med Univ Cent Ecuador ... Revista. Facultad de Ciencias Medicas. Universidad Central del Ecuador [*A publication*]

Rev Fac Cienc Med Univ Nac Cordoba ... Revista. Facultad de Ciencias Medicas. Universidad Nacional de Cordoba [*A publication*]

Rev Fac Cienc Med Univ Nac Rosario ... Revista. Facultad de Ciencias Medicas. Universidad Nacional de Rosario [*A publication*]

Rev Fac Cienc Nat Salta Univ Nac Tucuman ... Revista. Facultad de Ciencias Naturales de Salta. Universidad Nacional de Tucuman [*A publication*]

Rev Fac Cienc Quim Univ Nac La Plata ... Revista. Facultad de Ciencias Quimicas. Universidad Nacional de La Plata [*A publication*]

Rev Fac Cienc Univ Coimbra ... Revista. Faculdade de Ciencias. Universidade de Coimbra [*A publication*]

Rev Fac Cienc Univ Lisboa B ... Revista. Faculdade de Ciencias. Universidade de Lisboa. Serie B. Ciencias Fisico-Quimicas [*A publication*]

Rev Fac Cienc Univ Lisboa Ser B ... Revista. Faculdade de Ciencias. Universidade de Lisboa. Serie B. Ciencias Fisico Quimicas [*A publication*]

Rev Fac Cienc Univ Lisboa Ser C ... Revista. Faculdade de Ciencias. Universidade de Lisboa. Serie C. Ciencias Naturais [*A publication*]

Rev Fac Cienc Univ Lisb Ser C Cienc Nat ... Revista. Faculdade de Ciencias. Universidade de Lisboa. Serie C. Ciencias Naturais [*A publication*]

Rev Fac Cienc Univ Oviedo ... Revista. Facultad de Ciencias. Universidad de Oviedo [*A publication*]

Rev Fac Cienc Vet La Plata ... Revista. Facultad de Ciencias Veterinarias de La Plata [*A publication*]

Rev de la Fac de Derecho (Caraboba) ... Revista. Facultad de Derecho. Universidad de Caraboba [*Valencia, Venezuela*]   (DLA)

Rev de la Fac de Derecho (Caracas) ... Revista. Facultad de Derecho. Universidad Catolica Andres Bello Caracas   (DLA)

Rev de la Fac de Derecho y Cienc Soc ... Revista. Facultad de Derecho y Ciencias Sociales [*Montevideo, Uruguay*]   (DLA)

Rev de la Fac de Derecho de Mex ... Revista. Facultad de Derecho de Mexico [*A publication*]

Rev da Fac de Direito (Lisbon) ... Revista. Faculdade de Direito. Universidade de Lisboa Lisbon   (DLA)

Rev de Fac de Direito (Sao Paulo) ... Revista. Faculdade de Direito. Universidade de Sao Paulo [*Sao Paulo, Brazil*]   (DLA)

Rev Fac Eng Univ Porto ... Revista. Faculdade de Engenharia. Universidade do Porto [*A publication*]

Rev Fac Farm Bioquim Univ Cent Ecuador ... Revista. Facultad de Farmacia y Bioquimica. Universidad Central del Ecuador [*A publication*]

Rev Fac Farm Bioquim Univ Fed St Maria ... Revista. Faculdade de Farmacia e Bioquimica. Universidade Federal de Santa Maria [*A publication*]

Rev Fac Farm Bioquim Univ Nac Mayor San Marcos Lima ... Revista. Facultad de Farmacia y Bioquimica. Universidad Nacional Mayor de San Marcos Lima [*A publication*]

Rev Fac Farm Bioquim Univ Sao Paulo ... Revista. Faculdade de Farmacia e Bioquimica. Universidade de Sao Paulo [*A publication*]

Rev Fac Farm Odontol Araraquara ... Revista. Faculdade de Farmacia e Odontologia de Araraquara [*A publication*]

Rev Fac Farm Univ Cent Venez ... Revista. Facultad de Farmacia. Universidad Central de Venezuela [*A publication*]

Rev Fac Ing Quim Univ Nac Litoral ... Revista. Facultad de Ingenieria Quimica. Universidad Nacional del Litoral [*Argentina*] [*A publication*]

Rev Fac Med (Maracaibo) ... Revista. Facultad de Medicina (Maracaibo) [*A publication*]

Rev Fac Med (Mex) ... Revista. Facultad de Medicina (Mexico) [*A publication*]

Rev Fac Med (Tucuman) ... Revista. Facultad de Medicina (Tucuman) [*A publication*]

Rev Fac Med Univ Fed Ceara ... Revista. Faculdade de Medicina. Universidade Federal do Ceara [*A publication*]

Rev Fac Med Univ Fed Santa Maria ... Revista. Faculdade de Medicina. Universidade Federal de Santa Maria [*A publication*]

Rev Fac Med Univ Nac Colomb (Bogota) ... Revista. Facultad de Medicina. Universidad Nacional de Colombia (Bogota) [*A publication*]

Rev Fac Med Vet Univ Nac Mayor San Marcos ... Revista. Facultad de Medicina Veterinaria. Universidad Nacional Mayor de San Marcos [*A publication*]

Rev Fac Med Vet Univ Sao Paulo ... Revista. Faculdade de Medicina Veterinaria. Universidade de Sao Paulo [*A publication*]

Rev Fac Med Vet Zootec (Bogota) ... Revista. Facultad de Medicina, Veterinaria, y Zootecnia (Bogota) [A publication]

Rev Fac Med Vet Zootec Univ San Carlos ... Revista. Facultad de Medicina, Veterinaria, y Zootecnia. Universidad de San Carlos [A publication]

Rev Fac Med Vet Zootec Univ Sao Paulo ... Revista. Faculdade de Medicina Veterinaria e Zootecnia. Universidade de Sao Paulo [A publication]

Rev Fac Med Vet Zoot Univ Nac Colomb ... Revista. Facultad de Medicina, Veterinaria, y Zootecnia. Universidad Nacional de Colombia [A publication]

Rev Fac Nac Agron (Medellin) ... Revista. Facultad Nacional de Agronomia (Medellin) [A publication]

Rev Fac Nac Agron Univ Antioquia ... Revista. Facultad Nacional de Agronomia. Universidad de Antioquia [A publication]

Rev Fac Nac Agron Univ Nac (Colombia) ... Revista. Facultad Nacional de Agronomia. Universidad Nacional (Colombia) [A publication]

Rev Fac Odontol Aracatuba ... Revista. Faculdade de Odontologia de Aracatuba [A publication]

Rev Fac Odontol Pernambuco ... Revista. Faculdade de Odontologia de Pernambuco [A publication]

Rev Fac Odontol Port Alegre ... Revista. Faculdade de Odontologia de Port Alegre [A publication]

Rev Fac Odontol Sao Jose Dos Campos ... Revista. Faculdade de Odontologia de Sao Jose Dos Campos [A publication]

Rev Fac Odontol Sao Paulo ... Revista. Faculdade de Odontologia. Universidade de Sao Paulo [A publication]

Rev Fac Odontol Tucuman ... Revista. Facultad de Odontologia. Universidad Nacional de Tucuman [A publication]

Rev Fac Odontol Univ Sao Paulo ... Revista. Faculdade de Odontologia. Universidade de Sao Paulo [A publication]

Rev Fac Quim Farm Univ Cent Ecuador ... Revista. Facultad de Quimica y Farmacia. Universidad Central del Ecuador [A publication]

Rev Fac Sci Univ Istanbul Ser B Sci Nat ... Revue. Faculte de Sciences. Universite d'Istanbul. Serie B. Sciences Naturelles [A publication]

Rev Farm Bahia ... Revista Farmaceutica da Bahia [A publication]

Rev Farm (B Aires) ... Revista Farmaceutica (Buenos Aires) [A publication]

Rev Farm Bioquim ... Revista de Farmacia e Bioquimica [A publication]

Rev Farm Bioquim Amazonia ... Revista de Farmacia e Bioquimica da Amazonia [A publication]

Rev Farm Bioquim Univ Sao Paulo ... Revista de Farmacia e Bioquimica. Universidade de Sao Paulo [A publication]

Rev Farm (Bucharest) ... Revista Farmaciei (Bucharest) [A publication]

Rev Farm Cuba ... Revista Farmaceutica de Cuba [A publication]

Rev Farm Odontol ... Revista de Farmacia e Odontologia [A publication]

Rev Farm Peru ... Revista Farmaceutica Peruana [A publication]

Rev Farm Quim ... Revista de Farmacia y Quimica [A publication]

Rev Fed Am Hosp ... Review. Federation of American Hospitals [A publication]

Rev Fed Doct Cienc Filos Let (Havana) ... Revista. Federacion de Doctors en Ciencias y en Filosofia y Letras (Havana) [A publication]

Rev Fed Fr Soc Sci Nat ... Revue. Federation Francaise des Societes de Sciences Naturelles [A publication]

Rev Ferment Ind Aliment ... Revue des Fermentations et des Industries Alimentaires [A publication]

Rev F Gy Ob ... Revue Francaise de Gynecologie et d'Obstetrique [A publication]

Rev Filip Med Farm ... Revista Filipina de Medicina y Farmacia [A publication]

Rev Filol Istr Cl ... Revista di Filologia e di Isturzione Classica [A publication]

Rev Filosof (Argentina) ... Revista de Filosofia (Argentina) [A publication]

Rev Filosof Costa Rica ... Revista de Filosofia. Universidad de Costa Rica [A publication]

Rev Filosof (Mexico) ... Revista de Filosofia (Mexico) [A publication]

Rev Filosof (Spain) ... Revista de Filosofia (Spain) [A publication]

Rev Filoz .... Revista de Filozofie [A publication]

Rev Fis .... Revista de Fisica [A publication]

Rev Fis Quim Eng ... Revista de Fisica, Quimica, e Engenharia [A publication]

Rev Fis Quim Eng Ser A ... Revista de Fisica, Quimica, e Engenharia. Serie A [A publication]

Rev FITCE ... Revue FITCE [Federation des Ingenieurs des Telecommunications de la Communaute Europeenne] [A publication]

Rev Fiz Chim Ser A ... Revista de Fizica si Chimie. Seria A [A publication]

Rev Flora Med ... Revista da Flora Medicinai [A publication]

Rev Food Sci Technol (Mysore) ... Reviews in Food Sciences and Technology (Mysore) [A publication]

Rev Food Technol (Mysore) ... Reviews in Food Technology (Mysore) [A publication]

Rev Forest Venezolana ... Revista Forestal Venezolana [A publication]

Rev For Franc ... Revue Forestiere Francaise [A publication]

Rev For Fr (Nancy) ... Revue Forestiere Francaise (Nancy) [A publication]

Rev For Peru ... Revista Forestal del Peru [A publication]

Rev Fort Argent ... Revista Forestal Argentina [A publication]

Rev For Venez ... Revista Forestal Venezolana [A publication]

Rev Fr Alle ... Revue Francaise d'Allergologie [Later, Revue Francaise d'Allergologie et d'Immunologie Clinique] [A publication]

Rev Fr Allergol ... Revue Francaise d'Allergologie [Later, Revue Francaise d'Allergologie et d'Immunologie Clinique] [A publication]

Rev Fr Allergol Immunol Clin ... Revue Francaise d'Allergologie et d'Immunologie Clinique [A publication]

Rev Franc Agr ... Revue Francais de l'Agriculture [A publication]

Rev Francaise Automat Inform Rech Oper Ser Bleue ... Revue Francaise d'Automatique, Informatique, et Recherche Operationnelle. Serie Bleue [A publication]

Rev Francaise Automat Inform Rech Oper Ser Jaune ... Revue Francaise d'Automatique, Informatique, et Recherche Operationnelle. Serie Jaune [A publication]

Rev Franc de Droit Aer ... Revue Francaise de Droit Aerien [A publication]

Rev Fr Astronaut ... Revue Francaise d'Astronautique [France] [A publication]

Rev Fr Autom Inf Rech Oper ... Revue Francaise d'Automatique, Informatique, et Recherche Operationnelle [A publication]

Rev Fr de C ... Revue Francaise de Communication [A publication]

Rev Fr Corps Gras ... Revue Francaise des Corps Gras [A publication]

Rev Fr Electr ... Revue Francaise de l'Electricite [A publication]

Rev Fr Endocrinol ... Revue Francaise d'Endocrinologie [A publication]

Rev Fr Endocrinol Clin Nutr Metab ... Revue Francaise d'Endocrinologie Clinique, Nutrition, et Metabolisme [A publication]

Rev Fr Energ ... Revue Francaise de l'Energie [A publication]

Rev Fr Entomol ... Revue Francaise d'Entomologie [A publication]

Rev Fr Etud Clin Biol ... Revue Francaise d'Etudes Cliniques et Biologiques [A publication]

Rev Fr Geotech ... Revue Francaise de Geotechnique [A publication]

Rev Fr Gerontol ... Revue Francaise de Gerontologie [A publication]

Rev Fr Gynecol Obstet ... Revue Francaise de Gynecologie et d'Obstetrique [A publication]

Rev Fr Hist ... Revue Francaise d'Histoire d'Outre-Mer [A publication]

Rev Fr Hist Outre Mer ... Revue Francaise d'Histoire d'Outre Mer [A publication]

Rev Fr Inf and Rech Oper ... Revue Francaise d'Informatique et de Recherche Operationnelle [A publication]

Rev Frio ...... Revista del Frio [A publication]

Rev Fr Mal Respir ... Revue Francaise des Maladies Respiratoires [A publication]

Rev Fr Mec ... Revue Francaise de Mecanique [A publication]

Rev Fr Mkt ... Revue Francaise du Marketing [A publication]

Rev Fr Odonto Stomatol (Paris) ... Revue Francaise d'Odonto-Stomatologie (Paris) [A publication]

Rev Fr Pediatr ... Revue Francaise de Pediatrie [A publication]

Rev Fr Photogr Cinematogr ... Revue Francaise de Photographie et de Cinematographie [A publication]

Rev Fr Sci Polit ... Revue Francaise de Science Politique [A publication]

Rev Fr Sc P ... Revue Francaise de Science Politique [A publication]

Rev Fr Soc ... Revue Francaise de Sociologie [A publication]

Rev Fr Trait Inf ... Revue Francaise de Traitement de l'Information [A publication]

Rev Fr Tran ... Revue Francaise de Transfusion [Later, Revue Francaise de Transfusion et Immuno-Hematologie] [A publication]

Rev Fr Transfus ... Revue Francaise de Transfusion [Later, Revue Francaise de Transfusion et Immuno-Hematologie] [A publication]

Rev Fr Transfus Immuno-Hematol ... Revue Francaise de Transfusion et Immuno-Hematologie [A publication]

Rev Fund Serv Saude Publica (Braz) ... Revista. Fundacao Servicos de Saude Publica (Brazil) [A publication]

Rev Fund SESP ... Revista. Fundacao Servicos de Saude Publica [Brazil] [A publication]

Rev Fund SESP (Braz) ... Revista. Fundacao Servicos de Saude Publica (Brazil) [A publication]

rev'g .... Reversing (DLA)

Rev Gastroenterol ... Review of Gastroenterology [A publication]

Rev Gastroenterol Mex ... Revista de Gastroenterologia de Mexico [A publication]

Rev Gaucha Odontol ... Revista Gaucha de Odontologia [A publication]

Rev Gemmol AFG ... Revue de Gemmologie. Association Francaise de Gemmologie [A publication]

Rev Gen Assur Terr ... Revue Generale des Assurances Terrestres [A publication]

Rev Gen Bot ... Revue Generale de Botanique [A publication]

Rev Gen Caoutch Plast ... Revue Generale des Caoutchoucs et Plastiques [A publication]

Rev Gen Chem Fer ... Revue Generale des Chemins de Fer [A publication]

Rev Gen Chemins Fer ... Revue Generale des Chemins de Fer [A publication]

Rev Gen Chemins de Fer ... Revue Generale des Chemins de Fer [A publication]

Rev Gen Chim Pure Appl ... Revue Generale de Chimie Pure et Appliquee [A publication]

Rev Gen Clin et Therap ... Revue Generale de Clinique et de Therapeutique [A publication]

Rev Gen Colloides ... Revue Generale des Colloides [A publication]

Rev Gen Droit ... Revue Generale de Droit [A publication]

Rev Gen de Droit ... Revue Generale de Droit [A publication]

Rev Gen Elec ... Revue Generale de l'Electricite [A publication]

Rev Gen Electr ... Revue Generale de l'Electricite [A publication]

Rev Generale de Droit ... Revue Generale de Droit [A publication]

Rev Geneve ... Revue de Geneve [A publication]

Rev Gen de Legis y Jurispr ... Revista General de Legislacion y Jurisprudencia [*Madrid, Spain*] (DLA)
Rev Gen Mar ... Revista General de Marina [*A publication*]
Rev Gen Matieres Color Blanchiment Teint Impress Apprets ... Revue Generale des Matieres Colorantes du Blanchiment de la Teinture de l'Impression et des Apprets [*A publication*]
Rev Gen Matieres Plast ... Revue Generale des Matieres Plastiques [*A publication*]
Rev Gen Mec ... Revue Generale de Mecanique [*A publication*]
Rev Gen Med Vet (Toulouse) ... Revue Generale de Medecine Veterinaire (Toulouse) [*A publication*]
Rev Gen Nucl ... Revue Generale Nucleaire [*A publication*]
Rev Gen Reg ... Revised General Regulation, General Accounting Office [*United States*] (DLA)
Rev Gen Sci Pures Appl ... Revue Generale des Sciences Pures et Appliquees [*A publication*]
Rev Gen Sc Pures et Appliq ... Revue Generale des Sciences Pures et Appliquees [*A publication*]
Rev Gen Tech ... Revue Generale des Techniques [*France*] [*A publication*]
Rev Gen Therm ... Revue Generale de Thermique [*A publication*]
Rev Geofis ... Revista de Geofisica [*A publication*]
Rev Geog ... Revista Geografica [*A publication*]
Rev Geog Ph ... Revue de Geographie Physique et de Geologie Dynamique [*A publication*]
Rev Geogr Alpine ... Revue de Geographie Alpine [*A publication*]
Rev Geographie Alpine ... Revue de Geographie Alpine [*A publication*]
Rev Geographie Montreal ... Revue de Geographie de Montreal [*A publication*]
Rev Geogr Maroc ... Revue de Geographie du Maroc [*A publication*]
Rev Geogr Phys Geol Dyn ... Revue de Geographie Physique et de Geologie Dynamique [*A publication*]
Rev Geogr Pyrenees Sud-Ouest ... Revue Geographique des Pyrenees et du Sud-Ouest [*A publication*]
Rev Geol Chile ... Revista Geologica de Chile [*A publication*]
Rev Geol Dyn Geogr Phys ... Revue de Geologie Dynamique et de Geographie Physique [*A publication*]
Rev Geol Minas Ecuador Dir Gen Geol Minas ... Revista de Geologia y Minas. Ecuador. Direccion General de Geologia y Minas [*A publication*]
Rev Geologia ... Revista de Geologia [*A publication*]
Rev Geomorphol Dyn ... Revue de Geomorphologie Dynamique [*A publication*]
Rev Geophys ... Reviews of Geophysics [*Later, Reviews of Geophysics and Space Physics*] [*A publication*]
Rev Geophys ... Reviews of Geophysics and Space Physics [*A publication*]
Rev Geophysics ... Reviews of Geophysics [*Later, Reviews of Geophysics and Space Physics*] [*A publication*]
Rev Geophys and Space Phys ... Reviews of Geophysics and Space Physics [*A publication*]
Rev Geophys Space Phys ... Reviews of Geophysics and Space Physics [*A publication*]
Rev Geriatr ... Revue de Geriatrie [*A publication*]
Rev Germ... Revue Germanique [*A publication*]
Rev Gerontol Expression Fr ... Revue de Gerontologie d'Expression Francaise [*A publication*]
Rev of Ghana L ... Review of Ghana Law [*A publication*]
Rev Ginecol Obstet ... Revista de Ginecologia e d'Obstetricia [*A publication*]
Rev Goiana Med ... Revista Goiana de Medicina [*A publication*]
Rev Gospod Agr Stat (Bucharest) ... Revista Gospodariilor Agricole de Stat (Bucharest) [*A publication*]
Rev G Therm ... Revue Generale de Thermique [*A publication*]
Rev Guatem Estomatol ... Revista Guatemalteca de Estomatologia [*A publication*]
Rev Gynae et Chir Abd ... Revue de Gynaecologie et de Chirurgie Abdominale [*A publication*]
RevH.......... Revista de Historia [*Lisbon*] [*A publication*]
REVHA .... Reviews on Environmental Health [*A publication*]
Rev Hautes Temp Refract ... Revue des Hautes Temperatures et des Refractaires [*A publication*]
Rev Hebd Laryngol Otol Rhinol ... Revue Hebdomadaire de Laryngologie, d'Otologie, et de Rhinologie [*A publication*]
Rev Hellen de Droit Internat ... Revue Hellenique de Droit International [*A publication*]
Rev Hellenique de Dr Int'l ... Revue Hellenique de Droit International [*A publication*]
Rev Hematol ... Revue d'Hematologie [*A publication*]
Rev HF Electron Telecommun ... Revue HF, Electronique, Telecommunications [*A publication*]
Rev High-Temp Mater ... Reviews on High-Temperature Materials [*A publication*]
Rev Hig Med Esc ... Revista de Higiene y Medicina Escolares [*A publication*]
Rev Hig y San Pecuarias ... Revista de Higiene y Sanidad Pecuarias [*A publication*]
Rev Hig y San Vet (Madrid) ... Revista de Higiene y Sanidad Veterinaria (Madrid) [*A publication*]
Rev His A F ... Revue d'Histoire de l'Amerique Francaise [*A publication*]
Rev Hispan ... Revista Hispanica Moderna [*A publication*]
RevHist ...... Revista de Historia [*Sao Paulo*] [*A publication*]
Rev Hist...... Revue Historique [*A publication*]
Rev Hist Am ... Revue d'Histoire de l'Amerique Francaise [*A publication*]
Rev Hist Am Fr ... Revue d'Histoire de l'Amerique Francaise [*A publication*]

Rev Hist Canaria ... Revista de Historia Canaria [*A publication*]
Rev Hist Di ... Revue d'Histoire Diplomatique [*A publication*]
Rev Hist Econ Soc ... Revue d'Histoire Economique et Sociale [*A publication*]
Rev Hist L... Revue d'Histoire Litteraire de la France [*A publication*]
Rev Hist M ... Revue de l'Histoire Moderne et Contemporaine [*A publication*]
Rev Hist Nat Appliq ... Revue d'Histoire Naturelle Appliquee [*A publication*]
Rev Histoire Sci Appl ... Revue d'Histoire des Sciences et de Leurs Applications [*A publication*]
Rev Hist Rel ... Revue de l'Histoire des Religions [*A publication*] (OCD)
Rev Hist Relig ... Revue de l'Histoire des Religions [*A publication*]
Rev Hist Sci ... Revue d'Histoire des Sciences [*A publication*]
Rev Hist Sci Applic ... Revue d'Histoire des Sciences et de Leurs Applications [*A publication*]
Rev Hist Sci Leurs Appl ... Revue d'Histoire des Sciences et de Leurs Applications [*A publication*]
Rev Hist Textes ... Revue d'Histoire des Textes [*A publication*]
Rev Hist Th ... Revue d'Histoire du Theatre [*A publication*]
RevHL .... Revista de Historia. La Laguna de Tenerife [*A publication*]
RevHL .... Revista de Historia (Lisbon) [*A publication*]
Rev Hong Mines Metall Mines ... Revue Hongroise de Mines et Metallurgie. Mines [*A publication*]
Rev Hortic ... Revue Horticole [*A publication*]
Rev Hortic (Paris) ... Revue Horticole (Paris) [*A publication*]
Rev Hortic Suisse ... Revue Horticole Suisse [*A publication*]
Rev Hortic Vitic ... Revista de Horticultura si Viticultura [*A publication*]
Rev Hort Viticult ... Revista de Horticultura si Viticultura [*Romania*] [*A publication*]
Rev Hosp Clin Fac Med Univ Sao Paulo ... Revista. Hospital das Clinicas. Faculdade de Medicina. Universidade de Sao Paulo [*A publication*]
Rev Hosp Clin Fac Med Univ Sao Paulo Supl ... Revista. Hospital das Clinicas. Faculdade de Medicina. Universidade de Sao Paulo. Suplemento [*A publication*]
Rev Hosp Ninos (B Aires) ... Revista. Hospital de Ninos (Buenos Aires) [*A publication*]
Rev Hosp Psiquiatr Habana ... Revista. Hospital Psiquiatrico de la Habana [*A publication*]
RevHS .... Revista de Historia (Sao Paulo) [*A publication*]
Rev Hyg...... Revue d'Hygiene [*A publication*]
Rev Hyg et Med Prevent ... Revue d'Hygiene et de Medecine Preventive [*A publication*]
Rev Hyg Med Sc Univ ... Revue d'Hygiene et Medecine Scolaire et Universitaire [*A publication*]
Rev Hyg Med Soc ... Revue d'Hygiene et de Medecine Sociale [*A publication*]
Rev Hyg Trav ... Revue d'Hygiene du Travail [*A publication*]
Rev/I .... Revista/Review Interamericana [*A publication*]
Revlb .... Revista Iberoamericana [*A publication*]
Rev Iber Endocrinol ... Revista Iberica de Endocrinologia [*A publication*]
Rev Iberoam ... Revista Iberoamericana [*A publication*]
Rev Iberoam Educ Quim ... Revista Iberoamericana de Educacion Quimica [*A publication*]
Rev Iber Parasitol ... Revista Iberica de Parasitologia [*A publication*]
Rev IBYS .... Revista. IBYS [*Instituto de Biologia y Sueroterapia*] [*A publication*]
Rev ICIDCA ... Revista. ICIDCA [*Instituto Cubano de Investigaciones de los Derivados de la Cana de Azucar*] [*A publication*]
Rev IDIEM ... Revista. IDIEM [*Instituto de Investigaciones de Engoyes de Materiales*] [*A publication*]
RevIE .... Revista de Ideas Esteticas [*A publication*]
REVIEW ...... Recording and Video Playback of Electronic Warfare Information
Review .... Weekly Review [*A publication*]
Rev I F Pet ... Revue. Institut Francais du Petrole [*A publication*]
Rev Ig .... Revista. Igiena, Bacteriologie, Virusologie, Parazitologie, Epidemiologie, Pneumoftiziologie [*A publication*]
Rev Ig Bacteriol Virusol Parazitol Epidemiol Pneumoftiziol ... Revista. Igiena, Bacteriologie, Virusologie, Parazitologie, Epidemiologie, Pneumoftiziologie [*A publication*]
Rev Ig Soc ... Revista de Igiena Sociala [*A publication*]
RevIMA ...... Review of Indonesian and Malayan Affairs [*A publication*]
Rev Imagem ... Revista da Imagem [*A publication*]
Rev Immunol ... Revue d'Immunologie [*A publication*]
Rev Immunol Ther Antimicrob ... Revue d'Immunologie et de Therapie Antimicrobienne [*A publication*]
Rev Ind ...... Revue Industrielle [*A publication*]
Rev Ind Agric (Tucuman) ... Revista Industrial y Agricola (Tucuman) [*A publication*]
Rev Ind Aliment Prod Anim ... Revista Industriei Alimentare. Produse Animale [*A publication*]
Rev Ind Aliment Prod Veg ... Revista Industriei Alimentare. Produse Vegetale [*A publication*]
Rev Ind Anim ... Revista de Industria Animal [*A publication*]
Rev Ind Chim ... Revue Hebdomadaire des Industries Chimiques [*A publication*]
Rev Ind Elec ... Revue Hebdomadaire de l'Industrie Electrique et Electronique [*A publication*]
Rev Ind Fabril ... Revista Industrial y Fabril [*France*] [*A publication*]
Rev Indias ... Revista de las Indias [*A publication*]
Rev Ind Miner ... Revue de l'Industrie Minerale [*A publication*]

Rev Indon & Malayan Affairs ... Review of Indonesian and Malayan Affairs [*A publication*]

Rev Industr Agric (Tucuman) ... Revista Industrial y Agricola (Tucuman) [*A publication*]

Rev Inf & Autom ... Revista de Informatica y Automatica [*A publication*]

Rev Infect Dis ... Review of Infectious Diseases [*A publication*]

Rev Infirm ... Revue de l'Infirmiere [*A publication*]

Rev Inf Med ... Revue d'Informatique Medicale [*A publication*]

Rev Ing....... Revue des Ingenieurs des Ecoles Nationales Superieures des Mines [*A publication*]

Rev Ing (Buenos Aires) ... Revista de Ingenieria (Buenos Aires) [*A publication*]

Rev Ing Ind ... Revista de Ingenieria Industrial [*A publication*]

Rev Ing (Montevideo) ... Revista de Ingenieria (Montevideo) [*A publication*]

Rev Ing Quim ... Revista de Ingenieria Quimica [*A publication*]

Rev In Haut ... Revue Internationale des Hautes Temperatures et des Refractaires [*A publication*]

Rev Inst Adolfo Lutz ... Revista. Instituto Adolfo Lutz [*A publication*]

Rev Inst Agr Catalan San Isidro ... Revista. Instituto Agricola Catalan de San Isidro [*A publication*]

Rev Inst Antibiot (Recife) ... Revista. Instituto de Antibioticos. Universidade Federal de Pernambuco (Recife) [*A publication*]

Rev Inst Antibiot Univ Fed Pernambuco ... Revista. Instituto de Antibioticos. Universidade Federal de Pernambuco [*A publication*]

Rev Inst Antibiot Univ Recife ... Revista. Instituto de Antibioticos. Universidade do Recife [*A publication*]

Rev Inst Bacteriol Dep Nac Hig (Argent) ... Revista. Instituto Bacteriologico. Departamento Nacional de Higiene (Argentina) [*A publication*]

Rev Inst Bacteriol Malbran ... Revista del Instituto Bacteriologico Malbran [*A publication*]

Rev Inst Colomb Agropecu ... Revista. Instituto Colombiano Agropecuario [*A publication*]

Rev del Inst de Derecho Comparado ... Revista. Instituto de Derecho Comparado [*Barcelona, Spain*]   (DLA)

Rev Inst Franc Petrol ... Revue. Institut Francais du Petrole [*A publication*]

Rev Inst Fr Pet ... Revue. Institut Francais du Petrole [*A publication*]

Rev Inst Fr Pet ... Revue. Institut Francais du Petrole et Annales des Combustibles Liquides [*Later, Revue. Institut Francais du Petrole*] [*A publication*]

Rev Inst Fr Pet Ann Combust Liq ... Revue. Institut Francais du Petrole et Annales des Combustibles Liquides [*Later, Revue. Institut Francais du Petrole*] [*A publication*]

Rev Inst Geogr Geol (Sao Paulo) ... Revista. Instituto Geografico e Geologico (Sao Paulo) [*A publication*]

Rev Inst Geol Univ Nac Auton Mex ... Revista. Instituto de Geologia. Universidad Nacional Autonoma de Mexico [*A publication*]

Rev Inst Hyg Mines ... Revue. Institut d'Hygiene des Mines [*A publication*]

Rev Inst Hyg Mines (Hasselt) ... Revue. Institut d'Hygiene des Mines (Hasselt) [*A publication*]

Rev Inst Invest Tecnol (Bogota) ... Revista. Instituto de Investigaciones Tecnologicas (Bogota) [*A publication*]

Rev Inst Med Trop Sao Paulo ... Revista. Instituto de Medicina Tropical de Sao Paulo [*A publication*]

Rev Inst Mex Pet ... Revista. Instituto Mexicano del Petroleo [*A publication*]

Rev Inst Mex Petrol ... Revista. Instituto Mexicano del Petroleo [*A publication*]

Rev Inst Munic Bot (B Aires) ... Revista. Instituto Municipal de Botanica (Buenos Aires) [*A publication*]

Rev Inst Nac Geol Min (Argent) ... Revista. Instituto Nacional de Geologia y Mineria (Argentina) [*A publication*]

Rev Inst Nac Hig ... Revista. Instituto Nacional de Higiene [*A publication*]

Rev Inst Nacl Cancerol (Mex) ... Revista. Instituto Nacional de Cancerologia (Mexico) [*A publication*]

Rev Inst Nac Med Leg Colombia ... Revista. Instituto Nacional de Medicina Legal de Colombia [*A publication*]

Rev Inst Napoleon ... Revue de l'Institut Napoleon [*A publication*]

Rev Inst Pasteur Lyon ... Revue. Institut Pasteur de Lyon [*A publication*]

Rev Inst Salubr Enferm Trop ... Revista. Instituto de Salubridad y Enfermedades Tropicales [*A publication*]

Rev Int Bois ... Revue Internationale du Bois [*A publication*]

Rev Int Bois Matieres Premieres Prod Ind Origine Veg ... Revue Internationale du Bois et des Matieres Premieres et Produits Industriels d'Origine Vegetale [*A publication*]

Rev Int Bot Appl Agric Trop ... Revue Internationale de Botanique Appliquee et d'Agriculture Tropicale [*A publication*]

Rev Int Brass Malt ... Revue Internationale de Brasserie et de Malterie [*A publication*]

Rev Int Choc ... Revue Internationale de la Chocolaterie [*A publication*]

Rev Int Crim ... Revue Internationale du Criminalistique [*A publication*]

Rev Int Doc ... Revue Internationale de la Documentation [*A publication*]

Rev Interamer Cienc Soc ... Revista Interamericana de Ciencias Sociales [*A publication*]

Rev Interam Radiol ... Revista Interamericana de Radiologia [*A publication*]

Rev Internac y Diplom ... Revista Internacional y Diplomatica. Publicacion Mensual [*Mexico*]   (DLA)

Rev Internat de Droit Compare ... Revue Internationale de Droit Compare. Continuation du Bulletin de la Societe de Legislation Comparee [*A publication*]

Rev Internat de Droit Penal ... Revue Internationale de Droit Penal. Bulletin de l'Association Internationale de Droit Penal [*A publication*]

Rev Internat Franc du Droit des Gens ... Revue Internationale Francaise du Droit des Gens   (DLA)

Rev Internat Philos ... Revue Internationale de Philosophie [*A publication*]

Rev Int Falsif ... Revue Internationale des Falsifications [*A publication*]

Rev Int Falsif Anal Matieres Aliment ... Revue Internationale des Falsifications et d'Analyse des Matieres Alimentaires [*A publication*]

Rev Int Hautes Temp Refract ... Revue Internationale des Hautes Temperatures et des Refractaires [*A publication*]

Rev Int Heliotech ... Revue Internationale d'Heliotechnique [*France*] [*A publication*]

Rev Int Hepatol ... Revue Internationale d'Hepatologie [*A publication*]

Rev Int Hist Banque ... Revue Internationale d'Histoire de la Banque [*A publication*]

Rev Int Ind Agric ... Revue Internationale des Industries Agricoles [*A publication*]

Rev Int'l Comm Jurists ... Review. International Commission of Jurists [*A publication*]

Rev Int'l Dr Auteur ... Revue Internationale du Droit d'Auteur   (DLA)

Rev Int'l Droit Comp ... Revue Internationale de Droit Compare   (DLA)

Rev Int'l des Droits de l'Antiquite ... Revue Internationale des Droits de l'Antiquite   (DLA)

Rev Int'l Dr Penal ... Revue Internationale de Droit Penal   (DLA)

Rev Int Mus ... Revue Internationale de Musique [*A publication*]

Rev Int Oceanogr Med ... Revue Internationale d'Oceanographie Medicale [*A publication*]

Rev Int Pediatr ... Revue Internationale de Pediatrie [*A publication*]

Rev Int Ph ... Revue Internationale de Philosophie [*A publication*]

Rev Int Phil ... Revue Internationale de Philosophie [*A publication*]

Rev Int Prod Trop Mater Trop ... Revue Internationale des Produits Tropicaux et du Materiel Tropical [*A publication*]

Rev Int Psy ... Revue Internationale de Psychologie Appliquee [*A publication*]

Rev Int Sc ... Revista Internazionale di Scienze Economiche e Commerciali [*A publication*]

Rev Int Serv Sante Armees Terre Mer Air ... Revue Internationale des Services de Sante des Armees de Terre, de Mer, et de l'Air [*A publication*]

Rev Int Soja ... Revue Internationale du Soja [*A publication*]

Rev Int Tab ... Revue Internationale des Tabacs [*A publication*]

Rev Int Trach ... Revue Internationale du Trachome [*A publication*]

Rev Int Trach Pathol Ocul Trop Subtrop ... Revue Internationale du Trachome et de Pathologie Oculaire Tropicale et Subtropicale [*A publication*]

Rev Inv Cli ... Revista de Investigacion Clinica [*A publication*]

Rev Invest ... Revista de Investigacion [*A publication*]

Rev Invest Agr ... Revista de Investigaciones Agricolas [*A publication*]

Rev Invest Agric ... Revista de Investigaciones Agricolas [*A publication*]

Rev Invest Agropec Ser ... Revista de Investigaciones Agropecuarias. Serie [*A publication*]

Rev Invest Agropecuar Ser 2 ... Revista de Investigaciones Agropecuarias. Serie 2. Biologia y Produccion Vegetal [*A publication*]

Rev Invest Agropecuar Ser 5 ... Revista de Investigaciones Agropecuarias. Serie 5. Patologia Vegetal [*A publication*]

Rev Invest Agropecu Ser 6 ... Revista de Investigaciones Agropecuarias. Serie 6. Economia y Administracion Rural [*A publication*]

Rev Invest Agropecu Ser 1 Biol Prod Anim ... Revista de Investigaciones Agropecuarias. Serie 1. Biologia y Produccion Animal [*A publication*]

Rev Invest Agropecu Ser 2 Biol Prod Veg ... Revista de Investigaciones Agropecuarias. Serie 2. Biologia y Produccion Vegetal [*A publication*]

Rev Invest Agropecu Ser 3 Clima Suelo ... Revista de Investigaciones Agropecuarias. Serie 3. Clima y Suelo [*A publication*]

Rev Invest Agropecu Ser 4 Patol Anim ... Revista de Investigaciones Agropecuarias. Serie 4. Patologia Animal [*A publication*]

Rev Invest Agropecu Ser 5 Patol Veg ... Revista de Investigaciones Agropecuarias. Serie 5. Patologia Vegetal [*A publication*]

Rev Invest Clin ... Revista de Investigacion Clinica [*A publication*]

Rev Invest For ... Revista de Investigaciones Forestales [*A publication*]

Rev Invest Ganad ... Revista de Investigaciones Ganaderas [*A publication*]

Rev Invest Inst Nac Pesca ... Revista de Investigaciones. Instituto Nacional de la Pesca [*A publication*]

Rev Invest Salud Publica ... Revista de Investigacion en Salud Publica [*A publication*]

Rev Invest Univ Guadalajara (Mex) ... Revista de Investigacion. Universidad de Guadalajara (Mexico) [*A publication*]

Rev Ion....... Revista Ion [*A publication*]

Rev I Psych ... Revue Internationale de Psychologie Appliquee [*A publication*]

Rev IRE ...... Revue. IRE [*Institut National des Radioelements*] [*A publication*]

Rev I Soc.... Revue. Institut de Sociologie [*A publication*]

Revista CF ... Revista Colombiana de Folclor [*A publication*]

Rev Ivoirienne de Droit ... Revue Ivoirienne de Droit   (DLA)

Rev Jeumont-Schneider ... Revue Jeumont-Schneider [*A publication*]

Rev J Phil Soc Sci ... Review Journal of Philosophy and Social Science [*A publication*]

Rev J & PJ ... Revenue, Judicial, and Police Journal [*Bengal*]   (DLA)

Rev Jur....... Revista Juridica [*A publication*]
Rev de Jur ... Revue de Jurisprudence [*Quebec*] (DLA)
Rev Jur d'Alsace et de Lorraine ... Revue Juridique d'Alsace et de Lorraine (DLA)
Rev Jur de Buenos Aires ... Revista Juridica de Buenos Aires (DLA)
Rev Jur du Congo ... Revue Juridique du Congo (DLA)
Rev Jur del Peru ... Revista Juridica del Peru [*A publication*]
Rev Jur Themis ... Revue Juridique Themis [*A publication*]
Rev Jur U Inter PR ... Revista Juridica. Universidad Interamericana de Puerto Rico (DLA)
Rev Jur de la Univ de Puerto Rico ... Revista Juridica. Universidad de Puerto Rico [*A publication*]
Rev Jur UPR ... Revista Juridica. Universidad de Puerto Rico [*A publication*]
Rev Kobe Univ Merc Mar Part 2 ... Review. Kobe University of Mercantile Marine. Part 2 [*Japan*] [*A publication*]
Rev Kuba Med Trop Parasitol ... Revista Kuba de Medicina Tropical y Parasitologia [*A publication*]
RevL.......... Revista de Letras [*A publication*]
RevLA .... Revista de Letras (Assis) [*A publication*]
Rev Lang R ... Revue des Langues Romanes [*A publication*]
Rev Lang V ... Revue des Langues Vivantes/Tijdschrift voor Levende Talen [*A publication*]
Rev Lang Viv ... Revue des Langues Vivantes [*A publication*]
Rev Laryngol Otol Rhinol ... Revue de Laryngologie, Otologie, Rhinologie [*A publication*]
Rev Laryngol Otol Rhinol (Bord) ... Revue de Laryngologie, Otologie, Rhinologie (Bordeaux) [*A publication*]
Rev Laryngol Otol Rhino Suppl ... Revue de Laryngologie, Otologie, Rhinologie. Supplement [*France*] [*A publication*]
Rev Laser Eng ... Review of Laser Engineering [*Japan*] [*A publication*]
Rev Latam Microbiol ... Revista Latinoamericana de Microbiologia [*A publication*]
Rev Latam P ... Revista Latinoamericana de Psicologia [*A publication*]
Rev Latam Patol ... Revista Latinoamericana de Patologia [*A publication*]
Rev Latin de Filosof ... Revista Latinoamericana de Filosofia [*A publication*]
Rev Latinoam Anat Patol ... Revista Latinoamericana de Anatomia Patologica [*A publication*]
Rev Latinoam Cir Plast ... Revista Latinoamericana de Cirurgia Plastica [*A publication*]
Rev Latinoam Ing Quim Quim Apl ... Revista Latinoamericana de Ingenieria Quimica y Quimica Aplicada [*A publication*]
Rev Latinoam Microbiol ... Revista Latinoamericana de Microbiologia [*A publication*]
Rev Latinoam Microbiol Parasitol ... Revista Latinoamericana de Microbiologia y Parasitologia [*Later, Revista Latinoamericana de Microbiologia*] [*A publication*]
Rev Latinoam Microbiol Supl ... Revista Latinoamericana de Microbiologia. Suplemento [*A publication*]
Rev Latinoam Patol ... Revista Latinoamericana de Patologia [*A publication*]
Rev Latinoam Psicol ... Revista Latinoamericana de Psicologia [*A publication*]
Rev Latinoam Quim ... Revista Latinoamericana de Quimica [*A publication*]
Rev Latinoam Sider ... Revista Latinoamericana de Siderurgia [*A publication*]
Rev Leg ...... Revue Legale [*Canada*] (DLA)
Rev de Leg ... Revue de Legislation et de Jurisprudence [*Montreal*] (DLA)
Rev Leg ...... Revue de Legislation et de Jurisprudence [*Quebec*] (DLA)
Rev Legale ... Revue Legale (DLA)
Rev de Legis ... Revue de Legislation [*Canada*] (DLA)
Rev Leg NS ... Revue Legale. New Series [*Canada*] (DLA)
Rev Leg (OS) ... Revue Legale Old Series (DLA)
Rev Leprol Sao Paulo ... Revista de Leprologia de Sao Paulo [*A publication*]
Rev Liberale ... Revue Liberale [*A publication*]
Rev Ling Rom ... Revue de Linguistique Romane [*A publication*]
Rev Lit....... Revue de Litterature Comparee [*A publication*]
Rev de Lit Comp ... Revue de Litterature Comparee [*A publication*]
Rev Lit Comp ... Revue de Litterature Comparee [*A publication*]
Rev Louvre ... Revue du Louvre et des Musees de France [*A publication*]
Rev Lyon Med ... Revue Lyonnaise de Medecine [*A publication*]
RevM .... Revista (Madrid) [*A publication*]
Rev M .... Revue M [*Belgium*] [*A publication*]
Rev Macromol Chem ... Reviews in Macromolecular Chemistry [*A publication*]
Rev Madeira (Sao Paulo) ... Revista da Madeira (Sao Paulo) [*A publication*]
Rev du Marche Commun ... Revue du Marche Commun [*A publication*]
Rev Market & Ag Econ ... Review of Marketing and Agricultural Economics [*A publication*]
Rev Market Agric Econ ... Review of Marketing and Agricultural Economics [*A publication*]
Rev Market Agric Econ (Sydney) ... Review of Marketing and Agricultural Economics (Sydney) [*A publication*]
Rev Marketing Agr Econ ... Review of Marketing and Agricultural Economics [*A publication*]
Rev Mat Hisp-Amer ... Revista Matematica Hispano-Americana [*A publication*]
Rev Math Pures Appl ... Revue de Mathematiques Pures et Appliquees [*A publication*]
Rev MBLE ... Revue MBLE [*Manufacture Belge de Lampes et de Materiel*] [*Belgium*] [*A publication*]
Rev Mec Appl ... Revue de Mecanique Appliquee [*A publication*]

Rev Mec Tijdsch ... Revue Mecanique Tijdschrift [*Belgium*] [*A publication*]
Rev Med...... Revista Medicala [*A publication*]
Rev Med Accidents Mal Prof ... Revue de Medecine des Accidents et des Maladies Professionnelles [*A publication*]
Rev Med Aeronaut (Paris) ... Revue de Medecine Aeronautique (Paris) [*Later, Medecine Aeronautique et Spatial - Medecine Subaquatique et Hyperbare*] [*A publication*]
Rev Med Aeronaut Spat ... Revue de Medecine Aeronautique et Spatiale [*Later, Medecine Aeronautique et Spatial - Medecine Subaquatique et Hyperbare*] [*A publication*]
Rev Med Aliment ... Revista de Medicina y Alimentacion [*A publication*]
Rev Med Angola ... Revista Medica de Angola [*A publication*]
Rev Med ATM ... Revista de Medicina. ATM [*Associacao da Turma Medica*] [*A publication*]
Rev Med Bogota ... Revista Medica de Bogota [*A publication*]
Rev Med Brux ... Revue Medicale de Bruxelles [*A publication*]
Rev Med Bruxelles ... Revue Medicale de Bruxelles [*A publication*]
Rev Med Chi ... Revista Medica de Chile [*A publication*]
Rev Med Chil ... Revista Medica de Chile [*A publication*]
Rev Med Chile ... Revista Medica de Chile [*A publication*]
Rev Med Chir ... Revista Medico-Chirurgicala [*A publication*]
Rev Med-Chir (Iasi) ... Revue Medico-Chirurgicale (Iasi) [*A publication*]
Rev Med-Chir Mal Foie ... Revue Medico-Chirurgicale des Maladies du Foie [*A publication*]
Rev Med-Chir Mal Foie Rate Pancreas ... Revue Medico-Chirurgicale des Maladies du Foie, de la Rate, et du Pancreas [*France*] [*A publication*]
Rev Med-Chir Soc Med Nat din Iasi ... Revista Medico-Chirurgicala. Societatii de Medici si Naturalisti din Iasi [*A publication*]
Rev Med-Chir Soc Med Nat Iasi ... Revista Medico-Chirurgicala. Societatii de Medici si Naturalisti din Iasi [*A publication*]
Rev Med Cienc Afines ... Revista de Medicina y Ciencias Afines [*A publication*]
Rev Med Cir Habana ... Revista de Medicina y Cirugia de La Habana [*A publication*]
Rev Med Cir Sao Paulo ... Revista de Medicina e Cirurgia de Sao Paulo [*A publication*]
Rev Med y Cirug (Caracas) ... Revista de Medicina y Cirugia (Caracas) [*A publication*]
Rev Med y Cirug Habana ... Revista de Medicina y Cirugia de La Habana [*A publication*]
Rev Med Cordoba ... Revista Medica de Cordoba [*A publication*]
Rev Med Costa Rica ... Revista Medica de Costa Rica [*A publication*]
Rev Med Cubana ... Revista Medica Cubana [*A publication*]
Rev Med Dijon ... Revue Medicale de Dijon [*A publication*]
Rev Med Est ... Revue Medicale de l'Est [*A publication*]
Rev Med Estado Guanabara ... Revista Medica do Estado da Guanabara [*A publication*]
Rev Med Estado Rio De J ... Revista Medica do Estado do Rio De Janeiro [*A publication*]
Rev Med Estud Gen Navarro ... Revista de Medicina del Estudio General de Navarro [*A publication*]
Rev Med Exp ... Revista de Medicina Experimental [*A publication*]
Rev Med Exp (Lima) ... Revista de Medicina Experimental (Lima) [*A publication*]
Rev Med Fr ... Revue Medicale Francaise [*A publication*]
Rev Med Galicia ... Revista Medica de Galicia [*A publication*]
Rev Med (Hanoi) ... Revue Medicale (Hanoi) [*A publication*]
Rev Med Hondur ... Revista Medica Hondurena [*A publication*]
Rev Med Hosp Cent Empl Lima ... Revista Medica. Hospital Central del Empleado Lima [*A publication*]
Rev Med Hosp Colon Mex ... Revista Medica. Hospital Colonia Mexico [*A publication*]
Rev Med Hosp Ernesto Dornelles ... Revista de Medicina. Hospital Ernesto Dornelles [*A publication*]
Rev Med Hosp Gen Mex ... Revista Medica. Hospital General Mexico [*A publication*]
Rev Med Hosp Gen (Mexico City) ... Revista Medica. Hospital General (Mexico City) [*A publication*]
Rev Med Hosp Obrero ... Revista Medica del Hospital Obrero [*A publication*]
Rev Med Hosp Servidores Estado ... Revista Medica. Hospital dos Servidores do Estado [*A publication*]
Rev Med HSE ... Revista Medica. Hospital dos Servidores do Estado [*A publication*]
Rev Med Inst Mex Seguro Soc ... Revista Medica. Instituto Mexicano del Seguro Social [*A publication*]
Rev Med Inst Previdencia Serv Estado Minas Gerais ... Revista Medica. Instituto de Previdencia dos Servidores do Estado de Minas Gerais [*A publication*]
Rev Med Inst Previdencia Servidores Estado Minas Gerais ... Revista Medica. Instituto de Previdencia dos Servidores do Estado de Minas Gerais [*A publication*]
Rev Med Interna Med Interna ... Revista de Medicina Interna, Neurologie, Psihiatrie, Neurochirurgie, Dermato-Venerologie Seria. Medicina Interna [*A publication*]
Rev Med Interna Neurol Psihiatr ... Revista de Medicina Interna, Neurologie, Psihiatrie, Neurochirurgie, Dermato-Venerologie. Neurologie, Psihiatrie, Neurochirurgie [*A publication*]
Rev Med Interna Neurol Psihiatr Neurochir Dermato-Venerol ... Revista. Medicina Interna, Neurologie, Psihiatrie, Neurochirurgie, Dermato-Venerologie [*A publication*]

Rev Med Interne ... Revue de Medecine Interne [*A publication*]
Rev Mediterr Sci Med ... Revue Mediterraneenne des Sciences Medicales [*A publication*]
Rev Med Juiz de Fora ... Revista Medica de Juiz de Fora [*A publication*]
Rev Med Liege ... Revue Medicale de Liege [*A publication*]
Rev Med Liege Suppl ... Revue Medicale de Liege. Supplement [*A publication*]
Rev Med Limoges ... Revue de Medecine de Limoges [*A publication*]
Rev Med Mil ... Revista de Medicina Militar [*A publication*]
Rev Med Miniere ... Revue Medicale Miniere [*A publication*]
Rev Med Moyen-Orient ... Revue Medicale du Moyen-Orient [*A publication*]
Rev Med Nav ... Revue de Medecine Navale (Metropole et Outre-Mer) [*A publication*]
Rev Med Panama ... Revista Medica de Panama [*A publication*]
Rev Med Parag ... Revista Medica del Paraguay [*A publication*]
Rev Med (Paris) ... Revue de Medecine (Paris) [*A publication*]
Rev Med Prev ... Revue de Medecine Preventive [*A publication*]
Rev Med Psychosomat Psychol Med ... Revue de Medecine Psychosomatique et de Psychologie Medicale [*France*] [*A publication*]
Rev Med-Quir (Buenos Aires) ... Revista Medico-Quirurgica (Buenos Aires) [*A publication*]
Rev Med Rio Grande do Sul ... Revista de Medicina do Rio Grande do Sul [*A publication*]
Rev Med d Rosario ... Revista Medica del Rosario [*A publication*]
Rev Med Rosario ... Revista Medica del Rosario [*A publication*]
Rev de Med (Rosario) ... Revista de Medicina (Rosario) [*A publication*]
Rev Med (Sao Paulo) ... Revista de Medicina (Sao Paulo) [*A publication*]
Rev Med Sevilla ... Revista Medica de Sevilla [*A publication*]
Rev Med de S Paulo ... Revista Medica de Sao Paulo [*A publication*]
Rev de Med (S Paulo) ... Revista de Medicina (Sao Paulo) [*A publication*]
Rev Med Suisse Romande ... Revue Medicale de la Suisse Romande [*A publication*]
Rev Med (Tirgu-Mures) ... Revista Medicala (Tirgu-Mures) [*Romania*] [*A publication*]
Rev Med Toulouse ... Revue de Medecine de Toulouse [*A publication*]
Rev Med Toulouse Suppl ... Revue de Medecine de Toulouse. Supplement [*A publication*]
Rev Med Tours ... Revue de Medecine de Tours [*A publication*]
Rev Med Trav ... Revue de Medecine du Travail [*France*] [*A publication*]
Rev Med Trop ... Revista de Medicina Tropical [*A publication*]
Rev Med Univ Fed Ceara ... Revista de Medicina. Universidade Federal do Ceara [*A publication*]
Rev Med Univ Navarra ... Revista de Medicina. Universidad de Navarra [*A publication*]
Rev Med Uruguay ... Revista Medica del Uruguay [*A publication*]
Rev Med (Valparaiso) ... Revista de Medicina (Valparaiso) [*A publication*]
Rev Med Veracruz ... Revista Medica Veracruzana [*A publication*]
Rev Med Vet ... Revista de Medicina Veterinaria [*A publication*]
Rev Med Vet (B Aires) ... Revista de Medicina Veterinaria (Buenos Aires) [*A publication*]
Rev Med Vet (Bogota) ... Revista de Medicina Veterinaria (Bogota) [*A publication*]
Rev Med Vet Escuela Montevideo ... Revista de Medicina Veterinaria. Escuela de Montevideo [*A publication*]
Rev Med Vet (Montev) ... Revista de Medicina Veterinaria (Montevideo) [*A publication*]
Rev Med Vet Mycol ... Review of Medical and Veterinary Mycology [*A publication*]
Rev Med Vet Parasitol (Maracay) ... Revista de Medicina Veterinaria y Parasitologia (Maracay) [*A publication*]
Rev Med Vet (Santiago) ... Revista de Medicina Veterinaria (Santiago) [*A publication*]
Rev Med Vet (Sao Paulo) ... Revista de Medicina Veterinaria (Sao Paulo) [*A publication*]
Rev Med Vet (Toulouse) ... Revue de Medecine Veterinaire (Toulouse) [*A publication*]
Rev Med Yucatan ... Revista Medica de Yucatan [*A publication*]
Rev Mens Asoc Rural Urug ... Revista Mensual. Asociacion Rural del Uruguay [*A publication*]
Rev Mens Blanchissage Blanchiment Apprets ... Revue Mensuelle de Blanchissage, du Blanchiment, et des Apprets [*A publication*]
Rev Mens Mal Enf ... Revue Mensuelle des Maladies de l'Enfance [*A publication*]
Rev Metal ... Revista de Metalurgia [*A publication*]
Rev Metall ... Revue de Metallurgie [*Paris*] [*A publication*]
Rev Metall Cah Inf Tech ... Revue de Metallurgie. Cahiers d'Informations Techniques [*A publication*]
Rev Metall (Paris) ... Revue de Metallurgie (Paris) [*A publication*]
Rev Metall (Paris) Part 1 ... Revue de Metallurgie (Paris) Part 1. Memoires [*A publication*]
Rev Metall (Paris) Part 2 ... Revue de Metallurgie (Paris) Part 2. Extraits [*A publication*]
Rev Metal (Madrid) ... Revista de Metalurgia (Madrid) [*A publication*]
Rev Metaph ... Review of Metaphysics [*A publication*]
Rev Metaph Morale ... Revue de Metaphysique et de Morale [*A publication*]
Rev Metaphy ... Review of Metaphysics [*A publication*]
Rev Metaphys Morale ... Revue de Metaphysique et de Morale [*A publication*]
Rev Meteorol ... Revista Meteorologica [*A publication*]

Rev Met Lit ... Review of Metal Literature [*A publication*]
Rev Met (Madrid) ... Revista de Metalurgia (Madrid) [*A publication*]
Rev Met Mor ... Revue de Metaphysique et de Morale [*A publication*]
Rev Met (Paris) ... Revue de Metallurgie (Paris) [*A publication*]
Rev Metrol Prat Leg ... Revue de Metrologie Pratique et Legale [*A publication*]
Rev Met Technol ... Review of Metals Technology [*A publication*]
Rev Mex Anestesiol ... Revista Mexicana de Anestesiologia [*A publication*]
Rev Mex Astron Astrof ... Revista Mexicana de Astronomia y Astrofisica [*A publication*]
Rev Mex Astron Astrofis ... Revista Mexicana de Astronomia y Astrofisica [*A publication*]
Rev Mex Cienc Med Biol ... Revista Mexicana de Ciencias Medicas y Biologicas [*A publication*]
Rev Mex Cir Ginecol Cancer ... Revista Mexicana de Cirugia, Ginecologia, y Cancer [*A publication*]
Rev Mex Constr ... Revista Mexicana de la Construccion [*A publication*]
Rev Mex Electr ... Revista Mexicana de Electricidad [*A publication*]
Rev Mex Fis ... Revista Mexicana de Fisica [*A publication*]
Rev Mex Fis Supl Ensenanza ... Revista Mexicana de Fisica. Suplemento de Ensenanza [*A publication*]
Rev Mex Fis Supl Fis Apl ... Revista Mexicana de Fisica. Suplemento de Fisica Aplicada [*A publication*]
Rev Mex Fis Supl Reactor ... Revista Mexicana de Fisica. Suplemento del Reactor [*A publication*]
Rev Mexicana Astronom Astrofis ... Revista Mexicana de Astronomia y Astrofisica [*A publication*]
Rev Mexicana Fis ... Revista Mexicana de Fisica [*A publication*]
Rev Mex Lab Clin ... Revista Mexicana de Laboratorio Clinico [*A publication*]
Rev Mex Pediatr ... Revista Mexicana de Pediatria [*A publication*]
Rev Mex Radiol ... Revista Mexicana de Radiologia [*A publication*]
Rev Mex Sociol ... Revista Mexicana de Sociologia [*A publication*]
Rev Mex Tuberc Apar Respir ... Revista Mexicana de Tuberculosis y Aparto Respiratorio [*A publication*]
Rev Micr El ... Revista de Microscopia Electronica [*A publication*]
Rev Microbiol ... Revista de Microbiologia [*A publication*]
Rev Micropaleontol ... Revue de Micropaleontologie [*A publication*]
Rev Mil ... Revista Militar [*A publication*]
Rev Mil Med Vet ... Revista Militar de Medicina Veterinaria [*A publication*]
Rev Mil Remonta Vet ... Revista Militar de Remonta e Veterinaria [*A publication*]
Rev Mil Vet ... Revista Militar de Veterinaria [*A publication*]
Rev Mil Vet (Rio De Janeiro) ... Revista Militar de Veterinaria (Rio De Janeiro) [*A publication*]
Rev Min ... Revista Mineria [*A publication*]
REV/MIN .... Revolutions per Minute [*e.g., in reference to phonograph records*]
Rev Minas Hidrocarburos ... Revista de Minas e Hidrocarburos [*A publication*]
Rev Minelor (Bucharest) ... Revista Minelor (Bucharest) [*A publication*]
Rev Min Eng ... Revista Mineira de Engenharia [*A publication*]
Rev Mineral ... Reviews in Mineralogy [*A publication*]
Rev Minera y Petrolera ... Revista Minera y Petrolera [*A publication*]
Rev Min Geol Mineral ... Revista Minera, Geologia, y Mineralogia [*A publication*]
Rev M Mec ... Revue M - Mecanique [*A publication*]
Rev Modern Phys ... Reviews of Modern Physics [*A publication*]
Rev Mod Phys ... Reviews of Modern Physics [*A publication*]
Rev Moyen A ... Revue du Moyen-Age Latin [*A publication*]
Rev du Moyen-Age Latin ... Revue du Moyen-Age Latin [*A publication*]
Rev M Phys ... Reviews of Modern Physics [*A publication*]
Rev Mus ..... Revue Musicale [*A publication*]
Rev Mus Chilena ... Revista Musical Chilena [*A publication*]
Rev Mus Hist Nat Mendoza ... Revista. Museo de Historia Natural de Mendoza [*A publication*]
Rev Music ... Revue de Musicologie [*A publication*]
Rev Musical ... Revue Musicale [*A publication*]
Rev Music Chilena ... Revista Musical Chilena [*A publication*]
Rev Mus La Plata ... Revista. Museo de La Plata [*A publication*]
Rev Mus La Plata Secc Antropol ... Revista. Museo de La Plata. Seccion Antropologia [*A publication*]
Rev Mus La Plata Secc Bot ... Revista. Museo de La Plata. Seccion Botanica [*A publication*]
Rev Mus La Plata Secc Geol ... Revista. Museo de La Plata. Seccion Geologia [*A publication*]
Rev Mus La Plata Secc Paleontol ... Revista. Museo de La Plata. Seccion Paleontologia [*A publication*]
Rev Mus La Plata Secc Zool ... Revista. Museo de La Plata. Seccion Zoologia [*A publication*]
Rev Muz ..... Revista Muzeelor [*A publication*]
Rev Muz M Mon ... Revista Muzeelor si Monumentelor. Seria Monumente Istorice si Arta [*A publication*]
Rev Muz M Muz ... Revista Muzeelor si Monumentelor. Seria Muzee [*A publication*]
Rev Muz Monum Muz ... Revista Muzeelor si Monumentelor. Seria Muzee [*A publication*]
Rev Mycol ... Revue de Mycologie [*A publication*]
Rev Mycol (Paris) ... Revue de Mycologie (Paris) [*A publication*]
Rev Mycol (Paris) Suppl Colon ... Revue de Mycologie. Supplement Colonial (Paris) [*A publication*]
REVN .... Reversion (ROG)

RevN .... Revue Nouvelle [*Paris*] [*A publication*]
Rev Nac Agr ... Revista Nacional de Agricultura [*A publication*]
Rev Nac Agric (Bogota) ... Revista Nacional de Agricultura (Bogota) [*A publication*]
Rev Nat Lit ... Review of National Literatures [*A publication*]
Rev Neurol ... Revue Neurologique [*A publication*]
Rev Neurol B Aires ... Revista Neurologica de Buenos Aires [*A publication*]
Rev Neurol Clin (Madrid) ... Revista de Neurologia Clinica (Madrid) [*A publication*]
Rev Neurol (Paris) ... Revue Neurologique (Paris) [*A publication*]
Rev Neurops ... Revue de Neuropsychiatrie Infantile et d'Hygiene Mentale de l'Enfance [*A publication*]
Rev Neuro-Psiquiatr ... Revista de Neuro-Psiquiatria [*A publication*]
Rev Neuropsychiatr Infant ... Revue de Neuropsychiatrie Infantile et d'Hygiene Mentale de l'Enfance [*A publication*]
Rev Neuropsychiatr Infant Hyg Ment Enfance ... Revue de Neuropsychiatrie Infantile et d'Hygiene Mentale de l'Enfance [*A publication*]
Rev Neurosci ... Reviews of Neuroscience [*A publication*]
Rev Nickel ... Revue du Nickel [*A publication*]
Rev Nord.... Revue du Nord [*A publication*]
Rev du Not ... Revue du Notariat [*A publication*]
Rev Not ...... Revue du Notariat [*A publication*]
Rev Notariat ... Revue du Notariat [*A publication*]
Rev du Notariat ... Revue du Notariat [*A publication*]
Rev Nouv.... Revue Nouvelle [*Belgium*] [*A publication*]
REVNRY..... Revolutionary
RevNum ..... Revue Numismatique [*A publication*]
Rev Num Arg ... Revista Numismatica Argentina [*A publication*]
Rev Nutr Anim ... Revista de Nutricion Animal [*A publication*]
REVO......... Revoke (AABC)
REVO......... Revolution (DSUE)
Rev Oak Ridge Natl Lab (US) ... Review. Oak Ridge National Laboratory (United States) [*A publication*]
Rev Obras Pub ... Revista de Obras Publicas [*A publication*]
Rev Obras Publicas ... Revista de Obras Publicas [*A publication*]
Rev Obras Sanit Nac (B Aires) ... Revista de Obras Sanitarias de la Nacion (Buenos Aires) [*A publication*]
Rev Obstet Ginecol Venez ... Revista de Obstetricia y Ginecologia de Venezuela [*A publication*]
Rev Oc .... Revista de Occidente [*A publication*]
Rev O Chr ... Revue de l'Orient Chretien [*A publication*]
REVOCN ..... Revocation (ROG)
REVOCON ... Remote Volume Control
REVOCON ... Revocation
Rev Odontoestomatol ... Revista Odonto-Estomatologica [*A publication*]
Rev Odontoimplantol ... Revue Odonto-Implantologique [*A publication*]
Rev Odontol Circ Odontol Parag ... Revista Odontologica. Circulo de Odontologos del Paraguay [*A publication*]
Rev Odontol (Cordoba) ... Revista Odontologica (Cordoba) [*A publication*]
Rev Odontol Costa Rica ... Revista Odontologica de Costa Rica [*A publication*]
Rev Odontol Ecuat ... Revista Odontologica Ecuatoriana [*A publication*]
Rev Odontol Parana ... Revista Odontologica do Parana [*A publication*]
Rev Odonto Stomatol ... Revue d'Odonto-Stomatologie [*A publication*]
Rev Odonto-Stomatol (Bord) ... Revue d'Odonto-Stomatologie (Bordeaux) [*A publication*]
Rev Odonto-Stomatol Midi Fr ... Revue d'Odonto-Stomatologie du Midi de la France [*A publication*]
Rev Odonto-Stomatol (Paris) ... Revue d'Odonto-Stomatologie (Paris) [*A publication*]
Rev Of Fed Med Ecuador ... Revista Oficial. Federacion Medica del Ecuador [*A publication*]
Rev Oka ..... Revue d'Oka [*A publication*]
Revol Wld... Revolutionary World [*A publication*]
REVON....... Reversion
REVOP .... Random Evolutionary Operation
Rev Opt Theor Instrum ... Revue d'Optique Theorique et Instrumentale [*France*] [*A publication*]
Rev Ord...... Revised Ordinances (DLA)
Rev Ord NWT ... Revised Ordinances, Northwest Territories [*1888*] [*Canada*] (DLA)
Rev Orl .... Revista de Otorrinolaringologia [*A publication*]
Rev Orthop Dento-Faciale ... Revue d'Orthopedie Dento-Faciale [*A publication*]
Rev Ortop Traumatol Latinoam ... Revista de Ortopedia y Traumatologia Latinoamericana [*A publication*]
Rev Oto-Neuro-Oftalmol Cir Neurol Sud-Am ... Revista de Oto-Neuro-Oftalmologica y de Cirugia Neurologica Sud-Americana [*A publication*]
Rev Oto-Neuro-Ophtalmol ... Revue d'Oto-Neuro-Ophtalmologie [*A publication*]
Rev Oto-Neuro-Ophtalmol (Paris) ... Revue d'Oto-Neuro-Ophtalmologie (Paris) [*A publication*]
Rev Otorrinolaringol ... Revista de Otorrinolaringologia [*A publication*]
Rev Padurilor ... Revista Padurilor [*A publication*]
Rev Padurilor-Ind Lemnului Ser Ind Lemnului ... Revista Padurilor-Industria Lemnului. Seria Industria Lemnului [*Hungary*] [*A publication*]
Rev Padurilor-Ind Lemnului Ser Silvic Exploatarea Padurilor ... Revista Padurilor-Industria Lemnului. Seria Silvicultura si Exploatarea Padurilor [*A publication*]

Rev Palaeobot Palynol ... Review of Palaeobotany and Palynology [*A publication*]
Rev Palaeobot Palynology ... Review of Palaeobotany and Palynology [*A publication*]
Rev Palae P ... Review of Palaeobotany and Palynology [*A publication*]
Rev Palais Decouv ... Revue du Palais de la Decouverte [*France*] [*A publication*]
Rev Palud Med Trop ... Revue du Paludisme et de Medecine Tropicale [*A publication*]
Rev Path Comp ... Revue de Pathologie Comparee [*A publication*]
Rev Pathol Comp ... Revue de Pathologie Comparee [*A publication*]
Rev Pathol Comp Hyg Gen ... Revue de Pathologie Comparee et Hygiene Generale [*A publication*]
Rev Pathol Comp Med Exp ... Revue de Pathologie Comparee et de Medecine Experimentale [*France*] [*A publication*]
Rev Pathol Veg Entomol Agr France ... Revue de Pathologie Vegetale et d'Entomologie Agricole de France [*A publication*]
Rev Pathol Veg Entomol Agric Fr ... Revue de Pathologie Vegetale et d'Entomologie Agricole de France [*A publication*]
Rev Path Veg et Entom Agric ... Revue de Pathologie Vegetale et d'Entomologie Agricole [*A publication*]
Rev Patronato Biol Anim ... Revista del Patronato de Biologia Animal [*A publication*]
Rev Paul Med ... Revista Paulista de Medicina [*A publication*]
Rev Pediatr ... Revue de Pediatrie [*A publication*]
Rev Pediatr Obstet Ginecol ... Revista de Pediatrie, Obstetrica, si Ginecologie [*A publication*]
Rev Pediatr Obstet Ginecol Ser Obstet Ginecol ... Revista de Pediatrie, Obstetrica, si Ginecologie. Seria Obstetrica si Ginecologie [*A publication*]
Rev Pediatr Obstet Ginecol Ser Pediatr ... Revista de Pediatrie, Obstetrica, si Ginecologie. Seria Pediatria [*A publication*]
Rev Perinat Med ... Reviews in Perinatal Medicine [*A publication*]
Rev Peru Entomol ... Revista Peruana de Entomologia [*A publication*]
Rev Peru Entomol Agr ... Revista Peruana de Entomologia Agricola [*A publication*]
Rev Peru Entomol Agric ... Revista Peruana de Entomologia Agricola [*A publication*]
Rev Peru Salud Publica ... Revista Peruana de Salud Publica [*A publication*]
Rev Peru Tuberc Enferm Respir ... Revista Peruana de Tuberculosis y Enfermedades Respiratorias [*A publication*]
Rev Petrolifere ... Revue Petrolifere [*A publication*]
Rev Pet Technol (London) ... Reviews of Petroleum Technology (London) [*A publication*]
RevPF......... Revista Portuguesa de Filosofia [*A publication*]
Rev Pharmacol Ter Exp ... Revue de Pharmacologie et de Therapeutique Experimentale [*A publication*]
Rev Pharm Liban ... Revue Pharmaceutique Libanaise [*A publication*]
Rev Ph Ch J ... Review of Physical Chemistry of Japan [*A publication*]
Rev Phil ...... Revue de Philologie [*A publication*] (OCD)
Rev Phil...... Revue de Philologie, de Litterature, et d'Histoire Anciennes [*A publication*]
Rev Phil Fr ... Revue Philosophique de la France et de l'Etranger [*A publication*]
Rev Phil Louvain ... Revue Philosophique de Louvain [*A publication*]
Rev Philol... Revue de Philologie [*A publication*]
Rev Philos ... Revue Philosophique de Louvain [*A publication*]
Rev Philos Fr Etrang ... Revue Philosophique de la France et de l'Etranger [*A publication*]
Rev Philos Louv ... Revue Philosophique de Louvain [*A publication*]
Rev Phonet Appl ... Revue de Phonetique Appliquee [*A publication*]
Rev Phys Acad Repub Pop Roum ... Revue de Physique. Academie de la Republique Populaire Roumaine [*Romania*] [*A publication*]
Rev Phys Ap ... Revue de Physique Appliquee [*A publication*]
Rev Phys Appl ... Revue de Physique Appliquee [*A publication*]
Rev Phys Appl (Suppl J Phys) ... Revue de Physique Appliquee (Supplement to Journal de Physique) [*A publication*]
Rev Phys B ... Reviews of Physiology, Biochemistry, and Pharmacology [*A publication*]
Rev Phys Chem Jpn ... Review of Physical Chemistry of Japan [*A publication*]
Rev Physiol Biochem Exp Pharmacol ... Reviews of Physiology, Biochemistry, and Experimental Pharmacology [*A publication*]
Rev Physiol Biochem Pharmacol ... Reviews of Physiology, Biochemistry, and Pharmacology [*A publication*]
Rev Phys Technol ... Review of Physics in Technology [*United Kingdom*] [*A publication*]
Rev Plant Pathol ... Review of Plant Pathology [*A publication*]
Rev Plant Prot Res ... Review of Plant Protection Research [*A publication*]
Rev Plasma Phys ... Reviews of Plasma Physics [*A publication*]
Rev Plast (Madrid) ... Revista de Plasticos (Madrid) [*A publication*]
Rev Plast Mod ... Revista de Plasticos Modernos [*A publication*]
Rev Pol...... Review of Politics [*A publication*]
Rev Pol Acad Sci ... Review. Polish Academy of Sciences [*A publication*]
Rev Polarogr ... Review of Polarography [*A publication*]
Rev Polarogr (Jpn) ... Review of Polarography (Japan) [*A publication*]
Rev Policlin (Caracas) ... Revista de la Policlinica (Caracas) [*A publication*]
Rev of Polish Law and Econ ... Review of Polish Law and Economics [*Warsaw, Poland*] (DLA)
Rev Polit..... Review of Politics [*A publication*]

Rev Politec ... Revista Politecnica [*A publication*]
Rev Polym Technol ... Reviews in Polymer Technology [*A publication*]
Rev Polytech ... Revue Polytechnique [*Switzerland*] [*A publication*]
Rev Po Quim ... Revista Portuguesa de Quimica [*A publication*]
Rev Port Cienc Vet ... Revista Portuguesa de Ciencias Veterinarias [*A publication*]
Rev Port Estomatol Cir Maxilofac ... Revista Portuguesa de Estomatologia e Cirurgia Maxilofacial [*A publication*]
Rev Port Farm ... Revista Portuguesa de Farmacia [*A publication*]
Rev Port Filosof ... Revista Portuguesa de Filosofia [*A publication*]
Rev Port Pediatr ... Revista Portuguesa de Pediatria [*A publication*]
Rev Port Quim ... Revista Portuguesa de Quimica [*A publication*]
Rev Port Quim (Lisbon) ... Revista Portuguesa de Quimica (Lisbon) [*A publication*]
Rev Port Zool Biol Geral ... Revista Portuguesa de Zoologia e Biologia Geral [*A publication*]
Rev Powder Metall Phys Ceram ... Reviews on Powder Metallurgy and Physical Ceramics [*A publication*]
Rev PR .... Revista de Derecho Puertorriqueno [*A publication*]
Rev Prat ..... Revue du Praticien [*A publication*]
Rev Prat Biol Appl Clin Ther ... Revue Pratique de Biologie Appliquee a la Clinique et a la Therapeutique [*A publication*]
Rev Prat Controle Ind ... Revue Pratique du Controle Industriel [*France*] [*A publication*]
Rev Prat Froid ... Revue Pratique du Froid [*France*] [*Later, Journal RPF*] [*A publication*]
Rev Prat Froid Cond Air ... Revue Pratique du Froid et du Conditionnement de l'Air [*Later, Journal RPF*] [*A publication*]
Rev Prat Mal Pays Chands ... Revue Pratique des Maladies des Pays Chands [*A publication*]
REV PROC ... Revenue Procedure [*Internal Revenue Service*]
Rev Prod Chim ... Revue des Produits Chimiques [*A publication*]
Rev Prod Chim Actual Sci Reunis ... Revue des Produits Chimiques et l'Actualite Scientifique Reunis [*A publication*]
Rev Prog Color Relat Top ... Review of Progress in Coloration and Related Topics [*A publication*]
Rev Prot ..... Revue de la Protection [*France*] [*A publication*]
Rev Prum Obchodu ... Revue Prumyslu a Obchodu [*Czechoslovakia*] [*A publication*]
Rev Psicol ... Revista de Psicologia [*A publication*]
Rev Psicol Gen Apl ... Revista de Psicologia General y Aplicada [*A publication*]
Rev Psiquiatr ... Revista de Psiquiatria [*A publication*]
Rev Psiquiatr Peru ... Revista Psiquiatrica Peruana [*A publication*]
Rev Psy App ... Revue de Psychologie Appliquee [*A publication*]
Rev Pub Dat ... Review of Public Data Use [*A publication*]
Rev Pub Data Use ... Review of Public Data Use [*A publication*]
Rev Pure Appl Chem ... Reviews of Pure and Applied Chemistry [*A publication*]
Rev Pure Appl Pharmacol Sci ... Reviews in Pure and Applied Pharmacological Sciences [*A publication*]
Rev Quest Sci ... Revue des Questions Scientifiques [*A publication*]
Rev Quim Farm (Rio De Janeiro) ... Revista de Quimica e Farmacia (Rio De Janeiro) [*A publication*]
Rev Quim Farm (Santiago) ... Revista Quimico-Farmaceutica (Santiago) [*A publication*]
Rev Quim Farm (Tegucigalpa) ... Revista de Quimica y Farmacia (Tegucigalpa) [*A publication*]
Rev Quim Ind (Buenos Aires) ... Revista de Quimica Industrial (Buenos Aires) [*A publication*]
Rev Quim Ind (Rio De Janeiro) ... Revista de Quimica Industrial (Rio De Janeiro) [*A publication*]
Rev Quim Ing Quim ... Revista de Quimica e Ingenieria Quimica [*A publication*]
Rev Quim Pura Apl ... Revista de Quimica Pura e Aplicada [*A publication*]
Rev Quim Text ... Revista de Quimica Textil [*A publication*]
RevQum ..... Revue de Qumran [*A publication*]
REVR .... Receiver (AAG)
REVR .... Reversioner (ROG)
REVR .... Reviewer (AFM)
Rev R .... Revised Reports [*1759-1866*] [*England*] (DLA)
RevR .... Revue Romane [*A publication*]
Rev R Acad Cienc Exactas Fis Nat Madr ... Revista. Real Academia de Ciencias Exactas, Fisicas, y Naturales de Madrid [*A publication*]
Rev R Acad Farm Barcelona ... Revista. Real Academia de Farmacia de Barcelona [*A publication*]
Rev Radio Res Lab ... Review. Radio Research Laboratories [*A publication*]
Rev React Species Chem React ... Reviews on Reactive Species in Chemical Reactions [*A publication*]
Rev Real Acad Ci Exact Fis Natur Madrid ... Revista. Real Academia de Ciencias Exactas, Fisicas, y Naturales de Madrid [*A publication*]
Rev Reh ...... Reversed [*or Reversing*] on Rehearing [*Used in Shepard's Citations*] (DLA)
Rev Relig .... Review for Religious [*A publication*]
Rev Rel Res ... Review of Religious Research [*A publication*]
Rev Rep ...... Revised Reports [*England*] (DLA)
Rev Revs Australas Ed ... Review of Reviews. Australasian Edition [*A publication*]

Rev Rhum ... Revue du Rhumatisme et des Maladies Osteo-Articulaires [*A publication*]
Rev Rhum Mal Osteo-Artic ... Revue du Rhumatisme et des Maladies Osteo-Articulaires [*A publication*]
Rev River Plate ... Review of the River Plate [*A publication*]
Rev Ro Bioc ... Revue Roumaine de Biochimie [*A publication*]
Rev "Roche" Farm ... Revista "Roche" de Farmacia [*A publication*]
Rev Ro Chim ... Revue Roumaine de Chimie [*A publication*]
Rev Romande Agric Vitic Arboric ... Revue Romande d'Agriculture, de Viticulture, et d'Arboriculture [*A publication*]
Rev Romande Agr Viticult Arboricult ... Revue Romande d'Agriculture, de Viticulture, et d'Arboriculture [*A publication*]
Rev Ro Phys ... Revue Roumaine de Physique [*A publication*]
Rev Roumaine Linguist ... Revue Roumaine de Linguistique [*A publication*]
Rev Roumaine Math Pures Appl ... Revue Roumaine de Mathematiques Pures et Appliquees [*A publication*]
Rev Roumaine Sci Soc ... Revue Roumaine des Sciences Sociales. Serie de Sciences Juridiques [*A publication*]
Rev Roumaine Sci Tech Ser Electrotech Energet ... Revue Roumaine des Sciences Techniques. Serie Electrotechnique et Energetique [*A publication*]
Rev Roum Biochim ... Revue Roumaine de Biochimie [*A publication*]
Rev Roum Biol ... Revue Roumaine de Biologie [*A publication*]
Rev Roum Biol Ser Biol Veg ... Revue Roumaine de Biologie. Serie Biologie Vegetale [*Romania*] [*A publication*]
Rev Roum Biol Ser Bot ... Revue Roumaine de Biologie. Serie Botanique [*A publication*]
Rev Roum Biol Ser Zool ... Revue Roumaine de Biologie. Serie Zoologie [*A publication*]
Rev Roum Chim ... Revue Roumaine de Chimie [*A publication*]
Rev Roum Embryol ... Revue Roumaine d'Embryologie [*A publication*]
Rev Roum Embryol Cytol Ser Embryol ... Revue Roumaine d'Embryologie et de Cytologie. Serie d'Embryologie [*A publication*]
Rev Roum Endocrinol ... Revue Roumaine d'Endocrinologie [*A publication*]
Rev Roum Geol Geophys Geogr Ser Geogr ... Revue Roumaine de Geologie, Geophysique, et Geographie. Serie de Geographie [*A publication*]
Rev Roum Geol Geophys Geogr Ser Geol ... Revue Roumaine de Geologie, Geophysique, et Geographie. Serie de Geologie [*A publication*]
Rev Roum Geol Geophys Geogr Ser Geophys ... Revue Roumaine de Geologie, Geophysique, et Geographie. Serie de Geophysique [*A publication*]
Rev Roum Inframicrobiol ... Revue Roumaine d'Inframicrobiologie [*A publication*]
Rev Roum Math Pures Appl ... Revue Roumaine de Mathematiques Pures et Appliquees [*A publication*]
Rev Roum Med ... Revue Roumaine de Medecine [*A publication*]
Rev Roum Med Endocrinol ... Revue Roumaine de Medecine. Endocrinologie [*A publication*]
Rev Roum Med Interne ... Revue Roumaine de Medecine Interne [*Later, Revue Roumaine de Medecine. Medecine Interne*] [*A publication*]
Rev Roum Med Med Interne ... Revue Roumaine de Medecine. Medecine Interne [*A publication*]
Rev Roum Med Neurol Psychiatr ... Revue Roumaine de Medecine. Neurologie et Psychiatrie [*A publication*]
Rev Roum Med Virol ... Revue Roumaine de Medecine. Virologie [*A publication*]
Rev Roum Metall ... Revue Roumaine de Metallurgie [*A publication*]
Rev Roum Morphol Embryol ... Revue Roumaine de Morphologie et d'Embryologie [*A publication*]
Rev Roum Morphol Embryol Physiol Morphol Embryol ... Revue Roumaine de Morphologie, d'Embryologie, et de Physiologie. Morphologie et Embryologie [*A publication*]
Rev Roum Morphol Embryol Physiol Physiol ... Revue Roumaine de Morphologie, d'Embryologie, et de Physiologie. Physiologie [*A publication*]
Rev Roum Neurol ... Revue Roumaine de Neurologie [*Later, Revue Roumaine de Medecine. Serie Neurologie et Psychiatrie*] [*A publication*]
Rev Roum Neurol Psychiatr ... Revue Roumaine de Neurologie et de Psychiatrie [*Later, Revue Roumaine de Medecine. Serie Neurologie et Psychiatrie*] [*A publication*]
Rev Roum Phys ... Revue Roumaine de Physique [*A publication*]
Rev Roum Physiol ... Revue Roumaine de Physiologie [*Later, Revue Roumaine de Morphologie, d'Embryologie, et de Physiologie*] [*A publication*]
Rev Roum Sci Soc (Philos Logique) ... Revue Roumaine des Sciences Sociales (Philosophie et Logique) [*A publication*]
Rev Roum Sci Tech Ser Electrotech Energ ... Revue Roumaine des Sciences Techniques. Serie Electrotechnique et Energetique [*A publication*]
Rev Roum Sci Tech Ser Mec Appl ... Revue Roumaine des Sciences Techniques. Serie de Mecanique Appliquee [*A publication*]
Rev Roum Sci Tech Ser Met ... Revue Roumaine des Sciences Techniques. Serie de Metallurgie [*A publication*]
Rev Roum Virol ... Revue Roumaine de Virologie [*A publication*]
REV RUL .... Revenue Ruling [*Internal Revenue Service*]
REVS .... Reconnaissance Electro-Optical Viewing System
REVS .... Requirements Engineering and Validation System

REVS .... Rotor Entry Vehicle System [*Aerospace*]
Rev Sanid Fuerzas Policiales ... Revista de la Sanidad de las Fuerzas Policiales [*A publication*]
Rev Sanid Hig Publica ... Revista de Sanidad e Higiene Publica [*A publication*]
Rev Sanid Hig Publica (Madr) ... Revista de Sanidad e Higiene Publica (Madrid) [*A publication*]
Rev Sanid Mil (Argent) ... Revista de la Sanidad Militar (Argentina) [*A publication*]
Rev Sanid Polic ... Revista de la Sanidad de Policia [*A publication*]
Rev Sanit Mil ... Revista Sanitara Militara [*A publication*]
Rev San Mil (Buenos Aires) ... Revista de la Sanidad Militar (Buenos Aires) [*A publication*]
Rev Sao Paulo Braz Univ Fac Med Vet Zootec ... Revista. Sao Paulo Universidade. Faculdade de Medicina Veterinaria e Zootecnia [*A publication*]
Rev Saude ... Revista Saude [*A publication*]
Rev Saude Publica ... Revista de Saude Publica [*A publication*]
Rev Sci .... Revue Scientifique [*A publication*]
Rev Sci Bourbonnais Cent Fr ... Revue Scientifique du Bourbonnais et du Centre de la France [*A publication*]
Rev de Sci Criminelle et de Droit Penal Compare ... Revue de Science Criminelle et de Droit Penal Compare [*Paris, France*] (DLA)
Rev Scient (Paris) ... Revue Scientifique (Paris) [*A publication*]
Rev Sci Hum ... Revue des Sciences Humaines [*A publication*]
Rev Sci Ins ... Review of Scientific Instruments [*A publication*]
Rev Sci Instrum ... Review of Scientific Instruments [*A publication*]
Rev Sci Med ... Revue des Sciences Medicales [*A publication*]
Rev Sci Nat Auvergne ... Revue des Sciences Naturelles d'Auvergne [*A publication*]
Rev Sci Natur Auvergne ... Revue des Sciences Naturelles d'Auvergne [*A publication*]
Rev Sci Phil Theol ... Revue des Sciences Philosophiques et Theologiques [*A publication*]
Rev Sci Rel ... Revue des Sciences Religieuses [*A publication*]
RevScPhTh ... Revue des Sciences Philosophiques et Theologiques [*A publication*]
RevScR ...... Regue des Sciences Religieuses [*Strasbourg/Paris*] [*A publication*]
RevScRel ... Revue des Sciences Religieuses [*Strasbourg/Paris*] [*A publication*]
Rev Sel Code Leg ... Review of Selected Code Legislation (DLA)
Rev Serv Espec Saude Publica ... Revista. Servicio Especial de Saude Publica [*A publication*]
Rev Serv Nac Min Geol (Argent) ... Revista. Servicio Nacional Minero Geologico (Argentina) [*A publication*]
Rev Serv Nac Salud ... Revista. Servicio Nacional de Salud [*A publication*]
Rev SESP ... Revista. Servicio Especial de Saude Publica [*A publication*]
Rev Sifilogr Leprol Dermatol ... Revista de Sifilografia, Leprologia, y Dermatologia [*A publication*]
Rev Silicon Germanium Tin Lead Compd ... Reviews on Silicon, Germanium, Tin, and Lead Compounds [*A publication*]
Rev Sind Estad ... Revista Sindical de Estadistica [*A publication*]
Rev Soc Argent Biol ... Revista. Sociedad Argentina de Biologia [*A publication*]
Rev Soc Argent Neurol y Psiquiat ... Revista. Sociedad Argentina de Neurologia y Psiquiatria [*A publication*]
Rev Soc Biom Hum ... Revue. Societe de Biometre Humaine [*A publication*]
Rev Soc Boliv Hist Nat ... Revista. Sociedad Boliviana de Historia Natural [*A publication*]
Rev Soc Bras Agron ... Revista. Sociedade Brasileira de Agronomia [*A publication*]
Rev Soc Bras Med Trop ... Revista. Sociedade Brasileira de Medicina Tropical [*A publication*]
Rev Soc Bras Quim ... Revista. Sociedade Brasileira de Quimica [*A publication*]
Rev Soc Bras Zootec ... Revista. Sociedade Brasileira de Zootecnia [*A publication*]
Rev Soc Cient Parag ... Revista. Sociedad Cientifica del Paraguay [*A publication*]
Rev Soc Colomb Endocrinol ... Revista. Sociedad Colombiana de Endocrinologia [*A publication*]
Rev Soc Cubana Bot ... Revista. Sociedad Cubana de Botanica [*A publication*]
Rev Soc Cubana Ing ... Revista. Sociedad Cubana de Ingenieros [*A publication*]
Rev Soc Ec ... Review of Social Economy [*A publication*]
Rev Soc Entomol Argent ... Revista. Sociedad Entomologica Argentina [*A publication*]
Rev Soc L ... Review of Socialist Law [*A publication*]
Rev Soc Med Argent ... Revista. Sociedad Medica Argentina [*A publication*]
Rev Soc Med Cir Sao Jose Rio Preto ... Revista. Sociedade de Medicina e Cirurgia de Sao Jose Do Rio Preto [*A publication*]
Rev Soc Med Int ... Revista. Sociedad de Medicina Interna [*A publication*]
Rev Soc Med Vet (Buenos Aires) ... Revista. Sociedad de Medicina Veterinaria (Buenos Aires) [*A publication*]
Rev Soc Med Vet Chile ... Revista. Sociedad de Medicina Veterinaria de Chile [*A publication*]
Rev Soc Mex Hist Nat ... Revista. Sociedad Mexicana de Historia Natural [*A publication*]

Rev Soc Mex Hist Natur ... Revista. Sociedad Mexicana de Historia Natural [*A publication*]
Rev Soc Mex Lepidopterol AC ... Revista. Sociedad Mexicana de Lepidopterologia AC [*A publication*]
Rev Soc Pediatr Litoral ... Revista. Sociedad de Pediatria del Litoral [*A publication*]
Rev Soc Quim Mex ... Revista. Sociedad Quimica de Mexico [*A publication*]
Rev Soc R Belge Ing Ind ... Revue. Societe Royale Belge des Ingenieurs et des Industriels [*A publication*]
Rev Soc Rural Rosario ... Revista. Sociedad Rural de Rosario [*A publication*]
Rev Soc Sci Hyg Aliment Aliment Ration Homme ... Revue. Societe Scientifique d'Hygiene Alimentaire et de l'Alimentation Rationnelle de l'Homme [*A publication*]
Rev Soc Venez Cardiol ... Revista. Sociedad Venezolana de Cardiologia [*A publication*]
Rev Soc Venez Hist Med ... Revista. Sociedad Venezolana de Historia de la Medicina [*A publication*]
Rev Soc Venez Quim ... Revista. Sociedad Venezolana de Quimica [*A publication*]
Rev Soldadura ... Revista de Soldadura [*A publication*]
Rev Soudre Lastijdschrift ... Revue de la Soudure/Lastijdschrift [*A publication*]
Rev Soudure ... Revue de la Soudure/Lastijdschrift [*Brussels*] [*A publication*]
Rev Soudure Autogene ... Revue de la Soudure Autogene [*A publication*]
Rev Soudure/Lastijdschrift ... Revue de la Soudure/Lastijdschrift [*A publication*]
Rev Sov Med Sci ... Review of Soviet Medical Sciences [*A publication*]
Rev Sport Leisure ... Review of Sport and Leisure [*A publication*]
RevSR .... Revue des Sciences Religieuses [*Strasbourg/Paris*] [*A publication*]
Rev St .... Revised Statutes (DLA)
Rev Stat ..... Revised Statutes [*Various jurisdictions*] (DLA)
Rev Stat Ap ... Revue de Statistique Applique [*A publication*]
Rev Stomatol ... Revue de Stomatologie [*France*] [*Later, Revue de Stomatologie et de Chirurgie Maxillo-Faciale*] [*A publication*]
Rev Stomatol Chir Maxillo-Fac ... Revue de Stomatologie et de Chirurgie Maxillo-Faciale [*A publication*]
Rev Stomato-Odontol Nord Fr ... Revue Stomato-Odontologique du Nord de la France [*A publication*]
Rev Sudam Bot ... Revista Sudamericana de Botanica [*A publication*]
Rev Sud-Am Cien Med ... Revista Sud-Americana de Ciencias Medicas [*A publication*]
Rev Sud-Am Endocrin ... Revista Sud-Americana de Endocrinologia [*A publication*]
Rev Sud-Am Endocrinol Immunol Quimioter ... Revista Sud-Americana de Endocrinologia, Immunologia, y Quimioterapia [*A publication*]
Rev Sudam Morfol ... Revista Sudamericana de Morfologia [*A publication*]
Rev Suisse Agric ... Revue Suisse d'Agriculture [*A publication*]
Rev Suisse Dr Int'l Concurrence ... Revue Suisse du Droit International de la Concurrence [*Swiss Review of International Antitrust Law*] (DLA)
Rev Suisse Gynecol Obstet ... Revue Suisse de Gynecologie et d'Obstetrique [*A publication*]
Rev Suisse Gynecol Obstet Suppl ... Revue Suisse de Gynecologie et d'Obstetrique. Supplementum [*A publication*]
Rev Suisse Hydrol ... Revue Suisse d'Hydrologie [*A publication*]
Rev Suisse Med Sports ... Revue Suisse de Medecine des Sports [*A publication*]
Rev Suisse Psychol Pure Appl ... Revue Suisse de Psychologie Pure et Appliquee [*A publication*]
Rev Suisse Vitic Arboric ... Revue Suisse de Viticulture et Arboriculture [*A publication*]
Rev Suisse Vitic Arboric Hortic ... Revue Suisse de Viticulture et Arboriculture. Horticulture [*A publication*]
Rev Suisse Zool ... Revue Suisse de Zoologie [*A publication*]
Rev Surg .... Review of Surgery [*A publication*]
Rev Syniatrica ... Revista Syniatrica [*A publication*]
Revta Agric (Habana) ... Revista de Agricultura (Habana) [*A publication*]
Revta Agric (Piracicaba) ... Revista de Agricultura (Piracicaba) [*A publication*]
Revta Agron NE Argent ... Revista Agronomica del Noroeste Argentino [*A publication*]
Revta Biol ... Revista de Biologia [*A publication*]
Revta Biol Trop ... Revista de Biologia Tropical [*A publication*]
Revta Bras Biol ... Revista Brasileira de Biologia [*A publication*]
Revta Bras Ent ... Revista Brasileira de Entomologia [*A publication*]
Revta Ent (Rio De J) ... Revista de Entomologia (Rio De Janeiro) [*A publication*]
Revta Esp Fisiol ... Revista Espanola de Fisiologia [*A publication*]
Revta Fac Agron Univ Cent Venez ... Revista. Facultad de Agronomia. Universidad Central de Venezuela [*A publication*]
Revta Fac Agron Univ Nac La Plata ... Revista. Facultad de Agronomia y Veterinaria. Universidad Nacional de La Plata [*A publication*]
Revta Fac Agron Univ Repub (Urug) ... Revista. Facultad de Agronomia. Universidad de la Republica (Uruguay) [*A publication*]
Revta Fac Agron Vet Univ B Aires ... Revista. Facultad de Agronomia y Veterinaria. Universidad de Buenos Aires [*A publication*]

Revta Fac Cienc Agrar Univ Nac Cuyo ... Revista. Facultad de Ciencias Agrarias. Universidad Nacional de Cuyo [*A publication*]

Revta Fac Farm Bioquim S Paulo ... Revista. Faculdade de Farmacia e Bioquimica. Universidade de Sao Paulo [*A publication*]

Revta Floresta ... Revista Floresta [*A publication*]

Revta Hort Vitic ... Revista de Horticultura si Viticultura [*A publication*]

Revta Ind Agric (Tucuman) ... Revista Industrial y Agricola (Tucuman) [*A publication*]

Revta Interam Psicologia ... Revista Interamericana de Psicologia [*A publication*]

Revta Invest Agropec (B Aires) ... Revista de Investigaciones Agropecuarias (Buenos Aires) [*A publication*]

Revta Med Vet Parasit (Caracas) ... Revista de Medicina Veterinaria y Parasitologia (Caracas) [*A publication*]

Revta Mus Argent Cienc Nat Bernardina Rivadavia Zool ... Revista. Museo Argentino de Ciencias Naturales Bernardino Rivadavia. Zoologia [*A publication*]

Revta Padur ... Revista Padurilor [*A publication*]

Revta Univ Univ Catol Chile ... Revista Universitaria. Universidad Catolica de Chile [*A publication*]

Rev & TC .... Revenue and Taxation Code (DLA)

Rev Tec ...... Revista Tecnica [*A publication*]

Rev Tec Col Ing Agron Mex ... Revista Tecnica. Colegio de Ingenieros Agronomos de Mexico [*A publication*]

Rev Tech Batim Constr Ind ... Revue Technique du Batiment et des Constructions Industrielles [*France*] [*A publication*]

Rev Tech Ind Aliment ... Revue Technique de l'Industrie Alimentaire [*A publication*]

Rev Tech Ind Cuir ... Revue Technique des Industries du Cuir [*A publication*]

Rev Tech Luxemb ... Revue Technique Luxembourgeoise [*A publication*]

Rev Tech Thomson CSF ... Revue Technique Thomson - CSF [*A publication*]

Rev Tec Inst Nac Electron ... Revista Tecnica. Instituto Nacional de Electronica [*A publication*]

Rev Tec Intevep ... Revista Tecnica INTEVEP [*Instituto de Tecnologia Venezolana del Petroleo*] [*A publication*]

Rev Tec Sulzer ... Revista Tecnica Sulzer [*Switzerland*] [*A publication*]

Rev Tec Yacimientos Pet Fiscales Boliv ... Revista Tecnica. Yacimientos Petroliferos Fiscales Bolivianos [*A publication*]

Rev Tec Zulia Univ ... Revista Tecnica. Zulia University [*A publication*]

Rev Teilhard de Chardin ... Revue Teilhard de Chardin [*A publication*]

Rev Telecommun ... Revue des Telecommunications [*France*] [*A publication*]

Rev Telecomun (Madrid) ... Revista de Telecomunicacion (Madrid) [*A publication*]

Rev Telegr Electron ... Revista Telegrafica Electronica [*A publication*]

Rev Text (Ghent) ... Revue Textilis (Ghent) [*A publication*]

Rev Textile Progr ... Review of Textile Progress [*A publication*]

Rev Text (Paris) ... Revue Textile (Paris) [*A publication*]

Rev Text Tiba ... Revue Textile Tiba [*A publication*]

Rev Theobroma ... Revista Theobroma [*A publication*]

Rev Theol Phil ... Revue de Theologie et de Philosophie [*A publication*]

Rev Ther .... Revue Therapeutique [*A publication*]

Rev Therap Med-Chir ... Revue de Therapeutique Medico-Chirurgicale [*A publication*]

Rev Thomiste ... Revue Thomiste [*A publication*]

Rev Tisiol Neumonol ... Revista de Tisiologia y Neumonologia [*A publication*]

Rev Trab .... Revista de Trabajo [*A publication*]

Rev Trach ... Revue du Trachome [*A publication*]

Rev Transp Telecommun ... Revista Transporturilor si Telecommunicatiilor [*Romania*] [*A publication*]

Rev Trav Inst Peches Marit ... Revue des Travaux. Institut des Peches Maritimes [*A publication*]

Rev Trimest Can ... Revue Trimestrielle Canadienne [*A publication*]

Rev Trimestr de Droit Eur ... Revue Trimestrielle de Droit Europeen [*A publication*]

Rev Trimestrielle Canadienne ... Revue Trimestrielle Canadienne [*A publication*]

Rev Trimestr de Jurispr ... Revista Trimestral de Jurisprudencia [*Rio De Janeiro, Brazil*] (DLA)

Rev Tuberc ... Revue de Tuberculose [*A publication*]

Rev Tuberc Pneumol ... Revue de Tuberculose et de Pneumologie [*Later, Revue Francaise des Maladies Respiratoires*] [*A publication*]

Rev Tunisienne de Droit ... Revue Tunisienne de Droit [*Tunis, Tunisia*] (DLA)

Rev Turq Hyg Biol Exp ... Revue Turque d'Hygiene et de Biologie Experimentale [*A publication*]

Rev Tussock Grassl Mt Lands Inst ... Review. Tussock Grasslands and Mountain Lands Institute [*A publication*]

Revue Agric (Brux) ... Revue de l'Agriculture (Bruxelles) [*A publication*]

Revue Agric Nouv Caled ... Revue Agricole de la Nouvelle-Caledonie et Dependances [*A publication*]

Revue Can Biol ... Revue Canadienne de Biologie [*A publication*]

Revue Comp Anim ... Revue du Comportement Animal [*A publication*]

Revue Ferment Ind Aliment ... Revue des Fermentations et des Industries Alimentaires [*A publication*]

Revue Gen Bot ... Revue Generale de Botanique [*A publication*]

Revue Gen Gaz ... Revue Generale du Gaz [*Belgium*] [*A publication*]

Revue Geogr Phys Geol Dyn ... Revue de Geographie Physique et de Geologie Dynamique [*A publication*]

Revue Geol Dyn Geogr Phys ... Revue de Geologie Dynamique et de Geographie Physique [*France*] [*A publication*]

Revue Lux ... Revue Trimestrielle d'Etudes Linguistiques, Folkloriques, et Toponymiques (Luxembourg) [*A publication*]

Revue Med Liege ... Revue Medicale de Liege [*A publication*]

Revue Med Vet ... Revue Medicale et Veterinaire [*A publication*]

Revue Oka ... Revue d'Oka. Agronomie. Medicine. Veterinaire [*A publication*]

Revue Path Comp Hyg Gen ... Revue de Pathologie Comparee et Hygiene Generale [*A publication*]

Revue Path Gen Physiol Clin ... Revue de Pathologie Generale et de Physiologie Clinique [*A publication*]

Revue Path Veg Ent Agric Fr ... Revue de Pathologie Vegetale et d'Entomologie Agricole de France [*A publication*]

Revue Quest Scient ... Revue des Questions Scientifiques [*A publication*]

Revue Romande Agric Vitic Arboric ... Revue Romande d'Agriculture, de Viticulture, et d'Arboriculture [*A publication*]

Revue Roum Biochim ... Revue Roumaine de Biochimie [*A publication*]

Revue Roum Biol Ser Bot ... Revue Roumaine de Biologie. Serie Botanique [*A publication*]

Revue Zool Agric Appl ... Revue de Zoologie Agricole et Appliquee [*A publication*]

Revue Zool Bot Afr ... Revue de Zoologie et de Botanique Africaines [*A publication*]

Rev Un B .... Revue. Universite de Bruxelles [*A publication*]

Rev Uniao Pharm (Sao Paulo) ... Revista Uniao Pharmaceutica (Sao Paulo) [*A publication*]

Rev Union Mat Argent ... Revista. Union Matematica Argentina [*A publication*]

Rev Union Mat Argent Asoc Fis Argent ... Revista. Union Matematica Argentina y Asociacion Fisica Argentina [*A publication*]

Rev Univ Al I Cuza Inst Politeh Iasi ... Revista Universitati "Al. I. Cuza" si a Institutului Politehnic din Iasi [*A publication*]

Rev Univ Cauca ... Revista. Universidad del Cauca [*A publication*]

Rev Univ C I Parhon Politeh Bucuresti Ser Stiint Nat ... Revista Universitatii "C. I. Parhon" si a Politehnicii Bucuresti. Seria Stiintelor Naturii [*A publication*]

Rev Univers Mines Metall Mec ... Revue Universelle des Mines, de la Metallurgie, de la Mecanique, des Travaux Publics, des Sciences, et des Arts Appliques a l'Industrie [*A publication*]

Rev Univ Fed Para Ser II ... Revista. Universidade Federal do Para. Serie II [*A publication*]

Rev Univ Ind Santander ... Revista. Universidad Industrial de Santander [*A publication*]

Rev Univ Ind Santander Invest ... Revista. Universidad Industrial de Santander. Investigaciones [*A publication*]

Rev Univ Ind Santander Tecnolo ... Revista. Universidad Industrial de Santander. Tecnologia [*A publication*]

Rev Univ Los Andes (Bogota) ... Revista. Universidad de Los Andes (Bogota) [*A publication*]

Rev Univ Madrid ... Revista. Universidad de Madrid [*Spain*] [*A publication*]

Rev Univ Nac Cordoba ... Revista. Universidad Nacional de Cordoba [*A publication*]

Rev Univ Nac Tucuman Ser A ... Revista. Universidad Nacional de Tucuman. Serie A. Matematica y Fisica Teorica [*Argentina*] [*A publication*]

Rev Univ Ottawa ... Revue. Universite d'Ottawa [*A publication*]

Rev Univ Univ Nac Cuzco ... Revista Universitaria. Universidad Nacional del Cuzco [*A publication*]

Rev Univ Zulia (Maracaibo) ... Revista. Universidad del Zulia (Maracaibo) [*A publication*]

Rev Usem ... Revista Usem [*A publication*]

Rev Venez Cir ... Revista Venezolana de Cirugia [*A publication*]

Rev Venez Sanid Asist Soc ... Revista Venezolana de Sanidad y Asistencia Social [*A publication*]

Rev Venez Urol ... Revista Venezolana de Urologia [*A publication*]

Rev Ven Filosof ... Revista Venezolana de Filosofia [*A publication*]

Rev Ver Soie ... Revue du Ver a Soie [*A publication*]

Rev Vervietoise Hist Nat ... Revue Vervietoise d'Histoire Naturelle [*A publication*]

Rev Vet Can ... Revue Veterinaire Canadienne [*A publication*]

Rev Vet Zootec (Manizales) ... Revista de Veterinaria y Zootecnia (Manizales) [*A publication*]

Rev Vitic ..... Revue de Viticulture [*A publication*]

Rev Vivarais ... Revue du Vivarais [*A publication*]

REVW .... Review (NVT)

Rev World ... Revolutionary World [*A publication*]

Rev X .... Revue X [*Belgium*] [*A publication*]

REVY .... Reversionary (ROG)

Rev Zair Sci Nucl ... Revue Zairoise des Sciences Nucleaires [*Zaire*] [*A publication*]

Rev Zoo Agr ... Revue de Zoologie Agricole et de Pathologie Vegetale [*A publication*]

Rev Zool Afr ... Revue de Zoologie Africaine [*A publication*]

Rev Zool Agric Appl ... Revue de Zoologie Agricole et Appliquee [*A publication*]

Rev Zool Agric Pathol Veg ... Revue de Zoologie Agricole et de Pathologie Vegetale [*A publication*]

Rev Zool Bot Afr ... Revue de Zoologie et de Botanique Africaines [*A publication*]

Rev Zootec (B Aires) ... Revista Zootecnica (Buenos Aires) [*A publication*]

Rev Zooteh Med Vet ... Revista de Zootehnie si Medicina Veterinara [*A publication*]

REW .... Recycle Water [*Nuclear energy*]   (NRCH)
REW .... Redwood Valley, CA [*Location identifier*] [*FAA*]   (FAAL)
REW .... Reward   (AFM)
REW .... Rewind   (MDG)
REWDAC.... Retrieval by Title Words, Descriptors, and Classification   (DIT)
REWK .... Rework   (MSA)
REWRC ...... Report When Established Well to Right of Course
                       [*Aviation*]   (FAAC)
REWS .... Radio Electronic Warfare Service   (MCD)
REWSON.... Reconnaissance, Electronic Warfare, Special Operations, and
                       Naval Intelligence Processing Systems
REX .... Ram Air Freight, Inc. [*Hillsborough, NC*] [*FAA
                       designator*]   (FAAC)
REX .... Rare-Earth Exchanged [*Faujasite, a zeolite*]
REX .... Reactor Experimental [*USSR*]   (DEN)
REX .... Real-Time Executive Routine [*Data processing*]
REX .... Rechtswissenschaftliche Experten und Gutachter [*NOMOS
                       Datapool*] [*Database*]
REX .... Reduced Exoatmospheric Cross Section
REX .... Reentry Experiment
REX .... Reflector Erosion Experiment [*NASA*]
REX .... Requisition Exception Code [*Air Force*]   (AFIT)
R EX .... Review and Expositor [*A publication*]
REX .... Rex Silver Mines [*Vancouver Stock Exchange symbol*]
REX .... Rexburg [*Idaho*] [*Seismograph station code, US Geological
                       Survey*]   (SEIS)
REX .... Rexnord [*NYSE symbol*]
REX .... Reynosa [*Mexico*] [*Airport symbol*]   (OAG)
REX .... Robot Excavation [*Carnegie-Mellon Robotics Institute*]
REX .... Run Executive [*Data processing*]
REXC .... Reserve Exploration [*NASDAQ symbol*]   (NQ)
REXI .... Resource Exploration [*NASDAQ symbol*]   (NQ)
REXMIT ..... Retransmitted   (AABC)
REXN .... Rexon, Inc. [*NASDAQ symbol*]   (NQ)
Rexroth Inf ... Rexroth Informationen [*A publication*]
REXS........ Radio Exploration Satellite [*Japan*]
REY .... Reentry
REY .... Reyes [*Bolivia*] [*Airport symbol*]   (OAG)
REY .... Reykjavik [*Iceland*] [*Seismograph station code, US Geological
                       Survey*]   (SEIS)
REY .... Rush Ventures, Inc. [*Vancouver Stock Exchange symbol*]
Reyn.......... Reynolds, Reports [*40-42 Mississippi*]   (DLA)
REYNA ...... Reynolds & Reynolds [*NASDAQ symbol*]   (NQ)
Reynolds.... Reynolds, Reports [*40-42 Mississippi*]   (DLA)
Reynolds' Land Laws ... Reynolds' Spanish and Mexican Land Laws   (DLA)
Reyon Synth Zellwolle ... Reyon, Synthetica, Zellwolle [*A publication*]
Reyon Zellwolle Andere Chem Fasern ... Reyon, Zellwolle, und Andere
                       Chemie Fasern [*A publication*]
Reyrolle Parsons Rev ... Reyrolle Parsons Review [*A publication*]
REZ .... Mary Esther, FL [*Location identifier*] [*FAA*]   (FAAL)
Rezanie Instrum ... Rezanie i Instrument [*A publication*]
Re Zh Khim Neftepererab Polim Mashinostr ... Referativnyi Zhurnal.
                       Khimicheskoe. Neftepererabatyuayushchee i Polimerjnoe
                       Mashinostroenie [*A publication*]
Rezul't Issled Mezhdunar Geofiz Proektam ... Rezul'taty Issledovanyi po
                       Mezhdunarodny Geofizicheskim Proektam [*USSR*] [*A
                       publication*]
RF .... Franc [*Monetary unit in Rwanda*]
RF.............. Radial Fibers [*Ear anatomy*]
RF.............. Radial Flow   (AAG)
RF.............. Radical Force [*An association*]   (EA)
RF.............. Radio Facility
RF.............. Radio Frequency [*Transmission*]
RF.............. Rainform   (MCD)
RF.............. Raised Face   (MSA)
RF.............. Range-Finder [*Gunnery*]
R & F........ Rank and File
RF.............. Rapeseed Flour [*Food technology*]
RF.............. Rapid-Fire
RF.............. Rapports des Fouilles [*A publication*]
RF.............. Rating Factor   (IEEE)
RF.............. Razon y Fe [*A publication*]
RF.............. Read Forward
RF.............. Reason Foundation   (EA)
RF.............. Reception Fair [*Radio logs*]
RF.............. Receptive Field [*of visual cortex*]
RF.............. Reconnaissance Fighter   (MUGU)
RF.............. Reconnaissance Force
RF.............. Recovery Forces
RF.............. Recruitment for the Armed Forces [*British*]
RF.............. Red Fumes   (NATG)
RF.............. Reducing Flame
RF.............. Reef
RF.............. Reference [*Online database field identifier*]
RF.............. Reflight
RF.............. Refunding
RF.............. Regional Forces [*ARVN*]
RF.............. Register File
RF.............. Register Finder
RF .... Relative Flow [*Rate*]

Rf................ Relative to the Solvent Front [*Paper chromatography*]
                       [*Analytical chemistry*]
RF................ Release Factor   (NRCH)
RF................ Releasing Factor [*Also, RH*] [*Endocrinology*]
RF................ Reliability Factor
RF................ Renal Failure [*Medicine*]
RF................ Rent Free
RF................ Replacement Factor
RF................ Replicative Factor [*or Form*] [*Genetics*]
RF................ Reply Finding [*Nuclear energy*]   (NRCH)
RF................ Reporting File
RF................ Representative Fraction
RF................ Republique Francaise [*French Republic*]
RF................ Republique Francaise [*A publication*]
RF................ Reserve Force
RF................ Resistance Factor
RF................ Respectable Frere [*Worshipful Brother*] [*French*]
                       [*Freemasonry*]   (ROG)
RF................ Respiratory Failure [*Medicine*]
RF................ Response Factor
RF................ Retardation Factor
Rf................ Retention File [*IRS*]
RF................ Reticular Formation [*Sleep*]
RF................ Retroperitoneal Fibromatosis [*Oncology*]
RF................ Reverse Free
RF................ Revue de France [*A publication*]
RF................ Rex Francorum [*King of the Franks*] [*Latin*]
RF................ RFG Reiseflug und Industrieflug GmbH [*West Germany*] [*ICAO
                       designator*]   (FAAC)
RF................ Rheumatic Fever [*Medicine*]
RF................ Rheumatoid Factor [*Also known as IgM*] [*Immunology*]
RF................ Rhinal Fissure [*Anatomy*]
RF................ Rhodesian Front [*Later, Republican Front*]
RF................ Riboflavin [*Biochemistry*]
RF................ Rigging Fixtures   (MCD)
RF................ Right Field [*or Fielder*] [*Baseball*]
RF................ Right Foot
RF................ Right Forward [*Football*]
RF................ Right Front
RF................ Right Fullback [*Soccer*]
RF................ Rinforzando [*With Special Emphasis*] [*Music*]
RF................ Ring Frame
RF................ Ripple Factor
RF................ Rivista di Filologia e d'Istruzione Classica [*A publication*]
RF................ Rivista di Filosofia [*A publication*]
RF................ Rockefeller Foundation
RF................ Rodeo Foundation   (EA)
RF................ Roll Film [*Photography*]
RF................ Romanische Forschungen [*A publication*]
RF................ Rosicrucian Fellowship   (EA)
RF................ Rosicrucian Fraternity   (EA)
RF................ Rough Finish
RF................ Royal Fusiliers [*Military unit*] [*British*]
RF................ Ruch Filozoficzny [*A publication*]
RF................ Running Forward
Rf................ Rutherfordium [*Proposed name for chemical element 104*]
                       [*See also Ku*]
RF................ Sisters of St. Philip Neri Missionary Teachers [*Roman Catholic
                       religious order*]
RF1............. Federal Reserve Bank of Boston, Boston, MA [*OCLC
                       symbol*]   (OCLC)
RFA .... RADAR Filter Assembly
RFA .... Radiation Field Analyzer
RFA .... Radio Frequency Allocation   (MCD)
RFA .... Radio Frequency Amplifier
RFA .... Radio Frequency Attenuator   (MCD)
RFA .... Radio Frequency Authorizations [*Air Force*]
RFA .... Raleigh Flying Service, Inc. [*Morrisville, NC*] [*FAA
                       designator*]   (FAAC)
RFA .... Rapid Flow Analysis
RFA .... Recommendation for Acceptance   (AAG)
RFA .... Recurrent Fault Analysis [*Telecommunications*]   (TEL)
RFA .... Registered Fitness Appraiser [*Canadian Association of Sports
                       Sciences*]
RFA .... Regulatory Flexibility Act [*Environmental Protection Agency*]
RFA .... Relieved from Assigned [*Military*]
RFA .... Remote File Access
RFA .... Renewable Fuels Association   (EA)
RFA .... Request for Action   (KSC)
RFA .... Request for Alteration   (AAG)
RFA .... Request for Analysis
RFA .... Request Further Airways [*Aviation*]   (FAAC)
RFA .... Request for Grant Applications
RFA .... Reserve Forces Act
RFA .... Restrictive Fire Area [*Military*]   (AABC)
RFA .... Revue de la Franco-Ancienne [*A publication*]
RFA .... Right Femoral Artery [*Anatomy*]
RFA .... Right Frontoanterior [*A fetal position*] [*Obstetrics*]
RFA .... Rimfire Adapter   (MCD)
RFA .... Roll Follow-Up Amplifier
RFA .... Royal Field Artillery [*Military*] [*British*]

RFA .... Royal Fleet Auxiliary [*British*]
RFA .... Rural Forestry Assistance [*Program*] [*Forest Service*]
RFAA .... Relieved from Attached and Assigned [*Army*]
RFAAD ...... Revue Francaise d'Automatique, Informatique, et Recherche Operationnelle. Serie Automatique [*A publication*]
RFAC........ Royal Fine Art Commission [*British*]
RFACA .... Revista. Facultad de Ciencias Agrarias. Universidad Nacional de Cuyo [*A publication*]
R Fac Der (Caracas) ... Revista. Facultad de Derecho (Caracas) [*A publication*]
R Fac Der Mexico ... Revista. Facultad de Derecho de Mexico [*A publication*]
RFAD......... Released from Active Duty Not Result of Demobilization [*Navy*]
RFAD......... Request for Accelerated Delivery (MCD)
RFAED .... Readiness Forecast Authorization Equipment Data [*Air Force*] (AFM)
RFAF .... Request for Additional Fire (MCD)
RF/AFG..... Radio Frequency/Acoustic Firing Group [*Military*] (CAAL)
RFAGB ...... Riforma Agraria [*A publication*]
RFALA....... Revue Francaise d'Allergie [*A publication*]
RFALROU... Request Follow-Up Action on Listed Requisitions Indicated Still Outstanding in Unit [*Army*] (AABC)
RFAND ...... Revue Francaise d'Automatique, Informatique, et Recherche Operationnelle. Serie Analyse Numerique [*A publication*]
RFAO......... Rocky Flats Area Office [*Energy Research and Development Administration*]
RFAPA ...... Revista. Facultad de Agronomia. Universidad Nacional de La Plata [*A publication*]
RFAS......... Radio Frequency Attitude Sensor
RFASIX ..... Reserve Forces Act of 1955, Six Months Trainee
RFASS ...... Rapid Fire Artillery Support System (MCD)
RFAT .... Relieved from Attached [*Army*] (AABC)
RFATE ...... Radio Frequency Automatic Test Equipment (MCD)
RFATHREE ... Reserve Forces Act of 1955, Three Months Trainee
RFB .... Air-Cushion Vehicle built by Rhein Flugzeugbau [*West Germany*] [*Usually used in combination with numerals*]
RFB .... Ready for Baseline (NASA)
RFB .... Reason for Backlog [*Telecommunications*] (TEL)
RFB .... Recording for the Blind [*Princeton, NJ*] (EA)
RFB .... Recording for the Blind, Bethesda, MD [*OCLC symbol*] (OCLC)
RFB .... Reliability Functional Block
RFB .... Request for Bid (AFM)
RFB .... Retained Foreign Body [*Medicine*]
RFB .... Right Fullback [*Soccer*]
RFBA .... Reserve Forces Benefit Association [*Later, REA*] (EA)
RFBC......... River Forest Bancorp [*NASDAQ symbol*] (NQ)
RFBUB ...... Revista de Farmacia e Bioquimica. Universidade de Sao Paulo (Brazil) [*A publication*]
RFC .... Radio Facility Charts (MCD)
RFC .... Radio Frequency Chart (AAG)
RFC .... Radio Frequency Choke (AAG)
RFC .... Radio Frequency Compatibility
RFC .... Radio Frequency Crystal
RFC .... Railroad Freight Classification
RFC .... Rare Fruit Council [*Later, RFCI*] (EA)
RFC .... Reason for Change (MCD)
RFC .... Recirculation Flow Control [*Nuclear energy*] (NRCH)
RFC .... Reconstruction Finance Corporation [*Abolished, 1957*]
RFC .... Regenerative Fuel Cell
RFC .... Relative Force Capability (NATG)
RFC .... Religious Formation Conference (EA)
RFC .... Remote Food Carriers [*Army*] (INF)
RFC .... Request for Change (KSC)
RFC .... Request for Confirmation (MCD)
RFC .... Required Functional Capability [*Navy*]
RFC .... Research Facilities Center [*National Oceanic and Atmospheric Administration*]
RFC .... Residual Functional Capacity [*Social Security Administration*] (OICC)
RFC .... Resources for Communication [*Windsor, CA*] [*Information service*] (EISS)
RFC .... Retirement-for-Cause [*Program*] [*Air Force*]
RFC .... Revista de Folklore (Colombia) [*A publication*]
RFC .... River Forecast Center [*National Weather Service*] (NOAA)
RFC .... Rivista di Filologia Classica [*A publication*]
RFC .... Rivista di Filologia e d'Istruzione Classica [*A publication*]
RFC .... Rosette-Forming Cell [*Immunochemistry*]
RFC .... Royal Flying Corps [*Later, RAF*] [*British*]
RFC .... Rugby Football Club
RFCA......... Racing Fans Club of America (EA)
RFCA......... Reconstruction Finance Corporation Act [*Obsolete*]
RFCC......... Revista de Folklore. Organo de la Comision Nacional de Folklore (Colombia) [*A publication*]
RFCEA...... Revival Fires [*Christian Evangelizers Association*] (EA)
RFCG .... Radio Frequency Command Generator (MCD)
RFCI .... Rare Fruit Council International [*Formerly, RFC*] (EA)
RFCI .... Resilient Floor Covering Institute (EA)
RFCM........ Radio Frequency Control Monitor [*Formerly, RFU*] (MCD)
RFCMC ..... Reconstruction Finance Corporation Mortgage Company
RFCO .... Radio Frequency Checkout (AAG)
RFCO .... Revue des Facultes Catholiques de l'Ouest [*A publication*]
RFCP......... Radio Frequency Compatibility Program

RFCP........ Request for Computer Program (NASA)
RFCP........ Requests for Contractual Procurement (MUGU)
RFCR........ Refacer
RFCS........ Radio Frequency Carrier Shift (NVT)
RFCS........ Recirculation Flow Control System (NRCH)
RFCS........ Regenerative Fuel Cell Subsystem
RFCSEUSG ... Retirement Federation of Civil Service Employees of the United States Government [*Defunct*] (EA)
RFCT........ Report of Federal Cash Transactions (OICC)
RFD .... Radiation Flux Density
RFD .... Radio Frequency Demodulator
RFD .... Raised Face Diameter (MSA)
RFD .... Raised Foredeck
RFD .... Reactor Flight Demonstration
RFD .... Ready for Data (IEEE)
RFD .... Ready for Delivery (MUGU)
RFD .... Ready for Duty
RFD .... Reentry Flight Demonstration
RFD .... Refurbish for Delivery (MCD)
RFD .... Released for Delivery (NG)
RFD .... Reporting for Duty [*Air Force*]
RFD .... Request for Delivery
RFD .... Request for Deviation
RFD .... Request for Parts Disposition (MCD)
RFD .... Requirements Formulation Document [*NASA*] (NASA)
RFD .... Reserve Forces Duty [*Military*] (MCD)
RFD .... Residual Flux Density
RFD .... Rockford [*Illinois*] [*Airport symbol*] (OAG)
RFD .... Rural Free Delivery [*of mail*]
RFDA......... Request for Deviation Approval
RFDL......... Radio Frequency Data Link (MCD)
RFDS........ Royal Flying Doctor Service [*Australia*]
RFDT........ Reliability Failure Diagnostic Team (AAG)
RFDU........ Reconfiguration and Fault Detection Unit
RFE .... Radio Free Europe
RFE .... Radio Free Europe [*A publication*]
RFE .... Request for Effectivity (MCD)
RFE .... Request for Estimate (KSC)
RFE .... Request for Expenditure
RFE .... Revista de Filologia Espanola [*A publication*]
RFE .... Rutherfordton, NC [*Location identifier*] [*FAA*] (FAAL)
RFEA .... Radio Frequency Equipment Analyzer
RFEA .... Revue Francaise d'Etudes Americaines [*A publication*]
RFECA ...... Revue Francaise d'Etudes Cliniques et Biologiques [*A publication*]
RFED......... Research Facilities and Equipment Division [*NASA*] (MCD)
RFEHB...... Retired Federal Employees Health Benefits Program (MCD)
RFEI .... Request for Engineering Information (KSC)
RF/EMI...... Radio Frequency and Electromagnetic-Interference [*Telecommunications*]
RFEN........ Reef Energy Corp. [*NASDAQ symbol*] (NQ)
RFE/RL ..... Radio Free Europe/Radio Liberty [*Formerly, FEC, FEI, RLC*] [*Research center*] [*West Germany*] (EA)
RFF............ Radio Frequency Filter
RFF............ Radio Frequency Finder (NVT)
RFF............ Radio Frequency Fuze
RFF............ Random Force Field
RFF............ Ready for Ferry [*Navy*] (NVT)
RFF............ Recirculative Fluid Flow
RFF............ REFF, Inc. [*Toronto Stock Exchange symbol*]
RFF............ Refuge from Flood (ADA)
RFF............ Relative Failure Frequency
RFF............ Remote Fiber Fluorometer [*Instrumentation*]
RFF............ Research Flight Facility [*Air Force*]
RFF............ Resources for the Future
RFF............ Rift-Fracture-Fracture [*Geology*]
RFFD......... Radio Frequency Fault Detection
RFFLUP..... Revista. Faculdade de Filosofia e Letras. Universidade do Parana [*A publication*]
RFFO......... Request for Factory Order (MCD)
RFFSA....... Rede Ferroviaria Federal Sociedade Anonima [*Federal Railway Corporation*] [*Brazil*]
RFG .... RADAR Field Gradient (IEEE)
RFG .... Radio Frequency Generator
RFG .... Rapid-Fire Gun
RFG .... Rate and Free Gyro
RFG .... Receive Format Generator
RFG .... Refugio, TX [*Location identifier*] [*FAA*] (FAAL)
RFG .... Refunding [*Business and trade*]
RFG .... Reise und Industrieflug [*Airline*] [*West Germany*]
RFG .... Report Format Generator
RFG .... Roofing (AAG)
RFGN......... Refrigeration [*Charges*]
RFGND..... RoeFo. Fortschritte auf dem Gebiete der Roentgenstrahlen und der Nuklearmedizin [*A publication*]
RFGT........ Refrigerant (MSA)
RFH .... Radio Frequency Heating
RFH .... Raised Face Height (MSA)
RFH .... Revista de Filologia Hispanica [*A publication*]
RFH .... Royal Festival Hall [*London*]
RFH .... Royal Free Hospital (ROG)

RFHC......... Revista. Facultad de Humanidades y Ciencias [*A publication*]
RFHCO........ Rocket Fuel Handler Clothing Outfit [*Protective suit*]
RFHOM....... Revue Francaise d'Histoire d'Outre-Mer [*A publication*]
RFHSP........ Revista de Filologia e Historia (Sao Paulo) [*A publication*]
RFHT........... Radio Frequency Horn Technique
RFI............... RADAR Frequency Interferometer   (MCD)
RFI............... Radio Frequency Indicator
RFI............... Radio Frequency Interchange   (MDG)
RFI............... Radio Frequency Interference
RFI............... Rajneesh Foundation International   (EA)
RFI............... Ready for Installation   (MCD)
RFI............... Ready for Issue
RFI............... Regionalism and the Female Imagination [*A publication*]
RFI............... Relative Fluorescent Intensity [*Analytical chemistry*]
RFI............... Release for Issue   (MCD)
RFI............... Remote Facility Inquiry [*NASA*]   (KSC)
RFI............... Remote File Inquiry [*NASA*]   (NASA)
RFI............... Request for Information
RFI............... Request for Investigation
RFI............... Request for Issue
RFI............... Requested for Information
RFI............... Retail Floorcovering Institute [*Chicago, IL*]   (EA)
RFi............... Revista de Filosofia [*A publication*]
RFIC........... Rivista di Filologia e d'Istruzione Classica [*A publication*]
RFIF........... Refund Information File [*IRS*]
RFil............. Revista di Filosofia [*Torino*] [*A publication*]
RFil............. Russkaja Filologija [*A publication*]
R Filol Esp ... Revista de Filologia Espanola [*A publication*]
RFilos........ Rivista di Filosofia [*A publication*]
R Filoz .... Revista de Filozofie [*A publication*]
RFIM........... Radio Frequency Interference Meter
R Fins Publicas ... Revista de Financas Publicas [*A publication*]
RFIOA......... Revue Francaise d'Informatique et de Recherche Operationnelle [*A publication*]
RFIP .... Radio Frequency Impedance Probe
RF/IR.......... RADAR Frequency/Infrared Frequency   (IEEE)
RFISA........ Revista de Fisica [*A publication*]
RFIT........... Radio Frequency Interference Tests   (KSC)
RFJ.............. Radio Free Jazz [*A publication*]
RFJ.............. Radio Frequency Joint
RFJI............ Research Foundation for Jewish Immigration   (EA)
RFK .... Anguilla, MS [*Location identifier*] [*FAA*]   (FAAL)
RFK .... Radio Free Kabul   (EA-IO)
RFK .... Robert Francis Kennedy
RFKM .... Robert F. Kennedy Memorial [*An association*] [*Washington, DC*]   (EA)
RFL............. Radio Frequency Laboratories
RFL............. Radio Frequency Lens
RFL............. Reduced Focal Length
RFL............. Reflector
RFL............. Refuel   (AAG)
RFL............. Reports of Family Law [*A publication*]
RFL............. Requested Flight Level
RFL............. Reset Flux Level
RFL............. Resorcinol-Formaldehyde-Latex
RFL............. Restrictive Fire Line [*Military*]   (AABC)
RFL............. Revista. Faculdade de Letras. Universidade de Lisboa [*A publication*]
RFL............. Rough Field Landing
RFLD........... Radio Frequency Leakage Detector
RFL (2d) ..... Reports of Family Law Second Series [*A publication*]
RFLHGA..... Revue. Faculte de Langues, d'Histoire, et de Geographie. Universite d'Ankara [*A publication*]
RFLL........... Revista. Faculdade de Letras. Universidade de Lisboa [*A publication*]
RFLMN....... Rifleman   (AABC)
RFLP .... Restriction Fragment Length Polymorphism [*Genetics*]
R/FLR........ Rear Floor [*Automotive engineering*]
RFLUL........ Revista. Faculdade de Letras. Universidade de Lisboa [*A publication*]
RFLX .... Reflex   (MSA)
RFM............. Radio Frequency Management   (NOAA)
RFM............. Radio Frequency Monitoring [*Military*]   (CAAL)
RFM........... Reactive Factor Meter
RFM............ Refueling Mission [*Air Force*]
RFM........... Reserve Forces Modernization   (MCD)
RFM............ Revista de Filosofia (Madrid) [*A publication*]
RFM............ Roll Follow-Up Motor
RFM............ Roll Forming Machine
RFM............ Runway Friction Measurement [*Aviation*]
RFMA .... Reliability Figure of Merit Analysis
RFMC .... Regional Fishery Management Council [*Marine science*]   (MSC)
RFMO .... Radio Frequency Management Office   (MCD)
RFM Rev Fr Mec ... RFM, Revue Francaise de Mecanique [*A publication*]
RFMS .... Remote File Management System
RFMT .... Runway Friction Measurement Test [*Aviation*]
RFN .... Radio Frequency Noise
RFN .... Raufarhofn [*Iceland*] [*Airport symbol*]   (OAG)
RFN .... Registered Fever Nurse
RFN .... Remote Filter Niche   (NRCH)

RFN .... Rifleman
RFN .... Rivista di Filosofia Neo-Scolastica [*A publication*]
RFNA.......... Red Fuming Nitric Acid
RFNCC....... Regional Nuclear Fuel Cycle Centers
RFND.......... Refined   (MSA)
RFNG.......... Roofing
RFNM.......... Ready for Next Message
RFNS.......... Rivista di Filosofia Neo-Scolastica [*A publication*]
RFO............ Radio Frequency Oscillator
RFO .... Ready for Occupancy   (MCD)
RFO .... Reason for Outage   (FAAC)
RFO .... Regional Field Officer [*Civil Defense*]
RFO .... Request for Factory Order   (MCD)
RFO .... Retrofire Officer [*NASA*]   (KSC)
RFO .... Roll Follow-Up Operation
RFOFM....... Records for Our Fighting Men [*Collected phonograph records during World War II*]
RFolc.......... Revista de Folclor [*A publication*]
R Fomento Soc ... Revista de Fomento Social [*A publication*]
RF & OOA... Railway Fuel and Operating Officers Association [*Champaign, IL*]   (EA)
RFOP......... Regional Financial Operating Plan
R Format Perm ... Revue de la Formation Permanente [*A publication*]
RForsch ..... Romanische Forschungen [*A publication*]
RFOSA........ Revue Francaise d'Odonto-Stomatologie [*A publication*]
RFP............ Radio Finger Printing [*Identification of wireless radio operators by individual keying characteristics*]
RFP............ Radio Free People [*An association*] [*Defunct*]
RFP............ Radio Frequency Plasma
RFP............ Radio Frequency Pulse   (MCD)
RFP............ Raiatea [*French Polynesia*] [*Airport symbol*]   (OAG)
RFP............ Reactor Feed Pumps   (NRCH)
RFP............ Remaining Force Potential   (MCD)
RFP............ Reproductive Freedom Project [*ACLU*] [*Attempts to enforce the Supreme Court decisions guaranteeing a woman's right to choose abortion*]   (EA)
RFP............ Republicans for Progress [*Defunct*]
RFP............ Request for Programing [*Data processing*]
RFP............ Request for Proposal
RFP............ Request for Purchase
RFP............ Requirements and Formulation Phase   (MCD)
RFP............ Requirements for Production [*Army*]   (RDA)
RFP............ Requisition for Procurement [*DoD*]
RFP............ Retired on Full Pay [*Military*] [*British*]
RFP............ Reversed Field Pinch [*Plasma physics*]   (NRCH)
RFP............ Reviews for Physicians [*Elsevier Book Series*] [*A publication*]
RFP............ Revista de Filologia Portuguesa [*A publication*]
RFP............ Richmond, Fredericksburg & Potomac Railroad Co. [*AAR code*]
RFP............ Right Frontoposterior [*A fetal position*] [*Obstetrics*]
RFPA.......... Request for Part Approval   (MCD)
RFPA.......... Request for Proposal Authorization [*NASA*]   (NASA)
RFPB.......... Reserve Forces Policy Board [*DoD*]
RFPC.......... Reserve Flag Officer Policy Council [*Navy*]
RF/PF........ Regional Forces - Popular Forces [*Republic of Vietnam*] [*Army*]   (AABC)
RFPP.......... Radio Frequency Propagation Program   (NG)
RFPRA....... Reactor Fuel Processing [*A publication*]
RFPS .... Royal Faculty of Physicians and Surgeons of Glasgow [*Later, RCPS*]
RFPT .... Reactor Feed Pump Turbine [*Nuclear energy*]   (NRCH)
RFQ .... Radio-Frequency Quadrupole [*Accelerator for subatomic physics study*]
RFQ .... Request for Qualifications   (OICC)
RFQ .... Request for Quotation
RFR .... Radio Frequency Receiver
RFR .... Radio Frequency Relay
RFR .... Redfern Resources [*Vancouver Stock Exchange symbol*]
RFR .... Reject Failure Rate
RFr .... Revolution Francaise [*A publication*]
RFr .... Revue Francaise [*A publication*]
RFR .... Rio Frio [*Costa Rica*] [*Airport symbol*]   (OAG)
RFR .... Royal Fleet Reserve [*British*]
R Fr Affaires Socs ... Revue Francaise des Affaires Sociales [*A publication*]
R Franc Aff Soc ... Revue Francaise des Affaires Sociales [*A publication*]
R Francaise Hist Livre ... Revue Francaise d'Histoire du Livre [*A publication*]
R Francaise Hist Outre-Mer ... Revue Francaise d'Histoire d'Outre-Mer [*A publication*]
R Francaise Sci Pol ... Revue Francaise de Science Politique [*A publication*]
R Francaise Sociol ... Revue Francaise de Sociologie [*A publication*]
R Franc Comptab ... Revue Francaise de Comptabilite [*A publication*]
R Franc Dr Aer ... Revue Francaise de Droit Aerien [*A publication*]
R Franc Et Amer ... Revue Francaise d'Etudes Americaines [*A publication*]
R Franc Et Polit Afr ... Revue Francaise d'Etudes Politiques Africaines [*A publication*]
R Franc Et Polit Medit ... Revue Francaise d'Etudes Politiques Mediterraneennes [*A publication*]
R Franc Gestion ... Revue Francaise de Gestion [*A publication*]
R Franc Hist Outre-Mer ... Revue Francaise d'Histoire d'Outre-Mer [*A publication*]
R Franc Mkting ... Revue Francaise du Marketing [*A publication*]

R Franc Pedag ... Revue Francaise de Pedagogie [*A publication*]
R Franc Sci Polit ... Revue Francaise de Science Politique [*A publication*]
R Franc Sociol ... Revue Francaise de Sociologie [*A publication*]
RFRC......... Refractory (MSA)
R Fr Etud Pol Afr ... Revue Francaise d'Etudes Politiques Africaines [*A publication*]
RFRG.......... Revista de Filologie Romanica si Germanica [*Bucarest*] [*A publication*]
RFrign .... Rassegna Frignanese [*A publication*]
RFRJ........... Radio Frequency Rotary Joint
RFRR-A ...... Raumforschung und Raumordnung [*A publication*]
R Fr Sociol ... Revue Francaise de Sociologie [*A publication*]
RFS .... Radio Frequency Seal
RFS .... Radio-Frequency Shift (IEEE)
RFS .... Radio Frequency Subsystem [*NASA*]
RFS .... Random Filing System
RFS .... Range Frequency Synthesizer
RFS .... Ready for Sea [*Navy*]
RFS .... Ready for Service
RFS .... Refuse (FAAC)
RFS .... Regardless of Future Size (AAG)
RFS .... Regional Field Specialist [*Civil Defense*]
RFS .... Regional Frequency Supplies [*Telecommunications*] (TEL)
RFS .... Relapse-Free Survival [*Oncology*]
RFS .... Religion and Family Section [*Minneapolis, MN*] (EA)
RFS .... Renal Function Studies [*Medicine*]
RFS .... Render, Float, and Set [*Construction*]
RFS .... Request for Services [*Social Security Administration*]
RFS .... Request for Shipment (MCD)
RFS .... Resources Forecasting System
RFS .... Response Feedback System [*NASA*]
RFS .... Revue Francaise de Sociologie [*A publication*]
RFS .... Roll Follow-Up System
RFS .... Rossendorfer Forschungs-Reaktor [*Rossendorf Research Reactor*] [*German*]
RFS .... Rotational Flight Simulator [*Air Force*]
RFS .... Rover Flight Safety
RFSB.......... Regional Forward Scatter Branch [*Supreme Allied Commander, Europe*] (NATG)
RFSE .... Radio Frequency Shielded Enclosure
RFS/ECM... Radio Frequency Surveillance/Electronic Countermeasures (MCD)
RFSHA .... Reports. Liberal Arts and Science Faculty. Shizuoka University. Natural Science [*A publication*]
RFS/ISE .... Ready for Sea/Individual Ship Exercise (MCD)
RFSO-A ..... Revue Francaise de Sociologie [*A publication*]
RFSP .... Radioactive Fallout Study Program [*Canada*]
RFSP .... Revue Francaise de Science Politique [*A publication*]
RFSP .... Rigid Frame Selection Program
RFSS .... Radio Frequency Simulation System (MCD)
RFSS......... Radio Frequency Surveillance Subsystem
RFSS......... Reichsfuehrerschutzstaffel (BJA)
RFSTF .... Radio Frequency Systems Test Facility (KSC)
RFT............. Rapid Fermentation Technique
RFT............. Ready for Training [*Military*]
RFT............. Real Fourier Transform
RFT............. Reflectance, Fluorescence, Transmittance [*Densitometer*] [*Instrumentation*]
RFT............. Refresher Training [*Navy*] (NVT)
RFT............. Reinforcement
RFT............. Request for Tender (ADA)
RFT............. Right Frontotransverse [*A fetal position*] [*Obstetrics*]
RFT............. Rotary Feed-Through
RFTC.......... Radio Frequency Test Console
RFTD .... Radial Flow Torr Deposition System (IEEE)
RFTDS........ RADAR Frequency Target Discrimination System (MCD)
RF-TK........ Radio Frequency Tracking [*Military*] (MCD)
RFTL.......... Radio Frequency Transmission Line
RFTN.......... Reflectone, Inc. [*NASDAQ symbol*] (NQ)
RFTO.......... Ready for Takeoff [*Aviation*]
RFTOI........ Request for Test or Inspection (MCD)
RFTP.......... Request for Technical Proposal
RFTRA....... Revue Francaise de Traitement de l'Information [*A publication*]
RFTS .... Radio Frequency Test Set (AABC)
RFTY.......... Reformatory (AABC)
RFU .... Radio Frequency Unit [*Later, RFCM*] (MCD)
RFU .... Ready-for-Use (NG)
RFU .... Reliability Field Unit
RFU .... Remote Firing Unit (MCD)
RFU .... Returns File Unit [*IRS*]
RFU .... Rugby Football Union [*British*]
RFUA.......... Roll Follow-Up Amplifier
RFUM......... Roll Follow-Up Motor
RFUO......... Roll Follow-Up Operation
RFUS......... Reversible Follow-Up System
RFUS......... Roll Follow-Up System
RFV .... RADAR Film Viewer
RFV .... Regressing Friend Virus
RFV .... Resonant Frequency Vibration
RFVM......... Radio Frequency Voltmeter
RFW.......... Radio Free Women [*An association*] (EA)

RFW........... Radio Frequency Wave
RFW........... Rapid Filling Wave [*Cardiology*]
RFW........... Reactor Feedwater [*Nuclear energy*] (NRCH)
RFW........... Request for Waiver (MCD)
RFW........... Reserve Feed Water [*Technical drawings*]
RFW........... Reversible Full Wave
RFWAC ..... Reversible Full-Wave Alternating Current
RFWAR....... Requirements for Work and Resources (MUGU)
RFWDC ...... Reversible Full-Wave Direct Current
RFWF .... Radio Frequency Wave Form
RFX .... East Hartford, CT [*Location identifier*] [*FAA*] (FAAL)
RFX .... Reversed Field Experiment [*Nuclear energy*] (NRCH)
RFZ .... Restrictive Fire Zone [*Military*]
RFZ........... Rinforzando [*With Special Emphasis*] [*Music*]
R/G............ Radiation Guidance (MUGU)
RG .... Radio Direction Finding Station [*ITU designation*] (CET)
RG .... Radio Frequency Cables; Bulk [*JETDS nomenclature*] [*Military*] (CET)
RG .... Radio Guidance (AAG)
RG .... Radiogram (DEN)
R-G .... Radiologist-General
RG .... Range (AAG)
RG .... Rate Grown
RG .... Rate Gyroscope (KSC)
RG .... Re-Gummed [*Philately*]
RG .... Readers' Guide to Periodical Literature [*A publication*]
RG .... Readiness Group (AABC)
RG .... Reagent Grade
RG .... Real Gas
RG .... Rebuilding Grade [*Automotive engineering*] [*Polymer Steel Corp.*]
RG .... Reception Good [*Radio logs*]
RG .... Recherches Germaniques [*A publication*]
RG .... Rectangular Guide (CET)
R/G............ Red and Gold (Edges) [*Bookbinding*] (ROG)
RG .... Red-Green
RG .... Reduction Gear [*or Gearbox*] (NG)
RG .... Register (CET)
RG .... Regula Generalis [*General Rule or Order of Court*] [*Ontario*] (DLA)
RG .... Regulated Gallery (NRCH)
RG .... Regulatory Guide (NRCH)
RG .... Release Guard [*Telecommunications*] (TEL)
RG .... Remak's Ganglion [*Neurology*]
RG .... Remedial Gymnast [*British*]
RG .... Renable Gold Trust [*Formerly, Barrick-Cullation Gold Trust*] [*Toronto Stock Exchange symbol*]
RG .... Report Generator (CMD)
RG .... Report Guide
RG .... Reserve Grade [*Military*]
RG .... Reset Gate
RG .... Resettlement Grants [*British*] [*World War II*]
RG .... Resolving Gel [*Biochemistry*]
RG .... Reticulated Grating (AAG)
RG .... Reverse Gate
RG .... Revista de Guimaraes [*A publication*]
RG .... Revolutionary Government [*Vietnam*]
RG .... Revue Generale [*A publication*]
RG .... Revue Germanique [*A publication*]
RG .... Right Gluteus [*Anatomy*]
RG .... Right Guard [*Football*]
RG .... Right Gun
RG .... Ringing Generator [*Telecommunications*] (TEL)
R-G .... [*Alain*] Robbe-Grillet [*French author and film director*]
RG .... Robert Graham [*Designer's mark on US 1984 $1 Olympic commemorative coin*]
RG .... Rogers Group (EA)
RG .... Rolled Gold
RG .... Romana Gens [*A publication*]
RG .... Rueckgang [*Return*] [*Music*]
R & G .... Russell and Geldert's Nova Scotia Reports (DLA)
RG .... VEB Fahlberg-List [*East Germany*] [*Research code symbol*]
RG .... Viacao Aerea Rio-Grandense [*VARIG*] [*Brazil*] [*ICAO designator*] (FAAC)
RGA........... Rate Gyro Assembly
RGA........... Regal Petroleum [*Vancouver Stock Exchange symbol*]
RGA........... Republican Governors Association
RGA........... Residual Gas Analyzer
RGA........... Ring Guild of America [*Defunct*] (EA)
RGA........... Rio Grande [*Argentina*] [*Airport symbol*] (OAG)
RGA........... Royal Garrison Artillery [*British*]
RGA........... Rubber Growers' Association (EA-IO)
RGAA .... Radiochemical Gamma Activation Analysis
R Gabonaise Etud Pols Econs et Juridiques ... Revue Gabonaise d'Etudes Politiques. Economiques et Juridiques [*A publication*]
R Gad .... Raina Gadagramata [*A publication*]
RGAL......... Rate Gyro Assembly - Left Solid Rocket Booster (MCD)
RGand....... Romanica Gandensia [*A publication*]
RGAO........ Rate Gyro Assembly - Orbiter (MCD)
RGAP......... Rate Gyro Accelerometer Package (MCD)
RGAR .... Rate Gyro Assembly - Right Solid Rocket Booster (MCD)

RGAS .... Rocky Mountain Natural Gas Co. [*NASDAQ symbol*]　(NQ)
RGB .... Barry [*R. G.*] Corp. [*American Stock Exchange symbol*]
RGB .... Red Green Blue [*Video monitor*]
RGB .... Refractory Grade Bauxite [*Geology*]
RGB .... Revue Generale Belge [*A publication*]
RGB .... River Gunboat
RGBI .... Red Green Blue Intensity [*Video monitor*]
RGC .... Rangely [*Colorado*] [*Seismograph station code, US Geological Survey*]　(SEIS)
RGC .... Reconstructed Gas Chromatogram
RGC .... Reigate Resources (Canada) Ltd. [*Toronto Stock Exchange symbol*]
RGC .... Repair Group Category [*Military*]　(AFIT)
RGC .... Repository for Germinal Choice [*A sperm bank*]
RGC .... Republic Gypsum Company [*NYSE symbol*]
RGC .... Retinal Ganglion Cell [*Neurochemistry*]
RGC .... Rio Grande College [*Ohio*]
RGC .... Rio Grande College, Rio Grande, OH [*OCLC symbol*]　(OCLC)
RGC .... Rural Governments Coalition　(EA)
RGCR .... Renner's Gold Coast Colony Reports [*1868-1914*] [*Ghana*]　(DLA)
RGCY .... Regency Electronics [*NASDAQ symbol*]　(NQ)
RGD .... Ragged　(FAAC)
RGD .... Rarefied Gas Dynamics
RGD .... Regular Geophysical Day
RGD .... Revue Generale de Droit [*A publication*]
RGD .... Rigid　(MSA)
RGda .... Radio Grenada
RGDPD ...... Revue de Geologie Dynamique et de Geographie Physique [*A publication*]
RGDT .... Reliability Growth/Development Test
RGE .... Porgera [*Papua New Guinea*] [*Airport symbol*]　(OAG)
RGE .... Range [*Maps and charts*]　(MDG)
RGE .... Rat der Gemeinden Europas [*Council of European Municipalities*]
RGE .... Red under Gold Edges [*Books*]
RGE .... Reduced Gravity Environment
RGE .... Regroupement des Guineens a l'Exterieur [*Rally of Guineans Abroad*]　(PD)
R Gen .... Revue Generale [*A publication*]
R Gen Air Espace ... Revue Generale de l'Air et de l'Espace [*A publication*]
R Gen Assur Terr ... Revue Generale des Assurances Terrestres [*A publication*]
RGenBelge ... Revue General Belge [*A publication*]　(BJA)
R Gen Chem de Fer ... Revue Generale des Chemins de Fer [*A publication*]
R Gen Dr Int Publ ... Revue Generale de Droit International Public [*A publication*]
R Gen Sci ... Revue Generale des Sciences Pures et Appliquees [*A publication*]
R Gen Sci Pures et Ap ... Revue Generale des Sciences Pures et Appliquees [*A publication*]
R de Geog de Mtl ... Revue de Geographie de Montreal [*A publication*]
R Geogr Alpine ... Revue de Geographie Alpine [*A publication*]
R Geogr Est ... Revue Geographique de l'Est [*A publication*]
RGeogrH .... Revue de Geographie Humaine et d'Ethnologie [*A publication*]
R Geogr Lyon ... Revue de Geographie de Lyon [*A publication*]
R Geogr Maroc ... Revue de Geographie du Maroc [*A publication*]
R Geogr Pyrenees ... Revue Geographique des Pyrenees et du Sud-Ouest [*A publication*]
R Geogr (Rio De Janeiro) ... Revista Geografica (Rio De Janeiro) [*A publication*]
R Geog Soc Pr ... Royal Geographical Society. Proceedings [*A publication*]
RGEPS ...... Rucker-Gable Educational Programing Scale [*Psychology*]
RGer .... Recherches Germaniques [*A publication*]
RGF .... Range Gated Filter
RGF .... Rarefied Gas Field [*or Flow*]
RGF .... Roemisch-Germanische Forschungen [*A publication*]
RGFC .... Remote Gas Filter Correlation　(KSC)
RGFil .... Romano-Germanskaja Filologija [*A publication*]
RGG .... Religion in Geschichte und Gegenwart [*A publication*]
RGG .... Rotating Gravity Gradiometer
RGG .... Royal Grenadier Guards [*British*]
RGH .... Rare Gas Halogen [*Inorganic chemistry*]
RGH .... Rat Growth Hormone [*Endocrinology*]
RGH .... Rough　(AAG)
RGI .... Rangiroa [*French Polynesia*] [*Airport symbol*]　(OAG)
RGI .... Royal Glasgow Institute of Fine Arts [*Scotland*]
RGICC .... Region Internal Computer Code [*Data processing*]
RGIFA .... Royal Glasgow Institute of Fine Arts [*Scotland*]
RGIS .... Regis Corp. [*NASDAQ symbol*]　(NQ)
RGIT .... Robert Gordon Institute of Technology [*Scotland*]
RGJ .... Richmond, VA [*Location identifier*] [*FAA*]　(FAAL)
RGJ .... Royal Green Jackets [*Military unit*] [*British*]
RGJLond .... Royal Green Jackets, London [*Military unit*] [*British*]
RGJTAVR ... Royal Green Jackets Territorial and Army Volunteer Reserve [*Military unit*] [*British*]
RGK .... Red Wing, MN [*Location identifier*] [*FAA*]　(FAAL)
RGK .... Reserv Glavnogo Komandovaniia [*Reserve of the High Command*] [*USSR*]
RGKAI .... Roemisch-Germanische Kommission des Archaeologischen Instituts [*A publication*]

RGKNA ...... Rikagaku Kenkyusho Kenkyu Nempo [*A publication*]
RGKomm ... Roemisch-Germanische Kommission d'Arch Institut d'Deutschen Reichs [*A publication*]
RGL .... Rate Gyroscope Limit
RGL .... Reading Grade Level
RGL .... Regal International, Inc. [*NYSE symbol*]
RGL .... Regional Resources Ltd. [*Toronto Stock Exchange symbol*] [*Vancouver Stock Exchange symbol*]
RGL .... Regulate　(MSA)
RGL .... Report Generator Language [*Data processing*]　(IEEE)
RGL .... Review of Ghana Law [*A publication*]
RGL .... Revue de Geographie de Lyon [*A publication*]
RGL .... Rio Gallegos [*Argentina*] [*Airport symbol*]　(OAG)
RGL .... Wrangell, AK [*Location identifier*] [*FAA*]　(FAAL)
RGLR .... Regular　(MSA)
RGLT .... Regulating　(MSA)
RGLTD .... Regulated　(MSA)
RGLTR .... Regulator　(MSA)
RGM .... Radiogas Monitor [*Nuclear energy*]　(NRCH)
RGM .... Recorder Group Monitor
RGM .... Reliability Growth Management　(MCD)
RGM .... Remote Geophysical Monitor　(MCD)
RGM .... Reversible Gelatin Matrix
RGM .... Rounds per Gun per Minute
RGM .... Royex Gold Mining [*Toronto Stock Exchange symbol*] [*Vancouver Stock Exchange symbol*]
RGMI .... Regulations Governing the Meat Inspection [*of the USDA*]
RGMNA .... Chijil Kwangmul Chosa Yongu Pokoso [*A publication*]
RGMS .... Reversible Gelatin Matrix System
RGN .... Rangoon [*Burma*] [*Airport symbol*]　(OAG)
RGN .... Region　(AFM)
RGN .... Registered General Nurse
RGNEB .... Review of Compagnie Generale d'Electricite [*A publication*]
RGNG .... Rigging　(MSA)
R & G N Sc ... Russell and Geldert's Nova Scotia Reports　(DLA)
RGNUD .... Revue Generale Nucleaire [*A publication*]
RGO .... Akron, OH [*Location identifier*] [*FAA*]　(FAAL)
RGO .... Ranger Oil Ltd. [*Toronto Stock Exchange symbol*]
RGo .... Romanica Gothoburgensia [*A publication*]
RGO .... Royal Greenwich Observatory [*British*]
RGP .... Rate Gyro Package
RGP .... Regina Public Library [*UTLAS symbol*]
RGP .... Remote Graphics Processor
RGP .... Rhodesian Government Party
RGP .... Rolled Gold Plate [*Metallurgy*]
RGPF .... Royal Gunpowder Factory [*British*]
RGPGD .... Revue de Geographie Physique et de Geologie Dynamique [*A publication*]
RG PH .... Registered Pharmacist
RGPO .... Range Gate Pull Off　(NVT)
RGR .... Oklahoma City, OK [*Location identifier*] [*FAA*]　(FAAL)
RGR .... Range Gated Receiver
RGR .... Ranger
RGR .... Rare-Gas Recovery [*Nuclear energy*]　(NRCH)
RGr .... Rassegna Gregoriana [*A publication*]
RGR .... Rassemblement des Gauches Republicaines [*Assembly of the Republican Left*] [*French political party*]
RGR .... Receipt of Goods Received
RGR .... Regionair, Inc. [*Canada*] [*FAA designator*]　(FAAC)
RGR .... Regulus Resources, Inc. [*Vancouver Stock Exchange symbol*]
RGR .... Relative Growth Rate [*Entomology*]
RGR .... Revista Germanistilor Romani [*A publication*]
RGr .... Revue Gregorienne [*A publication*]
RGR .... Royal Garrison Regiment [*Military*] [*British*]　(ROG)
RGRCD .... Geothermal Resources Council. Special Report [*A publication*]
R Greenwich Obs Bull ... Royal Greenwich Observatory. Bulletins [*A publication*]
R Gregor .... Revue Gregorienne [*A publication*]
RGS .... RADAR Ground Stabilization
RGS .... Radio Guidance System
RGS .... Rate Gyro System
RGS .... Remote Ground Switching
RGS .... Rene Guyon Society [*Beverly Hills, CA*]　(EA)
RGS .... Restructured General Support [*Military*]
RGS .... River Gauging Station
RGS .... Rochester Gas & Electric Corp. [*NYSE symbol*]
RGS .... Rocket Guidance System　(KSC)
RGS .... Royal Geographical Society [*British*]
RGS .... Royal Gold & Silver Corp. [*Toronto Stock Exchange symbol*]
RGS .... Ruffed Grouse Society　(EA)
RGS .... Sisters of Our Lady of Charity of the Good Shepherd [*Roman Catholic religious order*]
RGSAT .... Radio Guidance Surveillance and Automatic Tracking　(AAG)
RGS Austsia SA Br Proc ... Royal Geographical Society of Australasia. South Australian Branch. Proceedings [*A publication*]
RGSC .... Ramp Generator and Signal Converter　(IEEE)
RGSDLR ...... Rigsdaler [*Numismatics*]
RGSIA .... Records. Geological Survey of India [*A publication*]
R G Soc Cornwall Tr ... Royal Geological Society of Cornwall. Transactions [*A publication*]

R G Soc Ireland J ... Royal Geological Society of Ireland. Journal [*A publication*]
RGSU .... Restructured General Support Unit   (MCD)
RGSWA ..... Records. Geological Survey of New South Wales [*A publication*]
Rgt............. Regent [*Record label*]
RGT .... Regent College Library [*UTLAS symbol*]
RGT .... Regiment
RGT .... Rengat [*Indonesia*] [*Airport symbol*]   (OAG)
RGT .... Resonant Gate Transistor [*Data processing*]
RGT .... Reverse Garbage Truck   (ADA)
RGT .... Rigging Template   (MCD)
RGT .... Right
RGTHA .... Revue Generale de Thermique [*A publication*]
RGTP .... Rough Template   (AAG)
RGTR .... Register
RgtT .... Ranger Tab [*Military decoration*]   (AABC)
RGU .... Rate Gyroscope Unit
R Guardia Fin ... Rivista della Guardia di Finanza [*A publication*]
RGuim .... Revista de Guimaraes [*A publication*]
RGV .... Relative Gas Vacuolation [*In algae*]
RGV .... Rio Grande Ventures Ltd. [*Vancouver Stock Exchange symbol*]
RGVV .... Religionsgeschichtliche Versuche und Vorarbeiten [*A publication*]
RGW .... Ramp Gross Weight [*Aviation*]
RGWS........ RADAR Guided Weapon System   (MCD)
RGY .... Regency Airlines [*Chicago, IL*] [*FAA designator*]   (FAAC)
RGZ .... Recommended Ground Zero   (AABC)
RGZM .... Roemisch-Germanische Zentralmuseum (Mainz) [*A publication*]
RH .... Air Rhodesia [*ICAO designator*]   (FAAC)
RH .... Rabbinic Hebrew   (BJA)
RH .... Radiant Heat
RH .... Radiation Homing   (AAG)
RH .... Radiological Health   (KSC)
r/h .... RADs [*Radiation Absorbed Doses*] per Hour   (DEN)
RH .... Rankine-Hugoniot [*Physics*]
RH .... Reactive Hyperemia [*Medicine*]
RH .... Receive Hub [*Telegraph*] [*Telecommunications*]   (TEL)
RH .... Regional Headquarters   (NOAA)
RH .... Relative Humidity
RH .... Releasing Hormone [*Also, RF*] [*Endocrinology*]
RH .... Religious Humanism [*A publication*]
r/h .... REMs [*Roentgen Equivalents, Man*] per Hour   (DEN)
RH .... Report Heading   (BUR)
RH .... Request-Response Header [*Data processing*]   (BUR)
RH .... Requesta Regni Hierosolymitani [*A publication*]   (BJA)
RH .... Research Highlights [*A publication*]   (DIT)
RH .... Residential Hotels [*Public-performance tariff class*] [*British*]
RH .... Restaurant Hospitality [*A publication*]
RH .... Revisionist History [*An association*]   (EA-IO)
R/H............ Revolutions per Hour   (DEN)
RH .... Revue Hebdomadaire [*A publication*]
RH .... Revue Hispanique [*A publication*]
RH .... Revue Historique [*A publication*]
RH .... Rheostat   (IEEE)
Rh............. Rhesus [*Blood factor*]
Rh............. Rhetorica [*of Aristotle*] [*Classical studies*]   (OCD)
Rh............. Rheumatism [*Medicine*]
RH .... Rhinitis [*Medicine*]
RH .... Rhinoceros   (ROG)
rh............... Rhodesia [*Southern Rhodesia*] [*MARC country of publication code*] [*Library of Congress*]   (LCCP)
Rh............. Rhodium [*Chemical element*]
RH .... Right Halfback [*Soccer*]
RH .... Right Hand
RH .... Right Hyperphoria [*Medicine*]
RH .... Road Haulage
RH .... Rochester History [*A publication*]
RH .... Rockwell Hardness
RH .... Roczniki Humanistyczne [*A publication*]
r/h............. Roentgens per Hour   (DEN)
RH .... Rosh Hashanah [*New Year*]   (BJA)
RH .... Rotuli Hundredorum [*Record Commission*] [*England*]   (DLA)
RH .... Round Head
RH .... Round House [*Maps and charts*]
RH .... Royal Highlanders [*Military unit*] [*British*]
RH .... Royal Highness
RH .... Royal Hospital [*London*]
RH .... Royal Hussars [*Military unit*] [*British*]
RH .... Rueckwaertiges Heeresgebiet [*Rear area of a group of armies*] [*German military*]
RH .... Runaway Hotline [*An association*] [*Austin, TX*]   (EA)
RH .... Ryan's Hope [*Television program*]
RH .... Southern Rhodesia [*Two-letter standard code*] [*Obsolete*]   (CNC)
RHA........... Records Holding Area
RHA........... Regional Health Authority [*British*]
RHA........... Reichold [*Alabama*] [*Seismograph station code, US Geological Survey*]   (SEIS)
RHA........... Reindeer Herders Association   (EA)

RHA .... Religious Heritage of America   (EA)
RHA .... Renewal and Housing Assistance Report [*HUD*]
RHA .... Revista de Historia de America [*A publication*]
RHA .... Revue Hittite et Asiatique [*A publication*]
RHA .... Reykholar [*Iceland*] [*Airport symbol*] [*Obsolete*]   (OAG)
RHA .... Rohm & Haas Co., Spring House, PA [*OCLC symbol*]   (OCLC)
RHA .... Rolled Homogeneous Armor [*Weaponry*]   (INF)
RHA .... Roman High Avoidance [*Behavior trait*]
RHA .... Rose Hybridizers Association   (EA)
RHA .... Royal Hawaiian Air Service [*Honolulu, HI*] [*FAA designator*]   (FAAC)
RHA .... Royal Hellenic Army   (NATG)
RHA .... Royal Hibernian Academy
RHA .... Royal Horse Artillery [*British*]
RHA .... Rural Housing Alliance [*Absorbed by RAI*]   (EA)
RHAB .... Random House AudioBooks [*Publisher*]
RHAB .... Rehab Hospital Services [*NASDAQ symbol*]   (NQ)
RHAF .... Revue d'Histoire de l'Amerique Francaise [*A publication*]
RHAF .... Royal Hellenic Air Force
Rh AI .... Rhetorica ad Alexandrum [*of Aristotle*] [*Classical studies*]   (OCD)
RHAM........ Rhammus [*Pharmacology*]   (ROG)
R Hanazono Coll ... Review of Hanazono College [*A publication*]
RHA(T)....... Regional Health Authority (Teaching) [*British*]
RHAV......... Rat Hepatoma-Associated Virus
RHAW .... RADAR Homing and Warning   (MCD)
RHAWR ..... RADAR Homing and Warning Receiver   (MCD)
RHAWS....... RADAR Homing and Warning System
RHB .... RADAR Homing Bomb [*Air Force*]
RHB .... Regional Hospital Boards [*British*]
RhB .... Rheinische Blaetter [*A publication*]
RHB .... Rheinische Heimatblaetter [*A publication*]
RHB .... Right Halfback [*Soccer*]
RHB .... Round Hole Broach
RHBA .... Racking Horse Breeders Association of America   (EA)
R & H Bank ... Roche and Hazlitt's Bankruptcy Practice [*2nd ed.*] [*1873*]   (DLA)
RHBNA .... Rehabilitation [*A publication*]
RHC........... Reactive Hydrocarbon [*Environmental science*]
RHC........... Reactor Head Cooling   (NRCH)
RHC........... Resetting Half-Cycle
RHC........... Respirations Have Ceased [*Medicine*]
RHC........... Revue d'Histoire Comparee [*A publication*]
RHC........... Right-Hand Circular [*NASA*]   (KSC)
RHC........... Right-Hand Console
RHC........... Right Hypochondrium [*Medicine*]
RHC........... Riverside Methodist Hospital Library, Columbus, OH [*OCLC symbol*]   (OCLC)
RHC........... Road Haulage Cases [*1950-55*] [*England*]   (DLA)
RHC........... Rosary Hill College [*New York*]
RHC........... Rotational Hand Controller [*NASA*]
RHC........... Royal Highlanders of Canada [*Military unit*] [*World War I*]
RHC........... Rubber Hydrocarbon
Rh CA........ Rhodesian Court of Appeal Law Reports [*1939-46*]   (DLA)
RHCC .... Reproductive Health Care Center
RHCC/PP.... Reproductive Health Care Center/Planned Parenthood
RHCFA .... Revista. Hospital das Clinicas. Faculdade de Medicina. Universidade de Sao Paulo [*A publication*]
RHCI.......... Radiant Heating and Cooling Institute
RHCM......... Revue d'Histoire et de Civilisation du Maghreb [*A publication*]
RHComp..... Revue d'Histoire Comparee [*A publication*]
RHCP .... Right-Hand Circularly Polarized [*LASER waves*]
RHCS .... Rocznik Historii Czasopismiennictwa Polskiego [*A publication*]
RHCSA....... Regional Hospitals Consultants' and Specialists' Association
RHD .... Archangelos [*Greece*] [*Seismograph station code, US Geological Survey*]   (SEIS)
RHD .... Radiological Health Data
RHD .... Railhead
RHD .... Random House Dictionary [*A publication*]
RHD .... Regional Health Director [*HEW*]
RHD .... Relative Hepatic Dullness [*Medicine*]
RHD .... Renal Hypertensive Disease [*Medicine*]
RHD .... Required Hangar Depth   (MCD)
RHD .... Return Head
RHD .... Revue d'Histoire Diplomatique [*A publication*]
RHD .... Revue d'Histoire du Droit [*A publication*]
RHD .... Revue Historique de Droit Francais et Etranger [*A publication*]
RHD .... Rheumatic Heart Disease [*Medicine*]
RHD .... Rhodes, Inc. [*NYSE symbol*]
RHD .... Right Hand Drive [*Automotive engineering*]
RHD .... Rural Housing Disaster
RHDFE .... Revue Historique de Droit Francais et Etranger [*A publication*]
R & H Dig... Robinson and Harrison's Digest [*Ontario*]   (DLA)
RHDip........ Revue d'Histoire Diplomatique [*A publication*]
RHD & R .... Radiological Health Data and Reports [*A publication*]
RHDS .... Rhodes, Inc. [*NASDAQ symbol*]   (NQ)
RHE .... Radiation Hazard Effects   (KSC)
RHE .... Random House Encyclopedia [*A publication*]
RHE .... Record Handling Electronics
RHE .... Reims [*France*] [*Airport symbol*]   (OAG)
RHE .... Reliability Human Engineering   (AAG)

RHE .... Reversible Hydrogen Electrode
RHE .... Revue d'Histoire Ecclesiastique [A publication]
RHEA .... Reentry Heating Energies Analyzer [Air Force]
RHEA .... Research into Higher Education. Abstracts [A publication]
RHeb .... Revue Hebdomadaire [A publication]
RHEB .... Right-Hand Equipment Bay [Apollo] [NASA]
RHEED ...... Reflected High-Energy Electron Diffraction [Spectroscopy]
RHEF .... Revue d'Histoire de l'Eglise de France [A publication]
Rhein Bienenztg ... Rheinische Bienenzeitung [A publication]
Rheinisch-Westfael Akad Wiss Nat- Ing- Wirtschaftswiss Vort ...
             Rheinisch-Westfaelische Akademie der Wissenschaften
             Natur-, Ingenieur-, und Wirtschaftswissenschaften.
             Vortraege [A publication]
Rheinstahl Tech ... Rheinstahl Technik [A publication]
Rhein Vb .... Rheinische Vierteljahresblaetter [A publication]
Rhein-Westfael Akad Wiss Vortr N ... Rheinisch-Westfaelische Akademie
             der Wissenschaften Natur-, Ingenieur-, und
             Wirtschaftswissenschaften. Vortraege [A publication]
RHel .... Romanica Helvetica [A publication]
RHEL .... Rutherford High Energy Laboratory (MCD)
R Hell Dr Int ... Revue Hellenique de Droit International [A publication]
RHEO .... Rheostat (AAG)
Rheol Abstr ... Rheology Abstracts [A publication]
Rheol Act ... Rheologica Acta [A publication]
Rheol Acta ... Rheologica Acta [A publication]
Rheol Bull ... Rheology Bulletin [A publication]
Rheol Leafl ... Rheology Leaflet [A publication]
Rheol Mem ... Rheological Memoirs [A publication]
Rheol Texture Food Qual ... Rheology and Texture in Food Quality [A
             publication]
RHES .... Revue d'Histoire Economique et Sociale [A publication]
Rhes .... Rhesus [of Euripides] [Classical studies] (OCD)
Rhet .... Ars Rhetorica [of Dionysius Halicarnassensis] [Classical
             studies] (OCD)
Rhet .... De Rhetoribus [of Suetonius] [Classical studies] (OCD)
Rhet .... Rhetores Graeci [A publication] (OCD)
RHET .... Rhetoric
Rhet Her ..... Rhetorica ad Herennium [First century BC] [Classical
             studies] (OCD)
Rhet Lat Min ... Rhetores Latini Minores [A publication] (OCD)
RHEUM ...... Rheumatism [Medicine]
Rheumatol Balneo Allergol ... Rheumatologia, Balneologia, Allergologia [A
             publication]
Rheumatol Phys Med ... Rheumatology and Physical Medicine [A
             publication]
Rheumatol Rehabil ... Rheumatology and Rehabilitation [A publication]
RHF .... Rarefied Hypersonic Flow
RHF .... Remembrance of the Holocaust Foundation (EA)
RHF .... Retired History File [Army]
RHF .... Revue d'Histoire Franciscaine [A publication]
RHF .... Right Heart Failure [Medicine]
RHF .... Roller Hockey Federation (EA)
RHF .... Royal Highland Fusiliers [Military unit] [British]
RHFEB .... Right-Hand Forward Equipment Bay [NASA] (KSC)
RHFS .... Receiving Hospital Field Station
RHFS .... Round Hill Field Station [MIT] (MCD)
RHG .... Royal Horse Guards [British]
rhGRF .... Rat Hypothalamus Growth Hormone-Releasing Factor
             [Endocrinology]
RHGSA .... Russian Historical and Genealogical Society in America [Later,
             Russian Nobility Association in America] (EA)
RHH .... Right-Hand Head
RHH .... Robertson [H. H.] Co. [NYSE symbol]
RHI .... Halmi [Robert], Incorporated [American Stock Exchange
             symbol]
RHI .... RADAR Height Indicator (CET)
RHI .... Range-Height Indicator [RADAR]
RHI .... Relative Humidity Indicator (AAG)
RHi .... Revue Hispanique [A publication]
RHI .... Rhinelander [Wisconsin] [Airport symbol] (OAG)
RHI .... Rhode Island
RHI .... Rhode Island Historical Society Library, Providence, RI [OCLC
             symbol] (OCLC)
RHi .... Rhode Island Historical Society, Providence, RI [Library
             symbol] [Library of Congress] (LCLS)
Rh I .... Rhode Island Reports (DLA)
Rh I .... Rhode Island Supreme Court Reports (DLA)
RHIA .... Radiation-Hardened Interfacing Amplifier
RHIB .... Rain and Hail Insurance Bureau [Defunct] (EA)
RHIC .... Relativistic Heavy Ion Collider [Nuclear physics]
RHiM .... Revista Hispanica Moderna [A publication]
RHIMO .... Agency for Navigation on the Rhine and the Moselle (NATG)
Rhin .... Rhinology [Medicine]
RHINO .... Range-Height Indicator Not Operating [Aviation] (FAAC)
RHINO .... Rhinoceros (DSUE)
RHINOL ...... Rhinology
RHIO .... Rank Has Its Obligations [Military slang]
RHIP .... Radiation Health Information Project (EA)
RHIP .... Rank Has Its Privileges [Military slang]
RHIR .... Rank Has Its Responsibilities [Military slang]
RHis .... Revue Historique [A publication]

RHi-Sh .... Rhode Island Historical Society, George L. Shepley Collection,
             Providence, RI [Library symbol] [Library of
             Congress] (LCLS)
RHisp .... Revue Hispanique [A publication]
R Hispan Mod ... Revista Hispanica Moderna [A publication]
R Hist .... Revista de Historia [A publication]
R d'Hist ...... Revue d'Histoire de l'Amerique Francaise [A publication]
R Hist .... Revue Historique [A publication]
RHist .... Roczniki Historyczne [A publication]
R Hist Am .... Revista de Historia de America [A publication]
R Hist Bul ... Revue Historique. Bulletins Critiques [A publication]
R Hist Deuxieme Geurre Mondiale ... Revue d'Histoire de la Deuxieme
             Guerre Mondiale [A publication]
R Hist Diplom ... Revue d'Histoire Diplomatique [A publication]
R Hist Droit ... Revue Historique de Droit Francais et Etranger [A publication]
R Hist Eccl ... Revue d'Histoire Ecclesiastique [A publication]
R Hist Fascisme ... Revue d'Histoire du Fascisme [A publication]
R Hist Litt France ... Revue d'Histoire Litteraire de la France [A publication]
RHistM .... Roemische Historische Mitteilungen [A publication]
R Hist Mem ... Revue Historique. Memoires et Etudes [A publication]
R Hist Mod & Contemp ... Revue d'Histoire Moderne et Contemporaine [A
             publication]
RHistorique ... Revue Historique [Paris] [A publication]
R Hist & Philos Rel ... Revue d'Histoire et de Philosophie Religieuses [A
             publication]
R Hist Ph Rel ... Revue d'Histoire et de Philosophie Religieuses [A
             publication]
R Hist Rel ... Revue de l'Histoire des Religions [A publication]
RHistS .... Royal Historical Society [British]
R Hist Sci & Ap ... Revue d'Histoire des Sciences et de Leurs Applications [A
             publication]
R Hist Spiritualite ... Revue d'Histoire de la Spiritualite [A publication]
RHittAs ...... Revue Hittite et Asianique [Paris] [A publication] (BJA)
RHJ .... Rubber Hose Jacket (MSA)
RhJbV .... Rheinisches Jahrbuch fuer Volkskunde [A publication]
RHJE .... Revue de l'Histoire Juive en Egypte [A publication]
RHK .... Radio Hong Kong
RHK .... Reefing Hook
RHKUL .... Roczniki Humanistyczne. Towarzystwo Naukowe Katolickiego
             Uniwersytetu Lubelskiego [A publication]
RHL .... Radiological Health Laboratory
RHL .... Residual Hazards List [NASA] (NASA)
RHL .... Rettie's Scotch Court of Session Cases, Fourth Series [House
             of Lords' Part] (DLA)
RHL .... Reverse Half-Line [Feed]
RHL .... Revista de Historia. La Laguna de Tenerife [A publication]
RHL .... Revue d'Histoire Litteraire de la France [A publication]
RHL .... Right Hepatic Lobe [Anatomy]
RHLB .... Revue d'Histoire Litteraire (Bucharest) [A publication]
RHLE .... Revista Critica de Historia y Literatura Espanolas [A
             publication]
RHLF .... Revue d'Histoire Litteraire de la France [A publication]
RHLG .... Radiometric Homing Level Gauge
Rh LJ .... Rhodesian Law Journal (DLA)
RHLP .... Revista de Historia Literaria de Portugal [A publication]
RHLR .... Revue d'Histoire et de Litterature Religieuse [A publication]
RHM .... Refractory Heavy Minerals [In sands used for glass making]
RHM .... Relative Humidity Meter
RHM .... Renewal and Housing Management [HUD]
RHM .... Revista Hispanica Moderna [A publication]
RHM .... Revue d'Histoire Moderne [A publication]
RHM .... Rhabdomyosarcoma [Also, RMS] [Oncology]
RhM .... Rheinische Merkur [A publication]
RhM .... Rheinisches Museum fuer Philologie [A publication]
RHM .... Rio Hardy [Mexico] [Seismograph station code, US Geological
             Survey] (SEIS)
RHM .... Roemische Historische Mitteilungen [A publication]
RHM .... Roentgen per Hour at One Meter
RHMC .... Revue d'Histoire Moderne et Contemporaine [A publication]
RHMH .... Revue d'Histoire de la Medicine Hebraique [Paris] [A
             publication]
RHMis .... Revue d'Histoire des Missions [A publication]
RhMP .... Rheinisches Museum fuer Philologie [A publication]
Rh M Ph..... Rheinisches Museum fuer Philologie [A publication]
RHMS .... Royal Hibernian Military School [Dublin]
RHMSA ...... Revue d'Hygiene et de Medecine Sociale [A publication]
Rh Mus ...... Rheinisches Museum fuer Philologie [A publication] (OCD)
RHN .... Royal Hellenic Navy [Obsolete] (NATG)
RHNL .... Reindeer Herders Newsletter. Institute of Arctic Biology.
             University of Alaska [A publication]
RHO .... Railhead Officer [Military] [Obsolete]
RHO .... Rhodes [Greece] [Seismograph station code, US Geological
             Survey] [Closed] (SEIS)
RHO .... Rhodes Island [Greece] [Airport symbol] (OAG)
RHO .... Rhodesia [Later, Zimbabwe]
RHO .... Rhombic [Antenna]
RHO .... Southern Rhodesia [Three-letter standard code]
             [Obsolete] (CNC)
RHOB .... Rayburn House Office Building (DLA)
RHOD .... Rhodium [Chemistry]
Rhod Agric J ... Rhodesia Agricultural Journal [A publication]

Rhod Beekeeping ... Rhodesian Beekeeping [*A publication*]
Rhod Bee News ... Rhodesian Bee News [*A publication*]
Rhod Bull For Res ... Rhodesia. Bulletin of Forestry Research [*A publication*]
Rhod Cotton Res Inst Annu Rep ... Rhodesia Cotton Research Institute. Annual Report [*A publication*]
Rhod Div Livest Pastures Annu Rep ... Rhodesia. Division of Livestock and Pastures. Annual Report [*A publication*]
Rhode Island Rep ... Rhode Island Reports (DLA)
Rhod Eng ... Rhodesian Engineer [*A publication*]
Rhodesia Ag J ... Rhodesia Agricultural Journal [*A publication*]
Rhodesia Agr J ... Rhodesia Agricultural Journal [*A publication*]
Rhodesian J Agr Res ... Rhodesian Journal of Agricultural Research [*A publication*]
Rhodesian J Econ ... Rhodesian Journal of Economics [*A publication*]
Rhodesian LJ ... Rhodesian Law Journal (DLA)
Rhodesian Min Jour ... Rhodesian Mining Journal [*A publication*]
Rhodesian Tob J ... Rhodesian Tobacco Journal [*A publication*]
Rhodesia Zambia Malawi J Agr Res ... Rhodesia, Zambia, and Malawi Journal of Agricultural Research [*A publication*]
Rhodes Univ Dep Ichthyol Ichthyol Bull ... Rhodes University. Department of Ichthyology. Ichthyological Bulletin [*A publication*]
Rhodes Univ Dep Ichthyol Occas Pap ... Rhodes University. Department of Ichthyology. Occasional Paper [*A publication*]
Rhodes Univ J L B Smith Inst Ichthyol Spec Publ ... Rhodes University. J. L. B. Smith Institute of Ichthyology. Special Publication [*A publication*]
Rhod Geol Surv Bull ... Rhodesia. Geological Survey. Bulletin [*A publication*]
Rhod Geol Surv Miner Resour Ser ... Rhodesia. Geological Survey. Mineral Resources Series [*A publication*]
Rhod Geol Surv Short Rep ... Rhodesia. Geological Survey. Short Report [*A publication*]
Rhod Grassl Res Stn Annu Rep ... Rhodesia Grasslands Research Station. Annual Report [*A publication*]
Rhod Hist ... Rhodesian History [*A publication*]
Rhod J Agric Res ... Rhodesia Journal of Agricultural Research [*A publication*]
Rhod Librn ... Rhodesian Librarian [*A publication*]
Rhod Lowveld Res Stn Annu Rep ... Rhodesia. Lowveld Research Station. Annual Report [*A publication*]
Rhod Minist Agric Dep Res Spec Serv Seed Serv Annu Rep ... Rhodesia. Ministry of Agriculture. Department of Research and Specialist Services. Seed Services. Annual Report [*A publication*]
Rhod Minist Agric Gatooma Res Stn Annu Rep ... Rhodesia. Ministry of Agriculture. Gatooma Research Station. Annual Report [*A publication*]
Rhod Minist Agric Grassl Res Stn Annu Rep ... Rhodesia. Ministry of Agriculture. Grasslands Research Station. Annual Report [*A publication*]
Rhod Nurse ... Rhodesian Nurse [*A publication*]
Rhod Sci News ... Rhodesia Science News [*A publication*]
Rhod Tob ... Rhodesian Tobacco [*A publication*]
Rhod Zambia Malawi J Agric Res ... Rhodesia, Zambia, and Malawi Journal of Agricultural Research [*A publication*]
RHOGI .... RADAR Homing Guidance Investigation (MCD)
RHOJ .... RADAR Home on Jam
RHOMB ..... Rhomboid [*Mathematics*]
RHOSP .... Registered Home Ownership Savings Plan
R Hospital France ... Revue Hospitaliere de France [*A publication*]
RHP .... Radiant Heat Pump
RHP .... Rated Horsepower
RHP .... Reduced Hard Pressure (MSA)
RHP .... Resource Holding Potential
RHP .... Resource Holding Power [*Fighting ability - animal defense*]
RHP .... Revue d'Histoire de la Philosophie et d'Histoire Generale de la Civilisation [*A publication*]
RHP .... Right Hand Panel (MCD)
RHP .... Right-Handed Pitcher [*Baseball*]
RHP .... Rural Health Program [*Military*] (CINC)
RHPA .... Reverse Hemolytic Plaque Assay [*Clinical chemistry*]
RHPC .... Rapid-Hardening Portland Cement
RHPH .... Revue d'Histoire de la Philosophie et d'Histoire Generale de la Civilisation [*A publication*]
RHPhC ...... Revue d'Histoire de la Philosophie et d'Histoire Generale de la Civilisation [*A publication*]
RHPhR .... Revue d'Histoire et de Philosophie Religieuses [*A publication*]
RHPhRel .... Revue d'Histoire et de Philosophie Religieuses [*A publication*]
RH PL .... Rhodium Plate (MSA)
RHPR .... Revue d'Histoire et de Philosophie Religieuses [*A publication*]
RHPS .... Radiation-Hardened Power Supply
RHQ .... Regimental Headquarters
RHR .... Receiver Holding Register
RHR .... Reheater (AAG)
RHR .... Rejectable Hazard Rate (IEEE)
RHR .... Residual Heat Removal [*Nuclear energy*] (NRCH)
RHR .... Resting Heart Rate [*Cardiology*]
RHR .... Revue de l'Histoire des Religions [*A publication*]
r/hr .... Roentgens per Hour (AABC)
RHR .... Rohr Industries, Inc. [*NYSE symbol*]
RHR .... Roughness Height Rating (MSA)
RHR .... Royal Highland Regiment [*Military unit*] [*British*]

RHRCA ...... Rehabilitation Record [*A publication*]
RHRP .... Residual Heat Removal Pump [*Nuclear energy*] (NRCH)
RHRS .... Residual Heat Removal System [*Nuclear energy*] (NRCH)
RHRSW ..... Residual Heat Removal Service Water [*Nuclear energy*] (NRCH)
RHS .... Rectangular Hollow Section [*Metal industry*]
RHS .... Revue d'Histoire des Sciences et de Leurs Applications [*A publication*]
RHS .... Revue d'Histoire de la Spiritualite [*A publication*]
RHS .... Right-Hand Side
RHS .... Rocketdyne Hybrid Simulator [*NASA*] (NASA)
RHS .... Rodeo Historical Society (EA)
RHS .... Rough Hard Sphere [*Model of liquids*]
RHS .... Royal Historical Society [*British*]
RHS .... Royal Historical Society. Transactions [*A publication*]
RHS .... Royal Horticultural Society [*British*] (ARC)
RHS .... Royal Humane Society [*British*]
RHSA .... Revue d'Histoire des Sciences et de Leurs Applications [*A publication*]
RHSC .... Right-Hand Side Console [*NASA*] (KSC)
RHSE .... Revue Historique du Sud-Est Europeen [*A publication*]
RHSEE ...... Revue Historique du Sud-Est Europeen [*A publication*]
RhSh .... Rosh Hashanah [*New Year*] (BJA)
RHSI .... Rubber Heel and Sole Institute [*Defunct*] (EA)
RHSJ .... Religious Hospitallers of St. Joseph [*Roman Catholic women's religious order*]
RhSNA .... National Archives of Rhodesia, Salisbury, Rhodesia [*Library symbol*] [*Library of Congress*] (LCLS)
RHSQ .... Royal Historical Society of Queensland. Journal [*A publication*]
RHSQJ .... Royal Historical Society of Queensland. Journal [*A publication*] (ADA)
RHSTr .... Royal Historical Society. Transactions [*A publication*]
RHT .... Radiant Heat Temperature (NASA)
RHT .... Revue d'Histoire des Textes [*A publication*]
RHT .... Revue d'Histoire du Theatre [*A publication*]
RHT .... Reynolds Hydrodynamic Theory [*Physics*]
RHT .... Right Hypertropia [*Ophthalmology*]
RHTe .... Revue d'Histoire des Textes [*A publication*]
RHTKA ...... Rheinstahl Technik [*A publication*]
RHTM .... Regional Highway Traffic Model [*Database*] [*No longer available online*]
RHTMA ...... Reviews on High-Temperature Materials [*A publication*]
RHTRB .... Revue des Hautes Temperatures et des Refractaires [*A publication*]
RHTS .... Reactor Heat Transport System (NRCH)
RHU .... Radioisotope Heater Unit (NASA)
RHU .... Registered Health Underwriter [*NAHU*]
RHUEA ...... Rheumatism [*England*] [*British*]
RHUL .... Revista de Historia. Universidad de La Laguna [*A publication*]
RHUL .... Roczniki Humanistyczne Uniwersitetu Lubelskiego [*A publication*]
RHUMA ...... Rhumatologie [*A publication*]
RHV .... Remnant Hepatic Volume [*Hematology*]
RHV .... Revue Historique Vaudoise [*A publication*]
RhV .... Rheinische Vierteljahresblaetter [*A publication*]
RhV .... Rheinische Vorzeit in Wort und Bild [*A publication*]
RHV .... Road Haulage Vehicle
RHV .... San Jose, CA [*Location identifier*] [*FAA*] (FAAL)
RhVJ .... Rheinische Vierteljahresblaetter [*A publication*]
RHW .... Required Hangar Width (MCD)
RHW .... Reversible Half-Wave
RHW .... Right Half Word
RHWAC ...... Reversible Half-Wave Alternating Current
RHWACDC ... Reversible Half-Wave Alternating Current - Direct Current
RHWB .... [*The*] Reverend Henry Ward Beecher [*American clergyman, 1813-1887*]
RHWDC ...... Reversible Half-Wave Direct Current
RHWR .... RADAR Homing and Warning Receiver (MCD)
RHX .... Atlanta, GA [*Location identifier*] [*FAA*] (FAAL)
RHX .... Regenerative Heat Exchanger [*Nuclear energy*] (NRCH)
RHY .... Rhyolite Resources [*Vancouver Stock Exchange symbol*]
RHYTHM .... Remember How You Treat Hazardous Materials [*E. I. du Pont de Nemours & Co. program*]
Rhythm ...... Rhythmica [*of Aristoxenus*] [*Classical studies*] (OCD)
Rhythmes Monde ... Rhythmes du Monde [*A publication*]
RI .... Member of the Royal Institute of Painters in Water Colours [*British*]
RI .... RADAR Input
RI .... Radiation Indicator (NRCH)
RI .... Radiation Intensity (AABC)
R & I .... Radical and Intense [*Extremely great*] [*Slang*]
RI .... Radicalist International (EA)
RI .... Radice Corp. [*NYSE symbol*]
RI .... Radio Inertial (MCD)
RI .... Radio Influence
RI .... Radio Inspector
RI .... Radio Interference (MCD)
RI .... Radioisotope
RI .... Radix Institute [*Ojai, CA*] (EA)
RI .... Rampart Institute (EA)
RI .... Random Interlace [*Television*]

RI .... Range Instrumentation (MCD)
RI .... Rassegna Italiana [*A publication*]
RI .... Re-Issue [*of a book or periodical*] [*Publishing*]
RI .... React International (EA)
RI .... Reactor Island (NRCH)
RI .... Read-In (DEN)
RI .... Reallocation Inventory (AFIT)
RI .... Receiving Inspection (AAG)
R & I .... Receiving and Inspection (KSC)
RI .... Recipe Index [*A publication*]
RI .... Recombinant Inbred [*Genetics*]
RI .... Recovery, Incorporated
RI .... Recruit Induction [*Military*]
RI .... Recruit Instruction [*Navy*]
RI .... Redheads International (EA)
RI .... Reflective Insulation [*Technical drawings*]
RI .... Refractive Index
RI .... Refugees International (EA)
R et I .... Regina et Imperatrix [*Queen and Empress*] [*Latin*]
RI .... Regina Imperatrix [*Queen Empress*] [*Latin*]
RI .... Regional Ileitis [*Medicine*]
RI .... Registro Italiano [*Italian ship classification society*]
RI .... Rehabilitation International [*New York, NY*] (EA)
RI .... Reinsurance (ADA)
RI .... Relative Intensity
RI .... Relaxation Instruction [*Psychology*]
RI .... Reliability Index
RI .... Religious Instruction (ADA)
RI .... Remission Induction [*Oncology*]
R & I .... Removal and Installation (NRCH)
RI .... Repeat Indication [*Telecommunications*] (TEL)
RI .... Report of Investigation
RI .... Repulsion Induction [*Motor*]
RI .... Request for Information (MCD)
RI .... Require Identification
RI .... Rescue, Incorporated (EA)
RI .... Resistance Index
RI .... Resistance Inductance (IEEE)
RI .... Resistance International (EA)
RI .... Resolve, Incorporated [*Belmont, MA*] (EA)
RI .... Resonance Integrals (NRCH)
RI .... Respiratory Illness [*Medicine*]
R & I .... Restaurants and Institutions [*A publication*]
RI .... Retention Index
RIA .... Retirement Income
RI .... Retreats International (EA)
RI .... Retroactive Inhibition [*Psychology*]
RI .... Reunite, Incorporated [*Reynoldsburg, OH*] (EA)
RI .... Reverberation Index
RI .... Revista Iberoamericana [*A publication*]
RI .... Revista de las Indias [*A publication*]
RI .... Rex Imperator [*King Emperor*] [*Latin*]
R et I .... Rex et Imperator [*King and Emperor*] [*Latin*]
RI .... Rhode Island [*Postal code*]
RI .... Rhode Island Music Educators Review [*A publication*]
Ri .... Ribosomal [*Protein*] [*Cytology*]
RI .... Rice Institute Pamphlet [*A publication*]
Ri .... Richardson Number [*Physics*]
RI .... Ring Index [*of chemical compounds*] [*A publication*]
RI .... Risorgimento Italiano [*A publication*]
RI .... Rivista Israelitica [*A publication*]
RI .... Rivista d'Italia [*A publication*]
RI .... Rock Island Lines [*Railroad*]
RI .... Rockwell International Corp. (MCD)
RI .... Rolf Institute [*Boulder, CO*] (EA)
RI .... Rotary International [*Evanston, IL*] (EA)
RI .... Routing Identifier [*or Indicator*] (AFM)
RI .... Royal Institution [*British*]
RI .... Royal Irish [*Military unit*] [*British*]
RI .... Rubber Insulation [*Technical drawings*]
RI .... Rulers of India [*A publication*]
RI .... Rutherford Institute (EA)
RIA .... Radioimmunoassay [*Clinical chemistry*]
RIA .... Railroad Insurance Association
RIA .... Rain in Area (ADA)
RIA .... Reactivity Initiated Accident [*Nuclear energy*] (NRCH)
RIA .... Registered Industrial and Cost Accountant
RIA .... Registered Investment Adviser [*Securities*]
RIA .... Regulatory Impact Analysis
RIA .... Religious Instruction Association [*Later, PERSC*]
RIA .... Remote Intelligence Acquisition
RIA .... Removable Instrument Assembly [*Nuclear energy*] (NRCH)
RIA .... Research Institute of America [*New York, NY*] [*Information service*] (EISS)
RIA .... Revista Iberoamericana [*A publication*]
RIA .... Rich International Airways, Inc. [*Miami, FL*] [*FAA designator*] (FAAC)
RIA .... Rivista. Istituto di Archeologia [*A publication*]
RIA .... Robotic Industries Association
RIA .... Rock Island Arsenal [*Illinois*] [*Army*]
RIA .... Royal Irish Academy

RIA .... Santa Maria [*Brazil*] [*Airport symbol*] (OAG)
RIAA .... Recording Industry Association of America [*Formerly, Record Industry Association of America*] [*New York, NY*] (EA)
RIAB .... Revista Interamericana de Bibliografia [*A publication*]
RIAC .... Regional Industry Advisory Committee [*Civil Defense*]
RIACS .... Research Institute for Advanced Computer Science [*University Space Research Association*] [*Research center*] (RCD)
RIAD .... Rencontres Internationales des Assureurs Defense (EA)
RIA-DA ...... Radioimmunoassay Double Antibody [*Test*] [*Clinical chemistry*]
RIAEC .... Rhode Island Atomic Energy Commission
RIAES........ Rhode Island Agricultural Experiment Station [*University of Rhode Island*] [*Research center*] (RCD)
RIAF .... Royal Indian Air Force
RIAF .... Royal Iraqi Air Force
RI Ag .... Rhode Island Agriculture [*A publication*]
RI Ag Exp ... Rhode Island. Agricultural Experiment Station. Publications [*A publication*]
RI Agr .... Rhode Island Agriculture. Rhode Island Agricultural Experiment Station [*A publication*]
RI Agric...... Rhode Island Agriculture [*A publication*]
RI Agric Exp Stn Bull ... Rhode Island. Agricultural Experiment Station. Bulletin [*A publication*]
RI Agric Exp Stn Res Q Rev ... Rhode Island. Agricultural Experiment Station. Research Quarterly Review [*A publication*]
RIAI .... Royal Institute of the Architects of Ireland
RIAL .... Religion in American Life (EA)
RIAL .... Revised Individual Allowance List [*Navy*] (NVT)
RIALF........ Flair Resources Ltd. [*NASDAQ symbol*] (NQ)
RIAM .... Royal Irish Academy of Music
RIAND .... Risk Analysis [*A publication*]
RIAR .... Requirements Inventory Analysis Report (AFM)
RIA-R........ Rock Island Arsenal General Thomas J. Rodman Laboratory [*Army*]
RIAS .... Research Initiation and Support [*National Science Foundation program*]
RIAS .... Research Institute for Advanced Studies [*Martin Marietta Corp.*]
RIAS .... Royal Incorporation of Architects in Scotland
RIAS .... Rundfunk im Amerikanischen Sektor Berlins [*Radio in American Sector*] [*West Berlin, Germany*]
RIASB........ Richerche Astronomiche [*A publication*]
RIASC .... Royal Indian Army Service Corps [*British*]
RIA Tax ...... Research Institute of America Tax Coordinator (DLA)
RIAX .... Rich International Airways, Inc. [*Air carrier designation symbol*]
RIB .... Railway Information Bureau
RIB .... Recoverable Item Breakdown
RIB .... Recyclable, Incineratable, Biodegradable [*Food packaging*]
RIB .... Review of International Broadcasting [*A publication*]
RIB .... Revista Iberoamericana de Bibliografia [*A publication*]
RIB .... Revue de l'Instruction Publique en Belgique [*A publication*]
RIB .... Ribbed (AAG)
RIB .... Riberalta [*Bolivia*] [*Airport symbol*] (OAG)
Rib........... Ribose [*Also, r*] [*A sugar*]
RIB .... Right Inboard (MCD)
Ri B........... Rivista Biblica [*A publication*]
RIB .... [*The*] Roman Inscriptions of Britain [*A publication*] (OCD)
RIB .... Rural Industries Bureau
RIBA .... Royal Institute of British Architects [*London, England*] (EISS)
RIBA J .... Royal Institute of British Architects. Journal [*A publication*]
RI Bd RC .... Rhode Island Board of Railroad Commission Reports (DLA)
R Iberoamer Segur Soc ... Revista Iberoamericana de Seguridad Social [*A publication*]
RIBI............ Ribi Immunochem Research, Inc. [*NASDAQ symbol*] (NQ)
RIBJ.......... Rhode Island Bar Journal [*A publication*]
RIBJD .... RIBA [*Royal Institute of British Architects*] Journal [*A publication*]
RIBS .... Restructured Infantry Battalion System (AABC)
RIBS .... Royal Institute of British Sculptors
RIBSS........ Research Institute for the Behavioral and Social Sciences [*Army*]
RI Bur Industrial Statistics An Rp Nat Res S B ... Rhode Island Bureau of Industrial Statistics. Annual Report. Natural Resources Survey. Bulletin [*A publication*]
Ric............ King Richard (DLA)
RIC .... RADAR Indicating Console [*FAA*]
RIC .... RADAR Input Control
RIC .... RADAR Intercept Calculator
RIC .... RADAR Intercept Control
RIC .... Radio Industry Council [*British*]
RIC .... Rafter Input Converter
RIC .... Range Instrumentation Conference (MUGU)
RIC .... Range Instrumentation Coordination (KSC)
RIC .... Raptor Information Center (EA)
RIC .... Rare-Earth Information Center [*Iowa State University*] [*Ames, IA*] (EISS)
RIC .... Read-In Counter
RIC .... Reconstructed Ion Chromatogram
RIC .... Record Identification Code [*Navy*]
RIC .... Regolamento Internazionale Carrozze [*International Carriage and Van Union*]

RIC .... Remote Information Center
RIC .... Repair Induction Code [*Module Maintenance Facility*]
RIC .... Repairable Identification Code
RIC .... Repairable Item Code
RIC .... Replaceable Item Code
RIC .... Request for Instrumentation Clarification [*NASA*]   (KSC)
RIC .... Resident Inspector-in-Charge
RIC .... Resistance, Inductance, and Capacitance   (NASA)
RIC .... Resource Identification Code [*Navy*]
RIC .... Resource Information Center System [*Search system*]
RIC .... Retirement Income Credit
RIC .... Review of International Cooperation [*A publication*]
RIC .... Richmond [*Florida*] [*Seismograph station code, US Geological Survey*] [*Closed*]   (SEIS)
RIC .... Richmond [*Virginia*] [*Airport symbol*]
RIC .... Ricks College, David O. McKay Learning Resources Center, Rexburg, ID [*OCLC symbol*]   (OCLC)
RIC .... Road Information Center [*Arab Contractors Co.*]   (EISS)
RIC .... Rockwell International Corporation   (NASA)
RIC .... Rodeo Information Commission   (EA)
RIC .... Roman Imperial Coinage [*A publication*]   (OCD)
RIC .... Routing Identification Code   (NATG)
RIC .... Royal Institute of Chemistry [*Later, RSC*] [*British*]
RIC .... Royal Irish Constabulary
RICA .... Railway Industry Clearance Association [*Omaha, NE*]   (EA)
RICAL........... Research Information Center and Library [*Foster Wheeler Corp.*] [*Information service*]   (EISS)
RICASIP ..... Research Information Center and Advisory Service on Information Processing [*National Bureau of Standards - National Science Foundation*]
Ric Autom ... Ricerche di Automatica [*A publication*]
RicBibRel ... Ricerche Bibliche e Religiose [*Milan*] [*A publication*]
Ric Biol Selvaggina ... Ricerche di Biologia della Selvaggina [*A publication*]
RICC........... Regional Interagency Coordinating Committee [*Department of Labor*]
RICC........... Remote Intercomputer Communications Interface   (MCD)
RICC........... Reportable Item Control Code [*Army*]   (AABC)
Ric Clin Lab ... Ricerca in Clinica e in Laboratorio [*A publication*]
Ric Demos ... Ricerche Demoscopiche [*A publication*]
Ric Doc Tess ... Ricerca e Documentazione Tessile [*A publication*]
RICE........... Recreational Industries Council on Exporting [*North Palm Beach, FL*]   (EA)
RICE........... Regional Information and Communications Exchange [*Rice University Library*] [*Houston, TX*]
RICE........... Relative Index of Combat Effectiveness [*Military*] [*British*]
RICE........... Research and Information Centre on Eritrea   (EA)
RICE........... Resources in Computer Education [*Northwest Regional Educational Laboratory Microcomputer Software and Information for Teachers*] [*Database*]
RICE........... Rest, Ice, Compression, Elevation [*Medicine*]
Rice........... Rice's South Carolina Law Reports [*1838-39*]   (DLA)
Rice Ch ...... Rice's South Carolina Equity Reports   (DLA)
Ric Econ..... Ricerche Economiche [*A publication*]
Rice Dig ..... Rice's Digest of Patent Office Decisions   (DLA)
Rice Eq...... Rice's South Carolina Equity Reports [*1838-39*]   (DLA)
Rice Ev ...... Rice's Law of Evidence   (DLA)
Rice Inst P ... Rice Institute Pamphlet [*A publication*]
Rice Inst Pam ... Rice Institute Pamphlet [*A publication*]
Rice J .... Rice Journal [*A publication*]
Rice L (SC) ... Rice's South Carolina Law Reports   (DLA)
Ricerca Scient ... Ricerca Scientifica [*A publication*]
Ricerca Scient Rc ... Ricerca Scientifica. Rendiconti [*A publication*]
Ricerche Automat ... Ricerche di Automatica [*A publication*]
Ricerche Mat ... Ricerche di Matematica [*A publication*]
Rice's Code ... Rice's Code of Practice [*Colorado*]   (DLA)
Rice Univ Aero-Astronaut Rep ... Rice University. Aero-Astronautic Report [*A publication*]
Rice Univ Stud ... Rice University. Studies [*A publication*]
RiceUS....... Rice University. Studies [*A publication*]
RicF........... Ricerche Filosofiche [*A publication*]
Rich........... King Richard   (DLA)
Rich........... Richardson's Reports [*2-5 New Hampshire*]   (DLA)
Rich........... [*J. S. G.*] Richardson's South Carolina Law Reports   (DLA)
RICH........... Richmond National Battlefield Park
Richardson Law Practice ... Richardson's Establishing a Law Practice   (DLA)
Richardson's S Ca Rep ... [*J. S. G.*] Richardson's South Carolina Law Reports   (DLA)
Rich Cas .... [*J. S. G.*] Richardson's South Carolina Cases [*1831-32*]   (DLA)
Rich Cas (SC) ... [*J. S. G.*] Richardson's South Carolina Equity Cases   (DLA)
Rich Ch ...... [*J. S. G.*] Richardson's South Carolina Equity Reports   (DLA)
Rich Ch Pr ... Richardson's Chancery Practice [*1838*]   (DLA)
Rich CP ...... Richardson's Practice Common Pleas [*England*]   (DLA)
Rich Ct Cl ... Richardson's Court of Claims Reports   (DLA)
RICHD .... Reviews in Inorganic Chemistry [*A publication*]
Richd E Repts ... [*J. S. G.*] Richardson's South Carolina Equity Reports   (DLA)
Rich Dict .... Richardson's New Dictionary of the English Language   (DLA)
Rich'd Law R ... [*J. S. G.*] Richardson's South Carolina Law Reports   (DLA)
RICHEL ...... Richmond - Cape Henry Environmental Laboratory [*NASA/ USGS*]

Rich Eq ...... [*J. S. G.*] Richardson's South Carolina Equity Reports [*1844- 46, 1850-68*]   (DLA)
Rich Eq Cas ... [*J. S. G.*] Richardson's South Carolina Equity Reports   (DLA)
Rich Eq Ch ... [*J. S. G.*] Richardson's South Carolina Equity Reports   (DLA)
Rich & H..... Richardson and Hook's Street Railway Decisions   (DLA)
Rich Land A ... Richey's Irish Land Act   (DLA)
Rich Law (SC) ... [*J. S. G.*] Richardson's South Carolina Law Reports   (DLA)
Rich L (SC) ... [*J. S. G.*] Richardson's South Carolina Law Reports   (DLA)
Rich NH ...... Richardson's Reports [*3-5 New Hampshire*]   (DLA)
Rich NS...... [*J. S. G.*] Richardson's South Carolina Reports, New Series   (DLA)
Rich PRCP ... Richardson's Practical Register of English Common Pleas   (DLA)
Rich Pr KB ... Richardson's Attorney's Practice in the Court of King's Bench [*8th ed.*] [*1792*]   (DLA)
Rich Pr Reg ... Richardson's Practical Register of English Common Pleas   (DLA)
Rich & S ..... Richardson and Sayles' Select Cases of Procedure without Writ [*Selden Society Publication 60*]   (DLA)
Rich & W .... Richardson and Woodbury's Reports [*2 New Hampshire*]   (DLA)
Rich Wills... Richardson's Law of Testaments and Last Wills   (DLA)
Rickia Arq Bot Estado Sao Paulo Ser Criptogam Supl ... Rickia Arquivos de Botanica do Estado de Sao Paulo. Serie Criptogamica [*A publication*]
Rickia Supl ... Rickia. Suplemento [*A publication*]
Rick & M..... Rickards and Michael's English Locus Standi Reports   (DLA)
Rickmansworth Hist ... Rickmansworth Historian [*A publication*]
Rick & S ..... Rickards and Saunders' English Locus Standi Reports   (DLA)
RicLing...... Ricerche Linguistiche [*A publication*]
RICM .... Registre International des Citoyens du Monde [*International Registry of World Citizens*]
RICM .... Right Intercostal Margin [*Medicine*]
Ric Mat ...... Ricerche di Matematica [*A publication*]
RICMO .... RADAR Input Countermeasures Officer [*Air Force*]
RICMT....... RADAR Input Countermeasures Technician [*Air Force*]
RICO......... Racketeer-Influenced and Corrupt Organizations [*Nickname of a 1970 law used by federal prosecutors to indict organized crime leaders*]
RICOA .... Rivista dei Combustibili [*A publication*]
RI Comp of Rules of St Agencies ... Rhode Island Compilation of Rules of State Agencies   (DLA)
RICP .... Revista. Instituto de Cultura Puertorriquena [*A publication*]
RicR......... Ricerche Religiose [*A publication*]
RicRel........ Ricerche Religiose [*A publication*]
RICS......... Range Instrumentation Control System
RICS......... Reports Index Control   (MCD)
RICS......... Respiratory Intensive Care System [*Medicine*]
Ric & S ...... Rickards and Saunders' English Locus Standi Reports [*1890- 94*]   (DLA)
RICS......... Royal Institute of Chartered Surveyors [*British*]
RICS......... Royal Institution of Chartered Surveyors [*British*]
RICS Abs Rev ... RICS [*Royal Institution of Chartered Surveyors*] Abstracts and Review [*A publication*]
Ric Sci....... Ricerca Scientifica [*A publication*]
Ric Sci Parte 2 Sez A ... Ricerca Scientifica. Parte 2. Rendiconti Sezione A. Biologica [*A publication*]
Ric Sci Parte 2 Sez B ... Ricerca Scientifica. Parte 2. Rendiconti Sezione B. Biologica [*A publication*]
Ric Sci Prog Tec ... Ricerca Scientifica ed il Progresso Tecnico [*A publication*]
Ric Sci Quad ... Ricerca Scientifica. Quaderni [*A publication*]
Ric Sci Rend Sez B ... Ricerca Scientifica. Serie Seconda. Parte II. Rendiconti. Sezione B. Biologica [*A publication*]
Ric Sci Ricostr ... Ricerca Scientifica e Ricostruzione [*A publication*]
Ric Sci Suppl ... Ricerca Scientifica. Supplemento [*A publication*]
RicSL........ Ricerche Slavistiche [*A publication*]
Ric Spettrosc ... Ricerche Spettroscopiche [*A publication*]
Ric Spettros Lab Astrofis Specola ... Ricerche Spettroscopiche. Laboratorio Astrofisico della Specola Vaticana [*A publication*]
RicSRel...... Ricerche di Storia Religiosa [*A publication*]
RicStRel..... Ricerche di Storia Religiosa [*Rome*] [*A publication*]
Ric Studi Med Sper ... Ricerche e Studi di Medicina Sperimentale [*A publication*]
Ric Termotecnica ... Ricerche di Termotecnica [*Italy*] [*A publication*]
RI Ct Rec.... Rhode Island Court Records   (DLA)
RICU.......... Respiratory Intensive Care Unit [*Medicine*]
Ric Zool Appl Caccia ... Ricerche di Zoologia Applicata alla Caccia [*A publication*]
Ric Zool Appl Caccia Suppl ... Ricerche di Zoologia Applicata alla Caccia. Supplemento [*A publication*]
RID .... RADAR Input Drum
RID .... Radial Immunodiffusion [*Analytical biochemistry*]
RID .... Radio Intelligence Division [*of the Federal Communications Commission*]
RID .... Range Instruments Development   (MCD)
RID .... Record Identity [*Military*]   (AFIT)
RID .... Records Issue Date [*Bell System*]   (TEL)
RID .... Reduced Ignition Relay   (MCD)
RID .... Refractive Index Detector [*Instrumentation*]
RID .... Regimented Inmate Discipline [*Mississippi State Penitentiary*]

RID .... Registry of Interpreters for the Deaf [*Silver Spring, MD*]   (EA)
RID .... Reglement International Concernant le Transport des Marchandises Dangereuses [*International Regulation Governing the Carriage of Dangerous Goods*]
RID .... Released to Inactive Duty
RID .... Reliability Index Determination   (MCD)
RID .... Remove Intoxicated Drivers [*An association*]
RID .... Research Institutes and Divisions [*of National Institutes of Health*]
RID .... Reset Inhibit Drive
RID .... Reset Inhibit Drum
RID .... Retrofit Installation Data   (MCD)
RID .... Reversible Intravas Device
RID .... Review Item Discrepancy   (MCD)
RID .... Review Item Disposition [*NASA*]   (NASA)
RID .... Richmond, IN [*Location identifier*] [*FAA*]   (FAAL)
RID .... Rider College Library, Lawrenceville, NJ [*OCLC symbol*]   (OCLC)
Rid .... Ridotto [*A publication*]
RID .... Rivista Italiana di Dialettologia [*A publication*]
RID .... Rivista Italiana del Drama [*A publication*]
RIDA .... Reverse Isotope Dilution Assay [*Chemical analysis*]
RIDA .... Revue Internationale des Droits de l'Antiquite [*A publication*]
RIDAC ...... Range Interference Detecting and Control
RIDAURA ... Remission Inducing Drug, Au [*Chemical symbol for gold*], Rheumatoid Arthritis [*Gold-based drug manufactured by SmithKline Beckman Corp.*]
RIDC .... Revue Internationale de Droit Compare [*A publication*]
RIDC .... Ryerson International Development Centre [*Ryerson Polytechnical Institute*] [*Canada*] [*Research center*]   (RCD)
Riddle's Lex ... Riddle's Lexicon   (DLA)
RIDE .... Research Institute for Diagnostic Engineering
RI Dec ...... Rhode Island Decisions   (DLA)
RIdeP .... Revue Internationale de Philosophie [*A publication*]
RIDEQ .... Revista Iberoamericana de Educacion Quimica [*A publication*]
RI Dev Counc Geol Bull ... Rhode Island Development Council. Geological Bulletin [*A publication*]
RI Devel Council Geol Bull Sci Contr ... Rhode Island Development Council. Geological Bulletin. Scientific Contribution [*A publication*]
RIDEX .... Ridexchange   (EA)
RIDF .... Random Input Describing Function [*Data processing*]
Ridg .... Ridgeway's Reports Tempore Hardwicke, Chancery and English King's Bench   (DLA)
RIDG .... Royal Inniskilling Dragoon Guards [*Military unit*] [*British*]
Ridg Ap ..... Ridgeway's Irish Appeal [*or Parliamentary*] Cases   (DLA)
Ridg Cas .... Ridgeway's Reports Tempore Hardwicke, Chancery and English King's Bench   (DLA)
Ridgew ...... Ridgeway's Reports Tempore Hardwicke, Chancery and English King's Bench   (DLA)
Ridgew Ir PC ... Ridgeway's Irish Parliamentary Reports [*1784-96*]   (DLA)
Ridgew L & S (Ir) ... Ridgeway, Lapp, and Schoales' Irish Term Reports   (DLA)
Ridgew T Hardw ... Ridgeway's Reports Tempore Hardwicke, Chancery [*27 English Reprint*] [*1744-46*]   (DLA)
Ridgew T Hardw (Eng) ... Ridgeway Tempore Hardwicke [*27 English Reprint*]   (DLA)
Ridg L & S ... Ridgeway, Lapp, and Schoales' Irish Term Reports   (DLA)
Ridg Parl Rep ... Ridgeway's Irish Parliamentary Reports [*1784-96*]   (DLA)
Ridg PC ...... Ridgeway's Irish Appeal [*or Parliamentary*] Cases   (DLA)
Ridg Pr Rep ... Ridgeway's Irish Appeal [*or Parliamentary*] Cases   (DLA)
Ridg Rep .... Ridgeway's Reports of State Trials in Ireland   (DLA)
Ridg St Tr .. Ridgeway's [*Individual*] Reports of State Trials in Ireland   (DLA)
Ridg Temp H ... Ridgeway's Reports Tempore Hardwicke, Chancery [*27 English Reprint*] [*1744-46*]   (DLA)
Ridg T H ... Ridgeway's Reports Tempore Hardwicke, Chancery [*27 English Reprint*] [*1744-46*]   (DLA)
Ridg T Hard ... Ridgeway's Reports Tempore Hardwicke, Chancery and English King's Bench [*27 English Reprint*]   (DLA)
Ridg T Hardw ... Ridgeway's Reports Tempore Hardwicke, Chancery and English King's Bench [*27 English Reprint*]   (DLA)
Ridgw Ir PC ... Ridgeway's Irish Parliamentary Cases   (DLA)
RIDI .... Receiving Inspection Detail Instruction [*NASA*]   (NASA)
RIDIT .... Relative to an Identified Distribution Transformation [*Pharmacology*]
RIDL .... Radiation Instrument Development Laboratory
RIDL .... Ridge Instrument Development Laboratory [*Navy*]
Ridley Civil & Ecc Law ... Ridley's Civil and Ecclesiastical Law   (DLA)
RIDP .... RADAR-IFF Data Processor   (MCD)
RIDP .... RNA-Instructed DNA Polymerase [*Later, RDDP*] [*An enzyme*]
RIDS .... Radio Information Distribution System   (MCD)
RIDS .... Range Information Display System   (MCD)
RIDS .... Receiving Inspection Data Status [*Report*]   (NRCH)
RIDS .... Regional Operations Control Centre Information Display System [*NORAD*]
RIDS .... Regulatory Information Distribution System [*Nuclear energy*]   (NRCH)
Rid Sup Proc ... Riddle's Supplementary Proceedings [*New York*]   (DLA)
RIE............ Range of Incentive Effectiveness
RIE............ Reactive Ion Etching [*Semiconductor technology*]
RIE............ Recognised Investment Exchange [*British*]

RIE............ Research in Education [*Monthly publication of ERIC*]
RIE............ Resources in Education [*Formerly, Research in Education*] [*National Institute of Education*] [*Database*]
RIE............ Retirement Income Endowment [*Insurance*]
RIE............ Revista de Ideas Esteticas [*A publication*]
RIE............ Revue Internationale de l'Enseignement [*A publication*]
RIE............ Rice Lake [*Wisconsin*] [*Airport symbol*]   (OAG)
RIE............ Right Inboard Elevon [*Aviation*]   (MCD)
RIE............ Royal Institute of Engineers [*British*]
RIEB.......... Revista. Instituto de Estudos Brasileiros [*A publication*]
RIEC .... Royal Indian Engineering College [*British*]
Riech Aromen Kosmet ... Riechstoffe, Aromen, Kosmetica [*A publication*]
Riechst Aromen ... Riechstoffe und Aromen [*A publication*]
Riechst Aromen Koerperpflegem ... Riechstoffe, Aromen, Koerperpflegemittel [*Later, Riechstoffe, Aromen, Kosmetica*] [*A publication*]
Ried........... Riedell's Reports [*68, 69 New Hampshire*]   (DLA)
RIEDAC...... Research in International Economics of Disarmament and Arms Control [*A program of Columbia University School of International Affairs*]
RIEEC........ Research Institute for the Education of Exceptional Children [*A publication*]
RIEF .... Recycling Isoelectric Focusing [*Preparative electrophoresis*]
RIEI .... Roofing Industry Educational Institute [*Englewood, CO*]   (EA)
RIEM .... Research Institute for Environmental Medicine [*Army*]   (MCD)
RIEMA....... Rapports et Proces-Verbaux des Reunions. Conseil International pour l'Exploration de la Mer [*A publication*]
RIES .... Research Institute for Engineering Sciences [*Wayne State University*] [*Research center*]   (RCD)
RIETCOM... Regional Interagency Emergency Transportation Committee
RIEtnN....... Revista. Instituto Etnologico Nacional [*A publication*]
RIEV .... Revista Internacional de Estudios Vascos [*A publication*]
RIF............ Radio-Influence Field   (IEEE)
RIF............ Radio Interference Filter
RIF............ Rate Input Form   (NVT)
RIF............ Reading Is Fundamental [*An association*]   (EA)
RIF............ Reduction in Force [*Military*]
RIF............ Refund Information File [*IRS*]
RIF............ Relative Importance Factor   (NASA)
RIF............ Release-Inhibiting Factor [*Endocrinology*]
RIF............ Reliability Improvement Factor
RIF............ Reportable Item File [*Military*]   (AFIT)
RIF............ Resistance Inducing Factor   (ADA)
RIF............ Richfield [*Utah*] [*Airport symbol*]   (OAG)
RIF............ Richfield, UT [*Location identifier*] [*FAA*]   (FAAL)
RIF............ Rifampin [*Also, R/AMP, RMP*] [*Bactericide*]
RIF............ Right Iliac Fossa [*Medicine*]
RIF............ Rodeo Information Foundation [*Later, Rodeo News Bureau*]
RIF............ Royal Inniskilling Fusiliers [*Military unit*] [*British*]
RIF............ Royal Irish Fusiliers [*Military unit*] [*British*]
RIFAA....... Revista Industrial y Fabril [*A publication*]
RIFC .... Radio In-Flight Correction
RIFC .... Radioactive Illuminated Fire Control   (MCD)
RIFC .... Rat Intrinsic Factor Concentrate
RIFD .... Rivista Internazionale di Filosofia del Diritto [*A publication*]
RIFFED...... Forced Out by a Reduction in Force
RIFI .... Radio Interference Field Intensity [*Meter*]   (NG)
RIFI .... Radio-Interference-Free Instrument
RIFIM .... Radio Interference Field Intensity Meter
RIFL.......... Random Item File Locater
RIFMA....... Roentgen-Isotope-Fluorescent Method of Analysis
RIFN .... Recombinant Interferon [*Biochemistry*]
Riforma Agrar ... Riforma Agraria [*Italy*] [*A publication*]
Riforma Med ... Riforma Medica [*A publication*]
RIFPA........ Revue. Institut Francais du Petrole et Annales des Combustions Liquides [*Later, Revue. Institut Francais du Petrole*] [*A publication*]
RIFS .... Radioisotope Field Support
RI/FS......... Remedial Investigation and Feasibility Study [*Environmental Protection Agency*]
RIFT.......... Reactor-in-Flight Test [*NASA*]
RIFT/S....... Reactor-in-Flight Test/System [*NASA*]   (AAG)
RIG .... Rabies Immune Globulin [*Immunology*]
RIG .... Radio Inertial Guidance   (AAG)
RIG .... Radio Interference Guard
RIG .... Rate Integrating Gyro
RIG .... Ridgeling [*Horse racing*]
RIG .... Rigging   (ROG)
RIG .... Rio Grande [*Brazil*] [*Airport symbol*]   (OAG)
RIG .... Roll-Imitation Gold
RIGAA ...... Rinsho Ganka [*A publication*]
Rigasche Ind Ztg ... Rigasche Industrie Zeitung [*A publication*]
Rigas Politehn Inst Zinatn Raksti ... Rigas Politehniskais Instituts. Rizskii Politehniceskii Institut. Ucenyi Zapiski. Rigas Politehniskais. Instituts Zinatniskie Raksti [*A publication*]
RIGB.......... Royal Institution of Great Britain
RI Gen Laws ... General Laws of Rhode Island   (DLA)
RIGFET ..... Resistive Insulated-Gate Field Effect Transistor
Rigg........... Select Pleas, Starrs, and Other Records from the Rolls of the Exchequer of the Jews, Edited by J. M. Riggs [*Selden Society Publications, Vol. 15*]   (DLA)

RIGGS .... Ross Ice Shelf Geophysical and Glaciological Survey [*Ross Ice Shelf Project*]

RIGHTS ...... Reforming Institutions to Guarantee Humane Treatment Standards [*Student legal action organization*]

RIGI .... Receiving Inspection General Instruction [*NASA*]   (NASA)

RIGI .... Rivista Indo-Greco-Italico [*A publication*]

RIGIB .... Radovi Instituta za Geolosko-Rudarska Istrazivanja i Ispitivanja Nuklearnih i Drugih Mineralnih Sirovina [*A publication*]

RIGPA .... Rezul'taty Issledovanyi po Mezhdunarodny Geofizicheskim Proektam [*A publication*]

RI Grad Sch Oceanogr Occas Publ ... Rhode Island Graduate School of Oceanography. Occasional Publication [*A publication*]

RIGS .... Radio Inertial Guidance System

RIGS .... Resonant Infrasonic Gauging System

RIGS .... Riggs National Corp. [*NASDAQ symbol*]   (NQ)

RIGS .... Runway Identifiers with Glide Slope [*Aviation*]

RIH .... Rhode Island History [*A publication*]

RIH .... Rhode Island Hospital, Providence, RI [*OCLC symbol*]   (OCLC)

RIH .... Right Inguinal Hernia [*Medicine*]

RIHAA .... Rivers and Harbors [*A publication*]

RIHANS ...... River and Harbor Aid to Navigation System [*Coast Guard*]

RIHED........ Regional Institute of Higher Education and Development

RIHGSP ..... Revista. Instituto Historico e Geographico de Sao Paulo [*A publication*]

RI Hist .... Rhode Island History [*A publication*]

RI Hist Soc Coll ... Rhode Island Historical Society. Collections [*A publication*]

RIHL .... Richton International [*NASDAQ symbol*]   (NQ)

RIHPC .... Revue Internationale d'Histoire Politique et Constitutionnelle [*A publication*]

RIHS .... Royal International Horse Show [*British*]

RIHT .... RIHT Financial Corp. [*NASDAQ symbol*]   (NQ)

RIHYA .... Rinsho Hinyokika [*A publication*]

RII .... RADAR Intelligence Information

RII .... Receiving Inspection Instructions   (NRCH)

RII .... Rivista Inguana et Intemelia [*A publication*]

RIIA .... Royal Institute of International Affairs [*British*]

RIIC .... Research Institute on International Change [*Columbia University*]

RIIES .... Research Institute on Immigration and Ethnic Studies [*Smithsonian Institution*]

RIIGA........ Rivista Italiana d'Igiene [*A publication*]

RIISA......... Report. Institute of Industrial Science. University of Tokyo [*A publication*]

RIISE .... Research Institute for Information Science and Engineering, Inc. [*Pittsburgh, PA*] [*Information service*]   (EISS)

Riista-Kalataloudes Tutkimuslaitos Kalantutkimusosasto Tied ... Riista- ja Kalataloudes Tutkimuslaitos Kalantutkimusosasto Tiedonantoja [*A publication*]

Riistatiet Julkaisuja ... Riistatieteellisia Julkaisuja [*A publication*]

RIJ .... Right Internal Jugular [*Vein*] [*Anatomy*]

RIJ .... Rioja [*Peru*] [*Airport symbol*]   (OAG)

RIJ .... Romano Internacionalno Jekhethanibe [*Romani Union*]   (EA)

RIJAZ .... Radovi Instituta Jugoslavenske Akademije Znanosti i Umjetnosti u Zadru [*A publication*]

RIJAZUZ .... Radovi Instituta Jugoslavenske Akademije Znanosti i Umjetnosti u Zadru [*A publication*]

RI Jew Hist Note ... Rhode Island Jewish Historical Notes [*A publication*]

RI Jewish Historical Notes ... Rhode Island Jewish Historical Notes [*A publication*]

RIJHN........ Rhode Island Jewish Historical Notes [*A publication*]

Rijksuniv Utrecht Jaarversl Wet Deel ... Rijksuniversiteit Utrecht Jaarverslag Wetenschappelijk Deel [*A publication*]

Rijksw Commun ... Rijkswaterstaat Communications [*A publication*]

RIJU.......... Riistatieteellisia Julkaisuja. Finnish Game Research [*A publication*]

RIK .... Replacement in Kind   (NG)

RIKAA .... Rinsho Kagaku [*A publication*]

RIKEB......... Rinsho Ketsueki [*A publication*]

RIKES........ Raman-Induced Kerr Effect Scattering [*Spectroscopy*]

RIL............ Radio Influence Level

RIL............ Radio Interference Level

RIL............ Recombinant Interleukin [*Immunotherapy*]

RIL............ Recoverable Item List

RIL............ Red Indicator Light

RIL............ Reduction in Leadtime   (MCD)

RIL............ Reliability Intensity Level   (CAAL)

RIL............ Rendiconti. Istituto Lombardo di Scienze e Lettere [*A publication*]

RIL............ Repairable Item List   (CAAL)

RIL............ Rifle, CO [*Location identifier*] [*FAA*]   (FAAL)

Ril .... Riley's South Carolina Chancery Reports [*1836-37*]   (DLA)

Ril .... Riley's South Carolina Equity Reports   (DLA)

RIL............ University of Rhode Island, Graduate Library School, Kingston, RI [*OCLC symbol*]   (OCLC)

RILA .... Rassegna Italiana di Linguistica Applicata [*A publication*]

RILA .... Repertoire International de la Litterature de l'Art [*International Repertory of the Literature of Art*] [*A publication*]

RILAMAC... Research in Laboratory Animal Medicine and Care

RILD .... Rivista Italiana di Letteratura Dialettale [*A publication*]

RILEM .... Reunion Internationale des Laboratoires d'Essais et de Recherches sur les Materiaux et les Constructions [*International Union of Testing and Research Laboratories for Materials and Structures*]   (EA-IO)

Riley .... Riley's Reports [*37-42 West Virginia*]   (DLA)

Riley .... Riley's South Carolina Chancery Reports   (DLA)

Riley .... Riley's South Carolina Law Reports   (DLA)

Riley Ch ..... Riley's South Carolina Equity Reports   (DLA)

Riley Eq...... Riley's South Carolina Equity Reports   (DLA)

Riley Eq (SC) ... Riley's South Carolina Equity Reports   (DLA)

Riley L (SC) ... Riley's South Carolina Law Reports   (DLA)

RILFC........ Rhode Island Library Film Cooperative [*Library network*]

Ril Harp ..... Riley's Edition of Harper's South Carolina Reports   (DLA)

RILKO........ Research into Lost Knowledge Organisation Trust   (EA-IO)

RILM.......... RILM [*Repertoire International de la Litterature Musicale*] Abstracts of Music Literature [*City University of New York*] [*Database*] [*A publication*]

RiLM.......... Rivista di Letterature Moderne [*A publication*]

RILOB........ Recherches Publiees sous la Direction de l'Institut de Lettres Orientales de Beyrouth [*A publication*]

RILOP........ Reclamation in Lieu of Procurement [*Navy*]   (NG)

RILS .... Ranging Integration Location System

RILS .... Rapid Integrated Logistic Support System   (AABC)

RILSA........ Resident Integrated Logistics Support Activity [*Military*]   (AFIT)

RILSD........ Resident Integrated Logistics Support Detachment [*Military*]   (MCD)

RILSL .... Rendiconti. Istituto Lombardo. Classe di Lettere, Scienze Morali, e Storiche [*A publication*]

RILST .... Remote Integrated Logistics Support Team [*Military*]   (MCD)

RILT........... Rabbit Ileal Loop Test [*for enterotoxins*]

RIM........... RADAR Input Mapper

RIM........... RADAR Input Monitor   (CET)

RIM........... RADAR Intelligence Map

RIM........... Radial Inlet Manifold

RIM........... Radiant Intensity Measurements   (MUGU)

RIM........... Radioisotope Medicine

RIM........... Reaction Injection Molding [*Plastics technology*]

RIM........... Read-In Mode

RIM........... Read Interrupt Mask [*Data processing*]

RIM........... Readiness Indicator Model   (MCD)

RIM........... Receipt, Inspection, and Maintenance [*Air Force*]

RIM........... Receiver Intermodulation [*Telecommunications*]   (TEL)

RIM........... Recreation Information Management [*Department of Agriculture*] [*Database*]

RIM........... Regulation Interpretation Memorandum [*Environmental Protection Agency*]

RIM........... Relative Intensity Measures [*of nursing care*]

RIM........... Resident Industrial Manager

RIM........... Resource Interface Module [*Datapoint*]

RIM........... Rim [*Hawaii*] [*Seismograph station code, US Geological Survey*]   (SEIS)

RIM........... Rimrock Airlines, Inc. [*Spokane, WA*] [*FAA designator*]   (FAAC)

RIM........... Rockridge Mining [*Vancouver Stock Exchange symbol*]

RIM........... Royal Indian Marine

RIM........... Rubber Insulation Material

RIMAS........ Russian Independent Mutual Aid Society

RIMB.......... Roche Institute of Molecular Biology

Rimba Indones ... Rimba Indonesia [*A publication*]

RIMC .... Reparable Item Movement Control [*Military*]   (AFIT)

RIMC .... Reportable Items of Major Combinations [*Army*]   (AABC)

RIMCS .... Reparable Item Movement Control System [*Military*]   (AFIT)

RIMD .... Resources and Institutional Management Division [*NASA*]

RIME .... Radio Inertial Missile Equipment

RIME .... Radio Inertial Monitoring Equipment   (KSC)

RIME .... Research Institute for Management Executives [*Washington, DC*]

RI Med J ..... Rhode Island Medical Journal [*A publication*]

RIMF.......... Reportable Item Master File [*Military*]   (AFIT)

RIMI.......... Research Improvement in Minority Institutions [*Program*] [*National Science Foundation*]

Rimini Stor Art Cult ... Rimini Storia Arte e Cultura [*A publication*]

RIMLF........ Rostral Interstitial Nucleus of Medial Longitudinal Fasciculus [*Neuroanatomy*]

RIMM.......... Report on Improved Manpower Management

RIMMS ...... RVNAF [*Republic of Vietnam Air Force*] Improvement and Modernization Management System

RIMOB....... Reserve Indication of Mobilization [*Army*]   (AABC)

RIMP.......... Minimum Range to Avoid Plumb Impingement   (MCD)

RIMP.......... Remote Input Message Processor

RIMP.......... Risk Management Program   (MCD)

RIMPAC ..... Rim of the Pacific [*Naval exercise; name refers to the four participating countries: Australia, Canada, New Zealand, and the United States*]

RIMPTF ...... Recording Industries Music Performance Trust Funds [*Later, MPTF*]   (EA)

RIMR.......... Rockefeller Institute for Medical Research

RIMS .... RADAR In-Flight Monitoring System

RIMS .... Radiant Intensity Measuring System

RIMS .... Radio Interference Measuring System

RIMS .... Record Information Movement Study   (KSC)

RIMS .... Remote Information Management System

RIMS .... Requirements Inventory Management System   (MCD)
RIMS .... Resonance Ionization Mass Spectrometry
RIMS .... Retarding Ion Mass Spectrometer [*Instrumentation*]
RIMS .... Risk and Insurance Management Society [*New York, NY*]   (EA)
RIMSTOP ... Retail Inventory Management/Stockage Policy [*DoD*]
RIN .... Radio Inertial   (MSA)
RIN .... Rassemblement pour l'Independance Nationale [*Quebec separatist party, 1960-1968*] [*Canada*]
RIN .... Rat Insulinoma [*A cell line*]
RIN .... Record Identification Number
RIN .... Redpath Industries Ltd. [*Toronto Stock Exchange symbol*]
RIN .... Reference Indication Number
RIN .... Regular Inertial Navigator   (MCD)
RIN .... Regulatory Identifier Number [*Environmental Protection Agency*]
RIN .... Report Identification Number [*Military*]   (AABC)
RIn .... Revista de las Indias [*A publication*]
Rin .... Rinascimento [*A publication*]
Rin .... Rinascita [*A publication*]
Rin .... Riner's Reports [*2 Wyoming*]   (DLA)
RIN .... Ringi Cove [*Solomon Islands*] [*Airport symbol*]   (OAG)
RIN .... Rivista Italiana di Numismatica e Scienze Affini [*A publication*]
RIN .... Rotor Impulsive Noise [*Helicopters*]
RIN .... Royal Indian Navy
RIN .... Royal Institute of Navigation
RIN .... Springfield, MO [*Location identifier*] [*FAA*]   (FAAL)
RINA .... Resident Inspector of Naval Aircraft
RINA .... Royal Institution of Naval Architects [*British*]
RINAB .... Research Institute Nethri As (Hveragerthi, Iceland). Bulletin [*A publication*]
RINAL .... RADAR Inertial Altimeter
RINASA ...... Rivista. Istituto Nazionale d'Archeologia e Storia dell'Arte [*A publication*]
Rinascenza Med ... Rinascenza Medica [*A publication*]
R Income Wealth ... Review of Income and Wealth [*A publication*]
RIND .... Reversible Ischemic Neurological Deficit [*Medicine*]
R Ind .... Revista de las Indias [*A publication*]
RINDA .... Revue Industrielle [*A publication*]
Rindertuberk Brucell ... Rindertuberkulose und Brucellose [*A publication*]
R Indias ...... Revista de las Indias [*A publication*]
RIndM .... Revista de las Indias (Madrid) [*A publication*]
R Indones Malay Aff ... Review of Indonesian and Malayan Affairs [*A publication*]
R Indones Malayan Aff ... Review of Indonesian and Malayan Affairs [*A publication*]
Riner .... Riner's Reports [*2 Wyoming*]   (DLA)
RINF .... Rinforzando [*With Special Emphasis*] [*Music*]
RINFZ .... Rinforzando [*With Special Emphasis*] [*Music*]
RING .... Ringer
Ring Bank ... Ringwood's Principles of Bankruptcy [*18th ed.*] [*1947*]   (DLA)
RINGDOC... Pharmaceutical Literature Documentation [*Derwent Publications Ltd.*] [*London, England*] [*Information service*]   (EISS)
Ringing Migr ... Ringing & Migration [*A publication*]
Ring Int Ornithol Bull ... Ring International Ornithological Bulletin [*A publication*]
RINM .... Resident Inspector of Naval Material
RINN .... Recommended International Nonproprietary Name [*Drug research*]
RINPA .... Rivista di Istochimica Normale e Patologica [*A publication*]
RINS .... Rand Information Systems [*NASDAQ symbol*]   (NQ)
RINS .... Research Institute for the Natural Sciences
RINS .... Resident Inspector
Rin S .... Rinascenza Salentina [*A publication*]
RINS .... Rotorace Inertial Navigation System   (MCD)
RINSMAT ... Resident Inspector of Naval Material   (MUGU)
RINSORD ... Resident Naval Inspector of Ordnance
RINSPOW... Resident Naval Inspector of Powder
R Inst Antropol Cordoba ... Revista. Instituto de Antropologia. Universidad de Cordoba [*A publication*]
R Inst Chem Lect Monogr Rep ... Royal Institute of Chemistry. Lectures, Monographs, and Reports [*A publication*]
R Inst Chem Lect Ser ... Royal Institute of Chemistry. Lecture Series [*A publication*]
R Inst Cienc Soc ... Revista. Instituto de Ciencias Sociales [*A publication*]
R Instit Europ ... Revista de Instituciones Europeas [*A publication*]
R Inst Nav Archit (London) Suppl Pap ... Royal Institution of Naval Architects (London). Supplementary Papers [*A publication*]
R Inst Nav Archit Q Trans ... Royal Institution of Naval Architects [*London*]. Quarterly Transactions [*A publication*]
R Inst Nav Archit Suppl Pap ... Royal Institution of Naval Architects [*London*]. Supplementary Papers [*A publication*]
R Inst Pr ..... Royal Institution of Great Britain. Proceedings [*A publication*]
R Inst Public Health Hyg J ... Royal Institute of Public Health and Hygiene. Journal [*A publication*]
R Inst Sociol ... Revue. Institut de Sociologie [*A publication*]
RINSUL ...... Rubber Insulation
RINT .... RADAR Intermittent   (MSA)
RINT .... Radiation Intelligence
RINT .... Revista. Instituto Nacional de la Tradicion [*A publication*]

R Int Commiss Jurists ... Review. International Commission of Jurists [*A publication*]
R Int Coop ... Review of International Cooperation [*A publication*]
R Int Croix Rouge ... Revue Internationale de la Croix Rouge [*A publication*]
R Int Cr Rouge ... Revue Internationale de la Croix Rouge [*A publication*]
R Int Dr Comp ... Revue Internationale de Droit Compare [*A publication*]
R Int Dr Penal ... Revue Internationale de Droit Penal [*A publication*]
R Integr ...... Revista de la Integracion [*A publication*]
R Interam Bibl ... Revista Interamericana de Bibliografia [*A publication*]
R Interam Bibliog ... Revista Interamericana de Bibliografia [*A publication*]
R Internat Hist Banque ... Revue Internationale d'Histoire de la Banque [*A publication*]
R Internat Rech Urbaine et Reg ... Revue Internationale de Recherche Urbaine et Regionale [*A publication*]
R Internaz Econ Trasporti ... Revista Internazionale del Trasporti [*A publication*]
R Internaz Scienze Econ e Commer ... Rivista Internazionale di Scienze Economiche e Commerciali [*A publication*]
R Internaz Scienze Soc ... Rivista Internazionale di Scienze Sociali [*A publication*]
R Int'l Arb Awards ... United Nations Reports of International Arbitral Awards   (DLA)
R Int Politcrim ... Revue Internationale de Politicriminelle [*A publication*]
R Int Sci Adm ... Revue Internationale des Sciences Administratives [*A publication*]
R Int Sci Soc ... Revue Internationale des Sciences Sociales [*A publication*]
R Int Secur Soc ... Revue Internationale de la Securite Sociale [*A publication*]
R Int Sociol ... Revue Internationale de Sociologie [*International Review of Sociology*] [*Rome*] [*A publication*]
R Int Sociol (Madrid) ... Revista Internacional de Sociologia (Madrid) [*A publication*]
R Int Trav ... Revue Internationale du Travail [*A publication*]
RINUA .... Rivista di Ingegneria Nucleare [*A publication*]
RINV .... Reliable Investors Corp. [*NASDAQ symbol*]   (NQ)
RIO .... RADAR-Intercept Officer [*Navy*]
RIO .... Ramus Infraorbitalis [*Anatomy*]
RIO .... Registry of Italian Oddities   (EA)
RIO .... Relocatable Input/Output
RIO .... Remain Intact Organization [*Larchwood, IA*]   (EA)
RIO .... Reporting In and Out [*Military*]
RIO .... Research Industry Office   (MCD)
RIO .... Reshaping the International Order [*Title of Club of Rome report*]
RIO .... Resident Inspector Office [*Coast Guard*]
RIO .... Resident Inspector of Ordnance   (AAG)
RIO .... Retail Issue Outlets   (NG)
RIO .... Revue Internationale d'Onomastique [*A publication*]
RIO .... Ride-It-Out
RIO .... Rio De Janeiro [*Brazil*] [*Airport symbol*]   (OAG)
RIO .... Rio Grant [*Caja Del Rio*] [*New Mexico*] [*Seismograph station code, US Geological Survey*] [*Closed*]   (SEIS)
RIO .... Rio Sierra Silver [*Vancouver Stock Exchange symbol*]
RIO .... Royal International Optical Corp. [*NYSE symbol*]
RIO .... Royal Italian Opera
RIOC .... Royal International Optical [*NASDAQ symbol*]   (NQ)
Rio De Janeiro Univ Federal Inst Geociencias Bol Geologia ... Universidade Federal do Rio De Janeiro. Instituto de Geociencias. Boletim Geologia [*A publication*]
RIOE .... Research in Ocean Engineering. University Sources and Resources [*A publication*]
RIOGD .... Rio Grande [*FAA*]   (FAAC)
Rio Grande Do Sul Inst Geocien Mapa Geol ... Universidade Federal do Rio Grande Do Sul. Instituto de Geociencias. Mapa Geologico da Folha de Morretes [*A publication*]
Rio Grande Do Sul Inst Pesqui Zootec Bol Tec ... Rio Grande Do Sul. Instituto de Pesquisas Zootecnicas. Boletim Tecnico [*A publication*]
RIOMETER ... Relative Ionospheric Opacity Meter
RIOno .... Revue Internationale d'Onomastique [*A publication*]
RIOPR .... Rhode Island Open Pool Reactor
RIOS .... Joint Working Group on River Inputs to Ocean Systems [*Marine science*]   (MSC)
RIOS .... ROM [*Read-Only Memory*] BIOS [*Pronounced "rye-ose"*] [*Data processing*]
RIOS .... Rotating Image Optical Scanner
RIOT .... RAM Input/Output Timer
RIOT .... Real-Time Input-Output Transducer [*or Translator*] [*Data processing*]
RIOT .... Remote Input/Output Terminal [*Data processing*]
RIOT .... Resolution of Initial Operational Techniques
RIOT .... Retrieval of Information by On-Line Terminal [*Atomic Energy Authority*] [*Data processing*] [*British*]
RIOV .... Rio Verde Energy Corp. [*NASDAQ symbol*]   (NQ)
RIP .... RADAR Identification Point   (AFM)
RIP .... RADAR Improvement Plan   (NATG)
RIP .... RADAR Improvement Program
RIP .... Radioimmunoprecipitation [*Clinical chemistry*]
RIP .... Radiological Information Plot   (NATG)
RIP .... Random Input Sampling [*Data processing*]
RIP .... Rapid Installation Plan

RIP .... Raster Image Processor [*Printer technology*]
RIP .... Rate-Invariant Path [*Economic theory*]
RIP .... Rays Initiating from a Point
RIP .... Reactor Instrument Penetration Valve   (IEEE)
RIP .... Readiness Improvement Program [*Military*]   (CAAL)
RIP .... Receiving Inspection Plan   (NRCH)
RIP .... Recoverable Item Program [*Marine Corps*]
RIP .... Reduction Implementation Panel [*DoD*]
RIP .... Register Indicator Panel
RIP .... Register of Intelligence Publications   (MCD)
RIP .... Reliability Improvement Program
RIP .... Remain in Place   (MCD)
RIP .... Remote Indicator Panel   (CAAL)
RIP .... Report on Individual Personnel   (MCD)
RIP .... Requiescat in Pace [*May He, or She, Rest in Peace*] [*Latin*]
RIP .... Research in Parapsychology [*A publication*]
RIP .... Research in Progress   (MCD)
RIP .... Respiratory Inversion Point [*Physiology*]
RIP .... Retired in Place [*Telecommunications*]   (TEL)
RIP .... Retirement Improvement Program [*Air Force*]   (AFM)
RIP .... Retirement Income Plan   (MCD)
RIP .... Revue Internationale de Philosophie [*A publication*]
RIP .... Ribosome Inactivating [*or Inhibiting*] Protein [*Biochemistry*]
RIP .... Rice Institute Pamphlet [*A publication*]
RIP .... Ripieno [*Additional*] [*Music*]
RIP .... Ripple Resources Ltd. [*Vancouver Stock Exchange symbol*]
RIP .... Routing Information Process [*Telecommunications*]   (TEL)
RIP .... Rural Industrialization Program [*Department of Agriculture*]
RIPA .... Radioimmunoprecipitation Assay [*Clinical chemistry*]
RIPA .... Royal Institute of Public Administration [*British*]
RIPB .... Revue de l'Instruction Publique en Belgique [*A publication*]
RIPC .... Rassegna Italiana di Politica e di Cultura [*A publication*]
RIPC .... Regroupement des Independants et Paysans Camerounais
              [*Regrouping of Independents and Farmers of the
              Cameroons*]
RIPE .... Range Instrumentation Performance Evaluation   (MUGU)
RIPEH .... Review of Iranian Political Economy and History [*A publication*]
RIPFCOMTF ... Rapid Item Processor to Facilitate Complex Operations on
              Magnetic Tape Files [*Data processing*]
RIPh .... Revue Internationale de Philosophie [*A publication*]
RIPH & H .... Royal Institute of Public Health and Hygiene [*British*]
RIPIS .... Rhode Island Pupil Identification Scale [*Psychology*]
RIPL .... Representation-Independent Programing Language
RIPOM .... Report [*command indicated*] If Present, Otherwise by Message
              [*Navy*]
RI Port Indus Devel Comm Geol Bull Sci Contr ... Rhode Island. Port and
              Industrial Development Commission. Geological Bulletin.
              Scientific Contribution [*A publication*]
RIPOSTE .... Restitution Incentive Program Operationalized as a Strategy
              Toward an Effective Learning Environment [*HEW*]
RIPP .... RADAR Intelligence Photo Producer
RIPPLE ...... Radioactive Isotope-Powered Pulse Light Equipment   (IEEE)
RIPPLE ...... Radioisotope-Powered Prolonged Life Equipment   (IEEE)
RIPR .... Recommended Immediate Procurement Records   (MCD)
RIPS .... RADAR Impact Prediction System   (CET)
RIPS .... Radio-Isotope Power Supply [*or System*]   (NG)
RIPS .... Range Instrumentation Planning Study [*AFSC*]
RI Pub Laws ... Public Laws of Rhode Island   (DLA)
RIPV .... Reactor Isolation Pressure Valve   (IEEE)
RIPWC .... Royal Institute of Painters in Water-Colours [*British*]
RIPY .... Ripley Co. [*NASDAQ symbol*]   (NQ)
RIQAP .... Reduced Inspection Quality Assurance Program
RIQS .... Remote Information Query System [*Information retrieval
              service*] [*Data processing*]
RIR .... RADAR Interface Recorder   (MCD)
RIR .... Range Illumination RADAR
RIR .... Receiving Inspection Report
RIR .... Redgrave Information Resources Corp. [*Publisher*]
RiR .... Redgrave Information Resources Corp., Westport, CT [*Library
              symbol*] [*Library of Congress*]   (LCLS)
RIR .... Reduction in Requirement [*Air Force*]   (AFM)
RIR .... Rehabilitation Information Round Table   (EA)
RIR .... Reliability Investigation Requests   (KSC)
RIR .... Reportable Item Report [*NASA*]   (NASA)
RIR .... Revista Istorica Romana [*A publication*]
RIR .... Rhode Island Red [*Poultry*]
RIR .... Riverside/Rubidoux, CA [*Location identifier*] [*FAA*]   (FAAL)
RIR .... ROM [*Read-Only Memory*] Instruction Register
RIRAA .... Russian Immigrants' Representative Association In America
RIRAB .... Rivista di Radiologia [*A publication*]
R Ir Acad Proc Sect B ... Royal Irish Academy. Proceedings. Section B [*A
              publication*]
R Iran Relat Int ... Revue Iranienne des Relations Internationales [*A
              publication*]
RIRB .... Railway Insurance Rating Bureau [*Defunct*]   (EA)
RIRCA .... Rhode Island Red Club of America   (EA)
RIRED .... Revue. IRE [*Institut National des Radioelements*] [*Belgium*] [*A
              publication*]
RI Rep .... Rhode Island Reports   (DLA)
RIRIG .... Reduced-Excitation Inertial Reference Integrating Gyro
R Irish Ac Pr ... Royal Irish Academy. Proceedings [*A publication*]

RIRJ .... Research Institute of Religious Jewry   (EA)
RIRMS .... Remote Information Retrieval and Management System [*Data
              processing*]   (BUR)
RIRO .... Roll-In/Roll-Out [*Storage allocation*] [*Data processing*]
RIRS .... Reliability Information Retrieval System   (MCD)
RIRT .... Rehabilitation Information Round Table [*Alexandria, VA*]   (EA)
RIRT .... Rhodium-Iron Resistance Thermometer
RIRTI .... Recording Infrared Tracking Instrument
RIS .... Kansas City, MO [*Location identifier*] [*FAA*]   (FAAL)
RIS .... RADIAC [*Radiation Detection, Indication, and Computation*]
              Instrument System
RIS .... Radio Interference Service [*Department of Trade*] [*British*]
RIS .... Ramjet Inlet System
RIS .... Range Information System [*For aircraft*]   (MCD)
RIS .... Range Instrumentation Ship
RIS .... Range Instrumentation Station
RIS .... Rassegna Italiana di Sociologia [*A publication*]
RIS .... Reblooming Iris Society   (EA)
RIS .... Receiving Inspection Segment
RIS .... RECON Information System   (MCD)
RIS .... Record Input Subroutine
RIS .... Recorded Information Service [*Telecommunications*]   (TEL)
RIS .... Redwood Inspection Service [*Mill Valley, CA*]   (EA)
RIS .... Regulatory Information Service [*Congressional Information
              Service, Inc.*] [*Bethesda, MD*] [*Telecommunications*]
RIS .... Reliability Information System
RIS .... Remote Information System
RIS .... Reports Identification Symbol [*Aviation*]
RIS .... Research Information Service [*John Crerar Library*]
              [*Information service*]   (EISS)
RIS .... Research Information Services [*Georgia Institute of
              Technology*] [*Atlanta*] [*Information service*]   (EISS)
RIS .... Research Information System [*Rehabilitation Services
              Administration*]   (EISS)
RIS .... Resonance Ionization Spectroscopy
RIS .... Retail Information System   (BUR)
RIS .... Retarded Infants Service [*An association*] [*New York,
              NY*]   (EA)
RIS .... Retransmission Identity Signal [*Telecommunications*]   (TEL)
RIS .... Revista Internacional de Sociologia [*A publication*]
RIS .... Revolution Indicating System   (MSA)
RIS .... Rise Resources, Inc. [*Vancouver Stock Exchange symbol*]
RIS .... Rishiri [*Japan*] [*Airport symbol*] [*Obsolete*]   (OAG)
Ris .... Risorgimento [*A publication*]
RIS .... Rivista Italiana di Sociologia [*A publication*]
RIS .... Rotatable Initial Susceptibility
RIS .... Rotating Image Scanner
RIS .... Routine Interest Shipping   (MCD)
RIS .... Russian Intelligence Service
RISA .... Radioimmunosorbent Assay [*Clinical chemistry*]
RISA .... Radioiodinated Serum Albumin [*Medicine*]
RISA .... Railway and Industrial Spring Association [*Later, RISRI*]
RISA .... Romani Imperii Semper Auctor [*Continual Increaser of the
              Roman Empire*] [*Latin*]
RISAA .... Rivista Italiana della Saldatura [*A publication*]
RIS-ALEX ... Research Information Services - Alexander Library
RISB .... Rotter Incomplete Sentences Blank [*Psychology*]
RISC .... Reduced Instruction Set Computer
RISC .... Refractive Index Sounding Central
RISC .... Remote Information Systems Center
RISC .... Rockwell International Science Center
RI Sch Des Bul ... Rhode Island School of Design. Bulletin [*A publication*]
RISD .... Requisition and Invoice Shipping Document
RISD .... Rhode Island School of Design
RISE .... Radiation Induced Surface Effect
RISE .... RAM [*Reliability, Availability, and Maintainability*] Improvement
              of Selected Equipment   (MCD)
RISE .... Readiness Improvement Status Evaluation   (MCD)
RISE .... Readiness Improvement Summary Evaluation   (MCD)
RISE .... Reform of Intermediate and Secondary Education   (OICC)
RISE .... Register for International Service in Education [*Institute of
              International Education*] [*New York, NY*]   (EISS)
RISE .... Reliability Improvement Selected Equipment   (AABC)
RISE .... Research and Information Services for Education [*Montgomery
              County Intermediate Unit*] [*King of Prussia, PA*]
RISE .... Research in Science Education [*National Science Foundation*]
RISE .... Research in Supersonic Environment
RISE .... Reusable Inflatable Salvage Equipment
RISE .... Rivista Internazionale di Scienze Economiche e Commerciali [*A
              publication*]
RISEAP ...... Regional Islamic Da'Wah Council of Southeast Asia and the
              Pacific   (EA-IO)
RISG .... Rivista Italiana di Scienze Giuridiche [*A publication*]
RISHE .... Research Institute for Supersensic Healing Energies
RISID .... Revista Padurilor-Industria Lemnului. Seria Industria Lemnului
              [*A publication*]
Rising Up ... Rising Up Angry [*A publication*]
RISK .... Rock Is Stoning Kids [*An association*]   (EA)
RISKA .... George Risk Industries Cl A [*NASDAQ symbol*]   (NQ)
RISKAC ..... Risk Acceptance   (NASA)
Risk Manage ... Risk Management [*A publication*]

Risk Mgmt ... Risk Management [*A publication*]
Risk Mgt ..... Risk Management [*A publication*]
RISL .... Residual Item Selection List
RiSL .... Rossija i Slavjanstvo [*A publication*]
RISM .... Reference Interaction Site Model [*Chemical physics*]
RISM .... Research Institute for the Study of Man [*Army*] (MCD)
RI/SME ...... Robotics International (EA)
RISO .... Range Instrumentation Systems Office [*White Sands Missile Range*]
RISO .... Revista Internacional de Sociologia [*A publication*]
RISoc .... Revue. Institut de Sociologie Solvay [*A publication*]
Risoe Inf ..... Risoe Information [*Denmark*] [*A publication*]
Risoe Natl Lab Rep Risoe-M (Den) ... Risoe National Laboratory. Report Risoe-M (Denmark) [*A publication*]
Risoe Rep (Den) Res Establ Risoe ... Risoe Report (Denmark) Research Establishment Risoe [*A publication*]
RISOL .... Risoluto [*Resolutely*] [*Music*] (ROG)
RISOP .... Red Integrated Strategic Offensive Plan [*Army*] (AABC)
Riso Rep ..... Risoe Report [*A publication*]
RISP .... Ross Ice Shelf Project [*International cooperative research project*]
RISPT .... Ross Ice Shelf Project. Technical Reports [*A publication*]
RISR .... Rassegna d'Informazioni. Istituto di Studi Romani [*A publication*]
RI-SR .... Removal Item - Ship's Record (MCD)
RiSR .... Ricerche di Storia Religiosa [*A publication*]
RISRI .... Railway and Industrial Spring Research Institute [*Defunct*] (EA)
RISS .... Range Instrumentation and Support Systems
RISS .... Refractive Index Sounding System
RISS .... Regional Information Sharing System [*Department of Justice*]
RISS .... Revue Internationale des Sciences Sociales [*A publication*]
RISSB .... Research Institute on the Sino-Soviet Bloc (EA)
RIST .... RADAR Installed System Tester (KSC)
RIST .... Radioimmunosorbent Technique [*Clinical chemistry*]
RIST .... Radioisotopic Sand Tracer [*Marine science*] (MSC)
RISTA .... Rivista Italiana di Stomatologia [*A publication*]
R Istituto Veneto Memorie ... Reale Istituto Veneto di Scienze, Lettere, ed Arti. Memorie [*A publication*]
RISULB .... Revue. Institut de Sociologie. Universite Libre de Bruxelles [*A publication*]
RISVD .... Risvegliato [*Reanimated*] [*Music*] (ROG)
RISW .... Registered Industrial Social Worker [*Designation awarded by the American Association of Industrial Social Workers*]
RISW .... Royal Institution of South Wales [*British*]
RISWR .... Regional Institute of Social Welfare Research [*Athens, GA*] (EA)
RIT .... RADAR Inputs Test
RIT .... Radio Information Test
RIT .... Radio Network for Inter-American Telecommunications
RIT .... Railway Inclusive Tour
RIT .... Rate of Information Throughput [*Data processing*] (BUR)
R & IT .... Rating and Income Tax Reports [*England*] (DLA)
RIT .... Receiver Incremental Tuning
RIT .... Reclamation Insurance Type [*Military*] (AFIT)
RIT .... Refining in Transit
RIT .... Relative Ignition Temperature
RIT .... Request for Interface Tool [*NASA*] (NASA)
RIT .... Retrieval Injury Threshold
RIT .... Rio Tigre [*Panama*] [*Airport symbol*] (OAG)
RIT .... Ritardando [*Gradually Slower*] [*Music*]
RIT .... Ritenuto [*Immediately Slower*] [*Music*]
rit .... Ritual (BJA)
RIT .... Rivista Italiana del Teatro [*A publication*]
RIT .... Rochester Institute of Technology [*New York*]
RIT .... Rochester Institute of Technology Library [*UTLAS symbol*]
RIT .... Rocket Interferometer Tracking
RIT .... Rotary Indexing Table
RIT .... Rothschild Investment Trust
RITA .... Rand Intelligent Terminal Agent
RITA .... Recoverable Interplanetary Transport Approach
RITA .... Refundable Income Tax Account
RITA .... Reseau Integre de Transmission Automatique [*French*]
RITA .... Reservation, Information, Tourist Accommodation [*Computerized system for booking hotel rooms*] [*British*]
RITA .... Resist Inside the Army [*Peace-movement slang*]
RITA .... Reusable Interplanetary Transport Approach Vehicle
RITA .... Rivera and Tamayo Fault Exploration [*Marine science*] (MSC)
RITA .... Romance Is Treasured Always [*Annual award bestowed by Romance Writers of America. Acronym selected to honor cofounder, Rita Clay Estrada*]
RITA .... Rural Industrial Technical Assistance [*Latin American building program*]
RITAA .... Revue d'Immunologie et de Therapie Antimicrobienne [*A publication*]
RITAC .... Retail Industry Trade Action Coalition (EA)
RitAcc .... Rituels Accadiens [*A publication*] (BJA)
RITAD .... Radiation-Induced Thermally Activated Depolarization [*Radiation dosimetry technique*]
R Ital Econ Demografia e Statis ... Rivista Italiana di Economia. Demografia e Statistica [*A publication*]

R Ital Mus ... Nuova Rivista Musicale Italiana [*A publication*]
R Ital Mus ... Rivista Italiana di Musicologia [*A publication*]
RITAR .... Ritardando [*Gradually Slower*] [*Music*]
RITARD ..... Ritardando [*Gradually Slower*] [*Music*]
RITARO ..... Ritardando [*Gradually Slower*] [*Music*] (ROG)
RITC .... Rhodamine Isothiocyanate [*Biochemistry*]
Ritch/ .... Ritchie's Cases Decided by Francis Bacon [*1617-21*] (DLA)
Ritch .... Ritchie's Equity Reports [*1872-82*] [*Nova Scotia*] (DLA)
Ritch Eq Dec ... Ritchie's Equity Decisions [*Nova Scotia*] (DLA)
Ritch Eq Rep ... Ritchie's Equity Reports [*Nova Scotia*] (DLA)
Ritchie .... Ritchie's Equity [*Canada*] (DLA)
RITE .... Rapid Information Technique for Evaluation
RITE .... Rapidata Interactive Text Editor (IEEE)
RITEA .... Rock Island Railroad Transportation and Employee Assistance Act [*1980*]
RITEN .... Ritenuto [*Immediately Slower*] [*Music*]
RITENA .... Reunion Internacional de Tecnicos de la Nutricion Animal [*International Meeting of Animal Nutrition Experts*] (EA-IO)
RITENO ...... Ritenuto [*Immediately Slower*] [*Music*] (ROG)
RiTh .... Revue Internationale de Theologie [*A publication*]
RITI .... Resident Inspection Test Instruction
RITL .... Revista de Istorie si Theori Literara [*A publication*]
RITMB .... Rayonnements Ionisants [*A publication*]
RITOP .... Red Integrated Tactical Operational Plan (CINC)
RITR .... Rework Inspection Team Report
RITREAD .... Rapid Iterative Reanalysis for Automated Design [*Computer program*]
RITS .... Rapid Information Transmission System
RITS .... Reconnaissance Intelligence Technical Squadron
Rits Int .... Ritso's Introduction to the Science (DLA)
RITU .... Research Institute of Temple University (KSC)
RIU .... Andalusia, AL [*Location identifier*] [*FAA*] (FAAL)
RIU .... RADAR Interface Unit [*Military*] (CAAL)
RIU .... Radioactive Iodine Uptake [*Medicine*]
RIU .... Railroad Insurance Underwriters [*Later, RTI*] (EA)
RIU .... Refractive Index Unit
RIU .... Remote Interface Unit [*NASA*] (NASA)
riu .... Rhode Island [*MARC country of publication code*] [*Library of Congress*] (LCCP)
RIU .... University of Rhode Island, Kingston, RI [*OCLC symbol*] (OCLC)
Riun Annu Assoc Elettrot Elettron Ital Rend ... Riunione Annuale della Associazione Elettrotecnica ed Elettronica Italiana. Rendiconti [*A publication*]
RI Univ Div Eng Res Dev Eng Repr ... Rhode Island University. Division of Engineering. Research and Development Engineering Reprint [*A publication*]
RI Univ Div Eng Res Dev Leafl ... Rhode Island University. Division of Engineering. Research and Development Leaflet [*A publication*]
RI Univ Eng Exp Stn Bull ... Rhode Island University. Engineering Experiment Station. Bulletin [*A publication*]
RI Univ Mar Tech Rep ... Rhode Island University. Marine Technical Report [*A publication*]
RIUSA .... Rehabilitation International USA
RIV .... Radio Influence Voltage
RIV .... Ramus Interventricularis [*First-order branch of coronary artery*] [*Medicine*]
RIV .... Regolamento Internazionale Veicoli [*Italian generic term meaning "International Regulation of Vehicles"*] [*Initialism also refers to International Wagon Union*]
RIV .... River
RIV .... Riverbend International [*American Stock Exchange symbol*]
RIV .... Riverside, CA [*Location identifier*] [*FAA*] (FAAL)
RIV .... Riverview [*Australia*] [*Seismograph station code, US Geological Survey*] (SEIS)
RIV .... Rivet (AAG)
Riv .... Riviera [*Record label*] [*France*]
Riv .... Rivista [*Review*] [*Italy*] (BJA)
Riv Aeronaut ... Rivista Aeronautica [*A publication*]
Riv Aeronaut Astronaut-Missil ... Rivista Aeronautica, Astronautica-Missilistica [*Italy*] [*A publication*]
Riv Agric Subtrop Trop ... Rivista di Agricoltura Subtropicale e Tropicale [*A publication*]
Riv Agron ... Rivista di Agronomia [*A publication*]
Riv Agr Subtrop Trop ... Rivista di Agricoltura Subtropicale e Tropicale [*A publication*]
Riv d'Alb .... Rivista d'Albania [*A publication*]
Riv Anat Patol Oncol ... Rivista di Anatomia Patologica e di Oncologia [*A publication*]
Riv Ann Reg ... Rivington's Annual Register (DLA)
Riv Antropol ... Rivista di Antropologia [*A publication*]
Riv d Arch Crist ... Rivista di Archeologia Cristiana [*A publication*] (OCD)
Riv Arte ...... Rivista d'Arte [*A publication*]
RivB .... Rivista Bibliografica [*A publication*]
RivBA .... Rivista delle Biblioteche e degli Archivi [*A publication*]
RIVBEA ...... [*Sam*] Rivers and Bea [*Rivers*] [*As in Rivbea Festival, jazz event named for saxophonist Sam Rivers and his wife, Bea*]
RivBibl .... Rivista Biblica [*A publication*]
Riv Biol .... Rivista di Biologia [*A publication*]

Riv Biol Norm Patol ... Rivista di Biologia Normale e Patologica [*A publication*]
Riv Biol (Perugia) ... Rivista di Biologia (Perugia) [*A publication*]
Riv Chir (Como) ... Rivista di Chirurgia (Como) [*A publication*]
Riv Clin Bologna ... Rivista Clinica di Bologna [*A publication*]
Riv Clin Med ... Rivista di Clinica Medica [*A publication*]
Riv Clin Pediatr ... Rivista di Clinica Pediatrica [*A publication*]
Riv Clin Tossicol ... Rivista di Clinica Tossicologia [*A publication*]
Riv Clin Univ Napoli ... Rivista Clinica. Universita di Napoli [*A publication*]
Riv Combust ... Rivista dei Combustibili [*A publication*]
Riv Coniglicolt ... Rivista di Coniglicoltura [*A publication*]
Riv Crit Clin Med ... Rivista Critica di Clinica Medica [*A publication*]
Riv Crit St ... Rivista Critica di Storia della Filosofia [*A publication*]
RivDal........ Rivista Dalmatica [*A publication*]
Riv Dir Agr ... Rivista di Diritto Agrario [*A publication*]
Riv Dir Europ ... Rivista di Diritto Europeo [*A publication*]
Riv Dir Finanz ... Rivista di Diritto Finanziaro e Scienza delle Finanze [*A publication*]
Riv Dir Int e Comp del Lavoro ... Rivista di Diritto Internazionale e Comparato del Lavoro [*Bologna, Italy*]   (DLA)
Riv Dir Int'le ... Rivista di Diritto Internazionale [*A publication*]
Riv Dir Int'le Priv & Proc ... Rivista di Diritto Internazionale Privato e Processuale [*Padova, Italy*]   (DLA)
Riv di Diritto Internaz ... Rivista di Diritto Internazionale [*A publication*]
Riv di Diritto Internaz e Comparato del Lavoro ... Rivista di Diritto Internazionale e Comparato del Lavoro [*Padua, Italy*]   (DLA)
RIVDIV....... River Assault Division [*Military*]
Riv Ecol...... Rivista di Ecologia [*A publication*]
Riv Econ Agr ... Rivista di Economia Agraria [*A publication*]
Riv Emoter Immunoematol ... Rivista di Emoterapia ed Immunoematologia [*A publication*]
River Plat ... Review of the River Plate [*A publication*]
RIVES........ Riverside Properties Investment Trust [*NASDAQ symbol*]   (NQ)
Riv Et........ Rivista di Etnografia [*A publication*]
Riv Etnogr ... Rivista di Etnografia [*A publication*]
RivFC .... Rivista di Filologia e d'Istruzione Classica [*A publication*]
RivFil .... Rivista di Filologia e d'Istruzione Classica [*A publication*]
Riv Filos ... Rivista de Filosofia [*A publication*]
Riv Filosof ... Rivista di Filosofia [*A publication*]
Riv Filosof Neo-Scolas ... Rivista di Filosofia Neo-Scolastica [*A publication*]
Riv Fis Mat Sci Nat ... Rivista di Fisica, Matematica, e Scienze Naturali [*A publication*]
Riv Fitosanit ... Rivista Fitosanitaria [*A publication*]
RIVFLOT .... River Flotilla [*Military*]
RIVFLOTONE ... River Flotilla One [*Military*]
Riv Fotogr Ital ... Rivista Fotografica Italiana [*A publication*]
Riv Freddo ... Rivista del Freddo [*A publication*]
Riv Frutti.... Rivista di Frutticoltura [*A publication*]
Riv Fruttic ... Rivista di Frutticoltura [*A publication*]
Riv Gastro Enterol ... Rivista di Gastro-Enterologia [*A publication*]
Riv Geofis Appl ... Rivista di Geofisica Applicata [*A publication*]
Riv Geogr Ital ... Rivista Geografica Italiana [*A publication*]
Riv Gerontol Geriatr ... Rivista di Gerontologia e Geriatria [*A publication*]
Riv Idrobiol ... Rivista di Idrobiologia [*A publication*]
RivIGI .... Rivista Indo-Greco-Italico di Filologia, Lingua, Antichita [*A publication*]
Riv Ig e San Pubb ... Rivista d'Igiene e Sanita Pubblica [*A publication*]
Riv Inf........ Rivista di Informatica [*A publication*]
Riv Inf........ Rivista dell'Informazione [*A publication*]
Riv Infort Mal Prof ... Rivista degli Infortuni e delle Malattie Professionali [*A publication*]
Riv Ing....... Rivista di Ingegneria [*A publication*]
Riv Ing Int... Rivista Inguana et Intemelia [*A publication*]
Riv Ing Nucl ... Rivista di Ingegneria Nucleare [*A publication*]
Riv Int Agric ... Rivista Internazionale di Agricoltura [*A publication*]
Riv Int Ec.... Rivista Internazionale di Scienze Economiche e Commerciali [*A publication*]
Riv Internaz di Filos del Diritto ... Rivista Internazionale di Filosofia del Diritto [*A publication*]
Riv Int Filosof Diritto ... Rivista Internazionale di Filosofia del Diritto [*A publication*]
Riv Int Filos Polit Soc Dir Comp ... Rivista Internazionale di Filosofia Politica e Sociale e di Diritto Comparato [*A publication*]
Riv Int Sci Econ Com ... Rivista Internazionale di Scienze Economiche e Commerciali [*A publication*]
Riv Int Sci Soc ... Rivista Internazionale di Scienze Sociali [*A publication*]
Riv Ist Arch ... Rivista del Reale Istituto d'Archeologia e Storia dell'Arte [*A publication*]
Riv Istochim Norm Patol ... Rivista di Istochimica Normale e Patologica [*A publication*]
Riv Ist Sieroter Ital ... Rivista. Istituto Sieroterapico Italiano [*A publication*]
Riv Ist Vaccinogeno Consorzi Prov Antituberc ... Rivista. Istituto Vaccinogeno e dei Consorzi Provinciali Antitubercolari [*A publication*]
Riv Ital Essenze ... Rivista Italiana delle Essenze [*A publication*]
Riv Ital Essenze Profumi ... Rivista Italiana delle Essenze e Profumi [*A publication*]
Riv Ital Essenze Profumi Piante Off ... Rivista Italiana delle Essenze dei Profumi e delle Piante Officinali [*A publication*]

Riv Ital Essenze Profumi Piante Off Aromi Saponi Cosmet ... Rivista Italiana delle Essenze dei Profumi e delle Piante Officinali Aromi Saponi Cosmetici [*A publication*]
Riv Ital Essenze Profumi Piante Offic Aromi Saponi Cosmet ... Rivista Italiana delle Essenze e Profumi Piante Officinali Aromi Saponi Cosmetici [*A publication*]
Riv Ital Essenze Profumi Piante Offic Olii Veg Saponi ... Rivista Italiana delle Essenze e Profumi Piante Officinali Olii Vegetali Saponi [*A publication*]
Riv Ital Ge ... Rivista Italiana di Geofisica e Scienze Affini [*A publication*]
Riv Ital Geofis ... Rivista Italiana di Geofisica [*Italy*] [*A publication*]
Riv Ital Geotec ... Rivista Italiana di Geotecnica [*A publication*]
Riv Ital Ginecol ... Rivista Italiana di Ginecologia [*A publication*]
Riv Italiana Paleontologia e Stratigrafia ... Rivista Italiana di Paleontologia e Stratigrafia [*A publication*]
Riv Ital Ig.... Rivista Italiana d'Igiene [*A publication*]
Riv Ital Ornitol ... Rivista Italiana di Ornitologia [*A publication*]
Riv Ital Paleontol Stratigr ... Rivista Italiana di Paleontologia e Stratigrafia [*A publication*]
Riv Ital Saldatura ... Rivista Italiana della Saldatura [*A publication*]
Riv Ital per le Sc Giur ... Rivista Italiana per le Scienze Giuridiche [*A publication*]   (OCD)
Riv Ital Sci Polit ... Rivista Italiana di Scienza Politica [*A publication*]
Riv Ital Sostanze Grasse ... Rivista Italiana delle Sostanze Grasse [*A publication*]
Riv Ital Sost Grasse ... Rivista Italiana delle Sostanze Grasse [*A publication*]
Riv Ital Stomatol ... Rivista Italiana di Stomatologia [*A publication*]
Riv Ital Trac Patol Ocul Virale Esotica ... Rivista Italiana del Tracoma e di Patologia Oculare, Virale, ed Esotica [*A publication*]
RIVL .... Rival Manufacturing [*NASDAQ symbol*]   (NQ)
RivL........... Rivista Letteraria per i Licei Classico, Scientifico, Artistico, e per l'Istituto Magistrale [*A publication*]
Riv Let Mod ... Rivista di Letteratura Moderne e Comparate [*A publication*]
Riv Lett Mod ... Rivista di Letteratura Moderne [*A publication*]
Riv Lig ...... Rivista di Studi Liguri [*A publication*]
Riv Malariol ... Rivista Malariologia [*A publication*]
Riv Maritt ... Rivista Marittima [*A publication*]
Riv Mat Sci Econom Social ... Rivista di Matematica per le Scienze Economiche e Sociali [*A publication*]
Riv Mat Univ Parma ... Rivista di Matematica. Universita di Parma [*A publication*]
Riv Mat Univ Parma 4 ... Rivista di Matematica. Universita di Parma. Serie 4 [*A publication*]
Riv Mecc .... Rivista di Meccanica [*A publication*]
Riv Med Aer ... Rivista di Medicina Aeronautica e Spaziale [*A publication*]
Riv Med Aeronaut ... Rivista di Medicina Aeronautica e Spaziale [*A publication*]
Riv Med Aeronaut Spaz ... Rivista di Medicina Aeronautica e Spaziale [*A publication*]
Riv Meteo A ... Rivista di Meteorologia Aeronautica [*A publication*]
Riv Meteorol Aeronaut ... Rivista di Meteorologia Aeronautica [*A publication*]
Riv Mineral Cristallogr Ital ... Rivista di Mineralogia e Cristallografia Italiana [*A publication*]
Riv Mineraria Sicil ... Rivista Mineraria Siciliana [*Italy*] [*A publication*]
Riv Min Sicil ... Rivista Mineraria Siciliana [*A publication*]
Riv Mus Italiana ... Rivista Musicale Italiana [*A publication*]
Riv Neurobiol ... Rivista di Neurobiologia [*A publication*]
Riv Neurol ... Rivista di Neurologia [*A publication*]
Riv Neuropsichiatr Sci Affini ... Rivista di Neuropsichiatria e Scienze Affini [*A publication*]
Riv Nuovo Cim ... Rivista del Nuovo Cimento [*A publication*]
Riv Nuovo Cimento Ser I ... Rivista del Nuovo Cimento. Serie I [*A publication*]
Riv Nuovo Cimento Soc Ital Fis ... Rivista del Nuovo Cimento. Societa Italiana di Fisica [*Italy*] [*A publication*]
Rivoluzione Ind ... Rivoluzione Industriale [*Italy*] [*A publication*]
Riv Osp Roma ... Rivista Ospedaliera Roma [*A publication*]
Riv Ostet Ginecol (Flor) ... Rivista di Ostetricia e Ginecologia (Florence) [*A publication*]
Riv Ostet Ginecol Prat ... Rivista di Ostetricia e Ginecologia Pratica [*A publication*]
Riv Ostet Ginecol Prat Med Perinat ... Rivista di Ostetricia e Ginecologia Pratica e di Medicina Perinatale [*A publication*]
Riv Oto-Neuro-Oftalmol ... Rivista Oto-Neuro-Oftalmologica [*A publication*]
Riv Oto-Neuro-Oftalmol Radio-Neuro-Chir ... Rivista Oto-Neuro-Oftalmologica e Radio-Neuro-Chirurgica [*A publication*]
Riv Parassit ... Rivista di Parassitologia [*A publication*]
Riv Parassitol ... Rivista di Parassitologia [*A publication*]
Riv Patol Appar Respir ... Rivista Patologia dell'Apparato Respiratorio [*A publication*]
Riv Patol Clin ... Rivista di Patologia e Clinica [*A publication*]
Riv Patol Clin Sper ... Rivista di Patologia Clinica e Sperimentale [*A publication*]
Riv Patol Clin Tuberc ... Rivista di Patologia e Clinica della Tubercolosi [*A publication*]
Riv Patol Clin Tuberc Pneumol ... Rivista di Patologia e Clinica della Tubercolosi e di Pneumologia [*A publication*]
Riv Patol Nerv Ment ... Rivista di Patologia Nervosa e Mentale [*A publication*]
Riv Patol Sper ... Rivista di Patologia Sperimentale [*A publication*]

Riv Patol Veg ... Rivista di Patologia Vegetale [*A publication*]
RivPed........ Rivista Pedagogica [*A publication*]
Riv Pediatr Sicil ... Rivista Pediatricia Siciliana [*A publication*]
Riv Per Lav Accad Sc Lett ed Arti Padova ... Rivista Periodica del Lavori. Accademia di Scienze, Lettere, ed Arti di Padova [*A publication*]
Riv Polit Agr ... Rivista di Politica Agraria [*A publication*]
Riv Polit Econ ... Rivista di Politica Economica [*A publication*]
RivR.......... Rivista delle Religioni [*A publication*]
Riv Radiol... Rivista di Radiologia [*A publication*]
Riv Rosmin Filos Cult ... Rivista Rosminiana di Filosofia e di Cultura [*A publication*]
Riv Sci Tecnol Alimenti Nutr Um ... Rivista di Scienza e Tecnologia degli Alimenti e di Nutrizione Umana [*A publication*]
Riv Sci Tecnol Aliment Nutr Umana ... Rivista di Scienza e Tecnologia degli Alimenti e di Nutrizione Umana [*A publication*]
Riv Sociol... Rivista di Sociologia [*A publication*]
Riv Sper Freniatr Med Leg Alienazioni Ment ... Rivista Sperimentale di Freniatria e Medicina Legale delle Alienazioni Mentali [*A publication*]
Riv Stor...... Rivista Storica Italiana [*A publication*]
Riv Stor Ital ... Rivista Storica Italiana [*A publication*]
Riv Stud Croci ... Rivista di Studi Crociani [*A publication*]
Riv Studi Polit Int ... Rivista di Studi Politici Internazionali [*A publication*]
RivStudOr ... Rivista degli Studi Orientali [*A publication*]
Riv Stud Orient ... Rivista degli Studi Orientali [*A publication*]
Riv Suinicolt ... Rivista di Suinicoltura [*A publication*]
Riv Svizz Apic ... Rivista Svizzera di Apicoltura [*A publication*]
Riv Svizz Med Sport ... Rivista Svizzera di Medicina dello Sport [*A publication*]
RIVT .... Rivulet　(ADA)
Riv Tec Elettr ... Rivista Tecnica d'Elettricita [*A publication*]
Riv Tec Ferrovie Ital ... Rivista Tecnica delle Ferrovie Italiane [*A publication*]
Riv Tess ..... Rivista Tessile [*A publication*]
Riv Tossicol Sper Clin ... Rivista di Tossicologia Sperimentale e Clinica [*A publication*]
Riv Trim Dir Pubbl ... Rivista Trimestrale di Diritto Pubblico [*A publication*]
Riv Trimest di Diritto Pubbl ... Rivista Trimestrale di Diritto Pubblico [*A publication*]
Riv Tuberc Mal App Resp ... Rivista della Tubercolosi e delle Malattie dell'Apparato Respiratorio [*A publication*]
Riv Veneta Sc Med ... Rivista Veneta di Scienze Mediche [*A publication*]
Riv Vet....... Rivista di Veterinaria [*A publication*]
Riv Vitic Enol ... Rivista de Viticoltura e di Enologia [*A publication*]
Riv World ... River World [*A publication*]
Riv Zootec ... Rivista di Zootecnia [*A publication*]
Riv Zootec ... Rivista di Zootecnia e Veterinaria [*A publication*]
Riv Zootec Vet ... Rivista di Zootecnia e Veterinaria [*A publication*]
RIW............ Recht der Internationalen Wirtschaft [*German*]　(DLA)
RIW............ Reliability Improvement Warranty [*Navy*]
RIW............ Review of Income and Wealth [*A publication*]
RIW............ Riverton [*Wyoming*] [*Airport symbol*]　(OAG)
RI Water Res Coordinating Board Geol Bull Hydrol Bull ... Rhode Island. Water Resources Coordinating Board. Geological Bulletin. Hydrologic Bulletin [*A publication*]
RI Water Resour Cent Annu Rep ... Rhode Island Water Resources Center. Annual Report [*A publication*]
RIWC......... Royal Institute of Painters in Water-Colours [*British*]　(ROG)
RIX............. Riga [*USSR*] [*Airport symbol*]　(OAG)
RIX............. University of Rhode Island, Extension Division Library, Providence, RI [*OCLC symbol*]　(OCLC)
RIXT .... Remote Information Exchange Terminal　(MCD)
RIY............. Renaissance of Italian Youth　(EA)
RIZ............. Radio Industry Zagreb [*Yugoslavia*]
RIZ............. Rio Alzucar [*Panama*] [*Airport symbol*]　(OAG)
Riz Rizicult Cult Vivr Trop ... Riz et Riziculture et Cultures Vivrieres Tropicales [*A publication*]
Rizsk Inst Inz Grazdan Aviacii ... Rizskii Institut Inzenerov Grazdanskoi Aviacii Imeni Leninskogo Komsomola [*A publication*]
R(J) .... Justiciary Cases [*In volumes of Session Cases*] [*1873-98*]　(DLA)
RJ .... La Reveil Juif. Sfax [*A publication*]　(BJA)
RJ .... New South Wales, Port Phillip District Judgments [*Australia*]　(DLA)
R & J.......... Rabkin and Johnson's Federal, Income, Gift, and Estate Taxation　(DLA)
RJ .... RADAR/Jimsphere
R & J.......... Rafique and Jackson's Privy Council Decisions [*India*]　(DLA)
RJ .... Ramjet
RJ .... Reform Judaism　(BJA)
RJ .... Reject
RJ .... Revista Javeriana [*A publication*]
RJ .... Revue Judiciaire, by Bruzard [*1843-44*] [*Mauritius*]　(DLA)
R de J .... Revue de Jurisprudence [*Quebec*]　(DLA)
RJ .... Revue de Jurisprudence　(DLA)
RJ .... [*The*] River Jordan [*A publication*]　(BJA)
RJ .... Road Junction [*Maps and charts*]
RJ .... Romanistisches Jahrbuch [*A publication*]
R & J.......... Romeo and Juliet [*Shakespearean work*]
RJ .... Rotary Joint

RJ .... Royal Jordanian Airlines Co. [*Arab Air Cargo*] [*Jordan*] [*ICAO designator*]　(FAAC)
RJ .... Rusky Jazyk [*A publication*]
RJ11........ Standard modular telephone jack for a single line instrument　(TSSD)
RJ 500........ Rolls-Japan 500 [*Type of Rolls-Royce engine*]
RJA............ Ramjet Addition　(AAG)
RJA............ Reform Jewish Appeal
RJA............ Retail Jewelers of America [*Later, JA*]　(EA)
RJA............ Rotary Joint Assembly
RJA............ Royal Jersey Artillery [*Military unit*] [*British*]
RJA............ Russko-Jewrejsky Archiw [*A publication*]　(BJA)
RJAF .... Royal Jordanian Air Force
RJaS........... Russkij Jazyk v Skole [*A publication*]
RJav .... Revista Javeriana [*A publication*]
RJaz .... Rusky Jazyk [*A publication*]
Rjazansk Gos Ped Inst Ucen Zap ... Rjazanskii Gosudarstvennyi Pedagogiceskii Institut. Ucenye Zapiski [*A publication*]
RJB............ Rajbiraj [*Nepal*] [*Airport symbol*] [*Obsolete*]　(OAG)
RJB............ Relay Junction Box　(KSC)
RJb............ Romanistisches Jahrbuch [*A publication*]
RJB............ Ruby Jewel Bearing
RJBE .... Relative Jostle Biological Effectiveness
RJC............ Ranger Junior College [*Texas*]
RJC............ Reaction Jet Control [*NASA*]　(NASA)
RJC............ Robinson Jeffers Committee　(EA)
RJC............ Rochester Junior College [*Minnesota*] [*Later, Rochester Community College*]
RJD............ Reaction Jet Device [*NASA*]　(NASA)
RJDA......... Rassemblement des Jeunesses Democratiques Africaines [*Rally of African Democratic Youth*]
RJDA......... Reaction Jet Driver - Aft [*NASA*]　(NASA)
RJDF .... Reaction Jet Driver - Forward [*NASA*]　(NASA)
R & J Dig ... Robinson and Joseph's Digest [*Ontario*]　(DLA)
RJE............ Ramjet Engine
RJE............ Rayleigh-Jeans Equation [*Physics*]
RJE............ Remote Job Entry [*Data processing*]
RJ/EC .... Reaction Jet/Engine Control [*NASA*]　(NASA)
RJETS .... Remote Job Entry Terminal System [*Data processing*]　(MCD)
RJF............ Les Rejaudoux [*France*] [*Seismograph station code, US Geological Survey*]　(SEIS)
RJF............ Raymond, James Financial Corp. [*NYSE symbol*]
RJFA .... Roumanian Jewish Federation of America　(EA)
RJFN .... RJ Financial Corp. [*NASDAQ symbol*]　(NQ)
RJICA........ Russian Journal of Inorganic Chemistry [*English Translation*] [*A publication*]
RJIS .... Regional Justice Information System
RJK............ Rijeka [*Yugoslavia*] [*Airport symbol*]　(OAG)
RJL............ Revue Juive de la Lorraine [*A publication*]
RJLI .... Royal Jersey Light Infantry [*Military unit*] [*British*]
RJM........... Reed, John M., San Antonio TX [*STAC*]
RJM........... Religious of Jesus-Mary [*Roman Catholic women's religious order*]
RJM........... Royal Jersey Militia [*Military unit*] [*British*]
RJM........... Warner Robins, GA [*Location identifier*] [*FAA*]　(FAAL)
RJMBA...... Roczniki Akademii Medycznej Imienia Juliana Marchlewskiego w Bialymstoku [*A publication*]
RJN............ Robinson Jeffers Newsletter [*A publication*]
RJO .... Remote Job Output [*Data processing*]
RJOD......... Reaction Jet OMS [*Orbital Maneuvering Subsystem*] Driver [*NASA*]　(NASA)
RJP............ Reaction Jet Pipe
RJP............ Remote Job Processing [*Data processing*]
RJP............ Rocket Jet Plume
RJPCA....... Russian Journal of Physical Chemistry [*English Translation*] [*A publication*]
RJ & PJ....... Revenue, Judicial, and Police Journal [*Calcutta*]　(DLA)
RJQ .... Rapports Judiciaires [*Quebec Law Reports*]　(DLA)
RJQ BR....... Rapports Judiciaires de Quebec, Cour du Banc du Roi [*Quebec Law Reports, King's Bench*]　(DLA)
RJQ CS ...... Rapports Judiciaires de Quebec, Cour Superieure [*Quebec Law Reports, Superior Court*]　(DLA)
RJR............ Mathieu's Quebec Revised Reports　(DLA)
RJR............ RJR Nabisco, Inc. [*NYSE symbol*]
RJR............ Rotary Joint Reed
RJR............ Russkij Jazyk za Rubezom [*A publication*]
RJRA .... Rotary Joint Reed Assembly
RJRQ .... Mathieu's Quebec Revised Reports　(DLA)
RJS............ Reaction Jet System　(KSC)
RJS............ Remote Job System [*Data processing*]　(MCD)
RJS............ Roberta Jo Society [*Circleville, OH*]　(EA)
RJS............ Russkij Jazyk v Skole [*A publication*]
RJS............ Ruth Jackson Society [*Worster, MA*]　(EA)
RJSFC........ R. J. Sutton Fan Club [*Nashville, TN*]　(EA)
RJT............ Rassemblement des Jeunes Togolais [*Togolese Youth Rally*]
RJT............ Reference Jet Transport
RJT............ Rejection Message [*Communications*]　(FAAC)
RJT............ Revue Juridique Themis [*A publication*]
RJT............ Royal Jubilee Trust [*Provides financial aid to start new businesses*] [*British*]
RJTV .... Ramjet Test Vehicle

R Jur	Revue Juridique [*A publication*]
R de Jur......	Revue de Jurisprudence [*Quebec*] (DLA)
R Juridique et Pol ...	Revue Juridique et Politique [*A publication*]
R Jur Polit ...	Revue Juridique et Politique, Independance et Cooperation [*A publication*]
RJV	Rheinisches Jahrbuch fuer Volkskunde [*A publication*]
RK	Rabbit Kidney
RK	Rack
R/K	Radial Keratotomy [*Ophthalmology*]
RK	Rassemblement Katangais [*Katanga Rally*] [*Elisabethville*]
RK	Rat Kidney
RK	Realkatalog der Aegyptologie [*A publication*] (BJA)
R-K	Redlich-Kwong [*Physics*]
RK	Rhodopsin Kinase [*An enzyme*]
RK	Right Kidney
RK	Right to Know [*An association*] [*Grand Prairie, TX*] (EA)
RK	Rock [*Maps and charts*] (MCD)
RK	Royal Knight [*British*]
RK	Run of Kiln
RK	Societe Air Afrique [*Cameroon*] [*ICAO designator*] (FAAC)
RKA	Rockdale, NY [*Location identifier*] [*FAA*] (FAAL)
RKAF..........	Royal Khmer Air Force [*Cambodia*] (CINC)
RKAF..........	Royal Khmere Air Force [*Cambodia*] (CINC)
RKANA......	Rost Kristallov [*A publication*]
RKB	Red Kidney Bean
RKCLA	Reaction Kinetics and Catalysis Letters [*A publication*]
RKCSN......	Rospravy Kralovske Ceske Spolecnosti Nauk [*A publication*]
RKD............	Rockland [*Maine*] [*Airport symbol*] (OAG)
RKE	Roskilde [*Denmark*] [*Airport symbol*] (OAG)
RKFJ	Rad Kongresa Folklorista Jugoslavije [*A publication*]
RKG............	Radiocardiogram
RKG............	Rockingham R. R. [*AAR code*]
RKG............	Royal Khmer Government [*Cambodia*]
RKH............	Rock Hill [*South Carolina*] [*Airport symbol*] (OAG)
RKH............	Rockingham Resources, Inc. [*Vancouver Stock Exchange symbol*]
RKHLit	Rocznik Komisji Historycznoliterackiej Pan [*A publication*]
RKHS	Register. Kentucky Historical Society [*A publication*]
RK II	Runge-Kutta Second Order [*Mathematics*]
RKJ	Ramsey, Kenneth J., Pittsburgh PA [*STAC*]
RKJ.............	Rozprawy Komisji Jezykowej Lodzkiego Towarzystwa Naukowego [*A publication*]
RKJL	Rozprawy Komisji Jezykowej Lodzkiego Towarzystwa Naukowego [*A publication*]
RKJW	Rozprawy Komisji Jezykowej Wroclawskiego Towarzystwa Naukowego [*A publication*]
RKKA	Raboche-Krest'ianskaia Krasnaia Armiia [*Workers' and Peasants' Red Army*] [*Redesignated Soviety Army*] [*USSR*]
RKKHA......	Rikagaku Kenkyusho Hokoku [*A publication*]
RKL	Ruskin Developments Limited [*Vancouver Stock Exchange symbol*]
RKLMF	Ruskin Development Limited [*NASDAQ symbol*] (NQ)
RKM	Runge-Kutta Method [*Mathematics*]
RKN............	Runge-Kutta-Nystroem [*Formula*] [*Mathematics*]
RKNFSYS ...	Rock Information System [*National Science Foundation*] [*Carnegie Institution*] [*Washington, DC*] [*Databank*] (EISS)
RKNKA.......	Rakuno Kagaku No Kenkyu [*A publication*]
RKO............	Radio-Keith-Orpheum [*Motion picture production and exhibition firm, also active in broadcasting*]
RKO............	Range Keeper Operator [*Navy*]
RKP	Rockport, TX [*Location identifier*] [*FAA*] (FAAL)
RKP	Routledge & Kegan Paul [*British publisher*]
RKPN..........	Rooms Katholieke Partij Nederland [*Roman Catholic Party of the Netherlands*] (PPE)
RKR............	Poteau, OK [*Location identifier*] [*FAA*] (FAAL)
RKr.............	Rakstu Krajums [*A publication*]
RKR	Rocker (AAG)
RKR	Rockspan Resources [*Vancouver Stock Exchange symbol*]
RKRA	Rocker Arm [*Mechanical engineering*]
RKS	Reko [*Solomon Islands*] [*Seismograph station code, US Geological Survey*] (SEIS)
RKS	Rock Springs [*Wyoming*] [*Airport symbol*] (OAG)
RKS	Rocket Stories [*A publication*]
RKSP..........	Rooms Katholieke Staatspartij [*Roman Catholic State Party*] [*The Netherlands*] (PPE)
RKT	Ras Al Khaymah [*United Arab Emirates*] [*Airport symbol*] (OAG)
RKT	Rikitea [*Tuamotu Archipelago*] [*Seismograph station code, US Geological Survey*] (SEIS)
RKT	Rocket (AAG)
RKTR..........	Rocketeer
RKTSTA......	Rocket Station
RKU............	Yule Island [*Papua New Guinea*] [*Airport symbol*] (OAG)
RKV	Rabbit Kidney Vacuolating Virus
RKV	Rose Knot Victor [*Gemini tracking ship*]
RKVA	Reactive Kilovolt-Ampere
RKVAM	Recording Kilovolt-Ampere Meter (MSA)
RKVP..........	Rooms Katholieke Volkspartij [*Roman Catholic People's Party*] [*The Netherlands*] (PPE)

RKW	Repertorium fuer Kunstwissenschaft [*A publication*]
RKW	Rockwood, TN [*Location identifier*] [*FAA*] (FAAL)
RKWD.........	Rockwood Holding Co. [*NASDAQ symbol*] (NQ)
RKX	Maxton, NC [*Location identifier*] [*FAA*] (FAAL)
RKX	Reako Explorations [*Vancouver Stock Exchange symbol*]
RKY	Rockaway Corp. [*American Stock Exchange symbol*]
Rky	Rocky [*Quality of the bottom*] [*Nautical charts*]
RKY	Roentgen Kymography
RKY	Rokeby [*Australia*] [*Airport symbol*] [*Obsolete*] (OAG)
RKZ	Reformierte Kirchenzeitung [*A publication*]
R & L...........	Bureau for Reference and Loan Services [*Library network*]
RL...............	LAR [*Liniile Aeriene Romane*] [*ICAO designator*] (FAAC)
RL...............	Master Cross-Reference List
RL...............	Radiation Laboratory
RL...............	Radio Liberty [*A publication*]
RL...............	Radio Liberty
RL...............	Radiolocation
RL...............	Radioluminescent
RL...............	Radionavigation land station using two separate loop antennas, and a single transmitter, and operating at a power of 150 watts or more [*ITU designation*] (CET)
RL...............	Rahmana Litslan (BJA)
RL...............	Rail (AAG)
R & L...........	Rail and Lake
RL...............	Raman LASER
RL...............	Random Lengths [*Lumber*]
RL...............	Random Logic
R/L.............	Rate/Limited (MCD)
RL...............	Rated Load
RL...............	Reactor Licensing (NRCH)
RL...............	Reader's Library [*A publication*]
RL...............	Reading List
RL...............	Receive Leg [*Telecommunications*] (TEL)
RL...............	Record Length
R/L.............	Redline (KSC)
RL...............	Reduced Level
RL...............	Reel
RL...............	Reeling Machines [*JETDS nomenclature*] [*Military*] (CET)
RL...............	Reference Library
RL...............	Reflection Loss [*Telecommunications*] (TEL)
RL...............	Reiz-Limen [*Stimulus threshold*] [*Psychology*]
RL...............	Relay Logic
RL...............	Release Load
RL...............	Religion Life [*A publication*]
R/L.............	Remote/Local (NASA)
RL...............	Report Immediately upon Leaving [*Aviation*] (FAAC)
RL...............	Research Laboratory
RL...............	Reserve List (ADA)
RL...............	Residential Lease (ADA)
RL...............	Resistor Logic (IEEE)
RL...............	Respectable Loge [*Worshipful Lodge*] [*French*] [*Freemasonry*] (ROG)
RL...............	Restaurant Liquor [*License*]
RL...............	Restricted Line Officer
RL...............	Retarded Learner [*Education*]
RL...............	Reticular Lamina [*Ear anatomy*]
RL...............	Retirement Loss
R/L.............	Return Link (MCD)
RL...............	Return Loss
RL...............	Revised Laws (DLA)
RL...............	Revista de Letras [*A publication*]
RL...............	Revista de Literatura [*A publication*]
RL...............	Revista Lusitana [*A publication*]
RL...............	Revue Legale [*Canada*] (DLA)
R de L........	Revue de Legislation et de Jurisprudence [*Canada*] (DLA)
RL...............	Revue de Lille [*A publication*]
RL...............	Rhumb Line
RL...............	Rial [*Monetary unit in Iran, Saudi Arabia, etc.*]
RL...............	Ricerche Linguistiche [*A publication*]
RL...............	Richland Operations Office [*Energy Research and Development Administration*]
RL...............	Right to Left
R/L.............	Right and Left
RL...............	Right Leg
RL...............	Right Line
RL...............	Right Lower [*Medicine*]
RL...............	Right Lung
RL...............	Ring Level (BUR)
RL...............	Ringer Lactated [*Medicine*]
RL...............	Rive'on Le-Khalkalah [*Tel Aviv*] (BJA)
RL...............	River Lines, Inc. [*AAR code*]
RL...............	Rivista Letteraria [*A publication*]
RL...............	Road Locomotive [*British*]
RL...............	Rocket Launcher
RL...............	Roll
RL...............	Roll Lift [*NASA*] (KSC)
RL...............	Rolland, Inc. [*Toronto Stock Exchange symbol*]
RL...............	Roman Law (DLA)
RL...............	Roof Leader (MSA)
RL...............	Royal (ROG)
RL...............	Royal Licence [*British*]

RL............... Ruch Literacki [*Krakow*] [*A publication*]
RL............... Russian Literature [*A publication*]
RLA............. Aeronautical Marker Beacon [*ITU designation*]   (CET)
RLA............. Reallexikon der Assyriologie [*Berlin*] [*A publication*]   (BJA)
RLA............. Receptive Language Age [*of the hearing-impaired*]
RLA............. Redevelopment Land Agency [*Washington, DC*]
RLA............. Regional Land Agent [*Ministry of Agriculture, Fisheries, and Food*] [*British*]
RLA............. Relay   (FAAC)
RLA............. Remote Line Adaptor
RLA............. Repair Level Analysis [*Military*]   (AFIT)
RLA............. Research Laboratory for Archeology [*British*]
RLA............. Responsible Local Agencies   (OICC)
RLA............. Restricted Landing Area [*Aviation*]
RLA............. Revista de Letras. Faculdade de Filosofia, Ciencias, e Letras (Assis) [*A publication*]
RLA............. Revista Liturgica Argentina [*A publication*]
RLA............. Roll Lock Actuator   (MCD)
RLA............. Royal Lao Army [*Laos*]
RLA............. Rui Lopes Associates, Inc. [*Sunnyvale, CA*] [*Telecommunications*]   (TSSD)
RLA............. Rural Land Alliance   (EA)
RLAC......... Reallexikon fuer Antike und Christentum [*A publication*]
RLAC......... Recycling Legislation Action Coalition   (EA)
RLADD....... RADAR Low-Angle Drogue Delivery   (AFM)
RLAF......... Royal Laotian Air Force
R Lang Rom ... Revue des Langues Romanes [*A publication*]
RLANO....... Relay Equipment Out of Operation [*Aviation*]   (FAAC)
RLAOK....... Relay Equipment Resumed Operation [*Aviation*]   (FAAC)
RLAQA....... Revista Latinoamericana de Quimica [*A publication*]
RLaR......... Revue des Langues Romanes [*A publication*]
RLAS......... Rocket Lunar Attitude System
RLAss........ Reallexikon der Assyriologie [*Berlin*] [*A publication*]   (BJA)
R Latinoamer Psicol ... Revista Latinoamericana de Psicologia [*A publication*]
R Latinoamer Sociol ... Revista Latinoamericana de Sociologia [*A publication*]
R Latinoam Estud Urbano Reg ... Revista Latinoamericana de Estudios Urbano Regionales [*A publication*]
RLaV......... Revue des Langues Vivantes [*A publication*]
RLB........... RACON Station [*ITU designation*]   (CET)
RLB........... Reliability [*or Reliable*]   (AAG)
RLB........... United States Railroad Labor Board Decisions   (DLA)
RLBCD....... Right Lower Border of Cardiac Dullness [*Cardiology*]
RLB Dec..... Railroad Labor Board Decisions   (DLA)
RLBG......... Relative Bearing [*Navigation*]   (FAAC)
RLBL......... Regional Laser and Biotechnology Laboratories [*University of Pennsylvania*] [*Research center*]   (RCD)
RLBM........ Rearward Launched Ballistic Missile
RLC........... Radio Launch Control System
RLC........... Radio Liberty Committee [*Later, RFE/RL*]   (EA)
RLC........... Rassegna Italiana di Lingue e Letteratura Classiche [*A publication*]
RLC........... Receive Logic Chassis
RLC........... Refund Litigation Coordinator [*IRS*]
RLC........... Remote Line Concentrator
RLC........... Remote Load Controller   (MCD)
RLC........... Report Landing Completed [*Aviation*]   (FAAC)
RLC........... Residual Lung Capacity [*Medicine*]
RLC........... Resistance Inductance Capacitance   (MSA)
RLC........... Revue de Litterature Comparee [*A publication*]
RLC........... Ribosome-Lamella Complex [*Physiology*]
RLC........... Right Line Contactor   (MCD)
RLC........... RLC Corp. [*NYSE symbol*]
RLC........... Robinson Little & Company Ltd. [*Toronto Stock Exchange symbol*]
RLC........... ROM [*Read-Only Memory*] Location Counter
RLC........... Rotating Litter Chair [*NASA*]   (KSC)
RLC........... Run Length Coding
RLCA......... National Rural Letter Carriers' Association
RLCA......... Religion and Labor Council of America [*Defunct*]   (EA)
RLCAD....... Revista Latinoamericana de Ciencias Agricolas [*A publication*]
RLCD......... Relocated
RLCR......... Railcar   (MSA)
RLCS......... Radio Launch Control System
RLCU......... Reference Link Control Unit [*Telecommunications*]   (TEL)
RLD........... RADAR Laydown Delivery   (AFM)
RLD........... Related Living Donor [*Medicine*]
RLD........... Relocation Dictionary
RLD........... Relocation List Directory
RLD........... Repetitive LASER Desorption
RLD........... Retail Liquor Dealer
RLD........... Richland [*Washington*] [*Airport symbol*] [*Obsolete*]   (OAG)
RLD........... Rolled   (AAG)
RLD........... Run Length Discriminator   (MCD)
RLD........... Ruptured Lumbar Disc [*Medicine*]
RLE........... Raleigh Energy [*Vancouver Stock Exchange symbol*]
RLE........... Relative Luminous Efficiency   (NATG)
RLE........... Request Loading Entry [*Data processing*]
RLE........... Research Laboratory of Electronics [*MIT*] [*Research center*]
RLE........... Right Lower Extremity [*Medicine*]

RLEA......... Railway Labor Executives Association   (EA)
RLeIt........ Rassegna della Letteratura Italiana [*A publication*]
RLEO......... Request Liaison Engineering Order [*NASA*]   (NASA)
R Let......... Revista de Letras [*A publication*]
RLETFL..... Report Leaving Each Thousand-Foot Level [*Aviation*]   (FAAC)
R Lett Mod ... Revue des Lettres Modernes [*A publication*]
RLF........... Relief   (AAG)
RLF........... Religion and Labor Foundation
RLF........... Religious Liberty Foundation   (EA)
RLF........... Remote Lift Fan [*Aviation*]
RLF........... Retrolental Fibroplasia [*Eye disease in premature babies*]
RLF........... Right Lateral Femoral [*Site of injection*] [*Medicine*]
RLF........... Royal Laotian Forces
RLF........... Royal Literary Fund [*British*]
RLFC......... Rebel Lee Fan Club   (EA)
RLFE......... Revista. Laboratorio de Fonetica Experimental [*A publication*]
RLG........... Glidepath [*Slope*] Station [*ITU designation*]   (CET)
RLG........... Kremmling, CO [*Location identifier*] [*FAA*]   (FAAL)
RLG........... Railing   (AAG)
RLG........... Regimental Landing Group
RLG........... Regional Liaison Group   (CINC)
RLG........... Release Guard [*Telecommunications*]   (TEL)
RLG........... Research Libraries Group, Inc. [*Stanford, CA*] [*Information service*]
RLG........... Research Libraries Group, Inc. [*Art Institute of Chicago*] [*Illinois*] [*Information service*]   (EISS)
RLG........... Ring LASER Gyro [*Navy*]
RLG........... Royal Laotian Government
RLGD......... Realigned
RLGM........ Remote Look Group Multiplexer   (MCD)
RLGM-CD .. Remote Look Group Multiplexer Cable Drive   (MCD)
RLH........... Run Like Hell [*Slang*]
RLHAS....... Revue de Litterature, Histoire, Arts, et Sciences [*A publication*]
RLHS......... Railway and Locomotive Historical Society   (EA)
RLHTE....... Research Laboratory of Heat Transfer in Electronics [*MIT*]   (MCD)
RLI........... Anniston, AL [*Location identifier*] [*FAA*]   (FAAL)
RLI........... Radiation Level Indicator
RLI........... Rassegna della Letteratura Italiana [*A publication*]
RLI........... Realtors Land Institute [*Chicago, IL*]   (EA)
RLI........... Retirement Life Item
RLI........... Revista de las Indias [*A publication*]
RLi........... Revue de Linguistique [*A publication*]
RLI........... Rhodesian Light Infantry [*Military unit*]
RLI........... Right/Left Indicator   (NVT)
RLI........... Rostral Length Index
RLIB......... Relocatable Library [*Data processing*]
RLIC......... RLI Corporation [*NASDAQ symbol*]   (NQ)
RLIEVDP ... Request Line Items Be Expedited for Vehicles [*or Equipment*] Deadlined for Parts [*Army*]   (AABC)
RLIF......... Reliable Life Insurance [*NASDAQ symbol*]   (NQ)
RLIN......... Research Libraries Information Network [*Pronounced "arlen"*] [*Formerly, BALLOTS*] [*Research Libraries Group, Inc.*] [*Stanford, CA*] [*Library network*] [*Information service*]
RLing........ Revue de Linguistique [*A publication*]
RLing........ Ricerche Linguistiche [*A publication*]
RLing........ Russian Linguistics [*A publication*]
RLir......... Realismo Lirico [*A publication*]
RLiR......... Revue de Linguistique Romane [*A publication*]
RLit........... Revista de Literatura [*A publication*]
RLit........... Russkaja Literatura [*A publication*]
RLitC......... Readings in Literary Criticism [*A publication*]
R Litt Comp ... Revue de Litterature Comparee [*A publication*]
RLiv......... Rivista di Livorno [*A publication*]
R de L et de J ... Revue de Legislation et de Jurisprudence   (DLA)
RLJ........... Rhodes-Livingstone Journal [*A publication*]
RLJ........... Rhodesian Law Journal   (DLA)
RLJ........... Russian Language Journal [*A publication*]
RLL........... Localizer Station [*ITU designation*]   (CET)
RLL........... Religion in Literature and Life [*A publication*]
RLL........... Relocating Linking Loader
RLL........... Representation-Language Language [*Data processing*]
RLL........... Reviews in Leukemia and Lymphoma [*Elsevier Book Series*] [*A publication*]
RLL........... Right Lower Limb [*Medicine*]
RLL........... Right Lower Lobe [*Lungs*]
RLL........... Rim of Lateral Lip
RLL........... Rocket Launcher Locator
RLL........... Rolla, ND [*Location identifier*] [*FAA*]   (FAAL)
RLL........... Royal LePage Capital Properties Partnership Units [*Formerly, A. E. LePage Capital Properties*] [*Toronto Stock Exchange symbol*]
RLL........... Run-Length-Limited [*Data processing*]
RLLB......... Right Long Leg Brace [*Medicine*]
RLLB......... Right Lower Leg Brace [*Medicine*]
RLLD......... Registered Laundry and Linen Director [*Designation awarded by National Association of Institutional Linen Management*]
RLLO......... Revue de Langue et Litterature d'Oc [*A publication*]
RLLP......... Revue de Langue et Litterature Provencales [*A publication*]
RLLProv ..... Revue de Langue et Litterature Provencales [*A publication*]

RLLR .... Revue de Louisiane/Louisiana Review [*A publication*]
RLLSC .... Right to Life League of Southern California　(EA)
R & LL & T ... Redman and Lyon on Landlord and Tenant [*8th ed.*] [*1924*]　(DLA)
RLM .... Marine Radio Beacon Station [*ITU designation*]　(CET)
RLM .... Rearward Launched Missile
RLM .... Regional Library of Medicine [*Pan American Health Organization*]
RLM .... Revista di Letterature Moderne e Comparate [*A publication*]
RLM .... Revue des Langues Modernes [*A publication*]
RLM .... Reynolds Metals Co. [*NYSE symbol*]
RLM .... Rivista di Letteratura Moderne e Comparate [*A publication*]
RLM .... Royal American Airways [*Tucson, AZ*] [*FAA designator*]　(FAAC)
RLM .... Royal London Militia
RLMA .... Roll Label Manufacturers Association　(EA)
RLMBA ...... Rendiconti. Istituto Lombardo. Accademia di Scienze e Lettere. Sezione B. Scienze Biologiche e Mediche [*A publication*]
RLMC .... Rivista di Letteratura Moderne e Comparate [*A publication*]
RLMF .... Revue du Louvre et des Musees de France [*A publication*]
RLMM .... Research Laboratory for Mechanics of Materials　(MCD)
RLMod ...... Revue des Lettres Modernes [*A publication*]
RLMPA .... Revista Latinoamericana de Microbiologia y Parasitologia [*Later, Revista Latinoamericana de Microbiologia*] [*A publication*]
RLMPB .... Proceedings. Reliability and Maintainability Conference [*A publication*]
RLMS .... RADAR Land Mass Simulation
RLMS .... Reproduction of Library Materials Section [*Resources and Technical Services Division of ALA*]
RLN .... LORAN Station [*ITU designation*]　(CET)
RLND .... Regional Lymph Node Dissection [*Medicine*]
RLNS .... Revue Legale. New Series [*Canada*]　(DLA)
RLO .... Omnidirectional Range Station [*ITU designation*]　(CET)
RLO .... RADAR Lock-On
RLO .... Regional Liaison Office [*Military*]　(AFM)
R & LO .... Reliability and Launch Operations　(MCD)
RLO .... Repairs Liaison Officer [*Landing craft and barges*] [*Navy*]
R/LO .... Response/Lockout　(MCD)
RLO .... Returned Letter Office
RLO .... Richland Operations Office [*Energy Research and Development Administration*]
RLO .... Rose Lookout Tower [*Oklahoma*] [*Seismograph station code, US Geological Survey*]　(SEIS)
RLOE .... Roemische Limes in Oesterreich [*A publication*]
RLOP .... Reactor Licensing Operating Procedure　(NRCH)
RLORA ...... Revue de Laryngologie, Otologie, Rhinologie [*A publication*]
RLOS .... Retention Level of Supply [*Navy*]　(NG)
RLOS .... Revue Legale. Old Series [*Canada*]　(DLA)
RLOSA ...... Revue de Laryngologie, Otologie, Rhinologie. Supplement [*A publication*]
R du Louvre ... Revue du Louvre et des Musees de France [*A publication*]
R Louvre .... Revue du Louvre et des Musees de France [*A publication*]
RLP .... Rail Loading Point　(NATG)
RLP .... Remote Line Printer　(MCD)
RLP .... Ribosome-Like Particle [*Cytology*]
RLP .... Roads and Landscape Planning [*British*]
RLP .... Rosella Plains [*Australia*] [*Airport symbol*] [*Obsolete*]　(OAG)
RLP .... Rotatable Log Periodic Antenna　(MCD)
RLP .... Rotating Linear Polarization
RLP .... Ruby LASER Pulse
RLPA .... Retail Loss Prevention Association [*New York, NY*]　(EA)
RLPA .... Rotating Log Periodic Antenna
RLPH .... Reflected Light Photohead
RLPL .... Railway Labor's Political League
RLQ .... Right Lower Quadrant [*of abdomen*] [*Medicine*]
RLQB .... Revue Legale Reports, Queen's Bench [*Canada*]　(DLA)
RLR .... Radio Range Station [*ITU designation*]　(CET)
RLR .... Radioactive Lighting Rod　(NRCH)
RL & R .... Rail, Lake, and Rail
RLR .... Record Length Register
RLR .... Retired Lives Reserve [*Insurance*]
RLR .... Revue des Langues Romanes [*A publication*]
RLR .... Revue de Linguistique Romane [*A publication*]
RLR .... Right Larval Retractor
RLR .... Right Lateral Rectus [*Eye anatomy*]
RLR .... Right Lateral Rotation [*Medicine*]
RLR .... Roller　(MSA)
RLR .... Rutgers Law Review [*A publication*]
RLRB .... Radio Liberty Research Bulletin [*A publication*]
RLRIU .... Radio Logic Routing Interface Unit　(MCD)
RLS .... Person who stammers, unable to enunciate the letters R, L, and S
RLS .... RADAR Line of Sight
RLS .... Radius of Landing Site [*NASA*]　(KSC)
RLS .... Raman LASER Source
RLS .... Regional Language Studies [*Newfoundland*] [*A publication*]
RLS .... Release　(FAAC)
RLS .... Remote Line Switch [*Telecommunications*]　(TEL)

RLS .... Research in the Life Sciences Committee [*National Academy of Sciences*]
RLS .... Reservoir Level Sensor　(MCD)
RLS .... Restricted Least Squares [*Statistics*]
RL & S .... Ridgeway, Lapp, and Schoales' Irish King's Bench Reports [*1793-95*]　(DLA)
RLS .... Rim Latch Set
RLS .... Ringer's Lactate Solution [*Physiology*]
RLS .... Riolos of Patras [*Greece*] [*Seismograph station code, US Geological Survey*]　(SEIS)
RLS .... Robert Louis Stevenson [*Nineteenth-century Scottish author*]
RLS .... Rocket Launching System
RLS .... Roll Limit Switch
RLS .... Rotary Limit Switch
RLS .... Ruby LASER System
RLS .... Surveillance RADAR Station [*ITU designation*]　(CET)
RLS .... Westerly, RI [*Location identifier*] [*FAA*]　(FAAL)
RLSA .... Republican Law Students Association of New York　(EA)
RLSC .... Revue Legale Reports, Supreme Court [*Canada*]　(DLA)
RLSD .... Received Line Signal Detector
RLSE .... Release　(MSA)
RLSP .... Ruby LASER Single Pulse
R L St .... Rackham Literary Studies [*A publication*]
RLST .... Realist, Inc. [*NASDAQ symbol*]　(NQ)
RLST .... Release Timer [*Telecommunications*]　(TEL)
RLSTA .... Regelungstechnik [*A publication*]
RLSTN .... Relay Station　(FAAC)
RLT .... Arlit [*Niger*] [*Airport symbol*]　(OAG)
RLT .... Regimental Landing Team [*Military*]
RLT .... Relating To　(AABC)
RLT .... Reliability Life Test
RLT .... Reorder Lead Time [*Navy*]　(NG)
RLT .... Repair Lead Time
RLT .... Return Line Tether　(MCD)
RLT .... Right Lateral Thigh [*Medicine*]
RLT .... Ring LASER Technique
RLT .... Rolling Liquid Transporter [*Army*]
RLT .... Russian Literature Triquarterly [*A publication*]
RLTA .... Reenlistment Leave Travel Allowance [*Military*]
RLTA .... Rhodesian Lawn Tennis Association
RLTK .... Rhumb Line Track　(FAAC)
RLTM .... Research Laboratories Technical Memorandum
RLTN .... Relation　(MSA)
RLTO .... Regional Lime Technical Officer [*Ministry of Agriculture, Fisheries, and Food*] [*British*]
RLTS .... Radio Linked Telemetry System
RLTV .... Relative　(AFM)
RLU .... RADAR Logic Unit　(MCD)
RLu .... Rassegna Lucchese [*A publication*]
RLU .... Relative Light Units [*Analysis of light intensity*]
RLU .... Remote Line Unit [*Telecommunications*]
RLU .... Waterville, ME [*Location identifier*] [*FAA*]　(FAAL)
RLub .... Rocznik Lubelski [*A publication*]
RLuc .... Rassegna Lucchese [*A publication*]
RLux .... Revue Trimestrielle d'Etudes Linguistiques, Folkloriques, et Toponymiques (Luxembourg) [*A publication*]
RLV .... Rauscher [*Murine*] Leukemia Virus
RLV .... Reallexikon der Vorgeschichte [*Berlin*] [*A publication*]　(BJA)
RLV .... Relieve　(AFM)
RLV .... Reusable Launch Vehicle [*Aerospace*]
RLV .... Revue des Langues Vivantes [*A publication*]
RLV .... Roving Lunar Vehicle　(AAG)
RLVDT .... Rotary Linear Variable Differential Transformer
RLVS .... Recoverable Launch Vehicle Structure　(KSC)
RLW .... Rajasthan Law Weekly [*India*]　(DLA)
RLW .... Real West Airlines [*Fargo, ND*] [*FAA designator*]　(FAAC)
RL & W .... Roberts, Leaming, and Wallis' County Court Reports [*1849-51*]　(DLA)
RLWL .... Reactor Low-Water Level　(IEEE)
RLWY .... Railway　(AAG)
RLXN .... Relaxation　(MSA)
RLY .... Railway
RLY .... Relay　(AAG)
RLY .... Worland, WY [*Location identifier*] [*FAA*]　(FAAL)
Rly Engng ... Railway Engineering Journal [*Incorporated in Railway Engineer International*] [*A publication*]
Rly Gaz .... Railway Gazette [*Later, Railway Gazette International*] [*A publication*]
RLz .... Radjans'ke Literaturoznavstvo [*Kiev*] [*A publication*]
R Lz .... Radjans'ke Literaturoznavstvo. Naukovo-Teoretycnyj Zurnal [*A publication*]
RM .... Journal of Recreational Mathematics [*A publication*]
RM .... Lab. Roland-Marie [*France*] [*Research code symbol*]
R & M .... Law Reporter, Montreal [*Canada*]　(DLA)
RM .... Maritime Radionavigation Mobile Station [*ITU designation*]　(CET)
RM .... McAlpine Aviation [*Great Britain*] [*ICAO designator*]　(FAAC)
RM .... Office of Resource Management [*Nuclear energy*]　(NRCH)
RM .... RADAR Mapper
RM .... RADAR Missile　(MUGU)
RM .... Radiation Measurement

R/M	Radiation/Meteoroid [*NASA satellite*]
RM	Radiation Monitor (NRCH)
RM	Radical Mastectomy [*Medicine*]
RM	Radio Marti [*Cuba*]
RM	Radio Material Officer (MCD)
RM	Radio Monitor
RM	Radioman [*Navy rating*]
RM	Range Marks
RM	Range of Movement [*Medicine*]
RM	Rassegna Monetaria [*A publication*]
RM	Rassegna Musicale [*A publication*]
RM	Raw Material
RM	Reaction Mass
RM	Reactor Manufacturer [*Nuclear energy*] (NRCH)
R/M	Read/Mostly [*Data processing*] (TEL)
RM	Readiness Manager [*DARCOM*] [*Army*]
RM	Readout Matrix
RM	Ready Money (ROG)
RM	Ream
RM	Receiver, Mobile
RM	Receiving Memo
RM	Record Mark (BUR)
RM	Red Marrow [*Hematology*]
R & M	Redistribution and Marketing (AFM)
RM	Redundancy Management (MCD)
RM	Reference Material
RM	Reference Method
RM	Reference Mission [*NASA*] (NASA)
RM	Refresh Memory (MCD)
RM	Regional Manager
RM	Regional Meetings [*Quakers*]
RM	Register Memory
RM	Reichsmark [*Later, DM*] [*Monetary unit in Germany*]
RM	Relais Musique [*Phonorecord series*] [*Canada*]
RM	Relative Mobility [*of ions*] [*Chemistry*]
R & M	Release and Material (MCD)
R & M	Reliability and Maintainability [*Navy*]
RM	Religionen der Menschheit [*A publication*]
RM	Remedial Maintenance (AFM)
Rm	Remission [*Medicine*]
RM	Remote Manipulator [*NASA*] (NASA)
RM	Remote Manual (NRCH)
RM	Remote Multiplexer [*Data processing*] (CAAL)
RM	Rendezvous Maneuver (MCD)
RM	Repair Manual
RM	Repetition Maximum [*Medicine*]
RM	Replaceable Module
RMAC	Remote Master Aircraft (MCD)
R & M	Reports and Memorandum (MCD)
RM	Rescue Module [*NASA*] (NASA)
RM	Research Materials [*National Bureau of Standards*]
RM	Research Memorandum
RM	Resident Magistrate
RM	Residential Member [*Designation awarded by American Institute of Real Estate Appraisers of the National Association of Realtors*]
RM	Resource Manager
RM	Respiratory Movement
RM	Response Memoranda [*Jimmy Carter administration*]
RM	Retail Manager
RM	Return Material [*Navy*] (NG)
RM	Review of Metaphysics [*A publication*]
R/M	Revolutions per Minute
RM	Revue de Metaphysique et de Morale [*A publication*]
RM	Revue Mondiale [*A publication*]
RM	Rhesus Monkey
RM	Riding Master [*British*]
RM	Ring Micrometer
RM	Risk Management [*A publication*]
RM	Rocket Management (MCD)
RM	Rollback Module [*Telecommunications*] (TEL)
RM	Roman Martyrology
rm	Romania [*MARC country of publication code*] [*Library of Congress*] (LCCP)
RM	Romans [*New Testament book*]
RM	Room (AAG)
RM	Routine Maintenance (AAG)
RM	Rowley Mile [*Horseracing*] [*British*]
RM	Rowohlts Monographien [*A publication*]
RM	Royal Mail [*British*]
RM	Royal Marines [*British*]
RM	Rubber Mold (MCD)
RM	Rule Making [*Nuclear energy*] (NRCH)
RM	Ruptured Membrane [*Medicine*]
RM	Rural Municipality (DLA)
R & M	Russell and Mylne's English Chancery Reports (DLA)
RM	Russkaja Mysl' [*A publication*]
R & M	Ryan and Moody's English Nisi Prius Reports (DLA)
RM1	Radioman, First Class [*Navy rating*]
RM2	Radioman, Second Class [*Navy rating*]
R & M/2	RON [*Research Octane Number*] and MON [*Motor Octane Number*] Averaged [*Antiknock index*] [*Fuel technology*]
RM3	Radioman, Third Class [*Navy rating*]
RMA	Racquetball Manufacturers Association (EA)
RMA	Radio-Labeled Monoclonal Antiglobulin [*Clinical chemistry*]
RMA	Radio Manufacturers Association [*Later, Electronic Industries Association*]
RMA	Radiometric Microbiological Assay
RMA	Random Multiple Access
RMA	Reactive Modulation Amplifier
RMA	Rear Maintenance Area [*Military*] [*British*]
RMA	Receiver Measurement Adapter (MCD)
RMA	Reclaim Managers Association [*Campbell, CA*] (EA)
RMA	Regional Manpower Administration
RMA	Registered Medical Assistants [*Formerly, ARMA*] [*Park Ridge, IL*] (EA)
RMA	Reliability, Maintainability, and Availability [*Standards*]
RMA	Reliability and Maintenance Analysis (CAAL)
RMA	Remote Manipulator Arm (MCD)
RMA	Research and Marketing Act [*1946*]
RMA	Reserve Military Aviator
RMA	Rhythmic Motor Activity [*Physiology*]
RMA	Rice Millers' Association [*Arlington, VA*] (EA)
RMA	Right Mentoanterior [*A fetal position*] [*Obstetrics*]
RMA	Robert Morris Associates [*National Association of Bank Loan Officers and Credit Men*] [*Philadelphia, PA*] (EA)
RMA	Rockefeller Mountains [*Antarctica*] [*Seismograph station code, US Geological Survey*] [*Closed*] (SEIS)
RMA	Rocky Mountain Airways [*Denver, CO*] [*FAA designator*] (FAAC)
RMA	Rocky Mountain Arsenal [*Army*] (AABC)
RMA	Rodeo Media Association [*Formerly, IRWA*] (EA)
RMA	Roma [*Australia*] [*Airport symbol*] (OAG)
RMA	Rosin Mildly Activated [*Standard material for soldering*]
RMA	Royal Malta Artillery [*Military unit*] [*British*]
RMA	Royal Marine Academy [*British*]
RMA	Royal Marine Artillery [*Obsolete*] [*British*]
RMA	Royal Military Academy [*For cadets of Royal Engineers and Royal Artillery; frequently referred to as Woolwich*] [*British*]
RMA	Royal Military Asylum [*British*]
RMA	Royal Musical Association [*British*]
RMA	Royal Musical Association. Proceedings [*A publication*]
RMA	Rubber Manufacturers Association [*Washington, DC*] (EA)
RMAAD	Revista Mexicana de Astronomia y Astrofisica [*A publication*]
RMAAS	Reactivity Monitoring and Alarm System [*Nuclear energy*] (NRCH)
RMab	Revue Mabillon [*A publication*]
RMAC	Remote Master Aircraft (MCD)
R-MAD	Reactor Maintenance, Assembly, and Disassembly
RMAF	Royal Moroccan Air Force
RMAFA	Revista. Union Matematica Argentina y Asociacion Fisica Argentina [*A publication*]
RMAL	Revised Master Allowance List [*Military*] (AFIT)
RMAL	Revue du Moyen-Age Latin [*Strasbourg*] [*A publication*]
RMALAN	Royal Malaysian Navy
RMA Proc	Royal Musical Association. Proceedings [*A publication*]
RMARC	Royal Musical Association. Research Chronicle [*A publication*]
R Marche Commun	Revue du Marche Commun [*A publication*]
RMA Res Chron	RMA [*Royal Musical Association*] Research Chronicle [*A publication*]
RMA Research	Royal Musical Association. Research Chronicle [*A publication*]
R Marketing & Ag Econ	Review of Marketing and Agricultural Economics [*A publication*]
R Marketing and Agric Econ	Review of Marketing and Agricultural Economics [*A publication*]
RMAS	Royal Military Academy Sandhurst [*British*]
R MAST	Radio Mast
RMATS-1	Remote Maintenance, Administration, and Traffic System-1 [*Telecommunications*] (TEL)
RMAX	Range, Maximum
RMB	Radio Marker Beacon
RMB	Rambler Oil Co. [*Toronto Stock Exchange symbol*]
RMB	Raw Materials Board [*of the Reconstruction Finance Corp.*]
RMB	Renminbi [*Monetary unit in China*]
RMB	Roadside Mailbox (ADA)
RMB	Rocky Mountain Motor Tariff Bureau, Inc., Denver CO [*STAC*]
RMB	Rombauer [*Missouri*] [*Seismograph station code, US Geological Survey*] (SEIS)
RMBC	Regional Marine Biological Centre [*Marine science*] (MSC)
RMBF	Required Myocardial Blood Flow [*Cardiology*]
RMBI	Canadian Risk Management and Business Insurance [*A publication*]
RMC	Captain of Royal Marines [*Military*] [*British*]
RMC	Chief Radioman [*Navy rating*]
RMC	R. M. Charlton's Georgia Reports (DLA)
RMC	Radiation Management Corporation (NRCH)
RMC	Radiation Material Corporation
RMC	Randolph-Macon College [*Virginia*]
RMC	Rat Mast Cell
RMC	Raytheon Manufacturing Company (MCD)
RM & C	Reactor Monitoring and Control (NRCH)

RMC .... Ready Mixed Concrete (ADA)
RMC .... Reduced Material Condition (NVT)
RMC .... Redundancy Management Control (MCD)
RMC .... Regional Media Center
RMC .... Regular Military Compensation (AABC)
RMC .... Regulated Motor Carriers
RMC .... Relative-Motion Control [*Microcopy*]
RMC .... Remote Manual Control (NRCH)
RMC .... Remote Multiplexer Combiner (MCD)
RMC .... Rendezvous Mercury Capsule [*NASA*] (AAG)
RMC .... Repair Manufacturer Codes
RMC .... Representative in Medical Council [*Royal College of
　　　　　　　Physicians*] [*British*] (ROG)
RMC .... Republican Mainstream Committee (EA)
RMC .... Residential Manpower Center [*Job Corps*]
RMC .... Resource Management Consultants [*Salem, NH*]
　　　　　　　[*Telecommunications*] (TSSD)
RMC .... Return to Military Control (AABC)
RMC .... Revista Musical Chilena [*A publication*]
RMC .... Revolutionary Military Council [*Grenada*]
RMC .... Revue du Marche Commun [*Review of the Common Market*]
　　　　　　　[*French*]
RMC .... Rocket Motor Case
RMC .... Rocky Mountain College [*Montana*]
RMC .... Rod Memory Computer [*NCR Corp.*]
RMC .... Rosemont College, Rosemont, PA [*OCLC symbol*] (OCLC)
RMC .... Rotary Mirror Camera
RMC .... Rotating Modulation Collimator
RMC .... Royal Marine Commandos [*British*]
RMC .... Royal Military College [*For army cadets; often referred to as
　　　　　　　Sandhurst*] [*British*]
RMC .... Rural Manpower Center [*Michigan State University*]
RMCA........ Right Middle Cerebral Artery [*Anatomy*]
RMCAT ..... Ralph Mayer Center for Artists' Techniques [*University of
　　　　　　　Delaware*] [*Newark*] [*Information service*] (EISS)
RMCB........ Registered Mail Central Bureau [*Later, RMIA*] (EA)
RMCB........ Reserve Mobile Construction Battalion
RMCB........ Royal Marine Commando Brigade [*British*]
RMCC .... RADAR Monitor and Control Console [*Military*] (CAAL)
RMCC .... Ryan and Moody's English Crown Cases (DLA)
R & MCC .... Ryan and Moody's English Crown Cases Reserved (DLA)
RMCCR ..... Ryan and Moody's English Crown Cases (DLA)
RMCCSC ... Raw Materials Committee of the Commonwealth Supply
　　　　　　　Council [*British*] [*World War II*]
RMCDC ...... Rocky Mountain Child Development Center [*University of
　　　　　　　Colorado*] [*Research center*] (RCD)
R & McG ..... Income Tax Decisions of Australasia (Ratcliffe and McGrath) [*A
　　　　　　　publication*]
R & McG Ct of Rev ... Court of Review Decisions [*Ratcliffe and McGrath*] [*A
　　　　　　　publication*]
R & McG Ct of Rev ... Court of Review Decisions (Ratcliffe and McGrath) [*A
　　　　　　　publication*]
R M Ch ...... R. M. Charlton's Georgia Reports [*1811-37*] (DLA)
R M Ch ...... Revista Musical Chilena [*A publication*]
R M Charlt (GA) ... R. M. Charlton's Georgia Reports [*1811-37*] (DLA)
RMCL .... Recommended Maximum Contaminant Levels
RMCLB...... Revue Medico-Chirurgicale [*A publication*]
RMCM .... Master Chief Radioman [*Navy rating*]
RMCM .... Reduced Material Condition Maintenance (MCD)
RMCM .... Return Material Credit Memo
RMCM .... Royal Manchester College of Music [*British*]
RMCMI ...... Rocky Mountain Coal Mining Institute [*Lakewood, CO*] (EA)
RMCO .... Raymond Manufacturing Company
RMCOEH.... Rocky Mountain Center for Occupational and Environmental
　　　　　　　Health [*University of Utah*] [*Research center*] (RCD)
RMCP........ Rat Mast Cell Protease [*An enzyme*]
RMCS........ Range Monitoring and Control Subsystem (MCD)
RMCS........ Reactor Manual Control System (NRCH)
RMCS........ Remote Monitoring and Control System [*Telecommunications*]
RMCS........ Royal Medical and Chirurgical Society [*British*] (ROG)
RMCS........ Royal Military College of Science [*British*]
RMCS........ Senior Chief Radioman [*Navy rating*]
RMCT .... Research Monographs in Cell and Tissue Physiology [*Elsevier
　　　　　　　Book Series*] [*A publication*]
RMCUSA.... Riley Motor Club USA (EA)
RMD .... Raw Materials Department [*Ministry of Supply*] [*British*]
RMD .... Ready Money Down [*Means immediate payment*]
RMD .... Repair and Modification Directive (AAG)
RMD .... Retromanubrial Dullness [*Medicine*]
RMDA........ Request for Manufacturing Development Authorization (AAG)
RMDAB ..... Revue de Medecine Aeronautique [*A publication*]
RMDI .... Radio Magnetic Deviation Indicator (AAG)
RM Dig ...... Rapalje and Mack's Digest of Railway Law (DLA)
RMDIR....... Remove Directory [*Data processing*]
RMDN........ Registered Mental Deficiency Nurse (ADA)
RMDP .... Rural Manpower Development Program
Rmdr .... Remainder (DLA)
RME .... Radiation Monitoring Equipment
RME .... Raw Materials (MCD)
RME .... Receptor Mediated Endocytosis [*Biochemistry*]
RME .... Request Monitor Entry [*Data processing*]

RME .... Resident Maintenance Engineer (NATG)
RME .... Rocket Mission Evaluator (MCD)
RME .... Rocky Mountain Energy [*Vancouver Stock Exchange symbol*]
RME .... Rome, NY [*Location identifier*] [*FAA*] (FAAL)
RME .... Royal Marine Engineers [*British*]
RMEA .... Revista Mexicana de Estudios Antropologicos y Historicos [*A
　　　　　　　publication*]
RMEC .... Refractory Metals Electrofinishing Corporation
RMED .... Recruit, Retrain, Reemploy Medics [*Program*]
RMed. .... Revue de la Mediterranee [*A publication*]
RMedSoc ... Royal Medical Society, Edinburgh
RMEL .... Rocky Mountain Educational Laboratory [*Closed*]
R Melbourne Hosp Clin Rep ... Royal Melbourne Hospital. Clinical Reports
　　　　　　　[*A publication*]
RMEMD...... Revue Roumaine de Morphologie, d'Embryologie, et de
　　　　　　　Physiologie. Serie Morphologie et Embryologie [*A
　　　　　　　publication*]
RMEPD....... Revue Roumaine de Morphologie, d'Embryologie, et de
　　　　　　　Physiologie. Serie Physiologie [*A publication*]
RMER .... Resource Management Expense Reporting System (MCD)
RMERA...... Rumanian Medical Review [*A publication*]
R Mercados ... Revista dos Mercados [*A publication*]
R Metaphys ... Review of Metaphysics [*A publication*]
R Met S ...... Royal Meteorological Society [*British*]
R Mex Agr ... Revista del Mexico Agrario [*A publication*]
R Mexic Sociol ... Revista Mexicana de Sociologia [*A publication*]
R Mexic Trab ... Revista Mexicana del Trabajo [*A publication*]
RMF........... Raw Materials Finance Department [*Ministry of Supply*]
　　　　　　　[*British*]
RMF........... Reactivity Measurement Facility [*Nuclear energy*]
RMF........... Reamfixture (MCD)
RMF........... Reflectivity Measuring Facility
RMF........... Residual Master File [*Data processing*]
RMF........... Resource Measurement Facility [*Data processing*]
RMF........... Reymann Memorial Farms [*West Virginia University*] [*Research
　　　　　　　center*] (RCD)
RMF........... Royal Munster Fusiliers [*Military unit*] [*British*]
RMFC........ Rachel Minke Fan Club (EA)
R M F C ...... Recherches sur la Musique Francaise Classique [*A publication*]
RMFC........ Ronnie Milsap Fan Club [*Nashville, TN*] (EA)
RMFEB...... Revista Mexicana de Fisica. Suplemento de Ensenanza [*A
　　　　　　　publication*]
RMFMA...... Rock Mechanics [*A publication*]
RMFSA...... Revista Mexicana de Fisica. Suplemento del Reactor [*A
　　　　　　　publication*]
RMFVR...... Royal Marine Forces Volunteer Reserve [*Obsolete*] [*British*]
RMG .... RADAR Mapper Gapfiller
RMG .... RAL Marketing Group, Inc. [*Vancouver Stock Exchange
　　　　　　　symbol*]
RMG .... Recommended for Medal and Gratuity [*British*]
RMG .... Relative-Motion Gauge
RMG .... Right Main Gear (MCD)
RMG .... Rome [*Georgia*] [*Airport symbol*] [*Obsolete*] (OAG)
RMG .... Rome [*Georgia*] [*Seismograph station code, US Geological
　　　　　　　Survey*] (SEIS)
RMG .... Royal Marine Gunner [*British*]
RMG .... Russkaya Muzikal'naya Gazeta [*A publication*]
RMGCA ..... Rocky Mountain Association of Geologists. Field Conference
　　　　　　　[*A publication*]
RMGF .... RADAR Mapper, Gap Filler (MSA)
RMGO .... Regional Military Government Officer [*World War II*]
RMH .... Refrigerator Mechanical Household (MSA)
RMH .... Riemann's Metrical Hypothesis [*Mathematics*]
RMHCSDI... Robert Maynard Hutchins Center for the Study of Democratic
　　　　　　　Institutions (EA)
RMHDDHG ... Regiere Mich Herr durch Deinen Heiligen Geist [*Rule Me, Lord,
　　　　　　　Through Thy Holy Spirit*] [*German*] [*Motto of Ann,
　　　　　　　Margravine of Brandenburg (1575-1612)*]
RMHI .... Religion and Mental Health Inventory
RMI............ Merrell-National Laboratories [*Research code symbol*]
RMI............ Rack Manufacturers Institute [*Pittsburgh, PA*] (EA)
RMI............ Radio Magnetic Indicator
RMI............ Radiological Monitoring for Instructors [*Civil Defense*]
RMI............ Rassegna Mensile di Israel [*A publication*]
RMI............ Reich Ministry of Interior
RMI............ Reliability Maturity Index [*Polaris*]
RMI............ Reliability Monitoring Index
RMI............ Religious of Mary Immaculate [*Roman Catholic women's
　　　　　　　religious order*]
RMI............ Renewable Materials Institute [*College of Environmental
　　　　　　　Science and Forestry at Syracuse*] [*Research
　　　　　　　center*] (RCD)
RMI............ Repair and Maintenance Instruction [*Military*]
RMI............ Research Monographs in Immunology [*Elsevier Book Series*]
　　　　　　　[*A publication*]
RMI............ Residential Mortgage Investments, Inc. [*American Stock
　　　　　　　Exchange symbol*]
RMI............ Richardson-Merrell, Incorporated [*Later, Richardson-Vicks,
　　　　　　　Inc.*]
RMI............ Rivista Mensile di Israel [*A publication*]
RMI............ Rivista Musicale Italiana [*A publication*]

RMI............ Rocket Motor Igniter
RMI............ Roll Manufacturers Institute   (EA)
RMI............ Route Monitoring Information [*Telecommunications*]   (TEL)
RMIA .... Rattan Manufacturers and Importers Association
RMIA .... Registered Mail Insurance Association [*Formerly, RMCB*] [*New York, NY*]   (EA)
RMIC .... Research Materials Information Center [*ORNL*]
RMICBM..... Road Mobile Intercontinental Ballistic Missile
RMII............ Reference Method Item Identification [*DoD*]
RMIIA .... Rassegna di Medicina Industriale e di Igiene del Lavoro [*A publication*]
R Mil Coll Can Civ Eng Res Rep ... Royal Military College of Canada. Civil Engineering Research Report [*A publication*]
R/MIN........ Revolutions per Minute
RMIND........ Reviews in Mineralogy [*A publication*]
RMIP.......... Reentry Measurements Instrumentation Package
RMIs .... Rassegna Mensile di Israel [*A publication*]
RMIS .... Readiness Management Information System [*Military*]   (AABC)
RMIS .... Resource Management Information System
RMJ............ Ramjet   (MSA)
RMJ............ Rumoi [*Japan*] [*Seismograph station code, US Geological Survey*]   (SEIS)
RMJM .... Recluse Missionaries of Jesus and Mary [*Roman Catholic women's religious order*]
RMJMA ...... Rocky Mountain Journal of Mathematics [*A publication*]
RMJSA ...... Roczniki Akademii Medycznej Imienia Juliana Marchlewskiego w Bialymstoku. Suplement [*A publication*]
RMK .... Remark   (AFM)
RMK .... Renmark [*Australia*] [*Airport symbol*]   (OAG)
RMK .... Retrofit Modification Kit
RMK .... Rhesus Monkey Kidney [*Medicine*]
RMK .... Robert-Mark [*American Stock Exchange symbol*]
RMK .... Roxmark Mines Ltd. [*Toronto Stock Exchange symbol*]
R Mkting Agric Econ ... Review of Marketing and Agricultural Economics [*A publication*]
RMKUA ...... Report. Research Institute for Applied Mechanics (Kyushu University) [*A publication*]
RML............ Lieutenant, Royal Marines [*Navy*] [*British*]   (ROG)
RML............ RADAR Mapper, Long Range
RML............ RADAR Microwave Link   (IEEE)
RML............ Range Measurements Laboratory [*Air Force*]
RML............ Refresher Maintenance Lab
RML............ Regional Medical Library
RML............ Relational Machine Language
RML............ Remote Maintenance Line [*Bell Laboratories*]
RML............ Remote Measurements Laboratory
RML............ Rescue Motor Launch [*Air/sea rescue*] [*Navy*]
RML............ Restricted Maximum Likelihood [*Statistics*]
RML............ Review of Metal Literature [*American Society for Metals*] [*A publication*]
RML............ Revista Mexicana de Literatura [*A publication*]
RML............ Rifled Muzzle-Loading [*Gun*]
RML............ Right Mediolateral [*Episiotomy*] [*Obstetrics*]
RML............ Right Mentolateral [*Episiotomy*] [*Obstetrics*]
RML............ Right Middle Lobe [*Lungs*]
RML............ Rock Mechanics Laboratory [*Pennsylvania State University*] [*Research center*]   (RCD)
RML............ Rocky Mountain Laboratories [*National Institutes of Health*]
RML............ Rotating Mirror LASER
RML............ Russell Corp. [*NYSE symbol*]
RMLI.......... Royal Marine Light Infantry [*Obsolete*] [*British*]
RML IV .... Mid-Atlantic Regional Medical Library Program [*Library network*]
RMLMA ...... Revue MBLE [*Manufacture Belge de Lampes et de Materiel*] [*A publication*]
RMLO .... Reports Management Liaison Officer [*Defense Supply Agency*]
RMLP .... Regional Medical Library Program
RMLR .... RADAR Mapper, Long Range   (MSA)
RMLR .... RADAR Microwave Link Repeater   (FAAC)
RMLR .... Rocky Mountain Law Review [*A publication*]
RMLT .... RADAR Microwave Link Terminal   (FAAC)
RMM .... RADAR Map Matching
RMM .... Rapid Micromedia Method [*Analytical biochemistry*]
RMM .... Read-Mostly Memory [*Data processing*]
RMM .... Read-Mostly Mode [*Data processing*]
RMM .... Remote Maintenance Monitor [*Data processing*]   (MCD)
RMM .... Revue de Metaphysique et de Morale [*A publication*]
RMM .... Revue du Monde Musulman [*A publication*]
RMM .... Rifle Marksman
RMM .... Ripple Mark Meter
RMMC .... Regiment Materiel Management Center [*Military*]   (AABC)
RMMC .... Rocky Mountain Mapping Center [*Colorado*]
RMMEA ...... Rolling Mill Machinery and Equipment Association [*Defunct*]   (EA)
RMMFA ...... Revue Medico-Chirurgicale des Maladies du Foie, de la Rate, et du Pancreas [*A publication*]
RMMI.......... Rocky Mountain Minerals [*NASDAQ symbol*]   (NQ)
RMMID .... Revue Roumaine de Medecine. Serie Medecine Interne [*A publication*]
RMMJA ...... Rocky Mountain Medical Journal [*A publication*]
RMMLF ...... Rocky Mountain Mineral Law Foundation   (EA)

RMMLR ..... Rocky Mountain Mineral Law Review   (DLA)
RMMND ..... Rocky Mountain Mineral Law Newsletter [*A publication*]
RM/MS & C ... Redundancy Management/Moding, Sequencing, and Control   (MCD)
RMMTB ..... Rocky Mountain Motor Tariff Bureau, Inc.
RMMU ..... Removable Media Memory Units
RMN .... Registered Mental Nurse
RMN .... Remain   (FAAC)
RMN .... Reserve Material [*Account*] Navy
RMN .... Roman Corp. Ltd. [*Toronto Stock Exchange symbol*]
RMNac ...... Revista. Museo Nacional [*A publication*]
R & MNP .... Ryan and Moody's English Nisi Prius Reports   (DLA)
RMNZA ...... Rudy i Metale Niezelazne [*A publication*]
RMO .... RADAR Master Oscillator
RMO .... RADAR Material Office [*Navy*]   (MCD)
RMO .... Radio Material Office [*or Officer*] [*Navy*]   (IEEE)
RMO .... Records Management Office [*or Officer*] [*Military*]   (AFM)
RMO .... Recruitment and Manning Organization [*WSA*]
RMO .... Regimental Medical Officer   (NATG)
RMO .... Regimental Munitions Officer [*Army*]
RMO .... Regional Management Officer [*Social Security Administration*]
RMO .... Regional Medical Officer [*British*]
RMO .... Reports Management Officer [*DoD*]
RMO .... Resident Medical Officer [*British*]
RMO .... Resources Management Office [*NASA*]   (KSC)
RMO .... Rochester-Mercier [*New York*] [*Seismograph station code, US Geological Survey*] [*Closed*]   (SEIS)
RMO .... Rocket Management Office [*Army*]   (RDA)
RMO .... Royal Marine Office [*British*]
RMOC .... Recommended Maintenance Operation Chart [*Army*]   (AABC)
RMod......... Revue Moderne [*A publication*]
RMOKHS.... Religious and Military Order of Knights of the Holy Sepulchre   (EA)
RMON........ Resident Monitor
RMOS........ Refractory Metal-Oxide Semiconductor   (IEEE)
RMP........... Radio Motor Patrol [*New York police cars*]
RMP........... Rainform Message Processing   (MCD)
RMP........... Raman Microprobe [*Spectrometer*]
RMP........... Rampart [*Alaska*] [*Airport symbol*]   (OAG)
RMP........... Rampart Resources Ltd. [*Vancouver Stock Exchange symbol*]
RMP........... Range Maintenance Plan   (MCD)
RMP........... Reduction of the Membrane Potential
RMP........... Reentry Measurement Program
RMP........... Refiner Mechanical Pulp [*Papermaking*]
RMP........... Regional Medical Program
RMP........... Registered Medical Practitioner [*British*]   (ROG)
RMP........... Research Management Plan
RMP........... Research and Microfilm Publications
RMP........... Resting Membrane Potential [*Neuroelectrochemistry*]
RMP........... Rheinisches Museum fuer Philologie [*A publication*]
RMP........... Rifampin [*Also, R/AMP, RIF*] [*Bactericide*]
RMP........... Right Mentoposterior [*A fetal position*] [*Obstetrics*]
RMP........... Rocket Motor Plume
RMP........... Rocket Motor Propellant   (MUGU)
RMP........... Rome [*Monte Porzio Catone*] [*Italy*] [*Seismograph station code, US Geological Survey*]   (SEIS)
RMP........... Round Maximum Pressure   (NATG)
RMP........... Royal Military Police [*British*]
RMPA........ Rocky Mountain Psychological Association   (MCD)
RMPA........ Royal Medico-Psychological Association [*British*]
RMPaul ..... Revista. Museu Paulista [*A publication*]
RMPF .... Rocky Mountain Poison Foundation
RMPI.......... Remote Memory Port Interface
RMPIA ...... Razrabotka Mestorozhdenii Poleznykh Iskopaemykh [*A publication*]
RMPM .... Rich Man, Poor Man [*Book title*]
RMPO........ Ramapo Financial Corp. [*NASDAQ symbol*]   (NQ)
RM & PP .... Raw Material and Purchase Parts   (MCD)
RMPPA....... Revue de Medecine Psychosomatique et de Psychologie Medicale [*A publication*]
RMPR .... Rassemblement Mahorais pour la Republique [*Mayotte Rally for the Republic*]   (PPW)
RMPR .... Rated Mobilization and Professional Resource   (MUGU)
RMPR .... Revised Maximum Price Regulation [*World War II*]
RMPS .... Regional Medical Programs Service [*Health Services and Mental Health Administration, HEW*]
RMQM........ Quarter-Master, Royal Marines [*Navy*] [*British*]   (ROG)
RMR .... Rapid Memory Reload   (MCD)
RMR .... Reamer [*Design engineering*]
RMR .... Reference Mixture Radio   (KSC)
RMR .... Reflector Moderated Reactor   (AAG)
RMR .... Regional Maintenance Representative
RMR .... Remote Map Reader
RMR .... Reserve Minority Report [*Army*]
RMR .... Resource Management Review [*Military*]
RMR .... Resting Metabolic Rate [*Physiology*]
RMR .... Right Medial Rectus [*Eye anatomy*]
RMR .... Rocky Mountain Law Review [*A publication*]
RMR .... Rocky Mountain Review [*A publication*]
RMR .... Rotation Magnitude Ratio
RMR .... Royal Marines Reserve [*British*]

RMR .... Royal Montreal Regiment [*Military unit*]
RMRHB ...... Rheumatology and Rehabilitation [*A publication*]
RMRM .... Radioactive Materials Reference Manual   (NRCH)
RMROCK ... Rocket Motors Records Office Center [*Navy*]
RMRS .... Remote Meter Resetting System [*Postage meter*]
RMS .... RADAR Maintenance Spares   (NG)
RMS .... RADAR Mapping Set [*or System*]
RMS .... Radian Means per Second   (NASA)
RMS .... Radiation and Meteoroid Satellite [*NASA*]
RMS .... Radio Marker Station
RMS .... Radiological Monitoring System
RMS .... Radiometric Sextant Subsystem
RMS .... Rail Mail Steamer
RMS .... Railway Mail Service
RMS .... Random Mass Storage [*Data processing*]
RMS .... Random Motion Simulator [*NASA*]   (NASA)
RMS .... Range Measuring System
RMS .... Range Modification System
RMS .... Rathkamp Matchcover Society   (EA)
RMS .... Reactor Monitor System   (IEEE)
RMS .... Record Management System
RMS .... Recovery Management Support [*Data processing*]
RMS .... Recruiting Main Station [*Military*]
RMS .... Redundancy Management System   (MCD)
RMS .... Reentry Measurement System
RMS .... Regulatory Manpower System   (NRCH)
RMS .... Regulatory Monitoring System   (NRCH)
RMS .... Rehabilitation Medicine Service [*Veterans Administration*]
RMS .... Reliability and Maintainability Simulator
RMS .... Remote Maintenance System
RMS .... Remote Manipulator Subsystem [*NASA*]   (NASA)
RMS .... Remote Manual Switch [*Nuclear energy*]   (NRCH)
RMS .... Remote Master Station   (MCD)
RMS .... Remote Missile Select
RMS .... Renaissance and Modern Studies [*A publication*]
RMS .... Reports Management System [*Office of Management and Budget*] [*Database*]
RMS .... Resources Management System [*Army*]
RMS .... Respiratory Muscle Strength [*Physiology*]
RMS .... Retromotor Simulator
RMS .... Revised Magnetic Standard
RMS .... Revista Mexicana de Sociologia [*A publication*]
RMS .... Rhabdomyosarcoma [*Also, RHM*] [*Oncology*]
RMS .... Rheometrics Mechanical Spectrometer
RMS .... RMS Electronics, Inc. [*American Stock Exchange symbol*]
RMS .... Rocket Management System   (MCD)
RMS .... Roll Microwave Sensor
RMS .... Romanian Missionary Society [*Wheaton, IL*]   (EA)
RMS .... Root Mean Square [*of transmission waves*]
RMS .... Royal Mail Service [*British*]
RMS .... Royal Mail Steamship [*British*]
RMS .... Royal Meteorological Society [*British*]
RMS .... Royal Microscopical Society [*British*]
RMS .... Royal Society of Miniature Painters, Sculptors, and Gravers [*British*]
RMS .... Rural Manpower Services   (OICC)
RMSA .... Seaman Apprentice, Radioman, Striker [*Navy rating*]
RMSCA .... Rivista Mineraria Siciliana [*A publication*]
RMSchMus ... Royal Marines School of Music [*British*]
RMSD .... Root Mean Square Deviation [*Statistical mathematics*]
RMSD .... Royal Mail Special Delivery [*British Post Office facility*]
RMSDS ...... Reserve Merchant Ship Defense System [*Navy*]   (MCD)
RMSE .... Root Mean Square Error
RMSF .... Rocky Mountain Spotted Fever
RMSFA .... Revista Mexicana de Fisica. Suplemento de Fisica Aplicada [*A publication*]
RMSG .... Resource Management Study Group [*Military*]
RMSM .... Royal Military School of Music [*British*]
RMSN .... Seaman, Radioman, Striker [*Navy rating*]
RMSP .... Refractory Metal Sheet Program [*Navy*]   (NG)
RMSP .... Resource and Mission Sponsor Plan [*Navy*]
RMSP .... Royal Mail Steam Packet Co.
RMSRA ...... Revue Medicale de la Suisse Romande [*A publication*]
RMSS .... Range Meteorological Sounding System   (MCD)
RMSS .... Religious Mercedarians of the Blessed Sacrament [*Roman Catholic women's religious order*]
RMSSJ .... Rocky Mountain Social Science Journal [*A publication*]
RMSU .... Remote Monitoring Sensor Unit   (MCD)
RMSVP ...... Remote Manipulation Subsystem Verification Plan   (MCD)
RMT .... Radiometric Moon Tracer
RMT .... Rapid Mass Transfer [*Physics*]
RMT .... Rectangular Midwater Trawl   (ADA)
RMT .... Registered Massage Therapist
RMT .... Registered Music Teacher
RMT .... Registered Music Therapist
RMT .... Registry of Medical Technologists
RMT .... Remote [*Telecommunications*]   (MSA)
RMT .... Research Methods and Techniques
RMT .... Resource Management Team   (MCD)
RMT .... Rework Monitoring Test
RMT .... Right Mentotransverse [*A fetal position*] [*Obstetrics*]

RMTB .... Reconfiguration Maximum Theoretical Bandwidth
RMTC .... RADAR Maintenance and Test Control   (MCD)
RMTC .... Rider Motorcycle Touring Club [*Commercial firm*]   (EA)
RMTE .... Remote   (AAG)
RMTF .... Ready Missile Test Facility [*Military*]   (CAAL)
RMTH .... Regular Member of the Third House [*Pseudonym used by Dr. Francis Bacon*]
RMTH .... River Mouth [*Board on Geographic Names*]
RMTK .... Ramtek Corp. [*NASDAQ symbol*]   (NQ)
RMTO .... Regional Motor Transport Officer [*British*]
RMTR .... Redesigned Missile Tracking RADAR [*Army*]   (AABC)
RMTRD .... Revue de Medicine du Travail [*A publication*]
RMTS .... Research Member of the Technical Staff
RMTSA .... Revista. Instituto de Medicina Tropical de Sao Paulo [*A publication*]
RMU .... Radio Maintenance Unit   (DEN)
RMU .... Rainbow Monument [*Utah*] [*Seismograph station code, US Geological Survey*]   (SEIS)
RMU .... Reference Measuring Unit   (MCD)
RMU .... Remote Maneuvering Unit [*NASA*]
RMU .... Remote Multiplexer Unit [*Data processing*]   (KSC)
RMu .... Revue Musicale [*A publication*]
R de MU ..... Revue de Musicologie [*Paris*] [*A publication*]
R-MuLV ...... Rauscher Murine Leukemia Virus
R Mus .... Revue Musicale [*A publication*]
R de Mus .... Revue de Musicologie [*A publication*]
R Mus Art Archeol ... Revue du Musee d'Art et d'Archeologie [*A publication*]
R Mus Chile ... Revista Musical Chilena [*A publication*]
R Mus Ital ... Nuova Rivista Musicale Italiana. Trimestrale di Cultura e Informazione Musicale [*A publication*]
R Mus Ital ... Rivista Musicale Italiana [*A publication*]
R Mus La Plata Antropol ... Revista. Museo de La Plata. Seccion Antropologia [*A publication*]
R Mus Nac ... Revista. Museo Nacional [*A publication*]
R Mus de Suisse Romande ... Revue Musicale de Suisse Romande [*A publication*]
RMV .... Reentry Measurement Vehicle
RMV .... Remotely Manned Vehicle
RMV .... Remove   (AAG)
RMV .... Respiratory Minute Volume [*Physiology*]
RMVBL .... Removable   (AAG)
RMVD .... Removed   (AAG)
RMVG .... Removing   (AAG)
RMVL .... Removal   (AAG)
RMVT .... Repetitive Monomorphic Ventricular Tachycardia [*Cardiology*]
RMW .... Rattlesnake Mountain [*Washington*] [*Seismograph station code, US Geological Survey*]   (SEIS)
RMW .... Reactor Makeup Water [*Nuclear energy*]   (NRCH)
R/M/W .... Read/Modify/Write
RMWAA ...... Roadmasters and Maintenance of Way Association of America [*Homewood, IL*]   (EA)
RMWC .... Randolph-Macon Woman's College [*Virginia*]
RMWO .... Warrant Officer, Royal Marines [*Navy*] [*British*]   (ROG)
RMWR .... Religious, Morale, Welfare, and Recreation [*Military*]   (AFM)
RMWS .... Reactor Makeup Water Storage   (NRCH)
RMWT .... Reactor Makeup Water Tank   (NRCH)
RMX .... Resource Management Executive   (MCD)
R & My .... Russell and Mylne's English Chancery Reports   (DLA)
RMZBA .... Rudarsko-Metalurski Zbornik [*A publication*]
RN .... Compagnia d'Exploitation de Lignes Aeriennes Interieures - Royal Air Inter [*Morocco*] [*ICAO designator*]   (FAAC)
RN .... Newport Public Library, Newport, RI [*Library symbol*] [*Library of Congress*]   (LCLS)
RN .... Radio Navigation
RN .... Radionuclide [*Radiology*]
Rn .... Radon [*Chemical element*]
RN .... Random Number   (IEEE)
RN .... Rassemblement National [*Canadian*]   (PPW)
RN .... Rattus Norvegicus [*The Norway or brown rat*]
RN .... Real Name [*British Library indexing for pseudonymous author*]
RN .... Reception Nil [*Radio logs*]
RN .... Reception Node
RN .... Record Number [*Online database field identifier*]
RN .... Red Nucleus [*Brain anatomy*]
RN .... Reference Noise
RN .... Reference Number
RN .... Registered Nurse
RN .... Rejection Notice   (AAG)
RN .... Renaissance News [*A publication*]
RN .... Renastera Noastra [*Rumania*] [*A publication*]   (BJA)
Rn .... Renumbered [*Existing article renumbered*] [*Used in Shepard's Citations*]   (DLA)
RN .... Research Note
RN .... Revision Notice   (KSC)
RN .... Revue du Nord [*A publication*]
R du N .... Revue du Notariat [*A publication*]
RN .... Revue Nouvelle [*A publication*]
RN .... Revue Numismatique [*A publication*]
RN .... Reynolds Number [*Also, R, Re*] [*Viscosity*]
R & N .... Rhodesia and Nyasaland Law Reports [*1956*]   (DLA)

RN .... Richard Nixon [*In book title "RN - The Memoirs of Richard Nixon"*]
RN .... River Name (BJA)
RN .... Roan (Leather) [*Bookbinding*] (ROG)
RN .... Rough Notes [*A publication*]
RN .... Royal Name (BJA)
RN .... Royal Navy [*British*]
RN .... Ruin (ROG)
RN .... Ruritan National [*Dublin, VA*] (EA)
RNA........... Radio Navigational Aids (NATG)
RNA........... Rassemblement National Arabe [*Arab National Rally*] [*Tunisian*] (PD)
RNA........... Rations Not Available [*Military*] (AABC)
RNA........... Recurring Nuisances Act [*British*]
RNA........... Regina Resources [*Vancouver Stock Exchange symbol*]
RNA........... Registered Nurse Anesthetist
RNA........... Registered Nursing Assistant
RNA........... Religion Newswriters Association (EA)
RNA........... Republic of New Africa [*Black separatist group*]
RNA........... Research Natural Area [*National Science Foundation*]
RNA........... Ribonucleic Acid [*Biochemistry, genetics*]
RNA........... Robbery Not Armed
RNA........... Rotatable Nozzle Assembly
RNA........... Rough, Noncapsulated, Avirulent [*With reference to bacteria*]
RNA........... Royal Neighbors of America (EA)
RNA........... Royal Netherlands Army (NATG)
RNA........... Royal Norwegian Army (MCD)
RNAA .... Radiochemical Neutron Activation Analysis
R/NAA .... Rocketdyne - North American Aviation [*Later, Rockwell International Corp.*] (AAG)
RNAA .... Russian Nobility Association in America [*Formerly, RHGSA*] (EA)
RNAAC...... Reference Number Action Activity Code (MCD)
RNAAF ...... Royal Norwegian Army and Air Force
RNAC .... Remote Network Access Controller
RNAC .... Royal Nepal Airlines Corporation
RNAD .... Royal Naval Armament Depot [*British*]
RNAF........ Royal Naval Air Force [*British*]
RNAF........ Royal Netherlands Air Force
RNAF........ Royal Norwegian Air Force
RNAL........ Radionuclear Applications Laboratory [*Pennsylvania State University*] [*Research center*] (RCD)
RNAMY ...... Royal Naval Aircraft Maintenance Yard [*British*]
RNAO News ... RNAO (Registered Nurses Association of Ontario) News [*A publication*]
RNap .... Revue Napoleonienne [*A publication*]
RNar .... Ragioni Narrative [*A publication*]
RNAS .... Royal Naval Air Service [*Precursor of Fleet Air Arm*] [*British*] [*Initialism also facetiously translated during World War I as "Really Not a Sailor"*]
RNAS .... Royal Naval Air Station [*British*]
RNase........ Ribonuclease [*An enzyme*]
RNATE ...... Royal Naval Air Training Establishment [*British*]
RNAV .... Area Navigation
R-NAV .... Random Navigation
RNAV .... Royal Naval Artillery Volunteers [*British*]
R Navig Fluv Europ ... Revue de la Navigation Fluviale Europeenne [*A publication*]
RNAW........ Royal Naval Aircraft Workshop [*British*]
RNAY .... Royal Naval Aircraft Yard [*British*]
RNaz........... Rassegna Nazionale [*A publication*]
RNB .... Millville, NJ [*Location identifier*] [*FAA*] (FAAL)
RNB .... Received, Not Billed (AFM)
RNB .... Renegotiation Board [*Terminated, 1979*] [*Federal government*]
RNB .... Republic New York Corp. [*NYSE symbol*]
RNB .... Ronneby [*Sweden*] [*Airport symbol*] (OAG)
RNB .... Royal Naval Barracks [*British*]
RNBC .... Royal Naval Beach Commando [*British*]
RNBLA .... Rivista de Neurobiologia [*A publication*]
RNBM .... Radio Noise Burst Monitor (MCD)
RNBM .... Royal Navy Ballistic Missile [*British*]
RNBT......... Royal Naval Benevolent Trust [*British*]
RNC .... Little Raleigh [*North Carolina*] [*Seismograph station code, US Geological Survey*] (SEIS)
RNC........... McMinnville, TN [*Location identifier*] [*FAA*] (FAAL)
RNC........... Radio Noncontingent
RNC........... Rainbow Network Communications [*Floral Park, NY*] [*Telecommunications*] (TSSD)
RNC........... Republican National Committee (EA)
RNC........... Request Next Character
RNC........... Romanian National Council (EA)
RNC........... Royal Naval College [*For future officers; often spoken of as Dartmouth*] [*British*]
RNC.......... Rumanian National Committee [*Later, Romanian National Tourist Office*] (EA)
RNCA .... Rhodesia and Nyasaland Court of Appeal Law Reports (DLA)
RNCC .... Reference Number Category Code (MCD)
RNCC .... Royal Naval College of Canada [*1911-1922*]
RNCF......... Read Natural Childbirth Foundation [*San Rafael, CA*] (EA)
RNCH .... Ranch (MCD)
RNCM........ Royal Northern College of Music [*British*]

RNColl........ Royal Naval College, Greenwich [*British*]
RN & CR ..... Ryde, Newport & Cowes Railway [*British*]
RNCT .... Reports of the Working Committees. Northeast Conference on the Teaching of Foreign Languages [*A publication*]
RNCVR...... Royal Naval Canadian Volunteer Reserve [*World War I*]
RND........... Radical Neck Dissection [*Medicine*]
RND........... Rassemblement National Democratique [*National Democratic Rally*] [*Senegalese*] (PPW)
RND........... Rocznik Naukowo-Dydaktyczny [*A publication*]
RND........... Round
RND........... Royal Naval Division [*British*]
RND........... San Antonio, TX [*Location identifier*] [*FAA*] (FAAL)
RNDM........ Random (MSA)
RNDPD...... Roundup [*United States*] [*A publication*]
RNDr .... Doctor of Natural Sciences
RNDZ........ Rendezvous (KSC)
RNE .... Aspen, CO [*Location identifier*] [*FAA*] (FAAL)
RNE .... Roanne [*France*] [*Airport symbol*] (OAG)
RNEC .... Royal Naval Engineering College [*British*]
RNEColl...... Royal Naval Engineering College [*British*]
RNEIAF ...... Royal Netherlands East Indies Air Force
RNEIN .... Royal Netherlands East Indies Navy
RNeosc ..... Revue Neo-Scolastique de Philosophie [*A publication*]
RNERL....... Radiochemistry and Nuclear Engineering Research Laboratory [*National Environmental Research Center*]
RNES......... Royal Naval Engineering Service [*British*]
RNF .... Radial Nerve Factor [*of sea urchin*]
RNF .... Radio Noise Figure (CET)
RNF .... Receiver Noise Figure
RNF .... Royal Northumberland Fusiliers [*Military unit*] [*British*]
RNFC........ Reference Number Format Code (MCD)
RNFL......... Rainfall (FAAC)
RNFP........ RADAR Not Functioning Properly [*Military*] (AFIT)
RNG........... Army National Guard (FAAC)
RNG........... Radio Range
RNG........... Random Number Generator [*Parapsychology*]
RNG........... Range [*or Ranging*] (AAG)
RNG........... Ranging Noise Generator
RNG........... Reference Noise Generator
RNG........... Regulations under the Natural Gas Act
RNG........... Running
RNGG........ Ringing (MSA)
RNGHQ ...... Royal Navy General Headquarters [*British*]
RNGMA...... Refiner and Natural Gasoline Manufacturer [*A publication*]
RNGT .... Renegotiate
RNGYA...... Rhinology [*A publication*]
RNH .... New Richmond, WI [*Location identifier*] [*FAA*] (FAAL)
RNH .... Royal Naval Hospital [*British*]
RNHi .... Newport Historical Society, Newport, RI [*Library symbol*] [*Library of Congress*] (LCLS)
RN-HSG ..... Radionuclide Hysterosalpingogram [*Medicine*]
RNI .... Kansas City, MO [*Location identifier*] [*FAA*] (FAAL)
RNI .... Research Notes (Ibadan) [*A publication*]
RNI .... Resident Navy Inspector
RNIB .... Royal National Institute for the Blind [*British*]
RNIC.......... Robinson Nugent [*NASDAQ symbol*] (NQ)
RN ID .... RN Idaho [*A publication*]
RNID .... Royal National Institute for the Deaf [*British*]
RNIE .... Royal Netherlands Institute of Engineers
RNIO .... Resident Naval Inspector of Ordnance
RNIR .... Reduction to Next Inferior Rank
RNIT .... Radio Noise Interference Test
RNJ........... Ramapo College of New Jersey, Mahwah, NJ [*OCLC symbol*] (OCLC)
RNJ........... Yoron-Jima [*Japan*] [*Airport symbol*] (OAG)
RNk .... North Kingstown Free Library, North Kingstown, RI [*Library symbol*] [*Library of Congress*] (LCLS)
RNKID ...... Rikuyo Nainen Kikan [*A publication*]
RNL .... Rainelle, WV [*Location identifier*] [*FAA*] (FAAL)
RNL .... Renewal (MSA)
RNL .... Rennell Island [*Solomon Islands*] [*Airport symbol*] (OAG)
RNL .... Review of National Literatures [*A publication*]
RNLAF...... Royal Netherlands Air Force
RNLBI........ Royal National Life-Boat Institution [*British*]
RNLI .... Royal National Life-Boat Institution [*British*]
RNLJ .... Rhodesia and Nyasaland Law Journal (DLA)
RNLO .... Royal Naval Liaison Officer [*British*]
R & NLR..... Rhodesia and Nyasaland Law Reports [*1956-64*] (DLA)
RNLT .... Running Light
RNM .... Radio-Navigation Mobile
RNM .... Radionuclide Migration
RNM .... Rassemblement National Malgache [*National Malagasy Rally*]
RNM .... Resistencia Nacional Mocambicana [*Mozambican National Resistance*] (PD)
RNM .... Revista Nacional (Montevideo) [*A publication*]
RNM .... University of Rochester, Miner Medical Library, Rochester, NY [*OCLC symbol*] (OCLC)
RN Mag ...... RN Magazine [*A publication*]
RNMC........ Royal Netherlands Marine Corps (CINC)
RNMCC..... Reference Number Mandatory Category Code [*DoD*]
RNMD........ Registered Nurse for Mental Defectives

RNMI .... Realtors National Marketing Institute [*Chicago, IL*] (EA)
RNMS........ Registered Nurse for the Mentally Subnormal [*British*]
RNN .... Naval War College, Newport, RI [*Library symbol*] [*Library of Congress*] (LCLS)
RNN.......... Ronne [*Denmark*] [*Airport symbol*] (OAG)
RNN.......... Royal Netherlands Navy
RNN.......... Royal Norwegian Navy
RNNAS....... Royal Netherlands Naval Air Service
RNNU .... United States Navy, Naval Underwater Systems Center, Technical Library, Newport, RI [*Library symbol*] [*Library of Congress*] (LCLS)
RN and O.... Raleigh News and Observer [*A publication*]
RNO........... Regional Nuclear Option (MCD)
RNO........... Regional Nursing Officer [*British*]
RNO........... Reno [*Nevada*] [*Airport symbol*] (OAG)
RNO........... Resident Naval Officer [*Followed by place name*] (NATG)
RNO........... Roan Selection Trust Ltd. [*Formerly, RHO; later, RST*] [*NYSE symbol*]
RNOA .... Royal Norwegian Army (NATG)
RNOAF....... Royal Norwegian Air Force (AFM)
RNOC .... Royal Naval Officers Club [*British*]
RNODC .... Responsible National Oceanographic Data Center [*Marine science*] (MSC)
RNON .... Royal Norwegian Navy (NATG)
RNORA .... Royal Norwegian Army (NATG)
R Nord........ Revue du Nord [*A publication*]
RNORN .... Royal Norwegian Navy (NATG)
R du Not ..... Revue du Notariat [*A publication*]
R Nouv .... Revue Nouvelle [*A publication*]
RNP .... Radio Navigation Point [*Military*] (MCD)
RNP .... Rassemblement National Populaire [*National People's Rally*] [*France*]
RNP .... Remote Network Processor
RNP .... Ribonucleoprotein [*Biochemistry*]
RNP .... Rongelap [*Marshall Islands*] [*Airport symbol*] (OAG)
RNP .... Royal National Park (ADA)
RNP .... Royal Naval Personnel Research Committee [*British*]
RNPL .... Royal Naval Physiological Laboratory [*British*]
RNPRC .... Royal Naval Personnel Research Committee [*British*] (MCD)
RNPS .... Royal Naval Patrol Service [*Obsolete*] [*British*]
RNPS......... Royal Navy Polaris School [*British*]
RNQ........... Waycross, GA [*Location identifier*] [*FAA*] (FAAL)
RNR .... Receive Not Ready [*Data processing*] (IEEE)
RNR .... Redwood Library and Athenaeum, Newport, RI [*Library symbol*] [*Library of Congress*] (LCLS)
RNR .... Robinson River [*Papua New Guinea*] [*Airport symbol*] (OAG)
RNR .... Royal Naval Reserve [*British*]
RNR .... Runner (MSA)
RNRB.......... Relative Navigational Reference Beacon [*Military*] (CAAL)
RNRF.......... Renewable Natural Resources Foundation (EA)
RNRLA .... Report of Naval Research Laboratory Progress [*United States*] [*A publication*]
RNS .... RADAR Netting Station (AABC)
RNS .... Ransom Resources Ltd. [*Vancouver Stock Exchange symbol*]
RNS .... Religious News Service
RNS .... Rennes [*France*] [*Airport symbol*] (OAG)
RNS .... Reusable Nuclear Shuttle [*NASA*]
RNS .... Reusable Nuclear Stage [*Aerospace*]
RNS .... Revue Neo-Scolastique de Philosophie [*A publication*]
RNS .... Royal Naval School [*British*]
RNS .... Royal Numismatic Society [*British*]
RNS .... Russian Numismatic Society (EA)
RNSA .... Royal Naval Sailing Association [*British*]
RNSC .... Reference Number Status Code (MCD)
RNSC .... Rocket/Nimbus Sounder Comparison [*NASA*]
RNSC .... Royal Naval Staff College [*British*]
RNSD .... Royal Naval Stores Depot [*British*]
RNSJA........ Rinsho Seijinbyo [*A publication*]
RNSP .... Revue Neo-Scolastique de Philosophie [*A publication*]
RNSQ .... Royal Naval Sick Quarters [*British*]
RNSR......... Royal Nova Scotia Regiment [*Military unit*]
RNSS......... Royal Naval Scientific Service [*British*] (DEN)
RNSS......... Royal Norwegian Society of Sciences
RNSTS .... Royal Naval Supply and Transport Service [*British*]
RNSYS .... Royal Nova Scotia Yacht Squadron
RNT .... Regensburger Neues Testament [*A publication*] (BJA)
RNT .... Registered Nurse Tutor [*British*]
RNT .... Renton, WA [*Location identifier*] [*FAA*] (FAAL)
RNTL .... Rockwood National Corp. [*NASDAQ symbol*] (NQ)
rNTP .... Ribonucleoside Triphosphate [*Biochemistry*]
RNTWPA .... Radio-Newsreel-Television Working Press Association (EA)
RNU........... RADAR Netting Unit (AABC)
RNU........... Ranau [*Malaysia*] [*Airport symbol*] (OAG)
RNum......... Rassegna Numismatica [*A publication*]
RNum .... Revue Numismatique [*A publication*]
RNV........... Cleveland, MS [*Location identifier*] [*FAA*] (FAAL)
RNV........... Radio Noise Voltage
RNV........... Radionuclide Ventriculography [*Medicine*]
RNV........... Random Noise Voltmeter
RNV........... Relative Nutritive Value [*Nutrition*]
RNV........... Replacement Naval Vessels

RNV........... Resistive Null Voltage
RNV........... Reusable Nuclear Vehicle [*Aerospace*] (KSC)
RNV........... Royal Naval Volunteer (Reserve) [*British*] (ROG)
RNVC .... Reference Number Variation Code (MCD)
RN(V)R...... Royal Naval (Volunteer) Reserve [*Obsolete*] [*World War II*] [*British*]
RNVSR .... Royal Naval Volunteer Supplementary Reserve [*Obsolete*] [*World War II*] [*British*]
RNWBL...... Renewable (MSA)
RNWMP..... Royal North West Mounted Police [*Later, RCMP*] [*Canada*]
RNWSD ..... Research News [*A publication*]
RNWY....... Runway (AABC)
RNX .... Renox Creek Resources [*Vancouver Stock Exchange symbol*]
RNX .... Rex-Noreco, Inc. [*American Stock Exchange symbol*]
RNXS........ Royal Naval Auxiliary Service [*British*]
RNY .... Rainier Energy Resources [*Vancouver Stock Exchange symbol*]
RNZ .... Radio New Zealand
RNZ .... Royal New Zealand
RNZAF ...... Royal New Zealand Air Force
RNZE........ Royal New Zealand Engineers
RNZN....... Royal New Zealand Navy
RNZN(V)R ... Royal New Zealand Naval (Volunteer) Reserve
Ro.............. Hoffmann-La Roche, Inc. [*Switzerland, USA*] [*Research code symbol*]
RO .... RADAR Observer
RO .... RADAR Operator
RO .... Radiation Office [*Environmental Protection Agency*]
RO .... Radio Operator
RO .... Radio Orchestra
RO .... Radionavigation Mobile Station [*ITU designation*] (CET)
RO .... Radioopaque
R & O .... Rail and Ocean
RO .... Railway Office [*British*] (ROG)
RO .... Range Only (CAAL)
RO .... Range Operation (AAG)
RO .... Rank Organisation PLC [*Toronto Stock Exchange symbol*]
RO .... Reactor Operator (NRCH)
RO .... Read Only [*Data processing*] (IBMDP)
RO .... Readout (KSC)
RO .... Reality Orientation
RO .... Receive Only
RO .... Receiving Office [*or Officer*]
RO .... Receiving Order [*Business and trade*]
RO .... Reconnaissance Officer
RO .... Recorders [*JETDS nomenclature*] [*Military*] (CET)
RO .... Records Office [*or Officer*] [*Air Force*] (AFM)
RO .... Recovery Operations [*NASA*]
RO .... Recruiting Officer [*Military*]
RO .... Recto [*Also, R*]
RO .... Reddish Orange
RO .... Regimental Orders [*Army*]
RO .... Regional Office [*or Officer*]
RO .... Register Output
RO .... Regulated Output (FAAC)
RO .... Relieving Officer (ROG)
RO .... Relocatable Output [*Data processing*]
RO .... Repair Order
R/O............ Repair and Overhaul (MCD)
RO .... Reportable Occurrence [*Nuclear energy*] (NRCH)
RO .... Reporting Officer [*Army*] (AABC)
RO .... Requirements Objective
R & O .... Requirements and Objectives
RO .... Requisitioning Objective [*Military*] (AABC)
R/O............ Requisitions/Objectives (CINC)
RO .... Research Objective (MCD)
RO .... Research Officer [*British*]
RO .... Reserve of Officers [*British*]
R of O .... Reserve of Officers [*British*]
RO .... Reserve Order
RO .... Restriction Orifice [*Nuclear energy*] (NRCH)
RO .... Retired Officer [*Military*] [*British*]
RO .... Retrofit Order [*Navy*] (NG)
RO .... Returning Officer (ROG)
RO .... Revenue Officer [*IRS*]
RO .... Reverse-Osmosis [*Physical chemistry*]
RO .... Revista de Occidente [*A publication*]
RO .... Revue Orientale [*A publication*]
RO .... Rework Order (MCD)
Ro............. Rhodium [*Correct symbol is Rh*] [*Chemical element*]
RO .... Right Outboard (MCD)
RO .... Roan [*Thoroughbred racing*]
RO .... Rocznik Orientalistyczny [*A publication*]
RO .... Roemisches Oesterreich. Jahresschrift der Oesterreichischen Gesellschaft fuer Archaeologie [*A publication*]
RO .... Roll
Ro............. Rolle's Abridgment (DLA)
R/O............ Rollout (MCD)
R & O .... Roma e l'Oriente [*A publication*]
Ro............. Romania [*A publication*]
RO .... Romania [*Two-letter standard code*] (CNC)

Ro .... Romanian (DLA)
RO .... Romanian Air Transport [*ICAO designator*] (FAAC)
RO .... Rood [*Unit of measurement*]
RO .... Roper Organization (EA)
RO .... Rose (ROG)
RO .... Rough
RO .... Rough Opening [*Technical drawings*]
RO .... Route Order [*Military*]
RO .... Routine Order
RO .... Routing Office [*or Officer*] [*Navy*]
RO .... Rowed Over [*Rowing*] [*British*] (ROG)
RO .... Royal Observatory [*British*]
RO .... Royal Octavo
R/O .... Rule Out [*Medicine*]
R-O .... Run-On [*Used in correcting manuscripts, etc.*]
RO .... Runoff Election
RO .... Runout (MSA)
RO .... Runover [*Publishing*]
RO .... Russian Obuckhoff Rifle
ROA .... Altimeter Station [*ITU designation*] (CET)
ROA .... Radiation Oncology Administrators [*Later, SROA*] (EA)
ROA .... Radio Operator's Aptitude Test [*Military*]
ROA .... Radius of Action (CAAL)
ROA .... Raman Optical Activity [*Spectrometry*]
ROA .... Reference Optical Alignment
ROA .... Rehabilitation of Offenders Act [*1974*] [*British*]
ROA .... Report on the ORT Activities [*Paris/Geneva*] [*A publication*]
ROA .... Reserve Officers Association of the United States (EA)
ROA .... Return on Assets [*Finance*]
ROA .... Right Occipitoanterior [*A fetal position*] [*Obstetrics*]
ROA .... Roanoke [*Virginia*] [*Airport symbol*]
ROA .... Robert Owen Association (EA)
roa .... Romance [*MARC language code*] [*Library of
        Congress*] (LCCP)
ROA .... Rules of the Air (AFM)
ROA .... Russian Orchestra of the Americas
ROAD .... Reorganization Objectives, Army Division [*Military*]
ROAD .... Retires on Active Duty [*Military*] (MCD)
ROAD .... Roadway Services, Inc. [*NASDAQ symbol*] (NQ)
Road Abstr ... Road Abstracts [*A publication*]
Road A R .... Road Apple Review [*A publication*]
Road Maps ... Economic Road Maps [*A publication*]
Road Res Bull ... Road Research Bulletin [*A publication*]
Road Res Lab (UK) RRL Rep ... Road Research Laboratory (United
        Kingdom). RRL Report [*A publication*]
Road Res Monogr ... Road Research Monographs [*A publication*]
Road Res Notes ... Road Research Notes [*A publication*]
Road Res Pap ... Road Research Papers [*A publication*]
ROADS ...... Real-Time Optical Alignment and Diagnostic System [*Module*]
ROADS ...... Roadway Analysis and Design System [*Data processing*]
Road Saf .... Road Safety [*A publication*]
Roads & Bridges ... Roads and Bridges [*A publication*]
Roads & Constr ... Roads and Construction [*A publication*]
Roads & Eng Constr ... Roads and Engineering Construction [*A publication*]
Roads Road Constr ... Roads and Road Construction [*A publication*]
Roads St .... Roads and Streets [*A publication*]
Road Transp of Aust ... Road Transporter of Australia [*A publication*]
Road Transp Aust ... Road Transporter of Australia [*A publication*]
ROAM .... RAN Energy, Inc. [*NASDAQ symbol*] (NQ)
ROAM .... Return on Assets Managed [*Finance*]
ROAMA ...... Rome Air Materiel Area [*Deactivated*] [*Air Force*]
ROANA ...... Rover Owners' Association of North America [*Defunct*] (EA)
ROAR .... Radio Operated Auto Racing
ROAR .... Regional Organization for Airways Restudy
ROAR .... Restore Our Alienated Rights [*Boston antibusing group*]
ROAR .... Return of Army Repairables (AABC)
ROAR .... Royal Optimizing Assembly Routing [*Royal McBee Corp.*] [*Data
        processing*]
ROAR .... Run for Aquino and Resignation [*Event organized by Philippine
        joggers to protest the assassination of Benigno Aquino*]
ROAT .... Radio Operator's Aptitude Test [*Military*]
Rob .... Christopher Robinson's Upper Canada Reports (DLA)
ROB .... Monrovia [*Liberia*] Roberts International Airport [*Airport
        symbol*] (OAG)
ROB .... RADAR Order of Battle
ROB .... RADAR Out of Battle (CET)
ROB .... Recovery Operations Branch [*NASA*] (KSC)
ROB .... Regional Office Building
ROB .... Relieve of Booty [*Crime term*]
RoB .... Religion och Bibel [*A publication*] (BJA)
ROB .... Remaining on Board
ROB .... Report on Board [*Navy*]
ROB .... Reserve on Board
ROB .... Reserveoffizier-Bewerber [*Reserve officer applicant*] [*German
        military - World War II*]
ROB .... Right of Baseline (MCD)
ROB .... Right Outboard (MCD)
ROB .... Rijksdienst voor het Oudheidkundig Bodemonderzoek [*A
        publication*]
Rob .... Robards' Reports [*12, 13 Missouri*] (DLA)
Rob .... Robards' Texas Conscript Cases (DLA)

ROB .... Robert Morris College, Coraopolis, PA [*OCLC symbol*] (OCLC)
ROB .... Roberts Airways [*Dallas, TX*] [*FAA designator*] (FAAC)
Rob. .... Roberts' Reports [*29-31 Louisiana Annual*] (DLA)
ROB .... Robertsfield [*Liberia*] [*Airport symbol*]
Rob. .... Robertson's English Ecclesiastical Reports (DLA)
Rob. .... Robertson's Reports [*24-30 New York Superior Court*] [*1863-
        68*] (DLA)
Rob. .... Robertson's Reports [*1 Hawaii*] (DLA)
Rob. .... Robertson's Scotch Appeal Cases [*1707-27*] (DLA)
ROB .... Robin International [*Toronto Stock Exchange symbol*]
Rob. .... Robinson's English Admiralty Reports [*1799-1809, 1838-
        1852*] (DLA)
Rob. .... Robinson's English Ecclesiastical Reports [*1844-53*] (DLA)
Rob. .... Robinson's Louisiana Reports [*1-4 Louisiana Annual*] [*1841-
        46*] (DLA)
Rob. .... Robinson's Reports [*40, 41 Virginia*] (DLA)
Rob. .... Robinson's Reports [*38 California*] (DLA)
Rob. .... Robinson's Reports [*2-9, 17-23 Colorado Appeals*] (DLA)
Rob. .... Robinson's Reports [*1 Nevada*] (DLA)
Rob. .... Robinson's Reports [*1-8 Ontario*] (DLA)
Rob. .... Robinson's Scotch Appeal Cases [*1840-41*] (DLA)
Rob. .... [*J. L.*] Robinson's Upper Canada Reports (DLA)
ROB .... Robotic Operating Buddy [*Nintendo video game system
        accessory*]
ROB .... Roburent [*Italy*] [*Seismograph station code, US Geological
        Survey*] (SEIS)
ROB .... Roburent [*Italy*] [*Geomagnetic observatory code*]
ROB .... Waco, TX [*Location identifier*] [*FAA*] (FAAL)
RoBA .... Academia R.S. Romania [*Academy of Romania*], Bucharest,
        Romania [*Library symbol*] [*Library of Congress*] (LCLS)
Rob A .... [*C.*] Robinson's Admiralty Reports [*1799-1809*] (DLA)
Rob Adm .... [*C.*] Robinson's Admiralty Reports [*England*] (DLA)
Rob Adm .... [*W.*] Robinson's English Admiralty Reports (DLA)
Rob Adm & Pr ... Roberts on Admiralty and Prize (DLA)
ROBAMP .... Rotational Base for Aviation Maintenance Personnel
Rob App ..... Robinson's Scotch Appeal Cases [*1840-41*] (DLA)
Robards ..... Robards' Reports [*12, 13 Missouri*] (DLA)
Robards ..... Robards' Texas Conscript Cases [*1862-65*] (DLA)
Robards & Jackson ... Robards and Jackson's Reports [*26-27 Texas*] (DLA)
Robb .... Robbins' New Jersey Equity Reports [*67-70 New
        Jersey*] (DLA)
Robb .... Robb's United States Patent Cases (DLA)
Rob Bank ... Robertson's Handbook of Bankers' Law (DLA)
Rob Bank ... Robson on Law and Practice in Bankruptcy [*7th ed.*]
        [*1894*] (DLA)
RoBBC .... Biblioteca Centrala de Stat a R.S. Romania [*Central State
        Library of Romania*], Bucharest, Romania [*Library
        symbol*] [*Library of Congress*] (LCLS)
Robb (NJ) ... Robbins' New Jersey Equity Reports (DLA)
Robb Pat Cas ... Robb's United States Patent Cases (DLA)
Rob Cal ...... Robinson's Reports [*38 California*] (DLA)
Rob Car V .. Robertson's History of the Reign of the Emperor Charles
        V (DLA)
Rob Cas ..... Robinson's Scotch Appeal Cases [*1840-41*] (DLA)
Rob Chr...... Robinson's Reports [*2-9, 17-23 Colorado Appeals*] (DLA)
ROBCO ...... Readiness Objective Code [*Military*] (AABC)
Rob Cons Cas (Tex) ... Robards' Texas Conscript Cases (DLA)
Rob Consc Cas ... Robards' Texas Conscript Cases (DLA)
ROBD .... Robot Defense Systems [*NASDAQ symbol*] (NQ)
Rob E .... Robertson's English Ecclesiastical Reports [*2 vols.*] [*1844-
        53*] (DLA)
Rob Ecc ..... Robertson's English Ecclesiastical Reports [*2 vols.*] [*1844-
        53*] (DLA)
Rob Eccl .... Robertson's English Ecclesiastical Reports [*2 vols.*] [*1844-
        53*] (DLA)
ROBEPS..... RADAR Operating below Prescribed Standards (FAAC)
Rob Eq .... Roberts' Principles of Equity (DLA)
Robert .... Robertson's Scotch Appeal Cases [*1707-27*] (DLA)
Robert App ... Robertson's Scotch House of Lords Appeals (DLA)
Robert App Cas ... Robertson's Scotch House of Lords Appeals (DLA)
Robert Morris Associates Bull ... Robert Morris Associates. Bulletin [*A
        publication*]
Roberts ...... Roberts' Reports [*29-31 Louisiana Annual*] (DLA)
Roberts Emp Liab ... Roberts on Federal Liabilities of Carriers (DLA)
Robertson ... Robertson's English Ecclesiastical Reports (DLA)
Robertson ... Robertson's Reports [*New York Marine Court*] (DLA)
Robertson ... Robertson's Reports [*1 Hawaii*] (DLA)
Robertson ... Robertson's Reports [*24-30 New York Superior Court*] (DLA)
Robertson ... Robertson's Scotch Appeal Cases [*1707-27*] (DLA)
Rob Fr .... Roberts on Frauds [*1805*] (DLA)
Rob Gav ..... Robinson's Common Law of Kent, or Custom on Gavelkind
        [*5th ed.*] [*1897*] (DLA)
Rob Hawaii ... Robinson's Reports [*1 Hawaii*] (DLA)
ROBIN .... Remote On-Line Business Information Network [*Data
        processing*] (IEEE)
ROBIN .... Rocket Balloon Instrument [*Air Force*]
Robin App ... Robinson's Scotch House of Lords Appeals (DLA)
ROBINS...... Roberts Information Services, Inc. [*Fairfax, VA*] [*Information
        service*] (EISS)
Robin Sc App ... Robinson's Scotch Appeal Cases [*1840-41*] (DLA)
Robinson ... Christopher Robinson's English Admiralty Reports (DLA)

Robinson ... [W.] Robinson's English Admiralty Reports (DLA)
Robinson ... Robinson's English Ecclesiastical Reports [1844-53] (DLA)
Robinson ... Robinson's Louisiana Reports [1841-46] (DLA)
Robinson ... Robinson's Louisiana Reports [1-12 Louisiana] (DLA)
Robinson ... Robinson's Ontario Reports (DLA)
Robinson ... Robinson's Reports [40-41 Virginia] (DLA)
Robinson ... Robinson's Reports [38 California] (DLA)
Robinson ... Robinson's Reports [17-23 Colorado] (DLA)
Robinson ... Robinson's Reports [1 Nevada] (DLA)
Robinson ... Robinson's Scotch House of Lords Appeals (DLA)
Robinson ... [J. L.] Robinson's Upper Canada Reports (DLA)
Robinson Sc App Cas ... Robinson's Scotch Appeal Cases [1840-41] (DLA)
Rob & J ...... Robards and Jackson's Reports [26, 27 Texas] (DLA)
Rob Jun ...... William Robinson's English Admiralty Reports [1838-52] (DLA)
Rob Jus ...... Robinson's Justice of the Peace [1836] (DLA)
Rob LA .... Robinson's Louisiana Reports [1-4 Louisiana Annual] [1841-46] (DLA)
Rob (LA Ann) ... Robinson's Louisiana Reports [1-4 Louisiana Annual] (DLA)
Rob Leg ..... Robertson's Legitimation by Subsequent Marriage [1829] (DLA)
Rob Louis ... Robinson's Louisiana Reports [1-12 Louisiana] (DLA)
Rob L & W ... Roberts, Leaming, and Wallis' County Court Reports [1849-51] (DLA)
Rob Mar (NY) ... Robertson and Jacob's New York Marine Court Reports (DLA)
Rob MO ...... Robards' Reports [12, 13 Missouri] (DLA)
ROBN .... Robbins & Meyers [NASDAQ symbol] (NQ)
Rob Nev ..... Robinson's Reports [1 Nevada] (DLA)
Rob (NY) .... Robertson's Reports [24-30 New York Superior Court] (DLA)
ROBO .... Rocket Orbital Bomber
ROBOMB .... Robot Bomb [Air Force]
Robotics T ... Robotics Today [A publication]
Robotron Tech Commun ... Robotron Technical Communications [A publication]
Rob Pat ...... Robinson on Patents (DLA)
Rob Per Suc ... Robertson's Law of Personal Succession [1836] (DLA)
R Obs Ann ... Royal Observatory Annals [A publication]
Robs Bank ... Robson on Law and Practice in Bankruptcy [7th ed.] [1894] (DLA)
Robs Bankr ... Robertson's Handbook of Bankers' Law (DLA)
R Obs Bull ... Royal Observatory Bulletins [A publication]
Rob Sc App ... Robinson's Scotch Appeal Cases (DLA)
Rob SI .... Robertson's Sandwich Island Reports [1 Hawaii] (DLA)
Robson .... Robson on Law and Practice in Bankruptcy [7 eds.] [1870-94] (DLA)
Rob Sr Ct ... Robertson's New York Superior Court Reports [24-30] (DLA)
Rob Super Ct ... Robertson's Reports [24-30 New York Superior Court] (DLA)
ROBT .... International Robomation/Intelligence [NASDAQ symbol] (NQ)
Robt Eccl ... Robertson's English Ecclesiastical Reports [163 English Reprint] [1844-53] (DLA)
Robt Eccl (Eng) ... Robertson's English Ecclesiastical Reports [163 English Reprint] (DLA)
Robt (NY) ... Robertson's Reports [24-30 New York Superior Court] (DLA)
Robt Sc App Cas ... Robertson's Scotch Appeal Cases (DLA)
Rob UC ...... Robinson's Upper Canada Reports (DLA)
ROBV .... Robotic Vision Systems [NASDAQ symbol] (NQ)
Rob VA .... Robinson's Reports [40, 41 Virginia] (DLA)
Rob Wm Adm ... [William] Robinson's English Admiralty Reports [3 vols.] [1838-50] (DLA)
Roc .... New Hampshire Reports (DLA)
ROC .... Railton Owners Club (EA)
ROC .... Range Operations Center [Western Test Range] (MCD)
ROC .... Range Operations Conference [NASA] (KSC)
ROC .... Rate of Climb [Aviation]
ROC .... Rate of Convergence (IEEE)
R/OC .... Receive-Only Center (FAAC)
ROC .... Receiver [or Relative] Operating Characteristics [Signal detection] [Psychophysics]
ROC .... Reconnaissance and Operations Center (NATG)
ROC .... Reconnaissance Optique de Caracteres [Optical Character Recognition] [French]
ROC .... Record of Comments (NASA)
ROC .... Redeem Our Country (EA)
ROC .... Reduce Operating Costs [Air Force project]
ROC .... Reduced Operational Capability Program [Navy] (NVT)
ROC .... Region One Cooperative Library Service Unit [Library network]
ROC .... Regional Operating Center [NATO Integrated Communications System] (NATG)
ROC .... Regroupement des Officiers Communistes [Political party] [Burkina Faso]
ROC .... Relative Operating Characteristics (MCD)
ROC .... Reliability Operating Characteristic
ROC .... Remote Operator's Console
ROC .... Republic of China (CINC)
ROC .... Republican Organizing Committee [Political organization in opposition to the NPL of North Dakota]

ROC .... Request of Change (NASA)
ROC .... Required Operational Capability [Military] (RDA)
ROC .... Reserve Officer Candidate
RO in C .... Resident Officer-in-Charge [Navy]
ROC .... Return on Capital
ROC .... Reusable Orbital Carrier [Aerospace] (MCD)
ROC .... Revue de l'Orient Chretien [A publication]
ROC .... Rochester [New York] [Airport symbol] (OAG)
ROC .... Rochester-Odenbach [New York] [Seismograph station code, US Geological Survey] (SEIS)
ROC .... Rochester Public Library, Rochester, MN [OCLC symbol] (OCLC)
Roc .... Rococo Records [Record label] [Canada, USA]
ROC .... Rotatable Optical Cube
ROC .... Rothmans Inc. [Formerly, Rothmans of Pall Mall Canada] [Toronto Stock Exchange symbol]
ROC .... Rothmans of Pall Mall Canada Ltd. [Toronto Stock Exchange symbol] [Vancouver Stock Exchange symbol]
ROC .... Royal Observer Corps [British civilian aircraft observers] [World War II]
ROC .... Royal Ordnance Corps [British]
ROCAF .... Republic of China Air Force (CINC)
ROCALDIS ... Routine Calls May Be Dispensed With
ROCAP ...... Regional Officer for Central American Programs [Department of State]
ROCAPPI ... Research on Computer Applications for the Printing and Publishing Industries
Rocas Miner ... Rocas y Minerales [A publication]
ROCAT ...... Rocket Catapult
ROCC .... Range Operations Conference Circuit (MUGU)
ROCC .... Range Operations Control Center (MCD)
ROCC .... Regional Oil Combating Center [Marine science] (MSC)
ROCC .... Regional Operations Control Center [AT & T]
Rocc .... Roccus' De Navibus et Naulo [Maritime law] (DLA)
ROCC .... Russell's Owl Collectors Club (EA)
Rocc De Nav et Nau ... Roccus' De Navibus et Naulo [Maritime law] (DLA)
R Occid Musul Mediterr ... Revue de l'Occident Musulman et de la Mediterranee [A publication]
Roccus Ins ... Roccus on Insurance (DLA)
ROCF .... Rockies Fund, Inc. [NASDAQ symbol] (NQ)
ROCH .... Rochester (ROG)
ROCH .... Ruch Oporu Chlopskiego [Movement of Peasant Resistance] [Poland] (PPE)
ROCHA ...... Roczniki Chemii [A publication]
Roche D & K ... Roche, Dillon, and Kehoe's Irish Land Reports [1881-82] (DLA)
Roche & H Bank ... Roche and Hazlitt's Bankruptcy Practice [2nd ed.] [1873] (DLA)
Roche Image Med Res ... Roche Image of Medicine and Research [A publication]
Roche Med Image Comment ... Roche Medical Image and Commentary [A publication]
Rochester Acad Sci Proc ... Rochester Academy of Science. Proceedings [A publication]
Rochester Conf Data Acquis Processing Biol Med Proc ... Rochester Conference on Data Acquisition and Processing in Biology and Medicine. Proceedings [A publication]
Rochester Hist ... Rochester History [A publication]
Rochester Hist Soc Publ Fund Ser ... Rochester Historical Society. Publication Fund Series [A publication]
Rochester Univ Lib Bul ... University of Rochester. Library Bulletin [A publication]
Roch Patr ... Rochester Patriot [A publication]
Roch Phil ... Rochester Philharmonic Orchestra Program Notes [A publication]
ROCI .... Rauschenberg Overseas Cultural Interchange [Retrospective exhibit of artist Robert Rauschenberg's work]
ROCI .... Rickman Owners Club International (EA)
ROCIA .... Rozhledy v Chirurgii [A publication]
ROCID .... Reorganization of Combat Infantry Division [Army] (AABC)
Rock .... New Hampshire Reports (DLA)
ROCK .... Rocket (MCD)
ROCK .... Rockor, Inc. [NASDAQ symbol] (NQ)
Rock .... Smith's New Hampshire Reports (DLA)
ROCKET .... Rand's Omnibus Calculator of the Kinetics of Earth Trajectories
Rocket News Lett ... Rocket News Letter [A publication]
Rocket Propul Technol ... Rocket Propulsion Technology [A publication]
ROCKEX .... Rocket Exercise [Military] (NVT)
Rockingham ... Smith's New Hampshire Reports (DLA)
Rock Magn Paleogeophys ... Rock Magnetism and Paleogeophysics [A publication]
Rock Mech ... Rock Mechanics [A publication]
Rock Mech Felsmech Mec Roches ... Rock Mechanics/Felsmechanik/ Mecanique des Roches [A publication]
ROCKOON ... Rocket Balloon [Navy]
Rock Prod ... Rock Products [A publication]
Rocks Miner ... Rocks and Minerals [A publication]
ROCKSTORE ... Rock Storage [Storage in excavated rock caverns]
Rocky Mountain J Math ... Rocky Mountain Journal of Mathematics [A publication]

Rocky Mt Bioeng Symp Proc ... Rocky Mountain Bioengineering Symposium. Proceedings [*A publication*]
Rocky Mt J Math ... Rocky Mountain Journal of Mathematics [*A publication*]
Rocky Mt L Rev ... Rocky Mountain Law Review [*A publication*]
Rocky Mt Med J ... Rocky Mountain Medical Journal [*A publication*]
Rocky Mt Miner Law Inst Annu Inst Proc ... Rocky Mountain Mineral Law Institute. Annual Institute Proceedings [*A publication*]
Rocky Mt Miner L Rev ... Rocky Mountain Mineral Law Review (DLA)
Rocky Mt Min L Inst Proc ... Rocky Mountain Mineral Law Institute. Proceedings [*A publication*]
Rocky Mtn L Rev ... Rocky Mountain Law Review [*A publication*]
Rocky Mtn Oil Reporter ... Rocky Mountain Oil Reporter [*A publication*]
Rocky Mt So ... Rocky Mountain Social Science Journal [*A publication*]
Rocky Mt Spectrosc Conf (Program Abstr) ... Rocky Mountain Spectroscopy Conference (Program and Abstracts) [*A publication*]
ROCL .... Rockwell Drilling [*NASDAQ symbol*] (NQ)
Rocla Pipes Ltd Tech J ... Rocla Pipes Limited. Technical Journal [*A publication*]
ROCMAGV ... Republic of China, Military Assistance Group, Vietnam
ROCMAS ... Russian Orthodox Catholic Mutual Aid Society of USA (EA)
ROCMC ..... Republic of China Marine Corps (CINC)
ROCMM ..... Regional Office of Civilian Manpower Management
ROCN .... Republic of China Navy (CINC)
ROCN .... Retraining Objective Control Number [*Air Force*] (AFM)
RocO .... Rocznik Orientalistyczny [*Warszawa*] [*A publication*]
ROCP .... RADAR Out of Commission for Parts [*ADC*]
ROCP .... Regional Occupation Center Program (OICC)
ROCPEX .... Republic of China Philatelic Exhibition
ROCR .... Recovery Operations Control Room [*NASA*] (KSC)
ROCR .... Remote Optical Character Recognition [*Data processing*]
ROCU .... Remote Operational Control Unit [*Military*] (CAAL)
ROCWMAS ... Russian Orthodox Catholic Women's Mutual Aid Society (EA)
Rocz Akad Med Bialymstoku ... Roczniki Akademii Medycznej Imienia Juliana Marchlewskiego w Bialymstoku [*A publication*]
Rocz Akad Med Bialymstoku Supl ... Roczniki Akademii Medycznej Imienia Juliana Marchlewskiego w Bialymstoku. Suplement [*A publication*]
Rocz Akad Med Juliana Marchlewskiego Bialymstoku ... Roczniki Akademii Medycznej Imienia Juliana Marchlewskiego w Bialymstoku [*A publication*]
Rocz Akad Med Juliana Marchlewskiego Bialymstoku Supl ... Roczniki Akademii Medycznej Imienia Juliana Marchlewskiego w Bialymstoku. Suplement [*A publication*]
Rocz Akad Roln Poznaniu ... Roczniki Akademii Rolniczej w Poznaniu [*Poland*] [*A publication*]
Rocz Bialostocki ... Rocznik Bialostocki [*A publication*]
Rocz Chem ... Roczniki Chemii [*A publication*]
Rocz Glebozn ... Roczniki Gleboznawcze [*A publication*]
RoczH .... Roczniki Humanistyczne Katolickiego Uniwersytetu [*A publication*]
Rocz Hist .... Roczniki Historyczne [*A publication*]
Rocz Inst Przem Mlecz ... Roczniki Instytutu Przemyslu Mleczarskiego [*Poland*] [*A publication*]
Rocz Jeleniogorski ... Rocznik Jeleniogorski [*A publication*]
Rocz Krakowski ... Rocznik Krakowski [*A publication*]
Rocz Muz Etnogr ... Rocznik Muzeum Etnograficznego w Krakowie [*A publication*]
Rocz Muz Narod Warszawie ... Rocznik Muzeum Narodowego w Warszawie [*A publication*]
Rocz Muz Swiet ... Rocznik Muzeum Swietokrzyskiego [*A publication*]
Rocz Muz Toruniu ... Rocznik Muzeum w Toruniu [*A publication*]
Roczn Akad Roln Poznan ... Roczniki Akademii Rolniczej w Poznaniu [*A publication*]
Rocz Nauk Roln ... Roczniki Nauk Rolniczych [*A publication*]
Rocz Nauk Roln Les ... Roczniki Nauk Rolniczych i Lesnych [*A publication*]
Rocz Nauk Roln Ser A ... Roczniki Nauk Rolniczych. Seria A [*A publication*]
Rocz Nauk Roln Ser A Prod Rosl ... Roczniki Nauk Rolniczych. Seria A. Produkcja Roslinna [*A publication*]
Rocz Nauk Roln Ser B ... Roczniki Nauk Rolniczych. Seria B. Zootechniczna [*A publication*]
Rocz Nauk Roln Ser B Zootech ... Roczniki Nauk Rolniczych. Seria B. Zootechniczna [*A publication*]
Rocz Nauk Roln Ser C Mech Roln ... Roczniki Nauk Rolniczych. Seria C. Mechnizacja Rolnictwa [*A publication*]
Rocz Nauk Roln Ser C Tech Roln ... Roczniki Nauk Rolniczych. Seria C. Technika Rolnicza [*Continues Seria C. Mechnizacja Rolnictwa*] [*A publication*]
Rocz Nauk Roln Ser D ... Roczniki Nauk Rolniczych. Seria D. Monografie [*A publication*]
Rocz Nauk Roln Ser D Monogr ... Roczniki Nauk Rolniczych. Seria D. Monografie [*A publication*]
Rocz Nauk Roln Ser E Ochr Rosl ... Roczniki Nauk Rolniczych. Seria E. Ochrona Roslin [*A publication*]
Rocz Nauk Roln Ser F Melio Vzytkow Zielonych ... Roczniki Nauk Rolniczych. Seria F. Melioracji i Vzytkow Zielonych [*A publication*]
Rocz Nauk Roln Ser H Rybactwo ... Roczniki Nauk Rolniczych. Seria H. Rybactwo [*A publication*]
Rocz Nauk Zootech ... Roczniki Naukowe Zootechniki [*A publication*]

Rocz Nauk Zootech Monogr Rozpr ... Roczniki Naukowe Zootechniki. Monografie i Rozprawy [*A publication*]
Rocz Nauk Zootech Pol J Anim Sci Technol ... Rocznik Naukowe Zootechniki. Polish Journal of Animal Science and Technology [*A publication*]
Roczn Chem ... Roczniki Chemii [*A publication*]
Roczniki Glebozn ... Roczniki Gleboznawcze [*A publication*]
Roczn Inst Handlu Wewn ... Roczniki Instytutu Handlu Wewnetrznego [*A publication*]
Roczn Nauk Roln A ... Roczniki Nauk Rolniczych. A. Produkcja Roslinna [*A publication*]
RoczOr .... Rocznik Orientalistyczny [*Warsaw*] [*A publication*]
Rocz Panstw Zakl Hig ... Roczniki Panstwowego Zakladu Higieny [*A publication*]
Rocz Panst Zakl Hig (Warszawa) ... Roczniki Panstwowego Zakladu Higieny (Warszawa) [*A publication*]
Rocz Pol Tow Geol ... Rocznik Polskiego Towarzystwa Geologicznego [*A publication*]
Rocz Pomor Akad Med Im Gen Karola Swierczewskiego Szczecin ... Roczniki Pomorska Akademia Medyczna Imeni Generala Karola Swierczewskiego w Szczecinia [*A publication*]
Rocz Pomor Akad Med Szczecinie ... Rocznik Pomorskiej Akademii Medycznej Imienia Generala Karola Swierczewskiego w Szczecinie [*Poland*] [*A publication*]
Rocz Pomor Akad Med Szczecinie ... Roczniki Pomorskiej Akademii Medycznej w Szczecinie [*A publication*]
Rocz Pomor Akad Med Szczecinie Supl ... Rocznik Pomorskiej Akademii Medycznej w Szczecinie. Suplement [*A publication*]
Rocz Sekc Dendrol Pol Tow Bot ... Rocznik Sekcji Dendrologicznej Polskiego Towarzystwa Botanicznego [*A publication*]
RoczSl .... Rocznik Slawistyczny [*A publication*]
Rocz Technol Chem Zywn ... Roczniki Technologii Chemii Zywnosci [*A publication*]
Rocz Wojsk Inst Hig Epidemiol ... Rocznik Wojskowego Instytutu Higieny i Epidemiologii [*Poland*] [*A publication*]
Rocz Wyzs Szkoly Roln Poznaniu ... Roczniki Wyzszej Szkoly Rolniczej w Poznaniu [*A publication*]
Rocz Wyzsz Roln Poznaniu ... Roczniki Wyzszej Szkoly Rolniczej w Poznaniu [*A publication*]
Rocz Wyzsz Szk Roln Poznaniu Pr Habilitacyjne ... Roczniki Wyzszej Szkoly Rolniczej w Poznaniu. Prace Habilitacyjne [*A publication*]
ROD .... Range of the Day [*Military*] (CAAL)
ROD .... Range Operations Directorate [*White Sands Missile Range*]
ROD .... Rate of Descent (KSC)
ROD .... Record of Discussion (MCD)
ROD .... Release Order Directive [*Later, ERO*] (NRCH)
ROD .... Remote Operated Door (MCD)
ROD .... Repair and Overhaul Directive (AAG)
ROD .... Required on Dock (KSC)
ROD .... Required Operational Date
ROD .... Reverse-Osmosis Desalination
R-O-D .... Rise-Off-Disconnect (AAG)
ROD .... Roddy Resources, Inc. [*Toronto Stock Exchange symbol*]
ROD .... Rosewood, OH [*Location identifier*] [*FAA*] (FAAL)
ROD .... Route Opening Detachment (MCD)
RODA .... Regardless of Destination Airport (FAAC)
RODA .... Sisters Oblates to Divine Love [*Roman Catholic religious order*]
RODAC ..... Reorganization Objectives, Army Division, Army and Corps [*Military*] (AABC)
RODATA .... Registered Organization Data Bank
RODC .... Regional Oceanographic Data Center [*Marine science*] (MSC)
RODC .... Registered Organization Development Consultant [*Designation awarded by Organization Development Institute*]
Rod and Gun and Canad Silver Fox News ... Rod and Gun and Canadian Silver Fox News [*A publication*]
RODIAC ..... Rotary Dual Input for Analog Computation
R-O Dis ...... Reality-Oriented Discussion
Rodm .... Rodman's Reports [*78-82 Kentucky*] (DLA)
Rodman ..... Rodman's Reports [*78-82 Kentucky*] (DLA)
RODMY ...... Rodime plc ADR [*NASDAQ symbol*] (NQ)
RODO .... Range Operations Duty Officer (MUGU)
Rodopskii Zbor ... Rodopskii Zbornik [*A publication*]
RODS .... Real-Time Operations, Dispatching, and Scheduling [*System*] [*TRW, Inc.*]
RODSB .... Revue d'Odonto-Stomatologie [*A publication*]
ROE .... Birmingham, AL [*Location identifier*] [*FAA*] (FAAL)
ROE .... Reflector Orbital Equipment
ROE .... Return on Equity [*Finance*]
ROE .... Roemisches Oesterreich [*A publication*]
ROE .... Roster of Exception (AABC)
ROE .... Round Off Error
ROE .... Royal Observatory, Edinburgh [*Scotland*]
ROE .... Rules of Engagement [*Military*] (AABC)
ROED .... Ridgeway Exco, Inc. [*NASDAQ symbol*] (NQ)
RoeFo Fortschr Geb Roentgenstr Nuklearmed ... RoeFo. Fortschritte auf dem Gebiete der Roentgenstrahlen und der Nuklearmedizin [*West Germany*] [*A publication*]
Roem Jahr Kunstges ... Roemisches Jahrbuch fuer Kunstgeschichte [*A publication*]
Roem Mitt ... Mitteilungen des Deutschen Archaeologischen Instituts. Roemische Abteilung [*A publication*]

Roem Q ...... Roemische Quartalschrift [*A publication*]
Roem Q ...... Roemische Quartalschrift fuer Christliche Altertumskunde und fuer Kirchengeschichte [*A publication*]
ROEND .... Roentgenstrahlen [*A publication*]
Roent .... Roentgenology [*Radiology*]
Roentgen Ber ... Roentgen Berichte [*A publication*]
Roentgen-BI ... Roentgen-Blaetter [*A publication*]
Roentgen Laboratoriumsprax ... Roentgen Laboratoriumspraxis [*A publication*]
Roentgenprax ... Roentgenpraxis [*A publication*]
Roentgen Technol ... Roentgen Technology. Official Journal of Indian Association of Radiological Technologists [*A publication*]
Roent M ..... Master of Roentgenology
ROF .... Rate of Fire [*In rounds per minute*] [*Military*]
ROF .... Reformed Ogboni Fraternity [*Nigerian*]
ROF .... Remote Operator Facility [*Honeywell, Inc.*]
ROF .... Reporting Organizational File [*Military*]   (AFM)
ROF .... Romanische Forschungen [*A publication*]
ROF .... Royal Oak Foundation   (EA)
ROF .... Royal Ordnance Factory [*British*]   (NATG)
ROFF .... Roffler Industries [*NASDAQ symbol*]   (NQ)
ROFFEN ..... Roffensis [*Signature of Bishop of Rochester*] [*Latin*]   (ROG)
ROFL .... Russian Orthodox Fraternity Lubov   (EA)
ROFOR ...... Route Forecast [*Aviation*]   (FAAC)
ROFR .... Repair of Repairables   (MCD)
ROFT .... RADAR Off Target
ROFT .... Rapid Optics Fabrication Technology   (MCD)
RofThPh ..... Review of Theology and Philosophy [*A publication*]
ROG .... Receipt of Goods
ROG .... Residency Operations Group
R-O-G .... Rise-Off-Ground [*Model airplane*]   (AAG)
ROG .... Rodale's Organic Gardening [*A publication*]
ROG .... Rogers, AR [*Location identifier*] [*FAA*]   (FAAL)
ROG .... Rogers Corp. [*American Stock Exchange symbol*]
ROG .... Rothchild Gold [*Vancouver Stock Exchange symbol*]
ROGAR ...... Review of Guard and Reserve Task Force   (MCD)
Rog CHR .... Rogers' City Hall Recorder [*1816-22*] [*New York*]   (DLA)
Rog Ecc L ... Rogers' Ecclesiastical Law [*5th ed.*] [*1857*]   (DLA)
Rog Ecc Law ... Rogers' Ecclesiastical Law   (DLA)
Rogers .... Rogers on Elections [*2 eds.*] [*1812, 1818-19*]   (DLA)
Rogers .... Rogers' Reports [*47-51 Louisiana Annual*]   (DLA)
Rog Hov ..... Roger De Hoveden's Chronica   (DLA)
ROGI .... Roberts Oil & Gas [*NASDAQ symbol*]   (NQ)
ROGOPAG ... Rossellini, Jr.; Godard, Pasolini, Gregoretti [*Title of episodic motion picture formed from surnames of its directors*]
Rog Rec ..... Rogers' New City Hall Recorder   (DLA)
R-O-H .... Receiver Off the Hook
ROH .... Regular Overhaul [*Navy*]   (NG)
ROH .... Returned on Hire
roh .... Rhaeto-Romance [*MARC language code*] [*Library of Congress*]   (LCCP)
ROH .... Robinhood [*Australia*] [*Airport symbol*] [*Obsolete*]   (OAG)
ROH .... Rohm & Haas Co. [*NYSE symbol*]
ROH .... Rohtak [*India*] [*Seismograph station code, US Geological Survey*] [*Closed*]   (SEIS)
RoH .... Roumeliotiko Hemerologio [*A publication*]
ROH .... Royal Opera House [*Covent Garden, London*]
Rohm Haas Rep ... Rohm and Haas Reporter [*A publication*]
ROHRA .... Rohre, Rohrleitungsbau, Rohrleitungstransport [*A publication*]
Rohre Rohrleitungsbau Rohrleitungstransp ... Rohre, Rohrleitungsbau, Rohrleitungstransport [*West Germany*] [*A publication*]
RoHum .... Roczniki Humanistyczne [*A publication*]
ROI .... Member of the Royal Institute of Oil Painters [*British*]
ROI .... Radio, Optical, Inertial
ROI .... Range Operations Instruction [*NASA*]   (KSC)
ROI .... Reactive Oxygen Intermediate [*Biochemistry*]
ROI .... Region of Interest   (NRCH)
ROI .... Reliability Organization Instruction   (AAG)
ROI .... Religious Observance Index   (BJA)
ROI .... Rendezvous Orbit Insertion [*Aerospace*]
ROI .... Report of Investigation   (AFM)
ROI .... Return on Investment
ROI .... River Oaks Industries, Inc. [*NYSE symbol*]
ROI .... Rotating Optical Interferometer
ROI .... Royal Institute of Oil Painters [*British*]
ROIC .... Resident Officer-in-Charge
ROICC .... Resident Officer-in-Charge of Construction
ROID .... Report of Item Discrepancy [*Army*]   (AABC)
ROII .... River Oaks Industries [*NASDAQ symbol*]   (NQ)
ROIL .... Reserve Oil & Mineral [*NASDAQ symbol*]   (NQ)
ROINST ...... Range Operations Instruction [*NASA*]   (MUGU)
ROIS .... Radio Operational Intercom System   (KSC)
ROJ .... Range of Jamming
ROJ .... Romanistisches Jahrbuch [*A publication*]
ROJ .... Royal Order of Jagie Ilo [*Later, SHOSJ*]   (EA)
ROK .... Republic of Korea
ROK .... Rockhampton [*Australia*] [*Airport symbol*]   (OAG)
ROK .... Rockwell International Corp. [*NYSE symbol*] [*Toronto Stock Exchange symbol*]
ROKA .... Republic of Korea Army   (AABC)
ROKAA .... Rodo Kagaku [*A publication*]

ROKAF .... Republic of Korea Air Force
ROKAP .... Republic of Korea Civic Action Program   (CINC)
ROKDTF .... Republic of Korea Division Task Force
ROKF .... Republic of Korea Forces
ROKFV ...... Republic of Korea Forces in Vietnam   (CINC)
ROKG .... Republic of Korea Government   (CINC)
ROKG .... Rocking
ROKIT .... Republic of Korea Indigenous Tank Program   (MCD)
ROKMC ..... Republic of Korea Marine Corps   (CINC)
ROKN .... Republic of Korea Navy   (CINC)
ROKPTN ..... Rockhampton   (ROG)
ROKPUC .... Republic of Korea Presidential Unit Citation Badge
ROKPUCE ... Republic of Korea Presidential Unit Citation
ROKUSCFC ... Republic of Korea and US Combined Forces Command   (MCD)
ROL .... RADAR Observer License
ROL .... Record of Oral Language   (ADA)
ROL .... Remote Operating Location   (MCD)
ROL .... Reordering Level
ROL .... Review de l'Orient Latin [*A publication*]
ROL .... Revue de l'Orient Latin [*A publication*]
ROL .... Right Occipitolateral [*Obstetrics*]
ROL .... Rolla [*Missouri*] [*Seismograph station code, US Geological Survey*]   (SEIS)
Rol .... Rolle's Abridgment [*2 vols.*]   (DLA)
Rol .... Rolle's English King's Bench Reports [*2 vols.*]   (DLA)
ROL .... Rollins, Inc. [*NYSE symbol*]
ROL .... Rotate Left [*Data processing*]
ROL .... Royal Overseas League [*London, England*]   (EA-IO)
Rol Ab .... Rolle's Abridgment   (DLA)
ROLAC ...... Regional Organization of Liaison for Allocation of Circuit   (NATG)
ROLADES ... Roland Air Defense System   (MCD)
ROLET .... Reference Our Letter   (NOAA)
ROLF .... Remotely Operated Longwall Face   (IEEE)
ROLF .... Rolfite Co. [*NASDAQ symbol*]   (NQ)
RoLit .... Romania Literara [*A publication*]
Roll .... Rolle's Abridgment [*2 vols.*]   (DLA)
Roll .... Rolle's English King's Bench Reports [*2 vols.*]   (DLA)
Roll Abr ..... Rolle's Abridgment   (DLA)
Rolle .... Rolle's Abridgment   (DLA)
Rolle .... Rolle's English King's Bench Reports [*2 vols.*] [*1614-25*]   (DLA)
Rolle Abr .... Rolle's Abridgment of the Common Law   (DLA)
Rolle R .... Rolle's English King's Bench Reports [*2 vols.*] [*1614-25*]   (DLA)
Roll Rep .... Rolle's English King's Bench Reports [*2 vols.*] [*1614-25*]   (DLA)
Rolls Ct Rep ... Rolls' Court Reports   (DLA)
Roll Stone ... Rolling Stone [*A publication*]
ROLR .... Receiving Objective Loudness Rating [*Telephones*]   (IEEE)
ROLS .... Recoverable Orbital Launch System
ROLSIM ..... Roland Simulation   (MCD)
ROM .... Priest, CA [*Location identifier*] [*FAA*]   (FAAL)
ROM .... Range of Motion [*or Movement*]
ROM .... Read-Only Memory [*Computer memory*] [*Data processing*]
ROM .... Read-Only Men [*On Board car window sign's version of the computer term, Read-Only Memory*]
ROM .... Readout Memory   (IEEE)
ROM .... Return on Market Value [*Finance*]
ROM .... Rio Algom Ltd. [*American Stock Exchange symbol*] [*Toronto Stock Exchange symbol*]
Rom .... Roemisch [*Roman*] [*German*]   (OCD)
ROM .... Roman [*Type*] [*Publishing*]
ROM .... Romance
Rom .... Romania [*A publication*]
Rom .... Romania [*Three-letter standard code*]   (CNC)
Rom .... Romans [*New Testament book*]
rom .... Romany [*MARC language code*] [*Library of Congress*]   (LCCP)
Rom .... Romany Records [*Record label*]
ROM .... Romberg [*Medicine*]
ROM .... Rome [*Italy*] [*Seismograph station code, US Geological Survey*] [*Closed*]   (SEIS)
ROM .... Rome [*Italy*] [*Airport symbol*]   (OAG)
Rom .... Romeo and Juliet [*Shakespearean work*]
Rom .... Romilly's Notes of English Chancery Cases [*1767-87*]   (DLA)
Rom .... Romulus [*of Plutarch*] [*Classical studies*]   (OCD)
ROM .... Rough Order of Magnitude [*Army*]   (AABC)
ROM .... Royal Ontario Museum [*Toronto, ON*] [*Research center*]
ROM .... Run of Mine
ROM .... Rupture of Membranes [*Medicine*]
ROMA .... Return on Managed Assets [*Business and trade*]
ROMAA ...... Rom-Amer Pharmaceuticals [*NASDAQ symbol*]   (NQ)
ROMAC ..... Range Operations Monitor Analysis Center   (MCD)
ROMAC ..... Range Operations Monitoring and Control
ROMACC ... Range Operational Monitoring and Control Center
ROMAD ..... Radio Operator/Maintenance Driver
Rom Adelsparteien ... Roemische Adelsparteien und Adelsfamilien [*A publication*]   (OCD)
Roma Econ ... Roma Economica [*A publication*]
Romagna Med ... Romagna Medica [*A publication*]
Romance Philol ... Romance Philology [*A publication*]
Roman Forsc ... Romanische Forschungen [*A publication*]
Roman Forsch ... Romanische Forschungen [*A publication*]

Roman Philol ... Romance Philology [*A publication*]
Roman R .... Romanic Review [*A publication*]
ROMANS.... Range-Only Multiple Aircraft Navigation System [*Air Force*]
ROMANS.... Remote Manipulation Systems [*NASA*]
Roman Z Lit ... Romanistische Zeitschrift fuer Literaturgeschichte - Cahiers d'Histoire des Litteratures Romanes [*A publication*]
RO(M)B...... Reduction of (Military) Budgets
ROMBI....... Results of Marine Biological Investigations [*Marine science*]   (MSC)
ROMBUS.... Reusable Orbital Module Booster and Utility Shuttle [*Aerospace*]
Rom Cas .... Romilly's Notes of English Chancery Cases [*1767-87*]   (DLA)
Rom Com Geol Dari Seama Sedin ... Romania Comitetul de Stat al Geologiei. Institutul Geologic. Dari de Seama ale Sedintelor [*A publication*]
Rom Cr Law ... Romilly's Observations on the Criminal Law [*3rd ed.*] [*1813*]   (DLA)
ROMD........ Remote Operations and Maintenance Demonstration [*Nuclear energy*]
ROMEMO... Reference Our Memorandum   (FAAC)
ROMES ...... Reference Our Message   (FAAC)
RomF .... Romanische Forschungen [*A publication*]
Rom Fgn Tr ... Romanian Foreign Trade [*A publication*]
Rom Forsch ... Roemische Forschungen [*A publication*]   (OCD)
Rom G .... Romanica Gandensia [*A publication*]
Rom Gesch ... Grundriss der Romischen Geschichte [*A publication*]   (OCD)
Rom Gesch ... Romische Geschichte bis zum Beginn der Punischen Kriege [*A publication*]   (OCD)
ROMI .... Rule Out Myocardial Infarction [*Medicine*]
Romilly NC (Eng) ... Romilly's Notes of English Chancery Cases   (DLA)
Rom Inst Geol Dari Seama Sedin ... Romania Institutul Geologic. Dari de Seama ale Sedintelor [*A publication*]
Rom Inst Geol Mem ... Romania Institutul Geologic. Memorii [*A publication*]
Rom Inst Geol Stud Teh Econ Ser B ... Romania Institutul Geologic. Studii Tehnice si Economice. Seria B. Prepararea Minereurilor [*A publication*]
Rom Inst Geol Stud Teh Econ Ser D ... Romania Institutul Geologic. Studii Tehnice si Economice. Seria D. Prospectiuni Geofizice [*A publication*]
Rom Inst Geol Stud Teh Econ Ser E ... Romania. Institutul Geologic. Studii Tehnice si Economice. Seria E [*A publication*]
Rom Inst Geol Stud Teh Econ Ser I ... Romania Comitetul de Stat al Geologiei. Institutul Geologic. Studii Tehnice si Economice. Seria I. Mineralogie-Petrografie [*A publication*]
Rom Inst Meteorol Hidrol Stud Hidrogeol ... Romania Institutul de Meteorologie si Hidrologie. Studii de Hidrogeologie [*A publication*]
RomJ.......... Romanistisches Jahrbuch [*A publication*]
Rom J Chem ... Romanian Journal of Chemistry [*A publication*]
Rom J Med Endocrinol ... Romanian Journal of Medicine. Endocrinology [*A publication*]
Rom J Med Intern Med ... Romanian Journal of Medicine. Internal Medicine [*A publication*]
Rom J Med Neurol Psychiatry ... Romanian Journal of Medicine. Neurology and Psychiatry [*A publication*]
Rom J Med Virol ... Romanian Journal of Medicine. Virology [*A publication*]
Rom Law .... Mackeldey's Handbook of the Roman Law   (DLA)
RomLit ...... Romania Literara [*Bucharest*] [*A publication*]
ROMM .... Read-Only Memory Module [*Data processing*]
Rom Med Rev ... Romanian Medical Review [*A publication*]
RomN .... Romance Notes [*A publication*]
ROMO .... Rocky Mountain National Park
ROMON...... Receiving-Only Monitor
ROMOSS.... Revised Officer Military Occupational Speciality System   (MCD)
ROMOTAR ... Range-Only Measurement of Trajectory and Recording
ROMP........ Report of Obligation Military Pay   (AFM)
ROMP........ Review of Management Practices [*or Processes*]
RomPh ...... Romance Philology [*A publication*]
Rom Pol ..... Roman Politics 220-150BC [*A publication*]   (OCD)
ROMPS ..... Regional Office Monthly Personnel Status [*Department of Labor*]
RomR .... Romanic Review [*A publication*]
Rom Rev .... [*The*] Roman Revolution [*1939*] [*A publication*]   (OCD)
Rom Rule Asia Min ... Roman Rule in Asia Minor [*A publication*]   (OCD)
ROMS........ Remote Ocean Surface Measuring System [*Navy*]   (CAAL)
RomSl .... Romanoslavica [*A publication*]
Rom Staatsr ... Roemisches Staatsrecht [*A publication*]   (OCD)
Rom Strafr ... Roemisches Strafrecht [*A publication*]   (OCD)
Rom Stud... Roemische Studien [*A publication*]   (OCD)
Rom Today ... Romania Today [*A publication*]
RON........... Receiving Only   (FAAC)
RON........... Remaining [*or Rest*] Overnight [*Aviation*]
RON........... Remote [*Alaska*] [*Seismograph station code, US Geological Survey*] [*Closed*]   (SEIS)
RON........... Research-Octane-Number [*Fuel technology*]
RON........... Rest Overnight [*Make a stopover in a traveling political campaign*]
RoN .... Romance Notes [*A publication*]
RON........... Rondon [*Colombia*] [*Airport symbol*] [*Obsolete*]   (OAG)

RON........... Squadron   (MUGU)
RONA .... Return on Net Assets
RONAG ..... Reserve Officers Naval Architecture Group
RONB .... Research-Octane-Number-Barrels [*Fuel technology*]
RONCO ..... Rock-Oldies-News-Commercials Operation [*Formula radio*]
RONCOM ... Ronald Como, Inc. [*Perry Como's production firm; Ronald is his son*]
RONEO...... Rotary and Neostyle [*Duplicating machine*] [*Acronym is trademark*]
RONLY ...... Receiver Only [*Radio*]
RONOA ..... Revue d'Oto-Neuro-Ophtalmologie [*A publication*]
RONS .... Reserve Officers of the Naval Service [*Later, ROA*]
R Ont Mus J ... Royal Ontario Museum. Journal [*A publication*]
R Ont Mus Life Sci Contrib ... Royal Ontario Museum. Life Sciences. Contributions [*A publication*]
R Ont Mus Life Sci Misc Publ ... Royal Ontario Museum. Life Sciences. Miscellaneous Publications [*A publication*]
R Ont Mus Life Sci Occas Pap ... Royal Ontario Museum. Life Sciences. Occasional Paper [*A publication*]
R Ont Mus Zool Paleontol Contrib ... Royal Ontario Museum of Zoology and Paleontology. Contributions [*A publication*]
R Ont Nickel Com ... Royal Ontario Nickel Commission [*A publication*]
RONWT ..... Revised Ordinances, Northwest Territories [*Canada*]   (DLA)
ROO........... Radio Optical Observatory
ROO........... Railhead Ordnance Officer
ROO........... Range Operations Officer
ROO........... Reserve of Officers [*British*]
ROO........... Resident Obstetric Officer [*British*]
ROO........... Richland Operations Office [*Energy Research and Development Administration*]
ROO........... Rondonopolis [*Brazil*] [*Airport symbol*]   (OAG)
ROOPH...... Readily Operative Overhead Protection by Hippos [*Facetious proposal for protection against nuclear attack*]
Roorkee Univ Res J ... Roorkee University Research Journal [*A publication*]
ROOSA ...... Roosevelt National Investment Co. [*NASDAQ symbol*]   (NQ)
ROOSCH.... Royal Order of Sputnik Chasers
Roosevelt Wild Life Bull ... Roosevelt Wild Life Bulletin [*A publication*]
ROOST...... Reusable One-Stage Orbital Space Truck [*Aerospace*]
ROOT .... Relaxation Oscillator Optically Tuned
Root........... Root's Connecticut Reports [*1774-89*]   (DLA)
Root........... Root's Connecticut Supreme Court Reports [*1789-98*]   (DLA)
Root Bt Laws ... Root's Digest of Law and Practice in Bankruptcy [*1818*]   (DLA)
Root R .... Root's Connecticut Reports   (DLA)
Roots......... Root's Connecticut Reports   (DLA)
Root's Rep ... Root's Connecticut Reports   (DLA)
ROP........... Re-Order Price
ROP........... Receive-Only Printer [*Data processing*]
ROP........... Receiving Operations Package [*DoD*]
ROP........... Record of Performance
ROP........... Record of Production
ROP........... Record of Purchase   (NRCH)
ROP........... Refined Oil Products
ROP........... Regional Operating Plan [*Department of Labor*]
ROP........... Registered Options Principal
ROP........... Reorder Point [*Navy*]   (NG)
ROP........... Repeat Offenders Project
ROP........... Republic of the Philippines   (CINC)
ROP........... Retinopathy of Prematurity [*Medicine*]
ROP........... Right Occipitoposterior [*A fetal position*] [*Obstetrics*]
ROP........... Right Outside Position [*Dancing*]
ROP........... Roll-Over Protection Equipment   (MCD)
ROP........... Romance Philology [*A publication*]
ROP........... Roper Corp. [*NYSE symbol*]
Rop........... Roper on Legacies [*4 eds.*] [*1799-1847*]   (DLA)
ROP........... Rota [*Mariana Islands*] [*Airport symbol*]   (OAG)
ROP........... Royal Order of Piast   (EA)
ROP........... Run of Paper [*Business and trade*]
ROP........... Run of Press [*i.e., on an unspecified page or plate in web press set-up*] [*Printing*]
ROP₃.......... Revision of Procurement Policy and Procedures
ROPA .... Reserve Officer Personnel Act of 1954
ROPAR...... Regional Operators Program for Aircraft Reliability
ROPB........ Reserve Officers Promotion Board [*Air Force*]
ROPER ...... Regional Operators Program for Engine Reliability
ROPES ...... Remote Online Print Executive System
ROPEVAL... Readiness/Operational Evaluation   (NVT)
ROPEVAL... Rim of the Pacific Evaluation   (MCD)
ROPF......... Research into One-Parent Families [*British*]
ROPHO...... Reference Our Telephone Call   (NOAA)
Rop Husb & Wife ... Roper's Law of Property between Husband and Wife   (DLA)
Rop H & W ... Roper's Law of Property between Husband and Wife [*2nd ed.*] [*1826*]   (DLA)
ROPK .... Ropak West, Inc. [*NASDAQ symbol*]   (NQ)
Rop Leg...... Roper on Legacies   (DLA)
ROPM........ Revue. Ordre de Premontre et de Ses Missions [*A publication*]
ROPP......... Receive-Only Page Printer
Rop Prop.... Roper's Law of Property between Husband and Wife [*2nd ed.*] [*1826*]   (DLA)
ROPRA .... Reserve Officer Performance Recording Activity

ROPRA .... Rock Products [*A publication*]
ROPS .... Range Operation Performance Summary
ROPS .... Roll Over Protection System [*for tractors*]
ROPS .... Roll Over Protective Structures [*NASA*]   (KSC)
ROPU .... RADAR Overheat Protection Unit   (MCD)
ROPXA ...... Roentgenpraxis [*A publication*]
ROQ .... Houghton Lake, MI [*Location identifier*] [*FAA*]   (FAAL)
ROQ .... Reordering Quality
ROR .... Koror [*Palau Islands*] [*Airport symbol*]   (OAG)
ROR .... Range-Only RADAR   (AABC)
ROR .... Rate of Read
ROR .... Rate of Return   (MCD)
ROR .... Released on Own Recognizance [*Law*]
ROR .... Repair, Overhaul, Restoration   (MCD)
ROR .... Repair of Repairables   (MCD)
RoR .... Review of Religion [*A publication*]
ROR .... Rochester Minerals [*Vancouver Stock Exchange symbol*]
ROR .... Rocket on Rotor
ROR .... Rockton & Rion Railway [*AAR code*]
RoR .... Romanian Review [*A publication*]
ROR .... Romanic Review [*A publication*]
ROR .... Rorer Group, Inc. [*NYSE symbol*]
ROR .... Rorschach [*Test*]
ROR .... Rotate Right [*Data processing*]
RORA .... Reliable Operate RADAR Altimeter
RORA .... Reserve Officer Recording Activity
RORC .... Royal Ocean Racing Club [*British*]
RORD .... Research Opportunities in Renaissance Drama [*A publication*]
RORD .... Return on Receipt of Document [*Business and trade*]
ROREF ...... Rosmac Resources Ltd. [*NASDAQ symbol*]   (NQ)
Ro Rep .... Robards' Texas Conscript Cases [*1862-65*]   (DLA)
Ro Rep .... Rolle's English King's Bench Reports   (DLA)
ROREQ .... Reference Our Requisition   (NOAA)
Rorer Jud Sales ... Rorer on Void Judicial Sales   (DLA)
Rorer RR .... Rorer on Railways   (DLA)
RORET .... Authorized Rotational Retention [*Navy*]
RO/RI .... Redistribution Out/Redistribution In   (CINC)
RORIS .... Remote Operated Radiographic Inspection System
RO/RO .... Roll-On/Roll-Off [*Cargo ships*]   (AFM)
RO-RO .... Rolls Royce [*Automobile*] [*Slang*]   (DSUE)
RORQN ...... Reference Our Requisition   (FAAC)
RORS .... Realignment of Resources and Services   (MCD)
RORSAT .... RADAR Ocean Reconnaissance Satellite   (MCD)
RORT .... Report on Reimbursable Transactions [*DoD*]
RORU .... Rest of Route Unchanged   (FAAC)
ROS .... RADAR Order Switch
ROS .... Range Operation Station
ROS .... Range Operations Supervisor   (MUGU)
ROS .... Range of Spares   (MCD)
ROS .... Rat Osteosarcoma [*Cell line*]
ROS .... Rate of Speed   (MCD)
ROS .... Reactive Oxygen Species
ROS .... Read-Only Storage [*Data processing*]
ROS .... Reduced Operational Status
ROS .... Reed Organ Society   (EA)
ROS .... Regulated Oxygen Supply   (MCD)
ROS .... Remote Optical Sight [*Military*]   (CAAL)
ROS .... Remote Optical System
ROS .... Removable Overhead Structure   (MCD)
ROS .... Report Originator System [*Military*]   (CAAL)
ROS .... Representative Observation Site [*Weather observing facility*]
             [*Air Force*]
ROS .... Requisition on Stores [*Nuclear energy*]   (NRCH)
ROS .... Resident Operating System
ROS .... Restored Oil Shales
ROS .... Return from Overseas [*Military*]
ROS .... Return on Sales
ROS .... Review of Systems [*Medicine*]
ROS .... Rod Outer Segments [*of the retina*]
ROS .... Rosa [*Rose*] [*Pharmacology*]   (ROG)
ROS .... Rosario [*Argentina*] [*Airport symbol*]   (OAG)
ROS .... Rosary
ROS .... Rose Resources Corp. [*Vancouver Stock Exchange symbol*]
ROS .... Roseneath [*New Zealand*] [*Seismograph station code, US
             Geological Survey*] [*Closed*]   (SEIS)
ROS .... Ross Aviation, Inc. [*Tulsa, OK*] [*FAA designator*]   (FAAC)
ROS .... Roswell Public Library, Roswell, NM [*OCLC symbol*]   (OCLC)
ROS .... Rotary on Stamps Fellowship   (EA)
ROS .... Rotating Optical Scanner
ROS .... Royal Order of Scotland   (EA)
ROS .... Run of Schedule [*Commercial announcement to be broadcast
             throughout the program schedule*]
ROS .... Rush Order Service
ROSA .... Record One Stop Association [*Defunct*]   (EA)
ROSA .... Recording Optical Spectrum Analyzer   (MCD)
ROSA .... Report of Supply Activity   (MCD)
ROSAR ...... Read-Only Storage Address Register
ROSAT ...... RADAR Ocean Surveillance Satellite   (NVT)
ROSAT ...... Roentgen Satellite [*Space research*]
ROSC .... Reserve Officers Sanitary Corps
ROSC .... Restoration of Spontaneous Circulation

ROSC .... Road Operators Safety Council [*British*]
Rosc .... Roscoe's Reports of the Supreme Court [*1861-78*] [*South
             Africa*]   (DLA)
ROSC .... Roscommon [*County in Ireland*]   (ROG)
Rosc Act .... Roscoe on Actions [*1825*]   (DLA)
Rosc Adm ... Roscoe's Admiralty Jurisdiction and Practice   (DLA)
Rosc Am .... Pro Sexto Roscio Amerino [*of Cicero*] [*Classical
             studies*]   (OCD)
Rosc Bdg Cas ... Roscoe's Digest of Building Cases [*4th ed.*] [*1900*]   (DLA)
Rosc Bills ... Roscoe's Bills of Exchange [*2nd ed.*] [*1843*]   (DLA)
Rosc Civ Pr ... Roscoe's Outlines of Civil Procedure [*2nd ed.*] [*1880*]   (DLA)
Rosc Cr ...... Roscoe's Law of Evidence in Criminal Cases [*16 eds.*] [*1835-
             1952*]   (DLA)
Rosc Crim Ev ... Roscoe's Law of Evidence in Criminal Cases [*16 eds.*]
             [*1835-1952*]   (DLA)
Rosc Ev ..... Roscoe's Nisi Prius Evidence [*20th ed.*] [*1934*]   (DLA)
Rosc Jur ..... Roscoe's Jurist [*England*]   (DLA)
Rosc Light ... Roscoe's Law of Light [*4th ed.*] [*1904*]   (DLA)
Rosc NP ..... Roscoe's Law of Evidence at Nisi Prius [*20 eds.*] [*1827-
             1934*]   (DLA)
ROSCOE .... RADAR and Optical Systems Code
Roscoe .... Roscoe's Reports of the Supreme Court of Cape Of Good
             Hope [*South Africa*]   (DLA)
Roscoe Bldg Cas ... Roscoe's Digest of Building Cases [*England*]   (DLA)
Roscoe Cr Ev ... Roscoe's Law of Evidence in Criminal Cases [*16 eds.*]
             [*1835-1952*]   (DLA)
Roscoe's BC ... Roscoe's Digest of Building Cases [*England*]   (DLA)
ROSCOM ... Roscommon [*County in Ireland*]
ROSCOP .... Report of Observations/Samples Collected by Oceanographic
             Programs [*Marine science*]   (MSC)
ROSCOPS ... Report of Observation/Samples Collected by Oceanographic
             Programs [*Bureau National des Donnees Oceaniques*]
             [*Database*]
Rosc PC ..... Roscoe's English Prize Cases [*1745-1859*]   (DLA)
Rosc Pl ...... Roscoe's Pleading [*1845*]   (DLA)
ROSDR .... Read-Only Storage Data Register
ROSE .... Reconstruction by Optimized Series Expansion [*Of large
             molecules*]
ROSE .... Remote Optical Sensing of Emissions [*Instrumentation*]
ROSE .... Remotely Operated Special Equipment [*Nuclear energy*]
ROSE .... Residuum Oil Supercritical Extraction [*Petroleum refining*]
ROSE .... Retrieval by Online Search [*Data processing*]
ROSE .... Rising Observational Sounding Equipment
ROSE .... Rivera Ocean Seismic Experiment
Rose .... Rose's English Bankruptcy Reports   (DLA)
Rose Annu R Natl Rose Soc ... Rose Annual. Royal National Rose Society [*A
             publication*]
Rose Bankr ... Rose's English Bankruptcy Reports [*1810-16*]   (DLA)
Rose Bankr (Eng) ... Rose's English Bankruptcy Reports   (DLA)
Rose BC ..... Rose's English Bankruptcy Reports   (DLA)
Rosenberger ... Street Railway Law [*United States*]   (DLA)
Rosenberger Pock LJ ... Rosenberger's Pocket Law Journal   (DLA)
Rose Notes ... Rose's Notes on United States Reports   (DLA)
Rose WC .... Rose. Will Case [*New York*]   (DLA)
ROSIE .... Reconnaissance by Orbiting Ship-Identification Equipment
ROSIE .... Rooters Organized to Stimulate Interest and Enthusiasm
             [*Women baseball fans, Cincinnati*]
ROSIE .... Rule Oriented System for Implementing Expertise   (MCD)
RoSlaw .... Rocznik Slawistyczny [*A publication*]
ROSM .... Revolutionary Organization of Socialist Muslims   (EA-IO)
ROSMAR ... Rosmarinus [*Rosemary*] [*Pharmacology*]   (ROG)
ROSO .... Relay-Operated Sampling Oscilloscope
RoSPA .... Royal Society for the Prevention of Accidents [*British*]
Ross Cont ... Ross on Contracts   (DLA)
Ross Conv ... Ross's Lectures on Conveyancing, Etc. [*Sc.*]   (DLA)
Ross LC ...... Ross's Leading Cases on Commercial Law [*England*]   (DLA)
Ross LC ...... Ross's Leading Cases in the Law of Scotland [*Land Rights*]
             [*1638-1840*]   (DLA)
Ross Ldg Cas ... Ross's Leading Cases on Commercial Law   (DLA)
Ross Ldg Cas ... Ross's Leading Cases in the Law of Scotland [*Land
             Rights*]   (DLA)
Ross Lead Cas ... Ross's Leading Cases [*England*]   (DLA)
Ross Lead Cas ... Ross's Leading Cases in the Law of Scotland [*Land
             Rights*] [*1638-1840*]   (DLA)
Ross V & P ... Ross on Vendors and Purchasers [*2nd ed.*] [*1826*]   (DLA)
ROST .... Regional Office of Science and Technology [*Marine
             science*]   (MSC)
ROSTA ...... Roads and Streets [*A publication*]
ROSTA Bull ... ROSTA [*Victoria. Road Safety and Traffic Authority*] Bulletin
             [*A publication*]
Rost Krist ... Rost Kristallov [*A publication*]
Rostl Vyroba ... Rostlinna Vyroba [*A publication*]
Rostl Vyroba Cesk Akad Zemed Ustav Vedeckotech Inf Zemed ...
             Rostlinna Vyroba-Ceskoslovenska Akademie Zemedelska.
             Ustav Vedeckotechnickych Informaci pro Zemedelstvi [*A
             publication*]
Rostocker Phys Manuskr ... Rostocker Physikalische Manuskripte [*A
             publication*]
Rostock Math Kolloq ... Rostocker Mathematisches Kolloquium [*A
             publication*]

Rostov Gidrometeorol Obs Sb Rab ... Rostovskaya Gidrometeorologicheskaya Observatoriya. Sbornik Rabot [*A publication*]
Rostov-na Donu Gos Ped Inst Fiz Mat Fak Ucen Zap ... Rostovskii-na Donu Gosudarstvennyi Pedagogiceskii Institut. Fiziko-Matematiceskii Fakultet Ucenye Zapiski [*A publication*]
Rostov-na-Donu Gos Univ Ucen Zap ... Rostovskii-na-Donu Gosudarstvennyi Universitet. Ucenyi Zapiski [*A publication*]
Rost Ustoich Rast ... Rost i Ustoichivost Rastenii [*A publication*]
Rost Ustoich Rast Respub Mezhved Sb ... Rost i Ustoichivost' Rastenii Respublikanskii Mezhvedomstvennyi Sbornik [*A publication*]
ROT .... RADAR on Target
ROT .... Range on Target
ROT .... Rate of Turn
ROT .... Red Oak Tannins [*in leaves*]
ROT .... Remaining Operating Time   (NASA)
ROT .... Remedial Occupation Therapy
ROT .... Reserve Oil Tank   (MSA)
ROT .... Reusable Orbital Transport [*Aerospace*]
ROT .... Right Occipitotransverse [*A fetal position*] [*Obstetrics*]
ROT .... Right Outer Thigh [*Injection site*]
ROT .... Rotary   (AAG)
ROT .... Rotate   (AAG)
ROT .... Rotating Light [*Navigation signal*]
ROT .... Rotor   (ADA)
ROT .... Rotorua [*New Zealand*] [*Seismograph station code, US Geological Survey*] [*Closed*]   (SEIS)
ROT .... Rotorua [*New Zealand*] [*Airport symbol*]   (OAG)
ROT .... Rule of Thumb
ROTAA .... Road Tar [*A publication*]
ROTAB .... Rotable Table
ROT ABCCC ... Rotational Airborne Command and Control Center   (CINC)
ROTAC ...... Rotary Oscillating Torque Actuators
ROTAD ...... Round Table [*A publication*]
Rotation Method Crystallogr ... Rotation Method in Crystallography [*A publication*]
ROT AWS ... Rotational Air Weather Squadron   (CINC)
ROT BS ..... Rotational Bomb Squadron   (CINC)
ROTC .... Reserve Officers Training Corps [*Separate units for Army, Navy, Air Force*]
ROTCC ...... Receiver-Off-Hook Tone Connecting Circuit
Rot Chart ... Rotulus Chartarum [*Charter Roll*] [*Latin*]   (DLA)
Rot Claus ... Rotuli Clause [*Close Roll*] [*Latin*]   (DLA)
ROTCM ..... Reserve Officers Training Corps Manual   (AABC)
ROTCR ...... Reserve Officers' Training Corps Region   (AABC)
Rot Cur Reg ... Rotuli Curiae Regis 1194-99   (DLA)
ROTE .... Range Optical Tracking Equipment   (AAG)
ROTE .... Role of Occupational Therapy with the Elderly [*Project*]
ROTE AREFS ... Rotating Air Refueling Squadron   (CINC)
ROTEL .... Reference Our Telegram   (FAAC)
ROTEL .... Rolling Hotel [*European bus-tour system*]
ROTEL .... Rotational Telemetry
Rotenburg Schr ... Rotenburger Schriften [*A publication*]
ROTERO ..... Roterodamum [*Rotterdam*]   (ROG)
ROTF .... Russian Orthodox Theological Fund   (EA)
ROT FIS ..... Rotating Fighter Interceptor Squadron   (CINC)
ROT FIS DET ... Rotating Fighter Interceptor Squadron Detachment   (CINC)
Rot Flor ...... Rotae Florentine [*Reports of the Supreme Court, of Florence*]   (DLA)
ROTG .... Rotating   (FAAC)
ROTH .... Read-Only Tape Handler
Rothamsted Exp Stn Rep ... Rothamsted Experimental Station. Report [*A publication*]
Rothamsted Exp Stn Rep Part 1 ... Rothamsted Experimental Station. Report. Part 1 [*A publication*]
Rothamsted Exp Stn Rep Part 2 ... Rothamsted Experimental Station. Report. Part 2 [*A publication*]
ROTHR .... Relocatable Over-the-Horizon RADAR
ROTI .... Range Optical Tracking Instrument
ROTI .... Recording Optical Tracking Instrument [*Missiles*]
ROTI .... Reinforced Oxide Throat Insert
RoTKan ...... Roczniki Teologiczno-Kanoniczne [*Lubin*] [*A publication*]
ROTL .... Remote Office Test Line [*Bell Laboratories*]
ROTLT/BCN ... Rotating Light or Beacon
ROTN .... Rotation   (ROG)
ROTOB .... Romania Today [*A publication*]
ROTOMT ..... Rotometer
ROTP .... Regular Officer Training Plan [*Canada*]
Rot Parl ..... Rotulae Parliamentariae   (DLA)
Rot Pat .... Rotuli Patenes   (DLA)
Rot Plac ..... Rotuli Placitorum   (DLA)
ROTR .... Receive-Only Typing Reperforator
ROTR .... Rotator [*Electromagnetics*]
ROT RCS .... Rotational RADAR Calibration Squadron   (CINC)
ROTR-S/P ... Receive-Only Typing Reperforator - Series to Parallel
ROTS .... RADAR Observer Testing System
ROTS .... Range on Target Signal
ROTS .... Remote Operator Task Station [*Air Force*]
ROTS .... Rotary Out Trunk Switch [*Telecommunications*]   (TEL)

ROTSAL .... Rotate and Scale [*Data processing*]
ROTT .... Rate of Turntable
ROTT .... Reorder Tone Trunks [*Telecommunications*]   (TEL)
ROT TAS ... Rotational Tactical Assault Squadron   (CINC)
ROT TBS ... Rotational Tactical Bomber Squadron   (CINC)
ROT TCS ... Rotational Troop Carrier Squadron   (CINC)   ʻ
ROTTER ..... Rotterdam   (ROG)
ROT TX ...... Rotating Transformer
Rotuli Curiae Reg ... Rotuli Curiae Regis [*England*]   (DLA)
ROTV .... Reusable Orbital Transport Vehicle [*Aerospace*]
ROTWX ..... Reference Our TWX [*Teletypewriter communications*]   (FAAC)
ROU .... Radio Officers Union [*British*]
ROU .... Rougiers [*France*] [*Seismograph station code, US Geological Survey*] [*Closed*]   (SEIS)
ROU .... Russe [*Bulgaria*] [*Airport symbol*]   (OAG)
ROUHA ...... Ropa a Uhlie [*A publication*]
ROUL .... Rouletted   (ROG)
Roum P ..... Roumanian Pharmacopoeia [*A publication*]
Round Dom ... Round's Law of Domicil [*1861*]   (DLA)
Round L & A ... Round's Right of Light and Air [*1868*]   (DLA)
Round Lien ... Round's Law of Lien [*1863*]   (DLA)
Round Tab ... Round Table [*A publication*]
ROUS .... [*The*] Rouse Co. [*NASDAQ symbol*]   (NQ)
Rouse Conv ... Rouse's Practical Conveyancer [*3rd ed.*] [*1867*]   (DLA)
Rouse Cop ... Rouse's Copyhold Enfranchisement Manual [*3rd ed.*] [*1866*]   (DLA)
Rouse Pr Mort ... Rouse's Precedents and Conveyances of Mortgaged Property   (DLA)
ROUT .... Routine   (AABC)
Roux Archiv EntwMech Organ ... Roux Archiv fuer Entwicklungsmechanik der Organismen [*A publication*]
ROV .... Refined Oil of Vitriol
ROV .... Remote Operated Valve   (KSC)
ROV .... Remote Optical Viewing
ROV .... Remotely Operated Vehicle [*Underwater robot*]
ROV .... Repairs to Other Vessels
ROV .... Report Over   (FAAC)
ROV .... Report of Visit [*LIMRA*]
ROV .... Restricted Overhaul   (MCD)
ROV .... Risk, Originality, and Virtuousity [*Scoring considerations in gymnastics competition*]
ROV .... Rostov [*USSR*] [*Airport symbol*]   (OAG)
ROVAC ...... Rotary Vane Air Cycle   (MCD)
ROVD .... Relay-Operated Voltage Divider
Rov Koezlem ... Rovartani Koezlemenyek [*A publication*]
ROVNITE .... Remaining Overnight
ROVS .... Remote Optical Viewing System
ROVYA ...... Rostlinna Vyroba [*A publication*]
ROW .... Relocate Out of Washington [*Navy*]   (NG)
ROW .... Requisition on Warehouse [*Nuclear energy*]   (NRCH)
ROW .... Rest of World
ROW .... Right of Way [*Also, RW*]
ROW .... Risk of War
ROW .... Roll Welding
ROW .... Roswell [*New Mexico*] [*Airport symbol*]   (OAG)
ROW .... Rowesville [*South Carolina*] [*Seismograph station code, US Geological Survey*]   (SEIS)
ROWE .... Rowe Furniture Corp. [*NASDAQ symbol*]   (NQ)
Rowe .... Rowe's Interesting Cases [*England and Ireland*] [*1798-1823*]   (DLA)
Rowe .... Rowe's Interesting Parliamentary and Military Cases   (DLA)
Rowell .... Rowell's Reports [*45-52 Vermont*]   (DLA)
Rowell El Cas ... Rowell's Contested Election Cases   (DLA)
Row Eng Const ... Rowland's Manual of the English Constitution [*1859*]   (DLA)
Rowe Rep ... Rowe's Irish Reports   (DLA)
Rowett Res Inst Annu Rep Stud Anim Nutr Allied Sci ... Rowett Research Institute. Annual Report. Studies in Animal Nutrition and Allied Sciences [*A publication*]
ROW/FEPA ... Riders of the Wind, the Field Events Player's Association   (EA)
ROWJ .... Records of Oceanographic Works in Japan [*A publication*]
ROWPE ...... Reverse Osmosis Water Purification Equipment   (MCD)
ROW & PF ... Rake Out, Wedge, and Point Flashings [*Construction*]
ROWPS ...... Reverse Osmosis Water Purification System   (MCD)
ROWPU ...... Reverse Osmosis Water Purification Unit [*Army*]   (RDA)
ROWS .... RADAR Ocean Wave Spectrometer
ROX .... Roseau, MN [*Location identifier*] [*FAA*]   (FAAL)
ROX .... Roxburgh [*New Zealand*] [*Seismograph station code, US Geological Survey*]   (SEIS)
ROXB .... Roxburghe [*Style of bookbinding*]   (ROG)
ROXB .... Roxburghshire [*County in Scotland*]
ROXL .... Rotate through X Left [*Data processing*]
ROXR .... Rotate through X Right [*Data processing*]
ROY .... Moultonboro, NH [*Location identifier*] [*FAA*]   (FAAL)
ROY .... Rio Mayo [*Argentina*] [*Airport symbol*]   (OAG)
ROY .... Royal
Roy .... Royale & Allegro-Royale [*Record label*]
Roy Aeronaut Soc J ... Royal Aeronautical Society. Journal [*A publication*]
Royal .... [*The*] Royal Magazine [*A publication*]

Royal Astron Soc Canada Jour ... Royal Astronomical Society of Canada. Journal [*A publication*]

Royal Astron Soc Geophys Jour ... Royal Astronomical Society. Geophysical Journal [*A publication*]

Royal Astron Soc Monthly Notices Geophys Supp ... Royal Astronomical Society. Monthly Notices. Geophysical Supplements [*A publication*]

Royal Astron Soc Quart Jour ... Royal Astronomical Society. Quarterly Journal [*A publication*]

Royal Aust Army Ed Corps News ... Royal Australian Army. Educational Corps. Newsletter [*A publication*]

Royal Aust Chem Inst J & Proc ... Royal Australian Chemical Institute. Journal and Proceedings [*A publication*]

Royal Aust Chem Inst Proc ... Royal Australian Chemical Institute. Proceedings [*A publication*]

Royal Aust Hist Soc J ... Royal Australian Historical Society. Journal and Proceedings [*A publication*]

Royal Aust Hist Soc J & Proc ... Royal Australian Historical Society. Journal and Proceedings [*A publication*]

Royalauto... Royalauto [*Royal Automobile Club of Victoria*] Journal [*A publication*]

Royal Bank Can Mo Letter ... Royal Bank of Canada. Monthly Letter [*A publication*]

Royal Empire Soc News ... Royal Empire Society. News [*A publication*]

Royal Geog Soc Asia SA Branch Proc ... Royal Geographical Society of Australasia. South Australian Branch. Proceedings [*A publication*]

Royal Hist Soc Q Hist Misc ... Royal Historical Society of Queensland. Historical Miscellanea [*A publication*]

Royal Hist Soc QJ ... Royal Historical Society of Queensland. Journal [*A publication*]

Royal Hist Soc Trans ... Royal Historical Society. Transactions [*A publication*]

Royal Hort Soc J ... Royal Horticultural Society. Journal [*A publication*]

Royal Inst of British Archts Trans ... Royal Institute of British Architects. Transactions [*A publication*]

Royal Microscopical Soc Proc ... Royal Microscopical Society. Proceedings [*A publication*]

Royal Ontario Mus Div Zoology and Palaeontology Contr ... Royal Ontario Museum. Division of Zoology and Palaeontology. Contributions [*A publication*]

Royal Perth Hospital J ... Royal Perth Hospital. Journal [*A publication*]

Royal Prince Alfred Hospital J ... Royal Prince Alfred Hospital. Journal [*A publication*]

Royal Soc Arts Jnl ... Royal Society of Arts. Journal [*A publication*]

Royal Soc Canada Proc ... Royal Society of Canada. Proceedings [*A publication*]

Royal Soc Hlth J ... Royal Society of Health. Journal [*A publication*]

Royal Soc NSW J & Proc ... Royal Society of New South Wales. Journal and Proceedings [*A publication*]

Royal Soc Q Proc ... Royal Society of Queensland. Proceedings [*A publication*]

Royal Soc SA Trans ... Royal Society of South Australia. Transactions [*A publication*]

Royal Soc Tasmania Papers and Proc ... Royal Society of Tasmania. Papers and Proceedings [*A publication*]

Royal Soc Tas Papers & Proc ... Royal Society of Tasmania. Papers and Proceedings [*A publication*]

Royal Soc Vic Proc ... Royal Society of Victoria. Proceedings [*A publication*]

Royal Soc Victoria Proc ... Royal Society of Victoria. Proceedings [*A publication*]

Royal Zoological Soc NSW Proc ... Royal Zoological Society of New South Wales. Proceedings [*A publication*]

Roy Arch Inst Can J ... Royal Architectural Institute of Canada. Journal [*A publication*]

Roy Astron Soc Mem ... Royal Astronomical Society. Memoirs [*A publication*]

Roy Aust Hist J ... Royal Australian Historical Society. Journal [*A publication*]

Roy Aust Hist Soc J Proc ... Royal Australian Historical Society. Journal and Proceedings [*A publication*]

Roy Can Inst Trans ... Royal Canadian Institute. Transactions [*A publication*]

Roy Dig ...... Royall's Digest Virginia Reports   (DLA)

Roy Eng J... Royal Engineers Journal [*A publication*]

ROYGBIV ... Red, Orange, Yellow, Green, Blue, Indigo, Violet [*Primary Colors*] [*Mnemonic aid*]

Roy His S.... Royal Historical Society. Transactions [*A publication*]

Roy Hist Soc Qld Hist Misc ... Royal Historical Society of Queensland. Historical Miscellanea [*A publication*]

Roy Hist Soc Qld J ... Royal Historical Society of Queensland. Journal [*A publication*]

Roy Hist Soc Trans ... Royal Historical Society. Transactions [*A publication*]

Roy Hist Soc Vic News ... Royal Historical Society of Victoria. Newsletter [*A publication*]

Roy Hort Soc J ... Royal Horticultural Society. Journal [*A publication*]

Roy Inst Brit Arch J ... Royal Institute of British Architects. Journal [*A publication*]

Roy Inst Nav Architects Quart Trans ... Royal Institution of Naval Architects [*London*]. Quarterly Transactions [*A publication*]

Roy Inst Ph ... Royal Institute of Philosophy. Lectures [*A publication*]

ROYLC .... Royalty Ventures [*NASDAQ symbol*]   (NQ)

Roy Meteorol Soc Q J ... Royal Meteorological Society. Quarterly Journal [*A publication*]

Roy Microscop Soc Proc ... Royal Microscopical Society. Proceedings [*A publication*]

Roy Micros Soc J ... Royal Microscopical Society. Journal [*A publication*]

Roy Soc Arts J ... Royal Society of Arts. Journal [*A publication*]

Roy Soc Can ... Royal Society of Canada. Proceedings and Transactions [*A publication*]

Roy Soc of Canada Trans ... Royal Society of Canada. Proceedings and Transactions [*A publication*]

Roy Soc Edinb Trans ... Royal Society of Edinburgh. Transactions [*A publication*]

Roy Soc of Edinburgh Trans ... Royal Society of Edinburgh. Transactions [*A publication*]

Roy Soc Hea ... Royal Society of Health. Journal [*A publication*]

Roy Soc of London Philos Trans ... Royal Society of London. Philosophical Transactions [*A publication*]

Roy Soc Lond Philos Trans ... Royal Society of London. Philosophical Transactions [*A publication*]

Roy Soc of New South Wales Jour and Proc ... Royal Society of New South Wales. Journal and Proceedings [*A publication*]

Roy Soc NSW J ... Royal Society of New South Wales. Journal [*A publication*]

Roy Soc NSW J & Proc ... Royal Society of New South Wales. Journal and Proceedings [*A publication*]

Roy Soc NZ J ... Royal Society of New Zealand. Journal [*A publication*]

Roy Soc NZ Proc ... Royal Society of New Zealand. Proceedings [*A publication*]

Roy Soc NZ Trans ... Royal Society of New Zealand. Transactions [*A publication*]

Roy Soc NZ Trans Bot ... Royal Society of New Zealand. Transactions. Botany [*A publication*]

Roy Soc NZ Trans Earth Sci ... Royal Society of New Zealand. Transactions. Earth Sciences [*A publication*]

Roy Soc NZ Trans Gen ... Royal Society of New Zealand. Transactions. General [*A publication*]

Roy Soc NZ Trans Geol ... Royal Society of New Zealand. Transactions. Geology [*A publication*]

Roy Soc NZ Trans Zool ... Royal Society of New Zealand. Transactions. Zoology [*A publication*]

Roy Soc Qld Proc ... Royal Society of Queensland. Proceedings [*A publication*]

Roy Soc SA Trans ... Royal Society of South Australia. Transactions [*A publication*]

Roy Soc Tas Papers ... Royal Society of Tasmania. Papers and Proceedings [*A publication*]

Roy Soc Vic Proc ... Royal Society of Victoria. Proceedings [*A publication*]

Roy Soc WA J ... Royal Society of Western Australia. Journal [*A publication*]

Roy Stat Soc J ... Royal Statistical Society. Journal [*A publication*]

Roy Telev Soc J ... Royal Television Society. Journal [*A publication*]

Roy Town Plan Inst ... Royal Town Planning Institute. Journal [*A publication*]

Roy West Aust Hist Soc J Proc ... Royal Western Australian Historical Society. Journal and Proceedings [*A publication*]

Roy Zool Soc NSW Proc ... Royal Zoological Society of New South Wales. Proceedings [*A publication*]

Roz Cesk Akad ... Rozpravy Ceskoslovenske Akademie Ved [*A publication*]

Rozhl Chir ... Rozhledy v Chirurgii [*A publication*]

Rozhl Tuberk Nemocech Plicn ... Rozhledy v Tuberkulose a v Nemocech Plicnich [*A publication*]

Roz Narod Tech Muz Praze ... Rozpravy Narodniho Technickeho Muzea v Praze [*A publication*]

Rozpr Akad Roln Szczecinie ... Rozprawy. Akademia Rolnicza w Szczecinie [*A publication*]

Rozpravy CSAV ... Rozpravy Ceskoslovenske Akademie Ved [*A publication*]

Rozprawy Elektrotech ... Rozprawy Elektrotechniczne. Polska Akademia Nauk. Instytut Technologii Elektronowej. [*A publication*]

Rozprawy Politech Poznan ... Rozprawy. Politechnika Poznanska [*A publication*]

Rozpr Cesk Akad Rada Tech Ved ... Rozpravy Ceskoslovenske Akademie Ved. Rada Technickych Ved [*Czechoslovakia*] [*A publication*]

Rozpr Cesk Akad Ved Rada Mat Prir Ved ... Rozpravy Ceskoslovenske Akademie Ved. Rada Matematickych a Prirodnich Ved [*A publication*]

Rozpr Cesk Akad Ved Rada Tech Ved ... Rozpravy Ceskoslovenske Akademie Ved. Rada Technickych Ved [*A publication*]

Rozpr Elektrotech ... Rozprawy Elektrotechniczne [*A publication*]

Rozpr Hydrotech ... Rozprawy Hydrotechniczne [*A publication*]

Rozpr Inz ... Rozprawy Inzynierskie [*A publication*]

Rozpr Politech Poznan ... Rozprawy. Politechnika Poznanska [*A publication*]

Rozpr Wydz Nauk Med Pol Akad Nauk ... Rozprawy Wydzialu Nauk Medyczynch Polska Akademia Nauk [*A publication*]

RP.............. Bristol-Myers Co. [*Research code symbol*]

RP.............. Problems of Reconstruction [*British*] [*World War II*]

RP.............. Providence Public Library, Providence, RI [*Library symbol*] [*Library of Congress*]   (LCLS)

RP.............. RADAR Plot   (DEN)

RP.............. Radial Artery Pressure [*Medicine*]

RP.............. Radial Pulse [*Medicine*]

RP.............. Radiation Pressure

RP.............. Radiation Protection

R-P .... Radiologist-Pediatric

RP .... Raid Plotter
RP .... Rally Point [*Air Force*]
RP .... Raphe Pallidus [*Anatomy*]
RP .... Rate Package   (AAG)
RP .... Rated Pressure   (NATG)
RP .... Raynaud's Phenomenon [*Medicine*]
RP .... Re-Geniusing Project   (EA)
RP .... Reactor Pressure [*Nuclear energy*]   (NRCH)
RP .... Reactor Projects   (NRCH)
RP .... Reader Printer
RP .... Reader Punch
RP .... Readiness Potential
RP .... Real Part [*of complex number*]   (DEN)
RP .... Real Property
RP .... Rear Projection [*Television*]
RP .... Receipt Pass   (AAG)
RP .... Receive Processor
RP .... Received Pronunciation [*of the English language*]
RP .... Reception Poor [*Radio logs*]
RP .... Receptor Potential
RP .... Recommended Practice
RP .... Recorder Point   (MCD)
RP .... Records of the Past [*A publication*]   (BJA)
RP .... Recovery Phase   (IEEE)
R & P .... Recruitment and Placement   (MCD)
RP .... Red Phosphorus [*Military*]   (RDA)
RP .... Reddish Purple
RP .... Reference Paper
RP .... Reference Pattern   (NATG)
RP .... Reference Point
RP .... Reference Publication   (MCD)
RP .... Reference Pulse
RP .... Refilling Point
RP .... Reformed Presbyterian
RP .... Refractory Period [*Medicine*]
RP .... Regimental Police [*British*]
RP .... Registered Plumbers [*British*]
RP .... Regius Professor [*The King's Professor*] [*British*]
RP .... Regulatory Peptides [*A publication*]
RP .... Reinforced Plastic
RP .... Relative Pressure   (KSC)
RP .... Relay Panel
RP .... Release Point [*Ground traffic*]
RP .... Relief Pitcher [*Baseball*]
RP .... Remote Pickup
RP .... Remote Printer   (BUR)
RP .... Renaissance Papers [*A publication*]
RP .... Rent Regulation [*Office of Price Stabilization*] [*Economic Stabilization Agency*]   (DLA)
RP .... Reorder Point [*Army*]
RP .... Repair Period   (NASA)
RP .... Repeater
RP .... Repetitively Pulsed   (MCD)
RP .... Replaceable Pad   (MCD)
RP .... Replacement Pilot [*Navy*]
RP .... Reply Paid
RP .... Report Immediately upon Passing [*Fix altitude*] [*Aviation*]   (FAAC)
RP .... Reporting Post [*RADAR*]
RP .... Reprint
RP .... Reproducers [*JETDS nomenclature*] [*Military*]   (CET)
RP .... Republic of Panama
RP .... Republic of the Philippines
RP .... Republican Party [*Iraq*]   (BJA)
RP .... Republikeinse Party van Suidwesafrika [*Republican Party of South West Africa*] [*Namibian*]   (PPW)
RP .... Repurchase Agreement [*Securities*]
RP .... Res Publica [*Latin*]
RP .... Research Paper
RP .... Research Publications
RP .... Reserve Personnel [*Air Force*]   (AFM)
R & P .... Reserve and Process   (NASA)
RP .... Reserve Purchase
RP .... Resistance Plate   (AAG)
RP .... Resolving Power [*of a lens*]
RP .... Respiratory Rate:Pulse Rate [*Index*] [*Medicine*]
RP .... Resting Pulse [*Physiology*]
RP .... Restoration Priority   (CET)
RP .... Resupply Provisions [*NASA*]   (KSC)
RP .... Retained Personnel
RP .... Retinitis Pigmentosa [*Eye disease*] [*Ophthalmology*]
RP .... Retinyl Palmitate [*Organic chemistry*]
RP .... Retrograde Pyelography [*Medicine*]
RP .... Retroperitoneal [*Medicine*]
R/P .... Return to Port [*for Orders*]
RP .... Return of Post
RP .... Return Premium
RP .... Reverend Pere [*Reverend Father*] [*French*]
RP .... Reverendus Pater [*Reverend Father*] [*Latin*]
R-P .... Reversed Phase [*Chromatography*]
RP .... Revertive Pulsing

RP .... Revision Proposal   (NG)
RP .... Revista de Portugal [*A publication*]
Rp .... Revoked or Rescinded in Part [*Existing regulation or order abrogated in part*] [*Used in Shepard's Citations*]   (DLA)
RP .... Revue de Paris [*A publication*]
RP .... Revue de Philologie, de Litterature, et d'Histoire Anciennes [*A publication*]
RP .... Revue Philosophique [*A publication*]
RP .... Revue de Phonetique [*Paris*] [*A publication*]
R/P .... Reward/Penalty
RP .... Rhone-Poulenc [*France*] [*Research code symbol*]
RP .... Right Traffic Pattern [*Aviation*]   (FAAC)
R/P .... Rise/Passive   (MCD)
RP .... Ristocetin-Polymyxin [*Antibacterial mixture*]
RP .... Rocket Projectile
RP .... Rocket Propellant [*Air Force*]
RP .... Rockland and Pollin [*Scale*] [*Psychology*]
RP .... Roll Pad   (MCD)
RP .... Rollback Process [*Telecommunications*]   (TEL)
RP .... Romance Philology [*A publication*]
RP .... Ron Pair!
RP .... Room and Pillar [*Coal mining*]
RP .... Rotatable Pool Quantity
RP .... Rotuli Parliamentorum [*1278-1533*] [*England*]   (DLA)
RP .... Round Punch
RP .... Route Package   (CINC)
RP .... Royal Panopticon   (ROG)
RP .... [*Member of*] Royal Society of Portrait Painters [*British*]
RP .... Rules of Procedure
R & P .... Rules and Procedures   (MSA)
RP .... Rupiah [*Monetary unit in Indonesia*]
RP .... Russow Aviation GmbH & Co. Luftfahrtunternehmen, Frankfurt [*West Germany*] [*ICAO designator*]   (FAAC)
RP .... Rust Preventive
RP .... Specia [*France*] [*Research code symbol*]
RPA .... Executive Air Travel [*Denver, CO*] [*FAA designator*]   (FAAC)
RPA .... Providence Athenaeum, Providence, RI [*Library symbol*] [*Library of Congress*]   (LCLS)
RPA .... RADAR Performance Analyzer
RPA .... Radium Plaque Adaptometer [*Navy*]
RPA .... Random Phase Approximation
RPA .... Rationalist Press Association   (EA-IO)
RPA .... Re-Entrant Process Allocator [*Telecommunications*]   (TEL)
RPA .... Real Property Administrator [*Designation awarded by Building Owners and Managers Institute*]
RPA .... Record and Playback Assembly   (MCD)
RPA .... Record of Procurement Action   (MCD)
RPA .... Redundancy Payments Act [*1965*] [*British*]
RPA .... Regional Plan Association   (EA)
RPA .... Regional Ports Authority [*British*]
RPA .... Registered Public Accountant
RPA .... Relative Peak Area [*Medicine*]
RPA .... Renal Physicians Association [*Washington, DC*]   (EA)
RPA .... Renewal Projects Administration [*HUD*]
RPA .... Request Present Altitude [*Aviation*]   (FAAC)
RPA .... Request for Procurement Action [*Authorization*] [*NASA*]   (NASA)
RPA .... Reserve Personnel, Army
RPA .... Resident Programer Analyst [*Data processing*]
RPA .... Resource Planning Associates, Cambridge, MA [*OCLC symbol*]   (OCLC)
RPA .... Response Profile Analysis [*National Demographics & Lifestyles, Inc.*]
RPA .... Resultant Physiological Acceleration
RPA .... Retarding Potential Analyzer [*NASA*]
RPA .... Retinoylphorbolacetate [*Biochemistry*]
RPa .... Revue de Paris [*A publication*]
RPA .... Revue de Phonetique Appliquee [*Paris*] [*A publication*]
RPA .... Revue Pratique d'Apologetique [*A publication*]
RPA .... Right Pulmonary Artery [*Medicine*]
RPA .... Rolpa [*Nepal*] [*Airport symbol*]   (OAG)
RPA .... RPA [*Royal Prince Alfred Hospital*] Magazine [*A publication*]
RPA .... Rubber Peptizing Agent
RPA .... Rust Prevention Association [*Later, Crop Quality Council*]
RPAA .... Rendiconti. Pontificia Accademia di Archeologia [*A publication*]
RPAA .... Rotating Phase Array Antenna
RPAB .... Brown University, Annmary Brown Memorial Library, Providence, RI [*Library symbol*] [*Library of Congress*]   (LCLS)
R Pac .... Revue du Pacifique. Etudes de Litterature Francaise [*A publication*]
RPACA ...... Reports on the Progress of Applied Chemistry [*A publication*]
RPAE .... Retarding Potential Analyzer Experiment [*NASA*]
RPAG .... Retired Professionals Action Group [*Formed by consumer-advocate Ralph Nader*] [*Absorbed by Gray Panthers*]
RPAH .... Royal Prince Alfred Hospital [*Australia*]
R Palaeobot & Palynol ... Review of Palaeobotany and Palynology [*A publication*]
RPall .... Revue Palladienne [*A publication*]

RPAM .... American Mathematical Society, Providence, RI [*Library symbol*] [*Library of Congress*] (LCLS)
RPAM .... Regional Public Affairs Manager [*Nuclear energy*] (NRCH)
RPAM .... Research in Public Administration and Management [*British*]
RPAO .... Radium Plaque Adaptometer Operator [*Navy*]
RPAODS .... Remotely Piloted Aerial Observation Detection System (MCD)
RPAPC .... Religious Press Associations Postal Coalition [*New York, NY*] (EA)
RPAR .... Rebuttable Presumption Against Regulation [*of pesticides*] [*Environmental Protection Agency*]
R Paraguaya Sociol ... Revista Paraguaya de Sociologia [*A publication*]
R de Paris .. Revue de Paris [*A publication*]
RPAS .... Audubon Society of Rhode Island, Providence, RI [*Library symbol*] [*Library of Congress*] (LCLS)
RPAS .... Reactor Protection Actuating Signal (NRCH)
RPAS .... Review. Polish Academy of Sciences [*A publication*]
RPASMC .... Rubber and Plastic Adhesive and Sealant Manufacturers Council [*Later, Adhesive and Sealant Council*] (EA)
R Pat Cas ... Reports of Patent, Design, and Trade Mark Cases (DLA)
RP-ATLF ... Roscoe Pound - American Trial Lawyers Foundation (EA)
RPaw .... Pawtucket Public Library, Pawtucket, RI [*Library symbol*] [*Library of Congress*] (LCLS)
R Pays Est ... Revue des Pays de l'Est [*A publication*]
RPB .... Belleville, KS [*Location identifier*] [*FAA*] (FAAL)
RPB .... Brown University, Providence, RI [*Library symbol*] [*Library of Congress*] (LCLS)
RPB .... RADAR Plotting Board
RPB .... Regional Preparedness Board [*Military*] (AABC)
RPB .... Research to Prevent Blindness [*An association*] [*New York, NY*] (EA)
RPB .... Resources Protection Board
RPB .... River Purification Board [*British*]
RPB .... Royal Palm Beach Colony Ltd. [*American Stock Exchange symbol*]
RPB .... Royal Protection Branch [*of the London Metropolitan Police*]
Rp B Bk R ... Reprint Bulletin. Book Reviews [*A publication*]
RPBG .... Revised Program and Budget Guidance
RPBH .... Butler Health Center, Providence, RI [*Library symbol*] [*Library of Congress*] (LCLS)
RPB-JH ...... Brown University, John Hay Library of Rare Books annd Special Collections, Providence, RI [*Library symbol*] [*Library of Congress*] (LCLS)
RPB-S .... Brown University, Sciences Library, Providence, RI [*Library symbol*] [*Library of Congress*] (LCLS)
RPBSC .... Rules Peculiar to the Business of the Supreme Court (DLA)
RPC .... Baltimore Regional Planning Commission [*Library network*]
RPC .... RADAR Planning Chart
RPC .... RADAR Processing Center
RPC .... Radiological Physics Center [*National Cancer Institute*]
RPC .... Rapeseed Protein Concentrate [*Food technology*]
RPC .... Real Property Cases [*1843-48*] [*England*] (DLA)
RPC .... Real Property Commissioner's Report [*1832*] [*England*] (DLA)
RPC .... Records Processing Center [*Veterans Administration*]
RPC .... Recruiting Publicity Center [*Military*]
RPC .... Reefed Parachute Canopy
RPC .... Refugee Processing Center (MCD)
RPC .... Regional Personnel Center
RPC .... Regional Planning Commission
RPC .... Regional Preparedness Committee [*Civil Defense*]
RPC .... Registered Protective Circuit
RPC .... Registered Publication Clerk [*or Custodian*] [*Navy*]
RPC .... Reliability Policy Committee (AAG)
RPC .... Remote Position Control
RPC .... Remote Power Controller
RPC .... Remote Process Cell [*Nuclear energy*] (NRCH)
RPC .... Remotely Piloted Craft [*Navy*]
RPC .... Renopericardial Canal [*Medicine*]
RPC .... Repair Parts Catalog
RPC .... Repair Parts Cost (MCD)
RPC .... Reparable Processing Center (AFM)
RPC .... Reply Postcard
RPC .... Report to Commander [*Military*]
RPC .... Reported Post Coastal (NATG)
RPC .... Reports of English Patent Cases (DLA)
RPC .... Reports of Patent Cases [*Legal*] [*British*]
RPC .... Reports of Patent, Design, and Trade Mark Cases [*England*] (DLA)
RPC .... Republican Policy Committee
RPC .... Request the Pleasure of Your Company [*On invitations*] (DSUE)
RPC .... Requisition Processing Cycle (MCD)
RPC .... Research Planning Conference [*LIMRA*]
RPC .... Resource Policy Center [*Dartmouth College*] [*Research center*] (RCD)
RPC .... Restrictive Practices Court [*Legal*] [*British*]
RPC .... Restructured Pork Chop [*Food industry*]
RPC .... Reticularis Pontis Caudalis [*Brain anatomy*]
RPC .... Revenue Properties Company Ltd. [*American Stock Exchange symbol*] [*Toronto Stock Exchange symbol*]
RPC .... Reverse-Phase Chromatography

RPC .... Reverse-Phase Column
RPC .... River Patrol Craft [*Military*] (CINC)
RPC .... Romanian Philatelic Club (EA)
RPC .... Row Parity Check (IEEE)
RPC .... Royal Pioneer Corps [*British*]
RPC .... Rules of Practice in Patent Cases [*A publication*]
RPC .... Rural Political Cadre [*Vietnam*]
RPC .... Russian People's Center (EA)
RPCA .... Reverse Passive Anaphylaxis [*Immunology*]
RPCAS .... Requisition Priority Code Analysis System [*Army*]
RPCC .... Reactor Physics Constants Center [*Argonne National Laboratory*]
RPCC .... Remote Process Crane Cave [*Nuclear energy*] (NRCH)
RPCCA ...... Red Poll Cattle Club of America [*Later, ARPA*] (EA)
RPCF .... Reiter Protein Complement Fixation [*Obsolete test for syphilis*]
RPCH .... Reformed Presbyterian Church
RPCH .... Rospatch Corp. [*NASDAQ symbol*] (NQ)
RPCI .... Regroupement des Partis de la Cote-D'Ivoire [*Regroupment of the Parties of the Ivory Coast*]
RP/CI .... Reinforced Plastics/Composites Institute (EA)
RPCK .... Renopericardial Canal, Kidney [*Medicine*]
RP/CL .... Reporting Post, Coastal Low [*RADAR*]
RPCM .... Rassemblement Populaire Caledonien et Metropolitain [*Caledonian and Metropolitan Popular Rally*] (PPW)
RP/CM ...... Reporting Post, Coastal Medium [*RADAR*]
RPCO .... Reclamation Program Control Officer [*Military*] (AFIT)
RPCO .... Repco, Inc. [*NASDAQ symbol*] (NQ)
RPCP .... Radioisotope-Powered Cardiac Pacemaker (MCD)
RPCP .... Renopericardial Canal, Pericardium [*Medicine*]
RPCR .... Rassemblement pour la Caledonie dans la Republique [*Popular Caledonian Rally for the Republic*] (PPW)
RPCRAAIO ... Receive and Process Complaints and Requests for Assistance, Advice, or Information Only [*Army*] (AABC)
RPC Rep.... Real Property Commissioner's Report [*1832*] [*England*] (DLA)
RPCRS .... Reactor Protection Control Rod System (IEEE)
RPCS .... Reactor Plant Control System (NRCH)
RPCSB .... Rivista di Patologia Clinica e Sperimentale [*A publication*]
RPCVCCA ... Returned Peace Corps Volunteers Committee on Central America (EA)
RPD .... RADAR Planning Device
RPD .... RADAR Prediction Device
RPD .... Radiation Protection Dosimetry [*A publication*]
RPD .... Radioisotope Power Device
RPD .... Rapid (AAG)
RPD .... Reactive Plasma Deposition
RPD .... Reactor Plant Designer (NRCH)
RPD .... Reflex Plasma Discharge
RPD .... Regius Professor of Divinity (ROG)
RPD .... Relative Power Density
RPD .... Renewal Parts Data (MSA)
RPD .... Repadre Resources Ltd. [*Vancouver Stock Exchange symbol*]
RPD .... Rerum Politicarum Doctor [*Doctor of Political Science*]
RPD .... Reserves Available to Support Private, Noninterbank Deposits [*Federal Reserve System*]
RPD .... Resistance Pressure Detector
RPD .... Respiratory Protective Device [*Medicine*]
RPD .... Retarding Potential Difference (IEEE)
RPD .... Retired Pay Defense (NVT)
RPD .... Rhode Island School of Design, Providence, RI [*Library symbol*] [*Library of Congress*] (LCLS)
RPD .... Rocket Propulsion Department [*Royal Aircraft Establishment*] [*British*]
RPDED ...... Revue du Palais de la Deouverte [*A publication*]
RPDES ...... Research Program Development and Evaluation Staff [*Department of Agriculture*]
RPDF .... Radiation Protection Design Features (NRCH)
RPDH .... Reserve Shutdown Planned Derated Hours [*Electronics*] (IEEE)
RPDL .... Radioisotope Process Development Laboratory [*ORNL*]
RPDL .... Rensselaer Polytechnic Institute Plasma Dynamics Laboratory [*Research center*] (RCD)
RPDL .... Repair Parts Decision List [*Military*] (CAAL)
RPDMRC ... Reference or Partial Description Method Reason Code (MCD)
RPDO .... Repair Parts Directive Order
RPDR .... Reproducer (MSA)
RPDS .... Rapids (MCD)
RPDS .... Retired Personnel Data System [*Air Force*]
RPDt .... Registered Professional Dietitian
RPDWR ..... Revised Primary Drinking Water Regulations
RPE .... Elmwood Public Library, Providence, RI [*Library symbol*] [*Library of Congress*] (LCLS)
RPE .... Radial Probable Error (IEEE)
RPE .... Range Planning Estimate (MUGU)
RPE .... Range Probable Error [*Formerly, Range Error Probable*] [*Air Force*] (NATG)
RPE .... Rating of Perceived Exertion
RPE .... Reformed Protestant Episcopal
RPE .... Registered Professional Engineer (IEEE)
RPE .... Related Payroll Expense

RPE .... Reliability Project Engineer   (NASA)
RPE .... Remote Peripheral Equipment   (IEEE)
RPE .... Repair Parts Estimate   (MCD)
RPE .... Report of Patients Evacuated [*Aeromedical evacuation*]
RPE .... Resource Planning and Evaluation   (NRCH)
RPE .... Retinal Pigment Epithelium
RPE .... Rocket Propulsion Establishment [*British*]   (KSC)
RPE .... Ron Pair Enterprises [*Division of Wilson, Inc.*]
RPE .... Rotating Platinum Electrode [*Electrochemistry*]
RPEA .... Regional Planning and Evaluation Agency [*California State Board of Education*]
RPed .... Revue Pedagogique [*A publication*]
RPEng .... Providence Engineering Society, Providence, RI [*Library symbol*] [*Library of Congress*]   (LCLS)
RPEP .... Register of Planned Emergency Procedures
R Pernambucana Desenvolvimento ... Revista Pernambucana de Desenvolvimento [*A publication*]
R Peruana Derecho Internac ... Revista Peruana de Derecho Internacional [*A publication*]
RPETY .... Royal Dutch Petroleum New York ADR [*NASDAQ symbol*]   (NQ)
RPF .... Radio Position Finding [*A term for RADAR before early 1942*]
RPF .... Radio Proximity Fuze
RPF .... Radiometer Performance Factor
RPF .... Rassemblement du Peuple Francais [*Rally of the French People*]
RPF .... Real Property Facilities [*Army*]   (AABC)
RPF .... Reduced Physical Fidelity   (MCD)
RPF .... Reformatorische Politieke Federatie [*Reformist Political Federation*] [*The Netherlands*]   (PPE)
RPF .... Region Peaking Factor [*Nuclear energy*]   (NRCH)
RPF .... Registered Professional Forester
RPF .... Relaxed Pelvic Floor [*Medicine*]
RPF .... Remote Processing Facility   (MCD)
RPF .... Renal Plasma Flow [*Medicine*]
RPF .... Repair Parts Facility   (MCD)
RPF .... Revista Portuguesa de Filologia [*A publication*]
RPF .... Revue de la Pensee Francaise [*A publication*]
RPF .... Right Panel Front [*Nuclear energy*]   (NRCH)
RPF .... Rotable Pool Factor   (MCD)
RPFC .... Ray Price Fan Club [*Harrisburg, PA*]   (EA)
RPFC .... Recurrent Peak Forward Current
RPFCA .... Revue Pratique du Froid et du Conditionnement de l'Air [*Later, Journal RPF*] [*A publication*]
RPFE .... Revue Philosophique de la France et de l'Etranger [*A publication*]
RPFFB .... RP [*Retinitis Pigmentosa*] Foundation Fighting Blindness [*Baltimore, MD*]   (EA)
RPFilos...... Revista Portuguesa de Filosofia [*A publication*]
RPFL .... Revue de Philologie Francaise et de Litterature [*A publication*]
RPFOD ...... Reported for Duty   (FAAC)
RPG .... Radiation Protection Guide [*AEC*]
RPG .... Radioisotopic Power Generator [*Navy*]
RPG .... Rampage Resources Ltd. [*Vancouver Stock Exchange symbol*]
RPG .... Rebounds per Game [*Basketball, hockey*]
RPG .... Reflection Phase Grating [*Acoustics*]
RPG .... Refugee Policy Group   (EA)
RPG .... Regional Planning Group   (NATG)
RPG .... Religion Publishing Group [*New York, NY*]   (EA)
RPG .... Report Processor Generator   (MCD)
RPG .... Report Program Generator [*Programing language*] [*1962*]
RPG .... Research Planning Guide   (MCD)
RPG .... Retrograde Pyelogram [*Medicine*]
RPG .... Right Pedal Ganglion
RPG .... Rocket-Propelled Grenade
RPG .... Role-Playing Game [*Video game*]
RPG .... Rotary Pulse Generator
RPG .... Rounds per Gun
RPGN .... Rapidly Progressive Glomerular Nephritis [*Medicine*]
RPGPM...... Rounds per Gun per Minute
RPH .... Raypath Resources Ltd. [*Vancouver Stock Exchange symbol*]
RPH .... Registered Pharmacist
RPH .... Remember Pearl Harbor [*Group*] [*World War II*]
RPH .... Remotely Piloted Helicopter
RP/H........... Repairs, Heavy
RPH .... Revista Portuguesa de Historia [*A publication*]
RPH .... Revolutions per Hour   (MCD)
RPh............ Revue de Philologie [*A publication*]
RPh............ Revue de Philologie, de Litterature, et d'Histoire Anciennes [*A publication*]
RPh............ Revue de Philosophie [*A publication*]
RPH .... Rhode Island Hospital, Peters House Medical Library, Providence, RI [*Library symbol*] [*Library of Congress*]   (LCLS)
RPH .... Rideout Pyrohydrolysis
RPh............ Romance Philology [*A publication*]
RPHA......... Reverse Passive Hemagglutination [*Clinical chemistry*]
R Ph F E ... Revue Philosophique de la France et de l'Etranger [*A publication*]
RPhil.......... Revue de Philosophie [*A publication*]
R Philos...... Revue Philosophique [*A publication*]

RPHJ .... Royal Perth Hospital Journal [*A publication*]   (ADA)
RPhL .... Revue Philosophique de Louvain [*A publication*]
RphLH........ Revue de Philologie, de Litterature, et d'Histoire Anciennes [*A publication*]
RP-HPLC.... Reversed-Phase High-Performance Liquid Chromatography
RPHST ...... Research Participation for High School Teachers [*National Science Foundation*]
RPI............. RADAR Precipitation Integrator [*National Weather Service*]
RPI............. Railway Progress Institute [*Alexandria, VA*]   (EA)
RPI............. Rapeseed Protein Isolate [*Food technology*]
RPI............. Rassemblement Populaire pour l'Independance [*People's Rally for Independence*] [*Djibouti*]   (PPW)
RPI............. Rated Position Identifier   (AFM)
RPI............. Read, Punch, and Interpret
RPI............. Real Property Inventory
RPI............. Registro de la Propiedad Industrial [*Spanish Patent Office*] [*Madrid, Spain*] [*Information service*]   (EISS)
RPI............. Relative Position Indication   (NRCH)
RPI............. Relay Position Indicator
RPI............. Remarried Parents, Incorporated [*An association*] [*Forest Hills, NY*]   (EA)
RPI............. Rensselaer Polytechnic Institute [*New York*]   (MCD)
RPI............. Republican Party of India   (PPW)
RPI............. Research Price Index
RPI............. Resource Policy Institute   (EA)
RPI............. Responsive Production Inventory
RPI............. Retail Prices Index [*British*]
RPI............. Reticulocyte Production Index [*Hematology*]
RPI............. Richmond Professional Institute [*Virginia*]
RPI............. Rod Position Indicator [*Nuclear energy*]   (NRCH)
RPI............. Roll Position Indicator   (MCD)
RPI............. Rose Polytechnic Institute [*Indiana*]
RPI............. Royal Polytechnic Institute   (ROG)
R & PI .... Rubber and Plastics Industry   (MCD)
RPIA .... Rocket Propellant Information Agency   (MCD)
RPIA .... Roll Position Indicator Assembly
RPIAC .... Retail Prices Index Advisory Committee [*Department of Employment*] [*British*]
RPIC .... Reagan Political Items Collectors   (EA)
RPIC .... Rock Properties Information Center [*Purdue University*] [*National Science Foundation*]   (EISS)
RPIE .... Real Property Installed Equipment [*Air Force*]   (MCD)
RPIE .... Replacement of Photography Imagery Equipment   (RDA)
RPIF .... Real Property Industrial Fund
RPIFC........ Robert Plant International Fan Club [*Seattle, WA*]   (EA)
RPIFC........ Ronnie Prophet International Fan Club [*Canada*]   (EA)
RPIO .... Registered Publication Issuing Office [*Military*]
RPIS .... Rod Position Indication System [*Nuclear energy*]   (NRCH)
RPIS .... Rod Position Information System [*Nuclear energy*]   (NRCH)
RPJ............. Revue de la Pensee Juive [*A publication*]
RPJ............. [*The*] Rise of Provincial Jewry [*A publication*]   (BJA)
RPJ............. Rotary Pressure Joint
RPJCB........ John Carter Brown Library, Providence, RI [*Library symbol*] [*Library of Congress*]   (LCLS)
RPK .... Ribophosphate Pyrophosphokinase [*An enzyme*]
RPK .... Roosevelt [*Washington*] [*Seismograph station code, US Geological Survey*]   (SEIS)
RPL............. RADAR Processing Language [*Data processing*]   (IEEE)
RPL............. Radiation Physics Laboratory [*National Bureau of Standards*]   (MCD)
RPL............. Radio-Photo Luminescent [*Dosimetry*]
RPL............. Ram Petroleums Limited [*Toronto Stock Exchange symbol*]
RPL............. Ramseur Pilot Light Teaching System
RPL............. Rapid Pole Line [*A type of pole line construction*]
RPL............. Rated Power Level   (NASA)
RPL............. Reactor Primary Loop
RPL............. Reading Public Library, Reading, PA [*OCLC symbol*]   (OCLC)
RPL............. Receive Replenishment From [*Navy*]   (NVT)
RPL............. Recommended Provisioning List
RPL............. Remote Program Load
RPL............. Renewal Parts Leaflet   (MSA)
RPL............. Repair Parts List [*Army*]   (AABC)
RP/L........... Repairs, Light
RPL............. Repetitive Flight Plan [*Aviation*]   (FAAC)
RPL............. Replenish   (MCD)
RPL............. Request Parameter List [*Data processing*]   (BUR)
RPL............. Requested Privilege Level [*Data processing*]
RPL............. Revue Philosophique de Louvain [*A publication*]
RPL............. Rhode Island State Law Library, Providence, RI [*Library symbol*] [*Library of Congress*]   (LCLS)
RPL............. Richmond Public Library [*UTLAS symbol*]
RPL............. Ripe Pulp Liquid [*A banana substrate*]
RPL............. Ripple
RPL............. Rocket Propulsion Laboratory [*Air Force*]
RPL............. Running Program Language [*Data processing*]
R Plan Desarr (Bogota) ... Revista de Planeacion y Desarrollo (Bogota) [*A publication*]
R Plastiq .... Revue Generale des Caoutchoucs et Plastiques [*A publication*]
RPLC......... Replace   (FAAC)
RPLC......... Reversed-Phase Liquid Chromatography

RPLHA........ Revue de Philologie, de Litterature, et d'Histoire Anciennes. Troisieme Serie [*A publication*]
RPLHD .... Revista Padurilor-Industria Lemnului. Celuloza si Hirtie. Seria Celuloza si Hirtie [*A publication*]
RPLLD .... Revista Padurilor-Industria Lemnului. Celuloza si Hirtie. Seria Industria Lemnului [*A publication*]
RPLN .... Retroperitoneal Lymph Nodes [*Medicine*]
RPLNG ...... Replenishing
RPLO........... Regal Petroleum Limited [*NASDAQ symbol*] (NQ)
RPLR .... Repeller (MSA)
RPLS .... Radionuclide Perfusion Lung Scan
RPLS .... Reactor Protection Logic System (IEEE)
RPLSN........ Repulsion (MSA)
RPLT .... Repellent (MSA)
RPLV .... Reentry Payload Launch Vehicle
RPM............ RADAR Performance Monitor
RPM............ Radiation Polarization Measurement
RPM............ Radio Programas de Mexico [*Radio network*]
RPM............ Rate per Minute
RPM............ Read Program Memory [*Data processing*] (MDG)
RPM............ Real Property Management
RPM............ Reclamation Program Manager [*Military*] (AFIT)
RPM............ Registered Publications Manual [*Navy*]
RPM............ Registered Publications Memorandum
RPM............ Registrants Processing Manual [*Selective Service System*]
RPM............ Regulated Power Module
RPM............ Relaxation Potential Model [*Physics*]
RPM............ Reliability Performance Measure [*QCR*]
RPM............ Reliability Planning and Management (MCD)
RPM............ Remote Performance Monitoring (CET)
RPM............ Remotely Piloted Munitions [*Army*]
RPM............ Resale Price Maintenance
R & PM ..... Research and Program Management [*NASA*]
RPM............ Research and Program Management [*NASA*]
R & PM ..... Resources and Program Management [*NASA*]
RPM............ Resupply Provisions Module [*NASA*] (KSC)
RPM............ Retail Price Maintenance
RPM............ Returns Program Manager [*IRS*]
RPM............ Revenue per Mile
RPM............ Revenue Passenger Mile
RPM............ Revolutions per Minute [*e.g., in reference to phonograph records*]
RPM............ Rhode Island Medical Society, Providence, RI [*Library symbol*] [*Library of Congress*] (LCLS)
RPM............ Rocket-Propelled Mines (NATG)
RPM............ Roll Position Mechanism (MCD)
RPM............ Rotations per Minute
RPM............ Royalty Payment Mechanism
RPMa.......... Masonic Temple Library, Providence, RI [*Library symbol*] [*Library of Congress*] (LCLS)
RPMA .... Real Property Maintenance Activities [*or Administration*] [*Army*] (AABC)
RPMC........ Remote Performance Monitoring and Control
RPMC........ Reserve Personnel, Marine Corps (MCD)
RPMD........ Resources Planning and Mobilization Division [*of OEP*]
RPMDA ...... Recenti Progressi in Medicina [*A publication*]
RPMI........... Radiant Power Measuring Instrument [*Geophysics*]
RPMI........... Revolutions-per-Minute Indicator
RPMI........... Roswell Park Memorial Institute [*State University of New York at Buffalo*] [*Research center*] (RCD)
RPMIO....... Registered Publication Mobile Issuing Office [*Military*]
RPMN .... Repairman (AABC)
RPMO........ Radio Projects Management Office
RPMOR ..... Rounds per Mortar
RPMORPM ... Rounds per Mortar per Minute
RPMP .... Register of Plan Mobilization Producers
RPMS .... Real Property Management System (MCD)
RPM/S ...... Revolutions per Minute/Second (DEN)
RPMS .... Royal Postgraduate Medical School [*British*]
RPN .... Registered Professional Nurse
RPN .... Registered Psychiatric Nurse (ADA)
RPN .... Reserve Personnel, Navy [*An appropriation*]
RPN .... Reverse Polish Notation [*Arithmetic evaluation*] [*Data processing*] (IEEE)
RPN .... Rosh-Pina [*Israel*] [*Airport symbol*] (OAG)
RPND......... Reprinting, No Date [*Publishing*]
R & P News ... Rubber and Plastics News [*A publication*]
RPNSM....... Replenishment
RPO .... Radiation Protection Officer [*NASA*] (NASA)
RPO .... Radiophare Omnidirectionnel [*Omnidirectional Radio Beacon*] (NATG)
RPO .... Railway Post Office
RPO .... Range Planning Office (MUGU)
RPO .... Regional Personnel Officer [*Social Security Administration*]
RPO .... Regional Pests Officer [*Ministry of Agriculture, Fisheries, and Food*] [*British*]
RPO .... Regional Program [*or Project*] Officer (OICC)
RPO .... Regional Purchasing Office [*Defense Supply Agency*]
RPO .... Regular Production Option [*Automotive engineering*]
RPO .... Regulating Petty Officer [*British*]
RPO .... Rejection Purchase Order (MCD)

RPO .... Repair Parts Order [*Navy*]
RPO .... Replacement Purchase Order
RPO .... Responsible Property Officer [*Military*] (AFIT)
RPO .... Revolution per Orbit
RPO .... Rotor Power Output
RPO .... Royal Philharmonic Orchestra [*British*]
RPOA .... Recognized Private Operating Agencies (NATG)
RPOC .... Remote Payload Operations Center [*NASA*] (MCD)
RPOC .... Report Proceeding on Course [*Aviation*] (FAAC)
RPOCN ...... Request for Purchase Order Change Notice (AAG)
R Pol........... Review of Politics [*A publication*]
R Pol Econ Terza Ser ... Revista di Politica Economica. Terza Serie [*A publication*]
R Pol Internac ... Revista de Politica Internacional [*A publication*]
R Polit .... Review of Politics [*A publication*]
R Politics.... Review of Politics [*A publication*]
R Polit Int .. Revue de Politique Internationale [*A publication*]
R Polit Int (Madrid) ... Revista de Politica Internacional (Madrid) [*A publication*]
R Polit et Litt ... Revue Politique et Litteraire [*A publication*]
R Polit Parl ... Revue Politique et Parlementaire [*A publication*]
R Polit Soc ... Revista de Politica Social [*A publication*]
R Pol et Litt ... Revue Politique et Litteraire [*A publication*]
R Pol et Parlementaire ... Revue Politique et Parlementaire [*A publication*]
RPOP......... Rover Preflight Operations Procedures [*NASA*] (KSC)
RPorP......... Portsmouth Priory, Portsmouth, RI [*Library symbol*] [*Library of Congress*] (LCLS)
RPOW....... RPM, Inc. [*NASDAQ symbol*] (NQ)
RPP .... RADAR Power Programer
RPP .... Radiation Protection Plan [*Nuclear energy*] (NRCH)
RPP .... Rassemblement Populaire pour le Progres [*Popular Rally for Progress*] [*Djibouti*] (PPW)
RPP .... Rate Pressure Product [*Cardiology*]
RPP .... Real Property Practice [*A publication*]
RPP .... Rechargeable Power Pack
R & PP .... Recreation and Public Purposes Act
RPP .... Reductive Pentose Phosphate [*Photosynthesis cycle*]
RPP .... Regional Priority Program [*Army*] (AABC)
RPP .... Regional Promotion Plan [*FAA*] (FAAC)
RPP .... Registered Postal Packet
RPP .... Reinforced Pyrolytic Plastic (NASA)
RPP .... Reliability Program Plan (MCD)
RPP .... Removable Patch Panel
RPP .... Rendezvous Point Position [*Aerospace*]
RPP .... Repair Parts Provisioning
RPP .... Repap Enterprises Corp. SV [*Toronto Stock Exchange symbol*]
RPP .... Reply Paid Postcard
RPP .... Republican People's Party [*Cumhuriyet Halk Partisi - CHP*] [*Turkey*] (PPW)
RPP .... Request Present Position [*Aviation*] (FAAC)
RPP .... Requisition Processing Point
RPP .... Retrograde Processing Point (MCD)
RPP .... Retropubic Prostatectomy [*Medicine*]
RPP .... Reverse Pulse Polarography [*Analytical chemistry*]
RPP .... Revue Politique et Parlementaire [*A publication*]
RPP .... Rivers Pollution Prevention (ROG)
RPP .... Roll-Pitch Pickoff
RPP .... Rules of Practices and Procedure
RPP .... Rural Practice Project [*An association*] [*Defunct*] (EA)
RPPA......... Republican Postwar Policy Association [*Encouraged Republican Party to drop its isolationist viewpoint and take a stand for an American share in international collaboration after the war*] [*World War II*]
RPPA......... Revue Politique et Parlementaire [*A publication*]
RPPC......... Providence College, Providence, RI [*Library symbol*] [*Library of Congress*] (LCLS)
RPPE .... Research, Program, Planning, and Evaluation
RPPI .... Remote Plan Position Indicator (MCD)
RPPI .... Repeater Plan Position Indicator (NVT)
RPPI .... Role Perception Picture Inventory
RPPJA .... Reports on Progress in Polymer Physics (Japan) [*A publication*]
RPPL .... Repair Parts Price List
RPPL .... Repair Parts Provisioning List
RPPM .... Park Museum Reference Library, Providence, RI [*Library symbol*] [*Library of Congress*] (LCLS)
RPPMP...... Repair Parts Program Management Plans
RPPO......... Regional Printing Procurement Office [*Army*]
RPPP .... Rules of Pleading, Practice, and Procedure (DLA)
RPPR......... Rooney Pace Group [*NASDAQ symbol*] (NQ)
RPPS......... Robotnicza Partia Polskich Socjalistow [*Workers Party of Polish Socialists*] (PPE)
RPPS-Lewica ... Robotnicza Partia Polskich Socjalistow - Lewica [*Workers Party of Polish Socialists - Left*] (PPE)
RPPTF........ Rotatable Porous-Prism Test Fixture
RPQ .... Rapports de Pratique de Quebec [*Quebec Practice Reports*] [*Canada*] (DLA)
RPQ .... Request for Price Quotation
RPR .... Federation Guadeloupeenne du Rassemblement pour la Republique [*Guadeloupe Federation of the Rally for the Republic*] (PPW)

RPR .... Radio Physics Research
RPR .... Raipur [*India*] [*Airport symbol*]   (OAG)
RPR .... Rapid Plasma Reagin [*Card test for venereal disease*]
RPR .... Rapid Power Reduction   (IEEE)
RPR .... Rassemblement pour la Republique [*Rally for the Republic*] [*French Guiana*]   (PPW)
RPR .... Rassemblement pour la Republique [*Rally for the Republic*] [*French Polynesian*]   (PPW)
RPR .... Rassemblement pour la Republique [*Rally for the Republic*] [*Wallis and Futuna Islander*]   (PD)
RPR .... Rassemblement pour la Republique [*Rally for the Republic*] [*Reunionese*]   (PPW)
RPR .... Rassemblement pour la Republique [*Rally for the Republic*] [*Martiniquais*]   (PPW)
RPR .... Read Printer
RPR .... Real Property Reports [*Canada*]   (DLA)
RPR .... Rear Projection Readout
RPR .... Rectangular Parallelepiped Resonant Method [*Crystal elasticity*]
RPR .... Rent Procedural Regulation [*Office of Rent Stabilization*] [*Economic Stabilization Agency*]   (DLA)
RPR .... Repair   (MSA)
RPR .... Repair Parts Requisition
RPR .... Rockport Resources Ltd. [*Vancouver Stock Exchange symbol*]
RPR .... Roger Williams College, Providence Campus, Providence, RI [*Library symbol*] [*Library of Congress*]   (LCLS)
RPR .... Roll-Pitch Resolver
RPRA .... Railroad Public Relations Association [*Washington, DC*]   (EA)
RPrag .... Romanistica Pragensia [*A publication*]
RPrat .... Revue Pratique d'Apologetique [*A publication*]
R Prat Dr Soc ... Revue Pratique de Droit Social [*A publication*]
RPRC .... Regional Primate Research Centers
RPRC .... Religious Public Relations Council   (EA)
RPRC .... Retired and Pioneer Rural Carriers of US   (EA)
RPRC .... Rhode Island College, Providence, RI [*Library symbol*] [*Library of Congress*]   (LCLS)
RPR-CT ...... Rapid Plasma Reagin Card Test [*Clinical chemistry*]
RPRD .... Research Policy and Review Division [*of OEP*]
rPRL .... Rat Prolactin [*Biochemistry*]
RPRL .... Regional Parasite Research Laboratory [*US Department of Agriculture*] [*Research center*]   (RCD)
RPRL .... Regional Poultry Research Laboratory [*Department of Agriculture*] [*Research center*]
RPRMN ...... Repairman
RPROP ...... Receiving Proficiency Pay [*Military*]
RPRRA .... Revue de Physique. Academie de la Republique Populaire Roumaine [*A publication*]
RPRRB .... Real Property Resource Review Board   (AFM)
RPRS .... Random-Pulse RADAR System   (AAG)
RPRS .... Roll-Pitch Resolver System
RPRT .... Report   (AFM)
RPRV .... Remotely Piloted Research Vehicle [*NASA*]
RPRWP ...... Reactor Plant River Water Pump   (IEEE)
RPS .... RADAR Position Symbol   (FAAC)
RPS .... Radiological Protection Service   (DEN)
RPS .... Range Pad Service
RPS .... Range Positioning System
RPS .... Rapid Photo Screening
RPS .... Reactor Protection Systems   (NRCH)
RPS .... Real-Time Programing System [*Data processing*]   (IEEE)
RPS .... Record and Playback Subsystem   (NASA)
RPS .... Records per Sector [*Data processing*]
RPS .... Registered Publications System
RPS .... Regulated Power Supply
RPS .... Regulatory Performance Summary [*Report*] [*Nuclear energy*]   (NRCH)
RPS .... Reinforced Porcelain System [*Dentistry*]
RPS .... Relative Performance Score [*Telecommunications*]   (TEL)
RPS .... Relay Power Supply   (MCD)
RPS .... Remittance Processing Systems [*IRS*]
RPS .... Remote Printing System
RPS .... Remote Processing Service   (BUR)
RPS .... Renal Pressor Substance [*Medicine*]
RPS .... Requirements Planning System [*Data processing*]
RPS .... Response-Produced Stimulation
RPS .... Retired Persons Services [*Alexandria, VA*]   (EA)
RPS .... Return Pressure Sensing   (MCD)
RPS .... Revolutions per Second   (AFM)
RPS .... Right Pedal Sinus
RPS .... Rigid Proctosigmoidoscopy [*Proctoscopy*]
RPS .... Ripe Pulp Solid [*A banana substrate*]
RPS .... Rochester Public Schools, Library Processing Center, Rochester, MN [*OCLC symbol*]   (OCLC)
RPS .... Rotary Precision Switch
RPS .... Rotating Passing Scuttle
RPS .... Rotational Position Sensing [*Data processing*]
RPS .... Royal Photographic Society [*British*]   (DEN)
RPS .... Rutile-Paper-Slurry [*Grade of titanium dioxide*]
RPSA .... Rudder Pedal Sensor Assembly   (MCD)
RPSBS .... Resources Pension Sh 2 [*NASDAQ symbol*]   (NQ)
RPSCTDY ... Return to Proper Station Upon Completion of Temporary Duty

RPS-DL ...... Registered Publications Section - District Library [*Navy*]
R & P SEC ... Radio and Panel Section [*Navy*]
RP (Ships) ... Registered Ships' Plumbers [*British*]
RPSI .... Roche Psychiatric Service Institute
R Psicol Gen Apl ... Revista de Psicologia General y Aplicada [*A publication*]
RPSIO .... Registered Publications Subissuing Office [*Military*]   (NVT)
RPSL .... Repair Parts Selective List
RPSL .... Rhode Island Department of State Library Services, Providence, RI [*Library symbol*] [*Library of Congress*]   (LCLS)
RPSM .... Registered Publication Shipment Memorandum
RPSM .... Resources Planning and Scheduling Method
RPSMG ...... Reactor Protective System Motor Generator   (IEEE)
RPSML .... Repair Parts Support Material List
RPsP .... Revue de Psychologie des Peuples [*A publication*]
RPS-PL ..... Registered Publications Section - Personnel Library [*Navy*]
RPSS .... Ryukyu Philatelic Specialist Society   (EA)
RPST .... Reaction Products Separator Tank [*Nuclear energy*]   (NRCH)
RPSTA .... Rivista di Parassitologia [*A publication*]
RPSTL .... Repair Parts and Special Tools List [*Army*]   (AABC)
RPT .... Congregation Sons of Israel and David, Temple Beth-El, Providence, RI [*Library symbol*] [*Library of Congress*]   (LCLS)
RPT .... Raluana Point [*New Britain*] [*Seismograph station code, US Geological Survey*]   (SEIS)
RPT .... Rapid Pull Through [*Gastroenterology*]
RPT .... Rassemblement du Peuple Togolais [*Rally of the Togolese People*]   (PPW)
RPT .... Reactor for Physical and Technical Investigations [*USSR*]   (DEN)
RPT .... Recirculation Pump Trip [*Nuclear energy*]   (NRCH)
RPT .... Reference Point Tracking
RPT .... Registered Physical Therapist
RPT .... Regular Public Transport   (ADA)
RPT .... Repair Parts Transporter   (MCD)
RPT .... Repeat   (AAG)
RPT .... Reply Paid Telegram
RPT .... Report
RPT .... Reprint
RPT .... RepublicBank Corp. [*Formerly, Republic of Texas Corp.*] [*NYSE symbol*]
RPT .... Request Programs Termination [*Data processing*]
RPT .... Resident Provisioning Team
R & PT .... Rifle and Pistol Team [*Navy*]
RPT .... Rocket-Powered Target
RPT .... Rocket Propulsion Technician [*Air Force*]
RPT .... Rotary Power Transformer
RPTA .... Rudder Pedal Transducer Assembly [*NASA*]   (NASA)
RPTC .... Repeating Coil   (MSA)
RPTD .... Repeated
RPTD .... Reported
RPTD .... Ruptured
RPTEA .... Reviews of Petroleum Technology [*A publication*]
RPTF .... Republican Presidential Task Force   (EA)
RPTF .... Rotatable Porro-Mirror Test Fixture
RPTGA .... Rocznik Polskiego Towarzystwa Geologicznego [*A publication*]
RPTLC .... Reverse Phase Thin-Layer Chromatography
RPTN .... Repetition   (AAG)
RPTOW ...... Rocznik Polskiego Towarzystwa [*A publication*]
RPTR .... Repeater   (MSA)
RPU .... RADAR Prediction Uncertainty
RPU .... Radio Phone Unit [*Navy*]
RPU .... Radio Propagation Unit [*Army*]   (MCD)
RPU .... Railway Patrolmen's International Union [*Later, BRAC*]   (EA)
RPu .... Rassegna Pugliese [*A publication*]
RPU .... Receiver Processor Unit [*Electronics*]
RPU .... Rectifier Power Unit
RPU .... Regional Planning Unit   (OICC)
RPU .... Regional Processing Unit
RPU .... Registered Publication Unit
RPU .... Remote Pickup Unit
RPU .... Remote Processing Unit   (KSC)
RPU .... Retention Pending Use [*Air Force*]
RPUSSR ..... Research Program of the USSR. New York Series [*A publication*]
RPV .... Reactor Pressure Vessel   (NRCH)
RPV .... Real Program Value   (CAAL)
RPV .... Recorder Processor Viewer
RPV .... Reduced Product Verification [*DoD*]
RPV .... Remote Positioning Valve
RPV .... Remotely Piloted Vehicle [*Aircraft*]
RPV .... Residual Pressure Valve [*Automotive engineering*]
RPV .... Rhopalosiphum padi Virus
RPV .... Right Pulmonary Vein [*Medicine*]
RPV .... United States Veterans Administration Hospital, Davis Park, Providence, RI [*Library symbol*] [*Library of Congress*]   (LCLS)
RPVI-ES ..... Remotely Piloted Vehicle Investigation - Emerging Sensors   (MCD)
RPVIO .... Registered Publication Van Issuing Office [*Military*]   (NVT)
RPVNTV ..... Rust Preventative

RPVT......... Relative Position Velocity Technique
RPVX........ Remote-Piloted Vehicle Experiment
RPW .... Rawle, Penrose, and Watts' Pennsylvania Reports [1828-40] (DLA)
RP & W ...... Rawle, Penrose, and Watts' Pennsylvania Reports [1828-40] (DLA)
RPWDA ...... Retail Paint and Wallpaper Distributors of America [Later, National Decorating Products Association]
RPX .... Roundup, MT [Location identifier] [FAA] (FAAL)
RPY .... Blythe, CA [Location identifier] [FAA] (FAAL)
RPY .... Roll, Pitch, and Yaw
RPZ .... Rada Pomocy Zydom [A publication]
RPZHA .... Roczniki Panstwowego Zakladu Higieny [A publication]
RQ .... Arab Wing Nigeria Ltd. [Nigeria] [ICAO designator] (FAAC)
RQ .... RASD Quarterly [American Library Association] [A publication]
RQ .... Recovery Quotient
RQ .... Renaissance Quarterly [A publication]
RQ .... Request (FAAC)
R/Q............. Request for Quotation (AAG)
R/Q............. Resolver/Quantizer (IEEE)
RQ .... Respiratory Quotient [Also, Q] [Physiology]
RQ .... Restoration Quarterly [A publication]
RQ .... Revue des Questions Historiques [A publication]
RQ .... Revue de Qumran [A publication]
RQ .... Riverside Quarterly [A publication]
RQ .... Roemische Quartalschrift fuer Christliche Altertumskunde und fuer Kirchengeschichte [A publication]
RQ .... RQ (Reference Quarterly) [American Library Association. Reference Services Division] [A publication]
RQA........... Recursive Queue Analyzer (IEEE)
R & QA ...... Reliability and Quality Assurance
RQA........... Roemische Quartalschrift fuer Christliche Altertumskunde und fuer Kirchengeschichte [A publication]
RQAHA...... Research Quarterly. American Association for Health, Physical Education, and Recreation [A publication]
RQAK .... Roemische Quartalschrift fuer Christliche Altertumskunde und fuer Kirchengeschichte [A publication]
RQAO........ Reliability and Quality Assurance Office [NASA]
RQC........... RADAR Quality Control
RQC........... Reliability and Quality Control (MCD)
RQCAK ...... Roemische Quartalschrift fuer Christliche Altertumskunde und fuer Kirchengeschichte [A publication]
RQCAKG.... Roemische Quartalschrift fuer Christliche Altertumskunde und fuer Kirchengeschichte [A publication]
R Q Ch A K ... Roemische Quartalschrift fuer Christliche Altertumskunde und fuer Kirchengeschichte [A publication]
RQCL......... Request Clearance [Aviation] (FAAC)
RQD........... Rock Quality Designation [Nuclear energy] (NRCH)
RQDCZ...... Request Clearance to Depart Control Zone [Aviation] (FAAC)
RQDP .... Request, Quandary and Deferment Plan
RQECZ....... Request Clearance to Enter Control Zone [Aviation] (FAAC)
RQH........... Revue des Questions Historiques [A publication]
RQHist....... Revue des Questions Historiques [A publication]
RQIAC........ Requires Immediate Action (NOAA)
RQIRA .... Revista de Quimica Industrial (Rio De Janeiro) [A publication]
RQK........... Roemische Quartalschrift fuer Kirchengeschichte [A publication]
RQL .... Reference Quality Level (IEEE)
RQL .... Rejectable Quality Level
RQMC .... Regimental Quartermaster-Corporal [British]
RQMD........ Richmond Quartermaster Depot [Virginia] [Merged with Defense General Supply Center]
RQMS........ Regimental Quartermaster-Sergeant [British]
RQMT........ Requirement (AFM)
RQN........... Radial Quantum Number
RQN........... Requisition (AFM)
RQO........... River Quality Objective [British]
RQP .... Request Permission (FAAC)
RQP .... Resistor Qualification Program
RQQPRI..... Recommended Qualitative and Quantitative Personnel Requirements Information [Military] (MCD)
RQR........... Require (AAG)
RQRD .... Required
RQRP........ Request Reply (FAAC)
RQS........... Rate Quoting System
RQS........... Ready Qualified for Standby
RQS........... Request Supplementary Flight Plan Message [Aviation code]
RQS........... Revue des Questions Scientifiques [A publication]
RQS........... River Quality Standard [British]
RQS........... Roemische Quartalschrift fuer Christliche Altertumskunde und fuer Kirchengeschichte [A publication]
RQT .... Reenlistment Qualification Test [Military] (MCD)
RQT .... Reliability Qualification Test (CAAL)
RQT .... Resistor Qualification Test
RQTAO...... Request Time and Altitude Over [Aviation] (FAAC)
RQTO .... Request Travel Order (NOAA)
RQTP......... Resistor Qualification Test Program
R/QTR........ Rear Quarter [Automotive engineering]
RQTS........ Requirements (KSC)
RQu .... Revue de Qumran [A publication]
R QUM....... Revue de Qumran [A publication]

RQUS .... Remote Query Update System [Data processing]
RQY........... Elkins, WV [Location identifier] [FAA] (FAAL)
RQY........... Relative Quantum Yield
RQZ........... Huntsville, AL [Location identifier] [FAA] (FAAL)
RR.............. Naval Research Reviews [A publication]
RR.............. Pike and Fischer's Radio Regulations (DLA)
RR.............. RADAR Range Station (FAAC)
RR.............. Radiation Reaction [Cells] [Medicine]
RR.............. Radiation Response
RR.............. Radiation Retinopathy [Ophthalmology]
R/R............. Radio and RADAR
RR.............. Radio Range
RR.............. Radio Recognition
RR.............. Radio Regulations
RR.............. Radio Relay (CINC)
RR.............. Radio Research
RR.............. Radioreceptor [Assay method] [Clinical chemistry]
RR.............. RAF-1 Group [Air Transport] [Great Britain] [ICAO designator] (FAAC)
RR.............. Railroad
RR.............. Rapid Rectilinear
RR.............. Rarely Reversed [Decisions in law]
RR.............. Rarissime [Very Rare]
RR.............. Raritan River Rail Road Co. [AAR code]
RR.............. Rate Rebate [British]
R & R .... Rate and Rhythm [of pulse]
RR.............. Rattus Rattus [The ship or black rat]
RR.............. Readiness Review (KSC)
RR.............. Readout and Relay
RR.............. Rear (AABC)
RR.............. Receive Ready [Data processing] (IEEE)
RR.............. Receiver Room [Navy] (CAAL)
RR.............. Receiving Report (AAG)
RR.............. Recipient Rights
RR.............. Recoilless Rifle
RR.............. Recommended for Re-Engagement [British]
RR.............. Record Rarities [Record label]
R/R............. Record/Retransmit (IEEE)
RR.............. Record Review [A publication]
RR.............. Records and Recording [A publication]
R & R .... Records and Reports
RR.............. Recovery Reliability (MCD)
RR.............. Recovery Room
RR.............. Recruit Roll [Navy]
RR.............. Recurrence Rate
RR.............. Redstone Resources, Inc. [Toronto Stock Exchange symbol]
RR.............. Redundancy Reduction (AAG)
RR.............. Reentry Range
RR.............. Reference Register [Data processing]
RR.............. Reflectors [JETDS nomenclature] [Military] (CET)
RR.............. Reformed Review [A publication]
R & R .... Refueling and Rearming [Air Force]
RR.............. Register to Register (MCD)
RR.............. Registered Representative [Wall Street stock salesman]
RR.............. Rehabilitation Record
R & R .... Reinstatement and Replacement (ADA)
RR.............. Relative Rank
RR.............. Relative Response
RR.............. Relative Risk [Medicine]
RR.............. Relay Rack [Telecommunications] (TEL)
RR.............. Relief Radii (MSA)
RR.............. Religious Roundtable [An association] (EA)
RR.............. Removal-Replacement
R & R .... Remove and Replace (KSC)
RR.............. Rendezvous RADAR [NASA]
RR.............. Renegotiation Regulations
RR.............. Rent Regulation [Office of Rent Stabilization] [Economic Stabilization Agency] (DLA)
R/R............. Repair/Rebuild (MCD)
R/R............. Repair or Replacement
R & R .... Repair and Return
RR.............. Repetition Rate
RR.............. Report Immediately upon Reaching [Aviation] (FAAC)
R & R .... Reporting and Requisitioning [Air Force]
RR.............. Required Reserves
RR.............. Requirements Review [NASA] (NASA)
RR.............. Reroute [Telecommunications] (TEL)
RR.............. Research Report
R & R .... Research and Reporting Committee [Interstate Conference of Employment Security Agencies] (OICC)
RR.............. Reservatis Reservandis [With All Reserve] [Latin]
RR.............. Resonance Raman
RR.............. Resource Report
RR.............. Respiratory Rate [Medicine]
RR.............. Responsible Receiver
R & R .... Rest and Recreation
R & R .... Rest and Recuperation [Military]
R & R .... Rest and Rehabilitation [Marine Corps]
RR.............. Retro-Rocket [Army] (AABC)
RR.............. Return Rate (IEEE)
RR.............. Return Register

RR.............. Revenue Release (DLA)
RR.............. Reverse Recovery [Electronics]
RR.............. Review of Religion [A publication]
RR.............. Review for Religious [A publication]
RR.............. Review of Reviews [London] [A publication]
RR.............. Revised Reports [Legal] [British]
RR.............. Revision Record (MSA)
RR.............. Rhymney Railway [Wales]
RR.............. Ricerche Religiose [A publication]
R & R .... Rich & Rare Canadian Whisky [Gooderham's]
RR.............. Ridge Regression [Statistics]
RR.............. Rifle Range
RR.............. Right Rear
RR.............. Right Reverend [Of an abbot, bishop, or monsignor]
RR.............. Rights Reserved
RR.............. Rigid-Rotor [Calculations]
RR.............. Risk Ratio
R & R .... Rock and Roll [Music]
R & R .... Rock and Rye
RR.............. Rodman & Renshaw Capital Group [NYSE symbol]
RR.............. Roemische Religions-Geschichte [A publication] (OCD)
RR.............. Roll Radius (MCD)
RR.............. Roll Roofing (AAG)
RR.............. Rolls-Royce [Automobile]
RR.............. Romanic Review [A publication]
RR.............. Ronald Reagan
RR.............. Rough Riders [The City of London Yeomanry] [Military unit]
                 [British]
RR.............. Round Robin (IEEE)
RR.............. Routine Relay (KSC)
R & R .... Routing and Record Sheet [Air Force]
RR.............. Running Reverse
RR.............. Rural Rehabilitation [United States] (DLA)
RR.............. Rural Resident (OICC)
RR.............. Rural Route
RR.............. Rush Release
R & R .... Russell and Ryan's English Crown Cases (DLA)
RR.............. Very Rare [Numismatics]
R of R's...... Review of Reviews [A publication]
RRA .... Dallas-Fort Worth, TX [Location identifier] [FAA] (FAAL)
RRA .... Race Relations Act [1976] [British]
RRA .... Radiation Research Associates, Inc. (NRCH)
RRA .... Radio Relay Aircraft (CET)
RRA .... Radioreceptor Assay [Clinical chemistry]
RRA .... Ranger Regimental Association (EA)
RRA .... Record Retention Agreement [IRS]
RRA .... Redmond, R. A., Los Angeles CA [STAC]
RRA .... Registered Record Administrator [American Medical Record
                 Association] [Medicine]
RRA .... Religious Research Association (EA)
RRA .... Remote Record Address
RRA .... Resident Research Associate
R & RA .... Retraining and Reemployment Administration [Terminated,
                 1947]
RRA .... Review of Reviews [United States] [A publication]
RRA .... Rubber Reclaimers Association [Later, NARI] (EA)
RRA .... Rubber Recyclers Association (EA)
RRAC .... Race Relations Advisory Committee [Trades Union Congress]
                 [British]
RRAC .... Regional Resources Advisory Committee (AABC)
RR et AC .... Rosea Rubeae et Aureae Crucis [The Order of the Rose of
                 Ruby and the Cross of Gold]
RRACD...... Ciencia e Cultura (Sao Paulo). Suplemento [A publication]
RRAD .... Red River Army Depot [Texas] (AABC)
RRAD .... Roll Ratio Adjust Device (MCD)
R Radical Pol Econ ... Review of Radical Political Economics [A publication]
R Radic Polit Econ ... Review of Radical Political Economics [A publication]
RRAEA ...... Rendiconti. Riunione Annuale. Associazione Elettrotecnica
                 Italiana [A publication]
RRAF......... Ready Reserve of the Armed Forces
RRAF......... Royal Rhodesian Air Force
RRAP......... Residential Rehabilitation Assistance Program [Canada]
RRAR........ ROM Return Address Register
RRB .... R. R. Bowker Co. [Publisher]
RRB .... RADAR Reflective Balloon
RRB .... Radio Research Board (DEN)
RRB .... Railroad Retirement Board
RRB .... Rubber Reserve Board [of the Reconstruction Finance Corp.]
RRBC .... Rat Red Blood Cell
RRBLB....... United States Railroad Retirement Board. Law Bulletin (DLA)
RRBN......... Round Robin (FAAC)
RRB Q Rev ... RRB [Railroad Retirement Board] Quarterly Review [A
                 publication]
RRB (Railroad Retirement Bd) Q R ... RRB (Railroad Retirement Board)
                 Quarterly Review [A publication]
RRBVD .... Revue Roumaine de Biologie. Serie Biologie Vegetale [A
                 publication]
RRC........... RADAR Return Code
RRC........... Radiation Recorder Controller (NRCH)
RRC........... Radiation Resistance Cable
RRC........... Radio Receptor Company

RRC........... Radio Relay Center (NATG)
RRC........... Radio Research Company
RRC........... Railroad Record Club [Commercial firm] (EA)
RRC........... Rainy River Community College, International Falls, MN [OCLC
                 symbol] (OCLC)
RRC........... Ravenroc Resources Ltd. [Vancouver Stock Exchange symbol]
RRC........... Reactor Recirculation Cooling [Nuclear energy] (NRCH)
R & RC....... Reactors and Reactor Control (MCD)
RRC........... Receiving Report Change (AAG)
RRC........... Reconstructionist Rabbinical College [Pennsylvania]
RR & C .... Records, Reports, and Control (AFM)
RRC........... Recreation Resources Center [University of Wisconsin]
                 [Research center] (RCD)
RRC........... Recruit Reception Center
RRC........... Red River Community College [UTLAS symbol]
RRC........... Reentry Rate Command [NASA]
RRC........... Refractories Research Center [Ohio State University]
                 [Research center] (RCD)
RRC........... Refugee Resource Center [Defunct] (EA)
RRC........... Regional Resource Center
RRC........... Regional Review Consultants [American Occupational Therapy
                 Association]
RRC........... Regular Route Carrier
R/RC .... Removal/Recertification
RRC........... Report Review Committee [National Academy of Sciences]
RRC........... Reports of Rating Cases [Legal] [British]
RRC........... Requirements Review Committee [Navy]
RRC........... Research Resources Center [University of Illinois at Chicago]
                 [Research center] (RCD)
RRC........... Residency Review Committee [Medicine]
RRC........... Resuscitation Research Center [University of Pittsburgh]
                 [Research center] (RCD)
RRC........... Retrograde River Crossing (MCD)
RRC........... Rheology Research Center [University of Wisconsin - Madison]
                 [Research center] (RCD)
RRC........... Road Runners Club of America
RRC........... Rocket Research Corporation (MCD)
RRC........... Rodale Research Center [Horticulture]
RRC........... Roll Ratio Controller (MCD)
RRC........... Rollin' Rock Club [Also, RRCOTAAOSOCOTWAOS]
RRC........... Routine Respiratory Care [Medicine]
RRC........... Royal Red Cross [British]
RRC........... Rubber Reserve Committee [Navy]
RRC........... Rubber Reserve Company [Dissolved, 1935, functions
                 transferred to Reconstruction Finance Corporation]
RRC........... Russell Research Center [Department of Agriculture]
RRC........... Ryde's Rating Cases (DLA)
RRCA .... Rhinelander Rabbit Club of America (EA)
RRCA .... Road Runners Club of America (EA)
RR & Can Cas ... Railway and Canal Cases [England] (DLA)
RRCC .... Reduced Rate Contribution Clause [Insurance]
R & RCC ..... Russell and Ryan's English Crown Cases Reserved (DLA)
RRCEM ...... Residency Review Committee for Emergency Medicine
                 [Chicago, IL] (EA)
RRCN .... Receiving Report Change Notice (AAG)
RR & Cn Cas ... Railway and Canal Cases [1835-54] (DLA)
RRCO .... Royal Resources Corporation [NASDAQ symbol] (NQ)
RRCOD....... Resource Recovery and Conservation [A publication]
RRCOTAAOSOCOTWAOS ... Rollin' Rock Club of Texas and Any Other
                 State or Country of the World and Outer Space [Also,
                 RRC]
RR Cr R ...... Revised Reports, Criminal Rulings [1862-75] [India] (DLA)
RRCS .... Railroad Communication System
RRCS .... Reentry RADAR Cross Section
RRCS .... Revenue Receipts Control Sheets [IRS]
RRCU .... Remote Range Control Unit (MCD)
RRCUS....... Rhodesian Ridgeback Club of the United States (EA)
RRCVR....... Remote Receiver (FAAC)
RRD .... Reactor Radiation Division [National Bureau of Standards]
RRD .... Reactor Research and Development
RRD .... Receive, Record, Display
RRD .... Reliability Requirements Directive
RR & D .... Reparations, Removal, and Demolition [Section] [Industry
                 Branch, US Military Government, Germany]
RRD .... Requisition Received Date [Bell System] (TEL)
RRD .... Resonant Reed Decoder
RRD .... Retendering Receipt Day (NRCH)
RRD .... Roosevelt Roads [Puerto Rico] [Seismograph station code, US
                 Geological Survey] (SEIS)
RRD .... Route/Route Destination [Telecommunications] (TEL)
RRDA .... Rendezvous Retrieval, Docking, and Assembly [of space
                 vehicle or orbital station] [NASA] (AAG)
RRDA .... Repetitive Report Distribution Audit (AAG)
RRDB......... Research Results Data Base [Department of Agriculture]
                 [Washington, DC] [Information service] (EISS)
RRDE......... Radio Research and Development Establishment (MCD)
RRDE......... Rotating Ring Disk Electrode
RRDFCS.... Redundant Reconfigurable Digital Flight Control
                 System (MCD)
RRDO .... Register of Rivers Discharging into the Oceans [Marine
                 science] (MSC)

RRDR.........	Raw RADAR Data Recorder
RRDS.........	Regents Renaissance Drama Series [*A publication*]
RRDS.........	Relative Record Data Set
RRDU.........	Recreation Research Demonstration Unit (RDA)
RRE	Marree [*Australia*] [*Airport symbol*] [*Obsolete*] (OAG)
RRE	RADAR Research Establishment [*British*]
R & RE	Radiation and Repair Engineering [*Nuclear energy*] (NRCH)
RRE	Railroad Enthusiasts
RRE	Range Rate Error
RRE	Receive Reference Equivalent [*Telecommunications*] (TEL)
RRE	Reg Resources [*Vancouver Stock Exchange symbol*]
RRE	Rolls-Royce Enthusiasts (EA)
RR & E	Round, Regular, and Equal [*With reference to pupils of eyes*]
RRE	Royal RADAR Establishment [*British*] [*Research center*]
RREA.........	Rendezvous RADAR Electronics Assembly (MCD)
RREC.........	Rehabilitation Record
RREC.........	Rice Research and Extension Center [*University of Arkansas*] [*Research center*] (RCD)
R Regional Econ and Bus ...	Review of Regional Economics and Business [*A publication*]
RRel...........	Review of Religion [*A publication*]
R Rel..........	Review for Religious [*A publication*]
R of Religion ...	Review of Religion [*A publication*]
R Relig Res ...	Review of Religious Research [*A publication*]
R Rel Res.....	Review of Religious Research [*A publication*]
RR/EO........	Race Relations/Equal Opportunity [*Military*] (AABC)
RRep	Records Repository [*Air Force*] (AFM)
RRERD	Resource Recovery and Energy Review [*A publication*]
R Rest DS...	Regents Restoration Drama Series [*A publication*]
RRETA	Reports. Research Institute of Electrical Communication. Tohoku University [*A publication*]
RREU.........	Rendezvous RADAR Electronics Unit (MCD)
RRev.........	Records Review [*Air Force*] (AFM)
RRev.........	Rijecka Revija [*A publication*]
RRF	Racing Research Fund [*Defunct*] (EA)
RRF	Rapid Reaction Forces [*Army*] (AABC)
RRF	Raptor Research Foundation (EA)
RRF	Reading Reform Foundation (EA)
RRF	Ready Reserve Fleet
RRF	Ready Reserve Force [*Military*]
RRF	Realty Refund Trust [*NYSE symbol*]
RRF	Red Resistance Front [*Netherlands*]
RRF	Reed Reactor Facility [*Reed College*] [*Research center*] (RCD)
RRF	Rehabilitation Research Foundation [*Columbia, MO*] (EA)
RRF	Resonant Reed Filter
RRF	Revised Recommended Findings
RRF	Rift-Rift-Fracture [*Geology*]
RRF	Riot Relief Fund [*New York, NY*] (EA)
RRF	Royal Regiment of Fusiliers [*Military unit*] [*British*]
RRFC.........	Rivista Rosminiana di Filosofia e di Cultura [*A publication*]
RRFC.........	Robert Redford Fan Club (EA)
RRFC.........	Robin Right Fan Club (EA)
RRFO.........	Rhine River Field Organization [*Post-World War II*]
RRFS.........	Range Rate Frequency Synthesizer
RRG...........	Point Mugu, CA [*Location identifier*] [*FAA*] (FAAL)
RRG...........	RADAR Range Gate
RRG...........	Requirements Review Group [*Air Staff*] [*Air Force*] (MCD)
RRG...........	Research Review Group (NRCH)
RRG...........	Resource Request Generator
RRG...........	Rodrigues Island [*Mauritius*] [*Airport symbol*] (OAG)
RRG...........	Roll Reference Gyro (AAG)
RRGA	Revue Roumaine de Geologie, Geophysique, et Geographie. Serie de Geographie [*Rumania*] [*A publication*]
RRGAB......	Rendiconti Romani di Gastroenterologia [*A publication*]
RRH...........	Rural Rental Housing [*Loans*] [*Farmers Home Administration*]
RRHFF.......	Rock and Roll Hall of Fame Foundation (EA)
RRHPF.......	Ronald Reagan Home Preservation Foundation (EA)
RRI............	Barora [*Solomon Islands*] [*Airport symbol*] (OAG)
RRI............	Radio Republik Indonesia [*Radio network*]
RRI............	Rate Range Indicator (MCD)
RRI............	Refugee Relief International (EA)
RRI............	Reimbursement Refund Indicator [*Military*] (AFIT)
RRI............	Reroute Inhibit [*Telecommunications*] (TEL)
RRI............	Resident Reactor Inspector [*Nuclear energy*] (NRCH)
RRI............	Revised Ring Index [*A publication*]
RRI............	Riverside Research Institute (MCD)
RRI............	Rocket Research Institute
RRI............	Romex Resources, Incorporated [*Vancouver Stock Exchange symbol*]
RRIC.........	Race Relations Information Center [*Defunct*]
RRIC.........	RADAR Repeater Indicator Console
RRIC (Rubber Res Inst Ceylon) Bull ...	RRIC (Rubber Research Institute of Ceylon) Bulletin [*A publication*]
RRIF.........	Registered Retirement Investment Fund [*Canada*]
RRIHS........	Regional Research Institute for Human Services [*Portland State University*] [*Research center*] (RCD)
RRIL	Rendiconti. Reale Istituto Lombardo di Scienze e Lettere [*Milan*] [*A publication*]
RR-IM	Office of Research and Reports, Intelligence Memoranda [*CIA*]
RRIM	Reinforced Reaction Injection Molding [*Plastics technology*]

RRIN	Readiness Risk Index Number (NG)
RRIPM........	Rapid Response Interference Prediction Model (MCD)
RRIS	Radiological Release Information System (MCD)
RRIS	Railway Research Information Service [*National Academy of Sciences*]
RRIS	Remote RADAR Integration Station
RRISL Bull ...	RRISL [*Rubber Research Institute of Sri Lanka*] Bulletin [*A publication*]
RRI Sri Lanka Bull ...	RRISL (Rubber Research Institute of Sri Lanka) Bulletin [*A publication*]
RRI & StL ...	Rockford, Rock Island & St. Louis Railroad
RRITA........	Report. Research Institute of Science and Technology. Nihon University [*A publication*]
RRJaNS.....	Rodnoj i Russkij Jazyki v Nacional'noj Skole [*A publication*]
RRK	Redaurum Red Lake Mines [*Toronto Stock Exchange symbol*]
RRK	Retaining Ring Kit
RRKM	Rice, Ramsperger, Kassel, Marcus [*Developers of a theorem in chemical kinetics, designated by the initial letters of their last names*]
RRL	Merrill, WI [*Location identifier*] [*FAA*] (FAAL)
RRL	Rabbit Reticulocyte Lysate [*Biochemistry*]
RRL	Radio Relay Link (NATG)
RRL	Radio Research Laboratory
RRL	Ralston Purina Co., Corporate Library, St. Louis, MO [*OCLC symbol*] (OCLC)
RRL	Ranchmen's Resources (1976) Limited [*Toronto Stock Exchange symbol*]
RRL	Rayleigh Radiation Law [*Physics*]
RRL	Regimental Reserve Line
RRL	Registered Record Librarian [*Medicine*]
RRL	Reserve Retired List [*Military*]
RRL	Revue Roumaine de Linguistique [*A publication*]
RRL	Road Research Laboratory [*British*]
RRL	Rocket Research Laboratories (KSC)
RRL	Ruby Rod LASER
RRL	Rudder Reference Line [*NASA*] (NASA)
RRL	Runway Remaining Lights [*Aviation*]
RRLC.........	Radiation-Resistant Linear Circuit
RRLC.........	Redwood Region Logging Conference (EA)
RRLR.........	Road Race Lincoln Register (EA)
RRLTD.......	Report. Research Laboratory of Engineering Materials. Tokyo Institute of Technology [*A publication*]
RRM	Rayleigh-Ritz Method [*Physics*]
RRM	Red Resource Monitoring (MCD)
RRM	Reliant Resources Ltd. [*Vancouver Stock Exchange symbol*]
RRM	Renegotiated-Rate Mortgage
RRM	Reports, Reviews, Meetings
RRM	Runaway Rotating Machine
RRMC........	Royal Roads Military College [*Royal Roads, BC*]
RRMF........	RADAR Reflectivity Measuring Facility
RRMG........	Reactor Recirculation Motor Generator (IEEE)
RRMRP......	Ready Reserve Mobilization Reinforcement Pool [*Army*]
RRMRS......	Ready Reserve Mobilization Reinforcement System [*Army*]
RRMTA......	Reactor Materials [*A publication*]
RRN	Rapid Reinforcement of NATO (MCD)
RRN	Relative Record Number [*Data processing*]
RRN	Serra Norte [*Brazil*] [*Airport symbol*] (OAG)
rRNA	Ribonucleic Acid, Ribosomal [*Biochemistry, genetics*]
RRNC........	Ranger Rick's Nature Club (EA)
RRNGA......	Razvedka i Razrabotka Neftyanykh i Gazovykh Mestorozhdenii [*A publication*]
RRNN........	Reproductive Rights National Network (EA)
RRNS........	Redundant Residue Number System (IEEE)
RRNS........	Related Returns Notification System [*IRS*]
RRO	Recipient Rights Officer
RRO	Regimental Reserve Officer (ADA)
RRO	Renegotiation Regional Office
RRO...........	Responsible Reporting Office [*Telecommunications*] (TEL)
RRO...........	Richport Resources [*Vancouver Stock Exchange symbol*]
RRo	Rivista Rosminiana [*A publication*]
RROA	Railroadians of America (EA)
RROC........	Rolls-Royce Owners' Club (EA)
RROS........	Resistive Read-Only Storage
R & ROTC...	Reserve and Reserve Officers' Training Corps [*Army*]
RROU	Remote Readout Unit
R Roumaine ...	Revue Roumaine d'Histoire de l'Art [*A publication*]
R Roumaine Hist ...	Revue Roumaine d'Histoire [*A publication*]
R Roumaine Hist Art ...	Revue Roumaine d'Histoire de l'Art [*A publication*]
R Roum Et Int ...	Revue Roumaine d'Etudes Internationales [*A publication*]
R Roum Sci Soc ...	Revue Roumaine des Sciences Sociales [*A publication*]
R Roum Sci Soc Ser Philos Logique ...	Revue Roumaine des Sciences Sociales. Serie de Philosophie et de Logique [*A publication*]
R Roum Sci Soc Ser Sci Econ ...	Revue Roumaine des Sciences Sociales. Serie de Sciences Economiques [*A publication*]
R Roum Sci Soc Ser Sci Jur ...	Revue Roumaine des Sciences Sociales. Serie de Sciences Juridiques [*A publication*]
R Roum Sci Soc Ser Sociol ...	Revue Roumaine des Sciences Sociales. Serie de Sociologie [*A publication*]
RRP	Radio Relay Pod
RRP	Range Ring Profile (MCD)

RRP .... Reactor Refueling Plug (NRCH)
RRP .... Ready Replacement Pilot
RRP .... Recommended Retail Price
RRP .... Recoverable Repair Parts
RRP .... Regional Project Research Program (EA)
RRP .... Regular Retail Price
RRP .... Relative Refractory Period [Medicine]
RRP .... Relay Rack Panel
RRP .... Religious Requirements and Practices [A publication]
RRP .... Republican Reliance Party [Cumhuriyetci Guven Partisi - CGP] [Turkey] (PPW)
RRP .... Reverse Repurchase Agreement [Securities]
RRP .... Reviews of Research and Practice. Institute for Research into Mental and Multiple Handicap [Elsevier Book Series] [A publication]
RRP .... Rock Hill, SC [Location identifier] [FAA] (FAAL)
RRP .... Roosevelt Roads [Puerto Rico] [Seismograph station code, US Geological Survey] [Closed] (SEIS)
RRP .... Rotterdam-Rhine Pipeline [Oil]
RRP .... Rough River Petroleum Corp. [Vancouver Stock Exchange symbol]
RRP .... Rudder Reference Plane [NASA] (NASA)
RRP .... Runway Reference Point [Aviation] (FAAC)
RRPA .... Ruhr Regional Planning Authority [Post-World War II]
RRPB .... Retraining and Reemployment Policy Board
RRPC .... Reserve Reinforcement Processing Center [Army] (AABC)
RRPD .... Runway Reference Point Downwind [Aviation] (FAAC)
RRPI .... Relative Rod Position Indication [Nuclear energy] (NRCH)
RRPI .... Rotary Relative Position Indicator [Nuclear energy] (NRCH)
RRPL .... Recommend Repair Parts List
RRPP .... Reverends Peres [Reverend Fathers] [French]
RRPRD ...... RTP. Regelungstechnische Praxis [A publication]
RRPS .... Ready Reinforcement Personnel Section [Air Force] (AFM)
RRPS .... Ronald Reagan Philatelic Society (EA)
RRPU .... Runway Reference Point Upwind [Aviation] (FAAC)
RRQ .... Rock Rapids, IA [Location identifier] [FAA] (FAAL)
RRQ .... Romanic Review Quarterly [A publication]
RRR .... Exceedingly Rare [Numismatics]
RRRA .... Railroad Reports [United States] (DLA)
RRR .... Raleigh Research Reactor
RRR .... Range and Range Rate
RRR .... Rapid Runway Repair
RRR .... Reader Railroad [AAR code]
RRR .... Readin', Ritin', and Rithmetic [Also, 3R's]
RRR .... Records, Racing, and Rallying [Sporting aviation]
RRR .... Red Red Rose [An association] (EA)
RRR .... Reduced Residual Radiation
RRR .... Relief, Recovery, Reform [Elements of the New Deal]
RRR .... Residual Resistance Ratio [Metal purity]
RRR .... Resistor-Reactor Rectifier
RRR .... Resource Requirements Request [Military] (MCD)
RRR .... Resurfacing, Restoration, and Rehabilitation [US Federal Highway Administration]
RRR .... Review of Religious Research [A publication]
RRR .... Rework Removal Rate
RRR .... Riverton Resources Corp. [Vancouver Stock Exchange symbol]
RRR .... Rum, Romanism, and Rebellion [Phrase coined during the Presidential campaign of 1884 to describe the Democratic party]
RRR .... University of Rochester, Rochester, NY [OCLC symbol] (OCLC)
RRRC .... Regulatory Requirements Review Committee [Nuclear energy] (NRCH)
RRRE .... RADAR Range-Rate Error
RRRED ...... Reclamation and Revegetation Research [A publication]
RR Rep ...... Railroad Reports (DLA)
RRRLC ...... Rochester Regional Research Library Council [Rochester, NY] [Library network]
RRRR .... Railroad Revitalization and Regulatory Reform Act [1976]
RRRRR ...... Receipt [British naval signaling]
RRRRRR .... Remedial Readin', Remedial Ritin', and Remedial Rithmetic [Also, 6R's] [Humorous interpretation of the three R's]
RRRS .... Route Relief Requirements System [Telecommunications] (TEL)
RRRV .... Rate of Rise of Restriking Voltage (IEEE)
RRS .... Dothan, AL [Location identifier] [FAA] (FAAL)
RRS .... RADAR Ranging System
RRS .... Radiation Research Society (EA)
RRS .... Radio Receiver Set
RRS .... Radio Recording Spectrophotometer
RRS .... Radio Relay Station
RRS .... Radio Relay System
RRS .... Radio Remote Set (CAAL)
RRS .... Radio Research Station [British]
RRS .... Range Rate Search (MCD)
RRS .... Reaction Research Society (EA)
RRS .... Reactor Recirculating System (NRCH)
RRS .... Reactor Refueling System (NRCH)
RRS .... Reactor Regulating System (NRCH)
RRS .... Readiness Reportable Status (NVT)

RRS .... Ready Reportable Status (MCD)
RRS .... Red River Settlement [Canada]
RRS .... Reed Relay Scanner
RRS .... Relay Radio Subsystem [NASA]
RRS .... Remaining Radiation Service (NATG)
RRS .... Remington's Revised Statutes (DLA)
RRS .... Rendezvous RADAR System [NASA] (MCD)
RRS .... Required Response Spectrum (IEEE)
RRS .... Research Referral Service [International Federation for Documentation] [Information service] (EISS)
RRS .... Resin Regeneration Subsystem [Nuclear energy] (NRCH)
RRS .... Resources and Referral Services (OICC)
RRS .... Restraint Release System (KSC)
RRS .... Retired Reserve Section
RRS .... Retransmission Request Signal [Telecommunications] (TEL)
RRS .... Retrograde Rocket System
RRS .... River and Rainfall Station [National Weather Service] (NOAA)
RRS .... Roll Rate Sensor
RRS .... Roo Rat Society (EA)
RRS .... Roros [Norway] [Airport symbol] (OAG)
RRS .... Royal Research Ship [British]
RRSCS ...... Rate Stabilization and Control System (MCD)
RRSP .... Registered Retirement Savings Plan
RRSTRAF ... Ready Reserve Strategic Army Forces
RRT .... Railroad Retirement Tax [IRS]
RRT .... Railroad Transport (NATG)
RRT .... Randomized Response Technique [Statistics]
RRT .... Ready Round Transporter (NATG)
RRT .... Reentry Reference Time [NASA]
RRT .... Registered Recreation Therapist
RRT .... Registered Respiratory Therapist
RRT .... Relative Retention Time
RR/T .... Rendezvous RADAR/Transponder [NASA] (KSC)
RRT .... Request for Review of Tooling
RRT .... Requirements Review Team
RRT .... Resources Rent Tax (ADA)
RRT .... Ring-Ring Trip [Telecommunications] (TEL)
RRT .... Robert Mines Ltd. [Vancouver Stock Exchange symbol]
RRTA .... Railroad Retirement Tax [IRS]
RRTCD ...... Tokyo Denki Daigaku Kenkyu Hokoku [A publication]
RRTD .... Rural Rehabilitation Technologies Database [University of North Dakota] [Grand Forks, ND] [Information service] (EISS)
RRTE .... Reroute (FAAC)
RRTIS .... Renewable Resources Technical Information System [Forest Service]
RRTS .... Range-Rate Tracking System
RRU .... Cedar Rapids, IA [Location identifier] [FAA] (FAAL)
RRU .... Radio Research Unit [Army] (AABC)
RRU .... Radiobiological Research Unit (IEEE)
RRU .... Remington-Rand UNIVAC
RRU .... Remote Readout Unit
RRU .... Remote Request Unit (CAAL)
RRU .... Resource Recycling Unit
RRU .... Retro-Rocket UNIVAC (MUGU)
RRV .... Denver, CO [Location identifier] [FAA] (FAAL)
RRV .... Rotor Reentry Vehicle
RRVRA ...... Revue Roumaine de Virologie [A publication]
RRVSGA .... Red River Valley Sugarbeet Growers Association (EA)
RRW .... Jacksonville, FL [Location identifier] [FAA] (FAAL)
RRW .... Radiation-Resistant Wire
RRW .... Royal Regiment of Wales [Military unit] [British]
RRWU .... Rhodesia Railway Workers' Union
RRX .... Railroad Crossing [Telecommunications] (TEL)
RRX .... Ronrico Explorations Ltd. [Vancouver Stock Exchange symbol]
R & Ry CC ... Russell and Ryan's English Crown Cases (DLA)
RS .... Aerotransportes [Argentina] [ICAO designator] (FAAC)
RS .... IEEE Reliability Society [New York, NY] (EA)
RS .... Rabbinic Supervisor (BJA)
RS .... Rabbinical School (BJA)
RS .... Rabbinical Seminary (BJA)
RS .... Rachmaninoff Society [Record label]
RS .... RADAR Scanner
RS .... RADAR Selector (MCD)
RS .... RADAR Simulator (CET)
RS .... RADAR Start (CET)
RS .... Radiated Susceptibility (IEEE)
RS .... Radiation Sensitive [Physiology]
RS .... Radiation Source (NRCH)
RS .... Radio Duties - Special
RS .... Radio Simulator
RS .... Radio Station [Maps and charts]
RS .... Radio Superviser [British]
RS .... Radio Switchboard (CAAL)
RS .... Radius of Safety (MCD)
RS .... Radular Sac
RS .... Ragtime Society (EA)
RS .... Railway Station (ROG)
RS .... Rain and Snow [Sleet] [Meteorology]
RS .... Random Saccades [Ophthalmology]
RS .... Random Splice [Telecommunications] (TEL)

RS............ Range Safety [*NASA*]   (KSC)
R & S .... Range and Safety   (AAG)
RS............ Range Selector
R/S............ Range Surveillance
RS............ Rapid Setting [*Asphalt grade*]
RS............ Ras Shamra   (BJA)
RS............ Rating Sheet [*Psychometrics*]
RS............ Rauwolfia Serpentina [*A plant, the root extract of which is used medicinally*]
RS............ Raw Stock
RS............ RAWINSONDE [*Radiosonde and RADAR Wind Sounding*] [*Upper air observation*]   (NASA)
RS............ Ray Society   (EA)
RS............ Reactor Safeguards   (NRCH)
RS............ Reader Stop [*Data processing*]   (BUR)
RS............ Reading of Standard
RS............ Ready Service   (AAG)
RS............ Real Storage
RS............ Realites Secretes [*A publication*]
RS............ Rebuild Standard [*Marine Corps*]
RS............ Receiver Station
RS............ Receiving Ship [*or Station*]
RS............ Reception Station
RS............ Recipient's Serum [*In blood matching*]
RS............ Reciprocating Steam   (MCD)
RS............ Recognition Structure [*Immunochemistry*]
RS............ Recommended Standard [*Telecommunications*]   (TEL)
RS............ Reconfiguration System   (MCD)
RS............ Reconnaissance Satellite
RS............ Reconnaissance Squadron [*Military*]
RS............ Reconnaissance-Strike [*Military*]
RS............ Reconnaissance Strip [*Military*]   (AFM)
R & S .... Reconnaissance and Surveillance   (MCD)
RS............ Reconstitution Site   (NVT)
RS............ Record Separator [*Control character*] [*Data processing*]
RS............ Recording Secretary
RS............ Recreation Supervisor [*Red Cross*]
RS............ Recruiting Service
RS............ Recruiting Station
RS............ Recruitment Surveys [*Army*] [*British*]
RS............ Rectal Sinus
RS............ Rectal Suppository [*Medicine*]
RS............ Rectified Spirits   (ROG)
RS............ Rectus-Sinister [*Nomenclature system*] [*Biochemistry*]
RS............ Reduced Strength   (MCD)
RS............ Reducing Sugar
RS............ Redundancy Status   (MCD)
RS............ Redundant Set   (MCD)
RS............ Reel Sequence [*Data processing*]
R & S .... Reenlistment and Separation [*Military*]   (AFM)
RS............ Reentry System   (AFM)
RS............ Reference Serum [*Clinical chemistry*]
RS............ Reference Standard
RS............ Reformed Spelling
RS............ Refrigeration System   (MCD)
RS............ Refurbishment Spare   (NASA)
RS............ Regional Authorities (Scotland)
RS............ Register Select
RS............ Register of Shipping of the USSR [*Ship classification society*]
RS............ Register and Storage   (MCD)
RS............ Registered Sanitarian
RS............ Regular Station [*Military*]
RS............ Regularly Scheduled [*Red Cross Volunteer*]
RS............ Regulating Station
RS............ Regulation Station [*Air Force*]
RS............ Reinforcing Stimulus
RS............ Reiter's Syndrome [*Medicine*]
R/S............ Rejection Slip   (ADA)
RS............ Relative Sweetness
R/S............ Relay Set [*Telecommunications*]   (TEL)
RS............ Reliability Summary   (KSC)
RS............ Religious Studies [*A publication*]
RS............ Relocation Site   (NVT)
RS............ Reminder Shock
R/S............ Remote Site [*NASA*]   (KSC)
RS............ Remote Station
RS............ Remotely Settable Fuze   (MCD)
RS............ Renal Specialist [*Medicine*]
RS............ Renin Substrate [*Biochemistry*]
R & S .... Renovation and Storage [*Military*]   (AFIT)
RS............ Rephael Society [*Brooklyn, NY*]   (EA)
RS............ Report of Survey
R & S .... Reports and Statistics Branch [*US Military Government, Germany*]
RS............ Reproductive Success [*Genetics*]
RS............ Republicains Sociaux [*Social Republicans*] [*French*]   (PPE)
RS............ Request to Send
RS............ Request for Services [*Social Security Administration*]
RS............ Request for Support   (MCD)
RS............ Research Scientist   (ADA)
R & S .... Research and Statistics   (IEEE)

RS............ Research on Steroids [*Elsevier Book Series*] [*A publication*]
RS............ Research Studies [*Pullman*] [*A publication*]
R & S .... Research and Study
RS............ Research Summary
RS............ Research Systems   (MCD)
RS............ Reset
RS............ Reset-Set [*Data processing*]
RS............ Reset Steering
RS............ Resident School   (MUGU)
RS............ Resistance Soldering
RS............ Resistant Sporangia [*Botany*]
RS............ Resources Section [*Resources and Technical Services Division*] [*American Library Association*]
RS............ Respiratory Syncytial [*Virus*]
RS............ Respiratory System [*Medicine*]
RS............ Response-Stimulus
RS............ Responsus [*To Answer*] [*Latin*]
RS............ Resume Sheet
RS............ Retail Shops and Stores [*Public-performance tariff class*] [*British*]
RS............ Return to Saturation
RS............ Revenue Sharing
RS............ Reverberation Strength
RS............ Reversal Shift [*Psychometrics*]
RS............ Review of Symptoms [*Medicine*]
RS............ Revised Statutes
R/S............ Revolutions per Second
RS............ Revue Suisse [*A publication*]
RS............ Revue de Synthese [*A publication*]
RS............ Reye's Syndrome [*Medicine*]
RS............ Ricerche Slavistiche [*A publication*]
RS............ Right Sacrum [*Medicine*]   (KSC)
RS............ Right Safety [*Sports*]
RS............ Right Side
RS............ Ringer's Solution [*Physiology*]
RS............ Ripon Society   (EA)
R/S............ Road Service
RS............ Road Space
RS............ [*The*] Roberval & Saguenay Railway Co. [*AAR code*]
RS............ Rochelle Salt [*Potassium Sodium Tartrate*] [*Organic chemistry*]
RS............ Rocket System   (MCD)
RS............ Rocznik Slawistyczny [*A publication*]
RS............ Rolling Stone [*A publication*]
RS............ Rolls Series   (DLA)
RS............ Romanische Studien [*A publication*]
RS............ Route Selector
RS............ Route Switching [*Telecommunications*]   (TEL)
RS............ Routing Slip [*Military*]
RS............ Royal Scots [*Military unit*]
RS............ Royal Society [*British*]
RS............ Rubble Stone   (AAG)
RS............ Rudder Station   (MCD)
RS............ Rural Sociology [*A publication*]
RS............ Syntex Laboratories, Inc. [*Research code symbol*]
3R's.......... Recognition, Reassurance, and Relaxation [*Military mental health technique*]   (INF)
RSA............ American Railway Supervisors Association [*Later, American Railway and Airline Supervisors Association*]   (EA)
RSA............ Rabbit Serum Albumin [*Immunology*]
RSA............ Rack Service Association   (EA)
RSA............ RADAR Service Area
RSA............ RADAR Signature Analysis [*Air Force*]
RSA............ Railway Supply Association [*Formed by a merger of Railway Electrical and Mechanical Supply Assocaiation and ARSA*] [*Wilmette, IL*]   (EA)
RSA............ Range Safety Approval   (MUGU)
RSA............ Rat Serum Albumin [*Immunology*]
RSA............ Rate Subsystem Analyst   (MUGU)
RSA............ Redstone Arsenal [*Huntsville, AL*] [*Army*]
RSA............ Regional Science Association   (EA)
RSA............ Regional Studies Association   (EA-IO)
RSA............ Regular Spiking Activity [*Electrophysiology*]
RSA............ Rehabilitation Services Administration [*Office of Special Education and Rehabilitive Services, Department of Education*]
RSA............ Relative Specific Activity
RSA............ Relative Standard Accuracy [*Testing methodology*]
RSA............ Remote Station Alarm
RSA............ Remote Storage Activities
RSA............ Renaissance Society of America   (EA)
RSA............ Rental Service Association   (EA)
RSA............ Repair Sevice Attendant [*Telecommunications*]   (TEL)
RSA............ Republic of South Africa
RSA............ Requirements Statement Analyzer
RSA............ Research Security Administrators
RSA............ Research Society on Alcoholism   (EA)
RSA............ Respiratory Sinus Arrhythmia [*Medicine*]
RSA............ Retire to Staging Area [*Military*]
RSA............ Revised Statutes of Alberta [*Canada*]   (DLA)
RSA............ Revised Statutes, Annotated   (DLA)
RSA............ Rhetoric Society of America   (EA)

RSA............ Rhythmic Slow Activity [*Electroencephalography*]
RSA............ Right Sacroanterior [*A fetal position*] [*Obstetrics*]
RSA............ Rivest-Shamir-Adleman [*Cryptography*]
RSA............ Rivista di Storia Antica [*A publication*]
RSA............ Rotary Servo Actuator
RSA............ Royal Scottish Academician [*or Academy*]
RSA............ [*The*] Royal Scottish Academy
RSA............ Royal Scottish Academy of Music and Drama
RSA............ Royal Society of Antiquaries
RSA............ Royal Society of Arts [*London*]
RSA............ Rubber Shippers Association [*Defunct*]
RSA............ Rural Sanitary Authority [*British*]
RSA............ Santa Rosa [*Argentina*] [*Airport symbol*]   (OAG)
RSAA........ Revue Suisse d'Art et d'Archeologie [*A publication*]
RSAAF...... Royal South African Air Force
RSAC........ RADAR Significance Analysis Code
RSAC........ Radiological Safety Analysis Computer   (MCD)
RSAC........ Recueil des Notices et Memoires. Societe Archeologique de Constantine [*A publication*]
RSAC........ Region, State, Area, County [*Code*] [*DoD*]
RSAC........ Remote Slave Aircraft   (MCD)
RSAF........ Royal Small Arms Factory [*British*]
RSAF........ Royal Swedish Air Force
RSAI......... Royal Society of Antiquaries of Ireland
RSAI......... Rutgers Social Attribute Inventory [*Psychology*]
RSALT....... Running, Signal, and Anchor Lights
RSAMC...... Royal Society of Arts, Manufacturing and Commerce [*London*]
R San I....... Royal Sanitary Institute [*Later, RSH*] [*British*]
R Sanit Inst J ... Royal Sanitary Institute. Journal [*A publication*]
RSAP......... Regional Science Association. Papers and Proceedings [*A publication*]
RSAP......... Revolutionaire Socialistische Arbeiders Partij [*Revolutionary Socialist Workers' Party*] [*The Netherlands*]   (PPE)
RSARR...... Republic of South Africa Research Reactor
RSAS........ Revenue Sharing Advisory Service   (EA)
RSAS........ Royal Sanitary Association of Scotland
RSAT......... Recueil. Societe de Prehistoire et d'Archeologie de Tebessa [*A publication*]
RSav.......... Revue de Savoie [*A publication*]
RSB............ Range Safety Beacon [*NASA*]   (AAG)
RSB............ Ravensbos [*Netherlands*] [*Seismograph station code, US Geological Survey*]   (SEIS)
RSB............ Reactor Service Building   (NRCH)
RSB............ Reconnaissance Strike Bomber
RSB............ Reduced-Size Blueprint   (NG)
RSB............ Reference Standards Book [*Military*]
RSB............ Regimental Stretcher-Bearer
RSB............ Regional Shipping Boards [*NATO*]   (NATG)
RSB............ Repair Service Bureau [*Telecommunications*]   (TEL)
RSB............ Reticulocyte Standard Buffer
RSB............ Revista. Sociedad Bolivariana [*A publication*]
RSB............ Rhondda & Swansea Bay Railway [*Wales*]
RSB............ Right Sternal Border [*Medicine*]
RSB............ Rivista Storica Benedettina [*A publication*]
RSB............ Rochester Subway Co. [*AAR code*]
RSB............ Roseberth [*Australia*] [*Airport symbol*] [*Obsolete*]   (OAG)
RSB............ Royal Swedish Ballet
RSB............ Rudder Speed Brake   (MCD)
RSBA........ Rail Steel Bar Association [*Later, SBMA*]   (EA)
RSB(E)...... Regional Shipping Board (East) [*NATO*]
R Sb Ekonom Promysl D ... Referativnyi Sbornik. Ekonomika Promyslennosti. D. Primenenie Matematiceskih Metodov v Ekonomiceskih Issledovanijah i Planirovanii [*A publication*]
RSBN......... Rivista di Studi Bizantini e Neoellenici [*A publication*]
RSBO......... Refined Soybean Oil
RSBRC....... Reference and Subscription Books Review Committee [*American Library Association*]
RSBS......... RADAR Safety Beacon System   (MCD)
RSB(W)..... Regional Shipping Board (West) [*NATO*]
RSC............ RADAR Scan Converter [*Military*]   (CAAL)
RSC............ RADAR Sea Clutter
RSC............ RADAR Set Control
RSC............ RADAR System Console [*Military*]   (CAAL)
RSC............ RADAR System Controller [*Military*]   (CAAL)
RSC............ Railway Systems Control [*A publication*]
RSC............ Range Safety Command [*or Control*] [*NASA*]
RSC............ Rat Skin Collagen
RSC............ Reactor Safety Commission [*German Federal Republic*]
RSC............ Reactor Safety Coordinator [*Nuclear energy*]   (NRCH)
RSC............ Reactor Steam Cycle
RSCT........ Reader Sentence Card
RSC............ Record Status Code   (AABC)
RSC......... Regional Service Center [*Military*]   (CINC)
RSC............ Regular, Slotted, Corrugated [*Container*]
RSC............ Reinforcement Support Category [*DoD*]
RSC............ Relative System Capability
RSC............ Religious Sisters of Charity [*Roman Catholic religious order*]
RSC............ Remote Sensing Center [*Texas A & M University*] [*Research center*]   (RCD)
RSC............ Remote Store Controller

R & SC....... Replacement and School Command [*Military*]
RSC............ Replacement and School Command [*Military*]
RSC............ Rescue Subcenter [*Aviation*]   (FAAC)
RSC............ Reserve Service Control [*Navy*]
RSC............ Residential Sales Council [*Chicago, IL*]   (EA)
RSC............ Residential Support Center   (OICC)
RSC............ Resort Air Service, Inc. [*Southern Pines, NC*] [*FAA designator*]   (FAAC)
RSC............ Restart Capability   (AAG)
RSC............ Reversible Sickled Cell [*Hematology*]
RSC............ Revised Statutes of Canada
RSC............ Riga [*USSR*] Skulte Airport [*Airport symbol*] [*Obsolete*]   (OAG)
RSC............ Right-Sided Colon Cancer [*Medicine*]
RSC............ Right Stage Center [*A stage direction*]
RSC............ Rivista di Studi Classici [*A publication*]
RSC............ Rivista di Studi Crociani [*A publication*]
RSC............ Road Safety Committee [*British police*]
RSC............ Royal Shakespeare Company [*British*]
RSC............ Royal Society of Canada
RSC............ Royal Society of Chemistry [*Formerly, CS, RIC*]
RSC............ Rules of the Supreme Court [*England*]   (DLA)
RSC............ Runway Surface Condition [*Aviation*]   (MCD)
RSC............ Rural Service Center [*Agency for International Development*]
RSC............ Russell Sage College [*New York*]
RSC............ Saint Charles Borromeo Seminary, Overbrook, PA [*OCLC symbol*]   (OCLC)
RSCA........ Religious Speech Communication Association   (EA)
RScA......... Right Scapulo-Anterior [*A fetal position*] [*Obstetrics*]
RSCAA...... Radio Shack Computer Alumni Association   (EA)
RSCAAL..... Remote Sensing Chemical Agent Alarm [*Army*]   (INF)
RSCC........ Remote-Site Command Computer [*NASA*]
RSCC........ Remote-Site Computer Complex [*NASA*]
RSCC........ Republican Senatorial Campaign Committee
RSCD........ Request to Start Contract Definition
RSCDSA.... Religion and Socialism Commission of the Democratic Socialists of America   (EA)
RSCG........ Radio Set Control Group
RSCH........ Range Scheduling   (MUGU)
RSCH........ Ready Spares Chassis
RSCH........ Research   (AFM)
R Sch Mines J ... Royal School of Mines. Journal [*England*] [*A publication*]
R Sci.......... Revue Scientifique [*A publication*]
RSCI.......... Rivista di Storia della Chiesa in Italia [*A publication*]
RSCIE........ Remote Station Communication Interface Equipment
R Sci Financ ... Revue de Science Financiere [*A publication*]
R Sci Hum ... Revue des Sciences Humaines [*A publication*]
R Sci Instr ... Review of Scientific Instruments [*A publication*]
R Sci Philos & Theol ... Revue des Sciences Philosophiques et Theologiques [*A publication*]
R Sci Ph Th ... Revue des Sciences Philosophiques et Theologiques [*A publication*]
R Sci Pol .... Revue des Sciences Politiques [*A publication*]
R Sci Rel .... Revue des Sciences Religieuses [*A publication*]
R Sci Soc France Est ... Revue des Sciences Sociales de la France de l'Est [*A publication*]
RSCJ.......... Society of the Sacred Heart [*Roman Catholic women's religious order*]
RSCL.......... Radioactive Sodium Chemistry Loop
RSCL.......... Rivista di Studi Classici [*A publication*]
RSCM........ Royal School of Church Music [*British*]
RSCN........ Registered Sick Children's Nurse [*British*]
RS Comp ... Statutes of Connecticut, Compilation of 1854   (DLA)
R Scott Mus Inf Ser Geol ... Royal Scottish Museum. Information Series. Geology [*A publication*]
RScP......... Right Scapuloposterior [*A fetal position*] [*Obstetrics*]
RScPhilT.... Revue des Sciences Philosophiques et Theologiques [*Paris*] [*A publication*]
RscPhTh .... Revue des Sciences Philosophiques et Theologiques [*Paris*] [*A publication*]
RSCR........ Range Safety Command Receiver [*NASA*]   (KSC)
RSCR........ Reserve Special Commendation Ribbon
RScR......... Revue des Sciences Religieuses [*A publication*]
RScRel....... Revue des Sciences Religieuses [*A publication*]
RSCS......... Range Safety Command System [*NASA*]   (AAG)
RSCS......... Rate Stabilization and Control System
RSCS......... Remote Spooling Communications Subsystem [*IBM Corp.*] [*Data processing*]   (IBMDP)
RSCS......... Rod Sequence Control System [*Nuclear energy*]   (NRCH)
RSCSA....... Railway Signal and Communications Suppliers Association [*Later, RSS*]   (EA)
RSCST....... Rivista Storico-Critica delle Scienze Teologiche [*A publication*]
RSCT......... Rohde Sentence Completions Test [*Psychology*]
RSCT......... Royal Society of Canada. Transactions [*A publication*]
RSCU........ Rescue   (FAAC)
RSCW........ Research Reactor, State College of Washington   (NRCH)
RSD............ Radiance Spectral Distribution
RSD............ Raised   (MSA)
RSD............ Raised Shelter Deck
RSD............ Rassemblement des Socialistes et des Democrates [*Rally of Socialists and Democrats*] [*Reunionese*]   (PPW)
RSD............ Ratoon Stunting Disease [*of sugarcane*]

RS & D .... Receipt, Storage, and Delivery [*Business and trade*]
RSD .... Reentry Systems Department
RSD .... Reference Services Division [*of ALA*] [*Later, RASD*]   (EA)
RSD .... Reflex Sympathetic Dystrophy [*Medicine*]
RSD .... Refueling Shutdown   (IEEE)
RSD .... Relative Standard Deviation [*Statistics*]
RSD .... Requirements and Specifications Document [*NASA*]   (NASA)
RSD .... Research Services Department [*United Way of Greater Indianapolis*] [*Indiana*] [*Information service*]   (EISS)
RSD .... Responsible System Designer   (NRCH)
RSD .... Roadside Delivery   (ADA)
RSD .... Rock Sound [*Bahamas*] [*Airport symbol*]   (OAG)
RSD .... Rolling Steel Door [*Technical drawings*]
RSD .... Royal Society, Dublin
RSDC .... Radiation Subprogramme Data Center [*Marine science*]   (MSC)
RSDG .... Raster Scan Display Generator   (MCD)
RSDI .... Rivista di Storia del Diritto Italiano [*A publication*]
RSDLP ...... Russian Social-Democratic Labor Party
RSDLP(B) ... Russian Social-Democratic Labor Party (Bolsheviks)
RSDP .... Remote Shutdown Panel   (IEEE)
RSDP .... Remote-Site Data Processor [*NASA*]
RSDr. .... Doctor of Social Sciences
RSDRP ...... Rossiiskaia Sotsial-Demokraticheskaia Rabochaya Partiia [*Russian Social Democratic Workers' Party*]   (PPE)
RSDS .... RADAR Systems Design Section
RSDS .... Range Safety Destruct System
RSDT .... Regulations of Office of the Secretary, Department of Transportation
RSDT .... Remote Station Data Terminal
RSDU .... RADAR Storm Detection Unit
RSDW .... Ross Sea Deep Water [*Marine science*]   (MSC)
RSDWP ...... Russian Social Democratic Workers Party
RSE .... RADAR Search Equipment
RSE .... Raid Size Estimate
RSE .... Rassegna di Studi Etiopici [*A publication*]
RSE .... Receiving Site Equipment [*NASA*]
RSE .... Reference Standards Equipment [*Deep Space Instrumentation Facility, NASA*]
RSE .... Renewable Sources of Energy [*A publication*]
RSE .... Request Select Entry [*Data processing*]
RSE .... Resistance Soldering Equipment
RSE .... Review of Social Economy [*A publication*]
RSE .... Revue des Sciences Ecclesiastiques [*A publication*]
RSE .... Rivista di Storia Economica [*A publication*]
RSE .... Royal Society of Edinburgh
RSE .... Sydney-Rose Bay [*Australia*] [*Airport symbol*]   (OAG)
RSEA .... Reference Sensing Element Amplifier
RSEA .... Revue de Sud-Est Asiatique [*A publication*]
R Se As Stud ... Review of Southeast Asian Studies [*Singapore*] [*A publication*]
RSEC .... Regional Science Experience Center
RSEC .... Regional Solar Energy Center
RSEC .... Representative Shuttle Environmental Control [*System*] [*NASA*]
RSECS ...... Representative Shuttle Environmental Control System [*NASA*]   (MCD)
RSED .... Refund Statute Expiration Date [*IRS*]
R Seneg Dr ... Revue Senegalaise de Droit [*A publication*]
RSEP .... Restraint System Evaluation Program [*Department of Transportation*]
RSEP .... [*H. B.*] Robinson Steam Electric Plant   (NRCH)
RSER .... Remote Sensing of Earth Resources
RSER .... Rotary Stylus Electronics Recorder
R Servizio Soc ... Rivista di Servizio Sociale [*A publication*]
RSES .... Refrigeration Service Engineers Society [*Des Plaines, IL*]   (EA)
RSES .... Rosenberg Self-Esteem Scale
RSEt .... Rassegna di Studi Etiopici [*A publication*]
RSEU .... Remote Scanner-Encoder Unit [*Bell Laboratories*]
RSEW .... Resistance Seam Welding
RSEW-HF ... Resistance Seam Welding - High Frequency
RSEW-I ...... Resistance Seam Welding - Induction
RSF .... Radial Structure Function [*of solid catalysts*]
RSF .... Rassegna di Scienze Filosofiche [*A publication*]
RSF .... Rassegna di Studi Francesi [*A publication*]
RSF .... Receiving-Safing Facility   (MCD)
RSF .... Reciprocal Cross Sterile Females [*Genetics*]
RSF .... Refurbish and Subassemblies Facilities [*NASA*]   (NASA)
RSF .... Reject Suspense File [*Army*]
RSF .... Relative Substitution Frequency [*of amino acids in proteins*]
RSF .... Remote Support Facility
RSF .... Research Systems Facility
RSF .... Residual Support Force [*After main force redeployment*] [*Military*]
RSF .... Rhododendron Species Foundation   (EA)
RSF .... Risk Studies Foundation   (EA)
RSF .... Rivista di Storia della Filosofia [*A publication*]
RSF .... Roll Sheet Feeder
RSF .... Rough Sunk Face [*Construction*]
RSF .... Royal Scots Fusiliers [*Military unit*]
RSF .... Russian Student Fund [*Defunct*]   (EA)

RSFA .... Roller Skating Foundation of America   (EA)
RSFC .... Ricky Skaggs International Fan Club   (EA)
RSFC .... Ronnie Smith Fan Club [*Herkimer, NY*]   (EA)
RSFFA .... Rendiconti. Scuola Internazionale di Fisica "Enrico Fermi" [*A publication*]
RSFMA ...... Rivista Sperimentale di Freniatria e Medicina Legale delle Alienazioni Mentali [*A publication*]
RSFPA .... Revista de la Sanidad de las Fuerzas Policiales del Peru [*A publication*]
RSFPP .... Retired Servicemen's Family Protection Plan
RSFR .... Rivista di Studi Filosofici e Religiosi [*A publication*]
RSFSA .... Rendiconti del Seminario. Facolta di Scienze. Universita di Cagliari [*A publication*]
RSFSR .... Russian Soviet Federated Socialist Republic
RSG .... Rabbi Saadia Gaon [*Jewish scholar, 882-942*]   (BJA)
RSG .... RADAR Set Group [*HAWK missile*]   (MCD)
RSG .... RADAR Signal Generator   (MCD)
RSG .... RADAR Systems Group [*of General Motors Corp.*]
RSG .... Range Safety Group [*Range Commanders Council*] [*NASA*]
RSG .... Rate Signal Generator   (AAG)
RSG .... Rate Support Grant [*British*]
RSG .... Rate Switching Gyro   (MCD)
RSG .... Reassign   (AABC)
RSG .... Receiving Stolen Goods
RSG .... Reenlistment Steering Group [*Military*]   (MCD)
RSG .... Reference Signal Generator
RSG .... Regional Seat of Government
RSG .... Relay Switch Group
RSG .... Research Study Group   (NATG)
RSG .... Resident Study Group [*Army*]   (MCD)
RSG .... Resource Service Group Ltd. [*Toronto Stock Exchange symbol*]
RSG .... Rising   (FAAC)
RSG .... Rocksprings, TX [*Location identifier*] [*FAA*]   (FAAL)
RSG .... Royal Scots Greys [*Military unit*]
RSGB .... Radio Society of Great Britain
RSGMT ...... Reassignment
RSGN .... Reassign
RSGPB ...... Rinsan Shikenjo Geppo [*A publication*]
RSGS .... Ranges and Space Ground Support   (AAG)
RSGS .... Royal Scottish Geographical Society
RSH .... RADAR Status History
RSH .... Resin Sluice Header   (NRCH)
RSh .... Revista Shell [*A publication*]
RSH .... Revue des Sciences Humaines [*A publication*]
RSH .... Revue de Synthese Historique [*A publication*]
RSH .... Ring Systems Handbook [*American Chemical Society*] [*A publication*]
RSH .... Royal Society of Health [*Formerly, R San I*] [*British*]
RSH .... Russian Mission [*Alaska*] [*Airport symbol*]   (OAG)
RSHA .... Reichssicherheitshauptampt [*Central Security Office of the Reich*] [*NAZI Germany*]
RSHC .... Research in the Sociology of Health Care [*A publication*]
RSHEA ...... Royal Society of Health. Journal [*A publication*]
RSHF .... Room Sensible Heat Factor
RSHG .... Revue. Societe Haitienne d'Histoire, de Geographie, et de Geologie [*A publication*]
RSHM .... Religious of the Sacred Heart of Mary [*Roman Catholic women's religious order*]
RSHS .... Railroad Station Historical Society   (EA)
RSHum ...... Revue des Sciences Humaines [*A publication*]
RSHX .... Recirculation Spray Heat Exchanger [*Nuclear energy*]   (NRCH)
RSI .... Air Sunshine, Inc. [*Ft. Lauderdale, FL*] [*FAA designator*]   (FAAC)
RSI .... East-West Resource Systems Institute [*East-West Center - Honolulu, HI*] [*Research center*]   (RCD)
RSI .... RADAR Scope Interpretation   (AAG)
RSI .... Rationalization, Standardization, and Interoperability [*Program*] [*Army*]   (INF)
RSI .... Reactor Siting Index   (NRCH)
RSI .... Realty South Investors, Inc. [*American Stock Exchange symbol*]
RSI .... Receipt, Storage, and Issue [*Army*]   (AABC)
R(SI) .... Reconstruction, Social Insurance [*British*] [*World War II*]
RSI .... Record Status Indicator   (AABC)
RSI .... Reflected Signal Indication [*Air Force*]
RSI .... Regional Safety Inspector [*Ministry of Agriculture, Fisheries, and Food*] [*British*]
RSI .... Register Sender Inward [*Telecommunications*]   (TEL)
RSI .... Religious Science International [*Formerly, IARSC*]   (EA)
RSI .... Remote Sensing Institute [*South Dakota State University*] [*Research center*]   (RCD)
RSI .... Replacement Stream Input [*Military*]
RSI .... Repressor-Sensitizer Index [*Psychology*]
RSI .... Repubblica Sociale Italiana [*Italian Socialist Republic*] [*Founded by Mussolini*] [*1943-1945*]
RSI .... Research Studies Institute
RSI .... Reusable Surface Insulation [*NASA*]
RSI .... Rio Sidra [*Panama*] [*Airport symbol*]   (OAG)
RSI .... Rivista Storica Italiana [*A publication*]
RSI .... Roll Stability Indicator [*NASA*]   (KSC)

RSI .... Roofing/Siding/Insulation [*A publication*]
RSI .... Rotary Shaft Indicator
RSI .... Royal Sanitary Institute   (ROG)
RSI .... Royal Signals Institution [*British*]   (DEN)
RS & I .... Rules, Standards, and Instructions
RSIC .... Radiation Shielding Information Center [*Department of Energy*] [*Oak Ridge, TN*]
RSIC .... Redstone Scientific Information Center [*Army*]
RSIC .... Responding Superior in Command   (MCD)
RSIC .... RSI [*Resource Services, Inc.*] Corporation [*NASDAQ symbol*]   (NQ)
RSID .... Resource Identification Table [*Data processing*]
RSIHM .... Reparation Society of the Immaculate Heart of Mary   (EA)
RSIJA .... Journal. Royal College of Surgeons in Ireland [*A publication*]
RSIM .... RADAR Simulator   (MSA)
RSIM .... Retrospective Single Ion Monitoring [*Analytical chemistry*]
R Sind Estadist ... Revista Sindical de Estadistica [*A publication*]
R Sindical Estadistica ... Revista Sindical de Estadistica [*A publication*]
RSIR .... International Statistical Institute. Review [*A publication*]
RSIS .... Radical Science Information Service [*News service attempting to interrelate radical politics and scientific issues*]
RSIS .... Rotorcraft Systems Integration Simulator [*Joint Army-NASA program*]   (RDA)
RSITA .... Reglement du Service International des Telecommunications de l'Aeronautique
RSITD .... Revue Francaise d'Automatique, Informatique, et Recherche Operationnelle. Serie Informatique Theorique [*A publication*]
R/SITU ...... Respiratory/Surgical Intensive Therapy Unit [*of a hospital*]
RSIUFL ...... Release Suspension for Issue and Use of Following Lots
RSIVP .... Rapid Sequence Intravenous Pyelogram [*Medicine*]
RSJ .... Rolled-Steel Joist
RSJ .... Rolling-Stock Jigsaws [*British*]
RSKU .... Reza Shah Kibur University [*Iran*]
RS KY Agric Exp Stn ... RS. Kentucky Agricultural Experiment Station [*A publication*]
RSL .... Radio Standards Laboratory [*National Bureau of Standards*]
RS or L .... Rated Same or Lower
RSL .... Received Signal Level [*Telecommunications*]   (TEL)
RSL .... Reconnaissance and Security Line
RSL .... Red Suisse de Languedoc   (EA)
RSL .... Reference Standards Laboratory [*Deep Space Instrumentation Facility, NASA*]
RSL .... Remote Sensing Laboratory [*University of Kansas, University of Minnesota*] [*Research center*]   (MCD)
RSL .... Remote Sprint Launching
RSL .... Requirements Statement Language
RSL .... Research Services Limited [*Database producer*] [*Wembley, Middlesex, England*]
RSL .... Resource Support List   (MCD)
RSl .... Revue des Etudes Slaves [*A publication*]
RSL .... Ricerche Slavistiche [*A publication*]
RSL .... Right Sacrolateral [*Obstetrics*]
RSL .... Ripe Skin Liquid [*A banana substrate*]
RSL .... Rivista di Sintesi Litteraria [*A publication*]
RSL .... Rivista di Studi Liguri [*A publication*]
RSL .... Road Service Licence [*British*]
RSl .... Rocznik Slawistyczny [*A publication*]
RSL .... Roselend [*France*] [*Seismograph station code, US Geological Survey*]   (SEIS)
RSL .... Royal Society of Literature [*British*]
RSL .... Royal Society, London [*British*]
RSL .... RSI Retail Solutions, Incorporated [*Vancouver Stock Exchange symbol*]
RSL .... Russell, KS [*Location identifier*] [*FAA*]   (FAAL)
RSLA .... Range Safety Launch Approval   (AFM)
RSlav .... Ricerche Slavistiche [*A publication*]
RSlav .... Romanoslavica [*A publication*]
RSLB .... Right Short Leg Brace [*Medicine*]
RSlI .... Radovi Slavenskog Instituta [*A publication*]
RSLig .... Rivista di Studi Liguri [*A publication*]
RSLit .... Riverside Studies in Literature [*A publication*]
RSLR .... Rivista de Storia e Letteratura Religiosa [*A publication*]
RSLS .... Receiver Side Lobe Suppression   (MCD)
RSLTS .... Results
RSlU .... Rocenka Slovanskeho Ustavu v Praze [*A publication*]
RSLVR .... Resolver   (MSA)
RSM .... Radiation Signature Measurement
RSM .... Radiation Survey Meter [*NASA*]
RSM .... Radio Squadron Mobile   (MUGU)
RSM .... Rapeseed Meal
RSM .... Real Storage Management [*Data processing*]   (IBMDP)
RSM .... Reconnaissance Strategic Missile
RSM .... Reed Switching Matrix
RSM .... Regimental Sergeant Major [*Army*]
RSM .... Response Surface Methodology
RSM .... Revised Statutes of Manitoba [*Canada*]   (DLA)
RSM .... Rivet Setting Machine
RSM .... Rivista Storico-Critica delle Scienze Mediche e Naturali [*A publication*]
RSM .... Robert Strange McNamara [*US Secretary of Defense, 1961-68*]

RSM .... Royal School of Mines [*British*]
RSM .... Royal School of Musketry [*Hythe*] [*Military*] [*British*]   (ROG)
RSM .... Royal Society of Medicine [*British*]
RSM .... Royal Society of Musicians [*British*]
RSM .... Sisters of Mercy [*Roman Catholic religious order*]
RSMA .... Radiological Systems Microfilm Associates [*Port Ewen, NY*]   (EA)
RSMA .... Railway Supply Manufacturers Association   (EA)
RSMA .... Railway Systems and Management Association [*Northfield, NJ*]   (EA)
RSMA .... Royal Society of Marine Artists [*Formerly, SMA*] [*British*]
RSMAS ...... Rosenstiel School of Marine and Atmospheric Science [*University of Miami*] [*Research center*]   (RCD)
RSMAS ...... Rosentiel School of Marine and Atmospheric Sciences [*Marine science*]   (MSC)
RSmB .... Bryant College, Smithfield, RI [*Library symbol*] [*Library of Congress*]   (LCLS)
RS & MD ..... Riots, Strikes, and Malicious Damage [*Insurance*]   (ADA)
RSMFA .... Rendiconti. Seminario Matematico e Fisico di Milano [*A publication*]
RSMG .... Rotorcraft Simulator Motion Generator [*Army*]   (RDA)
RSMJA .... Royal School of Mines. Journal [*A publication*]
RSMM .... Redundant System Monitor Model   (MCD)
Rs Mod Physics ... Reviews of Modern Physics [*A publication*]
RSMR .... Raw Stock Material Requirements
RSMS .... Radio Spectrum Measurement System [*National Telecommunications and Information Administration*]
RSMT .... Ras Shamra Mythological Texts   (BJA)
RSMT .... Red Sea Mission Team [*Minneapolis, MN*]   (EA)
RSN .... Radiation Surveillance Network [*Public Health Service*]
RSN .... Radio Supernovae [*Astrophysics*]
RSN .... Rassemblement pour le Salut National [*Rally for National Salvation*] [*Senegalese*]   (PD)
RSN .... Ready, Soon, Now (Approach) [*Marketing*]
RSN .... Reason   (AFM)
RSN .... Reject Sequence Number [*Data processing*]
RSN .... Report Serial Number [*Army*]
RSN .... Research Surveillance Network
RSN .... Resonate   (KSC)
RSN .... Revised Statutes of Newfoundland [*Canada*]   (DLA)
RSN .... Revue Suisse de Numismatique [*A publication*]
RSN .... Ruston, LA [*Location identifier*] [*FAA*]   (FAAL)
RSNA .... Radiological Society of North America [*Oak Brook, IL*]   (EA)
RSNA .... Royal Society of Northern Antiquaries   (ROG)
RSNB .... Revised Statutes of New Brunswick [*Canada*]   (DLA)
RSNF .... Royal Saudi Arabian Navy Forces   (MCD)
RSNGS ...... Rancho Seco Nuclear Generating Station   (NRCH)
RSNO .... Referral Service Network Office
RSNP .... Registered Student Nurse Program   (AABC)
RSNS .... Revised Statutes of Nova Scotia [*Canada*]   (DLA)
RSNT .... Revised Single Negotiating Text [*UN Law of the Sea Conference*]
RSO .... Radiation Safety Officer   (NRCH)
RSO .... Radio Symphony Orchestra
RSO .... Radiological Safety Office [*or Officer*]   (NASA)
RSO .... Radiosonde Observation   (MUGU)
RSO .... Railway Sorting Office
RSO .... Railway Suboffice
RSO .... Ramus Supraorbitalis [*Anatomy*]
RSO .... Range Safety Officer
RSO .... Range Support Operation
RSO .... Reactor Standards Office [*Oak Ridge National Laboratory*]
RSO .... Reactor System Outline   (NRCH)
RSO .... Reconnaissance and Survey Officer   (AABC)
RSO .... Reconnaissance System Officer   (MCD)
RSO .... Regimental Supply Officer [*Army*]
RSO .... Regional Safety Officer [*British*]
RSO .... Regional Security Officer [*Foreign Service*]
RSO .... Register Sender Outward [*Telecommunications*]   (TEL)
RSO .... Research Ship of Opportunity
RSO .... Resident Surgical Officer [*British*]
RSO .... Revenue Sharing Office [*Treasury*]   (OICC)
RSO .... Revised Statutes of Ontario [*Canada*]   (DLA)
RSO .... Revolutionaere Sozialisten (Oesterreichs) [*Revolutionary Socialists (Austria)*]   (PPE)
RSO .... Right Salpingo-Oophorectomy [*Medicine*]
RSO .... Rivista degli Studi Orientali [*A publication*]
RSO .... Runway Supervisory Officer [*Aviation*]   (MCD)
RSO .... Rural Suboffice [*British*]
RSOB .... Russell Senate Office Building [*Also, OSOB*]   (DLA)
RSOC .... Remote Sensing Oceanography [*Navy*]
RSoc .... Revue Socialiste [*A publication*]
R Soc .... Revue des Societes [*A publication*]
R Soc Can ... Royal Society of Canada. Transactions [*A publication*]
R Soc Can Proc ... Royal Society of Canada. Proceedings [*A publication*]
R Soc Econ ... Review of Social Economy [*A publication*]
R Soc Edinb Proc Sect B ... Royal Society of Edinburgh. Proceedings. Section B. Biology [*A publication*]
R Soc Esp Fis Quim Reun Bienal ... Real Sociedad Espanola de Fisica y Quimica. Reunion Bienal [*A publication*]
R Soc Et Expans ... Revue. Societe d'Etudes et d'Expansion [*A publication*]

R Soc Health J ... Royal Society of Health. Journal [*A publication*]
R Social Economy ... Review of Social Economy [*A publication*]
R Sociol...... Revija za Sociologiju [*A publication*]
R Soc Lond Philos Trans ... Royal Society of London. Philosophical Transactions [*A publication*]
R Soc Lond Philos Trans Ser A ... Royal Society of London. Philosophical Transactions. Series A [*A publication*]
R Soc Lond Philos Trans Ser B ... Royal Society of London. Philosophical Transactions. Series B [*A publication*]
R Soc Lond Proc Ser B ... Royal Society of London. Proceedings. Series B. Biological Sciences [*A publication*]
R Soc NZ Bull ... Royal Society of New Zealand. Bulletin [*A publication*]
R Soc NZJ ... Royal Society of New Zealand. Journal [*A publication*]
R Soc Queensl Proc ... Royal Society of Queensland. Proceedings [*A publication*]
R Soc S Aust Trans ... Royal Society of South Australia. Transactions [*A publication*]
R Soc Tasmania Pap Proc ... Royal Society of Tasmania. Papers and Proceedings [*A publication*]
R Soc Theory ... Review of Social Theory [*A publication*]
R Soc Victoria Proc ... Royal Society of Victoria. Proceedings [*A publication*]
R Soc West Aust J ... Royal Society of Western Australia. Journal [*A publication*]
RSOP......... Range Safety Operational Plan   (MUGU)
RSOP......... Readiness Standing Operating Procedures [*Military*]   (INF)
RSOP......... Reconnaissance, Selection, and Occupation of Position [*Military*]
RSOPN...... Resumed Operation   (FAAC)
RSOR .... Range Safety Operations Requirement
RSov.......... Rassegna Sovietica [*A publication*]
RSP .... RADAR Signal Processor
RSP .... Radii of Standard Parallels
RSP .... Radio Switch Panel
RSP .... Random Smooth Pursuit [*Ophthalmology*]
RSP .... Range Solar Panel
RSP .... Range Sorting Program
RSP .... Range Support Plan   (MUGU)
RSP .... Rapid Site Preparation
RSP .... Rapid Solidification Process   (MCD)
RSP .... Rate Sensing Package   (AAG)
RSP .... Reactivity Surveillance Procedures [*Nuclear energy*]   (NRCH)
RSP .... Reader/Sorter Processor
RSP .... Real-Time Signal Processor   (MCD)
RSP .... Receiving Stolen Property
RSP .... Reconnaissance and Security Positions
RSP .... Record Select Program [*Data processing*]
RSP .... Recoverable Sparoair Probe   (MUGU)
RSP .... Reinforced Structural Plastic
RSP .... Remote Shutdown Panel [*Nuclear energy*]   (NRCH)
RSP .... Render Safe Procedure
RSP .... Rendezvous Station Panel   (MCD)
RSP .... Replenishment Spare Part
RSP .... Replication Synchronization Process [*Telecommunications*]   (TEL)
RSP .... Reserve Stock Point
RSP .... Respirable Suspended Particulates
RSP .... Responder Beacon
RSP .... Restoration Priority [*Telecommunications*]   (TEL)
RSP .... Revolutionaire Socialistische Partij [*Revolutionary Socialist Party*] [*The Netherlands*]   (PPE)
RSP .... Revolutionary Socialist Party [*Indian*]   (PPW)
RSP .... Revue des Sciences Politiques [*A publication*]
RSP .... Right Sacroposterior [*A fetal position*] [*Obstetrics*]
RSP .... Rivista di Studi Pompeiani [*A publication*]
RSP .... Robotic Sample Processor [*Automation*]
RSP .... Roll Stabilization Platform
RSP .... Roscoe, Snyder & Pacific Railway Co. [*AAR code*]
RSP .... Rotating Shield Plug   (NRCH)
RSP .... Rotation in a Selected Plane
RSP .... Rural Satellite Program [*US Agency for International Development*] [*Washington, DC*] [*Telecommunications*]   (TSSD)
RSPA......... Railway Systems and Procedures Association [*Later, RSMA*]
RSPA......... Research and Special Programs Administration [*Department of Transportation*]
RSPA......... Royal Society for the Prevention of Accidents [*British*]
RSPB......... Retail Stockage Policy, Bulk Supplies   (MCD)
RSPB......... Royal Society for the Protection of Birds [*British*]
RSPCA...... Royal Society for the Prevention of Cruelty to Animals [*British*]
RSPD......... Rapid Solidification Plasma Deposition [*Metallurgy*]
RSPD......... Research and Special Project Division [*Bureau of National Affairs*] [*Information service*]   (EISS)
RSPD......... Respond   (MSA)
RSPE......... RADAR Signalling Processing Equipment
RSPE......... Retail Stockage Policy Evaluation   (MCD)
RSPh .... Revue des Sciences Philosophiques et Theologiques [*A publication*]
RSPhTh...... Revue des Sciences Philosophiques et Theologiques [*A publication*]
RSPI .... Ras Shamra Parallels. Vol. I [*A publication*]

RSPI .... Residential Space Planners International [*Minneapolis, MN*]   (EA)
RSPK .... Recurrent Spontaneous Psychokinesis [*Poltergeist*] [*Parapsychology*]
RSPL .... RADAR Significant Power Line
RSPL .... Recommended Spare Parts List
RSPMB...... Research in the Psychology of Music [*A publication*]
RSPMP...... Ready Store Positive Maintenance Program   (MCD)
RSPO......... Rail Services Planning Office [*Interstate Commerce Commission*]
RSPO......... Railway Station Police Officer [*British*]
RSPP .... Radio Simulation Patch Panel   (CET)
RSPP .... Royal Society of Portrait Painters [*British*]
RSPRT ...... Robust Sequential Probability Ratio Test [*Navy*]
RSPS .... Range Solar Panel Substrate
RSPS .... Response   (MSA)
RSPT .... Real Storage Page Table [*Data processing*]   (BUR)
RSPT .... Revue des Sciences Philosophiques et Theologiques [*A publication*]
RSPTA ...... Recherche Spatiale [*A publication*]
RSPTR....... Respirator   (MSA)
RSPV......... Respective   (AABC)
RSPWC ..... Royal Society of Painters in Water Colours [*British*]
RSQ........... Rescue   (AAG)
RSQ........... Revised Statutes of Quebec [*Canada*]   (DLA)
RSQ........... Rhetoric Society. Quarterly [*A publication*]
RSQBT....... Rescue Boat
RSQC......... Reliability, Safety, and Quality Control
RSR .... Congregation of Our Lady of the Holy Rosary [*Roman Catholic women's religious order*]
RSR .... En Route Surveillance RADAR
RSR .... Radiological Safety Review   (NRCH)
RSR .... Range Safety Report [*NASA*]   (AAG)
RSR .... Rapid Solidification Rate   (IEEE)
RSR .... Rassegna Storica del Risorgimento [*A publication*]
RSR .... Reactor Safety Research
RSR .... Ready Service Ring   (NG)
RSR .... Recherches de Science Religieuse [*A publication*]
RSR .... Red Sulfhydryl Reagent
RSR .... Reference Services Review [*A publication*]
RSR .... Refracted Surface-Reflected Ray
RSR .... Regular Sinus Rhythm [*Physiology*]
RSR .... Republica Socialista Romania [*Socialist Republic of Romania*]
RSR .... Request for Scientific Research   (AAG)
RSR .... Required Supply Rate   (AABC)
RSR .... Research Study Requests
RSR .... Resorufin [*Organic chemistry*]
RSR .... Resources Status Report
RSR .... Revised Supplementary Regulation
RSR .... Revue des Sciences Religieuses. Universite de Strasbourg [*A publication*]
RSR .... Rivista di Studi Religiosi [*A publication*]
RSR .... Rocket Scoring Reliability   (MCD)
RSR .... Rocket Stabilized Rod
RSR .... Rod Select Relay   (IEEE)
RSR .... Rotary Seal Ring
RSR .... Route Surveillance RADAR
RSR .... Royal Sussex Regiment [*Military unit*] [*British*]
RSR .... Worcester, MA [*Location identifier*] [*FAA*]   (FAAL)
RSRA .... Rotor Systems Research Aircraft [*Army/NASA*]
RSRC......... RSR Corporation [*NASDAQ symbol*]   (NQ)
RSRE......... Royal Signals and RADAR Establishment [*Malvern, England*] [*Computer chip designer*]
RSRel .... Revue des Sciences Religieuses. Universite de Strasbourg [*A publication*]
RSRis .... Rassegna Storica del Risorgimento [*A publication*]
RSRM .... Reduced Smoke Rocket Motor   (MCD)
RSROA...... Roller Skating Rink Operators Association of America [*Lincoln, NE*]   (EA)
RSROD...... Revue Francaise d'Automatique, Informatique, et Recherche Operationnelle. Serie Recherche Operationnelle [*A publication*]
RSRP......... Remote Sensing Research Program [*University of California*]
RSRP......... Rossica Society of Russian Philately   (EA)
RSRPB ...... Research and the Retarded [*A publication*]
RSRS......... Radio and Space Research Station [*Later, Appleton Laboratory*] [*British*]   (MCD)
RSRS......... Range Safety Receiving Station
RSRS......... Reser's Fine Foods [*NASDAQ symbol*]   (NQ)
RSRUS...... Revue des Sciences Religieuses. Universite de Strasbourg [*A publication*]
RSRV......... Rotor Systems Research Vehicle
RSRW........ Remote Short Range Wind Sensor   (MCD)
RSS .... RADAR Seeker Simulator [*Military*]   (CAAL)
RSS .... RADAR Sensing System [*Military*]   (CAAL)
RSS .... RADAR Signal Simulator
RSS .... Radiated Simulation System   (MCD)
RSS .... Radio Security Service [*British*]
RSS........... Radio Subsystem
RSS........... Railway Systems Suppliers   (EA)
RSS .... Range Safety Switch   (MCD)

RSS .... Range Safety System
RSS .... Rapid Scanning of Spectra [*Instrumentation*]
RSS .... Rashtriya Swayamsevak Sangh [*National Union of Selfless Servers*] [*Militant Hindu organization*] [*India*]
RSS .... Rassegna Storica Salernitana [*A publication*]
RSS .... Reactant Service System
RSS .... Reactants Supply System   (KSC)
RSS .... Reactor Safety Study
RSS .... Reactor Shutdown System   (NRCH)
RSS .... Ready Service Spares
RSS .... Real-Time Switching System
RS & S ...... Receiving, Shipping, and Storage   (NASA)
RSS .... Reed Stenhouse Companies Ltd. [*Toronto Stock Exchange symbol*] [*Vancouver Stock Exchange symbol*]
RSS .... Reference Sound Source
RSS .... Refrigeration System [*or Subsystem*] [*Skylab*] [*NASA*]
RSS .... Refrigeration System Shield   (MCD)
RSS .... Regiae Societatis Sodalis [*Fellow of the Royal Society*]
RSS .... Registered Shoeing Smith [*Blacksmith*] [*Scotland*]
RSS .... Rehabilitation Service Series
RSS .... Rehabilitation Support Schedule   (AFM)
RSS .... Relative System Sensitivity
RSS .... Relaxed Static Stability [*Aviation*]
RSS .... Remote Safing Switch
RSS .... Remote Sensing Society   (EA-IO)
RSS .... Remote Shutdown System   (IEEE)
RSS .... Remote Slave Station   (MCD)
RSS .... Remote Switching System [*Telecommunications*]
RSS .... Repeat Squawk Sheet   (MCD)
RSS .... Requirements Status System [*NASA*]
RSS .... Residual Sum of Squares [*Statistics*]
RSS .... Resource Survey Satellite
RSS .... Restricted Stepsize [*Statistics*]
RSS .... Retention Spermatemia Syndrome [*Medicine*]
RSS .... Revised Statutes of Saskatchewan   (DLA)
RSS .... Revue du Seizieme Siecle [*A publication*]
RSS .... Reye's Syndrome Society [*Formerly, NRSF*]   (EA)
RSS .... Rib Structure Station   (MCD)
RSS .... Ride Smoothing System [*Aviation*]
RSS .... Rifle Sharpshooter
RSS .... Rigid Space Structure
RSS .... Ripe Skin Solid [*A banana substrate*]
RSS .... Rivista di Scienze Storiche [*A publication*]
RSS .... Rockdale, Sandow & Southern Railroad Co. [*AAR code*]
RSS .... Romance of Science Series [*A publication*]
RSS .... Rome and the Study of Scripture [*A publication*]   (BJA)
RSS .... Root-Sum-Square
RSS .... Roseires [*Sudan*] [*Airport symbol*]   (OAG)
RSS .... Rotary Shaft Seal
RSS .... Rotary Stepping Switch
RSS .... Rotary Symbol Switch   (MCD)
RSS .... Rotating Service Structure [*Kennedy Space Center*]   (MCD)
RSS .... Routing and Switching System
RSS .... Rural Sociological Society   (EA)
RSSAA .... Revue Internationale des Services de Sante des Armees de Terre, de Mer, et de l'Air [*A publication*]
RSSal .... Rassegna Storica Salernitana [*A publication*]
RSSC .... Remote-Site Simulator Console [*NASA*]
RSSCW ...... Research Studies. State College of Washington [*Pullman*] [*A publication*]
RSSE .... Russian Spring-Summer Encephalitis [*Medicine*]
RSSEL .... Recommended Special Support Equipment List
RSSF .... Retrievable Surface Storage Facility [*Nuclear energy*]
RSSF .... Roller Speed Skating Federation   (EA)
RSSI .... Railway Systems Suppliers [*Formed by a merger of Railway Communications Suppliers Association and Signal Appliance Association*] [*Metuchen, NJ*]   (EA)
RSSJ .... Researches in the Social Sciences on Japan. East Asian Institute. Columbia University [*A publication*]
RSSJA .... Journal. Royal Statistical Society. Series C. Applied Statistics [*A publication*]
RSSK .... Rigid Seat Survival Kit   (NG)
RSSLI .... Radovi Staroslavenskog Instituta [*A publication*]
RSSMAP .... Reactor Safety Study Methodology Application Program [*Nuclear energy*]   (NRCH)
RSSMN ...... Rivista di Storia delle Scienze Mediche e Naturali [*A publication*]
RSSN .... Research Space Surveillance Network
RSSND ...... Roessing [*A publication*]
RSSP .... Range Single Shot Probability [*Military*]
RSSPCC .... Royal Scottish Society for Prevention of Cruelty to Children
RSSPL .... Recommended Spares and Spare Parts List
RSSPO ...... Resident Space Shuttle Project Office [*NASA*]   (NASA)
R & S SQ ... Repair and Salvage Squadron [*Military*]
RSSRT .... Russell Sage Social Relations Test [*Psychology*]
RSSS .... Rashtriya Swayamseyak Sangh [*National Union of Selfless Servers*] [*Militant Hindu organization*] [*India*]   (PD)
RSSS .... Reusable Space Shuttle System [*Aerospace*]   (KSC)
RSST .... Reserve Station Service Transformer [*Nuclear energy*]   (NRCH)
RSSU .... Remote-Site Simulation Unit [*Navy*]   (NVT)
RS Supp .... Supplement to the Revised Statutes   (DLA)

RSSW .... Ross Sea Shelf Water [*Ross Ice Shelf Project*]
RSSZ .... Rung Sat Special Zone [*Vietnam*]
RST .... RADAR Start   (MSA)
RST .... RADAR Systems Technician   (MCD)
RST .... Radiometric Sun Tracer
RST .... Range Search and Track   (MCD)
RST .... Rapid Solidification Technology
RST .... Read Symbol Table
RST .... Readability, Strength, Tone
RST .... Recognition Suppression Technique
RST .... Recovery Sequence Tester
RST .... Reentry System Technology [*Aerospace*]
RST .... Reflector Support Truss
RST .... Register and Self-Test
RST .... Reinforcing Steel [*Technical drawings*]
RST .... Religious of St. Andrew [*Roman Catholic religious order*]
RST .... Requirements for Scheduled Test   (MUGU)
RSt .... Research Studies [*A publication*]
RST .... Research Study Team
RST .... Reset [*Telecommunications*]   (TEL)
RST .... Reset-Set Trigger
RST .... Resin Skived Tape
RST .... Resistance   (AABC)
RST .... Resort Airlines [*Baltimore, MD*] [*FAA designator*]   (FAAC)
RST .... Rest
RST .... Restore   (MSA)
RST .... Rework/Scrap Tag   (MCD)
RST .... Right Sacrotransverse [*A fetal position*] [*Obstetrics*]
RST .... Rivista Storica Tincinese [*A publication*]
RST .... Rivista di Studi Teatrali [*A publication*]
RST .... Rochester [*Minnesota*] [*Airport symbol*]   (OAG)
RST .... Rolling Stock   (CINC)
RST .... Rough Saw Template   (MCD)
RST .... Routine Sequence Table
RST .... Royal Society of Teachers [*British*]
R Sta .... Radio Telegraph Station
RSTA .... Reconnaissance, Surveillance, and Target Acquisition   (MCD)
RStA .... Rivista di Storia Antica [*A publication*]
RSTAA .... Reconnaissance, Surveillance, and Target Acquisition Aircraft   (MCD)
RSTA & E ... Reconnaissance, Surveillance, Target Acquisition, and Engagement   (MCD)
R Statist (Bucuresti) ... Revista de Statistica (Bucuresti) [*A publication*]
RSTC .... RADAR Ship Target Classification [*Military*]   (CAAL)
RSTC .... Remote-Site Telemetry Computer [*NASA*]
RStCr .... Rivista Storico-Critica delle Scienze Teologiche [*A publication*]
RSTD .... Restricted
RSTG .... Roasting   (MSA)
RSTK .... Relay Servicing Tool Kit
RSTL .... Red Status Timeline
RSTL .... Relaxed Skin Tension Line [*Dermatology*]
R St Lig ..... Rivista di Studi Liguri [*A publication*]
RSTN .... Radio Solar Telescope Network   (MCD)
R St O .... Rivista degli Studi Orientali [*A publication*]
RSTO .... Rose's Stores [*NASDAQ symbol*]   (NQ)
R/STOL ..... Reduced/Short Takeoff and Landing [*Aircraft*]
R Storia Contemporanea ... Rivista di Storia Contemporanea [*A publication*]
RStorLettRel ... Rivista di Storia e Letteratura Religiosa [*Florence*] [*A publication*]   (BJA)
RSTP .... Real-Time Statistical and Terminal Profile [*IRS*]
RSTP .... Remote-Site Telemetry Processor [*NASA*]   (KSC)
RSTPF .... Rustproof   (MSA)
R St Pomp ... Rivista di Studi Pompeiani [*A publication*]
RSTR .... Resistor
RSTR .... Restrict   (MSA)
RSTRD .... Restricted
RSTS .... Resource-Sharing Time-Sharing System
RSTS .... Retirement Systems Testing Section [*Social Security Administration*]
R Stuart Pap ... Royal Stuart Papers [*A publication*]
RSTUD .... Rivista di Scienza e Tecnologia degli Alimenti e di Nutrizione Umana [*A publication*]
R Studi Eur ... Rivista di Studi Europei [*A publication*]
R Stud Liguri ... Rivista di Studi Liguri [*A publication*]
R Stud Or ... Revista degli Studi Orientali [*Rome*] [*A publication*]
RSTV .... Radiated Subscription Television   (ADA)
RSTY .... Rusty Pelicans Restaurants [*NASDAQ symbol*]   (NQ)
RSU .... Rating Scale Unit [*Acoustics*]
RSU .... Recorder Switch Unit
RSU .... Register Storage Unit
RSU .... Relay Storage Unit
RSU .... Remote Service Unit   (NASA)
RSU .... Remote Switching Unit [*Telecommunications*]
RSU .... Rescue Support Umbilical   (MCD)
RSU .... Rocenka Slovanskeho Ustavu [*A publication*]
RSU .... Runway Supervisory Unit [*Aviation*]   (FAAC)
RSUED .... Regional Science and Urban Economics [*A publication*]
R Suisse Zool ... Revue Suisse de Zoologie [*A publication*]
RSV .... Armored Reconnaissance Scout Vehicle [*Army*]   (RDA)
RSV .... Diesel Run Control Solenoid Valve   (IEEE)
RSV .... Random Sine Vibration

RSV	Rat Sarcoma Virus
RSV	Rat Seminal Vesicle
RSV	Recently Separated Veteran
RSV	Reconnaissance Scout Vehicle (MCD)
RSV	Remove Shutoff Valve (KSC)
RSV	Research Safety Vehicle [*Department of Transportation*]
RSV	Reserve (MSA)
RSV	Reservoir [*Board on Geographic Names*]
RSV	Respiratory Syncytial Virus
RSV	Revised Standard Version [*of the Bible, 1952*]
RSV	Revista Signos de Valparaiso [*A publication*]
RSV	Right Subclavian Vein [*Anatomy*]
RSV	Robinson, IL [*Location identifier*] [*FAA*] (FAAL)
RSV	Rous Sarcoma Virus [*Same as ASV*]
RSVA	Randolf-Sheppard Vendors of America [*Tampa, FL*] (EA)
RSV-Br	Rous Sarcoma Virus-Bryan [*Strain*]
RSVC	Resident Supervisor Call (BUR)
RSVN	Reservation (FAAC)
RSVP	Radiation Spectral Visual Photometer
RSVP	Rapid Sampling Vertical Profiler [*Oceanography*]
RSVP	Rapid Serial Visual Presentation [*Data processing*]
RSVP	Really Sexy Vamp Pants [*Slacks for evening wear by women*]
RSVP	Remote System Verification Program
RSVP	Repondez, S'il Vous Plait [*The Favor of an Answer Is Requested*] [*French*]
RSVP	Research Selected Vote Profile [*Election poll*]
RSVP	Research Society for Victorian Periodicals (EA)
RSVP	Response Segmentation and Validation Program [*Donnelley Marketing Information Services*] [*Stamford, CT*] [*Information service*] (EISS)
RSVP	Restartable Solid Variable Pulse [*Motor*] (MCD)
RSVP	Retired Senior Volunteer Program [*Washington, DC*] (EA)
RSVP	Ride Shared Vehicle Paratransit [*Transportation system*]
RSVR	Reservoir (AAG)
RSVR	Resolver (AAG)
RSVR	Roma. Rivista di Studi e di Vita Romana [*A publication*]
RSV(RV)	Revised Standard Version of the Bible [*A publication*] (BJA)
RSV-S-R	Rous Sarcoma Virus-Schmidt-Ruppin [*Strain*]
RSVTN	Reservation
RSW	Fort Myers [*Florida*] [*Airport symbol*] (OAG)
RSW	Fort Myers, FL [*Location identifier*] [*FAA*] (FAAL)
RSW	Rattlesnake Hills [*Washington*] [*Seismograph station code, US Geological Survey*] (SEIS)
RSW	Raw Service Water [*Nuclear energy*] (NRCH)
RSW	Refrigerated Seawater
RSW	Repeating Slide Wire
RSW	Resistance Spot Welding
RSW	Retarded Surface Wave
RSW	Royal Scottish Society of Painters in Water Colours
RSWB	Raumordnung, Stadtebau, Wohnungswesen, Bauwesen [*Regional Policy, Urban Development, Housing and Civil Engineering*] [*Database*] [*Stuttgart, West Germany*]
RSWC	Right Side Up with Care
RSWC	Royal Society of Painters in Water-Colours (ROG)
RSWS	Royal Scottish Water-Colour Society (ROG)
RSWSU	Research Studies. Washington State University [*Pullman*] [*A publication*]
RSWW	Ross Sea Winter Water [*Marine science*] (MSC)
RSY	Lumberton, NC [*Location identifier*] [*FAA*] (FAAL)
RSYCS	Rosy Cross [*Freemasonry*]
RSYN	Reactor Synthesis
RSyn	Revue de Synthese [*A publication*]
R Synd Suisse ...	Revue Syndicale Suisse [*A publication*]
RSYS	Restaurant Systems [*NASDAQ symbol*] (NQ)
RSZ	Phoenix, AZ [*Location identifier*] [*FAA*] (FAAL)
RT	Air Tungaru [*Great Britain*] [*ICAO designator*] (FAAC)
RT	Electric Current Relay
RT	Rachidian Tooth
RT	RADAR Transparency (MCD)
R/T	RADAR Trigger (CET)
RT	Radiation Therapy [*Medicine*]
RT	Radio Technician
RT	Radio Telegraphy (ADA)
RT	Radio Telephone (MSA)
RT	Radio/Television Repair Program [*Association of Independent Colleges and Schools specialization code*]
RT	[*The*] Radio Times [*A publication*]
RT	Radio Tracking (KSC)
RT	Radio Transmitter
RT	Radiographic Test (NRCH)
RT	Radiologic Technologist
RT	Radiotelegraphy
RT	Radiotelephone
R/T	Radiotelephony
RT	Radular Teeth
RT	Rail Tractor [*British*]
RT	Rail Transport
RT	Raintight (MSA)
RT	Randomized Trial [*Statistics*]

RT	Range Timing (AAG)
RT	Range Tracking
RT	Ranger Tab [*Military decoration*]
RT	Rate (AAG)
RT	Rate Transmitter
RT	Rated Time (IEEE)
RT	Ratio Transformer [*Unit*]
RT	Rational Therapy [*Short form for rational-emotive therapy*]
RT	Reaction Time
RT	Reactor Trip (NRCH)
RT	Reading Teacher [*A publication*]
RT	Reading Test
RT	Readout Technique
RT	Real Time [*Computer*]
RT	Receive-Transmit [*Radio*]
RT	Received Text (ROG)
R/T	Receiver/Transmitter [*Radio*] (KSC)
RT	Receiving Tube
R & T	Recherches et Travaux [*A publication*]
RT	Record Transfer
R/T	Record of Trial [*Army*] (AABC)
RT	Recovery Time [*Military*] (AFIT)
RT	Recreational Therapist [*or Therapy*]
RT	Recueil de Travaux [*A publication*]
RT	Recueil des Travaux Relatifs a la Philologie et a l'Archeologie Egyptiennes et Assyriennes [*A publication*]
RT	Recueillis Temporaires [*Temporarily Taken In*] [*Of unadoptable children*] [*French*]
RT	Red Tetrazolium [*Also, TPTZ, TTC*] [*Chemical indicator*]
RT	Reduction Tables
RT	Reference Trajectory [*NASA*] (KSC)
RT	Regional Treasurer [*British*]
RT	Register Ton
RT	Register Traffic [*Telecommunications*] (TEL)
RT	Register Transfer [*Data processing*]
R/T	Register Translator [*Telecommunications*] (TEL)
RT	Registered Technician [*American Registry of X-ray Technicians*]
RT	Regression Testing [*Data processing*] (IEEE)
RT	Rehabilitation Therapist [*or Therapy*]
RT	Rejection Tag (AAG)
RT	Related Terms [*Indexing*]
RT	Relaxation Time
RT	Relaxation Training [*Psychology*]
RT	Relay Tester
RT	Relay Transmitter
RT	Release Transmittal (MCD)
RT	Released Time
RT	Religious Theatre [*A publication*]
RT	Remote Terminal [*Data processing*]
RT	Renal Transplant [*Nephrology*]
R/T	Reperforator/Transmitter [*Teletypewriter*] [*Data processing*]
RT	Research and Technology
R & T	Research and Technology
RT	Reserve Training
RT	Reset Trigger
R-T	Resistance Test (NASA)
RT	Resistor Tolerance
RT	Resistor Transistor
RT	Resorts International, Inc. [*American Stock Exchange symbol*]
RT	Respiratory Therapy [*Medicine*]
RT	Response Time [*Data processing*]
RT	Resting Tension [*Biology*]
RT	Resuscitation Team
RT	Resuscitation Therapy
RT	Retention Time [*Data processing*]
RT	Retraining (OICC)
RT	Retro Table [*NASA*]
RT	Return Ticket
RT	Reverse Transcriptase [*An enzyme*]
RT	Revolving Radio Beacon [*ITU designation*] (CET)
RT	Revue Theatrale [*A publication*]
RT	Revue Thomiste [*Brussels*] [*A publication*]
RT	Revue Tunisienne [*A publication*]
R/T	Rho/Theta
RT	Rigging Tool (MCD)
RT	Right
RT	Right Tackle [*Football*]
RT	Right Turn after Takeoff [*Aviation*] (FAAC)
RT	Ring Trip [*Telecommunications*] (TEL)
RT	Ringing Tone [*Telecommunications*] (TEL)
RT	RISC [*Reduced-Instruction Set Computer*] Technology [*IBM Corp.*]
RT	Rise Time (DEN)
RT	[*The*] River Terminal Railway Co. [*AAR code*]
R & T	Road and Track [*A publication*]
RT	Road Traffic
RT	Road Transport (NATG)
RT	Road Truck
RT	Rocket Target
RT	Romain de Tirtoff [*Also known as ERTE*] [*Couturier*]

RT.............. Room Temperature
RT.............. Root [*Mathematics*] (ROG)
RT.............. Rotation Discrete Rate
rt................ Rotten [*Quality of the bottom*] [*Nautical charts*]
RT.............. Rough Terrain [*Military*] (AABC)
RT.............. Rough Times [*Formerly, Radical Therapist*] [*A publication*]
R & T .... Rough and Tumble Engineers' Historical Association (EA)
RT.............. Round Table
RT.............. Round Trip
RT.............. Route (AABC)
RT.............. Route Treatment [*Telecommunications*] (TEL)
RT.............. Router Template
RT.............. Royalty Trust
RT.............. Running Title
RT.............. Runup and Taxi [*Air Force*]
RT.............. Ruth [*Old Testament book*]
RT.............. Rye Terms [*Business and trade*]
Rt.............. Tetrachoric Correlation [*Psychology*]
RT.............. Total Reserves
RT.............. Transportes Aereos de Timor [*Portugal*] [*ICAO designator*] [*Obsolete*] (FAAC)
rT₃.............. Reverse Triiodothyronine [*Endocrinology*]
RTA .... RADAR Terrain Analysis
RTA .... Radically Tapered Antenna
RTA .... Radix Teachers Association [*Dallas, TX*] (EA)
RTA .... Rail Travel Authorization [*Military*]
RTA .... Railway Tie Association [*St. Louis, MO*] (EA)
RTA .... Reactivity Test Assembly [*Nuclear energy*]
RTA .... Real-Time Accumulator
RTA .... Real-Time Analyzer [*Electronics*]
RTA .... Reciprocal Trade Agreement
RTA .... Refrigeration Trade Association of America
RTA .... Reliability Test Assembly
RTA .... Reliable Test Analyzer [*Data processing*]
RTA .... Remote Test Access [*Telecommunications*] (TEL)
RTA .... Remote Trunk Arrangement [*Telecommunications*] (TEL)
RTA .... Renal Tubule Acidosis [*Medicine*]
RTA .... Request for Technical Action (MCD)
RTA .... Riberalta [*Bolivia*] [*Seismograph station code, US Geological Survey*] [*Closed*] (SEIS)
RTA .... Rise-Time Analyzer
RTA .... Road Traffic Accident [*British*]
RTA .... Road Traffic Act (DLA)
RTA .... Rotor Test Apparatus (MCD)
RTA .... Rotuma [*Fiji*] [*Airport symbol*] (OAG)
RTA .... Royal Thai Army
RTA .... Rubber Trade Association of New York [*New York, NY*] (EA)
RTAC .... Real-Time Adaptive Control
RTAC .... Regional Technical Aid Center [*Agency for International Development*]
RTAC .... Research and Technology Advisory Council [*Terminated, 1977*] [*NASA*] (EGAO)
RTAC .... Roads and Transportation Association of Canada [*Ottawa, ON*] [*Formerly, Canadian Good Roads Association*] [*Research center*]
RTACF .... Real-Time Auxiliary Computing Facility [*Apollo*] [*NASA*]
RTACS .... Real-Time Adaptive Control System [*Military*] (CAAL)
RTAD......... Router Adapter
RTAF .... Report to Armed Forces
RTAF .... Royal Thai Air Force
RTAFB .... Royal Thai Air Force Base (CINC)
RTAFCONV ... Royal Thai Air Force Contingent, Vietnam
RTAG .... Range Technical Advisory Group
RTAM .... Recherches de Theologie Ancienne et Medievale [*A publication*]
RTAM .... Remote Telecommunications Access Method [*Data processing*]
RTAM .... Remote Terminal Access Method [*Data processing*] (BUR)
RTAM .... Resident Terminal Access Method [*Data processing*]
RTANG....... Right Angle
RTAPS ...... Real-Time Terminal Application Program System [*Data processing*]
RTARF....... Royal Thai Armed Forces (CINC)
RTARP ...... Royal Thai Army Rebuild Plant (MCD)
RTASM....... Revue des Travaux. Academie des Sciences Morales et Politiques [*A publication*]
R Taxation Individuals ... Review of Taxation of Individuals [*A publication*]
RTB .... Radial Time Base
RTB .... Radio Television Brunei
RTB .... Radiodiffusion-Television Belge [*Belgian Radio Broadcasting and Television System*]
RTB .... Read Tape Binary [*Data processing*] (IEEE)
RTB .... Resistance Temperature Bulb
RTB .... Resolver Tracking Bridge
RTB .... Response/Throughput Bias [*Data processing*] (BUR)
RTB .... Return to Base [*Military*]
RTB .... Roatan [*Honduras*] [*Airport symbol*] (OAG)
RTB .... Rocket Test Base
RTB .... Rural Telephone Bank [*Department of Agriculture*]
RTBA......... Rate to Be Agreed [*Business and trade*]

RTBCA .... Revue Technique du Batiment et des Constructions Industrielles [*A publication*]
RTBISC ...... Radiodiffusion-Television Belge - Institut des Services Comuns [*Belgian Radio Broadcasting and Television - Common Services Institute*]
RTBM .... Real-Time BIT [*Binary Digit*] Mapping
RTBM .... Recoverable Test Bed Missile
RTBNA .... Recueil des Travaux Botaniques Neerlandais [*A publication*]
RTC .... RADAR Tracking Center [*or Control*]
RTC .... Radio Tecnica Colombiana [*Bogota*]
RTC .... Radio Transmission Control (NATG)
RTC .... Radio Tuned Circuit (DEN)
RTC .... Radiodiffusion-Television Congolaise [*Congolese Radio and Television*]
RTC .... Rails-to-Trails Conservancy [*Washington, DC*] (EA)
RTC .... Range Telemetry Central [*Aerospace*]
RTC .... Ratchet (AAG)
RTC .... Reader Tape Contact
RTC .... Real-Time Clock [*Data processing*] (MCD)
RTC .... Real-Time Command [*Data processing*]
RTC .... Real-Time Computer
RTC .... Real-Time Conference [*GEnie*] [*Telecommunications*]
RTC .... Real-Time Control [*Data processing*] (MCD)
RTC .... Real-Time Counter [*Data processing*]
RTC .... Reconstruction of Town and Country [*British*] [*World War II*]
RTC .... Recruit Training Center
RTC .... Recueil Tablettes Chaldeennes [*A publication*]
RTC .... Reference Test Chart
RTC .... Regional Term Contract
RTC .... Regional Transport Commissioner
RTC .... Rehabilitation Research and Training Centers [*Department of Health and Human Services*]
RTC .... Relative Time Clock [*Data processing*] (MDG)
RTC .... Remote Terminal Controller
RTC .... Removable Top Closure (NRCH)
RTC .... Replacement Training Center
RTC .... Required Technical Characteristic [*Military*] (CAAL)
RTC .... Requirements Type Contract [*Military*] (AABC)
RTC .... Reserve Training Corps
RTC .... Residential Training College [*for disabled people*] [*British*]
RTC .... Resort Timesharing Council (EA)
RTC .... Responsible Training Center [*Air Training Command*] (MCD)
RTC .... Return to Clinic [*Nursing*]
RTC .... Return to Control
RTC .... Reverse Transfer Capacitance
RTC .... Revue Trimestrielle Canadienne [*A publication*]
RTC .... Ridiculous Theatrical Company
RTC .... Rochester Telephone Corporation [*NYSE symbol*]
RTC .... Rocket Technique Committee
RTC .... Royal Tank Corps [*Military unit*] [*British*]
RTC-30 ...... Rehabilitation Research and Training Center in Blindness and Low Vision [*Mississippi State University*] [*Research center*] (RCD)
RTCA .... Race Track Chaplaincy of America (EA)
RTCA .... Radio Technical Commission for Aeronautics [*Washington, DC*] (EA)
RTCA .... Radio-Television Correspondents Association (EA)
RTCA .... Real-Time Casualty Assessment (MCD)
RTCA .... Ribofuranosyltriazolecarboxamide [*Ribavirin*] [*Antiviral compound*]
RTCANI...... Rav Tov Committee to Aid New Immigrants [*Later, RTIJRO*] (EA)
RTCB......... ROTI [*Recording Optical Tracking Instrument*] Tracker - Cocoa Beach [*NASA*] (KSC)
RTCB......... Run to Cladding Breach [*Nuclear energy*] (NRCH)
RTCC .... Radiant Technology [*NASDAQ symbol*] (NQ)
RTCC .... Real-Time Computer Center [*NASA*] (NASA)
RTCC .... Real-Time Computer Command [*NASA*] (NASA)
RTCC .... Real-Time Computer Complex
RTCDS ...... Real-Time Cinetheodolite Data System
RTCE .... Rotation/Translation Control Electronics (NASA)
RTCF .... Real-Time Combined File [*IRS*]
RTCF .... Real-Time Computer Facility
RTCH......... Radiation Technology [*NASDAQ symbol*] (NQ)
RTCH......... Rough Terrain Container Handler (MCD)
RTCL......... Reticle [*Optics*]
RTCM........ Radio Technical Commission for Maritime Services [*An association*] [*Washington, DC*] [*Information service*] (EA)
RTCMS ...... Radio Technical Commission for Marine Services [*Later, RTCM*]
RTCO .... Record Time Compliance Order
RTCOD...... [*The*] Research and Technology Coordinating Document [*Army*] (RDA)
RTCP......... Radio Transmission Control Panel (NATG)
RTCP......... Real-Time Communications Processor (NASA)
RTCP......... Resident Training and Counseling Programs (OICC)
RTCS......... Real-Time Communication System
RTCS......... Real-Time Computer Science Corp. [*Camarillo, CA*] [*Software manufacturer*]
RTCS......... Real-Time Computer System
RTCTO....... Record Time Compliance Technical Order (AAG)

RTCU	Real-Time Control Unit
RTCU	Router Cutter [*Tool*] (AAG)
RTD	Delayed [*Indicates delayed meteorological message*] (FAAC)
RTD	Radiodiffusion-Television de Djibouti
RTD	Range Time Decoder
RTD	Rate Dumping (MCD)
RTD	Read Tape Decimal
RTD	Real-Time Display
RTD	Reliability Technical Directive (AAG)
RTD	Remote Temperature Detector
RTD	Replacement Training Detachment (MCD)
RTD	Research and Technology Division [*Air Force*]
RTD	Residence Time Distribution [*Chemical engineering*]
RTD	Resistance Temperature Detector
RTD	Resistance Temperature Device [*Nuclear energy*] (NRCH)
RTD	Retard (MSA)
RTD	Retired
RTD	Return to Duty [*Military*]
RTD	Road Traffic Division [*British police*]
RTDA	Radio and Television Dealers' Association
RTDA	Retail Tobacco Dealers of America [*Rockville Centre, NY*] (EA)
RTDA	Returned Absentees
RTDAP	RADAR Target Data Analog Processor (MCD)
RTDC	Real-Time Data Channel (IEEE)
RTDC	Retardation Coil (MSA)
RTDC	Rocket-Thrown Depth Charge (NG)
RTDD	Real-Time Data Distribution
RTDD	Remote Timing and Data Distribution
RTDDC	Real-Time Digital Data Correction (MUGU)
RTDE	Range Time Data Editor [*NASA*] (KSC)
RTDE	Revue Trimestrielle de Droit Europeen [*A publication*]
RTDG	Radio and Television Directors Guild [*Later, DGA*]
RTDHS	Real-Time Data Handling System
RTDP	RADAR Target Data Processor (MCD)
RTDR	Reliability Test Data Report
RTDS	Real-Time Data System
RTDT	Real-Time Data Translator
RTDVA	Rechentechnik/Datenverarbeitung [*A publication*]
RTE	Radio Telefis Eireann [*Radio and television network*] [*Ireland*]
RTE	Radio Trans-Europe
RTE	Radio Trunk Extension (NATG)
RTE	RADOME [*RADAR Dome*] Test Equipment
RTE	Ready to Eat [*Cereals*]
RTE	Real-Time Executive [*Data processing*]
RTE	Receiver Test Equipment
RTE	Recovery Techniques Evaluation [*NASA*] (KSC)
RTE	Regenerative Turboprop Engines
RTE	Reliability Test Evaluation (AAG)
RTE	Remote Terminal Emulator [*For teleprocessing validation*]
RTE	Request to Expedite
RTE	Research Training and Evaluation (OICC)
RTE	Resident Training Equipment (MCD)
RTE	Residual Total Elongation [*Nuclear energy*] (NRCH)
RTE	Responsible Test Engineer [*NASA*] (NASA)
RTE	Return to Earth [*NASA*]
RTE	Return from Exception [*Data processing*]
RTE	Route (AFM)
RTE	RTE Corp. [*NYSE symbol*]
RTE-B	Real-Time Basic [*Data processing*] (MDG)
RTEC	Restec Systems, Inc. [*NASDAQ symbol*] (NQ)
RTECS	Registry of Toxic Effects of Chemical Substances [*National Library of Medicine*] [*Bethesda, MD*] [*Database*]
RTED	Return-to-Earth Digital [*NASA*]
RTEG	River Transport Escort Group (CINC)
RTEID	Revista Tecnica INTEVEP [*Instituto de Tecnologia Venezolana del Petroleo*] [*A publication*]
RTel	Radio Telemetry
RTEL	Radio Telephony (MSA)
R Telev Soc J	Royal Television Society. Journal [*A publication*]
RTEM	RADAR Tracking Error Measurement
RT & EPS	Rapid Transit and Electrical Power Systems
RTES	Radio and Television Executives' Society [*Later, IRTS*]
RTES	Real-Time Engine Simulation (MCD)
RTES	Real-Time Executive System [*SEMIS*]
RTF	Radio Transmission Facility
RTF	Radiodiffusion-Television Francaise [*French Radio Broadcasting and Television System*]
RTF	Radiotelephone
RTF	Ready to Fire (MCD)
RTF	Real-Time FORTRAN [*Data processing*]
RTF	Reconnaissance Task Force (AFM)
RTF	Reliability Task Force (MCD)
RTF	Religious Task Force (EA)
RTF	Reports Tempore Finch, English Chancery (DLA)
RTF	Resistance Transfer Factor [*of microorganisms to drugs*]
RTF	Respiratory Tract Fluid [*Medicine*]
RTF	Revue Theologique Francaise [*A publication*]
RTF	Rocket Test Facility
RTF	Rotational Test Facility [*NASA*]
RTF	Rubber-Tile Floor [*Technical drawings*]
RTFES	Religious Task Force on El Salvador (EA)

RTFL	Rough Terrain Front Loader (MCD)
RTFLT	Rough-Terrain Fork Lift Truck (MCD)
RTFM	Router Form
RTFMS	Radio Transmission Frequency Measuring System
RTFR	Reliability Trouble and Failure Report
RTFV	RADAR Target Folder Viewer
RTG	Radioactive Thermal Generator
RTG	Radioactive Thermoelectric Generator (NRCH)
RTG	Radiodiffusion-Television Gabonaise [*Gabonese radio and television network*]
RTG	Radiodiffusion-Television Guineenne [*Guinean radio and television network*]
RTG	Radioisotope Thermoelectric Generator
RTG	Radiotelegraph
RTG	Range to Go
RTG	Range to Ground (MCD)
RTG	Rare Tube Gas
RTG	Rating (MUGU)
RTG	Reglement Telegraphique [*Telegraph Regulations*] [*French*]
RTG	Requirements Tape Generator [*NASA*]
RTG	Reusable Training Grenade
RTG	Routing
RTG	Royal Thai Government
RTG	Ruteng [*Indonesia*] [*Airport symbol*] (OAG)
RTGB	Reactor Turbine Generator Board (NRCH)
RTGD	Real-Time Graphic Display
RTGD	Room Temperature Gamma Detector
RTGF	Rat Transforming Growth Factor [*Biochemistry*]
RTGp	Reconnaissance Technical Group [*Air Force*] (AFM)
RTGp	Reconnaissance Training Group [*Air Force*] (AFM)
RTGp	Retraining Group [*Air Force*] (AFM)
RTGU	Router Guide
RTGV	Real-Time Generation of Video
RTH	Houston Oil Royalty UBI [*NYSE symbol*]
RTH	New York, NY [*Location identifier*] [*FAA*] (FAAL)
RTh	Radio-Telephone (High Frequency) [*Telecommunications*]
RTH	Regional Telecommunications Hub [*Telecommunications*] (TEL)
RTH	Relay Transformer Header
RTH	Reports of Cases Concerning Settlements Tempore Holt [*England*] (DLA)
RTH	Reports Tempore Hardwicke [*England*] (DLA)
RTh	Revue de Theologie et de Philosophie [*A publication*]
RTh	Revue Thomiste [*A publication*]
RTH	Ridgeway's Reports Tempore Hardwicke, Chancery and English King's Bench (DLA)
RThAbstr	Religious and Theological Abstracts [*A publication*]
RThAM	Recherches de Theologie Ancienne et Medievale [*A publication*]
R T Hardw	Reports Tempore Hardwicke, English King's Bench (DLA)
RTHC	Rotation Translation Hand Controller (NASA)
R Theol Louvain	Revue Theologique de Louvain [*A publication*]
RTHK	Radio Television Hong Kong
RThL	Revue Theologique de Louvain [*A publication*]
R T Holt	Reports Tempore Holt, English King's Bench (DLA)
RThom	Revue Thomiste [*A publication*]
RtHon	Right Honourable
RThPh	Revue de Theologie et de Philosophie [*A publication*]
RThQr	Revue de Theologie et des Questions Religieuses [*A publication*] (BJA)
R Th R	Reformed Theological Review [*A publication*]
RTHS	Real-Time Hybrid System (NASA)
RTI	RADAR Target Identification
RTI	Radiation Transfer Index
RTI	Radiodiffusion-Television Ivoirienne [*Ivory Coast Radio and Television*]
RTI	Railroad Transportation Insurers [*Defunct*] (EA)
RTI	Referred-to-Input
RTI	Related Technical Instruction [*Bureau of Apprenticeship and Training*] [*Department of Labor*]
RTI	Request for Technical Information [*Military*]
RTI	Research Triangle Institutes [*Duke University, University of North Carolina at Chapel Hill, and North Carolina State University at Raleigh*] [*Research center*]
RTI	Resilient Tile Institute [*Later, RFCI*] (EA)
RTI	Respiratory Tract Infection [*Medicine*]
RTI	Rise-Time Indicator
RTI	Role Taking Inventory
RTI	Root Tolerance Index [*Botany*]
RTI	Roti [*Indonesia*] [*Airport symbol*] (OAG)
RTI	Round Table International [*Homeland, CA*] (EA)
RTIC	Rotor Temperature Indicator and Control [*Instrumentation*]
R Tiers-Monde	Revue Tiers-Monde [*A publication*]
RTIJRO	Rav Tov International Jewish Rescue Organization [*Brooklyn, NY*] (EA)
RTIO	Real-Time Input/Output Interface Subsystem [*Space Flight Operations Facility, NASA*]
RTIO	Remote Terminal Input/Output
RTI/OC	Real-Time Input/Output Controller [*Data processing*] (IEEE)
RTIP	RADAR Target Identification Point (AFM)
RTIP	Real-Time Interactive Processor (MCD)

RTIP .... Remote Terminal Interactive Processor (MCD)
RTIP .... Remote Terminal Interface Package
RTIR .... Reliability and Trend Indicator Reports (AAG)
RTIRS........ Real-Time Information Retrieval System
RTITB .... Road Transport Industry Training Board [*British*]
RTK .... Range Tracker (KSC)
RTK .... Record Test Kit
RTK .... Right to Know [*Laws*]
RTK .... Roanoke Rapids, NC [*Location identifier*] [*FAA*] (FAAL)
RTK .... Roczniki Teologiczno-Kanoniczne [*A publication*]
RTKHA .... Radiotekhnika (Kharkov) [*A publication*]
RTKKUL .... Roczniki Teologiczno-Kanoniczne. Katolickiego Uniwersytetu Lubelskiego [*A publication*]
RTKL .... Roczniki Teologiczno-Kanoniczne. Katolickiego Uniwersytetu Lubelskiego [*A publication*]
RTL............ RADAR Threshold Lobe Limit (CET)
RTL............ Radial Transmission Line
RTL............ Radio Television Luxembourgeoise [*Radio Television Luxembourg*] [*French*]
RTL............ Radioisotope Transport Loop [*Nuclear energy*] (NRCH)
RTL............ Radiomaritime Telex Letter
RTL............ Real-Time Language [*Data processing*] (IEEE)
RTL............ Refrigerated Transmission Line
RTL............ Regeneration Thermoluminescence
RTL............ Regimental Training Line [*Army*]
RTL............ Register Transfer Language [*Data processing*] (CSR)
RTL............ Register Transfer Level
RTL............ Register-Transistor Logic [*Data processing*]
RTL............ Reinforced Tile Lintel [*Technical drawings*]
RTL............ Relative Transcription Level [*Genetics*]
RTL............ Research and Technology Laboratories [*Army*] (RDA)
RTL............ Resistor-Transistor Logic [*Data processing*] (BUR)
RTL............ Resource Tie Line [*An association*]
RTL............ Run-Time Library [*Interdata*]
Rt Law Rep ... Rent Law Reports [*India*] (DLA)
RTLF .... Association of Railway Trainmen and Locomotive Firemen
RTLG......... Radio Telegraph (MSA)
RTLO......... Regional Training Liaison Officer [*Ministry of Agriculture, Fisheries, and Food*] [*British*]
RTLP .... Reference Transmission Level Point [*Telecommunications*]
RTLS .... Return to Launch Site [*NASA*]
RTLT .... Round-Trip Light Time
RTM.......... RADAR Target Materiel (AFM)
RTM.......... Radiation Test Model
RTm .... Radio-Telephone (Medium Frequency) [*Telecommunications*]
RTM.......... Radio Television Malaysia
RTM.......... Radio-Television Malgache [*Malagasy Radio and Television*]
RTM.......... Radio-Television Marocaine [*Moroccan Radio and Television*]
RTM.......... [*The*] Railway Transfer Co. of the City of Minneapolis [*AAR code*]
RTM.......... Rapid Tuning Magnetron
RTM.......... Real-Time Metric
RTM.......... Real-Time Monitor [*Systems Engineering Labs*]
RTM.......... Receiver-Transmitter-Modulator
RTM.......... Reconnaissance Tactical Missile
RTM.......... Recording Tachometer (IEEE)
RTM.......... Recovery Termination Management [*Data processing*]
RTM.......... Register Transfer Module [*Data processing*] (MDG)
RTM.......... Registered Trademark (DEN)
RTM.......... Regulatory Technical Memo [*Nuclear energy*] (NRCH)
RTM.......... Representative Town Meeting
RTM.......... Research Technical Memorandum
RTM.......... Resin Transfer Molding [*Plastics technology*]
RTM.......... Response Time Module
RTM.......... Revenue Ton-Miles
RTM.......... Rotterdam [*Netherlands*] [*Airport symbol*] (OAG)
RTM.......... Royal Trust Co. Mortgage Corp. [*Toronto Stock Exchange symbol*]
RTM.......... Running Time Meter (AAG)
RTMA .... Radio and Television Manufacturers Association
RTMAGV .... Royal Thai Military Assistance Group, Vietnam
RTMC........ Royal Thai Marine Corps (CINC)
RTMD........ Real-Time Multiplexer Display
RTMOS ...... Real-Time Multiprograming Operating System [*Data processing*] (IEEE)
RTMS .... RADAR Target Measuring System (MCD)
RTMS .... Real-Time Memory System
RTMS .... Real-Time Multiprograming System
RTMS .... Rocket Thrust Measuring System
RTMSW ...... Real-Time DSN [*Deep Space Network*] Monitor Software Assembly [*NASA*]
RTMTR....... Remote Transmitter (FAAC)
RTN .... North Country Library System, Watertown, NY [*OCLC symbol*] (OCLC)
RTN .... Radial, Tangential, Normal
RTN .... Radio Telescope Network
RTN .... Raton, NM [*Location identifier*] [*FAA*] (FAAL)
RTN .... Raytheon Co. [*NYSE symbol*]
RTN .... Registered Trade Name
RTN .... Relative Threat Number [*Military*] (CAAL)
RTN .... Remote Terminal Network

RTN .... Remote Tracking Network
RTN .... Renal Tubule Necrosis [*Medicine*]
RTN .... Report Test Number [*NASA*]
RTN .... Resistor Terminating Network
RTN .... Retain (KSC)
RTN .... Return (AAG)
RTN .... Return to Neuter
RTN .... Rota [*Nicaragua*] [*Seismograph station code, US Geological Survey*] (SEIS)
RTN .... Royal Thai Navy (CINC)
RTN .... RTN: Radio Television News [*A publication*]
RTNC .... Radio-Television Nationale Congolaise
RTND .... Retained (FAAC)
RTND .... Returned
RTNDA ...... Radio-Television News Directors Association
RTNE .... Routine (FAAC)
RTNEE .... Returnee [*Military*]
RTNF .... Recombinant Tumor Necrosis Factor [*Biochemistry*]
RTNG .... Retaining (MSA)
RTNOBE.... Round Table of National Organizations for Better Education (EA)
RTNP .... Red Tag News Publications [*Later, RTNPA*] (EA)
RTNPA ...... Red Tag News Publications Association [*Flossmoor, IL*] (EA)
RTNR .... Retainer (MSA)
RTNR .... Ringtone No Reply [*Telecommunications*] (TEL)
RTNS........ Rotating Target Neutron Source [*Nuclear physics*]
RTO........... Radiotelephone Operator
RTO .... Rail Transportation Officer [*Military*]
RTO .... Railway Traffic Officer [*Military*]
RTO .... Range Training Officer (MCD)
RTO .... Reactor Trip Override (NRCH)
RTO .... Real-Time Operation
rto............. Recto (BJA)
RTO .... Referred-to-Output
RTO .... Regional Team of Officers [*British*]
RTO .... Regional Telecommunications Office [*DoD*]
RTO .... Regional Training Officer (OICC)
RTO .... Rejected Takeoff [*Aviation*] (MCD)
RTO .... Reliability Test Outline (AAG)
RTO .... Report Time Over [*Aviation*] (FAAC)
RTO .... Responsible Test Organization (MCD)
RTO .... Road Traffic Officer [*British police*]
RTOG .... Radiation Therapy Oncology Group [*Philadelphia, PA*] (EA)
RTOK .... Retest OK (MCD)
RTOL......... Reduced Takeoff and Landing [*Aviation*]
RTOP......... Research and Technology Operating [*or Operations*] Plan [*NASA*]
RTOR........ Right Turn on Red [*i.e., on red traffic signal*]
RTor .... Rocznik Torunski [*A publication*]
RTOS......... Real-Time Operating System [*Control Data Corp.*]
RTOSA ...... Revue de Medecine de Toulouse. Supplement [*A publication*]
RTOT........ Range Track on Target [*Air Force*]
R Tourisme ... Revue de Tourisme [*A publication*]
RTOW........ Regulated [*or Restricted*] Takeoff Weight (MCD)
RTP .... Radio Televisao Portuguesa [*Portuguese Radio-Television System*]
RTP .... Reactor Thermal Power (IEEE)
RTP .... Real-Time Peripheral (IEEE)
RTP .... Real-Time Position (AAG)
RTP .... Real-Time Profiler [*Instrumentation*]
RTP .... Recruitment and Training Program
RTP .... Reference Telephonic Power (DEN)
RTP .... Reinforced Theatre Plan [*Military*] [*British*]
RTP .... Reinforced Thermoplastics
RTP .... Relative Threat Priority [*Military*] (CAAL)
RTP .... Reliability Test Plan (MCD)
RTP .... Remote Transfer Point
RTP .... Request to Purchase
RTP .... Request for Technical Proposal [*Military*]
RTP .... Requirement and Test Procedures
RTP .... Research Triangle Park [*North Carolina*]
RTP .... Resistor Test Program
RTP .... Resource Teaching Program (OICC)
RTP .... Reverse Tie Point (KSC)
RTP .... Revue de Theologie et de Philosophie [*A publication*]
RTP .... Room-Temperature Phosphorimetry [*Spectrometry*]
RTP .... Rotex Turret Punch
RTP .... Rutland Plains [*Australia*] [*Airport symbol*] [*Obsolete*] (OAG)
RTPA .... Rail Travel Promotion Agency [*Defunct*] (EA)
RTPC .... Restrictive Trade Practices Commission
RTPh .... Revue de Theologie et de Philosophie [*A publication*]
RTPH........ Round Trips per Hour (MSA)
RTPhil .... Revue de Theologie et de Philosophie [*A publication*]
RTPI .... Royal Town Planning Institute [*British*]
RTPL......... Real-Time Procedural Language [*Data processing*] (MDG)
RTPLRS .... Real-Time Position Location Reporting System (MCD)
RTPM .... Real-Time Program Management
RTPM .... Revista de Tradiciones Populares (Madrid) [*A publication*]
RTPR........ Reference Theta Pinch Reactor
RTQ........... Real-Time Quotes [*Information retrieval*]
RTQA .... Reports Tempore Queen Anne [*11 Modern*] [*England*] (DLA)

RTQC .... Real-Time Quality Control
R TR .... Radio Tower
RTR .... Reading Test and Reviews [*A publication*]
RTR .... Real-Time Readout
RTR .... Recovery Temperature Ratio
RTR .... Recreational Therapist Registered
RTR .... Reformed Theological Review [*A publication*]
RTR .... Reliability Test Requirements   (AAG)
RTR .... Remote Transmitter
RTR .... Repeater Test Rack   (DEN)
RTR .... Resonance Test Reactor
RTR .... Response Time Reporting
RTR .... Restoration and Eighteenth Century Theatre Research [*A publication*]
RTR .... Return and Restore Status Register [*Data processing*]
RTR .... Returning to Ramp [*Aviation*]   (FAAC)
RTR .... Ribbon-to-Ribbon Regrowth [*Of silicon for photovoltaic cells*]
RTr .... Rivista della Tripolitania [*A publication*]
RTR .... Rotor   (MSA)
RTR .... Royal Tank Regiment [*Military unit*] [*British*]
Rtr .... Ruth Rabbah   (BJA)
R Trab (Madrid) ... Revista de Trabajo (Madrid) [*A publication*]
R Trav Acad Sci Mor Polit ... Revue des Travaux. Academie des Sciences Morales et Politiques [*A publication*]
R Trav (Bruxelles) ... Revue du Travail (Bruxelles) [*A publication*]
RTRC .... Radio and Television Research Council   (EA)
RTRC .... Radiotelemetry and Remote Control   (MCD)
RTRC .... Regional Technical Report Centers [*Department of Commerce*]
RTRCDS ..... Real-Time Reconnaissance Cockpit Display System [*or Subsystem*]
RTRD .... Retard   (FAAC)
RT Regelungstech ... RT. Regelungstechnik [*West Germany*] [*A publication*]
R Tresor ..... Revue du Tresor [*A publication*]
RTREV .... Right Reverend [*Of an abbot, bishop, or monsignor*]
R Trim Dr Com ... Revue Trimestrielle de Droit Commercial [*A publication*]
R Trim Dr Europ ... Revue Trimestrielle de Droit Europeen [*A publication*]
R Trim Dr Sanit Soc ... Revue Trimestrielle de Droit Sanitaire et Social [*A publication*]
RTRN .... Return   (FAAC)
RTRO .... Real-Time Readout
RTRPAEA ... Receuil de Travaux Relatifs a la Philologie et a l'Archeologie Egyptiennes et Assyriennes [*Paris*] [*A publication*]
RTRPhAEA ... Receuil de Travaux Relatifs a la Philologie et a l'Archeologie Egyptiennes et Assyriennes [*Paris*] [*A publication*]
RTRS .... Real-Time Rescheduling Subsystem
RTRSW .... Rotary Switch   (MSA)
RTRV .... Retrieve   (MSA)
RT RV .... Right Reverend [*Of an abbot, bishop, or monsignor*]
RTRY .... Rotary
RTS .... RADAR Target Simulator
RTS .... RADAR Test Set
RTS .... RADAR Test Station   (MCD)
RTS .... RADAR Test System
RTS .... RADAR Tracking Station [*Military*]
RTS .... RADAR Tracking System
RTS .... Radial Tuned Suspension   (ADA)
RTS .... Radio-Television Scolaire [*French*]
RTS .... Radio Television Seychelles
RTS .... Radio-Television Singapore
RTS .... Radio Wire Broadcasting Network
RTS .... Radiodiffusion-Television du Senegal [*Radio and television network*] [*Senegal*]
RTS .... Radiotelemetry Subsystem
RTS .... Radioteletypewriter Set
RTS .... Rail Transfer System   (KSC)
RTS .... Range Time Signal
RTS .... Range Timing System
RTS .... Rapid Transit System
RTS .... Rapid Transmission and Storage [*Goldmark Corp.*] [*TV system*]
RTS .... Ratio Test Set
RTS .... Reactive Terminal Service [*International Telephone & Telegraph computer*]
RTr .... Reactor Trip System   (NRCH)
RTS .... Readiness Training Squadron [*Military*]   (NVT)
RTS .... Real-Time Simulation
RTS .... Real-Time Subroutines
RTS .... Real-Time Supply   (MCD)
RTS .... Real-Time System
RTS .... Reconnaissance Technical Squadron [*Air Force*]   (CINC)
RTS .... Recorded Time Signal
RT/S .... Refrigeration Technician/Specialist   (AAG)
RTS .... Refueling Water Transfer and Storage [*Nuclear energy*]   (NRCH)
RTS .... Regional Technical Support [*Military*]
RTS .... Relay Telemetry Subsystem [*NASA*]
RTS .... Relay Test System
RTS .... Religious Tract Society [*British*]
RTS .... Remember That Song [*An association*]   (EA)
RTS .... Remote Targeting System
RTS .... Remote Terminal Supervisor   (CMD)

RTS .... Remote Test System [*Bell System*]
RTS .... Remote Tracking Site [*Military*]
RTS .... Remote Tracking Station
RTS .... Repaired This Station   (AFM)
RTS .... Reparatur-Technische Station [*Repair and Technical Station*] [*German*]
RTS .... Request to Send
RTS .... Research and Technical Services [*Military*]
RTS .... Research Test Site   (AAG)
RTS .... Return to Search
RTS .... Return to Sender
RTS .... Return to Service [*Aviation*]
RTS .... Return to Stores
RTS .... Return from Subroutine [*Data processing*]
RTS .... Return to Supplier   (MCD)
RTS .... Rights [*Stock market term*]
RTS .... Rosner Television Systems, Inc. [*New York, NY*] [*Telecommunications*]   (TSSD)
RTS .... Rotary Thumbwheel Switch
RTS .... Rottnest Island [*Australia*] [*Airport symbol*]   (OAG)
RTS .... Royal Television Society [*British*]
RTS .... Royal Toxophilite Society [*British*]
RTS .... Russ Togs, Inc. [*NYSE symbol*]
RTSA .... RADAR Target Signature Analysis
RTSA .... Radio Tracking System Analyst   (MUGU)
RTSC .... Recommended Test Sequence Chart   (MCD)
RTSC .... Replacement and Training School Command [*Military*]
RTSD .... Resources and Technical Services Division [*American Library Association*]   (EA)
RTSD .... Royal Thai Survey Department   (CINC)
RTSD CCS ... RTSD [*Resources and Technical Services Division*] Cataloging and Classification Section
RTSD LRTS ... RTSD [*Resources and Technical Services Division*] Library Resources and Technical Services [*A publication*]
RTSD PLMS ... RTSD [*Resources and Technical Services Division*] Preservation of Library Materials Section
RTSD RLMS ... RTSD [*Resources and Technical Services Division*] Reproduction of Library Materials Section
RTSD RS .... RTSD [*Resources and Technical Services Division*] Resources Section
RTSDS .... Real-Time Scheduling Display System
RTSD SS .... RTSD [*Resources and Technical Services Division*] Serials Section
RTSF .... Real-Time Simulation Facility   (MCD)
RTSFR .... Rivista Trimestrale di Studi Filosofici e Religiosi [*A publication*]
RTSM .... Return to Stock Memo
RTSP .... Real-Time Signal Processor   (NVT)
RTSq .... Reconnaissance Technical Squadron [*Air Force*]   (AFM)
RTSS .... Real-Time Scientific System
RTSS .... Returning to School Syndrome
RTSS .... Revue Tunisienne de Sciences Sociales [*A publication*]
RTST .... Radio Technician Selection Test
RTSZA ...... Revista Tecnica Sulzer [*A publication*]
RTT .... Radet for Teknisk Terminologi [*Norwegian Council for Technical Terminology*] [*Oslo*] [*Information service*]   (EISS)
RTT .... Radiation Therapy Technician
RTT .... Radiation Tracking Transducer
RTT .... Radio Television Tunisien [*Tunisian Radio and Television*]
RTT .... Radiotelemetric Theodolite
RTT .... Radioteletypewriter
RTT .... Rate of Turntable
RTT .... Receiver Threshold Test   (CET)
RTT .... Rectangular Tongue Terminal
RTT .... Remote Tuning Technique
RTT .... Return Trip Time
RTT .... Ring Tongue Terminal
RTT .... Rocket-Thrown Torpedo
RTT .... Role-Taking Task
RTTA .... Range Tower Transfer Assembly   (KSC)
RTTAA ...... Railway Telegraph and Telephone Appliance Association
RTTD .... Real-Time Telemetry Data   (MCD)
RTTDS ...... Real-Time Telemetry Data System
RTTL .... Rattail [*Metallurgy*]
RTTL .... Running Telltale Light   (MSA)
RTTLA ...... Revista Transporturilor si Telecomunicatiilor [*A publication*]
RTTOS ...... Real-Time Tactical Operating System   (MCD)
RTTP .... Router Template   (AAG)
RTTS .... RADAR Telephone Transmission System
RTTS .... Reaction Torque Temperature Sensitivity
RTTS .... Real-Time Telemetry System
RTTV .... Real-Time Television
RTTV .... Research Target and Test Vehicle
RTTY .... Radioteletypewriter
RTU .... RADAR Timing Unit
RTU .... Railroad Telegraphers Union
RTU .... Range Transfer Unit   (MCD)
RTU .... Ready to Use
RTU .... Receiver/Transmitter Unit
RTU .... Recovery Task Unit
RTU .... Reinforcement Training Unit [*Army*]   (AABC)

RTU .... Remote Terminal Unit
RTU .... Replacement Training Unit [*Military*]
RTU .... Reserve Training Unit   (MCD)
RTU .... Response Test Unit
RTU .... Return to Unit [*Military*] [*British*]
RTU .... Right to Use [*Telecommunications*]   (TEL)
RT₃U .... Resin T₃ Uptake [*Endocrinology*]
RT₄U .... Resin T₄ Uptake [*Endocrinology*]
RTUA .... Recognition Technologies Users Association   (EA)
RTUM .... Revolutionary Trade Union Movement [*Czechoslovakia*]
R Tunisienne Sciences Socs ... Revue Tunisienne de Sciences Sociales [*A publication*]
R Tunis Sci Soc ... Revue Tunisienne de Sciences Sociales [*A publication*]
RTv .... Radio-Telephone (Very-High Frequency) [*Telecommunications*]
RTV .... Radiodiffusion-Television (Upper Volta) [*Radio and television network*]
RTV .... Real-Time Video
RTV .... Recovery Test Vehicle
RTV .... Reentry Test Vehicle [*Air Force*]
RTV .... Research Test Vehicle
RTV .... Retrieve Resources Ltd. [*Vancouver Stock Exchange symbol*]
RTV .... Returned to Vendor   (AAG)
RTV .... Rhodesian Television
RTV .... Rocket Test Vehicle   (MCD)
RTV .... Room Temperature Vulcanizing   (MCD)
RTVD .... Radiotelevision Dominicana [*Dominican Radio and Television*] [*Dominican Republic*]
RTVE .... Radiotelevision Espanola [*Spanish*]
RTVP .... Real-Time Video Processing
RTVS .... Radio/Television Services [*Washington State University*] [*Pullman*] [*Telecommunications service*]   (TSSD)
RTVS .... Real Time Velocimeter System [*Army*]   (RDA)
RTVS .... Relay Test and Verification System   (MCD)
RTW .... Manitoba Reports Tempore Wood   (DLA)
RTW .... Ready-to-Wear [*Clothing*]
RTW .... Right to Work
RTW .... Right Worshipful
RTW .... Round the World
RTWB .... Richardson's Theological Word Book [*A publication*]   (BJA)
RTWS .... Raw Type Write Submodule
RTWUS ...... Research and Technology Work Unit Summary
RTX .... Rapid Transit Experimental [*Gas-turbine bus*]
RTX .... Real-Time Executive
RTX .... Report Time Crossing [*Aviation*]   (FAAC)
RTX .... Revenue Canada Taxation Library [*UTLAS symbol*]
RTY .... Merty [*Australia*] [*Airport symbol*] [*Obsolete*]   (OAG)
RTY .... Muscatine, IA [*Location identifier*] [*FAA*]   (FAAL)
RTYC .... Royal Thames Yachting Club [*British*]
RTZ .... Radio Tanzania Zanzibar
RTZ .... Return-to-Zero [*Recording scheme*]
RTZ .... Rio Tinto Zinc Corp. [*Uranium mining company*] [*British, Namibian*]
RU .... Are You? [*Communication*]
RU .... Compagnie de Transport Aerien [*Switzerland*] [*ICAO designator*]   (FAAC)
Ru .... Gosudarstvennaia Biblioteka SSR Imeni V. I. Lenina [*Lenin State Library of the USSR*], Moscow, Soviet Union [*Library symbol*] [*Library of Congress*]   (LCLS)
RU .... RADAR Unit   (MCD)
RU .... Railway Underwriter
RU .... Rain Umbrella [*An association*]   (EA)
RU .... Range Unit
RU .... Range User
RU .... Rat Unit
RU .... Reading of Unknown
RU .... Ready Use [*British*]
RU .... Refrigeration Unit   (KSC)
RU .... Regular Unleaded [*Shell Oil Co.*]
RU .... Relative Unit [*Typography*]
RU .... Release Unit [*Army*]   (AABC)
RU .... Renaissance Universal [*An association*]   (EA)
R & U .... Repairs and Upkeep [*Military*]
R & U .... Repairs and Utilities
RU .... Repeat Unit [*Genetics*]
RU .... Replaceable Unit
RU .... Reproducing Unit
RU .... Request/Response Unit [*Data processing*]
RU .... Reserve Unit [*Equal to one US dollar*] [*International finance*]
RU .... Resin Uptake [*Endocrinology*]
RU .... Respiratory Unit [*Medicine*]
RU .... Retransmission Unit [*RADA*] [*Army*]   (RDA)
RU .... Revista Universitaria. Universidad Catolica de Chile [*A publication*]
RU .... Right Upper [*Medicine*]
RU .... Roentgen Unit [*Also, r*] [*Measuring X and gamma radiations*]
RU .... Roussel [*France*] [*Research code symbol*]
RU .... Rugby Union [*Controlling body of British rugby football*]
Ru .... Ruins
RU .... Runic [*Language, etc.*]   (ROG)
Ru .... Ruth [*Old Testament book*]
Ru .... Ruthenium [*Chemical element*]

ru .... Rutile [*CIPW classification*] [*Geology*]
RU .... Unborrowed Reserves
RU .... University of Rhode Island, Kingston, RI [*Library symbol*] [*Library of Congress*]   (LCLS)
RU .... Ursuline Nuns of the Congregation of Tildonk, Belgium [*Roman Catholic religious order*]
RU-486 ...... Roussel Uclaf "Once-a-Month" Pill [*Contraceptive*]
RUA .... Arua [*Uganda*] [*Airport symbol*]   (OAG)
RUA .... Retailer's Uniform Agency
RUA .... Right Upper Arm [*Medicine*]
RUA .... Royal Ulster Academy [*British*]
RUA .... Royal Ulster Academy of Painting, Sculpture, and Architecture [*Ireland*]
RUAGA .... Rubber Age [*A publication*]
Ruakura Farm Conf Proc ... Ruakura Farmers' Conference. Proceedings [*New Zealand*] [*A publication*]
Ruakura Farmers Conf Proc ... Ruakura Farmers' Conference. Proceedings [*A publication*]
RUAT .... Report upon Arrival Threat [*Army*]   (AABC)
RUB .... Revue. Universite de Bruxelles [*A publication*]
RUB .... Rubber   (AAG)
RUB .... Rubefacient [*Producing Heat and Redness of the Skin*] [*Medicine*]   (ROG)
RUB .... Ruber [*Red*] [*Pharmacy*]
RUB .... Ruble [*Monetary unit in the USSR*]
RuB .... Russkoe Bogatstvo [*A publication*]
RUBA .... Revista. Universidad de Buenos Aires [*A publication*]
Rubb Board Bull ... Rubber Board Bulletin [*India*] [*A publication*]
Rubb Dev ... Rubber Developments [*A publication*]
Rubber Age Synth ... Rubber Age and Synthetics [*A publication*]
Rubber Bul ... Rubber Statistical Bulletin [*A publication*]
Rubber Chem & Tech ... Rubber Chemistry and Technology [*A publication*]
Rubber Chem Technol ... Rubber Chemistry and Technology [*A publication*]
Rubber Dev ... Rubber Developments [*A publication*]
Rubber Devs ... Rubber Developments [*A publication*]
Rubber Devts ... Rubber Developments [*A publication*]
Rubber Ind ... Rubber Industry [*A publication*]
Rubber Ind (London) ... Rubber Industry (London) [*A publication*]
Rubber J .... Rubber Journal [*A publication*]
Rubber J Int Plast ... Rubber Journal and International Plastics [*A publication*]
Rubber Plast Age ... Rubber and Plastics Age [*A publication*]
Rubber Plastics Fire Flamm ... Rubber and Plastics Fire and Flammability [*A publication*]
Rubber Plast Wkly ... Rubber and Plastics Weekly [*A publication*]
Rubber Res Inst Ceylon Advis Circ ... Rubber Research Institute of Ceylon. Advisory Circular [*A publication*]
Rubber Res Inst Ceylon Annu Rep ... Rubber Research Institute of Ceylon. Annual Report [*A publication*]
Rubber Res Inst Ceylon Annu Rev ... Rubber Research Institute of Ceylon. Annual Review [*A publication*]
Rubber Res Inst Ceylon Bull ... Rubber Research Institute of Ceylon. Bulletin [*A publication*]
Rubber Res Inst Ceylon Q Circ ... Rubber Research Institute of Ceylon. Quarterly Circular [*A publication*]
Rubber Res Inst Ceylon Q J ... Rubber Research Institute of Ceylon. Quarterly Journal [*A publication*]
Rubber Res Inst Malaya Annu Rep ... Rubber Research Institute of Malaya. Annual Report [*A publication*]
Rubber Res Inst Malaya Plant Bull ... Rubber Research Institute of Malaya. Planters' Bulletin [*A publication*]
Rubber Res Inst Malaya Plant Man ... Rubber Research Institute of Malaya. Planting Manual [*A publication*]
Rubber Res Inst Malaya Q J ... Rubber Research Institute of Malaya. Quarterly Journal [*A publication*]
Rubber Res Inst Malaya Rep ... Rubber Research Institute of Malaya. Report [*A publication*]
Rubber Res Inst Malays Annu Rep ... Rubber Research Institute of Malaysia. Annual Report [*A publication*]
Rubber Res Inst Malays Plant Bull ... Rubber Research Institute of Malaysia. Planters' Bulletin [*A publication*]
Rubber Res Inst (Sri Lanka) ... Rubber Research Institute (Sri Lanka) [*A publication*]
Rubber Res Inst (Sri Lanka) Advis Circ ... Rubber Research Institute (Sri Lanka). Advisory Circular [*A publication*]
Rubber Res Inst (Sri Lanka) Annu Rev ... Rubber Research Institute (Sri Lanka). Annual Review [*A publication*]
Rubber Res Inst (Sri Lanka) Q J ... Rubber Research Institute (Sri Lanka). Quarterly Journal [*A publication*]
Rubber Wld ... Rubber World [*A publication*]
Rubb (India) ... Rubber (India) [*A publication*]
Rubb Plast Age ... Rubber and Plastics Age [*A publication*]
Rubb Plast News 2 ... Rubber and Plastics News 2 [*A publication*]
Rubb Statist Bull ... Rubber Statistical Bulletin [*A publication*]
Rubb Trends ... Rubber Trends [*A publication*]
Rubb World ... Rubber World [*A publication*]
Rub Conv ... Rubinstein on Conveyancing [*5th ed.*] [*1884*]   (DLA)
RUBD .... Rubberized   (AAG)

RuBeMiA.... Akademiia Nauk Belorusskaia SSR, Fundamemtalnaia Biblioteka Imeni Ia. Kolasa [*Academy of Sciences of the Belorussian SSR, J. Kolasa Fundamental Library*], Minsk, Belorussian SSR, Soviet Union [*Library symbol*] [*Library of Congress*] (LCLS)

RuBi .... Ruch Biblijny i Liturgiczny [*Cracow*] [*A publication*]

RUBISCO .. Ribulosebisphosphate Carboxylase/Oxygenase [*An enzyme*]

RUBN .... Russian, Ukrainian, and Belorussian Newspapers [*A bibliographic publication*]

RuBP .... Ribulosebisphosphate [*Also, RDP*] [*Biochemistry*]

RuBPCase ... Ribulosebisphosphate Carboxylase [*An enzyme*]

RuBPC/O ... Ribulosebisphosphate Carboxylase/Oxygenase [*Also, RUBISCO*] [*An enzyme*]

RUBruxelles ... Revue. Universite de Bruxelles [*Brussels*] [*A publication*]

RUBSG...... Recovery Unit and Base Support Group [*Air Force*]

RUBSH ...... Rubbish

RUBSSO .... Rossendale Union of Boot, Shoe, and Slipper Operatives [*British*]

Rub Trends ... Rubber Trends [*A publication*]

RUBWA ..... Rubber World [*A publication*]

RUC........... Reporting Unit Code [*Data processing*]

RUC .... Revista. Universidad de Cordoba [*A publication*]

RUC........... Riverine Utility Craft [*Vehicle for transporting through shallow water and snow*] [*Navy symbol*]

RUC .... Royal Ulster Constabulary [*British*]

RuC .... Ruperto-Carola [*A publication*]

RUCA .... Russell Cave National Monument

RUCAG ...... Residential Utility Consumer Action Group

RuchBL ...... Ruch Biblijny i Liturgiczny [*Cracow*] [*A publication*]

Ruch L....... Ruch Literacki [*A publication*]

Ruch Muz... Ruch Muzyczny [*A publication*]

Ruch Prawn Ekon Socjol ... Ruch Prawniczy Ekonomiczny i Socjologiczny [*A publication*]

Rucker ...... Rucker's Reports [*43-46 West Virginia*] (DLA)

RUCP .... Revista. Universidad Catolica del Peru [*A publication*]

RUCS .... Racial Unconscious [*Psychiatry*]

RUD........... Rudder (AAG)

RUDAEE.... Report of Unsatisfactory or Defective Airborne Electronic Equipment [*Navy*]

RUDAOE .... Report of Unsatisfactory or Defective Aviation Ordnance Equipment [*Navy*]

RUDAS...... Road Users Data Acquisition System (ADA)

Rud Glas ... Rudarski Glasnik [*A publication*]

RUDH .... Reserve Shutdown Unplanned Derated Hours [*Electronics*] (IEEE)

RUDI........... Regional Urban Defense Intercept

RUDI........... Report of Unsatisfactory or Defective Instrumentation [*Navy*]

RUDIM....... Rudimentary (ROG)

RUDIS .... Reference Your Dispatch (NOAA)

RUDM......... Report of Unsatisfactory or Defective Material [*Aircraft*] [*Navy*]

Rud-Metal Zb ... Rudarsko-Metalurski Zbornik [*A publication*]

Rud-Met Zb ... Rudarsko-Metalurski Zbornik [*A publication*]

RUDMIN ..... Report of Unsatisfactory or Defective Mine [*Navy*] (NG)

RUDMINDE ... Report of Unsatisfactory or Defective Mine, Depth Charge, or Associated Equipment [*Navy*] (NG)

Rudodobiv Metal ... Rudodobiv i Metalurgiya [*A publication*]

Rudodobiv Metal (Sofia) ... Rudodobiv i Metalurgiya (Sofia) [*Bulgaria*] [*A publication*]

Rudodob Metal ... Rudodobiv i Metalurgiya [*Bulgaria*] [*A publication*]

RUDTORPE ... Report of Unsatisfactory or Defective Torpedo Equipment [*Navy*] (NG)

RUDVA...... Rubber Developments [*A publication*]

Rudy Met Niezelaz ... Rudy i Metale Niezelazne [*A publication*]

RUE .... Right Upper Entrance [*A stage direction*]

RUE .... Right Upper Extremity [*Medicine*]

RUE .... Russellville, AR [*Location identifier*] [*FAA*] (FAAL)

Ruegg Emp L ... Ruegg on Employer's Liability [*9th ed.*] [*1922*] (DLA)

RUER......... SSRC [*Social Science Research Council*] Research Unit on Ethnic Relations [*Research center*] [*British*] (IRC)

RUF.......... Minocqua-Woodruff, WI [*Location identifier*] [*FAA*] (FAAL)

RUF .... Radiation Usage Factor (MCD)

RUF .... Resource Utilization Factor

RUF .... Rigid Urethane Foam

RUF .... Rough (FAAC)

RUFAS ...... Remote Underwater Fisheries Assessment System

RUFE......... Zeitschrift fuer Rundfunk und Fernsehen [*NOMOS Datapool*] [*Database*]

Ruff .... Ruffhead's Edition of the Statutes by Serjeant Runnington [*1235-1785*] (DLA)

Ruff .... Ruffin and Hawks' Reports [*8 North Carolina*] (DLA)

Ruff .... Statutes at Large, Ruffhead's Edition [*England*] (DLA)

Ruff & H...... Ruffin and Hawks' Reports [*8 North Carolina*] (DLA)

RUFF-PAC ... Ruff Political Action Committee (EA)

RUFORM..... Reference Your Form (FAAC)

RUFP......... Regulations under the Federal Power Act

RUG........... Recomp Users Group [*Data processing*]

RUG........... Regional User Group [*Data processing*]

RUG........... Retrograde Ureterogram [*Medicine*]

RUG........... ROSCOE User Group [*Princeton, NJ*] (CSR)

RUG........... Rugby, ND [*Location identifier*] [*FAA*] (FAAL)

RUG........... Rutgers-[*The*] State University, Graduate School of Library and Information Science, New Brunswick, NJ [*OCLC symbol*] (OCLC)

RUGED....... Rural Georgia [*A publication*]

RUGLA ...... Rudarski Glasnik [*A publication*]

RUH........... Range Users Handbook

RUH........... Riyadh [*Saudi Arabia*] [*Airport symbol*] (OAG)

RUHP......... Rescue Unit Home Port [*Navy*] (NVT)

RUI .... Research in Undergraduate Institutions [*A National Science Foundation program*]

RUI .... Royal University of Ireland

RUI .... Ruidoso [*New Mexico*] [*Airport symbol*] (OAG)

RUI .... Ruidoso, NM [*Location identifier*] [*FAA*] (FAAL)

RUIMB .... Ruimtevaart [*A publication*]

RUIN.......... Regional and Urban Information Network [*Washington, DC*]

RUISA .... Revista. Universidad Industrial de Santander [*A publication*]

RuJ............ Rusky Jazyk [*A publication*]

RUKBA ...... Royal United Kingdom Benevolent Institution

RuKiFrA ..... Akademiia Nauk Kirgizskoi SSR, Tsentralnaia Nauchaia Biblioteka [*Academy of Sciences of the Kirghiz SSR, Central Scientific Library*], Frunze, Kirghiz SSR, Soviet Union [*Library symbol*] [*Library of Congress*] (LCLS)

RuL .... Gosudarstvennaia Publichnaia Biblioteka Imeni Saltykova-Shchedrina [*State Saltikov-Shchedrin Public Library*], Leningrad, Soviet Union [*Library symbol*] [*Library of Congress*] (LCLS)

RUL .... Representative of the Senate of the University of London (ROG)

RUL .... Revue. Universite Laval [*Quebec*] [*A publication*]

RUL .... Revue. Universite de Lyon [*A publication*]

RUL .... Right Upper Eyelid [*Medicine*]

RUL .... Right Upper Limb [*Medicine*]

RUL .... Right Upper Lobe [*of lung*] [*Medicine*]

RUL .... Rikkyo University Library [*UTLAS symbol*]

RUL .... Rule Resources Limited [*Vancouver Stock Exchange symbol*]

RUL .... Ruled

RuLA .... Akademiia Nauk SSSR [*Academy of Sciences of the USSR*], Leningrad, Soviet Union [*Library symbol*] [*Library of Congress*] (LCLS)

Rul Cas ..... Campbell's Ruling Cases [*England*] (DLA)

RULE......... Restructuring the Undergraduate Learning Environment [*National Science Foundation*]

RULE........ Rule Industries, Inc. [*NASDAQ symbol*] (NQ)

Rules Sup Ct ... Rules of the Supreme Court (DLA)

RULET....... Reference Your Letter (NOAA)

RuLit .... Ruch Literacki [*Krakow*] [*A publication*]

RULP .... Revista. Universidad de La Plata [*A publication*]

Ru L T........ Russian Literature Triquarterly [*A publication*]

RuLU-N ...... Leningradskii Universitet, Nauchnaia Biblioteka Imeni Gor'kogo [*Leningrad State University, Gor'kii Scientific Library*], Leningrad, Soviet Union [*Library symbol*] [*Library of Congress*] (LCLS)

RUM .... Railwaymen's Union of Malaya

RUM .... Remote Underwater Manipulator [*Oceanography*]

RUM .... Remote Unit Monitor (MCD)

RUM .... Resource Unit Management

RUM .... Resource Utilization Monitor

RUM .... Revista. Universidad de Madrid [*A publication*]

rum............ Romanian [*MARC language code*] [*Library of Congress*] (LCCP)

RUM .... Rumangabo [*Zaire*] [*Seismograph station code, US Geological Survey*] (SEIS)

RUM .... Rumania

RUM .... Rumjartar [*Nepal*] [*Airport symbol*] [*Obsolete*] (OAG)

RUM .... San Marcos, TX [*Location identifier*] [*FAA*] (FAAL)

RUMC........ Ruby Mining Corporation [*NASDAQ symbol*] (NQ)

RUMEA ..... Rudodobiv i Metalurgiya [*A publication*]

RUMEM ..... Reference Your Memorandum (NOAA)

RUMEMO ... Reference Your Memorandum (FAAC)

RUMES...... Reference Your Message (FAAC)

RuMG .... Gosudarstvennaia Publichnaia Nauchno-Tekhnicheskaia Biblioteka SSSR [*State Public Scientific and Technical Library*], Moscow, Soviet Union [*Library symbol*] [*Library of Congress*] (LCLS)

RUMG........ Revista. Universidade de Minas Gerais [*A publication*]

RuMHi .... State Public Historical Library, Moscow, Soviet Union [*Library symbol*] [*Library of Congress*] (LCLS)

RUMIA........ Rundfunktechnische Mitteilungen [*A publication*]

RuMIN .... Institut Nauchnoi Informatsii po Obshchestvennym Naukam, Akademiia Nauk SSSR [*Institute of Scientific Information on Social Sciences, Academy of Sciences of the USSR*], Moscow, Soviet Union [*Library symbol*] [*Library of Congress*] (LCLS)

RuMLit .... Vsesoiuznaia Gosudarstvennaia Biblioteka Inostrannoi Literatury [*All-Union State Library of Foreign Literature*], Moscow, Soviet Union [*Library symbol*] [*Library of Congress*] (LCLS)

RUMMA...... Russian Metallurgy [*English Translation*] [*A publication*]

Rum Med Rev ... Rumanian Medical Review [*A publication*]

RUMOD ...... Regional Underground Monolith Disposal [*Hazardous wastes*]

RuMoKisA ... Akademiia Nauk Moldavskoi SSR, Tsentralnaia Nauchnaia Biblioteka [*Academy of Sciences of the Moldavian SSR, Central Scientific Library*], Kishivev, Moldavian SSR, Soviet Union [*Library symbol*] [*Library of Congress*]   (LCLS)
RUMP .... Radio-Controlled Ultraviolet Measurement Program   (MUGU)
RUMR .... Routine Unsatisfactory Material Report   (MCD)
RUM Rev Univers Mines ... RUM, Revue Universelle des Mines, de la Metallurgie, de la Mechanique des Travaux Publics des Sciences [*A publication*]
Rum Sci Abstr ... Rumanian Scientific Abstracts [*A publication*]
RUN .... Reduction Unlimited
RUN .... Reunion Island [*Airport symbol*]   (OAG)
RUN .... Rewind and Unload
RUN .... Rockmaster Resources [*Vancouver Stock Exchange symbol*]
run .... Rundi [*MARC language code*] [*Library of Congress*]   (LCCP)
RUN .... Runstream [*Data processing*]
RUN .... Ruthven [*California*] [*Seismograph station code, US Geological Survey*]   (SEIS)
RUNAA ...... Revista. Universidad Nacional de Tucuman. Serie A. Matematica y Fisica Teorica [*A publication*]
RUnBrux .... Revue. Universite de Bruxelles [*A publication*]
RUNC .... Revista. Universidad Nacional de Cordoba [*A publication*]
RUNCIBLE ... Revised Unified New Compiler with Its Basic Language Extended [*Data processing*]
Rundfunk & F ... Rundfunk und Fernsehen [*A publication*]
Rundfunktech Mitt ... Rundfunktechnische Mitteilungen [*A publication*]
RUNDH .... Reserve Shutdown Unit Derated Hours [*Electronics*]   (IEEE)
RUNEL .... Runway-End Lighting [*Aviation*]
RUNID .... Run Identification [*Data processing*]
R Union Ind ... Revista de la Union Industrial [*A publication*]
RUniv .... Revue Universelle [*A publication*]
R Univ .... Revue Universitaire [*A publication*]
R de l'Univ Laval ... Revue. Universite Laval [*A publication*]
R de l'Univ d'Ott ... Revue. Universite d'Ottawa [*A publication*]
R Univ Ottawa ... Revue. Universite d'Ottawa [*A publication*]
R de l'Univ de Sherbrooke ... Revue. Universite de Sherbrooke [*A publication*]
RUnLav ...... Revue. Universite Laval [*A publication*]
Runn .... Runnell's Reports [*38-56 Iowa*]   (DLA)
Runn .... Statutes at Large, Runnington's Edition [*England*]   (DLA)
Runn Eject ... Runnington on Ejectment [*2nd ed.*] [*1820*]   (DLA)
Runnell .... Runnell's Reports [*38-56 Iowa*]   (DLA)
Runn Times ... Running Times [*A publication*]
Runn World ... Runner's World [*A publication*]
RUnOtt .... Revue. Universite d'Ottawa [*A publication*]
RUNT .... Russian Underground Nuclear Test   (MCD)
RUO .... Revista. Universidad de Oviedo [*A publication*]
RUO .... Revue. Universite d'Ottawa [*A publication*]
RUO .... Right Ureteral Orifice [*Medicine*]
RUOQ .... Right Upper Outer Quadrant [*Site of injection*] [*Medicine*]
RUOt .... Revue. Universite d'Ottawa [*A publication*]
RUP .... Raza Unida Party   (EA)
RUP .... Rupertsland Resources Co. Ltd. [*Toronto Stock Exchange symbol*]
RUPAA ...... Rubber and Plastics Age [*A publication*]
RUPHO .... Reference Your Telephone Call   (NOAA)
RUPPERT ... Reserve Unit Personnel Performance Report
Ruppie .... Republican Urban Professional [*Lifestyle classification*]
RUPT .... Interrupt   (NASA)
RUPT .... Rupture   (NASA)
RUQ .... Rifle Unqualified [*Military*]
RUQ .... Right Upper Quadrant [*of abdomen*] [*Medicine*]
RUQ .... Salisbury, NC [*Location identifier*] [*FAA*]   (FAAL)
RUR .... Resin Uptake Ratio [*Endocrinology*]
RUR .... Rossum's Universal Robots [*Acronym is title of play by Karel Capek*]
RUR .... Royal Ulster Rifles [*Military unit*] [*British*]
RUR .... Rurutu Island [*French Polynesia*] [*Airport symbol*]   (OAG)
rur .... Russian SFSR [*MARC country of publication code*] [*Library of Congress*]   (LCCP)
RUR .... Russkaja Rech' [*A publication*]
Rur Advis Leafl Edinb Sch Agric ... Rural Advisory Leaflet. Edinburgh School of Agriculture [*A publication*]
Rur Afr .... Rural Africana [*A publication*]
Rural Am .... Rural America [*A publication*]
Rural Develop ... Rural Development [*A publication*]
Rural Dev Res Educ ... Rural Development. Research and Education [*A publication*]
Rural Dev Res Rep US Dep Agric Econ Stat Coop Serv ... Rural Development Research Report. United States. Department of Agriculture. Economics, Statistics, and Cooperatives Service [*A publication*]
Rural Elec Coop ... Rural Electric Cooperative   (DLA)
Rural Elec N ... Rural Electrification News [*A publication*]
Rural GA .... Rural Georgia [*United States*] [*A publication*]
Rural Life Res ... Rural Life Research [*A publication*]
Rural Newsl ... Rural Newsletter [*Central Coast Agricultural Research and Extension Committee*] [*A publication*]
Rural N Y .... Rural New Yorker [*A publication*]
Rural Res ... Rural Research [*Australia*] [*A publication*]

Rural Res ... Rural Research. Commonwealth Scientific and Industrial Research Organisation [*A publication*]
Rural Res CSIRO ... Rural Research. Commonwealth Scientific and Industrial Research Organisation [*A publication*]
Rural Socio ... Rural Sociology [*A publication*]
Rural Sociol ... Rural Sociology [*A publication*]
RURAX .... Rural Automatic Exchange [*Telecommunications*]   (TEL)
RURCA ...... Rural Research [*A publication*]
RUREQ .... Reference Your Requisition   (NOAA)
RURLAM ..... Replacement Unit Repair Level Analysis Model
Rur Newsl ... Rural Newsletter [*A publication*]
RURP .... Realised Ultimate Reality Piton [*Mountain climbing*]
RURPOP ..... Rural Population File   (MCD)
RURQN .... Reference Your Requisition   (FAAC)
Rur Res ...... Rural Research [*A publication*]
Rur Res CSIRO ... Rural Research. Commonwealth Scientific and Industrial Research Organisation [*A publication*]
Rur Sociol ... Rural Sociology [*A publication*]
RURTI .... Recurrent Upper Respiratory Tract Infection [*Medicine*]   (ADA)
RUS .... Marau [*Solomon Islands*] [*Airport symbol*]   (OAG)
RUS .... Rapid City, SD [*Location identifier*] [*FAA*]   (FAAL)
RUS .... Rice University. Studies [*A publication*]
RUS .... Rural Uplook Service [*Ithaca, NY*]
RUS .... Russ Berrie & Co. [*NYSE symbol*]
Rus .... Russell's Election Cases [*1874*] [*Nova Scotia*]   (DLA)
Rus .... Russell's English Chancery Reports   (DLA)
RUS .... Russia
rus .... Russian [*MARC language code*] [*Library of Congress*]   (LCCP)
RUS .... Rust College, Holly Springs, MS [*OCLC symbol*]   (OCLC)
RUSC .... Rusco Industries, Inc. [*NASDAQ symbol*]   (NQ)
RUSCA .... Rural Sociology [*A publication*]
Rus & C Eq Cas ... Russell and Chesley's Nova Scotia Equity Cases   (DLA)
RUSDIC ...... Russian Dictionary [*A publication*]
RUSE .... Rutgers University. Studies in English [*A publication*]
RUSEC .... Romanian-US Economic Council   (EA)
Rus EC .... Russell's Contested Election Cases [*Massachusetts*]   (DLA)
Rus EC .... Russell's Irish Election Reports   (DLA)
RUSEF .... Rational Use of the Sea Floor [*Marine science*]   (MSC)
Rus Elec Rep ... Russell's Election Cases [*1874*] [*Nova Scotia*]   (DLA)
RUSEng .... Rajasthan University. Studies in English [*A publication*]
Rus Eq Rep ... Russell's Nova Scotia Equity Decisions   (DLA)
Rus ER .... Russell's Election Cases [*1874*] [*Nova Scotia*]   (DLA)
RusF .... Russkij Fol'klor [*A publication*]
RUSH .... Remote User Shared Hardware [*Data processing*]
Rush-Presbyt-St Luke's Med Bull ... Rush-Presbyterian-St. Luke's Medical Center. Bulletin [*A publication*]
Rush-Presbyt-St Luke's Med Cent Res Rep ... Rush-Presbyterian-St. Luke's Medical Center. Research Report [*A publication*]
Rushw .... Rushworth's Historical Collections   (DLA)
RUSI .... Royal United Services Institute for Defence Studies [*British*]
RusL .... Russkaja Literatura [*A publication*]
Rus Ling ..... Russian Linguistics [*A publication*]
RUSNO ...... Resident United States Naval Officer
Rus P .... Russian Pharmacopoeia [*A publication*]
RusR .... Russian Review [*A publication*]
RusR .... Russkaja Rech' [*A publication*]
Rus Re .... Russkaja Rech' [*A publication*]
RUSS .... Remote User Service Station   (MCD)
Russ .... Russell's Contested Election Cases [*Massachusetts*]   (DLA)
Russ .... Russell's Election Cases [*1874*] [*Nova Scotia*]   (DLA)
Russ .... Russell's English Chancery Reports   (DLA)
RUSS .... Russet
RUSS .... Russia
Russ Arb ... Russell on Arbitrators   (DLA)
Russ & C ... Russell and Chesley's Nova Scotia Reports [*Nova Scotia Reports 10-12*] [*1875-79*]   (DLA)
Russ Cast Prod ... Russian Castings Production [*A publication*]
Russ & C Eq Cas ... Russell and Chesley's Nova Scotia Equity Cases   (DLA)
Russ Ch ..... Russell's English Chancery Reports   (DLA)
Russ Chem Rev ... Russian Chemical Reviews [*A publication*]
Russ & Ches ... Russell and Chesley's Nova Scotia Reports   (DLA)
Russ & Ches Eq ... Russell and Chesley's Nova Scotia Equity Reports   (DLA)
Russ Con El (Mass) ... Russell's Contested Election Cases [*Massachusetts*]   (DLA)
Russ Cr ...... Russell on Crimes and Misdemeanors   (DLA)
Russ Crim ... Russell on Crime [*12th ed.*] [*1964*]   (DLA)
Russ Crimes ... Russell on Crimes and Misdemeanors   (DLA)
Russ El Cas ... Russell's Election Cases [*1874*] [*Nova Scotia*]   (DLA)
Russ Elect Cas ... Russell's Contested Election Cases [*Massachusetts*]   (DLA)
Russ Elect Cas ... Russell's Election Cases [*Nova Scotia*]   (DLA)
Russell .... Russell's Nova Scotia Equity Decisions   (DLA)
Russell-Cotes Mus Bul ... Russell-Cotes Art Gallery and Museum Bulletin [*A publication*]
Russell NS ... Russell's Nova Scotia Equity Decisions   (DLA)
Russ Eng J ... Russian Engineering Journal [*A publication*]
Russ En J ... Russian Engineering Journal [*A publication*]
Russ & Eq ... Russell and Chesley's Nova Scotia Equity Reports   (DLA)
Russ Eq ...... Russell's Nova Scotia Equity Cases   (DLA)
Russ Eq Cas ... Russell's Nova Scotia Equity Cases   (DLA)
Russ Eq Rep ... Russell's Nova Scotia Equity Decisions   (DLA)

Russ Fact ... Russell on Factors and Brokers   (DLA)

Russ & G .... Russell and Geldert's Nova Scotia Reports [*Nova Scotia Reports 13-27*] [*1879-95*] [*Canada*]   (DLA)

Russ & Geld ... Russell and Geldert's Nova Scotia Reports   (DLA)

Russian Math Surveys ... Russian Mathematical Surveys [*A publication*]

Russian R ... Russian Review [*A publication*]

Russian Rev ... Russian Review [*A publication*]

Russ & Jap PC ... Russian and Japanese Prize Cases [*London*]   (DLA)

Russ J Inorg Chem ... Russian Journal of Inorganic Chemistry [*A publication*]

Russ J Phys Chem ... Russian Journal of Physical Chemistry [*A publication*]

Russkaia L ... Russkaia Literatura [*A publication*]

Russk Med ... Russkaia Meditsina [*A publication*]

Russ-K Min Ges St Petersburg Verh ... Russisch-Kaiserliche Mineralogische Gesellschaft zu St. Petersburg. Verhandlungen [*A publication*]

Russk Zhurnal Trop Med ... Russkii Zhurnal Tropicheskoi Meditsiny [*A publication*]

Russk Zool Zhurnal ... Russkii Zoologicheskii Zhurnal [*A publication*]

Russ Lit ..... Russkaja Literatura [*A publication*]

Russ Lit Tr ... Russian Literature Triquarterly [*A publication*]

Russ & M .... Russell and Mylne's English Chancery Reports [*1829-33*]   (DLA)

Russ Math Surv ... Russian Mathematical Surveys [*A publication*]

Russ Merc Ag ... Russell on Mercantile Agency   (DLA)

Russ Metall ... Russian Metallurgy [*A publication*]

Russ Met R ... Russian Metallurgy-USSR [*A publication*]

Russ & My ... Russell and Mylne's English Chancery Reports [*1829-33*]   (DLA)

Russ N Sc ... Russell's Nova Scotia Equity Cases   (DLA)

Russ Pharmacol Toxicol ... Russian Pharmacology and Toxicology [*A publication*]

Russ & R ..... Russell and Ryan's English Crown Cases Reserved [*1799-1823*]   (DLA)

Russ R .... Russian Review [*A publication*]

Russ & RCC ... Russell and Ryan's English Crown Cases Reserved [*168 English Reprint*] [*1799-1823*]   (DLA)

Russ & RCC (Eng) ... Russell and Ryan's English Crown Cases Reserved [*1799-1823*]   (DLA)

Russ & R Cr Cas ... Russell and Ryan's English Crown Cases Reserved   (DLA)

Russ Rev .... Russian Review [*A publication*]

Russ Rev Biol ... Russian Review of Biology [*A publication*]

Russ & Ry ... Russell and Ryan's English Crown Cases Reserved   (DLA)

Russ T Eld ... Russell's English Chancery Reports Tempore Elden   (DLA)

RUSSWO .... Revised Uniform Summary of Surveyed Weather Observations   (MCD)

Rust .... De Re Rustica [*of Varro*] [*Classical studies*]   (OCD)

RUSTA .... Rustica [*A publication*]

RUSTIC ...... Regional and Urban Studies Information Center [*Department of Energy*] [*Oak Ridge, TN*]   (EISS)

RUT .... Remote User Terminal [*Data processing*]   (CAAL)

RUT .... Room Usage Time

RUT .... Rooms Using Television [*Television ratings*]

RUT .... Ruta [*Rue*] [*Pharmacy*]   (ROG)

RUT .... Ruth [*Nevada*] [*Seismograph station code, US Geological Survey*] [*Closed*]   (SEIS)

RUT .... Rutland [*Vermont*] [*Airport symbol*]   (OAG)

RUT .... Rutland Railway Corp. [*AAR code*] [*Terminated*]

RUT .... Standard Regional Route Transmitting Frequencies [*Communications*]   (FAAC)

RUTD .... Rutlandshire [*County in England*]   (ROG)

RUTEL .... Reference Your Telegram   (FAAC)

Rutg Cas .... Rutger-Waddington Case [*1784*] [*New York City*]   (DLA)

Rutgers Camden L J ... Rutgers Camden Law Journal [*A publication*]

Rutgers Comput and Technol Law J ... Rutgers Computer and Technology Law Journal [*A publication*]

Rutgers J Comp & L ... Rutgers Journal of Computers and Law [*A publication*]

Rutgers J Computers & Law ... Rutgers Journal of Computers and the Law [*A publication*]

Rutgers J Comput & Law ... Rutgers Journal of Computers and the Law [*A publication*]

Rutgers J Comput Technol and Law ... Rutgers Journal of Computers, Technology, and the Law [*A publication*]

Rutgers L Rev ... Rutgers Law Review [*A publication*]

Rutgers State Univ Coll Eng Eng Res Bull ... Rutgers State University. College of Engineering. Engineering Research Bulletin [*A publication*]

Rutgers UL Rev ... Rutgers University. Law Review   (DLA)

Rutgers Univ Bur Biol Res Serol Mus Bull ... Rutgers University. Bureau of Biological Research. Serological Museum Bulletin [*A publication*]

Rutgers Univ Bur Eng Res Eng Res Publ ... Rutgers University. Bureau of Engineering Research. Engineering Research Publication [*A publication*]

Rutgers Univ Bur Miner Res Bull ... Rutgers University. Bureau of Mineral Research. Bulletin [*A publication*]

Rutgers Univ Coll Eng Eng Res Bull ... Rutgers University. College of Engineering. Engineering Research Bulletin [*A publication*]

Rutg L Rev ... Rutgers Law Review [*A publication*]

Rutherford Lab Rep ... Rutherford Laboratory Report [*A publication*]

Ruth Inst .... Rutherford's Institutes of Natural Law   (DLA)

RuthR .... Ruth Rabbah   (BJA)

RUTLDS ..... Rutlandshire [*County in England*]

RUTOP ...... Rutowski Optimization [*Computer program*]

RuTuAsA .... Akademiia Nauk Tarkmenskoi SSR, Tsentralnaia Nauchnaia Biblioteka [*Academy of Sciences of Turkmen SSR, Central Scientific Library*], Ashkhabad, Turkmen, SSR, Soviet Union [*Library symbol*] [*Library of Congress*]   (LCLS)

RUTWX ...... Reference Your TWX [*Teletypewriter Communications*]   (FAAC)

RUU .... Rijksuniversiteit Utrecht [*Netherlands*]

RuUk .... Gosudartsvennaia Publichnaia Biblioteka Ukrainskoi SSR [*State Public Library of the Ukrainian SSR*], Kiev, Soviet Union [*Library symbol*] [*Library of Congress*]   (LCLS)

RUUR .... Regrade Unclassified Upon Receipt [*Air Force*]

RUV .... Bellefontaine, OH [*Location identifier*] [*FAA*]   (FAAL)

RUV .... Rauvai [*Tuamotu Archipelago*] [*Seismograph station code, US Geological Survey*]   (SEIS)

RUWS .... Remote Unmanned Work System [*Navy*]

RUX .... Baltimore, MD [*Location identifier*] [*FAA*]   (FAAL)

RUY .... Revista. Universidad de Yucatan [*A publication*]

RV .... Rabies Virus

RV .... Radikale Venstre [*Radical Liberals*] [*Denmark*]   (PPE)

RV .... Radio Vehicle   (DEN)

RV .... Rahway Valley R. R. [*AAR code*]

R/V .... Range to Velocity [*Ratio of the RADAR platform*]

RV .... Rassegna Volterrana [*A publication*]

RV .... Rateable Value [*Property value*] [*British*]

RV .... Rated Voltage

RV .... Raven [*A publication*]

RV .... Reaction Voltage

RV .... Reactor Vessel [*Engineering*]

RV .... Reading and Vocabulary Test [*Also, RVT*] [*Military*]

R/V .... Rear View   (AAG)

RV .... Rear View [*Technical drawings*]

RV .... Recirculation Valve   (MCD)

RV .... Recovery Vehicle [*NASA*]   (NASA)

RV .... Recreational Vehicle

RV .... Recycling Valve

RV .... Reentry Vehicle [*Aerospace*]

RV .... Reeve Aleutian Airways, Inc. [*ICAO designator*]   (OAG)

RV .... Reeves MacDonald Mines [*Vancouver Stock Exchange symbol*]

RV .... Reference Voltage

RV .... Reinforcement Value [*Psychology*]

RV .... Release Valve   (NRCH)

RV .... Released Value [*Freight*]

RV .... Relief Valve

RV .... Renal Vessel [*Medicine*]

RV .... Rendezvous

RV .... Rendezvous Vehicle [*NASA*]   (KSC)

RV .... Rescue Vessel

RV .... Research Vehicle

RV .... Research Vessel

RV .... Residual Variance

RV .... Residual Volume [*Physiology*]

RV .... Retroversion

RV .... Retrovirus

Rv .... Revelation [*New Testament book*]

RV .... Reverberation Time

Rv .... Revised [*Regulation or order revised*] [*Used in Shepard's Citations*]   (DLA)

RV .... Revised Version [*of the Bible, 1881*]

RV .... Rheinische Vierteljahresblaetter [*A publication*]

RV .... Rifle Volunteers

RV .... Right Ventricle [*of heart*] [*Cardiology*]

RV .... Rod Valgallianse [*Red Electoral Alliance*] [*Norway*]   (PPE)

RV .... Roving Vehicle [*NASA*]

RV .... Rubella Virus

RV .... Runway Visibility [*Aviation*]   (AFM)

RV .... RV: Recreational Vehicles [*A publication*]

RVA .... Farafangana [*Madagascar*] [*Airport symbol*]   (OAG)

RVA .... Raven Air [*Anchorage, AK*] [*FAA designator*]   (FAAC)

RVA .... Reactive Volt-Ampere Meter

RVA .... Recorded Voice Announcement [*Telecommunications*]   (IBMDP)

RVA .... Regular Veterans Association of the United States   (EA)

RVA .... Relative Virtual Address

RVA .... Relative Volt-Ampere

RVA .... Reliability Variation Analysis

RVA .... Remote Voltage Adjustment

RVA .... Rib-Vertebra Angle [*Anatomy*]

RVA .... Right Ventricular Assistance [*Cardiology*]

RVA .... Right Visual Acuity [*Medicine*]

RVA .... Roberts Wesleyan College, K. B. Keating Library, Rochester, NY [*OCLC symbol*]   (OCLC)

RVAAP .... Ravenna Army Ammunition Plant   (AABC)

RVAD .... Rib-Vertebra Angle Difference [*Anatomy*]

RVAH .... Reconnaissance Attack Squadron [*Navy*]   (NVT)

RVAHA .... Revue d'Acoustique [*A publication*]

RVANCS .... Remote View Airborne Night Classification System
RVARM...... Recording Varmeter (MSA)
RVAS......... Records. Victorian Archaeological Survey [*A publication*]
RVASA .... Revue de l'Atherosclerose [*A publication*]
RVAT......... Retinal Visual Acuity Tester [*Ophthalmology*]
RVAV .... Regulating Valve Actuating Valve (KSC)
RVAW .... Readiness Patrol Squadron [*Navy*] (NVT)
RVB .... RADAR Video Buffer
RVB .... Rheinische Vierteljahresblaetter [*A publication*]
RVB .... Rochester Gas & Electric Corp., TIC Library, Rochester, NY
        [*OCLC symbol*] (OCLC)
RVBR .... Riveting Bar [*Tool*] (AAG)
RVBTA ...... Revue Belge des Transports [*A publication*]
RVC .... RADAR Video Controller [*Military*] (CAAL)
RVC .... Ramakrishna-Vivekananda Center [*An association*] (EA)
RVC .... Random Vibration Control
RVC .... Relative Velocity Computer
RVC .... Remote-Voice Control
RVC .... Reticulated Vitreous Carbon
RVC .... Rifle Volunteer Corps [*Military unit*] [*British*]
RVC .... Rochester General Hospital Library, Rochester, NY [*OCLC
        symbol*] (OCLC)
RVC .... Rotary Voice Coil [*Computer technology*]
RVC .... Royal Veterinary College [*British*]
RVC .... Royal Victorian Chain
RVCC .... Reeves Communications [*NASDAQ symbol*] (NQ)
RVCCB....... Reviews on Coatings and Corrosion [*A publication*]
RVCDA ...... Recreational Vehicle Club Directors of America (EA)
RVCF......... Remote Vehicle Checkout Facility [*NASA*] (NASA)
RVCI.......... Royal Veterinary College of Ireland
RVCM .... Recent Vertical Crustal Movement [*Geology*]
RVCM .... Republic of Vietnam Campaign Medal [*Military
        decoration*] (AFM)
RVCZA .... Revista de Coroziune [*A publication*]
RVD .... Dutchess County Mental Health Center, Poughkeepsie, NY
        [*OCLC symbol*] [*Inactive*] (OCLC)
RVD .... RADAR Video Digitizer
RVD .... Relative Vertebral Density
RVD .... Residual Vapor Detector (NATG)
RVD .... Right Ventricular Dimension [*Cardiology*]
RVD .... Royal Victoria Dock [*British*] (ROG)
RVDA .... Recreational Vehicle Dealers Association of North America
        [*Fairfax, VA*] (EA)
RVDP......... RADAR Video Data Processor
RVDP......... Relief Valve Discharge Piping (NRCH)
RVDT .... Rotary Variable Differential Transducer [*or Transformer*]
RVE .... RADAR Video Extractor
RVE .... Representative Volume Element
RVE .... Right Ventricular Enlargement [*Cardiology*]
RVE .... Rochester Institute of Technology, Wallace Memorial Library,
        Rochester, NY [*OCLC symbol*] (OCLC)
RVE .... Royce Ventures Ltd. [*Vancouver Stock Exchange symbol*]
RVE .... Saravena [*Colombia*] [*Airport symbol*] (OAG)
RVED-CMP ... Right Ventricular End-Diastolic Compliance [*Cardiology*]
RVEDP .... Right Ventricular End-Diastolic Pressure [*Cardiology*]
RVEDPI ...... Right Ventricular End-Diastolic Pressure Index [*Cardiology*]
RVEDV .... Right Ventricle End-Diastolic Volume [*Cardiology*]
RVELA........ Revista Electrotecnica [*A publication*]
RVENA .... Rivista di Viticoltura e di Enologia [*A publication*]
R Venez Folk ... Revista Venezolana de Folklore [*A publication*]
R Venezolana Estud Municipales ... Revista Venezolana de Estudios
        Municipales [*A publication*]
R Venezolana Sanidad y Asistencia Soc ... Revista Venezolana de Sanidad
        y Asistencia Social [*A publication*]
RVER......... Regional Veterans Employment Representative [*Department of
        Labor*]
RVESV .... Right Ventricular End-Systolic Volume [*Cardiology*]
RvEx .... Review and Expositor [*A publication*]
RVF .... Rate Variance Formula [*Air Force*]
RVF .... Revista Valenciana de Filologia [*A publication*]
RVF .... Revista Venezolana de Folklore [*A publication*]
RVF .... Rift Valley Fever
RVF .... Right Visual Field [*Psychometrics*]
RVF .... Rochester Psychiatric Center Library, Rochester, NY [*OCLC
        symbol*] (OCLC)
RVFN......... Report of Visit of Foreign Nationals (AAG)
RVFO......... Revista Venezolana de Folklore [*A publication*]
RVFX .... Rivet Fixture (AAG)
RVG........... Chicago, IL [*Location identifier*] [*FAA*] (FAAL)
RVG........... Reference-Voltage Generator
RVG........... Right Ventral Gluteal [*Injection site*]
RVG........... Right Visceral Ganglion [*Medicine*]
RVG........... Rotating Vertical Gradiometer
RVG........... Rumrill-Hoyt Corp., Library, Rochester, NY [*OCLC
        symbol*] (OCLC)
RVGA-A ..... Revue de Geographie Alpine [*France*] [*A publication*]
RV/GC........ Reentry Vehicle and Ground Control [*NASA*] (KSC)
Rv Gen Sciences ... Revue Generale des Sciences Pures et Appliquees [*A
        publication*]
RVGG .... Rotating Vertical Gravity Gradiometer
RVGPA....... Reviews of Geophysics [*A publication*]

RVH .... Renovascular Hypertension [*Medicine*]
RVH .... Right Ventricular Hypertrophy [*Cardiology*]
RVH .... St. Bernard's Seminary and College Library, Rochester, NY
        [*OCLC symbol*] (OCLC)
RVI............ Recorded Video Imaging (MCD)
RVI............ Recreational Vehicle Institute
RVI............ Renault Vehicules Industriels
RVI............ Reverse Interrupt Character [*Keyboard*]
RVI............ Saint Mary's Hospital, Medical Library, Rochester, NY [*OCLC
        symbol*] (OCLC)
RVIA .... Recreation Vehicle Industry Association [*Reston, VA*] (EA)
RVIMI .... Rubella Virus-Induced Mitotic Inhibitor
RVIS .... Reactor and Vessel Instrumentation System (NRCH)
RVJ............ Reidsville, GA [*Location identifier*] [*FAA*] (FAAL)
RVJ............ Sear-Brown Associates Information Center Library, Rochester,
        NY [*OCLC symbol*] (OCLC)
RVJS .... Reentry Vehicle Jamming Simulator [*Army*]
RVK .... Sybron Corp., Medical Products Division Library, Rochester,
        NY [*OCLC symbol*] (OCLC)
RVL .... Reedsville, PA [*Location identifier*] [*FAA*] (FAAL)
RVL .... Rolling Vertical Landing (MCD)
RVL .... Sybron Corp., Pfaudler Division Technical Library, Henrietta,
        NY [*OCLC symbol*] (OCLC)
RVLA .... Roanoke Valley Library Association [*Library network*]
RVLG......... Revolving
RVLG......... Right Ventrolateral Gluteal [*Site of injection*] [*Medicine*]
RVLI .... Raksti. Latvijas PSR Zinatnu Akademija. Valodas und
        Literaturas Instituta [*A publication*]
RVLIS .... Reactor Vessel Water Level Indication System (IEEE)
RVLR......... Revolver (AABC)
RVLV......... Revolve (MSA)
RVM .... Reactive Voltmeter
RVM .... Reentry Vehicle Module [*NASA*] (KSC)
RVM .... Repertoire de Vedettes-Matiere [*Laval Subject Authority
        Records*] [*UTLAS symbol*]
RVm .... Revised Version [*of the Bible*], Margin
RVM .... Rio Vista Mine [*California*] [*Seismograph station code, US
        Geological Survey*] (SEIS)
RVM .... Sybron Corp.; Taylor Division Research Library, Rochester, NY
        [*OCLC symbol*] (OCLC)
RVN .... Republic of Vietnam
RVN .... Requirements Verification Network [*NASA*] (NASA)
RVN .... Rogersville, TN [*Location identifier*] [*FAA*] (FAAL)
RVN .... Rovaniemi [*Finland*] [*Airport symbol*] (OAG)
RVN .... Women's Career Center Library, Rochester, NY [*OCLC
        symbol*] (OCLC)
RVNAF ...... Republic of Vietnam Air Force (AFM)
RVNAF ...... Republic of Vietnam Armed Forces
RVNAFHMFC ... Republic of Vietnam Armed Forces Honor Medal First Class
        [*Military decoration*] (AABC)
RVNAFHMSC ... Republic of Vietnam Armed Forces Honor Medal Second
        Class [*Military decoration*]
RVNCAMFC ... Republic of Vietnam Civil Actions Medal First Class [*Military
        decoration*] (AABC)
RVNCAMSC ... Republic of Vietnam Civil Actions Medal Second Class
        [*Military decoration*] (AABC)
RVNCM ...... Republic of Vietnam Campaign Medal [*Military
        decoration*] (AABC)
RVNF......... Republic of Vietnam Forces
RVNGCUCW/P ... Republic of Vietnam Gallantry Cross Unit Citation with
        Palm [*Military decoration*] (AABC)
RVNMC ...... Republic of Vietnam Marine Corps (CINC)
RVNN .... Republic of Vietnam Navy (CINC)
RVO .... Aquinas Institute Library, Rochester, NY [*OCLC
        symbol*] (OCLC)
RVO .... Lubbock, TX [*Location identifier*] [*FAA*] (FAAL)
RVO .... Regional Veterinary Officer [*British*]
RVO .... Relaxed Vaginal Outlet [*Medicine*]
RVO .... Royal Victorian Order
RVO .... Runway Visibility Observer [*Aviation*] (FAAC)
RVOOA....... Rivista Oto-Neuro-Oftalmologica [*A publication*]
RVOT......... Right Ventricular Outflow Tract [*Cardiology*]
RVP .... Avon Junior/Senior High School Library, Avon, NY [*OCLC
        symbol*] (OCLC)
RVP .... RADAR Video Processor [*Military*] (CAAL)
RVP .... Raster-to-Vector Processor [*Computer graphics technology*]
RVP .... Reid Vapor Pressure
RVP .... Reutilization Value Percentage [*DoD*]
RVP .... Rotary Vacuum Pump
RVPA .... Rivet Pattern (AAG)
RVPMB....... Review of Psychology of Music [*A publication*]
RVPTB........ Revue Polytechnique [*A publication*]
RVQ .... Benjamin Franklin High School Library, Rochester, NY [*OCLC
        symbol*] (OCLC)
RVR .... Bishop Kearney High School Library, Rochester, NY [*OCLC
        symbol*] (OCLC)
RVR .... RADAR Video Recorder
R & VR........ Rating and Valuation Reports [*Legal*] [*British*]
RVR .... Renal Vascular Resistance [*Medicine*]
RVR .... Reverse Velocity Rotor
RVR .... Rim Vent Release [*Safety device for aerosol containers*]

RVR .... River (FAAC)

RVR .... Riverside [*California*] [*Seismograph station code, US Geological Survey*] (SEIS)

RVR .... Runway Visual Range [*Aviation*]

RVRA .... Recreation Vehicle Rental Association [*Fairfax, VA*] (EA)

RV/RA .... Renal Vein/Renal Activity [*Ratio*] [*Medicine*]

RVRA .... Runway Visual Range Average [*Aviation*] (FAAC)

RVRANO .... Runway Visual Range Average Not Available [*Aviation*] (FAAC)

RVRC .... Renal Vein Renin Concentration [*Medicine*]

RVRM .... Runway Visual Range Midpoint [*Aviation*]

RVRNO .... Runway Visual Range Not Available [*Aviation*] (FAAC)

RVRR .... Runway Visual Range Rollout [*Aviation*] (FAAC)

RVRRNO .... Runway Visual Range Rollout Not Available [*Aviation*] (FAAC)

RVRT .... Runway Visual Range Touchdown [*Aviation*] (FAAC)

RVRTNO..... Runway Visual Range Touchdown Not Available [*Aviation*] (FAAC)

RVRU......... RADAR Video Recorder Unit

RVS .... Brighton High School Library, Rochester, NY [*OCLC symbol*] (OCLC)

RVS .... Radius Vector Subroutine

RVS .... Reentry Vehicle Separation [*Aerospace*] (MUGU)

RVS .... Reentry Vehicle Simulator [*Aerospace*] (AAG)

RVS .... Relative Value Scale [*or Schedule or Study*] [*Medicine*]

RVS .... Remote Viewing System

RVS .... Requirements Validation Study (MCD)

RVS .... Reverse (MSA)

RVS .... Revise (FAAC)

RVS .... Riverside Mountains [*California*] [*Seismograph station code, US Geological Survey*] (SEIS)

RVS .... Rocketborne Vacuum System

RVS .... Tulsa, OK [*Location identifier*] [*FAA*] (FAAL)

RVSBL....... Reversible (MSA)

Rv Scient .. Revue Scientifique [*A publication*]

RVSE......... Reverse (AABC)

RVSFC ...... Ricky and Vince Smith Fan Club [*Pottsville, PA*] (EA)

RVSS .... Reactor Vessel Support System (IEEE)

RVSSC...... Reverse Self Check (AAG)

RVST......... Russel Viper Serum Time [*Clinical chemistry*]

RVSVP ...... Repondez Vite, S'il Vous Plait [*Please Reply at Once*] [*French*]

RVSW .... Right Ventricular Stroke Work [*Cardiology*]

RVSWI....... Right Ventricular Stroke Work Index [*Cardiology*]

RVSZ......... Riveting Squeezer [*Tool*] (AAG)

RVT .... Brockport High School Library, Brockport, NY [*OCLC symbol*] (OCLC)

RVT .... Reading and Vocabulary Test [*Also, RV*] [*Military*]

RVT .... Reliability Verification Tests

RVT .... Renal Vein Thrombosis [*Medicine*]

RVT .... Resource Vector Table [*Data processing*] (IBMDP)

RVT .... Rivet (MSA)

RVT .... Royce Value Trust [*NYSE symbol*]

RVTD......... Riveted (MSA)

RVTO......... Reentry Vehicle Test and Observables [*Air Force*]

RVTOL ...... Rolling Vertical Takeoff and Landing [*Aviation*] (MCD)

Rv Trim Can ... Revue Trimestrielle Canadienne [*A publication*]

RVU .... Caledonia-Mumford Junior/Senior High School Library, Caledonia, NY [*OCLC symbol*] (OCLC)

RVU .... Relative Value Unit

RVU .... Relief Valve Unit

RVUXA ...... Revue X [*Belgium*] [*A publication*]

RVV .... Cardinal Mooney High School Library, Rochester, NY [*OCLC symbol*] (OCLC)

RVV .... Regional Vascular Volume [*Hematology*]

RVV .... Religionsgeschichtliche Versuche und Vorarbeiten [*A publication*]

RVV .... Romanistische Versuche und Vorarbeiten [*A publication*]

RVV .... Runway Visibility Values [*Aviation*]

RVVNO ...... Runway Visibility Not Available [*Aviation*] (FAAC)

RVW .... Charles H. Roth High School Library, Henrietta, NY [*OCLC symbol*] (OCLC)

RVW .... Ralph Vaughan Williams [*British composer, 1872-1958*]

RVX .... Charlotte Junior/Senior High School Library, Rochester, NY [*OCLC symbol*] (OCLC)

RVX .... Reentry Vehicle, Experimental [*Aerospace*]

RVY .... Churchville-Chili Senior High School Library, Rochester, NY [*OCLC symbol*] (OCLC)

RVY .... Clarksville Flying Service, Inc. [*Clarksville, AR*] [*FAA designator*] (FAAC)

RVY .... Rivera [*Uruguay*] [*Airport symbol*] (OAG)

RVZ .... Dansville Senior High School Library, Dansville, NY [*OCLC symbol*] (OCLC)

RW............. R. Warren [*Pseudonym used by Charles Ashton*]

RW............. Race Weight [*of a horse*]

RW............. Radiation Weapon (AAG)

RW............. Radical Women [*An association*] (EA)

RW............. Radiological Warfare

RW............. Radiological Warhead

RW............. Republican Weapons

RW............. Ragweed [*Immunology*]

RW............. Rail and Water [*Shipping*]

R & W .... Rail and Water [*Shipping*]

RW............. Railway

RW............. Rain Showers [*Meteorology*] (FAAC)

RW............. Ramo Wooldridge [*Later, TRW, Inc.*]

R/W .... Ramo-Wooldridge-Thompson Corp. [*Later, TRW, Inc.*] (AAG)

RW............. Random Walk

RW............. Random Widths [*Lumber*]

RW............. Raw Water [*Technical drawings*]

RW............. RAWINSONDE [*Radiosonde and RADAR Wind Sounding*] [*Upper air observation*]

R-W .... Read-Write [*Data processing*] (MSA)

R(W) .... Reconstruction, Workmen's Compensation [*British*] [*World War II*]

RW............. Recreation and Welfare [*Navy*]

RW............. Recruiting Warrant

RW............. Reduced Weight

RW............. Reel and Wheel [*Freight*]

RW............. Reformed World [*A publication*]

RW............. Regions of the World [*A publication*]

RW............. Relative Worth (MCD)

R/W .... Report Writer [*Data processing*]

RW............. Republic Airlines West, Inc. [*ICAO designator*] (FAAC)

RW............. Resistance Welding (IEEE)

RW............. Restaurant Wine [*License*]

R/W .... Returned to Work

RW............. Reverse Wound (MCD)

RW............. Rewind

RW............. Rideal-Walter Coefficient [*Pharmacy*]

RW............. Right of Way [*Also, ROW*]

RW............. Right Wing

RW............. Right Worshipful

RW............. Right Worthy

RW............. River Water [*Nuclear energy*] (NRCH)

RW............. Riveted and Welded [*Shipping*]

RW............. Rotary Wing [*Aircraft designation*]

RW............. Rough Weather [*A publication*]

R & W .... Routing and Work [*Military*]

RW............. Rowa-Wagner KG [*Germany*] [*Research code symbol*]

RW............. Royal Warrant [*British*] (ADA)

RW............. Royal Warwickshire Regiment [*Military unit*] [*British*]

RW............. Runway

rw .... Rwanda [*MARC country of publication code*] [*Library of Congress*] (LCCP)

RW............. Rwanda [*Two-letter standard code*] (CNC)

RWA .... E. J. Wilson High School Library, Spencerport, NY [*OCLC symbol*] (OCLC)

RWa........... George Hail Free Library, Warren, RI [*Library symbol*] [*Library of Congress*] (LCLS)

RWA .... RADWASTE Area (NRCH)

RWA .... Railway Wheel Association [*Defunct*] (EA)

RWA .... Raoul Wallenberg Association [*See also RWF*] (EA)

RWA .... Reaction Wheel Assembly (MCD)

RWA .... Rectangular Wave-Guide Assembly

RWA .... Regional Water Authority [*British*]

RWA .... Rippled Wall Amplifier

RWA .... Romance Writers of America (EA)

RWA .... Rotary Wing Aircraft

RWA .... Royal West of England Academy

RWA .... Rwanda [*Three-letter standard code*] (CNC)

RWAFF ...... Royal West African Frontier Force [*Military unit*] [*British*]

RWAGE ..... Ragweed Antigen E [*Immunology*]

RWAHSJ .... Royal Western Australian Historical Society. Journal [*A publication*] (ADA)

RWAMD ..... Radioactive Waste Management [*A publication*]

RWar .... Warwick Public Library, Warwick, RI [*Library symbol*] [*Library of Congress*] (LCLS)

RWarR .... Rhode Island Junior College, Knight Campus, Warwick, RI [*Library symbol*] [*Library of Congress*] (LCLS)

RWAVA ..... Rheinisch-Westfaelische Akademie der Wissenschaften Natur-, Ingenieur-, und Wirtschaftswissenschaften. Vortraege [*A publication*]

RWAW....... United Union of Roofers, Waterproofers, and Allied Workers

RWB .... Rear Wheel Brake

RWB .... Rod Withdrawal Block [*Nuclear energy*] (NRCH)

RWB .... Roger Williams College, Bristol, RI [*OCLC symbol*] (OCLC)

RWBH....... Records Will Be Handcarried [*Army*] (AABC)

RWBN....... Red and White Beacon [*Nautical charts*]

RWC .... East Junior/Senior High School Library, Rochester, NY [*OCLC symbol*] (OCLC)

RWC .... Radioactive Waste Campaign [*New York, NY*] (EA)

RWC .... Rainwater Conductor (AAG)

RWC .... Raw Water Cooling

RWC .... Reactor Water Cleanup (NRCH)

RWC .... Read, Write, and Compute

RWC .... Read-Write-Continue [*Data processing*]

RWC .... Relative Water Content

RWC .... Residential Wood Combustion

RWC .... Roberts Wesleyan College [*New York*]

RWCH....... Republican Women of Capitol Hill (EA)

RWCNEC ... Reports of the Working Committees. Northeast Conference [*A publication*]

RWCS........ Reactor Water Cleanup System (NRCH)

RWCS........ Red Wing Collectors Society (EA)

RWCU .... Reactor Water Cleanup (NRCH)
RWCUS ...... Raoul Wallenberg Committee of the United States (EA)
RWD .... Eastridge High School Library, Rochester, NY [OCLC symbol] (OCLC)
RWD .... Rear Wheel Drive
RWD .... Regular Way Delivery
RWD .... Regular World Day
RWD .... Rewind
RWD .... Right Wing Down [Aviation]
RWDCA ...... Red and White Dairy Cattle Association (EA)
RWDGM ..... Right Worshipful Deputy Grand Master [Freemasonry]
R/WDO ...... Rear Window [Automotive engineering]
RWDS .... RADWASTE Disposal System (NRCH)
RWDSU ..... Retail, Wholesale, and Department Store Union
RWE .... Edison Technical and Occupational Educational Center Library, Rochester, NY [OCLC symbol] (OCLC)
RWE .... Ralph Waldo Emerson [Initials used as pseudonym]
RWE .... Rheinisch-Westfaelisches Electrizitaetswerk [AG] [West Germany]
RWe .... Westerly Public Library, Westerly, RI [Library symbol] [Library of Congress] (LCLS)
RWEA .... Royal West of England Academy
RWED .... Read/Write Extend Delete
RWEL .... Rockwell Oil Co. [NASDAQ symbol] (NQ)
RWEMA ...... Ralph Waldo Emerson Memorial Association (EA)
RWES .... Resources West, Inc. [NASDAQ symbol] (NQ)
RWF........... Fairport High School Library, Fairport, NY [OCLC symbol] (OCLC)
RWF........... Raoul Wallenberg Foreningen [Raoul Wallenberg Association - RWA] (EA-IO)
RWF........... Redwood Falls, MN [Location identifier] [FAA] (FAAL)
RWF........... Roundtable for Women in Foodservice [Later, RWFBH] (EA)
RWF........... Roush, W. F., Miami FL [STAC]
RWF........... Royal Welch Fusiliers [Military unit] [British]
RWF........... Rozprawy Wydzialu Filologicznego Polskiej Akademyi Umiejetnosci [A publication]
RWFBH...... Roundtable for Women Food-Beverage-Hospitality [New York, NY] (EA)
RWFC........ Randy Wade Fan Club (EA)
RWG.......... Bakersfield Aviation Services [Bakersfield, CA] [FAA designator] (FAAC)
RWG.......... Gates-Chili Senior High School Library, Rochester, NY [OCLC symbol] (OCLC)
RWG.......... Radio Writers' Guild [Later, WGA]
RWG.......... Redwing Resources, Inc. [Vancouver Stock Exchange symbol]
RWG.......... Reliability Working Group (AAG)
RWG.......... Rigid Waveguide
RWG.......... Roebling Wire Gauge
RWGM....... Right Worshipful Grand Master [Freemasonry]
RWGR........ Right Worthy Grand Representative [Freemasonry]
RWGS........ Right Worthy Grand Secretary [Freemasonry] (ADA)
RWGT........ Right Worthy Grand Templar [Freemasonry]
RWGT........ Right Worthy Grand Treasurer [Freemasonry]
RWGW....... Right Worthy Grand Warden [Freemasonry]
RWGW....... Right Worthy Grand Worshipful [Freemasonry] (ROG)
RWH .... Geneseo Junior/Senior High School Library, Geneseo, NY [OCLC symbol] (OCLC)
RWH .... RADAR Warning and Homing
RWHD........ Rawhide (MSA)
RWI............ Greece-Arcadia Junior/Senior High School Library, Rochester, NY [OCLC symbol] (OCLC)
RWI............ RADAR Warning Installation (NATG)
RWI............ Radio Wire Integration [Military]
RWI............ Read-Write-Initialize [Data processing]
RWI............ Regular World Interval
RWI............ Remote Weight Indicator
RWI............ Rocky Mount [North Carolina] [Airport symbol] (OAG)
RWIB .... Rioja Wine Information Bureau (EA)
RWJ............ Greece-Athena Junior/Senior High School Library, Rochester, NY [OCLC symbol] (OCLC)
RWJGW...... Right Worthy Junior Grand Warden [Freemasonry]
RWK .... Greece-Olympia High School Library, Rochester, NY [OCLC symbol] (OCLC)
RWK .... Queen's Own Royal West Kent Regiment [Military unit] [British]
RWK .... Renwick Explorations Ltd. [Vancouver Stock Exchange symbol]
RWK .... Rework (AAG)
RWkEPA .... United States Environmental Protection Agency, National Marine Water Quality Laboratory, West Kingston, RI [Library symbol] [Library of Congress] (LCLS)
RWL........... H. W. Schroeder Junior/Senior High School Library, Webster, NY [OCLC symbol] (OCLC)
RWL........... Rawlins, WY [Location identifier] [FAA] (FAAL)
RWL........... Relative Water Level
RWLB .... Regional War Labor Board
RWLR .... Relative Water-Level Recorder
RWM.......... Hilton High School Library, Hilton, NY [OCLC symbol] (OCLC)
RWM.......... Read-Write Memory [Data processing] (MCD)
RWM.......... Rectangular Wave Modulation (IEEE)
RWM.......... Resistance Welding Machine
RWM.......... Right Worshipful Master [Freemasonry] (ROG)

RWM.......... Rod Worth Minimizer (NRCH)
RWM.......... Roll Wrapping Machine
RWMA .... Resistance Welder Manufacturers Association [Philadelphia, PA] (EA)
RWN .... Holly Junior/Senior High School Library, Holly, NY [OCLC symbol] (OCLC)
RWN .... Winamac, IN [Location identifier] [FAA] (FAAL)
RWNBH ..... Records Will Not Be Handcarried [Army] (AABC)
RWND........ Rewind (MSA)
RWO .... Honeoye Falls-Lima Senior High School Library, Honeoye Falls, NY [OCLC symbol] (OCLC)
RWO .... Kodiak, AK [Location identifier] [FAA] (FAAL)
RWO .... Reconnaissance Watch Officer (MCD)
RWO .... Regional Works Officer [British]
RWO .... Reimbursable Work Order [Navy] (NG)
RWO .... Riddare af Wasa Order [Knight of the Order of Vasa] [Sweden]
RWO .... Routine Work Order (KSC)
RWoH .... Harris Institute, Woonsocket, RI [Library symbol] [Library of Congress] (LCLS)
RWoU .... Union Saint-Jean-Baptiste d'Amerique, Woonsocket, RI [Library symbol] [Library of Congress] (LCLS)
RWP .... James Madison High School Library, Rochester, NY [OCLC symbol] (OCLC)
RWP .... Radiation Work Permit (NRCH)
RWP .... Radio Wave Propagation
RWP .... Radio Working Party
RWP .... RADWASTE Work Permit (NRCH)
RWP .... Rainwater Pipe [Construction]
RWP .... Rawalpindi/Islamabad [Pakistan] [Airport symbol] [Obsolete] (OAG)
RWP .... Reactor Work Permit (IEEE)
RWP .... Reformacja w Polsce [A publication]
RWP .... Rifle and Weapons Platoon [Army] [Obsolete] (AABC)
RWPC........ RADWASTE Process Cell (NRCH)
RWPG........ Real World Problem Generation
RWPH........ River Water Pumphouse [Nuclear energy] (NRCH)
RWQ .... James Monroe High School Library, Rochester, NY [OCLC symbol] (OCLC)
RWR .... James Sperry High School Library, Henrietta, NY [OCLC symbol] (OCLC)
RWR .... RADAR Warning Receiver (MCD)
RWR .... Radioactive Waste Reduction (NRCH)
R-W-R .... Rail-Water-Rail [Shipping]
RWR .... Read/Write Register
RWR .... Relative Weight Response
RWR .... Reward Resources Ltd. [Vancouver Stock Exchange symbol]
RWRC........ Remain Well to Right of Course [Aviation] (FAAC)
RWRS........ RADAR Warning System (MCD)
RWS .... Camp Springs, MD [Location identifier] [FAA] (FAAL)
RWS .... John Marshall High School Library, Rochester, NY [OCLC symbol] (OCLC)
RWS .... Radioactive Waste System (NRCH)
RWS .... Range While Search
RWS .... Reaction Wheel Scanner
RWS .... Reaction Wheel Systems (AAG)
RWS .... Regional Warning System
RWS .... Regional Weather Service (NOAA)
RWS .... Release with Service (OICC)
RWS .... Religionswissenschaftliche Studien [A publication]
RWS .... Royal Society of Painters in Water Colours [British]
RWS .... Royal West Surrey [Regiment] [Military unit] [British]
RWS .... Royal West Sussex [Regiment] [Military unit] [British]
RWSF .... RADWASTE Solidification Facility (NRCH)
RWSF .... Revolutionary War Studies Forum (EA)
RWSF .... Roosevelt Warm Springs Foundation [Atlanta, GA] (EA)
RWSGW ..... Right Worshipful Senior Grand Warden [Freemasonry]
RWSS........ RADWASTE Sample Station (NRCH)
RWSS........ River Water Supply System (IEEE)
RWST........ Refueling Water Storage Tank [Nuclear energy] (NRCH)
RWT .... Kendall High School Library, Kendall, NY [OCLC symbol] (OCLC)
RWT .... RADAR Warning Trainer (MCD)
RWT .... Read-Write Tape [Data processing]
RWT .... Refueling Water Tank [Nuclear energy] (NRCH)
RWTA........ River Water Treatment Area [Nuclear energy] (NRCH)
RWTS........ Regenerant Waste Treatment Subsystem [Nuclear energy] (NRCH)
RWU .... Keshequa Junior/Senior High School Library, Nunda, NY [OCLC symbol] (OCLC)
RWV .... L. C. Obourn High School Library, East Rochester, NY [OCLC symbol] (OCLC)
RWV .... Radioactive Waste Vent [Nuclear energy] (NRCH)
RWV .... Read-Write-Verify [Data processing]
RWVD........ Real World Visual Display
RWVR........ Real World Vehicular Rate
RWW .... Lester B. Forman Central Library, Fairport, NY [OCLC symbol] (OCLC)
RWX .... Letchworth Junior/Senior High School Library, Gainesville, NY [OCLC symbol] (OCLC)
RWY .... Livonia High School Library, Livonia, NY [OCLC symbol] (OCLC)

RWY .... Railway

RWY .... Royal Wiltshire Yeomanry [Military unit] [British]

RWY .... Runway   (AAG)

RWZ .... McQuaid Jesuit High School Library, Rochester, NY [OCLC symbol]   (OCLC)

RX .... Comite International de la Croix-Rouge [International Committee of the Red Cross] [ICAO designator]   (FAAC)

RX .... Excess Reserves

RX .... Rank Xerox

RX .... Receiver [or Reception] [Radio]   (NATG)

R$_x$ .... Recipe [Used as a symbol for medical prescriptions]

RX .... Reconnaissance-Experimental Aircraft

RX .... Register and Indexed Storage   (MCD)

RX .... Remote Exchange [Telecommunications]   (TEL)

RX .... Report Crossing [Aviation]   (FAAC)

RX .... Resolver-Transmitter

RX .... Rix-Dollar [British]   (ROG)

RX .... Rupees [Monetary unit]   (ROG)

RX .... Rush [on teletype messages]

RXA .... Mount Morris Junior/Senior High School Library, Mount Morris, NY [OCLC symbol]   (OCLC)

RXA .... Roxana Resources Ltd. [Vancouver Stock Exchange symbol]

RXB .... Nazareth Academy Library, Rochester, NY [OCLC symbol]   (OCLC)

RXC .... Our Lady of Mercy High School Library, Rochester, NY [OCLC symbol]   (OCLC)

RXCH .... Rexco Industries [NASDAQ symbol]   (NQ)

RXD .... Penfield High School Library, Penfield, NY [OCLC symbol]   (OCLC)

RXE .... Perry Junior/Senior High School Library, Perry, NY [OCLC symbol]   (OCLC)

RXF .... Pittsford-Medon High School Library, Pittsford, NY [OCLC symbol]   (OCLC)

RXF .... Rexford [Montana] [Seismograph station code, US Geological Survey]   (SEIS)

RXG .... Pittsford-Sutherland High School Library, Pittsford, NY [OCLC symbol]   (OCLC)

RXH .... R. L. Thomas High School Library, Webster, NY [OCLC symbol]   (OCLC)

RXH .... Rexham Corp. [NYSE symbol]

RXI .... Rexplore Resources International Ltd. [Vancouver Stock Exchange symbol]

RXI .... St. Agnes High School Library, Rochester, NY [OCLC symbol]   (OCLC)

RXJ .... Thomas Jefferson Junior/Senior High School Library, Rochester, NY [OCLC symbol]   (OCLC)

RXK .... Newark, OH [Location identifier] [FAA]   (FAAL)

RXK .... Warsaw High School Library, Warsaw, NY [OCLC symbol]   (OCLC)

RXL .... Rank Xerox Limited [Xerox subsidiary]

RXL .... Wayland Senior High School Library, Wayland, NY [OCLC symbol]   (OCLC)

RXLI .... Recessive X-Linked Ichthyosis [Medicine]

RXM .... Rexford Minerals Ltd. [Vancouver Stock Exchange symbol]

RXM .... West Irondequoit High School Library, Rochester, NY [OCLC symbol]   (OCLC)

RXN .... Islip, NY [Location identifier] [FAA]   (FAAL)

RXN .... Wheatland-Chili Junior/Senior High School Library, Scottsville, NY [OCLC symbol]   (OCLC)

RXO .... York High School Library, Retsof, NY [OCLC symbol]   (OCLC)

RXP .... American Baptist Historical Society Library, Rochester, NY [OCLC symbol]   (OCLC)

RXP .... Radix Point

RXQ .... Lincoln First Bank of Rochester Library Service, Rochester, NY [OCLC symbol]   (OCLC)

RXQ .... Washington, DC [Location identifier] [FAA]   (FAAL)

RXR .... Rainex Resources Ltd. [Vancouver Stock Exchange symbol]

RXS .... RADAR Cross Section

RXS .... Roxas City [Philippines] [Airport symbol]   (OAG)

RXT .... Right Exotropia [Ophthalmology]

RxTV .... Prescription Television

R du XVIe S ... Revue du Seizieme Siecle [A publication]

RXW .... Roxwell Gold Mines [Vancouver Stock Exchange symbol]

RXW .... Watersmeet, MI [Location identifier] [FAA]   (FAAL)

RXY .... Roxy Petroleum Ltd. [Toronto Stock Exchange symbol]

RXZ .... Chicago, IL [Location identifier] [FAA]   (FAAL)

RY .... Railway   (AFIT)

RY .... Relative Yield [Agriculture]

RY .... Relay   (DEN)

RY .... Roll Yoke

RY .... Rotterdam Airlines [Netherlands] [ICAO designator]   (FAAC)

RY .... Royal   (ROG)

RY .... Royal Bank of Canada [Toronto Stock Exchange symbol] [Vancouver Stock Exchange symbol]

RY .... Royal Yeomanry [Military unit] [British]

RY .... Runway   (FAAC)

ry .... Rydberg [Unit of energy] [Atomic physics] [Symbol]

ry .... Ryukyu Islands, Southern [ja (Japan) used in records cataloged after January 1978] [MARC country of publication code] [Library of Congress]   (LCCP)

RYA .... Railroad Yardmasters of America   (EA)

RYA .... Royal Yachting Association [British]

RYa .... Russkii Yazyk v Shkole [Moscow] [A publication]

Ry Age ...... Railway Age [A publication]

RYAL .... Royale Airline, Inc. [NASDAQ symbol]   (NQ)

RYALM ...... Relay Alarm   (AAG)

RYAN .... Ryan's Family Steak House [NASDAQ symbol]   (NQ)

Ryan Advis Health Serv Gov Boards ... Ryan Advisory for Health Services Governing Boards [A publication]

Ryan & M ... Ryan and Moody's English Nisi Prius Reports [171 English Reprint]   (DLA)

Ryan & M (Eng) ... Ryan and Moody's English Nisi Prius Reports [171 English Reprint]   (DLA)

RYB .... Raymond, MS [Location identifier] [FAA]   (FAAL)

RYB .... Rybachye [USSR] [Seismograph station code, US Geological Survey]   (SEIS)

RYBF .... Royal Business Group [NASDAQ symbol]   (NQ)

Rybn Khoz ... Rybnoe Khozyaistvo [A publication]

Rybn Khoz Resp Mezhved Temat Nauchn Sb ... Rybnoe Khozyaistvo Respublikanskii Mezhvedomstvennyi Tematicheskii Nauchnyi Sbornik [A publication]

Rybn Prom-st Dal'n Vost ... Rybnaya Promyshlennost' Dal'nego Vostoka [A publication]

RYC .... Raychem Corp. [NYSE symbol]

RYC .... Raymac Oil Corporation [Vancouver Stock Exchange symbol]

RyC .... Religion y Cultura [A publication]

RYC .... Rural Youth Corps [Defunct]   (EA)

Ry & Can Cas ... Railway and Canal Cases [England]   (DLA)

Ry & Can Traf Ca ... Railway and Canal Traffic Cases   (DLA)

Ry & Can Traffic Cas ... Railway and Canal Traffic Cases [England]   (DLA)

Ry & Can Tr Cas ... Reports of Railway and Canal Traffic Cases [1855-1950]   (DLA)

Ry Cas .... Reports of English Railway Cases   (DLA)

Ry & C Cas (Eng) ... Railway and Canal Cases [England]   (DLA)

RYCO .... Rynco Scientific Corp. [NASDAQ symbol]   (NQ)

Ry & Corp Law J ... Railway and Corporation Law Journal   (DLA)

Ry & Corp Law Jour ... Railway and Corporation Law Journal   (DLA)

Ry Corp Law Jour ... Railway and Corporation Law Journal   (DLA)

Ry & C Traffic Cas (Eng) ... Railway and Canal Traffic Cases [England]   (DLA)

RYD .... Real Year Dollars   (NASA)

Ryde .... Ryde's Rating Appeals [1871-1904]   (DLA)

Ryde & K .... Ryde and Konstam's Reports of Rating Appeals [1894-1904]   (DLA)

Ryde & K Rat App ... Ryde and Konstam's Reports of Rating Appeals [1894-1904]   (DLA)

Ryde Rat App ... Ryde's Rating Appeals [1871-1904]   (DLA)

Rydge's ...... Rydge's Business Journal [A publication]

Rydge's Constr Civ Eng & Min Rev ... Rydge's Construction, Civil Engineering, and Mining Review [A publication]

RYDMAR .... Reaction-Yield-Detected Magnetic Resonance [Also, RYDMR] [Spectroscopy]

RYDMR ...... Reaction-Yield-Detected Magnetic Resonance [Also, RYDMAR] [Spectroscopy]

RYE .... Retirement Year Ending [Army]   (AABC)

RYE .... Royalon Petroleum [Vancouver Stock Exchange symbol]

RYEJA....... Royal Engineers Journal [A publication]

RyF .... Razon y Fe [A publication]

Ry F .... Rymer's Fodera [20 vols.] [1704-35]   (DLA)

RyFab........ Razon y Fabula [A publication]

Ry Gaz Int ... Railway Gazette International [A publication]

RYK .... Relay Creek Resources Ltd. [Vancouver Stock Exchange symbol]

RYK .... Romulus, NY [Location identifier] [FAA]   (FAAL)

RYK .... Rykoff-Sexton, Inc. [NYSE symbol]

RYKHA ...... Rybnoe Khozyaistvo [A publication]

RYKOD...... Ryutai Kogaku [A publication]

RYL .... Royal Trustco Limited [Toronto Stock Exchange symbol] [Vancouver Stock Exchange symbol]

RYL .... Ryland Group, Inc. [NYSE symbol]

Ry Loco & Cars ... Railway Locomotives and Cars [A publication]

Ryl Plac Parl ... Ryley's Placita Parliamentaria [1290-1307] [England]   (DLA)

RYM .... Reference Your Message   (AABC)

RYM .... Revolutionary Youth Movement [Factions of Students for a Democratic Society. See RYM-I and RYM-II]

Ry & M .... Ryan and Moody's English Nisi Prius Reports   (DLA)

Ry MCC...... Ryan and Moody's English Crown Cases   (DLA)

Ry & MCC ... Ryan and Moody's English Crown Cases Reserved   (DLA)

Ry Mech & Elec Eng ... Railway Mechanical and Electrical Engineer [A publication]

Ry Mech Eng ... Railway Mechanical Engineer [A publication]

RYM-I .... Revolutionary Youth Movement I [Also known as "Weatherman"] [A faction of Students for a Democratic Society]

RYM-II........ Revolutionary Youth Movement II [A faction of Students for a Democratic Society]

Ry & MNP ... Ryan and Moody's English Nisi Prius Reports   (DLA)

Ry Mo .... Rythmes du Monde [A publication]

Ry & Moo.... Ryan and Moody [1823-26]   (DLA)

RYN .... Rayon

RYN .... Ryan Aviation Corp. [Wichita, KS] [FAA designator]   (FAAC)

RYN .... Ryan Homes, Inc. [NYSE symbol]

RYN............ Tucson, AZ [*Location identifier*] [*FAA*]   (FAAL)
RYNA .... Railroad Yardmasters of North America [*Absorbed by RYA*]   (EA)
RYNMS ...... Ryan Marketing Investors [*NASDAQ symbol*]   (NQ)
RYO............ Rio Turbio [*Argentina*] [*Airport symbol*]   (OAG)
Ryojun Coll Eng Publ ... Ryojun College of Engineering. Publications [*A publication*]
RYP .... Cumberland, MD [*Location identifier*] [*FAA*]   (FAAL)
R-Y-P .... Roll, Yaw, Pitch   (MCD)
RYPFA........ Revista YPF [*Yacimientos Petroliferos Fiscales*] (Argentina) [*A publication*]
RYR .... Radyr Junction [*Cardiff*] [*Welsh depot code*]
Ry R............ Railway Review [*A publication*]
RYR .... [*The*] Rymer Co. [*NYSE symbol*]
RYRKF .... Rayrock Resources [*NASDAQ symbol*]   (NQ)
RYRQD...... Reply Requested   (NOAA)
RYS .... Railway Stations [*Public-performance tariff class*] [*British*]
RYS .... Royal Yacht Squadron [*British*]
RYS .... Ryan Resources Ltd. [*Vancouver Stock Exchange symbol*]
RYT .... Ray-Net Communications Systems, Inc. [*Vancouver Stock Exchange symbol*]
RYT .... Relative Yield Total [*Agriculture*]
Ryt.............. Rytmi [*Record label*] [*Finland*]
Ry Track Struct ... Railway Track and Structures [*A publication*]
RYU .... Rosanky, TX [*Location identifier*] [*FAA*]   (FAAL)
RYU .... Ryukoku University [*UTLAS symbol*]
RYUSA .... Ryusan To Kogyo [*A publication*]
RYV .... Watertown, WI [*Location identifier*] [*FAA*]   (FAAL)
RYY .... Marietta, GA [*Location identifier*] [*FAA*]   (FAAL)
RZ............... Air Anjou Transports [*France*] [*ICAO designator*]   (FAAC)
RZ............... Rada Zydowska [*A publication*]
RZ............... Radostna Zeme [*A publication*]
RZ............... Radovi (Filozofski Fakultet-Zadar) [*A publication*]
R & Z .... Range and Zero   (KSC)
RZ............... Reaction Zone
RZ............... Reconnaissance Zone
RZ............... Recovery Zone   (MCD)
RZ............... Referativnyi Zhurnal. Informatika [*A publication*]
RZ............... Regal-Zonophone [*Record label*] [*Great Britain*]
RZ............... Regiment de Zouaves
RZ............... Resistance Zone
RZ............... Return-to-Zero Recording [*Data processing*]
RZ............... Revista Zurita Saragosse [*A publication*]
RZ............... Revolutionary Cells [*Revolutionary group*] [*West Germany*]
Rz .... Rhizome [*Botany*]
RZ............... Rueckenfallschirm mit Zwangsausloesung [*Static-line, backpack parachute*] [*German military - World War II*]
RZA .... Religious Zionists of America   (EA)
RZA .... Santa Cruz [*Argentina*] [*Airport symbol*]   (OAG)
R Z Avtomat Telemeh i Vycisl Tehn ...   Referativnyi Zhurnal. Avtomatika. Telemehanika i Vycislitelnaja Tehnika [*A publication*]
RZC .... Fayetteville, AR [*Location identifier*] [*FAA*]   (FAAL)
RZE .... Rzeszow [*Poland*] [*Airport symbol*]   (OAG)
RZETA........ Rozprawy Elektrotechniczne [*A publication*]
RZF............ Riemann Zeta Function [*Mathematics*]
R Z Fiz .... Referativnyi Zhurnal. Fizika [*A publication*]
RZh Avtomat Telemekh i Vychisl Tekhn ...   Akademiya Nauk SSSR. Institut Nauchnoi Informatsii. Referativnyi Zhurnal. Avtomatika. Telemekhanika i Vychislitel'naya Tekhnika [*A publication*]
RZh Mat ..... Akademiya Nauk SSSR. Institut Nauchnoi Informatsii. Referativnyi Zhurnal. Matematika [*A publication*]
RZINA........ Rozprawy Inzynierskie [*A publication*]
RZInformat ... Referativnyi Zhurnal. Informatika [*A publication*]
RZKibernet ... Referativnyi Zhurnal. Kibernetika [*A publication*]
RZL............ Rensselaer, IN [*Location identifier*] [*FAA*]   (FAAL)
RZL............ Return-to-Zero Level
RZM........... Return-to-Zero Mark
RZMA .... Rolled Zinc Manufacturers Association [*Defunct*]   (EA)
RZMat .... Referativnyi Zhurnal. Matematika [*A publication*]
RZMeh .... Referativnyi Zhurnal. Mehanika [*A publication*]
RZMVA...... Revista de Zootechnic si Medicina Veterinara [*A publication*]
RZNDA .... Razvedka Nedr [*A publication*]
RZ(NP)....... Nonpolarized Return-to-Zero Recording [*Data processing*]   (IBMDP)
RZO........... Demopolis, AL [*Location identifier*] [*FAA*]   (FAAL)
RZOOA...... Rivista di Zootecnia [*A publication*]
RZ(P).......... Polarized Return-to-Zero Recording [*Data processing*]   (IBMDP)
RZP .... Provincetown, MA [*Location identifier*] [*FAA*]   (FAAL)
RZS .... Rolled Zinc Sheet
RZS .... Royal Zoological Society [*British*]
RZSF .... Radovi Zavoda za Slavensku Filologiju [*A publication*]
RZSND .... Revue Zairoise des Sciences Nucleaires [*A publication*]
RZT .... Chillicothe, OH [*Location identifier*] [*FAA*]   (FAAL)
RZZ .... Roanoke Rapids, NC [*Location identifier*] [*FAA*]   (FAAL)

S

s .... Antisubmarine [*Designation for all US military aircraft*]
S .... Apparent Power [*Symbol*]   (DEN)
S .... Boltzmann Constant [*Statistical mechanics*]
S .... Codex Sinaiticus   (BJA)
S .... Entropy [*Symbol*] [*IUPAC*]
S .... Esses [*Phonetic alphabet*] [*Pre-World War II*]   (DSUE)
S .... Fun Fairs [*Public-performance tariff class*] [*British*]
S .... Isis-Chemie KG [*Germany*] [*Research code symbol*]
S .... Magnetic Solar Daily Variation
S .... New York Supplement   (DLA)
s .... Path, Length of Arc [*Symbol*] [*IUPAC*]
(S) .... Paymaster [*Navy*] [*British*]
S .... Permissible Working Stress
S .... Pitman-Moore Co. [*Research code symbol*]
S .... Pounds per Square Inch   (AAG)
S .... Poynting Vector [*Symbol*] [*Electromagnetism*]   (DEN)
S .... Reluctance [*Symbol*]   (DEN)
S .... Sabbath
S .... Sabin [*Unit of acoustic measurement*]   (DEN)
S .... Sable [*Heraldry*]
S .... Sacral
S .... Sacred
S .... Sacrifice [*Baseball*]
S .... Sacrum
S .... Saeculum
(S) .... Safe [*Task classification*] [*NASA*]   (NASA)
S .... Safety [*Football*]
S .... Sailing Ship
S .... Saint
S .... Saline
S .... Salvageable   (AAG)
S .... Same Case [*Same case as case cited*] [*Used in Shepard's
                    Citations*]   (DLA)
S .... Samuel [*Old Testament book*]   (BJA)
S .... San Francisco [*California*] [*Mint mark, when appearing on US
                    coins*]
S .... Sand [*Quality of the bottom*] [*Nautical charts*]
S .... Sandra [*Genotype of Phlox paniculata*]
S .... Saskatchewan   (DLA)
S .... Satang [*Monetary unit in Thailand*]
S .... Saturday
S .... Saturn
S .... Saxon
S .... Scalar [*Mathematics*]   (ROG)
S .... Scanning
S .... Scarce [*Numismatics*]
S .... Schedule
S .... Schilling [*Monetary unit in Austria*]
S .... [*Wolfgang*] Schmieder [*When used in identifying J. S. Bach's
                    compositions, refers to cataloging of his works by
                    musicologist Schmieder*]
S .... School
S .... Scilicet [*To Wit*] [*Latin*]   (DLA)
S .... Scot
S .... Scotland   (DLA)
S .... Scottish   (DLA)
S .... Scouting [*Naval aircraft designation*]
S .... Scribe
S .... Scuttle
S .... Sea   (ADA)
S .... Sea-Air Temperature Difference Correction
S .... Seaman [*Navy*]
S .... Seaplane [*Navy*]
S .... Search
S .... Searle's Cape Of Good Hope Reports [*South Africa*]   (DLA)
S .... Searle's Cases in the Supreme Court [*1850-67*] [*South
                    Africa*]   (DLA)
S .... Sears, Roebuck & Co. [*NYSE symbol*]
S .... Seasonal [*Business and trade*]   (OICC)
S .... Second [*or Secondary*]
s .... Second [*Symbol*] [*SI unit of time*]

s .... Secondary [*Preferred form is sec*] [*Chemistry*]
S .... Secondary [*or Shake*] Wave [*Earthquakes*]
S .... Secret [*Security classification*]
S .... Secretary
S .... Secretin [*Endocrinology*]
S .... Section
S .... Seder of Triennial Cycle   (BJA)
s .... Sedimentation Coefficient [*Physical chemistry*]
S .... See
S .... Seelenlaenge [*Barrel length*] [*German military - World War II*]
S .... Seite [*Page*] [*German*]
S .... Selvi [*Italy*] [*Research code symbol*]
S .... Semi
S .... Semi-Registered Tank [*Liquid gas carriers*]
S .... Semiannually
S .... Semis
S .... Sen [*Monetary unit in Japan*]
S .... Senate
S .... Senate Bill [*with number*]   (GPO)
S .... Senor [*Mister*] [*Spanish*]
S .... Sensation [*Psychology*]
S .... Sensitivity   (DEN)
S .... Sent [*Communications*]   (FAAC)
S .... Sentence [*Linguistics*]
S .... Senza [*Without*] [*Music*]
S .... Separation
S .... September
S .... September [*A publication*]
S .... Sepulchrum [*Sepulchre*] [*Latin*]
S .... Sepultus [*Buried*] [*Latin*]
S .... Series
S .... Serine [*One-letter symbol; see Ser*]
S .... Sermon
S .... Serum
S .... Service [*Military document classification*]   (INF)
S .... Servicing
S .... Servier [*France*] [*Research code symbol*]
S .... Sesquiplane [*Navy*]
S .... Set
S .... Set Meals [*School meals*] [*British*]
S .... Seven   (ROG)
S .... Seventy   (ROG)
S .... Sewage Disposal [*British Waterways Board sign*]
S .... Shaft Horsepower
S .... Shaft Main Engine
S .... Shape Descriptor [*S-curve, for example. The shape resembles
                    the letter for which it is named*]
S .... Shape Factor of a Structure [*Heat transmission symbol*]
S .... Shares [*Following a figure, indicates number of 100-share lots
                    in a transaction; e.g., 4s indicates 400 shares*] [*NYSE
                    symbol*]
S .... Sharp
S .... Shaw, Dunlop, and Bell's Scotch Court of Session Reports,
                    First Series   (DLA)
S .... Shaw's Scotch Appeal Cases, House of Lords   (DLA)
S .... Shaw's Scotch Court of Session Cases   (DLA)
S .... Shear [*Type of seismic wave*]
S .... Sheep   (ROG)
S .... Shell
S .... Sheltered [*Takeoff area for seaplanes*] [*For chart use only*]
S .... Shelters [*JETDS nomenclature*] [*Military*]   (CET)
S .... Shilling [*Monetary unit in Britain*] [*Obsolete*]
S .... Ship
S .... Shire   (ADA)
S .... Short Circuit
S .... Shunt Ahead [*Railroad signal arm*] [*British*]
S .... Sick
S .... Side
S .... Sidrah   (BJA)
S .... Siecle [*Century*] [*French*]
S .... Siemens [*Symbol*] [*SI unit of electric conductance*]

S................ Sierra [*Phonetic alphabet*] [*International*]   (DSUE)
S................ Sigma Mines (Quebec) Ltd. [*Toronto Stock Exchange symbol*]
S................ Sign [*or Signed*]
S................ Signa [*Write*] [*Pharmacy*]
S................ Signal [*Telecommunications*]   (TEL)
S................ Signal Strength [*Broadcasting*]
S................ Signature
/S/............ Signed [*Before signature on typed copy of a document, original of which was signed*]
S................ Signetur [*Let It Be Entitled*] [*Pharmacy*]   (ROG)
S................ Signor [*Mister*] [*Italian*]
S................ Silent [*Dance terminology*]
S................ Silicate
S................ Silk   (AAG)
S................ Silver
S................ Silversmith
S................ Simes [*Italy*] [*Research code symbol*]
S................ Simplex
S................ Simultaneous Transmission of Range Signals and Voice
S................ Sine [*Without*] [*Latin*]
S................ Single
S................ Single Silk [*Wire insulation*]
S................ Singular
(S)............ Sinister [*Counterclockwise configuration*] [*Biochemistry*] [*See RS*]
S................ Sinister [*Left*] [*Latin*]
S................ Sinistra [*Left Hand*] [*Music*]
S................ Sink
S................ Sire
S................ Sister
S................ Situs [*Placed*] [*Latin*]
S................ Sixteenmo [*Book from 15 to 17-1/2 centimeters in height*]
S................ Sixth Word Designator [*Data processing*]
S................ Skid   (AAG)
S................ Slate   (KSC)
S................ Slave [*LORAN stations*]
S................ Slavia [*A publication*]
S................ Sleeping [*Medicine*]
S................ Slewed [*Antenna*]
S................ Slip
S................ Slipped Up [*Horse racing*]
S................ Slope [*Technical drawings*]
S................ Slow
S................ Slow Muscle [*Skeletal muscle pharmacology*]
S................ Small [*Size designation for clothing, etc.*]
S................ Smooth [*Appearance of bacterial colony*]
S................ Smooth Sea [*Navigation*]
S................ Snow [*Meteorology*]
S................ Socialist
S................ Society
S................ Socius [*or Sodalis*] [*Fellow*]
S................ Soft
S................ Soiled [*Deltiology*]
S................ Sol [*Monetary unit in Peru*]
S................ Solar   (ADA)
S................ Solco Basel AG [*Switzerland*] [*Research code symbol*]
S................ Soldering
S................ Solicitor's Opinion   (DLA)
S................ Solid
(s)............ Solid [*Chemistry*]
S................ Solidus [*Shilling*] [*Latin*]
S................ Solo [*Music*]
S................ Solubility
S................ Somaliland Scouts [*Military unit*] [*British*]
S................ Son
S................ Song   (ROG)
S................ Soprano
S................ Sou [*Monetary unit in France*]
S................ Sough   (AAG)
S................ Sound Tape [*Films, television, etc.*]
S................ Source
S................ South [*or Southern*]
s------ .... South America [*MARC geographic area code*] [*Library of Congress*]   (LCCP)
S................ Southern Reporter   (DLA)
S................ Spacer
S................ Spade   (ADA)
S................ Spanish   (DLA)
S................ Spar [*Buoy*]
S................ Spares
S................ Spatial Ability [*Psychology*]
S................ Speak
S................ Special
s .... Special Abilities of an Individual [*Symbol*] [*Psychology*]
S................ Special Air Mission [*Military aircraft identification prefix*]   (FAAC)
S................ Species
S................ Specific Factor
S................ Specific Surface
S................ Specification
S................ Spectator [*A publication*]

S................ Speculum [*A publication*]
S................ Speech
S................ Speed
S................ Sphere [*or Spherical*]
s .... Spin Quantum Number [*Atomic physics*]   (DEN)
S................ Spinster
S................ Split [*In stock listings of newspapers*]
S................ Spoilers in Nozzle
S................ Sponsored
S................ Spontaneous
S................ Spool
S................ Sport [*In automobile model name "Honda Civic S"*]
S................ Spurs [*Horse racing*]
S................ Squadron
S................ Stackable Container
S................ Staff [*License plate code assigned to foreign diplomats in the US*]
S................ Staff
S................ Stand
S................ Standard
s .... Standard Deviation [*Also, SD*] [*Statistics*]
S................ Starboard
S................ Start   (KSC)
s .... Stat [*Unit of radioactive disintegration rate*]
S................ Static
S................ Station
S................ Statue   (ADA)
S................ Status Required [*Civil Service*]
S................ Statute
S................ Steamer
S................ Steel
S................ Stem
S................ Stere [*Metric*]
S................ Stimulus
S................ Stock
S................ Stolen Base [*Baseball*]
S................ Stopping Power
S................ Storage
S................ Straight
S................ Straight-In [*Aviation*]   (FAAC)
s .... Strange [*Quark*] [*Atomic physics*]
S................ Stratum   (BJA)
S................ Stratus Cloud [*Meteorology*]
S................ Streptomycin [*An antibiotic*]
S................ Streptozocin [*Also, STZ*] [*Antineoplastic drug*]
S................ Stroke of Piston in Inches [*Railroad term*]
S................ Studio [*A publication*]
S................ Stung [*by bees*] [*Medicine*]
S................ Subcompact [*Car size*]
S................ Subito [*Immediately; Suddenly*] [*Music*]
S................ Subject [*of a proposition in logic*]
S................ Subject [*Psychology*]
S................ Subluxation [*Chiropractic*]
S................ Submarine
s .... Submerged Pump [*Liquid gas carriers*]
S................ Substantive
S................ Substrate, Free [*Enzyme kinetics*]
S................ Succeeded
S................ Successor
S................ Sucre [*Monetary unit in Ecuador*]
S................ Sud [*South*] [*French*]   (ROG)
S................ Sugar [*Phonetic alphabet*] [*Royal Navy*] [*World War I*] [*Pre-World War II*] [*World War II*]   (DSUE)
S................ Suit
S................ Suitability   (CAAL)
S................ Sulfamethoxazole [*Also, SMX, SMZ*] [*Antibacterial compound*]
S................ Sulfur [*Chemical element*]
S................ Sumendus [*To Be Taken*] [*Pharmacy*]
S................ Summary
S................ Summer [*Vessel load line mark*]
S................ Summit Books [*Publisher's imprint*]
S................ Sun
S................ Sunday
S................ Sunny [*Meteorology*]   (ADA)
S................ Super
S................ Superb
S................ Superficial
S................ Superior
S................ Supernatant [*Protein*] [*Cytology*]
S................ Superseded [*New regulation or order substituted for an existing one*] [*Used in Shepard's Citations*]   (DLA)
S................ Supply [*Department aboard a carrier*] [*Navy*]
S................ Supreme Court Reporter   (DLA)
S................ Sur [*On*] [*French*]
S................ Surface Area
S................ Surfaced
S................ Surgeon [*Navy*] [*British*]   (ROG)
S................ Surgery [*Medical Officer designation*] [*British*]
S................ Surplus
S................ Surrogate
S................ Survey

S .... Susceptible
S .... Suus [*His*] [*Latin*]
S .... Svedberg Unit [*Physical chemistry*]
S .... Sweden
S .... Switch
S .... Switchboard [*Telecommunications*]   (TEL)
s .... Symmetrical [*Also, sym*] [*Chemistry*]
s .... Symmetry Number [*Symbol*] [*IUPAC*]
S .... Symposium [*A publication*]
S .... Synchronized Sleep
S .... Synoptic [*Meteorology*]
S .... Synthesis [*Phase in mitosis*] [*Cytology*]
s .... Thio [*or Mercapto*] [*As substituent on nucleoside*]
                   [*Biochemistry*]
S .... Thiouridine [*One-letter symbol; see Srd*]
S .... Wyeth Laboratories [*Research code symbol*]
S-1 .... Personnel Section [*in Army brigades or smaller units, and in
                   Marine Corps units smaller than a brigade; also, the
                   officer in charge of this section. Also refers to adjutant -
                   1st staff section, brigades, and lower units*]
S-2 .... Intelligence Section [*in Army brigades or smaller units, and in
                   Marine Corps units smaller than a brigade; also, the
                   officer in charge of this section*]
2-S .... Selective Service Class [*for Registrant Deferred Because of
                   Activity in Study*]
S-3 .... Operations and Training Section [*in Army brigades or smaller
                   units, and in Marine Corps units smaller than a brigade;
                   also, the officer in charge of this section*]
S3 .... Signal Selection Switchboard   (CAAL)
3S .... Simplification, Standardization, Specialization [*Economics*]
S³ .... Small Scientific Satellite [*NASA*]
3S .... Standard Supply System [*Army*]   (RDA)
S3 .... Systems and Software Simulator
S-4 .... Logistics Section [*in Army brigades or smaller units, and in
                   Marine Corps units smaller than a brigade; also, the
                   officer in charge of this section*]
4S .... Society for Social Studies of Science
S4 .... Stanford School Scheduling System
S5 .... Civil Affairs Officer [*Army*]   (AABC)
S7 .... Seller's Delivery in Seven Days [*New York Stock Exchange*]
                   [*Business and trade*]
4S's .... Sex, Silk, Swords, and Swash [*Elements of historical
                   romances*]
4S's .... Sun, Sand, Sea, Sex [*Used in advertising by travel agencies*]
S (Day) .... Day on which deployment to war stations of submarines is
                   ordered [*NATO exercises*]   (NATG)
S (DAY) ..... Submarine Deployment Day [*NATO*]
S (Test) ..... Suitability Test [*Military*]   (CAAL)
SA .... Air-Cushion Vehicle built by Societe National Industrielle
                   Aerospatiale [*France*] [*Usually used in combination with
                   numerals*]
sa----- .... Amazon River and Basin [*MARC geographic area code*]
                   [*Library of Congress*]   (LCCP)
S & A .... Bureau of Supplies and Accounts [*Later, NSUPSC*] [*Navy*]
SA .... Le Syllabaire Accadien [*A publication*]   (BJA)
SA .... Missionary Sisters of Our Lady of Africa [*White Sisters*]
                   [*Roman Catholic religious order*]
SA .... Sable [*Heraldry*]
S & A .... Safe-and-Arm   (KSC)
S/A .... Safe Arm
S/A .... Safe Arrival
SA .... Safety Analysis [*Nuclear energy*]   (NRCH)
S & A .... Safety and Arming Device
S & A .... Safing and Arming [*Mechanisms*]   (RDA)
SA .... Sail Area
SA .... Salicylic Acid [*Organic chemistry*]
SA .... Salt Acid
SA .... Salt Added
SA .... Salvation Army [*Verona, NJ*]   (EA)
Sa .... Samarium [*Obsolete form; see Sm*] [*Chemical element*]
SA .... Sample Array
SA .... Sample Assembly   (MCD)
Sa .... Samtiden [*A publication*]
SA .... Sandstorm
Sa .... Sanguinarine [*Biochemistry*]
SA .... Sanitary Authority [*British*]   (ROG)
SA .... Sarcastics Anonymous   (EA)
SA .... Sarcoma [*Medicine*]
SA .... Saturday
SA .... Saturn Apollo [*NASA*]   (KSC)
SA .... Saudi Arabia [*Two-letter standard code*]   (CNC)
S & A .... Saunders and Austin's Locus Standi Reports [*1895-
                   1904*]   (DLA)
SA .... Sausage Aerial [*Radio*]
SA .... Savannah & Atlanta Railway Co. [*AAR code*]
SA .... Savings Account
SA .... Scaling Amplifier
S/A .... Scheduled/Actual   (NASA)
SA .... Schizophrenics Anonymous   (EA)
SA .... Science Abstracts [*A publication*]
SA .... Science Advisors [*Army*]   (RDA)

S & A .... Science and Application   (NASA)
SA .... Scientific American [*A publication*]
SA .... Scientific Assistant [*Ministry of Agriculture, Fisheries, and
                   Food*] [*British*]
SA .... Scleroderma Association [*Lynnfield, MA*]   (EA)
SA .... Scoliosis Association [*New York, NY*]   (EA)
SA .... Seaman Apprentice [*Navy rating*]
SA .... Second Attack [*Men's lacrosse position*]
SA .... Secretary of the Army
SA .... Secundum Artem [*According to the Art*] [*Latin*]
SA .... Security Alarm Technician Program [*Association of
                   Independent Colleges and Schools specialization code*]
SA .... Security Assistance   (MCD)
SA .... See Also [*Indexing code*]
SA .... Seiners Association [*Later, PSVOA*]
SA .... Select Address
SA .... Selected Ammunition   (RDA)
SA .... Semen Analysis
SA .... Semiannual
SA .... Semiautomatic
SA .... Senior Advisor [*Military*]
SA .... Sense Amplifier
SA .... Sensitized Activated
SA .... Separat-Abdruck   (BJA)
SA .... Separated Atom [*Atomic physics*]
SA .... Sequential Automated
SA .... Serendipity Association [*Chicago, IL*]   (EA)
SA .... Serra
SA .... Serum Albumin [*Serology*]
S/A .... Service Action   (AAG)
SA .... Service Adviser [*or Attache*] [*British*]
SA .... Service Air [*Nuclear energy*]   (NRCH)
S/A .... Service Application [*Military*]   (AFIT)
SA .... Service Arm   (KSC)
SA .... Service Assistant [*Telecommunications*]   (TEL)
SA .... Servo Amplifier
SA .... Seventh Avenue [*New York City*]
SA .... Sex Appeal [*Slang*]
SA .... Sexaholics Anonymous [*Simi Valley, CA*]   (EA)
SA .... Shaft Angle [*Technical drawings*]
SA .... Shift Advance Driver
SA .... Ship Abstracts [*Helsinki University of Technology*]
                   [*Bibliographic database*]
SA .... Ship to Aircraft   (DEN)
S/A .... Ship Alteration   (MCD)
S/A .... Shipped Assembled
SA .... Shipping Authority
SA .... Shock Attenuation   (AAG)
SA .... Shop Accessory [*Drawing*]   (NG)
SA .... Sicanna Industries Ltd. [*Vancouver Stock Exchange symbol*]
S & A .... Sickness and Accident [*Insurance*]
SA .... Sideroblastic Anemia [*Hematology*]
SA .... Siegfried AG [*Switzerland*] [*Research code symbol*]
SA .... Sierra
SA .... Signal Analyzer
SA .... Signal Attenuation   (AAG)
SA .... Signature Analysis
SA .... Simple Alert   (NATG)
sa .... Sin Ano [*Without Year*] [*Publishing*] [*Spanish*]
SA .... Sine Anno [*Without Date of Publication*] [*Latin*]
SA .... Single Access   (MCD)
SA .... Single Action [*Firearm*]
SA .... Single Armor [*Telecommunications*]   (TEL)
SA .... Sinoatrial [*Medicine*]
SA .... Sinoauricular [*Medicine*]
SA .... Sinus Aestuum [*Bay of Billows*] [*Lunar area*]
SA .... Sister of Arts
SA .... Site Activation [*NASA*]   (MCD)
SA .... Situation Audit   (MCD)
SA .... Slow-Acting [*Pharmacy*]
SA .... Slugging Average [*Baseball*]
SA .... Small Arms [*All firearms other than cannon*]
SA .... Smithsonian Associates [*Later, Smithsonian Resident
                   Associate Program*]
SA .... Snap Action
SA .... Sociedad Anonima [*Stock company*] [*Spanish*]
S/A .... Societa Anonima [*Stock company*] [*Italian*]
SA .... Societas Adunationis [*Franciscan Friars or Sisters of the
                   Atonement*] [*Roman Catholic religious order*]
SA .... Societe Anonyme [*Stock company*] [*French*]
SA .... Society of Actuaries [*Formerly, ASA*]
SA .... Society of Alexandria [*Defunct*]   (EA)
SA .... Society of Antiquaries [*British*]
SA .... Society of Arts [*British*]
SA .... Sociological Abstracts [*Sociological Abstracts, Inc.*] [*San
                   Diego, CA*]
SA .... Sociological Analysis [*A publication*]
SA .... Solar Array   (KSC)
SA .... Soluble in Alkaline Solution
SA .... Son Altesse [*His or Her Highness*] [*French*]
SA .... Sonderabdruck   (BJA)

SA .... Soprano, Alto
SA .... Source Address
sa .... South Africa [MARC country of publication code] [Library of Congress]   (LCCP)
SA .... South Africa
SA .... South African Airways [ICAO designator]
SA .... South African Law Reports [A publication]
SA .... South America
SA .... South Arabian   (BJA)
SA .... South Atlantic
SA .... South Australia   (ADA)
SA .... South Australiana [A publication]
SA .... Southern Association [Baseball league]
SA .... Sovietskaia Archeologiia [A publication]
SA .... Space Aeronautics [A publication]
S/A .... Space Available   (ADA)
SA .... Spacecraft Adapter [NASA]
SA .... Speaker Amplifier
SA .... Special Action [Military]   (AFM)
S/A .... Special Activities [Air Force]
SA .... Special Agent   (AFM)
SA .... Special Area [RADAR]
SA .... Special Artificer [Navy]
SA .... Special Assignment [Navy]
SA .... Specific Activity
SA .... Spectrograph Assembly   (KSC)
SA .... Spectrum Analysis
SA .... Speech Activities [A publication]
SA .... Sperm Aster [Cytology]
SA .... Speronara [Ship's rigging]   (ROG)
SA .... Spin Axis   (AAG)
SA .... Splice Acceptor [Genetics]
SA .... Splitting Amplifier   (AFM)
SA .... Sponsored [or Sponsoring] Agency   (MCD)
SA .... Sports Ambassadors [An association]   (EA)
SA .... Spouse's Allowance [Canada]
SA .... Springfield Armory [Army]
SA .... Standard Accuracy [Analytical chemistry]
SA .... Standard Addition
SA .... Standard Agena [NASA]   (KSC)
SA .... Staphylococcus Aureus [Microbiology]
sA .... Statampere [Also, statA] [Unit of electric current]
SA .... State Agency [Formerly, the Disability Determination Services] [Social Security Administration]   (OICC)
S/A .... State Agent [Insurance]
SA .... State's Attorney
SA .... Station Address [Data processing]   (BUR)
SA .... Statocyst Anlage
S/A .... Status and Alert   (AAG)
SA .... Stokes-Adams [Syndrome] [Medicine]
SA .... Stone Arch [Bridges]
SA .... Storage Allocator [Telecommunications]   (TEL)
S/A .... Storage Area   (KSC)
SA .... Store Address
SA .... Store Automation
SA .... Stress Anneal   (KSC)
SA .... Structured Analysis [Programing language] [1977]   (CSR)
SA .... Students for America   (EA)
SA .... Studi Americani [Roma] [A publication]
SA .... Studies in Astronautics [Elsevier Book Series] [A publication]
SA .... Sturmabteilung [Political party] [German]   (PPE)
SA .... Styrene-Acrylonitrile [Also, SAN] [Organic chemistry]
SA .... Sub Anno [Under the Year] [Latin]
SA .... Subaccount (NASA)
SA .... Subarachnoid [Medicine]
SA .... Subassembly
SA .... Subcontract Agreement   (MCD)
SA .... Subject to Approval
SA .... Subsistence Allowance
SA .... Substitution Authorization   (AAG)
SA .... Successive Approximation   (IEEE)
S/A .... Such As
S & A .... Sugar and Acetone [Medicine]
SA .... Sugar Association
SA .... Sulfonamide
SA .... Summing Amplifier
SA .... Supervisory Authority
SA .... Superwomen Anonymous   (EA)
SA .... Supplemental Agreement   (NG)
S & A .... Supplies and Accounts
SA .... Supply Accountant [Navy] [British]
SA .... Support Activity   (MCD)
SA .... Support Agency [NASA]   (KSC)
SA .... Support Area   (MCD)
SA .... Supporting Arms [Navy] [A publication]
SA .... Surface/Air   (NATG)
SA .... Surface Area
SA .... Surgeon's Assistant [Medicine]
SA .... Surgical Anastomosis [Medicine]
S & A .... Surveillance and Accountability   (NRCH)
SA .... Surveillance Approach   (FAAC)

S/A .... Survivorship Agreement   (DLA)
SA .... Sustained Action [Pharmacy]
SA .... Sweet Adelines   (EA)
SA .... Swing Arm   (KSC)
SA .... Switching Devices [JETDS nomenclature] [Military]   (CET)
SA .... Symbolae Arctoae [A publication]
SA .... Symbolic Assembler   (IEEE)
SA .... Sympathetic Activity [Physiology]
SA .... Synchro Amplifier
SA .... Systemic Antibiotic [Medicine]
SA .... Systems Address
SA .... Systems Analysis
SA .... Systems Analyst
SA .... VEB Farbenfabrik Wolfen [East Germany] [Research code symbol]
SAA .... S-Band Acquisition Antenna [Deep Space Instrumentation Facility, NASA]
SAA .... Sakai [Japan] [Seismograph station code, US Geological Survey] [Closed]   (SEIS)
SAA .... Saratoga, WY [Location identifier] [FAA]   (FAAL)
SAA .... Satellite Attitude Acquisition
SAA .... Saturn Apollo Applications [NASA]   (KSC)
SAA .... Schweizer Anglistische Arbeiten [A publication]
SAA .... Senior Army Advisor
SAA .... Serum Amyloid A [Clinical chemistry]
SAA .... Service Action Analysis   (AAG)
SAA .... Servo-Actuated Assembly
SAA .... Sex Addicts Anonymous [Minneapolis, MN]   (EA)
SAA .... Sexual Abuse Anonymous   (EA)
SAA .... Shakespeare Association of America   (EA)
SAA .... Shelter Advertising Association [Minneapolis, MN]   (EA)
SAA .... Signal Appliance Association [Later, RSS]
SAA .... Simulated Accelerometer Assembly
SAA .... Single Article Announcement [American Chemical Society publication]
SAA .... Slot Array Antenna
SAA .... Small-Arms Ammunition
SAA .... Society for Academic Achievement   (EA)
SAA .... Society for American Archaeology   (EA)
SAA .... Society of American Archivists [Chicago, IL]   (EA)
SAA .... Society of Animal Artists
SAA .... Society of Archer-Antiquaries   (EA)
SAA .... Society of Architectural Administrators [North Hills, NY]   (EA)
SAA .... Society for Asian Art   (EA)
SAA .... Some American Artists [An association]   (EA)
SAA .... South African Airways
SAA .... South African Alliance   (PPW)
SAA .... South Atlantic Anomaly [NASA]   (KSC)
SAA .... Southern Ash Association [Defunct]   (EA)
SAA .... Special Arbitrage Account
SAA .... Special Assignment Airlift [Air Force]   (AFM)
SAA .... Specialty Advertising Association [Later, SAAI]
SAA .... Speech Association of America [Later, SCA]   (EA)
SAA .... Staff Administrative Assistant [Army]   (AABC)
SAA .... Standards Association of Australia
SAA .... State Approving Agency [Bureau of Apprenticeship and Training] [Department of Labor]
SAA .... Static Allegation Analyzer [Data processing]
SAA .... Step Adjustable Antenna
SAA .... Stepfamily Association of America [Baltimore, MD]   (EA)
SAA .... Summary Activity Account [Army]   (AABC)
SAA .... Sunflower Association of America [Later, National Sunflower Association]   (EA)
SAA .... Sunglass Association of America [Stamford, CT]   (EA)
SAA .... Supima Association of America   (EA)
SAA .... Surety Association of America [Iselin, NJ]   (EA)
SAA .... Surface Active Agents   (ADA)
SAA .... Survival Air-to-Air   (MCD)
SAA .... Suzuki Association of the Americas   (EA)
SAA .... Syrian Arab Airlines
SAAA .... Scottish Amateur Athletic Association
SAAARNG ... Senior Army Advisor, Army National Guard   (AABC)
SAAB .... Saudi Arabian Agricultural Bank
SAAB .... Svenska Aeroplan Aktiebolaget [Swedish automobile manufacturer; acronym used as name of its cars]
SAAC .... Schedule Allocation and Control   (NASA)
SA/AC .... Scientific Advisor to the Army Council [World War II]
SAAC .... Security Assistance Accounting Center [Military]   (AFIT)
SAAC .... Seismic Array Analysis Center [IBM Corp.]
SAAC .... Shelby American Automobile Club [Formerly, CC]   (EA)
SAAC .... Simulator for Air-to-Air Combat [Air Force]
SAAC .... Society for the Advancement of Ambulatory Care [Washington, DC]   (EA)
SAAC .... South American Athletic Confederation [Lima, Peru]   (EA-IO)
SAAC .... Space Applications Advisory Committee
SAAC .... Special Assistant for Arms Control [Military]
SAACI .... Salesmen's Association of the American Chemical Industry [Later, SACI]   (EA)
SAACONS ... Standard Army Automated Contracting System   (RDA)
SAACT ...... Surveillance and Accountability Control Team   (MCD)
SAAD .... Sacramento Army Depot [California]   (AABC)

SAAD .... San Antonio Air Depot [Air Force]
SAAD .... Small-Arms Ammunition Depot
SAAD .... Societe des Amis d'Alexandre Dumas   (EA)
SAAD .... Sperry Air Arm Division
SAAD Dig... SAAD [Society for the Advancement of Anaesthesia in
            Dentistry] Digest [A publication]
SA Advertiser (Newspr) ... South Australian Advertiser Reports
            (Newspaper) [A publication]
SAAEB ...... South African Atomic Energy Board
SAAF........ Sherman Army Airfield [Fort Leavenworth, KS]
SAAF........ Sino-American Amity Fund   (EA)
SAAF........ Small Arms Alignment Fixture [Weaponry]   (INF)
SAAF........ South African Air Force
SAAFA ...... Astrometriya i Astrofizika [A publication]
SAAG .... Science and Applications Advocacy Group
SAAHS...... Stability Augmentation Attitude Hold System [Aviation]
SAAI........ Specialty Advertising Association International [Irving,
            TX]   (EA)
SAAJA ...... Soviet Astronomy [English Translation] [A publication]
SAAL........ Single Address Assembly Machine Language [Data
            processing]   (MCD)
SAAL........ Single-Axis Acoustic Levitator
SA-ALC..... San Antonio Air Logistics Center [Formerly, SAAMA] [Air
            Force]   (NASA)
SAALCK .... State Assisted Academic Library Council of Kentucky [Library
            network]
SAAM........ Simulation Analysis and Modeling
SAAM........ Small-Animal Anesthesia Machine [Instrumentation]
SAAM........ Special Assignment Air Mission [Navy]   (NVT)
SAAM........ Special Assignment Airlift Movement [Army]   (AABC)
SAAMA ..... San Antonio Air Materiel Area [Later, SA-ALC] [Air Force]
SAAMI....... Sporting Arms and Ammunition Manufacturers Institute   (EA)
SAAMS ...... Special Airlift Assignment Missions [Military]
SAAN .... South African Associated Newspapers
SAANAn.... Societe Archeologique de l'Arrondissement de Nivelles.
            Annales [A publication]
SAAP......... Saranton Army Ammunition Plant   (AABC)
SAAP......... Saturn Apollo Applications Program [NASA]
SAAP......... Society for the Advancement of American Philosophy   (EA)
SAAP......... South Atlantic Anomaly Probe [NASA-CNAE]
SAAR .... Saw Arbor [Tool]
SA Arch J.. SA [South African] Archives Journal [A publication]
SAARF ...... Special Allied Airborne Reconnaissance Force [Teams
            parachuted into POW areas to take supplies to prisoners
            or to help them get out] [World War II]
SAAS .... Science Achievement Awards for Students
SAAS .... Shuttle Aerosurface Actuator Simulator   (MCD)
SAAS .... Society of African and Afro-American Students
SAAS .... Something about the Author Autobiography Series [A
            publication]
SAAS .... Southern Association of Agricultural Scientists   (EA)
SAAS .... Standard Army Ammunition System   (AABC)
SAASC...... San Antonio Air Service Command [Air Force]
SAASW ..... Sub-Antarctic Surface Water [Marine science]   (MSC)
SAAT .... Satellite Attitude Acquisition Technique
SAATAS.... South Australia & Territory Air Services   (FAAC)
SAATMS .... Satellite-Based Advanced Air Traffic Management System
            [Department of Transportation]
SAATSC ... San Antonio Air Technical Service Command [Air Force]
SAAU .... Selfreliance Association of American Ukrainians   (EA)
SAAU .... Swiss Association of Autonomous Unions
SAAUSAR ... Senior Army Advisor, United States Army Reserve   (AABC)
SAAVS ...... Submarine Acceleration and Velocity System
SAAWC..... Sector Antiair Warfare Coordinator [Center]   (NVT)
SAAX .... Saturn Airways, Inc. [Air carrier designation symbol]
SAB .... Saba [Netherlands Antilles] [Airport symbol]   (OAG)
SAB .... Sabbath
SAB .... Sabhawala [India] [Geomagnetic observatory code]
SAB .... Sabine Corp. [NYSE symbol]
SAB .... Sabotage [FBI standardized term]
SAB .... Sabouraud Dextrose Agar [Microbiology]
SAB .... Same as Basic   (KSC)
SAB .... Satellite Assembly Building   (MCD)
SAB .... School of American Ballet [New York]
SAB .... Science Advisory Board [Environmental Protection Agency]
SAB .... Scientific Advisory Board [Air Force]
SAB .... Shakespeare Association. Bulletin [A publication]
SAB .... Signal Aviation Branch
SAB .... Site Activation Board [NASA]   (KSC)
SAB .... Sitzungsberichte der Deutschen (Preussischen) Akademie der
            Wissenschaften zu Berlin. Philosophisch-Historische
            Klasse [Berlin] [A publication]
SAB .... Snap Action Bimetal [Automotive engineering]
SAB .... Societe Anonyme Belge d'Exploitation de la Navigation
            Aerienne [Sabena Belgian World Airlines]
SAB .... Society of American Bacteriologists [Later, ASM]
SAB .... Society for Applied Bacteriology   (EA)
SAB .... Solar Array Batteries
SAB .... Solid Assembly Building
SAB .... Soprano, Alto, Bass
SAB .... South Atlantic Bulletin [A publication]

SAB .... Space Applications Board [National Academy of Engineering]
SAB .... Spacecraft Assembly Building   (MCD)
SAB .... Special Assessment Bond
SAB .... Stack Access Block
SAB .... Statistics and Analysis Branch [Public Health Service]
            [Bethesda, MD] [Information service]   (EISS)
SAB .... Storage and Assembly Building [NASA]   (NASA)
SAB .... Structural Adhesive Bond
SAB .... Subject as Above   (AABC)
SAB .... Support Activities Building [National Security Agency]
SAB .... Supporting Assistance Bureau [Agency for International
            Development]
SAB .... System Advisory Board
SABA .... Serbian-American Bar Association   (EA)
SABA .... Societe Archeologique de Bruxelles. Annales [A publication]
SABA .... Society for the Advancement of Behavior Analysis   (EA)
SABA .... South African Black Alliance   (PPW)
Sabah For Rec ... Sabah Forest Record [A publication]
Sabah Soc J ... Sabah Society Journal [A publication]
SA Bank Officials J ... South Australian Bank Officials' Journal [A
            publication]
SABAR ...... Satellites, Balloons, and Rockets [Air Force program]
SABBA ...... System Analysis-Building Block Approach [Ge Cae
            International and Gen-Red Ltd.] [Software package]
SABC .... South African Broadcasting Corporation
Sabchota Med ... Sabchota Meditsina [A publication]
SABCO...... Society for the Area of Biological and Chemical Overlap
SABE......... Society for Automation in Business Education [Later,
            SDE]   (EA)
SABENA..... Societe Anonyme Belge d'Exploitation de la Navigation
            Aerienne [Belgian World Airlines]
SABER ...... SECNAV [Secretary of the Navy] Advisory Board on
            Educational Requirements   (NG)
SABET ...... SECNAV [Secretary of the Navy] Advisory Board on Education
            and Training [Pensacola, FL]   (EGAO)
SABEW ...... Society of American Business Editors and Writers [Formerly,
            SABW] [Columbia, MO]   (EA)
SABH .... Simultaneous Automatic Broadcast Homer   (FAAC)
SABHI .... Sabouraud Dextrose Agar and Brain-Heart Infusion
            [Microbiology]
SaBi........... La Sacra Bibbia [Turin] [A publication]   (BJA)
SABIC .... Saudi Basic Industries Corporation
SABIR ...... Semiautomatic Bibliographic Information Retrieval
SABIRS ...... Semiautomatic Bibliographic Information Retrieval
            System   (DIT)
SABLE....... Semiautomatic BOMARC Local Environment   (MCD)
SABM........ Set Asynchronous Balanced Mode
SA/BM ...... Systems Analysis and Battle Management [Military]   (RDA)
SABMAR... Service-Craft and Boats Machine Accounting Report
            [Navy]   (NG)
SABMIS ..... Seaborne [or Ship-Launched] Antiballistic Missile Intercept
            System [Navy]
SABNWTR ... Science Advisory Board of the Northwest Territories. Report
            [Canada] [A publication]
SABNWTRP ... Science Advisory Board of the Northwest Territories.
            Research Paper [Canada] [A publication]
SABNWTWP ... Science Advisory Board of the Northwest Territories.
            Working Paper [A publication]
SABO .... Sense Amplifier Blocking Oscillator
SABOA ...... Sabouraudia [A publication]
SABOD...... Same as Basic Operations Directive   (KSC)
SABOJ ...... South Australian Bank Officials' Journal [A publication]
SABOR...... Same as Basic Or   (MUGU)
SABP......... Skeletal Axis of Basal Piece
SABP......... Spontaneous Acute Bacterial Peritonitis [Medicine]
SABR......... Society for American Baseball Research [Members are called
            "Sabermetricians" and practice "sabermetrics", the
            study of baseball statistics]   (EA)
SABR......... Symbolic Assembler for Binary Relocatable Programs
Sabrao Newslett ... Sabrao Newsletter [A publication]
SABRB ...... Siemens-Albis Berichte [A publication]
SABRE ...... SAGE [Semiautomatic Ground Environment] Battery Routing
            Equipment
SABRE ...... Sales and Business Reservations Done Electronically
SABRE ...... Secure Airborne RADAR Equipment
SABRE ...... Self-Aligning Boost and Reentry [Air Force]
SABRE ...... Store Access Bus Recording Equipment
            [Telecommunications]   (TEL)
SABRE ...... Sweden and Britain Radar Auroral Experiment [Ionospheric
            physics]
SABRE ...... System for Autonomous Bodies Reporting and Evaluation
            [Joint project of the Government of Bangladesh and
            United Nations Department of Technical Co-operation for
            Development] [Information service]
SABRF ...... Skeletal Axis of Branchial Filament
SABRI......... Serikat Buruh Rokok Indonesia [Cigarette Workers' Union of
            Indonesia]
S/ABS .... Shock Absorber [Automotive engineering]
SABS......... South African Bureau of Standards [National standards
            organization]
SABS......... Stabilizing Automatic Bomb Sight

SABS Bull ... SABS [*South African Bureau of Standards*] Bulletin [*A publication*]
SABU .... Self-Adjusting Ball-Up [*A state of confusion which may, or may not, clear up of itself*] [*Military slang*]
SABW .... Society of American Business Writers [*Later, SABEW*]
Sac .... De Sacrificiis Abelis et Caini [*Philo*]   (BJA)
SAC .... Saccharin [*Sweetening agent*]
SAC .... Sacramento, CA [*Location identifier*] [*FAA*]   (FAAL)
SAC .... Sacrifice [*Baseball*]
Sac .... Sacris Erudiri. Jaarboek voor Godsdienstwetenschappen [*A publication*]
SAC .... Sacristan
SAC .... Safety Advisory Committee   (MCD)
SAC .... Sahali Resources, Inc. [*Vancouver Stock Exchange symbol*]
SAC .... Saint Ambrose College [*Davenport, IA*]
SAC .... Saint Anselm's College [*New Hampshire*]
SAC .... Saint Anselm's College, Manchester, NH [*OCLC symbol*]   (OCLC)
SAC .... Saint Augustine's College [*North Carolina*]
SAC .... Salute America Committee   (EA)
SAC .... San Andreas Lake [*California*] [*Seismograph station code, US Geological Survey*]   (SEIS)
SAC .... San Antonio College [*Texas*]
SAC .... Santa Ana College [*California*]
SAC .... Scene-of-Action Commander [*Navy*]   (NVT)
SAC .... School of Army Co-Operation [*Air Force*] [*British*]
SAC .... Scientific Advisory Committee [*Presidential*] [*Terminated*]
SAC .... Scientific Advisory Council [*Ministry of Supply*] [*British*] [*World War II*]
SAC .... Secondary Accountability Center   (AAG)
SAC .... Secondary Address Code
SAC .... Security Access Control [*Data processing*]
SAC .... Self-Adjusting Clutch
SAC .... Semiautomatic Coding
SAC .... Semiautomatic Controller   (CAAL)
SAC .... Senate Appropriations Committee   (NVT)
SAC .... Service Application Code [*Navy*]
SACCD .... Serving Area Concept [*Bell System*]
SAC .... Servo Adapter Coupler
SAC .... Shipbuilding Advisory Council [*British*]
SAC .... Ships Air Coordinator   (MCD)
SAC .... Side-Arm Controller [*Aviation*]
SAC .... Signature Authorization Card [*or Chart*]   (AAG)
SAC .... Single Acting Cylinder
SAC .... Single Address Code   (AAG)
SAC .... Sisters of the Holy Guardian Angels [*Roman Catholic religious order*]
SAC .... Sisters of Mary of the Catholic Apostolate [*Roman Catholic religious order*]
SAC .... Social and Athletic Club
SAC .... Societe Africaine de Culture [*Society of African Culture*]
SAC .... Society for American Cuisine   (EA)
SAC .... Society of the Catholic Apostolate [*Pallottines*] [*Roman Catholic men's religious order*]
SAC .... South-African Constabulary [*Military*] [*British*] [*Defunct*]   (ROG)
SAC .... South Atlantic Coast
SAC .... South Carolina Electric & Gas Co. [*NYSE symbol*]
SAC .... Southern Africa Committee   (EA)
SAC .... Special Agent in Charge [*FBI*]
SAC .... Special Area Code [*Bell System*]
SAC .... Specific Acoustic Capacitance
SAC .... Spectrum Analyzer Component   (MCD)
SAC .... Spiritual Advisory Council   (EA)
SAC .... Sport for All Clearing House   (EA-IO)
SAC .... Sprayed Acoustical Ceiling [*Technical drawings*]
S/AC .... Stabilization/Attitude Control [*NASA*]   (NASA)
SAC .... Standard Agena Clamshell [*NASA*]   (KSC)
SAC .... Standard Aircraft Characteristics
SAC .... Standing Armaments Committee [*NATO*]   (NATG)
SAC .... Starting Air Compressor   (CAAL)
SAC .... State Advisory Committee
SAC .... State Apprenticeship Council [*Bureau of Apprenticeship and Training*] [*Department of Labor*]
SAC .... Statistical Advisory Committee [*UN Food and Agriculture Organization*]
SAC .... Statistical Analysis Center   (OICC)
SAC .... Storage Access Channel   (CMD)
SAC .... Storage Access Control [*Data processing*]
SAC .... Store and Clear
SAC .... Store and Clear Accumulator [*Data processing*]
SAC .... Strategic Air Command
SAC .... Strategic Alert Cadre   (NVT)
SAC .... Studies in the Age of Chaucer [*A publication*]
SAC .... Studies in Ancient Civilization [*Elsevier Book Series*] [*A publication*]
SAC .... Submitting Activity Code
SAC .... Sugar Association of the Caribbean   (EA-IO)
SAC .... Sulfuric Acid Concentrate   (MCD)
SAC .... Sunbeam Alpine Club   (EA)
SAC .... Supplemental Air Carrier   (MCD)

SAC .... Supply Administration Center   (MCD)
SAC .... Supply Availability Card   (MCD)
SAC .... Support Action Center   (MCD)
SAC .... Supporting Arms Coordinator [*Air Force*]   (NVT)
SAC .... Supreme Allied Command [*or Commander*] [*Headquarters in London*] [*World War II*]
SAC .... Sussex Archaeological Collections [*A publication*]
SAC .... Sustained Abdominal Compression [*Gastroenterology*]
SAC .... Sveriges Arbetares Centralorganisation [*Central Organization of Swedish Workers*]
SAC .... Synchro Azimuth Converter
SAC .... System Automation Corporation [*Silver Spring, MD*] [*Information service*]   (EISS)
SAC .... Systems Acquisition Career
SAC .... Systems Auditability and Control [*Data processing*]
SACA .... Service Action Change Analysis   (AAG)
SACA .... Special Assistant for Consumer Affairs [*White House*] [*Obsolete*]
SACA .... Steam Automobile Club of America   (EA)
SACA .... Studebaker Automobile Club of America   (EA)
SACA .... Student Action Corps for Animals [*Washington, DC*]   (EA)
SACA .... Study Advisory Committee on Aeronautics [*National Academy of Engineering*]
SACA .... Subversive Activities Control Act of 1950
SACACCS ... Strategic Air Command Automated Command Control System   (AFM)
SACAM ...... Ship Acquisition Contract Administration Manual   (MCD)
SACAY .... SECNAV [*Secretary of the Navy*] Advisory Commission on Youth   (NG)
SACB .... Subversive Activities Control Board [*Later, Federal Internal Security Board*]
SACBC ...... Southern African Catholic Bishops' Conference [*Pretoria, South Africa*]   (EA-IO)
SACC .... Slovak-American Cultural Center   (EA)
SACC .... State Auditors Coordinating Committee   (EA)
SACC .... Supplemental Air Carrier Conference [*Defunct*]   (EA)
SACC .... Supporting Arms Coordination Center [*Air Force*]
SACCD ...... Saccharum [*A publication*]
SACCEI ...... Strategic Air Command Communications-Electronics Instruction
SACCH ...... Saccharatae [*Sugar-Coated*] [*Pharmacy*]
SACCOM ...... Strategic Air Command Communications   (MCD)
SACCOMNET ... Strategic Air Command Communications Network
SACCS ...... Strategic Air Command Communications [*or Control*] System
SACD .... Society of Americans of Colonial Descent   (EA)
SACDA ...... Surplus Agricultural Commodities Disposal Act of 1982
SACDIN ...... Strategic Air Command Digital Information Network   (MCD)
SACDM ...... Study and Action Course in District Management [*LIMRA*]
SACDNU .... Sudan African Closed Districts National Union
SAC(DP) .... Scientific Advisory Committee, Defence Services Panel [*British*] [*World War II*]
SacE .... Sacris Erudiri. Jaarboek voor Godsdienstwetenschappen [*A publication*]
SACE .... Semiautomatic Checkout Equipment [*DoD*]
SACE .... Serum Angiotensin Converting Enzyme [*Activity*] [*Serology*]
SACE .... Shore-Based Acceptance Checkout Equipment
SACEA ...... Sino-American Cultural and Economic Association
SACEM ...... Society for the Advancement of Continuing Education for Ministry   (EA)
SA Census & Statistics Bul ... Australia. Commonwealth Bureau of Census and Statistics. South Australian Office. Bulletin [*A publication*]
SA Cereb Palsy J ... SA [*South African*] Cerebral Palsy Journal [*A publication*]
SACEUR .... Supreme Allied Commander, Europe [*NATO*]
SACEUREP ... Supreme Allied Commander, Europe Representative [*NATO*]   (NATG)
SACFI .... Scholars and Citizens for Freedom of Information   (EA)
SACH .... Solid Ankle Cushion Heel [*Foot prosthesis*]
SACh .... Studies in Analytical Chemistry [*Elsevier Book Series*] [*A publication*]
SACHC ...... Soviet-American Committee on Health Cooperation
SACHQ ...... Strategic Air Command Headquarters   (AAG)
Sachs Akad d Wiss Philol-Hist Kl Ber u d Verhandl ... Saechsische Akademie der Wissenschaften. Philologisch-Historische Klasse. Berichte ueber die Verhandlungen [*A publication*]
Sachse NM ... Sachse's Minutes, Norwich Mayoralty Court   (DLA)
SACHY ...... Saatchi & Saatchi plc [*NASDAQ symbol*]   (NQ)
SACI .... Sales Association of the Chemical Industry [*New York, NY*]   (EA)
SACI .... Sales Association of the Chemistry Industry
SACI .... Secondary Address Code Indicator
SACI .... South Atlantic Cooperative Investigations [*Military*]
SACL .... South African Confederation of Labour
SACL .... Space and Component Log
SACL .... Standards and Calibration Laboratory   (KSC)
SACLA ...... Srpski Arhiv za Celokupno Lekarstvo [*A publication*]
SACLAMP ... Strategic Air Command Low-Altitude Missile Program [*Air Force*]
SACLANT ... Supreme Allied Commander, Atlantic [*NATO*]

SACLANTCEN ... Supreme Allied Commander, Atlantic, Antisubmarine Warfare Research Center [*NATO*]   (AABC)

SACLANTREPEUR ... Supreme Allied Commander, Atlantic, Representative in Europe [*NATO*]   (AABC)

SACLAU..... SACLANT [*Supreme Allied Commander, Atlantic*] Authentification System [*NATO*]   (NATG)

SACLEX..... SACLANT [*Supreme Allied Commander, Atlantic*] Standing Exercise Orders [*NATO*]   (NATG)

Sac Lit D .... Doctor of Sacred Literature

SACLO...... Strategic Air Command Liaison Officer

SACLOS .... Semiautomatic Command to Line of Sight [*Military*]

Sac M........ Sacred Music [*A publication*]

SACM........ School of Acquisition Management [*Army*]

SACM........ Simulated Aerial Combat Maneuver

SACMA ...... Suppliers of Advanced Composite Materials Association [*Arlington, VA*]   (EA)

SACMAP.... Selective Automatic Computational Matching and Positioning   (MCD)

SACMAPS ... Selective Automatic Computational Matching and Positioning System

SACMDR.... Site Activation Commander [*Army*]   (AABC)

SACMED.... Supreme Allied Commander, Mediterranean [*World War II*]

SAC/MEP ... Strategic Air Command/Minuteman Education Program   (AFM)

SACNA...... South Africa Club of North America [*Defunct*]   (EA)

SACNET..... Secure Automatic Communications Network

SACO .... Select Address and Contract Operate

SACO .... Service Administratif Canadien Outre-Mer [*Canadian Executive Service Overseas - CESO*]

SACO .... Sino-American Cooperative Organization [*Guerrilla and intelligence agency*] [*World War II*]

SACO .... Supporting Administrative Contracting Officer   (AFIT)

SACO .... Sveriges Akademikers Centralorganisation [*Swedish Confederation of Professional Associations*]

SACOA ..... Southern Appalachian Coal Operators Association   (EA)

SAC-OA .... Strategic Air Command Office of Operations Analysis

SACOD ..... South African Congress of Democrats

SACOM ..... SECNAV [*Secretary of the Navy*] Advisory Commission on Manpower   (NG)

SACOM ..... Southern Area Command [*Military*]   (AABC)

SACON ..... Shock-Absorbing Concretes   (RDA)

SACON ..... Structural Analysis Consultant   (MCD)

SACOPS .... Strategic Air Command Operational Planning System   (MCD)

SACP .... Society for Asian and Comparative Philosophy   (EA)

SACP .... South African Communist Party

SACP .... Strategic Air Command Project Office   (AAG)

SACPAN .... Stemming and Closure Panel [*DoD*]   (EGAO)

SACPB ...... South African Chemical Processing [*A publication*]

SACPG...... Senior Arms Control Planning Group [*Pronounced "sack pig"*] [*DoD*]

SACPO...... Saigon Area Civilian Personnel Office [*Vietnam*]

SACPO...... South African Colored People's Organization

SACR .... Sacrament   (ROG)

SACR .... Sacred   (ROG)

SACR .... Sacrifice   (ROG)

SACR .... Sacrist

SACR .... Strategic Air Command Regulations   (AAG)

SACRA...... Student Alliance for Christian Renewal in America

Sacred Mus ... Sacred Music [*A publication*]

SACROC ... Scurry Area Canyon Reef Operators Committee

SACS .... Satellite Attitude-Control Simulator [*NASA*]

SACS .... Scheduling Activity Control System [*PA Computers & Telecommunications Ltd.*] [*Software package*]

SACS .... Selective High-Frequency Antenna Coupler System [*Military*]   (CAAL)

SACS .... Sensor Accuracy Check Site   (MCD)

SACS .... Services After-Care Scheme [*British*]

SACS .... Ship Alteration Completion System

SACS .... Shipyard Accuracy Checksite   (MCD)

SACS .... Sino-American Cultural Society   (EA)

SACS .... Solar Altitude Control System

SACS .... SONAR Accuracy Check Site   (NVT)

SACS .... Southern Association of Colleges and Schools

SACS .... Structure and Composition System   (AABC)

SACS .... Synchronous Altitude Communications Satellite

SACS .... Systems Software Avionics Command Support   (MCD)

SACSA...... Special Assistant for Counterinsurgency and Special Activities [*Air Force*]   (AFM)

SACSA...... Standing Advisory Committee for Scientific Advice [*Oslo Commission*]

SACSEA .... Supreme Allied Command [*or Commander*], Southeast Asia

SACSIR...... South African Council for Scientific and Industrial Research

SAC/SSW .. Special Assistant to the Chief of Staff for Special Warfare [*Army*]

SACT .... Sinoatrial Conduction Time [*Cardiology*]

SACTO...... Sacramento Test Operations   (MCD)

SACTTYNET ... Strategic Air Command Teletype Network

SACTU...... South African Congress of Trade Unions

SACTW...... South African Council of Transport Workers

SACU .... Society for Anglo-Chinese Understanding

SACU .... South African Customs Union

SACUS...... Southern Association on Children under Six [*Little Rock, AR*]   (EA)

SACVAR .... Ship Alteration Cost Variance Account Report

SAD........... Saddle   (AAG)

SAD........... Saddleback Community College District, Mission Viejo Campus, Mission Viejo, CA [*OCLC symbol*]   (OCLC)

Sad .... Sadler's Pennsylvania Cases   (DLA)

SAD........... Safety Analysis Diagram   (NRCH)

SAD........... Safety, Arming, and Destruct   (MCD)

SAD........... Safety and Arming Device   (AABC)

SAD........... Safety Assurance Diagram   (NRCH)

SAD........... Safford, AZ [*Location identifier*] [*FAA*]   (FAAL)

sad .... Sandawe [*MARC language code*] [*Library of Congress*]   (LCCP)

S & AD....... Science and Applications Directorate [*NASA*]

SAD........... Search and Destroy   (MCD)

SAD........... Seasonal Affective Disorder [*Caused by long nights, short days*]

SAD........... Selected Area [*Electron*] Diffraction [*Also, SAED*] [*Analysis of solids*]

SAD........... Semiconductor Anticoincidence Detector

SAD........... Sentence Appraiser and Diagrammer

SAD........... Service Action Drawing   (AAG)

SAD........... Ship Acoustics Department [*David W. Taylor Naval Ship Research and Development Center*]

SAD........... Shuttle Authorized Document [*NASA*]   (NASA)

SAD........... Silverado Mines [*Vancouver Stock Exchange symbol*]

SAD........... Simple, Average, or Difficult   (AAG)

SAD........... Single Administrative Document [*European trade contract*] [*1986*]

SAD........... Sinoaortic Denervation [*Physiology*]

SAD........... Situation Attention Display

S-A-D .... Sleep Disturbance with Anxiety and Depression [*Combat behavior disorder*] [*Military*]   (INF)

SAD........... Social Avoidance Distress [*Scale*]

SAD........... Society of the Ark and the Dove   (EA)

SAD........... South American Datum

SAD........... South Atlantic Division [*Army Corps of Engineers*]

SAD........... Soviet Air Defense

SAD........... Soviet Air Demonstration

SAD........... Space Antennae Diversity [*Telecommunications*]   (TEL)

SAD........... Spacecraft Attitude Display   (MCD)

SAD........... Special Artificer, Special Synthetic Training Devices [*Navy*]

SAD........... Station Address Directory [*Army*]

SAD........... Store Address Director

SAD........... Submarine Anomaly Detection [*Navy*]   (NVT)

SAD........... Sugar, Acetone, Diacetic Acid [*Test*] [*Medicine*]

SAD........... Supervisory Aptitude Development [*In George Lee Walker novel "The Chronicles of Doodah"*]

SAD........... Support Air Direction [*Navy*]

SAD........... Survival Assistance Director [*Federal disaster planning*]

SAD........... Sympathetic Aerial Detonation [*Air Force*]

SAD........... System Allocation Document [*NASA*]   (NASA)

SAD........... System Analysis Drawing

SAD........... Systems Analysis Document   (MCD)

SADA .... Seismic Array Data Analyzer   (IEEE)

SADA .... Southern Appalachian Dulcimer Association   (EA)

SADAP ...... Simplified Automatic Data Plotter

SADAP...... State Alcoholism and Drug Abuse Profile [*Public Health Service*] [*Rockville, MD*] [*Information service*]   (EISS)

SADAR...... Satellite Data Reduction [*Processor system*]

SADARM.... Search and Destroy Armor [*Missile system*]   (RDA)

SADARM.... Selected Armor Defeating Artillery Munitions   (MCD)

SADARM.... Sense and Destroy Armor Missile   (MCD)

SAD Beng ... Select Cases, Sadr Diwani [*Bengal*]   (DLA)

SAD Bom ... Sadr Diwani Adalat Reports [*Bombay, India*]   (DLA)

SADBU....... Small and Disadvantaged Business Utilization [*Department of Commerce*]

SADC .... Sector Aid Defense Commander   (NATG)

SADC .... Sequential Analog-Digital Computer   (DIT)

SADC .... Sneak Attack Defense Coordinator [*Military*]   (CAAL)

SADD .... Semiautomatic Detection Device

SaDDC ...... Durban City Council, Durban, South Africa [*Library symbol*] [*Library of Congress*]   (LCLS)

SADE .... Superheat Advanced Demonstration Experiment

SADEC ...... Spin Axis Declination   (MCD)

SADELCA ... Sociedad Aerea del Caqueta [*Airline*] [*Colombian*]

SA Dep Agric Tech Bull ... South Australia. Department of Agriculture. Technical Bulletin [*A publication*]

SADF .... South African Defence Forces

SADH .... Succinic Acid - Dimethylhydrazide [*Plant growth retardant*]

SADI .... Secretarial Automated Data Index

SADIC .... Solid-State Analog-to-Digital Computer

SADIE .... Scanning Analog-to-Digital Input Equipment [*National Bureau of Standards*]

SADIE .... Secure Automatic Data Information Exchange [*System*]

SADIE .... Semiautomatic Decentralized Intercept Environment [*Air Force*]

SADIE .... Sterling and Decimal Invoicing Electronically   (IEEE)

Sadivn Resp Mizhvid Nauk-Temat Zb ... Sadivnytstvo Respublikanskyi Mizhvidomchyi Naukovo-Tematychnyi Zbirnik [*A publication*]
SADL......... Sadler [*William H.*], Inc. [*NASDAQ symbol*] (NQ)
SADL......... Ships Authorized Data List
SADL......... Spares Application Data List
SADL......... Special Automated Distribution List (AFIT)
SADL......... Sterilization Assembly Development Laboratory [*NASA*]
Sadler .... Sadler's Pennsylvania Cases (DLA)
Sadler (PA) ... Sadler's Cases [*Pennsylvania*] (DLA)
SADM........ Secretary of the Army Decision Memorandum [*Army*] (RDA)
SADM........ Solar Array Drive Motor
SADM........ Special Atomic Demolition Munitions (AABC)
SADM........ System Acquisition Decision Memorandum (MCD)
SADMG..... Special Artificer, Special Devices, Machine Gun Trainer [*Navy*]
SADNWF.... Sadr Diwani Adalat Cases, Northwest Frontier [*Pakistan*] (DLA)
SaDo .... Sacra Doctrina [*A publication*]
Sadovod .... Sadovodstvo [*A publication*]
Sadovod Vinograd Vinodel Mold ... Sadovodstvo Vinogradarstvo i Vinodelia Moldavii [*A publication*]
SADP......... Scandinavian Association of Directory Publishers [*Copenhagen, Denmark*] (EA-IO)
SADP......... Selected Area Electron Diffraction Pattern [*Analysis of solids*]
SADP......... Small Area Direct Path [*Military*] (CAAL)
SADP......... Structured Analysis, Design, and Programing [*Data processing*]
SADP......... Synthetic Array Data Processor
SADP......... System Architecture Design Package
Sad PA Cas ... Sadler's Pennsylvania Cases [*1885-88*] (DLA)
Sad PA Cs ... Sadler's Pennsylvania Cases [*1885-88*] (DLA)
SADPO...... Systems Analysis and Data Processing Office
SADR .... Saharan Arab Democratic Republic [*Moroccan*] (PD)
SADR .... Secure Acoustic Data Relay (NVT)
SADR .... Six Hundred Megacycle Air Defense RADAR
SADRAM... Seek and Destroy RADAR-Assisted Mission (MCD)
SADRI .... Social and Demographic Research Institute [*University of Massachusetts*] [*Research center*] (RCD)
SADRT ...... Secure Acoustic Data Relay Terminal (MCD)
SADS .... Schedule for Affective Disorders and Schizophrenia [*Psychological interview*]
SADS .... Semiautomatic Defense System (NG)
SADS .... Semiconductor Anticoincidence Detection System
SADS .... Senate Appropriations Defense Subcommittee
SADS .... Simulated Air Defense System [*RADAR*]
SADS .... Single Application Data Sheet
SADS .... Social Avoidance and Distress Scale [*Psychology*]
SADS .... Solar Array Drive System
SADS .... Swiss Air Defense System
SADS .... System Architecture Development Study [*NATO Integrated Communications System*] (NATG)
SADSAC .... Sampled Data Simulator and Computer
SADSAC .... Seiler ALGOL Digitally Simulated Analog Computer
SADSAC .... Small Acoustic Device Simulating Aircraft Carrier (NVT)
SADSACT ... Self-Assigned Descriptors from Self and Cited Titles [*Automatic indexing*]
SADT......... Self-Accelerating Decomposition Temperature
SADT......... Special Active Duty for Training [*Military*] (AABC)
SADT......... Structured Analysis and Design Technique [*Programing language*] [*1978*]
SADT......... Surface Alloy Diffused-Base Transistor
SADTC....... SHAPE [*Supreme Headquarters Allied Powers Europe*] Air Defense Technology Center [*Later, STC*] [*NATO*] (MCD)
Sadtler Commer Spectra ... Sadtler Commercial Spectra [*United States*] [*A publication*]
SADU .... Sea Search Attack Development Unit
SADV .... Semiannual Density Variation [*Geophysics*]
SAE .... Ogallala, NE [*Location identifier*] [*FAA*] (FAAL)
SAE .... Sable Resources Ltd. [*Vancouver Stock Exchange symbol*]
SaE............. Sanguinarine Extract [*Biochemistry*]
SAE .... Self-Addressed Envelope
SAE .... Semi-Actuator Ejector (MCD)
SAE .... Senior Assistant Editor [*Publishing*]
SAE .... Shaft Angle Encoder (KSC)
SAE .... Simple Arithmetic Expression
SAE .... Site Acceptance Evaluation [*Army*] (AABC)
SAE .... Society for the Advancement of Education (EA)
SAE .... Society of Automotive Engineers (EA)
SAE .... Son Altesse Electorale [*His Highness the Elector*] [*French*] (ROG)
SAE .... Soviet Antarctic Expedition
SAE .... Spiral Aftereffect [*Aerospace*]
SAE .... Stamped Addressed Envelope
SAE .... Standard Average European
SAE .... Steering Angle Error
SAE .... Stop at Expiration [*Magazine subscriptions*]
SAE .... Student Action for Education [*Defunct*] (EA)
SAE .... Subcortical Arteriosclerotic Encephalopathy [*Medicine*]
SAE .... Supersonic Aircraft Engine
SAEA......... Southwest Atomic Energy Associates

SAE Australas ... SAE [*Society of Automotive Engineers*] Australasia [*A publication*]
SAEB.......... Self-Adjusting Electric Brake
SAEB.......... Special Army Evaluation Board (AABC)
SAEBA .... Soviet Antarctic Expedition. Information Bulletin [*English Translation*] [*A publication*]
SAEC .... Saeculum [*Century*] [*Latin*] (ROG)
SAEC .... South American Explorers Club (EA)
SAEC .... Southern Agricultural Energy Center
SAEC .... Sumitomo Atomic Energy Commission [*Japan*]
Saechs Heimatbl ... Saechsische Heimatblaetter [*A publication*]
SAED .... Selected Area Electron Diffraction [*Also, SAD*] [*Analysis of solids*]
SA Ed .... South Australian Education [*A publication*]
SAED .... Systems Analysis and Engineering Development [*Naval Air Development Center*] (MCD)
SAEDA .... Subversion and Espionage Directed Against US Army and Deliberate Security Violations (AABC)
SAEDE .... Sensory Aids Evaluation and Development Center [*MIT*]
SAEDFR ..... Scholars Against the Escalating Danger of the Far Right [*New York, NY*] (EA)
SA Ed Gaz ... Education Gazette (South Australia. Education Department) [*A publication*]
SAEF......... Spacecraft Assembly and Encapsulation Facility [*NASA*] (NASA)
SAEF......... State Administrative Expense Funds
SAEH.......... Society for Automation in English and the Humanities [*Later, SDE*]
SAEI.......... Sumitomo Atomic Energy Industries Ltd. [*Japan*]
SAE J .... SAE [*Society of Automotive Engineers*] Journal [*A publication*]
SAEJA........ SAE [*Society of Automotive Engineers*] Journal [*A publication*]
SAE J Automot Eng ... SAE [*Society of Automotive Engineers*] Journal of Automotive Engineers [*A publication*]
SAE Meet Pap ... Society of Automotive Engineers. Meeting. Papers [*A publication*]
SAEMR....... Small-Arms Expert Marksmanship Ribbon [*Military decoration*] (AFM)
SAEND .... Save Energy [*A publication*]
SAEP.......... South African Education Program [*New York, NY*]
SAE Prepr ... SAE [*Society of Automotive Engineers*] Preprints [*A publication*]
SAE Proc ... Society of Automotive Engineers. Proceedings [*A publication*]
SAE Prog Technol ... SAE [*Society of Automotive Engineers*] Progress in Technology [*United States*] [*A publication*]
SAERB .... South African Electrical Review [*A publication*]
SAES......... Scanning Auger Electron Spectroscopy
SAES......... Special Assistant for Environmental Services [*Military*]
SAES......... State Agricultural Experiment Station
SAESA .... SAE [*Society of Automotive Engineers*] Special Publication [*A publication*]
SAE (Soc Automot Eng) Tech Pap ... SAE (Society of Automotive Engineers) Technical Papers [*A publication*]
SAE Spec Publ ... SAE [*Society of Automotive Engineers*] Special Publications [*A publication*]
SAETA ...... SA Ecuatoriana de Transportes Aereos [*Airline*] [*Ecuadorean*]
SAETA ...... SAETA. South Australian English Teachers Association [*A publication*]
SAETB ...... SAE [*Society of Automotive Engineers*] Technical Progress Series [*A publication*]
SAE Tech Lit Abstr ... SAE [*Society of Automotive Engineers*] Technical Literature Abstracts [*A publication*]
SAE Tech Prog Ser ... SAE [*Society of Automotive Engineers*] Technical Progress Series [*A publication*]
SAETO ...... Sociedad Aereo del Tolina [*Colombia*]
SAE Trans ... SAE [*Society of Automotive Engineers*] Transactions [*A publication*]
SAEW........ Ship's Advanced Electronic Warfare (MCD)
SAEWS ...... Ship's Advanced Electronic Warfare System (NVT)
SAF .... SAF [*Society of American Florists*]- The Center for Commercial Floriculture (EA)
SAF .... Safed [*Israel*] [*Seismograph station code, US Geological Survey*] [*Closed*] (SEIS)
SAF .... Safety (KSC)
SAF .... San Andreas Fault
SAF .... Santa Fe [*New Mexico*] [*Airport symbol*] (OAG)
SAF .... Scandinavian American Fraternity (EA)
SAF .... Scrapie-Associated Fibrils [*Neuroanatomy*]
SAF .... Second Amendment Foundation (EA)
SAF .... Secretary of the Air Force
SAF .... Secure Automated Fabrication [*Line*] [*Nuclear energy*]
SAF .... Segment Address Field
SAF .... Self-Articulating Femoral [*Medicine*]
SAF .... Shielding Analysis Form [*Civil Defense*]
SAF .... Single Action [*Maintenance*] Form (NVT)
SAF .... Society of American Florists [*Alexandria, VA*] (EA)
SAF .... Society of American Foresters (EA)
SAF .... Source Acquisitions File (MCD)
SAF .... South Africa
SAF .... South Africa Foundation (EA)
SAF .... Southern Attack Force [*Navy*]
SAF .... Spacecraft Assembly Facility [*NASA*]

SAF .... Spanish Air Force
SAF .... Special Action Force [*Military*]
SAF .... Specification Approval Form   (MCD)
SAF .... Spin Armed Fuze
SAF .... Stem Cell Activating Factor [*Biochemistry*]
SAF .... Sterilization Assembly Facility
SAF .... Strategic Air Force
SAF .... Students Against Fires [*International student engineering project for 1972-73 sponsored by Student Competitions on Relevant Engineering - SCORE*]
SAF .... Studies in American Fiction [*A publication*]
SAF .... Subject Authority File, Washington, DC [*UTLAS symbol*]
SAF .... Subject to the Availability of Funds   (MCD)
SAF .... Super Abrasion Furnace
SAF .... Support Action Form   (MCD)
SAF .... Suppressor Activating Factor [*Immunology*]
SAF .... Svenska Arbetsgivareforeningen [*An employers' confederation*] [*Sweden*]
SAF .... Switchable Acoustic Filter
SAF .... Symmetry-Adapted Function
SAF .... Symposium on Applications of Ferroelectrics [*IEEE*]
SAF .... Syrian Air Force   (BJA)
SAFA .... School Assistance in Federally Affected Areas
SAFA .... Service d'Aide aux Forces Alliees [*World War II*]
SAFA .... Society of Air Force Anesthesiologists [*Later, DMEF*]   (EA)
SAFA .... Society for Automation in the Fine Arts [*Later, SDE*]
SAFA .... Solar Array Failure Analysis
SAFA .... Soluble Antigen Fluorescent-Antibody [*Immunology*]
SAFAA .... Secretary of the Air Force, Administrative Assistant
SAFAD .... Small Arms for Air Defense   (MCD)
Saf Air Ammonia Plants ... Safety in Air and Ammonia Plants [*A publication*]
SAF/AL ...... Assistant Secretary of the Air Force, Research, Development, and Logistics
SAFARI ...... Semiautomatic Failure Anticipation Recording Instrumentation
SAFARI ...... South African Fundamental Atomic Reactor Installation
SAFARI ...... Spiro Agnew Fans and Rooters, Incorporated
SAFB .... Scott Air Force Base [*Illinois*]
SAFB .... Shaw Air Force Base [*South Carolina*]
SAFB .... Sheppard Air Force Base [*Texas*]   (AAG)
SAFC .... Safeco Corp. [*NASDAQ symbol*]
SAFCA .... Safeguard Communications Agency [*Army*]
SAFCB .... Secretary of the Air Force Correction Board
SAFCMD .... Safeguard Command [*Army*]   (AABC)
SAFCO .... Standing Advisory Committee on Fisheries of the Caribbean Organization
SAFCOM .... Safeguard System Command [*Obsolete*] [*Army*]
SAFCPM .... Safeguard Communications Program Manager [*Army*]   (AABC)
SAFCPMO ... Safeguard Communications Program Management Office [*Army*]   (AABC)
SAFCTF ..... Safeguard Central Training Facility [*Army*]   (AABC)
SAFD .... Plastics (Southern Africa) [*A publication*]
SAFD .... Society of American Fight Directors   (EA)
Saf Dig .... Safety Digest [*Japan*] [*A publication*]
SAFDL .... Specified Acceptable Fuel Design Limit [*Nuclear energy*]   (NRCH)
SAFE .... Safe Access to Files of Estate [*Howrex Corp.*] [*Moorestown, NJ*] [*Information service*]   (EISS)
SAFE .... Safeguards Analysis for Effluents
SAFE .... Safeguards Automated Facility Evaluation [*Nuclear energy*]   (NRCH)
SAFE .... San Andreas Fault Experiment
SAFE .... Satellite Alert Force Employment
SAFE .... Save Animals from Extinction [*An association*] [*Later, WPTI*]
SAFE .... Security American Finance [*NASDAQ symbol*]   (NQ)
S/AFE .... Seismic/Acoustic Feature Extraction   (MCD)
SAFE .... Selected Areas for Evasion [*Military*]   (MCD)
SAFE .... Self-Acceptance, Faulty Information, Effectiveness Counselling or Training [*Sex therapy*]
SAFE .... Sequential Analysis for Force Development   (MCD)
SAFE .... Settlement and Accelerated Funds Exchange [*Chicago*]
SAFE .... Shelter Available for Emergency
SAFE .... Simulation-Aided Fault Evaluation   (MCD)
SAFE .... Society to Advance Foreclosure Education   (EA)
SAFE .... Society for the Advancement of Fission Energy   (EA)
SAFE .... Society for the Application of Free Energy   (EA)
SAFE .... Society of Associated Financial Executives
SAFE .... Solvent Abuse Foundation for Education   (EA)
SAFE .... South America and Far East
SAFE .... Spectronix Automatic Fire Extinguishing [*System*] [*For armored vehicles*]
SAFE .... Stationary Attachment and Flexible Endoskeleton
SAFE .... Store and Forward Element [*Telecommunications*]   (TEL)
SAFE .... Strategy and Force Evaluation   (MCD)
SAFE .... Students Against Famine Everywhere [*Hanover, NH*]   (EA)
SAFE .... Suntanning Association for Education   (EA)
SAFE .... Support for the Analysts' File Environment   (MCD)
SAFE .... Survival [*formerly, Space*] and Flight Equipment Association [*Later, SAFE Association*]
SAFE .... System, Area, Function, Equipment
SAFEA .... Safety [*A publication*]

SAFEA .... Survival [*formerly, Space*] and Flight Equipment Association [*Later, SAFE Association*]   (EA)
Safe Manag ... Safety Management [*A publication*]
SAFER .... Sequential Action Flow Routine [*Military*] [*British*]
SAFER .... Special Aviation Fire and Explosion Reduction   (EGAO)
SAFER .... Systematic Aid to Flow on Existing Roads [*Traffic-control system*]
SAFE TRIP ... Students Against Faulty Tires Ripping in Pieces [*Student legal action organization*]
SAFETY ..... Safety Always Follows Everything You Do [*Sign*]
Safety Ed ... Safety Education [*A publication*]
Safety Educ ... Safety Education [*A publication*]
Safety Eng ... Safety Engineering [*A publication*]
Safety Maint ... Safety Maintenance [*A publication*]
Safety Maint & Prod ... Safety Maintenance and Production [*A publication*]
Safety Surv ... Safety Surveyor [*A publication*]
SAFF .... Safing, Arming, Fusing, and Firing [*Military*]   (MCD)
SAFF .... Store and Forward Facsimile
SAFFE .... Society of Americans for Firearms Elimination   (EA)
SAFFI .... Special Assembly for Fast Installations [*Telecommunications*]   (TEL)
SAFFM .... Secretary of the Air Force, Financial Management
SAFFUC ..... Sudan African Freedom Fighters' Union of Conservatives
SAFGC .... Secretary of the Air Force General Counsel
Saf Hyg (Osaka) ... Safety and Hygiene (Osaka) [*Japan*] [*A publication*]
SAFI .... Semiautomatic Flight Inspection [*FAA*]
SAFI .... Senior Air Force Instructor
SAFI .... Sholem Aleichem Folk Institute   (EA)
SAFIE .... Secretary of the Air Force, Special Assistant for Installations
SAFIL .... Secretary of the Air Force (Installations and Logistics)
SAFIMDA ... School Aid to Federally Impacted and Major Disaster Areas   (OICC)
SAFIN .... Secretary of the Air Force, Special Assistant for Intelligence
SAFIS .... Secretary of the Air Force, Office of Information Services
SAFITP ...... Safeguard Integrated Training Plan [*Army*]   (AABC)
SAFJB .... South African Forestry Journal [*A publication*]
SAFLL .... Secretary of the Air Force, Office of Legislative Liaison
SAFLOG ..... Safeguard Logistics Command [*Army*]   (AABC)
Saf Manage ... Safety Management [*A publication*]
SAFMem ..... Societe Nationale des Antiquaires de France. Memoires [*A publication*]
Saf Mines ... Safety in Mines [*A publication*]
SAFMP .... Assistant Secretary of the Air Force (Manpower and Personnel)
SAFMR .... Secretary of the Air Force, Manpower and Reserve Affairs
SAFMSC ..... Safeguard Materiel Support Command [*Army*]   (AABC)
Saf News Bull ... Safety News Bulletin [*A publication*]
Saf Newsl ... Safety Newsletter [*A publication*]
SAFO .... Secretary of the Air Force Order   (AFM)
SAFO .... Senior Acting Field Officer [*Military*] [*British*]   (ROG)
SAFO .... Senior Air Force Officer [*Present*]   (AFM)
SAFOC .... Semiautomatic Flight Operations Center
SAFOC .... Syndicat Autonome des Fonctionnaires d'Oubangi-Chari [*Autonomous Union of the Workers of Ubangi-Shari*]
SAFOH .... Society of American Florists and Ornamental Horticulturists [*Later, SAF*]
SAFOI .... Secretary of the Air Force, Office of Information
SAFP .... Society of Air Force Physicians [*Bolling AFB*] [*Washington, DC*]   (EA)
SAFPACC ... Safeguard Public Affairs Coordinating Committee [*Army*]   (AABC)
SAFPC .... Secretary of the Air Force Personnel Council
SAFPD .... Safety Practitioner [*A publication*]
SAFPLAN ... Submarine Area Frequency Plan [*Navy*]
SAFPO .... Safeguard Project Office   (MCD)
SAFR .... Senior Air Force Representative   (AFM)
SAFR .... Sodium Advanced Fast Reactor
SAFR .... Source Application of Funds Report   (MCD)
SAFR .... Supplementary Application Forms Required [*Civil Service*]
S Afr Archaeol Soc Goodwin Ser ... South African Archaeological Society. Goodwin Series [*A publication*]
S Afr Arch Ophthalmol ... South African Archives of Ophthalmology [*A publication*]
S-Afr Argief Oftalmol ... Suid-Afrikaanse Argief vir Oftalmologie [*A publication*]
SAFRAS ..... Self-Adaptive Flexible Format Retrieval and Storage System [*Data processing*]   (EISS)
S Afr Assoc Adv Sci Spec Publ ... South African Association for the Advancement of Science. Special Publication [*A publication*]
S Afr Assoc Mar Biol Res Bull ... South African Association for Marine Biological Research. Bulletin [*A publication*]
S Afr Bank ... South African Reserve Bank. Quarterly Bulletin [*A publication*]
S Afr Bankers J ... South African Bankers' Journal [*Cape Town, South Africa*]   (DLA)
S Afr Bee J ... South African Bee Journal [*A publication*]
S-Afr Bosbou Tydskr ... Suid-Afrikaanse Bosbou Tydskrif [*A publication*]
S Afr Build ... South African Builder [*A publication*]
S Afr Bur Stand Bull ... South African Bureau of Standards. Bulletin [*A publication*]
S Afr Cancer Bull ... South African Cancer Bulletin [*A publication*]

S Afr (Cape Good Hope) Dep Nat Conserv Rep ... South Africa (Cape of Good Hope) Department of Nature. Conservation Report [*A publication*]
S Afr Chart Account ... South African Chartered Accountant [*A publication*]
S Afr Chem Process ... South African Chemical Processing [*A publication*]
S Afr Corros J ... South African Corrosion Journal [*A publication*]
S Afr Counc Sci Ind Res Nat Bldg Res Inst Bull ... South Africa. Council for Scientific and Industrial Research. National Building Research Institute. Bulletin [*A publication*]
S Afr CSIR Air Pollut Group Annu Rep ... South Africa CSIR [*Council for Scientific and Industrial Research*] Air Pollution Group. Annual Report [*A publication*]
S Afr CSIR Air Pollut Res Group Annu Rep ... South Africa CSIR [*Council for Scientific and Industrial Research*] Air Pollution Research Group. Annual Report [*A publication*]
S Afr CSIR Annu Rep ... South Africa CSIR [*Council for Scientific and Industrial Research*] Annual Report [*A publication*]
S Afr CSIR Res Rep ... South Africa CSIR [*Council for Scientific and Industrial Research*] Research Report [*A publication*]
S Afr CSIR Spec Rep ... South Africa CSIR [*Council for Scientific and Industrial Research*] Special Report [*A publication*]
SAFRD .... Assistant Secretary of the Air Force (Research and Development)
SAFRD .... South African Food Review [*A publication*]
S Afr Dent J ... South African Dental Journal [*A publication*]
S Afr Dep Agric Tech Serv Bot Surv Mem ... South Africa Department of Agricultural Technical Services. Botanical Survey Memoir [*A publication*]
S Afr Dep Agric Tech Serv Bull ... South Africa Department of Agricultural Technical Services. Bulletin [*A publication*]
S Afr Dep Agric Tech Serv Entomol Mem ... South Africa Department of Agricultural Technical Services. Entomology Memoirs [*A publication*]
S Afr Dep Agric Tech Serv Sci Bull ... South Africa Department of Agricultural Technical Services. Scientific Bulletin [*A publication*]
S Afr Dep Agric Tech Serv Tech Commun ... South Africa Department of Agricultural Technical Services. Technical Communication [*A publication*]
S-Afr Dep Bosbou Jaarversl ... Suid-Afrika. Departement van Bosbou Jaarverslag [*A publication*]
S Afr Dep For Annu Rep ... South Africa Department of Forestry. Annual Report [*A publication*]
S Afr Dep For Bull ... South Africa Department of Forestry. Bulletin [*A publication*]
S-Afr Dep Landbou-Teg Dienste Teg Meded ... Suid-Afrika. Departement van Landbou-Tegniese Dienste Tegniese Mededeling [*A publication*]
S Afr Dep Mines Quart Inform Circ Miner ... South Africa. Department of Mines. Quarterly Information Circular. Minerals [*A publication*]
S Afr Div Sea Fish Annu Rep ... South Africa Division of Sea Fisheries. Annual Report [*A publication*]
S Afr Div Sea Fish Fish Bull ... South Africa Division of Sea Fisheries. Fisheries Bulletin [*A publication*]
S Afr Div Sea Fish Invest Rep ... South Africa Division of Sea Fisheries. Investigational Report [*A publication*]
S Afr Electr Rev ... South African Electrical Review [*A publication*]
S Afr Eng Electr Rev ... South African Engineer and Electrical Review [*A publication*]
S Afr Food Rev ... South African Food Review [*A publication*]
S Afr For J ... South African Forestry Journal [*A publication*]
S Afr Geol Surv Bibliogr Subj Index S Afr Geol ... South Africa. Geological Survey. Bibliography and Subject Index of South African Geology [*A publication*]
S Afr Geol Surv Bull ... South Africa Department of Mines. Geological Survey. Bulletin [*A publication*]
S Afr Geol Surv Mem ... South Africa Department of Mines. Geological Survey. Memoir [*A publication*]
S Afr Geol Surv Seismol Ser ... South Africa. Geological Survey. Seismologic Series [*A publication*]
S Afr Geol Surv South-West Afr Ser ... South Africa. Geological Survey. South-West Africa Series [*A publication*]
S African J Commun Disorders ... South African Journal of Communication Disorders [*A publication*]
S African J Psychol ... South African Journal of Psychology [*A publication*]
S African Lib ... South African Libraries [*A publication*]
S African Lib Q Bull ... South African Library Quarterly Bulletin [*A publication*]
S Afr Ind Chem ... South African Industrial Chemist [*A publication*]
S Afr Inst Mech Eng J ... South African Institution of Mechanical Engineers. Journal [*A publication*]
S Afr Inst Med Res Annu Rep ... South African Institute for Medical Research. Annual Report [*A publication*]
S Afr Inst Min Metall J ... South African Institute of Mining and Metallurgy. Journal [*A publication*]
S Afr Insur Mag ... South African Insurance Magazine [*A publication*]
S Afr Int ...... South Africa International [*A publication*]
S Afr J Agric Ext ... South African Journal of Agricultural Extension [*A publication*]

S Afr J Agric Sci ... South African Journal of Agricultural Science [*A publication*]
S Afr J Agr Sci ... South African Journal of Agricultural Science [*A publication*]
S Afr J Anim Sci ... South African Journal of Animal Science [*A publication*]
S Afr J Antarct Res ... South African Journal of Antarctic Research [*A publication*]
S Afr J Bot ... South African Journal of Botany [*A publication*]
S Afr J Chem ... South African Journal of Chemistry [*A publication*]
S Afr J Comm Disorders ... South African Journal of Communication Disorders [*A publication*]
S Afr J Contin Med Educ ... South African Journal of Continuing Medical Education [*A publication*]
S Afr J Crim L ... South African Journal of Criminal Law and Criminology [*A publication*]
S Afr J Crim Law Criminol ... South African Journal of Criminal Law and Criminology [*A publication*]
S Afr J Dairy Technol ... South African Journal of Dairy Technology [*A publication*]
S Afr J Ec ... South African Journal of Economics [*Suid-Afrikaanse Tydskrif vir Ekonomie*] [*A publication*]
S Afr J Econ ... South African Journal of Economics [*Suid-Afrikaanse Tydskrif vir Ekonomie*] [*A publication*]
S Afr J Hosp Med ... South African Journal of Hospital Medicine [*A publication*]
S Afr J Lab Clin Med ... South African Journal of Laboratory and Clinical Medicine [*A publication*]
S Afr J Labour Relat ... South African Journal of Labour Relations [*A publication*]
S Afr J Libr Inf Sci ... South African Journal for Librarianship and Information Science [*A publication*]
S Afr J Med Lab Technol ... South African Journal of Medical Laboratory Technology [*A publication*]
S Afr J Med Sci ... South African Journal of Medical Sciences [*A publication*]
S Afr J Musicology ... South African Journal of Musicology [*A publication*]
S Afr J Music Therap ... South African Journal of Music Therapy [*A publication*]
S Afr J Nutr ... South African Journal of Nutrition [*A publication*]
S Afr J Obstet Gynaecol ... South African Journal of Obstetrics and Gynaecology [*A publication*]
S Afr J Phys ... South African Journal of Physics [*A publication*]
S Afr J Physiother ... South African Journal of Physiotherapy [*A publication*]
S Afr J Radiol ... South African Journal of Radiology [*A publication*]
S Afr J Sci ... South African Journal of Science [*A publication*]
S Afr J Surg ... South African Journal of Surgery [*A publication*]
S Afr J Wild Res ... South African Journal of Wildlife Research [*A publication*]
S Afr J Zool ... South African Journal of Zoology [*A publication*]
SAfrL .... Studies in African Literature [*A publication*]
S Afr Labour Bull ... South African Labour Bulletin [*A publication*]
S Afr Lapid Mag ... South African Lapidary Magazine [*A publication*]
S Afr Law J ... South African Law Journal [*A publication*]
S Afr Libr ... South African Libraries [*A publication*]
S Afr LJ ...... South African Law Journal [*A publication*]
S Afr LR ...... South African Law Reports [*A publication*]
S Afr LR App ... South African Law Reports, Appellate (DLA)
S Afr Mach Tool Rev ... South African Machine Tool Review [*A publication*]
S Afr Mater Handl News ... South African Materials Handling News [*A publication*]
S Afr Mech Eng ... South African Mechanical Engineer [*A publication*]
S Afr Mech Engr ... South African Mechanical Engineer [*A publication*]
S Afr Med Equip News ... South African Medical Equipment News [*A publication*]
S Afr Med J ... South African Medical Journal [*A publication*]
S-Afr Med Tydskr ... Suid-Afrikaanse Mediese Tydskrif [*A publication*]
S Afr Min Eng J ... South African Mining and Engineering Journal [*A publication*]
S Afr Min J ... South African Mining Journal [*A publication*]
S Afr Mus Rep ... South African Museum Report [*A publication*]
S Afr Nurs J ... South African Nursing Journal [*A publication*]
S Afr Panorama ... South African Panorama [*A publication*]
S Afr Pneumoconiosis Rev ... South African Pneumoconiosis Review [*A publication*]
SAFRR .... Secretary of the Air Force, Requirements Review
S Afr Radiogr ... South African Radiographer [*A publication*]
S Afr Railw ... South African Railways [*A publication*]
S Afr Rep Secr Water Affairs ... South Africa. Report of the Secretary for Water Affairs [*A publication*]
S Afr Sci ..... South African Science [*A publication*]
S Afr Sea Fish Branch Invest Rep ... South Africa Sea Fisheries Branch. Investigational Report [*A publication*]
S Afr Shipp News Fish Ind Rev ... South African Shipping News and Fishing Industry Review [*A publication*]
S-Afr Spoorwee ... Suid-Afrikaanse Spoorwee [*South Africa*] [*A publication*]
S Afr Stat ... South African Statistical Journal [*A publication*]
S Afr Stat J ... South African Statistical Journal [*A publication*]
S Afr Sugar Assoc Exp Stn Annu Rep ... South African Sugar Association Experiment Station. Annual Report [*A publication*]
S Afr Sugar Assoc Exp Stn Bull ... South African Sugar Association Experiment Station. Bulletin [*A publication*]
S Afr Sugar J ... South African Sugar Journal [*A publication*]
S Afr Sug J ... South African Sugar Journal [*A publication*]

S Afr Surv J ... South African Survey Journal [*A publication*]
S Afr Tax Cas ... South African Tax Cases　(DLA)
S Afr Text... South African Textiles [*A publication*]
S Afr Transp ... South African Transport [*A publication*]
S Afr Treas ... South African Treasurer [*A publication*]
S Afr Tunnelling ... South African Tunnelling [*A publication*]
S-Afr Tydskr Antarkt Navors ... Suid-Afrikaanse Tydskrif vir Antarktiese Navorsing [*A publication*]
S Afr Tydskr Chem ... Suid-Afrikaanse Tydskrif vir Chemie [*A publication*]
S-Afr Tydskr Chir ... Suid-Afrikaanse Tydskrif vir Chirurgie [*A publication*]
S-Afr Tydskr Geneeskd ... Suid-Afrikaanse Tydskrif vir Geneeskunde [*A publication*]
S-Afr Tydskr Lab Kliniekwerk ... Suid-Afrikaanse Tydskrif Laboratorium en Kliniekwerk [*A publication*]
S-Afr Tydskr Landbouwet ... Suid-Afrikaanse Tydskrif vir Landbouwetenskap [*A publication*]
S-Afr Tydskr Med Lab Tegnol ... Suid-Afrikaanse Tydskrif vir Mediese Laboratorium-Tegnologie [*A publication*]
S-Afr Tydskr Obstet Ginekol ... Suid-Afrikaanse Tydskrif vir Obstetrie en Ginekologie [*A publication*]
S-Afr Tydskr Radiol ... Suid-Afrikaanse Tydskrif vir Radiologie [*A publication*]
S-Afr Tydskr Suiweltegnol ... Suid-Afrikaanse Tydskrif vir Suiweltegnologie [*A publication*]
S-Afr Tydskr Veekd ... Suid-Afrikaanse Tydskrif vir Veekunde [*A publication*]
S-Afr Tydskr Voeding ... Suid-Afrikaanse Tydskrif vir Voeding [*A publication*]
S-Afr Tydskr Wet ... Suid-Afrikaanse Tydskrif vir Wetenskap [*A publication*]
S-Afr Wet Nywerheid-Navorsingsraad Navorsingsversl ... Suid-Afrikaanse Wetenskaplike en Nywerheidnavorskingsraad. Navorsingsverslag [*A publication*]
S-Afr Wet Nywerheid-Navorsingsraad Spes Versl ... Suid-Afrikaanse Wetenskaplike en Nywerheidnavorskingsraad. Spesiale Verslag [*A publication*]
S Afr Wool Text Res Inst Annu Rep ... South African Wool Textile Research Institute. Annual Report [*A publication*]
S Afr Wool Text Res Inst Tech Rep ... South African Wool Textile Research Institute. Technical Report [*A publication*]
S Afr YIL..... South African Yearbook of International Law [*A publication*]
SAFS.......... Secondary Air Force Specialty
Saf Sci Abstr ... Safety Science Abstracts Journal [*A publication*]
SAFSCOM ... Safeguard System Command [*Obsolete*] [*Army*]　(AABC)
SAFSEA ... Safeguard System Evaluation Agency [*Army*]　(AABC)
Saf Ser IAEA ... Safety Series. IAEA [*International Atomic Energy Agency*] [*A publication*]
SAFSIM..... Safeguard System Simulation [*Missile system evaluation*] [*Army*]　(RDA)
SAFSL........ Secretary of the Air Force Space Liaison　(MCD)
SAFSM....... Safeguard System Manager [*Army*]
SAFSO ...... Safeguard System Office [*Army*]　(AABC)
SAFSR ...... Society for the Advancement of Food Service Research
SAFT........ Society for the Advancement of the Field Theory　(EA)
SAFTAC.... Semiautomatic Facility for Terminal Area Control
SAFTCP.... Safeguard Tactical Communications Plan [*Army*]　(AABC)
SAFTCS..... Safeguard Tactical Communications System [*Army*]　(AABC)
SAFTO ...... South African Foreign Trade Organisation
SAFTRANS ... Safeguard Transportation System [*Army*]　(AABC)
SAFTU .... South African Federation of Trade Unions
Safugetierkd Mitt ... Safugetierkundliche Mitteilungen [*A publication*]
SAFUS ...... Under Secretary of the Air Force
SAFWA ..... Southeastern Association of Fish and Wildlife Agencies [*Formerly, SAGFC*]　(EA)
SAFX.......... Saw Fixture [*Tool*]　(AAG)
s-ag---........ Argentina [*MARC geographic area code*] [*Library of Congress*]　(LCCP)
SAG............ Saga [*Japan*] [*Seismograph station code, US Geological Survey*]　(SEIS)
SAG............ Sage Energy Co. [*American Stock Exchange symbol*]
Sag............ Saggiatore [*A publication*]
SAG............ Sagwon, AK [*Location identifier*] [*FAA*]　(FAAL)
SAG............ Saint Anthony's Guild
SAG............ St. Apollonia Guild　(EA)
SAG............ Salicyl Acyl Glucuronide [*Organic chemistry*]
sag .... Sango [*MARC language code*] [*Library of Congress*]　(LCCP)
SAG............ Screen Actors Guild　(EA)
SAG............ Secretaria de Agricultura y Ganaderia [*Mexico*]
SAG............ Seismic Air Gun
SAG............ Semiautogenous Grinding System [*Ore-crushing process*]
SAG............ Service Advisory Group　(NATG)
SAG............ Signal Actuated Gate
SAG............ Significant Air Gap
SAG............ Society of Arthritic Gardeners
SAG............ Sowjetische Aktiengesellschaften [*Soviet Corporations*] [*East Germany*]
SAG............ Standard Address Generator　(IEEE)
SAG............ Strategic Communications Ltd. [*Vancouver Stock Exchange symbol*]
SAG............ Study Advisory Group [*Army*]
SAG............ Submarine Analysis Group [*Navy*]　(CAAL)

S/Ag.......... Supervised Agency　(DLA)
SAG............ Surface Action Group [*Military*]　(NVT)
SAG............ Surface Attack Group [*Navy*]　(CAAL)
SAG............ Systems Analysis Group
SAGA .... Saint-Gaudens National Historic Site
SAGA .... Sand and Gravel Association of Great Britain
SAGA .... Short-Arc Geodetic Adjustment [*Geophysics*]
SAGA .... Smocking Arts Guild of America　(EA)
SAGA .... Society of American Graphic Artists　(EA)
SAGA .... Software AG Systems Group [*NASDAQ symbol*]　(NQ)
SAGA .... Stage and Arena Guild of America
SAGA .... Studies, Analysis, and Gaming Agency [*Military*]
SAGA .... System for Automatic Generation and Analysis
Saga-Book ... Saga-Book of the Viking Society for Northern Research [*A publication*]
Saga S....... Saga och Sed [*A publication*]
SAGE .... Sage Drilling Co. [*NASDAQ symbol*]　(NQ)
SAGE .... Scientific Advisory Group on Effects [*DoD*]　(EGAO)
SAGE .... Semiautomatic Ground Environment [*US defense system*]
SAGE .... Senior Action in a Gay Environment [*New York, NY*]　(EA)
SAGE .... Skylab Advisory Group for Experiments [*NASA*]
SAGE .... Society for the Advancement of the George Economy [*Defunct*]　(EA)
SAGE .... Society for the Advancement of Good English　(EA)
SAGE .... Solar-Assisted Gas Energy [*Water heating*] [*NASA*]
SAGE .... South African General Electric Co.
SAGE .... Special Assistant for Growing Enterprises [*Division of National American Wholesale Grocer's Association*]
SAGE .... Sterilization Aerospace Ground Equipment　(KSC)
SAGE .... Strategic Analysis Guidance and Estimate　(MCD)
SAGE .... Stratospheric Aerosol Gas Experiment
Sage Annu R Communic Res ... Sage Annual Reviews of Communication Research [*A publication*]
Sage Elect Stud Yb ... Sage Electoral Studies Yearbook [*A publication*]
Sage Int Yb For Pol Stud ... Sage International Yearbook of Foreign Policy Studies [*A publication*]
SAGEM ...... Societe d'Applications Generals d'Electricite et de Mecanique [*France*]
SA Geol Atlas Ser ... South Australia. Geological Survey. Atlas Series [*A publication*]
SA Geol Surv Bull ... South Australia. Geological Survey. Bulletin [*A publication*]
SA Geol Surv Geol Atlas 1 Mile Ser ... South Australia. Geological Survey. Geological Atlas. 1 Mile Series [*A publication*]
SA Geol Surv Rep Invest ... South Australia. Geological Survey. Report of Investigations [*A publication*]
Sage Pap CP ... Sage Professional Papers in Comparative Politics [*A publication*]
Sage Pub Admin Abstr ... Sage Public Administration Abstracts [*A publication*]
SAGES .... Society American Gastrointestinal Endoscopic Surgeons [*Philadelphia, PA*]　(EA)
Sage Urb Stud Abstr ... Sage Urban Studies Abstracts [*A publication*]
Sage Yb Polit Publ Pol ... Sage Yearbooks in Politics and Public Policy [*A publication*]
Sage Yb Women's Pol ... Sage Yearbook in Women's Policy Studies [*A publication*]
SAGFC .... Southeastern Association of Game and Fish Commissioners [*Later, SAFWA*]　(EA)
SAGGE...... Synchronous Altitude Gravity Gradient Experiment
Saggi.......... Saggi e Ricerche di Letteratura Francese [*A publication*]
SAGI.......... South-African Garrisons Institutes [*Military*] [*British*]　(ROG)
SAGI.......... Specialty Advertising Guild International [*Later, SAA*]　(EA)
SAGM........ Separate Absorption, Grading, and Multiplication Layers [*Semiconductor technology*]
SAGMI....... Surface Attack Guided Missile　(MCD)
SAGMN...... Sudhoffs Archiv fuer Geschichte der Medizin und der Naturwissenschaften [*A publication*]
SAGMOS ... Self-Aligning Gate Metal Oxide Semiconductor　(IEEE)
SAGN .... Sagkeeng News [*Fort Alexander, MB*] [*A publication*]
SA-GOR ..... Security Assistance - General Operational Requirement [*Military*]　(AFIT)
SAGP .... Society for Ancient Greek Philosophy　(EA)
SAGS .... Semiactive Gravity-Gradient System [*NASA*]
SAGSET..... Society for Academic Gaming and Simulation in Education and Training
SAGU .... Saguaro National Monument
SAGW .... Surface-to-Air Guided Weapon [*British*]
SAH............ S-Adenosylhomocysteine [*Biochemistry*]
SaH .... Saat auf Hoffnung　(BJA)
SAH............ Sachem Exploration [*Vancouver Stock Exchange symbol*]
SAH............ Sanaa [*Yemen Arab Republic*] [*Airport symbol*]　(OAG)
SaH .... Sandoz Pharmaceuticals [*Research code symbol*]
SAH............ Semiactive Homer [*Missiles*]
SAH............ Sitzungsberichte. Heidelberg Akademie der Wissenschaften. Philosophisch-Historische Klasse [*A publication*]
SAH............ Society of American Historians　(EA)
SAH............ Society of Architectural Historians　(EA)
SAH............ Society of Automotive Historians　(EA)
SAH............ Standard Allowed Hours
SAH............ Stratford-On-Avon Herald [*A publication*]

SAH............ Subarachnoid Hemorrhage [*Medicine*]
SAH............ Supreme Allied Headquarters [*World War II*]
SAH............ Svenska Akademiens Handlingar [*A publication*]
SAHA.......... Society of American Historical Artists (EA)
SAHARA..... Synthetic Aperture High Altitude RADAR (AAG)
SAHC.......... S-Adenosylhomocysteine [*Biochemistry*]
SAHC.......... Self-Aligning Hydraulic Cylinder
SAHEA........ Sanitaer- und Heizungstechnik [*A publication*]
SAHF.......... Semiautomatic Height Finder
SAHG.......... Die Sumerischen und Akkadischen Hymnen und Gebete [*Zurich/Stuttgart*] [*A publication*]
SAHI............ Sagamore Hill National Historic Site
SAHLBull..... Societe d'Art et d'Histoire du le Diocese de Liege. Bulletin [*A publication*]
SAHOA........ Saiko To Hoan [*A publication*]
SA Homes & Gardens ... South Australian Homes and Gardens [*A publication*]
SAHPS........ Solar Energy Assisted Heat Pump System
SAHS.......... Swiss-American Historical Society (EA)
SAHS.......... Swiss American Historical Society. Newsletter [*A publication*]
SAHSA........ Servicio Aereo de Honduras, Sociedad Anonima
SAHYB........ Simulation of Analog and Hybrid Computers
SAI.............. Allstar Inns [*American Stock Exchange symbol*]
SAI.............. Saigo [*Japan*] [*Seismograph station code, US Geological Survey*] (SEIS)
SAI.............. Schizophrenics Anonymous International [*Later, Canadian Schizophrenia Foundation*] (EA)
SAI.............. Science Applications, Incorporated (NRCH)
SAI.............. Science Associates/International [*Publisher*] (EA)
SAI.............. Scientific Aid to Indochina [*Task force established 1973 by Scientists' Institute for Public Information*]
SAI.............. Scientific Associates, Incorporated (AAG)
SAI.............. Scriptwriters' Association International [*Defunct*] (EA)
SAI.............. Self-Analysis Inventory [*Psychology*]
SAI.............. Seltene Assyrische Ideogramme [*A publication*]
SAI.............. Senior Advocates International [*Defunct*] (EA)
SAI.............. Senior Army Instructor
SAI.............. Shoplifters Anonymous International [*Glen Mills, PA*] (EA)
SAI.............. Sigma Alpha Iota [*International professional music fraternity for women*] (EA)
SAI.............. Social Adequacy Index
SAI.............. Societa Anonima Italiana [*Stock company*] [*Italian*]
SAI.............. Software Access International, Inc. [*Information service*] (EISS)
SAI.............. Son Altesse Imperiale [*His or Her Imperial Highness*] [*French*]
sai.............. South American Indian [*MARC language code*] [*Library of Congress*] (LCCP)
SAI.............. Southern Alberta Institute of Technology [*UTLAS symbol*]
SAI.............. Special Accident Insurance (MCD)
SAI.............. Specific Acoustic Impedance
SAI.............. Spherical Attitude Indicator (MCD)
SAI.............. Standby Airspeed [*or Attitude*] Indicator (MCD)
SAI.............. State Agency Issuance [*Employment and Training Administration*] (OICC)
SAI.............. Statistical Abstracts of Israel [*A publication*]
SAI.............. Steering Axis Inclination [*Automotive engineering*]
SAI.............. Stern Activities Index [*Psychology*]
SAI.............. Subarchitectural Interface
SAI.............. Suburban Action Institute [*Later, MAI*] (EA)
SAI.............. Sudden Auroral Intensity
SAI.............. Sugar Association, Incorporated [*Washington, DC*] (EA)
SAI.............. Sun Air International [*Ft. Lauderdale, FL*] [*FAA designator*] (FAAC)
SAI.............. Surveillance Aided Intercept (NVT)
SAI.............. System Analysis Indicator (MCD)
SAIA.......... Survival of American Indians Association (EA)
SAIAS........ Ship Aircraft Inertial Alignment System (NG)
SAIB.......... Safe Area Intelligence Brief (MCD)
SAIB.......... Sucrose Acetate Isobutyrate [*Organic chemistry*]
SAIC.......... School of the Art Institute of Chicago
SAIC.......... Science Applications International Corporation [*Orlando, FL*]
SAIC.......... Small-Arms Interpost Competition [*Military*]
SAIC.......... South African Indian Congress (PD)
SAIC.......... Special Agent in Charge
SAIC.......... Switch Action Interrupt Count
SAICAR...... Succinoaminoimidazolecarboxamide Ribonucleotide [*Biochemistry*]
SAID.......... Safe Area Intelligence Description (MCD)
SAID.......... Safety Analysis Input Data (NRCH)
SAID.......... Semiautomatic Integrated Documentation
SAID.......... Specific Adaptation to Improved Demands [*Sports medicine*]
SAID.......... Speech Auto-Instructional Device
SAID.......... Supplementary Aviation Information Display
SAIDET...... Single-Axis Inertial Drift Erection Test
SAIDS........ Simian Acquired Immunodeficiency Syndrome [*Animal pathology*]
SAIDS........ Space Analyst Intervention Display System (MCD)
SAIE.......... Special Acceptance Inspection Equipment
SAIF.......... Standard Avionics Integrated Fuzing [*Air Force*]
SAIFER...... Safe Arm Initiation from Electromagnetic Radiation
SAIG.......... SAI Group, Inc. [*NASDAQ symbol*] (NQ)

SAIG.......... South Australian Industrial Gazette [*A publication*]
SAIGA........ Saishin Igaku [*A publication*]
SAIGB........ Sangyo Igaku [*A publication*]
SAIIC.......... South and Central American Indian Information Center (EA)
SAIL.......... Sea-Air Interaction Laboratory [*Oceanography*]
SAIL.......... Ship's Armament Inventory List [*Navy*]
SAIL.......... Shuttle Avionics Integration Laboratory [*NASA*]
SAIL.......... Simple Analytical Interactive Language [*Data processing*]
SAIL.......... Stanford Artificial Intelligence Laboratory [*Stanford University*]
SAILA........ Sail Assist International Liaison Association (EA)
SAILA........ Sault Area International Library Association [*Library network*]
SAILEDREP ... Sailing Report [*Navy*] (NVT)
SAILER...... Staffing of African Institutions for Legal Education and Research [*An association*] [*Later, International Legal Center*]
SAILORD.... Sailing Order [*Navy*] (NVT)
SAILREP ... Sailing Report
SAILS........ Seagoing Assembly-Integration-Launch System
SAILS........ Simplified Aircraft Instrument Landing System
SAILS........ Standard Army Intermediate Level System
SAIM.......... South America Indian Mission [*Later, SAM*] (EA)
SAIM.......... Systems Analysis and Integration Model (MCD)
SAIMR........ South African Institute for Medical Research
SAIMS........ Selected Acquisitions, Information, and Management System
SAIMS........ Supersonic Airborne Infrared Measurement System (MCD)
SAIN.......... Society for Advancement in Nursing [*New York, NY*] (EA)
SAIN.......... Systems Associates [*NASDAQ symbol*] (NQ)
Sainan-g-d .. Sainan-Gakuin-Daigaku (BJA)
Sains Malays ... Sains Malaysiana [*Malaysia*] [*A publication*]
SA Inst J .... South Australian Institutes. Journal [*A publication*]
Saint.......... Saint's Digest of Registration Cases [*England*] (DLA)
SAINT........ Salzburg Assembly: Impact of the New Technology
SAINT........ Satellite Array for International and National Telecommunications (MCD)
SAINT........ Satellite Inspection Technique (MCD)
SAINT........ Satellite Inspector and Satellite Interceptor [*Air Force spacecraft program*]
SAINT........ Satellite Interceptor (KSC)
SAINT........ Strategic Artificially Intelligent Nuclear Transport [*Robot series designation in 1986 movie "Short Circuit"*]
SAINT........ Symbolic Automatic Integrator
SAINT........ Systems Analysis of an Integrated Network of Tasks [*Air Force*]
Saint Lawrence Univ Geol Inf and Referral Service Bull ... Saint Lawrence University. Geological Information and Referral Service. Bulletin [*A publication*]
Saint Louis Univ LJ ... Saint Louis University. Law Journal [*A publication*]
SAINTS ..... Single Attack Integrated System
SAIORG...... Supreme Assembly, International Order of Rainbow for Girls [*Freemasonry*] (EA)
SAIP .... Ship Acquisition and Improvement Panel [*Navy*] (CAAL)
SAIP .... Societe d'Applications Industrielle de la Physique
SAIP .... Spares Acquisition Integrated with Production
SAIP .... Submarine Antenna Improvement Program [*Military*]
SAIPL........ Spares Acquisition Incorporated with Production List (MCD)
SAIR .... Saugus Ironworks National Historic Site
SAIR .... Semiannual Inventory Report [*Air Force*] (AFM)
SAIR .... South Australian Industrial Reports [*A publication*]
Sairaanh Vuosik ... Sairaanhoidon Vuosikirja [*A publication*]
SAIRR........ South African Institute of Racial Relations
SAIS.......... School of Advanced International Studies
SAIS.......... Societa Agricola Italo-Somala [*Italo-Somali Agricultural Society*]
SAIS.......... Society for American Indian Studies (EA)
SAIS.......... Southwestern American Indian Society [*Later, SAISR*] (EA)
SAISA........ South Atlantic Intercollegiate Sailing Association
SAISAC...... Ship's Aircraft Inertial System Alignment Console
SAISR........ Society for American Indian Studies and Research [*Formerly, SAIS*] (EA)
SAIS Rev.... SAIS [*School of Advanced International Studies*] Review [*A publication*]
SAIT .... Southern Alberta Institute of Technology [*Calgary, AB*]
SAIT News ... SAIT [*South Australian Institute of Teachers*] Newsletter [*A publication*]
Saito Ho-On Kai Mus Res Bull ... Saito Ho-On Kai Museum Research Bulletin [*A publication*]
SAITR........ Special Artificer, Instruments, Typewriter, and Office Equipment Repairman [*Navy*]
SAIWR........ Special Artificer, Instruments, Watch Repairman [*Navy*]
SAJ............ Golden Eagle Aviation [*Bedford, MA*] [*FAA designator*] (FAAC)
SAJ............ St. Joseph Light & Power Co. [*NYSE symbol*]
SAJ............ Salon Resources Corp. [*Vancouver Stock Exchange symbol*]
SAJ............ Society for the Advancement of Judaism (EA)
SAJA.......... Special Approaches to Juvenile Assistance [*An association*] [*Washington, DC*] (EA)
SAJAC........ South African Journal of Animal Science [*A publication*]
SAJAR........ South African Journal of Antarctic Research [*A publication*]
SAJCD........ South African Journal of Chemistry [*A publication*]
SAJE.......... South African Journal of Economics [*Suid-Afrikaanse Tydskrif vir Ekonomie*] [*A publication*]
SA J Educ Res ... South Australian Journal of Education Research [*A publication*]

SAJER .... South Australian Journal of Education Research [*A publication*]

SAJH .... San Juan Island National Historic Park

SAJI .... Saw Jig [*Tool*]

SAJIB .... Societe d'Animation du Jardin et de l'Institut Botaniques [*Canada*]

SAJL .... Studies in American Jewish Literature [*A publication*]

SAJMA .... South African Journal of Medical Sciences [*A publication*]

SAJ Res Sport Phys Educ Recreat ... SA [*South African*] Journal for Research in Sport. Physical Education and Recreation [*A publication*]

SAJS .... School for Advanced Jewish Studies   (BJA)

SAJSA .... South African Journal of Science [*A publication*]

SAJSB .... South African Journal of Surgery [*A publication*]

SAJTA .... South African Journal of Medical Laboratory Technology [*A publication*]

SAK .... Die Sumerischen und Akkadischen Koeningsinschriften [*A publication*]   (BJA)

SAK .... Kalispell, MT [*Location identifier*] [*FAA*]   (FAAL)

SAK .... Sakata [*Japan*] [*Seismograph station code, US Geological Survey*]   (SEIS)

SAK .... Saudarkrokur [*Iceland*] [*Airport symbol*]   (OAG)

SAK .... Stall Lake Mines [*Vancouver Stock Exchange symbol*]

SAK .... Stop Acknowledge   (CMD)

SAK .... Sveriges Arbetarepartiet Kommunisterna [*Swedish Workers' Communist Party*]   (PPW)

SAK .... University of Saskatchewan Libraries [*UTLAS symbol*]

SAKAD .... Sangyo To Kankyo [*A publication*]

SAKB .... Suider Afrikaanse Katolieke Biskopsraad [*Southern African Catholic Bishops' Conference - SACBC*] [*Pretoria, South Africa*]   (EA-IO)

Sakharth SSR Mecn Akad Gamothvl Centr Srom ... Sakharthvelos SSR Mecnierebatha Akademia Gamothvlithi Centris Sromebi [*A publication*]

Sakharth SSR Mecn Akad Marthw Sistem Inst Srom ... Sakharthvelos SSR Mecnierebatha Akademia. Marthwis Sistemebis Instituti Sromebi [*A publication*]

Sakharth SSR Mecn Akad Math Inst Srom ... Sakharthvelos SSR Mecnierebatha Akademia A. Razmadzis Sahelobis Thbilsis Mathematikis Institutis. Sromebi [*A publication*]

Sakharth SSR Mecn Akad Moambe ... Sakharthvelos SSR Mecnierebatha Akademia Moambe [*A publication*]

SAKHB .... Sangyo Anzen Kenkyusho Hokoku [*A publication*]

Sakh Prom ... Sakharnaya Promyshlennost [*A publication*]

Sakh Promst ... Sakharnaya Promyshlennost [*A publication*]

Sakh Svekla ... Sakharnaya Svekla [*A publication*]

SAKI .... Solatron Automatic Keyboard Instructor

SAKOD .... Sangyo Kogai [*A publication*]

SAKSO .... Collective name of Soren Frandsen, Asbjorn Jensen, Kurt Frederiksen, Soren Lundh, and Ole Rud Nielsen when writing in collaboration

Sakura X-Ray Photogr Rev ... Sakura X-Ray Photographic Review [*Japan*] [*A publication*]

SAL .... Anderson County Library, Anderson, SC [*OCLC symbol*]   (OCLC)

SAL .... Saharan Air Layer [*Meteorology*]

SAL .... Salary   (ADA)

Sal .... Salesianum [*A publication*]

sal. .... Salicylate [*Medicine*]

SAL .... Saline

Sal .... Salinger's Reports [*88-117 Iowa*]   (DLA)

SAL .... Salinometer   (KSC)

sal. .... Salishan [*MARC language code*] [*Library of Congress*]   (LCCP)

SAL .... Salivation [*Treatment for syphilis*] [*Slang*] [*British*]   (DSUE)

Sal .... Salmonella [*Bacteriology*]

SAL .... Salo [*Italy*] [*Seismograph station code, US Geological Survey*]   (SEIS)

SAL .... Saluting   (MSA)

SAL .... Salvation Army Shelter   (DSUE)

SAL .... Salvex Resources Ltd. [*Vancouver Stock Exchange symbol*]

SAL .... San Salvador [*El Salvador*] [*Airport symbol*]   (OAG)

SAL .... Sandhills Agriculture Laboratory [*University of Nebraska - Lincoln*] [*Research center*]   (RCD)

SAL .... Saperstein & Associates Limited [*Vancouver, BC*] [*Telecommunications*]   (TSSD)

SAL .... Scientific Airlock   (MCD)

SAL .... Seaboard Air Line R. R. [*Later, SCL*] [*AAR code*]

SAL .... Secundum Artis Leges [*According to the Rules of the Art*] [*Latin*]   (ADA)

SAL .... Selected Altitude Layer [*Decoder*]

SAL .... Semiactive LASER [*Military*]   (CAAL)

SAL .... Sensorineural Acuity Level [*Medicine*]

SAL .... Service Action Log   (AAG)

SAL .... Ship Authorized Leave   (NG)

SAL .... Shipboard Allowance List   (MSA)

SAL .... Short Approach Light [*Aviation*]

SAL .... Shuttle Avionics Laboratory [*NASA*]   (NASA)

SAL .... Solar Arc Lamp

SAL .... Solar Array Leaf

SAL .... Sons of the American Legion   (EA)

SAL .... South Atlantic League [*Nickname: Sally*] [*Baseball*]

SAL .... Southwestern American Literature [*A publication*]

SAL .... Space Astronomy Laboratory [*University of Florida*] [*Research center*]   (RCD)

SAL .... Special Ammunition Load [*Army*]   (AABC)

SAL .... Standard Acceptance Limits

SAL .... Station Allowance Unit   (NATG)

SAL .... Strategic Arms Limitation

SAL .... Structural Adjustment Loan [*World Bank*]

SAL .... Structured Assembly Language

SAL .... Studies in African Linguistics [*A publication*]

SAL .... Subject Authority List [*NASA*]

SAL .... Submarine Alerting and Loading System

SAL .... Supersonic Aerophysics Laboratory   (MCD)

SAL .... Surface Mail Air Lifted   (ADA)

SAL .... Symbolic Assembly Language [*Data processing*]   (DIT)

SAL .... Systems Assembly Language [*Data processing*]   (IEEE)

SALA .... Sammenslutningen af Landbrugets Arbejdsgiverforeninger [*Agricultural Employers' Federation*] [*Copenhagen, Denmark*]

SALA .... Scientific Assistant Land Agent [*Ministry of Agriculture, Fisheries, and Food*] [*British*]

SALA .... Servicios Aeronauticos Latina America

SALA .... Solar Arc Lamp Assembly

SALA .... Southwest Alliance for Latin America   (EA)

SALALM .... Seminars on the Acquisition of Latin American Library Materials

SA Law Reports CP ... South African Law Reports, Cape Provincial Division [*1910-46*]   (DLA)

SA Law Reports CPD ... South African Law Reports, Cape Provincial Division [*1910-46*]   (DLA)

SA Law Reports NPD ... South African Law Reports, Natal Province Division [*1910-46*]   (DLA)

SA Law Reports SWA ... Reports of the High Court of South-West Africa   (DLA)

SA Law Soc Bull ... South Australian Law Society. Bulletin [*A publication*]

SALB .... Studia Albanica [*A publication*]

SALC .... SAL Cable Communications [*NASDAQ symbol*]   (NQ)

SALC .... Special Associated Logistics Course   (MCD)

Sal Comp Cr ... Salaman's Liquidation and Composition with Creditors [*2nd ed.*] [*1882*]   (DLA)

SALCR .... South Australian Licensing Court. Reports [*A publication*]

Saldat Auto ... Saldatura Autogena [*A publication*]

SALDV .... Salvage Dives   (MUGU)

SALE .... Safeguards Analytical Laboratory Evaluation

SALE .... Silicon Avalanche Light Emitter

SALE .... Simple Algebraic Language for Engineers [*Data processing*]

SALEA .... Sanshi Kenkyu [*A publication*]

SALES .... Ship Aircraft Locating Equipment

Sales Mgt ... Sales Management [*Later, Sales and Marketing Management*] [*A publication*]

Sales & Mkt Mgt ... Sales and Marketing Management [*A publication*]

Sales TC .... Sales Tax Cases [*A publication*]

SALF .... Society of American Legion Founders   (EA)

SALF .... Somali Abo Liberation Front [*Ethiopian*]   (PD)

SALF .... Sudan African Liberation Front

SALG .... South American Liaison Group   (CINC)

SAL-GP ..... Semiactive LASER-Guided Projectile   (MCD)

SALI .... Suburban Airlines [*NASDAQ symbol*]   (NQ)

SALIC .... Salicional [*Music*]

SALINET ... Satellite Library Information Network

SALIS .... Salisbury [*England*]

SALIS .... Substance Abuse Librarians and Information Specialists   (EA)

Salisbury Med Bull ... Salisbury Medical Bulletin [*A publication*]

SALit .... Studies in American Literature [*A publication*]

SA L J .... South African Law Journal [*A publication*]

Salk .... Salkeld's English King's Bench Reports [*91 English Reprint*]   (DLA)

Salk (Eng) ... Salkeld's English King's Bench Reports [*91 English Reprint*]   (DLA)

SALL .... Sallust [*Roman historian, 86-34BC*] [*Classical studies*]   (ROG)

SALL .... Shore Activity Load List

SALLIE MAE ... Student Loan Marketing Association [*See also SLMA*]

Salm .... Salmagundi [*A publication*]

Salm .... Salmanassar   (BJA)

Salm .... Salmanticensis [*A publication*]

SALM .... Single Anchor Leg Mooring [*Oil platform*]

SALM .... Society of Air Line Meteorologists

Salm Abr ... Salmon's Abridgment of State Trials   (DLA)

Salmant ..... Salmanticensis [*Salmanca, Spain*] [*A publication*]   (BJA)

Salmon Trou Mag ... Salmon and Trout Magazine [*A publication*]

Salm St R ... Salmon's Edition of the State Trials   (DLA)

SALO .... Stop Authorization and Lift Order   (AAG)

SALOP ...... Shrewsbury [*British depot code*]

SALOP ...... Shropshire [*County in England*]

SALORS .... Structural Analysis of Layered Orthotropic Ring-Stiffened Shells [*Computer program*] [*NASA*]

SALP .... Sodium Aluminum Phosphate [*Inorganic chemistry*]

SALP .... South African Labour Party

SALP .... Systematic Assessment of Licensee Performance [*Nuclear energy*]   (NRCH)

SALR .... Saturation Adiabatic Lapse Rate [*Meteorology*]   (ADA)

SALR......... South African Law Reports [*A publication*]
SALR......... South Australian Law Reports [*A publication*]
SALR......... Synthetic Aperture LASER RADAR
SALRCP..... South African Law Reports, Cape Provincial Division [*1910-46*] (DLA)
SAL Reports OPD ... South African Law Reports, Orange Free State Provincial Division [*1910-46*] (DLA)
SALR SWA ... South African Law Reports, South West African Reports (DLA)
SALS......... Short Approach Light System [*Aviation*]
SALS......... Small-Angle Light Scattering
SALS......... Solid-State Acoustoelectric Light Scanner
SALS......... Southern Adirondack Library System [*Library network*]
SALS......... Standard Army Logistics System
SALSF....... Short Approach Light System with Sequenced Flashers [*Aviation*]
SALS-K..... Single Ammunition Logistics System - Korea (MCD)
SALSSAH ... Serials in Australian Libraries: Social Sciences and Humanities [*A publication*]
SALSSAH/NRT ... Serials in Australian Libraries: Social Sciences and Humanities/Newly Reported Titles [*A publication*]
SALSU ...... Singapore Admiralty Local Staff Union
SaLSUA ..... Sierra Leone Students Union of the Americas (EA)
Salt.......... De Saltatione [*of Lucian*] [*Classical studies*] (OCD)
SALT......... Salvation and Laughter Together (EA)
SALT......... Self-Contained All-Weather Landing and Taxiing (MCD)
SALT......... Serum Alanine Aminotransferase [*An enzyme*]
SALT......... Sisters All Learning Together [*Feminist group*]
SALT......... Skin-Associated Lymphoid Tissue [*Dermatology*]
SALT......... Society of American Law Teachers (EA)
SALT......... Society for Applied Learning Technology [*Warrenton, VA*] (EA)
SALT......... South African Law Times (DLA)
SALT......... State Agency Libraries of Texas [*Library network*]
SALT......... Strategic Arms Limitation Talks [*US/USSR*]
SALT......... Subscribers' Apparatus Line Tester [*Telecommunications*] (TEL)
SALT......... Symbolic Algebraic Language Translator [*Data processing*]
Salt C R..... New Salt Creek Reader [*A publication*]
SALTE....... Semiautomatic Line Test Equipment (NG)
SalTerz ...... Sal Terrae. Revista Hispanoamericana de Cultura Ecclesiastica [*Santander, Spain*] [*A publication*] (BJA)
SALTHQ.... Strike Command Alternate Headquarters [*Military*] (AABC)
SALTI........ Summary Accounting for Low-Dollar Turnover Items [*Army*]
Salt Lake M Rv ... Salt Lake Mining Review [*A publication*]
Salt Res Ind ... Salt Research and Industry [*A publication*]
SALTS....... Systems Alterations Status
Salud Publica Mex ... Salud Publica de Mexico [*A publication*]
SALUT .... Sea, Air, Land, and Underwater Targets [*Navy*]
SALUTE ..... Size, Activity, Location, Unit, Time, Equipment (MCD)
Salute Italia Med ... Salute Italia Medica [*A publication*]
SALV......... Duty Salvage Ship [*Navy*] (NVT)
SALV......... Salvador [*Brazil*] (ROG)
SALV......... Salvage (AFM)
Salv Div Bad ... Salvage Diver Badge [*Army*]
SALVDV..... Salvage Dives [*Army*]
SALVEX..... Salvage Exercise (MCD)
SALVOPS ... Salvage Operations [*Navy*] (NVT)
SALVTNG ... Salvage Training [*Navy*] (NVT)
SALWIS...... Shipboard Air-Launched Weapons Installation System (NG)
SALX......... Shamrock Airlines [*Air carrier designation symbol*]
SALY......... Salary (ROG)
Salzburger Jrbh Phil ... Salzburger Jahrbuch fuer Philosophie [*A publication*]
Salzburg Haus Nat Ber Abt B Geol-Mineral Samml ... Salzburg Haus der Natur. Berichte. Abteilung B. Geologisch-Mineralogische Sammlungen [*A publication*]
SAM .... S-Adenosylmethione [*Also, AdoMet, SAMe*] [*Biochemistry*]
SAM .... Safety Activation Monitor (IEEE)
SAM .... Salamo [*Papua New Guinea*] [*Airport symbol*] (OAG)
SAM .... Salicylamide [*Analgesic compound*]
Sam .... Samaria (BJA)
Sam............ Samaritan (BJA)
sam .... Samaritan Aramaic [*MARC language code*] [*Library of Congress*] (LCCP)
SAM .... Samarkand [*USSR*] [*Seismograph station code, US Geological Survey*] (SEIS)
Sam........... Samisdat [*A publication*]
Sam........... Sammlung [*A publication*]
SAM .... Sample and Analysis Management System [*Data processing*]
Sam........... Samson (BJA)
SAM .... Samson Energy Co. [*American Stock Exchange symbol*]
SAM .... Samsville, IL [*Location identifier*] [*FAA*] (FAAL)
Sam........... Samuel [*Old Testament book*]
SAM .... Scanning Acoustic Microscope
SAM .... Scanning Auger Microprobe [*Electron microscopy*]
SAM .... School of Aerospace Medicine [*Formerly, School of Aviation Medicine*]
SAM .... School in Agency Management [*LIMRA*]
SAM .... School Apperception Method [*Psychology*]

SAM .... School of Assets Management [*Army*] [*Later, School of Materiel Readiness*]
S Am .... Scientific American [*A publication*]
SAM .... Script Applier Mechanism [*Programing language*] [*1975*] (CSR)
SAM .... Sea Air Mariner
SAM .... Selective Automatic Monitoring
SAM .... Self-Propelled Anthropomorphic Manipulator [*Moon machine*]
SAM .... Semantic Analyzing Machine
SAM .... Semiautomatic Mathematics (IEEE)
SAM .... Semiautomatic Mounter [*3M Co.*]
SAM .... Send-a-Message (MCD)
SAM .... Sequential Access Memory [*Data processing*] (IEEE)
SAM .... Sequential Access Method [*IBM Corp.*] [*Data processing*]
SAM .... Serial Access Memory [*Data processing*]
SAM .... Service Attitude Measurement [*Bell System*]
Sam .... Serving Advertising in the Midwest [*Later, Adweek*] [*A publication*]
SAM .... Sex Arousal Mechanism [*Medicine*]
SAM .... Shared Appreciation Mortgage
SAM .... Shuttle Attachment Manipulator [*NASA*]
SAM .... Signal Analyzing Monitor (KSC)
SAM .... Signal [*System*] for Assessment and Modification [*of behavior*] [*Patented*]
SAM .... Simulated Assignment Model
SAM .... Simulation of Analog Methods [*Data processing*]
SAM .... Single Application Method [*College admissions*]
SAM .... Sinusoidal Amplitude Modulation [*Physics*]
SAM .... Sitzungsberichte der Bayerischen Akademie der Wissenschaften [*Munich*] [*A publication*]
SAM .... Sociedad Aeronautica de Medellin
SAM .... Sociedad Aeronautica de Medellin Consolidada [*Colombia*]
SAM .... Societe des Americanistes
SAM .... Society for Adolescent Medicine [*Granada Hills, CA*] (EA)
SAM .... Society for Advancement of Management [*Formed by a merger of Taylor Society and Society of Industrial Engineers*] [*Cincinnati, OH*] (EA)
SAM .... Society of American Magicians (EA)
SAM .... Society of Americanists (EA)
SAM .... Society of Antique Modelers (EA)
SAM .... Society for Asian Music (EA)
SAM .... Soldier, Sailor, Airman, Marine [*A publication*]
SAM .... Sort and Merge
SAM .... Sound Absorption Material [*Aviation*]
SAM .... Sourcebook in Applied Mathematics [*National Science Foundation project*]
SAM .... South America Mission (EA)
SAM .... Southern Appalachian Migrant [*Cincinnati slang*]
SAM .... Space Available Mail [*Military*] (AABC)
SAM .... Special Advisory Message
SAM .... Special Air Mission [*Aircraft*]
SAM .... Spills, Accidents, and Mixtures [*of Exxon Corp.'s "Stop SAM" safety program*]
SAM .... Squarewave Amplitude Modulation
SAM .... Stabilized Assay Meter (NRCH)
SAM .... Stage Assembly and Maintenance [*Building*]
SAM .... Standard Addition Method [*Mathematics*]
SAM .... Standard Arm Missile (MCD)
SAM .... Standard Assembly Module [*Eastman Kodak Co.*]
SAM .... Stimuli and Measurements (KSC)
SAM .... Strachey and McIlroy [*in SAM/76, a programing language named after its authors and developed in 1976*] (CSR)
SAM .... Stratospheric Aerosol Measurement [*or Monitor*] [*Meteorology*]
SAM .... Strela Antiaircraft Missiles
SAM .... Stroboscopic Analyzing Monitor [*Instrumentation*]
SAM .... Structural Acoustic Monitor
SAM .... Structural Assembly Model [*NASA*]
SAM .... Student Achievement Monitoring [*Vocational guidance*]
SAM .... Study of American Markets [*US News and World Report*]
SAM .... Subject Activity Monitor [*Device used in biological research*]
SAM .... Subsequent Address Message [*Telecommunications*] (TEL)
SAM .... Substitute Alloy Material [*Nuclear energy*]
SAM .... Substrate-Attached Material [*Cytology*]
SAM .... Subsynoptic Advection Model
SAM .... Subtraction, Addition, Multiplication
SAM .... Sulfur-Asphalt Module [*Road-paving technology*]
SAM .... Surface-Active Material
SAM .... Surface-to-Air Missile
SAM .... Symbolic and Algebraic Manipulation (IEEE)
SAM .... Synchronous Amplitude Modulation
SAM .... System Accuracy Model
SAM .... System Activity Monitor [*Data processing*]
SAM .... Systems Adapter Module
SAM .... Systems Analysis Module (IEEE)
SAM .... Systolic Anterior Motion [*Cardiology*]
SAMA........ Sacramento Air Materiel Area
SAMA........ Salem Maritime National Historic Site
SAMA........ Scientific Apparatus Makers Association [*Washington, DC*] (EA)
SAMA......... Serum Agar Measuring Aid

SAMA......... Site Approval and Market Analysis [*FHA*]
SAMA......... Specialty Automotive Manufacturers Association [*Newport Beach, CA*] (EA)
SAMA......... Student American Medical Association [*Later, AMSA*] (EA)
SAMAA ...... Special Assistant for Military Assistance Affairs [*Army*] (AABC)
SAMAC ...... Scientific and Management Advisory Committee [*Terminated, 1973*] [*Army Computer Systems Command*]
SAM Advanced Mgt J ... SAM [*Society for Advancement of Management*] Advanced Management Journal [*A publication*]
SAM Adv Man ... SAM [*Society for Advancement of Management*] Advanced Management Journal [*A publication*]
SAMAE ...... Southern Air Materiel Area, Europe
SAMANTHA ... System for the Automated Management of Text from a Hierarchical Arrangement
SAMAP ...... Southern Air Materiel Area, Pacific [*Army*] (AFIT)
SAMAR ...... Ship Activation, Maintenance, and Repair
SAMAR ...... Surface-to-Air Missile Availability Report (NG)
Samaru Agric Newsl ... Samaru Agricultural Newsletter [*A publication*]
Samaru Agr Newslett ... Samaru Agricultural Newsletter [*A publication*]
Samaru Inst Agric Res Soil Surv Bull ... Samaru Institute for Agricultural Research. Soil Survey Bulletin [*A publication*]
Samaru Misc Pap ... Samaru Miscellaneous Paper [*A publication*]
Samaru Res Bull ... Samaru Research Bulletin [*A publication*]
SAMAS ...... Security Assistance Manpower Accounting System (MCD)
SAM-B ...... School of Aviation [*later, Aerospace*] Medicine - Brooks
SAMB......... Secondary Aircraft Maintenance Base
SAMBA ...... Saudi American Bank
SAMBA ...... Special Agents Mutual Benefit Association [*FBI standardized term*]
SAMBA ...... Systems Approach to Managing BUSHIPS [*Bureau of Ships; later, NESC or ESC*] Acquisition [*Navy*] (MCD)
SAMBHist ... Societe des Antiquaires de la Morinie. Bulletin Historique [*A publication*]
SAMBO ...... Strategic Antimissile Barrage Objects
SAMBUD .... System for Automation of Materiel Plan for Army Materiel/ Budget (AABC)
SAMC......... South African Medical Corps
SAMC......... Southern Africa Media Center (EA)
SamChron ... Samaritan Chronology (BJA)
SAMCO ...... Sales Associates Management Corporation [*Palm Springs, CA*] (EA)
SAMCOS ... Senior Army Materiel Command Orientation Seminar
SAMCTT .... School of Aerospace Medicine Color Threshold Test
SAMCU ...... Special Airborne Medical Care Unit (MCD)
SAMD......... Surface-to-Air Missile Development
SAM-DC..... S-Adenosylmethionine Decarboxylase [*An enzyme*]
SAMe......... S-Adenosylmethionine [*Also, AdoMet, SAM*] [*Biochemistry*]
SAME......... [*The*] S & M Co. [*NASDAQ symbol*] (NQ)
SAME......... Sensory-Afferent/Motor-Efferent [*Neurology*]
SAME......... Society of American Military Engineers (EA)
SAME......... Students Against Misleading Enterprises [*Student legal action organization*]
SAMEA ...... South African Mechanical Engineer [*A publication*]
SAMEB....... SA [*South Africa*] Mining and Engineering Journal [*A publication*]
Same Day Surg ... Same-Day Surgery [*A publication*]
SA Methodist ... South Australian Methodist [*A publication*]
SAMEX....... Shuttle Active-Microwave Experiments (MCD)
SAMEX....... Surface-to-Air Missile Exercise (NVT)
SAMF......... Seaborne Army Maintenance Facilities
SAMF......... Ship's Air Maintenance Facility [*Navy*] (NVT)
SAMF......... Switchable Acoustic Matched Filter
SAMFU...... Self-Adjusting Military Foul-Up [*Slang*]
SAMHSJ .... South Australian Methodist Historical Society. Journal [*A publication*] (ADA)
SAMI......... Selling Areas-Marketing, Incorporated [*New York, NY*] [*Originator and database*] [*Information service*] (EISS)
SAMI......... Sequential Assessment of Mathematics Inventory
SAMI......... Single Action Maintenance Instruction (NG)
SAMI......... Socially Acceptable Monitoring Instruments [*Medicine*]
SAMICS .... Solar Array Manufacturing Industry Costing Standards
SAMICS ..... Systems Applications of Millimeter Wave Contact Seeker (MCD)
SAMID....... Ship Antimissile Integrated Defense [*Program*] [*Navy*]
SAMID....... Surface-to-Air Missile Intercept Development
SA Min Eng J ... SA [*South African*] Mining and Engineering Journal [*A publication*]
SAMIP....... Surface-to-Air Missile Improvement Program (MCD)
SAMIS....... Security Assistance Management Information System (MCD)
SAMIS....... Ship Alteration Management Information System [*Navy*] [*Discontinued*]
SAMIS....... Solar Array Manufacturing Industry Simulation
SAMIS....... Standard Army Management Information System (MCD)
SAMIS....... Structural Analysis and Matrix Inversion System (NRCH)
SAMJA....... South African Medical Journal [*A publication*]
SAML .... Nationella Samlingspartiet [*National Coalition Party*] [*Finland*] (PPE)
Saml.......... Samlaren [*A publication*]
SAML .... Sinus Histiocytes with Massive Lymphadenopathy [*Clinical chemistry*]
SAML .... Standard Army Management Language (AABC)

SAML .... Studies in American Literature [*The Hague*] [*A publication*]
SAMLA...... Southern Atlantic Modern Language Association
SAMM .... Standard Automated Material Management System [*DoD*]
SAMMA ...... Stores Account Material Management System (NG)
SAMMI ...... Signature Analysis Methods for Mission Identification
SAMMIE .... Scheduling Analysis Model for Mission Integrated Experiments [*NASA*] (KSC)
SAMMIE .... System for Aiding Man-Machine Interaction [*Prime Computer (UK) Ltd. and Prime Computers CAD/CAM Ltd.*] [*Software package*]
Samml Geol Fuehrer ... Sammlung Geologischer Fuehrer [*A publication*]
Samml Goeschen ... Sammlung Goeschen [*A publication*]
Samml Zwangl Abh Geb Psychiatr Neurol ... Sammlung Zwangloser Abhandlungen aus dem Gebiete der Psychiatrie und Neurologie [*A publication*]
SAMMS...... Ship Alteration Material Management System
SAMMS...... Standard Automated Materiel Management System [*DoD*]
SAMO......... Simulated Ab Initio Molecular Orbitals [*Atomic physics*]
SAMOA ...... Systematic Approach to Multidimensional Occupational Analysis (MCD)
Samoan Pac LJ ... Samoan Pacific Law Journal [*A publication*]
SAMOD ...... Secretary of the Army's Mobility, Opportunity, and Development Program (MCD)
Samoletostr Tekh Vozdushn Flota ... Samoletostroenie i Tekhnika Vozdushnogo Flota [*A publication*]
SAMOS ...... Satellite-Missile Observation Satellite [*or System*]
SAMOS ...... Silicon and Aluminum Metal-Oxide Semiconductor (ADA)
SA Motor ...... South Australian Motor [*A publication*]
SAMP......... Sample (AAG)
SAMP......... Shuttle Automated Mass Properties (MCD)
SAMP......... Stuntmen's Association of Motion Pictures [*North Hollywood, CA*] (EA)
SAMPAC.... Society of Advertising Musicians, Producers, Arrangers, and Composers
SAMPAM ... System for Automation of Materiel Plans for Army Material (MCD)
SAMPD ...... Science Analysis and Mission Planning Directorate [*NASA*]
SAMPE....... Society for the Advancement of Material and Process Engineering [*Formerly, Society of Aerospace Material and Process Engineers*]
SAMPE J.... SAMPE [*Society for the Advancement of Material and Process Engineering*] Journal [*A publication*]
SAMPE Q ... SAMPE [*Society for the Advancement of Material and Process Engineering*] Quarterly [*A publication*]
SAMPE Qtly ... SAMPE [*Society for the Advancement of Material and Process Engineering*] Quarterly [*A publication*]
SAMPLE..... Single Assignment Mathematical Programing Language [*1971*] [*Data processing*] (CSR)
SAMPSP .... Security Assistance Master Planning and Phasing (MCD)
SAMQA...... SAMPE [*Society for the Advancement of Material and Process Engineering*] Quarterly [*A publication*]
SAM & R..... Ship Activation, Maintenance, and Repair
SAMR......... Special Assistant for Material Readiness [*Army*]
SAMRA ...... Sino-American Medical Rehabilitation Association
SAMRAF .... South African Military Refugee Aid Fund (EA)
SAMRD....... South African Machine Tool Review [*A publication*]
SAMRT....... Shared Aperture Medium-Range Tracker (MCD)
SAMS......... Sample Method Survey [*for family housing requirements*] [*Military*] (AABC)
SAMS......... Sampling Analog Memory System
SAMS......... Sandia Air Force Material Study (MCD)
SAMS......... Satellite Automatic Monitoring System [*Programing language*]
SAMS......... Ship's Alteration Management System [*Navy*]
SAMS......... Shore Activity Management Support [*Navy*] (NVT)
SAMS......... Shuttle Attachment Manipulator System [*NASA*]
SAMS......... Society for Advanced Medical Systems [*Later, AAMSI*]
SAMS......... Standard Army Maintenance System (AABC)
SAMS......... Stratospheric and Mesospheric Sounder
SAMSA ...... Standard Army Management System - Supply Support Arrangement
SAM-SAC ... Specialized Aircraft Maintenance - Strategic Air Command (AAG)
SAMSARS ... Satellite-Based Maritime Search and Rescue System [*Telecommunications*] (TEL)
SAM/SAT ... South America/South Atlantic Regional Area [*Aviation*]
SAMSAT .... Surface-to-Air Missile Servicing, Assembly, and Test
SAMSEM ... Ship Antimissile System Engagement Model [*Navy*] (CAAL)
SAMSI....... Spacecraft Array for Michelson Spectral Inferometry
SAMSIM ..... Surface-to-Air Missile Simulation Model (MCD)
SAMSO ...... Space and Missile Systems Organization [*Merger of Ballistic Systems Division and Space Systems Division*] [*Air Force*]
SAMSO ...... Systems Analysis of Manned Space Operations (MCD)
SAMSOM ... Support Availability Multisystem Operational Model
SAMSON.... Strategic Automatic Message-Switching Operational Network [*Canada*] (MCD)
SAMSON.... System Analysis of Manned Space Operations (MCD)
SAMSOT.... SAMID [*Ship Antimissile Integrated Defense*] System Operational Test [*Navy*] (NVT)
SAMSq...... Special Air Mission Squadron [*Vietnam Air Force*] (AFM)
SAMT......... Simulated Aircraft Maintenance Trainer (MCD)
SAMT .... State of the Art Medium Terminal (MCD)

SAMT .... State-of-the-Art Medium Terminals
SAMTEC .... Space and Missile Test Center [*Air Force*]
SAMTECM ... Space and Missile Test Center Manual (MCD)
SAMTO ..... Space and Missile Test Organization
SA Museum Rec ... South Australian Museum. Records [*A publication*]
SA Mus Tcr ... South Africa Music Teacher [*A publication*]
SAN .... Gato, CA [*Location identifier*] [*FAA*] (FAAL)
SAN .... San Carlos Milling Co., Inc. [*American Stock Exchange symbol*]
SAN .... San Diego [*California*] [*Airport symbol*] (OAG)
SAN .... San Francisco Helicopter Airlines [*Air carrier designation symbol*]
SAN .... San Francisco Operations Office [*Energy Research and Development Administration*]
SAN .... SAN: Journal of the Society for Ancient Numismatics [*A publication*]
SAN .... Sanatorium
SAN .... Sandersville Railroad Co. [*AAR code*]
SAN .... Sandwich (MSA)
San .... Sanford's Reports [*59 Alabama*] (DLA)
SAN .... Sanitary (AAG)
san .... Sanskrit [*MARC language code*] [*Library of Congress*] (LCCP)
SAN .... Santiago [*Chile*] [*Seismograph station code, US Geological Survey*] (SEIS)
SAN .... School of Air Navigation [*British*]
SAN .... Servicios Aereos Nacionales [*Airline*] [*Ecuadorean*]
SAN .... Severe Acoustic Noise
SAN .... Ship Account Number [*Navy*]
SAN .... Shipping Accumulation Numbers (AAG)
SAN .... Sinoatrial Node [*Medicine*]
SAN .... Society for Ancient Numismatics (EA)
SAN .... Space Age News (AAG)
SAN .... Srpska Akademija Nauka i Umetnosti [*Belgrade, Yugoslavia*]
SAN .... Standard Address Number [*Publishing*]
SAN .... Styrene-Acrylonitrile [*Also, SA*] [*Organic chemistry*]
SAN .... Subsidiary Account Number
SANA .... Slavic American National Association (EA)
SANA .... Societa Anonima Navigazione Aerea [*Italy*]
SANA .... Soycrafters Association of North America (EA)
SANA .... Soyfoods Association of North America (EA)
SANA .... Specialty Advertising National Association [*Later, SAA*] (EA)
SANA .... State, Army, Navy, Air (AABC)
SANA .... Syrian Arab News Agency
SANAA .... Servicio Autonomo Nacional de Acueductos y Alcantarillados [*Honduras*]
SANACC .... State-Army-Navy-Air Force Coordinating Committee [*Terminated, 1949*] (EGAO)
SANAE .... South African National Antarctic Expedition
SANAFREQ ... Safety/NATOPS Frequency (MCD)
SANAn .... Societe Archeologique de Namur. Annales [*A publication*]
SANAT ...... Sanatorium
SA Nat .... South Australian Naturalist [*A publication*]
SA Naturalist ... South Australian Naturalist [*A publication*]
SANB .... South African National Bibliography
SANBAR .... Sanders Barotropic
SANBB .... Sankhya. Series B [*A publication*]
Sanb & B Ann St ... Sanborn and Berryman's Annotated Statutes [*Wisconsin*] (DLA)
San Bernardino County Med Soc Bull ... San Bernardino County Medical Society. Bulletin [*California*] [*A publication*]
SANC .... Sanctuary [*Naval cadet's hiding place for smoking*] [*Slang*] [*British*] (DSUE)
SANC .... Slovak American National Council (EA)
SANCAD ... Scottish Association for National Certificates and Diplomas
San Ch .... Sandford's New York Chancery Reports (DLA)
SANCIP ...... SACLANT [*Supreme Allied Commander, Atlantic*] Approved NATO Common Infrastructure Program (NATG)
San D .... Doctor of Sanitation
SAND .... Sampling Aerospace Nuclear Debris
Sand .... Sandford's New York Superior Court Reports [*3-7 New York*] (DLA)
SAND .... Site Activation Need Date [*NASA*] (NASA)
SAND .... Sorting and Assembly of New Data
SANDA ...... Supplies and Accounts
Sandars Just Inst ... Sandars' Edition of Justinian's Institutes (DLA)
SANDASO ... Bureau of Supplies and Accounts Shipment Order [*Obsolete*] [*Navy*]
Sand Ch .... Sandford's New York Chancery Reports [*1843-47*] (DLA)
Sand Ch R ... Sandford's New York Chancery Reports (DLA)
Sand Chy .... Sandford's New York Chancery Reports (DLA)
Sand Dune Res ... Sand Dune Research [*A publication*]
Sand Essays ... Sanders' Essays on Uses and Trusts [*5th ed.*] [*1844*] (DLA)
Sandf .... Sandford's New York Superior Court Reports [*3-7 New York*] (DLA)
Sandf Ch .... Sandford's New York Chancery Reports (DLA)
Sandf Ch (NY) ... Sandford's New York Superior Court Reports [*3-7 New York*] (DLA)
Sandf Ch Rep ... Sandford's New York Chancery Reports (DLA)
Sandf (NY) R ... Sandford's New York Superior Court Reports (DLA)
Sandford .... Sandford's New York Superior Court Reports (DLA)
Sandford's SCR ... Sandford's New York Superior Court Reports (DLA)

Sandford's Sup Ct R ... Sandford's New York Superior Court Reports (DLA)
Sandf R ...... Sandford's New York Superior Court Reports (DLA)
Sandf SC ... Sandford's New York Superior Court Reports (DLA)
Sandf SCR ... Sandford's New York Superior Court Reports (DLA)
Sandf Suc ... Sandford's Heritable Succession in Scotland (DLA)
Sandf Sup CR ... Sandford's New York Superior Court Reports (DLA)
Sandf Sup Ct ... Sandford's New York Superior Court Reports (DLA)
Sandf Superior Court R ... Sandford's New York Superior Court Reports (DLA)
Sand & H Dig ... Sandels and Hill's Digest of Statutes [*Arkansas*] (DLA)
Sandia SN ... Sandia Science News [*A publication*]
San Diego L Rev ... San Diego Law Review [*A publication*]
San Diego Soc Nat Hist Mem ... San Diego Society of Natural History. Memoirs [*A publication*]
San Diego Soc Nat History Occasional Paper Trans ... San Diego Society of Natural History. Occasional Papers. Transactions [*A publication*]
San Diego Soc Nat History Trans ... San Diego Society of Natural History. Transactions. [*A publication*]
San Diego Soc N H Tr ... San Diego Society of Natural History. Transactions [*A publication*]
Sand Inst Just Introd ... Sandars' Edition of Justinian's Institutes (DLA)
Sand I Rep ... Sandwich Islands Reports [*Hawaii*] (DLA)
San DLR ..... San Diego Law Review [*A publication*]
Sandl St Pap ... Sandler's State Papers (DLA)
SANDOCC ... San Diego Oceanic Coordinating Committee
Sandoz Bull ... Sandoz Bulletin [*A publication*]
Sand R ...... Sandford's New York Superior Court Reports (DLA)
SANDS .... Structural Analysis Numerical Design System
Sand SC .... Sandford's New York Superior Court Reports (DLA)
Sands Ch ... Sandford's New York Chancery Reports (DLA)
Sand SCR ... Sandford's New York Superior Court Reports (DLA)
Sand Sup Ct Rep ... Sandford's New York Superior Court Reports (DLA)
Sand Supr Ct R ... Sandford's New York Superior Court Reports (DLA)
Sand Uses and Trusts ... Sanders' Essays on Uses and Trusts (DLA)
SANE .... National Committee for a Sane Nuclear Policy [*"SANE" alone now used as organization name*] (EA)
San E .... Sanitary Engineer [*Academic degree*]
SANE .... Severe Acoustic Noise Environment
SANE .... Standard Apple Numerics Environment [*Software*] [*Apple Computers, Inc.*]
SANET .... Supplement to Ancient Near Eastern Texts [*A publication*]
SanF .... San Francisco Magazine [*A publication*]
SANF .... Sanford Recreation Area
Sanf .... Sanford's Reports [*59 Alabama*] (DLA)
SANF .... South African Naval Forces
San Fern VL Rev ... San Fernando Valley Law Review [*A publication*]
San FLJ ...... San Francisco Law Journal (DLA)
Sanf (NY) ... Sandford's New York Superior Court Reports [*3-7 New York*] (DLA)
Sanford's Ch R ... Sandford's New York Chancery Reports (DLA)
San Francisco Bus ... San Francisco Business [*A publication*]
San Francisco Micro Soc Tr ... San Francisco Microscopical Society. Transactions [*A publication*]
San Fran Law Bull ... San Francisco Law Bulletin (DLA)
San Fran LJ ... San Francisco Law Journal (DLA)
San Fr LB ... San Francisco Law Bulletin (DLA)
San Fr LJ ... San Francisco Law Journal (DLA)
SANG .... Saudi Arabian National Guard Modernization Program (RDA)
SANG .... Standardized Aeronautical Navigation/Guidance [*Program*] [*Air Force*]
SANGB .... Selfridge Army/Air National Guard Base (MCD)
SANGFPT ... Spherical Angles from Points (MCD)
Sang Natak ... Sangeet Natak [*New Delhi*] [*A publication*]
SANGruz .... Soobscenija Akademiji Nauk Gruzinskoj SSR [*A publication*]
Sanh .... Sanhedrin (BJA)
Sanh .... Sanherib (BJA)
SANH .... Somerset Archaeology and Natural History [*A publication*]
Sanid Aeronaut ... Sanidad Aeronautica [*A publication*]
Sanid Benef Munic ... Sanidad y Beneficiencia Municipal [*A publication*]
SANINSP ... Sanitation Inspector (AABC)
Sanit .... Sanitarium
Sanit .... Sanitary
Sanitary & Heat Eng ... Sanitary and Heating Engineering [*A publication*]
Sanit Eng Pap Colo State Univ ... Sanitary Engineering Papers. Colorado State University [*A publication*]
Sanit Heiz Tech ... Sanitaer- und Heizungstechnik [*A publication*]
Sanit Heizungstech (Duesseldorf) ... Sanitaer- und Heizungstechnik (Duesseldorf) [*A publication*]
Sanit Heizungstechnik ... Sanitaer- und Heizungstechnik [*West Germany*] [*A publication*]
Sanit Nytt ... Sanitets Nytt Utgitt av Forsvarets Sanitet [*A publication*]
Sanit Okh Vodoemov Zagryaz Prom Stochnymi Vodami ... Sanitarnaya Okhrana Vodoemov ot Zagryazneniya Promyshlennymi Stochnymi Vodami [*A publication*]
Sanit Tekh ... Sanitarnaya Tekhnika [*A publication*]
SANJA .... South African Nursing Journal [*A publication*]
San Jose Stud ... San Jose Studies [*A publication*]
San Just ..... Sandars' Edition of Justinian's Institutes (DLA)
SANKA ...... Sans Caffeine [*Acronym used as brand name*]
Sankhya A ... Sankhya. Series A. Indian Journal of Statistics [*A publication*]

Sankhya B ... Sankhya. Series B. Indian Journal of Statistics [*A publication*]
Sankhya C ... Sankhya. Series C. Indian Journal of Statistics [*A publication*]
Sankhya Indian J Stat Ser B ... Sankhya. Series B. Indian Journal of Statistics [*A publication*]
Sankhya Ser A ... Sankhya. The Indian Journal of Statistics. Series A [*A publication*]
Sankhya Ser B ... Sankhya. Series B. Indian Journal of Statistics [*A publication*]
SANLF....... Saudi Arabian National Liberation Front   (BJA)
SANM........ Synthetic Algal Nutrient Medium
SAN MIG ... San Miguel Beer   (DSUE)
SANNA...... Schweizer Archiv fuer Neurologie, Neurochirurgie, und Psychiatrie [*A publication*]
SANOVA .... Simultaneous Analysis of Variance
SANP......... Secondary Auxiliary Nuclear Power
SANR .... Subject to Approval No Risk
SANS .... Schedule for the Assessment of Negative Symptoms [*Psychometrics*]
SANS .... Simplified Account - Numbering System
SANS .... Small-Angle Neutron Scattering
SANS .... South African Naval Service
SANS .... Students Against Nuclear Suicide   (EA)
SAns .... Studia Anselmiana [*A publication*]
SANS .... Swimmer and Navigation System [*Navy*]   (CAAL)
SANSAN .... San Francisco, San Diego [*Proposed name for possible "super-city" formed by growth and mergers of other cities*]
SANSC...... Sanscrit
SANSK...... Sanskrit [*Language, etc.*]
SANSS....... Structure and Nomenclature Search System [*Formerly, SSS*] [*NIH-EPA*]
SANSS...... Substructure and Nomenclature Searching System [*Chemical Information Systems, Inc.*] [*Database*]
SANT......... Santa Monica Bank [*NASDAQ symbol*]   (NQ)
SANT......... Studien zum Alten und Neuen Testament [*A publication*]
S Ant .... Suomen Antropologi/Antropologi i Finland [*A publication*]
SANTA .... Souvenir and Novelty Trade Association [*Philadelphia, PA*]   (EA)
Santa Barbara Mus Nat History Dept Geology Bull ... Santa Barbara Museum of Natural History. Department of Geology. Bulletin [*A publication*]
Santa Barbara Soc N H B ... Santa Barbara Society of Natural History. Bulletin [*A publication*]
Santa Clara L ... Santa Clara Lawyer [*A publication*]
Santa Clara Law ... Santa Clara Lawyer [*A publication*]
Santa Clara L Rev ... Santa Clara Law Review [*A publication*]
Sante Publique (Bucur) ... Sante Publique. Revue Internationale (Bucuresti) [*A publication*]
Santerna De Ass ... Santerna. De Asse Curationibus et Sponsionibus Mercatorum   (DLA)
Sante Secur Soc ... Sante Securite Sociale [*A publication*]
Santo Domingo Univ Anales Pub ... Santo Domingo Universidad Anales. Publicaciones [*A publication*]
Santo Tomas J Med ... Santo Tomas Journal of Medicine [*A publication*]
SANU .... Sudan African National Union [*Political party*]
SA Nurs J... South African Nursing Journal [*A publication*]
SANWFZ .... South Asia Nuclear Weapons-Free Zone
Sanyal........ Sanyal's Criminal Cases between Natives and Europeans [*1796-1895*] [*India*]   (DLA)
SANYD...... Sanitets Nytt [*A publication*]
SANYY .... Sanyo Electric ADR [*NASDAQ symbol*]   (NQ)
SAO .... Saharan Air Outbreak [*Meteorology*]
SAO............ San Andreas Geological Observatory [*California*] [*Seismograph station code, US Geological Survey*]   (SEIS)
SAO............ Sandia Area Office [*Energy Research and Development Administration*]
SAO............ Sao Paulo [*Brazil*] [*Airport symbol*]   (OAG)
SAO............ Secret Army Organization [*English initialism for OAS, terrorist group in Algeria and metropolitan France*]
SAO............ Secretin-Stimulated Acid Output [*Clinical chemistry*]
SAO............ Select Address and Operate
SAO............ Selected Attack Option   (MCD)
SAO............ Single Airlift Organization   (CINC)
SAO............ Smithsonian Astrophysical Observatory
SAO............ Social Actions Office [*or Officer*] [*Air Force*]   (AFM)
SAO............ Sonobuoy Acoustic Operator [*Navy*]   (CAAL)
SAO............ Special Access Only   (MCD)
SAO............ Special Action Office [*Phased out, 1975*] [*Department of Justice*]
SAO............ Special Activities Office [*Air Force*]   (AFM)
SAO............ Special Air Operations
SAO............ Special Artificer, Optical [*Navy*]
SAO............ Special Astrophysics Observatory
SAO............ Splanchnic Artery Occlusion [*Medicine*]
SAO............ Squadron Accountant Officer [*Navy*] [*British*]
SAO............ Staff Administrative Office [*Military*]
SAO............ Studia et Acta Orientalia [*A publication*]
SAO............ Subsidiary/Affiliate Order   (MCD)
SAO............ Support Air Observation [*Navy*]
SAO............ Survey of Agency Opinion [*LIMRA*]

SAO............ Survivor's Assistance Officer [*Army*]   (AABC)
SAO............ Systems Acquisition Officer [*Military*]   (AFIT)
SAO............ Systems Analysis Office
SAOAS...... Secretary of the Army, Office of the Assistant Secretary
SAOAS...... Staff Association of the Organization of American States   (EA)
SAOB........ Svenska Akademiens Ordbok [*A publication*]
SAOC........ Space and Astronautics Orientation Course   (NG)
SAOC .... Studies in Ancient Oriental Civilization. The Oriental Institute of the University of Chicago [*A publication*]
SAOCS...... Submarine Air Optical Communications System   (MCD)
SAODAP .... Special Action Office for Drug Abuse Prevention [*Terminated, 1975*] [*FDA*]
SAO/MEX ... Special Action Office for Mexico [*Drug Enforcement Administration*]
Sao Paulo Brazil Inst Pesqui Tecnol Bol ... Sao Paulo, Brazil. Instituto de Pesquisas Tecnologicas. Boletin [*A publication*]
Sao Paulo Inst Agron (Campinas) Bol ... Sao Paulo Instituto Agronomico (Campinas). Boletim [*A publication*]
Sao Paulo Inst Agron (Campinas) Bol Tec ... Sao Paulo Instituto Agronomico (Campinas). Boletim Tecnico [*A publication*]
Sao Paulo Inst Agron (Campinas) Circ ... Sao Paulo Instituto Agronomico (Campinas). Circular [*A publication*]
Sao Paulo Inst Geogr Geol Bol ... Sao Paulo Instituto Geografico e Geologico. Boletim [*A publication*]
Sao Paulo Inst Geogr Geol Relat ... Sao Paulo Instituto Geografico e Geologico. Relatorio [*A publication*]
Sao Paulo Univ Inst Geocienc Bol ... Sao Paulo. Universidade. Instituto de Geociencias. Boletim [*A publication*]
Sao Paulo Univ Inst Geogr Geogr Planejamento ... Sao Paulo. Universidade. Instituto de Geografia. Geografia e Planejamento [*A publication*]
Sao Paulo Univ Inst Geogr Geomorfol ... Sao Paulo. Universidade. Instituto de Geografia. Geomorfologia [*A publication*]
Sao Paulo Univ Inst Geogr Ser Teses Monogr ... Sao Paulo. Universidade. Instituto de Geografia. Serie Teses e Monografias [*A publication*]
SA Ornithol ... South Australian Ornithologist [*A publication*]
SA Ornithologist ... South Australian Ornithologist [*A publication*]
SAOS .... Select Address [*and Provide*] Output Signal
SAOT .... Semiactive on Target
SAOTA...... Shrimp Association of the Americas   (EA)
SAP .... ASAP Air, Inc. [*Fort Worth, TX*] [*FAA designator*]   (FAAC)
SAP .... San Antonio Public Library, San Antonio, TX [*OCLC symbol*]   (OCLC)
SAP .... San Pedro Sula [*Honduras*] [*Airport symbol*]   (OAG)
SAP .... Sapporo [*Japan*] [*Seismograph station code, US Geological Survey*]   (SEIS)
SAP .... Scientific Advisory Panel [*Arlington, VA*] [*Environmental Protection Agency*]   (EGAO)
SAP .... Scorched Aluminum Powder
SAP .... Scouting Amphibian Plan [*Coast Guard*]
SAP .... Scruple Apothecaries
SAP .... Seaborne Aircraft Platform   (ADA)
SAP .... Second Audio Program
SAP .... Security Assistance Program   (MCD)
SAP .... Semi-Armor-Piercing [*Projectile*] [*Nickname: Sex-Appeal Pete*]
SAP .... Seminal Acid Phosphatase [*An enzyme*]
SAP .... Separate Audio Program [*Television broadcasting*]
SAP .... Serum Alkaline Phosphatase [*Clinical chemistry*]
SAP .... Serum Amyloid P [*Clinical chemistry*]
SAP .... Service Access Point
SAP .... Share Assembly Program [*Data processing*]
SAP .... Ship Acquisition Plan [*Navy*]
SAP .... Shipboard Acoustic Processor [*Navy*]   (CAAL)
SAP .... Shipboard Antenna Pedestal
SAP .... Single-Axis Platform
SAP .... Sintered Aluminum Powder
SAP .... Skeletal Axis of Pinnule
SAP .... Social Action Party [*Thailand*]
SAP .... Socialistische Arbeiderspartij [*Socialist Workers' Party*] [*The Netherlands*]   (PPW)
SAP .... Society for Adolescent Psychiatry   (EA)
SAP .... Society for American Philosophy [*Defunct*]   (EA)
SAP .... Sodium Acid Pyrophosphate [*Also, SAPP*] [*Leavening agent, meat additive*]
SAP .... Soon as Possible
SAP .... South African Party   (PPW)
SAP .... Soysal Adelet Partisi [*Social Justice Party*] [*Turkish Cypriot*]   (PPE)
SAP .... Special and Administrative Provisions [*of the Tariff Act of 1930*]
SAP .... Special Assistance Program   (ADA)
SAP .... Spot Authorization Plan [*WPB*] [*Obsolete*]
SAP .... Spy Against Pollution [*An association*]
SAP .... Squadron Aid Post   (ADA)
SAP .... Staphylococcus aureus Protease [*An enzyme*]
SAP .... State Association President [*American Occupational Therapy Association*]
SAP .... Strain Arrestor Plate [*NASA*]   (NASA)
SAP .... Strategic Advantages Profile

SAP	Strong Anthropic Principle [*Term coined by authors John Barrow and Frank Tipler in their book, "The Anthropic Cosmological Principle"*]
SAP	Structural Analysis Program (MCD)
SAP	Student Aid Project
SAP	Studia Anglica Posnaniensia [*A publication*]
SAP	Subassembly Precision (MCD)
SAP	Subject Access Project
SAP	Sumerian Animal Proverbs (BJA)
SAP	Supervisory Airplane Pilot
SAP	Sveriges Socialdemokratiska Arbetareparti [*Swedish Social Democratic Labor Party*] (PPW)
SAP	Symbolic Address Program
SAP	Symbolic Assembly Program [*Data processing*]
SAP	System Alignment Procedure (NATG)
SAP	Systemic Arterial Pressure [*Medicine*]
SAP	Systems Assurance Program [*IBM Corp.*]
SAPA	Sciences - A Process Approach [*National Science Foundation*]
SAPA	South African Press Association
SAPAI	Salesmen's Association of Paper and Allied Industries (EA)
SA Parl Deb	South Australia. Parliamentary Debates [*A publication*]
SA Parl Parl Deb	South Australia. Parliament. Parliamentary Debates [*A publication*]
SAPAT	South African Picture Analysis Test [*Psychology*]
SAPC	Shipowners Association of the Pacific Coast [*Defunct*] (EA)
SAPC	Small-Arms Post Competition
SAPC	Substance Abuse Problem Checklist
SAPC	Suspended Acoustical-Plaster Ceiling [*Technical drawings*]
SAPCHE	Semiautomatic Program Checkout Equipment (AAG)
SAPCO	Security Assistance Policy Coordinating Office [*Military*]
SAPDE	Social Activist Professors Defense Foundation (EA)
SAPDO	Special Accounts Property Disposal Officer [*Military*]
SAPE	Society for Automation in Professional Education [*Later, SDE*]
SAPE	Solenoid Array Pattern Evaluator
SAPEA	Sapere [*A publication*]
SAPEC	Savings Associations Political Education Committee
SAPED	Salt 'N' Pepper [*A publication*]
SAPENF	Societe Americaine pour l'Etude de la Numismatique Francaise (EA)
SAPFU	Surpassing All Previous Foul Ups [*Military slang*] [*Bowdlerized version*]
SAPhA	Student American Pharmaceutical Association [*Washington, DC*] (EA)
SAPHD	South African Journal of Physics [*A publication*]
SAPHE	Semi-Armor-Piercing High Explosive [*Projectile*] (MCD)
SAPHYDATA	Panel on the Acquisition, Transmission, and Processing of Hydrological Data [*Marine science*] (MSC)
SAPI	Sales Association of the Paper Industry [*New York, NY*] (EA)
SAPI	Semi-Armor-Piercing Incendiary [*Projectile*] (NATG)
SAPIENS	Spreading Activation Processor for Information Encoded in Network Structure [*Department of Education*]
SAPIR	System of Automatic Processing and Indexing of Reports
SAPIS	State Alcoholism Profile Information System [*Public Health Service*] (EISS)
SAPL	Seacoast Anti-Pollution League (EA)
SAPL	Service Action Parts List (AAG)
SAPL	Society for Animal Protective Legislation [*Washington, DC*] (EA)
SAPL	Spartan-Approved Parts List [*Missiles*] (MCD)
SAPNA	South African Panorama [*A publication*]
SAPNA	Succinyl-Alanyl-para-Nitroanilide [*Biochemistry*]
SaPNFB	National Film Board, Pretoria, South Africa [*Library symbol*] [*Library of Congress*] (LCLS)
SAPO	Sarawak People's Organization [*Malaysian*] (PPW)
SAPO	Silicoaluminophosphate [*Inorganic chemistry*]
SAPO	Special Aircraft Project Office (AAG)
SAPO	Subarea Petroleum Office
SAPOA	Savremena Poljoprivreda [*A publication*]
SAPON	Saponaria [*Soapwort*] [*Pharmacology*] (ROG)
SAPON	Saponification [*Analytical chemistry*]
SAPOV	Sub-Area Petroleum Office, Vietnam [*Military*]
SAPP	Security, Accuracy, Propriety, and Policy
S App	Shaw's Scotch Appeal Cases, House of Lords [*1821-24*] (DLA)
SAPP	Skeletal Axis of Palp
SAPP	Sodium Acid Pyrophosphate [*Also, SAP*] [*Leavening agent, meat additive*]
SAPP	Soul Assurance Prayer Plan (EA)
SAPP	Special Airfield Pavement Program (NATG)
SAPPHIRE	Synthetic Aperture Precision Processor High Reliability (MCD)
SAPPMA	San Antonio Procurement and Production Materiel Area [*Air Force*]
Sapporo Med J	Sapporo Medical Journal [*A publication*]
SAPR	Semiannual Progress Report
SAPR	South Australian Planning Reports [*A publication*]
SAPR	Summary Area Problem Report (AAG)
SAPRA	Sakharnaya Promyshlennost [*A publication*]
SAPRC	Security Assistance Program Review Commission
SAPS	Scandinavian Association of Paediatric Surgeons [*Copenhagen, Denmark*] (EA-IO)
SAPS	Selected Alternate Processing Separation (MCD)
SAPS	Servico de Alimentacao da Providencia Social [*Brazil*]

SAPS	Shippingport Atomic Power Station (NRCH)
SAPS	Signal Algorithmic Processing System [*Navy*]
SAPS	Small Area Plotting Sheet
SaPS	South African Council for Scientific and Industrial Research, Pretoria, South Africa [*Library symbol*] [*Library of Congress*] (LCLS)
SAPS	Surety Agents Promotional Society [*Defunct*] (EA)
SaPSL	State Library, Pretoria, South Africa [*Library symbol*] [*Library of Congress*] (LCLS)
SAPST	Special Assistant to the President for Science and Technology
SAPTA	SAE [*Society of Automotive Engineers*] Progress in Technology [*A publication*]
SA Pub Serv R	South Australian Public Service Review [*A publication*]
SAPUC	Sintered Aluminum Powder-Clad Uranium Carbide
SAPW	United Stone and Allied Products Workers of America [*Later, USWA*]
SAQ	Pittsburgh, PA [*Location identifier*] [*FAA*] (FAAL)
SAQ	San Andros [*Bahamas*] [*Airport symbol*] (OAG)
SAQ	Short Arc Quads [*Medicine*]
SAQ	South Atlantic Quarterly [*A publication*]
SAQ	Springbank Aviation Ltd. [*Canada*] [*FAA designator*] (FAAC)
SAQC	Statistical Analysis and Quality Control
SAQS	Single Agency Qualification Standards [*Aviation*] (FAAC)
SAQT	Sociedad Panamericana de Quimioterapia de la Tuberculosis [*Pan American Society for Chemotherapy of Tuberculosis - PASCT*] (EA)
SAR	National Society, Sons of the American Revolution (EA)
SAR	Safety Analysis Report
SAR	Safety Assessment Report (MCD)
SAR	Sales Authorization Request
SAR	Sample Acceptance Rate [*Statistics*]
SAR	Santa Anita Realty Enterprises, Inc. [*NYSE symbol*]
SAR	Santa Rosa Junior College, Santa Rosa, CA [*OCLC symbol*] (OCLC)
SAR	Sarajevo [*Yugoslavia*] [*Seismograph station code, US Geological Survey*] (SEIS)
SAR	Sarcoidosis [*Medicine*]
Sar	Sarcosine [*Biochemistry*]
Sar	Sarcosyl [*Biochemistry*]
SAR	Sardinia [*Italy*] (ROG)
Sar	Sarswati's Privy Council Judgments [*India*] (DLA)
SAR	Schedule Allocation Requirements (AAG)
SAR	Schedule and Request (MCD)
SAR	Sea-Air Rescue
SAR	Search and Release (AAG)
SAR	Search and Rescue
SAR	Segment Address Register [*Telecommunications*]
SAR	Selected Acquisition Report [*Military*]
SAR	Semiactive RADAR (MCD)
SAR	Semiannual Report
SAR	Semiautomatic Rifle [*Army*]
SAR	Service Analysis Report [*Telecommunications*] (TEL)
SAR	Service Analysis Request [*Telecommunications*] (TEL)
SAR	Service Aptitude Rating [*Military*] (NVT)
SAR	Service Assigned Requests (MCD)
SAR	Sexual Attitude Reassessment [*Medicine*]
SAR	Siemens Agronaut Reactor [*Germany*]
SAR	Significant Action Report [*Military*] (MCD)
SAR	Silver Acorn Developments [*Vancouver Stock Exchange symbol*]
SAR	Single-Axis Reference
SAR	Single-Bit Alternation Recording
SAR	Site Acceptance Review
SAR	Society for Animal Rights [*Later, ISAR*] (EA)
SAR	Society of Authors' Representatives [*New York, NY*] (EA)
SAR	Sodium-Adsorption-Ratio
SAR	Son Altesse Royale [*His or Her Royal Highness*] [*French*]
SAR	SONAR Acoustique Remorque [*Acoustic imaging system*] [*French*]
SAR	Sons of the American Revolution
SAR	Source Address Register [*Telecommunications*]
SAR	South African Railways
SAR	South African Republic
SAR	South African Republic High Court Reports (DLA)
SAR	South Asian Review [*A publication*]
SAR	South Australian Government Railways
SAR	South Australian Industrial Reports [*A publication*]
SAR	South Australian Reports (DLA)
SAR	Spacecraft Acceptance Review (MCD)
SAR	Sparta, IL [*Location identifier*] [*FAA*] (FAAL)
SAR	Special Aeronautical Requirement [*Navy*] (NG)
SAR	Specific Absorption Rate
SAR	Specific Acoustic Resistance
SAR	Specific Activity Report
SAR	Specification Approval Record (MCD)
SAR	Stable Auroral Red [*Arc*] [*Geophysics*]
SAR	Standardized Admissions Ratios [*Hospital activity analysis*]
SAR	Standing Authority Release [*For perishables*] [*Business and trade*]
SAR	Start Action Request [*Environmental Protection Agency*]
SAR	Starting Air Receiver (AAG)

SAR .... Stock Appreciation Relief [*British*]
SAR .... Stock Appreciation Rights
SAR .... Storage Address Register [*Telecommunications*]
SAR .... Street Address Record [*Telecommunications*]   (TEL)
SAR .... Structure Activity Relationship
SAR .... Studies in the American Renaissance [*A publication*]
SAR .... Study and Review [*Reports*]   (RDA)
SAR .... Subauroral Red [*Arc*] [*Geophysics*]
SAR .... Submarine Advanced Reactor
SAR .... Substitution Approval Request   (MCD)
SAR .... Successive Accelerated Replacement
SAR .... Successive Approximation Register [*Data processing*]
SAR .... Sulfuric Acid Regenerator   (MCD)
SAR .... Super-Abrasion-Resistant [*LUCITE glazing material*]
SAR .... Support Air Request [*Net*] [*Navy communications*]
SAR .... Symbol Acquisition Routine
SAR .... Synthetic Aperture RADAR [*NASA*]
SAR .... Syrian Arab Republic
SAR .... System Analysis Report
SAR .... System Array RADAR   (KSC)
SAR .... Systemic Arterial Resistance [*Medicine*]
SAR .... Systemic Availability Ratio [*Physiology*]
SAR .... Systems Assessment Review [*NASA*]   (KSC)
SARA .... Saralasin [*Antihypertensive*]
SARA .... Saratoga Mines, Inc. [*NASDAQ symbol*]   (NQ)
SARA .... Saratoga National Historical Park
SARA .... Saratoga Trunk   (DSUE)
SARA .... Search and Rescue Aid
SARA .... Sequential Automatic Recorder and Annunciator
SARA .... Sexual Assault Research Association   (EA)
SARA .... Society of American Registered Architects
SARA .... Still Another Response Averager
SARA .... Superfund Amendment and Reauthorization Act [*1986*]
SARA .... System for Anesthetic and Respiratory Analysis
SARA .... Systems Analysis and Resource Accounting [*Data processing system*]
SARAC ..... Steerable Array for RADAR and Communications   (CET)
SARAH ...... Search and Range Homing
SARAH ...... Search and Rescue and Homing
SARAH ...... Semiactive RADAR Alternate Head
SARAH ...... Semiautomatic Range Azimuth and Height [*Subsystem*]
SA Railways ... South Australian Railways Institute. Magazine [*A publication*]
SA Railways Institute Mag ... South Australian Railways Institute. Magazine [*A publication*]
SARARC .... Subauroral Red Arc [*Geophysics*]
Sarat Ch Sent ... Saratoga Chancery Sentinel [*1841-47*] [*New York*]   (DLA)
Saratov Gos-Ped Inst Ucen Zap ... Saratovskii Gosudarstvennyi-Pedagogiceskii Institut. Ucenye Zapiski [*A publication*]
SARAW ...... Sarawak [*Malaysia*]   (ROG)
SarawakMJ ... Sarawak Museum Journal [*A publication*]
Sarawak Mus J ... Sarawak Museum Journal [*A publication*]
Sarawak Res Branch Dep Agric Annu Rep ... Sarawak. Research Branch. Department of Agriculture. Annual Report [*A publication*]
SARB .... State Air Resources Board
Sarbah ...... Sarbah's Fanti Law Reports [*Gold Coast*]   (DLA)
Sarbah FC ... Sarbah's Fanti Customary Laws [*Gold Coast*]   (DLA)
SARBE ...... Search and Rescue-Beacon Equipment   (MCD)
SARC .... Sarcasm   (DSUE)
SARC .... Search and Rescue Center   (CINC)
SARC .... Secure Airborne RADAR Control
SARC .... System Acquisition Review Council [*Army*]
SARC .... Systems Analysis and Research Corporation
SARCALM ... Synthetic Array RADAR Command Air-Launched Missile
SARCAP .... Search and Rescue - Civil Air Patrol   (MCD)
SARCAR .... Smithsonian Archaeometric Research Collection and Records [*Facility*]
SARCC ...... Search and Rescue Coordination Center [*Air Force*]
SARCCUS ... South African Regional Committee for Conservation and Utilization of Soil
SARCEN .... Search and Rescue Central [*Navy*]
Sar Ch Sen ... Saratoga Chancery Sentinel [*New York*]   (DLA)
SARCOM .. Search and Rescue Communicator [*Navy*]
SARCUP .... Search and Rescue Capability Upgrade Project [*Canadian Navy*]
SARD .... Sardinia
SARD .... Simulated Aircraft RADAR Data
SARD .... Solar Array Release and Deployment   (MCD)
SARD .... Special Airlift Requirement Directive [*Air Force*]   (AFM)
SARD .... Special Airlift Requirement Document [*Army*]
SARD .... Support and Range Development   (MUGU)
SARDA ...... Society for Aid and Rehabilitation of Drug Addicts [*Hong Kong*]
SARDA ...... State and Regional Defense Airlift Plan [*FAA, Civil Defense*]
SARDC ...... Small-Arms Research and Development Center [*Army*]
SARDET .... Search and Rescue Detachment [*Navy*]   (NG)
SARDIP ..... Stricken Aircraft Reclamation and Disposal Program [*Navy*]   (NG)
SARDPO ... San Antonio Research and Development Procurement Office [*Air Force*]
SARDS ...... Special Air Route Designators   (CINC)
SARDX ...... Sardonyx [*Gemstone*]   (ROG)
SARE .... Safety Review [*A publication*]

SARE-A ...... Saturday Review [*A publication*]
SARED .... Supporting Applied Research and Exploratory Development [*National Weather Service*]
SAREF .... Safety Research Experiment Facility [*Nuclear energy*]
SA Regr ..... South Australian Register [*A publication*]
SA Regr (Newspr) ... South Australian Register Reports (Newspaper) [*A publication*]
SAREP .... Speech and Reading Enrichment Program
SA Res Service Bibliog ... South Australia. Public Library. Research Service. Bibliographies [*A publication*]
SAREX ...... Search and Rescue Exercise   (MCD)
SARF .... Semiautomated Reconstruction Facility [*Military*]   (CAAL)
Sar FCL ..... Sarbah's Fanti Customary Laws [*2nd ed.*] [*1904*] [*Ghana*]   (DLA)
Sar FLR ..... Sarbah's Fanti Law Cases [*1845-1903*] [*Ghana*]   (DLA)
Sar FNC .... Sarbah's Fanti National Constitution [*Ghana*]   (DLA)
Sarg .... Sargonic   (BJA)
SARG .... Synthetic Aperture RADAR Guidance   (MCD)
Sar Gaz ..... Sarawak Gazette [*Kuching*] [*A publication*]
Sargetia Ser Sci Nat ... Sargetia [*Acta Devensis*]. Series Scientia Naturae [*A publication*]
SARGUN .... Synthetic Aperture RADAR Gun [*NASA*]
SARI .... Share-a-Ride International [*Gaithersburg, MD*]   (EA)
SARI .... Standby Altitude Reference Indicator   (MCD)
SARIE .... Semiautomatic RADAR Identification Equipment   (MCD)
SARIPADI... Serikat Pamong Desa Indonesia [*Village Officials' Union of Indonesia*]
SARIS........ Synthetic Aperture RADAR Interpretation System [*NASA*]   (MCD)
SARISA ...... Surface Analysis by Resonance Ionization of Sputtered Atoms
SARK .... Saville Advanced Remote Keying   (MCD)
SARL .... Societe a Responsabilite Limitee [*Private Limited Company*] [*French*]
SARLA ...... South African Rock Lobster Association [*Defunct*]
SARLANT... Search and Rescue, Atlantic [*Coast Guard*]
SARM .... Set Asynchronous Response Mode
SARM .... Standard Antiradiation Missile   (MCD)
Sar Mus J .. Sarawak Museum Journal [*Kuching*] [*A publication*]
SARNI .... Serikat Nelajan Indonesia [*Sailors' Union of Indonesia*]
SAROAD .... Storage and Retrieval of Aerometric Data [*Environmental Protection Agency*]
Sarot Otd Gos Nauchno-Issled Inst Ozern Rechn Rybn Khoz Tr ... Sarotovskoe Otdelenie Gosudarstvennogo Nauchno-Issledovatel'skogo Instituta Ozernogo i Rechnogo Rybnogo Khozyaistva. Trudy [*A publication*]
SARP .... Safety Analysis Report for Packaging [*NASA*]   (NASA)
SARP .... Schedule, Analysis, and Review Procedure [*NASA*]   (KSC)
SARP .... Schedule and Resources Procedure [*NASA*]   (KSC)
SARP .... Scheduling and Reporting [*or Review*] Procedure [*NASA*]   (KSC)
SARP .... Severe Accident Research Plan [*Nuclear energy*]   (NRCH)
SARP .... Ship Alteration and Repair Package [*Navy*]   (CAAL)
SARP .... Shuttle Astronaut Recruitment Program [*NASA*]   (MCD)
SARP .... Signal Automatic RADAR Processing
SARP .... Small Autonomous Research Package
SARP .... Space Allocation Requirement Procedures   (MCD)
SARP .... Space Allocation and Reservation Program   (MCD)
SARP .... Standards and Recommended Practices
SARP .... Storage and Retrieval Processor   (MCD)
SARPF .... Strategic Air Relocatable Photographic Facility   (CINC)
SARPMA ... San Antonio Real Property Maintenance Agency [*Military*]
SARPS .... Standards and Recommended Practices [*International Civil Aviation Organization*]
SARRA ...... Short-Arc Reduction of RADAR Altimetry
SARRP ...... Severe Accident Risk Reduction Program [*Nuclear energy*]   (NRCH)
SARS .... Secretary of the Army Research and Study [*Fellowship*]
SARS .... Selected Acquisition Reports [*Military*]   (RDA)
SARS .... Semiautomated Reconstruction System [*Military*]   (CAAL)
SARS .... Sensor Analog Relay System
SARS .... Ship Attitude Record System
SARS .... Simulated Airborne RADAR System   (MCD)
SARS .... Single Allocation and Reservation Study   (MCD)
SARS .... Single-Axis Reference System
SARS .... Solar Array Reorientation System
SARS .... Spares Accounting Replenishment System [*NASA*]   (KSC)
SARS .... Stellar Attitude Reference Study
SARS .... Synthetic Array RADAR System
SARSA ...... Social Affairs Recreation and Sports Association
SARSAT.... Search and Rescue Satellite [*Navy*]
SARSAT.... Search and Rescue Satellite-Aided Tracking [*NASA*]
SARSEX..... Synthetic Aperture RADAR Signature Experiment [*Oceanography*]
SARSIM ..... Search and Rescue Simulation [*Coast Guard*]
SARSS ...... Search and Rescue Satellite System [*Navy*]   (MCD)
SART .... St. Alban's Repertory Theater [*Washington, DC*]
SART .... Seattle Army Terminal
SART .... Special Army Review Team   (MCD)
SART .... Standard Acid Reflux Test [*Clinical chemistry*]
SART .... Stimuli Analog Refresh Table   (MCD)
SARTACK ... Search AntiRADAR Tactical Aircraft, K-Band

SARTEL ..... Search and Rescue, Telephone [*Coast Guard*]
SARTOC .... Southern Africa Regional Tourism Council [*Blantyre, Malawi*]   (EA-IO)
SARTS ...... Satisfaction of Army Requirements through Space   (MCD)
SARTS ...... Small Arms Remote Target System   (MCD)
SARTS ...... Switched Access Remote Test System [*Bell System*]
SARUM ..... Bishop of Salisbury [*British*]
SARUS ...... Search and Rescue Using Satellites [*Air Force*]
SARV .... Satellite Aeromedical Research Vehicle
SAS .... Lithuanian Catholic Students' Association "Ateitis"   (EA)
SAS .... St. Andrew Goldfields Ltd. [*Toronto Stock Exchange symbol*]
SAS .... Salton City, CA [*Location identifier*] [*FAA*]   (FAAL)
SAS .... Sample Array System   (KSC)
SAS .... Saskatoon [*Saskatchewan*] [*Seismograph station code, US Geological Survey*] [*Closed*]   (SEIS)
SAS .... Satellite Attack Sensor
SAS .... Scandinavian Airlines System [*Sweden*]
SAS .... Schiapparelli [*Italy*] [*Research code symbol*]
SAS .... SEAL [*Subsea Equipment Associates Limited*] Atmospheric System
SAS .... Sealed Authentication System [*Military*]
SAS .... Secondary Alarm Station   (NRCH)
SAS .... Sections Administratives Specialisees [*French Army*]
SAS .... Security Agency Study   (NRCH)
SAS .... Segment Arrival Storage Area   (KSC)
SAS .... Self-Adaptive System
SA(S) .... Service Activity System
SA(S) .... Service Air (System)   (NRCH)
SAS .... Shakespearean Authorship Society   (EA)
SAS .... Sherwood Anderson Society   (EA)
SAS .... Ship Alteration Suite [*Navy*]   (CAAL)
SAS .... Side-Angle-Side (Rule) [*Geometry*]
SAS .... Signal Airways Service
SAS .... Signal Analysis System
SAS .... Silicon Avalanche Suppressor [*Telecommunications*]
SAS .... Single Anomalous Scattering [*Crystallography*]
SAS .... Single Audio System   (CAAL)
SAS .... Sklar Aphasia Scale [*Psychology*]
SAS .... Sleep Apnea Syndrome [*Medicine*]
SaS .... Slovo a Slovesnost [*A publication*]
SAS .... Small Applications Satellite   (KSC)
SAS .... Small Astronomy Satellite
SAS .... Small-Probe Atmospheric Structure [*NASA*]
SAS .... Snake Approach Scale [*Psychology*]
SAS .... Snap Action Switch
SAS .... Societatis Antiquariorum Socius [*Fellow of the Society of Antiquaries*] [*British*]
SAS .... Society for Applied Spectroscopy   (EA)
SAS .... Society for Armenian Studies   (EA)
SAS .... Society of Australasian Specialists [*Later, SASO*]
SAS .... Sodium Alkane Sulfonate [*Detergent intermediate*]
SAS .... Sodium Aluminum Sulfate [*Organic chemistry*]
SAS .... Solar Array Structure
SAS .... Solar Array System   (MCD)
SAS .... Solar Aspect Sensor
SAS .... Son Altesse Serenissime [*His or Her Serene Highness*] [*French*]
SAS .... Sound Amplification System
SAS .... South American Series [*A publication*]
SAS .... Southern Anthropological Society
SAS .... Southern Appalachian Studies [*Defunct*]   (EA)
SAS .... Soviet Academy of Sciences
SAS .... Space Activity Suit
SAS .... Space Adaptation Syndrome [*NASA*]
SAS .... Spacecraft Antenna System
SAS .... Special Access Space   (CAAL)
SAS .... Special Air Service [*British commando unit*]
SAS .... Special Ammunition Section [*Picatinny Arsenal*] [*Army*]
SAS .... Special Ammunition Site [*Army*]
SAS .... Special Ammunition Stockage [*Army*]   (AABC)
SAS .... Special Ammunition Storage   (RDA)
SAS .... Stability Augmentation System [*or Subsystem*] [*FAA*]
SAS .... Statement of Auditing Standards
SAS .... Station Air System [*Nuclear energy*]   (NRCH)
SAS .... Statistical Analysis System [*Programing language*] [*1966*]
SAS .... Sterile Aqueous Suspension
SAS .... Strategic Area Study   (MCD)
SAS .... Studia Academica Slovaca [*A publication*]
SAS .... Sum of Adjacent Spans
SAS .... Superior Atrial Septum [*Anatomy*]
SAS .... Supersonic Attack Seaplane
SAS .... Supravalvular Aortic Stenosis [*Cardiology*]
SAS .... Surface Active Substances   (IEEE)
SAS .... Survival Avionics System [*Military*]   (CAAL)
SAS .... Suspended Aluminosilicate
SAS .... Suspended Array System [*To detect submarines*]
SAS .... Sweden-America Foundation
SAS .... Switched Access System [*Telecommunications*]   (TEL)
SAS .... System Acquisition School   (MCD)
SAS .... System Analysis Study
SAS .... System Application Software [*Data processing*]   (BUR)

SASA .... Severe Accident Sequence Analysis [*Nuclear energy*]   (NRCH)
SASA .... Ski Area Suppliers Association [*Woodbury, CT*]   (EA)
SASA .... Small Arms Systems Agency [*Army*]
SASA .... Special Ammunition Supply Activity   (MCD)
SASAE ...... Supplements. Annales. Service des Antiquites de l'Egypt [*Cairo*] [*A publication*]
SASAR ...... Segmented Aperture-Synthetic Aperture RADAR
SASAT ...... Shipboard Antisubmarine Attack Teacher [*Navy*]
SASB .... Structural Analysis of Social Behavior
SASC .... Sasco Cosmetics [*NASDAQ symbol*]   (NQ)
SASC .... Semiautomatic Stock Control
SASC .... Senate Armed Services Committee
SASC .... Senior Appointments Selection Committee [*British*]
SASC .... Small Arms School Corps [*Military*] [*British*]
SASC .... Subject Analysis Systems Collection [*University of Toronto*] [*Toronto, ON*] [*Information service*]   (EISS)
SA Sch Post ... South Australian School Post [*A publication*]
SASCL .... St. Ansgar's Scandinavian Catholic League   (EA)
SASCOM ... Southern Atlantic Satellite Communication
SASCOM ... Special Ammunition Support Command [*Army*]   (AABC)
SASCON ... Southern African Solidarity Congress [*Zimbabwean*]   (PPW)
SASD .... Static Adjustable Speed Drive
SASDT .... Ships and Aircraft Supplemental Data Tables [*Navy*]
SASE .... Self-Addressed Stamped Envelope
SASE .... Small Arms Suppression Evaluation   (MCD)
SASE .... Space Adaptation Syndrome Experiment [*Pronounced "Sassy"*] [*Space shuttle experiment developed in Canada*]
SASF .... SIDPERS [*Standard Installation/Division Personnel System*] Authorized Strength File [*Military*]   (AABC)
SASG .... Security Assistance Steering Group [*Military*]
SASG .... Smoke/Aerosol Steering Group [*DARCOM*]   (RDA)
SASHA ...... Sanfujinka No Shimpo [*A publication*]
SASHEP .... Study of Accreditation of Selected Health Educational Programs
SA Shipp News ... South African Shipping News and Fishing Industry Review [*A publication*]
SASI .... Ships and Air Systems Integration [*Navy*]
SASI .... Shugart Associates Systems Interface
SASI .... Society of Air Safety Investigators [*Later, ISASI*]
SASI .... Southern Association of Science and Industry   (EA)
SASI .... Surface Air System Integration
SASI .... System Automation Software, Incorporated
SASI .... System on Automotive Safety Information [*General Motors Corp.*] [*Information service*]
S Asia R ..... South Asian Review [*A publication*]
SASIDS ...... Stochastic Adaptive Sequential Information Dissemination System
SASILO ...... Schriftenreihe des A. Stifer-Instituts des Landes Oberoesterreich [*A publication*]
SASJ .... Self-Aligning Swivel Joint
SASK .... Saskatchewan [*Canadian province*]
Sask .... Saskatchewan Law Reports [*1907-31*] [*Canada*]   (DLA)
Saskatchewan Dept Nat Res Ann Rept Mineral Res Br Misc Paper ... Saskatchewan. Department of Natural Resources. Annual Report. Mineral Resources Branch. Miscellaneous Paper [*A publication*]
Saskatchewan Geol Survey Rept ... Saskatchewan. Geological Survey. Report [*A publication*]
Saskatchewan L Rev ... Saskatchewan Law Review [*A publication*]
Sask Bar Rev ... Saskatchewan Bar Review [*A publication*]
Sask BR ..... Saskatchewan Bar Review [*A publication*]
Sask B Rev ... Saskatchewan Bar Review [*A publication*]
Sask Dep Miner Resour Geol Sci Br Precambrian Geol Div Rep ... Saskatchewan. Department of Mineral Resources. Geological Sciences Branch. Precambrian Geology Division. Report [*A publication*]
Sask Dep Miner Resour Pet Natural Gas Reservoir Ann ... Saskatchewan. Department of Mineral Resources. Petroleum and Natural Gas Reservoir. Annual [*A publication*]
Sask Dep Miner Resour Rep ... Saskatchewan. Department of Mineral Resources. Report [*A publication*]
Sask Dep Nat Resour Fish Branch Fish Rep ... Saskatchewan. Department of Natural Resources. Fisheries Branch. Fisheries Report [*A publication*]
Sask Dep Nat Resour Fish Wildl Branch Fish Rep ... Saskatchewan. Department of Natural Resources. Fisheries and Wildlife Branch. Fisheries Report [*A publication*]
Sask Gaz .... Saskatchewan Gazette [*A publication*]
Sask Geol Soc Spec Publ ... Saskatchewan Geological Society. Special Publication [*A publication*]
Sask Hist .... Saskatchewan History [*A publication*]
Sask L .... Saskatchewan Law   (DLA)
Sask Law Rev ... Saskatchewan Law Review [*A publication*]
Sask Libr .... Saskatchewan Library [*A publication*]
Sask LR ...... Saskatchewan Law Reports [*Canada*]   (DLA)
Sask L Rev ... Saskatchewan Law Review [*A publication*]
Sask Res Counc Eng Div Rep ... Saskatchewan Research Council. Engineering Division Report [*A publication*]
Sask Res Counc Geol Div Rep ... Saskatchewan Research Council. Geology Division. Report [*A publication*]

Sask Rev Stat ... Saskatchewan Revised Statutes [*Canada*]   (DLA)
Sask Stat ... Saskatchewan Statutes [*Canada*]   (DLA)
SaskTel...... Saskatchewan Telecommunications [*Regina*] [*Information service*]   (EISS)
SASM........ Smithsonian Air and Space Museum
SASM........ Society for Automation in the Sciences and Mathematics
SASM........ Special Assistant of Strategic Mobility [*Air Force*]   (AFM)
SASMS..... Special Assistant for Surface Missile System
SASN........ Special Assistant to the Secretary of the Navy
SASNA...... South African Shipping News and Fishing Industry Review [*A publication*]
SASO........ Senior Air Staff Officer [*British*]
SASO........ Society of Australasian Specialists/Oceania   (EA)
SASO........ South African Students' Organization   (PD)
SASOC...... School Administrators and Supervisors Organizing Committee [*Later, AFSA*]   (EA)
SASOP...... Sudan. Antiquities Service. Occasional Papers [*A publication*]
SASOY...... Sasol Ltd. ADR [*NASDAQ symbol*]   (NQ)
SASP........ Science and Application Space Platform   (MCD)
SASP........ Single Advanced Signal Processor [*Military*]   (CAAL)
SASP........ Site Activation and Support Plan   (MCD)
SASP........ Society for the Advancement of Social Psychology   (EA)
SASP........ Special Ammunition Supply Point [*Army*]
SASP........ Stand Alone Support Program
SASP........ State Agency for Surplus Property
SASP........ State Airport System Plan [*Department of Transportation*]
SASP........ Submarine Analytic Search Program [*Navy*]   (CAAL)
SASPS...... SAMMS [*Standard Automated Materiel Management System*] Automated Small Purchase System
SASR........ South Australian State Reports [*A publication*]
SASR........ State Reports (South Australia) [*A publication*]
SASRS...... Satellite-Aided Search and Rescue System [*Telecommunications*]
SASS........ Saturn Automatic Software System [*NASA*]
SASS........ Schedules and Status Summary [*NASA*]   (KSC)
SASS........ SEASAT-[*A*] Scatterometer System [*NASA*]
SASS........ Small Airbreathing System Synthesis   (MCD)
SASS........ Society for the Advancement of Scandinavian Study   (EA)
SASS........ Society for Automation in the Social Sciences [*Later, SDE*]
SASS........ Source Assessment Sampling Method [*Environmental Protection Agency*]
SASS........ South Australian Secrets Summary [*A publication*]
SASS........ South Australian Social Science [*A publication*]
SASS........ Special Aircraft Service Shop   (NG)
SASS........ SPEEDEX [*Systemwide Project for Electronic Equipment at Depots Extended*] Automatic Scheduling System [*Military*]
SASS........ Strategic Alerting Sound System   (AAG)
SASS........ Suspended Array Surveillance System [*To detect submarines*]
SASSAR.... Suid-Afrikaanse Spoorweg/South African Railways [*A publication*]
SASSC...... Senate Aeronautical and Space Sciences Committee   (AAG)
SASSE...... Synchronous Altitude Spin-Stabilized Experiment
SASSI....... Synthetic Amorphous Silica and Silicates Industry Association [*Haver De Grace, MD*]   (EA)
SASSIA...... Synthetic Amorphous Silica and Silicates Industry Association   (EA)
SASSIF..... Self-Adjusting System of Scientific Information Flow
SASSTIXS ... Satellite Air, Surface, Subsurface Tactical Information Exchange System [*Navy*]   (CAAL)
SASSY...... Small Angle Separator System [*Superheavy element research*]
SASSY...... Supported Activities Supply System [*Marine Corps*]
SAST........ Safety Standards
SAST........ Serum Aspartate Aminotransferase [*An enzyme*]
SAST........ Service Announcements in Science and Technology [*Later, GRTA, WGA*] [*National Technical Information Service*]   (EA)
SAST........ Single Asphalt Surface Treatment
SAST........ Society for the Advancement of Space Travel [*Defunct*]   (MCD)
SASTAJ .... SASTA [*South Australian Science Teachers Association*] Journal [*A publication*]
SASTAR.... Support Activities Staffing Review   (MCD)
SASTE...... Semiautomatic Shop Test Equipment   (NG)
SA Storekeepers J ... South Australian Storekeepers and Grocers Journal [*A publication*]
SASTP...... Stand-Alone Self-Test Program   (MCD)
SASTU...... Signal Amplitude Sampler and Totalizing Unit   (IEEE)
SASU........ Saturn Apollo Systems Utilization [*NASA*]
SASV........ Sisters of the Assumption of the Blessed Virgin [*Roman Catholic religious order*]
SASV........ Snap Action Spool Valve
SASWREC ... SACLANT [*Supreme Allied Commander, Atlantic*] Antisubmarine Warfare Research Center   (NATG)
SAT .... Die Schriften des Alten Testaments in Auswahl Neu Uebersetzt und fuer die Gegenwart Erklaert [*Goettingen*] [*A publication*]
SAT .... Safe Arming Time
SAT .... Sampler Address Translator
SAT .... San Antonio [*Texas*] [*Airport symbol*]
SAT .... Sang-Tuda [*USSR*] [*Seismograph station code, US Geological Survey*] [*Closed*]   (SEIS)

SAT............ Satellite
Sat............. Satellite Science Fiction [*A publication*]
Sat............. Satirae [*or Sermones*] [*of Horace*] [*Classical studies*]   (OCD)
SAT............ Satisfactory   (AABC)
Sat............. Satura [*of Petronius*] [*Classical studies*]   (OCD)
SAT............ Saturate   (AAG)
SAT............ Saturatus [*Saturated*] [*Pharmacy*]
SAT............ Saturday
SAT............ Saturn
SAT............ Saturn [*Rocket*]   (KSC)
Sat............. Saturn [*Record label*] [*France*]
Sat............. Saturnalia [*of Macrobius*] [*Classical studies*]   (OCD)
SAT............ Schafer Value Trust [*NYSE symbol*]
SAT .... Scholastic Aptitude Test [*Trademark of the College Entrance Examination Board*]
SAT .... School Ability Test [*Psychology*]
SAT .... School of Applied Tactics [*AAFSAT*]
SAT .... Scientific Advisory Team [*Navy*]   (MCD)
SAT .... Scientific and Technical   (MCD)
SAT .... Security Alert Team [*Military*]   (AFM)
SAT .... Security Assistance Team [*Military*]   (AABC)
SAT .... Semiarid Tropics [*Geography*]
SAT .... Semiautomatic Test Equipment [*NASA*]
SAT .... Sennacieca Asocio Tutmonda [*Nationless Worldwide Association*]   (EA-IO)
SAT .... Service Acceptance Trials   (NVT)
SAT .... Ship Acceptance Test [*Navy*]   (CAAL)
SAT .... Ship's Apparent Time [*Navigation*]
SAT .... Silicon Annular Transistor
SAT .... Sine Acido Thymonucleico [*Without Thymonucleic Acid*]
SAT .... Site Acceptance Test [*Military*]   (AABC)
SAT .... Site Alteration Tests
SAT .... Site Assignment Time
SAT .... Sitting Atop [*Molecular configuration*]
SAT .... Small Angle Tagger   (MCD)
SAT .... Snap Action Thermostat
SAT .... Societa Anonima Transadriatica [*Italy*]
SAT .... Sound-Apperception Test [*Psychology*]
SAT .... Southern African Territories
SAT .... Southern Air Transport, Inc.
SAT .... Space Available Travel
SAT .... Speaker Authentication Technique
SAT .... Special Assistance Team [*Navy*]   (NG)
SAT .... Specific Aptitude Test
SAT .... Spiral Aftereffect Test [*Psychology*]
SAT .... Stabilization Assurance Test   (IEEE)
SAT .... Standard Area of Tinplate [*100,000 square inches*]
SAT .... Stanford Achievement Test [*Education*]
SAT .... Staphylococcus Adherence Test [*Clinical chemistry*]
SAT .... Static Air Temperature
SAT .... Stepped Atomic Time [*National Bureau of Standards*]
SAT .... Strategic American Traveler
SAT .... Study of Appeal Tribunals [*British*]
SAT .... Subacute Thyroiditis [*Medicine*]
SAT .... Subassembly Template   (MCD)
SAT .... Subscriber Access Terminal
SAT .... Support Analysis Test
SAT .... Surface Antenna Terminal   (MCD)
SAT .... Surveillance, Acquisition, and Tracking [*Military*]   (RDA)
SAT .... System Access Technique [*Sperry UNIVAC*]
SAT .... System Alignment Test   (NVT)
SAT .... Systematic Assertiveness Training
SAT .... Systems Acceptance Tests   (KSC)
SAT .... Systems Approach to Training   (MCD)
SATA........ Die Schriften des Alten Testaments in Auswahl Neu Uebersetzt und fuer die Gegenwart Erklaert [*Goettingen*] [*A publication*]
SATA........ Safety and Arming Test Aid   (MCD)
SATA........ Satellite Automatic Tracking Antenna   (MCD)
SATA........ Sociedade Acoriana de Transportes Aereos Ltda. [*Airline*] [*Portuguese*]
SATA........ Something about the Author [*A publication*]
SATA........ Student Air Travel Association
SATA........ Subsonic Aerodynamic Testing Association   (MCD)
SATA......... Supervisory, Administrative, and Technical Association [*Union of Ship Distribution and Allied Workers*] [*British*]
SATAF...... Site Activity Task Force [*NASA*]   (KSC)
SATAM ...... Syndicat Autonome des Travailleurs de la Alimentation de Madagascar [*Autonomous Union of Food Workers of Madagascar*]
SATAN...... Satellite Active Nullifier [*Antisatellite weapon*]
SATAN...... Satellite Automatic Tracking Antenna
SATAN...... Sensor for Airborne Terrain Analysis
SATAN...... Strobes Against Troops at Night   (MCD)
SATANAS ... Semiautomatic Analog Setting   (IEEE)
SATANS..... Static and Transient Analysis, Nonlinear, Shells [*Computer program*] [*Navy*]
SATAR...... Satellite for Aerospace Research [*NASA*]
SA Tax Cas ... South African Tax Cases   (DLA)
SATB........ Simulated Air Training Bundle   (MCD)
SATB.......... Soprano, Alto, Tenor, Bass

SATB.........	Specific Aptitude Test Battery
SATC	Ship Automatic Torpedo Countermeasures (MCD)
SATC	South African Tax Cases (DLA)
SATC	Students Army Training Corps
SATC	Suspended Acoustical-Tile Ceiling [*Technical drawings*]
SATCA	Sino-American Technical Cooperation Association
SATCAMS ...	Semiautomatic Tactical Control and Airspace Management System (MCD)
SATCC......	Southern Air Traffic Control Centre [*British*]
SATCH.......	Salicylaldehyde Thiocarbohydrazone [*Organic chemistry*]
SATCHMO ...	Satchel Mouth [*Nickname of late trumpeter Louis Armstrong*]
SATCO......	Senior Air Traffic Control Officer (NATG)
SATCO......	Signal Automatic Air Traffic Control System
SATCO......	Supervisory Air Traffic Control Organization [*FAA*]
SATCOM....	Satellite Command
SATCOM....	Satellite Communications [*Military*]
SATCOM....	Scientific and Technical Communication
SATCOMA ...	Satellite Communications Agency [*AEC/DCA*]
SATCON	Satellite Condition (AABC)
SATCS.......	Scandinavian Association for Thoracic and Cardiovascular Surgery (EA)
SATD.........	Saturated
SATD.........	Seattle Army Terminal Detachment (AABC)
SATD.........	Strike Aircraft Test Directorate [*Military*] (CAAL)
SATDAT.....	Satellite Data (MCD)
SATDB......	Sangyo To Denki [*A publication*]
SATDPI......	Salesmen's Association of the Textile Dyeing and Printing Industry (EA)
SATE.........	Semiautomatic Test Equipment [*NASA*]
SATE.........	Special Acceptance Test Equipment (MCD)
SATE.........	Study of Army Test and Evaluation (MCD)
SATEA......	Soviet Atomic Energy [*English Translation*] [*A publication*]
SA Teachers J ...	SA [*South Australia*] Teachers' Journal [*A publication*]
SA Teach J ...	South Australian Teachers' Journal [*A publication*]
SATEC......	Semiautomatic Technical Control
SATEC......	Societe d'Aide Technique et de Cooperation [*An independent French company*]
SATELCO ...	Satellite Telecommunications Company [*Japanese-American firm*]
SATELDATA ...	Satellite Databank [*European Space Agency*] [*Database*]
Satell Commun ...	Satellite Communications [*A publication*]
Satellite	Satellite Communications [*A publication*]
SATELLITE ...	Scientific and Technological Library Literature [*Conference*]
Satel News ...	Satellite News [*A publication*]
SATENA.....	Servicio de Aeronavegacion a Territorios Nacionales [*Colombian airline*]
Sat E P	Saturday Evening Post [*A publication*]
Sat Eve Post ...	Saturday Evening Post [*A publication*]
SATF.........	Shortest Access Time First
SATF.........	Societe des Anciens Textes Francais [*A publication*]
SATF.........	Substituted Anilines Task Force [*Washington, DC*] (EA)
SATFAL.....	Satellite Data for Fallout (MCD)
SATFOR.....	Special Air Task Force [*Navy*]
SATFY........	Satisfactory (AFM)
SATGA.......	Societe Aerienne de Transport Guyane Antilles [*French Guiana Air Transport*]
SAT GCI.....	Satellite Ground Controlled Interception (NATG)
SATH..........	St. Thomas National Historic Site
SATH........	Society for the Advancement of Travel for the Handicapped (EA)
SATI	Siscom [*NASDAQ symbol*] (NQ)
SATI	Society for the Advancement of the Tourism Industry
SATIF........	Scientific and Technical Information Facility [*NASA*]
SATIN........	SAC [*Strategic Air Command*] Automated Total Information Network (MCD)
SATIN........	SAGE [*Semiautomatic Ground Environment*] Air Traffic Integration
SATIN........	Satellite Inspector System (AAG)
SATIR........	System for Evaluation of Tactical Information on Missile Destroyers
SATIRE	Scientific and Technical Information Reviewed and Exploited [*A publication*] (RDA)
SATIRE	Semiautomatic Technical Information Retrieval
SatireNL....	Satire Newsletter [*A publication*]
SATIS........	Satisfactory (AAG)
SATISFN....	Satisfaction (ROG)
SATISFY ...	Satisfactory (ROG)
SATIVA	Society for Agricultural Training through Integrated Voluntary Activities [*Viola, WI*] (EA)
SATK.........	Strike Attack
SATKA	Search Acquisition Tracking and Kill Assessment [*Antiballistic missile program*]
SATKA	Surveillance, Acquisition, Track, Kill, and Assessment [*Section of SDI - Strategic Defense Initiative*]
SATKB......	Sanitarnaya Tekhnika [*A publication*]
SATL.........	Satellite (AABC)
SATL.........	Science and Advanced Technology Laboratory [*Army*] (RDA)
SATL.........	South Atlantic
SATL.........	Surgical Achilles Tendon Lengthening [*Medicine*]
S Atlan Bull ...	South Atlantic Bulletin [*A publication*]
S Atlantic Q ...	South Atlantic Quarterly [*A publication*]
S Atl Q........	South Atlantic Quarterly [*A publication*]
S Atl Quart ...	South Atlantic Quarterly [*A publication*]
S Atl Rev	South Atlantic Review [*A publication*]
SAT-M.......	Scholastic Aptitude Test - Mathematics [*College Entrance Examination Board*]
SATM.........	Sodium Aurothiomalate [*Organometallic chemistry*]
SATM	Supply and Training Mission [*Military*] (CINC)
Sat Men.....	Saturae Menippeae [*of Varro*] [*Classical studies*] (OCD)
SATMO	Security Assistance Training Management Office [*Army*]
SATN.........	Saturation
Sat N	Saturday Night [*A publication*]
SATNAV....	Satellite Navigation (AABC)
SATNET....	Satellite Data Broadcast Networks, Inc. [*New York, NY*] [*Telecommunications*] (TSSD)
SATO	Scheduled Airlines Ticket Office
SATO	Self-Aligning Thick Oxide [*Process*]
SATO	Shuttle Attached Teleoperator [*NASA*] (NASA)
SATO	South American Travel Organization
SATO	Station Airline Ticket Office (MCD)
SATO	Supply and Transportation Operations [*NASA*] (NASA)
SATO	Synthetic Aircraft Turbine Oil
SATODP.....	Satellite Tracking Orbit Determination Program
SATON.....	Satisfaction (ROG)
SATOUR	South African Tourist Corp.
SATP........	Small-Arms Target Practice [*Navy*]
SATP........	Stabilization, Acquisition, Tracking, and Pointing
SATPATT...	Satellite Paper Tape Transfer
Sat R	Saturday Review [*A publication*]
SATR.........	Scheduled Air Transport Rating
SATR.........	So as to Reach [*Aviation*] (FAAC)
SATRA	Science and Technology Research Abstracts [*A publication*]
SATRA	Shoe and Allied Trades Research Association [*Later, Footwear Technology Centre*] [*British*] (EA)
SATRA	Soviet-American Trade Association
SATRA Bull ...	SATRA [*Shoe and Allied Trades Research Association*] Bulletin [*A publication*]
SATRAC....	Satellite Automatic Terminal Rendezvous and Coupling (MCD)
SATRACK ...	Satellite Tracking (MCD)
SATRAM	Systeme d'Atterrissage a Trajectoires Multiples [*Aviation*]
SATRAN....	Satellite Reconnaissance Advance Notice (MCD)
Sat R Arts ...	Saturday Review of the Arts [*A publication*]
Sat R Ed	Saturday Review of Education [*A publication*]
Sat Rev.....	Saturday Review [*A publication*]
Sat R Lit	Saturday Review of Literature [*A publication*]
SATROS....	Science and Technology Regional Organizations [*British*]
Sat R Sci ...	Saturday Review of the Sciences [*A publication*]
Sat R Soc ...	Saturday Review of Society [*A publication*]
Sat R/World ...	Saturday Review/World [*A publication*]
SATS.........	S. Allan Taylor Society (EA)
SATS.........	Satellite Antenna Test System [*NASA*]
SATS.........	Short Airfield Tactical Strip [*Military*]
SATS.........	Short Airfield for Tactical Support [*Marine Corps*]
SATS.........	Shuttle Avionics Test System [*NASA*] (NASA)
SATS.........	Simulated Airborne Transpondent System (MCD)
SATS.........	Single Array Test System (MCD)
SATS.........	Small Airfield for Tactical Support [*Air Force*]
SATS.........	Small Applications Technology Satellite (MCD)
SATS.........	Social and Technical Sciences
SATSA.......	Signal Aviation Test and Support Activity
SATSERV...	Service by Satellite
SATSIM.....	Satellite Simulation [*Military*] (CAAL)
SATSIM.....	Saturation Countermeasures Simulator
SATSLAM ...	Satellite-Tracked Submarine-Launched Antimissile (MCD)
SATT.........	Science, Applications, Technology Transfer, and Training [*System*] [*National Institutes of Health*]
SATT	Semiautomatic Transistor Tester [*NASA*]
SATT.........	Strowger Automatic Toll Ticketing [*Telecommunications*]
SATTR	Satisfactory to Transfer (NOAA)
SATU.........	Singapore Association of Trade Unions
SATU.........	South African Typographical Union
SATUC......	South African Trade Union Council
SATUR......	Saturate (AAG)
Saturday Rev ...	Saturday Review [*A publication*]
SATURN....	Simulation and Assignment of Traffic to Urban Road Networks [*Kins Developments Ltd.*] [*Software package*]
SAT-V	Scholastic Aptitude Test - Verbal [*College Entrance Examination Board*]
SATW........	Society of American Travel Writers [*Washington, DC*] (EA)
Sau............	All India Reporter, Saurashtra [*1950-57*] (DLA)
SAU............	Saltair [*Utah*] [*Seismograph station code, US Geological Survey*] (SEIS)
SAU............	Saudi Arabia [*Three-letter standard code*] (CNC)
SAU............	Saugeen Ontario Library Service [*UTLAS symbol*]
SAU............	Sausalito, CA [*Location identifier*] [*FAA*] (FAAL)
SAU............	Sawu [*Indonesia*] [*Airport symbol*] (OAG)
SAU............	Scandinavian Association of Urology (EA)
SAU............	Search Attack Unit
SAU............	Separate Administrative Unit [*Work Incentive Program*]
SAU............	Smallest Addressable Unit
SAU............	Spectrum Analysis Unit
SAU............	Sprawozdania Akademii Umiejetnosci [*A publication*]

SAU............ Standard Advertising Unit [*System introduced to make national newspaper advertising pages uniform in size and format and to replace the agate line with the inch as a unit of measure*]
SAU............ Statistical Analysis Unit
SAU............ Strap-Around Unit [*NASA*]   (NASA)
SAU............ Surface Attack Unit
SAU............ System [*or Subsystem*] Availability Unit
SAUCB....... Soviet Automatic Control [*English Translation*] [*A publication*]
SAUCERS ... Space and Unexplained Celestial Events Research Society
Saudi Arabia Dir Gen Miner Resour Geol Map ... Saudi Arabia. Directorate General of Mineral Resources. Geologic Map [*A publication*]
SAUFI........ Sindacato Autonomo Unificato Ferrovieri Italiani [*Autonomous Union of Italian Railroad Workers*]
SAU & G..... San Antonio, Uvalde & Gulf Railroad Co.
Saugertierkd Mitt ... Saugetierkundliche Mitteilungen [*A publication*]
Saugetierkundliche Mitt ... Saugetierkundliche Mitteilungen [*A publication*]
Sau LR .... Saurastra Law Reports [*India*]   (DLA)
Sauls.......... Reports Tempore Saulsbury [*5-6 Delaware*]   (DLA)
Saund .... Saunders' King's Bench Reports [*1666-73*]   (DLA)
Saund & A ... Saunders and Austin's Locus Standi Reports [*1895-1904*]   (DLA)
Saund Ass ... Saunders on Assault and Battery [*1842*]   (DLA)
Saund & Aust ... Saunders and Austin's Locus Standi Reports   (DLA)
Saund & B ... Saunders and Bidder's Locus Standi Reports [*England*]   (DLA)
Saund Bast ... Saunders on Affiliation and Bastardy [*11th ed.*] [*1915*]   (DLA)
Saund BC... Saunders and Cole's English Bail Court Reports [*82 RR*] [*1846-48*]   (DLA)
Saund & BC ... Saunders and Cole's English Bail Court Reports [*1846-48*]   (DLA)
Saund & C ... Saunders and Cole's English Bail Court Reports [*1846-48*]   (DLA)
Saund & M ... Saunders and Macrae's English County Courts and Insolvency Cases [*County Courts Cases and Appeals, II-III*]   (DLA)
Saund & Mac ... Saunders and Macrae's English County Court Cases   (DLA)
Saund Mag Pr ... Saunders' Magistrates' Courts Practice [*6th ed.*] [*1902*]   (DLA)
Saund Mil L ... Saunders' Militia Law [*4th ed.*] [*1855*]   (DLA)
Saund Mun Reg ... Saunders' Municipal Registration [*2nd ed.*] [*1873*]   (DLA)
Saund Neg ... Saunders on Negligence [*2nd ed.*] [*1878*]   (DLA)
Saund Pl & Ev ... Saunders' Pleading and Evidence   (DLA)
Saund Prec ... Saunders' Precedents of Indictments [*3rd ed.*] [*1904*]   (DLA)
Saund War ... Saunders on Warranties and Representations [*1874*]   (DLA)
SAUS .... Sausage   (DSUE)
SAUS .... Soccer Association of the United States   (EA)
SAus .... South Australia   (ADA)
Sau & Sc .... Sausse and Scully's Irish Rolls Court Reports [*1837-40*]   (DLA)
S Aus Nat Gal Bul ... South Australia National Gallery. Bulletin [*A publication*]
Sausse & Sc ... Sausse and Scully's Irish Rolls Court Reports [*1837-40*]   (DLA)
S Aust .... South Australia   (DLA)
S Aust .... South Australiana [*A publication*]
S Aust Clinics ... South Australian Clinics [*A publication*]
S Aust Coal Abstr Bull ... South Australian Coal Abstract Bulletin [*A publication*]
S Aust Dir Mines Gov Geol Annu Rep ... South Australia. Director of Mines and Government Geologist. Annual Report [*A publication*]
S Aust Geol Atlas Ser ... South Australia. Geological Survey. Atlas Series [*A publication*]
S Aust Geol Surv Bull ... South Australia. Geological Survey. Bulletin [*A publication*]
S Aust Geol Surv 1:250000 Geol Ser ... South Australia. Geological Survey. 1:250,000 Geological Series [*A publication*]
S Aust Geol Surv Rep Invest ... South Australia. Geological Survey. Report of Investigations [*A publication*]
S Aust L ..... South Australia Law   (DLA)
S Austl .... South Australia State Reports   (DLA)
S Austl LR ... South Australian Law Reports [*A publication*]
S Aust LR ... South Australian Law Reports [*A publication*]
S Austl St R ... South Australia State Reports   (DLA)
S Aust Miner Resour Rev ... South Australia Mineral Resources Review [*A publication*]
S Aust Nat ... South Australian Naturalist [*A publication*]
S Aust Nat ... South Australian Naturalist [*A publication*]
S Aust Orn ... South Australian Ornithologist [*A publication*]
S Aust Ornithol ... South Australia Ornithologist [*A publication*]
S Austr .... South Australia   (DLA)
S Australia Geol Surv Rep Invest ... South Australia. Geological Survey. Report of Investigations [*A publication*]
S Australiana ... South Australiana [*A publication*]
S Aust Rep Mus Board ... South Australia Report of the Museum Board [*A publication*]
S Austr L.... South Australia Law   (DLA)
SAV............ Savannah [*Tasmania*] [*Seismograph station code, US Geological Survey*]   (SEIS)
SAV............ Savannah [*Georgia*] [*Airport symbol*]   (OAG)
SAV............ Savannah Electric & Power Co. [*NYSE symbol*]
SAV............ Saveloy   (DSUE)
Sav............ Savile's English Common Pleas Reports   (DLA)

Sav............ Savings   (DLA)
SAV............ Savior
Sav............ Savremenik [*A publication*]
SAV............ Schweizerisches Archiv fuer Volkskunde [*A publication*]
SAV............ Service Availability [*AT & T*]
SAV............ Slovenska Akademia Vied [*A publication*]
SAV............ Society of American Ventriloquists   (EA)
SAV............ Spectra Ventures Ltd. [*Vancouver Stock Exchange symbol*]
SAV............ Statens Avtalsverk [*Sweden*]
SAV............ Stock at Valuation
SAV............ Strollad ar Vro [*Country Party*] [*French*]   (PPW)
SAV............ Student Alternatives to Violence [*Defunct*]   (EA)
SAV............ Submerged Aquatic Vegetation
SAVA......... Servicios do Aerotaxisa e Abastecimento do Vale Amazonica [*Airline*] [*Brazil*]
SAVA......... Sexual Abuse Victims Anonymous [*Canada*]
SAVAK....... Sazemane Attalat Va Anmiyate Keshvar [*Iranian security and intelligence organization*]
SAVASI...... Simple [*or Simplified*] Abbreviated Visual Approach Slope Indicator [*FAA*]
Sav Bank J ... Savings Bank Journal [*A publication*]
SAVBOND ... War Savings Bond [*Allotment for purchase*] [*Navy*]
SAVC .... Air-Cushion Vehicle built by Sealan Air Cushion Vehicles [*US*] [*Usually used in combination with numerals*]
SAVC .... Society for the Anthropology of Visual Communication   (EA)
Sav Conf Law ... Savigny's Conflict of Laws [*2nd ed.*] [*1880*]   (DLA)
Sav Dr Rom ... Savigny's Droit Romain   (DLA)
SAVE.......... Energy Resources of North Dakota, Inc. [*NASDAQ symbol*]   (NQ)
SAVE.......... Self-Learning Audio Visual Education [*National Foundation for the Prevention of Oral Disease*]
SAVE.......... Service Activities of Voluntary Engineers
SAVE.......... Shoppers Association for Value Economy [*New York, NY*]   (EA)
SAVE.......... Shortages and Valuable Excesses [*Navy*]   (NG)
SAVE.......... Society of American Value Engineers   (EA)
SAVE.......... Society of American Vintage-Radio Enthusiasts
SAVE.......... Society of Americans for Vashchenko Emigration   (EA)
SAVE.......... Stop Addiction through Voluntary Effort
SAVE.......... Student Action Voters for Ecology
SAVE.......... Students Against Volvo Exaggerations [*Student legal action organization*]
SAVE.......... System for Automatic Value Exchange [*Data processing*]
SAVER .... Stowable Aircrew Vehicle Escape Rotoseat   (MCD)
SAVER .... Study to Assess and Validate Essential Reports   (AABC)
SAVES ...... Sizing Aerospace Vehicle Structures [*NASA*]
SAVES ...... States Audiovisual Education Study
SAVICOM ... Society for the Anthropology of Visual Communication
Savigny Hist Rom Law ... Savigny's History of the Roman Law   (DLA)
Savigny System ... Savigny's System des Heutigen Roemischen Rechts   (DLA)
Savile .... Savile's English Common Pleas Reports [*123 English Reprint*] [*1580-94*]   (DLA)
SAVIM........ Survivability and Vulnerability Improvement Modification [*Army*]   (RDA)
Savings Bank J ... Savings Bank Journal [*A publication*]
SAVITAR.... Sanders Associates Video Input/Output Terminal Access Resource [*Data processing*]   (IEEE)
SAVL.......... Studien zur Allgemeinen und Vergleichenden Literaturwissenschaft [*A publication*]
Sav & Loan N ... Savings and Loan News [*A publication*]
Sav Loan News ... Savings and Loan News [*A publication*]
SAVMO ...... Service Audiovisual Management Office [*Army*]
SAVO .... Savoy Industries, Inc. [*NASDAQ symbol*]   (NQ)
SAVOR....... Single-Actuated Voice Recorder
Sav Pos ...... Savigny on Possessions [*6th ed.*] [*1848*]   (DLA)
Sav Priv...... Trial of the Savannah Privateers   (DLA)
SAVR.......... Savers Federal Savings & Loan [*NASDAQ symbol*]   (NQ)
Savremena Poljopr ... Savremena Poljoprivreda [*A publication*]
Savrem Med (Sofia) ... Savremenna Meditsina (Sofia) [*A publication*]
SAVS.......... Safeguards Area Ventilation System [*Nuclear energy*]   (NRCH)
SAVS.......... Status and Verification System [*NASA*]   (KSC)
SAVT.......... Save Area Table [*Data processing*]   (IBMDP)
SAVT.......... Secondary Address Vector Table [*Data processing*]   (IBMDP)
Sav Zeitschr ... Zeitschrift der Savigny-Stiftung fuer Rechtsgeschichte. Romanistische Abteilung [*A publication*]   (OCD)
SAW........... Gwinn, MI [*Location identifier*] [*FAA*]   (FAAL)
SAW........... St. Andrews [*Washington*] [*Seismograph station code, US Geological Survey*]   (SEIS)
SAW........... Sample Assignment Word
Saw............ Sawyer's United States Circuit Court Reports   (DLA)
SAW........... Semiautomatic Weapons
SAW........... Signal Aircraft Warning
SAW........... Sitzungsberichte der Akademie der Wissenschaft in Wien [*A publication*]
SAW........... Small-Arms Weapon
SAW........... Society of American Wars   (EA)
SAW........... Solar Array Wing   (MCD)
SAW........... South Albuquerque Works [*AEC*]
SAW........... Southern Army Worm [*Agronomy*]
SAW........... Special Air Warfare   (AFM)
SAW........... Squad Automatic Weapon

SAW	Strike Anywhere [*Match*]
SAW	Subantarctic Water
SAW	Submerged Arc Weld
SAW	Surface Acoustic Wave [*Microwave system*]
SAWA	Screen Advertising World Association (EA-IO)
SAWAS	South African Women's Auxiliary Services
SA Waterabstr ...	SA [*South Africa*] Waterabstracts [*A publication*]
SAWB	Sitzungsberichte der Akademie der Wissenschaften zu Berlin [*A publication*]
SAWBET	Supply Action Will Be Taken
SAWC	Special Air Warfare Center
SAWE	Society of Allied Weight Engineers (EA)
SAWF	Special Air Warfare Forces (AFM)
SAWG	Schedule and Allocations Working Group [*NASA*] (KSC)
SAWG	Special Advisory Working Group (NATG)
SAWg	Strategic Aerospace Wing [*Air Force*] (AFM)
SAWGUS ...	Standoff/Attack Weapons Guidance Utility Study (MCD)
SAWIC	South African Water Information Centre [*Pretoria, South Africa*] [*Information service*] (EISS)
SAWID	Shipboard Acoustic Warfare Integrated Defense (NVT)
SAWM	Sitzungsberichte der Akademie der Wissenschaften zu Muenchen [*A publication*]
SAWMARCS ...	Standard Aircraft Weapon Monitor and Release Control System (NG)
SAWO	Surface Acoustic Wave Oscillator [*Telecommunications*] (TEL)
SAWP	Society of American Wood Preservers [*Falls Church, VA*] (EA)
SAWPHK	Saechsische Akademie der Wissenschaften zu Leipzig. Philologisch-Historische Klasse [*A publication*]
SAWRS	Supplementary Aviation Weather Reporting Station [*National Weather Service*] (FAAC)
SAWS	Satellite Attack Warning System
SAWS	Seventh-Day Adventist World Service [*Superseded by ADRA*] (EA)
SAWS	Small-Arms Weapons System (NATG)
SAWS	Solar Array Wing Simulator (MCD)
SAWS	Special Airborne Weapon Subsystem (MCD)
SAWS	Subacoustic Warfare System
SAWS	Submarine Acoustic Warfare System [*Navy*] (MCD)
SAWW	Sitzungsberichte der Akademie der Wissenschaft in Wien [*A publication*]
Sawy	Sawyer's United States Circuit Court Reports (DLA)
Sawyer Circt ...	Sawyer's United States Circuit Court Reports (DLA)
Sawyer's Gas Turbine Int ...	Sawyer's Gas Turbine International [*A publication*]
Sawyer US Ct Rep ...	Sawyer's United States Circuit Court Reports (DLA)
SAX	Sambu [*Panama*] [*Airport symbol*] (OAG)
SAX	Saxon
SAX	Saxon Oil Development Partners [*American Stock Exchange symbol*]
SAX	Saxophone [*Music*]
Sax	Saxton's New Jersey Chancery Reports (DLA)
SAX	Small-Angle X-ray [*Instrumentation*]
SAX	Small Automatic Exchange [*Telecommunications*] (TEL)
SAX	Sparta, NJ [*Location identifier*] [*FAA*] (FAAL)
SAX	States Exploration [*Toronto Stock Exchange symbol*] [*Vancouver Stock Exchange symbol*]
SAXA	Slotted Array X-Band Antenna
SAXD	Small-Angle X-Ray Diffraction
SAXIF	Saxton Industries Ltd. [*NASDAQ symbol*] (NQ)
SAXL	Short-Arc Xenon Lamp
SAXLE	Single Cantilevered Axle
SAXS	Small-Angle X-Ray Scattering
Saxt	Saxton's New Jersey Chancery Reports (DLA)
Saxt Ch	Saxton's New Jersey Chancery Reports (DLA)
SAY	Salisbury [*Zimbabwe*] [*Airport symbol*] [*Obsolete*] (OAG)
Say	Sayer's English King's Bench Reports [*96 English Reprint*] (DLA)
SAY	Science Fiction Adventures Yearbook [*A publication*]
SAY	Soccer Association for Youth (EA)
SAY	Stanley Resources [*Vancouver Stock Exchange symbol*]
SAYE	Save as You Earn [*National Savings Plan*] [*British*]
Sayer	Sayer's English King's Bench Reports [*96 English Reprint*] (DLA) [*1751-56*]
Sayer (Eng) ...	Sayer's English King's Bench Reports [*96 English Reprint*] (DLA)
Sayles' Ann Civ St ...	Sayles' Annotated Civil Statutes [*Texas*] (DLA)
Sayles' Civ St ...	Sayles' Revised Civil Statutes [*Texas*] (DLA)
Sayles' Rev Civ St ...	Sayles' Revised Civil Statutes [*Texas*] (DLA)
Sayles' St ...	Sayles' Revised Civil Statutes [*Texas*] (DLA)
Sayles' Supp ...	Supplement to Sayles' Annotated Civil Statutes [*Texas*] (DLA)
Sayre Adm Cas ...	Sayre's Cases on Admiralty (DLA)
SAZ	Sasstown [*Liberia*] [*Airport symbol*] (OAG)
SAZ	Staples, MN [*Location identifier*] [*FAA*] (FAAL)
SAZO	Seeker Azimuth Orientation [*Air Force*]
SB	Bachelor of Science
SB	Beauval Public Library, Saskatchewan [*Library symbol*] [*National Library of Canada*] (NLC)
SB	International Standard Book Number [*Online database field identifier*]
SB	La Sacra Bibbia [*Turin*] [*A publication*] (BJA)

SB	La Sainte Bible [*A publication*] (BJA)
SB	S-Band (KSC)
SB	Salary Band [*British*]
SB	Sales Book
SB	Salomon, Inc. [*NYSE symbol*]
SB	Sarah Bernhardt [*French actress, 1844-1923*]
S & B	Saunders and Bidder's Locus Standi Reports [*1905-19*] (DLA)
SB	Save a Baby [*An association*] [*Orinda, CA*] (EA)
SB	Savings Bank
SB	Savings Bond [*Treasury Department security*]
SB	Schweizer Buch [*A publication*]
SB	Science Books [*A publication*]
SB	Science Books and Films [*A publication*]
SB	Scoring Booklet (MCD)
SB	Scouting-Bombing Plane [*When prefixed to Navy aircraft designation*]
SB	Scrieve Board
SB	Sea Base (MCD)
SB	Seaboard World Airlines, Inc. [*ICAO designator*]
SB	Secondary Battery [*Military*]
SB	Secondary Buffer [*Chemistry*]
SB	Section Base [*Military*]
SB	Securing Bands
SB	Selection Board [*Military*]
SB	Selective Bibliography (MCD)
SB	Selmer Bandwagon [*A publication*]
SB	Senate Bill [*in state legislatures*]
SB	Senior Beadle [*Ancient Order of Foresters*]
SB	Separately Binned
SB	Serial Binary (CET)
SB	Serial Block (MSA)
SB	Serum Bilirubin [*Clinical chemistry*]
SB	Service Bulletin
SB	Serving Brother [*Church of England*]
SB	Shaper Block (MCD)
SB	Shipbuilding [*Navy*]
SB	Shipping Board
SB	Short Bill
SB	Shortness of Breath [*Cardiology*]
S/B	Should Be
SB	Sick Bay
SB	Sideband [*Radio frequency*] (AAG)
SB	Signal Battalion [*Army*]
SB	Signal Boatswain
SB	Signature Book (ROG)
SB	Silver Braze (MSA)
SB	Simultaneous Broadcast
SB	Single Blind [*Experimental condition*]
SB	Single Braid (CET)
SB	Single-Breasted
SB	Single Breath
SB	Single Ended Boiler
SB	Sink Beater (ADA)
SB	Sinus Bradycardia [*Cardiology*]
SB	Sitzungsbericht [*Transaction*] [*German*]
SB	Skandinaviska Banken. Quarterly Review [*Later, Skandinaviska Enskilda Banken. Quarterly Review*] [*A publication*]
SB	Sleeve Bearing (KSC)
SB	Slow Burning
SB	Small Bonds
SB	Small Bore (ADA)
SB	Small Bowel
SB	Small Business
S & B	Smith and Batty's Irish King's Bench Reports [*1824-25*] (DLA)
SB	Smooth Bore [*Ballistics*]
SB	Social Biology Films [*National Science Foundation project*]
SB	Society for Biomaterials (EA)
SB	Sociologisch Bulletin [*A publication*]
SB	Sodium Bisulfite [*Inorganic chemistry*]
SB	Sodium Borate [*Inorganic chemistry*]
SB	Solid Body [*Technical drawings*]
SB	Solomon Islands [*Two-letter standard code*] (CNC)
SB	Soncino Blaetter [*A publication*]
SB	Sonobuoy (NVT)
SB	Soot Blower (AAG)
SB	Sources Bibliques [*Paris*] [*A publication*]
SB	South Britain [*England and Wales*]
SB	South Buffalo Railway Co. [*AAR code*]
SB	Southbound
SB	Sovetskaya Bibliografia [*A publication*]
SB	Space Base (KSC)
SB	Special Bibliography
SB	Special Billing [*Telecommunications*] (TEL)
SB	Special Branch [*British police*]
SB	Special Bulletin. New York Department of Labor (DLA)
SB	Speed Brake (MCD)
SB	Spin Block (MSA)
SB	Spina Bifida [*Medicine*]
SB	Splash Block
SB	Sports Bribery [*FBI standardized term*]

SB	Spring Back (ADA)
SB	Stabilized Breakdown
SB	Standard Babylonian (BJA)
SB	Standard Bead
SB	Standby Base [Air Force] (AFM)
SB	Stanford-Binet [Intelligence test] [Education]
SB	Statement of Billing
SB	Statistical Bulletin
SB	Status Board [Automated] (MCD)
SB	Statute Book (ADA)
SB	Steamboat
S & B	Sterilization and Bath
SB	Sternal Border [Anatomy]
Sb.	Stibium [Antimony] [Chemical element]
sb	Stilb [Unit of luminance]
SB	Stillborn [Medicine]
SB	Stockbroker
SB	Stolen Base [Baseball]
SB	Stove Bolt
Sb.	Strabismus [Medicine]
SB	Straight Binary
SB	Stretcher-Bearer
SB	Studi Baltici [A publication]
SB	Studi Bizantini [A publication]
SB	Studies in Bibliography [A publication]
SB	Stuffing Box
SB	Sub Branch [Banking]
SB	Subbituminous
SB	Submarine Base [Navy]
SB	Submarine Boat [British] (ROG)
SB	Submarine Fog Bell [Mechanical] [Maps and charts]
SB	Substantive
SB	Supplementary Benefits
SB	Supply Bulletin
SB	Support Box
SB	Supreme Bench (DLA)
SB	Surface Binding [Immunochemistry]
sb	Svalbard and Jan Mayen [MARC country of publication code] [Library of Congress] (LCCP)
SB	Switchboard
SB	Switchboard Operator [Navy]
SBA	Synchronization Base [NASA] (NASA)
SB	Synchronization Bit (MSA)
SBA	Saabruecker Beitraege zur Altertumskunde [Bonn] [A publication] (BJA)
SBA	Santa Barbara [California] [Airport symbol] (OAG)
SBA	Satellite Broadcasters Association (EA)
SBA	Sbarro, Inc. [American Stock Exchange symbol]
SBA	Scott Base [Antarctica] [Seismograph station code, US Geological Survey] (SEIS)
SBA	Scott Base [Antarctica] [Geomagnetic observatory code]
SBA	Seat Back Assembly (MCD)
SBA	Secondary Butyl Alcohol [Organic chemistry]
SBA	Shaped Beam Antenna
SBA	Shared Batch Area [Data processing] (IBMDP)
SBA	Show Business Association [New York, NY] (EA)
SBA	Siamese Breeders of America (EA)
SBA	Sick Bay Attendant [Navy]
SBA	Sitzungsberichte der Bayerischen Akademie der Wissenschaften [A publication]
SBA	Small Business Administration
SBA	Small Businesses' Association [British]
SB of A	Smaller Business of America [Defunct] (EA)
SBA	Society of Batik Artists
SBA	Soybean Agglutinin [Immunology]
SBA	Spirit and Breath Association [Skokie, IL] (EA)
SBA	Standard Beam Approach [British aircraft landing method]
SBA	Standing British Army
SBA	Structure Borne Acoustics (KSC)
SBA	Studies in Biblical Archaeology [A publication]
SBA	Sun Basin Airlines [Moses Lake, CA] [FAA designator] (FAAC)
SBA	Support Base Activation (AAG)
SBA	Susan B. Anthony Dollar
SBA	Sweet Bugger All [An exclamation] [Slang] [British] (DSUE)
SBA	Systems Builders Association [West Milton, OH] (EA)
SBAA	Spina Bifida Association of America [Chicago, IL] (EA)
SBAAM	Small Business Association of Apparel Manufacturers (EA)
SBAC	Small Business Assistance Center (EA)
SBAC	Society of British Aerospace Companies (MCD)
SBAC	Society of British Aircraft Constructors
SBAE	Stabilized Bombing Approach Equipment [Navy]
SBAFWP	Standby Auxiliary Feed Water Pump (IEEE)
SBAG	Schweizer Beitraege zur Allgemeinen Geschichte [A publication]
SBAH	Sodium Bis(methoxyethoxy)aluminum Hydride [Organic chemistry]
S-Bahn	Schnellbahn [High-Speed Railway] [German]
SbAk	Sbornik na Balgarskata Akademija na Naukite [A publication]
Sb Akad Nauk SSSR	Sbornik Rabot Akademiya Nauk SSSR [A publication]

SBAkWissWien	Sitzungsberichte der Oesterreichischen Akademie der Wissenschaften in Wien [A publication] (BJA)
SBAM	Space Based Antimissile
SBAMA	San Bernardino Air Materiel Area
SBAMP	Sea-Based Air Master Plan (MCD)
SBANE	Smaller Business Association of New England [Waltham, MA] (EA)
SBAP	Small Business Assistance Program
SBAP	Society of Business Advisory Professions (EA)
SBAR	San/Bar Corp. [NASDAQ symbol] (NQ)
S Bar J	State Bar Journal of California (DLA)
SBARMO Bull	SBARMO [Scientific Ballooning and Radiations Monitoring Organization] Bulletin [A publication]
SBAS	S-Band Antenna Switch (MCD)
SBASI	Single Bridgewire Apollo Standard Initiator [Explosive]
Sb Aspir Rab Kazan Gos Univ Estest Nauki	Sbornik Aspirantskikh Rabot Kazanskii Gosudarstvennyi Universitet Estestvennye Nauki [A publication]
Sb Aspir Rab Kazan Gos Univ Estest Nauki Biol	Sbornik Aspirantskikh Rabot Kazanskii Gosudarstvennyi Universitet Estestvennye Nauki Biologiya [A publication]
Sb Aspir Rab Kazan Univ Estestv Nauk	Sbornik Aspirantskikh Rabot Kazanskogo Universiteta Estestvennykh Nauk [A publication]
Sb Aspir Rab Voronezh Lesotekh Inst	Sbornik Aspirantskikh Rabot Voronezhskii Lesotekhnicheskii Institut [A publication]
Sb Aspir Rab Vses Nauchno Issled Inst Zhivotnovod	Sbornik Aspirantskikh Rabot Vsesoyuznyi Nauchno Issledovatel'skii Institut Zhivotnovodstva [A publication]
SBAW	Sitzungsberichte der Bayerischen Akademie der Wissenschaften [A publication]
SBAWW	Sitzungsberichte der Akademie der Wissenschaft in Wien [A publication]
SBB	Saddle Back Butte [California] [Seismograph station code, US Geological Survey] (SEIS)
SBB	Schweizerische Bundesbahnen [Swiss Federal Railways]
SBB	Self-Balancing Bridge
SBB	Serikat Buruh Batik [Batik Workers' Union] [Indonesia]
SBB	Single-Band Beaconry [RADAR]
SBB	Soncino Books of the Bible [London] [A publication] (BJA)
SBB	Studies in Bibliography and Booklore [A publication]
SBBA	Spanish-Barb Breeders Association (EA)
Sb Bakteriofagiya	Sbornik Bakteriofagiya [A publication]
SBBAW	Sitzungsberichte der Bayerischen Akademie der Wissenschaften [A publication]
Sb Biokhim Zerna Akad Nauk SSSR Inst Biokhim A N Bakha	Sbornik. Biokhimiya Zerna. Akademiya Nauk SSSR. Institut Biokhimii Imeni A. N. Bakha [A publication]
SBBKA	Seibutsu Butsuri Kagaku [A publication]
Sb Bot Rab Beloruss Otd Vses Bot Ova	Sbornik Botanicheskikh Rabot Belorusskoe Otdelenie Vsesoyuznogo Botanicheskogo Obshchestva [A publication]
Sb Bot Rabot Vses Bot Obshch Beloruss Otd	Sbornik Botanicheskikh Rabot. Vsesoyuznogo Botanicheskogo Obshchestva. Belorusskoe Otdelenie [A publication]
SBBPA	Studia Universitatis Babes-Bolyai. Series Physica [A publication]
SBBT	Short Basic Battery Test (NVT)
SBBUD	SBARMO [Scientific Ballooning and Radiations Monitoring Organization] Bulletin [A publication]
SBC	Baptist College at Charleston, Charleston, SC [OCLC symbol] (OCLC)
SBC	Ferrocarril Sonora Baja California SA de CV [AAR code]
SBC	Saint Basil's College [Stamford, CT]
SBC	Saint Benedict College [Indiana]
SBC	Saint Bernard College [Alabama]
SBC	Santa Barbara [California] [Seismograph station code, US Geological Survey] (SEIS)
SBC	Senate Budget Committee
SBC	Service Bureau Corporation
SBC	Sibasa [South Africa] [Airport symbol] (OAG)
SBC	Simpson Bible College [Later, Simpson College] [California]
SBC	Single Board Computer
SBC	Single Burst Correcting
SBC	Small Bayonet Cap
SBC	Small Business Centre [British]
SBC	Small Business Computer (BUR)
SBC	Solid Bowl Centrifuge
SBC	SONAR Breakout Cable
SBC	Southeastern Bible College [Lakeland, FL]
SBC	Southern Baptist College [Walnut Ridge, AR]
SBC	Southern Baptist Convention
SBC	Southwestern Bell Corporation [NYSE symbol]
SBC	Spaceborne Computer
SBC	Special Back Care [Medicine]
SBC	Standard Boundary Condition
SBC	Standard Buried Collector [Circuit]
SBC	Standing Balance: Eyes Closed [Test] [Occupational therapy]
SBC	Start Breguet Cruise [SST]
SBC	Statutes of British Columbia (DLA)
SBC	Strict Bed Confinement [Medicine]

SBC........... Styrene Block Copolymer [*Plastics technology*]
SBC........... Sue Bennett College [*London, KY*]
SBC........... Summary Billing Card (AFM)
SBC........... Supplementary Benefits Commission [*Department of Employment*] [*British*]
SBC........... Sweet Briar College [*Virginia*]
SBC........... Swiss Bank Corporation
SBC........... Swiss Broadcasting Corporation
SBCA........ Saint Bernard Club of America   (EA)
SBCA........ Satellite Broadcasting and Communications Association [*Formed by a merger of Satellite Television Industry Association and Direct Broadcast Satellite Association*] [*Alexandria, VA*]   (EA)
SBCA........ Seat Belt Control Apparatus
SBCA........ Sensor-Based Control Adapter
SBCA........ Small Business Council of America   (EA)
SBCA........ Soybean Council of America [*Defunct*]
SBCBA....... Sounding Brass and the Conductor [*A publication*]
SBCC........ St. Brendan Cup Committee   (EA)
SBCC....... Senate Bonding and Currency Committee   (OICC)
SBCC........ Separate Bias, Common Control
SBCC........ Southern Building Code Congress, International
SBCCA....... Still Bank Collectors Club of America   (EA)
SBCCI....... Southern Building Code Congress, International   (EA)
SB/CD....... Short Bed/Continuous Development [*Chamber for thin-layer chromatography*] [*Analytical biochemistry*]
SBCD........ Subtract BCD [*Binary Coded Decimal*] Number [*Data processing*]
SBCE........ Bachelor of Science in Civil Engineering
SBCED....... Scientific Bulletin. Canada Centre for Mineral and Energy Technology [*A publication*]
Sb Cesk Akad Zemed Ved ... Sbornik Ceskoslovenske Akademia Zemedelskych Ved [*A publication*]
Sb Cesk Akad Zemed Ved Lesn ... Sbornik Ceskoslovenske Akademie Zemedelskych Ved Lesnictvi [*A publication*]
Sb Cesk Akad Zemed Ved Rada A ... Sbornik Ceskoslovenske Akademie Zemedelskych Ved Rada A [*A publication*]
Sb Cesk Akad Zemed Ved Rada B ... Sbornik Ceskoslovenske Akademie Zemedelskych Ved Rada B [*A publication*]
Sb Cesk Akad Zemed Ved Rostl Vyr ... Sbornik Ceskoslovenske Akademie Zemedelskych Ved. Rostlinna Vyroba [*A publication*]
Sb Cesk Akad Zemed Ved Rostl Vyroba ... Sbornik Ceskoslovenske Akademie Zemedelskych Ved. Rostlinna Vyroba [*A publication*]
Sb Cesk Akad Zemed Ved Zivocisna Vyroba ... Sbornik Ceskoslovenske Akademie Zemedelskych Ved. Zivocisna Vyroba [*A publication*]
SBCF........ Southern Baptist Convention Flyers   (EA)
SBCJ........ Store Block Control Journal   (AABC)
SBCLS....... South Bay Cooperative Library System [*Library network*]
SBCO........ Shipbuilding Company
SBCORP .... Shipbuilding Corporation
SBCP........ Spanish Base Construction Program
SBCR........ Stock Balance and Consumption Report   (NASA)
SB & CR .... Stock Balance and Consumption Report   (AFM)
SBCS .... Series Book Collectors' Society   (EA)
SBCS .... Shore-Based Correlation Subsystem [*Navy*]   (CAAL)
SBCS .... Steam Bypass Control System   (NRCH)
Sb Csl Akad Zemed Ved Zemed Ekon ... Sbornik Ceskoslovenske Akademie Zemedelskych Ved Rada B. Zemedelska Ekonomika [*A publication*]
Sb Csl Akad Zemed Ved Ziv Vyroba ... Sbornik Ceskoslovenske Akademie Zemedelskych Ved Rada E. Zivocisna Vyroba [*A publication*]
SBCU .... Sensor-Based Control Unit [*Data processing*]
SBD........... "Dauntless" Single-Engine Scout-Bomber [*Navy symbol*]
S-BD.......... S-Band   (NASA)
SBD .... San Bernardino, CA [*Location identifier*] [*FAA*]   (FAAL)
SBD .... San Bernardino Public Library, San Bernardino, CA [*OCLC symbol*]   (OCLC)
SBD .... Savings Bond Division [*Navy*]
SBD........... Schematic Block Diagram [*NASA*]   (NASA)
SBD.......... Schottky Barrier Diode [*Electronics*]
SBD........... Space Business Daily [*A publication*]
SBD........... Standard Bibliographic Description
SBD........... Steel Beam Design [*Modray Ltd.*] [*Software package*]
SBD........... Subcontractor Bid Document   (MCD)
SBD........... Sunbird Airlines, Inc. [*Maiden, NC*] [*FAA designator*]   (FAAC)
SBD .... Surface Barrier Detector
SBDAW...... Sitzungsberichte der Deutschen Akademie der Wissenschaften zu Berlin. Klasse fuer Sprachen, Literatur, und Kunst [*A publication*]
SBDAWB.... Sitzungsberichte der Deutschen Akademie der Wissenschaften zu Berlin. Klasse fuer Sprachen, Literatur, und Kunst [*A publication*]
SBDC .... Shipbuilding and Drydock Company
SBDC .... Small Business Development Center [*Lehigh University, University of Alabama in Birmingham*] [*Research center*]

SBDC .... Small Business Development Corporation
SBDH .... Sociedade Brasileira de Discos Historicos J. Leon [*Record label*] [*Brazil*]
SBDL........ Solid Blank Delay Line
SBDO .... Space Business Development Operation   (AAG)
Sb Dokl Gidrotekh Vses Nauchno Issled Inst Gidrotekh ... Sbornik Dokladov po Gidrotekhnike. Vsesoyuznyi Nauchno-Issledovatel'skii Institut Gidrotekhniki [*A publication*]
SBDP......... Serikat Buruh Djawatan Perindustrian [*Department of Industry Workers' Union*] [*Indonesia*]
SBDPU .... Serikat Buruh Djawantan Pekerdjaan Umun [*Public Works' Union*] [*Indonesia*]
SBDT........ Surface Barrier Diffused Transistor
SBE .... S-Band Exciter [*System*] [*Also, SBES*]
SBE .... Sacred Books of the East [*A publication*]   (BJA)
SBE .... Selebi-Pikwe [*Botswana*] [*Later, PKW*] [*Airport symbol*]   (OAG)
SBE .... Self Breast Examination [*for cancer*]
SBE .... Semana Biblica Espanola [*A publication*]
SBE .... Shortness of Breath on Exertion [*Cardiology*]
SBE .... Simple Boolean Expression [*Mathematics*]
SBE .... Society of Broadcast Engineers   (EA)
SBE .... Society for Business Ethics   (EA)
SBE .... Solar Beam Experiment
SbE .... South by East
SBE .... State Board of Education   (OICC)
SBE .... Strategic Bomber Enhancement   (MCD)
SBE .... Sub BIT [*Binary Digit*] Encoder   (MCD)
SBE .... Subacute Bacterial Endocarditis [*Medicine*]
SBED........ Serial BIT [*Binary Digit*] Error Detector
SBEE........ Bachelor of Science in Electrical Engineering
SBEED ...... Storage Battery Electric Energy Demonstration
SBEI.......... SBE, Incorporated [*NASDAQ symbol*]   (NQ)
S Bell........ Bell's House of Lords Scotch Appeals Cases [*1842-50*]   (DLA)
Sb Ent Odd Nar Mus Praze ... Sbornik Entomologickeho Oddeleni Narodniho Musea v Praze [*A publication*]
SBER........ Self-Balancing Electronics Recorder
Sber .... Sitzungsbericht [*Transaction*] [*German*]   (BJA)
SBER......... Subbit Error Rate
Sber Bayer Akad Wiss ... Sitzungsberichte der Bayerische Akademie der Wissenschaften zu Muenchen [*A publication*]
Sber Dt Akad Landwwiss Berl ... Sitzungsberichte. Deutsche Akademie der Landwirtschaftswissenschaften zu Berlin [*A publication*]
Sber Ges Morph Physiol Muench ... Sitzungsberichte. Gesellschaft fuer Morphologie und Physiologie in Muenchen [*A publication*]
Sber Ges Naturf Freunde Berl ... Sitzungsberichte. Gesellschaft Naturforschender Freunde zu Berlin [*A publication*]
SBES........ S-Band Exciter System [*Also, SBE*]
SBET........ Society of Biomedical Equipment Technicians   (EA)
SBETC ...... Small Business Export Trade Corporation
SBEU........ Singapore Bank Employees' Union
SBEUA .... Small Business and Economic Utilization Advisor [*Army*]   (AABC)
SB & F .... Science Books and Films [*A publication*]
SBF .... Scientific Balloon Facility
SBF .... Serologic Blocking Factor [*Cardiology*]
SBF .... Short Backfire [*Antenna*]
SBF .... Silicone Brake Fluid   (MCD)
SBF .... Society of Business Folk [*Brown Deer, WI*]   (EA)
SBF .... Southern Baptist Foundation   (EA)
SBF .... Soy Base Formula [*Nutrition*]
SBF .... Splanchnic Blood Flow [*Physiology*]
SBF .... Studii Biblici Franciscani. Liber Annuus [*A publication*]
SBF .... Surface Burst Fuze
SBFA........ Set Back Front Axle [*Automotive engineering*]
SBFA........ Small Business Foundation of America [*Boston, MA*]   (EA)
Sb Faun Praci Ent Odd Nar Mus Praze ... Sbornik Faunistickych Praci Entomologickeho Oddeleni Narodniho Musea v Praze [*A publication*]
SBFAW...... Sitzungsberichte der Finnischen Akademie der Wissenschaften [*A publication*]
SBFC........ Standby for Further Clearance [*Aviation*]   (FAAC)
SBFLA....... Studii Biblici Franciscani. Liber Annuus [*A publication*]   (BJA)
SBFM........ Silver-Band Frequency Modulation   (IEEE)
SBFRA ...... Schriftenreihe des Bundesministers fuer Wissenschaftliche Forschung (Germany). Radionuklide [*A publication*]
SBFU........ Standby Filter Unit   (IEEE)
SBG........... School Board Gazette [*A publication*]
SBG........... Scottish Bus Group Ltd.
SBG........... Staatsbibliothek Preuss. Kulturbesitz - Gesamtkat. U. Dok., Berlin, Federal Republic of Germany [*OCLC symbol*]   (OCLC)
SBG........... Standard Battery Grade
SBG........... Steinberg, Inc. [*Toronto Stock Exchange symbol*]
SBG........... Strategic Bomber Group
SBG........... Universite de Sherbrooke, Publications Officielles [*UTLAS symbol*]
SBGA .... Serum Beta-Glucuronidase Activity [*Serology*]
SBGDA....... Spisanie na Bulgarskoto Geologichesko Druzhestvo [*A publication*]
Sb Geol Ved Geol ... Sbornik Geologickych Ved. Geologie [*A publication*]

Sb Geol Ved Hydrogeol Inz Geol ... Sbornik Geologickych Ved. Hydrogeologie, Inzenyrska, Geologie [*A publication*]

Sb Geol Ved Loziskova Geol ... Sbornik Geologickych Ved. Loziskova Geologie [*Czechoslovakia*] [*A publication*]

Sb Geol Ved Paleontol ... Sbornik Geologickych Ved. Paleontologie [*A publication*]

Sb Geol Ved Rada Loziskova Geol ... Sbornik Geologickych Ved. Rada Loziskova Geologie [*A publication*]

Sb Geol Ved Rada P Paleontol ... Sbornik Geologickych Ved. Rada P: Paleontologie [*A publication*]

Sb Geol Ved Rada Uzita Geofyz ... Sbornik Geologickych Ved. Rada Uzita Geofyzika [*A publication*]

Sb Geol Ved Uzita Geofyz ... Sbornik Geologickych Ved. Uzita Geofyzika [*Czechoslovakia*] [*A publication*]

SBGGAKOPR ... Sitzungsberichte der Gesellschaft fuer Geschichte und Altertumskunde der Ostseeprovinzen Russlands [*A publication*]

SBGGAKR ... Sitzungsberichte der Gesellschaft fuer Geschichte und Altertumskunde der Ostseeprovinzen Russlands [*A publication*]

SBGI.......... Serikat Buruh Gelas Indonesia [*Glass Workers' Union of Indonesia*]

SBGMA ...... Sitzungsberichte. Gesellschaft zur Befoerderung der Gesamten Naturwissenschaften zu Marburg [*A publication*]

SBGP .... Serikat Buruh Gula Proklamasi [*Sugar Workers' Union*] [*Indonesia*]

SBGP .... Strategic Bomber Group

SBGSN...... Serikat Buruh Garam dan Soda Negeri [*Salt Workers' Association*] [*Indonesia*]

SBGTS ...... Standby Gas Treatment System　(NRCH)

SBH............ St. Barthelemy [*Leeward Islands*] [*Airport symbol*]　(OAG)

SBH............ Sea Blue Histiocytosis [*Medicine*]

SBH............ Sodium Borohydride [*Inorganic chemistry*]

SBH............ State University of New York, Health Sciences Library, Buffalo, NY [*OCLC symbol*]　(OCLC)

SBH............ Strip-Buried Heterostructure [*Telecommunications*]　(TEL)

SBH............ Sumerisch-Babylonische Hymnen [*A publication*]　(BJA)

SBH............ Switch Busy Hour [*Telecommunications*]　(IEEE)

SBHAW ...... Sitzungsberichte. Heidelberge Akademie der Wissenschaft [*A publication*]

SBHC .... Society of the Bible in the Hands of Its Creators　(EA)

SBHC .... Speed Brake Hand Control　(NASA)

SBHC .... Studies in Browning and His Circle [*A publication*]

SBHEU ...... Singapore Business Houses Employees' Union

SBHRT ...... Serikat Buruh Hotel, Rumah-Makan dan Toko [*Hotel, Restaurant and Shops' Workers' Union*] [*Indonesia*]

SBHT.......... Studies in Burke and His Time [*A publication*]

SB-I............ Biblio Service Informatique [*Informatics Biblio Service*] [*Paris Informatics Administration*] [*France*] [*Information service*]　(EISS)

SBI .... Columbia Bible College, Columbia, SC [*OCLC symbol*]　(OCLC)

SBI .... Sabine Pass, TX [*Location identifier*] [*FAA*]　(FAAL)

SBI .... Santa Barbara Island　(MUGU)

SBI .... Scientific Bureau of Investigation [*In radio series "Armstrong of the SBI"*]

SBI .... Serikat Buruh Industri [*Industrial Workers' Union*] [*Indonesia*]

SBI .... Shares of Beneficial Interest [*Business and trade*]

SBI .... Shriners Burn Institute

SBI .... Single Byte Interleaved

SBI .... Small Business Institute [*Small Business Administration*]

SBI .... Somerville Belkin Industries Ltd. [*Toronto Stock Exchange symbol*]

SBI .... Soviet Bureau of Information

SBI .... Soybean (Trypsin) Inhibitor [*Biochemistry*]

SBI .... Special Background Investigation　(NVT)

SBI .... Steel Boiler Institute [*Defunct*]

SBI .... Sun Belt Institute　(EA)

SBI .... Synfuels Bibliography and Index [*A publication*]

SBIA.......... Small Business Innovation Development Act [*1982*]

SBIBD .... Symmetrical Balanced Incomplete Block Designs　(MCD)

SBIC.......... Small Business Investment Company [*Generic term*]

SBICo......... Small Business Investment Company [*Generic term*]

SBIE .... Shared Bibliographic Input Experiment [*Special Libraries Association*]

SBIG.......... Seibels Bruce Group [*NASDAQ symbol*]　(NQ)

SBILS........ Scanning Beam Instrument Landing System　(KSC)

SBIN.......... Fort Battleford National Historic Park, Parks Canada [*Parc Historique National Fort Battleford, Parcs Canada*] [*Battleford, Saskatchewan*] [*Library symbol*] [*National Library of Canada*]　(NLC)

Sb Inf Obogashch Briket Uglei ... Sbornik Informatsii po Obogashcheniyu i Briketirovaniyu Uglei [*USSR*] [*A publication*]

Sb Inst Neorg Khim Elektrokhim Akad Nauk Gruz SSR ... Sbornik Institut Neorganicheskoi Khimii i Elektrokhimii Akademii Nauk Gruzinskoi SSR [*A publication*]

SBIO.......... Synbiotics Corp. [*NASDAQ symbol*]　(NQ)

SBIR.......... Small Business Innovation Research

SBIR.......... Storage Bus in Register

SBiz........... Studi Bizantini [*A publication*]

Sb "Izme Pochv Okul'turiv Klassifik Diagnostika" ... Sbornik. "Izmenenie Pochv pri Okul'turivanii, Ikh Klassifikatsiya i Diagnostika" [*A publication*]

SBJ............ Journal. State Bar of California　(DLA)

SBJ............ Schottky Barrier Junction [*Electronics*]

SBJ............ Solberg, NJ [*Location identifier*] [*FAA*]　(FAAL)

Sb Jihoceskeho Muz Cesk Budejovicich Prir Vedy ... Sbornik Jihoceskeho Muzea v Ceskych Budejovicich Prirodni Vedy [*A publication*]

SBK .... St. Brieuc [*France*] [*Airport symbol*]　(OAG)

SBK .... Serikat Buruh Kehutanan [*National Forestry Workers' Union*] [*Indonesian*]

SBK .... Serikat Buruh Kependjaaran [*Prisons Workers' Unions*] [*Indonesian*]

SBK .... Signet Banking Corp. [*NYSE symbol*]

SBK .... Single-Beam Klystron　(MSA)

SBK .... Society for Behavioral Kinesiology

SBK .... South Brooklyn Railway Co. [*AAR code*]

SBK .... Universite de Sherbrooke, Bibliotheque [*UTLAS symbol*]

Sb Karantinu Rast ... Sbornik po Karantinu Rastenii [*A publication*]

SBKAW ...... Sitzungsberichte der K. Akademie der Wissenschaften in Wien [*A publication*]

SBKAWW ... Sitzungsberichte der K. Akademie der Wissenschaften in Wien [*A publication*]

Sb Klubu Prirodoved Brno ... Sbornik Klubu Prirodovedeckeho v Brno [*A publication*]

SBKP.......... Serikat Buruh Kementerian Pertahanan [*Defense Ministry Union*] [*Indonesian*]

Sb Kratk Soobshch Fiz AN SSSR Fiz Inst NN Lebedeva ... Sbornik Kratkie Soobshcheniya po Fizike. Akademiya Nauk SSSR. Fizicheskii Institut Imeni N. N. Lebedeva [*A publication*]

Sb Kratk Soobshch Fiz AN SSSR Fiz Inst PN Lebedeva ... Sbornik Kratkie Soobshcheniya po Fizike. AN SSSR. Fizicheskii Institut Imeni P. N. Lebedeva [*A publication*]

Sb Kratk Soobshch Kazan Univ Zool ... Sbornik Kratkikh Soobshchenii Kazanskogo Universiteta po Zoologii [*A publication*]

s-bl---.......... Brazil [*MARC geographic area code*] [*Library of Congress*]　(LCCP)

SBL .... Santa Ana [*Bolivia*] [*Airport symbol*] [*Obsolete*]　(OAG)

SBL .... Sealed Beam Lamp

SBL .... Serikat Buruh Logam [*Metal Workers' Union*] [*Indonesian*]

SBL .... Society of Biblical Literature [*Formerly, SBLE*]　(EA)

SBL .... Soybean Lecithin [*Biochemistry*]

SBL .... Space-Based LASER

SBL .... Staphylococcal Bacteriophage Lysate

SBL .... State University of New York at Buffalo, Law Library, Buffalo, NY [*OCLC symbol*]　(OCLC)

SBL .... Studies in Black Literature [*A publication*]

SBL .... Styrene-Butadiene Latexes [*Organic chemistry*]

SBLA.......... Small Business Loans Act [*Canada*]

SBLC.......... Small Business Legislative Council [*Washington, DC*]　(EA)

SBLC.......... Standby Liquid Control　(NRCH)

SBLE .... Society of Biblical Literature and Exegesis [*Later, SBL*]　(EA)

SBLEA .... Sbornik Lekarsky [*A publication*]

Sb Lek........ Sbornik Lekarsky [*A publication*]

Sb Lekar .... Sbornik Lekarsky [*A publication*]

Sb Leningr Inst Inzh Zheleznodorozhn Transp ... Sbornik Leningradskogo Instituta Inzhenerov Zheleznodorozhnogo Transporta [*A publication*]

SBLI............ Savings Bank Life Insurance

SBLO.......... Strong Black Liquor Oxidation [*Papermaking*]

SBLOCA .... Small-Break Loss of Coolant Accident [*Nuclear energy*]　(NRCH)

SBLP.......... Simplified Bank Loan Participation Plan [*Small Business Administration*]

SBLSA .... Small Business and Labor Surplus Advisor　(AABC)

SBM .... College of Charleston, Charleston, SC [*OCLC symbol*]　(OCLC)

SBM .... St. Louis, Brownsville & Mexico [*AAR code*]

SBM .... School in Basic Management [*LIMRA*]

SBM .... Sheboygan [*Wisconsin*] [*Airport symbol*]　(OAG)

SBM .... Sheboygan, WI [*Location identifier*] [*FAA*]　(FAAL)

SBM .... Single Black Male [*Classified advertising*]

SBM .... Single-Buoy Mooring [*Oil tanker*]

SBM .... Societe des Bains de Mer [*Monte Carlo*]

SBM .... Society of Behavioral Medicine [*Knoxville, TN*]　(EA)

SBM .... Speed-O-Print Business Machines Corp. [*American Stock Exchange symbol*]

SBM .... Stuttgarter Biblische Monographien [*Stuttgart*] [*A publication*]

SBM .... Submerge [*or Submersible*]　(KSC)

SBM .... Submit　(AABC)

SBM .... System Balance Measure　(BUR)

SBMA........ SINS [*Ship Inertial Navigational System*] Bedplate Mirror Assembly

SBMA........ Steel Bar Mills Association [*St. Louis, MO*]　(EA)

SBMDL....... Submodel

SBME........ Society of Business Magazine Editors [*Later, ASBPE*]

SBMI.......... School Bus Manufacturers Institute [*Bethesda, MD*]　(EA)

Sb Mikroelementy i Produktivn Rast ... Sbornik. Mikroelementy i Produktivnost Rastenii [*A publication*]

SBMMB...... Studia Universitatis Babes-Bolyai. Series Mathematica-Mechanica [*A publication*]

Sb Mosk Inst Stali Splavov ... Sbornik. Moskovskii Institut Stali Splavov [*USSR*] [*A publication*]
SBMPL .... Simultaneous Binaural Midplane Localization [*Audiometry*]
SBMSI .... Serikat Buruh Minjak Shell Indonesia [*Union of Oil Workers for Shell of Indonesia*]
Sb Muz Antropol Etnogr ... Sbornik Muzeja Antropologii i Etnografii [*A publication*]
SBMV .... Southern Bean Mosaic Virus
SBMW .... Serikat Buruh Maclaine, Watson [*Maclaine Watson Company Workers' Union*] [*Indonesia*]
SBN .... Buffalo Narrows Public Library, Saskatchewan [*Library symbol*] [*National Library of Canada*]   (NLC)
SBN .... Sheridan Broadcasting Network
SBN .... Small Business Network [*Baltimore, MD*]   (EA)
SBN .... South Bend [*Indiana*] [*Airport symbol*]   (OAG)
SBN .... Spaceborne   (KSC)
SBN .... Standard Book Number
SBN .... Studi Bizantini e Neoellenici [*A publication*]
SBN .... Suburban Airlines [*Red Bank, NJ*] [*FAA designator*]   (FAAC)
SBN .... Sunbelt Nursery Group, Inc. [*American Stock Exchange symbol*]
SBN₂ .... Single Breath Nitrogen [*Test*] [*Medicine*]
Sb Nar Mus Praze Rada B Prir Vedy ... Sbornik Narodniho Muzea v Praze Rada B: Prirodni Vedy [*A publication*]
Sb Nauchni Tr ... Sbornik Nauchni Trudove [*A publication*]
Sb Nauchno Issled Inst Osn Podzemn Sooruzh ... Sbornik Nauchno-Issledovatel'skii Institut Osnovanii i Podzemnykh Sooruzhenii [*A publication*]
Sb Nauchno-Issled Rab Adygeisk Oblast Opyt Sta ... Sbornik Nauchno-Issledovatel'skikh Rabot Adygeikaya Oblast Opytnaya Stantsiya [*A publication*]
Sb Nauchno-Issled Rab Azovo-Chernomorsk S-Kh Inst ... Sbornik Nauchno-Issledovatel'skikh Rabot Azovo-Chernomorskogo Sel'skokhozyaistvennogo Instituta [*A publication*]
Sb Nauchno-Issled Rab Gor'k Obl Opytn Stn Zhivotnovod ... Sbornik Nauchno-Issledovatel'skikh Rabot Gor'kovskoi Oblastnoi Opytnoi Stantsii Zhivotnovodstva [*A publication*]
Sb Nauchno-Issled Rab Orlov Gos Sel'-khoz Opyt Sta ... Sbornik Nauchno-Issledovatel'skikh Rabot. Orlovskoi Gosudarstvennoi Sel'skokhozyaistvennoi Opytnoi Stantsii [*A publication*]
Sb Nauchno Issled Rab Tashk Tekst Inst ... Sbornik Nauchno-Issledovatel'skikh Rabot Tashkentskogo Tekstil'nogo Instituta [*A publication*]
Sb Nauchno-Issled Rab Vses Nauchno-Issled Inst Tab Makhorki ... Sbornik Nauchno-Issledovatel'skikh Rabot. Vsesoyuznogo Nauchno-Issledovatel'skii Institut Tabaka i Makhorki [*A publication*]
Sb Nauchno-Issled Rab Vses Nauchno-Issled Inst Tab Makhorki ... Sbornik Nauchno-Issledovatel'skikh Rabot Vsesoyuznogo Nauchno-Issledovatel'skogo Instituta Tabaka i Makhorki [*A publication*]
Sb Nauchn Rab Angar Nauchno-Issled Inst Gig Tr Prof Zabol ... Sbornik Nauchnykh Rabot Angarskogo Nauchno-Issledovatel'skogo Instituta Gigieny Truda i Professional'nykh Zabolevanii [*A publication*]
Sb Nauchn Rab Beloruss Nauchno-Issled Kozhnovenerol Inst ... Sbornik Nauchnykh Rabot Belorusskogo Nauchno-Issledovatel'skogo Kozhnovenerologicheskogo Instituta [*A publication*]
Sb Nauchn Rab Kazan Gos Med Inst ... Sbornik Nauchnykh Rabot Kazanskogo Gosudarstvennogo Meditsinskogo Instituta [*A publication*]
Sb Nauchn Rab Khar'k Gos Med Inst ... Sbornik Nauchnykh Rabot Khar'kovskii Gosudarstvennyi Meditsinskii Institut [*A publication*]
Sb Nauchn Rab Khar'k Gos Med Inst ... Sbornik Nauchnykh Rabot Khar'kovskogo Gosudarstvennogo Meditsinskogo Instituta [*A publication*]
Sb Nauchn Rab Khar'k Nauchno-Issled Inst Vaktsin Syvorot ... Sbornik Nauchnykh Rabot Khar'kovskogo Nauchno-Issledovatel'skogo Instituta Vaktsin i Syvorotok [*A publication*]
Sb Nauchn Rab Kiev Voen Gosp ... Sbornik Nauchnykh Rabot Kievskii Voennyi Gospital [*A publication*]
Sb Nauchn Rab Kirg Med Inst ... Sbornik Nauchnykh Rabot Kirgizskii Meditsinskii Institut [*A publication*]
Sb Nauchn Rab Kirg Nauchno-Issled Inst Okhr Materin Det ... Sbornik Nauchnykh Rabot Kirgizskii Nauchno-Issledovatel'skii Institut Okhrany Materinstva Detstva [*A publication*]
Sb Nauchn Rab Kirg Nauchno-Issled Inst Tuberk ... Sbornik Nauchnykh Rabot Kirgizskogo Nauchno-Issledovatel'skogo Instituta Tuberkuleza [*A publication*]
Sb Nauchn Rab Kurgan Gos S-kh Inst ... Sbornik Nauchnykh Rabot Kurganskii Gosudarstvennyi Sel'skokhozyaistvennyi Institut [*A publication*]
Sb Nauchn Rab Leningr Gos Inst Usoversh Vrachei ... Sbornik Nauchnykh Rabot Leningradskii Gosudarstvennyi Institut Usovershenstvovaniya Vrachei [*A publication*]

Sb Nauchn Rab Leningr Khim-Farm Inst ... Sbornik Nauchnykh Rabot Leningradskogo Khimiko-Farmatsevticheskogo Instituta [*A publication*]
Sb Nauchn Rab Minsk Gos Med Inst ... Sbornik Nauchnykh Rabot Minskogo Gosudarstvennogo Meditsinskogo Instituta [*A publication*]
Sb Nauchn Rab Nauchno-Issled Sadov Im I V Michurina ... Sbornik Nauchnykh Rabot Nauchno-Issledovatel'skogo Instituta Sadov Imeni I. V. Michurina [*A publication*]
Sb Nauchn Rab Rizh Med Inst ... Sbornik Nauchnykh Rabot Rizhskogo Meditsinskogo Instituta [*A publication*]
Sb Nauchn Rab Rostov Med Inst ... Sbornik Nauchnykh Rabot Rostovskogo Meditsinskogo Instituta [*A publication*]
Sb Nauchn Rab Ryazan S-kh Inst ... Sbornik Nauchnykh Rabot Ryazanskii Sel'skokhozyaistvennyi Institut [*A publication*]
Sb Nauchn Rab Sarat Med Inst ... Sbornik Nauchnykh Rabot Saratovskii Meditsinskii Institut [*A publication*]
Sb Nauchn Rab Sib Zon Nauchno-Issled Vet Inst ... Sbornik Nauchnykh Rabot Sibirskogo Zonal'nogo Nauchno-Issledovatel'skogo Veterinarnogo Instituta [*A publication*]
Sb Nauchn Rab Stud Stalingr S-Kh Inst ... Sbornik Nauchnykh Rabot Studentov Stalingradskogo Sel'skokhozyaistvennogo Instituta [*A publication*]
Sb Nauchn Rab Sverdl Med Inst ... Sbornik Nauchnykh Rabot Sverdlovskogo Meditsinskogo Instituta [*A publication*]
Sb Nauchn Rab Sverdl Otd Vses O-va Anat Gistol Embriol ... Sbornik Nauchnykh Rabot Sverdlovskogo Otdeleniya Vsesoyuznogo Obshchestva Anatomov, Gistologov, i Embriologov [*A publication*]
Sb Nauchn Rab Tsentr Nauchno-Issled Lab Rostov Med Inst ... Sbornik Nauchnykh Rabot Tsentral'naya Nauchno-Issledovatel'skaya Laboratoriya Rostov'skogo Meditsinskogo Instituta [*A publication*]
Sb Nauchn Rab Voen-Med Fak Kuibyshev Med Inst ... Sbornik Nauchnykh Rabot Voenno-Meditsinskogo Fakul'teta Kuibyshevskogo Meditsinskogo Instituta [*A publication*]
Sb Nauchn Rab Volgogr Gos Med Inst ... Sbornik Nauchnykh Rabot Volgogradskoi Gosudarstvennyi Meditsinskii Institut [*A publication*]
Sb Nauchn Rab Volgogr Med Inst ... Sbornik Nauchnykh Rabot Volgogradskogo Meditsinskogo Instituta [*A publication*]
Sb Nauchn Rab Volgogr Obl Klin Boln ... Sbornik Nauchnykh Rabot Volgogradskoi Oblastnoi Klinicheskoi Bol'nitsy [*A publication*]
Sb Nauchn Rab Volgogr Pedagog Inst ... Sbornik Nauchnykh Rabot Volgogradskogo Pedagogicheskogo Instituta [*A publication*]
Sb Nauchn Rab Vses Nauchno-Issled Inst Lek Rast ... Sbornik Nauchnykh Rabot Vsesoyuznyi Nauchno-Issledovatel'skii Institut Lekarstvennykh Rastenii [*A publication*]
Sb Nauchn Rab Vses Nauchno-Issled Inst Sadovod ... Sbornik Nauchnykh Rabot Vsesoyuznyi Nauchno-Issledovatel'skii Institut Sadovodstva [*A publication*]
Sb Nauchn Rab Vses Nauchno-Issled Inst Zhivotnovod ... Sbornik Nauchnykh Rabot Vsesoyuznyi Nauchno-Issledovatel'skii Institut Zhivotnovodstva [*A publication*]
Sb Nauchn Rab Yarosl Gorzdravotdela ... Sbornik Nauchnykh Rabot Yaroslavskogo Gorzdravotdela [*A publication*]
Sb Nauchn Rab Yarosl Med Inst ... Sbornik Nauchnykh Rabot Yaroslavskogo Meditsinskogo Instituta [*A publication*]
Sb Nauchn Rab Zaochn Inst Sov Torg ... Sbornik Nauchnykh Rabot Zaochnyi Institut Sovetskoi Torgovli [*A publication*]
Sb Nauchn Soobshch Kafedry Org Fizk Khim Dagest Gos Univ ... Sbornik Nauchnykh Soobshchenii Kafedry Organicheskoi i Fizkolloidnoi Khimii. Dagestanskii Gosudarstvennyi Universitet [*A publication*]
Sb Nauchn Soobshch Sarat Avtomob Dorozhn Inst ... Sbornik Nauchnykh Soobshchenii Saratovskii Avtomobil'no Dorozhnyi Institut [*A publication*]
Sb Nauchn Tr Andizh Med Inst ... Sbornik Nauchnykh Trudov Andizhanskogo Meditsitskogo Instituta [*A publication*]
Sb Nauchn Tr Arm Gos Zaochn Pedagog Inst ... Sbornik Nauchnykh Trudov Gosudarstvennogo Zaochnogo Pedagogicheskogo Instituta [*A publication*]
Sb Nauchn Tr Arm Otd Vses Bot Ova ... Sbornik Nauchnykh Trudov Armyanskogo Otdelnykh Vsesoyuznogo Botanicheskoi Obshchestva [*A publication*]
Sb Nauchn Tr Arm S-kh Inst ... Sbornik Nauchnykh Trudov Armyanskogo Sel'skokhozyaistvennogo Instituta [*A publication*]
Sb Nauchn Tr Azerb Nauchno Issled Inst Gematol Pereliv Krovi ... Sbornik Nauchnykh Trudov Azerbaidzhanskogo Nauchno-Issledovatel'skogo Instituta Gematologii i Perelivaniya Krovi [*A publication*]
Sb Nauchn Tr Azerb Nauchno-Issled Inst Pereliv Krovi ... Sbornik Nauchnykh Trudov Azerbaidzhanskogo Nauchno-Issledovatel'skogo Instituta Perelivanya Krovi [*A publication*]
Sb Nauchn Tr Azerb Nauchno Issled Inst Perel Krovi ... Sbornik Nauchnykh Trudov Azerbaidzhanskogo Nauchno-Issledovatel'skogo Instituta Perelivaniya Krovi [*A publication*]

Sb Nauchn Tr Bashk Gos Med Inst ... Sbornik Nauchnykh Trudov Bashkirskogo Gosudarstvennogo Meditsinskogo Instituta [*A publication*]

Sb Nauchn Tr Bashk Med Inst ... Sbornik Nauchnykh Trudov Bashkirskogo Meditsinskogo Instituta [*A publication*]

Sb Nauchn Tr Bashk Nauchno-Issled Trakhomatoznogo Inst ... Sbornik Nauchnykh Trudov Bashkirskogo Nauchno-Issledovatel'skogo Trakhomatoznogo Instituta [*A publication*]

Sb Nauchn Tr Beloruss Inst Mekh Selsk Khoz ... Sbornik Nauchnykh Trudov Belorusskii Institut Mekhanizatsii Sel'skogo Khozyaistva [*A publication*]

Sb Nauchn Tr Beloruss Lesotekh Inst ... Sbornik Nauchnykh Trudov Belorusskogo Lesotekhnicheskogo Instituta [*A publication*]

Sb Nauchn Tr Beloruss Nauchno-Issled Inst Pochvoved Agrokhim ... Sbornik Nauchnykh Trudov Belorusskii Nauchno-Issledovatel'skii Institut Pochvovedeniya i Agrokhimii [*A publication*]

Sb Nauchn Tr Beloruss Nauchno-Issled Inst Zemled ... Sbornik Nauchnykh Trudov Belorusskii Nauchno-Issledovatel'skii Institut Zemledeliya [*A publication*]

Sb Nauchn Tr Beloruss Politekh Inst ... Sbornik Nauchnykh Trudov Belorusskii Politekhnicheskii Institut [*A publication*]

Sb Nauchn Tr Beloruss S-kh Akad ... Sbornik Nauchnykh Trudov Belorusskoi Sel'skokhozyaistvennoi Akademii [*A publication*]

Sb Nauchn Tr Chelyab Politekh Inst ... Sbornik Nauchnykh Trudov Chelyabinskii Politekhnicheskii Institut [*USSR*] [*A publication*]

Sb Nauchn Tr Chit Gos Med Inst ... Sbornik Nauchnykh Trudov Chitinskii Gosudarstvennyi Meditsinskii Institut [*A publication*]

Sb Nauchn Tr Chuv Nauchno-Issled Trakhomatoznogo Inst ... Sbornik Nauchnykh Trudov Chuvashskogo Nauchno-Issledovatel'skogo Trakhomatoznogo Instituta [*A publication*]

Sb Nauchn Tr Donskogo S-kh Inst ... Sbornik Nauchnykh Trudov Donskogo Sel'skokhozyaistvennogo Instituta [*A publication*]

Sb Nauchn Tr Erevan Politekh Inst ... Sbornik Nauchnykh Trudov. Erevanskii Politekhnicheskii Institut [*Armenian SSR*] [*A publication*]

Sb Nauchn Tr Est Nauchno-Issled Inst Zemled Melior ... Sbornik Nauchnykh Trudov Estonskogo Nauchno-Issledovatel'skogo Instituta Zemledeliya i Melioratsii [*A publication*]

Sb Nauchn Tr Est S-kh Akad ... Sbornik Nauchnykh Trudov Estonskaya Sel'skokhozyaistvennaya Akademiya [*A publication*]

Sb Nauchn Tr Fiz Tekh Inst Akad Nauk B SSR ... Sbornik Nauchnykh Trudov. Fiziko-Tekhnicheskii Institut. Akademiya Nauk Belorusskoi SSR [*A publication*]

Sb Nauchn Tr Fiz Tekh Inst Nizk Temp Akad Nauk Ukr SSR ... Sbornik Nauchnykh Trudov. Fiziko-Tekhnicheskii Institut Nizkikh Temperatur. Akademiya Nauk Ukrainskoi SSR [*Ukrainian SSR*] [*A publication*]

Sb Nauchn Tr Gazov Khromatogr ... Sbornik Nauchnykh Trudov po Gazovoi Khromatografii [*A publication*]

Sb Nauchn Tr Gos Nauchno Issled Inst Elektrodnoi Promsti ... Sbornik Nauchnykh Trudov. Gosudarstvennyi Nauchno-Issledovatel'skii Institut Elektrodnoi Promyshlennosti [*A publication*]

Sb Nauchn Tr Gos Nauchno-Issled Inst Keramzitu ... Sbornik Nauchnykh Trudov. Gosudarstvennyi Nauchno-Issledovatel'skii Institut po Keramzitu [*A publication*]

Sb Nauchn Tr Gos Nauchno-Issled Inst Tsvetn Met ... Sbornik Nauchnykh Trudov Gosudarstvennogo Nauchno-Issledovatel'skogo Instituta Tsvetnykh Metallov [*A publication*]

Sb Nauchn Tr Inst Metallofiz Akad Ukr SSR ... Sbornik Nauchnykh Trudov Instituta Metallofiziki. Akademiya Nauk Ukrainskoi SSR [*Ukrainian SSR*] [*A publication*]

Sb Nauchn Tr Irkutsk Gos Nauchno-Issled Inst Redk Met ... Sbornik Nauchnykh Trudov Irkutskii Gosudarstvennyi Nauchno-Issledovatel'skii Institut Redkikh Metallov [*A publication*]

Sb Nauchn Tr Ivanov Energ Inst ... Sbornik Nauchnykh Trudov Ivanovskogo Energeticheskogo Instituta [*A publication*]

Sb Nauchn Tr Ivanov Gos Med Inst ... Sbornik Nauchnykh Trudov Ivanovskogo Gosudarstvennogo Meditsinskogo Instituta [*A publication*]

Sb Nauchn Tr Ivanov Med Inst ... Sbornik Nauchnykh Trudov Ivanovskogo Meditsinskogo Instituta [*A publication*]

Sb Nauchn Tr Ivanov S-kh Inst ... Sbornik Nauchnykh Trudov Ivanovskogo Sel'skokhozyaistvennogo Instituta [*A publication*]

Sb Nauchn Tr Kalinin Gos Skh Opytn Stant ... Sbornik Nauchnykh Trudov Kalininskaya Gosudarstvennaya Sel'skokhozyaistvennaya Opytnaya Stantisiya [*A publication*]

Sb Nauchn Tr Kamenets Podolsk Skh Inst ... Sbornik Nauchnykh Trudov Kamenets-Podol'skogo Sel'skokhozyaistvennogo Instituta [*A publication*]

Sb Nauchn Tr Kar'k Gos Med Inst ... Sbornik Nauchnykh Trudov Khar'kovskogo Gosudarstvennogo Meditsinskogo Instituta [*A publication*]

Sb Nauchn Tr Kaz Gorno-Metall Inst ... Sbornik Nauchnykh Trudov Kazakhskii Gorno-Metallurgicheskii Institut [*A publication*]

Sb Nauchn Tr Khar'k Med Inst ... Sbornik Nauchnykh Trudov Khar'kovskogo Meditsinskogo Instituta [*A publication*]

Sb Nauchn Tr Kiev Inst Inzh Grazhd Aviats ... Sbornik Nauchnykh Trudov Kievskogo Instituta Inzhenerov Grazhdanskoi Aviatsii [*Ukrainian SSR*] [*A publication*]

Sb Nauchn Tr Kiev Inzh Stroit Inst ... Sbornik Nauchnykh Trudov Kievskogo Inzhenerno-Stroitel'nogo Instituta [*A publication*]

Sb Nauchn Tr Kirg Med Inst ... Sbornik Nauchnykh Trudov Kirkizskogo Meditsinskogo Instituta [*A publication*]

Sb Nauchn Tr Krasnoyarsk Gos Med Inst ... Sbornik Nauchnykh Trudov Krasnoyarskogo Gosudarstvennogo Meditsinskogo Instituta [*A publication*]

Sb Nauchn Tr Kuibyshev Nauchno Issled Inst Epidemiol Gig ... Sbornik Nauchnykh Trudov Kuibyshevskogo Nauchno-Issledovatel'skogo Instituta Epidemiologii i Gigieny [*A publication*]

Sb Nauchn Tr Kuibyshev Nauchno Issled Inst Gig ... Sbornik Nauchnykh Trudov. Kuibyshevskii Nauchno-Issledovatel'skii Institut Gigeny [*A publication*]

Sb Nauchn Tr Kuibyshev Nauchno Issled Vet Stn ... Sbornik Nauchnykh Trudov Kuibyshevskoi Nauchno-Issledovatel'noi Veterinarnoi Stantsii [*A publication*]

Sb Nauchn Tr Kuzbasskii Politekh Inst ... Sbornik Nauchnykh Trudov. Kuzbasskii Politekhnicheskii Institut [*A publication*]

Sb Nauchn Tr Leningr Inst Usoversh Vet Vrachei ... Sbornik Nauchnykh Trudov Leningradskogo Instituta Usovershenstvovaniya Veterinarnykh Vrachei [*A publication*]

Sb Nauchn Tr Leningr Inst Usoversh Vrachei ... Sbornik Nauchnykh Trudov Leningradskogo Instituta Usovershenstvovaniya Vrachei [*A publication*]

Sb Nauchn Tr Leningr Inzh-Stroit Inst ... Sbornik Nauchnykh Trudov Leningradskii Inzhenerno-Stroitel'nyi Institut [*A publication*]

Sb Nauchn Tr Leningr Nauchno-Issled Inst Pereliv Krovi ... Sbornik Nauchnykh Trudov Leningradskogo Nauchno-Issledovatel'skogo Instituta Perelivanya Krovi [*A publication*]

Sb Nauchn Tr Lugansk S-kh Inst ... Sbornik Nauchnykh Trudov Luganskogo Sel'skokhozyaistvennogo Instituta [*A publication*]

Sb Nauchn Tr Magnitogorsk Gornometall Inst ... Sbornik Nauchnykh Trudov. Magnitogorskii Gornometallurgicheskii Institut [*USSR*] [*A publication*]

Sb Nauchn Tr Mogilev Obl Gos Skh Opytn Stn ... Sbornik Nauchnykh Trudov Mogilevskaya Oblastnaya Gosudarstvennaya Sel'skokhozyaistvennaya Opytnaya Stantsiya [*A publication*]

Sb Nauchn Tr Morfol Kafedry Bashk Med Inst ... Sbornik Nauchnykh Trudov Morfologicheskoi Kafedry Bashkirskogo Meditsinskogo Instituta [*A publication*]

Sb Nauchn Tr Mosk Inst Tsvetn Met Zolota ... Sbornik Nauchnykh Trudov Moskovskii Institut Tsvetnykh Metallov i Zolota [*A publication*]

Sb Nauchn Tr Mosk Poligr Inst ... Sbornik Nauchnykh Trudov Moskovskii Poligraficheskii Institut [*A publication*]

Sb Nauchn Tr Mosk Tekhnol Inst Pishch Promsti ... Sbornik Nauchnykh Trudov Moskovskii Tekhnologicheskii Institut Pishchevoi Promyshlennosti [*A publication*]

Sb Nauchn Tr Nauchno-Issled Inst Pereliv Krovi Arm SSR ... Sbornik Nauchnykh Trudov Nauchno-Issledovatel'skogo Instituta Gematologii i Perelivaniya Krovi Armyanskoi SSR [*A publication*]

Sb Nauchn Tr Nauchno-Issled Inst Zemled Echmiadzin (Arm SSR) ... Sbornik Nauchnykh Trudov Nauchno-Issledovatel'skii Institut Zemledeliya. Echmiadzin (Armenian SSR) [*A publication*]

Sb Nauchn Tr Permsk Gorn Inst ... Sbornik Nauchnykh Trudov. Permskii Gornyi Institut [*A publication*]

Sb Nauchn Tr Permsk Gos Med Inst ... Sbornik Nauchnykh Trudov Permskii Gosudarstvennyi Meditsinskii Institut [*A publication*]

Sb Nauchn Tr Permsk Gos Skh Opytn Stn ... Sbornik Nauchnykh Trudov. Permskaya Gosudarstvennaya Sel'skokhozyaistvennaya Opytnaya Stantsiya [*A publication*]

Sb Nauchn Tr Permsk Politekh Inst ... Sbornik Nauchnykh Trudov Permskij Politekhnicheskij Institut [*A publication*]

Sb Nauchn Tr Primorsk S-kh Inst ... Sbornik Nauchnykh Trudov Primorskogo Sel'skokhozyaistvennogo Instituta [*A publication*]

Sb Nauchn Tr Rostov Donu Gos Med Inst ... Sbornik Nauchnykh Trudov Rostovskogo na Donu Gosudarstvennogo Meditsinskogo Instituta [*A publication*]

Sb Nauchn Tr Rostov Nauchno-Issled Inst Akad Kommunaln Khoz ... Sbornik Nauchnykh Trudov Rostovskii Nauchno-Issledovatel'skii Institut Akademii Kommunal'nogo Khozyaistva [*A publication*]

Sb Nauchn Tr Ryazan Med Inst ... Sbornik Nauchnykh Trudov Ryazanskogo Meditsinskogo Instituta [*A publication*]

Sb Nauchn Tr Ryazan S-kh Inst ... Sbornik Nauchnykh Trudov Ryazanskogo Sel'skokhozyaistvennogo Instituta [*A publication*]

Sb Nauchn Tr Samark Gos Med Inst ... Sbornik Nauchnykh Trudov Samarkandskogo Gosudarstvennogo Meditsinskogo Instituta [*A publication*]

Sb Nauchn Tr Sanit Tekh ... Sbornik Nauchnykh Trudov po Sanitarnoi Tekhnike [*A publication*]

Sb Nauchn Tr Sev-Oset Gos Med Inst ... Sbornik Nauchnykh Trudov Severo-Osetinskii Gosudarstvennyi Meditsinskii Institut [*A publication*]

Sb Nauchn Tr Sverdl Fil Mosk Inst Nar Khoz ... Sbornik Nauchnykh Trudov Sverdlovskii Filial Moskovskogo Instituta Narodnogo Khozyaistva [*A publication*]

Sb Nauchn Tr Tashk Gos Med Inst ... Sbornik Nauchnykh Trudov Tashkentskogo Gosudarstvennogo Meditsinskogo Instituta [*A publication*]

Sb Nauchn Tr Tomsk Inzh Stroit Inst ... Sbornik Nauchnykh Trudov Tomskii Inzhenerno-Stroitel'nyi Institut [*USSR*] [*A publication*]

Sb Nauchn Tr Tsentr Aptechn Nauchno-Issled Inst ... Sbornik Nauchnykh Trudov Tsentral'nogo Aptechnogo Nauchno-Issledovatel'skogo Instituta [*A publication*]

Sb Nauchn Tr Ukr Inst Usoversh Vrachei ... Sbornik Nauchnykh Trudov Ukrainskogo Instituta Usovershenstvovaniy Vrachei [*A publication*]

Sb Nauchn Tr Ukr Nauchno-Issled Inst Ogneuporov ... Sbornik Nauchnykh Trudov Ukrainskii Nauchno-Issledovatel'skii Institut Ogneuporov [*Ukrainian SSR*] [*A publication*]

Sb Nauchn Tr Ukr Nauchno-Issled Uglekhim Inst ... Sbornik Nauchnykh Trudov Ukrainskii Nauchno-Issledovatel'skii Uglekhimcheskii I nstitut [*Ukrainian SSR*] [*A publication*]

Sb Nauchn Tr Vinnitsk Gos Med Inst ... Sbornik Nauchnykh Trudov Vinnitskogo Gosudarstvennogo Meditsinskogo Instituta [*A publication*]

Sb Nauchn Tr Vitebsk Med Inst ... Sbornik Nauchnykh Trudov Vitebskogo Meditsinskogo Instituta [*A publication*]

Sb Nauchn Tr Vladimir Vech Politekh Inst ... Sbornik Nauchnykh Trudov Vladimirskii Vechernii Politekhnicheskii Institut [*A publication*]

Sb Nauchn Tr Vladivost Med Inst ... Sbornik Nauchnykh Trudov Vladivostokskii Meditsinskii Institut [*A publication*]

Sb Nauchn Tr Voen Med Fak Sarat Medinst ... Sbornik Nauchnykh Trudov Voenno-Meditsinskii Fakul'tet Saratovskom Medinstitut [*A publication*]

Sb Nauchn Tr Vses Nauchno-Issled Gorno-Metall Inst Tsvet Met ... Sbornik Nauchnykh Trudov Vsesoyuznogo Nauchno-Issledovatel'skogo Gorno-Metallurgiceskogo Instituta Tsvetnykh Metallov [*USSR*] [*A publication*]

Sb Nauchn Tr Vses Nauchno Issled Gornometall Inst Tsvetn Met ... Sbornik Nauchnykh Trudov Vsesoyuznyi Nauchno-Issledovatel'skii Gornometallurgicheskii Institut Tsvetnykh Metallov [*A publication*]

Sb Nauchn Tr Vses Nauchno Issled Inst Metall Teplotekh ... Sbornik Nauchnykh Trudov Vsesoyuznyi Nauchno-Issledovatel'skii Institut Metallurgicheskoi Teplotekhniki [*A publication*]

Sb Nauchn Voen-Med Fak Kuibyshev Med Inst ... Sbornik Nauchnykh Rabot Voenno-Meditsinskogo Fakul'teta Kuibyshevskogo Meditsinskogo Instituta [*USSR*] [*A publication*]

Sb Nauch Tr Beloruss Nauch-Issled Inst Zemled ... Sbornik Nauchnykh Trudov Belorusskii Nauchno-Issledovatel'skii Institut Zemledeliya [*A publication*]

Sb Nauch Tr Eston Sel'skokhoz Akad ... Sbornik Nauchnykh Trudov Estonskoi Sel'skokhozyaistvennoi Akademii [*A publication*]

Sb Nauch Trud Eston Nauch Inst Zeml Melior ... Sbornik Nauchnykh Trudov Estonskogo Nauchnogo Instituta Zemledeliya i Melioratsii [*A publication*]

Sb Nauch Trud Eston Sel'khoz Akad ... Sbornik Nauchnykh Trudov Estonskoi Sel'skokhozyaistvennoi Akademii [*A publication*]

Sb Nauch Trud Leningr Inst Usoversh Vet Vrach ... Sbornik Nauchnykh Trudov Leningradskogo Instituta Usovershenstvovaniya Veterinarnykh Vrachei [*A publication*]

Sb Naucn Soobsc Dagestan Gos Univ ... Sbornik Naucnyh Soobscenii. Dagestanskii Gosudarstvennyi Universitet Imeni V. I. Lenina [*A publication*]

Sb Nauc Trud Jaroslav Pedag Inst ... Sbornik Naucnyh Trudov Jaroslavskogo Pedagogiceskij Institut [*A publication*]

SBND .... Southbound [*FAAC*]

SBNH .... Society for the Bibliography of Natural History (EA)

SBNL .... Submarine Base, New London [*Connecticut*] [*Navy*]

SBNO .... Senior British Naval Officer

SBNOWA ... Senior British Naval Officer, Western Atlantic

SBNT .... Single-Breath Nitrogen Test [*Physiology*]

SbNU .... Sbornik za Narodni Umotvorenija i Narodopis [*A publication*]

s-bo--- .... Bolivia [*MARC geographic area code*] [*Library of Congress*] (LCCP)

SBO .... Salina [*Utah*] [*Airport symbol*] (OAG)

SBO .... Showboat, Inc. [*American Stock Exchange symbol*]

SBO .... Small Business Office

SBO .... Specific Behavioral Objectives [*Aviation*]

SBO .... Standing Balance: Eyes Open [*Test*] [*Occupational therapy*]

SBO .... Studia Biblica et Orientalia [*Rome*] [*A publication*] (BJA)

SBO .... Swainsboro, GA [*Location identifier*] [*FAA*] (FAAL)

SBOA .... Specialty Bakery Owners of America [*New York, NY*] (EA)

SBOAA .... Soobshcheniya Byurakanskoi Observatorii. Akademiya Nauk Armyanskoi SSR [*A publication*]

SbOAW ...... Sitzungsberichte der Oesterreichischen Akademie der Wissenschaften in Wien. Philosophisch-Historische Klasse [*A publication*]

SBoc .... Studi sul Boccaccio [*A publication*]

SBol .... Strenna Bolognese [*A publication*]

SBOLS .... Shadow Box Optical Landing System

SBOM .... Soybean Oil Meal

SBON .... Siboney Corp. [*NASDAQ symbol*] (NQ)

SBOOM ...... Sonic Boom [*Computer program*] [*NASA*]

Sbor Arch Praci ... Sbornik Archivnich Praci [*A publication*]

Sbor Narod Muz Praze ... Sbornik Narodniho Muzea v Praze [*Acta Musei Nationalis Pragae*]. Series A: Historia [*A publication*]

Sborn Rabot v Pam I M Sadovskago (S Peterburg) ... Sbornik Rabot v Pamiat Professora Ivana Mikhailovicha Sadovskago (S Peterburg) [*A publication*]

Sborn Ved Lesn Ust Vysoke Skoly Zemed ... Sbornik Vedeckeho Lesnickeho Ustavu Vysoke Skoly Zemedelske v Praze [*A publication*]

Sbor Praci Filos Fak ... Sbornik Praci Filosoficke Fakulty Brnenske University [*A publication*]

Sbor Vlast Prac Podblanicka ... Sbornik Vlastivednych Praci z Podblanicka [*A publication*]

SBOS .... South Boston Savings Bank [*NASDAQ symbol*] (NQ)

SBOSI .... Serikat Buruh Obat Seluruh Indonesia [*All Indonesian Medicinal Factory Workers' Union*]

SBOST .... Slavonic Benevolent Order of the State of Texas (EA)

SBOT .... Sacred Books of the Old Testament [*The "Rainbow Bible"*] [*A publication*] (BJA)

SBP .... San Luis Obispo [*California*] [*Airport symbol*] (OAG)

SBP .... Sec-Butyl Percarbonate [*Organic chemistry*]

SBP .... Serikat Buruh Pegadaian [*Pawnshop Workers' Union*] [*Indonesia*]

SBP .... Serikat Buruh Penerbangan [*Airways' Unions*] [*Indonesia*]

SBP .... Service Benefit Plan (AABC)

SBP .... Societe Beneluxienne de Phlebologie [*Benelux Phlebology Society - BPS*] (EA)

SBP .... Society of Biological Psychiatry [*Los Angeles, CA*] (EA)

SBP .... Sonic Boom Panel (MCD)

SBP .... Soziale Buergerpartei [*Social Citizen's Party*] [*West Germany*] (PPW)

SBP .... Spaceborne Programer

SBP .... Special Block Purchase

SBP .... Special Businessowners Policy [*Insurance*]

SBP .... Spontaneous Bacterial Peritonitis [*Medicine*]

SBP .... Squalene-Binding Protein [*Biochemistry*]

SBP .... Standard Brands Paint Co. [*NYSE symbol*]

SBP .... Standard Businessowners Policy [*Insurance*]

SBP .... Subic Bay [*Philippines*] [*Seismograph station code, US Geological Survey*] [*Closed*] (SEIS)

SBP .... Sumerian and Babylonian Psalms [*A publication*] (BJA)

SBP .... Survivor Benefit Plan [*For survivors of retired military personnel*]

SBP .... Systolic Blood Pressure [*Medicine*]

SBPA .... Southern Baptist Press Association

Sb Pathofysiol Traveni Vyz ... Sbornik pro Pathofysiologii Traveni a Vyzivy [*A publication*]

SBPAW ...... Sitzungsberichte der K. Preussischen Akademie der Wissenschaften [*Berlin*] [*A publication*]

SBPAWB .... Sitzungsberichte der K. Preussischen Akademie der Wissenschaften (Berlin) [*A publication*]

SBPD .... Society of Business Publication Designers [*Later, SPD*] (EA)

Sb Pedagog Fak Plzni Ser Chem ... Sbornik Pedagogicke Fakulty v Plzni. Serie. Chemie [*A publication*]

SBPG .... Serikat Buruh Perusahaan Gula [*Sugar Workers' Union*] [*Indonesia*]

SBPH .... Single Burst Probability of Hit (AABC)

SBPI .... Serikat Buruh Pelabuhan Indonesia [*Dockworkers' Union of Indonesia*]

SBPI .... Serikat Buruh Pendjahit Indonesia [*Tailors' Union of Indonesia*]

SBPI .... Southern Baptist Periodical Index [*A publication*]

SBPKB .... Serikat Buruh Persuahaan Kaju and Bangunan [*Building, Road and Irrigation Workers' Union*] [*Indonesia*]

SBPP .... Serikat Buruh Pelabuhan dan Pelajaran [*Dockworkers' Union*] [*Indonesia*]

SBPPK .... Serikat Buruh Pendidikan, Pengadjaran dan Kebudjaan [*Department of Education Workers' Union*] [*Indonesia*]

Sb Prac Chem Fak SVST ... Sbornik Prac Chemickej Fakulty Slovenskej Vysokej Skoly Technickej [*A publication*]

Sb Praci Ped Fak v Ostrave Ser A ... Sbornik Praci Pedagogicke Fakulty v Ostrave. Seria A [*A publication*]

Sb Praci Prirodoved Fak Univ Palackeho v Olomouci ... Sbornik Praci Prirodovedecki Fakulty University Palackeho v Olomouci [*A publication*]

Sb Praci Prirodoved Fak Univ Palackeho v Olomouci Fyz ... Sbornik Praci Prirodovedecke Fakulty University Palackeho v Olomouci. Obor Fyzika [*A publication*]

Sb Praci Prirodoved Fak Univ Palackeho v Olomouci Mat ... Sbornik Praci Prirodovedecke Fakulty University Palackeho v Olomouci. Obor Matematika [*A publication*]

Sb Prazhskogo Khim Tekhnol Inst Sekts Protsessy Appar ... Sbornik Prazhskogo Khimiko Tekhnologicheskogo Instituta Sektsiya. Protsessy i Apparaty [*A publication*]

SBPR Bol ... SBPR Boletin [*A publication*]

Sb Prednasek Prac Vyzk Ustavu Tepelne Tech ... Sbornik Prednasek Pracovniku Vyzkumneho Ustavu Tepelne Techniky [*A publication*]

Sb Pr Pedagog Fak Ostrave Rada A ... Sbornik Praci Pedagogicke Fakulty v Ostrave. Rada A. Matematika Fizika [*A publication*]

Sb Pr Pedagog Fak Ostrave Rada E ... Sbornik Praci Pedagogicke Fakulty v Ostrave. Rada E [*Czechoslovakia*] [*A publication*]

Sb Pr Pedagog Inst Ostrave Prir Vedy Mat ... Sbornik Praci Pedagogickeho Instituta i Ostrave Prirodni Vedy a Matematika [*A publication*]

Sb Pr Ustavu Vyzk Rud (Prague) ... Sbornik Praci Ustavu pro Vyzkum Rud (Prague) [*A publication*]

Sb Pr UVP ... Sbornik Praci UVP [*A publication*]

Sb Pr Vyzk Chem Vyuziti Uhli Dehtu Ropy ... Sbornik Praci z Vyzkumu Chemickeho Vyuziti Uhli. Dehtu a Ropy [*Czechoslovakia*] [*A publication*]

SBPS .... Savings Bank of Puget Sound [*NASDAQ symbol*]   (NQ)

SBPT .... Serikat Buruh Perhubungan dan Transport [*Communications and Transportation Workers' Union*] [*Indonesia*]

SBPT .... Serikat Buruh Pertambangan Timah [*Tin Mine Labor Union*] [*Indonesia*]

SBPU .... Serikat Buruh Pekerdjaan Umum [*Public Workers' Ministry Union*] [*Indonesia*]

SBQ .... Grenada, MS [*Location identifier*] [*FAA*]   (FAAL)

SBQ .... Serikat Buruh Qantas [*Qantas Labor Union*] [*Indonesia*]

SBR .... Saber Aviation, Inc. [*Charlotte, NC*] [*FAA designator*]   (FAAC)

SBR .... Sabine Royalty Trust UBI [*NYSE symbol*]

SBR .... Sale by Reference

SBR .... Seat Bucket Read   (NG)

SBR .... Segment Base Register   (BUR)

SBR .... Sequencing Batch Reactor [*Chemical engineering*]

SBR .... Service Billing Record

SBR .... Signal to Background Ratio [*Instrumentation*]

SBR .... Society of Bead Researchers   (EA)

SBR .... Society for Biological Rhythm

SBR .... Soviet Breeder Reactor

SBR .... Space-Based RADAR   (MCD)

SBR .... Standard Busy Rate   (NATG)

SBR .... Starburst Energy [*Vancouver Stock Exchange symbol*]

SBR .... Stimulus-Bound Repetition [*Medicine*]

SBR .... Storage Buffer Register

SBR .... Strict Bed Rest [*Medicine*]

SBR .... Styrene-Butadiene Rubber [*Also, GR-S*] [*Synthetic rubber*]

SBR .... Supplemental Budget Request

Sb Rab Ashkhab Gidrometeorol Obs ... Sbornik Rabot Ashkhabadskoi Gidrometeorologicheskoi Observatorii [*A publication*]

Sb Rab Basseinovoi Gidrometeorol Obs Chern Azovskogo Morei ... Sbornik Rabot Basseinovoi Gidrometeorologicheskoi Chernogo i Azovskogo Morei [*A publication*]

Sb Rab Gidrol Leningr Gos Gidrol Inst ... Sbornik Rabot po Gidrologii Leningradskogo Gosudarstvennogo Gidrologicheskogo Instituta [*A publication*]

Sb Rab Gor'k Volzh Rybinsk Gidrometeorol Obs ... Sbornik Rabot Gor'kovskoi. Volzhskoi i Rybinskoi Gidrometeorologicheskikh Observatorii [*A publication*]

Sb Rab Ikhtiol Gidrobiol ... Sbornik Rabot po Ikhtiologii i Gidrobiologii [*A publication*]

Sb Rab Inst Prikl Zol Fitopatol ... Sbornik Rabot Instituta Prikladnoi Zoologii i Fitopatologii [*A publication*]

Sb Rab Inst Prikl Zool Fitopatol ... Sbornik Rabot Instituta Prikladnoi Zoologii i Fitopatologii [*A publication*]

Sb Rab Inst Tsitol Akad Nauk SSSR ... Sbornik Rabot Instituta Tsitologii Akademii Nauk SSSR [*A publication*]

Sb Rab Kafedry Fak Khir Sverdl Med ... Sbornik Rabot Kafedry i Fakul'tete Khirurgii Sverdlovskogo Meditsinskogo [*A publication*]

Sb Rab Kaz Resp Nauchn Ova Anat Gistol Embriol ... Sbornik Rabot Kazakhskogo Respublikanskogo Nauchnogo Obshchestva Anatomov Gistologiv i Embriologov [*A publication*]

Sb Rab Kaz Resp Nauchn O-va Anat Gistol Embriol ... Sbornik Rabot Kazakhskogo Respublikanskogo Nauchnogo Obshchestva Anatomov, Gistologov, i Embriologov [*A publication*]

Sb Rab Khim Istochnikam Toka ... Sbornik Rabot po Khimicheskim Istochnikam Toka [*A publication*]

Sb Rab Kursk Gidrometeorol Obs ... Sbornik Rabot Kurskoi Gidrometeorologicheskoi Observatorii [*A publication*]

Sb Rab Lab Yuzhn Morei Gos Okeanogr Inst ... Sbornik Rabot Laboratoriya Yuzhnykh Morei Gosudarstvennyi Okeanograficheskii Institut [*A publication*]

Sb Rab Leningr Vet Inst ... Sbornik Rabot Leningradskii Veterinarnyi Institut [*A publication*]

Sb Rab Lesn Khoz Mold Mold Lesn Opytn Stn ... Sbornik Rabot po Lesnomu Khozyaistva Moldavii Moldavskaya Lesnaya Opytnaya Stantsiya [*A publication*]

Sb Rab Maslichn Kult ... Sbornik Rabot po Maslichnym Kul'turam [*A publication*]

Sb Rab Mezhdunar Geofiz Godu ... Sbornik Rabot po Mezhdunarodnomu Geofizicheskom Godu [*A publication*]

Sb Rab Mikol Algol Akad Kirg SSR ... Sbornik Rabot po Mikologii i Al'gologii Akademii Kirgizskoi SSR [*A publication*]

Sb Rab Mikol Al'gol Kirg SSR ... Sbornik Rabot po Mikologii i Al'gologii Akademii Kirgiszkoi SSR [*A publication*]

Sb Rab Molodykh Uch Akad Nauk Mold SSR ... Sbornik Rabot Molodykh Uchenykh Akademii Nauk Moldavskoi SSR [*A publication*]

Sb Rab Molodykh Vses Sel Genet Inst ... Sbornik Rabot Molodykh Vsesoyuznogo Selektsii Genetiki Instituta [*A publication*]

Sb Rabot Nauch Inst Udobr Insektofungits (Moscow) ... Sbornik Rabot Nauchnyi Institut po Udobreniyam i Insektofungitsidam (Moscow) [*A publication*]

Sb Rab Rostov Gidrometeorol Obs ... Sbornik Rabot Rostovskoi Gidrometeorologicheskoi Observatorii [*A publication*]

Sb Rab Rybinsk Gidrometeorol Obs ... Sbornik Rabot Rybinskoi Gidrometeorologicheskoi Observatorii [*A publication*]

Sb Rab Silikozu ... Sbornik Rabot po Silikozu [*A publication*]

Sb Rab Silikozu Ural Fil Akad Nauk SSSR ... Sbornik Rabot po Silikozu Ural'skii Filial Akademii Nauk SSSR [*A publication*]

Sb Rab Sverdl Gos Med Inst ... Sbornik Rabot Sverdlovskii Gosudarstvennyi Meditsinskii Institut [*A publication*]

Sb Rab Sverdl Med Inst ... Sbornik Rabot Sverdlovskogo Meditsinskogo Instituta [*A publication*]

Sb Rab Sverdl Nauchno Issled Kozhno Venerol Inst ... Sbornik Rabot Sverdlovskii Nauchno Issledovatel'skii Kozhno Venerologicheskii Institut [*A publication*]

Sb Rab Tsentr Muz Pochvoved Im V ... Sbornik Rabot Tsentral'nogo Muzeya Pochvovedeniya Imeni V. V. Dokuchaeva [*A publication*]

Sb Rab Tsentr Muz Pochvoved Im V V Dokuchaeva ... Sbornik Rabot Tsentral'nogo Muzeya Pochvovedeniya Imeni V. V. Dokuchaeva [*A publication*]

Sb Rab Tsentr Nauchno Issled Inst Kozh Obuvn Promsti ... Sbornik Rabot Tsentral'nyi Nauchno Issledovatel'skii Institut Kozhevenno Obuvnoi Promyshlennosti [*A publication*]

Sb Rab Ukr Nauchno Issled Inst Ogneuporov ... Sbornik Rabot Ukrainskii Nauchno Issledovatel'skii Institut Ogneuporov [*A publication*]

Sb Rab Vologod Nauchno-Issled Vet Opytn Stn ... Sbornik Rabot Vologodskoi Nauchno-Issledovat' Skoi Veterinarnoi Opytnoi Stantsii [*A publication*]

Sb Rab Vopr Proizvod Primen Biol Prep ... Sbornik Rabot Voprosov Proizvodstva i Primeneniya Biologicheskikh Preparatov [*A publication*]

Sb Rab Vses Nauchno Issled Inst Okhr Tr ... Sbornik Rabot Vsesoyuznyi Nauchno Issledovatel'skii Institut Okhrany Truda [*A publication*]

Sb Rab Vses Zaochn Inst Pishch Promsti ... Sbornik Rabot Vsesoyuznyi Zaochnyi Institut Pishchevoi Promyshlennosti [*A publication*]

Sb Rab Vychisl Tsentra Mosk Gos Univ ... Sbornik Rabot Vychislitel'nogo Tsentral'nogo Moskovskogo Gosudarstvennogo Universiteta [*A publication*]

SBRC .... Santa Barbara Research Center [*Hughes Aircraft Co.*]

SBRC .... Southwest Border Regional Commission [*Department of Commerce*]

SBRI .... Serikat Buruh Rokok Indonesia [*Cigarette Workers' Union of Indonesia*]

SBRI .... Southwest Biomedical Research Institute [*Arizona State University*] [*Research center*]   (RCD)

SBRI .... Space Biomedical Research Institute [*Houston, TX*]

SB-RK ...... Bomber [*Russian aircraft symbol*]

Sb Rost Ustoichivost Rast Akad Nauk Ukr SSR Respub Mezhved ... Sbornik. Rost i Ustoichivost' Rastenii. Akademiya Nauk Ukrainskoi SSR. Respublikanskii Mezhvedomstvennyi [*A publication*]

SBRP .... Sonic Boom Research Program

SBRRI .... Serikat Buruh Radio Republik Indonesia [*Broadcasting Workers' Association of Indonesia*]

SBRU .... Subaru of America [*NASDAQ symbol*]   (NQ)

SBS .... Salem Corp. [*American Stock Exchange symbol*]

SBS .... Samuel Butler Society [*Defunct*]   (EA)

SBS .... Satellite Business Systems [*McLean, VA*] [*Telecommunications*]   (MCD)

SBS .... Scarborough Board of Education [*UTLAS symbol*]

SBS .... Semiconductor Bilateral Switch   (MSA)

SBS .... Sensor Based System   (BUR)

SBS .... Serially Balanced Sequence [*Statistics*]

SBS .... Sidi-Bou-Said [*Tunisia*] [*Seismograph station code, US Geological Survey*]   (SEIS)

SBS .... Silicon Bilateral Switch

SBS .... Single-Business Service

SBS .... Sisters of the Blessed Sacrament [*Roman Catholic religious order*]

SBS .... Small Business Sourcebook [*A publication*]

SBS .... Small Business Specialist [*DoD*]

SBS .... Small Business System   (ADA)

SBS .... Solid Bleached Sulphate [*Fiber for paperboard packaging*]

SBS .... Southern Base Section [*England*]
SBS .... Spaniel Breeders Society (EA)
SBS .... Spanish Benevolent Society "La Nacional" (EA)
SBS .... Special Block Sale
SBS .... Special Boat Squadron [*British commando unit*]
SBS .... Standby Status (AAG)
SBS .... Steamboat Springs [*Colorado*] [*Airport symbol*] (OAG)
SBS .... Steel Building System
SBS .... Stimulated Brillouin Scattering (IEEE)
SBS .... Straight Binary Second
SBS .... Strategic Balkan Services [*World War II*]
SBS .... Strategic Bombing Survey
SBS .... Strategic Business Segment
SBS .... Stuttgarter Bibelstudien. Katholisches Bibelwerk [*Stuttgart*] [*A publication*] (BJA)
SBS .... Styrene-Butadiene-Styrene [*Copolymer*]
SBS .... Superburn Systems Ltd. [*Formerly, Bluegrass Petroleums, Inc.*] [*Vancouver Stock Exchange symbol*]
SBS .... Sweep Back Station (MCD)
SBS .... Swiss Benevolent Society of New York (EA)
SBS .... System Breakdown Structure [*Military*] (AFIT)
SBSA .... Society of Basque Studies in America [*Brooklyn, NY*] (EA)
SBSanE ..... Bachelor of Science in Sanitary Engineering
SBSAW ...... Sitzungsberichte der Saechsischen Akademie der Wissenschaften zu Leipzig. Philologisch-Historische Klasse [*A publication*]
SBSAWL .... Sitzungsberichte der Saechsischen Akademie der Wissenschaften zu Leipzig. Philologisch-Historische Klasse [*A publication*]
SBSB .... Small Business Service Bureau (EA)
SBSBA ...... Scottish Blackface Sheep Breeders Association (EA)
SBSC .... Saint Bernardine of Siena College [*New York*]
SBSC .... Saint Bernard's Seminary and College [*New York*]
SBSC .... Separate Bias, Single Control
SBSCA ...... Small Business Support Center Association [*Houston, TX*] (EA)
SBSD .... Subside (FAAC)
Sb Severocesk Mus Prir Vedy Sci Nat ... Sbornik Severoceskeho Musea Prirodni Vedy Scientiae Naturales [*A publication*]
SBSG .... Small Business Systems Group [*Westford, MA*] [*Telecommunications*] (TSSD)
SBSI .... Serikat Buruh Seluruh Indonesia [*All Indonesian Laborers' Union*]
SBSK .... Samodzielna Brygada Strzelcow Karpackich [*Poland*]
SBSKK ...... Serikat Buruh Sepatu Keradjinan Kulit Karet [*Shoe Workers' Union*] [*Indonesia*]
SBSM .... Sisterhood of Black Single Mothers (EA)
SBSP .... Single Base Solid Propellant (MSA)
SBSS .... Space-Based Space Surveillance (MCD)
SBSS .... Spare Band Surveillance System (MCD)
SBSS .... Standard Base Supply System [*Military*] (AFIT)
Sb Statei Aspir Kirg Gos Univ ... Sbornik Statei Aspirantov Kirgizskogo Gosudarstvennogo Universiteta [*A publication*]
Sb Statei Aspir Kirg Univ Fiz-Mat Estestv Nauk ... Sbornik Statei Aspirantov Kirgizskogo Universiteta Fiziko-Matematicheskikh. Estestvennykh Nauk [*A publication*]
Sb Statei Erevan Gos Univ ... Sbornik Statei Erevanskii Gosudarstvennyi Universitet [*A publication*]
Sb Statei Geol Gidrogeol ... Sbornik Statei po Geologii i Gidrogeologii [*A publication*]
Sb Statei Gidrogeol Geoterm ... Sbornik Statei po Gidrogeologii i Geotermii [*A publication*]
Sb Statei Makeev Nauchno Issled Inst Bezop Rab Gorn Promsti ... Sbornik Statei Makeevskii Nauchno Issledovatel'skii Institut Bezopasnykh Rabot Gornoi Promyshlennosti [*A publication*]
Sb Statei Mosk Inzh-Fiz Inst ... Sbornik Statei Moskovskii Inzhenerno-Fizicheskii Institut [*USSR*] [*A publication*]
Sb Statniho Geol Ustavu Cesk Repub ... Sbornik Statniho Geologickeho Ustavu Ceskoslovenski Republiky [*A publication*]
Sb Statniho Vyzk Ustavu Tepelne Tech ... Sbornik Statniho Vyzkumneho Ustavu Tepelne Techniky [*A publication*]
SBStJ .... Serving Brother, Order of St. John of Jerusalem [*British*]
SBSTR .... Substrate [*Electronics*]
Sb Stud Nauchn Issled Rab Arkhang Lesotekh Inst ... Sbornik Studencheskikh Nauchno Issledovatel'skikh Rabot Arkhangel'skii Lesotekhnicheskii Institut [*A publication*]
Sb Stud Nauchn Issled Rab Mosk Vet Akad ... Sbornik Studencheskikh Nauchno Issledovatel'skikh Rabot Moskovskaya Veterinarnaya Akademiya [*A publication*]
Sb Stud Nauchno-Issled Rab Kirg S-kh Inst ... Sbornik Studencheskikh Nauchno-Issledovatel'skikh Rabot Kirgizskogo Sel'skokhozyaistvennogo Instituta [*A publication*]
Sb Stud Nauchn Rab Alma-At Zoovet Inst ... Sbornik Studencheskikh Nauchnykh Rabot Alma-Atinskogo Zooveterinarnogo Instituta [*A publication*]
Sb Stud Nauchn Rab Kabard Balkar Gos Univ ... Sbornik Studencheskikh Nauchnykh Rabot Kabardino Balkarskii Gosudarstvennyi Universitet [*A publication*]

Sb Stud Rab Krasnodar Gos Pedagog Inst ... Sbornik Studencheskikh Rabot Krasnodarskogo Gosudarstvennogo Pedagogicheskogo Instituta [*A publication*]
Sb Stud Rab Mosk Tekhnol Inst Myasn Molochn Promsti ... Sbornik Studencheskikh Rabot Moskovskogo Tekhnologicheskogo Instituta Myasnoi i Molochnoi Promyshlennosti [*A publication*]
Sb Stud Rab Rostov Gos Univ ... Sbornik Studencheskikh Rabot Rostovskogo Gosudarstvennogo Universiteta [*A publication*]
Sb Stud Rab Sredneaziat Gos Univ ... Sbornik Studencheskikh Rabot Sredneaziatskogo Gosudarstvennogo Universiteta [*A publication*]
SBSUSA..... Sport Balloon Society of the United States of America (EA)
SBT .... Salina Board of Trade (EA)
SBT .... San Benito [*California*] [*Seismograph station code, US Geological Survey*] (SEIS)
SBT .... San Bernardino, CA [*Location identifier*] [*FAA*] (FAAL)
SBT .... Screening Breath Tester [*Drunken driving*]
SBT .... Seabright Resources, Inc. [*Toronto Stock Exchange symbol*]
SBT .... Segregated Ballast Tank [*Shipping construction*]
SBT .... Serikat Buruh Tambang [*Mine Workers' Union*] [*Indonesia*]
SBT .... Serikat Buruh Teknik [*Technicians' Union*] [*Indonesia*]
SBT .... Serikat Buruh Textil [*Textile Workers' Union*] [*Indonesia*]
SBT .... Serum Bactericidal Titer [*Clinical chemistry*]
SBT .... Shakespeare Birthplace Trust (EA)
SBT .... Shanghai Book Traders
SBT .... Side Buoyancy Tank
SBT .... Simultaneous Baseband Transmission [*of information*]
SBT .... Six BIT [*Binary Digit*] Transcode (CMD)
SBT .... Small Boat
SBT .... Sodium Bitartrate [*Inorganic chemistry*]
SBT .... Space-Based Tug [*NASA*]
SBT .... Studies in Biblical Theology [*A publication*]
SBT .... Submarine Bathythermograph
SBT .... Surface Barrier Transistor
SBT .... System Burning Time
SBTC......... Speedbrake Thrust Control (MCD)
SBTDA .... Sbornik Trudov Vsesoyuznogo Zaochnogo Politekhnicheskogo Instituta [*A publication*]
SBTG......... Sabotage (AABC)
SBTG......... SBT Corp. [*NASDAQ symbol*] (NQ)
SBTI .... Soybean Trypsin Inhibitor
SBTOW ..... Standby Towship [*Navy*] (NVT)
SBTP .... Serikat Buruh Teknik dan Pelabuhan [*Technical and Harbour Workers' Union*] [*Indonesia*]
Sb Tr Agron Fiz ... Sbornik Trudov po Agronomicheskoi Fizike [*A publication*]
Sb Tr Arm Nauchno-Issled Lesn Opytn Stn ... Sbornik Trudov Armyanskoi Nauchno-Issledovatel'skoi Lesnoi Opytnoi Stantsii [*A publication*]
Sb Tr Aspir Tadzh Univ Estest Nauk ... Sbornik Trudov Aspirantov Tadzhikskogo Universiteta Estestvennykh Nauk [*A publication*]
Sb Tr Astrakh Gos S-kh Opytn Stn ... Sbornik Trudov Astrakhanskoi Gosudarstvennoi Sel'skokhozyaistvennoi Opytnoi Stantsii [*A publication*]
Sb Tr Astrakh Protivochumn Stn ... Sbornik Trudov Astrakhanskoi Protivochumnoi Stantsii [*A publication*]
Sb Tr Azerb Gos Med Inst ... Sbornik Trudov Azerbaidzhanskogo Gosudarstvennogo Meditsinskogo Instituta [*A publication*]
Sb Tr Azerb Nauchno-Issled Inst Kurortol Fiz Metod Lech ... Sbornik Trudov Azerbaidzhanskogo Nauchno-Issledovatel'skogo Instituta Kurortologii i Fizicheskikh Metodov Lecheniya [*A publication*]
Sb Tr Bashk Gos Zapov ... Sbornik Trudov Bashkirskogo Zapovednika [*A publication*]
Sb Tr Bryansk Inst Transp Mashinostr ... Sbornik Trudov Bryanskii Institut Transportnogo Mashinostroeniya [*A publication*]
Sb Tr Chelyab Elektrometall Komb ... Sbornik Trudov Chelyabinskogo Elektrometallurgicheskogo Kombinata [*A publication*]
Sb Tr Chelyabinsk Elektrometal Komb ... Sbornik Trudov Chelyabinsk Elektrometallurgicheskogo Kombinata [*USSR*] [*A publication*]
Sb Tr Dal'nevost Nauchno-Issled Inst Lesn Khoz ... Sbornik Trudov Dal'nevostochnyi Nauchno-Issledovatel'skii Institut Lesnogo Khozyaistva [*A publication*]
Sb Tr Donetsk Nauchno-Issled Inst Cher Metall ... Sbornik Trudov Donetskii Nauchno-Issledovatel'skii Institut Chernoi Metallurgii [*A publication*]
Sb Tr Donets Nauchno-Issled Inst Chern Metall ... Sbornik Trudov Donetskii Nauchno-Issledovatel'skii Institut Chernoi Metallurgii [*USSR*] [*A publication*]
Sb Tr Geobot Eksped L'vov Univ ... Sbornik Trudov Geobotanicheskoi Ekspeditsii L'vovskogo Universiteta [*A publication*]
Sb Tr Glavniiproekt Energ Inst (USSR) ... Sbornik Trudov. Glavniiproekt Energeticheskii Institut (USSR) [*A publication*]

Sb Tr Gos Inst Proekt Zavodov Sanit Tekh Oborudovaniya ... Sbornik Trudov Gosudarstvennyi Institut po Proektirovaniyu Zavodov Sanitarno Tekhnicheskogo Oborudovaniya [*A publication*]

Sb Tr Gos Nauchno-Issled Energ Inst Im G M Krzhizhanovskogo ... Sbornik Trudov. Gosudarstvennyi Nauchno-Issledovatel'skii Energeticheskii Institut Imeni G. M. Krzhizhanovskogo [*A publication*]

Sb Tr Gos Vses Nauchno-Issled Inst Stroit Mater Konstr ... Sbornik Trudov. Gosudarstvennyi Vsesoyuznyi Nauchno-Issledovatel'skii Institut Stroitel'nykh Materialov i Konstruktsii [*A publication*]

Sb Tr Gruz Zootekh Vet Inst ... Sbornik Trudov Gruzinskii Zootekhnichesko Veterinarnyi Institut [*A publication*]

Sb Tr Gruz Zootekh-Vet Uchebn-Issled Inst ... Sbornik Trudov Gruzinskogo Zootekhnichesko-Veterinarnogo Uchebno-Issledovatel'skogo Instituta [*A publication*]

Sb Tr Inst Mashinoved Avtom Akad Nauk B SSR ... Sbornik Trudov Institut Mashinovedeniya i Avtomatizats Akademii Nauk Belorusskoi SSR [*A publication*]

Sb Tr Inst Neftekhim Protsessov Akad Nauk Az SSR ... Sbornik Trudov Institut Neftekhimicheskikh Protsessov Akademiya Nauk Azerbaidzhanskoi SSR [*A publication*]

Sb Tr Inst Stroit Mekh Seismostoikosti Akad Nauk Gruz SSR ... Sbornik Trudov Institut Stroitel'noi Mekhaniki i Seismostoikosti Akademiya Nauk Gruzinskoi SSR [*A publication*]

Sb Tr Inst Urol Akad Med Nauk SSSR ... Sbornik Trudov Instituta Urologii Akademii Meditsinskikh Nauk SSSR [*A publication*]

Sb Tr Inst Urol Gruz SSR ... Sbornik Trudov Instituta Urologii Gruzinskoi SSR [*A publication*]

Sb Tr Ivanov Med Inst ... Sbornik Trudov Ivanovskogo Meditsinskogo Instituta [*A publication*]

Sb Tr Izhevsk Med Inst ... Sbornik Trudov Izhevskogo Meditsinskogo Instituta [*A publication*]

Sb Tr Kafedry Mikrobiol Orenb Med Inst ... Sbornik Trudov Kafedry Mikrobiologii Orenburgskogo Meditsinskogo Instituta [*A publication*]

Sb Tr Kirg Nauchno-Issled Inst Epidemiol Mikrobiol Gig ... Sbornik Trudov Kirgizskii Nauchno-Issledovatel'skii Institut Epidemiologii, Mikrobiologii, i Gigieny [*A publication*]

Sb Tr Klyuchevskogo Zavoda Ferrosplavov ... Sbornik Trudov Klyuchevskogo Zavoda Ferrosplavov [*A publication*]

Sb Tr Klyuchevsk Zavoda Ferrosplavov ... Sbornik Trudov Klyuchevskogo Zavoda Ferrosplavov [*USSR*] [*A publication*]

Sb Tr Krym Med Inst ... Sbornik Trudov Krymskogo Meditsinskogo Instituta [*A publication*]

Sb Tr Kursk Gos Med Inst ... Sbornik Trudov Kurskii Gosudarstvennyi Meditsinskii Institut [*A publication*]

Sb Tr Kursk Med Inst ... Sbornik Trudov Kurskogo Meditsinskogo Instituta [*A publication*]

Sb Tr Latv Fil Vses Ova Pochvovedov ... Sbornik Trudov Latviiskii Filial Vsesoyuznogo Obshchestva Pochvovedov [*A publication*]

Sb Tr Leningr Gos Inst Usoversh Vrachei ... Sbornik Trudov Leningradskii Gosudarstvennyi Institut Usovershenstvaniya Vrachei [*A publication*]

Sb Tr Leningr Inst Inzh Zheleznodorozhn Transp ... Sbornik Trudov Leningradskii Institut Inzhenerov Zheleznodorozhnogo Transporta [*A publication*]

Sb Tr Leningr Inst Sov Torg ... Sbornik Trudov Leningradskii Institut Sovetskoi Torgovli [*A publication*]

Sb Tr Leningr Inzh-Stroit Inst ... Sbornik Trudov. Leningradskii Inzhenerno-Stroitel'nyi Institut [*A publication*]

Sb Tr Leningr Nauchno Issled Inst Gematol Pereliv Krovi ... Sbornik Trudov. Leningradskii Nauchno-Issledovatel'skii Institut Gematologii i Perelivaniya Krovi [*A publication*]

Sb Tr Leningr Nauchno-Issled Inst Gematol Pereliv Krovi ... Sbornik Trudov Leningradskogo Nauchno-Issledovatel'skogo Instituta Gematologii i Perelivaniya Krovi [*A publication*]

Sb Tr Leningr Nauchn O-va Nevropatol Psikhiatr ... Sbornik Trudov Leningradskogo Nauchnogo Obshchestva Nevropatologov i Psikhiatrov [*A publication*]

Sb Tr Leningr Nauchn Ova Nevropatol Psikhiatrov ... Sbornik Trudov Leningradskogo Nauchnogo Obshchestva Nevropatologov i Psikhiatrov [*A publication*]

Sb Tr Lesn Khoz (Kazan) ... Sbornik Trudov po Lesnomu Khozyaistvu (Kazan) [*A publication*]

Sb Tr Med Uchrezhd Mosk Oksko Volzh Vozdravotdela ... Sbornik Trudov Meditsinskikh Uchrezhdenii Moskovsko-Oksko-Volzhskogo Vozdravotdela [*A publication*]

Sb Tr Mold Stn Vses Inst Zashch Rast ... Sbornik Trudov Moldavskoi Stantsii Vsesoyuznogo Instituta Zashchity Rastenii [*A publication*]

Sb Tr Mosk Inzh-Stroitel Inst Im V V Kuibysheva ... Sbornik Trudov. Moskovskii Inzhenerno-Stroitel'nyi Institut Imeni V. V. Kuibysheva [*USSR*] [*A publication*]

Sb Tr Mosk Inzh Stroit Inst ... Sbornik Trudov Moskovskii Inzhenerno-Stroitel'nyi Institut [*A publication*]

Sb Tr Mosk Tekhnol Inst ... Sbornik Trudov. Moskovskii Tekhnologicheskii Institut [*A publication*]

Sb Tr Mosk Vech Metall Inst ... Sbornik Trudov. Moskovskii Vechernii Metallurgicheskii Institut [*USSR*] [*A publication*]

Sb Tr Mosk Zaochn Poligr Inst ... Sbornik Trudov Moskovskii Zaochnyi Poligraficheskii Institut [*A publication*]

Sb Tr MVTU ... Sbornik Trudov MVTU [*A publication*]

Sb Tr Nauchn Issled Inst Kurortol Fizioter (Tiflis) ... Sbornik Trudov. Nauchno-Issledovatel'skii Institut Kurortologii i Fizioterapii (Tiflis) [*A publication*]

Sb Tr Nauchn Issled Inst Probl Kursk Magn Anomalii ... Sbornik Trudov. Nauchno-Issledovatel'skii Institut po Problemam Kurskoi Magnitnoi Anomalii [*A publication*]

Sb Tr Nauchno-Issled Inst Eksp Klin Ter ... Sbornik Trudov Nauchno-Issledovatel'skii Institut Eksperimental'noi i Klinicheskoi Terapii [*A publication*]

Sb Tr Nauchno-Issled Inst Eksp Klin Ter Gruz SSR ... Sbornik Trudov Nauchno-Issledovatel'skii Instituta Eksperimental'noi Klinicheskoi Terapii Gruzinskoi SSR [*A publication*]

Sb Tr Nauchno-Issled Inst Gematol Pereliv Krovi Gruz SSR ... Sbornik Trudov Nauchno-Issledovatel'skogo Instituta Gematologii i Perelivaniya Krovi Gruzinskoi SSR [*A publication*]

Sb Tr Nauchno-Issled Inst Gig Tr Profzabol Gruz SSR ... Sbornik Trudov Nauchno-Issledovatel'skii Institut Gigieny Truda i Profzabolevanii Gruzinskoi SSR [*A publication*]

Sb Tr Nauchno Issled Inst Gig Tr Profzabol (Tiflis) ... Sbornik Trudov. Nauchno-Issledovatel'skii Institut Gigieny Truda i Profzabolevanii (Tiflis) [*A publication*]

Sb Tr Nauchno Issled Inst Kurortol Fizioter Abkhazskii Fil ... Sbornik Trudov. Nauchno-Issledovatel'skii Institut Kurortologii i Fizioterapii. Abkhazskii Filial [*A publication*]

Sb Tr Nauchno Issled Inst Med Parazitol Trop Med Gruz SSR ... Sbornik Trudov. Nauchno-Issledovatel'skogo Instituta Meditsinskoi Parazitologii i Tropicheskoi Meditsiny Gruzinskoi SSR [*A publication*]

Sb Tr Nauchno-Issled Inst Prom Stroit Ufa ... Sbornik Trudov. Nauchno-Issledovatel'skii Institut Promyshlennogo Stroitel'stva Ufa [*A publication*]

Sb Tr Nauchno-Issled Inst Rentgenol Med Radiol Gruz SSR ... Sbornik Trudov Nauchno-Issledovatel'skogo Instituta Rentgenologii i Meditsinskoi Radiologii Gruzinskoi SSR [*A publication*]

Sb Tr Nauchno Issled Inst Rentgenol Med Radiol (Tiflis) ... Sbornik Trudov. Nauchno-Issledovatel'skii Institut Rentgenologii i Meditsinskoi Radiologii (Tiflis) [*A publication*]

Sb Tr Nauchno-Issled Inst Sanit Gig Gruz SSR ... Sbornik Trudov Nauchno-Issledovatel'skogo Instituta Sanitarii i Gigieny Gruzinskoi SSR [*A publication*]

Sb Tr Nauchno-Issled Inst Travmatol Ortoped Gruz SSR ... Sbornik Trudov Nauchno-Issledovatel'skogo Instituta Travmatologii i Ortopedii Gruzinskoi SSR [*A publication*]

Sb Tr Nauchnoizsled Inst Tr Khig Prof Bol ... Sbornik Trudov na Nauchnoizsledovatelskiya Instituta po Trudova-Khigienna i Professionalni Bolesti [*A publication*]

Sb Tr Nauchnoizsled Proekt Inst Rudodobiv Obogat Obogat ... Sbornik ot Trudov na Nauchnoizsledovatelskiya i Proektantski Institut za Rudodobiv i Obogatyavane. Obogatyavane [*A publication*]

Sb Tr Nauchno-Izzled Inst Okhr Tr ... Sbornik Trudov na Nauchno-Izzledovatelskiya Instituta po Okhrana na Truda [*A publication*]

Sb Tr Novosb Vseross O-va Otolaringol ... Sbornik Trudov Novosibirskogo Otdeleniya Vserossiiskogo Obshchestva Otolaringologov [*A publication*]

Sb Tr Novosib Otd Vseross Ova Otolaringol ... Sbornik Trudov Novosibirskogo Otdeleniya Vserossiiskogo Obshchestva Otolaringologov [*A publication*]

Sb Tr Odess Inzh Stroit Inst ... Sbornik Trudov Odesskii Inzhenerno-Stroitel'nyi Institut [*A publication*]

Sb Tr Odess Med Inst ... Sbornik Trudov Odesskii Meditsinskii Institut [*A publication*]

Sb Tr Osvo Terskokumskikh Peskov ... Sbornik Trudov Osvoeniyu Terskokumskikh Peskov [*A publication*]

Sb Tr Permsk Gor Psikhiatr Boln ... Sbornik Trudov Permskoi Gorodskoi Psikhiatricheskoi Bol'nitsy [*A publication*]

Sb Tr Povolzh Lesotekh Inst ... Sbornik Trudov Povolzhskogo Lesotekhnicheskogo Instituta [*A publication*]

Sb Tr Proektn Nauchno-Issled Inst Ural Promstroiniiproekt ... Sbornik Trudov. Proektnyi i Nauchno-Issledovatel'skii Institut "Ural'skii Promstroiniiproekt" [*A publication*]

Sb Tr Resp Kostno Tuberk Bol'n Im Lenina ... Sbornik Trudov Respubliki Kostno Tuberkuleznaya Bol'nitsa Imeni Lenina [*A publication*]

Sb Tr Resp Nauchno-Issled Inst Mestnykh Stroit Mater ... Sbornik Trudov Respublikanskii Nauchno-Issledovatel'skii Institut Mestnykh Stroitel'nykh Materialov [*A publication*]

Sb Tr Resp Nauchno-Issled Inst Okhr Materin Det ... Sbornik Trudov Respublikanskii Nauchno-Issledovatel'skii Institut Okhrany Materinstva Detstva [*A publication*]

Sb Tr Samark Med Inst ... Sbornik Trudov Samarkandskogo Meditsinskogo Instituta [*A publication*]

Sb Tr Sekt Radiobiol Akad Nauk Arm SSR ... Sbornik Trudov Sektor Radiobiologii Akademiya Nauk Armyanskoi SSR [*A publication*]

Sb Tr Sev Nauchno-Issled Inst Promsti ... Sbornik Trudov Severnyi Nauchno-Issledovatel'skii Institut Promyshlennosti [*A publication*]

Sb Tr Stalingr Inst Inzh Gor Khoz ... Sbornik Trudov Stalingradskii Institut Inzhenerov Gorodskogo Khozyaistva [*A publication*]

Sb Tr Stavrop Gos Pedagog Inst ... Sbornik Trudov. Stavropol'skii Gosudarstvennyi Pedagogicheskii Institut [*A publication*]

Sb Tr Sud Med Sud Khim ... Sbornik Trudov po Sudebnoi Meditsine i Sudebnoi Khimii [*A publication*]

Sb Tr Sverdl Gor Klin Bol'n No 1 ... Sbornik Trudov Sverdlovskoi Gorodskoi Klinicheskoi Bol'nitsy No. 1 [*A publication*]

Sb Tr Sverdl Nauchno Issled Inst Pererab Drev ... Sbornik Trudov. Sverdlovskii Nauchno-Issledovatel'skii Institut Pererabotki Drevesiny [*A publication*]

Sb Tr Sverdl Nauchno-Issled Inst Stroit ... Sbornik Trudov Sverdlovskii Nauchno-Issledovatel'skii Institut po Stroitel'stvu [*A publication*]

Sb Tr Tadzh Nauchno-Issled Inst Zemled ... Sbornik Trudov Tadzhikskogo Nauchno-Issledovatel'skogo Instituta Zemledeliya [*A publication*]

Sb Tr Tbilis Gos Nauchno Issled Inst Stroit Mater ... Sbornik Trudov Tbilisskii Gosudarstvennyi Nauchno-Issledovatel'skii Institut Stroitel'nykh Materialov [*A publication*]

Sb Tr Tbilis Inst Usoversh Vrachei ... Sbornik Trudov Tbilisskogo Instituta Usovershenstvovaniya Vrachei [*A publication*]

Sb Tr Tsent Nauchno-Issled Inst Chern Metall ... Sbornik Trudov Tsentral'nogo Nauchno-Issledovatel'skogo Instituta Chernoj Metallurgii [*USSR*] [*A publication*]

Sb Tr Tsentr Nauchno-Issled Inst Chern Metall ... Sbornik Trudov Tsentral'nogo Nauchno-Issledovatel'skogo Instituta Chernoj Metallurgii [*A publication*]

Sb Tr Tsentr Nauchno-Issled Inst Olovyannoi Promsti ... Sbornik Trudov Tsentral'nyi Nauchno-Issledovatel'skii Institut Olovyannoi Promyshlennosti [*A publication*]

Sb Trud Agron Fiz ... Sbornik Trudov po Agronomicheskoi Fizike [*A publication*]

Sb Trud Moskov Obl Pedag Inst ... Sbornik Trudov Moskovskogo Oblastskogo Pedagogiceskij Institut [*A publication*]

Sb Trud Nauc-Issled Inst Hudoz Promys ... Sbornik Trudov Nauchno-Issledovatel'skogo Instituta Hudozestvennoi Promyshlennosti [*A publication*]

Sb Trudov Inst Problem Upravlen ... Sbornik Trudov Institut Problem Upravlenina [*A publication*]

Sb Trudov Odess Elektrotehn Inst Svjazi ... Sbornik Trudov Odesskogo Elektrotehniceskogo Instituta Svjazi Imeni A. S. Popova [*A publication*]

Sb Trudov Vsesojuz Zaocn Politehn Inst ... Sbornik Trudov Vsesojuznogo Zaocnogo Politehniceskogo Instituta [*A publication*]

Sb Trud Vopros Zool Kazansk Gos Pedagog Inst ... Sbornik Trudov Vopros Zool Kazanskii Gosudarstvennyi Pedagogiceskij Institut [*A publication*]

Sb Trud Zool Muz ... Sbornik Trudov Zoologicheskogo Muzeya [*A publication*]

Sb Tr Ufim Neft Inst ... Sbornik Trudov Ufimskogo Neftyanogo Instituta [*A publication*]

Sb Tr Ukr Nauchno-Issled Inst Met ... Sbornik Trudov Ukrainskij Nauchno-Issledovatel'skij Institut Metallov [*A publication*]

Sb Tr Ukr Nauchno Issled Inst Pishch Promsti ... Sbornik Trudov. Ukrainskii Nauchno-Issledovatel'skii Institut Pishchevoi Promyshlennosti [*A publication*]

Sb Tr Ukr Nauchno Issled Inst Poligr Promsti ... Sbornik Trudov Ukrainskogo Nauchno-Issledovatel'skogo Instituta Poligraficheskoi Promyshlennosti [*A publication*]

Sb Tr Ukr Tsentr Nauchno-Issled Inst Ortop Travmatol ... Sbornik Trudov Ukrainskogo Tsentral'nogo Nauchno-Issledovatel'skogo Instituta Ortopedii i Travmatologii [*A publication*]

Sb Tr Voronezh Otd Vses Khim Ova ... Sbornik Trudov Voronezhskogo Otdeleniya Vsesoyuznogo Khimicheskogo Obshchestva [*A publication*]

Sb Tr Voronezh S-kh ... Sbornik Trudov Voronezhskogo Sel'skohozyaistvennogo Instituta [*A publication*]

Sb Tr Voronezh S-Kh Inst ... Sbornik Trudov Voronezhskogo Sel'skohozyaistvennogo Instituta [*A publication*]

Sb Tr Vrachei Dorogi ... Sbornik Trudov Vrachei Dorogi [*A publication*]

Sb Tr Vrachei Pribalt Zhelezn ... Sbornik Trudov Vrachei Pribaltiiskogo Zheleznodorozhiya [*A publication*]

Sb Tr Vses Inst Rastenievod ... Sbornik Trudov Vsesoyuznyi Institut Rastenievodstva [*A publication*]

Sb Tr Vses Nauchno-Issled Eksp-Konstr Inst Tary Upakovki ... Sbornik Trudov Vsesoyuznyi Nauchno-Issledovatel'skii i Eksperimental'no-Konstruktorskii Institut Tary i Upakovki [*A publication*]

Sb Tr Vses Nauchno-Issled Inst Bolezn Ptits ... Sbornik Trudov Vsesoyuznogo Nauchno-Issledovatel'skogo Instituta po Boleznyam Ptits [*A publication*]

Sb Tr Vses Nauchno-Issled Inst Gidroliza Rastit Mater ... Sbornik Trudov. Vsesoyuznyi Nauchno-Issledovatel'skii Institut Gidroliza Rastitel'nykh Materialov [*USSR*] [*A publication*]

Sb Tr Vses Nauchno Issled Inst "Goznaka" ... Sbornik Trudov. Vsesoyuznyi Nauchno-Issledovatel'skii Institut "Goznaka" [*A publication*]

Sb Tr Vses Nauchno-Issled Inst Nov Stroit Mater ... Sbornik Trudov. Vsesoyuznyi Nauchno-Issledovatel'skii Institut Novykh Stroitel'nykh Materialov [*USSR*] [*A publication*]

Sb Tr Vses Nauchno-Issled Inst Stroit Mater Konstr ... Sbornik Trudov. Vsesoyuznyi Nauchno-Issledovatel'skii Institut Stroitel'nykh Materialov i Konstruktsii [*A publication*]

Sb Tr Vses Nauchno Issled Inst Tverd Splavov ... Sbornik Trudov. Vsesoyuznyi Nauchno-Issledovatel'skii Institut Tverdykh Splavov [*A publication*]

Sb Tr Vses Nauchno-Issled Proekt Inst Titana ... Sbornik Trudov. Vsesoyuznyi Nauchno-Issledovatel'skii i Proektnyi Institut Titana [*USSR*] [*A publication*]

Sb Tr Vses Nauchno-Issled Proektn Inst Teplotekh Sooruzh ... Sbornik Trudov. Vsesoyuznyi Nauchno-Issledovatel'skii i Proektnyi Institut po Teplotekhnicheskim Sooruzheniyam [*A publication*]

Sb Tr Vses Zaochn Inzh Stroit Inst ... Sbornik Trudov. Vsesoyuznyi Zaochnyi Inzhenerno-Stroitel'nyi Institut [*A publication*]

Sb Tr Vses Zaochn Politekh Inst ... Sbornik Trudov Vsesoyuznogo Zaochnogo Politekhnicheskogo Instituta [*A publication*]

Sb Tr Yuzhn Nauchno Issled Inst Prom Stroit ... Sbornik Trudov. Yuzknyi Nauchno-Issledovatel'skii Institut Promyshlennogo Stroitel'stva [*A publication*]

Sb Tr Zool Muz Mosk Univ ... Sbornik Trudov Zoologicheskogo Muzeya Moskovskogo Universiteta [*A publication*]

SBTS .... Shore-Based Tracking System

SBTS .... Stretch Block Template Set   (MCD)

SBTT .... Serikat Buruh Tambang Timah [*Tin Mine Laborers' Union*] [*Indonesia*]

SBTT .... Southern Bell Telephone & Telegraph Co.   (KSC)

SBTU .... Serikat Buruh Teknik Umum [*Indonesia*]

SBU .... Blue Earth, MN [*Location identifier*] [*FAA*]   (FAAL)

SBU .... Saint Bonaventure University [*New York*]

SBU .... Silver Brazing Union   (MSA)

SBU .... Small Base Unit [*Telecommunications*]

SBU .... Small Battle Unit [*Navy*]   (NVT)

SBU .... Small Business United [*Later, NSBU*]   (EA)

SBU .... Springbok [*South Africa*] [*Airport symbol*]   (OAG)

SBU .... Stansbury Island [*Utah*] [*Seismograph station code, US Geological Survey*] [*Closed*]   (SEIS)

SBU .... Station Buffer Unit [*Data processing*]

SBU .... Strategic Business Unit

SBU .... Svensk Biblisk Uppslagverk [*A publication*]   (BJA)

SBU .... Symbolae Biblicae Upsalienses [*A publication*]

SBUE .... Switch-Backup Entry [*NASA*]   (KSC)

SBURCS .... Six-BIT [*Binary Digit*] Universal Random Character Set [*Data processing*]

Sb Ustav Vedeckotech Inf Genet Slechteni ... Sbornik Ustav Vedeckotechnickych Informaci. Genetika a Slechteni [*A publication*]

Sb Ustav Vedeckotech Inf Melior ... Sbornik Ustav Vedeckotechnickych Informaci. Rada. Meliorace [*A publication*]

Sb Ustav Vedeckotech Inf Zemed Genet Slechteni ... Sbornik Ustav Vedeckotechnickych Informaci pro Zemedelstvi, Genetika, a Slechteni [*A publication*]

Sb Ustav Vedeckotech Inf Zemed Melior ... Sbornik Ustav Vedeckotechnickych Informaci pro Zemedelstvi. Rada. Meliorace [*A publication*]

Sb Ustred Ustavi Geol ... Sbornik Ustredniho Ustavi Geologickeho [*A publication*]

SBUV .... Solar and Backscatter Ultraviolet Spectrometer   (MCD)

Sb UVTI Genet Slechteni ... Sbornik UVTI [*Ustav Vedeckotechnickych Informaci*] Genetika a Slechteni [*A publication*]

Sb UVTI Melior ... Sbornik UVTI [*Ustav Vedeckotechnickych Informaci*] Meliorace [*A publication*]

Sb UVTI Ochr Rostl ... Sbornik UVTI [*Ustav Vedeckotechnickych Informaci*] Ochrana Rostlin [*A publication*]

Sb UVTI Ustav Vedeckotech Inf Zahradnictvi ... Sbornik UVTI-Ustav Vedeckotechnickych Informaci. Zahradnictvi [*A publication*]

SBUV/TOMS ... Solar and Backscattered Ultraviolet and Total Ozone Mapping System

SBV .... Sabah [*Papua New Guinea*] [*Airport symbol*]   (OAG)

SBV .... Semiautomatic Bleeder Valve

SBV .... Single Binocular Vision

SBV .... South Boston, VA [*Location identifier*] [*FAA*]   (FAAL)

SBVC .... San Bernardino Valley College [*California*]

SBVE .... State Board of Vocational Education [*State Board of Education*]   (OICC)

Sb Ved Lesn Ustav Vys Sk Zemed Praze ... Sbornik Vedeckeho Lesnickeho Ustavu Vysoke Skoly Zemedelske v Praze [*A publication*]

Sb Ved Praci Ustred Statniho Ust Praze ... Sbornik Vedeckych Praci Ustredniho Statniho Ustavu v Praze [*A publication*]

Sb Ved Pr Lek Fak Karlovy Univ Hradci Kralove Suppl ... Sbornik Vedeckych Praci Lekarske Fakulty Karlovy University v Hradci Kralove. Supplementum [*A publication*]

Sb Ved Pr Lek Fak Univ Karlovy Hradci Kralove ... Sbornik Vedeckych Praci Lekarske Fakulty. Karlovy University v Hradci Kralove [*A publication*]

Sb Ved Pr VLVDU Hradci Kralove ... Sbornik Vedeckych Praci VLVDU [*Vojenskeho Lekarskeho Vyzkumneho a Doskolovaciho Ustavu*] v Hradci Kralove [*A publication*]

Sb Ved Pr Vys Sk Banske Ostrave Rada Horn-Geol ... Sbornik Vedeckych Praci Vysoke Skoly Banske v Ostrave. Rada Hornicko-Geologicka[*Czechoslovakia*] [*A publication*]

Sb Ved Pr Vys Sk Bransk Ostrave ... Sbornik Vedeckych Praci Vysoke Skoly Banske v Ostrave [*A publication*]

Sb Ved Pr Vys Sk Chem-Technol (Pardubice) ... Sbornik Vedeckych Praci. Vysoka Skola Chemickotechnologicka (Pardubice) [*A publication*]

Sb "Vop Issled Izpol'z Pochv Moldavii" ... Sbornik "Voprosy Issledovaniya i Izpol'zovaniya Pochv Moldavii" [*A publication*]

SBVS.......... Saga-Book of the Viking Society for Northern Research [*A publication*]

SBVS.......... Shield Building Ventilation System   (NRCH)

Sb Vses Inst Zashch Rast ... Sbornik Vsesoyuznogo Instituta Zashchity Rastenii [*A publication*]

Sb Vses Sov Nauchno-Tekh Obshchestv Kom Korroz Zashch Met ... Sbornik Vsesoyuznyi Sovet Nauchno-Tekhnickeskikh Obshchestv. Komitet po Korrozi i Zashchite Metallov [*A publication*]

Sb Vynalezu ... Sbirka Vynalezu [*A publication*]

Sb Vys Chem Technol Praze Ekon Rizeni Chem Prum ... Sbornik Vysoke Skoly Chemicko-Technologicke v Praze. Ekonomika a Rizeni Chemickeho Prumyslu [*A publication*]

Sb Vysk Pr Odboru Celul Pap ... Sbornik Vyskumnych Prac z Odboru Celulozy a Papiera [*A publication*]

Sb Vysk Sk Chem-Technol Praze (Oddil) Chem Inz ... Sbornik Vysoke Skoly Chemicko-Technologicke v Praze (Oddil). Chemicke Inzenyrstvi [*A publication*]

Sb Vysk Sk Chem-Technol Praze (Oddil) Chem Inz Autom ... Sbornik Vysoke Skoly Chemicko-Technologicke v Praze (Oddil). Chemicke Inzenyrstvi a Automatizace [*A publication*]

Sb Vysk Sk Chem Technol Praze (Oddil) K ... Sbornik Vysoke Skoly Chemicko-Technologicke v Praze (Oddil). K [*A publication*]

Sb Vysoke Uceni Tech v Brne ... Sbornik Vysokeho Uceni Technickeho v Brne [*A publication*]

Sb Vys Sk Chem-Technol Praze ... Sbornik Vysoke Skoly Chemicko-Technologicke v Praze [*A publication*]

Sb Vys Sk Chem Technol Praze Anal Chem ... Sbornik Vysoke Skoly Chemicko-Technologicke v Praze. Analyticka Chemie [*A publication*]

Sb Vys Sk Chem Technol Praze Anorg Chem Technol ... Sbornik Vysoke Skoly Chemicko-Technologicke v Praze. Anorganicka Chemie a Technologie [*A publication*]

Sb Vys Sk Chem Technol Praze Anorg Org Technol ... Sbornik Vysoke Skoly Chemicko-Technologicke v Praze. Anorganicka a Organicka Technologie [*A publication*]

Sb Vys Sk Chem Technol Praze Anorg Technol ... Sbornik Vysoke Skoly Chemicko-Technologicke v Praze. Anorganicka Technologie [*A publication*]

Sb Vys Sk Chem Technol Praze Chem Inz Autom ... Sbornik Vysoke Skoly Chemicko-Technologicke v Praze. Chemicke Inzenyrstvi a Automatizace [*A publication*]

Sb Vys Sk Chem Technol Praze Chem Technol Silik ... Sbornik Vysoke Skoly Chemicko-Technologicke v Praze. Chemie a Technologie Silikatu [*A publication*]

Sb Vys Sk Chem Technol Praze Mineral ... Sbornik Vysoke Skoly Chemicko-Technologicke v Praze. Mineralogie [*A publication*]

Sb Vys Sk Chem Technol Praze Oddil Fak Anorg Technol ... Sbornik Vysoke Skoly Chemicko-Technologicke v Praze. Oddil Fakult Anorganicke a Organicke Technologie [*A publication*]

Sb Vys Sk Chem Technol Praze Oddil Fak Potravin Technol ... Sbornik Vysoke Skoly Chemicko-Technologicke v Praze. Oddil Fakulty Poetravinarske Technologie [*A publication*]

Sb Vys Sk Chem-Technol Praze (Oddil) Fak Technol Paliv Vody ... Sbornik Vysoke Skoly Chemicko-Technologicke v Praze (Oddil). Fakulty Technologie Paliv a Vody [*A publication*]

Sb Vys Sk Chem Technol Praze Org Chem Technol ... Sbornik Vysoke Skoly Chemicko-Technologicke v Praze. Organicka Chemie a Technologie [*A publication*]

Sb Vys Sk Chem-Technol Praze Rada B ... Sbornik Vysoke Skoly Chemicko-Technologicke v Praze. Rada B. Anorganicka Chemie a Technologie [*A publication*]

Sb Vys Sk Chem Technol Praze Technol Paliv ... Sbornik Vysoke Skoly Chemicko-Technologicke v Praze. Technologie Paliv [*Czechoslovakia*] [*A publication*]

Sb Vys Sk Chem-Technol Praze Technol Vody ... Sbornik Vysoke Skoly Chemicko-Technologicke v Praze. Technologie Vody [*A publication*]

Sb Vys Sk Chem-Technol Pr Potraviny ... Sbornik Vysoke Skoly Chemicko-Technologicke v Praze. Potraviny [*A publication*]

Sb Vys Skola Chem-Technol Fak Potrav Technol ... Sbornik Vysoka Skola Chemicko-Technologicka. Fakulta Potravinarske Technologie [*A publication*]

Sb Vys Skoly Polnohospod Nitre Prevadzkovo-Ekon Fak ... Sbornik Vysokej Skoly Polnohospodarskej v Nitre Prevadzkovo-Ekonomicka Fakulta [*A publication*]

Sb Vys Skoly Zemed Brne Rada A ... Sbornik Vysoke Skoly Zemedelske v Brne. Rada A [*A publication*]

Sb Vys Skoly Zemed Brne Rada B ... Sbornik Vysoke Skoly Zemedelske v Brne. Rada B [*A publication*]

Sb Vys Skoly Zemed Praze ... Sbornik Vysoke Skoly Zemedelske v Praze [*A publication*]

Sb Vys Sk Zemed Brne ... Sbornik Vysoke Skoly Zemedelske v Brne [*A publication*]

Sb Vys Sk Zemed v Brne A ... Sbornik Vysoke Skoly Zemedelske v Brne. A [*A publication*]

Sb Vys Sk Zemed Brne Rada C Spisy Fak Lesn ... Sbornik Vysoke Skoly Zemedelske v Brne. Rada C. Spisy Fakulty Lesnicke [*A publication*]

Sb Vys Sk Zemed Lesn Fak Brne Rada C Spisy ... Sbornik Vysoke Skoly Zemedelske a Lesnicke Fakulty v Brne. Rada C. Spisy Fakulty Lesnicke [*A publication*]

Sb Vys Sk Zemed Praze ... Sbornik Vysoke Skoly Zemedelske v Praze [*A publication*]

Sb Vys Sk Zemed Praze Fak Agron Rada A ... Sbornik Vysoke Skoly Zemedelske v Praze. Fakulta Agronomicka. Rada A. Rostlinna Vyroba [*A publication*]

Sb Vys Uceni Tech Brne ... Sbornik Vysokeho Uceni Technickeho v Brne [*A publication*]

Sb Vys Zemed Lesn Fak Brne B Spisy Fak Vet ... Sbornik Vysoke Skoly Zemedelske a Lesnicke Fakulty v Brne. Rada B. Spisy Fakulty Veterinarni [*A publication*]

SBW .... Shebandowan Resources [*Vancouver Stock Exchange symbol*]

SBW .... Sibu [*Malaysia*] [*Airport symbol*]   (OAG)

SbW .... South by West

SBW .... Spectral Bandwidth

SBW .... Spruce Budworm

SBW .... Steel Basement Window

SBW .... Submarine Warfare   (MCD)

SbWAk .... Sitzungsberichte der Wiener Akademie [*A publication*]

SBWFA .... Schriftenreihe des Bundesministers fuer Wissenschaftliche Forschung (Germany). Strahlenschutz [*A publication*]

SBWG .... Strategic Bomb Wing [*Military*]

SBWU .... Singapore Bus Workers' Union

SBWX .... Seaboard World Airlines, Inc. [*Air carrier designation symbol*]

SBX .... S-Band Transponder

SBX .... Shelby, MT [*Location identifier*] [*FAA*]   (FAAL)

SBX .... Student Book Exchange

SBX .... Subsea Beacon/Transponder

SBY .... Salisbury [*Maryland*] [*Airport symbol*]   (OAG)

SBY .... Salisbury, MD [*Location identifier*] [*FAA*]   (FAAL)

SBY .... Sand Bay [*Alaska*] [*Seismograph station code, US Geological Survey*] [*Closed*]   (SEIS)

SBY .... Shapiro, Barney, Newark NJ [*STAC*]

SBY .... Standby [*Airlines*]

SBZ .... Sibiu [*Romania*] [*Airport symbol*]   (OAG)

SBZ .... Sowjetische Besatzungszone [*Soviet Occupation Zone*] [*East Germany*]

SBZ Sanit Heiz Klimatech ... SBZ Sanitaer-, Heizungs-, und Klimatechnik [*West Germany*] [*A publication*]

SC .... All India Reporter, Supreme Court Reports   (DLA)

SC .... Cape Of Good Hope Reports [*South Africa*]   (DLA)

SC .... Catalan Solidarity   (PPW)

SC .... Christian Scientist

SC .... Congregation of the Servants of Christ [*Anglican religious community*]

SC .... Court of Session Cases [*Scotland*]   (DLA)

SC .... Cruiser Submarine [*Navy symbol*] [*Obsolete*]

SC .... Juta's Supreme Court Reports [*1880-1910*] [*Cape Of Good Hope, South Africa*]   (DLA)

SC .... Manetti Roberts [*Italy*] [*Research code symbol*]

SC .... Quebec Official Reports, Superior Court [*Canada*]   (DLA)

SC .... Sacra Congregatio [*Sacred Congregation*] [*Latin*]

SC .... Sacrococcygeal [*Anatomy*]

SC .... Sacrosanctam Concilium [*Constitution on the Sacred Liturgy*] [*Vatican II document*]

SC .... Sad Case [*An unpopular person*] [*Teen slang*]

SC .... Safe Custody [*Banking*]

SC .... Saffery Champness International [*British accounting firm*]

S/C .... Sales Code

SC .... Sales Costs

SC .... Salesianorum Congregatio [*Congregation of St. Francis of Sales*] [*Salesian Fathers*] [*Roman Catholic religious order*]

SC .... Salmagundi Club

SC .... Salvage Charges

SC .... Same Case [*Law*]

SC .... Same Coupling [*Music*]

SC .... Sandia Corporation

SC .... Sanitary Corps

SC .... Satellite Communications [*Military*]

SC .... Satellite Computer

SC .... Saturable Core   (MSA)

S & C .... Saunders and Cole's English Bail Court Reports   (DLA)

Sc. .... Scaccaria [*Exchequer*] [*Latin*]   (DLA)

SC .... Scale

Sc. .... Scammon's Reports [*2-5 Illinois*]   (DLA)

SC .... Scandinavian
Sc .... Scandium [*Chemical element*]
SC .... Scapula
SC .... Scarce [*Bookselling*]   (ROG)
SC .... Scavenge   (AAG)
SC .... Scene
SC .... Scented Cape [*Tea trade*]   (ROG)
SC .... Schilling [*Monetary unit*]   (ROG)
Sc .... Schmidt Number [*IUPAC*]
SC .... School Certificate
SC .... School Construction   (OICC)
SC .... Schools Council [*British*]
SC .... Schooner   (ROG)
SC .... Schwann Cell [*Biology*]
SC .... Science
SC .... Science and Culture [*A publication*]
Sc .... Scientia. Organo Internazionale di Sintesi Scientifica [*A publication*]
SC .... Scilicet [*Namely*] [*Latin*] [*Legal term*]
SC .... Scope Change   (MCD)
SC .... Score   (AABC)
Sc .... Scoriae [*Quality of the bottom*] [*Nautical charts*]
SC .... Scoring Criteria   (MCD)
Sc .... Scotch   (DLA)
Sc .... Scotland   (DLA)
SC .... Scots
Sc .... Scottish   (DLA)
SC .... Scottish Constitution   (ADA)
Sc .... Scott's English Common Pleas Reports   (DLA)
SC .... Screen Coordinator [*Military*]   (CAAL)
SC .... Screen Flag [*Navy*] [*British*]
SC .... Screw
S/C .... Screwed and Coupled
SC .... Script [*Films, television, etc.*]
Sc .... Scriptorium [*A publication*]
SC .... Scruple
SC .... Sculpsit [*He, or She, Engraved It*] [*Latin*]
SC .... Sculptor
SC .... Sculpture Center   (EA)
SC .... Scuola Cattolica [*A publication*]
Sc .... Scutum [*of Hesiod*] [*Classical studies*]   (OCD)
SC .... [*The*] Seal Cylinders of Western Asia [*A publication*]   (BJA)
SC .... Seamen's Center [*Later, Seamen and International House*]   (EA)
S & C .... Search and Clear [*Military*]
SC .... Search Control   (IEEE)
SC .... Searchlight Carrier [*British*]
SC .... Searle [*G. D.*] & Co. [*Research code symbol*]
SC .... Seat Cabs
SC .... Seco-Cemp Ltd. [*Toronto Stock Exchange symbol*]
SC .... Secondary Code
SC .... Secondary Confinement [*Nuclear energy*]   (NRCH)
SC .... Secondary Containment   (IEEE)
S-C .... Secret and Confidential Files [*Navy*]
SC .... Secretory Component [*Supersedes SP, TP*] [*Immunology*]
SC .... Secular College
SC .... Security Call [*Economics*]
SC .... Security Council of the United Nations
SC .... See Comments [*Routing slip*]
SC .... See Copy
SC .... Select Cases [*Oudh, India*]   (DLA)
SC .... Select Committee
SC .... Self-Care [*Medicine*]
SC .... Self-Check   (AAG)
SC .... Self-Closing
SC .... Self Compatible
SC .... Self-Contained
S/C .... Self-Contained [*English housing term*]
SC .... Semiclosed [*Anatomy*]
SC .... Semiconductor
SC .... Senatus Consulto [*By the Decree of the Senate*] [*Latin*]
SC .... Senatus Consultum [*Classical studies*]   (OCD)
SC .... Sending Complete [*Telecommunications*]   (TEL)
SC .... Senior Cameraman
SC .... Senior Counsel [*Ireland*]
S/C .... Sensor Controller   (MCD)
SC .... Separate Cover
SC .... Sequence Charts   (AAG)
SC .... Sequence Controller
SC .... Sequence Counter
SC .... Servants of Charity [*Roman Catholic men's religious order*]
S/C .... Service Ceiling
SC .... Service Center [*IRS*]
SC .... Service Certificate [*Military*] [*British*]
SC .... Service Change
SC .... Service Charge [*Banking*]
SC .... Service Club [*Military enlisted men's club*]
SC .... Service Code [*Telecommunications*]   (TEL)
SC .... Service Command [*Marine Corps*]
SC .... Service Connected [*Medicine*]

SC .... Servicos Aereos Cruzeiro do Sul SA [*Brazil*] [*ICAO designator*]   (FAAC)
SC .... Session Cases [*Legal*] [*British*]
SC .... Session Control [*Data processing*]   (IBMDP)
SC .... Set/Clear [*Flip-flop*] [*Data processing*]
SC .... Set Clock
S/C .... Set Course [*Navigation*]
SC .... Severest Critic [*Initialism used by E. B. White to describe his wife*]
SC .... Seychelles [*Two-letter standard code*]   (CNC)
SC .... Shaft Center   (MSA)
SC .... Shakespearean Criticism [*A publication*]
SC .... Shaped Charge [*of explosive*]
SC .... Sharp Cash [*Prompt payment*]
SC .... Shell Transport & Trading Company Ltd. [*NYSE symbol*]
SC .... Shift Control Counter [*Data processing*]   (MDG)
S & C .... Shipper and Carrier [*Business and trade*]
SC .... Shipping Container
SC .... Shipping Contract   (MCD)
SC .... Ship's Cook [*Navy*]
SC .... Shire Council   (ADA)
SC .... Shop Call   (MCD)
SC .... Shopping Concourses [*Public-performance tariff class*] [*British*]
SC .... Short Circuit
SC .... Short Course [*of instruction*]
SC .... Should Cost   (MCD)
SC .... Sickle Cell [*Medicine*]
SC .... Side Cabin
SC .... Side Contact [*Valves*]   (DEN)
SC .... Sierra Club   (EA)
SC .... Signal Comparator
SC .... Signal Conditioner
S & C .... Signal and Conditioning   (KSC)
SC .... Signal Corps [*Later, Communications and Electronics Command*] [*Army*]
SC .... Significant Characteristics   (MCD)
SC .... Silicone Coated
SC .... Silvered Copper [*Wire*]   (IEEE)
SC .... Simulation Coordinator
SC .... Simulator Control   (MCD)
SC .... Sine Correction [*Without lenses*] [*Ophthalmology*]
SC .... Sine-Cosine
SC .... Single Case
SC .... Single Cell
SC .... Single Circuit [*Electricity*]
SC .... Single Column
SC .... Single Comb
SC .... Single Contact [*Switch*]
SC .... Single Counter
SC .... Single Crochet
SC .... Single Crystal
SC .... Sinusoidal Collagen [*Anatomy*]
SC .... Sisters of Charity [*Roman Catholic religious order*]
SC .... Sisters of Charity [*Anglican religious community*]
SC .... Site Contingency [*Nuclear energy*]   (NRCH)
SC .... Sized and Calendered [*Paper*]
S & C .... Sized and Calendered [*Paper*]
SC .... Skill Component
SC .... Skin Conductance
SC .... Slow Component
SC .... Slow Curing [*Asphalt grade*]
SC .... Small Capitals [*Typography*]
SC .... Small Compact [*Car size*]
SC .... Small Craft
SC .... Smooth Contour [*Technical drawings*]
SC .... Snow Cover [*Meteorology*]
SC .... So-Called
SC .... Social Casework [*A publication*]
SC .... Social Compass [*A publication*]
SC .... Social Credit Party [*British*]
SC .... Socialist Commentary [*A publication*]
S en C .... Sociedad en Comandita [*Limited partnership company*] [*Spanish*]
SC .... Societas Fratrum Sacris Cordis [*Brothers of the Sacred Heart*] [*Roman Catholic religious order*]
SC .... Society of the Cincinnati   (EA)
SC .... Society for Cryobiology   (EA)
S/C .... Software Contractor [*NASA*]   (NASA)
SC .... Soil Characteristics
SC .... Soil Conservation [*A publication*]
SC .... Solar Cell
SC .... Soldier Capabilities
SC .... Sole Charge [*Ecclesiastical*] [*British*]   (ROG)
SC .... Solid-State Circuit   (MCD)
S/C .... Son Compte [*His or Her Account*] [*French*]
SC .... SONAR Channel [*Navy*]   (CAAL)
SC .... Soncino Chumash [*A publication*]   (BJA)
SC .... Songwriters Club [*Later, SLC*]   (EA)
SC .... Sound Channel [*Navy*]   (CAAL)
SC .... Source Code

SC	Sources Chretiennes [*Paris*] [*A publication*]
SC	South Carolina [*Postal code*]
SC	South Carolina Musician [*A publication*]
SC	South Carolina Reports (DLA)
Sc	South Carolina State Library, Columbia, SC [*Library symbol*] [*Library of Congress*] (LCLS)
SC	Southern California
SC	Southern Classification
SC	Southern Conference (EA)
SC	Spacecraft (MCD)
S/C	Spacecraft/Capsule
SC	Spark Control
SC	Special Access, Compartmented (MCD)
SC	Special Care [*Medicine*]
SC	Special Circuit
SC	Special Circular
S/C	Special Conditions (MCD)
SC	Special Constable
SC	Specialty Code
SC	Specific Cueing
SC	Specification Change
SC	Speed Controller (NRCH)
SC	Spermatocyte
SC	Sports Club (ADA)
SC	Spot Check (AAG)
SC	Spread Correlation
SC	Spreading Coefficient
SC	Spring Conditions [*Skiing*]
SC	Squamous Cell Carcinoma [*Also, SCC*] [*Medicine*]
S & C	Stabilization and Control (KSC)
SC	Stack (Pipe) Cut [*Sanitation*] [*British*] (ROG)
SC	Staff Captain [*Military*] [*British*]
SC	Staff Car [*British*]
SC	Staff College [*Military*]
SC	Staff Corps
SC	Stage Center [*A stage direction*]
SC	Standard Candle [*Power*]
SC	Standard Conditions
S & C	Standards and Control
SC	Standing Committee (ADA)
SC	Star of Courage [*Award*] [*British*]
SC	Start Computer
SC	Start Conversion [*Data processing*]
sC	Statcoulomb [*Also, Fr, statC*] [*Unit of electric charge*]
SC	Statement of Capability
S/C	Statement of Charges [*Army*]
SC	Statement of Compatibility (MCD)
SC	Statistical Control
SC	Statistics Canada
SC	Status Statement [*Online database field identifier*]
SC	Statutes of Canada
S of C	Statutes of Canada (DLA)
SC	Steel Casting
SC	Steel Cored [*Conductors*]
SC	Steering Committee (NATG)
SC	Stellar Camera
SC	Stendhal Club [*A publication*]
SC	Stepped Care [*Medicine*]
SC	Sternoclavicular [*Joint*] [*Anatomy*]
SC	Stop-Continue (DEN)
SC	Storage Capacity (AAG)
SC	Stored Command
S/C	Stowage Container
S & C	Strategic and Critical Raw Material [*Military*]
SC	Stratocumulus [*Meteorology*]
SC	Strike Command [*Military*]
S/C	Strip Chart [*Recorder*] [*NASA*] (NASA)
SC	Stronnictwo Chlopskie [*Peasants' Party*] [*Poland*] (PPE)
SC	Studi Colombiani [*A publication*]
SC	Studia Catholica [*A publication*]
SC	Studia Celtica [*A publication*]
SC	Su Cuenta [*Your Account*] [*Business and trade*] [*Spanish*]
S/C	Subcable (KSC)
S/C	Subcarrier (AAG)
SC	Subcommittee
SC	Subcontractor (NATG)
SC	Subcours
SC	Subcutaneous [*Beneath the Skin*] [*Medicine*]
SC	Subject Classification [*Library science*]
SC	Submarine Chaser [*110 foot*]
SC	Sudden Commencement
SC	Sugar-Coated [*Pharmacy*]
SC	Suisse Contemporaine [*A publication*]
SC	Summary Court [*Navy*]
SC	Sumter & Choctaw Railway Co. [*AAR code*]
SC	Supercalendered [*Paper*]
S/C	Superconducting Magnetic (MCD)
SC	Supercritical Chromatography
SC	Superimposed Coding [*Data processing*] (DIT)
SC	Superimposed Current
SC	Superintending Cartographer [*Navy*] [*British*]

SC	Superior Colliculus [*Eye anatomy*]
SC	Superior Court (DLA)
SC	Supervisor's Console
SC	Supervisory Control
SC	Supplemental Contract (AAG)
SC	Supplementary Information [*Telecommunications*] (TEL)
SC	Supply Catalog [*Military*] (AABC)
SC	Supply Control [*Military*]
SC	Supply Corps
SC	Support Chief
SC	Support Command [*Army*]
SC	Support Concept Manual [*Marine Corps*]
SC	Support Contractor (MCD)
SC	Support Controller [*NASA*] (KSC)
SC	Support Coordinator (AAG)
SC	Suppressed Carrier (IEEE)
SC	Supreme Council [*Freemasonry*] (ROG)
SC	Supreme Court
SC	Supreme Court Reporter [*National Reporter System*] (DLA)
SC	Surface Combustion [*Reducing gas process*]
SC	Surface Command (MCD)
SC	Surgeon-Captain [*British*]
SC	Surgeon-Commander [*Navy*] [*British*]
SC	Surveillance Compliance [*Nuclear energy*] (NRCH)
S & C	Swan and Critchfield's Revised Statutes [*Ohio*] (DLA)
SC	Swimming Club
SC	Switching Cell (IEEE)
SC	Symbolic Code (AAG)
SC	Synanon Church [*An association*] [*Badger, CA*] (EA)
SC	Synaptonemal Complex [*Botanical cytology*]
SC	Synchro-Cyclotron
SC	Synchronization Coefficient
SC	System Controller [*Military*] (CAAL)
SC	Systems Command [*Air Force*]
SC	Systolic Click [*Cardiology*]
S1C	Seaman, First Class [*Navy*]
SCA............	Air Weather Service, Technical Library, Scott AFB, IL [*OCLC symbol*] (OCLC)
SCA............	Archibald Library, Caronport, Saskatchewan [*Library symbol*] [*National Library of Canada*] (NLC)
SCA............	SAAB Clubs of America (EA)
SCA............	Saluki Club of America (EA)
SCA............	Samoyed Club of America (EA)
SCA............	Santa Cruz [*Argentina*] [*Seismograph station code, US Geological Survey*] [*Closed*] (SEIS)
SCA............	Satellite Committee Agency [*Army*] (MCD)
SCA............	Satellite Communications Agency [*Army*]
SCA............	Save the Children Alliance (EA-IO)
Sca............	Scala [*Record label*]
Sca............	Scandinavica [*A publication*]
SCA............	Scarborough Public Library [*UTLAS symbol*]
SCA............	Schedule Change Authorization [*NASA*] (NASA)
SCA............	Schipperke Club of America (EA)
SCA............	School and College Ability [*Test*] [*of ETS*]
SCA............	Science Clubs of America (EA)
SCA............	Science Fiction Classics Annual [*A publication*]
SCA............	Screen Composers of America (EA)
SCA............	Sebright Club of America (EA)
SCA............	Secondary Communications Authorization (IEEE)
SCA............	Secondary Control Assembly [*Nuclear energy*] (NRCH)
SCA............	Selectivity Clear Accumulator
SCA............	Senior Citizens of America [*Defunct*] (EA)
SCA............	Sequence Control Area [*NASA*] (KSC)
SCA............	Sequencer Control Assembly
SCA............	Service Cinematographique des Armees [*France*]
SCA............	Service and Compliance Administration [*US wage/price controls agency*]
SCA............	Service Contract Act [*1965*]
SCA............	Service Cryptologic Agencies [*Military*]
SCA............	Servo Corporation of America [*American Stock Exchange symbol*]
SCA............	Sex Chromosome Abnormality
SCA............	Shareholder Credit Accounting
SCA............	Shields Class Association (EA)
SCA............	Ship Cost Adjustment [*Navy*]
SCA............	Shipbuilders Council of America [*Washington, DC*] (EA)
SCA............	Shipping Control Authority (NVT)
SCA............	Shooters Club of America [*Defunct*]
SCA............	Should Cost Analysis (MCD)
SCA............	Shuttle Carrier Aircraft [*NASA*] (NASA)
SCA............	Sickle Cell Anemia [*Medicine*]
SCA............	Signal Conditioning Assembly [*NASA*] (KSC)
SCA............	Simulated Core Assembly [*Nuclear energy*] (NRCH)
SCA............	Simulation Control Area (MCD)
SCA............	Simulation Conversion Assembly [*Deep Space Instrumentation Facility, NASA*]
SCA............	Single Channel Analyzer
SCA............	Ski Council of America [*New York, NY*] (EA)
SCA............	Small-Caliber Ammunition (MSA)
SCA............	Smithsonian Contributions to Anthropology [*A publication*]
SCA............	Smoke Control Association [*Buckingham, PA*] (EA)

SCA............ Sneak Circuit Analysis [*NASA*]   (NASA)
SCA............ Society of Canadian Artists [*Formerly, Society of Co-Operative Artists*]
SCA............ Society for Cardiac Angiography [*Cleveland, OH*]   (EA)
SCA............ Society of Cardiovascular Anesthesiologists [*Richmond, VA*]   (EA)
SCA............ Society for Commercial Archeology   (EA)
SCA............ Society for Creative Anachronism   (EA)
SCA............ Society for Cultural Anthropology [*American Anthropological Association*]   (EA)
SCA............ Software Control Authorization [*NASA*]   (KSC)
SCA............ Sonar Class Association   (EA)
S Ca.......... South Carolina Reports   (DLA)
SCA............ South Central Air, Inc. [*Kenai, AK*] [*FAA designator*]   (FAAC)
SCA............ Southern Communications Area [*Military*]
SCA............ Southern Cotton Association [*Memphis, TN*]   (EA)
SCA............ Soybean Council of America [*Defunct*]   (EA)
SCA............ Spacecraft Adapter [*NASA*]   (KSC)
SCA............ SPALTRA [*Special Projects Alterations, Training*] Control Activity
SCA............ Specific Combining Ability
SCA............ Specification Compliance Agreement   (MCD)
SCA............ Speech Communication Association
SCA............ Speed Coaches Association   (EA)
SCA............ Spinach Carbonic Anhydrase [*An enzyme*]
SCA............ Standard Consolidated Area [*Bureau of Census*]
SCA............ Steel-Cored-Aluminium
SCA............ Sterba Curtain Antenna
SCA............ Stevengraph Collectors' Association   (EA)
SCA............ Stock Company Association [*Defunct*]   (EA)
SCA............ Stock Control Activity   (AFIT)
SCA............ Student Conservation Association
SCA............ Subcarrier Authorization   (MSA)
SCA............ Subcarrier Channel [*Telecommunications*]
SCA............ Subchannel Adapter
SCA............ Subcontract Authorization   (AAG)
SCA............ Subcritical Assembly   (DEN)
SCA............ Subsequent Coupons Attached
SCA............ Subsidiary Communications Authorization [*Facilities used to transmit background music to subscribing customers*]
SCA............ Summary Cost Account   (AABC)
SCA............ Surface Coatings Abstracts [*Paint Research Association of Great Britain*] [*Bibliographic database*]
SCA............ Swedish Council of America [*Minneapolis, MN*]   (EA)
SCA............ Switch Control Assembly
SCA............ Switzerland Cheese Association [*New York, NY*]   (EA)
SCA............ Synagogue Council of America   (EA)
SCA............ Synchronous Communications Adapter
SCA............ System Comparison Analysis [*Bell System*]
SCA............ System Control Area
SCAA.......... Skin Care Association of America   (EA)
SCAA .... Specialty Coffee Association of America [*New York, NY*]   (EA)
SCAA .... Spill Control Association of America [*Formerly, OSCAA*] [*Southfield, MI*]   (EA)
SCAA .... Sussex Cattle Association of America   (EA)
SCAAN...... System for Computerized Application Analysis [*Automotive engineering*]
SCAAP...... Special Commonwealth African Assistance Plan
SCAB .... Streptozocin, CCNU [*Lomustine*], Adriamycin, Bleomycin [*Antineoplastic drug regimen*]
SCABG...... Single Coronary Artery Bypass Graft [*Cardiology*]
Scac.......... Scaccaria Curia [*Court of Exchequer*] [*Latin*]   (DLA)
SCAC .... School and College Advisory Center [*Later, EGASCAC*]   (EA)
SCAC .... Self-Cleaning Air Cleaner
SCAC .... Standard Carriers Alpha Code   (MCD)
SC Acad Sci Bull ... South Carolina Academy of Science. Bulletin [*A publication*]
SC (ACT) ... Supreme Court [*Australian Capital Territory*]   (DLA)
SC Acts...... Acts and Joint Resolutions of the State of South Carolina   (DLA)
SCAD .... Savannah College of Art and Design [*Georgia*]
SCAD .... Scan Converter and Display [*Systems*]
SCAD .... Schenectady Army Depot   (AABC)
SCAD .... Small Current Amplifying Device
SCAD .... State Commission Against Discrimination
SCAD .... Strategic Bomber Penetration Decoy [*Air Force*]
SCAD .... Subsonic Cruise Armed Decoy [*Air Force*]
SCADA...... Student Coalition Against Drug Abuse
SCADA...... Supervisory Control and Data Acquisition   (IEEE)
SCADAR .... Scatter Detection and Ranging
SCADC...... Standard Central Air Data Computer
SCADS...... SAS Census Access and Display System [*University of Missouri, St. Louis*] [*Information service*]   (EISS)
SCADS...... Scanning Celestial Attitude Determination System
SCADS...... Shipborne Containerized Air Defense System
SCADS...... Simulation of Combined Analog Digital Systems [*Data processing*]   (IEEE)
SCADS...... Sioux City Air Defense Sector [*ADC*]
Sc Advocate ... Science Advocate [*A publication*]
SCAE .... Society for Computer-Aided Engineering [*Rockford, IL*]   (EA)
SCAEC....... Submarine Contact Analysis and Evaluation Center   (NVT)

SCAEF .... Supreme Commander, Allied Expeditionary Force [*World War II*]
Scaen Rom Frag ... Scaenicorum Romanorum Fragmenta [*A publication*]   (OCD)
SCAEPA..... Society for Computer Applications in Engineering, Planning, and Architecture [*Formerly, CEPA*]   (EA)
SCAF........ Self-Centred-Altruism Fad
SCAF........ Supersonic Cruise Attack Fighter   (MCD)
SCAF........ Suppressor Cell Activating Factor [*Biochemistry*]
SCAF........ Supreme Commander of Allied Forces   (ADA)
SCAFB .... Schilling Air Force Base   (AAG)
SCAFEDS ... Space Construction Automated Fabrication Experiment Definition Study   (MCD)
SCAG........ Saigon Civil Assistance Group [*Vietnam*]
SCAG........ Southern California Association of Governments
SCAG........ Special COMSEC Advisory Group [*US Army Communications Command*]   (MCD)
SC Ag Dept ... South Carolina. Department of Agriculture, Commerce, and Industries. Publications [*A publication*]
SC Ag Exp ... South Carolina. Agricultural Experiment Station. Publications [*A publication*]
SC Agric Exp Stn Bull ... South Carolina. Agricultural Experiment Station. Bulletin [*A publication*]
SC Agric Exp Stn Circ ... South Carolina. Agricultural Experiment Station. Circular [*A publication*]
SC Agric Exp Stn Tech Bull ... South Carolina. Agricultural Experiment Station. Technical Bulletin [*A publication*]
SC Agr Res ... South Carolina Agricultural Research [*A publication*]
SCAHR...... School of Community and Allied Health Resources
ScAi .... Aiken-Bamberg-Barnwell-Edgefield Regional Library, Aiken, SC [*Library symbol*] [*Library of Congress*]   (LCLS)
ScAiD........ E. I. DuPont de Nemours & Co., Aiken, SC [*Library symbol*] [*Library of Congress*]   (LCLS)
SCAIF........ Sertoli-Cell Androgenic Inhibitory Factor [*Endocrinology*]
SCAJAP..... Shipping Control Administrator Japan
SCAL......... Silver City Airways Limited
SCAL......... STAR [*Self Testing and Reporting*] Computer Assembly Language
S Cal Ac Sc B ... Southern California Academy of Sciences. Bulletin [*A publication*]
SCALD .... Structural Computer-Aided Logic Design
SCALE .... Space Checkout and Launch Equipment
SCALE .... Statutes and Cases Automated Legal Enquiry   (ADA)
SCALER..... Statistical Calculation and Analysis of Engine Removal [*Navy*]
S Calif Law Rev ... Southern California Law Review [*A publication*]
S Cal Law R ... Southern California Law Review [*A publication*]
S Cal L Rev ... Southern California Law Review [*A publication*]
SCALO...... Scanning Local Oscillator   (NG)
SCALP .... Students Concerned about Legal Prices [*Student legal action organization*]
S CA LR ..... Southern California Law Review [*A publication*]
Scam.......... Scammon's Reports [*2-5 Illinois*]   (DLA)
Sc Am .... Scientific American [*A publication*]
SCAM........ Selection Classification Age Maturity Program [*Medical screening procedure for athletes*]
SCAM........ Soil Classification and Mapping Branch [*Department of Agriculture*]   (EISS)
SCAM........ Spectrum Characteristics Analysis and Measurement [*FAA*]
SCAM........ Station Control and Monitoring
SCAM........ Strike Camera   (MCD)
SCAM........ Study Course in Agency Management [*LIMRA*]
SCAM........ Subsonic Cruise Armed Missile/Decoy [*Air Force*]   (MCD)
SCAM........ Synchronous Communications Access Method
SCAMA ...... Scientific American [*A publication*]
SCAMA ...... Service Central des Approvisionements et Materiels Americains [*Central Office of American Supplies and Equipment*] [*World War II*]
SCAMA ..... Skewed Circular Arc Method of Analysis
SCAMA ...... Station Conferencing and Monitoring Arrangement [*NASA*]
SCAMA ...... Switching, Conferencing, and Monitoring Arrangement [*NASA*]
SCAMC...... Symposium on Computer Applications in Medical Care [*Baltimore, MD*]
SCAMP ...... Sectionalized Carrier and Multipurpose Vehicle [*Military*]
SCAMP ...... Self-Contained Airborne Multipurpose Pod   (MCD)
SCAMP ...... Self-Contained Ancillary Modular Platform [*Woods Hole Oceanographic Institution*]
SCAMP ...... Self-Propelled Crane for Aircraft Maintenance and Positioning   (MCD)
SCAMP ...... Sensor Control and Management Platoon [*Marine Corps*]
SCAMP ...... Signal Conditioning Amplifier
SCAMP ...... Single Channel Amplitude Monopulse Processing
SCAMP ...... Small-Caliber Ammunition Modernization Program [*Army*]   (RDA)
SCAMP ...... Space-Controlled Army Measurements Probe
SCAMP ...... Sperry Computer-Aided Message Processor [*British*]
SCAMP ...... Standard Configuration and Modification Program
SCAMP ...... Succinyl CAMP [*Biochemistry*]
SCAMP ...... Summer Campus, Advanced Mathematics Program [*Institute for Defense Analysis*]
SCAMPERS ... Standard Corps-Army-MACOM Personnel System   (AABC)

SCAMPS.... Small Computer Analytical and Mathematical Programing System (IEEE)
SCAMPTME ... Succinyl CAMP Tyrosine Methyl Ester [*Biochemistry*]
SCAMS ...... Scanning Microwave Spectrometer
Sc Am Sup ... Scientific American. Supplement [*A publication*]
ScAn .... Anderson County Library, Anderson, SC [*Library symbol*] [*Library of Congress*] (LCLS)
SCAN .... Satellite Cable Audio Networks [*Cable-television service*]
SCAN .... Savings Comparative Analysis [*Federal Home Loan Bank Board*] [*Database*]
SCAN .... Scandinavian
Scan .... Scandinavian Studies [*A publication*]
Scan .... Scandinavica [*A publication*]
SCAN .... Scanner Association of North America (EA)
SCAN .... Scintiscan [*Medicine*]
SCAN .... Seismic Computerized Alert Network [*For warning of an earthquake*]
SCAN .... Selected Current Aerospace Notices [*NASA*]
SCAN .... Self-Correcting Automatic Navigator
SCAN .... Service Center Advantage Network [*Federal-Mogul Corp.*]
SCAN .... Service Center for Aging Information [*Department of Health and Human Services*] [*Information service*] (EISS)
SCAN .... Short Current Abstracts and Notes (DIT)
SCAN .... Signal Corps Administrative Network [*Obsolete*] [*Army*]
SCAN .... Silent Communication Alarm Network [*NASA*]
SCAN .... Southern California Answering Network [*Electronic link of many libraries, communities, etc.*] [*Los Angeles Public Library*] [*Los Angeles, CA*]
SCAN .... Spares Change Advance Notice (MCD)
SCAN .... Stock Control and Analysis (BUR)
SCAN .... Stock Market Computer Answering Network [*British*]
SCAN .... Student Career Automated Network (IEEE)
SCAN .... Suspected Child Abuse and Neglect
SCAN .... Switched Circuit Automatic Network [*Army*]
SCAN .... System for Collection and Analysis of Near-Collision Reports (AAG)
SCANA ...... Self-Contained Adverse-Weather Night Attack
SCAND ...... Scandinavia
Scand .... Scandinavica [*A publication*]
SCAND ...... Single Crystal Automatic Neutron Diffractometer
Scand Actuar J ... Scandinavian Actuarial Journal [*A publication*]
SCANDAL ... Select Committee to Arrange a New Deal to Avoid Litigation [*Toledo, OH, group formed in 1973 to humorously protest results of the Michigan-Toledo "War of 1835"*] [*See also FAT CHANCE*]
Scand Audiol ... Scandinavian Audiology [*A publication*]
Scand Audiol Suppl ... Scandinavian Audiology. Supplement [*A publication*]
Scand Ec Hist Rev ... Scandinavian Economic History Review [*A publication*]
Scand Econ Hist Rev ... Scandinavian Economic History Review [*A publication*]
SCANDEFA ... Scandinavian Dental Fair [*Danish Dental Association*] (TSPED)
SCANDI ...... Surveillance Control and Driver Information [*Traffic system*]
Scandinavian Publ Libr Q ... Scandinavian Public Library Quarterly [*A publication*]
Scandinav J Econ ... Scandinavian Journal of Economics [*A publication*]
Scand J Clin Lab Invest ... Scandinavian Journal of Clinical and Laboratory Investigation [*A publication*]
Scand J Clin Lab Invest Suppl ... Scandinavian Journal of Clinical and Laboratory Investigation. Supplement [*A publication*]
Scand J Dent Res ... Scandinavian Journal of Dental Research [*A publication*]
Scand J Econ ... Scandinavian Journal of Economics [*A publication*]
Scand J Gastroenterol ... Scandinavian Journal of Gastroenterology [*A publication*]
Scand J Gastroenterol Suppl ... Scandinavian Journal of Gastroenterology. Supplement [*A publication*]
Scand J Haematol ... Scandinavian Journal of Haematology [*A publication*]
Scand J Haematol Suppl ... Scandinavian Journal of Haematology. Supplement [*A publication*]
Scand J Haematol Suppl Ser Haematol ... Scandinavian Journal of Haematology. Supplement. Series Haematological [*A publication*]
Scand J Immunol ... Scandinavian Journal of Immunology [*A publication*]
Scand J Immunol Suppl ... Scandinavian Journal of Immunology. Supplement [*A publication*]
Scand J Infect Dis ... Scandinavian Journal of Infectious Diseases [*A publication*]
Scand J Infect Dis Suppl ... Scandinavian Journal of Infectious Diseases. Supplement [*A publication*]
Scand J Metall ... Scandinavian Journal of Metallurgy [*A publication*]
Scand J Plast Reconstr Surg ... Scandinavian Journal of Plastic and Reconstructive Surgery [*A publication*]
Scand J Plast Reconstr Surg Suppl ... Scandinavian Journal of Plastic and Reconstructive Surgery. Supplement [*A publication*]
Scand J Plast Recon Surg ... Scandinavian Journal of Plastic and Reconstructive Surgery [*A publication*]
Scand J Psychol ... Scandinavian Journal of Psychology [*A publication*]
Scand J Rehabil Med ... Scandinavian Journal of Rehabilitation Medicine [*A publication*]

Scand J Rehabil Med Suppl ... Scandinavian Journal of Rehabilitation Medicine. Supplement [*A publication*]
Scand J Respir Dis ... Scandinavian Journal of Respiratory Diseases [*A publication*]
Scand J Respir Dis Suppl ... Scandinavian Journal of Respiratory Diseases. Supplement [*A publication*]
Scand J Rheumatol ... Scandinavian Journal of Rheumatology [*A publication*]
Scand J Rheumatol Suppl ... Scandinavian Journal of Rheumatology. Supplement [*A publication*]
Scand J Soc Med ... Scandinavian Journal of Social Medicine [*A publication*]
Scand J Soc Med Suppl ... Scandinavian Journal of Social Medicine. Supplement [*A publication*]
Scand J St ... Scandinavian Journal of Statistics [*A publication*]
Scand J Statist ... Scandinavian Journal of Statistics. Theory and Applications [*A publication*]
Scand J Thorac Cardiovasc Surg ... Scandinavian Journal of Thoracic and Cardiovascular Surgery [*A publication*]
Scand J Thorac Cardiovasc Surg Suppl ... Scandinavian Journal of Thoracic and Cardiovascular Surgery. Supplement
Scand J Urol Nephrol ... Scandinavian Journal of Urology and Nephrology [*A publication*]
Scand J Urol Nephrol Suppl ... Scandinavian Journal of Urology and Nephrology. Supplement [*A publication*]
Scand J Work Envir Hlth ... Scandinavian Journal of Work Environment and Health [*A publication*]
Scand J Work Environ Health ... Scandinavian Journal of Work Environment and Health [*A publication*]
SCANDOC ... Scandinavian Documentation Center [*Washington, DC*]
Scand Oil-Gas Mag ... Scandinavian Oil-Gas Magazine [*A publication*]
Scand Paint Printing Ink Res Inst Rept ... Scandinavian Paint and Printing Ink Research Institute. Reports [*A publication*]
Scand Pol Stud ... Scandinavian Political Studies [*A publication*]
Scand Public Lib Q ... Scandinavian Public Library Quarterly [*A publication*]
Scand R ..... Scandinavian Review [*A publication*]
Scand Refrig ... Scandinavian Refrigeration [*Norway*] [*A publication*]
Scand Stud ... Scandinavian Studies [*A publication*]
Scand Stud Criminol ... Scandinavian Studies in Criminology (DLA)
Scand Stud in L ... Scandinavian Studies in Law [*A publication*]
Scand Stud Law ... Scandinavian Studies in Law [*A publication*]
Scand Yb ... Scandinavian Yearbook [*A publication*]
Scan Electron Microsc ... Scanning Electron Microscopy [*A publication*]
SCANIIR ..... Surface Composition by Analysis of Neutral and Ion Impact Radiation [*Qualitative analysis*]
SCAN MAG ... Scandalum Magnatum [*Defamation of Dignity*] [*Latin*] (ROG)
Scanning Electron Microsc ... Scanning Electron Microscopy [*A publication*]
SCANO .... Automatic Scanning Unit Inoperative [*Aviation*] (FAAC)
SCANP .... Scandinavian Periodicals Index in Economics and Business [*Database*] [*Sweden*]
SCANS ...... Scheduling and Control by Automated Network System
SCANS ...... System Checkout Automatic Network Simulator
SCANSAR ... Scanning Synthetic Aperture RADAR
SCAN-Test ... Scandinavian Pulp, Paper, and Board Testing Committee [*Stockholm, Sweden*] (EA-IO)
SCAO .... Senior Civil Affairs Officer
SCAO .... Standing Committee on Army Organization [*British*]
SCAO .... Standing Conference of Atlantic Organisations (EA-IO)
SCAOK ...... Automatic Scanning Unit Operative [*Aviation*] (FAAC)
SCAO(P).... Senior Civil Affairs Office, Police [*British*]
SCAP .... Service Center Audit Program [*IRS*]
SCAP .... Silent Compact Auxiliary Power
SCAP .... Silicon Capacitance Absolute Pressure Sensor
SCAP .... Small Communications Augmentation Package (MCD)
SCAP .... Space Charge Atomizing Precipitaters (KSC)
SCAP .... Supreme Commander, Allied Powers [*World War II*] (MUGU)
SCAPA ...... Society for Checking the Abuses of Public Advertising [*British*]
SCAPE ...... Self-Contained Atmospheric Personnel [*or Protective*] Ensemble [*Suit*] [*Aerospace*]
SCAPE ...... System Compatibility and Performance Evaluation [*Military*] (CAAL)
SCAPS ...... Small Capitals [*Typography*]
SCAR .... Satellite Capture and Retrieval (AFM)
SCAR .... Scandinavian Council for Applied Research
SCAR .... Scandinavian Review [*A publication*]
SCAR .... Scientific Committee on Antarctic Research [*ICSU*] (EA-IO)
SCAR .... Signal Conditioner Assembly Request (MCD)
S Car .... South Carolina (DLA)
S Car .... South Carolina Reports (DLA)
SCAR .... Spacecraft Assessment Report [*NASA*] (KSC)
SCAR .... Special Committee on Atlantic Research
SCAR .... Special Committee on Atomic Research [*Pugwash Conference*]
SCAR .... Special International Committee on Antarctic Research
SCAR .... Status Control Alert and Reporting (MCD)
SCAR .... Strike Control and Reconnaissance [*Aircraft*]
SCAR .... Structure-Carcinogenic Activity Relationship [*Biochemistry*]
SCAR .... Subcaliber Aircraft Rocket
SCAR .... Submarine Celestial Altitude Recorder [*Navy*]
SCAR .... Subsequent Contrast Application Review (MCD)
SCAR .... Supersonic Cruise Aircraft [*or Airplane*] Research [*NASA*]
SCAR .... Supplier Corrective Action Request
SCARA ...... Selective Compliance Assembly Robot Arm [*IBM Corp.*]

SCARAB .... Submersible Craft Assisting Repair and Burial [*Autonomous underwater vehicle*]
Scarborough Dist Archaeol Soc Res Rep ... Scarborough District Archaeological Society. Research Reports [*A publication*]
SCARDE .... Study Committee on Analysis of Research, Development, and Engineering
SCAReU ..... Stanford Community Against Reagan University [*Group opposed to proposed Ronald Reagan presidential library at Stanford University*]
SCARF ...... Santa Cruz Acoustic Range Facility
SCARF ...... Side-Looking Coherent All-Range Focused
SCARF ...... Special Committee on the Adequacy of Range Facilities   (MUGU)
SCARF ...... Survey of Change and Residential Finance [*Census Bureau*]
SCARF ...... System Control Audit Review File [*Data processing*]
SCARP ...... Society for Comic Art Research and Preservation
S Car R ..... South Carolina Law Reports   (DLA)
SCARS ...... SACEUR [*Supreme Allied Commander, Europe*] Command Alerting Reporting System [*Army*]
SCARS ...... Serialized Control and Reporting System   (MCD)
SCARS ...... Software Configuration Accounting and Reporting System
SCARS ...... Status Control Alert Reporting System   (NATG)
SCART ...... Sperry Continuity and Resistance Tester
SCARWAF ... Special Category Army with Air Force
SCAS .... Signal Corps Aviation School [*Obsolete*] [*Army*]
SCAS .... Southwest Center for Advanced Studies [*Later, University of Texas at Dallas*]
SCAS .... Stability Control Augmentation System   (NVT)
SCAS .... State Cost Accounting System   (OICC)
SCAS .... Subsystem Computer Application Software   (MCD)
SCASG ...... SONAR Calibration and Alignment Steering Group
SCASS ...... Signal Corps Aircraft Signal Service [*Obsolete*] [*Army*]
Sc As Trinidad Pr ... Scientific Association of Trinidad. Proceedings [*A publication*]
SCAT .... Scatterometer
SCAT .... Scatula [*Package*] [*Pharmacy*]
SCAT .... School and College Ability Test [*of ETS*]
SCAT .... Schottky Cell Array Technology
SCAT .... Scout-Attack [*Helicopter*]   (MCD)
SCAT .... Security Control of Air Traffic [*FAA*]
SCAT .... Selected Calibration and Alignment Test   (MCD)
SCAT .... Self-Contained Automatic Transmitter   (MCD)
SCAT .... Sequential Component Automatic Testing   (MSA)
SCAT .... Service Code Automatic Tester [*Automotive engineering*]
SCAT .... Service Command Air Transportation
SCAT .... Share Compiler-Assembler, Translator
SCAT .... Sheep Cell Agglutination Test
SCAT .... Small Car Automatic Transit [*System*]
SCAT .... Solid Catalysts   (KSC)
SCAT .... Solution to Customer Aircraft Troubles   (MCD)
SCAT .... South Pacific Combat Air Transport [*World War II*]
SCAT .... Space Communications and Tracking
SCAT .... Special Advisory Committee on Telecommunications
SCAT .... Speed Command Attitude/Target [*FAA*]
SCAT .... Speed Control Approach/Takeoff
SCAT .... Sperry Canada Automatic Tester
SCAT .... State Change Algorithm Translator
SCAT .... Storage, Checkout, and Transportation [*Rack*] [*Aerospace*]
SCAT .... Submarine Classification and Tracking
SCAT .... Supersonic Commercial Air Transport [*NASA*]
SCAT .... Surface-Controlled Avalanche Transistor
SCAT .... Systems Consolidation of Accessions and Trainees   (AABC)
SCATA ...... Survival Sited Casualty Treatment Assemblage   (AFM)
SCATANA ... Security Control of Air Traffic and Air Navigation Aids [*FAA*]
SCATE ...... Self-Checking Automatic Testing Equipment
SCATE ...... Space Chamber Analyzer - Thermal Environment [*NASA*]
SCATE ...... Stromberg-Carlson Automatic Test Equipment
SCATER ..... Security Control of Air Traffic and Electromagnetic Radiations [*During an air defense emergency*] [*FAA*]
Scates' Comp St ... Treat, Scates, and Blackwell's Compiled Illinois Statutes   (DLA)
SCATHA .... Spacecraft Charging at High Altitudes [*Satellite*]
SCathol ..... Studia Catholica [*A publication*]
SCAT ORIG ... Scatula Originalis [*Original Package*] [*Pharmacy*]
SCATS ...... Scheduling and Tracking System   (MCD)
SCATS ...... Self-Contained Automatic Test System
SCATS ...... Sequentially Controlled Automatic Transmitter Start
SCATS ...... Simulation, Checkout, and Training System
SCATT ...... Scientific Communication and Technology Transfer [*System*] [*University of Pennsylvania*]
SCATT ...... Shared Catalog Accessed Through Terminals [*Data processing system*]
SCAUA ...... Scientific Australian [*A publication*]
SCauc .... Studia Caucasica [*A publication*]
SCAUL ...... Standing Conference of African University Libraries
SCAULWA ... Standing Conference of African University Libraries [*Lagos, Nigeria*]   (EA-IO)
SCA(UN) .... Department of Security Council Affairs of the United Nations
Scaur .... Pro Scauro [*of Cicero*] [*Classical studies*]   (OCD)
SCAV .... Scavenge   (AAG)
SCAW .... Scientists' Center for Animal Welfare [*Bethesda, MD*]   (EA)

SCAW .... Supreme Camp of the American Woodmen   (EA)
SCAWNA ... Self-Contained Adverse-Weather Night Attack   (MCD)
SCAWU ..... Singapore Clerical and Administrative Workers' Union
Sc Azione ... Scuola in Azione [*A publication*]
Sc B .... Bachelor of Science
ScB .... Beaufort County Library, Beaufort, SC [*Library symbol*] [*Library of Congress*]   (LCLS)
SCB .... Sample Collection Bag [*NASA*]
SCB .... Scarborough [*Ontario*] [*Seismograph station code, US Geological Survey*] [*Closed*]   (SEIS)
SCB .... Schedule Change Board [*NASA*]   (NASA)
SCB .... Scholarly Book Center [*ACCORD*] [*UTLAS symbol*]
Sc B .... Scientiae Baccalaureus [*Bachelor of Science*] [*Latin*]
SCB .... Scribner, NE [*Location identifier*] [*FAA*]   (FAAL)
SCB .... Secondary Carpet Backing
SCB .... Segment Control BIT [*Binary Digit*]
SCB .... Selection Control Board [*NASA*]   (NASA)
SCB .... Selector Control Box   (MCD)
SCB .... Session Control Block [*Data processing*]   (BUR)
SCB .... Ship Characteristics Board
SCB .... Shipowners Claims Bureau [*New York, NY*]   (EA)
SCB .... Ships Characteristics Board
SCB .... Ship's Cook, Butcher [*Navy*]
SCB .... Silicon Cell Bridge
SCB .... Silver Cadmium Battery
SCB .... Software Control Board [*Apollo*] [*NASA*]
SCB .... South Central Bulletin [*A publication*]
SCB .... Specification Control Board [*NASA*]   (NASA)
SCB .... Stack Control Block
SCB .... Station Control Block [*Data processing*]   (IBMDP)
SCB .... Statistiska Centralbyran [*Statistics Sweden*] [*Stockholm*] [*Information service*]   (EISS)
SCB .... Strictly Confined to Bed [*Medicine*]
SCB .... Studi si Cercetari de Bibliologie [*A publication*]
ScBa .... Lexington County Circulating Library, Batesburg, SC [*Library symbol*] [*Library of Congress*]   (LCLS)
SCBA .... Self-Contained Breathing Apparatus
SCBA .... Supreme Circle Brotherhood of America   (EA)
Sc BAM ..... Bachelor of Science in Applied Mathematics
SC in Banco ... Supreme Court in Banco [*Canada*]   (DLA)
S & C Bank ... Standard and Chartered Review [*Formerly, Standard Bank Review*] [*Later, Standard Chartered Review*] [*A publication*]
Sc BC .... Bachelor of Science in Chemistry
SCBCA ...... Small Claims Board of Contract Appeals
SCBD .... Scan Conversion and Bright Display
Sc BE .... Bachelor of Science in Engineering
SCBF .... Sacred Cat of Burma Fanciers   (EA)
SCBF .... Spinal Cord Blood Flow
SCBL .... Scotts Bluff and Agate Fossil Beds National Monuments
SCBNP ...... Society for the Collection of Brand-Name Pencils [*Inactive*]   (EA)
SCBOA ...... Studii si Cercetari de Biologie. Seria Botanica [*A publication*]
Sc BP .... Bachelor of Science in Physics
SCBR .... Seller's Approved Configuration Baseline Document [*NASA*]   (NASA)
SCBR .... Serum Cholesterol-Binding Reserve [*Medicine*]
SCBR .... Steam-Cooled Breeder Reactor
SCBS .... Saint Charles Borromeo Seminary [*Pennsylvania*]
SCBS .... Society for the Conservation of Bighorn Sheep   (EA)
SC/BSE ..... Scientific Co-Operation Bureau for the European and North American Region   (EA)
SCBU .... Special Care Baby Unit [*Medicine*]
SCBW .... Society of Children's Book Writers
SCBZA ...... Studii si Cercetari de Biologie. Seria Zoologie [*A publication*]
SCC .... Cameron's Supreme Court Cases [*Canada*]   (DLA)
ScC .... Charleston Library Society, Charleston, SC [*Library symbol*] [*Library of Congress*]   (LCLS)
SCC .... Deadhorse [*Alaska*] [*Airport symbol*]   (OAG)
SCC .... Deadhorse, AK [*Location identifier*] [*FAA*]   (FAAL)
SCC .... Sacra Congregatio Concilii [*Sacred Congregation of the Council*] [*Latin*]
SCC .... SAGE [*Semiautomatic Ground Environment*] Control Center
SCC .... Salivary Caffeine Clearance [*Physiology*]
SCC .... Santa Cruz [*California*] [*Seismograph station code, US Geological Survey*] [*Closed*]   (SEIS)
SCC .... Satellite Communication Concentrator
SCC .... Satellite Communications Controller
SCC .... Satellite Control Center
SCC .... Satellite-Controlled Clock
SCC .... Scandinavian Collectors Club
SCC .... Scarborough Campus, University of Toronto [*UTLAS symbol*]
SCC .... Science Council of Canada
SCC .... Science Fiction Chronicle [*A publication*]
SCC .... Sea Cadet Corps [*Navy*] [*British*]
SCC .... Sears Canada, Inc. [*Toronto Stock Exchange symbol*]
SCC .... Secondary Containment Cooling   (IEEE)
SCC .... Security Capital Corporation [*American Stock Exchange symbol*]
SCC .... Security Commodity Code   (AAG)
SCC .... Security Control Center [*NASA*]   (KSC)

SCC............ Security Coordination Committee (NATG)
SCC............ Select Cases in Chancery [Legal] [British]
SCC............ Select Cases in Chancery Tempore King, Edited by Macnaghten [England] (DLA)
SCC............ Self-Contained Canister (MCD)
SCC............ Senate Children's Caucus [Washington, DC] (EA)
SCC............ Senate Copper Caucus (EA)
SCC............ Sequence Control Chart
SCC............ Sequential Control Counter [Data processing] (BUR)
scc .... Serbo-Croatian (Cyrillic) [MARC language code] [Library of Congress] (LCCP)
SCC............ Serial Communications Controller
SCC............ Service Change Committee [Military]
SCC............ Services for Crippled Children
SCC............ Servo Control Cabinet [Military] (CAAL)
SCC............ Set Conditionally [Data processing]
SCC............ Ship Control Center
SCC............ Short-Circuit Current
SCC............ Short-Course Chemotherapy [Medicine]
SCC............ Signaling Conversion Circuit [Telecommunications] (TEL)
SCC............ Simplified Computer Code
SCC............ Simulation Control Center [NASA] (KSC)
SCC............ Single Conductor Cable (MSA)
SCC............ Single Copy Complexity [Genetics]
SCC............ Single Cotton-Covered [Wire insulation]
SCC............ Sisters of Christian Charity [Roman Catholic religious order]
SCC............ Slidell Computer Complex [NASA]
SCC............ Small Cause Court [India] (DLA)
SCC............ Small Cell Cancer [Oncology]
SCC............ Small Center Contact
SCC............ Small Compressor Colorimeter (MCD)
SCC............ Societe Chimique des Charbonnages [France]
SCC............ Society for Children With Craniosynostosis [Arvada, CO] (EA)
SCC............ Society for the Christian Commonwealth
SCC............ Society of Cosmetic Chemists
SCC............ Source Classification Code [Environmental Protection Agency]
SCC............ Southern Connecticut State College, Division of Library Science, New Haven, CT [OCLC symbol] (OCLC)
SCC............ Spacecraft Control Center [NASA] (KSC)
SCC............ Special Coordinating Committee [National Security Council]
SCC............ Specialized Common Carrier [Telecommunications] (NRCH)
SCC............ Specific Clauses and Conditions (NATG)
SCC............ Squadron Control Center (AAG)
SCC............ Squamous Cell Carcinoma [Also, SC] [Medicine]
SCC............ Standard Commodity Classification
SCC............ Standard Commodity Codes (MCD)
SCC............ Standard Consultative Commission [for resolving compliance disputes arising from SALT 1 accord]
SCC............ Standard Cubic Centimeter (KSC)
SCC............ Standardized Cost Categories
SCC............ Standards Council of Canada [See also CCNO]
SCC............ Standing Consultative Commission [SALT agreements] [US/USSR]
SCC............ Standing Interdepartmental Committee on Censorship [War Cabinet] [British]
SCC............ Starcraft Campers Club (EA)
SCC............ State Coordination Committee [Responsible for administering the Work Incentive Program at the state level]
SCC............ State Corporation Commission
SCC............ Steel Carriers Conference [An association] (EA)
SCC............ Stock Control Center [Army]
SCC............ Storage Connecting Circuit [Teletype]
SCC............ Strategic Communications Command [Army] (MCD)
SCC............ Stress Corrosion Cracking [Metals]
SCC............ Student of Codrington College [Barbados]
SCC............ Studio Collector's Club (EA)
SC(C)......... Submarine Chaser (Control) [110 foot] [Obsolete]
SCC............ Submission Control Code (MCD)
SCC............ Sunbeam Car Club (EA)
SCC............ Supervisor Control Console
SCC............ Supervisory Control Conference (KSC)
SCC............ Supply Control Center
SCC............ Supreme Court of Canada
SCC............ Supreme Court Cases [India] (DLA)
SCC............ Surveillance Coordination Center (NATG)
SCC............ Switching Control Center [Bell System]
SCC............ Synchronous Communications Controller
SCC............ System Command Center (FAAC)
SCC............ System Communication Controller
SCC............ System Coordinate Center [Military] (CAAL)
SCC............ Systems Control Center
SCCA......... Single Cell Cytotoxicity Assay [Clinical chemistry]
SCCA......... Southeastern Cottonseed Crushers Association (EA)
SCCA......... Specification Compliance Concept Agreements (MCD)
SCCA......... Sports Car Club of America (EA)
SCCA......... Subcontract Change Authorization (AAG)
SCCAC...... Society for Conceptual and Content Analysis by Computer [Bowling Green University] [Bowling Green, OH] [Association for Computers and the Humanities special interest group] (EA)

SCC-ACO ... Strategic Communications Command Advanced Concepts Office [Army]
SC Cas....... Supreme Court Cases (DLA)
ScCatt........ Scuola Cattolica [A publication]
ScCB......... Baptist College at Charleston, Charleston, SC [Library symbol] [Library of Congress] (LCLS)
SCCB .... Safety Change Control Board (MCD)
SCCB .... Software Configuration Control Board (KSC)
SCCBS....... Science Council of Canada. Background Study [A publication]
ScCC......... College of Charleston, Charleston, SC [Library symbol] [Library of Congress] (LCLS)
SCCC......... Satellite Communications Control Centre [British]
SCCC......... System Casualty Control Console [Military] (CAAL)
SCCCE...... Society of Certified Consumer Credit Executives (EA)
ScCCit .... Citadel, Charleston, SC [Library symbol] [Library of Congress] (LCLS)
ScCDHHi.... Dalcho Historical Society of the Episcopal Diocese of South Carolina, Charleston, SC [Library symbol] [Library of Congress] (LCLS)
SCCE .... Satellite Configuration Control Element (MCD)
SCCE .... School and College Conference on English
SCCE .... Society of Certified Credit Executives [St. Louis, MO] (EA)
SCCEA...... Strategic Communications Command Equipment Applications Directorate [Army]
ScCF .... Charleston County Library, Charleston, SC [Library symbol] [Library of Congress] (LCLS)
SCCF .... Satellite Communication Control Facility
SCCF .... Security Clearance Case Files (AABC)
SCCF .... Service Center Control File [IRS]
SCCG .... Station Communications Control Group [Ground Communications Facility, NASA]
SCCH .... Society of Cinema Collectors and Historians (EA)
SCCH .... Standard Cubic Centimeters per Hour (MCD)
ScChwC..... Chesterfield-Marlboro Technical College, Cheraw, SC [Library symbol] [Library of Congress] (LCLS)
SCC(I)....... Special Coordination Committee (Intelligence) (MCD)
SCCL .... Small Cell (Anaplastic) Carcinoma of the Lung [Oncology]
ScCleU...... Clemson University, Clemson, SC [Library symbol] [Library of Congress] (LCLS)
ScCliJ .... Jacobs Library, Clinton, SC [Library symbol] [Library of Congress] [Obsolete] (LCLS)
ScClP .... Presbyterian College, Clinton, SC [Library symbol] [Library of Congress] (LCLS)
ScClTO ...... Thornwell Orphanage, Clinton, SC [Library symbol] [Library of Congress] (LCLS)
ScCM .... Medical University of South Carolina, Charleston, SC [Library symbol] [Library of Congress] (LCLS)
SCCM .... Sertoli Cell Culture Medium [Clinical chemistry]
SCCM .... Single Chamber Controllable Motor (MCD)
SCCM .... Society of Critical Care Medicine [Fullerton, CA] (EA)
SCCM .... Standard Cubic Centimeters per Minute (NASA)
SCCM .... Standing Commission on Church Music [General Convention of the Protestant Episcopal Church] (EA)
ScCMP....... Middleton Place, Charleston, SC [Library symbol] [Library of Congress] (LCLS)
ScCMu ...... Charleston Museum Library, Charleston, SC [Library symbol] [Library of Congress] (LCLS)
SCCN........ Subcontract [or Subcontractor] Change Notice (KSC)
SCCO........ Security Classification Control Officer
ScCoAH .... South Carolina Department of Archives and History, Columbia, SC [Library symbol] [Library of Congress] (LCLS)
ScCoB........ Benedict College, Columbia, SC [Library symbol] [Library of Congress] (LCLS)
ScCoB........ Columbia Bible College, Columbia, SC [Library symbol] [Library of Congress] (LCLS)
ScCoC .... Columbia College, Columbia, SC [Library symbol] [Library of Congress] (LCLS)
SC Code .... Code of Laws of South Carolina (DLA)
SC Code Ann ... Code of Laws of South Carolina, Annotated (DLA)
ScCoGS..... Church of Jesus Christ of Latter-Day Saints, Genealogical Society Library, Columbia Branch, Columbia, SC [Library symbol] [Library of Congress] (LCLS)
ScCon .... Horry County Memorial Library, Conway, SC [Library symbol] [Library of Congress] (LCLS)
Sc Conspectus ... Science Conspectus [A publication]
ScCoR........ Richland County Library, Columbia, SC [Library symbol] [Library of Congress] (LCLS)
Sc Costs .... Scott's ABC Guide to Costs [2nd ed.] [1910] (DLA)
ScCoT........ Lutheran Theological Southern Seminary, Columbia, SC [Library symbol] [Library of Congress] (LCLS)
ScCoV........ United States Veterans Administration Hospital, Columbia, SC [Library symbol] [Library of Congress] (LCLS)
SCCP .... Systems Change Control Procedure [Social Security Administration]
SCCPG....... Satellite Communications Contingency Planning Group (NATG)
SCCR .... Science Council of Canada. Report [A publication]
SCCR .... Society for Cross-Cultural Research (EA)
SCCR .... Subcontractor Change Request (MCD)

ScCRC .... Charleston Diocesan Archives, Roman Catholic Church, Charleston, SC [*Library symbol*] [*Library of Congress*] (LCLS)
SCCRI .... Swedish Cement and Concrete Research Institute (MCD)
SCCS .... Satellite Communications Control System (MCD)
SCCS .... Secondary Chemical Control System (NRCH)
SCCS .... Sodium Chemistry Control System [*Westinghouse Corp.*] (IEEE)
SCCS .... Source Code Control System [*Data processing*]
SCCS .... Souvenir Card Collectors Society (EA)
SCCS .... Special Consultative Committee on Security [*OAS*]
SCCS .... Standard Commodity Classification System (NG)
SCCS .... Standard Cubic Centimeters per Second (NASA)
SCCS .... Standby Core Cooling System [*Nuclear energy*] (NRCH)
SCCS .... STRICOM [*Strike Command*] Command and Control System [*Army*] (AABC)
SCCS .... Switching Control Center System [*Telecommunications*] (TEL)
SCCSA .... Sports Car Collectors Society of America (EA)
ScCSM .... Old Slave Mart Museum, Charleston, SC [*Library symbol*] [*Library of Congress*] (LCLS)
SCC Spec ... Soap/Cosmetics/Chemical Specialties [*A publication*]
SCCSS ...... Science Council of Canada. Special Study [*A publication*]
ScCT .... Trident Technical College, Palmer Campus, Charleston, SC [*Library symbol*] [*Library of Congress*] (LCLS)
SCC-TED ... Strategic Communications Command - Test and Evaluation Directorate [*Army*]
SCCTR ...... Standing Committee for Controlled Thermonuclear Research [*Terminated, 1973*] [*AEC*] (EGAO)
SCCTSD .... Society of Catholic College Teachers of Sacred Doctrine [*Later, CTS*] (EA)
SCCU .... Single Channel Control Unit
SCCU .... Spacecraft Command Control Unit (KSC)
SCCUS ...... Swedish Chamber of Commerce of the United States [*Later, Swedish-American Chamber of Commerce*]
ScCV .... United States Veterans Administration Hospital, Charleston, SC [*Library symbol*] [*Library of Congress*] (LCLS)
SCCW .... Scarritt College for Christian Workers [*Tennessee*]
SCCWRP TR ... SCCWRP (Southern California Coastal Water Research Project). TR [*A publication*]
SCD............ Darlington County Library, Darlington, SC [*OCLC symbol*] (OCLC)
SCD............ Doctor of Commercial Science
Sc D .... Doctor of Science
SCD............ S-Band Cassegrain Diplexer
SCD............ Satellite Control Department
SCD............ Schedule (AABC)
SCD............ Schneider Corp. [*Toronto Stock Exchange symbol*]
SCD............ Science Communication Division [*George Washington University Medical Center*] [*Information service*] (EISS)
Sc D .... Scientiae Doctor [*Doctor of Science*] [*Latin*]
SCD............ Scientific Computer Division [*Army Tank-Automotive Command*]
ScD .... Scintillation Detector (IEEE)
SCD........... Screen Door
SCD........... Screwed (MDG)
SCD........... Secondary Current Distribution [*Electroplating*]
SCD........... Security Coding Device (NATG)
SCD........... Senior Citizen Discount
SCD........... Service Computation Date [*Military*] (AFM)
SCD........... Service Control Drawing
SCD........... Servo Chart Drive
SCD........... Ship's Center Display [*Navy*] (NVT)
SCD........... Sickle Cell Disease [*Medicine*]
SCD........... Signal Canceling Device
SCD........... Significant Construction Deficiency [*Nuclear energy*] (NRCH)
SCD........... Society of Craft Designers [*Columbus, GA*] (EA)
SCD........... Software Conceptual Design [*Data processing*]
SCD........... Soil Conservation District [*Agriculture*]
SCD........... Source Control Drawing
SCD........... Space Control Document [*NASA*] (KSC)
SCD........... Specification Control Document [*NASA*] (NASA)
SCD........... Specification Control Drawing
SCD........... Spreading Cortical Depression
SCD........... State Civil Defense
SCD........... Sterile Connection Device [*Medicine*]
SC & D .... Stock Control and Distribution (AFM)
SCD........... Streaming Current Detector
SCD........... Subacute Combined Degeneration [*of spinal cord*] [*Medicine*]
SCD........... Subcarrier Discriminator
SCD........... Subcontract Deviation
SCD........... Subject Captain's Discretion [*Aviation*] (FAAC)
SCD........... Sudden Cardiac Death [*Medicine*]
SCD........... Supply, Commissary, and Disbursing [*Navy*]
SCD........... Surrey Commercial Dock [*British*]
SCD........... Surveillance Criticality Designator [*DoD*]
SCD........... Sylacauga, AL [*Location identifier*] [*FAA*] (FAAL)
SCD........... System Coordination Document
ScDa .... Darlington County Library, Darlington, SC [*Library symbol*] [*Library of Congress*] (LCLS)
Sc DA .... Right Scapuloanterior Position [*of the fetus*] [*Obstetrics*]

SCDA .... Safing, Cool Down, and Decontamination Area [*NASA*] (NASA)
SCDA .... SEATO [*Southeast Asia Treaty Organization*] Central Distribution Agency (NATG)
SCDAP....... Severe Core Damage Analysis Package [*Nuclear energy*] (NRCH)
SCDC .... Service Coding and Data Collection (AAG)
SCDC .... Societe des Comptables de Direction au Canada [*Society of Management Accountants of Canada - SMAC*]
SCDC .... Source Coding and Data Collection
SCDC......... Supreme Court Reports, District of Columbia (DLA)
SCDCNS .... Supreme Court Reports, District of Columbia, New Series (DLA)
SC/DDS ..... Sensor Control/Data Display Set (MCD)
Sc D in Ed ... Doctor of Science in Education
SC Dent J.... South Carolina Dental Journal [*A publication*]
ScDeV .... Voorhees College, Denmark, SC [*Library symbol*] [*Library of Congress*] (LCLS)
SCDFGNY ... Sickle Cell Disease Foundation of Greater New York [*Superseded by Foundation for Research and Education in Sickle Cell Disease*] [*New York, NY*] (EA)
Sc D Govt... Doctor of Science in Government
Sc D in Hyg ... Doctor of Science in Hygiene
SCDI........... Science Dimension [*A publication*]
SC Dig........ Cassel's Supreme Court Digest [*Canada*] (DLA)
Sc & Div ..... Law Reports, Scotch and Divorce Appeals (DLA)
Sc & Div App ... Scotch and Divorce Appeals [*English Law Reports*] (DLA)
SC Div Bad ... Second Class Diver Badge [*Army*]
SC Div Geol Geol Notes ... South Carolina. Division of Geology. Geologic Notes [*A publication*]
SC Div Geol Miner Resour Ser ... South Carolina. Division of Geology. Mineral Resources Series [*A publication*]
SC Div Geol Misc Rep ... South Carolina. Division of Geology. Miscellaneous Report [*A publication*]
SC Div Geology Mineral Industries Lab Monthly Bull ... South Carolina. Division of Geology. Mineral Industries Laboratory. Monthly Bulletin [*A publication*]
SCDL......... Saturated Current Demand Logic
SCDL......... Ship Configuration Detail List [*Navy*]
SCDL......... Stabilized Carbon Dioxide LASER
Sc D (Med) ... Doctor of Medical Science
SCDMR ...... Steam-Cooled D$_2$O Moderated Reactor
SCD OCSA ... Staff Communications Division, Office, Chief of Staff [*Army*] (AABC)
SCD OC of SA ... Staff Communications Division, Office, Chief of Staff [*Army*] (AABC)
Sc DP .... Right Scapuloposterior Position [*of the fetus*] [*Obstetrics*]
SCDP .... Sedimentary Chlorophyll Degradation Product [*Paleontology*]
SCDP .... Simulation Control Data Package [*NASA*] (NASA)
SCDP .... Society of Certified Data Processors [*Superseded by AICCP*] (EA)
SCDP .... Southern Cooperative Development Program [*Sponsored by Southern Consumers Education Foundation*]
SCDP .... Steel Cadmium Plated
SCDR .... Screwdriver (MSA)
SCDR .... Seller Critical Design Review [*NASA*] (NASA)
SCDR .... Shuttle Critical Design Review [*NASA*] (NASA)
SCDR .... Software Critical Design Review [*NASA*] (NASA)
SCDR .... Subcontractor Critical Design Review
SCDR .... Subsystem Controller Definition Record [*Data processing*] (IBMDP)
SCDS .... Scan Converter Display System (MCD)
SCDS .... Sensor Communication and Display System (MCD)
SCDS .... Shipboard Chaff Decoy System [*Navy*]
SCDS .... Signal Circuits Design Section
SCDS .... Staff of Chief of Defence Staff [*British*]
SCDSB........ Suppressed-Carrier Double Sideband
SCDSD...... Scientific Clearinghouse and Documentation Services Division [*National Science and Technology Authority*] [*Manila, Philippines*] [*Information service*] (EISS)
SCD (St V) ... Supreme Court Decisions [*St. Vincent*] [*1928-36*] (DLA)
SCDU .... Signal Conditioning and Display Unit [*NASA*] (NASA)
S & CDU ..... Switch and Cable Distribution Unit (AAG)
ScDwE ...... Erskine College, Due West, SC [*Library symbol*] [*Library of Congress*] (LCLS)
ScDwE-T.... Erskine College, Erskine Theological Seminary, Due West, SC [*Library symbol*] [*Library of Congress*] (LCLS)
ScE........... Edgefield County Library, Edgefield, SC [*Library symbol*] [*Library of Congress*] (LCLS)
SCE........... Saturated Calomel Electrode [*Electrochemistry*]
SCE........... Scan Conversion Equipment [*Television*]
SCE........... Schedule Compliance-Evaluation [*Polaris*]
SCE........... Schlegeis [*Austria*] [*Seismograph station code, US Geological Survey*] (SEIS)
ScE........... Sciences Ecclesiastiques [*Montreal-Brussels*] [*A publication*]
SCE........... Scottish Certificate of Education
SCE........... Scribe Ezra [*Freemasonry*]
SCE........... Secretory Carcinoma of Endometrium
SCE........... Select Cases Relating to Evidence Strange (DLA)
SCE........... Selection Control Element
SCE........... Separated Career Employee

SCE .... Signal Conditioning Equipment
SCE .... Signal Conversion Electronics [*Telecommunications*] (TEL)
SCE .... Single Cotton-Covered Enameled [*Wire insulation*] (DEN)
SCE .... Single Cycle Execute
SCE .... Sister Chromatid Exchange [*Cytology*]
SCE .... Situationally Caused Error
SCE .... Small Current Element
SCE .... Societe Canadienne d'Esthetique [*Canadian Society for Aesthetics - CSAC*]
SCE .... Society of Carbide Engineers [*Later, Society of Carbide and Tool Engineers*] (EA)
SCE .... Society of Christian Engineers (EA)
SCE .... Society of Christian Ethics (EA)
SCE .... Society for Clinical Ecology [*Later, AAEM*] (EA)
SCE .... Society for Creative Ethics [*Later, SPC*] (EA)
SCE .... Solar Corona Explorer [*Project*] [*NASA*]
SCE .... Solder Circuit Etch
SCE .... Source (MSA)
SCE .... Southern California Edison Co. [*NYSE symbol*]
SCE .... Space Cabin Environment [*Skylab*] [*NASA*]
SCE .... Spacecraft Command Encoder (MCD)
SCE .... Special Conditioning Equipment
SCE .... Stabilization Control Electronics
SCE .... Standard Calomel Electrode
SCE .... State College [*Pennsylvania*] [*Airport symbol*] (OAG)
SCE .... State College, PA [*Location identifier*] [*FAA*] (FAAL)
SCE .... Stored Controlled Energy
SCE .... Stratified-Charge Engine [*Auto engine*]
SCE .... Superintending Civil Engineer [*British*]
SCE .... United States Air Force, Armament Laboratory, Technical Library, Eglin AFB, FL [*OCLC symbol*] (OCLC)
ScEA .... John R. Abney Collection, Edgefield County Library, Edgefield, SC [*Library symbol*] [*Library of Congress*] (LCLS)
ScEa .... Pickens County Library, Easley, SC [*Library symbol*] [*Library of Congress*] (LCLS)
SCEA .... Service Children's Education Authority [*Ministry of Defence*] [*British*]
SCEA .... Signal Conditioning Electronics Assembly
SCEA .... Society of Communications Engineers and Analysts
SCEAR ...... Scientific Committee on the Effects of Atomic Radiation
SCEB .... SHAPE [*Supreme Headquarters Allied Powers Europe*] Communications Electronics Board [*NATO*] (NATG)
SCEB .... Societe Canadienne des Etudes Bibliques [*Canadian Society of Biblical Studies - CSBS*]
SCEB .... Syndicat Canadien des Employes de Bureau [*Canadian Office Employees Union - COEU*]
SCEC .... Societe Canadienne des Etudes Classiques [*Classical Association of Canada - CAC*]
SCEC .... Spaceborne Computer Engineering Conference (MCD)
SCECC ...... Societe Canadienne pour l'Etude Comparee des Civilisations [*Canadian Society for the Comparative Study of Civilizations - CSCSC*]
ScEccl ...... Sciences Ecclesiastique [*A publication*]
Sc Ed D ..... Doctor of Science in Education
SCEE .... Societe Canadienne pour l'Etude de l'Education [*Canadian Society for the Study of Education - CSSE*]
SCEE .... Student Committee for Economic Education (EA)
SCEEB ...... Scottish Certificate of Education Examination Board [*British*]
SCEEE ...... Southeastern Center for Electrical Engineering Education [*Air Force*]
SCEERR .... Sacra Congregatio Episcoporum et Regularium [*Sacred Congregation of Bishops and Regulars*] [*Latin*]
SCEES ...... Service Central des Enquetes et Etudes Statistiques [*Central Service for Statistical Inquiries and Studies*] [*Ministry of Agriculture*] [*Paris, France*]
SCEES ...... Societe Canadienne pour l'Etude de l'Enseignement Superieur [*Canadian Society for the Study of Higher Education - CSSHE*]
SCEET ...... Support Concept Economic Evaluation Technique (MCD)
SCEF .... Southern Conference Educational Fund (EA)
SCEH .... Society for Clinical and Experimental Hypnosis [*Liverpool, NY*] (EA)
SCEI .... Safe Car Educational Institute
SCEI .... Societe Canadienne pour les Etudes Italiennes [*Canadian Society for Italian Studies - CSIS*]
SCEI .... Special Committee on Environmental Information [*Special Libraries Association*]
SCEIL .... Service Ceiling
SCEKS ...... Spectrum Clear Except Known Signals (MUGU)
SCEL .... Signal Corps Engineering Laboratories [*Obsolete*] [*Army*]
SCEL .... Small Components Evaluation Loop (NRCH)
SCEL .... Standing Committee on Education in Librarianship
SCELBAL... Scientific Elementary Basic Language [*1963*] [*Data processing*] (CSR)
Scen .... Scenario [*A publication*]
SCEN .... Societe Canadienne pour l'Etude des Noms [*Canadian Society for the Study of Names - CSSN*]
SCEN .... South Central
SCENE ...... Studies of Coastal and Estuarine Environments [*Marine science*] (MSC)
SCENIC ..... Scientific Engineering Information Center (KSC)

Scenic Trips Geol Past ... Scenic Trips to the Geologic Past [*A publication*]
SCEO .... Senior Chief Executive Officer [*Civil Service*] [*British*]
SCEO .... Station Construction Engineering Officer
SCEP .... Secure Communications Equipment Program [*Air Force*] (CET)
SCEP .... Significant Criminal Enforcement Project [*Bureau of Alcohol, Tobacco, and Firearms*]
SCEP .... Study of Critical Environmental Problems [*MIT*]
SCEPC ...... Senior Civil Emergency Planning Committee [*NATO*] (NATG)
SCEPS ...... Solar Cell Electric Power System (RDA)
SCEPS ...... Stored Chemical Energy Propulsion System
SCEPTR... Suitcase Emergency Procedures Trainer (MCD)
SCEPTRE... System for Circuit Evaluation and Prediction of Transient Radiation Effect (MCD)
SCEPTRE... System Computerized for Economical Performance, Tracking, Recording and Evaluation [*North Central Airlines*]
SCEPTRE... System for Constant Elevation Precipitation Transmission and Recording
SCEPTRON ... Spectral Comparative Pattern Recognizer
SC Eq........ South Carolina Equity Reports (DLA)
SCER .... Societe Canadienne pour l'Etude de la Religion [*Canadian Society for the Study of Religion - CSSR*]
SCER .... Societe Canadienne d'Etudes de la Renaissance [*Canadian Society for Renaissance Studies - CSRS*]
SCER .... Standing Commission on Ecumenical Relations of the Episcopal Church [*New York, NY*] (EA)
SCERT ...... Systems and Computers Evaluation and Review Technique [*Data processing*]
ScEs.......... Science et Esprit [*A publication*]
SCES .... State Cooperative Extension Service
SCESWUN ... Standing Committee on the Economic and Social Work of the United Nations
SCET .... Spacecraft Event Time
SCETA ...... Societe de Controle et d'Exploitation de Transports Auxiliaires [*France*]
SCETV ...... South Carolina Educational Television [*Columbia*] [*Telecommunications*] (TSSD)
SCEU .... Selector Channel Emulation Unit
SCEWA ..... Society for Citizen Education in World Affairs [*Later, CEA*]
SCF .... Florence County Library, Florence, SC [*OCLC symbol*] (OCLC)
SCF .... Phoenix [*Arizona*] Scottsdale [*Airport symbol*] (OAG)
SCF .... S-Band Composite Feed
SCF .... Sampled Channel Filter
SCF .... Satellite Control Facility [*Sunnyvale, CA*] [*NASA*]
SCF .... Save the Children Federation [*Westport, CT*] (EA)
SCF .... Scandinavia Fund, Inc. [*American Stock Exchange symbol*]
SCF .... Schematic Concept Formation
SCF .... Science Fantasy [*A publication*]
SCF .... Scientific Computing Facility
SCF .... Secondary Checkpoint File
SCF .... Sectional Center Facility [*Air Force*] (AFM)
SCF .... Sectional Center Facility [*First three digits of the ZIP code*] [*US Postal Service*]
SCF .... Self-Consistent Field [*Quantum mechanics*]
SCF .... Senior Chaplain to the Forces [*British*]
SCF .... Sequential Compatibility Firing
SCF .... Single Catastrophic Failure (AAG)
SCF .... Single Cost Factor
SCF .... Single Crystal Filament
SCF .... Skin Cancer Foundation [*Formerly, NSCF*] [*New York, NY*] (EA)
SCF .... Slovak Catholic Federation [*Formerly, SCFA*] (EA)
SCF .... SNAP [*Systems for Nuclear Auxiliary Power*] Critical Facility (NRCH)
SCF .... Sociedad Centroamericana de Farmacologia [*Central American Society of Pharmacology - CASP*] [*San Jose, Costa Rica*] (EA-IO)
SCF .... Society of the Compassionate Friends [*Later, TCF*] (EA)
SCF .... Sodium Cleaning Facility (NRCH)
SCF .... Spacecraft Checkout Facility
SCF .... Spacecraft Control Facility (MCD)
SCF .... Spherical Cavity Flow
SCF .... Spinning Continuous Filament
SCF .... Spinning Crucible Furnace
SCF .... Standard Cubic Foot
SCF .... Station Code File
SCF .... Steinbeck Center Foundation (EA)
SCF .... Stress Concentration Factor (MCD)
SCF .... Subchorionic Fibrin [*Obstetrics*]
SCF .... Supercritical Fluid
SCF .... Support Carrier Force
SCFA .... Segmented Continuous Flow Analysis [*Analytical chemistry*]
SCFA .... Short-Chain Fatty Acids [*Biochemistry*]
SCFA .... Slovak Catholic Federation of America [*Later, Slovak Catholic Federation*] (EA)
SCFBR ...... Steam-Cooled Fast Breeder Reactor
SCFC .... Southern California Film Circuit [*Library network*]
SCFD .... Standard Cubic Feet per Day
SC & FE..... Sierra Club and Friends of the Earth [*Marine science*] (MSC)
SCFEL .... Standard COMSEC [*Communications Security*] Facility Equipment List

SCFF......... Scotopic Critical Flicker Frequency [*Magnetic environment*]
SCFGVPT ... Southern California Figure-Ground Visual Perception Test
SCFH......... Standard Cubic Feet per Hour   (AAG)
SCFI.......... Streptococcal Chemotactic Factor Inhibitor
                  [*Immunochemistry*]
ScFI........... Florence County Library, Florence, SC [*Library symbol*]
                  [*Library of Congress*]   (LCLS)
ScFlM........ Francis Marion College, Florence, SC [*Library symbol*] [*Library
                  of Congress*]   (LCLS)
ScFIT........ Florence-Darlington Technical College Library, Florence, SC
                  [*Library symbol*] [*Library of Congress*]   (LCLS)
SCFM........ Scanforms, Inc. [*NASDAQ symbol*]   (NQ)
SCFM........ Standard Cubic Feet per Minute
SCFM........ Subcarrier Frequency Modulation
                  [*Telecommunications*]   (TEL)
SCFMA ...... Summer and Casual Furniture Manufacturers Association
                  [*High Point, NC*]   (EA)
SCFO .... Science Forum [*A publication*]
SCFP.......... Science Career Facilitation Project [*National Science
                  Foundation*]
SCFP.......... Syndicat Canadien de la Fonction Publique [*Canadian Union of
                  Public Employees - CUPE*]
SCFPA .... Structural Cement-Fiber Products Association [*Formerly,
                  SWFPA*] [*Washington, DC*]   (EA)
SCFS......... S-Band Composite Feed System
SCFS......... Slip-Cast-Fused Silica   (RDA)
SCFS......... Standard Cubic Feet per Second   (AAG)
SCFSEC..... Standing Committee of French-Speaking Ethnical
                  Communities   (EA)
SCG........... Air Force Geophysics Laboratory Research Library, Hanscom
                  AFB, MA [*OCLC symbol*]   (OCLC)
ScG .... Greenville County Library, Greenville, SC [*Library symbol*]
                  [*Library of Congress*]   (LCLS)
SCG........... St. Claude [*Guadeloupe*] [*Seismograph station code, US
                  Geological Survey*]   (SEIS)
SCG........... SCANA Corp. [*NYSE symbol*]
Sc G .... Science Gossip [*A publication*]
SCG........... Scientific Computing Group [*University of Toronto*] [*Research
                  center*]   (RCD)
SCG........... Scoring   (ADA)
SCG........... Screen Cartoonists Guild [*Defunct*]   (EA)
SCG........... Security Classification Guide   (AFM)
SCG........... Self Changing Gear
SCG........... SEMMS [*Solar Electric Multiple-Mission Spacecraft*]
                  Coordinating Group [*NASA*]
SCG........... Sequential Control Guidance   (KSC)
SCG........... Shipcraft Guild   (EA)
SCG........... Sliding-Coil Gauge   (RDA)
SCG........... Society of the Classic Guitar   (EA)
SCG........... Sodium Cromoglycate [*Pharmacology*]
SCG........... Solution Crystal Growth
SCG........... Space Charge Grid
SCG........... Space and Communications Group [*of General Motors Corp.*]
SCG........... Special Consultative Group [*NATO*]
SCG........... Steel Carriers Group [*Alexandria, VA*]   (EA)
SCG........... Stored Cold Gas
SCG........... Superior Cervical Ganglion [*Anatomy*]
ScGa .... Cherokee County Public Library, Gaffney, SC [*Library symbol*]
                  [*Library of Congress*]   (LCLS)
SCGA .... Sodium-Cooled Graphite Assembly [*Nuclear energy*]
SCGA .... Southern Cotton Ginners Association [*Memphis, TN*]   (EA)
SCGA .... Synergistic Communications [*NASDAQ symbol*]   (NQ)
ScGaL .... Limestone College, Gaffney, SC [*Library symbol*] [*Library of
                  Congress*]   (LCLS)
ScGBJ .... Bob Jones University, Greenville, SC [*Library symbol*] [*Library
                  of Congress*]   (LCLS)
SCGC .... Society of Carnival Glass Collectors
SCGD .... Specification Control Group Directive   (KSC)
SCGDL....... Signal Corps General Development Laboratory [*Obsolete*]
                  [*Army*]
SCGE .... Sioux City Grain Exchange   (EA)
ScGeo .... Georgetown County Memorial Library, Georgetown SC
                  [*Library symbol*] [*Library of Congress*]   (LCLS)
ScGF .... Furman University, Greenville, SC [*Library symbol*] [*Library of
                  Congress*]   (LCLS)
SCGGA ..... Sonoma County Grape Growers Association [*Santa Rosa,
                  CA*]   (EA)
SCGGA ...... Studii si Cercetari de Geologie, Geofizica, si Geografie. Seria
                  Geologie [*A publication*]
SCGP .... Scrabble Crossword Game Players   (EA)
SCGP .... Self-Contained Guidance Package   (AAG)
ScGrw .... Abbeville-Greenwood Regional Library, Greenwood, SC
                  [*Library symbol*] [*Library of Congress*]   (LCLS)
ScGrwL...... Lander College, Greenwood, SC [*Library symbol*] [*Library of
                  Congress*]   (LCLS)
ScGrwP...... Piedmont Technical College, Greenwood, SC [*Library symbol*]
                  [*Library of Congress*]   (LCLS)
SCGSS...... Signal Corps Ground Signal Service [*Obsolete*] [*Army*]
SCGSS...... Super-Critical Gas Storage System   (KSC)
SCGT .... Stanford's Compendium of Geography and Travel [*A
                  publication*]

SCH........... AFSC Technical Information Center, Washington, DC [*OCLC
                  symbol*]   (OCLC)
SCH........... Schedule   (AAG)
SCH........... Schefferville [*Quebec*] [*Seismograph station code, US
                  Geological Survey*]   (SEIS)
SCH........... Scheme   (ADA)
SCH........... Schenectady, NY [*Location identifier*] [*FAA*]   (FAAL)
SCH........... Schering [*Italy*] [*Research code symbol*]
SCH........... Schering-Plough Corp. [*Research code symbol*]
SCH........... Scherl and Roth Orchestra News [*A publication*]
SCH........... Schiller [*German poet, 1759-1805*]   (ROG)
SCH........... Schilling [*Monetary unit in Austria*]
Sch............. Schist [*Quality of the bottom*] [*Nautical charts*]
SCH........... Schoenaur Rifle
SCH........... Scholar
Sch............. Scholastik [*A publication*]
SCH........... Scholium [*Note*] [*Latin*]
Sch............. School [*Toronto*] [*A publication*]
SCH........... School   (AFM)
SCH........... Schooner
SCH........... Schreiber Resources Ltd. [*Vancouver Stock Exchange symbol*]
Sch............. Schultz Number
SCH........... Search   (MCD)
SCH........... Seizures per Circuit per Hour [*Telecommunications*]   (TEL)
SCH........... Sequencer Chassis
SCH........... Shelter Complex Headquarters [*Civil Defense*]
SCH........... Sisters of Charity of St. Vincent de Paul, Halifax [*Roman
                  Catholic religious order*]
SCH........... Societe Canadienne d'Hermeneutique [*Canadian Society for
                  Hermeneutics - CSH*]
SCH........... Society for Calligraphy and Handwriting   (EA)
SCh............ Society of Christ [*Roman Catholic men's religious order*]
SCH........... Society for Colonial History [*Defunct*]   (EA)
SCH........... Socket Head   (AAG)
Sch .... Sources Chretiennes [*A publication*]
SCH........... Square Cartridge Heater
SCH........... Student Credit Hours
SCH........... Studia ad Corpus Hellenisticum Novi Testamenti   (BJA)
SCh............ Succinylcholine [*Biochemistry*]
SCH........... Supporting Checkout
ScHaC....... Coker College, Hartsville, SC [*Library symbol*] [*Library of
                  Congress*]   (LCLS)
Sch Activities ... School Activities [*A publication*]
Schalk....... Schalk's Jamaica Reports   (DLA)
Sch Aq R.... Schultes' Aquatic Rights [*1811*]   (DLA)
Sch Arts..... School Arts Magazine [*A publication*]
Sch Arts M ... School Arts Magazine [*A publication*]
SCHASE .... Steeplechase
Schatzkammer ... Schatzkammer der Deutschen Sprachlehre. Dichtung und
                  Geschichte [*A publication*]
SCHAVMED ... School of Aviation Medicine [*Later, School of Aerospace
                  Medicine*]   (MCD)
SChB......... Small Chemical Businesses [*American Chemical Society*]
Sch Bailm ... Schouler on Bailments   (DLA)
Sch Bell ..... School Bell [*A publication*]
SCHC .... Society of the Companions of the Holy Cross [*Byfield,
                  MA*]   (EA)
Sch Coach ... Scholastic Coach [*A publication*]
Sch & Com ... School and Community [*A publication*]
Sch Community News ... School and Community News [*A publication*]
Sch Counsel ... School Counselor [*A publication*]
SCHD .... Scheduling
Sch Days.... School Days [*A publication*]
Sch Dom Rel ... Schouler on Domestic Relations   (DLA)
SCHE......... Scheme   (ROG)
SChE......... Serum Cholinesterase [*An enzyme*]
SCHE .... Societe Canadienne de l'Histoire de l'Eglise [*Canadian Society
                  of Church History - CSCH*]
SCHEC....... Societe Canadienne de l'Histoire de l'Eglise Catholique
                  [*Canadian Catholic History Association - CCHA*]
SCHED...... Schedule   (KSC)
Sch Ed ...... School and Home Education [*Illinois*] [*A publication*]
Sched Discounts Differentials Serv Charges Applying Wheat ... Schedule
                  of Discounts, Differentials, and Service Charges Applying
                  to Wheat [*A publication*]
SCHEDE..... Schedule   (ROG)
Sch (El Ed) ... School (Toronto) (Elementary Edition) [*A publication*]
SCHEM ...... Schematic
Sch Eng Bull NC State Univ ... School of Engineering. Bulletin. North
                  Carolina State University [*A publication*]
Scher .... Scherer's New York Miscellaneous Reports [*22-47*]   (DLA)
SCHERZ..... Scherzando [*Playful*] [*Music*]
Sch Exec .... School Executive [*A publication*]
Sch Executives M ... School Executives Magazine [*A publication*]
SchF.......... Schultexte aus Fara [*A publication*]
SCHG........ Supercharge
SCHGM...... South Carolina Historical and Genealogical Magazine [*A
                  publication*]
SChH......... Studies in Church History [*A publication*]
Sch Health Rev ... School Health Review [*A publication*]
Sch and Home ... School and Home [*A publication*]

Sch H & W ... Schouler on Husband and Wife (DLA)

ScHi .... South Carolina Historical Society, Charleston, SC [Library symbol] [Library of Congress] (LCLS)

Schiffstechnik ... Schiffstechnik. Forschungshefte fuer Schiffbau und Schiffsmaschinenbau [A publication]

Schild Steier ... Schild von Steier. Beitraege zur Steierischen Vor- und Fruehgeschichte und Muenzkunde [A publication]

SC His M .... South Carolina Historical and Genealogical Magazine [A publication]

SC Hist Assn Proc ... South Carolina Historical Association. Proceedings [A publication]

SC Hist Mag ... South Carolina Historical Magazine [A publication]

SCHIZ .... Schizophrenia [Medicine]

schizo .... Schizophrenia [Psychology]

Schizophr Bull ... Schizophrenia Bulletin [A publication]

Schizophr Syndr ... Schizophrenic Syndrome [A publication]

Schizophr Syndr Annu Rev ... Schizophrenic Syndrome: An Annual Review [A publication]

SCHJ .... Societe Canadienne de l'Histoire Juive [Canadian Jewish Historical Association - CJHS]

SCHL .... Court of Session Cases, House of Lords [Scotland] (DLA)

SCHL .... Scholastic, Inc. [NASDAQ symbol] (NQ)

SCHL .... Scholl, Inc. [NASDAQ symbol]

SC(HL) .... Sessions Cases (House of Lords) [Legal] [British]

SCHL .... Societe Canadienne d'Hypotheques et de Logement [Central Mortgage and Housing Corporation - CMHC]

SCHLA .... School for Latin America [Military] (AFM)

Schlachtofwes Lebensmittelueberwach ... Schlachtofwesen Lebensmittelueberwachung [A publication]

Sch L Bull ... School Law Bulletin [A publication]

Sch & Lef ... Schoales and Lefroy's Irish Chancery Reports (DLA)

Sch Leg Rec ... Schuylkill's Pennsylvania Legal Record (DLA)

Schleif Polier Oberflaechentech ... Schleif-, Polier-, und Oberflaechentechnik [A publication]

Schleif Poliertech (Hoya Weser Ger) ... Schleif- und Poliertechnik (Hoya-Weser, Germany) [A publication]

Schles Ges Jber ... Schlesische Gesellschaft fuer Vaterlaendische Kultur. Jahres-Bericht [A publication]

Schlesw-Holst Bienenztg ... Schleswig-Holsteinisches Bienenzeitung [A publication]

Schleswig Holsteinisches Aerztebl ... Schleswig-Holsteinisches Aerzteblatt [A publication]

Sch Lib .... School Librarian [A publication]

Sch Lib .... School Libraries [A publication]

Sch Lib Assn Calif Bul ... School Library Association of California. Bulletin [A publication]

Sch Lib J .... School Library Journal [A publication]

Sch Libn .... School Librarian [A publication]

Sch Libr ..... School Librarian [A publication]

Sch Lib R ... School Library Review and Educational Record [A publication]

Sch Libr Bull ... School Library Bulletin [A publication]

Sch Librn ... School Librarian and School Library Review [Later, School Librarian] [A publication]

Schlief-Poliertech ... Schlief- und Poliertechnik [West Germany] [A publication]

Sch Life...... School Life [A publication]

Sch LR ...... Schuylkill's Pennsylvania Legal Record (DLA)

SCHLS ...... Schluszsatz [Finale] [Music]

SCHLSHIP ... Schoolship [Navy] (NVT)

SCHLSHP ... Scholarship

SCHLT ...... Searchlight (MSA)

SCHM........ Schematic (AAG)

Schm......... Schoolmaster [Navy] [British]

Sch M .... Schweizer Monatshefte [A publication]

SCHM........ Societe Canadienne d'Histoire de la Medecine [Canadian Society for the History of Medicine - CSHM]

SCHM........ South Carolina Historical and Genealogical Magazine [A publication]

Sch Manag ... School Management [A publication]

Sch Manage ... School Management Bulletin [A publication]

Sch Management ... School Management [A publication]

Sch Management Bul ... School Management Bulletin [A publication]

Schm Civil Law ... Schmidt's Civil Law of Spain and Mexico (DLA)

Sch Media Q ... School Media Quarterly [A publication]

Sch Mgt ..... School Management [A publication]

Schmidt Civ Law ... Schmidt's Civil Law of Spain and Mexico (DLA)

Schmierstoffe Schmierungstech ... Schmierstoffe und Schmierungstechnik [East Germany] [A publication]

Schmiertech Tribol ... Schmiertechnik und Tribologie [A publication]

Sch Mines Q ... School of Mines Quarterly [A publication]

Schm LJ..... Schmidt's Law Journal [New Orleans] (DLA)

Schmollers Jahrb ... Schmollers Jahrbuch fuer Gesetzgebung, Verwaltung und Volkswirtschaft im Deutschen Reiche [A publication]

SCHMOO ... Space Cargo Handler and Manipulator for Orbital Operations

SCHMR ...... Schoolmaster (ROG)

Sch Mus ..... School Music [A publication]

Sch Mus B ... Bachelor of School Music

Sch MZ....... Schweizerische Musikzeitung [A publication]

Schneeberger Hb ... Schneeberger Heimatbuechlein [A publication]

Schnell Inf Hydraul & Pneum ... Schnell Informationen Hydraulik und Pneumatik [A publication]

SCHO .... Scholar [or Scholarship] (ROG)

SCHO .... Societe Canadienne d'Histoire Orale [Canadian Oral History Association - COHA]

SCHO .... Standard Controlled Heteroydne Oscillator

Schoales & L ... Schoales and Lefroy's Irish Chancery Reports (DLA)

Schoenberg Inst ... Arnold Schoenberg Institute. Journal [A publication]

SCHOL .... Scholarship

Schol........ Scholastik. Vierteljahresschrift fuer Theologie und Philosophie [A publication]

Schol........: Scholia [Classical studies] (OCD)

Schol........ Scholiast [Classical studies] (OCD)

SCHOL....... Scholium [Note] [Latin] (ROG)

SCHOLAR ... Schering-Oriented Literature Analysis and Retrieval System [Schering-Plough Corp.] [Bloomfield, NJ] [Information service] (EISS)

Scholarly Pub ... Scholarly Publishing [A publication]

Scholastic ... Senior Scholastic [Teacher Edition] [A publication]

Scholastic D ... Scholastic Debater [A publication]

Schol Bern ... Scholia Bernensia ad Vergilii Bucolica et Georgica [A publication] (OCD)

Schol Bob ... Scholia Bobiensia [Classical studies] (OCD)

Schol Coach ... Scholastic Coach [A publication]

Schol Cruq ... Scholia Cruquiana [Classical studies] (OCD)

Schol Flor Callim ... Scholia Florentina in Callimachum [Classical studies] (OCD)

Schol S ...... Scholia Satyrica [A publication]

Schol Teach ... Scholastic Teacher [A publication]

Schol Teach JH/SH Ed ... Scholastic Teacher. Junior/Senior High Teacher's Edition [A publication]

Schomberg Mar Laws Rhodes ... Schomberg's Treatise on the Maritime Laws of Rhodes (DLA)

School of Advanced Studies Rev ... School of Advanced International Studies. Review (DLA)

School Arts M ... School Arts Magazine [A publication]

School & Col ... School and College [A publication]

School Fam ... School Family [A publication]

School Lib ... School Libraries [A publication]

School of LR ... School of Law. Review. Toronto University [Canada] (DLA)

Schoolmens W Univ PA Proc ... Schoolmen's Week. University of Pennsylvania. Proceedings [A publication]

School Mus ... School Musician [A publication]

School and Soc ... School and Society [A publication]

Schopenhauer-Jahr ... Schopenhauer-Jahrbuch [A publication]

Schopenhauer-Jahrb ... Schopenhauer-Jahrbuch [A publication]

Schott Inf ... Schott Information [A publication]

Schouler Bailm ... Schouler on Bailments (DLA)

Schouler Dom Rel ... Schouler on Domestic Relations (DLA)

Schouler Pers Prop ... Schouler on the Law of Personal Property (DLA)

Schouler US Hist ... Schouler's History of the United States under the Constitution (DLA)

SchP .... Ordo Clericorum Regularium Pauperum Matris Dei Scholarum Piarum [Roman Catholic men's religious order]

SchP .... Scholarly Publishing [A publication]

Sch & Parent ... School and Parent [A publication]

Sch Per Prop ... Schouler on the Law of Personal Property (DLA)

Sch Pharm Bull Univ Wis Ext Div ... School of Pharmacy. Bulletin. University of Wisconsin. Extension Division [A publication]

SCHPM ...... Societe Canadienne d'Histoire et de Philosophie des Mathematiques [Canadian Society for the History and Philosophy of Mathematics - CSHPM]

SCHPS ...... Societe Canadienne d'Histoire et de Philosophie des Sciences [Canadian Society for the History and Philosophy of Science - CSHPS]

Sch R.......... School Review [A publication]

SCHR .... Schooner

SchR .... Schweizer Rundschau [A publication]

SCHR .... Societe Canadienne d'Histoire de la Rhetorique [See also CSHR] [Canada]

Sch Reg ..... Schuylkill's Pennsylvania Register (DLA)

Sch Rev...... School Review [A publication]

Schr Geb Brennst Geol ... Schriften aus dem Gebiet der Brennstoff-Geologie [A publication]

Schriftenr Agrarwiss Fak Univ Kiel ... Schriftenreihe der Agrarwissenschaftlichen Fakultaet der Universitaet Kiel [A publication]

Schriftenr Bundesminist Wiss Forsch Forsch Bild ... Schriftenreihe des Bundesministers fuer Wissenschaftliche Forschung. Forschung und Bildung [West Germany] [A publication]

Schriftenr Bundesminist Wiss Forsch (Ger) Radionuklide ... Schriftenreihe des Bundesministers fuer Wissenschaftliche Forschung (West Germany). Radionuklide [A publication]

Schriftenr Bundesminist Wiss Forsch (Ger) Strahlenschutz ... Schriftenreihe des Bundesministers fuer Wissenschaftliche Forschung (West Germany). Strahlenschutz [A publication]

Schriftenr Bundesminist Wiss Forsch Kernenergierecht ... Schriftenreihe des Bundesministers fuer Wissenschaftliche Forschung. Kernenergierecht [West Germany] [A publication]

Schriftenr Bundesminist Wiss Forsch Strahlenschutz ... Schriftenreihe des Bundesministers fuer Wissenschaftliche Forschung. Strahlenschutz [A publication]

Schriftenr Bundesverb Dtsch Kalkind ... Schriftenreihe des Bundesverbandes der Deutschen Kalkindustrie [*A publication*]

Schriftenr Dtsch Atomforums ... Schriftenreihe des Deutschen Atomforums [*A publication*]

Schriftenreihe Rechenzentrum Univ Koeln ... Schriftenreihe des Rechenzentrums. Universitaet zu Koeln [*A publication*]

Schriftenreihe Zentralinst Math Mech ... Schriftenreihe. Zentralinstitut fuer Mathematik und Mechanik [*A publication*]

Schriftenr Forschungsgem Schweiz Lackfabr ... Schriftenreihe. Forschungsgemeinschaft Schweizerischer Lackfabrikanten [*A publication*]

Schriftenr Forstl Fak Univ Goettingen ... Schriftenreihe der Forstlichen Fakultaet der Universitaet Goettingen und Mitteilungen der Niedersaechsischen Forstlichen Versuchsanstalt [*A publication*]

Schriftenr Intensivmed Notfallmed Anaesthesiol ... Schriftenreihe Intensivmedizin, Notfallmedizin, Anaesthesiologie [*A publication*]

Schriftenr Int Ges Nahr Vitalst Forsch eV ... Schriftenreihe. Internationale Gesellschaft fuer Nahrungs- und Vitalstoff-Forschung eV [*A publication*]

Schriftenr Landesanst Immissionisschutz ... Schriftenreihe der Landesanstalt fuer Immissionisschutz [*West Germany*] [*A publication*]

Schriftenr Landschaftspflege Naturschutz ... Schriftenreihe fuer Landschaftspflege und Naturschutz [*A publication*]

Schriftenr Neurol ... Schriftenreihe Neurologie [*A publication*]

Schriftenr Neurol-Neurol Ser ... Schriftenreihe Neurologie-Neurology Series [*A publication*]

Schriftenr Oesterr Wasserwirtschaftsverb ... Schriftenreihe. Oesterreichischen Wasserwirtschaftsverbandes [*A publication*]

Schriftenr Schweissen Schneiden Ber ... Schriftenreihe Schweissen Schneiden. Bericht [*A publication*]

Schriftenr Theor Prax Med Psychol ... Schriftenreihe zur Theorie und Praxis der Medizinischen Psychologie [*A publication*]

Schriftenr Vegetationskd ... Schriftenreihe fuer Vegetationskunde [*A publication*]

Schriftenr Versuchstierkd ... Schriftenreihe Versuchstierkunde [*A publication*]

Schriftenr Ver Wasser Boden Lufthyg ... Schriftenreihe des Vereins fuer Wasser, Boden, und Lufthygiene [*A publication*]

Schriftenr Zementind ... Schriftenreihe der Zementindustrie [*A publication*]

Schrift Naturf Gesellsch Kopenhagen ... Schriften der Naturforschenden Gesellschaft zu Kopenhagen [*A publication*]

Schrifttum Agrarwirt ... Schrifttum der Agrarwirtschaft [*A publication*]

Schr Math Inst Univ Muenster 2 ... Schriftenreihe des Mathematischen Instituts der Universitaet Muenster. 2 Serie [*A publication*]

Schr Math Inst Univ Munster ... Schriftenreihe des Mathematischen Instituts der Universitaet Muenster [*A publication*]

Schr Naturwiss Ver Schleswig-Holstein ... Schriften des Naturwissenschaftlichen Vereins fuer Schleswig-Holstein [*A publication*]

Schrreihe Forstl Fak Univ Goettingen ... Schriftenreihe. Forstliche Fakultaet. Universitaet Goettingen [*A publication*]

SCHRUB .... Schmidt Rubin Rifle

SCHS .... Small Component Handling System   (NRCH)

SCHS .... Supreme Court Historical Society

Sch Sci & Math ... School Science and Mathematics [*A publication*]

Sch Sci Rev ... School Science Review [*England*] [*A publication*]

Sch (Sec Ed) ... School (Toronto) (Secondary Edition) [*A publication*]

Sch Shop ... School Shop [*A publication*]

Sch & Soc ... School and Society [*A publication*]

Schupo ...... Schutzpolizist [*Policeman*] [*German*]

Schuy Leg Rec (PA) ... Schuylkill's Pennsylvania Legal Record   (DLA)

Schuyl Legal Rec ... Schuylkill Legal Record [*Pa.*]   (DLA)

Schuyl Leg Rec ... Schuylkill's Pennsylvania Legal Record   (DLA)

Schuy Reg (PA) ... Schuylkill's Pennsylvania Register   (DLA)

SCHVD .... Sachverhalte [*A publication*]

Schw A Neur ... Schweizer Archiv fuer Neurologie, Neurochirurgie, und Psychiatrie [*A publication*]

SchwArchV ... Schweizerisches Archiv fuer Volkskunde [*A publication*]

Schwarz Int L ... Schwarzenberger's International Law   (DLA)

Schweiz Aerzteztg ... Schweizerische Aerztezeitung [*A publication*]

Schweiz Alum Rundsch ... Schweizer Aluminium Rundschau [*A publication*]

Schweiz Anst Forstl Versuchswes Mitt ... Schweizerische Anstalt fuer das Forstliche Versuchswesen Mitteilungen [*A publication*]

Schweiz Apoth Ztg ... Schweizerische Apotheker-Zeitung [*A publication*]

Schweiz Arch ... Schweizer Archiv [*A publication*]

Schweiz Arch Angew Wiss Tech ... Schweizer Archiv fuer Angewandte Wissenschaft und Technik [*A publication*]

Schweiz Archiv f Volksk ... Schweizerisches Archiv fuer Volkskunde [*A publication*]

Schweiz Arch Neurol Neurochir Psychiatr ... Schweizer Archiv fuer Neurologie, Neurochirurgie, und Psychiatrie [*A publication*]

Schweiz Arch Neurol Psychiatr ... Schweizer Archiv fuer Neurologie und Psychiatrie [*A publication*]

Schweiz Arch Tierh ... Schweizer Archiv fuer Tierheilkunde [*A publication*]

Schweiz Arch Tierh (Bern) ... Schweizerisches Archiv fuer Tierheilkunde und Tierzucht (Bern) [*A publication*]

Schweiz Arch Tierheilkd ... Schweizer Archiv fuer Tierheilkunde [*A publication*]

Schweiz Arch Verkehrswiss und Verkehrspol ... Schweizerlisches Archiv fuer Verkehrswissenschaft und Verkehrspolitik [*A publication*]

Schweiz Bauztg ... Schweizerische Bauzeitung [*A publication*]

Schweiz Beitr Dendrol ... Schweizerische Beitrage zur Dendrologie [*A publication*]

Schweiz Bienen-Ztg ... Schweizerische Bienen-Zeitung [*A publication*]

Schweiz Bl Heiz Lueft ... Schweizerische Blaetter fuer Heizung und Lueftung [*Switzerland*] [*A publication*]

Schweiz Brau-Rundsch ... Schweizerische Brauerei-Rundschau [*A publication*]

Schweiz Chem Ztg ... Schweizerische Chemiker-Zeitung [*A publication*]

Schweiz Chem Ztg Tech Ind ... Schweizer Chemiker-Zeitung Technik-Industrie [*A publication*]

Schweiz Elektrotech Z ... Schweizerische Elektrotechnische Zeitschrift [*A publication*]

Schweizer Archiv Verkehrswiss u -Polit ... Schweizerisches Archiv fuer Verkehrswissenschaft und Verkehrspolitik [*A publication*]

Schweizer Arch Tierheilk ... Schweizer Archiv fuer Tierheilkunde [*A publication*]

Schweizer Arch Volksk ... Schweizer Archiv fuer Volkskunde [*A publication*]

Schweizer Mineralog u Petrog Mitt ... Schweizerische Mineralogische und Petrographische Mitteilungen [*A publication*]

Schweizer Natschutz ... Schweizer Naturschutz [*A publication*]

Schweizer Palaeont Abh Mem Suisses Paleontologie ... Schweizerische Palaeontologische Abhandlungen. Memoires Suisses de Palaeontologie [*A publication*]

Schweizer Z Soziol ... Schweizerische Zeitschrift fuer Soziologie [*A publication*]

Schweizer Z Volkswirtsch u Statist ... Schweizerische Zeitschrift fuer Volkswirtschaft und Statistik [*A publication*]

Schweiz Gaertnerztg ... Schweizerische Gaertnerzeitung [*A publication*]

Schweiz Ing & Archit ... Schweizer Ingenieur und Architekt [*A publication*]

Schweiz Jb f Internat Recht ... Schweizerisches Jahrbuch fuer Internationales Recht/Annuaire Suisse de Droit International [*Zurich, Switzerland*]   (DLA)

Schweiz Landtech ... Schweizer Landtechnik [*A publication*]

Schweiz Landw Forsch ... Schweizerische Landwirtschaftliche Forschung [*A publication*]

Schweiz Landwirtsch Monatsh ... Schweizerische Landwirtschaftliche Monatshefte [*A publication*]

Schweiz Landw Mh ... Schweizerische Landwirtschaftliche Monatshefte [*A publication*]

Schweiz Med Wochenschr ... Schweizerische Medizinische Wochenschrift [*A publication*]

Schweiz Med Wochenschr Suppl ... Schweizerische Medizinische Wochenschrift. Supplementum [*A publication*]

Schweiz Med Wschr ... Schweizerische Medizinische Wochenschrift [*A publication*]

Schweiz Mh ... Schweizer Monatshefte [*A publication*]

Schweiz Milchwirtsch Forsch ... Schweizerische Milchwirtschaftliche Forschung [*A publication*]

Schweiz Milchztg ... Schweizerische Milchzeitung [*A publication*]

Schweiz Mineral Petrogr Mitt ... Schweizerische Mineralogische und Petrographische Mitteilungen [*A publication*]

Schweiz Monatsschr Zahnheilkd ... Schweizerische Monatsschrift fuer Zahnheilkunde [*A publication*]

Schweiz Muenzbl ... Schweizer Muenzblaetter [*Switzerland*] [*A publication*]

Schweiz Mus ... Schweizerische Musikzeitung [*A publication*]

Schweiz Naturf Ges Verh ... Schweizerische Naturforschende Gesellschaft. Verhandlungen [*A publication*]

Schweiz Naturschutz Prot Nat ... Schweizer Naturschutz. Protection de la Nature [*A publication*]

Schweiz Palaeontol Abh ... Schweizerische Palaeontologische Abhandlungen [*A publication*]

Schweiz Palaeontol Abh-Mem Suisse Palaeontol ... Schweizerische Palaeontologische Abhandlungen. Memoires Suisses de Palaeontologie [*A publication*]

Schweiz Photorundsch ... Schweizerische Photorundschau [*A publication*]

Schweiz Photo Ztg ... Schweizerische Photo-Zeitung [*A publication*]

Schweiz Rdsch ... Schweizer Rundschau [*A publication*]

Schweiz Strahler ... Schweizer Strahler [*A publication*]

Schweiz Tech ... Schweizerische Technikerzeitung [*Switzerland*] [*A publication*]

Schweiz Tech Z ... Schweizerische Technische Zeitschrift [*Switzerland*] [*A publication*]

Schweiz Ver Atomenerg Bull ... Schweizerische Vereinigung fuer Atomenergie. Bulletin [*Switzerland*] [*A publication*]

Schweiz Ver Gas-Wasserfachmaennern Monatsbull ... Schweizerische Verein von Gas- und Wasserfachmaennern Monatsbulletin [*Switzerland*] [*A publication*]

Schweiz Wohnschr Chem u Pharm ... Schweizerische Wochenschrift fuer Chemie und Pharmacie [*A publication*]

Schweiz Z Allg Pathol Bakterol ... Schweizerische Zeitschrift fuer Allgemeine Pathologie und Bakteriologie [*A publication*]

Schweiz Z Forstwes ... Schweizerische Zeitschrift fuer Forstwesen [*A publication*]

Schweiz Z Gesch ... Schweizerische Zeitschrift fuer Geschichte [*A publication*]

Schweiz Z Gynaekol Geburtshilfe ... Schweizerische Zeitschrift fuer Gynaekologie und Geburtshilfe [*A publication*]

Schweiz Z Gynaekol Geburtshilfe Suppl ... Schweizerische Zeitschrift fuer Gynaekologie und Geburtshilfe. Supplementum [*A publication*]

Schweiz Z Hydrol ... Schweizerische Zeitschrift fuer Hydrologie [*A publication*]

Schweiz Z Obst-u Weinb ... Schweizerische Zeitschrift fuer Obst- und Weinbau [*A publication*]

Schweiz Z Obst-Weinbau ... Schweizerische Zeitschrift fuer Obst- und Weinbau [*A publication*]

Schweiz Z Pathol Bakteriol ... Schweizerische Zeitschrift fuer Pathologie und Bakteriologie [*A publication*]

Schweiz Z Pharm ... Schweizerische Zeitschrift fuer Pharmacie [*A publication*]

Schweiz Z Pilzkd ... Schweizerische Zeitschrift fuer Pilzkunde [*A publication*]

Schweiz Z Psychol Anwend ... Schweizerische Zeitschrift fuer Psychologie und Ihre Anwendungen [*A publication*]

Schweiz Z Sportmed ... Schweizerische Zeitschrift fuer Sportmedizin [*A publication*]

Schweiz Z f Strafrecht ... Schweizerische Zeitschrift fuer Strafrecht/Revue Penale Suisse [*Berne, Switzerland*]   (DLA)

Schweiz Z Tuberk Pneumonol ... Schweizerische Zeitschrift fuer Tuberkulose und Pneumonologie [*A publication*]

Schweiz Z Vermess Photogramm Kulturtech ... Schweizerische Zeitschrift fuer Vermessung, Photogrammetrie, und Kulturtechnik [*A publication*]

Schwenk.... Schwenckfeldiana [*A publication*]

Schwest Rev ... Schwestern Revue [*A publication*]

Schwiez Z Path Bakt ... Schweizerische Zeitschrift fuer Pathologie und Bakteriologie [*A publication*]

SchwKiZ .... Schweizerische Kirchenzeitung [*Lucerne*] [*A publication*]

SchwKZ ...... Schweizerische Kirchenzeitung [*Lucerne*] [*A publication*]

SchwM ...... Schweizer Monatshefte [*A publication*]

Schw Med Wo ... Schweizerische Medizinische Wochenschrift [*A publication*]

SchwMH .... Schweizer Monatshefte [*Zurich*] [*A publication*]

Schw Musikz ... Schweizerische Musikzeitung/Revue Musicale Suisse [*A publication*]

SCHWR ...... Steam-Cooled Heavy-Water Reactor

SchwRundschau ... Schweizer Rundschau [*A publication*]

SchwV....... Schweizer Volkskunde [*A publication*]

Schw Z Gesc ... Schweizerische Zeitschrift fuer Geschichte [*A publication*]

Schw Z Psyc ... Schweizerische Zeitschrift fuer Psychologie und Ihre Anwendungen [*A publication*]

Schw Z Soz ... Schweizerische Zeitschrift fuer Sozialversicherung [*A publication*]

SCI .... Council for the Securities Industry [*Levy*] [*British*]

SCI .... Sacra Congregatio Indicis [*Sacred Congregation of the Index*] [*Latin*]

SCI .... Safari Club International   (EA)

SCI .... San Clemente Island [*California*] [*Seismograph station code, US Geological Survey*]   (SEIS)

SCI .... San Clemente Island

SCI .... Santa Cruz Island   (MUGU)

SCI .... Savio Club International   (EA)

SCI .... Schedule-Cost Index   (MCD)

SCI .... SCI Satellite Conferencing International Corp. [*Formerly, Valclair Resources, Ltd.*] [*Vancouver Stock Exchange symbol*]

SCI .... Science [*A publication*]

SCI .... Science   (AFM)

SCI .... Science Citation Index [*A publication*]

SCI .... Science of Creative Intelligence [*Transcendental meditation*]

SCI .... Science Curriculum Improvement [*Study*] [*Education*]

SCI .... Scientific Computers, Incorporated   (MCD)

SCI .... Scripta Classica Israelica [*A publication*]

Scl .... Scripta Islandica [*A publication*]

SCI .... Seamen's Church Institute of New York/New Jersey   (EA)

SCI .... Security Container Institute [*Inactive*] [*Glendale, CA*]   (EA)

SCI .... Selected Configured Item   (MCD)

SCI .... Seminar Clearinghouse International, Inc. [*St. Paul, MN*] [*Information service*]   (EISS)

SCI .... Sensitive Compartmented Information [*Reagan administration*]

SCI .... Sequential Comparison Index [*Measures effect of chemical pollution in lakes and streams*]

SCI .... Service Change Information   (MCD)

SCI .... Service Civil International [*International Voluntary Service*]

SCI .... Ship Controlled Intercept [*RADAR*] [*Navy*]

SCI .... Shipping Container Institute

SCI .... Shipping Corporation of India Ltd.

SCI .... Ship's Capability Impaired [*Navy*]

SCI .... Short Circuit

SCI .... Signal Corps Item [*Obsolete*] [*Army*]   (NATG)

SCI .... Simulation Councils, Incorporated

SCI .... Single Column Inch   (ADA)

SCI .... Sister Cities International [*An association*]   (EA)

SCI .... Slot Cell Inserter

SCI .... Small Craft Instructor [*Red Cross*]

SCI .... Societe de Chimie Industrielle   (EA)

SCI .... Society of Chemical Industry   (EA)

SCI .... Soft Cast Iron

SCI .... Source Code Indicator   (MCD)

SCI .... Special Customs Invoice

SCI .... Spinal Cord Injury [*Medicine*]

SCI .... Sponge and Chamois Institute [*New York, NY*]   (EA)

SCI .... Stein Collectors International   (EA)

SCI .... Stratospheric Circulation Index [*Geophysics*]

SCI .... Stroke Club International [*Galveston, TX*]   (EA)

SCI .... Structured Clinical Interview

SCI .... Supervisory Cost Inspector [*Navy*]

SCI .... Switch Closure In   (MCD)

SCI .... System Consultants, Incorporated [*Mason, MI*] [*Software manufacturer*]

SCI .... System Control Interface

SciA .... Scientific American [*A publication*]

SCIA .... Signal Corps Intelligence Agency [*Obsolete*] [*Army*]

SCIA .... Social Competence Inventory for Adults [*Psychology*]

SCIA .... Studii si Cercetari de Istoria Artei. Seria Arta Plastica [*A publication*]

SCIA .... Systems Change Impact Analysis [*Social Security Administration*]

SciAb .... Science Abstracts [*A publication*]

Sci Abstr China Biol Sci ... Science Abstracts of China. Serie Biological Sciences [*A publication*]

Sci Abstr China Chem Chem Technol ... Science Abstracts of China. Chemistry and Chemical Technology [*A publication*]

Sci Abstr China Math Phys Sci ... Science Abstracts of China. Mathematical and Physical Sciences [*A publication*]

Sci Abstr China Med ... Science Abstracts of China. Medicine [*A publication*]

Sci Abstr China Tech Sci ... Science Abstracts of China. Technical Sciences [*A publication*]

Sci Adv Mater Process Eng Proc ... Science of Advanced Materials and Process Engineering. Proceedings [*A publication*]

Sci Adv Mater Process Eng Q ... Science of Advanced Materials and Process Engineering. Quarterly [*United States*] [*A publication*]

Sci Aer Aerotech ... Science Aerienne et l'Aerotechnique [*A publication*]

Sci Ag .... Scientific Agriculture [*A publication*]

Sci Agr .... Scientific Agriculture [*A publication*]

Sci Agric.... Science in Agriculture [*A publication*]

Sci Agric Bohemoslov ... Scientia Agriculturae Bohemoslovaca [*A publication*]

Sci Agric PA State Univ Agric Exp Stn ... Science in Agriculture. Pennsylvania State University. Agricultural Experiment Station [*A publication*]

Sci Agron Rennes ... Sciences Agronomiques Rennes [*A publication*]

Sci Alaska Proc Alaskan Sci Conf ... Science in Alaska. Proceedings. Alaskan Science Conference [*A publication*]

Sci Aliment ... Scienza dell'Alimentazione [*A publication*]

Sci Am .... Scientific American [*A publication*]

Sci Amer ..... Scientific American [*A publication*]

Sci Am Monthly ... Scientific American Monthly [*A publication*]

Sci Am S .... Scientific American. Supplement [*A publication*]

Sci Appliance ... Science and Appliance [*A publication*]

SCIAPS ..... Senate Comprehensive Integrated Automated Printing System

SciArch...... Science and Archaeology [*A publication*]

Sci & Archaeol ... Science and Archaeology [*A publication*]

SCIAS .... Society of Chemical Industry, American Section   (EA)

SCIAS .... Supreme Council of the Independent Associated Spiritualists   (EA)

Sci Aust ..... Scientific Australian [*A publication*]

Sci & Aust Technol ... Science and Australian Technology [*A publication*]

Sci Aust Technol ... Science and Australian Technology [*A publication*]

Sci Avenir ... Sciences et Avenir [*France*] [*A publication*]

SCIB .... Significant Counterintelligence Briefs   (AFM)

Sci Basis Med ... Scientific Basis of Medicine [*A publication*]

Sci Basis Med Annu Rev ... Scientific Basis of Medical Annual Reviews [*A publication*]

Sci Biol J.... Science of Biology Journal [*A publication*]

Sci Biol Ser ... Science of Biology Series [*A publication*]

Sci Bk........ Science Books and Films [*A publication*]

Sci Bks....... Science Books [*A publication*]

Sci Bks & Films ... Science Books and Films [*A publication*]

SCIBP .... Special Committee for the International Biological Program [*National Research Council*]

Sci Bul........ Science Bulletin for Teachers in Secondary Schools [*A publication*]

Sci Bull Academ Min Metall (Krakow) Geol ... Scientific Bulletins. Academy of Mining and Metallurgy (Krakow). Geology [*A publication*]

Sci Bull Acad Min Metall (Krakow) Ceram ... Scientific Bulletins. Academy of Mining and Metallurgy (Krakow). Ceramics [*A publication*]

Sci Bull Acad Min Metall (Krakow) Electrif Mech Min Metall ... Scientific Bulletins. Academy of Mining and Metallurgy (Krakow). Electrification and Mechanization in Mining and Metallurgy [*A publication*]

Sci Bull Acad Min Metall (Krakow) Math Phys Chem ... Scientific Bulletins. Academy of Mining and Metallurgy (Krakow). Mathematics, Physics, Chemistry [*A publication*]

Sci Bull Acad Min Metall (Krakow) Metall Foundry Pract ... Scientific Bulletins. Academy of Mining and Metallurgy (Krakow). Metallurgy and Foundry Practice [*A publication*]

Sci Bull Acad Min Metall (Krakow) Min ... Scientific Bulletins. Academy of Mining and Metallurgy (Krakow). Mining [*A publication*]

Sci Bull Acad Min Metall (Krakow) Spec Ser ... Scientific Bulletins. Academy of Mining and Metallurgy (Krakow). Special Series [*A publication*]

Sci Bull At Energy New Energ Organ ... Scientific Bulletin. Atomic Energy and New Energies Organization [*A publication*]

Sci Bull Can Cent Miner Energy Technol ... Scientific Bulletin. Canada Centre for Mineral and Energy Technology [*A publication*]

Sci Bull Coll Agric Univ Ryukyus Okinawa ... Science Bulletin. College of Agriculture. University of Ryukyus. Okinawa [*A publication*]

Sci Bull Cotton Res Inst Sindos ... Science Bulletin. Cotton Research Institute. Sindos [*A publication*]

Sci Bull Dep Agric For Un S Afr ... Science Bulletin. Department of Agriculture and Forestry. Union of South Africa [*A publication*]

Sci Bull Dep Agric NSW ... Science Bulletin. Department of Agriculture. New South Wales [*A publication*]

Sci Bull Dept Agr NSW ... Science Bulletin. Department of Agriculture. New South Wales [*A publication*]

Sci Bull Dept Agr S Afr ... Science Bulletin. Department of Agriculture. South Africa [*A publication*]

Sci Bull Fac Agric Kyushu Univ ... Science Bulletin. Faculty of Agriculture. Kyushu University [*A publication*]

Sci Bull Fac Agr Kyushu Univ ... Science Bulletin. Faculty of Agriculture. Kyushu University [*A publication*]

Sci Bull Fac Ed Nagasaki Univ ... Science Bulletin. Faculty of Education. Nagasaki University [*A publication*]

Sci Bull Fac Educ Nagasaki Univ ... Science Bulletin. Faculty of Education. Nagasaki University [*A publication*]

Sci Bull Repub S Afr Dept Agr Tech Serv ... Science Bulletin. Republic of South Africa. Department of Agricultural Technical Services [*A publication*]

Sci Bull Stanislaw Staszic Univ Min Metall Ceram ... Scientific Bulletins. Stanislaw Staszic University of Mining and Metallurgy. Ceramics [*A publication*]

Sci Bull Stanislaw Staszic Univ Min Metall Geol ... Scientific Bulletins. Stanislaw Staszic University of Mining and Metallurgy. Geology [*A publication*]

Sci Bull Stanislaw Staszic Univ Min Metall Math Phys Chem ... Scientific Bulletins. Stanislaw Staszic University of Mining and Metallurgy. Mathematics, Physics, Chemistry [*A publication*]

Sci Bull Stanislaw Staszic Univ Min Metall Min ... Scientific Bulletins. Stanislaw Staszic University of Mining and Metallurgy. Mining [*A publication*]

Sci Bull Stanislaw Staszic Univ Min Metall Sozol Sozotech ... Scientific Bulletins. Stanislaw Staszic University of Mining and Metallurgy. Sozology and Sozotechnics [*A publication*]

Sci Bull Stanislaw Staszic Univ Min Metall Spec Ser ... Scientific Bulletins. Stanislaw Staszic University of Mining and Metallurgy. Special Series [*A publication*]

Sci Bull Univ Kans ... Science Bulletin. University of Kansas [*A publication*]

SCIC .... Semiconductor Integrated Circuit

SCIC .... Single-Column Ion Chromatography

SCICC .... Service Center Internal Computer Code [*Data processing*]

Sci Ceram ... Science of Ceramics [*England*] [*A publication*]

SCICF .... Safari Club International Conservation Fund   (EA)

SCICFNDT ... Standing Committee for International Cooperation within the Field of Non-Destructive Testing   (EA)

Sci & Child ... Science and Children [*A publication*]

Sci Chron (Karachi) ... Science Chronicle (Karachi) [*A publication*]

Sci Cit Ind ... Science Citation Index [*A publication*]

SCICLOPS ... Systems Control, Incorporated Computerized Library Operations [*Information service*]   (EISS)

Sci Counc Afr South Sahara Publ ... Scientific Council for Africa South of the Sahara. Publication [*A publication*]

Sci Counc Jap Annu Rep ... Science Council of Japan. Annual Report [*A publication*]

Sci Couns ... Science Counselor [*A publication*]

SCICS .... Spinal Cord Injury Care System [*University of Alabama in Birmingham*] [*Research center*]   (RCD)

Sci and Cult ... Science and Culture [*A publication*]

Sci Cult ...... Science and Culture [*A publication*]

Sci Cult (New Delhi) ... Science and Culture (New Delhi) [*A publication*]

Sci D .... Doctor of Science

SCID .... Severe Combined Immune Deficiency [*Immunology*]

SCID .... Small Column Insulated Delays   (MCD)

SCID .... Subcommutator Identification [*NASA*]

SCID-A .... Studies in Comparative International Development [*A publication*]

SCIDE .... Servicio Cooperativo Interamericano de Educacion

Sci Dep Bull United Plant Assoc South India ... Scientific Department Bulletin. United Planters' Association of Southern India [*A publication*]

Sci Dig .... Science Digest [*A publication*]

Sci Digest ... Science Digest [*A publication*]

Sci Dimens ... Science Dimension [*A publication*]

Sci Dimension ... Science Dimension [*A publication*]

SCIDNT ...... System Control Incorporated Identification Program [*Navy*]

SCIE .... Scientific Computers [*NASDAQ symbol*]   (NQ)

SCIE .... Stolen Children Information Exchange   (EA)

SCIEA .... Science [*A publication*]

Sci Ed .... Science Education [*A publication*]

Sci Ed News ... Science Education Newsletter [*A publication*]

Sci Educ .... Science Education [*A publication*]

Sci 80 (Eighty) ... Science 80 (Eighty) [*A publication*]

Sci Elec ...... Scientia Electrica [*A publication*]

Science ...... Science for People [*A publication*]

Science Ed ... Science Education [*A publication*]

Science N L ... Science News Letter [*A publication*]

Science Prog ... Science Progress [*A publication*]

Sciences Pol ... Sciences Politiques [*A publication*]

Sciencia Med ... Sciencia Medica [*A publication*]

Sci Eng ...... Science and Engineering [*A publication*]

Sci and Eng Rep Def Acad ... Scientific and Engineering Reports. Defense Academy [*A publication*]

Sci and Eng Rep Natl Def Acad (Jpn) ... Scientific and Engineering Reports. National Defense Academy (Japanese) [*A publication*]

Sci & Eng Rep Saitama Univ C ... Science and Engineering Reports. Saitama University. Series C [*A publication*]

Sci and Eng Rep Saitama Univ Ser C ... Science and Engineering Reports. Saitama University. Series C [*A publication*]

Sci Eng Rev Doshisha Univ ... Science and Engineering Review. Doshisha University [*A publication*]

Sci Enseign Sci ... Sciences et l'Enseignement des Sciences [*A publication*]

SCIENT ...... Scientific

Scient Agric ... Scientific Agriculture [*A publication*]

Scient Am ... Scientific American [*A publication*]

Scient Amer ... Scientific American [*A publication*]

Scient Am Suppl ... Scientific American. Supplement [*A publication*]

Scient Hort ... Scientific Horticulture [*A publication*]

Scientia Genet ... Scientia Genetica [*A publication*]

Scientiarum Hist ... Scientiarum Historia [*A publication*]

Scient Instrum ... Scientific Instruments [*A publication*]

Scient Mon ... Scientific Monthly [*A publication*]

Scient Month ... Scientific Monthly [*A publication*]

Scient Pap Coll Gen Educ Tokyo ... Scientific Papers. College of General Education. University of Tokyo [*A publication*]

Scient Papers Civil Vet Dept (Madras) ... Scientific Papers. Civil Veterinary Department (Madras) [*A publication*]

Scient Proc R Dubl Soc ... Scientific Proceedings. Royal Dublin Society [*A publication*]

Scient Rep Fac Agric Okayama Univ ... Scientific Reports. Faculty of Agriculture. Okayama University [*A publication*]

Scient Rep Govt Inst Infect Dis Tokyo Imp Univ ... Scientific Reports. Government Institute for Infectious Diseases. Tokyo Imperial University [*A publication*]

Scient Rep Kyoto Prefect Univ Agric ... Scientific Reports. Kyoto Prefectural University. Agriculture [*A publication*]

Scient Res (Bangladesh) ... Scientific Researches (Bangladesh) [*A publication*]

Scienza Aliment ... Scienza dell'Alimentazione [*A publication*]

Scienza Tecnol Aliment ... Scienza e Tecnologia degli Alimenti [*A publication*]

Sci Esprit ... Science et Esprit [*A publication*]

SCIF .... Daughters of the Sacred Heart of Jesus [*Bethlehemite Sisters*] [*Roman Catholic religious order*]

SCIF .... Science Forum [*A publication*]

SCIF .... Static Column Isoelectric Focusing [*Materials processing*]

SCIF .... Systems Certification and Integration Facility

SCI FA .... Scire Facias [*Please make known*] [*A writ to enforce, annul, or vacate a judgment, patent, charter or other matter of record*] [*Legal term*] [*Latin*]

Sci Fa ad Dis Deb ... Scire Facias ad Disprobandum Debitum   (DLA)

Sci Farmer ... Science for the Farmer [*A publication*]

SCI-FI .... Science Fiction [*Also, SF*]

Sci Fiction Bk Rev Ind ... Science Fiction Book Review Index [*A publication*]

Sci Forum ... Science Forum [*A publication*]

SCIGB .... Sicherheitsingenieur [*A publication*]

Sci Geol Bull ... Sciences Geologiques. Bulletin [*A publication*]

Sci Geol Bull Inst Geol Univ Louis Pasteur Strasbourg ... Sciences Geologiques. Bulletin. Institut de Geologie. Universite Louis Pasteur de Strasbourg [*France*] [*A publication*]

Sci Geol S ... Scientia Geologica Sinica [*A publication*]

Sci Geol Sin ... Scientia Geologica Sinica [*A publication*]

Sci Gov Rep ... Science and Government Report [*United States*] [*A publication*]

Sci Govt Rep ... Science and Government Report [*A publication*]

Sci Hist ...... Scientiarum Historia [*A publication*]

Sci Hort ...... Scientific Horticulture [*A publication*]

Sci Hortic ... Scientia Horticulturae [*A publication*]

Sci Hum Life ... Science of Human Life [*A publication*]

SCII .... Science in Iceland [*A publication*]
SCII .... Southland Capital Investment [*NASDAQ symbol*] (NQ)
SCII .... Strong-Campbell Interest Inventory [*Vocational guidance*]
Sci Icel ...... Science in Iceland [*A publication*]
Sci Ilus .... Science Illustrated [*A publication*]
Sci Ind .... Science and Industry [*A publication*]
Sci Ind Equip Bull ... Scientific and Industrial Equipment Bulletin [*A publication*]
Sci Ind (Karachi) ... Science and Industry (Karachi) [*A publication*]
Sci in Ind (Lond) ... Science in Industry (London) [*A publication*]
Sci Ind (Philips) ... Science and Industry (Philips) [*The Netherlands*] [*A publication*]
Sci Ind Photogr ... Science et Industries Photographiques [*A publication*]
Sci Ind Spat ... Sciences et Industries Spatiales [*Switzerland*] [*A publication*]
Sci Ind Spatiales Space Res Eng Weltraumforsch Ind ... Sciences et Industries Spatiales, Space Research and Engineering, Weltraumforschung und Industrie [*A publication*]
Sci Inf Notes ... Scientific Information Notes [*A publication*]
Sci Info N ... Scientific Information Notes [*A publication*]
Sci Insect Control (Kyoto) ... Scientific Insect Control (Kyoto) [*A publication*]
Sci Instr ...... Scientific Instruments [*A publication*]
Sci Instrum ... Journal of Physics. E: Scientific Instruments [*A publication*]
Sci Invest Freshw Salmon Fish Res Scott Home Dep ... Scientific Investigations. Freshwater and Salmon Fisheries Research. Scottish Home Department [*A publication*]
SCI-IVS ...... SCI-International Voluntary Service [*Formerly, IVS*] (EA)
Sci J .... Science Journal [*A publication*]
Sci Jour ...... Science Journal [*A publication*]
Sci J Shivaji Univ ... Science Journal. Shivaji University [*A publication*]
SCIL .... Scilicet [*Namely*] [*Latin*]
SCIL .... Ship's Construction Item List (MCD)
SCIL .... Small Computers in Libraries [*A publication*]
SCIL .... Soft Consumable Item List
SCIL .... Support Center International Logistics [*Army*]
Sci Leafl ...... Science Leaflet [*A publication*]
SCILF .... Studii si Cercetari de Istorie Literara si Folclor [*A publication*]
Sci Life ...... Science and Life [*A publication*]
Sci Light ...... Science of Light [*A publication*]
SCILL .... Southern California Interlibrary Loan Project [*Library network*]
Sci Lubr ..... Scientific Lubrication [*A publication*]
Sci Lubr Liq Fuel ... Scientific Lubrication and Liquid Fuel [*A publication*]
SCIM .... Congregation des Soeurs Servantes du Coeur Immaculae de Marie [*Servants of the Immaculate Heart of Mary*] [*Good Shepherd Sisters*] [*Roman Catholic religious order*]
SCIM .... Selected Categories in Microfiche [*National Technical Information Service*]
SCIM .... Speech Communications Index Meter
SCIM .... Standard Cubic Inches per Minute (AAG)
SCIM .... Subject Codes for Intelligence Management (MCD)
Sci Mac ...... Science of Machine [*Japan*] [*A publication*]
Sci March ... Science on the March [*A publication*]
Sci Mat...... Scienze Matematiche [*A publication*]
Sci Mech...... Science and Mechanics [*A publication*]
Sci Med ...... Sciences Medicales [*A publication*]
Sci Med Ital ... Scientia Medica Italica [*A publication*]
Sci Med Ital (Engl Ed) ... Scientia Medica Italica (English Edition) [*A publication*]
Sci Meet..... Scientific Meetings [*A publication*]
SCIMITAR ... System for Countering Interdiction Missiles and Targets RADARs (MCD)
Sci Mo........ Scientific Monthly [*A publication*]
Sci Monogr Wyo Expl Stn ... Science Monograph. Wyoming Experimental Station [*A publication*]
SCIMP........ Self-Contained Imaging Micro-Profiler [*Instrumentation*]
SCIMPEX ... Syndicat des Commercants Importateurs et Exportateurs de l'Ouest African [*Union of Commercial Importers and Exporters of West Africa*]
Sci N .... Science News [*A publication*]
Sci Nat .... Science et Nature [*A publication*]
Sci New Guinea ... Science in New Guinea [*A publication*]
Sci News.... Science News [*A publication*]
Sci News (Harmondsworth) ... Science News (Harmondsworth) [*A publication*]
Sci News Lett ... Science News Letter [*United States*] [*A publication*]
Sci Nourishment ... Science of Nourishment [*A publication*]
SCINT .... Scintillator [*Nucleonics*]
SCIO .... Staff Counterintelligence Officer [*Military*] (NVT)
SCIOP .... Social Competence Inventory for Older Persons [*Psychology*]
Sci Opin .... Scientific Opinion [*A publication*]
SCIP .... Scanning for Information Parameters
SCIP .... Sea Counterinfiltration Patrol (CINC)
SCIP .... Self-Contained Instrument Package (KSC)
SCIP .... Ship's Capability Impaired for Lack of Parts [*Navy*]
SCIP .... Society of Competitor Intelligence Professionals (EA)
SCIP .... Special Crisis Intervention Program (OICC)
SCIP .... Stanford Center for Information Processing [*Stanford University*] [*Database*]
Sci Paed Ex ... Scientia Paedagogica Experimentalis [*A publication*]
Sci Pap Coll Gen Educ Univ Tokyo ... Scientific Papers. College of General Education. University of Tokyo [*A publication*]

Sci Pap Coll Gen Educ Univ Tokyo (Biol Part) ... Scientific Papers. College of General Education. University of Tokyo (Biological Part) [*A publication*]
Sci Papers College Gen Ed Univ Tokyo ... Scientific Papers. College of General Education. University of Tokyo [*A publication*]
Sci Papers Prague ICT C ... Scientific Papers. Prague Institute of Chemical Technology. Part C. Organic Chemistry and Technology [*A publication*]
Sci Pap Fac Eng Tokushima Univ ... Scientific Papers. Faculty of Engineering. Tokushima University [*A publication*]
Sci Pap Imp Fuel Res Inst (Jpn) ... Scientific Papers. Imperial Fuel Research Institute (Japan) [*A publication*]
Sci Pap Inst Algol Res Fac Sci Hokkaido Univ ... Scientific Papers. Institute of Algological Research. Faculty of Science. Hokkaido University [*A publication*]
Sci Pap Inst Chem Technol (Prague) Chem Eng Autom ... Scientific Papers. Institute of Chemical Technology (Prague). Chemical Engineering and Automation [*A publication*]
Sci Pap Inst Phys and Chem Res ... Scientific Papers. Institute of Physical and Chemical Research [*A publication*]
Sci Pap Inst Phys Chem Res (Jpn) ... Scientific Papers. Institute of Physical and Chemical Research (Japan) [*A publication*]
Sci Pap Inst Phys Chem Res (Tokyo) ... Scientific Papers. Institute of Physical and Chemical Research (Tokyo) [*A publication*]
Sci Pap Osaka Univ ... Scientific Papers. Osaka University [*A publication*]
Sci Pap Prague Inst Chem Technol Sect Chem Eng ... Scientific Papers. Prague Institute of Chemical Technology. Section: Chemical Engineering [*A publication*]
Sci Peche... Science et Peche [*A publication*]
Sci Peopl ... Science for People [*A publication*]
Sci Pest Contr ... Scientific Pest Control [*A publication*]
Sci Pest Control ... Scientific Pest Control [*A publication*]
Sci Pharm ... Scientia Pharmaceutica [*A publication*]
Sci Pharm Biol Lorraine ... Sciences Pharmaceutiques et Biologiques de Lorraine [*A publication*]
Sci Pict ...... Science Pictorial [*People's Republic of China*] [*A publication*]
SCIPIO .... Sales Catalog Index Project Input On-Line [*Art Institute of Chicago, Cleveland Museum of Art, Metropolitan Museum of Art*] [*Information service*] (EISS)
SCIPMIS .... Standard Civilian Personnel Management Information System [*Army*]
Sci Pro .... Science Progress [*A publication*]
Sci Pro .... Scientific Progress [*London*] [*A publication*]
Sci Proc Cardiff Med Soc ... Scientific Proceedings. Cardiff Medical Society [*A publication*]
Sci Proc R Dublin Soc ... Scientific Proceedings. Royal Dublin Society [*A publication*]
Sci Proc R Dublin Soc A ... Scientific Proceedings. Royal Dublin Society. Series A [*A publication*]
Sci Proc R Dublin Soc Ser A ... Scientific Proceedings. Royal Dublin Society. Series A [*A publication*]
Sci Proc R Dublin Soc Ser B ... Scientific Proceedings. Royal Dublin Society. Series B [*A publication*]
Sci Proc Roy Dublin Soc Ser B ... Scientific Proceedings. Royal Dublin Society. Series B [*A publication*]
Sci Prog ..... Science Progress [*A publication*]
Sci Prog Decouverte ... Science Progres Decouverte [*A publication*]
Sci Prog (Lond) ... Science Progress (London) [*A publication*]
Sci Prog (London) ... Science Progress (London) [*A publication*]
Sci Prog Nat ... Science Progres la Nature [*A publication*]
Sci Prog (New Haven) ... Science in Progress (New Haven) [*A publication*]
Sci Prog (Oxf) ... Science Progress (Oxford) [*A publication*]
Sci Progr.... Science Progress [*A publication*]
Sci Progr Decouverte ... Science Progres Decouverte [*A publication*]
Sci Psychoanal ... Science and Psychoanalysis [*A publication*]
Sci Publ Af ... Science and Public Affairs. Bulletin of the Atomic Scientists [*A publication*]
Sci Publ Fuji Photo Film Co Ltd ... Scientific Publications. Fuji Photo Film Company Limited [*Japan*] [*A publication*]
Sci Public Policy ... Science and Public Policy [*A publication*]
Sci Publ Pol ... Science and Public Policy [*A publication*]
Sci Publ Sci Mus Minn ... Scientific Publications. Science Museum of Minnesota [*A publication*]
Sci Publ Sci Mus (St Paul) ... Scientific Publications. Science Museum of Minnesota (St. Paul) [*A publication*]
Sci Q Natl Univ Peking ... Science Quarterly. National University of Peking [*A publication*]
SCIR.......... Society of Cardiovascular and Interventional Radiology (EA)
SCIR.......... Subsystem Capability Impact Reporting [*Military*] (NVT)
SCIRA .... Snipe Class International Racing Association (EA)
SCIRA .... Stable Carbon Isotope Ratio Analysis [*For determining material source*]
SCIRA .... State Central Information Reception Agency
SCIRC .... Spinal Cord Injury Research Center [*Ohio State University*] [*Research center*] (RCD)
S Circular ... South Circular [*A publication*]
Sci Rec...... Science Record [*A publication*]
Sci Rec (Chin Ed) ... Science Record (Chinese Edition) [*People's Republic of China*] [*A publication*]
Sci Rec (Peking) ... Science Record (Peking) [*A publication*]

Sci Rep Agric Coll Norway ... Scientific Reports. Agricultural College of Norway [*A publication*]
Sci Rep Cent Res Inst Kasauli ... Scientific Report. Central Research Institute. Kasauli [*A publication*]
Sci Rep College Gen Ed Osaka Univ ... Science Reports. College of General Education. Osaka University [*A publication*]
Sci Rep Coll Gen Educ Osaka Univ ... Science Reports. College of General Education. Osaka University [*Japan*] [*A publication*]
Sci Rep Fac Agr Ibaraki Univ ... Scientific Report. Faculty of Agriculture. Ibaraki University [*A publication*]
Sci Rep Fac Agric Ibaraki Univ ... Scientific Reports. Faculty of Agriculture. Ibaraki University [*A publication*]
Sci Rep Fac Agric Kobe Univ ... Science Reports. Faculty of Agriculture. Kobe University [*A publication*]
Sci Rep Fac Agric Meijo Univ ... Scientific Reports. Faculty of Agriculture. Meijo University [*A publication*]
Sci Rep Fac Agr Okayama Univ ... Scientific Report. Faculty of Agriculture. Okayama University [*A publication*]
Sci Rep Fac Educ Fukushima Univ ... Science Reports. Faculty of Education. Fukushima University [*Japan*] [*A publication*]
Sci Rep Fac Educ Gunma Univ ... Science Reports. Faculty of Education. Gunma University [*A publication*]
Sci Rep Fac Liberal Art Educ Gifu Univ Natur Sci ... Science Report. Faculty of Liberal Arts and Education. Gifu University. Natural Science [*A publication*]
Sci Rep Fac Sci Ege Univ ... Scientific Reports. Faculty of Science. Ege University [*A publication*]
Sci Rep Fac Sci Kyushu Univ Geol ... Science Reports. Faculty of Science. Kyushu University. Geology [*Japan*] [*A publication*]
Sci Rep Gov Inst Infect Dis Tokyo Imp Univ ... Scientific Reports. Government Institute for Infectious Diseases. Tokyo Imperial University [*A publication*]
Sci Rep Hirosaki Univ ... Science Reports. Hirosaki University [*A publication*]
Sci Rep Hokkaido Fish Exp Stn ... Scientific Reports. Hokkaido Fisheries Experimental Station [*A publication*]
Sci Rep Hokkaido Salmon Hatchery ... Scientific Reports. Hokkaido Salmon Hatchery [*A publication*]
Sci Rep Hoyo Univ Agr ... Scientific Report. Hoyo University of Agriculture [*A publication*]
Sci Rep Hyogo Univ Agr Fac Agr Kobe Univ ... Science Reports. Hyogo University of Agriculture and Faculty of Agriculture. Kobe University [*A publication*]
Sci Rep Hyogo Univ Agric ... Science Reports. Hyogo University of Agriculture [*A publication*]
Sci Rep Hyogo Univ Agric Ser Agric ... Science Reports. Hyogo University of Agriculture. Series Agriculture [*A publication*]
Sci Rep Hyogo Univ Agric Ser Agric Chem ... Science Reports. Hyogo University of Agriculture. Series Agricultural Chemistry [*A publication*]
Sci Rep Hyogo Univ Agric Ser Agric Hortic ... Science Reports. Hyogo University of Agriculture. Series Agriculture and Horticulture [*A publication*]
Sci Rep Hyogo Univ Agric Ser Agric Technol ... Science Reports. Hyogo University of Agriculture. Series Agriculture Technology [*A publication*]
Sci Rep Hyogo Univ Agric Ser Nat Sci ... Science Reports. Hyogo University of Agriculture. Series Natural Science [*A publication*]
Sci Rep Hyogo Univ Agric Ser Plant Prot ... Science Reports. Hyogo University of Agriculture. Series Plant Protection [*A publication*]
Sci Rep Hyogo Univ Agric Ser Zootech Sci ... Science Reports. Hyogo University of Agriculture. Series Zootechnical Science [*A publication*]
Sci Rep (India) ... Science Reporter (India) [*A publication*]
Sci Rep Indian Agric Res Inst ... Scientific Reports. Indian Agricultural Research Institute [*A publication*]
Sci Rep Inter-Union Comm Geodyn ... Scientific Report. Inter-Union Commission on Geodynamics [*A publication*]
Sci Rep Ist Super Sanita ... Scientific Reports. Istituto Superiore di Sanita [*A publication*]
Sci Rep Kagoshima Univ ... Science Reports. Kagoshima University [*A publication*]
Sci Rep Kanazawa Univ ... Science Reports. Kanazawa University [*A publication*]
Sci Rep Kanazawa Univ Part II Biol Geol ... Science Reports. Kanazawa University. Part II. Biology and Geology [*A publication*]
Sci Rep Kyoto Prefect Univ Agric ... Scientific Reports. Kyoto Prefectural University. Agriculture [*A publication*]
Sci Rep Kyoto Prefect Univ Nat Sci Life Sci ... Scientific Reports. Kyoto Prefectural University. Natural Science and Life Science [*Japan*] [*A publication*]
Sci Rep Kyoto Prefect Univ Nat Sci Living Sci Welfare Sci ... Scientific Reports. Kyoto Prefectural University. Natural Science, Living Science, and Welfare Science [*Japan*] [*A publication*]
Sci Rep Kyoto Pref Univ ... Scientific Report. Kyoto Prefectural University [*A publication*]
Sci Rep Meiji Seika Kaisha ... Scientific Reports. Meiji Seika Kaisha [*A publication*]

Sci Rep Miyagi Agr Coll ... Scientific Report. Miyagi Agricultural College [*A publication*]
Sci Rep Natl Univ Peking ... Science Reports. National University of Peking [*A publication*]
Sci Rep Niigata Univ Ser A ... Science Reports. Niigata University. Series A. Mathematics [*A publication*]
Sci Rep Niigata Univ Ser B ... Science Reports. Niigata University. Series B. Physics [*A publication*]
Sci Rep Niigata Univ Ser C ... Science Reports. Niigata University. Series C. Chemistry [*A publication*]
Sci Rep Niigata Univ Ser D Biol ... Science Reports. Niigata University. Series D. Biology [*A publication*]
Sci Rep Niigata Univ Ser E ... Science Reports. Niigata University. Series E. Geology and Mineralogy [*A publication*]
Sci Rep Niigata Univ Ser F Geol Mineral ... Science Reports. Niigata University. Series F. Geology and Mineralogy [*A publication*]
Sci Rep Osaka Univ ... Science Reports. Osaka University [*A publication*]
Sci Rep Res Inst Engrg Kanagawa Univ ... Science Reports. Kanagawa University. Research Institute for Engineering [*A publication*]
Sci Rep Res Inst Theor Phys Hiroshima Univ ... Scientific Reports. Research Institute for Theoretical Physics. Hiroshima University [*Japan*] [*A publication*]
Sci Rep Res Inst Tohoku Univ ... Science Reports. Research Institutes. Tohoku University [*A publication*]
Sci Rep Res Inst Tohoku Univ A ... Science Reports. Research Institutes. Tohoku University. Series A. Physics, Chemistry, and Metallurgy [*A publication*]
Sci Rep Res Inst Tohoku Univ Med ... Science Reports. Research Institutes. Tohoku University. Series C. Medicine [*A publication*]
Sci Rep Res Inst Tohoku Univ Ser A ... Science Reports. Research Institutes. Tohoku University. Series A. Physics, Chemistry, and Metallurgy [*A publication*]
Sci Rep Res Inst Tohoku Univ Ser B ... Science Reports. Research Institutes. Tohoku University. Series B. Technology [*A publication*]
Sci Rep Res Inst Tohoku Univ Ser C ... Science Reports. Research Institutes. Tohoku University. Series C. Medicine [*A publication*]
Sci Rep Res Inst Tohoku Univ Ser C Med ... Science Reports. Research Institutes. Tohoku University. Series C. Medicine [*A publication*]
Sci Rep Res Inst Tohoku Univ Ser D ... Science Reports. Research Institutes. Tohoku University. Series D [*A publication*]
Sci Rep Res Inst Tohoku Univ Ser D Agric ... Science Reports. Research Institutes. Tohoku University. Series D. Agriculture [*A publication*]
Sci Rep Saitama Univ Ser A ... Science Reports. Saitama University. Series A. Mathematics, Physics, and Chemistry [*A publication*]
Sci Rep Saitama Univ Ser B Biol Earth Sci ... Science Reports. Saitama University. Series B. Biology and Earth Sciences [*A publication*]
Sci Rep Shiga Pref Jr Coll ... Scientific Report. Shiga Prefectural Junior College [*A publication*]
Sci Rep Shima Marinel ... Science Report. Shima Marineland [*A publication*]
Sci Rep Soc Res Phys Chem ... Science Reports. Society for the Research of Physics Chemistry [*A publication*]
Sci Rep Tohoku Imp Univ Ser 1 ... Science Reports. Tohoku Imperial University. Series 1. Mathematics, Physics, Chemistry [*A publication*]
Sci Rep Tohoku Imp Univ Ser 3 ... Science Reports. Tohoku Imperial University. Series 3. Mineralogy, Petrology, Economic Geology [*A publication*]
Sci Rep Tohoku Imp Univ Ser 4 ... Science Reports. Tohoku Imperial University. Series 4. Biology [*A publication*]
Sci Rep Tohoku Univ ... Science Reports. Tohoku University [*A publication*]
Sci Rep Tohoku Univ Eighth Ser Phys and Astron ... Science Reports. Tohoku University. Eighth Series. Physics and Astronomy [*A publication*]
Sci Rep Tohoku Univ First Ser ... Science Reports. Tohoku University. First Series [*Japan*] [*A publication*]
Sci Rep Tohoku Univ Fourth Ser (Biol) ... Science Reports. Tohoku University. Fourth Series. Biology [*A publication*]
Sci Rep Tohoku Univ I ... Science Reports. Tohoku University. First Series [*A publication*]
Sci Rep Tohoku Univ Second Ser (Geol) ... Science Reports. Tohoku University. Second Series. Geology [*A publication*]
Sci Rep Tohoku Univ Ser 5 ... Science Reports. Tohoku University. Series 5. Geophysics [*Japan*] [*A publication*]
Sci Rep Tohoku Univ Ser IV ... Scientific Report. Tohoku University. Series IV. Biology [*A publication*]
Sci Rep Tohoku Univ Seventh Ser ... Science Reports. Tohoku University. Seventh Series [*Japan*] [*A publication*]
Sci Rep Tohoku Univ Third Ser ... Science Reports. Tohoku University. Third Series. Mineralogy, Petrology, and Economic Geology [*Japan*] [*A publication*]
Sci Rep Tohoku Univ 8th Series ... Science Reports. Tohoku University. 8th Series [*Japan*] [*A publication*]
Sci Rep Tokyo Bunrika Daigaku Sect B ... Science Reports. Tokyo Bunrika Daigaku. Section B [*A publication*]

Sci Rep Tokyo Bunrika Daigaku Sect C ... Science Reports. Tokyo Bunrika Daigaku. Section C [*A publication*]
Sci Rep Tokyo Kyoiku Daigaku Sect A ... Science Reports. Tokyo Kyoiku Daigaku. Section A [*A publication*]
Sci Rep Tokyo Kyoiku Daigaku Sect B ... Science Reports. Tokyo Kyoiku Daigaku. Section B [*A publication*]
Sci Rep Tokyo Kyoiku Daigaku Sect C ... Science Reports. Tokyo Kyoiku Daigaku. Section C [*A publication*]
Sci Rep Tokyo Woman's Christian College ... Science Reports. Tokyo Woman's Christian College [*A publication*]
Sci Rep Whales Res Inst (Tokyo) ... Scientific Reports. Whales Research Institute (Tokyo) [*A publication*]
Sci Rep Yamaguchi Univ ... Science Reports. Yamaguchi University [*A publication*]
Sci Rep Yokohama Natl Univ I ... Science Reports. Yokohama National University. Section I. Mathematics, Physics, and Chemistry [*A publication*]
Sci Rep Yokohama Natl Univ Sect II Biol Geol Sci ... Science Reports. Yokohama National University. Section II. Biological and Geological Sciences [*A publication*]
Sci Rep Yokohama Nat Univ Sect 2 ... Science Reports. Yokohama National University. Section 2. Biological and Geological Sciences [*A publication*]
Sci Rep Yokohama Nat Univ Sect I ... Science Reports. Yokohama National University. Section I. Mathematics and Physics [*A publication*]
Sci Rep Yokosuka City Mus ... Science Report. Yokosuka City Museum [*A publication*]
Sci Res Abstr ... Science Research Abstracts [*A publication*]
Sci Res Br Univ Coll ... Scientific Research in British Universities and Colleges [*A publication*]
Sci Res Counc Jam J ... Scientific Research Council of Jamaica. Journal [*A publication*]
Sci Res (Dacca) ... Scientific Research (Dacca) [*Pakistan*] [*A publication*]
Sci Res (Dacca, Bangladesh) ... Scientific Researches (Dacca, Bangladesh) [*A publication*]
Sci Res Natl Sci Ed ... Scientific Research. Natural Science Edition [*People's Republic of China*] [*A publication*]
Sci Res (NY) ... Scientific Research (New York) [*A publication*]
Sci Resour Lett ... Science Resource Letter [*A publication*]
Sci Rev ... Scienca Revuo [*A publication*]
Sci Rev ... Science Review [*A publication*]
Sci Rondo ... Scienca Rondo [*A publication*]
Sci R Toh A ... Science Reports. Research Institutes. Tohoku University. Series A. Physics, Chemistry, and Metallurgy [*A publication*]
SCIS .... Safety Containment Isolation System   (IEEE)
SCIS .... SCI Systems, Inc. [*NASDAQ symbol*]   (NQ)
SCIS .... Science Curriculum Improvement Study [*Education*]
SC Is .... Selected Judgments of the Supreme Court of Israel   (DLA)
SCIS .... Social Change in Sweden [*A publication*]
SCIS .... Spacecraft Interface Specification   (MCD)
SCIS .... Spinal Cord Injury Service [*Medicine*]
SCIS .... Standard Cubic Inches per Second   (NASA)
SCISEARCH ... Science Citation Index Search [*Institute for Scientific Information*] [*Philadelphia, PA*] [*Bibliographic database*]
Sci Serves Farm ... Science Serves Your Farm [*A publication*]
Sci Silvae ... Scientia Silvae [*A publication*]
Sci Sin ...... Scientia Sinica [*A publication*]
Sci Sinica ... Scientia Sinica [*A publication*]
Sci Sinica ... Scientia Sinica/Zhongguo Kexue [*A publication*]
Sci Sinica Ser B ... Scientia Sinica. Series B. Chemical, Biological, Agricultural, Medical, and Earth Sciences [*A publication*]
Sci Sinica Suppl ... Scientia Sinica. Supplement [*A publication*]
Sci Sinter ... Science of Sintering [*A publication*]
Sci Sintering ... Science of Sintering [*A publication*]
SCISO .... Supreme Court, Individual Slip Opinions
Sci & Soc ... Science and Society [*A publication*]
Sci Soc ...... Science and Society [*A publication*]
Sci Soc ...... Sciences Sociales [*A publication*]
Sci Sol .... Science du Sol [*A publication*]
Sci Sol (1922-28) ... Science du Sol (1922-28) [*A publication*]
SCISRS ...... Sigma Center Information Storage and Retrieval System
Sci Stud ..... Science Studies [*A publication*]
Sci Stud St Bonaventure Univ ... Science Studies. St. Bonaventure University [*A publication*]
SCIT .... Science Teacher [*A publication*]
SCIT .... Scientific, Inc. [*NASDAQ symbol*]   (NQ)
SCIT .... Small Craft Instructor Trainer [*Red Cross*]
SCIT .... Special Commissions of Income Tax [*British*]
SCIT .... Standard Change Integration and Tracking   (NASA)
SCIT .... Subcommittee on Interzonal Trade [*Allied German Occupation Forces*]
Sci Teach ... Science Teacher [*A publication*]
Sci Teach (New Delhi) ... Science Teacher (New Delhi) [*A publication*]
Sci Teach News ... Science Teachers News [*A publication*]
SCITEC ...... [*The*] Association of the Scientific, Engineering, and Technological Community of Canada
Sci Tec ...... Scienza e Tecnica [*A publication*]
Sci Tech ..... Science and Australian Technology [*A publication*]
Sci & Tech ... Science and Technology [*A publication*]

Sci Tech ..... Science and Technology [*A publication*]
Sci Tech Aerosp Rep ... Scientific and Technical Aerospace Reports [*NASA*] [*A publication*]
Sci & Tech Aerosp Reports ... Scientific and Technical Aerospace Reports [*A publication*]
Sci Tech Armement ... Sciences et Techniques de l'Armement [*A publication*]
Sci Tech Human Values ... Science, Technology, and Human Values [*A publication*]
Sci Tech Inf Process ... Scientific and Technical Information Processing [*A publication*]
Sci Tech Inf Process (Engl Transl) ... Scientific and Technical Information Processing (English Translation) [*A publication*]
Sci Tech Inf Process (Eng Transl Nauchno-Tekh Inf Ser I) ... Scientific and Technical Information Processing (English Translation of Nauchno-Tekhnicheskaya Informatsiya Seriya I) [*A publication*]
Sci Technol ... Science and Technology [*A publication*]
Sci Technol ... Sciences and Technologies. Korea University [*Republic of Korea*] [*A publication*]
Sci Technol Aliment ... Science et Technologie Alimentaire [*People's Republic of China*] [*A publication*]
Sci Technol China ... Science and Technology in China [*A publication*]
Sci Technol Jpn ... Science and Technology of Japan [*A publication*]
Sci Technol Ser ... Science Technology Series [*United States*] [*A publication*]
Sci Tech (Paris) ... Sciences et Techniques (Paris) [*A publication*]
Sci Tec Latt-Casearia ... Scienza e Tecnica Lattiero-Casearia [*A publication*]
Sci Tecnol Alimenti ... Scienza e Tecnologia degli Alimenti [*A publication*]
SCITEC-PAC ... Science and Technology Political Action Committee   (EA)
Sci Terre .... Sciences de la Terre [*A publication*]
Sci Terre Inf Geol ... Sciences de la Terre. Informatique Geologique [*A publication*]
Sci Terre Mem ... Sciences de la Terre. Memoires [*A publication*]
Sci Today (Bombay) ... Science Today (Bombay) [*A publication*]
Sci Tools .... Science Tools [*A publication*]
Sci Total Environ ... Science of the Total Environment [*A publication*]
Sci Tree Top ... Scientific Tree Topics [*A publication*]
SCIU .... Selector Control Interface Unit   (MCD)
SCI-USA .... Service Civil International - United States of America [*Crozet, VA*]   (EA)
SCIV .... Studii si Cercetari de Istorie Veche [*Later, Studii si Cercetari de Istorie Veche si Arheologie*] [*A publication*]
SCIV .... Subclavian Intravenous Injection [*Medicine*]
SCIVA .... Studii si Cercetari de Istorie Veche si Arheologie [*A publication*]
Sci Vie .... Science et Vie [*A publication*]
SCIWE .... Synthesis Center of the Institute for Wholistic Education   (EA)
Sci Works High Med Inst Pleven ... Scientific Works. Higher Medical Institute of Pleven [*A publication*]
Sci Works Res Inst Epidemiol Microbiol (Sofia) ... Scientific Works. Research Institute of Epidemiology and Microbiology (Sofia) [*A publication*]
Sci World ... Scholastic Science World [*A publication*]
Sci World ... Scientific World [*England*] [*A publication*]
SCIXF .... Scitex Corp. [*NASDAQ symbol*]   (NQ)
Sci Yearb Vet Fac (Thessalonica) ... Scientific Yearbook. Veterinary Faculty (Thessalonica) [*A publication*]
SCJ .... Congregatio Sacerdotum a Corde Jesu [*Congregation of the Priests of the Sacred Heart of Jesus*] [*Roman Catholic religious order*]
SC J .... Court of Justiciary Cases [*Scotland*]   (DLA)
SC J .... Nebraska Supreme Court Journal   (DLA)
SCJ .... Science Council of Japan   (MCD)
SC(J) .... Sessions Cases (Judiciary Reports) [*Legal*] [*British*]
SCJ .... Siberian Chemistry Journal [*A publication*]
SC & J .... Signal Collection and Jamming
SCJ .... Sisters of the Child Jesus [*Roman Catholic religious order*]
SCJ .... Sixteenth Century Journal [*A publication*]
SCJ .... Society for Collegiate Journalists   (EA)
SCJ .... Spertus College of Judaica [*Chicago, IL*]   (BJA)
SCJ .... Stretch Chuck Jaws   (MCD)
SCJ .... Super Cobra Jet [*Automotive engineering*]
SC J .... Supreme Court Journal [*India*]   (DLA)
SCJ .... Supreme Court of Justice [*British*]   (ROG)
SCJ .... Sydney Cinema Journal [*A publication*]
S C Jap ...... Studia Celtica Japonica [*A publication*]
SCJB .... Jamaica Supreme Court Judgment Books   (DLA)
SCJC .... Saint Catharine Junior College [*Kentucky*]
Sc J Cl Inv ... Scandinavian Journal of Clinical and Laboratory Investigation [*A publication*]
Sc J Dent R ... Scandinavian Journal of Dental Research [*A publication*]
Sc J Gastr ... Scandinavian Journal of Gastroenterology [*A publication*]
Sc J Haemat ... Scandinavian Journal of Haematology [*A publication*]
Sc J Immun ... Scandinavian Journal of Immunology [*A publication*]
Sc J In Dis ... Scandinavian Journal of Infectious Diseases [*A publication*]
Sc J Plast ... Scandinavian Journal of Plastic and Reconstructive Surgery [*A publication*]
Sc J Psycho ... Scandinavian Journal of Psychology [*A publication*]
Sc J Re Med ... Scandinavian Journal of Rehabilitation Medicine [*A publication*]

Sc J Resp D ... Scandinavian Journal of Respiratory Diseases [*A publication*]
Sc J Rheum ... Scandinavian Journal of Rheumatology [*A publication*]
SCJS .... Seminary College of Jewish Studies (BJA)
Sc J S Med ... Scandinavian Journal of Social Medicine [*A publication*]
ScJTh .... Scottish Journal of Theology [*Edinburgh*] [*A publication*]
Sc J Thor C ... Scandinavian Journal of Thoracic and Cardiovascular Surgery [*A publication*]
SCJUA .... Science Journal Incorporating Discovery [*A publication*]
Sc Jur .... Scottish Jurist (DLA)
Sc J Urol N ... Scandinavian Journal of Urology and Nephrology [*A publication*]
SCK .... Air Force Weapons Laboratory, Kirtland AFB, NM [*OCLC symbol*] (OCLC)
s-ck--- .... Colombia [*MARC geographic area code*] [*Library of Congress*] (LCCP)
SCK .... Serum Creatine Kinase [*An enzyme*]
SCK .... Sisters of Christ the King [*Roman Catholic religious order*]
SCK .... SS Airways, Inc. [*Mission, KS*] [*FAA designator*] (FAAC)
SCK .... Stockton [*California*] [*Airport symbol*] (OAG)
SCK .... Stockton, CA [*Location identifier*] [*FAA*] (FAAL)
SCK .... Studiecentrum voor Kernenergie [*Also, CEEN, NERC*] [*Nuclear energy*] [*Belgium*] (NRCH)
SCKD .... Society of Certified Kitchen Designers [*Hackettstown, NJ*] (EA)
SCKLS .... South Central Kansas Library System [*Library network*]
SCKTPT .... Southern California Kinesthesia and Tactile Perception Tests
ScKW .... Williamsburg Technical College, Kingstree, SC [*Library symbol*] [*Library of Congress*] (LCLS)
s-cl--- .... Chile [*MARC geographic area code*] [*Library of Congress*] (LCCP)
SCL .... Great Falls, MT [*Location identifier*] [*FAA*] (FAAL)
SCL .... Santa Clara Lawyer [*A publication*]
SCL .... Santa Clara - Ricard [*California*] [*Seismograph station code, US Geological Survey*] [*Closed*] (SEIS)
SCL .... Santiago [*Chile*] [*Airport symbol*] (OAG)
SCL .... Save a Cat League (EA)
SCL .... Scale
SCL .... Scarlet (ROG)
SCL .... Scrap Classification List [*DoD*]
Scl .... Sculptor [*Constellation*]
SCL .... Seaboard Coast Line Railroad Co. [*Subsidiary of Seaboard Coast Line Industries*] [*Later, CSX Corp.*] [*AAR code*]
SCL .... Secondary Coolant Loop [*NASA*] (NASA)
SCL .... Select Cases in Chancery Tempore King [*25 English Reprint*] [*1724-33*] (DLA)
SCL .... Selectively Cross Linked
SCL .... Senior Citizens League [*Defunct*] (EA)
SCL .... Sequential Control Logic
SCL .... Shaped Charge Liner
SCL .... Shaw Cablesystems Limited [*Toronto Stock Exchange symbol*]
SCL .... Ship Configuration List [*Navy*] (CAAL)
SCL .... Signal Corps Laboratory [*Obsolete*] [*Army*]
SCL .... Signal Corps Letter (MCD)
SCL .... Simmons College, Boston, MA [*OCLC symbol*] (OCLC)
SCL .... Single Composition Lathe-Cut [*Dental alloy*]
SCL .... Sinus Cycle Length [*Cardiology*]
SCL .... Sisters of Charity (of Leavenworth) [*Roman Catholic religious order*]
SCL .... Site Concurrence Letter (AFM)
SCL .... Skin Conductance Level [*Physiology*]
SCL .... Society for Caribbean Linguistics (EA-IO)
SCL .... Sofati Container Line [*Shipping line*]
SCL .... Soft Contact Lens
SCL .... Software Career Link [*Database producer*] [*Burlington, MA*]
SCL .... South Carolina Law Reports [*Pre-1868*] (DLA)
SCL .... South Central Regional Library System [*UTLAS symbol*]
SCL .... Southeastern Composers' League (EA)
SCL .... Space Charge Limited
SCL .... Specification Change Log [*NASA*] (NASA)
SCL .... Spontaneous Cycle Length
SCL .... Standard Classification List
SCL .... Stendhal Club [*A publication*]
SCL .... Stepan Co. [*American Stock Exchange symbol*]
SCL .... Stock Corporation Law (DLA)
SCL .... String Control Language [*Data processing*]
SCL .... Student of the Civil Law
SCL .... Studies in Canadian Literature [*A publication*]
SCL .... Studii si Cercetari Lingvistice [*A publication*]
SCL .... Super Chevys Limited [*An association*] (EA)
SCL .... Symbolic Correction Loader
SCL .... Symmetric Clipper
SCL .... Symphony Command Language [*Data processing*]
SCL .... System Command Language [*Data processing*]
SCL .... Systems Component List (KSC)
SCL .... Systems Control Language [*Data processing*]
Sc LA .... Left Scapuloanterior Position [*of the fetus*] [*Obstetrics*]
ScLangU .... United Merchants Research Center, Langley, SC [*Library symbol*] [*Library of Congress*] (LCLS)
Sc La R .... Scottish Land Court Reports [*Supplementary to Scottish Law Review*] (DLA)
Sc La Rep ... Report by the Scottish Land Court (DLA)

Sc La Rep Ap ... Appendices to the Report of the Scottish Land Court (DLA)
Sc La Rep App ... Appendices to the Report of the Scottish Land Court (DLA)
SClas .... Studii Clasice [*A publication*]
ScLau .... Laurens County Library, Laurens, SC [*Library symbol*] [*Library of Congress*] (LCLS)
SCLAV .... Sclavonic [*Language, etc.*] (ROG)
SCLC .... Small-Cell Lung Cancer [*Oncology*]
SCLC .... Southern Christian Leadership Conference (EA)
SCLC .... Space-Charge-Limited Current
SCLCS ...... Ship Command-Launch Control Subsystem [*Navy*] (CAAL)
SCLDF ...... Sierra Club Legal Defense Fund (EA)
SCLE .... Society and Leisure [*Czechoslovakia*] [*A publication*]
SCLE .... Subacute Cutaneous Lupus Erythematosus [*Medicine*]
SCLEC .... Signal Corps Logistics Evaluation Committee [*Obsolete*] [*Army*] (KSC)
SCLER ...... Scleroscope
SCLER ...... Sclerosis [*Medicine*]
SCLERA ..... Santa Catalina Laboratory for Experimental Relativity by Astrometry [*University of Arizona*] [*Research center*] (RCD)
SCLERO ..... Scleroderma [*Medicine*]
SC Libn ..... South Carolina Librarian [*A publication*]
Sc LJ .... Scottish Law Journal and Sheriff Court Record (DLA)
Sc L J .... Scottish Literary Journal [*A publication*]
SCLJ .... South Carolina Law Journal (DLA)
SCLK .... Ship's Clerk
SCLL .... Sandia Corporation, Livermore Laboratory
SCLL .... Supreme Committee for Liberation of Lithuania (EA)
SC LM .... Scottish Law Magazine and Sheriff Court Reporter (DLA)
SCLM .... Stability, Control, and Load Maneuvers (MCD)
SCLN .... Semicolon (FAAC)
SCLO .... Self-Consistent Local Orbital [*Method*] [*Mathematics*]
SCLO .... Statistical Clearance Liaison Officer [*Army*] (AABC)
SCLOG ...... Security Log [*Telecommunications*] (TEL)
Sc LP .... Left Scapuloposterior Position [*of the fetus*] [*Obstetrics*]
SC L Q .... South Carolina Law Quarterly [*A publication*]
Sc LR .... Scottish Law Reporter (DLA)
Sc LR .... Scottish Law Review and Sheriff Court Reports (DLA)
SCLRA ...... School Review [*A publication*]
Sc L Rep ... Scottish Law Reporter [*Edinburgh*] (DLA)
SC L Rev ... South Carolina Law Review [*A publication*]
SCLS .... Serra Cooperative Library System [*Library network*]
SCLS .... South Central Library System [*Library network*]
Sc LT .... Scots Law Times (DLA)
SCLY .... Scullery (MSA)
Sc M .... Master of Science
SCM .... S-Band Cassegrain Monopulse
SCM .... Sacra Caesarea Majestas [*Sacred Imperial Majesty*] [*Latin*]
SCM .... Samarium Cobalt Magnet
SCM .... Sanctae Memoriae [*Of Holy Memory*] [*Latin*]
SCM .... Scammon Bay [*Alaska*] [*Airport symbol*] (OAG)
SCM .... Scammon Bay, AK [*Location identifier*] [*FAA*] (FAAL)
SCM .... School Musician. Director and Teacher [*A publication*]
SCM .... SCM Corp. [*Formerly, Smith-Corona Marchant, Inc.*] [*NYSE symbol*]
SCM .... Selective Complement Accumulator
SCM .... Sender's Composition Message [*Cable*]
SCM .... Service Command Module [*Aerospace*] (MCD)
SCM .... Sheep Creek Mountain [*Alaska*] [*Seismograph station code, US Geological Survey*] (SEIS)
SCM .... Signal Conditioning Module
SCM .... Simulated Core Mock-Up [*or Model*] [*Nuclear energy*] (NRCH)
SCM .... Single-Channel MODEM [*Telecommunications*] (TEL)
SCM .... Single Crystal Meteorite
SCM .... Site Configuration Message
SCM .... Small-Core Memory [*Data processing*]
SCM .... Society for Computer Medicine [*Later, AAMSI*] (EA)
SCM .... Software Configuration Management [*Data processing*] (IEEE)
SCM .... Solar Cell Module
SCM .... Soluble Cytotoxic Mediator [*Immunology*]
SCM .... Special Court-Martial
SCM .... Specification Change Memorandum
SCM .... Stamp Cancelling Machine
SCM .... Standard Cubic Meter
SCM .... State-Certified Midwife [*British*]
SCM .... Steam Condensing Mode (NRCH)
SCM .... Sternocleidomastoid [*Anatomy*]
SCM .... Stillman College, Tuscaloosa, AL [*OCLC symbol*] (OCLC)
S & CM ...... Strategic and Critical Materials [*Military*]
SCM .... Strategic Cruise Missile (MCD)
SCM .... Streamline Curvature Method [*Computer program*]
SCM .... Streptococcal Cell Membrane [*Microbiology*]
SCM .... Strouds Creek & Muddlety Railroad [*AAR code*]
SCM .... Student Christian Movement [*British*]
SCM .... Subscribers' Concentration Module [*Telecommunications*] (TEL)
SCM .... Subsystem Configuration Management [*NASA*] (NASA)
SCM .... Summary Court-Martial
SCM .... Superconducting Magnet (IEEE)
SCM .... Supervision Control Module [*Telecommunications*] (TEL)

SCM .... Supply Categories of Material (MCD)
SCM .... Suppressed-Carrier Modulation
SCM .... Sussex County Magazine [*A publication*]
SCM .... Sustained Competitive Motivation
SCMA .... Silk Commission Manufacturers Association [*Defunct*] (EA)
SCMA .... Southern Cypress Manufacturers Association [*Memphis, TN*] (EA)
SCMAI .... Staff Committee on Mediation, Arbitration, and Inquiry [*American Library Association*]
SCMAT ..... Southern California Motor Accuracy Test
SCMB .... Seaby's Coin and Medal Bulletin [*A publication*]
SCMC .... S-Carboxymethylcysteine [*An amino acid*]
SCMC .... Sisters of Charity of Our Lady, Mother of the Church [*Roman Catholic religious order*]
SCMC .... Sodium(carboxymethyl)cellulose [*Organic chemistry*]
SCME .... American Federation of State, County, and Municipal Employees
SCME .... Service Center Math Error [*IRS*]
SCME .... Society of Clinical and Medical Electrologists [*Formed by a merger of Electrolysis Society of America and National Electrolysis Organization*] [*Seaford, NY*] (EA)
SCMF .... Single Contact Midge Flange
Sc M in Hyg ... Master of Science in Hygiene
SCMI .... Society to Conquer Mental Illness [*Defunct*] (EA)
SCMM .... Sisters of Charity of Our Lady, Mother of Mercy [*Roman Catholic religious order*]
SCMM .... Society of Catholic Medical Missionaries, Inc. [*Medical Mission Sisters*] [*Roman Catholic religious order*]
SCMO .... Senior Clinical Medical Officer [*British*]
SCMO .... Societe Canadienne de Meteorologie et d'Oceanographie [*Canadian Meteorological and Oceanographic Society - CMOS*]
SCMO .... Societe pour une Confederation au Moyen-Orient [*Society for Middle East Confederation - SMEC*] [*Haifa, Israel*] (EA-IO)
SCMO .... Studie- en Informatiecentrum TNO voor Milieu-Onderzoek [*TNO Study and Information Center on Environmental Research*] [*Delft, Netherlands*] [*Information service*] (EISS)
SCMO .... Subsidiary Communications Multiplex Operation [*FM radio frequency unused portion*]
SCMO .... Summary Court-Martial Order
SCMOD ...... Scale Model
SCMP .... Second-Class Mail Publications [*Later, ASCMP*] (EA)
SCMP .... Service Craft Modernization Program [*Navy*] (CAAL)
SCMP .... Society of Company Meeting Planners [*Monterey, CA*] (EA)
SCMP .... Support Center Management Plan (AAG)
SCMP .... System Contractor Management Plan [*NASA*] (NASA)
SCMPT ..... Sperm Cervical Mucus Penetration Test [*Clinical chemistry*]
SCMR .... Secretary's Committee on Mental Retardation [*Department of Health and Human Services*]
SCMR .... Special Committee on Migration and Resettlement [*Department of State*] [*World War II*]
SCMR .... Surface Composition Mapping Radiometer [*NASA*]
SCMS .... Signal Command Management System (AABC)
SCMS .... Somali Current Monitoring System [*Marine science*] (MSC)
SCMS .... Standard Configuration Management Systems [*Military*] (AFIT)
Sc Mun App Rep ... Scotch Munitions Appeals Reports [*Edinburgh and Glasgow*] (DLA)
SCN .... Citadel, Daniel Library, Charleston, SC [*OCLC symbol*] (OCLC)
SCN .... Saarbrucken [*West Germany*] [*Airport symbol*] (OAG)
SCN .... Satellite Communications Network, Inc. [*Edison, NJ*] [*Telecommunications*] (TSSD)
SCN .... Satellite Conference Network, Inc. [*NYSE symbol*] [*Telecommunications service*] (TSSD)
SCN .... Satellite Control Network
SCN .... Schematic Change Notice
SCN .... Scribe Nehemiah [*Freemasonry*]
SCN .... Search Control Number (MCD)
SCN .... Self-Checking Number
SCN .... Self-Compensating Network [*Telecommunications*] (TEL)
SCN .... Self-Contained Navigation [*NASA*]
SCN .... Sensitive Command Network
SCN .... Seventeenth-Century News [*A publication*]
SCN .... Shipbuilding and Conversion, Navy
SCN .... Ships Construction, Navy [*Funding*]
SCN .... Shortest Connected Network
SCN .... Show Cause Notice
SCN .... Silent Canyon Resources Ltd. [*Vancouver Stock Exchange symbol*]
SCN .... Single Crystal Needle
SCN .... Sisters of Charity (of Nazareth) [*Roman Catholic religious order*]
SCN .... Sorting Code Number
SCN .... Special Change Notice (KSC)
SCN .... Specific Control Number
SCN .... Specification Change Notice
SCN .... Stock Control Number
SCN .... Studii si Cercetari de Numismatica [*A publication*]
SCN .... Summary and Charge Number

SCN .... Sunset Crater National Monument [*Arizona*] [*Seismograph station code, US Geological Survey*] (SEIS)
SCN .... Supply Corps, Navy
SCN .... Suprachiasmatic Nucleus [*or Nuclei*] [*of the hypothalamus*] [*Anatomy*]
SCN .... Sylvania-Corning Nuclear Corp.
SCN .... System Change Notice
SCN .... System Control Number
SCNA .... Self-Contained Night Attack (MCD)
SCNA .... Sudden Cosmic-Noise Absorption
SCNAWAF ... Special Category Navy with Air Force
SCNB .... Societe Nationale des Chemins de Fer Belges [*Belgian National Railways*]
ScNC .... Newberry College, Newberry, SC [*Library symbol*] [*Library of Congress*] (LCLS)
SCNC .... South Carolina National [*NASDAQ symbol*] (NQ)
SCND .... Scientific Industries [*NASDAQ symbol*] (NQ)
SCND .... Second (FAAC)
scnDNA .... Deoxyribonucleic Acid, Single Copy Nuclear [*Biochemistry, Genetics*]
SCNG .... Scanning (MSA)
SCNI .... Select Committee on Nationalised Industries [*British*]
SC (Nig) ..... Judgments of the Supreme Court of Nigeria (DLA)
SCNN .... Scan-Tron Corp. [*NASDAQ symbol*] (NQ)
SCNO .... Savio Club National Office (EA)
ScNoaSH ... North Augusta Senior High School, North Augusta, SC [*Library symbol*] [*Library of Congress*] (LCLS)
SCNPWC ... Standing Committee for Nobel Prize Winners' Congresses (EA)
SCNR .... Scanner (MSA)
SCNR .... Scientific Committee of National Representatives [*NATO*]
Sc NR .... Scott's New English Common Pleas Reports (DLA)
SCNR .... Sequence Control Number Register [*Data processing*]
SCNR .... Solid-Core Nuclear Rocket [*NASA*]
SCNR .... Supreme Council for National Reconstruction [*South Korea*]
SCNS .... Self-Contained Navigation System [*NASA*]
SCNS .... Subcutaneous Nerve Stimulation [*For treatment of pain*]
SCN/SIN ... Sensitive Command Network/Sensitive Information Network (CET)
SCNTN ...... Self-Contained
SCNUL ...... Standing Conference on National and University Libraries [*British*]
SC Nurs ..... South Carolina Nursing [*A publication*]
SCO .... Converse College, Spartanburg, SC [*OCLC symbol*] (OCLC)
SCO .... Manetti Roberts [*Italy*] [*Research code symbol*]
SCO .... Sales Contracting Officer [*Army*]
SCO .... Sarawak Communist Organization [*Malaya*]
ScO .... Scientific Officer [*Also, SO*] [*Ministry of Agriculture, Fisheries, and Food*] [*British*]
SCO .... Scobey, MT [*Location identifier*] [*FAA*] (FAAL)
SCO .... Score Resources [*Vancouver Stock Exchange symbol*]
SCO .... Scoresbysund [*Greenland*] [*Seismograph station code, US Geological Survey*] [*Closed*] (SEIS)
Sco .... Scorpius [*Constellation*]
SCO .... Scottish (ROG)
Sco .... Scott's English Common Pleas Reports (DLA)
SCO .... Selective Conscientious Objection
SCO .... Service Cryptologic Organizations (MCD)
SCO .... Single Crystal Orthoferrites
SCO .... Sisters of Charity of Ottawa [*Grey Nuns of the Cross*] [*Roman Catholic religious order*]
SCO .... Society of Commissioned Officers
SCO .... Southern College of Optometry [*Tennessee*]
S/CO .... Spacecraft Observer (KSC)
SCO .... Spacecraft Operations [*NASA*] (KSC)
SCO .... Squadron Command Officer (AAG)
SCO .... Squadron Constructor Officer [*Navy*] [*British*]
SCO .... Staff Communications Office [*Army*]
SCO .... Start Checkout [*NASA*] (NASA)
SCO .... State Coordinating Officer [*Federal disaster planning*]
SCO .... Statistical Control Office [*or Officer*]
SCO .... Studi Classici e Orientali [*A publication*]
SCO .... Subcarrier Oscillator
SCO .... Subcommissural Organ [*Neuroanatomy*]
SCO .... Subcontract Consignment Order
SCO .... Successor Contracting Officer (MCD)
SCO .... Supercritical Oxygen (MCD)
SCO .... Switch Closure Out (MCD)
SCO .... Synthetic Crude Oil [*Fuel technology*]
SCO .... System Counterpart Officer [*Military*] (AFIT)
SCOA .... Sample Cave Operating Area [*Nuclear energy*] (NRCH)
SCOA .... Supreme Council Order of the Amaranth (EA)
SCOBA .... Standing Conference of the Canonical Orthodox Bishops in the Americas (EA)
SCOBO ..... Satellite Collection Buoy Observations
SCOBOL .... Structured COBOL
SCOC .... Sediment Community Oxygen Consumption [*Marine biology*]
SCOC .... Short-Circuit Output Current
SCOC .... Support Command Operations Center [*Military*]
SCOCE .... Special Committee on Compromising Emanations (AABC)

SCOCLIS ... Standing Conference of Co-Operative Library and Information Services [British]
Sco Costs ... Scott's Costs in the High Court [4th ed.] [1880]   (DLA)
SCOD .... Societe Cooperative Oecumenique de Developpement [Ecumenical Development Cooperative Society - EDCS] [Amersfoort, Netherlands]   (EA-IO)
SCOD .... South Coast One Design [Cruising boat]
SCODA ...... Scan Coherent Doppler Attachment
SCODS ...... Study Commission on Ocean Data Stations [Marine science]   (MSC)
SCOE .... Special Checkout Equipment [NASA]   (NASA)
SCOFA ...... Shipping Control Office, Forward Area [Navy]
SCOFOR ... Scottish Forces [World War II]
SCOFOR ... Scouting Force [Navy]
ScoGaelS .. Scottish Gaelic Studies [A publication]
ScoGS .... Scottish Gaelic Studies [A publication]
S and COH ... Son and Coheir [Genealogy]
SCOHR ...... Students Committee on Human Rights
SCOL .... School   (NVT)
SCOLA .... Second Consortium of Local Authorities
SCOLAG Bull ... Scottish Legal Action Group. Bulletin   (DLA)
Scol Anon ... Scolia Anonyma [Classical studies]   (OCD)
SCOLAR .... Standard Costing of Laboratory Resources
Scol Att ...... Scolia Attica [Classical studies]   (OCD)
SCOLAVNMED ... School of Aviation Medicine [Later, School of Aerospace Medicine]
SCOLCAP ... Scottish Libraries Cooperative Automation Project
SCOLE .... Standing Committee on Library Education [American Library Association]
SCOLMA .... Standing Conference on Library Materials on Africa [British]
SCOLSHIP ... Schoolship [Navy]   (NVT)
SCOM .... Scientific Committee [NATO]   (NATG)
SCOM .... Site Cutover Manager [Telecommunications]   (TEL)
SCOM .... Spacecraft Communicator
SCOMA ...... Shipping Control Office, Marianas [Navy]
SCOMO ...... Satellite Collection of Meteorological Observations
S/COMPT ... Side Compartment [Automotive engineering]
SCON .... Syscon Corp. [NASDAQ symbol]   (NQ)
Scone & Upper Hunter Hist Soc J ... Scone and Upper Hunter Historical Society. Journal [A publication]
Sco NR .... Scott's New English Common Pleas Reports   (DLA)
SCONRES ... Senate Concurrent Resolution   (AFIT)
SCONS .... Shipment Control System [Military]
SCONT .... Ship Control
SCONUL .... Standing Conference on National and University Libraries [British]
SCOOP .... Scientific Computation of Optimal Programs   (IEEE)
SCOOP .... Scientific Computation of Optimum Procurement [Air Force]
SCOOP .... Stop Crapping on Our Premises [New York City project opposing the litter caused by dog dirt]
SCOOP .... Strategic Confirmation of Optical Phenomenology
SCOOP .... Support Plan to Continuity of Operations Plan
SCOP .... Ferrocarril del Sureste [AAR code]
SCOP .... Scopolamine [Anticholinergic compound]
SCOP .... Single Copy Order Plan [Later, STOP] [Bookselling]
SCOP .... Steering Committee on Pilotage
SCOPE .... Schedule-Cost-Performance   (IEEE)
SCOPE .... Scientific Committee on Problems of the Environment [International Council of Scientific Unions]   (EA)
SCOPE .... Scripps Cooperative Oceanic Productivity Expedition [1956]
SCOPE .... Senior Citizens' Opportunities for Personal Enrichment [Federal antipoverty program]
SCOPE .... Sequential Customer Order Processing Electronically
SCOPE .... Service Center of Private Enterprise
SCOPE .... Simple Checkout-Oriented Program Language
SCOPE .... Southern Coastal Plains Expedition [Marine science]   (MSC)
SCOPE .... Special Committee on Paperless Entries [California interbank group]
SCOPE .... Special Committee on Problems of the Environment [of International Council of Scientific Unions]
SCOPE .... Stromberg Central Operations Panel - Electric
SCOPE .... Student Council on Pollution and the Environment [Association conceived in late 1969 by then Secretary of the Interior Walter J. Hickel]
SCOPE .... Subsystem for the Control of Operations and Plan Evaluation
SCOPE .... Summer Community Organization and Political Education Program
SCOPE .... Supervisory Control of Program Execution   (MCD)
SCOPE .... Supportive Council on Preventive Effort [Ohio]
SCOPE .... System to Coordinate the Operation of Peripheral Equipment
SCOPES .... Squad Combat Operations Exercise, Simulation [Military]
SCOPP ...... School-College Orientation Program of Pittsburgh
SCOPS ...... Select Committee on Ocean Policy Study [Federal Council for Science and Technology]
SCOR .... Scientific Committee on Oceanic Research [ICSU] [Nova Scotia, Canada]   (EA-IO)
Scor .... Scorpius [Constellation]
SCOR .... Self-Calibrating Omnirange
SCOR .... Small Cycle Observation Recording
SCOR .... Special Center of Research [HEW]
SCOR .... Special Committee on Oceanographic Research

SCOR .... Specialized Center of Research in Atherosclerosis [University of Chicago] [Research center]   (RCD)
SCOR .... Status Control of Rejections   (MCD)
SCOR .... Syncor International Corp. [NASDAQ symbol]   (NQ)
SCORAN .... Scorer and Analyzer [Computerized educational testing]
ScOrC .... Claflin College, Orangeburg, SC [Library symbol] [Library of Congress]   (LCLS)
SCORDES ... Sferics Correlation Detection System
SCORE ...... Satellite Computer-Operated Readiness Equipment [SSD]
SCORE ...... Scientific Cooperative Operational Research Expedition [Marine science]   (MSC)
SCORE ...... Selection Copy and Reporting   (IEEE)
SCORE ...... Selective Conversion and Retention [Navy]
SCORE ...... Service Corps of Retired Executives Association [Small Business Administration] [Washington, DC]   (EA)
SCORE ...... Short Course Off-Road Event [Off-road vehicle racing]
SCORE ...... Signal Communication by Orbiting Relay Equipment [Radio]
Score .... Simulated Combat Operations Range Equipment   (MCD)
SCORE ...... Space Communications for Orbiting Relay Equipment   (MCD)
SCORE ...... Special Claim on Residual Equity
SCORE ...... Spectral Combinations for Reconnaissance Exploitation [Photography]
SCORE ...... Standing Committee on Regulatory Effectiveness [Nuclear Regulatory Commission]   (NRCH)
SCORE ...... Stratified Charge, Omnivorous Rotary Engine [Automotive engineering]
SCORE ...... Street Corner Offense Reduction Experiment
SCORE ...... Student Competitions on Relevant Engineering
SCORE ...... Subsystem Control of Required Equipment   (MCD)
SCORE ...... System for Computerized Olympic Results and Events [Texas Instruments, Inc.]
SCORE ...... System Cost and Operational Resource Evaluation   (MCD)
SCORE ...... Systematic Communications of Range Effectiveness   (MUGU)
SCORE ...... Systems Coordinative Reporting   (MCD)
SCORES ..... Scenario Oriented Recurring Evaluation System [Military]
SCORN ...... Special Committee Opposing Resurgent Nazism
SCORON .... Scouting Squadron
SCOROR .... Secretary's Committee on Research on Reorganization [Navy]
SCORP ...... Statewide Comprehensive Outdoor Recreation Plan
SCORPI ..... Subcritical Carbon-Moderated Reactor Assembly for Plutonium Investigations   (MCD)
SCORPIO ... Subcritical Carbon-Moderated Reactor Assembly for Plutonium Investigations [British]   (DEN)
SCORPIO ... Subject-Content-Oriented Retriever for Processing Information On-Line [Congressional Research Service]
ScOrS .... South Carolina State College, Orangeburg, SC [Library symbol] [Library of Congress]   (LCLS)
SCORU ...... Statistical Control and Operations Records Unit [Air Force]
SCOS .... Scottish Certificate in Office Studies
ScoS .... Scottish Studies [A publication]
SCOS .... Small Computer and Office Systems [Honeywell, Inc.]
SCOS .... Subsystem Computer Operating System [NASA]   (NASA)
SCOSA ...... Sadtler Commercial Spectra [A publication]
SCOST .... Special Committee on Space Technology   (KSC)
SCOSTEP ... Scientific Committee on Solar Terrestrial Physics   (EA)
SCOT .... Satellite Communication Terminal [Navy] [British]   (MCD)
SCOT .... Satellite Communications Overseas Transmission
SCOT .... Scotland [or Scottish]
SCOT .... Scottish [or Scotsman]   (ROG)
SCOT .... Shipborne SATCOM Terminal [British]
SCOT .... Standby Compatible One-Tape [System]
SCOT .... Steel Car of Tomorrow
SCOT .... Supplementary Checkout Trailer
SCOT .... Support-Coated Open-Tubular [Column] [Chromatography]
SCOTAC .... Speech-Compatible Tactile Communicant   (MCD)
Scot Agr .... Scottish Agriculture [A publication]
Scot AL ...... Scottish Art and Letters [A publication]
SCOTAPLL ... Standing Conference on Theological and Philosophical Libraries in London
Scot App Rep ... Scottish Appeal Reports   (DLA)
Scot Archaeol Forum ... Scottish Archaeological Forum [A publication]
Scot Art R ... Scottish Art Review [A publication]
Scot Art Rev ... Scottish Art Review [A publication]
SCOTBEC ... Scottish Business Education Council
SCOTBUILD ... Scottish Building and Public Works Exhibition [Scottish Exhibitions Ltd.]   (TSPED)
SCOTCH .... Summer Cultural Opportunities for Teams and Children [National music program]
Scot Edu St ... Scottish Educational Studies [A publication]
SCOTENG ... Scottish Engineering Exhibition for Design, Production, and Automation [Scottish Exhibitions Ltd.]   (TSPED)
SCOTF .... Scottie Gold Mines [NASDAQ symbol]   (NQ)
Scot Geog M ... Scottish Geographical Magazine [A publication]
Scot Geogr Mag ... Scottish Geographical Magazine [A publication]
Scot GM ..... Scottish Geographical Magazine [A publication]
Scot Hist R ... Scottish Historical Review [A publication]
Scot Hist Riv ... Scottish Historical Review [A publication]
SCOTHOT ... Scottish Hotel, Catering, and Licensed Trade Exhibition [Scottish Exhibitions Ltd.]   (TSPED)

SCOTICE ... Scotland to Iceland Submarine Cable System [*Telecommunications*]   (TEL)
Scot J Geol ... Scottish Journal of Geology [*A publication*]
Scot J Pol Econ ... Scottish Journal of Political Economy [*A publication*]
Scot J Poli ... Scottish Journal of Political Economy [*A publication*]
Scot J Rel... Scottish Journal of Religious Studies [*A publication*]
ScotJt ...... Scottish Journal of Theology [*A publication*]
Scot J Th.... Scottish Journal of Theology [*A publication*]
Scot J Theo ... Scottish Journal of Theology [*A publication*]
Scot Jur ..... Scottish Jurist   (DLA)
SCOTL .... Scotland   (ROG)
Scot Law J ... Scottish Law Journal [*Glasgow*]   (DLA)
Scotl Dep Agric Fish Mar Res ... Scotland Department of Agriculture and Fisheries. Marine Research [*A publication*]
Scotl Dep Agric Fish Tech Bull ... Scotland Department of Agriculture and Fisheries. Technical Bulletin [*A publication*]
Scot Lit J.... Scottish Literary Journal [*A publication*]
Scot LJ...... Scottish Law Journal and Sheriff Court Record   (DLA)
Scot LM ..... Scottish Law Magazine and Sheriff Court Reporter   (DLA)
Scot L Mag ... Scottish Law Magazine [*Edinburgh, Scotland*]   (DLA)
Scot LR ...... Scottish Law Reporter   (DLA)
Scot LR ...... Scottish Law Review [*A publication*]
Scot L Rep ... Scottish Law Reporter   (DLA)
Scot L Rev ... Scottish Law Review [*A publication*]
Scot LT ...... Scots Law Times   (DLA)
Scot Med J ... Scottish Medical Journal [*A publication*]
ScotNAE .... Scottish National Antarctic Expedition [*1902-04*]
SCOTNATS ... Scottish Nationalists
Scot R .... Scottish Review [*A publication*]
SCOTRACEN ... Scouting Training Center [*Navy*]
SCOTS .... Surveillance and Control of Transmission Systems [*Bell Laboratories*]
SCOTS .... System Checkout Test Set   (MCD)
Scots LTR ... Scots Law Times Reports   (DLA)
Scots Mag ... Scots Magazine [*A publication*]
Scots RR ..... Scots Revised Reports [*1707-1873*]   (DLA)
Scot Stud... Scottish Studies [*A publication*]
Scott .... Scott's English Common Pleas Reports   (DLA)
Scott .... Scott's Reports [*25, 26 New York Civil Procedure*]   (DLA)
SCOTT ...... Single Channel Objective Tactical Terminal [*Army*]   (RDA)
SCOTT ...... Synchronous Continuous Orbital Three-Dimensional Tracking
Scott Agric ... Scottish Agriculture [*A publication*]
Scott Australas ... Scottish Australasian [*A publication*]
Scott Bee J ... Scottish Bee Journal [*A publication*]
Scott Beekeep ... Scottish Beekeeper [*A publication*]
Scott Beekpr ... Scottish Beekeeper [*A publication*]
Scott Birds ... Scottish Birds [*A publication*]
Scott Birds J Scott Ornithol Club ... Scottish Birds. Journal. Scottish Ornithologists' Club [*A publication*]
Scott Econ Bull ... Scottish Economic Bulletin [*A publication*]
Scott Econ Soc Hist ... Scottish Economic and Social History [*A publication*]
Scott Educ Rev ... Scottish Educational Review [*A publication*]
Scott Elect Engr ... Scottish Electrical Engineer [*A publication*]
Scott (Eng) ... Scott's English Common Pleas Reports   (DLA)
Scott Field ... Scottish Field [*A publication*]
Scott Fish Bull ... Scottish Fisheries Bulletin [*A publication*]
Scott Fish Res Rep ... Scottish Fisheries Research Report [*A publication*]
Scott Fmr... Scottish Farmer and Farming World [*A publication*]
Scott For.... Scottish Forestry [*A publication*]
Scott For J ... Scottish Forestry Journal [*A publication*]
Scott Geogr Mag ... Scottish Geographical Magazine [*A publication*]
Scottish Art R ... Scottish Art Review [*A publication*]
Scottish Bankers M ... Scottish Bankers Magazine [*A publication*]
Scottish Econ Bul ... Scottish Economic Bulletin [*A publication*]
Scottish Ednl J ... Scottish Educational Journal [*A publication*]
Scottish Ednl Studies ... Scottish Educational Studies [*A publication*]
Scottish Geog Mag ... Scottish Geographical Magazine [*A publication*]
Scottish J Pol Economy ... Scottish Journal of Political Economy [*A publication*]
Scottish Mus ... Scottish Music and Drama [*A publication*]
Scott J........ Reporter, English Common Bench Reports   (DLA)
Scott J Geol ... Scottish Journal of Geology [*A publication*]
Scott J Polit Econ ... Scottish Journal of Political Economy [*A publication*]
Scott J Theology ... Scottish Journal of Theology [*A publication*]
Scott Labour Hist Soc J ... Scottish Labour History Society Journal [*A publication*]
Scott Lit J ... Scottish Literary Journal [*A publication*]
Scott Mar Biol Assoc Annu Rep ... Scottish Marine Biological Association. Annual Report [*A publication*]
Scott Marxist ... Scottish Marxist [*A publication*]
Scott Med J ... Scottish Medical Journal [*A publication*]
Scott Nat.... Scottish Naturalist [*A publication*]
Scott NR ..... Scott's New English Common Pleas Reports   (DLA)
SCOTT-R ... Super-Critical, Once-Thru Tube Reactor [*Experiment*] [*General Electric Co.*]
Scott Trade Union Rev ... Scottish Trade Union Review [*A publication*]
Scott Tradit ... Scottish Tradition [*A publication*]
SCOU .... Ship Course
SC Oudh .... Oudh Select Cases [*India*]   (DLA)
SCOUS...... Spectrum Clear of Unknown Signals   (MUGU)
SCOUT...... Surface-Controlled Oxide Unipolar Transistor

Scouting in NSW ... Scouting in New South Wales [*A publication*]
SCOWAH ... Schmulowitz Collection of Wit and Humor [*San Francisco Public Library*]
SCOWR...... Special Committee on Water Research [*International Council of Scientific Unions*]
SCP............ Brotherhood of Sleeping Car Porters [*Later, BRAC*]   (EA)
SCP............ SAGE [*Semiautomatic Ground Environment*] Computer Program
SCP............ St. Catharines Public Library [*UTLAS symbol*]
SCP............ Satellite Cloud Photograph
SCP............ Scanner Control Power   (MCD)
SCP............ Scanning Phased Array
SCP............ Schematic Change Proposal
SCP............ Scoops [*A publication*]
SCP............ Scope Industries [*American Stock Exchange symbol*]
SCP............ Scrip   (ROG)
SCP............ Script [*Films, television, etc.*]
SCP............ Secondary Control Point
SCP............ Sector Command Post [*Military*]
SCP............ Secure Conferencing Project
SCP............ Security Classification Procedure
SCP............ Self-Consistent Phonon
SCP............ Senior Companion Program [*Washington, DC*]   (EA)
SCP............ Service Control Point [*DoD*]   (AFIT)
SCP............ Servo-Controlled Positioner
SCP............ Sheep Choroid Plexus
SCP............ Short-Circuit Protection
SCP............ Silver Cup Resources Ltd. [*Vancouver Stock Exchange symbol*]
SCP............ Simulation Control Program [*Military*]   (CAAL)
SCP............ Simulator Control Panel [*NASA*]
SCP............ Single-Cell Protein
SCP............ Small Cardioactive Peptide [*Biochemistry*]
SCP............ Smaller Communities Program [*Department of Labor*]
SCP............ Social Credit Party of Canada [*Parti Credit Social du Canada*]   (PPW)
SCP............ Societe Canadienne de la Population [*Canadian Population Society - CPS*]
SCP............ Societe Culinaire Philanthropique   (EA)
SCP............ Society of California Pioneers   (EA)
SCP............ Society for Czechoslovak Philately [*Formerly, CZPS*]   (EA)
SCP............ Sodium Cellulose Phosphate [*Kidney-stone drug*]
SCP............ Software Change Proposal   (MCD)
SCP............ Solar Cell Panel
SCP............ Sonobuoy Control Panel
SCP............ Spacecraft Platform [*NASA*]
SCP............ Spanish Communist Party
SCP............ Special Category Patient [*Aeromedical evacuation*]
SCP............ Specific Candlepower   (NASA)
SCP............ Spherical Candlepower
SCP............ Spiritual Counterfeits Project   (EA)
SCP............ Standardized Care Plans [*for hospitals*]
SCP............ State College [*Pennsylvania*] [*Seismograph station code, US Geological Survey*]   (SEIS)
SCP............ Station Communications Processor
SCP............ Sterol Carrier Protein
SCP............ Stromberg-Carlson Practices [*Telecommunications*]   (TEL)
SCP............ Structural Ceramic Panel
SCP............ Subcontract Proposal   (AAG)
SCP............ Sudanese Communist Party   (PD)
SCP............ Supervisor's Control Panel
SCP............ Supervisory Control Program [*Burroughs Corp.*]
SCP............ Supplier's Contract Property   (MCD)
SCP............ Supply Cataloging Program
SCP............ Supply Control Plan [*World War II*]
SCP............ Survey Control Point
SCP............ Symbolic Conversion Program   (BUR)
SCP............ Synthetic Fuels Commercialization Program [*Also, SFCP*] [*Energy Resources Council*]
SCP............ Syrian Communist Party   (PPW)
SCP............ System Change Package
SCP............ System Communication Pamphlet   (IEEE)
SCP............ System Concept Paper [*Army*]   (RDA)
SCP............ System Control Processor [*Honeywell, Inc.*]
SCP............ System Control Programing [*Data processing*]
SCP............ Systems Change Proposal   (AFM)
s̄CP............ Without Chest Pain [*Medicine*]
SCPA .... Solar Cell Panel Assembly
SCPA .... Southern Coal Producers Association [*Defunct*]   (EA)
SCPA .... Spacecraft Payload Adapter   (MCD)
Sc Parliament ... Science in Parliament [*A publication*]
SCPC .... Signal Corps Pictorial Center [*Obsolete*] [*Army*]
SCPC .... Single-Channel-per-Carrier [*Telecommunications*]
SCPCU ...... Society of Chartered Property and Casualty Underwriters   (EA)
SCPD .... Staff Civilian Personnel Division [*Army*]
S & CP Dec ... Ohio Decisions   (DLA)
SCPD OC of SA ... Staff Civilian Personnel Division, Office, Chief of Staff [*Army*]   (AABC)
SCPD OCSA ... Staff Civilian Personnel Division, Office, Chief of Staff [*Army*]   (AABC)
SCPE.......... Scope, Inc. [*NASDAQ symbol*]   (NQ)

SCPE......... Specialized Customer Premises Equipment [*for the handicapped*]
Sc for People ... Science for People [*A publication*]
SCPF......... Sacra Congregatio de Propaganda Fide [*Sacred Congregation for the Propagation of the Faith*] [*Latin*]
SCPGB...... Revista. Sociedad Cientifica del Paraguay [*A publication*]
SCPI......... Scientists' Committee for Public Information [*Defunct*]
SCPI......... Small Computer Program Index [*ALLM Books*] [*Information service*] [*A publication*] [*British*] (EISS)
SCPI......... Structural Clay Products Institute [*Later, BIA*] (EA)
SCPL......... Signal Corps Photographic Laboratory [*Obsolete*] [*Army*]
SCPM......... Sample Collection and Preparation Module [*X-ray spectrometry*]
SCPM......... Semiautomatic Circuit Performance Monitor [*Navy*] (MCD)
SCPMT...... Southern California Perceptual Motor Tests
SCPNT...... Southern California Postrotary Nystagmus Test
SCPO......... Second-Class Post Office
SCPO......... Senior Chief Petty Officer [*Navy rating*]
SCPP......... Sierra Cooperative Pilot Project [*Department of the Interior*]
SCPP......... Supreme Court, Preliminary Prints
SCPP......... Surveyor Command Preparation Program [*Aerospace*]
SCPPS...... Secondary Containment Purge and Pressure Control System [*Nuclear energy*] (NRCH)
SCPR......... Semiconductor Parameter Retrieval [*Information Handling Services*] [*Database*]
SCPR......... Standard Cardiopulmonary Resuscitation
SCPRF...... Structural Clay Products Research Foundation [*Absorbed by BIA*] (EA)
SCPS......... Scopas Technology [*NASDAQ symbol*] (NQ)
SCPS......... Servo-Controlled Positioning System
SCPS......... Society of Civil and Public Servants [*A union*] [*British*]
SCP(S)...... Subscribers' Call Processing (Subsystem) [*Telecommunications*] (TEL)
SCPSC...... South Carolina Public Service Commission Reports (DLA)
SCPT......... SAGE [*Semiautomatic Ground Environment*] Computer Programing Training
SCPT......... Security Control Point (MUGU)
SCPT......... Self-Consistent Perturbation Theory [*Physics*]
SCPTR...... Standing Committee on Personnel Training and Readiness [*Navy*]
SCQ......... Hanscom Air Force Base, Base Library, Hanscom AFB, MA [*OCLC symbol*] (OCLC)
SCQ......... Saco Resources [*Vancouver Stock Exchange symbol*]
SCQ......... Santiago De Compostela [*Spain*] [*Airport symbol*] (OAG)
SCQ......... Sisters of Charity of Quebec [*Grey Nuns*] [*Roman Catholic religious order*]
SCQC......... Scout Crew Qualification Course [*Army*]
SCQE......... Squad Combat Qualification Exercise [*Army*] (INF)
SCR......... Cape Colony Supreme Court Reports (DLA)
SCR......... Chinook Regional Library, Swift Current, Saskatchewan [*Library symbol*] [*National Library of Canada*] (NLC)
SCR......... Juta's Supreme Court Cases [*1880-1910*] [*Cape Of Good Hope, South Africa*] (DLA)
SCR......... Law Reports of Supreme Court of Sarawak, North Borneo, and Brunei (DLA)
SCR......... San Cristabal [*Chile*] [*Seismograph station code, US Geological Survey*] [*Closed*] (SEIS)
SCR......... Scanning Control Register
SCR......... Schedule Change Request [*NASA*] (NASA)
SCR......... Score (ROG)
SCR......... Scourer[*s*] [*or Scouring*] [*Freight*]
SCR......... Scranton Public Library, Scranton, PA [*OCLC symbol*] (OCLC)
Scr......... Scrapie [*Animal pathology*]
SCR......... Scratch
SCR......... Screw (AAG)
scr......... Scribe [*MARC relator code*] [*Library of Congress*]
Scr......... Scrinium [*A publication*]
SCR......... Scrip (ADA)
Scr......... Scripture (BJA)
SCR......... Scruple
SCR......... Scrutiny [*A publication*]
SCR......... Scurry-Rainbow Oil Ltd. [*Toronto Stock Exchange symbol*]
SCR......... Sea Containers Ltd. [*NYSE symbol*]
SCR......... Section Cross Reference (MCD)
SCR......... Security Airways & Freight Express, Inc. [*Glen Burnie, MD*] [*FAA designator*] (FAAC)
SCR......... Selective Catalytic Reduction
SCR......... Selective Chopper Radiometer
SCR......... Selenium Control Rectifier (NRCH)
SCR......... Semiconductor
SCR......... Semiconductor-Controlled Rectifier
SCR......... Senior Common Room [*in British colleges and public schools*]
SCR......... Sequence Checking Routine
scr......... Serbo-Croatian (Roman) [*MARC language code*] [*Library of Congress*] (LCCP)
SCR......... Series Control Relay
SCr......... Serum Creatinine [*Hematology*]
SCR......... Set Complete Radio
SCR......... Shift Count Register
SCR......... Ship to Component Record [*Navy*]
SCR......... Short-Circuit Ratio

SCR......... Signal Conditioning Rack
SCR......... Signal Conversion Relay [*Telecommunications*] (TEL)
SCR......... Signal Corps Radio [*Followed by model number*] [*Obsolete*] [*Army*]
SCR......... Silicon-Controlled Rectifier [*Electronics*]
SCR......... Single-Channel Reception (DEN)
SCR......... Single Character Recognition
SCR......... Skin Conductance Response
SCR......... Sneak Circuit Report [*NASA*] (NASA)
SCR......... Society of Cardiovascular Radiology [*Later, SCVIR*] (EA)
SCR......... Society for Cultural Relations between the Peoples of the British Commonwealth and the USSR
SCR......... Sodium-Cooled Reactor
SCR......... Software Change Request [*NASA*]
SCR......... Software Correction Report (CAAL)
SCR......... Software Cost Reduction [*Data processing*]
SCR......... Solar Cosmic Radiation [*or Ray*]
SCR......... [*Department of*] Soldiers' Civil Reestablishment [*Canada*]
SCR......... SONAR Control Room
SCR......... South Carolina Reports (DLA)
SCR......... South Carolina Review [*A publication*]
SCR......... Soviet Cybernetics Review [*A publication*]
SCR......... Spacecraft Received Time
SCR......... Spanish Communication Region [*Air Force*] (MCD)
SCR......... Specification Clarification Request (MCD)
SCR......... Speed Change Rate
SCR......... Static Card Reader
SCR......... Strip Chart Recorder [*NASA*]
S Cr......... Strumenti Critici [*A publication*]
SCR......... Studies in Comparative Religion [*A publication*]
SCR......... Sub-Chief Ranger [*Ancient Order of Foresters*]
SCR......... Summary Control Report [*Planning and Production*] [*Navy*]
SCR......... Supersonic Combustion Ramjet
SCR......... Support Control Room [*NASA*] (KSC)
SCR......... Supreme Court Reports [*India*] (DLA)
SCR......... Supreme Court Reports [*1928-41, 1946-51*] [*Sarawak*] (DLA)
SCR......... Supreme Court Reports [*Canada*] (DLA)
SCR......... Supreme Court Reports [*1862-76*] [*New South Wales, Australia*] (DLA)
SCR......... Surface-Contour RADAR
SCR......... Syrene-Chloroprene Rubber
SCR......... System Change Request
SCR......... System Control Registers [*Data processing*]
SCR......... System Control Routine
SCRA......... Single Channel Radio Access Subsystem (MCD)
SC & RA...... Specialized Carriers and Rigging Association [*Alexandria, VA*] (EA)
SCRA......... Stanford Center for RADAR Astronomy
SCRA......... Steel Can Recycling Association [*Pittsburgh, PA*] (EA)
SCRA......... Supreme Council of the Royal Arcanum (EA)
SCRAC...... Standing Conference of Regional Advisory Councils for Further Education
SCRAG...... Senior Civilian Representative, Attorney General [*Department of Justice civil disturbance unit*]
SCRAM...... Safety Control Rod Axe Man [*Nuclear energy*] (IEEE)
SCRAM...... Selective Combat Range Artillery Missile
SCRAM...... Self-Corrected Remedial Aid and Media [*Teaching method*]
SCRAM...... Service Change Release and Manufacture (MCD)
SCRAM...... Several Compilers Reworked and Modified
SCRAM...... Short-Range Attack Missile
SCRAM...... Space Capsule Regulator and Monitor
SCRAM...... Spares Components Reidentification and Modification [*Program*] [*DoD*]
SCRAM...... Spares Control, Release, and Monitoring
SCRAM...... Special Criteria for Retrograde of Army Materiel (AABC)
SCRAM...... Supersonic Combustion Ramjet Missile
SCRAM...... Synanon Committee for Responsible American Media [*Later, SCRAP*]
SCRAMJET ... Supersonic Combustion Ramjet
SCRAMM... System Calibration, Repair, and Maintenance Model [*Military*] (CAAL)
SCraneN...... Stephen Crane Newsletter [*A publication*]
SCRAP...... Selective Curtailment of Reports and Paperwork [*Navy*]
SCRAP...... Series Computation of Reliability and Probability [*Data processing*]
SCRAP...... Simple Complex Reaction-Time Apparatus
SCRAP...... Society for Completely Removing All Parking Meters
SCRAP...... Students Challenging Regulatory Agency Proceedings [*Student legal action organization*]
SCRAP...... Super-Caliber Rocket-Assisted Projectile (IEEE)
SCRAP...... Synanon Committee for a Responsible American Press [*Formerly, SCRAM*] (EA)
SCRAPE..... Screening Country Requirements Against Plus Excess [*DoD*]
Scrat Bdg Soc ... Scratchley's Building Societies [*5th ed.*] [*1883*] (DLA)
Scrat & Bra ... Scratchley and Brabook's Building Societies [*2nd ed.*] [*1882*] (DLA)
SCRATCHPAD ... [*A*] programing language (CSR)
Scrat Life Ass ... Scratchley's Life Assurance [*13th ed.*] [*1887*] (DLA)
SCRB......... Software Configuration Review Board (CAAL)
SCRB......... Structured Case Review Blank
SCRBA...... Student Committee for the Right to Bear Arms [*Defunct*] (EA)

SCRD .... Scientific Radio Systems [*NASDAQ symbol*]   (NQ)
SCRD .... Secondary Control Rod Driveline [*Nuclear energy*]   (NRCH)
SCRD .... Student Coalition for the Right to Drink   (EA)
SCRDB ...... Screwed Bonnet
SCRDE ...... Stores and Clothing Research and Development Establishment
            [*British*]
Scr Demolinguist ... Scritti Demolinguistici [*A publication*]
SCRDM ...... Secondary Control Rod Drive Mechanism [*Nuclear
            energy*]   (NRCH)
SCRDN ...... Screw Down
SCRE .... Scandinavian Review [*A publication*]
SCRE .... Supreme Cossack Representation in Exile   (EA)
SCREB .... Scientific Research [*A publication*]
Screen Ed ... Screen Education [*A publication*]
Screen Ed Notes ... Screen Education Notes [*A publication*]
SCREENEX ... Screening Exercise [*Military*]   (NVT)
SC Rep .... Juta's Supreme Court Cases [*1880-1910*] [*Cape Of Good
            Hope, South Africa*]   (DLA)
SC Res .... Senate Concurrent Resolution   (DLA)
SC Research Plan Devel Board Bull ... South Carolina Research Planning
            and Development Board. Bulletin [*A publication*]
SC Resour Cent Tech Rep ... South Carolina Marine Resources Center.
            Technical Report [*A publication*]
Sc Rev Rept ... Scots Revised Reports [*A publication*]
S & C Rev St ... Swan and Critchfield's Revised Statutes [*Ohio*]   (DLA)
SCREWS .... Solar Cosmic Ray Early Warning System   (MUGU)
SCRF .... Small Craft Repair Facility [*Navy*]   (NVT)
Scr Fac Sci Nat Univ Purkynianae Bru Biol ... Scripta Facultatis Scientiarum
            Naturalium Universitatis Purkynianae Brunensis. Biologia
            [*A publication*]
SCRG .... Stationary Cosmic Ray Gas
Scr Geobot ... Scripta Geobotanica [*A publication*]
Scr Geogr ... Scripta Geographica [*A publication*]
Scr Geol (Leiden) ... Scripta Geologica (Leiden) [*A publication*]
ScrH .... Scripta Hierosolymitana [*A publication*]
ScrHier .... Scripta Hierosolymitana [*Jerusalem*] [*A publication*]
ScrHierosol ... Scripta Hierosolymitana [*Jerusalem*] [*A publication*]
Scr Hierosolymitana ... Scripta Hierosolymitana [*A publication*]
Scr Hierosolymitana Publ Heb Univ (Jerus) ... Scripta Hierosolymitana.
            Publications of the Hebrew University (Jerusalem) [*A
            publication*]
ScRhW .... Winthrop College, Rock Hill, SC [*Library symbol*] [*Library of
            Congress*]   (LCLS)
SCRI .... Science Court and Research Institute   (EA)
SCRI .... Scientists' Committee for Radiation Information   (EA)
SCRI .... South Central Reservoir Investigation [*Department of the
            Interior*]
SCRI .... Southern Center for Research and Innovation, Inc. [*University
            of Southern Mississippi*] [*Research center*]   (RCD)
SCRI .... Supercomputer Computations Research Institute [*Florida
            State University*] [*Research center*]   (RCD)
Scrib .... Scribner's Monthly [*A publication*]
Scrib Com ... Scribner's Commentator [*A publication*]
Scrib Dow ... Scribner on the Law of Dower   (DLA)
Scrib M ..... Scribner's Magazine [*A publication*]
SCRIM .... Supersonic Cruise Intermediate Range Missile   (MCD)
SCRIMP ..... Save Cash, Reduce Immediately Meat Prices [*Boston, MA,
            group protesting high cost of food, 1973*]
Scrip .... Scriptorium [*A publication*]
SCRIP .... Scriptum [*Something Written*] [*Latin*]   (ROG)
SCRIP .... Scripture
SCRIP .... System for Controlling Returns in Inventory and Production
            Data [*IRS*]
Scrip Metal ... Scripta Metallurgica [*A publication*]
Scripps Inst Oceanogr Contrib ... Scripps Institution of Oceanography.
            Contributions [*A publication*]
SCRIPT ...... Scientific and Commercial Subroutine Interpreter and Program
            Translator
Script .... Scriptorium [*A publication*]
SCRIPT ...... Scripture
SCRIPT ...... System Controlling Research Image Processing Tasks   (MCD)
Scripta Fac Sci Natur UJEP Brunensis Biol ... Scripta Facultatis
            Scientiarum Naturalium Universita JE Purkyne Brunensis.
            Biologia [*A publication*]
Scripta Fac Sci Natur UJEP Brunensis Chem ... Scripta Facultatis
            Scientiarum Naturalium Universita JE Purkyne Brunensis.
            Chemia [*A publication*]
Scripta Fac Sci Natur UJEP Brunensis Math ... Scripta Facultatis
            Scientiarum Naturalium Universita JE Purkyne Brunensis.
            Mathematica [*A publication*]
Scripta Fac Sci Natur UJEP Brunensis Phys ... Scripta Facultatis
            Scientiarum Naturalium Universita JE Purkyne Brunensis.
            Physica [*A publication*]
Scripta Math ... Scripta Mathematica [*A publication*]
ScriptB .... Scripture Bulletin [*London*] [*A publication*]
SCRIS .... Southern California Regional Information Study [*Bureau of
            Census*]
Scriv Cop ... Scriven on the Law of Copyholds [*7th ed.*] [*1896*]   (DLA)
Scriven ..... Scriven on the Law of Copyholds   (DLA)
SCRJ .... Supersonic Combustion Ramjet
ScrJud .... Scripta Judaica [*Oxford*] [*A publication*]

SCRL .... Sensory Communication Research Laboratory [*Gallaudet
            College*] [*Research center*]   (RCD)
SCRL .... Signal Corps RADAR Laboratory [*Obsolete*] [*Army*]
SCRL .... Skill Components Research Laboratory [*Air Force*]   (MCD)
SCRL .... Station Configuration Requirement List   (MCD)
SCR (L) ..... Supreme Court Reports (Law) [*New South Wales*] [*A
            publication*]
SCRLC ...... South Central Research Library Council [*Ithaca, NY*] [*Library
            network*]   (EISS)
SCRLF .... Sceptre Resources Limited [*NASDAQ symbol*]   (NQ)
Scr LT .... Scranton Law Times [*Pennsylvania*]   (DLA)
SCRM .... Secondary Certified Reference Material   (NRCH)
Scr Med (Brno) ... Scripta Medica (Brno) [*A publication*]
Scr Med Fac Med Univ Brun Olomuc ... Scripta Medica Facultatum
            Medicinae Universitatum Brunensis et Olomucencis
            [*Czechoslovakia*] [*A publication*]
Scr Met ...... Scripta Metallurgica [*A publication*]
Scr Metall ... Scripta Metallurgica [*A publication*]
Scr Minora ... Scripta Minora-Regiae Societatis Humaniorum Litterarum
            Lundensis [*A publication*]
SCRN .... Screen[*s*] [*or Screening*] [*Freight*]
scRNP .... Ribonucleoprotein, Small Cytoplasmic
SCR (NS) (NSW) ... Supreme Court Reports (New Series) (New South Wales)
            [*A publication*]
SCRNSW .... New South Wales Supreme Court Reports   (DLA)
SCR (NSW) ... Supreme Court Reports (New South Wales) [*A publication*]
SCR (NSW) Eq ... Supreme Court Reports (Equity) (New South Wales) [*A
            publication*]
SCROLL ..... String and Character Recording Oriented Logogrammatic
            Language [*1970*] [*Data processing*]   (CSR)
SCROOGE ... Society to Curtail Ridiculous, Outrageous, and Ostentatious
            Gift Exchange   (EA)
SCRP .... Scripps-Howard Broadcasting [*NASDAQ symbol*]   (NQ)
SCRP .... Supplemental Conventional Reading Program [*Education*]
SCR (Q) ...... Queensland Supreme Court. Reports [*A publication*]
Sc RR .... Scotch Revised Reports   (DLA)
SCRS .... Secondary Control Rod System   (NRCH)
SCRS .... Service Center Replacement System [*Data processing*]
SCRS .... Society of Collision Repair Specialists [*Blue Springs, MO*]   (EA)
SCRS .... Strip Chart Recorder System [*NASA*]
Scr Sci Med Annu Sci Pap ... Scripta Scientifica Medica. Annual Scientific
            Papers [*A publication*]
SCRT .... Sealed Cathode Ray Tube
SCRT .... Subscribers' Circuit Routine Tester
            [*Telecommunications*]   (TEL)
SCRTC ...... Signal Corps Replacement Training Center [*Obsolete*] [*Army*]
SCRTERM ... Screw Terminal
ScrTheol .... Scripta Theologica [*Pamplona*] [*A publication*]
SCRTY .... Security
Scrut Charter ... Scrutton on Charter-Parties [*18th ed.*] [*1974*]   (DLA)
Scrutton ..... Scrutton on Charter-Parties [*16 eds.*] [*1886-1955*]   (DLA)
SCRWC ...... Sierra Club Radioactive Waste Campaign [*Later, RWC*]   (EA)
ScS .... Reflected S Wave [*Earthquakes*]
SCS .... Safety Control Switch
SCS .... Saint Charles Seminary [*Later, SCBS*] [*Pennsylvania*]
SCS .... Santa Clara Systems, Inc. [*San Jose, CA*]
            [*Telecommunications service*]   (TSSD)
SCS .... Satellite Control Satellite [*Telecommunications*]   (TEL)
SCS .... Satellite Test Center Communications Subsystem   (MCD)
SCS .... Scan Converter [*or Counter*] System
ScS .... Scandinavian Studies and Notes [*A publication*]
SCS .... Scientific Civil Service [*British*]
SCS .... Scientific Control Systems   (DIT)
ScS .... Scottish Studies [*A publication*]
SCS .... Screening and Costing Staff [*NATO*]   (NATG)
SCS .... Sea Control Ship [*Navy*]   (NVT)
SCS .... Secondary Control Ship [*Navy*]   (NVT)
SCS .... Secondary Control System   (MCD)
SCS .... Secondary Coolant System [*Nuclear energy*]   (NRCH)
SCS .... Secret Control Station [*NASA*]   (KSC)
SCS .... Secret Cover Sheet   (AAG)
SCS .... Section Control Station [*RADAR*]
SCS .... Secure Communications System [*Military*]   (CAAL)
SCS .... Security Container System [*Army*]   (AABC)
SCS .... Semiconductor Controlled Switch   (MSA)
SCS .... Septuagint and Cognate Studies   (BJA)
SCS .... Sequence Control System   (KSC)
SCS .... Sequencing and Command Systems Specialist [*NASA*]
SCS .... Ship Control Station [*Navy*]   (CAAL)
SCS .... Short-Circuit-Stable
SCS .... Shutdown Cooling System [*Nuclear energy*]   (NRCH)
SCS .... Sicasica [*Bolivia*] [*Seismograph station code, US Geological
            Survey*] [*Closed*]   (SEIS)
SCS .... Signal Center and School [*Army*]   (MCD)
SCS .... Signal Communications System [*Air Force*]
SCS .... Signal Conditioning System   (KSC)
SCS .... Silicon-Controlled Switch
SCS .... Simulation Control Subsystem   (KSC)
SCS .... Single Channel Simplex
SCS .... Single Composition Spherical [*Dental alloy*]
SCS .... Single Control Support   (BUR)

SCS........... Slaving Control System
SCS........... Slovak Catholic Sokol   (EA)
SCS........... Slow Code Scanner
SCS........... Small Components Structural
SCS........... Small Computer System
SCS........... Societe en Commandite Simple [Simple Partnership] [Belgium]
SCS........... Society for Ch'ing Studies   (EA)
SCS........... Society for Cinema Studies
SCS........... Society of Civil Servants [British]
SCS........... Society of Clinical Surgery [Defunct]   (EA)
SCS........... Society for Computer Simulation [La Jolla, CA]
SCS........... Society for Conservative Studies [Later, YAF]   (EA)
SCS........... Society of Construction Superintendents   (EA)
SCS........... Sodium Cellulose Sulfate [Organic chemistry]
SCS........... Sodium Characterization System   (NRCH)
SCS........... Software Communications Service
SCS........... Soil Conservation Service [Department of Agriculture]
SCS........... Solar Collector Subassembly   (MCD)
SCS........... SONAR Calibration Set
SCS........... SONAR Communications Set
SCS........... Space Cabin Simulator   (IEEE)
SCS........... Space Command Station   (AAG)
SCS........... Spacecraft System [NASA]   (KSC)
SCS........... Spanish Colonial Style [Cigars]
SCS........... Special Communications System   (MCD)
SCS........... Special Contingency Stockpile [Military]   (AABC)
SCS........... Speed Class Sequencing
SCS........... Spinal Cord Society [Fergus Falls, MN]   (EA)
SCS........... Stabilization and Control System [or Subsystem] [NASA]
SCS........... Standard Coordinate System   (KSC)
SCS........... Stationing Capability System [Army]   (AABC)
SCS........... Statistical Control System
SCS........... Stiffened Cylindrical Shell
SCS........... Stimulated Compton Scattering [Spectroscopy]
SCS........... Stop Control Braking System [Lucas Girling]
SC & S........ Strapped, Corded, and Sealed [As, of a package or bale]
SCS........... Student's Confidential Statement [Education]
SCS........... Suit Communication System [for spacesuits] [NASA]
SCS........... Superintendent of Car Service
SCS........... Supervisory Control System   (MCD)
SCS........... Supply Control Study
SCS........... Surface Composition Strengthened
SCS........... Swedish Colonial Society   (EA)
SCS........... Sweeping Current Supply
SCS........... University of South California, School of Library Science, Los
              Angeles, CA [OCLC symbol]   (OCLC)
SCSA........ Siamese Cat Society of America   (EA)
SCSA........ Soil Conservation Society of America   (EA)
SCSA........ Sports Car Collectors Society of America   (EA)
SCSA........ Standard Consolidated Statistical Area [Census Bureau]
SCSA........ Supreme Council for Sport in Africa
SCSB........ Standard Capital Superannuation Benefit [British]
SCSBM...... Society for Computer Science in Biology and Medicine
SCSC........ Secondary Curriculum Study Center [of NASSP]
SCSC........ Sorores a Caritate Sanctae Crucis [Sisters of Mercy of the Holy
              Cross] [Roman Catholic religious order]
SCSC........ South Carolina State College
Sc-SC........ South Carolina Supreme Court, Columbia, SC [Library symbol]
              [Library of Congress]   (LCLS)
SCSC........ Southern Connecticut State College [New Haven]
SCSC........ Strategic Conventional Standoff Capability   (MCD)
SCSC........ Summer Computer Simulation Conference
SCSCCL .... Sellin Center for Studies in Criminology and Criminal Law
              [Philadelphia, PA]   (EA)
SCSCLC .... Single-Carrier Space-Charge-Limited Current
SCSCO...... Secure Submarine Communications   (KSC)
SC (Scot)... Scottish Court of Session Cases, New Series   (DLA)
Sc SD........ Doctor of Social Sciences
SCSD........ School Construction Systems Development [Project] [of
              Educational Facilities Laboratories]
SCSD........ Simulation and Control Systems Division [General Electric
              Co.]   (MCD)
SCSE........ Smooth Curve - Smooth Earth
SCSE........ State Commission for Space Exploration [USSR]
SCSEP...... Senior Community Service Employment Program   (EA)
Sc Sess Cas ... Scotch Court of Session Cases   (DLA)
SCSFI........ Studii si Cercetari Stiintifice. Filologie (Iasi) [A publication]
SCSG........ Signal Conditioning Subsystem Group   (MCD)
SCSG........ Superior Cervical Sympathetic Ganglia [Anatomy]
SCSGIG ..... Supreme Council Sovereign Grand Inspectors General
              [Freemasonry]
SCSH........ Sisters of Charity of St. Hyacinthe [Grey Nuns] [Roman
              Catholic religious order]
SCSH........ Structural Carbon Steel Hard
SCSH........ Survey of the Chronic Sick and Handicapped [British]
SCSHX...... Shutdown Cooling System Heat Exchange [Nuclear
              energy]   (NRCH)
SCSI.......... Small Computer System Interface [Pronounced "scuzzy"]
SCSIT........ Southern California Sensory Integration Tests

SCSJA .... Sisters of Charity of St. Joan Antida [Roman Catholic religious
              order]
SCSL......... Sandia Corporation, Sandia Laboratory   (AABC)
ScSl .... Scandoslavica [A publication]
SCSL......... Sisters of Charity of St. Louis [Roman Catholic religious order]
SCSL......... Standing Lenticular Stratocumulus [Meteorology]   (FAAC)
SCSLP....... Smithsonian Center for Short-Lived Phenomena
SCSM........ Structural Carbon Steel Medium
SCSMHPS ... Special Constituency Section for Mental Health and
              Psychiatric Services [American Hospital Association]
              [Chicago, IL]   (EA)
SCSN .... Standard Computer Software Number
ScSo .... Science and Society [A publication]
SCSO .... Space Communications Station Operation
SCSO .... Superconducting Cavity Stabilized Oscillator [For clocks]
ScSocD...... Doctor of Social Science
ScSocL ...... Licence in Social Science [British]
SCSP......... Secretariat of the Council for Scientific Policy [British]
SCSP......... Serum Cancer-Suppressive Peptide [Oncology]
SCSP......... Smaller Communities Services Program [Department of Labor]
ScSp .... Spartanburg County Public Library, Spartanburg, SC [Library
              symbol] [Library of Congress]   (LCLS)
SC/SP....... Supracondylar/Suprapatellar [Prosthesis]
SCSP......... System Calibration Support Plan [Air Force]   (CET)
ScSpC....... Converse College, Spartanburg, SC [Library symbol] [Library
              of Congress]   (LCLS)
S & C Spec ... Soap/Cosmetics/Chemical Specialties [A publication]
ScSpM .... Milliken Research Corp., Research Library, Spartanburg, SC
              [Library symbol] [Library of Congress]   (LCLS)
ScSpW .... Wofford College, Spartanburg, SC [Library symbol] [Library of
              Congress]   (LCLS)
ScSpW-MHi ... Methodist Historical Society, South Carolina Conference of
              the Methodist Church, Wofford College, Spartanburg, SC
              [Library symbol] [Library of Congress]   (LCLS)
SCSR .... Self-Contained Self-Rescuer [Breathing device]
SCSR .... Ship Construction Subsidy Regulations [Canada]
SCSRS-S ... Standard Command Supply Review System - SAILS
SCSS .... Satellite Communications System Control   (NATG)
SCSS .... Self-Contained Starting System [NASA]
SCSS .... Structural Carbon Steel Soft
SCST .... Scan Converter Storage Tube
ScSt .... Scandinavian Studies [A publication]
SCST .... Society of Commercial Seed Technologists   (EA)
SC State Devel Board Div Geology Bull Geol Notes ... South Carolina State
              Development Board. Division of Geology. Bulletin.
              Geologic Notes [A publication]
SCSTC...... Senior Citizen Ski Touring Committee   (EA)
Sc Stud ..... Scandinavian Studies [A publication]
Sc Stud Criminol ... Scandinavian Studies in Criminology [1965]   (DLA)
Sc Stud Law ... Scandinavian Studies in Law [A publication]
SCSU .... St. Cloud State University
ScSu .... Sumter County Library, Sumter, SC [Library symbol] [Library
              of Congress]   (LCLS)
ScSuM .... Morris College, Sumter, SC [Library symbol] [Library of
              Congress]   (LCLS)
ScSum .... Timrod Library, Summerville, SC [Library symbol] [Library of
              Congress]   (LCLS)
SCSZ......... Sbornik Ceskoslovenske Spolecnosti Zemepisne [A
              publication]
SCT........... Air Force Institute of Technology, Wright-Patterson AFB, OH
              [OCLC symbol]   (OCLC)
SCT........... S-Band Cassegrain Transmit
SCT........... Sacrococcygeal Teratoma [Oncology]
SCT........... Salmon Calcitonin [Endocrinology]
SCT........... Sample Control Tape [Data processing]
SCT........... Satellite Communication Terminal   (MCD)
SCT........... Scan Conversion Tube
SCT........... Scanning Telescope   (KSC)
SCT........... Scattered
SCT........... Schottky Clamped Transistor
SCT........... Scintrex Ltd. [Toronto Stock Exchange symbol]
SCT........... Scorpion Toxin [Immunology]
SCT........... Scotty Lake [Alaska] [Seismograph station code, US
              Geological Survey]   (SEIS)
SCT........... Scout   (AABC)
Sct............ Scutum [Constellation]
SCT........... Semiconductor Curve Tracer
SCT........... Sentence Completion Technique [or Test]
SCT........... Sequence Checking Tape
SCT........... Service Counter Terminal [Banking]
SCT........... Single-Cell Test   (MCD)
SCT........... Single Channel Transponder   (MCD)
SCT........... Sioux City Terminal Railway [AAR code]
SCT........... Skylab Communication Terminal [NASA]   (KSC)
SCT........... Societe Canadienne de Theologie [Canadian Theological
              Society - CTS]
SCT........... Society for Clinical Trials [Baltimore, MD]   (EA)
SCT........... SONAR Certification Test

SCT............ Sous-Commission des Cartes Tectoniques [*Subcommission for Tectonic Maps of the Commission for the Geological Map of the World - STMCGMW*] [*Moscow, USSR*]   (EA-IO)

SCT............ South Central Air Transport, Inc. [*Natchez, MS*] [*FAA designator*]   (FAAC)

SCT............ Special Characters Table [*Data processing*]   (IBMDP)

SCT............ Spectral Control Technique

SCT............ Spectrographic Telescope

SCT............ Step Control Table   (CMD)

SCT............ Structural Clay Tile [*Technical drawings*]

SCT............ Student Coalition for Truth   (EA)

SCT............ Subroutine Call Table [*Data processing*]

SCT............ Subscriber Carrier Terminal [*Telecommunications*]   (TEL)

SCT............ Sugar-Coated Tablet

S Ct............ Supreme Court Reporter   (DLA)

SCt............ Supreme Court Reports

SCT............ System Circuit Test

SCT............ System Compatibility Tests

SCTA........ Secondary Container Transfer Area   (NRCH)

SCTA........ Southern California Timing Association   (EA)

SCTA........ Steel Carriers Tariff Association, Inc.

SCTB........ Santa Cruz Test Base   (MCD)

ScTB........ Scottish Tourist Board

S Ct Bull (CCH) ... United States Supreme Court Bulletin [*Commerce Clearing House*]   (DLA)

SCTC........ Small Craft Training Center

SCTC........ Submarine Chaser Training Center [*Navy*]

SCTC........ Systems & Computer Technology Corporation [*NASDAQ symbol*]   (NQ)

SC (T & C) ... Thompson and Cook's New York Supreme Court Reports   (DLA)

SCTD........ Scattered

SCTD........ Subcaliber Training Device   (AABC)

SCTE........ Science of the Total Environment [*A publication*]

SCTE........ Society of Cable Television Engineers   (EA)

SCTE........ Society of Carbide and Tool Engineers [*Formerly, SCE*]   (EA)

SCTE........ Spacecraft Central Timing Equipment [*NASA*]

SCTF........ SHAPE [*Supreme Headquarters Allied Powers Europe*] Centralized Training Facility [*NATO*]   (NATG)

SCTF........ Sodium Chemical Technology Facility   (NRCH)

SCTH........ Service Center for Teachers of History   (EA)

SCTHA....... Ssu Ch'uan Ta Hsueh Hsueh Pao - Tzu Jan K'o Hsueh [*A publication*]

SCTI.......... Scott Instruments Corp. [*NASDAQ symbol*]   (NQ)

SCTI.......... Sodium-Components Test Installation

SCTI.......... Solid Carbide Tool Institute   (EA)

SCTI.......... University of Southern California Tax Institute   (DLA)

SCTL......... Short-Circuited Transmission Line

SCTL......... Small Components Test Loop [*Nuclear energy*]

SCTN......... Service Center Taxpayer Notice [*IRS*]

SCTOC...... Satellite Communications Test Operations Center

Sc Total Env ... Science of the Total Environment [*A publication*]

SCTP......... Ship Construction Test Plan [*Navy*]   (CAAL)

SCTP......... Straight Channel Tape Print [*Data processing*]   (KSC)

SCTP......... Syndicat Canadien des Travailleurs du Papier [*Canadian Paperworkers Union - CPU*]

SCTPP....... Straight Channel Tape Print Program [*Data processing*]   (KSC)

SCTR......... Scooter   (AAG)

SCTR......... Sector   (MSA)

SCTR......... Signal Corps Technical Requirements   (MCD)

SCTRACEN ... Submarine Chaser Training Center [*Navy*]

S Ct Rev..... Supreme Court Review [*A publication*]

SCTS.......... SFOF [*Space Flight Operations Facility*] Communications Terminal Subsystem [*NASA*]

SCTS.......... System Components Test Station   (MCD)

SCTTU...... Scottish Council of Textile Trade Unions

SCTV......... Second City Television [*Television program, the title of which was later changed to its initialism*]

SCTV......... Standing Conference on Television Viewing [*British*]

SCTV-GDHS ... Spacecraft Television - Ground Data Handling System [*NASA*]

S Ct Vict..... Reports of Cases in the Supreme Court of Victoria [*1861-69*] [*Australia*]   (DLA)

SCTY......... Security   (AFM)

SCU........... 6585th Test Group Technical Information Center, Holloman AFB, NM [*OCLC symbol*]   (OCLC)

SCU........... S-Band Cassegrain Ultra

SCU........... Santiago [*Cuba*] [*Airport symbol*]   (OAG)

SCU........... Scanner Control Unit

SCU........... Scottish Church Union

SCU........... Secondary Control Unit   (AAG)

SCU........... Selector Checkout Unit

SCU........... Sensor Control Unit   (MCD)

SCU........... Sequence Control Unit   (KSC)

SCU........... Service Command Unit

SCU........... Service and Cooling Umbilical   (MCD)

SCU........... Servicing Control Unit [*Telecommunications*]   (TEL)

SCU........... Sheep Canyon [*Utah*] [*Seismograph station code, US Geological Survey*] [*Closed*]   (SEIS)

SCU........... Single Conditioning Unit

scu .... South Carolina [*MARC country of publication code*] [*Library of Congress*]   (LCCP)

SCU........... Special Care Unit

SCU........... Static Checkout Unit   (KSC)

SCU........... Station Control Unit

SCU........... Statistical Control Unit [*Military*]

SCU........... Storage Control Unit

SCU........... Subscribers' Concentrator Unit [*Telecommunications*]   (TEL)

SCU........... Sulfur-Coated Urea [*Chemical technology*]

SCU........... Surface Control Unit

SCU........... Switch Control Unit   (MCD)

SCU........... Synchronous Controller Unit

SCU........... System Control Unit

ScU........... University of South Carolina, Columbia, SC [*Library symbol*] [*Library of Congress*]   (LCLS)

SCUA........ Suez Canal Users Association   (NATG)

SCUAE...... State Committee on the Utilization of Atomic Energy [*USSR*]

ScUB........ Scandinavian University Books [*A publication*]

SCUBA...... Self-Contained Underwater Breathing Apparatus

SCUCC Dec ... South Carolina Unemployment Compensation Commission Decisions   (DLA)

SCUCCR.... South Carolina Unemployment Compensation Commission Reports of Hearings   (DLA)

SCUD .... Subsonic Cruise Unarmed Decoy [*Air Force*]   (MCD)

SCUDS...... Simplification, Clarification, Unification, Decimalization, Standardization

Scul............ Sculptor [*Constellation*]

SCUL......... Simulation of the Columbia University Libraries [*Data processing research*]

SCUL......... Soundings. University of California. Library [*Santa Barbara*] [*A publication*]

ScU-L........ University of South Carolina, Law School, Columbia, SC [*Library symbol*] [*Library of Congress*]   (LCLS)

SCULL ...... Serial Communication Unit for Long Links

SCULP ...... Sculpsit [*He, or She, Engraved It*] [*Latin*]

SCULP ...... Sculptor

SCULP ...... Sculpture   (ROG)

Sculp Int .... Sculpture International [*A publication*]

SCULPS..... Sculpsit [*He, or She, Engraved It*] [*Latin*]

SCULPT ..... Sculptor [*or Sculpture*]

Sculpt Hellenist Age ... Sculpture of the Hellenistic Age [*A publication*]   (OCD)

Sculpt R ..... Sculpture Review [*A publication*]

SCUM........ Society for Cutting Up Men

ScU-M....... University of South Carolina, School of Medicine, Columbia, SC [*Library symbol*] [*Library of Congress*]   (LCLS)

SCUMRA.... Societe Central de l'Uranium et des Minerals et Metaux Radioactifs [*France*]

SC(UN) ...... Security Council of the United Nations

SC Univ Pubs Phys Sci Bull ... South Carolina University. Publications. Physical Sciences Bulletin [*A publication*]

SCUP .... School Computer Use Plan   (IEEE)

SCUP .... Scupper

SCUP .... Service Center Unpostable [*IRS*]

SCUP .... Society for College and University Planning   (EA)

SCUPU...... Self-Contained Underwater Pinger Unit [*SONAR*]

SCUS .... Supreme Court of the United States

ScU-S....... University of South Carolina, Science Library, Columbia, SC [*Library symbol*] [*Library of Congress*]   (LCLS)

SCUSA...... Student Conference on United States Affairs

SCUSE...... Special Committee for United States Exports   (EA)

ScU-Su ...... University of South Carolina at Sumter, Sumter, SC [*Library symbol*] [*Library of Congress*]   (LCLS)

Scut........... Scutum [*of Hesiod*] [*Classical studies*]   (OCD)

Scut........... Scutum [*Constellation*]

SCUU .... Southern College University Union

SCV........... Eglin Regional Hospital Library, Eglin AFB, FL [*OCLC symbol*]   (OCLC)

SCV........... St. Croix [*Virgin Islands*] [*Seismograph station code, US Geological Survey*]   (SEIS)

SCV........... Seaclutter Visibility [*Navy*]   (CAAL)

SCV........... Side Control Valves

SCV........... Simultaneous Chest Compression and Ventilation [*Medicine*]

SCV........... Smooth, Capsulated, Virulent [*Bacteriology*]

SCV........... Sons of Confederate Veterans   (EA)

SCV........... South Atlantic Ltd. [*Vancouver Stock Exchange symbol*]

SCV........... Speed Control Valve

SCV........... Steel Containment Vessel   (NRCH)

SCV........... Stock Change Voucher [*Military*]   (AFIT)

SCV........... Strip Chart Viewer

SCV........... Sub Center Visibility   (MCD)

SCV........... Sub Clutter Visibility

SCV........... Suceava [*Romania*] [*Airport symbol*]   (OAG)

SCV........... Supersonic Cruise Missile

SCV........... System Compatibility Vehicle

SCV........... System Component Verification

SCVIR .... Society of Cardiovascular and Interventional Radiology [*Pittsburgh, PA*]   (EA)

SCVTR .... Scan Converting Video Tape Recorder   (MCD)

SCW.......... AFWAL [*Air Force Wright Aeronautical Laboratories*] Technical Information Center, Wright-Patterson AFB, OH [*OCLC symbol*] (OCLC)
SCW.......... Sherman Crater - Mount Baker [*Washington*] [*Seismograph station code, US Geological Survey*] [*Closed*] (SEIS)
SCW.......... Silicone Carbide Whisker
SCW.......... Society of Colonial Wars
SCW.......... State College of Washington
SCW.......... Super-Critical Wing
SCW.......... Superintendent of Contract Work [*Navy*]
SCWA........ St. Clair Paint & Wallpaper Class A SV [*Toronto Stock Exchange symbol*]
SC (WA).... Supreme Court [*Western Australia*] (DLA)
ScWal........ Oconee County Library, Walhalla, SC [*Library symbol*] [*Library of Congress*] (LCLS)
SC Water Resour Comm Rep ... South Carolina. Water Resources Commission. Report [*A publication*]
SCWC .... Special Commission on Weather Modification
SCWCU..... Supreme Council of the Western Catholic Union [*Later, Western Catholic Union*] (EA)
SCWDS..... Southeastern Cooperative Wildlife Disease Study [*University of Georgia*] [*Research center*] (RCD)
SCWEP ..... Spinnable Cotton Waste Equalization Program
SCWG .... Satellite Communications Working Group [*NATO*] (NATG)
SCWGA..... Sonoma County Wine Growers Association [*Santa Rosa, CA*] (EA)
SCWIA .... South Carolina Wildlife [*A publication*]
SC Wildl..... South Carolina Wildlife [*A publication*]
SCWPH ..... Students Concerned with Public Health [*Defunct*] (EA)
SCWPLR .... Special Committee for Workplace Product Liability Reform [*Washington, DC*] (EA)
SCWR......... Supercritical Water Reactor
SCWS........ Scottish Co-Operative Wholesale Society
SCWSL ..... Small Caliber Weapon Systems Laboratory (MCD)
SCWT........ System Cold Wire Tests
SCX.......... Oneida, TN [*Location identifier*] [*FAA*] (FAAL)
SCX.......... Single-Charge Exchange
SCX.......... Solar Coronal X-Ray
SCX.......... Starrett [*L. S.*] Company [*NYSE symbol*]
SCY.......... Scan Converter Yoke
SCY.......... Scurry, TX [*Location identifier*] [*FAA*] (FAAL)
SCYL......... Single-Cylinder
SCZ.......... Santa Cruz [*Solomon Islands*] [*Airport symbol*] (OAG)
SD .... Decisions of the Sadr Court [*1845-62*] [*Bengal, India*] (DLA)
SD .... Diamant [*France*] [*Research code symbol*]
SD .... Doctor of Science
SD .... Sadr Diwani Adalat Court [*Bengal, India*] (DLA)
SD .... Safe Deposit [*Business and trade*]
SD .... Safety Destructor (NG)
SD .... Said (ROG)
SD .... Sailed
SD .... Sailing Directions [*British*]
S/D............ Salaried Direct [*Ratio*]
SD .... Salutem Dicit [*Sends Greetings*] [*Latin*]
SD .... Same Day
SD .... Sammlung Dieterich [*A publication*]
SD .... Sample Data (NG)
SD .... Sample Delay
SD .... Sans Date [*No Date*] [*French*]
SD .... Sash Door
SD .... Saturation Deficit
SD .... Scandinavian Delegation [*British*]
SD .... Schematic Diagram
SD .... Scientiae Doctor [*Doctor of Science*] [*Latin*] (ADA)
SD .... Scientific Design [*Group*]
SD .... Scientific Detective Monthly [*A publication*]
SD .... Scottish District [*Council*]
SD .... Scram Discharge [*Nuclear energy*] (NRCH)
SD .... Sea Damaged [*Grain trade*]
S/D............ Seadrome
SD .... Search Depth [*Navy*] (NVT)
S & D .... Search and Destroy [*Army*] (AABC)
SD .... Seasonal Derating (IEEE)
SD .... Second Defense [*Men's lacrosse position*]
SD .... Secretary of Defense
SD .... Segregation Distorter [*Genetics*]
SD .... Seismic Detector (MCD)
SD .... Seize Detector
SD .... Selenium Diode
SD .... Self-Destroying [*Projectile*]
SD .... Self-Destruct
SD .... Semantic Differential
SD .... Semidetached (ADA)
SD .... Semidiameter
SD .... Senate Document
SD .... Senatus Decreto [*By Decree of the Senate*] [*Latin*]
SD .... Send Data [*Data processing*]
SD .... Send Digits [*Telecommunications*] (TEL)
SD .... Senile Dementia [*Medicine*]
SD .... Senior Deacon [*Masonry*]
SD .... Senior Director [*FAA*] (FAAC)

SD .... Septal Defect [*Medicine*]
SD .... Serializer/Deserializer
SD .... Serine Dehydratase [*An enzyme*]
SD .... Serologically Defined [*Immunology*]
SD .... Serologically Determined [*Medicine*]
SD .... Service Dated (ROG)
SD .... Service Dress
SD .... Servicing Diagram
SD .... Servus Dei [*Servant of God*] [*Latin*]
SD .... Several Dates
SD .... Sewed
SD .... Shakedown [*Nuclear energy*] (NRCH)
S & D .... Shaw, Dunlop, and Bell's Scotch Court of Session Reports, First Series [*1821-38*] (DLA)
SD .... Shell-Destroying [*Device*]
SD .... Shield of David (BJA)
SD .... Shop Drawing (AAG)
SD .... Short Day [*Botany*]
SD .... Short Delay
SD .... Short Delivery
SD .... Short Duration
SD .... Shoulder Dislocation
SD .... Shower Drain (AAG)
S/D............ Shut Down
SD .... Sicherheitsdienst [*Police Duty*] [*NAZI Germany*]
S-D............ Sickle Cell Hemoglobin D [*Disease*] [*Medicine*]
SD .... Side Deck
SD .... Side Door
SD .... Side Drum
SD .... Siegfried AG [*Switzerland*] [*Research code symbol*]
SD .... Sight Draft [*Business and trade*]
SD .... Significant Digit [*Mathematics*]
SD .... Simple Design
SD .... Sine Dato [*Undated book*] [*Latin*]
SD .... Sine Die [*Without Day*] [*Latin*]
SD .... Single Deck [*Navigation*]
SD .... Single Determination
SD .... Single Distilled
SD .... Single Domain [*Grains in rocks*] [*Geophysics*]
S & D .... Single and Double [*Reduction gears*]
SD .... Site Defense [*Military*] (AABC)
SD .... Situation Display
SD .... Skid
SD .... Skin Destruction [*Medicine*]
SD .... Skin Dose
SD .... Slope Difference [*Statistics*]
SD .... Slowdown
SD .... Small-Scale Disturbance Field
SD .... Social Democratic Party [*West Germany*]
SD .... Socialdemokratiet i Danmark [*Social Democratic Party of Denmark*] (PPE)
SD .... Soft Drawn
SD .... Solid Drawn
S & D .... Song and Dance Act [*Slang*]
SD .... Sort File Description [*Data processing*]
SD .... Sorties per Day [*Air Force*] (AFIT)
SD .... Sound [*Board on Geographic Names*]
SD .... Sound [*Films, television, etc.*]
SD .... Sounding Doubtful [*Nautical charts*]
SD .... Source/Destination [*Inspection/Acceptance Point*] (MCD)
SD .... Source Document [*Data processing*]
SD .... South Dakota [*Postal code*]
SD .... South Dakota Compiled Laws, Annotated (DLA)
SD .... South Dakota Musician [*A publication*]
SD .... South Dakota Reports (DLA)
Sd............. South Dakota State Library Commission, Pierre, SD [*Library symbol*] [*Library of Congress*] (LCLS)
SD .... South Division (ROG)
SD .... Southern District (DLA)
SD .... Space Digest [*A publication*]
SD .... Space Division [*Air Force*]
SD .... Spare Disposition (MCD)
SD .... Special Delivery
SD .... Special Document
SD .... Special Duty
SD .... Specially Denatured
SD .... Specification for Design
SD .... Specification Document [*NASA*] (NASA)
SD .... Spectacle Dispenser [*Navy technician*]
SD .... Spectral Distribution
SD .... Spin Device
SD .... Splice Donor [*Genetics*]
SD .... Spontaneous Delivery [*Obstetrics*]
Sd............. Sprachdienst [*A publication*]
SD .... Sprache und Dichtung [*A publication*]
SD .... Staff Duties [*Military*] [*British*]
SD .... Stage Direction
SD .... Stage Door [*Theatrical slang*]
SD .... Standard Decision (MCD)
SD .... Standard Deduction
SD .... Standard Deviation [*Also, s*]

SD .... Standard Dress [*Military*] [*British*]
SD .... Standard Oil Co. of California [*NYSE symbol*] [*Delisted*] [*Vancouver Stock Exchange symbol*]
SD .... Standardization Data
SD .... Standardization Directory
SD .... Standards Development   (IEEE)
SD .... Stands Detached [*Freight*]
SD .... State Department
SD .... State Director
S/D .... Statement of Differences
SD .... Station Director [*Deep Space Instrumentation Facility, NASA*]
SD .... Statutory Declaration [*British*]
SD .... Steel Deck   (ADA)
SD .... Stein & Day [*Publishers*]
SD .... Stereo Directional
SD .... Stern Discharge
SD .... Steward [*Navy rating*]
SD .... Stone Disintegration [*Urology*]
S/D .... Storage or Distribution
S & D .... Storage and Distribution
SD .... Storm Data [*A publication*]
SD .... Storm Detection [*RADAR*]
SD .... Stowage Drawer
SD .... Straight Duty
SD .... Strength Differential [*Steel*]
SD .... Strength-Duration (Curve) [*Prosthesis*]
SD .... Streptodornase [*An enzyme*]
SD .... Stronnictwo Demokratyczne [*Democratic Party*] [*Poland*]   (PPE)
SD .... Structural Detail   (AAG)
SD .... Structural Dynamics   (KSC)
SD .... Studi Danteschi [*A publication*]
SD .... Studia Delitschiana [*A publication*]
SD .... Studia et Documenta ad Iura Orientis Antiqui Pertinenta [*Leiden*] [*A publication*]   (BJA)
SD .... Study Director   (MCD)
SD .... Subdural [*Anatomy*]
SD .... Submarine Detector [*ADA*]
SD .... Sudan [*Two-letter standard code*]   (CNC)
SD .... Sudan Airways [*ICAO designator*]   (FAAC)
S-D .... Sudden Death [*Tiebreaking in sports*]
SD .... Sudden Death [*Medicine*]
SD .... Sugar Determination
SD .... Sun's Declensions [*Astronomy*]   (ROG)
SD .... Super Duty [*Automotive engineering*]
SD .... Superintendent of Documents [*US Government Printing Office*]
SD .... Supply Department [*Navy*]
SD .... Supply Depot
SD .... Supply Ducts   (NRCH)
SD .... Support Directive   (KSC)
SD .... Support [*or Supporting*] Document   (KSC)
SD .... Surface Duct [*Navy*]   (CAAL)
SD .... Surveillance Drone [*Air Force*]
SD .... Survival Dose
Sd .... Suspended [*Regulation or order suspended*] [*Used in Shepard's Citations*]   (DLA)
SD .... Swaziland
SD .... Sweep Driver
SD .... Switch Driver
SD .... Syllable Duration [*Entomology*]
SD .... System Demonstration
SD .... System Description
SD .... System Designator   (AFIT)
SD .... System Drawer
SD .... Systems Development   (MCD)
S/D .... Systems Directorate [*Army*]   (RDA)
SD1 .... Systolic Discharge [*Cardiology*]
SD1 .... Steward, First Class [*Navy rating*]
S 2d .... New York Supplement, Second Series   (DLA)
SD2 .... Steward, Second Class [*Navy rating*]
SD3 .... Steward, Third Class [*Navy rating*]
SDA .... Augustana College, Sioux Falls, SD [*OCLC symbol*]   (OCLC)
SDA .... Baghdad-Saddam [*Iraq*] [*Airport symbol*]   (OAG)
SDA .... Sacrodextra Anterior [*A fetal position*] [*Obstetrics*]
SDA .... Sadr Diwani Adalat Reports [*India*]   (DLA)
SD & A ...... San Diego & Arizona Railway
SDA .... Scottish Diploma in Agriculture
SDA .... Screw Displacement Axis
SDA .... Section Department Authority
SDA .... Semidehydroascorbate [*Biochemistry*]
SDA .... Sequential Degradation Analysis
SDA .... Service Delivery Area [*Job Training and Partnership Act*]   (OICC)
SDA .... Seventh-Day Adventist
SDA .... Sex Discrimination Act [*1975*] [*British*]
SDA .... Shaft Drive Axis   (KSC)
SDA .... Shenandoah, IA [*Location identifier*] [*FAA*]   (FAAL)
SDA .... Ship's Destination Authority   (NVT)
SDA .... Significant Digit Arithmetic
SDA .... Simple Doublet Antenna
SDA .... Sleeve Dipole Antenna

SDA .... Slowdown Area
SDA .... Soap and Detergent Association [*Formerly, AAS & GP*] [*New York, NY*]   (EA)
SDA .... Social Democratic Alliance [*British*]
SDA .... Software Design Associates, Inc. [*New York, NY*] [*Software manufacturer*]
SDA .... Source Data Acquisition   (BUR)
SDA .... Source Data Automation
SDA .... Special Disbursing Agent, Bureau of Indian Affairs [*United States*]   (DLA)
SDA .... Special Duty Assignment   (AFM)
SDA .... Specially Denatured Alcohol
SDA .... Specific Dynamic Action [*of foods*] [*Physiology*]
SDA .... Spectral Distribution Analyzer
SDA .... Spontaneous Divergent Academic [*Test*] [*Education*]
SDA .... Stacked Dipole Array
SDA .... Standard Gold Mines [*Vancouver Stock Exchange symbol*]
SDA .... Statistical Distribution Analyzer
SDA .... Step Down Amplifier
SDA .... Stepwise Discriminant Analysis
SDA .... Steroid-Dependent Asthmatic [*Medicine*]
SDA .... Stevens-Duryea Associates   (EA)
SDA .... Students for Democratic Action
SDA .... Subcarrier Demodulator Assembly [*Deep Space Instrumentation Facility, NASA*]
SDA .... Succinic Dehydrogenase Activity
SDA .... Sulfadiazine [*Antibiotic*]
SDA .... Superficial Distal Axillary [*Lymph node*]
SDA .... Supplier Data Approval   (NRCH)
SDA .... Supporting Data Analysis
SDA .... Surface Design Association [*Fayetteville, TN*]   (EA)
SDA .... Sweet Damn All [*Nothing At All*] [*Slang*]
SDA .... Symbolic Device Address
SDA .... Symbolic Disk Address   (AFM)
SDA .... Symbols-Digits-Alphabetics
SDA .... System Design Agency   (MCD)
SDA .... Systems Data Analysis
SDA .... Systems Dynamic Analyzer
SDAA .... Salt Distributors Association of America   (EA)
SDAA .... Servicemen's Dependents Allowance Act
SDAA .... Skein Dyers Association of America [*Later, SRPDAA*]   (EA)
SDAA .... Stacked Dipole Aerial Array
SdAbA .... Alexander Mitchell Library, Aberdeen, SD [*Library symbol*] [*Library of Congress*]   (LCLS)
SdAbN .... Northern State College, Aberdeen, SD [*Library symbol*] [*Library of Congress*]   (LCLS)
SdAbP........ Presentation College, Aberdeen, SD [*Library symbol*] [*Library of Congress*]   (LCLS)
SDAC .... Seismic Data Analysis Center
SDAC .... Shelby Dodge Automobile Club   (EA)
SDAD .... Satellite Digital and Analog Display
SDAD .... Special Domestically Available Documents [*NASA*]   (KSC)
SDADA ...... Seventh-Day Adventist Dietetic Association [*Loma Linda, CA*]   (EA)
SD Admin R ... Administrative Rules of South Dakota   (DLA)
SD Admin Reg ... South Dakota Register   (DLA)
SDADS....... Satellite Digital and Display System
SDAE .... San Diego & Arizona Eastern Railway Co. [*AAR code*]
SDAE .... Source Data Automation Equipment
SDAF........ Special Defense Acquisition Fund
SD Ag Exp ... South Dakota. Agricultural Experiment Station. Publications [*A publication*]
SD Agric Exp Stn Bull ... South Dakota. Agricultural Experiment Station. Bulletin [*A publication*]
S DAK .... South Dakota
S Dak .... South Dakota Reports   (DLA)
S Dak Agr Expt Sta Tech Bull ... South Dakota. Agricultural Experiment Station. Technical Bulletin [*A publication*]
S Dak Farm Home Res ... South Dakota Farm and Home Research [*A publication*]
S Dak Geol Surv Bull ... South Dakota. Geological Survey. Bulletin [*A publication*]
S Dak Geol Surv Circ ... South Dakota. Geological Survey. Circular [*A publication*]
S Dak His R ... South Dakota Historical Review [*A publication*]
S Dak His S ... South Dakota State Historical Society. Collections [*A publication*]
S Dak J Med ... South Dakota Journal of Medicine [*A publication*]
S Dak Lib Bull ... South Dakota Library Bulletin [*A publication*]
S Dak Rev ... South Dakota Review [*A publication*]
S Dak State Geologist Bienn Rept ... South Dakota State Geologist. Biennial Report [*A publication*]
S Dak State Univ Coop Ext Serv ... South Dakota State University. Cooperative Extension Service [*A publication*]
SdAl .... Alcester Public Library, Alcester, SD [*Library symbol*] [*Library of Congress*]   (LCLS)
SDAL........ Switched Data Access Line
SD Ala .... United States District Court for the Southern District of Alabama   (DLA)
SdAle .... Alexandria Public Library, Alexandria, SD [*Library symbol*] [*Library of Congress*]   (LCLS)

SDAM......... Standard Deviation above the Mean [*Statistics*]
SDA Mad.... Madras Sadr Diwani Adalat Reports [*1805-62*] [*India*]   (DLA)
SDAML........ Send by Airmail   (NOAA)
SDANA....... Shrine Directors Association of North America   (EA)
SDAP......... Sociaal-Democratische Arbeiders Partij [*Social Democratic Workers' Party*] [*The Netherlands*]   (PPE)
SDAP......... System Development and Performance
SDAP......... Systems Development and Acquisition Plan   (MCD)
SDAP......... Systems Development Analysis Program
SDAPP........ Special Duty Assignment Proficiency Pay [*Air Force*]
SdAr.......... Arlington Public Library, Arlington, SD [*Library symbol*] [*Library of Congress*]   (LCLS)
SdArm........ Armour Public Library, Armour, SD [*Library symbol*] [*Library of Congress*]   (LCLS)
SDAS .... Scientific Data Automation System   (IEEE)
SDAS .... Shared Demand Assignment Signaling   (MCD)
SDAS .... Simplified Directional Approach System [*Aviation*]
SDAS .... Source Data Automation System   (AABC)
SDAS .... Systems Data Analysis Section
SDAT........ Senile Dementia of the Alzheimer Type [*Medicine*]
SDAT........ Spacecraft Data Analysis Team [*NASA*]
SDAT........ Stanford Diagnostic Arithmetic Test
SDAT........ Stationery Digital Audio Tape
SDAU........ SDA [*Software Design Associates*] Users' Group
SDAUG....... SDA [*Software Design Associates*] Users' Groups [*Formerly, IUG*]   (EA)
SDAW........ Sitzungsberichte der Deutschen Akademie der Wissenschaften zu Berlin [*A publication*]
SDAWB ...... Sitzungsberichte der Deutschen Akademie der Wissenschaften zu Berlin [*A publication*]
SDB .... Sa Da Bandeira [*Angola*] [*Seismograph station code, US Geological Survey*]   (SEIS)
SDB .... Salesians of Don Bosco [*Roman Catholic men's religious order*]
SDB .... Sandberg, CA [*Location identifier*] [*FAA*]   (FAAL)
SDB .... Securities Data Base System [*Capital Market Systems, Inc.*] [*Information service*]   (EISS)
SDB .... Segment Descriptor Block
SDB .... Shakespeare Data Bank, Inc. [*Evanston, IL*] [*Information service*]   (EISS)
SDB .... Shallow Draft Barge   (MCD)
SD & B .... Shaw, Dunlop, and Bell's Scotch Court of Session Reports, First Series [*1821-38*]   (DLA)
SDB .... Skill Development Base [*Army*]   (AABC)
SDB .... Sociaal-Democratische Bond [*Social Democratic League*] [*The Netherlands*]   (PPE)
SDB .... Society for Developmental Biology
SDB .... South Dakota State University, Brookings, SD [*OCLC symbol*]   (OCLC)
SdB .... South Dakota State University, Brookings, SD [*Library symbol*] [*Library of Congress*]   (LCLS)
SDB .... Spacecraft Design Book
SDB .... Special District Bond
SDB .... Square Die Bushing
SDB .... Storage Data Bus
SDB .... Strength and Dynamics Branch [*Air Force*]
SDB .... Supplement au Dictionnaire de la Bible [*A publication*]
SDB .... System Data Buffer   (MCD)
SDBC .... San Diego Bancorp [*NASDAQ symbol*]   (NQ)
SDBCS .... Steam Dump Bypass Control System   (NRCH)
SdBer........ Beresford Public Library, Beresford, SD [*Library symbol*] [*Library of Congress*]   (LCLS)
SdBf .... Belle Fourche Public Library, Belle Fourche, SD [*Library symbol*] [*Library of Congress*]   (LCLS)
SDBF......... System Development Breadboard Facility
SDBGC....... Seventh Day Baptist General Conference   (EA)
SDBHS....... Seventh Day Baptist Historical Society   (EA)
SD Bird Notes ... South Dakota Bird Notes [*A publication*]
SDB Jo .... South Dakota Bar Journal   (DLA)
SDBL......... Sight Draft Bill of Lading Attached [*Business and trade*]
SdB-M........ South Dakota State University, Minuteman Graduate Center Library, Ellsworth AFB, Rapid City, SD [*Library symbol*] [*Library of Congress*]   (LCLS)
SDBMS ...... Seventh Day Baptist Missionary Society   (EA)
SdBo .... Bonesteel Public Library, Bonesteel, SD [*Library symbol*] [*Library of Congress*]   (LCLS)
SDBO .... Societe de Banque Occidentale [*Paris, France*]
SDBP......... Supine Diastolic Blood Pressure [*Medicine*]
Sd-BPH ..... South Dakota State Library for the Handicapped, Pierre, SD [*Library symbol*] [*Library of Congress*]   (LCLS)
SdBro........ Brookings Public Library, Brookings, SD [*Library symbol*] [*Library of Congress*]   (LCLS)
SdBrS .... Bristol Independent School District Library, Bristol, SD [*Library symbol*] [*Library of Congress*]   (LCLS)
SD & B Sup ... Shaw, Dunlop, and Bell's Supplement, Containing House of Lords Decisions   (DLA)
SD & B Supp ... Shaw, Dunlop, and Bell's Supplement, Containing House of Lords Decisions [*Scotland*]   (DLA)
SdBu .... Burke Public Library, Burke, SD [*Library symbol*] [*Library of Congress*]   (LCLS)

SDBU/CR... Office of Small and Disadvantaged Business Utilization and Civil Rights   (NRCH)
SDBWF ...... Seventh Day Baptist World Federation   (EA)
SDBY......... Standby
SDC........... Chief Steward [*Later, MSC*] [*Navy rating*]
SDC........... Salivary Duct Carcinoma [*Oncology*]
SDC........... Sample Data Collection
SDC........... San Diego - Robinson [*California*] [*Seismograph station code, US Geological Survey*] [*Closed*]   (SEIS)
SDC........... Sands Minerals [*Vancouver Stock Exchange symbol*]
SDC........... Scientific Data Center   (MCD)
SDC........... Scientific Documentation Center Ltd. [*Dunfermline, Fife, Scotland*]
SDC........... Seaward Defense Craft   (NATG)
SDC........... Secondary Distribution Center   (AAG)
SDC........... Seismological Data Center [*Environmental Science Services Administration*]
SDC........... Seize Detector Control
SDC........... Self-Defense Corps [*Vietnam*]
SDC........... September Days Club [*Atlanta, GA*]   (EA)
SDC........... Serum Digoxin Concentration [*Clinical chemistry*]
SDC........... Shaft-Driven Counter
SDC........... Shield Design Code   (NRCH)
SDC........... Shipment Detail Card
SDC........... Shutdown Cooling [*Nuclear energy*]   (NRCH)
SDC........... Signal Data Converter
SDC........... Single Drift Correction
SDC........... Situation Display Converter
SDC........... Society of Daily Communicants [*Defunct*]   (EA)
SDC........... Society of the Divine Compassion [*Anglican religious community*]
SDC........... Society of Dyers and Colourists   (EA-IO)
SDC........... Sodium Deoxycholate [*Organic chemistry*]
SDC........... Software Development Computer [*NASA*]   (NASA)
SDC........... Solid Dielectric Cable
SDC........... SONAR Data Computer [*Navy*]   (CAAL)
SDC........... Southern Defense Command [*Army*]
SDC........... Space Data Corporation
SDC........... Space Defense Center   (MCD)
SDC........... Space Defense Corporation   (MCD)
SDC........... Space Development Corporation
SDC........... Spacecraft Data Simulator [*NASA*]   (KSC)
SDC........... Spares Disposition Code [*NASA*]   (NASA)
SDC........... Special Devices Center [*Navy*]
SDC........... Specific Damping Capacity [*Metals*]
SDC........... Stabilization Data Computer
SDC........... Standard Data Chain
SDC........... State Defense Council
SDC........... Static Dielectric Constant
SDC........... Structural Design Criteria
SDC........... Studebaker Driver's Club
SDC........... Subcontractor's Data Catalog   (MCD)
SDC........... Submersible Decompression Chamber [*Underwater tank*]
SDC........... Submersible Diving Capsule [*Oceanography*]
SDC........... Sundance Airways, Inc. [*San Antonio, TX*] [*FAA designator*]   (FAAC)
SDC........... Supply Distribution Center [*Military*]   (AFIT)
SDC........... Support Design Change
SDC........... Sydney Dance Company [*Australia*]
SDC........... System for Data Calculation [*Information retrieval*]
SDC........... System Designator Code   (AFM)
SDC........... System Development Corporation [*Santa Monica, CA*] [*Information service*]
SDC........... System Development Corporation [*Uxbridge, Middlesex, England*] [*Information service*]   (EISS)
SDC........... Systems Development District   (AAG)
SDC........... Yankton College, Yankton, SD [*OCLC symbol*]   (OCLC)
SdCa......... Canton Carnegie Public Library, Canton, SD [*Library symbol*] [*Library of Congress*]   (LCLS)
SDCA .... Scottish Deerhound Club of America   (EA)
SD Cal....... United States District Court for the Southern District of California   (DLA)
SdCan........ Canova Public Library, Canova, SD [*Library symbol*] [*Library of Congress*]   (LCLS)
SdCar........ Carthage Public Library, Carthage, SD [*Library symbol*] [*Library of Congress*]   (LCLS)
SDCC .... Simulation Data Conversion Center [*Space Flight Operations Facility, NASA*]
SDCC .... Small-Diameter Component Cask [*Nuclear energy*]   (NRCH)
SDCC .... Society of the Descendants of the Colonial Clergy   (EA)
SDCD .... [*Adjusted*] Sea Duty Commencement Date
SDCE .... Scientific Data Collection Exercise
SDCE .... Society of Die Casting Engineers   (EA)
SDCF .... Sampled Data Channel Filter
SdCh .... Chamberlain Public Library, Chamberlain, SD [*Library symbol*] [*Library of Congress*]   (LCLS)
SDCH .... Society of Descendants of Colonial Hispanics   (EA)
SDCIS .... Supplier Data Control Information System   (MCD)
SdCl........... Clark Public Library, Clark, SD [*Library symbol*] [*Library of Congress*]   (LCLS)

SdCla	Claremont Public Library, Claremont, SD [*Library symbol*] [*Library of Congress*] (LCLS)
SDCM	Master Chief Steward [*Later, MSCM*] [*Navy rating*]
SdCo	Colome Public Library, Colome, SD [*Library symbol*] [*Library of Congress*] (LCLS)
SD Comm	Doctor of Science in Commerce
SD Compiled Laws Ann	South Dakota Compiled Laws, Annotated (DLA)
SD Comp Laws Ann	South Dakota Compiled Laws, Annotated (DLA)
SDCP	Summary Development Cost Plan [*NASA*] (NASA)
SDCP	Supply Demand Control Points
SDCR	Source Data Communication Retrieval
SDCS	SAIL [*Shuttle Avionics Integration Laboratory*] Data Communications System [*NASA*] (NASA)
SDCS	Sample Data Control System (MCD)
SDCS	Science Data Conditioning System
SDCS	Senior Chief Steward [*Navy rating*] [*Later, MSCS*]
SDCS	Shutdown Cooling System [*Nuclear energy*] (NRCH)
SDCS	Simulation Data Conversion System [*Space Flight Operations Facility, NASA*]
SDCS	Single Differential Cross Section
SDCT	Slosson Drawing Coordination Test
SdCu	Custer County Library, Custer, SD [*Library symbol*] [*Library of Congress*] (LCLS)
SDCW	San Diego College for Women [*California*]
SDD	Lubango [*Angola*] [*Airport symbol*] (OAG)
SDD	Santo Domingo [*Ciudad Trujillo*] [*Dominican Republic*] [*Seismograph station code, US Geological Survey*] (SEIS)
SDD	Scottish Development Department
SDD	Scottish Diploma in Dairying
SDD	Second Development Decade [*United Nations*]
SDD	Selected Dissemination of Documents
SD/D	Service Deputy/Director (MUGU)
SDD	Shuttle Design Directive [*NASA*] (NASA)
SDD	Sierra Nevada Gold [*Vancouver Stock Exchange symbol*]
SDD	Signal Data Demodulator
SDD	Sioux Falls Public Library, Sioux Falls, SD [*OCLC symbol*] (OCLC)
SDD	Slowdown Density
SDD	Sodium Dimethyldithiocarbamate [*Also, SDDC*] [*Organic chemistry*]
SDD	Software Description Document [*NASA*] (NASA)
SDD	Software Design Description [*Data processing*] (IEEE)
SDD	Software Design Document [*NASA*] (NASA)
SDD	Specially Designated Distributor [*Liquor*]
SDD	Standard Delivery Date
SDD	Store Door Delivery
SDD	Stored Data Description
SDD	Stress Degree Day [*Crop inventory*]
SDD	Subchannel Data Distributor (KSC)
SDD	Subsystem Design Description (MCD)
SDD	System Design Description (NRCH)
SDD	System Design Document (MCD)
SDD	Systems Definition Directive (AFM)
SDD	Systems Development Department [*David W. Taylor Naval Ship Research and Development Center*]
SDDC	Self Determination for DC [*District of Columbia*] [*Formerly, WHRC*] [*An association*] (EA)
SDDC	Silver Diethyldithiocarbamate [*Organic chemistry*]
SDDC	Sodium Dimethyldithiocarbamate [*Organic chemistry*] [*Also, SDD*]
SDDC	Sterile Disposable Device Committee [*Defunct*]
SdDel	Dell Rapids Carnegie Public Library, Dell Rapids, SD [*Library symbol*] [*Library of Congress*] (LCLS)
SDDL	Stored Data Definition Language
SDDM	Secretary of Defense Decision Memorandum
SDD-NU	Summaries of Doctoral Dissertations. Northwestern University [*A publication*]
SDDP	Sight Draft Documents Against Payment [*Business and trade*]
SdDr	Draper Public Library, Draper, SD [*Library symbol*] [*Library of Congress*] (LCLS)
SDDRA	Showa Densen Denran Rebyu [*A publication*]
SdDs	De Smet Public Library, De Smet, SD [*Library symbol*] [*Library of Congress*] (LCLS)
SDDS	Secondary Data Display System (MCD)
SDDS	Signal Data Demodulator Set [*or System*]
SD/DS	Synchro-Digital/Digital-Synchro (CAAL)
SDDTTG	Stored Data Definition and Translation Task Group
SDDU	Simplex Data Distribution Unit
SDDUW	Summaries of Doctoral Dissertations. University of Wisconsin [*A publication*]
SDE	Santiago Del Estero [*Argentina*] [*Airport symbol*] (OAG)
SDE	Self-Disinfecting Elastomer
SDE	Simple Designational Expression
SDE	Societe de Droits d'Execution du Canada [*Performing Rights Organization of Canada - PROC*]
SDE	Society of Data Educators [*Memphis, TN*]
SDE	Software Development Environment [*NCR Corp.*]
SDE	Source Data Entry
SDE	Space Division Evaluator [*NASA*] (NASA)
SDE	Specific Dynamic Effect [*Medicine*]
SDE	Standard Data Element [*Army*] (AABC)
SDE	Steam Distillation Extracton
SDE	Students for Data Education (IEEE)
SDE	Support Data Engineering (MCD)
SDE & C	Standard Data Element and Codes [*Air Force*]
SDECE	Service de Documentation Exterieure et de Contre-Espionage [*Pronounced "suh-deck"*] [*Intelligence organization*] [*France*] [*Later, DGSE*]
SdEd	Edgemont Public Library, Edgemont, SD [*Library symbol*] [*Library of Congress*] (LCLS)
SdEdH	Edgemont High School, Edgemont, SD [*Library symbol*] [*Library of Congress*] (LCLS)
S/DEFL	Stone Deflector [*Automotive engineering*]
SDEG	Special Doctrine Equipment Group [*Army*]
SdEl	Elkton Public Library, Elkton, SD [*Library symbol*] [*Library of Congress*] (LCLS)
Sdelovaci Tech	Sdelovaci Technika [*A publication*]
SdEs	Estelline Public Library, Estelline, SD [*Library symbol*] [*Library of Congress*] (LCLS)
SDES	Submarine Data Extraction System [*Navy*] (CAAL)
SDESG	Strapdown Electrically Suspended Gyro (KSC)
SdEu	Eureka Public Library, Eureka, SD [*Library symbol*] [*Library of Congress*] (LCLS)
SDF	Louisville [*Kentucky*] [*Airport symbol*] (OAG)
SDF	Louisville [*Kentucky*] Standiford Airport [*Airport symbol*]
SDF	Sanatana Dharma Foundation (EA)
SDF	Satellite Distribution Frame [*Telecommunications*] (TEL)
SDF	Screen Definition Facility [*Data processing*]
SDF	Seasonal Derating Factor (IEEE)
SDF	Self-Defense Force [*Japan*]
SDF	Simplified Directional Facility [*Aviation*]
SDF	Single Defruit [*Aviation*] (FAAC)
SDF	Single Degree of Freedom [*Also, SDOF*] [*Acoustics*]
SDF	Sioux Falls College, Sioux Falls, SD [*OCLC symbol*] (OCLC)
SDF	Slow Death Factor [*Medicine*]
SDF	Social Democratic Federation [*Later, SDP*] [*Early British political party, members of which were sometimes referred to as "Silly Damn Fools"*]
SDF	Social Democratic Federation [*Icelandic*] (PPW)
SDF	Social Democratic Federation [*Shaminren*] [*Japan*] (PPW)
SDF	Social Democratic Front [*Ghanaian*] (PPW)
SDF	Software Development Facility [*Military*] (CAAL)
SDF	Sonic Depth Finder
SDF	Source Development Fund [*Supply and Services Canada*]
SDF	Source Document Folders [*IRS*]
SDF	Southern Development Foundation [*Lafayette, LA*] (EA)
SDF	Special Denatured Formula [*Applied to alcohol*]
SDF	Spectral Density Function
SDF	Standard Distribution Format [*Data processing*]
SDF	Standard Drug File [*Derwent Publications Ltd.*] [*Database*]
SDF	Static Direction Finder
SDF	Stopping Distance Factor (MCD)
SDF	Stowe-Day Foundation (EA)
SDF	Strategic Defensive Forces [*Army*] (AABC)
SDF	Student Description Form [*Psychology*]
SDF	Sudan Defence Force [*British*]
SDF	Sundorph Aeronautical Corp. [*Cleveland, OH*] [*FAA designator*] (FAAC)
SDF	Supergroup Distribution Frame [*Telecommunications*] (TEL)
SDF	Surface Direct Fire [*Navy*] (CAAL)
SDF	Swedish Defense Forces
SDF	System Data Format [*Data processing*]
SDF	System Development Facility (KSC)
SD Farm Home Res	South Dakota Farm and Home Research [*A publication*]
SDFAUS	State Defense Force Association of the United States (EA)
SDFC	Space Disturbance Forecast Center [*Environmental Science Services Administration*] (IEEE)
SDFC	Standardized Discriminant Function Coefficient
SDFL	Schottky Diode FET [*Field Effect Transistor*] Logic
SD Fla	United States District Court for the Southern District of Florida (DLA)
SDFN	SONAR Dome Flow Noise
SdFr	Freeman Public Library, Freeman, SD [*Library symbol*] [*Library of Congress*] (LCLS)
SDFRA	Reports. Faculty of Science. Shizuoka University [*A publication*]
SD/FS	Smoke Detector/Fire Suppression (MCD)
SDFS	Standard Disk Filing System
SDFTN	Soda Fountain
SDG	Sacred Dance Guild (EA)
SDG	Scan Display Generator
SDG	Schriften der Droste-Gesellschaft [*A publication*]
SDG	Screen Directors' Guild of America [*Later, DGA*]
SDG	Siding (AAG)
SDG	Simulated Data Generator
SDG	Situation Display Generator
SDG	Soli Deo Gloria [*Glory to God Alone*] [*Latin*]
SDG	Special Development Groups [*Navy*]
SdG	Studii de Gramatica [*A publication*]
SDG	Subminiature Displacement Gyroscope

SDG........... Sucrose Density Gradients
SDG........... Sundance Gold Mining Ltd. [*Vancouver Stock Exchange symbol*]
SDG........... System Design Group (MCD)
SDGA....... Single Degaussing Cable
SDGA....... Sucrose Density Gradient Analysis [*Clinical chemistry*]
SD GA .... United States District Court for the Southern District of Georgia (DLA)
SDGC........ Simulated Distillation Gas Chromatography
SDGC........ Sun-Diamond Growers of California (EA)
SDGE .... Situation Display Generator Element
SdGe.......... Sully-Potter County Library, Gettysburg, SD [*Library symbol*] [*Library of Congress*] (LCLS)
SD Geol Surv Bull ... South Dakota. Geological Survey. Bulletin [*A publication*]
SD Geol Surv Misc Invest ... South Dakota. Geological Survey. Miscellaneous Investigations [*A publication*]
SD Geol Surv Rep Invest ... South Dakota. Geological Survey. Report of Investigations [*A publication*]
SD Geol Surv Spec Rep ... South Dakota. Geological Survey. Special Report [*A publication*]
SDGH .... Sweet Dough
SDGW .... Structural Design Gross Weight
SDH........... Scottish Diploma in Horticulture
SDH........... Seasonal Derated Hours (IEEE)
SDH........... Single Dad's Hotline (EA)
SDH........... Slavistische Drukken en Herdrukken [*A publication*]
SDH........... Software Development Handbook [*NASA*] (NASA)
SDH........... Sorbitol Dehydrogenase [*Also, Sorb D*] [*An enzyme*]
SDH........... South Dakota Historical Resource Center, Pierre, SD [*OCLC symbol*] (OCLC)
SDH........... Spinal Dorsal Horn [*Anatomy*]
SDH........... Structured Document Handbook [*Data processing*]
SDH........... Styling Data Handling
SDH........... Subdural Hematoma [*Medicine*]
SDH........... Succinic Dehydrogenase [*An enzyme*]
SDH........... Support Dogs for the Handicapped [*Grove City, OH*] (EA)
SDHD .... Society of Daughters of Holland Dames (EA)
SDHD .... Sudden-Death Heart Disease [*Medicine*]
SDHE........ Spacecraft Data Handling Equipment
SdHi .... South Dakota Department of Cultural Affairs, Historical Resources Center, Pierre, SD [*Library symbol*] [*Library of Congress*] (LCLS)
SDHI.......... Studia et Documenta Historiae et Iuris [*A publication*]
SdHig .... Hyde County Library, Highmore, SD [*Library symbol*] [*Library of Congress*] (LCLS)
SDHIRS ...... Subdistrict Headquarters Induction and Recruiting Station [*Navy*]
SdHM .... Minnehaha County Rural Library, Hartford, SD [*Library symbol*] [*Library of Congress*] (LCLS)
SdHow .... Howard Public Library, Howard, SD [*Library symbol*] [*Library of Congress*] (LCLS)
SDHS .... Society of Dance History Scholars (EA)
SdHsV .... United States Veterans Administration Center, Hot Springs, SD [*Library symbol*] [*Library of Congress*] (LCLS)
SdHuro....... Huron Public Library, Huron, SD [*Library symbol*] [*Library of Congress*] (LCLS)
SdHuroC .... Huron College, Huron, SD [*Library symbol*] [*Library of Congress*] (LCLS)
SDI .... Saidor [*Papua New Guinea*] [*Airport symbol*] (OAG)
SDI .... Saudi Arabian Airlines
SDI .... Selected Descriptive Item
SDI .... Selective Dissemination of Information [*System*] [*Data processing*]
SDI .... Serial Dilution Indicator [*Clinical chemistry*]
SDI .... Service de Documentation Interministerielle [*Interministerial Documentation Service*] [*National Telecommunications Research Center*] [*Issy Les Moulineaux, France*] [*Information service*] (EISS)
SDI .... Services Delivery Improvement
SDI .... Source Data Information
SDI .... Standard Data Interface [*Data processing*]
SDI .... Standard Deviation Interval [*Medicine*]
SDI .... Standardized Discharge Instructions [*for hospital patients*]
SDI .... State Disability Insurance
SDI .... Steel Deck Institute [*Canton, OH*] (EA)
SDI .... Steel Door Institute [*Cleveland, OH*] (EA)
SDI .... Strategic Defense Initiative [*Reagan administration*] [*Facetiously translated as "Silly Damn Idea"*]
SDI .... Subcontractor Data Item
SDI .... Supplier Data Item (MCD)
SDI .... Support Directive Instruction (KSC)
SDI .... Symbolic Displays, Incorporated (MCD)
SD & I .... System Development and Integration (MCD)
SDIA.......... Small Defense Industries Association [*Later, Strategic Industries Association*]
SDICC........ Societe de Developpement de l'Industrie Cinematographique Canadienne [*Canadian Film Development Corporation - CFDC*]
SDID.......... Supplier Data Item Description (MCD)
SDIE .... Special Defense Intelligence Estimate (MCD)

SDIF .... Software Development and Integration Facility [*NASA*] (NASA)
SDIG.......... Screen Directors International Guild [*Absorbed by Directors Guild of America*] (EA)
SDIHD .... Sudden-Death Ischemic Heart Disease [*Medicine*]
SDILINE ..... Selective Dissemination of Information Online [*National Library of Medicine*] [*Bethesda, MD*] [*Bibliographic database*]
SD III .... United States District Court for the Southern District of Illinois (DLA)
SDIM .... System of Documentation and Information for Metallurgy [*Commission of the European Communities*] [*Database*] [*Information service*] (EISS)
SDIM1 .... System fuer Dokumentation und Information der Metallurgie [*System for Documentation and Information in Metallurgy*] [*Fachinformationszentrum Werkstoffe*] [*Database*] [*German*]
SDIM1 .... Systeme de Documentation et d'Information en Metallurgie [*System for Documentation and Information in Metallurgy*] [*Database*] [*French*]
SDIN.......... Special Defence Intelligence Notice (MCD)
SD Ind .... United States District Court for the Southern District of Indiana (DLA)
SDIO.......... Serial Digit Input/Output [*Data processing*]
SDIO.......... Strategic Defense Initiative Organization [*Military*] (RDA)
SDIOA .... Studia et Documenta ad Iura Orientis Antiqui Pertinenta [*A publication*]
SDIOAP...... Studia et Documenta ad Iura Orientis Antiqui Pertinenta [*A publication*]
SD Iowa...... United States District Court for the Southern District of Iowa (DLA)
SDIP .... Specifically Designated Intelligence Position (AFM)
SDIP .... Strengthening Developing Institutions Program [*HEW*]
SDIP .... System Description and Implementation Plan [*Navy*]
SDIS.......... Ship Distance
SDIS.......... Ship Draft Indicating System (MSA)
SDIT.......... Service de Documentation et d'Information Techniques de l'Aeronautique
SDIT .... Ship Draft Indicator Transmitter (MSA)
SDI/UC ..... State Disability Insurance - Unemployment Compensation
SDIZ .... Submarine Defense Identification Zone
SDJ .... Greensboro, NC [*Location identifier*] [*FAA*] (FAAL)
SDJ .... Sanada [*Japan*] [*Seismograph station code, US Geological Survey*] (SEIS)
SDJ .... Sendai [*Japan*] [*Airport symbol*] (OAG)
SDJ .... Society of the Devotees of Jerusalem (EA)
SD J Med ... South Dakota Journal of Medicine [*A publication*]
SD J Med Pharm ... South Dakota Journal of Medicine and Pharmacy [*A publication*]
S & DJR...... Somerset & Dorset Joint Railway [*British*]
SDK........... Sandakan [*Malaysia*] [*Airport symbol*] (OAG)
SDK........... Seljacko-Demokratska Koalicija [*Peasant-Democratic Coalition*] [*Yugoslav*] (PPE)
SDK........... Shelter Deck
SDK........... Si De Ka Quarterly [*Ann Arbor, MI*] (DLA)
SDK........... Sigma Delta Kappa [*Fraternity*]
SDK........... Studebaker's Resource Development Ltd. [*Formerly, Rio Blanco Resources Ltd.*] [*Vancouver Stock Exchange symbol*]
SDK........... System Design Kit
SdKJ .... Jackson-Washabaugh County Library, Kadoka, SD [*Library symbol*] [*Library of Congress*] (LCLS)
SDKK........ Studia z Dziejow Kosciola Katolickiego [*A publication*]
SDKOD ..... Saitama Daigaku Kiyo. Kogakubu [*A publication*]
SDKSB....... Saitama Daigaku Kiyo. Shizenkagaku-Hen [*A publication*]
SdL............ Hearst Free Library, Lead, SD [*Library symbol*] [*Library of Congress*] (LCLS)
SDL .... National Council, Sons and Daughters of Liberty (EA)
SDL .... Saddle (MSA)
SDL .... Scenario Development Language [*Military*] (CAAL)
SDL .... Scientific DataLink [*Comtex Scientific Corp.*] [*New York, NY*] [*Information service*] (EISS)
SDL .... Scottie Gold Mines [*Vancouver Stock Exchange symbol*]
SDL .... Scottsdale, AZ [*Location identifier*] [*FAA*] (FAAL)
SDL .... Semiconductor Diode LASER [*Also, TDL*]
SDL .... Shaft Driver, Left
SDL .... Slowdown Length
SDL .... Software Design Language
SDL .... Software Development Laboratory [*NASA*] (NASA)
SDL .... Software Development Language [*Burroughs Corp.*]
SDL .... Sonic Delay Line
SDL .... Space Dynamics Laboratories [*Utah State University*] [*Research center*] (RCD)
SDL .... Specification and Description Language [*Telecommunications*] (TEL)
SDL .... Standard Distribution List [*NASA*]
SDL .... Stark County District Library, Canton, OH [*OCLC symbol*] (OCLC)
SDL .... Strip Delay Line
SDL .... Sundsvall [*Sweden*] [*Airport symbol*] (OAG)
SDL .... Supporting Document List
SDL .... Surplus Distribution List (AAG)
SDL .... System Descriptive Language [*Data processing*] (IEEE)

SDL .... System Design Language
SDL .... System Development Language [*1971*] [*Data processing*] (CSR)
SDL .... System Directory List [*Data processing*] (BUR)
SDL .... Systematic Design Language [*Data processing*]
SDL .... Systems Development Laboratories (MCD)
SDLC .... Synchronous Data-Link Control [*Telecommunications*]
SDLC .... System Data Link Control [*Telecommunications*]
SDLC .... System Development Life Cycle
SdLeH .... Lennox High School Library, Lennox, SD [*Library symbol*] [*Library of Congress*] (LCLS)
SdLem .... Lemmon Public Library, Lemmon, SD [*Library symbol*] [*Library of Congress*] (LCLS)
SdLemH ..... Lemmon High School Library, Lemmon, SD [*Library symbol*] [*Library of Congress*] (LCLS)
SDLM .... Standard Depot Level Maintenance (MCD)
SDLO .... State, Defense Liaison Office
SDLP .... Social Democratic and Labour Party [*Northern Ireland*] (PPW)
SDLP .... Societe de Developpement du Livre et du Periodique [*Society for the Development of Books and Periodicals*] [*Canada*]
SD L Rev .... South Dakota Law Review [*A publication*]
SdM .... Mitchell Public Library, Mitchell, SD [*Library symbol*] [*Library of Congress*] (LCLS)
SDM .... National Association of Special Delivery Messengers [*Later, APWU*] [*AFL-CIO*]
SDM .... Samsonov Density Meter [*Gravimetrics*]
SDM .... San Diego, CA [*Location identifier*] [*FAA*] (FAAL)
SDM .... Santiago De Maria [*El Salvador*] [*Seismograph station code, US Geological Survey*] (SEIS)
SDM .... School in District Management [*LIMRA*]
SDM .... Selective Dissemination of Microfiche
SDM .... Semiconductor Disk Memory
SDM .... Sensory Detection Method [*for measuring blood pressure*]
SDM .... Sequency-Division Multiplexing (IEEE)
SDM .... Short-Delay Monostable [*Circuitry*]
SDM .... Shutdown Margin [*Nuclear energy*] (NRCH)
SDM .... Shutdown Mode (IEEE)
SDM .... Shuttle Data Management [*NASA*] (MCD)
SdM .... Siglo de las Misiones [*A publication*]
SDM .... Simulated Dynamic Missile [*Military*] (CAAL)
SDM .... Site Defense of Minuteman [*Missiles*] (MCD)
SDM .... Slowdown Model
SDM .... Soma Dendrite Membrane
SDM .... Sons and Daughters of Malta (EA)
SDM .... Space Division Multiplexing [*Physics*]
SDM .... Spares Determination Method [*Bell System*]
SDM .... Specially Designated Merchant [*Liquor sales*]
SDM .... Standardization Design Memoranda (IEEE)
SDM .... STARAN Debug Module
SDM .... Statistical Delta Modulation
SDM .... Statistical-Dynamical Model
SDM .... Structures, Structural Dynamics, and Materials (MCD)
SDM .... Subdivision Manager
SDM .... Subsystem Design Manual (MCD)
SDM .... Synchronous Digital Machine
SDM .... System Definition Manual [*NASA*] (NASA)
SdMa .... Bennett County Library, Martin, SD [*Library symbol*] [*Library of Congress*] (LCLS)
SDMA .... Sam Davis Memorial Association (EA)
SDMA .... Shared Direct Memory Access [*Sperry UNIVAC*]
SDMA .... Sodium Dihydrobis(methoxyethoxy)aluminate [*Organic chemistry*]
SDMA .... Space Division Multiple Access
SdMadT ..... Dakota State College, Madison, SD [*Library symbol*] [*Library of Congress*] (LCLS)
SdMar .... Dakota Wowapipahi Library, Marty, SD [*Library symbol*] [*Library of Congress*] (LCLS)
SDME .... Synchronous Data Modern Equipment
SDMEA .... South Dakota Journal of Medicine [*A publication*]
SdMeS .... Menno Public School Library, Menno, SD [*Library symbol*] [*Library of Congress*] (LCLS)
SD (Met) .... Doctor of Science in Metallurgy
SDMH .... Symmetrical-Dimthylhydrazine [*Organic chemistry*]
SdMi .... Hand County Library, Miller, SD [*Library symbol*] [*Library of Congress*] (LCLS)
S-DMICC ... State-Defense Military Information Control Committee (AFM)
SdMil .... Milbank Carnegie Library, Milbank, SD [*Library symbol*] [*Library of Congress*] (LCLS)
SDMIS .... Standardization Data Management Information System
SD Miss ...... United States District Court for the Southern District of Mississippi (DLA)
SDMIX .... South Dakota Medical Information Exchange [*University of South Dakota*] [*Sioux Falls*] [*Telecommunications*] (TSSD)
SDMJ .... September, December, March, and June [*Denotes quarterly payments of interest or dividends in these months*] [*Business and trade*]
SdMo .... A. H. Brown Public Library, Mobridge, SD [*Library symbol*] [*Library of Congress*] (LCLS)
SDMO .... Subcommand Data Management Office [*Military*] (AFIT)
SDMS .... Shipboard Data Multiplex System (MCD)

SDMS .... Society of Diagnostic Medical Sonographers [*Dallas, TX*] (EA)
SDMS .... Spatial Data Management System (MCD)
SDMS .... Supplier Data Management System (MCD)
SDMT .... Stanford Diagnostic Mathematics Test [*Education*]
SDMT .... Stress and Degraded Mode Test (CAAL)
SdMW .... Dakota Wesleyan University, Mitchell, SD [*Library symbol*] [*Library of Congress*] (LCLS)
SDN .... North American Baptist Seminary, Sioux Falls, SD [*OCLC symbol*] (OCLC)
SDN .... Sandane [*Norway*] [*Airport symbol*] (OAG)
SDN .... Satellite Data Network [*AgriData Resources, Inc.*] [*Milwaukee, WI*] [*Telecommunications service*] (TSSD)
SDN .... Secret Document Number
SDN .... Separation Designation Number
SDN .... Service Dealer's Newsletter [*Lynott Associates*] [*Abington, PA*] [*A publication*] [*Information service*] (EISS)
SDN .... Sexually Dimorphic Nucleus [*Brain anatomy*]
SDN .... Societe Demographique Nordique [*Nordic Demographic Society - NDS*] (EA-IO)
SDN .... Societe des Nations [*League of Nations*]
SDN .... Software Development Note [*NASA*] (NASA)
SDN .... Subdeacon
SDN .... Subscriber's Directory Number [*Telecommunications*] (TEL)
SDN .... Sudan [*Three-letter standard code*] (CNC)
SDN .... Swindon [*British depot code*]
SDN .... Synchronized Digital Network [*Telecommunications*] (TEL)
SDNCO ...... Staff Duty Noncommissioned Officer [*Army*]
SdNe .... Newell Public Library, Newell, SD [*Library symbol*] [*Library of Congress*] (LCLS)
SdNeu .... New Underwood Public Library, New Underwood, SD [*Library symbol*] [*Library of Congress*] (LCLS)
SDNIA .... Saga Daigaku Nogaku Iho [*A publication*]
SDNRIU ..... Secure Digital Net Radio Interface Unit [*Army*] (RDA)
SDN & SU ... Step-Down and Step-Up (MSA)
SDNT .... Student
SD Nurse .... South Dakota Nurse [*A publication*]
SDNY .... United States District Court for the Southern District of New York (DLA)
SDO .... Oglala Sioux Community College, Learning Resources Center, Pine Ridge, SD [*OCLC symbol*] (OCLC)
SdO .... Onida Public Library, Onida, SD [*Library symbol*] [*Library of Congress*] (LCLS)
SDO .... Salado [*Chile*] [*Seismograph station code, US Geological Survey*] [*Closed*] (SEIS)
SDO .... San Diego Gas & Electric Co. [*NYSE symbol*]
SDO .... Schedules Duty Officer (KSC)
SDO .... Senior Duty Officer [*Air Force*] [*British*]
SDO .... Serra Dor [*A publication*]
SDO .... Shielded Diatomic Orbitals [*Atomic physics*]
SDO .... Ship Development Objective [*Navy*]
SDO .... Shipboard Distribution Only [*Navy*] (CAAL)
SDO .... Sod House, NV [*Location identifier*] [*FAA*] (FAAL)
SDO .... SONAR Detection Opportunity [*Navy*] (CAAL)
SDO .... Source Data Operation (MDG)
SDO .... Special Duty Officer (MCD)
SDO .... Special Duty Only [*Military*]
SDO .... Specialist Duty Only [*Navy personnel designation*]
SDO .... Squadron Duty Officer [*Navy*] (NVT)
SDO .... Staff Duty Officer [*Army*]
SDO .... Station Duty Officer [*Navy*]
SDO .... Synthetic Drying Oil
SDO .... Systems Development Office [*National Weather Service*]
SDOB .... Scaled Depth of Burst (MCD)
S Doc .... Senate Document (DLA)
SDOC .... Specific Direct Operating Costs
SDOE .... State Department of Education (OICC)
SDOF .... Single Degree of Freedom [*Also, SDF*] [*Acoustics*]
SDOG .... Sendschrift der Deutschen Orient-Gesellschaft [*Leipzig*] [*A publication*]
SD Ohio ...... United States District Court for the Southern District of Ohio (DLA)
SDOM .... Society of Dirty Old Men (EA)
SDOP .... Sons and Daughters of Oregon Pioneers (EA)
SDOPR .... Sound Operator [*Navy*]
SDP .... National Society, Sons and Daughters of the Pilgrims (EA)
SDP .... Sacrodextra Posterior [*A fetal position*] [*Obstetrics*]
SDP .... Sand Point [*Alaska*] [*Airport symbol*] (OAG)
SDP .... Sand Point, AK [*Location identifier*] [*FAA*] (FAAL)
SDP .... Scottish Diploma in Poultry Husbandry
SDP .... Sea Duty Pay [*Navy*]
SDP .... Sentry Dog Patrol (AFM)
SDP .... Set-Down Pool [*Nuclear energy*] (NRCH)
SDP .... Seychelles Democratic Party
SDP .... Shelf Dynamics Program [*CUE*] (MSC)
SDP .... Ship Development Plan [*Navy*]
SDP .... Short-Day Plant [*Botany*]
SDP .... Shuttle Data Processor [*NASA*] (MCD)
SDP .... Signal Data Processor
SDP .... Signal Dispatch Point [*Telecommunications*] (TEL)
SDP .... Silicon Diode Pellet
SDP .... Singapore Democratic Party (PPW)

SDP .... Single Department Purchasing [*Agency*]
SDP .... Sirotherm Demineralization Process
SDP .... Site Data Processors
SDP .... Slowdown Power
SDP .... Small Distribution Phenomena
SDP .... Smoke Dispersion Pod
SDP .... Social Democratic Party [*British*]
SDP .... Social Democratic Party [*West Germany*]
SDP .... Social Democratic Party [*Philippine*]   (PPW)
SDP .... Social Democratic Party [*Trinidadian and Tobagan*]   (PPW)
SDP .... Social Democratic Party [*Sangkhom Prachatipatai*] [*Thai*]   (PPW)
SDP .... Social Democratic Party [*Althyduflokkurinn*] [*Icelandic*]   (PPW)
SDP .... Software Development Plan [*NASA*]   (NASA)
SDP .... Solar Desalination Plant
SDP .... Source Data Processing
SDP .... Sozial Demokratesch Partei [*Social Democratic Party*] [*Luxembourg*]   (PPE)
SDP .... Spectral Dependence Photocurrent
SDP .... State Data Program [*University of California, Berkeley*] [*Information service*]   (EISS)
SDP .... Station Data Processing
SDP .... Storage and Distribution Point [*Military*]   (AFM)
SdP .... Sudetendeutsche Partei [*Sudeten German Party*] [*Czechoslovak*]   (PPE)
SDP .... Sulfonyldiphenol [*Organic chemistry*]
SDP .... Sun Distributors, Inc. [*NYSE symbol*]
SDP .... Supply Distribution Point
SDP .... Surface Deformation Pattern
SDP .... Survey Data Processing
Sdp .... Suspended in Part [*Regulation or order suspended in part*]   (DLA)
SDP .... Swaziland Democratic Party
SDP .... System Design Proposal [*Navy*]
SDP .... Systems Development Package [*or Plan*]   (NG)
SdPa .... Parker Public Library, Parker, SD [*Library symbol*] [*Library of Congress*]   (LCLS)
SDPA......... Small Defense Plants Administration [*Terminated, 1953*]
SDPC......... Shuttle Data Processing Complex   (MCD)
SDPC......... Social Democratic Party of Canada
SDPD .... Special Defense Projects Department
SDPDA...... Special Defense Property Disposal Account [*DoD*]
SdPEC ...... South Dakota Department of Education and Cultural Affairs, Historical Resources Center, Pierre, SD [*Library symbol*] [*Library of Congress*]   (LCLS)
SDPF......... Sensor Data Processing Facility   (MCD)
SDPF......... Social-Democratic Party of Finland
SdPiO........ Oglala Sioux Community College, Pine Ridge, SD [*Library symbol*] [*Library of Congress*]   (LCLS)
SdPl .... Plankinton City Library, Plankinton, SD [*Library symbol*] [*Library of Congress*]   (LCLS)
SDPL......... Safeguard Data Processing Laboratory [*Army*]   (AABC)
SDPL......... Sensor Data Processing Laboratory   (MCD)
SDPL......... Servomechanisms and Data Processing Laboratory [*Massachusetts Institute of Technology*]   (MCD)
SDPO .... Site Defense Project Office [*Military*]   (AABC)
SDPO .... Space Defense Project Office [*AMC*]
SdPr .... Presho Public Library, Presho, SD [*Library symbol*] [*Library of Congress*]   (LCLS)
SDPR......... Sons and Daughters of Pioneer Rivermen   (EA)
SDPR......... System Design and Performance Requirements
SDPS......... Signal Data Processing System
SDPT......... Structured Doll Play Test [*Psychology*]
SDQ........... Santo Domingo [*Dominican Republic*] [*Airport symbol*]   (OAG)
SDQ........... Student Description Questionnaire
SDQFC...... Sir Douglas Quintet Fan Club   (EA)
SDR........... New York State Department Reports   (DLA)
SdR .... Rapid City Public Library, Rapid City, SD [*Library symbol*] [*Library of Congress*]   (LCLS)
SDR........... Santander [*Spain*] [*Airport symbol*]   (OAG)
SDR........... Schlumberger-Doll Research Center, Ridgefield, CT [*OCLC symbol*]   (OCLC)
SDR........... Scientific Data Recorder
SDR........... Search Decision Rule [*Data processing*]
SDR........... Seismic Detection and Ranging
SDR........... Self-Decoding Readout
SDR........... Sender   (KSC)
SDR........... Sensor Data Record [*For spacecraft*]
SDR........... Service Difficulty Report   (MCD)
SDR........... Sezione Demografia e Razza [*A publication*]
SDR........... Shaft Driver, Right
SDR........... Sheffield District Railway   (ROG)
SDR........... Ship Destination Room   (NATG)
SDR........... Ship Diversion Room   (NATG)
SDR........... Shipment Document Release [*Military*]   (AFIT)
SDR........... Signal Data Recorder   (MCD)
SDR........... Signal Distribution Room [*NASA*]   (KSC)
SDR........... Significant Deficiency Report   (IEEE)
SDR........... Simple Detection Response
SDR........... Single-Drift Region   (IEEE)

SDR........... Sisters of the Divine Redeemer [*Roman Catholic religious order*]
SDR........... Sloane, Donald R., New York NY [*STAC*]
SDR........... Small Development Requirement [*Military*]
SDR........... SNAP [*Systems for Nuclear Auxiliary Power*] Development Reactor
SDR........... Snyder, TX [*Location identifier*] [*FAA*]   (FAAL)
SDR........... Sodium Deuterium Reactor
SDR........... Software Design Requirement [*NASA*]   (NASA)
SDR........... Software Design Review   (MCD)
SDR........... Solution Development Record
S & DR....... Somerset & Dorset Joint Railway [*British*]   (ROG)
SDR........... SONAR Data Recorder
SDR........... Sophisticated Data Research, Inc. [*Atlanta, GA*] [*Information service*]   (EISS)
SDR........... Sounder   (MSA)
SDR........... South Dakota Review [*A publication*]
SDR........... South Devon Railway   (ROG)
SDR........... Spacelab Disposition Record [*NASA*]   (NASA)
SDR........... Special Despatch Rider
SDR........... Special Drawing Rights [*International Monetary Fund*]
SDR........... Spin Dependent Resonance [*Physics*]
SDR........... Splash Detection RADAR
SDR........... Statistical Data Recorder [*Data processing*]   (MDG)
SDR........... Storage Data Register   (MCD)
SDR........... Strip Domain Resonance
SDR........... Stroud Resources Ltd. [*Toronto Stock Exchange symbol*]
SDR........... Successive Discrimination Reversal
SDR........... Suddeutscher Rundfunk [*South German Radio Network*]
SDR........... Survey of Doctorate Recipients [*National Research Council*] [*Database*]
SDR........... System Data Record
SDR........... System for Data Retrieval [*Information retrieval*]
SDR........... System Definition Record [*Data processing*]   (IBMDP)
SDR........... System Definition Requirement
SDR........... System Design Report [*NATO*]   (NATG)
SDR........... System Design Review [*NASA*]   (NASA)
SDR........... System Development Requirement [*Air Force*]
SDR........... System Discrepancy Report
S DRAKE.... Second Dynamic Response and Kinematics Experiment [*Marine science*]   (MSC)
SDRB........ Software Design Review Board [*NASA*]   (NASA)
SDR & C ..... Shipment Document Release and Control [*Military*]   (AFIT)
SDRC Ops ... South Dakota Board of Railroad Commissioners Opinions   (DLA)
SdRe .... Redfield Carnegie Library, Redfield, SD [*Library symbol*] [*Library of Congress*]   (LCLS)
SDRL........ Subcontractor Data Requirements List
SdRM .... South Dakota School of Mines and Technology, Rapid City, SD [*Library symbol*] [*Library of Congress*]   (LCLS)
SdRN.......... National College of Business, Rapid City, SD [*Library symbol*] [*Library of Congress*]   (LCLS)
SDRNG...... Sound Ranging   (MUGU)
SDRP........ Simulated Data Reduction Program
SdRS .... Saint Martins Academy, Rapid City, SD [*Library symbol*] [*Library of Congress*]   (LCLS)
SDRS........ Signal Data Recording Set   (MCD)
SDRS........ Splash Detection RADAR System   (MCD)
SDRSA....... Shimane Daigaku Ronshu: Shizen Kagaku [*A publication*]
SDRT........ Stanford Diagnostic Reading Test [*Education*]
SDRW........ SONAR Dome Rubber Window   (NVT)
S-DRY .... Surfaced Dry [*Lumber*]
SDS .... Safety Data Sheet   (KSC)
SDS .... St. David's Society of the State of New York   (EA)
SDS .... Same Day Surgery [*Medicine*]
SDS .... Samostalna Demokratska Stranka [*Independent Democratic Party*] [*Yugoslav*]   (PPE)
SDS .... Sample Display Service [*Department of Commerce*]
SDS .... Sanatorio Duran [*Costa Rica*] [*Seismograph station code, US Geological Survey*]   (SEIS)
SDS .... Satellite Data System [*Air Force*]
SDS .... School Dental Service
SDS .... Scientific Data System [*Later, XDS*]
SDS .... Self-Directed Search
SDS .... Self-Rating Depression Scale [*Psychology*]
SDS .... Sensory Deprivation Syndrome [*Medicine*]
SDS .... Servo Drive System
SDS .... Sexual Differentiation Scale [*Psychometrics*]
SDS .... Ship Defense System
SDS .... Shop Distribution Standards   (KSC)
SDS .... Short Distance Swimmer
SDS .... Shuttle Dynamic Simulation [*NASA*]   (NASA)
SDS .... Sign-Digit Subtractor
SDS .... Signal Distribution System
SDS .... Simulating Digital Systems
SDS .... Simulation Data Subsystem   (KSC)
SDS .... Sisters of the Divine Saviour [*Roman Catholic religious order*]
SDS .... Smoke Destruction System
SDS .... Societas Divini Salvatoris [*Society of the Divine Saviour*] [*Salvatorians*] [*Roman Catholic men's religious order*]
SDS .... Sodium Dodecyl Sulfate [*Also, SLS*] [*Organic chemistry*]

SDS .... Software Design Specification [*NASA*] (NASA)
SDS .... Software Development System
SDS .... Solar Disk Simulator
SDS .... Sons and Daughters of the Soddies (EA)
SDS .... South Dakota State Library Commission, Pierre, SD [*OCLC symbol*] (OCLC)
SDS .... Sozialistischer Deutscher Studentenbund [*Student political organization*] [*Germany*]
SDS .... Space Defense System (AAG)
SDS .... Space Division Switching [*Telecommunications*]
SDS .... Space Documentation Service [*NASA/ESRO*] (DIT)
SDS .... Spacecraft Design Specification
SDS .... Special Distress Signal (DEN)
SDS .... Special Docking Simulator [*NASA*] (KSC)
SDS .... Spectrometer Digital System
SDS .... Splash Detection System
SDS .... Status Display Support (MCD)
SDS .... Steam Dump System [*Nuclear energy*] (NRCH)
SDS .... Steering Damping System (MCD)
SDS .... Stimulator of DNA Synthesis [*Immunochemistry*]
SDS .... Students for a Democratic Society (EA)
SDS .... Submerged Demineralizer System [*Water purification*]
SDS .... Sudden Death Syndrome [*in children*] [*Medicine*]
SDS .... Sudden Drowning Syndrome
SDS .... Supplemental Data Sheet
SDS .... Supplier Data Sheet
SDS .... Sweet Dough Stabilizer [*Brand of bakery product from H. C. Brill Co., Inc.*]
SDS .... Swimmer Distress Signal [*Navy*] (CAAL)
SDS .... Sydsvenska Dagbladet Snaellposten [*A publication*]
SDS .... System Data Synthesizer (KSC)
SDS .... System Design Specification
SDS .... Systematic Design Language [*Data processing*]
SDSAM ...... Specifically Designated Special Air Mission [*Aircraft*] [*Air Force*]
SDSBE .... San Diego Symposium for Biomedical Engineering
SDSC .... San Diego State College [*California*]
SDSC .... San Diego Supercomputer Center
Sd-SC .... South Dakota Supreme Court Library, Pierre, SD [*Library symbol*] [*Library of Congress*] (LCLS)
SD Sch Mines Bull ... South Dakota. School of Mines. Bulletin [*A publication*]
SDSD .... Saco Defense Systems Division [*Maremont Corp.*] (RDA)
SDSD .... Satellite Data Services Division [*National Oceanic and Atmospheric Administration*] [*Washington, DC*] [*Information service*] (EISS)
SDSD .... Single Disk Storage Device [*Data processing*] (BUR)
SDSD .... Studi e Documenti di Storia e Diritto [*A publication*]
SDSE .... Society of the Descendants of the Schwenkfeldian Exiles (EA)
SD Sess Laws ... South Dakota Session Laws (DLA)
SDSH .... Society Devoted to the Sacred Heart [*Roman Catholic women's religious order*]
SDSI .... Shared Data Set Integrity
SdSi .... Sisseton Library, Sisseton, SD [*Library symbol*] [*Library of Congress*] (LCLS)
SdSif .... Sioux Falls Carnegie Free Public Library, Sioux Falls, SD [*Library symbol*] [*Library of Congress*] (LCLS)
SdSifA .... Augustana College, Sioux Falls, SD [*Library symbol*] [*Library of Congress*] (LCLS)
SdSifB .... North American Baptist Seminary, Sioux Falls, SD [*Library symbol*] [*Library of Congress*] (LCLS)
SdSifC ...... Sioux Falls College, Sioux Falls, SD [*Library symbol*] [*Library of Congress*] (LCLS)
SdSifH .... Coolidge High School Library, Sioux Falls, SD [*Library symbol*] [*Library of Congress*] (LCLS)
SdSifV .... United States Veterans Administration Center, Sioux Falls, SD [*Library symbol*] [*Library of Congress*] (LCLS)
SDSL .... Sail Dynamics Simulation Laboratory (MCD)
SDSL .... Subject Directory of Special Libraries [*A publication*]
SD SMS CLSD ... Side Seams Closed [*Freight*]
SdSpe .... Grace Balloch Memorial Library, Spearfish, SD [*Library symbol*] [*Library of Congress*] (LCLS)
SdSpen ..... Hanson-McCook County Regional Library, Spencer, SD [*Library symbol*] [*Library of Congress*] (LCLS)
SdSpeT ...... Black Hills State College, Spearfish, SD [*Library symbol*] [*Library of Congress*] (LCLS)
SdSpU .... University of South Dakota at Springfield, Springfield, SD [*Library symbol*] [*Library of Congress*] (LCLS)
SDS & RU ... Soil Data Storage and Retrieval Unit [*Department of Agriculture*] (EISS)
SDSS .... Satellite Data System Spacecraft [*Air Force*]
SDSS .... Self-Deploying Space Station
SDSS .... Space Division Shuttle Simulator [*NASA*] (NASA)
SDSSE ...... Science Data System Support Equipment
SdSt .... Sturgis Public Library, Sturgis, SD [*Library symbol*] [*Library of Congress*] (LCLS)
SD St BJ ..... South Dakota State Bar Journal (DLA)
SDSVF ...... State Dependent State Variable Feedback [*Rocket engine*] [*NASA*]
SDSW .... Sense Device Status Word
SDT .... National College Library, Rapid City, SD [*OCLC symbol*] (OCLC)

SDT .... Sacrodextra Transversa [*A fetal position*] [*Obstetrics*]
SDT .... Saidu Sharif [*Pakistan*] [*Airport symbol*] (OAG)
SDT .... Saturated Discharge Temperature [*Refrigeration*]
SDT .... Science Data Team
SDT .... Scientific Distribution Technique
SDT .... Sea Depth Transducer
SDT .... Second Destination Transportation (MCD)
SDT .... Serial Data Transmission
SDT .... Serum Dilution Test [*Clinical chemistry*]
SDT .... Shell-Destroying Tracer [*Ammunition*]
SDT .... Shipboard Data Terminal (MCD)
SDt .... Sifre on Deuteronomy [*A publication*] (BJA)
SDT .... Signal Detection Theory
SDT .... Simulated Data Tape
SDT .... Simulated Dynamic Target [*Military*] (CAAL)
SDT .... Skylab Data Task [*NASA*]
SDT .... Source Distribution Technique
SDT .... Speedy Drill Template (MCD)
SDT .... Start-Data-Traffic [*Data processing*] (IBMDP)
SDT .... Steered Directional Transmission (MCD)
SDT .... Step-Down Transformer
SDT .... Stromberg Dexterity Test [*Education*]
SDT .... Structural Dynamic Test [*NASA*] (NASA)
SD/T .... Surface Detector/Tracker [*Navy*] (CAAL)
SDT .... Surveillance Data Transmission
SDT .... System Dynamic Tester
SDTA .... Scottish Dance Teacher's Alliance (EA-IO)
SDTA .... Stewardsman Apprentice, Steward, Striker [*Navy rating*]
SDTA .... Structural Dynamic Test Article [*NASA*] (NASA)
SD Tex ...... United States District Court for the Southern District of Texas (DLA)
SDTGA ...... Staedtetag [*A publication*]
SDTI .... Selective Dissemination of Technical Information [*Data processing*]
SDTK .... Supported Drift Tube Klystron
SDTN .... Stewardsman, Steward, Striker [*Navy rating*]
SDTP .... Startover Data Transfer and Processing [*Program*]
SDTR .... Serial Data Transmitter/Receiver [*Telecommunications*] (TEL)
SDTS .... Satellite Data Transmission System (DIT)
SDTT .... Silicon Diode Target Tube
SDU .... Huron College, Huron, SD [*OCLC symbol*] (OCLC)
SDU .... Memphis, TN [*Location identifier*] [*FAA*] (FAAL)
SDU .... Rio De Janeiro-Dumont [*Brazil*] [*Airport symbol*] (OAG)
SDU .... Self-Destruct Unit
SDU .... Shelter Decontamination Unit
SDU .... Signal Distribution Unit (AAG)
SDU .... Source Data Utility
sdu .... South Dakota [*MARC country of publication code*] [*Library of Congress*] (LCCP)
SDU .... Soziale Demokratische Union [*Social Democratic Union*] [*West Germany*] (PPW)
SDU .... Spectrum Display Unit
SDU .... Station Display Unit
SDU .... Students for a Democratic University [*Canada*]
SDU .... Subcarrier Delay Unit
SDU .... Surface Drone Unit [*Navy*] (CAAL)
SdU .... University of South Dakota, Vermillion, SD [*Library symbol*] [*Library of Congress*] (LCLS)
SDUK .... Society for the Diffusion of Useful Knowledge
SdU-L .... University of South Dakota, Law Library, Vermillion, SD [*Library symbol*] [*Library of Congress*] (LCLS)
SdU-M .... University of South Dakota, Medical School, Vermillion, SD [*Library symbol*] [*Library of Congress*] (LCLS)
SDUN .... Standun, Inc. [*NASDAQ symbol*] (NQ)
SD Uniform Prob Code ... South Dakota Uniform Probate Code (DLA)
SDUSA ...... Social Democrats, USA (EA)
SDV .... Santo Domingo [*Venezuela*] [*Seismograph station code, US Geological Survey*] (SEIS)
SDV .... Scram Discharge Volume [*Nuclear energy*] (NRCH)
SDV .... Shuttle Derived Vehicle (MCD)
SDV .... Slowed-Down Video [*RADAR*]
SDV .... Society of Divine Vocations [*Vocationist Fathers*] [*Roman Catholic religious order*]
SDV .... Solar Daily Variation
SDV .... Specific Desensitizing Vaccine [*Medicine*] (ADA)
S Dv .... Sprache und Datenverarbeitung [*A publication*]
SDV .... Swimmer Delivery Vehicle [*Navy symbol*] [*Obsolete*] (MCD)
SDV .... Tel Aviv/Yafo [*Israel*] [*Airport symbol*] (OAG)
SdV .... Vermillion Public Library, Vermillion, SD [*Library symbol*] [*Library of Congress*] (LCLS)
S-DVB .... Styrene-Divinylbenzene [*Organic chemistry*]
SDVF .... Software Development and Verification Facilities [*NASA*] (NASA)
SDVI .... Service Disabled Veterans Insurance
SDW .... Dakota Wesleyan University, Layne Library, Mitchell, SD [*OCLC symbol*] (OCLC)
SDW .... S. D. Warren [*Paper manufacturer*]
SDW .... Segment Descriptor Word
SDW .... Six-Day War [*Arab-Israeli War, 1967*] (BJA)
SDW .... Southdown, Inc. [*NYSE symbol*]
SDW .... Spin-Density Wave [*Physics*]

SDW .... Standing Detonation Wave
SDW .... Swept Delta Wing
SdW .... Watertown Regional Library, Watertown, SD [*Library symbol*] [*Library of Congress*] (LCLS)
SDWA .... Safe Drinking Water Act [*1974*] [*Environmental Protection Agency*]
SdWa .... Wagner Public Library, Wagner, SD [*Library symbol*] [*Library of Congress*] (LCLS)
SdWau .... Waubay Public Library, Waubay, SD [*Library symbol*] [*Library of Congress*] (LCLS)
SdWe .... Webster Public Library, Webster, SD [*Library symbol*] [*Library of Congress*] (LCLS)
SdWes .... Wessington Springs Carnegie Public Library, Wessington Springs, SD [*Library symbol*] [*Library of Congress*] (LCLS)
SdWinT ...... Tripp County Library, Winner, SD [*Library symbol*] [*Library of Congress*] (LCLS)
SD W Va ..... United States District Court for the Southern District of West Virginia (DLA)
SDX .... Satellite Data Exchange
SDX .... Sedona [*Arizona*] [*Airport symbol*] (OAG)
SDX .... Sigma Delta Chi [*Later, SPJ*]
S + DX ...... Speech with Duplex Telegraph
SDY .... Mount Marty College, Yankton, SD [*OCLC symbol*] (OCLC)
SDY .... Sandy Corp. [*American Stock Exchange symbol*]
SDY .... Sidney [*Montana*] [*Airport symbol*] (OAG)
SDY .... Sidney, MT [*Location identifier*] [*FAA*] (FAAL)
SdY .... Yankton Community Library, Yankton, SD [*Library symbol*] [*Library of Congress*] (LCLS)
SdYC .... Yankton College, Yankton, SD [*Library symbol*] [*Library of Congress*] (LCLS)
SdYM .... Mount Marty College, Yankton, SD [*Library symbol*] [*Library of Congress*] (LCLS)
SDYN .... Staodynamics, Inc. [*NASDAQ symbol*] (NQ)
SDZ .... Southern Pines, NC [*Location identifier*] [*FAA*] (FAAL)
SDZ .... Stimmen der Zeit (BJA)
SE .... Ferrocarriles Unidos del Sureste, SA de CV [*AAR code*]
SE .... Safety Evaluation (NRCH)
S & E .... Salaries and Expenses
SE .... Sales Engineer
SE .... Saline Enema [*Medicine*]
SE .... Sanford & Eastern Railroad [*AAR code*] [*Terminated*]
SE .... Sanitary Engineer [*Academic degree*]
SE .... Saorstat Eireann [*Irish Free State*]
SE .... Saponification Equivalent [*Analytical chemistry*]
SE .... School of Engineering (MCD)
SE .... Sciences Ecclesiastiques [*A publication*]
S & E .... Scientific and Engineering
S & E .... Scientists and Engineers (RDA)
SE .... Sea [*Maps and charts*]
SE .... Second Entrance [*Theatrical slang*]
SE .... Secretarial, Word Processing, and/or Medical Office Assistant Programs [*Association of Independent Colleges and Schools specialization code*]
SE .... Securities Transaction [*Banking*]
SE .... Seeing Eye [*An association*] [*Morristown, NJ*] (EA)
SE .... Selenium [*Chemical element*]
SE .... Seleucid Era (BJA)
SE .... Self Employment [*Social Security Administration*] (OICC)
SE .... Self-Evident Statement [*Used in correcting manuscripts, etc.*]
Se .... Semeia [*A publication*]
Se .... Semiotica [*A publication*]
SE .... Senior Editor [*Publishing*]
SE .... September (ADA)
SE .... Sequence of Events
SE .... Series
SE .... Series Statement [*Online database field identifier*]
SE .... Service Engineer
SE .... Service Equipment (AAG)
S & E .... Services and Equipment
SE .... Set
se .... Seychelles [*bi (British Indian Ocean Territory) used in records cataloged before January 1978*] [*MARC country of publication code*] [*Library of Congress*] (LCCP)
SE .... Shareholders' Equity [*Business and trade*]
SE .... Sherritt Gordon Mines Ltd. [*Toronto Stock Exchange symbol*]
SE .... Shielding Effectiveness (IEEE)
SE .... Shift Engineer (NRCH)
SE .... Signal Excess (NVT)
SE .... Single End
SE .... Single-Ended, Cylindrical Boiler [*Navy*]
SE .... Single Engine
SE .... Single Entry [*Bookkeeping*]
SE .... Slovenski Etnograf [*A publication*]
SE .... Smoke Extract
SE .... Social Education [*A publication*]
SE .... Social Emotional
SE .... Society of Engineers
SE .... Software Engineering (MCD)
SE .... Soil Extract
SE .... Solanaceae Enthusiasts (EA)

SE .... Solar Ecliptic
SE .... Solar Explorer [*NASA*]
SE .... Solid Extract [*Pharmacy*]
SE .... Solidaridad Espanola [*Spanish Solidarity*] (PPW)
SE .... Sonic Extract [*Cytology*]
SE .... Southeast
SE .... Southeastern Reporter [*National Reporter System*] (DLA)
SE .... Southern Europe (NATG)
SE .... Space Exploration (AAG)
SE .... Spanish Solidarity (PD)
SE .... Spatial Emotional (Stimuli)
SE .... Special Edition [*Car model designation*]
SE .... Special Equipment
SE .... Spectral Edge [*Cardiology*]
SE .... Sphenoethmoidal [*Suture*] [*Medicine*]
SE .... Spherical Equivalent
SE .... Spin-Echo Scan [*Roentgenology*]
SE .... Split End [*Football*]
SE .... Stable Element
SE .... Staff Engineer [*Navy*] [*British*] (ROG)
SE .... Stage of Exhaustion [*of gas*] [*Medicine*]
SE .... Stamped Envelope
SE .... Standard English
SE .... Standard Error
S/E .... Standardization/Evaluation (AFM)
SE .... Starch Equivalent
SE .... Starter Electrode
SE .... Stationary Eddy
SE .... Status Enquiry [*British*]
SE .... Status Epilepticus [*Medicine*]
SE .... Steam Emulsion
SE .... Stock Exchange
SE .... Studi Etruschi [*A publication*]
SE .... Studia Estetyczne [*A publication*]
SE .... Studies in English [*A publication*]
SE .... Subcontract Engineers (MCD)
SE .... Subcritical Experiment [*Nuclear energy*]
SE .... Summer Emergency [*Vessel load line mark*]
SE .... Sun Electric Corp. [*NYSE symbol*]
SE .... Superintending Engineer (ADA)
S & E .... Supplies and Equipage [*Military*] (CINC)
SE .... Support Equipment [*Military*] (AFM)
S & E .... Surveillance and Entry
SE .... Sustainer Engine (AAG)
SE .... Sustaining Engineering
SE .... Sweden [*Aircraft nationality and registration mark*] (FAAC)
SE .... Sweden [*Two-letter standard code*] (CNC)
SE .... System Effectiveness [*Army*] (AABC)
SE .... System Element (NASA)
SE .... Systems Engineer [*or Engineering*] [*Data processing*]
S1E .... Surfaced One Edge [*Technical drawings*]
SE2 .... Scientists and Engineers for Secure Energy (EA)
SEA .... Clemson University, Clemson, SC [*OCLC symbol*] (OCLC)
SEA .... Marine Manufacturers Safety Equipment Association (EA)
SEA .... Safety Engineering Analysis (AFM)
SEA .... Sailing Education Association
Sea .... Sankt Eriks Arsbok [*A publication*]
SEA .... Scandinavian Endodontic Association [*Molndal, Sweden*] (EA-IO)
SEA .... Scanning Electrostatic Analysis (NASA)
SEA .... Science and Education Administration [*Department of Agriculture*]
SEA .... Scientific Exchange Agreement
SEA .... Sea Echelon Area [*Navy*] (NVT)
SEA .... Sea Education Association (EA)
SEA .... Seashore Environmental Alliance
SEA .... Seasonal Employees in Agriculture
SEA .... Seattle [*Washington*] [*Seismograph station code, US Geological Survey*] [*Closed*] (SEIS)
SEA .... Seattle/Tacoma [*Washington*] [*Airport symbol*] (OAG)
SEA .... Securities Exchange Act [*1934*]
SEA .... Senior Enlisted Academy [*Navy*]
SEA .... Senior Enlisted Advisor [*Navy*]
SEA .... Senior Executives Association (EA)
SEA .... Service Educational Activities [*Military*] (AABC)
SEA .... Service Employers Association [*Formerly, BMEA, BSL*] [*New York, NY*] (EA)
SEA .... Sheep Erythrocyte Agglutination [*Test*]
SEA .... Ship/Equipment/Alterations [*Navy*] (NG)
SEA .... Ships Editorial Association [*Navy*]
SEA .... Silicon Elastimeter Ablator (NASA)
SEA .... Sindicato de Escritores y Artistas [*Ecuador*]
SEA .... Societe d'Electronique et d'Automatique [*Became part of Compagnie Internationale d'Informatique*]
SEA .... Society for the Elimination of Acronyms
SEA .... Society of Evangelical Agnostics (EA)
SEA .... Sociology of Education Association (EA)
SEA .... SONAR Evaluation and Assistance [*Teams*]
SEA .... Southeast Air, Inc. [*New Bedford, MA*] [*FAA designator*] (FAAC)
SEA .... Southeast Asia

SEA .... Southern Economic Association   (EA)
SEA .... SPALT [*Special Projects Alterations*] Evaluation Area
SEA .... Special Equipment Authorization   (AAG)
SEA .... Specific Energy Absorption
SEA .... Spherical Electrostatic Analyzer
SEA .... Standard Electronic Assembly
SEA .... Staphylococcal Enterotoxin A [*Medicine*]
SEA .... State Economic Area
SEA .... State Education Agency
SEA .... Static Error Analysis
SEA .... Statistical Energy Analysis [*or Approach*] [*Vibration analysis*]
SEA .... Students for Ecological Action
SEA .... Studies in Educational Administration [*A publication*]
SEA .... Studies in English and American [*A publication*]
SEA .... Subterranean Exploration Agency
SEA .... Sudden Enhancement of Atmospherics [*NASA*]
SEA .... Sulphur Extended Asphalt [*Paving material*]
SEA .... Survival Education Association   (EA)
SEA .... Susquehanna Environmental Advocates   (NRCH)
SEA .... Svensk Exegetisk Arsbok [*A publication*]
SEA .... System Engineering Analysis
SEA .... System Error Analysis
SEA .... Systems Effectiveness Analyzer   (IEEE)
SEAAC ...... South-East Asia Air Command   (ADA)
SEAAC ...... Southeast Asian Art and Culture [*Foundation*]
SEAADSA ... Sea Automated Data Systems Activity [*Navy*]
SEABEE .... Construction Battalion [*CB*] [*Acronym is a phonetic reference to a member of this Naval unit*]
SEABT ...... SEABEE Team [*Navy*]   (NVT)
SEABU ...... Southeast Asia Buildup   (CINC)
SEAC .... Seacoast
SEAC .... Social and Economic Archive Centre [*British*]
SEAC .... Society for Economic, Social, Cultural Study and Expansion in Central Africa
SEAC .... Society for Electroanalytical Chemistry
SEAC .... Southeast Archeological Center [*US Department of the Interior*] [*Research center*]   (RCD)
SEAC .... Southeast Asia Center [*Chicago, IL*]   (EA)
SEAC .... Southeast Asia Command
SEAC .... Specialized Employability Assistance to Claimants   (OICC)
SEAC .... Standards Eastern [*or Electronic*] Automatic Computer [*National Bureau of Standards*]
SEAC .... Submarine Exercise Area Coordinator [*Navy*]   (NVT)
SEACAD .... Sea Cadet Cruise [*Navy*]   (NVT)
SEACDT ..... Southeast Asia Collective Defense Treaty   (AABC)
SEACF ...... Support Equipment Assembly and Checkout Facility [*NASA*]   (NASA)
SEACOM .... Southeast Asia Commonwealth
SEACOM .... Southeast Asia Communications   (MCD)
SEACON .... Seafloor Construction Experiment [*Navy*]
SEACOORD ... Southeast Asia Coordination Council [*Military*]
SEACOP .... Strategic Sealift Contingency Planning System [*Army*]   (AABC)
SEACORE ... Southeast Asia Communications Research   (MCD)
SEACS ...... Search of Enemy Air Defense   (MCD)
SEACS ...... Ship Equipment Accounting System   (MCD)
SE/ACT ..... Southern Europe - ACTISUD [*Authority for the Coordination of Inland Transport in Southern Europe*] [*NATO*]   (NATG)
SEAD .... Seneca Army Depot [*New York*]   (AABC)
SEAD .... Suppression of Enemy Air Defenses   (AABC)
SEAD .... Survivable Electronic Air Defense
SEADAB .... Southeast Asia DataBase   (MCD)
SEADAC .... Seakeeping Data Analysis Center [*Navy*]
SEADAG .... Southeast Asia Development Advisory Group [*Department of State*]
SEADCUG ... NAVSEA Data Communications Users Group [*Navy*]
SEADEX ..... Seaward Defense Exercise [*NATO*]   (NATG)
SEADROP ... Small Expendable Air-Dropped Remote Ocean Platform [*Marine science*]   (MSC)
SEADS ...... Shuttle Entry Air Data Sensor   (MCD)
SEADS ...... Survivable and Effective Airbreathing Defense [*Study*]   (MCD)
SEADU ...... Sea Duty
SEA-EX ..... Sealift Express [*Military*]
SEAFDEC ... Southeast Asian Fisheries Development Center [*Thailand*]
Sea Fish Res Stn (Haifa) Bull ... Sea Fisheries Research Station (Haifa). Bulletin [*A publication*]
Seafood Bus ... Seafood Business [*A publication*]
Seafood Export J ... Seafood Export Journal [*A publication*]
Seafood Merch ... Seafood Merchandising [*A publication*]
SEAFRON ... Sea Frontier
Sea Front ... Sea Frontiers [*A publication*]
SEAG .... Sea Galley Stores [*NASDAQ symbol*]   (NQ)
Sea Grant Coll Tech Rep Univ Wis ... Sea Grant College Technical Report. University of Wisconsin [*A publication*]
SEAIC .... Southeast Asia Information Center   (NG)
SEAID .... Support Equipment Abbreviated Items Description [*NASA*]   (NASA)
SEAIG .... Southeast Asia Information Group   (AFM)
SEAIMP ..... Solar Eclipse Atmospheric and Ionospheric Measurements Project   (IEEE)
SEAISI .... South East Asia Iron and Steel Institute   (EA)
SEAITACS ... Southeast Asia Integrated Tactical Air Control System   (CINC)

SEAJS .... Southeast Asian Journal of Sociology [*Singapore*] [*A publication*]
SEAJT .... South East Asia Journal of Theology [*A publication*]
SEAK .... Seahawk Oil International [*NASDAQ symbol*]   (NQ)
SEAL .... Sea, Air, and Land
SEAL .... Sea, Air, and Land Capability [*Refers to Navy personnel trained in unconventional warfare*]
SEAL .... Ship's Electronics Allowance List [*Navy*]
SEAL .... Signal Evaluation Airborne Laboratory [*FAA*]
SEAL .... Solar Energy Applications Laboratory [*Colorado State University*] [*Research center*]   (RCD)
SEAL .... Standard Electronic Accounting Language [*Data processing*]   (BUR)
SEAL .... Subsea Equipment Associates Limited [*Bermuda*]
SEALA ...... Seal Fleet Cl A [*NASDAQ symbol*]   (NQ)
SEALAB .... Sea Laboratory
SEALF .... Semiempirical Absorption Loss Formula [*Radio*]
SEALF .... Southeast Asia Land Forces [*British*]
SEALITE .... Systematic Evaluation and Analysis of a LASER in a Test Environment   (MCD)
SEALLINC ... Southeast Louisiana Library Network Cooperative [*Library network*]
SEALOB .... Sealift Obligation Report [*Army*]
SEALOCK ... Search, Locate, Communications, or Kill   (MCD)
SEALR .... Southeast Asia Logistic Requirement   (AFM)
SEALS .... Sea, Air, Land Teams
SEALS .... Severe Environmental Air Launch Study   (KSC)
SEALS .... Stored Energy Actuated Lift System
SEAM .... Sidewinder Expanded Acquisition Mode   (MCD)
SEAM .... Society for the Emancipation of the American Male
SEAM .... Software Engineering and Management
SEAM .... Southeast Asia Microfilm Project [*Library network*]
SEAM .... Subset Extraction and Association Measurement
SEAM .... Surface Environment and Mining Program
SEAMAP .... Scientific Exploration and Mapping Program   (MCD)
SEAMAP .... Systematic Exploration and Mapping Program [*Marine science*]   (MSC)
SeaMARCI ... Sea Mapping and Remote Characterization I [*Oceanography*]
SEAMARF ... Southeast Asia Military Air Reservation Facility   (CINC)
SEAMEC .... Southeast Asian Ministers of Education Council
Seamens J ... Seamen's Journal [*A publication*]
SEAMES .... Southeast Asian Ministers of Education Secretariat [*Thailand*]
SEAMEX .... Seamanship Exercise   (NVT)
SEAMIC ..... Southeast Asia Management Information Center [*Navy*]
SEAMINFO ... Surface Mining and Environment Information System [*University of Arizona*]   (EISS)
SEAMIST ... Seavan Management Information System
SEAMORE ... Southeast Asia Mohawk Revision Program [*Army aviation*]
SEAMS .... Southeast Asian Mathematical Society
SEAMS .... System Effectiveness Assurance Management System   (MCD)
SEAMUS .... Society for Electro-Acoustic Music in the United States   (EA)
SEAN .... Scientific Event Alert Network [*Smithsonian Institution*] [*Washington, DC*]   (MCD)
SEAN .... Strapdown Electrically Suspended Gyro Aerospace Navigation [*System*]
SEAN .... Syndicat des Enseignants Africains du Niger [*African Union of Teachers of Niger*]
SEANC .... Southeast Asia NOTAM [*Notice to Airmen*] Center [*Military*]
Seance Pub Ann Acad Pharm ... Seance Publique Annuelle. Academie de Pharmacie [*A publication*]
SEANITEOPS ... Southeast Asia Night Operations [*Army*]
Sean O Cas ... Sean O'Casey Review [*A publication*]
SEAOC .... Structural Engineers Association of California   (EA)
SEAONC .... Structural Engineers Association of Northern California   (NRCH)
SEAOPSS ... Southeast Asia Operational Sensor System   (MCD)
SEAOR ...... Southeast Asia Operational Requirements   (MCD)
SEAP .... SEATO [*Southeast Asia Treaty Organization*] Administrative Publication
SEAPA ...... Spectrothermal Emission Aerosol Particle Analyzer
SEAPAC ..... Sea Activated Parachute Automatic Crew Release   (MCD)
SEAPEX ..... Southeast Asia Petroleum Exploration Society
SEAPRO ..... Southeast Asia Programs Directorate
SEAPT .... Seaport
SeAQ .... Southeast Asia Quarterly [*A publication*]
SEAQ .... Stock Exchange Automated Quotations [*London, England*]
SEAR .... Safeguard Emergency Action Report [*Army*]   (AABC)
SEAR .... Safety Evaluation Audit Report   (NRCH)
SEAR .... Summary Engineering Assessment Report   (MCD)
SEAR .... System Engineering Analysis Report
SEAR .... Systematic Effort to Analyze Results
SEARA ...... Stockpile Evaluation and Reliability Assessment Program
SEARAM .... Semiactive RADAR Missile
Seara Med ... Seara Medica [*A publication*]
Seara Med Neurocir ... Seara Medica Neurocirurgica [*A publication*]
SEA RARE ... Sea Reinforcement and Resupply of Europe   (MCD)
SEARC .... Southeast Asia Regional Council
SEARCA .... Southeast Asian Regional Center for Graduate Study and Research in Agriculture [*Information service*] [*Philippines*]   (EISS)

SEARCC .... SouthEast Asia Regional Computer Confederation (EA)
SEARCH .... Science, Engineering, and Related Career Hints [*A publication*] [*Scientific Manpower Commission*]
SEARCH .... Scientific Evaluation and Research of Charismatic Healing [*An association*] (EA)
SEARCH .... Scientific Exploration and Research [*Seventh-Day Adventist foundation*]
SEARCH .... System for Electronic Analysis and Retrieval of Criminal Histories [*Project succeeded by National Crime Information Center*] [*Department of Justice*]
SEARCH .... System Evaluation and Reliability Checker
SEARCH .... System for Exploring Alternative Resource Commitments in Higher Education [*Data processing*]
Search Agric Ent (Ithaca NY) ... Search Agriculture. Entomology (Ithaca, New York) [*A publication*]
Search Agric (Geneva NY) ... Search Agriculture (Geneva, New York) [*A publication*]
SEARCHEX ... Sea/Air Search Exercise [*NATO*] (NATG)
Search & Seizure L Rep ... Search and Seizure Law Report [*A publication*]
SEAREQ..... Sea Requirement [*Canadian Navy*]
SEAREX..... Sea/Air Chemical Exchange [*Marine science*] (MSC)
Searle........ Searle's Supreme Court Reports [*1850-67*] [*Cape Colony*] (DLA)
Searle Dig ... Searle's Minnesota Digest (DLA)
Searle Sm ... Searle and Smith's English Probate and Divorce Reports (DLA)
Searle & Sm ... Searle and Smith's English Probate & Divorce Reports [*1859-60*] (DLA)
Sears Found Marine Research Mem ... Sears Foundation for Marine Research. Memoir [*A publication*]
SEAS......... Sea Environment Acquisition System
SEAS......... Sea School [*Marine Corps*]
SEAS......... Seasons. Federation of Ontario Naturalists [*A publication*]
SEAS......... Selected Effects Armament Subsystem [*Army*] (RDA)
SEAS......... Ship/Equipment/Alterations Summary [*Navy*] (NG)
SEAS......... Shipboard Environmental Data Acquisition System [*Marine science*] (MSC)
SEAS......... Strategic Environmental Assessment System [*Environmental Protection Agency*]
SEAS......... Support Equipment Avionics System
SEAS......... Surveillance Environmental Acoustic Support [*Military*] (CAAL)
SEAS......... System Enhancement and Support [*Military*] (CAAL)
Se As Aff.... Southeast Asian Affairs [*Singapore*] [*A publication*]
SEASAME ... Southeast Asian Science and Mathematics Experiment [*RECSAM*]
SEASAT..... Sea Satellite [*NASA*]
SEASC...... Scientific Exploration of the Atlantic Shelf Committee
Se As Chron ... Southeast Asia Chronicle [*A publication*]
SEASCO ..... Southeast Asia Science Cooperation Office
SEASET..... Separate Effects and Systems Effects Tests (NRCH)
SEASIA ..... Southeast Asia (NG)
SE Asia ..... Southeast Asia Chronicle [*A publication*]
SE Asia J Th ... Southeast Asia Journal of Theology [*A publication*]
Se As Iron Steel Inst Q ... Southeast Asia Iron and Steel Institute Quarterly [*Singapore*] [*A publication*]
Se As J Soc Sci ... Southeast Asian Journal of Social Science [*Singapore*] [*A publication*]
Se As J Theo ... South East Asia Journal of Theology [*Singapore*] [*A publication*]
Sea & Sm ... Searle and Smith's English Probate & Divorce Reports (DLA)
S E As R ..... South East Asian Review [*India*] [*A publication*]
S E As Stud ... South East Asian Studies [*Kyoto*] [*A publication*]
SEASTAG ... Southeast Asia Treaty Organization Standardization Agreement
SEAT......... Sociedad Espanol de Automoviles de Turismo [*Spanish automobile manufacturer; acronym used as name of its cars*] [*Madrid*]
SEATAC..... Southeast Asian Agency for Regional Transport and Communications Development [*Kuala Lumpur, Malaysia*] (EA-IO)
SEATAF ..... Southern European Atomic Task Force
SEATAR..... Studies on East Asia Tectonics and Resources [*Marine science*] (MSC)
SEATEC..... Sea Test and Evaluation Capability [*Navy*] (CAAL)
Sea Technol ... Sea Technology [*A publication*]
SEATELCOM ... Southeast Asia Telecommunications System (AABC)
SEATIC ...... Southeast Asia Translation and Interrogation Center [*Navy*]
SEATO Med Res Monogr ... Southeast Asia Treaty Organization. Medical Research Monograph [*A publication*]
SEATS .... Shubert Entertainment and Arts Ticketing System [*National computerized theatre-ticket selling system*]
SEATS .... Special Education Administration Task Simulation Game
Seattle Sym ... Seattle Symphony Orchestra. Program Notes [*A publication*]
Sea Vend ... Seaborne on Vendors and Purchasers [*9th ed.*] [*1926*] (DLA)
Sea View Hosp Bull ... Sea View Hospital. Bulletin [*A publication*]
SEAWARS ... Seawater Activated Release System [*Navy*] (CAAL)
Seaway Rev ... Seaway Review [*A publication*]
SEAWBS .... Southeast Asia Wideband System [*Military*]
SEAWEA.... Sea and Weather Observations [*Navy*] (NVT)
SEAX......... Span East Airlines, Inc. [*Air carrier designation symbol*]

SEB .... Scientific Equipment Bay [*NASA*] (KSC)
SEB .... Scottish Examining Board
SEB .... Seaboard Corp. [*American Stock Exchange symbol*]
SEB .... Sebenico [*Yugoslavia*] [*Seismograph station code, US Geological Survey*] [*Closed*] (SEIS)
SEB .... Sebha [*Libya*] [*Airport symbol*] (OAG)
Seb. .... Sebir [*or Sebirin*] (BJA)
SEB .... Secondary Education Board
SEB .... Selective Enlistment Bonus [*Navy*] (NVT)
SEB .... Skandinaviska Enskilda Banken [*Sweden*]
SEB .... Social and Emotional Behavior
SEB .... Society for Economic Botany (EA)
SEB .... Socio-Economic Benefit
SEB .... Source Evaluation Board [*NASA*]
SEB .... South Equatorial Belt [*Planet Jupiter*]
SEB .... Special Enlistment Bonus (MCD)
SEB .... Staphylococcal Enterotoxin B [*Medicine*]
SEB .... Strip Electron Beam
SEB .... Support Equipment Bulletin (MCD)
SEB .... System Error Bridge
SEBA .... Staphylococcal Enterotoxin B Antisera [*Medicine*]
SEBAn ...... Societe d'Emulation de Bruges. Annales [*A publication*]
SEBBETSI ... Serikat Buruh Beras dan Seluruh Indonesia [*Rice and Tapioca Workers' Union of Indonesia*]
SEBC .... South-Eastern Bible College [*Florida*]
SEBD.......... Software Engineering Bibliographic Data Base [*Data and Analysis Center for Software*] [*Database*]
SEBDA .... Serikat Buruh Daehrah Autonoom [*Civil Servants' Union*] [*Indonesia*]
SEbE .... Southeast by East
SEBIC .... Sustained Electron Bombardment-Induced Conductivity
SEBL .... Self-Emptying Blind Loop [*Gastroenterology*]
SEBM .... Society for Experimental Biology and Medicine (EA)
SEBQ .... Senior Enlisted Bachelor Quarters [*Army*] (AABC)
SEbS .... Southeast by South
SEBS......... Submarine Emergency Buoyancy System
Seb Trade-Marks ... Sebastian on Trade-Marks (DLA)
Seb Tr M ... Sebastian on Trade-Marks [*5th ed.*] [*1911*] (DLA)
SEBUA ...... Seibutsu Butsuri [*A publication*]
SEBUMI ..... Serikat Buruh Minjak, Stanvac [*Oil Workers' Union, Stanvac*] [*Indonesia*]
SEBV .... Solder End Ball Valve
s-ec--- .... Ecuador [*MARC geographic area code*] [*Library of Congress*] (LCCP)
SEC .... Safeguards Equipment Cabinet (IEEE)
SEC .... Sanitary Engineering Center
SEC .... Scandinavian Episcopal Conference [*Oslo, Norway*] (EA-IO)
SEC .... Scientific and Engineering Computation
SEC .... Scientific Estimates Committee (AABC)
SeC .... Scuola e Cultura del Mondo [*A publication*]
SEC .... SEC: Bi-Monthly Magazine for Employees of the State Electricity Commission of Victoria [*A publication*]
SEC .... Secant
SEC .... Second (AFM)
Se C .... Second Coming [*A publication*]
Sec .... Secondary [*Chemistry*]
SEC .... Secondary
SEC .... Secondary Electron Conduction [*Television camera system*]
SEC .... Secondary Emission Conductivity
SEC .... Secret (AFM)
SEC .... Secretariat
SEC .... Secretary [*A publication*]
SEC .... Secretary
SEC .... Section
SEC .... Sector
SEC .... Secular
SEC .... Secundum [*According To*] [*Latin*]
SEC .... Secure (KSC)
Sec .... Securities (DLA)
S & EC ...... Securities and Exchange Commission
SEC .... Securities and Exchange Commission
SEC .... Securities and Exchange Commission Decisions and Reports (DLA)
SEC .... Securities and Exchange Commission, Washington, DC [*OCLC symbol*] (OCLC)
SEC .... Security (AAG)
SEC .... Sensormatic Canada Ltd. [*Toronto Stock Exchange symbol*]
SEC .... Sequential Events Controller [*NASA*] (NASA)
SEC .... Shaftless Expander-Compressor
SEC .... Simple Electronic Computer [*Birkbeck College*] [*London, England*] (DEN)
SEC .... Single Error Correcting
SEC .... Size Exclusion Chromatography
SEC .... Social Economic Council [*Sociaal Economische Raad*] [*Netherlands*]
SEC .... Societe de l'Ecole des Chartes [*A publication*]
SEC .... Societe des Ecrivains Canadiens [*Society of Canadian Writers*]
SEC .... Societe Europeenne de Culture [*European Society of Culture - ESC*] (EA-IO)
SEC .... Society for Educative Communication (EA)
SEC .... Society of Exchange Counselors [*Sacramento, CA*] (EA)

SEC .... Soft Elastic Capsule [*Pharmacy*]
SEC .... Solar Energy Collector
SEC .... Solar Energy Concentrator
SEC .... Solid Electrolyte Capacitor
SEC .... Source Evaluation Committee [*NASA*] (NASA)
SEC .... South Equatorial Current [*Oceanography*] (MSC)
SEC .... Southeastern Command
SEC .... Southeastern Commuter Airlines [*Auburn, AL*] [*FAA designator*] (FAAC)
SEC .... Southeastern Conference [*College sports*]
SEC .... Space Environmental Chamber (AAG)
SEC .... Special Emergency Campaign [*Red Cross fund-raising*]
SEC .... Spectroelectrochemistry
SEC .... Staff Evaluation Coordinators (MCD)
SEC .... Standard Error of Calibration
SEC .... Standards and Ethics Commission [*American Occupational Therapy Association*]
SEC .... Standing with Eyes Closed [*Equilibrium test*]
SEC .... Sterling Electronics Corporation [*American Stock Exchange symbol*]
SEC .... Stevens Creek [*California*] [*Seismograph station code, US Geological Survey*] (SEIS)
SEC .... Structural Engineers Councils (KSC)
SEC .... Submarine Element Coordinator (NVT)
SEC .... Sulphur Export Corporation [*An association*] (EA)
SEC .... Supply Executive Committee [*NATO*] (NATG)
SEC .... Support Equipment Change (MCD)
SEC .... Switching Equipment Congestion [*Telecommunications*] (TEL)
SECA .... Self-Employment Contributions Act of 1954 [*under which self-employed persons contribute to OASDI coverage for themselves*]
SECA .... Shiatsu Education Center of America [*Later, Ohashi Institute - OI*] (EA)
SECA .... Solar Energy Construction Association (EA)
SECA .... Southern Educational Communications Authority [*Television network*]
SECA .... Sportbike Enthusiast Club of America (EA)
SECAC ...... Sectional Aeronautical Chart
SECAD .... Services Engineering Computer-Aided Design [*Pierce Management Services*] [*Software package*]
SECAD ...... Support Equipment Concept Approval Data
SECAL ...... Selected Calling System [*Military*] (AFM)
SECAM ...... Sequence Electronique Couleur avec Memoire [*Color Sequence with Memory*] [*French color television system*]
SECAN .... Standing Group Communication Security and Evaluation Agency Washington
SECANT ..... Separation and Control of Aircraft Using Nonsynchronous Techniques [*Collision avoidance*] [*RCA*]
SECAP ...... Systems Experiment Correlation and Analysis Program (MCD)
SECAR ...... Secondary RADAR (IEEE)
SECARMY ... Secretary of the Army
SEC ART.... Secundum Artem [*According to the Art*] [*Latin*]
SECAS ...... Ship Equipment Configuration Accounting System (NVT)
SECB .... Security Bancorp [*NASDAQ symbol*] (NQ)
Sec Bk Judg ... Second Book of Judgments [*Huxley*] [*England*] (DLA)
SECC .... Safe Energy Communications Council (EA)
SECC .... Scientific and Engineering Computing Council (MCD)
SECC .... South Equatorial Countercurrent [*Oceanography*] (MSC)
SECC .... Studies in Eighteenth-Century Culture [*A publication*]
SECC .... Sun Equities Corporation [*NASDAQ symbol*] (NQ)
SECC .... Survivable Enduring Command and Control
Sec City ..... Second City [*A publication*]
SEC Compl (P-H) ... Securities and Exchange Commission Compliance [*Prentice-Hall, Inc.*] (DLA)
SECD .... Secondary (AABC)
SECD .... Secured (ROG)
SECDA....... Southeastern Community Development Association (EA)
SECDED .... Single-BIT [*Binary Digit*] Error Correction and Double-BIT [*Binary Digit*] Error Detection
SECDEF..... Secretary of Defense
Sec D & M ... Security Distributing and Marketing [*A publication*]
SEC Docket ... Securities and Exchange Commission Docket (DLA)
Secd Pt Edw III ... Year Books, Part III [*England*] (DLA)
Secd Pt H VI ... Year Books, Part VIII [*England*] (DLA)
SECDY ...... Secondary
SECE......... Selfhelp of Emigres from Central Europe (EA)
Sec Ed........ Secondary Education [*A publication*]
SECEM ...... Support Equipment Cost Effectiveness Model (MCD)
Sec & Ex C ... Securities and Exchange Commission (DLA)
SECFLT ..... Second Fleet [*Atlantic*] [*Navy*]
SECGF .... Silver Eureka Corporation [*NASDAQ symbol*] (NQ)
SECGRUHQ ... Security Group Headquarters
SECH......... Secant, Hyperbolic
Sechenov Physiol J USSR ... Sechenov. Physiological Journal of the USSR [*A publication*]
SECHT .... Scoping Emergency Cooling Heat Transfer (KSC)
Sec Ind Digest ... Secondary Industries Digest [*A publication*]
SECINSP.... Security Inspection [*Military*] (NVT)
Sec Int........ Secretary of the Interior (DLA)
SECIR .... Semiautomatic Encoding of Chemistry for Information Retrieval (DIT)

SECIT........ Syndicat des Employes Indigenes du Commerce du Togo [*Union of Indigenous Employees of Commerce of Togo*]
SECJA....... Southern Economic Journal [*United States*] [*A publication*]
SEC Jud Dec ... Securities and Exchange Commission Judicial Decisions (DLA)
SECLA ...... Southeastern Connecticut Library Association [*Library network*]
SEC LEG.... Secundum Legem [*According to Law*] [*Latin*]
SECLT....... Second Lieutenant [*Army*]
SECM........ School of English Church Music [*Later, RSCM*]
SEC Mag.... SEC Magazine: Journal of the State Electricity Commission of Victoria [*A publication*]
SECMem.... Societe d'Emulation de Cambrai. Memoires [*A publication*]
Sec Mgmt ... Security Management [*A publication*]
Sec Mgt...... Security Management [*A publication*]
SECMR ...... Sector Manager [*Aviation*] (FAAC)
SECN .... Section (ROG)
SECN .... Sex Education Coalition News [*A publication*]
SEC NAT.... Secundum Naturam [*According to Nature*] [*Latin*]
SECNAV .... Secretary of the Navy
SECNAVINST ... Secretary of the Navy Instruction
SEC News ... SEC [*US Securities and Exchange Commission*] News Digest [*A publication*]
SECNY....... Sales Executives Club of New York [*New York, NY*] (EA)
SECO .... Securities and Exchange Commission
SECO .... Self-Regulating Error-Correct Coder-Decoder
SECO .... Sequential Coding
SECO .... Sequential Control [*Teletype*] [*Data processing*]
SECO .... Station Engineering Control Office [*Telecommunications*] (TEL)
SECO .... Steam and Electric Cogeneration [*Power source*]
SECO .... Sustainer-Engine Cutoff
SECOBI...... Servicio de Consulta a Bancos de Informacion [*Data Base Consultation Service*] [*Information service*] [*Mexico*] (EISS)
SECOFF..... Section Office
SECOIN...... Security Consultants International
SECOL ...... Southeastern Conference on Linguistics
SECOLAS ... Southeastern Conference on Latin American Studies [*United States*]
SECOM ...... School Emergency Communication
SECON...... Secondary Electron Conduction [*Television camera system*]
Secondary Teach ... Secondary Teacher [*A publication*]
S Econ J..... Southern Economic Journal [*A publication*]
SECOR...... Sequential Collation of Range [*Army program*]
SECOR...... Sequential Correlation
SECOR...... Sequential Cosine Ranging [*System*] (MUGU)
SECORD .... Secure Voice Cord Board [*Telecommunications*] (TEL)
SECP......... [*Division of*] Shore Establishment and Civilian Personnel [*Navy*]
SECP......... State Energy Conservation Program
SECPR .... Standard External Cardiopulmonary Resuscitation
SECPS .... Secondary Propulsion System [*NASA*] (KSC)
SECR........ Secretariat
SE & CR ..... Southeastern & Chatham Railway [*Nickname: Seldom Ever Caught Running*]
SECRA ...... Secondary RADAR [*RADAR beacon*]
SEC REG.... Secundum Regulam [*According to Rule*] [*Latin*]
Sec Reg Guide ... Securities Regulation Guide [*Prentice-Hall, Inc.*] (DLA)
Sec Reg & L Rep ... Securities Regulation and Law Reports [*Bureau of National Affairs*] [*A publication*]
Sec Reg & Trans ... Securities Regulations and Transfer Report [*A publication*]
SECREP..... Regional Representative of the Secretary of Transportation
SECRG....... Securing
SECRL .... Secretarial
Secr Pap Int Wheat Counc ... Secretariat Papers. International Wheat Council [*A publication*]
SECS .... Seagrass Ecosystems Component Study [*Marine science*] (MSC)
SECS .... Selective Electron-Capture Sensitization [*Analytical chemistry*]
SECS .... Sequential Events Control System [*NASA*] (KSC)
SECS .... Shuttle Events Control Subsystem [*NASA*] (NASA)
SECS .... Simulation and Evaluation of Chemical Synthesis [*Data processing*]
SECS .... Solar Electric Communication Satellite
SECS .... Space Environmental Control System (AAG)
SECS .... Stem Elevated Camera System
SECSTA ..... Naval Security Station
SECSW ...... Science and Engineering Committee for a Secure World (EA)
SECSY ...... Spin-Echo Correlated Spectroscopy
SECT......... Secretariat
SECT......... Section (KSC)
SECT......... Submarine Emergency Communications Transmitter
SECTAM .... Sterile Environmental Control Technology Applications to Medicine
SECTASKFLT ... Second Task Fleet
SECTBASE ... Section Base [*Navy*]
Sec Teach ... Secondary Teacher [*A publication*]
Sec Teacher ... Secondary Teacher [*A publication*]
SECTL........ Secretarial

SECTLZD... Sectionalized
SECTY ...... Secretary
SECU .... Slave Emulator Control Unit
SEC(UN).... Secretariat of the United Nations
Secur Med Trav ... Securite et Medecine du Travail [*A publication*]
Secur R Law ... Securities Regulation Law Journal [*A publication*]
SECUS....... Supreme Emblem Club of the United States   (EA)
SECWAR.... Secretary of War [*Obsolete*]
Sec World ... Security World [*A publication*]
SECY......... Secretary
SECY......... Security
SED .... Sanitary Engineering Division [*MIT*]   (MCD)
SED .... Saturn Electrostatic Discharges [*Planetary science*]
SED .... Scarborough Board of Education [*Professional Education Library*] [*UTLAS symbol*]
SED .... Scottish Education Department
SED .... Sedan   (AAG)
SED .... Sedative [*Medicine*]   (ROG)
SED .... Seddin [*German Democratic Republic*] [*Later, NGK*] [*Geomagnetic observatory code*]
Sed............ Sedes [*A Stool*] [*Medicine*]
SED .... Sediment
SED .... Sedition [*FBI standardized term*]
SED .... Sedona Air Center [*West Sedona, AZ*] [*FAA designator*]   (FAAC)
SED .... Segmented Expanding Die   (MCD)
SED .... Sensor Evolutionary Development   (MCD)
SED .... Seriously [*or Severely*] Emotionally Disturbed
SED .... Shipper's Export Declaration
SED .... Shore Establishments Division [*Navy*]
SED .... Skin Erythema Dose [*Medicine*]
SED .... Software Engineering Data [*Data Analysis Center for Software*] [*Database*]
SED .... Solar Energy Density
SED .... Sound Energy Density
SED .... Sozialistische Einheitspartei Deutschlands [*Socialist Unity Party of Germany*] [*East Germany*]   (PPW)
SED .... Space Environment Division [*NASA*]
SED .... Special Electrical Devices   (AABC)
SED .... Spectral Energy Distribution
SED .... Spondyloepiphysial Dysplasia [*Medicine*]
SED .... Staphylococcal Enterotoxin D [*Medicine*]
SED .... State Executive Director
SED .... Status Entry Device [*Telecommunications*]   (TEL)
SED .... Stray Energy Detector
SED .... Students for Economic Democracy   (EA)
SED .... Swansea East Dock [*Welsh depot code*]
SED .... System Engineering Division [*Apollo Spacecraft Program Office*]
SED .... System Entry Date [*Military*]   (AFIT)
SED .... Systems Effectiveness Demonstration   (NG)
SE 2d......... Southeastern Reporter, Second Series   (DLA)
SEDA .... Safety Equipment Distributors Association [*Chicago, IL*]   (EA)
SEDA .... Side Effects of Drugs. Annual [*Elsevier Book Series*] [*A publication*]
SEDA .... State Emergency Defense Airlift
SEDA .... Structured Exploratory Data Analysis
Sedalia N H Soc B ... Sedalia Natural History Society. Bulletin [*A publication*]
SEDAM ...... Societe d'Etudes et de Development des Aeroglisseurs Marins Terrestres et Amphibies [*French*]   (MCD)
SEDAR ...... Shipborne Electronic Deflection Array RADAR   (MCD)
SEDAS ...... Spurious Emission Detection Acquisition System   (MCD)
SEDC .... Steam Engine Direct Connected   (MSA)
SEDCOR .... Specialty Electronics Development Corporation
SEDD .... Systems Evaluation and Development Division [*NASA*]
SEDES ...... Societe d'Editions d'Enseignement Superieur [*A publication*]
SEDES ...... Societe d'Etudes pour le Developpement Economique et Social [*Society for the Study of Economic and Social Development*] [*Paris, France*] [*Information service*]   (EISS)
SEDFRE ..... Scholarship, Education, and Defense Fund for Racial Equality
Sedg Dam ... Sedgwick on the Measure of Damage   (DLA)
Sed Geol .... Sedimentary Geology [*A publication*]
Sedg L Cas ... Sedgwick's Leading Cases on Damages   (DLA)
Sedg L Cas ... Sedgwick's Leading Cases on Real Property   (DLA)
Sedg Stat Law ... Sedgwick on Statutory and Constitutional Law   (DLA)
Sedg St & Const Law ... Sedgwick on Statutory and Constitutional Law   (DLA)
Sedg & W Tit ... Sedgwick and Wait on the Trial of Title to Land   (DLA)
Sedg & W Tr Title Land ... Sedgwick and Wait on the Trial of Title to Land   (DLA)
SEDIC .... Sociedad Espanola de Documentacion e Informacion Cientifica [*Spanish Society for Documentation and Information Sciences*] [*Information service*]   (EISS)
Sediment Ge ... Sedimentary Geology [*A publication*]
Sediment Geol ... Sedimentary Geology [*A publication*]
SEDIS......... Service Information-Diffusion [*Information Dissemination Office*] [*National Institute for Research in Informatics and Automation*] [*Le Chesnay, France*] [*Information service*]   (EISS)

SEDIS........ Surface Emitter Detection, Identification System [*Navy*]
SEDIT........ Sophisticated String Editor   (IEEE)
SEDL......... Southwest Educational Development Laboratory
SEDM........ Society for Experimental and Descriptive Malacology   (EA)
SEDM........ Status Entry Device Multiplexer [*Telecommunications*]   (TEL)
SEDME....... Surveying Equipment Distance Measuring Electronic   (MCD)
SEDOR...... Spin Echo Double Resonance [*Physics*]
SEDP......... Support for Engineer Development Priorities   (MCD)
SEDPC...... Scientific and Engineering Data Processing Center
SEDR......... Science Education Development and Research Division [*National Science Foundation*]
SEDR......... Supplementary Experiment Data Record [*Aerospace*]
SEDR......... System Effective Data Rate   (BUR)
SEDR......... Systems Engineering Department Report   (IEEE)
SEDS......... Social and Economic Development Strategy
SEDS......... Society for Educational Data Systems [*Later, SDE*]
SEDS......... Space Electronics Detection System   (KSC)
SEDS......... State Energy Data System [*Department of Energy*] [*Database*]
SEDS......... Students for the Exploration and Development of Space
SEDS......... Support Equipment Data System
SEDS......... System Effectiveness Data System [*Air Force*]
SEDSCAF ... Standard ELINT Data System Codes and Format   (NVT)
SEE .... San Diego/Santee, CA [*Location identifier*] [*FAA*]   (FAAL)
SEE .... Sealed Air Corp. [*NYSE symbol*]
SEE .... Secondary Electron Emission
SEE .... Senior Environmental Employment Program [*Environmental Protection Agency*]
SEE .... Societe d'Etudes et d'Expansion [*Studies and Expansion Society - SES*]   (EA-IO)
SEE .... Society of Environmental Engineers [*Later, Institute of Environmental Sciences*]
SEE .... Society of Explosives Engineers
SEE .... Southeastern Electric Exchange
SEE .... Special Purpose End Effector   (MCD)
SEE .... Sun Earth Explorer [*Satellite*] [*NASA*]
SEE .... Survival, Evasion, and Escape [*Military*]
SE & E .... Survival, Evasion, and Escape [*Military*]   (AABC)
SEE .... Systems Effectiveness Engineering   (MCD)
SEE .... Systems Effectiveness Evaluation   (NG)
SEE .... Systems Efficiency Expert
SEE .... Systems Equipment Engineer [*Telecommunications*]   (TEL)
SEEA .... Societe Europeenne d'Energie Atomique
SEEA .... Software Error Effects Analysis
SEEAPAC ... Shore Electronic Engineering Activity, Pacific
SEEB........ Seeburg Industries, Inc. [*NASDAQ symbol*]
SEECA ...... Solar Energy and Energy Conservation Act of 1980
SEECA ...... State Environmental Education Coordinators Association   (EA)
SEECL ...... Solar Energy and Energy Conversion Laboratory [*University of Florida*] [*Research center*]   (RCD)
SEED........ Safe Eye Exposure Distance [*Air Force*]
SEED........ Scientists and Engineers in Economic Development [*National Science Foundation*]
SEED........ Self Electrooptic Effect Device [*Optical analog of a transistor*]
SEED........ Sewall Early Education Developmental Profiles
SEED........ Skill Escalation Employment Development   (EA)
SEED........ Special Elementary Education for the Disadvantaged
SEED........ Supply of Essential Engineering Data
Seed Bull ... Seed Bulletin [*A publication*]
SEEDIS ...... Socio-Economic Demographic Information System [*Lawrence Berkeley Laboratory*] [*Database*]
Seed and Nursery Tr ... Seed and Nursery Trader [*A publication*]
Seed Res (New Delhi) ... Seed Research (New Delhi) [*A publication*]
SEEDS ...... Space Exposed Experiment Developed for Students
Seed Sci Technol ... Seed Science and Technology [*A publication*]
Seed Trade Rev ... Seed Trade Review [*A publication*]
SEEE .... Studies in Electrical and Electronic Engineering [*Elsevier Book Series*] [*A publication*]
SEEF .... Scientists and Engineers Emigrant Fund
SEEHRL ..... Sanitary Engineering and Environmental Health Research Laboratory [*University of California, Berkeley*] [*Research center*]   (RCD)
SEEI .... Special Essential Elements of Information   (MCD)
SEEJ .... Slavic and East European Journal [*A publication*]
SEEK........ Search for Education, Elevation, and Knowledge [*Program*]
SEEK........ Survival, Escape, and Evasion Kit [*Navy*]   (NG)
SEEK........ Systems Evaluation and Exchange of Knowledge [*Data processing*]
SEEN........ Syndicat d'Etudes de l'Energie Nucleaire [*Belgium*]
SEEO........ Salvis Erroribus et Omissis [*Errors and Omissions Excepted*] [*Latin*]
SEEO........ Shore Electronic Engineering Office [*Navy*]
SEEP......... Sex Equity in Education Program [*Women's Action Alliance*]   (EA)
SEEP......... Sixth Fleet Escort Evaluation Program [*Navy*]
SEEP......... Stimulated Emission of Energetic Particles [*Experiment for study of radio waves*]
SEEQ........ SEEQ Technology, Inc. [*NASDAQ symbol*]   (NQ)
SEER........ Seasonal Energy-Efficiency Ratio [*of heat pumps, air conditioners, etc.*]
SEER........ Slavonic and East European Review [*A publication*]
SEER........ Student Exposition on Energy Resources [*Project*]

SEER......... Submarine Explosive Echo Ranging
SEER......... Supervisory Electronic Engineer [*Radio*]
SEER......... Surveillance, Epidemiology, and End-Results [*Program*] [*National Cancer Institute*]
SEER......... System for Electronic Evaluation and Retrieval [*Data processing*]
SEER......... Systems Engineering, Evaluation, and Research (MCD)
SEEREP .... Ships' Essential Equipment Requisition Expediting Program [*Navy*] (NVT)
SEERS ...... Senior Enlisted Evaluation Reports [*Military*] (INF)
SEES........ Slavic and East European Studies [*A publication*]
SEES........ Standard Entry/Exit System [*Army*]
SEES........ System Effectiveness Engineering Section
SEET........ Science End-to-End Test [*Space*]
SEETB....... South East England Tourist Board
SE Eur...... Southeastern Europe [*A publication*]
SEEX........ Systems Evaluation Experiment (MCD)
SEF .... SALT Education Fund [*Defunct*] (EA)
SEF .... Sebring, FL [*Location identifier*] [*FAA*] (FAAL)
Sef............ Sefarad [*A publication*]
SEF .... Self-Extinguishing Fiber [*Monsanto Co. trademark*]
SEF .... Sequential Excitation Fluorescence [*Aviation*] [*Navy*]
SEF .... Shielding Effectiveness Factor
SEF .... Simple Environment Factor
SEF .... Simulated Engine Failure (ADA)
SEF .... Small-End Forward [*of command module*]
SEF .... Software Engineering Facility
SEF .... Solar Energy Flux
SEF .... Somatically Evoked Field [*Neurophysiology*]
SEF .... Sound Energy Flux
SEF .... Southern Education Foundation (EA)
SEF .... Space Education Foundation [*Later, AEF*]
SEF .... Special Entry Flying List [*Navy*] [*British*]
SEF .... Standard External File
SEF .... Staphylococcus Aureus Enterotoxin F [*Toxic shock toxin*]
SEF .... Surface Effect Ship
SEF .... Systems Engineering Facility [*Defense Communications Agency*] (RDA)
SE/FAC..... Support Equipment/Facility [*NASA*] (NASA)
SEFACAN ... Segregator, Facer, Canceller Machine
SEFAR....... Sonic End Fire for Azimuth and Range
SE & FBR ... Science Fiction and Fantasy Book Review [*A publication*]
SEFC........ Southeast Fisheries Center [*Marine science*] (MSC)
SEFCL....... Southeastern Fish Control Station [*Department of the Interior*]
SEFD......... Solar Energy Flux Density
SEFEL....... Secretariat Europeen des Fabricants d'Emballages Metalliques Legers [*European Secretariat of Manufacturers of Light Metal Packages*] (EA)
SEFES....... Southeastern Forest Experiment Station [*Department of Agriculture*]
SEFI .... Societe Europeenne pour la Formation des Ingenieurs [*European Society for Engineering Education*] (EA)
SEFIC....... Seventh Fleet Intelligence Center [*Navy*]
SEFIP....... Statistical Estimation Fault Isolation Procedure (MCD)
SEFLO....... Sequence Flow [*Tracing technique*]
SEFM .... Support Equipment Field Modification (AAG)
SEFOR ...... Southwest Experimental Fast Oxide Reactor [*for commercial atomic power*]
SEFR......... Shielding Experiment Facility Reactor
SEFR........ System Effectiveness Forecast Report
SEFS........ Special Elite Forces Society (EA)
SefT .... Sefer Torah. Post-Talmudic Tractate (BJA)
SEFT .... Single Engine Flight Training
SEG.......... Screen Extras Guild (EA)
SEG.......... Sealing
Seg........... Segismundo [*A publication*]
SEG.......... Segment (AAG)
SEG.......... Segno [*Sign*] [*Music*]
SEG.......... Segue [*Follows*] [*Music*]
SEG.......... Selinsgrove, PA [*Location identifier*] [*FAA*] (FAAL)
SEG.......... Sequence of Events Generator
SEG.......... Side Entry Goniometer
SEG.......... Sliding Electron Gun
SEG.......... Society of Economic Geologists (EA)
SEG.......... Society of Exploration Geophysicists (EA)
SEG.......... Special Effect Generator [*Video technology*]
SEG.......... Standardization Evaluation Group (AFM)
SEG.......... Subesophageal Ganglion [*Anatomy*]
SEG.......... Supplementum Epigraphicum Graecum [*A publication*]
SEG.......... System Engineering Groundrule [*NASA*] (NASA)
SEG.......... Systems Engineering Group [*Air Force*]
SEG.......... Systems Evaluation Group
SEGBA....... Servicios Electricos del Gran Buenos Aires, SA [*Electrical utility*] [*Argentina*]
SEGD .... Society of Environmental Graphics Designers [*Sausalito, CA*] (EA)
SEGEA...... Orthopaedic Surgery [*A publication*]
SEGH .... Society for Environmental Geochemistry and Health [*University of Missouri*] [*Rolla, MO*] (EA)
SEGM......... Segment

SEG/R & T ... Systems Engineering Group/Research and Technology [*Air Force*]
Seguranca Desenvolv ... Seguranca e Desenvolvimento. ADESG [*Revista da Associacao dos Diplomados da Escola Superior de Guerra*] [*Brazil*] [*A publication*]
SEH .... Sehore [*India*] [*Seismograph station code, US Geological Survey*] (SEIS)
SEH .... Shuttle Electronic Hardware [*NASA*]
SEH .... Single-Engined Helicopter (MCD)
SEH .... Societe Europeenne d'Hematologie
SEH .... Solar Equivalent Hours
SEH .... Star/Earth Horizon Sightings
SEH .... Strobel, E. H., Saint Louis MO [*STAC*]
SEH .... Subependymal Hemorrhage [*Medicine*]
SEHAB ...... Sea Rehabilitation [*Navy*] (NVT)
SE-HPLC.... Size Exclusion-High Performance Liquid Chromatography
SEHR........ Scandinavian Economic History Review [*A publication*]
SEI........... Safety Equipment Institute [*Arlington, VA*] (EA)
SEI........... Seis Pros, Inc. [*American Stock Exchange symbol*]
SEI........... Self Employment Income [*Social Security Administration*] (OICC)
SEI........... Senhor Do Bonfim [*Brazil*] [*Airport symbol*] (OAG)
SEI........... Societa Editrice Internazionale [*Italy*] [*Publisher*]
SEI........... Societas Ergophthalmologica Internationalis [*International Ergophthalmological Society*] (EA-IO)
SEI........... Society of Engineering Illustrators
SEI........... Software Engineering Institute [*DoD*]
SEI........... Special Engineering Investigation (MCD)
SEI........... Special Equipment Item (MCD)
SEI........... Special Experience Identifier [*Military*]
SEI........... Statistical Engineering Institute (MCD)
SEI........... Stern Environment Indexes [*Psychology*]
SEI........... Stockpile Entry Inspection [*Navy*] (NG)
SEI........... Stray Energy Indicator
SEI........... Support Equipment Installation [*NASA*] (NASA)
SEI........... System/Equipment Inventory
SE & I ...... Systems Engineering and Integration [*Social Security Administration*]
SEIA .... Security Equipment Industry Association [*Santa Monica, CA*] (EA)
SEIA .... Solar Energy Industries Association
SEIA .... Solar Energy Institute of America (MCD)
SEIAC .... Science Education Information Analysis Center [*ERIC*]
SEIB .... Service des Etudes et Inventaires Bio-Physiques [*Quebec*]
SEIB .... Statistical and Economic Information Bulletin for Africa [*A publication*]
SEIC .... SEI Corporation [*NASDAQ symbol*] (NQ)
SEIC .... Solar Energy Information Center
SEIC .... System Effectiveness Information Central
SEICO .... Support Equipment Installation and Checkout [*NASA*] (NASA)
SEIDB........ Solar Energy Information Data Bank [*Department of Energy*]
SEIE .... Solvent Extraction and Ion Exchange [*A publication*]
SEIE .... Submarine Escape Immersion Equipment
Seifen Fachbl ... Seifen Fachblatt [*A publication*]
Seifen Ole ... Seifen, Oele, Fette, Waesche [*A publication*]
Seifensieder Ztg ... Seifensieder Zeitung [*A publication*]
Seifensieder Ztg Allg Oel Fett Ztg ... Seifensieder-Zeitung in Gemeinschaft auf Kriegsdauer mit Allgemeine Oel- und Fett-Zeitung [*A publication*]
SEIGA .... Seishin Igaku [*A publication*]
Seign Rep ... Lower Canada Seignorial Questions Reports (DLA)
SEIJD .... Seijinbyo [*A publication*]
SEIL .... Science Experiments Integration Laboratories
SEIMC....... Special Education Instructional Materials Centers [*Office of Education*] [*Albany, NY*] [*Database producer*] (EISS)
SEIMS .... State Economic Information Management System [*State Department*] [*Database*]
SEINAM ..... Solar Energy Institute of North America (EA)
SEIOD .... Spogli Elettronici dell'Italiano delle Origini e del Duecento [*A lexical, morphological, and syntactical inventory of Old Italian texts*]
SEIP .... System Engineering Implementation Plan
SEIRS........ Suppliers and Equipment Information Retrieval System [*International Civil Aviation Organization*] [*Databank*] [*Information service*] (EISS)
SEIS .... Solar Energy Information Services (EISS)
SEIS .... Submarine Emergency Identification Signal (NG)
SEISA....... South Eastern Intercollegiate Sailing Association
SEISMOG... Seismographic
SEISMOL ... Seismologic
Seismol Bull ... Seismological Bulletin [*A publication*]
Seismol and Geol ... Seismology and Geology [*A publication*]
Seismolog Soc Am Bull ... Seismology Society of America. Bulletin [*A publication*]
Seismol Ser Earth Phys Branch ... Seismological Series of the Earth Physics Branch [*A publication*]
Seismol Ser Geol Surv (S Afr) ... Seismologic Series. Geological Survey (South Africa) [*A publication*]
Seismol Serv Can Seismol Ser ... Seismological Service of Canada. Seismological Series [*A publication*]

Seismol Soc Am Bul ... Seismological Society of America. Bulletin [*A publication*]
Seismostoikost Sooruzh ... Seismostoikost Sooruzhenii [*USSR*] [*A publication*]
Seism Prib Instrum Sredstva Seism Nabl ... Seismichiskie Pribory. Instrumental'naye Sredstva Seismicheskikh Nablyudenii [*A publication*]
SEIT .... Satellite Educational and Informational Television
SEIT .... Supervisory Electronic Installation Technician
SEIT .... System Evaluation, Integration, and Test   (MCD)
SEITA Ann Dir Etud Equip Sect 2 ... SEITA [*Service d'Exploitation Industrielle des Tabacs et des Allumettes*] Annales de la Direction des Etudes de l'Equipement. Section 2 [*A publication*]
SEITA Annls ... Service d'Exploitation Industrielle des Tabacs et des Allumettes. Annales de la Direction des Etudes et de l'Equipement [*A publication*]
SEIU .... Service Employees International Union   (EA)
SE/IWT ...... Southern Europe - Inland Waterways Transport [*NATO*]   (NATG)
SEJ .... Australian Stock Exchange Journal [*A publication*]
SEJ .... Sliding Expansion Joint [*Technical drawings*]
SEJ .... Southern Economic Journal [*A publication*]
SEJCR .... Societe Europeenne des Jeunes de la Croix-Bleue [*European Society for Blue Cross Youth - ESBCY*]   (EA-IO)
SEJG .... Sacris Erudiri. Jaarboek voor Godsdienstwetenschappen [*A publication*]
SEK .... Synomospondia Ergaton Kyprou [*Cyprus Workers' Confederation*] [*"Free Labour Syndicats"*]
SEKF .... Sister Elizabeth Kenny Foundation [*Later, SKI*]
SEKLS ...... Southeast Kansas Library System [*Library network*]
SEKRLC ..... Southeastern Kentucky Regional Library Cooperative [*Library network*]
Sel .... Ducretet-Thomson [*Formerly, Ducret Selmer*] [*Record label*] [*France*]
SEL .... Satellite Experiment Laboratory [*National Oceanic and Atmospheric Administration*]
SEL .... Scouts' Esperanto League   (EA)
SEL .... Select [*or Selection*]   (AAG)
SEL .... Selected Equipment List   (NVT)
SEL .... Selector   (DEN)
Sel .... Seleucid Era   (BJA)
SEL .... Selkirk College Library [*UTLAS symbol*]
sel .... Selkup [*MARC language code*] [*Library of Congress*]   (LCCP)
SEL .... Semlyachik [*USSR*] [*Seismograph station code, US Geological Survey*]   (SEIS)
SEL .... Seoul [*South Korea*] [*Airport symbol*]   (OAG)
SEL .... Seton Co. [*American Stock Exchange symbol*]
SEL .... Signal Engineering Laboratories
SEL .... Skolta Esperanto-Ligo [*Scouts' Esperanto League*]   (EA-IO)
SEL .... Socialist Electoral League [*Norway*]   (PPW)
SEL .... Solar Environmental Laboratory [*National Oceanic and Atmospheric Administration*]
SEL .... Southeastern Educational Laboratory
SEL .... Space Environment Laboratory [*National Oceanic and Atmospheric Administration*]
SEL .... Spontaneously Emitted Light
SEL .... Standard Elektrik Lorenz [*Germany*]
SEL .... Stanford Electronics Laboratory [*Stanford University*] [*Research center*]   (MCD)
SEL .... Star/Earth Landmark Sightings
SEL .... Studies in English Literature [*A publication*]
SEL .... Super Einspritz Lang [*Fuel-injection, long wheelbase*] [*As in 450 SEL, the model number of a Mercedes-Benz automobile*]
SEL .... Support Equipment List [*Navy*]
SEL .... System Engineering Laboratories   (MCD)
SELA .... Sistema Economico Latinoamericano [*Latin American Economic System*]   (EA-IO)
Sel Annu Rev Anal Sci ... Selected Annual Reviews of the Analytical Sciences [*A publication*]
Sel App Beng ... Selected Appeals, Sadr Diwani Adalat [*Bengal, India*]   (DLA)
SELAVIP .... Servicio Latinoamericano y Asiatico de Vivienda Popular [*Latin American and Asian Low Income Housing Service*]   (EA-IO)
SelBab .... Babylonian Seleucid Era   (BJA)
Sel Bibliogr Algae ... Selected Bibliography on Algae [*A publication*]
Sel Bibliogr Middle East Geol ... Selected Bibliography of Middle East Geology [*A publication*]
SELCAL ..... Selective Calling [*Radio*]
Sel Cas .... Select Cases, Central Provinces [*India*]   (DLA)
Sel Cas Ch ... Select Cases in Chancery [*England*]   (DLA)
Sel Cas Ch (T King) ... Select Cases in Chancery Tempore King [*25 English Reprint*] [*1724-33*]   (DLA)
Sel Cas DA ... Select Cases, Sadr Diwani Adalat [*India*]   (DLA)
Sel Cas Ev ... Select Cases in Evidence [*Strange*] [*England*]   (DLA)
Sel Cas KB Edw I ... Select Cases in King's Bench under Edward I [*Sayles*] [*England*]   (DLA)
Sel Cas NF ... Select Cases, Newfoundland   (DLA)
Sel Cas NWP ... Select Cases, Northwest Provinces [*India*]   (DLA)

Sel Cas NY ... Yate's Select Cases [*1809*] [*New York*]   (DLA)
Sel Cas with Opin ... Select Cases with Opinions by a Solicitor   (DLA)
Sel Cas SDA ... Select Cases, Sadr Diwani Adalat [*Bengal, Bombay, India*]   (DLA)
Sel Cas T Br ... Cooper's Select Cases Tempore Brougham   (DLA)
Sel Cas T King ... Select Cases in Chancery Tempore King [*England*]   (DLA)
Sel Cas T Nap ... Select Cases Tempore Napier [*Ireland*]   (DLA)
Sel Ca T King ... Select Cases in Chancery Tempore King [*25 English Reprint*] [*1724-33*]   (DLA)
Sel Ch Cas ... Select Cases in Chancery Tempore King, Edited by Macnaghten [*England*]   (DLA)
Sel Col Cas ... Select Collection of Cases [*England*]   (DLA)
SELCOM .... Select Committee [*Army Materiel Command*]
Seld .... Selden's New York Reports [*5-10 New York*]   (DLA)
SELDADS ... Space Environment Laboratory Data Acquisition and Display System [*National Oceanic and Atmospheric Administration*]
Sel Dec Bomb ... Select Cases, Sadr Diwani Adalat [*Bombay, India*]   (DLA)
SEL DECK ... Select Decking [*Lumber*]
Sel Dec Madr ... Select Decrees, Sadr Adalat [*Madras, India*]   (DLA)
Selden .... Selden's New York Court of Appeals Reports   (DLA)
Selden Notes ... Selden's New York Court of Appeals Notes of Cases [*1st ed.*] [*1853*]   (DLA)
Seld JP .... Selden's Judicature in Parliaments [*1681*]   (DLA)
Seld Mare Claus ... Selden's Mare Clausum [*The Sea Closed*] [*Refutation of Grotius' Mare Liberum*]   (DLA)
Seld Notes ... Selden's New York Court of Appeals Notes   (DLA)
Seld R .... Selden's New York Court of Appeals Reports   (DLA)
Seld Soc ...... Selden Society   (DLA)
Seld Soc Yrbk ... Selden Society Yearbook [*United States*]   (DLA)
Seld Tit Hon ... Selden's Titles of Honor   (DLA)
SELEC .... Select   (ROG)
SELEC .... Superelastic LASER Energy Conversion   (MCD)
Selec Ed R ... Selections from the Edinburgh Review [*A publication*]
Selected Water Resources Abstr ... Selected Water Resources Abstracts [*A publication*]
Select J ...... Select Journal [*A publication*]
Selek Semenovod ... Selektsiya i Semenovodstvo [*A publication*]
SelEnv .... Selected References on Environmental Quality [*A publication*]
Selez Tec Molit ... Selezione di Tecnica Molitoria [*A publication*]
SELF .... National Citizens Committee to Save Education and Library Funds
SELF .... Self-Eject Launch Facility [*NASA*]   (MCD)
SELF .... Short Expeditious Landing Field   (CINC)
SELF .... Societe des Ecrivains Luxembourgeois de Langue Francaise
Self Rel ...... Self-Reliance [*A publication*]
SELFTAV ... Self-Conducted Tender Availability [*Navy*]   (NVT)
SELGEM .... Self-Generating Master [*Information management system*] [*Data processing*]
SE Libn ..... Southeastern Librarian [*A publication*]
SELID .... Serials Librarian [*A publication*]
SELit .... Studies in English Literature [*Japan*] [*A publication*]
SELJ .... Studies in English Literature (Japan) [*A publication*]
SELK .... Selkirkshire [*County in Scotland*]
Sel'Khoz Beloruss ... Sel'skoe Khozyaistvo Belorussii [*A publication*]
Sel'-khoz Biol ... Sel'skokhozyaistvennaya Biologiya [*A publication*]
Sel'Khoz Kirgizii ... Sel'skoe Khozyaistvo Kirgizii [*A publication*]
Sel'Khoz Povol ... Sel'skoe Khozyaistvo Povolzh'ya [*A publication*]
Sel'Khoz Sev Kavkaz ... Sel'skoe Khozyaistvo Severnogo Kavkaza [*A publication*]
Sel'Khoz Sev-Zapad Zony ... Sel'skoe Khozyaistvo Severo-Zapadnoi Zony [*A publication*]
Sel Khoz Sev Zap Zony ... Sel'skoe Khozyaistvo Severo-Zapadnoi Zony [*A publication*]
Sel'Khoz Sib ... Sel'skoe Khozyaistvo Sibiri [*A publication*]
Sel'Khoz Tadzhikistana ... Sel'skoe Khozyaistvo Tadzhikistana [*A publication*]
Sel Khoz Turkmen ... Sel'skoe Khozyaistvo Turkmenistana [*A publication*]
SELL .... Sales Environment Learning Laboratory [*Computer-based marketing game*]
SELL .... Studies in English Literature and Language [*Japan*] [*A publication*]
SELL .... Suomi, Eesti, Latvija, Lietuva [*Finland, Estonia, Latvia, Lithuania*]
Sel L Cas ... Select Law Cases [*England*]   (DLA)
Sell Pr .... Sellon's Practice in the King's Bench   (DLA)
Sell Prac .... Sellon's Practice in the King's Bench   (DLA)
SE/LM .... Systems Engineering/Logistics Management   (MCD)
SelMac ...... Macedonian Seleucid Era   (BJA)
Sel Math Sov ... Selecta Mathematica Sovietica [*A publication*]
SEL MERC ... Select Merchantable [*Lumber*]
SELMOUS ... Special English Language Materials for Overseas University Students
SELN .... Selection   (AAG)
Sel NP .... Selwyn's Law of Nisi Prius   (DLA)
Sel Off Ch ... Selden's Office of Lord Chancellor [*1671*]   (DLA)
SELOR .... Ship Emitter Location Report [*Navy*]   (CAAL)
Sel Org Transform ... Selective Organic Transformations [*A publication*]
Sel Pap Environ Isr ... Selected Papers on the Environment in Israel [*A publication*]
Sel Pr .... Sellon's Practice   (DLA)

Sel PRC Mag ... Selections from People's Republic of China Magazines [*Hong Kong*] [*A publication*]
SELR .... Saturn Engineering Liaison Request [*NASA*]   (KSC)
SELR .... Selector   (AAG)
Sel Rand Abstr ... Selected Rand Abstracts [*A publication*]
SELREC ..... Shore Electronics Reconnaissance System
SELREFTRA ... Selected Refresher Training [*Navy*]   (NVT)
SELRES ..... Selected Reserve [*Military*]
SELRFT ..... Selected Refresher Training [*Navy*]   (NVT)
SELS .... Selective Service
SELS .... Severe Local Storm [*National Weather Service*]
SELSA .... Southeast Library Service Area [*Library network*]
Sel Sci Pap Ist Super Sanita ... Selected Scientific Papers. Istituto Superiore di Sanita [*A publication*]
Sel Semenovod (Mosc) ... Selekstsiya i Semenovodstvo (Moscow) [*A publication*]
Sel Semenovod Resp Mezhved Temat Sb ... Selekstsiya i Semenovodstvo Respublikanskii Mezhvedomstvennyi Tematicheskii Sbornik [*A publication*]
Sel Serv L Rep ... Selective Service Law Reporter   (DLA)
Sel Serv L Rptr ... Selective Service Law Reporter   (DLA)
Sel'sk Khoz ... Sel'skoe Khozyaistvo [*A publication*]
Sel'sk Khoz Kaz ... Sel'skoe Khozyaistvo Kazakhstana [*A publication*]
Sel'sk Khoz Kirg ... Sel'skoe Khozyaistvo Kirgizii [*A publication*]
Sel'sk Khoz Mold ... Sel'skoe Khozyaistvo Moldavii [*A publication*]
Sel'sk Khoz Povolzh'ya ... Sel'skoe Khozyaistvo Povolzh'ya [*A publication*]
Sel'sk Khoz Rubezhom Rastenievod ... Sel'skoe Khozyaistvo za Rubezhom. Rastenievodstvo [*A publication*]
Sel'sk Khoz Sev Zapadn Zony ... Sel'skoe Khozyaistvo Severo-Zapadnoi Zony [*A publication*]
Sel'sk Khoz Tadzh ... Sel'skoe Khozyaistvo Tadzhikistana [*A publication*]
Sel'sk Khoz Tatar ... Sel'skoe Khozyaistvo Tatarii [*A publication*]
Sel'sk Khoz Tatarii ... Sel'skoe Khozyaistvo Tatarii [*A publication*]
Sel'sk Khoz Turkm ... Sel'skoe Khozyaistvo Turkmenistana [*A publication*]
Sel'skokhoz Biol ... Sel'skokhozyaistvennaya Biologiya [*A publication*]
Sel'skokhoz Proizv Nechernozem Zony ... Sel'skokhozyaistvennoe Proizvodstvo Nechernozemnoi Zony [*A publication*]
Sel'skokhoz Proizv Povol ... Sel'skokhozyaistvennoe Proizvodstvo Povolzh'ya [*A publication*]
Sel'skokhoz Proizv Sev Kavkaza TSCHO ... Sel'skokhozyaistvennoe Proizvodstvo Severnogo Kavkaza i TSCHO [*A publication*]
Sel'skokhoz Proizv Sib Dal'nego Vostoka ... Sel'skokhozyaistvennoe Proizvodstvo Sibiri i Dal'nego Vostoka [*A publication*]
Sel'skokhoz Proizv Urala ... Sel'skokhozyaistvennoe Proizvodstvo Urala [*A publication*]
Selskostop Misal ... Selskostopanska Misal [*A publication*]
Selskostop Misul ... Selskostopanska Misul [*A publication*]
Selskostop Nauka ... Selskostopanska Nauka [*A publication*]
Selskostop Tekh ... Selskostopanska Tekhnika [*A publication*]
Sel Sortoizuch Agrotekh Plodovykh Yagodnykh Kul't ... Selektsiya, Sortoizuchenie, Agrotekhnika Plodovykh i Yagodnykh Kul'tur [*A publication*]
SEL STR ..... Select Structural [*Lumber*]
SELSW .... Selector Switch   (MCD)
SELSYN ..... Self-Synchronous [*Trade name*] [*Motor*]
SELT .... SAGE [*Semiautomatic Ground Environment*] Evaluation Library Tape
SELT .... Select Information Systems [*NASDAQ symbol*]   (NQ)
SELT .... Self-Eject Launch Technique [*NASA*]   (KSC)
SELT .... Sheet Explosive Loading Technique
Sel Top Solid State Phys ... Selected Topics in Solid State Physics [*A publication*]
Sel Vet Ist Zooprofil Sper Lomb Emilia ... Selezione Veterinaria-Istituto Zooprofilattico Sperimentale della Lombardia e dell'Emilia [*A publication*]
SELW .... Selwyn College [*Cambridge*] [*British*]   (ROG)
Sel Water Res Abstr ... Selected Water Resources Abstracts [*A publication*]
Selw & Barn ... Barnewall and Alderson's English King's Bench Reports [*1st part*]   (DLA)
Selw NP ..... Selwyn's Law of Nisi Prius [*England*]   (DLA)
SELY .... Southeasterly [*Meteorology*]   (FAAC)
SEM .... Scanning Electron Microscope [*or Microscopy*]
SEM .... Secondary Emission Microscope
SEM .... Secondary Emission Monitor
SEM .... Secondary Enrichment Medium [*Microbiology*]
SEM .... Security Environmental Systems, Inc. [*Vancouver Stock Exchange symbol*]
SEM .... Seller's Engineering Memo [*NASA*]   (NASA)
SEM .... Selma, AL [*Location identifier*] [*FAA*]   (FAAL)
Sem .... Semahoth   (BJA)
Sem .... Semana [*A publication*]
SEM .... Semaphore
SEM .... Semble [*It Seems*]
SEM .... Semel [*Once*]
SEM .... Semi [*One-Half*] [*Pharmacy*]
SEM .... Semicolon
SEM .... Semienriched Minimal [*Agar*]
Sem .... Seminar [*A publication*]
SEM .... Seminary
SEM .... Semipalatinsk [*USSR*] [*Seismograph station code, US Geological Survey*]   (SEIS)

SEM .... Semitic
sem .... Semitic [*MARC language code*] [*Library of Congress*]   (LCCP)
Sem .... Semitica [*Paris*] [*A publication*]
SEM .... Semo Aviation, Inc. [*Malden, MO*] [*FAA designator*]   (FAAC)
SEM .... Sempre [*Throughout*] [*Music*]
SEM .... Singularity Expansion Method   (IEEE)
SEM .... Society for Ethnomusicology   (EA)
SEM .... Society for Experimental Mechanics [*Formerly, SESA*]   (EA)
SEM .... Solar Environment Monitor
SEM .... Sortie Effectiveness Model [*NASA*]   (MCD)
SEM .... Southeast Missouri State University, Cape Girardeau, MO [*OCLC symbol*]   (OCLC)
SEM .... Southern Illinois University at Carbondale Center for Electron Microscopy [*Research center*]   (RCD)
SEM .... Space Environment Monitor [*NASA*]
SEM .... Standard Electronic Module   (CAAL)
SEM .... Standard Error of the Mean
SEM .... Standard Error of Measurement [*Testing*]
SEM .... Standard Estimating Module   (IEEE)
SEM .... Station Engineering Manual [*Telecommunications*]   (TEL)
SEM .... Stereoscan Electron Microscope
SEM .... Stray Energy Monitor
SEM .... Structural Econometric Model [*Statistics*]
SEM .... Subarray Electronics Module [*Data processing*]
SEM .... Subcontractor Engineering Memorandum   (MCD)
S-EM .... Suck-Egg Mule [*A publication*]
SEM .... System Effectiveness Model   (CAAL)
SEM .... System Engineering Management
SEM .... Systems Engineering & Manufacturing Corp. [*American Stock Exchange symbol*]
S-E-M .... Systems/Equipment/Munitions [*Army*]   (AFIT)
SEM .... Systolic Ejection Murmur [*Cardiology*]
SEMA .... Societe d'Etudes de Mathematiques Appliquees [*France*]
SEMA .... Special Electronic Mission Aircraft   (RDA)
SEMA .... Specialty Equipment Market Association [*Whittier, CA*]   (EA)
SEMAA ...... Safety Equipment Manufacturers Agents Association   (EA)
Semaine Med ... Semaine Medicale [*A publication*]
Semaine Vet ... Semaine Veterinaire [*A publication*]
Sem Anal ... Seminaire d'Analyse [*A publication*]
Sem Anal Moderne ... Seminaire d'Analyse Moderne [*A publication*]
Semana Med ... Semana Medica [*A publication*]
SemBEsp ... Semana Biblica Espanola [*Madrid*] [*A publication*]
SEMCC ...... Southeastern Massachusetts Health Sciences Libraries Consortium [*Library network*]
SEMCIP ..... Shipboard Electromagnetic Capability Improvement Program [*Navy*]   (NVT)
SEMCOG ... Southeast Michigan Council of Governments [*Detroit, MI*]
SEMCOR .... Semantic Correlation [*Machine-aided indexing*]
SEMD .... Stray Energy Monitor Device
SEME .... Semicon, Inc. [*NASDAQ symbol*]   (NQ)
SEMEL in D ... Semel in Die [*Once a Day*] [*Pharmacy*]
Semen Elette ... Sementi Elette [*A publication*]
SEMET .... Self-Evident Meteorological Code   (NATG)
SEMG .... Scanning Electron Micrograph
SEMH .... Service Engineering Man-Hours
Sem Hematol ... Seminars in Hematology [*A publication*]
SEMHI .... Southeastern Manufactured Housing Institute [*Later, Manufactured Housing Institute*]   (EA)
Sem Hop .... Semaine des Hopitaux [*A publication*]
Sem Hop Inf ... Semaine des Hopitaux. Informations [*A publication*]
Sem Hop Paris ... Semaine des Hopitaux de Paris [*A publication*]
Sem Hop-The ... Semaine des Hopitaux-Therapeutique [*A publication*]
SEMI .... Self-Evacuating Multilayer Insulation [*System*]
SEMI .... Semiconductor Equipment and Materials Institute [*Mountain View, CA*]   (EA)
SEMI .... Shipboard Electromagnetic Interference [*Navy*]   (CAAL)
SEMI .... Societe d'Etudes de Marche et d'Informatique [*Society for the Study of Marketing and Informatics*] [*Marseille, France*] [*Information service*]   (EISS)
SEMI .... Special Electromagnetic Interference   (MCD)
SEMICOND ... Semiconductor
Semicond Insul ... Semiconductors and Insulators [*A publication*]
Semicond and Insul ... Semiconductors and Insulators [*A publication*]
Semicond Prod ... Semiconductor Products [*A publication*]
Semicond Semimet ... Semiconductors and Semimetals [*A publication*]
SEMIDR ..... Semidrachma [*Half a Drachma*] [*Pharmacy*]
SEMIH .... Semihora [*Half an Hour*] [*Pharmacy*]
SEMIKON ... Seminare/Konferenzen [*Seminars/Conferences*] [*Society for Business Information*] [*Munich, West Germany*] [*Information service*]   (EISS)
Semin Arthritis Rheum ... Seminars in Arthritis and Rheumatism [*A publication*]
Semin Chim Etat Solide ... Seminaires de Chimie de l'Etat Solide [*A publication*]
Semin Drug Treat ... Seminars in Drug Treatment [*A publication*]
Semin Estratigrafia ... Seminarios de Estratigrafia [*Madrid*] [*A publication*]
SEMINEX ... Seminary in Exile [*Liberal-oriented Lutheran seminary*]
Semin Hematol ... Seminars in Hematology [*A publication*]
Semin Nucl Med ... Seminars in Nuclear Medicine [*A publication*]
Semin Oncol ... Seminars in Oncology [*A publication*]
Semin Perinatol ... Seminars in Perinatology [*A publication*]

Semin Psychiatry ... Seminars in Psychiatry [*A publication*]
Semin Roentgenol ... Seminars in Roentgenology [*A publication*]
Sem Inst Prikl Mat Annotac Dokladov ... Seminar Instituta Prikladnoi Matematiki. Annotacii Dokladov [*A publication*]
Semin Thromb Hemostas ... Seminars in Thrombosis and Hemostasis [*A publication*]
Semin Thromb Hemostasis ... Seminars in Thrombosis and Hemostasis [*A publication*]
SEMIRAD ... Secondary Electron-Mixed Radiation Dosimeter (IEEE)
SEMIS .... Solar Energy Monitor in Space [*NASA*] (MCD)
SEMIS .... State Extension Management Information System [*Department of Agriculture*]
Sem Judiciaire ... La Semaine Judiciaire (DLA)
SEMKA ...... Semento Kogyo [*A publication*]
Sem Kond ... Seminarium Kondakovianum [*A publication*]
SEMLAM ..... Semiconductor LASER Amplifier
SEMLAT .... Semiconductor LASER Array Techniques
SEMM .... Smoke Effectiveness Manual Model (MCD)
SEMM .... Solar Electric Multiple-Mission (MCD)
Sem Math Sci ... Seminar on Mathematical Sciences [*Yokohama*] [*A publication*]
Sem Math Sup ... Seminaire de Mathematiques Superieures [*A publication*]
Sem Math Superieures ... Seminaire de Mathematiques Superieures [*Montreal*] [*A publication*]
Sem Med ... Semana Medica [*A publication*]
SEMMS ...... Solar Electric Multiple-Mission Spacecraft
SEMN .... Slow Extension Motoneuron [*Neurology*]
SEMN .... Superficial Extensor Motoneuron [*Neurology*]
SEMO .... Systems Engineering and Management Operations [*Military*]
Semon .... Semonides [*Seventh century BC*] [*Classical studies*] (OCD)
SEMOPS ..... Sequential Multiobjective Problem Solving
SEMP .... Sempre [*Throughout*] [*Music*]
SEMP .... Simplified Early Maturities Participation Plan [*Small Business Administration*]
SEMP .... Societe d'Editions Medico-Pharmaceutiques [*Medical-Pharmaceutical Publishing Co.*] [*Information service*] [*France*] (EISS)
SEMP .... Socioeconomic Military Program (CINC)
SEMP .... Standard Electronics Module Program (MCD)
SEMP .... System Engineering Management Plan
SEMPA .... Scanning Electron Microscope and Particle Analyzer
SEMPA .... Scanning Electron Microscopy with Polarization Analysis
SEMPB .... Schiffli Embroidery Manufacturers Promotion Board [*Union City, NJ*] (EA)
SEMRE .... SPRINT Electromagnetic Radiation Evaluation [*Army*] (AABC)
SEMRFL ..... Michigan Regional Libraries Film Program at Monroe [*Library network*]
Sem Roentg ... Seminars in Roentgenology [*A publication*]
Sem S .... Semiotic Scene [*A publication*]
SEMS .... Severe Environment Memory Series [*or System*] [*Data processing*]
SEMS .... Space Environment Monitor System [*NASA*] (NASA)
SEMS .... Stray Energy Monitor System
SEMS .... Support Engineering Manhour Summary (MCD)
SEMS .... System Engineering Management Standard
SEMT .... Science, Engineering, Medicine, and Technology [*Series*]
SEMTA .... Southeastern Michigan Transportation Authority
SEMTEC .... Southeastern Marine Trades Exhibit and Conference [*National Marine Manufacturers Association*] (TSPED)
Sem Ther ... Semaine Therapeutique [*France*] [*A publication*]
SEMTR ...... SPRINT Early Missile Test RADAR [*Army*] (AABC)
SEMTR ...... Supervisory Electronic Maintenance Technician [*Relief*]
SEMTSA ..... Structural Econometric Modeling Time Series Analysis [*Statistics*]
Se Mulli (New Phys) ... Se Mulli (New Physics) [*A publication*]
Sem Vitivinic ... Semana Vitivinicola [*Spain*] [*A publication*]
SEMY .... Seminary
Sen .... De Senectute [*of Cicero*] [*Classical studies*] (OCD)
SEN .... Lexington, KY [*Location identifier*] [*FAA*] (FAAL)
SEN .... Science Engineering News [*National Oceanic and Atmospheric Administration*]
SeN .... Seara Nova [*A publication*]
SEN .... Semienclosed
SEN .... Senate
SEN .... Senator
SEN .... Sendai [*Mukaiyama*] [*Japan*] [*Seismograph station code, US Geological Survey*] (SEIS)
Sen .... Seneca [*the Elder*] [*First century BC*] [*Classical studies*] (OCD)
Sen .... Seneca [*the Younger*] [*First century AD*] [*Classical studies*] (OCD)
SEN .... Senegal [*Three-letter standard code*] (CNC)
SENU .... Senior
SEN .... Senlac Resources, Inc. [*Toronto Stock Exchange symbol*]
SEN .... Sennae [*Of Senna*] [*Pharmacy*] (ROG)
SEN .... Sensitive
SEN .... Sensor (AAG)
SEN .... Senza [*Without*] [*Music*]
SEN .... Single Edge Notched
SEN .... Societe Europeenne de Neuroscience [*European Neuroscience Association - ENA*] (EA)
SEN .... Software Error Notification [*Data processing*]

SEN .... Sports Exchange Network [*Cable TV programing service*]
SEN .... State Enrolled Nurse [*British*]
SEN .... Steam Emulsion Number
SEN .... System Error Notification [*Data processing*]
SEN .... Systems Engineering Notice
SENA .... Seaport Navigation Co. [*AAR code*] [*Later, SNCO*]
SENA .... Societe d'Energie Nucleaire Franco-Belge des Ardennes [*Belgian-French power consortium*]
SENA .... Sympathetic Efferent Nerve Activity
SENAV ...... Senior Naval Aviator (NVT)
SENAVAV ... Senior Naval Aviator
SENAVOMAC ... Senior Naval Officer, Military Airlift Command (MCD)
SenCh .... Senior Chaplain [*Navy*] [*British*]
Senckenb Biol ... Senckenbergiana Biologica [*A publication*]
Senckenbergische Nat Ges Frankfurt Ber ... Senckenbergische Naturforschende Gesellschaft in Frankfurt Am Main. Bericht [*A publication*]
Senckenberg Marit ... Senckenbergiana Maritima [*A publication*]
Senckenb Lethaea ... Senckenbergiana Lethaea [*A publication*]
Senckenb Marit ... Senckenbergiana Maritima [*A publication*]
Senckenb Naturforsch Ges Abh ... Senckenbergische Naturforschende Gesellschaft Abhandlungen [*A publication*]
SEND .... Scientists and Engineers for National Development [*Scholarship program*]
SEND .... Securities and Exchange Commission News Digest [*A publication*]
SEND .... Sentry Data, Inc. [*NASDAQ symbol*] (NQ)
SEND .... Shared Equipment Need Date (NASA)
Sendai Astron Rap ... Sendai Astronomiaj Raportoj [*A publication*]
Sen Doc .... Senate Document (DLA)
Senegal Cent Rech Oceanogr Dakar-Thiaroye Arch ... Senegal. Centre de Recherches Oceanographiques de Dakar-Thiaroye. Archive [*A publication*]
Senegal Cent Rech Oceanogr Dakar-Thiaroye Doc Sci ... Senegal. Centre de Recherches Oceanographiques de Dakar-Thiaroye. Document Scientifique [*A publication*]
Senegal Dir Mines Geol Bull ... Senegal. Direction des Mines et de la Geologie. Bulletin [*A publication*]
SENEGAMBIA ... Senegal and Gambia
SENEL .... Single Noise Exposure Level
SENET .... Scientific and Engineering Computer Network (MCD)
SENG .... Single Engine
S in Eng ..... Studies in English [*A publication*]
SEngL .... Studies in English Literature [*The Hague*] [*A publication*]
Sen J .... Senate Journal (DLA)
Sen Jo .... Senate Journal (DLA)
SENL .... Standard Equipment Nomenclature List
SENLOG .... Sentinel Logistics Command
Senn .... Sennaherib (BJA)
SE'NNIGHT ... Seven Nights [*A week*] (ROG)
SENO .... Steam Emulsion Number
SENPD .... Senpaku [*A publication*]
SENPO .... Sentinel Project Office [*Army*] (MCD)
Sen R .... Seneca Review [*A publication*]
SENR .... Senior
Sen Rep .... Senate Report (DLA)
Sen Rep .... United States Senate Committee Report (DLA)
Sens .... De Sensu [*of Aristotle*] [*Classical studies*] (OCD)
SENS .... Sensitive (MSA)
SENS .... Social England Series [*A publication*]
Sens and Actuators ... Sensors and Actuators [*A publication*]
SENSB .... Sense Processes [*A publication*]
Sen Schol ... Senior Scholastic [*A publication*]
SENSCOM ... Sentinel Systems Command [*Army*] (MCD)
SENSD .... Studies in Environmental Science [*A publication*]
SENSEA ..... Sentinel System Evaluation Agency [*DoD*]
Sensibilizirovannaya Fluoresta Smesej Parov Met ... Sensibilizirovannaya Fluorestsentsiya Smesej Parov Metallov [*A publication*]
SENSO .... Sensor Operator (MCD)
SENSO .... Sentinel Systems Office [*Military*]
Sens Process ... Sensory Processes [*A publication*]
SENT .... Sentence (AABC)
SENTA .... Societe d'Etudes Nucleaires et de Techniques Avancees [*France*]
SENTAC ..... Society for Ear, Nose, and Throat Advances in Children [*Santa Barbara, CA*] (EA)
SENTOS ..... Sentinel Operating System (IEEE)
SENTRAB ... Syndicat des Travailleurs des Entreprises, Privees, Travaux Publics et Batiments [*Union of Workers of Private Enterprises, Public Works and Buildings*] [*Togo*]
SENTRE ..... Sensor of Tail Region Emitters (MCD)
SENU .... Spectrum Efficient Network Unit (MCD)
SENYLRC ... Southeastern New York Library Resources Council [*Highland, NY*] [*Library network*]
SEO .... Salvage Engineering Order (MCD)
SEO .... Seaport Corp. [*American Stock Exchange symbol*]
SEO .... Seguela [*Ivory Coast*] [*Airport symbol*] (OAG)
SEO .... Senior Engineer Officer [*Navy*]
SEO .... Senior Executive Officer [*Civil Service*] [*British*]
SEO .... Senior Experimental Officer [*Also, SExO, SXO*] [*Ministry of Agriculture, Fisheries, and Food*] [*British*]

SEO............ Seoul [*Keizyo*] [*South Korea*] [*Seismograph station code, US Geological Survey*] (SEIS)
SEO............ Serial Engineering Order (MCD)
SEO............ Shoulder-Elbow Orthosis [*Medicine*]
SEO............ Sin Errores y Omisiones [*Errors and Omissions Excepted*] [*Business and trade*] [*Spanish*]
SEO............ Special Engineering Order [*NASA*] (NASA)
SEO............ State Energy Office
SEO............ Synchronous Equatorial Orbit [*or Orbiter*] [*NASA*] (KSC)
SEOC.......... Submarine Extended Operating Cycle (NVT)
SEOCS...... Sun-Earth Observatory and Climatology Satellite
SEODSE..... Special Explosive Ordnance Disposal Supplies and Equipment [*Army*] (AABC)
SEOG......... Supplemental Educational Opportunity Grants
SEON......... Solar Electro-Optical Network (MCD)
SEOO......... Sauf Erreur ou Omission [*Errors and Omissions Excepted*] [*French*]
SEOO......... State Economic Opportunity Office
SEOP.......... SHAPE [*Supreme Headquarters Allied Powers Europe*] Emergency Operating Procedures [*NATO*] (NATG)
SEOPSN..... Select-Operate-Sense
S/EOS........ Standard Earth Observation Satellite (MCD)
SEOS......... Symmetric Exchange of Symmetry [*Spectrometry*]
SEOS......... Synchronous Earth Observatory Satellite [*NASA*]
Seoul J Med ... Seoul Journal of Medicine [*A publication*]
Seoul Natl Univ Eng Rep ... Seoul National University. Engineering Reports [*A publication*]
Seoul Nat Univ Fac Pap Bio Agric Ser ... Seoul National University. Faculty Papers. Biology and Agriculture Series [*A publication*]
Seoul Nat Univ Fac Pap Med Pharm Ser ... Seoul National University. Faculty Papers. Medicine and Pharmacy Series [*A publication*]
Seoul Nat Univ Fac Pap Sci Technol Ser ... Seoul National University. Faculty Papers. Science and Technology Series [*A publication*]
Seoul University J Pharm Sci ... Seoul University. Journal of Pharmaceutical Sciences [*A publication*]
Seoul Univ Fac Pap Ser C ... Seoul University Faculty Papers. Series C. Science and Technology [*A publication*]
Seoul Univ Fac Pap Ser D ... Seoul University Faculty Papers. Series D. Medicine and Pharmacy [*A publication*]
Seoul Univ Fac Pap Ser E ... Seoul University. Faculty Papers. Series E. Biology and Agriculture [*A publication*]
Seoul Univ J Biol Agric Ser (B) ... Seoul University. Journal. Biology and Agriculture. Series (B) [*A publication*]
Seoul Univ J Biol Agr Ser (B) ... Seoul University. Journal. Biology and Agriculture. Series (B) [*A publication*]
Seoul Univ J Med Pharm Ser (C) ... Seoul University. Journal. Medicine and Pharmacy. Series (C) [*A publication*]
Seoul Univ J Nat Sci Ser A ... Seoul University. Journal. Natural Science. Series A [*A publication*]
Seoul Univ J Nat Sci Ser B ... Seoul University. Journal. Natural Science. Series B [*A publication*]
Seoul Univ J Nat Sci Ser C ... Seoul University. Journal. Natural Science. Series C [*A publication*]
Seoul Univ J Sci Technol Ser (A) ... Seoul University. Journal. Science and Technology. Series (A) [*A publication*]
SEOW........ Society of Engineering Office Workers (EA)
SEP............ Samenwerkende Elektriciteit Produktie Bedrijven [*Electric utility*] [*Netherlands*]
SEP............ Saturday Evening Post [*A publication*]
SEP............ Scientific and Engineering Personnel
SEP............ Secretaria de Educacion Publica [*Mexico*] [*A publication*]
SE(P).......... Security Executive, Control at Ports [*British*] [*World War II*]
SEP............ Selective Employment Payments [*British*]
SEP............ Self-Elevating Platform
SEP............ Sensory Evoked Potential [*Neurophysiology*]
SEP............ Separate (AFM)
SEP............ Separation Parameter
SEP............ Sepia [*Stamp collecting*] (ROG)
SEP............ September (AFM)
SEP............ Septuagint [*Version of Bible*]
SEP............ Sepultus [*Buried*] [*Latin*]
SEP............ Serial Entry Printer
SEP............ Shepherd Products Ltd. [*Toronto Stock Exchange symbol*]
SEP............ Simplified Employee Pension
SEP............ Site Emergency Plan (NRCH)
SEP............ Slow Electrical Process [*Human brain*]
SEP............ Slug Ejector Punch
SEP............ Society of Engineering Psychologists [*Later, DAEEP*] (EA)
SEP............ Society for Exact Philosophy (EA)
SEP............ Society of Experimental Psychologists (EA)
SEP............ Solar Electric Power [*or Propulsion*]
SEP............ Somatically Evoked Potential [*Neurophysiology*]
SEP............ SOSUS Estimated Position (NVT)
SEP............ Southern Education Program [*Defunct*] (EA)
SEP............ Space Electronic Package
SEP............ Special Education Programs [*Department of Education*] [*Formerly, BEH*]
SEP............ Special Emphasis Program [*DoD*]
SEP............ Specific Excess Power (MCD)

SEP............ Sperm Entry Point [*into egg*]
SEP............ Spherical Error Probability
SEP............ Stable Element Panel
SEP............ Standard Electronic Package
SEP............ Standard Engineering Practice (AAG)
SEP............ Standard Error of Prediction
SEP............ Star Epitaxial Planar (MSA)
SEP............ Stephenville, TX [*Location identifier*] [*FAA*] (FAAL)
SEP............ Strong Equivalence Principle [*Thermodynamics*]
SEP............ Student Expense Program [*Civil Defense*]
SEP............ Studiegroup voor Europese Politiek (EA)
SEP............ Supervisor Executive Program [*NASA*] (KSC)
SEP............ Support Equipment Package [*NASA*] (NASA)
SEP............ Surface Electrical Property [*Apollo*] [*NASA*]
SEP............ Surface Experiments [*NASA*]
SEP............ Surrendered Enemy Personnel
SEP............ Survey of Eastern Palestine [*A publication*] (BJA)
SEP............ Systematic Evaluation Program [*Nuclear Regulatory Commission*]
SEP............ Systems Effectiveness Plan
SEP............ Systems Engineering Process
SEP............ Systems Extension Plan
SEP............ Systolic Ejection Period [*Cardiology*]
SEPA......... Southeast Pacific Area
SEPA......... Southeastern Power Administration [*Department of Energy*]
SEPA......... Southeastern Psychological Association (MCD)
SEPA......... Soviet Extended Planning Annex (MCD)
SEPA......... Spanish Evangelical Publishers Association [*Miami, FL*] (EA)
SEP & A...... Special Equipment Parts and Assemblies Section (AAG)
SEPA......... System Evaluation Planning and Assessment Model (MCD)
SEPAC....... Space Experiments with Particle Accelerators [*Spacelab mission*]
SEPACFOR ... Southeast Pacific Force [*later, Command*] [*Navy*]
SEPAK....... Suspension of Expendable Penetration Aids by Kite [*Military*]
SEPAR....... Shuttle Electrical Power Analysis Report [*NASA*] (NASA)
SEPARON ... Separation (ROG)
Separ Sci ... Separation Science [*Later, Separation Science and Technology*] [*A publication*]
SEPAWG.... Save EPA [*Environmental Protection Agency*] Working Group (EA)
SE/PB........ Southern Europe - Ports and Beaches [*NATO*] (NATG)
SEPC.......... Space Exploration Program Council [*NASA*]
SEPCEN..... Separation Center [*Navy*]
SEPCOR..... Separate Correspondence (MCD)
SEPD.......... Separated
SEPD.......... State Emergency Planning Director [*Civil Defense*]
SEPE.......... Seattle Port of Embarkation
SEPE.......... Separate (ROG)
SEPE.......... Societe d'Edition et de Publications en Exlusivite
SEPEA....... Societe Europeene de Psychiatrie de l'Enfant et de l'Adolescent [*European Society of Child and Adolescent Psychiatry - ESCAP*] (EA-IO)
SEPEA....... Societe Europeenne de Psychiatrie de l'Enfant et de l'Adolescent [*European Society of Child and Adolescent Psychiatry - ESCAP*] (EA-IO)
SEPEL........ Southeastern Plant Environment Laboratories [*Duke University and North Carolina State University*]
SEPEMIAG ... Societe d'Etudes pour l'Equipement Miniere, Agricole, et Industrial du Gabon [*Gabon Society for Study of Mining, Agricultural, and Industrial Equipment*]
SEPG.......... Separating
SEPGA....... Southeastern Pecan Growers Association (EA)
Seph.......... Sephardic [*Jews from Spain, Portugal, North Africa, and the Mediterranean*] (BJA)
SEPI.......... Silicon Electro-Physics, Inc. [*NASDAQ symbol*] (NQ)
SEPI.......... Sylvania Electric Products, Incorporated (KSC)
SEPIL......... Selective Excitation of Probe Ion Luminescence [*Analytical chemistry*]
SEPL......... South European Pipeline [*Oil*]
SEPM........ Society of Economic Paleontologists and Mineralogists (EA)
SEPM Core Workshop ... Society of Economic Paleontologists and Mineralogists. Core Workshop [*A publication*]
SEPN.......... Separation (AAG)
SEPO......... Space Electric Power Office [*AEC*]
SEPOL........ Settlement Problem-Oriented Language [*Data processing*] (IEEE)
SEPOL....... Soil Engineering Problem-Oriented Language [*Data processing*]
SEPORT..... Supply and Equipment Report [*Army*] (AABC)
SEPOS....... Selected Enlisted Personnel for Overseas Service (AABC)
SEPP.......... Seppyo. Journal. Japanese Society of Snow and Ice [*A publication*]
Sep Purif M ... Separation and Purification Methods [*A publication*]
Sep Purif Methods ... Separation and Purification Methods [*A publication*]
SEPRD....... Sensory Processes [*A publication*]
SEPRL........ Southeast Poultry Research Laboratory [*University of Georgia*] [*Research center*] (RCD)
SEPROS..... Separation Processing
SEPS.......... Service Module Electrical Power System [*NASA*] (KSC)
SEPS.......... Severe Environment Power System (IEEE)
SEPS.......... Smithsonian Earth Physics Satellite

SEPS.......... Socio-Economic Planning Sciences [*A publication*]
SEPS.......... Solar Electric-Propelled Spacecraft (MCD)
SEPS.......... Solar Electronic Propulsion System (MCD)
SEPS.......... System/Equipment Population Summary
SEPSA ...... Society of Educational Programmers and Systems Analysts [*Later, SDE*]
SEPS-B ...... Socio-Economic Planning Sciences [*A publication*]
Sep Sci ...... Separation Science [*Later, Separation Science and Technology*] [*A publication*]
Sep Sci Technol ... Separation Science and Technology [*A publication*]
SEPSME .... Social Economic and Political Studies of the Middle East [*A publication*] (BJA)
SEPST....... Solar Electric Propulsion System Technology
SEPT .... Separate
Sept .... Septem Contra Thebas [*of Aeschylus*] [*Classical studies*] (OCD)
SEPT .... September
Sept .... Septuagint (BJA)
SEPTA....... Southeastern Pennsylvania Transportation Authority
SEPTAR ..... Seaborne Powered Target [*Navy*] (NVT)
SEPTD .... Separated
SEPTEL..... Separate Telegram
SEPTG ...... Separating
SEPTLA ..... Southeastern Pennsylvania Theological Library Association [*Library network*]
SEPTR....... Separator
SEPTR....... September (ROG)
SEPULT ..... Sepultus [*Buried*] [*Latin*] (ROG)
SEQ........... Scientific Equipment (KSC)
SEQ........... Seguin, TX [*Location identifier*] [*FAA*] (FAAL)
SEQ........... Sequel
SEQ........... Sequence (AABC)
SEQ........... Sequente [*And in What Follows*] [*Latin*]
SEQ........... Sequential Pulse Counting [*Spectrometry*]
SEQ........... Sequestrum [*Medicine*]
SEQ........... Sequitur [*It Follows*] [*Latin*]
SEQ........... Storage Equities, Inc. [*American Stock Exchange symbol*]
SEQ........... String Education Quarterly [*A publication*]
SEQ LUCE ... Sequenti Luce [*The Following Day*] [*Latin*] (ADA)
SEQOPT..... Sequential Optimization (MCD)
SEQP......... Supreme Equipment & Systems [*NASDAQ symbol*] (NQ)
SEQQ .... Sequentia [*The Following*] [*Plural form*] [*Latin*]
SEQQ .... Sequentibus [*In the Following Places*] [*Latin*] (ADA)
SEQR .... Sequencer (AAG)
SEQS .... Simultaneous Equation Solver [*Computer program*]
SEQU .... Sequoia and Kings Canyon National Parks
SEQUEL ..... Structured English Query Language [*1974*] [*Data processing*] (CSR)
SEQUIN..... Sequential Quadrature Inband [*Television system*] (DEN)
SEQUIP ..... Study of Environmental Quality Information Programs (KSC)
SEQUR...... Safety Equipment Requirements
SER .... Cataloging Services Department, OCLC [*Online Computer Library Center*], Inc., Columbus, OH [*OCLC symbol*] (OCLC)
SER .... Safety Evaluation Report (NRCH)
SER .... Sandia Engineering Reactor
SER .... Seder Eliyahu Rabbah (BJA)
SER .... Sequential Events Recorder
SER .... Serial (AFM)
SER .... Series (AAG)
Ser .... Serine [*Also, S*] [*An amino acid*]
SER .... Sermon
Ser .... Serpens [*Constellation*]
SER .... Servant
Ser .... Service [*A publication*]
SER .... Service (NATG)
SER .... Service, Employment, Redevelopment [*Operation for Mexican-Americans*] [*Later, SER - Jobs for Progress*]
SeR............ Sewanee Review [*A publication*]
SER .... Seymour, IN [*Location identifier*] [*FAA*] (FAAL)
SER .... Shore Establishment Realignment [*Navy*] (NVT)
SER .... Sierracin Corp. [*American Stock Exchange symbol*]
SER .... Significant Event Report (IEEE)
SER .... Simultaneous Evoked [*Cortical*] Response [*Neurophysiology*]
SER .... Site Evaluation Report (MCD)
SER .... Smooth [*Surfaced*] Endoplasmic Reticulum [*Cytology*]
SER .... SNAP [*Systems for Nuclear Auxiliary Power*] Experimental Reactor
SER .... Sociedad Espanola de Radiodifusion [*Broadcasting organization*]
SER .... Society for Educational Reconstruction (EA)
SER .... Society for Epidemiologic Research [*Baltimore, MD*] (EA)
SER .... Somatosensory Evoked Response [*Neurophysiology*]
SER .... South-Eastern Railway [*British*]
SeR............ Studi e Ricerche [*A publication*]
SER .... Sua Eccellenza Reverendissima [*His Eminence*]
SER .... Support Equipment Requirement
SER .... Surface Electrical Resistivity
SER .... System Environment Recording (BUR)
SERA.......... Sierra Railroad Co. [*AAR code*]

SERA.......... Society for Entrepreneurship Research and Application [*Defunct*] (EA)
SERA.......... Stop Equal Rights Amendment [*Alton, IL*] (EA)
SERAA ...... Seramikkusu [*A publication*]
SERAC ...... Southeastern Regional Arts Council
SERANAK ... Serge and Natalie Koussevitzky [*Acronym was name of summer home of Boston Symphony Orchestra conductor and his first wife*]
SERANDA ... Service Record, Health Record, Pay Account, and Personal Effects [*Military*]
SERAPE ..... Simulator Equipment Requirements for Accelerating Procedural Evolution
SERAPHIM ... Systems Engineering Respecting Acquisition and Propagation of Heuristic Instructional Materials [*Chemistry*]
Ser Astron Uniw Adama Mickiewicza Poznaniu ... Seria Astronomia. Uniwersytet Imeni Adama Mickiewicza w Poznaniu [*A publication*]
SERB.......... Selective Early Retirement Board [*Army*] (INF)
SERB.......... Serbia
SERB.......... Shuttle Engineering Review Board [*NASA*] (NASA)
SERB.......... Study of the Enhanced Radiation Belt [*NASA*]
SERB.......... Systems Engineering Review Board [*NASA*] (NASA)
Serb Acad Sci Arts Bull ... Serbian Academy of Sciences and Arts. Bulletin [*A publication*]
Serb Acad Sci Arts Glas ... Serbian Academy of Sciences and Arts. Glas [*A publication*]
SERBAUD ... Serikat Buruh Angkutan Udara [*Airways' Union*] [*Indonesia*]
Ser Bibliogr INTA (Pergamino) ... Serie Bibliografica. Instituto Nacional de Tecnologia Agropecuaria (Pergamino, Argentina) [*A publication*]
Ser Biol Uniw Adama Mickiewicza Poznaniu ... Seria Biologia. Uniwersytet Imeni Adama Mickiewicza w Poznaniu [*A publication*]
SERBIUM ... Serikat Buruh Industri dan Umum [*Industrial and General Workers' Union*] [*Indonesia*]
SERBU ...... Serikat Buruh Umum [*General Workers' Union*] [*Indonesia*]
SERBUHI.... Serikat Buruh Harian Indonesia [*Newspaper Employees' Union of Indonesia*]
SERBUMAMI ... Serikat Buruh Makanan dan Minuman [*Food Workers' Union*] [*Indonesia*]
SERBUMIKSI ... Serikat Buruh Minjak Kelapa Seluruh [*Coconut Oil Workers' Union*] [*Indonesia*]
SERBUMIT ... Serikat Buruh Minjak dan Tambang [*Oil and Minerals Workers' Union*] [*Indonesia*]
SERBUMUSI ... Serikat Buruh Muslimin Indonesia [*Moslem Workers' Union of Indonesia*]
SERBUNI.... Serikat Buruh Unilever Indonesia [*Unilever Employees' Union of Indonesia*]
SERBUPI.... Serikat Buruh Perkebunan Indonesia [*Plantation Workers' Union of Indonesia*]
SERBUPRI ... Serikat Buruh Pertambangan Indonesia [*Mining Workers' Union of Indonesia*]
SERC.......... Science and Engineering Research Council [*British*]
SERC.......... Smithsonian Environmental Research Center
SERC.......... Southeastern Electric Reliability Council [*Regional power council*]
SERC.......... Sussex European Research Centre [*Research center*] [*British*] (IRC)
Ser Chem Uniw Adama Mickiewicza Poznaniu ... Seria Chemia. Uniwersytet Imeni Adama Mickiewicza w Poznaniu [*A publication*]
Ser Conf Union Math Internat ... Serie des Conferences. Union Mathematique Internationale [*A publication*]
SERD.......... Stored Energy Rotary Drive
SERD........ Support Equipment Recommendation Data [*NASA*] (KSC)
SERDA....... Signals and Electronic Warfare Research and Development Act
Ser Defects Cryst Solids ... Series Defects in Crystalline Solids [*A publication*]
SERDES..... Serializer, Deserializer
Ser Didact Univ Nac Tucuman Fac Agronom Zooteh ... Serie Didactica. Universidad Nacional de Tucuman. Facultad de Agronomia y Zootecnia [*A publication*]
Ser Div Ind Chem CSIRO ... Serial. Division of Industrial Chemistry. Commonwealth Scientific and Industrial Research Oganisation [*A publication*]
Ser Divulg Agron Angolana ... Serie Divulgacao Agronomia Angolana [*A publication*]
SERE.......... Services Electronic Research Establishment [*British*] (DEN)
SERE.......... Survival, Evasion, Resistance, and Escape [*School*] [*Military*] (AFM)
Ser Emp..... Service Employee [*A publication*]
SERENDIP ... Search for Extraterrestrial Radio Emission from Nearby Developed Intelligent Populations
Serengeti Res Inst Annu Rep ... Serengeti Research Institute. Annual Report [*A publication*]
Ser Entomol (The Hague) ... Series Entomologica (The Hague) [*A publication*]
SEREP........ System Environment Recording, Editing, and Printing [*Data processing*]
SEREP....... System Error Record Editing Program [*Data processing*]
SERF .... Sandia Engineering Reactor Facility
SERF .... Service Fracturing Co. [*NASDAQ symbol*] (NQ)

SERF .... Solar and Energy Research Facility [*University of Arizona*] [*Research center*] (RCD)
SERF .... Space Environmental Research Facility
SERF .... Special Environmental Radiometallurgy Facility [*Nuclear energy*] (NRCH)
SERFE ...... Selection of Exempt Organization Returns for Examination [*IRS*]
SERFORSOPACSUBCOM ... Service Force, South Pacific, Subordinate Command
SERG .... Sergeant
SERG .... Serving (MSA)
SERGE ...... Socially and Ecologically Responsible Geographers (EA)
Serg Land Laws PA ... Sergeant on the Land Laws of Pennsylvania (DLA)
Serg & Lowb ... English Common Law Reports, Edited by Sergeant and Lowber (DLA)
Serg & Lowb Rep ... English Common Law Reports Edited by Sergeant and Lowber [*American Reprint*] (DLA)
Serg & R ..... Sergeant and Rawle's Pennsylvania Reports (DLA)
Serg & Raw ... Sergeant and Rawle's Pennsylvania Reports (DLA)
Serg & Rawl ... Sergeant and Rawle's Pennsylvania Supreme Court Reports [*1814-28*] (DLA)
SERGT .... Sergeant
SERH .... Secretaria de Estado de Recursos Hidricos [*Argentina*]
Ser Haematol ... Series Haematologica [*A publication*]
SERI .... Society for the Encouragement of Research and Invention (EA)
SERI .... Solar Energy Research Institute [*Golden, CO*] [*Department of Energy*]
Serials BLL ... Serials in the British Lending Library [*A publication*]
Sericult Res ... Sericultural Research [*Japan*] [*A publication*]
Ser Inf Conf Cursos Reun Interam Inst Agric Sci ... Serie Informes de Conferencias. Cursos y Reuniones-Inter-American Institute of Agricultural Sciences [*A publication*]
SER-IV .... Supination, External Rotation - Type IV Fracture
SERIX .... Swedish Environmental Research Index [*Swedish National Environmental Protection Board*] [*Database*] (EISS)
SERJ .... Serjeant [*Military*] [*British*] (ROG)
SERJ .... Space Electric Ramjet [*Air Force*]
SERJ .... Supercharged Ejector Ramjet [*Aircraft engine*]
SERJT-MAJ ... Serjeant-Major [*Military*] [*British*] (ROG)
SERL .... Sanitary Engineering Research Laboratory [*University of California*] (MCD)
Ser L .... Serie Linguistica [*A publication*]
SERL .... Services Electronic Research Laboratory [*British*]
SERLANT ... Service Forces, Atlantic [*Navy*]
Ser Lib .... Serials Librarian [*A publication*]
Ser Libr ...... Serials Librarian [*A publication*]
SERLINE ... Serials On-Line [*National Library of Medicine*] [*Bethesda, MD*] [*Database*]
SERM .... Sermon (ROG)
SERM .... Society of Early Recorded Music (EA)
SERM .... Syncrude Environmental Research Monograph [*A publication*]
Ser Mat Fis ... Serie di Matematica e Fisica [*A publication*]
SERMCE .... Amalgamated Association of Street, Electric Railway, and Motor Coach Employees of America [*Later, ATU*]
SERME ...... Sign Error Root Modulus Error
SERMLP ..... Southeastern Regional Medical Library Program [*Emory University*] [*Atlanta, GA*] [*Library network*] (EISS)
Ser Monogr Inst Zootec ... Serie Monografias. Instituto de Zootecnia [*A publication*]
SERN .... Southeastern [*Meteorology*] (FAAC)
SERNO ...... Serial Number
SERNO ...... Service Number [*Military*]
SERO .... Service Employment Redevelopment Operation (OICC)
SERO .... System Engineering Release Order (MCD)
Serol Mus Bull ... Serological Museum Bulletin [*A publication*]
SERON ...... Service Squadron [*Navy*]
Serono Symp Proc ... Serono Symposia. Proceedings [*A publication*]
SERP .... Self-Employed Retirement Plan [*Keogh plan*]
Serp .... Serpens [*Constellation*]
SERP .... Simulated Ejector Ready Panel
SERP .... Software Engineering Research Projects [*Data Analysis Center for Software*] [*Database*]
SERP .... Standardization/Evaluation Review Panel (AFIT)
SERPA ...... Southeastern Resource Policy Association (EA)
SERPAC .... Service Forces, Pacific [*Navy*]
Ser Paedopsychiatr ... Series Paedopsychiatrica [*A publication*]
Ser Poeyana Inst Biol Acad Cienc Cuba ... Serie Poeyana. Instituto de Biologia. Academia de Ciencias de Cuba [*A publication*]
Ser Poeyana Inst Zool Acad Cienc Cuba ... Serie Poeyana. Instituto de Zoologia. Academia de Ciencias de Cuba [*A publication*]
SERPS ...... Service Propulsion System [*or Subsystem*] [*NASA*] (KSC)
SERPS .... State Earnings-Related Pension Scheme [*British*]
Ser R .... Serials Review [*A publication*]
SERR .... Serrate (MSA)
SerrC .... Serraika Chronika [*A publication*]
SERRON ..... Service Squadron [*Navy*]
SE/RRT ...... Southern Europe - Railroad Transport [*NATO*] (NATG)
SERS .... Seaborne Environmental Reporting System
SERS .... Shuttle Equipment Record System [*NASA*] (NASA)
SERS .... Southern Education Reporting Service

SERS .... State Employees Retirement System
SERS .... Support Equipment Requirements Sheet
SERS .... Surface-Enhanced Raman Spectroscopy
Ser SI .... Serial Slants [*A publication*]
Sert .... Sertorius [*of Plutarch*] [*Classical studies*] (OCD)
SERT .... Shipboard Electronic Readiness Team [*Navy*] (CAAL)
SERT .... Single-Electron Rise Time [*Scintillation counting*] (IEEE)
SE/RT .... Southern Europe - Road Transport [*NATO*] (NATG)
SERT .... Space Electric [*or Electronic*] Rocket Test
SERT .... Special Education Resource Teacher
SERT .... Special Education Review Team
SERT .... Spinning Satellite for Electric Rocket Test
SERT .... Sustained Ethanol Release Tube [*Pharmacology*]
SERTH ...... Satisfactory Evidence Received This Headquarters
SERT J ...... SERT [*Society of Electronic and Radio Technicians*] Journal [*A publication*]
SERTOMA ... Service to Mankind [*Meaning of name of Sertoma International Organization*]
SERUG .... SII [*Systems Integrators, Incorporated*] Eastern Regional Users Group [*Scranton, PA*] (EA)
Ser Universitaria ... Serie Universitaria [*A publication*]
SERV .... Servant
SERV .... Servian (ROG)
SERV .... Service (AAG)
Serv .... Service: A Review of Agricultural and Chemical Progress [*A publication*]
SERV .... Single-Stage Earth-Orbital Reusable Vehicle (MCD)
SERV .... Space Emergency Reentry Vehicle [*NASA*]
SERV .... Surface Effect Rescue Vessel [*Coast Guard*]
Serv Can Faune Cah Biol ... Service Canadien de la Faune. Cahiers de Biologie [*A publication*]
SERVCOMFMFPAC ... Service Command, Fleet Marine Force, Pacific
SERVDIV .... Service Division [*Navy*]
SERVE .... Serve and Enrich Retirement by Volunteer Experience [*Staten Island, NY, project*]
SERVE .... Service (ROG)
Serv Esp Saude Publica Rev (Brazil) ... Servico Especial de Saude Publica. Revista (Brazil) [*A publication*]
Serv Farm Ranch Home ... Serving Farm, Ranch, and Home. Quarterly. University of Nebraska. College of Agriculture and Home Economics. Agricultural Experiment Station [*A publication*]
SERVFOR ... Service Force [*Navy*]
Serv Geol Ital Mem Descr Carta Geol Ital ... Servizio Geologico d'Italia Memorie Descrittive della Carta Geologica d'Italia [*A publication*]
Serv Geol Port Mem ... Servicos Geologics de Portugal. Memoria [*A publication*]
SERVHEL ... Service Record and Health Record [*Military*]
SERVLANT ... Service Force, Atlantic Fleet
SERVLANTSUBORDCOMD ... Service Force, Atlantic Fleet, Subordinate Command
SERVMART ... Service Mart
Serv Nac Min Geol (Argent) Rev ... Servicio Nacional Minero Geologico (Argentina). Revista [*A publication*]
SERVNO ..... Service Number [*Navy*]
SERVO ...... Service Office
SERVO ...... Servomechanism
SERVON ..... Service Squadron [*Navy*]
SERVPA ...... Service Record and Pay Record [*Military*]
SERVPAC ... Service Force, Pacific Fleet
SERVPAHEL ... Service Record, Pay Record, and Health Record [*Military*]
SERVREC ... Service Record
SERVSCOLCOM ... Service School Command [*Navy*]
Serv Shell Agric Ser A ... Servicio Shell para el Agricultor. Serie A [*A publication*]
Serv Shell Agr Ser A ... Servicio Shell para el Agricultor. Serie A. Informe [*A publication*]
Serv Soc (Bruxelles) ... Service Social (Bruxelles) [*A publication*]
Serv Soc Monde ... Service Social dans le Monde [*A publication*]
Serv Soc (Quebec) ... Service Social (Quebec) [*A publication*]
SERVSOWESPAC ... Service Force, Southwest Pacific Fleet
SERVT .... Servant
Serv World ... Service World International [*A publication*]
SES .... Group Psychotherapy Suitability Evaluation Scale [*Psychology*]
SES .... Satellite Earth Station
SES .... Scandinavian Packaging Association (EA)
SES .... Schriften far Ekonomik un Statistik [*A publication*]
SES .... Scientific Exploration Society (EA)
SES .... Seafarers Education Service [*British*]
SES .... Seagrass Ecosystem Study [*Marine science*] (MSC)
SES .... Secondary Electron Scattering
SES .... Section d'Eclaireurs-Skieurs [*of Chasseurs Alpins, French Army*]
SES .... Seismic Electric Signal
SES .... Senior Executive Service [*Civil Service*]
SES .... Sequential Environmental Stress
SES .... Service Evaluation System [*Telecommunications*] (TEL)
SES .... Sesone [*Herbicide*] [*Trademark of Union Carbide Corp.*]
SES .... Shuttle Engineering Simulation [*NASA*] (NASA)
SES .... Sight Erection Support

SES .... Signal Enhancement Seismograph
SES .... Signals Exploitation Space   (MCD)
SES .... Small Edison Screw
SES .... Social and Economic Studies [*A publication*]
SES .... Societe des Etudes Socialistes [*Society for Socialist Studies - SSS*]
SES .... Societe Europeenne des Satellites [*Luxembourg*]
SES .... Society of Educators and Scholars   (EA)
SES .... Society of Engineering Science
SES .... Society for Environmental Stabilization [*Defunct*]   (EA)
SES .... Society of Eye Surgeons [*Bethesda, MD*]   (EA)
SES .... Socioeconomic Status [*or Strata*]
SES .... Soil Erosion Service [*Became Soil Conservation Service, 1935*]
SES .... Solar Eclipse Sensor   (MCD)
SES .... Solar Energy Society [*Later, International Solar Energy Society*]   (EA)
SES .... Solar Environment Simulator
SES .... SONAR Echo Simulator
SES .... Space Environment Simulator [*NASA*]
SES .... Space Erectable Structure
SES .... Special Emphasis Study   (NASA)
SES .... Special Exchange Service [*Telecommunications*]   (TEL)
SES .... SPRINT Engagement Simulation [*Missile system evaluation*] [*Army*]   (RDA)
SES .... Standards Engineering Society   (EA)
SES .... State Experiment Stations Division [*of ARS, Department of Agriculture*]
SES .... Steam Electric Station [*Nuclear energy*]   (NRCH)
SES .... Steam Engine Systems Corp.
SES .... Story of Exploration Series [*A publication*]
SES .... Strategic Engineering Survey [*Navy*]
SES .... Studies in Environmental Science [*Elsevier Book Series*] [*A publication*]
SES .... Studies and Expansion Society [*See also SEE*]   (EA-IO)
SES .... Study of Education at Stanford [*Stanford University*]
SES .... Suffield [*Alberta*] [*Seismograph station code, US Geological Survey*]   (SEIS)
SES .... Supervisory Electronics Specialist
SES .... Surface Effects Ship [*Navy symbol*]
SES .... Sustaining Engineering Services
SES .... System External Storage
SESA .... Signal Equipment Support Agency
SESA .... Social and Economic Statistics Administration [*Terminated, 1975*] [*Department of Commerce*]
SESA .... Society for Experimental Stress Analysis [*Later, SEM*]   (EA)
SESA .... Solar Energy Society of America   (EA)
SESA .... Standard Electrica, SA [*Brazilian affiliate of ITT*]
SESA .... State Employment Security Agency
SESA .... Story of the Empire Series [*A publication*]
SESAC ...... Society of European Stage Authors and Composers
SESAC ...... Space and Earth Science Advisory Committee [*NASA*]
SESAME .... Search for Excellence in Science and Mathematics Education [*Graduate program at University of California at Berkeley*]
SESAME .... Service, Sort and Merge [*Data processing*]
SESAME .... Severe Environmental Storms and Mesoscale Experiment [*National Science Foundation/National Oceanic and Atmospheric Administration*]
SESA Pap ... SESA [*Society for Experimental Stress Analysis*] Papers [*A publication*]
SESC .... Selective Elution Solvent Chromatography
SESC .... Shuttle Events Sequential Control   (MCD)
SESC .... South Eastern State College [*Oklahoma*]
SESC .... Space Environment Services Center [*National Oceanic and Atmospheric Administration*] [*Boulder, CO*]   (KSC)
SESC .... Surface Environmental Sample Container [*Apollo*] [*NASA*]
SESCO ...... Secure Submarine Communications
SESDA ...... Serikat Sekerdja Departemen Agama [*Brotherhood of Employees of Department of Religious Affairs*] [*Indonesia*]
SESDA ...... Small Engine Servicing Dealers Association [*St. Petersburg, FL*]   (EA)
SESDAQ .... Stock Exchange of Singapore Dealing and Automated Quotation System
SESE .... Secure Echo-Sounding Equipment [*SONAR*] [*Navy*]
SE/SE .... Single Entry/Single Exit
SESE .... Space Electronics Support Equipment   (MCD)
SESEF .... Ship Electronics System Evaluation Facility [*Navy*]   (CAAL)
SESG .... Southern Europe Shipping Group [*NATO*]   (NATG)
SESL .... Self-Erecting Space Laboratory   (AAG)
SESL .... Space Environment Simulation Laboratory [*NASA*]
SeSL .... Studi e Saggi Linguistici [*A publication*]
SESLP .... Sequential Explicit Stochastic Linear Programing [*Data processing*]
SESMI .... Systems Engineering Support and Management Integration   (MCD)
SESO .... Senior Equipment Staff Officer [*Air Force*] [*British*]
SESOC ...... Surface Effect Ship for Ocean Commerce
SESOME .... Service, Sort, and Merge [*Data processing*]   (IEEE)
SESP .... Society of Experimental Social Psychology   (EA)
SESP .... Space Experiment Support Program   (MCD)
SESPA ...... Scientists and Engineers for Social and Political Action [*Later, SFTP*]   (EA)

SESPENDO ... Serikat Buruh Pegawai Negeri dan Daeran Otonom [*Civil Servants Workers' Union*] [*Indonesia*]
SESPO .... Surface Effect Ships Project Office [*Navy*]
SESQUIH ... Sesquihora [*An Hour and a Half*] [*Pharmacy*]   (ROG)
SESQUIHOR ... Sesquihora [*An Hour and a Half*] [*Pharmacy*]
SESR......... Selected Equipment Status Report [*Navy*]   (NG)
SESR......... Societe Europeenne de Sociologie Rurale [*European Society for Rural Sociology*]
SESR......... Special Environmental Storage Requirements   (MCD)
SES Rep CSIRO Sol Energy Stud ... SES Report. Solar Energy Studies Unit. Commonwealth Scientific and Industrial Research Organisation [*A publication*]
SESS......... Session
SESS......... Society of Ethnic and Special Studies   (EA)
SESS......... Space Environmental Support System
SESS......... Summer Employment for Science Students
Sess Ca..... Scotch Court of Session Cases   (DLA)
Sess Ca..... Sessions Cases, King's Bench [*1710-48*] [*England*]   (DLA)
Sess Cas.... Scotch Court of Session Cases   (DLA)
Sess Cas.... Session Cases [*Scotland*]   (DLA)
Sess Cas.... Session Cases, High Court of Justiciary Section [*1906-16*] [*Scotland*]   (DLA)
Sess Cas.... Sessions Cases, King's Bench [*England*]   (DLA)
Sess Cas KB ... Sessions Settlement Cases, King's Bench [*England*]   (DLA)
Sess Cas Sc ... Scotch Court of Session Cases   (DLA)
Sess N....... Session Notes [*Scotland*]   (DLA)
Sess Pap CCC ... Central Criminal Court Cases, Sessions Papers [*England*]   (DLA)
Sess Pap OB ... Old Bailey's Sessions Papers   (DLA)
Sest........... Pro Sestio [*of Cicero*] [*Classical studies*]   (OCD)
SESTM....... Societe Europeenne de la Science et de la Technologie des Membranes [*European Society of Membrane Science and Technology - ESMST*]   (EA)
SESUNC .... Sesuncia [*An Ounce and a Half*] [*Pharmacy*]   (ROG)
Set............. English Settlement and Removal Cases [*Burrow's Settlement Cases*]   (DLA)
SET .... Satellite Experimental Terminal   (NATG)
SET .... Scientists, Engineers, Technicians
SET .... Securities Exchange of Thailand
SET .... Security Escort Team [*Military*]
SET .... Selective Electronic Training [*Navy*]   (NG)
SET .... Selective Employment Tax [*British*]
SET .... Self-Employment Tax [*IRS*]
SET .... Self-Extending Translator   (IEEE)
SET .... Senior Electronic Technician [*National Weather Service*]
SET .... Sensory Evaluation Test [*Army*]
SET .... Service Evaluation Telemetry   (AAG)
SET .... Setif [*Algeria*] [*Seismograph station code, US Geological Survey*]   (SEIS)
SET .... Setting   (MSA)
SET .... Settlement   (ROG)
SET .... Settling
SET .... Sheraton Executive Traveler [*Sheraton Corp.*]
SET .... Simplified Engineering Technique
SET .... Simulated Emergency Test
SET .... Single-Electron-Transfer [*Organic chemistry*]
SET .... Single Escape Tower
SET .... Society for the Eradication of Television   (EA)
SET .... Software Engineering Technology
SET .... Software Engineering Terminology [*Data processing*]   (IEEE)
SET .... Solar Energy Thermionic [*Program*] [*NASA*]
SET .... Space Electronics and Telemetry   (MCD)
SET .... Spacecraft Elapsed Time
SET .... Stack Entry Time [*Aviation*]   (FAAC)
SET .... Standard d'Exchange et de Transfert [*Computer graphics*] [*French*]
SET .... Stepped Electrode Transistor
SeT............. Studi e Testi [*Rome*] [*A publication*]
SET .... Studies in English (University of Texas) [*A publication*]
SET .... Submarine Engineering Technical
SET .... Suitability Evaluation Team   (MCD)
SE & T .... Supplies, Equipment, and Training [*Civil Defense*]
SET .... Symbol Elaboration Test [*Psychology*]
SET .... Synchro Error Tester
SET .... Syndicat des Enseignants du Togo [*Union of Togolese Teachers*]
SET .... System Effectiveness Test   (MCD)
SET .... Systems Engineering Test   (CET)
SETA......... Simplified Electronic Tracking Apparatus [*Air Force*]
SETA......... Systems Engineering and Technical Assistance   (MCD)
Seta Artif ... Seta Artificiale [*A publication*]
SETAB....... Sets Tabular Material [*Phototypesetting computer*]
SETAC ...... Sector TACAN [*Tactical Air Navigation*] System
SETAC ...... Society of Environmental Toxicology and Chemistry   (EA)
SETAC ...... Specially Equipped Traffic Accident Car [*British police*]
SETAD ...... Secure Transmission of Acoustic Data   (NVT)
SETAF....... Southern European Task Force [*NATO*]
SETAR ...... Serial Event Timer and Recorder

SETA-UITA ... Syndicat Europeen des Travailleurs de l'Alimentation, de l'Hotellerie, et des Branches Connexes dans l'UITA [*European Committee of Food, Catering, and Allied Workers' Unions within the IUF - ECF-IUF*] (EA-IO)
SETB .... Secondary Education Text-Books [*A publication*]
SETB .... Set Theoretic Language - BALM [*1973*] [*Data processing*] (CSR)
SETC .... Solid Electrolyte Tantalum Capacitor
SETC .... Southeastern Theatre Conference (EA)
SETD .... Sledborne Event Time Digitizer
SETD .... Space Environment Test Division [*NASA*]
SE & TD ...... Systems Engineering and Technical Direction (AAG)
SETE .... Secretariat for Electronic Test Equipment [*DoD*]
SETE .... Status of Electronic Test Equipment (MCD)
SETE .... Support and Electronic Test Equipment
SETE .... System Evaluation Test Equipment [*Military*] (CAAL)
SETEL .... Societe Europeenne de Teleguidage [*Five European firms organized in 1958 under French law to act as European prime contractor for production of HAWK missiles*] [*NATO*]
SETEP .... Science and Engineering Technician Education Program [*National Science Foundation*]
SETF .... SNAP [*Systems for Nuclear Auxiliary Power*] Experimental Test Facility
SETF .... STARAN Evaluation and Training Facility
SET-GO ...... Support and Encouragement for Talent - Gateway to Opportunity [*Project*] (EA)
SETI .... Search for Extraterrestrial Intelligence
SETI .... Societe Europeenne pour le Traitement de l'Information [*European Society for the Processing of Information*]
SETINA ...... Southeast Texas Information Network Association
SETIS .... Societe Europeenne pour l'Etude et l'Integration des Systemes Spatiaux
SETL .... Science Experiment Test Laboratory [*NASA*]
SETL .... Set Theoretic Language [*1971*] [*Data processing*] (CSR)
SETLG .... Settling (MSA)
SETM .... Societe d'Etudes et de Travaux Mecanographiques
SET Manpower Comments ... Scientific Engineering. Technical Manpower Comments [*A publication*]
SETOLS ..... Surface Effect Takeoff and Land System [*Naval aviation*]
Seto Mar Biol Lab Publ ... Seto Marine Biological Laboratory. Publications [*A publication*]
Seton .... Seton's Forms of Decrees, Judgments, and Orders in Equity [*7 eds.*] [*1830-1912*] (DLA)
Seton Dec ... Seton's Forms of Decrees, Judgments, and Orders in Equity [*7th ed.*] [*1912*] (DLA)
Seton Hall Leg J ... Seton Hall Legislative Journal [*A publication*]
Seton Hall L Rev ... Seton Hall Law Review [*A publication*]
SETP .... Society for Experimental Test Pilots (EA)
SETR .... Setter (MSA)
SETS .... Seeker Evaluation Test System [*Military*]
SETS .... Set Equation Transformation System [*1970*] [*Data processing*] (CSR)
SETS .... Skylab End-to-End Test System [*NASA*]
SETS .... Solar Electric Test Satellite
SETS .... Solar Energy Thermionic Conversion System [*NASA*]
SETS .... Special Electron Tube Section
SETS .... Standardized Environmental Technical Specifications (NRCH)
Sett .... Settlement Cases (DLA)
SETT .... Submarine Escape Training Tank
SETTA .... Southeastern Test and Training Area [*Military*] (MCD)
Sett Cas ..... Burrow's English Settlement Cases (DLA)
Sett Cas ..... Settlement and Removal, Cases in English King's Bench (DLA)
Settim Med ... Settimana Medica [*Italy*] [*A publication*]
Settim Osp ... Settimana Ospitaliera [*A publication*]
SETTL .... Settler [*Genealogy*]
SETTLET ..... Settlement (ROG)
Sett & Rem ... Settlement and Removal Cases in English King's Bench (DLA)
SETTT .... Settlement (ROG)
SEU .... Saint Edward's University [*Texas*]
SEU .... Sales Education Units
SEU .... Solar Energy Update [*A publication*]
SEU .... Source Entry Utility
SEU .... Southeastern University [*Washington, DC*]
SEU .... Subjective Expected Utility [*Concept*] [*Theory used for decision making*]
SEUG .... Screaming Eagles Users Group (EA)
SEURE .... Systems Evaluation Code Under Radiation Environment (IEEE)
SEUS .... Single Event Upsets [*Astronautics*]
SEUS .... Southeastern United States
SEUSSN ...... Southeastern United States Seismic Network (NRCH)
SEV .... Scout Evaluation Vehicle
SEV .... Sensor Equivalent Visibility
SEV .... Service City, AK [*Location identifier*] [*FAA*] (FAAL)
SEV .... Sevastopol [*USSR*] [*Seismograph station code, US Geological Survey*] [*Closed*] (SEIS)
SEV .... Seven
SEV .... Several
SEV .... Severe [*Used to qualify weather phenomena*]
SEV .... Severed

Sev .... Severus [*of Scriptores Historiae Augustae*] [*Classical studies*] (OCD)
SEV .... Sevres [*China*] (ROG)
SEV .... Ship Exercise Vehicle
SEV .... Simcoe Erie Investors Ltd. [*Toronto Stock Exchange symbol*]
SEV .... Societe d'Ethologie Veterinaire [*Society for Veterinary Ethology - SVE*] (EA-IO)
SEV .... Special Equipment Vehicle
SEV .... Split End Vector [*System for plant cell transformation*]
SEV .... State Equalized Value [*Real estate*]
SEV .... Surface Effects Vehicle [*Military*]
SEVA .... Skylab Extravehicular Visor Assembly [*NASA*]
SEVA .... Standup Extravehicular Activity [*Aerospace*]
SEVA .... Surface Extravehicular Activity [*Lunar exploration*]
SEVAC .... Secure Voice Access Console [*Army*] (AABC)
SEVAL .... Senior Evaluator (MCD)
Sev App Cas ... Sevestre's Bengal High Court Appeal Cases [*1864-68*] [*India*] (DLA)
SEVAS .... Secure Voice Access Systems [*Army*] (AABC)
Sev Cent N ... Seventeenth-Century News [*A publication*]
Seven Ct N ... Seventeenth-Century News [*A publication*]
SEVENTHFLT ... Seventh Fleet [*Navy*]
Sevestre ..... Calcutta Reports of Cases in Appeal (DLA)
SEVFLT ...... Seventh Fleet [*Pacific*] [*Navy*]
Sev HC .... Sevestre's Bengal High Court Reports [*India*] (DLA)
SEVL .... Several (ROG)
SEVOCOM ... Secure Voice Communications (AFM)
Sev-Oset Gos Pedagog Inst Uch Zap ... Severo-Osetinskii Gosudarstvennyi Pedagogicheskii Institut. Uchenye Zapiski [*A publication*]
SEVP .... Severance Pay [*Military*]
SEVPEN ..... Service d'Edition et de Vente des Publications de l'Education Nationale [*A publication*]
Sev SDA ..... Sevestre's Sadr Diwani Adalat Reports [*Bengal, India*] (DLA)
Sev-Vost Kompleks Nauch-Issled Inst Akad Nauk SSSR Sib Otd ... Severo-Vostochnyy Kompleksnyy Nauchno-Issledovatel'skiy Institut. Akademiya Nauk SSSR. Sibirskoye Otdeleniye [*A publication*]
Sev Zapad Evr Chasti SSSR ... Severo-Zapad Evropeiskoi Chasti SSSR [*A publication*]
SEW .... Sewage [*or Sewer*] (AAG)
Sew .... Sewanee Review [*A publication*]
SEW .... Seward [*Alaska*] [*Seismograph station code, US Geological Survey*] (SEIS)
SEW .... Shipboard Electronics Warfare [*Navy*]
SEW .... Silicon Epitaxial Wafer
SEW .... SONAR Early Warning
SEW .... Sozialistische Einheitspartei Westberlins [*Socialist Unity Party of West Berlin*] [*West Germany*] (PPW)
SE & W .... Start Early and Walk [*Fictitious railroad initialism used to indicate one of the most reliable modes of rural transportation*]
SEW .... Surface Electromagnetic Wave
Sewage Ind Waste Eng ... Sewage and Industrial Waste Engineering [*A publication*]
Sewage Ind Wastes ... Sewage and Industrial Wastes [*A publication*]
Sewage Purif Land Drain Water River Eng ... Sewage Purification. Land Drainage. Water and River Engineering [*A publication*]
Sewage Works Eng Munic Sanit ... Sewage Works Engineering and Municipal Sanitation [*A publication*]
Sewage Works J ... Sewage Works Journal [*A publication*]
Sewanee R ... Sewanee Review [*A publication*]
Sewanee Rev ... Sewanee Review [*A publication*]
Sewan R ..... Sewanee Review [*A publication*]
SEWC .... SIGINT/Electronic Warfare Coordination Element (MCD)
S/EWCC .... Signal Intelligence/Electronic Warfare Coordination Center (NVT)
Sew Cor ..... Sewell on Coroners [*1843*] (DLA)
Sewell Sheriffs ... Sewell on the Law of Sheriffs (DLA)
SEWHO ...... Shoulder-Elbow-Wrist-Hand Orthosis [*Medicine*]
SEWL .... Southeast Water Laboratory [*Environmental Protection Agency*]
SEWMRPG ... Southern European Western Mediterranean Regional Planning Group [*NATO*] (NATG)
SEWO .... Shoulder-Elbow-Wrist Orthosis [*Medicine*]
SEWPS ...... Safety Weather Probability Study (MCD)
Sew R .... Sewanee Review [*A publication*]
SEWS .... Satellite Early Warning System
SEWS .... Sun-End Work Station [*NASA*] (KSC)
SEWS .... Surface Electromagnetic Wave Spectroscopy
Sew Sh .... Sewell on the Law of Sheriffs [*1842*] (DLA)
SEWT .... Simulator for Electronic Warfare Training
SEWY .... Seaway Food Town [*NASDAQ symbol*] (NQ)
Sex .... Sextans [*Constellation*]
SEX .... Shipment Exception Code [*Military*] (AFIT)
SEX .... Summer Experiment Group [*Summer work for engineering undergraduates*]
SEXAFS ..... Surface-Extended X-Ray Absorption Fine Structure
SEXC .... Sierra Exploration Company [*NASDAQ symbol*] (NQ)
S/EXH .... Single Exhaust [*Automotive engineering*]
SEXLF .... States Explorations Limited [*NASDAQ symbol*] (NQ)

SExO .... Senior Experimental Officer [*Also, SEO, SXO*] [*Ministry of Agriculture, Fisheries, and Food*] [*British*]
Sex Prob Ct Dig ... Sex Problems Court Digest   (DLA)
SEXR .... Shoulder External Rotation [*Sports medicine*]
Sext .... Sextans [*Constellation*]
SEXT .... Shoulder Extension [*Sports medicine*]
Sext Emp ... Sextus Empiricus [*Third century AD*] [*Classical studies*]   (OCD)
Sex Transm Dis ... Sexually-Transmitted Diseases [*A publication*]
SEY .... Block Island, RI [*Location identifier*] [*FAA*]   (FAAL)
SEY .... Secondary Electron Yield
SEY .... Selibaby [*Mauritania*] [*Airport symbol*]   (OAG)
SEY .... Seymchan [*USSR*] [*Seismograph station code, US Geological Survey*]   (SEIS)
SEY .... Southeastern Yiddish   (BJA)
SEY .... Starlight Energy [*Vancouver Stock Exchange symbol*]
SEY .... Summer Employment Youth [*DoD*]
Seychelles Dep Agric Annu Rep ... Seychelles Department of Agriculture. Annual Report [*A publication*]
Seych LR .... Seychelles Law Reports   (DLA)
SEYF .... Scottish Episcopal Youth Fellowship
SEYM .... Secondary Electron Yield Measurement
Sey Merch Sh ... Seymour's Merchant Shipping Acts [*2nd ed.*] [*1857*]   (DLA)
SEYMS .... Secondary Electron Yield Measurement System
SEYS .... Secondary Electron Yield System
SEZ .... Mahe Island [*Seychelles Islands*] [*Airport symbol*]   (OAG)
SEZ .... Sedona, AZ [*Location identifier*] [*FAA*]   (FAAL)
SEZ .... Special Economic Zone
SF .... E. R. Squibb & Sons [*Research code symbol*]
SF .... Fleet Submarine [*Navy symbol*] [*Obsolete*]
SF .... Meiji Seika Kaisha Ltd. [*Japan*] [*Research code symbol*]
SF .... Provisional Sinn Fein [*Northern Ireland*]   (PPW)
SF .... Sabre Foundation   (EA)
SF .... Sacrifice Fly [*Baseball*]
SF .... Safety Factor
SF .... Safety, Reliability, and Quality Assurance, and Protective Services [*Kennedy Space Center*] [*NASA*]   (NASA)
SF .... Salt Free [*Diet*]
SF .... Sampled Filter   (IEEE)
SF .... San Francisco [*California*]
sf .... Sao Tome and Principe [*MARC country of publication code*] [*Library of Congress*]   (LCCP)
SF .... Satiety Factor [*Physiology*]
SF .... Saw Fixture   (MCD)
SF .... Sbornik Filologicky [*A publication*]
SF .... Scale Factor
SF .... Scarlet Fever [*Medicine*]
SF .... School of Chiropody Full Time [*British*]
SF .... Science Fiction [*A publication*]
SF .... Science Fiction [*Also, SCI-FI*]
SF .... Scleroderma Federation [*Formerly, International Scleroderma Foundation - ISF*] [*Washington, DC*]   (EA)
SF .... Scouting Force [*Navy*]
SF .... Sea Flood
SF .... Seasonal Food [*Department of Employment*] [*British*]
SF .... Secondary Failure [*NASA*]   (KSC)
SF .... Secure Facility   (MCD)
S & F .... Security and Facilities [*DoD*]
SF .... Security Forces [*Japanese army*]
Sf .... Sefire Inscriptions   (BJA)
SF .... Select Frequency
SF .... Selection Filter   (MCD)
SF .... Semifinished [*Steel or other material*]
SF .... Semifixed [*Ammunition*]   (NATG)
SF .... Seminal Fluid [*Medicine*]
SF .... Senate File   (OICC)
SF .... Senior Fellow
SF .... Separation Factor [*Chemical analysis*]
SF .... Service Factor   (MSA)
SF .... Seva Foundation [*Chelsea, MI*]   (EA)
SF .... Sexagesimo-quarto [*Book up to 7-1/2 centimeters in height*] [*Bibliography*]
Sf .... Sforzando [*With Additional Accent*] [*Music*]
SF .... Sherwood Foresters [*Military unit*] [*British*]
SF .... Shift Forward
SF .... Shipfitter [*Navy*]
SF .... Short Format
SF .... Side Frequency   (DEN)
SF .... Signal Frequency
SF .... Single Feeder
SF .... Single-Fronted   (ADA)
SF .... Sinking Fund [*Finance*]
SF .... Sinn Fein [*Political front of the Irish Republican Army*]
SF .... Skin Fibroblast [*Clinical chemistry*]
SF .... Skip Flag [*Data processing*]   (MDG)
SF .... Slip Fit   (MSA)
SF .... Slow Fire [*Military*]
SF .... Social Forces [*A publication*]
SF .... Socialisticki Front [*A publication*]
SF .... Societe Aerienne Francaise [*France*] [*ICAO designator*]   (FAAC)
SF .... Society Farsarotul   (EA)

SF .... Soft [*Horse racing*]
SF .... Soils and Fertilizers [*A publication*]
SF .... Solar Flare [*Astronomy*]
SF .... Solid Fuel   (ADA)
SF .... SONAR Frequency [*Military*]   (CAAL)
SF .... Sons of the Holy Family [*Roman Catholic men's religious order*]
SF .... Sosialistisk Folkepartiet [*Socialist People's Party*] [*Norway*]   (PPE)
SF .... Sound and Flash [*Military*]
S & F .... Sound and Flash [*Military*]
SF .... Source Factor   (NRCH)
SF .... Source and Fissionable [*Material*] [*Obsolete; see SS*] [*Nuclear energy*]
SF .... South Following [*Astronomy*]
SF .... Southern Forest Products Association
SF .... Space Filler [*Philately*]
SF .... Space Flight [*A publication*]
SF .... Spacial Factor
SF .... Special Facilities
SF .... Special Fixtures   (MCD)
SF .... Special Forces [*Military*]
SF .... Spent Fuel [*Nuclear energy*]   (NRCH)
SF .... Spinal Fluid [*Medicine*]
SF .... Spiritus Frumenti [*Whisky*] [*Pharmacy*]   (ROG)
SF .... Spontaneous Fission [*Radioactivity*]
SF .... Sports Foundation [*Mount Prospect, IL*]   (EA)
SF .... Spot Face
Sf .... Sprachforum [*A publication*]
SF .... Squadron or Flotilla Flag [*Navy*] [*British*]
SF .... Square Foot
SF .... Stainless Steel Fastenings
SF .... Standard Form [*Military*]
SF .... Standard Frequency
SF .... Stanton Foundation   (EA)
SF .... Star Field   (MCD)
SF .... Starlight Foundation [*Los Angeles, CA*]   (EA)
SF .... Startled Falcon [*Book written by Thomas Dunn English (1844)*]
SF .... Statement of Functions   (NATG)
sF .... Statfarad [*Also, statF*] [*Unit of capacitance*]
SF .... Static Firing [*NASA*]   (NASA)
SF .... Sterile Females [*Genetics*]
SF .... Stifel Financial Corp. [*NYSE symbol*]
S & F .... Stock and Fixtures
SF .... Stock Fund   (AFM)
SF .... Stopped-Flow [*Spectroscopy*]
S/F .... Store-and-Forward [*Data communications*]
SF .... Stowage Factor [*Shipping*]
SF .... Streptococcus faecilis [*Microbiology*]
SF .... Stress Formula
SF .... Structure Function
SF .... Studi Francesi [*A publication*]
SF .... Studia Fennica [*A publication*]
SF .... Studia Filozoficzne [*A publication*]
SF .... Su Favor [*Your Favor*] [*Spanish*]
SF .... Sub Finem [*Near the End*] [*Latin*]
SF .... Subcontractor Furnished [*NASA*]   (NASA)
SF .... Subframe
SF .... Success Factor
SF .... Successful Flight   (MCD)
SF .... Sufficient Funding   (MCD)
SF .... Sugar-Free [*Pharmacy*]
SF .... Sulfation Factor [*of blood serum*]
SF .... Sun Factor   (ADA)
SF .... Sunk Face [*Construction*]
SF .... Sunshine Foundation [*Philadelphia, PA*]   (EA)
SF .... Supply Fan   (AAG)
SF .... Surface Foot
SF .... Sustaining Fiber
SF .... Swedenborg Foundation   (EA)
SF .... Swiss Franc [*Monetary unit*]
SF .... Symbral Foundation [*Washington, DC*]   (EA)
SF .... Syndicat des Fonctionnaires [*Lao Civil Servants' Union*]
SF .... Synovial Fluid [*Medicine*]
SF1 .... Shipfitter, First Class [*Navy*]
SF2 .... Shipfitter, Second Class [*Navy*]
SF3 .... Shipfitter, Third Class [*Navy*]
SF3 .... Society for the Furtherance and Study of Fantasy and Science Fiction   (EA)
SF-4 .... Shipping Fever [*An influenza serotype*]
SFA .... Sadr Foujdaree Adalat Reports [*India*]   (DLA)
SFA .... Saks Fifth Avenue [*Retail clothing store*]
SFA .... Scandinavian Fraternity of America   (EA)
SFA .... Science Fiction Adventures [*1952-1954*] [*A publication*]
SFA .... Scientific-Atlanta, Inc. [*NYSE symbol*]
SFA .... Screw Focusing Adjustment [*Optical*]   (ROG)
SFA .... Segment Frequency Algorithm
SFA .... Segmented Flow Analysis
SFA .... Selected Financial Assistance [*British*]
SFA .... Sempervivum Fanciers Association   (EA)
SFA .... Service-Factor Amperes   (MSA)

SFA .... Seven Falls [*Quebec*] [*Seismograph station code, US Geological Survey*] [*Closed*]   (SEIS)
SFA .... Sfax [*Tunisia*] [*Airport symbol*]   (OAG)
S & FA ...... Shipping and Forwarding Agent
SFA .... Short Field Aircraft
SFA .... Show Folks of America   (EA)
SFA .... Sigmund Freud Archives [*New York, NY*]   (EA)
SFA .... Simulated Flight - Automatic
SFA .... Single Failure Analysis   (NRCH)
SFA .... Single-Frequency Approach [*Aviation*]   (FAAC)
SFA .... Slide Fastener Association [*Columbia, SC*]   (EA)
SFA .... Slow Flying Aircraft
SFA .... Snack Food Association [*Alexandria, VA*]   (EA)
SFA .... Societe Francaise d'Acoustique [*French Society of Acoustics - FSA*]   (EA-IO)
SFA .... Society of Filipino Accountants   (EA)
SFA .... Soil-Derived Fulvic Acid
SFA .... Solid Fuels Administration [*Terminated, 1954*]
SFA .... Soroptimist Federation of the Americas [*Later, Soroptimist International of the Americas*]   (EA)
SFA .... Southeastern Fabric Association [*Atlanta, GA*]   (EA)
SFA .... Southeastern Fisheries Association [*Tallahassee, FL*]   (EA)
SFA .... Southern Freight Association
SFA .... Spatial Frequency Analyzer
SFA .... Special Forces Association   (EA)
SFA .... Special Forces Auxiliary [*Military*]
SFA .... Special Foreign Activities [*Military*]   (AABC)
SFA .... Standard Fuel Assembly [*Nuclear energy*]   (NRCH)
SFA .... Stopped-Flow Analyzer [*Chemical analysis*]
SFA .... Subcommittee on Frequency Allocations
SFA .... Sunfinder Assembly
SFA .... Superficial Femoral Artery [*Anatomy*]
SFA .... Supplementary Failure Analysis [*NASA*]   (KSC)
SFA .... Surface Fibroblast Antigen [*Cytochemistry*]
SFA .... Symphony Foundation of America   (EA)
SFAA .... Society for Applied Anthropology   (EA)
SFAA .... Society for French-American Affairs   (EA)
SFAAP ...... Sunflower Army Ammunition Plant   (AABC)
SFAAW ...... Stove, Furnace, and Allied Appliance Workers International Union of North America [*AFL-CIO*]
SFAB .... Science Fiction Adventures [*1958-1963*] [*A publication*]
SFAC .... Science Fiction Adventure Classics [*A publication*]
SFACA ...... Solid Fuel Advisory Council of America   (EA)
SFACI .... Software Flight Article Configuration Inspection [*NASA*]   (NASA)
SFAD .... Science Fiction Adventures [*1956-1958*] [*A publication*]
SFAD .... Society of Federal Artists and Designers [*Later, FDC*]   (EA)
SFADS ...... San Francisco Air Defense Sector [*ADC*]
SFAF .... San Francisco AIDS Foundation [*San Francisco, CA*]   (EA)
SFAHD ...... Society of the Friends of Ancient and Historical Dubrovnik [*Dubrovnik, Yugoslavia*]   (EA-IO)
SFAL .... Samuel Feltman Ammunition Laboratory [*Army*]
SFAOD ...... Superficial-Femoral Artery Occlusive Disease [*Medicine*]
SFAP .... Society for Folk Arts Preservation   (EA)
SFAPS ...... Space Flight Acceleration Profile Simulator [*NASA*]
SFAR .... Sound Fixing and Ranging
SFAR .... Special Federal Aviation Regulation [*FAA*]
SFAR .... System Failure Analysis Report   (IEEE)
SFARG ...... SIOP [*Single Integrated Operations Plan*] Force Application Review Group   (CINC)
SFAS .... Safety Features Actuation Signal   (NRCH)
SFAV .... Surrogate Fast Attack Vehicle [*Two-passenger wheeled vehicle*]   (INF)
SFAW .... Solid Fuel Administration for War [*World War II*] [*Terminated, 1947*]
SFAW .... Stove, Furnace, and Allied Appliance Workers International Union of North America [*AFL-CIO*]
SFB .... San Francisco [*California*] [*Seismograph station code, US Geological Survey*] [*Closed*]   (SEIS)
SFB .... San Francisco Ballet
SFB .... Sanford, FL [*Location identifier*] [*FAA*]   (FAAL)
SFB .... Sbornik Filosoficke Fakulty v Bratislave [*A publication*]
SFB .... Science Fantasy [*A publication*]
SFB .... Semiconductor Functional Block   (IEEE)
SFB .... Sender Freies Berlin [*Radio network*] [*West Germany*]
SFB .... Solid Fiberboard
SFB .... Southwestern Freight Bureau, St. Louis MO [*STAC*]
SFB .... Spinning Form Block   (MCD)
SFB .... Standard Federal Bank [*NYSE symbol*]
SFB .... Structural Feedback
SFB .... Sugarcane Farmers Bulletin [*Quezon City*] [*A publication*]
SFBA .... Steamship Freight Brokers Association
SFBARTD... San Francisco Bay Area Rapid Transit District
SF Bay ...... San Francisco Bay Guardian [*A publication*]
SF Bay Gdn ... San Francisco Bay Guardian [*A publication*]
SFBC .... San Francisco Bancorp [*NASDAQ symbol*]   (NQ)
SFBCS ...... Special Forces Burst Communications Systems [*Army*]   (RDA)
SFBI .... Spent Fuel Building Isolation [*Nuclear energy*]   (NRCH)
SFBL .... Self-Filling Blind Loop [*Gastroenterology*]
SFBNS ...... San Francisco Bay Naval Shipyard
SFBRI........ Science Fiction Book Review Index 1923-1973 [*A publication*]

SFC .... Chief Shipfitter [*Navy rating*]
SFC .... Colorado Springs, CO [*Location identifier*] [*FAA*]   (FAAL)
SFC .... S-Band Frequency Converter
SFC .... St. Francis Center [*Washington, DC*]   (EA)
SFC .... Saint Francis College [*Indiana; Maine; New York; Pennsylvania; Wisconsin*]
SFC .... San Francisco [*California*] [*Seismograph station code, US Geological Survey*]   (SEIS)
SFC .... San Francisco Examiner and Chronicle [*This World Section*] [*A publication*]
SFC .... School Facilities Council of Architecture, Education, and Industry [*Later, ASBO*]   (EA)
SFC .... Science Fiction Adventure Classics [*A publication*]
SFC .... Sectored File Controller
SFC .... Selection Filter Control   (MCD)
SFC .... Selector File Channel
SFC .... Sergeant First Class
SFC .... Serial Frame Camera   (CAAL)
SFC .... SF Commentary [*A publication*]
SFC .... Ship Fire Control   (AAG)
SFC .... Shipborne Fighter Control [*Navy*]   (CAAL)
SFC .... Shoes Fan Club   (EA)
SFC .... Sight Fire Control
SFC .... Sioux Falls College [*South Dakota*]
SFC .... Societe Frederic Chopin [*Frederic Chopin Society - FCS*]   (EA-IO)
SfC .... Society for Calligraphy [*Los Angeles, CA*]   (EA)
SFC .... Society of Flavor Chemists   (EA)
SFC .... Solar Forecast Center [*Air Force*]   (IEEE)
SFC .... Solid Fat Content [*Food analysis*]
SFC .... Soluble Fibrin-Fibrinogen Complex [*Hematology*]
SFC .... Space Flight Center [*NASA*]
SFC .... Special Flight Charts [*Air Force*]
SFC .... Special Foreign Currency [*US counterpart funds*]
SFC .... Specific Fuel Consumption
SFC .... Spinal Fluid Count [*Medicine*]
SFC .... Star Field Camera [*NASA*]
SFC .... State Fund Chairmen [*Red Cross*]
SFC .... Subcritical Fluid Chromatography
SFC .... Supercritical Fluid Chromatography
SFC .... Superior Fine Cognac
SFC .... Surface   (AFM)
SFC .... Switching Filter Connector
SFC .... Sylvia Fan Club [*Nashville, TN*]   (EA)
SFC .... Synchronized Framing Camera
SFC .... Synthetic Fuels Corporation [*Sponsored by the federal government*]
SFCB .... Shipfitter, Construction Battalion [*Navy*]
SFCBB ...... Shipfitter, Construction Battalion, Blacksmith [*Navy*]
SFCBM...... Shipfitter, Construction Battalion, Mechanical Draftsman [*Navy*]
SFCBP ...... Shipfitter, Construction Battalion, Pipe Fitter and Plumber [*Navy*]
SFCBR ...... Shipfitter, Construction Battalion, Rigger [*Navy*]
SFCBS ...... Shipfitter, Construction Battalion, Steelworker [*Navy*]
SFCBW ...... Shipfitter, Construction Battalion, Welder [*Navy*]
SFCC .... Sisters for a Christian Community
SFCD......... Safecard Services, Inc. [*NASDAQ symbol*]   (NQ)
SFCD......... Stopped-Flow Circular Dichroism [*Spectroscopy*]
SFCE .... Surface
SFCH .... Society of Freight Car Historians [*Monrovia, CA*]   (EA)
SFCHD ...... Solid Fuel Chemistry [*English translation*] [*A publication*]
SFCM .... Master Chief Shipfitter [*Later, HTCM*] [*Navy rating*]
SFCMP...... Self-Rising Flour and Corn Meal Program [*Chicago, IL*]   (EA)
SFCO .... Special Forces Company [*Military*]   (CINC)
SFCP .... Shore Fire Control Party [*Navy*] [*NATO*]
SFCP......... Special Foreign Currency Program [*National Bureau of Standards*]
SFCP......... Synthetic Fuels Commercialization Program [*Also, SCP*] [*Energy Resources Council*]
SFCPTNG ... Shore Fire Control Party Training [*Navy*]   (NVT)
SFCR .... Storage Facility Control Room   (NRCH)
SFCRS ...... State-Federal Crop Reporting Service
SFCS......... Saint Fidelis College and Seminary [*Pennsylvania*]
SFCS......... Secondary Flow Control System [*Nuclear energy*]   (NRCH)
SFCS......... Senior Chief Shipfitter [*Later, HTCS*] [*Navy rating*]
SFCS......... Spent Fuel Cooling System [*Nuclear energy*]   (NRCH)
SFCS......... Surveyor Flight Control Section
SFCS......... Survivable Flight Control System [*Military*]
SFCSI........ Special Foreign Currency Science Information [*Program*] [*National Science Foundation*]
SFCSIP ...... Special Foreign Currency Science Information Program [*National Science Foundation*]
SFCSR ...... Storage Facility Cable Spreading Room   (NRCH)
SFCW........ San Francisco College for Women [*California*]
SFCW........ Search for Critical Weakness [*Aerospace*]   (AAG)
SFCW........ Sweep Frequency, Continuous Wave
SFD .... Florence-Darlington Technical College Library, Florence, SC [*OCLC symbol*]   (OCLC)
SFD .... San Fernando [*Venezuela*] [*Airport symbol*]   (OAG)
SFD .... Science Fiction Digest [*A publication*]

SFD .... Signal Flow Diagram   (MCD)
SFD .... Single Family Dwelling [*Economics*]
SFD .... Solar Flux Density
SFD .... Source-to-Film Distance [*Radiology*]
SFD .... Sudden Frequency Deviation
SFD .... Sympathetic Firing Device [*Military*]   (CAAL)
SFD .... System Function Description   (IEEE)
SFD .... System Functional Diagram [*or Drawing*]   (KSC)
SFD .... Systems Flexowriter Double Case
SFDA .... Shakey's Franchised Dealers Association [*Los Angeles, CA*]   (EA)
SFDE .... Staff and Faculty Development Elements
SFDH .... Schriften des Freien Deutschen Hochstifts [*A publication*]
SFDI .... Solar Facility Design Integration   (MCD)
SFDR .... Single-Feeder
SFDR .... Standard Flight Data Recorder
SFDS .... Smithfield Foods, Inc. [*NASDAQ symbol*]   (NQ)
SFDS .... Standby Fighter Director Ship [*Navy*]
SFDS .... Strike Force Data System   (NVT)
SFDS .... System Functional Design Specification   (MCD)
SFDT .... Signal Format Development Team [*France*]
SFDT .... Site Format Dump Tape   (MCD)
SFDW .... Special Friends of Dottie West   (EA)
SFE .... Safeguard Scientifics, Inc. [*NYSE symbol*]
SFE .... Scale Factor Error   (KSC)
SFE .... Seismic Feature Extraction   (MCD)
SFE .... Seller-Furnished Equipment   (MCD)
SFE .... Smart Front End
SFE .... Societe Financiere Europeenne
SFE .... Society of Financial Examiners
SFE .... Society of Fire Engineers
SFE .... Solar-Flare Effect [*Physics*]
SFE .... Solid Fuel Engine
SFE .... Special Furnished Equipment   (MCD)
SFE .... Stacking Fault Energy [*Alloy*]
SFE .... Student-Faculty Evaluation
SFE .... Students in Free Enterprise   (EA)
SFE .... Studies in Financial Economics [*Elsevier Book Series*] [*A publication*]
SFE .... Surface-Free Energy
SFE .... Synthetic Fermented Egg [*Animal repellent*]
SFEA .... Squib Fuse Electrical Assembly   (KSC)
SFEA .... Survival [*formerly, Space*] and Flight Equipment Association [*Later, SAFE Association*]
SFEC .... Standard Facility Equipment Card [*Electronics*]
SFEL .... Standard Facility Equipment List [*Electronics*]
SFELT .... Societe Francaise d'Editions Litteraires et Techniques [*A publication*]
SFEM .... Segner's Fortified Edd Meat [*Growth medium for phage*]
SFEM .... SFE Technologies [*NASDAQ symbol*]   (NQ)
SFEM .... Southern Farm Equipment Manufacturers [*Atlanta, GA*]   (EA)
SFEMG ...... Single Fiber Electromyography [*Neurophysiology*]
SFen .... Studia Fennica [*A publication*]
SFENA .... Societe Francaise d'Equipements pour la Navigation Aerienne   (MCD)
SFER .... Siata/Fiat 8V Register   (EA)
SFERC .... San Francisco Energy Research Center [*Energy Research and Development Administration*]
SFERICS .... Atmospherics   (FAAC)
SFERT .... Systeme Fundamental Europeen de Reference pour la Transmission Telephonique [*European master telephone reference system*]   (DEN)
SFF .... Science Fiction Foundation   (EA)
SFF .... Sea Frontier Force [*Navy*]
SFF .... Self-Forging Fragment [*Warhead*]   (MCD)
SFF .... Sheffield [*Tasmania*] [*Seismograph station code, US Geological Survey*]   (SEIS)
SFF .... Site Field Force [*Army*]   (AABC)
SFF .... Slocan Forest Products Ltd. [*Toronto Stock Exchange symbol*] [*Vancouver Stock Exchange symbol*]
SFF .... Solar Forecast Facility [*Air Force*]   (MCD)
SFF .... Spiritual Frontiers Fellowship   (EA)
SFF .... Spokane, WA [*Location identifier*] [*FAA*]   (FAAL)
SFF .... Standard File Format
SFF .... Step Family Foundation [*New York, NY*]   (EA)
SFF .... Supplementary Financing Facility [*International Monetary Fund*]
SFFA .... Fireman Apprentice, Shipfitter [*Navy rating*]
SFFBU .... Sbornik Praci Filosoficke Fakulty Brnenske University [*A publication*]
SFFF .... Scandinavian Association of Zone-Therapeutists [*Herlev, Denmark*]   (EA-IO)
SFFF .... Sedimentation Field Flow Fractionation [*For separation of colloids*]
SFFF .... Societas pro Fauna et Flora Fennica [*A publication*]
SFFFM .... Societas pro Fauna et Flora Fennica. Memoranda [*A publication*]
SF/FIA ...... Stock Fund/Financial Inventory Accounting
SFFMP .... State/Federal Fisheries Management Program [*National Marine Fisheries Service*]
SFFN .... Fireman, Shipfitter, Striker [*Navy rating*]

SFFS .... Satellite Frost Forecast System [*Department of Agriculture*]
SFFS .... Save the Flags of Fort Sumter   (EA)
SFFUK .... Sbornik Filozofickej Fakulty Univerzity. Komenskeho. Philologica [*A publication*]
SFFUP .... Sbornik Filozofickej Fakulty Univerzity. P. J. Safarika v Presove [*A publication*]
SFFUR .... Safety and Flight Failure/Unsatisfactory Report
SFFV .... Spleen Focus Formation Virus
s-fg--- .... French Guiana [*MARC geographic area code*] [*Library of Congress*]   (LCCP)
SFG .... Saint Maarten [*Netherlands Antilles*] [*Airport symbol*]   (OAG)
SFG .... Serial Publications of Foreign Governments [*A bibliographic publication*]
SFG .... SF Greats [*A publication*]
SFG .... Signal Flow Graph
SFG .... Spanische Forschungen der Gorresgesellschaft [*A publication*]
SFG .... Special Forces Group [*Military*]
SFG .... Staircase Function Generator
SFG .... Sum Frequency Generation
SFGD .... Safeguard   (AABC)
SFGD .... Safeguard Health Enterprises [*NASDAQ symbol*]   (NQ)
SFGD .... Shell's Flue Gas Desulfurization
SFGE .... San Francisco Grain Exchange [*Defunct*]   (EA)
SFGEP .... Space Flight Ground Environment Panel [*NASA*]   (KSC)
SFGS .... Southwestern Federation of Geological Societies
SFH .... SF Horizons [*A publication*]
SFH .... Simulated Flight Hour   (MCD)
SFH .... Slow Frequency Hopping   (MCD)
SFH .... Standard Fading Hour [*National Bureau of Standards*]
SFH .... Super Flux Harness
SFHb .... Stroma-Free Hemoglobin [*Hematology*]
SFHC .... Society of Folk Harpers and Craftsmen   (EA)
SFHF .... Society of the Friends of the Holy Father
SFHS .... Society for French Historical Studies   (EA)
SFI .... Sequential Fuel Injection [*Automotive engineering*]
SFI .... SF Impulse [*A publication*]
SFI .... Sindacato Ferrovieri Italiani [*Union of Italian Railroad Workers*]
SFI .... Small Flow Indicator
SFI .... Societe Financiere Internationale [*International Finance Society*]
SFI .... Society of Friends of Icons [*Hanover, West Germany*]   (EA-IO)
SFI .... Solid Fat Index [*Food analysis*]
SFI .... Southern Forest Institute [*Defunct*]   (EA)
SFI .... Space Flight Instrumentation   (AAG)
SFI .... Spendthrift Farm, Incorporated [*American Stock Exchange symbol*]
SFI .... Sport Fishing Institute   (EA)
SFI .... Starfire Resources Ltd. [*Vancouver Stock Exchange symbol*]
SFI .... Step Function Input
SFI .... Studi di Filogia Italiana [*A publication*]
SFIB .... SFI [*Sport Fishing Institute*] Bulletin [*A publication*]
SFIB .... Southern Freight Inspection Bureau
SFIC .... San Francisco Information Center [*Army Air Warning Service*]
SFICEC ...... State-Federal Information Clearinghouse for Exceptional Children
S Fict R ..... Science Fiction Review [*A publication*]
SFID .... Section Francaise de l'Internationale Ouvriere [*French Section of the Workers International*]
SFil .... Studime Filologjike [*A publication*]
SFIMR .... Stock Fund Inventory Management Record [*Military*]   (AFIT)
S-FIN .... Semi-Finished [*Automotive engineering*]
SFIN .... Southland Financial Corp. [*NASDAQ symbol*]   (NQ)
SFIO .... Section Francaise de l'Internationale Ouvriere [*French Socialist Party*]
SFIQ .... Science Fiction Quarterly [*1951-1958*] [*A publication*]
SFIR .... Specific Force Integrating Receiver [*Air Force*]
SFIREG ...... State FIFRA Issues Research and Evaluation Group [*Sacramento, CA*]   (EGAO)
SFIS .... Stanford French and Italian Studies [*A publication*]
SFIT .... Simplified Fault Isolation Test   (MCD)
SFIT .... Standard Family Interaction Test [*Psychology*]
SFJ .... Sondre Stromfjord [*Greenland*] [*Airport symbol*]   (OAG)
SFJ .... Swept Frequency Jamming
SFK .... Special Function Key [*Calculators*]
SFK .... Stonyfork, PA [*Location identifier*] [*FAA*]   (FAAL)
SFKGA ...... Sprechsaal fuer Keramik, Glas, Email, Silikate [*A publication*]
SFL .... Salt Flat, TX [*Location identifier*] [*FAA*]   (FAAL)
SFL .... San Felipe [*California*] [*Seismograph station code, US Geological Survey*]   (SEIS)
SFL .... Sao Filipe [*Cape Verde Islands*] [*Airport symbol*]   (OAG)
SFL .... Secondary Freon Loop [*NASA*]   (NASA)
SFL .... Sequence Flash Lights [*FAA*]
SFL .... Sexual Freedom League   (EA)
SFL .... Short Flashing Light [*Navigation signal*]
SFL .... Society of Federal Linguists   (EA)
SFL .... Studies in French Literature [*A publication*]
SFL .... Substrate Fed Logic
SFL .... Surinam Florin [*Monetary unit in Surinam*]
SFLC .... San Francisco Laser Center [*University of California, Berkeley*] [*Research center*]   (RCD)
SFLIS .... Sloga Fraternal Life Insurance Society   (EA)

SFLJ........... San Francisco Law Journal   (DLA)
SFLM........... Southern Film Extruders [*NASDAQ symbol*]   (NQ)
SFLR .... University of San Francisco. Law Review [*A publication*]
SFLRP .... Society of Federal Labor Relations Professionals   (EA)
SFLS .... Semiflush
SFLX .... Shoulder Flexion [*Sports medicine*]
SFM .... Francis Marion College, Florence, SC [*OCLC symbol*]   (OCLC)
SFM .... San Francisco - Josephine D. Randall Junior Museum
                [*California*] [*Seismograph station code, US Geological
                Survey*]   (SEIS)
SFM .... San Francisco Movers Tariff Bureau, San Francisco CA [*STAC*]
SFM .... Sanford, ME [*Location identifier*] [*FAA*]   (FAAL)
SFM .... Serum Free Medium
SFM .... SFM Corp. [*American Stock Exchange symbol*]
SFM .... Shepherds Fold Ministries [*Formerly, CANA*] [*An association*]
                [*Santa Cruz, CA*]   (EA)
SFM .... Shipfitter, Metalsmith [*Navy*]
SFM .... Simulated Flight - Manual
SFM .... Simulated Flow Method
SFM .... Sinai Field Mission [*US government*]
SFM .... Sinusoidal Frequency Modulation [*Physics*]
SFM .... Society for the Family of Man   (EA)
SFM .... Society for Foodservice Management [*Formed by a merger of
                National Institute Cafeteria Managers Association and
                AFSM*] [*Louisville, KY*]   (EA)
SFM .... Spectrophotofluorometer
SFM .... Storage Facility Manual   (MCD)
SFM .... Surface Feet per Minute
SFM .... Swept Frequency Modulation
SFM .... Switching Mode Frequency Multipliers
SFM .... Symposia. Fondation Merieux [*Elsevier Book Series*] [*A
                publication*]
SFMA .... Soda Fountain Manufacturers Association
SFMA .... Southern Furniture Manufacturers Association [*Later,
                AFMA*]   (EA)
SFMA .... Subscription Fulfillment Managers Association [*Later,
                FMA*]   (EA)
SFMF......... Student Foreign Missions Fellowship [*Formerly, SMF*]   (EA)
SFMG......... Franciscan Missionary Sisters of Assisi [*Roman Catholic
                religious order*]
SFMI........... Soft Fibre Manufacturers' Institute [*Defunct*]   (EA)
S 8 Fmkr .... Super 8 Filmaker [*A publication*]
SFML......... Standard Facility Material List [*Electronics*]
SFMN .... Slow Flexor Motoneuron [*Neurology*]
SFMN .... Superficial Flexor Motoneuron [*Neurology*]
SFMP .... Surplus Facilities Management Program [*Department of
                Energy*]
SFMR .... Stepped-Frequency Microwave Radiometer [*For measuring
                rain rate and wind speed*]
SFN .... San Francisco Naval Shipyard
SFN .... Santa Fe [*Argentina*] [*Airport symbol*]   (OAG)
SFN .... Seattle First National Bank, Seattle, WA [*OCLC
                symbol*]   (OCLC)
SFN .... See Footnote   (ROG)
SFN .... SFRA Newsletter [*A publication*]
SFN .... Ships and Facilities, Navy   (NG)
SFN .... Stefan Resources, Inc. [*Vancouver Stock Exchange symbol*]
SFNA .... Stabilized Fuming Nitric Acid
SFNCTU..... Swiss Federation of National-Christian Trade Unions
SFNFC ...... Sally Field National Fan Club [*Sacramento, CA*]   (EA)
SFNSY ...... San Francisco Naval Shipyard
SFNYA ...... Southern Florist and Nurseryman [*United States*] [*A
                publication*]
SFO .... Defense Solid Fuels Order [*United States*]   (DLA)
SFO .... San Fernando Observatory [*California State University,
                Northridge*] [*Research center*]   (RCD)
SFO .... San Francisco [*California*] [*Airport symbol*]
SFO .... San Francisco/Oakland [*California*] [*Airport symbol*]   (OAG)
SFO .... Sector Field Office [*Aviation*]   (FAAC)
SFO .... Sector Frequency Only [*Military*]   (CAAL)
SFO .... Secular Franciscan Order [*Roman Catholic religious order*]
                [*Formerly, TOSF*]
SFO .... Serious Fraud Office [*Proposed*] [*British government*]
SFO .... Service Fuel Oil
SFO .... SFO [*San Francisco and Oakland*] Helicopter Airlines, Inc. [*Air
                carrier designation symbol*]
SFO .... Simulated Flame Out [*Aviation*]
SFO .... Single-Frequency Outlet
SFO .... Space Flight Operations [*NASA*]
SFO .... Spot Face Other Side [*Technical drawings*]   (MSA)
SFO .... Sterling Forest [*New York*] [*Seismograph station code, US
                Geological Survey*]   (SEIS)
SFO .... Strathfield Oil & Gas Ltd. [*Toronto Stock Exchange symbol*]
SFO .... Subfornical Organ [*Brain anatomy*]
SFO .... Submarine Fog Oscillator [*Maps and charts*]
S & FO .... Supply and Fiscal Officer
SFOB .... Special Forces Operational Base [*Army*]
SFOBB .... San Francisco-Oakland Bay Bridge
SFOC .... Space Flight Operations Complex [*NASA*]
SFOD .... San Francisco Ordnance District [*Military*]
SFOD .... Space Flight Operations Director [*NASA*]

SFOD .... Special Forces Operational Detachment [*Army*]   (AABC)
SFOD-D...... [*First*] Special Forces Operational Detachment - Delta
                [*Military*]   (INF)
SFOF .... Space Flight Operations Facility [*NASA*]
SFOG .... South Fork Oil & Gas [*NASDAQ symbol*]   (NQ)
SFOK .... Sooner Federal Savings & Loan Association [*NASDAQ
                symbol*]   (NQ)
SFOLDS ..... Ship Form Online Design System [*British Ship Research
                Association*] [*Software package*]
SFOM .... Shuttle Flight Operations Manual   (MCD)
SFOM .... Space Flight Operations Memorandum [*NASA*]
SFOMS ...... Ships Force Overhaul Management Systems [*Navy*]
SFOO .... San Francisco Operations Office [*Energy Research and
                Development Administration*]
SFOP......... Safety Operating Procedure [*Kennedy Space Center*]
                [*NASA*]   (NASA)
SFOP......... Space Flight Operations Plan [*NASA*]
Sforz .... Sforzando [*With Additional Accent*] [*Music*]
SFP .... Franciscan Sisters of the Poor [*Roman Catholic religious
                order*]
SFP .... San Felipe [*Mexico*] [*Seismograph station code, US Geological
                Survey*]   (SEIS)
SFP .... Santa Fe Energy Partners [*NYSE symbol*]
SFP .... Santa Fe Public Library, Santa Fe, NM [*OCLC symbol*]   (OCLC)
SFP .... Science Fiction Plus [*A publication*]
SFP .... Security Filter Processor
SFP .... Sforzato Piano [*Sudden change from forte to piano*]
                [*Music*]   (ROG)
SFP .... Shipfitter, Pipefitter [*Navy*]
SFP .... Shungwayah Freedom Party [*Kenya*]
SFP .... Simultaneous Foveal Perception [*Ophthalmology*]
SFP .... Single Failure Point [*NASA*]   (MCD)
SFP .... Sintered Ferrous Part
SFP .... Skeleton Flight Plan
SFP .... Slack Frame Program
SFP .... Solar Flare Proton
SFP .... Spartan-Furnished Property [*Missiles*]   (MCD)
SFP .... Special Furnished Property   (MCD)
SFP .... Spent Fuel Pit [*Nuclear energy*]   (NRCH)
SFP .... Spent Fuel Pool [*Nuclear energy*]   (NRCH)
SFP .... Spinal Fluid Pressure [*Medicine*]
SFP .... Stopped Flow Pressure
SFP .... Straight Fixed Price
SFP .... Strike for Peace [*Later, WDFP*]   (EA)
SFP .... Students for Peace   (EA)
SFP .... Summary Financial Program
SFP .... Summary Flight Plan   (MCD)
SFP .... Super Flat Pack
SFP .... Sustainer Firing Package
SFP .... Svenska Folkpartiet [*Swedish People's Party*] [*Finland*]   (PPE)
SFPA......... Science Fiction Poetry Association   (EA)
SFPA......... Single Failure Point Analysis [*NASA*]   (KSC)
SFPA......... Southern Forest Products Association [*New Orleans, LA*]   (EA)
SFP-ANGS ... Standardization Field Panel for Artillery and Naval Gunfire
                Support [*Army*]   (AABC)
SFPAVS ..... Spent Fuel Pool Area Ventilation System [*Nuclear
                energy*]   (NRCH)
SFPCCS ..... Spent Fuel Pool Cooling and Cleanup System [*Nuclear
                energy*]   (NRCH)
SFPCS ...... Spent Fuel Pool Cooling System [*Nuclear energy*]   (NRCH)
SFPE .... San Francisco Port of Embarkation [*Military*]
SFPE .... Society of Fire Protection Engineers   (EA)
SFPE Technol Rep ... SFPE [*Society of Fire Protection Engineers*]
                Technology Report [*A publication*]
SFPM .... Surface Feet per Minute
SFPOE .... San Francisco Port of Embarkation [*Military*]
SFPOMMPAB ... Society for the Prevention of Married Men Posing as
                Bachelors
SFPP .... Spruce Fall Power & Paper [*AAR code*]
SFPPL .... Short Form Provisioning Parts List [*NASA*]   (NASA)
SFPPS .... Shore Facilities Planning and Programing System [*Navy*]
SFPRF........ Semifireproof   (MSA)
SFPRL .... Spartan-Furnished Property Request List [*Missiles*]   (MCD)
SFPS .... Single Failure Point Summary [*NASA*]   (NASA)
SFPS .... Studia z Filologii Polskiej i Slowianskiej [*A publication*]
SFPT .... Society of Fire Protection Technicians   (EA)
SFPTU........ Swiss Federation of Protestant Trade Unions
SFQ .... Science Fiction Quarterly [*1940-1943*] [*A publication*]
SFQ .... Southern Folklore Quarterly [*A publication*]
SFQ .... Suffolk, VA [*Location identifier*] [*FAA*]   (FAAL)
SFR .... Safety of Flight Requirements   (AFM)
SFR .... San Fernando, CA [*Location identifier*] [*FAA*]   (FAAL)
SFR .... San Francisco Review [*A publication*]
SFR .... San Francisco - Rincon [*California*] [*Seismograph station code,
                US Geological Survey*]   (SEIS)
SFR .... Santa Fe Regional Library [*Gainsville Public Library*] [*UTLAS
                symbol*]
SF & R .... Scholars' Facsimiles and Reprints [*A publication*]
SfR .... Scholars' Facsimiles & Reprints, Inc., Delmar, NY [*Library
                symbol*] [*Library of Congress*]   (LCLS)
SFR .... Science Fiction Review [*A publication*]

SFR .... Selective File Retrieval
SFR .... Semi-Fire-Resistive Construction
SFR .... Sequenced Flashing Lights
SFR .... Solar Flare Radiation
SFR .... Space Frame RADOME
SFR .... Special Federal Responsibilities   (OICC)
SFR .... Spin Flip Raman [*LASER*]
SFR .... Stanford French Review [*A publication*]
S Fr .... Studi Francesi [*A publication*]
SFR .... Submarine Fleet Reactor
S FR........... Swiss Franc [*Monetary unit*]
SFRA .... Science Fiction Research Association   (EA)
S and FRAN ... San Francisco [*California*] [*Navy*]
SFran .... Studi Francescani [*A publication*]
SFRB.......... [*The*] Atchison, Topeka & Santa Fe Railway Co. - DF Loaders
              [*AAR code*]
SFRB.......... San Francisco Review of Books [*A publication*]
SFRC.......... Soya Food Research Council
SFRCS .... Steam and Feedwater Line Rupture Control System [*Nuclear
              energy*]   (NRCH)
SFRD.......... [*The*] Atchison, Topeka & Santa Fe Railway Co. - Refrigerator
              Cars [*AAR code*]
SFRD.......... Safe Functional Requirements Document   (MCD)
SFRD.......... Secret Formerly Restricted
SF Rev Bks ... San Francisco Review of Books [*A publication*]
SFRF .... Sport Fishery Research Foundation   (EA)
SFRJ.......... Solid Fuel Ramjet
SFrL .... Studies in French Literature [*A publication*]
SFRM .... Science Fiction Review. Monthly [*A publication*]
SFrQ.......... San Francisco Quarterly [*A publication*]
SFRS .... Search for Random Success [*Aerospace*]   (AAG)
SFRS .... Swept Frequency Radiometer System
SFRY......... Socialist Federal Republic of Yugoslavia
SFS .... S-Band Feed System
SFS .... Saint Francis Seminary [*Wisconsin*]
SFS .... San Fernando [*Spain*] [*Geomagnetic observatory code*]
SFS .... San Fernando [*Spain*] [*Seismograph station code, US
              Geological Survey*]   (SEIS)
SFs .... Saybolt Furol Seconds [*Oil viscosity*]
SFS .... Science Fiction Stories [*A publication*]
SFS .... Science for Schools [*Manila*] [*A publication*]
SFS .... Sektion fuer Systementwicklung [*GID*] [*Information retrieval*]
SFS .... Senior Flight Surgeon [*Army*]   (AABC)
SFS .... Serial Focal Seizures [*Medicine*]
SFS .... Shuttle Flight Status   (MCD)
SFS .... Simplified Flight System
SFS .... Sine Fraude Sua [*Without Fraud on His Part*] [*Latin*]   (DLA)
SFS .... Society for Foodservice Systems   (EA)
SFS .... Society for Freedom in Science
SFS .... Sodium Formaldehyde Sulfoxylate [*Organic chemistry*]
SFS .... Software Facilities and Standards [*Data processing*]   (TEL)
SFS .... Sonic Frequency System
SFS .... South San Francisco, CA [*Location identifier*] [*FAA*]   (FAAL)
SFS .... Space Futures Society   (EA)
SFS .... Star Field Sensor
SFS .... Steam and Feedwater System [*Nuclear energy*]   (NRCH)
SFS .... Suomen Standardisoimisliitto [*Finnish Standards Association*]
              [*Helsinki*] [*Information service*]   (EISS)
SFS .... Super Food Services, Inc. [*American Stock Exchange symbol*]
SF & S .... Supporting Facilities and Services
SFS .... Surfaced Four Sides [*Technical drawings*]
SFS .... Symbolic File Support
SFS .... System Failure Summaries [*NASA*]   (KSC)
SFSA .... Steel Founders' Society of America [*Des Plaines, IL*]   (EA)
SFSAFBI ..... Society of Former Special Agents of the Federal Bureau of
              Investigation   (EA)
SFSAS .... Standard Fuel Savings Advisor System
SFSC .... San Francisco State College [*Later, California State University*]
SFSCL .... Shunt Feedback Schottky Clamped [*Electronics*]
SFSCPD..... San Francisco Signal Corps Procurement District
SFSCT ...... Smooth-Face Structural Clay Tile [*Technical drawings*]
S & FSD ...... Sea and Foreign Service Duty [*A Navy pay status*]
SFSD.......... Star Field Scanning Device
S & FSD(A) ... Sea and Foreign Service Duty (Aviation) [*A Navy pay status*]
S & FSD(S) ... Sea and Foreign Service Duty (Submarine) [*A Navy pay
              status*]
SFSE .... San Francisco Stock Exchange
SFSI .... Sunwest Financial Services [*NASDAQ symbol*]   (NQ)
SFSL .... Science Fiction. Review of Speculative Literature [*A
              publication*]
SFSLA........ Sbornik Trudov po Agronomicheskoi Fizike [*A publication*]
SFSMD...... Studia Fransisci Scholten Memorial Dicata   (BJA)
SFSN.......... Society of French-Speaking Neurosurgeons   (EA)
SFSO.......... San Francisco Symphony Orchestra
SFSP .... Spent Fuel Storage Pool [*Nuclear energy*]   (NRCH)
SFSR .... Shipfitter, Ship Repair [*Navy*]
SFSRC .... Shipfitter, Ship Repair, Chipper-Caulker [*Navy*]
SFSRD .... Shipfitter, Ship Repair, Diver [*Navy*]
SFSRF....... Shipfitter, Ship Repair, Steelworker-Anglesmith [*Navy*]
SFSRL .... Shipfitter, Ship Repair, Driller-Reamer [*Navy*]
SFSRP........ Shipfitter, Ship Repair, Pipe Fitter-Plumber [*Navy*]

SFSRR......... Shipfitter, Ship Repair, Riveter [*Navy*]
SFSRS......... Shipfitter, Ship Repair, Shipfitter [*Navy*]
SFSRW........ Shipfitter, Ship Repair, Welder [*Navy*]
SFSS......... Satellite Field Services Stations [*National Weather Service*]
SFSS......... Svenska Fornskriftssaellskapets Skrifter [*A publication*]
SFST......... Scherenfernrohrstand [*Emplacement of battery commander's
              telescope*] [*German military - World War II*]
SFST......... Science Fiction Studies [*A publication*]
SFSU......... Singapore Federation of Services' Unions
SFSV......... Svenska Forfattare Utgivna av Svenska Vitterhetssamfundet [*A
              publication*]
SF Sym ...... San Francisco Symphony Program Notes [*A publication*]
SF & T .... Sawyer, Finn & Thatcher [*Advertising agency*]
SFT........... Shaft   (MSA)
SFT........... Simulated Flight Tests
SFT........... Skelleftea [*Sweden*] [*Airport symbol*]   (OAG)
SFT........... Skinfold Thickness [*Medicine*]
SFT........... Skyfreight, Inc. [*Seattle, WA*] [*FAA designator*]   (FAAC)
sft........... Soft [*Quality of the bottom*] [*Nautical charts*]
SFT........... Soviet and Eastern European Foreign Trade [*A publication*]
SFT........... Special Flight Test
SFT........... Specific Financial Transactions
SFT........... Spiral Fin Tubing
SFT........... Squeeze Film Test
SFT........... Stacking Fault Tetrahedra [*Metals*]
SFT........... Stanford [*California*] [*Seismograph station code, US
              Geological Survey*]   (SEIS)
SFT........... Static Firing Test [*NASA*]   (NASA)
SFT........... Stockpile Flight Tests
SFT........... Stop for Tea [*British*]
SFT........... Structural Firing Test [*Military*]   (CAAL)
SFT........... Studi di Filologia Todeska [*A publication*]
SFT........... Superfast Train
SFT........... Supplemental Flight Test
SFT........... Swift Independent Corp. [*American Stock Exchange symbol*]
SFT........... System Fault Tolerant [*Novell, Inc.*] [*Orem, UT*]
              [*Telecommunications*]
SFTA......... Spent Fuel Transportation Accident [*Nuclear energy*]   (NRCH)
SFTA......... Structural Fatigue Test Article [*NASA*]   (NASA)
SFTB......... Science Fiction Times [*A publication*]
SFTB......... Southern Freight Tariff Bureau
SFTC......... Sherman Fairchild Technology Center   (MCD)
SFTCD...... Senior Fellow, Trinity College, Dublin   (ROG)
SFTE........ Society of Flight Test Engineers   (MCD)
SFTF .... Static Firing Test Facility [*NASA*]   (NASA)
SFTFC....... Search for Tomorrow Fan Club [*Mahopac, NY*]   (EA)
SFTI .... Special Flight Test Instrumentation   (MCD)
SFTIP .... Special Flight Test Instrumentation Pool   (NG)
SFTL .... Sonic Fatigue Test Laboratory   (AAG)
SFTO......... San Diego Field Test Operations [*Aerospace*]   (AAG)
SFTP......... Science for the People [*Formerly, SESPA*]
SFTR......... Shipfitter   (AAG)
SFTR......... Summary Flight Test Report   (MCD)
SFTS .... San Francisco Theological Seminary [*San Anselmo, CA*]
SFTS .... Scale Factor Temperature Sensitivity
SFTS .... Service Flying Training School [*British*]
SFTS .... Space Flight Test System   (MCD)
SFTS .... Standard Frequency and Time Signals   (IEEE)
SFTS .... Synthetic Flight Training System [*Army*]
SFTT .... Spent Fuel Transfer Tubes [*Nuclear energy*]   (NRCH)
SFTU......... Swiss Federation of Trade Unions
SFTW......... Stamps for the Wounded
SFTWR...... Software [*Data processing*]   (MCD)
SFTY .... Safety
SFU .... Furman University, Greenville, SC [*OCLC symbol*]   (OCLC)
SFU .... Safia [*Papua New Guinea*] [*Airport symbol*]   (OAG)
SFU .... Sector Field Unit [*Aviation*]   (FAAC)
SFU .... Signals Flying Unit [*British*]
SFU .... Simon Fraser University [*Canada*]
SFU .... Simon Fraser University Library [*UTLAS symbol*]
SFU .... Societe de Fluoration de l'Uranium [*An international nuclear
              fuel company*]
SFU .... Special Function Unit
SFU .... Standard Firing Unit [*NASA*]   (NASA)
SFU .... Status Fill-In Unit [*Telecommunications*]   (TEL)
SFU .... Suriname Freedom Union   (EA)
SFU .... Synthetic Fuels Update [*A publication*]
SFUGE ...... Singapore Federation of Unions of Government Employees
SF/UIS ...... Space Frame and Unit Integrating System
SFUK .... Sbornik Filozofickej Fakulty Univerzity. Komenskeho [*A
              publication*]
SFUPD ...... Synthetic Fuels Update [*A publication*]
SFUS .... Sbornik Filozofickej Fakulty Univerzity. P. J. Safarika [*A
              publication*]
SFUS .... Sovetskoe Finno-Ugrovedenie/Soviet Fenno-Ugric Studies [*A
              publication*]
SF/USA..... Stopped-Flow/Unsegmented Storage Analyzer [*Chemical
              analysis*]
SFV .... Semliki Forest Virus
SFV .... Sight Feed Valve
SFVC......... State Fund Vice Chairmen [*Red Cross*]

SFVCS	San Francisco Vocational Competency Scale
SFVK........	Svenska Folkskolans Vaenner. Kalender [*A publication*]
SFW	Sante Fe [*Panama*] [*Airport symbol*] (OAG)
SFW	Shell Fragment Wound [*Medicine*]
SFW	Special Filter Wheel [*Military*] (CAAL)
SFW	Williston, ND [*Location identifier*] [*FAA*] (FAAL)
SFWA	Science Fiction Writers of America
SFWA	Sierra Foothill Winery Association [*Somerset, CA*] (EA)
SFWB	Single Fronted Weatherboard (ADA)
SFWC	Supreme Forest Woodmen Circle [*Later, Woodmen of the World Life Insurance Society*] (EA)
SFWEM	Static Feed Water Electrolysis Module [*NASA*]
SFWLI	Ship's Force Worklist Instruction
SFWM	Swiss Federation of Watch Manufacturers (EA)
SFWR	Stewardesses for Women's Rights
SFWS	Stopped-Flow Wavelength Scanning [*Spectrometry*]
SFX	St. Francis Xavier University Library [*UTLAS symbol*]
SFX	Santa Fe Southern Pacific Corp. [*NYSE symbol*]
SFX	Sound Effects [*Script code*]
SFXD	Semifixed
SFXR	Super Flash X-Ray (MCD)
SFY	Savanna, IL [*Location identifier*] [*FAA*] (FAAL)
SFY	Science Fiction Yearbook [*A publication*]
SFY	Standard Facility Years [*FAA*]
SFY	Swift Energy Company [*American Stock Exchange symbol*]
SFZ	Pawtucket, RI [*Location identifier*] [*FAA*] (FAAL)
Sfz............	Sforzando [*With Additional Accent*] [*Music*]
SG	Command Surgeon [*AFSC*]
SG	Sa Grace [*His or Her Grace*] [*French*]
SG	Sa Grandeur [*His or Her Highness*] [*French*]
SG	Sabah Air [*Malaysia*] [*ICAO designator*] (FAAC)
SG	Sachs-Georgi [*Test for syphilis*] [*Also, S-GT*] [*Obsolete*]
SG	Safety Guide (NRCH)
SG	Salutis Gratia [*For the Sake of Safety*] [*Latin*]
SG	Sample Gas
SG	Sawtooth Generator
SG	Scanning Gate
SG	Schutzgemeinschaft Gegen Meinungsterror [*Guard Society Against Opinion Terror*] [*Germany*]
SG	Scientific Leasing, Inc. [*American Stock Exchange symbol*]
SG	Scots Guards [*Military unit*] [*British*]
SG	Screen Grid [*Electrode or vacuum tube*]
SG	Sculptors Guild (EA)
SG	Sea Grant
SG	Seaman Gunner [*British*] [*Obsolete*]
SG	Secretary-General [*United Nations*]
sg	Senegal [*MARC country of publication code*] [*Library of Congress*] (LCCP)
SG	Senior Gleaners [*North Highlands, CA*] (EA)
SG	Senior Grade
SG	Service Group (MUGU)
SG	Set Gate
SG	Shell Gland
SG	Shell Gun
SG	Sheller-Globe Corp.
SG	Sherrgold Units [*Toronto Stock Exchange symbol*]
SG	Ship and Goods [*British*] (ROG)
SG	Shipcraft Guild (EA)
SG	Siculorum Gymnasium [*A publication*]
SG	Signal Generator
SG	Signal Ground (BUR)
SG	Silica Gel [*Analytical chemistry*]
SG	Singapore [*Two-letter standard code*] (CNC)
SG	Singing
SG	Single Gourmet [*An association*] (EA)
SG	Single Groove [*Insulators*]
Sg	Singular (BJA)
SG	Sinte Geertruydtsbronne [*A publication*]
SG	Skin Graft [*Medicine*]
S/G............	Slaved Gyro (MCD)
S & G	Smale and Giffard's English Vice-Chancery Reports (DLA)
S/G............	Smith/Greenland [*Advertising agency*]
SG	Smoke Generator
SG	Snow Grains [*Meteorology*] (FAAC)
SG	Society of Genealogists (EA)
SG	Soft Gelatin [*Pharmacy*]
SG	Solicitor General
SG	Soluble Gelatin
Sg	Song of Songs [*Old Testament book*] [*Roman Catholic canon*] (BJA)
SG	Sort Generator (BUR)
SG	Sound Generation (MCD)
SG	South Georgia Railway Co. [*AAR code*] [*Terminated*]
SG	Spark Gap (DEN)
SG	Special Group [*NATO*]
SG	Specific Gravity [*Also, SPG, SPGR*]
SG	Spheroidal Graphite [*Ductile iron*]
SG	Sprach der Gegenwart [*A publication*]
SG	Stacking Gel [*Biochemistry*]
SG	Standardization Group [*Air Force*] (AFM)
SG	Standing Group

SG	Steam Generator (NRCH)
SG	Steel Girder [*Bridges*]
SG	Steering Group (MCD)
SG	Stellate Ganglion [*Neuroanatomy*]
S & G	Stone and Graham's Court of Referees Reports [*England*] (DLA)
S & G	Stone and Graham's Private Bills Reports [*England*] (DLA)
SG	Strain Gauge (KSC)
SG	Structural Gene
SG	Structural Glass
SG	Student Guide
SG	Studi Genuesi [*A publication*]
SG	Studi Germanici [*A publication*]
SG	Studi Goriziani [*A publication*]
SG	Studium Generale [*A publication*]
SG	Su Giro [*Your Draft*] [*Banking*] [*Spanish*]
SG	Substantia Gelatinosa [*Anatomy*]
SG	Summation Gallop [*Cardiology*]
SG	Sun Gate
SG	Sunkist Growers (EA)
SG	Sunset Gun [*Military ceremonial*]
SG	Sunsweet Growers (EA)
SG	Super Group (NATG)
SG	Super Guppy (KSC)
Sg	Supplementing [*New matter added to an existing regulation or order*] [*Used in Shepard's Citations*] (DLA)
SG	Surgeon
SG	[*The*] Surgeon General [*Army and Air Force*]
SG	Swamp Glider
SG	Sweep Generator
SG	Sydney Gazette [*A publication*]
SG	Symbol Generator
SG	System Gain
1SG	First Sergeant [*Army*]
SGA	Savoonga, AK [*Location identifier*] [*FAA*] (FAAL)
SGA	Scientific Glass Apparatus Co., Inc.
SGA	Sea Grant Association (EA)
SG & A	Selling, General, and Administrative Expenses
SGA	Shirtsleeve Garment Assembly [*NASA*]
SGA	Sigma Security, Inc. [*Vancouver Stock Exchange symbol*]
SGA	Single-Monitor Graphic Adaptor [*Computer graphics*]
SGA	Slave Gyro Assembly
SGA	Small for Gestational Age [*Pediatrics*]
SGA	Societe de Geologie Appliquee aux Gites Mineraux [*Society for Geology Applied to Mineral Deposits*] [*ICSU*] (EA-IO)
SGA	Society of Gastrointestinal Assistants [*Rochester, NY*] (EA)
SGA	Society of Governmental Appraisers [*Later, Association of Governmental Appraisers*] (EA)
SGA	Society of Graphic Art [*British*]
SGA	Solar Greenhouse Association (EA)
SGA	Songwriters Guild of America [*New York, NY*] (EA)
SGA	Soybean Growers of America (EA)
SGA	Spectrometric Gas Analysis
SGA	Split Group Aperture
SGA	Spouses of Gays Association [*Philadelphia, PA*] (EA)
SGA	Standards of Grade Authorization
SGA	Stephens Glacier [*Alaska*] [*Seismograph station code, US Geological Survey*] [*Closed*] (SEIS)
SGA	Substantial Gainful Activity [*Social Security Administration*] (OICC)
SGA	Switch Group Assembly
SGAA	Sporting Goods Agents Association [*Formerly, SGRA*] [*Morton Grove, IL*] (EA)
SGAA	Stained Glass Association of America [*St. Louis, MO*] (EA)
SGAC	Silvermine Guild Arts Center [*New Canaan, CT*] (EA)
SGAC	State Governmental Affairs Council [*Washington, DC*] (EA)
SGACC	Secretariat General de l'Aviation Civile et Commerciale [*France*]
SGAD	Safeguard Army Depot (AABC)
SGAE	Studiengesellschaft fuer Atomenergie [*Implements Austria's nuclear program*] (NRCH)
SGAHRS	Steam Generator Auxiliary Heat Removal System (NRCH)
SGAIG	Scholars Group Against the Invasion of Grenada (EA)
SGA J	SGA [*Society of Gastrointestinal Assistants*] Journal [*A publication*]
SGAK	Studien zur Germanistik, Anglistik und Komparatistik [*A publication*]
SGAL.........	Sage-Allen & Co. [*NASDAQ symbol*] (NQ)
SGA of M-A ...	Sod Growers Association of Mid-America (EA)
SGAOR.......	Sitzungsberichte der Gesellschaft fuer Geschichte und Altertumskunde der Ostseeprovinzen Russlands [*A publication*]
SGAS	Society for German-American Studies (EA)
SGAS	Space Geodesy Altimetry Study [*Raytheon Co.*]
SGAS	Steam Generator Available Signal [*Nuclear energy*] (NRCH)
SGAT	Seagate Technology [*NASDAQ symbol*] (NQ)
SGAUG	Scitex Graphic Arts Users Group
SGAUSA	St. George Association of the USA (EA)
sGAW........	Specific Airway Conductance
SGAW	Subgroup on Assessment of Weapons [*NATO*] (NATG)
SGB............	Santa Fe, NM [*Location identifier*] [*FAA*] (FAAL)

SGB........... Schlesische Geschichtsblaetter (Breslau) [*A publication*]
SGB........... Schweizerischer Gewerkschaftsbund [*Swiss Federation of Trade Unions*]
SGB........... Societe Generale de Banque [*Bank Society*] [*Brussels, Belgium*] [*Information service*]   (EISS)
SGB........... Steam Generator Blowdown [*Nuclear energy*]   (NRCH)
SGB........... Steam Generator Building   (NRCH)
SGB........... Stellate Ganglion Blockade [*Anesthesiology*]
SGB........... Strain Gauge Bridge
SGB........... Studien und Mitteilungen zur Geschichte des Benediktiner-Ordens [*A publication*]
SGB........... Switchgear Block   (MSA)
SGBD........ Steam Generator Blowdown [*Nuclear energy*]   (NRCH)
SGBI......... Santa Gertrudis Breeders International   (EA)
SGBIP....... Subject Guide to Books in Print [*A publication*]
SGBPS....... Steam Generator Blowdown Processing System [*Nuclear energy*]   (NRCH)
SGBS........ Steam Generator Blowdown System [*Nuclear energy*]   (NRCH)
SGC........... Saint Gregory College [*Oklahoma*]
SGC........... Salivary Gland Choristoma [*Medicine*]
SGC........... Screen Grid Current
SGC........... Simulated Generation Control
SGC........... Solicitor General Canada
SGC........... South Georgia College [*Douglas*]
SGC........... Southern Governors Conference
SGC........... Space General Corporation   (MCD)
SGC........... Spartan Guidance Computer [*Missiles*]   (AABC)
SGC........... Spherical Gear Coupling
SGC........... Stabilized Ground Cloud   (MCD)
SGC........... Stabilizer Gyro Circuit
SGC........... Standard Geographical Classification [*Canada*]
SGC........... Strata Energy Corporation [*Vancouver Stock Exchange symbol*]
SGC........... Supergroup Connector [*Telecommunications*]   (TEL)
SGC........... Superior Geocentric Conjunction
SGC........... Superior Surgical Manufacturing Company, Inc. [*American Stock Exchange symbol*]
SGC........... Washington, DC [*Location identifier*] [*FAA*]   (FAAL)
SGCA........ Silvermine Guild Center for the Arts [*Later, SGAC*]   (EA)
SGCD........ Society of Glass and Ceramic Decorators [*Port Jefferson, NY*]   (EA)
SGCE........ Ship Gyrocompass Equipment [*Navy*]   (CAAL)
SGCEC....... Standing Group Communications-Electronics Committee [*Later, MCEWG*] [*NATO*]   (NATG)
SGCF........ SNAP [*Systems for Nuclear Auxiliary Power*] Generalized Critical Facility
SGCL......... Studies in General and Comparative Literature [*A publication*]
SGCMG...... Single Gimbal Control Moment Gyro [*Navigation*]
SGCS........ Silicon Gate-Controlled Switch
SGCS........ Slave Gyro Control System
SGD........... Napa, CA [*Location identifier*] [*FAA*]   (FAAL)
SGD........... Self-Generating Dictionary
SGD........... Senior Grand Deacon [*Freemasonry*]
SGD........... Shogun Developments Corp. [*Vancouver Stock Exchange symbol*]
SGD........... Signaling Ground [*Telecommunications*]   (TEL)
SGD........... Signed
SGD........... Sliding Glass Door   (ADA)
SGD........... Society of Glass Decorators [*Later, SGCD*]   (EA)
SGD........... Solar-Geophysical Data [*A publication*]
SGD........... Sonderborg [*Denmark*] [*Airport symbol*]   (OAG)
SGD........... Sui Generis Degree
SGDCTO.... Sangre de Cristo [*FAA*]   (FAAC)
SGDE........ Steering Gear Dual Emergency   (MSA)
SGDE........ System Ground Data Equipment [*RADAR*]
SGDF........ Supergroup Distribution Frame [*Telecommunications*]   (TEL)
SGDG........ Sans Garantie du Gouvernement [*Without Government Guarantee*] [*French*]   (ROG)
SGDI......... Sammlung der Griechischen Dialekt-Inschriften [*A publication*]   (BJA)
SGDI......... Swaging Die [*Tool*]
SGDI......... Switched Ground Discrete Input   (MCD)
SGDO........ Switched Ground Discrete Output   (MCD)
SGDPS....... Second Generation Data Processing System   (MCD)
Sge........... Sagitta [*Constellation*]
SGE........... Secondary Grid Emission
SGE........... Severable Government Equipment
SGE........... Sigma Gamma Epsilon [*Society*]
SGE........... Society of Government Economists   (EA)
SGEG........ Syndicat General de l'Education en Guadeloupe   (PD)
SGEM........ Study Group on Environmental Monitoring [*National Research Council*]
SGEMP...... System-Generated Electromagnetic Pulse [*Army*]
SGen......... Studium Generale [*A publication*]
SGer.......... Studia Germanica [*A publication*]
S Ger S...... Stanford German Studies [*A publication*]
SGES........ Society of Grain Elevator Superintendents [*Later, GEAPS*]
SGET......... Spacecraft Ground Elapsed Time
SGEU........ Singapore General Employees' Union
SGF........... Sample Gas Flow
SGF........... Sarcoma Growth Factor

SGF........... Skeletal Growth Factor [*Genetics*]
SGF........... Small Gene Fragment [*Genetics*]
SGF........... Southern Group of Forces [*USSR*]   (NATG)
SGF........... Springfield [*Missouri*] [*Airport symbol*]   (OAG)
SGF........... Springfield, MO [*Location identifier*] [*FAA*]   (FAAL)
SGF........... Stockholmer Germanistische Forschungen [*A publication*]
SGFID....... Seventh Generation Fund for Indian Development [*Formerly, TSP*]   (EA)
SGFMV...... Sammendrag af Groenlands Fangstlister MV [*A publication*]
SGFNT....... Significant   (FAAC)
SGFP........ Steam Generator Feed Pump   (IEEE)
SGF Publ.... SGF [*Sveriges Gummitekniska Foerening*] Publicerande [*A publication*]
SGG........... Saint George Island, AK [*Location identifier*] [*FAA*]   (FAAL)
SGG........... St. George Minerals [*Vancouver Stock Exchange symbol*]
SGG........... South Georgia [*United Kingdom*] [*Geomagnetic observatory code*]
SGG........... Studia Germanica Gandensia [*A publication*]
SGG.......... Sustainer Gas Generator
SGGAOPR ... Sitzungsberichte der Gesellschaft fuer Geschichte und Altertumskunde der Ostseeprovinzen Russlands [*A publication*]
SGH........... Serum Growth Hormone [*Endocrinology*]
SGH........... Seth G. Huntington [*Designer's mark on US bicentennial half dollar*]
SGH........... Signal Hill Energy Corp. [*Vancouver Stock Exchange symbol*]
SGH........... Springfield, OH [*Location identifier*] [*FAA*]   (FAAL)
SGh........... Studia Ghisleriana [*Pavia*] [*A publication*]
SGH........... Sud-Ghoubbet [*Djibouti*] [*Seismograph station code, US Geological Survey*]   (SEIS)
SGHLA........ Surgical Hospital [*Medicine*]
SGHLA........ Stadt- und Gebaeudetechnik [*A publication*]
SGHW........ Steam-Generating, Heavy-Water [*Reactor*] [*British*]   (NRCH)
SGHWR...... Steam-Generating, Heavy-Water Reactor [*British*]   (NRCH)
SGI........... Sea Grant Institute [*University of Wisconsin*] [*Research center*]   (RCD)
SGI........... Search Group, Incorporated [*An association*]   (EA)
SGI........... Servicio Geodesico Interamericano [*Inter-American Geodetic Survey - IAGS*] [*United States*]
SGI........... Slattery Group, Incorporated [*NYSE symbol*]
SGI........... Society for Gynecologic Investigation [*Washington, DC*]   (EA)
SGI........... Specific Gravity Indicator
SGI........... Spring Garden Institute
SGI........... Standard Graphic Interface [*XOR Systems*]
SGI........... Studi di Grammatica Italiana [*A publication*]
SGIA........ Sun Glass Institute of America [*Defunct*]   (EA)
SGIG........ Sovereign Grand Inspector-General [*Freemasonry*]   (ROG)
SGINDEX ... System Generation Cross-Reference Index [*NASA*]
SGIS........ Safeguards Initiation Signal [*Nuclear energy*]   (NRCH)
SGIS........ Steam Generator Isolation Signal   (IEEE)
SGIS........ Student Government Information Service   (EA)
SGIT........ Special Group Inclusive Tour [*Airline fare*]
SGJ........... Sagarai [*Papua New Guinea*] [*Airport symbol*]   (OAG)
SGJ........... St. Augustine, FL [*Location identifier*] [*FAA*]   (FAAL)
SGJ........... Supersonic Gas Jet
SGJA........ Sporting Goods Jobbers Association [*Later, NASGW*]
SGJP........ Satellite Graphic Job Processor [*Data processing*]
SGK........... Hsinkong [*Republic of China*] [*Also, HSI*] [*Seismograph station code, US Geological Survey*]   (SEIS)
SGK........... Knoxville, TN [*Location identifier*] [*FAA*]   (FAAL)
SGKA........ Studien zur Geschichte und Kultur des Alterums [*A publication*]   (BJA)
SGL........... Mount Signal [*California*] [*Seismograph station code, US Geological Survey*]   (SEIS)
SGL........... Signal
SGL........... Single   (MSA)
SGL........... Society of Gas Lighting
SGL........... South State Cooperative Library System, Los Angeles, CA [*OCLC symbol*]   (OCLC)
SGL........... Space-Ground Link   (MCD)
SGL........... Studies in German Literature [*A publication*]
SGl........... Sumerisches Glossar [*A publication*]   (BJA)
SGL........... Sunglasses
SGL........... Supermarkets General Corp. [*NYSE symbol*]
SGLC........ Strain Gauge Load Cell
SGLE........ Single   (AAG)
SGLF........ Scottish Grand Lodge of Freemasons
SGLF........ Symposia. Giovanni Lorenzini Foundation [*Elsevier Book Series*] [*A publication*]
SGLI........ Servicemen's Group Life Insurance
SGLI........ Slave Gyro Leveling Integrator
SGLI........ Societe Geographique de Liege. Bulletin [*Belgium*] [*A publication*]
SGLIC....... Steam Generator Level Instrumentation Cabinet [*Nuclear energy*]   (NRCH)
SGLL........ Studies in the Germanic Languages and Literatures [*A publication*]
SGLO........ Standing Group Liaison Officer to the North Atlantic Council
SGLP........ Standing Group Representative Liaison Paper to the International Staff [*Obsolete*] [*NATO*]   (NATG)
SGLS........ Satellite Grand Link System   (NATG)

SGLS .... Space-to-Ground Link Subsystem [*NASA*]
SGLWCH .... Study Group on Labor and Working Class History   (EA)
SGM .... College Mathieu, Gravelbourg, Saskatchewan [*Library symbol*] [*National Library of Canada*]   (NLC)
SGM .... Scottish Geographical Magazine [*A publication*]
SGM .... Screen Grid Modulation
SGM .... Sea Gallantry Medal [*Navy*] [*British*]
SGM .... Sergeant Major   (AABC)
SGM .... Silver Gate [*Montana*] [*Seismograph station code, US Geological Survey*]   (SEIS)
SGM .... Society for General Microbiology [*British*]
SGM .... Society for General Music   (EA)
SGM .... Soeurs Grises de Montreal [*Sisters of Charity, Grey Nuns of Montreal*] [*Roman Catholic religious order*]
SGM .... Spark Gap Modulation
SGM .... Standing Group Memorandum [*Obsolete*] [*NATO*]   (NATG)
SGM .... Strategic Guidance Memo [*Navy*]
SGMA .... Sigmaform Corp. [*NASDAQ symbol*]   (NQ)
SGMA .... Sporting Goods Manufacturers Association [*North Palm Beach, FL*]   (EA)
SGMAA ..... Sporting Goods Manufacturers Agents Association [*Later, SGRA*]
SGMC .... Standing Group Meteorological Committee [*Obsolete*] [*NATO*]   (NATG)
SGMCI ...... Sporting Goods Manufacturers' Credit Interchange [*Buffalo, NY*]   (EA)
SGMD .... Swaging Mandel
SGME .... Service Generale des Moyens de l'Enseignement [*Canada*]
SGMH .... Study Group. Institute for Research into Mental and Multiple Handicap [*Elsevier Book Series*] [*A publication*]
SGMIA .... S-G Metals Industries CI A [*NASDAQ symbol*]   (NQ)
SGML .... Standard Generalized Markup Language [*International Standards Organisation*]
SGML .... Study Group for Mathematical Learning [*Urbana, IL*]   (EA)
SGMP .... Society of Government Meeting Planners [*Washington, DC*]   (EA)
SGMS .... Shipboard Gravity Measuring System
SGMSR ..... Steam Generator Maximum Steam Rate   (NRCH)
SGMT .... Simulated Greenwich Mean Time   (MCD)
SGMT .... Subgroup Modern Terminal
SGN .... Ho Chi Minh [*Vietnam*] [*Airport symbol*]   (OAG)
SGN .... Saigon [*Vietnam*]
SGN .... Scan Gate Number
SGN .... Self-Generated Noise [*Oceanography*]
SGN .... Service Geologique National [*National Geological Survey*] [*Bureau of Geological and Mining Research*] [*Orleans, France*] [*Information service*]   (EISS)
sgn .... Signer [*MARC relator code*] [*Library of Congress*]
SGN .... Simulation Gaming News [*A publication*]
SGN .... Standing Group, North Atlantic Treaty Organization
SGN .... Surgeon General of the Navy
SGNAD ...... Shoni Geka Naika [*A publication*]
SGNET .... Sea Grant Network [*National Oceanic and Atmospheric Administration*] [*Narragansett, RI*] [*Information service*]   (EISS)
SGNLD ...... Signalled   (ROG)
SGNLS ...... Sequential Generalized Nonlinear Least Squares [*Statistics*]
SGNMOS ... Screen-Grid N-Channel Metal Oxide Semiconductor
SGNR .... Signature   (AABC)
SGO .... Saint George [*Australia*] [*Airport symbol*]   (OAG)
SGO .... Sea Gold Oil Corp. [*Vancouver Stock Exchange symbol*]
SGO .... Seagull Energy Corp. [*NYSE symbol*]
SGO .... Society of Geriatric Ophthalmology [*Canton, OH*]   (EA)
SGO .... Society of Gynecologic Oncologists [*Chicago, IL*]   (EA)
SGO .... Squadron Gunnery Officer
SGo .... Studi Goriziani [*A publication*]
SGO .... Surgeon General's Office
SGO .... Sydney Godolphin Osborne [*Literary signature of 19th-century British writer*]
SGOBA ...... Surgery, Gynecology, and Obstetrics [*A publication*]
SGOG .... Steam Generators Owners Group [*Nuclear energy*]   (NRCH)
SGOG .... Suppressor Grid Orbitron Gauge
SGoldoniani ... Studi Goldoniani [*A publication*]
SGOLY .... St. Helena Gold Mines [*NASDAQ symbol*]   (NQ)
SGOR .... Solution Gas-Oil Ratio
SGor .... Studi Goriziani [*A publication*]
SGOS .... Shuttle Ground Operations Simulator [*NASA*]   (NASA)
SGOT .... Serum Glutamic Oxaloacetic Transaminase [*An enzyme*]
SGP .... San Gregorio [*Peru*] [*Seismograph station code, US Geological Survey*] [*Closed*]   (SEIS)
SGP .... Schering-Plough Corp. [*NYSE symbol*]
SGP .... Secondary Gun Pointer [*Navy*]
SGP .... Seminiferous Growth Factor [*Biochemistry*]
SGP .... Singapore [*Three-letter standard code*]   (CNC)
SGP .... Single Ground Point   (MCD)
SGP .... Society of General Physiologists   (EA)
SGP .... Society of Ghana Philatelists [*Defunct*]   (EA)
SGP .... Solicitor General, Prairies [*UTLAS symbol*]
SGP .... South Galactic Pole
SGP .... Specialty Glass Products, Inc.

SGP .... Staatkundig Gereformeerde Partij [*Political Reformed Party*] [*The Netherlands*]   (PPE)
SGP .... Stabilized Gyro Platform
SGP .... Standard Guidance Package
SGP .... Stephen Greene Press
SGP .... Sudeten German Party
SGP .... Sulfated Glycoprotein [*Biochemistry*]
SGPA .... Stained Glass Professionals Association [*Inactive*] [*Jensen Beach, FL*]   (EA)
SGPC .... Soviet Government Purchasing Commission [*World War II*]
SGPI .... Superintendent of Government Printing, India   (ROG)
SGPM .... Saint-Gobain-Pont-A-Mousson [*French industrial giant*]
SgpNL .... National Library, Singapore, Singapore [*Library symbol*] [*Library of Congress*]   (LCLS)
SgpNU .... Nangang University, Singapore, Singapore [*Library symbol*] [*Library of Congress*]   (LCLS)
SGPO .... Standing Group Representative Communication to the Private Office of the NATO Secretary General [*Obsolete*]   (NATG)
SGPT .... Serum Glutamic-Pyruvic Transaminase [*An enzyme*]
SgpU .... University of Singapore, Singapore, Singapore [*Library symbol*] [*Library of Congress*]   (LCLS)
SGR .... Greenville County Library, Greenville, SC [*OCLC symbol*]   (OCLC)
SGR .... Houston, TX [*Location identifier*] [*FAA*]   (FAAL)
Sgr .... Sagittarius [*Constellation*]
SGR .... Saturn Energy [*Vancouver Stock Exchange symbol*]
SGR .... School of General Reconnaissance [*Air Force*] [*British*]
SGR .... Science and Government Report [*A publication*]
SGR .... Seismic Group Recorder [*Geophysics*]
SGR .... Self-Generation Reactor   (NRCH)
SGR .... Seminal Groove
SGR .... Sodium Graphite Reactor
SGR .... Steam Gas Recycle [*Shale oil process*]
S/GR .... Steering Gear [*Automotive engineering*]
SGr .... Studii de Gramatica [*A publication*]
SGR .... Submandibular Gland Renin [*Endocrinology*]
SGR .... Sugar Land [*Texas*] [*Airport symbol*]   (OAG)
SGRA .... Sporting Goods Representatives Association [*of SIRA*] [*Later, Sporting Goods Agents Association*]   (EA)
SGRAC ...... Supreme Grand Royal Arch Chapter [*Freemasonry*]   (ROG)
SGram .... Studii de Gramatica [*A publication*]
SGRCA ...... Sodium Graphite Reactor Critical Assembly   (IEEE)
SGRD .... Signal Ground   (AAG)
SGRD .... State Government Research Directory [*A publication*]
SGREP .... Standing Group Representative [*NASA*]
S-GRN .... Surfaced Green [*Lumber*]
SGRS .... Stockton Geriatric Rating Scale [*Psychology*]
SGRT .... Soviet Geography. Review and Translation [*A publication*]
SGS .... Sage Resources Ltd. [*Vancouver Stock Exchange symbol*]
SGS .... St. George [*South Carolina*] [*Seismograph station code, US Geological Survey*]   (SEIS)
SGS .... Scottish Gaelic Studies [*A publication*]
SGS .... Scottish Guild of Servers [*Episcopalian*]
SGS .... Secretary of the General Staff [*Army*]
SGS .... Segmented Gamma Scanner [*Nuclear energy*]   (NRCH)
SGS .... Signal Generating Station   (CET)
SGS .... Single Green Silk-Covered [*Wire insulation*]
SGS .... Sisters of the Good Samaritan   (ADA)
SGS .... Society of the Golden Section   (EA)
SGS .... Society of the Good Shepherd [*Anglican religious community*]
SGS .... Statistics Gathering System [*NASA*]
SGS .... Steam Generator System [*Nuclear energy*]   (NRCH)
SGS .... Stream Generation Statement [*Data processing*]
SGS .... Stretch Glass Society   (EA)
SGS .... Swiveling Gunner's Station
SGS .... Symbol Generation and Storage [*Data processing*]
SGSC .... Samuel Gompers Stamp Club   (EA)
SGSC .... Standing Group Security Committee [*Obsolete*] [*NATO*]   (NATG)
SGSC .... Strain Gauge Signal Conditioner   (MCD)
SGSE .... Standard Ground Support Equipment
SGSFU ..... Salt-Glazed Structural Facing Units [*Technical drawings*]
SGSHA ...... Shigen Gijutsu Shikenjo Hokoku [*A publication*]
SGSI .... Stabilized Glide Slope Indicator   (NVT)
SGSN .... Skylab Ground Support Network [*NASA*]
SGSNY ...... St. George's Society of New York   (EA)
SGSO .... Space Ground Support Operations [*NASA*]   (KSC)
SGSP .... Salt Gradient Solar Ponds [*Energy source*]
SGSP .... Single Groove, Single Petticoat [*Insulators*]
SGSP .... Society of Glass Science and Practices [*Clarksburg, WV*]   (EA)
SGSR .... Society for General Systems Research [*Washington, DC*]   (EA)
SGSS .... Study Group on Social Security   (EA)
SGSUB ..... Salt-Glazed Structural Unit Base [*Technical drawings*]
SGSVDV .... Steam Generator Stop Valve Dump Valve   (IEEE)
S-GT .... Sachs-Georgi Test [*for syphilis*] [*Also, SG*] [*Obsolete*]
SGT .... Satellite Ground Terminal
SGT .... Schriften der Gesellschaft fuer Theatergeschichte [*A publication*]
SGT .... Seagram's Gin and Tonic
SGT .... Segment Table [*Data processing*]   (IBMDP)
SGT .... Sergeant   (AABC)

SGT .... Small Gas Turbine
SGT .... Small Group Therapy
SGT .... Special Gas Taper [*Thread*]
SGT .... Stuttgart, AR [*Location identifier*] [*FAA*]   (FAAL)
SGT .... Subsystem Ground Test   (MCD)
SGTA .... Servo Gear Train Assembly
Sgte .... Sagitta [*Constellation*]
SGTF .... Steam Generator Test Facility [*Nuclear energy*]   (NRCH)
SGTIA ...... Standing Group Technical Intelligence Agency [*NATO*]   (NATG)
SGTID .... Sawyer's Gas Turbine International [*A publication*]
Sgtl .... Sightlines [*A publication*]
SGTM .... Strain Gauge Thrust Meter
SGTMAJ ...... Sergeant Major
SGTPA ...... Sbornik Trudov. Nauchno-Issledovatel'skii Institut Gigieny Truda i Profzabolevanii Imeni N. I. Makhviladze [*A publication*]
Sgtr .... Sagittarius [*Constellation*]
SGTR .... Standard Government Travel Request
SGTR .... Standardized Government Travel Regulations
SGTR .... Steam Generator Test Rig [*Nuclear energy*]   (NRCH)
SGTR .... Steam Generator Tube Rupture [*Nuclear energy*]   (NRCH)
SGTS .... Satellite Ground Terminal System
SGTS .... Standby Gas Treatment System   (NRCH)
SGTS .... Swing Grip Thermal Stripper
SGU .... Saint George [*Utah*] [*Airport symbol*]   (OAG)
SGU .... Saint George, UT [*Location identifier*] [*FAA*]   (FAAL)
SGU .... Sammelbuch Griechischer Urkunden aus Aegypten [*A publication*]   (BJA)
SGU .... Sidewinder Generator Unit   (NG)
SGU .... Studia Germanistica Upsaliensia [*A publication*]
SGU .... Sveriges Geologiska Undersokning [*Geological Survey of Sweden*] [*Uppsala*] [*Information service*]   (EISS)
SGULF ...... Seagull Resources [*NASDAQ symbol*]   (NQ)
S-G(UN) ..... Secretary-General of the United Nations
SGUS .... Slovak Gymnastic Union Sokol of the USA   (EA)
SGV .... Salivary Gland Virus
SGV .... Sierra Grande [*Argentina*] [*Airport symbol*]   (OAG)
SGV .... Small Granular Vesicle [*Cytology*]
SGV .... Summlung Gemeinverstaendlicher Vortraege und Schriften aus dem Gebiet der Theologie und Religionsgeschichte [*Tuebingen*] [*A publication*]
SGVGA ...... Sbornik Geologickych Ved. Geologie [*A publication*]
SGVLA ...... Sbornik Geologickych Ved. Loziskova Geologie [*A publication*]
SGVS .... Summlung Gemeinverstaendlicher Vortraege und Schriften aus dem Gebiet der Theologie und Religionsgeschichte [*Tuebingen*] [*A publication*]
SGVUA ...... Sbornik Geologickych Ved, Uzita Geofyzika [*A publication*]
SGW .... Salt-Glazed Ware
SGW .... Security Guard Window   (AAG)
SGW .... Senior Grand Warden [*Freemasonry*]
SGW .... South Carolina State College, Orangeburg, SC [*OCLC symbol*]   (OCLC)
SGWLC ..... Steam Generator Water Level Control   (NRCH)
SGWM .... Standing Group Working Memorandum [*NATO*]   (NATG)
SGX .... Selector Group Matrix [*Telecommunications*]   (TEL)
SGX .... Songea [*Tanzania*] [*Airport symbol*]   (OAG)
s-gy--- ...... Guyana [*MARC geographic area code*] [*Library of Congress*]   (LCCP)
SGY .... Skagway [*Alaska*] [*Airport symbol*]   (OAG)
SGY .... Skagway, AK [*Location identifier*] [*FAA*]   (FAAL)
SGY .... Sooner Energy Corp. [*Vancouver Stock Exchange symbol*]
SGym .... Siculorum Gymnasium [*A publication*]
SGZ .... Green Bay, WI [*Location identifier*] [*FAA*]   (FAAL)
SGZ .... Signet Resources, Inc. [*Vancouver Stock Exchange symbol*]
SGZ .... Surface Ground Zero
SGZAB ...... Sanyo Gijutsu Zasshi [*A publication*]
SH .... Air-Cushion Vehicle built by Sealand Hovercraft [*England*] [*Usually used in combination with numerals*]
SH .... Sa Hautesse [*His, or Her, Highness*] [*French*]
SH .... Sacred Heart   (ROG)
SH .... Sacrifice Hit [*Baseball*]
SH .... St. Helena [*Two-letter standard code*]   (CNC)
SH .... Samaritan Free Hospital [*British*]   (ROG)
S/H .... Sample and Hold   (IEEE)
SH .... Schering AG [*Germany*] [*Research code symbol*]
SH .... Schistosoma Hematobium [*A parasitic fluke*]
SH .... Schoolhouse
SH .... Scleroscope Hardness
SH .... Scratch Hardness [*Aerospace*]
SH .... Scripophila Helvetica   (EA)
SH .... Scripta Hierosolymitana   (BJA)
SH .... Second Harvest, the National Food Bank Network [*An association*] [*Chicago, IL*]   (EA)
SH .... Secondhand   (ADA)
SH .... Section Heading Code [*Online database field identifier*]
SH .... Sefer ha-Shanah   (BJA)
SH .... Sekira Hodshit [*Tel Aviv*]   (BJA)
SH .... Semester Hour
SH .... Send Hub [*Telegraphy*]   (TEL)
SH .... Sequence History
SH .... Serum Hepatitis [*Medicine*]

SH .... Service Hours [*Electronics*]   (IEEE)
SH .... Servicio Aereo de Honduras, Sociedad Anonima [*ICAO designator*]   (FAAC)
SH .... Session Handler
SH .... Severely Handicapped
SH .... Sexual Harassment
SH .... Shackle   (AAG)
Sh .... Shadforth's Reserved Judgements [*A publication*]
Sh .... Shadforth's Reserved Judgments [*Australia*]   (DLA)
SH .... Shale [*Lithology*]
SH .... Shall
Sh .... Shand's Reports [*11-41 South Carolina*]   (DLA)
SH .... Shanghai
SH .... Share
Sh .... Shauri   (BJA)
Sh .... [*W. G.*] Shaw's Reports [*30-35 Vermont*]   (DLA)
Sh .... [*G. B.*] Shaw's Reports [*10, 11 Vermont*]   (DLA)
Sh .... Shaw's Scotch Appeal Cases   (DLA)
Sh .... Shaw's Scotch Justiciary Cases   (DLA)
Sh .... Shaw's Scotch Session Cases   (DLA)
Sh .... Shaw's Scotch Teind [*Tithe*] Court Reports   (DLA)
SH .... Sheep   (ROG)
SH .... Sheep Skin [*Bookbinding*]   (ROG)
SH .... Sheet   (AAG)
Sh .... Sheldon's Superior Court Reports [*Buffalo, New York*]   (DLA)
SH .... Shell Development Co. [*Research code symbol*]
sh .... Shells [*Quality of the bottom*] [*Nautical charts*]
Sh .... Shepherd's Alabama Reports   (DLA)
Sh .... Shepley's Reports [*13-18, 21-30 Maine*]   (DLA)
Sh .... Sheriff   (DLA)
SH .... Sherwood Number
SH .... Shield   (MSA)
Sh .... Shiel's Cape Times Law Reports [*South Africa*]   (DLA)
SH .... Shilling [*Obsolete*] [*Monetary unit in Britain*]
SH .... Ship
Sh .... Shipp's Reports [*66-67 North Carolina*]   (DLA)
SH .... Ship's Head [*Heading*] [*Navigation*]
SH .... Ship's Serviceman [*Navy rating*]
SH .... Shipwright
Sh .... Shirley's Reports [*49-55 New Hampshire*]   (DLA)
SH .... Shoal   (ROG)
SH .... Shooting [*FBI standardized term*]
SH .... Short   (ROG)
S/H .... Shorthand
sh .... Shoulder
SH .... Showers   (AAG)
Sh .... Shower's English King's Bench Reports   (DLA)
Sh .... Shower's English Parliamentary Cases   (DLA)
SH .... Shunt [*Electricity*]
SH .... Shuttle   (MCD)
SH .... Sick in Hospital
SH .... Single Heterostructure   (MCD)
SH .... Sinus Histiocytosis [*Medicine*]
S H .... Slovenska Hudba [*A publication*]
SH .... Social History
SH .... Socially Housed [*Experimental animals*]
SH .... Society for HematoPathology [*Memphis, TN*]   (EA)
SH .... Society for the Humanities   (EA)
SH .... Soldiers' Home [*Later, US Soldiers' and Airmen's Home*] [*Government agency*]
SH .... Somatotrophic [*Growth*] Hormone [*Also, GH, STH*] [*Endocrinology*]
S and H ...... Son and Heir [*Genealogy*]
SH .... Source Handshake
SH .... Southern Hemisphere
sh .... Spanish Territories in Northern Morocco [*Spanish North Africa*] [*MARC country of publication code*] [*Library of Congress*]   (LCCP)
SH .... Special Hazards
SH .... Specified Hours
SH .... Specified Hours of Operation [*Broadcasting term*]
S & H .... Speech and Hearing [*Medicine*]
SH .... Speighel Historiael van de Bond van Gentse Germanisten [*A publication*]
S & H .... Sperry & Hutchinson Co.
SH .... Spontaneously Hypertensive [*Medicine*]
sH .... Stathenry [*Also, statH*] [*Unit of inductance*]
SH .... Station Hospital [*Military*]
SH .... Station House
SH .... Stationary High-Power [*Reactor*]   (NRCH)
SH .... Steel Heads
SH .... Steelton & Highspire Railroad Co. [*AAR code*]
S & H .... Steering and Hydroplane [*British*]
SH .... Stored Heading   (MCD)
SH .... Studia Hellenistica [*A publication*]
SH .... Studia Hibernica [*Dublin*] [*A publication*]
SH .... Sulfhydryl [*Chemistry*]
SH .... Sun-Herald [*A publication*]
S & H .... Sundays and Holidays
SH .... Super-High-Frequency [*Radio wave*]   (NG)
SH .... Surgical History [*Medicine*]

SH .... Switch Handler [*Telecommunications*] (TEL)
SH .... Sydney Herald [*A publication*]
SH1 .... Ship's Serviceman, First Class [*Navy rating*]
SH2 .... Ship's Serviceman, Second Class [*Navy rating*]
SH₂ .... Supercritical Hydrogen [*NASA*] (NASA)
SH3 .... Ship's Serviceman, Third Class [*Navy rating*]
SHA .... Ozark, AL [*Location identifier*] [*FAA*] (FAAL)
SHA .... Safety Hazard Analysis (MCD)
SHA .... Sailplane Homebuilders Association (EA)
SHA .... Sample and Hold Amplifier
SHA .... Scriptores Historiae Augustae [*Classical studies*] (OCD)
SHA .... Secretariat for Hispanic Affairs (National Conference of
　　　　　　　Catholic Bishops) [*Washington, DC*] (EA)
SHA .... Shakwak Exploration Co. [*Vancouver Stock Exchange symbol*]
SHA .... Shanghai [*China*] [*Airport symbol*] (OAG)
ShA .... Shulhan 'Arukh (BJA)
SHA .... Sidereal Hour Angle
SHA .... Sitzungsberichte. Heidelberg Akademie der Wissenschaft [*A
　　　　　　　publication*]
SHA .... Smith-Hurd's Illinois Annotated Statutes (DLA)
SHA .... Societe Historique Acadienne [*Acadian Historical Society*]
　　　　　　　[*Canada*] (EA)
SHA .... Society for Historical Archaeology
SHA .... Society for Humane Abortion (EA)
SHA .... Society for Humanistic Anthropology [*American
　　　　　　　Anthropological Association*] (EA)
SHA .... Sodium Hydroxide Addition (NRCH)
SHA .... Solid Homogeneous Assembly [*Nuclear energy*]
SHA .... Southern Historical Association (EA)
SHA .... Spherical Harmonic Analysis [*Geophysics*]
SHA .... Spring Hill [*Alabama*] [*Seismograph station code, US
　　　　　　　Geological Survey*] (SEIS)
SHA .... Station Housing Allowance (MCD)
SHa .... Sulgi Hymn A (BJA)
SHA .... Support Harness Assembly
SHA .... System Hazard Analyses [*NASA*] (NASA)
SHAA .... Schaak Electronics, Inc. [*NASDAQ symbol*] (NQ)
SHAA .... Sealed Head Access Area [*Nuclear energy*] (NRCH)
SHAA .... Serum Hepatitis Associated Antigen [*Hematology*]
SHAA .... Society of Hearing Aid Audiologists [*Later, NHAS*] (EA)
SHAA-Ab ... Serum Hepatitis Associated Antigen-Antibody [*Hematology*]
SHA-Ab ...... Serum Hepatitis Associated Antibody [*Hematology*]
Shab .... Shabbath (BJA)
SHABS ...... Shock Absorber
SHAC .... Society for the History of Alchemy and Chemistry (EA)
SHAC .... Solar Heating and Air Conditioning
SHACC ...... Servicing Hotels and the Caribbean Community
SHACO ..... Shorthand Coding
SHACOB .. Solar Heating and Cooling of Buildings [*Energy Research and
　　　　　　　Development Administration*]
Shad .... Shadforth's Reports [*Australia*] [*A publication*] (DLA)
SHAD .... Shallow Habitat Air Dive [*Navy*]
SHAD .... Sharpe Army Depot [*California*]
SHAD .... Shipboard Hazards Appraisal and Defense (CINC)
SHADCOM ... Shipping Advisory Committee [*NATO*]
SHADE ...... Shielded Hot-Air-Drum Evaporator [*Concentrator for
　　　　　　　hazardous wastes*]
SHADO ...... Supreme Headquarters, Alien Defense Organization [*in
　　　　　　　television program "UFO"*]
SHADRAC ... Shelter Housed Automatic Digital Random Access [*Data
　　　　　　　processing*]
SHAEF ...... Supreme Headquarters, Allied Expeditionary Force [*Europe*]
　　　　　　　[*World War II*]
SHAF .... Staying Healthy after Fifty [*Project*] [*AARP*]
SHAFB ...... Sheppard Air Force Base [*Texas*] (AAG)
SHAFR ...... Society for Historians of American Foreign Relations
SHAFT ...... Second Home All-Inclusive First Trust [*Real estate*]
SHAG .... Simplified High-Accuracy Guidance [*NASA*] (NASA)
SHAGAn ... Societe d'Histoire et d'Archeologie de Gand. Annales [*A
　　　　　　　publication*]
SHAGBull... Societe d'Histoire et d'Archeologie de Gand. Bulletin [*A
　　　　　　　publication*]
SHAH .... Shire National Corp. [*NASDAQ symbol*] (NQ)
SHAK .... Shakespeare
Shakes Jah ... Shakespeare-Jahrbuch [*A publication*]
Shakespeare-Jahrb ... Shakespeare-Jahrbuch [*A publication*]
Shakespeare Q ... Shakespeare Quarterly [*A publication*]
Shakespeare S ... Shakespeare Survey [*A publication*]
Shakes Q ... Shakespeare Quarterly [*A publication*]
Shakes Surv ... Shakespeare Survey [*A publication*]
Shakhtnoe Stroit ... Shakhtnoe Stroitel'stvo [*USSR*] [*A publication*]
Shak-Jahrb ... Shakespeare-Jahrbuch [*A publication*]
ShakS .... Shakespeare Studies [*A publication*]
SHAL .... Subject Heading Authority List [*Data processing*]
Shale .... Decrees and Judgments in Federal Anti-Trust Cases [*United
　　　　　　　States*] (DLA)
Shale Ctry ... Shale Country [*A publication*]
Shalm .... Shalmaneser (BJA)
SHALOM.... Synchronous Halo Monitor [*NASA*]
SHALPub ... Societe Historique et Archeologique dans le Duche de
　　　　　　　Limbourg. Publications [*A publication*]

SHAM .... Salicylhydroxamic Acid [*Chelating agent*]
SHAME ...... Save, Help Animals Man Exploits [*Connecticut organization*]
SHAME ...... Society to Humiliate, Aggravate, Mortify, and Embarrass
　　　　　　　Smokers
SHAMYR .... Shomrei Mitzvot Yotzei Russia (BJA)
SHAN .... Shannon Oil & Gas [*NASDAQ symbol*] (NQ)
Shan .... Shannon's Unreported Tennessee Cases (DLA)
Shan Cas ... Shannon's Tennessee Cases (DLA)
Shand .... Shand's Reports [*11-41 South Carolina*] (DLA)
Shand Pr ... Shand's Practice, Scotch Court of Sessions (DLA)
SHANE ...... Steerable Hydrophone Array, Nonlinear Element
SHANICLE ... Short-Range Navigation Vehicle [*System*] [*Air Force*]
Shankland's St ... Shankland's Tennessee Public Statutes (DLA)
Shannon Cas (Tenn) ... Shannon's Unreported Tennessee Cases (DLA)
Shannon's Code ... Shannon's Tennessee Annotated Code (DLA)
SHANT ...... Shantung [*Province in China*] (ROG)
Shantung Med J ... Shantung Medical Journal [*People's Republic of China*]
　　　　　　　[*A publication*]
SHAP .... Ship Acquisition Plan [*Navy*] (CAAL)
SHAPE ...... Simulated Hospital Administration and Planning Exercise
SHAPE ...... Supersonic High-Altitude Parachute Experiment [*NASA*]
SHAPE ...... Supreme Headquarters, Allied Powers Europe [*NATO*]
SHAPEX .... SHAPE [*Supreme Headquarters Allied Powers Europe*] Annual
　　　　　　　Command Exercise [*NATO*] (NATG)
SHAPM ...... Ship Acquisition Project Manager [*Navy*]
Sh App ...... Shaw's Scotch Appeal Cases, House of Lords (DLA)
ShAr .... Shulhan 'Arukh (BJA)
SHAR .... Simplified Hourly Absence Reporting (MCD)
SHAR .... Sriharikota Island Launch Complex [*India*]
SHARE ...... Salvadorean Humanitarian Aid, Research, and Education [*In
　　　　　　　association name, SHARE Foundation*] (EA)
SHARE ...... Share Happily and Reap Endlessly [*Hollywood women's charity
　　　　　　　organization*]
SHARE ...... Shared Area Resources Exchange [*Library network*]
SHARE ...... So Handicapped All Read Easily
SHARE ...... Society to Help Avoid Redundant Effort [*in data processing*]
SHARE ...... Systems for Heat and Radiation Energy
SHAREM .... Ship ASW [*Antisubmarine Warfare*] Readiness Effectiveness
　　　　　　　Measuring Program
SHARES.... Shared Acquisitions and Retention System
Shark Elec ... Sharkey's Practice of Election Committees [*2nd ed.*]
　　　　　　　[*1866*] (DLA)
SHARP ...... School Health Additional Referral Program [*Public Health
　　　　　　　Service*]
SHARP ...... Ships Analysis and Retrieval Program [*Navy*]
Sharpe ...... Calendar of Coroners Rolls of the City of London (DLA)
Sharpe ...... Sharpe's London Magazine [*A publication*]
SHARPS.... Ship/Helicopter Acoustic Range-Prediction System
　　　　　　　[*Navy*] (NVT)
Shars Black ... Sharswood's Edition of Blackstone's Commentaries (DLA)
Shars Bl Comm ... Sharswood's Edition of Blackstone's
　　　　　　　Commentaries (DLA)
Shars & B Lead Cas Real Prop ... Sharswood and Budd's Leading Cases on
　　　　　　　Real Property (DLA)
Shars Comm L ... Sharswood's Commercial Law (DLA)
Shars Law Lec ... Sharswood's Lectures on the Profession of the Law (DLA)
Shars Leg Eth ... Sharswood's Legal Ethics (DLA)
Shars Tab Ca ... Sharswood's Table of Cases, Connecticut (DLA)
SHAS .... Shared Hospital Accounting System [*Data processing*]
SHAS .... Shawmut Corp. [*NASDAQ symbol*] (NQ)
ShaS .... Shishah Sedarim (BJA)
SHAT .... Shatterproof Glass [*NASDAQ symbol*] (NQ)
SHATAn ..... Societe Historique et Archeologique de Tournai. Annales [*A
　　　　　　　publication*]
SHATC ...... SHAPE [*Supreme Headquarters Allied Powers Europe*]
　　　　　　　Technical Center [*Formerly, SADTC*] [*NATO*] (NATG)
SHAVE ...... Sugar Hotel Alpha Victor Echo [*Apollo 10 astronauts' code for
　　　　　　　shaving operation*]
Shaw .... [*W. G.*] Shaw's Reports [*30-35 Vermont*] (DLA)
Shaw .... [*G. B.*] Shaw's Reports [*10, 11 Vermont*] (DLA)
Shaw .... Shaw's Scotch Appeal Cases (DLA)
Shaw .... Shaw's Scotch Court of Session Cases, First Series (DLA)
Shaw .... Shaw's Scotch Justiciary Cases (DLA)
Shaw .... Shaw's Scotch Teind [*Tithe*] Court Reports (DLA)
SHAW........ Sitzungsberichte. Heidelberg Akademie der Wissenschaft [*A
　　　　　　　publication*]
Shaw App ... Shaw's Scotch Appeal Cases, English House of Lords (DLA)
ShawB....... Shaw Bulletin [*A publication*]
SHAWCO ... Students' Health and Welfare Centers Organization
Shaw Crim Cas ... Shaw's Criminal Cases, Scotch Justiciary Court (DLA)
Shaw & D ... Shaw and Dunlop's Scotch Court of Session Reports, First
　　　　　　　Series (DLA)
Shaw D & B ... Shaw, Dunlop, and Bell's Scotch Court of Session Reports,
　　　　　　　First Series (DLA)
Shaw D & B Supp ... Shaw, Dunlop, and Bell's Supplement, Containing
　　　　　　　House of Lords Decisions [*Scotland*] (DLA)
Shaw Dec... Shaw's Decisions in Scotch Court of Sessions, First
　　　　　　　Series (DLA)
Shaw Dig ... Shaw's Digest of Decisions [*Scotland*] (DLA)
Shaw & Dunl ... Shaw and Dunlop's Scotch Court of Session Reports, First
　　　　　　　Series (DLA)

Shaw Dunl & B ... Shaw, Dunlop, and Bell's Scotch Court of Session Cases, First Series [1821-38] (DLA)
Shaw (G B) ... [G. B.] Shaw's Reports [10, 11 Vermont] (DLA)
Shaw HL ..... Shaw's Scotch Appeal Cases, House of Lords [1821-24] (DLA)
Shaw J .... John Shaw's Justiciary Cases [1848-52] [Scotland] (DLA)
Shaw Jus .... [John] Shaw's Justiciary Cases [1848-52] [Scotland] (DLA)
SHAWL ...... Special Hard-Target Assault Weapon LAW (RDA)
Shaw & M ... Shaw and Maclean's Scotch Appeal Cases (DLA)
Shaw & Macl ... Shaw and Maclean's Scotch Appeal Cases (DLA)
Shaw & M Sc App Cas ... Shaw and Maclean's Scotch Appeal Cases [1835-38] (DLA)
Shaw P ...... Patrick Shaw's Justiciary Cases [1819-31] [Scotland] (DLA)
Shaw PL ..... Shaw's Parish Law (DLA)
Shaw R ...... Shaw Review [A publication]
Shaw Sc App Cas ... Shaw's Scotch Appeal Cases, House of Lords [1821-24] (DLA)
Shaw TC .... Shaw's Scotch Teind [Tithe] Cases [1821-31] (DLA)
Shaw T Cas ... Shaw's Scotch Teind [Tithe] Court Reports (DLA)
Shaw Teind ... Shaw's Scotch Teind [Tithe] Court Decisions [1821-31] (DLA)
Shaw (VT) ... [G. B.] Shaw's Reports [10, 11 Vermont] (DLA)
Shaw (VT) ... [W. G.] Shaw's Reports [30, 35 Vermont] (DLA)
Shaw W & C ... Shaw, Wilson, and Courtenay's Scotch Appeals Reports, House of Lords (DLA)
Shaw (W G) ... [W. G.] Shaw's Reports [30-35 Vermont] (DLA)
SHAZAM .... [Grace of] Selena, [Strength of] Hippolyta, [Skill of] Ariadne, [Fleetness of] Zephyrus, [Beauty of] Aurora, [Wisdom of] Minerva [Word used to change Mary Batson into Mary Marvel in the comic book series]
SHAZAM ... [Wisdom of] Solomon, [Strength of] Hercules, [Stamina of] Atlas, [Power of] Zeus, [Courage of] Achilles, [Speed of] Mercury [Word used to change Billy Batson into Captain Marvel in the comic book series]
SHB .... Nakashibetsu [Japan] [Airport symbol] (OAG)
SHB .... Scotty's, Inc. [NYSE symbol]
SHB .... Second-Harmonic Band
SHB .... Shelbyville, IN [Location identifier] [FAA] (FAAL)
SHB .... Silhouette Harness Board (MCD)
SHB .... Sodium Hydroxybutyrate [Organic chemistry]
SHB .... Subacute Hepatitis with Bridging [Medicine]
SHBD .... Serum Hydroxybutyrate Dehydrogenase [An enzyme]
SHBG .... Sex-Hormone-Binding Globulin [Endocrinology]
SHBG .... Sexual Hormone Binding Globulin [Clinical chemistry]
SHBLDR ..... Shipbuilder (MSA)
S and H Bull ... Smoking and Health Bulletin [A publication]
SHC .... Chief Ship's Serviceman [Navy rating]
SHC .... Mount St. Helena [California] [Seismograph station code, US Geological Survey] (SEIS)
SHC .... Sacred Heart College [Alabama]
SHC .... Seton Hill College [Pennsylvania]
SHC .... Shaklee Corporation [NYSE symbol]
SHC .... Shell Canada Ltd. [Toronto Stock Exchange symbol] [Vancouver Stock Exchange symbol]
SHC .... Shipping Coordinating Committee [Coast Guard]
SHC .... Shire Indaselassie [Ethiopia] [Airport symbol] (OAG)
SHC .... Siena Heights College [Michigan]
SHC .... Silicones Health Council [Washington, DC] (EA)
SHC .... Sky Harbor Air Service, Inc. [Cheyenne, WY] [FAA designator] (FAAC)
SHC .... Societe Historique du Canada [Canadian Historical Association - CHA]
SHC .... Sodium Hypochlorite [Inorganic chemistry]
SHC .... Southern Humanities Conference (EA)
SHC .... Spherical Harmonic Coefficient [Geophysics]
SHC .... Spring Hill College [Mobile, AL]
SHC .... Stanford Humanities Center [Stanford University] [Research center] (RCD)
SHC .... Superheat Control [Boilers]
SHC .... Superhybrid Composite [Laminate]
SHC .... Superior Heliocentric Conjunction
SHC .... Surveillance Helicopter Company [Army] (AABC)
SHCA .... Safety Helmet Council of America [Los Angeles, CA] (EA)
SHCA .... Siberian Husky Club of America
SHCA .... Solid Homogeneous Critical Assembly [Nuclear reactor] [Japan]
SHC-BRC ... Small Homes Council-Building Research Council [University of Illinois] [Research center] (RCD)
SHCC .... Statewide Health Coordinating Council
SHCGSAS ... Shrimp Harvesters Coalition of the Gulf and South Atlantic States (EA)
Shchorichnyk Ukrains'ke Bot Tov ... Shchorichnyk. Ukrayins'ke Botanichne Tovarystvo [A publication]
SHCJ .... Society of the Holy Child Jesus [Roman Catholic women's religious order]
SHCM .... Master Chief Ship's Serviceman [Navy rating]
SHCOS ...... Supreme Headquarters, Chief of Staff [World War II]
SHCPP .... Sanitation Handbook of Consumer Protection Programs
SHCR .... Shipping Container
SHCR .... Skyline Hikers of the Canadian Rockies (EA)
Sh Crim Cas ... Shaw's Justiciary Court, Criminal Cases [Scotland] (DLA)
SHCRT ...... Short Circuit (AAG)

SHCS .... Senior Chief Ship's Serviceman [Navy rating]
SHCS .... Springer Series on Health Care and Society [A publication]
SHCSR .... Spicilegium Historicum Congregationis Smi Redemptoris [A publication]
SHCS USAF ... School of Health Care Sciences, United States Air Force (AFM)
SHCT .... Sheriff Court [Legal] [British]
SHCT .... Studies in the History of Christian Thought [A publication] (BJA)
Sh Ct Rep .. Sheriff Court Reports [Scotland] (DLA)
Sh Ct of Sess ... Shaw's Scotch Court of Session Cases (DLA)
SHCW .... Scottish History from Contemporary Writers [A publication]
SHD .... Shade
SHD .... Shahrud [Iran] [Seismograph station code, US Geological Survey] (SEIS)
SHD .... Shield Development [Vancouver Stock Exchange symbol]
SHD .... Ship's Diver [Navy] [British]
SHD .... Shode
SHD .... Should (ROG)
SHD .... Shroud (AAG)
SHD .... Silo Hardsite Defense
SHD .... Society for the History of Discoveries
SHD .... Special Handling Designator (MCD)
SHD .... Staunton [Virginia] [Airport symbol] (OAG)
SHD .... Staunton/Waynesboro/Harrisonburg, VA [Location identifier] [FAA] (FAAL)
SHd .... Sulgi Hymn D (BJA)
SHDA .... Selenaheptadecanoic Acid [Organic chemistry]
SHDC .... Sacred Heart Dominican College [Texas]
SHDC .... Subject Headings Used in the Dictionary Catalog [Later, LCSH] [A publication]
SHDI .... Supraoptic-Hypophyseal Diabetes Insipidus [Endocrinology]
Sh Dig .... Shaw's Digest of Decisions [Scotland] (DLA)
SHDPS .... St. Helena and Dependencies Philatelic Society (EA)
SHDR .... Service and Hardware Difficulty Reports (MCD)
SHDS .... Second Harmonic Discrimination System (MCD)
Sh & Dunl ... Shaw and Dunlop's Scotch Court of Session Reports, First Series (DLA)
SHE .... Securities Hazards Expert [In film title]
SHE .... Self-Help Enterprises [An association] [Visalia, CA] (EA)
SHE .... Semihomogeneous Experiment
SHE .... Sheba Copper Mines [Vancouver Stock Exchange symbol]
SHE .... Shemkha [USSR] [Seismograph station code, US Geological Survey] (SEIS)
SHE .... Shenyang [China] [Airport symbol] (OAG)
SHE .... Siderphile Superheavy Element [Physics]
SHE .... Signal Handling Equipment (AAG)
SHE .... Society for History Education (EA)
SHE .... Sodium Heat Engine
SHE .... Spares Handling Expense
SHE .... Special Handling Equipment
SHE .... Standard Hydrogen Electrode [Electrochemistry]
SHE .... Subject Headings for Engineering [A publication]
S/HE .... Sundays and Holidays Excepted
SHE .... Supercritical Helium (KSC)
SHE .... Superheavy Element [Nuclear physics]
SHE .... Syrian Hamster Embryonic [Cells]
SHEAR .... Society for Historians of the Early American Republic (EA)
Shear Cont ... Shearwood on Contract [1897] (DLA)
Shearm & Red Neg ... Shearman and Redfield on the Law of Negligence (DLA)
Shear Pers Pr ... Shearwood on Personal Property [1882] (DLA)
Shear & R Neg ... Shearman and Redfield on the Law of Negligence (DLA)
Shear R Pr ... Shearwood on Real Property [3rd ed.] [1885] (DLA)
Sheb .... Shebi'it (BJA)
Shebi .... Shebi'it (BJA)
Shebu .... Shebu'oth (BJA)
SHED .... Settlement Houses Employment Development [Large group of settlement houses]
SHEDS .... Ship Helicopter Extended Delivery System [Navy] (NVT)
SHEEO .... State Higher Education Executive Officers Association (EA)
Sheepfarming Annu ... Sheepfarming Annual [A publication]
Sheepfarming Annu Massey Agr Coll ... Sheepfarming Annual. Massey Agricultural College [A publication]
Sheet Met Ind ... Sheet Metal Industries [A publication]
Sheet Met Platework News ... Sheet Metal and Plateworking News [A publication]
SHEF .... Sandwich Chef, Inc. [NASDAQ symbol] (NQ)
SHEFD .... Sheffield [England]
SHEH .... Stanford Honors Essays in the Humanities [A publication]
SHEIA .... Steric Hindrance Enzyme Immunoassay [Clinical chemistry]
Sheil Ir Bar ... Sheil's Sketches of the Irish Bar (DLA)
SHEK .... Schweizer Hilfswerk fuer Emigrationskinder (BJA)
Shek .... Shekalim (BJA)
SHEL .... Sheldahl Co. [NASDAQ symbol] (NQ)
SHEL .... Shore ELINT [Electromagnetic Intelligence] System [Navy] (NG)
Shel Bank ... Shelford's Bankrupt and Insolvency Law [3rd ed.] [1862] (DLA)
Shel Ca ..... Shelley's Cases in Vol. 1 of Coke's Reports (DLA)
Sheld .... Sheldon's Superior Court Reports [Buffalo, New York] (DLA)
Sheldon ..... Sheldon's Superior Court Reports [Buffalo, New York] (DLA)

Sheld Subr ... Sheldon on Subrogation   (DLA)
SHELF .... Super-Hard Extremely-Low Frequency   (MCD)
Shelf Lun ... Shelford on Lunacy   (DLA)
Shelf Mar & Div ... Shelford on Marriage and Divorce   (DLA)
Shel High ... Shelford on Highways [4th ed.] [1869]   (DLA)
Shel J St Com ... Shelford on Joint Stock Companies [2nd ed.] [1870]   (DLA)
Shell Agric ... Shell in Agriculture [A publication]
Shell Aviat News ... Shell Aviation News [A publication]
Shell Bitum Rev ... Shell Bitumin Review [A publication]
Shell Devel Co Explor and Production Research Div Pub ... Shell Development Company. Exploration and Production Research Division. Publication [A publication]
Shellfish ..... Shellfish. Market Review and Outlook [A publication]
Shell House J ... Shell House Journal [A publication]
Shell J .... Shell Journal [A publication]
Shell Mag .... Shell Magazine [England] [A publication]
Shell Polym ... Shell Polymers [A publication]
SHELLREP ... Shelling Report [Military]   (NATG)
Shel Lun ..... Shelford on Lunacy [2nd ed.] [1847]   (DLA)
Shel M & D ... Shelford on Marriage and Divorce [1841]   (DLA)
Shel Mort ... Shelford on Mortmain and Charitable Uses [1836]   (DLA)
Shel Prob ... Shelford on Probate, Legacy, Etc. [2nd ed.] [1861]   (DLA)
SHELREP ... Shelling Report [Military]
SHELREPT ... Shelling Report [Military]   (MUGU)
Shel R Pr St ... Sheldon's Real Property Statutes [9th ed.] [1893]   (DLA)
Shel Ry ...... Shelford on Railways [4th ed.] [1869]   (DLA)
Shelter ...... Shelterforce [A publication]
Shel Will ... Shelford on Wills [1838]   (DLA)
SHEMA ...... Steam Heating Equipment Manufacturers Association [Defunct]   (EA)
S-HEMP ..... System - Hydraulic, Electrical, Mechanical, Pneumatic
Shen .... Shenandoah [A publication]
SHEN .... Shenandoah National Park
Shep .... Select Cases [37-39 Alabama]   (DLA)
Shep .... Shepherd's Alabama Reports   (DLA)
Shep .... Shepley's Reports [13-18, 21-30 Maine]   (DLA)
SHEP .... Shock Hydrodynamic Elastic Plastic   (MCD)
SHEP .... Solar High-Energy Particles
Shep Abr ... Sheppard's Abridgment   (DLA)
Shepherd ... Shepherd's Reports [19-21, 24-41, 60, 63, 64 Alabama]   (DLA)
Sheph Sel Cas ... Shepherd's Select Cases [Alabama]   (DLA)
Shepley ..... Shepley's Reports [13-18, 21-30 Maine]   (DLA)
Shep Prec ... Sheppard's Precedent of Precedents [9th ed.] [1825]   (DLA)
Shep Sel Cas ... Shepherd's Select Cases [Alabama]   (DLA)
SHERB ...... Sandia Human Error Rate Bank [NASA]   (NASA)
Sher Ct Rep ... Sheriff Court Reports [Scotland]   (DLA)
SHERK .... [The] New Schaff-Herzog Encyclopaedia of Religious Knowledge [A publication]   (BJA)
SHERLOC ... Something to Help Everyone Reduce Load on Computers [Army]
Sherst Delo ... Sherstyanoe Delo [A publication]
SHERVICK ... Sherman Tanks Converted into Tractors by Vickers Armstrong
Shev .... Shevi'it   (BJA)
Shevu .... Shevu'ot   (BJA)
SHEX .... Sundays and Holidays Excepted [Business and trade]
S & H/exct ... Sundays and Holidays Excepted in Lay Days
SHF .... Schiffner Oilfield & Technology Corp. [Vancouver Stock Exchange symbol]
SHF .... Self Help Foundation [Waverly, IA]   (EA)
SHF .... Shawinigan Falls [Quebec] [Seismograph station code, US Geological Survey] [Closed]   (SEIS)
SHF .... Shift   (MSA)
SHF .... Sisters of the Holy Faith [Roman Catholic religious order]
SHF .... Sisters of the Holy Family [Roman Catholic religious order]
SHF .... Societe de l'Histoire de France [A publication]
SHF .... Soil and Health Foundation [Later, SHS]   (EA)
SHF .... Storage-Handling Facility [Nuclear energy]   (NRCH)
SHF .... Structures Heating Facility
SHF .... Super-High-Frequency [Radio wave]
SHF .... University of Sheffield, Postgraduate School of Librarianship, Sheffield, England [OCLC symbol]   (OCLC)
SHFA .... Single Conductor, Heat and Flame Resistant, Armor [Cable]
SHFABull ... Societe de l'Histoire de France. Annuaire Bulletin [A publication]
SHF/EHF .... Super-High Frequency/Extremely-High Frequency   (MCD)
SHFF .... Societe Historique et Folklorique Francaise   (EA)
SHFG .... Society for History in the Federal Government   (EA)
SHF-GMFSC ... Super-High-Frequency - Ground Mobile Forces Satellite Communications   (MCD)
SHFL .... Shoulder Horizontal Flexion [Sports medicine]
SHFS .... Superhyperfine Structure
SHFT .... Shift   (FAAC)
SHF-TDMA-MODEM ... Super-High-Frequency - Time Division Multiple Access - MODEM   (MCD)
SHFTG .... Shafting [Freight]
SHFTGR ...... Shaft Gear
SHFXF .... Shadowfax Resources Ltd. [NASDAQ symbol]   (NQ)
SHG .... Second-Harmonic Generation [LASER]
SHG .... Selected Honor Guards   (MCD)
SHG .... Sharpe Energy and Resources Ltd. [Vancouver Stock Exchange symbol]

SHG .... Shirttail Gulch [California] [Seismograph station code, US Geological Survey]   (SEIS)
SHG .... Short-Handed Goal [Hockey]
SHG .... Shungnak [Alaska] [Airport symbol]   (OAG)
SHG .... Shungnak, AK [Location identifier] [FAA]   (FAAL)
SHG .... Sister Servants of the Holy Ghost and Mary Immaculate [Roman Catholic religious order]
SHG .... Special High Grade [Zinc metal]
SHGED .... Shoni Geka [A publication]
SHGM .... Society for the History of the Germans in Maryland
SHGNA ...... Shigen [A publication]
SHGO .... Shop & Go, Inc. [NASDAQ symbol]   (NQ)
SHH .... Shenandoah Resources Ltd. [Vancouver Stock Exchange symbol]
SHH .... Shishmaref [Alaska] [Airport symbol]   (OAG)
SHH .... Shishmaref, AR [Location identifier] [FAA]   (FAAL)
SHH .... Sociedad Honoraria Hispanica   (EA)
SHHC .... Scherer [R. P.] Corporation [NASDAQ symbol]   (NQ)
Shhh .... Self-Help for Hard of Hearing People [An association] [Bethesda, MD]   (EA)
SHHPB ...... Shu-Hsueh Hsueh-Pao [A publication]
SHHV .... Society for Health and Human Values   (EA)
SHI .... Sheet Iron
SHI .... Shimojishima [Japan] [Airport symbol]   (OAG)
SHI .... Shiraz [Iran] [Seismograph station code, US Geological Survey]   (SEIS)
S-HI .... System-Human Interaction
SHib .... Studia Hibernica [A publication]
SHID .... Spartan Hardware Inspection Discrepancy [Missiles]   (MCD)
SHIEF .... Shared Information Elicitation Facility [Data processing]
Shiel .... Cape Times Law Reports, Edited by Shiel   (DLA)
Shiel .... Shiel's Cape Colony Reports   (DLA)
SHIELD ...... Supreme Headquarters, International Espionage Law-Enforcement Division [Organization in comic book "Nick Fury, Agent of SHIELD"]
SHIELD ...... Sylvania High-Intelligence Electronic Defense   (MCD)
Shig .... Shigella [Bacteriology]
Shikoku Acta Med ... Shikoku Acta Medica [A publication]
Shikoku Agr Res ... Shikoku Agricultural Research [A publication]
SHIL .... Shillelagh [Army surface-to-surface missile]   (AABC)
SHIL .... Shiloh National Military Park
Shill WC ... Shillman's Workmen's Compensation Cases [Ireland]   (DLA)
Shimadzu Rev ... Shimadzu Review [A publication]
Shinagawa Tech Rep ... Shinagawa Technical Report [A publication]
SHIN BET ... Israel General Security Service [Acronym represents Hebrew phrase]
SHINC .... Sundays and Holidays Included [Business and trade]
SHINCOM ... Ship Integrated Communications System [Canadian Navy]
SHINCOM ... Shipboard Integrated Interior Communication System   (MCD)
Shingle ..... [The] Shingle. Philadelphia Bar Association   (DLA)
Shinko Electr J ... Shinko Electric Journal [A publication]
SHINMACS ... Shipborne Integrated Machinery Control System [Canadian Navy]
Shinn Repl ... Shinn's Treatise on American Law of Replevin   (DLA)
Shinshu Med J ... Shinshu Medical Journal [Japan] [A publication]
Shinshu Univ Fac Sci J ... Shinshu University. Faculty of Science. Journal [A publication]
SHIO .... Sveriges Hantverks- och Industriorganisation-Familjefoeretagen [Federation of Trades, Industries, and Family Enterprises] [Stockholm, Sweden]
SHIOER ...... Statistical Historical Input/Output Error Rate Utility [Sperry UNIVAC]
SHIP .... Self-Help Improvement Program
SHIP .... Self-Help Issue Point [Army]
SHIP .... Separator for Heavy Ion Reaction Products
SHIP .... Shipment
SHIP .... Slater Hall Information Products [Washington, DC] [Information service]   (EISS)
SHIP .... Special Handling Inventory Procedure   (MCD)
SHIP .... Standard Hardware Interface Program
SHIPACS ..... Ship Acquisition Study [Navy]
SHIPALT .... Ship Alteration [Navy]
Shipbldg Mar Engng Int ... Shipbuilding and Marine Engineering International [A publication]
Shipbldg Shipp Rec ... Shipbuilding and Shipping Record [A publication]
Ship Boat ... Ship and Boat [A publication]
Ship and Boat ... Ship and Boat International [A publication]
Ship & Boat Int ... Ship and Boat International [A publication]
Shipbuild Mar Engine Build ... Shipbuilder and Marine Engine Builder [England] [A publication]
Shipbuild Mar Eng Int ... Shipbuilding and Marine Engineering International [A publication]
Shipbuild & Mar Engng Int ... Shipbuilding and Marine Engineering International [A publication]
Shipcare Marit Manage ... Shipcare and Maritime Management [A publication]
Ship Com Aviation ... Shipping, Commerce, and Aviation of Australia [A publication]
SHIPCON ... Shipping Control [NATO]   (NATG)
SHIPDA ...... Shipping Data
SHIPDAFOL ... Shipping Data Follows

SHIPDAT.... Shipping Date
SHIPDTO.... Ship on Depot Transfer Order
Ship Gaz .... Shipping Gazette [*London*]   (DLA)
SHIPGO..... Shipping Order
SHIPIM....... Ship Immediately
Shipp........ Shipp's Reports [*66-67 North Carolina*]   (DLA)
Shipping Statis ... Shipping Statistics [*A publication*]
Shipping Statis and Econ ... Shipping Statistics and Economics [*A publication*]
Shipp Weekly ... Shipping Weekly [*A publication*]
Shipp Wld Shipbldr ... Shipping World and Shipbuilder [*A publication*]
Shipp World & Shipbuild ... Shipping World and Shipbuilder [*A publication*]
SHIPREQ.... Ship to Apply on Requisition
SHIPS........ Shipment Planning System [*Military*]
SHIPSYSCOM ... Ship Systems Command
SHIPT........ Shipment
SHIR........ Ship History and Inventory Record [*Navy*]   (NG)
SHIRAN...... S-Band High-Accuracy Ranging and Navigation
Shir Cr L ... Shirley's Sketch of the Criminal Law [*2nd ed.*] [*1889*]   (DLA)
Shire & Munic R ... Shire and Municipal Record [*A publication*]
Shire Munic Rec ... Shire and Municipal Record [*A publication*]
Shire & Munic Rec ... Shire and Municipal Record [*A publication*]
Shirl .... Shirley's Reports [*49-55 New Hampshire*]   (DLA)
Shirley .... Shirley's Reports [*49-55 New Hampshire*]   (DLA)
Shirley Inst Bull ... Shirley Institute. Bulletin [*A publication*]
Shirley Inst Mem ... Shirley Institute. Memoirs [*A publication*]
Shirl LC..... Shirley's Leading Crown Cases [*England*]   (DLA)
Shir Mag L ... Shirley on Magisterial Law [*2nd ed.*] [*1896*]   (DLA)
SHIRTDIF ... Storage, Handling, and Retrieval of Technical Data in Image Formation [*Data processing*]   (IEEE)
SHIU........ Steering Hover Indicator Unit   (MCD)
Shivaji Univ J ... Shivaji University. Journal [*A publication*]
Shivaji Univ Sci J ... Shivaji University. Science Journal [*A publication*]
Shizenshi-Kenkyu Occas Pap Osaka Mus Nat Hist ... Shizenshi-Kenkyu Occasional Papers. Osaka Museum of Natural History [*A publication*]
Sh-J.......... Shakespeare-Jahrbuch [*A publication*]
SHJ........... Sharjah [*United Arab Emirates*] [*Airport symbol*]   (OAG)
SHJ........... Shionomisaki [*Japan*] [*Seismograph station code, US Geological Survey*]   (SEIS)
SHJ........... Society for Humanistic Judaism   (EA)
Sh-Jb .... Shakespeare-Jahrbuch [*A publication*]
SHJC........ Sacred Heart Junior College [*North Carolina; Pennsylvania*]
SHJM .... Sisters of the Sacred Hearts of Jesus and Mary [*Roman Catholic religious order*]
SHJP .... [*A*] History of the Jewish People in the Time of Jesus Christ [*Emil Schurer*] [*A publication*]   (BJA)
SHJR .... Senate-House Joint Reports   (DLA)
Sh Jus .... Shaw's Scotch Justiciary Cases   (DLA)
Sh Just....... [*P.*] Shaw's Justiciary Decisions [*Scotland*]   (DLA)
SHK.......... Sehonghong [*Lesotho*] [*Airport symbol*]   (OAG)
SHK.......... Shank   (AAG)
Shk.......... Shikimic Acid [*Biochemistry*]
SHK.......... Shiraki [*Japan*] [*Seismograph station code, US Geological Survey*]   (SEIS)
SHK.......... Shock [*A publication*]
SHK.......... Shock   (MSA)
SHK.......... Speaker of the House of Keys [*British*]   (ROG)
SHK.......... Systems Housekeeping
SHKDN...... Shakedown   (AABC)
SHKKA...... Shika Kiso Igakkai Zasshi [*A publication*]
SHL .... Sacred Heart League   (EA)
SHL .... Sensorineural Hearing Loss [*Medicine*]
SHL .... Shaw Industries Limited [*Toronto Stock Exchange symbol*]
SHL .... Sheldon, IA [*Location identifier*] [*FAA*]   (FAAL)
SHL .... Shell   (AAG)
SHL .... Shell Canada Limited [*UTLAS symbol*]
SHL .... Shellac   (MSA)
SHL .... Shillong [*India*] [*Seismograph station code, US Geological Survey*]   (SEIS)
SHL .... Shillong [*India*] [*Geomagnetic observatory code*]
SHL .... Shoal
SHL .... Southall [*British depot code*]
SHL .... Southern Hockey League
SHL .... Student Homophile League [*Superseded by Gay People at Columbia*]   (EA)
SHLB......... Simulation Hardware Load Boxes   (NASA)
SHLD........ Shield   (AAG)
SHLD........ Shoulder   (AAG)
SHLDR ...... Shoulder   (MSA)
ShLH .... Shne Luhot Ha-Berit   (BJA)
Sh Litt .... Shortt on Works of Literature [*2nd ed.*] [*1884*]   (DLA)
SHLM........ Schulman [A.], Inc. [*NASDAQ symbol*]   (NQ)
SHLMA...... Southern Hardwood Lumber Manufacturers Association [*Later, HMA*]   (EA)
SHLN........ Shoreline   (MSA)
SHLS........ Shawnee Library System [*Library network*]
SHLS........ Shoals   (MCD)
SHLW ...... Shallow   (FAAC)
SHM .... Nanki Shirahama [*Japan*] [*Airport symbol*]   (OAG)

SHM .... Shimizu [*Japan*] [*Seismograph station code, US Geological Survey*]   (SEIS)
SHM .... Ship Heading Marker [*Navigation*]
SHM .... Simple Harmonic Motion
SHM .... Sinusoidal Hydrodynamic Modulation [*Electrochemistry*]
SHM .... Stage Handling Manual [*NASA*]   (KSC)
Sh & Macl .. Shaw and Maclean's Scotch Appeal Cases   (DLA)
SHMD........ Shore Manning Document [*Navy*]   (NVT)
SHMED ...... State Hazardous Materials Enforcement Development [*Nuclear energy*]   (NRCH)
Sh Metal Inds ... Sheet Metal Industries [*A publication*]
SHMI .... Saddlery Hardware Manufacturers Institute [*Defunct*]   (EA)
SHMKR ...... Shoemaker   (MSA)
SHMN .... Subacute Hepatitis with Multilobular Necrosis [*Medicine*]
SHMO........ Senior Hospital Medical Officer [*British*]
SHMO........ Shadow Mountain National Recreation Area
SHMO........ Social/Health Maintenance Organization [*Department of Health and Human Services*]
SHMP .... Sodium Hexametaphosphate [*Inorganic chemistry*]
SHN........... St. Helena [*Three-letter standard code*]   (CNC)
SHN........... Sclerosing Hyaline Necrosis [*Medicine*]
ShN .... Shakespeare Newsletter [*A publication*]
shn .... Shan [*MARC language code*] [*Library of Congress*]   (LCCP)
SHN........... Shandon Resources, Inc. [*Vancouver Stock Exchange symbol*]
SHN........... Shelton, WA [*Location identifier*] [*FAA*]   (FAAL)
SHN........... Shimonoseki [*Japan*] [*Seismograph station code, US Geological Survey*]   (SEIS)
SHN........... Shorthand Note
SHN........... Shown   (AAG)
SHN........... Spontaneous Hemorrhagic Necrosis [*Medicine*]
SHNA .... SHARAF Name Authority [*UTLAS symbol*]
SHNAD ...... Shoni Naika [*A publication*]
SHNC .... Scottish Higher National Certificate
SHND .... Scottish Higher National Diploma
SHNG .... Shingle
S/HNP .... Skagit/Hanford Nuclear Project   (NRCH)
SHNS .... Shoney's South, Inc. [*NASDAQ symbol*]   (NQ)
SHNS .... Society of Head and Neck Surgeons [*Manchester, MA*]   (EA)
SHO........... Scenic Hudson, Incorporated [*An association*]   (EA)
SHO........... Schedule Order   (MCD)
SHO........... Secondary Hypertrophic Osteoarthropathy [*Medicine*]
SHO........... Senate Historical Office
SHO........... Senior House Officer [*British*]
SHO........... Shikotan [*USSR*] [*Seismograph station code, US Geological Survey*]   (SEIS)
sho .... Shona [*MARC language code*] [*Library of Congress*]   (LCCP)
SHO........... Shore
SHO........... Shutout [*Sports*]
SHO........... Starrett Housing Corp. [*American Stock Exchange symbol*]
SHO........... Student Health Organizations [*Defunct*]
SHOA .... Superannuation, Home, and Overseas Allowances [*Civil Service*] [*British*]
SHOB .... Shore-Based   (CINC)
SHOBOM ... Shore Bombardment [*Navy*]   (NVT)
SHOBOMTNG ... Shore Bombardment Training [*Navy*]   (NVT)
SHOC .... SHAPE [*Supreme Headquarters Allied Powers Europe*] Operations Center [*NATO*]   (NATG)
SHOC .... Software/Hardware Operational Control
SHOCK ...... Students Hot on Conserving Kilowatts [*Student legal action organization*]
Shock Vib Bull ... Shock and Vibration Bulletin [*A publication*]
Shock Vib Dig ... Shock and Vibration Digest [*A publication*]
SHODOP .... Short-Range Doppler
Shoe Leather Rep ... Shoe and Leather Reporter [*A publication*]
Shokubai Suppl ... Shokubai. Supplement [*Japan*] [*A publication*]
SHOMADS ... Short-to-Medium-Range Air Defense System [*Army*]   (RDA)
Shome LR ... Shome's Law Reporter [*India*]   (DLA)
SHON .... Shoney's, Inc. [*NASDAQ symbol*]   (NQ)
SHOND ...... Shoni No Noshinkei [*A publication*]
S'HONG ..... Souchong [*Tea trade*]   (ROG)
SHOP .... Shell Higher Olefin Process [*Petrochemistry*]
SHOP .... Shopsmith, Inc. [*NASDAQ symbol*]   (NQ)
SHOPAIR ... Short Path Infrared   (MCD)
SHOPAT..... Shore Patrol [*Navy*]   (NVT)
SHOR .... Shorewood Corp. [*NASDAQ symbol*]   (NQ)
SHORAD .... Short-Range Air Defense [*Army*]   (NATG)
SHORAD C² ... Short-Range Air Defense Command and Control
SHORADS ... Short-Range Air Defense System [*Army*]   (RDA)
SHORAN .... Short-Range Navigation
SHORDU .... Shore Duty [*Navy*]
SHOREALT ... Shore Alteration
SHOROC .... Shore-Required Operational Capability [*Navy*]
SHOROUTPUBINST ... Shore Duty Beyond the Seas Is Required by the Public Interest [*Navy*]
SHORPUBINT ... Shore Duty Is Required by the Public Interest [*Navy*]
SHORSTAMPS ... Shore Requirements, Standards, and Manpower Planning System [*Navy*]
SHORTD .... Shortened   (ROG)
Short Rep Rhod Geol Surv ... Short Report. Rhodesia Geological Survey [*A publication*]

Shortt Inf ... Shortt on Informations, Criminal, Quo Warranto, Mandamus, and Prohibition [1887] (DLA)

Shortt Inform ... Shortt on Informations, Criminal, Quo Warranto, Mandamus, and Prohibition (DLA)

Shortt Lit ... Shortt on Literature and Art [2nd ed.] [1884] (DLA)

SHORVEY ... Shore Duty Survey

SHOS .... Southern Hospitality Corp. [NASDAQ symbol] (NQ)

SHOSJ ...... Sovereign Hospitaller Order of St. John (EA)

SHOT .... Shooting, Hunting, Outdoor Trade Show

SHOT .... Society for the History of Technology

Show .... Shower's English King's Bench Reports (DLA)

Show .... Shower's English Parliamentary Cases (DLA)

Showa Wire Cable Rev ... Showa Wire and Cable Review [Japan] [A publication]

Shower KB ... Shower's English King's Bench Reports [89 English Reprint] [1678-95] (DLA)

Shower KB (Eng) ... Shower's English King's Bench Reports [89 English Reprint] (DLA)

Shower PC (Eng) ... Shower's English Parliamentary Cases [1 English Reprint] (DLA)

Show KB .... Shower's English King's Bench Reports (DLA)

Show-Me ... Show-Me News and Views [Missouri] [A publication]

Show Me Lib ... Show-Me Libraries [A publication]

Show Parl Cas ... Shower's English Parliamentary Cases [1 English Reprint] (DLA)

Show PC .... Shower's English Parliamentary Cases [1 English Reprint] (DLA)

SHP .... Santa Helena [Peru] [Seismograph station code, US Geological Survey] [Closed] (SEIS)

SHP .... Securities Shipped as Instructed

SHP .... Seeker Head Position

SHP .... Shaft Horsepower

SHP .... Shaker Heights Public Library, Shaker Heights, OH [OCLC symbol] (OCLC)

ShP .... Shakespeare Pictorial [A publication]

SHP .... Shape (MSA)

SHP .... Shearon Harris Plant [Nuclear energy] (NRCH)

SHP .... Shoal Petroleum [Vancouver Stock Exchange symbol]

SHP .... Single Highest Peak [Aerospace]

SHP .... Society for Hospital Planning of the American Hospital Association [Later, SHPM] (EA)

SHP .... Society for Hungarian Philately (EA)

SHP .... Southern Hardwood Producers [Later, SHLMA, HMA]

ShP .... Southern Historical Press, Easley, SC [Library symbol] [Library of Congress] (LCLS)

SHP .... Standard Hardware Program [Military]

SHP .... Standard Holding Pattern [Aviation]

SHP .... Standard Holding Procedure [Aviation]

Shp. .... Starship. The Magazine about Science Fiction [A publication]

SHP .... [The] Stop & Shop Companies, Inc. [NYSE symbol]

SHP .... Wichita Falls, TX [Location identifier] [FAA] (FAAL)

SHPA .... Prairie Agricultural Machinery Institute, Humboldt, Saskatchewan [Library symbol] [National Library of Canada] (NLC)

SHPA .... Shelf Paper. Alaska Outer Continental Shelf Office [A publication]

SHPBD .... Shipboard (MSA)

SHPC .... Scenic Hudson Preservation Conference [Later, SHI] (EA)

SHPCL .... Ship Class

SHPD .... Seeker Head Position Display [Military] (CAAL)

SHPDA .... State Health Planning and Development Agency

SHPE .... Society of Hispanic Professional Engineers (EA)

SHPG .... Shipping

SHPHG .... Shipment of Household Goods (NOAA)

SHPHUJ ..... Scripta Hierosolymitana. Publications of the Hebrew University (Jerusalem) [A publication]

SHPM .... Society for Hospital Planning and Marketing of the American Hospital Association [Chicago, IL] (EA)

SHPMT ...... Shipment (AABC)

SHPNG .... Shipping

SHPO .... State Historic Preservation Office

SHPR .... Shipper

SHPRF .... Shakeproof (MSA)

SHPS .... Seahead Pressure Simulator

SHPS .... Sodium Hydroxide Purge System (IEEE)

SHPSD .... Shipside (AABC)

SHPT .... Shipment (AAG)

SHPTARBY ... Ship to Arrive by _____

Sh Q .... Shakespeare Quarterly [A publication]

SHQ .... Southwestern Historical Quarterly [A publication]

SHQ .... Station Headquarters

SHQ .... Supreme Headquarters

SHQUN ...... Shasper Industries Units [Toronto Stock Exchange symbol]

SHR .... Scottish Historical Review [A publication]

ShR .... Shakespeare Review [A publication]

SHR .... Share [Business and trade]

SHR .... Sheridan [Wyoming] [Airport symbol] (OAG)

SHR .... Sheridan, WY [Location identifier] [FAA] (FAAL)

SHR .... Shirakawa [Japan] [Seismograph station code, US Geological Survey] (SEIS)

SHR .... Shore (MCD)

SHR .... Sisters of the Holy Redeemer [Roman Catholic religious order]

SHR .... Solar Heat Reflecting (KSC)

SHR .... Southern Humanities Review [A publication]

SHR .... Spontaneously Hypertensive Rats

SHR .... Step-Height Ratio [Crystallography]

Shr .... [The] Taming of the Shrew [Shakespearean work]

SHRAM ...... Short-Range Air-to-Surface Missile

SHRAP .... Shrapnel

SHRC .... Safety and Health Regulations for Construction [Bureau of Reclamation]

SHRC .... Shared Housing Resource Center [Later, NSHRC] (EA)

SHRD .... Shredded [Freight]

SHRD .... Shroud [Engineering]

SHRD .... Supplemental Heat Rejection Devices (NASA)

SHRDF .... Shroud Fin [Engineering]

SHRDR .... Shredder (MSA)

SHRF .... Ship Regular Freight (AABC)

SHRI .... Sciences and Humanities Research Institute [Iowa State University] [Research center] (RCD)

SHRM .... SAB Harmon Industries, Inc. [NASDAQ symbol] (NQ)

SHRNG .... Shearing (MSA)

SHROPS ..... Shropshire [County in England]

SHRP .... Sharpener (MSA)

SHRS .... Shores (MCD)

SHRS .... Shutdown Heat Removal System [Nuclear energy] (NRCH)

SHRS .... Supplementary Heat Removal System (IEEE)

SHRT .... Short (FAAC)

SHRTA .... Scientia Horticulturae (Amsterdam) [A publication]

SHRTG .... Shortage (AABC)

SHRTWV .... Short Wave (FAAC)

SHRW .... Sherwood Diversified Services, Inc. [NASDAQ symbol] (NQ)

SHS .... Galveston, TX [Location identifier] [FAA] (FAAL)

SHS .... Sacred Heart Seminary [Michigan]

SHS .... Sayer Head Sling [Medicine]

SHS .... Scandinavian Herpetological Society [Jyllinge, Denmark] (EA-IO)

SHS .... Scottish History Society (EA)

SHS .... Senior High School

SHS .... Shaer Shoe Corp. [American Stock Exchange symbol]

ShS .... Shakespeare Survey [A publication]

SHS .... Shares [Business and trade]

SHS .... Shashi [China] [Airport symbol] (OAG)

SHS .... Shasta Dam [California] [Seismograph station code, US Geological Survey] [Closed] (SEIS)

SHS .... Sheep Hemolyzate Supernatant

SHS .... Ship's Heading Servo

SHS .... Simulation Hardware System (MCD)

SHS .... Small Hydro Society (EA)

SHS .... Societas Heraldica Scandinavica [Bagsvaerd, Denmark] (EA-IO)

SHS .... Societatis Historiae Socius [Fellow of the Historical Society] [Latin]

SHS .... Sod House Society [Formerly, SHSN] (EA)

SHS .... Sodium Hexadecyl Sulfate [Organic chemistry]

SHS .... Soil and Health Society (EA)

SHS .... Soviet Hydrometeorological Service

SHS .... Spartan Homing Sensor [Missiles]

SHS .... Sports Hall of Shame (EA)

SHS .... Square Hollow Section [Metal industry]

SHS .... Standard Heavy Spanwire [Military] (CAAL)

SHS .... Superheated Steam

SHS .... Surveyors Historical Society (EA)

SHS .... Systemhouse Ltd. [Toronto Stock Exchange symbol]

SHS .... University of Sheffield, Postgraduate Librarianship, Sheffield, England [OCLC symbol] (OCLC)

SHSA .... Saint Hubert Society of America (EA)

SHSA .... Seaman Apprentice, Ship's Serviceman, Striker [Navy rating]

SHSA .... Southern Hardwood Square Association (EA)

SHSAC ...... Supreme Headquarters, Supreme Allied Commander [World War II]

Sh Sc App ... Shaw's Scotch Appeals Cases, House of Lords (DLA)

SHSDY .... Shiseido Co. ADR [NASDAQ symbol] (NQ)

SHSGS .... Supreme Headquarters, Secretary General Staff [World War II]

ShSh .... Shomer Shabbat (BJA)

SHSLB .... Street and Highway Safety Lighting Bureau [Defunct] (EA)

SHSLC .... Siouxland Health Sciences Consortium [Library network]

SHSN .... Seaman, Ship's Serviceman, Striker [Navy rating]

SHSN .... Sod House Society of Nebraska [Later, SHS] (EA)

SHSPB .... Soviet Hydrology. Selected Papers [A publication]

SHSS .... Stanford Hypnotic Susceptibility Scale [Psychology]

SHSTF .... Scout Helicopter Special Task Force (MCD)

SHSTS .... Ship Status

ShStud ...... Shakespeare Studies [Tokyo] [A publication]

SHSWD ..... Society for Hospital Social Work Directors [Chicago, IL] (EA)

SHT .... Sheet (AAG)

SHT .... Sholia Resources Ltd. [Vancouver Stock Exchange symbol]

SHT .... Short (MSA)

SH & T .... Shower and Toilet (AAG)

SHT .... Sidi Hakoma Tuff [Geology]

SHT .... Simple Hypocalcemic Tetany [Medicine]

SHT .... Society for the History of Technology (EA)

SHT	Society of the Most Holy Trinity [*Anglican religious community*]
SHT	Space Hand Tool [*NASA*]
SHT	Svensk Humanistisk Tidsskrift [*A publication*]
SHT	Swansea Harbour Trust [*Wales*]
SHTC	Short Time Constant (MSA)
SHTDN	Shutdown (FAAC)
Sh Teind Ct	Shaw's Scotch Teind [*Tithe*] Court Decisions (DLA)
SHTG	Sheeting [*Freight*]
SHTG	Shortage (AFM)
SHTHG	Sheathing (MSA)
SHT IRN	Sheet Iron [*Freight*]
SHT IRN STL	Sheet Iron or Steel [*Freight*]
SHTL	Shuttle (MSA)
SHTL	Small Heat-Transfer Loop [*Nuclear energy*] (NRCH)
SHT MTL	Sheet Metal [*Freight*]
SHTN	Short Ton [*2000 lbs.*]
SHTPB	Saturated Hydroxy-Terminated Polybutadiene
SHTR	Shutter (AAG)
SHTSD	Short Side
SHT STL WRE	Sheet Steel Ware [*Freight*]
SHTT	Sequential Headturn Test
SHU	Sacred Heart University, Library, Bridgeport, CT [*OCLC symbol*] (OCLC)
SHU	Seton Hall University [*New Jersey*]
SHU	Shoe-Town, Inc. [*NYSE symbol*]
SHU	Shuyak Island [*Alaska*] [*Seismograph station code, US Geological Survey*] (SEIS)
SHU	Skyhigh Resources Ltd. [*Vancouver Stock Exchange symbol*]
SHum	Studies in the Humanities [*A publication*]
S Hum Rev	Southern Humanities Review [*A publication*]
SHUR	Selected History Update and Reporting (MCD)
SHUR	System for Hospital Uniform Reporting
SHUSA	Scottish Heritage USA (EA)
Shuttle	Shuttle, Spindle, and Dyepot [*A publication*]
SHV	Shavano Air, Inc. [*Poncha Springs, CO*] [*FAA designator*] (FAAC)
SHV	Sheave (MSA)
SHV	Shreveport [*Louisiana*] [*Airport symbol*] (OAG)
SHV	Shreveport, LA [*Location identifier*] [*FAA*] (FAAL)
SHV	Solenoid Hydraulic Valve
SHV	Standard Havens, Inc. [*American Stock Exchange symbol*]
SHV	Sub Hoc Voce [*Under This Word*] [*Latin*]
SHVE	Sammelblatt der Historischer Verein Eichstatt [*A publication*]
SHVF	Sammelblatt der Historischer Verein Freising [*A publication*]
SHVG	Shaving[s] [*Freight*]
SHVI	Sammelblatt der Historischer Verein Ingolstadt [*A publication*]
SHVSCE	Shuttle Versus Current Expendable Launch Vehicle [*NASA*] (KSC)
SHVSNE	Shuttle Versus New Expendable Launch Vehicle [*NASA*] (KSC)
SHW	Mount St. Helens [*Washington*] [*Seismograph station code, US Geological Survey*] (SEIS)
SHW	Shararah [*Saudi Arabia*] [*Airport symbol*] (OAG)
SHW	Sherwin-Williams Co. [*NYSE symbol*]
Sh W & C	Shaw, Wilson, and Courtenay's Scotch Appeals Reports [*Wilson and Shaw's Reports*] (DLA)
SHWPA	Sheng Wu Hua Hsueh Yu Sheng Wu Wu Li Hsueh Pao [*A publication*]
SHWR	Shower (FAAC)
SHWY	Super Highway (TEL)
SHWY	Superhighway (TEL)
SHX	Shageluk [*Alaska*] (OAG)
SHX	Shageluk, AK [*Location identifier*] [*FAA*] (FAAL)
SHX	Shaw Industries, Inc. [*NYSE symbol*]
SHY	Kaiser, MO [*Location identifier*] [*FAA*] (FAAL)
SHY	Sharon Energy Ltd. [*Vancouver Stock Exchange symbol*]
SHY	Shinyanga [*Tanzania*] [*Airport symbol*] (OAG)
SHYDF	Sharon Energy Ltd. [*NASDAQ symbol*] (NQ)
SHZ	Seshute's [*Lesotho*] [*Airport symbol*] (OAG)
SHZ	Shizuoka [*Japan*] [*Seismograph station code, US Geological Survey*] (SEIS)
SHZ	Steelhead Resources Ltd. [*Vancouver Stock Exchange symbol*]
SI	Arab Wings Co. [*ICAO designator*] (FAAC)
SI	Sacroiliac [*Medicine*]
SI	Safety Injection [*Nuclear energy*] (NRCH)
SI	Safety Inspection (IEEE)
SI	Sailmakers Institute (EA)
SI	Saintpaulia International
SI	Saline Injection [*Abortion technique*]
SI	Salinity Indicator
SI	Salmon Institute [*Formerly, CSI*] (EA)
SI	Salt Institute [*Alexandria, VA*] (EA)
SI	Sample Interval
SI	Sandwich Islands
SI	Sanitary Inspector [*British*] (ROG)
SI	Saturation Index [*Chemistry*]
SI	Saturday Inspection [*Slang*]
SI	Save It [*Energy-saving campaign*] [*British*]
SI	School Inventory [*Psychology*]
SI	Scientific Instrument (NASA)
SI	Screen Grid Input
SI	Scuola Italiana [*A publication*]
SI	Security Identity
SI	Seine Island [*Island off the coast of France*] (ROG)
SI	Selected Item (MCD)
SI	Selective Identification
SI	Self Incompatible
SI	Semi-Insulating
S-I	Sensation-Intuition [*Jungian psychology*]
SI	Sensitive Information (MCD)
SI	Sensory Integration
SI	Sergeant Instructor [*Military*] [*British*]
SI	Serial Input
SI	Seriously Ill [*Military*] (AABC)
SI	Serra International (EA)
SI	Sertoma International [*Kansas City, MO*] (EA)
SI	Serum Iron [*Serology*]
SI	Service Indicator [*Telecommunications*] (TEL)
SI	Service Instruction
SI	Service Interruption
SI	Sex Inventory [*Psychology*]
SI	Sexual Intercourse (ADA)
SI	Shetland Isles
SI	Shift-In Character [*Keyboard*] [*Data processing*]
SI	Ship Item (MCD)
SI	Shipping Instructions (AFM)
SI	Ship's Installation [*Navy*]
SI	Short Interest [*Brokerage*]
SI	Signal Intelligence (MCD)
SI	Signal Interface
S/I	Signal-to-Interference
SI	Signal-to-Intermodulation [*Ratio*]
SI	Silence [*Navigation*]
Si	Silicon [*Chemical element*]
SI	Silver Institute [*Washington, DC*] (EA)
SI	Similarity Index
SI	Simulator Initiation (MCD)
SI	Sinai (BJA)
SI	Sing Out [*A publication*]
si	Singapore [*MARC country of publication code*] [*Library of Congress*] (LCCP)
SI	Single Silk [*Wire insulation*] (AAG)
SI	Sinus Iridum [*Bay of Rainbows*] [*Lunar area*]
SI	Sirach [*Ecclesiasticus*] [*Old Testament book*]
Si	Sistema [*A publication*]
SI	Slaved Illuminator [*Military*] (CAAL)
SI	Small Inclusions [*Diamond clarity grade*]
S/I	Smectite-Illite [*Clay mineral*]
SI	Smithsonian Institution
SI	Socialist International
SI	Society of Illustrators (EA)
SI	Solar Inertial (MCD)
SI	Solidarity International (EA)
SI	Solubility Index [*Water*]
SI	Soluble Insulin
SI	Soroptimist International (EA-IO)
SI	Source Impedance
SI	Southeast Institute (EA)
SI	Southpaw's International [*Birmingham, AL*] (EA)
SI	Space Institute [*University of Tennessee*] [*Research center*] (RCD)
SI	Space Intelligence [*Parapsychology*]
SI	Spark Ignition
SI	Speaker Intercom
SI	Special Inquiry [*Classification system used by doctors on Ellis Island to detain, re-examine, and possibly deny entry to certain immigrants*]
SI	Special Inspection (MCD)
SI	Special Instruction
SI	Special Intelligence [*Army*] (AABC)
SI	Special Intervention [*Medicine*]
SI	Spectrum Index
SI	Speech Interpolation [*Telecommunications*] (TEL)
SI	Spettatore Italiano [*A publication*]
SI	Spokane International Railroad Co. [*AAR code*]
SI	Sponsor Identification [*Television*]
SI	Sports Illustrated [*A publication*]
SI	Spot Inspection [*Military*] (AFM)
SI	Spot Inventory
SI	Spratly Islands [*Two-letter standard code*] (CNC)
SI	Square Inch (MCD)
SI	Staff Inspector
SI	Standardization and Interoperability
SI	Standing Instruction (MSA)
SI	Star of India
SI	Staten Island
SI	Station Identification
SI	Statutory Instruments [*Legal*] [*British*]
SI	Steering Intelligence (MCD)
SI	Stimulation Index [*Cytochemistry*]
S & I	Stocked and Issued (AFM)

SI .... Storage Immediate
SI .... Straight-In Approach [*Aviation*]
SI .... Straight, Incorporated [*An association*] [*St. Petersburg, FL*] (EA)
SI .... Stretch Inhibitor
S/I .... Strike/Interdiction (MCD)
SI .... Structure-of-Intellect [*Model*]
SI .... Student Investigator (KSC)
SI .... Studia Islamica [*A publication*]
SI .... Studii Italiene [*A publication*]
S/I .... Subject Issue
SI .... Sulphur Institute [*Washington, DC*] (EA)
SI .... Sundance Institute (EA)
SI .... Superimpose (MDG)
SI .... Supply Instruction [*Marine Corps*]
SI .... Support Installation (MCD)
SI .... Surveillance Inspection [*Nuclear energy*] (NRCH)
S & I .... Surveillance and Inspection (AAG)
S & I .... Surveys and Investigation
SI .... Survival International (EA-IO)
SI .... Svizzera Italiana [*A publication*]
SI .... Symbolic Input [*Data processing*]
SI .... System Integration
SI .... Systeme International d'Unites [*International System of Units*] [*Also, SIU*]
SIA .... Sailing Industry Association [*Chicago, IL*] (EA)
SIA .... San Francisco, CA [*Location identifier*] [*FAA*] (FAAL)
SIA .... Sanitary Institute of America [*Later, IAWCM*]
SIA .... Sasquatch Investigations of Mid-America [*An association*] (EA)
SIA .... Scaffold Industry Association [*Van Nuys, CA*] (EA)
SIA .... Science Information Association
SIA .... Scottish Island Area [*Council*]
SIA .... Securities Industry Association [*Formed by a merger of Investment Bankers Association of America - IBA and ASEF*] [*New York, NY*] (EA)
SIA .... Self-Insurers Association
SIA .... Self-Interstitial Atom
SIA .... Semiconductor Industry Association [*San Jose, CA*] (EA)
SIA .... Sensor Interface Assembly
SIA .... Serial Input Adapter
SIA .... Service in Information and Analysis [*Host*] [*British*] (BUR)
SIA .... Shelter Oil & Gas Ltd. [*Toronto Stock Exchange symbol*]
SIA .... Sialic Acid [*Biochemistry*]
SIA .... Sian [*Republic of China*] [*Seismograph station code, US Geological Survey*] [*Closed*] (SEIS)
SIA .... Signal Apparel [*NYSE symbol*]
SIA .... Singapore Airlines
SIA .... Ski Industries America [*McLean, VA*] (EA)
SIA .... Societa Italiana di Agopuntura [*Italy*]
SIA .... Societe Internationale d'Acupuncture [*International Society of Acupuncture*]
SIA .... Societe Internationale Arthurienne [*International Arthurian Society*]
SIA .... Society for Industrial Archeology
SIA .... Society of Insurance Accountants [*Formed by a merger of ACAS and IAA*] [*Crozet, VA*] (EA)
SIA .... Software Impact Assessment [*NASA*] (NASA)
SIA .... Software Institute of America [*Andover, MA*] [*Telecommunications*] (TSSD)
SIA .... Solar Inertial Altitude (MCD)
SIA .... Soroptimist International of the Americas [*Philadelphia, PA*] (EA)
SIA .... Speaker Intercom Assembly [*NASA*]
SIA .... Special Investor Account [*Stock purchasing*]
SIA .... Sprinkler Irrigation Association [*Later, IA*] (EA)
S/I .... Standard Instrument Approach [*RADAR*] [*Aviation*]
SIA .... Standard Interface Adapter
SIA .... Station of Initial Assignment
SIA .... Storage Instantaneous Audimeter [*Measures television viewing*]
SIA .... Strategic Industries Association (EA)
SIA .... Stress-Induced Analgesia [*Reaction to pain*]
SIA .... Structural Inventory and Appraisal [*Of roads and bridges*]
SIA .... Subminiature Integrated Antenna
SIA .... Synalbumin-Insulin Antagonism [*Medicine*]
SIA .... System Integration Area (MCD)
SIA .... Xian [*China*] [*Airport symbol*] (OAG)
SIABA .... Sindacato Italiano Artisti Belle Arti [*Italian Union of Fine Arts*]
SIAC .... Secretariat International des Artistes Catholiques
SIAC .... Securities Industry Automation Corporation [*NYSE/ASE*] [*New York, NY*]
SIAC .... Societe Internationale des Artistes Chretiens [*International Society for Christian Artists*] (EA-IO)
SIAC .... Southeastern Intercollegiate Athletic Association (MCD)
SIAC .... Special Interest Auto Club (EA)
SIAC .... State Industry Advisory Committee [*Civil Defense*]
SIAC .... Studies in Automation and Control [*Elsevier Book Series*] [*A publication*]
SIAC .... Submarine Integrated Attack Center (MCD)
SIAD .... Sierra Army Depot [*California*] (AABC)

SIADH .... Syndrome of Inappropriate Antidiuretic Hormone [*Endocrinology*]
SIADS .... Sensor Integration and Display Sharing [*Military*] (CAAL)
SIAE .... Scottish Institute of Agricultural Engineering [*British*] (ARC)
SIAF .... Service Indicator Associated Field [*Telecommunications*] (TEL)
SIAF .... Small Independent Action Force [*Military*]
SIAGL .... Survey Instrument, Azimuth Gyroscope, Lightweight (MCD)
SIA J .... SIA [*Societe des Ingenieurs de l'Automobile*] Journal [*France*] [*A publication*]
SIAJ .... SIAJ: Singapore Institute of Architects. Journal [*A publication*]
SIAL .... Salon International de l'Alimentation [*World Food Fair*]
SIAL .... Sialagogue [*Promoting Flow of Saliva*] [*Medicine*] (ROG)
SIAL .... Sigma-Aldrich Corp. [*NASDAQ symbol*] (NQ)
SIAL .... Southeast Iowa Academic Libraries [*Library network*]
SIALON ..... Silicon, Aluminum, Oxygen, and Nitrogen [*A ceramic*]
SIAM .... Self-Initiating Antiaircraft Munition [*ARPA*]
SIAM .... Separate Index Access Method [*Data processing*] (BUR)
SIAM .... Signal Information and Monitoring Service [*American radio monitoring service*]
SIAM .... Society for Industrial and Applied Mathematics [*Philadelphia, PA*]
SIAM .... Strategic Impact and Assumptions Identification Method
SIAMA .... Society for Interests of Active Missionaries in Asia, Africa, and America (EA-IO)
SIAM J Algebraic and Discrete Methods ... SIAM [*Society for Industrial and Applied Mathematics*] Journal of Algebraic and Discrete Methods [*A publication*]
SIAM J Algebraic Discrete Methods ... SIAM [*Society for Industrial and Applied Mathematics*] Journal on Algebraic and Discrete Methods [*A publication*]
SIAM J A Ma ... SIAM [*Society for Industrial and Applied Mathematics*] Journal on Applied Mathematics [*A publication*]
SIAM J Appl Math ... SIAM [*Society for Industrial and Applied Mathematics*] Journal of Applied Mathematics [*A publication*]
SIAM J App Math ... SIAM [*Society for Industrial and Applied Mathematics*] Journal on Applied Mathematics [*A publication*]
SIAM J Comput ... SIAM [*Society for Industrial and Applied Mathematics*] Journal on Computing [*A publication*]
SIAM J Cont ... SIAM [*Society for Industrial and Applied Mathematics*] Journal on Control [*A publication*]
SIAM J Control ... SIAM [*Society for Industrial and Applied Mathematics*] Journal on Control [*A publication*]
SIAM J Control Optim ... SIAM [*Society for Industrial and Applied Mathematics*] Journal on Control and Optimization [*A publication*]
SIAM J Control and Optimiz ... SIAM [*Society for Industrial and Applied Mathematics*] Journal on Control and Optimization [*A publication*]
SIAM J Control Optimization ... SIAM [*Society for Industrial and Applied Mathematics*] Journal on Control and Optimization [*A publication*]
SIAM J Math ... SIAM [*Society for Industrial and Applied Mathematics*] Journal on Mathematical Analysis [*A publication*]
SIAM J Num ... SIAM [*Society for Industrial and Applied Mathematics*] Journal on Numerical Analysis [*A publication*]
SIAM J Sci Statist Comput ... SIAM [*Society for Industrial and Applied Mathematics*] Journal on Scientific and Statistical Computing [*A publication*]
SIAM R .... SIAM [*Society for Industrial and Applied Mathematics*] Review [*A publication*]
SIAM Rev ... SIAM [*Society for Industrial and Applied Mathematics*] Review [*A publication*]
SIAM Stud Appl Math ... SIAM [*Society for Industrial and Applied Mathematics*] Studies in Applied Mathematics [*A publication*]
SIAM Studies in Appl Math ... SIAM [*Society for Industrial and Applied Mathematics*] Studies in Applied Mathematics [*A publication*]
SIAN .... Societe Industrielle et Agriculturelle du Niari [*Industrial and Agricultural Society of Niari*]
SIANM .... Special Inspection, Army Nuclear Matters (MCD)
SI/AO .... Smithsonian Institution/Astrophysical Observatory (KSC)
SIAP .... Sociedad Interamericana de Planeficacion [*Inter-American Planning Society*] [*Mexico*]
SIAP .... Standard Instrument Approach Procedure [*Aviation*]
SIAP .... Standard-Italo Americana Petroli
SIAP .... Straight-In Approach [*Aviation*]
SIAR .... Small, Irregular, Agglutinated Rooms [*Architecture*]
SIAS .... Safety Injection Actuation Signal [*Nuclear energy*] (NRCH)
SIAS .... Signals Intelligence Analysis System (MCD)
SIAS .... Submarine Integrated Antenna System (MCD)
SIASP .... Society for Italian-American Scientists and Physicians (EA)
SIAT .... Single Integrated Attack Team
SIAT .... Societa Italiana Assicurazioni Trasporti [*Genova, Italy*]
SIAT .... Synthesis of Impact Acceleration Technology (MCD)
SIAU .... Seminario Internacional de Administracao Universitaria
SIB .... Satellite Integrated Buoy
SIB .... Satellite Ionospheric Beacons [*Military*]
SIB .... Saudi International Bank
SIB .... Scales of Independent Behavior [*Occupational therapy*]

SIB .... Securities and Investments Board [*Great Britain*]
SIB .... Selection Interview Blueprint [*LIMRA*]
SIB .... Self-Injurious Behavior [*Abnormal psychology*]
SIB .... Serial Interface Board
SIB .... Ship Information Booklet [*Navy*]
SIB .... Shipbuilding Industry Board [*British*]
SIB .... Siberia
SIB .... Sibiti [*Congo*] [*Airport symbol*]   (OAG)
Sib............. Sibling
SIB .... Sibola Mines Ltd. [*Vancouver Stock Exchange symbol*]
Sib............. Sibyllines   (BJA)
SIB .... SIDPERS [*Standard Installation/Division Personnel System*] Interface Branch [*Military*]
SIB .... Sistema de Informacion Bursatil [*Stock Exchange Information System*] [*Madrid Stock Exchange*] [*Madrid, Spain*] [*Information service*]   (EISS)
SIB .... Special Investigation Branch [*Army*] [*British*]
SIB .... Standard Iron Bar   (MSA)
SIB .... Subject Interface Box   (KSC)
SIB .... Systems Information Bulletin [*Data processing*]
SIBC.......... Saudi Investment Banking Corporation
SIBC.......... Societe Internationale de Biologie Clinique [*World Association of Anatomic and Clinical Pathology Societies*]
Sibelius...... Sibelius-Mitteilungen [*A publication*]
Siberian Math J ... Siberian Mathematical Journal [*A publication*]
SIBEX........ Second International BIOMASS Experiment
SIBEX........ Singapore International Building Exhibition   (TSPED)
Sib Geogr Sb ... Sibirskii Geograficheskii Sbornik [*A publication*]
SIBH.......... Salicylideniminobenzohydroxamic Acid [*Biochemistry*]
SIBIL .... Systeme Integre pour les Bibliotheques Universitaires de Lausanne [*Integrated System for the University of Lausanne Libraries*] [*Switzerland*] [*Information service*]   (EISS)
Sibirsk Mat Z ... Sibirskii Matematiceskii Zurnal [*A publication*]
Sibirsk Mat Zh ... Akademiya Nauk SSSR. Sibirskoe Otdelenie. Sibirskii Matematiceskii Zhurnal [*A publication*]
Sibirsk Vrach Viedom ... Sibirskiia Vrachebnyia Viedomosti [*A publication*]
SIBL .... Separate Infantry Brigade Light   (INF)
SIBMAS ..... Societe Internationale des Bibliotheques et Musees des Arts du Spectacle [*International Association of Libraries and Museums of the Performing Arts*]   (EA-IO)
Sib Mat Zh ... Sibirskij Matematicheskij Zhurnal [*A publication*]
SIB-MIBOC ... Securities and Investment Board and the Marketing of Investments Board Organisation Commission [*London, England*]
SibOr.......... Sibylline Oracles   (BJA)
SIBOR .... Singapore Interbank Offered Rate
SIBS .... Salk Institute for Biological Studies
SIBS .... Stellar Inertial Bombing System
SIBTN........ Something Is Better than Nothing
Sib Vest Sel'Khoz Nauki ... Siberskii Vestnik Sel'skokhozyaistvennoi Nauki [*A publication*]
SIC .... Covington/Cincinnati, OH [*Location identifier*] [*FAA*]   (FAAL)
SIC .... High School Student Information Center   (EA)
SIC .... Safety Information Center [*National Safety Council*]   (EISS)
SIC .... Sakharov International Committee   (EA)
SIC .... Science Information Council [*National Science Foundation*]
SIC .... Scientific Information Center
SIC .... Second Pilot in Command [*Aviation*]   (FAAC)
SIC .... Security Intelligence Centre [*British*] [*World War II*]
SICU .... Security Intelligence Corps
SIC .... Semiconductor Integrated Circuit
SIC .... Sept-Iles [*Quebec*] [*Seismograph station code, US Geological Survey*]   (SEIS)
SIC .... Serial Interface Chip
SIC .... Service, Inc., Omaha NE [*STAC*]
SIC .... Servicio Informativo Continental [*Press agency*] [*Argentina*]
SIC .... Siccus [*Dry*] [*Latin*]   (ADA)
SIC .... Sicily
SIC .... Sico, Inc. [*Toronto Stock Exchange symbol*]
SIC .... Silicon-Insulating Compound
SIC .... Silicon Integrated Circuit
SIC .... Simulated Interface Calibration
SIC .... Skills Inventory Coordinator
SIC .... Societa Italiana Cauzioni [*Rome, Italy*]
SIC .... Societe Internationale de Cardiologie [*International Society of Cardiology*]
SIC .... Societe Internationale de Chirurgie [*International Society of Surgery - ISS*]   (EA)
SIC .... Societe Internationale de Criminologie [*International Society of Criminology*]   (EA)
SIC .... Society of Inkwell Collectors   (EA)
SIC .... SONAR Information Center   (NVT)
SIC .... Sorties per Inspection Cycle [*Air Force*]   (AFIT)
SIC .... Special Information Center   (MCD)
SIC .... Special Interest Committee
SIC .... Specific Inductive Capacity
SIC .... Standard Industrial Classification [*File indexing code*]
SIC .... Standard Inspection Criteria
SIC .... States Information Center [*Council of State Governments*]   (EISS)

SIC .... Status of Implementation Chart
SIC .... Structural Influence Coefficient
SIC .... Survey Information Center
SIC .... Systeme Informatique pour la Conjoncture [*Information System for the Economy*] [*France*] [*Information service*] [*Databank*]   (EISS)
SIC .... Systems Integration Contractor
SICA.......... Secondary Inventory Control Activity   (MCD)
SICA.......... Society of Industrial and Cost Accountants of Canada
SICAC........ Society of Inter-Celtic Arts and Culture   (EA)
SICAM........ Sex Information Council of America [*Later, CSIE*]   (EA)
SICAVS..... Societes d'Investissement a Capital Variable [*French mutual funds*]
SICBM........ Small Intercontinental Ballistic Missile   (MCD)
SICC.......... Safeguard Inventory Control Center [*Army*]   (AABC)
SICC.......... Service Inventory Control Center [*DoD*]
SICDOC ..... Special Interest Committee on Program Documentation [*Association for Computing Machinery*]
SICEA .... Steel Industry Compliance Extension Act of 1981
SICF .... Societe des Ingenieurs Civils de France
SicG .... Siculorum Gymnasium [*A publication*]
Sicherheit Chem Umwelt ... Sicherheit in Chemie und Umwelt [*A publication*]
Sicilia Arch ... Sicilia Archaeologica. Rassegna Periodica di Studi, Notizie e Documentazione [*A publication*]
SICJA........ Siberian Chemistry Journal [*English Translation*] [*A publication*]
Sick........... Sickels' Reports [*46-85 New York*]   (DLA)
Sick........... Single Income, Couple of Kids [*Lifestyle classification*]
Sick Min Dec ... Sickels' United States Mining Laws and Decisions   (DLA)
Sick Op ..... Sickels' Opinions of the New York Attorneys-General   (DLA)
SICL .... Sampling Inspection Checklist
SICL .... Self-Interview Checklist [*Navy*]   (NVT)
SICM .... Scheduled Input Control Method   (MCD)
SICM .... Small Intercontinental Ballistic Missile   (MCD)
SICM .... Soybean Integrated Crop Management Model
SICO .... Signal Control   (DEN)
SICO .... Switched in for Checkout [*NASA*]   (KSC)
SICO .... Systems Integration and Checkout
SICOB .... Salon International de l'Informatique, de la Communication, et de l'Organisation du Bureau [*Business equipment exhibition*]
SICOM .... Securities Industry Communication [*Western Union Corp.*] [*Information service*]
SI COMMS ... Special Intelligence Communications   (MCD)
S Icon........ Studies in Iconography [*A publication*]
SICOT .... Societe Internationale de Chirurgie Orthopedique et de Traumatologie [*International Society of Orthopaedic Surgery and Traumatology*]   (EA-IO)
SICOVAM ... Societe Interprofessionnelle pour la Compensation des Valeurs Mobilieres [*French depository body*]
SICP.......... Selected Ion Current Profile [*Spectrometry*]
SICP.......... Society of Indochina Philatelists   (EA)
SICR.......... Selected Item Configuration Record   (MCD)
SICR.......... Specific Intelligence Collection Requirements   (AFM)
SICR.......... Supply Item Change Record
SICRI........ Substances Immunologically Cross-Reactive with Insulin
SICS.......... Safety Injection Control System [*Nuclear energy*]   (NRCH)
SICS.......... Secondary Infrared Calibration System
SICS.......... Ships Integrated Communications System   (MCD)
SICU .... Surgical Intensive Care Unit [*Medicine*]
SID .... Doctor of Industrial Science
SID .... Sal Island [*Cape Verde Islands*] [*Airport symbol*]   (OAG)
SID .... Scheduled Issue Date [*Telecommunications*]   (TEL)
SID .... Seal-In Device   (MSA)
SID .... Security and Intelligence Service [*Army*]
SID .... Seismic Intrusion Detector [*Army*]
sid .... Semel in Die [*Once a Day*] [*Pharmacy*]
SID .... Sequence Information Data
SID .... Serial Input Data [*Data processing*]
SID .... Servizio Informazioni Difesa [*Defense Intelligence Service*] [*Italy*]
SID .... Shuttle Integration Device [*NASA*]   (NASA)
SID .... Sida [*Iceland*] [*Seismograph station code, US Geological Survey*]   (SEIS)
sid .... Sidamo [*MARC language code*] [*Library of Congress*]   (LCCP)
Sid............. Siderfin's King's Bench Reports [*82 English Reprint*]   (DLA)
SID .... Silicon Imaging Device   (IEEE)
SID .... Silver Iodine Generator
SID .... Simulator Interface Devices   (MCD)
SID .... Situation Display
SID .... Situation Information Display
SID .... Sketch-In-Depth [*Parthorn*] [*Software package*]
SID .... Skin Inserted Detonator   (MCD)
SID .... Slew-Induced Distortion
SID .... Society for Information Display [*Playa Del Rey, CA*]   (EA)
SID .... Society for International Development
SID .... Society for Investigative Dermatology [*San Francisco General Hospital*] [*San Fracisco, CA*]   (EA)
SID .... Sodium Ionization Detector [*Nuclear energy*]   (NRCH)
SID .... Software Interface Document   (MCD)

SID .... Sound Interface Device [*Computer chip*]
SID .... Source Image Distortion
SID .... Space and Information Systems Division [*NASA*]
SID .... Space Intruder Detector [*Burglar alarm*]
SID .... Special Intelligence Detachment [*Military*]   (CINC)
SID .... Specification Interpretation Documentation   (MCD)
SID .... Spiritus in Deo [*Spirit Rests in God*] [*Latin*]
SID .... Sports Information Director
SID .... Standard Instrument Departure [*RADAR*] [*Aviation*]
SID .... Strategic Intelligence Digests [*Military*]   (AABC)
SID .... Subcontract Item Definition
SID .... Subject Identification Module [*NASA*]
SID .... Subscriber Identification   (CAAL)
SID .... Sudden Infant Death [*Syndrome*] [*Medicine*]
SID .... Sudden Ionospheric Disturbance [*Telecommunications*]
SID .... Surface Ionization Detector [*Instrumentation*]
S & ID .... Surveillance and Identification
SID .... SWIFT [*Society for Worldwide Interbank Financial
                Telecommunications*] Interface Device
SID .... Syntax Improving Device   (IEEE)
SID .... System Interface Document [*NASA*]   (NASA)
SID .... Systems Integration Demonstrator [*Aircraft*]
SID .... Systems Integration and Deployment [*Program*] [*Department
                of Transportation*]
SIDA .... Societa Italiana di Assicurazioni, SpA [*Rome, Italy*]
SIDA .... Societe Internationale Fernand de Vischer pour l'Histoire des
                Droits de l'Antiquite   (EA)
SIDA .... Swedish International Development Agency
SIDAC .... Single Integrated Damage Anaysis Capability   (MCD)
Sida Contrib Bot ... Sida Contributions to Botany [*A publication*]
Sid Apoll .... Sidonius Apollinaris [*Fifth century AD*] [*Classical
                studies*]   (OCD)
SIDAR .... Selective Information Dissemination and Retrieval [*Data
                processing*]   (DIT)
SIDAR .... Symposium on Image Display and Recording
SIDASE ...... Significant Data Selection
SIDC .... Slaved Illuminator Data Converter [*Military*]   (CAAL)
SIDC .... Supply Item Design Change [*Navy*]   (NG)
SIDC .... Support Issue Development Committee [*Military*]   (CAAL)
SIDC .... Systems Identification Data Cost
SIDD .... Scientific Information and Documentation Division [*Later,
                ESIC*]
SIDE .... Suprathermal-Ion-Detector Experiment [*Apollo*] [*NASA*]
SIDEC .... Stanford International Development Education Center
                [*Stanford University*]
Side Eff Drugs Annu ... Side Effects of Drugs. Annual [*A publication*]
SIDEFCOOP ... Sociedad Interamericana de Desarrollo de Financiamiento
                Cooperativo [*Inter-American Society for the Development
                of Cooperative Financing*]   (EA-IO)
Sid (Eng) ... Siderfin's King's Bench Reports [*82 English Reprint*]   (DLA)
SIDES .... Source Input Data Edit System
SIDF .... Sinusoidal Input Describing Function [*Data processing*]
SIDFA .... Senior Industrial Development Field Adviser [*United Nations*]
SID J .... SID [*Society for Information Display*] Journal [*A publication*]
SIDL .... System Identification Data List [*Navy*]   (NG)
SIDM .... Syndicat International des Debardeurs et Magasiniers
                [*International Longshoremen's and Warehousemen's
                Union - ILWU*] [*Canada*]
Sid Mess .... Sidereal Messenger [*A publication*]
SIDN .... Small Industry Development Network [*Georgia Institute of
                Technology*]
SIDO .... Societe Internationale pour le Developpement des
                Organisations [*International Society for the Development
                of Organizations*]   (EA-IO)
SIDOR .... Siderurgica del Orinoco [*Government steel company*]
                [*Venezuela*]
SIDP .... Seed Industry Development Program [*UN Food and Agriculture
                Organization*]
SIDP .... Sheep Industry Development Program   (EA)
SIDPE .... Sensing, Identifying, Predicting, Deciding, and
                Executing   (MCD)
SIDPERS ... Standard Installation/Division Personnel System
                [*Military*]   (AABC)
SIDS .... Satellite Imagery Dissemination System   (MCD)
SIDS .... Sensor Interface Data System [*Military*]   (CAAL)
SIDS .... Ships Integrated Defense System
SIDS .... Shrike Improved Display System [*Military*]   (NVT)
SIDS .... Societe Internationale de Defense Sociale [*International
                Society for Social Defence - ISSD*]   (EA-IO)
SIDS .... Societe Internationale de Droit Sociale
SIDS .... Space Investigations Documentation System [*NASA*]
SIDS .... Spares Integrated Data System   (MCD)
SIDS .... Specification Interpretation Documents   (MCD)
SIDS .... Standard Information Display System [*Military*]   (CAAL)
SIDS .... Stellar Inertial Doppler System
SIDS .... Sudden Infant Death Syndrome [*Medicine*]
SIDSA .... Support Integrated Data System   (MCD)
SIDSA .... Sudden Infant Death Syndrome Act of 1974
SIDTC .... Single Integrated Development Test Cycle
SIDTEC ..... Single Integrated Development Test Cycle   (MCD)
SIDY .... Science Dynamics Corp. [*NASDAQ symbol*]   (NQ)

SIDZD .... Saitama Ika Daigaku Zasshi [*A publication*]
SIE............. Science Information Exchange [*Later, SSIE*] [*Smithsonian
                Institution*]
SIE............. Sea Isle, NJ [*Location identifier*] [*FAA*]   (FAAL)
SIE............. Select Information Exchange [*Information service*]   (EISS)
SIE............. Selected Inertial Equipment
SIE............. Selected Item Exchange   (MCD)
SIE............. Servizio Informazioni Esercito [*Italy*] [*Forces Intelligence
                Service*]
SIE............. Shanell International Energy Corp. [*Vancouver Stock
                Exchange symbol*]
SIE............. Shuttle Interface Equipment [*NASA*]   (NASA)
Sie............. Siemens [*Unit of electric conductance*]
SIE............. Siena [*Italy*] [*Seismograph station code, US Geological
                Survey*]   (SEIS)
SIE............. Sierra Express [*Reno, NV*] [*FAA designator*]   (FAAC)
SIE............. Sierra Health Services, Inc. [*American Stock Exchange
                symbol*]
SIE............. Single Instruction Execute
SIE............. Societe Internationale d'Electrochimie [*International Society of
                Electrochemistry*]
SIE............. Society of Industrial Engineers [*Later, SAM*]
SIE............. Studies in International Economics [*Elsevier Book Series*] [*A
                publication*]
SIE............. Surface Ionization Engine
SIE............. System Integration Equipment   (KSC)
SIE............. System Investigation Equipment   (KSC)
SIEA .... Sensor Interface Electronics Assembly   (MCD)
SIEB .... Satellite Interrogated Environmental Buoy
SIEC .... Societe Internationale pour l'Enseignement Commercial
                [*International Society for Business Education*]   (EA-IO)
SIEC .... Suicide Information and Education Centre [*Canadian Mental
                Health Association*] [*Information service*] [*Calgary,
                AB*]   (EISS)
SIECCAN ... Sex Information and Education Council of Canada
SIECD .... Societe Internationale d'Education Continue en Dentisterie
                [*International Society of Continuing Education in Dentistry
                - ISCED*]   (EA-IO)
SIECOP ...... Scientific Information and Education Council of
                Physicians   (EA)
SIECUS ...... Sex Information and Education Council of the US [*New York,
                NY*]   (EA)
SIED .... Supplier Item Engineering Order   (MCD)
SIEDS........ Societe Internationale d'Etude du Dix-Huitieme Siecle
                [*International Society for Eighteenth-Century Studies -
                ISECS*]   (EA-IO)
SIEF .... Societe Internationale d'Ethnographie et de Folklore
                [*International Society for Ethnology and Folklore*]
SIEFA .... Source Inventory and Emission Factor Analysis [*Environmental
                Protection Agency*]
SIEGE .... Simulated EMP [*Electromagnetic Pulse*] Ground Environment
                [*Air Force*]
Siemens Electron Components Bull ... Siemens Electronic Components
                Bulletin [*A publication*]
Siemens Energietech ... Siemens Energietechnik [*West Germany*] [*A
                publication*]
Siemens Forsch Entwickl ... Siemens Forschungs- und
                Entwicklungsberichte. Research and Development
                Reports [*A publication*]
Siemens Forsch Entwicklungsber ... Siemens Forschungs- und
                Entwicklungsberichte [*A publication*]
Siemens Forsch- und Entwicklungsber ... Siemens Forschungs- und
                Entwicklungsberichte [*A publication*]
Siemens Forsch Entwicklungsber Res Dev Rep ... Siemens Forschungs-
                und Entwicklungsberichte. Research and Development
                Reports [*A publication*]
Siemens Power Eng ... Siemens Power Engineering [*West Germany*] [*A
                publication*]
Siemens Rev ... Siemens Review [*A publication*]
Siemens-Z ... Siemens-Zeitschrift [*A publication*]
SIEND .... Saiensu [*A publication*]
SIEP .... Screening Inspection for Electronic Parts [*NASA*]
SIEPM .... Societe Internationale pour l'Etude de la Philosophie
                Medievale [*International Society for the Study of Medieval
                Philosophy*]   (EA-IO)
SIERNEV .... Sierra Nevada [*FAA*]   (FAAC)
Sierra......... Sierra Club. Bulletin [*A publication*]
Sierra Club B ... Sierra Club. Bulletin [*A publication*]
Sierra Ed News ... Sierra Educational News [*A publication*]
Sierra Leone Agric Div Minist Agric Nat Resour Rep ... Sierra Leone
                Agricultural Division. Ministry of Agriculture and Natural
                Resources. Report [*A publication*]
Sierra Leone Fish Div Tech Pap ... Sierra Leone Fisheries Division. Technical
                Paper [*A publication*]
Sierra Leone Rep Geol Surv Div ... Sierra Leone. Report on the Geological
                Survey Division [*A publication*]
SIES .... Ship Integrated Electronic System
SIES .... Sobek's International Explorer's Society [*Commercial
                firm*]   (EA)
SIES .... Society of the Incarnation of the Eternal Son [*Anglican religious
                community*]

SIESC .... Secretariat International des Enseignants Secondaires Catholiques [*International Secretariat of Catholic Secondary School Teachers*] [*Acronym used in association name, SIESC Pax Romana*] (EA-IO)
SIESTA ...... Silent Energy Sources for Tactical Applications (MCD)
SIETAR ...... Society for Intercultural Education, Training, and Research (EA)
SIEUSE ...... Secretariat International de l'Enseignement Universitaire des Sciences de l'Education
SI/EW .... Special Intelligence/Electronic Warfare (MCD)
SIF .... Reidsville, NC [*Location identifier*] [*FAA*] (FAAL)
SIF .... Salvo in Flight [*Military*] (CAAL)
SIF .... Science Information Facility [*FDA*]
SIF .... Scleroderma International Foundation [*New Castle, PA*] (EA)
SIF .... Scotch-Irish Foundation (EA)
SIF .... Scott Industrial Foam
SIF .... Secure Identification Feature
SIF .... Security and Intelligence Fund (EA)
SIF .... Selective Identification Feature [*Military decoder modification*]
SIF .... Short-Intrusion Fuze (RDA)
SIF .... SIFCO Industries, Inc. [*American Stock Exchange symbol*]
SIF .... Signaling Information Field [*Telecommunications*] (TEL)
SIF .... Simra [*Nepal*] [*Airport symbol*] (OAG)
SIF .... Single-Face
SIF .... Small Intensely Fluorescent [*Cytology*]
SIF .... Social Investment Forum [*Boston, MA*] (EA)
SIF .... Sound Intermediate Frequency
SIF .... Storage Interface Facility
SIF .... Studi Internazionali di Filosofia [*A publication*]
SIF .... Switched In-Flight (KSC)
SIF .... Synthetic Interstitial Fluid [*Biochemistry*]
SIFA .... Society of Independent Financial Advisors [*Englewood, CO*] (EA)
SIFAD .... Separate Ion Formation and Drift
SIFAR .... Surveillance Imagery Fast Access Recording (MCD)
SIFAT .... Servants in Faith and Technology (EA)
SIFC .... Saskatchewan Indian Federated College [*University of Regina*]
SIFC .... Sparks International Official Fan Club [*Gainsborough, Lincolnshire, England*] (EA-IO)
SIFC .... Studi Italiani di Filologia Classica [*A publication*]
SIFCC .... Senate Interstate and Foreign Commerce Committee
SIFCS .... Sideband Intermediate Frequency Communications System (AAG)
SifDeut ...... Sifrei Deuteronomy (BJA)
SIF/IFF .... Selective Identification Feature/Identification Friend or Foe [*Military*] (AFM)
SifNum .... Sifrei Numbers (BJA)
SIFO .... Societa Italiana di Farmacia Ospedaliera [*Italy*]
SIFO .... Svenska Institutet foer Opinionsundersoekningar
SIFR .... Simulated Instrument Flight Rules (AAG)
SIFR .... Sun-Improved Frequency Response
SIFT .... Selected-Ion Flow Tube [*Instrumentation*]
SIFT .... Share Internal FORTRAN Translator [*Data processing*] (IEEE)
SIFT .... Simplified Input for Toss [*Data processing*]
SIFT .... Software Implemented Fault Tolerance [*NASA*]
SIFTOR ...... Sifting of Information for Technology of Reactors [*MIT-AEC study*]
SIFX .... Simulated Installation Fixture (AAG)
SifZut .... Sifrei Zuta (BJA)
SIG .... San Juan-Isla Grand [*Puerto Rico*] [*Airport symbol*] (OAG)
SIG .... San Juan, PR [*Location identifier*] [*FAA*] (FAAL)
SIG .... Senior Interagency Group [*Federal government*]
SIG .... Senior Interdepartmental Group [*Department of State*]
SIG .... Serum Immune Globulin [*Immunochemistry*]
SIG .... Ship Improvement Guide
SIG .... Signa [*Write*] [*Pharmacy*]
SIG .... Signal
SIG .... Signalman [*Navy rating*] [*British*]
SIG .... Signature (AFM)
SIG .... Signetur [*Let It Be Labelled*] [*Pharmacy*]
sig .... Significant
SIG .... Signifying (ROG)
SIG .... Signore
SIG .... Silicon-Insulated Gate
SIG .... Silver-Intensified Gold [*Biological stain*]
SIG .... Silver Ridge Resources, Inc. [*Vancouver Stock Exchange symbol*]
SIG .... Simplicity Is Greatness [*See also GIS*]
SIG .... Simplified Inertial Guidance
SIG .... South Ingalls [*Colorado*] [*Seismograph station code, US Geological Survey*] [*Closed*] (SEIS)
SIG .... Southern Indiana Gas & Electric Co. [*NYSE symbol*]
SIG .... Special Interest Group
SIG .... Special Investigative Group [*DoD*]
SIG .... Starfield Image Generator
SIG .... State Implementation Grant
SIG .... Stellar Inertial Guidance Signal
SIG .... Strapdown Inertial Guidance
sIg .... Surface Immunoglobulin [*Immunochemistry*]
SIG .... Sylloge Inscriptionum Graecarum [*A publication*]
S-IgA .... Secretory Immunoglobulin A [*Immunology*]

Siga .... Signora [*Madam*] [*Italy*]
SIGAB .... Saigai Igaku [*A publication*]
SIGACC ..... Special Interest Group on Academic and Associated Computing [*Formerly, SIGUCC*] [*Association for Computing Machinery*] (CSR)
SIGACT ...... Special Interest Group on Automata and Computability Theory [*Association for Computing Machinery*]
SIGADA ..... Special Interest Group on Ada [*Association for Computing Machinery*] [*New York, NY*] (EA)
SIG/AH ...... Special Interest Group/Arts and Humanities [*of the American Society for Information Science*]
SIG/ALP .... Special Interest Group/Automated Language Processing [*American Society for Information Science*]
SIGAP .... Surrey Investigation Group into Aerial Phenomena [*British*]
SIGAPL ...... Special Interest Group on APL Programing Language [*Association for Computing Machinery*] [*New York, NY*] (EA)
SIGARCH ... Special Interest Group for Architecture of Computer Systems [*Association for Computing Machinery*] [*New York, NY*] (CSR)
SIGART ...... Special Interest Group on Artificial Intelligence [*Association for Computing Machinery*] [*New York, NY*] (EA)
SIGBAT ...... Signal Battalion [*Army*]
SIG/BC ...... Special Interest Group/Biological and Chemical Information Systems [*of the American Society for Information Science*]
SIGBDP ...... Special Interest Group for Business Data Processing and Management [*New York, NY*] (EA)
SIGBIO .... Special Interest Group on Biomedical Computing [*Association for Computing Machinery*] [*Formed by a merger of Biomedical Computing Society and Special Interest Group for Biomedical Information Processing*] [*New York, NY*] (EA)
SIG/BSS .... Special Interest Group/Behavioral and Social Sciences [*of the American Society for Information Science*]
SIGC .... Signal Corps [*Later, Communications and Electronics Command*] [*Army*]
SIGCAPH ... Special Interest Group for Computers and the Physically Handicapped [*Association for Computing Machinery*] [*New York, NY*]
SIGCAS ...... Special Interest Group on Computers and Society [*Association for Computing Machinery*] [*New York, NY*] (CSR)
SIG/CBE ... Special Interest Group/Costs, Budgeting, and Economics [*of the American Society for Information Science*]
SIGCEN ...... Signal Center [*Military*] (AABC)
SIGCHI .... Special Interest Group on Computer and Human Interaction [*Association for Computing Machinery*] [*Northwestern University*] [*Evanston, IL*] (EA)
SIGCLD ...... Significant Clouds [*Aviation*] (FAAC)
SIGCOMM ... Special Interest Group on Data Communication [*Association for Computing Machinery*]
SIGCONDR ... Signal Conditioner (MCD)
SIGCOR ..... Signal Corps [*Later, Communications and Electronics Command*] [*Army*]
SIGCOSIM ... Special Interest Group on Computer Systems, Installation Management [*Association for Computing Machinery*]
SIGCPR ...... Special Interest Group on Computer Personnel Research [*Association for Computing Machinery*] [*Indiana University*] [*Bloomington, IN*]
SIG/CR ...... Special Interest Group/Classification Research [*of the American Society for Information Science*]
SIGCS .... Special Interest Group for Computers and Society [*Association for Computing Machinery*] (EA)
SIG/CSE ... Special Interest Group for Computer Science Education [*Association for Computing Machinery*] [*New York, NY*]
SIGCUE ...... Special Interest Group for Computer Uses in Education [*Association for Computing Machinery*] [*New York, NY*]
SIG-D .... Simplified Inertial Guidance-Demonstration [*Army*] (RDA)
SIGDA .... Special Interest Group for Design Automation [*Association for Computing Machinery*] [*New York, NY*]
SIGDIV .... Signal Division [*SHAPE*] (NATG)
SIGDOC ..... Special Interest Group on Documentation [*Association for Computing Machinery*]
SIGE .... Silicon Germanium
SIGE .... Societe Internationale de Gastro-Enterologie
SIG/ES .... Special Interest Group/Education for Information Science [*of the American Society for Information Science*]
SIGEX .... Signal Exercise (NATG)
SIGFIDET ... Special Interest Group on File Description and Translation [*Association for Computing Machinery*] [*Later, Special Interest Group on the Management of Data*]
SIG/FIS ...... Special Interest Group/Foundations of Information Science [*of the American Society for Information Science*]
SIGGEN ...... Signal Generator (IEEE)
SIGGRAPH ... Special Interest Group on Computer Graphics [*Association for Computing Machinery*] [*New York, NY*]
Sight & S .. Sight and Sound [*A publication*]
Sight-Sav R ... Sight-Saving Review [*A publication*]
Sight-Sav Rev ... Sight-Saving Review [*A publication*]

SIGI	System for Interactive Guidance and Information [*Computerized career-counseling service offered by the Educational Testing Service*] [*Princeton, NJ*]
SIG/IAC	Special Interest Group/Information Analysis Centers [*of the American Society for Information Science*]
SIGINT	Signal Intelligence [*Military*] (AABC)
SIGIR	Special Interest Group on Information Retrieval [*Association for Computing Machinery*] [*New York, NY*]
SIGIRD	Systeme Integre de Gestion Informatise des Ressources Documentaires [*Integrated System for the Management of Documentary Resources*] [*University of Quebec, Montreal*] [*Montreal, PQ*] [*Information service*] (EISS)
SIG/ISE	Special Interest Group/Information Services to Education [*of the American Society for Information Science*]
SIG/LA	Special Interest Group/Library Automation and Networks [*of the American Society for Information Science*]
SIGLASH	Special Interest Group on Language Analysis and Studies in the Humanities [*Association for Computing Machinery*]
SIGLE	System for Information on Grey Literature in Europe [*European Association for Grey Literature Exploitation*] [*Database*] [*Kirchberg, Luxembourg*] (EISS)
SIGLEX	Special Interest Group on Lexicography [*National Security Agency*]
SIGLINT	Signal Intelligence [*US surveillance satellite*]
Siglo Med....	Siglo Medico [*A publication*]
SIGMA........	Sealed Insulating Glass Manufacturers Association [*Chicago, IL*] (EA)
SIGMA........	Site Information Generation and Material Accountability Plan [*Army*] (AABC)
SIGMA........	Society of In-Plant Graphics Management Associations
SIGMA........	Society of Independent Gasoline Marketers of America [*Washington, DC*] (EA)
SIGMA........	Society of Inventors of Games and Mathematical Attractions [*British*]
SIGMA........	Standardized Inertial Guidance Multiple Application
SIGMALOG ...	Simulation and Gaming Method for Analysis of Logistics [*Army*]
SIGMAP	Special Interest Group for Mathematical Programing [*Association for Computing Machinery*] [*Washington, DC*]
SIGMAS	Signal Measurement and Analysis System
Sigma Ser Pure Math ...	Sigma Series in Pure Mathematics [*A publication*]
SIGMET	Significant Meteorological Information [*Aviation*] (FAAC)
SIGMETRICS ...	Special Interest Group on Measurement and Evaluation [*Association for Computing Machinery*] (CSR)
SIGMICRO ...	Special Interest Group on Microprograming [*Association for Computing Machinery*] [*New York, NY*]
SIGMINI	Special Interest Group on Minicomputers [*Later, SIGSMALL*] [*Association for Computing Machinery*] (CSR)
SIGMN	Signalman
sigmo	Sigmoidoscopy [*Medicine*]
SIGMOD	Special Interest Group on Management of Data [*Association for Computing Machinery*]
SIGN...........	Signa [*Label*] [*Pharmacy*] (ROG)
SIGN...........	Strapdown Inertial Guidance and Navigation (MCD)
SIGNA	Signora [*Madam*] [*Italy*] (ROG)
Signa........	Signorina [*Miss*] [*Italy*]
SIGNA	Species Iris Group of North America (EA)
Signalmans J ...	Signalman's Journal [*A publication*]
Signal Process ...	Signal Processing [*A publication*]
SIGNCE.....	Significance (ROG)
SIGNE	Signature
SIGNF	Signify (ROG)
Sign Lang Stud ...	Sign Language Studies [*A publication*]
SIGN N P	Signetur Nomine Proprio [*Let It Be Written Upon with the Proper Name*] [*Pharmacy*] (ROG)
SIG/NPM.....	Special Interest Group/Nonprint Media [*of the American Society for Information Science*]
Sig n pro	Signa Nomine Proprio [*Label with the Proper Name*] [*Pharmacy*]
SIGNRE.....	Signature (ROG)
SIGNUM	Special Interest Group for Numerical Mathematics [*Association for Computing Machinery*] (CSR)
SIGO	Signal Officer
SIGOA.......	Special Interest Group on Office Automation [*Later, SIGOIS*]
SIGOIS	Special Interest Group on Office Information Systems [*Pittsburgh, PA*] (EA)
SIGOP	Signal Optimization Program [*Federal Highway Administration*]
SIGOPS.....	Special Interest Group on Operating Systems [*Association for Computing Machinery*]
SIGPC	Special Interest Group on Personal Computing [*Association for Computing Machinery*]
SIGPLAN.....	Special Interest Group on Programing Languages [*Association for Computing Machinery*] [*New York, NY*]
SIGPRAD ...	Special Interest Group on Phobias and Related Anxiety Disorders [*New York, NY*] (EA)
SIGR..........	Sigma Research, Inc. [*NASDAQ symbol*] (NQ)
SIGRAM	Sound Intensity Diagram (MCD)
SIGREAL....	Special Interest Group on Real Time Processing [*Association for Computing Machinery*]
SIG/RT	Special Interest Group/Reprographic Technology [*of the American Society for Information Science*]

SIGS...........	Sandia Interactive Graphics System
SIGS...........	Simplified Inertial Guidance System (MCD)
SIGS...........	Stellar Inertial Guidance System [*Air Force*] (AAG)
SIGSAC......	Special Interest Group on Security, Audit, and Control [*Association for Computing Machinery*] [*New York, NY*]
SIGSAM	Special Interest Group for Symbolic and Algebraic Manipulation [*Association for Computing Machinery*]
SIGSCSA ...	Special Interest Group on Small Computing Systems and Applications [*Later, SIGSMALL*] [*Association for Computing Machinery*] [*New York, NY*] (EA)
SIG/SDI	Special Interest Group/Selective Dissemination of Information [*American Society for Information Science*]
SIGSEC......	Signal Security [*Military*] (AABC)
SIGSIM.......	Special Interest Group on Simulation [*Association for Computing Machinery*] [*New York, NY*]
SIGSMALL ...	Special Interest Group on Small Computing Systems and Applications [*Formerly, SIGSCSA*] [*Association for Computing Machinery*] (EA)
SIGSOC	Special Interest Group on Social and Behavioral Science Computing [*Association for Computing Machinery*]
SIGSOFT....	Special Interest Group on Software Engineering [*Association for Computing Machinery*] [*New York, NY*]
SIGSOP......	Signals Operator (ADA)
SIGSPAC ...	Special Interest Group on Urban Data Systems, Planning, Architecture, and Civil Engineering [*Association for Computing Machinery*]
SIGSPACE ...	Senior Interagency Group (Space)
Sig Sta ...	Signal Station [*Nautical charts*]
SIGSTN......	Signal Station [*Navigation*]
SIGTRAN ...	Special Interest Group on Translation [*National Security Agency*]
SIGUCCS...	Special Interest Group for University and College Computing Services [*Association for Computing Machinery*] [*Later, Special Interest Group on Academic and Associated Computing*] [*Drake University*] [*Des Moines, IA*]
Sigurnost Rudn ...	Sigurnost u Rudnicima [*A publication*]
SIGVOICE ...	Special Interest Group on Voice [*National Security Agency*]
SIH	Schweizerisches Institut fuer Hauswirtschaft
SIH	Seamen and International House (EA)
SIH	Silgarhi Doti [*Nepal*] [*Airport symbol*] (OAG)
SIH	Societe Internationale d'Hematologie [*International Society of Hematology - ISH*] (EA)
SIH	Society for Italic Handwriting (EA)
SIH	Sun Ice [*Toronto Stock Exchange symbol*]
SIHED	Sanitaer-Installateur und Heizungsbauer [*A publication*]
SIHS..........	SI Handling Systems [*NASDAQ symbol*] (NQ)
SIHS..........	Society for Italian Historical Studies (EA)
SIHT..........	Space Impact Hand Tool [*NASA*]
SIHW	Society for Italic Handwriting (EA)
SII..............	School Interest Inventory [*Psychology*]
SII..............	Security-Insecurity Inventory [*Psychology*]
SII..............	Self-Interview Inventory [*Psychology*]
SII..............	Short Interval Identification
SII..............	Sitkinak Island [*Alaska*] [*Seismograph station code, US Geological Survey*] (SEIS)
SII..............	Smith International, Incorporated [*NYSE symbol*]
SII..............	Space Industries, Incorporated
SII..............	Special Interest Items (MCD)
SII..............	Standard Identification for Individuals [*Social security*] [*American National Standards Institute*]
SII..............	Statement of Intelligence Interest [*Army*] (RDA)
SII..............	Sugar Information, Incorporated [*Defunct*] (EA)
SII..............	Supervisory Immigrant Inspector [*Immigration and Naturalization Service*]
SIIA	Self-Insurance Institute of America [*Santa Ana, CA*] (EA)
SIIAEC	Secretariat International des Ingenieurs, des Agronomes, et des Cadres Economiques Catholiques [*International Secretariat of Catholic Technologists, Agriculturists, and Economists*] (EA-IO)
SIIC	Secretariat International des Groupements Professionnels des Industries Chimiques des Pays de la CEE
SIIC	Special Interest Item Code (AABC)
SIINC.........	Scientific Instrumentation Information Network and Curricula [*National Science Foundation*]
SIIR	Spares Item Inventory Record (MCD)
SIIRS	Smithsonian Institution Information Retrieval System (DIT)
SIJ..............	Minneapolis, MN [*Location identifier*] [*FAA*] (FAAL)
SIJ..............	Sacroiliac Joint
SIJ..............	Siglufjordur [*Iceland*] [*Airport symbol*] (OAG)
SIJ..............	Small Industry Journal [*Quezon City*] [*A publication*]
SIK	Sikeston, MO [*Location identifier*] [*FAA*] (FAAL)
SIK	Silknit Ltd. [*Toronto Stock Exchange symbol*]
Sik.............	Single Income, Kids [*Lifestyle classification*]
SIK	Studi Italici (Kyoto) [*A publication*]
SiK	Sztuka i Krytyka [*A publication*]
Sikh R	Sikh Review [*Calcutta*] [*A publication*]
SIL.............	Ile a la Crosse Public Library, Saskatchewan [*Library symbol*] [*National Library of Canada*] (NLC)
SIL.............	Safety Information Letter (IEEE)
SIL.............	Scanner Input Language
SIL.............	Schedule Interface Log

SIL............. Selected Item List
SIL............. Semiconductor Injector LASER
SIL............. Seriously Ill List [*Military*]
SIL............. Service Information Letter
SIL............. Silcorp Ltd. [*Toronto Stock Exchange symbol*]
SIL............. Silence   (MSA)
Sil............. Silius Italicus [*First century AD*] [*Classical studies*]   (OCD)
SIL............. Sillimanite [*Mineralogy*]
SIL............. Silurian [*Period, era, or system*] [*Geology*]
SIL............. Silver   (AAG)
Sil............. Silver Tax Division [*Internal Revenue Bulletin*]   (DLA)
SIL............. Slidel, LA [*Location identifier*] [*FAA*]   (FAAL)
SIL............. Smithsonian Institution Information Leaflets
SIL............. Smithsonian Institution Libraries
SIL............. SNOBOL Implementation Language Reimplemented [*1974*] [*Data processing*]   (CSR)
SIL............. Societas Internationalis Limnologiae Theoreticae et Applicae [*International Association of Theoretical and Applied Limnology*]
SIL............. Societe Internationale de la Lepre [*International Leprosy Association*]
SIL............. Society for Individual Liberty   (EA)
SIL............. Sound Intensity Level
SIL............. Sound Interference Level [*NASA*]   (NASA)
SIL............. Special Interest Launch [*Military*]   (AFIT)
SIL............. Speech Interference Level
SIL............. Steam Isolation Line   (IEEE)
SIL............. Store Interface Link
SIL............. Studies in Linguistics [*A publication*]
SIL............. Summer Institute of Linguistics
SIL............. Supply Information Letter   (MCD)
SIL............. Support Items List   (MCD)
SIL............. Surge Impedance Loading
SIL............. Systems Integration Laboratory   (MCD)
SILA......... Scientific Laboratories, Inc. [*NASDAQ symbol*]   (NQ)
SILAD....... Siderurgia Latinoamericana [*A publication*]
SILAF........ Sindacato Italiano Lavoratori Appalti Ferroviari [*Italian Union of Railroad Contract Workers*]
SILAP........ Sindacato Nazionale Dipendenti Ministero del Lavori Pubblici [*National Union of Employees in the Ministry of Public Welfare*] [*Italy*]
SILAT........ Subionospheric Latitude
SILCA........ Sindacato Italiano Lavoratori Cappellai ed Affini [*Italian Federation of Hat and Allied Workers*]
Sil (Ct of Ap) ... Silvernail's New York Court of Appeals Reports   (DLA)
Silent Pic ... Silent Picture [*A publication*]
SILF........... Societe Internationale de Linguistique Fonctionelle [*International Society of Functional Linguistics*]   (EA-IO)
SILG.......... Silencing   (MSA)
SILI........... Siliconix, Inc. [*NASDAQ symbol*]   (NQ)
SILI........... Sindacato Nazionale Lavoratori Italcable [*National Union of Cable Workers*] [*Italy*]
SILI........... Standard Item Location Index
SILICA....... System for International Literature Information on Ceramics and Glass [*Fachinformationszentrum Werkstoffe*] [*Database*]
Silicates Indus ... Silicates Industriels [*A publication*]
Silik........... Silikaty [*A publication*]
Silk Rayon Ind India ... Silk and Rayon Industries of India [*A publication*]
Silkworm Inf Bull ... Silkworm Information Bulletin [*A publication*]
Silliman J... Silliman Journal [*A publication*]
SILN.......... Silicon General, Inc. [*NASDAQ symbol*]   (NQ)
SILO.......... Security Intelligence Liaison Office [*Central Mediterranean Forces*] [*Navy*]
SILON........ Subionospheric Longitude
SILOP........ Studies in Linguistics. Occasional Papers [*A publication*]
SILP.......... Section of International Law and Practice [*American Bar Association*]   (EA)
SILP.......... Sindacato Italiano Lavoratori del Petrolio [*Italian Union of Oil Workers*]
SILP.......... Sindacato Italiano Lavoratori Postelegrafonici [*Italian Union of Postal and Telegraph Workers*]
SILS.......... Shipboard Impact Locator System
SILS.......... Shipley-Institute of Living Scale for Measuring Intellectual Impairment [*Psychology*]
SILS.......... Silver Solder
SILSP........ Safeguard Integrated Logistics Support Plan [*Army*]   (AABC)
Sil (Sup Ct) ... Silvernail's New York Supreme Court Reports   (DLA)
SILT.......... Stored Information Loss Tree
SILTA........ Studi Italiani di Linguistica Teorica ed Applicata [*A publication*]
SILTE........ Sindacato Italiano Lavoratori Telecomunicazioni [*Italian Union of Telecommunications Workers*]
SILTS........ Shuttle Infrared Leeside Temperature Sensing [*NASA*]   (NASA)
SILTS........ Sindacato Italiano Lavoratori Telefoni di Stato [*Italian Union of Government Telephone Workers*]
SILULAP .... Sindacato Italiano Lavoratori Uffici Locali ed Agenzie Postelegrafonici [*Italian Union of Local Post and Telegraph Office Workers*]
Silv............ Silvae [*of Statius*] [*Classical studies*]   (OCD)
SILV.......... Silver   (ROG)
SILV.......... Silver King Mines [*NASDAQ symbol*]   (NQ)

Silv .... Silvernail's New York Criminal Reports [*9-14 New York*]   (DLA)
Silv .... Silvernail's New York Reports [*1886-92*]   (DLA)
Silv .... Silvernail's New York Supreme Court Reports [*1889-90*]   (DLA)
Silv A.......... Silvernail's New York Court of Appeals Reports   (DLA)
Silvaecult Trop Subtrop ... Silvaecultura Tropica et Subtropica [*A publication*]
Silvae Genet ... Silvae Genetica [*A publication*]
Silva Fenn ... Silva Fennica [*A publication*]
Silv App ...... Silvernail's New York Court of Appeals Reports   (DLA)
Silv Cit ...... Silvernail's New York Citations   (DLA)
Silv Ct App ... Silvernail's New York Court of Appeals Reports   (DLA)
Silv Ct App (NY) ... Silvernail's New York Court of Appeals Reports   (DLA)
Silvernail's NY Rep ... Silvernail's New York Court of Appeals Reports   (DLA)
Silvic Sao Paulo ... Silvicultura em Sao Paulo [*A publication*]
Silv Notes Ont Dep Lds For ... Silvicultural Notes. Ontario Department of Lands and Forests [*A publication*]
Silv Res Note (Tanz) ... Silviculture Research Note (Tanzania) [*A publication*]
Silv Sup ..... Silvernail's New York Supreme Court Reports   (DLA)
Silv (Sup Ct) ... Silvernail's New York Supreme Court Reports   (DLA)
Silv Unrep ... Silvernail's New York Unreported Cases   (DLA)
SIM............ SACLANT [*Supreme Allied Commander, Atlantic*] Staff Instruction Manual   (NATG)
SIM............ Scanning Ion Microscope
SIM............ School of Industrial Management [*MIT*]   (MCD)
SIM............ Scientific Instrument Module [*NASA*]
SIM............ Sclerite-Inducing Membrane [*Entomology*]
SIM............ Selected Inventory Management [*Military*]   (CAAL)
SIM............ Selected Ion Monitoring [*Chromatography*]
SIM............ Selected Item Management
SIM............ Sequential Inference Machine [*Data processing*]
SIM............ Sergeant Instructor of Musketry
SIM............ Service Instructions Message [*Telecommunications*]   (TEL)
SIM............ Service International de Microfilm, Paris, France [*Library symbol*] [*Library of Congress*]   (LCLS)
SIM............ Servicio Intelligencia Militar [*Military Intelligence Service*] [*Dominican Republic*]
SIM............ Servizio Informazioni Militaire [*Military Intelligence Service*] [*Italy*]
SIM............ Set Interrupt Mask [*Data processing*]
SIM............ Shima Resources [*Vancouver Stock Exchange symbol*]
SIM............ Ship Instrumentation Manager   (KSC)
SIM............ Simbai [*Papua New Guinea*] [*Airport symbol*]   (OAG)
SIM............ Simferopol [*USSR*] [*Seismograph station code, US Geological Survey*]   (SEIS)
SIM............ Similar   (AAG)
SIM............ Simile [*In a Similar Manner*] [*Music*]
Sim............ Simmons' Reports [*95-97, 99 Wisconsin*]   (DLA)
Sim............ Simons' English Chancery Reports [*57-60 English Reprint*] [*1826-50*]   (DLA)
SIM............ Simplex
SIM............ Simposio Internacional de Macromoleculas [*International Symposium on Macromolecules*]
SIM............ Simulated [*or Simulation*]   (AABC)
SIM............ Small Intestine Metaplasia [*Medicine*]
SIM............ Societa Italiana di Metapsichica [*Italy*]
SIM............ Societe Internationale de la Moselle [*International Moselle Company*]
SIM............ Societe Internationale de Musicologie [*International Musicological Society*]
SIM............ Society for Industrial Microbiology   (EA)
SIM............ Society for Information Management [*Chicago, IL*]   (EA)
SIM............ Solar Interplanetary Model
SIM............ Space Interceptor Missile   (MCD)
SIM............ Stage Inert Mass
SIM............ Steatite Insulation Material
SIM............ Stellar Image Monitor
SIM............ Student Interracial Ministry [*Defunct*]
SIM............ Submarine Intended Movement   (NVT)
SIM............ Subsystem Interface Module
SIM............ Subtotal Integration Mode
SIM............ Sucrose-Isomaltose Deficiency [*Medicine*]
SIM............ Sudan Interior Mission
SIM............ Sulfide Production, Indole Production, and Motility [*Growth medium*]
SIM............ Surveillance Intelligence and Reconnaissance Mission [*Military*]   (CAAL)
SIM............ Synchronous Interface Module
SIM............ Systems Integration Model   (MCD)
SIMA .... Salon International de la Machine Agricole
SIMA .... Scientific Instrument Manufacturers' Association [*British*]
SIMA .... Shore Intermediate Maintenance Activity [*Navy*]   (NVT)
SIMA .... Studies in Mediterranean Archaeology [*A publication*]
SIMAC....... Sonic Instrument Measurement and Control   (AAG)
SIMAJ .... Scientific Instrument Manufacturers' Association of Japan
SIMArsbok ... Svenska Israels-Missionens Arsbok [*Stockholm*] [*A publication*]
SIMAS........ Shuttle Information Management Accountability System [*NASA*]   (NASA)
SIMAS........ SONAR-in-Situ Mode Assessment System [*Marine science*]   (MSC)

SIMBAD ..... Simulation as a Basis for Social Agents' Decisions [*Data processing*]

SIMBAY ..... Scientific Instrumentation Module Bay [*NASA*]   (KSC)

SIMC .... Silicon Integrated Monolithic Circuit

Sim & C ..... Simmons and Conover's Reports [*99-100 Wisconsin*]   (DLA)

SIMC .... Societe Internationale de Medecine de Catastrophe [*International Society for Disaster Medicine - ISDM*]   (EA)

SIMC .... Societe Internationale de Medecine Cybernetique [*International Society of Cybernetic Medicine*]

SIMC .... Societe Internationale pour la Musique Contemporaine [*International Society for Contemporary Music*]

SIMC .... Syndicat International des Marins Canadiens [*Seafarers' International Union of Canada - SIU*]

SIMCA .... Societe Industrielle de Mecanique et de Carrosserie Automobile [*French automobile manufacturer; acronym used as name of its cars*]

SIMCANSOC ... Simulated Canadian Society [*Simulation game*]

SIMCAP ..... Simulation, Corps Automated Procedures   (MCD)

SIMCE .... Simulation Communications Electronics [*Group of computer programs*] [*Army*]

SIMCEN ..... Simulation Center [*Deep Space Network, NASA*]

SIMCHE ..... Simulation and Checkout Equipment [*NASA*]   (KSC)

SIMCO .... Sea Ice Microbial Colony

SIMCOM .... Simulation and Computer [*Data processing*]

SIMCOM .... Simulator Compiler [*Computer*]

SIMCON ..... Scientific Inventory Management and Control

SIMCON ..... Simplified Control

SIMCON ..... Simulation Controller

SIMD .... Single Instruction, Multiple Data   (IEEE)

SIMDEP ...... Simulation Development Program [*DASA*]

Sim Dig ...... Simmons' Wisconsin Digest   (DLA)

Sim Dig Pat Dec ... Simonds' Digest of Patent Office Decisions [*United States*]   (DLA)

SIME .... Security Intelligence, Middle East [*Navy*]

SIME .... Studies in Mechanical Engineering [*Elsevier Book Series*] [*A publication*]

Sim (Eng) ... Simons' English Chancery Reports [*57-60 English Reprint*]   (DLA)

Simes & S Future Interests ... Simes and Smith on the Law of Future Interests   (DLA)

SIMEX .... Secondary Item Materiel Excess [*DoD*]

SIMFAC ..... Simulation Facility

SIMFAR ..... Simulated Frequency Analysis and Recording   (MCD)

SIMG .... Sammelbaende der Internationalen Musik Gesellschaft [*A publication*]

SIMG .... Societas Internationalis Medicinae Generalis [*International Society of General Practice*]   (EA-IO)

SIMHA .... Societe Internationale de Mycologie Humaine et Animale [*International Society for Human and Animal Mycology - ISHAM*]   (EA)

SIMICORE ... Simultaneous Multiple Image Correlation

SIMILE ...... Simulator of Immediate Memory in Learning Experiments

SIML .... Similar   (AAG)

Simla .... All India Reporter, Simla 1951   (DLA)

SIMLALY .... Simultaneously   (ROG)

SIMLR .... Similar   (ROG)

SIMM .... Single In-Line Memory Module [*Data processing*]

SIMM .... Studies in Indo-Muslim Mysticism [*A publication*]

SIMM .... Symbolic Integrated Maintenance Manual   (MCD)

SIMNET ..... Simulation Network

Sim NS ...... Simons' English Vice-Chancery Reports, New Series [*61 English Reprint*]   (DLA)

SIMNS .... Simulated Navigation Systems

Sim NS (Eng) ... Simons' English Vice-Chancery Reports, New Series [*61 English Reprint*]   (DLA)

SIMO .... Special Items Management Office

SIMOBS ..... Simultaneous Observations [*RADAR and optical*]

SIMOC .... Simulated Occupant [*People Machine*] [*Office of Civil Defense*]

Simon .... Simonides [*Fifth century BC*] [*Classical studies*]   (OCD)

Simon's Town Hist Soc ... Simon's Town Historical Society [*A publication*]

SIMOP .... Simultaneous Operation

SIMOS .... Space Imbalanced Military Occupational Specialty

SIMP .... Satellite Information Message Protocol

SIMP .... Shipboard Integrated Maintenance Program [*Navy*]   (NG)

SIMP .... Simpleton   (DSUE)

Simp .... Single Income, Money Problems [*Lifestyle classification*]

SIMP .... Societa Italiana di Medicina Psicosomatica [*Italy*]

SIMP .... Specific Impulse   (MSA)

SIMPAC ..... Simplified Programing for Acquisition and Control   (IEEE)

SIMPAC ..... Simulation Package [*Data processing*]

Simp Inf ..... Simpson on Infants [*4th ed.*] [*1926*]   (DLA)

SIMPL .... Simulation Implementation Machine Programing Languages   (KSC)

SIMPL/1 ..... Simulation Language Based on Programing Language, Version One

SIMPLAN ... Simple Modeling and Planning [*SIMPLAN Users Group*] [*New York, NY*]   (CSR)

SIMPLAN ... Simplified Modeling and Planning [*Programing language*] [*1973*]   (CSR)

SIMPLE ...... Simulation of Industrial Management Problems [*Program*] [*1958*] [*Data processing*]   (CSR)

SIMPLE ...... Solver for Implicit Equations [*Computer language*]

SIMPLE ...... System for Integrated Maintenance and Program Language Extension

SIMPO .... Simulation of Personnel Operations [*Army Research Institute for the Behavioral and Social Sciences*]   (RDA)

Simp Otlalennoi Gibrid Rast ... Simpozium po Otlalennoi Gibridizatsii Rastenii [*A publication*]

SIMPP .... Society of Independent Motion Picture Producers

SIMPU .... Simulation Punch

SIMR .... Schenley Instant Market Reports

SIMR .... Simulator   (AAG)

SIMR .... Societe Internationale de Mecanique des Roches [*International Society for Rock Mechanics - ISRM*]   (EA-IO)

SIMR .... Systems Integration Management Review   (MCD)

SIMRAND ... Simulation of Research and Development

Sim Ry Acc ... Simon's Law Relating to Railway Accidents [*1862*]   (DLA)

SIMS .... Secondary Ion Mass Spectrometer [*or Spectrometry*]

SIMS .... Sedna Information Management System [*Sedna Corp.*] [*St. Paul, MN*] [*Information service*]   (EISS)

SIMS .... Selected Item Management System   (AABC)

SIMS .... Selective Interference Modulation Spectrometer

SIMS .... Shuttle Imaging Microwave System [*NASA*]   (NASA)

SIMS .... Shuttle Inventory Management System [*NASA*]   (NASA)

SIMS .... Siam Institute for Mathematics and Society

Sim & S ...... Simons and Stuart's English Chancery Reports [*57 English Reprint*]   (DLA)

SIMS .... Single Item, Multisource   (IEEE)

SIMS .... Skandinaviska Simuleringssaellskapet [*Scandinavian Simulation Society*]   (EA)

SIMS .... Stellar Inertial Measurement System [*NASA*]

SIMS .... Strategic Integrated Management System [*American Occupational Therapy Association*]

SIMS .... Students' International Meditation Society

SiMS .... Studier i Modern Sprakvetenskap [*A publication*]

SIMS .... Symbolic Integrated Maintenance System

SIMSA .... Savings Institutions Marketing Society of America

SIMSCRIPT ... [*A*] simulation programing language [*1963*] [*Data processing*]

SIMSEP ..... Simulation of Solar Electric Propulsion [*NASA*]

SIMSI .... Selective Inventory Management of Secondary Items [*Navy*]

SIMSIN ...... Simulated Strapdown Inertial Navigation   (MCD)

SIMSLIN .... Safety in Mines Scattered Light Instrument   (ADA)

SIMSOC ..... Simulated Society

Sim & St ..... Simons and Stuart's English Chancery Reports [*57 English Reprint*]   (DLA)

Sim & Stu ... Simons and Stuart's English Vice-Chancery Reports [*57 English Reprint*]   (DLA)

Sim & Stu (Eng) ... Simons and Stuart's English Chancery Reports [*57 English Reprint*]   (DLA)

SIMSUP ...... Simulation Supervisor

SIMS-X ...... Selected Items Management System - Expanded   (MCD)

SIMSYS ..... Simulated System   (CAAL)

SIMTOS ..... Simulated Tactical Operations Systems [*Army*]   (RDA)

SIMUL .... Simultaneous   (AABC)

SIMULA ...... Simulation Language [*1964*] [*Data processing*]

Simulat Gam ... Simulation and Games [*A publication*]

Simulat & Games ... Simulation and Games [*A publication*]

Simulations Councils Proc ... Simulations Councils. Proceedings [*A publication*]

Simul and Games ... Simulation and Games [*A publication*]

SIMUPOL ... Simulative Procedure Oriented Language   (MCD)

SIN .... Salpingitis Isthmica Nodosum

SIN .... Scientific Information Notes [*A publication*]

SIN .... Security Information Network

SIN .... Sensitive Information Network

SIN .... Simultaneous Interpenetrating Networks [*Organic chemistry*]

SiN .... Sin Nombre [*A publication*]

SIN .... Sinagawa [*Japan*] [*Seismograph station code, US Geological Survey*] [*Closed*]   (SEIS)

SIN .... Sinclair Community College, Dayton, OH [*OCLC symbol*]   (OCLC)

SIN .... Sine [*Mathematics*]

SIN .... Sine [*Without*] [*Latin*]

SIN .... Sinecure   (ROG)

SIN .... Singapore [*Singapore*] [*Airport symbol*]   (OAG)

SIN .... Single Identifying Number

SIN .... Sinistra [*Left Hand*] [*Music*]

Sin .... Sinter [*Record label*] [*Brazil*]

SIN .... Social Insurance Number [*Canada*]

SIN .... Society for International Numismatics   (EA)

SIN .... Spanish International Network [*Cable-television system*]

SIN .... Stop Inflation Now [*Variation on the anti-inflation WIN slogan of President Gerald Ford*]

SIN .... Study Item Number [*Army*]   (AABC)

S IN .... Sub Initio [*Towards the Beginning*] [*Latin*]   (ROG)

SIN .... Subject Indication Number

SIN .... Support Information Network

SIN .... Symbolic Integrator

SINA .... Scheduling Information Not Available   (KSC)

SINA .... Shellfish Institute of North America [*Also known as Oyster Growers and Dealers Association of North America*] [*Washington, DC*]   (EA)

SINA.......... Society for Indecency to Naked Animals [*A hoax association*]
SINACMA ... Sindacato Nazionale Dipendenti Corte dei Conti e Magistrature Amministrative [*National Union of General Accounting Office Employees*] [*Italy*]
SINAD .... Signal Plus Noise and Distortion
SINADIMID ... Sindacato Nazionale Dipendenti Ministero Difesa [*National Union of Ministry of Defense Employees*] [*Italy*]
SINAF......... Sindacato Nazionale Dipendenti Ministero Agricoltura e Foreste [*National Union of Ministry of Agriculture and Forestry Employees*] [*Italy*]
SINAMAI .... Sindacato Nazionale e Dipendenti Ministero Africa Italiana [*National Union of Former Italian Employees of African Ministry*] [*Italy*]
SINAMIL..... Sindacato Nazionale Dipendenti Ministero del Lavoro e Previdenza Sociale [*National Union of Ministry of Labor and Social Security Employees*] [*Italy*]
SINAMN ..... Sindacato Nazionale Dipendenti Marina Mercantile [*National Union of Merchant Marine Workers*] [*Italy*]
SINAP .... Satellite Input to Numerical Analysis and Prediction [*National Weather Service*]
SINAP .... Sinapis [*Mustard*] [*Pharmacology*]   (ROG)
SINAPI .... Sindacato Nazionale Ministero Pubblica Istruzione [*National Union of Ministry of Public Instructors*] [*Italy*]
SINASCEL ... Sindacato Nazionale Scuola Elementare [*National Union of Elementary School Teachers*] [*Italy*]
SINB.......... Southern Interstate Nuclear Board
SINC.......... Nicaraguan International Rescue from Communism   (PD)
SINC.......... Seal, Incorporated [*NASDAQ symbol*]   (NQ)
SINCGARS ... Single-Channel Ground and Airborne Radio System   (MCD)
SINCGARS-V ... Single-Channel Ground and Airborne Radio System, Very High Frequency
Sinclair ...... Sinclair's Manuscript Decisions, Scotch Session Cases   (DLA)
SINCOE...... Sindacato Nazionale Dipendenti Ministero Industria e Commercio Estero [*National Union of Ministry of Industry and Foreign Commerce Employees*] [*Italy*]
SINCTRAC ... Single Channel Tactical Radio Communications [*Army*]   (RDA)
Sind........... All India Reporter, Sind [*1914-50*]   (DLA)
Sind........... Indian Rulings, Sind Series [*1929-47*]   (DLA)
SIND.......... Saskatchewan Indian [*A publication*]
SIND.......... Satellite Inertial Navigation Determination   (MCD)
SIND.......... Southern Indiana Railway, Inc. [*AAR code*]
SIND.......... Strobe Intersection Deghoster
SINDAF ...... Sindacato Nazionale Dipendenti Amministrazioni Finanziarie [*National Union of Financial Administration Employees*] [*Italy*]
S Ind Stud ... Southern Indian Studies [*A publication*]
Sind Univ Res J Sci Ser ... Sind University Research Journal. Science Series [*A publication*]
SIN-ETH..... Swiss Institute of Nuclear Research - Eidgenoessische Technische Hochschule
SINEWS ..... Ship Integrated Electronic Warfare System
SINF .... Sinfonia [*Symphony*] [*Music*]
SINFDOK ... Statens Rad for Vetenskaplig Information och Dokumentation [*Swedish Council for Scientific Information and Documentation*]   (EISS)
SINFUB ...... Skrifter Utgitt av Instituttet foer Nordisk Filologi. Universitetet i Bergen [*A publication*]
SING.......... Singapore
SING.......... Singular
SING.......... Singulorum [*Of Each*] [*Pharmacy*]
SINGAN ..... Singularity Analyzer [*Data processing*]
Singapore J Primary Ind ... Singapore Journal of Primary Industries [*A publication*]
Singapore Lib ... Singapore Libraries [*A publication*]
Singapore L Rev ... Singapore Law Review [*A publication*]
Singapore Med J ... Singapore Medical Journal [*A publication*]
Singapore Natl Inst Chem Bull ... Singapore National Institute of Chemistry. Bulletin [*A publication*]
Singapore Statist Bull ... Singapore Statistical Bulletin [*A publication*]
Singer Prob Cas (PA) ... Singer's Probate Cases [*Pennsylvania*]   (DLA)
Singers ...... Singer's Probate Court [*Pennsylvania*]   (DLA)
Sing Kir...... Singende Kirche [*A publication*]
Sing LR ...... Singapore Law Review [*A publication*]
Sing Pub Health B ... Singapore Public Health Bulletin [*A publication*]
SINGR .... Singular
Sing Stat B ... Singapore Statistical Bulletin [*A publication*]
SINH.......... Sine, Hyperbolic
SINIST....... Sinister [*Left*] [*Latin*]
Sinister ...... Sinister Wisdom [*A publication*]
Sink.......... Single Income, No Kids [*Lifestyle classification*]
Sin N .... Sin Nombre [*A publication*]
SIN Newsl ... SIN [*Schweizerisches Institut fuer Nuklearforschung*] Newsletter [*A publication*]
Sino........... Thioinosine [*Also, Sno, M*] [*A nucleoside*]
Sino-Am Rels ... Sino-American Relations [*Taiwan*] [*A publication*]
Si non val ... Si Non Valeat [*If It Is Not Effective*] [*Pharmacy*]
Sinop Odontol ... Sinopse de Odontologia [*A publication*]
SINR.......... Shoulder Internal Rotation [*Sports medicine*]
SINR.......... Signal to Interference plus Noise Ratio   (MCD)
SINR.......... Swiss Institute for Nuclear Research
SINS.......... Satellite Interceptor Navigation System [*Navy*]   (CAAL)

SINS.......... Ship Inertial Navigational System
SINS.......... Sindacato Scuola non Statale [*Union of Private Schools' Employees*] [*Italy*]
SINSU .... Skrifter Utgivna av Institutionen foer Nordiska Sprak Vid Uppsala Universitet [*A publication*]
SINSUU...... Skrifter Utgivna av Institutionen foer Nordiska Sprak Vid Uppsala Universitet [*A publication*]
S INT .... Senza Interruzione [*Without Interruption*] [*Music*]
SINT .... System Integrators [*NASDAQ symbol*]   (NQ)
Sint Almazy ... Sinteticheskie Almazy [*A publication*]
Sint Anal Strukt Org Soedin ... Sintez, Analiz, i Struktura Organicheskikh Soedinenii [*USSR*] [*A publication*]
S INTER ..... Senza Interruzione [*Without Interruption or Pause*] [*Music*]   (ROG)
Sintesi Econ ... Sintesi Economica [*A publication*]
Sint Fiz-Khim Polim ... Sintez i Fiziko-Khimiya Polimerov [*A publication*]
Sint Org Soedin ... Sintezy Organicheskikh Soedinenij [*A publication*]
SI N VAL..... Si Non Valeat [*If It Does Not Answer*] [*Pharmacy*]   (ROG)
SIO .... Sacroiliac Orthosis [*Medicine*]
SIO .... Scripps Institution of Oceanography [*La Jolla, CA*] [*Research center*]
SIO .... Senior Information Officer
SIO .... Senior Intelligence Officer   (MCD)
SIO .... Serial Input/Output   (MCD)
SIO .... Ship's Information Officer [*Navy*]
SIO .... Sindacato Italiano Ostetriche [*Italian Union of Midwives*]
sio .... Siouan [*MARC language code*] [*Library of Congress*]   (LCCP)
SIO .... Smithton [*Australia*] [*Airport symbol*]   (OAG)
SIO .... Sorting It Out [*An association*]   (EA)
SIO .... Southern Union Resources [*Vancouver Stock Exchange symbol*]
SIO .... Special Inquiry Officer
SIO .... Special Intelligence Officer [*Military*]   (NVT)
SIO .... Staged in Orbit
SIO .... Start Input/Output
SIO .... Systems Integration Office [*NASA*]   (NASA)
SIOA......... System Input/Output Adapter   (CAAL)
SIOATH..... Source Identification and Ordering Authorization [*DoD*]
SIOBA .... Sbornik Informatsii po Obogashcheniyu i Briketirovaniyu Uglei [*A publication*]
SIOC .... Serial Input/Output Channel
SIOD.......... Sindacato Italiano Odonototecnici Diplomati [*Italian Union of Odontotechnicians*]
SIOE .... Special Issue of Equipment
SIOH.......... Supervision, Inspection, and Overhead   (AFM)
SIOP.......... Secure Identification Operating Procedure
SIOP.......... Selector Input/Output Processor [*Data processing*]   (IEEE)
SIOP.......... Single Integrated Operations Plan [*Military*]   (AFM)
SIOP.......... Societe Internationale d'Oncologie Pediatrique [*International Society of Pediatric Oncology*]   (EA-IO)
SIOP.......... Strategic Integrated Operational Plan
SIOP-ESI.... Single Integrated Operational Plan - Extremely Sensitive Information [*Security level above Top Secret*]
SI OP SIT ... Si Opus Sit [*If There Be Occasion*] [*Pharmacy*]   (ROG)
SIOUX .... Sequential and Iterative Operation Unit X   (IEEE)
SIP............. Safety Injection Pump   (IEEE)
SIP............. Safety Instrumentation Package   (MCD)
SIP............. Sampling Inspection Procedures
SIP............. Saskatchewan Institute of Pedology [*University of Saskatchewan*] [*Research center*]   (RCD)
SIP............. Satellite Information Processor
SIP............. Satellite Inspector Program   (AAG)
SIP............. Schedule-Induced Polydipsia [*Psychology*]
SIP............. Scientific Information [*or Instruction*] Processor [*Honeywell, Inc.*]
SIP............. Scientific Instrument Package [*NASA*]   (KSC)
SIP............. Securities Investor Protection Corp.
SIP............. Selma [*Alabama*] Interreligious Project   (EA)
SIP............. Senior Intensified Program [*Education*]
SIP............. Separation Instrument Package   (MCD)
SIP............. Shinkiari [*Pakistan*] [*Seismograph station code, US Geological Survey*]   (SEIS)
SIP............. Ship Improvement Program
SIP............. Ship in Production
SIP............. Short Interval Plan [*Management principles*]
SIP............. Short Irregular Pulses
SIP............. Sickness Impact Profile
SIP............. Simferopol [*USSR*] [*Airport symbol*]   (OAG)
SIP............. Simulated Input Processor [*Data processing*]
SIP............. Sindacato Italiano Pescatori [*Italian Union of Fishermen*]
SIP............. Single In-Line Package [*Data processing*]
SIP............. Sipald Resources [*Vancouver Stock Exchange symbol*]
Sip............. Sipario [*A publication*]
SIP............. Skill Improvement Program [*Bureau of Apprenticeship and Training*] [*Department of Labor*]
SIP............. Slow Inhibitory Potential [*Electrophysiology*]
SIP............. Sociedad Interamericana de Prensa [*Inter-American Press Association*]
SIP............. Sociedad Interamericana de Psicologia [*Interamerican Society of Psychology*]   (EA-IO)

SIP	Societa Italiana per l'Esercizio Telefonico [*Italian Society for Telephone Use*] [*Rome, Italy*] [*Information service*] (EISS)
SIP	Society of Indiana Pioneers (EA)
SIP	Society for Invertebrate Pathology (EA)
SIP	Society of Israel Philatelists
SIP	Sodium Iron Pyrophosphate [*Inorganic chemistry*]
SIP	Software Instrumentation Package [*Sperry UNIVAC*] [*Data processing*]
SIP	Software in Print [*Technique Learning*] [*Dobbs Ferry, NY*] [*Information service*] (EISS)
SIP	Solar Instrument Probe (MUGU)
SIP	SPALT [*Special Projects Alterations*] Improvement Program
SIP	Special Impact Program (OICC)
SIP	Standard Initial Provisioning System (MCD)
SIP	Standard Inspection Procedure
SIP	Standard Interest Profile
SIP	Standardization Instructor Pilot (AABC)
SIP	State Implementation Plan [*Environmental Protection Agency*]
SIP	Step in Place
SIP	Strain Isolator Pad [*Aerospace*]
SIP	Student Insurance Producers Association (EA)
SIP	Studies in Process [*Jet Propulsion Laboratory, NASA*]
SIP	Subject Index to Periodicals [*A publication*]
SIP	Submerged Injection Process [*Steelmaking*]
SIP	Supersonic Infantry Projectile
SIP	Supply Improvement Program
SIP	Symbolic Input Program [*Data processing*] (BUR)
SIPA	Securities Investor Protection Act [*1970*]
SIPAG	Syndicat des Instituteurs, Professeurs, et Agents de la Guadeloupe (PD)
SIPAMA	Servico de Inspecao dos Produtos Agropecuarios e Materiais Agricolas [*Brazil*]
SIPB	Safety Injection Permissive Block (IEEE)
SIPC	Securities Investor Protection Corporation [*Government insurance agency for brokerage accounts*] [*Pronounced "sipic"*]
SIPC	Stationing and Installations Planning Committee [*Military*]
SIPCO	Signal Processor Checkout (CAAL)
SIPD	Supply Item Provisioning Document [*Navy*] (NG)
SIPE	Scientific Information Program on Eutrophication [*University of Wisconsin*]
SIPE	Societe Internationale de Psychopathologie de l'Expression [*International Society of Art and Psychopathology*]
SIPES	Society of Independent Professional Earth Scientists (EA)
SIPG	Societe Internationale de Pathologie Geographique [*International Society of Geographical Pathology*] (EA-IO)
SIPG	Special Intercept Priorities Group [*Armed Forces Security Agency*]
SIPI	Scientists' Institute for Public Information (EA)
SIPI	Southwestern Indian Polytechnic Institute [*New Mexico*]
SIPI	Supervisory Immigration Patrol Inspector [*Immigration and Naturalization Service*]
SIPL	Seeley's Illustrated Pocket Library [*A publication*]
SIPM	Star Identification Program, Mariner [*NASA*]
SIPN	Security Industry and Product News [*A publication*]
SIPN	Semi-Interpenetrating Polymer Network [*Organic chemistry*]
SIPO	Serial-In, Parallel-Out [*Telecommunications*] (TEL)
SIPO	Sicherheitspolizei [*Security Police*] [*NAZI*] (BJA)
SIPO	Soobshcheniia Imperatorskovo Pravoslavnovo Palestinskovo Obshchestva [*A publication*]
SIPO	Spacecraft Integration Project Office
SIPO	Swiss Intellectual Property Office [*Bern*] [*Information service*] (EISS)
SIPOA	Servico de Inspecao de Produtos de Origem Animal [*Brazil*]
SIPOP	Satellite Information Processor Operational Program (AFM)
SIPOS	Semi-Insulating Polycrystalline Silicon [*Photovoltaic energy systems*]
SIPP	Sodium Iron Pyrophosphate [*Organic chemistry*]
SIPP	Survey on Income and Program Participation [*Census Bureau, Department of Health and Human Services*]
SIPP	System Information Processing Program (MCD)
SIPPS	System of Information Processing for Professional Societies
Sippy	Senior Independent Pioneer [*Lifestyle classification*]
SIPR	Special In-Process Review (MCD)
SIPRA	Societa Italiana Pubblicita Per Azioni [*Italian radio and television advertising company*]
SIPRE	Snow, Ice, and Permafrost Research Establishment
SIPRI	Stockholm International Peace Research Institute [*Sweden*] (EA-IO)
SIPROS	Simultaneous Processing Operation System [*Control Data Corp.*] [*Data processing*]
SIPS	Simulated Input Preparation System (IEEE)
SIPS	Small Instrument Pointing System (MCD)
SIPS	Societa Internazionale di Psicologia della Scrittura [*International Society of Psychology of Handwriting - ISPH*] (EA-IO)
SIPS	Spartan Improved Performance Study [*Missiles*] (AABC)
SIPS	State Implementation Plan System [*Environmental Protection Agency*]
SIPS	Statistical Interactive Programing System
SIPSDE	Society of Independent and Private School Data Education [*Later, SDE*] (EA)
SIPT	Sensory Integration and Praxis Test [*Occupational therapy*]
SIPT	Simulating Part (AAG)
SIPTH	Serum Immunoreactive Parathyroid Hormone [*Endocrinology*]
SIPU	Selective Inactivation Photodynamic Unit
SIQ	Sick in Quarters
SIQ	Social Intelligence Quotient [*In book title*]
SIQ	Student Interests Quarterly [*A publication*]
SIQR	Studies: An Irish Quarterly Review of Letters, Philosophy, and Science [*A publication*]
SIR	Safeguards Implementation Report (NRCH)
SIR	Scientific Information Retrieval, Inc. [*Database management system*] [*Information service*] (EISS)
SIR	Search, Inspection, and Recovery (NVT)
SIR	Segment Identification Register
SIR	Selected Item Reporting
SIR	Selective Information Retrieval [*Data processing*]
SIR	Self-Indication Ratio
SIR	Semantic Information Retrieval [*Massachusetts Institute of Technology*] [*Data processing*] (DIT)
SIR	Semiannual Inventory Report [*Navy*] (NVT)
SIR	Serious Incident Report [*Military*] (AFM)
SIR	Service International de Recherches [*International Tracing Service*] [*Red Cross*]
SIR	Shipboard Intercept Receiver [*Navy*]
SIR	Shuttle Imaging RADAR [*of earth's surface*] [*NASA*]
SIR	Signal-to-Interference Ratio
SIR	Simultaneous Impact Rate (AFM)
SIR	Sinclair, WY [*Location identifier*] [*FAA*] (FAAL)
SIR	Single Isomorphous Replacement [*Crystallography*]
SIR	Single Item Release
SIR	Sion [*Switzerland*] [*Airport symbol*]
Sir	Sirach [*Old Testament book*] [*Roman Catholic canon*]
SIR	Siria [*Venezuela*] [*Seismograph station code, US Geological Survey*] (SEIS)
Sir	Sirius [*Record label*] [*Sweden*]
SIR	Size Up, Interview, Rate [*Mnemonic used by Responsible Beverage Service in its bartender training program*]
SIR	Small Intestine Rinse [*Physiology*]
SIR	Snow and Ice on Runways [*Aviation*] (FAAC)
SIR	Societa Italiana Resine [*Italy*]
SIR	Societe Rorschach Internationale [*International Rorschach Society*] [*Originally, Societe Internationale du Test de Rorschach et Autres Methodes Projectives*]
SIR	Society for Individual Responsibility [*Defunct*] (EA)
SIR	Society of Industrial Realtors [*Association name and designation awarded by this group*] [*Washington, DC*] (EA)
SIR	Society of Insurance Research [*Appleton, WI*] (EA)
SIR	Software Incident Report (MCD)
SIR	Sound Isolation Room
SIR	Special Information Retrieval
SIR	Special Inspection Requirement
SIR	Special Investigative Requirement (AFM)
SIR	Specific Insulation Resistance
SIR	Specification Information Retrieval System [*Data processing*] (MCD)
SIR	Stable Isotopes Resource
SIR	Standarization, Interoperability, and Readiness [*NATO*] (MCD)
SIR	Staten Island Rapid Transit Railway Co. [*Later, SIRC*] [*AAR code*]
SIR	Statistical Information Retrieval
SIR	Stratified Indexing and Retrieval [*Japan*] [*Data processing*] (DIT)
SIR	Studies in Romanticism [*A publication*]
SIR	Styrene-Isoprene Rubber
SIR	Subcontractor Information Request
SIR	Submarine Intermediate Reactor
SIR	Supersonic Infantry Rocket
SIR	Suppliers Information Request
SIR	Symbolic Input Routine [*Data processing*] (DIT)
SIR	Synthetic-Aperture Imaging RADAR [*System*]
SIR	System Initialization Routine
SIR	System Integration Receiver [*System*]
SIR	Systems Integration Review [*NASA*] (NASA)
SIRA	Safety Investigation Regulations (IEEE)
SIRA	Scientific Instrument Research Association [*British*]
SIRA	Social Issues Research Associates (EA)
SIRA	Sports Industries Representatives Association (EA)
SIRA	Stable Isotope Ratio Analysis
SIRA	Strapdown Inertial Reference Assembly (MCD)
SIRA	Strategic Intelligence Research and Analysis
SIRA	System for Instructional Response Analysis
Sirag	Sirag. Amsagir Grakanut ean ew Aruesdi [*A publication*]
SIRAP	System of Information Retrieval and Analysis, Planning [*Army*] [*Fort Belvoir, VA*] [*Information service*] (EISS)
SIRAS	Single Isomorphous Replacement, Anomalous Scattering [*Crystallography*]
SIRB	Sintered Iron Rotating Band

SIRC .... Science Information Resource Center [*Harper & Row*] [*Information service*]
SIRC .... Sirco International Corp. [*NASDAQ symbol*] (NQ)
SIRC .... Spares Integrated Reporting and Control [*System*]
SIRC .... Sport Information Resource Centre [*Coaching Association of Canada*] [*Database*] [*Ottawa, ON*] (EISS)
SIRC .... [*The*] Staten Island Railroad Corporation [*AAR code*]
SIR(CICR) ... Service International de Recherches (du Comite International de la Croix-Rouge) [*International Tracing Service of the International Committee of the Red Cross*]
SIRCS .... Shipboard Intermediate Range Combat System [*Navy*]
SIRCULS .... San Bernardino-Inyo-Riverside Counties United Library Services [*Library network*]
SIRCUS ..... Standard Information Retrieval Capability for Users [*Army*]
SIRD .... Shore-Based Interfare Requirement Date
SIRD .... Support Instrumentation Requirements Document [*NASA*]
SIRE .... Satellite Infrared Experiment (MCD)
SIRE .... Society for the Investigation of Recurring Events
SIREA .... SIAM [*Society for Industrial and Applied Mathematics*] Review [*A publication*]
SIREMAR ... Sicilia Regionale Marittima SpA [*Palermo, Italy*]
SIREN .... SIGSEC Resources and Equipment Needs (MCD)
SIREWS .... Shipboard Infrared Electronic Warfare System
SIRF .... System Information Reports Formatting (MCD)
SIRI .... Societe Internationale pour la Readaptation des Invalides
SIRIC .... Soybean Insect Research Information Center [*University of Illinois*] [*Champaign, IL*]
SIRIN .... Single Readiness Information System [*NORRS*]
SIRIS .... Sputter-Initiated Resonance Ionization Spectrometry
SIRIS .... Sylloge Inscriptionum Religionis Isiacae et Sarapiacae [*A publication*] (BJA)
SIRIVS .... Spaceborne Intensified Radiometer for Imaging Vetroviolet Spectroscopy (MCD)
Sir JS .... Sir John Strange's English Reports (DLA)
SIRL .... Site Installation Requirements List (AAG)
SIRL .... Support Item Requirement List (MCD)
SIRLEJ .... Societe Internationale de Recherche en Litterature d'Enfance et de Jeunesse [*International Research Society for Children's Literature - IRSCL*] (EA)
Sir L Jenk... Wynne's Life of Sir Leoline Jenkins [*1724*] (DLA)
SIRLS .... Information Retrieval System for the Sociology of Leisure and Sport [*University of Waterloo*] [*Waterloo, ON*] [*Information service*] (EISS)
SIRLS .... Southwest Idaho Regional Library System [*Library network*]
SIRM .... Saturation Isothermal Remanent Magnetization [*Paleomagnetics*]
SIRM .... Sterile Insect Release Method
SIRMA .... Small Independent Record Manufacturers Association [*Stanford, CT*] (EA)
SIRMCE ..... Societe Internationale pour la Recherche sur les Maladies de Civilisation et l'Environnement [*International Society for Research on Civilization Diseases and Environment*] (EA-IO)
SIROW .... Southwest Institute for Research on Women [*University of Arizona*] [*Research center*] (RCD)
SIRR .... Section on Individual Rights and Responsibilities [*American Bar Association*] [*Washington, DC*] (EA)
SIRR .... Software Integration Readiness Review [*NASA*] (NASA)
SIRR .... Southern Industrial Railroad, Inc. [*AAR code*]
SIRS .... Salary Information Retrieval System (IEEE)
SIRS .... Satellite Infrared Spectrometer [*NASA*]
SIRS .... Scheduled Issue Release System
SIRS .... Ship Installed Radiac System (NATG)
SIRS .... Skills Inventory Retrieval System (MCD)
SIRS .... Social Issues Resources Series [*A publication*]
SIRS .... Soils Information Retrieval Systems [*Database*] [*Army Corps of Engineers*]
SIRS .... Soluble Immune Response Suppressor [*Immunology*]
SIRS .... Specification, Instrumentation, and Range Safety
SIRS .... Statewide Individual Referral System (OICC)
SIRS .... System Integration Receiver System (MCD)
SIRSA .... Special Industrial Radio Service Association [*Land Mobile Communications Council*] [*Rosslyn, VA*] (EA)
SIRT .... Signaling Information Receiver/Transmitter (MCD)
SIRT .... Staten Island Rapid Transit Railway Co. [*Later, SIRC*]
SIRTF .... Shuttle Infrared Telescope Facility [*NASA*]
SIRTF .... Space [*formerly, Shuttle*] Infrared Telescope Facility
Sir TJ.......... Sir Thomas Jones' English King's Bench and Common Pleas Reports (DLA)
Sir T Ray .... Sir T. Raymond's English King's Bench Reports (DLA)
SIRU .... Strapdown Inertial Reference Unit [*Navigation*]
SIRW .... Safety Injection and Refueling Water [*Nuclear energy*] (NRCH)
SIRWT .... Safety Injection and Refueling Water Tank [*Nuclear energy*] (NRCH)
SIRWT .... Safety Injection Reserve Water Tank (IEEE)
SIS .... Canadian Security Intelligence Service [*UTLAS symbol*]
SIS .... Naval Intelligence Service [*Italy*]
SIS .... Safety Information System [*Department of Transportation*]
SIS .... Safety Injection System (NRCH)
SIS .... SAGE [*Semiautomatic Ground Environment*] Interceptor Simulator

SIS .... Satellite Infrared Spectrometer [*NASA*]
SIS .... Satellite Interceptor System (AFM)
SIS .... Savage Information Services [*Rolling Hills Estates, CA*] (EISS)
SIS .... Scanning Image Spectrometer
SIS .... Science Information Service (EA)
SIS .... Science Information Services [*Franklin Institute*]
SIS .... Scientific Instruction Set
SIS .... Scientific Instrument Society (EA)
SIS .... Scotch-Irish Society of the United States of America (EA)
SIs .... Scripta Islandica [*A publication*]
SIS .... Secondary Injection System
SIS .... Secret Intelligence Service [*British*]
SIS .... Semiautomatic Imagery Screening Subsystem (MCD)
SIS .... Semiconductor-Insulator-Semiconductor
SIS .... Senior Intelligence Service [*CIA personnel*]
SIS .... Sensor Image Simulator (MCD)
SIS .... Serial Input System (MCD)
SIS .... Serving the Indigent Sick
SIS .... Share Information Service [*British*]
SIS .... Shared Information Service (CMD)
SIS .... Shipping Instruction Sheet
SIS .... Shock-Isolation Support
SIS .... Short Interval Scheduling [*Quality control*]
SIS .... Shut-In Society
SIS .... Shuttle Information System (MCD)
SIS .... Shuttle Interface Simulator [*NASA*] (NASA)
SIS .... Signal Intelligence Service [*Later, Army Security Agency*]
SIS .... Signaling Interworking Subsystem [*Telecommunications*] (TEL)
SIS .... Silicon of Insulating Substrate (MCD)
SIS .... Simian Sarcoma Virus [*Oncology*]
SIS .... Simulation Interface Subsystem (KSC)
SIS .... Single Item Squawk Sheet
SIS .... Singles in Service [*An association*] [*Santa Clara, CA*] (EA)
SIS .... Sino-Indian Studies [*A publication*]
SIS .... Sion [*Switzerland*] [*Seismograph station code, US Geological Survey*] [*Closed*] (SEIS)
SIS .... Sishen [*South Africa*] [*Airport symbol*] (OAG)
SIS .... Sister
SIS .... Societa Internazionale Scotista [*International Scotist Society - ISS*] (EA-IO)
SIS .... Society of International Secretaries
SIS .... Society for Iranian Studies (EA)
SIS .... Software Implementation Specifications [*NASA*] (NASA)
SIS .... Software Integrated Schedule [*NASA*] (NASA)
SIS .... Space and Information System
SIS .... SPALT [*Special Projects Alterations*] Information Shut
SIS .... Spark Ignition System
SIS .... Speaker Intercom System (KSC)
SIS .... Special Industrial Services [*United Nations Industrial Development Organization*]
SIS .... Special Information System (MCD)
SIS .... Special Intelligence Service
SIS .... Special Interest Sessions
SIS .... Special Isotope Separation [*Physics*]
SIS .... Specification Information System
SIS .... Spectral Imaging Sensor
SIS .... Spuria Iris Society (EA)
SIS .... Stage Interface Substitute
SIS .... Stand-Alone Information System [*National Library of Medicine*]
SIS .... Standard Indexing System [*DoD*]
SIS .... Standard Instruction Set (MSA)
SIS .... Standards Information Service [*National Bureau of Standards*] (EISS)
SIS .... Standards Information Service [*Standards Council of Canada*] [*Ottawa, ON*] [*Information service*] (EISS)
SIS .... Station Identification Store [*Bell Laboratories*]
SIS .... Stator Interstage Seal
SIS .... STEP [*Scientific and Technical Exploitation Program*] Information Subsystem
SIS .... Sterile Injectable Suspension
SIS .... Strategic Intelligence School [*Military*]
SIS .... Strategic Intelligence Summary [*Military*] (NATG)
SIS .... Student Instruction Sheet [*Military*]
SIS .... Student International Service [*Foundation*]
SIS .... Styrene-Isoprene-Styrene [*Organic chemistry*]
SIS .... Submarine Integrated SONAR
SIS .... Superconductor-Insulator-Superconductor [*Transistor technology*]
SIS .... Supplier Identification System [*London Enterprise Agency*] [*London, England*] [*Information service*] (EISS)
SIS .... Supply Item Status
SIS .... Surgical Infection Society [*Montreal, PQ*] (EA)
S & IS .... Survey and Investigation Staff [*Navy*] (NVT)
SIS .... Sveriges Standardiseringskommission [*Sweden*] [*National standards organization*]
SIS .... Swedish Standards Institution [*Stockholm*] [*Information service*] (EISS)
SIS .... Synchronous Identification System (MCD)
SIS .... System Integration Schedule [*NASA*] (NASA)
SIS .... System Integration Support

SIS .... System Interrupt Supervisor
SISAC .... Serials Industry Systems Advisory Committee [*Book Industry Study Group*] [*New York, NY*] [*Information service*] (EISS)
SISAM .... Spectrometer with Interference Selective Amplitude Modulation [*Physics*]
SI/SAO ...... Special Intelligence/Special Activities Office (MCD)
SISB .... SIS Corp. [*NASDAQ symbol*] (NQ)
SISC .... Single Screw
SISC .... Statewide Information Steering Committee [*California*]
SISC .... Stewart Information Services [*NASDAQ symbol*] (NQ)
SISCO .... Special Inter-Departmental Selection Committee [*UN Food and Agriculture Organization*]
SISCON ..... Science in Social Context
SISD .... Scientific Information Systems Department [*Merrell Dow Pharmaceuticals, Inc.*] [*Information service*] (EISS)
SISD .... Single Instruction, Single Data (IEEE)
SISH .... Societe Internationale de la Science Horticole [*International Society for Horticultural Science - ISHS*] (EA-IO)
SISI .... Short Increment Sensitivity Index [*Medicine*]
SISI .... Surveillance and In-Service Inspection [*Nuclear energy*] (NRCH)
SISIMS ...... Say It So It Makes Sense [*A publication*]
SISIR .... Singapore Institute of Standards and Industrial Research
SISKY .... Siskiyou [*FAA*] (FAAC)
S Isl .... Sandwich Islands
SISL .... Sons of Italy Supreme Lodge (EA)
SIsI .... Studia Islamica [*A publication*]
SISMS .... Standard Integrated Support Management System [*Joint Chiefs of Staff*]
SISO .... Science Information Services Organization [*Franklin Institute*] (EISS)
Si & So .... Sight and Sound [*A publication*]
SISO .... Single-Input, Single-Output [*Process engineering*]
SISORS ..... Supply Item Status and Order Reporting System
SISP .... Sudden Increase of Solar Particles
SISR .... Selected Items Status Report [*Army*] (AABC)
SISS .... Second International Science Study [*International Association for the Evaluation of Educational Achievement*]
SISS .... Semiconductor-Insulator-Semiconductor System
SISS .... Sensory Integration Special Interest Section [*American Occupational Therapy Association*]
SISS .... Single Item, Single Source (IEEE)
SISS .... Societe Internationale de la Science du Sol
SISS .... Sources of Information on Social Security [*British*]
SISS .... Standoff Imaging Sensor System (MCD)
SISS .... Submarine Improved SONAR System
SISS .... Submarine Integrated SONAR System
SISS .... Synchronous Identification System Study
SISS .... System Integration Support Service
SISSC .... Special Interest Sections Steering Committee [*American Occupational Therapy Association*]
SIST .... Self-Inflating Surface Target
SIST .... Sister
Sist e Autom ... Sistemi e Automazione [*A publication*]
Sist Avtom Nauchn Issled ... Sistemy Avtomatisatsii Nauchnykh Issledovanii [*A publication*]
Sistema ..... Sistema Revista de Ciencias Sociales [*A publication*]
Sistem Metod Sovrem Nauka ... Sistemnyj Metod i Sovremennaja Nauka [*A publication*]
SISTER ...... Special Institution for Scientific and Technological Education and Research [*In proposal stage, 1964, in Great Britain*]
Sisters .... Sisters Today [*A publication*]
SISTM .... Simulation by Incremental Stochastic Transition Matrices (MCD)
SISTMS ..... Standard Integrated Supply/Transportation Manifest System (AABC)
Sist Nerv .... Sistema Nervoso [*A publication*]
Sistole Rev Urug Cardiol ... Sistole. Revista Uruguaya de Cardiologia [*A publication*]
SISTRAN.... System for Information Storage and Retrieval and Analysis
SISUSA ...... Scotch-Irish Society of the United States of America (EA)
SiSV .... Simian Sarcoma Virus [*Also, SSV*]
SIT .... Safety Injection Tank [*Nuclear energy*] (NRCH)
SIT .... Safety Injection Transmitter [*Nuclear energy*] (NRCH)
SIT .... Sensory Integration Training
SIT .... Separation-Initiated Timer
SIT .... Sequential Interval Timer
SIT .... Serum Inhibitory Titer [*Clinical chemistry*]
SIT .... Serum Inhibitory Titers [*Serology*]
SIT .... Shuttle Integrated Test [*NASA*] (NASA)
SIT .... Silicon Intensifier Target
SIT .... Silicon Intensifier Tube
SIT .... Simulation Input Tape
sit .... Sino-Tibetan [*MARC language code*] [*Library of Congress*] (LCCP)
SIT .... Sitka [*Alaska*] [*Airport symbol*] (OAG)
SIT .... Sitka [*Alaska*] [*Geomagnetic observatory code*]
SIT .... Sitka [*Alaska*] [*Seismograph station code, US Geological Survey*] (SEIS)
SIT .... Sitka, AK [*Location identifier*] [*FAA*] (FAAL)

SIT .... Situation (AFM)
SIT .... Slosson Intelligence Test
SIT .... Social Intelligence Test [*Psychology*]
SIT .... Society of Instrument Technology [*British*]
SIT .... Software Integrated Test [*NASA*] (KSC)
SIT .... Space Impact Tool [*NASA*]
SIT .... Spaceborne Infrared Tracker
SIT .... Sperm Immobilization Test [*Clinical chemistry*]
SIT .... Spontaneous Ignition Temperature
SIT .... Statement of Inventory Transaction
SIT .... Static Induction Transistor [*Telecommunications*] (TEL)
SIT .... Stevens Institute of Technology [*New Jersey*]
SIT .... Stop Immorality on Television [*An association*]
SIT .... Stopping in Transit
SIT .... Storage Inspection Test [*Navy*] (NG)
SIT .... Storage in Transit
SIT .... Structurally Integrated Thruster (MCD)
SIT .... Sugar Industry Technologists
SIT .... System Integration Test
SIT .... Systems Interface Test (NVT)
SI3T .... Association of French Telephone, Telegraph, and Related Telematics Industries [*Paris*] [*Telecommunications service*] (TSSD)
SITA .... Sociedade Internacional de Trilogia Analitica [*International Society of Analytical Trilogy - ISAT*] (EA-IO)
SITA .... Societe Internationale des Telecommunications Aeronautiques [*International Society of Aeronautical Telecommunications*] [*London, England*]
SITA .... Students' International Travel Association
SITA .... System International Tinplate Area
SITAR .... Societa Incremento Turismo Aereo [*Italy*]
SITC .... Satellite International Television Center [*Telecommunications*] (TEL)
SITC .... Standard Industrial Trade Classification [*United Nations*]
SITC .... Standard International Trade Classification
SITCA .... Secretaria de Integracion Turistica Centroamericana
SITCEN ...... Situation Center [*NATO*] (NATG)
SITCOM ...... Situation Comedy [*Television*]
SITE .... Sample Instruction Test Exercise (MCD)
SITE .... Satellite Instructional Television Experiment [*NASA/Indian Space Research Organization, 1974*]
SITE .... Sculpture in the Environment [*In Best by SITE, Inc.*]
SITE .... Search Information Tape Equipment
SITE .... Shipboard Information, Training, and Education [*System*] [*Navy*] (NVT)
SITE .... Situate (ROG)
SITE .... Society of Incentive Travel Executives [*New York, NY*] (EA)
SITE .... Society of Insurance Trainers and Educators [*Columbus, OH*] (EA)
SITE .... Spacecraft Instrumentation Test Equipment
SITE .... Suction Infusion Tissue Extractor [*Ophthalmology*]
SITE .... Superfund Innovative Technologies Evaluation Program [*Environmental Protection Agency*]
S-ITED .... Superimposed Integrated Trajectory Error [*Aviation*]
SITEL .... Societe des Ingenieurs do Telecommunication [*Belgium*] (MCD)
SITES .... Smithsonian Institution Traveling Exhibition Service
Site Sel Hdbk ... Site Selection Handbook [*A publication*]
SITI .... Swiss Institute for Technical Information [*Information service*] (EISS)
SITIM .... Societe Internationale des Techniques d'Imagerie Mentals [*International Society for Mental Imagery Techniques in Psychotherapy and Psychology*] (EA-IO)
SITK .... Sitka National Monument
SITL .... Southwestern Industrial Traffic League (EA)
SITMAP ..... Situation Map (MCD)
SITN .... Situation (ROG)
SITOR .... Simplex TELEX over Radio
SITP .... Scheduled into Production
SITP .... Shipyard Installation Test Procedure [*or Program*]
SITP .... Site Inspection and Test Procedure [*Nuclear energy*] (NRCH)
SITP .... System Integration Test Program
SITP .... Systems Integrated Test Plan [*Military*] (CAAL)
SITPB .... System Integration Test Program Board
SITPRO ...... Simplification of International Trade Procedures [*Committee*] [*British*]
SITRAM ...... Societe Ivoirienne de Transport Maritime [*The Ivorian national shipping industry*]
SITREP....... Situation Report
SITS .... IEEE Social Implications of Technology Society [*New York, NY*] (EA)
SITS .... SAGE [*Semiautomatic Ground Environment*] Intercept Target Simulation
SITS .... Scientists in the Sea [*Marine science*] (MSC)
SITS .... Secure Imagery Transmission System [*Military*] (CAAL)
SITS .... Societe Internationale de Transfusion Sanguine [*International Society of Blood Transfusion - ISBT*] (EA)
SITS .... System Integration Test Service
SITS .... System Integration Test Site [*Military*] (CAAL)
SITSUM...... Situation Summary [*Military*] (NVT)
SITU .... Society for the Investigation of the Unexplained (EA)

SITU .... South India Teachers' Union
SITU .... Surgical Intensive Therapy Unit
SITU .... Systeme d'Information des Trajets Urbains [*Computerized transit routing information service in Paris*]
SITV .... System Integration Test Vehicle
SITVC .... Secondary Injection Thrust Vector Control
Sitz .... Sitzungsberichte [*Proceedings*] [*German*] (OCD)
Sitzungsber Akad Wiss DDR Math-Naturwiss-Tech Jahrgang 1977 ... Sitzungsberichte der Akademie der Wissenschaften der DDR. Mathematik-Naturwissenschaften-Technik. Jahrgang 1977 [*A publication*]
Sitzungsber Berl Ges Naturforsch Freunde ... Sitzungsberichte der Berlinische Gesellschaft Naturforschender Freunde [*A publication*]
Sitzungsber Deut Akad Landwirt Wiss Berlin ... Sitzungsberichte. Deutsche Akademie der Landwirtschaftswissenschaften zu Berlin [*A publication*]
Sitzungsber Deut Akad Wiss Berlin Kl Math Phys Tech ... Sitzungsberichte der Deutschen Akademie der Wissenschaften zu Berlin. Klasse fuer Mathematik, Physik, und Technik [*A publication*]
Sitzungsber Finn Akad Wiss ... Sitzungsberichte der Finnischen Akademie der Wissenschaften [*A publication*]
Sitzungsber Ges Befoerd Ges Naturwiss Marburg ... Sitzungsberichte. Gesellschaft zur Befoerderung der Gesamten Naturwissenschaften zu Marburg [*West Germany*] [*A publication*]
Sitzungsber Ges Naturforsch Freunde Berlin ... Sitzungsberichte. Gesellschaft Naturforschender Freunde zu Berlin [*A publication*]
Sitzungsber Heidelb Akad Wiss Math-Naturwiss Kl ... Sitzungsberichte. Heidelberg Akademie der Wissenschaften. Mathematisch-Naturwissenschaftliche Klasse [*A publication*]
Sitz Wien ... Sitzungsberichte der Akademie der Wissenschaften in Wien [*A publication*] (OCD)
SIU .... Saturn Instrumentation [*NASA*]
SIU .... Seafarers' International Union of North America [*AFL-CIO*]
SIU .... Sequence Initiate Update
SIU .... Shiloh Resources Ltd. [*Vancouver Stock Exchange symbol*]
SIU .... Signal Interface Unit (MCD)
SIU .... Simushir [*USSR*] [*Seismograph station code, US Geological Survey*] (SEIS)
SIU .... Slide-In Unit [*Telecommunications*] (TEL)
SIU .... Societe Internationale d'Urologie [*International Society of Urology - ISU*] (EA-IO)
SIU .... Sonobuoy Interface Unit [*Navy*] (CAAL)
SIU .... Southern Illinois University
SIU .... System [*or Subsystem*] Interface Unit
SIU .... Systeme International d'Unites [*International System of Units*] [*Also, SI*]
SIU-AGLI.... Seafarers' International Union of North America [*AFL-CIO*]; Atlantic, Gulf, Lakes and Inland Waters District
SIU-AGLIW ... Seafarers' International Union of North America - Atlantic, Gulf, Lakes, and Inland Water District
SIUC.......... Southern Illinois University, Carbondale
SIUCB .... Societa Italiana della Union Chimique Belge [*Italy*]
SIUFL .... Suspend Issue and Use of Following Lots
SIU-IUP ...... Seafarers' International Union of North America [*AFL-CIO*]; Inlandboatmen's Union of the Pacific
SIU-IUPW... Seafarers' International Union of North America [*AFL-CIO*]; International Union of Petroleum Workers
SIU-MCS.... Seafarers' International Union of North America [*AFL-CIO*]; Marine Cooks and Stewards' Union
SIU-MFOW ... Seafarers' International Union of North America [*AFL-CIO*]; Pacific Coast Marine Firemen, Oilers, Watertenders and Wipers Association
SIUNA .... Seafarers' International Union of North America [*AFL-CIO*]
SIUP .... Southern Illinois University Press
SIUPA........ Solomon Islands United Party (PPW)
SIUSA .... Survival International USA [*An association*] (EA)
SIUSM .... Suspend from Issue and Use as Suspect Material
SIU-SUP..... Seafarers' International Union of North America [*AFL-CIO*]; Sailors' Union of the Pacific
SIU-TSAW ... Seafarers' International Union of North America [*AFL-CIO*]; Transporation Services and Allied Workers
SIV .... Silicon Videcon [*TV system*]
SIV .... Silver Cloud Mines [*Vancouver Stock Exchange symbol*]
SIV .... Simian Immunodeficiency Virus
SIV .... Societa Italiana Vetro [*Glass manufacturer*] [*Italy*]
SIV .... Spectrum Identification Voltage [*Military*] (CAAL)
SIV .... Sullivan, IN [*Location identifier*] [*FAA*] (FAAL)
SIV .... Survey of Interpersonal Values [*Psychology*]
SIVD .... Spacecraft Information Viewing Device
SIVE .... Shuttle Interface Verification Equipment [*NASA*] (NASA)
SI VIR PERM ... Si Vires Permittant [*If the Strength Will Bear It*] [*Pharmacy*] (ROG)
SIW .... Congregation of the Incarnate Word and the Blessed Sacrament [*Roman Catholic women's religious order*]
SIW .... Self-Inflicted Wound [*Military*]
SIW .... Serum Samples from Infertile Women [*Immunochemistry*]
SIW .... Socialist International Women (EA)

SIW............ Strassburger Israelitisch Wochenschrift [*A publication*] (BJA)
SIW............ Strategic Intelligence Wing (MCD)
SIW............ Subpolar Intermediate Water [*Oceanography*]
SIWDR....... Sidewinder [*Naval ordnance*]
SIWL .... Single Isolated Wheel Load [*Aviation*] (FAAC)
SIX............. Motel 6, Inc. [*NYSE symbol*]
SIX............. Singleton [*Australia*] [*Airport symbol*] (OAG)
Six .... Sixties [*A publication*]
SIXATAF .... Sixth Allied Tactical Air Force, Southeastern Europe [*NATO*] (NATG)
Six Circ ...... Cases on the Six Circuits [*1841-43*] [*Ireland*] (DLA)
Six Ct J ...... Sixteenth Century Journal [*A publication*]
SIXEP......... Site Ion Exchange Effluent Plant [*Nuclear energy*]
SIXFLT .... Sixth Fleet [*Atlantic*] [*Navy*]
SIXPAC ...... System for Inertial Experiment Priority and Attitude Control (MCD)
Sixteen Cent J ... Sixteenth Century Journal [*A publication*]
SIXTHFLT ... Sixth Fleet [*Atlantic*] [*Navy*]
SIY .... Montague, CA [*Location identifier*] [*FAA*] (FAAL)
SIZ............. Security Identification Zone
SIZ............. Sizeler Property Investment [*NYSE symbol*]
SIZSA........ Sapporo Igaku Zasshi [*A publication*]
SIZZ .... Sizzler Restaurants [*NASDAQ symbol*] (NQ)
SJ .... Saalburg-Jahrbuch [*A publication*]
SJ .... Samuel Johnson [*Initials used as pseudonym*]
SJ .... San Juan [*Puerto Rico*]
SJ .... Scottish Jurist [*1829-73*] (DLA)
SJ .... Service Junior
SJ .... Shakespeare-Jahrbuch [*A publication*]
SJ .... Side Judge [*Football*]
SJ .... Silliman Journal [*A publication*]
SJ .... Simulation Journal [*A publication*]
SJ .... Single Jewish [*Classified advertising*]
SJ .... SJ Huvudkontor [*Swedish State Railways*]
SJ .... Slip Joint [*Technical drawings*]
SJ .... Sloppy Joe [*Sandwich*]
SJ .... Slovensky Jazyk [*A publication*]
SJ .... Societas Jesu [*Society of Jesus*] [*Jesuits*] [*Roman Catholic men's religious order*]
SJ .... Solicitors' Journal [*A publication*] (DLA)
SJ .... Source Jamming
SJ .... Southern Air Transport, Inc. [*ICAO designator*] (FAAC)
SJ .... Statens Jaernvaeger [*Sweden*]
SJ .... Sub Judice [*Under Consideration*] [*Latin*]
sj .... Sudan [*MARC country of publication code*] [*Library of Congress*] (LCCP)
SJ .... Supersonic Jet [*Gas stream*]
SJ .... Svalbard and Jan Mayen Islands [*Two-letter standard code*] (CNC)
SJA............ San Juan Airlines [*Port Angeles, WA*] [*FAA designator*] (FAAC)
SJA............ Service Job Analysis [*A publication*]
SJA............ Southwestern Journal of Anthropology [*A publication*]
SJA............ Staff Judge Advocate [*Air Force*]
SJAA.......... Swedish Journalists Association of America (EA)
SJAE.......... Steam Jet Air Ejector (NRCH)
SJAnth........ Southwestern Journal of Anthropology [*A publication*]
SJART........ San Jacinto Army Terminal
SJB............ St. Joseph Belt Railway Co. [*AAR code*]
SJB............ Society of Jewish Bibliophiles (EA)
SJB............ Westfield, MA [*Location identifier*] [*FAA*] (FAAL)
SJBA.......... Sephardic Jewish Brotherhood of America (EA)
SJBC......... Saint John the Baptist, Clewer
SJC............ Saint John's College [*California; Kansas; Maryland*]
SJC............ Saint Joseph College [*West Hartford, CT*]
SJC .... Saint Joseph's College [*California; Indiana; Maine; New Jersey; New York, Pennsylvania*]
SJC .... San Javier [*Chile*] [*Seismograph station code, US Geological Survey*] [*Closed*] (SEIS)
SJC .... San Jose [*California*] [*Airport symbol*] (OAG)
SJC .... San Jose, CA [*Location identifier*] [*FAA*] (FAAL)
SJC .... Sayre Junior College [*Oklahoma*]
SJC .... Sisters of St. Joseph of Cluny [*Roman Catholic religious order*]
SJC .... Snead Junior College [*Boaz, AL*]
SJC .... Society of Jews and Christians
SJC .... Southerland, J. C., Dearborn MI [*STAC*]
SJC .... Standing Joint Committee
SJC .... Supreme Judicial Court
SJCC......... Cayey [*Puerto Rico*] [*Seismograph station code, US Geological Survey*] (SEIS)
SJCC......... Saint John College of Cleveland [*Ohio*]
SJCC......... San Jose City College [*California*]
SJCC......... Scott Joplin Commemorative Committee (EA)
SJCC......... Spring Joint Computer Conference [*American Federation of Information Processing Societies*]
SJCLA....... Scandinavian Journal of Clinical and Laboratory Investigation [*A publication*]
SJCOA ...... SIAM [*Society for Industrial and Applied Mathematics*] Journal of Control [*A publication*]
SJCOD...... SIAM [*Society for Industrial and Applied Mathematics*] Journal on Control and Optimization [*A publication*]

SJCPS....... Society of Jewish Composers, Publishers, and Songwriters [*Defunct*] (EA)
SJCS.......... Secretary Joint Chiefs of Staff (MCD)
SJCT.......... SJC Today. Sheldon Jackson College [*Sitka, AK*] [*A publication*]
SJCW......... Saint Joseph's College for Women [*Later, SJC*] [*New York*]
SJD............ Doctor of Juridical Science [*or Doctor of the Science of Jurisprudence or Doctor of the Science of Law*]
SJD............ Los Cabos [*Mexico*] [*Airport symbol*] (OAG)
SJD............ St. Joseph's College, Philadelphia, PA [*OCLC symbol*] (OCLC)
SJDBA....... Soviet Journal of Developmental Biology [*A publication*]
SJE............ San Jose Del Guaviaro [*Colombia*] [*Airport symbol*] (OAG)
SJE............ Swedish Journal of Economics [*A publication*]
SJE............ Swiveling Jet Engine
SJECA....... Soviet Journal of Ecology [*English Translation*] [*A publication*]
SJER.......... Scandinavian Journal of Educational Research [*A publication*]
SJF............ Saint John [*Virgin Islands*] [*Airport symbol*] (OAG)
SJF............ Shortest Job First [*Data processing*]
SJF............ Single Jewish Female [*Classified advertising*]
SJF............ Supersonic Jet Flow
SJFC.......... Saint John Fisher College [*New York*]
SJFMA....... Soviet Journal of Non-Ferrous Metals [*English Translation*] [*A publication*]
SJFT.......... Svenska Jerusalems-Foereningens Tidskrift [*A publication*]
SJG............ St. Joe Gold Corp. [*American Stock Exchange symbol*] [*Toronto Stock Exchange symbol*]
SJG............ San Juan [*Puerto Rico*] [*Geomagnetic observatory code*]
SJG............ San Juan [*Puerto Rico*] [*Seismograph station code, US Geological Survey*] (SEIS)
SJG............ South Jersey Gas Co. [*Later, SJI*] [*NYSE symbol*]
SJGE.......... St. Joseph Grain Exchange (EA)
SJGHA....... Sumitomo Jukikai Giho [*A publication*]
SJGRA....... Scandinavian Journal of Gastroenterology [*A publication*]
SJH............ St. Joseph Seminary [*California*] [*Seismograph station code, US Geological Survey*] (SEIS)
SJH............ San Juan Del Cesar [*Colombia*] [*Airport symbol*] (OAG)
SJH............ Shakespeare-Jahrbuch (Heidelberg) [*A publication*]
SJHAA....... Scandinavian Journal of Haematology [*A publication*]
SJI............ Mobile, AL [*Location identifier*] [*FAA*] (FAAL)
SJI............ San Jose [*Philippines*] [*Airport symbol*] (OAG)
SJI............ Society for Japanese Irises (EA)
SJI............ South Jersey Industries, Inc. [*NYSE symbol*]
SJI............ Steel Joist Institute [*Myrtle Beach, SC*] (EA)
SJIA.......... Saint Joan's International Alliance [*See also AIJA*] (EA-IO)
SJIS........... State Judicial Information System (OICC)
SJJ............ Sarajevo [*Yugoslavia*] [*Airport symbol*] (OAG)
SJJC.......... Sheldon Jackson Junior College [*Sitka, AK*] [*Later, Sheldon Jackson College*]
SJJR.......... Societe Jean-Jacques Rousseau (EA-IO)
SJJRA........ Standard Jack and Jennet Registry of America (EA)
SJK............ Sao Jose Dos Campos [*Brazil*] [*Airport symbol*] (OAG)
SJK............ Steam-Jacketed Kettle
SJL............ St. Jude's League (EA)
SJL............ San Joaquin Valley Library System, Fresno, CA [*OCLC symbol*] (OCLC)
SJL............ Semitic Journal of Linguistics [*A publication*]
SJL............ Slovensky Jazyk a Literatura v Skole [*A publication*]
SJLA.......... Studies in Judaism in Late Antiquity [*A publication*]
SJLAC....... Soviet Jewry Legal Advocacy Center (EA)
SJLB.......... Selected Judgments, Lower Burma (DLA)
SJLC.......... St. Johnsbury & Lamoille County R. R. [*AAR code*]
SJLC.......... Single Junction Latching Circulator
SJLR.......... St. John's Law Review [*A publication*]
SJM........... San Jose De Maipo [*Chile*] [*Seismograph station code, US Geological Survey*] [*Closed*] (SEIS)
SJM........... Single Jewish Male [*Classified advertising*]
SJM........... Smucker [*J. M.*] Co. [*NYSE symbol*]
SJM........... Special Joint Meeting
SJM........... Svalbard and Jan Mayen Islands [*Three-letter standard code*] (CNC)
SJM........... System Junction Module [*Deep Space Instrumentation Facility, NASA*]
SJMAA....... SIAM [*Society for Industrial and Applied Mathematics*] Journal of Mathematical Analysis [*A publication*]
SJMC........ Signed Judgments of the Military Courts in the Administered Territories [*Israel*] (BJA)
SJMS......... Speculum [*A publication*]
SJN............ St. Johns, AZ [*Location identifier*] [*FAA*] (FAAL)
SJN............ San Juan [*Peru*] [*Seismograph station code, US Geological Survey*] [*Closed*] (SEIS)
SJN............ Supersonic Jet Noise
SJNAA....... SIAM [*Society for Industrial and Applied Mathematics*] Journal on Numerical Analysis [*A publication*]
SJNCA....... Soviet Journal of Nuclear Physics [*English Translation*] [*A publication*]
SJNTA....... Soviet Journal of Nondestructive Testing [*English Translation*] [*A publication*]
SJO............ Jahrbuch der Deutschen Shakespeare-Gesellschaft Ost [*A publication*]
SJO............ San Jose [*Costa Rica*] [*Airport symbol*] (OAG)
SJO............ Service Junior - Oil-Resistant

SJOJ.......... Savez Jevrejskih Opstina Jugoslavije (BJA)
SJOTB....... Soviet Journal of Optical Technology [*English Translation*] [*A publication*]
SJP............ San Jose Public Library, San Jose, CA [*OCLC symbol*] (OCLC)
SJP............ San Juan [*Puerto Rico*] [*Seismograph station code, US Geological Survey*] [*Closed*] (SEIS)
SJP............ Sao Jose Do Rio Preto [*Brazil*] [*Airport symbol*] (OAG)
SJP............ Serialized Job Processor
SJP............ Singapore Justice Party (PPW)
SJP............ Southern Journal of Philosophy [*A publication*]
SJP............ Special Job Procedure [*Navy*] (NG)
SJP............ Standard Jet Penetration [*Aviation*]
SJP............ Sun-Jupiter-Probe [*Angle*]
SJPE.......... Scottish Journal of Political Economy [*A publication*]
S J Phil...... Southern Journal of Philosophy [*A publication*]
SJPS.......... Saint John's Provincial Seminary [*Michigan*]
SJPYA........ Scandinavian Journal of Psychology [*A publication*]
SJQ............ San Joaquin Reservoir [*California*] [*Seismograph station code, US Geological Survey*] [*Closed*] (SEIS)
SJR............ San Jose [*Costa Rica*] [*Seismograph station code, US Geological Survey*] [*Closed*] (SEIS)
SJR............ San Juan Racing Association, Inc. [*NYSE symbol*]
SJR............ Senate Joint Resolution
SJR............ Social Justice Review [*A publication*]
SJRB.......... Soviet Jewry Research Bureau (EA)
SJRES........ Senate Joint Resolution (AFIT)
SJRMF....... Senator Joseph R. McCarthy Foundation (EA)
SJRT.......... St. Johns River Terminal [*AAR code*]
SJS............ Saint John's Seminary [*Brighton, MA*]
SJS............ St. Johns Tracking Station [*Newfoundland*]
SJS............ Saint Joseph's Seminary [*Illinois; New York*]
SJS............ San Jose [*Costa Rica*] [*Seismograph station code, US Geological Survey*] (SEIS)
SJS............ San Jose Studies [*A publication*]
SJS............ Search Jam System
SJS............ Secretary, Joint Staff [*Military*] (CINC)
SJS............ Society of Jewish Science (EA)
SJS............ Sunshine-Jr. Stores, Inc. [*American Stock Exchange symbol*]
SJSC.......... San Jose State College [*California*] [*Later, San Jose State University*]
SJSD.......... Soviet Jewry Solidarity Day (BJA)
SJSS.......... Saint Joseph's Seraphic Seminary [*New York*]
SJSUD....... Science Journal. Shivaji University [*A publication*]
SJT............ St. Joseph Terminal Railroad Co. [*AAR code*]
SJT............ San Angelo [*Texas*] [*Airport symbol*] (OAG)
SJT............ San Angelo, TX [*Location identifier*] [*FAA*] (FAAL)
SJT............ San Juan Basin Royalty Trust [*NYSE symbol*]
SJT............ Scottish Journal of Theology [*A publication*]
SJT............ Service Junior - Thermoplastic
SJT............ Southwestern Journal of Theology [*A publication*]
SJT............ Subsonic [*or Supersonic*] Jet Transport
SJTCC....... State Job Training Coordinating Council (OICC)
SJTh.......... Scottish Journal of Theology [*A publication*] (BJA)
SJU............ St. John's University [*Minnesota; New York*]
SJU............ St. John's University, Division of Library and Information Science, Jamaica, NY [*OCLC symbol*] (OCLC)
SJU............ San Juan [*Puerto Rico*] [*Airport symbol*] (OAG)
SJUF.......... Skandinavisk Jodisk Ungdomsforbund (BJA)
S Jur.......... Sirey. Jurisprudence [*France*] (DLA)
S Jur I........ Sirey. Jurisprudence, Cour de Cassation [*France*] (DLA)
S Jur II....... Sirey. Jurisprudence, Other Courts [*France*] (DLA)
S Jur III...... Sirey. Jurisprudence, Jurisprudence Administrative [*France*] (DLA)
S Just........ Shaw's Scotch Justiciary Cases (DLA)
SJV............ Kyoto University. Jimbun Kagaku Kenkyu-sho. Silver Jubilee Volume [*A publication*]
SJV............ St. John [*Virgin Islands*] [*Seismograph station code, US Geological Survey*] (SEIS)
SJV............ Sharing Joint Venture
SjV............ Sirp ja Vasar [*A publication*]
SJV............ Societe Jules Verne (EA-IO)
SJVLS........ San Joaquin Valley Library System [*Library network*]
SJVWGA.... San Joaquin Valley Wine Growers Association [*Madera, CA*] (EA)
SJW........... St. Louis, MO [*Location identifier*] [*FAA*] (FAAL)
SJW........... Shakespeare-Jahrbuch (Weimar) [*A publication*]
SJW........... Single Jewish Woman [*Classified advertising*]
SJW........... SJW Corp. [*American Stock Exchange symbol*]
SJWCP....... Skid Jacket Water Cooling Pump [*Nuclear energy*] (NRCH)
SJ(Weimar) ... Shakespeare-Jahrbuch (Weimar) [*A publication*]
SJWVUSA ... Sons of Jewish War Veterans of the United States of America (EA)
SJX............ St. James, MI [*Location identifier*] [*FAA*] (FAAL)
SJX............ Sartaneja [*Belize*] [*Airport symbol*] (OAG)
SJY............ San Jacinto, CA [*Location identifier*] [*FAA*] (FAAL)
SJZ............ Angola, IN [*Location identifier*] [*FAA*] (FAAL)
SJZ............ Sao Jorge Island [*Azores*] [*Airport symbol*] (OAG)
SJZ............ Schweizerische Juristen-Zeitung [*A publication*]
SJZ............ Selected Judgments, Zambia (DLA)
SK .... Sack
SK .... Safe Keeping

SK .... Safety-Kleen Corp. [*NYSE symbol*]
SK .... Sanitaetskompanie [*Medical company*] [*German military - World War II*]
SK .... Santa Klaus (ROG)
SK .... Saskatchewan [*Canadian province, postal code*]
SK .... Scandinavian Airlines System [*Sweden*] [*ICAO designator*] (OAG)
SK .... Seminarium Kondakovianum [*A publication*]
SK .... Service Kit
SK .... Sick
SK .... Sikes Corp. [*American Stock Exchange symbol*]
sk .... Sikkim [*ii (India) used in records cataloged after January 1978*] [*MARC country of publication code*] [*Library of Congress*] (LCCP)
SK .... Sinclair-Koppers Co. [*Later, Arco Polymers, Inc.*]
SK .... Sink (AAG)
SK .... Skein
SK .... Skeletals
SK .... Sketch (AAG)
S & K .... Skills and Knowledges
SK .... Skimmed
SK .... Skinned (MSA)
sk .... Skot [*Unit of luminance*]
SK .... Smack (ROG)
SK .... Socket (DEN)
SK .... Sonic Key (MCD)
SK .... South Kensington [*District of London*] (ROG)
SK .... Sovetskii Kollektsioner [*A publication*]
SK .... Sovetskyaya Kolonia [*Soviet Colony*]
SK .... Station-Keeping
SK .... Storekeeper [*Navy rating*]
SK .... Streptokinase [*An enzyme*]
Sk .... Strike [*or Stroke*]
SK .... Substance K [*Biochemistry*]
SK .... Sumerische Kultlieder aus Altbabylonischer Zeit [*A publication*] (BJA)
SK1 .... Storekeeper, First Class [*Navy rating*]
SK2 .... Storekeeper, Second Class [*Navy rating*]
SK3 .... Storekeeper, Third Class [*Navy rating*]
SKA .... Skalstugan [*Sweden*] [*Seismograph station code, US Geological Survey*] (SEIS)
SKA .... Skills, Knowledge, and Abilities [*Employment*]
SKA .... Spokane, WA [*Location identifier*] [*FAA*] (FAAL)
SKA .... Switchblade Knife Act
SKAD .... Survival Kit Air-Droppable [*Military*] [*Canada*]
SKAMP ...... Station-Keeping and Mobile Platform [*Robot sailboat*]
Skand .... Skandinavistik [*A publication*]
Skand Ensk Bank Quart R ... Skandinaviska Enskilda Banken. Quarterly Review [*A publication*]
Skandia Int Symp ... Skandia International Symposia [*A publication*]
Skandinavis ... Skandinavistik [*A publication*]
Skandinaviska Enskilda Banken Q R ... Skandinaviska Enskilda Banken. Quarterly Review [*A publication*]
Skand Numis ... Skandinavisk Numismatik [*A publication*]
SKAP .... Skills, Knowledge, Abilities, and Personnel [*Attributes*] (MCD)
SKAT .... Kommentar zum Alten Testament [*A publication*] (BJA)
SKAT .... Sex Knowledge and Aptitude [*Test*]
SKATI .... Skills, Knowledges, Aptitudes, Temperaments, Interests (OICC)
Skat Mag .... Skating Magazine [*A publication*]
SKAWW ...... Sitzungsberichte der Kaiserlichen Akademie der Wissenschaften in Wien [*A publication*]
SKB .... Saint Kitts [*Leeward Islands*] [*Airport symbol*] (OAG)
SKB .... Skew Buffer
SKB .... Skybridge International, Inc. [*Vancouver Stock Exchange symbol*]
SKB .... SmithKline Beckman Corp. [*Formerly, SKL*] [*NYSE symbol*]
SKB .... Wichita Falls, TX [*Location identifier*] [*FAA*] (FAAL)
SKBF .... Schweizerische Koordinationsstelle fuer Bildungsforschung [*Swiss Coordination Center for Research in Education*] [*Information service*] (EISS)
SKBGD ...... Sangyo Kogai Boshi Gijutsu [*A publication*]
SKC .... Sky Clear [*Meteorology*] (FAAC)
SKC .... Suki [*Papua New Guinea*] [*Airport symbol*] (OAG)
SKC .... Waukesha, WI [*Location identifier*] [*FAA*] (FAAL)
SKCATL ...... South Korea Conventional Air Target List (MCD)
SKCB .... Storekeeper, Construction Battalion, Stevedore [*Navy rating*]
SKCM .... Master Chief Storekeeper [*Navy rating*]
SKCM .... Society of King Charles the Martyr (EA)
SKCMA .... Steel Kitchen Cabinet Manufacturers Association (EA)
SKCS .... Senior Chief Storekeeper [*Navy rating*]
SKD .... St. Katherine's Dock [*Shipping*] [*British*] (ROG)
SKD .... Samarkand [*USSR*] [*Airport symbol*] (OAG)
SKD .... Selve-Kornbegel-Dornheim [*Name of a German small arms ammunition factory*] [*World War II*]
SKD .... Sitkalidak Island [*Alaska*] [*Seismograph station code, US Geological Survey*] (SEIS)
SKD .... Skid
SKD .... Skilled (MSA)
SKD .... Skirted

SKD .... Skyworld Resources & Development Ltd. [*Vancouver Stock Exchange symbol*]
SKD .... Storekeeper, Disbursing [*Navy rating*]
SKDGQ ...... Sammlung Ausgewaehlter Kirchen- und Dogmengeschichtlichen Quellenschriften [*A publication*]
SKDH .... Shikimate Dehydrogenase [*An enzyme*]
SKDL .... Suomen Kansan Demokraattinen Liitto [*Finnish People's Democratic League*] (PPW)
SKDN .... Shakedown [*Navy*] (NVT)
SKDNC .... Shakedown Cruise [*Navy*]
SKDNCRU ... Shakedown Cruise [*Navy*] (NVT)
SKDU .... Ship's Keyboard Display Unit
SKE .... Belleville, IL [*Location identifier*] [*FAA*] (FAAL)
SKE .... Skeena Resources Ltd. [*Vancouver Stock Exchange symbol*]
SKE .... Skien [*Norway*] [*Airport symbol*] (OAG)
SKE .... Sky Tours, Inc. [*Port Clinton, OH*] [*FAA designator*] (FAAC)
SKE .... Station-Keeping Equipment
SKED .... Schedule (NG)
SKED .... Sort Key Edit [*Library of Congress*]
SKEDCON ... Schedule Conference [*Military*] (NVT)
SKEIA .... Sanshi Kagaku Kenkyusho Iho [*A publication*]
SKEL .... Skeletal (AAG)
Skeletal Radiol ... Skeletal Radiology [*A publication*]
Skene .... [*Sir John*] Skene's De Verborum Significatione [*of the Signification of Words*] [*7 eds.*] [*1597-1683*] (DLA)
Skene De Verb Sign ... Skene. De Verborum Significatione [*of the Signification of Words*] (DLA)
SKET .... Skeleton Key (DSUE)
SKF .... San Antonio, TX [*Location identifier*] [*FAA*] (FAAL)
SKF .... Skycraft, Inc. [*Seattle, WA*] [*FAA designator*] (FAAC)
SKF .... SmithKline Corp. [*Formerly, Smith, Kline & French Co.*] [*Research code symbol*]
SKF .... Svenska Kullagerfabriken AB [*Swedish manufacturer, especially of ball bearings; active in many countries*]
SKFB .... S & K Famous Brands [*NASDAQ symbol*] (NQ)
SkFi .... Skandinavskaga Filologija [*A publication*]
SKF Psychiatr Rep ... SK and F [*Smith, Kline, and French*] Psychiatric Reporter [*A publication*]
SkFx .... Skull Fracture [*Medicine*]
SKG .... Srpski Knjizevni Glasnik [*A publication*]
SKG .... Thessaloniki [*Greece*] [*Airport symbol*] (OAG)
SKGG .... Schriften der Koenigsberger Gelehrten-Gesellschaft [*A publication*]
SKGGD ...... Sammlung Kurzer Grammatiken Germanischer Dialekte [*A publication*]
SKGND ...... Sanup Kwahak Gisul Yeonguso Nonmunjip (Inha University) [*A publication*]
SKGSA .... Sekiyu Gakkaishi [*A publication*]
SKH .... Selkirk Communications Ltd. [*Toronto Stock Exchange symbol*]
SKH .... Surkhet [*Nepal*] [*Airport symbol*] (OAG)
S-kh Biol .... Sel'skokhozyaistvennaya Biologiya [*A publication*]
S-kh Proizvod Urala ... Sel'skokhozyaistvennoe Proizvodstvo Urala [*A publication*]
S-kh Rub Rastenievod ... Sel'skokhozyaistvo za Rubezhom Rastenievodstvo [*A publication*]
SKHVL .... Skrifter Utgivna av Kungliga Humanistiska Vetenskapssamfundet i Lund [*A publication*]
SkHVSU ..... Skrifter Utgivna av Humanistiska Vetenskapssamfundet i Upsala [*A publication*]
SKI .... Sac City, IA [*Location identifier*] [*FAA*] (FAAL)
SKI .... St. Kitts [*St. Kitts*] [*Seismograph station code, US Geological Survey*] (SEIS)
SKI .... Sister Kenny Institute [*Formerly, SEKF*] [*Minneapolis, MN*] (EA)
SKI .... Sloan-Kettering Institute for Cancer Research
SKIF .... Social Security Number Key Index File [*IRS*]
SKIF .... Sotsyalistisher Kinder Farband (BJA)
SKIL .... Scanner Keyed Input Language
SKILA .... Southern Korean Interim Legislative Assembly
SKILL .... Satellite Kill
Skillings' Min Rev ... Skillings' Mining Review [*A publication*]
Skill Pol Rep ... Skillman's New York Police Reports (DLA)
Skil Mining ... Skillings' Mining Review [*A publication*]
Skin .... Skinner's English King's Bench Reports (DLA)
Skin Diver Mag ... Skin Diver Magazine [*A publication*]
Skinker ...... Skinker's Reports [*65-79 Missouri*] (DLA)
Skinner ...... Skinner's English King's Bench Reports [*90 English Reprint*] [*1681-98*] (DLA)
Skinner (Eng) ... Skinner's English King's Bench Reports [*90 English Reprint*] (DLA)
Skin Res ..... Skin Research [*A publication*]
SKINS .... Supplemental Knowledge Incentive Notes [*Scrip offered to students for good performance*] [*Experimental learning program*]
SKIP .... Sick Kids Need Involved People [*Severna Park, MD*] (EA)
SKIP .... Skinner Investigation Platform
SKIP .... Skippers, Inc. [*NASDAQ symbol*] (NQ)
SKIPI .... Super Knowledge Information Processing Intelligence [*Data processing*]
SKJ .... Sitkinak Island, AK [*Location identifier*] [*FAA*] (FAAL)

SKK .... Shaktoolik [*Alaska*] [*Airport symbol*]   (OAG)
SKK .... Shaktoolik, AK [*Location identifier*] [*FAA*]   (FAAL)
SKK .... Sikka [*USSR*] [*Seismograph station code, US Geological Survey*] [*Closed*]   (SEIS)
SKK .... Sowjetische Kontrollkommission
SKKCA ...... Supreme Knight of the Knights of Columbus of America
SKKOA ...... Shin Kinzoku Kogyo [*A publication*]
SKL .... Isle Of Skye [*Scotland*] [*Airport symbol*]   (OAG)
SKL .... Skilak [*Cooper Landing*] [*Alaska*] [*Seismograph station code, US Geological Survey*]   (SEIS)
SKL .... Skill Level
SKL .... Stackpool Resources Limited [*Vancouver Stock Exchange symbol*]
SKL .... Suomen Kristillinen Liitto [*Finnish Christian League*]   (PPE)
SKM .... Fayette Flying Service & Scheduled Skyways System [*Fayetteville, AR*] [*FAA designator*]   (FAAC)
SKM .... Schuster-Kubelka-Munk [*Optics*]
SKM .... Sine-Kosine Multiplier
SkMG .... Sulfate of Potash Magnesia Export Association [*Northbrook, IL*]   (EA)
SKN .... Skaneateles [*New York*] [*Seismograph station code, US Geological Survey*]   (SEIS)
SKN .... Skein   (ROG)
SKN .... Skyline Aviation Service, Inc. [*Beaver Falls, PA*] [*FAA designator*]   (FAAC)
SKN .... Smithville, TN [*Location identifier*] [*FAA*]   (FAAL)
SKN .... Stokmarknes [*Norway*] [*Airport symbol*]   (OAG)
SKNSB ...... Shokuhin Shosha [*A publication*]
S/KNU ...... Steering Knuckle [*Automotive engineering*]
SKO .... Deadhorse, AK [*Location identifier*] [*FAA*]   (FAAL)
SKO .... Saskatchewan Oil and Gas Common [*Toronto Stock Exchange symbol*]
SKO .... Sets, Kits, and Outfits   (MCD)
SKO .... Skopje [*Yugoslavia*] [*Seismograph station code, US Geological Survey*]   (SEIS)
SKO .... Society of Kastorians "Omonoia"   (EA)
SKO .... Sokoto [*Nigeria*] [*Airport symbol*]   (OAG)
Skoda Rev ... Skoda Review [*A publication*]
Skogshoegsk Inst Skogstek Rapp Uppsats Res Notes ... Skogshoegskolan, Institutionen foer Skogsteknik, Rapporter och Uppsatser. Research Notes [*Sweden*] [*A publication*]
Skogs-Lantbruksakad Tidskr ... Skogs- och Lantbruksakademiens Tidskrift [*A publication*]
SKOR .... Score Exploration Corp. [*NASDAQ symbol*]   (NQ)
Skoteys ...... Spoiled Kids of the Eighties [*Lifestyle classification*] [*Offspring of the Yuppies*]
SKP .... Skip   (BUR)
SKP .... Skopje [*Yugoslavia*] [*Airport symbol*]   (OAG)
SKP .... Station-Keeping Position
SKP .... Suomen Kommunistinen Puolue [*Communist Party of Finland*]   (PPW)
SKP .... Sveriges Kommunistiska Partiet [*Communist Party of Sweden*]   (PPE)
S-K-P's ...... Escapees [*An association*]   (EA)
SKPanKr .... Sprawozdania z Posiedzen Komisji Pan. Oddzial w Krakowie [*A publication*]
SKPI .... Super Knowledge, Processing Interaction [*Concept advanced by Timothy Leary*]
SKPL .... Sketch Pad Layout   (MCD)
SKQ .... Sekakes [*Lesotho*] [*Airport symbol*]   (OAG)
SKQ .... Sexual Knowledge Questionnaire
SKR .... Bedford, MA [*Location identifier*] [*FAA*]   (FAAL)
S KR .... Krona [*Monetary unit in Sweden*]
SKR .... Sanskrit [*Language, etc.*]
SKR .... Saskatchewan Regional Libraries [*UTLAS symbol*]
SKR .... Saturn Kilometer-Wave Radiation [*Planetary science*]
SKR .... Separator-Key Generator-Recombiner   (MCD)
SKR .... Severo-Kurilsk [*USSR*] [*Seismograph station code, US Geological Survey*]   (SEIS)
SKR .... Shaker Heights City School District, Shaker Heights, OH [*OCLC symbol*]   (OCLC)
Skr .... Skipper [*Navy*] [*British*]
SKR .... Skylark Resources Ltd. [*Vancouver Stock Exchange symbol*]
SKR .... South Korea Republic
SKR .... Station-Keeping RADAR
SKRAD ...... Skeletal Radiology [*A publication*]
Skriftser Roskilde Universitetsbibl ... Skriftserie fra Roskilde Universitetsbibliotek [*A publication*]
Skr Lund .... Skrifter Utgivna av Vetenskaps-Societeten i Lund [*A publication*]
Skr Norske Vid-Akad Oslo I ... Skrifter Utgitt av det Norske Videnskaps-Akademi i Oslo I. Matematisk-Naturvidenskapelig Klasse [*A publication*]
Skr Nor Vidensk-Akad Oslo I Mat-Naturvidensk Kl ... Skrifter av det Norske Videnskaps-Akademi i Oslo I Matematisk-Naturvidenskapelig Klasse [*A publication*]
Skr Szk Gl Gospod Wiejsk-Akad Roln Warszawie Ogrod ... Skrypty Szkoly Glownej Gospodarstwa Wiejskiego-Akademii Rolniczej w Warszawie. Ogrodnictwo [*A publication*]
Skr Udgivet Univ Zool Mus (Kbh) ... Skrifter Udgivet af Universitetets Zoologiske Museum (Kobenhavn) [*A publication*]

Skr Uppsala ... Skrifter Utgivna av Kungliga Humanist. Vetenskaps-Samfundet i Uppsala [*A publication*]
SKS .... Career Development Center, Shaker Heights, OH [*OCLC symbol*]   (OCLC)
SKS .... Savezna Komisija za Standardizacija [*Federal Commission for Standardization*] [*Yugoslavia*]
SKS .... Skrydstrup [*Denmark*] [*Airport symbol*]   (OAG)
SKS .... Soren Kierkegaard Society   (EA)
SKS .... Sound Air Aviation [*Ronkonkoma, NY*] [*FAA designator*]   (FAAC)
SKS .... Specialist Knowledge Services [*British organization for occult research*]
SKS .... Station-Keeping Ship
SKSA .... Suomalainen Kirjallisuuden Seura [*A publication*]
SKSA .... Seaman Apprentice, Storekeeper, Striker [*Navy rating*]
SkSb .... Skandinavskij Sbornik [*A publication*]
SKSD .... Streptokinase Streptodornase [*An enzyme mixture*] [*Medicine*]
SKSL .... Skaneateles Short Line Railroad Corp. [*Later, SSL*] [*AAR code*]
SKSN .... Seaman, Storekeeper, Striker [*Navy rating*]
SKSS .... Stoleczny Komitet Samopomocy Spolecznej [*Warsaw*]   (BJA)
SKT .... Sanskrit
SKT .... Saskatchewan Trust Co. SV [*Toronto Stock Exchange symbol*]
SKT .... Skill Knowledge Tests
SKT .... Skirt   (MSA)
SKT .... Skwentna [*Alaska*] [*Seismograph station code, US Geological Survey*]   (SEIS)
SKT .... Socket   (MSA)
SKT .... Specialty Knowledge Test [*Military*]   (AFM)
SKT .... Storekeeper, Technical [*Navy rating*]
SKT .... Tropical International, Inc. [*Miami, FL*] [*FAA designator*]   (FAAC)
SKU .... Newburgh, NY [*Location identifier*] [*FAA*]   (FAAL)
SKU .... Sakura [*Japan*] [*Seismograph station code, US Geological Survey*] [*Closed*]   (SEIS)
SKU .... Stores Keeping Unit
SKV .... Santa Katarina [*Egypt*] [*Airport symbol*]   (OAG)
SKV .... Skewing the Pitch Angle
SKV .... Storekeeper, Aviation [*Navy rating*]
SKVV .... Schweizerischer Katholischer Volksverein
SKW .... Shichikawa [*Japan*] [*Seismograph station code, US Geological Survey*]   (SEIS)
SKW .... Skwentna, AK [*Location identifier*] [*FAA*]   (FAAL)
SKW .... Sky West Aviation, Inc. [*St. George, UT*] [*FAA designator*]   (FAAC)
SKW .... Suddeutsche Kalkstickstoffwerke [*AG*]
SKWKA ...... Sanop Kwa Kisul [*A publication*]
SKX .... Skyline Explorations [*Vancouver Stock Exchange symbol*]
SKX .... Taos, NM [*Location identifier*] [*FAA*]   (FAAL)
SKY .... Sandusky, OH [*Location identifier*] [*FAA*]   (FAAL)
SKY .... Sky Flite, Inc. [*Tulsa, OK*] [*FAA designator*]   (FAAC)
SKY .... Skyline Corp. [*NYSE symbol*]
SKY .... Skyrocket Exploration [*Vancouver Stock Exchange symbol*]
Sky .... Skywriting [*A publication*]
SKYBET .... Skylab Best Estimate of Trajectory [*NASA*]
SKYCAV ... Sky Cavalry
SKYCOM ... Skylab Communications Engineer [*NASA*]
SKYP .... Suomen Kansan Yhtenaeisyyden Puolue [*People's Unity Party*] [*Finland*]   (PPW)
Sky & Tel. ... Sky and Telescope [*A publication*]
Sky Telesc ... Sky and Telescope [*A publication*]
SKZ .... Schweizerische Kirchenzeitung [*A publication*]
SKZ .... Sukkur [*Pakistan*] [*Airport symbol*]   (OAG)
SL .... Antares SpA [*ICAO designator*]   (FAAC)
SL .... Large-Scale Disturbance Field
SL .... Lloydminster Public Library, Saskatchewan [*Library symbol*] [*National Library of Canada*]   (NLC)
SL .... Safe Locker   (AAG)
SL .... Safety Level [*Army*]
SL .... Safety Limit   (NRCH)
S & L .... Sale and Leaseback
SL .... Sales Letter
SL .... Salvage Loss
SL .... Sample Laboratory   (MCD)
SL .... San Luis Obispo [*Mexican state; city and county in California*]
SL .... Sand-Loaded [*Technical drawings*]
SL .... Satellite-Like [*Virus*]
S & L .... Savings and Loan [*Association*]
SL .... Savings and Loan [*Association*]
SL .... Scanning Slit   (MCD)
S & L .... Schoales and Lefroy's Irish Chancery Reports [*1802-06*]   (DLA)
SL .... School Leavers [*Department of Employment*] [*British*]
SL .... Scientists for Life [*An association*] [*Defunct*]   (EA)
SL .... Scottish Liturgy [*Episcopalian*]
SL .... Sea Level
SL .... Searchlight
SL .... Second Lieutenant
SL .... Section Leader   (NRCH)
SL .... Section List   (MCD)
SL .... Secundum Legem [*According to Law*] [*Latin*]
SL .... Seditious Libeler

SL	Send Leg [*Telegraphy*] (TEL)
SL	Sendero Luminoso [*Shining Path*] [*Peruvian*] (PD)
SL	Sensation Level [*Audiometry*]
SL	Sensu Lato [*In a Broad Sense*] [*Latin*]
SL	Separate Lead [*Cables*]
SL	Sergeant-at-Law
SL	Service Letter (MCD)
SL	Servomechanisms Laboratory [*MIT*] (MCD)
SL	Session Laws (DLA)
SL	Shear Layer [*or Load*]
SL	Shelf Life (NASA)
SL	Shift Left
SL	Ship-of-the-Line
S-of-L	Ship-of-the-Line
SL	Shipowner's Liability [*Business and trade*]
S/L	Shops and Labs [*NASA*] (NASA)
SL	Short Landed [*Tea trade*] (ROG)
SL	Short Lengths [*Construction*]
SL	Short Letter
S-L	Short-Long [*as of a signal light's flash cycle*]
SL	Sick Leave (AFM)
SL	Side Load (AAG)
SL	Sidelobe (CAAL)
sl	Sierra Leone [*MARC country of publication code*] [*Library of Congress*] (LCCP)
SL	Sierra Leone [*Two-letter standard code*] (CNC)
SL	Sigillo Locus [*Place for the Seal*] [*Latin*] (ROG)
SL	Signal Level
SL	Significance Level
SL	Silicon Lacquer
SL	Silver Library [*A publication*]
SL	Simulation Language [*Data processing*] (BUR)
SL	Sine Loco [*Without Place*] [*Latin*]
SL	Single Ledger [*Accounting*]
SL	Single Line
SL	Single-Locus [*Light flashes*]
SL	Sisters of Loretto at the Foot of the Cross [*Roman Catholic religious order*]
SL	Skill Level
SL	Skylab [*NASA*] (KSC)
SL	SL Industries, Inc. [*NYSE symbol*]
SL	Slain (ROG)
SL	Slate (AAG)
Sl	Slavia [*A publication*]
SL	Slesvigske Parti [*Schleswig Party*] [*Denmark*] (PPE)
SL	Slide (AAG)
SL	Slightly
SL	Slip [*Knitting*]
SL	Slit Lamp [*Instrumentation*]
Sl	Slovene (DLA)
SL	Slow [*Track condition*] [*Thoroughbred racing*]
SL	Small Lymphocytes [*Hematology*]
SL	Small Lymphoma [*Oncology*]
SL	Societas Liturgica (EA)
SL	Society of Limerents (EA)
SL	Sockellafette [*Pedestal mount*] [*German military - World War II*]
SL	Soft Landing (MCD)
SL	Solar Lobby [*An association*] (EA)
SL	Sold
SL	Solicitor-at-Law
SL	Sonic Log
SL	Sons of Liberty (EA)
SL	Sortie Lab [*NASA*]
SL	Sound Level (NASA)
SL	Sound Locator [*Military*]
SL	Source Language [*Data processing*] (BUR)
SL	Source Level
SL	South Latitude
SL	Southeast Airlines, Inc. [*ICAO designator*] [*Obsolete*] (OAG)
SL	Soviet Life [*A publication*]
S/L	Soviet Literature [*A publication*]
S/L	Space Laboratory (KSC)
SL	Spacelab [*NASA*] (NASA)
SL	Spartacist League (EA)
SL	Special Layout (MCD)
SL	Special Libraries [*A publication*]
SL	Special Linear [*Group theory, mathematics*]
S/L	Speedletter
SL	Split Level [*Home*] [*Classified advertising*]
SL	Spool
SL	Sprinkler Leakage [*Insurance*]
SL	Squadron Leader [*RAF*] [*British*]
SL	Stage Left [*A stage direction*]
SL	Stagnation Line
SL	Standard Label [*Data processing*]
SL	Standard Length
SL	Standard of Living
SL	Standard Location [*Civil Defense*]
S & L	Standards and Limits
SL	Star Line

SL	Start Line
SL	Stationary Low-Power [*Reactor*] [*Dismantled*] (NRCH)
SL	Statistical List
S/L	Statute of Limitations (OICC)
SL	Stern Loading
SL	Stock Length [*Construction or manufacturing materials*]
SL	Stock Level (AFM)
SL	Stock List (MCD)
SL	Stomodeal Lip [*Endocrinology*]
SL	Storage Location
SL	Straight Line
SL	Streamline
SL	Streptolysin [*Hematology*]
SL	Stronnictwo Ludowe [*Peasant Party (1944-1949)*] [*Poland*] (PPE)
SL	Stronnictwo Ludowe [*Peasant Party (1931-1945)*] [*Poland*] (PPE)
SL	Structures Laboratory [*Army*]
SL	Studia Linguistica [*Lund*] [*A publication*]
SL	Studies in Linguistics [*A publication*]
SL	Studio Location
SL	Sub-Lieutenant [*Navy*] [*British*]
SL	Suberin Lamella [*Botany*]
SL	Sublingual [*Medicine*]
SL	Submarine Qualification Lapsed [*Navy*]
SL	Subscriber's Loop [*Telecommunications*] (TEL)
SL	Sumerian Laws (BJA)
SL	Sumerisches Lexikon [*Rome*] [*A publication*]
SL	Sunday League (EA)
SL	Superlattice [*Solid state physics*]
SL	Supplementary List [*Navy*] [*British*]
SL	Supplier Letter (MCD)
S & L	Supply and Logistics
SL	Support Line [*Military*]
SL	Surface Launch (MUGU)
SL	Svenska Landsmal och Svenskt Folkliv [*A publication*]
SL	Sydney & Louisburg Railway Co. [*AAR code*]
SL	Synchronous Line Medium Speed (BUR)
SL	Syria and Lebanon
SL	System Language
S & L	System and Logistics
SLA	La Ronge Public Library, Saskatchewan [*Library symbol*] [*National Library of Canada*] (NLC)
SLA	Left Sacroanterior Position [*of the fetus*] [*Obstetrics*]
SLA	Salta [*Argentina*] [*Airport symbol*] (OAG)
SLA	San Lorenzo [*Argentina*] [*Seismograph station code, US Geological Survey*] (SEIS)
SLA	Sandia Laboratories, Albuquerque (AABC)
SLA	Saturn LM [*Lunar Module*] Adapter [*NASA*]
SLA	School Library Association
SLA	Scott Library [*A publication*]
SLA	Scottish Library Association
SLA	Sequential Launch Adapter [*Missiles*] (RDA)
SLA	Shared Line Adapter
SLA	Short and Long Arm [*Automotive engineering*]
SLA	Showmen's League of America (EA)
SLA	Side-Looking LASER Altimeter (RDA)
SLA	Sierra Leone Airlines
SL & A	Sine Loco et Anno [*Without Place and Year*] [*Latin*]
SLA	Single-Line Approach
Sla	Slavia [*A publication*]
sla	Slavic [*MARC language code*] [*Library of Congress*] (LCCP)
SLA	Sleep-Learning Association (EA)
SLA	Slovak League of America (EA)
SLA	Society for Linguistic Anthropology [*American Anthropological Association*] (EA)
SLA	South Lebanon Army
SLA	Spacecraft LM [*Lunar Module*] Adapter [*NASA*]
SLA	Special Libraries Association (EA)
SLA	Specific Leaf Area [*Botany*]
SLA	Sports Lawyers Association (EA)
SLA	Square Loop Antenna
SLA	Standard Life Association (EA)
SLA	Standard Location Area [*Civil Defense*]
SLA	State Liquor Authority
SLA	Stored Logic Array
SLA	Stripline
SLA	Studies in Linguistic Analysis [*Elsevier Book Series*] [*A publication*]
SLA	Sulfur-Lead Analyzer
SLA	Supplies in Liberated Areas [*British*] [*World War II*]
SLA	Supply Loading Airfield
SLA	Support and Logistics Areas (MCD)
SLA	Symbionese Liberation Army [*Radical California group; kidnapped newspaper heiress Patricia Hearst in 1974*]
SLA	Synchronous Line Adapter
SLAA	Society for Latin American Anthropology (EA)
SLAA	State and Local Assistance Act
SLA Adv & Mkt Div Bul	Special Libraries Association. Advertising and Marketing Division. Bulletin [*A publication*]

SLA Alabama Chap Bul ... Special Libraries Association. Alabama Chapter. Bulletin [*A publication*]

SLAAP .... St. Louis Army Ammunition Plant

SLAAS .... Supersonic Low-Altitude Attack Aircraft System   (MCD)

SLAB........ Sage Laboratories [*NASDAQ symbol*]   (NQ)

SLAB.......... Students for Labeling of Alcoholic Beverages [*Student legal action organization*]

SLA Biol Sci Div Reminder ... Special Libraries Association. Biological Sciences Division. Reminder [*A publication*]

Slaboproudy Obz ... Slaboproudy Obzor [*Czechoslovakia*] [*A publication*]

SLA Bus & Fin Div Bul ... Special Libraries Association. Business and Financial Division. Bulletin [*A publication*]

SLAC........ Special Committee on Latin American Coordination

SLAC.......... Stanford Linear Accelerator Center [*Stanford University*] [*AEC*] [*Research center*]

SLAC......... Stowage Launch Adapter Container

SLAC......... Straight-Line (Linear) Accelerator [*Nuclear energy*]

SLAC......... Support List Allowance Card   (MCD)

SLAD......... Salon Litteraire, Artistique, et Diplomatique

SLAD......... Shipboard Landing Assist Device

SLAD......... SONAR Locator, Altimeter, and Depthometer

SLAD......... System Logic and Algorithm Development

Slade........ Slade's Reports [*15 Vermont*]   (DLA)

SLADE .... Society of Lithographic Artists, Designers, and Engineers [*British*]

SLAE......... Standard Lightweight Avionics Equipment [*Army*]   (RDA)

SLAET....... Society of Licensed Aircraft Engineers and Technologists   (EA-IO)

SLA Fin Div Bul ... Special Libraries Association. Financial Division. Bulletin [*A publication*]

SLAFRS ..... Southwestern Livestock and Forage Research Station [*Oklahoma State University*] [*Research center*]   (RCD)

SLAG......... Safe Launch Angle Gate

SLAG......... Side-Looking Air-to-Ground [*RADAR*]

SLA GA Chap Bul ... Special Libraries Association. Georgia Chapter. Bulletin [*A publication*]

SLA Geog & Map Div Bul ... Special Libraries Association. Geography and Map Division. Bulletin [*A publication*]

SLA Geog and Map Div Bull ... Special Libraries Association. Geography and Map Division. Bulletin [*A publication*]

SLAHF....... Slovak League of America Heritage Foundation   (EA)

SLAHTS ..... Stowage List and Hardware Tracking System   (MCD)

SLA Ind Chap Slant ... Special Libraries Association. Indiana Chapter. Slant [*A publication*]

SLAIS........ School of Library Archival and Information Studies [*University of British Columbia, Vancouver*] [*Canada*]

SLAIT .... Study Group on Legal Aspects of Intermodal Transportation [*National Research Council*]

SLAKSJ ..... Supreme Ladies Auxiliary Knights of St. John   (EA)

SLAL .... Stowage Launch Adapter, Lower

SLAM .... S. L. A. Marshall [*Military author and commentator*]

SLAM .... Scanning LASER Acoustic Microscope

SLAM .... Sea-Launched Air Missile   (NVT)

SLAM .... Seeking, Locating, Annihilating, Monitoring [*Army project, Vietnam*]

SLAM .... Short LOFAR [*Low-Frequency Acquisition and Ranging*] Alerting Message   (NVT)

SLAM .... Side Load Arresting Mechanism   (KSC)

SLAM .... Sierra Leone Alliance Movement   (PD)

SLAM .... Simulation Language for Alternative Modeling [*Data processing*]   (CSR)

SLAM .... Society's League Against Molestation [*Arcadia, CA*]   (EA)

SLAM .... Space-Launched Air Missile   (MCD)

SLAM .... Spares Level Activity Model   (MCD)

SLAM .... Stowage Launch Adapter, Middle

SLAM .... Submarine-Launched Air Missile

SLAM .... Supersonic Low-Altitude Missile [*Later, LASV*] [*NATO*]   (NATG)

SLAM .... Surface-Launched Air Missile

SLAM .... Symbolic Language Adapted for Microcomputers

SLA Metals Div News ... Special Libraries Association. Metals Division. News [*A publication*]

SLAMEX .... Submarine-Launched Assault Missile Exercise   (NVT)

SLA Mich Chap Bul ... Special Libraries Association. Michigan Chapter. Bulletin [*A publication*]

SLA Montreal Chap Bul ... Special Libraries Association. Montreal Chapter. Bulletin [*A publication*]

SLAMS...... Simplified Language for Abstract Mathematical Structures [*Data processing*]   (IEEE)

SLAMS....... State and Local Air Monitoring Stations [*Environmental Protection Agency*]

SLAMS....... Surface Look-Alike Mine System   (MCD)

SLA Museum Div Bul ... Special Libraries Association. Museum Division. Bulletin [*A publication*]

SLAN.......... Shock Landing Analysis   (MCD)

SLAN.......... Sine Loco, Anno, vel Nomine [*Without Place, Year, or Name*] [*Latin*]

SLAN.......... Slander [*or Slanderous*] [*FBI standardized term*]

SLA News ... SLA [*Scottish Library Association*] News [*A publication*]

S Lang....... Studies in Language [*A publication*]

SLANG....... Systems Language

SLANT .... Simulator Landing Attachment for Night Landing Training

SlAnt.......... Slavia Antiqua [*A publication*]

Slants Khim Prom-st ... Slantsevaya i Khimicheskaya Promyshlennost [*Estonian SSR*] [*A publication*]

SLAO.......... Committee on Supply Questions in Liberated Areas (Official) [*World War II*]

SLAP .... Office of State and Local Assistance Programs [*Department of Energy*]

SLAP .... Saboted Light Armor Penetrator [*Weaponry*]   (MCD)

SLAP .... Sandia-Livermore Aeroheating Program

SLAP .... Simplified Labor and Performance   (MCD)

SLAP .... Symbolic Language Assembly Program [*Data processing*]   (KSC)

SLA Picture Div Picturescope ... Special Libraries Association. Picture Division. Picturescope [*A publication*]

SLA Pittsburgh Chap Bul ... Special Libraries Association. Pittsburgh Chapter. Bulletin [*A publication*]

SLAPN .... Succinyl-L-alanyl-L-alanyl-L-alanine-p-nitroanilide [*Biochemistry*]

SLAPS........ Subscriber Loop Analysis Program System [*Bell System*]

SLAR.......... Select ADC [*Analog-to-Digital Converter*] Register [*Data processing*]   (MDG)

SLAR.......... Senior Logistics Aviation Representative   (MCD)

SLAR.......... Side-Looking Aerial [*or Airborne*] RADAR

SLAR.......... Slant Range

SLAR.......... Slargando [*Slackening*] [*Music*]   (ROG)

SLAR.......... Steerable LASER Radiometer   (MCD)

SLARD....... Saskatchewan Law Review [*A publication*]

SLARF....... Slant Range Fuze   (NG)

SLARG....... Slargando [*Slackening*] [*Music*]

SLASC....... St. Louis Area Support Center [*Military*]   (MCD)

SLA Sci-Tech News ... Special Libraries Association. Science-Technology Division. News [*A publication*]

SLASH .... Seiler Laboratory ALGOL Simulated Hybrid [*Data processing*]

SLASH .... Small Light Antisubmarine Helicopter

Slaski Kwar Hist Sobotka ... Slaski Kwartalnik Historyczny Sobotka [*A publication*]

SLAST........ Submarine-Launched Antiship Torpedo

SLAT......... Sample Lot Acceptance Testing

SLAT .... Sindacato Lavoratori Amministrativi e Technichi [*Union of Administration and Technical Workers*] [*Somalia*]

SLAT .... Slater Electric [*NASDAQ symbol*]   (NQ)

SLAT .... South Latitude

SLAT .... Special Logistics Actions, Thailand   (AABC)

SLAT .... Supersonic Low Activities Target   (MCD)

SLAT .... Support List Allowance Tape   (MCD)

SLAT .... Surface Launcher Air-Targeted [*Weapon*]   (MCD)

SLATE......... Organization of campus activists at the University of California, Berkeley [*Name, although capitalized, is not an acronym but is instead derived from the group's founding in 1958, when it ran a slate of candidates for student government*]

SLATE....... Ship-Launched ASW [*Antisubmarine Warfare*] Two-Way Expendable [*Buoy*] [*Navy*]   (CAAL)

SLATE....... Small, Lightweight Altitude-Transmission Equipment [*FAA*]

SLATE....... Stimulated Learning by Automated Typewriter Environment

SLATE....... Submarine-Launched Two-Way Expendable   (NVT)

SLA Texas Chap Bul ... Special Libraries Association. Texas Chapter. Bulletin [*A publication*]

SLATO .... Secretariado Latinamericano de Trotskismo Orthodoxo [*Peru*]

SLA Toronto Chap Bul ... Special Libraries Association. Toronto Chapter. Bulletin [*A publication*]

SLAU.......... Stowage Launch Adapter, Upper

Slav .... Slavia [*A publication*]

SLAV.......... Slavic [*Language, etc.*]   (ROG)

SLAV.......... Slavonian [*Language, etc.*]   (ROG)

SLAV.......... Slavonic [*Language, etc.*]

SLAV.......... Special Logistics Actions, South Vietnam   (CINC)

SlavA.......... Slavia Antiqua [*A publication*]

SLAVCA..... Sindacato Nazionale Lavoratori Vetro e Ceramica [*National Union of Glass and Ceramics' Workers*] [*Italy*]

Slav E Eur ... Slavic and East European Journal [*A publication*]

SlavEnoch ... Slavic Book of Enoch   (BJA)

SlavF.......... Slavjanskaja Filologija [*A publication*]

Slavia Ant ... Slavia Antiqua [*A publication*]

Slavic E Eu ... Slavic and East European Journal [*A publication*]

Slavic & E Eur J ... Slavic and East European Journal [*A publication*]

Slavic R..... Slavic Review [*A publication*]

Slavon E Eu ... Slavonic and East European Review [*A publication*]

Slavon & E Eur R ... Slavonic and East European Review [*A publication*]

Slavonic & E Eur R ... Slavonic and East European Review [*A publication*]

Slavonic R ... Slavonic Review [*A publication*]

SlavP.......... Slavica Pragensia [*A publication*]

SlavR.......... Slavic Review [*A publication*]

Slav R......... Slavische Rundschau [*A publication*]

SlavR.......... Slavisticna Revija [*A publication*]

SLAVR....... Slavonic Review [*A publication*]

SlavRev....... Slavisticna Revija [*A publication*]

SlavS.......... Slavica Slovaca [*A publication*]

Slav S........ Slavisticki Studii [*A publication*]

SLAW .... Conference on the Sociology of the Languages of American Women [*1976*]

SLAW .... St. Lawrence Railroad [*Division of National Railway Utilization Corp.*] [*AAR code*]
SLA Western NY Chap Bul ... Special Libraries Association. Western New York Chapter. Bulletin [*A publication*]
SLB .... Schlumberger Ltd. [*NYSE symbol*]
SLB .... Self-Lubricating Bearing
SLB .... Short Leg Brace [*Medicine*]
SLB .... Side-Lobe Blanking [*RADAR*]
SLB .... Signal Light Bare [*MSA*]
SLB .... Sintered Lead Bronze
SLB .... Solomon Islands [*Three-letter standard code*] (CNC)
SLB .... Southland Aviation, Inc. [*Destin, FL*] [*FAA designator*] (FAAC)
SLB .... Steam Line Break (NRCH)
SLB .... Storm Lake, IA [*Location identifier*] [*FAA*] (FAAL)
SLB .... Studia ad Tabulas Cuneiformes Collecta a de Liagre Boehl Pertinentia [*A publication*]
SLBL .... Soluble (MSA)
SLBM .... Sea-Launched Ballistic Missile [*Navy*] (CAAL)
SLBM .... Submarine-Launched Ballistic Missile [*Navy*] [*Obsolete*]
SLBMDWS ... Submarine-Launched Ballistic Missile Detection and Warning System (IEEE)
SLBP .... Spring-Loaded Ball Plunger
SLBR .... Slaughter Brothers [*NASDAQ symbol*] (NQ)
SLBS .... Sierra Leone Broadcasting Service
SLC .... Salt Lake City [*Utah*] [*Airport symbol*] (OAG)
SLC .... Salt Lake City [*Utah*] [*Seismograph station code, US Geological Survey*] (SEIS)
SLC .... Salt Lake City, UT [*Location identifier*] [*FAA*] (FAAL)
SLC .... [*The*] San Luis Central Railroad Co. [*AAR code*]
SLC .... Sarah Lawrence College [*New York*]
SLC .... Scottish Land Court Reports (DLA)
SLC .... Scottish Land Courts (DLA)
SLC .... Scottish Leaving Certificate
SLC .... Sea-Level Canal Study (EISS)
SLC .... Searchlight Control [*Military*]
SLC .... Selector Channel
SLC .... Set Location Counter (CMD)
SLC .... Shelf Life Code (MCD)
SLC .... Shift Left and Count Instructions [*Data processing*] (MDG)
SL & C .... Shipper's Load and Count [*Bills of lading*]
SLC .... Side-Lobe Cancellation [*RADAR*]
SLC .... Side-Lobe Clutter
SLC .... Simulated Linguistic Computer
SLC .... Single Launch Contractor (KSC)
SLC .... Single Line Control (BUR)
SLC .... Slice (MSA)
SLC .... Small Library Computing, Inc. [*Holbrook, NY*] [*Information service*] (EISS)
SLC .... Smith's Leading Cases (DLA)
SLC .... Songwriters and Lyricists Club [*Brooklyn, NY*] (EA)
SLC .... Sonobuoy Launch Container (NVT)
SLC .... Southland Corporation [*NYSE symbol*]
SLC .... Space Launch Complex
SLC .... Spanish Literature Committee [*Grand Rapids, MI*] (EA)
SLC .... Special Libraries Cataloguing, Inc. [*North Vancouver, BC*] [*Information service*] (EISS)
SLC .... Standard Launch Complex (KSC)
SLC .... Standard Location Codes
SLC .... Standby Liquid Control (NRCH)
SLC .... Standing Liaison Committee
SLC .... Stanford Linear Collider [*High-energy physics*]
SLC .... State Library of Ohio, Catalog Center, Columbus, OH [*OCLC symbol*] (OCLC)
SLC .... State Line Airport [*Leawood, KS*] [*FAA designator*] (FAAC)
SLC .... Stockage List Code (AABC)
SLC .... Straight-Line Capacitance [*or Capacity*]
SLC .... Strategic LASER Communications [*Military*] (CAAL)
SLC .... Stuart's Lower Canada Appeal Cases [*1810-35*] (DLA)
SLC .... Sublingual Cleft [*Medicine*]
SLC .... Submarine LASER Communications
SLC .... Subscriber Loop Carrier [*Telecommunications*] (TEL)
SLC .... Sue and Labor Clause [*Business and trade*]
SLC .... Surgeon Lieutenant-Commander [*Navy*] [*British*]
SLC .... Susquehanna Library Cooperative [*Library network*]
SLC .... Sustained Load Crack [*Titanium alloy*]
SLC .... Synchro Loop Closure
SLC .... Synchronous Line Medium Speed with Clock (BUR)
SLC .... System Life Cycle
SLC App .... Stuart's Lower Canada Appeal Cases (DLA)
SLCB .... Single-Line Color Bar (IEEE)
SLCC .... Saturn Launch Control Computer [*NASA*] (KSC)
SLCD .... Surplus Land for Community Development
SLCL .... Shop/Lab Configuration Layout (MCD)
SLCL .... Sierra Leone Council of Labour
SLCL .... Small Lymphocyte Cell Lymphoma [*Oncology*]
SLCM .... Sea-Launched Cruise Missile [*Pronounced "slick-em"*] (AABC)
SLCM .... Ship Life-Cycle Management
SLCM .... Software Life Cycle Management
SLCM .... Submarine-Launched Cruise Missile (IEEE)
SLCM .... Surface Launch Cruise Missile

SLCN .... Silicon Systems, Inc. [*NASDAQ symbol*] (NQ)
SL Co .... Appendices of Proceedings of the Scottish Land Court (DLA)
SL Co R ..... Appendices of Proceedings of the Scottish Land Court (DLA)
SL Council Phila & Vicinity Bul ... Special Libraries Council of Philadelphia and Vicinity. Bulletin [*A publication*]
SLCP .... Ship's Loading Characteristics Pamphlet [*Navy*] (NVT)
SLCR .... Salem Carpet Mills [*NASDAQ symbol*] (NQ)
SLCR .... Scottish Land Court Reports (DLA)
SLCRM ...... Ship Life-Cycle Reference Matrix [*Navy*]
SLCRS ...... Supplementary Leak Collection and Release System [*Nuclear energy*] (NRCH)
SLCS .... Standby Liquid Control System [*Nuclear energy*] (NRCH)
SLCT .... Select (FAAC)
SLCU .... Standard Landing Craft Unit [*Military*]
SLCU .... Synchronous Line Control Unit
SLD .... Sailed
SLD .... San Luis Dam [*California*] [*Seismograph station code, US Geological Survey*] (SEIS)
SLD .... Sea Landing Division [*NATO*]
SLD .... Sealed
SLD .... Serum Lactate Dehydrogenase [*Also, SLDH*] [*An enzyme*]
SLD .... Shutdown Logic Diagram [*Nuclear energy*] (NRCH)
SLD .... Simulated Launch Demonstration [*NASA*] (KSC)
SLD .... Sliac [*Czechoslovakia*] [*Airport symbol*] (OAG)
SLD .... Slide
SLD .... Sliding Door (AAG)
SLD .... Slowdown (AAG)
SLD .... Slumber Lodge Development Corp. Ltd. [*Vancouver Stock Exchange symbol*]
SLD .... Sold
SLD .... Solder
SLD .... Solid (FAAC)
SLD .... Solid Logic Dense (BUR)
SLD .... Sonic Layer Depth (NVT)
SLD .... Source Language Debug [*Data processing*] (IEEE)
SLD .... Source-Level Debugger [*Motorola, Inc.*]
SLD .... Specific Language [*or Learning*] Disability [*Education*]
SLD .... Square Law Detection
SLD .... Straight Line Depreciation [*Telecommunications*] (TEL)
SLD .... Studia Litteraria (University of Debrecen) [*A publication*]
SLD .... Synchronous Line Driver
SLDAA ...... SACLANT [*Supreme Allied Commander, Atlantic*] Distributing and Accounting Agency (NATG)
SLD CARB DI ... Solidified Carbon Dioxide [*Freight*]
SLDD .... Scientific Library and Documentation Division [*National Science and Technology Authority*] [*Philippines*] [*Information service*] (EISS)
SLDG .... Sliding
SLDH .... Serum Lactate Dehydrogenase [*Also, SLD*] [*An enzyme*]
SLDPF .... Spacelab Data Processing Facility (MCD)
SLDR .... Solder (MSA)
SLDR .... Soldier
SLDS .... Scanning LASER Doppler System [*NASA*]
SLDS .... Skylab Launch Data System [*NASA*] (KSC)
SLDTSS ..... Single Language Dedicated Time-Sharing System
SLDVS ...... Scanning LASER Doppler Vortex System [*NASA*]
SLE .... Saint Louis Encephalitis [*Medicine*]
SLE .... Salem [*Oregon*] [*Airport symbol*] (OAG)
SLE .... Salem, OR [*Location identifier*] [*FAA*] (FAAL)
SLE .... Sara Lee Corp. [*NYSE symbol*]
SLE .... Service Life Evaluation
SLE .... Shuttle Transport [*New York, NY*] [*FAA designator*] (FAAC)
SLE .... Sierra Leone [*Three-letter standard code*] (CNC)
SLE .... Small Lattice Experiment
SLE .... Small Local Exchange [*Telecommunications*] (TEL)
SLE .... Smith, Leland C., Oakland CA [*STAC*]
SLE .... Societas Linguistica Europaea (EA-IO)
SLE .... Society of Logistics Engineers (MCD)
SLE .... Station Liaison Engineer [*NASA*]
SLE .... Student Letter Exchange (EA)
SLE .... Studio Lighting Equipment
SLE .... Superheat Limit Explosion
SLE .... Systemic Lupus Erythematosus [*Medicine*]
SLEC .... Southland Energy Corporation [*NASDAQ symbol*] (NQ)
SLED .... Special Learning Education [*In company name, SLED Software*] [*Minneapolis, MN*] [*Software manufacturer*]
SLED .... State Level Electricity Demand [*Model*] [*Nuclear Regulatory Commission*]
SLEDGE .... Simulating Large Explosive Detonable Gas Experiments
SLEEP .... Scanning Low-Energy Electron Probe (IEEE)
SLEEP .... Silent, Lightweight, Electric Energy Plant (RDA)
SLEEP .... Swedish Low-Energy Experimental Pile [*Nuclear energy*]
Sleep Sick Bureau Bull ... Sleeping Sickness Bureau. Bulletin [*A publication*]
SLEICC ...... Statue of Liberty - Ellis Island Centennial Commission (EA)
SLEIF .... Statue of Liberty - Ellis Island Foundation (EA)
SLEM .... Solution of Linearized Equations of Motion
SLEMA ...... Schiffli Lace and Embroidery Manufacturers Association [*Union City, NJ*] (EA)
SLEMU ...... Spacelab Engineering Model Unit (MCD)
SLENT .... Slentando [*Slackening*] [*Music*] (ROG)

SLEP .... Second Large ESRO [*European Space Research Organization*] Project
SLEP .... Service Life Extension Program (MCD)
SLESP .... Suplemento Literario do Estado de Sao Paulo [*A publication*]
Sleszky Num ... Sleszky Numismatik [*A publication*]
SLet .... Sestante Letterario [*A publication*]
SLEUTH ...... UNIVAC 1108 Assembly Language
SLEV .... St. Louis Encephalitis Virus
SLEV .... Salaried Legal Expense Voucher
SLEW .... Static Load Error Washout
SLF .... Saturn Launch Facility [*NASA*]
SLF .... Savings and Loan Foundation [*Later, FSI*] (EA)
SLF .... Scientific Laboratory Facility
SLF .... Shuttle Landing Facility (MCD)
SLF .... Skandinaviska Lackteknikers Forbund [*Federation of Scandinavian Paint and Varnish Technicians*]
SLF .... Society of the Little Flower (EA)
SLF .... South Luzon Force [*Army*] [*World War II*]
SLF .... Southwestern Legal Foundation (DLA)
SLF .... Special Landing Forces [*Marine Corps*]
SLF .... Straight-Line Frequency
SLF .... Suction Line Filter
SLF .... Super-Low-Frequency (MCD)
SLF .... Svenska Litteratursaellskapet i Finland [*A publication*]
SLF .... System Library File [*Data processing*] (BUR)
SLFA .... Svensklaerarfoereningens Arsskrift [*A publication*]
SLFC .... Sierra Leone Full Court Reports (DLA)
SLFC .... Survivable Low-Frequency Communications [*Air Force*]
SLFCLN ..... Self-Cleaning [*Engineering*]
SLFCS .... Survivable Low-Frequency Communications System [*Air Force*]
SLFD .... Steam Lava Flow Deflector (MCD)
SLFGEN ..... Self-Generating
SLFIA .... Substrate-Labeled Fluorescent Immunoassay
SLFIND ...... Self-Indicating
S-LFL .... Short-Long Flashing Light [*Navigation signal*]
SLFLKG ..... Self-Locking [*Engineering*]
SLFOEAMTMTS ... St. Louis Field Office, Eastern Area, Military Traffic Management and Terminal Service [*Army*] (AABC)
SLFP .... Sri Lanka Freedom Party (PPW)
SLFSE .... Self-Sealing [*Engineering*]
SLFTPG ..... Self-Tapping [*Screw*] [*Design engineering*]
SLFU .... Skrifter Utgivna. Genom Landsmals-och Folk-Minnesarkivet i Uppsala [*A publication*]
SLG .... Community of the Sisters of the Love of God [*Anglican religious community*]
SLG .... Lander College, Larry A. Jackson Library, Greenwood, SC [*OCLC symbol*] (OCLC)
SLG .... Scottish Law Gazette [*A publication*]
SLG .... Seligman & Associates, Inc. [*American Stock Exchange symbol*]
SLG .... Siloam Springs, AK [*Location identifier*] [*FAA*] (FAAL)
SLG .... Sludge (MSA)
SLG .... Slugger [*Percentage*] [*Baseball*]
SLG .... Soda Lime Glass
SLG .... Southern Lights [*Vancouver Stock Exchange symbol*]
SLG .... State or Local Government
SLG .... Studia Linguistica Germanica [*A publication*]
SLGB .... Synchronous Line Group (BUR)
SLGB .... Society of Local Government Barristers [*British*] (DLA)
SLGM .... Surface-Launched Guided Missile
SLGP .... Student Loan Guaranty Program
SLGR .... Slinger
SLGT .... Slight (FAAC)
SLGW .... Salt Lake, Garfield & Western Railway Co. [*AAR code*]
SLH .... Sola [*Vanuatu*] [*Airport symbol*] (OAG)
SLHR .... Society for Life History Research [*Formerly, SLHRP*] [*Los Angeles, CA*] (EA)
SLHRP .... Society for Life History Research in Psychopathology [*Later, SLHR*] (EA)
SLI .... Los Alamitos, CA [*Location identifier*] [*FAA*] (FAAL)
SLI .... St. Lucia [*St. Lucia*] [*Seismograph station code, US Geological Survey*] [*Closed*] (SEIS)
SLI .... Sea-Level Indicator (KSC)
SLI .... Seal and Label Institute
SLI .... Shelf Life Item [*Military*] (AABC)
SLI .... Signal Line Isolator
SLI .... Silver Hill Mines [*Vancouver Stock Exchange symbol*]
SLI .... Slick Airways, Incorporated
SLI .... Slide Lobe Indicator
SLI .... Society for Louisiana Irises (EA)
SLI .... Somatostatin-Like Immunoreactivity
SLI .... Somerset Light Infantry [*Military unit*] [*British*]
SLI .... Sound Level Indicator
SLI .... Spacelab Integration (MCD)
SLI .... Starting, Lighting, and Ignition [*Automobile system*]
SLI .... Steam Line Isolation [*Nuclear energy*] (NRCH)
SLI .... Studi Linguistici Italiani [*A publication*]
SLI .... Studies in the Literary Imagination [*A publication*]
SLI .... Suppress Length Indication (BUR)
SLI .... Synchronous Line Interface

SL & I .... System Load and Initialization [*NASA*] (NASA)
SLIA .... Spiritual Life Institute of America
SLIB .... Subsystem Library [*Data processing*] (IBMDP)
SLIC .... School Libraries in Canada [*A publication*]
SLIC .... Search of the Library Information Collection [*Search system*]
SLIC .... Second Life Insurance of Georgia [*NASDAQ symbol*] (NQ)
SLIC .... Selective Letters [*or Listing*] in Combination
SLIC .... Signature Library Intelligence Catalogue
SLIC .... Subscriber's Line Interface Circuit [*Telecommunications*] (TEL)
SLIC .... System Line Image Composer
SLICB .... Sea-Launched Intercontinental Ballistic Missile (MUGU)
SLICE .... Source Label Indicating and Coding Equipment
SLICE .... Southwestern Library Interstate Cooperative Endeavor
SLICE .... Students Litigating Against Injurious Can Edges [*Student legal action organization*]
SLICE .... System Life Cycle Estimation
SLID .... Scanning Light Intensity Device
SLID .... Students League for Industrial Democracy [*Later, Students for a Democratic Society*]
SLIDE .... [*A*] programing language (CSR)
SLif .... Slovjans'ke Literaturoznavstvo i Fol'klorystyka [*A publication*]
SLIG .... Sucker, Low-Brow, Idiot, Goodwill-Buster [*Acronym used as word meaning "act of discourtesy or stupid criticism"*] [*World War II*]
SLIGO .... Sand Lake Irish Gatherings Organization
SLIH .... Second Level Interrupt Handler (CMD)
SLIM .... Saint Louis Institute of Music
SLIM .... Simplified Logistics and Improved Maintenance (MCD)
SLIM .... Slewed-Launch Interceptor Missile
SLIM .... Standards Laboratory Information Manual (NG)
SLIM .... Submarine-Launched Inertial Missile
SLIMS .... Supply Line Inventory Management System [*Bell System*]
SLIN .... Standard Library Identification Number
SLIN .... Standard Line Item Number [*Army*] (AABC)
SLIN .... Sub-Line Item Number (MCD)
SLIN .... System Line Item Number (MCD)
SLIP .... Self Leisure Interest Profile
SLIP .... Skills Level Improvement Program
SLIP .... Symbolic List Processor
SLIP .... Symmetric List Interpretive Program [*Data processing*]
SLIP .... Symmetric List Processor [*FORTRAN extension*]
SLIPR .... Source Language Input Program
SLIR .... School of Labor and Industrial Relations [*Michigan State University*] [*Research center*] (RCD)
SLIRBM ..... Sea-Launched Intermediate-Range Ballistic Missile (MUGU)
SLIS .... Shared Laboratory Information System
SLIS .... Social Legislation Information Service [*Washington, DC*] (EA)
SLit .... Slovenska Literatura [*A publication*]
SLit .... Studies in Literature [*A publication*]
SLitI .... Studies in the Literary Imagination [*A publication*]
S Liv .... Southern Living [*A publication*]
SLIV .... Steam Line Isolation Valve [*Nuclear energy*] (NRCH)
SLJ .... Hattiesburg, MS [*Location identifier*] [*FAA*] (FAAL)
SLJ .... School Library Journal [*A publication*]
SLJ .... Scottish Law Journal [*Edinburgh*] (DLA)
SLJ .... Silly Little Job (DSUE)
SLJ .... Southern Literary Journal [*A publication*]
SLJ .... Southwestern Law Journal [*A publication*]
SLJ .... Straits Law Journal [*1888-92*] [*Malasia*] (DLA)
SLJR .... Sudan Law Journal and Reports (DLA)
SLK .... Atlanta Skylark Club, Inc. [*Atlanta, GA*] [*FAA designator*] (FAAC)
SLK .... Magicsilk, Inc. [*American Stock Exchange symbol*]
SLK .... Saranac Lake [*New York*] [*Airport symbol*] (OAG)
SLK .... Saranac Lake, NY [*Location identifier*] [*FAA*] (FAAL)
SLK .... Schwerpunkte Linguistik und Kommunikationswissenschaft [*A publication*]
SLK .... Slick (MCD)
SLK .... Superior Limbic Keratoconjunctivitis [*Ophthalmology*]
SLKP .... Supreme Lodge Knights of Pythias (EA)
SLL .... La Loche Public Library, Saskatchewan [*Library symbol*] [*National Library of Canada*] (NLC)
SLL .... Salalah [*Oman*] [*Airport symbol*] (OAG)
SLL .... Sandia Laboratories, Livermore (AABC)
SLL .... Sandwell Swan Wooster, Inc. [*Toronto Stock Exchange symbol*] [*Vancouver Stock Exchange symbol*]
SLL .... Shelf Life Limit (MCD)
SLL .... Signal Long Lines
SLL .... Skrifter Utgivna. Genom Landsmalsarkivet i Lund [*A publication*]
SLL .... Society for Libertarian Life (EA)
SLL .... Station List Publishing Company, St. Louis MO [*STAC*]
SLL .... Sterling Lord Literistic, Inc. [*Literary agency*] [*British*]
SLL .... Stollet [*Sweden*] [*Seismograph station code, US Geological Survey*] (SEIS)
SLL .... Suffolk University, Law Library, Boston, MA [*OCLC symbol*] (OCLC)
SLLL .... Synchronous Line, Low, Load (BUR)
SLLR .... Sierra Leone Language Review [*A publication*]
SLLR .... Sierra Leone Law Recorder (DLA)

SLLS .... Snap Lock Limit Switch
SLLS .... Solid-State LASER Light Source
SLM .... St. Louis [*Missouri*] [*Seismograph station code, US Geological Survey*] (SEIS)
SLM .... School for Latin America [*Military*]
SLM .... Sea-Launched Missile
SLM .... Sealift Magazine [*A publication*]
SLM .... Senior Level Management
SLM .... Simulated Laboratory Module
SLM .... Snow Lake Mines Ltd. [*Vancouver Stock Exchange symbol*]
SLM .... Sound Level Meter
SLM .... Southern Literary Messenger [*A publication*]
SLM .... Statistical Learning Model (IEEE)
SLM .... Student Loan Marketing Association [*NYSE symbol*]
SLM .... Submarine-Launched Missile
SLM .... Subscriber Loop Multiplex [*Bell System*]
SLM .... Surface-Launched Missile [*Navy*] (CAAL)
SLM .... Synchronous Line Module
SLMA .... Shoe Lace Manufacturers Association [*Defunct*] (EA)
SLMA .... Southeastern Lumber Manufacturers Association [*Forest Park, GA*] (EA)
SLMA .... Student Loan Market Association [*NASDAQ symbol*] (NQ)
SLMA .... Student Loan Marketing Association [*Government-chartered private corporation*] [*Nickname: "Sallie Mae"*]
SLMAB ...... Single-Line Missile Assembly Building
SLME .... Select Manual Entry Switch
SLMM .... Simultaneous Compass Locator at Middle Marker [*Aviation*] (FAAC)
SLMM .... Submarine-Launched Mobile Mine (MCD)
SlMov .... Sloc'jans'ke Movoznavstvo [*A publication*]
SLMP .... School Library Manpower Project [*American Association of School Librarians*] (EA)
SLMR .... Sailmaker [*Navy*] [*British*]
SLMS .... Sound Level Measuring Set
SLMS .... Surface-Launched Missile System
SLN .... Salena Research Corp. [*Vancouver Stock Exchange symbol*]
SLN .... Salina [*Kansas*] [*Airport symbol*] (OAG)
SLN .... Salina, KS [*Location identifier*] [*FAA*] (FAAL)
SLN .... Salinas [*Chile*] [*Seismograph station code, US Geological Survey*] (SEIS)
SLN .... Santiago Library System, Orange, CA [*OCLC symbol*] (OCLC)
SLN .... Section List Number (MCD)
SLN .... Service Link Network [*Bell Laboratories*]
SLN .... Sinclair Lewis Newsletter [*A publication*]
SLN .... Solution
SLN .... Southeastern Library Network [*Library network*]
SLN .... Sri Lanka Navy
SLN .... Statement of Logistical Needs [*Air Force*]
SLN .... Superior Laryngeal Nerve [*Neuroanatomy*]
SLND .... Sine Loco Nec Data [*Without Place or Date of Printing*] [*Latin*]
SLNK .... Satellink Corp. [*NASDAQ symbol*] (NQ)
SLNS .... Department of Northern Saskatchewan, La Ronge, Saskatchewan [*Library symbol*] [*National Library of Canada*] (NLC)
SLO .... Salem, IL [*Location identifier*] [*FAA*] (FAAL)
SLO .... Segment Limits Origin
SLO .... Shark Liver Oil
SLO .... Ship Liaison Officer [*Navy*] (CAAL)
SLO .... Single Loop Operation [*Nuclear energy*] (NRCH)
SLO .... Slavia Orientalis [*A publication*]
SLO .... Sligo [*County in Ireland*] (ROG)
SLO .... Slocum Air, Inc. [*Miami, FL*] [*FAA designator*] (FAAC)
SLO .... Slough [*British depot code*]
slo .... Slovak [*MARC language code*] [*Library of Congress*] (LCCP)
SLO .... Slow Lift-Off (MCD)
SLO .... State Liaison Officer
SLO .... Stop-Limit Order [*Business and trade*]
SLO .... Stop-Loss Order [*Business and trade*]
SLO .... Streptolysin O [*Hematology*]
SLO .... Submarine Liaison Officer [*Navy*] (NVT)
SLO .... Swept Local Oscillator (IEEE)
Sloan .... Sloan Management Review [*A publication*]
Sloan Leg Reg ... Sloan's New York Legal Register (DLA)
Sloan Manag ... Sloan Management Review [*A publication*]
Sloan Manage Rev ... Sloan Management Review [*A publication*]
Sloan Mgmt Rev ... Sloan Management Review [*A publication*]
Sloan Mgt R ... Sloan Management Review [*A publication*]
SLOB .... Satellite Low-Orbit Bombardment
SLOB .... Strategic Low-Orbit Bomber (AAG)
SLOB .... Supplemental Layoff Benefits (MCD)
SLOB .... Supply Left of Baseline (MCD)
SLOC .... Sea Lines of Communication [*NATO*] (NATG)
SLOc .... Slavia Occidentalis [*A publication*]
SLOcc .... Slavia Occidentalis [*A publication*]
SLOCOP .... Specific Linear Optimal Control Program [*Hydrofoil*] [*Grumman Aerospace Corp.*]
SLOE .... Special List of Equipment [*Air Force*]
SLOH .... Skylab Operations Handbook [*NASA*] (MCD)
Slo L .... Slovo Lektora [*A publication*]
SLOM .... Simultaneous Compass Locator at Outer Marker [*Aviation*] (FAAC)

SLOMAR .... Space Logistics, Maintenance, and Rescue
SLON .... Sloan Technology Corp. [*NASDAQ symbol*] (NQ)
SLoP .... Slovansky Prehled [*A publication*]
SLOPE ...... Study of Lunar Orbiter Photographic Evaluation (MCD)
SLOR .... Simultaneous Line Over-Relaxation [*Nuclear energy*]
SLOR .... Slavia Orientalis [*A publication*]
SLOR .... Swept Local Oscillator Receiver (NG)
SLORV ...... Structural Loads on Reentry Vehicles (MCD)
SLOS .... Scanning Line of Sight (KSC)
SLOS .... Secondary Line of Sight [*Sextants*]
SLOS .... Sierra Leone Organization Society
SLOS .... Star Line-of-Sight (MCD)
SLOS .... Sun Line-of-Sight
SLOSH ...... Sea, Lake, Overland Surge from Hurricanes [*National Oceanic and Atmospheric Administration*]
SLOSJ .... State and Local Officials for Soviet Jews (EA)
SLO/SRI .... Shift Left Out/Shift Right In
SLOT .... Submarine-Launched One-Way Tactical [*Buoy*] (NVT)
SLOTH ...... Suppressing Line Operands and Translating to Hexadecimal [*Telecommunications*] (TEL)
Slov Akad Znan Umet Razred Prirodosl Vede Dela ... Slovenska Akademija Znanosti in Umetnosti. Razred za Prirodoslovne Vede. Dela [*A publication*]
Slovak Mus ... Slovak Musik [*A publication*]
Slov Arch ... Slovenska Archeologia [*A publication*]
Slov Archeol ... Slovenska Archeologia [*A publication*]
Slov Ceb ... Slovenski Cebelar [*A publication*]
Slov Etnogr ... Slovenski Etnografi [*A publication*]
Slov Hud .... Slovenska Hudba [*A publication*]
Slov Lit ...... Slovenska Literatura [*A publication*]
SlovN .... Slovensky Narodopis [*A publication*]
Slov Numiz ... Slovenske Numizmatika [*A publication*]
SlovP .... Slovensky Pohl'ady [*A publication*]
Slov Preh ... Slovansky Prehled [*A publication*]
Slow Learn ... Slow Learning Child [*A publication*]
Slow Learn Child ... Slow Learning Child [*A publication*]
SLOWPOKE ... Safe Low-Power Critical Experiment [*Nuclear energy*]
SLP .... Left Sacroposterior Position [*of the fetus*] [*Obstetrics*]
SLP .... St. Lucie Plant [*Nuclear energy*] (NRCH)
SLP .... School Lunch Program
SLP .... Scintilore Explorations Ltd. [*Toronto Stock Exchange symbol*]
SLP .... Scottish Labour Party (PPW)
SLP .... Scouting Landplane
SLP .... Sea-Level Pressure
SLP .... Secretary for Logistics Planning [*Air Force*]
SLP .... Segmented Level Programing [*Data processing*] (IEEE)
SLP .... Serie Linguistica Peruana [*A publication*]
SLP .... Sex-Limited Protein [*Immunology*]
SLP .... Shelby, NC [*Location identifier*] [*FAA*] (FAAL)
SLP .... Silicon Light Pulser
SLP .... Sine Legitima Prole [*Without Lawful Issue*] [*Latin*]
SLP .... Sleep
SLP .... Slip (ADA)
SLP .... Sloop
SLP .... Slope (MSA)
SLP .... Slovansky Prehled [*A publication*]
SLP .... Slovensky Pohl'ady [*A publication*]
SLP .... Slovensky Porocevalec [*A publication*]
SLP .... Socialist Labor Party [*Egyptian*] (PPW)
SLP .... Socialist Labor Party of America
SLP .... Soft Lander Probe [*Aerospace*]
SLP .... Sound Level Plot [*Military*] (CAAL)
SLP .... Source Language Processor [*Data processing*] (BUR)
SLP .... Spring-Loaded Pulley
SLP .... Stock List Price [*Military*] (AFIT)
S/LP .... Stop Lamp [*Automotive engineering*]
SLP .... Strategic Locations Planning [*San Jose, CA*] [*Information service*] (EISS)
SLP .... Sun Energy Partners [*NYSE symbol*]
SLP .... Supersonic Local Pressure
SLP .... Supplier Loaned Property (MCD)
SLP .... Surface Launch Platform (NVT)
SLPA .... Selected Legally Protected Animals [*Marine science*] (MSC)
SLPA .... Silicon Light Pulser Array
SLPB .... Spacelab Program Board [*NASA*] (NASA)
SLPC .... St. Louis Production Center
SLPC .... Socialist Labour Party of Canada
SLPC .... Supported Liquid Phase Catalyst
SLPD .... Skylab Program Directive [*NASA*] (KSC)
SLPH .... Seat Lock Pin Handle
SLPHR .... Sulphur
SLPL .... Sea Loading Pipe Line [*Technical drawings*]
SLPM .... Selected List of Published Material [*Her Majesty's Stationery Office*] [*British*]
SLPM .... Silicon Light Pulser Matrix
SLPMS ...... Single Level Power Management System
SLPO .... Skylab Program Office [*NASA*] (KSC)
SLPo .... Slovensky Pohl'ady [*A publication*]
SLPoh .... Slovensky Pohl'ady [*A publication*]
SLPP .... Serum Lipophosphoprotein [*Serology*]
SLPP .... Sierra Leone People's Party (PD)

SLPP .... Sri Lanka People's Party (PPW)
SLPR .... Sidelobe Pulse Rejection [*Military*] (CAAL)
SLPr .... Slavica Pragensia [*A publication*]
SLPR .... Slavistic Printings and Reprintings [*A publication*]
SLPR .... Supplier Loaned Property Request (MCD)
SLPRB .... Steroids and Lipids Research [*A publication*]
SLPRF .... Fisheries Branch, Parks and Renewable Resources, La Ronge, Saskatchewan [*Library symbol*] [*National Library of Canada*] (NLC)
SLPS .... Sonobuoy Launcher Pneumatic System
SLPS .... State and Local Program Support [*Nuclear energy*] (NRCH)
SLPT .... Socialist Labor Party of Turkey [*Turkiye Sosyalist Isci Partisi*] (PPW)
SLPTF .... Scintilore Explorations [*NASDAQ symbol*] (NQ)
SLPW .... Sloop-of-War
SLQ .... Saint Louis Quarterly [*Baguio City*] [*A publication*]
SLQ .... Sleetmute [*Alaska*] [*Airport symbol*] (OAG)
SLQ .... Sleetmute, AK [*Location identifier*] [*FAA*] (FAAL)
SLQ .... Surface Layer Quality
SLR .... Radcliffe College, Schlesinger Library, Cambridge, MA [*OCLC symbol*] (OCLC)
SLR .... Sales Letter Report
SLR .... Saskatchewan Law Reports (DLA)
SLR .... Satellite LASER Ranging [*for geodetic and geophysical measurements*]
SLR .... Scottish Land Court Reports (DLA)
SLR .... Scottish Law Reporter [*Edinburgh*] (DLA)
SLR .... Scottish Law Review and Sheriff Court Reports [*1885-1963*] (DLA)
SLR .... Sealer
SLR .... Self-Loading Rifle (MCD)
SLR .... Sense Line Register
SLR .... Service Level Reporter [*IBM Corp.*]
SL & R .... Shop Order Load Analysis and Reporting [*IBM Corp.*]
SLR .... Side-Looking RADAR (AFM)
SLR .... Simple Left to Right [*Data processing*]
SLRr .... Sind Law Reporter [*India*] (DLA)
SLR .... Singapore Law Reports [*1946-49, 1953-56*] (DLA)
SLR .... Single-Lens Reflex [*Camera*]
SLR .... Skylab Rescue [*NASA*] (KSC)
SLR .... Slavische Rundschau [*A publication*]
SLR .... Slavisticna Revija [*A publication*]
SLR .... Slavonic and East European Review [*A publication*]
SLR .... Slush on Runway [*Aviation*] (FAAC)
SLR .... Solar (AAG)
SLR .... Sound Level Recorder
SLR .... South Lancashire Regiment [*British*]
SLR .... Southern Law Review [*St. Louis, MO*] (DLA)
SLR .... Special Light Rifle (NATG)
SLR .... Specific Lung Resistance
SLR .... Spin Lattice Relaxation
SLR .... Stabell Resources [*Vancouver Stock Exchange symbol*]
SLR .... Static Line Regulation
SLR .... Statute Law Revision (DLA)
SLR .... Storage Limits Register
SLR .... Straight Leg Raising [*Medicine*]
SLR .... Streptococcus lactis R Factor [*Biochemistry*]
SLR .... Sulphur Springs, TX [*Location identifier*] [*FAA*] (FAAL)
SLR .... Sydney Law Review [*A publication*]
SLR .... System Level Requirement [*Military*] (CAAL)
SLRA .... Soviet Long-Range Air (MCD)
SLRA .... Suede and Leather Refinishers of America [*Defunct*] (EA)
SLRAAA ..... Sprache und Literatur. Regensburger Arbeiten zur Anglistik und Amerikanistik [*A publication*]
SLRAP .... Standard Low-Frequency Range Approach
SLRB .... State Labor Relations Board
SLRC .... San Luis Rey College [*California*]
SLRC/MILO ... State Library Resource Center - Maryland Interlibrary Organization [*Library network*]
SLRD .... Searchlight RADAR
SLRec .... Slovenska Rec [*A publication*]
SL Rev .... Scottish Law Review and Sheriff Court Reports (DLA)
SLRev .... Slavonic and East European Review [*A publication*]
SLRev .... Slavonic Review [*A publication*]
SLRI .... Shipboard Long-Range Input
SLRJ .... St. Louis University. Research Journal of the Graduate School of Arts and Sciences [*A publication*]
SLR Leic .... Leicester's Straits Law Reports [*Malaya*] (DLA)
SLR Leicester ... Leicester's Straits Law Reports [*1827-77*] [*Malaya*] (DLA)
SLRN .... Select Read Numerically
SLRN .... Solaron Corp. [*NASDAQ symbol*] (NQ)
SL RNG ...... Slope Range
SLRNS .... Straits Law Reports, New Series [*Malasia*] (DLA)
SLRP .... Society for Strategic and Long Range Planning (EA-IO)
SLRRB .... Senior Logistics Readiness Review Board [*Fort Lewis*] (MCD)
SLRS .... Satellite LASER Ranging System
SLRT .... Straight Leg Raising Test [*or Tenderness*] [*Medicine*]
SLRTB .... Saskatchewan Department of Tourism and Small Business, La Ronge, Saskatchewan [*Library symbol*] [*National Library of Canada*] (NLC)

SlRund .... Slavische Rundschau [*A publication*]
SLRV .... Standard Light Rail Vehicle [*Mass transit*]
SLRV .... Surveyor Lunar Roving Vehicle [*Aerospace*] (MCD)
SLS .... Saint Lawrence Seaway Development Corporation [*Department of Transportation*]
SLS .... Saint Lawrence Seminary [*Wisconsin*]
SLS .... Santiago Library System [*Library network*]
SLS .... Saturn Longitude System [*Planetary science*]
SLS .... School of Logistics Science [*Army*]
SLS .... Sea-Land Service, Inc. [*AAR code*]
SLS .... Sea Level, Standard Day
SLS .... Sea-Level Static
SLS .... Secondary Landing Site [*NASA*] (NASA)
SLS .... Selas Corp. of America [*American Stock Exchange symbol*]
SLS .... Serra Cooperative Library System, San Diego, CA [*OCLC symbol*] (OCLC)
SLS .... Side-Lobe Suppression
SLS .... Side-Looking SONAR
SLS .... Sign Language Studies [*A publication*]
SLS .... Signaling Link Selection [*Telecommunications*] (TEL)
SLS .... Silicon Light Source
SLS .... Silistra [*Bulgaria*] [*Airport symbol*] (OAG)
SLS .... Sindacato Lavoratori della Somalia [*Workers Union of Somalia*]
SLS .... Skylab Simulator [*NASA*] (KSC)
SLS .... Slightly Soluble
SLS .... Slovenska Ljudska Stranka [*Slovene People's Party*] [*Yugoslav*] (PPE)
SL'S .... Slovenska L'Udova Strana [*Slovak People's Party*] [*Also, HSL'S*] (PPE)
SLS .... So-Luminaire System [*Vancouver Stock Exchange symbol*]
SLS .... Sodium Lauryl Sulfate [*Also, SDS*] [*Organic chemistry*]
SLS .... Soengei Langka [*Sumatra*] [*Seismograph station code, US Geological Survey*] [*Closed*] (SEIS)
SLS .... Sonobuoy Localization System (NVT)
SLS .... Sortie Lab Simulator [*NASA*] (NASA)
SLS .... Source Library System
SLS .... Space Launch System
SLS .... Spacecraft Landing Strut
SLS .... Specific Living Space (AAG)
SLS .... Spoken Language Services, Inc.
SLS .... Standard Light Spanwire [*Military*] (CAAL)
SLS .... Statement Level Simulator [*NASA*] (NASA)
SLS .... Stores Locator System (MCD)
SLS .... Strained-Layer Superlattices [*Crystalline materials*]
SLS .... Student Lesson Sheets
SLS .... Students for a Libertarian Society (EA)
SLS .... Suburban Library System [*Library network*]
SLS .... Surface Laboratory System [*NASA*] (KSC)
SLS .... SWALCAP Library Services Ltd. [*Bristol, England*] [*Information service*] (EISS)
SLSA .... St. Lawrence Seaway Authority [*Canada*] [*See also AVMS*]
SLSA .... Secondary Lead Smelters Association [*Atlanta, GA*] (EA)
SLSA .... Shuttle Logistics Support Aircraft (MCD)
SLSA .... Slotting Saw
SLSA .... Svenska Linne-Sallskapet Arsskrift [*Uppsala*] [*A publication*]
SLSAC .... Saint Lawrence Seaway Authority of Canada
SLSADJ ..... Stores Locator System Adjustment (MCD)
SlSb .... Slezsky Sbornik [*A publication*]
SLSDC .... Saint Lawrence Seaway Development Corporation [*Department of Transportation*]
SLSF .... St. Louis-San Francisco Railway Co. [*AAR code*]
SLSF .... Sodium Loop Safety Facility [*Nuclear energy*]
SLSF .... Svenska Landsmal och Svenskt Folkliv [*Uppsala*] [*A publication*]
SLSI .... Super Large-Scale Integration
SLSL .... Statutory Long Service Leave (ADA)
SLSM .... Silver Life Saving Medal
SLSMS ...... Spacelab Support Module Simulator (MCD)
SLSO .... Shipyard Labour Supply Officer [*British*]
SLSP .... SACLANT Scheduled Program (MCD)
SLSp .... Slovensky Spisovatel [*A publication*]
SLSP .... Slow Speed
SLSS .... Secondary Life Support System [*NASA*]
SLSS .... Shuttle Launch Support System (MCD)
SL-SS .... Spacelab Subsystem [*NASA*] (NASA)
SLSS .... Swimmer Life Support System [*Navy*] (CAAL)
SLSS .... Systems Library Subscription Service [*Data processing*] (IBMDP)
SLSSM ...... Submerged Launched Surface-to-Surface Missile (MCD)
SL-SSS ..... Spacelab Subsystem Segment [*NASA*] (NASA)
SLST .... St. Louis, San Francisco & Texas Railway Co. [*AAR code*]
SLST .... Slightly Staining
SLST .... Slip Stitch [*Knitting*]
SLT .... Salta [*Argentina*] [*Seismograph station code, US Geological Survey*] [*Closed*] (SEIS)
SLT .... Scots Law Times [*A publication*]
SLT .... Searchlight
SLT .... Second Law of Thermodynamics
SLT .... Self-Loading Tape (AFM)
SLT .... Sellectek Industries, Inc. [*Vancouver Stock Exchange symbol*]

SLT............ Shiga-Like Toxin [*Biochemistry*]
SLT............ Ship Letter Telegram
SL & T .... Shipper's Load and Tally [*Bills of lading*]
SLT............ Shuttle Loop Transit [*NASA*]
SLT............ Simulated Launch Test [*NASA*]   (KSC)
SLT............ Skylight   (AAG)
SLT............ Slate   (MSA)
SLT............ Slate Run, PA [*Location identifier*] [*FAA*]   (FAAL)
SLT............ Sleet [*Meteorology*]   (FAAC)
SLT............ Slit
SLT............ Solid Logic Technique [*Data processing*]   (IEEE)
SLT............ Solid Logic Technology
SLT............ Sonobuoy Launch Tube [*Navy*]   (CAAL)
SLT............ Special [*or Specific*] Launch Trajectory   (AFM)
SLT............ Spotlight   (MSA)
SLT............ Stockpile Laboratory Tests
SLT............ Stress Limit Tests
SLT............ Structured Learning Therapy
SLT............ Svensk Litteraturtidskrift [*A publication*]
SLTB......... Switchman's Local Test [*Telecommunications*]   (TEL)
SLTB......... Society for Low Temperature Biology   (EA)
SLTC......... Siltec Corp. [*NASDAQ symbol*]   (NQ)
SLTD......... Salted
SLTD......... Slotted   (MSA)
SLTDP........ Special LASER Technology Development Program
SLTEA....... Sheffield Lighter Trades Employers' Association [*British*]
SLTerm..... Slavjanska Lingvisticna Terminologija [*A publication*]
SLTF .... Shortest Latency Time First
SLTF .... Silo-Launch Test Facility
SLTG......... Sterner Lighting Systems [*NASDAQ symbol*]   (NQ)
SLT (Lyon Ct) ... Scots Law Times Lyon Court Reports   (DLA)
SLTM .... Selecterm, Inc. [*NASDAQ symbol*]   (NQ)
SLTM .... Standard Lap Turn Method   (NVT)
SLTM .... Storia delle Letteratura di Tutto il Mondo [*A publication*]
SLTM .... Structural Lander Test Model
SLT (Notes) ... Scots Law Times Notes of Recent Decisions   (DLA)
SLTO......... Sea-Level Takeoff
SLTR .... Service Life Test Report   (AAG)
SLT & SDL ... Searchlight and Sound Locator [*Navy*]
SLT (Sh Ct) ... Scots Law Times Sheriff Court Reports   (DLA)
SLTUF........ Sri Lanka Trade Union Federation [*Sri Lanka Vurthiya Samithi Sammelanaya*]
SLTV .... St. Lucia Television Service
SLTX .... Sales Tax
SLU .... Pavlovsk [*USSR*] [*Later, LNN*] [*Geomagnetic observatory code*]
SLU .... Saint Lawrence University [*New York*]
SLU .... St. Louis University [*Missouri*]
SLU .... St. Louis University, Law Library, St. Louis, MO [*OCLC symbol*]   (OCLC)
SLU .... St. Lucia [*West Indies*] [*Airport symbol*]   (OAG)
SLU .... Serial Line Unit
Slu............. Slough [*Maps and charts*]
SLU .... Slutsk [*USSR*] [*Later, LNN*] [*Geomagnetic observatory code*]
SLU .... Source Library Update
SLU .... Southern Labor Union
SLU .... Special Liaison Unit [*Military intelligence*] [*World War II*]
SLU .... Studii de Literatura Universala [*Bucharest*] [*A publication*]
SLU .... Subscriber Line Use [*Telecommunications*]
SLU .... Svenska Litteratursaellskapet i Uppsala [*A publication*]
SLU .... Switching Logic Unit   (CAAL)
SLUC......... Standard Level User Charges
SLUF......... Short Little Ugly Feller [*Nickname for A-7 aircraft*]   (MCD)
SLUFAE ..... Surface-Launched Unit, Fuel-Air Explosive Mine Neutralizer [*Army*]   (RDA)
SLUG......... Superconducting Low-Inductance Undulatory Galvanometer
SLULJ .... St. Louis University. Law Journal [*A publication*]
SLUMA...... Southern Lumberman [*United States*] [*A publication*]
SLURBS ..... Sleazy Suburbs
SLURJ .... Saint Louis University. Research Journal [*Baguio City*] [*A publication*]
SLURP........ Self Leveling Unit for Removing Pollution [*Marine science*]   (MSC)
SLURP........ Spiny Lobster Undersea Research Project
SLURREX... Slurry Reactor Experiment
SLUS......... Subscriber's Line Use System [*AT & T*] [*Telecommunications*]   (TEL)
SI UVAN .... Slavistica. Praci Institutu Slov'janoznavstva Ukrajins'koji Vil'noji Akademiji Nauk [*A publication*]
SLV .... El Salvador [*Three-letter standard code*]   (CNC)
SLV .... Federal Carriers, Inc. [*White Lake, NY*] [*FAA designator*]   (FAAC)
SLV .... Salivate   (KSC)
SLV .... San Jose, CA [*Location identifier*] [*FAA*]   (FAAL)
SLV .... Satellite Launching Vehicle [*Air Force*]
SLV .... Saturn Launch Vehicle [*NASA*]   (KSC)
SLV .... Seldovia [*Alaska*] [*Seismograph station code, US Geological Survey*]   (SEIS)
SLv............ Sifra on Leviticus [*A publication*]   (BJA)
SLV .... Silvercrest Corp. [*American Stock Exchange symbol*]
SLV .... Simulated Launch Vehicle   (MCD)

SLV .... Sleeve   (AAG)
slv.............. Slovenian [*MARC language code*] [*Library of Congress*]   (LCCP)
SLV .... Soft Landing Vehicle [*NASA*]
SLV .... Space Launch Vehicle
SLV .... Space-Like Vector
SLV .... Standard Launch Vehicle
SLVC......... Selvac Corp. [*NASDAQ symbol*]   (NQ)
SLVG......... Sleeving [*Electricity*]
SLVG......... Special Launch Vehicle Group [*NASA*]   (KSC)
SLVRF....... Silverado Mines Ltd. [*NASDAQ symbol*]   (NQ)
SLVRJ....... Surface-Launched Low-Volume Ramjet
SLVT........ Solvent   (MSA)
SLVY......... Silvey Corp. [*NASDAQ symbol*]   (NQ)
SLW.......... Single Line Working [*Railway engineering term*]
SLW.......... Sisters of the Living Word [*Roman Catholic religious order*]
SLW.......... Slow
SLW.......... Space-Based LASER Weapon   (MCD)
SLW.......... Specific Leaf Weight [*Botany*]
SLW.......... Spectral Line Width
SLW.......... Store Logical Word
SLW.......... Straight-Line Wavelength
SLW.......... Wooster, OH [*Location identifier*] [*FAA*]   (FAAL)
SLWL........ Straight-Line Wavelength   (MSA)
SLWMS...... Secondary Liquid Waste Management System [*Nuclear energy*]   (NRCH)
SL-Wola Ludu ... Stronnictwo Ludowe-Wola Ludu [*Peasant Party-People's Will*] [*Poland*]   (PPE)
SLWT........ Side Loadable Warping Tug [*Navy*]   (CAAL)
SLX .... Salt Cay [*British West Indies*] [*Airport symbol*]   (OAG)
SLX .... Siltronics Ltd. [*Toronto Stock Exchange symbol*]
SLX .... Slate Creek, AK [*Location identifier*] [*FAA*]   (FAAL)
SLY .... Hayward, WI [*Location identifier*] [*FAA*]   (FAAL)
SLY .... Safety, Liquidity, Yield
SLY .... Skelly Resources Ltd. [*Vancouver Stock Exchange symbol*]
SLY .... Sloppy [*Horse racing*]
SLY .... Southerly
SLYP......... Short Leaf Yellow Pine [*Lumber*]
SLZ .... Sao Luiz [*Brazil*] [*Airport symbol*]   (OAG)
SLZ .... Suppress Leading Zero [*Data processing*]
SM............ Altair Linee Aeree SpA [*Italy*] [*ICAO designator*]   (FAAC)
SM............ Dr. Schwarz Arzneimittelfabrik GmbH [*Germany*] [*Research code symbol*]
SM............ Master of Science
SM............ Medal of Service of the Order of Canada
SM............ Meteorological Aids Station [*ITU designation*]
SM............ Misericorde Sisters [*Roman Catholic religious order*]
SM............ Sa Majeste [*His or Her Majesty*] [*French*]
SM............ Sacred to the Memory of --- [*Epitaphs*]   (ROG)
S & M........ Sadism and Masochism
SM............ St. Marys Railroad Co. [*AAR code*]
SM............ Sales Management [*Later, Sales and Marketing Management*] [*A publication*]
SM............ Sales Manager
SM............ Salvage Mechanic [*Navy*]
Sm............ Samarium [*See Sa*] [*Chemical element*]
SM............ Sammlung Metzler [*A publication*]
Sm............ Samuel [*Old Testament book*]
SM............ San Marco [*Satellite*] [*NASA/Italy*]
sm .... San Marino [*MARC country of publication code*] [*Library of Congress*]   (LCCP)
SM............ San Marino [*Two-letter standard code*]   (CNC)
SM............ Sanctae Memoriae [*Of Holy Memory*] [*Latin*]
SM............ Scheduled Maintenance   (MCD)
SM............ Schistosoma Mansoni [*A parasitic fluke*]
S of M .... School of Musketry [*Military*] [*British*]   (ROG)
S-M .... Schuetzenmine [*Antipersonnel mine*] [*German military - World War II*]
SM............ Schwarz/Mann [*Supply company in biochemistry and chemistry*]
SM............ Schweizer Muenzblaetter [*Gazette Numismatique Suisse*] [*A publication*]
SM............ Scientific Memorandum
SM............ Scientific Monthly [*A publication*]
SM............ Seat Mile
SM............ Secondary Memory [*Data processing*]   (BUR)
SM............ Secretary's Memorandum [*Military*]
SM............ Security Manual   (AAG)
SM............ Security Monitor   (AAG)
Sm............ Semahot   (BJA)
SM............ Semiconductor Memory
SM............ Semimonthly
SM............ Senior Magistrate
S/M........... Sensory-to-Motor [*Ratio*]
SM............ Sentence Modifier [*Linguistics*]
S & M......... September and March [*Denotes semiannual payments of interest or dividends in these months*] [*Business and trade*]
SM............ Sequence Monitor
S & M......... Sequencer and Monitor   (KSC)
SM............ Sergeant Major

SM	Serious Music [*Canadian Broadcasting Corporation record series prefix*]
SM	Serratia marcescens [*Biological warfare with bacteria*]
S & M	Service and Maintenance
S/M	Service/Maintenance (NASA)
SM	Service Manual
SM	Service Mark [*Trademarks*]
SM	Service Member (AABC)
SM	Service Module [*NASA*]
SM	Service Monitoring [*Telecommunications*] (TEL)
SM	Set Mode (BUR)
SM	Sewage Microparticulates [*Oceanography*]
SM	Sewing Machine
S & M	Sexton and Malone [*Comic book*] [*CBC TV series*]
SM	Sexual Myths [*Scale*]
SM	Shape Memory [*Metallurgy*]
SM	Shared Memory [*Data processing*] (BUR)
S & M	Shaw and Maclean's House of Lords Cases (DLA)
SM	Sheet Metal
SM	Shell Model
SM	Shelter Management [*Civil Defense*]
SM	Shipment Memorandum [*Navy*]
SM	Ship's Manifest (ADA)
SM	Shock Mount
SM	Shop Manual [*Air Force*] (AAG)
SM	Short Meter [*Music*]
SM	Short Module [*NASA*] (NASA)
SM	Shuttle Management [*Kennedy Space Center*] [*NASA*] (NASA)
SM	Siam
SM	Signaling Module [*Telecommunications*] (TEL)
SM	Signalman [*Navy rating*]
SM	Silver Medalist
SM	Silver Methenamine [*Biological stain*]
SM	Silver Mica [*Capacitor*]
SM	Simple Maintenance
SM	Simple Mastectomy [*Medicine*]
SM	Simulated Missile (AAG)
SM	Simulators [*JETDS nomenclature*] [*Military*] (CET)
SM	Single Manager [*Defense*]
SM	Sinistra Mano [*Left Hand*]
SM	Sinus Medii [*Central Bay*] [*Lunar area*]
SM	Sisters of Mercy [*Roman Catholic religious order*]
S de M	Sisters Servants of Mary [*Roman Catholic religious order*]
SM	Slow Moving
SM	Small (AAG)
SM	Small Pica
S & M	Smedes and Marshall's Mississippi Chancery Reports (DLA)
S & M	Smedes and Marshall's Mississippi Reports [*9-22 Mississippi*] [*1843-50*] (DLA)
Sm	Smena [*Moscow*] [*A publication*]
Sm	Smith (DLA)
Sm	Smith Collection. British Museum [*London*] (BJA)
Sm	Smithsonian [*A publication*]
SM	SMM Enterprises Ltd. [*Vancouver Stock Exchange symbol*]
SM	Smooth (MSA)
SM	Socially Maladjusted
SM	Societas Mariae [*Congregation of Mary*] [*Marists*] [*Roman Catholic religious order*]
SM	Society of Mary [*Marianists*] [*Roman Catholic men's religious order*]
SM	Society of Medalists
S of M	Society of Metaphysicians (EA)
SM	Society of Miniaturists (EA)
SM	Soil Mechanics
SM	Solar Magnetic [*System*] [*NASA*]
SM	Solar Magnetospheric
SM	Soldier's Manual
SM	Soldier's Medal
SM	Solicitor's Memorandum, United States Internal Revenue Bureau (DLA)
SM	Solid Measure (ROG)
SM	Somatomedin [*Biochemistry*]
SM	Song of Moses (BJA)
SM	Sons of Malta
SM	Southern Minnesota Railroad
SM	Southmark Corp. [*NYSE symbol*]
SM	Spanish Moss
SM	Spawning Mark
SM	Special Memorandum
SM	Specification Memo (AAG)
SM	Speculative Masonry [*Freemasonry*]
SM	Speech Monographs [*A publication*]
SM	SpenderMenders [*An association*] (EA)
SM	Sphingomyelin [*Also, Sph*] [*Biochemistry*]
SM	Sports Medicine [*A publication*]
SM	Stabilized Member [*NASA*] (KSC)
SM	Staff Manager [*Insurance*]
SM	Staff Memorandum
SM	Stage Manager
SM	Standard Matched
SM	Standard Memoranda (AAG)
SM	Standard Missile
SM	Standards Manual
SM	Staphylococcus Medium [*Microbiology*]
SM	State Militia [*e.g., NJSM - New Jersey State Militia*]
SM	Station Manager [*Deep Space Instrumentation Facility, NASA*]
SM	Stationary Medium-Power [*Reactor*]
SM	Statistical Multiplexer (MCD)
SM	Statistiske Meddelelser [*Denmark*]
SM	Statute Mile
SM	Stipendiary Magistrate
S & M	Stock and Machinery
SM	Stock Market
SM	Strategic Missile (NATG)
SM	Streptomycin [*Antibiotic compound*]
SM	Stria Medullaris [*Neuroanatomy*]
SM	Strip Mine
SM	Structural Mechanical (MCD)
SM	Structure Memory
S & M	Structures and Materials (MCD)
SM	Structures Memorandum
SM	Student Manual [*Civil Defense*]
SM	Studi Medievali [*A publication*]
S M	Studia Musicologica. Academiae Scientiarum Hungaricae [*A publication*]
SM	Studio SM [*Record label*] [*France*]
S/M	Submarine [*British*]
SM	[*Officer Qualified for*] Submarine Duties [*British*]
SM	Submarine Flag [*Navy*] [*British*]
SM	Submarine, Minelaying [*Obsolete*]
S/M	Submarine Pay
SM	Substitute Materials [*British*]
SM	Suckling Mice
SM	Sumerian Mythology [*S. N. Kramer*] [*A publication*] (BJA)
SM	Summary Memorandum
SM	Summer [*A publication*]
S & M	Sun and Moon [*A publication*]
S/M	Super Mare [*On Sea*] [*In place names*] [*Latin*] (ROG)
S & M	Supply and Maintenance [*Army*] (AABC)
SM	Supply Manual
SM	Support Module [*NASA*] (NASA)
SM	Surface Measure
SM	Surface Missile (AAG)
S & M	Surfaced and Matched [*Lumber*]
SM	Surgeon Major
SM	Sustained Medication [*Pharmacology*]
SM	Sydney Mail [*A publication*]
SM	Synchronous MODEM
SM	System Manager [*Air Force*] (AFM)
SM	System Mechanics
SM	System Monitor
SM	Systema Malykh [*Small System*] [*Russian*] [*Data processing*]
SM	Systemic Mastocytosis [*Medicine*]
SM	Systems Management (MCD)
SM	Systems Memory [*Data processing*] (BUR)
SM	Systolic Mean [*Cardiology*]
SM	Systolic Murmur [*Cardiology*]
SM1	Signalman, First Class [*Navy rating*]
SM2	Signalman, Second Class [*Navy rating*]
SM3	Signalman, Third Class [*Navy rating*]
SMA	Andreafsky/St. Marys, AK [*Location identifier*] [*FAA*] (FAAL)
SMA	Sa Majeste Aulique [*His, or Her, Austrian Majesty*] [*French*] (ROG)
SMA	Safe Manufacturers' Association
SMA	Saigon Mission Association (EA)
SMA	Salad Manufacturers Association [*Atlanta, GA*] (EA)
SMA	San Manuel Arizona Railroad Co. [*AAR code*]
SMA	Santa Maria [*Azores*] [*Airport symbol*] (OAG)
SMA	Scale Manufacturers Association [*Rockville, MD*] (EA)
SMA	Screen Manufacturers Association [*Chicago, IL*] (EA)
SMA	Semimajor Axis
SMA	Senior Marine Advisor
SMA	Senior Military Attache
SMA	Sergeant Major of the Army (AABC)
SMA	Service Merchandisers of America [*Later, NASM*] (EA)
SMA	Shape Memory Alloy (RDA)
SMA	Shelving Manufacturers Association [*Pittsburgh, PA*] (EA)
SMA	Shielded Metal Arc [*Nickel and alloy welding*]
SMA	Ship's Material Account
SMA	Simultaneous Multiphasic Analysis [*Medicine*]
SMA	Site Maintenance Area (AAG)
SMA	Skymark Airlines (FAAC)
SMA	Slave Manipulator Arm [*Astronautics*]
SMA	Small Arms (NATG)
SMA	Social Maturity Age
SMA	Society of African Missions [*Roman Catholic men's religious order*]
SMA	Society of Management Accountants
SMA	Society of Manufacturer's Agents [*Later, SMR*] (EA)
SMA	Society of Maritime Arbitrators (EA)
SMA	Society of Medical Administrators [*Brea, CA*] (EA)
SMA	Society for Medical Anthropology (EA)

SMA .... Society for Medieval Archaeology   (EA)
SMA .... Society of Missionaries of Africa   (EA)
SMA .... Society of Municipal Arborists   (EA)
SMA .... Software Maintenance Association   (EA)
SMA .... Somatomedin A [*Biochemistry*]
SMA .... Southern Maryland Aviation, Inc. [*FAA designator*]   (FAAC)
SMA .... Soviet Military Administration
SMA .... Special Miscellaneous Account
SMA .... Spinal Muscular Atrophy [*Medicine*]
SMA .... Spontaneous Motor Activity [*Neurophysiology*]
SMA .... Squadron Maintenance Area
SMA .... Stabilized Member Assembly [*NASA*]
SMA .... Standard Maintenance Allowance
SMA .... Standard Methods Agar [*Microbiology*]
SMA .... State Mutual of America [*An insurance company*]
SMA .... Steatite Manufacturers Association [*Later, DPCSMA*]   (EA)
SMA .... Stoker Manufacturers Association   (EA)
SMA .... Stucco Manufacturers Association [*Sherman Oaks, CA*]   (EA)
S M (A) ...... Studies in Music (Australia) [*A publication*]
SMA .... Stylomastoid Artery [*Anatomy*]
SMA .... Styrene-Maleic Anhydride [*Organic chemistry*]
SMA .... Subject Matter Area   (AFM)
SMA .... Suggested for Mature Audiences [*Motion pictures*]
SMA .... Summerton [*South Carolina*] [*Seismograph station code, US Geological Survey*] [*Closed*]   (SEIS)
SMA .... Superior Mesenteric Artery [*Anatomy*]
SMA .... Superplastic Metal Alloy
SMA .... Supplementary Motor Area [*Anatomy*]
S & MA ...... Supply and Maintenance Agency [*System*] [*Army*]
SMA .... Support Management Area [*Mission Control Center*] [*NASA*]
SMA .... Surface Modulating Assembly [*Cytology*]
SMA .... Syrie et Monde Arabe [*Damascus*] [*A publication*]
SMAA .... Submarine Movement Advisory Authority   (NVT)
SMAB .... Solid Motor Assembly Building [*for Missiles*]
SMAB .... Spartan Management Action Board [*Missiles*]   (MCD)
SMAC .... Scene Matching Area Correlator [*Navy*]   (MCD)
SMAC .... Science and Mathematics Analysis Center [*ERIC*]
SMAC .... Scientific Machine Automation Corporation
SMAC .... Serial Memory Address Counter [*Computer*]
SMAC .... Shielded Metal Arc Cutting [*Welding*]
SMAC .... Simulation, Manual and Computerized
SMAC .... Society of Management Accountants of Canada
SMAC .... Special Mission Attack Computer
SMAC .... Striated Microtubule-Associated Components [*Botanical cytology*]
SMAC .... Submicron Aerosol Collector
SMACH ...... Sounding Machine [*Engineering*]
SMACK ...... Society of Males Who Appreciate Cute Knees [*Group opposing below-the-knee fashions introduced in 1970*]
SMACNA ... Sheet Metal and Air Conditioning Contractors' National Association [*Merrifield, VA*]   (EA)
SMACRATRACEN ... Small Craft Training Center
SMACS ...... Serialized Missile Accounting and Control System
SMACS ...... Simulated Message Analysis and Conversion Subsystem
Sm Act ...... Smith's Action at Law [*12th ed.*] [*1876*]   (DLA)
SMAD .... Solvated Metal Atom Dispersion [*Chemistry*]
SMAD .... Sowjetische Militaeradministration
Sm Adm Pr ... Smith's Admiralty Practice [*4th ed.*] [*1892*]   (DLA)
SMAE .... Sbornik Muzeia Antropologii i Etnografii [*A publication*]   (BJA)
SMAE .... Society of Model Aeronautical Engineers [*British*]
SMAE .... Superior Mesenteric Artery Embolus [*Medicine*]
SMAF .... Special Mission Aircraft Flights   (NATG)
SMAF .... Specific Macrophage Arming Factor [*Hematology*]
SMAF .... Superior Mesenteric Artery Flow
SMAG .... Simulator Missile Airborne and Ground   (MCD)
SMAG .... Systems Management Analysis Group   (MCD)
Sma & Giff ... Smale and Giffard's English Vice-Chancellors' Reports   (DLA)
SMAIL .... Source Mail [*Electronic mail*]
SMAJ .... Sergeant Major
SMAL .... Single Mode Alignment   (CAAL)
SMAL .... Structural Macroassembly Language
SMAL .... System Material Analysis List
SMALC ...... Sacramento Air Logistics Center   (MCD)
Smale & G ... Smale and Giffard's English Vice-Chancellors' Reports   (DLA)
SMALGOL ... Small Computer Algorithmic Language
Small Bus ... Small Business Reporter [*A publication*]
Small Bus Comput ... Small Business Computers [*A publication*]
Small Bus Comput News ... Small Business Computer News [*A publication*]
Small Business ... Small Business Report [*A publication*]
Small Gr B ... Small Group Behavior [*A publication*]
Small Group Behav ... Small Group Behavior [*A publication*]
Small Mamm Newsl ... Small Mammal Newsletters [*A publication*]
Small Pr ..... Small Press Review [*A publication*]
Small Stock Mag ... Small Stock Magazine [*A publication*]
Small Sys ... Small Systems World [*A publication*]
Small Sys Soft ... Small Systems Software [*A publication*]
Small Syst Software ... Small Systems Software [*A publication*]
Small Syst World ... Small Systems World [*A publication*]
SMALLTALK ... [*A*] programing language   (CSR)
SMAMA ...... Sacramento Air Materiel Area   (KSC)
SMAME ...... Society of Marine Architects and Marine Engineers   (EA)

SMAP .... Systems Management Analysis Project   (MCD)
SMAR .... Sheet Metal Assembler Riveter   (MCD)
S & Mar ...... Smedes and Marshall's Mississippi Reports [*9-22 Mississippi*]   (DLA)
SMARC ...... Survivable-MOS [*Metal-Oxide Semiconductor*] Array Computer [*Air Force*]
SM Arch .... Solid Mechanics Archives [*A publication*]
SMART ...... Salton's Magical Automatic Retriever of Texts [*Data processing*]
SMART ...... Satellite Maintenance and Repair Techniques [*Air Force*]
SMART ...... Scheduled Maintenance and Reliability Team   (MCD)
SMART ...... Science, Mathematics, and Related Technologies
SMART ...... Selected Methods for Attracting the Right Targets [*Bombing system*]   (AFM)
SMART ...... Sequential Mechanism for Automatic Recording and Testing
SMART ...... Socony Mobil Automatic Real Time   (DIT)
SMART ...... Sort Merge and Reduction Tapes   (CAAL)
SMART ...... Space Maintenance and Repair Techniques
SMART ...... Space Management and Retail Tracking System [*Information Resources, Inc.*]
SMART ...... Spacesaver Material Accounting Resource Terminal [*Spacesaver Corp.*]
SMART ...... Stop Merchandising Alcohol on Radio and Television
SMART ...... Structural Maintenance and Repair Team   (MCD)
SMART ...... Supersonic Military Air Research Track
SMART ...... Supersonic Missile and Rocket Track
SMART ...... System Malfunction Analysis Reinforcement Trainer
SMART ...... System for Management and Allocation of Resources Technique [*Data processing*]
SMART ...... System for the Mechanical Analysis and Retrieval of Text
SMART ...... Systems Management Analysis, Research, and Testing   (MCD)
SMART ...... Systems Managers Administrative Rating Test [*Simulation game*]
SMART ...... University of Saskatchewan Libraries Machine-Assisted Reference Teleservices [*University of Saskatchewan Library*] [*Saskatoon, SK*] [*Information service*]   (EISS)
SMARTS .... Selective Multiple Addresses Radio and Television Service [*A program delivery service introduced by RCA*]
SMARTS .... Sport Management Art and Science Society [*Defunct*]   (EA)
SMARTS .... Status Memory and Real Time System [*AT & T*]
SMAS .... Servicemaster Industries [*NASDAQ symbol*]   (NQ)
SMAS .... Submuscular Aponeurotic System [*Medicine*]
SMAS .... Superficial Musculoaponeurotic System [*Plastic surgery*]
SMAS .... Switched Maintenance Access System [*Bell System*]
SMASF ...... Servicemen's Mutual Aid and Savings Fund [*South Vietnam*]
SMASH ..... Southeast Asia Multisensor Armed Surveillance Helicopter
SMASH ..... Step-by-Step Monitor and Selector Hold [*Telecommunications*]   (TEL)
SMASH ...... Students Mobilizing on Auto Safety Hazards [*Student legal action organization*]   (EA)
SMASHEX ... Search for Simulated Submarine Casualty Exercise [*Navy*]   (NVT)
Smaskrift Landbruksdep Opplysningstjenesten ... Smaskrift-Norway. Landbruksdepartementet. Opplysningstjenesten [*A publication*]
SMAT .... Superior Mesenteric Artery Thrombosis [*Medicine*]
SMATH ...... Satellite Materials Hardening   (MCD)
SMATS ...... Speed-Modulated Augmented Thrust System   (NG)
SMATV ...... Satellite Master Antenna Television
SMAW .... Second Marine Aircraft Wing
SMAW .... Shielded Metal Arc Welding
SMAW .... Shoulder-Launched Multipurpose Assault Weapon   (MCD)
SMAW .... Submerged Metal Arc Weld [*Nuclear energy*]   (NRCH)
SMAWT ...... Short-Range Man-Portable Antitank Weapons Technology
SMB .... Bachelor of Sacred Music
SMB .... Sa Majeste Britannique [*His or Her Britannic Majesty*] [*French*]
SMB .... Samaipata [*Bolivia*] [*Seismograph station code, US Geological Survey*] [*Closed*]   (SEIS)
SMB .... Simba Resources, Inc. [*Vancouver Stock Exchange symbol*]
SMB .... Small and Medium-Sized Businesses
SMB .... Societas Missionaria Bethlehem [*Society of Bethlehem Missionaries*] [*Roman Catholic men's religious order*]
SMB .... Standard Mineral Base [*Medium*] [*Medicine*]
SMB .... Steve Miller Band [*Pop music group*]
SMB .... System Monitor Board
SMBA .... Slovenian Mutual Benefit Association [*Later, AMLA*]   (EA)
Sm & Bat ... Smith and Batty's Irish King's Bench Reports   (DLA)
SMBC .... Studien und Mitteilungen aus dem Benediktiner- und dem Cistercienser-Orden [*A publication*]
SMBCO ...... Studien und Mitteilungen aus dem Benediktiner- und dem Cistercienser-Orden [*A publication*]
SMBCOZ .... Studien und Mitteilungen aus dem Benediktiner- und dem Cistercienser-Orden [*A publication*]
SMBD .... Stat'i Materialy po Bolgarskoj Dialektologii [*A publication*]
SMBDB ...... Structural Margin Beyond Design Basis [*Nuclear energy*]   (NRCH)
SMBF .... Superior Mesenteric Blood Flow [*Physiology*]
SMBFT .... Small Bowel Follow-Through [*Medicine*]
SMBG .... Self-Monitoring of Blood Glucose [*Medicine*]
SMBJ .... Style Manual for Biological Journals
SMBL .... Semimobile

SMBL	Symbol Technologies [*NASDAQ symbol*] (NQ)
Sm & BRR Cas	Smith and Bates' American Railway Cases (DLA)
SMBS	Safeguard Material Balance Simulator
SMC	Chief Signalman [*Navy rating*]
SMC	Medical University of South Carolina Library, Charleston, SC [*OCLC symbol*] (OCLC)
SMC	Sa Majeste Catholique [*His or Her Catholic Majesty*] [*of Spain*] [*French*]
SMC	SAGE [*Semiautomatic Ground Environment*] Maintenance Control
SMC	Saint Martin's College [*Washington*]
SMC	Saint Mary's College [*Indiana; Kansas; Michigan; Minnesota*]
SMC	Saint Michael's College [*Vermont*]
SMC	Scientific Manpower Commission (EA)
SMC	Segmented Maintenance Cask [*Nuclear energy*] (NRCH)
SMC	Senior Medical Consultant
SMC	Senior Mission Controller (MCD)
SMC	Sequential Machine Controller [*Programing language*] [*1977-78*] (CSR)
SMC	Service Men's Center [*World War II*]
SMC	Sheet Molding Compound [*Plastics technology*]
SMC	Silicon Monolithic Circuit
SMC	Silva Mind Control [*Psychic system*]
SMC	Single Mothers by Choice [*New York, NY*] (EA)
SMC	Small Magellanic Cloud [*Astronomy*]
SMC	Smith [*A. O.*] Corporation [*American Stock Exchange symbol*]
SMC	Smithsonian Miscellaneous Collections [*A publication*]
SMC	Smooth Muscle Cell [*Cytology*]
SMC	Societe Mediterraneenne de Chimiotherapie [*Mediterranean Society of Chemotherapy - MSC*] [*Milan, Italy*] (EA-IO)
SMC	Society of Marine Consultants [*Rockville Centre, NY*] (EA)
SMC	Soil and Moisture Conservation
SMC	Somatomedin C [*Biochemistry*]
SMC	Somerset [*Colorado*] [*Seismograph station code, US Geological Survey*] (SEIS)
SmC	Southern Microfilm Corporation, Houston, TX [*Library symbol*] [*Library of Congress*] (LCLS)
SMC	Southern Missionary College [*Tennessee*]
SMC	Southern Motor Carriers Rate Conference, Atlanta GA [*STAC*]
SMC	Spanish Music Center [*Commercial firm*] (EA)
SMC	Special Mouth Care [*Medicine*]
S-M-C	Sperm [*or Spore*] Mother-Cell
SMC	Squared Multiple Correlation [*Psychology*]
SMC	Squawk Mode Code (FAAC)
SMC	Staff Message Control [*Military*]
SMC	Standard-Modern Technologies [*Formerly, Baxter Technologies*] [*Toronto Stock Exchange symbol*]
SMC	Standard Molding Corporation
SMC	Station-Control and Monitor Console Subsystem [*Deep Space Instrumentation Facility, NASA*]
SMC	Stepper Motor Control
SMC	Storage Module Controller
SMC	Student Mobilization Committee [*to End the War in Vietnam*] [*Defunct*] (EA)
SMC	Studies in Medieval Culture [*A publication*]
SMC	Sunnybrook Medical Centre, Toronto [*UTLAS symbol*]
SMC	Super-Multi-Coating [*Camera lenses*]
SMC	Supply and Maintenance Command [*Army*]
SMC	Surface Movement Control [*Aviation*]
SMC	Switch Maintenance Center [*Telecommunications*] (TEL)
SMC	Synchronized Maneuver Countermeasures Model (MCD)
SMC	System Monitor Console (CAAL)
SMC	Systems, Man, and Cybernetics (MCD)
SMCA	Single Manager for Conventional Ammunition [*DoD*]
SMCA	Sodium Monochloroacetate [*Organic chemistry*]
SMCA	Suckling Mouse Cataract Agent [*Microbiology*]
SMCAF	Society of Medical Consultants to the Armed Forces [*Bethesda, MD*] (EA)
SMCC	Saint Mary's College of California
SMCC	Santa Monica City College [*California*]
SMCC	Shuttle Mission Control Center [*NASA*] (NASA)
SMCC	Simulation Monitor and Control Console (KSC)
SMCC	Society of Memorial Cancer Center
SMCC	Standard Machinery Control Console [*Canadian Navy*]
SMCC	State Manpower Coordinating Committee [*Department of Labor*]
SMCC	Succinimidyl (Maleimidomethyl)cyclohexanecarboxylate [*Organic chemistry*]
Sm CCM	Smith's Circuit Courts-Martial Reports [*Maine*] (DLA)
SMCD	Supreme Military Council Decree [*Ghana*] (DLA)
SMCE	Master of Science in Civil Engineering
SMCE	Sociedad Mexicana de Computacion Electronica [*Mexico*]
SMCG	Stuart McGuire Co. [*NASDAQ symbol*] (NQ)
SMCH	Service Merchandise [*NASDAQ symbol*] (NQ)
S & M Ch	Smedes and Marshall's Mississippi Chancery Reports (DLA)
Sm Ch Pr	Smith's Chancery Practice [*7th ed.*] [*1862*] (DLA)
S & M Ch R	Smedes and Marshall's Mississippi Chancery Reports (DLA)
S & M Ch Rep	Smedes and Marshall's Mississippi Chancery Reports (DLA)
S & M Chy	Smedes and Marshall's Mississippi Chancery Reports (DLA)

SMCL	Southeastern Massachusetts Cooperating Libraries [*Library network*]
SMCLN	Semicolon (AABC)
SMCM	Master Chief Signalman [*Navy rating*]
SMCN	Selective Myocardial Cell Necrosis [*Cardiology*]
SMCO	SAGE [*Semiautomatic Ground Environment*] Maintenance Control Office
Sm Com L	Smith's Manual of Common Law [*12th ed.*] [*1905*] (DLA)
Sm Con	Smith on Contracts [*8th ed.*] [*1885*] (DLA)
Sm Cond Ala	Smith's Condensed Alabama Reports (DLA)
SMCP	San Marino Communist Party
SMCPCF	Fort Walsh National Historic Park, Parks Canada [*Parc Historique National Fort Walsh, Parcs Canada*] Maple Creek, Saskatchewan [*Library symbol*] [*National Library of Canada*] (NLC)
SMCPSTC	Supply and Maintenance Command Packaging Storage and Transportability Center [*Army*]
SMCR	Selected Marine Corps Reserve
SMCR	Society for Menstrual Cycle Research [*Rochester, NY*] (EA)
SMCRA	Surface Mining Control and Reclamation Act
SMCRC	Southern Motor Carriers Rate Conference
SMCS	IEEE Systems, Man, and Cybernetics Society [*New York, NY*] (EA)
SMCS	Senior Chief Signalman [*Navy rating*]
SMCS	Separation Monitor and Control System (MCD)
SMCS	Simulation Monitor and Control System (CAAL)
SMCS	Structural Mode Control System (MCD)
SMCSG	Special Military Construction Study Group (AABC)
SMCU	Separation Monitor Control Unit (MCD)
SMD	Doctor of Sacred Music
SMD	Fort Wayne, IN [*Location identifier*] [*FAA*] (FAAL)
SMD	Saint Michael's College, Library, Winooski, VT [*OCLC symbol*] (OCLC)
SMD	Sauter Mean Diameter (KSC)
SMD	Scheduling Management Display
SMD	Senile Macular Degeneration [*Medicine*]
SMD	Serum Malic Dehydrogenase [*An enzyme*]
SMD	Ship Manning Document [*Navy*]
SMD	Short Meter Double [*Music*]
SMD	Silicon Multiplier Detector
SMD	Singular Multinomial Distribution [*Statistics*]
SMD	Society of Medical-Dental Management Consultants (EA)
SMD	Spacelab Mission Development (MCD)
SMD	Special Measuring Device (NASA)
SMD	Statistical Methods Division [*Census*] (OICC)
SMD	Stop Motion Detector
SMD	Storage Module Drive
SMD	Structures and Mechanics Division [*NASA*]
SMD	Submanubrial Dullness [*Medicine*]
SMD	Submarine Mine Depot
SMD	Submersible Mining Device
SMD	Surface Mounted Device [*Microelectronics*]
SMD	Susceptor Meus Dominus [*God Is My Protector*] [*Latin*] [*Motto of Jacob, Margrave of Baden-Hochberg (1562-90); Georg Friedrich, Margrave of Baden-Hochberg (1573-1638)*]
SMD	Symptom Medication Diary [*Medicine*]
SMD	Synchronous Modulator-Demodulator (MCD)
SMD	System Management Directive (AFM)
SMD	Systems Manufacturing Division [*IBM Corp.*]
SMD	Systems Measuring Device (KSC)
SMD	Systems Monitor Display
SMDA	Second Marine Division Association (EA)
SMDA	State Medicaid Directors Association [*Washington, DC*] (EA)
SMDC	Saint Mary's Dominican College [*Louisiana*]
SMDC	Shielded Mild Detonating Cord
SMDC	Sisters of Mercy, Daughters of Christian Charity of St. Vincent de Paul [*Roman Catholic religious order*]
SMDC	Sodium Methyldithiocarbamate [*Fungicide*]
SMDC	Superconductive Materials Data Center (KSC)
SMDE	Static Mercury Drop Electrode [*Electrochemistry*]
SM Dendrol	Master of Science in Dendrology
SMDF	SCATS [*Simulation, Checkout, and Training System*] Main Distributing Frame
SMDI	Surface Miss Distance Indicator [*Navy*] (CAAL)
SMDL	Stoff- und Motivgeschichte der Deutschen Literatur [*A publication*]
SMDL	Subminiature Microwave Delay Line
SMDMC	Society of Medical-Dental Management Consultants [*Minneapolis, MN*] (EA)
SMDO	Special Microwave Devices Operation [*Raytheon Co.*]
SMD, OCOFS	Staff Management Division, Office, Chief of Staff [*Army*]
SMD OCSA	Staff Management Division, Office, Chief of Staff [*Army*] (AABC)
SMD OC of SA	Staff Management Division, Office, Chief of Staff [*Army*] (AABC)
SMDPL	Supply Management Date and Price List [*Navy*]
SMDPS	Service Module Deluge Purge System [*NASA*] (KSC)
SMDR	Selected Management Data Report [*DoD*]
SMDR	Station Message Detail Recording [*Formerly, MDR*] [*Telecommunications*]
SMDR	Summary Management Data Report [*DoD*]

SMDT .... Shore Mode Data Transmitter (MCD)
SMDTB ...... School Musician. Director and Teacher [*A publication*]
SME .... Sales and Marketing Executives-International (EA)
SME .... Sancta Mater Ecclesia [*Holy Mother Church*] [*Latin*]
SME .... Scale Model Engineering [*Initialism is brand name of tone arm*]
SME .... School of Military Engineering
SME .... Semiconductor Manufacturing Equipment [*Sumitomo Metals*]
SME .... Shape Memory Effect [*Metal alloy property*]
SME .... Sheet Metal Enclosure
SME .... Shell Metal Extractant
SME .... Shipbuilding and Marine Engineering [*Department of Employment*] [*British*]
SME .... Singleton Materials Engineering Laboratories [*Tennessee Valley Authority*]
SME .... Small and Medium-Size Enterprises
SME .... Society of Manufacturing Engineers [*Dearborn, MI*] (MCD)
SME .... Society of Military Engineers (KSC)
SME .... Society of Mining Engineers [*of American Institute of Mining, Metallurgical, and Petroleum Engineers*]
SME .... Soil Mechanics Experiment [*NASA*]
SME .... Solar Mesosphere Explorer (MCD)
SME .... Somerset, KY [*Location identifier*] [*FAA*] (FAAL)
SME .... Spartan Missile Equipment [*Missiles*] (MCD)
SME .... Stalk Median Eminence [*Anatomy*]
SME .... Standard Medical Examination [*Military*]
SME .... Stellar Mass Ejection
SMe .... Studi Medievali [*A publication*]
SME .... Subject Matter Experts (NVT)
SME .... Surface Measuring Equipment
SME .... Surface Movement Element (AFIT)
SMEA .... Studi Micenei ed Egeo-Anatolici [*A publication*]
SMEA .... Sun Marine Employees Association [*Aston, PA*] (EA)
SMEAC ...... Science, Mathematics, and Environmental Education Information Analysis Center
SMEADO .... Selected Major Exploratory Advanced Development Objective (MCD)
SME of AIME ... Society of Mining Engineers of American Institute of Mining, Metallurgical, and Petroleum Engineers (EA)
SMEAT .... Skylab Medical Experiments Altitude Test [*NASA*]
SMEC .... Society for Middle East Confederation [*Haifa, Israel*] (EA-IO)
SMEC .... Strategic Missile Evaluation Committee [*Air Force*]
Sm Ecc Cts ... Smith on Ecclesiastical Courts [*7th ed.*] [*1920*] (DLA)
SMEC Mag ... SMEC [*Snowy Mountains Engineering Corporation*] Magazine [*A publication*]
SME Collect Pap ... Society of Manufacturing Engineers. Collective Papers [*A publication*]
SME Creative Mfg Semin Tech Pap ... Society of Manufacturing Engineers. Creative Manufacturing Seminars. Technical Papers [*A publication*]
SMECTYMNUS ... Steven Marshall, Edward Calamy, Thomas Young, Matthew Newcomen, William Spurstow [*Collective author of 17th-century antiepiscopal tract*]
SMED .... Shared Medical Systems [*NASDAQ symbol*] (NQ)
Sm E D ...... [*E. D.*] Smith's New York Common Pleas Reports (DLA)
SMed .... Studi Medievali [*A publication*]
Smedes and Marshall's Chy Repts ... Smedes and Marshall's Mississippi Chancery Reports (DLA)
Smedes & M Ch ... Smedes and Marshall's Mississippi Chancery Reports (DLA)
Smedes & M (Miss) ... Smedes and Marshall's Mississippi Reports (DLA)
Smed & M ... Smedes and Marshall's Mississippi Reports (DLA)
Smed & M Ch ... Smedes and Marshall's Mississippi Chancery Reports (DLA)
Smee .... Collection of Abstracts of Acts of Parliament (DLA)
SMEE .... Master of Science in Electrical Engineering
SME-I .... Sales and Marketing Executives International [*Cleveland, OH*] (EA)
SMEK .... Summary Message Enable Keyboard
SMELLS ..... Someone Must Eliminate Libby Lagoon Smells [*Hartford, Wisconsin, organization*]
Sme & M .... Smedes [*W. C.*] and Marshall [*T. A.*] [*Mississippi*] (DLA)
Sm Eng ...... Smith's English King's Bench Reports (DLA)
SMEP .... Society of Multivariate Experimental Psychology (EA)
Sm Eq .... [*J. W.*] Smith's Manual of Equity (DLA)
Sm Eq .... Smith's Principles of Equity (DLA)
SMER .... Skylab Mission Evaluation Report [*NASA*] (MCD)
SM-ER .... Surface Missile, Extended Range
SMERC ...... San Mateo Educational Resources Center [*San Mateo County Office of Education*] [*Redwood City, CA*] [*Information service*] (EISS)
SMERE .... SPRINT Missile Electromagnetic Radiation Evaluation [*Army*] (AABC)
SMERF .... Social, Military, Ethnic, Religious, and Fraternal Groups [*Market segment*]
SMERSH .... Smert' Shpionam [*Russian phrase meaning "Death to the Spies," and name of a special division of USSR state security organizations charged with elimination of internal opposition to the regime from 1942 into postwar years*] [*Best known outside of USSR for role of its agents in the popular James Bond series of espionage stories*]
SMES .... Shuttle Mission Engineering Simulator [*NASA*] (NASA)

SMES .... Shuttle Mission Evaluation Simulation [*NASA*] (NASA)
SMES .... Superconducting Magnetic Energy Storage (NASA)
SME/SC .... SPRINT Missile Engineering/Service Course [*Army*] (AABC)
SMET .... Simulated Mission Endurance Test (MCD)
SMET .... Spacecraft Maneuver Engine Transients [*Apollo program*] [*NASA*]
SMETC ...... Swiss Mouse Embryo Tissue Culture
SMETDS .... Standard Message Trunk Design System [*Telecommunications*] (TEL)
SME Tech Pap ... Society of Manufacturing Engineers. Technical Papers [*A publication*]
SME Tech Pap Ser EE ... Society of Manufacturing Engineers. Technical Paper. Series EE (Electrical Engineering) [*A publication*]
SME Tech Pap Ser EM ... Society of Manufacturing Engineers. Technical Paper. Series EM (Engineering Materials) [*A publication*]
SME Tech Pap Ser FC ... Society of Manufacturing Engineers. Technical Paper. Series FC (Finishing and Coating) [*A publication*]
SME Tech Pap Ser MF ... Society of Manufacturing Engineers. Technical Paper. Series MF (Material Forming) [*A publication*]
SME Tech Pap Ser MR ... Society of Manufacturing Engineers. Technical Paper. Series MR (Material Removal) [*A publication*]
Smeth LS ... Smethurst on Locus Standi [*1867*] (DLA)
SMETO ...... Staff Meteorological Officer [*NATO*] (NATG)
SME West Metal Tool Expos Conf Tech Pap ... Society of Manufacturing Engineers. Western Metal and Tool Exposition and Conference. Technical Papers [*A publication*]
SMF .... S-Band Multifrequency
SMF .... S & M Photolabels [*Toronto Stock Exchange symbol*]
SMF .... Sacramento [*California*] [*Airport symbol*] (OAG)
SMF .... Sacramento, CA [*Location identifier*] [*FAA*] (FAAL)
SMF .... Sales Manpower Foundation (EA)
SMF .... Saticon Mixed-Field [*Video technology*]
SMF .... Saw Machine Fixture (MCD)
SMF .... Schumann Memorial Foundation (EA)
SMF .... Scientific Marriage Foundation [*Mellot, IN*] (EA)
SMF .... Screw Machine Feeder
SMF .... Senior Management Forum [*Information Industry Association*]
SMF .... Service to Military Families [*Red Cross*]
SMF .... Shaker Museum Foundation (EA)
SMF .... Signal De Mont [*France*] [*Seismograph station code, US Geological Survey*] (SEIS)
SMF .... [*The*] Singer Co. [*NYSE symbol*]
SMF .... Site Modification Facility
SMF .... Skrifter Utgivna av Modernsmalslararnas Forening [*A publication*]
SMF .... Snell Memorial Foundation, Inc.
SMF .... Societe Mathematique de France
SMF .... Society for the Maintenance of the Faith [*British*]
SMF .... Software Maintenance Function [*Data processing*] (TEL)
SMF .... Solar Magnetic Field
SMF .... Space Manufacturing Facility
SMF .... Spar Material Factor [*Yacht racing regulation*]
SMF .... Special Modifying Factor (DEN)
SMF .... Spectral Multilayer Filter
SMF .... Stable Matrix Form
SMF .... Static Magnetic Field
SMF .... Streptozocin, Mitomycin C, Fluorouracil [*Antineoplastic drug regimen*]
SMF .... Student Missions Fellowship [*Later, SFMF*] (EA)
SMF .... Switchable Matched Filter
SMF .... System Management Facility [*IBM Corp.*]
SMF .... System Measurement Facility [*Data processing*] (IEEE)
SMFA .... Simplified Modular Frame Assignment System [*Telecommunications*] (TEL)
SMFAS ...... Simplified Mainframe Administration System (MCD)
SMFAS ...... Simplified Modular Frame Assignment System [*Bell System*]
SMFG .... Stearns Manufacturing Co. [*NASDAQ symbol*] (NQ)
SMFL .... Science, Mathematics, Foreign Languages
SMFMA ...... Sprayed Mineral Fiber Manufacturers Association (EA)
Sm For Med ... Smith on Forensic Medicine [*10th ed.*] [*1955*] (DLA)
SMFP .... Systems Maintenance Field Party [*Aviation*] (FAAC)
SMFR .... Service to Military Families Representative [*Red Cross*]
SMFW .... Society of Medical Friends of Wine (EA)
SMG .... Megilot Genuzot [*E. L. Sukenik*] [*A publication*] (BJA)
SMG .... San Miguel [*Portugal*] [*Geomagnetic observatory code*]
SMG .... School of Military Government [*World War II*]
SMG .... Schweizerische Musikforschende Gesellschaft Mitteilungsblatt [*A publication*]
SMG .... Science Management Corp. [*American Stock Exchange symbol*]
SMG .... Seismocardiogram
SMG .... Sisters Poor Servants of the Mother of God [*Roman Catholic religious order*]
Sm & G ...... Smale and Giffard's English Vice-Chancery Reports (DLA)
Sm & G ...... Smith and Guthrie's Missouri Appeal Reports [*81-101 Missouri*] (DLA)
SMG .... Software Message Generator [*Data processing*] (TEL)
SMG .... Solids Moisture Gauge
SMG .... Space Missions Group [*Ford Aerospace & Communications Corp.*] [*Detroit, MI*] [*Telecommunications service*] (TSSD)
SMG .... Spacecraft Meteorology Group (KSC)

SMG .... Speed Made Good [*Navy*]　(NVT)
SMG .... Submachine Gun
SMGB......... Studien und Mitteilungen zur Geschichte des Benediktiner-Ordens und Seiner Zweige [*A publication*]
SMGBOZ.... Studien und Mitteilungen zur Geschichte des Benediktiner-Ordens und Seiner Zweige (Salzburg) [*A publication*]
SMGD........ Supply Management Grouping Designator [*Navy*]　(NG)
SM Geol ..... Master of Science in Geology
SMGO .... Senior Military Government Officer [*World War II*]
SMGP........ Strategic Missile Group [*Air Force*]
SMGS .... Southeastern Michigan Gas [*NASDAQ symbol*]　(NQ)
SMH .... St. Michael's Hospital, Toronto [*UTLAS symbol*]
SMH .... Scheduled Man-Hours　(MCD)
SMH .... Section for Metropolitan Hospitals [*American Hospital Association*] [*Chicago, IL*]　(EA)
SMH .... Semtech Corp. [*American Stock Exchange symbol*]
SMH .... Standard Mirror Hybrid　(MCD)
SMH .... Sydney Morning Herald [*A publication*]
SMHA........ Southern Mutual Help Association [*Jeanerette, LA*]　(EA)
SMHE........ Selected Material Handling Equipment [*Army*]　(RDA)
SMH (Newspr) (NSW) ... Sydney Morning Herald Reports (Newspaper) (New South Wales) [*A publication*]
SMHR........ Smoking and Health Reporter [*A publication*]
SMHS .... Superstition Mountain Historical Society　(EA)
SM in Hyg ... Master of Science in Hygiene
SMI .... Sa Majeste Imperiale [*His or Her Imperial Majesty*] [*French*]
SMI .... Sales Method Index [*LIMRA*]
SMI .... Samos Island [*Greece*] [*Airport symbol*]　(OAG)
SMI .... Secondary Metal Institute　(EA)
SMI .... Self-Metering Instrumentation
SMI .... Senior Medical Investigator
SMI .... Service at Military Installations [*Red Cross*]
SMI .... Shelter Management Instructor [*Civil Defense*]
SMI .... Simla [*India*] [*Seismograph station code, US Geological Survey*] [*Closed*]　(SEIS)
SMI .... Simulation of Machine Indexing
SMI .... Smithsonian Institution, Washington, DC [*OCLC symbol*]　(OCLC)
SMI .... Soldier-Machine Interface [*Army*]　(RDA)
SMI .... Sorptive Minerals Institute [*Washington, DC*]　(EA)
SMI .... Spectrametrics, Incorporated
SMI .... SpenderMenders International [*San Francisco, CA*]　(EA)
SMI .... Spring Manufacturers Institute [*Wheeling, IL*]　(EA)
SMI .... Springs Industries, Incorporated [*Formerly, Springs Mills, Incorporated*] [*NYSE symbol*]
SMI .... Standard Measuring Instrument
SMI .... Static Memory Interface [*Data processing*]　(MDG)
SMI .... Statute Miles
SMI .... Style of Mind Inventory [*Psychology*]
SMI .... Success Motivation Institute
SMI .... Super Market Institute [*Later, FMI*]　(EA)
SMI .... Supplementary Medical Insurance
SMI .... Supply Management Inspection　(NVT)
SMI .... Sustained Maximal Inspiration [*Physiology*]
SMI .... System Memory Interface [*Data processing*]
SMI .... Systems Management, Incorporated [*Rosemont, IL*] [*Software manufacturer*]
SMI .... Systems Measurement Instrument [*Data processing*]
SMIA .... Social Marketing International Association　(EA-IO)
SMIA .... Steel Management in Action [*Bethlehem Steel Co.*]
SMIAC....... Soil Mechanics Information Analysis Center [*Army Corps of Engineers*] [*Vicksburg, MS*]　(EISS)
SMIAT .... Special Military Intelligence Activities Team　(CINC)
Smi & Bat... Smith and Batty's Irish King's Bench Reports　(DLA)
SMIC .... Missionary Sisters of the Immaculate Conception of the Mother of God [*Roman Catholic religious order*]
SMIC .... Sorghum and Millets Information Center [*ICRISAT*] [*India*]
SMIC .... Special Material Identification Code
SMIC .... Study of Man's Impact on Climate
SMIC .... Superior Manufacturing & Instrument Corporation [*NASDAQ symbol*]　(NQ)
SMIC .... Supply Management Information Center [*Military*]　(CAAL)
SMICBM..... Semimobile Intercontinental Ballistic Missile
SMID .... Semiconductor Memory Integrated Device　(MCD)
SMIDA....... Small Business Innovation Development Act [*1982*]
SMIEEE...... Senior Member of Institute of Electrical and Electronic Engineers
SMIER .... Societe Medicale Internationale d'Endoscopie et de Radiocinematographie [*International Medical Society for Endoscopy and Radiocinematography*]
Smlg .... Surface Membrane Immunoglobulin [*Immunochemistry*]
SMIIS .... Solar Microwave Interferometer Imaging System
SMIJA .... South African Mining and Engineering Journal [*A publication*]
SMIL .... Solidaritet med Israel
SMIL .... Statistical Methods in Linguistics [*A publication*]
SMIL .... Statistics and Market Intelligence Library [*Department of Trade*] [*British*]
SMILE .... Safe Military Infrared LASER Equipment
SMILE .... Ship's Master Index Listing of Equipment　(MCD)
SMILE .... Significant Milestone Integration Lateral Evaluation [*Data processing*]

SMILE .... South Central Minnesota Interlibrary Exchange [*Library network*]
SMI²LE ...... Space Migration, Intelligence Increase, Life Extension [*Idea advanced by Timothy Leary, 1960's counterculture figure*]
SMILS .... Sonobuoy Missile Impact Location System [*Navy*]　(CAAL)
SM/IM .... System Manager or Item Manager　(AFIT)
Sm Ind ...... Smith's Reports [*1-4 Indiana*]　(DLA)
SMIO .... Spares Multiple Item Order　(AAG)
SMIP .... Ship's 3-M Improvement Plan [*Navy*]　(NVT)
SMIP .... Structure Memory Information Processor
SMIPP .... Sheet Metal Industry Promotion Plan [*Cleveland, OH*]　(EA)
SMIPS .... Small Interactive Image Processing System [*NASA*]
SMIRE .... Senior Member of the Institution of Radio Engineers
SMIRR .... Shuttle Multispectral Infrared Radiometer [*NASA*]
SMIRS .... School Management Information Retrieval Service [*University of Oregon*] [*Eugene, OR*]
SMIS .... Safeguard Management Information System [*Army*]　(AABC)
SMIS .... School of Management Information Systems [*Army*]
SMIS .... Ship Management Information System　(MCD)
SMIS .... Society for Management Information Systems [*Chicago, IL*]　(EA)
SMIS .... Supply Management Information System
SMIS .... Survey Methodology Information System [*Inter-University Consortium for Political & Social Research*] [*Database*]
SMIS .... Symbolic Matrix Interpretation System
SMIS INC ... Societe de Microelectronique Industrielle de Sherbrooke, Inc. [*University of Sherbrooke*] [*Canada*] [*Research center*]　(RCD)
SMISOP ..... Safeguard Management Information System Operating Program [*Army*]　(AABC)
SMiss .... Studia Missionalia [*A publication*]
SMIT.......... Sherman Mental Impairment Test [*Psychology*]
SMIT.......... Simulated Midcourse Interaction Test [*NASA*]
SMIT.......... Spin Motor Interruption Technique
SMIT.......... Submit　(ROG)
SMITE .... Simulated Mechanical Impact Test Equipment　(MCD)
SMITE .... Simulation Model of Interceptor Terminal Effectiveness
Smith .... Smith on English Registration　(DLA)
Smith .... Smith, Reporter [*7, 12 Heiskell's Tennessee Reports*]　(DLA)
Smith .... [*E. P.*] Smith's Court of Appeals Reports [*15-27 New York*]　(DLA)
Smith .... [*E. H.*] Smith's Court of Appeals Reports [*147-162 New York*]　(DLA)
Smith .... [*J. P.*] Smith's English King's Bench Reports　(DLA)
Smith .... Smith's Indiana Reports　(DLA)
Smith .... Smith's New Hampshire Reports　(DLA)
Smith .... [*E. D.*] Smith's New York Common Pleas Reports　(DLA)
Smith .... [*P. F.*] Smith's Pennsylvania State Reports　(DLA)
Smith .... [*C. L.*] Smith's Registration Cases [*1895-1914*]　(DLA)
Smith .... Smith's Reports [*81-83 Missouri Appeals*]　(DLA)
Smith .... Smith's Reports [*61-84 Maine*]　(DLA)
Smith .... Smith's Reports [*54-62 California*]　(DLA)
Smith .... Smith's Reports [*2-4 South Dakota*]　(DLA)
Smith .... Smith's Reports [*1-11 Wisconsin*]　(DLA)
Smith .... [*E. B.*] Smith's Reports [*21-47 Illinois Appeals*]　(DLA)
Smith .... Smithsonian [*A publication*]
Smith Act.... Smith's Actions at Law　(DLA)
Smith & B... Smith and Bates' American Railway Cases　(DLA)
Smith & B... Smith and Batty's Irish King's Bench Reports　(DLA)
Smith & Bat ... Smith and Batty's Irish King's Bench Reports　(DLA)
Smith & BRRC ... Smith and Bates' American Railway Cases　(DLA)
Smith CCM ... Smith's Circuit Courts-Martial Reports [*Maine*]　(DLA)
Smith Ch Pr ... Smith's Chancery Practice　(DLA)
Smith Coll ... Smith College. Studies in Social Work [*A publication*]
Smith Coll Mus Bul ... Smith College. Museum of Art. Bulletin [*A publication*]
Smith Coll Stud Social Work ... Smith College. Studies in Social Work [*A publication*]
Smith Com Law ... Smith's Manual of Common Law　(DLA)
Smith Cond Rep ... Smith's Condensed Alabama Reports　(DLA)
Smith Cong Election Cases ... Smith's Election Cases [*United States*]　(DLA)
Smith Cont ... Smith on Contracts　(DLA)
Smith CP ... [*E. D.*] Smith's New York Common Pleas Reports　(DLA)
Smith Ct App ... [*E. P.*] Smith's Court of Appeals Reports [*15-27 New York*]　(DLA)
Smith De Rep Angl ... [*Sir Thomas*] Smith. De Republica Anglica [*The Commonwealth of England and the Manner of Government Thereof*] [*1621*]　(DLA)
Smith Dict Antiq ... Smith's Dictionary of Greek and Roman Antiquities　(DLA)
Smith E D... [*E. D.*] Smith's New York Common Pleas Reports [*1850-58*]　(DLA)
Smith E H... [*E. H.*] Smith's Court of Appeals Reports [*147-162 New York*]　(DLA)
Smith E P... [*E. P.*] Smith's Court of Appeals Reports [*15-27 New York*]　(DLA)
Smith Ext Int ... Smith on Executory Interest　(DLA)
Smith & G ... Smith and Guthrie's Missouri Appeal Reports [*81-101 Missouri*]　(DLA)
Smith & H... Smith and Heiskell [*Tennessee*]　(DLA)
Smith-Hurd ... Smith-Hurd's Illinois Annotated Statutes　(DLA)

Smith-Hurd Ann St ... Smith-Hurd's Illinois Annotated Statutes (DLA)
Smith Ind ... Smith's Indiana Reports (DLA)
Smith J P ... [*J. P.*] Smith's English King's Bench Reports (DLA)
Smith KB ... Smith's English King's Bench Reports (DLA)
Smith Laws PA ... Smith's Laws of Pennsylvania (DLA)
Smith LC ... Smith's Leading Cases (DLA)
Smith Lead Cas ... Smith's Leading Cases (DLA)
Smith LJ .... Smith's Law Journal (DLA)
Smith Man Eq Jur ... Smith's Manual of Equity Jurisprudence (DLA)
Smith ME ... Smith's Reports [*61-84 Maine*] (DLA)
Smith Merc Law ... Smith on Mercantile Law (DLA)
Smith NH ... Smith's New Hampshire Reports (DLA)
Smith NY ... Smith's Court of Appeals Reports [*15-27, 147-162 New York*] (DLA)
Smith PA .... [*P. F.*] Smith's Pennsylvania State Reports (DLA)
Smith P F ... P. F. Smith's Pennsylvania State Reports (DLA)
Smith Reg ... [*C. L.*] Smith's Registration Cases [*England*] (DLA)
Smith Reg Cas ... [*C. L.*] Smith's Registration Cases [*England*] (DLA)
Smith's (Ind) R ... Smith's Indiana Reports (DLA)
Smiths Inst ... Smithsonian Institution [*A publication*]
Smith's Laws ... Smith's Laws of Pennsylvania (DLA)
Smith's Lead Cas ... Smith's Leading Cases (DLA)
Smithson Ann Flight ... Smithsonian Annals of Flight [*A publication*]
Smithson Contr Bot ... Smithsonian Contributions to Botany [*A publication*]
Smithson Contrib Anthropol ... Smithsonian Contributions to Anthropology [*A publication*]
Smithson Contrib Bot ... Smithsonian Contributions to Botany [*A publication*]
Smithson Contrib Earth Sciences ... Smithsonian Contributions to Earth Sciences [*A publication*]
Smithson Contrib Paleobiol ... Smithsonian Contributions to Paleobiology [*A publication*]
Smithson Contrib Zool ... Smithsonian Contributions to Zoology [*A publication*]
Smithson Contr Zool ... Smithsonian Contributions to Zoology [*A publication*]
Smithson Inst Annu Rep ... Smithsonian Institution. Annual Report [*A publication*]
Smithson Inst Cent Short-Lived Phenom Annu Rep Rev Events ... Smithsonian Institution. Center for Short-Lived Phenomena. Annual Report and Review of Events [*A publication*]
Smithson Misc Colins ... Smithsonian Miscellaneous Collections [*A publication*]
Smithson Misc Collect ... Smithsonian Miscellaneous Collections [*A publication*]
Smithson Rep ... Smithsonian Institution. Annual Report [*A publication*]
Smithson Rept ... Smithsonian Institution. Reports [*A publication*]
Smith's R ... Smith's Indiana Reports (DLA)
Smith Wealth Nat ... Smith's Inquiry into the Nature and Causes of the Wealth of Nations (DLA)
Smith Wis ... Smith's Reports [*1-11 Wisconsin*] (DLA)
SMIU .... Stove Mounters International Union of North America [*Later, Stove, Furnace, Allied Appliance Workers International Union of North America*]
SMIU .... Studies by Members of the Istanbul University English Department [*A publication*]
SMIZD .... Sei Marianna Ika Daigaku Zasshi [*A publication*]
SMJ .... Moose Jaw Public Library, Saskatchewan [*Library symbol*] [*National Library of Canada*] (NLC)
SMJ .... Sarawak Museum Journal [*A publication*]
SMJ .... Siberian Mathematical Journal [*A publication*]
SMJ .... Sim [*Papua New Guinea*] [*Airport symbol*] (OAG)
SMJ .... Society of Medical Jurisprudence [*Scarsdale, NY*] (EA)
SMJC .... Saint Mary's Junior College [*Minnesota; Missouri; North Carolina*]
SMJC .... Service Module Jettison Controller [*NASA*] (MCD)
SM-JDCC ... Sunshine Music - Jan and Dean Collectors Club [*Parsons, KS*] (EA)
SMJMA ...... SIAM [*Society for Industrial and Applied Mathematics*] Journal on Applied Mathematics [*A publication*]
SMJOA .... Southern Medical Journal [*United States*] [*A publication*]
SMJP .... Palliser Regional Library, Moose Jaw, Saskatchewan [*Library symbol*] [*National Library of Canada*] (NLC)
SMJT .... Saskatchewan Technical Institute, Moose Jaw, Saskatchewan [*Library symbol*] [*National Library of Canada*] (NLC)
SMK .... Saint Michael [*Alaska*] [*Airport symbol*] (OAG)
SMK .... St. Michael, AK [*Location identifier*] [*FAA*] (FAAL)
SMK .... Sanmark-Stardust, Inc. [*American Stock Exchange symbol*]
SMH .... Smack [*Ship*]
SMK .... Smoke (AAG)
Sm KB .... Smith's English King's Bench Reports (DLA)
SMKLS .... Smokeless (AAG)
SMKR .... Sim-Kar Lighting Fixture Co., Inc. [*NASDAQ symbol*] (NQ)
SMKSTK .... Smokestack[*s*] [*Freight*]
SML .... CV Sportsmark International, Inc. [*Vancouver Stock Exchange symbol*]
SML .... Montreal Lake Library, Saskatchewan [*Library symbol*] [*National Library of Canada*] (NLC)
SML .... Saluda Motor Lines [*AAR code*]

SML .... Sawmill [*Alaska*] [*Seismograph station code, US Geological Survey*] (SEIS)
SML .... Search Mode Logic
SML .... Semantic-Meta-Language
SML .... Serials Master List
SML .... Simulator Load
SML .... Skylab Mobile Laboratory [*NASA*] (KSC)
SML .... Small (FAAC)
SML .... Software Master Library [*Data processing*] (TEL)
SML .... Southern Maine Library District, Portland, ME [*OCLC symbol*] (OCLC)
SML .... Spartan Material List [*Missiles*] (MCD)
SML .... Spool Multileaving [*Data processing*] (IBMDP)
SML .... Standard Markup Language [*Data processing*]
SML .... States Marine Lines
SML .... Statistical Methods in Linguistics [*Stockholm*] [*A publication*]
SML .... Stella Maris [*Bahamas*] [*Airport symbol*] (OAG)
SML .... Stimmen aus Maria-Laach [*A publication*]
SML .... Structure Mold Line (MCD)
SML .... Support Material List
SML .... Symbolic Machine Language [*Data processing*]
SMLB .... Smith Laboratories [*NASDAQ symbol*] (NQ)
Sm LC .... Smith's Leading Cases (DLA)
SMLC .... Southwest Michigan Library Cooperative [*Library network*]
Sm L Cas Com L ... Smith's Leading Cases on Commercial Law (DLA)
SMLD .... Suckling Mouse Mean Lethal Dose [*Microbiology*]
SMLE .... Short Magazine Lee-Enfield Rifle
SMLE .... Small-Medium Local Exchange [*Telecommunications*] (TEL)
SMLF .... Skrifter Utgivna av Modernsmalslararnas Forening [*A publication*]
SMLI .... Space Microwave Laboratories [*NASDAQ symbol*] (NQ)
Sm LJ .... Law Journal (Smith) [*England*] (DLA)
SMLJ .... St. Mary's Law Journal [*A publication*]
SMLM .... Simple-Minded Learning Machine (IEEE)
SMLM .... Soviet Military Liaison Mission [*Army*]
SMLO .... Senior Military Liaison Officer
SMLR .... Stepwise Multiple Linear Regression [*Mathematics*]
SMLS .... Saint Mary of the Lake Seminary [*Mundelein, IL*]
SMLS .... Scimed Life Systems [*NASDAQ symbol*] (NQ)
SMLS .... Sea-Based Mobile Logistics Supply [*Navy*] (CAAL)
SMLS .... Seamless (AAG)
SMLV .... Studi Mediolatini e Volgari [*A publication*]
SMM .... Master of Sacred Music (BJA)
SMM .... Safeguards and Materials Management [*AEC*]
SMM .... Saigon Military Mission [*Vietnam*]
SMM .... Sancta Mater Maria [*Holy Mother Mary*] [*Latin*]
SMM .... Scattering Matrix Method [*Materials research*]
SMM .... Secondary Mortgage Market (ADA)
SMM .... Semiconductor Memory Module
SMM .... Semporna [*Malaysia*] [*Airport symbol*] (OAG)
SMM .... Shared Multiport Memory
SMM .... Ship, Machinery, Marine Technology International Exhibition (TSPED)
Sm & M ...... Smedes and Marshall's Mississippi Reports [*9-22 Mississippi*] (DLA)
SMM .... Societas Mariae Montfortana [*Missionaries of the Company of Mary*] [*Montfort Fathers*] [*Roman Catholic religious order*]
SMM .... Solar Maximum Mission (MCD)
SMM .... Specially Meritorious Medal
SMM .... Spectral Matrix Method (KSC)
SMM .... Standard Method of Measurement (IEEE)
SMM .... Start of Manual Message (BUR)
SMM .... Stress Memo Manual
SMM .... Subsystem Measurement Management [*NASA*] (NASA)
SMM .... Summit Airlines [*Philadelphia, PA*] [*FAA designator*] (FAAC)
SMM .... Supervisory Middle Management
SMM .... Supplemental Minimal Medium [*Microbiology*]
SMM .... System Maintenance Manual
SMM .... Systems Maintenance Management [*Data processing*]
SMMA .... Small Motor Manufacturers Association [*Libertyville, IL*] (EA)
SMMART .... Society for Mass Media and Resource Technology. Journal [*A publication*]
SMMB .... Stores Management Multiplex Bus [*Data processing*] (MCD)
SMMC .... System Maintenance Monitor Console [*FAA*]
Sm & M Ch ... Smedes and Marshall's Mississippi Reports [*9-22 Mississippi*] (DLA)
SMMD .... Specimen Mass Measurement Device [*NASA*] (KSC)
Sm ME .... Smith's Reports [*61-84 Maine*] (DLA)
Sm Merc L ... Smith on Mercantile Law [*13th ed.*] [*1931*] (DLA)
SMMH .... Scheduled Maintenance Man-Hours (MCD)
SMMI .... El Senoussi Multiphasic Marital Inventory [*Psychology*]
S & MMIS ... Supply and Maintenance Management Information System [*Army*]
SMMP .... Screw Machine Metal Part
SMMP .... Standard Methods of Measuring Performance (IEEE)
SMMR .... Scanning Multichannel [*or Multifrequency or Multispectral*] Microwave Radiometer
SMMR .... Specific Mobilization Material Requirement [*Military*] (AFIT)
SM-MR .... Surface Missile, Medium Range
SMMRT Journal ... Society for Mass Media and Resource Technology. Journal [*A publication*]

SMMS .... Shipbuilding Material Management Systems [*Navy*]   (NG)
Sm M & S ... Smith on Master and Servant [*8th ed.*] [*1931*]   (DLA)
SMMS .... Standard Maintenance Management System [*Military*]   (CAAL)
SMMS .... Support Maintenance Management System [*Army*]
SMMT .... Society of Motor Manufacturers and Traders [*Defunct*]   (EA)
SMMT .... Strategic Missiles Materials Technology   (MCD)
SMMT .... Summit Savings Association [*NASDAQ symbol*]   (NQ)
SMN .... Nuzi Texts in the Semitic Museum [*Harvard*]   (BJA)
SMN .... Salmon, ID [*Location identifier*] [*FAA*]   (FAAL)
SMN .... Seamen's Corp. [*American Stock Exchange symbol*]
SMN .... Sleeping Mountain [*Nevada*] [*Seismograph station code, US
                  Geological Survey*] [*Closed*]   (SEIS)
SMN .... Studia Musicologica Norvegica [*A publication*]
SMNA .... Safe Manufacturers' National Association   (EA)
SMNC .... Splenic Mononuclear Cell [*Cytology*]
Sm Neg ...... Smith on Negligence [*2nd ed.*] [*1884*]   (DLA)
SMNK .... Smooth Neck
SMNO .... Singapore Malays National Organization [*Pertubohan
                  Kebangsaan Melayu Singapore*]   (PPW)
SMNRY ...... Seminary
SMNSA .... Soviet Mining Science [*English Translation*] [*A publication*]
SMO .... Santa Maria Resources Ltd. [*Toronto Stock Exchange symbol*]
SMO .... Santa Monica, CA [*Location identifier*] [*FAA*]   (FAAL)
SMO .... Sea Airmotive, Inc. [*Anchorage, AK*] [*FAA designator*]   (FAAC)
SMO .... Secondary Market Operation
SMO .... Senior Medical Officer [*Military*]
SMO .... Service Module Oxidizer [*NASA*]
SMO .... Small Magnetospheric Observatory [*Satellite*] [*NASA*]
SMO .... Smoke
SMO .... So Much Of
SMO .... Society of Military Ophthalmologists [*Rockville, MD*]   (EA)
SMO .... Society of Military Otolaryngologists [*Later, SMO-HNS*]   (EA)
SMO .... Sovereign Military Order [*British*]
SMO .... Squadron Medical Officer
SMO .... Stabilized Master Oscillator
SMO .... State Maintenance Office [*or Officer*] [*Military*]
SMO .... Supplementary Meteorological Office   (FAAC)
SMO .... Supply Management Office [*Air Force*]   (AFM)
SMO .... Surface Mining Office [*Department of the Interior*]   (OICC)
SMO .... System Management Office   (AFIT)
SMOA .... Ships Material Office, Atlantic
SMOA .... Single-Manager Operating Agency
SMOC .... Simulation Mission Operation Computer   (MCD)
SMOC .... Submodule and Operator Controller [*For sequence of
                  telephonic operations*]
SMOG .... Sales Management Organization Game
SMOG .... Save Me, Oh God
SMOG .... Smelost', Mysl', Obraz, Glubina [*Boldness, Thought, Image,
                  Depth*] or Samoye Molodoye Obyedinenie Geniev
                  [*Youngest Federation of Geniuses*] [*Clandestine group of
                  writers in Moscow, USSR*]
SMOG .... Smoke and Fog
SMOG .... Special Monitor Output Generator   (IEEE)
SMOG .... Sprite-Midget Owners Group   (EA)
SMOG .... Structural Modeling Oriented Graphics [*Module*]
SMO-HNS ... Society of Military Otolaryngologists - Head and Neck
                  Surgeons [*San Antonio, TX*]   (EA)
SMOKE ..... Surface Magnetooptic Kerr Effect [*Surface analysis*]
SMOLANT ... Ships Material Office, Atlantic   (MCD)
Smolensk Gos Ped Inst Ucen Zap ... Smolenskii Gosudarstvennyi
                  Pedagogiceskii Institut. Ucenye Zapiski [*A publication*]
SMOM .... Sovereign Military Order of Malta   (EA)
SMon .... Studia Monastica [*A publication*]
SMON .... Subacute Myelooptic Neuropathy [*Medicine*]
SMOP .... Ships Material Office, Pacific
SMOP .... So Much of Paragraph
SMOPAC .... Ships Material Office, Pacific   (MCD)
SMOPS ..... School of Maritime Operations [*British*]
SMORG ..... Senior Marketing Officers Research Group [*LIMRA*]
SMORZ ..... Smorzando [*Slower and Softer*] [*Music*]
SMOS .... Secondary Military Occupational Specialty
SMOS .... Senior Marketing Officers Seminar [*LIMRA*]
SMOS .... Society of Military Orthopaedic Surgeons [*Walter Reed Army
                  Medical Center*] [*Washington, DC*]   (EA)
SMOSC ..... Secondary Military Occupational Specialty Code   (AABC)
SMOT .... Free Interprofessional Association of Soviet Workers   (PD)
SMOTE ...... Simulation of Turbofan Engine [*Air Force*]
Smoult .... Notes of Cases in Smoult's Collection of Orders [*Calcutta,
                  India*]   (DLA)
SMOW .... Standard Mean Ocean Water
SMP .... Sacred Music Press   (BJA)
SMP .... St. Martin's Press
SMP .... Saint Mary's Press [*Record label*] [*New York*]
SMP .... Sampler   (DEN)
SMP .... Santa Monica Public Library, Santa Monica, CA [*OCLC
                  symbol*]   (OCLC)
SMP .... Scanning and Measuring Projector
SMP .... Scheduled Maintenance Program   (MCD)
SMP .... See Me Please
SMP .... Sensitized Material Print   (MSA)
SMP .... Servo Meter Panel   (AAG)

SMP .... Ship's Mission Profile [*Navy*]   (CAAL)
SMP .... Simplon Resources Ltd. [*Vancouver Stock Exchange symbol*]
SMP .... Simultaneous Macular Perception [*Ophthalmology*]
SMP .... Sine Mascula Prole [*Without Male Issue*] [*Latin*]
SMP .... Sisters of St. Mary of the Presentation [*Roman Catholic
                  religious order*]
SMP .... Skimmed Milk Powder   (ADA)
SMP .... Smudge Pot
SMP .... Social Marginal Productivity
SMP .... Society of Miniature Painters [*British*]   (ROG)
SMP .... Software Management Plan   (MCD)
SMP .... Somplago [*Italy*] [*Seismograph station code, US Geological
                  Survey*] [*Closed*]   (SEIS)
SMP .... Sound Motion Picture Technician [*Navy*]
SMP .... Special Maintenance Project [*FAA*]
SMP .... Special Manufacturing Procedure
SMP .... Special Marketing Program [*Business*]
SMP .... Special Multi-Peril [*Insurance*]
SMP .... Stampede Pass, WA [*Location identifier*] [*FAA*]   (FAAL)
SMP .... Standard Maintenance Procedure
SMP .... Standard Motor Products, Inc. [*NYSE symbol*]
SMP .... Standards, Methods, and Planning
SMP .... Stores Management Process   (MCD)
SMP .... Submitochondrial Particle [*Cytology*]
SMP .... Sulfamethoxypyridazine [*Antimicrobial compound*]
SMP .... Summary Maneuver Plan
SMP .... Suomen Maaseudun Puolue [*Finnish Rural Party*]   (PPW)
SMP .... Symmetric Multiprocessing
SMP .... System Modification Program [*Data processing*]
SMP .... Systems Maintenance Procedure   (MCD)
SMP .... Systems Modernization Plan [*Social Security Administration*]
SMP .... Systems Monitoring Panel   (NVT)
SMPA .... Solid Motor Processing Area [*NASA*]   (KSC)
SMPAD ..... Society of Motion Picture Art Directors [*Later, Society of
                  Motion Picture and Television Art Directors*]   (EA)
Sm Pat ...... Smith on Patents [*2nd ed.*] [*1854*]   (DLA)
SMPC .... Saint Mary of the Plains College [*Dodge City, KS*]
SMPD .... Ship Maintenance Planning Data   (MCD)
SMPD .... Surface Missile Processing Description   (MCD)
SMPE .... Society of Marine Port Engineers [*New York, NY*]   (EA)
SMPF .... Scientific & Medical Publications of France, Inc.
SMPG .... Small Magazine Publishers Group [*Freedom, ME*]   (EA)
SMPG .... Standardization Management Policy Group
SMPI .... Surface Missile Proficiency Inspection   (MCD)
SMPKA ...... Sempaku [*A publication*]
Sm Pl......... Somersetshire Pleas [*Civil and Criminal*], Edited by Chadwyck-
                  Healey and Landon [*Somerset Record Society
                  Publications, Vol. 11, 36, 41, 44*]   (DLA)
SMPLG ...... Sampling   (MSA)
SMPM .... Structural Materials Property Manual [*NASA*]   (NASA)
SM/PM .... System Management/Performance Monitor [*NASA*]   (NASA)
SMPO .... SEATO [*Southeast Asia Treaty Organization*] Military Planning
                  Office   (CINC)
SMPO .... Sound Motion Picture Operator [*Navy*]
S-MPR .... Semimonthly Progress Reports [*Navy*]
SMPR .... Supply and Maintenance Plan and Report [*Army*]   (AABC)
Sm Pr R ..... Small Press Review [*A publication*]
SMPS .... Simplified Message Processing Simulation   (IEEE)
SMPS .... Simpson Industries, Inc. [*NASDAQ symbol*]   (NQ)
SMPS .... Society for Marketing Professional Services [*Alexandria,
                  VA*]   (EA)
SMPSA ...... Solid Motor Processing and Storage Car
SMPTAD .... Society of Motion Picture and Television Art Directors
                  [*Formerly, SMPAD*]   (EA)
SMPTE ...... Society of Motion Picture and Television Engineers [*Formerly,
                  Society of Motion Picture Engineers*] [*Scarsdale,
                  NY*]   (EA)
SMPTE J .... Society of Motion Picture and Television Engineers. Journal [*A
                  publication*]
SMPTRB .... Shuttle Main Propulsion Test Requirement Board   (MCD)
SMQ .... School Media Quarterly [*A publication*]
SMQ .... Silvermaque Mining Ltd. [*Toronto Stock Exchange symbol*]
SMQ .... Social Maturity Quotient
SMQ .... Structure Module Qualification Test   (MCD)
SMQS .... Societe de Mary Queen de Scots [*Mary Queen of Scots Society
                  - MQSS*] [*Scarborough, ON*]   (EA-IO)
SMR .... Great Falls, MT [*Location identifier*] [*FAA*]   (FAAL)
SMR .... Midrash Rabbah [*H. Freedman and Maurice Simon*] [*A
                  publication*]   (BJA)
SMR .... Sa Majeste Royale [*His, or Her, Royal Majesty*] [*French*]
SMR .... San Marino [*Three-letter standard code*]   (CNC)
SMR .... Santa Marta [*Colombia*] [*Airport symbol*]   (OAG)
SMR .... Scheduled Maintenance Replacement
SMR .... School of Materiel Readiness [*Formerly, SAM*] [*Army*]   (RDA)
SMR .... Secret Marriage Rite   (BJA)
SMR .... Semeru [*Java*] [*Seismograph station code, US Geological
                  Survey*] [*Closed*]   (SEIS)
SMR .... Seminarians for Ministerial Renewal [*Later, NFCS*]   (EA)
SMR .... Sensorimotor Rhythm [*Neurophysiology*]
SMR .... Series Mode Rejection
SMR .... Severely Mentally Retarded

SMR .... Sheffield and Midland Railway [*British*] (ROG)
SMR .... Shield Mock-Up Reactor
S & MR ...... Shire and Municipal Record [*A publication*]
SMR .... Side-Looking Mapping RADAR
SMR .... Skeletal Muscle Relaxant [*Drug*]
SMR .... Small Missile Range (MCD)
SMR .... Society of Manufacturers' Representatives [*Birmingham, MI*] (EA)
SMR .... Society of Mary Reparatrix [*Roman Catholic women's religious order*]
SMR .... Solid Moderated Reactor
SMR .... Somnolent Metabolic Rate [*Medicine*]
SMR .... Source, Maintenance, and Recoverability (MCD)
SM & R ...... Source, Maintenance, and Recoverability (NG)
SMR .... Spanish Mustang Registry (EA)
SMR .... Special Money Requisition
SMR .... Specialized Mobile Radio
SMR .... Standard Mortality Rate
SMR .... Standardized Mortality Ratio
SMR .... Stanmar Resources Ltd. [*Vancouver Stock Exchange symbol*]
SMR .... Statement of Material Requirements
SMR .... Status Monitoring Routine
SMR .... Statute Mile Radius (FAAC)
SMR .... Steam-Methane Reforming [*Chemical engineering*]
SMR .... Stock Management Report
SMR .... Submucous Resection [*Medicine*]
SMR .... Super-Metal Rich [*Astronomy*]
SMR .... Supplemental Medical Report
SMR .... Supply Management Report
SMR .... Surface Movement RADAR
SMR .... Switching Mode Regulator
SMR .... System Malfunction Report
SMRA........ Simultaneous Multicomponent Rank Annihilation [*Mathematics*]
SMRAS ..... Safeguard Maintenance and Reporting Analysis System [*Army*] (AABC)
SMRB........ Simmons Market Research Bureau, Inc. [*New York, NY*] [*Database producer*]
SMRC........ Silver Marten Rabbit Club (EA)
SMRC........ Society of Miniature Rifle Clubs [*British*] (ROG)
SMRCS ..... Service Module Reaction Control System [*NASA*] (KSC)
SMRD........ Spin Motor Rotation Detector (MCD)
SMRD........ Spin Motor Run Discrete (NASA)
SMRE........ Submerged Repeater Monitoring Equipment [*RADAR*]
S & M Record ... Shire and Municipal Record [*A publication*]
SMRF........ Salvadoran Medical Relief Fund (EA)
SMRGC ..... Sun-Maid Raisin Growers of California (EA)
SMRI .... Society for Magnetic Resonance Imaging [*McLean, VA*] (EA)
SMRI .... Solution Mining Research Institute [*Woodstock, IL*] (EA)
SMRIS ...... Soviet Missile Range Instrumented Ship (CINC)
SMRL .... Stanford Magnetic Resonance Laboratory [*Stanford University*] [*Research center*] (RCD)
SMRL .... Submarine Medical Research Laboratory
SMRLA....... Southern Maryland Regional Library Resource Center [*Library network*]
SMRLH...... Soldier's Mail, Rush Like Hell [*On correspondence*]
SMR/MIS ... Supply, Maintenance and Readiness Management Information System [*Logistics Management Information System*] (AABC)
SMRP........ Society for Medieval and Renaissance Philosophy (EA)
SMRP........ Strategic Mobilization Requirements and Program (MCD)
SMRR........ Supplier Material Review Record (MCD)
SMRRA ...... Report. Saskatchewan Department of Mineral Resources [*A publication*]
SMRS .... Specialized Mobile Radio System
SMRS .... Specific Mobilization Reserve Stock [*Military*] (AFIT)
SM/RSF .... Ammunition Stores Management and Remote Set Fuzing (MCD)
SMRT .... Scheduled Maintenance Replacement Time
SMRT .... Single Message Rate Timing
SMRU .... Sea Mammal Research Unit [*British*] (ARC)
SMRV .... Squirrel Monkey Retravirus
SMRVA....... Sloan Management Review [*A publication*]
SMRVS....... Small Modular Recovery Vehicle System [*Nuclear energy*]
SMRY .... Summary (FAAC)
SMS .... Marine Service Squadron
SMS .... Sa Majeste Suedoise [*His, or Her, Swedish Majesty*] [*French*] (ROG)
SMS .... Saint Marie [*Madagascar*] [*Airport symbol*] (OAG)
SMS .... Saint Mary's Seminary [*Connecticut; Missouri; Ohio; Vermont*]
SMS .... Samos [*Greece*] [*Seismograph station code, US Geological Survey*] [*Closed*] (SEIS)
SMS .... Satellite Motion Simulator
SMS .... Scandinavian Migraine Society (EA)
SMS .... Scientific Mission Support
SMS .... Screen Management System [*Computer technology*]
SMS .... Semiconductor-Metal-Semiconductor
SMS .... Sensor Monitoring Set (MCD)
SMS .... Separation Mechanism Subsystem [*NASA*] (NASA)
SMS .... Sequence Milestone System
SMS .... Serial Motor Seizures [*Medicine*]

SMS .... Shared Mass Storage
SMS .... Ship Motion Simulator
SMS .... Ship's Missile System (MCD)
SMS .... Shuttle Mission Simulator [*NASA*] (NASA)
SMS .... Signal Messenger Service (NATG)
SMS .... Signal Missile Support [*Air Force*] (MUGU)
SMS .... Silane to Molten Silane [*Photovoltaic energy systems*]
SMS .... Silico-Manganese Steel
SMS .... Skandinavisk Migraeneselskab [*Scandinavian Migraine Society*] (EA-IO)
SMS .... Small Magnetospheric Satellite [*NASA*]
Sm & S ...... Smith and Sager's Drainage Cases [*Canada*] (DLA)
SMS .... Solar Maximum Satellite (MCD)
SMS .... Spanish Market Selection [*Cigars*]
SMS .... Spares Management System
SMS .... Special Mint Set [*Numismatics*]
SMS .... Spin Motor Supply
SMS .... Standard Material Specification (MCD)
SMS .... Standard Modular System
SMS .... Standard Molecular System
SMS .... Startling Mystery Stories [*A publication*]
SMS .... State Mutual Securities Trust [*NYSE symbol*]
SMS .... Stationary Meteorological Satellite [*NASA*]
SMS .... Stores Management System (MCD)
SMS .... Strategic Missile Squadron [*Air Force*]
SMS .... Structures and Mechanical System [*Skylab*] [*NASA*]
SMS .... Student Monitoring System [*Vocational guidance*]
SMS .... Studier i Modern Sprakvetenskap [*A publication*]
SMS .... Subject Matter Specialist
SMS .... Sumter, SC [*Location identifier*] [*FAA*] (FAAL)
SMS .... Surface Missile Ship (MUGU)
SMS .... Surface Missile System [*NASA*]
SMS .... SURTASS Measurement System [*Navy*] (CAAL)
SMS .... Suspended Maneuvering System [*McDonnell Douglas Corp.*] (MCD)
SMS .... Switching and Maintenance Set
SMS .... Synchronous Meteorological Satellite [*NASA*]
SMS .... Synoptic Meteorological Sounding
SMS .... Syro-Mesopotamian Studies [*Malibu, CA*] [*A publication*] (BJA)
SMS .... System Migration Section [*Social Security Administration*]
SMS .... Systems Maintenance Sector [*Electronics*] (FAAC)
SMS .... Systems Maintenance Service (MCD)
SMSA........ Seaman Apprentice, Signalman, Striker [*Navy rating*]
SMSA........ Shop Missile Assembly and Maintenance
SMSA........ Signal Missile Support Agency [*Air Force*] (AAG)
SMSA........ Standard Metropolitan Statistical Area [*Later, MSA*] [*Census Bureau*]
SMSA........ Super-Cooled Infrared Multispectral Survey and Analysis [*Traces mineral deposits*]
SMSAE...... Surface Missile System Availability Evaluation [*NASA*] (KSC)
SMSanE.... Master of Science in Sanitary Engineering
SMSB........ Strategic Missile Support Base [*Air Force*] (AFM)
SMSC........ Service Module Sequence Controller [*NASA*]
SMSC........ Southeastern Missouri State College
SMSC........ Standard Microsystems Corporation [*NASDAQ symbol*] (NQ)
SMSC........ Standard Modular System Card [*Data processing*] (BUR)
SMSC........ State Manpower Service Council [*Department of Labor*]
SMSCC...... Shuttle Mission Simulator Computer Complex [*NASA*] (MCD)
SMSD........ Ship Magnetic Submarine Detector
SMSE........ Systems Maintenance Sector Electronics (FAAC)
SMSF........ Special Maintenance Support Facility (MCD)
SMSG........ School Management Study Group (EA)
SMSG........ Self-Mutilators Support Group [*Chicago, IL*] (EA)
SMSGT ...... Senior Master Sergeant
SMSH........ Sisters of Sainte Marthe [*of St. Hyacinthe*] [*Roman Catholic religious order*]
SMSI .... Standard Manned Space Flight Initiator [*NASA*] (NASA)
SMSI .... State Microscopical Society of Illinois (EA)
SMSI .... Strong Metal-Support Interaction [*Catalysis*]
SMSIP .... Surface Missile Ship Improvement Program (MCD)
SMSJ........ Scott's Monthly Stamp Journal [*A publication*]
SMSM .... Missionary Sisters of the Society of Mary [*Marist Sisters*] [*Roman Catholic religious order*]
SMSMS ..... Strategic Missile Squadron Munitions Section [*Air Force*] (AAG)
SMSN........ Seaman, Signalman, Striker [*Navy rating*]
SMSO........ Subcontract Material Sales Order
Sm & Sod L & T ... Smith and Soden on Landlord and Tenant [*2nd ed.*] [*1878*] (DLA)
SMSP........ St. Peter's Abbey and College, Muenster, Saskatchewan [*Library symbol*] [*National Library of Canada*] (NLC)
SMSP........ Security Military Space Program (MUGU)
SMSP........ Soil Moisture Strength Prediction [*Army*]
SMSpr........ Studier i Modern Sprakvetenskap [*A publication*]
SMSR........ Studi e Materiali di Storia della Religioni [*A publication*]
SMS Report ... Socioeconomic Monitoring System Report [*A publication*]
SMSRL....... Sarah Mellon Scaife Radiation Laboratory [*University of Pittsburgh*] (MCD)
SMSRS....... Shipboard Meteorological Satellite Readout Station

SMSS .... School of Management and Strategic Studies [*Founded 1982 by Richard Farson, offers a two-year management program through GTE Telenet*]
SMSS .... Studies in Management Science and Systems [*Elsevier Book Series*] [*A publication*]
SMSV .... San Miguel Sea Lion Virus
SMT .... S-Band Megawatt Transmit
SMT .... Sacred Marriage Texts   (BJA)
SMT .... Samuel Manu-Tech, Inc. [*Toronto Stock Exchange symbol*]
SMT .... Saturn Missile Test [*NASA*]
SMT .... Segmented Mirror Telescope [*Astronomy*]
SMT .... Senior Medical Technician
SMT .... Service Module Technician [*NASA*]   (KSC)
SMT .... Sexual Medicine Today [*A publication*]
SMT .... Shelter Management Training [*Civil Defense*]
SMT .... Ship Maintenance Test
SMT .... Shipboard Marriage Test
SMT .... Ship's Mean Time [*Navigation*]
SMT .... Shop Mechanic's Test
SMT .... Small Missile Telecamera
SMT .... South Dakota School of Mines and Technology, Rapid City, SD [*OCLC symbol*]   (OCLC)
SMT .... Square Mesh Tracking [*Air Force*]
SMT .... Stabilized March Technique
SMT .... Standard Measurement Technique [*Navy*]
SMT .... Studies in Modern Thermodynamics [*Elsevier Book Series*] [*A publication*]
SMT .... Submit   (FAAC)
SMT .... Sultan-Mazar [*USSR*] [*Seismograph station code, US Geological Survey*] [*Closed*]   (SEIS)
SMT .... Summit   (MCD)
SMT .... Supermedial Thigh [*Flap for plastic surgery*]
SMT .... Supplementary Monophonic Transmission   (ADA)
SMT .... Supply, Maintenance, and Transportation [*Directorate*] [*Army*]   (RDA)
SMT .... Surface Missile Test [*Navy*]   (CAAL)
SMT .... Surface Mount Technology [*Electronics*]
SMT .... System Maintenance Test
SMT .... System Maintenance Trainer   (MCD)
SMT .... System Modulation Transfer [*Acutance*] [*Photography*]
SMT .... Systems Manufacturing Technology [*San Marcos, CA*]
SMTA .... Sewing Machine Trade Association [*Stamford, CT*]   (EA)
SMTA .... Surface Mount Technology Association [*Los Gatos, CA*]   (EA)
SMTAS ...... Shuttle Module Test and Analysis System   (MCD)
SMTC .... Sa Majeste Tres Chretienne [*His, or Her, Most Christian Majesty*] [*French*]
SMTD .... Short Take-Off and Landing and Maneuvering Technology Demonstrator [*Air Force*]
SMTE .... Society for Music Teacher Education   (EA)
SMTF .... Sa Majeste Tres Fidele [*His, or Her, Most Faithful Majesty*] [*French*]
SMTF .... Spacecraft Magnetic Test Facility [*Goddard Space Flight Center*] [*NASA*]
SMTG .... Solid-State and Molecular Theory Group [*MIT*]   (MCD)
SMTH .... Smooth   (FAAC)
SMTI .... Selective Moving Target Indicator   (IEEE)
SMTI .... Sodium Mechanisms Test Installation [*Nuclear energy*]   (NRCH)
SMTI .... Southeastern Massachusetts Technological Institute [*Later, Southeastern Massachusetts University*]
SMTK .... Sump Tank
SMTM .... Sometime   (FAAC)
SMTN .... Smoky Mountain R. R. [*AAR code*]
SMTS .... Synchronous Meteorological Test Satellite [*NASA*]
SMTT .... Small Bowel Transit Time [*Gastroenterology*]
SMU .... St. Mary's University Library [*UTLAS symbol*]
SMU .... Scottish Mothers' Union [*Episcopalian*]
SMU .... Secondary Multiplexing Unit
SMU .... Self-Maneuvering Unit [*Air Force*]
SMU .... Sheep Mountain, AK [*Location identifier*] [*FAA*]   (FAAL)
SMU .... Single Motor Unit
SMU .... Sociedadas Mexicanas Unedas   (EA)
SMU .... Soft Mockup   (MCD)
SMU .... Southeastern Massachusetts University [*North Dartmouth*]
SMU .... Southeastern Massachusetts University, North Dartmouth, MA [*OCLC symbol*]   (OCLC)
SMU .... Southern Methodist University [*Texas*]
SMU .... Spectrum Monitoring Unit
SMU .... Store Monitor Unit
SMU .... Sunnyside Mine [*Utah*] [*Seismograph station code, US Geological Survey*] [*Closed*]   (SEIS)
SMU .... Super-Module Unit [*Telecommunications*]   (TEL)
SMU .... System Maintenance Unit [*Data processing*]
SMU .... System Monitoring Unit
SMUC .... Societe de Musique des Universites Canadiennes [*Canadian University Music Society - CUMS*]
SMUD .... Sacramento Municipal Utility District [*Photovoltaic energy systems*]
SMUG .... Smuggling [*FBI standardized term*]
SMus .... Studia Musicologica [*Budapest*] [*A publication*]
S Mus D ...... Doctor of Sacred Music

SMUSE .... Socialist Movement for the United States of Europe
SMUT .... Shrink Mock-Up Template   (MSA)
SMV .... Samovar Hills, AK [*Location identifier*] [*FAA*]   (FAAL)
SMV .... Samsville [*Illinois*] [*Seismograph station code, US Geological Survey*]   (SEIS)
SMV .... Santa Maria Valley Railroad Co. [*AAR code*]
SMV .... Satellite Mutual Visibility
SMV .... Sinusoidal Membrane Vesicle [*Anatomy*]
SMV .... Slow Moving Vehicle [*Emblem to prevent rear-end collisions*]
SM/V .... Squared-Mean to Variance
SMV .... Studi Mediolatini e Volgari [*A publication*]
SMV .... Superior Mesenteric Vein [*Anatomy*]
SMVH .... Service in Military and Veterans Hospitals [*Red Cross*]
SMVMA ...... Sbornik Trudov. Moskovskii Vechernii Metallurgicheskii Institut [*A publication*]
SMVP .... Shuttle Master Verification Plan [*NASA*]   (NASA)
SMVRD ..... Shuttle Master Verification Requirements Document [*NASA*]   (NASA)
SMW .... Second Main Watch
SMW .... Sheet Metal Workers' International Association   (EA)
SMW .... Simpatico Wines [*Vancouver Stock Exchange symbol*]
SMW .... Slotted Metal Window
SMW .... Smara [*Morocco*] [*Airport symbol*]   (OAG)
SMW .... Society of Magazine Writers [*Later, ASJA*]   (EA)
SMW .... Society of Military Widows   (EA)
SMW .... South Mountain [*Washington*] [*Seismograph station code, US Geological Survey*]   (SEIS)
SMW .... Standard Materials Worksheet [*NASA*]   (NASA)
SMW .... Strategic Missile Wing [*Air Force*]
S Mw .... Studien zur Musikwissenschaft [*A publication*]
SMWC .... Saint Mary-of-the-Woods College [*Indiana*]
SMWDSEP ... Single, Married, Widowed, Divorced, Separated
SMWG .... Strategic Missile Wing [*Air Force*]
SMWIA .... Sheet Metal Workers' International Association
SMWP .... Strategic Mobility Work Project [*Army*]   (AABC)
SMX .... Santa Maria [*California*] [*Airport symbol*]   (OAG)
SMX .... Santa Maria, CA [*Location identifier*] [*FAA*]   (FAAL)
SMX .... Semi-Micro Xerography
SMX .... Submultiplexer Unit
SMX .... Sulfamethoxazole [*Also, S, SMZ*] [*Antibacterial compound*]
SMY .... Ark Valley Airways [*Arkansas City, KS*] [*FAA designator*]   (FAAC)
SMY .... Marianna, FL [*Location identifier*] [*FAA*]   (FAAL)
SMY .... Scientist-Man Year
SMY .... Shemya [*Alaska*] [*Seismograph station code, US Geological Survey*]   (SEIS)
SMY .... Simenti [*Senegal*] [*Airport symbol*]   (OAG)
SMY .... Smyrna Public Library, Smyrna, DE [*OCLC symbol*]   (OCLC)
Smy .... Smythe's Irish Common Pleas Reports [*1839-40*]   (DLA)
SMY .... Solar Maximum Year [*August, 1979-February, 1981*]
SMY .... Summary   (MSA)
Smy & B ..... Smythe and Bourke's Irish Marriage Cases [*1842*]   (DLA)
SMYS .... Specified Minimum Yield Strength
Smythe .... Smythe's Irish Common Pleas Reports [*1839-40*]   (DLA)
S Mz .... Schweizerische Musikzeitung/Revue Musicale Suisse [*A publication*]
SMZ .... Stoelmanseiland [*Suriname*] [*Airport symbol*]   (OAG)
SMZ .... Sulfamethoxazole [*Also, S, SMX*] [*Antibacterial compound*]
sn----- .... Andean Area [*MARC geographic area code*] [*Library of Congress*]   (LCCP)
SN .... Parke, Davis & Co. [*Research code symbol*]
SN .... Sacramento Northern Railway [*AAR code*]
SN .... Safety Notice   (MCD)
SN .... Sample Name
SN .... San
SN .... Santa [*Saint*] [*Italian*]
SN .... Santo
SN .... Saponification Number [*Analytical chemistry*]
SN .... Saturday Night [*A publication*]
SN .... Science News [*A publication*]
SN .... Scientific Note
SN .... Seaman [*Navy rating*]
SN .... Secretary of the Navy
SN .... Sector Number   (MUGU)
SN .... Secundum Naturam [*Naturally*] [*Latin*]
SN .... See Note   (ROG)
SN .... Semiconductor Network   (IEEE)
SN .... Senegal [*Two-letter standard code*]   (CNC)
S/N .... Sequence Number
SN .... Sergeant Navigator [*British*]
SN .... Serial Number
SN .... Service Note   (MSA)
SN .... Service Number [*Military*]
SN .... Session Notes [*Scotland*]   (DLA)
SN .... Shakespeare Newsletter [*A publication*]
SN .... Shalom Network   (EA)
SN .... Shaping Network   (MCD)
Sn .... Shingle [*Quality of the bottom*] [*Nautical charts*]
SN .... Shipping Note [*Business and trade*]
S/N .... Shipping Number
SN .... Side Note

SN .... Sigma Nu [*A national fraternity*]
SN .... Sign (BUR)
SN .... Signal Node
S/N .... Signal to Noise Ratio [*Unweighted*] (CMD)
SN .... Sine [*Without*] [*Latin*]
SN .... Sine of the Amplitude (IEEE)
SN .... Sinoatrial Node [*Medicine*]
SN .... Siren
SN .... Slovensky Narodopis [*A publication*]
SN .... Small-Probe Nephelometer [*NASA*]
SN .... Snellen [*Test types*] [*Ophthalmology*]
SN .... Snow [*Meteorology*] (FAAC)
SN .... Societe Anonyme Belge d'Exploitation de la Navigation
 Aerienne [*Sabena Belgian World Airlines*] [*ICAO
 designator*] (FAAC)
SN .... Society for Neuroscience (EA)
SN .... Solid Neutral
S/N .... Sons of Norway (EA)
SN .... Sovetskaja Nauka [*A publication*]
SN .... Special Nuclear [*Material*]
S/N .... Speech/Noise [*Ratio*] [*Electronics*]
SN .... Sponsoring Agency [*Online database field identifier*]
SN .... Sporting News [*A publication*]
SN .... Standard Nomenclature
SN .... Standard Oil Co. (Indiana) [*NYSE symbol*] [*Toronto Stock
 Exchange symbol*]
Sn .... Stannum [*Tin*] [*Chemical element*]
S & N .... Statesman and Nation [*A publication*]
SN .... Stationing Flag [*Navy*] [*British*]
sn .... Stereospecifically Numbered [*Biochemistry*]
SN .... Sterling Nuclear Plant (NRCH)
sn .... Sthene [*Absolute unit of force*]
SN .... Stock Number (MCD)
SN .... Story of the Nations [*A publication*]
S-N .... Stress Number (NASA)
SN .... Stronnictwo Narodowe [*Nationalist Party*] [*Poland*] (PPE)
SN .... Strouhal Number [*Sound*]
SN .... Student Nurse
SN .... Studia Neophilologica [*A publication*]
SN .... Subnormal
SN .... Substantia Nigra [*Brain anatomy*]
SN .... Supernatant [*Chemistry*]
SN .... Supernova
SN .... Suprasternal Notch [*Anatomy*]
SN .... Survey Number
SN .... Syllable Number [*Entomology*]
SN .... Synchronizers [*JETDS nomenclature*] [*Military*] (CET)
SN .... Systems/Strategic Navigation [*Aviation*] (FAAC)
S-N (Plane) ... Sella Turcica-Nasion [*Plane that passes through these points*]
 [*Cephalometrics*]
SNA .... Orange County [*California*] [*Airport symbol*] (OAG)
SNA .... Sadr Nizamut Adalat Reports [*India*] (DLA)
SNA .... Sanae [*Antarctica*] [*Geomagnetic observatory code*]
SNA .... Sanae [*Antarctica*] [*Seismograph station code, US Geological
 Survey*] (SEIS)
SNA .... Santa Ana, CA [*Location identifier*] [*FAA*] (FAAC)
SNA .... Santana Petroleum [*Vancouver Stock Exchange symbol*]
SNA .... Satellite Networking Associates, Inc. [*New York, NY*]
 [*Telecommunications*] (TSSD)
SNA .... Saudi News Agency (BJA)
SNA .... Scandinavian Neurological Association (EA)
SNA .... Schlaraffia Nordamerika (EA)
SNA .... Sella, Nasion, A [*Anthropometric landmark*]
SNA .... Shakespeariana [*A publication*]
SNA .... Snap-On Tools Corp. [*NYSE symbol*]
SNa .... Sot la Nape [*A publication*]
SNA .... Soviet Naval Aviation
SNA .... Student Naval Aviator
SNA .... Suburban Newspapers of America [*An association*] [*Formed by
 a merger of AHNA and Suburban Section of the National
 Newspaper Association*] [*Chicago, IL*] (EA)
SNA .... Sudan News Agency (BJA)
SNA .... Syrian News Agency (BJA)
SNA .... System of National Accounts [*United Nations*]
SNA .... Systems Network Architecture [*IBM Corp.*] [*Data processing*]
SNAB .... Stock Number Action Bulletin
SNA Beng ... Sadr Nizamut Adalat Reports [*1805-50*] [*Bengal, India*] (DLA)
SNA Beng (NS) ... Sadr Nizamut Adalat Reports, New Series [*1851-59*]
 [*Bengal, India*] (DLA)
SNACC ...... Society of Neurosurgical Anesthesia and Critical Care
 [*Richmond, VA*] (EA)
SNACS ...... Share News on Automatic Coding Systems [*Data processing*]
SNACS ...... Single Nuclear Attack Case Study [*DoD*]
SNACS ...... Stock Number Assignment Control System [*Air Force*] (AFM)
SNADIGC ... Sindacato Nazionale Dipendenti Ministero Grazia e Giustizia
 [*National Union of Ministry of Justice Employees*] [*Italy*]
SNAF........ Soviet Naval Air Force
SNAFU .... Situation Normal, All Fouled Up [*Military slang*] [*Bowdlerized
 version*]
SNAG .... Short Notes on Alaskan Geology. Alaska Department of
 Natural Resources. Geologic Report [*A publication*]

SNAG .... Society of North American Goldsmiths (EA)
SNagg .... Serum Normal Agglutinator [*Hematology*]
SNAIAS ...... Ship's Navigation and Aircraft Inertial Alignment System
 [*Navy*] (NG)
SNAKE .... Stochastic Network Adaptive Kinematics Evaluator
SNAME ..... Society of Naval Architects and Marine Engineers (EA)
SNANSC ... Society of Neurosurgical Anesthesia and Neurological
 Supportive Care [*Later, SNACC*] (EA)
SNAP......... Sarawak National Party [*Malaysian*] (PPW)
SNAP......... Satellite Nuclear Auxiliary Power [*Military*] (CAAL)
SNAP......... Selective Niobium Anodization Process [*Semiconductor
 technology*]
SNAP......... Senior Naval Aviator Present
SNAP......... Sensory Nerve Action Potential [*Neurophysiology*]
SNAP......... Shelter Neighborhood Action Project
SNAP......... Shielded Neutron Assay Probe [*Nuclear energy*] (NRCH)
SNAP......... Shipboard Nontactical ADP Program [*Navy*] (CAAL)
SNAP......... Short Notice Annual Practice [*Military*]
SNAP......... Simplified Needs Assessment Profile System [*Developed by
 Texas Instruments, Inc.*]
SNAP......... Simplified Numerical Automatic Programer [*Data processing*]
SNAP......... Single Number Access Plan [*Telecommunications*] (TEL)
SNAP......... Six Node Averaging Program [*Data processing*]
SNAP......... Small Nuclear Adapted Power Source
SNAP......... Small Nuclear Auxiliary Power
SNAP......... Society of National Association Publications [*Washington,
 DC*] (EA)
SNAP......... Soviet Nuclear Artillery Projectile (MCD)
SNAP......... Space Nuclear Auxiliary Power
SNAP......... Staffing Needs Assessment Process
SNAP......... Standard Navy Accounting Procedures
SNAP......... Standard Network Access Protocol [*Data processing*]
SNAP......... Steerable Null Antenna Processor (RDA)
SNAP......... Sterile Nitrogen Atmosphere Processing
SNAP......... Structural Network Analysis Program
SNAP......... Student Naval Aviation Pilot
SNAP......... Summary of Navy Approved Programs
SNAP......... Supersonic Nonequilibrium Analysis Program (MCD)
SNAP......... Switching Network Analysis Program [*Bell System*]
SNAP......... System Network Activity Program [*Sperry UNIVAC*]
SNAP......... Systematic National Acquisitions Programme [*Public Archives
 of Canada*]
SNAP......... Systems for Nuclear Auxiliary Power
SNAP(G).... Student Naval Aviation Pilot (Glider)
SNAPS .... Standard Notes and Parts Selection (TEL)
SNAPS .... State and National Apprenticeship Program Statistics [*Bureau
 of Apprenticeship and Training*] [*Department of Labor*]
SNAPS .... Switching Node and Processing Sites [*ITT*] (TEL)
SNAPTRAN ... Systems for Nuclear Auxiliary Power Transient
SNARE .... Sandia Nuclear Assembly for Reactor Experiments
SNARL .... Suggested No Adverse Risk Levels [*Environmental Protection
 Agency*]
SNAS .... Student Need Analysis System
SNASE ...... Sindacato Nazionale Autonomo Scuola Elementare [*Primary
 teachers association*] [*Rome, Italy*]
SNASOR .... Static Nonlinear Analysis of Shells of Revolution [*Computer
 program*]
SNAT......... Serotonin N-Acetyltransferase [*An enzyme*]
SNAT......... Southern National Corp. [*NASDAQ symbol*] (NQ)
SNAV .... Sindacato Nazionale Attrazionisti Viaggianti [*National Union of
 Traveling Entertainers*] [*Italy*]
SNB........... Lakeland Library Region, North Battleford, Saskatchewan
 [*Library symbol*] [*National Library of Canada*] (NLC)
SNB........... Scalene Node Biopsy [*Medicine*]
SNB........... Sella, Nasion, B [*Anthropometric landmark*]
SNB........... Sierra Nevada Batholith [*Geology*]
SNB........... Snake Bay [*Australia*] [*Airport symbol*] (OAG)
SNB........... Soviet News Bureau
SNB........... Spinal Nucleus of the Bulbocavernosus [*Neuroanatomy*]
SNB........... Sunbird, Inc. D/B/A Sunbird Airlines, Inc. [*Murray, KY*] [*FAA
 designator*] (FAAC)
SNB........... Swiss National Bank
SNBL......... Second National Building & Land [*NASDAQ symbol*] (NQ)
SNBL......... Sioux City & New Orleans Barge Line [*AAR code*]
SNBNK....... Snowbank (FAAC)
SNBR........ Snubber [*Mechanical engineering*]
SNBU .... Switched Network Backup [*Data processing*] (IBMDP)
SNC........... Apollo Airways, Inc. D/B/A Pacific Coast Airlines [*Goleta, CA*]
 [*FAA designator*] (FAAC)
SNC........... Saint Norbert College [*Wisconsin*]
SNC........... San Antonio College, San Antonio, TX [*OCLC symbol*] (OCLC)
SNC........... San Nicolas Island [*California*] [*Seismograph station code, US
 Geological Survey*] [*Closed*] (SEIS)
SNC........... Sanitary Corps [*Army*]
snc .... Saskatchewan [*MARC country of publication code*] [*Library of
 Congress*] (LCCP)
SNC........... Satellite News Channel [*Cable-television system*] [*Went off the
 air October, 1983*]
S/NC......... Satisfactory/No Credit [*University grading system*]
SNC........... School of Naval Co-Operation [*Air Force*] [*British*]
SNC........... Scottish National Certificate

SNC............ Shergottites, Nakhlites, and Chassignites [*Meteorite components*]
SNC............ Shipped Not Credited [*Military*]   (AFIT)
SNC............ Standard Navigation Computer
SNC............ Submarine Net Controller   (MCD)
SNC............ Sunatco Development Corporation [*Vancouver Stock Exchange symbol*]
SNC............ Swiss Nonvaleurs Club   (EA-IO)
SNC............ Syndicat National du Cinema [*National Syndicate of Motion Pictures*]
SNCA......... Seneca Oil [*NASDAQ symbol*]   (NQ)
SNCC........ Student National [*formerly, Nonviolent*] Coordinating Committee [*Pronounced "snick"*]   (EA)
SNCC........ System Network Computer Center [*Louisiana State University*] [*Research center*]   (RCD)
SNCCDIPP ... Selected Non-Communist Countries Defense Intelligence Projection for Planning   (MCD)
SNCF......... Societe Nationale des Chemins de Fer Francais [*French National Railways*]
SNCFA....... Societe Nationale des Chemins de Fer Algeriens [*Algerian Railways*]
SNCI.......... Societe Nationale de Credit et d'Investissement [*Credit institution*] [*Luxembourg*]
SNCL......... Serial Number Configuration List   (MCD)
SNCLAR.... University of Santa Clara School of Law   (DLA)
SNCLF....... Societe de Neuro-Chirurgie de Langue Francaise [*Society of French-Speaking Neurosurgeons - SFSN*]   (EA)
SNCM........ Second Nicaraguan Campaign Medal
SNCO........ Seaport Navigation Co. [*AAR code*]
SNCO........ Second National Corporation [*NASDAQ symbol*]   (NQ)
SNCO........ Senior Noncommissioned Officer
SNCO........ Staff Noncommissioned Officer [*Military*]
SNCOC...... Senior Noncommissioned Officer Course
SNCP......... Salem National Corporation [*NASDAQ symbol*]   (NQ)
SNCP......... Special Navy Control Program   (MCD)
SND........... San Diego - College [*California*] [*Seismograph station code, US Geological Survey*]   (SEIS)
SND........... Sand   (FAAC)
SND........... Sanford, FL [*Location identifier*] [*FAA*]   (FAAL)
SND........... Sanfred Resources [*Vancouver Stock Exchange symbol*]
SND........... Sap No Defect
SND........... Scottish National Dictionary [*A publication*]
SND........... Scottish National Diploma
SND........... Second Class Passengers [*Shipping*] [*British*]
SND........... Selected Natural Diamond
SND........... Self-Powered Neutron Detector
SND........... Semiconductor Neutron Dosimeter
snd........... Sindhi [*MARC language code*] [*Library of Congress*]   (LCCP)
SND........... Sisters of Notre Dame [*Roman Catholic religious order*]
SND........... Sisters of Notre Dame de Namur [*Roman Catholic religious order*]
SND........... Society of Newspaper Design   (EA)
SND........... Sound   (AAG)
SND........... Standardized Normal Distribution
SND........... Static No Delivery
SNDA......... Scottish National Dictionary Association
SNDA......... Student National Dental Association   (EA)
SNDC......... Serbian National Defense Council   (EA)
SNDG......... Sending   (MSA)
SNDG......... Sounding   (MSA)
SNDL......... Sandale R. R. [*AAR code*]
SNDL......... Standard Navy Distribution List
SNDL......... Studienausgaben zur Neueren Deutschen Literatur [*A publication*]
SNDLF....... Societe de Nutrition et de Dietetique de Langue Francaise [*French-Language Society of Nutrition and Dietetics - FLSND*] [*Paris, France*]   (EA-IO)
SND-MB..... Selected Natural Diamond - Metal Bond
SNDO........ Standard Nomenclature of Diseases and Operations
SNDPRF..... Soundproof   (MSA)
SNDR........ Shimane Daigaku Ronshu: Jinbun Kagaku [*Journal of the Shimane University: Humanistic Sciences*] [*A publication*]
SNDS......... Stock Number Data Section   (MCD)
SNDSB....... Sonderschule [*A publication*]
SNDT......... Shreemati Nathibai Domodar Thackersey Women's University [*India*]
SNDT......... Society for Nondestructive Testing [*Later, ASNT*]   (KSC)
SNDV........ Strategic Nuclear Delivery Vehicles [*Army*]   (AABC)
SNE........... Santa Elena, TX [*Location identifier*] [*FAA*]   (FAAL)
SNE........... Sao Nicolau [*Cape Verde Islands*] [*Airport symbol*]   (OAG)
SNE........... Severe Noise Environment
SNE........... Shawnee Airlines [*Orlando, FL*] [*FAA designator*]   (FAAC)
SNE........... Society for Nutrition Education [*Oakland, CA*]   (EA)
SNE........... Sony Corp. [*NYSE symbol*] [*Toronto Stock Exchange symbol*] [*Vancouver Stock Exchange symbol*]
SNE........... Spatial Nonemotional (Stimuli)
SNE........... Subacute Necrotizing Encephalomyelopathy [*Medicine*]
SNE........... Syndicat National de l'Edition [*French publishers' association*]
SNEA......... Societe Nationale Elf Aquitaine [*National Elf Aquitaine Company*] [*Paris, France*] [*Information service*]   (EISS)
SNEA......... Student National Education Association   (EA)

SNEC......... Saxton Nuclear Engineering Corporation
SNECI....... Sindicato Nacional dos Empregados do Comercio e da Industria da Provincia de Mocambique [*National Union of Commercial and Industrial Workers of Mozambique*]
SNECIPA ... Sindicato Nacional dos Empregados do Comercio e da Industria da Provincia de Angola [*National Syndicate of Workers of Commerce and Industry of the Province of Angola*]
SNECMA.... Societe Nationale d'Etude et de Construction de Moteurs d'Avion [*Paris, France*]
Sneed........ Sneed's Kentucky Decisions [*2 Kentucky*]   (DLA)
Sneed........ Sneed's Tennessee Reports [*33-37 Tennessee*]   (DLA)
Sneed Dec ... Sneed's Kentucky Decisions [*2 Kentucky*]   (DLA)
Sneed Tenn ... Sneed's Tennessee Reports   (DLA)
Sneed (Tenn) Rep ... Sneed's Tennessee Reports   (DLA)
SNEFU .... Situation Normal - Everything Fouled Up [*Bowdlerized version*] [*Obsolete*]   (DSUE)
SNEG .... Syndicat National des Enseignants de Guinee [*National Union of Guinean Teachers*]
SNEI.......... Societe Nouvelle d'Editions Industrielles [*Industrial News Publishing Company*] [*Paris, France*] [*Information service*]   (EISS)
SNEIA .... Sbornik Nauchnykh Trudov Ivanovskogo Energeticheskogo Instituta [*A publication*]
SNEL........ Snelling & Snelling [*NASDAQ symbol*]   (NQ)
SNEL......... Societe Nationale d'Electricite
SNEL........ Special Nuclear Effects Laboratory
Snell Eq .... Snell's Principles in Equity   (DLA)
SNELPIF .... Sindacato Nazionale Esperti Laureati Propagandisti Industrie Farmaceutiche [*National Union of University Graduated Experts for Propaganda in Pharmaceutical Industries*] [*Italy*]
SNEMSA.... Southern New England Marine Sciences Association
SNEPT .... Space Nuclear Electric Propulsion Test
SNES......... Syndicat National de l'Enseignement Secondaire [*National Union of Secondary Schoolteachers*] [*France*]
SNET......... Syndicat National de l'Enseignement Technique [*National Union of Technical School Teachers*] [*France*]
SNF .... Secret - No Foreigners [*Security classification*]
SNF .... Selskab foer Nordisk Filologi Arsberetning [*A publication*]
SNF .... Serb National Federation   (EA)
SNF .... Short-Range Nuclear Forces
SNF .... Silicon Nitride Film
SNF .... Skilled Nursing Facility
SNF .... Solids Not Fat
SNF .... Spent Nuclear Fuel
SNF .... Spot Noise Figure
SNF .... Sudanese National Front   (PD)
SNF .... System Noise Figure
SNFCC....... Shippers National Freight Claim Council [*Huntington, NY*]   (EA)
SNFL......... Standing Naval Force, Atlantic   (MCD)
SNFLD....... Secret - Limited Distribution - Not Releasable to Foreigners [*Security classification*]
SNFLK....... Snowflake   (FAAC)
SNFO .... Student Naval Flight Officer
SNFPP....... Syndicat National de la Fonction Publique Provinciale [*National Union of Provincial Government Employees - NUPGE*] [*Canada*]
SNFR......... Small-Probe Net Flux Radiometer [*NASA*]
SNFS......... Student Naval Flight Surgeon
SNG.......... San Ignacio De Velasco [*Bolivia*] [*Airport symbol*]   (OAG)
SNG.......... Sans Notre Garantie [*Without Our Guarantee*] [*Business and trade*] [*French*]
SNG.......... Solidified Nitroglycerol [*or Nitroglycerin*] [*Explosive*]
SNG.......... Songkhla [*Thailand*] [*Seismograph station code, US Geological Survey*]   (SEIS)
SNG.......... [*The*] Southern New England Telephone Co. [*NYSE symbol*]
SNG.......... Stabilization Network Group
SNG.......... Sterling Energy Corp. [*Vancouver Stock Exchange symbol*]
SNG.......... Substitute [*or Synthetic*] Natural Gas
Sng.......... Synagogue   (BJA)
SNG.......... Synthetic Natural Gas   (IEEE)
SNGA .... Sodium N-Glycoloylarsanilic [*or N-Glycolylarsanilic*] Acid [*Pharmacology*]
SNGFR .... Single Nephron Glomerular Filtration Rate
SNGL........ Single
SNGN .... Segmental Necrotizing Glomerulonephritis [*Medicine*]
SNGOD ...... Special NGO [*Nongovernmental Organization*] Committee on Disarmament   (EA)
SNGRA...... Sangre [*A publication*]
SNGS .... Salem Nuclear Generating Station   (NRCH)
SNH.......... Savannah, TN [*Location identifier*] [*FAA*]   (FAAL)
SNH.......... Signtech [*Toronto Stock Exchange symbol*]
snh .... Sinhalese [*MARC language code*] [*Library of Congress*]   (LCCP)
SNH.......... Skilled Nursing Home
SNH.......... Snatch [*Block*] [*Design engineering*]
SNH.......... Society for Nursing History [*Columbia University*] [*New York, NY*]   (EA)

SNH............ Sunshine Point [*Alaska*] [*Seismograph station code, US Geological Survey*]   (SEIS)
SNI............. National Intelligence Service [*Zairian*]   (PD)
SNI............. San Nicolas Island
SNI............. Selective Notification of Information
SNI............. Sequence Number Indicator
SNI............. Signal-to-Noise Improvement [*Data transmission*]   (IEEE)
SNI............. Sinoe [*Liberia*] [*Airport symbol*]   (OAG)
SNI............. Sistema Nacional de Informacion [*National Information System*] [*Colombia*]   (EISS)
SNI............. Sonor Investments Ltd. [*Toronto Stock Exchange symbol*]
SNI............. Sports Network, Incorporated [*Later, HSN*]
SNI............. Standard Network Interconnection [*Telecommunications*]
SNI............. Sun City Industries, Inc. [*American Stock Exchange symbol*]
SNI............. Syndicat National des Instituteurs [*National Union of Teachers*] [*France*]
SNIC Bull ... SNIC [*Singapore National Institute of Chemistry*] Bulletin [*A publication*]
SNIE.......... Sindacato Nazionale Insegnanti Elementari [*National Union of Elementary Teachers*] [*Italy*]
SNIE.......... Special National Intelligence Estimates [*See also SNIE's*]   (MCD)
SNIE's .... Special National Intelligence Estimates [*Summaries of foreign policy information and advice prepared for the president*] [*Known informally as "sneeze"*]
SNIFFEX .... Sniffer [*Exhaust trail indicator*] Exercise [*Military*]   (NVT)
SNIMOG..... Sustained Noninflationary Market-Oriented Growth
SNIP.......... Single Net Information and Position [*Reporting procedures*] [*Navy*]   (NVT)
SNIP.......... Single Net Integrated Procedure [*Military*]   (CAAL)
SNIPE........ Soviet Naval Interdiction Possibilities, Europe
SNIR........... Signal-to-Noise Plus Interference Ratio
SNIRD........ Supposedly Noiseless Infrared Detector
SNIT .... Stock Number Identification Table
SNIVT........ Society of Non-Invasive Vascular Technology [*Columbus, OH*]   (EA)
SNJ .... Everett, WA [*Location identifier*] [*FAA*]   (FAAL)
SNJ .... Sinj [*Yugoslavia*] [*Seismograph station code, US Geological Survey*] [*Closed*]   (SEIS)
SNJM .... Sisters of the Holy Names of Jesus and Mary [*Roman Catholic religious order*]
SNK........... Shannock Corp. [*Vancouver Stock Exchange symbol*]
SNK........... Snyder, TX [*Location identifier*] [*FAA*]   (FAAL)
SNK........... Student-Newman-Keuls [*Statistical procedure*]
SNK........... Swank, Inc. [*NYSE symbol*]
SNKL........ Snorkel   (MSA)
SNL .... Department of State Newsletter [*A publication*]
SNL .... Sample Noise Level
SNL .... Sandia National Laboratories [*Department of Energy*]
SNL .... Satire Newsletter [*A publication*]
SNL .... Saturday Night Live [*Television program*]
SNL .... Selected Nodes List [*Telecommunications*]   (TEL)
SNL .... Seminole Resources, Inc. [*Vancouver Stock Exchange symbol*]
SNL .... Sevenhill [*Australia*] [*Seismograph station code, US Geological Survey*] [*Closed*]   (SEIS)
SNL .... Shakespeare Newsletter [*A publication*]
SNL .... Shawnee, OK [*Location identifier*] [*FAA*]   (FAAL)
SNL .... Somali National League
SNL .... Soonair Lines, Inc. [*Tulsa, OK*] [*FAA designator*]   (FAAC)
SNL .... Spore Newsletter [*A publication*]
SNL .... Standard Name Line
SNL .... Standard Nomenclature List [*Military*]
SNL .... State Narcotic Law
SNL .... Stock Not Listed   (AAG)
SNL .... Sun Chemical Corp. [*NYSE symbol*]
SNLA........ Sandia National Laboratory (Albuquerque)
SNLC......... Senior NATO Logistician Conference   (NATG)
SNLG........ Signaling   (MSA)
SNLN......... Saskatchewan Native Library Services Newsletter [*A publication*]
SNLR......... Services No Longer Required
SNLS........ Society for New Language Study   (EA)
SNLT......... Sunlite, Inc. [*NASDAQ symbol*]   (NQ)
SNM .... Saint Mary's University, San Antonio, TX [*OCLC symbol*]   (OCLC)
SNM .... Satellite Navigation Map
SNM .... Sbornik Narodniho Muzea [*A publication*]
SNM .... Senior Naval Member
SNM .... Signal-to-Noise Merit
SNM .... Sindacato Nazionale Medici [*Doctors association*] [*Rome, Italy*]
SNM .... Society of Nuclear Medicine [*New York, NY*]   (EA)
SNM .... Socorro [*New Mexico*] [*Seismograph station code, US Geological Survey*]   (SEIS)
SNM .... Somali National Movement   (PD)
SNM .... Special Nuclear Materials
SNM .... Spent Nuclear Material   (IEEE)
SNM .... Square Nautical Mile   (NVT)
SNM .... Subject Named Member   (NVT)
SNM .... Sulfanilamide [*Antimicrobial compound*]
SNM .... Sunmask Petroleum [*Vancouver Stock Exchange symbol*]
SNMA........ Sonoma Vineyards [*NASDAQ symbol*]   (NQ)

SNMA......... Student National Medical Association   (EA)
SNMCB ...... Scheduled Not Mission Capable Both [*Maintenance and supply*]   (MCD)
SNMCM ..... Scheduled Not Mission Capable Maintenance   (MCD)
SNMD........ Sunrise Medical, Inc. [*NASDAQ symbol*]   (NQ)
SNMDCS... Standard Navy Maintenance Data Collection System
SNMMMIS ... Standard Navy Maintenance and Material Management Information System
SNMMMS.. Standard Navy Maintenance and Material Management System
SNMP .... Spent Nuclear Material Pool   (IEEE)
SNMS........ Secondary Neutrals Mass Spectrometry
SNMT......... Society of Nuclear Medical Technologists [*Defunct*]   (EA)
SNN........... Shannon [*Ireland*] [*Airport symbol*]   (OAG)
SNN........... Shared Nearest Neighbor   (MCD)
SNN........... Sienna Resources Ltd. [*Toronto Stock Exchange symbol*] [*Vancouver Stock Exchange symbol*]
SNN........... Sining [*Republic of China*] [*Seismograph station code, US Geological Survey*]   (SEIS)
SNN........... Smith College, Northampton, MA [*OCLC symbol*]   (OCLC)
SNN........... Structure-Nomenclature Notation [*Chemistry*]
SNNG .... Schakels Nederlands Nieuw Guinea [*A publication*]
SNNTS .... Studies in the Novel (North Texas State University) [*A publication*]
SNO .... Senior Naval Officer
SNO .... Senior Navigation Officer [*Air Force*] [*British*]
SNO .... Senior Nursing Officer [*British*]
SNO .... Serial Number   (MDG)
SNO .... Special Naval Operations   (NVT)
SNO .... Stock Number   (MSA)
Sno............ Thioinosine [*Also, SIno, M*] [*A nucleoside*]
SNOAD...... Senior Naval Officer Adriatic [*British*]
SNOB .... Senior Naval Officer on Board
S Nob .... Sine Nobilitate [*Without Nobility*] [*Notation used at Oxford University to indicate that a student was untitled. This abbreviation is claimed to have acquired its present connotation when commoners at the university put on more airs than did their titled counterparts*] [*Latin*]
SNOBOL .... String-Oriented Symbolic Language [*1963*] [*Data processing*]
SNOE .... Smart Noise Equipment [*RADAR jammer*] [*Air Force*]
SNoF .... Studier i Nordisk Filologi [*A publication*]
SNOINCR ... Snow Depth Increase in Past Hour [*Meteorology*]   (FAAC)
SNOK .... Secondary Next of Kin [*Army*]   (AABC)
SNOL .... Senior Naval Officer, Landings [*British*]
SNOMed .... Systematized Nomenclature of Medicine
SNOO .... Small Nonoverlapping Offset [*Oceanography*]
SNOOP...... Students Naturally Opposed to Outrageous Prying [*Student legal action organization*]   (EA)
SNOOPI..... System Network Online Operations Information [*Suggested name for the Library of Congress computer system*]
SNOP .... Senior Naval Officer Present
SNOP .... Standard Nomenclature of Pathology [*College of American Pathologists*]
SNOP .... Systematized Nomenclature of Pathology [*NCI*]
SNORE...... Self-Noise Reduction
SNORE...... Signal-to-Noise Ratio Estimator
SNORKEX ... Snorkel Detection Exercise [*Military*]   (NVT)
SNORT .... Supersonic Naval Ordnance Research Track [*China Lake, CA*]
SNOTEL ..... Snow Survey Telemetry Network [*Department of Agriculture*]
SNov .... Seara Nova [*A publication*]
Snow .... Snow's Reports [*3 Utah*]   (DLA)
SNOW .... Standard Normal Ocean Water
SNOWCAT ... Support of Nuclear Operations with Conventional Air Tactics   (NATG)
SNOWFLEX ... Field Exercise under Snow Conditions [*Military*]   (NVT)
SNOWI ...... Senior Naval Officer, West Indies [*British*]
Snow Revel ... Snow Revelry [*A publication*]
SNOW TIME ... SAC-NORAD [*Strategic Air Command - North American Air Defense*] Operational Weapons Test Involving Military Electronics
SNP .... Saint Paul Island [*Alaska*] [*Airport symbol*]   (OAG)
SNP .... St. Paul Island, AK [*Location identifier*] [*FAA*]   (FAAL)
SNP .... School Nurse Practitioner
SNP .... Scottish National Party   (PPW)
SNP .... Skagit Nuclear Project   (NRCH)
SNP .... Society for Natural Philosophy   (EA)
SNP .... Sodium Nitroprusside [*A vasodilator*]
SNP .... Soluble Nucleoprotein
SNP .... Sonepat [*India*] [*Seismograph station code, US Geological Survey*] [*Closed*]   (SEIS)
SNP .... Space Nuclear Propulsion
SNP .... Statistical Network Processor
SNP .... Studia Neophilologica [*A publication*]
SNP .... Suspected, Not Proved
SNP .... Synchro Null Pulse
SNP .... Synchronous Network Processor
SNP .... System Network Processor
SNPA......... Southern Newspaper Publishers Association
SNPh......... Studia Neophilologica [*A publication*]
SNPJ .... Slovene National Benefit Society   (EA)
SNPM......... Standard and Nuclear Propulsion Module

SNPO .... Society for Nonprofit Organizations [*Madison, WI*]   (EA)
SNPO .... Space Nuclear Propulsion Office [*Later, Division of Space Nuclear Systems, of Energy Research and Development Administration*] [*AEC-NASA*]
SNPOA ...... Space Nuclear Propulsion Office, Albuquerque [*See SNPO*]
SNPOC ...... Space Nuclear Propulsion Office, Cleveland [*See SNPO*]
SNPON ...... Space Nuclear Propulsion Office, Nevada [*See SNPO*]
SNPP .... Sequoyah Nuclear Power Plant   (NRCH)
SNPR .... Screen Print   (AAG)
SNPRI .... Selected Nonpriority List Item
SNPS .... Shoreham Nuclear Power Station   (NRCH)
SNQ .... Scottish Notes and Queries [*A publication*]
SNQ .... Sea-1 Aquafarms Ltd. [*Vancouver Stock Exchange symbol*]
SNQ .... Sussex Notes and Queries [*A publication*]
SNR .... Saint Nazaire [*France*] [*Airport symbol*]   (OAG)
SNR .... Schaffner Ranch [*California*] [*Seismograph station code, US Geological Survey*]   (SEIS)
SNR .... Schenectady Naval Reactors Office [*Energy Research and Development Administration*]
SNR .... Schweizerische Numismatische Rundschau [*A publication*]
SNR .... Senior
SNR .... Senior National Representatives SONAR [*Four Power Army*]   (MCD)
SNR .... Senor [*Mister*] [*Spanish*]
SNR .... Service Not Required
SNR .... Signal-to-Noise Ratio
SNR .... Slow Neutron Reactor   (NRCH)
SNR .... SONAR
SNR .... Supernova Remnant [*Astronomy*]
SNR .... Supplier Nonconformance Report   (NRCH)
SNRA .... Sawtooth National Recreation Area [*Idaho*]
SNRA .... Senora [*Mrs.*] [*Spanish*]
SNRAFU .... Situation Normal, Really All Fouled Up [*Military slang*] [*Bowdlerized version*]
SNRC .... Sudanese National Research Council
SNRG .... Synergex Corp. [*NASDAQ symbol*]   (NQ)
SNRLTCS .. Skilled Nursing and Related Long Term Care Services   (EA)
snRNA .... Ribonucleic Acid, Small Nuclear [*Biochemistry, genetics*]
snRNP .... Ribonucleoprotein, Small Nuclear [*Biochemistry*]
SNRS .... Sunrise [*Meteorology*]   (FAAC)
SNRSA ...... Sunrise Savings & Loan Association of Florida CI A [*NASDAQ symbol*]   (NQ)
SNRT .... Sinus Node Recovery Time [*Cardiology*]
SNRTC ...... Sinus Node Recovery Time Corrected [*Cardiology*]
SNS .... Salinas, CA [*Location identifier*] [*FAA*]   (FAAL)
SNS .... Samarbeidsnemden for Nordisk Skogforskning [*Nordic Forest Research Cooperation Committee*] [*Oslo, Norway*]   (EA-IO)
SNS .... San Onofre [*California*] [*Seismograph station code, US Geological Survey*]   (SEIS)
SNS .... Scandinavian Neurosurgical Society   (EA)
SNS .... Seabrook Nuclear Station   (NRCH)
SNS .... Senior Nursing Sister [*Navy*] [*British*]
SNS .... Sensorstat System [*Vancouver Stock Exchange symbol*]
SNS .... Simulated Network Simulations   (KSC)
SNS .... Skyline Network Service [*Satellite Business Systems*] [*McLean, VA*] [*Telecommunications*]   (TSSD)
SNS .... Slovo na Storozi [*A publication*]
SNS .... Small Nuclear Stage   (KSC)
SNS .... Society of Neurological Surgeons [*Charleston, SC*]   (EA)
SNS .... Somatic Nervous System
SNS .... Space Nuclear System
SNS .... Spallation Neutron Source
SNS .... Special Night Squads [*Palestine*]   (BJA)
SNS .... Stabilized Night Sight
SNS .... Sundstrand Corp. [*NYSE symbol*]
SNS .... Sympathetic Nervous System [*Physiology*]
SN/SC .... Stock Number Source Code   (MCD)
SNSCNY .... St. Nicholas Society of the City of New York   (EA)
SNSE .... Society of Nuclear Scientists and Engineers [*Defunct*]
SNSH .... Snow Showers [*Meteorology*]
SNSL .... Standard Navy Stock List
SNSL .... Stock Number Sequence Listing   (MSA)
SNSM .... Sindacato Nazionale Scuola Media [*National Union of Intermediate School Teachers*] [*Italy*]
SNSN .... Standard Navy Stock Number
SNSO .... Space Nuclear Systems Office [*AEC/NASA*]
SNSR .... Sensor   (AAG)
SNSR .... Sensormatic Electronics [*NASDAQ symbol*]   (NQ)
SNSS .... Skrifter Utgivna av Namnden foer Svensk Sprakvard [*A publication*]
SNST .... Sunset [*Meteorology*]   (FAAC)
SNSTA ...... Sonesta International Hotels [*NASDAQ symbol*]   (NQ)
SNT .... Saint
SNT .... [*The*] Scrolls and the New Testament [*K. Stendahl*] [*A publication*]   (BJA)
SNT .... Sears Point [*California*] [*Seismograph station code, US Geological Survey*]   (SEIS)
SNT .... Selective Nuclear Transfer
SNT .... Silicon Needle Transducer

SNT .... Sindacato Nazionale Tabacchine [*National Union of Women Tobacco Workers*] [*Italy*]
SNT .... Single Negotiating Text [*UN Law of the Sea Conference*]
SNT .... Society for Nondestructive Testing [*Later, ASNT*]   (EA)
SNT .... Sonat, Inc. [*NYSE symbol*]
SNT .... Supplements. Novum Testamentum [*Leiden*] [*A publication*]
SNT .... System Noise Temperature
SNTA .... Sodium Nitrilotriacetate
SNTA .... Syndicat National des Transporteurs Aeriens [*Airlines association*] [*Paris, France*]
SNTC .... Sentry Manufacturing Company [*NASDAQ symbol*]   (NQ)
SNTC .... Syndicat National des Transporteurs de Cameroun [*National Union of Cameroonese Transportation Workers*]
SNTC .... Syndicat National des Travailleurs Congolais [*National Union of Congolese Workers*] [*Leopoldville*]
SNTCC ...... Simplified Neutron Transport Computer Code
SNTE .... Santec Corp. [*NASDAQ symbol*]   (NQ)
SNTF .... Special Navy Task Force   (MUGU)
SNTFC ...... Special Navy Task Force Commander
SNTF(SMS) ... Special Navy Task Force for Surface Missile Systems   (MUGU)
SNTO .... Swiss National Tourist Office [*Zurich*]   (EA)
SNTR .... Sinter [*Metallurgy*]
SNTS .... Short-Length, Nonbuoyant Torpedo System
SNTS .... Society for New Testament Study   (EA)
SNTS .... Studiorum Novi Testamenti Societas [*Society for the Study of the New Testament*]
SNTSB ...... Studiorum Novi Testamenti Societas. Bulletin [*A publication*]
SNTSMS .... Studiorum Novi Testamenti Societas. Monograph Series [*A publication*]
SNTZD ...... Sensitized   (MSA)
SNTZG ...... Sensitizing   (MSA)
SNu .... Sifre on Numbers   (BJA)
SNU .... SNC Group [*Toronto Stock Exchange symbol*]
SNU .... Solar Neutrino Unit [*Astrophysics*]
SNU .... Somali National Union
SNUB .... Show Nothing Unless Bad
SNUD .... Stock Number User Directory [*Air Force*]   (AFM)
SNUJ .... Singapore National Union of Journalists
SNUPPS .... Standardized Nuclear Unit Power Plant System [*Nuclear reactor combine*]
SNUR .... Significant New Use Rules [*Environmental Protection Agency*]
SNURP ...... Small Nuclear Ribonucleoprotein Particle [*Genetics*]
SNV .... Santa Elena [*Venezuela*] [*Airport symbol*]   (OAG)
SNV .... Spleen Necrosis Virus
SNV .... Statens Naturvardsverk [*National Environmental Protection Board*] [*Solna, Sweden*] [*Information service*]   (EISS)
SNV .... Suneva Resources [*Vancouver Stock Exchange symbol*]
SNV .... Systema Nervosum Vegetativo [*Obsolete term for the autonomic nervous system*] [*Medicine*]
SNVAO ...... Skrifter Utgitt av Det Norske Videnskaps-Akademi i Oslo [*A publication*]
SNVKB ...... Sbornik Nauchnykh Rabot Voenno-Meditsinskogo Fakul'teta Kuibyshevskogo Meditsinskogo Instituta [*A publication*]
SNVO .... Skrifter det Norske Videnskaps-Akademi i Oslo [*A publication*]
SNVT .... Short No-Voltage Tester [*Ground surveillance RADAR system*]   (MCD)
SNW .... Sandoway [*Burma*] [*Airport symbol*]   (OAG)
S/N)w .... Signal-to-Noise, Weighted
SNW .... Snow [*Meteorology*]   (FAAC)
SNW .... Snowwater Resources Ltd. [*Vancouver Stock Exchange symbol*]
SNW .... Stanwood Corp. [*American Stock Exchange symbol*]
SNW .... Strategic Nuclear Weapon
SNW .... Sun West Airlines [*Scottsdale, AZ*] [*FAA designator*]   (FAAC)
Sn & W Ch ... Snow and Winstanley's Chancery Practice   (DLA)
SNWFL ...... Snowfall   (FAAC)
SNWS .... Shipboard Nuclear Weapon Security [*Navy*]   (CAAL)
SNWTH ..... Sources for NWT [*Northwest Territory*] History. Prince of Wales Northern Heritage Centre [*Canada*] [*A publication*]
SNX .... Sunburst Exploration Ltd. [*Toronto Stock Exchange symbol*]
SNY .... Sidney [*Nebraska*] [*Airport symbol*]   (OAG)
SNY .... Southern New York Railway [*AAR code*]
SNY .... Spanish Navy
SNY .... Sunny   (MSA)
Snyder Mines ... Snyder on Mines and Mining   (DLA)
SNYK .... Security New York State Corp. [*NASDAQ symbol*]   (NQ)
SNZ .... Senzan [*Japan*] [*Seismograph station code, US Geological Survey*]   (SEIS)
SNZ .... Shipping Corporation of New Zealand (CDA) [*Toronto Stock Exchange symbol*]
SNZO .... South Karori [*New Zealand*] [*Seismograph station code, US Geological Survey*]   (SEIS)
SO .... Sail Only   (CINC)
SO .... Sales Order
SO .... Salpingo-Oophorectomy [*Medicine*]
SO .... Salvis Omissis [*Omissions Excepted*] [*Latin*]
SO .... Saturdays Only [*British railroad term*]
SO .... Saturn Orbiter [*NASA*]
SO .... Schenectady Operation [*Energy Research and Development Administration*]   (MCD)

SO .... Scientific Officer [*Ministry of Agriculture, Fisheries, and Food*] [*Also, ScO*] [*British*]
SO .... Scottish [*Communion*] Office [*Episcopalian*]
SO .... Scouting-Observation Plane [*When prefixed to Navy aircraft designation*]
SO .... Second Class Open [*Train ticket*]
SO .... Second Opinion [*An association*] [*Defunct*] (EA)
SO .... Secretary's Office [*Navy*]
SO .... Secretary's Order
SO .... Secure Operations (MCD)
SO .... Security Office
SO .... Seder 'Olam (BJA)
SO .... Sell-Off (AAG)
SO .... Seller's Option [*Business and trade*]
SO .... Send Only
SO .... Senior Officer [*Military, police*]
SO .... Serial Output
SO .... Service Order
SO .... Sex Offender
SO .... Sheriff's Office [*or Officer*] (ROG)
SO .... Shift-Out Character [*Keyboard*] [*Data processing*]
SO .... Shipment [*or Shipping*] Order [*Business and trade*]
SO .... Ship's Option
SO .... Shop Order
SO .... Shot
S-O .... Shut-Off (AAG)
SO .... Shutout [*Sports*]
SO .... Sibirskie Ogni [*A publication*]
S/O .... Sign Off
SO .... Signal Officer
SO .... Significant Other [*Term for members of unmarried couples*]
SO .... Slavia Occidentalis [*A publication*]
SO .... Sleepout (ADA)
SO .... Slope Occurrence
SO .... Slow Operate [*Relay*]
SO .... Slow Oxidative [*Fibers*] [*Neuroanatomy*]
SO .... Small Oocyte
So .... Societa [*A publication*]
SO .... Society (ROG)
So .... Sojourner [*A publication*]
So .... Sokrates [*A publication*]
SO .... Sold Out (ADA)
SO .... Solicitor's Opinion (DLA)
SO .... Somali [*Two-letter standard code*] (CNC)
so .... Somali [*MARC country of publication code*] [*Library of Congress*] (LCCP)
S/O .... Son Of [*Genealogy*]
SO .... SONARman [*Navy*]
So .... Sophia: Studies in Western Civilization and the Cultural Interaction of East and West [*Tokyo*] [*A publication*]
SO .... Sorrel Resources Ltd. [*Toronto Stock Exchange symbol*]
SO .... Sorting Office [*British*] (ROG)
S/O .... Sound Off
So .... Soundings [*A publication*]
SO .... Source [*Online database field identifier*]
SO .... South [*or Southern*]
SO .... Southern Airways [*ICAO designator*]
SO .... Southern Co. [*NYSE symbol*]
SO .... Southern Oscillation [*Meteorology*]
So .... Southern Reporter [*National Reporter System*] (DLA)
SO .... Special Olympics [*An association*] (EA)
SO .... Special Operations
SO .... Special Orders
SO .... Spheno-Occipital [*Synchondrosis*] [*Medicine*]
SO .... Spiracular Organ [*Fish anatomy*]
SO .... Spring Opening
SO .... Staff Officer
SO .... Stamp Office [*British*] (ROG)
SO .... Standing Orders
SO .... Station Officer [*British police*]
SO .... Stationery Office [*British*]
SO .... Stay Out [*Official leave from Eton College*] [*British*]
SO .... Stock Order (AAG)
SO .... Stock Outboard [*Powerboat*]
SO .... Stockage Objectives
SO .... Stop Order (MCD)
SO .... Stopover [*Slang*]
SO .... Strategic Outline Chart [*Air Force*]
SO .... Strikeouts [*Baseball*]
SO .... Studia Oliveriana [*A publication*]
SO .... Studia Orientalia [*A publication*]
SO .... Submarine Oscillator (DEN)
SO .... Suboffice
S/O .... Substance Of
SO .... Superior Oblique [*Muscle*] [*Anatomy*]
SO .... Superior Old [*Spirits*]
SO .... Supply Officer
SO .... Support Operations
SO .... Surface Operations [*Navy*] (CAAL)
SO .... Surveillance Officer
SO .... Switching Oscilloscope

SO .... Switchover
SO .... Symbolae Osloenses [*A publication*]
SO .... Symbolic Output [*Data processing*]
SO .... Sympathetic Ophthalmia [*Medicine*]
SO .... Symphony Orchestra
SO .... System Override (AAG)
SO .... Systems Orientation
SO1 .... SONARman First Class [*Navy*]
SO2 .... SONARman Second Class [*Navy*]
SO3 .... SONARman Third Class [*Navy*]
SOA............ Safe Operating Area (IEEE)
SOA............ Sales Order Authority (AAG)
SOA............ Scandinavian Orthopaedic Association (EA)
SOA............ Self-Optimizing and Adaptive
SOA............ Senate Operating Agency (MCD)
SOA............ Separate Operating Agency [*Air Force*] (AFM)
SOA............ Serial Output Adapter
SOA............ Shelby Owners of America (EA)
SOA............ Ship Operating Automation
SOA............ Shipyard Overhaul Availability
SOA............ Shuttle Orbital Application [*NASA*]
SOA............ Smithsonian Office of Anthropology
SOA............ Society of Actuaries [*Formed by a merger of Actuarial Society of America and American Institute of Actuaries*] [*Itasca, IL*] (EA)
SOA............ Sonora, TX [*Location identifier*] [*FAA*] (FAAL)
SOA............ Soundness of Approach (MCD)
SOA............ Source of Assignment (MCD)
SOA............ Southern Airways (MCD)
SOA............ Special Open Allotment (AABC)
SOA............ Special Operating Agency (AABC)
SOA............ Speed of Advance [*Military*]
SOA............ Speed of Approach
SOA............ Spirit of Adventure (EA)
SOA............ Standardbred Owners Association (EA)
SOA............ Start of Address
SOA............ State of the Art
SOA............ Statement of Assurance
SOA............ Stimulus Onset Asynchrony [*Psychology*]
SOA............ Student Orientation Assistant
SOA............ Superoxide Anion [*Chemistry*]
SOA............ Switch Off Assembly (MCD)
SOA............ Sydsvenska Ortnamnssaellskapets Arsskrift [*A publication*]
SOAA .... Signed Out Against Advice [*Medicine*]
SOAA .... Staff Officers Association of America (EA)
SoAB .... South Atlantic Bulletin [*A publication*]
SOAC .... State-of-the-Art Car [*Transit*] [*Department of Transportation*]
SoAF .... Soviet Air Force
SOAF........ Sultanate of Oman Air Force
SOAFQ ...... South Atlantic Financial [*NASDAQ symbol*] (NQ)
So Africa .... Southern Africa [*A publication*]
So African L ... South African Law Reports [*A publication*]
So African LJ ... South African Law Journal [*A publication*]
So Afr LJ .... South African Law Journal [*A publication*]
So Afr LR ... South African Law Reports [*A publication*]
So Afr LT .... South African Law Times (DLA)
So Afr Prize Cas ... South African Prize Cases [*Juta*] (DLA)
SoAfrStJ .... South African Statistical Journal [*A publication*]
SOAI........ Service des Organisations Aeronautiques Internationales [*France*]
SOAL........ Search Optical Augmentation LASER (MCD)
SOAMB ...... Soviet Applied Mechanics [*English Translation*] [*A publication*]
SOAMUS.... Study of One-Atmosphere Manned Underwater Structures
SoANGr...... Soobscenija Akademiji Nauk Gruzinskoj SSR [*A publication*]
SOAP .... Sarnia Olefins and Aromatics Project [*Canadian ethylene project*]
SOAP .... Self-Optimizing Automatic Pilot
SOAP .... Ship Overhaul Assistance Program (MCD)
SOAP .... Simplify Obscure ALGOL [*Algorithmic Language*] Programs (MCD)
SOAP .... Society of Airway Pioneers (EA)
SOAP .... Society for Obstetric Anesthesia and Perinatology [*Halifax, NS*] (EA)
SOAP .... Society of Office Automation Professionals [*Willow Grove, PA*] [*Telecommunications service*] (EA)
SOAP .... Spectrochemical [*or Spectrographic, Spectrometric, or Spectroscopic*] Oil Analysis Program [*Air Force*]
SOAP .... Students Opposed to Advertised Pollutants [*Student legal action organization*]
SOAP .... Subjective, Objective, Assessment, and Plan [*Medicine*]
SOAP .... Supply Operations Assistance Program [*Military*]
SOAP .... Symbolic Optimum Assembly Programing [*IBM Corp.*] [*Data processing*]
SOAP .... Symptoms, Observations, Assessment, Plan
SOAP .... Systems Operational Analysis Plan
Soap Chem Spec ... Soap and Chemical Specialties [*Later, Soap/ Cosmetics/Chemical Specialties*] [*A publication*]
Soap & Chem Spec ... Soap and Chemical Specialties [*Later, Soap/ Cosmetics/Chemical Specialties*] [*A publication*]
Soap Cosmet ... Soap/Cosmetics/Chemical Specialties [*A publication*]

Soap/Cosmet/Chem Spec ... Soap/Cosmetics/Chemical Specialities [*A publication*]
SOAPD ...... Southern Air Procurement District
Soap Perfum Cosmet ... Soap, Perfumery, and Cosmetics [*A publication*]
Soap Prf Cos ... Soap, Perfumery, and Cosmetics [*A publication*]
Soap & San Chem ... Soap and Sanitary Chemicals [*A publication*]
SOAR .... Safe Operating Area
SOAR .... Save Our American Resources [*Boy Scout project*]
SOAR .... Seminars on Aeroanxiety Relief
SOAR .... Shuttle Orbital Applications and Requirements [*NASA*]
SOAR .... Simulation of Airlift Resources [*Air Force*]
SOAR .... Simulation of Apollo Reliability [*NASA*] (KSC)
SOAR .... State-of-the-Art Report [*Navy*]
SOAR .... Stress on Analytical Reasoning
SOARS ...... Second Order Attitude Reference Set (MCD)
SOARS ...... Shuttle Operations Automated Reporting System [*NASA*] (NASA)
SOAS .... School of Oriental and African Studies [*University of London*]
So AS .... Somersetshire Archaeological and Natural History Society. Proceedings [*Later, Somerset Archaeology and Natural History*] [*A publication*]
SOASC(I) ... Senior Officer Assault Ships and Craft (India) [*British*]
SOase .... Sulfite Oxidase [*An enzyme*]
SOAS JLCR ... School of Oriental and African Studies. Jordan Lectures in Comparative Religion [*A publication*]
So Assn Q ... Southern Association Quarterly [*A publication*]
SOAS ULLOS ... School of Oriental and African Studies. University of London. London. Oriental Series [*A publication*]
So Atlan Bul ... South Atlantic Bulletin [*A publication*]
So Atlan Q ... South Atlantic Quarterly [*A publication*]
So Atl Quar ... South Atlantic Quarterly [*A publication*]
SOATS ...... Support Operations Automated Training System [*NASA*] (NASA)
So Aus Bul ... National Gallery of South Australia. Bulletin [*A publication*]
So Aus LR ... South Australian Law Reports [*A publication*]
So Aust LR ... South Australian Law Reports [*A publication*]
So Austr L ... South Australian Law Reports [*A publication*]
So Austr St ... South Australian State Reports [*A publication*]
SOAW .... Sitzungsberichte der Oesterreichischen Akademie der Wissenschaften in Wien. Philosophisch-Historische Klasse [*A publication*]
Sob. .... De Sobrietate [*of Philo*] (BJA)
SOB .... Second Overtone Band
SOB .... Senate Office Building
SOB .... Service Observance Bureau [*A telephone-monitoring section of the Bell System*]
SOB .... Shortness of Breath [*Cardiology*]
SOB .... Silly Old Bugger [*Officer over the age of 39*] [*British*] (DSUE)
SOB .... Son of a Bitch
SOB .... Souls on Board [*Aviation slang*] (FAAC)
SOB .... Space Orbital Bomber (AAG)
SOB .... Start of Block
SOB .... Sub-Occipito Bregma [*Medicine*] (ROG)
SOB .... Sudost-Bahn [*Swiss Southeastern Railway*]
SOB .... Superior Official Bureaucrat [*Satirical bureaucracy term*]
SOB's .... Silly Old Buggers [*Wardroom officers over the "advanced" age of 39*] [*British naval slang*]
SOB's .... Sons of Bosses International [*An association*] [*Superseded by NFBC*] (EA)
SOB's .... South of Broad Street [*Reference is to residents of the historic and aristocratic section of Charleston, South Carolina*]
SOBA .... 605th Ordnance Battalion Association (EA)
SOBASSPIFTAGE ... Society of Beer and Sordid Sex Professional Invitational Fishing Tournament and Gastronomical Extravaganza
SOBC .... Save Our Barns Committee (EA)
SOBECOV ... Societe de Stockage et de Commercialisation des Produits Vivriers [*Development organization*] [*Bujumbura, Burundi*]
SOBELAIR ... Societe Belge de Transports Pan Air [*Belgian airline*]
SOBIGM ..... Sign Off Brother, I've Got Mine [*Remark used by seamen who avoided risky assignments during World War II*] [*Also used as hoax by National Maritime Union for name of organization issuing pamphlet about low state of merchant marine service*]
So Biv .... Southern Bivouac [*A publication*]
SOBK .... Southwest Bank [*NASDAQ symbol*] (NQ)
SOBLIN ...... Self-Organizing Binary Logical Network [*OTS*]
So Bod .... Sounding Board [*A publication*]
SOBP .... Sentral Organisasi Buruh Pantjasila [*Central Organization of Pantjasila Labor*] [*Indonesian*]
Sobre Deriv Cana Azucar ... Sobre los Derivados de la Cana de Azucar [*Cuba*] [*A publication*]
SOBS .... Scanning Ocean Bottom SONAR
SOBS .... Society for Office-Based Surgery [*Later, ASOS*] (EA)
SOBU .... Student Organization for Black Unity
SOC .... Chief SONARman [*Navy rating*] [*Obsolete*]
SOC .... Saint Olaf College [*Minnesota*]
SOC .... Satellite Operations Center [*Cape Kennedy*]
SOC .... Satellite Orbit Control
SOC .... Scene of Crime
SOC .... Schedule of Organizational Change [*Air Force*] (AFM)

SOC .... Sector Operations Center [*Air Force*]
SOC .... Self-Organizing Control
SOC .... Separated Orbit Cyclotron (IEEE)
SOC .... Service and Overhaul Change (MSA)
SOC .... Servicemen's Opportunity College [*DoD*]
SOC .... Set Overrides Clear (IEEE)
SOC .... Shop Order Control
SOC .... Silicon on Ceramic [*Technique for producing solar cells*]
SOC .... Simulated Operational Computer (KSC)
SOC .... Simulation Operation Computer (MCD)
SOC .... Simulation Operations Center [*NASA*] (KSC)
SOC .... Singer Owners Club (EA)
SOC .... Single Orbit Computation
SOC .... Sochi [*USSR*] [*Seismograph station code, US Geological Survey*] (SEIS)
SOC .... Social
SOC .... Socialist
Soc .... Societas [*A publication*]
Soc .... Society [*A publication*]
SOC .... Society
SOC .... Society of Cinematologists [*Later, SCS*] (EA)
Soc .... Sociological (DLA)
Soc .... Sociology (DLA)
SOC .... Socket (AAG)
SOC .... Socrates [*Greek philosopher, 470-399BC*] (ROG)
SOC .... Solo [*Indonesia*] [*Airport symbol*] (OAG)
SOC .... Somerset County College, Somerville, NJ [*OCLC symbol*] (OCLC)
So C .... South Carolina Reports (DLA)
SOC .... South Coast Airways [*Nederland, TX*] [*FAA designator*] (FAAC)
SOC .... Southern Oregon College
SOC .... Space Operations Center
SOC .... Space Operations Controller
SOC .... Special Operations Command [*Military*] (AABC)
SOC .... Specialized Oceanographic Center [*Marine science*] (MSC)
SOC .... Specific Optimal Control
SOC .... Squadron Operations Center [*Air Force*]
SOC .... Standard Occupational Classifications (OICC)
SOC .... Standard Oil Company
SOC .... Standards of Official Conduct (DLA)
SOC .... Standing Order Confirmation [*Publishing*]
SOC .... Standing Orders Committee [*British*]
SOC .... Start of Construction [*Military*] (AFIT)
SOC .... Start of Conversion [*Navy*]
SOC .... State of Charge
SoC .... State of Consciousness
SOC .... Statement of Capability (MCD)
SOC .... Station Operations Console (MCD)
SOC .... Strike Operations Coordinator [*Navy*] (NVT)
SOC .... Strike Options Comparison (MCD)
SOC .... Studies in Organic Chemistry [*Elsevier Book Series*] [*A publication*]
SOC .... Superior Oil Company [*Nevada*] [*NYSE symbol*] [*Delisted*] [*Toronto Stock Exchange symbol*]
SOC .... Superposition of Configuration [*Atomic physics*]
SOC .... Supply Overhaul Coordinator (MCD)
SOC .... Synthetic Organic Chemical
SOC .... System Operational Concept
SOC .... System Option Controller [*NASA*] (NASA)
SOC .... Systems Operation Center
Soc A .... Sociological Abstracts [*A publication*]
SOCA .... Staff Officer for Civil Affairs [*British*] [*World War II*]
SocAb .... Sociological Abstracts [*A publication*]
SOCABU .... Societe du Caoutchouc Butyl [*France*]
Soc Act .... Social Action [*A publication*]
Soc Act & L ... Social Action and the Law [*A publication*]
Soc Actuar Trans ... Society of Actuaries. Transactions [*A publication*]
SOCAD ...... Serviceman's Opportunity for College Associate Degree (MCD)
Soc Adv Electrochem Sci Technol Trans ... Society for the Advancement of Electrochemical Science and Technology. Transactions [*A publication*]
Soc African J ... Societe des Africanistes. Journal [*A publication*]
Soc Agric Alger Bull ... Societe des Agricultures d'Algerie. Bulletin [*Algeria*] [*A publication*]
SOCAL ...... Southern California [*Military*] (NVT)
SOCAL ...... Standard Oil Co. of California
So Calif L Rev ... Southern California Law Review [*A publication*]
So Calif Q ... Southern California Quarterly [*A publication*]
So Calif Quar ... Southern California Quarterly [*A publication*]
So Calif Tax Inst ... University of Southern California School of Law Tax Institute (DLA)
Soc Alp Giulie Comm Grotte Eugenio Boegan Atti Mem ... Societa Alpina delle Giulie. Club Alpino Italiano. Sezione di Trieste. Commissione Grotte "Eugenio Boegan." Atti e Memorie [*A publication*]
SOCALSEC ... Southern California Sector, Western Sea Frontier
Soc Altern ... Social Alternatives [*A publication*]
Soc Alternatives ... Social Alternatives [*Australia*] [*A publication*]

Soc d Americanistes J ... Societe des Americanistes de Paris. Journal [*A publication*]

Soc Amer J ... Societe des Americanistes de Paris. Journal [*A publication*]

Soc Am For ... Society of American Foresters. Proceedings [*A publication*]

Soc Anal .... Sociological Analysis [*A publication*]

Soc Anarc ... Social Anarchism [*A publication*]

Soc Anthropol Paris Bull Mem ... Societe d'Anthropologie de Paris. Bulletins et Memoires [*A publication*]

SOCAP....... Society of Consumer Affairs Professionals in Business [*Alexandria, VA*] (EA)

Soc Appl Bacteriol Symp Ser ... Society for Applied Bacteriology. Symposium Series [*A publication*]

Soc Appl Bacteriol Tech Ser ... Society for Applied Bacteriology. Technical Series [*A publication*]

SOCAR....... Shuttle Operational Capability Assessment Report (MCD)

So Car....... South Carolina (DLA)

So Car....... South Carolina Reports (DLA)

So Ca R ..... South Carolina Review [*A publication*]

SOCAR....... Statement of Condition and Recommendation [*Military*] (AABC)

SOCAR....... Systems Operational Compatibility Assessment Review [*NASA*]

So Car BA Rep ... South Carolina Bar Association Reports (DLA)

Soc Archeol & Hist Limousin Bul ... Societe Archeologique et Historique du Limousin. Bulletin [*A publication*]

Soc Arch Hist J ... Society of Architectural Historians. Journal [*A publication*]

Soc Arch Hist Poitou Arch ... Societe des Archives Historiques du Poitou. Archives [*A publication*]

Soc Archit Hist J ... Society of Architectural Historians. Journal [*A publication*]

So Car Const ... South Carolina Constitutional Reports [*by Treadway, by Mill, or by Harper*] (DLA)

Soc Argent Cancerol Bol Trab ... Sociedad Argentina de Cancerologia. Boletines y Trabajos [*A publication*]

Soc Argent Cir Jornadas Quir ... Sociedad Argentina de Cirujanos Jornadas Quirurgicas [*A publication*]

So Car Hist Assoc Proc ... South Carolina Historical Association. Proceedings [*A publication*]

So Car Hist Mag ... South Carolina Historical and Genealogical Magazine [*A publication*]

So Car LJ ... South Carolina Law Journal [*Columbia*] (DLA)

So Car LQ ... South Carolina Law Quarterly [*A publication*]

So Car L Rev ... South Carolina Law Review [*A publication*]

Soc Army Hist Research Jour ... Society for Army Historical Research. Journal [*London*] [*A publication*]

So Car R..... South Carolina Law Reports (DLA)

Soc Arts J ... Society of Arts. Journal [*A publication*]

SOCAS....... Subcommittee on Chemical Abstracts Service [*American Chemical Society*]

Soc Astron Ital Mem ... Societa Astronomica Italiana. Memorie [*A publication*]

SOCATS .... Scenario Oriented Corps Area Training System (MCD)

Soc Auto Eng J ... Society of Automotive Engineers. Journal [*A publication*]

SOCB .... Shop Order Control Board

SoCB.......... South Central Bulletin [*A publication*]

Soc Behav Pers ... Social Behavior and Personality [*A publication*]

Soc Beh Per ... Social Behavior and Personality [*A publication*]

Soc Belge d'Etudes Geog Bull ... Societe Belge d'Etudes Geographiques. Bulletin [*A publication*]

Soc Belge G B ... Societe Belge de Geologie. Bulletin [*A publication*]

Soc Belge Geol Bull ... Societe Belge de Geologie. Bulletin [*A publication*]

Soc Biol ... Social Biology [*A publication*]

Soc Bot France B ... Societe Botanique de France. Bulletin [*A publication*]

Soc Brotheriana Bol ... Sociedade Brotheriana. Boletim [*A publication*]

SOCC......... Salvage Operational Control Center [*On submarine rescue ship during salvage operation*]

SOCC........ Satellite Oceanic Control Center

SOCC........ Satellite Operations Control Center [*NASA*] (NASA)

SOCC........ Spacecraft Operations Control Center

SOCC........ Special Opportunities Counties and Cities Program [*Tennessee Valley Authority*]

SOCC........ Submarine Operations Control Center [*Navy*] (CAAL)

SOCC........ Subordinate Operations Control Center

Soc Casework ... Social Casework [*A publication*]

SOCCER .... SMART's Own Concordance Constructor, Extremely Rapid [*Cornell University*] [*Data processing*]

Soccer J..... Soccer Journal [*A publication*]

Soc Chem Ind J ... Society of Chemical Industry. Journal [*A publication*]

Soc Chem Ind (Lond) Monogr ... Society of Chemical Industry (London). Monograph [*A publication*]

Soc Cient Ant Alz Mem ... Sociedad Cientifica "Antonio Alzate." Memorias y Revista [*A publication*]

Soc Cient Parag Rev ... Sociedad Cientifica del Paraguay. Revista [*A publication*]

SOC Coll .... Studia Orientalia Christiana. Collectanea [*A publication*]

SOCCOM ... Southern Command (MCD)

Soc Comp ... Social Compass [*A publication*]

Soc Compass ... Social Compass [*A publication*]

SOCCS ...... Summary of Component Control Status (NRCH)

Soc Cubana Historia Nat Mem ... Sociedad Cubana de Historia Natural. Memorias [*A publication*]

Soc Cubana Ingenieros Rev ... Sociedad Cubana de Ingenieros. Revista [*A publication*]

Soc Cubana Ing Rv ... Sociedad Cubana de Ingenieros. Revista [*A publication*]

SOCD......... Source Control Drawing

Soc Def ...... Social Defence [*New Delhi*] [*A publication*]

SOCDS...... Source Codes (MCD)

Soc Dyers & Col J ... Society of Dyers and Colourists. Journal [*A publication*]

SOCE .... Staff Officer Construction Engineering

Soc Econ ... Social Economist [*A publication*]

Soc Econ Admin ... Social and Economic Administration [*A publication*]

Soc Econ Paleontol Mineral Pac Sect Guideb ... Society of Economic Paleontologists and Mineralogists. Pacific Section. Guidebooks [*A publication*]

Soc Econ Paleontol Mineral Permian Basin Sect Publ ... Society of Economic Paleontologists and Mineralogists. Permian Basin Section. Publication [*A publication*]

Soc Econ Paleontol Mineral Repr Ser ... Society of Economic Paleontologists and Mineralogists. Reprint Series [*A publication*]

Soc Econ Paleontol Mineral Spec Publ ... Society of Economic Paleontologists and Mineralogists. Special Publication [*A publication*]

Soc Econ Paleontologists and Mineralogists Special Pub ... Society of Economic Paleontologists and Mineralogists. Special Publication [*A publication*]

Soc Econ Paleontologists and Mineralogists Spec Pub ... Society of Economic Paleontologists and Mineralogists. Special Publication [*A publication*]

Soc-Econ Plan Sci ... Socio-Economic Planning Sciences [*A publication*]

Soc & Econ Stud ... Social and Economic Studies [*A publication*]

Soc Econ Stud ... Social and Economic Studies [*A publication*]

Soc Econ Wetgeving ... Social Economisch Wetgeving. Tijdschrift voor Europees en Economisch Recht (DLA)

Soc Ed .... Social Education [*A publication*]

Soc Educ ... Social Education [*A publication*]

SOCELEX ... Society Against Elephant Exploitation (EA)

Soc Eng (London) J ... Society of Engineers (London). Journal [*A publication*]

Soc Espan Hist Nat Bol Secc Geol ... Sociedad Espanola de Historia Natural [*Real*] Boletin. Seccion Geologica [*A publication*]

Soc Espanola H N An ... Sociedad Espanola de Historia Natural. Anales [*A publication*]

Soc d'Etudes Sc d'Angers B ... Societe d'Etudes Scientifiques d'Angers. Bulletin [*A publication*]

Soc Etud et Expansion R ... Societe d'Etudes et d'Expansion Revue [*A publication*]

Soc Etud Indochinoises Bul ... Societe des Etudes Indochinoises. Bulletin [*A publication*]

Soc Exp Biol Semin Ser ... Society for Experimental Biology. Seminar Series [*A publication*]

Soc Explor Geophys Annu Int Meet Abstr ... Society of Exploration Geophysicists. Annual International Meeting. Abstracts [*A publication*]

Soc Exp Stress Anal Pap ... Society for Experimental Stress Analysis. Papers [*A publication*]

SOCF .... Spacecraft Operations and Checkout Facility (AAG)

Soc Fauna Flora Fenn Flora Fenn ... Societas pro Fauna et Flora Fennica. Flora Fennica [*A publication*]

Soc Forces ... Social Forces [*A publication*]

Soc Francaise Mineralogie et Cristallographie Bull ... Societe Francaise de Mineralogie et de Cristallographie. Bulletin [*A publication*]

Soc Franc Miner B ... Societe Francaise de Mineralogie. Bulletin [*A publication*]

Soc Fr Dermatol Syphiligr Bull ... Societe Francaise de Dermatologie et de Syphiligraphie. Bulletin [*A publication*]

Soc Fr Gynecol C R ... Societe Francaise de Gynecologie. Comptes Rendus [*A publication*]

Soc Fribourgeoise Sc Nat B Mem ... Societe Fribourgeoise des Sciences Naturelles. Bulletin. Memoires [*A publication*]

Soc Fr Mineral Cristallogr Bull ... Societe Francaise de Mineralogie et de Cristallographie. Bulletin [*A publication*]

Soc F TV Arts J ... Society of Film and Television Arts. Journal [*A publication*]

Soc G Belgique An ... Societe Geologique de Belgique. Annales [*A publication*]

Soc Gen Physiol Ser ... Society of General Physiologists. Series [*A publication*]

Soc Geog Fenniae Acta Geog ... Societas Geographica Fenniae. Acta Geographica [*A publication*]

Soc Geog Lima Bol ... Sociedad Geografica de Lima. Boletin [*A publication*]

Soc Geog Mex B ... Sociedad de Geografia y Estadistica de la Republica Mexicana. Boletin [*A publication*]

Soc Geog (Paris) B ... Societe de Geographie (Paris). Bulletin [*A publication*]

Soc Geog Que B ... Societe de Geographie de Quebec. Bulletin [*A publication*]

Soc Geogr Bol (Madrid) ... Sociedad Geografica. Boletin (Madrid) [*A publication*]

Soc Geol Belg Ann ... Societe Geologique de Belgique. Annales [*A publication*]

Soc Geol Belgique Annales ... Societe Geologique de Belgique. Annales [*A publication*]

Soc Geol France Bull ... Societe Geologique de France. Bulletin [*A publication*]

Soc Geol Fr Bull ... Societe Geologique de France. Bulletin [*A publication*]

Soc Geol Fr Mem ... Societe Geologique de France. Memoires [*A publication*]

Soc Geol Fr Mem Hors Ser ... Societe Geologique de France. Memoire Hors Serie [*A publication*]

Soc Geol Mex Bol ... Sociedad Geologica Mexicana. Boletin [*A publication*]

Soc Geol Mexicana Bol ... Sociedad Geologica Mexicana. Boletin [*A publication*]

Soc Geol Mineral Bretagne Bull ... Societe Geologique et Mineralogique de Bretagne. Bulletin [*A publication*]

Soc Geol et Mineralog Bretagne Bull ... Societe Geologique et Mineralogique de Bretagne. Bulletin [*A publication*]

Soc Geol Nord Ann ... Societe Geologique du Nord. Annales [*A publication*]

Soc Geol Normandie Bull ... Societe Geologique de Normandie. Bulletin [*A publication*]

Soc Geol Peru Bol ... Sociedad Geologica del Peru. Boletin [*A publication*]

Soc Geol Port Bol ... Sociedade Geologica de Portugal. Boletim [*A publication*]

Soc G France B Mem ... Societe Geologique de France. Bulletin. Memoires [*A publication*]

Soc G Italiana B ... Societa Geologica Italiana. Bollettino [*A publication*]

Soc Glass Technology Jour ... Society of Glass Technology. Journal [*A publication*]

Soc G Mex B ... Sociedad Geologica Mexicana. Boletin [*A publication*]

Soc G Nord An Mem ... Societe Geologique du Nord. Annales. Memoires [*A publication*]

Soc G Normandie B ... Societe Geologique de Normandie. Bulletin [*A publication*]

SOCH .... Spacelab Orbiter Common Hardware   (MCD)

Soc Haitienne Histoire Geographie Geologie Revue ... Societe Haitienne d'Histoire de Geographie et de Geologie. Revue [*A publication*]

SOCHINAFOR ... South China Force [*World War II*]

Soc Hist ..... Social History [*A publication*]

So C Hist Mag ... South Carolina Historical Magazine [*A publication*]

Soc Hist Nat Toulouse Bull ... Societe d'Histoire Naturelle de Toulouse. Bulletin [*A publication*]

Soc Hongroise Geog Abrege B ... Societe Hongroise de Geographie. Abrege du Bulletin [*A publication*]

Soc Hygiene ... Social Hygiene [*A publication*]

SOCI .... Society Corp. [*NASDAQ symbol*]   (NQ)

Social Biol ... Social Biology [*A publication*]

Social Case ... Social Casework [*A publication*]

Social Comp ... Social Compass [*A publication*]

Social en Democr ... Socialisme en Democratie [*A publication*]

Social Ec A ... Social and Economic Administration [*A publication*]

Social Econ ... Social and Economic Studies [*A publication*]

Social and Econ Admin ... Social and Economic Administration [*A publication*]

Social & Econ Stud ... Social and Economic Studies [*A publication*]

Social Educ ... Social Education [*A publication*]

Social Forc ... Social Forces [*A publication*]

Social Ind... Social Indicators Research [*A publication*]

Social Indicators Res ... Social Indicators Research [*A publication*]

Social Pol... Social Policy [*A publication*]

Social Prax ... Social Praxis [*A publication*]

Social Prob ... Social Problems [*A publication*]

Social Psy ... Social Psychiatry [*A publication*]

Social Psychol Q ... Social Psychology Quarterly [*A publication*]

Social Res ... Social Research [*A publication*]

Social Revol ... Socialist Revolution [*A publication*]

Social Sci... Social Science Quarterly [*A publication*]

Social Scie ... Social Science [*A publication*]

Social Science J (Fort Collins) ... Social Science Journal (Fort Collins) [*A publication*]

Social Science Q ... Social Science Quarterly [*A publication*]

Social Sci Inf ... Social Science Information [*A publication*]

Social Sci Q ... Social Science Quarterly [*A publication*]

SOCIAL SCISEARCH ... Social Science Citation Index Search [*Database*]

Social Sc M ... Social Science and Medicine [*A publication*]

Social Sec ... Social Security Bulletin [*US*] [*A publication*]

Social Security Bul ... Social Security Bulletin [*A publication*]

Social Se R ... Social Service Review [*A publication*]

Social Services J ... Social Services Journal [*A publication*]

Social St S ... Social Studies of Science [*A publication*]

Social Stud ... Social Studies [*A publication*]

Social Theor Pract ... Social Theory and Practice [*A publication*]

Social Trud ... Socialisticeskij Trud [*A publication*]

Societe d'Etudes et d'Expansion Revue ... Societe d'Etudes et d'Expansion. Revue [*A publication*]

SOCIM .... Society of Connoisseurs in Murder   (EA)

Soc Imp Nat Moscou B ... Societe Imperiale des Naturalistes de Moscou. Bulletin [*A publication*]

Soc Indep Prof Earth Sci Bull ... Society of Independent Professional Earth Scientists. Bulletin [*A publication*]

Soc Indicators Res ... Social Indicators Research [*A publication*]

Soc Indic Res ... Social Indicators Research [*A publication*]

Soc Ind Min B C R Men ... Societe de l'Industrie Minerale. Bulletin. Comptes Rendus Mensuels des Reunions [*A publication*]

Soc Ind Res ... Social Indicators Research [*A publication*]

Soc l'Industrie Minerale Cong Cent ... Societe de l'Industrie Minerale. Congres du Centenaire [*A publication*]

Soc Ing Civils France Mem ... Societe des Ingenieurs Civils de France. Memoires [*A publication*]

Socio-Econ ... Socio-Economic Planning Sciences [*A publication*]

Socioecon Newsletter ... Socioeconomic Newsletter [*A publication*]

Socio-Econ Plann Sci ... Socio-Economic Planning Sciences [*A publication*]

Socioecon Rep ... Socioeconomic Report. California Medical Association [*A publication*]

SOCIOL ...... Sociology

Sociol Anal ... Sociological Analysis [*A publication*]

Sociol Anal Theory ... Sociological Analysis and Theory [*A publication*]

Sociol B (Bombay) ... Sociological Bulletin (Bombay) [*A publication*]

Sociol Bull ... Sociological Bulletin [*A publication*]

Sociol Cas ... Sociologicky Casopis [*A publication*]

Sociol Contemp ... Sociologie Contemporaine [*A publication*]

Sociol of Ed ... Sociology of Education [*A publication*]

Sociol Educ ... Sociology of Education [*A publication*]

Sociol Educ Abstr ... Sociology of Education Abstracts [*A publication*]

Sociol Focu ... Sociological Focus [*A publication*]

Sociol Fors ... Sociologisk Forskning [*A publication*]

Sociol Gids ... Sociologische Gids [*A publication*]

Sociol Health Illness ... Sociology of Health and Illness [*A publication*]

Sociol Inq... Sociological Inquiry [*A publication*]

Sociol Inquiry ... Sociological Inquiry [*A publication*]

Sociol Int (Berlin) ... Sociologia Internationalis (Berlin) [*A publication*]

Sociol Issled (Moskva) ... Sociologiceskie Issledovanija (Moskva) [*A publication*]

Sociol Issled (Sverdlovsk) ... Sociologiceskie Issledovanija (Sverdlovsk) [*A publication*]

Sociol Law ... Sociology of Law [*A publication*]

Sociol Meddel ... Sociologiske Meddelelser [*A publication*]

Sociol Meth ... Sociological Methods and Research [*A publication*]

Sociol Methods & Res ... Sociological Methods and Research [*A publication*]

Sociol Neer ... Sociologia Neerlandica [*A publication*]

Sociological R ... Sociological Review [*A publication*]

Sociologus ... Sociologus Zeitschrift fuer Empirische Soziologie, Sozialpsychologische, und Ethnologische Forschung [*A publication*]

Sociol Org ... Sociologia dell'Organizzazione [*A publication*]

Sociol Q ..... Sociological Quarterly [*A publication*]

Sociol Quart ... Sociological Quarterly [*A publication*]

Sociol R ...... Sociological Review [*A publication*]

Sociol Rev ... Sociological Review [*A publication*]

Sociol Rev Monogr ... Sociological Review. Monograph [*A publication*]

Sociol R Mg ... Sociological Review. Monograph [*A publication*]

Sociol R NS ... Sociological Review. New Series [*A publication*]

Sociol Rur ... Sociologia Ruralis [*A publication*]

Sociol Ruralis ... Sociologia Ruralis [*A publication*]

Sociol Sela ... Sociologija Sela [*A publication*]

Sociol et Soc ... Sociologie et Societes [*A publication*]

Sociol Soc ... Sociology and Social Research [*A publication*]

Sociol Soci ... Sociologie et Societes [*A publication*]

Sociol & Social Res ... Sociology and Social Research [*A publication*]

Sociol & Soc Res ... Sociology and Social Research [*A publication*]

Sociol Symp ... Sociological Symposium [*A publication*]

Sociol Trav ... Sociologie du Travail [*A publication*]

Sociol Wk Occupat ... Sociology of Work and Occupations [*A publication*]

Sociol W Oc ... Sociology of Work and Occupations [*A publication*]

Sociol Yb Relig Britain ... Sociological Yearbook of Religion in Britain [*A publication*]

Sociom ...... Sociometry [*A publication*]

Socio Meth ... Sociological Methodology [*A publication*]

Socio R ...... Sociological Review [*A publication*]

Socio-Tech B ... Social-Technological Bulletin [*Quezon City*] [*A publication*]

Soc Isl .... Society Islands

SO Cist .... Sacer Ordo Cisterciensis [*Order of Cistercians*] [*Roman Catholic men's religious order*]

Soc Italiana Sc Nat Milano Atti ... Societa Italiana di Scienze Naturali in Milano. Atti [*A publication*]

Soc Ital Sci Farm Doc ... Societa Italiana di Scienze Farmaceutiche Documento [*A publication*]

Soc Ital Sci Nat Mus Civ Stor Nat Milano Atti ... Societa Italiana di Scienze Naturali e Museo Civico di Storia Naturale di Milano. Atti [*A publication*]

Soc Jus R ... Social Justice Review [*A publication*]

SocJust ...... Social Justice Review [*A publication*]

SOCK .... Save Our Cute Knees [*Detroit group opposing below-the-knee fashions introduced in 1970*]

Socker Handli ... Socker Handlingar [*A publication*]

Soc Languedoc Geogr ... Societe Languedocienne de Geographie [*A publication*]

Soc Languedocienne Geogr Bull ... Societe Languedocienne de Geographie. Bulletin [*A publication*]

SOCLD .... Solar Cells [*A publication*]

Soc and Leisure ... Society and Leisure [*A publication*]

SOCLGY .... Sociology

Soc Ligustica Sc Nat Geog Atti ... Societa Ligustica di Scienze Naturali e Geografiche. Atti [*A publication*]

Soc Linn Bord Bull ... Societe Linneenne de Bordeaux. Bulletin [*A publication*]

Soc Linneenne Normandie Bull ... Societe Linneenne de Normandie. Bulletin [*A publication*]

Soc Linn Lyon Bull ... Societe Linneenne de Lyon. Bulletin Mensuel [*A publication*]

SOCM .... Master Chief SONARman [*Navy rating*]

SOCM .... Shanley Oil Company [*NASDAQ symbol*] (NQ)

SOCM .... Stand-Off Cluster Munitions

SOCMA ..... Synthetic Organic Chemical Manufacturers Association [*Washington, DC*] (EA)

Soc Maandbl Arb ... Sociaal Maandblad Arbeid [*A publication*]

Soc Malac Belgique An ... Societe Malacologique de Belgique. Annales [*A publication*]

Soc Malacologica Rev ... Sociedad Malacologica. Revista [*A publication*]

Soc Malawi J ... Society of Malawi Journal [*A publication*]

Soc Manuf Eng Tech Pap Ser AD ... Society of Manufacturing Engineers. Technical Paper. Series AD (Assembly Division) [*A publication*]

Soc Manuf Eng Tech Pap Ser EE ... Society of Manufacturing Engineers. Technical Paper. Series EE (Electrical Engineering) [*A publication*]

Soc Manuf Eng Tech Pap Ser EM ... Society of Manufacturing Engineers. Technical Paper. Series EM (Engineering Materials) [*A publication*]

Soc Manuf Eng Tech Pap Ser FC ... Society of Manufacturing Engineers. Technical Paper. Series FC (Finishing and Coating) [*A publication*]

Soc Manuf Eng Tech Pap Ser IQ ... Society of Manufacturing Engineers. Technical Paper. Series IQ (Inspection and Quality) [*A publication*]

Soc Manuf Eng Tech Pap Ser MF ... Society of Manufacturing Engineers. Technical Paper. Series MF (Material Forming) [*A publication*]

Soc Manuf Eng Tech Pap Ser MR ... Society of Manufacturing Engineers. Technical Paper. Series MR (Material Removal) [*A publication*]

Soc Manuf Eng Tech Pap Ser MS ... Society of Manufacturing Engineers. Technical Paper. Series MS [*A publication*]

Soc Mass Media Resour Technol J ... Society for Mass Media and Resource Technology. Journal [*A publication*]

SOCMC ...... Special Order of the Commandant of the Marine Corps

Soc Med-Chir Hop Form Sanit Armees ... Societe Medico-Chirurgicale des Hopitaux et Formations Sanitaires des Armees [*A publication*]

Soc Med Mil Franc Bull ... Societe de Medecine Militaire Francaise. Bulletin [*A publication*]

Soc Mex Geog Estadistica B ... Sociedad Mexicana de Geografia y Estadistica. Boletin [*A publication*]

Soc Mexicana Geografia y Estadistica Bol ... Sociedad Mexicana de Geografia y Estadistica. Boletin [*A publication*]

Soc Mexicana Historia Nat Rev ... Sociedad Mexicana de Historia Natural. Revista [*A publication*]

Soc Micros Can Bull ... Societe de Microscopie du Canada. Bulletin [*A publication*]

Soc Miner France ... Societe Mineralogique de France. Bulletin [*A publication*]

SocN .... Sociolinguistics Newsletter [*A publication*]

SOCN .... Source Control Number

Soc Nat Luxemb Bull ... Societe des Naturalistes Luxembourgeois. Bulletin [*A publication*]

Soc Nat Pet Aquitaine Bull Cent Rech Pau ... Societe Nationale des Petroles d'Aquitaine. Bulletin de Centres de Recherches de Pau [*A publication*]

Soc Nav Architects Mar Eng Tech Res Bull ... Society of Naval Architects and Marine Engineers. Technical and Research Bulletin [*New York*] [*A publication*]

Soc Nav Architects Mar Eng Trans ... Society of Naval Architects and Marine Engineers of New York. Transactions [*A publication*]

Soc Nav Archit Mar Eng Trans ... Society of Naval Architects and Marine Engineers. Transactions [*United States*] [*A publication*]

Soc Nematol Spec Publ ... Society of Nematologists. Special Publication [*A publication*]

Soc Neuchatel Geogr Bull ... Societe Neuchateloise de Geographie. Bulletin [*A publication*]

Soc Neurosci Symp ... Society for Neuroscience. Symposia [*A publication*]

Soc Nucl Med Southeast Chapter Contin Educ Lect ... Society of Nuclear Medicine. Southeastern Chapter. Continuing Education Lectures [*A publication*]

Soc Num Mexico Bol ... Sociedad Numismatica de Mexico. Boletin [*A publication*]

SOCO .... Scenes-of-the-Crime Officer [*Scotland Yard*]

SOCO .... Standard Oil Company of California

SOCO .... Summit Oilfield Corporation [*NASDAQ symbol*] (NQ)

SOCO .... Switched out for Checkout [*NASA*] (KSC)

Soc Occup Medicine J ... Society of Occupational Medicine. Journal [*A publication*]

Soc Ocean J ... Societe des Oceanistes. Journal [*A publication*]

SOCOM ...... Society and Commerce Publications

SOCOM ...... Solar Communications

SOCOM ...... Southern Command (MCD)

SOCOM ...... Special Operations Command

SOCONY .... Standard Oil Company of New York [*Socony Mobil is now official name of firm*]

SOCORICO ... Society of Costa Rica Collectors [*Philately*] (EA)

SOCPAC .... Special Operations Center, Pacific Command (CINC)

Soc Paleontol Ital Boll ... Societa Paleontologica Italiana. Bollettino [*A publication*]

Soc Pet E J ... Society of Petroleum Engineers. American Institute of Mining, Metallurgical, and Petroleum Engineers. Journal [*A publication*]

Soc Pet Eng AIME Improv Oil Recovery Field Rep ... Society of Petroleum Engineers. American Institute of Mining, Metallurgical, and Petroleum Engineers. Improved Oil Recovery Field Reports [*A publication*]

Soc Pet Eng AIME J ... Society of Petroleum Engineers. American Institute of Mining, Metallurgical, and Petroleum Engineers. Journal [*A publication*]

Soc Pet Eng AIME Pap ... Society of Petroleum Engineers. American Institute of Mining, Metallurgical, and Petroleum Engineers. Papers [*A publication*]

Soc Pet Eng AIME Trans ... Society of Petroleum Engineers. American Institute of Mining, Metallurgical, and Petroleum Engineers. Transactions [*A publication*]

Soc Pet Eng J ... Society of Petroleum Engineers. American Institute of Mining, Metallurgical, and Petroleum Engineers. Journal [*A publication*]

Soc Pet Engr J ... Society of Petroleum Engineers. American Institute of Mining, Metallurgical, and Petroleum Engineers. Journal [*A publication*]

Soc Pet Engrs J ... Society of Petroleum Engineers. American Institute of Mining, Metallurgical, and Petroleum Engineers. Journal [*A publication*]

Soc Petrol Eng J ... Society of Petroleum Engineers. American Institute of Mining, Metallurgical, and Petroleum Engineers. Journal [*A publication*]

Soc Petrol Eng Trans ... Society of Petroleum Engineers. American Institute of Mining, Metallurgical, and Petroleum Engineers. Transactions [*A publication*]

Soc Petroleum Engineers AIME Trans ... Society of Petroleum Engineers. American Institute of Mining, Metallurgical, and Petroleum Engineers. Transactions [*A publication*]

Soc Petroleum Engineers Jour ... Society of Petroleum Engineers. American Institute of Mining, Metallurgical, and Petroleum Engineers. Journal [*A publication*]

Soc Photo-Opt Instrum Eng Proc ... Society of Photo-Optical Instrumentation Engineers. Proceedings [*United States*] [*A publication*]

Soc Plast Eng Div Tech Conf Tech Pap ... Society of Plastics Engineers. Divisional Technical Conference. Technical Papers [*A publication*]

Soc Pol .... Social Policy [*A publication*]

Soc Policy ... Social Policy [*A publication*]

Soc-Polit Soc-Ekon Probl Razvit Social Obsc ... Social'no-Politiceskie i Social'no-Ekonomiceskie Problemy Razvitogo Socialisticeskogo Obscestva [*A publication*]

Soc Pr .... Social Progress [*A publication*]

Soc Prax .... Social Praxis [*A publication*]

Soc Prehist Francais Bull ... Societe Prehistorique Francaise. Bulletin [*A publication*]

Soc Prehist Francaise Bul ... Societe Prehistorique Francaise. Bulletin [*A publication*]

Soc Prehist Fr Bull ... Societe Prehistorique Francaise. Bulletin [*A publication*]

Soc Prob .... Social Problems [*A publication*]

Soc Probl Nauc-Tehn Revol ... Social'nye Problemy Naucno-Tehniceskogo Revoljucii [*A publication*]

Soc Promotion Agr Sc Pr ... Society for the Promotion of Agricultural Science. Proceedings of the Annual Meeting [*A publication*]

Soc Psichol Filos ... Social'naja Psichologija i Filosofija [*A publication*]

Soc Psychiatry ... Social Psychiatry [*A publication*]

Soc Psychol ... Social Psychology [*A publication*]

Soc Psychol Q ... Social Psychology Quarterly [*A publication*]

Soc Psych Res Proc ... Society for Psychical Research. Proceedings [*A publication*]

Soc Que Prot Plant Rapp ... Societe de Quebec pour la Protection des Plantes. Rapport [*A publication*]

Soc Quim Mexico Rev ... Sociedad Quimica de Mexico. Revista [*A publication*]

SOCR .... Scan-Optics, Inc. [*NASDAQ symbol*] (NQ)

Soc R .... Social Research [*A publication*]

Soc R .... Sociological Review [*A publication*]

SoCR :......... South Carolina Review [*A publication*]

SOCR .... Special Operational Contract Requirements (AAG)

SOCR .... Sustained Operations Control Room [*NASA*] (KSC)

SOCR .... Synchronous Orbit Communication Relay (MCD)

SOCRATES ... Storage and Retrieval of Carrier Rates [*Military shipments*]

SOCRATES ... System for Organizing Content to Review and Teach Educational Subjects

SOCRATES ... System for Organizing Current Reports to Aid Technology and Science

SOCRED .... Social Credit Party [*British*]

Soc Regis... Socialist Register [*A publication*]

Soc Res...... Social Research [*A publication*]

Soc Res...... Social Reserve [*A publication*]

Soc Res Child Devel Monogr ... Society for Research in Child Development. Monographs [*A publication*]

Soc Research Administrators J ... Journal. Society of Research Administrators [*A publication*]

Soc Rev...... Socialist Review [*A publication*]

Soc Revol... Socialist Revolution [*A publication*]

Soc R di Nap Accad di Archeol Atti ... Societa Reale di Napoli. Accademia di Archeologia, Lettere, e Belle Arti. Atti [*A publication*]

Soc R di Nap Accad di Sci Mor e Pol Atti ... Societa Reale di Napoli. Accademia di Scienze Morali e Politiche. Atti [*A publication*]

Soc R di Napoli Accad di Archeol Atti ... Societa Reale di Napoli. Accademia di Archeologia, Lettere, e Belle Arti. Atti [*A publication*]

Soc R di Napoli Accad d Sci Fis e Mat Atti ... Societa Reale di Napoli. Accademia delle Scienze, Fisiche, e Matematiche. Atti [*A publication*]

SOC ROS ... Societas Rosicruciana [*Freemasonry*]

Soc Royale Econ Pol Belgique Seance ... Societe Royale d'Economie Politique de Belgique Seances [*A publication*]

Soc Roy Belge de Geog B ... Societe Royale Belge de Geographie. Bulletin [*A publication*]

Soc Roy Econ Polit Belgique ... Societe Royale d'Economie Politique de Belgique [*A publication*]

SOCS .... Senior Chief SONARman [*Navy rating*]

SOCS .... Spacecraft-Orientation-Control System

SOCS .... Subsystem Operating and Checkout System   (MCD)

Soc Sci ...... Social Sciences [*A publication*]

Soc Scientist ... Social Scientist [*A publication*]

Soc Sci Fenn Arsb-Vuosik ... Societas Scientiarum Fennicae. Arsbok-Vuosikirja [*A publication*]

Soc Sci Fenn Commentat Phys-Math ... Societas Scientiarum Fennica. Commentationes Physico-Mathematicae [*A publication*]

Soc Sci Fenn Comment Phys-Math ... Societas Scientiarum Fennica. Commentationes Physico-Mathematicae [*A publication*]

Soc Sci Fennica Arsb ... Societas Scientiarum Fennica. Arsbok [*A publication*]

Soc Sci Fennica Commentationes Phys-Math ... Societas Scientiarum Fennica. Commentationes Physico-Mathematicae [*A publication*]

Soc Sci Ind ... Social Sciences Index [*A publication*]

Soc Sci Inf ... Social Science Information [*A publication*]

Soc Sci Inform ... Social Science Information [*A publication*]

Soc Sci J.... Social Science Journal [*A publication*]

Soc Sci Lettres & Arts Pau Bul ... Societe des Sciences, Lettres, et Arts. Pau Bulletin [*A publication*]

Soc Sci Lodz Acta Chim ... Societatis Scientiarum Lodziensis. Acta Chimica [*A publication*]

Soc Sci Med ... Social Science and Medicine [*A publication*]

Soc Sci Med A ... Social Science and Medicine. Part A. Medical Sociology [*A publication*]

Soc Sci Med B ... Social Science and Medicine. Part B. Medical Anthropology [*A publication*]

Soc Sci Med C ... Social Science and Medicine. Part C. Medical Economics [*A publication*]

Soc Sci Med D ... Social Science and Medicine. Part D. Medical Geography [*A publication*]

Soc Sci Medic ... Social Science and Medicine [*A publication*]

Soc Sci Med (Med Anthropol) ... Social Science and Medicine (Medical Anthropology) [*A publication*]

Soc Sci Med (Med Geogr) ... Social Science and Medicine (Medical Geography) [*A publication*]

Soc Sci Med Med Psychol Med Sociol ... Social Science and Medicine. Medical Psychology and Medical Sociology [*A publication*]

Soc Sci Monographs ... Social Science Monographs [*A publication*]

Soc Sci Nat Ouest Fr Bull ... Societe des Sciences Naturelles de l'Ouest de la France. Bulletin [*A publication*]

Soc Sci Q ... Social Science Quarterly [*A publication*]

Soc Sci R ... Social Science Review [*Bangkok*] [*A publication*]

Soc Sci Res ... Social Science Research [*A publication*]

Soc Sci Res Council Bull ... Social Science Research Council. Bulletin [*A publication*]

Soc Sci (Winfield) ... Social Science (Winfield) [*A publication*]

Soc & Sci Res ... Sociology and Social Research [*A publication*]

Soc Sc Nat Neuchatel B ... Societe des Sciences Naturelles de Neuchatel. Bulletin [*A publication*]

Soc Sec Bull ... Social Security Bulletin [*US*] [*A publication*]

Soc Sec Rep ... Social Security Reporter [*A publication*]

Soc Secur Bull ... Social Security Bulletin [*A publication*]

Soc Serbe Geographie Mem ... Societe Serbe de Geographie. Memoires [*A publication*]

Soc Ser Rev ... Social Service Review [*A publication*]

Soc Serv .... Social Service [*A publication*]

Soc Serv J ... Social Services Journal [*A publication*]

Soc Serv Q ... Social Service Quarterly [*A publication*]

Soc Serv R ... Social Service Review [*A publication*]

Soc Serv Rev ... Social Service Review [*A publication*]

Soc de Statist de Paris J ... Societe de Statistique de Paris. Journal [*A publication*]

Soc Statist Paris J ... Societe de Statistique de Paris. Journal [*A publication*]

Soc Stud .... Social Studies [*A publication*]

Soc Studies ... Social Studies [*A publication*]

Soc Stud Sci ... Social Studies of Science [*United Kingdom*] [*A publication*]

Soc Sur ...... Social Survey [*A publication*]

Soc Surv ...... Social Survey [*A publication*]

Soc Survey ... Social Survey [*A publication*]

SOCTAP .... Sulfur Oxide Control Technology Assessment Panel [*Federal interagency committee*]

Soc Theory & Pract ... Social Theory and Practice [*A publication*]

Soc Thought ... Social Thought [*A publication*]

Soc Thr ...... Socialist Theory and Practice [*A publication*]

Soc Trends ... Social Trends [*A publication*]

Soc Tss ...... Socialt Tidsskrift [*A publication*]

Soc Vac Coaters Proc Annu Conf ... Society of Vacuum Coaters. Proceedings. Annual Conference [*A publication*]

Soc Vaudoise Sci Nat Bull ... Societe Vaudoise des Sciences Naturelles. Bulletin [*A publication*]

Soc Venez Cienc Nat Bol ... Sociedad Venezolana de Ciencias Naturales. Boletin [*A publication*]

Soc Venezolana Ciencias Natur Bol ... Sociedad Venezolana de Ciencias Naturales. Boletin [*A publication*]

Soc Ven Sci Nat Lav ... Societa Veneziana di Scienze Naturali Lavori [*A publication*]

Soc W......... Social Work [*A publication*]

Soc Welfare ... Social Welfare [*A publication*]

Soc Wetensch ... Sociale Wetenschappen [*A publication*]

Soc Wk (Albany) ... Social Work (Albany) [*A publication*]

Soc Work ... Social Work [*A publication*]

Soc Work Health Care ... Social Work in Health Care [*A publication*]

Soc Work Lect ... Social Work Lectures [*New Zealand*] [*A publication*]

Soc Workr ... Social Worker [*A publication*]

Soc Work Res Abstr ... Social Work Research and Abstracts [*A publication*]

Soc Work Today ... Social Work Today [*A publication*]

SOCY .... Society   (ROG)

SOCY .... Sociology   (ROG)

SOCYA...... Society [*A publication*]

Soc Zemes Ukis ... Socialistinis Zemes Ukis [*A publication*]

Soc Zemjod ... Socijalisticko Zemjodelstvo [*A publication*]

Soc Zool France B ... Societe Zoologique de France. Bulletin [*A publication*]

Soc Zool Fr Bull ... Societe Zoologique de France. Bulletin [*A publication*]

SOD........... Sediment Oxygen Demand [*of water bodies*]

SOD........... Sell-Off Date   (AAG)

SOD........... Seller's Option to Double [*Business and trade*]

SOD........... Serial Output Data [*Data processing*]

SOD........... Shorter Oxford Dictionary [*A publication*]

SOD........... Shuttle Operational Data   (MCD)

SOD........... Small Object Detector

SOD........... Society of Dismas   (EA)

SOD........... Sodankyla [*Finland*] [*Geomagnetic observatory code*]

SOD........... Sodankyla [*Finland*] [*Seismograph station code, US Geological Survey*]   (SEIS)

SOD........... Sodomy [*FBI standardized term*]

SOD........... Soldier Orientation and Development   (MCD)

SOD........... Solitron Devices, Inc. [*American Stock Exchange symbol*]

SOD........... Sons of the Desert   (EA)

SOD........... Sound-on-Disk   (DEN)

SOD........... Special Operations Detachment [*Military*]   (AABC)

SOD........... Special Operations Division [*Office of Preparedness, General Services Administration*]

SOD........... Special Order Discharge

SOD........... Staff Operations Division [*NASA*]   (MCD)

SOD........... Superintendent of Documents [*US Government Printing Office*]

SOD........... Superoxide Dismutase [*An enzyme*]

SOD........... Sustained Operational Date   (AFM)

SOD........... Systems Operational Description [*or Design*]

So 2d.......... Southern Reporter, Second Series   (DLA)

SODA .... Source Oriented Data Acquisition

SODA .... Stamp Out Drug Addiction

SODAC ...... Source Data Collection

So Dak B Jo ... South Dakota Bar Journal   (DLA)

So Dak Hist ... South Dakota History [*A publication*]

So Dak Hist Coll ... South Dakota Historical Collections [*A publication*]

So Dak L Rev ... South Dakota Law Review [*A publication*]

So Dakota Lib Bul ... South Dakota Library Bulletin [*A publication*]

So Dak R ...... South Dakota Review [*A publication*]

SODAR....... Sound Detecting and Ranging

SODAS...... Structure-Oriented Description and Simulation   (IEEE)

SODAS...... Synoptic Oceanographic Data Acquisition System [*Marine science*]   (MSC)

SODB .... Science Organization Development Board [*National Academy of Sciences*]

SODB .... Shuttle [*or Spacecraft*] Operational Data Book [*NASA*]

SODB .... Start of Data Block   (MCD)

Sodep .... Social Democratic Party [*Turkey*]   (PPW)

SODEPALM ... Societe pour le Developpement et l'Exploitation du Palmier a Huile [*Ivory Coast*]
SODEPAX ... Committee on Society, Development, and Peace [*of the Roman Catholic Church and the World Council of Churches*] [*Defunct*] (EA)
SODEX ...... Social Data Exchange Association [*Council for Community Services*] [*Information service*] (EISS)
SODPAL ...... Social Democrat Party and Liberal [*British*]
SODRE .... Servicio Oficial de Difusion Radio Electrica [*Radio and television network*] [*Uruguay*]
SODRS ...... Synchronous Orbit Data Relay Satellite
SODS .... Saturn Operational Display System [*NASA*]
SODS .... Shuttle Operational Data System (MCD)
SODS .... Skylab Orbit-Deorbit System (MCD)
SODS .... Subordinate Operations Data System (NVT)
SODT .... Scope Octal Debugging Tape
SODTICIOAP ... Special Ordnance Depot Tool Identification, Classification, Inventory, and Obsolescence Analysis Program [*Popularly called "Soda Cap"*]
SODU .... Screen Oriented Disk Utility [*Data processing*]
SOE .... Sequence of Events
SOE .... Significant Operating Experience (IEEE)
SOE .... Silver Oxide Electrode
SOE .... Skylab Operational Environment [*NASA*]
SOE .... Slater Orbital Exponents [*Atomic physics*]
SOE .... Souanke [*Congo*] [*Airport symbol*] (OAG)
SOE .... Special Operations Executive [*British research unit corresponding to OSS*] [*World War II*]
SOE .... Stage Operations Engineer
SOE .... Start of Entry [*Data processing*]
SOE .... Status of Equipment [*Army*] (AABC)
SOE .... Summary of Engagements (MCD)
SOE .... Super Orbit Entry
SOEAP ...... Summary of Effective Allowance Parts List [*Navy*]
SOEASTPAC ... Southeast Pacific Command [*Navy*]
So East Rep ... Southeastern Reporter (DLA)
SOEBT ...... Stationery and Office Equipment Board of Trade [*Great Neck, NY*] (EA)
SOEC .... Statistical Office of the European Communities
SOECA ...... Soviet Electrochemistry [*English Translation*] [*A publication*]
So Econ J ... Southern Economic Journal [*A publication*]
SOED .... Shorter Oxford English Dictionary [*A publication*]
So Educ Report ... Southern Education Report [*A publication*]
SOEEA ...... Soviet Electrical Engineering [*English Translation*] [*A publication*]
SOEH .... Society for Occupational and Environmental Health [*Washington, DC*] (EA)
SOEMC ...... Senior Officer Executive Management Course [*Naval War College*]
SOEMD ...... Solar Energy Materials [*A publication*]
SOEND ...... Solar Engineering [*A publication*]
SOEP .... Solar-Oriented Experimental Package [*NASA*]
SOER .... Significant Operating Event Report (IEEE)
SOERO ...... Small Orbiting Earth Resources Observatory (IEEE)
SOES .... Station Operations and Engineering Squadron [*Marine Corps*]
SOE/SO ..... Special Operations Executive, Special Operations [*British*] [*World War II*]
Soester Z ... Soester Zeitschrift [*A publication*]
So Expose ... Southern Exposure [*A publication*]
SOF .... Safety of Flight [*NASA*] (NASA)
SoF .... Samtid och Framtid [*A publication*]
SOF .... Satisfactory Operation Factor [*Telecommunications*] (TEL)
SOF .... Secretary's Open Forum (EA)
Sof. .... Soferim (BJA)
SOF .... Sofia [*Bulgaria*] [*Airport symbol*] (OAG)
SOF .... Sofia [*Bulgaria*] [*Seismograph station code, US Geological Survey*] (SEIS)
SOF .... Soldiers of Fortune
SOF .... Sound on Film
SOF .... Special Operations Force [*Military*]
SOF .... Spillover Factor
SOF .... Spreading Ocean Floor
SOF .... Start of Frame
SOF .... Status of Forces
SOF .... Storage Oscilloscope Fragments
SOF .... Strategic Offensive Forces [*Army*] (AABC)
SOF .... Sub-Occipito Frontal [*Medicine*] (ROG)
SOF .... Suedost-Forschungen [*A publication*]
SOF .... Superior Orbital Fissure [*Eye anatomy*]
SOF .... Supervisor of Flying (MCD)
SOFA .... Bench Craft, Inc. [*NASDAQ symbol*] (NQ)
SOFA .... Status of Forces Agreement [*International treaty*]
SOFA .... Student Overseas Flights for Americans
SOFAR ...... Sound Fixing and Ranging [*Navy underground sound system*]
SOFAS ...... Survivable Optical Forward Acquisition System (MCD)
SOFC .... Saturn Operational Flight Control [*NASA*]
SOFC .... Solid Oxide Fuel Cell [*Energy source*]
SOFCS ...... Self-Organizing Flight Control System
SofD .... Sons of David (BJA)
SOFEX ...... Southern Ocean Float Experiment [*Marine science*] (MSC)
S/OFF .... Sign Off [*Data processing*] (MDG)

SOFI .... Spray-On Foam Insulation (NASA)
SOFIE .... Sources de Financement des Entreprises [*CCMC Informatique de Gestion*] [*Database*]
SOFIX .... Software Fix [*NASA*]
SOFNET ..... Solar Observing and Forecasting Network [*Air Force*]
SOFOA ...... Social Forces [*A publication*]
So Folklore Q ... Southern Folklore Quarterly [*A publication*]
SOFPAC ..... Special Operating Forces, Pacific
SOFRECOM ... Societe Francaise d'Etudes et de Realisations d'Equipements de Telecommunications [*French communications engineering company*] [*Telecommunications*] (TEL)
SOFRES ..... Societe Francaise d'Enquetes par Sondages [*French opinion-polling organization*]
SOFT .... Simple Output Format Translator (IEEE)
SOFT .... Society of Forensic Toxicologists (EA)
SOFT .... SofTech, Inc. [*NASDAQ symbol*] (NQ)
SOFT .... Space Operations and Flight Techniques [*NASA*] (NASA)
SOFT .... Special Operational Forces Taiwan (CINC)
SOFT .... Status of Forces Treaty
SOFT 18/13 ... Support Organization for Trisomy 18/13 [*Midvale, UT*] (EA)
SOFTA .... Shippers Oil Field Traffic Association [*Irving, TX*] (EA)
SOFTCON ... Software Conference [*Trademark*]
Soft Eng ..... IEEE. Transactions on Software Engineering [*A publication*]
Software .... Software: Practice and Experience [*A publication*]
Software Pract and Exper ... Software: Practice and Experience [*A publication*]
Software Pract Exper ... Software: Practice and Experience [*A publication*]
Software Rev ... Software Review [*A publication*]
Software Tools Commun ... Software Tools Communications [*A publication*]
Softw Newsl ... Software Newsletter [*A publication*]
Soft World ... Software World [*A publication*]
SOFTY .... Southern Federation of Temple Youth
SOG .... Same Output Gate [*Data processing*] (AAG)
SOG .... Seat of Government [*Washington, DC*]
SOG .... Second-Order Gradient
sog .... Sogdian [*MARC language code*] [*Library of Congress*] (LCCP)
SOG .... Sogenannt [*So-Called*] [*German*]
SOG .... Sogndal [*Norway*] [*Airport symbol*] (OAG)
SOG .... Special Operations Group [*Navy*]
SOG .... Speed Made Good Over the Ground (NATG)
SOG .... Straits Oil & Gas [*Vancouver Stock Exchange symbol*]
SOG .... Studies and Observations Group [*Military*]
SOGAT ...... Supraoesophageal Ganglion [*Invertebrate nuerology*]
SOGAT ...... Society of Graphical and Allied Trades [*British*]
SOGEA ...... Southeastern Geology [*United States*] [*A publication*]
SOGEB ...... Soviet Genetics [*English Translation*] [*A publication*]
SOGLF .... Shelter Oil & Gas [*NASDAQ symbol*] (NQ)
SOGp .... Special Operations Group [*Air Force*] (AFM)
SOGWPIP ... Silly Old Grandmother with Pictures in Purse
SOH .... Skylab Operations Handbook [*NASA*]
SOH .... Southern Ohio Aviation Sales Co. [*West Carrollton, OH*] [*FAA designator*] (FAAC)
SOH .... Standard Oil Co. (Ohio) [*NYSE symbol*]
SOH .... Start of Heading [*Transmission control character*] [*Data processing*]
SOH .... Supply Overhaul (MCD)
SOHAM ...... Southampton [*City in England*] (ROG)
SOHI .... Sponsors of Open Housing Investment [*Later, Fund for an Open Society*] (EA)
SOHIO .... Standard Oil Co. (Ohio)
So His S ..... Southern Historical Society [*A publication*]
So Hist Pap ... Southern Historical Society. Papers [*A publication*]
SOHO .... Solar and Heliospheric Observatory [*European Space Agency*]
SoHo .... South of Houston Street [*See also NoHo, SoSo, TriBeCa*] [*Artists' colony in New York City*]
SOHR .... Solar Hydrogen Rocket Engine
SoHR .... Southern Humanities Review [*A publication*]
SOI .... Scientific and Optical Instruments
SOI .... Signal Operation Instructions
SOI .... Silicon-on-Insulator
SOI .... Snyder Oil Partners [*NYSE symbol*]
SOI .... South Molle Island [*Australia*] [*Airport symbol*] (OAG)
SOI .... Southern Illinois University at Carbondale, Carbondale, IL [*OCLC symbol*] (OCLC)
SOI .... Southern Indiana Railway, Inc. [*Later, SIND*] [*AAR code*]
SOI .... Space Object Identification (AFM)
SOI .... Specific Operating Instruction (AFM)
SOI .... Sphere of Influence
SOI .... Standard Operating Instruction (KSC)
SOI .... State of Stimulus Overinclusion [*Schizophrenia*]
SOI .... Statistics of Income [*IRS*]
SOI .... Stimulus Onset Interval
SOI .... Surety and Operational Inspection [*Military*] (AFIT)
SOIC .... Supply Officer-in-Command [*Military*]
SOICC .... State Occupational Information Coordinating Committee
SOICS .... Summary of Installation Control Status (NRCH)
SOID .... Shipboard Ordnance Infrared Decoy (MCD)
Soil Assoc Inf Bull Advis Serv ... Soil Association. Information Bulletin and Advisory Service [*England*] [*A publication*]
Soil Biochem ... Soil Biochemistry [*A publication*]

Soil Biol B ... Soil Biology and Biochemistry [*A publication*]
Soil Biol and Biochem ... Soil Biology and Biochemistry [*A publication*]
Soil Biol Biochem ... Soil Biology and Biochemistry [*A publication*]
Soil Biol Microbiol ... Soil Biology and Microbiologie [*A publication*]
Soil Cons ... Soil Conservation [*A publication*]
Soil Conser ... Soil Conservation [*A publication*]
Soil Conserv ... Soil Conservation [*A publication*]
Soil Cons Serv NSW J ... Soil Conservation Service of New South Wales. Journal [*A publication*]
Soil Crop Sci Soc Fla Proc ... Soil and Crop Science Society of Florida. Proceedings [*A publication*]
Soil Fert .... Soils and Fertilizers [*A publication*]
Soil Fert Taiwan ... Soils and Fertilizers in Taiwan [*A publication*]
Soil Ld-Use Surv Br Caribb ... Soil and Land-Use Surveys of the British Caribbean [*A publication*]
So III LJ ...... Southern Illinois University. Law Journal [*A publication*]
Soil Mech Found Eng ... Soil Mechanics and Foundations Engineering [*A publication*]
Soil Mech Found Engng ... Soil Mechanics and Foundation Engineering [*A publication*]
Soil Mech Found Eng Reg Conf Afr Proc ... Soil Mechanics and Foundation Engineering. Regional Conference for Africa. Proceedings [*A publication*]
Soil Publ .... Soil Publication. Commonwealth Scientific and Industrial Research Organisation [*Australia*] [*A publication*]
Soil Publ CSIRO ... Soil Publication. Commonwealth Scientific and Industrial Research Organisation [*Australia*] [*A publication*]
Soils Bull FAO ... Soils Bulletin. Food and Agriculture Organization [*A publication*]
Soil Sci .... Soil Science [*A publication*]
Soil Sci Agron ... Soil Science and Agronomy [*A publication*]
Soil Sci Plant Nutr ... Soil Science and Plant Nutrition [*A publication*]
Soil Sci Plant Nutr (Tokyo) ... Soil Science and Plant Nutrition (Tokyo) [*A publication*]
Soil Sci Pl Nutr ... Soil Science and Plant Nutrition [*A publication*]
Soil Sci So ... Soil Science Society of America. Proceedings [*A publication*]
Soil Sci Soc America Proc ... Soil Science Society of America. Proceedings [*A publication*]
Soil Sci Soc Am J ... Soil Science Society of America. Journal [*A publication*]
Soil Sci Soc Am Proc ... Soil Science Society of America. Proceedings [*A publication*]
Soil Sci Soc Fla Proc ... Soil Science Society of Florida. Proceedings [*A publication*]
Soil Ser Dep Soil Sci Minnesota Univ ... Minnesota University. Department of Soil Science. Soil Series [*A publication*]
Soil Ser Minn Univ Agr Ext Serv ... Soil Series. Minnesota University. Agriculture Extension Service [*A publication*]
Soils Fert ... Soils and Fertilizers [*England*] [*A publication*]
Soils Fertil ... Soils and Fertilizers [*A publication*]
Soils Fertil Taiwan ... Soils and Fertilizers in Taiwan [*A publication*]
Soils Found ... Soils and Foundations [*A publication*]
Soils Land Use Ser Div Soils CSIRO ... Soils and Land Use Series. Division of Soils. Commonwealth Scientific and Industrial Research Organisation [*A publication*]
Soils Ld Use Ser Div Soils CSIRO ... Soils and Land Use Series. Division of Soils. Commonwealth Scientific and Industrial Research Organisation [*A publication*]
Soils Rep Manitoba Soil Surv ... Soils Report. Manitoba Soil Survey [*A publication*]
Soil Surv Invest Rep ... Soil Survey Investigations. Report [*A publication*]
Soil Surv Pap Neth Soil Surv Inst ... Soil Survey Papers. Netherlands Soil Survey Institute [*A publication*]
Soil and Water Conser News ... Soil and Water Conservation News [*A publication*]
Soil and Water Conserv Jour ... Soil and Water Conservation Journal [*A publication*]
SOINC .... Supply Officer-in-Charge [*Navy*]
SOIP .... Sell-Off Impact Prognosticator [*Aerospace*] (AAG)
SOIP .... Ship Overhaul Improvement Program [*Navy*]
SOIP .... Sphere of Influence People
SOIS .... Space Object Identification System
SOIS .... Spacelab/Orbiter Interface Simulator [*NASA*] (NASA)
SOISCUM ... Space Object Identification Summary (MCD)
SOJ .... Sea of Japan (NVT)
SOJ .... Sorkjosen [*Norway*] [*Airport symbol*] (OAG)
SOJ .... Standoff Jammer (NVT)
SoJA .... Soviet Jewish Affairs [*A publication*]
So Jersey LS Dictum ... South Jersey Law School Dictum (DLA)
SOJS .... Standoff Jammer Suppression (MCD)
SOJT .... Structured On-the-Job Training (MCD)
SOJT .... Supervised On-the-Job Training
SOJTA .... State On-the-Job Training Agencies [*Department of Labor*]
SOK .... American Sokol Educational and Physical Culture Organization
SOK .... Semongkong [*Lesotho*] [*Airport symbol*] [*Obsolete*] (OAG)
Sok .... Sokrates [*A publication*]
SOK .... South Kauai, HI [*Location identifier*] [*FAA*] (FAAL)
SOK .... Sprog og Kultur [*A publication*]
SOK .... Suomen Osuuskauppojen Keskuskunta [*Co-Operative Wholesale Society*] [*Helsinki, Finland*]
SOK .... Supply OK [*i.e., Authorized*]
SOKAB ...... Sosei To Kako [*A publication*]

SOKSI .... Sentral Organisasi Karyawan Sosialis Indonesia [*Central Organization of Indonesian Socialist Workers*]
SOL .... Safe Operating Limit
SOL .... Sasko Oil & Gas [*Toronto Stock Exchange symbol*] [*Vancouver Stock Exchange symbol*]
SOL .... School of Living [*An association*] (EA)
SOL .... Secretary of Labor (OICC)
SOL .... Senior Operator License [*Nuclear energy*] (NRCH)
SOL .... Shipowner's Liability [*Business and trade*]
SOL .... Short of Luck (DSUE)
SOL .... Simulation Oriented Language [*Data processing*]
SOL .... Sisters of Our Lady [*Roman Catholic religious order*]
SOL .... Social Organisation Limited
SOL .... Solar (AAG)
SOL .... Solder
SOL .... Soldier out of Luck [*Military slang*]
SOL .... Solenoid (AAG)
SOL .... Soleus Muscle [*Anatomy*]
SOL .... Soliciting [*FBI standardized term*]
SOL .... Solicitor
Sol .... Solicitor [*A publication*]
SOL .... Solicitor of Labor [*Department of Labor*]
SOL .... Solid (MSA)
Sol .... Solidarity [*Manila*] [*A publication*]
SOL .... Solitaire [*Jewelry*] (ROG)
Sol .... Soloman's Court of Request Appeals [*Ceylon*] (DLA)
SOL .... Solomon [*Biblical king*] (ROG)
SOL .... Solomon, AK [*Location identifier*] [*FAA*] (FAAL)
Sol .... Solon [*of Plutarch*] [*Classical studies*] (OCD)
SOL .... Solubilis [*Soluble*] [*Pharmacy*]
SOL .... Soluble
SOL .... Solutio [*Solution*] [*Pharmacy*]
SOL .... Solution
SOL .... Solve [*or Solutus*] [*Dissolve or Dissolved*] [*Pharmacy*] (ROG)
SOL .... Southern Illinois University, School of Law Library, Carbondale, IL [*OCLC symbol*] (OCLC)
SOL .... Space-Occupying Lesion [*Medicine*]
SOL .... Strictly Out of Luck [*Bowdlerized version*] [*Slang*]
SOL .... Substitute Optical Landing System (NG)
SOL .... Sure out of Luck [*Bowdlerized version*]
SOL .... System Oriented Language
SOLA .... Selected Objects for Living Actively [*Commercial firm specializing in home furnishings for the elderly*]
Sol Age ...... Solar Age [*A publication*]
Solaire 1 Mag ... Solaire 1 Magazine [*France*] [*A publication*]
SOLAN .... Solid Angles
SOLANT ..... South Atlantic Force [*Later, Command*] [*Navy*] [*World War II*]
SOLANTFOR ... South Atlantic Force [*Later, Command*] [*Navy*] [*World War II*]
SOLAR .... Sandel On-Line Automated Reference [*Information service*]
SOLAR .... Semantically Oriented Lexical Archive
SOLAR .... Serialized On-Line Automatic Recording [*Data processing*] (IEEE)
SOLAR .... Shop Operations Load Analysis Reporting
SOLAR .... Sociedad Latinoamericana de Estudios sobre America Latina y el Caribe [*International Association of Latin American and Caribbean Studies - IALACS*] [*Mexico City, Mexico*] (EA-IO)
SOLAR .... Society of Loose Actors Revolving [*SOLAR Theater, Inc.*]
Solar E D ... Solar Energy Digest [*A publication*]
Solar En D ... Solar Energy Digest [*A publication*]
Solar Energ ... Solar Energy [*A publication*]
Solar Intel ... Solar Energy Intelligence Report [*A publication*]
SOLARIS .... Submerged Object Locating and Retrieving Identification System
SOLAR MAX ... Solar Maximum Mission Satellite
Solar Phys ... Solar Physics [*A publication*]
Solar Syst Res ... Solar System Research [*A publication*]
SOLAS .... Safety of Life at Sea Conference [*Marine science*] (MSC)
SOLAT .... Style of Learning and Thinking [*Occupational therapy*]
So Law ...... Southern Lawyer (DLA)
SOLB .... Start of Line Block (CET)
Sol Cells .... Solar Cells [*A publication*]
SOLCHEM ... Solar-Chemical [*Energy conversion process*]
Sol Cl Gaz ... Solicitors' Clerks' Gazette [*1921-40*] (DLA)
SOLD .... Simulation of Logic Design
SOLE .... Society of Logistics Engineers
SOLEC .... Stand on Leg, Eyes Closed [*Equilibrium test*]
Sol Energy ... Solar Energy [*A publication*]
Sol Energy Intell Rep ... Solar Energy Intelligence Report [*A publication*]
Sol Energy Mater ... Solar Energy Materials [*Netherlands*] [*A publication*]
Sol Energy Prog Aust NZ ... Solar Energy Progress in Australia and New Zealand [*A publication*]
Sol Energy Res Dev Rep ... Solar Energy Research and Development Report [*A publication*]
Sol Energy Res Rep Univ Queensl ... Solar Energy Research Report. University of Queensland [*A publication*]
Sol Energy Update ... Solar Energy Update [*A publication*]
Sol Eng ...... Solar Engineering [*A publication*]
Sol Eng Mag ... Solar Engineering Magazine [*A publication*]

SOLF......... Southern Oregon Library Federation [*Library network*]
SOLFEAS... Solar Energy System Economic Feasibility Program [*Army*] (RDA)
Sol G.......... Solicitor General (DLA)
Sol Gen...... Solicitor General (DLA)
Sol Heat Cool ... Solar Heating and Cooling [*A publication*]
SOLI........... Soviet Life [*A publication*]
SOLI........... Symphony Orchestra Library Information [*Sinfonia Software*] [*Piedmont, CA*]
SOLICO...... Sorenson Lighted Controls, Inc.
SOLID .... Self-Organizing Large Information Dissemination System (IEEE)
SOLID .... Simulation of Life Insurance Decisions [*Game*]
Solid Fuel Chem ... Solid Fuel Chemistry [*English translation of Khimiya Tverdogo Topliva*] [*A publication*]
Solid Fuel Chem (Engl Transl) ... Solid Fuel Chemistry (English Translation) [*A publication*]
Solid Mech Arch ... Solid Mechanics Archives [*A publication*]
Solid St Abstr ... Solid State Abstracts [*A publication*]
Solid Stat... Solid State Technology [*A publication*]
Solid State Commun ... Solid State Communications [*A publication*]
Solid-State Electron ... Solid-State Electronics [*A publication*]
Solid State J ... Solid State Journal [*A publication*]
Solid State Phys ... Solid State Physics [*A publication*]
Solid State Phys Chem ... Solid State Physics and Chemistry [*Japan*] [*A publication*]
Solid State Phys (New York) ... Solid State Physics. Advances in Research and Applications (New York) [*A publication*]
Solid State Technol ... Solid State Technology [*A publication*]
Solid St Commun ... Solid State Communications [*A publication*]
Solid Wastes Manage ... Solid Wastes Management [*Later, World Wastes*] [*England*] [*A publication*]
Solid Wastes Manage Refuse Removal J ... Solid Wastes Management/ Refuse Removal Journal [*Later, World Wastes*] [*A publication*]
Solid Wastes Mgmt ... Solid Wastes Management [*Later, World Wastes*] [*A publication*]
Solid Waste Syst ... Solid Waste Systems [*A publication*]
Solid WM ... Solid Wastes Management [*Later, World Wastes*] [*A publication*]
SOLINET.... Southeastern Library Network [*Atlanta, GA*] [*Library network*]
SOLINEWS.... Southeastern Library Network. Newsletter [*A publication*]
SOLION...... Solution of Ions [*Office of Naval Research*]
SOLIS........ Social Sciences Literature Information System [*Informationszentrum Sozialwissenschaften*] [*Database*]
SOLIS........ Symbionics On-Line Information System [*Data processing*]
SOLISTRON ... Solid-State Klystron
So Lit J....... Southern Literary Journal [*A publication*]
SOliv .... Studia Oliveriana [*A publication*]
Sol J .... Solicitors' Journal [*A publication*]
So LJ.......... Southern Law Journal and Reporter (DLA)
SoLJ.......... Southern Literary Journal [*A publication*]
Sol Jo (Eng) ... Solicitors' Journal [*England*] [*A publication*]
Sol J & R.... Solicitors' Journal and Reporter (DLA)
Sol Law Rep ... Solar Law Reporter [*A publication*]
Sol Life...... Solar Life [*A publication*]
SOLM .... Sisters of Our Lady of Mercy [*Mercedarians*] [*Roman Catholic religious order*]
Sol Man Cl Gaz ... Solicitor's Managing Clerks' Gazette [*1941-62*] (DLA)
SOLN.......... Solution
Soln Dannye ... Solnechnye Dannye [*USSR*] [*A publication*]
Sol News Int ... Solar News International [*West Germany*] [*A publication*]
SOLO .... Selective Optical Lock-On [*Sighting device*]
SOLO .... Senior Officer Legal Orientation (MCD)
SOLO .... Southeastern Ohio Library Organization [*Library network*]
SOLO .... Status of Logistics Offensive (AABC)
SOLO .... Supply On-Line Option [*IMS America Ltd.*] [*Database*]
SOLO .... System for Ordinary Life Operations [*Insurance*]
SOLOC...... Southern Line of Communications [*World War II*]
Solo Cent Acad "Luiz De Queiroz" Univ Sao Paulo ... Solo Centro Academico "Luiz De Queiroz." Universidade de Sao Paulo [*A publication*]
SOLOG...... Standardization of Certain Aspects of Operations and Logistics
SOLOMON ... Simultaneous Operation Linked Ordinal Modular Network
Sol Op .... Solicitor's Opinion [*Especially of Internal Revenue Bureau*] [*United States*] (DLA)
Sol Phys.... Solar Physics [*A publication*]
Sol Q .... Solicitor Quarterly [*1962-65*] (DLA)
So LQ .... Southern Law Quarterly (DLA)
SOLQA....... Sociological Quarterly [*A publication*]
SOLR.......... Applied Solar Energy [*NASDAQ symbol*] (NQ)
SOLR.......... Sidetone Objective Loudness Rating [*of telephone connections*] (IEEE)
SOLR.......... Solicitor
So LR .... Southern Law Review [*Nashville, TN*] (DLA)
SOLRAD..... Solar Radiation [*Satellite system*] [*Navy*]
SOLRAD-HI ... Solar Radiation - High-Altitude [*Satellite system*] [*Navy*]
SOL Rev..... School of Law. Review [*Canada*] (DLA)
So L Rev.... Southern Law Review [*St. Louis, MO*] (DLA)
So L Rev.... Southern Law Review [*Nashville, TN*] (DLA)
So L Rev NS ... Southern Law Review, New Series [*St. Louis, MO*] (DLA)

So LRNS .... Southern Law Review, New Series [*St. Louis, MO*] (DLA)
Solrs.......... Solicitors (DLA)
SOLS.......... Solicitors
Sols Afr ...... Sols Africains [*A publication*]
SOL-SAL..... Solar Scientific Airlock
Sol St Comm ... Solid State Communications [*A publication*]
Sol-St Elec ... Solid-State Electronics [*A publication*]
Sol St Tech ... Solid State Technology [*A publication*]
Sol Syst Res ... Solar System Research [*A publication*]
So LT.......... Southern Law Times (DLA)
Sol Terr Environ Res Jpn ... Solar Terrestrial Environmental Research in Japan [*A publication*]
Sol Therm Components ... Solar Thermal Components [*A publication*]
Sol Therm Energy Util ... Solar Thermal Energy Utilization [*A publication*]
Sol Therm Heat Cool ... Solar Thermal Heating and Cooling [*A publication*]
Sol Therm Power Gener ... Solar Thermal Power Generation [*A publication*]
Sol Therm Rep ... Solar Thermal Report [*A publication*]
Sol Times... Solar Times [*A publication*]
SOLTRAN ... Solar Spectrum and Transmittance [*Solar energy research*]
SOL U/T...... Solicitor's Undertaking
SOLUT........ Solutus [*Dissolved*] [*Pharmacy*] (ROG)
SOLV......... Solenoid Valve [*Mechanical engineering*]
SOLV......... Solv-Ex [*NASDAQ symbol*] (NQ)
SOLV......... Solve [*Dissolve*] [*Pharmacy*]
SOLV......... Solvent
SOLV......... Super-Open-Frame Low Voltage (IEEE)
SOLVE C CAL ... Solve Cum Calore [*Dissolve by Heating*] [*Pharmacy*]
Solvent Extr Ion Exch ... Solvent Extraction and Ion Exchange [*A publication*]
Solvent Extr Rev ... Solvent Extraction Reviews [*A publication*]
SOLY.......... Solubility
Som............ De Somniis [*of Philo*] (BJA)
SOM .... SACLANT [*Supreme Allied Commander, Atlantic*] Staff Organization Manual (NATG)
SOM .... San Tome [*Venezuela*] [*Airport symbol*] (OAG)
SOM .... Scanning Optical Microscope
SOM .... Securities Order Matching [*Data processing*]
SOM .... See Our Message
SOM .... Self-Organizing Machine
SOM .... Sensitivity-of-Method [*FDA*]
SOM .... Serous Otitis Media [*Ear inflammation*]
SOM .... Share of Market [*Advertising*]
SOM .... Shift Operations Manager (NRCH)
SOM .... Ship Operations Manager [*NASA*] (KSC)
SOM .... Skidmore, Owings & Merrill [*Architectural firm*]
SOM .... Small Office Microfilm
som .... Somali [*MARC language code*] [*Library of Congress*] (LCCP)
SOM .... Somali [*Three-letter standard code*] (CNC)
SOM .... Somatostatin [*Biochemistry*]
SOM .... Somatotrophin [*Endocrinology*]
SOM .... Sombrero [*Chile*] [*Seismograph station code, US Geological Survey*] (SEIS)
SOM .... Somerset [*County in England*]
SOM .... Somerset County Library, Bridgewater, NJ [*OCLC symbol*] (OCLC)
Som............ Somerset Legal Journal [*Pennsylvania*] (DLA)
SOM .... Somersetshire [*County in England*]
SOM .... Somnus [*Sleep*] [*Latin*] (ROG)
SOM .... SONARman [*Navy*]
SOM .... Sound of Music [*Dolls by Alexander*] [*Doll collecting*]
So M .... Southern Magazine [*A publication*]
SOM .... Spacecraft Operations Manual
SOM .... Spares Optimization Model [*NASA*] (NASA)
SOM .... Stage Operating Manual [*NASA*] (KSC)
SOM .... Standard Operating Manual [*NASA*] (NASA)
SOM .... Standoff Missile (MCD)
SOM .... Start-of-Message
SOM .... Superior Oblique Muscle [*Eye anatomy*]
SOM .... Superior Old Marsala
SOM .... Survivability Optimization Model (MCD)
SOM .... Sustained Operations Model
SOM .... System Operator Manual [*Military*] (CAAL)
SOMA........ Services to Ongoing Mature Aging [*Counseling group*]
SOMA........ Signed Out Against Medical Advice
SOMA........ Soobscenija Otdela Machanizacii i Avtomatizacii Informacionnych Rabot [*A publication*]
SoMa......... South of Market [*District of San Francisco*]
SOMA........ Student Osteopathic Medical Association [*Philadelphia, PA*] (EA)
SOMADA ... Self-Organizing Multiple-Access Discrete Address [*Data processing*] (IEEE)
SOMARPI... Supplemental Maintenance and Repair Parts Instruction (MCD)
Somatic Cell Genet ... Somatic Cell Genetics [*A publication*]
SOMBA...... Southern Medical Bulletin [*United States*] [*A publication*]
Som Cell G... Somatic Cell Genetics [*A publication*]
SOMDA...... Southwestern Medicine [*United States*] [*A publication*]
SOME........ Secretary's Office, Management Engineer [*Navy*]
SOME........ So Others Might Eat [*Washington, DC, soup kitchen and social-service center*]
SOMEA ..... Sovetskaya Meditsina [*A publication*]

SOMEG to ADV ... Something to Advantage [*Advertising*] [*Legal*]
Somerset Archaeol Natur Hist ... Somerset Archaeology and Natural History [*A publication*]
Somerset Arch Nat Hist ... Somerset Archaeology and Natural History [*A publication*]
Somerset Industrial Archaeology Soc Jnl ... Somerset Industrial Archaeology Society. Journal [*A publication*]
Somerset Levels Pap ... Somerset Levels Papers [*A publication*]
Somerset LJ ... Somerset Legal Journal (DLA)
SOMET ...... Sometimes
SOMF .... SIDPERS [*Standard Installation/Division Personnel System*] Organization Master File [*Military*] (AABC)
SOMF .... Start of Minor Frame (MCD)
SOMH .... SONARman Harbor Defense [*Navy*]
SOM-H ...... Start-of-Message - High Precedence (CET)
SOMI .... Sternal-Occipital-Mandibular Immobilization [*Medicine*]
SOMIEX ..... Societe Malienne d'Importation et d'Exportation [*Malian Import Export Co.*]
SOMISA ..... Sociedad Mixta Siderurgia Argentina [*Steel producer in Argentina*]
SOMISS ..... Study of Management Information Systems Support [*Army*]
SOM-L .... Start-of-Message - Low Precedence (CET)
Som Leg J (PA) ... Somerset Legal Journal [*Pennsylvania*] (DLA)
SOM-LI .... Somatostatin-Like Immunoreactivity
Som LJ .... Somerset Legal Journal [*Pennsylvania*] (DLA)
Som LR ...... Somalia Law Reports (DLA)
Somogyi Muesz Sz ... Somogyi Mueszaki Szemle [*Hungary*] [*A publication*]
SOM-P .... Start-of-Message - Priority
SOMP .... Sydney Ocean Meeting Point [*Navy*]
SOMPA ...... System of Multicultural Pluralistic Assessment [*Psychological and educational testing*]
Som Pl .... Somersetshire Pleas [*Civil and Criminal*], Edited by Chadwyck-Healey and Landon [*Somerset Record Society Publications, Vols. 11, 36, 41, 44*] (DLA)
SOMRB ...... Senior Officers Materiel Review Board [*Army*] (AABC)
SOMS .... Service Order Mechanization [*or Mechanized*] System [*AT & T*]
SOMS .... Shuttle Orbiter Medical System (MCD)
SOMS .... Synchronous, Operational Meteorological Satellite
SOMSA ...... Soviet Materials Science [*English Translation*] [*A publication*]
SOMST ...... Somersetshire [*County in England*] (ROG)
SOMT .... Soldier Operator Maintainer Testing (MCD)
SOMTO ...... Subversive Operations, Mediterranean Theatre of Operations [*World War II*]
SOMTS ...... Division of Ship Operations and Marine Technical Support [*University of California, San Diego*] [*Research center*] (RCD)
SON .... Espiritu Santo [*Vanuata*] [*Airport symbol*] (OAG)
S/ON .... Sign On [*Data processing*] (MDG)
SON .... Slovenske Odborne Nazvoslovie [*A publication*]
SON .... Society of Nematologists
son .... Songhai [*MARC language code*] [*Library of Congress*] (LCCP)
SON .... Sonneberg [*Federal Republic of Germany*] [*Seismograph station code, US Geological Survey*] [*Closed*] (SEIS)
Son .... Sonnets [*Shakespearean work*]
Son .... Sonora [*Record label*] [*Sweden*]
SON .... Sonora Gold Corp. [*Toronto Stock Exchange symbol*] [*Vancouver Stock Exchange symbol*]
SON .... Statement of Operational Need
SON .... Support of Other Nations [*Military support furnished certain nations and funded by the Air Force*]
SON .... Supraoptic Nucleus [*Brain anatomy*]
SONA .... School of Naval Administration, Leland Stanford University
SONAC ..... SONAR Nacelle [*Sonacelle*]
SONAD ...... Sonic Azimuth Detector (MCD)
SONAD ...... Speech-Operated Noise Adjusting Device [*Telecommunications*] (TEL)
SONAR .... Sound Navigation and Ranging
SONARRAY ... SONAR Array [*Sounding system*] [*Navy*]
SONATRACH ... Societe Nationale de Transport et de Commercialisation des Hydrocarbures
SONB .... Sonobuoy
Sonc .... Soncino (BJA)
SoncinoB ... [*The*] Soncino Books of the Bible (Bornemouth) [*A publication*] (BJA)
SONCM ..... SONAR Countermeasures and Deception
SONCR ...... SONAR Control Room (MSA)
SOND .... Secretary's Office, Navy Department
Sonderdr Internist Welt ... Sonderdruck aus Internistische Welt [*West Germany*] [*A publication*]
Sonderh Bayer Landw Jb ... Sonderhefte. Bayerisches Landwirtschaftliches Jahrbuch [*A publication*]
Sonderh Landw Forsch ... Sonderheft zur Zeitschrift "Landwirtschaftliche Forschung" [*A publication*]
Sonderh Z PflKrankh PflPath PflSchutz ... Sonderheft. Zeitschrift fuer Pflanzenkrankheiten, Pflanzenpathologie, und Pflanzenschutz [*A publication*]
Sonderjydsk M-skr ... Sonderjydsk Manedsskrift [*A publication*]
Song .... Song of Songs [*Old Testament book*] [*Roman Catholic canon*]
SongCh ...... Song of the Three Children [*Old Testament book*] [*Apocrypha*] (BJA)

Song 3 Childr ... Song of the Three Children [*Old Testament book*] [*Apocrypha*]
Song Hits Mag ... Song Hits Magazine [*A publication*]
SongR .... Song of Songs Rabbah (BJA)
SONGS ...... San Onofre Nuclear Generating Station (NRCH)
Song Sol .... Song of Solomon [*Old Testament book*]
Song of Three Childr ... [*The*] Song of the Three Holy Children [*Apocrypha*]
Songwriter ... Songwriter Magazine [*A publication*]
Songwriters R ... Songwriter's Review [*A publication*]
SONIC .... System-Wide On-Line Network for Information Control [*Data processing*]
SONM .... Sonoma International [*NASDAQ symbol*] (NQ)
SONNA .... Somali National News Agency
Sonnenenerg ... Sonnenenergie [*A publication*]
SONO .... Satellite Object Number (MUGU)
SONO .... Sonobuoy
SONO .... Sonoco Products Co. [*NASDAQ symbol*] (NQ)
SONOAN ... Sonic Noise Analyzer
SOnoM ...... Studia Ononmastica Monacensia [*A publication*]
SONOSW ... Sonoswitch
SONP .... Solid Organs Not Palpable [*Medicine*]
So NQ .... Somerset Notes and Queries [*A publication*]
SONRD ...... Secretary's Office, Office of Research and Development [*Navy*]
SONRES ..... Saturated Optical Nonresonant Emission Spectroscopy
SONS .... Seek Out New Suppliers
SONS .... Society of Non-Smokers (EA)
SONS .... Statistics of Naval Shipyards
Son Spec ... Sonorum Speculum [*A publication*]
SOO .... Sault Meadows Energy [*Vancouver Stock Exchange symbol*]
SOO .... Schenectady Operations Office [*Energy Research and Development Administration*]
SOO .... Songo [*Mozambique*] [*Airport symbol*] (OAG)
SOO .... Soo Line Corp. [*NYSE symbol and AAR code*]
SOO .... Staff Officer Operations [*British*]
Soob A N Gruz SSR ... Soobshcheniia Akademii Nauk Gruzinskoi SSR [*A publication*]
Soob G Ermitazh ... Soobshcheniia Gosudarstvennogo Ermitazha [*A publication*]
Soob G Muz Izob Isk Pushkin ... Soobshcheniia Gosudarstvennyi Muzei Izobrazitel'nykh Iskusstv Imeni A. S. Pushkina [*A publication*]
Soob Kherson Muz ... Soobshcheniia Khersonnesskogo Muzeia [*Sebastopol*] [*A publication*]
SoobMP ..... Soobscenija du Musee d'Art Pouchkine [*A publication*]
Soobscenija Akad Nauk Gruz SSR ... Soobscenija Akademiji Nauk Gruzinskoj SSR [*A publication*]
Soobsc Gosud Russk Muz ... Soobscenija Gosudarstvennogo Russkogo Muzeja [*A publication*]
Soobsc Muz Isk Nar Vostoka ... Soobscenija Muzeja Iskusstva Narodov Vostoka [*A publication*]
Soobsc Vycisl Mat ... Soobscenija po Vychislitel noi Matematike [*A publication*]
Soobshch Akad Nauk Gruzin SSR ... Soobshcheniya Akademiya Nauk Gruzinskoi SSR [*A publication*]
Soobshch Akad Nauk Gruz SSSR ... Soobshcheniya Akademiya Nauk Gruzinskoi SSSR [*A publication*]
Soobshch Byurakan Obs Akad Nauk Arm SSR ... Soobshcheniya Byurakanskoj Observatorii. Akademiya Nauk Armyanskoj SSR [*A publication*]
Soobshch Dal'Nevost Fil Sib Otd Aka Nauk SSSR ... Soobshcheniya Dal'Nevostochnogo Filiala Sibirskogo Otdla Akademii Nauk SSSR [*A publication*]
Soobshch Inst Agrokhim Probl Gidroponiki Akad Nauk Arm SSR ... Soobshcheniya Instituta Agrokhimicheskikh Problem i Gidroponiki. Akademiya Nauk Armyanskoi SSR [*Armenian SSR*] [*A publication*]
Soobshch Inst Lesa Akad Nauk SSSR ... Soobshcheniya Instituta Lesa Akademii Nauk SSSR [*A publication*]
SoobshchIPPO ... Soobshcheniia Imperialnovo Pravoslavnovo Palestinskavo Obshchestva [*A publication*]
Soobshch Obshch Lab Agrokhim Akad Nauk Armyan SSR ... Soobshcheniya Obshchestvoi Laboratorii Agrokhimii Akademii Nauk Armyanskoi SSR [*A publication*]
Soobshch Sakhalin Fil Akad Nauk SSSR ... Soobshcheniya Sakhalinskogo Filiala Akademii Nauk SSSR [*A publication*]
Soobshch Shemakhinskoi Astrofiz Obs Akad Nauk Azerb SSR ... Soobshcheskoi Shemakhinskoi Astrofizicheskoi Observatorii. Akademiya Nauk Azerbaidzhan SSR [*Azerbaidzhan SSR*] [*A publication*]
Soochow J Hum ... Soochow Journal of Humanities [*Taipei*] [*A publication*]
Soochow J Lit Soc Stud ... Soochow Journal of Literature and Social Studies [*Taipei*] [*A publication*]
Soochow J Math Natur Sci ... Soochow Journal of Mathematical and Natural Sciences [*Later, Soochow Journal of Mathematics*] [*A publication*]
SOOM .... Saigon Officers Open Mess [*Vietnam*]
SOON .... Sequence for Opportunities and Negatives [*Rand Corp.*]
SOON .... Solar Observing Optical Network [*Air Force*]
SOON .... Sooner Defense of Florida [*NASDAQ symbol*] (NQ)
Soon Chun Hyang J Med ... Soon Chun Hyang Journal of Medicine [*Republic of Korea*] [*A publication*]

SOOP .... Special Old Oil Price
SOOP .... Submarine Oceanographic Observation Program
SOP .... Pinehurst [*North Carolina*] [*Airport symbol*] (OAG)
SOP .... Safety Operating Plan
SOP .... Saturn Orbiter Probe [*NASA*]
SOP .... Scavenging, Oil Pump (MSA)
SOP .... Scented Orange Pekoe [*Tea trade*] (ROG)
SOP .... Seat of the Pants
SOP .... Second Opinion Program [*Health Benefits Research Center, New York Hospital, Cornell Medical Center*] [*Later, NSOP*] (EA)
SOP .... Secondary Operation
SOP .... Secondary Oxygen Pack [*NASA*]
SOP .... Semiopen Position [*Dancing*]
SOP .... Semiorganic Polymer
SOP .... Senior Officer Present
SOP .... Ship's Operational Program [*Navy*] (NVT)
SOPSA .... Shop Overload Parts (AAG)
SOP .... Simulated Output Program [*Data processing*]
SOP .... Simulation Operations Plan [*NASA*] (KSC)
SOP .... Sleeping-Out Pass [*British armed forces*]
SOP .... Soprano
SOP .... Sopron [*Hungary*] [*Seismograph station code, US Geological Survey*] (SEIS)
SOP .... Southern Pines, NC [*Location identifier*] [*FAA*] (FAAL)
SOP .... Spacelab Opportunity Payload (MCD)
SOP .... Spares Order Processing (MCD)
SOP .... Special Operating Procedure (IEEE)
SOP .... Special Order Price
SOP .... Staff Officer of Pensioners [*Army*] [*British*] (ROG)
SOP .... Standard Operating Plan (OICC)
SOP .... Standard [*or Standing*] Operating Procedure
SOP .... Statewide Operating Plan
SOP .... Station Operating Plan (AAG)
SOP .... Stock Option Plan
SOP .... Strategic Objectives Plan
SOP .... Strategic Orbit Point (KSC)
SOP .... Study Organization Plan (BUR)
SOP .... Subsystems Operating Procedure [*NASA*] (NASA)
SOP .... Successive Organization of Perception [*Pilot behavior*]
SOP .... Sulfate of Potash [*Fertilizer*]
SOP .... Supplemental Oxygen Package (MCD)
SOP .... Supplier Operating Procedure (MCD)
Sor .... Surface Oil Pickup
SOP .... Surgical Outpatient [*Medicine*]
SOP .... Symbolic Optimum Program
SOP .... Systems Operation Plan [*NASA*] (KSC)
SOPA .... Senior Officer Present Afloat
SOP(A) .... Senior Officer Present (Ashore) [*Navy*]
SOPA .... Society of Professional Archeologists (EA)
SOPA .... Standoff Precision Attack [*Military*] (CAAL)
SOPAA .... Soviet Physics. Acoustics [*English Translation*] [*A publication*]
SOPAC ...... Joint CCOP/IOC Program of Research on the South Pacific [*Marine science*] (MSC)
SOPAC ...... South Pacific Command [*Navy*]
SOPAC ...... Southern Pacific Railroad Co.
SOPACBACOM ... South Pacific Base Command [*Navy*] [*World War II*]
SOPACCOMS ... South Pacific Communications [*Navy*]
SOPAD ...... SOPA [*Senior Officer Present Afloat*] Administrative Duties [*Military*] (NVT)
SOPAD ...... Summary of Proceedings and Debate [*of House of Representatives*]
SOPAG ...... Societe des Participations Gardinier [*French fertilizer firm*]
SOPAT ...... South China Patrol [*Navy*] [*World War II*]
SOPC .... Sales Operations Planning and Control [*Management*]
SOPC .... Shuttle Operations and Planning Center (MCD)
SOPDOSS ... Submersible Oriented Platform for Deep Ocean Sediment Studies [*Marine science*] (MSC)
SOPE .... Simulated Off-the-Pad Ejection [*NASA*]
SO-PE .... Sodium Pentathol [*Nickname*]
Soph .... Sopherim (BJA)
Soph .... Sophista [*of Plato*] [*A publication*] (OCD)
SOPH .... Sophister [*British*] (ROG)
SOPH .... Sophocles [*Greek poet, 496–406BC*] [*Classical studies*] (ROG)
SOPH .... Sophomore
Soph .... Sophonias [*Old Testament book*] [*Douay version*]
SOPH .... Starboard Out, Port Home [*Variation of POSH*]
SOPHE ...... Society for Public Health Education [*San Francisco, CA*] (EA)
Soph El ...... Sophistici Elenchi [*of Aristotle*] [*Classical studies*] (OCD)
Sophia Econ R ... Sophia Economic Review [*Tokyo*] [*A publication*]
Sophia:T .... Sophia: Studies in Western Civilization and the Cultural Interaction of East and West (Tokyo) [*A publication*]
SOPI .... Superintendent of Public Instruction (OICC)
SOPJA .... Soviet Physics Journal [*English Translation*] [*A publication*]
SOPLA .... Soviet Plastics [*English Translation*] [*A publication*]
SOPLASCO ... Southern Plastics Company
SOPLC ...... Senior Officer Preventive Logistics Course (MCD)
SOPM .... Standard Orbital Parameter Message [*NASA*] (KSC)
SOPMET .... Standing Operating Procedure - Meteorological Plan (NATG)
SOPO .... Society of Oral Physiology and Occlusion

SOPODA .... Social Planning, Policy & Development Abstracts [*Sociological Abstracts, Inc.*] [*Database*]
SOPONATA ... Sociedade Portuguesa de Navios Tanques [*Shipping company*] [*Lisbon, Portugal*]
SOPP .... Sodium Ortho-Phenylphenoxide [*Organic chemistry*]
SOPP .... Special Order Perfect Price [*for undamaged merchandise*]
SOPP .... Statement of Provisioning Policy [*Military*] (AFIT)
SOPPA .... Soviet Plant Physiology [*English Translation*] [*A publication*]
SOPPC .... Special Operations Photo Processing Cell (MCD)
SOPR .... South Pierce Railroad [*AAR code*]
SOPR .... Spanish Open Pool Reactor
SOPR .... Special Officer Personnel Requirements [*Military*]
SOPR .... Standing Operating Procedure Regulation [*Navy*] (MCD)
SOPS .... Shot Noise Optical Optimization Communication System with Stops [*NASA*]
S Op S .... Si Opus Sit [*If Needed*] [*Pharmacy*]
SOPS .... Spacecraft Operations Planning Section
SOPSA ...... Shuttle Orbit-Injection Propulsion System Analysis [*NASA*]
SOPT .... Science Operations Planning Team
SOPUA ...... Soviet Physics. Uspekhi [*English Translation*] [*A publication*]
SOPUS ...... Senior Officer Present, United States Navy
SOQ .... Senior Officers' Quarters
SOQ .... Sick Officer Quarters
Soq .... Soqotri (BJA)
SOQ .... Sorong [*Indonesia*] [*Airport symbol*] (OAG)
So Q .... Southern Quarterly Review [*A publication*]
SOQ .... System Optical Quality (MCD)
SOQAS ...... Statement of Quality and Support (MCD)
SOQUEM... Societe Quebecoise d'Exploration Miniere [*Quebec Mining Exploration Co.*]
SOQUIJ ...... Societe Quebecoise d'Information Juridique [*Quebec Society for Legal Information*] [*Montreal, PQ*] [*Information service*] (EISS)
SOR .... Sale or Return [*Business and trade*] (ADA)
SOR .... Sampling Oscilloscope Recorder
SOR .... Saxon Owners Registry (EA)
SOR .... Seder 'Olam Rabbah (BJA)
SOR .... Sensor Operation Room (AFM)
SOR .... Serie Orientale Roma [*A publication*]
SOR .... Service Operational Requirement
SOR .... Single Order Release (MCD)
SoR .... Society of Rheology
SOR .... Sonor Petroleum Corp. [*Toronto Stock Exchange symbol*]
Sor .... Soria [*Record label*]
SOR .... Soroa [*Cuba*] [*Seismograph station code, US Geological Survey*] (SEIS)
SOR .... Source Capital, Inc. [*NYSE symbol*]
SOR .... Source of Repair (MCD)
So R .... Southern Review [*US*] [*A publication*]
SoR .... Southern Review: An Australian Journal of Literary Studies [*A publication*]
SOR .... Specific Operational Requirement
SOR .... Spilled Oil Research [*Marine science*] (MSC)
SOR .... Squadron Operational Report
SOR .... Stable-Orbit Rendezvous [*NASA*]
SOR .... Stand-Off Range (MCD)
SOR .... Standard Operating Report
SOR .... Standard Operating Rules
SOR .... Start of Record (MUGU)
SOR .... State of Readiness (MCD)
SOR .... Statement of Requirement [*Military*] (AFIT)
SOR .... Status or Operating Resources (MCD)
SOR .... Statutory Order and Regulation [*Canada*]
SOR .... Stephens Owners Registry (EA)
S-O-R .... Stimulus-Organism-Response
SOR .... Students of Origins Research [*A publication*]
SOR .... Subcarrier Oscillator Rack
SOR .... Successive Overrelaxation
SOR .... Systems Operational Requirement
SOR .... Winfield/Arkansas City, KS [*Location identifier*] [*FAA*] (FAAL)
SORA .... Secretary's Office, Records Administration [*Navy*]
SORA .... Sorgento Rapido [*Reactor*] (NRCH)
So R A .... Southern Review: An Australian Journal of Literary Studies [*A publication*]
SORAD....... Sonic Ranging and Detection (KSC)
SORAFOM ... Societe de Radiodiffusion de la France d'Outre-Mer [*Society for Radio Broadcasting of Overseas France*]
SORAP ...... Signature Overlap Range Prediction
SORAP ...... Standard Omnirange Approach
SORB .... Subsistence Operations Review Board [*Military*] (AABC)
Sorb D .... Sorbitol Dehydrogenase [*Also, SDH*] [*An enzyme*]
SORC .... Signal Officers' Reserve Corps
SORC .... Sound Ranging Control
SORC .... Southern Ocean Racing Conference
SORC .... Station Operations Review Committee [*Nuclear energy*] (NRCH)
SORCS...... Shipboard Ordnance Requirement Computer System [*Navy*]
SORD .... Society of Record Dealers of America
SORD .... Southwestern Order Retrieval and Distribution [*Southwest Bell Telephone Co.*]
SORD .... Submerged Object Recovery Device

SORDC....... Southwest Ohio Regional Data Center [*University of Cincinnati*] [*Research center*]   (RCD)
SORE .... Stamp Out Regulatory Excesses [*An association*]   (EA)
SOREL ...... Sun-Orbiting Relativity Experiment Satellite
SOREM ...... Sleep-Onset REM [*Rapid Eye Movement*]
SOREMA.... Societe de Reassurance des Assurances Mutuelles Agricoles [*Paris, France*]
So Rep ...... Southern Reporter   (DLA)
So Repr ..... Southern Reporter   (DLA)
S O Rev ..... Sean O'Casey Review [*A publication*]
SORG .... Sorg Printing Co. [*NASDAQ symbol*]   (NQ)
SORG .... Submarine Operations Research Group [*Navy*]
SORI .... Southern Research Institute   (AAG)
SORIN .... Societa Ricerche Impianti Nucleari [*Italy*]
SORM........ Set-Oriented Retrieval Module
SORNE(I) ... Senior Officer, Royal Naval Establishment (India) [*British*] [*World War II*]
SORNG...... Sound Ranging
So R ns ..... Southern Review: New Series [*US*] [*A publication*]
SORO .... Scan on Receive Only   (MCD)
SORO .... Special Operations Research Office
SORP......... Signature Overlay Range Prediction   (MCD)
SORPTR..... South Repeater   (MCD)
SORR .... SIGINT [*Signal Intelligence*] Operations Readiness Review [*Military*]   (AABC)
SORR .... Submarine Operations Research Report [*Navy*]
SORRAT..... Society for Research on Rapport and Telekinesis
SORS .... Shipboard Operational Readiness System [*Navy*]   (CAAL)
SORS .... Spacecraft Oscillograph Recording System
SORSI .... Sacro Occipital Research Society International [*Sedan, KS*]   (EA)
SORT......... Senior Officer Refresher Training
SORT......... Ship's Operational Readiness Test
SORT......... Simulated Optical Range Target   (MCD)
SORT......... Slosson Oral Reading Tests
SORT......... Special Operations Response Team [*Prison management*]
SORT......... Spilled Oil Response Team [*Marine science*]   (MSC)
SORT......... Staff Organizations Round Table [*American Library Association*]
SORT......... Structured-Objective Rorschach Test [*Psychology*]
SORT...... Structures for Orbiting Radio Telescope   (MCD)
SORT......... System Operational Readiness Test   (MCD)
SORTE .... Summary of Radiation Tolerant Electronics
SORTI........ Satellite Orbital Track and Intercept [*ARPA*]
SORTI........ Star-Oriented Real-Time Teaching Instrument   (AAG)
SORTIE ..... Simulation of Reentry Target Interceptor Endgame   (MCD)
SORTIE ..... Super-Orbital Reentry Test Integrated Environment   (MUGU)
SORTS ...... Shipboard Organizational Troubleshooting System   (MCD)
SORWUC ... Service, Office, and Retail Workers Union of Canada
SOS........... Coalition to Protect Social Security   (EA)
SOS........... Congress of Scientists on Survival [*Inactive*]
SOS........... Safety Observation Station
SOS........... Safety on the Streets [*Project of National Safety Council*]
SoS............ Saga och Sed [*A publication*]
SOS........... Same Old Sludge [*Slang phrase used to describe television programing*]
SOS........... Same Old Stew [*Military slang*] [*Bowdlerized version*]
SOS........... Same Old Stuff [*Reference to the weather*]
SOS........... Same Only Softer [*Band leader's signal*] [*Slang*]
SOSC......... Sanity on Sex [*Group opposing sex education in schools*]
SOS........... Satellite Observation System
SOS...... Save Our Seas   (EA)
SOS........... Save Our Ship [*or Souls*] [*Popular explanation of Morse code letters used as a signal for extreme distress*]
SOS........... Save Our Shores   (EA)
SOS......... Save Our Strays [*An association*] [*Brooklyn, NY*]   (EA)
SOS........... [*Anatoly*] Scharansky, [*Yuri*] Orlov, and [*Andrei*] Sakharov [*Organization named after dissident Soviet scientists*]   (EA)
SOS........... Scheduled Oil Sampling [*Automotive engineering*]
SOS........... Science of Survival
SOS........... Scientists for Sakharov, Orlov, and Scharansky
SOS........... Secretary of State
SOS........... Self-Opening Sack [*Paper bag*]
SOS........... Self-Organizing System
SOS........... Send Out Succor
SOS........... Senior Opportunities and Services [*OEO*]
SOS........... Sentinel on Station
SOS........... Serial Output Special   (MCD)
SOS........... Service Order System [*Telecommunications*]   (TEL)
SOS...... Service of Supply [*Later, ASF*] [*Army*]
SOS........... Shakespeare Oxford Society   (EA)
SOS........... Share Operating System [*Data processing*]
SOS........... Share Our Strength [*An association*] [*Washington, DC*]   (EA)
SOS........... Ships Ordnance Summary
SOSPA....... Si Opus Sit [*If Needed*] [*Pharmacy*]
SOS........... Signed-Off Sick
SOS........... Silicon-on-Sapphire [*Integrated circuit*]
SOS........... Simultaneous Oral Spelling [*Gillingham method*] [*Education*]
SOS........... Sisters of Service [*Roman Catholic religious order*]
SOS........... Slip on Show [*Indicates a woman's slip is showing*]   (DSUE)

SOS........... Slum on a Shingle [*Army breakfast dish*] [*Bowdlerized version*]
SOS........... Sniping, Observation, and Scouting [*Course*] [*Military*] [*British*] [*World War I*]
SOS........... Society for Occlusal Studies [*Georgetown Dental Clinic*] [*Washington, DC*]   (EA)
SOS........... Society of Scribes   (EA)
SoS .... Song of Songs [*Old Testament book*] [*Roman Catholic canon*]   (BJA)
SOS........... Sophisticated Operating System [*Apple III microcomputer*] [*Data processing*]
SOS........... Sostenuto [*Sustained*] [*Music*]
SOS........... Source of Supply
SOS........... Soviet Oceanographic Surveillance   (MCD)
SOS........... Space Ordnance Systems, Inc.   (MCD)
SOS........... Spare Operation Support
SOS........... Special Organizational Services [*An association*]   (EA)
SOS........... Speed of Service [*Telecommunications*]   (TEL)
SOS........... Speed of Sound
SOS........... Squadron Officers School [*Air Force*]
SOS........... Squadron Operational Support [*Military*]   (AFIT)
SOS........... Stabilized Optical Sight
SOS........... Stamp Out Stupidity [*Student group opposing drug abuse*]
SOS........... Start of Significance [*Data processing*]   (BUR)
SOS........... Station Operating Supervisor [*IEEE*]
SOS........... Stock Order Shipment
SOS........... Strategic Orbital System   (AAG)
SOS........... Student-Originated Studies [*National Science Foundation*]
SOS........... Suborbital Sequence [*NASA*]
SOS........... Sum-of-the-Squares
SOS........... Supervisor of Shipbuilding [*Navy*]
SOS........... Supplemental Oxygen System   (MCD)
SOS........... Supplementary Ophthalmic Service [*Medicine*]
SOS........... Support Our Soldiers [*Network of antiwar-oriented coffee houses located near military bases*]   (EA)
SOS........... Supporters of Silkwood   (EA)
SOS........... Survivors of Sacrifice   (EA)
SOS........... Survivors of Suicide
SOS........... Suspend Other Service [*Business and trade*]
SOS........... Suspension of Service [*Pilots' strike*]
SOS........... Symbolic Operating System [*Data processing*]
SOS........... Symmetry, Orbitals, and Spectra [*Atomic physics*]
SoS .... Syn og Segn [*A publication*]
SOS........... Synchronous Orbit Satellite   (AAG)
SOS........... System Operational Specification [*Military*]   (CAAL)
SOSA .... Sell Overseas America, the Association of American Export [*Redondo Beach, CA*]   (EA)
SOSA .... Sustained Operations Support Area [*NASA*]   (KSC)
Sos Aikakausk ... Sosiaalinen Aikakauskirja [*A publication*]
SOSAL ...... School of Systems and Logistics [*Military*]
SOSAT ...... Submarine One-Way Satellite [*Navy*]   (CAAL)
SOSC .... Safety Observation Station Display Console
SOSC .... Smithsonian Oceanographic Sorting Center
SOSC .... Source of Supply Code
So School News ... Southern School News [*A publication*]
SOSCU....... Stamps on Stamps - Centenary Unit [*American Topical Association*]   (EA)
SOSD........ Spatial Operational Sequence Diagram
SOSE .... Science Operations Support Equipment
SOSE .... Silicon-on-Something-Else [*Telecommunications*]   (TEL)
SOSEC....... Satellite Ocean Surveillance Evaluation Center
SOSED...... Secretary's Office, Shore Establishments Division [*Incorporated into SECP, 1944*] [*Navy*]
SO SH .... Somali Shilling [*Monetary unit in the Somali Democratic Republic*]
SOSI.......... Shift In, Shift Out   (IEEE)
SOSI.......... Sippican Ocean Systems [*NASDAQ symbol*]   (NQ)
SOS Intl ..... Society of Saunterers, International [*Gaylord, MI*]   (EA)
SOSK .... Squadron Operational Support Kit   (MCD)
SO/SL .... Saturn Orbiter Satellite Lander [*NASA*]
SOSM....... Ship Overhaul Schedule Milestone [*Navy*]
SOSM....... Source of Supply Modifier
SOSO .... Safety and Operating Systems Office [*NASA*]
SoSo .... South of SoHo [*See also NoHo, SoHo, TriBeCa*] [*Artists' colony in New York City*]
SOSO .... Synchronous Orbiting Solar Observatory
SOSP .... Squadron Operational Support Package [*Military*]   (AFIT)
SOSQ .... Special Operations Squadron
SOSR .... Spin on Straight Rail
SOSS .... Satellite Optical Surveillance Station   (MCD)
SOSS .... Shipboard Oceanographic Survey System
SOSS .... SONAR Schoolship [*Navy*]   (NVT)
SOSS .... Soviet Ocean Surveillance System   (MCD)
SOSS .... Strategic Orbital System Study   (AAG)
SOSS .... Structurally Oriented Simulation System [*NASA*]
SOSSI .... Scouts on Stamps Society International   (EA)
SOSSPA..... Service of Supply, South Pacific Area [*Navy*] [*World War II*]
SOSSUS .... Study on Surgical Services in the United States [*Medicine*]
SOST........ Sostenuto [*Sustained*] [*Music*]
So St .... Southern Studies [*A publication*]
SOST......... Special Operator Service Traffic [*Telecommunications*]   (TEL)
SOSTEL ..... Solid-State Electric Logic   (NG)

SOSTEN..... Sostenuto [*Sustained*] [*Music*]
SOSU .... Scout Observation Service Unit [*Navy*]
SOSU .... Ships on Stamps Unit [*American Topical Association*]   (EA)
SOSUMO ... Societe Sucriere du Moso [*Development organization*]
                 [*Bujumbura, Burundi*]
SOSUS...... SONAR Surveillance System [*Military*]
SOSUS...... Sound and Surveillance System   (MSA)
SOSUS...... Sound Surveillance Undersea   (MCD)
SOT .... Same Old Thing [*Slang*]
SOT .... Secretary of Transportation   (NATG)
SOT .... Sensation of Transcendence
SOT .... Shower over Tub [*Real estate*]
SoT .... Sloejd och Ton [*A publication*]
SOT .... Snowbird, TN [*Location identifier*] [*FAA*]   (FAAL)
SOT .... Society of Ornamental Turners   (EA)
SOT .... Society of Toxicology   (EA)
SOT .... Solar Optical Telescope
SOT .... Son of Temperance [*A heavy drinker*] [*Slang*]
Sot.............. Sotah   (BJA)
SOT .... Sound on Tape [*Videotape*]
SOT .... Sounds of Our Times, Cook Studio [*Record label*]
SOT .... South Omaha Terminal Railway Co. [*AAR code*]
SOT .... Soviet Orientation Team   (MCD)
SOT .... Spatial Orientation Trainer [*Air Force*]
SOT .... SRO Entertainment [*Vancouver Stock Exchange symbol*]
SOT .... Start of Tape
SOT .... Start of Text
SOT .... State of Termination [*Telecommunications*]   (TEL)
S-o-T .... Stoke-On-Trent [*City in England*]
SOT .... Strap-On Tank [*NASA*]   (NASA)
SOT .... Subscriber Originating Trunk [*Telecommunications*]   (TEL)
SOT .... Syntax-Oriented Translator   (IEEE)
SOT .... Systems Operating Test
SOTA .... State of the Art
SOTA .... Students Older than Average
SOTAC...... State-of-the-Art Car [*Transit*] [*Department of Transportation*]
SOTARSS ... Stand-Off Target Acquisition Reconnaissance Surveillance
                 System   (MCD)
SOTAS...... Stand-Off Target Acquisition/Attack System
SOTB.......... Secretary's Office, Transportation Branch [*Navy*]
SOTCA...... Soudage et Techniques Connexes [*A publication*]
SOTDAT..... Source Test Data System [*Environmental Protection Agency*]
SOTE.......... Standard Optical Test Equipment
So Tex LJ... Southern Texas Law Journal   (DLA)
SOTFE .... Special Operations Task Force, Europe
SOTG .... Sales Other than Gasoline [*Business and trade*]
SOTI .... [*A*] Survey of Old Testament Introductions [*Gleason L. Archer*]
                 [*A publication*]   (BJA)
Sotilaslaak Aikak ... Sotilaslaaketieteellinen Aikakauslehti [*A publication*]
SOTIM....... Sonic Observation of the Trajectory and Impact of Missiles
SOTP.......... Ship Overhaul Test Program
SOTP.......... Shipyard Overhaul Test Program
SOTP.......... System Overhaul Test Program
SOTR.......... Southtrust Corp. [*NASDAQ symbol*]   (NQ)
SOTS.......... Special Operations Team [*Military*]   (CINC)
SOTS.......... Suborbital Tank Separation   (MCD)
SOTS.......... Synchronous Orbiting Tracking Stations   (MCD)
Sots Pollum ... Sotsialistik Pollumajandus [*A publication*]
Sots Sel'Khoz Azerb ... Sotsialisticheskoe Sel'skoe Khozyaistvo
                 Azerbaidzhana [*A publication*]
Sots Sel'Khoz Uzbek ... Sotsialisticheskoe Sel'skoe Khozyaistvo
                 Uzbekistana [*A publication*]
Sots Sel'sk Khoz Azerb ... Sotsialisticheskoe Sel'skoe Khozyaistvo
                 Azerbaidzhana [*A publication*]
Sots Sel'sk Khoz Uzb ... Sotsialisticheskoe Sel'skoe Khozyaistvo
                 Uzbekistana [*A publication*]
Sots Trud... Sotsialisticheskiy Trud [*USSR*] [*A publication*]
Sots Tvarinnit ... Sotsialistichne Tvarinnitstvo [*A publication*]
Sots Tvarynnytstvo ... Sotsialistychne Tvarynnytstvo [*A publication*]
SOTT.......... Second-Order Transition Temperature
SOTT.......... Synthetic Medium Old Tuberculin Trichloroacetic Acid
                 Precipitated [*Later, PPD, Purified Protein Derivative*]
                 [*Immunology*]
SOTUS...... Sequentially Operated Teletypewriter Universal Selector
SOU........... Souchong [*Tea trade*]   (ROG)
SOU........... Sources Public Library [*UTLAS symbol*]
SOU........... South   (ROG)
SOU........... Southampton [*England*] [*Airport symbol*]   (OAG)
SOU........... Southern Airways [*Air carrier designation symbol*]
SOU........... Southern California Gas Co. [*American Stock Exchange
                 symbol*]
SOU........... Southern Petroleum Corp. [*Vancouver Stock Exchange
                 symbol*]
SOU........... Southern Railway System [*AAR code*]
SOU........... Statens Offentlige Utredningar [*Sweden*]
Sou Aus LR ... South Australian Law Reports [*A publication*]
Soudage Tech Connexes ... Soudage et Techniques Connexes [*A
                 publication*]
Soud Lek ... Soudni Lekarstvi [*A publication*]
SOUL.......... Studies of Ocean Upper Layers [*Marine science*]   (MSC)
Soule Syn ... Soule's Dictionary of English Synonyms   (DLA)

Soul Il........ Soul Illustrated [*A publication*]
So U L Rev ... Southern University Law Review [*A publication*]
Soun........... Soundings [*A publication*]
Sound .... Soundings [*A publication*]
Sound Brass ... Sounding Brass and the Conductor [*A publication*]
Sound (Can) ... Sound (Canada) [*A publication*]
Sound & Vib ... Sound and Vibration [*A publication*]
Sound Vib ... Sound and Vibration [*A publication*]
Sound Vis Broadc ... Sound and Vision Broadcasting [*A publication*]
So Univ L Rev ... Southern University Law Review [*A publication*]
SOUP .... Solar Optical Universal Polarimeter
SOUP .... Students Opposed to Unfair Practices [*in advertising*] [*Student
                 legal action organization*]
SOUP .... Submarine Operational Update Program [*Canadian Navy*]
SOUQAR .... Section d'Oceanographie d'Universite de Quebec a Rimouski
                 [*Canada*]   (MSC)
SOUR .... Sourdough Journal. Alaska Library Association [*A publication*]
SouR .... Southern Review [*US*] [*A publication*]
SOURCE ...... Simulation of Utilization, Resources, Cost, and Efficiency
Sources Hist Math Phys Sci ... Sources in the History of Mathematics and
                 Physical Sciences [*A publication*]
Sources in Hist of Math and Phys Sci ... Sources in the History of
                 Mathematics and Physical Sciences [*A publication*]
Sources Sci ... Sources of Science [*A publication*]
Sources Stud Hist Arabic Math ... Sources and Studies in the History of
                 Arabic Mathematics [*A publication*]
SOURS....... Subcommittee on Use of Radioactivity Standards [*National
                 Research Council*]
SOUSAFE ... Status of United States Air Force Equipment
SOUSSA .... Steady, Oscillatory, and Unsteady, Subsonic, and Supersonic
                 Aerodynamics [*NASA*]
SOUTB....... Statens Offentliga Utredningar [*A publication*]
SOUTC....... Satellite Operators and Users Technical Committee [*McLean,
                 VA*]   (EA)
South .... Southern Reporter [*National Reporter System*]   (DLA)
South Afr Archaeol B ... South African Archaeological Bulletin [*A
                 publication*]
South Afr Georg J ... South African Geographical Journal [*A publication*]
South African J African Affairs ... South African Journal of African Affairs [*A
                 publication*]
South African J Econ ... South African Journal of Economics [*Suid-
                 Afrikaanse Tydskrif vir Ekonomie*] [*A publication*]
South African Med Rec ... South African Medical Record [*A publication*]
South African Min Eng Jour ... South African Mining and Engineering
                 Journal [*A publication*]
South African Statist J ... South African Statistical Journal [*A publication*]
South Afr Int Quart ... South Africa International Quarterly [*A publication*]
South Afr J Afr Aff ... South African Journal of African Affairs [*A publication*]
South Afr J Econ ... South African Journal of Economics [*Suid-Afrikaanse
                 Tydskrif vir Ekonomie*] [*A publication*]
South Afr J Sci ... South African Journal of Science [*A publication*]
South Afr LJ ... South African Law Journal [*A publication*]
Southard.... Southard's New Jersey Law Reports [*4-5 New Jersey*]   (DLA)
South As Dig Reg Writ ... South Asian Digest of Regional Writing
                 [*Heidelberg*] [*A publication*]
South Asian R ... South Asian Review [*A publication*]
South Asian Stud ... South Asian Studies [*A publication*]
South As Stud ... South Asian Studies [*Jaipur*] [*A publication*]
South As Surv ... South Asian Survey [*New Delhi*] [*A publication*]
South Atlan Q ... South Atlantic Quarterly [*A publication*]
South Aus LR ... South Australian Law Reports [*A publication*]
South Aust Dep Agric Fish Agron Bran Rep ... South Australia. Department
                 of Agriculture and Fisheries. Agronomy Branch. Report [*A
                 publication*]
South Aust Dep Mines Miner Resour Rev ... South Australia. Department of
                 Mines. Mineral Resources Review [*A publication*]
South Aust Fish Ind Counc ... SAFIC. South Australia Department of
                 Fisheries and Australian Fisheries Industry Council [*A
                 publication*]
South Aust Geol Surv Bull ... South Australia. Geological Survey. Bulletin [*A
                 publication*]
South Aust Geol Surv 1:250000 Geol Ser ... South Australia. Geological
                 Survey. 1:250,000 Geological Series [*A publication*]
South Aust Geol Surv Q Geol Notes ... South Australia. Geological Survey.
                 Quarterly Geological Notes [*A publication*]
South Aust Geol Surv Rep Invest ... South Australia. Geological Survey.
                 Report of Investigations [*A publication*]
South Aust Mot ... South Australian Motor [*A publication*]
South Aust Nat ... South Australian Naturalist [*A publication*]
South Aust Orn ... South Australian Ornithologist [*A publication*]
South Aust Rep Mus Board ... South Australia Report of the Museum Board
                 [*A publication*]
South Bus ... South Business [*A publication*]
South Calif Coastal Water Res Proj Annu Rep ... Southern California
                 Coastal Water Research Project. Annual Report [*A
                 publication*]
South Calif L Rev ... Southern California Law Review [*A publication*]
South Calif Q ... Southern California Quarterly [*A publication*]
South Car ... South Carolina   (DLA)
South Car ... South Carolina Reports   (DLA)

South Carolina Acad Sci Bull ... South Carolina Academy of Science. Bulletin [*A publication*]
South Carolina Div Geology Geol Notes ... South Carolina. Division of Geology. Geologic Notes [*A publication*]
South Carolina Div Geology Misc Rept ... South Carolina. Division of Geology. Miscellaneous Report [*A publication*]
South Carolina L Rev ... South Carolina Law Review [*A publication*]
South Car R ... South Carolina Review [*A publication*]
SOUTHCOM ... Southern Command [*Military*] (AFM)
South Conf Gerontol Rep ... Southern Conference on Gerontology. Report [*A publication*]
South Coop Ser Bull ... Southern Cooperative Series Bulletin [*A publication*]
South Corn Impr Conf Rep ... Southern Corn Improvement Conference. Report [*A publication*]
South Dairy Prod J ... Southern Dairy Products Journal [*A publication*]
South Dak L Rev ... South Dakota Law Review (DLA)
South Dakota Geol Survey Guidebook ... South Dakota. Geological Survey. Guidebook [*A publication*]
South Dakota Geol Survey Rept Inv ... South Dakota. Geological Survey. Report of Investigations [*A publication*]
South Dakota Geol Survey Spec Rept ... South Dakota. Geological Survey. Special Report [*A publication*]
South Dakota Geol Survey Water Resources Rept ... South Dakota Geological Survey and South Dakota Water Resources Commission. Water Resources Report [*A publication*]
South Dakota L Rev ... South Dakota Law Review [*A publication*]
Southeast Asia Bldg Materials & Equipment ... Southeast Asia Building Materials and Equipment [*A publication*]
Southeast Asia J Theol ... Southeast Asia Journal of Theology [*A publication*]
Southeast Asian Conf Soil Eng Proc ... Southeast Asian Conference on Soil Engineering. Proceedings [*A publication*]
Southeast Asian J Soc Sci ... Southeast Asian Journal of Social Science [*A publication*]
Southeast Asian J Trop Med Public Health ... Southeast Asian Journal of Tropical Medicine and Public Health [*A publication*]
South East Asian Stud ... South East Asian Studies [*A publication*]
Southeast Asia Pet Explor Soc Proc ... Southeast Asia Petroleum Exploration Society. Proceedings [*A publication*]
Southeastcon Reg 3 (Three) Conf Proc ... Southeastcon Region 3 (Three) Conference Proceedings [*United States*] [*A publication*]
Southeastern Geology Spec Pub ... Southeastern Geology. Special Publication [*A publication*]
Southeastern Rep ... South Eastern Reporter (DLA)
Southeast Geol ... Southeastern Geology [*A publication*]
Southeast Geol Soc Field Conf Guideb ... Southeastern Geological Society. Field Conference Guidebook [*A publication*]
Southeast Geol Spec Publ ... Southeastern Geology. Special Publication [*A publication*]
South Econ ... Southern Economist [*Bangalore*] [*A publication*]
South Econ J ... Southern Economic Journal [*A publication*]
South Econ Jour ... Southern Economic Journal [*A publication*]
Southern.... Southern Reporter (DLA)
Southern Calif Acad Sci Bull ... Southern California Academy of Sciences. Bulletin [*A publication*]
Southern Econ J ... Southern Economic Journal [*A publication*]
Southern Folklore Q ... Southern Folklore Quarterly [*A publication*]
Southern H R ... Southern Humanities Review [*A publication*]
Southern Hum R ... Southern Humanities Review [*A publication*]
Southern J Med Phys Sc ... Southern Journal of the Medical and Physical Sciences [*A publication*]
Southern Lit J ... Southern Literary Journal [*A publication*]
Southern P R ... Southern Poetry Review [*A publication*]
Southern Pulp Paper Mfr ... Southern Pulp and Paper Manufacturer [*A publication*]
Southern R ... Southern Review [*A publication*]
Southern Rep ... Southern Reporter (DLA)
Southern Rev ... Southern Review [*A publication*]
South Exposure ... Southern Exposure [*United States*] [*A publication*]
South Florist Nurseryman ... Southern Florist and Nurseryman [*United States*] [*A publication*]
South Folkl Quart ... Southern Folklore Quarterly [*A publication*]
South Folk Q ... Southern Folklore Quarterly [*A publication*]
South Food Process ... Southern Food Processor [*A publication*]
SOUTHFORNET ... Southern Forestry Information Network [*Forest Service*] [*Athens, GA*] (EISS)
South Hist Assoc Publ ... Southern Historical Association. Publications [*A publication*]
South Hist Soc Papers ... Southern Historical Society. Papers [*A publication*]
South Hortic ... Southern Horticulture [*A publication*]
South Hosp ... Southern Hospitals [*A publication*]
South Ill ULJ ... Southern Illinois University. Law Journal [*A publication*]
South Indian Hortic ... Southern Indian Horticulture [*A publication*]
South J Agric Econ ... Southern Journal of Agricultural Economics [*A publication*]
South J Appl For ... Southern Journal of Applied Forestry [*A publication*]
South Law J ... Southern Law Journal [*Tuscaloosa, AL*] (DLA)
South Law J & Rep ... Southern Law Journal and Reporter (DLA)
South Law Rev ... Southern Law Review (DLA)
South Law Rev NS ... Southern Law Review, New Series (DLA)

South Liv ... Southern Living [*A publication*]
South LJ ... Southern Law Journal (DLA)
South LJ & Rep ... Southern Law Journal and Reporter (DLA)
South L Rev ... Southern Law Review (DLA)
South L Rev NS ... Southern Law Review, New Series (DLA)
South Lumberman ... Southern Lumberman [*A publication*]
South M ... South Magazine [*A publication*]
South Med ... Southern Medicine [*A publication*]
South Med Bull ... Southern Medical Bulletin [*A publication*]
South Med J ... Southern Medical Journal [*A publication*]
South Med Surg ... Southern Medicine and Surgery [*A publication*]
South Methodist Univ Inst Stud Earth Man Rep ... Southern Methodist University. Institute for the Study of Earth and Man. Reports of Investigations [*A publication*]
SOUTHN .... Southampton [*City in England*] (ROG)
South Pac Bull ... South Pacific Bulletin [*A publication*]
South Pac Comm Tech Pap ... Southern Pacific Commission. Technical Paper [*A publication*]
South Pacific B ... South Pacific Bulletin [*A publication*]
South Pacific Bul ... South Pacific Bulletin [*A publication*]
South Pacific J Ed ... South Pacific Journal of Education [*A publication*]
South Pac J Teach Educ ... South Pacific Journal of Teacher Education [*A publication*]
South Pharm J ... Southern Pharmaceutical Journal [*A publication*]
South Plast Chem ... Southern Plastics and Chemicals [*A publication*]
South Power Ind ... Southern Power and Industry [*A publication*]
South Power J ... Southern Power Journal [*A publication*]
South Pract ... Southern Practitioner [*A publication*]
South Pulp Pap J ... Southern Pulp and Paper Journal [*A publication*]
South Pulp Pap Manuf ... Southern Pulp and Paper Manufacturer [*A publication*]
South Q...... Southern Quarterly [*A publication*]
South Quar ... Southern Quarterly Review [*A publication*]
South Quart ... Southern Quarterly [*A publication*]
South R ... South Carolina Review [*A publication*]
South R ...... Southern Review [*A publication*]
South Rag ... Southern Rag [*A publication*]
South Res Inst Bull ... Southern Research Institute. Bulletin [*United States*] [*A publication*]
South Rhod Geol Surv Bull ... Southern Rhodesia. Geological Survey. Bulletin [*A publication*]
South Seedsman ... Southern Seedsman [*A publication*]
South Speech Comm J ... Southern Speech Communication Journal [*A publication*]
South Stars ... Southern Stars [*A publication*]
South Texas Geol Soc Bull ... South Texas Geological Society. Bulletin [*A publication*]
South Texas LJ ... South Texas Law Journal [*A publication*]
South Text Bull ... Southern Textile Bulletin [*A publication*]
South UL Rev ... Southern University Law Review [*A publication*]
SOUTHW.... Southwell [*City in England*] (ROG)
Southwest Afr Ann ... Southwest Africa Annual [*A publication*]
Southwest Bull ... Southwest Bulletin [*United States*] [*A publication*]
Southwest Entomol ... Southwestern Entomologist [*A publication*]
Southwestern As Petroleum G B ... Southwestern Association of Petroleum Geologists. Bulletin [*A publication*]
Southwestern LA Jour ... Southwestern Louisiana Journal [*A publication*]
Southwestern LJ ... Southwestern Law Journal [*A publication*]
Southwestern UL Rev ... Southwestern University. Law Review [*A publication*]
Southwestern Univ L Rev ... Southwestern University. Law Review [*A publication*]
Southwest Hist Q ... Southwestern Historical Quarterly [*A publication*]
Southwest J ... Southwest Journal [*A publication*]
Southwest J Anthropol ... Southwestern Journal of Anthropology [*A publication*]
Southwest Med ... Southwestern Medicine [*United States*] [*A publication*]
Southwest Miller ... Southwestern Miller [*A publication*]
Southwest Mus Paper ... Southwest Museum. Papers [*A publication*]
Southwest Nat ... Southwestern Naturalist [*A publication*]
Southwest Pet Short Course Proc Annu Meet ... Southwestern Petroleum Short Course. Proceedings of the Annual Meeting [*United States*] [*A publication*]
Southwest UL Rev ... Southwestern University. Law Review [*A publication*]
Southwest Vet ... Southwestern Veterinarian [*United States*] [*A publication*]
Southwest Water Works J ... Southwest Water Works Journal [*A publication*]
Southw His Q ... Southwestern Historical Quarterly [*A publication*]
Southw Hist Quar ... Southwestern Historical Quarterly [*A publication*]
SouthWJTh ... Southwestern Journal of Theology [*Fort Worth, TX*] [*A publication*]
Southw LJ ... Southwestern Law Journal and Reporter (DLA)
Southw Lore ... Southwestern Lore [*A publication*]
Southw Pol Sci Quar ... Southwest Political Science Quarterly [*A publication*]
Southw Pol and Soc Sci Q ... Southwestern Political and Social Science Quarterly [*A publication*]
Southw Rev ... Southwest Review [*A publication*]
Southw Soc Sci Quar ... Southwestern Social Science Quarterly [*A publication*]
SOV............ Seldovia, AK [*Location identifier*] [*FAA*] (FAAL)

SOV............ Sham Ovariectomy [*Endocrinology*]
SOV............ Share of Voice [*Advertising*]
SOV............ Shut-Off Valve
SOV............ Simulated Operational Vehicle (MCD)
SOV............ Solenoid-Operated Valve
SOV............ Somerset County Vocational and Technical School,
        Bridgewater, NJ [*OCLC symbol*] (OCLC)
SOV............ Sovereign
SOV............ Soviet
SOV............ Study of Values
SOV............ Subjective Optical Vertical
SOVAC....... Software Validation and Control System (MCD)
SovAE........ Soviet Antarctic Expedition [*1955-*]
Sov Aeronaut ... Soviet Aeronautics [*English Translation of Izvestia VUZ.*
        Aviatsionnaya Teknika] [*A publication*]
Sov Antarct Exped Inform Bull ... Soviet Antarctic Expedition. Information
        Bulletin [*A publication*]
Sov Antarkt Eksped Inform Byull ... Sovetskaya Antarkticheskaya
        Ekspeditsiya Informatsionnyy Byulletin [*A publication*]
Sov Anthr A ... Soviet Anthropology and Archeology [*A publication*]
Sov Anthro Arch ... Soviet Anthropology and Archeology [*New York*] [*A*
        publication]
Sov Appl Mech ... Soviet Applied Mechanics [*A publication*]
Sov Arh ..... Sovetskie Arhivi [*A publication*]
Sov Arkh ..... Sovetskie Arkhivy [*A publication*]
Sov Arkheol ... Sovetskaya Arkheologiya [*A publication*]
Sov Astron ... Soviet Astronomy [*A publication*]
Sov Astron Lett ... Soviet Astronomy. Letters [*A publication*]
Sov Astron Lett (Engl Transl) ... Soviet Astronomy. Letters (English
        Translation) [*A publication*]
Sov At Energy ... Soviet Atomic Energy [*A publication*]
Sov At En R ... Soviet Atomic Energy (USSR) [*A publication*]
Sov Atom Energy ... Soviet Atomic Energy [*A publication*]
Sov Automat Contr ... Soviet Automatic Control [*A publication*]
Sov Autom Control ... Soviet Automatic Control [*A publication*]
Sov Bibliog ... Sovetskaya Bibliografia [*A publication*]
Sov Bibliotekov ... Sovetskaia Bibliotekovedenie [*A publication*]
Sov Chem Ind ... Soviet Chemical Industry [*A publication*]
Sov Cybern Rev ... Soviet Cybernetics Review [*A publication*]
SOVEA....... Southwestern Veterinarian [*United States*] [*A publication*]
Sov East Europ For Trade ... Soviet and Eastern European Foreign Trade [*A*
        publication]
Sov Educ ... Soviet Education [*A publication*]
Sov E E For ... Soviet and Eastern European Foreign Trade [*A publication*]
Sov & E Eur For Tr ... American Review of Soviet and Eastern European
        Foreign Trade (DLA)
Sov Elec Eng ... Soviet Electrical Engineering [*A publication*]
Sov Electr Eng ... Soviet Electrical Engineering [*English Translation of*
        Elektrotekhnika] [*A publication*]
Sov Electrochem ... Soviet Electrochemistry [*A publication*]
Sov Eng J... Soviet Engineering Journal [*A publication*]
Sov Engng Res ... Soviet Engineering Research [*A publication*]
Sov Eng Res ... Soviet Engineering Research [*A publication*]
SovEt .... Sovetskaya Etnografija [*A publication*]
Sovet Geol ... Sovetskaya Geologiya [*A publication*]
Sovet Geologiya ... Sovetskaya Geologiya [*A publication*]
Sovet Muz ... Sovetskaya Muzyka [*A publication*]
SovEtn .... Sovetskaya Etnografija [*A publication*]
Sov Etnogr ... Sovetskaja Etnografija [*A publication*]
Sovetskoe Bibl ... Sovetskoe Bibliotekovedenie [*A publication*]
Sov Export ... Soviet Export [*A publication*]
Sov Farm ... Sovetskaya Farmatsiya [*A publication*]
Sov Film..... Soviet Film [*A publication*]
Sov Finno-Ugroved ... Sovetskoje Finno-Ugrovedenie [*A publication*]
Sov Fluid Mech (Engl Transl) ... Soviet Fluid Mechanics (English
        Translation) [*A publication*]
Sov Foto..... Sovetskoe Foto [*A publication*]
SovFU........ Sovetskoje Finno-Ugrovedenie [*A publication*]
Sov Genet ... Soviet Genetics [*A publication*]
Sov Genet (Engl Transl Genetika) ... Soviet Genetics (English Translation of
        Genetika) [*A publication*]
Sov Geogr ... Soviet Geography. Review and Translations [*A publication*]
Sov Geogr R ... Soviet Geography. Review and Translations [*A publication*]
Sov Geol .... Sovetskaya Geologiya [*A publication*]
Sov Geol and Geophys ... Soviet Geology and Geophysics [*A publication*]
Sov Geol Geophys ... Soviet Geology and Geophysics [*A publication*]
Sov Geol Geophys (Engl Transl) ... Soviet Geology and Geophysics (English
        Translation) [*A publication*]
Sov Gos Pravo ... Sovetskoe Gosudarstvo i Pravo [*A publication*]
SovH .... Sovetish Heymland [*A publication*]
Sov Hydrol ... Soviet Hydrology. Selected Papers [*A publication*]
Sov Hydrol Sel Pap ... Soviet Hydrology. Selected Papers [*A publication*]
SOVIA .... Sound and Vibration [*A publication*]
Soviet Aeronaut ... Soviet Aeronautics [*A publication*]
Soviet Agric Sci ... Soviet Agricultural Science [*A publication*]
Soviet Appl Mech ... Soviet Applied Mechanics [*A publication*]
Soviet Astronom ... Soviet Astronomy [*A publication*]
Soviet Automat Control ... Soviet Automatic Control [*A publication*]
Soviet Ed ... Soviet Education [*A publication*]
Soviet F...... Soviet Film [*A publication*]
Soviet J Ecol ... Soviet Journal of Ecology [*A publication*]

Soviet J Nuclear Phys ... American Institute of Physics. Soviet Journal of
        Nuclear Physics [*A publication*]
Soviet J Particles and Nuclei ... Soviet Journal of Particles and Nuclei [*A*
        publication]
Soviet Law and Govt ... Soviet Law and Government [*A publication*]
Soviet L & Govt ... Soviet Law and Government [*A publication*]
Soviet Lit ... Soviet Literature [*A publication*]
Soviet Math Dokl ... Soviet Mathematics. Doklady [*A publication*]
Soviet Math (Iz VUZ) ... Soviet Mathematics (Izvestija Vyssih Ucebnyh
        Zavedenii. Matematika) [*A publication*]
Soviet Phys Acoust ... Soviet Physics. Acoustics [*A publication*]
Soviet Physics J ... Soviet Physics Journal [*A publication*]
Soviet Phys J ... Soviet Physics Journal [*A publication*]
Soviet Phys JETP ... Soviet Physics. JETP [*A publication*]
Soviet Phys Uspekhi ... Soviet Physics. Uspekhi [*A publication*]
Soviet Plant Physiol ... Soviet Plant Physiology [*A publication*]
Soviet Pl Physiol ... Soviet Plant Physiology [*A publication*]
Soviet Soil Sci ... Soviet Soil Science [*A publication*]
Soviet Stud ... Soviet Studies [*A publication*]
Soviet Stud Phil ... Soviet Studies in Philosophy [*A publication*]
SOVIN .... Samenwerkingsverband voor Opleiding en Vorming op het
        Terrein van de Inforatieverzorging via Netwerken
        [*Collective for Training and Education in Connection with*
        Information Provision via Networks] [*The Hague,*
        Netherlands] [*Information service*] (EISS)
Sov Instrum & Control J ... Soviet Journal of Instrumentation and Control [*A*
        publication]
Sovistva At Yader ... Sovistva Atomnykh Yader [*USSR*] [*A publication*]
SovJa .... Sovetska Jazykoveda [*A publication*]
Sov J At...... Soviet Journal of Atomic Energy [*A publication*]
Sov J Coord Chem (Engl Transl) ... Soviet Journal of Coordination
        Chemistry (English Translation) [*A publication*]
Sov J Dev Biol (Engl Transl Ontogenez) ... Soviet Journal of Developmental
        Biology (English Translation of Ontogenez) [*A publication*]
Sov J Ecol ... Soviet Journal of Ecology [*A publication*]
Sov J Ecol (Engl Transl Ekologiya) ... Soviet Journal of Ecology (English
        Translation of Ekologiya) [*A publication*]
Sov Jew Aff ... Soviet Jewish Affairs [*A publication*]
Sov J Glass Phys Chem ... Soviet Journal of Glass Physics and Chemistry [*A*
        publication]
Sov J Glass Phys and Chem ... Soviet Journal of Glass Physics and
        Chemistry [*A publication*]
Sov J Glass Phys Chem (Engl Transl) ... Soviet Journal of Glass Physics
        and Chemistry (English Translation) [*A publication*]
Sov J Instrum Control ... Soviet Journal of Instrumentation and Control [*A*
        publication]
Sov J Low Temp Phys ... Soviet Journal of Low Temperature Physics [*A*
        publication]
Sov J Low Temp Phys (Engl Transl) ... Soviet Journal of Low Temperature
        Physics (English Translation) [*A publication*]
Sov J Mar Biol ... Soviet Journal of Marine Biology [*A publication*]
Sov J Mar Biol (Engl Transl) ... Soviet Journal of Marine Biology (English
        Translation) [*A publication*]
Sov J Nondestr Test ... Soviet Journal of Nondestructive Testing [*A*
        publication]
Sov J Nondestruct Test ... Soviet Journal of Nondestructive Testing [*A*
        publication]
Sov J Non-Ferrous Met ... Soviet Journal of Non-Ferrous Metals [*A*
        publication]
Sov J Nucl Phys ... Soviet Journal of Nuclear Physics [*A publication*]
Sov J Nuc R ... Soviet Journal of Nuclear Physics (USSR) [*A publication*]
Sov J Opt Technol ... Soviet Journal of Optical Technology [*A publication*]
Sov J Part Nucl ... Soviet Journal of Particles and Nuclei [*A publication*]
Sov J Plasma Phys ... Soviet Journal of Plasma Physics [*A publication*]
Sov J Quant Electron ... Soviet Journal of Quantum Electronics [*A*
        publication]
Sov J Quantum Electron ... Soviet Journal of Quantum Electronics [*A*
        publication]
Sov Khlopok ... Sovetskii Khlopok [*A publication*]
Sov Kino Fotopromst ... Sovetskaya Kino-Fotopromyshlennost [*A*
        publication]
SovKniga ... Sovetskaya Kniga [*A publication*]
Sov Krasnyi Krest ... Soveti Krasnyi Krest [*USSR*] [*A publication*]
SovL........... Soviet Literature [*A publication*]
Sov Law Gov ... Soviet Law and Government [*A publication*]
Sov Lit........ Soviet Literature [*A publication*]
Sov M........ Sovetskaya Muzyka [*A publication*]
Sov Mater Sci ... Soviet Materials Science [*A publication*]
Sov Mater Sci (Engl Transl) ... Soviet Materials Science (English Translation
        of Fiziko-Khimicheskaya Mekhanika Materialov) [*A*
        publication]
Sov Math.... Soviet Mathematics [*A publication*]
Sov Med.... Sovetskaya Meditsina [*A publication*]
SOVMEDRON ... Soviet Mediterranean Squadron [*NATO*] (NATG)
Sovmestnaya Sov-Mong Nauchno-Issled Geol Eksped ... Sovmestnaya
        Sovetsko-Mongol'skaya Nauchno-Issledovatel'skaya
        Geologicheskaya Ekspeditsiya [*A publication*]
Sovmestnaya Sov-Mong Nauchno-Issled Geol Eksped Tr ... Sovmestnaya
        Sovetsko-Mongol'skaya Nauchno-Issledovatel'skaya
        Geologicheskaya Ekspeditsiya. Trudy [*A publication*]
Sov Metall ... Sovetskaya Metallurgiya [*A publication*]

Sov Meteorol Hydrol ... Soviet Meteorology and Hydrology [*English translation of Meteorologiya i Gidrologiya*] [*A publication*]

Sov Meteorol Hydrol (Engl Transl) ... Soviet Meteorology and Hydrology (English Translation) [*A publication*]

Sov Min Sci ... Soviet Mining Science [*A publication*]

SOVN .... Sovran Financial Corp. [*NASDAQ symbol*] (NQ)

Sov Nauka ... Sovetskaya Nauka [*A publication*]

Sov Neurol Psychiatry ... Soviet Neurology and Psychiatry [*A publication*]

Sov Neur R ... Soviet Neurology and Psychiatry (USSR) [*A publication*]

Sov Non-Ferrous Met Res ... Soviet Non-Ferrous Metals Research [*A publication*]

Sov Non-Ferrous Met Res (Engl Transl) ... Soviet Non-Ferrous Metals Research (English Translation) [*A publication*]

Sov Oceanogr ... Soviet Oceanography [*A publication*]

SOVOG ...... Sozialistische Volksorganisation [*Socialist National Community*] [*Lithuanian*] (PPE)

Sov Pedag ... Soviet Pedagogy [*A publication*]

Sov Ph Ac R ... Soviet Physics. Acoustics (USSR) [*A publication*]

Sov Ph Se R ... Soviet Physics. Semiconductors (USSR) [*A publication*]

Sov Phys Acoust ... Soviet Physics. Acoustics [*A publication*]

Sov Phys Collect ... Soviet Physics. Collection [*A publication*]

Sov Phys Coll (Engl Transl) ... Soviet Physics. Collection (English Translation) [*A publication*]

Sov Phys Cryst ... Soviet Physics. Crystallography [*A publication*]

Sov Phys Crystallogr ... Soviet Physics. Crystallography [*A publication*]

Sov Phys Dokl ... Soviet Physics. Doklady [*A publication*]

Sov Phys J ... Soviet Physics Journal [*A publication*]

Sov Phys JETP ... Soviet Physics. JETP [*Journal of Experimental and Theoretical Physics of the Academy of Sciences of the USSR*] [*A publication*]

Sov Phys Lebedev Inst Rep ... Soviet Physics. Lebedev Institute Reports [*English Translation of Sbornik Kratkie Soobshcheniya po Fizike*] [*A publication*]

Sov Phys Lebedev Inst Rep (Engl Transl) ... Soviet Physics. Lebedev Institute Reports (English Translation) [*A publication*]

Sov Phys Semicond ... Soviet Physics. Semiconductors [*A publication*]

Sov Phys Solid State ... Soviet Physics. Solid State [*English translation of Fizika Tverdogo Tela*] [*A publication*]

Sov Phys Sol St ... Soviet Physics. Solid State Physics [*A publication*]

Sov Phys Tech Phys ... Soviet Physics. Technical Physics [*A publication*]

Sov Phys Tech Phys Lett ... Soviet Physics. Technical Physics. Letters [*A publication*]

Sov Phys T P ... Soviet Physics. Technical Physics [*A publication*]

Sov Phys Usp ... Soviet Physics. Uspekhi [*A publication*]

Sov Phys Uspekhi ... Soviet Physics. Uspekhi [*A publication*]

Sov Plant Physiol ... Soviet Plant Physiology [*A publication*]

Sov Plant Physiol (Engl Transl Fiziol Rast) ... Soviet Plant Physiology (English Translation of Fiziologiya Rastenii) [*A publication*]

Sov Plast.... Soviet Plastics [*A publication*]

Sov Powder Metall Met Ceram ... Soviet Powder Metallurgy and Metal Ceramics [*A publication*]

Sov Powder Metall and Met Ceram ... Soviet Powder Metallurgy and Metal Ceramics [*A publication*]

Sov Powder Met Metal Ceram ... Soviet Powder Metallurgy and Metal Ceramics [*A publication*]

Sov Power Eng ... Soviet Power Engineering [*A publication*]

Sov Power Eng (Engl Transl) ... Soviet Power Engineering (English Translation of Elektricheskie Stantsii) [*A publication*]

Sov Prog Chem ... Soviet Progress in Chemistry [*A publication*]

Sov Psikhonevrol ... Sovetskaya Psikhonevrologiya [*A publication*]

Sov Psychol ... Soviet Psychology [*A publication*]

Sov Psyco R ... Soviet Psychology (USSR) [*A publication*]

Sov Public Health ... Soviet Public Health [*A publication*]

SOVR .... Sovereign Corp. [*NASDAQ symbol*] (NQ)

SovR.......... Soviet Review [*A publication*]

Sov Radiochem ... Soviet Radiochemistry [*A publication*]

Sov Radio Eng ... Soviet Radio Engineering [*A publication*]

Sov Radiophys ... Soviet Radiophysics [*A publication*]

Sov Radiophys (Engl Transl) ... Soviet Radiophysics (English Translation of Izvestiya Vysshikh Uchebnykh Zavedenii Radiofizika) [*A publication*]

Sovrem Probl Gastroenterol ... Sovremennye Problemy Gastroenterologii [*A publication*]

Sovrem Probl Gastroenterol Resp Mezhved Sb ... Sovremennye Problemy Gastroenterologii Respublikanskii Mezhvedomstvennyi-Sbornik [*A publication*]

Sovrem Probl Gematol Pereliv Krovi ... Sovremennye Problemy Gematologii i Perelivaniya Krovi [*A publication*]

Sovrem Probl Onkol ... Sovremennye Problemy Onkologii [*A publication*]

Sovrem Probl Org Khim ... Sovremennye Problemy Organicheskoi Khimii [*A publication*]

Sovrem Probl Otolaringol Resp Mezhved Sb ... Sovremennye Problemy Otolaringologii Respublikanskoi Mezhvedomstvennyi Sbornik [*A publication*]

Sovrem Probl Radiobiol ... Sovremennye Problemy Radiobiologii [*USSR*] [*A publication*]

Sovrem Psikhotropnye Sredstva ... Sovremennye Psikhotropnye Sredstva [*A publication*]

Sovrem Vopr Endokrinol ... Sovremennye Voprosy Endokrinologii [*A publication*]

Sovrem Vopr Sud Med Ekspertnoi Prak ... Sovremennye Voprosy Sudebnoi Meditsiny i Ekspertnoi Praktiki [*A publication*]

Sovrem Zadachi Tochn Naukakh ... Sovremennye Zadachi v Tochnykh Naukakh [*A publication*]

Sov Rubber Technol ... Soviet Rubber Technology [*A publication*]

SOVS .... Sovereigns [*Monetary unit*]

SovS.......... Soviet Studies [*A publication*]

SovS.......... Soviet Survey [*A publication*]

Sov Sci........ Soviet Science [*A publication*]

Sov Sci (Engl Transl) ... Soviet Science (English Translation) [*A publication*]

Sov Sci Rev ... Soviet Science Review [*England*] [*A publication*]

Sov Shakhtior ... Sovetskii Shakhtior [*USSR*] [*A publication*]

SovSlav...... Sovetskoe Slavjanovedenie [*A publication*]

Sov Soc....... Soviet Sociology [*A publication*]

Sov Sociol ... Soviet Sociology [*A publication*]

Sov Soil Sci ... Soviet Soil Science [*A publication*]

Sov Soil Sci Suppl ... Soviet Soil Science. Supplement [*A publication*]

Sov Stat & Dec ... Soviet Statutes and Decisions [*A publication*]

Sov St Phil ... Soviet Studies in Philosophy [*A publication*]

Sov Stud ... Soviet Studies [*A publication*]

Sov Stud Hist ... Soviet Studies in History [*A publication*]

Sov Subtrop (Sukhumi USSR) ... Sovetskie Subtropiki (Sukhumi, USSR) [*A publication*]

Sov Tech Phys Lett ... Soviet Technical Physics. Letters [*A publication*]

Sov Tech Phys Lett (Engl Transl) ... Soviet Technical Physics. Letters (English Translation) [*A publication*]

Sov Tjurkolog ... Sovetskaja Tjurkologija [*A publication*]

Sov T P Lett ... Soviet Technical Physics. Letters [*A publication*]

Sov Veda Chem ... Sovetska Veda. Chemie [*A publication*]

SovVo .... Sovetskoje Vostokovedenije [*A publication*]

Sov Vrach Zh ... Sovetskii Vrachebnyi Zhurnal [*A publication*]

SOVX .... Sham Ovariectomized [*Endocrinology*]

Sov Zdravookhr ... Sovetskoe Zdravookhranenie [*A publication*]

Sov Zdravookhr Kirg ... Sovetskoe Zdravookhranenie Kirgizii [*A publication*]

Sov Zdravookhr Turkm ... Sovetskoe Zdravookhranenie Turkmenii [*A publication*]

Sov Zootekh ... Sovetskaya Zootekhniya [*A publication*]

SOW.......... Scope of Work (MCD)

SOW.......... Show Low [*Arizona*] [*Airport symbol*] [*Obsolete*] (OAG)

SOW.......... Skylab Orbital Workshop [*NASA*]

SOW.......... Special Operations Wing [*Military*] (MCD)

SOW.......... Standoff Weapons (MCD)

SOW.......... Start of Word

SOW.......... Statement of Work (MCD)

SOW.......... Subdivision of Work [*NASA*] (NASA)

SOW.......... Sunflower Ordnance Works [*Military*]

SOW.......... Synthetic Ocean Water

SOWA .... Stock Option Writers Association (EA)

SOWC .... Senior Officers' War Course [*British*]

SOWESPAC ... Southwest Pacific Command [*Navy*]

SOWESSEAFRON ... Southwest Sea Frontier [*Navy*]

SOWESTDIVDOCKS ... Southwest Division, Bureau of Yards and Docks [*Navy*] (MUGU)

So West LJ ... Southwestern Law Journal [*A publication*]

So West Rep ... South Western Reporter (DLA)

SOWETO.... Southwestern Townships [*South Africa*]

SOWg........ Special Operations Wing [*Air Force*] (AFM)

SOWIDOK ... Sozialwissenschaftliche Dokumentation [*Social Sciences Documentation Center*] [*Vienna Chamber of Labor*] [*Vienna, Austria*] [*Information service*] (EISS)

Sowjetw Ges ... Sowjetwissenschaft Gesellschaft [*A publication*]

Sowjetwiss ... Sowjetwissenschaft [*A publication*]

So Workm ... Southern Workman [*A publication*]

SOWP........ Society of Wireless Pioneers [*Santa Rosa, CA*] (EA)

SoWS .... Southern Writers Series [*A publication*]

SOW/S & D ... Statement of Work/Specifications and Design

SOX.......... Sentry Oil & Gas [*Vancouver Stock Exchange symbol*]

SOX.......... Solid Oxygen

SOX.......... Supercritical Oxygen [*NASA*] (KSC)

SOXP........ Southeast Explorations Corp. [*NASDAQ symbol*] (NQ)

SOY.......... Sioux Center, IA [*Location identifier*] [*FAA*] (FAAL)

SOY.......... SO Resources [*Vancouver Stock Exchange symbol*]

SOY.......... Stronsay [*Scotland*] [*Airport symbol*] (OAG)

Soybean Dig ... Soybean Digest [*A publication*]

SOYD .... Sum of the Years' Digits Method [*Finance*]

SOYO .... Society of Orthodox Youth Organizations (EA)

SOZ.......... Seder 'Olam Zuta (BJA)

SOZ.......... Somerset, PA [*Location identifier*] [*FAA*] (FAAL)

SOZ.......... Soviet Occupied Zone (NATG)

SoZ.......... Sovremennye Zapiski [*A publication*]

SOZDA....... Sovetskoe Zdravookhranenie [*A publication*]

Sozialdemokr Pressedienst ... Sozialdemokratische Pressedienst [*A publication*]

Sozial Forstw ... Sozialistische Forstwirtschaft [*A publication*]

Sozialistische Arbeitswiss ... Sozialistische Arbeitswissenschaft [*A publication*]

Sozialistische Finwirt ... Sozialistische Finanzwirtschaft [*A publication*]

Sozialmed Paedagog Jugendkd ... Sozialmedizinische und Paedagogische Jugendkunde [*A publication*]

Sozial Polit ... Sozialistische Politik [*A publication*]

Soz Kommun ... Sozialisation und Kommunikation [*A publication*]

Soz- Praeventivmed ... Sozial- und Praeventivmedizin [*A publication*]
Soz Sicherheit ... Soziale Sicherheit [*A publication*]
Soz Welt..... Soziale Welt [*A publication*]
Soz und Wirtpol MSpiegel ... Sozial- und Wirtschaftspolitischer
　　　　　Monatsspiegel aus Zeitungen und Zeitschriften [*A
　　　　　publication*]
Soz Wiss Jb Polit ... Sozialwissenschaftliches Jahrbuch fuer Politik [*A
　　　　　publication*]
Sp.............. Biblioteca Nacional, Madrid, Spain [*Library symbol*] [*Library of
　　　　　Congress*]   (LCLS)
SP.............. Error in Spelling [*Used in correcting manuscripts, etc.*]
SP.............. International Society of Philology
sp----- .... La Plata River and Basin [*MARC geographic area code*]
　　　　　[*Library of Congress*]   (LCCP)
SP.............. Motor Patrol Boat [*Navy symbol*] [*Obsolete*]
Sp.............. [*The*] New Testament of Our Lord and Saviour Jesus Christ
　　　　　(1937) (Francis Aloysius Spencer) [*A publication*]   (BJA)
SP.............. Office of State Programs [*Nuclear energy*]   (NRCH)
SP.............. Poland [*Aircraft nationality and registration mark*]   (FAAC)
SP.............. Sacra Pagina [*Paris-Gembloux*] [*A publication*]   (BJA)
S & P .... Salt and Pepper
SP.............. Sample Part
SP.............. Sampling Point   (NRCH)
SP.............. San Pedro [*California*]
SP.............. Sanctissime Pater [*Most Holy Father*] [*Latin*]
SP.............. Satellite Processor [*Data transmission*]
SP.............. Schering-Plough Corp. [*Commercial firm*]
SP.............. Scholarly Publishing [*A publication*]
SP.............. Schools of Philosophy [*A publication*]
SP.............. Science Pilot
SP.............. Science Press [*Ephrata, PA*] [*Information service*]   (EISS)
SP.............. Scientific Paper
SP.............. Scientific Processor   (BUR)
S/P............ Scientific Products
SP.............. Scottish Peer   (ROG)
SP.............. Sea Platform   (MCD)
S/P............ Seaplane
SP.............. Secretory Piece [*Superseded by SC, Secretory Component*]
　　　　　[*Immunology*]
SP.............. Secretory Protein [*Endocrinology*]
SP.............. Section Patrol [*Navy*]
SP.............. Security Police [*Air Force*]   (AFM)
SP.............. Security Procedure   (NRCH)
SP.............. Security Publication [*Navy*]
SP.............. Self Potential [*Log*]
SP.............. Self-Powered [*Gun*]   (MCD)
SP.............. Self-Propelled [*Military*]
SP.............. Selling Price
SP.............. Seminar Press
SP.............. Semipostal
S/P............ Semiprivate [*Room*]
SP.............. Semipublic [*Telecommunications*]   (TEL)
SP.............. Send Processor
SP.............. Senile Plaque [*Neurology*]
SP.............. Senior Partner
SP.............. Sensor Processor   (BUR)
Sp.............. Senterpartiet [*Center Party*] [*Norway*]   (PPE)
SP.............. Senza Pedale [*Without Pedals*] [*Music*]
SP.............. Septum Pellucidum [*Brain anatomy*]
SP.............. Sequence Programer [*Data processing*]   (AAG)
S-P............ Sequential-Phase   (CET)
SP.............. Sequential Processor
S/P............ Serial to Parallel   (KSC)
SP.............. Servants of the Holy Paraclete [*Roman Catholic men's religious
　　　　　order*]
SP.............. Service Panel
SP.............. Service Phase   (MCD)
SP.............. Service Processor   (IEEE)
SP.............. Service Publications   (AAG)
SP.............. Session of Peace [*Legal*] [*British*]   (ROG)
SP.............. Set Point
SP.............. Severely, Profoundly Handicapped   (OICC)
SP.............. Sewer Pipe [*Telecommunications*]   (TEL)
SP.............. Shanti Project [*An association*] [*Counseling service to those
　　　　　facing illness or grief*] [*San Francisco, CA*]   (EA)
SP.............. Shear Plate [*Technical drawings*]
SP.............. Shift Pulses
SP.............. Shipping Port
SP.............. Shore Party [*Navy*]
SP.............. Shore Patrol
SP.............. Shore Police [*Navy*]
SP.............. Shoreline Protection [*Type of water project*]
SP.............. Short Page
SP.............. Short Perforation [*Philately*]
SP.............. Short Period
SP.............. Short Persistence
SP.............. Short Pulse
SP.............. Shoulder Pitch   (MCD)
SP.............. Shuttle Projects Office [*Kennedy Space Center*]
　　　　　[*NASA*]   (NASA)
SP.............. Sic Porro [*So Forth*] [*Latin*]

SP.............. Sieve Pore [*Botany*]
SP.............. Sign Post
S/P............ Signal Processor   (NASA)
SP.............. Signal Publication [*British*]
SP.............. Signaling Projector [*British*]
SP.............. Signed Photograph
SP.............. Sikkim Parishad [*Political party*] [*Indian*]   (PPW)
SP.............. Silver Plate
SP.............. Silver Protein [*An antiseptic*]
SP.............. Simple Printing
SP.............. Sine Prole [*Died Without Issue*] [*Latin*]
SP.............. Singing Point [*Telecommunications*]   (TEL)
SP.............. Single Particle
SP.............. Single-Phase
SP.............. Single-Pole [*Switch*]
SP.............. Single Programer
SP.............. Single Purpose
SP.............. Sisters of the Presentation of Mary [*Roman Catholic religious
　　　　　order*]
SP.............. Sisters of Providence [*Roman Catholic religious order*]
SP.............. Skin Prick [*Immunology*]
SP.............. Sloop   (ROG)
SP.............. Slovansky Prehled [*A publication*]
SP.............. Slugging Percentage [*Baseball*]
SP.............. Small Packet
SP.............. Small Paper [*Printing*]
SP.............. Small Pica
SP.............. Small Plaque
SP.............. Small Premises [*Hairdressers, doctors, dentists, etc.*] [*Public-
　　　　　performance tariff class*] [*British*]
SP.............. Smokeless Powder
SP.............. Smokeless Propellant   (NATG)
SP.............. Smoki People [*An association*]   (EA)
SP.............. Snow Pellets [*Meteorology*]   (FAAC)
SP.............. Socialist Party
SP.............. Socialistische Partij [*Socialist Party*] [*Belgium*]   (PPW)
SP.............. Sociedade Acoriana de Transportes Aereos Ltda.
　　　　　[*Portugal*]   (FAAC)
SP.............. Society of Philaticians   (EA)
SP.............. Society of Protozoologists   (EA)
SP.............. Sociolinguistics Program   (EA)
SP.............. Soil Pipe
SP.............. Soil Pit
SP.............. Solar Panel
SP.............. Solar Physics   (NASA)
SP.............. Soldiers for Peace   (EA)
SP.............. Solid Propellant
S of P........ Sons of Phoenix [*Freemasonry*]   (ROG)
S/P............ Sotto Protesto [*Under Protest*] [*Italian*]
SP.............. Sound Powered   (CAAL)
SP.............. South Pacific
SP.............. South Pole [*Also, PS*]
SP.............. South Proceeding [*Astronomy*]
SP.............. Southern Pacific Transportation Co. [*AAR code*]
SP.............. Southern Pine [*Utility pole*] [*Telecommunications*]   (TEL)
SP.............. Space Character [*Keyboard*]   (AAG)
SP.............. Space Patrol   (AAG)
SP.............. Space and Power
SP.............. Space Propulsion [*A publication*]
sp .... Spain [*MARC country of publication code*] [*Library of
　　　　　Congress*]   (LCCP)
SP.............. Spain
SP.............. Spanish   (ROG)
SP.............. Spare   (AAG)
SP.............. Spare Part
SP.............. Spares Planning   (AAG)
SP.............. Spark   (AAG)
SP.............. Spartan Program [*Missiles*]   (MCD)
Sp.............. Spear's South Carolina Law Reports [*1842-44*]   (DLA)
SP.............. Special   (AFM)
Sp.............. Special Branch [*Navy*] [*British*]
SP.............. Special Paper
SP.............. Special Performance
SP.............. Special Planning   (AAG)
SP.............. Special Product   (MCD)
SP.............. Special Progress [*Program*] [*Education*]
SP.............. Special Projects
SP.............. Special Propellants
SP.............. Special Publication
SP.............. Special Purchase   (ADA)
SP.............. Special Purpose
SP.............. Specialist   (ADA)
SP.............. Species [*Also, sp*]
SP.............. Specific   (AAG)
SP.............. Specimen
Sp.............. Spectator [*A publication*]
Sp.............. Speculum [*A publication*]
SP.............. Speech Pathologist
SP.............. Speed   (MSA)
SP.............. Spelling

SP..............	Spelling [*Aaron*] Productions, Inc. [*American Stock Exchange symbol*]
SP..............	Spherical [*Buoy*]
SP..............	Spherical Polar
sp..............	Spherical Tank [*Liquid gas carriers*]
SP..............	Spinal
sp..............	Spinel [*CIPW classification*] [*Geology*]
Sp..............	Spinks' English Admiralty Prize Cases [*164 English Reprint*] [*1854-56*] (DLA)
Sp..............	Spinks' English Ecclesiastical and Admiralty Reports (DLA)
SP..............	Spirit
SP..............	Spirometry
SP..............	Spitze [*Point*] [*Music*]
SP..............	Splash Plate
SP..............	Splashproof (MSA)
SP..............	Splitting [*Electronics*]
Sp..............	Spontaneous
SP..............	Spontaneous Potential [*Log*]
SP..............	Spool (MSA)
SP..............	Spore Plasma [*Botany*]
SP..............	Sport
SP..............	Sports for the People (EA)
SP..............	Sprague-Dawley [*Rat variety*]
SP..............	Spring [*A publication*]
Sp..............	Spring Tide
SP..............	Sputnik [*Moscow*] [*A publication*]
SP..............	Square Punch
SP..............	Stable Platform
SP..............	Stack Pointer [*Data processing*]
S/P..............	Staff Paymaster [*Navy*] [*British*] (ROG)
S & P..............	Stake and Platform [*Technical drawings*]
SP..............	Standard Holding Pattern [*Aviation*]
SP..............	Standard or Peculiar (NASA)
SP..............	Standard Pile [*Nuclear reactor*]
SP..............	Standard Play [*Video technology*]
S & P..............	Standard & Poor's Corp.
SP..............	Standard Practice [*or Procedure*]
SP..............	Standard Price
SP..............	Standard Program [*Data processing*] (BUR)
SP..............	Standing Procedure (NATG)
SP..............	Standpipe (MSA)
SP..............	Start Permission (KSC)
SP..............	Starting Point
SP..............	Starting Price
SP..............	State Plan (OICC)
SP..............	Static Pointer [*Data processing*]
SP..............	Static Pressure
SP..............	Station Pressure [*Meteorology*] (FAAC)
S/P..............	Status Panel (CAAL)
S/P..............	Status Post [*Medicine*]
SP..............	Stern Post
SP..............	Stirrup Pump
SP..............	Stool Preservative [*Medicine*]
SP..............	Stop Payment [*Banking*]
SP..............	Stop Press (ADA)
SP..............	Storage Protein [*Food industry*]
SP..............	Straight Partners [*An association*] [*Rockville, MD*] (EA)
SP..............	Strategic Planning Chart [*Air Force*]
S & P..............	Strategy and Policy Group [*War Department*] [*World War II*]
SP..............	Street Price (ROG)
SP..............	Stretcher Party
SP..............	Structured Programing [*Data processing*] (BUR)
SP..............	Studia Papyrologica [*A publication*]
SP..............	Studia Patristica [*A publication*]
SP..............	Studies in Philology [*A publication*]
SP..............	Study Plan
SP..............	Subject-Predicate
SP..............	Subliminal Perception
SP..............	Submarine Patrol [*Navy*]
SP..............	Subprofessional [*Civil Service employees designation*]
SP..............	Substance P [*A peptide*] [*Biochemistry*]
SP..............	Successive Planometric [*A discrimination task*]
SP..............	Sugar Phosphate [*Biochemistry*]
SP..............	Suisse Primitive [*A publication*]
SP..............	Sumerian Proverbs (BJA)
SP..............	Summary Plotter [*RADAR*]
SP..............	Summating Potential [*Hearing*]
SP..............	Summus Pontifex [*Supreme Pontiff, Pope*] [*Latin*]
SP..............	Sunlit Period
SP..............	Sun's Parallax [*Astronomy*] (ROG)
SP..............	Superficial Pineal Organ [*Neuroanatomy*]
SP..............	Superseded in Part [*New matter substituted for part of an existing regulation or order*] [*Used in Shepard's Citations*] (DLA)
SP..............	Supervisory Process [*Telecommunications*] (TEL)
SP..............	Supplement
SP..............	Supply Point [*Military*] (NATG)
SP..............	Support
SP..............	Support Plan (MCD)
SP..............	Support Publications (AAG)
SP..............	Supraprotest
SP..............	Suprapubic [*Medicine*]
SP..............	Surveillance Procedure (NRCH)
SP..............	Suspicious Person
SP..............	Sustainer Pitch (AAG)
SP..............	Swelling Power [*Food technology*]
SP..............	Switch Panel
SP..............	Syllable Period [*Entomology*]
SP..............	Symbol Programer (MUGU)
SP..............	Symphysis Pubica [*Anatomy*]
SP..............	System Parameter (KSC)
S-P..............	System Processor (IEEE)
S-P..............	Systems and Procedures
SP..............	Systolic Pressure [*Cardiology*]
SP4..............	Specialist 4 [*Army*]
SP5..............	Specialist 5 [*Army*]
SP6..............	Specialist 6 [*Army*]
SP7..............	Specialist 7 [*Army*]
SP8..............	Specialist 8 [*Obsolete*] [*Army*]
SP9..............	Specialist 9 [*Obsolete*] [*Army*]
SPA..............	Greenville/Spartanburg [*South Carolina*] Downtown [*Airport symbol*] (OAG)
SPA..............	S-Band Power Amplifier
SPA..............	Sacrum Palatium Apostolicum [*Sacred Apostolic Palace, Vatican, Quirinal*] [*Latin*]
SPA..............	Salt-Poor Albumin [*Medicine*]
SPA..............	Salt Producers Association [*Later, SI*] (EA)
SPA..............	Satellite Personnel Activity [*Military*]
SPA..............	Scatter Propagation Antenna
SPA..............	Science and Public Affairs. Bulletin of the Atomic Scientists [*A publication*]
SPA..............	Sea Photo Analysis [*Navy*]
SPA..............	Seaplane Pilots Association [*Frederick, MD*] (EA)
SPA..............	Self-Phasing Array
SPA..............	Semipermanently Associated [*Telecommunications*] (TEL)
SPA..............	Service Pay and Allowances [*Military*] [*British*]
SPA..............	Servo Power Assembly (MCD)
SPA..............	Servo Preamplifier
SPA..............	Shared Peripheral Area (NASA)
SPA..............	Sierra Pacific Airlines [*North Hollywood, CA*] [*FAA designator*] (FAAC)
SPA..............	Signal Processor Assembly [*NASA*]
SPA..............	Silicon Pulser Array
SPA..............	Singapore People's Alliance
SPA..............	Single Parameter Analysis
SPA..............	Single Position Automatic [*Tester*]
SPA..............	Sitzungsberichte der Preussischen Akademie der Wissenschaften [*A publication*]
SPA..............	Skill Performance Aid [*Army*] (RDA)
SPA..............	Small-Particle Aerosol
SPA..............	Socialist Party of Australia
SpA..............	Societa per Azioni [*Corporation*] [*Italian*] [*Business and trade*]
SPA..............	Society of Participating Artists [*Record label*]
SPA..............	Society for Personality Assessment (EA)
SPA..............	Society for Personnel Administration [*Later, IPMA*] (EA)
SPA..............	Society of Philatelic Americans (EA)
SPA..............	Society of Professional Assessors
SPA..............	Society for Psychological Anthropology (EA)
SPA..............	Society for Public Administration
SPA..............	Sociological Practice Association [*Chester, NY*] (EA)
SPA..............	Sodium Polyacrylate [*Organic chemistry*]
SPA..............	Software Publishers Association [*Washington, DC*] (EA)
SPA..............	Solar Power Array
SPA..............	Songwriters Protective Association [*Later, AGAC*]
SPA..............	SOSUS Probability Area (NVT)
SPA..............	South Pacific Area [*World War II*]
SPA..............	South Pole [*Antarctica*] [*Seismograph station code, US Geological Survey*] (SEIS)
SPA..............	Southeastern Peanut Association (EA)
SPA..............	Southern Pine Association [*Later, SFPA*] (EA)
SPA..............	Southwestern Power Administration [*Department of Energy*]
SPA..............	Space Processing Applications [*Program*] [*NASA*]
SPA..............	Spade [*Freight*]
SPA..............	Spanish
spa..............	Spanish [*MARC language code*] [*Library of Congress*] (LCCP)
SPA..............	Spartanburg, SC [*Location identifier*] [*FAA*] (FAAL)
SPA..............	Sparton Corp. [*NYSE symbol*]
SPA..............	Special Project Activities (MCD)
SPA..............	Special Public Assistance
SPA..............	Special-Purpose Aircraft [*Drone vehicle*] [*Military*]
SPA..............	Special Purpose Alteration (MCD)
SPA..............	Specialist, Physical Training Instructor [*Navy rating*]
SPA..............	Spectrum Analyzer
SPA..............	Splice Plug Assembly
SPA..............	Sportsman Pilots Association
SPA..............	Standard Practice Amendment (AAG)
SPA..............	Staphylococcal Protein A [*Immunochemistry*]
SPA..............	State Planning Agency [*Department of Justice*]
SPA..............	Sterile Preparation Area (MCD)
SPA..............	Stimulation-Produced Analgesia
SPA..............	Strategic Planning Associates [*Singapore*]
SPA..............	Strategic Posture Analysis [*Army*] (AABC)

SPA .... Subject to Particular Average [*Insurance*]
SPA .... Submarine Patrol Area [*Navy*]   (NVT)
SPA .... Subpoena
SPA .... Substitute Part Authorization   (AAG)
SPA .... Sudden Phase Anomaly [*Radio engineering*]
SPA .... Sundry Persons' Account [*Banking*]
SPA .... Superphosphoric Acid [*Fertilizer*]
SPA .... Supervisory Performance Appraisal [*Civil Service*]
SPAS .... Suprapubic Aspiration [*Medicine*]
SPA .... Surface Vehicle Power Adapter
SPA .... SURTASS Probability Area [*Navy*]   (CAAL)
SPA .... Survey of Personal Attitude [*Psychology*]
SPA .... System Performance Analyzer [*Motorola, Inc.*]
SPA .... Systems and Procedures Association [*Later, ASM*]   (EA)
SPAA .... Sage Public Administration Abstracts [*A publication*]
SPAA .... Spacecraft Performance Analysis Area
SPAAC .... Syndicat du Personnel Africain de l'Aeronautique Civile
              [*African Union for Civil Aviation Employees*]
SPAAMFAA ... Society for the Preservation and Appreciation of Antique
              Motor Fire Apparatus in America
SPAASS ..... Synod Office, Diocese of Saskatchewan, Angelican Church of
              Canada, Prince Albert, Saskatchewan [*Library symbol*]
              [*National Library of Canada*]   (NLC)
SPAB .... Society for the Protection of Ancient Buildings   (EA)
SPAB .... Society of Psychologists in Addictive Behaviors [*Louisville,
              KY*]   (EA)
SPAB .... Supply, Priorities, and Allocations Board [*World War II*]
SPABH .... Society for the Preservation of American Business
              History   (EA)
SPAC .... Secretary's Pesticide Advisory Committee [*HEW*]
SPAC .... Signal Programer and Conditioner [*Air Force Eastern Test
              Range*]
S Pac .... South Pacific [*A publication*]
SPAC .... Space Program Advisory Council [*Terminated, 1977*] [*NASA*]
SPAC .... Spacecraft Performance Analysis and Command [*NASA*]
SPAC .... Spacious   (ADA)
SPAC .... Spatial Computer
SPACA .... Spectrochimica Acta [*A publication*]
SPACCS .... Space Command and Control System
SPACDocRap ... Societe Paleontologique et Archeologique de
              l'Arrondissement Judiciare de Charleroi. Documents et
              Rapports [*A publication*]
SPACE .... Council of AFL-CIO Unions for Scientific, Professional, and
              Cultural Employees [*Later, Department for Professional
              Employees, AFL-CIO*]
SPACE .... Sales Profitability and Contribution Evaluator [*Data
              processing*]
SPACE .... Self-Programing Automatic Circuit Evaluator
SPACE .... Sequential Position and Covariance Estimation   (IEEE)
SPACE .... Sidereal Polar Axis Celestial Equipment
SPACE .... Society for Private and Commercial Earth Stations
              [*Washington, DC*] [*Telecommunications*] [*Information
              service*]   (EA)
SPACE .... Space Program American Citizens' Effort
SPACE .... Spacecraft Prelaunch Automatic Checkout Equipment
SPACE .... Special Political Agricultural Community Education [*Milk
              cooperative trust fund*]
SPACE .... Sperry Program for Advancing Careers through Education
SPACE .... Support Package for Aerospace Computer Emulation   (MCD)
SPACE .... Symbolic Programing Anyone Can Enjoy
Space/Aeronaut ... Space/Aeronautics [*A publication*]
Space Biol Med (Engl Transl) ... Space Biology and Medicine (English
              Translation) [*A publication*]
Space Cit ... Space City News [*A publication*]
SPACECOM ... Space Communications
Space Congr Proc ... Space Congress. Proceedings [*United States*] [*A
              publication*]
Space Life Sci ... Space Life Sciences [*A publication*]
Space Res ... Space Research [*A publication*]
Space Res Bulg ... Space Research in Bulgaria [*A publication*]
SPACES ..... Saving and Preserving Arts and Cultural Environments   (EA)
Space Sci Instrum ... Space Science Instrumentation [*A publication*]
Space Sci R ... Space Science Reviews [*A publication*]
Space Sci Rev ... Space Science Reviews [*A publication*]
Space Sol Power Rev ... Space Solar Power Review [*A publication*]
SPACETAC ... Space and Tactical System Corporation   (MCD)
SPACETRACK ... Space Tracking System [*Air Force*]   (MCD)
SPACG .... Syndicat du Personnel de l'Aeronautique Civile du Gabon
              [*Union of Civil Aviation Employees of Gabon*]
S Pacific..... South Pacific [*A publication*]
S Pacific Bull ... South Pacific Bulletin [*A publication*]
SPACLALS ... South Pacific Association for Commonwealth Literature and
              Language Studies [*Christchurch, New Zealand*]   (EA-IO)
S Pac LR ... South Pacific Law Review [*Australia*]   (DLA)
SPACON .... Space Control
SPACS .... Sodium Purification and Characterization System   (NRCH)
SPAD .... Satellite Position Prediction and Display
SPAD .... Satellite Protection for Area Defense [*ARPA*]
SPAD .... Scratch Pad Memory [*Data processing*]
SPAD .... Seaway Port Authority of Duluth
SPAD .... Shuttle Payload Accommodation Document   (MCD)

SPAD .... Societe pour Aviation et ses Derives [*France*] [*World War I
              airplane*]
SPAD .... Space Patrol Active Defense
SPAD .... Space Patrol for Air Defense
SPAD .... Space Principles, Applications, and Doctrine [*Air Force
              Systems Command*]
SPAD .... SPRINT Air-Directed Defense [*Army*]
SPAD .... Submarine Patrol Area Definition   (MCD)
SPADATS ... Space Detection and Tracking System [*Air Force*]
SPADATSC ... Space Detection and Tracking System Center [*Air Force*]
SPADATSS ... Space Detection and Tracking System Sensors [*Air Force*]
SPADCCS ... Space Defense Command and Control System   (MCD)
SPADE ...... Signal Processing and Display Equipment
SPADE ...... Single-Channel-per-Carrier, Pulse-Code-Modulation, Multiple-
              Access, Demand-Assignment Equipment
              [*Telecommunications*]
SPADE ...... Small Portable Analysis and Diagnostic Equipment [*Aircraft
              maintenance*]
SPADE ...... Spare Parts Analysis, Documentation, and Evaluation
SPADE ...... Sparta Acquisition Digital Equipment   (MCD)
SPADE ...... Sperry Air Data Equipment
SPADE ...... Strike Planning and Damage Estimator [*Military*]
SPADES ..... Solar Perturbation and Atmospheric Density Measurement
              Satellite
SPADETS ... Space Detection Network [*Military*]
SPADL .... Spare Parts Application Data List
SPADNS .... (Sulfophenylazo)dihydroxynaphthalene-disulfonate [*Organic
              chemistry*]
SPADOC ... Space Defense Operations Center [*DoD*]
SPADS ...... Satellite Position and Display System
SPADS ...... Shuttle Problem Analysis Data System [*NASA*]   (NASA)
SPADS ...... SPRINT Air-Directed Defense System [*Army*]   (AABC)
SPA DT ..... Subpoena Duces Tecum [*Legal*] [*Latin*]   (ROG)
SPAEF....... Societe des Petroles d'Afrique Equatoriale Francaise [*French
              Equatorial African Petroleum Co.*]
SPAEF....... Southern Public Administration Education Foundation   (EA)
SPAF......... Forestry Branch, Saskatchewan Department of Natural
              Resources, Prince Albert, Saskatchewan [*Library symbol*]
              [*National Library of Canada*]   (NLC)
SP-AF........ Shuttle Projects - Air Force Liaison Office [*Kennedy Space
              Center*] [*NASA*]   (NASA)
SPAF......... Simulation Processor and Formatter   (MCD)
SPAFA ...... SEAMEO [*Southeast Asia Ministers of Education Organization*]
              Project in Archaeology and Fine Arts   (EA)
SPAFA ...... Sports Afield [*A publication*]
SPAG .... South Plains Association of Governments
SPAG .... Spaghetti   (DSUE)
SPAG .... Special Program/Analysis Guidance [*DoD*]
SPAH........ Society for the Preservation and Advancement of the
              Harmonica   (EA)
SPAH........ Spacelab Payload Accommodations Handbook   (MCD)
SPAI .... Screen Printing Association International [*Fairfax, VA*]   (EA)
SPAID .... Sheffield Package Analysis and Identification of Data
              [*Commercial & Industrial Development Bureau*] [*Software
              package*]
SPAIN .... Indian and Northern Affairs Canada [*Affaires Indiennes et du
              Nord Canada*] Prince Albert, Saskatchewan [*Library
              symbol*] [*National Library of Canada*]   (NLC)
Spain Estac Cent Ecol Bol ... Spain. Estacion Centro de Ecologia. Boletin [*A
              publication*]
Spain Inst Geol Min Bol Geol Min ... Spain. Instituto Geologico y Minero.
              Boletin Geologico y Minero [*A publication*]
Spain Inst Geol Min Mem ... Spain. Instituto Geologico y Minero. Memorias
              [*A publication*]
Spain Junta Energ Nucl Rep ... Spain. Junta de Energia Nuclear. Report [*A
              publication*]
SpAk .... Spisanie na Balgarskata Akademija na Naukite [*A publication*]
SPAL......... Simulator, Projectile, Airburst, Liquid [*Chemical defense
              device*] [*Military*]   (RDA)
SPAL......... Stabilized Platform Airborne LASER   (RDA)
SPAL......... Succinyl-poly-DL-alanine Poly-L-lysine [*Biochemical analysis*]
S & P (Ala) Rep ... Stewart and Porter's Alabama Reports   (DLA)
SPALT....... Special Projects Alterations [*Navy*]
SPALTRA.. Special Projects Alterations, Training [*Navy*]
SPAM........ S-Parameter Acquisition and Manipulation [*Computer software
              program*] [*General Motors Corp.*]
SPAM........ Satellite Processor Access Method
SPAM........ Scanning Photoacoustic Microscopy
SPAM........ Search Pattern Assessment Model [*Military*]   (CAAL)
SPAM........ Ship Position and Attitude Measurement   (IEEE)
SPAM........ Society for the Publication of American Music [*Record label*]
SPAM........ Soil-Plant-Atmosphere [*Computer simulation model*]
SPAM........ Sonobuoy Placement Assortment Model   (MCD)
SPAM........ Special Aeronautical Material [*Navy*]   (NG)
SPAM........ Spiced Ham
SPAMA ..... Spanish Air Materiel Area
SPAMAG ... Space Medicine Advisory Group   (MCD)
SPAMF...... Seychelles Popular Anti-Marxist Front   (PD)
SPAMMER ... Space Hammer
SPAMS...... Ship Position and Altitude Measurement System   (MCD)
SPAN......... Society of Philatelists and Numismatists

SPAN......... Solar Particle Alert Network [*National Oceanic and Atmospheric Administration*]
SPAN......... South Pacific Action Network
SPAN......... Space Communications Network
SPAN......... Space Navigation
SPAN......... Spacecraft Analysis (KSC)
SPAN......... Span-America Medical Systems [*NASDAQ symbol*] (NQ)
SPAN......... SPAN. Shell Public Health and Agricultural News [*A publication*]
SPAN......... SPAN: State Planning Authority News [*A publication*]
SPAN......... Spaniard (ROG)
SPAN......... Spanish
SPAN......... Statistical Processing and Analysis [*Data processing*]
SPAN......... Storage Planning and Allocation [*Data processing*]
SPAN......... Stored Program Alphanumerics [*FAA*]
SPAN......... Successive, Proportionate, Additive Numeration [*Decision making*]
SPAN......... System for Projection and Analysis
SPANAT..... Systems Planning Approach - North Atlantic [*FAA*]
SPANC....... Wapiti Regional Library, Prince Albert, Saskatchewan [*Library symbol*] [*National Library of Canada*] (NLC)
SPAND....... Solar Proton Albedo Neutron Decay
SPANDAR ... Space and Range RADAR [*NASA*]
SPANGLISH ... Spanish and English
SPANNER ... Special Analysis of Net Radio [*Study*]
SPANNER ... Special Analysis of Net Radios (MCD)
SPANRAD ... Superimposed Panoramic RADAR Display
SPANS ...... Sealift Procurement and National Security [*Study*]
SPAOPSUP ... Space Operations Support (NVT)
SPAP......... Serum Prostatic Acid Phosphatase [*An enzyme*]
SPAP......... Special Package Auto Policy [*Insurance*]
SPap .... Studia Papyrologica [*A publication*]
SPAQUA ..... Sealed Package Quality Assurance (IEEE)
SPAR......... SAC [*Strategic Air Command*] Peacetime Airborne Reconnaissance
SPAR......... Seagoing Platform for Acoustic Research [*NOL*]
SPAR......... Semper Paratus [*Always Ready*] [*Coast Guard motto*]
SPAR......... Sensitivity Prediction from the Acoustic Reflex [*Audiometry*]
SPAR......... Society of Photographers and Artist Representatives [*New York, NY*] (EA)
SPAR......... Soil-Plant-Atmosphere-Research [*Agriculture*]
SPAR......... Space Precision Altitude Reference System (MCD)
SPAR......... Space Processing Applications Rocket [*NASA*]
SPAR......... SPALT [*Special Projects Alterations*] Planning and Authorization Report
SPAR......... Special Prelaunch Analysis Request [*NASA*] (KSC)
SPAR......... Spelling and Reading Tests
SPAR......... Staff Procurement Activity Requirement [*Military*]
SPAR......... Super-Precision Approach RADAR
SPAR......... Surveillance and Precision Approach RADAR (NATG)
SPAR......... Symbolic Program Assembly Routine [*Data processing*]
SPAR......... Synchronous Position Altitude Recorder
SPAR......... System Program Assessment Review [*Air Force*]
SPARC...... Shore-Establishment Planning Analysis and Review Cooperation [*or Coordination*] [*Navy*] (NG)
SPARC...... Slab Penetration and Reflection Calculation
SPARC...... Space Air Relay Communications (MCD)
SPARC...... Space Program Analysis and Review Council [*Air Force*]
SPARC...... Space Research Capsule [*or Conic*] [*NASA*]
SPARC...... Spectral Analysis and Recognition Computer [*NASA*]
SPARC...... Standards Planning and Requirements Committee [*ANSI*]
SPARC...... Steam Plant Automation and Results Computer
SPARC...... Support Planning Analysis Reporting and Control [*Navy*] (NG)
SPARC...... Sustainability Predictions for Army Spare Component Requirements for Combat (RDA)
SPARC...... System Parametric Allocation of Resources and Cost (MCD)
SPARCS..... Solar Pointing Aerobee Rocket Control System
SPARCS..... Statewide Planning and Research Cooperative System [*New York State Department of Health*] [*Albany*] [*Information service*] (EISS)
SPARD ...... Sparkasse [*A publication*]
SPARE ...... Save Pound Animals from Research Experiments [*Costa Mesa, CA*] (EA)
SPARES ..... Space Radiation Evaluation System [*NASA*] (KSC)
SPARK ...... Saboteurs for a Philistine America Redeemed from Kultur [*From book, "Bringing Down the House," by Richard P. Brickner*]
SPARK ...... Screen Pattern Analyzer and Rescreening Key [*Printing process*]
SPARK ...... Seminars on Practical Applications of Research Knowledge [*Advertising Research Foundation*]
SPARK ...... Solid Propellant Advanced Ramjet Kinetic Energy (MCD)
SPARK ...... Systematic Pulmono/Cardiac Anaphylaxis Resusitation Kit (MCD)
Sparks ...... Sparks' Reports [*British Burma*] (DLA)
Spark's Am Biog ... Spark's Library of American Biography [*A publication*]
SPARM...... Solid-Propellant Augmented Rocket Motor [*Navy*]
SPARM...... Sparrow Antiradiation Missile (MCD)
SPARMIS ... Standard Police Automated Resource Management Information System
SPARMO .... Solar Particles and Radiations Monitoring Organization

SPARMO Bull ... SPARMO [*Solar Particles and Radiation Monitoring Organization*] Bulletin [*A publication*]
SPARPS..... Spares and Repair Parts Support [*Navy*] (NG)
SPARS .... Semper Paratus [*US Coast Guard Women's Auxiliary; name taken from Coast Guard motto*]
SPARS ...... Site Production and Reduction System
SPARS ...... Society of Professional Audio Recording Studios [*Beverly Hills, CA*] (EA)
SPARS ...... Society of Professional Recording Studios (EA)
SPARS ...... Space Precision Altitude [*or Attitude*] Reference System
SPARSA..... Sferics, Position [*or Pulse*], Azimuth, Rate, and Spectrum Analyzer
SPARSIM ... Spartan Simulation [*Missile system evaluation*] (RDA)
SPART ...... Space Research and Technology [*Report*] [*NASA*] (KSC)
SPART ...... Sunny Point Army Terminal
SPARTA ..... Sequential Programed Automatic Recording Transistor Analyzer
SPARTA ..... Special Antimissile Research Tests in Australia
SPARTAN ... Shuttle-Pointed Autonomous Research Tool for Astronomy [*NASA*]
SPARTAN ... Special Proficiency at Rugged Training and Nation Building [*Training program for Green Berets*] [*Army*]
SPARTAN ... System for Personnel Automated Reports, Transactions, and Notices [*Census Bureau, NASA*]
SPAS......... Shipboard Pollution Abatement System [*Navy*] (CAAL)
SPAS......... Shuttle Pallet Satellite [*NASA*]
SPAS......... Skill Performance Aids
SPAS......... Social Service Department, Prince Albert, Saskatchewan [*Library symbol*] [*National Library of Canada*] (NLC)
SPA-S ...... Societa Prodotti Antibiotici [*Italy*] [*Research code symbol*]
SPAS......... Societatis Philosophicae Americanae Socius [*Member of the American Philosophical Society*]
SPAS......... Solar Proton Alpha Spectrometer
SPASCOMT ... Space Assignment Committee
SPASEP ..... Secretaria Permanente del Acuerdo Sudamericano de Estupefacientes y Psicotropicos [*Permanent Secretariat of the South American Agreement on Narcotic Drugs and Psychotropic Substances - PSSAANDPS*] [*Buenos Aires, Argentina*] (EA-IO)
SPASM....... Self-Propelled Air-to-Surface Missile (MCD)
SPASM....... Smithsonian Package for Algebra and Symbolic Mathematics (MCD)
SPASM...... Space Propulsion Automated Synthesis Modeling [*Program*]
SPASM...... System Performance and Activity Software Monitor [*Data processing*] (IEEE)
SPAST ...... Special Assistant [*Navy*]
SPASUR..... Space Surveillance System [*Navy*]
SPAT......... Self-Propelled Antitank Gun (MCD)
SPAT......... Silicon Precision Alloy Transistor
SPAT......... Spleen Antigen [*Complement Fixation*] Test [*Immunology*]
SPat .... Studia Patavina [*A publication*]
SPATA ...... Society of Polish-American Travel Agents [*Niles, IL*] (EA)
SPATE....... Sergeant Production Automatic Test Equipment
SPATE....... South Pacific Association for Teacher Education (EA)
SPATE....... Student Personnel Association for Teacher Education [*Later, AHEAD*] (EA)
SPA ad TEST ... Subpoena ad Testificandum [*Subpoena to Testify*] [*Latin*] (ROG)
S Patriot ... Southern Patriot [*A publication*]
SPATS ...... South Pacific Air Transportation Service [*Navy*]
SPAU......... Signal Processing [*or Processor*] Arithmetic Unit [*Navy*]
SPAU......... Stable Platform Alignment Unit
Spaulding ... Spaulding's Reports [*71-73 Maine*] (DLA)
SPAW........ Sitzungsberichte der Preussischen Akademie der Wissenschaften [*A publication*]
Spawanie Ciecie Met ... Spawanie i Ciecie Metali [*A publication*]
SPAWG ..... Special Activity Wing (MUGU)
SPAWN ...... Salmon Protection Association of Western Newfoundland [*Canada*] (ASF)
SPAYZ ...... Spatial Property Analyzer
SPB .... St. Thomas [*Virgin Islands*] Seaplane Base [*Airport symbol*] (OAG)
SPB .... Scottish Prayer Book [*Episcopalian*]
SPB .... Seaplane Base
SPB .... Ship's Plotting Board
SPB .... Silver-Plated Bronze
SPB .... Society of the Precious Blood [*Anglican religious community*]
SPB .... Solar Particle Beams
SPB .... Sotheby Parke Bernet [*Formerly, PB*] [*Manhattan art auction house*]
SPB .... Special Pathogens Branch [*Centers for Disease Control*]
SPB .... Spindle Pole Body [*Cell biology*]
SpB .... Sprakliga Bidrag [*Lund*] [*A publication*]
SPB .... Springboard Resources Ltd. [*Vancouver Stock Exchange symbol*]
SPB .... Standard Practice Bulletin (MCD)
SPB .... Standardized Performance Battery [*Acoustics*]
SPB .... Stored Program Buffer
SPB .... Studia Post-Biblica [*Leiden*] [*A publication*]
SPB .... Surplus Property Board

SPBA......... Society of Professional Benefit Administrators [*Washington, DC*] (EA)
SPBA......... Specialty Paper and Board Affiliates [*Later, API*] (EA)
SpBA........ Spisanie na Balgarskata Akademija na Naukite [*A publication*]
SPBAA...... Spisanie na Bulgarskata Akademiya na Naukite [*A publication*]
SpBAN...... Spisanie na Bulgarskata Akademiya na Naukite [*A publication*]
SpBaU........ Universidad de Barcelona, Biblioteca Universitaria y Provincal, Barcelona, Spain [*Library symbol*] [*Library of Congress*] (LCLS)
SPBC........ Saint Paul Bible College [*Minnesota*]
SPBC........ Society of Professional Business Consultants [*Chicago, IL*] (EA)
SPBC........ South Pacific Base Command [*Navy*] [*World War II*]
SPBD........ Springboard (NVT)
SPBE........ Service de Presse Baptiste Europeen [*European Baptist Press Service - EBPS*] [*Ruschlikon, Switzerland*] (EA-IO)
SPBGY ...... Sotheby Parke Bernet [*NASDAQ symbol*] (NQ)
SPBI........ Serikat Buruh Pertjetakan Indonesia [*Printing Workers' Union of Indonesia*]
SPBI........ Society for Proclaiming Britain in Israel
SPBK........ Speed Brake (NASA)
SPBM........ Single Point Buoy Mooring [*Oil platform*]
SPBOT .... Stationers and Publishers Board of Trade [*Later, Stationery and Office Equipment Board of Trade*]
SPBP........ Society for the Preservation of Birds of Prey (EA)
SPBR........ Speed Brake (MCD)
SPBS........ Schweizerische Partei der Behinderten und Sozialbenachteiligten [*Swiss Party of the Handicapped and Socially Disadvantaged*] (PPW)
SPBS........ Standard Property Book System [*Army*]
SPC........... IEEE. Spectrum [*A publication*]
SPC........... Institute for Studies of Destructive Behaviors and the Suicide Prevention Center of Los Angeles [*California*] (EA)
SPC........... Political Committee at Senior Level [*NATO*] (NATG)
SPC........... St. Paul's Cathedral [*London, England*]
SPC........... Saint Paul's College [*Missouri; Virginia; Washington, DC*]
SPC........... Saint Paul's College, Lawrenceville, VA [*OCLC symbol*] (OCLC)
SPC........... Saint Peter College [*Maryland; New Jersey*]
SPC........... Saint Procopius College [*Illinois*]
SPC........... Salicylamide, Phenacetin [*Acetophenetidin*], and Caffeine [*Pharmacy*]
SPC........... Santa Cruz La Palma [*Canary Islands*] [*Airport symbol*] (OAG)
SPC........... Saratoga Processing [*Vancouver Stock Exchange symbol*]
SPC........... Seattle Pacific College [*Washington*]
SPC........... Security Pacific Corporation [*NYSE symbol*]
SPC........... Self-Programming Compiler [*Software*] [*Data processing*]
SPC........... Set Point Controller
SPC........... Shipping and Packing Cost (NASA)
SPC........... Shuttle Pin Clutch
SPC........... Silver-Plated Copper
SPC........... Simultaneous Prism and Cover (Test) [*Ophthalmology*]
SPC........... Single Prime Contractor [*Weapon system procurement*] [*Air Force*] (AAG)
SPC........... Site Programer Course
SPC........... Size-Press Coated [*Publishing*]
SPC........... Skalnate-Pleso [*Czechoslovakia*] [*Seismograph station code, US Geological Survey*] (SEIS)
SPC........... Small Peripheral Controller
SPC........... Soap Perfumery and Cosmetics [*A publication*]
SPC........... Socialist Party of Chile
SPC........... Society for Philosophy of Creativity
SPC........... Society for the Prevention of Crime [*New York, NY*] (EA)
SPC........... Solar Pointing Control
SPC........... Solid-Propellant Combustion
SPC........... Solid-Propellant Conference
S/P/C........ Sotto Protesto per Mettere in Conto [*Under Protest to Place to Account*] [*Italy*]
SPC........... South Pacific Commission [*See also CPS*] [*Noumea, New Caledonia*] (EA-IO)
SPC........... South Pacific Island Airways, Inc. [*Pago Pago, American Samoa*] (FAAC)
SPC........... Southern Pacific Communications Corp.
SPC........... Southern Ports Foreign Committee, Chicago IL [*STAC*]
SPC........... Soy Protein Council [*Formerly, FPC*] [*Washington, DC*] (EA)
SPC........... Space Projects Center [*NASA*]
SpC........... Spanish Columbia, San Sebastian [*Record label*] [*Spain*]
SPC........... Spare Parts Catalog
Sp C........ Special Commissioner (DLA)
SPC........... Special Common [*Projectile*]
SPC........... Special Program Code [*Navy*]
SPC........... Special Project Code [*IRS*]
SPC........... Special Purpose Chaff [*Navy*] (CAAL)
SPC........... Specialist, Classification Interviewer [*Navy rating*]
SPC........... Specific Propellant Consumption
SPC........... Standard Plate Count [*Microbiology*]
SPC........... Standard Products Committee [*Navy*]
SPC........... Standby Pressure Control [*Nuclear energy*] (NRCH)
SPC........... Starting Point Code (NASA)
SPC........... Static Power Conservers (MCD)
SPC........... Static Pressure Compensation

SPC........... Station Program Cooperative [*Public television*]
SPC........... Statistical Process Control
SPC........... Sterilizable Potting Compound
SPC........... Stockage Priority Code [*Military*] (AFIT)
SPC........... Stored Program Command [*or Control*] [*Data processing*]
SPC........... Strategy and Planning Committee [*Military*]
SPC........... Subcontract Plans Committee
SPC........... Sucrose-Phosphate-Citrate [*A culture medium*]
SPC........... Sugar Packet Club (EA)
SPC........... Supplemental Planning Card (AAG)
SPC........... Suspended Plaster Ceiling [*Technical drawings*]
SPC........... Switching and Processing Center [*EFTS*] [*Banking*]
SPC........... Syndicat des Postiers du Canada [*Canadian Union of Postal Workers - CUPW*]
SPC........... Synoptic Properties Code (MCD)
SPCA........ School Projectionist Club of America (EA)
SPCA........ Serum Prothrombin Conversion Accelerator [*Factor VII*] [*Also, PPCA*] [*Hematology*]
SPCA........ Society for the Prevention of Cruelty to Animals
SPCA........ Southern Pulpwood Conservation Association [*Later, SFI*] (EA)
SPCA........ Spark Plug Collectors of America (EA)
SPCA........ Special-Purpose Cable Assembly
SPCAT...... Special Category (MSA)
SPCC........ Servo Pressure Control Console
SPCC........ Ship's Parts Control Center
SPCC........ Society for the Prevention of Cruelty to Children
SPCC........ Southern Pacific Communications Corporation
SPCC........ Space Parts Control Center (MUGU)
SPCC........ Spill Prevention Control and Countermeasure [*Petroleum industry*]
SPCC........ Staggered Phase Carrier Cancellation
SPCC........ Standardization, Policy, and Coordination Committee [*NATO*] (NATG)
SPCC........ Stored Program CAMAC [*Computer-Aided Measurement and Control*] Channel [*Data processing*]
SPCC........ Strength Power and Communications Cable
SPCC........ Study Planning and Coordinating Committee [*Army*]
SPCCS...... Spill Prevention Control and Countermeasure System [*Environmental Protection Agency*] [*Information service*] [*No longer exists*] (EISS)
SPCDS...... Small Permanent Communications and Display Segment (MCD)
SPCEC...... Stereo Photographers, Collectors, and Enthusiasts Club (EA)
SPCF........ Special Project Control File [*IRS*]
Sp Ch........ Spears' South Carolina Chancery Reports (DLA)
SPCH........ Speech
SPCHB...... Soviet Progress in Chemistry [*English Translation*] [*A publication*]
SPCHG...... Supercharge
SPCHGR...... Supercharger (AAG)
SPCK........ Society for Promoting Christian Knowledge [*Publisher*] [*British*]
SPCL........ Special (MSA)
SPCLASGN ... Special Assignment [*Military*] (NVT)
SPCLN ...... Special Cleaning
SPCLY ...... Especially (FAAC)
SPCM........ Master Chief Steam Propulsionman [*Navy rating*]
SPCM........ Spanish Campaign Medal
SPCM........ Special Court-Martial
SPCM........ Specialty Composites [*NASDAQ symbol*] (NQ)
SPCMO...... Special Court-Martial Order
SPCMWOMJ ... Special Court-Martial without a Military Judge (AFM)
SPCN........ Stored Program Controlled Network [*Telecommunications*]
SPCNI...... Society for Pacific Coast Native Irises (EA)
SPCO........ Southern Pacific Company
SPCONV .... Speed Converter
SPCP........ Single Prime Contractor Policy [*Air Force*] (AAG)
SPCP........ Society of Professors of Child Psychiatry [*Washington, DC*] (EA)
SPCQB...... SPC [*South Pacific Commission*] Quarterly Bulletin [*A publication*]
SPC Quart Bull ... SPC [*South Pacific Commission*] Quarterly Bulletin [*A publication*]
SPCR........ Spacer
SPCR........ Spare Parts Change Request
Sp Cr Ct..... Special Criminal Court (DLA)
SPCS........ Schedule Planning and Control System (MCD)
SPCS........ Selective Paging Communications System
SPCS........ Static Power Conversion System
SPCS........ Storage and Processing Control System
SPCS........ Surgical Postcaval Shunt [*Medicine*]
SPC/SQC ... Statistical Process/Statistical Quality Control
SPCT........ Studi e Problemi di Critica Testuale [*A publication*]
SPCTG...... Spherical Cartridge
Sp Ct RRRA ... Special Court Regional Railroad Reorganization Act (DLA)
SPCTYS...... Society for the Prevention of Cruelty to Young Singers
SPCU........ Simulation Process Control Unit (MCD)
SPCU .... Skylab Process Control Unit [*NASA*]
SPCUS...... Sweet Potato Council of the United States (EA)
SPCW........ Specialist, Chemical Warfare [*Navy rating*]

SPD	Doctor of Political Science
SPD	S-Band Polarization Diversity
SPD	Safety Program Directive [*NASA*]
SPD	Saidpur [*Bangladesh*] [*Airport symbol*] (OAG)
SPD	St. Peter's Dome Lookout [*New Mexico*] [*Seismograph station code, US Geological Survey*] (SEIS)
SPD	Salutem Plurimam Dicit [*He Wishes Much Health*] [*Latin*]
SPD	Sampled [*Tea trade*] (ROG)
SPD	Scientific Passenger Pod (MCD)
SPD	Seaplane Depot Ship
SPD	Semipermeable Dressing [*Medicine*]
SPD	Separation Program Designator (AABC)
SPD	Service Project Drawing
SPD	Shearing, Piling, and Disking [*Forest management*]
SPD	Ship Performance Department [*David W. Taylor Naval Ship Research and Development Center*]
SPD	Ship Project Directive [*Navy*]
SPD	Sigma Phi Delta (EA)
SPD	Silicon Photo Diode [*Photography*]
SPD	Single Path Doppler [*RADAR*] (AAG)
SPD	Situation Projected Display
SPD	Skylab Program Directive [*NASA*] (KSC)
SPD	Society for Pediatric Dermatology [*University of Michigan Medical Center*] [*Ann Arbor*] (EA)
SPD	Society of Professional Drivers [*Paoli, PA*] (EA)
SPD	Society of Publication Designers [*New York, NY*] (EA)
SPD	South Pacific Division [*Army*] [*World War II*]
SPD	South Polar Distance
SPD	Southern Procurement Division [*Navy*]
SPD	Sozialdemokratische Partei Deutschlands [*Social Democratic Party of Germany*] [*West Germany*]
SpD	Spanish Decca, San Sebastian [*Record label*] [*Spain*]
SPD	Spectral Power Distribution (MCD)
SPD	Speech Processing Device
SPD	Speed (AABC)
Spd	Spermidine [*Biochemistry*]
SPD	Standard Practice Directive [*NASA*] (NASA)
SPD	Standard Products Co. [*American Stock Exchange symbol*]
SPD	Static Pressure Distribution
SPD	Statistical Policy Division [*Office of Management and Budget*]
SPD	Steamer Pays Dues [*Shipping*]
SPD	Stick Positioning Device (MCD)
SPD	Storage Pool Disease
SPD	Stored Program Decoder [*or Decommutation*]
SPD	Strategic Posture Display (MCD)
SPD	Subjective Probability Distribution
SPD	Supplemental Program Directive (AFIT)
SPD	Supplementary Petroleum Duty [*Tax*] [*British*]
SPD	Surge Protective Device (MCD)
SPD	Synchronizer for Peripheral Devices
SPD	Synchronous Phase Demodulator
SPD	System Program Directive (AFIT)
SPD	System Program Director [*Air Force*] (MCD)
SPD	Systems Parameters Document (AAG)
SPD	Systems Program Documentation
SPDA	Single-Premium Deferred Annuity [*Insurance*]
SPDB	Subsystem Power Distribution Box (MCD)
SPDBK	Speed Brake (MCD)
SPDC	S-P Drug Company [*NASDAQ symbol*] (NQ)
SPDC	Spare Parts Distributing Center [*Navy*]
SPDCU	Subsurface Probe Data and Control Unit
SPDF	Special Projects Data Facility
SPDF	Swedish Post Defense Forces
SPDG	Spiral Point Drill Geometry
SPDHF	Special Pay for Duty Subject to Hostile Fire [*Military*]
SPDI	Special Discriminant (CAAL)
SPDL	Spindle (MSA)
SPDLTR	Speedletter
SPDM	Subprocessor with Dynamic Microprograming
SPDOM	Speedometer (MSA)
SPDP	Stored Program Data Processor (KSC)
SPDP	Succinimidyl(pyridyldithio)propionate [*Organic chemistry*]
SPDR	Software Preliminary Design Review [*NASA*] (NASA)
SPDR	Special Drill [*Tool*] (AAG)
SPDR	Spider [*Engineering acoustics*]
SP/DR	Systems Performance/Design Requirements
SPDRAB	Society for the Prevention of Disparaging Remarks about Brooklyn
SPDS	Safe-Practice Data Sheet (MSA)
SPDS	Safety Parameter Display System [*Instrumentation*]
SPDS	Sequential Payload Delivery System (MCD)
SPDS	Suggestion Program Data System [*Military*]
SPDT	Single-Pole, Double-Throw [*Switch*]
SPDTDB	Single-Pole, Double-Throw, Double-Break [*Switch*]
SPDTNCDB ...	Single-Pole, Double-Throw, Normally-Closed, Double-Break [*Switch*]
SPDTNO	Single-Pole, Double-Throw, Normally-Open [*Switch*]
SPDTNODB ...	Single-Pole, Double-Throw, Normally-Open, Double-Break [*Switch*]
SPDTSW	Single-Pole, Double-Throw Switch
SPDW	South Pacific Deep Water

SPDWY	Speedway
SPDY	Spectradyne, Inc. [*NASDAQ symbol*] (NQ)
s-pe---	Peru [*MARC geographic area code*] [*Library of Congress*] (LCCP)
SPE	Senior Project Engineer
SPE	Serum Protein Electrophoresis
SPE	Shaft Position Encoder
SPE	Sian [*Republic of China*] [*Seismograph station code, US Geological Survey*] (SEIS)
SPE	Signal Processing Element [*Navy*]
SPE	Sliding Padeye (MCD)
SPE	Small Processing Element [*Data processing*]
SPE	Society of Petroleum Engineers [*of AIME*]
SPE	Society for Photographic Education (EA)
SPE	Society of Plastic Engineers (EA)
SPE	Society of Professors of Education [*Formerly, NSCTE*] (EA)
SPE	Society for Pure English
SPE	Solid-Phase Extraction
SPE	Solid Polymer Electrolyte
SPE	Space Processing Equipment [*Astronautics*]
SPE	Special-Purpose Equipment
SPE	Sperry UNIVAC Information Center, Blue Bell, PA [*OCLC symbol*] (OCLC)
SPe	Spettatore Italiano [*A publication*]
SPE	Spherical Probable Error
SPE	Static Phase Error [*NASA*]
SPE	Station Project Engineer [*NASA*]
SPE	Stepped Potential Electrode [*Electrode chemistry*]
SPE	Stop Project ELF (EA)
SPE	Stored Program Element
SPE	Studies in Public Economics [*Elsevier Book Series*] [*A publication*]
SPE	Subport of Embarkation
SPE	Sucrose Polyester [*Pharmacology*]
SPE	Sun-Planet-Earth [*Astronomy*]
SPE	Supercritical Fluid Extraction [*Chemical engineering*]
SPE	System Performance Evaluation (KSC)
SPE	Systems Performance Effectiveness
SPE	Unilabo [*France*] [*Research code symbol*]
SPEA	Sales Promotion Executives Association [*Later, MCEI*] (EA)
SPEA	Southeastern Poultry and Egg Association (EA)
SPEAC	Selma Project Education Alternatives Center [*Alabama*] (EA)
SPEAC	Solar Photovoltaic Energy Advisory Committee [*Inactive since 1982*] (EGAO)
SPEAHR	Society for the Protection of East Asians' Human Rights/USA (EA)
SPE of AIME ...	Society of Petroleum Engineers of American Institute of Mining, Metallurgical, and Petroleum Engineers (EA)
SPEAK	Society for Promoting and Encouraging the Arts and Knowledge of the Church (EA)
SPEAKEASY ...	[*An*] information retrieval system
SPEAL	Special-Purpose Engineering Analysis Language (MCD)
SPEAR	Signal Processing, Evaluation, Alert, and Report [*Navy*] (NVT)
SPEAR	SLAC Positron-Electron Asymmetric Ring
SPEAR	Small Payload Ejection and Recovery for the Space Shuttle [*NASA*] (MCD)
SPEAR	Source Performance Evaluation and Reporting
SPEAR	Spaceborne Earth Applications Ranging System (MCD)
SPEAR	Squadron Performance Effectiveness Analysis Representation (MCD)
SPEAR	Stanford Positron-Electron Accumulation Ring
SPEAR	Statistical Property Estimation and Regeneration (MCD)
SPEAR	Supplier Performance Evaluation and Reporting [*or Review*] [*General Motors quality award*]
Spear Ch....	Spears' South Carolina Chancery Reports (DLA)
Spear Eq....	Spears' South Carolina Equity Reports (DLA)
Spear High ...	Spearman on Highways [*1881*] (DLA)
SPEARS	Satellite Photoelectric Analog Rectification System
Spears	Spears' South Carolina Equity Reports (DLA)
Spears	Spears' South Carolina Law Reports (DLA)
Spears Eq ...	Spears' South Carolina Equity Reports (DLA)
SPEBSQSA ...	Society for the Preservation and Encouragement of Barber Shop Quartet Singing in America (EA)
Spec	De Specialibus Legibus [*of Philo*] (BJA)
SPEC	Scientific Pollution and Environmental Control Society
SPEC	Society of Professional Engineering Checkers
SPEC	South Pacific Bureau for Economic Co-Operation [*Suva, Fiji*]
SPEC	Special (KSC)
SPEC	Specialist
SPEC	Specific
SPEC	Specification (AFM)
SPEC	Specimen (AAG)
Spec	Spectator [*A publication*]
Spec	Spectrum [*A publication*]
SPEC	Spectrum
SPEC	Spectrum Control [*NASDAQ symbol*] (NQ)
Spec	Speculation [*A publication*]
Spec	Speculum [*A publication*]
SPEC	Speech Predictive Encoded Communications [*Telephone channels*]

SPEC......... Staff of the Production Executive Committee [*of the WPB*] [*Obsolete*]
SPEC......... Stored Program Educational Computer
SPEC......... Studies in the Political Economy of Canada [*Society*]
SPEC......... Systems and Procedures Exchange Center [*Association of Research Libraries*]
SPECA....... Society for the Preservation and Enjoyment of Carriages in America   (EA)
SPECAN..... Spectral Analysis
SPECAT..... Special Category   (AABC)
Spec Bull Coll Agric Utsunomiya Univ ... Special Bulletin. College of Agriculture. Utsunomiya University [*A publication*]
Spec Bull Coll Agr Utsunomiya Univ ... Special Bulletin. College of Agriculture. Utsunomiya University [*A publication*]
Spec Bull Dep Agric S Aust ... Special Bulletin. Department of Agriculture. South Australia [*A publication*]
Spec Bull Dep Agric South Aust ... Special Bulletin. Department of Agriculture. South Australia [*A publication*]
Spec Bull First Agron Div Tokai-Kinki Natl Agric Exp Stn ... Special Bulletin. First Agronomy Division. Tokai-Kinki National Agricultural Experiment Station [*A publication*]
Spec Bull Mich Agric Exp Stn ... Special Bulletin. Michigan Agricultural Experiment Station [*A publication*]
Spec Bull Mich State Univ Agr Exp Sta ... Special Bulletin. Michigan State University. Agricultural Experiment Station [*A publication*]
Spec Bull Okayama Agr Exp Sta ... Special Bulletin. Okayama Agricultural Experiment Station [*A publication*]
Spec Bull Rehovot Nat Univ Inst Agr ... Special Bulletin. Rehovot. National and University Institute of Agriculture [*A publication*]
Spec Bull Taiwan For Res Inst ... Special Bulletin. Taiwan Forestry Research Institute [*A publication*]
Spec Bull Tottori Agric Exp Stn ... Special Bulletin. Tottori Agricultural Experiment Station [*A publication*]
Sp Ecc & Ad ... Spinks' English Ecclesiastical and Admiralty Reports [*164 English Reprint*] [*1853-55*]   (DLA)
Spec Ceram ... Special Ceramics [*A publication*]
Spec Circ Mass Ext Serv ... Special Circular. Massachusetts Extension Service [*A publication*]
Spec Circ Ohio Agr Exp Sta ... Special Circular. Ohio Agricultural Experiment Station [*A publication*]
Spec Circ Ohio Agric Res Dev Cent ... Special Circular. Ohio Agricultural Research and Development Center [*A publication*]
Spec Circ PA State Univ Coll-Agric Ext Serv ... Special Circular. Pennsylvania State University. College of Agriculture. Extension Service [*A publication*]
Spec Circ Univ Wis Coll Agr Ext Serv ... Special Circular. University of Wisconsin. College of Agriculture. Extension Service [*A publication*]
Spec Contrib Geophys Inst Kyoto Univ ... Special Contributions. Geophysical Institute. Kyoto University [*Japan*] [*A publication*]
Spec Courses Fd Ind ... Specialist Courses for the Food Industry [*A publication*]
Spec Courses Food Ind ... Specialist Courses for the Food Industry [*Food Industry News*] [*A publication*]
SPECD....... Specification Data Base
SPECDEVCEN ... Special Devices Center [*Navy*]
Spec Educ ... Special Education. Forward Trends [*A publication*]
Spec Educ Bull ... Special Education Bulletin [*A publication*]
Spec Educ Forward Trends ... Special Education. Forward Trends [*A publication*]
Spec Eng ... Specifying Engineer [*A publication*]
SPECHNDLG ... Special Handling   (MCD)
SPECI........ Specimen   (DSUE)
Special Bull Univ Minnesota Agric Exten Div ... Special Bulletin. University of Minnesota. Agricultural Extension Division [*A publication*]
Special Ed ... Special Education [*A publication*]
Speciality Chem ... Speciality Chemicals [*A publication*]
Special Lib ... Special Libraries [*A publication*]
Special Rep Ser Med Research Com (London) ... Special Report Series. Medical Research Committee (London) [*A publication*]
Special Sch Bul (NT) ... Special Schools Bulletin (Northern Territory) [*A publication*]
Special Sch Bul (Qld) ... Special Schools Bulletin (Queensland Department of Education) [*A publication*]
SPECIFD.... Specified   (ROG)
Specif Eng ... Specifying Engineer [*A publication*]
Specif Engr ... Specifying Engineer [*A publication*]
SPECIFN.... Specification   (ROG)
Spec Int ..... Specialties International [*A publication*]
Spec Issue Plant Cell Physiol ... Special Issue of Plant and Cell Physiology [*A publication*]
SPECL........ Special   (ROG)
SPECL........ Specialize
Spec Libr ... Special Libraries [*A publication*]
Spec Libr Ass Toronto Chapter Bull ... Special Libraries Association. Toronto Chapter. Bulletin [*A publication*]
SPECLST... Specialist
SPECMAP ... Spectral Mapping
SPECO........ Steel Products Engineering Company

SPECOL..... Special Customer-Oriented Language
SPECOM.... Special Command
SPECOMALT ... Special Communications Alteration
SPECOMME ... Specified Command Middle East
SPECON .... Systems Performance Effectiveness Conference
SPECOPS ... Special Operations [*Navy*]   (NVT)
SPECOR..... Spectral Correlation RADAR   (MCD)
Spec Pap Dep Nat Resour (QD) ... Special Papers. Department of Natural Resources (Queensland) [*A publication*]
Spec Pap Palaeontol ... Special Papers in Palaeontology [*A publication*]
Spec Period Rep Aliphatic Chem ... Specialist Periodical Reports. Aliphatic Chemistry [*A publication*]
Spec Period Rep Alkaloids ... Specialist Periodical Reports. Alkaloids [*A publication*]
Spec Period Rep Amino-Acids Peptides Proteins ... Specialist Periodical Reports. Amino-Acids, Peptides, and Proteins [*A publication*]
Spec Period Rep Biosynth ... Specialist Periodical Reports. Biosynthesis [*A publication*]
Spec Period Rep Carbohydr Chem ... Specialist Periodical Reports. Carbohydrate Chemistry [*A publication*]
Spec Period Rep Catal ... Specialist Periodical Reports. Catalysis [*A publication*]
Spec Period Rep Foreign Compd Metab Mamm ... Specialist Periodical Reports. Foreign Compound Metabolism in Mammals [*A publication*]
Spec Period Rep Gas Kinet Energy Transfer ... Specialist Periodical Reports. Gas Kinetics and Energy Transfer [*A publication*]
Spec Period Rep Gen Synth Methods ... Specialist Periodical Reports. General and Synthetic Methods [*A publication*]
Spec Period Rep Mol Struct Diffr Methods ... Specialist Periodical Reports. Molecular Structure by Diffraction Methods [*A publication*]
Spec Period Rep React Kinet ... Specialist Periodical Reports. Reaction Kinetics [*A publication*]
Spec Period Rep Terpenoids Steroids ... Specialist Periodical Reports. Terpenoids and Steroids [*A publication*]
Spec Publ Acad Nat Sci Phila ... Special Publication. Academy of Natural Sciences. Philadelphia [*A publication*]
Spec Publ Am Littoral Soc ... Special Publication. American Littoral Society [*A publication*]
Spec Publ Am Soc Agron ... Special Publication. American Society of Agronomy [*A publication*]
Spec Publ Am Soc Mammal ... Special Publication. American Society of Mammalogists [*A publication*]
Spec Publ Aust Conserv Fdn ... Special Publication. Australian Conservation Foundation [*A publication*]
Spec Publ Aust Conserv Found ... Special Publication. Australian Conservation Foundation [*A publication*]
Spec Publ Br Ceram Res Assoc ... Special Publication. British Ceramics Research Association [*A publication*]
Spec Publ Chicago Acad Sci ... Special Publications. Chicago Academy of Science [*A publication*]
Spec Publ Coll Agric Natl Taiwan Univ ... Special Publication. College of Agriculture. National Taiwan University [*A publication*]
Spec Publ Coll Agr Nat Taiwan U ... Special Publications. College of Agriculture. National Taiwan University [*A publication*]
Spec Publ Geol Soc Aust ... Special Publication. Geological Society of Australia [*A publication*]
Spec Publ Geol Soc London ... Special Publication. Geological Society of London [*A publication*]
Spec Publ Geol Surv S Afr ... Special Publications. Geological Survey of South Africa [*A publication*]
Spec Publ (Isr) Agric Res Org ... Special Publication (Israel). Agricultural Research Organization [*A publication*]
Spec Publ KY Geol Surv ... Special Publication. Kentucky Geological Survey [*A publication*]
Spec Publ NM Geol Soc ... Special Publication. New Mexico Geological Society [*A publication*]
Spec Publ S Afr Assoc Adv Sci ... Special Publication. South African Association for the Advancement of Science [*A publication*]
Spec Publs Am Ass Econ Ent ... Special Publications. American Association of Economic Entomology [*A publication*]
Spec Publ Ser Soil Sci Soc Amer ... Special Publication Series. Soil Science Society of America [*A publication*]
Spec Publ US Bur Mines ... Special Publications. United States Bureau of Mines [*A publication*]
Spec Publ US Natn Bur Stand ... Special Publications. United States National Bureau of Standards [*A publication*]
Spec Publ West Aust Mus ... Special Publication. Western Australian Museum [*A publication*]
Spec Pub R Soc Tasm ... Royal Society of Tasmania. Special Publications [*A publication*]
Spec Rep Agric Exp Stn Coop Ext Serv Univ Arkansas ... Special Report. Agricultural Experiment Station. Cooperative Extension Service. University of Arkansas [*A publication*]
Spec Rep Agric Exp Stn Oreg State Univ ... Special Report. Agricultural Experiment Station. Oregon State University [*A publication*]
Spec Rep Arctic Inst N Am ... Special Report. Arctic Institute of North America [*A publication*]

Spec Rep Ark Agr Exp Sta ... Special Report. Arkansas Agricultural Experiment Station [*A publication*]

Spec Rep Ark Agric Exp Stn ... Special Report. Arkansas Agricultural Experiment Station [*A publication*]

Spec Rep Colo Dep Game Fish Parks ... Special Report. Colorado Department of Game, Fish, and Parks [*A publication*]

Spec Rep Colo Div Game Fish Parks ... Special Report. Colorado Division of Game, Fish, and Parks [*A publication*]

Spec Rep Colo Div Wildl ... Special Report. Colorado Division of Wildlife [*A publication*]

Spec Rep Commonw Exp Bldg Stn ... Special Report. Commonwealth Experimental Building Station [*A publication*]

Spec Rep EPRI SR Electr Power Res Inst (Palo Alto Calif) ... Special Report EPRI SR [*Electric Power Research Institute. Special Report*] Electric Power Research Institute (Palo Alto, California) [*A publication*]

Spec Rep Geol Soc Lond ... Special Reports. Geological Society of London [*A publication*]

Spec Rep ICSU Comm Data Sci Technol ... Special Report. International Council of Scientific Unions. Committee on Data for Science and Technology [*A publication*]

Spec Rep Indiana Geol Surv ... Special Report. Indiana Geological Survey [*A publication*]

Spec Rep Iowa State Univ Coop Ext Serv ... Special Report. Iowa State University. Cooperative Extension Service [*A publication*]

Spec Rep Johns Hopkins Univ Appl Phys Lab ... Special Report. Johns Hopkins University. Applied Physics Laboratory [*A publication*]

Spec Rep Nebr Agr Exp Sta ... Special Report. Nebraska Agricultural Experiment Station [*A publication*]

Spec Rep (Oregon) Agric Exp Stn ... Special Report (Oregon). Agricultural Experiment Station [*A publication*]

Spec Rep Oreg State Coll Agr Exp Sta ... Special Report. Oregon State College Agricultural Experiment Station [*A publication*]

Spec Rep Robert Wood Johnson Foundation ... Special Report. Robert Wood Johnson Foundation [*A publication*]

Spec Rep Ser Indian Counc Med Res ... Special Report Series. Indian Council of Medical Research [*A publication*]

Spec Rep Univ Ill Urbana Champaign Water Resour Cent ... Special Report. University of Illinois at Urbana-Champaign. Water Resources Center [*A publication*]

Spec Rep Univ Minn Agr Ext Serv ... Special Report. University of Minnesota. Agricultural Extension Service [*A publication*]

Spec Rep Univ MO Coll Agr Exp Sta ... Special Report. University of Missouri. College of Agriculture. Experiment Station [*A publication*]

Spec Rep Wood Res Lab VA Polyt Inst ... Special Report. Wood Research Laboratory. Virginia Polytechnic Institute [*A publication*]

SPECS .... Spectacles　(ROG)

Spec Sci Rep FL Dep Nat Resour Mar Res Lab ... Special Scientific Report. Florida Department of Natural Resources. Marine Research Laboratory [*A publication*]

Spec Sci Rep Wildlife US Fish Wildlife Serv ... Special Scientific Report. Wildlife. United States Fish and Wildlife Service [*A publication*]

Spec Ser Fla Dep Agric ... Special Series. Florida Department of Agriculture [*A publication*]

Spec Steel ... Special Steel [*Japan*] [*A publication*]

Spec Steels Rev ... Special Steels Review [*A publication*]

Spec Steels Tech Rev (Sheffield) ... Special Steels Technical Review (Sheffield) [*A publication*]

SPECT .... Single Photon Emission Computed Tomography

Spect .... Spectacula [*of Martial*] [*Classical studies*]　(OCD)

Spect .... Spectator [*A publication*]

SPECT .... Spectrograph

SPECT .... Spectrometer　(NASA)

Spect Act A ... Spectrochimica Acta. Part A. Molecular Spectroscopy [*A publication*]

Spect Act B ... Spectrochimica Acta. Part B. Atomic Spectroscopy [*A publication*]

Spec Tech Assoc Publ ... Special Technical Association. Publication [*A publication*]

Spec Tech Publs Am Soc Test Mater ... Special Technical Publications. American Society for Testing Materials [*A publication*]

Spect Lett ... Spectroscopy Letters [*A publication*]

SPECTNG ... Specialist Training [*Navy*]　(NVT)

Spec Transp Plann Practice ... Specialized Transportation Planning and Practice [*A publication*]

SPECTRE ... Special Executive for Counterintelligence, Terrorism, Revenge, and Extortion [*Fictitious organization whose agents were characters in the late Ian Fleming's "James Bond" mysteries*]

Spectrochim Acta ... Spectrochimica Acta [*A publication*]

Spectrochim Acta A ... Spectrochimica Acta. Part A. Molecular Spectroscopy [*A publication*]

Spectrochim Acta B ... Spectrochimica Acta. Part B. Atomic Spectroscopy [*A publication*]

Spectrochim Acta Part A Mol Spectrosc ... Spectrochimica Acta. Part A. Molecular Spectroscopy [*A publication*]

Spectrochim Acta Part B At Spectrosc ... Spectrochimica Acta. Part B. Atomic Spectroscopy [*A publication*]

SPECTROL ... Scheduling, Planning, Evaluation, and Cost Control [*Air Force*]

Spectrosc Lett ... Spectroscopy Letters [*A publication*]

Spectrosc Mol ... Spectroscopia Molecular [*A publication*]

Spectros Prop Inorg Organomet Compd ... Spectroscopic Properties of Inorganic and Organometallic Compounds [*A publication*]

Spectrum Int ... Spectrum International [*A publication*]

Specu .... Speculum [*A publication*]

Specul Sci Technol ... Speculations in Science and Technology [*Switzerland*] [*A publication*]

SPECVER ... Specification Verification [*Data processing*]　(IEEE)

SPED .... Special Education Director

Sp Ed .... Specialist in Education [*Academic degree*]

SPED .... Sulfur, Phosphorus, Emission Detector [*Chromatograph accessory*]

SPED .... Supersonic Planetary Entry Decelerator　(KSC)

SPEDA ...... Special Education [*A publication*]

SPEDAC ..... Solid-State, Parallel, Expandable, Differential Analyzer Computer

SPEDCO ..... Southeastern Pennsylvania Development Corporation

SPEDE .... System for Processing Educational Data Electronically

SPEDIAT .... Special Diary Transcript [*Military*]

SPEDTAC ... Stored Program Educational Transistorized Automatic Computer

SPEDY .... Summer Program for Economically Disadvantaged Youth [*Department of Labor*]

SPEE .... Society for the Promotion of Engineering Education [*Later, ASEE*]

SPEE .... Special Purpose End Effector　(MCD)

SPEE .... Studies in Production and Engineering Economics [*Elsevier Book Series*] [*A publication*]

Speech Mon ... Speech Monographs [*A publication*]

Speech Monogr ... Speech Monographs [*A publication*]

Speech Teac ... Speech Teacher [*A publication*]

SPEED .... Scheduled Procurement of Essential Equipment Deliveries [*US Postal Service*]

SPEED ...... Self-Programed Electronic Equation Delineator

SPEED ...... Signal Processing in Evacuated Electronic Devices

SPEED ...... Single-Point Emergency Equipment Divestment

SPEED ...... Special Procedures for Expediting Equipment Development　(MCD)

SPEED ...... Study and Performance Efficiency in Entry Design

SPEED ...... Subsistence Preparation by Electronic Energy Diffusion

SPEED ...... Systematic Plotting and Evaluation of Enumerated Data [*National Bureau of Standards*] [*Data processing*]

SPEED ...... Systems Planning and Effectiveness Evaluation Device　(MCD)

SPEED ...... Systemwide Project for Electronic Equipment at Depots [*Military*]　(AABC)

SPEEDEX ... Systemwide Project for Electronic Equipment at Depots Extended [*Military*]　(AABC)

SPEEDO ..... Speedometer [*Automotive engineering*]

SPEEDX ..... Society to Preserve the Engrossing Enjoyment of Dxing　(EA)

SPEEL .... Shore Plant Electronic Equipment List　(MUGU)

Speers ...... Speers' South Carolina Law Reports　(DLA)

Speers Eq ... Speers' South Carolina Equity Reports　(DLA)

Speers Eq (SC) ... Speers' [*or Spears'*] South Carolina Equity Reports　(DLA)

Speers L (SC) ... Speers' [*or Spears'*] South Carolina Law Reports　(DLA)

SPEF .... Single Program Element Funding　(AABC)

SPEF .... Student Performance Evaluation Form

SPEG .... Serum Protein Electrophoretogram [*Clinical chemistry*]

SPEG .... Spencerville & Elgin Railroad Co. [*AAR code*]

SPEG .... Staff Planning Evaluation Group　(AAG)

SPEJ .... Society of Petroleum Engineers. American Institute of Mining, Metallurgical, and Petroleum Engineers. Journal [*A publication*]

SPE J .... SPE [*Society of Plastics Engineers*] Journal [*A publication*]

SPEJA .... SPE [*Society of Plastics Engineers*] Journal [*A publication*]

SPEJ Soc Pet Eng J ... SPEJ. Society of Petroleum Engineers [*of AIME*] Journal [*United States*] [*A publication*]

Spektrum Wiss ... Spektrum der Wissenschaft [*German Federal Republic*] [*A publication*]

SPELD .... Specific Learning Disability　(ADA)

SPELD Info ... SPELD [*Societe de Promotion a l'Etranger du Livre de Droit*] Information [*A publication*]

SPELEOL ... Speleological

Speleol Abstr ... Speleological Abstracts [*A publication*]

Speleol Biul Speleoklubu Warsz ... Speleologia Biuletyn Speleoklubu Warszawskiego [*A publication*]

Spel Feuds ... Spelman on Feuds　(DLA)

Spel Gl .... Spelman's Glossarium Archaiologicum　(DLA)

SPELL .... Society for the Preservation of English Language and Literature　(EA)

Spell Extr Rel ... Spelling on Extraordinary Relief in Equity and in Law　(DLA)

Spell Extr Rem ... Spelling's Treatise on Injunctions and Other Extraordinary Remedies　(DLA)

Spel LT ...... Spelman's Law Tracts　(DLA)

Spelm .... Spelman's Glossarium Archaiologicum [*3 eds.*] [*1626-87*]　(DLA)

Spelman .... Spelman's Glossarium Archaiologicum [*3 eds.*] [*1626-87*]　(DLA)

SPELPAT ... Spelling Patterns
Spel Rep .... Spelman's Reports, Manuscript, English King's Bench   (DLA)
SPEM .... Sindacato Petrolieri e Methanieri [*Union of Oil and Methane Gas Workers*] [*Italy*]
SPEMS ...... Self-Propelled Elevated Maintenance Stand   (MCD)
SPENAVO ... Special Naval Observer
Spenc .... Spencer's Law Reports [*20 New Jersey*]   (DLA)
Spenc .... Spencer's Reports [*10-20 Minnesota*]   (DLA)
Spence Ch ... Spence's Equitable Jurisdiction of the Court of Chancery   (DLA)
Spence Eq Jur ... Spence's Equitable Jurisdiction of the Court of Chancery   (DLA)
Spence Pat Inv ... Spence on Patentable Inventions [*1851*]   (DLA)
Spencer ..... Spencer's Law Reports [*20 New Jersey*]   (DLA)
Spencer ..... Spencer's Reports [*10-20 Minnesota*]   (DLA)
SPEND .... Specifying Engineer [*A publication*]
Spen (NJ) ... Spencer's Law Reports [*20 New Jersey*]   (DLA)
Spenser St ... Spenser Studies [*A publication*]
Spens Sel Cas ... Spens' Select Cases [*Bombay, India*]   (DLA)
SPEOPT .... Special Optical Tracking System [*NASA*]
SPEP .... Serum Protein Electrophoresis [*Clinical chemistry*]
SPEP .... Society for Phenomenology and Existential Philosophy
SPEPD ...... Space Power and Electric Propulsion Division [*Formerly, Nuclear Systems and Space Power Division*] [*NASA*]
SPEPS .... Specialist, Motion Picture Service - Booker [*Navy rating*]
Sp Eq .... Spears' South Carolina Equity Reports   (DLA)
SPEQ .... Special Equipment   (AAG)
SPER .... Sperti Drug Products [*NASDAQ symbol*]   (NQ)
SPERA ...... Sperimentale [*A publication*]
Sper Arch Biol Norm Patol ... Sperimentale. Archivio di Biologia Normale e Patologica [*A publication*]
SPERDVAC ... Society to Preserve and Encourage Radio Drama, Variety, and Comedy   (EA)
SPE Reg Tech Conf Tech Pap ... SPE [*Society of Plastics Engineers*] Regional Technical Conference. Technical Papers [*A publication*]
SPE Repr Ser ... Society of Petroleum Engineers. American Institute of Mining, Metallurgical, and Petroleum Engineers. Reprint Series [*United States*] [*A publication*]
SPERM ...... Secret Paper Reconstitution Mechanism [*Device to reclaim documents that have been inadvertently shredded*]
Sperry Technol ... Sperry Technology [*A publication*]
SPERT .... Schedule Performance Evaluation and Review Technique
SPERT .... Short Pulse Experimental RADAR Techniques   (MCD)
SPERT .... Simplified Program Evaluation and Review Technique [*Trademark*]
SPERT .... Special Power Excursion Reactor Test [*US reactor facilities*]
SPERW ...... Specialist, Recreation and Welfare Assistant [*Navy rating*]
SPES .... Servico de Propaganda e Educacao Sanitaria [*Brazil*]
SPES .... Stored Program Element System [*Data processing*]   (IEEE)
SPESS .... Stored Program Electronic Switching System [*Telecommunications*]   (TEL)
SPET .... Single Photon Emission Tomography
SPET .... Solid-Propellant Electric Thruster [*Aerospace*]
SPET .... Super Power Electron Tube
SPETE .... Special Purpose Electronic Test Equipment [*Military*]   (CAAL)
SPETERL ... Ship Portable Electrical/Electronic Test Equipment Requirement List [*Navy*]   (CAAL)
SPetr .... Studi Petrarcheschi [*A publication*]
Spets Stali Splavy ... Spetsial'nye Stali Splavy [*USSR*] [*A publication*]
Spettatore Int ... Spettatore Internazionale [*A publication*]
SPEX .... Small and Specialists Publishers Exhibition
SPEX .... Special Exercise [*Navy*]   (NVT)
SPEX .... Spex Industries [*NASDAQ symbol*]   (NQ)
SPF .... St. Paul-En-Foret [*France*] [*Seismograph station code, US Geological Survey*]   (SEIS)
SPF .... St. Photios Foundation   (EA)
SPF .... Science Policy Foundation [*British*]
SPF .... Service Publication Form   (AAG)
SPF .... SIDPERS [*Standard Installation/Division Personnel System*] Personnel File [*Military*]   (AABC)
SPF .... Single Project Funding   (MCD)
SPF .... Site Population Factor [*Nuclear energy*]   (NRCH)
SPF .... Skin Protection Factor [*Medicine*]
SPF .... Society for the Propagation of the Faith   (EA)
SPF .... Space Power Facility
SPF .... Space Science Fiction [*A publication*]
SPF .... Space Science Fiction Magazine [*A publication*]
SPF .... Spacelab Processing Facility [*NASA*]   (NASA)
SPF .... Spearfish, SD [*Location identifier*] [*FAA*]   (FAAL)
SPF .... Special Purpose Force   (MCD)
SPF .... Specialist, Firefighter [*Navy rating*]
SPF .... Specific-Pathogen Free [*Medicine*]
SPF .... Spectrophotofluorometer
SPF .... Spinning Form   (MCD)
Spf .... Sprachforum [*A publication*]
SPF .... Springfield Resources [*Vancouver Stock Exchange symbol*]
SPF .... Standard-Pacific Corp. [*NYSE symbol*]
SPF .... Standard Pesticide File [*Derwent Publications Ltd.*] [*Database*]
SPF .... Standard Project Flood   (NRCH)
SPF .... Strategic Protection Force

SPF .... Stressed Panel Fasteners
SPF .... Structured Programing Facility [*Data processing*]
SPF .... Subscriber Plant Factor [*Telecommunications*]
SPF .... Suburban Press Foundation [*Later, SNA*]   (EA)
SPF .... Sun-Protection Factor [*Cosmetics industry*]
SPF .... Surrogate Parent Foundation [*New York, NY*]   (EA)
SPF .... Survival Probability Function
SPF .... Synthetic Phenolic Foam
SPF .... System Performance Factor [*Telecommunications*]   (TEL)
SPF .... System Productivity Facility [*Data processing*]
SPFA .... Single-Point Failure Analysis   (KSC)
SPFA .... Societe des Professeurs Francais et Francophones en Amerique   (EA)
SPFA .... Steel Plate Fabricators Association [*Geneva, IL*]   (EA)
SPFB .... Sbornik Pedagogicke Fakulty v Brne [*A publication*]
SPFB .... Sbornik Praci Filosoficke Fakulty Brnenske University [*A publication*]
SPFC .... Site Peculiar Facility Change   (AAG)
SPFC .... Society for the Parents of Fugitive Children [*Fictional organization in film "Taking Off"*]
Spfdr .... Springfielder [*A publication*]
SpFest .... Spanish Festival [*Record label*]
SPFFBU .... Sbornik Praci Filosoficke Fakulty Brnenske University [*A publication*]
SPFFC .... Southern Ports Foreign Freight Committee
SP-FGS ..... Shuttle Projects - Flight and Ground Systems Office [*Kennedy Space Center*] [*NASA*]   (NASA)
SPFL .... Southern Philippines Federation of Labor
SPFLA .... Spaceflight [*A publication*]
SPFM .... Society for the Preservation of Film Music   (EA)
SPFM .... Society of Priests for a Free Ministry   (EA)
SPFM .... Spinning Form [*Tool*]   (AAG)
SPFO .... Sbornik Pedagogicke Fakulty (Ostrava) [*A publication*]
SPFOL .... Sbornik Pedagogicke Fakulty (Olomouci) [*A publication*]
SPFP .... Single Pass Fit Program   (MCD)
SPFP .... Single-Point Failure Potential   (KSC)
SPFPAD .... Spacecraft Performance and Flight Path Analysis Directorate [*NASA*]
SPFT .... Single-Pedestal Flat-Top [*Desk*]
SPFW .... Single-Phase Full Wave
SPFX .... Special Effects [*Filmmaking*]
SPG .... Saint Paul Guild   (EA)
SPG .... Saint Petersburg, FL [*Location identifier*] [*FAA*]   (FAAL)
SPG .... Salicyl Phenolic Glucuronide [*Organic chemistry*]
SPG .... Scan Pattern Generator
SPG .... Screen Producers Guild [*Later, PGA*]   (EA)
SPG .... Seed Pea Group [*Defunct*]   (EA)
SPG .... Shift Pattern Generator [*Automotive engineering*]
SPG .... Short Pulse Generator
SPG .... Silver Spring Mining [*Vancouver Stock Exchange symbol*]
SPG .... Simple Phrase Grammar
SPG .... Single-Point Ground   (MCD)
SPG .... Sinusoidal Pressure Generator
SPG .... Society for the Propagation of the Gospel [*Later, USPG*] [*British*]
SPG .... Sort Program Generator [*Data processing*]   (BUR)
SPG .... Source Power Gain
SPG .... Special Patrol Group [*of the London Metropolitan Police, providing protection for public figures*]
SPG .... Special Project Group [*DoD*]
SPG .... Specialist, Gunnery [*Navy rating*]
SPG .... Specific Gravity [*Also, SP, SPGR*]
SPG .... Spiroglycol [*Organic chemistry*]
Spg .... Sponge [*Quality of the bottom*] [*Nautical charts*]
SPG .... Spooling   (MSA)
SPG .... Spring   (AAG)
SPG .... Stereophotogrammetry [*Medicine*]
SPG .... Study Planning Guide   (MCD)
SPG .... Sucrose, Phosphate, Glutamate [*A culture medium*]
SPG .... System Phasing Group   (MCD)
SPGA .... Southeastern Pecan Growers Association
SPGA .... Southwestern Peanut Growers Association   (EA)
SPGB .... Socialist Party of Great Britain   (PPW)
SPGCPS .... Senior Policy Group for Canadian Production Sharing
SPGD .... Self-Powered Gamma Detector [*Nuclear energy*]   (NRCH)
SPGG .... Solid-Propellant Gas Generator   (AAG)
SPGH .... Society for the Preservation of the Greek Heritage   (EA)
SPGJ .... Society for the Propagation of the Gospel among the Jews [*British*]
SPGKA .... Senpaku Gijutsu Kenkyujo Hokoku [*A publication*]
SPGL .... Studien zur Poetik und Geschichte der Literatur [*A publication*]
Sp Glos ...... Spelman's Glossarium Archaiologicum   (DLA)
SPGM .... Specialist, Gunnery, Aviation Free Gunnery Instructor [*Navy rating*]
SPGN .... Specialist, Gunnery, Antiaircraft Gunnery Instructor [*Navy rating*]
SPGN .... Sympathetic Post-Ganglionic Neurone [*Neurology*]
SPGPM .... Shots per Gun per Minute [*Military*]   (NVT)
SPGR .... Specific Gravity [*Also, SG, SPG*]
SPGS .... Spare Guidance System
SPGS .... Springs   (MCD)

SPGT.......... Springfield Terminal Railway Co. [*Later, ST*] [*AAR code*]
SPH .... San Pedro Hill [*California*] [*Seismograph station code, US Geological Survey*] [*Closed*] (SEIS)
SPH .... Self-Propelled Howitzer (MCD)
SPH .... Severely and Profoundly Handicapped
SPH .... Social Process in Hawaii [*A publication*]
SPH .... Soy Protein Hydrolyzate
SPH .... Space Heater (KSC)
SPH .... Special Psychiatric Hospital [*USSR*]
SPH .... Spherical (ROG)
SPH .... Spherical Lens [*Ophthalmology*]
Sph. .... Sphingosine [*Also, SM*] [*Biochemistry*]
SPH .... Springhill, LA [*Location identifier*] [*FAA*] (FAAL)
SPH .... Stable Platform Housing
SPH .... Statement of Personal History
S in Ph .... Studies in Philology [*A publication*]
Sph .... Studies in Philology [*A publication*]
SPHCA .... Soviet Physics. Crystallography [*English Translation*] [*A publication*]
SPHD .... Special Pay for Hostile Duty [*Military*] (AFM)
SP/Hd .... Spool Piece Head (NRCH)
SPHDA .... Soviet Physics. Doklady [*English Translation*] [*A publication*]
SPHE .... Society of Packaging and Handling Engineers (EA)
SPHER .... Small-Particle Heat-Exchange Receiver [*Solar energy technology*]
SPHER .... Spherical
SPHERE ..... Scientific Parameters for Health and the Environment, Retrieval and Estimation [*Environmental Protection Agency*] [*Washington, DC*] [*Database*]
SPHF .... Spin-Polarized Hartree-Fock [*Atomic wave-function*]
SPHINX ...... Space Plasma High-Voltage Interaction Experiment [*Spacecraft*] [*NASA*]
SPHINX ...... Survival Probability Hazard in a Nuclear Exchange
SPHJA .... Soviet Physics. JETP [*Journal of Experimental and Theoretical Physics of the Academy of Sciences of the USSR*] [*English translation*] [*A publication*]
SP-HL .... Sun Present - Horizon Lost
SPHN .... Siphon (MSA)
SPhNC .... Studies in Philology. University of North Carolina [*A publication*]
SPhon .... Studia Phonologica [*Kyoto*] [*A publication*]
SPhP .... Symbolae Philologorum Posnaniensium [*A publication*]
SPHQ .... Shore Patrol Headquarters
SPHQ .... Swedish Pioneer Historical Quarterly [*A publication*]
SPHS .... Society for the Promotion of Hellenic Studies (EA)
SPHS .... Swedish Pioneer Historical Society (EA)
SP/HT .... Specific Heat
SPHT .... Super Pressure - High Temperature
SPHW .... Single-Phase Half Wave
SPI .... Die Sprache der Palmyrenischen Inschriften [*Leipzig*] [*A publication*] (BJA)
SPI .... Illinois State Library, Springfield, IL [*OCLC symbol*] (OCLC)
SPI .... St. Paul Island [*Alaska*] [*Seismograph station code, US Geological Survey*] [*Closed*] (SEIS)
SPI .... Sandusky Plastics, Incorporated [*American Stock Exchange symbol*]
SPI .... Scanning Pulse Immobilization
SPI .... Schedule Performance Index (MCD)
SPI .... Secretariats Professionnels Internationaux
SPI .... Self-Paced Instruction (IEEE)
SPI .... Senior Patrol Inspection [*Immigration and Naturalization Service*]
SPI .... Sequence of Pulse Intervals
SPI .... Serum Precipitable Iodine [*Serology*]
SPI .... Service Pedalogique Interafricain
SPI .... Service Publication Instruction (AAG)
SPI .... Severely and Profoundly Impaired
SPI .... Share Price Index (ADA)
SPI .... Shared Peripheral Interface
SPI .... Ship's Plan Index
SPI .... Signal Presence Indicator (CAAL)
SPI .... Single Processor Interface
SPI .... Single Program Initiation [*Data processing*]
SPI .... Site Peculiar Interference (AAG)
SPI .... Site Population Index [*Nuclear energy*] (NRCH)
SPI .... Smoke Point Improvement [*Petroleum refining*]
SPI .... Societe pour l'Informatique [*Company for Informatics*] [*Information service*] [*Defunct*] (EISS)
SPI .... Society of Photographic Illustrators (EA)
SPI .... Society of the Plastics Industry [*Washington, DC*] (EA)
SPI .... Society of Professional Investigators
SPI .... Solid Propellant Information
SPI .... South Pacific Island Airways, Inc. [*Pago Pago, American Samoa*] [*FAA designator*] (FAAC)
SPI .... Soy Protein Isolate [*Food technology*]
SPI .... Spanish Paprika Institute (EA)
SPI .... Special Position Identification
SPI .... Specialist, Punched Card Accounting Machine Operator [*Navy rating*]
SPI .... Specific Productivity Index (IEEE)
Spi .... Spicules [*Quality of the bottom*] [*Nautical charts*]

SPI .... Sports Philatelists International (EA)
SPI .... Springfield [*Illinois*] [*Airport symbol*] (OAG)
SPI .... Standard Performance Indicator [*Army*]
SPI .... Standard Practice Instructions (MCD)
SPI .... Standard Protective Item
SPI .... Statement of Policy or Interpretation [*Food and Drug Administration*]
SPI .... Station Program Identification [*Telecommunications*] (TEL)
SPI .... Storage Protein Isolate [*Food industry*]
SPI .... Strategic Planning Institute [*Cambridge, MA*]
SPI .... Surface Position Indicator (NASA)
SPI .... Synergy Power Institute [*Formerly, CSP*] (EA)
SPI .... Synthetic Phase Isolation [*Telemetry*]
SPIA .... Solid Propellant Information Agency [*Air Force*]
SPIAM .... Sodium Purity In-Line Analytical Module [*Nuclear energy*] (NRCH)
SPIB .... Scripta Pontificii Instituti Biblici [*A publication*] (BJA)
SPIB .... Shetland Pony Identification Bureau
SPIB .... Social and Prevocational Information Battery
SPIB .... Society of Power Industry Biologists (EA)
SPIB .... Southern Pine Inspection Bureau [*Pensacola, FL*] (EA)
SPIBB .... Sbornik Pedagogickeho Institutu v Banskej Bystrici [*A publication*]
SPIBS .... Satellite Positive-Ion-Beam System [*Air Force*] (MCD)
SPIC .... Ship Position Interpolation Computer
SPIC .... Sisters of Providence and of the Immaculate Conception [*Roman Catholic religious order*]
SPIC .... Society of the Plastics Industry of Canada
SPIC .... Standard and Poor's Index - Composite [*Stock market*]
SPIC .... Students for Promotion of Identity on Campus [*New York group promoting ethnic pride among Latin American students*]
SPIC .... Summary Punch IBM [*International Business Machines*] Collector
SPICE .... Sales-Point Information Computing Equipment [*Merchandising*]
SPICE .... Solar Particle Intensity Composition Experiment [*NASA*]
SPICE .... Space Power Internal Combustion Engine (MCD)
SPICE .... Spacelab Payload Integration and Coordination in Europe [*NASA*] (NASA)
SPICE .... Special Programs Increasing Counseling Effectiveness [*Pennsylvania State Department of Public Instruction*]
SPID .... Standard Performance Indicator Dictionary [*Army*]
SPID .... Submersible Portable Inflatable Dwelling
SPID .... Sum of Pain Intensity Differences
SPIDAC ...... Specimen Input to Digital Automatic Computer
SPIDER ...... Smokeless Propellant in Demonstration Experimental Rocket (KSC)
SPIDER ...... Sonic Pulse-Echo Instrument Designed for Extreme Resolution (IEEE)
SPIDER ...... Systematic Planning for the Integration of Defense Engineering and Research [*Program*]
SPIDER CHART ... Systematic Planning for the Integration and Direction of Engineering and Research Chart (MCD)
SPIDF .... Support Planning Identification File (MCD)
SPIDR .... Society of Professionals in Dispute Resolution
SPIE .... Scavenging-Precipitation-Ion Exchange (IEEE)
SPIE .... Secretariat Professionnel International de l'Enseignement [*International Federation of Free Teachers' Unions - IFFTU*] (EA-IO)
SPIE .... Self-Programed Individualized Education (IEEE)
SPIE .... Ships Precise Identification Emitter (MCD)
SPIE .... Simulated Problem Input Evaluation
SPIE .... Society of Photo-Optical Instrumentation Engineers [*Bellingham, WA*] (EA)
SPIE .... Society of Political Item Enthusiasts (EA)
SPIE .... Special Patrol Insertion/Extraction (MCD)
SPIEC .... Proceedings. Society of Photo-Optical Instrumentation Engineers [*A publication*]
SPIE J .... SPIE [*Society of Photo-Optical Instrumentation Engineers*] Journal [*Later, Optical Engineering*] [*A publication*]
SPIE Semin Proc ... SPIE [*Society of Photo-Optical Instrumentation Engineers*] Seminar Proceedings [*A publication*]
SPIE Vol .... SPIE [*Society of Photo-Optical Instrumentation Engineers*] Volume [*United States*] [*A publication*]
SPIF .... School Practices Information File [*Educational testing service*] [*Database*]
SPIF .... Standard Payload Interface (MCD)
SPIFDA ...... South Pacific Island Fishery Development Agency [*Marine science*] (MSC)
SPIG .... Sbornik Praci Pedagogickeho Institutu v Gottwaldove [*A publication*]
SPII .... Shuttle Program Implementation Instruction [*NASA*] (NASA)
SPII .... Standard and Poor's Index - Industrials [*Stock market*]
SPIIN .... Supplemental Procurement Instrument Identification Number [*DoD*]
Spike M & S ... Spike on Master and Servant [*3rd ed.*] [*1872*] (DLA)
SPIL .... Sensitive Projects and Installation List (MCD)
SPIL .... Ship's Parts Integration List
SPILA .... Sports Illustrated [*A publication*]
SPILB .... Spiegel [*A publication*]

SP-ILS....... Shuttle Projects - Integrated Logistics Support [*Kennedy Space Center*] [*NASA*]   (NASA)
SPIM .... Service de Previsions Ionospherique Militaire
SPIMD .... Siauliu Pedagoginio Instituto Mokslo Darbai [*A publication*]
SPIMS .... Shuttle Program Information Management System [*NASA*]
SPIN .... Sbornik Pedagogickeho Institutu v Nitre [*A publication*]
SPIN .... School Practices Information Network [*Bibliographic Retrieval Services*] [*Information service*]   (EISS)
SPIN .... Science Procurement Information Network [*Canada*]
SPIN .... Searchable Physics Information Notices [*American Institute of Physics*] [*New York, NY*] [*Bibliographic database*]
SPIN .... Service Parts Information Notice
SPIN .... Southern California Police Information Network
SPIN .... Space Inspection
SPIN .... Spinster   (ADA)
SPIN .... Standard & Poor's 500 Index Subordinated Notes
SPIN .... Standard Procedure Instructions   (KSC)
SPIN .... Strategies and Policies for Informatics [*Intergovernmental Bureau for Informatics*]
SPIN .... Submarine Program Information Notebook
SPIN .... Superconductive Precision Inertial Navigation
SPINAL ...... Stimulator, Planetary Instrument Alignment
SPINDEX .... Selective Permutation Indexing [*Library of Congress*]
SPINDEX .... Subject Profile Index [*Computer-based*]
SPINE .... Simulated Program for Investigation of Nuclear Effects
SPINES ...... Science and Technology Policies Information Exchange System [*UNESCO*] [*Paris, France*] [*Bibliographic database*]   (EISS)
Spinks....... Spinks' English Ecclesiastical and Admiralty Reports [*164 English Reprint*]   (DLA)
Spinks Eccl & Adm (Eng) ... Spinks' English Ecclesiastical and Admiralty Reports [*164 English Reprint*]   (DLA)
Spinks PC ... Spinks' English Admiralty Prize Cases   (DLA)
Spinks Prize Cas ... Spinks' English Admiralty Prize Cases [*164 English Reprint*]   (DLA)
Spinks Prize Cas (Eng) ... Spinks' English Admiralty Prize Cases [*164 English Reprint*]   (DLA)
Spinner Weber Textilveredl ... Spinner, Weber, Textilveredlung [*A publication*]
SPINSTRE ... Spencer Information Storage and Retrieval System   (DIT)
SPINT........ Special Intelligence   (MCD)
SPINTAC.... Special Interest Aircraft   (NVT)
SPINTCOMM ... Special Intelligence Communications [*Later, DIN/DSSCS*]   (CET)
SPINVESWG ... Special Investigation Wing   (MUGU)
SPIO .... Sbornik Praci Pedagogickeho Institutu v Ostrave [*A publication*]
SPIOL........ Sbornik Pedagogickeho Institutu v Olomouci [*A publication*]
SPIP .... Sbornik Pedagogickeho Institutu v Plzni [*A publication*]
spIP .... Special Position Identification Pulse   (CET)
SPIP .... SPI Pharmaceuticals [*NASDAQ symbol*]   (NQ)
SPIPA........ Scientific Papers. Institute of Physical and Chemical Research [*A publication*]
S'PIPE .... Standpipe
SPIPL........ Sbornik Pedagogickeho Institutu v Plzni [*A publication*]
SPIR .... Search Program for Infrared Spectra [*Canadian Scientific Numeric Database Service*] [*Database*]
SPIR .... Spiral
SPIR .... Spire Corp. [*NASDAQ symbol*]   (NQ)
SPIR .... Spiritoso [*With Animation*] [*Music*]
SPIR .... Spiritus [*Spirit*] [*Pharmacy*]
SPIR .... Standard and Poor's Index - Rails [*Stock market*]
SPIR .... Student Project for International Responsibility
SPIRAL ...... Sperry Inertial RADAR Altimeter
SPIRBM...... Solid-Propellant Intermediate Range Ballistic Missile   (AAG)
SPIRE .... Spatial Inertial Reference Equipment
SPIREP...... Spot Intelligence Report [*Air Force*]
SPIRES ..... Standard Personnel Information Retrieval System [*Military*]
SPIRES ..... Stanford Public Information Retrieval System [*Stanford University Libraries*] [*Stanford, CA*] [*Bibliographic database management system*] [*Information service*]
SPIRIT .... Sales Processing Interactive Real-Time Inventory Technique [*NCR Corp. trademark*]
SPIRIT .... Sensible Policy in Information Resources and Information Technology   (EA)
Spirit.......... Spirit That Moves Us [*A publication*]
SPIRIT....... Spiritoso [*With Animation*] [*Music*]
SPIRIT....... Spiritus [*Latin*]   (ROG)
Spirit Mis ... Spirit of Missions [*A publication*]
Spirit Pilg... Spirit of the Pilgrims [*A publication*]
SPIRO .... Students Protesting Illegal Real Estate Operators [*Student legal action organization*]   (EA)
SPIRT........ Short Path Infrared Tester   (KSC)
SPIRT........ Stock Point Interrogation/Requirements Technique
Spirto Vodochn Promst ... Spirto-Vodochnaya Promyshlennost [*A publication*]
Spirt Prom-st' ... Spirtovaya Promyshlennost' [*A publication*]
SPIS .... Senate Permanent Investigating Subcommittee   (AAG)
SPIS .... Space Philatelists International Society   (EA)
Spis B'lg Akad Nauk ... Spisanie na B'lgarskata Akademiya na Naukite [*A publication*]

Spis B'lg Geol Druzh ... Spisania na B'lgarsoto Geologichesko Druzhestvo [*A publication*]
Spis Bulg Akad Nauk ... Spisanie na Bulgarskata Akademiya na Naukite [*Bulgaria*] [*A publication*]
Spis Bulg Geol Druzh ... Spisanie na Bulgarskoto Geologichesko Druzhestvo [*A publication*]
SPISE......... Special Projects in Science Education
Spis Nauchno-Issled Inst Minist Zemed Gorite ... Spisanie na Nauchno-Issledovatelskite Instituti pri Ministerstvata na Zemedelete i Gorite [*A publication*]
Spis Nauchnoizsled Inst Minist Zemed (Bulg) ... Spisanie na Nauchnoizsledovatelskite Instituti pri Ministerstvoto na Zemedelieto (Bulgaria) [*A publication*]
SPISS........ Spissus [*Dried*] [*Pharmacy*]
Spisy Lek Fak Masaryk Univ (Brno) ... Spisy Lekarske Fakulty Mesarykovy University (Brno) [*A publication*]
Spisy Prir Fak Univ Brne ... Spisy Prirodovedecke Fakulty Universita v Brne [*Czechoslovakia*] [*A publication*]
Spisy Priroved Fak Univ J E Purkyne Brne ... Spisy Prirodovedecke Fakulty University J. E. Purkyne v Brne [*A publication*]
Spisy Vydavane Prirodoved Fak Massarykovy Univ ... Spisy Vydavane Prirodovedeckou Fakultou Massarykovy University [*A publication*]
SPIT........... Secondary Power Integration Test   (MCD)
SPIT .... Selective Printing of Items from Tape [*Data processing*]
SPITS........ Scan Platform Inertial Thermal Simulator
SPIU .... Sbornik Praci Pedagogickeho Institutu, Usti Nad Labem [*A publication*]
SPIU .... Ship Position Interpolation Unit
SPIU .... Standard and Poor's Index - Utilities [*Stock market*]
SPIW .... Special-Purpose Individual Weapon [*A rifle that fires flechettes or darts*] [*Pronounced "spew"*]
SPJ............. Socialist Party of Japan [*Nikon Shakaito*]   (PPW)
SPJ............. Society of Professional Journalists, Sigma Delta Chi [*Formerly, SDX*]
SPJ............. Socijalisticka Partija Jugoslavije [*Socialist Party of Yugoslavia*]   (PPE)
SPJ............. Sparta [*Greece*] [*Airport symbol*] [*Obsolete*]   (OAG)
SPJ............. Special Purpose Jammer [*Military*]   (CAAL)
SPJC......... St. Petersburg Junior College [*Clearwater, FL*]
SPJSDX ..... Society of Professional Journalists, Sigma Delta   (EA)
SPK .... Reno, NV [*Location identifier*] [*FAA*]   (FAAL)
SPK .... Saporamean Kampuchea News Agency [*Cambodia*]
SPK .... Sapporo [*Japan*] [*Airport symbol*]   (OAG)
SPK .... Scotts Peak [*Tasmania*] [*Seismograph station code, US Geological Survey*]   (SEIS)
SPK .... Silver Tusk Mines [*Vancouver Stock Exchange symbol*]
SPK .... Spare Parts Kit
SPK .... Spark   (MSA)
spk .... Speckled [*Quality of the bottom*] [*Nautical charts*]
SPK .... Spike   (MSA)
SPK .... Spinnbarkheit [*With reference to cervical mucus*] [*Medicine*]
SPK .... Superficial Punctate Keratitis [*Ophthalmology*]
SPKL......... Sprinkle   (FAAC)
SPKP......... Suomen Perustuslaillinen Kansanpuolue [*Finnish Constitutional People's Party*]   (PPW)
SPKR......... Speaker   (AAG)
SPKT......... Sprocket
SPKYB .... Shih P'in Kung Yeh [*A publication*]
SPL............. Airspur Helicopters, Inc. [*Huntington Beach, CA*] [*FAA designator*]   (FAAC)
SPL............. Saskatoon Public Library [*UTLAS symbol*]
SPL............. Scott Paper Limited [*Toronto Stock Exchange symbol*] [*Vancouver Stock Exchange symbol*]
SPL............. Scratch Pad Line   (MCD)
SPL............. Separate Parts List   (MSA)
SPL............. Serialized Parts List   (MCD)
SPL............. Service Priority List   (BUR)
SPL............. Signal Processing Language [*Data processing*]   (CSR)
SPL............. Signature and Propagation Laboratory [*Army*]   (RDA)
SPL............. Simple Phrase Language [*Data processing*]
SPL............. Simple Programing Language [*Data processing*]
SPL............. Simulation Programing Language [*Data processing*]
SPL............. Sine Prole Legitima [*Without Legitimate Issue*] [*Latin*]
SPL............. Single Pet Lover
SPL............. Single Propellant Loading   (AFM)
SPL............. Skin Potential Level
SPL............. Sloane Physics Laboratory [*Yale*]   (MCD)
SPL............. Software Parts List [*Data processing*]   (TEL)
SPL............. Software Programing Language [*Data processing*]   (IEEE)
SPL............. Sound Power Level [*Acoustics*]
SPL............. Sound Pressure Level [*Acoustics*]
SPL............. Source Program Library
SPL............. Space Physics Laboratory [*Aerospace corporation*]
SPL............. Space Programing Language [*Data processing*]
SPL............. Spare Parts List
SPL............. Spartanburg County Public Library, Spartanburg, SC [*OCLC symbol*]   (OCLC)
SPL............. Special   (AAG)
SPL............. Special-Purpose Language [*Data processing*]
SPL............. Speed Phase Lock

SPL .... Spermatophore Length
SpL .... Spiegel der Letteren [*A publication*]
SPL .... Spiral   (MSA)
SPL .... Spiridon Lake [*Alaska*] [*Seismograph station code, US Geological Survey*]   (SEIS)
SPL .... Splice [*Telecommunications*]   (TEL)
SPL .... Spritsail [*Ship's rigging*]   (ROG)
SPL .... Standard Pulse LASER
SPL .... Standards Parts Listing   (MCD)
SPL .... Staphylococcal Phage Lysate [*Biochemistry*]
SPL .... Studie a Prace Linguisticke [*A publication*]
SPL .... Succinyl-poly-L-lysine [*Biochemical analysis*]
SPL .... Summary Parts List
SPL .... Sun Pumped LASER   (MCD)
SPL .... Superior Parietal Lobule [*Neuroanatomy*]
Spl .... Supplement   (BJA)
SPL .... Supplementary Flight Plan Message [*Aviation code*]
SPL .... Swiss Party of Labour
SPL .... System Program Loader
SPL .... System Programing Language [*Data processing*]   (NASA)
SPLA .... Special-Purpose Lead Azide   (MCD)
SPLA .... Sudan People's Liberation Army
SPLAASH... Spacecraft Protective Landing Area for the Advancement of Science and Humanities [*Landing zone for flying saucers near Mt. Rainier, WA*]
SPLAN .... Support Plan   (MCD)
SPLANCH ... Split-Level Ranch [*House*]
SPLASH ..... Shipboard Platforms for Landing and Servicing Helicopters
SPLASH ..... Special Program to List Amplitudes of Surges from Hurricanes
SPLAT .... Simplified Programing Language for Artists [*1978*] [*Data processing*]   (CSR)
SPLAT .... Student Potential Life Achievement Test [*Parody of Scholastic Aptitude Test preparation books*]
Sp Laws ..... Spirit of the Laws Montesquieu   (DLA)
SPLC .... Ship Program Life Cycle [*Navy*]
SPLC .... Southern Poverty Law Center
SPLC .... Spare Parts List for Codification
SPLC .... Splice
SPLC .... Standard Point Location Code [*American Trucking Association and Association of American Railroads*]
SPLC .... Student Press Law Center   (EA)
SPLEB .... Spectroscopy Letters [*A publication*]
SPLHC .... Sgt. Pepper's Lonely Hearts Club   (EA)
SPLI .... Spermatophore Length Index
SPLI .... Substance P-Like Immunoreactivity
Sp Lib .... Special Libraries [*A publication*]
SPLIT .... Space Program Language Implementation Tool   (KSC)
SPLIT .... Sundstrand Processing Language Internally Translated
SPLK .... Studie Prazskeho Linguistickeho Krouzku [*A publication*]
SPLKA ...... Spacelink Ltd. Cl A [*NASDAQ symbol*]   (NQ)
SPLL .... Self-Propelled Launcher Loader   (MCD)
SPLL .... Standard Phase-Locked Loop
SPLLG .... Stable Production Low Leach Glass [*For nuclear wastes*]
SPLM .... Space Programing Language Machine
SPLN .... Spline [*Engineering*]
SPLNS .... South Plains [*FAA*]   (FAAC)
SPLSA .... Space Life Sciences [*A publication*]
SPLT .... Specialist, Link Trainer Instructor [*Navy rating*]
SPLTR .... Splitter
SPLTRK ..... Special Tracker [*Military*]   (CAAL)
SPLV .... Stable Plurilamellar Vesicle [*Pharmacology*]
SPLX .... Simplex [*Mathematics*]
SPLY .... Supply   (MSA)
SPM .... St. Philips Marsh [*Bristol*] [*British depot code*]
SPM .... St. Pierre and Miquelon [*Three-letter standard code*]   (CNC)
SPM .... Salud Publica de Mexico [*A publication*]
SPM .... Scanning Photon Microscope
SPM .... Scratch Pad Memory [*Data processing*]   (BUR)
SPM .... Scripture Press Ministries   (EA)
SPM .... Sedimentary Phosphate Method
SPM .... Self-Propelled Mount
SPM .... Semipermeable Membrane
SPM .... Sequential Processing Machine   (DIT)
SPM .... Short Particular Metre [*Music*]
SPM .... Shots per Minute [*Military*]   (RDA)
SPM .... Significant Probability Mapping
SPM .... Sine Prole Mascula [*Without Male Issue*] [*Latin*]
SPM .... Single-Point Mooring [*Oil platform*]
SPM .... Single Program Manager [*Air Force*]
SPM .... Six Point Mooring [*Oil platform*]
SPM .... Smaller Profit Margin
SPM .... Societas Patrum Misericordiae [*Fathers of Mercy*] [*Roman Catholic religious order*]
SPM .... Society for Policy Modeling   (EA)
SPM .... Society of Pragmatic Mysticism   (EA)
SPM .... Society of Prospective Medicine [*Indianapolis, IN*]   (EA)
SPM .... Solar Polar Mission   (MCD)
SPM .... Solar Power Module
SPM .... Solar Proton Monitor
SPM .... Sound-Powered Microphone
SPM .... Source Program Maintenance [*IBM Corp.*]

SPM .... South Pacific Mail [*A publication*]
SPM .... Special-Purpose Materials   (MCD)
SPM .... Specialist, Mail Clerk [*Navy rating*]
SPM .... Spectrophosphorimeter
SPM .... Spectrum Industrial Resources [*Vancouver Stock Exchange symbol*]
Sp M .... Spicilegio Moderno [*A publication*]
SpM .... Spiriformis Medialis Nucleus [*Brain anatomy*]
SPM .... Split Phase Motor
SPM .... Standard Payload Module   (MCD)
SPM .... Standard Practice Memo   (MCD)
SPM .... Standard Procedure Manual   (AAG)
SPM .... Standard Process Manual
SPM .... Static Presentation Mode
SPM .... Stationary Plasma Motor
SPM .... Strokes per Minute
SPM .... Subscriber's Private Meter [*Telecommunications*]   (TEL)
SPM .... Subsystem Project Manager [*NASA*]   (NASA)
SPM .... Sun Probe-Mars [*NASA*]
SPM .... Superparamagnetic [*Fraction in rock*] [*Geophysics*]
SPM .... Support Program Management
SPM .... Suspended Particulate Matter
SPM .... Symbol Processing Machine   (IEEE)
SPM .... Synaptic Plasma Membrane [*Neurophysiology*]
SPM .... Synaptosomal Plasma Membrane [*Neurobiology*]
SPM .... Synthetic Plasma Membrane [*Biochemistry*]
SPM .... Systems Program Manager
SPMA .... Shoe Pattern Manufacturers Association [*Formed by a merger of National Shoe Pattern Manufacturers Association and Shoe Pattern Manufacturers Association of New England*] [*Boston, MA*]   (EA)
SPMA .... Soda Pulp Manufacturers Association [*Defunct*]   (EA)
SPMA .... Southwest Parks and Monuments Association   (EA)
SPMA .... Sump Pump Manufacturers Association [*Later, SSPMA*]   (EA)
SPMB .... Strong Partial Maternal Behavior [*Psychology*]
SPMC .... Society of Paper Money Collectors
SPMC .... Society of Professional Management Consultants [*Association name and designation awarded by this group*] [*Englewood, NJ*]   (EA)
SPMC .... Special Machine [*Tool*]   (AAG)
SPMCA ...... Soviet Powder Metallurgy and Metal Ceramics [*English Translation*] [*A publication*]
SPMEA ...... Sulfate of Potash Magnesia Export Association   (EA)
SPMGA ...... Speech Monographs [*A publication*]
SPML .... Special Meal [*Diabetic, low-cholesterol, low-calorie, hypoglycemic, or gluten-free*] [*Airline notation*]   (ADA)
SPMLF ...... Societe de la Psychologie Medicale de Langue Francaise [*French-Language Society of Medical Psychology - FLSMP*]
SPMM .... Society for the Promotion of Mohammedan Missions [*Defunct*]   (EA)
SPMO .... SAMMS [*Standard Automated Materiel Management System*] Program Management Office [*DoD*]
SPMOL ...... Source Program Maintenance Online
Sp Mon ...... Speech Monographs [*A publication*]
SPMP .... Special-Purpose Multiprocessor [*Data processing*]
SP-MPC ..... Shuttle Projects - Management Planning and Control Office [*Kennedy Space Center*] [*NASA*]   (NASA)
SPMR .... Sub Postmaster [*British*]
SPMRL ...... Sulphite Pulp Manufacturers' Research League [*Indianapolis, IN*]   (EA)
SPMS .... Sine Prole Mascula Superstite [*Without Surviving Male Issue*] [*Latin*]   (ADA)
SPMS .... Solar Particle Monitoring System [*NASA*]   (KSC)
SPMS .... Special-Purpose Manipulator System [*NASA*]   (NASA)
SPMS .... Special-Purpose Monitoring Station [*Environmental Protection Agency*]
SPMS .... Suppression Pool Makeup System [*Nuclear energy*]   (NRCH)
SPMS .... Surveyor Payload Mechanism Section
SPMS .... System Program Management Surveys [*Air Force*]
SPMXA ...... Salud Publica de Mexico [*A publication*]
SPN .... Cape Shipunski [*USSR*] [*Seismograph station code, US Geological Survey*]   (SEIS)
SPN .... Pelican Narrows Public Library, Saskatchewan [*Library symbol*] [*National Library of Canada*]   (NLC)
SPN .... Saipan [*Mariana Islands*] [*Airport symbol*]   (OAG)
SPN .... Satellite Programming Network [*Cable-television system*]
SPN .... School Product News [*A publication*]
SPN .... Secretariado da Propaganda Nacional [*Portugal*]
SPN .... Separation Program Number [*Military*]
SPN .... Shipment/Performance Notification [*DoD*]
SPN .... Shuttle Project Notice [*Kennedy Space Center*] [*NASA*]   (NASA)
SPN .... Sparton Resources, Inc. [*Toronto Stock Exchange symbol*]
SPN .... Special Program Number   (MUGU)
SPN .... Sponsor Program Number [*Military*]
SPN .... Sympathetic Preganglionic Neuron [*Anatomy*]
SPND .... Self-Powered Neutron Detector   (NRCH)
SPNEA ...... Society for the Preservation of New England Antiquities   (EA)
SPNF .... Shot Peening Fixture   (MCD)
SPNG .... Sponge

SPN/GEANS ... Standard Precision Navigator/Gimbolled Electrostatic Aircraft Navigation System (MCD)
SPNI .... Societe pour la Protection de la Nature en Israel [*Society for the Protection of Nature in Israel*] [*Tel Aviv*] (EA-IO)
SPNI .... Society for the Protection of Nature in Israel [*Tel Aviv*] (EA-IO)
S/PNL .... Side Panel [*Automotive engineering*]
SPNM .... Society for the Promotion of New Music [*British*]
sp nov .... Species Nova [*New Species*] [*Biology*]
SPNR .... Spanner (AAG)
SPNS .... Spoons (ROG)
SPNS .... Switched Private Network Service [*ITT service mark*]
SPNSN ...... Suspension (MSA)
SPNZ .... Socialist Party of New Zealand (PPW)
SPO .... Denver, CO [*Location identifier*] [*FAA*] (FAAL)
SPO .... Sacramento Peak Observatory
SPo. .... Sao Paulo. Revista do Arquivo Municipal [*A publication*]
SPO .... Saturn Program Office [*NASA*] (KSC)
SPO .... Sausages, Potatoes, and Onions [*Meaning a cheap restaurant that specializes in these*] [*British slang*]
SPO .... Sea Post Office
SPO .... Senate Post Office
SPO .... Separate Partition Option
SPO .... Shore Patrol Officer [*Navy*]
SPO .... Short Period Oscillation
SPO .... Shuttle Project Office [*NASA*] (KSC)
SPO .... Signal Property Office
SPO .... Single Pickle Ordinary [*Metal industry*]
SPO .... Slaving Pick-Off
SPO .... Society of Planning Officials
SPO .... Sozialdemokratische Partei Oesterreichs [*Social Democratic Party of Austria*]
SPO .... Sozialistische Partei Oesterreichs [*Socialist Party of Austria*] (PPW)
SPO .... Spacelab Program Office [*NASA*]
SPO .... Spare Parts Order [*NASA*] (NASA)
SPO .... Special Placement Officer (ADA)
SP & O .... Special Plans and Operation [*Military*]
SPO .... Special Projects Office [*Navy*]
SPO .... Specialist, Inspector of Naval Material [*Navy rating*]
SPO .... Spokane [*Washington*] [*Seismograph station code, US Geological Survey*] [*Closed*] (SEIS)
SPO .... Spooner Mines & Oils Ltd. [*Toronto Stock Exchange symbol*]
SPO .... Stoker Petty Officer [*Navy*] [*British*] (DSUE)
SPO .... Subpurchase Order (AAG)
SPO .... Supplemental Production Order (AAG)
SPO .... Surplus Property Office [*Transferred to War Assets Administration, 1947*]
SPO .... System Program [*or Project*] Office [*Air Force*]
SPOA .... Les Sagesses du Proche-Orient Ancien. Colloque de Strasbourg [*1962*]. Travaux du Centre d'Etudes Superieurs Specialise d'Histoire des Religions de Strassbourg [*Paris*] [*A publication*] (BJA)
SPOA .... Soviet Panorama [*A publication*]
SPOAV ...... Specialist, Inspector of Aviation Material [*Navy rating*]
SPOBS ...... Special Observer [*US Army group in London*] [*World War II*]
SPOC .... Shuttle Payload Opportunity Carrier
SPOC .... Shuttle Portable Onboard Computer [*NASA*]
SPOC .... Single-Point Orbit Calculator
SPOC .... Spacecraft Oceanography Project [*Navy*]
SPOC .... Special Projects Operations Center [*Allied Force Headquarters*] [*World War II*]
SPOC .... Systems Program Office Cadre (MCD)
SPOCK ...... Simulated Procedure for Obtaining Common Knowledge
SPOCM ..... Society for the Preservation of Old Mills (EA)
SPOCN ...... Subpurchase Order Change Notice (AAG)
SPOD .... Seaports of Debarkation (MCD)
SpOd .... Spanish Odeon, Barcelona [*Record label*] [*Spain*]
SPODA ...... Society for the Prevention of Drug Addiction
SPODAC .... SITS [*SAGE Intercept Target Simulation*] Probability of Detection and Conversion (MCD)
SPODP ...... Single Precision Orbit Determination Program [*NASA*]
SPOE .... Seaports of Embarkation (MCD)
SPOE .... Society of Post Office Engineers [*Pronounced "spowee"*] [*British*]
SPOE .... Sozialistische Partei Oesterreichs [*Socialist Party of Austria*]
SPOEN ...... Specialist, Engineering Inspector [*Navy rating*]
SPOG .... Sales of Products Other than Gasoline
SPol. .... Storia e Politica [*A publication*]
Spold Kwartal Nauk ... Spoldzielczy Kwartalnik Naukomy [*A publication*]
Spolia Zeylan ... Spolia Zeylanica [*A publication*]
Spolia Zool Mus Haun ... Spolia Zoologica Musei Hauniensis [*A publication*]
SPOM .... Suspended Particulate Organic Material [*Environmental chemistry*]
SPOMCUS ... Selective Prepositioning of Materiel Configured to Unit Sets [*Army*] (AABC)
SpomSAN ... Spomenik Srpske Akademije Nauka [*A publication*]
SPON .... Sponsor (AFM)
SPON .... Statistical Profile of Old Norse
SPONT ...... Spontaneous
SPOOF ...... Society for the Protection of Old Fishes (EA)
SPOOF ...... Structure and Parity Observing Output Function

SPOOFS ..... Society for the Promotion of Otherwise Overlooked Football Scores
SPOOK ...... Supervisor Program Over Other Kinds [*Data processing*]
SPOOL .... Simultaneous Peripheral Operation Online [*Data processing*] (MCD)
Spoon .... Spooner's Reports [*12-15 Wisconsin*] (DLA)
Spooner .... Spooner's Reports [*12-15 Wisconsin*] (DLA)
SPOOR ...... Specialist, Ordnance Inspector [*Navy rating*]
SPOP .... Scan Platform Operations Program
SPOPE ...... Specialist, Petroleum Technician [*Navy rating*]
SP-OPN ..... Shuttle Projects - Operations Planning Office [*Kennedy Space Center*] [*NASA*] (NASA)
SPO-PO ..... System Program Office/Project Office [*Air Force*] (AFIT)
SPOPS .... Special Operations
SPORT .... St. Petersburg [*Florida*] Olympic Regatta Training
SPORT .... Space Probe Optical Recording Telescope [*Army*]
SPORT .... Sporting (ROG)
Sportarzt Sportmed ... Sportarzt Sportmedizin [*A publication*]
SPORTFOR ... Support Force
Sport Leis ... Sport and Leisure [*A publication*]
Sport Rec ... Sport and Recreation [*A publication*]
Sports Ill ... Sports Illustrated [*A publication*]
Sports Illus ... Sports Illustrated [*A publication*]
Sports Turf Bull ... Sports Turf Bulletin [*A publication*]
Sport es Testn ... Sport es Testneveles [*A publication*]
SPOS .... Strong Point/Obstacle System [*Military*] (NVT)
Sposoby Zap Inf Besserebr Nositelyakh ... Sposoby Zapisi Informatsii na Besserebryanykh Nositelyakh [*A publication*]
SPOSS .... Society for the Promotion of Science and Scholarship [*Palo Alto, CA*] (EA)
SPOT .... Satellite Positioning and Tracking
SPOT .... Simulated Pave Penny Omnidirectional Target (MCD)
SPOT .... Skill in Personnel through On-Site Training [*Department of Labor*]
SPOT .... Smithsonian Precision Optical Tracking
Spot .... Spotlight [*Record label*] [*Australia*]
SPOT .... Symptom Pattern Observation Technique [*Aviation*]
SPOTREP. .... Spot Report [*Military*] (NVT)
SPOTS .... Sikorsky Program Operations Tracking System (MCD)
Spott Eq Rep ... Spottiswoode's English Equity Reports (DLA)
Spottis .... [*R.*] Spottiswoode's Scotch Court of Session Reports (DLA)
Spottis CL & Eq Rep ... Common Law and Equity Reports, Published by Spottiswoode (DLA)
Spottis Eq ... Spottiswoode's Equity [*Scotland*] (DLA)
Spottis Pr ... Spottiswoode's Practices [*Scotland*] (DLA)
Spottis St ... Spottiswoode's Styles [*Scotland*] (DLA)
Spottisw .... Spottiswoode's Equity [*Scotland*] (DLA)
Spottisw Eq ... Spottiswoode's Equity [*Scotland*] (DLA)
SPOTY ...... Single Parent of the Year
SPOUT .... System Peripheral Output Utility (NRCH)
SPP .... Menongue [*Angola*] [*Airport symbol*] (OAG)
SPP .... New York Society for the Prevention of Pauperism
SPP .... Peace Corps School Partnership Program [*Later, PCPP*] (EA)
SPP .... Safe-Practice Procedure (MCD)
SPP .... St. Paul [*Alaska*] [*Seismograph station code, US Geological Survey*] [*Closed*] (SEIS)
SPP .... St. Paul Public Library, St. Paul, MN [*OCLC symbol*] (OCLC)
SPP .... Sclerosing Papillomatous Pattern [*Medicine*]
SPP .... Scott Paper Co. [*NYSE symbol*]
SPP .... Secular Periodic Perturbation
SPP .... Severe Parental Punishment
SPP .... Sexuality Preference Profile
SPP .... Signal Processing Peripheral
SPP .... Society for Pediatric Psychology [*Iowa City, IA*] (EA)
SPP .... Society of Private Printers
SPP .... Solar Photometry Probe (AAG)
SPP .... Solar Physics Payload (MCD)
SPP .... Soluble Protein Preparation [*Biochemistry*]
SPP .... Southwest Power Pool [*Regional power council*]
SPP .... Spare Parts Provisioning
SPP .... Special Purpose Processor
SPP .... Specialist, Photographic Specialist [*Navy rating*]
SPP .... Species [*Plural form*] [*Also, spp*]
SPP .... Sponsor Program Proposal (MCD)
SPP .... Standard Practice Procedures (MCD)
SPP .... Still Picture Projector (MSA)
SPP .... Straight Path Penetration
SPP .... Suprapubic Prostatectomy [*Medicine*]
SPP .... Surplus Personal Property
SPP .... Swaziland Progressive Party
SPP .... System Package Plan [*or Program*]
SPPA .... Screen Process Printing Association [*Later, SPAI*] (EA)
SPPA .... Society for Philosophy and Public Affairs (EA)
SPPA .... Society for the Preservation of Poultry Antiquities (EA)
SPPAY ...... Semipost-Pay, Pay-Station [*Telecommunications*] (TEL)
SP-PAY ..... Shuttle Projects - Payload Integration Office [*Kennedy Space Center*] [*NASA*] (NASA)
SPPB .... Sodium Pyrophosphate Buffer [*Analytical chemistry*]
SPPB .... Statens Psykologisk-Pedagogiska Bibliotek [*National Library for Psychology and Education*] [*Stockholm, Sweden*] [*Information service*] (EISS)

SPPC......... Spare Parts Provisioning Card
SPPD......... Space Propulsion and Power Division [*NASA*]
SPPF......... Seychelles People's Progressive Front   (PPW)
SPPF......... Solid-Phase Pressure Forming [*Shell Chemical Co.*]
SPPI......... Southern Production Program, Incorporated
SPPI......... Symposium on the Preventability of Perinatal Injury
SPPIL....... Shuttle Preferred Pyrotechnic Items List [*NASA*]   (NASA)
SPPK......... Studien zur Palaeographie und Papyruskunde [*C. Wessely*] [*A publication*]   (BJA)
SPPL .... Spare Parts Provisioning List [*NASA*]   (NASA)
SPPL .... Spark Plug
SPPL .... Statewide Public Library Interlibrary Loan and Reference Network [*Library network*]
SPPLB....... Specialist, Photographer, Laboratory [*Navy rating*]
SPPLITT..... Southern Pacific Pipelines and International Tank Terminals [*Two companies jointly building deepwater port to accomodate outsize oil carriers*]
SpPm .... Biblioteca Publica, Palma De Mallorca, Spain [*Library symbol*] [*Library of Congress*]   (LCLS)
SPPMA....... Southern Pulp and Paper Manufacturer [*United States*] [*A publication*]
SPPMP....... Specialist, Motion Picture Production [*Navy rating*]
SPPO......... Scheduled Program Printout   (NATG)
SPPO......... Spacelab Payload Project Office [*NASA*]
SPPO......... Special Projects Program Order   (AAG)
SPPP......... Superior Performance Proficiency Pay   (MCD)
SPPPA....... Spartan Potential Production Problem Analysis [*Missiles*]   (MCD)
SPPPA....... Spartan Production Program Producibility Analysis [*Missiles*]   (MCD)
SPPPG ...... Specialist, Photogrammetry [*Navy rating*]
SPPPM ...... Surveyor Project Policy and Procedure Manual [*NASA*]
SPPR........ Special Peacetime Program Requirements [*DoD*]
SPPR........ Specialist, Public Relations [*Coast Guard*]
Sp Pr Cas... Spinks' English Admiralty Prize Cases [*1854-56*]   (DLA)
SPPS......... Semipost-Pay, Pay-Station [*Telecommunications*]   (TEL)
SPPS......... Solid-Phase Peptide Synthesis [*Biochemistry*]
SPPS......... Specialist, Port Security [*Coast Guard*]
SPPS......... Stable Plasma Protein Solution [*Medicine*]
SPPS......... Subsystem Program Preparation Support [*Programing language*] [*Data processing*]
SPPTY....... Southern Pacific Petroleum [*NASDAQ symbol*]   (NQ)
SPPVM....... Specialist, V-Mail [*Navy rating*]
SPQ .... Memphis, TN [*Location identifier*] [*FAA*]   (FAAL)
SPQ .... San Pedro [*California*] [*Airport symbol*] [*Obsolete*]   (OAG)
SPQ .... Stanford Parent Questionnaire [*Psychology*]
SPQCR...... Specialist, Communications Specialist, Cryptographer [*Navy rating*]
SPQIN .... Specialist, Communications Specialist, Radio Intelligence [*Navy rating*]
SPQR........ Selected Product Quality Review [*DoD*]
SPQR......... Senatus Populusque Romanus [*The Senate and People of Rome*] [*Latin*]
SPQR........ Small Profits, Quick Returns
SPQRP ...... Specialist, Communications Specialist, Registered Publication Clerk [*Navy rating*]
SPQTE ...... Specialist, Communications Specialist, Technician [*Navy rating*]
SPR .... Puerto Rico Reports, Spanish Edition   (DLA)
SPR .... S-Band Planetary RADAR
SPR .... St. Pierre [*Quebec*] [*Seismograph station code, US Geological Survey*] [*Closed*]   (SEIS)
SPR .... San Pedro [*Belize*] [*Airport symbol*]   (OAG)
SPR .... Sandia Pulsed Reactor
SPR .... Sapper [*Military*]
SPR .... Satellite Parametric Reduction
SPR .... Scientific Process & Research, Inc. [*Somerset, NJ*] [*Information service*]   (EISS)
SPR .... Seal Pressure Ratio
SPR .... Seconds per Revolution [*or Rotation*]   (NVT)
SPR .... Secretary of the Air Force Program Review   (MCD)
SPR .... Semipermanent Repellent   (ADA)
SPR .... Send Priority and Route Digit [*Telecommunications*]   (TEL)
SPR .... Sense Printer
SPR .... Sequential Probability Ratio [*Statistics*]
SPR .... Serial Probe Recognition [*Psychometrics*]
SPR .... Shock Position Ratio
SPR .... Shortest Possible Route   (MCD)
SPR .... Silicon Power Rectifier
SPR .... Simplified Practice Recommendation
SPR .... Single-Ply Roofing
SPR .... Single-Point Refueling   (MCD)
SPR .... Skin Potential Response [*Physiology*]
SPR .... Slavistic Printings and Reprintings [*A publication*]
SPR .... Society of Patient Representatives [*Later, NSPR*]   (EA)
SPR .... Society for Pediatric Radiology [*Durham, NC*]   (EA)
SPR .... Society for Pediatric Research [*Albuquerque, NM*]   (EA)
SPR .... Society for Philosophy of Religion   (EA)
SPR .... Society for Psychical Research [*British*]
SPR .... Society for Psychophysiological Research
SPR .... Software Problem Report [*NASA*]   (NASA)

SPR .... Solid-Phase Reactor
SPR .... Solid-Propellant Rocket
SPR .... South Polar Region
SPR .... Southern Poetry Review [*A publication*]
SPR .... Spacer   (AAG)
SPR .... Spare [*Telecommunications*]   (TEL)
SPR .... Special Program Requirement   (AFM)
SPR .... Special Program Review [*Army*]   (RDA)
SPR .... Special Project Report
SPR .... Special-Purpose RADAR
SPR .... Special-Purpose Requirements [*Army*]
SPR .... Specialist, Recruiter [*Navy rating*]
SPR .... Spinster
SPR .... Sponsor
Spr .... Sprache [*A publication*]
Spr .... Sprague's United States District Court [*Admiralty*] Decisions   (DLA)
SPR .... Spratly Islands [*Three-letter standard code*]   (CNC)
SPR .... Spring   (MSA)
SPR .... Sprinkler   (AAG)
SPR .... Statement of Procedural Rules   (DLA)
SPR .... Sterling Capital Corp. [*American Stock Exchange symbol*]
SPR .... Storage Protection Register
SPR .... Strategic Petroleum Reserve
SPR .... Sub Petito Remissionis [*With Request for Return*] [*Latin*]
SPR .... Subcontractor Performance Review [*NASA*]   (NASA)
SPR .... Sudden Pressure Relay
SPR .... Sun Protection Required [*Identification system for heat-sensitive cargo*] [*Shipping*]
SPR .... Supplementary Progress Report
SPR .... Supply Performance Report   (CINC)
SPR .... Support Plans and Requirements
SPR .... System Parameter Record [*Data processing*]   (IBMDP)
SPR .... System Performance Rating
SPR .... System Problem Report   (MCD)
SPR .... System Program Review   (AABC)
SPR's .... Small Parcels and Rolls [*Postal Service*]
SPRA........ Space Probe RADAR Altimeter   (KSC)
SPRA........ Special-Purpose Reconnaissance Aircraft [*Navy*]
SPRACAY ... Society for Prevention of Rock and Roll and Corruption of American Youth [*Organization in 1956 movie "Shake, Rattle and Roll"*]
Sprache Tech Zeit ... Sprache im Technischen Zeitalter [*A publication*]
SPRAG...... Spray Arrester Gear   (MCD)
SPRAG...... STS [*Space Transportation System*] Payload Requirements and Analysis Group [*NASA*]   (NASA)
Sprague ..... Sprague's United States District Court [*Admiralty*] Decisions   (DLA)
Sprague's J ME His ... Sprague's Journal of Maine History [*A publication*]
Sprakvetensk Sallsk i Uppsala Forhandl ... Sprakvetenskapliga Sallskapets i Uppsala Foerhandlingar [*A publication*]
SPRAM...... Sao Paulo. Revista do Arquivo Municipal [*A publication*]
SPRAT ...... Small Portable RADAR Torch
Spraw...... Sprawozdania [*A publication*]
Spraw Opolskie Tow Przyj Nauk Wydz Nauk Med ... Sprawozdania Opolskie Towarzystwo Przyjaciol Nauk. Wydzial Nauk Medycznych [*A publication*]
Sprawozdania Kom Nauk PAN ... Sprawozdania z Posiedzen Komisji Naukowych. Polskiej Akademii Nauk [*A publication*]
Spraw Poznan Tow Przyj Nauk ... Sprawozdania Poznanskiego Towarzystwa Przyjaciol Nauk [*A publication*]
Spraw Pr Pol Tow Fiz ... Sprawozdania i Prace Polskiego Towarzystwa Fizycznego [*A publication*]
Spraw Tow Nauk Lwowie ... Sprawozdania Towarzystwa Naukowego we Lwowie [*A publication*]
Spraw Tow Nauk Toruniu ... Sprawozdania Towarzystwa Naukowego w Toruniu [*A publication*]
Spraw Wroclaw Tow Nauk ... Sprawozdania Wroclawskiego Towarzystwa Naukowego [*A publication*]
Spraw Wroclaw Tow Nauk Ser A ... Sprawozdania Wroclawskiego Towarzystwa Naukowego. Seria A [*A publication*]
Spraw Wroclaw Tow Nauk Ser B ... Sprawozdania Wroclawskiego Towarzystwa Naukowego. Seria B [*A publication*]
SprB.......... Sprakliga Bidrag [*A publication*]
SPR BOG.... Springender Bogen [*Bouncing Bow*] [*Music*]
SPRC......... Seafood Products Research Center [*Public Health Service*]
SPRC......... Self-Propelled Robot Craft   (IEEE)
SPRC......... Society of Public Relations Counsellors
SPRD......... Science Policy Research Division [*of Congressional Research Service, Library of Congress*]
SPRD......... Spread   (FAAC)
SPRDNG .... Spreading [*Freight*]
SPRDR ...... Spreader   (MSA)
SPRDS ...... Steam Pipe Rupture Detector System   (IEEE)
SPRE......... Society of Park and Recreation Educators   (EA)
SPRE......... Solid-Propellant Rocket Engine
SPRE......... Special Prefix Code [*Northern Telecom*] [*Telecommunications*]
SPREAD..... Spring Evaluation Analysis and Design   (MCD)
SPREAD.... Supercomputer Project Research Experiment in Advanced Development [*Lawrence Livermore Laboratory, Los Alamos National Laboratory, and SRI*]

SPREC .... Specular Reflection Computer Program   (MCD)
SPREE .... Solid-Propellant Exhaust Effects   (MCD)
SPREG .... Speed Regulator
S & P RES DIS ... Severn and Potomac Reserve District [*Marine Corps*]
SPRF .... Sandia Pulsed Reactor Facility
SPRF .... Societe de Publications Romanes et Francaises [*A publication*]
SPRF .... Space Propulsion Research Facility   (AAG)
SPRF .... Special-Purpose Receiving Facility
SPRG .... Social Policy Research Group, Inc. [*Boston, MA*] [*Information service*]   (EISS)
SPRG .... Spring
SPRG .... Sprinkling   (MSA)
SPRH .... Spearhead Industries, Inc. [*NASDAQ symbol*]   (NQ)
SPRI .... Scott Polar Research Institute [*Cambridge, England*]
SPRI .... Single Ply Roofing Institute [*Glenview, IL*]   (EA)
SPRI .... Social Problems Research Institute [*University of South Carolina at Columbia*] [*Research center*]   (RCD)
SPRI .... Social Process Research Institute [*University of California, Santa Barbara*] [*Research center*]   (RCD)
SPRI .... Social Psychiatry Research Institute [*New York, NY*]   (EA)
SPRI .... Sperm Reservoir Length Index
SPRI .... Sugar Processing Research, Incorporated
SPRIA .... Solid-Phase Radioimmunoassay [*or Radioimmunoprecipitation Assay*] [*Clinical medicine*]
Springer Semin Immunopathol ... Springer Seminars in Immunopathology [*A publication*]
Springer Ser Electrophys ... Springer Series in Electrophysics [*A publication*]
Springer Ser Inform Sci ... Springer Series in Information Sciences [*A publication*]
Springer Ser Optical Sci ... Springer Series in Optical Sciences [*A publication*]
Springer Ser Opt Sci ... Springer Series in Optical Sciences [*A publication*]
Springer Tracts Mod Phys ... Springer Tracts in Modern Physics [*A publication*]
Springer Tracts Nat Philos ... Springer Tracts in Natural Philosophy [*A publication*]
SPRINT ...... Selective Printing [*Data processing*]
SPRINT ...... Solid-Propellant Rocket Intercept Missile [*ARPA/AMC*]
SPRINT ...... Southern Pacific Communications' Switched Long Distance Service [*Telecommunications*]   (TEL)
SPRINT ...... Spare Parts Review Initiatives [*Army*]   (RDA)
SPRINT ...... Special Police Radio Inquiry Network [*New York City*]
SPRINT ...... Strategic Programme for Innovation and Technology Transfer [*European Commission*]
SPRINTER ... Specification of Profits with Interaction under Trial and Error Response
SPRITE ...... Signal Processing in the Element   (MCD)
SPRITE ...... Solid-Propellant Rocket Ignition Test and Evaluation   (KSC)
SPRITE ...... Surveillance, Patrol, Reconnaissance, Intelligence Gathering, Target Designation, and Electronic Warfare [*Unmanned aircraft*] [*Military*]
SPRJ .... Self-Powered Reference Junction
SPRK .... Sparkman Producing Co. [*NASDAQ symbol*]   (NQ)
SprKJ .... Sprawozdania z Posiedzen Komisji Jezykowej Towarzystwa Naukowego Warszawskiego [*A publication*]
SPRKLG ..... Sprinkling [*Freight*]
SPRKT .... Sprocket   (MSA)
SprKUL ...... Sprawozdania z Czynnosci Wydawniczej i Posiedzen Naukowych Oraz Kronika Towarzystwa Naukowego Katolockiego Uniwersytetu Lubelskiego [*A publication*]
SPRL .... Space Physics Research Laboratory [*University of Michigan*] [*Research center*]   (RCD)
SPRL .... Spiral   (FAAC)
SprLTN ...... Sprawozdania z Czynnosci i Posiedzen Lodzkiego Towarzystwa Naukowego [*A publication*]
SPRM .... Special Reamer [*Tool*]   (AAG)
Spr Miedzyn ... Sprawy Miedzynarodowe [*A publication*]
S-P/ROM ... Slave Programable Read-Only Memory
SPROM ..... Switched Programable Read-Only Memory
SPROPS ..... Section Properties [*Camutek*] [*Software package*]
SprPAUm ... Sprawozdania z Czynnosci i Posiedzen Polskiej Akademii Umiejetnosci [*A publication*]
SprPTPN ... Sprawozdania Poznanskiego Towarzystwa Przyjaciol Nauk [*A publication*]
SPRRS .... Southern Plains Range Research Station [*Oklahoma State University*] [*Research center*]   (RCD)
SPRS .... Single Passenger Reservation System [*DoD*]
SPRS .... Special-Purpose RADAR Set
SPRS .... Student Proficiency Rating Scale
SPRS .... Sublime Power of the Royal Secret [*Freemasonry*]   (ROG)
SprSUF ..... Sprakvetenskapliga Sallskapets i Uppsala Foerhandlingar [*A publication*]
SPRT .... Sequential Probability Ratio Test [*Statistics*]
SPRT .... Standard Platinum Resistance Thermometer
SPRT .... Support   (MSA)
SPRT .... System Performance and Repeatability Test [*Military*]   (CAAL)
SprTNW ..... Sprawozdania z Posiedzen Towarzystwa Naukowego Warszawskiego [*A publication*]
SprTT .... Sprawozdania Towarzystwa Naukowego w Toruniu [*A publication*]

SPRUCE ..... Special Programs and Rehabilitation under Unemployment Compensation [*Department of Labor*]
SprV .... Sprachkunst (Vienna) [*A publication*]
SPS .... St. Patrick's Missionary Society [*Roman Catholic men's religious order*]
SPS .... Saint Patrick's Seminary [*Menlo Park, CA*]
SPS .... Samples per Second
SPS .... San Pedro De Poas [*Costa Rica*] [*Seismograph station code, US Geological Survey*]   (SEIS)
SPS .... Satellite and Production Services [*Tallahassee, FL*] [*Telecommunications*]   (TSSD)
SPS .... Saturn Parts Sales [*NASA*]
SPS .... Saturn Propulsion System [*NASA*]
SPS .... Scene per Second   (MCD)
SPS .... Schedule Promulgated Separately [*Navy*]   (NVT)
SPS .... School of Practical Science
SPS .... Scientific Power Switching
SPS .... Secondary Plant System   (NRCH)
SPS .... Secondary Power Source
SPS .... Secondary Power System [*or Subsystem*]   (MCD)
SPS .... Secondary Propulsion System [*NASA*]
SPS .... Sekcja Pracy Spolecznej [*A publication*]   (BJA)
SPS .... Self Protection System   (MCD)
SPS .... Series-Parallel-Serial Configuration [*Electronics*]   (MDG)
SPS .... Service Propulsion System [*or Subsystem*] [*NASA*]
SPS .... Servo Parameter Shift
SPS .... Set Point Station
SpS .... Sharpshooter [*Military decoration*]   (AABC)
SPS .... Ship Planning System
SPS .... Ship Program Schedule
SPS .... Shipping/Production Scheduling
SPS .... Shuttle Procedures Simulator [*NASA*]   (NASA)
SPS .... Signal Processing System   (KSC)
SPS .... Silent Propulsion System   (MCD)
SPS .... Simple Phrase System
SPS .... Simplified Processing Station   (MCD)
SPS .... Simulated Parts Sketch   (MCD)
SPS .... Simulator Panel Set   (MCD)
SPS .... Sine Prole Superstite [*Without Surviving Issue*] [*Latin*]
SPS .... Single-Pole Switch
SPS .... Social Problems Series [*A publication*]
SPS .... Socialistische Partij Suriname [*Suriname Socialist Party*]   (PPW)
SPS .... Society of Pelvic Surgeons [*Jackson, MS*]   (EA)
SPS .... Society for Pentecostal Studies   (EA)
SPS .... Society of Physics Students   (EA)
SPS .... Sodium Polyanetholesulfonate [*Analytical biochemistry*]
SPS .... Sodium Polystyrene Sulfonate [*Organic chemistry*]
SPS .... Soft Particle Spectrometer [*Geophysics*]
SPS .... Software Products Scheme [*Data processing*]
SPS .... Solar Panel Substrate
SPS .... Solar Power Satellite [*NASA*]
SPS .... Solar Power System   (MCD)
SPS .... Solar Probe Spacecraft [*Pioneer satellite*]
SPS .... Soluble Polysaccharide of Soybean [*Food technology*]
SPS .... SONAR Phase Shifter
SPS .... South Pole Station [*National Weather Service*]
SPS .... Southwestern Public Service Co. [*NYSE symbol*]
SPS .... Sozialdemokratische Partei der Schweiz [*Social Democratic Party of Switzerland*]   (PPE)
SPS .... Sozialdemokratische Partei Suedtirols [*Social Democratic Party of South Tirol*]   (PPE)
SPS .... Space Planning System [*Applied Research of Cambridge Ltd.*] [*Software package*]
SPS .... Space Power System   (CET)
SPS .... Space Stories [*A publication*]
SPS .... Spacecraft Propulsion System   (AAG)
SPS .... Special-Purpose SONAR   (MCD)
SPS .... Special Services [*Military*]
SPS .... Specialist, Personnel Supervisor [*Women's Reserve*] [*Navy rating*]
SPS .... Specialist, Shore Patrol and Security [*Navy rating*]
SPS .... Specimina Philologiae Slavicae [*A publication*]
SPS .... Spectrum Planning Subcommittee [*FCC*]
SPS .... Speed Switch   (IEEE)
SPS .... Spokane, Portland & Seattle Railway System [*AAR code*]
SPS .... SPS Technologies, Inc. [*Formerly, Standard Pressed Steel Co.*]   (MCD)
SPS .... Stabilized Platform Subsystem   (KSC)
SPS .... Standard Pipe Size
SPS .... Standard Port System   (MCD)
SPS .... Standard Process Specification   (MCD)
SPS .... Standard Project Storm [*Nuclear energy*]   (NRCH)
SPS .... Standby Power Source [*Electronics*]
SPS .... Statement of Prior Submission   (NASA)
SPS .... Static Power System
SPS .... Static Pressure System
SPS .... Statistical Performance Standards [*Navy*]   (NG)
SPS .... Stator Pivot Seal
SPS .... Steady Potential Shift
SPS .... Steampipe Survey

SPS .... Stereo Photographic System
SPS .... Stichting Plurale Samenlevingen [*Foundation for the Study of Plural Societies - FSPS*]   (EA-IO)
SPS .... Stored Program Simulator
SPS .... Strategic Planning Society [*Formerly, Society for Strategic and Long Range Planning*]   (EA)
SPS .... Strategic Planning Staff [*Social Security Administration*]
SPS .... Strategical Planning Section [*Joint Planning Staff*] [*World War II*]
SPS .... String Processing System [*Word processing software*]
SPS .... Student Profile Section [*of the American College Testing Test Battery*]
SPS .... Submarine Piping System
SPS .... Submerged Production System [*Deepwater platform*] [*Humble Oil*]
SPS .... Subsea Production System [*Petroleum technology*]
SPS .... Sucrose-Phosphate Synthase [*An enzyme*]
SPS .... Sulfite-Polymyxin-Sulfadiazine [*Agar*] [*Microbiology*]
SPS .... Summit Power Station [*Nuclear energy*]   (NRCH)
SPS .... Super Proton Synchrotron [*Atom smasher*]
SPS .... Supplementary Protection System   (NRCH)
SPS .... Supply Point Simulation   (MCD)
SPS .... Symbolic Programing System [*Data processing*]
SPS .... Symbols per Second [*Data processing*]
SPS .... System Performance Score [*Telecommunications*]   (TEL)
SPS .... Wichita Falls [*Texas*] [*Airport symbol*]   (OAG)
SPSA........ Senate Press Secretaries Association   (EA)
SPSA........ Society of Philippine Surgeons in America [*Chesapeake, VA*]   (EA)
SPSA........ Special Projects School for Air
SpSAG ...... Archivo General de Indias [*Archives of the Indies*], Seville, Spain [*Library symbol*] [*Library of Congress*]   (LCLS)
SPSC........ Saharan People's Support Committee   (EA)
SP/SC .... Shield Plug/Support Cylinder   (NRCH)
SPSC........ Signal Processing and Spectral Control
SPSC........ Space Power Systems Conference
SPSC........ Standard Performance Summary Charts   (AAG)
SPSCR ...... Special Screw
SPSD........ Space Power Systems Division [*NASA*]
SPSDC....... Surface and Defect Properties of Solids [*A publication*]
SP-SDF ..... Socialist Party - Social Democratic Federation [*Later, Socialist Party of the United States of America*]   (EA)
SPSDM...... Society for the Philosophical Study of Dialectical Materialism   (EA)
SPSDS .... Ship's Passive Surveillance and Detection System [*Navy*]   (CAAL)
SPSE........ Society of Photographic Scientists and Engineers   (EA)
SPSEA ...... Soviet Physics. Semiconductors [*English translation*] [*A publication*]
Sp & Sel Cas ... Special and Selected Law Cases [*1648*] [*England*]   (DLA)
SPSF .... Self-Propagating-Star Formation [*Galactic science*]
SPSF .... Society of the President Street Fellows   (EA)
SP/SHLD .. Splash Shield [*Automotive engineering*]
SPSHP ...... Special Shaped
SPSHS ...... Stanford Profile Scales of Hypnotic Susceptibility [*Psychology*]
SPSI .... Serikat Pelajaran Seluruh Indonesia [*Sailors' Union of Indonesia*]
SPSI .... Society for the Promotion of Scientific Industry [*British*]
SPSL .... Socialist Party of Sri Lanka
SPSL .... Society for the Philosophy of Sex and Love   (EA)
SPSL .... Spare Parts Selection List
SPSM .... Society for the Philosophical Study of Marxism   (EA)
SPSM .... Supply Point Simulation Model   (MCD)
SPSME...... Spacelab Payload Standard Modular Electronics   (MCD)
SPSN .... Submitted Package Sequence Number   (MCD)
SPSO .... Senior Personnel Staff Officer [*Air Force*] [*British*]
SPSO .... Senior Principal Scientific Officer [*Ministry of Agriculture, Fisheries, and Food*] [*British*]
SPSP .... St. Peter and St. Paul [*The Papal seal*]
SPSP .... Solid-Propellant Surveillance Panel [*Military*]
SPSP .... Spare Parts Support Package
SPsp.......... Sprachspiegel. Schweizerische Zeitschrift fuer die Deutsche Muttersprache [*A publication*]
SPSPS ...... Specialist, Personnel Supervisor, V-10 [*Navy rating*]
SpsQualBad ... Sharpshooter Qualification Badge [*Military decoration*]   (AABC)
SPSRA ...... Space Science Reviews [*A publication*]
SPSS......... Shield Plug Storage Station   (NRCH)
SPSS......... Single Pulse Selection System
SPSS......... Statistical Package for the Social Sciences [*Programing language*] [*1970*]
SPS-SCWG ... Spanish Philatelic Society Spanish Civil War Study Group [*Defunct*]   (EA)
SPSSI........ Society for the Psychological Study of Social Issues   (EA)
Sp St .... Private and Special Laws   (DLA)
SPST .... Single-Pole, Single-Throw [*Switch*]
SPST .... Symonds Picture-Story Test [*Psychology*]
SPSTNC..... Single-Pole, Single-Throw, Normally-Closed [*Switch*]
SPSTNO..... Single-Pole, Single-Throw, Normally-Open [*Switch*]
SPSTNODM ... Single-Pole, Single-Throw, Normally-Open, Double-Make [*Switch*]

SPSTP........ Solid-Propellant Rocket Static Test Panel [*Military*]
SPSTSW ... Single-Pole, Single-Throw Switch
SPSU .... Studia Philologiae Scandinavicae Upsaliensia [*A publication*]
SPSW .... Single-Pole Switch
SPSWO ...... Spare Parts Sales Work Order
SPT .... Albuquerque, NM [*Location identifier*] [*FAA*]   (FAAL)
SPT .... Piedmont Technical College, Greenwood, SC [*OCLC symbol*]   (OCLC)
SPT .... Scaled-Particle Theory
SPT .... School of Physical Training [*British*]
SPT .... Scientist-Pilot [*NASA*]   (KSC)
SPT .... Seaport
SPT .... Sectors per Track
SPT .... Septic [*Classified advertising*]   (ADA)
SPT .... Septuple   (MSA)
SPT .... Shaft Position Transducer
SPT .... Ship Position Transmitter
SPT .... Shipper Pays Taxes
SPT .... Silicon Planar Transistor
SPT .... Silicon-Powered Transistor
SPT .... Skin Prick Test [*Immunology*]
SPT .... Small Perturbation Theory
SPT .... Society of Painters in Tempera   (EA)
SPT .... Society of Photo-Technologists [*Denver, CO*]   (EA)
SPT .... Society of Projective Techniques [*Later, SPA*]   (EA)
SPT .... Sodium Pyridinethione [*Organic chemistry*]
SPT .... Sogepet Ltd. [*Toronto Stock Exchange symbol*]
SPT .... Sound-Powered Telephone
SPT .... South Point [*Hawaii*] [*Seismograph station code, US Geological Survey*]   (SEIS)
SPT .... Space Power Tool
SPT .... Space Travel [*A publication*]
SPT .... Span East Airlines, Inc. [*Miami, FL*] [*FAA designator*]   (FAAC)
SpT .... Spanish Telefunken [*Record label*]
SPT .... Spare Parts Transfer
SPT .... Special Perishable Tool   (MCD)
SPT .... Special Purpose Tests   (NRCH)
SPT .... Specialist, Teacher [*Navy rating*]
SpT .... Speech Teacher [*A publication*]
SPT .... Spirit
SPT .... Split   (MSA)
SPT .... Spraytight
Spt .... Spritsail
SPT .... Sputum
SPT .... Standard Penetration Test [*Nuclear energy*]   (NRCH)
SPT .... Static Pressure Transducer
SPT .... Structural Programing Technique
SPT .... Support   (AFM)
SPT .... Symbolic Program Tape [*Data processing*]   (IEEE)
SPT .... Symbolic Program Translator [*Data processing*]   (IEEE)
SPT .... System Page Table [*Telecommunications*]   (TEL)
SPT .... System Parameter Table [*Data processing*]   (IBMDP)
SPT .... System Planning Team [*Military*]   (AFIT)
SP3T......... Single-Pole, Triple-Throw [*Switch*]   (IEEE)
SP4T......... Single-Pole, Quadruple-Throw [*Switch*]   (IEEE)
SPTA........ Southern Paper Trade Association [*Biloxi, MS*]   (EA)
SPTA........ Southern Pressure Treaters Association [*Shreveport, LA*]   (EA)
Sp Tax Rul ... Special Tax Ruling [*Internal Revenue Service*] [*United States*]   (DLA)
SPTC........ Share-Purchase Tax Credit [*Canada*]
SPTC........ Specified Period of Time Contract
SPTC........ Studies in Physical and Theoretical Chemistry [*Elsevier Book Series*] [*A publication*]
SPTD........ Signal Processor Techniques Department
SPTD........ Supplemental Provisioning Technical Documentation [*NASA*]   (NASA)
SPTE .... Special Purpose Test Equipment   (MCD)
SPTEA....... Single Persons for Tax Equality Association   (EA)
SPTF .... Screen Printing Technical Foundation [*Fairfax, VA*]   (EA)
SPTF .... Signal Processing Test Facility
SPTF .... Social Progress Trust Fund [*Inter-American Development Bank*]
SPTF .... Sodium Pump Test Facility [*Energy Research and Development Administration*]
SPTL .... Society of Public Teachers of Law [*British*]   (DLA)
SPTL .... Support Line [*Military*]
SPTM .... Spectrum Laboratories, Inc. [*NASDAQ symbol*]   (NQ)
SPTN........ Spartech Corp. [*NASDAQ symbol*]   (NQ)
SPTN........ Spill Technology Newsletter [*A publication*]
SPTP......... Special-Purpose Test Program   (MCD)
SPT & PA ... Society for Projective Techniques and Personality Assessment [*Later, SPA*]
SPTPA....... Soviet Physics. Technical Physics [*English Translation*] [*A publication*]
SPTPN........ Sprawozdania Poznanskiego Towarzystwa Przyjaciol Nauk [*A publication*]
SP(TR) .... Specialist (Transportation) [*Coast Guard*]
SPTR......... Spectran Corp. [*NASDAQ symbol*]   (NQ)
SPTRJ........ Self-Powered Thermocouple Reference Junction
SPTS......... Spirits
SPTS......... Sport's Restaurants [*NASDAQ symbol*]   (NQ)

SPTS .... Stock Positioning and Transportation Study [*DoD*]
SPTT .... Single-Pole, Triple-Throw [*Switch*]   (CET)
SPTUF .... South Pacific Trade Union Forum [*14-nation group opposed to nuclear testing and dumping in the Pacific*]
SPTW .... Single-Pedestal Typewriter [*Desk*]
SPTWC ...... Salle Palasz and Tri-Weapon Club   (EA)
SPU .... Mount Spur [*Alaska*] [*Seismograph station code, US Geological Survey*]   (SEIS)
SPU .... S-Band Polar Ultra
SPU .... Salinas Public Library, Salinas, CA [*OCLC symbol*]   (OCLC)
SPU .... School Personnel Utilization
SPU .... Service Propulsion Unit
SPU .... Signal Processing Unit
SPU .... Slave Processing Unit
SPU .... Society for Pediatric Urology [*Gainesville, FL*]   (EA)
SPU .... Southeast Airmotive Corp. [*Charlotte, NC*] [*FAA designator*]   (FAAC)
SPU .... Specialist, Utility [*Women's Reserve*] [*Navy rating*]
SPU .... Split [*Yugoslavia*] [*Airport symbol*]   (OAG)
SPU .... Statutes of Practical Utility [*A publication*]
SPU .... Student Peace Union [*Defunct*]   (EA)
SPU .... Subsurface Propulsion Unit
SPU .... System Partitioning Unit [*Data processing*]
SPUC .... Society for the Protection of Unborn Children   (EA)
SPUD .... One Potato 2, Inc. [*NASDAQ symbol*]   (NQ)
SPUD .... St. Paul Union Depot Co. [*AAR code*]
SPUD .... Society for Prevention of Unwholesome Diet [*National Potato Council*]
SPUD .... Solar Power Unit Demonstrator
SPUD .... Stored Program Universal Demonstrator
SPUK .... Special Projects, United Kingdom
SPUN .... Society for the Protection of the Unborn through Nutrition   (EA)
SPUP .... Seychelles People's United Party   (PPW)
SPUR .... San Francisco Planning and Urban Research Association [*California*] [*Information service*]   (EISS)
SPUR .... Single Precision Unpacked Rounded [*floating-point package*] [*Computer program system*] [*Sperry Rand Corp.*]
SPUR .... Source Program Utility Routine
SPUR .... Space Power Unit Reactor [*Air Force*]
SPUR .... Special Purchase Office [*DoD*]
SPUR .... Support for Promoting the Utilization of Resources [*Esso Education Foundation*]
SPURM ...... Special Purpose Unilateral Repetitive Modulation   (IEEE)
SPURT ...... Small Primate Unrestrained Test
SPURT ...... Spinning Unguided Rocket Trajectory
SPURV ...... Self-Propelled Underwater Research Vehicle
SP-USA ..... Socialist Party of the United States of America   (EA)
SPUTA ...... Scientific Papers. College of General Education. University of Tokyo [*A publication*]
SPV .... Sa-Pa [*Vietnam*] [*Seismograph station code, US Geological Survey*]   (SEIS)
SPV .... Sensor Payload Vehicle
SPV .... Shope Papilloma Virus
SPV .... Slow-Phase Velocity [*Ophthalmology*]
SPV .... Space Adventures [*A publication*]
SpV .... Spanish RCA Victor [*Record label*]
SPV .... Special-Purpose Vehicles
SPV .... Specialist, Transport Airman [*Navy rating*]
SPV .... Specification Performance Validation [*Military*]   (CAAL)
SPV .... Split-Product Vaccine [*Immunology*]
SPV .... STN Shop Television Network Ltd. [*Vancouver Stock Exchange symbol*]
SPV .... Storage Process Vent   (NRCH)
SPV .... Storage Protect Violation   (CMD)
SPV .... Sulfophosphovanillin (Reaction) [*Clinical chemistry*]
SPV .... Sun Probe near Limb of Venus [*Angle*]
SPV .... Surface Photovoltage [*Photovoltaic energy systems*]
SPV .... Survey of Personal Values [*Psychology*]
SPVA .... Society for the Preservation of Variety Arts   (EA)
SPVEA ...... Superintendencia do Plano de Valorizacao Economica da Amazonia [*Brazil*]
SPVLI .... Single Premium Variable Life Investment [*Insurance*]
SPVN .... Supervision   (MSA)
SPVOL ...... Specific Volume   (DEN)
SPVPF ...... Shuttle Payload Vertical Processing Facility   (MCD)
SPVR .... Storage Process Vent Room   (NRCH)
Spvry Mgt ... Supervisory Management [*A publication*]
SPW .... Sealed Power Corp. [*NYSE symbol*]
SPW .... Self-Protection Weapon
SPW .... Seward Park [*Washington*] [*Seismograph station code, US Geological Survey*]   (SEIS)
SPW .... Shipment Planning Worksheet
SPW .... Spaceway Science Fiction [*A publication*]
SPW .... Spare Parts Withdrawal   (MCD)
SPW .... Special Warfare   (NVT)
SPW .... Specialist, Chaplain's Assistant [*Navy rating*]
SPW .... Spencer [*Iowa*] [*Airport symbol*]   (OAG)
SPW .... Wofford College, Spartanburg, SC [*OCLC symbol*]   (OCLC)
SPWA .... Southern Peanut Warehousemen's Association   (EA)
SPWA .... Steel Products Warehouse Association

SPWAO ...... Small Press Writers and Artists Organization   (EA)
SPWAR ...... Special Warfare
SPWC .... Society for the Punishment of War Criminals   (EA)
SPWG .... Space Parts Working Group
SPWL .... Single Premium Whole Life Insurance Policy
SPWLA ..... Society of Professional Well Log Analysts   (EA)
SPWM .... Single-Sided Pulse Width Modulation [*Telecommunications*]
SPWR .... Small Pressurized Water Reactor
SPWS .... Shipment Planning Worksheet   (MCD)
SPWSM ..... Spanish War Service Medal
SPWWIII .... Society for the Prevention of World War III [*Defunct*]
SPX .... League City, TX [*Location identifier*] [*FAA*]   (FAAL)
SPX .... Simplex Circuit
SPX .... Simplex Instrument [*Telegraphy*]
SPX .... Spirit Petroleum [*Vancouver Stock Exchange symbol*]
SPX .... Superheat Power Experiment
SPXAC ...... Specialist, Archivist [*Navy rating*]
SPXAR ...... Specialist, Artist [*Navy rating*]
SPXBL .... Specialist, Ballistics [*Navy rating*]
SPXCC ...... Specialist, Cable Censor [*Navy rating*]
SPXCG ...... Specialist, Crystal Grinder [*Navy rating*]
SPXCT ...... Specialist, Cartographer [*Navy rating*]
SPXDI .... Specialist, Discharge Interviewer [*Navy rating*]
SPXED ...... Specialist, Engineering Draftsman [*Navy rating*]
SPXFP ...... Specialist, Fingerprint Expert [*Navy rating*]
SPXGU ...... Specialist, Gauge Specialist [*Navy rating*]
SPXID .... Specialist, Intelligence Duties [*Navy rating*]
SPXIR .... Specialist, Interpreter [*Navy rating*]
SPXJO .... Specialist, Journalist [*Navy rating*]
SPXKP ...... Specialist, Key Punch Operator and Supervisor [*Navy rating*]
SPXNC ...... Specialist, Naval Correspondent [*Navy rating*]
SPXOP ...... Specialist, Special Project [*Navy rating*]
SPXPC ...... Specialist, Position Classifier [*Navy rating*]
SPXPI .... Specialist, Pigeon Trainer [*Navy rating*]
SPXPL .... Specialist, Plastic Expert [*Navy rating*]
SPXPR ...... Specialist, Public Information [*Navy rating*]
SPXQM ...... Specialist, Operations - Plotting and Chart Work [*Navy rating*]
SPXRL .... Specialist, Research Laboratory [*Navy rating*]
SPXRS ...... Specialist, Armed Forces Radio Service and Special Naval Radio Units [*Navy rating*]
SPXSB ...... Specialist, Telephone Switchboard Operator and Supervisor [*Navy rating*]
SPXST .... Specialist, Strategic Services [*Navy rating*]
SPXTD ...... Specialist, Topographic Draftsman [*Navy rating*]
SPXTS .... Specialist, Air Stations Operations Desk - Time Shack [*Navy rating*]
SPXVA ...... Specialist, Visual Training Aids [*Navy rating*]
s-py--- .... Paraguay [*MARC geographic area code*] [*Library of Congress*]   (LCCP)
SPY .... Saint Paul Island, AK [*Location identifier*] [*FAA*]   (FAAL)
SPY .... San Pedro [*Ivory Coast*] [*Airport symbol*]   (OAG)
SPY .... Spectra-Physics, Inc. [*NYSE symbol*]
SPYR .... Sprayer   (MSA)
SPZ .... Spar Aerospace Ltd. [*Toronto Stock Exchange symbol*]
SPZ .... Springdale [*Arkansas*] [*Airport symbol*]   (OAG)
SPZ .... Submarine Patrol Zone [*Navy*]   (NVT)
SPZ .... Sulfinpyrazone [*Uricosuric compound*]
SQ .... E. R. Squibb & Sons [*Research code symbol*]
SQ .... Safety Quotient
SQ .... Sequens [*Following*] [*Latin*]
SQ .... Shakespeare Quarterly [*A publication*]
SQ .... Sick Quarters [*Navy*] [*British*]
SQ .... Singapore Airlines Ltd. [*ICAO designator*]   (FAAC)
SQ .... Situation Questionnaire
SQ .... Social Quotient [*Psychology*]
SQ .... Southern Quarterly [*A publication*]
SQ .... Squadron
SQ .... Squall [*Meteorology*]
SQ .... Squamous [*Cell*] [*Oncology*]
SQ .... Square
sq .... Square Tank [*Liquid gas carriers*]
SQ .... Staff Qualified [*Military*] [*British*]
SQ .... Stereoquadraphonic [*Record playing system*] [*CBS*]
SQ .... Subcutaneous [*Beneath the Skin*] [*Medicine*]
SQ .... Superquick [*Fuse*]
SQ .... Survival Quotient   (ADA)
sq .... Swaziland [*MARC country of publication code*] [*Library of Congress*]   (LCCP)
SQA .... Software Quality Assurance [*Data processing*]   (IEEE)
SQA .... Sparrevohn, AK [*Location identifier*] [*FAA*]   (FAAL)
SQA .... Squaring Amplifier
SQA .... Supplier Quality Assurance
SQA .... Surveyor Quality Assurance
SQA .... System Queue Area [*Data processing*]   (BUR)
SQAD .... Surveyor Quality Assurance Directive
SQAI .... Square Industries [*NASDAQ symbol*]   (NQ)
SQAL .... Squall [*Meteorology*]
SQAP .... Supplemental Quality Assurance Provision
SQAR .... Supplier Quality Assurance Representative
SQAT .... Ship's Qualification Assistance Team [*Navy*]
SQB .... Space Qualified Booster

SQB............ Squibb Corp. [*NYSE symbol*]
SQBC......... Space Qualified Booster Charger
SQC............ Self-Quenching Control
SQC............ Southern Cross [*Australia*] [*Airport symbol*]   (OAG)
SQC............ Station Quality Control [*RADAR*]
SQC............ Statistical Quality Control
SQCG......... Squirrel Cage [*Electricity*]
SQCM........ Square Centimeter   (MSA)
SQCP......... Statistical Quality Control Procedure
SQD........... Self-Quenching Detector
SQD........... Signal Quality Detector
SQD........... Social Questions of Today [*A publication*]
SQD........... Squad   (AABC)
SQD........... Squadron   (NVT)
SQD........... Square D Co. [*NYSE symbol*]
SQDC........ Special Quick Disconnect Coupling
SQDN......... Squadron   (AAG)
SQE............ Supplier Quality Engineering   (MCD)
SQF............ Cleveland, OH [*Location identifier*] [*FAA*]   (FAAL)
SQFT......... Square Foot   (MSA)
SQH........... Ford-Aire [*Sidney, NY*] [*FAA designator*]   (FAAC)
SQH........... Square Head [*Bolt*]
SQHA........ Standard Quarter Horse Association   (EA)
SQI............ Skill Qualifications Identifier [*Army*]   (INF)
SQI............ Special Qualifications Identifiers [*Army*]   (AABC)
SQI............ Sterling/Rock Falls [*Illinois*] [*Airport symbol*]   (OAG)
SQIC......... Suppliers Quality Identification Classification
SQIN......... Square Inch   (MSA)
SQKM....... Square Kilometer   (MSA)
SQL........... San Carlos, CA [*Location identifier*] [*FAA*]   (FAAL)
SQL........... School Quota Letter
SQL........... Space Qualified LASER
SQL........... Squelch
SQL........... Standard High-Level Query Language
SQL/DS...... Structured Query Language/Data System [*IBM Corp.*]
SQLN......... Squall Line [*Meteorology*]   (FAAC)
SQM.......... Level Island, AK [*Location identifier*] [*FAA*]   (FAAL)
SQM.......... Sao Miguel Do Araguaia [*Brazil*] [*Airport symbol*]   (OAG)
SQM.......... Square Meter
SQMD........ Squadron Manning Document   (NVT)
SQMS........ Squadron Quartermaster-Serjeant [*Military*] [*British*]   (ROG)
SQMS........ Staff Quartermaster Sergeant
SQN........... Sanana [*Indonesia*] [*Airport symbol*]   (OAG)
SQN........... School Quota Number
SQN........... Spin Quantum Number [*Atomic physics*]
SQN........... Squadron   (NATG)
SQN........... Susquehanna Corp. [*American Stock Exchange symbol*]
SQNA......... Squadron Airfield   (NATG)
SQO........... Squadron Officer
SQP........... Shippensburg State College, Shippensburg, PA [*OCLC symbol*]   (OCLC)
SQPD........ Super Quick Point Detonating
SQPN........ Staggered Quadriphase Pseudorandom Noise   (MCD)
SQQ........... San Quentin Quail [*A minor female*] [*Slang*]
SQQ........... Sequentibus [*In the Following Places*] [*Latin*]
SQR........... Sequence Relay   (KSC)
SQR........... Sequoia Resources Ltd. [*Vancouver Stock Exchange symbol*]
SQR........... Soroako [*Indonesia*] [*Airport symbol*]   (OAG)
SQR........... Square
SQR........... Square Root [*Data processing*]
SQR........... State Reports [*Queensland*] [*A publication*]
SQR........... Supplier Quality Rating
SQR........... Supplier Quality Representative   (NRCH)
SQ3R......... Survey, Question, Read, Review, Recite [*Psychology*]
SQRT......... Seismic Qualification Review Team [*Nuclear energy*]   (NRCH)
SQRT......... Square Root
SQS........... Skill Qualification Score [*Military*]   (AABC)
SQS........... Statistische Quellenwerke der Schweiz [*Switzerland*]
SQS........... Stochastic Queuing System
SQS........... Superquick Sensor   (MCD)
SQ/SD....... Special Qualifications/Special Designation   (NVT)
SQSSE....... Supplier Quality System Survey Evaluations   (MCD)
SQT........... Melbourne, FL [*Location identifier*] [*FAA*]   (FAAL)
SQT........... Queensland State Reports   (DLA)
SQT........... Ship Qualification Test [*or Trial*] [*Navy*]
SQT........... Skill Qualification Test [*Army*]
SQT........... Soldier Qualification Test   (MCD)
SQT........... Sterilization Qualification Tests
SQT........... System Qualification Tests
SQTIPT...... Ship Qualification Trials in Port [*Navy*]   (NVT)
SQTNG...... Squadron Training   (NVT)
SQTT......... Ship Qualification Trial Team [*Navy*]   (NG)
SQU........... E. R. Squibb & Sons, Princeton, NJ [*OCLC symbol*]   (OCLC)
Squ............ Square   (BJA)
SQU........... Squaw Peak [*Utah*] [*Seismograph station code, US Geological Survey*]   (SEIS)
SQUAD...... Squadron
SQUADEX ... Squadron Exercises [*Canadian Navy*]
SQUAF...... Sonobuoy Qualification Facility [*Navy*]   (CAAL)
SQUALL..... Salary Quotient at Lower Limits [*Business and trade*]
SQUAP....... Supplementary Quality Assurance Provisions

SQUARE .... Specifying Queries as Relational Expressions [*Programing language*] [*1973*] [*Data processing*]   (CSR)
S Quart....... Southern Quarterly [*A publication*]
Squibb Abstr Bull ... Squibb Abstract Bulletin [*A publication*]
Squibb Auc ... Squibb on Auctioneers [*2nd ed.*] [*1891*]   (DLA)
SQUID........ Sperry Quick Updating of Internal Documentation   (IEEE)
SQUID........ Superconducting Quantum Interference Detector [*or Device*] [*For studying changes in the Earth's magnetic field*]
SQUIRE...... Submarine Quickened Response
SQUO........ Squadron-Officer [*Air Force*] [*British*]   (DSUE)
SQUOD ...... Selected Quantile Output Device [*Electronics*]
SQUOFF.... Squadron-Officer [*Air Force*] [*British*]   (DSUE)
SQW.......... Squarewave   (MSA)
SQWV....... Squarewave
SQX........... Sulfaquinoxaline [*or (Sulfanilamido)quinoxaline*] [*Animal antibiotic*]
SQZGR...... Squeeze Grip
SR.............. Air-Cushion Vehicle built by Saunders Roe [*England*] [*Usually used in combination with numerals*]
SR.............. Air Search RADAR Receiver [*Shipborne*]
SR.............. General Society, Sons of the Revolution   (EA)
SR.............. New South Wales State Reports [*A publication*]
SR.............. New York State Reporter   (DLA)
SR.............. Partiia Sotsialistov Revolyutsionerov [*Socialist Revolutionary Party*] [*Russian*]   (PPE)
SR.............. Regina Public Library, Saskatchewan [*Library symbol*] [*National Library of Canada*]   (NLC)
SR.............. Saarlandischer Rundfunk [*Radio network*] [*West Germany*]
SR.............. Safety Recommendation   (AAG)
SR.............. Safety Release [*Army*]
S/R............. Safety Relief Valve   (NRCH)
S/R............. Safety Representative [*Insurance*]
SR.............. Safety Rods   (NRCH)
SR.............. Saidi Riyal [*Monetary unit in Oman*]
SR.............. Salva Ratificatione [*On Condition of Ratification*] [*Latin*]
SR.............. Sample Rate
SR.............. Sarcoplasmic Reticulum [*Anatomy*]
SR.............. Saturable Reactor
SR.............. Saturation Recovery [*NMR imaging*]
SR.............. Saturday Review [*A publication*]
SR.............. Saudi Riyal   (BJA)
SR.............. Savannah River Test Pile [*Nuclear energy*]   (NRCH)
SR.............. Sawyer Rifle
SR.............. Scan Radius
SR.............. Scan Ratio   (MCD)
SR.............. Scanning Radiometer
SR.............. Schooner [*Shipping*]   (ROG)
SR.............. Schweizer Rundschau [*A publication*]
SR.............. Sciences Religieuses [*A publication*]
SR.............. Scientific Report
SR.............. Scientific Research
SR.............. Scoring Reliability   (MCD)
SR.............. Scottish Regional [*Council*]
SR.............. Scottish Rifles [*Military unit*] [*British*]
SR.............. Scripture Reader   (ROG)
SR.............. Seaman Recruit [*Navy*]
SR.............. Seaplane Reconnaissance Aircraft
SR.............. Search RADAR
SR.............. Search and Reconnaissance [*Air Force*]
SR.............. Search and Recovery [*Military*]
SR.............. Search and Rescue
SR.............. Second Harmonic Resonance   (MCD)
SR.............. Secretion Rate [*Endocrinology*]
SR.............. Section Report
SR.............. Sedimentation Rate
SR.............. Selective Ringing
SR.............. Selenium Rectifier [*Electronics*]
SR.............. Self-Rectifying
SR.............. Semantic Reaction
SR.............. Senate Report
SR.............. Senate Resolution
SR.............. Send and Receive
SR.............. Senior
SR.............. Senior Registrar
SR.............. Senior Reviewer
SR.............. Senor [*Mister*] [*Spanish*]
SR.............. Sensitivity Ratio
SR.............. Sensitivity Response [*Cell*] [*Radiology*]
SR.............. Sensitization Response
SR.............. Sensory Rhodopsin [*Biochemistry*]
SR.............. Separate Rations
S & R......... Sergeant and Rawle's Pennsylvania Reports [*1824-28*]   (DLA)
SR.............. Series Number [*Online database field identifier*]
SR.............. Service Record
SR.............. Service Report
S-R............. Set-Reset [*Flip-Flop*] [*Data processing*]
SR.............. Settlement Register [*Data processing*]
SR.............. Severe, Right-Moving [*Thunderstorm*]
SR.............. Sewanee Review [*A publication*]
SR.............. Sex Ratio
SR.............. Shaft Rate   (NVT)

SR.............. Sharpened Romberg [*Equilibrium*]
SR.............. Shift Register
SR.............. Shift Reverse
SR.............. Shift Right
SR.............. Ship Repair Ratings
SR.............. Ship-to-Shore RADAR [*or Radio*]   (DEN)
SR.............. Shipment [*or Shipping*] Request
S/R............. Shipper/Receiver [*Difference*]
SR.............. Shipping Receipt [*Business and trade*]
S/R............. Shipping Request   (NG)
SR.............. Ships Records   (MCD)
SR.............. Shock Related
SR.............. Shock Resistance
SR.............. Short Range
SR.............. Short Rate
SR.............. Short Run [*Economics*]
SR.............. Shutdown Request [*NASA*]   (KSC)
SR.............. Side Rails [*On a bed*] [*Medicine*]
SR.............. Sigma Reaction
SR.............. Signor [*Mister*] [*Italy*]
SR.............. Silicon Rectifier
SR.............. Silicon Rubber
SR.............. Simulation Report
SR.............. Single Reduction
SR.............. Sinus Rhythm [*Medicine*]
SR.............. Sinus Roris [*Bay of Dew*] [*Lunar area*]
SR.............. Sir
SR.............. Sister
SR.............. Skeleton Records [*Army*]
SR.............. Skywave Synchronization   (DEN)
SR.............. Slant Range
SR.............. Slave River Journal [*Fort Smith, Northwest Territory*] [*A publication*]
SR.............. Slavonic Review [*A publication*]
SR.............. Slew Rate
SR.............. Slip Ring [*Electricity*]
SR.............. Sloane Ranger [*Member of a British social set satirized in "The Official Sloane Ranger Handbook, The First Guide to What Really Matters in Life"*] [*Name is derived from Sloane Square in Chelsea*]
SR.............. Slovenska Rec [*A publication*]
SR.............. Slow Release [*Electronics*]
SR.............. Small Ring
SR.............. Social Register
SR.............. Social Research [*A publication*]
SR.............. Socialist Revolutionary [*USSR*]
SR.............. Society of Rheology [*Later, SoR*]   (EA)
SR.............. Society of Rosicrucians   (EA)
SR.............. Sociologia Religiosa [*A publication*]
SR.............. Solar Radiation
SR.............. Solar Reference
SR.............. Solicitor's Recommendation [*Internal Revenue Bureau*] [*United States*]   (DLA)
SR.............. Solid Rocket
SR.............. Soluble, Repository [*With reference to penicillin*]
SR.............. Soror [*Sister*]
SR.............. Sorter Reader
SR.............. Sortie Rate   (MCD)
SR.............. Sound Ranging
SR.............. Sound Rating   (IEEE)
SR.............. Sound Recordings [*US Copyright Office class*]
SR.............. Sound Report
SR.............. Source Range [*Nuclear energy*]   (NRCH)
SR.............. Southern Railway Co. [*NYSE symbol*]
SR.............. Southern Review [*US*] [*A publication*]
SR.............. Southern Rhodesia [*Later, Zimbabwe*]
SR.............. Southern Rhodesia High Court Reports   (DLA)
SR.............. Southwest Review [*A publication*]
SR.............. Spares Requirement
SR.............. Special Register
SR.............. Special Regulations [*Military*]
SR.............. Special Report
SR.............. Special Reserve
SR.............. Specific Range
SR.............. Specification Requirement
SR.............. Speech Recognition
SR.............. Speed Recorder   (IEEE)
SR.............. Speed Regulator
SR.............. Spelling Reform   (ADA)
SR.............. Split Ring [*Technical drawings*]
SR.............. Spontaneous Discharge Rate [*Audiology*]
S/R............. Spotter Reconnaissance [*Air Force*] [*British*]
SR.............. Square [*Ship's rigging*]   (ROG)
SR.............. Stable Recipient [*Medicine*]
SR.............. Staff Report
SR.............. Stage of Resistance [*in General-Adaptation Syndrome*]
SR.............. Stage Right [*A stage direction*]
SR.............. Standard Range Approach [*Aviation*]
SR.............. Standard Repair   (AAG)
SR.............. Standard Requirement
SR.............. Standardization Report

SR.............. Star Route [*A type of rural postal delivery route*]
SR.............. Starting Relay   (DEN)
SR.............. State Register
SR.............. Statement of Requirements   (MCD)
SR.............. Stateroom   (MSA)
SR.............. Station Radio [*British*]
SR.............. Station Regulation
SR.............. Stationery Request   (MCD)
SR.............. Statistical Reporter [*Manila*] [*A publication*]
SR.............. Statstjanstemannens Riksforbund [*National Association of Salaried Employees in Government Service*] [*Sweden*]
SR.............. Status Register
SR.............. Status Report
SR.............. Status Review [*NASA*]   (NASA)
SR.............. Statutes Revised   (DLA)
SR.............. Statutory Rule   (ADA)
SR.............. Steep Rock Resources, Inc. [*Toronto Stock Exchange symbol*]
sr .... Steradian [*Symbol*] [*SI unit of solid angle*]
SR.............. Stereo Review [*A publication*]
SR.............. Steroid Receptor [*Endocrinology*]
S-R............. Stimulus-Response
SR.............. Stock Replacement   (AAG)
SR.............. Stock Report
SR.............. Storage Register
SR.............. Storage and Repair   (MCD)
S & R......... Storage and Retrieval [*Data processing*]
SR.............. Storage Room
SR.............. Stove or Range
S & R......... Stowage and Repair
SR.............. Strategic Research   (MCD)
SR.............. Stress-Rupture   (MCD)
SR.............. Strike Rate   (ADA)
Sr .... Strontium [*Chemical element*]
Sr .... Strouhal Number [*IUPAC*]
SR.............. Studia Rosenthaliana [*Assen*] [*A publication*]
SR.............. Studies in Religion [*A publication*]
SR.............. Studies and Reports. Ben-Zvi Institute [*Jerusalem*] [*A publication*]
SR.............. Studies in Romanticism [*A publication*]
SR.............. Study Regulation   (MCD)
SR.............. Study Requirement [*Air Force*]
SR.............. Styrene Rubber
SR.............. Su Remesa [*Your Remittance*] [*Business and trade*] [*Spanish*]
SR.............. Subject Ratio
SR.............. Subroutine [*Data processing*]   (AAG)
SR.............. Subscriber Register
SR.............. Sugar Requirements and Quotas
SR.............. Sulfonamide-Resistant [*Microbiology*]
SR.............. Summary Report
SR.............. Sunrise [*Meteorology*]   (FAAC)
SR.............. Supervisor   (TEL)
SR.............. Supplemental Report
SR.............. Supplementary Regulation
SR.............. Supply Room
SR.............. Support Reaction Load   (NRCH)
SR.............. Support Request [*or Requirement*]   (KSC)
SR.............. Support Room   (MCD)
SR.............. Supporting Research
SR.............. Supreme Court of Quebec, Reports   (DLA)
sr .... Surinam [*MARC country of publication code*] [*Library of Congress*]   (LCCP)
SR.............. Surinam [*Two-letter standard code*]   (CNC)
SR.............. Surveillance RADAR [*Air Force*]
SR.............. Surveying Recorder [*Navy rating*] [*British*]
SR.............. Sustained Release [*Pharmacy*]
SR.............. Sveriges Radio
SR.............. Swissair [*Airline*] [*ICAO designator*]
SR.............. Switch Register
SR.............. Synchrotron Radiation [*High-energy physics*]
SR.............. Systems Review [*Medicine*]
SR-11 .... Sapporo Rat (Virus)
SRA............ Sair Aviation [*Syracuse, NY*] [*FAA designator*]   (FAAC)
SRA............ San Ramon [*Costa Rica*] [*Seismograph station code, US Geological Survey*]   (SEIS)
SRA............ Saskatchewan Archives, Regina, Saskatchewan [*Library symbol*] [*National Library of Canada*]   (NLC)
SRA............ Saturday Review of the Arts [*A publication*]
SRA............ Science Research Associates, Inc. [*Chicago, IL*] [*Software manufacturer*]
SRA............ Screw Research Association   (EA)
SRA............ Selective Restricted Availability   (MCD)
SRA............ Self-Regulatory Agency [*Securities*] [*British*]
SRA............ Senior Residential Appraiser [*Designation awarded by Society of Real Estate Appraisers*]
SRA............ Service and Regulatory Announcement, Department of Agriculture   (DLA)
SRA............ Servicemen's Readjustment Act
SRA............ Ship Radio Authorization [*Army*]   (AABC)
SRA............ Ship Replaceable Assembly   (MCD)
SRA............ Shipyard Restricted Availability [*Navy*]   (CAAL)

SRA .... Shop-Replaceable Assembly [*NASA*]
SRA .... Short-Range Acquisition   (MCD)
SRA .... Short Reflex Arc
SRA .... Simultaneous Range Adcock Antenna [*Military RADAR*]
SRA .... Small, Replaceable Assembly   (RDA)
SRA .... Social Research and Applications [*Missoula, MT*] [*Research center*]   (RCD)
SRA .... Society of Research Administrators   (EA)
SRA .... Society of Residential Appraisers [*Later, SREA*]
SRA .... Society for Risk Analysis [*McLean, VA*]   (EA)
SRA .... Sociological Research Association
SRA .... Southern Rural Action, Inc.
SRA .... Spanish Refugee Aid [*New York, NY*]   (EA)
SRA .... Special Refractories Association [*Defunct*]   (EA)
SRA .... Special Repair Activity   (MCD)
SRA .... Special Rules Area
SRA .... Specialized Repair Activity
SRA .... Spin Reference Axis   (KSC)
SRA .... Standards of Readiness and Availability   (NATG)
SRA .... Station Representatives Association [*New York, NY*]   (EA)
SRA .... Stock Record Account   (AFM)
SRA .... Strand Oil & Gas Ltd. [*Toronto Stock Exchange symbol*]
SRA .... Structures Research Associates
SRA .... Subminiature Rotary Actuator
SRA .... Sugar Rationing Administration [*Department of Agriculture*] [*Ceased functions, 1948*]
SRA .... Sulforicinoleic Acid [*Organic chemistry*]
SRA .... Sun's Right Ascension [*Astrology*]   (ROG)
SRA .... Supplemental Retirement Annuities
SRA .... Support Requirements Analysis [*NASA*]   (NASA)
SRA .... Surgeon Rear-Admiral [*British*]
SRA .... Surveillance RADAR Approach
SRA .... Syria. Revue d'Art Oriental et d'Archeologie [*A publication*]
SRA .... System Reaction Analysis [*Bell System*]
SRA .... System Requirements Analysis
SRAA .... Scholastic Rowing Association of America   (EA)
SRAA .... Senior Army Advisor   (AABC)
SRAAG ...... Senior Army Advisor, Army National Guard   (AABC)
SRAAM ..... Short-Range Air-to-Air Missile   (MCD)
SRAAR ...... Senior Army Advisor, Army Reserve   (AABC)
SRAB .... Allan Blair Memorial Clinic, Regina, Saskatchewan [*Library symbol*] [*National Library of Canada*]   (NLC)
SRAC .... Alcoholism Commission of Saskatchewan, Regina, Saskatchewan [*Library symbol*] [*National Library of Canada*]   (NLC)
SRAC .... Safe Return Amnesty Committee   (EA)
SRAC .... Sears Roebuck Acceptance Corporation
SRAC .... Short Run Average Costs
SrAcftCrmnBad ... Senior Aircraft Crewman Badge [*Military decoration*]   (AABC)
SR-ACK ..... Service Request Acknowledgment [*Air Force*]   (CET)
SR/AD .... Supporting Research and Advanced Development
SRAE .... Solar Radio Astronomy Experiment
SRAEL .... Labour Market Planning and Information Resource Centre, Saskatchewan Department of Advanced Education and Manpower, Regina, Saskatchewan [*Library symbol*] [*National Library of Canada*]   (NLC)
SRAEN ...... Systeme de Reference pour la Determination de l'Affaiblissement Equivalent pour la Nettete [*Master telephone transmission reference system*]   (DEN)
SRAEW ...... Women's Services Branch, Saskatchewan Department of Advanced Education and Manpower, Regina, Saskatchewan [*Library symbol*] [*National Library of Canada*]   (NLC)
SRAF .... Archibald Foundation, Regina, Saskatchewan [*Library symbol*] [*National Library of Canada*]   (NLC)
SRAF .... Social Revolutionary Anarchist Federation   (EA)
SRAF .... Standby Reserve of the Armed Forces
SRAG .... Saskatchewan Department of Agriculture, Regina, Saskatchewan [*Library symbol*] [*National Library of Canada*]   (NLC)
SRAG .... Semiactive RADAR Antiair Guidance System
SRAGE ...... Economics Branch, Agriculture Canada [*Direction de l'Economie, Agriculture Canada*] Regina, Saskatchewan [*Library symbol*] [*National Library of Canada*]   (NLC)
SRAGR ...... Research Station, Agriculture Canada [*Station de Recherches, Agriculture Canada*] Regina, Saskatchewan [*Library symbol*] [*National Library of Canada*]   (NLC)
SRAI .... Soybean Research Advisory Institute [*Terminated, 1984*]   (EGAO)
SRAI .... Supercat Race Association International [*Mahtomedi, MN*]   (EA)
SRA-J Soc R ... SRA - Journal of the Society of Research Administrators [*A publication*]
SRAM .... Semirandom Access Memory
SRAM .... Short-Range Attack Missile [*Navy*]
SRAM .... Skill Qualification Test Requirements Alert Message
SRAM .... Some Remarks on Abstract Machines [*Data processing*]
SRAM .... Static Random Access Memory [*Data processing*]
SRAN .... Short-Range Aids to Navigation [*Navy*]
SRAN .... Skill Qualification Test Requirements Alert Notice

SRAN .... Stock Record Account Number   (AFM)
SRANA ...... Shrine Recorders Association of North America   (EA)
SRANC .... Southern Rhodesia African National Congress
SRAO .... Supplemental Recreational Activities Overseas [*Red Cross*]
SRAP .... Service Record and Allied Papers
SRAP .... Slow Response Action Potentials [*Neurophysiology*]
SRAP .... Standard Range Approach [*Aviation*]
SRARAV ..... Senior Army Aviator   (AABC)
Sr Ar Av Bad ... Senior Army Aviator Badge [*Military decoration*]
SRARM .... Short-Range Antiradiation Missile
SR Arts ...... Saturday Review of the Arts [*A publication*]
SRAS .... Albert South Library, Regina, Saskatchewan [*Library symbol*] [*National Library of Canada*]   (NLC)
SRAT .... Search RADAR Alignment Test [*Military*]   (CAAL)
SRAT .... Short-Range Applied Technology
SRATC .... Short-Run Average Total Cost [*Economics*]
SRATS .... Solar Radiation and Thermospheric Structure [*Japanese satellite*]
SRATUC ..... Southern Rhodesian African Trade Union Congress
Sr Autobahn ... Strasse und Autobahn [*A publication*]
SRAVC .... Short-Run Average Variable Costs [*Economics*]
SRaw .... Specific Resistance, Airway [*Medicine*]
SRAX .... Southern Air Transport, Inc. [*Air carrier designation symbol*]
SRAZ .... Studia Romanica et Anglica Zagrabiensia [*A publication*]
SRB .... Safety Review Board   (NRCH)
SRB .... Schilpp, Reed B., Los Angeles CA [*STAC*]
SRB .... Scurry-Rainbow Oil Ltd. [*American Stock Exchange symbol*]
SRB .... Seaplane Repair Base
SRB .... Selective Reenlistment Bonus [*Military*]   (AABC)
SRB .... Self-Retaining Bolt
SRB .... Service Record Book [*Military*]
SRB .... Service Request Block [*Data processing*]   (BUR)
SRB .... Sheftall Record Book [*A publication*]   (BJA)
SRB .... Sky Ranch for Boys [*Sky Ranch, SD*]   (EA)
SRB .... Solar Reflectory Beacon
SRB .... Solid-Rocket Booster [*NASA*]
SRB .... Sorter Reader Buffer
SRB .... Sparta, TN [*Location identifier*] [*FAA*]   (FAAL)
SRB .... Special Review Board [*Military*]   (INF)
SRB .... Spherical Roller Bearing
SRB .... State Research Bureau [*Secret police*] [*Uganda*]
SRB .... Styrene Rubber Butadiene   (NG)
SRB .... Support Research Branch [*Springfield Armory*]
SRB .... System Review Board   (MCD)
SRBA .... Students for the Right to Bear Arms   (EA)
SRBAB .... Solid-Rocket Booster Assembly Building [*NASA*]   (NASA)
SRBC .... Serum-Treated Red Blood Cell [*Clinical chemistry*]
SRBC .... Sheep Red Blood Cell[*s*] [*Also, SRC*]
SRBC .... Susquehanna River Basin Compact [*Maryland, Pennsylvania, New York*]
SRBDF .... Solid-Rocket Booster Disassembly Building [*NASA*]   (NASA)
SRBE .... Societe Royale Belge des Electriciens [*Belgium*]   (MCD)
SRBM .... Short-Range Ballistic Missile
SRBMI .... BMI Finance, Regina, Saskatchewan [*Library symbol*] [*National Library of Canada*]   (NLC)
SRBOC ...... Super Rapid Bloom Off Board Chaff [*Navy*]   (NVT)
SRBT .... Single-Rod Burst Test [*Nuclear energy*]   (NRCH)
SRBUC ...... Scientific Research in British Universities and Colleges [*Later, RBUPC*] [*British Library*]
SRC .... AMF Sunfish Racing Class Association   (EA)
SRC .... Richland County Library, Columbia, SC [*OCLC symbol*]   (OCLC)
SRC .... Sacra Rituum Congregatio [*Sacred Congregation of Rites*] [*Latin*]
SRC .... Safety Research Center [*Bureau of Mines*]
SRC .... Salinas Road [*California*] [*Seismograph station code, US Geological Survey*]   (SEIS)
SRC .... Sample Recovery Container [*NASA*]   (KSC)
SRC .... Sample Rock Container [*NASA*]
SRC .... Sarcoma
SRC .... Saskatchewan Research Council [*University of Saskatchewan*] [*Research center*]   (RCD)
SRC .... Saturable Reactor Coil
SRC .... Scheduled Removal Component   (MCD)
SRC .... Science Research Council [*Later, SERC*] [*British*]
SRC .... Scleroderma Renal Crisis [*Medicine*]
SRC .... Scott's Hospitality, Inc. [*Toronto Stock Exchange symbol*]
SRC .... Se Ruega Contestacion [*The Favor of a Reply Is Requested*] [*Spanish*]
SRC .... Searcy, AR [*Location identifier*] [*FAA*]   (FAAL)
SRC .... Secured Returns Code [*IRS*]
SRC .... Securities Research Company
SRC .... Semiconductor Research Cooperative
SRC .... Senate Rail Caucus   (EA)
S/RC .... Send/Receive Center   (FAAC)
SRC .... Send Register Control [*Data processing*]
SRC .... Servants of Our Lady Queen of the Clergy [*Roman Catholic women's religious order*]
SRC .... Service Resources Corporation [*NYSE symbol*]
SRC .... Sheep Red Cell[*s*] [*Also, SRBC*]
SRC .... Shutdown Reactor Cooling   (NRCH)

SRC............ Signal Reserve Corps
SRC............ Silicon Readout Cell
SRC............ Silicon Rectifier Column
SRC............ Ski Retailers Council [*New York, NY*] (EA)
SRC............ Slow-Recovery Capsules [*Pharmacy*]
SRC............ Social Rehabilitation Clinic [*New York, NY*] (EA)
SRC............ Societe Royale du Canada [*Royal Society of Canada - RSC*]
SRC............ Solvent-Refined Coal
SRC............ Sound Ranging Control
SRC............ Sound Recording Company [*Record label*]
SRC............ Source Range Channel (IEEE)
SRC............ Southeast Asia Resource Center (EA)
SRC............ Southern Regional Council (EA)
SRC............ Southwest Radio Church [*An association*]
SRC............ Southwest Research Corporation
SRC............ Space Research Council [*British*]
SRC............ Spares Receiving Checklist (NRCH)
SRC............ Special Regular Commissions [*Army*] [*British*]
SRC............ Specific Reactant Consumption [*Engine*]
SRC............ Speech Recognition Computer
SRC............ Standard Requirements Code [*Military*]
SRC............ Standards Review Committee [*American Occupational Therapy Association*]
SRC............ Station Reliability Coordinator
SRC............ Sterility Research Center [*Public Health Service*]
SRC............ Stock Record Card [*Military*]
SRC............ Strasburg Railroad Company [*AAR code*]
SRC............ Stray Radiation Chamber
SRC............ Stuart's Lower Canada Reports (DLA)
SRC............ Studies in Religion: A Canadian Journal [*A publication*]
SRC............ Subject-Field Reference Code (ADA)
SRC............ Submarine Rescue Chamber (MCD)
SRC............ Support Review Code (MCD)
SRC............ Survey Research Center [*University of Kentucky*] [*Research center*] (RCD)
SRC............ Survey Research Center [*Oregon State University*] [*Research center*] (RCD)
SRC............ Sustained-Release Capsule [*Pharmacology*]
SRC............ Swiss Red Cross
SRC............ Synchronous Remote Control
SRC............ Synchrotron Radiation Center [*University of Wisconsin - Madison*] [*Research center*] (RCD)
SRC............ Syracuse Research Corporation [*New York*] [*Information service*] (EISS)
SRC............ Systems Release Certification [*Social Security Administration*]
SRC............ Systems Research Configuration
SRCA........ Saskatchewan Department of Consumer Affairs, Regina, Saskatchewan [*Library symbol*] [*National Library of Canada*] (NLC)
SRCA........ Slovenian Research Center of America [*Willoughby Hills, OH*] (EA)
SRCA........ Specific Red Cell Adherence [*Test*] [*Clinical chemistry*]
SRCAS...... Safety-Related Control Air System (NRCH)
SRCB........ Canadian Bible College, Regina, Saskatchewan [*Library symbol*] [*National Library of Canada*] (NLC)
SRCB........ Software Requirements Change Board [*NASA*] (NASA)
SRCBD...... Software Requirements Change Board Directive [*NASA*] (NASA)
SRCC........ Senior Control Center [*Air Force*]
SRCC........ Sensor Referenced and Computer Controlled [*For remote manipulators*]
SRCC........ Simplex Remote Communications Central
SR & CC.... Strikes, Riots, and Civil Commotions [*Insurance*]
SRCC........ Strikes, Riots, and Civil Commotions [*Insurance*]
SRCD........ Set-Reset Clocked Data [*Data processing*]
SRCD........ Society for Research in Child Development (EA)
SRCE........ First Source Corp. [*NASDAQ symbol*] (NQ)
SR-CEF..... Schmidt-Ruppin Chick Embryo Fibroblast[*s*]
SRCH........ Search (AAG)
SRCH........ Search Natural Resources [*NASDAQ symbol*] (NQ)
SRCI.......... Safety-Related Controls and Instrumentation (NRCH)
SRCI.......... Survey Research Consultants International, Inc. [*Information service*] [*Williamstown, MA*] (EISS)
SRCL.......... Security Requirements Check List (MCD)
SRCM........ Savonius Rotor Current Meter
SRCM........ Sisters of Reparation of the Congregation of Mary [*Roman Catholic religious order*]
SRCNET..... Science and Engineering Research Council Network [*Later, SERCNET*]
SRCP......... Short Range Construction Program [*Military*]
SRCP......... Society of Retired Catholic Persons (EA)
SRCP......... Special Reserve Components Program
SRCR......... SONAR Control Room
SRCR......... Stability Regulated Controlled Rectifier
SRCR......... System Run Control Record
SRCRC...... Snake River Conservation Research Center [*University of Idaho*] [*Research center*] (RCD)
SRCS......... Sustancia. Revista de Cultura Superior [*A publication*]
SRCT.......... Standard Recovery Completion Time
SRCU......... Credit Union Central, Regina, Saskatchewan [*Library symbol*] [*National Library of Canada*] (NLC)

SRCU........ Secretary's Records Correspondence Unit [*Department of Labor*]
SRD............ San Andres [*Colombia*] [*Seismograph station code, US Geological Survey*] (SEIS)
SRD............ Satellite Racing Development [*British*]
SRD............ Scheduled Release Date (MCD)
SRD............ Secret - Restricted Data [*Security classification*]
SRD............ Seldom Reaches Destination
SRD............ Selective Radiation Detector
SRD............ Self-Reading Dosimeter (IEEE)
SRD............ Serous Retinal Detachment [*Ophthalmology*]
SRD............ Service Revealed Deficiency [*or Difficulty*]
SRD............ Shift Register Drive
S-RD.......... Shipper-Receiver Difference (NRCH)
SRD............ Shuttle Requirements Definition [*NASA*] (NASA)
SRD............ Shuttle Requirements Document [*NASA*] (NASA)
SRD............ Single Radial Diffusion [*or Immunodiffusion*] [*Analytical biochemistry*]
SRD............ Small Rigid Dome
SRD............ Society for the Relief of Distress [*British*]
SRD............ Society for the Right to Die [*New York, NY*] (EA)
SRD............ Software Requirements Document [*Data processing*]
SRD............ Special Research Detachment [*Army*]
SRD............ Stafford Road [*Wolverhampton*] [*British depot code*]
SRD............ [*The*] Standard Oil Co. [*NYSE symbol*]
SRD............ Standard Reference Data
SRD............ Standard Repair Design [*Navy*] (MCD)
SRD............ Standard Reporting Designator (MCD)
SRD............ State Registered Dietitian
SRD............ Statistical Research Division [*Census*] (OICC)
SRD............ Step Recovery Diode
SRD............ Sutherland Resources [*Vancouver Stock Exchange symbol*]
SRD............ Systems Requirement Document
Srd .... Thiouridine [*Also, S, SU*] [*A nucleoside*]
SRDA .... Dunlop Art Gallery, Regina, Saskatchewan [*Library symbol*] [*National Library of Canada*] (NLC)
SRDA .... Search RADAR Designation Alignment (MCD)
SRDA .... Sodium Removal Development Apparatus [*Nuclear energy*] (NRCH)
SRDAS...... Service Recording and Data Analysis System (IEEE)
SRDC .... Standard Reference Data Center
SRDE .... Signals Research and Development Establishment [*British*]
SRDE .... Smallest Replaceable Defective Element
SRDG .... Software Research and Development Group [*University of Calgary*] [*Research center*] (RCD)
SRDH .... Subsystems Requirements Definition Handbook [*NASA*] (NASA)
SRDI.......... Safety-Related Display Instrumentation (NRCH)
SRDL........ Saskatchewan Department of Labour, Regina, Saskatchewan [*Library symbol*] [*National Library of Canada*] (NLC)
SRDL........ Signals Research and Development Laboratory [*Army*] [*British*]
SRDM........ Subrate Data Multiplexer [*Telecommunications*] (TEL)
SRDS........ Shop Repair Data Sheets
SRDS........ Single Requirements Determination System
SRDS........ Standard Rate and Data Service, Inc. [*Wilmette, IL*] (MCD)
SRDS........ Standard Reference Data System (DIT)
SRDS........ Systems Research and Development Service [*FAA*] (MCD)
SRDT........ Single Rotating Directional Transmission [*Military*] (CAAL)
SRE............ Sancta Romana Ecclesia [*Most Holy Roman Church*] [*Latin*]
SRE............ Sanctae Romanae Ecclesiae [*Of the Most Holy Roman Church*] [*Latin*]
SRE............ Saskatchewan Department of the Environment, Regina, Saskatchewan [*Library symbol*] [*National Library of Canada*] (NLC)
SRE............ Saturday Review of Education [*A publication*]
SRE............ Schedule of Recent Experience [*Psychometrics*]
SRe............ Science Review [*Manila*] [*A publication*]
SRE............ Seminole, OK [*Location identifier*] [*FAA*] (FAAL)
SRE............ Send Reference Equivalent, Search RADAR [*Telecommunications*] (TEL)
SRE............ Series Relay [*Electronics*]
SRE............ Shelby's Rabbit Eater [*In model name Omni SRE, proposed for Dodge car designed by Carroll Shelby*]
SRE............ Signaling Range Extender [*Telecommunications*] (TEL)
SRE............ Single Region Execution
SRE............ Single Round Effectiveness (NATG)
SRE............ Single Rural Eligible [*Classified advertising*]
SRE............ Site Resident Engineer [*Telecommunications*] (TEL)
SRE............ Society of Relay Engineers [*British*]
SRE............ Society of Reliability Engineers (EA)
SRE............ Society of Reproduction Engineers [*Later, IAVCM*] (EA)
SRE............ Sodium Reactor Experiment
SRE............ Sound Reproduction Equipment (DEN)
SRE............ Special Re-Education
SRE............ Srednekan [*USSR*] [*Later, MGD*] [*Geomagnetic observatory code*]
SRE............ Standard RADAR Environment
SRE............ Statistical Reporter [*A publication*]
SRE............ Stray Radiant Energy
SRE............ Sucre [*Bolivia*] [*Airport symbol*] (OAG)
SRE............ Surveillance RADAR Element

SREA.......... Senior Real Estate Analyst [*Designation awarded by Society of Real Estate Appraisers*]
SREA.......... Society of Real Estate Appraisers [*Chicago, IL*] (EA)
SREA.......... Street Rod Equipment Association [*Whittier, CA*] (EA)
SREAE....... AES Regina Weather Office, Environment Canada [*Bureau Meteorologique du SEA de Regina, Environnement Canada*] Saskatchewan [*Library symbol*] [*National Library of Canada*] (NLC)
SREB.......... Southern Regional Educational Board
SREC.......... Executive Council, Regina, Saskatchewan [*Library symbol*] [*National Library of Canada*] (NLC)
SREC.......... Southern Rice Export Corporation (EA)
SRED.......... Saskatchewan Department of Education, Regina, Saskatchewan [*Library symbol*] [*National Library of Canada*] (NLC)
SREEP....... Environmental Protection Service, Environment Canada [*Service de la Protection de l'Environnement, Environnement Canada*] Regina, Saskatchewan [*Library symbol*] [*National Library of Canada*] (NLC)
SREG .... Standard Register Co. [*NASDAQ symbol*] (NQ)
SREG .... Standing Register [*Civil Service*]
SREI .... Student Role Expectation Inventory
SREIW .... Inland Waters Directorate, Environment Canada [*Direction Generale des Eaux Interieures, Environnement Canada*] Regina, Saskatchewan [*Library symbol*] [*National Library of Canada*] (NLC)
SREL .... Savannah River Ecology Laboratory [*Energy Research and Development Administration*] [*Aiken, SC*]
SREL .... Space Radiation Effects Laboratory [*Langley, VA*] [*NASA*]
S-REM....... Sleep with Rapid Eye Movement
SREM .... Software Requirements Engineering Methodology
SREM .... Sound Ranging Evaluation Model (MCD)
SRen .... Studies in the Renaissance [*A publication*]
S Rep .... Senate Reports (DLA)
S Rep .... Southern Reporter (DLA)
SREPT....... Senate Committee Report (AFIT)
SRES.......... Senate Resolution (AFIT)
SRES.......... Senores [*Sirs, Gentlemen*] [*Spanish*]
SRES.......... Sierra Resources [*NASDAQ symbol*] (NQ)
SRES.......... Southern Railway Employees' Sangh [*India*]
S Res .... United States Senate Resolution (DLA)
SRET.......... Satellite de Recherches et d'Environment Technique [*Satellite for Environmental and Technical Research*] [*France*]
SRev.......... School Review [*A publication*]
SRev.......... Slavic Review [*A publication*]
SRev.......... Southwest Review [*A publication*]
S Rev (Adel) ... Southern Review (Adelaide) [*A publication*]
S Rev (Baton) ... Southern Review (Baton Rouge) [*A publication*]
SRF .... S-Band Receiver Filter
SRF .... Salmonellosis-Resistance Factor
SRF .... Sam Rayburn Foundation
SRF .... San Rafael, CA [*Location identifier*] [*FAA*] (FAAL)
SRF .... Scleroderma Research Foundation [*Columbus, NJ*] (EA)
SRF .... Seal Rescue Fund (EA)
SRF .... Secure Reserve Forces [*Military*] (MCD)
SRF .... Selected Reserve Force [*Units*] [*of Army National Guard*] [*Discontinued, 1969*]
SR & F .... Selection, Referral, and Followup
SRF .... Self-Realization Fellowship (EA)
SRF .... Self-Referenced Fringe (MCD)
SRF .... Self-Resonant Frequency
SRF .... Semireinforced Furnace
SRF .... Ship Repair Facility [*Navy*] (NVT)
SRF .... Shuttle Refurbish Facility [*NASA*] (NASA)
SRF .... Sido, Robert F., Edwardsville IL [*STAC*]
SRF .... Skin Reactive Factor [*Immunochemistry*]
SRF .... Skin Respiratory Factor [*Physiology*]
SRF .... Slovak Relief Fund (EA)
SRF .... Snake Ranch Flats [*New Mexico*] [*Seismograph station code, US Geological Survey*] [*Closed*] (SEIS)
SRF .... Software Recording Facility
SRF .... Software Recovery Facility [*Data processing*] (IBMDP)
SRF .... Solar Radiation Flux
SRF .... Somatotrophin-Releasing Factor [*Endocrinology*]
SRF .... Sorter Reader Flow
SRF .... Space Requirement Forms (AAG)
SRF .... Spacecraft Research Foundation [*Inactive*] (EA)
SRF .... Special Reporting Facility [*Department of State*]
SRF .... Stable Radio Frequency
SRF .... Strategic Reserve Forces (MCD)
SRF .... Strategic Retaliatory Forces (AAG)
SRF .... Strategic Rocket Forces (MCD)
SRF .... Submarine Range-Finder
SRF .... Submarine Repair Facility
SRF .... Sun River Gold Corp. [*Vancouver Stock Exchange symbol*]
SRF .... Supported Ring Frame
SRF .... Surface Roughness Factor [*Telecommunications*] (TEL)
SRF .... Survival Research Foundation (EA)
SRF .... System Recovery Factor
SRFB.......... Space Research Facilities Branch [*National Research Council of Canada*]

SRFD.......... Society for the Rehabilitation of the Facially Disfigured [*Later, National Foundation for Facial Reconstruction*] [*New York, NY*] (EA)
SRFF .... Set-Reset Flip-Flop [*Data processing*]
SRFI .... Self-Rising Flour Institute [*Later, SFCMP*]
SRFI .... Sugar Research Foundation, Incorporated [*Later, ISRF*] (EA)
SRFI .... Super Rite Foods, Incorporated [*NASDAQ symbol*] (NQ)
SrFltSurgBad ... Senior Flight Surgeon Badge [*Military decoration*] (AABC)
SRFM .... Source Range Flux Monitoring (NRCH)
SRFTL .... Secure Resource Force Target List (MCD)
SRG.......... Regina General Hospital, Saskatchewan [*Library symbol*] [*National Library of Canada*] (NLC)
SRG.......... Santa Sarita Mining [*Vancouver Stock Exchange symbol*]
SRG.......... Schering-Plough Corp. [*Research code symbol*]
SRG.......... Schriften der Raabe-Gesellschaft [*A publication*]
SRG.......... Semarang [*Indonesia*] [*Airport symbol*] (OAG)
SRG.......... Servomotor Rate Generator
SRG.......... Short Range (FAAC)
SRG.......... Sine-Random Generator
SRG.......... Social Research Group [*George Washington University*] [*Research center*] (RCD)
SRG.......... Society of Remedial Gymnasts (EA)
SRG.......... Sorg, Inc. [*American Stock Exchange symbol*]
SRG.......... Sound Ranging
SRG.......... Statistical Research Group [*Princeton University*] (MCD)
SRG.......... Stimulated Raman Gain [*Spectroscopy*]
SRG.......... Surge (MSA)
SRG.......... System Routing Guide [*Military*] (CAAL)
SRG.......... Systems Research Group (CINC)
SRGA .... Stable Reactor, General, Atomic
SRGD .... Gabriel Dumont Institute, Regina, Saskatchewan [*Library symbol*] [*National Library of Canada*] (NLC)
SRGE .... Saskatchewan Government Employees Association, Regina, Saskatchewan [*Library symbol*] [*National Library of Canada*] (NLC)
SRGH .... Pasqua Hospital, Regina, Saskatchewan [*Library symbol*] [*National Library of Canada*] (NLC)
SRGI.......... Saskatchewan Government Insurance, Regina, Saskatchewan [*Library symbol*] [*National Library of Canada*] (NLC)
SRGM........ Super Rapid Gun Mounting [*Military*]
SRGMF...... Santa Sarita Mining [*NASDAQ symbol*] (NQ)
SRGR .... Short-Range Guided Rocket
SRGS .... St. Rosalie Generating Station (NRCH)
SRGS .... Saskatchewan Genealogical Society, Regina, Saskatchewan [*Library symbol*] [*National Library of Canada*] (NLC)
SRGS .... Survivable Radio Guidance System [*Military*]
SRGY .... American Surgery Centers Corp. [*NASDAQ symbol*] (NQ)
SRH .... Secretaria de Recursos Hidraulicos [*Mexico*]
SRH .... Sequential Rough Handling (MCD)
SRH .... Single Radial Hemolysis [*Immunochemistry*]
SRH .... Smith, R. H., Minneapolis MN [*STAC*]
SRH .... [*A*] Social and Religious History of the Jews [*S. W. Baron*] [*A publication*] (BJA)
SRH .... Spontaneously Responding Hyperthyroidism [*Endocrinology*]
SRH .... Stigmata of Recent Hemorrhage [*Medicine*]
SRH .... Strathcona Resources Industries Ltd. [*Toronto Stock Exchange symbol*]
SRH .... Subsystems Requirements Handbook [*NASA*] (NASA)
SRH .... Supply Railhead
SRH .... Switchyard Relay House [*Nuclear energy*] (NRCH)
SRHB.......... Society for Research into Hydrocephalus and Spina Bifida (EA)
SRHC .... Shutdown Reactor Head Cooling (NRCH)
SR HCR ..... Southern Rhodesia High Court Reports [*1911-55*] (DLA)
SRHE .... Society for Religion in Higher Education [*Later, SVHE*] (EA)
SRHIT........ Small RADAR-Homing Interceptor Technology
SRHJ .... [*A*] Social and Religious History of the Jews [*S. W. Baron*] [*A publication*] (BJA)
SRHL .... Southwestern Radiological Health Laboratory [*HEW*]
S Rhodesia Geol Surv Bull ... Southern Rhodesia. Geological Survey Bulletin [*A publication*]
SRHP.......... Planning Branch, Saskatchewan Department of Highways and Transportation, Regina, Saskatchewan [*Library symbol*] [*National Library of Canada*] (NLC)
SRHP.......... Section for Rehabilitation Hospitals and Programs [*American Hospital Association*] [*Chicago, IL*] (EA)
SRHS.......... Health Sciences Library, Plains Health Centre, Regina, Saskatchewan [*Library symbol*] [*National Library of Canada*] (NLC)
SRHSB .... Society for Research into Hydrocephalus and Spina Bifida (EA)
SRI .... Sacrum Romanum Imperium [*The Holy Roman Empire*] [*Latin*]
SRI .... Samarinda [*Indonesia*] [*Airport symbol*] (OAG)
SRI .... Scholarly Resources, Incorporated, Wilmington, DE [*Library symbol*] [*Library of Congress*] (LCLS)
SRI .... Sefid-Roud [*Iran*] [*Seismograph station code, US Geological Survey*] (SEIS)
SRI .... Selective Retention Indicators (NVT)
SRI .... Senior Resident Inspector [*Nuclear energy*] (NRCH)
SRI .... Servo Repeater Indicator
SRI .... Severe Renal Insufficiency [*Medicine*]

SRI .... Signal Routing and Interface (MCD)
SRI .... Silicon Rubber Insulation
SRI .... Ski Retailers International (EA)
SRI .... Social Research Institute [*University of Utah*] [*Research center*] (RCD)
SRI .... Society for Rational Individualism [*Later, SIL*] (EA)
SRI .... Sorry [*Communications operator's procedural remark*]
SRI .... Southeastern Reservoir Investigation [*Department of the Interior*]
SRI .... Southern Research Institute
SRI .... Southwest Research Institute
SRI .... Space Research Institute [*Defunct*] (EA)
SRI .... Spalling Resistance Index (IEEE)
SRI .... Special Recreation, Incorporated [*Iowa City, IA*] (EA)
SRI .... Spectrum Resolver Integrator
SRI .... Spectrum Resources, Incorporated [*St. Charles, MO*] [*Telecommunications*] (TSSD)
SRI .... Speech Rehabilitation Institute (EA)
SRI .... Spring Research Institute (EA)
SRI .... Standard Research Institute (MCD)
SRI .... Standby Request for Information (AABC)
SRI .... Standing Request for Information (MCD)
SRI .... Stanford Research Institute [*Later, SRI International*] [*Databank originator*]
SRI .... Stick to Rudder Interconnect (MCD)
SRI .... Surface Roughness Indicator
SRI .... Sveriges Runinskrifter [*A publication*]
SRI .... Swiss Radio International
SRI .... Syllable Repetition Interval [*Entomology*]
SRIA .... Saskatchewan Intergovernmental Affairs, Regina, Saskatchewan [*Library symbol*] [*National Library of Canada*] (NLC)
SRIA .... State and Regional Indicators Archive [*University of New Hampshire*] [*Durham*] [*Information service*] (EISS)
SRIAER ...... Scientific Research Institute for Atomic Energy Reactors [*USSR*]
SRIB .... Strike Route Information Book [*Strategic Air Command*] (AABC)
SRIC .... Short-Run Incremental Costs (ADA)
SRIC .... Southwest Research and Information Center (EA)
SRIC .... SRI Corporation [*NASDAQ symbol*] (NQ)
SRID .... Search RADAR Input Device (MCD)
SRIELA ...... Selected Reports: Publication of the Institute of Ethnomusicology of the University of California at Los Angeles [*A publication*]
SRIF .... Somatotrophin-Releasing Inhibiting Factor [*Also, GH-RIF, GH-RIH, GRIF, SS*] [*Endocrinology*]
SRIF .... Special Risk Insurance Fund [*Federal Housing Administration*]
SRIFC .... Saskatchewan Indian Federated College, Regina, Saskatchewan [*Library symbol*] [*National Library of Canada*] (NLC)
SRIH .... Somatostatin [*Biochemistry*]
SRI J .... SRI [*Stanford Research Institute*] Journal [*A publication*]
Sri Lan J Hum ... Sri Lanka Journal of Humanities [*Peradeniya*] [*A publication*]
Sri Lanka Assoc Adv Sci Proc Annu Sess ... Sri Lanka Association for the Advancement of Science. Proceedings of the Annual Session [*A publication*]
Sri Lanka Geol Surv Dep Econ Bull ... Sri Lanka. Geological Survey Department. Economic Bulletin [*A publication*]
Sri Lanka Lab Gaz ... Sri Lanka Labour Gazette [*A publication*]
SRILTA ...... Stanford Research Institute Lead Time Analysis
SR-IM .... Office of Strategic Research, Intelligence Memoranda [*CIA*]
SRIM .... Selected Research in Microfiche [*National Technical Information Service*] (MCD)
SRIM .... Short-Range Intercept Missile (MCD)
SRIM .... Standing Order Microfiche Service
SRIP .... Selected Reserve Incentive Program [*Army*]
SRIP .... Ship Readiness Improvement Plan [*Navy*] (NG)
SRIP .... Short-Range Impact Point (MUGU)
SRIP .... Society for the Research and Investigation of Phenomena (EA-IO)
SRIP .... Specification Review and Improvement Program [*Navy*] (NG)
SRI Pestic Res Bull ... SRI [*Stanford Research Institute*] Pesticide Research Bulletin [*A publication*]
SRIS .... Safety Recommendation Information System [*Database*]
SRIS .... Safety Research Information Service [*National Safety Council*] [*Chicago, IL*] (EISS)
SRISP .... Interprovincial Steel & Pipe Corp. Ltd., (IPSCO), Regina, Saskatchewan [*Library symbol*] [*National Library of Canada*] (NLC)
SRISS .... Scientia: Revista Internazionale di Sintesi Scientifica [*A publication*]
SRIT .... Service and Repair Identification Tag (MCD)
SRJ............. San Borja [*Bolivia*] [*Airport symbol*] (OAG)
SRJ............. Self-Restraint Joint
SRJ............. Short Run Job (MCD)
SRJ............. Standard-Range Juno [*Survey meter for radiation*]
SRJ............. Static Round Jet

SRJC .... Communications Policy Branch, Saskatchewan Department of Justice, Regina, Saskatchewan [*Library symbol*] [*National Library of Canada*] (NLC)
SRJC .... Santa Rosa Junior College [*California*]
SRK .... Spirit Lake, IA [*Location identifier*] [*FAA*] (FAAL)
SRK .... Sredniy Kalar [*USSR*] [*Seismograph station code, US Geological Survey*] (SEIS)
SRK .... Stralak Resources [*Vancouver Stock Exchange symbol*]
SRKN .... Single Rotating Knife
SRL .... Legislative Library of Saskatchewan, Regina, Saskatchewan [*Library symbol*] [*National Library of Canada*] (NLC)
SRL .... Santa Rosalia [*Mexico*] [*Seismograph station code, US Geological Survey*] [*Closed*] (SEIS)
SRL .... Saturday Review of Literature [*A publication*]
SRL .... Savannah River Laboratory [*Energy Research and Development Administration*]
SRL .... Save-the-Redwoods League (EA)
SRL .... Sceptre Resources Limited [*American Stock Exchange symbol*] [*Toronto Stock Exchange symbol*]
SRL .... Schema Representation Language [*Artificial intelligence*]
SRL .... Scientific Research Laboratory (AAG)
SRL .... Screwworm Research Laboratory [*Department of Agriculture*]
SRL .... Seiler Research Laboratory [*Air Force*] (MCD)
SRL .... Singing Return Loss [*Telecommunications*] (TEL)
SRL .... Skin Resistance Level [*Physiology*]
SRL .... Society of Romance Linguistics (EA-IO)
SRL .... Sonobuoy Receiver Logic [*Navy*] (CAAL)
SRL .... Sound Reference Laboratory [*Orlando, FL*] [*Navy*]
SRL .... Spares Recommendation List (MCD)
SRL .... Stability Return Loss [*Telecommunications*] (TEL)
SRL .... Standard Reference Library
SRL .... Stress Relieving Liner (KSC)
SRL .... Structural Return Loss [*Telecommunications*] (TEL)
SRL .... Student Religious Liberals [*Later, SRL, A Free Religious Fellowship*] [*Defunct*]
SRL .... Study Reference List (AFM)
SRL .... Summary Requirements List (MCD)
SRL .... Support Requirements Letter (CET)
SRL .... Survey Research Laboratory [*University of Illinois*] [*Urbana*] [*Information service*] (EISS)
SRL .... Systems Research Laboratory
SRLC .... Luther College, Regina, Saskatchewan [*Library symbol*] [*National Library of Canada*] (NLC)
SRLD .... Small Rocket Lift Device
SRLF .... Saggi e Ricerche di Letteratura Francese [*A publication*]
SRLP .... Leader-Post Ltd., Regina, Saskatchewan [*Library symbol*] [*National Library of Canada*] (NLC)
SRLP .... Socialist and Revolutionary Labour Party [*Gambian*] (PD)
SRLR .... Securities Regulation and Law Report [*A publication*]
Sr LS .... Senior Life Saving [*Red Cross*]
SRLS .... Starved Rock Library System [*Library network*]
SRLY .... Series Relay (IEEE)
SRM .... Schedule Request Message (MCD)
SRM .... Scrim-Reinforced Material [*Nonwoven sheets*]
SRM .... Secretory Rate Maximum [*Physiology*]
SRM .... Sensor Response Model
SRM .... Service Repair Manual
SRM .... Shift Register Memory
SRM .... Ship Repair and Maintenance [*National Shipping Authority*]
SRM .... Short-Range Missile [*Projected; not to be confused with SRAM*]
SRM .... Short Range MODEM
SRM .... Single Register Machine
SRM .... Smokeless Rocket Motor (MCD)
SRM .... Snowmelt-Runoff Model [*Hydrology*]
SRM .... Society for Range Management
SRM .... Socorro - La Joya [*New Mexico*] [*Seismograph station code, US Geological Survey*] [*Closed*] (SEIS)
SRM .... Solid-Rocket Motor
SRM .... Source-Range Monitors (NRCH)
SRM .... Specific Repair Methods [*Boeing*]
SRM .... Specification Requirements Manual [*NASA*] (NASA)
SRM .... Speed of Relative Movement
SRM .... Spiritual Regeneration Movement [*Foundation of America*] (EA)
SRM .... Square Root Mode [*Data processing*]
SRM .... Standard Reference Material [*National Bureau of Standards*]
SRM .... Standard Reference Module
SRM .... Standard Repair Manual (MCD)
SRM .... Strategic Reconnaissance Missile
SRM .... Superior Rectus Muscle [*Eye anatomy*]
SRM .... System Resource Manager [*IBM Corp.*] (BUR)
SRM .... System for Resources Management [*Jet Propulsion Laboratory, NASA*]
SRMA .... Silk and Rayon Manufacturers Association [*Defunct*] (EA)
SRMC .... Society of Risk Management Consultants [*Formed by a merger of Insurance Consultants Society and Institute of Risk Management*] [*Baton Rouge, LA*] (EA)
SRMC .... Specification Requirements Manual (MCD)
SRMCASE ... Symmetry-Restricted-Multiconfiguration Annihilation of Single Excitations [*Physics*]

SRML .... Short-Range Missile Launcher
SRMP .... Supply Readiness Milestone Plan [*Military*] (CAAL)
SRMR .... Saskatchewan Department of Mineral Resources, Regina, Saskatchewan [*Library symbol*] [*National Library of Canada*] (NLC)
SRMS .... Scheduling and Resource Management System [*Tymshare UK*] [*Software package*]
SRMS .... Ships Records Management System (MCD)
SRMT .... Southern Rock Mountain Trench [*Geology*]
SRN .... Sabine River & Northern Railroad Co. [*AAR code*]
SRN .... Saskatchewan Registered Nurses Association, Regina, Saskatchewan [*Library symbol*] [*National Library of Canada*]
SRN .... Saturn Science Fiction and Fantasy [*A publication*]
SRN .... Serial Reference Number
SRN .... Simulation Reference Number
SRN .... Software Release Notice [*NASA*] (NASA)
SRN .... Southern Air Transport, Inc.
SRN .... Specification Revision Notice (MCD)
SRN .... State Registered Nurse [*British*]
SRN .... Strathearn House Group Ltd. [*Toronto Stock Exchange symbol*]
SRN .... Stretch Receptor Neuron
sRNA .... Ribonucleic Acid, Soluble [*Replaced by tRNA*] [*Biochemistry, genetics*]
SRNB .... Sociology. Reviews of New Books [*A publication*]
SRNC .... Severn River Naval Command
SRND .... Surround (FAAC)
S & R on Neg ... Shearman and Redfield on the Law of Negligence (DLA)
S & R Neg ... Shearman and Redfield on the Law of Negligence (DLA)
SRNFC ...... Source Range Neutron Flux Channel (IEEE)
SRNG .... Syringe
SRNR .... Stock Request Number
SRNS .... Steroid-Responsive Nephrotic Syndrome [*Medicine*]
SRNS .... Surveyor Retro Nozzle Structure
SRNSW ...... New South Wales State Reports [*A publication*]
SR (NSW) ... State Reports (New South Wales) [*A publication*]
SR (NSW) B & P ... State Reports (New South Wales). Bankruptcy and Probate [*A publication*]
SR (NSW) Eq ... State Reports (New South Wales). Equity [*A publication*]
SRNV .... Subretinal Neovascularization [*Ophthalmology*]
SRO .... S-Band RADAR Operational
SRO .... Safety Recall Order (MCD)
SRO .... Sales Release Order
SRO .... Saskatchewan Oil Co., Regina, Saskatchewan [*Library symbol*] [*National Library of Canada*] (NLC)
SRO .... Savannah River Operation [*Office*] [*Energy Research and Development Administration*]
SRO .... Scarboro Resources Ltd. [*Toronto Stock Exchange symbol*]
SRO .... Self-Regulatory Organization
SRO .... Senior Range Officer
SRO .... Senior Reactor Operator (NRCH)
SRO .... Senior Research Officer [*Ministry of Agriculture, Fisheries, and Food*] [*British*]
SRO .... Sex-Ratio Organism [*Entomology*]
SRO .... Shakespearean Research Opportunities [*A publication*]
SRO .... Shop Repair Order
SRO .... Short-Range Order [*Solid state physics*]
SRO .... Shrobarova [*Czechoslovakia*] [*Seismograph station code, US Geological Survey*] (SEIS)
SRO .... Single-Room Occupancy [*New York housing term*]
SRO .... Singly Resonant Oscillator (IEEE)
SRO .... Society of Radio Operators
SRO .... Solar Radio Observatory
SRO .... Southern Airlines, Inc. [*West Palm Beach, FL*] [*FAA designator*] (FAAC)
SRO .... Spares Requirement Order
SRO .... Special Rate Order [*Business and trade*]
SRO .... Special Regional Operations (NATG)
SRO .... Specification Release Order (NRCH)
SRO .... Squadron Recreation Officer [*Navy*] [*British*]
SRO .... Standing Room Only [*Theater*]
SRO .... Standing Route Order [*Army*] (AABC)
SRO .... Statutory Rules and Orders
SR & O .... Statutory Rules and Orders [*England*] (DLA)
SRO .... Steele-Richardson-Olszewski Syndrome [*Medicine*]
SRo .... Studi Romani [*Rome*] [*A publication*]
SRo .... Studia Rosenthaliana [*A publication*] (BJA)
SRO .... Superintendent [*or Supervisor*] of Range Operations [*NASA*]
SRO .... Supplementary Reserve of Officers [*Military*] [*British*]
SRO .... Systems Reproduction Order (MCD)
SROA .... Safety-Related Operator Action [*Nuclear energy*] (NRCH)
SROA .... Society for Radiation Oncology Administrators [*Philadelphia, PA*] (EA)
SROB .... Short-Range Omnidirectional Beacon [*Aerospace*]
SROD .... Stove Rod
SROE .... [*Shipboard*] Satellite Readout Equipment (MCD)
SROEQ .... Selected References on Environmental Quality as It Relates to Health [*A publication*]
SROF .... Self-Renewal Occupational Field

SROH .... Occupational Health Library, Regina, Saskatchewan [*Library symbol*] [*National Library of Canada*] (NLC)
SROKA ...... Second Republic of Korea Army
SRom .... Studi Romani [*Rome*] [*A publication*]
SROTC ...... Senior Reserve Officers' Training Corps (AABC)
SROTS ...... Superficial Rays of the Sun [*In reference to suntanning, supposedly occuring before 10am and after 2pm*] [*See also BROTS*]
SRP .... Safeguard Readiness Posture [*Army*] (AABC)
SRP .... Salary Reduction Plan [*Business and trade*]
SRP .... Saskatchewan Library and Union Catalogue, Regina, Saskatchewan [*Library symbol*] [*National Library of Canada*] (NLC)
SRP .... Saskatchewan Provincial Library [*UTLAS symbol*]
SRP .... Savannah River Plant [*Energy Research and Development Administration*]
SRP .... Scientific Research Proposal (AAG)
SRP .... Sealift Readiness Program [*Military*]
SRP .... Seat Reference Point
SRP .... Seismic Reflection Profile [*Marine science*] (MSC)
SRP .... Selective Reenlistment Program [*Air Force*]
SRP .... Self-Recording Penetrometer
SRP .... Sensor Reporting Post
SRP .... Shags Rocks Passage [*Oceanography*]
SRP .... Ship's Repair Party [*Navy*] [*British*]
SRP .... Short Ragweed Pollen [*Immunology*]
SRP .... Sierra Pacific Resources [*NYSE symbol*]
SRP .... Signal Recognition Particle [*Biochemistry*]
SRP .... Small Rotating Plug [*Nuclear energy*] (NRCH)
SRP .... Socialist Revolution Party [*Sosyalist Devrim Partisi*] [*Turkey*] (PPW)
SRP .... Socialist Revolutionary Party [*Indian*] (PPW)
SRP .... Socialist Revolutionary Party [*USSR*]
SRP .... Socialisticka Radnicka Partija Jugoslavije [*Socialist Workers' Party of Yugoslavia*] (PPE)
SRP .... Society for Radiological Protection [*British*] (DEN)
SRP .... Solar Radiation Pressure
SRP .... Solicitation Review Panel [*Air Force*]
SRP .... Sonobuoy Referenced Position [*Navy*] (NG)
SRP .... Source Record Punch
SRP .... Sozialistische Reichspartei [*Socialist Reich Party*] [*West Germany*] (PPE)
SRP .... Space Requirement Program (MCD)
S & RP .... Spares and Repair Parts [*Navy*]
SRP .... Spin Recovery Parachute
SRP .... Standard Relative Power
SRP .... Standard Repair Procedures
SRP .... Standard Review Plan (NRCH)
SRP .... Start Rendezvous Point (MCD)
SRP .... State Registered Physiotherapist [*British*]
SRP .... Stratospheric Research Program
SRP .... Stray Radiant Power
SRP .... Studia Rossica Posnaniensia [*A publication*]
SRP .... Suggested Retail Price
SRP .... Supply Readiness Program [*Air Force*]
SRP .... Supply Refuelling Point [*Air Force*] [*British*]
SRP .... Traverse City, MI [*Location identifier*] [*FAA*] (FAAL)
SRPA .... Senior Real Property Appraiser [*Designation awarded by Society of Real Estate Appraisers*]
SRPA .... Spherical Retarding Potential Analyzer (MCD)
Srp Akad Nauka Umet Od Prir-Mat Nauka Glas ... Srpska Akademija Nauka i Umetnosti Odeljenje Prirodno-Matematichkikh Nauka Glas [*A publication*]
Srp Akad Nauka Umet Posebna Izdan Od Prir Mat Nauka ... Srpska Akademija Nauka i Umetnosti Posebna Izdanja Odeljenje Prirodno-Matematichkikh Nauka [*A publication*]
SRPARABAD ... Senior Parachutist Badge [*Military decoration*]
Srp Arh Celok Lek ... Srpski Arhiv za Celokupno Lekarstvo [*A publication*]
Srp Arkh Tselok Lek ... Srpski Arkhiv za Tselokupno Lekarstvo [*A publication*]
SRPC .... Saskatchewan Power Corp., Regina, Saskatchewan [*Library symbol*] [*National Library of Canada*] (NLC)
SRPC .... Sulphate Resisting Portland Cement
SRPCRD ..... Research and Development Center, Saskatchewan Power Corp., Regina, Saskatchewan [*Library symbol*] [*National Library of Canada*] (NLC)
SRPD .... System Research and Planning Division [*NASA*] (KSC)
SRPDAA ..... Silk and Rayon Printers and Dyers Association of America [*Wayne, NJ*] (EA)
SRPG .... Scraping
SRPH .... Saskatchewan Department of Health, Regina, Saskatchewan [*Library symbol*] [*National Library of Canada*] (NLC)
SRPI .... Scrap Rubber and Plastics Institute (EA)
SRPI .... Silk and Rayon Print Institute [*Defunct*] (EA)
SRPIS .... Southern Regional Plant Introduction Station [*University of Georgia*] [*Research center*] (RCD)
SRPJ .... Self-Restraining Pipe Joint
SRPN .... Special Requisition Priority Number
SRPO .... Science Resources Planning Office [*National Science Foundation*]

SRPO.........	Soobchtcheniia Russkago Palestinskago Obchtshestva [*A publication*]
SRPP.........	Skeletal Rod of Palp
SRPR.........	Scraper
SRPR.........	Stray Radiant Power Ratio
SRPR.........	Surtsey Research Progress Report [*A publication*]
Sr Prcht Bad ...	Senior Parachutist Badge [*Military decoration*]
SRPS.........	Saskatchewan Public Service Commission, Regina, Saskatchewan [*Library symbol*] [*National Library of Canada*] (NLC)
SRPS.........	Scientific Research Project Support [*National Science Foundation*]
SRPS.........	Secure Record and Playback System (MCD)
SRPS.........	Sensor-Referenced Positioning System
SR/PS.......	Shipping Request/Packing Sheet (MCD)
Srpsko Hem Drus Bull ...	Srpsko Hemiskog Drustvo. Bulletin [*A publication*]
SRPV.........	Stationary Remotely Piloted Vehicle (MCD)
SRPW........	Savannah River Plant - Well DRB-10 [*South Carolina*] [*Seismograph station code, US Geological Survey*] (SEIS)
SR & Q.......	Safety, Reliability, and Quality (NASA)
SRQ...........	Sarasota/Bradenton [*Florida*] [*Airport symbol*]
SRQ...........	State Reports (Queensland) [*A publication*]
SR & QA.....	Safety, Reliability, and Quality Assurance (NASA)
SRR...........	Central New York Library Resources Council, Syracuse, NY [*OCLC symbol*] (OCLC)
SRR...........	Scots Revised Reports (DLA)
SRR...........	Search and Range RADAR
SRR...........	Search and Rescue Region [*Aviation*] (FAAC)
SRR...........	Seastar Resource Corp. [*Vancouver Stock Exchange symbol*]
SRR...........	Security Rules and Regulations
srr..............	Serer [*MARC language code*] [*Library of Congress*] (LCCP)
SRR...........	Shift Register Recognizer (IEEE)
SRR...........	Short-Range RADAR
SRR...........	Short-Range Recovery (IEEE)
SRR...........	Shuttle Requirements Review (MCD)
SRR...........	Site Readiness Review [*NASA*] (NASA)
SRR...........	Skin Resistance Response [*Physiology*]
SRR...........	Slow Rotation Room [*NASA*]
SRR...........	Socialist Republic of Romania
SRR...........	Sound Recorder-Reproducer (MSA)
SRR...........	Special Reimbursement Rate (AFM)
SRR...........	Special Report Writer [*NASA*]
SRR...........	Spurious Response Rejection
SRR...........	Steering Reversal Rate
SRR...........	Strategic Ready Reserve [*Military*]
SRR...........	Stride Rite Corp. [*NYSE symbol*]
SRR...........	Supplementary Reserve Regulations [*Army*] [*British*]
SRR...........	Support Requirements Records [*Navy*] (NG)
SRR...........	Survival, Recovery, and Reconstitution [*Military*] (AFM)
SRR...........	Systems Requirement Review
SRRA........	Sage Race Relations Abstracts [*A publication*]
SRRB........	Search and Rescue Radio Beacon
SRRC........	Resource Centre, RCMP Academy, Regina, Saskatchewan [*Library symbol*] [*National Library of Canada*] (NLC)
SRRC........	Scottish Reactor Research Centre (DEN)
SRRC........	Southern Regional Research Center [*Department of Agriculture*]
SRRC........	Sperry Rand Research Center (MCD)
SRRC........	Standing Results Review Committee [*Nuclear energy*] (NRCH)
SRRCS......	Surface Raid Reporting Control Ship [*Navy*] (NVT)
SRRE........	Prairie Farm Rehabilitation Administration, Agriculture Canada [*Administration du Retablissement Agricole des Prairies, Agriculture Canada*] Regina, Saskatchewan [*Library symbol*] [*National Library of Canada*] (NLC)
SRRI..........	Wascana Institute of Applied Arts and Sciences, Regina, Saskatchewan [*Library symbol*] [*National Library of Canada*] (NLC)
SRRS........	Social Readjustment Rating Scale [*Psychometrics*]
SR-RSV......	Rous Sarcoma Virus, Schmidt-Ruppin Strain
SRRT.........	Social Responsibilities Round Table [*American Library Association*]
SRS...........	Saskoil, Regina, Saskatchewan [*Library symbol*] [*National Library of Canada*] (NLC)
SRS...........	Satellite RADAR Station (NATG)
SRS...........	Satellite Readout Station (MCD)
SRS...........	Satellite Receiving Station
SRS...........	Scandinavian Radiological Society (EA)
SRS...........	Science Requirements Strategy [*Viking lander mission*] [*NASA*]
SRS...........	Scientific Reference Service [*HEW*]
SRS...........	Scientific Research Society of America [*Later, Sigma XI, The Scientific Research Society of America*] (AAG)
SRS...........	Scottish Record Society (EA)
SRS...........	Search and Rescue Ship (KSC)
SRS...........	Second Readiness State (AAG)
SRS...........	Secondary RADAR System
SRS...........	Secondary Recovery Ships [*NASA*] (KSC)
SRS...........	Secure Range Safety [*NASA*] (KSC)
SRS...........	Segment Ready Storage
SRS...........	Seismic Recording System

SRS...........	Selenium Rectifier Stack
SRS...........	Senate Recording Studio
SRS...........	Series [*Deltiology*]
SRS...........	Shakespeare Recording Society [*Commercial firm*] (EA)
SRS...........	Shipboard RADAR System
SRS...........	Short-Range Search (MCD)
SRS...........	Side-Looking RADAR System
SRS...........	Sight Restoration Society (EA)
SRS...........	Silent Running Society (EA)
SRS...........	Silver-Russell Syndrome [*Medicine*]
SRS...........	Simple Random Sample [*Statistics*]
SRS...........	Simulated Raman Scattering
SRS...........	Simulated Remote Sites [*NASA*] (KSC)
SRS...........	Simulated Remote Station
SRS...........	Slave Register Set
SRS...........	Sleep Research Society [*La Jolla, CA*] (EA)
SRS...........	Slippery Rock State College, Slippery Rock, PA [*OCLC symbol*] (OCLC)
SRS...........	Slow-Reacting Substance [*of anaphylaxis*] [*Leukotriene C*] [*Immunology*]
SRS...........	Small Research Satellite (KSC)
SRS...........	Social and Rehabilitation Service [*Abolished, 1977*] [*HEW*]
SRS...........	Social and Rehabilitation Service. Publications [*A publication*]
SRS...........	Societatis Regiae Socius [*Fellow of the Royal Society*]
SRS...........	Society for Romanian Studies [*Huntington College*] [*Huntington, IN*] (EA)
SRS...........	Sodium Removal Station [*Nuclear energy*] (NRCH)
SRS...........	Software Requirements Specification [*NASA*] (NASA)
SRS...........	Solar Radiation Simulator
SRS...........	Solid RADWASTE System [*Nuclear energy*] (NRCH)
SRS...........	Songwriters Resources and Services [*Later, NAS*] (EA)
SRS...........	Sonobuoy Reference System [*Navy*] (CAAL)
SRS...........	Sound Ranging Set
SRS...........	Sound Recordings Specialists [*Record label*]
SRS...........	Sounding Rocket System
SRS...........	Southern Railway System (MCD)
SRS...........	Space Recovery Systems (KSC)
SRS...........	Spaceborne Reconnaissance System
SRS...........	Spares Recommendation Sheet (MCD)
SRS...........	Special Revenue Sharing (OICC)
SRS...........	Specification Requirement Sheet (RDA)
SRS...........	Specification Revision Sheet [*NASA*] (NASA)
SRS...........	Speech Reinforcement System
SRS...........	Splenorenal Shunt [*Medicine*]
SRS...........	Squad Radio Set
SRS...........	Srpska Radikalna Stranka [*Serbian Radical Party*] [*Yugoslav*] (PPE)
S/RS.........	Staff Returns [*Marine Corps*]
SRS...........	Standard Reference Section
SRS...........	Standard Repair Specification (MCD)
SRS...........	State Revenue Society (EA)
SRS...........	Statistical Reporting Service [*Later, ESCS*] [*Department of Agriculture*]
SRS...........	Stimulated Raman Scattering [*Spectrometry*]
SRS...........	Strange Stories [*A publication*]
SRS...........	Strategic Reconnaissance Squadron (MCD)
SRS...........	Strike Reporting System
SRS...........	Structural Research Series
SRS...........	Student Response System [*Automated group instruction*]
SRS...........	Submarine Reactor Small
SRS...........	Subscriber-Response System [*Study of cable television*] [*Hughes Aircraft Co.*]
SRS...........	Substitute Route Structure
SRS...........	Sunrise Metals [*Vancouver Stock Exchange symbol*]
SRS...........	Supplementary Restraint System [*In cars*]
SRS...........	Supply Response Section [*Navy*]
SRS...........	Support Requirement System [*NASA*] (NASA)
SRS...........	Surveillance RADAR Station
SRS...........	Survey Research Service [*National Opinion Research Center, University of Chicago*] [*Research center*]
SRS...........	Synchronous Relay Satellite [*Telecommunications*] (TEL)
SRS...........	Synchrotron Radiation Source [*High-energy physics*]
SRS...........	System Requirements Specification (MCD)
SRSA........	Saskatchewan Arts Board, Regina, Saskatchewan [*Library symbol*] [*National Library of Canada*] (NLC)
SRSA........	Scientific Research Society of America [*Later, Sigma XI, The Scientific Research Society of America*]
SRS-A.......	Slow-Reacting Substance of Anaphylaxis [*Immunology*]
SR SATSIM ...	Search RADAR Satellite Simulation [*Military*] (CAAL)
SRSC........	Safety Railway Services [*NASDAQ symbol*] (NQ)
SRSC........	Saturday Review of the Sciences [*A publication*]
SRSC........	Slippery Rock State College [*Pennsylvania*]
SRSC........	Sul Ross State College [*Later, SRSU*] [*Texas*]
SRSC........	System Centre, Saskatchewan Revenue Supply and Services, Regina, Saskatchewan [*Library symbol*] [*National Library of Canada*] (NLC)
SRSCC......	Simulated Remote Station Control Center
Sr Schol....	Senior Scholastic [*A publication*]
SR-Sci.......	Saturday Review of the Sciences [*A publication*]
Sr Sci........	Senior Science [*A publication*]
SRSD.........	Saturday Review of Society [*A publication*]

SRSEM....... Saskatchewan Department of Energy and Mines, Regina, Saskatchewan [*Library symbol*] [*National Library of Canada*] (NLC)
SRSEMG .... Geological Laboratory, Saskatchewan Department of Energy and Mines, Regina, Saskatchewan [*Library symbol*] [*National Library of Canada*] (NLC)
SRSG .... Search RADAR Simulation Group [*Military*] (CAAL)
SRSG .... Subsurface Geological Laboratory, Regina, Saskatchewan [*Library symbol*] [*National Library of Canada*] (NLC)
SRSH......... Wascana Hospital, Regina, Saskatchewan [*Library symbol*] [*National Library of Canada*] (NLC)
SRSI .... Sikh Religious Studies Information [*A publication*]
SRSIB......... Salt Research and Industry [*A publication*]
SRSK .... Short-Range Station Keeping (NG)
SRSNY ...... Stockholder Relations Society of New York (EA)
SRSO .... Saturday Review of Society [*A publication*]
SRSO .... Scoliosis Research Society [*Park Ridge, IL*] (EA)
SR-Soc..... Saturday Review of Society [*A publication*]
SR Sq .... Strategic Reconnaissance Squadron
SRSR......... Schedule and Resources Status Report [*NASA*] (NASA)
SRSS......... Resource Centre, Saskatchewan Department of Social Services, Regina, Saskatchewan [*Library symbol*] [*National Library of Canada*] (NLC)
SRSS.......... Scientia: Revista Sintesi di Scientifica [*A publication*]
SRSS.......... Simulated Remote Sites Subsystem [*NASA*] (KSC)
SRSS.......... Sociological Resources for Social Studies [*Project of American Sociological Association*]
SRSS.......... Solar Radiation Simulator System
SRSS.......... Square Root of the Sum of the Squares (NRCH)
SRSSP .... Planning & Evaluation Library, Saskatchewan Department of Social Services, Regina, Saskatchewan [*Library symbol*] [*National Library of Canada*] (NLC)
SRSSPT .... Personnel & Training Library, Saskatchewan Department of Social Services, Regina, Saskatchewan [*Library symbol*] [*National Library of Canada*] (NLC)
SRST......... SASK TEL Corporate Library, Regina, Saskatchewan [*Library symbol*] [*National Library of Canada*] (NLC)
SRST......... Speed Reading Self-Taught [*Learning International*]
SRSTA........ Society of Roller Skating Teachers of America (EA)
SRSU......... Sul Ross State University [*Texas*]
SRSUE .... Studies in Regional Science and Urban Economics [*Elsevier Book Series*] [*A publication*]
SRT .... S-Band Radio Transmitter
SRT .... Sagittal Ray Trace
SRT .... Sarutani [*Japan*] [*Seismograph station code, US Geological Survey*] (SEIS)
SRT .... Scarlet Energy, Inc. [*Vancouver Stock Exchange symbol*]
SRT .... Science Recommendation Team
SRT .... Science, Research, and Technology
SRT .... Search RADAR Terminal
SRT .... Sedimentation Rate Test
SRT .... Self-Repair Technique
SRT .... Serials Round Table [*Later, RTSD*] [*American Library Association*]
SRT .... Short-Range Transport [*Aircraft*] (NATG)
SRT .... Shuttle Requirements Traceability (MCD)
SRT .... Silica RADOME Technique
SRT .... Simple Reaction Time [*Psychometry*]
SRT .... Single Requesting Terminal [*Data processing*] (IBMDP)
SRT .... Slow-Run-Through Trials [*Navy*] (NG)
SRT .... Social Relations Test [*Psychology*]
SRT .... Solar Radiation Test
SRT .... Solar Radio Telescope
SRT .... Solids Retention Time [*Water pollution*]
SRT .... Soroti [*Uganda*] [*Airport symbol*] (OAG)
SRT .... Special Rated Thrust (MCD)
SRT .... Special Real-Time Command (MCD)
SRT .... Special Review Team [*Nuclear energy*] (NRCH)
SRT .... Specification Requirements Table [*NASA*] (NASA)
SRT .... Speech Reception Thresholds [*Audiometry*]
SRT .... Spent Resin Tank (NRCH)
SRT .... Spousal Remainder Trust [*Banking*]
SRT .... Standard Rate Turn (NVT)
SRT .... Standard Remote Terminal
SRT .... Station Readiness Test
SRT .... Step Recovery Transistor
SRT .... Strategic Rocket Troops (NATG)
SRT .... Subcaliber Rocket Trainer [*Army*] (INF)
SRT .... Supply Response Time
SRT .... Supporting Research and Technology (MCD)
SR & T .... Supporting Research and Technology
SRT .... Surface Recording Terminal (MCD)
SRT .... Sustained Release Theophylline [*Medicine*]
SRT .... Synchro and Resolver Transmission
SRT .... System Reaction Time (KSC)
SRT .... System Reliability Test
SRT .... Systems Readiness Test (KSC)
SRTA.......... Senorita [*Miss*] [*Spanish*]
SRTC......... Scientific Research Tax Credit [*Canada*]
SRTC......... Search RADAR Terrain Clearance (NG)
SRTC......... Society of Ration Token Collectors (EA)

SRTC......... Special Real-Time Command (KSC)
SRTC......... Stored Program Real-Time Commands (MCD)
SRTD......... Sorted (MCD)
SRTF .... Short-Range Task Force
SRTF .... Shortest Remaining Time First [*Data processing*]
SRTGA ...... Science Reports. Tohoku University. Seventh Series [*A publication*]
SRTG-A..... Science Reports. Tohoku University. Seventh Series. Geography [*Japan*] [*A publication*]
SRTN .... Solar Radio Telescope Network
SRTN......... Special Representative for Trade Negotiations [*Later, USTR*] [*Executive Office of the President*]
SRTP .... Sensitized Room Temperature Phosphorescence
SRTS .... Scaled Range Target System (MCD)
SRTS .... Science Research Temperament Scale [*Psychology*]
SRTU .... Ship Repair Training Unit
SRTUC ...... Southern Rhodesian Trade Unions Congress
SRTVM....... Short-Range Track via Missile [*Military*] (CAAL)
SRU .... Santa Cruz, CA [*Location identifier*] [*FAA*] (FAAL)
SRU .... Seaplane Reconnaissance Unit
SRU .... Secondary Replaceable Unit
SRU .... Selective Reserve Unit [*Navy*] (NVT)
SRU .... Sensor Readout Unit (MCD)
SRU .... Servo Repeater Unit
SRU .... Ship Repair Unit
SRU .... Shop-Replaceable Unit [*NASA*] (NASA)
SRU .... Signal Responder Unit (AAG)
SRU .... Silver Recovery Unit
SRU .... Societe de Raffinage d'Uranium [*France*]
SRU .... Space Replaceable Unit (MCD)
SRU .... Structural Repeating Unit [*Polymer nomenclature system*]
SRu .... Studi Rumeni [*Rome*] [*A publication*]
SRU .... Subassembly Repairable Unit (MCD)
SRU .... Submarine Repair Unit
SRU .... Support Resource Unit (MCD)
SRU .... Suspension and Release Units (AFM)
SRU .... System Replaceable Unit
SRU .... University of Regina, Saskatchewan [*Library symbol*] [*National Library of Canada*] (NLC)
SRU .... University of Scranton, Scranton, PA [*OCLC symbol*] (OCLC)
SRUC .... Regina Campus, Campion College, University of Saskatchewan, Saskatchewan [*Library symbol*] [*National Library of Canada*] (NLC)
SRUFA ...... Faculty of Fine Arts, University of Regina, Saskatchewan [*Library symbol*] [*National Library of Canada*] (NLC)
SRUG .... Department of Geography, University of Regina, Saskatchewan [*Library symbol*] [*National Library of Canada*] (NLC)
SRUNM ...... Norman MacKenzie Art Gallery, University of Regina, Saskatchewan [*Library symbol*] [*National Library of Canada*] (NLC)
SRUTA ...... Soviet Rubber Technology [*English translation*] [*A publication*]
SRV .... Executive Air Services, Inc. [*Jacksonville, FL*] [*FAA designator*] (FAAC)
SRV .... Safety Relief Valve (NRCH)
SRV .... Saline Retention Value
SRV .... Satellite Reentry Vehicle
SRV .... Service Corp. International [*NYSE symbol*]
SRV .... Short-Range Viewer
SRV .... Socialist Republic of Vietnam
SRV .... Society of Russian Veterans of the World War (EA)
SRv.......... Southwest Review [*A publication*]
SRV .... Space Rescue Vehicle
SRV .... Step Recovery Varactor
SRV .... Stony River [*Alaska*] [*Airport symbol*] (OAG)
SRV .... Submerged Research Vehicle
SRV .... Surface Recombination Velocity (DEN)
SRV .... Surface Roving Vehicle [*NASA*] (KSC)
SRV .... Surrogate Research Vehicle [*Army Tank-Automotive Command*]
SRV .... System Readiness Verification
SRVC .... Sine-Random Vibration Control
SRVCLG..... Service Ceiling [*Aerospace engineering*]
SRVDL ...... Safety/Relief Valve Discharge Line [*Nuclear energy*] (NRCH)
SRVEILOPS ... Surveillance Operations [*Military*] (NVT)
SRVI.......... Servico, Inc. [*NASDAQ symbol*] (NQ)
SRVL .... Survival (MSA)
SRW .... Salisbury, NC [*Location identifier*] [*FAA*] (FAAL)
SRW .... Saskatchewan Wheat Pool, Regina, Saskatchewan [*Library symbol*] [*National Library of Canada*] (NLC)
SRW .... Saturday Review/World [*A publication*]
SRW .... Short Ragweed [*Immunology*]
SRW .... Silenced Reconnaissance Weapon (MCD)
SRW .... Strategic Reconnaissance Wing [*Air Force*] (MCD)
SR (WA).... State Reports (Western Australia) [*A publication*]
SRWBR ...... Short-Range Wideband Radio (MCD)
SRWD......... South Saskatchewan Committee for World Development, Regina, Saskatchewan [*Library symbol*] [*National Library of Canada*] (NLC)
SRWg .... Strategic Reconnaissance Wing [*Air Force*] (AFM)
SRW Nachr ... SRW [*Siemens-Reiniger-Werke*] Nachricht [*West Germany*] [*A publication*]

SR/World ... Saturday Review/World [*A publication*]
SRWP .... Collection Split in/Collection Partagee Entre SRSSP & SRSSPT, Saskatchewan [*Library symbol*] [*National Library of Canada*]   (NLC)
SRWR .... Saskatchewan Water Resources Commission, Regina, Saskatchewan [*Library symbol*] [*National Library of Canada*]   (NLC)
SRWS .... Simplified and Regularized Writing System
SRWS .... Solid Radioactive Waste System [*Nuclear energy*]   (NRCH)
SRWS .... Standard Reference Water Sample [*US Geological Survey*]
SRWU .... Sudan Railways Workers' [*Trade*] Union
SRX .... Sert [*Libya*] [*Airport symbol*] [*Obsolete*]   (OAG)
SRX .... SR Telecom [*Toronto Stock Exchange symbol*]
SRY .... Sherwood Rangers Yeomanry [*Military unit*] [*British*]
SRY .... Ship Repair Yard   (CINC)
SRY .... Shiroyama [*Japan*] [*Seismograph station code, US Geological Survey*]   (SEIS)
SRY .... Stryker Resources Ltd. [*Vancouver Stock Exchange symbol*]
SRZ .... San Marcos, TX [*Location identifier*] [*FAA*]   (FAAL)
SRZ .... Santa Cruz [*Bolivia*] [*Airport symbol*]   (OAG)
SRZ .... Satz Rechen Zentrum [*Computer Composition Center*] [*Hartmann & Heenemann*] [*Information service*] [*Berlin, West Germany*]   (EISS)
SRZ .... Special Rules Zone
SRZ .... Stratas Corp. [*Vancouver Stock Exchange symbol*]
SRZ .... Studia Romanica Zagrabiensia [*A publication*]
SRZF .... Synchro Resolver Zeroing Fixture
SRZLO ...... Supreme Royal Zuanna, Ladies of the Orient [*Defunct*]   (EA)
SS .... Aerolineas Dominicanas SA [*Dominican Republic*] [*ICAO designator*]   (FAAC)
SS .... Faulty Sentence Structure [*Used in correcting manuscripts, etc.*]
SS .... Passing Stop Sign [*Traffic offense charge*]
SS .... Royal Statistical Society [*British*]
SS .... Sa Saintete [*His Holiness*] [*The Pope*] [*French*]
SS .... Sa Seigneurie [*His Lordship*] [*French*]
SS .... Saccharin Sodium [*Sweetening agent*]
SS .... Sacred Scripture
SS .... Safe Shutdown [*Nuclear energy*]   (NRCH)
SS .... Safety Services [*Red Cross*]
SS .... Safety Supervisor   (MUGU)
SS .... Safety Supplements [*Air Force*]
SS .... Sagittal Sinus [*Anatomy*]
SS .... Saint-Sacrement [*Blessed Sacrament*] [*French*]
SS .... Saints [*as in "SS Peter and Paul"*]
SS .... Saline Soak
SS .... Salmonella-Shigella [*Microbiology*]
SS .... Salt-Sensitive
SS .... Same Size [*Photography, publishing*]
SS .... Sample Sink   (NRCH)
SS .... Sample Station   (NRCH)
S/S .... Samples per Second   (KSC)
SS .... Sampling System   (NRCH)
SS .... Sancti [*Saints*] [*Latin*]
SS .... Sanctissimus [*Most Holy*] [*Latin*]
SS .... Sanctum Sanctorum [*Holy of Holies*] [*Latin*] [*Freemasonry*]
SS .... Sand Springs Railway Co. [*AAR code*]
SS .... Sandstone [*Lithology*]
SS .... Sartre Society [*Purdue University*] [*West Lafayette, IN*]   (EA)
SS .... Saskatoon Public Library, Saskatchewan [*Library symbol*] [*National Library of Canada*]   (NLC)
SS .... Satellite-Switched
SS .... Satellite System
SS .... Saturated Solution [*Pharmacy*]
S & S .... Sausse and Scully's Irish Rolls Court Reports [*1837-40*]   (DLA)
SS .... Scandinavian Seminar   (EA)
S & S .... Scandinavian Studies [*A publication*]
S & S .... Schleicher & Schuell [*Filter-paper company*]
S & S .... School and Society [*A publication*]
SS .... School and Society [*A publication*]
SS .... Schutzstaffel [*Elite Guard*] [*NAZI Germany*]
SS .... Schwab Safe Co. [*American Stock Exchange symbol*]
SS .... Science Service
S & S .... Science and Society [*A publication*]
SS .... Scientific Services   (KSC)
SS .... Scilicet [*Namely*] [*Legal term*] [*Latin*]
SS .... Scintiscanning [*Medicine*]
SS .... Screw Steamer
SS .... Sea Scout - Nonrigid Airship [*Royal Naval Air Service*] [*British*]
SS .... Sea State
S & S .... Searle and Smith's English Probate & Divorce Reports [*1859-60*]   (DLA)
SS .... Second Stage
SS .... Secondary School
SS .... Secret Service
SS .... Secretary for Scotland
SS .... Secretary of State
S of S .... Secretary of State
S of S .... Secretary of State for Defence [*British*]   (RDA)
SS .... Secretary of State Department [*Canada*]
SS .... Sections   (ADA)

SS .... Security Service
SS .... Security Systems, Inc. [*In TV series "Max Headroom"*]
SS .... Selden Society   (EA)
SS .... Select Standby
SS .... Selective Service
SS .... Selective Signaling
SS .... Selector Switch   (IEEE)
SS .... Semifinal Splice [*Telecommunications*]   (TEL)
SS .... Semis [*One-Half*] [*Pharmacy*]
SS .... Semisteel
SS .... Semisubmersible [*Drilling unit*]
SS .... Sempervivium Society   (EA-IO)
SS .... Senior Scholars   (EA)
SS .... Senior Scholastic [*A publication*]
S & S .... Sense and Sensibility [*Novel by Jane Austen*]
SS .... Sensor [*Genetics*]
SS .... Sensor Supervisor [*Military*]   (CAAL)
SS .... Sensu Stricto [*In a Narrow Sense*] [*Latin*]
SS .... Sentence Suspended
SS .... Senza Sordini [*Without Mutes*] [*Music*]
SS .... Sequentia [*What Follows*] [*Latin*]   (ROG)
SS .... Sequential Switch
SS .... Serials Section [*Resources and Technical Services Division*] [*American Library Association*]
SS .... Series Separate
Ss .... Serum Serologic [*Immunochemistry*]
SS .... Serum Sickness [*Medicine*]
SS .... Service Sink   (MSA)
SS .... Service Squadron   (AAG)
SS .... Service Structure   (KSC)
SS .... Sessions
SS .... Set Screw [*Technical drawings*]
SS .... Set Steering
S & S .... Sex and Shopping [*Themes of Judith Krantz's novels*]
SS .... Sezary Syndrome [*Dermatology*]
SS .... Shackamaxon Society   (EA)
SS .... Shakespeare Survey [*A publication*]
SS .... Sharpshooter [*Marine Corps*]
SS .... Shear Strength   (AAG)
SS .... Shelf Stock
SS .... Shell Shock
SS .... Shift Supervisor   (IEEE)
SS .... Shimmy Showing [*From one girl to another, in reference to dress disarrangement*]
SS .... Ship Service
S/S .... Ship-to-Shore   (MUGU)
SS .... Ship Station
SS .... Ship System
SS .... Shipping Situation [*British*]
S & S .... Shipping and Storage
SS .... Shipside
SS .... Shomrim Society [*An association*] [*New York, NY*]   (EA)
SS .... Shop Steward
SS .... Short Sight   (ADA)
SS .... Short Sleeves
SS .... Shortstop
SS .... Shosin Society   (EA)
SS .... Shuttle System   (MCD)
SS .... Side Seam
SS .... Side to Side
SS .... Side by Side   (AAG)
SS .... Side Slip   (MCD)
SS .... Sidestream Smoke [*from cigarettes*]
S & S .... Sight and Sound [*A publication*]
SS .... Sight and Sound [*A publication*]
S/S .... Sign Signature   (AAG)
SS .... Signal Selector   (DEN)
SS .... Signal Strength [*Broadcasting*]   (KSC)
SS .... Signaling System [*Telecommunications*]   (TEL)
SS .... Signed and Sealed
S & S .... Signs and Symptoms [*Medicine*]
S/S .... Silk Screen   (ADA)
SS .... Silver Standard [*Vancouver Stock Exchange symbol*]
SS .... Silver Star [*Military award*]
SS .... Silvernail's New York Supreme Court Reports   (DLA)
S & S .... Simon & Schuster [*Publisher*]
S & S .... Simons and Stuart's English Vice-Chancellors' Reports [*1822-26*]   (DLA)
SS .... Simple Spike
SS .... Simplified Spelling
SS .... Single Scan
SS .... Single Seated
SS .... Single Shot
SS .... Single Sideband
SS .... Single Signal
SS .... Single Stout [*Beer*]   (ROG)
SS .... Single-Stranded [*or ss*] [*Genetics*]
SS .... Single Strength [*Citrus juices*]
SS .... Single Dtring   (MCD)
SS .... Sinistral Sig   (EA)
SS .... Sinner Saved [*Pseudonym used by William Huntington*]

SS	Site Safety (NRCH)
SS	Site Suitability (NRCH)
SS	Sjoegren's Syndrome [*Medicine*]
SS	Skid Strip (KSC)
SS	Sliding Scale (AAG)
SS	Slocum Society (EA)
SS	Slop Sink
SS	Slovo a Slovesnost [*A publication*]
SS	Slow Setting [*Asphalt grade*]
SS	Small Signal
SS	Small Subcompact [*Car size*]
SS	Smoke Stand (MSA)
SS	Smokeshop [*A publication*]
SS	Soap Solution
SS	Soapsuds
SS	Social Science
SS	Social Security
SS	Social Service
SS	Social Shopper
SS	Social Studies [*A publication*]
SS	Social Surveys
SS	Society of St. Sulpice [*Sulpicians*] [*Roman Catholic men's religious order*]
SS	Society of Separationists (EA)
SS	Society of Signalmen (EA)
SS	Society of the Silurians [*New York, NY*] (EA)
SS	Society for Strings (EA)
SS	Sociological Studies [*A publication*]
SS	SoftSearch, Inc. [*Denver, CO*] [*Information service*] (EISS)
SS	Solid Shield (MCD)
SS	Solid State
SS	Soluble Solids [*Chemistry*]
SS	Somatics Society [*Commercial firm*] [*Novato, CA*] (EA)
SS	Somatostatin [*Also, GH-RIF, GH-RIH, GRIF, SRIF*] [*Endocrinology*]
S of S	Song of Solomon [*Old Testament book*]
SS	Songsmith Society (EA)
SS	Sonneck Society (EA)
SS	Soprano Saxophone
SS	Sound and Sense [*Baguio City*] [*A publication*]
SS	Sound System
SS	Source Selection (MCD)
S/S	Source/Sink [*Data processing*] (IBMDP)
SS	Source/Source [*Inspection/Acceptance point*] (MCD)
SS	Source and Special [*Material*] [*Nuclear energy*]
SS	Source of Supply (AFM)
SS	South Saxon (ROG)
SS	Souvenir Sheet [*Philately*]
SS	Space Shuttle [*NASA*] (KSC)
SS	Space Simulator (IEEE)
SS	Space Station (AAG)
SS	Space Switch [*Telecommunications*] (TEL)
ss...............	Spanish Sahara [*Western Sahara*] [*MARC country of publication code*] [*Library of Congress*] (LCCP)
SS	Sparingly Soluble
SS	Special Series
SS	Special Service [*Vessel load line mark*]
SS	Special Session
SS	Special Settlement
SS	Special Source Materials (NRCH)
SS	Special Staff
SS	Special Strike (NATG)
SS	Special Study
SS	Special Subjects
SS	Specification for Structure
S/S	Spectrum Signature (NG)
SS	Speed Sensor (NRCH)
SS	Spenser Society (EA)
SS	Spherical Symmetry
S & S	Spigot and Socket
SS	Spin-Stabilized [*Rockets*]
SS	Spiral to Spiral
SS	Spore Surface [*Immunology*]
SS	Spread Spectrum (CET)
SS	Squawk Sheet (KSC)
SS	Stabilization System (AAG)
SS	Stack Segment [*Data processing*]
SS	Staff Sergeant [*Military*] [*British*] (ROG)
SS	Staff Specialist
SS	Staff Surgeon
SS	Stainless Steel
SS	Standard Frequency Station [*ITU designation*]
SS	Standard Score [*Psychology*]
SS	Standard Size (ADA)
SS	Standardized Solution [*Pharmacy*]
SS	Starlight Scope
S & S	Stars & Stripes [*A publication*]
S/S	Start/Stop
SS	Startling Stories [*A publication*]
SS	State School (ADA)
SS	State Supervisor

S/S............	Statement of Service [*Military*]
SS	Statesman Series [*A publication*]
SS	Station Set [*NASA*] (NASA)
S to S	Station to Station
SS	Station Supervision
SS	Statistical Standards
SS	Statistics Sources [*A publication*]
sS	Statsiemens [*Also, statS*] [*Unit of electric conductance, admittance, and susceptance*]
SS	Steady State
SS	Steamship
SS	Steel Sash
SS	Steering System
SS	Stereoscopic Society - American Branch (EA)
SS	Sterile Solution
SS	Steroid Score [*Immunology*]
SS	Stimulator Substance [*Liver regeneration*]
SS	Storage to Storage (MCD)
SS	Straight Shank [*Screw*]
SS	Straight Sided
SS	Straits Settlements [*in Malaya*]
SS	Strategic Study [*Military*]
SS	Strong Safety [*Football*]
SS	Student at Staff College [*Army*] [*British*] (ROG)
SS	Studi Sardi [*A publication*]
SS	Studi Semitici [*A publication*]
SS	Studi Storici [*A publication*]
SS	Studia Serdicensia [*A publication*]
SS	Stumpwork Society (EA)
SS	Style Sac
SS	Subject-Subject [*Education of the hearing-impaired*]
SS	Subliminal Self [*Psychical research*]
SS	Submarine [*Navy symbol*]
SS	Submarine Qualification [*Navy*]
SS	Submarine Scout
SS	Submarine Studies [*SORG*]
SS	Subsagittal [*Medicine*]
SS	Subscriber Switching [*Telecommunications*] (TEL)
SS	Subsolar [*NASA*] (KSC)
SS	Substitutes [*Sports*]
ss...............	Substructure [*Data processing*]
SS	Subsystem (AAG)
SS	Successive Stereometric [*A discrimination task*]
SS	Sugar Series [*Elsevier Book Series*] [*A publication*]
SS	Sum-of-the-Squares
SS	Summary Sheet
SS	Summation Sound
SS	Summing Selector (MSA)
SS	Summons (ROG)
SS	Sun Seeker (AAG)
SS	Sun Sensor
SS	Sun Simulator (MCD)
SS	Sunday School
SS	Sunset [*Meteorology*] (FAAC)
SS	Super Search (MCD)
SS	Super Speed
SS	Super Sport [*In automobile model name*]
SS	Superintending Scientist [*British*] (ADA)
SS	Superintending Sister [*Navy*] [*British*]
SS	Supersensitive (AAG)
SS	Supersonic
SS	Supervisors Section [*American Association of School Librarians*]
S & S	Supply and Service [*Army*] (AABC)
SS	Supply Ship (MCD)
SS	Support Services (MCD)
SS	Support System [*Air Force*]
SS	Supportive Service (OICC)
SS	Supra Scriptum [*Written Above*] [*Latin*]
SS	Surface-Sized [*Paper*]
SS	Surface-to-Surface (NATG)
SS	Surveillance Station [*RADAR*]
SS	Suspended Sentence
SS	Suspended Solids [*Wastewater treatment*]
S & S	Swan and Sayler's Revised Statutes of Ohio (DLA)
SS	Swedish Society, Discofil [*Record label*] [*Sweden*]
SS	Switch Selector (KSC)
S & S	Sword and Sorcery
SS	Sworn Statement
SS	Sympathetically Stimulated [*Physiology*]
SS	Syn og Segn [*A publication*]
SS	Synchro Standard
SS	Synergetic Society (EA)
SS	Synopsis Series of the United States Treasury Decisions (DLA)
S & S	Syntax and Semantics [*A publication*]
SS	System Segment (MCD)
SS	System Sensitivity
SS	System Software (MCD)
SS	System Summary (MCD)
SS	System Supervisor
SS	Systems Specifications (NG)

S1S............ Surfaced or Dressed One Side [*Technical drawings*]
S2S............ Surfaced or Dressed Two Sides [*Technical drawings*]
S4S............ Surfaced or Dressed Four Sides [*Technical drawings*]
SSA........... Associate in Secretarial Science
SSA........... Cargo Submarine [*Navy symbol*] [*Obsolete*]
SSA........... First Soprano, Second Soprano, and Alto [*in all-women choral groups*]
SSA........... S-Band Single Access   (MCD)
SSA........... Salsalate [*Anti-inflammatory drug*]
SSA........... Salvador [*Brazil*] [*Airport symbol*]   (OAG)
SSA........... Saskatchewan Archives Office, Saskatoon, Saskatchewan [*Library symbol*] [*National Library of Canada*]   (NLC)
SSA........... Sauna Society of America [*Washington, DC*]   (EA)
SSA........... Scandinavian Society of Anaesthesiologists   (EA)
SSA........... Scandinavian Sociological Association   (EA)
SSA........... Secretary of State for Air [*British*]
SS of A...... Secular Society of America [*Defunct*]
SSA........... Security Supporting Assistance [*US government program for promoting economic and political stability in areas of strategic interest*]
SSA........... Segment Search Argument [*Data processing*]   (BUR)
SSA........... Seismological Society of America   (EA)
SSA........... Selective Service Act
SSA........... Semiotic Society of America   (EA)
SSA........... Senior Scientific Assistant [*Ministry of Agriculture, Fisheries, and Food*] [*British*]
SSA........... Sensat Technologies Ltd. [*Vancouver Stock Exchange symbol*]
SSA........... Sequential Spectrometer Accessory [*Instrumentation*]
SSA........... Series of Standard Additions
SSA........... Shakespeare Society of America   (EA)
SSADH...... Shan State Army [*Burmese*]   (PD)
SSA........... Shaw Society of America [*Defunct*]   (EA)
SSA........... Sheath of Skeletal Axis
SSA........... Ship's Stores Ashore [*Navy*]
SSA........... Shuttle Simulation Aircraft [*NASA*]   (NASA)
SSA........... Signal Security Agency [*Later, Army Security Agency*]
SSA........... Signal Supply Agency
SSA........... Simian Society of America [*Phoenix, AZ*]   (EA)
SSA........... Simpler Spelling Association [*Later, PSC*]   (EA)
SSA........... Single Line Synchronous Adapter   (MCD)
SSA........... Sisters of St. Ann of Providence [*Roman Catholic religious order*]
SSA........... Sisters of St. Anne [*Roman Catholic religious order*]
SS-A.......... Sjogren's Syndrome A [*Medicine*]
SSA........... Slaving Signal Amplifier
SSA........... Sleeve Stub Antenna
SSA........... Slovak Studies Association   (EA)
SSA........... Soaring Society of America   (EA)
SSA........... Social Science Abstracts [*A publication*]
SSA........... Social Security Act [*1935*] [*Also, SSACT*]
SSA........... Social Security Administration [*of HEW*]
SSA........... Social Security Administration. Publications [*A publication*]
SSA........... Society of Security Analysts
SSA........... Solid-State Abstracts
SSA........... Sommelier Society of America [*New York, NY*]   (EA)
SSA........... Source Selection Activity [*or Authority*] [*Military*]
SSA........... Space Suit Assembly   (KSC)
SS & A....... Space Systems and Applications [*NASA*]   (NASA)
SSA........... Spanish-Surnamed American
SSA........... Spatial Sound Around [*Acoustics*]
SSA........... Special Service Agreement [*UN Food and Agriculture Organization*]
SSA........... Sportswear Salesmen's Association [*New York, NY*]   (EA)
SSA........... Spring Service Association [*Medina, OH*]   (EA)
SSA........... Staff Supply Assistant [*Military*]   (AABC)
SSA........... Staff Support Agencies [*Military*]
SSA........... Staging and Support Area [*NASA*]   (KSC)
SSA........... Standard Single Account   (INF)
SSA........... Stars of the Stage [*A publication*]
SSA........... Steuben Society of America   (EA)
SSA........... Stratford Public Library, Stratford, CT [*OCLC symbol*]   (OCLC)
SSA........... Student Ski Association
SSA........... Studio Suppliers Association [*Sea Cliffe, NY*]   (EA)
SSA........... Style Sac Artery
ssa........... Sub-Saharan African [*MARC language code*] [*Library of Congress*]   (LCCP)
SSA........... Subterranean Sociological Association   (EA)
SSA........... Sulfite Sensitive Asthmatic
SSA........... Sulfosalicylic Acid [*Organic chemistry*]
SSA........... Sumi-E Society of America   (EA)
SSA........... Supply Support Activity   (AABC)
SSA........... Supply Support Arrangements [*A bilateral agreement between the United States and a friendly foreign government*]
SSA........... Support Services Alliance [*Nanuet, NY*]   (EA)
SSA........... Survival Surface-to-Air   (MCD)
SSA........... Symbol Synchronizer Assembly [*NASA*]
SSA........... Synchro Signal Amplifier
SSAA......... Salzburger Studien zur Anglistik und Amerikanstik [*A publication*]

SSAA......... Saskatchewan Institute of Applied Arts, Saskatoon, Saskatchewan [*Library symbol*] [*National Library of Canada*]   (NLC)
SSAA......... Shoe Suppliers Association of America [*East Bridgewater, MA*]   (EA)
SSAA......... Skate Sailing Association of America   (EA)
SSAA......... Social Security Acts Amendments   (DLA)
SSAA......... Space Science Analysis Area [*Space Flight Operations Facility, NASA*]
SSAAII...... Ses Altesses Imperiales [*Their Imperial Highnesses*] [*French*]   (ROG)
SSAAT...... Sun Sensor Attitude Angle Transducer
SSAC......... Armak Chemicals, Saskatoon, Saskatchewan [*Library symbol*] [*National Library of Canada*]   (NLC)
SSAC......... Secondary School Admissions Center [*Defunct*]   (EA)
SSAC......... Social Security Advisory Committee [*British*]
SSAC......... Society for the Study of Architecture in Canada [*Established 1974*]
SSAC......... Source Selection Advisory Council   (AFM)
SSAC......... Space Science Analysis and Command [*Team*] [*NASA*]
SSAC......... Sponsors' Standards Advisory Committee [*American National Standards Institute*]
SSAC......... Standing State Advisory Committee [*Terminated, 1977*] [*of Water Resources Council*]   (EGAO)
SSAC......... Suprasellar Arachnoid Cyst [*Medicine*]
SSAC......... Suspended Sprayed Acoustical Ceiling [*Technical drawings*]
SSACT...... Social Security Act [*1935*] [*Also, SSA*]
SSADARS ... Social Security Administration Data Acquisition and Response System
SSADC...... Solid-State Air Data Computer   (MCD)
SSADH...... Succinate-Semialdehyde Dehydrogenase [*An enzyme*]
SSAF......... Standard Single Account File [*Number*]   (MCD)
SSAG......... Single-Step Acidulation Granulation [*Fertilizer technology*]
SSAG......... Strategic Studies Advisory Group [*Army*]   (AABC)
SSAGR...... Research Station, Agriculture Canada [*Station de Recherches, Agriculture Canada*] Saskatoon, Saskatchewan [*Library symbol*] [*National Library of Canada*]   (NLC)
SSAJ......... Sweep Stop Alarm Jam   (MCD)
SSAL......... Scientific Serials in Australian Libraries [*A publication*]
SSAL......... Simplified Short Approach Light [*Aviation*]
S-SAL........ Solar Scientific Airlock   (MCD)
SSALF....... Simplified Short ALS [*Approach Light System*] with Sequenced Flashers [*Aviation*]
SSALR...... Simplified Short ALS [*Approach Light System*] with Runway Alignment Indicator Lights [*Aviation*]
SSALS...... Simplified Short Approach Light System [*Aviation*]
SSALSR..... Simplified Short Approach Light System with Runway Alignment Indicator Lights [*Aviation*]
SSAL Supp't ... SSAL [*Scientific Serials in Australian Libraries*] Supplement [*A publication*]
SSAN........ Social Security Account Number
SSAO........ Semicarbazide-Sensitive Amine Oxidase [*Biochemistry*]
SSAO........ Solid-State Audio Oscillator
SSAOA...... Soobshcheniya Shemakhinskoi Astrofizicheskoi Observatorii, Akademiya Nauk Azerbaidzhanskoi SSR [*A publication*]
SSAP......... Source Service Access Point
SSAP......... Statement of Standard Accounting Practice
SSAP......... Survival Stabilator Actuator Package [*Hydraulic power*]
SSAPD...... Symposium on Salt. Proceedings [*A publication*]
S-SAR........ Secret - Special Access Required [*Security classification*]   (MCD)
SSAR......... Site Safety Analysis Report [*Nuclear energy*]   (NRCH)
SSAR......... Society for the Study of Amphibians and Reptiles   (EA)
SSAR......... Spin-Stabilized Aircraft Rocket
SSAR......... Standard Safety Analysis Report [*Nuclear energy*]   (NRCH)
SSAR......... Steady State Adiabatic Reactor [*Chemical engineering*]
SSar.......... Studi Sardi [*A publication*]
SSARB...... Sassar [*A publication*]
SSARR...... Streamflow Synthesis and Reservoir Regulation
SSAS......... Salzburg Seminar in American Studies   (EA)
SSAS......... Searchless Self-Adjusting System
SSAS......... Signal Security Assessment System [*Military*]   (CAAL)
SSAS......... Small Sample Assay System [*Nuclear energy*]   (NRCH)
SSAS......... Special Signal Analysis System [*Electronic countermeasures system*]
SSAS......... Static Stability Augmentation System [*Aviation*]
SSAS......... Station Signaling and Announcement Subsystem [*Telecommunications*]   (TEL)
SSASH...... Studia Slavica. Academiae Scientiarum Hungaricae [*A publication*]
SSAT......... Secondary School Admission Test Board   (EA)
SSAT......... Shuttle Service and Access Tower [*NASA*]   (NASA)
SSAT......... Social Security Appeals Tribunal   (ADA)
SSAT......... Society for Surgery of the Alimentary Tract [*Los Angeles, CA*]   (EA)
SSAT......... Space Shuttle Access Tower   (MCD)
SSAT......... Sweep Stop Alarm Target [*Military*]   (CAAL)
SSATB...... Secondary School Admission Test Board
SSAU......... Submarine Search Attack Unit   (NVT)
SSAV......... Shoreline Savings Association [*NASDAQ symbol*]   (NQ)
SSAV......... Simian Sarcoma Associated Virus

SSAWL....... Sitzungsberichte der Saechsischen Akademie der Wissenschaften zu Leipzig. Philologisch-Historische Klasse [*A publication*]
SSAWV ...... Sons of Spanish American War Veterans   (EA)
SSB .... Cave Junction, OR [*Location identifier*] [*FAA*]   (FAAL)
SSB .... Fleet Ballistic Submarine [*Navy symbol*]
SSB .... St. Croix [*Virgin Islands*] Seaplane Base [*Airport symbol*]   (OAG)
SSB .... St. Sauveur Badole [*France*] [*Seismograph station code, US Geological Survey*]   (SEIS)
SSB .... Security Screening Board [*Army*]
SSB .... Selective Service Board
SSB .... Single Sideband
SSB .... Single-Strand Break [*Genetics*]
SSB .... Sino-Soviet Bloc
SS-B .... Sjogren's Syndrome B [*Medicine*]
SSb .... Skandinavskij Sbornik [*A publication*]
SSB .... Social Security Board [*Abolished, 1946*]
SSB .... Social Security Bulletin [*US*] [*A publication*]
SSB .... Society for the Study of Blood [*Cornell University Medical College*] [*New York, NY*]   (EA)
SSB .... Source Selection Board
SSB .... Space Science Board [*National Research Council*]
SSB .... Special Studies Branch [*Supreme Headquarters Allied Powers Europe*]   (NATG)
SSB .... Spontaneous Symmetry Breaking [*Physics*]
SSB .... Standard Software Base   (MCD)
SSB .... Submarine, Ballistic Missile [*Diesel*] [*NATO*]
SSB .... Subscriber Busy [*Telecommunications*]   (TEL)
SSB .... Swimmer Support Boat
SSBA .... Sons of Scotland Benevolent Association   (EA)
SSBAM ..... Single Sideband Amplitude Modulation   (KSC)
SSBC .... Stock Status Balance Card   (NG)
SSBC .... Summary Sheet Bar Chart [*NASA*]   (NASA)
SSBD .... Single-Sideboard   (IEEE)
SSB/DPUT ... Serikat Sekerdja Biro/Dinas Pembangunan Usaha Tani [*Agricultural Development Service Workers' Union*] [*Indonesia*]
SSBE.......... Saskatoon Board of Education, Saskatchewan [*Library symbol*] [*National Library of Canada*]   (NLC)
SSBF .... Single Sideband Filter
SSBFH .... Star-Spangled Banner Flag House   (EA)
SSBFM ...... Single Sideband Frequency Modulation   (IEEE)
SSBG .... Sex Steroid Binding Globulin [*Endocrinology*]
SSBG .... Single Sideband Generator
SSBG .... Social Services Block Grant
SSB/GP ..... Source Selection Board/General Procurement   (MCD)
SSBKD .... Serikat Sekerdja/Buruh Ketapradja Djakarta Raja [*General Union of Government Officials of Greater Djakarta*] [*Indonesia*]
SSBKTN..... Serikat Sekerdja Bank Koporasi, Tani dan Nelajan Disingkat [*Cooperative, Farmers and Fishers Bank Employees' Union*] [*Indonesia*]
SSB/L .... Steamship Bill of Lading [*Business and trade*]
SSBLA .... Sel'skokhozyaistvennaya Biologiya [*A publication*]
SSBM........ Single Sideband Modulation
SSBMA ..... Students to Save Baltic and Mediterranean Avenues   (EA)
SSBN .... Fleet Ballistic Missile Submarine (Nuclear powered) [*Navy symbol*]
SSBO .... Single Swing Blocking Oscillator   (MSA)
SSBPI........ Serikat Sekerdja Bank Pembangunan Indonesia [*Indonesian Development Bank Employees' Union*]
SSBPS ...... Social Security Benefit Protection Service [*Detroit, MI*]   (EA)
SSBPT....... Serikat Sekerdja Balai Penelitian Tekstil [*Textile Research Institute Workers' Union*] [*Indonesia*]
SSBR........ Smooth-Surface Built-Up Roof [*Technical drawings*]
SSBR........ Solid Strand Burning Rate   (KSC)
SSBS......... Sisters Servants of the Blessed Sacrament [*Roman Catholic religious order*]
SSBSC....... Single Sideband Suppressed Carrier
SSBSCOM ... Single Sideband Suppressed Carrier Optical Modulator
SSBUS ...... South Slavic Benevolent Union Sloga [*Later, Sloga Fraternal Life Insurance Society*]   (EA)
SSC........... Co-Operative College of Canada, Saskatoon, Saskatchewan [*Library symbol*] [*National Library of Canada*]   (NLC)
SSC........... Cruiser Submarine [*Navy symbol*] [*Obsolete*]
SSC........... Missionary Sisters of St. Columban [*Roman Catholic religious order*]
SSC........... Naval Service School Command
SSC........... St. Sauveur De Carouges [*Seismograph station code, US Geological Survey*]   (SEIS)
SSC........... Saline Sodium Citrate [*Clinical chemistry*]
SSC........... Salisbury State College, Salisbury, MD [*OCLC symbol*]   (OCLC)
SS & C...... Same Sea and Country [*or Coast*]
SSC........... Sample Survey Centre [*University of Sydney*] [*Australia*] [*Information service*]   (EISS)
SSC........... Sandford's New York Superior Court Reports   (DLA)
SSC........... Sarawak Supreme Court Reports   (DLA)
SSC........... Satellite Systems Corporation [*Virginia Beach, VA*] [*Telecommunications*]   (TSSD)
S & Sc ...... Sausse and Scully's Irish Rolls Court Reports   (DLA)

SSC........... Savannah State College [*Georgia*]
SSC........... Scan-to-Scan Correlation
SSC........... Scotch Session Cases   (DLA)
SSC........... Sculptors Society of Canada
SSC........... Sea-State Correction [*Doppler navigation*]   (DEN)
SSC........... Sea Systems Command [*Also, NSSC*] [*Navy*]
SSC........... Second-Stage Conduit
SSC........... Sector Switching Center [*Telecommunications*]   (TEL)
SSC........... Secure Systems Corporation [*Manassas, VA*] [*Telecommunications*]   (TSSD)
SSC........... Security Classification Code   (MCD)
SSC........... Selector Subchannels
SSC........... Senate Staff Club   (EA)
SSC........... Senate Steel Caucus   (EA)
SSC........... Senior Service College [*Army*]   (AABC)
SSC........... Sensor Signal Conditioner
SSC........... Sequential Subsystem Controllers   (MCD)
SSC........... Serial Shift Counter [*Data processing*]
SSC........... Service Schools Command   (MCD)
SSC........... Seven Springs Center [*An association*]   (EA) ·
SSC........... Ship Structure Committee   (EA)
SSC........... Shipbuilding Stabilization Committee [*World War II*]
SSC........... Ship's Speed Converter   (MCD)
SSC........... Short Segmented Cask [*Nuclear energy*]   (NRCH)
SSC........... Short Service Commissions [*Army*] [*British*]
SSC........... Shuttle System Contractor [*NASA*]   (NASA)
SSC........... Siblings for Significant Change [*New York, NY*]   (EA)
SSC........... Side-Stick Controller
SSC........... Signaling and Supervisory Control
SSC........... Silver Star Citation [*Military award*]
SSC........... Simulated Spacecraft [*NASA*]
SSC........... Single Silk-Covered [*Wire insulation*]
SSC........... Sisters of St. Casimir [*Roman Catholic religious order*]
SSC........... Site Selection Criteria   (AAG)
S & SC ...... Sized and Supercalendered [*Paper*]
SSC........... Skill Specialty Code   (MCD)
SSC........... Social Sciences Center [*University of Nevada*] [*Research center*]   (RCD)
SSC........... Socialist Scholars Conference   (EA)
SSC........... Societas Sanctae Crucis [*Society of the Holy Cross*] [*Latin*]
SSC........... Society of the Sacred Cross [*Anglican religious community*]
SSC........... Society of Silver Collectors   (EA)
SSC........... Society for the Study of Caucasia   (EA)
SSC........... Sodium Chloride-Sodium Citrate [*Analytical chemistry*]
SSC........... Software Support Center [*Army*]   (RDA)
SSC........... Solar Stabilization Computer
SSC........... Soldier Support Center
SSC........... Solicitor, Supreme Court
SSC........... Solid-Solution CERMET [*NASA*]   (NASA)
SSC........... Solid-State Circuit
SSC........... Solid-State Computer
SSC........... Soluble Solids Content [*Analytical chemistry*]
SSC........... Southeastern Simulation Council
SSC........... Southeastern State College [*Later, Southeastern Oklahoma State University*]
SSC........... Southern State College [*Arkansas; South Dakota*]
SSC........... Space Science Committee [*Formerly, Provisional Space Science Advisory Board for Europe*]   (EA)
SSC........... Space Suit Communicator [*Apollo*] [*NASA*]
SSC........... Space Systems Center
SSC........... Spacecraft System Console
SSC........... Special Service Center [*Bell System*]
SSC........... Special Service Clergyman [*Church of England*]
SSC........... Spin Synchronous Clock
SSC........... Squadron Supervisory Console [*Air Force*]
SSC........... Squadron Support Center   (AAG)
SSC........... Squib Simulator Console
SSC........... Staff Selection Committee [*UN Food and Agriculture Organization*]
SSC........... Staff Service Center   (MCD)
SSC........... Standard Saline Citrate
SSC........... Standardization Status Code [*DoD*]
SSC........... Standards Steering Committee [*ANSI*]
SSC........... State Superfund Contract [*Environmental Protection Agency*]
SSC........... Static Standby Computer [*Mission Control Center*] [*NASA*]
SSC........... Station Selection Code [*Western Union*]   (BUR)
SSC........... Statistical Society of Canada [*Societe Statistique du Canada*]
SSC........... Stepping Switch Counter   (AAG)
SSC........... Stores Stock Catalog
SSC........... Structures, Systems, and Components   (NRCH)
SSC........... Submarine Supply Center
SSC........... Subsystem Computer   (MCD)
SSC........... Subsystem Sequence Controller [*NASA*]   (NASA)
SSC........... Sudden Storm Commencement [*Physics*]
SSC........... Sumter, SC [*Location identifier*] [*FAA*]   (FAAL)
SSC........... Sunshine Mining Company [*NYSE symbol*]
SSC........... Super Serial Card [*Apple Computer, Inc.*]
SSC........... Super System Code   (NRCH)
SSC........... Superconducting Super Collider [*Particle accelerator*]
SS & C........ Supersized and Calendered [*Paper*]
SSC........... Supply and Services Canada

SSC............ Supply Status Code [*Army*]   (AABC)
SSC............ Supply Support Center [*Navy*]
SSC............ Supply System Command [*Navy*]   (MCD)
SSC............ Systems Science and Cybernetics   (MCD)
SSC............ Systems Support Center   (BUR)
SSCA......... Seven Seas Cruising Association   (EA)
SSCA......... Southern Speech Communication Association   (EA)
SSCA......... Spray System Compressed Air [*Nuclear energy*]   (NRCH)
SSCA......... Standard Schnauzer Club of America   (EA)
SSCA......... Stockholm Studies in Classical Archaeology [*A publication*]
SSCA......... Surface Sampler Control Assembly [*NASA*]   (NASA)
SSCAG...... Research Station, Agriculture Canada [*Station de Recherches, Agriculture Canada*] Swift Current, Saskatchewan [*Library symbol*] [*National Library of Canada*]   (NLC)
SSCATS..... Skylab Simulation, Checkout, and Training System [*NASA*]
SSCB......... SCB Restaurant Systems [*NASDAQ symbol*]   (NQ)
SSCC......... Common Channel Signaling System [*Telecommunications*]   (TEL)
SSCC......... Congregatio Sacrorum Cordium [*Fathers of the Sacred Heart*] [*Picpus Fathers*] [*Roman Catholic religious order*]
SSCC......... IEEE Solid-State Circuits Council [*New York, NY*]   (EA)
SSCC......... Salt Shaker Collectors Club   (EA)
SSCC......... SATCOM System Control Center   (KSC)
SSCC......... Second-Stage Conduit Container
SSCC......... Sisters of the Sacred Hearts and of Perpetual Adoration [*Roman Catholic religious order*]
SSCC......... Sound Surveillance System Control Center   (MCD)
SSCC......... Space Surveillance Control Center
SSCC......... Spin-Scan Cloud Camera [*NASA*]
SSCC......... Support Services Control Center   (MCD)
SSCCB...... Safeguard System Configuration Control Board [*Army*]   (AABC)
SSCCS...... Solid State Component Control System   (NRCH)
SSCD......... Society of Small Craft Designers [*Boyne City, MI*]   (EA)
SSCD......... Start Sample Command Delayed
SSCD......... Superheated Superconducting Colloid Detector [*Particle physics*]
SSCD......... Support System Concept Document
SSCDS...... Small Ship Combat Data System
SSCE......... Silver/Silver Chloride Electrode
SSCE......... Sodium Chloride Calomel Electrode
SSCES...... Stanford Studies in the Civilizations of Eastern Asia [*A publication*]
SS/CF....... Signal Strength, Center Frequency [*Broadcasting*]
SSCF......... Space Subsystem Control Facility   (NATG)
SSCF......... Stress/Strain Controlled Fatigue   (MCD)
SSCH......... Sisters of Ste. Chretienne [*Roman Catholic religious order*]
SSCHS...... Space Shuttle Cargo Handling System [*NASA*]   (NASA)
SSCI........... Sanitation Suppliers and Contractors Institute [*Largo, FL*]   (EA)
SSCI........... Saskatoon Collegiate Institute, Saskatchewan [*Library symbol*] [*National Library of Canada*]   (NLC)
SSCI........... Senate Select Committee on Intelligence   (MCD)
SSCI........... Social Sciences Citation Index [*Institute for Scientific Information*] [*Database*] [*A publication*]
SSCI........... Steel Service Center Institute [*Cleveland, OH*]   (EA)
SSCI........... Steel Shipping Container Institute [*Union, NJ*]   (EA)
SSCISAM... Settimane di Studio del Centro Italiano di Studi sull'Alto Medioevo [*A publication*]
SSCJ......... Sorores a Sacro Corde Jesus [*Sisters of the Sacred Heart of Jesus*] [*Roman Catholic religious order*]
SSCJ......... Southern Speech Communication Journal [*A publication*]
SSCK........ Sister Servants of Christ the King [*Roman Catholic religious order*]
SSCL......... Shuttle System Commonality List [*NASA*]   (NASA)
SSCL......... Social Science Computing Laboratory [*University of Western Ontario*] [*London, ON*] [*Information service*]   (EISS)
SSCM....... Servants of the Holy Heart of Mary [*Roman Catholic women's religious order*]
SSCM....... Sisters of Saints Cyril and Methodius [*Roman Catholic religious order*]
SSCMA..... Special Supplementary Clothing Monetary Allowance [*Military*]
SSCN........ Nuclear Cruise Missile Submarine   (MCD)
SSCN........ Scotts Seaboard Corporation [*NASDAQ symbol*]   (NQ)
SSCNS...... Ship's Self-Contained Navigation System
SSCO........ Shipper Service Control Office [*Military*]   (AABC)
SSCP......... School Science Curriculum Project
SSCP......... Standard Saline Citrate Phosphate [*A buffer*]
SSCP......... State Service Center Program   (OICC)
SSCP......... System Services Control Point [*Data processing*]
SSCQT...... Selective Service College Qualifying Test
SSCR........ Set Screw
SSCR........ Sind Sadr Court Reports [*India*]   (DLA)
SSCR........ Spectral Shift Control Reactor
SSCr......... Stainless Steel Crown [*Dentistry*]
SSCRI....... Social Science Computer Research Institute [*University of Pittsburgh*] [*Pennsylvania*] [*Information service*]   (EISS)
SSCRN...... Silkscreen   (MSA)
SSCS......... Sea Shepherd Conservation Society   (EA)
SSCS......... Shipboard Satellite Communications System
SS & CS.... Ship's Stores and Commissary Stores [*Navy*]

SSCS......... Side-Stick Control System
SSCS......... Single Sideband Communications System
SSCS......... Southern Signal Corps School
SSCS......... Space Suit Communications System   (MCD)
SSCS......... Standards and Security Compliance Section [*Social Security Administration*]
SSCS......... Steep-Spectrum Compact Sources [*of galactic radio waves*]
SSCS......... Submarine SONAR Calibration Set
SSCS......... Synchronous Satellite Communications System
SSCSP...... Space Shuttle Crew Safety Panel [*NASA*]   (NASA)
SSCT......... Shipboard Communications Terminal
SSCT......... Solid-State Celestial Tracker
SSCT......... Solid-State Control Transformer
SSCU......... Soil Sampler Control Unit
SSCU......... Spacecraft Systems Controller Unit [*NASA*]   (KSC)
SSCU......... Special Signal Conditioning Unit
SSCU......... Store Station Control Unit   (MCD)
SSCV......... Semisubmersible Crane Vessel
SSCX......... Solid-State Control Transformer
SSD............ Doctor of Sacred Scripture
SSD............ Institute of the Sisters of St. Dorothy [*Roman Catholic religious order*]
SSD............ Safe Separation Device
SSD............ Sanctissimus Dominus [*Most Holy Lord*] [*Latin*]
SSD............ Scrap Salvage Division [*Navy*]
SSD............ SDC Sydney Development Corp. [*Vancouver Stock Exchange symbol*]
SSD............ Security Support Detachment   (MCD)
SSD............ Seize Signal Detector
SSD............ Semiconductor Silicon Detector
SSD............ Separation Systems Division [*Energy Research and Development Administration*]
SSD............ Sequence Switch Driver
S & SD....... Sewerage and Sewage Disposal
SSD............ Signal Seeking Device
SSD............ Single-Station DOVAP [*Doppler, Velocity, and Position*]
SSD............ Social Security Disability
SSD............ Software System Design [*Data processing*]
SSD............ Solid-State Detector
SSD............ Solid-State Dosimeter
SSD............ Solid-State Storage Device [*Data processing*]
SSD............ Source-to-Skin [*or -Surface*] Distance [*Radiology*]
SSD............ Space Sciences Division [*Jet Propulsion Laboratory*]
SSD............ Space Shuttle Display [*NASA*]
SSD............ Space Systems Division [*Air Force*]
SSD............ Special Service Division [*Army Services Forces*] [*World War II*]
SSD............ Specialized Storage Depot
SSD............ Specialized Support Department [*Air Force*]   (AFM)
SSD............ Specialized Support Depot [*Army*]   (AABC)
SSD............ Split-Screen Display
SSD............ Split Stage Demonstrator   (MCD)
SSD............ Squared Successive Differences [*Data processing*]
SSD............ Staatssicherheitsdienst [*State Security Service*] [*East Germany*]
SSD............ Stabilized Ship Detector [*Navy*]
SSD............ Subsoil Drain [*Technical drawings*]
SSD............ Sun Shadow Device
SSD............ Support Software Documentation   (MCD)
SSD............ Surface Sampler Device [*NASA*]
SSD............ Surveillance Situation Display
SSD............ Survival Support Device   (NVT)
SS & D....... Synchronization Separator and Digitizer
SSD............ System Status Display
SSD............ System Summary Display   (MCD)
SSD............ Systems Support Division [*Air Force*]
SSDA......... Sequential Similarity Detection Algorithm
SSDA......... Service Station Dealers of America [*Formerly, NCPR*] [*Washington, DC*]   (EA)
SSDA......... Social Science Data Archive [*Carleton University*] [*Ottawa, ON*] [*Information service*]   (EISS)
SSDA......... Social Science Data Archive [*University of Iowa*] [*Iowa City*] [*Information service*]   (EISS)
SSDA......... Social Science Data Archives [*Australian National University*] [*Canberra, ACT*] [*Information service*]   (EISS)
SSDA......... Social Science Data Archives [*University of California, Los Angeles*] [*Information service*]   (EISS)
SSDA......... Synchronous Serial Data Adapter
SSDB......... Shore Station Development Board
SSDC......... Sclerosing Sweat Duct Carcinoma [*Oncology*]
SSDC......... Signal Source Distribution Center   (AAG)
SSDC......... Social Science Data Center [*University of Connecticut*] [*Research center*]   (EISS)
SSDC......... Social Science Data Center [*University of Pennsylvania*] [*Philadelphia*] [*Information service*]   (EISS)
SSDC......... Social Science Documentation Centre [*Indian Council of Social Science Research*] [*New Delhi, India*] [*Information service*]   (EISS)
SSDC......... Social Science Documentation Centre [*UNESCO*]   (EISS)
SSDC......... Social Self-Defense Committee [*Poland*]   (PD)
SSDC......... Society of Stage Directors and Choreographers   (EA)
SSDC......... Space Science Data Center [*NASA*]   (MCD)

SSDC .... Synoptic-Scale Subprogramme Data Centre [*Marine science*]　(MSC)
SSDD .... Single-Sided, Double-Density Disk [*Magnetic disk*] [*Data processing*]
SSDD .... Software System Design Document　(MCD)
SSDG .... Ship Service Diesel Generator [*Navy*]　(CAAL)
SSDG .... Society for the Study of Development and Growth [*Later, SDB*]　(EA)
SSDH .... Subsystem Data Handbook [*NASA*]　(NASA)
SSDHPER ... Society of State Directors of Health, Physical Education, and Recreation　(EA)
SSDI .... Social Security Disability Insurance
SSDI .... Support System Design Integration　(AAG)
SSDK .... Savannah State Docks Railroad Co. [*AAR code*]
SSDL .... Secondary Standard Dosimetry Laboratory
SSDL .... Social Science Data Center [*Hunter College of City University of New York*] [*Research center*]　(RCD)
SSDL .... Social Science Data Library [*University of North Carolina*] [*Chapel Hill*] [*Information service*]　(EISS)
SSDL .... Society for the Study of Dictionaries and Lexicography [*Later, DSNA*]　(EA)
SSDM .... Shielding Standard Design Method　(MCD)
SSDMIC .... Secretariat State-Defense Military Information Control Committee
SSDN .... Sanctissimus Dominus Noster [*Our Most Holy Lord, Jesus Christ*] [*Latin*]
ssDNA .... Deoxyribonucleic Acid, Single-Stranded [*Biochemistry, genetics*]
SSDP .... Serikat Sekerdja Djawalan Padjak [*Brotherhood of Tax Office Employees*] [*Indonesia*]
SSDP .... Standard Source Data Package　(AFIT)
SSDP .... Suomen Sosialidemokraattinen Puolue [*Finnish Social Democratic Party*]　(PPW)
SSDPA .... Soft-Serv Dairy Products Association　(EA)
SSDPS ...... Solar System Data Processing System
SSDR .... Satellite Situation Display Room
SSDR .... SIGINT/SIGSEC Facilities Data Reporting System　(MCD)
SSDR .... Species Specific Defense Reaction
SSDR .... Steady State Determining Routine
SSDR .... Subsystem Development Requirement　(AFM)
SSDR .... Supermarket Subsystem Definition Record [*Data processing*]　(IBMDP)
SSDRS ...... Safeguard System Design Release Schedule [*Army*]　(AABC)
SSDS .... Small Ship Data System　(MUGU)
SSDS .... Space Shuttle Display and Simulation [*NASA*]
SSDS .... Surface-Supported Diving System　(CAAL)
SSDSA ...... Solomon Schecter Day School Association　(EA)
SSDSG ...... Special State Defense Study Group [*Military*]
SSDT .... Society of Soft Drink Technologists　(EA)
SSDVOR .... Single Sideband Doppler Very-High-Frequency Omnidirectional Range [*FAA*]
SSE .... North-Holland Series in Systems Science and Engineering [*Elsevier Book Series*] [*A publication*]
SSE .... Safe Shutdown Earthquake [*Nuclear energy*]　(NRCH)
SSE .... Safety System Engineering　(MCD)
SSE .... Salvador Society of Engineers
SSE .... Satellite Systems Engineering, Inc. [*Bethesda, MD*] [*Information service*]　(TSSD)
SSE .... Scale of Socio-Egocentrism [*Psychology*]
SSE .... Schick Shaving Experience [*Advertising slogan*]
SSE .... Scuola de Sviluppo Economico [*Italy*]
SSE .... Sector Scan Engagement [*Military*]　(CAAL)
SSE .... Seed Savers Exchange [*Formerly, TSX*]　(EA)
SSE .... Self-Sustained Emission
SSE .... SIGINT Support Element　(MCD)
SSE .... Signal Security Element　(AABC)
SSE .... Single Sideband Exciter
SSE .... Single Silk Covering over Enamel Insulation [*Telecommunications*]　(TEL)
SSE .... Sisters of St. Elizabeth [*Roman Catholic religious order*]
SSE .... Skin Self Examination [*Medicine*]
SSE .... Soap Suds Enema [*Medicine*]
SSE .... Society of St. Edmund [*Roman Catholic men's religious order*]
SSE .... Society for the Study of Evolution　(EA)
SSE .... Solid-State Electronics
SSE .... South-Southeast
SSE .... Southeastern Stock Exchange
SSE .... Southwest Semiconductor and Electronics Exposition　(TSPED)
SSE .... Space Shuttle Engines　(MCD)
SSE .... Special Support Equipment
SSE .... Squared Sum of Errors
SSE .... Stage Systems Engineer
SSE .... Stateside Energy [*Vancouver Stock Exchange symbol*]
SSE .... Strangest Stories Ever Told [*A publication*]
SSe .... Studi Secenteschi [*A publication*]
SSE .... Subsystem Element [*NASA*]　(NASA)
SSE .... Subsystem Support Equipment　(MCD)
SSE .... Sum of Squared Errors [*Statistics*]
SSE .... Support System Evaluation
SSE .... Support Systems Engineering [*Boeing*]

SSE .... Surface Support Equipment
SSE .... Sydney Stock Exchange [*Australia*]　(ADA)
SSE .... System Safety Engineering　(AFM)
SSE .... System Status Evaluation [*Army*]　(AABC)
SSE .... System Support Engineering
SSE .... System Support Equipment
S1S1E .... Surfaced or Dressed One Side and One Edge [*Technical drawings*]
SSEA .... Sentinel System Evaluation Agency [*DoD*]
SSEA .... Separate Sampling and Excitation Analysis [*Spectroscopy*]
SSEA .... Stage-Specific Embryonic Antigen [*Immunology*]
SSEA .... System Safety Engineering Analysis　(MCD)
SSEAM ...... Ship Systems Equipment Acquisition Manual　(MCD)
SSEAT .... Surveyor Scientific Evaluation Advisory Team [*NASA*]
SSEB .... Source Selection Evaluation Board　(AFM)
SSEC .... Selective Sequence Electronic Calculator [*Data processing*]
SSEC .... Social Science Education Consortium　(EA)
SSEC .... Society for the Study of Early China　(EA)
SSEC .... Solar System Exploration Committee [*NASA*]
SSEC .... Solid-State Electronic Chronograph
SSEC .... Sound Surveillance Evaluation Center [*Navy*]　(NVT)
SSEC .... Space Science and Engineering Center [*University of Wisconsin - Madison*] [*Research center*]　(RCD)
SSEC .... Static Source Error Correction
SSECF .... Stateside Energy Corporation [*NASDAQ symbol*]　(NQ)
SSECO ...... Second-Stage Engine Cutoff
SSECS ...... Space Station Environmental Control System
SSECW ...... Prairie Migratory Bird Research Centre, Canadian Wildlife Service, Environment Canada [*Centre de Recherches sur les Oiseaux Migrateurs des Prairies, Service Canadien de la Faune, Environnement Canada*] Saskatoon, Saskatchewan [*Library symbol*] [*National Library of Canada*]　(NLC)
SSEE .... Standing-Shock Equilibrium Expansion
SSE/EWE ... SIGINT [*Signal Intelligence*] Support Element/Electronic Warfare Element [*Military*]　(AABC)
SSEF .... Solid-State Electro-Optic Filter
SSEG .... Ship System Engineering Group [*British*]
SSEG .... System-Segment [*Data processing*]
SSEH .... National Hydrology Rsearch Centre, Environment Canada [*Centre National de Recherche en Hydrologie, Environnement Canada*] Saskatoon, Saskatchewan [*Library symbol*] [*National Library of Canada*]　(NLC)
SSEIP .... Special Stockpile Engineering Investigation Program　(MCD)
SSEKP ...... Single Shot Engagement Kill Probability　(MCD)
SSEL .... Solid-State Electronics Laboratory [*Stanford University*]　(MCD)
SSEL .... Space Science and Engineering Laboratory [*Pennsylvania State University*]
SSEL .... Standard Statistical Establishment List [*Bureau of the Census*]
SSEL .... Stockholm Studies in English Literature [*A publication*]
SSEM .... Solid State Extended Memory　(MCD)
SSEM .... Space System Effectiveness Model
SSEM .... Supply Support Element Manager
SSEO .... SEABEE Support and Equipment Office [*Navy*]
SSEOS ...... Space Shuttle Engineering and Operations Support [*NASA*]　(MCD)
SSEP .... Somatosensory Evoked Potential [*Neurophysiology*]
SSEP .... Submarine Surveillance Equipment Program　(NVT)
SSEP .... System Safety Engineering Plan　(AFM)
SSEPA .... Society of Spanish Engineers, Planners, and Architects　(EA)
SSept .... Studia Septentrionalia [*A publication*]
SSER .... Site Safety Evaluation Report　(NRCH)
SSER .... Somatosensory Evoked Response [*Neurophysiology*]
SSER .... Supplement to Safety Evaluation Report [*Nuclear energy*]　(NRCH)
SSERN .... South-Southeastern [*Meteorology*]　(FAAC)
SSES .... Ship Signals Exploitation Space [*Navy*]　(CAAL)
SSES .... Shipboard Signal Exploration System　(MCD)
SSES .... Single Strip Engine System
SSES .... Special Signal Exploitation Spaces　(NVT)
SSES .... Susquehanna Steam Electric Station　(NRCH)
SSESC ...... College of Emmanuel and St. Chad, Saskatoon, Saskatchewan [*Library symbol*] [*National Library of Canada*]　(NLC)
SSESM ...... Spent Stage Experimental Support Module　(KSC)
SSESS ...... Soviet Space Event Support Ships　(CINC)
SSET .... State Science, Engineering, and Technology Program [*National Science Foundation*]
SSEU .... System Selector Extension Unit
SSEWD ...... South-Southeastward [*Meteorology*]　(FAAC)
SSF .... Congregation of the Sisters of the Family [*Roman Catholic religious order*]
SSF .... Safe Shutdown Facility [*Nuclear energy*]　(NRCH)
SSF .... Saint Saulge [*France*] [*Seismograph station code, US Geological Survey*]　(SEIS)
SSF .... San Antonio, TX [*Location identifier*] [*FAA*]　(FAAL)
SSF .... Saybolt Seconds Furol [*Oil viscosity*]
SSF .... Service Storage Facility
SSF .... Service Support Force [*Military*]
SSF .... Ship's Service Force [*Navy*]
SSF .... Simulated Spinal Fluid [*Medicine*]

SSF .... Single-Seated Fighter
SSF .... Single Sideband Filter
SSF .... Single Sided Frame [*Telecommunications*]   (TEL)
SSF .... Single Solar Flare
SSF .... Single-Stage Fan
SSF .... Sjogren's Syndrome Foundation [*Great Neck, NY*]   (EA)
SSF .... Society of St. Francis [*Anglican religious community*]
SSF .... Society for the Study of Fertility [*British*]
SSF .... Sodium Silicofluoride [*Inorganic chemistry*]
SSF .... Software Support Facility   (MCD)
SSF .... Soluble Suppressor Factor [*Immunology*]
SSF .... Somali Salvation Front   (PD)
SSF .... Sona Systems Ltd. (Canada) [*Vancouver Stock Exchange symbol*]
SSF .... Space Simulation Facility   (AAG)
SSF .... Special Security Facility
SSF .... Special Service Force [*Canadian and US troops under combined command*] [*World War II*]
SSF .... Spun Soy Fiber [*Food technology*]
SSF .... Stainless Steel Fiber
SSF .... Standard Saybolt Furol [*Oil viscosity*]
SSF .... Standby Shutdown Facility [*Nuclear energy*]   (NRCH)
SSF .... Studies in Short Fiction [*A publication*]
SSF .... Style Sac Flap
SSF .... Super Science Fiction [*A publication*]
SSF .... Supply Status File   (MCD)
SSF .... Symmetrical Switching Function
SSF .... System Support Facility
SSFC .... Sequential Single Frequency Code System [*Telecommunications*]   (TEL)
SSFC .... Social Science Federation of Canada [*Research center*]   (IRC)
SSFC .... Solid State Frequency Changer [*Military*]   (CAAL)
SSF CHL .... Societas Scientiarum Fennicae. Commentationes Humanarum Litterarum [*A publication*]
SSFF .... Scholastic Science Fiction Federation   (EA)
SSFGSS ..... Space Shuttle Flight and Ground System Specification [*NASA*]   (NASA)
SSFI .... Scaffolding, Shoring, and Forming Institute [*Formerly, SSSI, SSI*] [*Cleveland, OH*]   (EA)
SSFL .... Santa Susana Field Laboratory [*NASA*]   (NASA)
SSFL .... Steady-State Fermi Level
SSFM .... Scandinavian Society of Forensic Medicine   (EA)
SSFM .... Single Sideband Frequency Modulation
SSFN .... Solidarity: A Socialist-Feminist Network   (EA)
SSFO .... Scandinavian Society of Forensic Odontology   (EA)
SSFO .... Simultaneous Single Frequency Outlet
SS & FO .... Specialized Safety and Flight Operations
SSFR .... Safety Services Field Representative [*Red Cross*]
SSFS .... Samlingar Utgivna av Svenska Fornskriftssallskapet (Stockholm) [*A publication*]
SSFS .... Space Shuttle Functional Simulator [*NASA*]   (KSC)
SSFS .... Special Services Forecasting System [*Telecommunications*]   (TEL)
SSFT .... Scientific Software [*NASDAQ symbol*]   (NQ)
SSFT .... Self-Sealing Fuel Tank
SSFVT .... Subsystems Functional Verification Test [*NASA*]
SSG .... Guided Missile Submarine [*Navy symbol*]
SSG .... Malabo [*Equatorial Guinea*] [*Airport symbol*]   (OAG)
SSG .... Safety Study Group   (MCD)
SSG .... Schriften der Theodor-Storm-Gesellschaft [*A publication*]
SSG .... Science Steering Group [*NASA*]
SSG .... Search Signal Generator
SSG .... Senior Savers Guide Publishing, Inc. [*Vancouver Stock Exchange symbol*]
SSG .... Shuttle Support Group   (MCD)
SSG .... Single Sideband Generator
SSG .... Small Signal Gain   (IEEE)
SSG .... Southern Society of Genealogists   (EA)
SSG .... Special Security Group   (MCD)
SSG .... Special Studies Group [*Joint Chiefs of Staff*] [*Military*]
SSG .... Special Support Group [*FBI*]   (CINC)
SSG .... Staff Sergeant [*Army*]   (AABC)
SSG .... State Services Group [*Information service*]   (EISS)
SSG .... Stonehenge Study Group   (EA)
SSG .... Supply Spectrum Generator
SSG .... Sweep Signal Generator
SSG .... Symbolic Stream Generator [*Data processing*]
SSG .... System Safety Group [*Air Force*]
SSGA .... Society of St. Gregory of America [*Later, CMAA*]   (EA)
SSGA .... Sterling Silversmiths Guild of America [*Baltimore, MD*]   (EA)
SSGA .... Swordsmen and Sorcerers' Guild of America   (EA)
SSGC .... Saskatoon Gallery and Conservatory, Saskatchewan [*Library symbol*] [*National Library of Canada*]   (NLC)
SSGC .... Short System Ground Check
SSGD .... Smoke Screen Generative Device
SSGDFB ..... Second Sight-Guide Dog Foundation for the Blind [*Also known as GDFB*]   (EA)
SSGED .... Seikei-Saigai Geka [*A publication*]
SSGJ .... Single Strength Grapefruit Juice
SSGJ .... Supersonic Gas Jet

SSGM .... Service Station & Garage Management [*Canada*] [*A publication*]
SSGMB ..... Sbornik Nauchnogo Studencheskogo Obshchestva, Geologicheskii Fakul'tet, Moskovskii Gosudarstvenyi Universitet [*A publication*]
SSGN .... Guided Missile Submarine (Nuclear Propulsion) [*Navy symbol*]
SSGP .... Spin Stabilized Guided Projectile   (MCD)
SSGp .... System Safety Group [*Air Force*]   (AFM)
SSGS .... Solid-State Gamma Switch
SSGS .... Standard Space Guidance System
SSGS .... Stanford Studies in Germanics and Slavics [*A publication*]
SSGT .... Ship Service Gas Turbine [*Navy*]   (CAAL)
SSGT .... Small-Scale Gap Test [*Explosive*]
SSGT .... Staff Sergeant [*Military*]
SSGT .... Subsystem Ground Test   (MCD)
SSGTG ..... Ship's Service Gas Turbine Generator [*Navy*]   (NVT)
SSGW .... Sitzungsberichte der Saechsischen Gesellschaft der Wissenschaften [*Leipzig*] [*A publication*]
SSGW .... Surface-to-Surface Guided Weapon   (NATG)
SSH .... Schwartz-Slawsky-Herzfeld [*Theory*] [*Chemical kinetics*]
SSH .... Second-Stage Hydraulics
SSH .... Sharm E Sheikh [*Israel*] [*Airport symbol*]   (OAG)
SSH .... Skytteanska Samfundets Handlinger [*A publication*]
SSH .... Small-Scale Hydroelectric Project
SSH .... Snowshoe Hare
SSH .... Social Sciences and Humanities Index [*A publication*]
SSH .... Social Sciences and Humanities Research Council of Canada [*UTLAS symbol*]
SSH .... Social Service Handbooks [*A publication*]
SSH .... South Shore [*AAR code*]
SSH .... Studia Slavica. Academiae Scientiarum Hungaricae [*A publication*]
SSH .... Studies in Society and History [*A publication*]
SSH .... Substantial Stockholder
SSH .... Sunshine [*Alaska*] [*Seismograph station code, US Geological Survey*]   (SEIS)
SSHA .... Subsystem Hazard Analysis
SSHA .... Survey of Study Habits and Attitudes [*Education*]
SSHB .... Society for the Study of Human Biology   (EA)
SSHB .... Stainless Steel Helium Bottle
SSHB .... Station Set Handbook [*NASA*]   (NASA)
SSHCG ...... Students' Series of Historical and Comparative Grammars [*A publication*]
SSHD .... Single-Silo Hardsite Defense
SSHE .... Scraped-Surface Heat Exchanger [*Process engineering*]
SSHJM ...... Sisters of the Sacred Hearts of Jesus and Mary [*Roman Catholic religious order*]
SSHJP .... Servants of the Sacred Heart of Jesus and of the Poor [*Roman Catholic women's religious order*]
S/SHLD ..... Side Shield [*Automotive engineering*]
SSHM .... Society for the Social History of Medicine   (EA-IO)
SSHP .... Single-Shot Hit Probability
SSHR .... Social Systems and Human Resources [*National Science Foundation*]   (MCD)
SSHR .... Spartan Safety Hazard Report [*Missiles*]   (MCD)
SSHRC ...... Social Sciences and Humanities Research Council of Canada
SSHRCC .... Social Sciences and Humanities Research Council of Canada [*Pronounced "sherk"*] [*See also CRSHC*]
SSHS .... Stainless Steel Helium Sphere
SSHSA ...... Steamship Historical Society of America   (EA)
SSHum ...... Social Sciences and Humanities Index [*A publication*]
SSI .... Brunswick, GA [*Location identifier*] [*FAA*]   (FAAL)
SSI .... Safe Shutdown Impoundment [*Nuclear energy*]   (NRCH)
SSI .... Safeway Stores, Incorporated
SSI .... Satellite Services, Incorporated [*Houston, TX*] [*Telecommunications*]   (TSSD)
SSI .... Scaffolding and Shoring Institute [*Later, SSFI*]   (EA)
SSI .... Scientific Software-Intercomp, Inc. [*Denver, CO*] [*Software manufacturer*]
SSI .... Second-Stage Ignition
SSI .... Sector Scan Indicator
SSI .... Security Systems, Incorporated [*In TV series "Max Headroom"*]
SSI .... Seismic Survival Indicator [*Earthquake analysis program*] [*Data processing*]
SSI .... Semisopochnoi Island [*Alaska*] [*Seismograph station code, US Geological Survey*] [*Closed*]   (SEIS)
SSI .... Service Social International [*International Social Service - ISS*]   (EA-IO)
SSI .... Service Software, Incorporated [*Cherry Hill, NJ*] [*Software manufacturer*]
SSI .... Shaft Speed Indicator
SSI .... Short Story International [*A publication*]
SSI .... Shoulder Sleeve Insignia [*Military*]   (AABC)
SSI .... Significant Structural Item   (NASA)
SSI .... Single Service Institute [*Washington, DC*]   (EA)
SSI .... Site of Special Scientific Interest [*Great Britain*]
SSI .... Skill Speciality Identifier   (MCD)
SSI .... Sky Survey Instrument
SSI .... Slater Steel Industries Ltd. [*Toronto Stock Exchange symbol*]

SSI .... Slater Steels Corp. [*Formerly, Slater Steel Industries*] [*Toronto Stock Exchange symbol*]
SSI .... Small-Scale Integration
SSI .... Smart Set International [*Program to discourage drug abuse*] [*Defunct*]   (EA)
SSI .... Social Science Information [*A publication*]
SSI .... Social Science Institute [*Washington University*] [*Research center*]   (RCD)
SSI .... Social Security Information
SSI .... Society of Saunterers, International [*Gaylord, MI*]   (EA)
SSI .... Society of Scribes and Illuminators   (EA)
SSI .... Society for Siberian Irises   (EA)
SSI .... Society for the Study of Internationalism   (EA)
SSI .... Solid-State Inverter
SSI .... Space Studies Institute   (EA)
SSI .... Spacecraft System Integration
SSI .... Spares Status Inquiry   (AAG)
SSI .... Special Subject for Inspection [*DoD*]
SSI .... Special Surveillance Inspection   (MCD)
SSI .... Specialty Skill Identifier   (AABC)
SSI .... Specific Searching Image [*Tendency of birds to select prey of the color to which they have been accustomed*]
SSI .... Staff Sergeant Instructor [*Military*] [*British*]
SSI .... Standing Signal Instructions
SSI .... Start Signal Indicator [*Telecommunications*]   (TEL)
SSI .... Steady-State Irradiation   (NRCH)
SSI .... Stockpile Surveillance Inspection
SSI .... Storage-to-Storage Instruction   (IEEE)
SSI .... Strategic Studies Institute   (MCD)
SSI .... Structural Significant Item   (MCD)
SSI .... Student/Supervisor Instructions [*Army Training Extension Course*]   (INF)
SSI .... Sucro-Sac-Ologists Society International [*Defunct*]   (EA)
SSI .... Supplemental Security Income [*Social Security Administration*]
SSI .... Supplemental Security Insurance [*Program*]
SSI .... Supply Support Index   (CAAL)
SSI .... Surprise Security Inspection [*Navy*]   (NVT)
SSI .... Survey Sampling, Incorporated [*Westport, CT*] [*Information service*]   (EISS)
SSI .... Symptom Sign Inventory [*Psychology*]
SSI .... Synchronous Systems Interface
SSI .... System Science Institute [*IBM Corp.*]
SSI .... System Status Indicator [*Bell System*]
SSIA .... Scottish Society for Industrial Archaeology   (EA)
SSIA .... Shoe Service Institute of America [*Chicago, IL*]   (EA)
SSIA .... Specification Serial of Individual Assigned
SSIAM .... Structured and Scaled Interview to Assess Maladjustment [*Psychometrics*]
SSIB .... Shop Stock Items Bin   (MCD)
SSIBD .... Shuttle System Interface Block Diagram [*NASA*]   (NASA)
SSIC .... Saskatchewan Indian Cultural College, Saskatoon, Saskatchewan [*Library symbol*] [*National Library of Canada*]   (NLC)
SSIC .... Small-Scale Integrated Circuit
SSIC .... Southern States Industrial Council [*Later, USIC*]   (EA)
SSIC .... Standard Subject Identification Code   (NVT)
SSID .... Ship Systems Integration Data   (MCD)
SSIDS .... Siblings of Sudden Infant Death Syndrome Victims [*Medicine*]
SSIE .... Skylab Systems Integration Equipment [*NASA*]   (MCD)
SSIE .... Smithsonian Science Information Exchange [*Smithsonian Institution*] [*Washington, DC*] [*Database*]
SSIE .... Solid Surface Interaction Experiment
SSIEM .... Society for the Study of Inborn Errors of Metabolism   (EA-IO)
SSIG .... Single Signal   (IEEE)
SSIG .... State Student Incentive Grants
S Sig Sta .... Storm Signal Station [*Nautical charts*]
SSII .... Solid-State Image Intensifier
SSII .... Specialized Systems [*NASDAQ symbol*]   (NQ)
SSIL .... Supply Significant Items List   (MCD)
SSILS .... Solid State Instrument Landing System   (MCD)
SSIM .... Statistical, Sampling Inventory Method   (AABC)
SSINA .... Scientia Sinica [*English Edition*] [*A publication*]
SSIOD .... Solid State Ionics [*A publication*]
SSIP .... Secondary Students Information Press [*A publication*]
SSIP .... Ship Support Improvement Program [*DoD*]
SSIP .... Shuttle Student Involvement Project [*NASA*]
SSIP .... Standard Systems Improvement Program
SSIP .... Subsystem Integration Plan
SSIP .... Subsystems Integration Program [*or Project*] [*NATO*]   (NATG)
SSIP .... System Setup Indicator Panel
SSIP .... Systems Software Interface Processing   (MCD)
SSIPL .... Support and Sustaining Implications of Increased POMCUS Levels [*Military*]
SSIR .... Soil Survey Investigations Report
SSIR .... Special Security Investigation Requirement   (AFM)
SSIS .... Society for South India Studies   (EA)
SSIS .... Spacecraft System Integration Support
SSISS .... Spacecraft System Integration Support Service
SSITP .... Shuttle System Integrated Test Plan [*NASA*]   (NASA)
SSIU .... Subsystem Interface Unit   (MCD)
SSIUL .... Social Sciences Information Utilization Laboratory

SSIUS .... Specialty Steel Industry of the United States [*Washington, DC*]   (EA)
SSIX .... Submarine Satellite Information Exchange [*Geosynchronous communications satellite*]
SSIXS .... Submarine Satellite Information Exchange System   (MCD)
SSJ............. Sandnessjoen [*Norway*] [*Airport symbol*]   (OAG)
SSJ............. Savez Sindikata Jugoslavije [*Yugoslavia Federation of Trade Unions*]
SSJ............. Self-Aligning Swivel Joint
SSJ............. Self-Screening Jammer   (MCD)
SSJ............. Sequential Spot Jamming [*Military*]   (CAAL)
SSJ............. Servo Summing Junction
SSJ............. Shinshu-Shinmachi [*Japan*] [*Seismograph station code, US Geological Survey*]   (SEIS)
SSJ............. Side-Support Jack
SSJ............. Sinatra Society of Japan [*Tokyo*]   (EA-IO)
SSJ............. Single Subsonic Jet
SSJ............. Sisters of St. Joseph [*Roman Catholic religious order*]
SSJ............. Sisters of St. Joseph of the Third Order of St. Francis [*Roman Catholic religious order*]
SSJ............. Societas Sancti Joseph Sanctissimi Cordis [*St. Joseph's Society of the Sacred Heart*] [*Josephites*] [*Roman Catholic men's religious order*]
SSJ............. Solid-State Jammer
SSJ............. Southern Speech Journal [*A publication*]
SSJC .... Southern Seminary and Junior College [*Virginia*]
SSJD .... Society of St. John the Divine [*Anglican religious community*]
SSJE .... Society of St. John the Evangelist [*Anglican religious community*]
SSJSM .... Sisters of St. Joseph of St. Mark [*Roman Catholic religious order*]
SSK .... Antisubmarine Submarine [*Navy symbol*]
SSK .... Softkey Software Products, Inc. [*Vancouver Stock Exchange symbol*]
SSK .... Soil Stack
SSKDN .... Serikat Sekerdja Kementerian Dalam Negeri [*Union of Workers in the Department of Interior*] [*Indonesia*]
SSKI .... Saturated Solution of Potassium Iodide [*Medicine*]
SSKIL .... Library Technician Program, Kelsey Institute of Applied Arts & Sciences, Saskatoon, Saskatchewan [*Library symbol*] [*National Library of Canada*]   (NLC)
SSKP .... Serikat Sekerdja Kementerian Pertaganan [*Ministry of Defense Workers' Unions*] [*Indonesia*]
SSKP .... Single-Shot Kill Probability
SSKPS .... Solid-State Klystron Power Supply
SSKY......... Super Sky International [*NASDAQ symbol*]   (NQ)
SSL .... Congregation of Sisters of St. Louis [*Roman Catholic religious order*]
SSL .... Licentiate of Sacred Scripture
SSL .... Safety Systems Laboratory [*Formerly, Office of Vehicle Systems Research*] [*Department of Transportation*]
SSL .... Scandoslavica [*Copenhagen*] [*A publication*]
SSL .... School of Systems and Logistics [*Military*]
SSL .... Scientific Subroutine Library
SSL .... Scientific Support Laboratory [*CDEC*]   (MCD)
SSL .... Seattle, WA [*Location identifier*] [*FAA*]   (FAAL)
SSL .... Selected Source List   (AAG)
SSL .... Shift and Select [*Data processing*]   (MDG)
SSL .... Ship Shortage Log   (AAG)
SSL .... Shop Stock List   (MCD)
SSL .... Skaneateles Short Line Railroad Corp. [*AAR code*]
SSL .... Social Security Administration Library, Baltimore, MD [*OCLC symbol*]   (OCLC)
SSL .... Sociosystem Laboratory
SSL .... Sodium Stearoyl Lactylate
SSL .... Software Sciences Limited [*British*]
SSL .... Software Slave Library [*Data processing*]   (TEL)
SSL .... Software Specification Language
SSL .... Solid-State Lamp
SSL .... Solid-State LASER
SSL .... Source Statement Library [*Data processing*]
SSL .... Southern Star Resources Limited [*Vancouver Stock Exchange symbol*]
SSL .... Space Sciences Laboratory [*University of California, Berkeley*] [*Research center*] [*NASA*]   (MCD)
SSL .... Space Simulation Laboratory
SSL .... Special Sensor-Lightning
SSL .... Spent Sulfite Liquor [*Papermaking*]
SSL .... Storage Structure Language
SSL .... Studi e Saggi Linguistici [*A publication*]
SSL .... Studies in Scottish Literature [*A publication*]
SSL .... Studies in Semitic Languages and Linguistics [*A publication*]
SSL .... Sunset Lake [*Pennsylvania*] [*Seismograph station code, US Geological Survey*] [*Closed*]   (SEIS)
SSL .... Support Status List   (MCD)
SSL .... System Specification Language
SSL .... System Stock List   (NATG)
SSlav.......... Studia Slavica. Academiae Scientiarum Hungaricae [*A publication*]
SSLC.......... Ship System Life Cycle [*Navy*]

SSLC......... Society of Savings and Loan Controllers [*Later, Financial Managers Society*]   (EA)
SSLC......... Synchronous Single-Line Controller
SSLE......... Subacute Sclerosing Leukoencephalitis [*Medicine*]
SSLF......... Skrifter Utgivna av Svenska Litteratursallskapet i Finland [*A publication*]
SSLF......... Southern Sudan Liberation Front   (BJA)
SSLH......... Society for the Study of Labour History   (EA)
SSLI......... Serum Sickness-Like Illness [*Medicine*]
SSLI......... Society of School Librarians International   (EA)
SSLI......... Studies in Semitic Languages and Linguistics [*A publication*]
SSLIA....... Southern Second Life Cl A [*NASDAQ symbol*]   (NQ)
SSLL........ Stanford Studies in Language and Literature [*A publication*]
SSLO........ Solid-State Local Oscillator
SSLORAN ... Skywave Synchronized Long-Range Aid to Navigation
SSLP......... Transport Submarine   (MCD)
SSL-POW/MIA ... Seaside Support League - POW/MIA   (EA)
SSLPS....... Solid-State Logic Protection System [*Nuclear energy*]   (NRCH)
SSLR......... Straits Settlements Law Reports   (DLA)
SSLR Supp ... Straits Settlements Law Reports, Supplement [*1897-99*] [*Malasia*]   (DLA)
SSLS......... Solid-State LASER System
SSLS......... Standard Space Launch System [*BSD*]
SSLSM....... Single Service Logistics Support Manager   (MCD)
SSLSN ...... Skrifter Utgivna av Svenska Litteratursallskapet Studier i Nordisk Filologi [*A publication*]
SSLT......... Solid-State Logic Timer
SSLT......... Starboard Side Light   (MCD)
SSLT......... Stock Status Lag Time   (AABC)
SSLV......... Southern San Luis Valley Railroad Co. [*AAR code*]
SSLV......... Standard Space Launch Vehicle
SSM .... St. Thomas More College, Saskatoon, Saskatchewan [*Library symbol*] [*National Library of Canada*]   (NLC)
SSM .... Sault Ste. Marie [*Michigan*] [*Airport symbol*]   (OAG)
SSM .... School in Sales Management [*LIMRA*]
S & Sm ...... Searle and Smith's English Probate & Divorce Reports   (DLA)
SSM .... Second-Stage Motor
SSM .... Second Surface Mirror
SSM .... Self-Sterilizing-Material [*Pharmacology*]
SSM .... Semiconductor Storage Module
SSM .... Seminaire St. Martial [*Haiti*] [*Seismograph station code, US Geological Survey*] [*Closed*]   (SEIS)
SSM .... Serum-Supplemented Medium [*Microbiology*]
SSM .... Sesquiterpenoid Stress Metabolite [*Plant physiology*]
SSM .... Ship Simulation Model [*Navy*]
SSM .... Signal Strength Monitor [*Broadcasting*]
SSM .... Silver Star Medal [*Military decoration*]
SSM .... Single Sideband Modulation
SSM .... Single Sideband Signal Multiplier [*Telecommunications*]
SSM .... Sisters of St. Mary of the Third Order of St. Francis [*Roman Catholic religious order*]
SSM .... Sisters of the Sorrowful Mother [*Third Order of St. Francis*] [*Roman Catholic religious order*]
SSM .... Small Semiconductor Memory
SSM .... Society of the Sacred Mission [*Anglican religious community*]
SSM .... Society of St. Margaret [*Anglican religious community*]
SSM .... Society of the Servants of Mary [*Anglican religious community*]
SSM .... Solar Simulation Module
SSM .... Solar Stereoscopic Mission [*NASA*]
SSM .... Solid-State Materials   (CET)
SSM .... Space Science Fiction Magazine [*A publication*]
SSM .... Space Station Module [*NASA*]   (KSC)
SSM .... Spacecraft Systems Monitor   (MCD)
SSM .... Spark Source Mass Spectroscopy
SSM .... Special Safeguarding Measures [*Telecommunications*]   (TEL)
SSM .... Spread Spectrum Modulation   (NATG)
SSM .... Squadron Sergeant Major
SSM .... SSMC, Inc. [*NYSE symbol*]
SSM .... Staff Sergeant Major [*Military*]
SSM .... Standard Surfacing Mat [*Fiberglass*]
SSM .... Subsynaptic Membrane [*Anatomy*]
SSM .... Subsystem Manager [*NASA*]   (NASA)
SSM .... Superficial Spreading Melanoma [*Oncology*]
SSM .... Supply Support Management
SSM .... Support Systems Module [*NASA*]
SSM .... Surface-to-Surface Missile
SSM .... System Support Management [*or Manager*]   (AFM)
SSM .... System Support Module   (MCD)
SSMA....... School Science and Mathematics Association   (EA)
SSMA....... Soldiers, Sailors, Marines, and Airmen's Club [*Washington, DC*]
SSMA....... Solid-State Microwave Amplifier
SSMA....... Southwest Spanish Mustang Association   (EA)
SSMA....... Spread-Spectrum Multiple Access [*Satellite communications*]
SSMB....... Ship's Serviceman, Barber [*Navy rating*]
SSMB....... Space Shuttle Maintenance Baseline   (MCD)
SSMB....... Special Services Management Bureau [*Telecommunications*]   (TEL)
SSMC....... Second-Stage Motor Container
SSMC....... Ship's Serviceman, Cobbler [*Navy rating*]
SSMC....... Silver State Mining [*NASDAQ symbol*]   (NQ)

SSMCIS ..... Secondary School Mathematics Curriculum Improvement Study [*National Science Foundation*]
SSMCNP.... Safeguard System Management Communications Network Program [*Army*]   (AABC)
SSMCS ..... Synchronous Satellite Military Communication System
SSMD........ Saskatchewan Mining Development Corp., Saskatoon, Saskatchewan [*Library symbol*] [*National Library of Canada*]   (NLC)
SSMD........ Silicon Stud-Mounted Diode
SSME....... Satellite System Monitoring Equipment
SSME....... Space Shuttle Main Engine [*NASA*]
SSME....... Spread Spectrum Modulation Equipment [*NATO*]   (MCD)
SSMEC ..... Space Shuttle Main Engine Controller   (MCD)
SSMECA.... Space Shuttle Main Engine Controller Assembly [*NASA*]   (NASA)
SSMF .... Symbol Sink - Matched Filter
SSMG....... Satellite Systems Monitoring Group [*INTELSAT*]
SSMG....... Ship's Service Motor Generator [*Navy*]   (NVT)
SSMHRC.... Spanish Speaking Mental Health Research Center [*Public Health Service*] [*University of California, Los Angeles*] [*Research center*]   (RCD)
SSMI .... Sister Servants of Mary Immaculate [*Roman Catholic religious order*]
SSMIF & G ... Squadron Sergeant-Major Instructor in Fencing and Gymnastics [*Military*] [*British*]   (ROG)
SSM/IM..... System Support Manager/Inventory Manager   (MCD)
SSMIMA..... Scissor, Shear, and Manicure Implement Manufacturers Association [*Later, National Association of Scissors and Shears Manufacturers*]   (EA)
SSMIS ...... Support Services Management Information System [*Army*]
SSML .... Shaped Substrata Meanderline   (MCD)
SSML .... Ship's Serviceman, Laundryman [*Navy rating*]
SSMLN...... Society for the Study of Midwestern Literature. Newsletter [*A publication*]
SSMM ...... Space Station Mathematical Model
SSMMA..... Staple and Stapling Machine Manufacturers Association [*Defunct*]
SSMN....... Sisters of St. Mary of Namur [*Roman Catholic religious order*]
SSMO....... Sisters of St. Mary of Oregon [*Roman Catholic religious order*]
SSMO........ Summary of Synoptic Meteorological Observations [*Marine science*]   (MSC)
SSMOB ..... Surface-to-Surface Missile Order of Battle   (MCD)
SSMP .... Safeguard System Master Plan [*Army*]   (AABC)
SSMP .... Stockholm Studies in Modern Philology [*A publication*]
SSMP .... Supply Support Management Plan [*Military*]   (CAAL)
SSMPP...... Society for the Study of Male Psychology and Physiology   (EA)
SSMRP...... Seismic Safety Margins Research Program [*Nuclear Regulatory Commission*]
SSMS .... Solid-State Mass Spectrometer
SSMS .... Sons of Sherman's March to the Sea
SSMS .... Spark Source Mass Spectroscopy
SSMS .... Submarine Safety Monitoring System
SSMSN ..... Surface-to-Surface Mission   (AABC)
S SMS N CLSD ... Side Seams Not Closed [*Freight*]
SSMT .... Salvage Sales Material Transfer
SSMT .... Ship's Serviceman, Tailor [*Navy rating*]
SSMT .... Society for the Study of Myth and Tradition   (EA)
SSMTG ..... Solid-State and Molecular Theory Group [*MIT*]   (MCD)
SSMV .... Single-Shot Multivibrator
SSN.......... Romulus, NY [*Location identifier*] [*FAA*]   (FAAL)
SSN.......... Samson Gold Corp. [*Vancouver Stock Exchange symbol*]
SSN.......... San Juan Del Sur [*Nicaragua*] [*Seismograph station code, US Geological Survey*]   (SEIS)
SSN.......... Scandinavian Studies and Notes [*A publication*]
SSN.......... Segment Stack Number
SSN.......... Senior Security Network [*An association*] [*Washington, DC*]   (EA)
SSN.......... Severely Subnormal
SSN.......... Ship, Submersible (Nuclear-Powered)
SSN.......... Social Security Number   (AABC)
SSN.......... Soviet Sciences in the News [*A publication*]
SSN.......... Space Surveillance Network
SSN.......... Specification Serial Number
SSN.......... Standard Serial Numbers   (DIT)
SSN.......... Standard Study Number [*Military*]
SSN.......... Station Serial Number   (CET)
SSN.......... Stock Segregation Notice [*DoD*]
SSN.......... Studia Semitica Neerlandica [*Assen*] [*A publication*]
SSN.......... Submarine (Nuclear-Powered) [*Navy symbol*]   (NVT)
SSN.......... Switched Service Network [*Telecommunications*]
SSN.......... Sykepleiernes Samarbeid i Norden [*Northern Nurses Federation - NNF*]   (EA-IO)
SSNAP...... Single Seat Night Attack Program   (MCD)
SSNCHK .... Social Security Number Check
SSND .... School Sisters of Notre Dame [*Roman Catholic religious order*]
SSND .... Solid-State Neutral Dosimeter
SSN(DS) .... Submarine (Nuclear-Powered) in Direct Support [*Navy symbol*]   (NVT)
SSNF........ Source Spot Noise Figure
SSNJ........ Self-Screening Noise Jammer   (MCD)

SSNLO .... Shan State Nationalities Liberation Organization [*Burmese*]　(PD)
SSNM .... Strategic Special Nuclear Materials
SSNMH ...... Scipio Society of Naval and Military History　(EA)
SSNP .... Syrian Social Nationalist Party　(BJA)
SSNPP .... Small-Size Nuclear Power Plant
SSNS .... Standard Study Numbering System　(AABC)
SSNW .... Social Scientists Against Nuclear War　(EA)
SSNY .... Swiss Society of New York　(EA)
SSO .... Safety/Security Officer [*Military*]　(AABC)
SSO .... Safety Significant Operations
SSO .... San Simon, AZ [*Location identifier*] [*FAA*]　(FAAL)
SSO .... Schweizerische Monatsschrift fuer Zahnheilkunde [*A publication*]
SSO .... Security System Organization
SSO .... Self-Sustained Outlet　(FAAC)
SSO .... Senior Safety Officer [*Navy*]　(CAAL)
SSO .... Senior Scientific Officer [*Ministry of Agriculture, Fisheries, and Food*] [*British*]
SSO .... Senior Staff Officer [*Military*] [*British*]
SSO .... Senior Supply Officer [*Military*] [*British*]
SSO .... Ship Safety Officer
SSO .... Simosato [*Japan*] [*Later, HTY*] [*Geomagnetic observatory code*]
SSO .... Single Sweep Operation
SSO .... Society of Surgical Oncology [*Manchester, MN*]　(EA)
SSO .... Solid-State Oscillator
sso .... Southern Sotho [*MARC language code*] [*Library of Congress*]　(LCCP)
SSO .... Space Shuttle Orbiter [*NASA*]　(RDA)
SSO .... Spares Shipping Order
SSO .... Special Security Office [*or Officer*] [*Military*]　(CINC)
SSO .... Special Service Officer [*Military*]
SSO .... Squadron Signals Officer [*Navy*] [*British*]
SSO .... Srednee Spetsial'noe Obrazovanie [*Moscow*] [*A publication*]
SSO .... Staff Security Officer　(AAG)
SSO .... Statistical Service Office [*Military*]
SSO .... Steady-State Oscillation
SSO .... Studier fra Sprog- og Oldtidsforskning [*A publication*]
SSO .... Submarine Oiler [*Navy ship symbol*]
SSO .... Submarine Supply Office
SSO .... Subsystem Operation [*in Spacelab*]　(MCD)
SSO .... Sunflower Seed Oil
SSO .... System Service Order [*Bell System*]
SSOA .... System Staff Office
SSOA .... Software Services of America [*NASDAQ symbol*]　(NQ)
SSOA .... Subsurface Ocean Area　(NVT)
SSOB .... Senior Scientist on Board [*Navy*]
SSOC .... Southern Student Organizing Committee [*Defunct*]
SSOC .... Switching Service Operations Center [*Telecommunications*]
SSOCA .... Senior Staff Officer for Civil Affairs [*British*] [*World War II*]
SSOD .... Solid-State Optical Detector
SSOD .... Special Session on Disarmament [*A special session of the UN General Assembly held from May 23 to June 28, 1978*]
SSODCM ... Space Systems Operational Design Criteria Manual [*NASA*]
SSODIA ...... Special Security Office, Defense Intelligence Agency　(CINC)
SSOE .... Special Subject Operational Evaluation
SSOFS .... Smiling Sons of the Friendly Shillelaghs
SSOG .... Satellite Systems Operations Guide [*INTELSAT*]
SSOG .... Scandinavian Association of Obstetricians and Gynaecologists　(EA)
SSOG .... Spur Stepover Gear
SSOJ .... Savez Socialisticke Omladine Jugoslavije [*League of Socialist Youth of Yugoslavia*]　(PPE)
SSOJ .... Single Strength Orange Juice
S of Sol ..... Song of Solomon [*Old Testament book*]　(ROG)
SSOM .... Solid-State Optical MASER
SSOM .... [*The*] Space Shuttle Operator's Manual
SSOO .... Satellite Supply Operations Officer [*Military*]　(AFIT)
SSOP .... Satellite Systems Operations Plan [*INTELSAT*]
SSOP .... Space Systems Operating Procedures　(MCD)
SSOR .... Ship Systems Operational Requirements
SSORD ...... Senza Sordini [*Without Mutes*] [*Music*]
S SORD ..... Software Review [*A publication*]
SSORM ..... Standard Ship's Organization and Regulations Manual [*Navy*]　(NVT)
SSORT .... Ship's Systems Operational Readiness Test　(MCD)
SSORT .... Ships Systems Operational Requirements
SSOS .... Single Source of Supply　(MCD)
SSOSM .... Studi Storici dell'Ordine dei Servi de Maria [*A publication*]
SSOT .... Special Session of Oyer and Terminer [*Legal*] [*British*]　(ROG)
SSOU1 .... System Output Unit 1 [*IBM Corp.*]　(MDG)
SSOWSJ .... Supreme Shrine of the Order of the White Shrine of Jerusalem　(EA)
SSP .... Association of the Sons of Poland　(EA)
SSP .... Petroleum Air Transport, Inc. [*Lafayette, LA*] [*FAA designator*]　(FAAC)

SSP .... Plant Biotechnology Institute, National Research Council Canada [*Institut de Biotechologie des Plantes, Conseil National de Recherches Canada*] Saskatoon, Saskatchewan [*Library symbol*] [*National Library of Canada*]　(NLC)
SSP .... Prairie Regional Laboratory, National Research Council [*Laboratoire Regional des Prairies, Conseil National de Recherches*] Saskatoon, Saskatchewan [*Library symbol*] [*National Library of Canada*]　(NLC)
SSP .... SACEUR [*Supreme Allied Commander, Europe*] Schedule Program [*Army*]　(AABC)
SSP .... Sagittal Sinus Pressure [*Medicine*]
SSP .... St. Philip's College, San Antonio, TX [*OCLC symbol*]　(OCLC)
SSP .... Salt Soluble Protein [*Food industry*]
SSP .... Scientific Services Program [*Army Research Office*]　(RDA)
SSP .... Scientific Software Products, Inc. [*Indianapolis, IN*] [*Information service*]　(EISS)
SSP .... Scientific Subroutine Package [*Data processing*]
SSP .... Scouting Seaplane
SSP .... Seismic Section Profiler
SSP .... Selected Topics in Solid State Physics [*Elsevier Book Series*] [*A publication*]
SSP .... Sensor Select Panel　(MCD)
SSP .... Sentence Synthesizing Program
SS & P .... Service, Supply, and Procurement [*Military*]
SSP .... Ship Speed
SSP .... Ship's Stores Profit [*Navy*]
SSP .... Shortage Specialty Pay [*Navy*]　(NVT)
SSP .... Shoshone Peak [*Nevada*] [*Seismograph station code, US Geological Survey*]　(SEIS)
SSP .... SIGINT Support Plan　(MCD)
SSP .... Simulation Support Processor
SSP .... Single-Shot Probability
SSP .... Single Stock Point [*Military*]　(AFIT)
SSP .... Skylab Student Project [*NASA*]
SSP .... Small Sortie Payload [*NASA*]　(NASA)
SSP .... Society of St. Paul for the Apostolate of Communications [*Pauline Fathers*] [*Roman Catholic religious order*]
SSP .... Society of Satellite Professionals [*Washington, DC*] [*Telecommunications*] [*Information service*] [*An association*]　(EA)
SSP .... Society for Scholarly Publishing [*Washington, DC*]　(EA)
SSP .... Sodium Sampling Package [*Nuclear energy*]　(NRCH)
SSP .... Solid-State Photodiode
SSP .... Solid-State Pneumatic
SSP .... Solid-State Preamplifier
SSP .... SONAR Signal Processor
SSP .... Source Selection Plan
SSP .... South Simpson, AK [*Location identifier*] [*FAA*]　(FAAL)
SSP .... Space Shuttle Program [*NASA*]　(NASA)
SSP .... Special Services Protection [*Telecommunications*]　(TEL)
SSP .... Special Session of Peace [*Legal*] [*British*]　(ROG)
SSP .... Species Survival Plans [*Program sponsored by the American Association of Zoological Parks and Aquariums to protect certain endangered species*]
SSP .... Staff Site Position　(NRCH)
SSP .... Standard Shop Practice　(MCD)
SSP .... Standard Switch Panel　(MCD)
SSP .... Standby Status Panel
SSP .... State Supplementary Payment [*Social Security Administration*]
SSP .... Static Sodium Pots [*Nuclear energy*]　(NRCH)
SSP .... Steam Service Pressure
SSP .... Stores Stressed Platform [*Military*] [*British*]
SSP .... Strategic Systems Project [*Office*] [*Navy*]
SSP .... Submarine Transport [*Navy symbol*] [*Obsolete*]
SSP .... Subsatellite Point [*Telecommunications*]　(TEL)
SSP .... Subsolar Point [*Aerospace*]
SSP .... Subspecies [*Also, ssp*]
S/SP .... Subsystem Software Program　(MCD)
SSP .... Supersensitivity Perception
SSP .... Supervisory Surveillance Program [*DoD*]
SSP .... Supplemental Standard Practice　(AAG)
SSP .... Support Software Package　(MCD)
SSP .... Sustained Superior Performance
SSP .... System Safety Plan　(MCD)
SSP .... System Status Panel
SSP .... System Support Program　(AFM)
SSPA .... Social Security Pensions Act [*1975*] [*British*]
SSPA .... Society of St. Peter Apostle [*Formerly, SSPANC*]　(EA)
SSPA .... Solid State Phased Array　(MCD)
SSPANC .... Society of St. Peter the Apostle for Native Clergy [*Later, SSPA*]　(EA)
SSPB .... Socket Screw Products Bureau [*Defunct*]　(EA)
SSPB .... Swedish State Power Board [*Nuclear energy*]
SSPC .... Missionary Sisters of St. Peter Claver [*Roman Catholic religious order*]
SSPC .... Solid-State Power Controller [*NASA*]
SSPC .... Spacelab Stored Program Command　(MCD)
SSPC .... Steel Structures Painting Council [*Pittsburgh, PA*]　(EA)
SSPCL .... System Software Package Component List　(MCD)
SSPCL .... System Support Package Component List　(MCD)

SSPCP .... Shipboard Signal Processing Control Program [*Navy*] (CAAL)
SSPCT .... Technical Library, Potash Corp. of Saskatchewan, Saskatoon, Saskatchewan [*Library symbol*] [*National Library of Canada*] (NLC)
SSPD .... Shuttle System Payload Data [*NASA*] (NASA)
SSPD .... Shuttle System Payload Definition Study [*NASA*] (NASA)
S/SPD .... Single Speed [*Automotive engineering*]
SSPDA .... Space Shuttle Payload Data Activity [*NASA*] (NASA)
SSPDA .... Surface Sampler Processing and Distribution Assembly
SSPDB .... Subsystem Power Distribution Box (MCD)
SSPDS .... Space Shuttle Payload Data Study [*NASA*] (NASA)
SSPE .... Subacute Sclerosing Panencephalitis [*Medicine*]
SSPE .... Support System Project Engineer
S Speech Commun J ... Southern Speech Communication Journal [*A publication*]
SSPF .... Structured Soy Protein Fiber [*Food industry*]
SSPFC .... Stainless Steel Plumbing Fixture Council [*Defunct*] (EA)
SSPHS .... Society for Spanish and Portuguese Historical Studies (EA)
SSPI .... Sight System Passive Infrared [*Sensor*] [*Army*]
SSpJ .... Southern Speech Journal [*A publication*]
SSPK .... Single Shot Probability of Kill [*Military*]
SSPL .... Saturation Sound Pressure Level
SSPL .... Solid-State Pneumatic Logic
SSPL .... Steady-State Power Level (IEEE)
SSPL .... System Support Package List (MCD)
SSPM .... Single Strokes per Minute (MSA)
SSPM .... Space Shuttle Program Manager [*NASA*] (NASA)
SSPMA .... Sump and Sewage Pump Manufacturers Association [*Formerly, SPMA*] [*Chicago, IL*] (EA)
SSPMO ...... SONAR Systems Project Management Office
SSPN .... Satellite System for Precise Navigation [*Air Force*]
SSPN .... Ship's Stores and Profit, Navy
SSPN .... System for Precise Navigation [*Later, DNSS*] (MCD)
ssp nov ..... Subspecies Nova [*New Subspecies*] [*Biology*]
SSPO .... Space Shuttle Program Office [*NASA*] (KSC)
SSPO .... Strategic Systems Project Office [*Navy*]
SSPP .... POS Pilot Plant Corp., University of Saskatchewan Campus, Saskatoon, Saskatchewan [*Library symbol*] [*National Library of Canada*] (NLC)
SSPP .... Sancti Patres [*Holy Fathers*] [*Latin*]
SSPP .... Scandinavian Society for Plant Physiology (EA-IO)
SSPP .... Schedule Status Preprocessor (MCD)
SSPP .... Serikat Sekerdja Pamong Pradja [*Public Officials' Union*] [*Indonesia*]
SSPP .... Society for the Study of Process Philosophies (EA)
SSPP .... Solar Sea Power Plant [*NASA*]
SSPP .... Subspecies [*Plural form*] [*Also, sspp*]
SSPP .... Subsynaptic Plate Perforation [*Neurophysiology*]
SSPP .... System Safety Program Plan [*Navy*]
SSPPSG ..... Space Shuttle Payload Planning Steering Group [*NASA*] (NASA)
SSPRO .... Space Shuttle Program Resident Office [*NASA*] (NASA)
SSPS .... Satellite Solar Power Station [*or System*] [*NASA*]
SSPS .... Sheffield Sawmakers' Protection Society [*A union*] [*British*]
SSPS .... Silver/Somatostatin Positive Structure [*Anatomy*]
SSPS .... Solar-Based Solar Power Satellite
SSPS .... Solid-State Protection System (IEEE)
SSPS .... Space Shuttle Program Schedule [*NASA*] (NASA)
SSPS .... Spacecraft Support Planning Section
SSPSG ...... Science and Public Policy Studies Group [*Newsletter*]
SSPSM .... Serikat Sekerdja Pabrik Sendjata dan Mesiu [*Armaments' Union*] [*Indonesia*]
SSPTF .... Santa Susana Propulsion Test Facility [*NASA*] (NASA)
SSPTT .... Serikat Sekerdja Pos, Telegrap dan Telepon [*National Postal, Telegraph and Telephone Employees' Union*] [*Indonesia*]
SSPU .... Ship's Service Power Unit [*Navy*] (CAAL)
SSPWR ...... Small-Size Pressurized Water Reactor
SSQ .... Shell Lake, WI [*Location identifier*] [*FAA*] (FAAL)
SSQ .... Simple Sinusoidal Quantity
SSQ .... Social Science Quarterly [*A publication*]
SSQ .... Station Sick Quarters
SSQTA .... Social Science Quarterly [*A publication*]
SSR .... RADAR Picket Submarine [*Navy symbol*]
SSR .... SACEUR [*Supreme Allied Commander, Europe*] Strategic Reserve [*Army*] (NATG)
SSR .... Safety Services Representative [*Red Cross*]
SSR .... Saskatchewan Research Council, Saskatoon, Saskatchewan [*Library symbol*] [*National Library of Canada*] (NLC)
SSR .... Satellite Situation Report (AAG)
SSR .... Schedule Shipment Record (MCD)
SSR .... Seal Steam Regulator (NRCH)
SSR .... Secondary Surveillance RADAR
SSR .... Security Survey Report [*Nuclear energy*]
SSR .... Seek-Storm RADAR
SSR .... Selenium Stack Rectifier
SSR .... Self-Sufficiency Ratio [*Business and trade*]
SSR .... Separate Superheater Reactor
SSR .... Shipbuilding and Ship Repair [*Department of Employment*] [*British*]
SSR .... Shop Support Request [*NASA*] (NASA)
SSR .... Sisters Island, AK [*Location identifier*] [*FAA*] (FAAL)

SSR .... Site Suitability Report [*Nuclear energy*] (NRCH)
SSR .... Slate-Shingle Roof [*Technical drawings*]
SSR .... Social Security Rulings [*on Old Age, Survivors, and Disability Insurance*] [*US*] [*A publication*]
SSR .... Societe Suisse de Radiodiffusion et Television [*Radio and television network*] [*Switzerland*]
SSR .... Society for the Study of Reproduction [*Champaign, IL*] (EA)
SSR .... Sociology and Social Research [*A publication*]
SSR .... Solid State Relay (IEEE)
SSR .... South Staffordshire Regiment [*Military unit*] [*British*]
SSR .... Soviet Socialist Republic
SSR .... Special Scientific Report
SSR .... Spin-Stabilized Rockets
SSR .... Spotted Swine Record [*Later, National Spotted Swine Record*] (EA)
SSR .... Staff Support Room
SSR .... Static Shift Register
SSR .... Static Squelch Range
SSR .... Station Set Requirement [*NASA*] (NASA)
SSR .... Statistical Summary Report (AAG)
SSR .... Steady-State Rate [*of production*] [*Medicine*]
SSR .... Stock Status Report
SSR .... Students for Social Responsibility (EA)
SSR .... Studi e Materiali di Storia della Religioni [*A publication*]
SSR .... Subsynchronous Resonance (IEEE)
SSR .... Sum of the Squared Residuals [*Econometrics*]
SSR .... Summarized Spares Requirement
SSR .... Supplementary Statement Required [*Civil Service*]
SSR .... Supply Support Request [*Military*] (AFM)
SSR .... Surface Slip Resistance
s-sr--- .... Surinam [*MARC geographic area code*] [*Library of Congress*] (LCCP)
SSR .... Susara [*Romania*] [*Seismograph station code, US Geological Survey*] (SEIS)
SSR .... Synchronous Stable Relaying (IEEE)
SSR .... System Status Report
SSR .... System Study Requirement (AAG)
SSR .... System Support Record
SSRA .... Spread Spectrum Random Access System [*Telecommunications*] (TEL)
SSRB .... Sole Source Review Board (MCD)
SSRC .... Social Science Research Center [*Mississippi State University*] [*Research center*] (RCD)
SSRC .... Social Science Research Council (EA)
SSRC .... Society for the Study of Religion and Communism (EA)
SSRC .... Structural Stability Research Council [*Formerly, CRC*]
SSRC .... Swedish Space Research Committee
SSRCA ...... Super Sunfish Racing Class Association (EA)
SSRCC ...... Social Sciences Research Council of Canada [*See also CCRSS*] [*Later, SSHRCC*]
SSRC Newsl ... SSRC [*Social Science Research Council*] Newsletter [*A publication*]
SSRCR ...... Suggested State Regulations for the Control of Radiation (NRCH)
SSRD .... Station Set Requirements Document [*NASA*] (NASA)
SSREA .... Sight-Saving Review [*A publication*]
SSREX .... Canada Department of Regional Industrial Expansion [*Ministere de l'Expansion Industrielle Regionale*] Saskatoon, Saskatchewan [*Library symbol*] [*National Library of Canada*] (NLC)
SSRF .... Shell-Supported Ring Frame
SSRF .... Small-Scale Raiding Force [*Military*]
SSR-F .... Special Scientific Report - Fisheries
SSRFC ...... Social Science Research Facilities Center [*University of Minnesota*] [*Research center*] (RCD)
SSRG .... Selective Service Regulations
SSRG .... Simple Shift Register Generator
SSRH .... General Constituency Section for Small or Rural Hospitals [*American Hospital Association*] [*Chicago, IL*] (EA)
SSRI .... Social Science Research Institute [*of CRESS*] [*University of Hawaii at Manoa*] [*Research center*] (RDA)
SSRI .... Social Science Research Institute [*University of Maine at Orono*] [*Research center*] (RCD)
SSRI .... Social Systems Research Institute [*University of Wisconsin - Madison*] [*Research center*] (RCD)
SSRL .... Stanford Synchrotron Radiation Laboratory [*Department of Energy*] [*Research center*]
SSRL .... Stockholm Studies in Russian Literature [*A publication*]
SSRL .... Systems Simulation Research Laboratory
SSRM .... Second-Stage Rocket Motor
SSRN .... RADAR Picket Submarine (Nuclear Powered) [*Navy symbol*] [*Obsolete*]
SSRN .... Service Shop Requirement Notice
SSRN .... System Software Reference Number [*NASA*] (NASA)
SSRNJ .... Socijalisticka Savez Radnog Naroda Jugoslavije [*Socialist Alliance of Working People of Yugoslavia - SAWPY*] (PPE)
SSRP .... Single Shot Kill Probability (MCD)
SSRP .... Somali Socialist Revolutionary Party
SSRP .... Stanford Synchrotron Radiation Project
SSRPW .... Southwest Realty Wts [*NASDAQ symbol*] (NQ)

SSRR......... Social Service Reporting Requirements [*HEW*]
SSRR......... Station Set Requirements Review [*NASA*] (NASA)
SSRS......... SIGINT Surveillance and Reporting System (MCD)
SSRS......... Society for Social Responsibility in Science (EA)
SSRS......... Start-Stop-Restart System [*NASA*] (KSC)
SSRS......... Submarine Sand Recovery System
SSRSB...... Safety and Special Radio Services Bureau [*of FCC*]
SSRT......... Subsystem Readiness Test (KSC)
SSRWA ..... Soviet Science Review [*A publication*]
SSS........... MSA Realty Corp. [*American Stock Exchange symbol*]
SSS........... Safeguard Spartan System [*Aerospace*] (MCD)
SSS........... San Salvador [*El Salvador*] [*Seismograph station code, US Geological Survey*] (SEIS)
SSS........... Satellite Syndicated Systems [*Douglasville, GA*] [*Cable TV programing service*] [*Telecommunications*]
SSS........... Sauna - Swimming Pool - Storage Area [*Key fitting those locks in apartment complex*]
SSS........... Scene Storage System (MCD)
SSS........... Scientific Subroutine System [*Data processing*] (BUR)
SSS........... Secondary Sampling System (NRCH)
S/SS .... Sector/Subsector
SSS........... Selective Service System
SSS........... Self-Service Store
SSS........... Semitic Study Series [*A publication*] (BJA)
SSS........... Senior Service School [*Military*] (AFM)
SSS........... Sensitized Stainless Steel (NRCH)
SSS........... Sentinel-Spartan System (MCD)
SSS........... Shevchenko Scientific Society (EA)
SSS........... Shield and Seismic Support [*Nuclear energy*] (NRCH)
SSS........... Ship's Service Stores
SSS........... Shnat Sherut Scheme (BJA)
SSS........... Siassi [*Papua New Guinea*] [*Airport symbol*] (OAG)
SSS........... Sick Sinus Syndrome [*Medicine*]
SSS........... Signal Switching System
SSS........... Signature Security Service [*DoD*]
SSS........... Silicon-Symmetrical Switch (CET)
SSS........... Simplified Spelling Society (EA)
SSS........... Simulation Study Series (KSC)
SSS........... Single Screw Ship
SSS........... Single Signal Superheterodyne [*Radio*]
SSS........... Single Signal Supersonic [*Heterodyne*] (DEN)
SSSA......... Sisters of Social Service [*Roman Catholic religious order*]
SSS........... Site Security Supervisor (AFM)
SSS........... Skills Support System [*Education*]
SSS........... Small Scientific Satellite [*NASA*]
SSS........... Small Solar Satellite [*NASA*]
SSS........... Small Starlight Scope [*Light-intensifying device*]
SSS........... Small Structures Survey [*Civil Defense*]
SSS........... Social Science Series [*A publication*]
SSS........... Social Status Study [*Psychology*]
SSS........... Societas Sanctissimi Sacramenti [*Congregation of the Blessed Sacrament*] [*Roman Catholic men's religious order*]
SSS........... Society for Slovene Studies (EA)
SSS........... Society for Socialist Studies [*Canada*] [*See also SES*]
SSS........... Society for the Suppression of Speculative Stamps [*Defunct*]
SSS........... Software Staging Section [*Social Security Administration*]
SSS........... Solid-State Spectrometer
SSS........... Solid-State Switching (NG)
SSS........... Solid-State System
SSS........... SONAR Signal Simulator
SSS........... Sortie Support System (MCD)
SSS........... Southern Satellite Systems, Inc. [*Tulsa, OK*] [*Telecommunications*] (TSSD)
SSS........... Space Shuttle Simulation [*NASA*]
SSS........... Space Shuttle System [*NASA*] (KSC)
SSS........... Space Station Simulator
SSS........... Space Surveillance System [*Navy*] (MCD)
SSS........... Spacecraft System Support
SSS........... Special Safeguards Study (NRCH)
SSS........... Special Safety Safeguards (NRCH)
SSS........... Specific Soluble Substance [*Polysaccharide hapten*]
SSS........... Spin-Stabilized Spacecraft
SSS........... Spinning Space Station
SSS........... Stabilized Sighting System
SSS........... Staff Summary Sheet (MCD)
SSS........... Stage Separation Subsystem [*NASA*] (NASA)
SSS........... Stainless Steel Sink [*Classified advertising*] (ADA)
SSS........... Standard Scratch Score [*Golf*]
SSS........... Standard Supply System [*Army*] (AABC)
SSS........... Station Set Specification [*NASA*] (NASA)
SSS........... Stepping Switch Scanner
SSS........... Sterile Saline Soak
SSS........... Stockholders Sovereignty Society (EA)
SSS........... STOL Support Ship [*Navy*] (CAAL)
SSS........... Storage Serviceability Standard [*Army*]
SSS........... Strategic Satellite System (MCD)
SSS........... Strategic Support Squadron [*Air Force*]
SSS........... Stratum Super Stratum [*Layer Over Layer*] [*Latin*]
SSS........... Strike Support Ship [*Navy*] (NVT)
SSS........... Strong Soap Solution
SSS........... Structures Subsystem (KSC)

SSS .... Subject Specialists Section [*Association of College and Research Libraries*]
SSS .... Subjective Stress Scale
SSS .... Subscribers' Switching Subsystem [*Telecommunications*] (TEL)
SSS .... Substructure Search System [*Later, SANSS*] [*NIH/EPA*]
SSS .... Subsystem Segment [*NASA*] (NASA)
SSS .... Subsystem Support Service (BUR)
SSS .... Super Science Stories [*A publication*]
SSS .... Supply Screening Section [*Navy*]
SSS .... Survivable Satellite System (MCD)
SSS .... Symbolic Shorthand System
SSS .... System Safety Society [*Irvine, CA*] (EA)
SSS .... Systems Science and Software (MCD)
SSS .... Trois Fois Salut [*Thrice Greeting*] [*French*] [*Freemasonry*] (ROG)
SSSA......... St. Andrew's College, Saskatoon, Saskatchewan [*Library symbol*] [*National Library of Canada*] (NLC)
SSSA......... Self-Service Storage Association [*Eureka Springs, AR*] (EA)
SSSA......... Soil Science Society of America (EA)
SSSA......... Submarine SONAR Subjective Analysis (NVT)
SSSAS...... Society of Spanish and Spanish-American Studies (EA)
SSSA Spec Publ ... SSSA [*Soil Science Society of America*] Special Publication [*A publication*]
SSSA Spec Publ Ser ... SSSA [*Soil Science Society of America*] Special Publication Series [*A publication*]
SSSB......... Society for the Study of Social Biology [*Formerly, AES*] (EA)
SSSB......... System Source Selection Board [*Air Force*]
SSSBCR.... Star, Starling, Stuart, and Briton Car Register (EA)
SSSBP ...... System Source Selection Board Procedure [*Air Force*]
SSSC .... Self-Service Supply Centers (AFIT)
SSSC .... Single Sideband Suppressed Carrier
SSSC .... Soft-Sized Super-Calendered [*Paper*]
SSSC .... Space Science Steering Committee
SSSC .... Special Spectrum Study Committee
SSSC .... Stainless Steel Sink Council [*Defunct*] (EA)
SSSC .... Studies in Surface Science and Catalysis [*Elsevier Book Series*] [*A publication*]
SSSC .... Surface/Subsurface Control [*Navy*] (CAAL)
SSSC .... Surface/Subsurface Surveillance Center [*Navy*] (NVT)
SSSC .... Surface/Subsurface Surveillance Coordinator [*Navy*]
SSSCA....... Soviet Soil Science [*English translation*] [*A publication*]
SSSCD....... Social Studies of Science [*A publication*]
SSSD .... Second-Stage Separation Device
SSSD .... Single-Sided, Single-Density Disk [*Magnetic disk*] [*Data processing*]
SSSD .... Solid-State Solenoid Driver
SSSD .... Space Shuttle Simulation Display [*NASA*]
SSSEDA..... Aerospace Products Division, SED Systems Ltd., Saskatoon, Saskatchewan [*Library symbol*] [*National Library of Canada*] (NLC)
SSSF......... Stationary Source Simulator Facility [*Environmental science*]
SSSG .... SLCM [*Sea-Launched Cruise Missile*] Survivability Steering Group [*Navy*] (CAAL)
SSSI.......... Kelsey Institute of Applied Arts and Sciences, Saskatoon, Saskatchewan [*Library symbol*] [*National Library of Canada*] (NLC)
SSSI.......... Servamatic Solar Systems [*NASDAQ symbol*] (NQ)
SSSI.......... Site of Special Scientific Interest [*British*]
SSSI.......... Society for the Study of Symbolic Interaction (EA)
SSSI.......... Special Steel Summary Invoice [*International Trade Administration*]
SSSI.......... Steel Scaffolding and Shoring Institute [*Later, SSFI*] (EA)
SSSJ......... Single Subsonic Jet
SSSJ......... Student Struggle for Soviet Jewry
SSSJD....... Soil Science Society of America. Journal [*A publication*]
SSS Journal ... State Shipping Service of Western Australia. Journal [*A publication*]
SSSL......... Society for the Study of Southern Literature (EA)
SSSL......... Supersonic Split Line (KSC)
SSSLF....... South Slavonian Socialist Labor Federation [*Defunct*] (EA)
SSSM........ Site Space Surveillance Monitor (AFM)
SSSM........ South Street Seaport Museum (EA)
SSSM........ Subset-Specified Sequential Machine [*Air Force*]
SSSMP...... Surface Ship SONAR Modernization Program (MCD)
SSSN........ Satellite Syndicated Systems [*NASDAQ symbol*] (NQ)
SSSN........ Secondary Social Security Number
S/S/SN ..... System/Subsystem/Subject Number (MCD)
SSSO........ Specialized Surplus Sales Office
SSSP......... Society for the Study of Social Problems [*Buffalo, NY*] (EA)
SSSP......... Space Shuttle Synthesis Program [*National Academy of Sciences*]
SSSP......... Station to Station Send Paid [*Telecommunications*] (TEL)
SSSP......... Stockholm Studies in Scandinavian Philology [*A publication*]
SSSP......... System Source Selection Procedure [*Air Force*]
SSSQ .... McCarron-Dial Street Survival Skills Questionnaire [*Occupational therapy*]
SS/SR .... Safety Standdown/Safety Review (MCD)
SSSR......... SAGE [*Semiautomatic Ground Environment*] System Status Report
SSSR.......... Smallest Set of Smallest Rings [*Organic chemistry*]

SSSR......... Social Sciences Services and Resources (EA)
SSSR......... Society for the Scientific Study of Religion (EA)
SSSR......... Southwestern Social Science Review [*A publication*]
SSSR......... Soyuz Sovetskikh Sotsialisticheskikh Respublik [*Union of Soviet Socialist Republics*]
SSSR......... Syracuse Scales of Social Relations [*Education*]
SSSS......... Shallow Spherical Sandwich Shell
SSSS......... Society for the Scientific Study of Sex [*Philadelphia, PA*] (EA)
SSSS......... Space Shuttle System Segment (MCD)
SSSS......... Space Shuttle System Specification [*NASA*] (NASA)
SSSS......... Staphylococcal Scalded Skin Syndrome [*Medicine*]
SSSSC........ Stewart & Stevenson [*NASDAQ symbol*] (NQ)
SSSSC....... Surface/Subsurface Surveillance Coordinator [*Navy*] (CAAL)
SSSST....... Subscale Subsonic Targets (MCD)
SSST......... S-Band Spread Spectrum Transponder (MCD)
SSST......... Site Suitability Source Term (NRCH)
SSST......... Solid-State Silicon Target
SSStJ......... Serving Sister, Order of St. John of Jerusalem [*British*]
SSSV......... Scientific Systems Services, Inc. [*NASDAQ symbol*] (NQ)
SSSW........ Surface/Subsurface Warfare [*Navy*] (CAAL)
SST .... Safe Secure Trailer [*For transporting nuclear materials*]
SST .... Safe Separate/Timing (CINC)
SST .... Saskatchewan Teachers' Federation Saskatoon, Saskatchewan [*Library symbol*] [*National Library of Canada*] (NLC)
SST .... Satellite-to-Satellite Tracking
SST .... Saturated Suction Temperature [*Refrigeration*]
SST .... Saturn Systems Test [*NASA*]
SST .... Science Stories [*A publication*]
SST .... Sea Surface Temperature [*Oceanography*]
SST .... Seaplane Shuttle Transport [*New York-Philadelphia air-link*]
SST .... Secondary Surge Tank [*Nuclear energy*] (NRCH)
SST .... Serviceability Self-Test (MCD)
SST .... Shakespeare Studies (Tokyo) [*A publication*]
SST .... Shipboard [*Weapon*] Suitability Test [*Navy*] (NG)
SST .... Ships Service Turbine (MCD)
SST .... Sideways-Spinning Tube [*Spectrometry*]
SST .... Sight, Sound, and Touch [*Ways to identify proper belt tension*] [*Automotive engineering*]
SST .... Silver Sceptre Resources [*Vancouver Stock Exchange symbol*]
SST .... Simulated Structural Test (KSC)
SST .... Single Sideband Transmission [*Telecommunications*] (TEL)
SST .... Single Subscriber Terminal [*Army*] (RDA)
SST .... Single Systems Trainer (MCD)
SST .... Slide, Script, and Tape
SST .... Social Security Tax Ruling [*Internal Revenue Bulletin*] (DLA)
SST .... Solid-State Transmitter (MCD)
SST .... SONAR Signaling (NVT)
SST .... Soviet Science and Technology [*Plenum Publishing Corp.*] [*Alexandria, VA*] [*Information service*] (EISS)
SSt .... Sowjet Studien [*A publication*]
SST .... Spacecraft System Test [*NASA*]
SST .... Special Strike Teletype (NATG)
SST .... Split Second Timing
SST .... Stainless Steel
SST .... Station Service Transformer (NRCH)
SS/T......... Steady-State/Transient Analysis [*Nuclear energy*] (NRCH)
SST .... Stiffened Super-Tough [*Polymer technology*]
SST .... Stream Support Team (MCD)
SST .... Structural Static Test [*NASA*] (NASA)
SST .... Student Science Training [*Program*] [*National Science Foundation*] [*Defunct*]
SST .... Subscriber Transferred [*Telecommunications*] (TEL)
SST .... Subsystem Terminal on Spacelab (MCD)
SST .... Subsystems Test (KSC)
SST .... Superficial Spreading Type (Melanoma) [*Oncology*]
SST .... Supersonic Transport
SST .... Supplementary Service Tariff [*British*]
SST .... Susitna [*Alaska*] [*Seismograph station code, US Geological Survey*] [*Closed*] (SEIS)
SST .... Synchronous System Trap
SST .... System Segment Table
SST .... System Survey Team [*Military*] (AFIT)
SST .... Systems Support Tape
SST .... Target and Training Submarine [*Self-propelled*] [*Navy symbol*]
SSTA......... Secondary School Theatre Association [*Later, SSTC*] (EA)
SSTA......... Support System Task Analysis (AAG)
SSTADS..... Small Ship Typhoon Air Defense System (MCD)
SSTAR ...... Society for Sex Therapy and Research (EA)
SSTC......... Secondary School Theatre Conference [*Later, SSTA*] (EA)
SSTC......... Ship System Test Contractor (MCD)
SSTC......... Single-Sideband Transmitted Carrier (IEEE)
SSTC......... Solid-State Timer-Controller
SSTC......... Space Shuttle Test Conductor [*NASA*] (NASA)
SSTC......... Spacecraft System Test Console [*NASA*]
SSTC......... Specialized System Test Contractor
SSTC......... Summary of Supplemental Type Certificates
SSTD......... Surface Ship Torpedo Defense [*Navy*] (CAAL)
SSTDC...... Society of Stage Directors and Choreographers (EA)
SST-DMA... Satellite Switched Time Division Multiple Access
SS/TDMA ... Spread Spectrum/Time Division Multiple Access (MCD)

SSTDS .... Small Ship Tactical Data System [*Navy*] (CAAL)
SSTEP....... System Support Test Evaluation Program
SSTF .... Saturn Static Test Facility [*NASA*]
SSTF .... Shortest Seek Time First
SSTF .... Space Shuttle Task Force [*NASA*]
SSTF .... Space Simulation Test Facility (AAG)
SSTF .... Space Station Task Force [*NASA*]
SSTG......... Ship Service Turbo Generator (MSA)
SSTG......... Space Shuttle Task Group [*NASA*] (KSC)
SSTG......... Special Service Training Group [*World War II*]
SSTI .... Serikat Sekerdja Topografi Indonesia [*Indonesian Topography Employees' Union*]
SSTIR .... Sea Surface Temperature Imaging Radiometer
SSTIXS ...... Small Ship Teletype Information Exchange System [*or Subsystem*] (MCD)
SSTL .... Solid State Track Link [*TOW*] (MCD)
SSTM .... SAGE [*Semiautomatic Ground Environment*] System Training Mission
SSTM .... Single Service Training Manager (MCD)
SSTM .... System Support Technical Manager [*Navy*] (NG)
SSTMS...... Standard Supply Transportation Manifest System
SSTO........ Single Stage to Orbit [*NASA*]
SSTP......... Student Science Training Program [*National Science Foundation*] [*Defunct*]
SSTP......... Subsystems Test Procedure (KSC)
SSTP......... Supersonic Transport Panel [*International Civil Aviation Organization*]
SSTR......... Senior Staff Technical Representative (MCD)
SSTRD...... Special Steels Technical Review [*A publication*]
SSTS......... Signaling and Supervision Techniques Study
SST-T-T..... Sound, Sense, Today, Tomorrow, Thereafter [*Teacher's Guide, published by Department of Transportation, for promoting supersonic travel*]
SSTU........ SAGE [*Semiautomatic Ground Environment*] System Training Unit
SSTU........ Seamless Steel Tubing
SStud........ Shakespeare Studies [*A publication*]
SSTV......... Congregation of Sisters of St. Thomas of Villanova [*Roman Catholic religious order*]
SSTV......... Sea Skimming Test Vehicles
SSTV......... Slow-Scan Television
SSTV......... Submarine Shock Test Vehicle
SStW......... Synoptische Studien fuer A. Wikenhauser [*1953*] [*A publication*] (BJA)
SSU........... San Pedro Sula [*Honduras*] [*Seismograph station code, US Geological Survey*] (SEIS)
SSU........... Saybolt Seconds Universal [*Oil viscosity*]
SSU........... Self-Service Unit
SSU........... Semiconductor Storage Unit [*Data processing*]
SSU........... Sensor Simulator Unit
SSU........... Single Signaling Unit [*Telecommunications*] (TEL)
SSU........... Solvent Service Unit
SSU........... Source Resources Ltd. [*Vancouver Stock Exchange symbol*]
SSU........... Spacecraft Support Unit
SSU........... Special Service Unit [*Military*]
SSU........... Squadron Service Unit [*Aircraft*]
SSU........... Stabilized Sight Unit (MCD)
SSU........... Standard Saybolt Universal [*Oil viscosity*]
SSU........... Statistical Service Unit [*Military*]
SSU........... Strategic Services Unit [*Formerly, OSS*]
SSU........... Stratospheric Sounding Unit [*Telecommunications*] (TEL)
SSU........... Subscriber Switching Unit [*Telecommunications*] (TEL)
SSU........... Subsequent Signal Unit [*Group of BITS*] [*Telecommunications*] (TEL)
SSU........... Sunday School Union
SSU........... Surface Screen Unit [*Navy*] (NVT)
SSU........... Switch Selector Update
SSU........... System Selector Unit
SSU........... System Support Unification (MCD)
SSU........... University of Saskatchewan, Saskatoon, Saskatchewan [*Library symbol*] [*National Library of Canada*] (NLC)
SSU........... White Sulphur Springs, WV [*Location identifier*] [*FAA*] (FAAL)
SSUEM...... Uranerz Exploration & Mining Ltd., Saskatoon, Saskatchewan [*Library symbol*] [*National Library of Canada*] (NLC)
SSUF......... Sprakvetenskapliga Sallskapets i Uppsala Foerhandlingar [*A publication*]
SSUGP...... Government Publications, University of Saskatchewan, Saskatoon, Saskatchewan [*Library symbol*] [*National Library of Canada*] (NLC)
SSUJD...... [*The*] Right Honourable John G. Diefenbaker Centre, University of Saskatchewan, Saskatoon, Saskatchewan [*Library symbol*] [*National Library of Canada*] (NLC)
SSUL........ Law Library, University of Saskatchewan, Saskatoon, Saskatchewan [*Library symbol*] [*National Library of Canada*] (NLC)
SSULS ...... Lutheran Seminary, University of Saskatchewan, Saskatoon, Saskatchewan [*Library symbol*] [*National Library of Canada*] (NLC)

SSUM......... Medical Library, University of Saskatchewan, Saskatoon, Saskatchewan [*Library symbol*] [*National Library of Canada*] (NLC)
SSUMC...... Ukrainian Museum of Canada, Saskatoon, Saskatchewan [*Library symbol*] [*National Library of Canada*] (NLC)
SSUR......... Springfield Sunday Union and Republican [*A publication*]
SSURADS ... Shipboard Surveillance RADAR System (MCD)
SSUS......... Spin-Stabilized Upper Stage [*NASA*] (NASA)
SSUS......... Spinning Solid Upper Stage (RDA)
SSUS......... System Support Unification Subsystem (MCD)
SSUSA...... Special Staff, United States Army
SSUS-A...... Spinning Solid Upper Stage - Atlas Class (MCD)
SSUS-D...... Spinning Solid Upper Stage - Delta Class (MCD)
SSUSN...... Society of Sponsors of the United States Navy (EA)
SSUSP...... Spinning Solid Upper Stage Project (MCD)
SSUTC...... Special Service Unit Training Center [*World War II*]
SSV.......... Satellite Servicing Vehicle
SSV.......... Seraphic Society for Vocations [*Defunct*] (EA)
SSV.......... Sheep Seminal Vesicle
SSV.......... Ship-to-Surface Vessel
SSV.......... Simian Sarcoma Virus [*Also, SiSV*]
SSV.......... Small Synaptic Vesicle [*Neurobiology*]
SSV.......... Space Shuttle Vehicle [*NASA*]
SSV.......... Spool Selector Valve
SSV.......... Static Self-Verification
SSV.......... Sub Signo Veneni [*Under a Poison Label*] [*Pharmacy*]
SSV.......... Subjective Scale Value
SSV.......... Sumac Ventures, Inc. [*Vancouver Stock Exchange symbol*]
SSV.......... Supersatellite Vehicle
SSV.......... Supersonic Test Vehicles
SSV.......... Sydslesvigsk Vaelgerforening [*South Schleswig Voters' Association*] [*Also, SSW*] [*West Germany*] (PPW)
SSVA......... Signal Susceptibility and Vulnerability Assessment [*Military*] (CAAL)
SSVC......... Selective Service
SSVE......... Subacute Spongiform Virus Encephalopathies [*Medicine*]
SSV/GC & N ... Space Shuttle Vehicle/Guidance, Control, and Navigation [*NASA*]
SSVM........ Self-Scaling Variable Metric [*Algorithms*] [*Data processing*]
SsvOA....... Sydsvenska Ortnamnssaellskapets Arsskrift [*A publication*]
SSVP......... Society of St. Vincent De Paul (EA-IO)
SSVP......... Soviet Ship Vulnerability Program
SSVS......... Slow-Scan Video Simulator
SSV-SSAV ... Simian Sarcoma Virus-Simian Sarcoma Associated Virus [*Complex*]
SSW.......... Safety Switch
SSW.......... St. Louis Southwestern Railway Co. [*AAR code*]
SSW.......... Secretary of State for War [*British*]
SSW.......... Sense Switch [*Military*] (AFIT)
SSW.......... Siemens-Schuckert Werke [*Germany*]
SSW.......... Solid-State Welding
SSW.......... South-Southwest
SSW.......... Space Switch [*Telecommunications*] (TEL)
SSW.......... Staggered Spondaic Word
SSW.......... Standby Service Water [*Nuclear energy*] (NRCH)
SSW.......... Sterling Software, Inc. [*American Stock Exchange symbol*]
SSW.......... Suedschleswigscher Waehlerverband [*South Schleswig Voter's League*] [*Also, SSV*] [*West Germany*] (PPE)
SSW.......... Surface Science Western [*University of Western Ontario*] [*Research center*] (RCD)
SSW.......... Surface Strike Warfare [*Navy*] (CAAL)
SSW.......... Swept Square Wave (MCD)
SSW.......... Synchro Switch [*Electronics*]
SSW.......... Systems West Consultants Ltd. [*Vancouver Stock Exchange symbol*]
SSW.......... Wheatland Regional Library, Saskatoon, Saskatchewan [*Library symbol*] [*National Library of Canada*] (NLC)
SSWA........ Sanitary Supply Wholesalers Association [*Indianapolis, IN*] (EA)
SSWC........ Surface/Subsurface Warfare Coordinator [*Navy*] (CAAL)
SSWD........ Single, Separated, Widowed, or Divorced
SSWD........ Western Development Museum, Saskatoon, Saskatchewan [*Library symbol*] [*National Library of Canada*] (NLC)
SSWF........ Sudden Shortwave Fade
SSWG........ System Safety Working Group
SSWLH...... Society for the Study of Women in Legal History (EA)
SSWM........ Standing Spin Wave Mode (MCD)
SSWM........ Superimposed Surface Wave Modes
SSWO........ Special Service Work Order [*Telecommunications*] (TEL)
SSWP........ Station Service Water Pump [*Nuclear energy*] (NRCH)
SSWRN...... South-Southwestern [*Meteorology*] (FAAC)
SSWS........ Standby Service Water System (NRCH)
SSWU........ Singapore Sawmill Workers' Union
SSWWD..... South-Southwestward [*Meteorology*] (FAAC)
SSWWS...... Seismic Sea-Wave Warning System
SSX.......... Samsun [*Turkey*] [*Airport symbol*] (OAG)
SSX.......... SS1 [*Nevada*] [*Seismograph station code, US Geological Survey*] [*Closed*] (SEIS)
SSX.......... Submarines, Experimental
SSX.......... Sulfisoxazole [*An antibiotic*]

SSXBT....... Submarine Expendable Bathythermograph [*Marine science*] (MSC)
SSY.......... M'Banza Congo [*Angola*] [*Airport symbol*] (OAG)
SSY.......... Silver Strike Resources [*Vancouver Stock Exchange symbol*]
S/SYS....... Subsystem (NASA)
SSZ.......... Pocket Submarine (NATG)
SSZ.......... Saigon Special Zone [*Military*]
SSZ.......... Sea Scout Zero - Nonrigid Airship [*Royal Naval Air Service*] [*British*]
SSZ.......... Society of Systematic Zoology (EA)
SSZ.......... Specified Strike Zone [*Army*] (AABC)
SSZBA...... Sbornik Vysoke Skoly Zemedelski v Brne. Rada B [*A publication*]
St.............. C. H. Boehringer Sohn, Ingelheim [*Germany*] [*Research code symbol*]
St.............. E. Merck AG [*Germany*] [*Research code symbol*]
ST.............. Missionarii Servi Sanctissimae Trinitatis [*Missionary Servants of the Most Holy Trinity*] [*Roman Catholic men's religious order*]
ST.............. Saddle Tank [*Trains*] [*British*]
ST.............. Safety Tool (MCD)
ST.............. Saint
ST.............. St. Lawrence Cement, Inc. [*Toronto Stock Exchange symbol*] [*Vancouver Stock Exchange symbol*]
ST.............. Sainte
ST.............. Sales Tax Branch, United States Internal Revenue Bureau (DLA)
ST.............. Sales Tax Rulings, United States Internal Revenue Bureau (DLA)
ST.............. Sanitary Towel [*British*] (DSUE)
ST.............. Sao Tome and Principe [*Two-letter standard code*] (CNC)
ST.............. Save the Theaters (EA)
ST.............. Sawtooth [*Architecture*]
ST.............. Scalar Totalizer
ST.............. Scalloped Tinned [*Configuration*] (MCD)
ST.............. Schmitt Trigger [*Electronics*]
ST.............. Schuler Tuning
S & T......... Science and Technology (NATG)
ST.............. Sclerotherapy [*Medicine*]
ST.............. Screw Terminal
ST.............. Seaman Torpedoman [*Obsolete*] [*Navy*]
S/T............ Search/Track
ST.............. Seat
ST.............. Secretary/Treasurer [*or Secretary and Treasurer*]
ST.............. Sedimentation Time
ST.............. Self-Test
ST.............. Self-Toning [*Paper*] [*Photography*] (ROG)
ST.............. Semitendinosus [*Muscle*]
ST.............. Sensitivity Training
ST.............. Senza Tempo [*Without Regard to Time*] [*Music*]
ST.............. Sequence Timer
ST.............. Service Tabulating (AAG)
ST.............. Service Test
ST.............. Service Tools (AAG)
ST.............. Set Trigger
ST.............. Shares Time with [*Broadcasting term*]
S/T............ Shelter Taxi [*NASA*] (KSC)
ST.............. Ship Trial (MCD)
ST.............. Shipping Ticket [*Military*]
ST.............. Shock Tube
ST.............. Shock Tunnel
ST.............. Short-Term Stay [*in hospital*] [*British*]
ST.............. Short Ton [*2000 lbs.*]
ST.............. Shrink Template
ST.............. Sidetone [*Telecommunications*] (TEL)
ST.............. Sigma Tau [*Later, Tau Beta Pi Association*]
ST.............. Signes du Temps [*A publication*]
ST.............. Silent [*Films, television, etc.*]
ST.............. Silicon Tube
ST.............. Silicotungstate [*Inorganic chemistry*]
ST.............. Simhat Torah (BJA)
ST.............. Simplification Task (MCD)
S & T......... Simulation and Training
ST.............. Simulator Training
st.............. Sine Tempore [*At the Time Announced*] [*Latin*]
ST.............. Single Throw [*Switch*]
ST.............. Single Tire
ST.............. Single Turn (MSA)
ST.............. Sinus Tachycardia [*Cardiology*]
ST.............. Skill Technical (INF)
ST.............. Skin Test
ST.............. Skin Track (MUGU)
S & T......... Sky and Telescope [*A publication*]
ST.............. Sleeping Time
ST.............. Slide and Tape
ST.............. Slight Trace
ST.............. Slovo a Tvar [*A publication*]
ST.............. Societe Theosophique [*Theosophical Society*]
ST.............. Society for Theriogenology [*Hastings, NE*] (EA)
ST.............. Solar Thermal [*Energy source*]
ST.............. SONAR Technician [*Navy rating*]

S/T.............. Sonic Telegraphy
S of T.......... Sons of Temperance
ST.............. Sons of Temperance
ST.............. Sounding Tube
ST.............. Space Telescope [*NASA*]
ST.............. Space-Time
ST.............. Spacelab Technology [*NASA*]   (NASA)
ST.............. Special Test
ST.............. Special Text
ST.............. Special Tools
ST.............. Special Translation
ST.............. Speech Teacher [*A publication*]
ST.............. Speech Therapist
ST.............. Speed Transmitter   (NRCH)
ST.............. Springfield Terminal Railway Co. [*AAR code*]
ST.............. SPS Technologies, Inc. [*Formerly, Standard Pressed Steel Co.*]
              [*NYSE symbol*]
ST.............. Stage
St.............. Stair's Decisions, Scotch Court of Session   (DLA)
St.............. Stair's Institutes [*5th ed.*] [*1832*]   (DLA)
St.............. Stamen [*Botany*]
ST.............. Stamped [*Stock exchange term*]
ST.............. Standard
ST.............. Standard Time
ST.............. Standardized Test [*Psychology*]
ST.............. Standby Time   (MCD)
St.............. Stanton Number [*IUPAC*]
ST.............. Stanza
ST.............. Star Tracker   (AAG)
ST.............. Starboard Flag [*Navy*] [*British*]
ST.............. Start
S/T.............. Start Tank   (AAG)
ST.............. Start Timing
ST.............. Starter   (MCD)
ST.............. State
ST.............. State Trials [*Legal*] [*British*]
ST.............. Static   (KSC)
ST.............. Static Test
ST.............. Static Thrust
ST.............. Statim [*Immediately*] [*Latin*]   (ROG)
ST.............. Station [*Medicine*]
ST.............. Statistisk Tabelvaerk [*Denmark*]
ST.............. Statsoekonomisk Tidsskrift [*A publication*]
ST.............. Statt [*Instead Of*] [*German*]
ST.............. Status
ST.............. Statute
ST.............. Steam   (AAG)
ST.............. Steam Tanker
ST.............. Steam Trawler
ST.............. Steam Tug
ST.............. Steam Turbine   (MCD)
ST.............. Steamer   (ROG)
ST.............. Steel Truss [*Bridges*]
ST.............. Stem [*Linguistics*]
ST.............. Stencil
S & T.......... Stenographer and Typist [*Examination*] [*Civil Service
              Commission*]
st.............. Stere [*Unit of volume*]
St.............. Stereo Review [*A publication*]
ST.............. Sternothyroid [*Anatomy*]
ST.............. Sternotomy [*Medicine*]
ST.............. Stet [*Let It Stand*] [*Latin*]
ST.............. Sticky Type [*Bomb*]
ST.............. Stimulus [*Medicine*]
ST.............. Stitch
ST.............. Stock Transfer
St.............. Stokes [*Unit of kinematic viscosity*]
ST.............. Stone [*Unit of weight*]
St.............. Stones [*Quality of the bottom*] [*Nautical charts*]
ST.............. Storage Tube
ST.............. Store   (AAG)
ST.............. Stored Time
S & T.......... Storm and Tempest   (ADA)
ST.............. Story   (ROG)
St.............. Story's United States Circuit Court Reports   (DLA)
ST.............. Stotinki [*Monetary unit*] [*Bulgarian*]
ST.............. Strad [*A publication*]
S/T.............. Straight Time
ST.............. Strait
St.............. Strannik: Dukhovnyi, Ucheno-Literaturnyi Zhurnal [*A
              publication*]
ST.............. Straps [*JETDS nomenclature*] [*Military*]   (CET)
ST.............. Strategic Transport [*Aircraft*] [*Military*]
S & T.......... Strategy and Tactics [*A publication*]
St.............. Stratosphere
ST.............. Stratus [*Meteorology*]
ST.............. Street
ST.............. Stress Testing [*Medicine*]
ST.............. Strict [*Medicine*]
S-T.............. Strip-Tin   (MSA)
ST.............. Stroma [*Medicine*]

ST.............. Strophe [*Poetry*]   (ROG)
ST.............. Structural   (NASA)
ST.............. Structure Tee   (AAG)
St.............. Stuart, Milne, and Peddie's Scotch Court of Session
              Cases   (DLA)
ST.............. Student's t-Test [*Statistical mathematics*]
ST.............. Studi Tassiani [*A publication*]
ST.............. Studia Taiwanica [*A publication*]
ST.............. Studia Theologica [*A publication*]
St.............. Studies [*A publication*]
ST.............. Studies in Theology [*A publication*]
St.............. Studium [*A publication*]
ST.............. Stumped [*Cricket*]
St.............. Styrene [*Also, Sty*] [*Organic chemistry*]
ST.............. Substitution Theorem [*Logic*]
ST.............. Subtentacular [*Zoology*]
ST.............. Sudan [*Aircraft nationality and registration mark*]   (FAAC)
ST.............. Sulfotransferase [*An enzyme*]
ST.............. Summer Time [*Daylight saving time*]
ST.............. Sunday Telegraph [*A publication*]
ST.............. [*The*] Sunday Times [*London, England*] [*A publication*]
ST.............. Super Tampella [*Explosive*]   (INF)
ST.............. Superintendent of Transportation
S of T.......... Superintendent of Transportation
ST.............. Supplementary Term [*Online database field identifier*]
S & T.......... Supply and Transport
ST.............. Supporting Technologies [*Military*]   (RDA)
ST.............. Surface Target [*Navy*]   (CAAL)
ST.............. Surface Tension
ST.............. Surface Tracker [*Navy*]   (CAAL)
ST.............. Surgical Technician
ST.............. Surveillance Test   (NATG)
ST.............. Survival Time
ST.............. Svensk Tidskrift [*A publication*]
S & T.......... Swabey and Tristram's Probate and Divorce Reports [*1858-
              65*]   (DLA)
ST.............. Swept Tone
ST.............. Symmetrical TOKAMAK
ST.............. System Test
ST.............. Szondi Test [*Psychology*]
ST.............. Tradewinds Pte. Ltd. [*Great Britain*] [*ICAO designator*]   (FAAC)
St.............. United States Statutes at Large   (DLA)
ST1............. SONAR Technician, First Class [*Navy rating*]
ST2............. SONAR Technician, Second Class [*Navy rating*]
ST3............. SONAR Technician, Third Class [*Navy rating*]
ST's........... Sanitary Towels
STA............ S-Band Test Antenna
STA............ Sail Training Association   (EA)
STA............ Santa [*Saint*] [*Italian*]
STA............ Satara [*India*] [*Seismograph station code, US Geological
              Survey*] [*Closed*]   (SEIS)
STA............ Satellite Tracking Annex   (MUGU)
STA............ Serum Thrombotic Accelerator [*Serology*]
STA............ Serum Thymic-Like Activity [*Biochemistry*]
STA............ Servico des Transportes Aereos [*Portuguese West Africa*]
STA............ Shift Technical Adviser   (NRCH)
STA............ Shipboard Transmitting Antenna
STA............ Shore-Based Transmitting Antenna
STA............ Short-Term Arrangements [*Department of State*]
STA............ Short-Term Averaging   (CAAL)
STA............ Short-Terms Abroad
STA............ Shuttle Training Aircraft [*NASA*]
STA............ Sialyltransferase Activity [*Medicine*]
STA............ Single Target Attack
STA............ Slaving Torquer Amplifier
STA............ Slurry Technology Association [*Washington, DC*]   (EA)
STA............ Society of Typographic Arts [*Chicago, IL*]   (EA)
STA............ Softening Temperature of Ash
STA............ Solution Treat and Age [*Metals*]
STA............ Southern Textile Association [*Cary, NC*]   (EA)
STA............ Space Technology Applications
STA............ Special Temporary Authorization [*FCC*]
STA............ Staff Training Assistant [*Army*]   (AABC)
STA............ Stagger Tuned Antenna
STA............ Staley Continental, Inc. [*NYSE symbol*]
STA............ Stamped
STA............ Star Aviation Corp. [*Denver, CO*] [*FAA designator*]   (FAAC)
STA............ Stara Dala [*Czechoslovakia*] [*Later, HRB*] [*Geomagnetic
              observatory code*]
STA............ State Technical Assistance   (OICC)
STA............ Static Test Article   (NASA)
STA............ Station [*Telecommunications*]
STA............ Stationary   (MSA)
STA............ Status [*Online database field identifier*]   (AABC)
STA............ Stauning [*Denmark*] [*Airport symbol*]   (OAG)
STA............ Steel Carriers Tariff Association, Inc., East Riverdale MD
              [*STAC*]
STA............ Steel Tape Armored [*Cables*]
STA............ Stock Transfer Association [*New York, NY*]   (EA)
STA............ Store Accumulator

STA .... Straight-In Approach [*Aviation*]   (FAAC)
STA .... Strange Adventures [*A publication*]
STA .... Structural Test Article   (NASA)
StA .... Studi Anselmiana [*A publication*]
STA .... Submarine Tender Availability
STA .... Superficial Temporal Artery [*Anatomy*]
STA .... Supersonic Tunnel Association   (EA)
STA .... Survival in Target Area   (MCD)
STA .... Swedish Telecommunications Administration [*Farsta*] [*Telecommunications*]   (TSSD)
STA .... Systems Test Area
STA .... University of Santa Clara, Orradre Library, Santa Clara, CA [*OCLC symbol*]   (OCLC)
STAA .... Staar Surgical Co. [*NASDAQ symbol*]   (NQ)
STAA .... Surface Transportation Assistance Act [*1978*]
STAACT J ... STAACT [*Science Teachers Association of the Australian Capital Territory*] Journal [*A publication*]
STAAD ...... Submarine Tender Availability Arrival/Departure [*Obsolete*]
STAAF ...... Study to Align AMC [*Now DAR COM*] Functions   (MCD)
STAAS ...... Surveillance and Target Acquisition Aircraft System   (AFM)
Staat u Recht ... Staat und Recht [*A publication*]
Staatsanz Baden-Wuerttemb ... Staatsanzeiger fuer Baden-Wuerttemberg [*A publication*]
Staatsanz Rheinl-Pfalz ... Staatsanzeiger fuer Rheinland-Pfalz [*German Federal Republic*] [*A publication*]
Staatsbl Koninkrijk Ned ... Staatsblad van het Koninkrijk der Nederlanden [*A publication*]
Staatsbuerger-Beil Bayer Staatsztg ... Staatsbuerger-Beilage der Bayerischen Staatszeitung [*A publication*]
Staatsverw ... Roemische Staatsverwaltung [*A publication*]   (OCD)
Staat und Wirt in Hessen ... Staat und Wirtschaft in Hessen [*A publication*]
STAB .... Squadron Tactical Analysis Board [*Military*]   (CAAL)
STAB .... Stabilize [*or Stabilizer*]   (AAG)
STAB .... Standby Advisory Board [*Army*]   (INF)
St Ab .... Statham's Abridgment   (DLA)
STAB .... Strike Assault Boat [*Navy symbol*]
STAB .... Supersonic Tests of Aerodynamic Bombs   (MUGU)
STAB .... Supersonic Transport Advisory Board
STABEX .... Stabilization of Export Earnings [*Program of the EEC*]
StAbs .... Status Absolutus
STABS .... Suinn Test Anxiety Behavior Scale [*Psychology*]
Sta Bull Oreg State Coll Agr Exp Sta ... Station Bulletin. Oregon State College. Agricultural Experiment Station [*A publication*]
Sta Bull Univ Minn Agr Exp Sta ... Station Bulletin. University of Minnesota. Agricultural Experiment Station [*A publication*]
STABY .... Stability   (MSA)
STAC .... Science and Technology Advisory Committee [*NASA*]   (MCD)
STAC .... Software Timing and Control
STAC .... Southern Technology Applications Center [*NASA*] [*University of Florida*] [*Gainesville*] [*Information service*]   (EISS)
STAC .... Staccato [*Detached, Distinct*] [*Music*]
STAC .... Standard Tariff Agents Code
STAC .... Submarine-to-Aircraft Communications
STAC .... Surface Target Attack Comparison Model   (MCD)
STACC ...... Staccato [*Detached, Distinct*] [*Music*]
Sta Circ Wash Agr Exp Sta ... Station Circular. Washington Agricultural Experiment Station [*A publication*]
STACO ...... Standing Committee for the Study of Scientific Principles of Standardization [*ISO*]
STACOM .... State Criminal Justice Communications
STACRES ... Standing Committee on Research and Statistics [*UN Food and Agriculture Organization*]
STACS .... Subtropical Atlantic Climate Studies [*National Oceanic and Atmospheric Administration*]
STAD .... Start Address [*Telecommunications*]   (TEL)
STAD .... Submarine Tender Availability Document
STADAC ..... Station Data Acquisition and Control [*NASA*]   (NASA)
STADACOL ... Statistical Data Collection Program
STADAD .... Satellite Tracking and Data Acquisition Department
STADAN .... Satellite Tracking and Data Acquisition Network [*Later, STDN*]
STADD ...... Ship-Towed Acoustic Deception Device   (MCD)
Staden-Jb .... Staden-Jahrbuch [*A publication*]
STADES ..... Standard Army Data Elements Systems   (MCD)
STADES ..... Standard Data Elements System   (MCD)
STADIN ..... Standing Administrative Instruction for Army Attaches   (AABC)
STADINAIR ... Standing Administrative Instruction for Air Attaches   (AFM)
Stadler Genet Symp ... Stadler Genetics Symposia [*A publication*]
St Adm NS ... Stuart's Lower Canada Vice-Admiralty Reports, New Series   (DLA)
STADMR .... Station Administrator [*Aviation*]   (FAAC)
Stadt- Gebaeudetech ... Stadt- und Gebaeudetechnik [*German Democratic Republic*] [*A publication*]
Stadt (Wien) ... Informationsdienst der Stadt (Wien) [*A publication*]
STADU ...... System Termination and Display Unit   (MCD)
STA-DYNULSIMU ... Static-Dynamic Ullage Simulation Unit
STAE .... Second Time Around Echo
STAE .... Specify Task Asynchronous Exit [*Data processing*]
STAEP .... Scientific and Technical Assessment of Environmental Pollutants [*Marine science*]   (MSC)
STAF .... St. Thomas Aquinas Foundation of the Dominican Fathers of the United States   (EA)

STAF .... Science Team Analysis Facility [*NASA*]
STAF .... Scientific and Technical Application Forecasts
STAF .... Staff Builders [*NASDAQ symbol*]   (NQ)
STA/F .... Standard Access and Format [*Reference Technology, Inc. software*]
STAFDA ..... Specialty Tools and Fasteners Distributors Association [*Elm Grove, WI*]   (EA)
STAFEX .... Staff Exercises [*NATO*]   (NATG)
STAFF .... Small Target Activated Fire and Forget [*Projectile*]   (MCD)
STAFF .... Smart Target-Activated Fire and Forget [*Antitank weapon system*]   (RDA)
STAFF .... Staffordshire [*County in England*]
STAFF .... Stellar Acquisition Flight Feasibility
Staff J (University of Reading) ... Staff Journal (University of Reading) [*A publication*]
Stafford ...... Stafford's Reports [*69-71 Vermont*]   (DLA)
Staff Pap .... Staff Papers [*A publication*]
STAFFS ..... Staffordshire [*County in England*]
STAFS .... Sugar, Tobacco, Alcohol, Fat, and Salt
STAFT .... Steerable Antenna Focusing Technique
STAG .... Security Tag Systems [*NASDAQ symbol*]   (NQ)
STAG .... Shuttle Turnaround Analysis Group [*NASA*]   (NASA)
STAG .... Skills Training Adjustment Group [*Educational project sponsored by The Hartford*]
STAG .... Special Task Air Group
STAG .... Standards Technical Advisory Group
STAG .... Steam and Gas [*Turbine*]
STAG .... Straight-Talking American Government [*Comedian Pat Paulsen's political party*]
STAG .... Strategy and Tactics Analysis Group [*Later, Concepts Analysis Agency*] [*Army*]   (KSC)
STAG .... Student Agitation [*FBI*]
STAG .... Submarine-Rocket Technical Advisory Group
STAGD ...... Syndicat des Travailleurs de l'Administration Generale du Dahomey [*Dahomean Union of General Administration Workers*]
STAGE ...... Simulated Total Atomic Global Exchange [*DoD*]
STAGG ...... Small-Turbine Advanced Gas Generator
STAG-MAG ... Stage Manager [*Theater term*]   (DSUE)
STAGN ...... Stagnation [*Meteorology*]   (FAAC)
STAGS ...... Simulated Tank and Antiarmor Gunnery System   (INF)
STAGS ...... Structural Analysis of General Shells
STAGS ...... Swedish Tank Agility/Survivability Test   (MCD)
STAGS-D ... Simulated Tank Antiarmor Gunnery System - Dragon [*Army*]   (INF)
St A H .... Studies in American Humor [*A publication*]
STAHA ...... Stahlbau [*A publication*]
Stahlbau Rundsch ... Stahlbau Rundschau [*Austria*] [*A publication*]
Stahlia Misc Pap ... Stahlia Miscellaneous Papers [*A publication*]
STAI .... State-Trait Anxiety Inventory [*Psychology*]
STAI .... Subtask ABEND [*Abnormal End*] Intercept [*Data processing*]   (BUR)
STAIC .... State-Trait Anxiety Inventory for Children [*Psychology*]
STAID .... Station Identification
Stainless Steel Ind ... Stainless Steel Industry [*A publication*]
Stainl Steel ... Stainless Steel [*South Africa*] [*A publication*]
Stain Tech ... Stain Technology [*A publication*]
Stain Technol ... Stain Technology [*A publication*]
Stair .... Stair's Decisions of the Lords of Council and Session [*1661-81*] [*Scotland*]   (DLA)
STAIR .... Structural Analysis Interpretive Routine
Stair I .... Stair's Institutes [*5 eds.*] [*1681-1832*]   (DLA)
Stair Inst ... Stair's Institutes [*5 eds.*] [*1681-1832*]   (DLA)
Stair Prin ... Stair's Principles of the Laws of Scotland   (DLA)
Stair Rep .... Stair's Decisions, Scotch Court of Session   (DLA)
STAIRS ..... Storage and Information Retrieval System [*IBM Corp.*]
STAIRS/VS ... Storage and Information Retrieval System/Virtual Storage [*IBM Corp.*]
STAK .... Steak N Shake, Inc. [*NASDAQ symbol*]   (NQ)
STAL .... Stalactite/Stalagmite Formation   (DSUE)
STALAG ...... Stammlager [*Prisoner-of-war camp*] [*German*]
STALAGLUFT ... Stammlagerluft [*Prisoner-of-war camp for airmen*] [*German*]
STALAS ...... Stationary LASER Site [*NASA*]
Stal Elect ... Stalman on Election and Satisfaction [*1827*]   (DLA)
Stal in Engl ... Stal in English [*A publication*]
Staleplavil'n Proizvod ... Staleplavil'noe Proizvodstvo [*A publication*]
Staleplavil'n Proizvod (Moscow) ... Staleplavil'noe Proizvodstvo (Moscow) [*A publication*]
Stal Nemet Vklyucheniya ... Stal'e Nemetallicheskie Vklyucheniya [*A publication*]
STALO .... Stabilized Local Oscillator [*RADAR*]
STALOG ..... Study of Automation of the Logistic System [*Military*]
STALOS ..... Stabilized Tunable Local Oscillator
STALPETH ... Steel, Aluminum, Polyethylene [*Components of a type of telecommunications cable*]
STAL Sci Tech Anim Lab ... STAL. Sciences et Techniques de l'Animal de Laboratoire [*A publication*]
STaM .... Sefer Torah. Tefillin. Mezuzah
STAM .... Shared Tape Allocation Manager
STAM .... Statistics in Medicine [*A publication*]

STAM......... Submarine Tactical Advanced Missile (MCD)
STAM......... Superintendent of Technical Applications of Metals [*Ministry of Supply*] [*British*] [*World War II*]
STAM......... Surface Target Acquisition Model (MCD)
STAM......... System Telecommunications Access Method [*NCR Corp.*]
STAMIC..... Set Theory Analysis and Measure of Information Characteristics
STAMINRQ ... Status During Minimize Required (MCD)
STAMIS...... Standard Army Management Information Systems
STAMM...... Systematic Teaching and Measuring Mathematics [*Education*]
STAMMIS ... Standard Army Multicommand Management Information System (MCD)
STAMNI ..... Sonic True Airspeed and Mach Number Indicator
STAMO ...... Stable Master Oscillator
STAMOS.... Sortie Turn Around Maintenance Operations Simulation [*NASA*] (KSC)
STAMP....... Satellite Telecommunications Analysis and Modeling Program
STAMP....... Small Tactical Aerial Mobility Platform [*Proposed*] [*Marine Corps*]
STAMP....... Space Technology Analysis and Mission Planning (MCD)
STAMP....... Standard Air Munitions Package
STAMP....... Systems Tape Addition and Maintenance Program [*Data processing*] (IEEE)
STAMPED ... Size, Temperature, Application, Material, Pressure, Ends, and Delivery [*To aid selection of industrial hose*]
STAN......... Selectable Two-Area Nozzle (MCD)
STAN......... Stanchion
Stan........... Stanford (DLA)
STAN......... Sum Total and Nosegear (MCD)
STANA....... Statistics on the North Atlantic [*Fisheries*] [*UN Food and Agriculture Organization*]
STANAG .... Standardization Agreement [*NATO*]
STANAVFORCHAN ... Standing Naval Force, Channel [*NATO*] (NATG)
STANAVFORLANT ... Standing Naval Force, Atlantic [*Activated 1968*] [*NATO*]
STANAVITO ... Syndicat des Travailleurs de Transport et de la Navigation du Togo [*Union of Transport and Navigation Workers of Togo*]
STANCAL .... Standard Oil Co. of California
STANCIB ... State-Army-Navy Communications Intelligence Board [*Later, USCIB*]
STAND .... Standard
Standard Chartered R ... Standard Chartered Review [*A publication*]
Stand Ass Aust Aust Stand ... Standards Association of Australia. Australian Standard [*A publication*]
Stand Ass Aust Commercial Stand ... Standards Association of Australia. Commercial Standard [*A publication*]
Stand Ass Aust Miscell Pub ... Standards Association of Australia. Miscellaneous Publication [*A publication*]
Stand Ex Prof Tax Rep ... Standard Excess Profits Tax Reporter [*Commerce Clearing House*] (DLA)
Stand Fed Tax Rep ... Standard Federal Tax Reporter [*Commerce Clearing House*] (DLA)
Stand GA Prac ... Standard Georgia Practice (DLA)
Stan Dig ..... Stanton's Kentucky Digest (DLA)
Stand Methods Clin Chem ... Standard Methods of Clinical Chemistry [*A publication*]
Stand News ... Standardization News [*A publication*]
Stand PA Prac ... Standard Pennsylvania Practice (DLA)
Stand Philip Per Ind ... Standard Philippine Periodicals Index [*A publication*]
Stand Qual ... Standardisierung und Qualitaet [*German Democratic Republic*] [*A publication*]
St Andrew Univ Sociol R ... St. Andrew's University. Sociological Review [*A publication*]
Stan Env't Ann ... Stanford Environmental Law Annual [*A publication*]
STANFINS ... Standard Financial System (AABC)
Stanf J Int ... Stanford Journal of International Studies [*A publication*]
Stanford..... Stanford's English Pleas of the Crown (DLA)
Stanford Ichthyol Bull ... Stanford Ichthyological Bulletin [*A publication*]
Stanford J Internat Law ... Stanford Journal of International Law [*A publication*]
Stanford J Internat Studies ... Stanford Journal of International Studies [*A publication*]
Stanford J Int'l Stud ... Stanford Journal of International Studies [*A publication*]
Stanford J Int Stud ... Stanford Journal of International Studies [*A publication*]
Stanford La ... Stanford Law Review [*A publication*]
Stanford Law Rev ... Stanford Law Review [*A publication*]
Stanford L Rev ... Stanford Law Review [*A publication*]
Stanford Med Bull ... Stanford Medical Bulletin [*A publication*]
Stanford Research Inst Jour ... Stanford Research Institute Journal [*A publication*]
Stanford Stud Psychol ... Stanford Studies in Psychology [*A publication*]
Stanford Univ Dep Civ Eng Tech Rep ... Stanford University. Department of Civil Engineering. Technical Report [*A publication*]
Stanford Univ Dep Mech Eng Tech Rep ... Stanford University. Department of Mechanical Engineering. Technical Report [*A publication*]
Stanford Univ Publ Geol ... Stanford University Publications in the Geological Sciences [*A publication*]

Stanford Univ Publ Univ Ser Biol Sci ... Stanford University. Publications. University Series. Biological Sciences [*A publication*]
Stanford Univ Publ Univ Ser Eng ... Stanford University. Publications. University Series. Engineering [*A publication*]
Stanford Univ Publ Univ Ser Math Astron ... Stanford University. Publications. University Series. Mathematics and Astronomy [*A publication*]
Stanford Univ Publ Univ Ser Med Sci ... Stanford University. Publications. University Series. Medical Sciences [*A publication*]
STANINE.... Standard Nine Score [*Military*]
Stan J Int'l Stud ... Stanford Journal of International Studies [*A publication*]
Stanki i Instrum ... Stanki i Instrument [*A publication*]
Stanki Rezhushchie Instrum ... Stanki i Rezhushchie Instrumenty [*A publication*]
STANLANCRU ... Standard Landing Craft Unit [*Military*]
Stan L Rev ... Stanford Law Review [*A publication*]
STANO...... Surveillance, Target Acquisition, and Night Observation [*DoD*]
STANOC .... Surveillance, Target Acquisition, Night Observation, and Counter - Surveillance [*British*] (MCD)
STANOLIND ... Standard Oil Co. (Indiana)
STANORD ... Standardization Order [*Navy*] (NG)
Sta Note For Exp Sta (Idaho) ... Station Note. Forest, Wildlife, and Range Experiment Station (Moscow, Idaho) [*A publication*]
Stan PA Prac ... Standard Pennsylvania Practice (DLA)
STANS ...... Soviet Tactical Nuclear Study (MCD)
STANS ...... Standard Army Nonappropriated System (MCD)
StAns .... Studia Anselmiani [*Rome*] [*A publication*]
STANSM .... STANO [*Surveillance, Target Acquisition, and Night Observation*] System Manager [*Army*] (RDA)
StANT .... Studien zum Alten und Neuen Testament [*Munich*] [*A publication*]
STANTEC ... Standard Telephones Electronic Computer (MCD)
St Anth....... St. Anthony Messenger [*A publication*]
Stanton ...... Stanton's Reports [*11-13 Ohio*] (DLA)
Stanton's Rev St ... Stanton's Revised Kentucky Statutes (DLA)
STANVAC ... Standard Vacuum Oil Co.
STANY .... Security Traders Association of New York
STAP......... Scientific and Technical Analysis and Programs Directorate
STAP......... Shipbuilding Temporary Assistance Program
STAP......... Special Technical Assistance Program (EA)
STAP......... Survivability Test Advisory Panel [*Military*] (CAAL)
Sta Pap For Exp Sta (Idaho) ... Station Paper. Forest, Wildlife, and Range Experiment Station (Moscow, Idaho) [*A publication*]
STAPFUS... Stable Axis Platform Follow-Up System
STAPH ...... Staphylococcus [*Medicine*]
STAPHS ...... Staphylococci
STAPL....... SIGPLAN Technical Committee on APL [*A Programming Language*] [*Association for Computing Machinery*] (CSR)
STAPLAN... Status, Time, Attrition, Planning Methodology
STAPP...... Simulation Tape Print Program
STAPP....... Single-Thread All-Purpose Program
STAPPA..... State and Territorial Air Pollution Program Administrators (EA)
Stapp Car Crash Conf Proc ... Stapp Car Crash Conference. Proceedings [*A publication*]
STAPRC.... Scientific and Technical Association of the People's Republic of China
STAQ .... Security Traders Automated Quotation [*System*]
STAQ .... Student Teachers' Attitude Questionnaire
STAQC...... Statistical Quality Control System [*Military*]
STAR........ Safe Teenage Rocketry
St A R........ St. Andrews Review [*A publication*]
STAR......... San Clemente 3-D Acoustic Range (MCD)
STAR......... Satellite Telecommunications Automatic Routing
STAR......... Satellite Transponder Addressable Receiver
STAR......... Satellites for Telecommunications, Applications, and Research [*Consortium*]
STAR......... Science Teaching Achievement Recognition
STAR......... Scientific and Technical Aerospace Reports [*NASA*] [*A publication*]
STAR......... Score, Teach, and Record [*Teaching machine*]
STAR......... Second Time Around Racers [*Car racing*]
STAR......... Selective Training and Retention [*Navy*]
STAR......... Self-Test Antenna Radiation [*Military*] (CAAL)
STAR......... Self-Test Automatic Readout
STAR......... Self-Testing and Repairing [*Computer self-repair*]
STAR......... Serials Titles Automated Records [*US National Agricultural Library*] [*Beltsville, MD*] [*A publication*]
STAR......... Shell Transient Asymmetric Response
STAR......... Shield Test Air Reactor
STAR......... Ship-Tended Acoustic Relay [*Military*]
STAR......... Shipboard Tactical Airborne Remote Piloted Vehicle [*Navy*] (CAAL)
STAR......... Shuttle Turnaround Analysis Report [*NASA*] (NASA)
STAR......... Simple Test Approach for Readability [*General Electric*]
STAR......... Simulation of Tactical Alternative Responses (MCD)
STAR......... Simultaneous Temperature Alarm Readout
STAR......... Sled Towed Array (MCD)
STAR......... Societe de Transport Aerien du Rwanda [*Airline*] (FAAC)
STAR......... Society for Test Anxiety Research (EA)
STAR......... Space Technology and Advanced Research

STAR.........	Space Thermionic Auxiliary Reactor
STAR.........	Space-Time Autoregressive [*Statistics*]
STAR.........	Special Tasks and Rescue (ADA)
STAR.........	Special Treatment and Review [*Navy*] (NG)
STAR.........	Special Tube Analyzing Recorder
STAR.........	Specialized Training and Reassignment [*Military*]
STAR.........	Spectral Technology and Applied Research
STAR.........	Speed through Aerial Resupply [*Air Force*]
STAR.........	Sport, Travel, Art, and Recreation
STAR.........	Standard Instrument Arrival [*Aviation*] (FAAC)
STAR.........	Standard Telecommunications Automatic Recognizer [*Data processing*]
STAR.........	Standard Tensioned Alongside Receiver [*Navy*] (NVT)
STAR.........	Standard Terminal Arrival Route [*Aviation*]
STAR.........	Standard Test Authorization and Report System [*Navy*]
STAR.........	Starcom, Inc. [*NASDAQ symbol*] (NQ)
Star	Starkie's English Nisi Prius Reports (DLA)
Star	Starship [*A publication*]
Star	Starship. The Magazine about Science Fiction [*A publication*]
STAR.........	Statistical Table Assembly and Retrieval System [*Proposed for Social Security Administration*]
STAR.........	Statistical Treatment of Aircraft Returns (MCD)
STAR.........	Steerable Array RADAR
STAR.........	Stellar Attitude Reference
STAR.........	Steps to Abstract Reasoning
STAR.........	Sting Array [*Computer system*] (MCD)
STAR.........	Stock Technical Analysis Reports [*Innovest Systems, Inc.*] [*Database*]
STAR.........	Stop the Arms Race [*Women's International League for Peace and Freedom*]
STAR.........	Strike, Transfers, Acquisitions, or Removals [*Navy*] (NG)
STAR.........	String Array Processor
STAR.........	Submarine Test and Research (MCD)
STAR.........	[*The*] Sunday Times Atlantic Riband [*Award offered by a London newspaper to any sailboat beating the 1905 record for a transatlantic crossing*]
STAR.........	Supplier Transmittal and Approval Request (MCD)
STAR.........	Surface-to-Air Recovery
STAR.........	Surveillance, Target Acquisition, and Reconnaissance
STAR.........	Swedish Tactical Attack RADAR
STAR.........	System for Telephone Administrative Response [*Data processing*]
STAR.........	System for Time and Accomplishment Reporting (MCD)
STAR.........	System Training Application Requirements
STARAD.....	Starfish Radiation [*Satellite*] [*NASA*]
STARAN....	Stellar Attitude Reference and Navigation
STARC	State Area Commands (MCD)
Star Ch Ca ...	Star Chamber Cases [*1477-1648*] [*England*] (DLA)
Star Ch Cas ...	Star Chamber Cases [*1477-1648*] [*England*] (DLA)
Starchroom Laundry J ...	Starchroom Laundry Journal [*A publication*]
STARCIPS ..	Standard Army Civilian Pay System
STARCOM ...	Strategic Army Command Network
STARCOM ...	Strategic Army Communications System [*Military*]
STARD	Starch/Staerke [*A publication*]
STARE	Scandinavian Twin Auroral RADAR Experiment [*Ionospheric science*]
STARE	Steerable Telemetry Antenna Receiving Equipment
STARFIARS ...	Standard Army Financial Inventory Accounting and Reporting System
STARFIRE ...	System to Accumulate and Retrieve Financial Information with Random Extraction [*Data processing*]
STARIMAR ...	Space-Time Autoregressive Integrated Moving Average [*Statistics*]
Stark	Starkie's English Nisi Prius Reports [*1815-22*] (DLA)
Stark CL.....	Starkie's Criminal Law (DLA)
Stark Cr Pl ...	Starkie's Criminal Pleading (DLA)
Stark Ev	Starkie on Evidence (DLA)
Starkie	Starkie's English Nisi Prius Reports (DLA)
Starkie (Eng) ...	Starkie's English Nisi Prius Reports [*171 English Reprint*] (DLA)
Starkie Ev ...	Starkie on Evidence (DLA)
Starkie's	English Nisi Prius Reports [*171 English Reprint*] (DLA)
Stark Jury Tr ...	Starkie on Trial by Jury (DLA)
Stark Lib ...	Starkie on Libel (DLA)
Stark NP ...	Starkie's English Nisi Prius Reports (DLA)
Stark Sl & L ...	Starkie on Slander and Libel (DLA)
STARLAB...	Space Technology Applications and Research Laboratory [*NASA*]
STARLO	Special Test Army Reserve Limited Objective
STARP	Supplemental Training and Readiness Program
STARR	Schedule, Technical, and Resources Report [*NASA*] (NASA)
STARR	Staff Assessment of Readiness Report (MCD)
STARR	Study Techniques for Advanced RADAR Requirements
Starr & C Ann St ...	Starr and Curtis' Annotated Statutes [*Illinois*] (DLA)
STARS	Satellite Telemetry Automatic Reduction System [*NASA*]
STARS	Satellite Transmission and Reception Specialists [*Houston, TX*] [*Telecommunications*] (TSSD)
STARS	Seaborne Tracking and Ranging Station
STARS	Sealink Ticket and Reservation System [*Sealink UK Ltd.*] [*London, England*] [*Information service*] (EISS)

STARS	Shell Theory Automated for Rotational Structures
STARS	Short-Term Auction-Rate Stock
STARS	Short Track Auto Racing Series [*Car racing*]
STARS	Silent Tactical Attack Reconnaissance System
STARS	Simulation and Training Advanced Research System [*Air Force*]
STARS	Software Technology for Adaptable, Reliable Systems [*Data processing*]
STARS	Software Technology for Adaptable, Reliable Systems Program [*DoD*] (RDA)
STAR(S)	Specialized Training and Reassignment (Student) [*Military*]
STARS	Stabilized Twin-Gyro Attitude Reference System
STARS	Standard Terminal Arrival Routes [*Aviation*] (MCD)
STARS	Standard, TRADOC Automated Retrieval System (MCD)
STARS	Stationary Automotive Road Simulator
STARS	Stellar Tracking Attitude Reference System
STARS	Study of Tactical Airborne RADAR System
STARS	Support Tracking Analysis Reporting Systems (MCD)
STARS	Surface-to-Air Recovery System
STARS	Surveillance Target Attack RADAR System
STARS	Synchronized Time, Automated Reporting System
STARS	System Test and Astronaut Requirement Simulation
STARS	System Thermal Air Platform Reconnaissance Signature (MCD)
Star SC	Star Session Cases [*1824-25*] (DLA)
STARS II	Shell Theory Automated for Rotational Structures - II (MCD)
START	Safety Technology Applied to Rapid Transit [*Committee*] [*American Public Transit Association*]
START	Selection to Activate Random Testing [*Module*] [*NASA*]
START	Service Technician Advancement, Recruitment, and Training
START	Space Test and Reentry Technology
START	Space Transport and Reentry Tests
START	Spacecraft Technology and Advanced Reentry Tests [*Air Force*]
START	Special Treatment and Rehabilitative Training [*Prisons project*]
START	Story-Telling Automatic Reading Tutor
START	Strategic Arms Reduction Talks
START	Summary Tape Assistance, Research, and Training
START	System of Transportation Applying Rendezvous Technique (MCD)
START	Systematic Tabular Analysis of Requirements Technique (IEEE)
STARTEX...	Start of the Exercise (MCD)
STARTLE ...	Surveillance and Target Acquisition RADAR for Tank Location and Engagement [*Army*] (MCD)
STARUTE...	Stable Parachute
STAS.........	Safe-to-Arm Signal
STAS.........	Safe-to-Arm System (MUGU)
STAS.........	Short Term Analysis Services [*Scientific Services Program*] [*Army*] (RDA)
STAS.........	Startel Corp. [*NASDAQ symbol*] (NQ)
STAS.........	Statutes
STASD	Stainless Steel [*A publication*]
STASH	Student Association for the Study of Hallucinogens [*Defunct*] (EA)
STASHIP....	Station Ship [*Navy*] (NVT)
Sta Sper Maiscolt (Bergamo) ...	Stazione Sperimentale di Maiscoltura (Bergamo) [*A publication*]
STASS	Submarine-Towed Array Surveillance System (NVT)
STAT.........	SEABEE Technical Assistance Team [*Navy*]
Stat	Stat. Bulletin of the Wisconsin Nurses' Association [*A publication*]
STAT.........	Static (AAG)
STAT.........	Statim [*Immediately*] [*Latin*]
STAT.........	Station
STAT.........	Stationery Office [*British*]
STAT.........	Statistic (AFM)
Stat	Statius [*First century AD*] [*Classical studies*] (OCD)
Stat	Stative (BJA)
STAT.........	Statuary
STAT.........	Status (MSA)
STAT.........	Statute
STAT.........	Statutory Tenant (DSUE)
STATA	Stata Corp. Cl A [*NASDAQ symbol*] (NQ)
statA	Statampere [*Also, sA*] [*Unit of electric current*]
Stat Ab (NZ) ...	Monthly Abstract of Statistics (New Zealand) [*A publication*]
Stat Bull Metrop Life Insur Co ...	Statistical Bulletin. Metropolitan Life Insurance Company [*A publication*]
Stat Bull Metropol Life Ins Co ...	Statistical Bulletin. Metropolitan Life Insurance Company [*A publication*]
statC	Statcoulomb [*Also, sC*] [*Unit of electric charge*]
StatCan......	Statistics Canada
STATCAT ...	Statistical Context-Aided Testing [*North-Holland Publishing Co.*] [*Software package*]
StatConst ...	Status Constructus (BJA)
Stat Def......	Statutory Definition (DLA)
STATE.......	Simplified Tactical Approach and Terminal Equipment
STATE.......	Simulation for Tank/Antitank Evaluation (NATG)
State Agric Coll Oreg Eng Exp Stn Circ ...	State Agricultural College of Oregon. Engineering Experiment Station. Circular [*A publication*]

State Court J ... State Court Journal [*A publication*]
State Dept Bull ... United States State Department. Bulletin   (DLA)
State Fish Chief Secr Dep NSW Res Bull ... State Fisheries Chief. Secretary's Department. New South Wales. Research Bulletin [*A publication*]
State Geologists Jour ... State Geologists Journal [*A publication*]
State Gov ... State Government [*A publication*]
State Govt ... State Government [*A publication*]
State Govt News ... State Government News [*A publication*]
State Hortic Assoc PA Proc ... State Horticultural Association of Pennsylvania. Proceedings [*A publication*]
State Libn ... State Librarian [*A publication*]
State Locl & Urb L Newsl ... State, Local, and Urban Law Newsletter [*A publication*]
STATEM .... Shipment Status System   (AABC)
State Mot Carr Guide ... State Motor Carrier Guide [*Commerce Clearing House*]   (DLA)
Staten Island As Pr ... Staten Island Association of Arts and Sciences. Proceedings [*A publication*]
Staten Island Inst Arts Sci Proc ... Staten Island Institute of Arts and Sciences. Proceedings [*A publication*]
Statens Inst Byggnadsforsk Handl (Trans) ... Statens Institut foer Byggnadsforskning. Handlingar (Translations) [*A publication*]
Statens Inst Byggnadsforsk Natl Swedish Bldg Res Doc ... Statens Institut foer Byggnadsforskning. National Swedish Building Research Document [*A publication*]
Statens Lantbrukskem Kontrollanst Medd ... Statens Lantbrukskemiska Kontrollanstalt. Meddelande [*A publication*]
Statens Lantbrukskem Lab Medd ... Statens Lantbrukskemiska Laboratorium. Meddelande [*A publication*]
Statens Naturvetensk Forskningsrad Ekologikomm Bull ... Statens Naturvetenskapliga Forskningsrad Ekologikommitter Bulletin [*A publication*]
Statens Offentliga Utredn ... Statens Offentliga Utredningar [*A publication*]
Statens Skadedyrlab Arsberet ... Statens Skadedyrlaboratorium Arsberetning [*A publication*]
Statens Vaeginst (Swed) Medd ... Statens Baeginstitut (Sweden). Meddelande [*A publication*]
Statens Vaeginst (Swed) Rapp ... Statens Vaeginstitut (Sweden). Rapport [*A publication*]
Statens Vaxtskyddsanst Medd ... Statens Vaxtskyddsanstalt Meddelanden [*A publication*]
State Plann and Environ Comm Tech Bull ... State Planning and Environment Commission. Technical Bulletin [*A publication*]
State R .... New York State Reporter   (DLA)
State Rep ... New York State Reporter   (DLA)
State Tax Cas Rep ... State Tax Cases Reporter [*Commerce Clearing House*]   (DLA)
State Tr ...... State Trials [*Howell*] [*England*]   (DLA)
State Tr NS ... State Trials, New Series, Edited by Macdonell [*England*]   (DLA)
State Wash Dep Fish Res Div Inf Bkl ... State of Washington. Department of Fisheries. Research Division. Information Booklet [*A publication*]
State Wash Dep Fish Res Div Inf Booklet ... State of Washington. Department of Fisheries. Research Division. Information Booklet [*A publication*]
statF .... Statfarad [*Also, sF*] [*Unit of capacitance*]
Stat Glo ...... Statute of Gloucester [*First statute to give costs in actions*]   (DLA)
statH .... Stathenry [*Also, sH*] [*Unit of inductance*]
Stath Abr ... Statham's Abridgment   (DLA)
STATIC ...... Student Taskforce Against Telecommunication Information Concealment [*Student legal action organization*]
Stat ICJ ...... Statute of the International Court of Justice   (DLA)
Stat Inst ...... Statutory Instruments   (DLA)
Stat Instrum (Lond) ... Statutory Instrument (London) [*A publication*]
STATIS ...... Statistics
Statis et Etud Fins (Ser Bleue) ... Statistiques et Etudes Financieres (Serie Bleue) [*A publication*]
Statis et Etud Fins (Ser Orange) ... Statistiques et Etudes Financieres (Serie Orange) [*A publication*]
Statis et Etud Fins (Ser Rouge) ... Statistiques et Etudes Financieres (Serie Rouge) [*A publication*]
Statis et Etud Midi Pyrenees ... Statistiques et Etudes Midi-Pyrenees [*A publication*]
Statis Neerl ... Statistica Neerlandica [*Netherlands*] [*A publication*]
Statist Abstr US ... Statistical Abstract. United States [*A publication*]
Statist Anal Donnees ... Statistique et Analyse des Donnees. Bulletin de l'Association des Statisticiens Universitaires [*A publication*]
Statist Bull USDA ... Statistical Bulletin. United States Department of Agriculture [*A publication*]
Statist Canad Consumpt Prodn Invent Rubb ... Statistics Canada. Consumption. Production Inventories of Rubber and other Selected Sections [*A publication*]
Statist Decisions Econom ... Statistique et Decisions Economiques [*Paris*] [*A publication*]

Statist et Develop Loire ... Statistique et Developpement Pays de la Loire [*A publication*]
Statist Econ Normande ... Statistiques pour l'Economie Normande [*A publication*]
Statist i Elektron-Vycisl Tehn v Ekonom ... Statistika i Elektronno-Vycislitel'naja Tehnika v Ekonomike. Naucno-Issledovatel'skii Institut po Proektirovanija Vycislitel'nyh Centrov i Sistem Ekonomiceskoi Informacii CSU SSSR [*A publication*]
Statist Et Finance Et Econ Ser Orange ... Statistiques et Etudes Financieres. Etudes Economiques (Serie Orange) [*A publication*]
Statist Et Financ Ser Bleue ... Statistiques et Etudes Financieres (Serie Bleue) [*A publication*]
Statist Et Financ Ser Rouge ... Statistiques et Etudes Financieres (Serie Rouge) [*A publication*]
Statist Et Midi-Pyrenees ... Statistiques et Etudes Midi-Pyrenees [*A publication*]
Statist Hefte ... Statistische Hefte [*A publication*]
Statistical Register of SA ... Statistical Register of South Australia [*A publication*]
Statistical Register of WA ... Statistical Register of Western Australia [*A publication*]
Statist M L ... Statistical Methods in Linguistics [*A publication*]
Statist Neerlandica ... Statistica Neerlandica [*A publication*]
Statist Newslett Abstr ... Statistical Newsletter and Abstracts. Indian Council of Agricultural Research [*A publication*]
Statist Paper ... Statistics of Paper [*A publication*]
Statist R (Beograd) ... Statisticka Revija (Beograd) [*A publication*]
Statist Sect Pap For Comm (Lond) ... Statistics Section Paper. Forestry Commission (London) [*A publication*]
Statist Theory Method Abstracts ... Statistical Theory and Method Abstracts [*A publication*]
Statist Trav Suppl B Mens ... Statistiques du Travail. Supplement au Bulletin Mensuel [*A publication*]
Statiszt Szle ... Statisztikai Szemle [*A publication*]
Stat at L ..... United States Statutes at Large   (DLA)
STATLIB .... Statistical Computing Library [*Bell System*]
Stat Local ... Governments Statute of Local Governments   (DLA)
Stat LR .... Statute Law Review [*A publication*]
Stat Marl .... Statute of Marlbridge   (DLA)
Stat Mech ... Statistical Mechanics [*A publication*]
Stat Mer ..... Statute of Merton   (DLA)
Stat Mert .... Statute of Merton   (DLA)
Stat Mod Lev Fin ... Statute Modus Levandi Fines   (DLA)
STATNET .... Statistical Analysis of Network
STAT News ... Science Teachers Association of Tasmania. Newsletter [*A publication*]
Stat News Lett (New Delhi) ... Statistical News Letter (New Delhi) [*A publication*]
Statni Tech Knih Praze Vymena Zkusenosti ... Statni Technicka Knihovna v Praze. Vymena Zkusenosti [*A publication*]
Statni Vyzk Ustav Sklarsky Kradec Kralove Inf Prehl ... Statni Vyzkumny Ustav Sklarsky. Kradec Kralove. Informativni Prehled [*A publication*]
Stat Notes Health Plann ... Statistical Notes for Health Planners [*A publication*]
Stat NSW ... Statutes of New South Wales [*Australia*]   (DLA)
Stat NZ ...... Statutes of New Zealand   (DLA)
Stat O & R ... Statutory Orders and Regulations [*Canada*]   (DLA)
Stato Soc ... Stato Sociale [*A publication*]
STATPAC ... Statistics Package [*Computer program*]   (IEEE)
STATRAFO ... Standard Transfer Order
Stat Realm ... Statutes of the Realm [*England*]   (DLA)
Stat Reg NZ ... Statutory Regulations [*New Zealand*]   (DLA)
STATREP .... Advise Present Grade, Status, Physical Condition, and Mailing Address of Following Named [*Military*]
Stat Rep ... Statistical Reporter [*A publication*]
Stat R & O ... Statutory Rules and Orders [*1890-1947*] [*England*]   (DLA)
Stat R & ONI ... Statutory Rules and Orders of Northern Ireland   (DLA)
Stat R & O & Stat Inst Rev ... Statutory Rules and Orders and Statutory Instruments Revised [*England*]   (DLA)
Stat Rptr ... Statistical Reporter [*A publication*]
STATS ...... Stationary Tank Automatic Target System   (MCD)
statS .... Statsiemens [*Also, sS*] [*Unit of electric conductance, admittance, and susceptance*]
STATSBOBP ... Scale of Teacher Attitudes toward Selective Behavior of Boy Pupils [*Satirical*]
Stats Can ... Statistics Canada
STAT-SEL ... Status Select [*Army*]
STATSERVOFF ... Statistical Service Office [*Supreme Headquarters Allied Powers Europe*]   (NATG)
Statsokon Tss ... Statsoekonomisk Tidsskrift [*A publication*]
Statsvet Ts ... Statsvetenskaplig Tidskrift [*A publication*]
STATSVS ... Statistical Services   (MUGU)
STATT .... Statement
statT .... Stattesla [*Unit of magnetic flux density*]
Stat Textb Monogr ... Statistics Textbooks and Monographs [*A publication*]
Stat Theor Meth Abstr ... Statistical Theory and Method Abstracts [*A publication*]
Stat Tidskr ... Statistisk Tidskrift [*A publication*]

Stat Tidskrift ... Statistick Tidskrift [*A publication*]
STATTS ..... Stationary Automatic Tank Target System   (MCD)
Stat Use Radiat Jpn ... Statistics on the Use of Radiation in Japan [*A publication*]
statV.......... Statvolt [*Also, sV*] [*Electrostatic unit of potential difference*]
statWb .... Statweber [*Unit of magnetic flux*]
Stat Westm ... Statute of Westminster   (DLA)
Stat Winch ... Statute of Winchester   (DLA)
STATY .... Statutory   (ROG)
Staub J....... Staub Journal [*A publication*]
Staub-Reinhalt Luft ... Staub, Reinhaltung der Luft [*A publication*]
Staundef .... Staundeforde's Exposition of the King's Prerogative   (DLA)
Staundef PC ... Staundeforde's Les Plees del Coron [*Pleas of Crown*]   (DLA)
Staundf Pl Cor ... Staundeforde's Placita Coronae [*Pleas of Crown*]   (DLA)
Staundf Prerog ... Staundeforde's Exposition of the King's Prerogative   (DLA)
Staund Pl ... Staundeforde's Pleas of Crown [*1557*] [*England*]   (DLA)
St Autobahn ... Strasse und Autobahn [*A publication*]
Stavby Jadrovej Energ ... Stavby Jadrovej Energetiky [*Supplement to Inzenyrske Stavby*] [*Czechoslovakia*] [*A publication*]
Stavebnicky Cas ... Stavebnicky Casopis [*A publication*]
STAVRA ..... Supreme High Command of the Soviet Armed Forces [*Russian*]   (MCD)
STAX.......... Sludge Tracking Acoustical Experiment [*Marine science*]   (MSC)
STB .... Bachelor of the Science of Theology
StB .... Kommentar zum Neuen Testament aus Talmud und Midrasch (H. L. Strack - F. Billerbeck) [*A publication*]   (BJA)
STB .... Sacrae Theologiae Baccalaureus [*Bachelor of Sacred Theology*] [*Latin*]
STB .... St. Blazey [*British depot code*]
STB .... Santa Barbara [*Venezuela*] [*Airport symbol*]   (OAG)
STB .... Scan True Bearing   (NVT)
STB .... Segment Tag BITS [*Binary Digits*]
STB .... September Resources Ltd. [*Vancouver Stock Exchange symbol*]
STB .... Shore Terminal Box   (MSA)
STB .... Signal Training Brigade   (MCD)
STB .... Soprano, Tenor, Bass
STB .... Southeast Banking Corp. [*NYSE symbol*]
STB .... Southern Tourist Board [*British*]
STB .... Special Tax Bond
STB .... Stable   (MSA)
STB .... Standard Torsion Bar   (MCD)
STB .... Steinbach [*Federal Republic of Germany*] [*Seismograph station code, US Geological Survey*]   (SEIS)
StB .... Stenografische Berichte der Fuenf Hauptversammlungen des Verbandes der Deutschen Juden [*A publication*]
STB .... Stillborn
STB .... Stourbridge [*British depot code*]
STB .... Stretch Block   (MCD)
StB .... Studi sul Boccaccio [*A publication*]
STB .... Subsystems Test Bed   (IEEE)
STB .... Sun's True Bearing [*Navigation*]
STB .... Supertropical Bleach [*Sanitizing agent*]
STB .... System [*or Subsystem*] Test Bed [*NASA*]   (KSC)
STB .... Systems Testing Branch [*Social Security Administration*]
STBA.......... Selective Top-to-Bottom Algorithm   (DIT)
St Barbara Mus Nat Hist Contrib Sci ... Santa Barbara Museum of Natural History. Contributions in Science [*A publication*]
St Bar Rev ... State Bar Review   (DLA)
STBCP .... Southeast Banking Corporation [*NASDAQ symbol*]   (NQ)
STBD......... Standard-Bred Pacers & Trotters [*NASDAQ symbol*]   (NQ)
STBD......... Starboard
StBFranc.... Studii Biblici Franciscani [*Jerusalem*] [*A publication*]
StBFranc LA ... Studii Biblici Franciscani. Liber Annuus [*Jerusalem*] [*A publication*]
sTBG .... Slow Thyroxine-Binding Globulin [*Endocrinology*]
StBiz .... Studi Bizantini e Neoellenici [*A publication*]
STBK......... State Street Boston [*NASDAQ symbol*]   (NQ)
STBL......... Stable   (FAAC)
STBLN....... Stabilization   (MSA)
STBLZ........ Stabilize   (AABC)
StBM......... Stuttgarter Biblische Monographien [*A publication*]
STBN......... Southern Bancorp, Inc. [*NASDAQ symbol*]   (NQ)
St Bonaventure Sci Stud ... St. Bonaventure Science Studies [*A publication*]
StBoT........ Studien zu den Bogazkoey-Texten [*Wiesbaden*] [*A publication*]
STBR......... Star Brite Corp. [*NASDAQ symbol*]   (NQ)
St Brown .... Stewart-Brown's Cases in the Court of the Star Chamber [*1455-1547*]   (DLA)
STBSCP..... Stroboscope [*Engineering*]
StBSt .... Stuttgarter Bibelstudien [*Stuttgart*] [*A publication*]
StBt .... Steamboat   (ADA)
STBT......... Subcaliber Tracer Bullet Trainer [*Army*]   (INF)
STBU......... Statistical Bulletin
STBY......... Standby   (AAG)
STC .... Chief SONAR Technician [*Navy rating*]
STC .... Sacramento Test Center   (MCD)
STC .... Saint Cloud, MN [*Location identifier*] [*FAA*]   (FAAL)
STC .... Sales Tax Cases [*A publication*]
STC .... Sales Tax Cases [*India*]   (DLA)

STC .... Samuel Taylor Coleridge [*Nineteenth-century British poet*]
STC .... Satellite Television Corporation [*Washington, DC*] [*Telecommunications*]   (TSSD)
STC .... Satellite Test Center [*Air Force*]
STC .... Satellite Tracking Center [*Sunnyvale, CA*]
STC .... Satellite Tracking Committee [*Military*]
STC .... Scandinavian Travel Commission [*Later, Scandinavian National Travel Offices*]   (EA)
STC .... Security Time Control
STC .... Security Training Center
STC .... Senate Tourism Caucus   (EA)
STC .... Senior Training Corps [*British*]
STC .... Sensitivity-Time Control [*RADAR*]
STC .... Serum Theophylline Concentration [*Clinical chemistry*]
STC .... Service to Chapters [*Red Cross*]
STC .... Service to Claimants [*Unemployment Insurance Service*] [*Department of Labor*]
STC .... Service Technology Corporation [*of Ling-Temco-Vought, Inc.*]
STC .... Serving Test Center [*Bell System*]
STC .... Set Carry
STC .... [*The*] Seven Tablets of Creation [*L. W. King*] [*A publication*]   (BJA)
STC .... SHAPE [*Supreme Headquarters Allied Powers Europe*] Technical Center [*Formerly, SADTC*] [*The Hague, Netherlands*] [*NATO*]
STC .... Short Time Constant
STC .... Short Title Catalog [*A publication*]
STC .... Simulation Tape Conversion
STC .... Single-Trip Container
STC .... Ski Touring Council
STC .... Slow Time Constant   (MCD)
STC .... Smokeless Tobacco Council [*Washington, DC*]   (EA)
STC .... Society for Technical Communication [*Washington, DC*]   (EA)
STC .... Society of Telecommunications Consultants [*New York, NY*] [*Telecommunications*] [*Information service*] [*An association*]   (EA)
STC .... Soft Tissue Calcification [*Medicine*]
STC .... Sound Transmission Class [*Followed by number, indicates FHA rating of sound insulating quality of a partition construction*]
STC .... Source Telecomputing Corporation [*McLean, VA*] [*Telecommunications*]   (TSSD)
STC .... Space Technology Center
STC .... Space Test Center [*Air Force*]
STC .... Space-Time Continuum
STC .... Spacecraft Test Conductor [*NASA*]   (KSC)
STC .... Specialists Training Center
STC .... Specific Taste Changes
STC .... Specific Thermal Capacity
STC .... Spectral Transfer Coefficient
STC .... Standard Telephone and Cable [*IT & T affiliate*] [*British*]
STC .... Standard Test Configuration [*NASA*]   (NASA)
STC .... Standard Transmission Code [*Data processing*]
STC .... Standing Technical Committee [*British*]
STC .... State Tax Cases [*Commerce Clearing House*]   (DLA)
STC .... State Teachers College
STC .... Station Technical Control [*Telecommunications*]   (TEL)
STC .... Station Test and Calibration
StC .... Status Constructus   (BJA)
STC .... Stepchild
St C .... Stephen's Commentaries on the Laws of England [*21st ed.*] [*1950*]   (DLA)
STC .... Stereo Tape Club of America
STC .... Stern Telecommunications Corporation [*New York, NY*] [*Telecommunications*]   (TSSD)
STC .... Stewart, Tabori & Chang [*Publisher*]
STC .... Stock Trust Certificate [*Business and trade*]
STC .... Stone Canyon Observatory [*California*] [*Seismograph station code, US Geological Survey*]   (SEIS)
STC .... Storage Container   (MCD)
STC .... Storage Technology Corporation [*In company name, STC Systems, Inc.*] [*Waldwick, NJ*] [*Software manufacturer*]
STC .... Stored Time Command
STC .... Streamtube Curvature
StC .... Studia Catholica [*A publication*]
StC .... Studia Celtica [*A publication*]
STC .... Subtropical Convergence [*Oceanography*]
STC .... Summit Technical Center [*Celanese Research Co.*]
STC .... Supplemental Type Certificate
STC .... Synthetic Turf Council   (EA)
STC .... System Test Configuration
STC .... System Test Console
STC .... System Transfer Constant
STC .... Systems Test Complex [*NASA*]
STCA .... Scottish Terrier Club of America   (EA)
STCA .... Silky Terrier Club of America   (EA)
STCA .... Skye Terrier Club of America   (EA)
STCA .... Sodium Trichloroacetate [*Organic chemistry*]
STCA .... Staffordshire Terrier Club of America   (EA)
St Can Lit ... Studies in Canadian Literature [*A publication*]
St Cas .... Stillingfleet's English Ecclesiastical Cases   (DLA)

StCath....... Studia Catholica [*Nijmegen*] [*A publication*] (BJA)
StCau........ Studia Caucasica [*A publication*]
STCB........ Subtask Control Block [*Data processing*] (IBMDP)
STCC .... Spacecraft Technical Control Center (MDG)
STCC .... Springfield Technical Community College [*Massachusetts*]
STCC .... Standard Transportation Commodity Classification [*or Code*]
STCC .... Standards Council of Canada [*See also CCNO*]
STCC .... Syndicat des Travailleurs en Communication, Electronique,
           Electricite, Techniciens, et Salaries du Canada
           [*Communications, Electronic, Electrical, Technical, and
           Salaried Workers of Canada - CWC*]
STCDHS .... Spacecraft Telemetry Command Data Handling System
STCDS ...... System Test Complex Data System
STCDSS..... Standing Technical Committee on Disposal of Sewage Sludge
           [*British*]
STCE......... System Test Complex Equipment
STCFEO..... Science and Technology Center, Far East Office
           [*Army*] (AABC)
STCH .... Stitch (MSA)
St Ch Cas... Star Chamber Cases [*England*] (DLA)
STCI.......... Siebert Telecommunications Consulting, Incorporated
           [*Cincinnati, OH*] [*Telecommunications*] (TSSD)
STCICS..... Strike Command Integrated Communications System [*British*]
StCILF ...... Studii si Cercetari de Istorie Literara si Folclor [*A publication*] (NRCH)
STCL......... Source-Term Control Loop [*Nuclear energy*] (NRCH)
StCL......... Studii si Cercetari Lingvistice [*A publication*]
STCLB ...... Start Climb [*Aviation*] (FAAC)
St Clem ..... St. Clement's Church Case [*Philadelphia, PA*] (DLA)
StClOr....... Studi Classici e Orientali [*A publication*]
STCM........ Master Chief SONAR Technician [*Navy rating*]
STCO .... Supervisor Training Conference Outline [*Air Force*] (MCD)
STCOL...... Steel Column [*Camutek*] [*Software package*]
STCP........ Short-Term Cost Plan [*NASA*] (NASA)
STCR........ Solar Thermal Central Receiver
StCrN .... Stephen Crane Newsletter [*A publication*]
STCS........ Senior Chief SONAR Technician [*Navy rating*]
St CS .... Studies in Contemporary Satire [*A publication*]
STCS........ Surveyor Thermal Control Section
StCSF .... Studii si Cercetari Stiintifice. Filologie [*A publication*]
STCT......... Small Transportable Communications Terminal
STCW........ System Time Code Word
STD .... Doctor of the Science of Theology
STD .... Sacrae Theologiae Doctor [*Doctor of Sacred Theology*] [*Latin*]
STD .... Safety Topic Discussion (AAG)
STD .... Salinity/Temperature/Density [*or Depth*] [*Oceanography*]
STD .... Schools of Theology in Dubuque [*Library network*]
STD .... Servo Tape Display
STD .... Sexually Transmitted Disease [*Medicine*]
STD .... Ship Training Detachment
STD .... Shuttle Test Director (MCD)
STD .... Skin Test Dose
STD .... Sledborne Time Digitizer
STD .... Society for Theological Discussion [*Defunct*] (EA)
STD .... Spacecraft Technology Division [*NASA*] (KSC)
STD .... Standard (AFM)
STD .... Standard Airways [*El Paso, TX*] [*FAA designator*] (FAAC)
STD .... Standard Test Dose
STD .... Standard Trustco Ltd. [*Toronto Stock Exchange symbol*]
STD .... Standing (AABC)
STD .... Started (ADA)
STD .... Steward [*British*]
ST D .... Stopped Diapason [*Organ stop*] [*Music*]
STD .... Storage Tube Display
STD .... Strain Gauge Transient Dosimetry
STD .... Stripline Tunnel Diode
StD .... Studi Danteschi [*A publication*]
StD .... Studies and Documents [*A publication*]
STD .... Subscriber Trunk Dialing [*Telephone communications*]
STD .... Supporting Technology Development (KSC)
STD .... Synopsis Series of the United States Treasury Decisions (DLA)
STD .... System Technology Demonstration Program (RDA)
S-TDA .... Selenium-Tellurium Development Association
STDA........ Steward's Assistant [*Navy*]
STDA........ Stripline Tunnel Diode Amplifier
STDB........ Steward's Branch [*Marine Corps*]
STDBY ...... Standby (NVT)
STDC .... Southern Travel Directors Council
STDC .... Standards Council of Canada [*See also CCNO*]
STD/DEV ... Standard Deviation (MCD)
STDDS ...... Submarine Tactical Data Display Subsystem (MCD)
STDE........ Standard Energy Corp. [*NASDAQ symbol*] (NQ)
St Dept....... State Department Reports (DLA)
STDF......... Standoff
STDHA...... Staedtehygiene [*A publication*]
ST DIAP ..... Stopped Diapason [*Organ Stop*]
STDJ .... Studies on the Texts of the Desert of Judah [*A publication*]
STDL......... Standard Logic [*NASDAQ symbol*] (NQ)
STDL......... Submarine Tactical Data Link (NVT)
STDM........ Statistical Time-Division Multiplexer [*or Multiplexing*]
STDM........ Synchronous Time-Division Multiplexing [*Data
           processing*] (MDG)

STDN......... Set the Date Now [*Association supporting the end of US
           military involvement in Indochina*] [*Defunct*] (EA)
STDN......... Spaceflight Tracking and Data Network [*Formerly, STADAN*]
           [*NASA*]
STDN......... Standardization (AFM)
Std Obraztsy Chern Metall ... Standartnye Obraztsy v Chernoi Metallurgii [*A
           publication*]
STDP........ Short-Term Dynamic Psychotherapy
STDP........ Special Training Devices Program (AFM)
STDS......... Snake Torpedo Destruction System
STDS......... Standards [*Timber measurement*]
STDS......... Submarine Tactical Data System (MCD)
STDST ...... Start Descent [*Aviation*] (FAAC)
STDV........ Start Tank Discharge Valve (KSC)
STDVG...... Stern Diving
STDWN ..... Stand Down (MCD)
STDY........ Saturday
STDY........ Steady (MSA)
STDZN...... Standardization (AABC)
STE .... Sainte [*Female*]
STE .... Segment Table Entry [*Data processing*] (MDG)
STE .... Shield Test Experiment [*Nuclear energy*] (NRCH)
STE .... Shift Technical Engineer (NRCH)
STE .... [*The*] Simplified Test Equipment [*Army*] (INF)
STE .... Societe [*Company*] [*French*]
STE .... Society of Tractor Engineers [*Later, SAE*]
STE .... Spacecraft Test Engineering [*NASA*] (KSC)
STE .... Span Terminating Equipment [*Telecommunications*] (TEL)
STE .... Special Test Equipment
STE .... Special-Type Ellipsometer
STE .... Specific Temperature Excursion
STE .... Star Tracker Electronics [*Apollo*] [*NASA*]
STE .... Station Test Equipment [*Deep Space Instrumentation Facility,
           NASA*]
STE .... Statute
Ste .... Steaua [*A publication*]
STE .... Stelco, Inc. [*Toronto Stock Exchange symbol*] [*Vancouver
           Stock Exchange symbol*]
STE .... Stepanavan [*USSR*] [*Seismograph station code, US Geological
           Survey*] [*Closed*] (SEIS)
STE .... Stevens Point [*Wisconsin*] [*Airport symbol*] [*Obsolete*] (OAG)
STE .... Stockton Terminal & Eastern Railroad [*AAR code*]
St E .... Studienreihe Englisch [*A publication*]
STE .... Suitability Test Evaluation (AAG)
STE .... Supergroup Translation Equipment
STE .... Support Test Equipment (MCD)
STE .... System Test Engineer [*NASA*] (NASA)
STEA......... Surveyor Test Equipment Assembly
STEA......... System Test, Evaluation, and Assembly
STEAG...... Steinkohlen-Elektrizitaet AG [*West Germany*]
STEAM...... Department of Science, Technology, Energy, and Materials
           [*Proposed Cabinet department*]
STEAM...... Sensor Technology as Applied to the Marine Corps
STEAM...... Standard Towing Equipment for Aircraft Maintenance (MCD)
Steam Eng ... Steam Engineer [*A publication*]
Steam Fuel Users J ... Steam and Fuel Users' Journal [*A publication*]
Steam Heat Eng ... Steam and Heating Engineer [*A publication*]
Steam and Heat Eng ... Steam and Heating Engineer [*A publication*]
Steam Heat Engr ... Steam and Heating Engineer [*A publication*]
Steam Plant Eng ... Steam Plant Engineering [*A publication*]
Steamusers Fuel Users J ... Steamusers' and Fuel Users' Journal [*A
           publication*]
STEAP........ Simulated Trajectories Error Analysis Program [*NASA*]
Stearns Real Act ... Stearn's Real Actions (DLA)
STEC......... Solar Thermal Electric Conversation (MCD)
STEC......... Syndicat des Travailleurs de l'Energie et de la Chimie [*Energy
           and Chemical Workers Union - ECWU*] [*Canada*]
St Eccl Cas ... Stillingfleet's English Ecclesiastical Cases (DLA)
Stecher Agency & Partnership ... Stecher's Cases on Agency and
           Partnership (DLA)
Stechert-Hafner Bk News ... Stechert-Hafner Book News [*A publication*]
STECR ...... Ships Tactical Environmental Control Receiver
STECS ...... Software Technology and Engineering Center Staff [*Social
           Security Administration*]
STED......... Science, Technology, and Economic Development
STED......... Standard Technical Equipment Development Division
           [*Obsolete*] [*National Security Agency*]
STEDBAC ... Stearyldimethylbenzylammonium Chloride [*Organic chemistry*]
STEDI........ Space Thrust Evolution and Disposal Investigation [*Air Force*]
STEDMIS ... Ships Technical Data Management Information System [*Navy*]
STEDMIS ... Standard Technical Data Management Information
           System (CAAL)
STEEG ...... Scanned Topographic Electroencephalograph
Steel Const ... Steel Construction [*A publication*]
Steel Constr ... Steel Construction [*A publication*]
Steel Fabric J ... Steel Fabrication Journal [*A publication*]
Steel Fabr J ... Steel Fabrication Journal [*A publication*]
STEELFACTS ... Materials Database Steel and Iron [*German Iron and Steel
           Engineers Association*] [*Dusseldorf, West Germany*]
           [*Information service*] (EISS)
Steel Furn Mon ... Steel Furnace Monthly [*A publication*]

Steel Int ..... Steel International [*A publication*]
Steel Met Int ... Steels and Metals International [*A publication*]
Steel Process ... Steel Processing [*A publication*]
Steel Rev ... Steel Review [*A publication*]
Steel Times Int ... Steel Times International [*England*] [*A publication*]
STEEP........ Safety Training for the Execution of Emergency Procedures [*NASA*]
STEEP........ Shock Two-Dimensional Eulerian Elastic Plastic [*Computer code*]
STEEP........ Solution to Environmental and Economic Problems
Steer PL..... Steer on Parish Law [*6th ed.*] [*1899*]   (DLA)
STEG.......... Staatliche Gesellschaft zur Erfassung von Ruestungsgut [*German Public Corporation for the Collection and Distribution of War Materials*]
STEG.......... Supersonic Transport Evaluation Group
STEIA........ Stahl und Eisen [*A publication*]
STE/ICE..... Simplified Test Equipment for Internal Combustion Engines   (RDA)
STE/ICEPM ... Simplified Test Equipment for Internal Combustion Engine Powered Material   (MCD)
STEIN......... System Test Environment Input
Steinbeck M ... Steinbeck Monograph Series [*A publication*]
Steinbeck Q ... Steinbeck Quarterly [*A publication*]
S Tein ...... Shaw's Scotch Teind [*Tithe*] Cases   (DLA)
Steinind Steinstrassenbau ... Steinindustrie und Steinstrassenbau [*A publication*]
Stein-Ind Strassenbau ... Stein-Industrie und -Strassenbau [*A publication*]
Steinkohlenbergbauver Kurznachr ... Steinkohlenbergbauverein Kurznachrichten [*A publication*]
SteiQ.......... Steinbeck Quarterly [*A publication*]
Steirische Beitr Hydrogeol ... Steirische Beitraege zur Hydrogeologie [*A publication*]
Steklo Keram ... Steklo i Keramika [*A publication*]
Steklo Sitally Silik Mater ... Steklo, Sitally, i Silikatnye Materialy [*Belorussian SSR*] [*A publication*]
Stekol'naya Prom-st ... Stekol'naya Promyshlennost [*USSR*] [*A publication*]
STEL .... Satelco, Inc. [*NASDAQ symbol*]   (NQ)
STEL .... Short-Term Exposure Limit [*To air pollutants*]
STEL .... Society of Telegraphic Engineers [*British*]
STEL .... Studenta Tutmonda Esperantista Liga [*World League of Esperanto-Speaking Students*]
STELB....... Stereo Review [*A publication*]
STELCO...... Steel Company of Canada
STELLA...... Structural Thinking Experiential Learning Laboratory with Animation [*Software*]
STELLAR ... Star Tracker for Economical Long Life Attitude Reference [*NASA*]
Stellenbosse Stud ... Stellenbosse Student [*A publication*]
STEM .... Scanning Transmission Electron Microscope
STEM ..... SEABEE Tactical Equipment Management [*Navy*]
STEM .... Searching Together Educational Ministries   (EA)
STEM .... Shaped Tube Electrolytic Machining [*GE*]
STEM .... Shoplifters Take Everybody's Money
STEM .... Society for Teachers of Emergency Medicine [*Dallas, TX*]   (EA)
STEM .... Socio-Technological-Economic-Military [*DoD*]
STEM .... Solar-Terrestrial Environment Model [*to predict the terrestrial effects of solar events*]
STEM .... Special Technical and Economic Mission
STEM .... Special Telemetry Equipped Missile
STEM .... Stay Time Extension Module [*NASA*]
STEM .... Stellar Tracker Evaluation Missile
STEM .... Storable Tubular Extendable Member
STEM .... System Test Equipment Mission [*NASA*]   (KSC)
STEM .... Systems for Tools and Equipment Management [*Military*]   (AFIT)
STEM .... Systems Training and Exercise Module   (MCD)
STEMFAB ... Storable Tubular Extendable Member Fabrication
STEMS...... Small Terminal Evasive Missile System   (MCD)
STEMS...... Society to Encourage Miniskirts [*New York group opposing below-the-knee fashions introduced in 1970*]
STEN.......... Sheppard-Turpin-England [*Machine carbine codesigned by Sheppard and Turpin*]
STEN.......... Stencil
STEN.......... Stenographer
STENCH..... Society to Exterminate Neo-Communist Harbingers
Stendhal Cl ... Stendhal Club [*A publication*]
ST-ENDOR ... Special Triple-Electron Nuclear Double Resonance [*Spectroscopy*]
STENO ...... Stenographer   (MUGU)
STENS ...... Standard Terrestrial Navigation System   (MCD)
STEO .... Special Test Equipment Order   (MCD)
STeol.......... Studii Teologice [*A publication*]
STEP ..... Safeguard Test and Evaluation Program [*Army*]   (AABC)
STEP .... Safety Test Engineering Program [*AEC*]
STEP .... School to Employment Program
STEP .... Scientific and Technical Exploitation Program   (AFM)
STEP .... Selective Traffic Enforcement Program [*Department of Transportation*]
STEP .... Self-Teaching Exportable Package
STEP .... Sensitivity Temperature Error Program   (MCD)

STEP .... Sequential Tests of Educational Progress [*of ETS; given in 10th and 12th grades*]
STEP .... Ship Type Electronics Plan [*Navy*]   (NG)
STEP .... Short Term Enrichment Program [*of US Information Agency*]
STEP .... Simple Transition to Economical Processing   (IEEE)
STEP .... Simple Transition to Electronic Processing
STEP .... Software Test and Evaluation Process [*DoD*]
STEP .... Solutions to Employment Problems [*A program of National Association of Manufacturers*]
STEP .... Space Technology Experiments Platform
STEP .... Space Terminal Evaluation Program
STEP .... Special Training Enlistment Program
STEP .... Special Training Equipment Program Document   (AFIT)
STEP .... Staff Training Extramural Programs [*National Institutes of Health*]
STEP .... Standard Tape Executive Package [*or Program*] [*NCR Corp.*]
STEP .... Standard Terminal Program [*Data processing*]   (IEEE)
STEP .... Standard Test Equipment Procedure   (NG)
STEP .... Statistical Trajectory Estimation Program [*NASA*]
STEP .... Student Education Program
STEP .... Student Transfer Education Plan [*Defunct*] [*National Urban League*]
STEP .... Students toward Environmental Participation [*UNESCO and National Park Service*]
STEP .... Summer Training Employment Program   (MCD)
STEP .... Supervisory Tape Executive Program [*Data processing*]
STEP .... Supplemental Training and Employment Program   (OICC)
STEP .... System for Testing Evaluation of Potential [*Employee evaluation software*] [*London House, Inc.*]
STEP .... Systematic Training for Effective Parenting
Steph .... Stephens' Supreme Court Decisions [*1774-1923*] [*Jamaica*]   (DLA)
Steph Cl.... Stephens on Clergy [*1848*]   (DLA)
Steph Com ... Stephen's Commentaries on the Laws of England   (DLA)
Steph Comm ... Stephen's Commentaries on the Laws of England   (DLA)
Steph Const ... Stephens on the English Constitution   (DLA)
Steph Cr .... Stephen's Digest of the Criminal Law   (DLA)
Steph Crim Dig ... Stephen's Digest of the Criminal Law   (DLA)
Steph Cr L ... Stephen's General View of the Criminal Law [*9 eds.*] [*1877-1950*]   (DLA)
Steph Cr Law ... Stephen's General View of the Criminal Law   (DLA)
Steph Dig.... Stephen's Digest, New Brunswick Reports   (DLA)
Steph Dig Cr L ... Stephen's Digest of the Criminal Law   (DLA)
Steph Dig Ev ... Stephen's Digest of the Law of Evidence   (DLA)
Steph Elect ... Stephens on Elections [*1840*]   (DLA)
Stephen F Austin State Coll Sch For Bull ... Stephen F. Austin State College. School of Forestry. Bulletin [*A publication*]
Stephen HCL ... Stephen's History of Criminal Law   (DLA)
Stephens ... Supreme Court Decisions, by J. E. R. Stephens   (DLA)
Steph Ev .... Stephen's Digest of the Law of Evidence   (DLA)
Steph Lect ... Stephen's Lectures on the History of France   (DLA)
Steph NP.... Stephen's Law of Nisi Prius   (DLA)
Steph Pl.... Stephen on Pleading   (DLA)
STEPR........ Saturation Transfer Electron Paramagnetic Resonance [*Physics*]
STEPS........ Science and Technology Evaluation and Prioritization System [*Program*]   (RDA)
STEPS........ Ships Technical Publication System [*Navy*]
STEPS........ Solar Thermionic Electrical Power System
STEPS........ Stored Thermal Energy Propulsion System
STER......... Seater
STER......... Stereotype
STER......... Sterilize   (AABC)
STER......... Sterling
STER......... Sterna [*A publication*]
STER......... Successively Truncated Expectation of the Reciprocal [*Statistics*]
STER......... System Training Equipment Requirement
Stereo .... Stereo Review [*A publication*]
STEREO.... Stereophonic   (MSA)
STEREO.... Stereoscope
STEREO.... Stereoscopic   (DSUE)
STEREO.... Stereotype [*Refers to old news*] [*Slang*]   (DSUE)
Stereochem Fundam Methods ... Stereochemistry. Fundamentals and Methods [*A publication*]
Stereo R..... Stereo Review [*A publication*]
STERF....... Special Test Equipment Repair Facility
STERL....... Sterling   (ADA)
STERNUT... Sternutamentum [*Snuff*] [*Pharmacy*]
Steroids Lipids Res ... Steroids and Lipids Research [*A publication*]
Steroids Suppl ... Steroids. Supplement [*A publication*]
STES .... Solar Thermal Energy System
STES Newsl ... STES [*Seasonal Thermal Energy Storage*] Newsletter [*United States*] [*A publication*]
STET .... Specialized Technique for Efficient Typesetting
STET .... Steward, Technical [*Marine Corps*]
STET .... System Test Experiments Tape
STETF........ Solar Total Energy Test Facility [*Energy Research and Development Administration*]
StEtr.......... Studi Etruschi [*A publication*]
Stettin Ent Ztg ... Stettiner Entomologische Zeitung [*A publication*]

STEV .... Stevedore
StEv .... Studia Evangelica [*Berlin*] [*A publication*]
Stev Arb.... Stevens on Arbitration [*2nd ed.*] [*1835*] (DLA)
Stev Av ...... Stevens on Average [*5th ed.*] [*1835*] (DLA)
Stev Dig ..... Stevens' New Brunswick Digest (DLA)
STEVE....... Space Tool for Extravehicular Emergencies
Stevens & G ... Stevens and Graham's Reports [*98-139 Georgia*] (DLA)
Stevens Ind ... Stevens Indicator [*A publication*]
Stevens Inst Technol (Hoboken NJ) Davidson Lab Rep ... Stevens Institute
     of Technology (Hoboken, New Jersey). Davidson
     Laboratory. Report [*A publication*]
STEVS....... Spartan Tactical Equipment Verification Site [*Missiles*] (MCD)
STEW .... Stewart Sandwiches [*NASDAQ symbol*] (NQ)
Stew .... Stewart's Alabama Reports [*1827-31*] (DLA)
Stew .... Stewart's Equity Reports [*28-45 New Jersey*] (DLA)
Stew .... Stewart's Nova Scotia Admiralty Reports (DLA)
Stew .... Stewart's Reports [*1-10 South Dakota*] (DLA)
Stew Adm ... Stewart's Nova Scotia Vice-Admiralty Reports [*1803-
     13*] (DLA)
Stew Admr ... Stewart's Nova Scotia Admiralty Reports (DLA)
Stew (Ala) ... Stewart's Alabama Reports (DLA)
Stew Ans ... Stewart's Answers to Dirleton's Doubts [*2 eds.*] [*1715, 1762*]
     [*Scotland*] (DLA)
Stewart ...... Stewart's Alabama Reports [*1827-31*] (DLA)
Stewart ...... Stewart's Equity Reports [*28-45 New Jersey*] (DLA)
Stewart ...... Stewart's Nova Scotia Admiralty Reports (DLA)
Stewart ...... Stewart's Reports [*1-10 South Dakota*] (DLA)
Stewart (Ala) ... Stewart's Alabama Reports (DLA)
Stewart-Brown ... Stewart-Brown's Lancashire and Cheshire Cases in the
     Court of Star Chamber (DLA)
Stewart R... Stewart's Alabama Reports (DLA)
Stew Eq ..... Stewart's Equity Reports [*28-45 New Jersey*] (DLA)
Stew N Sc ... Stewart's Nova Scotia Admiralty Reports (DLA)
Stew & P .... Stewart and Porter's Alabama Supreme Court Reports [*1831-
     34*] (DLA)
Stew and Porter ... Stewart and Porter's Alabama Reports (DLA)
Stew & P Rep ... Stewart and Porter's Alabama Reports (DLA)
STEWS....... Shipboard Tactical Electronic Warfare System [*Navy*]
Stewt Rep ... Stewart's Alabama Reports (DLA)
Stew VA ..... Stewart's Nova Scotia Vice-Admiralty Reports (DLA)
STE-X......... Simplified Test Equipment Expandable [*Army*] (RDA)
STEX .... Statute Expired [*IRS*]
S Texas LJ ... South Texas Law Journal [*A publication*]
STeZ .... South Temperate Zone
STF............ S-Band Temperature Fahrenheit
STF............ S-Band Transmit Filter
STF............ Safety Test Facility [*Nuclear energy*]
STF............ Satellite Tracking Facility [*Air Force*]
STF............ Service Tabulating Form (AAG)
STF............ Signal Tracking Filter
STF............ Software Test Facility [*NASA*] (MCD)
STF............ Space Track Facility
STF............ Spacecraft Test Facility
STF............ Special Task Force [*Army*]
STF............ Special Technical Factors (MCD)
STF............ Special Tube Feeding [*Medicine*]
STF............ Spin Test Facility [*NASA*]
STF............ Staff (AFM)
STF............ Standardized Test of Fitness [*Canadian Association of Sports
     Sciences*]
STF............ Stanford Resources Ltd. [*Toronto Stock Exchange symbol*]
St F .... Starch-Free [*Pharmacy*]
STF............ Starkville, MS [*Location identifier*] [*FAA*] (FAAL)
STF............ Static Test Facility (KSC)
stf.............. Stiff [*Quality of the bottom*] [*Nautical charts*]
STF............ Strange Fantasy [*A publication*]
STF............ Stratiform [*Meteorology*] (FAAC)
STF............ Structural Fatigue Test (MCD)
STF............ Subject to Finance (ADA)
STF............ Subjective Transfer Function (MCD)
STF............ Supervisory Time Frame
STF............ System Test Facility
STF............ Systems Technology Forum [*Burke, VA*]
     [*Telecommunications*] (TSSD)
STFAS....... Support to Total Force Analysis [*TRADOC*] (MCD)
STFF .... Safeguard Tactical Field Force [*Army*] (AABC)
STFG......... Staffing Guides [*Army*] (AABC)
STFG......... Stuffing (MSA)
StFil .... Studia Filozoficzne [*A publication*]
STFL .... Stifel Financial Corp. [*NASDAQ symbol*] (NQ)
STFM .... Societe des Textes Francais Modernes [*A publication*]
STFM .... Society of Teachers of Family Medicine [*Kansas City,
     MO*] (EA)
STFM .... Stretcher Form [*Tool*] (AAG)
St Form Sp ... Studies in Formative Spirituality [*A publication*]
St For Note Calif Div For ... State Forest Notes. California Division of
     Forestry [*A publication*]
STFR .... Stratus Fractus [*Meteorology*] (FAAC)
StFr .... Studi Francescani [*A publication*]
STFRM .... Stratiform [*Meteorology*] (FAAC)
STFSGT ..... Staff Sergeant [*Marine Corps*]

STFT .... Stray Field Test (NVT)
STG........... Saint George Island [*Alaska*] [*Airport symbol*] (OAG)
STG........... Satellite Terminal Guidance
Stg .... Sea-Tangle [*Nautical charts*]
STG........... Sedalia, Marshall, Boonville Stage Line, Inc. [*Des Moines, IA*]
     [*FAA designator*] (FAAC)
STG........... SONAR Technician, Ground [*Navy rating*]
STG........... Space Task Group [*Later, Manned Spacecraft Center*] [*NASA*]
STG........... Space Telescope Guidance [*NASA*]
STG........... Special Technology Group [*National Technical Information
     Service*] (MCD)
STG........... Split Thickness Graft [*Medicine*]
STG........... Staging (AABC)
STG........... Standing [*Numismatics*]
STG........... Starting (MSA)
STG........... Steego Corp. [*Formerly, Sterling Precision Corp.*] [*NYSE
     symbol*]
STG........... Steering Task Group
STG........... Sterling
STG........... Stomatogastric Ganglion [*Neuroanatomy*]
STG........... Storage
STG........... Storage Triacylglycerol [*Biochemistry*]
STG........... Strathgordon [*Tasmania*] [*Seismograph station code, US
     Geological Survey*] (SEIS)
STG........... Strong (FAAC)
StG........... Studi Germanici [*A publication*]
StG........... Studium Generale [*Heidelberg*] [*A publication*]
STG........... Study Group [*NATO*]
STG........... Sydney Tourist Guide [*A publication*]
STGAA...... Shade Tobacco Growers Agricultural Association (EA)
StGAK....... Studien zur Germanistik, Anglistik und Komparatistik [*A
     publication*]
STGAR....... Staging Area [*Military*]
STGB......... Staging Base [*Military*]
StGB......... Strafgesetzbuch [*Penal Code*] [*German*]
STGC........ Secure Task Group, Common (MCD)
STGE........ Storage
STGEA...... Studium Generale [*A publication*]
STGEN...... Steam Generator
STGG .... Staging (AAG)
STGH .... Stang Hydronics [*NASDAQ symbol*] (NQ)
STGHT ...... Straight
StGKA....... Studien zur Geschichte und Kultur des Altertums [*A
     publication*]
St Gloc ...... Statute of Gloucester [*First statute to give costs in
     actions*] (DLA)
STGM........ Status Game Corp. [*NASDAQ symbol*] (NQ)
STGO .... Star-Glo Industries [*NASDAQ symbol*] (NQ)
STGP........ Subcontract Task Group Procurement
STGR......... Steiger Tractor [*NASDAQ symbol*] (NQ)
STGR......... Stringer (AAG)
Stgr .... Studia Grammatica [*A publication*]
St Gr I........ Studi di Grammatica Italiana [*A publication*]
STG/STF ... Special Task Group/Special Task Force [*Army*] (MCD)
STGT........ Secondary Target
StGThK ..... Studien zur Geschichte der Theologie und der Kirche [*A
     publication*]
S Th .... Scholar in Theology [*British*]
STH .... Seton Hall University, South Orange, NJ [*OCLC
     symbol*] (OCLC)
STH .... Somatotrophic [*Growth*] Hormone [*Also, GH, SH*]
     [*Endocrinology*]
STH .... South
STH .... Stanhome, Inc. [*NYSE symbol*]
STH .... Stoney Hill [*Jamaica*] [*Seismograph station code, US
     Geological Survey*] (SEIS)
STH .... Stray Horse Resources, Inc. [*Vancouver Stock Exchange
     symbol*]
STh........... Studia Theologica [*A publication*]
STh........... Subthalamus [*Anatomy*]
STH .... Subtotal Hysterectomy [*Medicine*]
STH .... Toronto School of Theology Library, University of Toronto
     [*UTLAS symbol*]
Sth Afr Rep ... South African Republic High Court Reports (DLA)
SThB .... Sacrae Theologiae Baccalaureus [*Bachelor of Sacred
     Theology*]
SThD .... Sacrae Theologiae Doctor [*Doctor of Sacred Theology*]
StHefte...... Statistische Hefte [*A publication*]
Sthen .... Stheneboea [*of Euripides*] [*Classical studies*] (OCD)
STHEST... Southeast
STHESTN... Southeastern
S ThL......... Sacrae Theologiae Lecentiatus [*Licentiate in Sacred Theology*]
STHMK ...... Stanhome, Inc. [*NASDAQ symbol*] (NQ)
STHMPN.... Southampton [*England*]
STHN........ Southern
Sthn Afr Fam Pract ... Southern African Family Practice [*A publication*]
STHP......... Shih-Ta Hsueh-Pao [*Bulletin of Taiwan Normal University*] [*A
     publication*]
STHPD ...... Shih-Ta Hsueh-Pao [*A publication*]
StHR.......... Stress Hypertensive Rats
SThU .... Schweizerische Theologische Umschau [*A publication*]

St Hum .... Studies in the Humanities [*A publication*]
STHV .... Science, Technology, and Human Values [*A publication*]
STHWST .... Southwest
STHWSTN ... Southwestern
SThZ .... Schweizerische Theologische Zeitschrift [*Zurich*] [*A publication*]
STI .... Mountain Home, ID [*Location identifier*] [*FAA*] (FAAL)
STI .... St. Thomas Institute [*Cincinnati, OH*] [*Research center*] (RCD)
STI .... Santiago [*Dominican Republic*] [*Airport symbol*] (OAG)
STI .... Saskatoon Technical Institute [*UTLAS symbol*]
STI .... Saxton Industries [*Vancouver Stock Exchange symbol*]
STI .... Scientific and Technical Information [*System*] [*Canada*]
STI .... Scientific and Technical Information [*Facility*] [*NASA*]
STI .... Screw Thread Insert
STI .... Serum Trypsin Inhibitor [*Serology*]
STI .... Server Technology, Incorporated [*Sunnyvale, CA*] [*Information service*] (EISS)
STI .... Service Tools Institute [*Later, HTI*] (EA)
STI .... Short-Term Integration (CAAL)
STI .... Silicon Target Intensifier
STI .... Single Tooth Indexer
STI .... Small Towns Institute (EA)
STI .... Soybean Trypsin Inhibition [*Biochemistry*]
STI .... Space Technology, Incorporated (MCD)
STI .... Specifications Technology, Incorporated
STI .... Speech Transmission Index
STI .... Star Valley [*Idaho*] [*Seismograph station code, US Geological Survey*] (SEIS)
STI .... State Technical Institute
STI .... Steel Tank Institute [*Northbrook, IL*] (EA)
STI .... Stem Tolerance Index [*Botany*]
Sti .... Stinson [*Record label*]
StI .... Studi Ispanici [*A publication*]
StI .... Studi Italiani [*A publication*]
StI .... Studia Islandica [*A publication*]
StI .... Studies: An Irish Quarterly Review of Letters, Philosophy, and Science [*A publication*]
STI .... SunTrust Banks, Incorporated [*NYSE symbol*]
STI .... Surface Targets of Interest (MCD)
STI .... Survive Tomorrow, Incorporated [*Commercial firm*] (EA)
STI .... Systolic Time Interval [*Cardiology*]
STIA .... Scientific, Technological, and International Affairs Directorate [*National Science Foundation*]
STIAP .... Standard Instrument Approach [*RADAR*] [*Aviation*]
STIB .... Stimulus Train-Induced Bursting [*Neuroscience*]
STIBOKA ... Stichting voor Bodemkartering [*Netherlands Soil Survey Institute*] [*Wageningen*] [*Information service*] (EISS)
STIC .... Science and Technology Information Center [*National Science Council*] [*Taipei, China*] (EISS)
STIC .... Scientific and Technical Intelligence Center [*DoD*]
STIC .... Solid-State Transducer Intercompartmental Catheter [*Instrumentation*]
STIC .... Space Technical Information Control (MCD)
STIC .... Space Toy Information Center (EA)
STICAP ..... Stiff Circuit Analysis Program [*Data processing*]
STICEC ...... Special Travel Industry Council on Energy Conservation
Stich .... Stichus [*of Plautus*] [*Classical studies*] (OCD)
Sticht Bosbouwproefsta "Dorschkamp" Ber ... Stichting Bosbouwproefstation "De Dorschkamp." Berichten [*A publication*]
Sticht Bosbouwproefsta "Dorschkamp" Korte Meded ... Stichting Bosbouwproefstation "De Dorschkamp." Korte Mededelingen [*A publication*]
Sticht Bosbouwproefsta "Dorschkamp" Uitv Versl ... Stichting Bosbouwproefstation "De Dorschkamp." Uitvoerige Verslagen [*A publication*]
Sticht Bosbouwproefstn De Dorschkamp Korte Meded ... Stichting Bosbouwproefstation "De Dorschkamp." Korte Mededeling [*A publication*]
Sticht Coord Cult Onderz Broodgraan Jaarb ... Stichting voor Coordinate van Cultuur en Onderzoek van Broodgraan Jaarboekje [*A publication*]
Sticht Energieonderz Cent Ned Rep ... Stichting Energieonderzoek Centrum Nederland. Report [*A publication*]
Sticht Inst Pluimveeonderz "Het Spelderholt" Jaarversl ... Stichting Instituut voor Pluimveeonderzoek "Het Spelderholt" Jaarverslag [*A publication*]
Sticht Inst Pluimveeonderz Spelderholt Jaarversl ... Stichting Instituut voor Pluimveeonderzoek "Het Spelderholt" Jaarverslag [*A publication*]
STICTION ... Static Friction
STID .... Scientific and Technical Information Dissemination [*NASA*]
STID .... Scientific and Technical Information Division [*NASA*] (IEEE)
STIDAS ...... Speech Transmission Index Device [*Using*] Artificial Signals
STIF .... Scientific and Technical Information Facility [*NASA*]
STIF .... Short-Term Irradiation Facility (NRCH)
STIF .... Spectral Transmission Interference Filter
STIF .... Stiffener [*Civil engineering*]
STIFC .... Space Track Interim Fire Control
STII .... Stanford Telecommunications [*NASDAQ symbol*] (NQ)
St I I .... Studien zur Indologie und Iranistik [*A publication*]

Stiinta Sol ... Stiinta Solului [*A publication*]
STIL .... Software Test and Integration Laboratory [*NASA*] (NASA)
STIL .... Statistical Interpretive Language [*Data processing*] (MDG)
Stil .... Stillingfleet's English Ecclesiastical Cases [*1702-04*] (DLA)
Stiles .... Stiles' Reports [*22-29 Iowa*] (DLA)
Stiles (IA) .. Stiles' Reports [*22-29 Iowa*] (DLA)
STILLAT .... Stillatim [*By Drops or In Small Quantities*] [*Pharmacy*]
STILLB ...... Stillborn [*Medicine*]
Still Eccl Cas ... Stillingfleet's English Ecclesiastical Cases (DLA)
STILS .... Stinger Launch Simulator (MCD)
STIM .... Sensitivity Training Impact Model
STIM .... Stimulant (DSUE)
STIM .... Stimulating (ROG)
stim .... Stimulus
Stim Gloss ... Stimson's Law Glossary (DLA)
Stim Law Gloss ... Stimson's Law Glossary (DLA)
Stimm Zeit ... Stimmen der Zeit [*A publication*]
STIMS .... Scientific and Technical Information Modular System [*NASA*] (MCD)
Stimson ..... Stimson's Law Glossary (DLA)
STIMU .... Stimutech, Inc. Uts [*NASDAQ symbol*] (NQ)
Stimul Newsl ... Stimulation Newsletter [*A publication*]
Stiness .... Stiness' Reports [*20-34 Rhode Island*] (DLA)
STINFO ...... Scientific and Technical Information Office [*Army*]
STING .... Swift Target Identification Notification Grid (MCD)
STINGER .... SEABEE Tactically Installed, Navy Generated, Engineer Resources [*System*] [*Navy*] (NVT)
STINGS ...... Stellar Inertial Guidance System [*Air Force*]
STIO .... Scientific and Technical Information Office [*NASA*]
STIP .... Scientific and Technical Information Program (MCD)
STIP .... Skill Training Improvement Program [*Department of Labor*]
STIP .... Solar Technical Information Program [*Solar Energy Research Institute*] [*Golden, CO*] [*Information service*] (EISS)
STIP .... Stipend [*or Stipendiary*]
STIPE .... Stipendiary Magistrate [*British*] (DSUE)
STIPIS .... Scientific, Technical, Intelligence, and Program Information System [*HEW*]
STIR .... Scientific and Technical Intelligence Register (AFM)
STIR .... Separate Track and Illumination RADAR [*Military*] (CAAL)
STIR .... Shield Test and Irradiation Reactor
STIR .... Signal Track and Illuminating RADAR [*Canadian Navy*]
STIR .... SNAP [*Systems for Nuclear Auxiliary Power*] Shield Test Irradiation Reactor
STIR .... Surplus to Immediate Requirements (ADA)
Stirling E N ... Stirling Engine Newsletter [*A publication*]
STIRS .... Self-Training Interpretive Retrieval System
STIS .... Scientific & Technical Information Services, Inc. [*Information service*] (EISS)
STIS .... Silicon Target Image Sensor
STIS .... Specialized Textile Information Service
STIS .... Sumika Technical Information Service, Inc. [*Information service*] [*Osaka, Japan*] (EISS)
STISA .... Sbornik Nauchnykh Trudov Tomskii Inzhenerno-Stroitel'nyi Institut [*A publication*]
STISEC ...... Scientific and Technological Information Services Enquiry Committee [*Australia*]
StIsl .... Studia Islandica [*A publication*]
StIslam ...... Studia Islamica [*Paris*] [*A publication*]
Sti Solului ... Stiinta Solului [*A publication*]
StIsp .... Studi Ispanici [*A publication*]
STIT .... Signal Technical Intelligence Team [*Army*] (AABC)
StIt .... Studi Italici [*Kyoto*] [*A publication*]
St Ital .... Studi Italiani di Filologia Classica [*A publication*]
STIT-CONUS ... Scientific and Technical Information Team, Continental United States [*Army*] (AABC)
STIT-EUR ... Scientific and Technical Information Team, Europe [*Army*] (AABC)
STIT-FE ...... Scientific and Technical Information Team, Far East [*Army*] (AABC)
STIV .... Silicon Target Intensifier Vidicon
StiZ .... Stimmen der Zeit [*A publication*] (BJA)
STIZ .... Submarine Transit Identification Zones (NVT)
STJ .... St. John's [*Newfoundland*] [*Geomagnetic observatory code*]
STJ .... St. John's [*Newfoundland*] [*Seismograph station code, US Geological Survey*] (SEIS)
STJ .... Saint Joseph College, West Hartford, CT [*OCLC symbol*] (OCLC)
STJ .... St. Joseph, MO [*Location identifier*] [*FAA*] (FAAL)
StJ .... St. Joseph Railway
STJ .... Series Tee Junction
STJ .... Severn Tunnel Junction [*British depot code*]
STJ .... Society of St. Teresa of Jesus [*Roman Catholic women's religious order*]
STJ .... Special Trial Judge [*US Tax Court*]
STJ .... Subtropical Jet Stream (ADA)
StJb .... Stifter-Jahrbuch [*A publication*]
STJM .... St. Jude Medical, Inc. [*NASDAQ symbol*] (NQ)
St J MO PUC ... St. Joseph, Missouri, Public Utilities Commission Reports (DLA)
St John's L Rev ... St. John's Law Review [*A publication*]
STJU .... St. John's University [*Minnesota; New York*]

StJud .... Studia Judaica. Forschungen zur Wissenschaft des Judentums [*Berlin*] [*A publication*]
STJW .... Stretcher Jaws [*Tool*] (AAG)
stk .... Scotland [*MARC country of publication code*] [*Library of Congress*] (LCCP)
STK .... Single Tone Keying
STK .... Situation Track Display
STK .... Soiuz Trudovogo Krest'ianstva [*Union of Working Peasantry*] [*Russian*]
STK .... Stack (MSA)
STK .... Stakes Race [*Horse racing*]
STK .... Standard Test Key [*Data processing*]
STK .... Stephens Creek [*Australia*] [*Seismograph station code, US Geological Survey*] (SEIS)
STK .... Sterling, CO [*Location identifier*] [*FAA*] (FAAL)
stk .... Sticky [*Quality of the bottom*] [*Nautical charts*]
STK .... Stock (AAG)
STK .... Strake [*Mining engineering*]
STK .... Sturmkanone [*Self-propelled assault gun*] [*German military - World War II*]
STK .... Svensk Teologisk Kvartalskrift [*A publication*]
STKAB ...... Standarty i Kachestvo [*A publication*]
STKC .... Stanwick Corporation [*NASDAQ symbol*] (NQ)
STKD .... Stockade (AABC)
STK EX ...... Stock Exchange
STKF .... Stock Fund
STKFA .... Stock Fund Accounting
STKFS .... Stock Fund Statement
STKG .... Sturzkampfgeschwader [*Dive-bomber wing*] [*German military - World War II*]
STKM .... Storm King Mines [*NASDAQ symbol*] (NQ)
STKR .... Stocker & Yale [*NASDAQ symbol*] (NQ)
STKR .... Stockroom (AABC)
STKS .... Stakes (ROG)
STKv .... Svensk Teologisk Kvartalskrift [*A publication*]
STL .... Bibliotheque Municipale de Saint-Laurent [*UTLAS symbol*]
STL .... Sacrae Theologiae Lector [*Reader in Sacred Theology*] [*Latin*]
STL .... Sacrae Theologiae Licentiatus [*Licentiate in Sacred Theology*] [*Latin*]
STL .... Safe Tow Length
STL .... St. Louis [*Missouri*] [*Airport symbol*]
STL .... Santa Lucia [*Chile*] [*Seismograph station code, US Geological Survey*] [*Closed*] (SEIS)
STL .... Satellite
STL .... Schottky Transistor Logic (IEEE)
STL .... Seatrain Lines, Inc. [*AAR code*]
STL .... Sequential Table Lookup
STL .... Short Term Leaflet. Ministry of Agriculture, Fisheries, and Food [*A publication*]
STL .... Simulated Tape Load
STL .... Site Team Leader [*Nuclear energy*] (NRCH)
STL .... Southern Traffic League
STL .... Southern Transportation League [*Arlington, VA*] (EA)
STL .... Space Technology Laboratories [*of TRW Group*]
STL .... Special Tool List
STL .... Standard Telegraph Level [*Telecommunications*] (TEL)
STL .... Startling Stories [*A publication*]
STL .... Steel (KSC)
STL .... Step-Through Latencies
STL .... Sterling Bancorp [*NYSE symbol*]
STL .... Stockage List
STL .... Stol Air Commuter [*San Rafael, CA*] [*FAA designator*] (FAAC)
StL .... Studia Linguistica [*A publication*]
StL .... Studies on the Left [*A publication*]
StL .... Studies in Logic and the Foundations of Mathematics [*Elsevier Book Series*] [*A publication*]
STL .... Studio-Transmitter Link
STL .... Sunday Times (London) [*A publication*]
STL .... Supersonic Transition Locus [*Galactic winds*]
STL .... Support Table Load
STL .... Suppressor T Lymphocyte [*Immunology*]
STL .... Swelling, Tenderness, Limitation of Movement [*Medicine*]
STL .... Synchronous Transistor Logic (MDG)
STL .... System Test Loop (IEEE)
STL .... Systems Techniques Laboratory [*Stanford University*] (MCD)
STLA .... Strip Transmission Line Adapter [*or Assembly*]
StLAR .... St. Lawrence & Atlantic Railway
St at Large ... Statutes at Large (DLA)
St Law .... Loughborough's Digest of Statute Law [*Kentucky*] (DLA)
STLB & M ... St. Louis, Brownsville & Mexico [*Railway*]
STLC .... Sequence Thin-Layer Chromatography
STLC .... Soluble Threshold Limit Concentration [*Environmental chemistry*]
STLF .... Southern Troops and Landing Force
STLI .... Statue of Liberty National Monument
STLI .... Stockage List Item
StLI .... Studi di Letteratura Ispano-Americana [*A publication*]
St Lim .... Statute of Limitations (DLA)
StLIM & S... St. Louis, Iron Mountain & Southern Railway
StLing .... Studies in Linguistics [*A publication*]
S T L J .... South Texas Law Journal [*A publication*]

STLJD .... South Texas Law Journal [*A publication*]
St L J Th..... St. Luke's Journal of Theology [*A publication*]
STLL .... Submarine Tender Load List
STLM .... Safeguard Tactical Logistics Management
St L M........ Studien zur Literatur der Moderne [*A publication*]
St Lngst .... Statistical Methods in Linguistics [*A publication*]
STLO .... St. Louis Steel Casting [*NASDAQ symbol*] (NQ)
STLO .... Scientific and Technical Liaison Office [*AFSC*]
StLo .... Studia Logica [*A publication*]
St & Loc Taxes (BNA) ... State and Local Taxes [*Bureau of National Affairs*] (DLA)
St & Loc Tax Serv (P-H) ... State and Local Tax Service [*Prentice-Hall, Inc.*] (DLA)
StLog .... Studia Logica [*A publication*]
StL & OR .... St. Louis & Ohio River Railroad
STLOS ...... Star Line-of-Sight (KSC)
St Louis L Rev ... St. Louis Law Review (DLA)
St Louis Metropol Med ... St. Louis Metropolitan Medicine [*A publication*]
St Louis Mus Bul ... St. Louis City Art Museum Bulletin [*A publication*]
St Louis U L J ... St. Louis University. Law Journal [*A publication*]
St Louis Univ B ... St. Louis University. Bulletin [*A publication*]
St Louis U Res J ... Saint Louis University. Research Journal [*Baguio City*] [*A publication*]
St Lou ULJ ... St. Louis University. Law Journal [*A publication*]
St L P........ Studia Linguistica et Philologica [*A publication*]
STL-QPSR ... Speech Transmission Laboratory. Royal Institute of Technology. Stockholm. Quarterly Progress and Status Reports [*A publication*]
STLR .... Semitrailer
STLS .... South Texas Library System [*Library network*]
STLS .... Southern Tier Library System [*Library network*]
STLS .... Stinger Training Launch Simulator (MCD)
STL-SF...... St. Louis-San Francisco Railway Co.
STL-SF & T ... St. Louis, San Francisco & Texas Railway Co.
STL STL and WD ... Steel or Steel and Wood [*Freight*]
StL & SW.... St. Louis & South Western Railway
STLSW of T ... St. Louis Southwestern Railway Co. of Texas
STLT .... Satellite (FAAC)
STLT .... Small Transportable Link Terminal
STLT .... Stellite [*Metallurgy*]
STLT .... Studio-Transmitter Link-Television
STLU .... St. Louis University [*Missouri*]
St LU Intra L Rev ... St. Louis University. Intramural Law Review (DLA)
St Luke J.... St. Luke's Journal of Theology [*A publication*]
St Luke's Hosp Gaz ... St Luke's Hospital Gazette [*A publication*]
STLV .... Simian T-Cell Lymphotropic Virus
STLV .... Simian T-Lymphotropic Virus
STL WD..... Steel or Wood [*Freight*]
STL WI ...... Steel or Wire [*Freight*]
STM........... Groupement International d'Editeurs Scientifiques, Techniques, et Medicaux [*International Group of Scientific, Technical, and Medical Publishers*] (EA-IO)
STM........... Master of Arts in Theology
STM........... Master of the Science of Theology
STM........... Sacrae Theologiae Magister [*Master of Sacred Theology*]
STM........... Safety Test Missile (MCD)
STM........... Santarem [*Brazil*] [*Airport symbol*] (OAG)
STM........... Satellite Technology Management, Inc. [*Torrance, CA*] [*Telecommunications*] (TSSD)
STM........... Save the Manatee Club (EA)
STM........... Scanning Tunneling Microscope
STM........... Scientific, Technical, and Medical
STM........... Screened Through Matching [*Parapsychology*]
STM........... Section Technical Manual [*Jet Propulsion Laboratory, NASA*]
STM........... Send Test Message (AAG)
STM........... Service Technique Militaire [*Switzerland*]
STM........... Service Test Model (NG)
STM........... Shielded Tunable Magnetron
STM........... Short-Term Memory
STM........... Signal Termination Module [*NASA*] (NASA)
STM........... Slate Mountain [*Nevada*] [*Seismograph station code, US Geological Survey*] [*Closed*] (SEIS)
STM........... Society for Traditional Music (EA)
STM........... Southam, Inc. [*Toronto Stock Exchange symbol*] [*Vancouver Stock Exchange symbol*]
STM........... Special Test Missile
STM........... Specialized Trade Mission [*Department of Commerce*]
STM........... Specification Test Material (MCD)
STM........... Spin Tuned Magnetron
STM........... Standard Type Material (MCD)
STM........... Standards Tool Master (MCD)
STM........... State Transition Matrix
STM........... Static Test Model (MCD)
STM........... Statistical Multiplexing [*Telecommunications*]
STM........... Statute Mile
STM........... Steam
STM........... Steward's Mate [*Navy rating*]
STM........... Storm (FAAC)
STM........... Strategic Mortgage Investments, Inc. [*NYSE symbol*]
STM........... Stream [*Board on Geographic Names*]
STM........... Structural Test Model

StM............. Studi e Materiali di Storia delle Religioni [*A publication*]
StM............. Studia Monastica [*A publication*]
STM............. Subject to Mortgage   (ADA)
STM............. Supersonic Tactical Missile   (MCD)
STM............. Supplementary Technical Manual [*Military*]
STM............. Surface-to-Target-to-Missile
STM............. Synthetic Timing Mode
STM............. System Training Mission   (AFM)
STMA......... Space-Time Moving Average [*Statistics*]
STMA......... Sports Turf Managers Association [*Defunct*]   (EA)
STMA......... Statistical Theory and Method Abstracts [*A publication*]
STMA......... Stuffed Toy Manufacturers Association
STMAF....... Stampede International Resources Cl A [*NASDAQ
                 symbol*]   (NQ)
St Marianna Med J ... St. Marianna Medical Journal [*Japan*] [*A publication*]
St Mark ...... St. Mark's Church Case [*Philadelphia, PA*]   (DLA)
St Mark Rev ... St. Mark's Review [*A publication*]
St Marks R ... St. Mark's Review [*A publication*]
St Marks Rev ... St. Mark's Review [*A publication*]
St Marlb..... Statute of Marlbridge   (DLA)
St Mary's L J ... St. Mary's Law Journal [*A publication*]
StMBC .... Studien und Mitteilungen aus dem Benediktiner- und dem
                 Cistercienser-Orden [*A publication*]
STMCGMW ... Subcommission for Tectonic Maps of the Commission for the
                 Geological Map of the World [*Moscow, USSR*]   (EA-IO)
STME .... Stellar Television Monitor Equipment
St Med ...... Studi Medievali [*A publication*]
StMed .... Studia Mediewistyczne [*A publication*]
St Mert ...... Statute of Merton   (DLA)
STMEV....... Storm Evasion [*Navy*]   (NVT)
S T Mf........ Svensk Tidskrift foer Musikforskning [*A publication*]
STMG .... Steaming   (MSA)
STMGA ...... Salmon and Trout Magazine [*A publication*]
StMGB .... Studien und Mitteilungen zur Geschichte des Benediktiner-
                 Ordens [*A publication*]
STMGR ...... Station Manager [*Aviation*]   (FAAC)
St Mi.......... Statute Mile [*Nautical charts*]
St Mis........ Studia Missionalia [*A publication*]
STMIS........ System Test Manufacturing Information System   (IEEE)
St Misc....... Studi Miscellanei, Seminario di Archeologia e Storia dell'Arte
                 Greca e Romana dell'Universita di Roma [*A publication*]
STML .... Sindicato de Trabajadores Mineros de Llallagua
STML .... Stimulate   (MSA)
St Mod Lev Fin ... Statute Modus Levandi Fines   (DLA)
StMon .... Studia Monastica [*A publication*]
St Mot Carr Guide (CCH) ... State Motor Carrier Guide [*Commerce Clearing
                 House*]   (DLA)
STMP .... Ship Test Management Plan [*Navy*]   (CAAL)
STMP .... System Training Management Plan   (MCD)
STMR .... Steamer
S/T-MR ..... Surplus Termination Material Requisition   (MCD)
STMS .... St. Thomas More Society   (EA)
STMS .... Scottish Tramway Museum Society
StMSR....... Studi e Materiali di Storia delle Religioni [*Rome/Bologna*] [*A
                 publication*]
STMT .... Statement   (AFM)
STMU .... Special Test and Maintenance Unit
STMW .... Subtropical Mode Water [*Oceanography*]
STMYA...... Stomatologiya [*A publication*]
STN .... SAC [*Strategic Air Command*] Telephone Net
St N .... St. Nicholas [*A publication*]
STN .... Satellite Television Network [*Washington, DC*]
                 [*Telecommunications*]   (TSSD)
STN .... Satellite Tracking Network   (MCD)
STN .... Saturn Airways, Inc.   (MCD)
STN .... Scientific and Technical Information Network
STN .... Seatoun [*New Zealand*] [*Seismograph station code, US
                 Geological Survey*] [*Closed*]   (SEIS)
STN .... Software Trouble Note [*NASA*]   (NASA)
STN .... Solar Telescope Network
STN .... Solitary Tract Nucleus [*Also, NST*] [*Anatomy*]
STN .... Special Traffic Notice [*British*]
STN .... Specification Transmittal Notice   (MCD)
STN .... Stain [*Deltiology*]
STN .... Stainless
STN .... Stansted [*England*] [*Airport symbol*]   (OAG)
STN .... Statement of Technology Needs [*Air Force*]
STN .... Station
STN .... Stevens [*J. P.*] & Co., Inc. [*NYSE symbol*]
STN .... Stone [*Unit of weight*]   (AAG)
StN .... Studia Neotestamentica [*Paris/Bruges*] [*A publication*]
STN .... Subthalamic Nucleus [*Neurobiology*]
STN .... Switched Telecommunications Network
STNA......... Sons of Temperance of North America [*Wilmot, NS*]   (EA)
STNA......... Stanadyne, Inc. [*NASDAQ symbol*]   (NQ)
Stn Biol Mar Grande Riviere Que Rapp Annu ... Station de Biologie Marine.
                 Grande Riviere, Quebec. Rapport Annuel [*A publication*]
Stn Bull Agric Exp Stn Univ Minn ... Station Bulletin. Minnesota Agricultural
                 Experiment Station [*A publication*]

Stn Bull New Hamps Agric Exp Stn ... Station Bulletin. Agricultural
                 Experiment Station. University of New Hampshire [*A
                 publication*]
Stn Bull Ore Agric Exp Stn ... Station Bulletin. Oregon Agricultural
                 Experiment Station [*A publication*]
StNeerla..... Statistica Neerlandica [*A publication*]
St Neophil ... Studia Neophilologica [*A publication*]
StNF......... Studier i Nordisk Filologi [*A publication*]
Stn Fed Essais Agric (Lausanne) Publ ... Stations Federales d'Essais
                 Agricoles (Lausanne). Publication [*A publication*]
STNG .... Sustaining
STNI .... Subtotal Nodal Irradiation [*Oncology*]
Stn L......... Stanford Law Review [*A publication*]
STNLS........ Stainless   (MSA)
STNR......... Stationary
Stn Rep Hort Res Stn (Tatura) ... Station Report. Horticultural Research
                 Station (Tatura) [*A publication*]
STNRY .... Stationary   (FAAC)
Stns Circ Wash Agric Exp Stns ... Stations Circular. Washington
                 Agricultural Experiment Stations [*A publication*]
Stn Sper Agrar Ital ... Stazione Sperimentali Agrarie Italiane [*A publication*]
STNT......... Sprawozdania Towarzystwa Naukowego w Toruniu [*A
                 publication*]
StNT......... Studien zum Neuen Testament [*A publication*]
STNV......... Satellite Tobacco Necrosis Virus
STNWRE .... Stoneware [*Freight*]
StO............ St. Olaf [*Record label*]
STO............ Science and Technology Objectives   (MCD)
STO............ Sea Transport Officer
STO............ Segment Table Origin
STO............ Service du Travail Obligatoire [*French labor force*] [*World War
                 II*]
STO............ Short Takeoff   (MCD)
STO............ Short-Term Objective
STO............ Slater-Type Orbital [*Atomic structure*]
STO............ Small-Time Operator [*Slang*]
STO............ Sojourner Truth Organization   (EA)
STO............ Standard Transfer Order
STO............ Standing Order [*Business and trade*]
StO............ Standing Tool Order   (KSC)
StO............ Stimmen des Orients [*A publication*]
STO............ Stockholm [*Sweden*] [*Airport symbol*]   (OAG)
STO............ Stoker [*Navy*] [*British*]
STO............ Stone Container Corp. [*NYSE symbol*]
STO............ Stonehill College, North Easton, MA [*OCLC symbol*]   (OCLC)
STO............ Stonyhurst [*Blackburn*] [*England*] [*Seismograph station code,
                 US Geological Survey*] [*Closed*]   (SEIS)
STO............ Storage Processor
STO............ Storekeeper [*Coast Guard*]
Sto............ Storey's Delaware Reports   (DLA)
Sto............ Story's United States Circuit Court Reports   (DLA)
StO............ Studia Oliveriana [*A publication*]
STO............ Swedish Trade Office   (EA)
STO............ System Test Objectives
STOAD...... Scientific and Technical Organizations and Agencies Directory
                 [*A publication*]
Sto Ag .... Story on Agency   (DLA)
STOAL ...... Short Takeoff Arrested Landing   (MCD)
Sto Att Lien ... Stokes on Lien of Attorneys and Solicitors [*1860*]   (DLA)
STOB......... Standard Commercial Tobacco Co. [*NASDAQ symbol*]   (NQ)
Sto Bailm ... Story on Bailments   (DLA)
Sto Bills ..... Story on Bills   (DLA)
STOC .... Standard Tactical Operating Condition
STOC .... Systems for Test Output Consolidation [*Data processing*]
Sto CC .... Story's United States Circuit Court Reports   (DLA)
Stoch Processes Appl ... Stochastic Processes and Their Applications [*A
                 publication*]
Stock .... Stockton's New Brunswick Vice-Admiralty Reports [*1879-
                 91*]   (DLA)
Stock .... Stockton's New Jersey Equity Reports   (DLA)
Stock Adm ... Stockton's New Brunswick Vice-Admiralty Reports   (DLA)
Stockett ..... Stockett's Reports [*27-53 Maryland*]   (DLA)
STOCKH .... Stockholmia [*Stockholm*] [*Imprint*]   (ROG)
Stockh Contrib Geol ... Stockholm Contributions in Geology [*A publication*]
Stockholm Contrib Geol ... Stockholm Contributions in Geology [*A
                 publication*]
Stockholm Tek Hogsk Avh ... Stockholm. Tekniska Hogskolan. Avhandling
                 [*A publication*]
Stockholm Tek Hogsk Handl ... Stockholm. Tekniska Hogskolan.
                 Handlingar [*Transactions*] [*A publication*]
Stockt .... Stockton's New Jersey Equity Reports [*9-11 New
                 Jersey*]   (DLA)
Stockt Ch... Stockton's New Jersey Equity Reports [*9-11 New
                 Jersey*]   (DLA)
Stockton .... Stockton's New Brunswick Vice-Admiralty Reports   (DLA)
Stockton Adm (New Br) ... Stockton's New Brunswick Vice-Admiralty
                 Reports   (DLA)
Stockt Vice-Adm ... Stockton's New Brunswick Vice-Admiralty
                 Reports   (DLA)
Sto Comm ... Story's Commentaries on the Constitution of the United
                 States   (DLA)

Sto Con ...... Story on Contracts (DLA)
Sto Conf Law ... Story on Conflict of Laws (DLA)
Sto Const ... Story's Commentaries on the Constitution of the United States (DLA)
Sto Const Cl B ... Story's Constitutional Class Book (DLA)
Sto Cont ..... Story on Contracts (DLA)
StocProc .... Stochastic Processes and Their Applications [*A publication*]
STOCS ...... South Texas Outer Continental Shelf
Sto Eq Jur ... Story on Equity Jurisprudence (DLA)
Sto Eq Pl .... Story on Equity Pleadings (DLA)
STOG .... Science and Technology Objectives Guide (MCD)
Sto & G .... Stone and Graham's Private Bills Decisions [*1865*] (DLA)
STOGW ...... Short Takeoff Gross Weight [*Aviation*]
STOIAC ...... Strategic Technology Office Information Analysis Center [*Battelle Memorial Institute*] (MCD)
STOIIP .... Stock Tank Oil Initially in Place [*Petroleum technology*]
STOL .... Saturn Test Oriented Language [*NASA*]
STOL .... Short Takeoff and Landing [*Aviation*]
STOL .... Standing Operating and Landing
STOL .... Systems Test and Operation Language
Stolport ...... Short Takeoff and Landing Airport [*London, England*]
STOM .... Safe Transport of Munitions (MCD)
STOM .... Stomachic [*To Strengthen the Stomach*] [*Medicine*] (ROG)
STOM .... System Test and Operations Manual
Stomach Intest ... Stomach and Intestine [*Japan*] [*A publication*]
S Tomas Nurs J ... Santo Tomas Nursing Journal [*A publication*]
Stomatol DDR ... Stomatologie der DDR [*East Germany*] [*A publication*]
Stomatol Glas Srb ... Stomatoloski Glasnik Srbije [*A publication*]
Stomatol Zpr ... Stomatologicke Zpracy [*A publication*]
STON .... Short Ton [*2000 lbs.*] (AABC)
Stone .... Stone's Justices' Manual [*Annual*] (DLA)
Stone Ben Bdg Soc ... Stone's Benefit Building Societies [*1851*] (DLA)
Stone C ...... Stone Country [*A publication*]
Stone D ...... Stone Drum [*A publication*]
Stone Just Man ... Stone's Justices' Manual [*Annual*] (DLA)
Stony .... Stony Hills [*A publication*]
STOP .... Save the Oppressed People Committee (EA)
STOP .... Selected Test Optimization Program (MCD)
STOP .... Ship's Toxicological Protective System
STOP .... Single Title Order Plan [*Formerly, SCOP*] [*Bookselling*]
STOP .... Society that Opposes Pornography
STOP .... Stable Ocean Platform
STOP .... Start Tromping on Pedal [*Facetious interpretation of the traffic sign*]
STOP .... Stop forced busing; Teach children, not bus them; Operate neighborhood schools for those in the neighborhood wishing to attend them; Put an end to government interference in the parent-child relationship [*In association name, S.T.O.P. Forced Busing*] (EA)
STOP .... Stop the Oil Profiteers [*Antioil price slogan*]
STOP .... Stop the Olympic Prison [*Lake Placid Olympics, 1980*] [*Opposed possible later use of an Olympic building as a prison*] [*Defunct*]
STOP .... Stop This Outrageous Purge [*Group opposed to extremist measures used by segregationists in Arkansas; opposed by CROSS*]
STOP .... Strategic Orbit Point (AFM)
STOP .... Strategic Talks on Prevention [*of accidental atomic war and nuclear weapons proliferation*] [*Proposed by Sen. Gary Hart, 1982*]
STOP .... Student/Teacher Organization to Prevent Nuclear War (EA)
STOP .... Supersonic Transport Optimization Program [*NASA*]
Sto Part ..... Story on Partnership (DLA)
Sto Pl .... Story's Civil Pleading (DLA)
STOP-NSA ... Students to Oppose Participation in the National Student Association (EA)
STOPP ...... Society of Teachers Opposed to Physical Punishment
STOPP ...... Society of Teachers of Professional Photography (EA)
Stop Pregl ... Stopanski Pregled [*A publication*]
STOPPS ...... Standard Transportation Operations Personnel Property (MCD)
STOPS ...... Shipboard Toxicological Operational Protective System [*Navy*]
STOPS ...... Stability Operations
STOPS ...... Stabilized Terrain Optical Position Sensor [*Army*]
STOPS ...... Supreme Temple Order Pythian Sisters (EA)
STOQ .... Storage Queue
STOR .... Scripps Tuna Oceanographic Research
STOR .... Segment Table Origin Register [*Data processing*] (BUR)
STOR .... Storage (AFM)
StOr .... Studia Orientalia. Edidit Societas Orientalis Fennica [*Helsinki*] [*A publication*]
STOR .... Summary Tape Operations Rental [*Bureau of the Census*]
STOR .... System Test and Operations Report
STORAD .... Stored Address [*Data processing*]
STORADS ... Site Tactical Optimized Range Air Defense System
Storage Handl Distrib ... Storage Handling Distribution [*A publication*]
Stor Art ..... Storia dell'Arte [*A publication*]
STORC .... Self-Ferrying Trans-Ocean Rotary-Wing Crane [*Helicopter*]
StOrChrColl ... Studia Orientalia Christiana. Collectanea [*Cairo*] [*A publication*]
Stor Dict .... Stormouth's Dictionary of the English Language (DLA)

STORE .... Storage Technology for Operational Readiness
STORE .... Students to Observe Retail Establishments [*Student legal action organization*] (EA)
Stor Ebr It ... Storia dell'Ebraismo in Italia. Sezione Toscana [*A publication*]
Storefront ... Storefront Classroom [*A publication*]
STORES ...... Syntactic Tracer Organized Retrospective Enquiry System [*Instituut voor Wiskunde, Informatiewerk, en Statistiek*] [*Data processing*] [*The Netherlands*]
STORET ..... Storage and Retrieval [*Data processing*]
STORET ..... Storage and Retrieval for Water Quality Data [*Environmental Protection Agency*] [*Databank*] (MSC)
Storia e Polit ... Storia e Politica [*A publication*]
STORLAB .. Space Technology Operations and Research Laboratory (IEEE)
STORM ...... Safe Transport of Munitions Project (MCD)
STORM ...... Sensor, Tank, Off-Route Mine (MCD)
STORM ...... Statistically Oriented Matrix Program (IEEE)
STORM ..... Stormscale Operational and Research Meteorology [*National Oceanic and Atmospheric Administration*]
STORMS .... Standardized Operation Research Management System (MCD)
STORMSAT ... Storm Satellite (MCD)
STORW ..... Storer Communications Wts [*NASDAQ symbol*] (NQ)
Story .... Story on Equity Jurisprudence [*1836-1920*] (DLA)
Story .... Story's United States Circuit Court Reports (DLA)
Story Ag ..... Story on Agency (DLA)
Story Bailm ... Story on Bailments (DLA)
Story Comm Const ... Story's Commentaries on the Constitution of the United States (DLA)
Story Confl Laws ... Story on Conflict of Laws (DLA)
Story Const ... Story's Commentaries on the Constitution of the United States (DLA)
Story Cont ... Story on Contracts (DLA)
Story Eq Jur ... Story on Equity Jurisprudence (DLA)
Story Eq Pl ... Story's Equity Planning (DLA)
Story Laws ... Story's Laws of the United States (DLA)
Story Merchants ... Abbott's Merchant Ships and Seamen, by Story (DLA)
Story Partn ... Story on Partnership (DLA)
Story Prom Notes ... Story on Promissory Notes (DLA)
Story R .... Story's United States Circuit Court Reports [*First Circuit*] (DLA)
Story Sales ... Story on Sales of Personal Property (DLA)
Story's Circuit CR ... Story's United States Circuit Court Reports [*First Circuit*] (DLA)
Story's Laws ... Story's United States Laws (DLA)
Story's Rep ... Story's United States Circuit Court Reports (DLA)
Story US Laws ... Story's Laws of the United States (DLA)
STOS .... Space Test Operations Section
Sto Sales ..... Story on Sales of Personal Property (DLA)
STOSY .... Santos Ltd. ADR [*NASDAQ symbol*] (NQ)
STOT .... Scheduled Time Over Target (AFM)
STOT .... Stockpile-to-Target (AFM)
STOTINS ..... Stand-Off Techniques for Parachute Insertion (MCD)
StOTPr .... Studies in Old Testament Prophecy Presented to T. H. Robinson [*A publication*] (BJA)
Stotz-Kontakt-Roemmler Nachr ... Stotz-Kontakt-Roemmler Nachrichten [*A publication*]
StOU .... Stimmen Orient und Uebersee [*A publication*] (BJA)
STOVL .... Short Take-Off and Vertical Landing (MCD)
STO/VL .... Short Takeoff/Vertical Landing (MCD)
STOW .... Side Transfer Optimum Warehousing
STOW .... Stowage (AAG)
STOW .... Swim the Ontario Waterways [*Personal incentive program for fitness swimmers*] [*Ontario Masters Swimming Club*]
STOW .... System for Takeoff Weight
STP .... North-Holland Studies in Theoretical Poetics [*Elsevier Book Series*] [*A publication*]
STP .... Sacrae [*or Sacrosanctae*] Theologiae Professor [*Professor of Sacred Theology*]
STP .... SAGE [*Semiautomatic Ground Environment*] System Training Program
STP .... St. Paul, MN [*Location identifier*] [*FAA*] (FAAL)
STP .... Saint Peter's College, Jersey City, NJ [*OCLC symbol*] (OCLC)
STP .... Sao Tome and Principe [*Three-letter standard code*] (CNC)
STP .... Satellite Ticket Printer [*Travel industry*]
STP .... Satellite Tracking Program [*of the Smithsonian Institution's Astrophysical Observatory*]
STP .... Save the Tallgrass Prairie [*An association*] (EA)
STP .... Scientifically Treated Petroleum [*A motor fuel oil additive*] [*Initials reported, by extension of meaning, also to stand for a hallucinogenic drug, DOM*]
STP .... Sea Test Phase [*Navy*] (CAAL)
STP .... Selective Tape Print
STP .... Self-Test Program (MCD)
STP .... Sewage Treatment Plant
STP .... Short Term Program (NRCH)
STP .... Short Term Projections [*Townsend-Greenspan & Co., Inc.*] [*Database*]
STP .... Shuttle Technology Panel [*NASA*] (NASA)
STP .... Signal Transfer Point [*Telecommunications*] (TEL)
STP .... Simultaneous Test Procedure [*Statistics*]

STP	Simultaneous Track Processor
STP	Singing Tree Press [*Publisher's imprint*]
STP	Society of Television Pioneers (EA)
STP	Society for Thai Philately (EA)
STP	Sodium Triphosphate [*or Sodium Tripolyphosphate*] [*Also, STPP*] [*Inorganic chemistry*]
STP	Solar-Terrestrial Physics (EISS)
STP	Solar-Terrestrial Probe [*NASA*]
STP	South Texas Project [*Nuclear energy*] (NRCH)
STP	Space Technology Payload (MCD)
STP	Space Test Program [*Air Force*]
STP	Special Technical Publication (MCD)
STP	Special Tool Production
STP	Spectrum of Time Project [*Astronomy*]
STP	Stamp (MSA)
STP	Standard Temperature and Pressure
STP	Standard [*Normal*] Temperature and Pulse [*Medicine*]
STP	Standard Test Procedure
STP	Standard Type Process (MCD)
STP	Standardized Test Program
St P	State Papers (DLA)
STP	Sterilization Test Program
St & P	Stewart and Porter's Alabama Reports (DLA)
STP	Stop the Pentagon/Serve the People (EA)
STP	Stoppage (AABC)
STP	Storage Tube Processor
STP	Storm Track Prediction (MCD)
STP	Strength, Toughness, Pride
STP	Strip
StP	Studi Petrarcheschi [*A publication*]
StP	Studia Palmyrenskie [*Warsaw*] [*A publication*]
StP	Studia Patristica [*A publication*]
STP	Subsystem Test Plan [*NASA*] (NASA)
STP	Supracondylar Tibial Prosthesis [*Medicine*]
STP	Sycamore Test Procedure [*Aerospace*] (AAG)
STP	System Test Plan
STP	System Test Program [*Navy*] (CAAL)
STP	Systems Technology Program (MCD)
STP	Systems Training Program [*RADAR*]
StPa	Studia Patristica [*A publication*]
StPapyr......	Studia Papyrologica [*Barcelona*] [*A publication*]
StPatrist....	Studia Patristica [*Berlin-Ost*] [*A publication*]
St Paul Med J ...	St. Paul Medical Journal [*A publication*]
StPB	Studia Post-Biblica [*A publication*]
St P Brook ...	Staff Papers. Brookings Institution [*A publication*]
STPCS	Scientific and Technical Personnel Characteristic System [*National Science Foundation*]
StPCyRy.....	St. Paul City Railway
StP & D......	St. Paul & Duluth Railroad
STPD.........	Stamped (ROG)
STPD.........	Standard Temperature and Pressure, Dry
STPD.........	Stripped (MSA)
STPDN	Stepdown
St Petersb Med Wchnschr ...	St. Petersburger Medicinische Wochenschrift [*A publication*]
STPF	Shield Test Pool Facility [*Nuclear energy*]
STPG.........	Spare-Time Production for Gain [*FAO*]
STPG.........	Stamping (ROG)
STPG.........	Stepping (MSA)
STPGA	Steel Processing [*A publication*]
STPH.........	Static Phase Error [*NASA*] (NASA)
St Philon ...	Studia Philonica [*A publication*]
STPI	Science and Technology Policy Implementation [*Project*]
STPL	[*The*] St. Paul Companies, Inc. [*NASDAQ symbol*] (NQ)
STPL	Sidetone Path Loss [*Telecommunications*] (TEL)
STPL	Stern Plane
St Pl Cr......	Staundeforde's Pleas of Crown [*England*] (DLA)
STPM	Syndicat Togolais du Personnel de la Meteorologie [*Togolese Union of Meteorological Personnel*]
StPM & M...	St. Paul, Minneapolis & Manitoba Railway
STPNG......	Stopping (MSA)
STPO.........	Science and Technology Policy Office [*Supersedes OST*] [*National Science Foundation*]
St and Port ...	Stewart and Porter's Alabama Reports (DLA)
StP & P......	St. Paul & Pacific Railroad
STPP.........	Sodium Tripolyphosphate [*Also, STP*] [*Inorganic chemistry*]
STPP.........	Student Teacher Performance Profile
STPR........	Semiannual Technical Progress Report
STPR........	Stepper [*Motor*] [*Electronics*]
STPR........	Stripper
STPR........	Stumper [*Freight*]
St Pr Reg....	Style's Practical Register [*England*] (DLA)
STPS.........	Stern Teacher Preference Schedule
STPSA	Studia Psychologica [*A publication*]
StP & SC ...	St. Paul & Sioux City Railroad
STPST.......	Stop-Start [*Telecommunications*] (TEL)
STPTC	Standardization of Tar Products Test Committee
StPUD	St. Paul Union Depot
StPUSY.....	St. Paul Union Stock Yards Co.
STPX	Systems Training Program Exercise (AABC)
STQ............	Society of Translators of Quebec [*Canada*]
STQ...........	Streator, IL [*Location identifier*] [*FAA*] (FAAL)
STR	Questar Corp. [*NYSE symbol*]
STR	Scientific Technical Report
STR	Scientific and Technological Research (DEN)
STR	Sea Test Range (MUGU)
STR	Search and Track RADAR
STR	Seater (ADA)
STR	Segment Table Register
STR	Service Test Review
STR	Service Trouble Report
STR	Sidetone Reduction [*Telecommunications*] (TEL)
STR	Society for Theatre Research (EA)
STR	Society of Thoracic Radiology [*Norcross, GA*] (EA)
STR	Software Trouble Report (MCD)
STR	Soul-Taehakkyo Ronmunjip. Inmun-Sahoe-Kwahak [*Seoul University Journal. Humanities and Social Sciences*] [*A publication*]
STR	Spacecraft Telemetry Regenerator (MCD)
STR	Special Theory of Relativity
STR	Special Trade Representative
STR	Speed Tolerant Recording [*Electronic Processors, Inc.*]
STR	Standard Broadcasting Corp. Ltd. [*Toronto Stock Exchange symbol*]
STR	Standard Taxiway Routing
STR	Standard Tool Request
STR	Standard Training Requirements [*Navy*] (NVT)
STR	Star Science Fiction [*A publication*]
STR	Steamer
STR	Stereo Review [*A publication*]
STR	Storage Rack (MCD)
STR	Store
STR	Straight (AAG)
STR	Strainer (AAG)
STR	Strait [*Maps and charts*]
Str	Strange's Cases of Evidence [*1698-1732*] [*England*] (DLA)
Str	Strange's English King's Bench Reports [*1716-49*] (DLA)
STR	Strasbourg [*France*] [*Seismograph station code, US Geological Survey*] (SEIS)
STR	Strasse [*Street*] [*German*]
Str	Strategemata [*of Frontinus*] [*Classical studies*] (OCD)
STR	Strategic Training Range (MCD)
STR	Streak
str	Streaky [*Quality of the bottom*] [*Nautical charts*]
STR	Stream [*Maps and charts*]
STR	Street
STR	Streichinstrumente [*Stringed Instruments*] [*Music*]
STR	Strength (AFM)
STR	Streptococcus [*Medicine*]
STR	Stretch [*Horse racing*]
Str	Striatum [*Brain anatomy*] [*Also, ST*]
STR	String
STR	Stringendo [*Hastening*] [*Music*]
STR	Strings [*of an orchestra*]
STR	Strip (AAG)
STR	Stroke
STR	Strophe [*Classical studies*] (OCD)
STR	Structural [*Lumber*]
St R	Stuart's Lower Canada Appeal Cases [*Quebec*] (DLA)
StR	Studi Religiosi [*A publication*]
StR	Studi Romagnoli [*A publication*]
STr	Studi Trentini [*A publication*]
STr	Studi Trentini di Scienze Storiche [*A publication*]
StR	Studia Romanica [*A publication*]
StR	Studie o Rukopisech [*A publication*]
STR	Stuttgart [*West Germany*] [*Airport symbol*] (OAG)
STR	Subject Terminal Control Release [*Aviation*] (FAAC)
STR	Submarine Test Reactor
STR	Submarine Thermal Reactor
STR	Submersible Test Rack
STR	Summary Technical Report
STR	Super Transportable RADAR
STR	Surplus to Requirements (ADA)
STR	Synchronous Transmitter Receiver [*Data processing*]
STR	System Test Review [*NASA*] (NASA)
STR	Systems Technology RADAR (MCD)
STRA.........	Stratus Computer, Inc. [*NASDAQ symbol*] (NQ)
STRA.........	Supply and Training Mission [*Military*] (CINC)
STRAAD....	Special Techniques Repair Analysis Aircraft Damage [*Navy*] (NVT)
STRAB	Strabismus [*Medicine*]
Strab	Strabo [*First century BC*] [*Classical studies*] (OCD)
STRABAD ...	Strategic Base Air Defense (AABC)
STRAC	Standards in Training Commission [*Army*] (INF)
STRAC	Strategic Army Corps [*Acronym has come to mean "ordered" or "neat"*]
STRACS.....	Small Transportable Communications Stations
STRACS.....	Surface Traffic Control System (MCD)
STRAD	Signal Transmission Reception and Distribution (IEEE)
Strad	Stradivari [*Record label*]
STRAD	Stradivarius Violin [*Music*] (DSUE)
STRAD	Strategic Aerospace Division [*Air Force*] (AFM)

STRAD .... Switching, Transmitting, Receiving, and Distribution
STRADAP ... Storm RADAR Data Processor [*ESD*]
STRAF .... Strategic Army Forces
STRAFE ..... Students Resisting Aerosol Flurocarbon Emissions [*Student legal action organization*] (EA)
Strafford .... Smith's New Hampshire Reports (DLA)
STRAFIP .... Strategic Army Forces Readiness Improvement Program (AABC)
STRAFPOA ... Strategic Air Force, Pacific Ocean Area
STRAGL ..... Straggler Line [*Military*]
Strahan ...... Strahan's Reports [*19 Oregon*] (DLA)
Strahlenschutz Forsch Prax ... Strahlenschutz in Forschung und Praxis [*West Germany*] [*A publication*]
Strahlenthe ... Strahlentherapie [*A publication*]
Strahlenther Sonderb ... Strahlentherapie. Sonderbaende [*A publication*]
STRAIN ..... Structural Analytical Interpreter
STRAIRPOA ... Strategic Air Force, Pacific Ocean Area
Straits Times A ... Straits Times Annual [*Singapore*] [*A publication*]
STRAM ...... Synchronous Transmit Receive Access Method (CMD)
Strand .... Strand Magazine [*A publication*]
Strand (Lond) ... Strand Magazine (London) [*A publication*]
Strand (NY) ... Strand Magazine (New York) [*A publication*]
STRANGE ... SAGE [*Semiautomatic Ground Environment*] Tracking and Guidance Evaluation System
Strange ...... Strange's English Court Reports (DLA)
Strange (Eng) ... Strange's English Courts Reports [*93 English Reprint*] (DLA)
Strange Madras ... Strange's Notes of Cases, Madras (DLA)
STRAP .... SCAR Team Report Analysis Program (MCD)
STRAP .... Simplified Transient Radiation Analysis Program (MCD)
STRAP .... Simultaneous Transmission and Recovery of Alternating Pictures [*TV system*]
STRAP .... Sonobuoy Thinned Random Array Program [*Navy*] (CAAL)
STRAP .... Star [*or Stellar*] Tracking Rocket Attitude Positioning [*System*] [*NASA*]
STRAP .... Stretch Assembly Program [*IBM Corp.*]
STRAP .... Structural Analysis Package
STRAPP ...... Standard Tanks, Racks, Adapter, and Pylon Packages (MCD)
STRASB ..... Strasbourg [*Imprint*] (ROG)
Strasb Med ... Strasbourg Medical [*A publication*]
STRAT .... Strategic (AFM)
STRAT .... Stratigraphic
STRATAD ... Strategic Aerospace Division [*Air Force*]
STRATCOM ... Strategic Communications Command [*Army*] (RDA)
STRATCOM ... Stratospheric Composition (MCD)
Strateg Anal ... Strategic Analysis [*India*] [*A publication*]
Strategic Dig ... Strategic Digest [*A publication*]
Strategic R ... Strategic Review [*A publication*]
Strateg Manage J ... Strategic Management Journal [*A publication*]
Strathclyde Bioeng Semin ... Strathclyde Bioengineering Seminars [*A publication*]
STRATMAS ... Strategic Mobility [*Planning and*] Analysis System [*Military*] (NVT)
STRATO ..... Stratosphere (AFM)
Strat R .... Strategic Review [*Washington, DC*] [*A publication*]
STRATSAT ... Strategic Satellite System [*Air Force*] [*Telecommunications*] (TEL)
Stratton ..... Stratton's Reports [*12-14 Oregon*] (DLA)
STRATWARM ... Stratospheric Warming
Strauss ...... Internationale Richard-Strauss-Gesellschaft Mitteilungen [*A publication*]
Str Autobahn ... Strasse und Autobahn [*A publication*]
STRAW ...... Simultaneous Tape Read and Write
STRBK ...... Strongback
STRC .... Science and Technology Research Center [*North Carolina*] (MCD)
STRC .... Scientific and Technical Research Centres in Australia [*A publication*]
STRC .... Scientific, Technical, and Research Commission
STRC .... Society of Traditional Roman Catholics [*Charlotte, NC*] (EA)
STRC .... Switch Tail Ring Counter
Str Cas Ev ... Strange's Cases of Evidence [*"Octavo Strange"*] (DLA)
STRCH ...... Stretch (AAG)
STRC-IVS ... STRC [*Science and Technology Research Center*] Inverted File Search System [*Search system*]
STRD .... Short Tour Return Date [*Military*]
STRD .... Stored
STRD .... Strand [*Engineering*]
STRE .... Specialist Teams Royal Engineers [*Military*] [*British*]
STREAM ..... Standard Tensioned Replenishment Alongside Method [*Military*] (NVT)
Street Ry Rep ... Street Railway Reports (DLA)
StRel/ScRel ... Studies in Religion/Sciences Religieuses [*A publication*]
Strem Chem ... Strem Chemiker [*A publication*]
St Ren .... Studies in the Renaissance [*A publication*]
STRENGTHD ... Strengthened (ROG)
Strength Mater ... Strength of Materials [*A publication*]
STREP .... Ship's Test and Readiness Evaluation Procedure
STREP .... Space Trajectory Radiation Exposure Procedure
St Rep .... State Reporter (DLA)
St Rep .... State Reports (DLA)

STREP .... Status Report [*IRS*]
STREP .... Streptococcus [*Medicine*]
St Rep NSW ... State Reports [*New South Wales*] [*A publication*]
St Rep Queensl (Austr) ... Queensland State Reports [*Australia*] (DLA)
STREPS ...... Streptococci
STREPTO .... Streptomycin (DSUE)
STRES .... Store Release Evaluation System (MCD)
STRESS ..... Satellite Transmission Effects Simulation (MCD)
STRESS ..... Stop the Robberies, Enjoy Safe Streets [*Detroit police unit*] [*Disbanded*]
STRESS ..... Structural Engineering Systems Solver [*Programing language*] [*1962*]
STRETCH ... [*An*] early large computer [*IBM 7030*]
STRETCH ... Space Technology Requirements Engineering Test of Component Hardware [*NASA*] (KSC)
Str Ev .... Strange's Cases of Evidence [*1698-1732*] [*England*] (DLA)
STRF .... Sea Turtle Rescue Fund (EA)
STRFLD ..... Star Field (MCD)
STRG .... Steering (AAG)
STRG .... Strong (MSA)
STRG WND ... String or Wind [*Freight*]
Str & HC ..... Streets and Highways Code (DLA)
STRI .... Smithsonian Tropical Research Institute
STRI .... Stones River National Battlefield
Strick Ev .... Strickland on Evidence [*1830*] (DLA)
STRICOM ... Strike Command [*Military*]
STRIDE ..... Standard Reactor Island Design (NRCH)
STRIDE ...... System to Retrieve Information from Drug Evidence [*Drug Enforcement Administration*]
STRIKEOPS ... Strike Operations [*Military*] (NVT)
STRIKEX .... Strike Exercise [*Navy*] [*NATO*] (NATG)
STRIKFLTLANT ... Striking Fleet Atlantic
STRIKFORSOUTH ... Striking and Support Forces Southern Europe [*Navy*]
STRIKFTLANTREPEUR ... Striking Fleet Atlantic Representative in Europe [*NATO*] (NATG)
STRING ..... Stringendo [*Hastening*] [*Music*]
Stringf .... Stringfellow's Reports [*9-11 Missouri*] (DLA)
Stringfellow ... Stringfellow's Reports [*9-11 Missouri*] (DLA)
STRINO ...... Stringendo [*Hastening*] [*Music*] (ROG)
STRIP .... Specification Technical Review and Improvement Program [*Navy*] (NG)
STRIP .... Standard Requisition and Issue Procedures [*Military*] (CINC)
STRIP .... Standard Taped Routines for Image Processing [*National Bureau of Standards*]
STRIP .... Stock Turn-In and Replenishment Invoicing Procedures
STRIP .... String Processing Language [*Data processing*] (DIT)
STRIVE ...... Standard Techniques for Reporting Information on Value Engineering
St Riv Wat Supply Comm Tech Bull ... Victoria. State Rivers and Water Supply Commission. Technical Bulletin [*A publication*]
STRJ .... Self-Powered Thermocouple Reference Junction
STRK .... Stroke (MSA)
STRKA .... Staerke [*A publication*]
STRKR .... Striker [*Automotive engineering*]
STRL .... Sea Trials [*Navy*] (NVT)
STR L .... Straight Line [*Freight*]
STRL .... Structural
STR LGTHS ... Straight Lengths [*Freight*]
STRLN .... Streamline (MSA)
STRM .... Storeroom (MSA)
STR M .... Strand Magazine [*A publication*]
STRM .... Stream
STRM .... Sturm Ruger & Co. [*NASDAQ symbol*] (NQ)
STRN .... Standard Technical Report Number
STRN .... Strength (AAG)
STRN .... Sutron Corp. [*NASDAQ symbol*] (NQ)
Str NC .... [*Sir T.*] Strange's Notes of Cases [*Madras*] (DLA)
STRNG .... Steering
STRNR .... Strainer (AAG)
STRO .... Scandinavian Tire and Rim Organization (EA)
STRO .... Stereo Routes (FAAC)
StRo .... Studi Romani [*Rome*] [*A publication*]
Strob .... Strobhart's South Carolina Law Reports [*1846-50*] (DLA)
Strob Ch .... Strobhart's South Carolina Equity Reports (DLA)
STROBE ..... Satellite Tracking of Balloons and Emergencies
STROBE ..... Stroboscopic (MSA)
Strob Eq .... Strobhart's South Carolina Equity Reports [*1846-50*] (DLA)
STROBES ... Shared-Time Repair of Big Electronic Systems [*Data processing*]
Strobh Eq (SC) ... Strobhart's South Carolina Equity Reports (DLA)
Strobh L (SC) ... Strobhart's South Carolina Law Reports (DLA)
Stroemungsmech Stroemungsmasch ... Stroemungsmechanik und Stroemungsmaschinen [*A publication*]
Stroezh Funkts Mozuka ... Stroezh i Funktsii na Mozuka [*A publication*]
STROFAC .... Stabilized Routing for Afloat Commands (MCD)
STR OFF FIXT ... Store or Office Fixture[*s*] [*Freight*]
Stroit Alyum Konstr ... Stroitel'nye Alyuminievye Konstruktsii [*A publication*]
Stroit Arkhit Leningrada ... Stroitel'stvo i Arkhitektura Leningrada [*A publication*]
Stroit Arkhit Uzb ... Stroitel'stvo i Arkhitektura Uzbekistana [*A publication*]
Stroit Dorog ... Stroitel'stvo Dorog [*A publication*]

Stroit Dorozhn Mash ... Stroitel'nye i Dorozhnye Mashiny [*A publication*]
Stroit Keram ... Stroitel'naya Keramika [*A publication*]
Stroit Konstr ... Stroitel'nye Konstruktsii [*A publication*]
Stroit Konstr Alyum Splavov ... Stroitel'nye Konstruktsii iz Alyuminievkh Splavov [*A publication*]
Stroit Mater ... Stroitel'nye Materialy [*A publication*]
Stroit Mater (1929-32) ... Stroitel'nye Materialy (1929-32) [*A publication*]
Stroit Mater (1933-38) ... Stroitel'nye Materialy (1932-38) [*A publication*]
Stroit Mater Betony ... Stroitel'nye Materialy i Betony [*A publication*]
Stroit Mater Izdeliya Konstr ... Stroitel'nye Materialy. Izdeliya i Konstruktsii [*A publication*]
Stroit Mater Konstr ... Stroitel'nye Materialy i Konstruktsii [*A publication*]
Stroit Mater Silik Prom-st ... Stroitelni Materiali i Silikatna Promishlenost [*Bulgaria*] [*A publication*]
Stroit Mekh Raschet Sooruz ... Stroitel'naya Mekhanika i Raschet Sooruzheniy [*USSR*] [*A publication*]
Stroit Truboprovodov ... Stroitel'stvo Truboprovodov [*USSR*] [*A publication*]
Strojir Vyroba ... Strojirenska Vyroba [*A publication*]
Strojnicky Cas ... Strojnicky Casopis [*Czechoslovakia*] [*A publication*]
Strojniski Vestn ... Strojniski Vestnik [*A publication*]
Strom ... Stromateis [*of Clemens Alexandrinus*] [*Classical studies*]　(OCD)
STROM ... Stromberg [*Automotive engineering*]
StRom ... Studia Romanica [*A publication*]
StRom ... Studies in Romanticism [*A publication*]
Stromprax ... Strompraxis [*A publication*]
STRP ... Strap
STRP ... Striker Petroleum [*NASDAQ symbol*]　(NQ)
St RQ ... Queensland State Reports [*Australia*]　(DLA)
St R (Q) ... State Reports (Queensland) [*A publication*]
St R Qd ... Queensland State Reports [*Australia*]　(DLA)
St R (QD) ... State Reports (Queensland) [*A publication*]
St R Queensl ... State Reports, Queensland [*A publication*]
STRS ... Steamers
STRT ... [*The*] Stewartstown Railroad Co. [*AAR code*]
STRT ... Strait [*Board on Geographic Names*]
Str Tiefbau ... Strassen- und Tiefbau [*A publication*]
STRTL ... Structural
STRTR ... Starter [*Automotive engineering*]
STRU ... Styrelserepresentationsutredningen [*Sweden*]
STRUBAL ... Structured Basic Language [*Data processing*]　(CSR)
STRUC ... Structure　(AABC)
Struc Rev ... Structuralist Review [*A publication*]
STRUCT ... Structure　(AAG)
Struct Bonding ... Structure and Bonding [*A publication*]
Struct Concr ... Structural Concrete [*A publication*]
Struct Eng ... Structural Engineer [*A publication*]
Struct Engr ... Structural Engineer [*A publication*]
Struct Funct Brain ... Structure and Functions of the Brain [*A publication*]
Struct Glass ... Structure of Glass [*A publication*]
Struct Mater Note Aust Aeronaut Res Lab ... Australia. Department of Supply. Aeronautical Research Laboratories. Structures and Materials Note [*A publication*]
Struct Mater Rep Aust Aeronaut Res Lab ... Australia. Aeronautical Research Laboratories. Structures and Materials Report [*A publication*]
Struct Note Aust Aeronaut Res Lab ... Australia. Aeronautical Research Laboratories. Structures Note [*A publication*]
Struct Rep Aust Aeronaut Res Lab ... Australia. Aeronautical Research Laboratories. Structures Report [*A publication*]
Struct Rep Dep Archit Sci Syd Univ ... Structures Report. Department of Architectural Science. University of Sydney [*A publication*]
Struct Saf ... Structural Safety [*A publication*]
Struct Surv ... Structural Survey [*A publication*]
STRUDL ... Structural Design Language [*Data processing*]　(MCD)
STRUFO ... Structural Formula [*Data processing*] [*Chemistry*]
Strukt Funkts Fermentov ... Struktura i Funktsiya Fermentov [*A publication*]
Strukt Modif Khlopk Tsellyul ... Struktura i Modifikatsiya Khlopkovoi Tsellyulozy [*A publication*]
Strukt Rol Vody Zhivom Org ... Struktura i Rol Vody v Zhivom Organizme [*A publication*]
Strukt Svoistva Krist ... Struktura i Svoistva Kristallov [*A publication*]
Strukt Svoistva Litykh Splavov ... Struktura i Svoistva Litykh Splavov [*A publication*]
Strukturn i Mat Lingvistika ... Strukturnaja i Matematiceskaja Lingvistika [*A publication*]
Strum Crit ... Strumenti Critici [*A publication*]
Strum una Nuova Cultur Guida e Manual ... Strumenti per una Nuova Cultura. Guida e Manuali [*A publication*]
Struve ... Struve's Washington Territory Reports [*1854-88*]　(DLA)
Str Verkehr ... Strasse und Verkehr [*A publication*]
STRW ... Strawbridge & Clothier [*NASDAQ symbol*]　(NQ)
STRX ... Syntrex, Inc. [*NASDAQ symbol*]　(NQ)
STRY ... Stryker Corp. [*NASDAQ symbol*]　(NQ)
STRYCH ... Strychnina [*Strychnine*] [*Pharmacy*]　(ROG)
St Ry Rep ... Street Railway Reports [*United States*]　(DLA)
STrZ ... South Tropical Zone [*Planet Jupiter*]
STS ... Office of State Technical Services [*Also, OSTS*] [*Abolished, 1970*] [*Department of Commerce*]
STS ... S-Band Transmitter System

STS ... Saint Thomas Seminary [*Colorado; Connecticut; Kentucky*]
Sts ... Saints
STS ... Santa Rosa [*California*] [*Airport symbol*]　(OAG)
STS ... Santiago [*Spain*] [*Seismograph station code, US Geological Survey*]　(SEIS)
STS ... Satellite-to-Satellite　(CET)
STS ... Satellite Tracking Station
STS ... Satellite Transmissions Systems, Inc. [*Hauppauge, NY*] [*Telecommunications*]　(TSSD)
STS ... Scheduled Truck Service [*Army*]
STS ... School-to-School [*Red Cross Youth*]
STS ... School Television Service
STS ... Science Talent Search　(EA)
STS ... Science, Technology, and Society
STS ... Science of To-Day Series [*A publication*]
STS ... Scottish Tartans Society　(EA)
STS ... Scottish Text Society [*A publication*]
STS ... Sea Training Staff [*Canadian Navy*]
STS ... Security Termination Statement [*Military*]　(AFM)
STS ... Self-Test Select
STS ... Seminex [*Concordia Seminary in Exile*] Library, St. Louis, MO [*OCLC symbol*]　(OCLC)
STS ... Serological Test for Syphilis [*Medicine*]
STS ... Servo Test System
STS ... Sewage Treatment System [*Navy*]　(CAAL)
STS ... Ship-to-Shore
STS ... Shuttle Transportation System　(MCD)
STS ... Siltstone [*Lithology*]
STS ... Simulator Test Set　(CAAL)
STS ... Skaggs Telecommunications Service [*Salt Lake City, UT*] [*Telecommunications*]　(TSSD)
STS ... Skylab Terminal System [*NASA*]
STS ... Society for Textual Scholarship　(EA)
STS ... Society of Thoracic Surgeons [*Chicago, IL*]　(EA)
STS ... Socio-Technical Systems [*Management technique*]
STS ... Sodium Tetradecyl Sulfate [*Organic chemistry*]
STS ... Sodium Thiosulfate [*Inorganic chemistry, biochemistry*]
STS ... Soft Tissue Sarcoma [*Oncology*]
STS ... Solar Tracking System
STS ... SONAR Technician, Submarine [*Navy rating*]
STS ... SONAR Test System
STS ... Sonic Telex System [*Sonicair*] [*Phoenix, AZ*] [*Telecommunications*]　(TSSD)
STS ... Space-Time-Space [*Digital switching structure*] [*Telecommunications*]　(TEL)
STS ... Space Transportation System
STS ... Spacecraft Telecommunications System
STS ... Spacecraft Tracking Station [*NASA*]　(KSC)
STS ... Special Task Stores [*Military*] [*British*]
STS ... Special Test System [*Air Force*]　(AFM)
STS ... Special Training Standard [*Air Force*]　(AFM)
STS ... Special Treatment Steel
STS ... Specialty Training Standard　(MCD)
STS ... Specialty Training System
STS ... Specific Tensile Strength
STS ... Spring Trapmakers' Society [*British*]
STS ... Stabilized Telescope System
StS ... Stamp Seal　(BJA)
STS ... Standard (Galilean) Telescopes [*Instrumentation*]
STS ... Standard Technical Specifications　(NRCH)
STS ... Standard Test for Syphilis [*Medicine*]
STS ... State Technical Services [*Abolished, 1970*]
STS ... Static Test Stand
STS ... Station to Station
STS ... Stationary Time Series
STS ... Sterol-sulphatase [*An enzyme*]
STS ... Stirring Science Stories [*A publication*]
STS ... Stockpile-to-Target Sequence
STS ... Strategic Technical Service　(CINC)
STS ... Strategic Training Squadron　(MCD)
STS ... Structural Transition Section　(MCD)
StS ... Studia Slavica [*A publication*]
STS ... Supersonic Target System
STS ... Supplementary Test Site [*Nuclear energy*]　(EISS)
STS ... Surveillance Test Set　(MCD)
STS ... Survey Tabulation Services, Inc. [*Cambridge, MA*] [*Information service*]　(EISS)
STS ... System Test Set
STS ... System Test Software　(CAAL)
STS ... System Trouble Shooting
STS ... System Trouble Survey　(CET)
STSA ... Seaman Apprentice, SONAR Technician, Striker [*Navy rating*]
STSA ... Southern Thoracic Surgical Association　(EA)
STSA ... State Technical Services Act
StSa ... Studi Salentini [*A publication*]
STSALV ... Standby Salvage Ship [*Navy*]　(NVT)
STSB ... Seattle Trust & Savings Bank [*NASDAQ symbol*]　(NQ)
STSC ... Scientific Time Sharing Corporation [*Host*] [*Information service*]　(EISS)
ST SCI ... Space Telescope Science Institute [*Johns Hopkins University*] [*Research center*]　(RCD)

STSCM ...... Space Transportation System Cost Model [*NASA*]   (KSC)
StSec .... Studi Secenteschi [*A publication*]
StSem .... Studi Semitici [*A publication*]
StSemNeerl ... Studia Semitica Neerlandica [*Assen*] [*A publication*]
STSG .... Space Topics Study Group [*American Philatelic Society*]   (EA)
STSG .... Split Thickness Skin Graft
STSH .... Stabilized Shunt [*Electricity*]
STSI .... Space Telescope Science Institute [*NASA*]
STSK .... Scandinavian Committee for Satellite Communications
                  [*Telecommunications*]   (TEL)
StSl .... Studia Slavica [*A publication*]
StSLL .... Studies in Semitic Languages and Linguistics [*A publication*]
STSM .... Surface-to-Target-to-Surface-to-Missile
STSN .... Seaman, SONAR Technician, Striker [*Navy rating*]
STSN .... Set-and-Test-Sequence-Number [*Data processing*]   (IBMDP)
STSO .... Senior Technical Staff Officer [*British*]
ST & SP ...... Start and Stop
STSR .... System Test Summary Report [*NASA*]   (NASA)
STSS .... Sensitive Thrust Stand System
STSS .... Society for Traumatic Stress Studies   (EA)
STSS .... Studi Trentini di Scienze Storiche [*A publication*]
Ststcian ...... Statistician [*A publication*]
STT .... Charlotte Amalie, VI [*Location identifier*] [*FAA*]   (FAAL)
STT .... Saigon Transportation Terminal Command [*Republic of
                  Vietnam Armed Forces*]
STT .... St. Thomas [*Virgin Islands*] [*Airport symbol*]
STT .... Science Stories [*A publication*]
STT .... Seattle - Marshall [*Washington*] [*Seismograph station code,
                  US Geological Survey*] [*Closed*]   (SEIS)
STT .... Seek Time per Track
STT .... Semitendinosus Tendon [*Anatomy*]
STT .... Sensitization Test
STT .... Ship Turn Transmitter
STT .... Shore Targeting Terminal [*Navy*]   (CAAL)
STT .... Signal Tracing Tester
STT .... Single Target Track [*Navy*]   (NG)
STT .... Skid-to-Turn
STT .... Skin Temperature Test [*Physiology*]
STT .... Spacecraft Terminal Thrust
STT .... Spade Tongue Terminal
STT .... Standard Triple Therapy [*For hypertension*]
STT .... Stenographer, Medical [*Navy*]
STT .... Strange Tales of Mystery and Terror [*A publication*]
StT .... Studi Tassiani [*A publication*]
STT .... Sutton Resources Ltd. [*Vancouver Stock Exchange symbol*]
STT .... Syndicat des Travailleurs en Telecommunications
                  [*Telecommunications Workers Union - TWU*] [*Canada*]
St Tax Rep (CCH) ... State Tax Reporter [*Commerce Clearing House*]   (DLA)
STTC .... Sheppard Technical Training Center   (AFM)
StTCL .... Studies in Twentieth-Century Literature [*A publication*]
StTDJ .... Studies on the Texts of the Desert of Judah [*J. Van Der Ploeg*]
                  [*Leiden*] [*A publication*]   (BJA)
ST & TE ...... Special Tools and Test Equipment   (MCD)
STTE .... Special Tools and Test Equipment
STTEA .... Stain Technology [*A publication*]
StTeol .... Studii Teologice [*Bucharest*] [*A publication*]
StTEstmatn ... Statistical Theory of Estimation [*A publication*]
STTF .... SONAR Test Tower Facility
STTF .... Special Tank Task Force   (MCD)
STTF .... System Technology Test Facility   (MCD)
STT-FNB .... Suomen Tietotoimisto-Finska Notisbyran [*Press agency*]
                  [*Finland*]
STTG .... Statesman Group [*NASDAQ symbol*]   (NQ)
StTh .... Studia Theologica [*A publication*]
StTheol ...... Studia Teologica [*A publication*]
StThL .... Studia Theologica Lundensia. Skrifter Utgivna av Teologiska
                  Fakulteten i Lund [*A publication*]
StThVars .... Studia Theologica Varsaviensia [*Warsaw*] [*A publication*]
S/TTL .... Schottky Transistor-Transistor Logic
STTL .... Sit Tibi Terra Levis [*May the Earth Lie Light on Thee*] [*Letters
                  found on Roman tombs*] [*Latin*]
STTM .... Stabilized Tracking Tripod Module   (RDA)
STTO .... Sawtooth Timing Oscillator   (DEN)
STTO .... Staking Tool   (AAG)
St Tomas J Med ... Santo Tomas Journal of Medicine [*A publication*]
STTOT .... Single Target Track on Target [*Navy*]
St Tr .... Howell's English State Trials [*1163-1820*]   (DLA)
STTR .... Stator
St Tri .... State Trials   (DLA)
St Tr NS ..... Macdonell's State Trials [*1820-58*]   (DLA)
STTS .... S-Band Transponder Test Set   (MCD)
STTS .... Shipboard Target Tracking System
STTT .... Space Telescope Task Team [*NASA*]
St Twen Ct ... Studies in Twentieth-Century Literature [*A publication*]
STU .... Schweizerische Theologische Umschau [*A publication*]
STU .... Secure Telephone Unit [*Data processing*]
STU .... Seeker Test Unit   (MCD)
STU .... Service Trials Unit
STU .... Servo Test Unit
STU .... Short Ton Unit
STU .... Signal Transfer Unit

STU .... Skin Test Unit
STU .... Space-Time Unit [*Computer*]
STU .... Special Test Unit   (CET)
STU .... Special Training Unit
STU .... Star Tracker Unit   (MCD)
STU .... Static Test Unit   (KSC)
STU .... Stepup
STU .... Stuart   (ROG)
STU .... Stuart [*D. A.*] Ltd. [*Toronto Stock Exchange symbol*]
STU .... Student   (AFM)
Stu .... Studia [*A publication*]
Stu .... Studium [*A publication*]
STU .... Stuttgart [*Federal Republic of Germany*] [*Seismograph station
                  code, US Geological Survey*]   (SEIS)
STU .... Styrelsen foer Teknisk Utveckling [*Swedish Board for
                  Technical Development*]
STU .... Submarine Test Unit
STU .... Submersible Test Unit [*Navy*]
STU .... Subscribers' Trunk Unit [*Telecommunications*]   (TEL)
STU .... System Timing Unit
STU .... System Transition Unit [*Data processing*]
STU .... Systems Test Unit   (KSC)
STU .... University of Steubenville, Steubenville, OH [*OCLC
                  symbol*]   (OCLC)
Stu Adm ..... Stuart's Lower Canada Vice-Admiralty Reports   (DLA)
Stu Adm NS ... Stuart's Lower Canada Vice-Admiralty Reports, New
                  Series   (DLA)
Stu Ap .... Stuart's Lower Canada King's Bench Reports, Appeal
                  Cases   (DLA)
Stuart .... Stuart, Milne, and Peddie's Scotch Court of Session
                  Cases   (DLA)
Stuart .... Stuart's Lower Canada Reports   (DLA)
Stuart .... Stuart's Lower Canada Vice-Admiralty Reports   (DLA)
Stuart Adm NS ... Stuart's Lower Canada Vice-Admiralty Reports, New
                  Series   (DLA)
Stuart Beng ... Stuart's Select Cases [*1860*] [*Bengal, India*]   (DLA)
Stuart KB ... Stuart's Lower Canada King's Bench Reports [*1810-25*]
                  [*Quebec*]   (DLA)
Stuart KB (Quebec) ... Stuart's Lower Canada King's Bench Reports
                  [*Quebec*]   (DLA)
Stuart LCKB ... Stuart's Lower Canada King's Bench Reports   (DLA)
Stuart LCVA ... Stuart's Lower Canada Vice-Admiralty Reports   (DLA)
Stuart M & P ... Stuart, Milne, and Peddie's Scotch Court of Session Cases
                  [*1851-53*]   (DLA)
Stuart & Por ... Stuart [*or Stewart*] and Porter's Alabama Reports   (DLA)
Stuart & Porter ... Stuart [*or Stewart*] and Porter's Alabama Reports   (DLA)
Stuart's Adm ... Stuart's Lower Canada Vice-Admiralty Reports [*1836-74*]
                  [*Quebec*]   (DLA)
Stuart's R ... Stuart's Lower Canada King's Bench Reports, Appeal Cases
                  [*Quebec*]   (DLA)
Stuart Vice-Adm ... Stuart's Lower Canada Vice-Admiralty Reports   (DLA)
STUB .... Stadt- und Universitaetsbibliothek Frankfurt [*Database
                  producer*]
Stubbs CH ... Stubb's Constitutional History   (DLA)
Stubbs Sel Ch ... Stubb's Select Charters   (DLA)
STUC .... Sarawak Trade Union Congress
STUC .... Scottish Trades Union Congress
STUC .... Singapore Trade Union Congress
Stu Cer Fiz ... Studii si Cercetari de Fizica [*A publication*]
STUD .... Standard Tractor, Universal with Dozer [*Army*]
STUD .... Student
Stud .... Studien [*A publication*]
Stud .... Studies [*A publication*]
STUD .... Studies
Stud Acta Orient ... Studia et Acta Orientalia [*A publication*]
StudActOr ... Studia et Acta Orientalia [*A publication*]
StudAeg ..... Studia Aegyptiaca [*Rome*] [*A publication*]
Stud Afr Linguist ... Studies in African Linguistics [*A publication*]
Stud Ag Econ ... Stanford University Food Research Institute Studies in
                  Agricultural Economics, Trade, and Development [*A
                  publication*]
Stud Alb ..... Studia Albanica [*A publication*]
Stud Algebra Anwendungen ... Studien zur Algebra und Ihre Anwendungen
                  [*A publication*]
Stud Aliment Apa ... Studii de Alimentari cu Apa [*A publication*]
Stud Am Fic ... Studies in American Fiction [*A publication*]
Stud Anc Technol ... Studies in Ancient Technology [*A publication*]   (OCD)
Stud Angew Wirtschaftsforsch Statist ... Studien zur Angewandten
                  Wirtschaftsforschung und Statistik [*A publication*]
Stud Appl M ... Studies in Applied Mathematics [*A publication*]
Stud Appl Math ... Studies in Applied Mathematics [*A publication*]
Stud Art Ed ... Studies in Art Education [*A publication*]
Stud Art Educ ... Studies in Art Education [*A publication*]
Stud Bibliog ... Virginia University. Bibliographical Society. Studies in
                  Bibliography [*A publication*]
Stud Bibliog & Bklore ... Studies in Bibliography and Booklore [*A
                  publication*]
Stud Biol .... Studies in Biology [*A publication*]
Stud Biol Acad Sci Hung ... Studia Biologica. Academiae Scientiarum
                  Hungaricae [*A publication*]
Stud Biophy ... Studia Biophysica [*A publication*]

Stud Biophys ... Studia Biophysica [*A publication*]
Stud Black Lit ... Studies in Black Literature [*A publication*]
Stud Bot Hung ... Studia Botanica Hungarica [*A publication*]
Stud Br His ... Studies in British History and Culture [*A publication*]
Stud Broadcast ... Studies of Broadcasting [*A publication*]
Stud Brown ... Studies in Browning and His Circle [*A publication*]
StudBT .... Studia Biblica et Theologica [*New Haven, CT*] [*A publication*]
Stud Burke Time ... Studies in Burke and His Time [*A publication*]
Stud Can ... Studia Canonica [*A publication*]
StudCath ... Studia Catholica [*A publication*]
Stud Cerc Buzan ... Studii si Cercetari de Istorie Buzoiana [*A publication*]
Stud Cerc Docum ... Studii si Cercetari de Documentare [*A publication*]
Stud Cerc Econom ... Studii si Cercetari Economice [*A publication*]
Stud Cercet Agron Acad Rep Pop Romine Fil (Cluj) ... Studii si Cercetari de Agronomie. Academia Republicii Populare Romine Filiala (Cluj) [*A publication*]
Stud Cercet Antropol ... Studii si Cercetari de Antropologie [*A publication*]
Stud Cercet Astron ... Studii si Cercetari de Astronomie [*A publication*]
Stud Cercet Biochim ... Studii si Cercetari de Biochimie [*A publication*]
Stud Cercet Biol ... Studii si Cercetari de Biologie [*A publication*]
Stud Cercet Biol Acad Rep Pop Romine Fil (Cluj) ... Studii si Cercetari de Biologie. Academia Republicii Populare Romine Filiala (Cluj) [*A publication*]
Stud Cercet Biol Acad Rep Pop Romine Ser Biol Veg ... Studii si Cercetari de Biologie. Academia Republicii Populare Romine. Seria Biologi Vegetala [*A publication*]
Stud Cercet Biol Ser Bot ... Studii si Cercetari de Biologie. Seria Botanica [*A publication*]
Stud Cercet Biol Ser Zool ... Studii si Cercetari de Biologie. Seria Zoologie [*A publication*]
Stud & Cercet Calcul Econ & Cibern Econ ... Studii si Cercetari de Calcul Economic si Cibernetica Economica [*A publication*]
Stud Cercet Chim ... Studii si Cercetari de Chimie [*A publication*]
Stud & Cercet Doc ... Studii si Cercetari de Documentare [*A publication*]
Stud Cercet Embriol Citol Ser Embriol ... Studii si Cercetari de Embriologie si Citologie. Seria Embriologie [*Romania*] [*A publication*]
Stud Cercet Endocrinol ... Studii si Cercetari de Endocrinologie [*A publication*]
Stud Cercet Energ ... Studii si Cercetari de Energetica [*A publication*]
Stud Cercet Energ Electroteh ... Studii si Cercetari de Energetica si Electrotehnica [*A publication*]
Stud Cercet Fiz ... Studii si Cercetari de Fizica [*A publication*]
Stud Cercet Fiziol ... Studii si Cercetari de Fiziologie [*Romania*] [*A publication*]
Stud Cercet Geol Geofiz Geogr Ser Geofiz ... Studii si Cercetari de Geologie, Geofizica, si Geografie. Seria Geofizica [*A publication*]
Stud Cercet Geol Geofiz Geogr Ser Geogr ... Studii si Cercetari de Geologie, Geofizica, si Geografie. Seria Geografie [*A publication*]
Stud Cercet Geol Geofiz Geogr Ser Geol ... Studii si Cercetari de Geologie, Geofizica, si Geografie. Seria Geologie [*A publication*]
Stud Cercet Ig Sanat Publica ... Studii si Cercetari de Igiena si Sanatate Publica [*A publication*]
Stud Cercet Inframicrobiol ... Studii si Cercetari de Inframicrobiologie [*A publication*]
Stud Cercet Inframicrobiol Microbiol Parazitol ... Studii si Cercetari de Inframicrobiologie, Microbiologie, si Parazitologie [*A publication*]
Stud Cercet Inst Cercet Piscic ... Studii si Cercetari. Institutul de Cercetari Piscicole [*A publication*]
Stud Cercet Inst Cercet Proiect Piscic ... Studii si Cercetari. Institutul de Cercetari si Proiectari Piscicole [*A publication*]
Stud Cercet Inst Meteorol Hidrol Partea 1 ... Studii si Cercetari. Institutul de Meteorologie si Hidrologie. Partea 1. Meteorologie [*A publication*]
Stud Cercet Inst Meteorol Hidrol Partea 2 ... Studii si Cercetari. Institutul de Meteorologie si Hidrologie. Partea 2. Hidrologie [*A publication*]
Stud Cercet Mec Apl ... Studii si Cercetari de Mecanica Aplicata [*A publication*]
Stud Cercet Med (Cluj) ... Studii si Cercetari de Medicina (Cluj) [*A publication*]
Stud Cercet Med Interna ... Studii si Cercetari de Medicina Interna [*A publication*]
Stud Cercet Metal ... Studii si Cercetari de Metalurgie [*Romania*] [*A publication*]
Stud Cercet Metal Comun Stiint ... Studii si Cercetari de Metalurgie. Comunicari Stiintifice [*A publication*]
Stud Cercet Neurol ... Studii si Cercetari de Neurologie [*A publication*]
Stud Cercet Piscic Inst Cercet Proiect Aliment ... Studii si Cercetari. Piscicole Institutul de Cercetari si Proiectari Alimentare [*A publication*]
Stud Cercet Silvic ... Studii si Cercetari de Silvicultura [*A publication*]
Stud Cercet Virusol ... Studii si Cercetari de Virusologie [*A publication*]
Stud Cerc Inst Cerc For (Industr Lemn) ... Studii si Cercetari. Institutul de Cercetari Forestiere (Industrializarea Lemnului) [*A publication*]
Stud Cerc Inst Cerc For (Mec Lucr For) ... Studii si Cercetari. Institutul de Cercetari Forestiere (Mecanizarea Lucrarilor Forestiere) [*A publication*]

Stud Cerc Inst Cerc For Silv ... Studii si Cercetari. Institutul de Cercetari Forestiere. Silvicultura [*A publication*]
Stud Cerc Mat ... Studii si Cercetari Matematice [*A publication*]
Stud Cerc Mec Apl ... Studii si Cercetari de Mecanica Aplicata [*A publication*]
Stud Chemother Inst Med Res ... Studies. Chemotherapeutic Institute for Medical Research [*Japan*] [*A publication*]
Stud Ch G P ... Studies in Chinese Government and Politics [*A publication*]
Stud Cl ... Studii Clasice [*A publication*]
StudClas .... Studii Clasice [*A publication*]
Stud Class ... Studies of Classical India [*A publication*]
Stud Com Co ... Studies in Comparative Communism [*A publication*]
Stud Com I D ... Studies in Comparative International Development [*A publication*]
Stud Com L G ... Studies in Comparative Local Government [*A publication*]
Stud Comm R ... Studies in Communism, Revisionism, and Revolution [*A publication*]
Stud Comp Com ... Studies in Comparative Communism [*Los Angeles*] [*A publication*]
Stud Comp Commun ... Studies in Comparative Communism [*A publication*]
Stud Comp Communism ... Studies in Comparative Communism [*A publication*]
Stud Comp Int Dev ... Studies in Comparative International Development [*New Jersey*] [*A publication*]
Stud Comp Int Develop ... Studies in Comparative International Development [*A publication*]
Stud in Comp Local Govt ... Studies in Comparative Local Government [*A publication*]
Stud Comp R ... Studies in Comparative Religion [*A publication*]
Stud Comp Relig ... Studies in Comparative Religion [*A publication*]
Stud Comun (Brukenthal) ... Studii si Comunicari (Brukenthal) [*A publication*]
Stud Comun (Pitesti) ... Studii si Comunicari (Pitesti) [*A publication*]
Stud Comun (Satu Mare) ... Studii si Comunicari (Satu Mare) [*A publication*]
Stud Conserv ... Studies in Conservation [*A publication*]
Stud in Contin Educ ... Studies in Continuing Education [*A publication*]
Stud Cosmic Ray ... Studies of Cosmic Ray [*Japan*] [*A publication*]
Stud Demogr ... Studia Demograficzne [*A publication*]
Stud Dipl .... Studia Diplomatica [*Brussels*] [*A publication*]
Stud Diplom ... Studia Diplomatica [*A publication*]
Stud & Doc His Jur ... Studia et Documenta Historiae et Juris [*A publication*]
Stud Doc Hist Iur ... Studia et Documenta Historiae et Iuris [*Rome*] [*A publication*] (OCD)
Stud Docum Asian Docum ... Studies and Documents. Asian Documentation and Research Center [*A publication*]
STUDE .... Studebaker [*Automotive engineering*]
Stud Econ ... Studi Economici [*A publication*]
Stud Ed ...... Studies in Education [*A publication*]
Stud Engl Lit ... Studies in English Literature [*A publication*]
Stud Engl Phil ... Studien zur Englischen Philologie [*A publication*]
Stud Engl (T) ... Studies in English Literature (Tokyo) [*A publication*]
Studente Vet ... Studente Veterinario [*A publication*]
Student Law J ... Student Lawyer Journal (DLA)
Student L Rev ... Student Law Review (DLA)
Student Musicol ... Student Musicologists at Minnesota [*A publication*]
Stud Entomol ... Studia Entomologica [*A publication*]
Student Q J Instn Elec Engrs ... Institution of Electrical Engineers. Student Quarterly Journal [*A publication*]
Students'ky Nauk Pratsi Kyyv Derzh Unyv ... Students'ky Naukovi Pratsi Kyyivs'kyyi Derzhavnyyi Unyversytet [*A publication*]
Stud Epurarea Apelor ... Studii de Epurarea Apelor [*A publication*]
Stud Etr ..... Studi Etruschi [*Firenze*] [*A publication*] (OCD)
Stud Europ Soc ... Studies in European Society [*A publication*]
Stud Fam Pl ... Studies in Family Planning [*A publication*]
Stud Fam Plann ... Studies in Family Planning [*A publication*]
Stud Fauna Curacao Other Caribb Isl ... Studies on the Fauna of Curacao and Other Caribbean Islands [*A publication*]
Stud Fauna Suriname Other Guyanas ... Studies of the Fauna of Suriname and Other Guyanas [*A publication*]
Stud Fenn ... Studia Fennica [*A publication*]
Stud Filol ... Studime Filologjike [*A publication*]
Stud Finans ... Studia Finansowe [*A publication*]
Stud Form Spir ... Studies in Formative Spirituality [*A publication*]
Stud For Suec ... Studia Forestalia Suecica [*A publication*]
Stud For Suec (Skogshogsk) ... Studia Forestalia Suecica (Skogshogskolan) [*A publication*]
Stud Found Methodol Philos Sci ... Studies in the Foundations, Methodology, and Philosophy of Science [*A publication*]
Stud Gen .... Studium Generale [*A publication*]
Stud Genet ... Studies in Genetics [*A publication*]
Stud Geol Mineral Inst Tokyo Univ Educ ... Studies from the Geological and Mineralogical Institute. Tokyo University of Education [*A publication*]
Stud Geol Pol ... Studia Geologica Polonica [*A publication*]
Stud Geol (Tulsa Okla) ... Studies in Geology (Tulsa, Oklahoma) [*A publication*]
Stud Geomorphol Carpatho-Balcanica ... Studia Geomorphologica Carpatho-Balcanica [*A publication*]
Stud Geoph ... Studia Geophysica et Geodaetica [*A publication*]
Stud Geophys Geod ... Studia Geophysica et Geodaetica [*A publication*]

Stud Geophys Geod (Cesk Akad Ved) ... Studia Geophysica et Geodaetica (Ceskosloven-Akademie Ved) [*A publication*]
Stud Geotech ... Studia Geotechnica. Politechnika Wroclawaka [*A publication*]
Stud Gesch Akad Wiss DDR ... Studien zur Geschichte der Akademie der Wissenschaften der DDR [*A publication*]
Stud Gesch Kult Alt ... Studien zur Geschichte und Kultur des Altertums [*A publication*] (OCD)
Stud Gr Rom Hist ... Studies in Greek and Roman History [*A publication*] (OCD)
Stud H Art ... Studies in the History of Art [*A publication*]
Stud Helminthol ... Studia Helminthologica [*A publication*]
Stud Hist.... Studies in History, Economics, and Public Law (DLA)
Stud Hist.... Studime Historike [*A publication*]
Stud Hist Art ... Studies in the History of Art [*A publication*]
Stud Hist Biol ... Studies in History of Biology [*A publication*]
Stud Hist Math Phys Sci ... Studies in the History of Mathematics and Physical Sciences [*A publication*]
Stud Hist Med ... Studies in History of Medicine [*A publication*]
Stud Hist P ... Studies in History and Philosophy of Science [*A publication*]
Stud Hist Philos Sci ... Studies in History and Philosophy of Science [*A publication*]
Stud Hist & Soc ... Studies in History and Society [*A publication*]
Studia Alban ... Studia Albanica [*A publication*]
Studia Automat ... Studia z Automatiki [*A publication*]
Studia Forest Suecica ... Studia Forestalia Suecica [*A publication*]
Studia For Suec ... Studia Forestalia Suecica [*A publication*]
Studia I ...... Studia Iranica [*A publication*]
Studia Leibnitiana Suppl ... Studia Leibnitiana. Supplementa [*A publication*]
Studia M .... Studia Missionalia [*A publication*]
Studia Math ... Studia Mathematica [*A publication*]
Studia Math/Math Lehrbuecher ... Studia Mathematica/Mathematische Lehrbuecher [*A publication*]
Studia Mus ... Studia Musicologica [*A publication*]
Studia Mus Nor ... Studia Musicologica Norvegica [*A publication*]
Studia Neophil ... Studia Neophilologica [*A publication*]
Studia Sci Math Hungar ... Studia Scientiarum Mathematicarum Hungarica [*A publication*]
Studia Univ Babes-Bolyai Ser Math-Mech ... Studia Universitatis Babes-Bolyai. Series Mathematica-Mechanica [*A publication*]
Studia Univ Babes-Bolyai Ser Phys ... Studia Universitatis Babes-Bolyai. Series Physica [*A publication*]
Studia Zool R Scient Univ Hung Budapest ... Studia Zoologica Regiae Scientiarum Universitatis Hungaricae Budapestensis [*A publication*]
Studi Cl Orient ... Studi Classici e Orientali [*A publication*]
Studiecent TNO Scheepsbouw Navig Commun ... Studiecentrum TNO [*Toegepast Natuurwetenschappelijk Onderzoek*] voor Scheepsbouw en Navigatie. Communication [*A publication*]
Studiecent TNO Scheepsbouw Navig Rep ... Studiecentrum TNO [*Toegepast Natuurwetenschappelijk Onderzoek*] voor Scheepsbouw en Navigatie. Report [*A publication*]
Studi Emigr ... Studi Emigrazione [*A publication*]
Studienb Naturwiss Tech ... Studienbuecher Naturwissenschaft und Technik [*A publication*]
Studies App Math ... Studies in Applied Mathematics [*A publication*]
Studies in Art Ed ... Studies in Art Education [*A publication*]
Studies in Aust Bibliog ... Studies in Australian Bibliography [*A publication*]
Studies Conserv ... Studies in Conservation [*A publication*]
Studies Crim L ... Studies in Criminal Law and Procedure (DLA)
Studies Econ Analysis ... Studies in Economic Analysis [*A publication*]
Studies Hum ... Studies in the Humanities [*A publication*]
Studies L & Econ Develop ... Studies in Law and Economic Development [*A publication*]
Studies Mus ... Studies in Music [*A publication*]
Studies Parasitol and Gen Zool ... Studies in Parasitology and General Zoology [*A publication*]
Studies Philol ... Studies in Philology [*A publication*]
Studies Pol Economy ... Studies in Political Economy [*A publication*]
Studies Zool Lab Univ Nebr ... Studies from the Zoological Laboratory. University of Nebraska [*A publication*]
Studii Cerc Biol ... Studii si Cercetari de Biologie [*A publication*]
Studii Cerc Biol Biol Anim ... Studii si Cercetari de Biologie. Seria Biologie Animala [*A publication*]
Studii Cerc Biol Zool ... Studii si Cercetari de Biologie. Seria Zoologie [*A publication*]
Studii Cercet Chim ... Studii si Cercetari de Chimie [*A publication*]
Studii Cercet Econ ... Studii si Cercetari Economice [*A publication*]
Studii Cerc Stiint Iasi Biol Stiint Agric ... Studii si Cercetari Stiintifice. Filiala Iasi. Academia RPR. Biologice si Stiinte Agricole [*A publication*]
StudiItalFilol Class ... Studi Italiani di Filologia Classica [*Florence*] [*A publication*]
Studii Teh Econ Inst Geol Rom ... Studii Tehnice si Economice Institutului Geologic al Romaniei. Stiinta Solului [*A publication*]
Studijni Inform Lesnictyi ... Studijni Informace. Lesnictyi [*A publication*]
Stud Indo-As Art Cult ... Studies in Indo-Asian Art and Culture [*New Delhi*] [*A publication*]
Stud In Relat ... Studies on International Relations [*A publication*]

Stud Inst Med Res (Malaya) ... Studies from the Institute for Medical Research (Malaya) [*A publication*]
Stud Int ...... Studio International [*A publication*]
Stud & Intel Obs ... Student and Intellectual Observer [*A publication*]
Studio ...... Studio International [*A publication*]
Studio Int ... Studio International [*A publication*]
Studio Intl ... Studio International [*A publication*]
Studi Sassaresi Sez II Arch Bimest Sci Med Nat ... Studi Sassaresi. Sezione II. Archivio Bimestrale di Scienze Mediche e Naturali [*A publication*]
Studi Sassar Sez 2 ... Studi Sassaresi. Sezione 2. Archivio Bimestrale di Scienze Mediche e Naturali [*A publication*]
Stud Islam ... Studia Islamica [*A publication*]
Studi Stor ... Studi Storici per l'Antichita Classica [*A publication*] (OCD)
Studi Stor ... Studi Storici Instituto Gramisci Editor [*A publication*]
Stud Ital ..... Studi Italiani di Filologia Classica [*A publication*] (OCD)
Studi Teh Econ Inst Geol Rom ... Studii Tehnice si Economice Institutului Geologic al Romaniei [*A publication*]
Studi Trentini Sci Nat Sez B Biol ... Studi Trentini di Scienze Naturali. Sezione B. Biologica [*A publication*]
Studi Urbinati Fac Farm ... Studi Urbinati. Facolta di Farmacia [*A publication*]
Stud J Inst Electron and Telecommun Eng ... Students' Journal. Institution of Electronics and Telecommunication Engineers [*A publication*]
Stud J Inst Electron Telecommun Eng ... Students' Journal. Institution of Electronics and Telecommunication Engineers [*A publication*]
Stud Kulturkunde ... Studien zur Kulturkunde [*A publication*]
Stud Lang C ... Studies in Language. Companion Series [*A publication*]
Stud Leibn ... Studia Leibnitiana [*A publication*]
Stud Leibnit ... Studia Leibnitiana [*A publication*]
Stud Leibnitiana ... Studia Leibnitiana [*A publication*]
Stud Ling ... Studies in Linguistics [*A publication*]
Stud Ling Sci ... Studies in the Linguistic Sciences [*Urbana*] [*A publication*]
Stud Lit ...... Studia Liturgica [*A publication*]
Stud Lit Im ... Studies in the Literary Imagination [*A publication*]
Stud Log ...... Studia Logica [*A publication*]
Stud Magr ... Studi Magrebini [*A publication*]
Stud Mater Weiterbild Med Tech Laborassistenten ... Studien-Material zur Weiterbildung Medizinisch-Technischer Laborassistenten [*A publication*]
Stud Math ... Studia Mathematica [*A publication*]
Stud Math Appl ... Studies in Mathematics and Its Applications [*A publication*]
Stud Math Managerial Econom ... Studies in Mathematical and Managerial Economics [*A publication*]
Stud Mat Ist Medie ... Studii si Materiale de Istorie Medie [*A publication*]
Stud Mat Muz Ist Mil ... Studii si Materiale de Muzeografie si Istorie Militara [*A publication*]
Stud Mat Suceava ... Studii si Materiale Muzeul Judetean. Suceava. Romania [*A publication*]
Stud Med Geogr ... Studies in Medical Geography [*A publication*]
Stud Med Szeged ... Studia Medica Szegedinensia [*A publication*]
Stud Med Szegedinensia ... Studia Medica Szegedinensia [*A publication*]
Stud Microbiol ... Studia Microbiologica [*A publication*]
StudMon.... Studia Monastica [*A publication*]
Stud Mycol ... Studies in Mycology [*A publication*]
Stud Myst ... Studia Mystica [*A publication*]
Stud Nakamura Gakuin Univ ... Studies in Nakamura Gakuin University [*A publication*]
Stud Nat Sci ... Studies in the Natural Sciences [*A publication*]
Stud Nat Sci (Portales NM) ... Studies in Natural Sciences (Portales, New Mexico) [*A publication*]
Stud Nauchno Issled Rab Sib Tekhnol Inst ... Studencheskie Nauchno-Issledovatel'skie Raboty. Sibirskii Tekhnologicheskii Institut [*A publication*]
Stud Nauk Polit ... Studia Nauk Politycznych [*A publication*]
Stud Neoph ... Studia Neophilologica [*A publication*]
StudNeot ... Studia Neotestamentica [*Paris/Bruges*] [*A publication*]
Stud Neotrop Fauna ... Studies on the Neotropical Fauna [*Later, Studies on the Neotropical Fauna and Environment*] [*A publication*]
Stud Neotrop Fauna Environ ... Studies on the Neotropical Fauna and Environment [*A publication*]
Stud Neuro Anat ... Studies in Neuro-Anatomy [*A publication*]
Stud Niger Lang ... Studies in Nigerian Languages [*A publication*]
Stud Novel ... Studies in the Novel [*A publication*]
StudNT ...... Studien zum Neuen Testament [*Guetersloh*] [*A publication*]
StudOr ...... Studia Orientalia [*Helsinki*] [*A publication*]
Stud Orient ... Studia Orientalia [*Helsinki*] [*A publication*]
Stud Ov ...... Studium Ovetense [*A publication*]
Stud Pac Lang Cult ... Studies in Pacific Languages and Cultures in Honour of Bruce Biggs [*A publication*]
Stud Paint (Osaka) ... Studies in Paint (Osaka) [*Japan*] [*A publication*]
StudPal ..... Studien zur Palaeographie und Papyruskunde [*Leipzig*] [*A publication*]
StudPap ..... Studia Papyrologica [*A publication*]
Stud Papyrol ... Studia Papyrologica [*A publication*]
Stud Patr ... Studia Patristica [*A publication*]
Stud Person Psychol ... Studies in Personnel Psychology [*A publication*]
Stud Pers P ... Studies in Personnel Psychology [*A publication*]

Stud Phil Christ ... Studia Philosophiae Christiane [*A publication*]
Stud Phil E ... Studies in Philosophy and Education [*A publication*]
Stud Phil & Ed ... Studies in Philosophy and Education [*A publication*]
Stud Phil H ... Studies in Philosophy and the History of Philosophy [*A publication*]
Stud Phil Hist Phil ... Studies in Philosophy and the History of Philosophy [*A publication*]
Stud Phil Ling ... Studies in Philippine Linguistics [*Manila*] [*A publication*]
Stud Philol ... Studies in Philology [*A publication*]
Stud Philos ... Studies in Philosophy [*The Hague*] [*A publication*]
Stud Philos & Educ ... Studies in Philosophy and Education [*A publication*]
Stud Philos Med ... Studies in Philosophy of Medicine [*A publication*]
Stud Phil (Switzerland) ... Studia Philosophica (Switzerland) [*A publication*]
Stud Phonol ... Studia Phonologica [*A publication*]
Stud Phys Anthropol ... Studies in Physical Anthropology [*A publication*]
Stud Picena ... Studia Picena [*A publication*]
Stud Pneumol Phtiseol Cech ... Studia Pneumologica et Phtiseologica Cechoslovaca [*A publication*]
Stud Prawno-Ekon ... Studia Prawno-Ekonomiczne [*A publication*]
Stud Prot Epurarea Apelor ... Studii de Protectia si Epurarea Apelor [*A publication*]
Stud Psycho ... Studia Psychologica [*Bratislava*] [*A publication*]
Stud Psychol ... Studia Psychologiczne [*A publication*]
Stud Psychol (Bratisl) ... Studia Psychologica (Bratislava) [*A publication*]
Stud Q J Inst Electr Eng ... Students Quarterly Journal. Institution of Electrical Engineers [*England*] [*A publication*]
Stud Radiat Eff Solids ... Studies in Radiation Effects in Solids [*A publication*]
Stud Rel ..... Studies in Religion [*Ontario*] [*A publication*]
Stud Relig ... Studies in Religion [*A publication*]
Stud Res Inst Meteorol Hydrol Part 2 ... Studies and Research. Institute of Meteorology and Hydrology. Part 2. Hydrology [*A publication*]
Stud Ric Ist Mineral Petrogr Univ Pavia ... Studi e Ricerche. Istituto di Mineralogia e Petrografia. Universita di Pavia [*A publication*]
StudRom .... Studi Romani [*Rome*] [*A publication*]
StudRom .... Studi Romanzi [*Padua*] [*A publication*]
Stud Romagn ... Studi Romagnoli [*A publication*]
Stud Roman ... Studies in Romanticism [*A publication*]
Stud Romant ... Studies in Romanticism [*A publication*]
Stud Romanticism ... Studies in Romanticism [*A publication*]
StudSal ...... Studi Salentini [*A publication*]
StudSard ... Studi Sardi [*A publication*]
Stud Sassar Sez 1 ... Studi Sassaresi. Sezione 1 [*A publication*]
Stud Sci Math Hung ... Studia Scientiarum Mathematicarum Hungarica [*Hungary*] [*A publication*]
StudSemNeerl ... Studia Semitica Neerlandica [*Assen*] [*A publication*]
Stud Short Fict ... Studies in Short Fiction [*A publication*]
Stud Sociol ... Studi di Sociologia [*A publication*]
Stud Socjol ... Studia Socjologiczne [*A publication*]
Stud Soc Li ... Studies in Social Life [*A publication*]
Stud Soc Sci Torun Sect B ... Studia Societatis Scientiarum Torunensis. Sectio B (Chemie) [*A publication*]
Stud Soc Sci Torun Sect C (Geogr Geol) ... Studia Societatis Scientiarum Torunensis. Sectio C (Geographia et Geologia) [*A publication*]
Stud Soc Sci Torun Sect D (Bot) ... Studia Societatis Scientiarum Torunensis. Sectio D (Botanica) [*A publication*]
Stud Soc Sci Torun Sect E (Zool) ... Studia Societatis Scientiarum Torunensis. Sectio E (Zoologia) [*A publication*]
Stud Soc Sci Torun Sect F ... Studia Societatis Scientiarum Torunensis. Sectio F (Astronomia) [*Poland*] [*A publication*]
Stud Soc Sci Torun Sect G (Physiol) ... Studia Societatis Scientiarum Torunensis. Sectio G (Physiologia) [*A publication*]
Stud Soc Wk ... Studies on Social Work [*A publication*]
Stud Solid Phys Chem ... Studies on Solid State Physics and Chemistry [*Japan*] [*A publication*]
Stud Sov Th ... Studies in Soviet Thought [*A publication*]
Stud Sov Thought ... Studies in Soviet Thought [*A publication*]
Stud Spelaeol ... Studies in Spelaeology [*A publication*]
Stud Speleol ... Studies in Speleology [*A publication*]
Stud Statist Mech ... Studies in Statistical Mechanics [*A publication*]
Stud Stat Mech ... Studies in Statistical Mechanics [*A publication*]
Stud Surf Sci Catal ... Studies in Surface Science and Catalysis [*Netherlands*] [*Elsevier Book Series*] [*A publication*]
Stud Teh Econ Inst Geol (Rom) Ser C ... Studii Tehnice si Economice. Institutul Geologic (Romania). Seria C. Pedologie [*A publication*]
Stud Teh Econ Inst Geol (Rom) Ser D ... Studii Tehnice si Economice. Institutul Geologic (Romania). Seria D. Prospectiuni Geofizice [*A publication*]
Stud Teh Econ Inst Geol (Rom) Ser E ... Studii Tehnice si Economice. Institutul Geologic (Romania). Seria E. Hidrogeologie [*A publication*]
Stud Teh Econ Inst Geol Ser E ... Studii Tehnice si Economice. Institutul Geologic (Romania). Seria E. Hidrogeologie [*A publication*]
Stud Teh Econ Inst Geol Ser I ... Studii Tehnice si Economice. Institutul Geologic (Romania). Seria I. Mineralogie-Petrografie [*A publication*]

Stud Teh Econ Ser D Inst Geol Geofiz (Bucharest) ... Studii Tehnice si Economice. Seria D. Prospectiuni Geofizice. Institutul de Geologie si Geofizica (Bucharest) [*Romania*] [*A publication*]
Stud Teh Econ Ser E Inst Geol Geofiz ... Studii Tehnice si Economice. Seria E. Hidrogeologie. Institutul de Geologie si Geofizica [*A publication*]
Stud Th ...... Studia Theologica [*A publication*]
Stud Third World Soc ... Studies in Third World Societies [*Williamsburg*] [*A publication*]
Stud Tokugawa Inst ... Studies from the Tokugawa Institute [*A publication*]
Stud Tour Rep Dep Prim Ind Queensl ... Study Tour Report. Department of Primary Industries. Queensland [*A publication*]
Stud Trop Oceanogr Inst Mar Sci Univ Miami ... Studies in Tropical Oceanography. Institute of Marine Science. University of Miami [*A publication*]
Stud Trop Oceanogr (Miami) ... Studies in Tropical Oceanography (Miami) [*A publication*]
Stud Univ Babes-Bolyai Biol ... Studia Universitatis Babes-Bolyai. Series Biologia [*A publication*]
Stud Univ Babes-Bolyai Chem ... Studia Universitatis Babes-Bolyai. Series Chemia [*A publication*]
Stud Univ Babes-Bolyai Geol-Geogr ... Studia Universitatis Babes-Bolyai. Series Geologia-Geographia [*A publication*]
Stud Univ Babes-Bolyai Math ... Studia Universitatis Babes-Bolyai. Series Mathematica [*A publication*]
Stud Univ Babes-Bolyai Phys ... Studia Universitatis Babes-Bolyai. Series Physica [*A publication*]
Stud Univ Babes-Bolyai Ser Biol ... Studia Universitatis Babes-Bolyai. Series Biologia [*A publication*]
Stud Univ Babes-Bolyai Ser Chem ... Studia Universitatis Babes-Bolyai. Series Chemia [*A publication*]
Stud Univ Babes-Bolyai Ser Geol-Minerol ... Studia Universitatis Babes-Bolyai. Series Geologia-Mineralogia [*A publication*]
Stud Univ Babes-Bolyai Ser Math-Phys ... Studia Universitatis Babes-Bolyai. Series Mathematica-Physica [*A publication*]
Stud Univ Babes-Bolyai Ser Phys ... Studia Universitatis Babes-Bolyai. Series Physica [*A publication*]
Stud Urb .... Studi di Urbanistica Antica [*A publication*]   (OCD)
Stud Urb .... Studi Urbinati di Storia, Filosofia, e Letteratura [*A publication*]
Stud Urb (Ser A) ... Studi Urbinati di Scienze Giuridiche ed Economiche (Ser. A) [*A publication*]
Stud Venez ... Studi Veneziani [*A publication*]
Stud Voltaire Eighteenth Century ... Studies on Voltaire and the Eighteenth Century [*A publication*]
Stud VT Geol ... Studies in Vermont Geology [*A publication*]
Stud W .... Student World [*A publication*]
Study Elem Particles ... Study of Elementary Particles [*Japan*] [*A publication*]
Study of Soc ... Study of Society [*A publication*]
Study Tea ... Study of Tea [*A publication*]
Stud Zrodloznawcze ... Studia Zrodloznawcze. Commentationes [*A publication*]
StudzumAuNT ... Studien zum Alten und Neuen Testament [*Munich*] [*A publication*]
STUF .... Stuff Yer Face, Inc. [*NASDAQ symbol*]   (NQ)
STUFF .... System to Uncover Facts Fast
STUG .... Sturmgeschuetz [*Self-propelled assault gun*] [*German military - World War II*]
STUH .... Stuart Hall Co. [*NASDAQ symbol*]   (NQ)
STUK .... Sturmkanone [*Self-propelled assault gun*] [*German military - World War II*]
STUKA .... Sturzkampfflugzeug [*Dive bomber*] [*German military - World War II*]
Stu KB .... Stuart's Lower Canada King's Bench Reports [*1810-35*]   (DLA)
Stu LC .... Stuart's Lower Canada King's Bench Reports [*1810-35*]   (DLA)
Stu Mil & Ped ... Stuart, Milne, and Peddie's Scotch Court of Sessions Reports   (DLA)
Stu Mon ..... Studia Monastica [*A publication*]
Stu M & P ... Stuart, Milne, and Peddie's Scotch Court of Sessions Reports   (DLA)
StUmwNT ... Studien zur Umwelt des Neuen Testament [*Goettingen*] [*A publication*]
StUNT .... Studien zur Umwelt des Neuen Testament [*Goettingen*] [*A publication*]
STUOA .... Sbornik Nauchnykh Trudov Ukrainskii Nauchno-Issledovatel'skii Institut Ogneuporov [*A publication*]
STUP .... Spinning Tubular Projectile   (MCD)
Stu Pat .... Studia Patavina [*A publication*]
STUPID ...... Simulation of the Underlying Processes in Decisions   (MCD)
Stu Prob & St ... Studies in Probability and Statistics [*A publication*]
Sturg Ins D ... Sturgeon's Insolvent Debtors Act [*1842*]   (DLA)
Stu Ros .... Studia Rosenthaliana [*A publication*]
STURP .... Shroud of Turin Research Project   (EA)
Stur & Porter ... Stuart [*or Stewart*] and Porter's Alabama Reports   (DLA)
StuSta .... Studia Staropolskie [*A publication*]
StuTC .... Studies in the Twentieth Century [*A publication*]
Stutt Beitr Naturk ... Stuttgarter Beitraege zur Naturkunde [*A publication*]
Stuttg Beitr Naturkd ... Stuttgarter Beitraege zur Naturkunde [*A publication*]
Stuttg Beitr Naturkd Ser A (Biol) ... Stuttgarter Beitraege zur Naturkunde. Serie A (Biologie) [*A publication*]

Stuttg Beitr Naturkd Ser B (Geol Palaeontol) ... Stuttgarter Beitraege zur Naturkunde. Serie B (Geologie und Palaeontologie) [*A publication*]
Stuttg Beitr Naturk Ser C Allg Aufsaetze ... Stuttgarter Beitraege zur Naturkunde. Serie C. Allgemeinverstaendliche Aufsaetze [*A publication*]
STUVAC..... Study Vacation [*Australian*] [*Slang*]   (DSUE)
STV .... Santa Anna Di Valdieri [*Italy*] [*Seismograph station code, US Geological Survey*]   (SEIS)
STV .... Separation Test Vehicle
STV .... Short-Tube Vertical [*Evaporator*]
STV .... Single Transferable Vote
STV .... Small Test Vessel   (NRCH)
STV .... Solar Thermal Vacuum
STV .... Solidaridad de Trabajadores Vascos [*Solidarity of Basque Workers*] [*In exile*] [*Spain*]
STV .... Space Test Vehicle [*NASA*]   (KSC)
STV .... Special Test Vehicle
STV .... Standard Test Vehicle
STV .... Stikine Silver [*Vancouver Stock Exchange symbol*]
STV .... Stonewall, TX [*Location identifier*] [*FAA*]   (FAAL)
STV .... Stove [*Classified advertising*]   (ADA)
STV .... Structural Test Vehicle [*NASA*]   (KSC)
StV .... Studies on Voltaire and the Eighteenth Century [*A publication*]
STV .... Submarine Target Vessel   (NVT)
STV .... Subscription Television
STV .... Supersonic Test Vehicle   (AAG)
STV .... Surveillance Television   (AFM)
STVA......... Self-Tuning Vibration Absorber [*Navy*]   (CAAL)
Stva........... Stvaranje [*A publication*]
STVA......... Subscription Television Association [*Defunct*]   (EA)
STVC......... Sumerian Texts of Varied Context [*E. Chiera*] [*A publication*]
STVD........ Spacecraft Television Video Data
STVFB....... Samoletostroenie i Tekhnika Vozdushnogo Flota [*A publication*]
STVI .... STV Engineers, Incorporated [*NASDAQ symbol*]   (NQ)
StVladSemQ ... St. Vladimir's Seminary Quarterly [*New York*] [*A publication*]
STVM .... Semitrailer Van Mount
STVS.......... Short-Term Visual Storage [*or Store*] [*Psychophysiology*]
STVS.......... Surinaamse Televisie Sichtung [*Television network*] [*Surinam*]
STVTF....... Sterivet Laboratories Ltd. [*NASDAQ symbol*]   (NQ)
STW .... Save the Whales   (EA)
STW .... Southwest Tech [*Vancouver Stock Exchange symbol*]
STW .... Speed Made Good Through the Water   (NATG)
STW .... Star Trek Welcommittee   (EA)
STW .... Stillwater, NJ [*Location identifier*] [*FAA*]   (FAAL)
STW .... Stillwater Public Library, Stillwater, OK [*OCLC symbol*]   (OCLC)
STW .... Storm Water
STW .... Striped Peak [*Washington*] [*Seismograph station code, US Geological Survey*]   (SEIS)
STW .... Subtropical Water
ST. WAPNIACL ... State, Treasury, War, Attorney General, Postmaster General, Navy, Interior, Agriculture, Commerce, Labor [*Pre-1947 mnemonic guide to names of the departments in the President's Cabinet, in order of creation*] [*Obsolete*]
STWB........ Statewide Bancorp [*NASDAQ symbol*]   (NQ)
STWBRD.... Strawboard [*Freight*]
STWD........ Steward   (FAAC)
STWE........ Society of Technical Writers and Editors [*Later, STWP, STC*]
St Westm ... Statute of Westminster   (DLA)
STWG........ Stowage   (MSA)
STWP........ Society of Technical Writers and Publishers [*Formerly, STWE*] [*Later, STC*]   (EA)
STWP........ Steam Working Pressure   (MSA)
STWS........ Stewardess   (FAAC)
STWY........ Stairway   (AAG)
STWY........ Stopway   (FAAC)
STX .... Christiansted, St. Croix, VI [*Location identifier*] [*FAA*]   (FAAL)
STX .... St. Croix [*Virgin Islands*] [*Airport symbol*]
STX .... Saxitoxin [*A neurotoxin*]
STX .... Situational Training Exercise [*Army*]   (INF)
STX .... Starrex Mining Corp. Ltd. [*Toronto Stock Exchange symbol*]
STX .... Start of Text Character [*Keyboard*] [*Data processing*]
STX .... Station 2 [*Nevada*] [*Seismograph station code, US Geological Survey*] [*Closed*]   (SEIS)
STX .... Stewart-Warner Corp. [*NYSE symbol*]
STY .... Salto [*Uruguay*] [*Airport symbol*]   (OAG)
StY .... Standard Yiddish   (BJA)
STY .... Sterling Drug, Inc. [*NYSE symbol*]
STY .... Stony River [*Alaska*] [*Seismograph station code, US Geological Survey*]   (SEIS)
Sty............. Style's English King's Bench Reports [*1646-55*]   (DLA)
Sty............. Styrene [*Also, St*] [*Organic chemistry*]
Style.......... Style's English King's Bench Reports   (DLA)
Style Pr Reg ... Style's Practical Register   (DLA)
STYP.......... Styptic [*Stopping Bleeding*] [*Medicine*]   (ROG)
Sty Pr Reg ... Style's Practical Register [*1657-1710*]   (DLA)
Styr Tek Utveckling Inf Energitek ... Styrelsen foer Teknisk Utveckling Informerar om Energiteknik [*Sweden*] [*A publication*]
STZ .... Santa Terezinha [*Brazil*] [*Airport symbol*]   (OAG)

STZ .... Schweizerische Theologische Zeitschrift [*Zurich*] [*A publication*]   (BJA)
STZ .... Serum-Treated Zymosan [*Clinical chemistry*]
STZ .... Southern Transgressive Zone [*Geology*]
STZ .... Sprache im Technischen Zeitalter [*A publication*]
STZ .... Stallion Resources Ltd. [*Vancouver Stock Exchange symbol*]
STZ .... Stratford [*New Zealand*] [*Seismograph station code, US Geological Survey*] [*Closed*]   (SEIS)
STZ .... Streptozocin [*Also, S*] [*Antineoplastic drug*]
SU .... AEROFLOT [*Aero Flotilla*] [*USSR*] [*ICAO designator*]   (FAAC)
Su.............. Ciba-Geigy Corp. [*Research code symbol*]
SU .... Optical Device [*JETDS nomenclature*] [*Military*]   (CET)
SU .... Salicyluric Acid [*Also, SUA*] [*Biochemistry*]
SU .... Salmon Unlimited   (EA)
SU .... Samostijna Ukraina [*Independent Ukraine*] [*A publication*]
su.............. Saudi Arabia [*MARC country of publication code*] [*Library of Congress*]   (LCCP)
SU .... Savings Unit
SU .... Scorable Unit
SU .... Selectable Unit   (BUR)
SU .... Sensation Units
SU .... Separation Ullage
SU .... Service Unit [*Military*]
SU .... Set Up [*Freight*]
SU .... Shipment Unit [*Army*]
SU .... Siemens Unit
SU .... Sigma Units
SU .... Signaling Unit
SU .... Sindicato Unitario [*United Syndicate*] [*Trade union*] [*Madrid, Spain*]
SU .... Single Uptake [*Boilers*]
SU .... Single User [*The military activity that has the sole interest in an item of supply*] [*DoD*]
SU .... Society of the Sisters of St. Ursula of the Blessed Virgin [*Roman Catholic religious order*]
SU .... Somogyi Unit [*of amylase*] [*Clinical chemistry*]
SU .... Sonics and Ultrasonics   (MCD)
SU .... Soviet Union [*The USSR*]
SU .... Space Unit [*American Topical Association*]   (EA)
SU .... Special Unitary [*Algebra*]
SU .... Standard Upkeep
SU .... Stanford University [*California*]
SU .... Start Up [*of a relay, power switchgear*]   (IEEE)
S/U .... Startup [*Nuclear energy*]   (NRCH)
SU .... Storage Unit [*Data processing*]
SU .... Stripers Unlimited   (EA)
SU .... Strontium Units [*Nuclear energy*]
SU .... Student Union
SU .... Studi Urbinati [*A publication*]
SU .... Stunts Unlimited   (EA)
SU .... Subject [*Online database field identifier*]
SU .... Subscriber Unit [*RADA*] [*Army*]   (RDA)
Su.............. Sufentanil [*or Sulfentanyl*] [*An analgesic*]
SU .... Sukhoy [*Aircraft*]
Su.............. Sumet [*Let Him, or Her, Take*] [*Pharmacy*]
SU .... Suncor, Inc. [*Toronto Stock Exchange symbol*]
SU .... Sunday
SU .... Super Unleaded (Gasoline)
Su.............. Superior Court   (DLA)
SU .... Supply
SU .... Support Unit [*NASA*]   (NASA)
SU .... Suppressor [*Electronics*]   (MDG)
SU .... Switching Unit
SU .... Syracuse University
SU .... Thiouridine [*Two-letter symbol; see Srd*]
SU .... Union of Soviet Socialist Republics [*Two-letter standard code*]   (CNC)
SU .... United Arab Republic [*Aircraft nationality and registration mark*]   (FAAC)
SUA............ Salicyluric Acid [*Also, SU*] [*Biochemistry*]
SUA............ Satellite Unfurlable Antenna
SUA............ Serum Uric Acid [*Clinical chemistry*]
SUA............ Silver Users Association [*Washington, DC*]   (EA)
SUA............ Small Unit Action [*Military*]   (CINC)
SUA............ Standard Unit of Accounting [*Data processing*]
SUA............ State Universities Association [*Later, NASULGC*]
SUA............ Stuart [*Florida*] [*Airport symbol*]   (OAG)
SUA............ Stuart, FL [*Location identifier*] [*FAA*]   (FAAL)
SUA............ Summit Tax Exempt Bond [*American Stock Exchange symbol*]
SUA............ Superior Acceptance Corp. Ltd. [*Toronto Stock Exchange symbol*]
SUA............ Supplemental Unemployment Assistance
SUA............ Susitna [*Alaska*] [*Seismograph station code, US Geological Survey*]   (SEIS)
SUAB .... Svenska Utvecklingsaktiebolaget [*Swedish Corporation for Development*]
SUADPS..... Shipboard Uniform Automatic Data Processing System [*Navy*]
SUAEWICS ... Soviet Union Airborne Early Warning and Interceptor Control System   (MCD)
SUAR .... Start Unload Address Register
Suas.......... Suasoriae [*of Seneca the Elder*] [*Classical studies*]   (OCD)

SUAS .... System for Upper Atmosphere Sounding (MCD)
SUAWACS ... Soviet Union Airborne Warning and Control System (MCD)
SUB .... Scandinavian University Books [*A publication*]
SUB .... Student Union Building [*Canada*]
SUB .... Subaltern
SUB .... Subaud [*Understand*] [*Latin*]
Sub .... Subcommittee (DLA)
SUB .... Subeditor
SUB .... Subject
SUB .... Subjunctive [*Grammar*]
SUB .... Submarine (AFM)
SUB .... Submerged
SUB .... Subordinate (DSUE)
Sub. .... Subordinated (DLA)
SUB .... Subroutine
Sub. .... Subscriber
SUB .... Subscription
SUB .... Substitute Character [*Keyboard*] (AFM)
SUB .... Substratum
SUB .... Subtract
SUB .... Subtract Binary Number [*Data processing*]
SUB .... Suburban
SUB .... Subway (AAG)
SUB .... Supplemental Unemployment Benefits
SUB .... Surabaya [*Indonesia*] [*Airport symbol*] (OAG)
SUBACLANT ... Submarine Allied Command, Atlantic [*NATO*] (NATG)
SUBACS ...... Submarine Advanced Combat System
SUBAD .... Submarine Air Defense
SUBAD ...... Submarine Force, Pacific Fleet Administration
SUBADMI ... Submarine Force, Pacific Fleet Administration, Mare Island
SUBASE ..... Submarine Base [*Navy*]
SUBASELANT ... Submarine Bases, Atlantic [*Navy*]
SUBASEPAC ... Submarine Bases, Pacific [*Navy*]
SUBASSY ... Subassembly
SUBASWEX ... Submarine-Antisubmarine Warfare Exercise (NVT)
SUBB .... Studia Universitatis Babes-Bolyai. Series Philologia [*A publication*]
SUB-BELL ... Submarine Fog Bell [*Mechanical*]
SUBBP .... Studia Universitatis Babes-Bolyai. Series Philologia [*A publication*]
SUBC .... Subler, Carl, Agent, Versailles OH [*STAC*]
SUBC .... Suburban Bancorp [*NASDAQ symbol*] (NQ)
SUBCAL ..... Subcaliber
Sub-Cell Bi ... Sub-Cellular Biochemistry [*A publication*]
Sub-Cell Biochem ... Sub-Cellular Biochemistry [*A publication*]
SUBCOM ..... Subcommittee
SUBCOM ... Subordinate Command, Service Force, Pacific Fleet
SUBCOMNELM ... Subordinate Command, [*US*] Naval Forces, Eastern Atlantic and Mediterranean
subcrep ...... Subcrepitant [*Medicine*]
SUBCU ...... Subcutaneous [*Beneath the Skin*] [*Medicine*]
subcut .... Subcutaneous [*Beneath the Skin*] [*Medicine*]
Subd .... Subdivision (DLA)
SUBDEVGRUONE ... Submarine Development Group One [*San Diego*]
SUBDEVGRUTWO ... Submarine Development Group Two [*FPO New York 09501*]
SUBDIV ...... Submarine Division [*Navy*]
SUBDIZ ...... Submarine Defense Identification Zone
SUBEASTLANT ... Submarine Force, Eastern Atlantic [*NATO*]
SUBED .... Submarine Electromagnetic Deception System
SUBEX .... Submarine Exercise (NATG)
SUBFIN COCT ... Sub Finem Coctionis [*When the Boiling Is Nearly Finished*] (ROG)
SUBFIX ...... We Forward Subject to Correction [*Code*] (FAAC)
SUBFLOT ... Submarine Flotilla [*Navy*]
SUBGEN .... Subgenus
SUBH .... Scripta Universitatis atque Bibliotecae Hierosolymitanarum Jerusalem [*A publication*] (BJA)
SUBIC .... Submarine Integrated Control Systems
SUBINSURV ... Inspection and Survey Board Sub Board [*Navy*]
SUBJ .... Subject (AFM)
SUBJ .... Subjective (ROG)
SUBJ .... Subjunctive [*Grammar*]
Subj of Day ... Subject of the Day [*A publication*]
SUBL .... Sublime [*or Subliming*]
SUBLANT .. Submarine Force, Atlantic Fleet
Sub Life ..... Suburban Life [*A publication*]
subling ...... Sublingual [*Medicine*]
SUBM .... Submerged
SUBM .... Submission [*or Submit*] (AFM)
SUBMACOM ... Major Army Subcommand (AABC)
submand .... Submandibular [*Medicine*]
SUBMD ...... Studia Universitatis Babes-Bolyai. Series Mathematica [*A publication*]
SUBMED .... Submarines Mediterranean [*NATO*] (NATG)
SUBMEDCEN ... Submarine Medical Center [*Navy*]
SUBMEDNOREAST ... Submarines Northeast Mediterranean [*NATO*] (NATG)
SUBMG ...... Submerged (MSA)
SUBMIN ..... Subminiature
SUBMISS ... Submarine Missing [*Navy*] (NVT)

SUBMIS/SUBSUNK ... Submarine Missing/Presumed Sunk [*Navy*]
SUBMON .... Submission (ROG)
Subm W ..... Submerged Well [*Nautical charts*]
SUBN .... Summit Bancorp [*NASDAQ symbol*] (NQ)
SUBNO .... Substitutes Not Desired
sub nom ..... Sub Nomine [*Under the Name*] [*Latin*] (DLA)
SUBNOT .... Submarine Notice (MCD)
SUBNOTE ... Submarine Notice [*Navy*] (NVT)
Subnucl Ser ... Subnuclear Series [*A publication*]
SUBOK .... Substitution Acceptable
SUBOPAUTH ... Submarine Operating Authority [*Navy*] (NVT)
SUBOR .... Subordinate (AFM)
SUBORCOM ... Subordinate Command
SUBORCOMDSERVLANT ... Subordinate Command, Service Force, Atlantic Fleet
SUBORCOMDSERVPAC ... Subordinate Command, Service Force, Pacific Fleet
SUBORD .... Subordinate [*Linguistics*]
SUB-OSC ... Submarine Oscillator
SUBPA .... Antisubmarine Warfare Barrier Submarine Patrol Area [*Navy*] (NVT)
SUBPAC .... Submarine Force, Pacific Fleet
SUBPACAD ... Submarine Force, Pacific Fleet, Administrative Command
SUBPACSUBORDCOM ... Submarine Force, Pacific Fleet, Subordinate Command
Subpar .... Subparagraph (DLA)
SUBPARA ... Subparagraph
SUBPZ .... Antisubmarine Warfare Barrier Submarine Patrol Zone [*Navy*] (NVT)
SUB Q .... Subcutaneous [*Beneath the Skin*] [*Medicine*]
SUBQ .... Subsequent (AABC)
SUBRAP ..... Submarine Range Prediction System [*Navy*] (NVT)
SUBRO ...... Subrogation
SUBROC .... Submarine Rocket
SUBRON .... Submarine Squadron [*Navy*]
SUBRPIO .... Sub-Registered Publications Issuing Office
SUBRQMT ... Subrequirement
SUBRU .... Submarine Repair Unit
SUBS .... Subscriptions
SUBS .... Subsidiary [*Business and trade*]
SUBS .... Subsistence (AABC)
SUBS .... Substantive [*Grammar*]
SUBS .... Substitute
SUBSAFE ... Submarine Safety [*Program*]
SUBSAFECEN ... Submarine Safety Center [*Navy*]
Subsc .... Subscription (DLA)
SUBSCD .... Subscribed (ROG)
SUBSCOFOR ... Submarines Scouting Force [*Pacific Fleet*]
SUBSCR ..... Subscription (ROG)
SUBSCRON ... Subscription (ROG)
SUBSEC ..... Subsection
SUBSELS ... Subsisting Elsewhere
SUBSEQ .... Subsequent (ROG)
Subser Optical Sci Engrg ... Subseries on Optical Science and Engineering [*A publication*]
SUBSET ..... Subscriber Set (CET)
SUBSID ..... Subsidiary (ROG)
Subsidia Med ... Subsidia Medica [*A publication*]
SUBSIS ...... Subsistence (AFM)
SUBSLANT ... Submarines, Atlantic Fleet
SUBSLY ..... Subsequently (ROG)
SUBSP .... Subspecies
SUBSPAC ... Submarines, Pacific Fleet
SUBSQ .... Subsequently (ADA)
SUBSS .... Submarine Schoolship [*Navy*] (NVT)
SUBSSOWESPAC ... Submarines, Southwest Pacific Force
SUBST .... Substance (ROG)
SUBST .... Substantive (ROG)
SUBST .... Substitute (AAG)
SUBSTA ..... Substation
Subst Alcohol Actions Misuse ... Substance and Alcohol Actions/Misuse [*A publication*]
SUBSTD .... Substituted (ROG)
SUBSTG .... Substituting (AAG)
SUBSTN ..... Substitution
SUBSTR ..... Substructure (AAG)
SUBSTTD ... Substituted
SUBSUNK ... Submarine Sunk [*Navy*] (NVT)
SUBSYS ..... Subsystem (AAG)
SUBTACGRU ... Submarine Tactical Group [*NATO*] (NATG)
SUBTAG .... Submarine Tactics Analysis Group
Sub Torg .... Sovetskaya Torgovlya [*A publication*]
SUBTR .... Subtraction (MSA)
SUBTRAFAC ... Submarine Training Facility
SUBTRAP .. Submersible Training Platform [*Marine science*] (MSC)
Subtrop Kul't ... Subtropicheskie Kul'tury [*A publication*]
Subtrop Kul't Min Sel'Khoz SSSR ... Subtropicheskie Kul'tury. Ministerstvo Sel'skogo Khozyaistva SSSR [*A publication*]
SUBV .... Subversion (AABC)
Sub Vol ...... Submarine Volcano [*Nautical charts*]

SUBWESTLANT ... Submarine Force, Western Atlantic Area [*NATO*] (NATG)
SUC........... Saggi di Umanismo Cristiano [*A publication*]
SUC........... Southern Union College [*Wadley, AL*]
SUC........... Succeeding (MSA)
SUC........... Successor (ADA)
Suc........... Succinoyl [*Biochemistry*]
SUC........... Succus [*Juice*] [*Pharmacy*]
SUC........... Sucre [*Bolivia*] [*Seismograph station code, US Geological Survey*] [*Closed*] (SEIS)
SUC........... Suction (ADA)
SUC........... Suncoast Petroleum [*Vancouver Stock Exchange symbol*]
SUC........... Sundance, WY [*Location identifier*] [*FAA*] (FAAL)
SUC........... University of South Carolina, Columbia, SC [*OCLC symbol*] (OCLC)
SUCC........ State University Computation Center [*Iowa State University*] [*Research center*] (RCD)
SUCC........ Succentor [*Ecclesiastical*] (ROG)
SUCC........ Successor (ROG)
SUCC........ Succinate
SUCC........ Succinum [*Amber*] [*Latin*] (ROG)
Success Farming ... Successful Farming [*A publication*]
Successful F ... Successful Farming [*A publication*]
SUCCN........ Succession (ROG)
SUCCON.... Succession
SUCCR....... Successor
SUCEE....... Socialist Union of Central and Eastern Europe (PD)
Suc Farm ... Successful Farming [*A publication*]
SUCHTRANS ... Such Transportation as Command Indicated Designates
SUCHTRANSAVAIL ... Such Transportation as Available
SUCI........... Socialist Unity Center of India (PPW)
SUCKER .... Society for Understanding Cats, Kangaroos, Elks, and Reptiles [*Slang*]
SUCL......... Set Up in Carloads [*Freight*]
SUCL......... Stetson University College of Law (DLA)
SUCO........ Service Universitaire Canadien Outre-Mer [*Canadian University Service Overseas - CUSO*]
SUCR......... Sunset Crater National Monument
SUCT........ Suction (AAG)
Su Ct Cir .... Supreme Court [*Ceylon*] (DLA)
SuD........... Sprache und Dichtung [*A publication*]
SUD........... Stroud, OK [*Location identifier*] [*FAA*] (FAAL)
SUD........... Sudbury [*Ontario*] [*Seismograph station code, US Geological Survey*] (SEIS)
SUD........... Sudbury Board of Education [*UTLAS symbol*]
SUD........... Sudbury Contact Mines Ltd. [*Toronto Stock Exchange symbol*]
SUD........... Sudden Unexpected [*or Unexplained*] Death [*Medicine*]
SUD........... Sudorific [*Causing Sweat*] [*Pharmacy*] (ROG)
SUDAER.... Stanford University, Department of Aeronautics and Astronautics (MCD)
SUDAM...... Editorial Sudamericana, BA [*A publication*]
SUDAM...... Sunk or Damaged [*Navy*]
Sudan Geol Surv Dep Bull ... Sudan. Geological Survey Department. Bulletin [*A publication*]
Sudan J Econ and Social Studies ... Sudan Journal of Economic and Social Studies [*A publication*]
Sudan J Vet Sci Anim Husb ... Sudan Journal of Veterinary Science and Animal Husbandry [*A publication*]
Sudan LJ & Rep ... Sudan Law Journal and Reports [*Khartoum*] (DLA)
Sudan Notes ... Sudan Notes and Records [*A publication*]
Sudan Notes Rec ... Sudan Notes and Records [*A publication*]
Sudan Soc ... Sudan Society [*A publication*]
SUDAP....... Superintendencia da Agricultura e Producao [*Brazil*]
Sud Dew Ad ... Sudder Dewanny Adawlut [*or Sadr Diwani Adalat*] Reports [*India*] (DLA)
Sud Dew Rep ... Sudder Dewanny [*or Sadr Diwani*] Reports, Northwest Province [*India*] (DLA)
Sudebno-Med Ekspert ... Sudebno-Meditsinskaya Ekspertiza [*A publication*]
SUDEC....... Superintendencia do Desenvolvimento Economico e Cultural [*Brazil*]
SUDEL .... Groupe Regional pour la Coordination de la Production et du Transport de l'Energie Electrique entre l'Autriche, la Grece, l'Italie et la Yougoslavie [*Regional Group for Coordinating the Production and Transmission of Electricity between Austria, Greece, Italy, and Yugoslavia*] (EA)
SUDENE..... Superintendencia do Desenvolvimento do Nordeste [*Brazil*]
SUDENE Bol Recur Nat ... SUDENE [*Superintendencia do Desenvolvimento do Nordeste*] Boletim do Recursos Naturais [*A publication*]
Sudhoffs Arch ... Sudhoffs Archiv fuer Geschichte der Medizin und der Naturwissenschaften [*A publication*]
Sudhoffs Arch ... Sudhoffs Archiv. Zeitschrift fuer Wissenschaftsgeschichte [*A publication*]
SUDI........... State Unemployment Disability Insurance (AAG)
Sud Inform Econ Provence-Cote D'Azur-Corse ... Sud Information Economique Provence-Cote D'Azur-Corse [*A publication*]
Sud-Med Ekspert ... Sudebno-Meditsinskaya Ekspertiza [*A publication*]
Su Doc .... Superintendent of Documents, Government Printing Office (DLA)

SUDOSAT ... Sudanian Satellite
SUDS .... Satellite Undetected Duds
SUDS .... Silhouetting Underwater Detecting System
SUDS .... Small Unit Delivery System (MCD)
SUDS .... State's Urban Development Something-or-Other [*Slang for Urban Development Corporation, New York*]
SUDS .... Subjective Units of Disturbance
SUDS .... Submarine Detecting System
SUDT .... Silicon Unilateral Diffused Transistor
SUE .... Sahara Upwelling Experiment [*US, Spain*] (MSC)
SUE .... Seismic Underwater Explorer
SUE .... Servants' United Effort [*Lemonade*] [*Slang*] [*British*] (DSUE)
SUE .... Shuttle Unique Equipment (MCD)
SUE .... Significantly Underutilized Employee Program [*DoD*]
SUE .... Skylab Upwelling Experiment [*Marine science*] (MSC)
SUE .... Strontium Unit Equivalent
SUE .... Sturgeon Bay, WI [*Location identifier*] [*FAA*] (FAAL)
SUE .... Sub-Unit Evaluation (MCD)
SUE .... Sudden Expansion
SUE .... Suzie Mining Exploration [*Vancouver Stock Exchange symbol*]
SuedA .... Suedostdeutsches Archiv [*A publication*]
Sueddt Mh ... Sueddeutsche Monatshefte [*A publication*]
Sueddtsch Ztg ... Sueddeutsche Zeitung [*A publication*]
SUEDE ...... Surface Evaluation and Definition
SuedoA ...... Suedostdeutsches Archiv [*A publication*]
Suedost-Forsch ... Suedost-Forschungen. Internationale Zeitschrift fuer Geschichte, Kultur, und Landeskunde Sued-Osteuropas [*A publication*]
SUEL.......... Sperry Utah Engineering Laboratory (MCD)
Suelos Ecuat ... Suelos Ecuatoriales [*A publication*]
SUEM.......... Syndicat Unique des Enseignants de Mauritanie [*Unitary Union of Mauritanian Teachers*]
SUEOTU..... Supreme Unsurpassable Engineers of the Universe [*Rank in Junior Woodchucks organization mentioned in Donald Duck comic by Carl Barks*]
SUERF........ Societe Universitaire Europeenne de Recherches Financieres (EA-IO)
SUET.......... Small Unit Evaluation and Training (MCD)
Suet........... Suetonius [*First century AD*] [*Classical studies*] (OCD)
SUF............ Lametia-Terme [*Italy*] [*Airport symbol*] (OAG)
SuF............ Sinn und Form [*A publication*]
SUF............ Socialist Unity Front [*Romanian*] (PPW)
SUF .... Sufficient (AFM)
SUF .... Suffolk University, Boston, MA [*OCLC symbol*] (OCLC)
SUF .... Swaziland United Front
SUFF .... Sufficient
SUFF .... Sufficit [*Suffices*] [*Latin*]
SUFF .... Suffix (AAG)
SUFF .... Suffolk [*County in England*]
SUFF .... Suffragan [*Ecclesiastical*] (ROG)
SUFFER ..... Save Us from Formaldehyde Environmental Repercussions [*Later, Cure Formaldehyde Poisoning Association*] (EA)
SUFFER ..... System Utility Facility for Easy Recovery [*NASA*]
Suffolk U L Rev ... Suffolk University. Law Review [*A publication*]
Suffolk Univ L Rev ... Suffolk University. Law Review [*A publication*]
SUFFT........ Sufficient
SUFFTY ..... Sufficiently (ROG)
SUFPAC ..... Surface Force Pacific (MCD)
SUFSW....... Small Unit Fire Support Weapon (MCD)
SUG............ Asheville, NC [*Location identifier*] [*FAA*] (FAAL)
SUG............ Sell Under the Guise of Market Research [*Marketing*] [*British*]
SUG............ Southern Union Co. [*Formerly, Southern Union Gas Co.*] [*NYSE symbol*]
SuG .... Sprache und Gemeinschaft [*A publication*]
SUG............ Sugar
SUG............ Sugar Island [*Michigan*] [*Seismograph station code, US Geological Survey*] [*Closed*] (SEIS)
SUG............ Suggest (AFM)
SUG............ Surigao [*Philippines*] [*Airport symbol*] (OAG)
Sugar .... Sugar y Azucar [*A publication*]
Sugar Beet J ... Sugar Beet Journal [*A publication*]
Sugar Bul... Sugar Bulletin [*A publication*]
Sugar Bull ... Sugar Bulletin [*United States*] [*A publication*]
Sugarcane Breed Newsl ... Sugarcane Breeders' Newsletter [*A publication*]
Sugar Ind Abstr ... Sugar Industry Abstracts [*A publication*]
Sugar J... Sugar Journal [*A publication*]
Sugar Mol ... Sugar Molecule [*A publication*]
Sugar Technol Rev ... Sugar Technology Reviews [*A publication*]
Sugd Powers ... Sugden on Powers (DLA)
Sugd Vend ... Sugden on Vendors and Purchasers (DLA)
SUGEND .... Sugendus [*To Be Sucked*] [*Pharmacy*]
Sug Est ..... Sugden on the Law of Estates (DLA)
SUGG.......... Suggestion (ROG)
Sug Hd Bk ... Sugden's Hand-Book of Property Law (DLA)
SUGI........... SAS [*Statistical Analysis System*] Users Group International (EA)
Sug Pow..... Sugden on Powers [*8 eds.*] [*1808-61*] (DLA)
Sug Pr .... Sugden on the Law of Property (DLA)
Sug Prop.... Sugden on the Law of Property as Administered by the House of Lords (DLA)
Sug Pr St.... Sugden on Property Statutes (DLA)

Sug Vend ... Sugden on Vendors and Purchasers (DLA)
Sug V & P... Sugden on Vendors and Purchasers [14 eds.] [1805-62] (DLA)
SUH .... Rockland, ME [Location identifier] [FAA] (FAAL)
SUHL .... Sylvania Ultrahigh-Level Logic (IEEE)
SUHS .... Susitna Hydro Studies [A publication]
SUI .... Safe Use Instructions [General Motors Corp.]
SUI .... Standard Universal Identifying Number
SUI .... State University of Iowa [Later, University of Iowa]
SUI .... Suihwa [Republic of China] [Seismograph station code, US Geological Survey] (SEIS)
SUI .... Summit Resources [Toronto Stock Exchange symbol]
SUIAP .... Simplified Unit Invoice Accounting Plan
SUICA .... Soul Uitae Chapchi [A publication]
Suicide Life Threat Behav ... Suicide and Life-Threatening Behavior [A publication]
SUID .... Sudden Unexpected Infant Death [Medicine]
Suid-Afr Tydskr Geneesk ... Suid-Afrikaanse Tydskrif vir Geneeskunde [A publication]
Suid-Afr Tydskr Landbouwetenskap ... Suid-Afrikaanse Tydskrif vir Landbouwetenskap [A publication]
SUIP .... Support Unit Improvement Program (MCD)
SUIV .... Suivant [Following] [French]
SUJ .... Satu Mare [Romania] [Airport symbol] (OAG)
SUJ .... Side Upset Jaw (MSA)
SUJB .... Southern Universities Joint Board [for school examinations] [British]
SUK .... Suckling Hill [Alaska] [Seismograph station code, US Geological Survey] (SEIS)
Suk .... Sukkah (BJA)
suk .... Sukuma [MARC language code] [Library of Congress] (LCCP)
SUKGA ...... Sumitomo Kikai Giho [A publication]
SUKLO ...... Senior United Kingdom Liaison Officer [Later, BJSM] [British]
SUKUA ...... Subtropicheskie Kul'tury [A publication]
SUL .... Per lo Studio e l'Uso del Latino [A publication]
SUL .... Simplified User Logistics (AABC)
SUL .... Small University Libraries
SUL .... Sophia University [UTLAS symbol]
SuL .... Sprache und Literatur [A publication]
SUL .... Standard User Labels [Data processing]
SUL .... State University of New York, Union List of Serials, Albany, NY [OCLC symbol] (OCLC)
SUL .... Sui [Pakistan] [Airport symbol] (OAG)
SUL .... Sulpetro Ltd. [Toronto Stock Exchange symbol]
SUL .... Sulphur Creek [New Britain] [Seismograph station code, US Geological Survey] (SEIS)
SULBF .... Sulpetro Ltd. Cl B [NASDAQ symbol] (NQ)
SULCL .... Set Up in Less than Carloads [Freight]
SuLEXCo ... Sulphur Export Corporation [An association] (EA)
SULF .... Southern United Life Insurance [NASDAQ symbol] (NQ)
SULF .... Speedball Up-Range Launch Facility [Army] (AABC)
Sulfuric Acid Ind ... Sulfuric Acid and Industry [Japan] [A publication]
SULINAC ... Super Linear Accelerator [Space flight simulator]
SULIS .... Syracuse University Libraries Information System [Syracuse University Libraries] [New York] [Information service] (EISS)
Sull .... Pro Sulla [of Cicero] [Classical studies] (OCD)
Sull .... Sulla [of Plutarch] [Classical studies] (OCD)
Sullivan ..... Smith's New Hampshire Reports (DLA)
Sull Lect ..... Sullivan's Lectures on Constitution and Laws of England (DLA)
Sulphur Inst J ... Sulphur Institute. Journal [A publication]
Su LR .... Suffolk University. Law Review [A publication]
SULT .... Sultan
Sulzer Tech Rev ... Sulzer Technical Review [A publication]
Sum. .... Hale's Summary of the Pleas of the Crown [England] (DLA)
SUM .... Saturn Umbilical Maintenance [NASA]
SUM .... Save Uganda Movement
SUM .... Servicio Universitario Mundial [World University Service]
SUM .... Set-Up [Control] Module [Telecommunications] (TEL)
SUM .... Shallow Underwater Missile
SUM .... Socialist Unionist Movement [Al Haraka at Tawhidiyya al Ishtirakiyya] [Syrian] (PPW)
SUM .... Solar Ultraviolet Monitor (MCD)
SUM .... Sullivan Mines, Inc. [Toronto Stock Exchange symbol]
SUM .... Sume [Take] [Pharmacy]
Sum. .... Sumerian (BJA)
SUM .... Summary (AABC)
SUM .... Summer
SUM .... Summing
SUM .... Summit Energy, Inc. [American Stock Exchange symbol]
SUM .... Summoned
Sum. .... Sumner's United States Circuit Court Reports (DLA)
SUM .... Sumoto [Japan] [Seismograph station code, US Geological Survey] (SEIS)
SUM .... Sumter [South Carolina] [Airport symbol] (OAG)
SUM .... Surface-to-Underwater Missile
SUM .... System Check and Utility Master (MCD)
SUM .... System Utilization Monitor [Data processing]
SUM .... University of South Carolina, School of Medicine, Columbia, SC [OCLC symbol] (OCLC)
SUMA .... Summa Medical [NASDAQ symbol] (NQ)

Sumatra Res B ... Sumatra Research Bulletin [A publication]
SUMC .... Space Ultrareliable Modular Computer
SUMCA ..... Summer & Company Cl A [NASDAQ symbol] (NQ)
SUMCM ..... Summary Court-Martial
SUMCMO ..... Summary Court-Martial Order
Sum Dec .... Summary Decisions [Bengal, India] (DLA)
SUMED ...... Suez-Mediterranean [Pipeline]
SUMEX ...... Stanford University Medical Experimental Computer Project [Stanford University] [Research center] (RCD)
SUMH .... Summit Health Ltd. [NASDAQ symbol] (NQ)
SUMI .... Sumitomo Bank of California [NASDAQ symbol] (NQ)
SUMIT .... Standard Utility Means for Information Transformation [Data processing]
Sumitomo ... Sumitomo Bank Review [A publication]
Sumitomo Bull Ind Health ... Sumitomo Bulletin of Industrial Health [A publication]
Sumitomo Elec Tech Rev ... Sumitomo Electric Technical Review [A publication]
Sumitomo Electr Rev ... Sumitomo Electric Review [Japan] [A publication]
Sumitomo Electr Tech Rev ... Sumitomo Electric Technical Review [A publication]
Sumitomo Light Metal Tech Rep ... Sumitomo Light Metal Technical Reports [A publication]
Sumitomo Mach ... Sumitomo Machinery [Japan] [A publication]
Sumitomo Met ... Sumitomo Metals [A publication]
Sum Jur ..... Sumarios Juridicos. Compilacao de Doutrina e Jurisprudencia dos Tribunais Comuns e Especiais [Lousa, Portugal] (DLA)
Sum List .... Sumarski List [A publication]
SUMM .... Summary
SUMM .... Summer
SUMM .... Summitatis [Summits or Tops] [Pharmacy] (ROG)
SUMMA ..... Superconducting Magnetic Mirror Apparatus
SUMMAC ... Stanford University Modified Markers and Cell Method
Summa Phytopathol ... Summa Phytopathologica [A publication]
SUMMCO ... Summary Court-Martial Order
Summer Comput Simul Conf Proc ... Summer Computer Simulation Conference. Proceedings [A publication]
Summerfield ... Summerfield's Reports [21 Nevada] (DLA)
Summerfield S ... S. Summerfield's Reports [21 Nevada] (DLA)
Summer Inst Part Phys Proc ... Summer Institute on Particle Physics. Proceedings [A publication]
SUMMIT ..... Sperry UNIVAC Minicomputer Management of Interactive Terminals
SUMMIT ..... Supervisor of Multiprograming, Multiprocessing, Interactive Time Sharing [Data processing] (IEEE)
Summit Mag ... Summit Magazine [A publication]
Summ Proc Aust Conf Nucl Tech Anal ... Australian Conference on Nuclear Techniques of Analysis. Summary of Proceedings [A publication]
Summ Proc West Cotton Prod Conf ... Summary of Proceedings. Western Cotton Production Conference [A publication]
Summ Rep Electrotech Lab ... Summary Reports of the Electrotechnical Laboratory [Japan] [A publication]
Sumn .... Sumner's United States Circuit Court Reports (DLA)
Sumner ...... Sumner's United States Circuit Court Reports (DLA)
SUMNS ...... Summons (ROG)
Sumn Ves ... Sumner's Edition of Vesey's Reports (DLA)
SUMPAC .... Southampton University Man-Powered Aircraft [British]
SUMPM ...... Summary Performance Measure (MCD)
Sum Proc Soil Sci Soc NC ... Summary of Proceedings. Soil Science Society of North Carolina [A publication]
Sum Rep .... Sumner's United States Circuit Court Reports (DLA)
Sum Rep Electrotech Lab (Tokyo Japan) ... Summaries of Reports. Electrotechnical Laboratory (Tokyo, Japan) [A publication]
SUMS .... Shuttle Upper-Atmosphere Mass Spectrometer (MCD)
SUMS .... Specialized Unit Maintenance Support (MCD)
SUMS .... Sperry UNIVAC Material System
SUMS .... Summons (ROG)
SUMSTAT ... Summary Statistical Data [Federal government]
SUMT .... Sequential Unconstrained Minimization Technique
SUM TAL ... Sumat Talem [Take One Like This] [Pharmacy]
Sum UCCR ... Sumner's United States Circuit Court Reports (DLA)
Sum Ves .... Sumner's Edition of Vesey's Reports (DLA)
SUN .... Hailey, ID [Location identifier] [FAA] (FAAL)
SUN .... OPTEVFOR Detachment, Sunnyvale CA [Navy] (CAAL)
SUN .... Serum Urea Nitrogen [Clinical medicine]
SUN .... Spanish Universal Network [Cable-television system]
SUN .... Spiritual Unity of Nations [An association]
SUN .... Standard Units and Nomenclature (MCD)
SUN .... State University of Nebraska
SUN .... Sun Aire Lines [Palm Springs, CA] [FAA designator] (FAAC)
SUN .... Sun Co., Inc. [NYSE symbol]
SUN .... Sun Life Assurance Company of Canada [UTLAS symbol]
SUN .... Sun Valley [Idaho] [Airport symbol] (OAG)
sun .... Sundanese [MARC language code] [Library of Congress] (LCCP)
SUN .... Sunday (AFM)
SUN .... Sundstrand-Turbo (AAG)
SUN .... Sunnyside [Utah] [Seismograph station code, US Geological Survey] [Closed] (SEIS)

SUN............ Sunset Railway Co. [*AAR code*]
SUN............ Suntec Ventures Ltd. [*Vancouver Stock Exchange symbol*]
SUN............ Suntech Library and Information Center, Marcus Hook, PA
     [*OCLC symbol*]   (OCLC)
SUN............ Switching Unit
SUN............ Symbols, Units, and Nomenclature [*Commission*] [*IUPAC*]
SUN............ Symphony for United Nations   (EA)
SUN............ Union of Soviet Socialist Republics [*Three-letter standard
     code*]   (CNC)
SUNA........ Seafarers' International Union of North America [*AFL-
     CIO*]   (EA)
SUNA........ Sudan News Agency
SUNA........ Switchmen's Union of North America [*Later, United
     Transportation Union*]
SUNAT....... Scandinavian Union for Non-Alcoholic Traffic   (EA)
SUnBH....... Scripta Universitatis atque Bibliotecae Hierosolymitanarum
     Jerusalem   (BJA)
SUNCOR.... Sun Oil Company of Radnor [*Pennsylvania*]
SUND........ Sunday
SUND........ Sundries
SUNDAE.... Stanford University Division of Aero Engineering   (AAG)
Sunday M... Sunday Magazine [*A publication*]
Sund M...... Sunday Magazine [*A publication*]
SUNDS........ Sundries   (ROG)
SUNF........ Sunstar Foods [*NASDAQ symbol*]   (NQ)
SUNFED..... Special United Nations Fund for Economic Development
SUNI.......... Southern Universities Nuclear Institute
SUNI.......... Suncoast Plastics, Incorporated [*NASDAQ symbol*]   (NQ)
SUNIST...... Serveur Universitaire National de l'Information Scientifique et
     Technique [*Online service*]
Sunk.......... Single, Unemployed, No Kids [*Lifestyle classification*]
SUNN........ SunGroup, Inc. [*NASDAQ symbol*]   (NQ)
SUNO........ Southern University in New Orleans
SUNOCO.... Sun Oil Company [*Later, Sun Co., Inc.*]
SUNSAT..... Sun-Energy Collecting Satellite
Sunshine State Agric Res Rep ... Sunshine State Agricultural Research
     Report [*A publication*]
Sunshine State Agr Res Rep ... Sunshine State Agricultural Research
     Report. Florida University Agricultural Experiment Station
     [*A publication*]
SUNSPOT ... Study of Utilization Systems, Policies, and Techniques   (MCD)
SUNSW...... Sunshine Mining Wts [*NASDAQ symbol*]   (NQ)
SUNT.......... Studien zur Umwelt des Neuen Testament [*Goettingen*] [*A
     publication*]
SunT .... Sunday Times [*A publication*]
Sun Times ... Sunday Times [*A publication*]
SUNWACD ... Swaleureniddwharfeairecalderdon [*British town*]
Sun Wld ..... Sun World [*A publication*]
Sun Work Br ... Sun at Work in Britain [*A publication*]
SUNX.......... Sunbelt Exploration [*NASDAQ symbol*]   (NQ)
SUNY........ State University of New York [*Computer retrieval and control
     projects*] [*Albany, NY*]
SUNYA....... State University of New York at Albany
SUNYAB.... State University of New York at Buffalo
SUNY BCN ... State University of New York Biomedical Communication
     Network   (EA)
SUNY/OCLC ... State University of New York Online Computer Library
     Center [*Library network*]
SunyP......... State University of New York Press, Albany, NY [*Library
     symbol*] [*Library of Congress*]   (LCLS)
SUO............ Senior Under-Officer [*Royal Military Academy*] [*British*]   (ROG)
SUO............ Shell Oil Co. [*Toronto Stock Exchange symbol*]
SUO............ Society of University Otolaryngologists [*Later, SOU-
     HNS*]   (EA)
SUO............ Sun River [*Oregon*] [*Airport symbol*] [*Obsolete*]   (OAG)
SUO-HNS... Society of University Otolaryngologists - Head and Neck
     Surgeons [*Chicago, IL*]   (EA)
Suom Elainlaakaril ... Suomen Elainlaakarilehti [*A publication*]
Suomen Elainlaakril Fin Veterinartidskr ... Suomen Elainlaakarilehti. Finsk
     Veterinartidskrift [*A publication*]
Suomen Kem A B ... Suomen Kemistilehti (A, B) [*A publication*]
Suomen Kemistil A ... Suomen Kemistilehti A [*A publication*]
Suomen Maataloust Seura Maataloust Aikakausk ... Suomen
     Maataloustieteellinen Seura. Maataloustieteellinen
     Aikakauskirj [*A publication*]
Suomen Maataloust Seuran Julk ... Suomen Maataloustieteellisen Seuran
     Julkaisuja [*A publication*]
Suom Hammaslaak Toim ... Suomen Hammaslaakariseuran Toimituksia [*A
     publication*]
Suom Hammaslaak Toimi ... Suomen Hammaslaakariseuran Toimituksia [*A
     publication*]
Suom Hyonteistiet Aikak ... Suomen Hyonteistieteellinen Aikakauskirja [*A
     publication*]
Suom Kalatalous ... Suomen Kalatalous [*A publication*]
Suom Kemistil A ... Suomen Kemistilehti A [*A publication*]
Suom Kemistil B ... Suomen Kemistilehti B [*A publication*]
Suom Kemistiseuran Tied ... Suomen Kemistiseuran Tiedonantoja [*A
     publication*]
Suom Maataloustiet Seuran Julk ... Suomen Maataloustieteellisen Seuran
     Julkaisuja [*A publication*]

Suom Maatal Seur Julk ... Suomen Maataloustieteellisen Seuran Julkaisuja
     [*A publication*]
Suom Psykiatr ... Suomalaista Psykiatriaa [*A publication*]
SUP............ ABC Airlines, Inc. [*DFW Airport*] [*Mesquite, TX*] [*FAA
     designator*]   (FAAC)
SUP............ Sailors' Union of the Pacific
SUP............ Single Unit Pack [*for vehicles*]
SUP............ Single Unit Package [*Pharmacy*]
SUP............ Single Unit Parameter
SUP............ Special Utility Program [*NASA*]   (KSC)
SUP............ Spisy University J. E. Purkyne [*A publication*]
SUP............ Standard Unit of Processing [*Data processing*]
SUP............ Statistical Utility Program
SUP............ Superfine
SUP............ Superior   (AFM)
SUP............ Superior Industries International, Inc. [*American Stock
     Exchange symbol*]
SUP............ Superior Oil Co., Exploration Library, Houston, TX [*OCLC
     symbol*]   (OCLC)
SUP............ Superlative
SUP............ Supine
SUP............ Supplement   (AFM)
SUP Ct J..... Supply   (AFM)
SUP............ Support
SUP............ Suppress   (DEN)
SUP............ Supra [*Above*] [*Latin*]
Sup............ Supraphon [*Record label*] [*Czechoslovakia*]
SUP............ Supreme
SUP............ Supreme Resources, Inc. [*Vancouver Stock Exchange symbol*]
SUP............ System Utilization Procedure
SUPA......... Society of University Patent Administrators   (EA)
SUPAD....... Supplementary Address   (MCD)
SUPADS.... Suppression of Air Defense System   (MCD)
SUPANX.... Supply Annex
SUPARCO ... Space and Upper Atmospheric Research Committee
     [*Pakistan*]
SUPCE....... Syracuse University Publications in Continuing Education   (EA)
SUPCEN..... Supply Center
SUPCHG... Supercharge   (FAAC)
SUPCOM.... Support Command [*Army*]
SUPCOM.... Supreme Command
SUPCON ... Superintending Constructor
SUPCOSTINS ... Supervisory Cost Inspector [*Navy*]
Sup Court Rep ... Supreme Court Reporter   (DLA)
SUPCRIT.... Super Critical   (MCD)
Sup Ct....... Supreme Court   (DLA)
Sup Ct....... Supreme Court Reporter [*National Reporter System*]   (DLA)
Sup Ct App ... Supreme Court Appeals [*India*]   (DLA)
Sup Ct Hist Soc'y YB ... Supreme Court Historical Society. Yearbook   (DLA)
Sup Ct J ... Supreme Court Journal [*India*]   (DLA)
Sup Ct L Rev ... Supreme Court Law Review   (DLA)
Sup Ct MR ... Supreme Court Monthly Review [*India*]   (DLA)
Sup Ct Pr ... Supreme Court Practice   (DLA)
Sup Ct R.... Supreme Court Reports [*India*]   (DLA)
Sup Ct R..... United States Supreme Court Rule   (DLA)
Sup Ct Rep ... Supreme Court Reporter   (DLA)
Sup Ct Repr ... Supreme Court Reporter   (DLA)
Sup Ct Rev ... Supreme Court Review [*A publication*]
Sup Ct R (NY) ... New York Supreme Court Reports   (DLA)
SUPCUR .... Superimposed Current
SUPD......... Supradur Companies [*NASDAQ symbol*]   (NQ)
SUPDEP ... Supply Depot
SUPDIV...... Supervisor of Diving [*Navy*]
SUPDT ...... Superintendent   (ADA)
SUPE......... Superior Electric Co. [*NASDAQ symbol*]   (NQ)
SUPER ...... Superannuation Pension [*Australian*]   (DSUE)
SUPER ...... Superficial
SUPER ...... Superfine
SUPER ...... Superimpose
SUPER ...... Superintendent
SUPER ...... Superior
Super .... Superior Court   (DLA)
Super .... Superior Court Reports   (DLA)
SUPER ...... Supernumerary
SUPER ...... Supersede   (MUGU)
SUPER ...... Supervisor   (DSUE)
Super Ct .... Superior Court   (DLA)
Super Ct App Div ... Superior Court, Appellate Division   (DLA)
Super Ct Ch Div ... Superior Court, Chancery Division   (DLA)
Super Ct Law Div ... Superior Court, Law Division   (DLA)
Super Ct Rep ... Superior Court Reports [*New York, Pennsylvania,
     etc.*]   (DLA)
Super Ct (RI) ... Rhode Island Superior Court   (DLA)
SUPERFL ... Superficial   (ROG)
SUPERHET ... Superheterodyne
SUPERL ..... Superlative
Super Mgt ... Supervisory Management [*A publication*]
Supermkt Bus ... Supermarket Business [*A publication*]
Super News ... Supermarket News [*A publication*]
SUPERNOVA ... [*A*] NOVA Computer [*Data General Corp.*]
Superphosphat-Mitt ... Superphosphat-Mitteilungen [*A publication*]

SUPERSTR ... Superstructure
Superv Manage ... Supervisory Management [*A publication*]
Superv Nurse ... Supervisor Nurse [*A publication*]
SUPF .... Superior Foods, Inc. [*NASDAQ symbol*]   (NQ)
SUPG .... System Utilization Procedural Guide
SUP GOSSYP ... Super Gossypium [*On Cotton Wool*] [*Pharmacy*]
SUPHTD ..... Superheated   (AAG)
SUPHTR ..... Superheater   (AAG)
SUPIER ...... Supply Pier [*Navy*]
SUPINSMAT ... Supervising Inspector of Naval Material
SUPINSP .... Supply Inspection [*Navy*]   (NVT)
SUPINTREP ... Supplementary Intelligence Report   (AABC)
SUPIR .... Supplementary Photographic Interpretation Report [*Military*]
Sup Jud Ct ... Supreme Judicial Court [*Massachusetts*]   (DLA)
Supl Antropol ... Suplemento Antropologico [*A publication*]
SUP LINT ... Super Linteum [*On Lint*] [*Pharmacy*]
SUPMG ...... Southern University Press Marketing Group [*Acronym is pronounced "soupmug"*]
SUPMTL ..... Supplemental
SUPNZ .... Socialist Unity Party of New Zealand
SUPO .... Super Power [*Water boiler*] [*Nuclear reactor*]
SUPO .... Supply Officer
SUPOHDU ... Supply from Stock on Hand or Due In
SUPOPS ..... Supply Operations [*DoD*]
Supp .... New York Supplement Reports   (DLA)
SUPP .... Sarawak United People's Party [*Malaysian*]   (PPW)
SUPP .... Supplement   (KSC)
Supp .... Supplices [*of Euripides*] [*Classical studies*]   (OCD)
Supp .... Supplices Contra Thebas [*of Aeschylus*] [*Classical studies*]   (OCD)
SUPP .... Supply
SUPP .... Support   (AAG)
SUPP .... Suppositorium [*Suppository*] [*Pharmacy*]
supp .... Suppurative [*Medicine*]
SUPPACT ... Support Activity
Supp Aesch ... Supplementum Aeschyleum [*A publication*]   (OCD)
SUPPL .... Supplement   (AABC)
Suppl .... Supplementary   (DLA)
Suppl Acta Agric Scand ... Acta Agriculturae Scandinavica. Supplementum [*A publication*]
Suppl Acta Univ Carol Biol ... Supplementum. Acta Universitatis Carolinae. Biologica [*A publication*]
Suppl Agrokem Talajt ... Supplementum. Agrokemia es Talajtan [*A publication*]
Suppl Annls Agric Fenn ... Annales Agriculturae Fenniae. Supplementum [*A publication*]
Suppl Annls Gembloux ... Supplement. Annales de Gembloux [*A publication*]
Suppl Annls Inst Pasteur (Paris) ... Supplement. Annales de l'Institut Pasteur (Paris) [*A publication*]
Suppl Certif Eng ... Supplement. Certificated Engineer [*A publication*]
Suppl Collect Sci Works Charles Univ Fac Med Hradec Kralove ... Supplement to Collection of Scientific Works. Charles University Faculty of Medicine. Hradec Kralove [*A publication*]
Suppl For Rep (Sixth) Discuss Meet (Edinb) ... Supplement to Forestry. Report of the Sixth Discussion Meeting (Edinburgh) [*A publication*]
Suppl Geophys ... Supplement. Geophysics [*A publication*]
Suppl Israel J Bot ... Supplement. Israel Journal of Botany [*A publication*]
Suppl J Phys Soc Jap ... Supplement. Journal of the Physical Society of Japan [*A publication*]
Suppl LC Subj Head ... Supplement. LC [*United States Library of Congress*] Subject Headings [*A publication*]
Suppl Nord Jordbrforsk ... Nordisk Jordbrugsforskning. Supplement [*A publication*]
SUPPLOT ... Supplemental Plot   (MCD)
Suppl Prog Theor Phys ... Supplement. Progress of Theoretical Physics [*A publication*]
Suppl Ric Biol Selvaggina ... Supplemento alle Ricerche di Biologia della Selvaggina [*A publication*]
Suppl Ric Sci ... Supplemento a la Ricerca Scientifica [*A publication*]
Suppl Sb Ved Pr Lek Fak Univ Karlovy Hradci Kralove ... Supplementum. Sborniku Vedeckych Praci Lekarske Fakulty University Karlovy. Hradci Kralove [*A publication*]
Supplta Ent ... Supplementa Entomologica [*A publication*]
Sup Pop Sci Mo ... Supplement. Popular Science Monthly [*A publication*]
SUPPOS ..... Suppository [*Pharmacy*]
Supp Pr T P ... Supplement. Progress of Theoretical Physics [*A publication*]
SUPPR .... Suppression   (MSA)
Supp Rev ... Supplement to the Revision   (DLA)
Supp Rev St ... Supplement to the Revised Statutes   (DLA)
SUPPS .... Regional Supplementary Procedures [*Aviation code*]
SUPPS .... Supplementary Procedures   (MCD)
SUPPT .... Supply Point [*Military*]
Supp Ves Jun ... Supplement to Vesey, Junior's, Reports   (DLA)
SUPR .... Superintendent   (ROG)
SUPR .... Superior   (AABC)
SUPR .... Supervisor
SUPR .... Suppress
SUPR .... Supreme

SUPRAD ..... Supplementary Radio   (NG)
Supr Court ... Supreme Court Review [*A publication*]
Supr Ct ...... Pennsylvania Superior Court Reports   (DLA)
Supr Ct Rep ... Supreme Court Reporter   (DLA)
Supreme Court Rev ... Supreme Court Review [*A publication*]
SUPRN .... Suppression
SUPROX ..... Successive Approximation   (IEEE)
SUPRSTR ... Superstructure   (AAG)
SUPSAL ...... Supervisor of Salvage [*Navy*]
SUPSALV ... Supervisor of Salvage [*Navy*]
SUPSD .... Supersede   (AFM)
SUPSENS ... Supersensitive
SUPSGT ..... Supply Sergeant [*Marine Corps*]
SUPSHIP ... Supervisor of Shipbuilding [*Navy*]
Sup Stud .... Superior Student [*A publication*]
SUPSYSCOM ... Supply System Command [*Navy*]
SUPT .... Specialized Undergraduate Pilot Training [*Air Force*]
SUPT .... Superintendent
SUPT .... Support   (CINC)
SUPTG .... Supporting   (AAG)
SUPTNAVOBSY ... Superintendent, Naval Observatory
Sup Trib ..... Supremo Tribunal [*Supreme Court of Appeal*]   (DLA)
SUPUSLL ... Stanford University. Publications. University Series. Languages and Literatures [*A publication*]
SUPV .... Supervisor   (AAG)
SUPVR .... Supervisor   (AFM)
Supvry Mgmt ... Supervisory Management [*A publication*]
SUPVSN ..... Supervision
SUPWB ...... Socialist Unity Party of West Berlin [*Germany*]
SUPX .... Supertex, Inc. [*NASDAQ symbol*]   (NQ)
SUPY .... Supervisory   (DEN)
Sur .... Revista Sur [*A publication*]
SUR .... Seemingly Unrelated Regression [*Statistics*]
SUR .... Small Unit Radio [*Military*]   (INF)
SUR .... Speech Understanding Research
SUR .... Start-Up Rate   (NRCH)
SUR .... State University Railroad Co. [*AAR code*]
SUR .... Sul Ross State University, Library, Alpine, TX [*OCLC symbol*]   (OCLC)
Sur .... Sural Nerve
SUR .... Surcharge   (ROG)
Sur .... Surety   (DLA)
SUR .... Surface   (AABC)
SUR .... Surgery
SUR .... Surinam [*Three-letter standard code*]   (CNC)
SUR .... Surlari [*Romania*] [*Geomagnetic observatory code*]
SUR .... Surplus [*Business and trade*]
SUR .... Surround
SUR .... Sutherland [*South Africa*] [*Seismograph station code, US Geological Survey*]   (SEIS)
Sur .... Thiouracil [*Also, SUra*] [*Biochemistry*]
SURA .... Shan United Revolutionary Army [*Burmese*]   (PD)
SUra .... Thiouracil [*Also, Sur*] [*Biochemistry*]
SURANO ..... Surface RADAR and Navigation Operation
SURBAT ..... Simultaneous Unlimited Rigorous Block Analytical Triangulation [*Apollo program*] [*NASA*]
SURC .... Syracuse University Research Corporation
SURCAL ..... Surveillance Calibration Satellite
SURCAP .... Surviving Capability Plan [*Military*]
SURCO ...... State University Research Center at Oswego [*State University College at Oswego*] [*Research center*]   (RCD)
Sur Ct .... Surrogate's Court   (DLA)
SURE .... Sensor Upgrade and Refurbishment Effort [*Marine Corps*]   (MCD)
SURE .... Shuttle Users Review and Evaluation [*NASA*]   (NASA)
SURE .... Simplicity, Useability, Reliability, Economy
SURE .... Subsystem Replacement
SURE .... Sulphate Regional Experiment [*Electric Power Research Institute*]
SURE .... Surgicare Corp. [*NASDAQ symbol*]   (NQ)
SURE .... Symbolic Utilities Revenue Environment [*IBM Corp.*]
SUREJ .... Surface Ship Electromagnetic Jammer
SUREPI ...... Surface Ship Electromagnetic Passive Intercept System
SUREQ .... Submit Requisition   (NOAA)
SURF .... Antisubmarine Warfare Barrier Surface Patrol Ship [*Navy*]   (NVT)
SURF .... Standard UNREP [*Underway Replenishment*] Receiving Fixture [*Navy*]   (NVT)
SURF .... Support of User Records and Files [*Data processing*]
SURF .... Surface
surf .... Surfactant
SURF .... Synchrotron Ultraviolet Radiation Facility [*National Bureau of Standards*]
SURFAC ..... Surveillance Facility [*Navy*]
Surface Sci ... Surface Science [*A publication*]
Surface Techn ... Surface Technology [*A publication*]
Surfacing J ... Surfacing Journal [*United Kingdom*] [*A publication*]
Surfactant Sci Ser ... Surfactant Science Series [*A publication*]
Surf Coat ... Surface Coatings [*A publication*]
Surf Colloid Sci ... Surface and Colloid Science [*A publication*]

Surf Defect Prop Solids ... Surface and Defect Properties of Solids [*A publication*]
SURF DET TRKR ... Surface Detector/Tracker [*Navy*] (CAAL)
Surf Interface Anal ... Surface and Interface Analysis [*A publication*]
Surf J .... Surfacing Journal [*A publication*]
Surf Min Reclam Symp ... Surface Mining and Reclamation Symposia [*A publication*]
SURFPA ..... Antisubmarine Warfare Barrier Surface Patrol Area [*Navy*] (NVT)
SURFPZ ..... Antisubmarine Warfare Barrier Surface Patrol Zone [*Navy*] (NVT)
Surf Sci ...... Surface Science [*A publication*]
SURFSIDE ... Small Unified Reactor Facility Systems for Isotopes, Desalting, and Electricity [*Nuclear energy*]
Surf Tech ... Surface Technology [*A publication*]
Surf Technol ... Surface Technology [*A publication*]
SURFWARDEVGRU ... Surface Warfare Development Group [*Also, SWDG*] [*Navy*]
SURG .... Surgeon [*or Surgery or Surgical*] (AFM)
SURG .... Surgery Centers Corp. [*NASDAQ symbol*] (NQ)
Surg Annu ... Surgery Annual [*A publication*]
Surg Bus .... Surgical Business [*A publication*]
Surg Clin N Am ... Surgical Clinics of North America [*A publication*]
Surg Clin North Am ... Surgical Clinics of North America [*A publication*]
Surg Cl NA ... Surgical Clinics of North America [*A publication*]
SURGE .... SEASAT Users Group of Europe (MSC)
SURGE .... Sorting, Updating, Report Generating, Etc. [*IBM Corp.*] [*Data processing*]
SURGEN .... [*The*] Surgeon General [*Army, Air Force*]
Surg Forum ... Surgical Forum [*A publication*]
Surg Gastroenterol ... Surgical Gastroenterology [*A publication*]
Surg Gynec and Obst ... Surgery, Gynecology, and Obstetrics [*A publication*]
Surg Gynecol Obstet ... Surgery, Gynecology, and Obstetrics [*A publication*]
Surg Gyn Ob ... Surgery, Gynecology, and Obstetrics [*A publication*]
Surgical ..... Surgical Business [*A publication*]
Surg Ital ..... Surgery in Italy [*A publication*]
Surg Neurol ... Surgical Neurology [*A publication*]
Surg Technol ... Surgical Technologist [*A publication*]
Surg Ther ... Surgical Therapy [*Japan*] [*A publication*]
SURI .... Syracuse University Research Institute (MCD)
SURIC .... Surface Ship Integrated Control System [*Obsolete*] [*Navy*]
Surinaam ... Surinaamse Landbouw [*A publication*]
SURISS ..... Sheffield Urban and Regional Instructional Simulation System [*British*]
SURMAC .... Surface Magnetic Confinement (MCD)
SUROB .... Surf Observation Report [*Navy*] (NVT)
SURP .... Submerged Unmanned Recovery Platform (NVT)
SURPIC ..... Surface Picture [*AMVER*] [*Coast Guard*]
SURR .... Surrender
SURR .... Surrey [*County in England*]
SURR .... Surrogate
Surr Ct Proc Act ... Surrogate's Court Procedure Act (DLA)
SURRD .... Surrendered (ROG)
Surrey Arch Coll ... Surrey Archaeological Collections [*A publication*]
SURRO .... Surrogate (ADA)
SURS .... Surface Export Cargo System [*Military*] (AABC)
SURS .... Surface Export Traffic System
SURSAN .... Superintendencia de Urbanizacao e Saneamento [*Brazil*]
SURSAT ..... Satellite Surveillance Program [*Canada*] (MSC)
SURSAT ..... Survey Satellite [*NASA*]
SURTAC ..... NORAD Surveillance and Tactical Network (MCD)
SURTASS ... Surveillance Towed Array SONAR System
SURTEMS ... Surface Temperature Measuring System
SURTOPS ... Surveillance Training and Operating Procedures Standardization [*Military*] (CAAL)
Surtsey Res Prog Rep ... Surtsey Research Progress Report [*A publication*]
SURV .... Standard Underwater Research Vehicle
SURV .... Surveillance (AAG)
SURV .... Survey (AABC)
SURV .... Surveyor
SURV .... Survival (AFM)
SURV .... Survival Technology [*NASDAQ symbol*] (NQ)
SURV .... Surviving
SURVAL ..... Simulator Universal Radio Variability Library
Surv Biol Prog ... Survey of Biological Progress [*A publication*]
Surv Bus .... Survey of Business [*United States*] [*A publication*]
Surv Cur Bus ... Survey of Current Business [*A publication*]
Surv Curr Bus ... Survey of Current Business [*A publication*]
Surv Curr Busin ... Survey of Current Business [*A publication*]
Survey Bus (Univ Tenn) ... Survey of Business (University of Tennessee) [*A publication*]
Survey Calif L ... Survey of California Law (DLA)
Survey Cur Bus ... Survey of Current Business [*A publication*]
Survey Current Bus ... Survey of Current Business [*A publication*]
Survey G .... Survey Graphic [*A publication*]
Survey Progr Chem ... Survey of Progress in Chemistry [*A publication*]
Surv High Energy Phys ... Surveys in High Energy Physics [*Switzerland*] [*A publication*]
SURVIAC ... Survivability/Vulnerability Information Analysis Center (MCD)
SURVL .... Surveillance (AFM)

Surv-Local Gov Technol ... Surveyor-Local Government Technology [*A publication*]
SURVM ...... Surveillance and Maintenance [*Army*] (AABC)
Surv & Map ... Surveying and Mapping [*A publication*]
Surv Mapp ... Surveying and Mapping [*A publication*]
Surv Munic Cty Eng ... Surveyor and Municipal and County Engineer [*A publication*]
Surv Ophthalmol ... Survey of Ophthalmology [*A publication*]
SURVOPS ... Survey Operations [*Navy*] (NVT)
SURVOR ..... Survivor
Surv Pap Horace Lamb Centre Oceanogr Res ... Survey Paper. Horace Lamb Centre for Oceanographical Research. Flinders University of South Australia [*A publication*]
Surv Prog Chem ... Survey of Progress in Chemistry [*A publication*]
SURVR .... Surveyor
SURVR .... Survivor (AAG)
SURVRAP ... Surveillance Range Acoustics Prediction System (MCD)
SURVSA ..... Survivable Satellite Communications System (MCD)
SURVSATCOM ... Survivable Satellite Communications System
SURVSUM ... Surveillance Summary Reports (NVT)
SURWAC ... Surface Water Automatic Computer (AAG)
SUS .... St. Louis [*Missouri*] Spirit of St. Louis Airport [*Airport symbol*] [*Obsolete*] (OAG)
SUS .... Saybolt Universal Seconds [*Oil viscosity*]
SUS .... Semiconductor Unilateral Switch (MSA)
SUS .... Signal Underwater Sound
SUS .... Silicon Unilateral Switch
SUS .... Small Ultimate Size [*Telecommunications*] (TEL)
SUS .... Society of University Surgeons [*Denver, CO*] (EA)
SUS .... Sound Underwater Source [*Navy*] (CAAL)
SUS .... Speech Understanding System
SUS .... Startup System [*Nuclear energy*] (NRCH)
SUS .... Stop Unnecessary Spending
SUS .... Studi Urbinati di Storia, Filosofia, e Letteratura [*A publication*]
SUS .... Suit Umbilical System (MCD)
SUS .... Sunshine Columbia [*Vancouver Stock Exchange symbol*]
SUS .... Susaki [*Mitsui*] [*Japan*] [*Seismograph station code, US Geological Survey*] [*Closed*] (SEIS)
Sus .... Susanna [*Apocrypha*] (BJA)
SUS .... Suspect
SUS .... Suspense [*A publication*]
SUS .... Suspicion Law [*Statute permitting policemen to detain individuals suspected of criminal activity*] [*British*]
SUS .... Susquehanna University, Selinsgrove, PA [*OCLC symbol*] (OCLC)
SUS .... Susquehanna University. Studies [*A publication*]
Sus .... Susreti [*A publication*]
SUS .... Sustainer (AAG)
sus .... Susu [*MARC language code*] [*Library of Congress*] (LCCP)
SUSA .... Seventh United States Army
SUSAFFS ... Society of United States Air Force Flight Surgeons
SUSAN ...... System Utilizing Signal-Processing for Automatic Navigation (MCD)
SUSC .... Religieuses de la Sainte - Union des Sacres - Coeurs de Jesus et Marie [*Religious of the Holy Union of the Sacred Hearts*] [*Roman Catholic women's religious order*]
SUS per COLL ... Suspensa per Collum [*Hanging by the Neck*] [*Legal*] [*Latin*] (ROG)
SUS per COLL ... Suspensio per Collum [*Hanged by the Neck*] [*Latin*]
SUSD .... State University of South Dakota
SUSEME .... Superintendencia de Servicos Medicos [*Brazil*]
SUSF .... Samlingar Utgivna av Svenska Fornskriftssallskapet [*A publication*]
SUSFL .... Studi Urbinati di Storia, Filosofia, e Letteratura [*A publication*]
SUSFU .... Situation Unchanged, Still Fouled Up [*Military slang*] [*Bowdlerized version*]
SUSGR .... Southwestern Union for the Study of Great Religions (EA)
SUSH .... Set-Up Sheet
SUSIE .... Stock Updating Sales Invoicing Electronically (IEEE)
SUSIM .... Solar Ultraviolet Spectral Irradiance Monitor (MCD)
SUSIS .... Sport und Sportwissenschaftliche Informationssystem [*Sport and Sports-Scientific Information System*] [*West Germany*] (EISS)
Sus Leg Chron ... Susquehanna Legal Chronicle [*Pennsylvania*] (DLA)
SUSLO ...... Senior United States Liaison Officer [*National Security Agency*]
SUSMOP .... Senior United States Military Observer Palestine
SUSNO .... Senior United States Naval Officer
SUSP .... Suspected [*Passage or line of a work*] [*Literary criticism*] (ROG)
SUSP .... Suspend [*or Suspension*] (AFM)
SUSP .... Suspicion [*FBI standardized term*]
SUSPD .... Suspended
SUSPDNG ... Suspending [*Freight*]
SUSP L .... Suspecta Lectio [*Double Reading*] [*Latin*] (ROG)
Susq LC .... Susquehanna Leading Chronicle [*Pennsylvania*] (DLA)
Susq L Chron ... Susquehanna Legal Chronicle [*Pennsylvania*] (DLA)
Susq Legal Chron ... Susquehanna Legal Chronicle [*Pennsylvania*] (DLA)
Susq Leg Chron ... Susquehanna Legal Chronicle [*Pennsylvania*] (DLA)
Susquehanna Leg Chron (PA) ... Susquehanna Legal Chronicle [*Pennsylvania*] (DLA)
SUSRA .... Steel in the USSR [*A publication*]

SUSREP..... Senior United States Representative to Defense Production Board [*NATO*] (NATG)
SUSS......... Sound Underwater Signal Source (MCD)
SUSS........ Submarine Schoolship [*Navy*] (NVT)
SUSS........ Sussex [*County in England*]
Sussex Arch Coll ... Sussex Archaeological Collections Relating to the Antiquities of the County [*A publication*]
SUST......... Sustainer
SUSTD ...... Sustained [*Legal*] (ROG)
SUSTN ...... Sustain [*Legal*] (ROG)
SUSTN ...... Sustentation [*Ecclesiastical*] (ROG)
SuSu .... Suomalainen Suomi [*A publication*]
SuSuomi..... Suomalainen Suomi [*A publication*]
SuSuV .... Suomalainen Suomi. Kulttuuripolittinen Aikakauskirja/Valvoja [*A publication*]
SUSV......... Small Unit Support Vehicle [*Military*] (RDA)
SUSY's...... Supersymmetric Theories [*Particle physics*]
SUT .... Satellite under Test
SUT .... Set-Up Time
SUT .... Small Unit Transceiver [*Military*] (INF)
SUT .... Society for Underwater Technology [*British*] (EA)
SUT .... Southport, NC [*Location identifier*] [*FAA*] (FAAL)
SUT .... Start-Up Transformer (NRCH)
SUT .... State Unemployment Tax (MCD)
SUT .... Subunit Test
SUT .... Suttsu [*Japan*] [*Seismograph station code, US Geological Survey*] (SEIS)
SUT .... Syndicat Uni du Transport [*United Transportation Union - UTU*] [*Canada*]
SUT .... System under Test (AAG)
SUTARS..... Search Unit Tracing and Recording System
SUTD......... Soviet Union Today [*A publication*]
SUTEC ...... Seneca Underwater Test and Evaluation Center
SUTH......... Sutherland [*County in Scotland*]
Suth .... Sutherland's Calcutta Reports [*India*] (DLA)
Suth App.... Sutherland's Appeal Reports, Small Causes Court [*1861-65*] [*Bengal, India*] (DLA)
Suth Bengal ... Sutherland's Bengal High Court Reports [*India*] (DLA)
Suth Dam.... Sutherland on the Law of Damages (DLA)
Suth FBR.... Sutherland's Bengal Full Bench Reports [*India*] (DLA)
Suth Mis..... India Weekly Reporter, Miscellaneous Appeals (DLA)
Suth PCA... Sutherland's Privy Council Appeals (DLA)
Suth PCJ.... Sutherland's Privy Council Judgments (DLA)
Suth Sp N ... Full Bench Rulings [*Calcutta*] (DLA)
Suth Sp N ... Sutherland's Special Number of Weekly Reporter (DLA)
Suth Stat Const ... Sutherland on Statutes and Statutory Construction (DLA)
Suth St Const ... Sutherland on Statutes and Statutory Construction (DLA)
Suth WR..... Sutherland's Weekly Reporter, Calcutta [*1864-76*] (DLA)
Suth WR Mis ... Sutherland's Weekly Reports, Miscellaneous Appeals [*India*] (DLA)
SUTRASFCO ... Sindicato Unificado de Trabajadores de la Standard Fruit Company [*Honduras*]
SUTT......... Small Unit Training Team [*Military*]
Sutton .... Sutton on Personal Actions at Common Law (DLA)
SUU.......... Fairfield, CA [*Location identifier*] [*FAA*] (FAAL)
SUU.......... Santaquin Canyon [*Utah*] [*Seismograph station code, US Geological Survey*] (SEIS)
SUU.......... Society of University Urologists [*Houston, TX*] (EA)
SUU.......... Suspension Unit (AFM)
SUV .... Small Unilamellar Vesicle [*Pharmacy*] [*Biochemistry*]
SUV .... Sociacated Unilamellar Vesicles
SUV .... Sport-Utility Vehicle [*Type of truck*]
SUV .... Sumpter Valley Railway [*AAR code*]
SUV .... Suva [*Fiji*] [*Seismograph station code, US Geological Survey*] (SEIS)
SUV .... Suva [*Fiji*] [*Airport symbol*] (OAG)
SUVAT ...... Support Unit Vehicle Automatic Tester
SUVCW ...... Sons of Union Veterans of the Civil War (EA)
SUVI.......... Strong Ultraviolet Index
Suvrem Med ... Suvremenna Meditsina [*Bulgaria*] [*A publication*]
SUVSL .... Skrifter Utgivna av Vetenskaps-Societeten i Lund [*A publication*]
SUW .... Struthers Wells Corp. [*American Stock Exchange symbol*]
SUW .... Superior, WI [*Location identifier*] [*FAA*] (FAAL)
SUW .... Surface Warfare (NVT)
SUWC .... Surface Warfare Coordinator [*Also, SWC*] (NVT)
SUWU........ Skilled and Unskilled Workers' Union - Somali Republic
SUX .... Sioux City [*Iowa*] [*Airport symbol*] (OAG)
sux .... Sumerian [*MARC language code*] [*Library of Congress*] (LCCP)
SUY .... State University Railroad Co. [*Later, SUR*] [*AAR code*]
SUY .... Sudureyri [*Iceland*] [*Airport symbol*] (OAG)
s-uy--- .... Uruguay [*MARC geographic area code*] [*Library of Congress*] (LCCP)
SUYR.......... Southampton University Yacht Research Group [*British*]
SUZ .... Suez Petroleum Corp. [*Vancouver Stock Exchange symbol*]
SUZ .... Suria [*Papua New Guinea*] [*Airport symbol*] (OAG)
SV.............. El Salvador [*Two-letter standard code*] (CNC)
SV.............. Safety Valve (AAG)
SV........ Sailing Vessel

SV.............. Sales Voucher [*Business and trade*]
SV.............. Sancta Virgo [*Holy Virgin*] [*Latin*]
SV.............. Sanctitas Vestra [*Your Holiness*] [*Latin*]
SV.............. Saponification Value [*Organic analytical chemistry*]
SV.............. Satellite Virus
SV.............. Saudi Arabian Airlines [*ICAO designator*] (FAAC)
SV.............. Saves [*Baseball*]
SV.............. Savings Transfer [*Banking*]
SV.............. Scalp Vein [*Medicine*]
SV.............. Schedule Variance (MCD)
SV.............. Schweizer Volkskunde [*A publication*]
SV.............. Scuola e Vita [*A publication*]
SV.............. Secondary Valve
SV.............. Secular Variation [*Geophysics*]
SV.............. Security Violation (AAG)
SV.............. Selecta Vision [*RCA brand name for tape cartridges of TV programs*]
SV.............. Selective Volunteer [*Navy*]
SV.............. Selenoid Valve (MCD)
SV.............. Self-Ventilated (MSA)
SV.............. Self Verification
SV.............. Seminal Vesicle [*Anatomy*]
SV.............. Service
SV.............. Set Value
S & V .... Shock and Vibration
SV.............. Shuttle Vehicle [*NASA*] (NASA)
SV.............. Side Valve [*Automotive engineering*]
SV.............. Side View (MSA)
SV.............. Sieve
Sv.............. Sievert [*SI unit for radioactive dose equivalent*]
SV.............. Silicone Varnish
SV.............. Simian Virus
SV.............. Simulated Video (MCD)
SV.............. Single Silk Varnish [*Wire insulation*] (AAG)
SV.............. Single Value
SV.............. Single Vibrations [*Half cycles*]
SV.............. Sinus Venosus [*Anatomy*]
SV.............. Siste, Viator [*Stop, Traveller*] [*Latin*] (ROG)
SV.............. Slide Valve
SV.............. Slovesna Veda [*A publication*]
SV.............. Slowed-Down Video [*RADAR*] (CET)
SV.............. Sluice [*or Stop*] Valve
SV.............. Snake Venom [*Medicine*]
SV.............. Sodium Vapor
SV.............. Soft Valve
SV.............. Solenoid Valve (KSC)
SV.............. Solicited Volunteer [*In drug studies*]
SV.............. Sons of Veterans
SV.............. Sophisticated Vocabulary (AAG)
SV.............. Sosialistisk Valgforbund [*Socialist Electoral Alliance*] [*Norway*] (PPE)
SV.............. Sosialistisk Venstreparti [*Socialist Left Party*] [*Norway*] (PPE)
SV.............. Sotto Voce [*In an Undertone*] [*Music*]
SV.............. Sovetskaia Vostokovedenie [*A publication*]
SV.............. Space Vehicle
SV.............. Space Visualization [*Visual perception*]
SV.............. Specified Value (MCD)
SV.............. Spiritus Vinosus [*Ardent Spirit*] [*Pharmacy*] (ROG)
SV.............. Star of Valour [*British*] (ADA)
SV.............. State Vector (KSC)
SV.............. Status Valid
sV.............. Statvolt [*Also, statV*] [*Electrostatic unit of potential difference*]
SV.............. Stimulation Value [*Psychology*]
SV.............. Stop Valve (NRCH)
SV.............. Stripping Voltammetry [*Electroanalytical chemistry*]
SV.............. Stroke Volume [*Physiology*]
SV.............. Study of Values [*Psychology*]
SV.............. Sub Verbo [*or Sub Voce*] [*Under the Word*] [*Latin*]
SV.............. Subclavian Vein [*Cardiology*]
SV.............. Subdivision Flag [*Navy*] [*British*]
SV.............. Subject-Verb [*Education of the hearing-impaired*]
SV.............. Subjective Vertical [*Neurology*]
S/V .... Supply Valve (MCD)
SV.............. Supraventricular [*Cardiology*]
SV.............. Surface Vessel
S/V .... Surface/Volume [*Ratio*]
S/V .... Surrender Value
S/V .... Survivability/Vulnerability [*Applied to ability of weapon systems to survive attacks*] [*Military*]
SV.............. Suvaguq. Pond Inlet [*A publication*]
sv.............. Swan Islands [*ho (Honduras) used in records cataloged after January 1978*] [*MARC country of publication code*] [*Library of Congress*] (LCCP)
SV.............. Swept Volume
SV.............. Symptomatic Volunteer [*In drug studies*]
SV.............. Synaptic Vesicle [*Neurobiology*]
SVA........... Savoonga [*Alaska*] [*Airport symbol*] (OAG)
SVA........... SEABEE Veterans of America (EA)
SVA........... Sectionalized Vertical Antenna
SVA........... Security and Vulnerability Analysis (MCD)
SVA........... Shared Virtual Area [*Data processing*]

SVA............ Single-Valve First-Actuation [*Nuclear energy*] (NRCH)
SVA............ Solar Vane Actuators
SVA............ Statistical Vibration Analysis
SVA............ Stock Valuation Adjustment [*Business and trade*] (ADA)
SVA............ Sun Valley Airlines (FAAC)
SVA............ Suva [*Fiji*] [*Seismograph station code, US Geological Survey*] (SEIS)
SVAA .... Super Vernier Auto Alert [*Military*] (CAAL)
SVAB.......... Shuttle Vehicle Assembly Building [*NASA*] (NASA)
SVA & C ..... Shuttle Vehicle Assembly and Checkout [*NASA*] (NASA)
SVAD .... Savanna Army Depot [*Illinois*] (AABC)
SVADA....... Savanna Army Depot Activity (AABC)
Sv Aeroplan Ab SAAB Tech Notes ... Svenska Aeroplan Aktiebolaget. Linkoping, Sweden. SAAB Technical Notes [*A publication*]
SVALC .... Sangamon Valley Academic Library Consortium [*Library network*]
SVAN .... Savannah Foods & Industries [*NASDAQ symbol*] (NQ)
SVAO .... Service at Veterans Administration Offices [*Red Cross*]
SVAPA ...... Svarochnoe Proizvodstvo [*A publication*]
SVAR.......... Stuart's Lower Canada Vice-Admiralty Reports [*1836-74*] [*Quebec*] (DLA)
Svarka Vzryvom Svoistva Svarnykh Soedin ... Svarka Vzryvom i Svoistva Svarnykh Soedinenii [*A publication*]
Svar Proizvod ... Svarochnoe Proizvodstvo [*A publication*]
SVAT.......... Standard Version Acceptance Test (MCD)
SVB............ Sambava [*Madagascar*] [*Airport symbol*] (OAG)
SVB............ Savin Corp. [*NYSE symbol*]
SVB............ Shuttle Vehicle Booster [*NASA*] (NASA)
SVB............ Space Vehicle Booster (MCD)
SV:B.......... Study of Values: British Edition [*Psychology*]
SVBEEQV ... Si Vales, Bene Est; Ego Quoque Valeo [*I Hope You're Well; I Am*] [*Latin*]
SVBP.......... Single-Variable Bypass Program [*DoD*]
SVBSA .... Sivilt Beredskap [*A publication*]
SVBT.......... Space Vehicle Booster Test (AAG)
SVBUA ...... Shock and Vibration Bulletin [*A publication*]
SVC............ Saint Vincent College [*Pennsylvania*]
SVC............ Selective Venous Catheterization [*Cardiology*]
SVC............ Service (AFM)
SVC............ Service Command [*Army*]
SVC............ Service Message [*Aviation code*]
SVC............ Silver City [*New Mexico*] [*Airport symbol*] (OAG)
SVC............ Silver Creek [*California*] [*Seismograph station code, US Geological Survey*] (SEIS)
SVC............ Sine Vibration Control
SVC............ Single Variable Control
SVC............ Society of Vacuum Coaters [*Washington, DC*] (EA)
SVC............ Space Vehicle Code
SVC............ Spiroplasmavirus citri [*Microbiology*]
SVC............ Spring Viremia of Carp
SVC............ Stokely-Van Camp, Inc. [*NYSE symbol*]
SVC............ Superior Vena Cava [*Anatomy*]
SVC............ Supervisor Call (NASA)
SVC............ Switched Virtual Circuit
SVCAB...... Saphenous Vein Coronary Artery Bypass [*Cardiology*]
SVCBL .... Serviceable
SVCE........ Service
SVCG .... Spatial Vectorcardiogram [*Cardiology*]
SVCIA .... Soviet Chemical Industry [*English Translation*] [*A publication*]
SVCMN ...... Service Man (NVT)
SVCP......... Special Virus Cancer Program [*National Cancer Institute*]
SVCS .... Superior Vena Caval Syndrome [*Medicine*]
Svc Strs ..... Service Stars [*Army*]
SVCU .... Space Visualization Contralateral Use [*Occupational therapy*]
SVD............ St. Vincent [*Windward Islands*] [*Airport symbol*] (OAG)
SVD............ Simple Vertex Delivery [*Medicine*]
SVD............ Simplified Vapor Detector
SVD............ Simultaneous Voice/Data
SVD............ Singular Value Decomposition [*Mathematics*]
SVD............ Societas Verbi Divini [*Society of the Divine Word*] [*Roman Catholic men's religious order*]
SVD............ Space Vehicles Division [*NASA*] (MCD)
SVD............ Spontaneous Vaginal Delivery [*Gynecology*]
SVD............ Surveyor Vehicle Department
SvD .... Svenska Dagbladet [*A publication*]
SVD............ Sverdlovsk [*USSR*] [*Geomagnetic observatory code*]
SVD............ Swine Vesicular Disease
SVDF......... Segmented Virtual Display File
SVDI.......... Serie de Vocabularios y Diccionarios Indigenas [*A publication*]
SVDP.......... Saint Vincent de Paul (ADA)
SVDP.......... Skylab Video Documentation Project [*NASA*] (KSC)
SVDS.......... Space Vehicle Dynamic Simulator [*NASA*] (NASA)
SVE............ Secure Voice Equipment (NATG)
SVE............ Seminal Vesicle Epithelium [*Anatomy*]
SVE............ Severide Resources, Inc. [*Vancouver Stock Exchange symbol*]
SVE............ Society of Vector Ecologists (EA)
SVE............ Society for Veterinary Ethology [*See also SEV*] (EA-IO)
SVE............ Supraventricular Ectopic [*Beat*] [*Cardiology*]
SVE............ Susanville, CA [*Location identifier*] [*FAA*] (FAAL)
SVE............ Sverdlovsk [*Ekaterinburg*] [*USSR*] [*Seismograph station code, US Geological Survey*] (SEIS)

SVE .... Swept Volume Efficiency [*Air Force*]
SVE .... System Valve Engineering
s-ve--- .... Venezuela [*MARC geographic area code*] [*Library of Congress*] (LCCP)
SVEA.......... Schweizerischer Verband Evangaelischer Arbeitnehmer [*A union*] [*Swiss*]
SVEA........ Supplemental Vocational Education Assistance (OICC)
SvEA .... Svensk Exegetisk Arsbok [*A publication*]
SVEAA ...... Schweizerischer Verband Evangelischer Arbeiter und Angestellter [*Swiss Federation of Protestant Trade Unions*]
SVEAD .... State Variable Estimation and Accuracy Determination
SVEC.......... Studies on Voltaire and the Eighteenth Century [*A publication*]
Sven Bot Tidskr ... Svensk Botanisk Tidskrift [*A publication*]
Sven Bryggeritidskr ... Svensk Bryggeritidskrift [*A publication*]
Sven Farm Tidskr ... Svensk Farmaceutisk Tidskrift [*A publication*]
Sven Farm Tidskr Sci Ed ... Svensk Farmaceutisk Tidskrift. Scientific Edition [*A publication*]
Sven Foerfattningssaml ... Svensk Foerfattningssamling [*A publication*]
Sven Forskningsinst Cem Betong K Tek Hoegsk Stockholm Medd ... Svenska Forskningsinstitutet foer Cement och Betong vid Kungliga Tekniska Hoegskolan i Stockholm. Meddelanden [*A publication*]
Sven Forskningsinst Cem Betong K Tek Hoegsk Stockholm Saertr ... Svenska Forskningsinstitutet foer Cement och Betong vid Kungliga Tekniska Hoegskolan i Stockholm. Saertryck [*A publication*]
Sven Forskningsinst Cem Betong K Tek Hoegsk Stockholm Utredn ... Svenska Forskningsinstitutet foer Cement och Betong vid Kungliga Tekniska Hoegskolan i Stockholm. Utredningar [*A publication*]
Sven Forskningsinst Cem Betong K Tek Hogsk ... Svenska Forskningsinstitutet foer Cement och Betong vid Kungliga i Stockholm. Meddelanden Tekniska Hoegskolan [*Sweden*] [*A publication*]
Sven Fotogr Tidskr ... Svensk Fotografisk Tidskrift [*A publication*]
Sven Frotidn ... Svensk Froetidning [*A publication*]
Sven Kem Tidskr ... Svensk Kemisk Tidskrift [*A publication*]
Sven Kraftverksfoeren Publ ... Svenska Kraftverksfoereningens Publikationer [*A publication*]
Sven Kraftverksfoeren Publ Medd ... Svenska Kraftverksfoereningens Publikationer Meddelande [*A publication*]
Sven Laekartidn ... Svenska Laekartidningen [*A publication*]
Sven Linne-SallskArsskr ... Svenska Linne-Sallskapet Arsskrift [*A publication*]
Sven Mejeriernas Riksfoeren Produkttek Avd Medd ... Svenska Mejeriernas Riksfoerening. Produkttekniska Avdelningen. Meddelande [*A publication*]
Sven Mejeritidn ... Svenska Mejeritidningen [*A publication*]
Sven Mosskulturfoeren Tidskr ... Svenska Mosskulturfoereningens Tidskrift [*A publication*]
Sven Naturvetensk ... Svensk Naturvetenskap [*A publication*]
Sven Papperfoeraedlingstidskr ... Svensk Pappersfoeraedlingstidskrift [*A publication*]
Sven Papperstidn ... Svensk Papperstidning [*A publication*]
Svensk Bot Tidskr ... Svensk Botanisk Tidskrift [*A publication*]
Svensk Geog Arsbok ... Svensk Geografisk Arsbok [*A publication*]
Svensk Jur-Tidn ... Svensk Juristtidning [*Stockholm, Sweden*] (DLA)
Sven Skogsvardsforen Tidskr ... Svenska Skogsvardsforeningens Tidskrift [*A publication*]
SvenskPapr ... Svensk Papperstidning [*A publication*]
Svensk Teol Kvartalskr ... Svensk Teologisk Kvartalskrift [*A publication*]
Svensk Tid ... Svensk Tidskrift foer Musikforskning [*A publication*]
Svensk Travarutidn ... Svensk Traevaru-och Pappersmassetidning [*A publication*]
Svensk Vet-tidskr ... Svensk Veterinaertidskrift [*A publication*]
Svens Pap T ... Svensk Papperstidning Tidskrift [*A publication*]
Sven Tandlakareforb Tidn ... Svensk Tandlakareforbunds Tidning [*Sweden*] [*A publication*]
Sven Tandlak Tidskr ... Svensk Tandlakare Tidskrift [*A publication*]
Sven Tids M ... Svensk Tidskrift foer Musikforskning [*A publication*]
Sven Traevaru-Tidn ... Svensk Traevaru-Tidning [*A publication*]
Sven Vall Mosskulturfoeren Medd ... Svenska Vall- och Mosskulturfoereningens Meddelanden [*A publication*]
Sven Vattenkraftfoeren Publ ... Svenska Vattenkraftforeningens Publikationer [*A publication*]
SVER.......... State Veterans Employment Representative [*Department of Labor*]
Sverdlovsk Gos Ped Inst Ucen Zap ... Sverdlovskii Gosudarstvennyi Pedagogiceskii Institut. Ucenye Zapiski [*A publication*]
Sver Geol Unders Arsb Ser C Avh Uppsatser ... Sveriges Geologiska Undersoekning Arsbok. Serie C. Avhandlingar och Uppsatser [*A publication*]
Sver Gummitek Foren Publ ... Sveriges Gummitekniska Forening. Publicerande [*A publication*]
Sveriges Geol Unders Ser C ... Sveriges Geologiska Undersoekning Arsbok. Serie C. Avhandlingar och Uppsatser [*A publication*]
Sveriges Riksbank Q R ... Sveriges Riksbank. Quarterly Review [*A publication*]
Sveriges Skogsvforb Tidskr ... Sveriges Skogsvardsfoerbunds Tidskrift [*A publication*]

Sveriges Utsaedesfoer Tidskr ... Sveriges Utsaedesfoerenings Tidskrift [*A publication*]
Sver Mekanforb Mekanresult ... Sveriges Mekanforbund, Mekanresultat [*A publication*]
Sver Nat ..... Sveriges Natur [*A publication*]
Sver Nat Arsb ... Sveriges Natur Arsbok [*A publication*]
Sver Off Stat Bergshantering ... Sveriges Officiella Statistik Bergshantering. Statistika Centralbyran [*Stockholm*] [*A publication*]
Sver Pomol Foeren Arsskr ... Sveriges Pomologiska Foerening Arsskrift [*A publication*]
Sver Skogsvardsfoerbunds Tidskr ... Sveriges Skogsvardsfoerbunds Tidskrift [*A publication*]
Sver Skogsvardsforb Tidskr ... Sveriges Skogsvardsfoerbunds Tidskrift [*A publication*]
SVERT........ Subvert   (ROG)
Sver Utsadesforen Tidskr ... Sveriges Utsaedesfoerenings Tidskrift [*A publication*]
Svetotekh ... Svetotekhnika [*A publication*]
Svetsaren Weld Rev ... Svetsaren: A Welding Review [*A publication*]
SvExAb ..... Svensk Exegetisk Arsbok [*A publication*]
SvExArsb ..... Svensk Exegetisk Arsbok [*A publication*]
SVF .... Save [*Benin*] [*Airport symbol*]   (OAG)
SVF .... Silverleaf Resources Ltd. [*Vancouver Stock Exchange symbol*]
SVF .... Standard Vented Furnace
SVF .... State Variable Filter
SVF .... Stoicorum Veterum Fragmenta [*A publication*]   (OCD)
Sv Farm Tid ... Svensk Farmaceutisk Tidskrift [*A publication*]
SVF Fachorgan Textilveredl ... SVF Fachorgan fuer Textilveredlung [*A publication*]
SVFR .... Special Visual Flight Rules [*Aviation*]
SVG .... Saphenous Vein Graft [*Cardiology*]
SVG .... Sauvagine [*A polypeptide*]
SVG .... Servicing
SVG .... Spiritus Vini Gallici [*Brandy*] [*Pharmacy*]   (ROG)
SVG .... Stavanger [*Norway*] [*Airport symbol*]   (OAG)
SVG .... Sun Valley Gold Mines Ltd. [*Vancouver Stock Exchange symbol*]
SVGC .... Secure Voice and Graphic Conferencing   (MCD)
SV/GC .... Secure Voice/Graphics Conferencing   (MCD)
SVGI .... Silicon Valley Group [*NASDAQ symbol*]   (NQ)
SVGLA ...... Sovetskaya Geologiya [*A publication*]
SVGS .... Savings
SVGU .... Sveriges Geologiska Undersoekning [*A publication*]
SVH .... Seven Mile High Resources, Inc. [*Vancouver Stock Exchange symbol*]
SVH .... Severely Handicapped
SVH .... Statesville, NC [*Location identifier*] [*FAA*]   (FAAL)
SVHE........ Society for Values in Higher Education   (EA)
SVI .... St. Vincent [*St. Vincent*] [*Seismograph station code, US Geological Survey*] [*Closed*]   (SEIS)
SVI .... San Vincente Del Caguan [*Colombia*] [*Airport symbol*]   (OAG)
SVI .... Service Interception [*Telecommunications*]   (TEL)
SVI .... Single Vendor Integrity   (MCD)
SVI .... Sludge Volume Index [*Wastewater treatment*]
SVI .... Sound Velocity Indicator
SVI .... Spiritus Vini Industrialis [*Industrial Alcohol*] [*Pharmacy*]
SVI .... Stroke Volume Index [*Medicine*]
Svl .... Svizzera Italiana [*A publication*]
SVI .... System Verification Installation
SVIA .... Specialty Vehicles Institute of America [*Costa Mesa, CA*]   (EA)
SVIB .... Strong Vocational Interest Blank [*Psychology*]
SVIC.......... Shock and Vibration Information Center [*Navy*] [*Washington, DC*]   (MCD)
SVICLC ...... Shenandoah Valley Independent College Library Cooperative [*Library network*]
SVIL .... Seville Energy Corp. [*NASDAQ symbol*]   (NQ)
Svinovod.... Svinovodstvo [*A publication*]
SVIO .... Superintendent Veterinary Investigation Officer [*Ministry of Agriculture, Fisheries, and Food*] [*British*]
SVIP .... Secure Voice Improvement Program [*DoD*]
SVIPA........ Swiss Videotex Industry Association [*Zurich*] [*Information service*]   (EISS)
SVIPA........ Swiss Viewdata Information Providers Association [*Zurich*] [*Telecommunications*]   (TSSD)
SVITA........ Spectravideo, Inc. Cl A [*NASDAQ symbol*]   (NQ)
SVJ............. Lompoc, CA [*Location identifier*] [*FAA*]   (FAAL)
SVJ............. Sovetska Veda. Jazykoveda [*A publication*]
SVJ............. Steed Ventures Corp. [*Formerly, Poney Explorations Ltd.*] [*Vancouver Stock Exchange symbol*]
SVJ............. Svolvaer [*Norway*] [*Airport symbol*]   (OAG)
SvJerTs...... Svenska Jerusalems-Foereningens Tidskrift [*Uppsala*] [*A publication*]
Sv JT .... Svensk Juristtidning [*Sweden*]   (DLA)
Sv Kraftverksforen Publ ... Svenska Kraftverksfoereningens Publikationer [*A publication*]
SVL .... Sapphire Vacuum Lens
SVL .... Savonlinna [*Finland*] [*Airport symbol*]   (OAG)
SVL .... Scripps Visibility Laboratory
SVL .... Silver Lake Resources, Inc. [*Toronto Stock Exchange symbol*]
SVL .... Snout-to-Vent Length [*Biometry*]
SVL .... Studien zur Vergleichenden Literaturgeschichte [*A publication*]

SVLA......... Steered Vertical Line Array [*Military*]   (CAAL)
SVLAA....... Svenska Laekartidningen [*A publication*]
SVLB .... Sapphire Vacuum Lens Blank
SVLF .... Shipboard Very Low Frequency [*Navy*]   (NG)
SVLL .... Short Vertical Lower Left
SvLm......... Svenska Landsmal och Svenskt Folkliv [*A publication*]
SVLOG ...... Servicing Log [*Telecommunications*]   (TEL)
SVLP .... Special Virus Leukemia Program [*National Cancer Institute*]
SVLR .... Short Vertical Lower Right
SVLTE........ Services Valve Life Test Establishment [*British*]   (MCD)
SVM .... Salem, MI [*Location identifier*] [*FAA*]   (FAAL)
SVM .... Seminal Vesicle Mesenchyme [*Anatomy*]
SVM .... Seminal Vesicle Microsome [*Anatomy*]
SVM .... Semitrailer Van Mount
SVM .... Service Volontaire Mennonite [*Mennonite Voluntary Service*]
SVM .... ServiceMaster [*NYSE symbol*]
SVM .... Ship Vulnerability Model   (MCD)
SVM .... Silicon Video Memory
SVm .... Silver City [*New Mexico*] [*Seismograph station code, US Geological Survey*]   (SEIS)
SVM .... Silver Hart Minerals [*Vancouver Stock Exchange symbol*]
SVM .... Sisters of the Visitation of the Congregation of the Immaculate Heart of Mary [*Roman Catholic religious order*]
SVM .... Spiritus Vini Methylatus [*Methylated Spirit*] [*Pharmacy*]
SVM .... Stamp Vending Machine
SvM .... Svensk Missionstidskrift [*A publication*]
SVM .... System Validation Model   (NVT)
SVMA........ Space Vehicle Mission Analysis
SVMPCG.... Grasslands National Park, Parks Canada [*Parc National Grasslands, Parcs Canada*] Val Marie, Saskatchewan [*Library symbol*] [*National Library of Canada*]   (NLC)
SVMTR....... Servomotor [*Control systems*]
SVN........... Savannah, GA [*Location identifier*] [*FAA*]   (FAAL)
SVN........... South Vietnam   (CINC)
SVNAB....... Svensk Naturvetenskap [*A publication*]
SVNESE..... South Vietnamese
SVNM........ St. Vincent National Movement   (PPW)
SVNRF .... State of Vietnam Ribbon of Friendship [*Military decoration*]   (AABC)
SVNVAC .... Sunny Von Bulow National Victim Advocacy Center [*Fort Worth, TX*]   (EA)
SVO........... Moscow [*USSR*] Sheremetyevo Airport [*Airport symbol*]   (OAG)
SVO........... Servo   (KSC)
SVO........... Silver Talon Mines Ltd. [*Vancouver Stock Exchange symbol*]
SVO........... Space Vehicle Operations   (MCD)
SVO........... Special Vehicle Operation [*Ford Motor Co.*]
SVO........... Subject-Verb-Object [*Education of the hearing-impaired*]
SVOD .... Soviet Aircraft Navigation and Landing System   (MCD)
Svoista Veshchestv Str Mol ... Svoistva Veshchestv i Stroenie Molekul [*A publication*]
SVP .... Bie [*Angola*] [*Airport symbol*]   (OAG)
SVP .... St. Louis Public Library, St. Louis, MO [*OCLC symbol*]   (OCLC)
SVP .... Security Vehicle Patrol [*Air Force*]   (AFM)
SVP .... Seminal Vesicle Protein [*Biochemistry*]
SVP .... Senior Vice President
SVP .... Service Processor   (BUR)
SVP .... S'il Vous Plait [*If You Please*] [*French*]
SVP .... Silver Princess Resources [*Vancouver Stock Exchange symbol*]
SVP .... Snake Venom Phosphodiesterase [*An enzyme*]
SVP .... Society of St. Vincent de Paul
SVP .... Society of Vertebrate Paleontology   (EA)
SVP .... Sound Velocity Profile
SVP .... Specific Vocational Preparation [*US Employment Service*] [*Department of Labor*]
SVP .... Supplemental Vacation Plan
SVPB......... Supraventricular Premature Beats [*Cardiology*]
SVPIA........ Surface and Vacuum Physics Index [*A publication*]
SVPM........ Small Vehicles, Program Manager
SVPP .... Schweizerischen Vereinigung fuer Parapsychologie
SVQ........... Seville [*Spain*] [*Airport symbol*]   (OAG)
SVR .... Severe   (FAAC)
SVR .... Slant Visual Range
SVR .... Society of Vietnamese Rangers   (EA)
SVR .... Spiritus Vini Rectificatus [*Rectified Spirit of Wine*] [*Pharmacy*]
SVR .... Super Video Recorder
SVR .... Supply-Voltage Rejection   (IEEE)
SVR .... Systemic Vascular Resistance [*Medicine*]
SVRA......... State Vehicular Recreation Area
SVRB......... Supervisor Request Block [*Data processing*]   (BUR)
SVRD......... Silicon Voltage Reference Diode
SVRDA....... Soviet Radiochemistry [*English Translation*] [*A publication*]
SVREP....... Southwest Voter Registration and Education Project   (EA)
SVRI.......... Systemic Vascular Resistance Index
SVRL......... Several   (FAAC)
SVRN......... Sovereign Thoroughbred [*NASDAQ symbol*]   (NQ)
SVRR......... Software Verification Readiness Review [*NASA*]   (NASA)
SVS........... Eastern Commuter, Inc. [*Hasbrouck Heights, NJ*] [*FAA designator*]   (FAAC)

SVS	Saga-Book of the Viking Society for Northern Research [*A publication*]
SVS	Schedule Visibility System (AAG)
SVS	Secure Voice Switch
SVS	Secure Voice System [*Telecommunications*]
SVS	Service School [*Military*]
SVS	Silverside Resources, Inc. [*Toronto Stock Exchange symbol*] [*Vancouver Stock Exchange symbol*]
SVS	Single Virtual Storage [*IBM Corp.*] [*Data processing*]
SVS	Slandsville [*South Carolina*] [*Seismograph station code, US Geological Survey*] (SEIS)
SVS	Society for Vascular Surgery [*Manchester, MA*] (EA)
SVS	Sound Velocity Structure
SVS	Space Vehicle Simulator (AAG)
SVS	Spectroradiometer Visible System
SVS	Spinning Vehicle Simulator
SVS	Stabilized Viewing System
SVS	Stevens Village [*Alaska*] [*Airport symbol*] (OAG)
SVS	Still-Camera Video System [*Canon, Inc.*]
SVS	Suit Ventilation System (MCD)
SVS	Synthetic Vision Systems, Inc.
SVSC	Space Vehicle Sectoring Code
SVSHKG	Schriften des Vereins fuer Schleswig-Holsteinische Kirchengeschichte [*A publication*]
SVSL	Skrifter Utgivna av Vetenskaps-Societeten i Lund [*A publication*]
SVSO	Superintending Victualling Stores Officer [*British*]
S V Sound Vib	S V, Sound and Vibration [*A publication*]
SVSP	School Volunteer Services Program
SVSPO	Sbornik Vysoke Skoly Pedagogicke v Olomouci [*A publication*]
SVSPO(JL)	Sbornik Vysoke Skoly Pedagogicke v Olomouci. Jazyka a Literatura [*A publication*]
SVSPP	Sbornik Vysoke Skoly Pedagogicke v Praze. Jazyka a Literatura [*A publication*]
SVSS	Sprague Voltage-Sensitive Switch
SVSThR	Sammlung Gemeinverstaendlicher Vortraege und Schriften aus dem Gebiet der Theologie und der Religionsgeschichte [*A publication*]
SVT	St. Vincent [*St. Vincent*] [*Seismograph station code, US Geological Survey*] (SEIS)
SVT	Secure Voice Terminal (MCD)
SVT	Self Valuation Test [*Psychology*]
SVT	Servotronics, Inc. [*American Stock Exchange symbol*]
SVT	Silicon Vidicon Target
SVT	Silverton Resources Ltd. [*Toronto Stock Exchange symbol*]
SVT	Solar Vacuum Telescope
SVT	Space Vehicle Test
SVT	Space Visualization Test
SVT	Spiritus Vini Tenuis [*Proof Spirit of Wine*] [*Pharmacy*]
SVT	Stray Voltage Tester
SVT	Supplements. Vetus Testamentum [*Leiden*] [*A publication*]
SVT	Supraventricular Tachycardia [*Cardiology*]
SvT	Svenska Texter [*A publication*]
SVT	System Validation Testing
SvTK	Svensk Teologisk Kvartalskrift [*A publication*]
SvTKv	Svensk Teologisk Kvartalskrift [*A publication*]
SVTL	Semivital
SVTL	Services Valve Test Laboratory [*British*] (NATG)
SVTM	Shielded Voltage Tunable Magnetron
S/VTOL	Short/Vertical Takeoff and Landing [*Aviation*] (NATG)
SVTP	Sound, Velocity, Temperature, Pressure
SVTP	Studia in Veteris Testamenti Pseudepigrapha [*A publication*]
SVTQ	St. Vladimir's Theological Quarterly [*A publication*]
SVT(S)	Space Vehicle Test (Supervisor)
SvTs	Svensk Tidskrift [*A publication*]
SVTT	Surface Vessel Torpedo Tube (NVT)
SVU	Savusavu [*Fiji*] [*Airport symbol*] (OAG)
S/VU	Sound/Video Unlimited
SVU	Super Valu Stores, Inc. [*NYSE symbol*]
SVU	Surface Vehicular Unit
SVU	System Verification Unit
SVUL	Short Vertical Upper Left
SVUL	Suomen Valtakunnan Uhreiluliitto [*Finnish Central Sports Federation*]
SVUOJ	Sri Venkateswara University. Oriental Journal [*A publication*]
SVUR	Short Vertical Upper Right
SVV	Sit Venia Verbo [*Forgive the Expression*] [*Latin*]
SVW	Silverhawk Resources [*Vancouver Stock Exchange symbol*]
SVW	Sparrevohn [*Alaska*] [*Seismograph station code, US Geological Survey*] (SEIS)
SVW	Sparrevohn, AK [*Location identifier*] [*FAA*] (FAAL)
SVXUN	Socanav Units [*Toronto Stock Exchange symbol*]
SVY	Survey
SVZ	San Antonio [*Venezuela*] [*Airport symbol*] (OAG)
SVZ	Sisters of Charity of St. Vincent de Paul [*Roman Catholic religious order*]
SW	Methylphosphonous Dichloride [*Toxic compound*] [*Army symbol*]
SW	Namib Air (Pty) Ltd. [*South Africa*] [*ICAO designator*] (FAAC)
Sw	Royal Swedish Library (Kungl. Biblioteket), Stockholm, Sweden [*Library symbol*] [*Library of Congress*] (LCLS)
SW	Sadler's Wells Theatre [*London*]
SW	Salt Water
SW	Sandwich-Wound (DEN)
SW	Satan Worship
SW	Science Wonder Stories [*A publication*]
SW	Seaboard World Airlines, Inc.
SW	Seawater
S/W	Seaworthy (ADA)
SW	Secret Writing [*Espionage*]
SW	Secretary of War [*Obsolete*]
SW	Security Watch
SW	Semiweekly
SW	Senior Warden [*Freemasonry*]
SW	Senior Wolf [*An accomplished philanderer*] [*Slang*]
SW	Senior Woodward [*Ancient Order of Foresters*]
SW	Sent Wrong [*i.e., misdirected*]
SW	Service Water [*Nuclear energy*] (NRCH)
SW	Sewing Machine Repair Program [*Association of Independent Colleges and Schools specialization code*]
SW	Shallow Water Attack Craft [*Navy symbol*]
SW	Shelter Warden [*British Home Defence*] [*World War II*]
SW	Shipper's Weights [*Bills of lading*]
SW	Ship's Warrant [*Marine Corps*]
SW	Shirl J. Winter [*Designer's mark when appearing on US coins*]
SW	Short Weight
SW	Shortwave [*Electronics*]
SW	Shotgun Wedding [*Forced marriage*] [*Slang*]
SW	Side Wheel
SW	Sidewinder
SW	Simple Wear
SW	Single Wall (AAG)
SW	Single Weight
SW	Slavic Word [*A publication*]
SW	Slow Wave [*Electroencephalograph*]
S & W	Smith and Wesson (MCD)
SW	Snow [*Ship's rigging*] (ROG)
SW	Snow Showers [*Meteorology*] (FAAC)
S & W	Soap and Water [*Enema*] [*Medicine*]
SW	Social Work [*or Worker*]
SW	Socialist Worker [*A publication*]
SW	Socket Weld
SW	Software [*Data processing*]
SW	Solar Wing (MCD)
SW	Son of a Witch [*An association*] (EA)
SW	Sound Whistle [*British railroad term*]
SW	South Wales
SW	South and West [*A publication*]
S & W	South and West [*A publication*]
SW	South Western Reporter [*National Reporter System*] (DLA)
SW	Southwest
SW	Southwest Africa (MCD)
SW	Special Warfare
SW	Special Weapon
SW	Specific Weight
SW	Spontaneous Swallows [*Gastroenterology*]
SW	Spore Wall [*Botany*]
SW	Spotweld [*Technical drawings*]
SW	Stall Warning System (MCD)
SW	Standby-Service Water (NRCH)
SW	Station Wagon [*Car*]
SW	Status of Women [*Canada*]
SW	Status Word
SW	Steam Wagon [*British*]
SW	Steelworker [*Navy rating*]
SW	Stenciled Weight
SW	Sterile Water
SW	Stewart-Warner Corp.
SW	Stock Width [*Construction or manufacturing materials*]
SW	Stone & Webster, Inc. [*NYSE symbol*]
SW	Store Ward
SW	Strategic Warning (MCD)
SW	Stud-Arc Welding
SW	Subjective Weakness [*Medicine*]
SW	Surface Warfare (MCD)
Sw	Swabey's English Admiralty Reports (DLA)
Sw	Swabey's English Ecclesiastical Reports [*1855-59*] (DLA)
sw	Swamp [*Maps and charts*]
SW	Swamp (ROG)
Sw	Swann [*Blood group*]
Sw	Swan's Tennessee Reports [*31, 32 Tennessee*] (DLA)
Sw	Swanston's English Chancery Reports (DLA)
SW	Swash
SW	Swear
sw	Sweden [*MARC country of publication code*] [*Library of Congress*] (LCCP)
SW	Sweden
Sw	Sweeney's New York Superior Court Reports (DLA)
SW	Swell Organ
Sw	Swinton's Scotch Justiciary Cases (DLA)
SW	Swiss
SW	Switch (AAG)

SW.............	Switchband Wound [*Relay*]
SW.............	Switzerland
SW1...........	Steelworker, First Class [*Navy rating*]
SW2...........	Steelworker, Second Class [*Navy rating*]
SW3...........	Steelworker, Third Class [*Navy rating*]
SWA..........	Reports of the High Court of South-West Africa [*1920-46*] (DLA)
SWA..........	Scheduler Work Area [*Data processing*] (IBMDP)
SWA..........	Scope of Word Addendum (MCD)
SWA..........	Seriously Wounded in Action [*Military*]
SWA..........	Shallow Water Acoustics
SWA..........	Shantou [*China*] [*Airport symbol*] (OAG)
SWA..........	Single Wire Armored [*Cables*]
SWA..........	Sitzungsberichte der Wiener Akademie [*A publication*]
SWA..........	Southern Water Authority [*British*]
SWA..........	Southern Wholesalers Association [*Atlanta, GA*] (EA)
SWA..........	Southern Woodwork Association [*Athens, GA*] (EA)
SWA..........	Southwest Africa
SWA..........	Southwest Airlines Co. [*San Antonio, TX*] [*FAA designator*] (FAAC)
SWA..........	Southwest Asia
SWA..........	Specialty Wire Association [*Later, AWPA*]
SWA..........	Standing Wave Apparatus
SWA..........	State Welfare Agency [*Social Security Administration*] (OICC)
SWA..........	Straight Wire Antenna
SWA..........	Stunt Women of America [*Pacific Palisades, CA*] (EA)
SWA..........	Superwomen's Anonymous [*San Francisco, CA*] (EA)
SWA..........	Support Work Authorization (MCD)
swa...........	Swahili [*MARC language code*] [*Library of Congress*] (LCCP)
SWA..........	Swan Island [*Swan Island*] [*Seismograph station code, US Geological Survey*] [*Closed*] (SEIS)
SWA..........	Swissair [*Airline*]
SWA..........	System Work Area
SWAA........	Slovak Writers and Artists Association (EA)
Swab.........	Swabey's English Ecclesiastical Reports [*1855-59*] (DLA)
Swab Admr ...	Swabey's English Admiralty Reports [*166 English Reprint*] (DLA)
Swab Div....	Swabey on Divorce and Matrimonial Causes [*3rd ed.*] [*1859*] (DLA)
Swabey Adm ...	Swabey's English Admiralty Reports [*166 English Reprint*] [*1855-59*] (DLA)
Swabey Adm (Eng) ...	Swabey's English Admiralty Reports [*166 English Reprint*] (DLA)
Swabey & T (Eng) ...	Swabey and Tristram's Probate and Divorce Reports [*164 English Reports*] (DLA)
Swab & T ...	Swabey and Tristram's Probate and Divorce Reports [*164 English Reprint*] (DLA)
Swab & Tr ...	Swabey and Tristram's Probate and Divorce Reports [*164 English Reprint*] (DLA)
SWAC	Shallow Water Attack Craft, Light (MCD)
SWAC	Special Warhead Arming Control (AFM)
SWAC	Spotweld Accessory [*Tool*] (AAG)
SWAC	Standards Western Automatic Computer [*National Bureau of Standards*]
SWACS.....	Space Warning and Control System [*NORAD*]
SWAD........	Special Warfare Aviation Detachment [*Army*]
SWAD........	Subdivision of Work Authorization Document [*NASA*] (NASA)
SWADE.....	Second Wives of America Demanding Equality
SWADS.....	Scheduler Work Area Data Set [*IBM Corp.*] (MCD)
SWAFAC...	Southwest Atlantic Fisheries Advisory Commission
SWAG	Standard Written Agreement [*Military*]
SWAGS.....	Scientific Wild-Aim Guess [*Bowdlerized version*] (MCD)
SWAK........	Sealed with a Kiss [*Correspondence*]
SWAK........	Spinners and Weavers Association of Korea [*Defunct*] (EA)
SWAL........	Shallow Water Attack Craft, Light [*Navy symbol*] (NVT)
SwAL	Southwestern American Literature [*A publication*]
SWALC	Southwest Academic Library Consortium [*Library network*] (EISS)
SWALCAKWS ...	Sealed with a Lick 'Cause a Kiss Won't Stick [*Correspondence*] (DSUE)
SWALK	Sealed with a Loving Kiss [*Correspondence*]
SWALM.....	Switch Alarm (AAG)
SWAM.......	Shallow Water Attack Craft, Medium [*Navy symbol*] (NVT)
SWAM.......	Sine Wave Amplitude Modulation
SWAMI.....	Software-Aided Multiform Input [*Software*] [*Data processing*]
SWAMI......	Speech with Alternating Masking Index [*Discrimination test*]
SWAMI......	Stall Warning and Margin Indicator
SWAMI......	Standing Wave Area Monitor Indicator (MUGU)
SWAMI......	Stanford Worldwide Acquisition of Meteorological Information [*Weather prediction system*]
SWAN........	Second Wives Association of North America [*Toronto, ON*] (EA)
Swan	Swan's Tennessee Supreme Court Reports [*1851-53*] (DLA)
Swan	Swanston's English Chancery Reports (DLA)
Swan Ch	Swanston's English Chancery Reports (DLA)
Swan & CR St ...	Swan and Critchfield's Revised Statutes [*Ohio*] (DLA)
Swan Eccl C ...	Swan's Ecclesiastical Courts [*1830*] (DLA)
SWANK......	Sealed with a Nice Kiss [*Correspondence*]
Swank.......	Single Woman and No Kids [*Lifestyle classification*]
Swan Pl & Pr ...	Swan on Pleading and Practice [*Ohio*] (DLA)
Swan Pr	Swan on Practice [*Ohio*] (DLA)

SWANS	State Wildlife Advisory News Service [*A publication*]
Swan's	Swan's Tennessee Reports (DLA)
Swans	Swanston's English Chancery Reports (DLA)
Swansea Coll Fac Ed J ...	University College of Swansea. Collegiate Faculty of Education. Journal [*A publication*]
Swan's R	Swan's Tennessee Reports (DLA)
Swan & S St ...	Swan and Sayler's Supplement to the Revised Statutes [*Ohio*] (DLA)
Swan's St...	Swan's Ohio Statutes (DLA)
Swanst......	Swanston's English Chancery Reports [*36 English Reprint*] (DLA)
Swanst (Eng) ...	Swanston's English Chancery Reports [*36 English Reprint*] (DLA)
Swan Tr	Swan's Ohio Treatise (DLA)
SWANU......	South West Africa National Union [*Namibian*] (PPW)
SWANY......	Swan Resources ADR [*NASDAQ symbol*] (NQ)
SWAP........	Sampling Work Action Patrol
SWAP........	Senior Worker Action Program
SWAP........	Severe Weather Avoidance Plan (FAAC)
SWAP........	Society for Wang Applications and Programs (CSR)
SWAP........	Standard Wafer Array Programing
SWAP........	Stress Wave Analyzing Program
SWAP........	Student Woodlawn Area Project [*Chicago, IL*]
SWAP........	SWAP [*Salesmen with a Purpose*] Club International [*Arvada, CO*] (EA)
SWAP........	Systems Worthiness Analysis Program [*FAA*]
SWAPO......	South West Africa People's Organization [*Namibian*] (PD)
SWAPS	Ship Workload and Priority Systems [*Navy*]
SWAPS	Special Wire Assembly Planning System (MCD)
SWAR.......	Schwartz Brothers, Inc. [*NASDAQ symbol*] (NQ)
Swarajya A ...	Swarajya Annual Number [*Madras*] [*A publication*]
SWARK......	Southwark [*Borough of London*] (ROG)
SWARM......	Southwestern and Rocky Mountain Division [*AAAS division*]
SWARMS ...	Small Warhead and Reentry Multiple System
SWAS........	Slim Whitman Appreciation Society of the United States (EA)
SWASG	Submarine Sensor to Weapon Alignment Steering Group
SWASS	Screwworm Adult Suppression System [*Medicine*]
SWAT........	Secure Wire Access Terminal (MCD)
SWAT........	Service Weapons Acceptability Tests
SWAT........	Sidewinder Acquisition Track (IEEE)
SWAT........	Sidewinder Angle Tracking [*Missiles*] (NG)
SWAT........	Special Warfare Armored Transporter [*A vehicle*]
SWAT........	Special Weapons and Tactics [*Police*]
SWAT........	Squad Weapon Analytical Trainer (MCD)
SWAT........	Stress Wave Analysis Technique
SWATCH....	Swiss Watch
SWATH	Small Waterplane Area Twin Hull [*Ship*] [*Navy*]
SWATH	Small Wetted Area Twin-Hulled Ship (MCD)
SWATM......	Shallow Water Antitraffic Mine [*Military*]
SWATS	Shallow Water Acoustic Tracking System [*Navy*] (CAAL)
SWATT......	Simulator for Antitank Tactical Training [*Army*] (INF)
SWAW.......	Sitzungsberichte der Wiener Akademie der Wissenschaften [*A publication*]
SWAX........	Southwest Airlines Co. [*Air carrier designation symbol*]
Swaziland Geol Surv Mines Dep Annu Rep ...	Swaziland. Geological Survey and Mines Department. Annual Report [*A publication*]
SWB	Sandia Wind Balloon (MUGU)
SWB	Scheduled Weather Broadcast (FAAC)
SWB	Short Wheelbase
SWB	Single with Bath [*Hotel room*]
SWB	South Wales Borderers [*Military unit*] [*British*]
SWB	South Westchester BOCES [*Boards of Cooperative Educational Services*] [*UTLAS symbol*]
SWB	Southwest Bancorp [*American Stock Exchange symbol*]
SWB	Southwestern Motor Freight Bureau, Dallas TX [*STAC*]
SWB	Summary of World Broadcasts [*British Broadcasting Corporation*]
SWB	Switchboard (NATG)
SWBB........	Windmere Corp. [*NASDAQ symbol*] (NQ)
SWBD........	Switchboard (AAG)
SWBHD......	Swash Bulkhead
SWBP........	Service Water Booster Pump [*Nuclear energy*] (IEEE)
SWBRD	Sun at Work in Britain [*A publication*]
SWBS........	Ship Work Breakdown Structure [*Navy*] (CAAL)
SWBS........	Software Work Breakdown Structure (MCD)
SWBS........	Solid Waste Barrel Storage (NRCH)
SWbS........	Southwest by South
SWBS........	Subcontract Work Breakdown Structure (MCD)
SWbW.......	Southwest by West
SWC..........	Chief Steelworker [*Navy rating*]
SWC..........	Omaha, NE [*Location identifier*] [*FAA*] (FAAL)
SWC..........	Saline Water Conversion (MCD)
SWC..........	Second Wives Coalition (EA)
SWC..........	Semi-Wadcutter [*Ammunition*]
SWC..........	Senate Wine Caucus (EA)
SWC..........	Share the Work Coalition (EA)
SWC..........	Ship Weapon Coordinator (NVT)
SWC..........	Shock Wave Control
SWC..........	Shortwave Converter
SWC..........	Signals Warfare Center [*Army*]
SWC..........	Simon Wiesenthal Center [*An association*] (EA)

SWC .... Single Wire Connector
SWC .... Skywave Correction [*Aircraft navigation*]
SWC .... Slovak World Congress   (EA-IO)
SWC .... Soil and Water Conservation Research Division [*of ARS, Department of Agriculture*]
SWC .... Solar Wind Compensator [*or Composition*] [*Apollo 11*] [*NASA*]
SWC .... Solid Wastes Cask [*Nuclear energy*]   (NRCH)
SWC .... Southwest Conference [*College sports*]
SWC .... Southwestern Connecticut Library Council, Bridgeport, CT [*OCLC symbol*]   (OCLC)
SWC .... Special Warfare Center [*Later, J. F. Kennedy Center for Special Warfare*] [*Army*]
SWC .... Special Warfare Craft [*Navy*]   (CAAL)
SWC .... Special Weapons Center [*or Command*]
SWC .... Stall Warning Computer   (MCD)
SWC .... Stawell [*Australia*] [*Airport symbol*]   (OAG)
SWC .... Submersible Work Chamber
SWC .... Superior White Crystal [*Sugar*]
SWC .... Supreme War Council [*World War II*]
SWC .... Surewin Resources Corporation [*Vancouver Stock Exchange symbol*]
SWC .... Surface Warfare Coordinator [*Also, SUWC*]   (NVT)
SWC .... Surface Weapons Control
SWC .... Surface Weapons Coordinator [*Navy*]   (CAAL)
SWC .... Surge Withstand Capability   (IEEE)
SWC .... System Weapons Coordinator [*Navy*]   (CAAL)
SWCA .... Constructionman Apprentice, Steelworker, Striker [*Navy rating*]
SWCA .... Silver Wyandotte Club of America   (EA)
SWCEL ...... Southwestern Cooperative Educational Laboratory
SWCENT .... Switching Central [*Telecommunications*]   (AABC)
SWCH .... Switch   (MCD)
SWCL .... Seawater Conversion Laboratory   (KSC)
SWCL .... Special Warfare Craft, Light [*Navy symbol*]
SWCL .... State Worker's Compensation Law   (OICC)
SWCLR ..... Southwest Council of La Raza [*Mexican-American organization*]   (EA)
SWCM .... Master Chief Steelworker [*Navy rating*]
SW/CM ...... Software Configuration Management   (MCD)
SWCM .... Special Warfare Craft, Medium [*Navy symbol*]
SWCN .... Constructionman, Steelworker, Striker [*Navy rating*]
SWCP .... Saline Water Conversion Program [*Department of the Interior*]
SWCP .... Salt-Water Circulating Pump   (MSA)
SWCP .... Society of the War of 1812 in the Commonwealth of Pennsylvania
SWCPI...... Solid Waste Council of the Paper Industry [*Washington, DC*]   (EA)
SWCS........ SAC Warning and Control System   (MCD)
SWCS........ Salt Water Cooling System [*Nuclear energy*]   (NRCH)
SWCS........ Senior Chief Steelworker [*Navy rating*]
SWCST ..... Saturn Workshop Cockpit Simulation Trainer [*NASA*]
SWD .... Self-Wiring Data [*Telecommunications*]   (TEL)
SWD .... Senior Weapon Director [*Air Force*]
SWD .... Seward, AK [*Location identifier*] [*FAA*]   (FAAL)
SWD .... Sewed
SWD .... Short-Wave Diathermy [*Medicine*]
SWD .... Side Water Depth
SWD .... Single Word Dump
SWD .... Sliding Watertight Door
SWD .... Smaller Word
SWD .... Southwestern Division [*Army Corps of Engineers*]
SWD .... Standard Shares, Inc. [*American Stock Exchange symbol*]
SWD .... Standing Wave Detector
SWD .... Submarine Wire Dispenser
SWD .... Sun, Wind, Dust [*Goggles*]   (MCD)
SWD .... Surface Wave Dielectrometer
SWD .... Swaziland [*Swaziland*] [*Seismograph station code, US Geological Survey*]   (SEIS)
SWD .... Synchronous Wave Device
SW 2d........ South Western Reporter, Second Series   (DLA)
SWDA........ Solid Waste Disposal Act [*1965*] [*Environmental Protection Agency*]
SWDA........ Step-Wise Discriminant Analysis
SWDB........ Special Weapons Development Board
SWDC........ Shock Wave Data Center [*Lawrence Radiation Laboratory*]
SWDG .... Surface Warfare Development Group [*Also, SURFWARDEVGRU*] [*Navy*]
SWDL........ Safe Winter Driving League   (EA)
SWDL........ Surface Wave Delay Line
SWDS........ Scrolls from the Wilderness of the Dead Sea. Smithsonian Institution Exhibit Catalogue [*Washington, DC*]   (BJA)
SWDS........ Software Development System   (MCD)
SWDVS ..... Software Development and Verification System [*NASA*]
SWDYN...... Single-Wheel Dynamometer
SWE .... Scalar Wave Equation
SWE .... Shift Word, Extracting
SWE .... Simulated Work Experience
SWE .... Society of Wine Educators   (EA)
SWE .... Society of Women Engineers   (EA)
SWE .... Solar Wind Experiment [*NASA*]   (KSC)
SWE .... Spherical Wave Expansion [*Telecommunications*]   (TEL)

SWE .... Status Word Enable
SWE .... Steelworker Erector [*Navy rating*]
SWE .... Stress Wave Emission
SWE .... Sweden [*Three-letter standard code*]   (CNC)
swe........... Swedish [*MARC language code*] [*Library of Congress*]   (LCCP)
SWE .... Swensen's Inc. [*Vancouver Stock Exchange symbol*]
SWEA....... Swedish Women's Educational Association   (EA)
SWEAT...... Student Work Experience and Training
SWECS ..... Small Wind Energy Conversion Systems
SWED....... Sweden [*or Swedish*]
SWED........ Swedlow, Inc. [*NASDAQ symbol*]   (NQ)
SwedAE ..... Swedish Antarctic Expedition [*1901-04*]
Swed Dent J ... Swedish Dental Journal [*A publication*]
Swed Dent J (Suppl) ... Swedish Dental Journal (Supplement) [*A publication*]
Swed Foersvarets Forskningsanst FOA Rep ... Sweden. Foersvarets Forskningsanstalt. FOA Report [*A publication*]
Swed Geol Unders Ser Ae Geol Kartbl 1:50000 ... Sweden. Geologiska Undersoekning. Serie Ae. Geologiska Kartblad i Skala 1:50,000 [*A publication*]
Swed Geotech Inst Proc ... Swedish Geotechnical Institute. Proceedings [*A publication*]
SWEDIS ..... Swedish Drug Information System [*Swedish National Board of Health and Welfare*] [*Databank*] [*Sweden*]   (EISS)
Swedish Aust & Swedish NZ Trade J ... Swedish-Australian and Swedish-New Zealand Trade Journal [*A publication*]
Swedish Deep-Sea Expedition Repts ... Swedish Deep-Sea Expedition. Reports [*A publication*]
Swedish Econ ... Swedish Economy [*A publication*]
Swedish Hist Soc Yearbook ... Swedish Historical Society. Yearbook [*A publication*]
Swedish J Econ ... Swedish Journal of Economics [*A publication*]
Swed J Agric Res ... Swedish Journal of Agricultural Research [*A publication*]
Swed J Econ ... Swedish Journal of Economics [*A publication*]
SWEDL....... Southwest Educational Development Laboratory
Swed State Shipbuild Exp Tank Report ... Swedish State Shipbuilding Experiment Tank. Report [*A publication*]
SWEDTEL ... Swedish Telecoms International AB [*Stockholm*] [*Telecommunications*]   (TSSD)
Swed Weed Conf ... Swedish Weed Conference [*A publication*]
Swed Weed Conf Rep ... Swedish Weed Conference. Reports [*A publication*]
SWEE........ Southwest Electronic Exhibit
Sween........ Sweeny's New York Superior Court Reports [*31-32 New York*] [*1869-70*]   (DLA)
Sweeney (NY) ... Sweeny's New York Superior Court Reports [*31-32 New York*]   (DLA)
Sweeny ...... Sweeny's New York Superior Court Reports [*31-32 New York*]   (DLA)
SWEEP...... Structures with Error Expurgation Program
SWEET...... Stay at Work, Earn Extra Time [*United Auto Workers*]
Sweet........ Sweet on the Limited Liability Act   (DLA)
Sweet........ Sweet on Wills   (DLA)
Sweet........ Sweet's Law Dictionary   (DLA)
Sweet........ Sweet's Marriage Settlement Cases   (DLA)
Sweet........ Sweet's Precedents in Conveyancing   (DLA)
Sweet LD ... Sweet's Dictionary of English Law [*1882*]   (DLA)
Sweet M Sett Cas ... Sweet's Marriage Settlement Cases [*England*]   (DLA)
Sweet Pr Conv ... Sweet's Precedents in Conveyancing [*4th ed.*] [*1886*]   (DLA)
SWEFCO.... Special Weapons Ferry Control Office [*or Officer*]
SWEHO ...... Scandinavian Journal of Work Environment and Health [*A publication*]
SWEIA....... Studies in Wind Engineering and Industrial Aerodynamics [*Elsevier Book Series*] [*A publication*]
SWEJDFC ... Sing with the Earth John Denver Fan Club [*Denver, CO*]   (EA)
SWEL .... Southwestern Electric Service Co. [*NASDAQ symbol*]   (NQ)
SWEL .... Special Weapons Equipment List
Swell .... Single Woman Earning Lots in London [*Lifestyle classification*]
SWELSTRA ... Special Weapons Equipment List Single Theater Requisitioning Agency
Swen .... Sweeney's New York Superior Court Reports [*31-32 New York*]   (DLA)
SWENU ...... Swensen's, Inc. Uts [*NASDAQ symbol*]   (NQ)
SWES........ Southwest Leasing Corp. [*NASDAQ symbol*]   (NQ)
SWESS....... Special Weapons Emergency Separation System   (AFM)
SWESSAR ... Stone and Webster Standard Safety Analysis Report [*Nuclear energy*]   (NRCH)
SWET........ Simulated Water Entry Test
SWETS....... Solid Waste Engineering Transfer System
SWETTU ... Special Weapons Experimental Tactical Test Unit
SWF .... Newburgh [*New York*] [*Airport symbol*]   (OAG)
SWF .... Seawater Feed
SWF .... Shortwave Fadeouts
SWF .... Silver Wing Fraternity   (EA)
SWF .... Single White Female [*Classified advertising*]
SWF .... Southwest Folklore [*A publication*]
SWF .... Southwest Forest Industries, Inc. [*NYSE symbol*]
SWF .... Special Warning Function   (MCD)
SWF .... Special Weapons Facility [*Navy*]
SWF .... Steelworker Fabricator [*Navy rating*]

SWF .... Still Waters Foundation [*Pensacola, FL*] (EA)
SWF .... Suedwestfunk [*Radio network*] [*West Germany*]
SWFB .... Southwestern Freight Bureau
SWFC .... Southwest Fisheries Center
SWFC .... Surface Weapons Fire Control
SWFG .... Secondary Waveform Generator [*Telecommunications*] (TEL)
SWFPA ...... Structural Wood Fiber Products Association [*Later, Structural Cement - Fiber Products Association*] (EA)
SWFR .... Slow Write, Fast Read [*Data processing*] (IEEE)
SWFT .... Swift Energy Co. [*NASDAQ symbol*] (NQ)
SWFTU ...... Sudan Workers Federation of Trade Unions
SWFX .... Spotweld Fixture [*Tool*]
SWG .... Salam-Weinberg-Glashow [*One unified field theory in physics*]
SWG .... Scientific Working Group [*EXAMETNET*]
SWG .... Shock Wave Generator
SWG .... Shuttle Working Group [*NASA*] (MCD)
SWG .... Sine Wave Generator
SWG .... Slotted Waveguide
SWG .... Society of Woman Geographers (EA)
SWG .... South-West Gold Corp. [*Vancouver Stock Exchange symbol*]
SWG .... Special Working Group
SWG .... Squarewave Generator
SWG .... Staff Working Group
SWG .... Standard Wire Gauge [*Telecommunications*]
SWG .... Standard/Working Group (MCD)
SWG .... Stubs Wire Gauge
SWG .... Swing (MSA)
SWGD .... Swinging Door
SWGH .... Schriften der Strassburger Wissenschaftlichen Gesellschaft in Heidelberg [*A publication*]
SWGM .... Spanish World Gospel Mission (EA)
SWGR .... Switchgear
SwGU .... Goteborgs Universititsbibliotek, Goteborg, Sweden [*Library symbol*] [*Library of Congress*] (LCLS)
SWH .... Seaway Multi-Corp Ltd. [*Toronto Stock Exchange symbol*]
SWH .... Significant Wave Height [*Oceanography*]
SWHA .... Social Welfare History Archives Center [*University of Minnesota*] [*Research center*] (RCD)
SWHG .... Social Welfare History Group [*Western Michigan University*] [*Kalamazoo*] (EA)
SW Hist Q... Southwestern Historical Quarterly [*A publication*]
SWHQ .... Southwestern Historical Quarterly [*A publication*]
SWI .... Salt-Water Igniter
SWI .... Sealant and Waterproofers Institute [*Kansas, MO*] (EA)
SWI .... Seawind Resources, Incorporated [*Vancouver Stock Exchange symbol*]
SWI .... Seaworthiness Impairment (NVT)
SWI .... Sherman [*Texas*] [*Airport symbol*] (OAG)
SWI .... Shock Wave Interaction
SWI .... Sine Wave Inverter
SWI .... Software Interrupt [*Data processing*]
SWI .... Special Weather Intelligence (MCD)
SWI .... Special World Intervals
SWI .... Stall Warning Indicator
SWI .... Standing Wave Indicator
SWI .... Steel Window Institute [*Cleveland, OH*] (EA)
SWI .... Stroke Work Index [*Neurology*]
SWI .... Sunworld International Airways, Inc. [*Las Vegas, NV*] [*FAA designator*] (FAAC)
SWICA ...... Self Winding Clock Association (EA)
SWID .... Southwest India Docks [*Shipping*] [*British*] (ROG)
SWIDOC..... Sociaal-Wetenschappelijk Informatie-en Documentatiecentrum [*Social Science Information and Documentation Center*] [*Netherlands*] [*Information service*] (EISS)
SWIFT .... Significant Word in the Full Title [*Data processing*] (DIT)
SWIFT .... Society for World-Wide International Funds Transfer
SWIFT .... Society for Worldwide Interbank Financial Telecommunication [*La Hulpe, Belgium*] [*Banking network*]
SWIFT .... Software Implemented Friden Translator [*Data processing*]
SWIFT ...... Stored Wave Inverse Fourier Transform [*Spectrometry*]
SWIFT ...... Strength of Wings Including Flutter
SWIFT ...... System Workshops in Forecasting Techniques [*Bell System*]
Swift Dig .... Swift's Connecticut Digest (DLA)
SWIFT LASS ... Signal Word Index of Field and Title - Literature Abstract Specialized Search (DIT)
SWIFT SIR ... Signal Word Index of Field and Title - Scientific Information Retrieval (DIT)
SWIG .... Southwestern Irrigated Cotton Growers Association
SWIM .... Sea Warfare Interim Model (CINC)
SWIM .... Sperm-Washing Insemination Method
Swimm World Jun Swimm ... Swimming World and Junior Swimmer [*A publication*]
SWIMS ...... Serialized Weapons Information Management System [*Navy*]
SWIMS ...... Ship Weapon Installation Manuals
Swin .... Swinburne on Wills [*10 eds.*] [*1590-1803*] (DLA)
Swin .... Swinton's Scotch Justiciary Reports [*1835-41*] (DLA)
Swinb Desc ... Swinburne on Descents [*1825*] (DLA)
Swinb Mar ... Swinburne on Married Women [*1846*] (DLA)
Swinb Wills ... Swinburne on Wills (DLA)

SWINE........ Students Wildly Indignant about Nearly Everything [*Group in "L'il Abner" comic strip*]
Swine Day Univ Calif ... Swine Day. University of California [*A publication*]
Swine Rep Univ Hawaii Coop Ext Serv ... Swine Report. University of Hawaii. Cooperative Extension Service [*A publication*]
SWINGR..... Sweep Integrator (AAG)
Swin Jus Cas ... Swinton's Scotch Justiciary Cases (DLA)
Swin Reg App ... Swinton's Scotch Registration Appeal Cases [*1835-41*] (DLA)
Swint.......... Swinton's Scotch Justiciary Cases (DLA)
SWIO .... SACLANT [*Supreme Allied Commander, Atlantic*] War Intelligence Organization (NATG)
SWIP .... Secret Work in Process (MCD)
SWIP .... Society for Women in Philosophy (EA)
SWIP .... Soil-Wheel Interaction Performance
SWIP .... Standing Wave Impedance Probe [*Geophysical instrument*]
SWIP .... Super-Weight Improvement Program [*Navy*] (NG)
SWIPMD.... Society for Women in Philosophy, Midwest Division (EA)
SWIR .... Shortwave Infrared
SWIR .... Special Weapons Inspection Report
SWIRL....... South Western Industrial Research Limited [*British*] (ARC)
SWIRLS..... Southwest Regional Library System [*Library network*]
SWIRS....... Solid Waste Information Retrieval System [*Environmental Protection Agency*]
SWIS .... Sensitive Wildlife Information System [*Army*] [*Vicksburg, MS*] (EISS)
SWIS .... Swiss Wildlife Information Service [*Zurich*] [*Information service*] (EISS)
SWISSAIR ... Swiss Air Transport Co. Ltd.
Swiss Credit Bank Bul ... Swiss Credit Banking Bulletin [*A publication*]
Swiss J Hydrol ... Swiss Journal of Hydrology [*A publication*]
Swiss News ... Swiss Economic News [*A publication*]
Swiss R Wld Aff ... Swiss Review of World Affairs [*A publication*]
SWIT .... Switzerland
SWITL .... Southwestern Industrial Traffic League [*Lubbock, TX*] (EA)
SWITT .... Surface Wave Independent Tap Transducer (IEEE)
SWITZ .... Switzerland
SWIX .... Shelby Williams Industries [*NASDAQ symbol*] (NQ)
SWJ........... Single Wire Junction
SWJ........... Socket Wrench Joint
SW J Anthrop ... Southwestern Journal of Anthropology [*A publication*]
SW J Phil.... Southwestern Journal of Philosophy [*A publication*]
Sw J T .... Southwestern Journal of Theology [*A publication*]
SW J Th...... Southwestern Journal of Theology [*A publication*]
SWK........... [*The*] Stanley Works [*NYSE symbol*]
SW KR .... Swedish Krona [*Monetary unit*]
SWL........... Safe Working Load [*Shipping*]
SWL........... Short Wavelength LASER
SWL........... Short Wavelength Limit
SWL........... Shortwave Listener [*Radio*]
SWL........... Signals Warfare Laboratory [*Army*] (RDA)
SWL........... Single-Wheel Loading [*Aviation*]
SWL........... Snow Hill, MD [*Location identifier*] [*FAA*] (FAAL)
SWL........... Solid Waste Litter
SWL........... South West Air Ltd. [*Windsor, ON, Canada*] [*FAA designator*] (FAAC)
SWL........... Southwest Realty [*American Stock Exchange symbol*]
SWL........... Still Water Level
SWL........... Sulfite Waste Liquor
SWL........... Surface Wave Line
SWLA .... Southwestern Library Association
SW Law J ... Southwestern Law Journal [*A publication*]
SWLC .... Southwestern Connecticut Library Council [*Library network*]
SWLDG ..... Socket Welding
Sw Legal Found Inst on Oil & Gas L & Tax ... Southwestern Legal Foundation. Institution on Oil and Gas Law and Taxation [*A publication*]
SWLF .... Southwestern Legal Foundation (EA)
SWLG........ Swelling (FAAC)
SWLG........ SWLG Corp. [*NASDAQ symbol*] (NQ)
SW L J .... Southwestern Law Journal [*A publication*]
SWL Rev .... Southwestern Law Review (DLA)
SwLU .... Lunds Universitet [*University of Lund*], Lund, Sweden [*Library symbol*] [*Library of Congress*] (LCLS)
SWLY .... Southwesterly [*Meteorology*] (FAAC)
SWM.......... Sawmill [*California*] [*Seismograph station code, US Geological Survey*] [*Closed*] (SEIS)
SWM.......... Serber-Wilson Method [*Nuclear energy*] (NRCH)
SWM.......... Shipboard Wave Meter
SWM.......... Single White Male [*Classified advertising*]
SwM .... Southwest Microfilm, Inc., El Paso, TX [*Library symbol*] [*Library of Congress*] (LCLS)
SWM.......... Special Warfare Mission (AABC)
SWM.......... Spotweld Machine [*Tool*]
SWM.......... Stan West Mining Corp. [*Toronto Stock Exchange symbol*]
SWM.......... Suia-Missu [*Brazil*] [*Airport symbol*] (OAG)
SWM.......... Surface Wave Mode
SWMA .... Society of Women in Military Aviation (EA)
SWMA .... Solid Waste Management Association
SWMA .... Southwestern Monuments Association [*Later, SPMA*] (EA)
SWMAT...... Switch Matrix (MCD)

SWMC........ Stan West Mining Corporation [*NASDAQ symbol*]   (NQ)
SWMCCS... Standard Weather Messages Command and Control System   (MCD)
SWMFB...... Southwestern Motor Freight Bureau
SWMO........ Solid Waste Management Office [*Later, Office of Solid Waste Management Programs*] [*Environmental Protection Agency*]
SWMS .... Solid Waste Management System [*Nuclear energy*]   (NRCH)
SW Musician ... Southwestern Musician [*A publication*]
SWN .... Leadville, CO [*Location identifier*] [*FAA*]   (FAAL)
SWN .... Notre Dame College, Wilcox, Saskatchewan [*Library symbol*] [*National Library of Canada*]   (NLC)
SWN .... Southwestern Energy Co. [*NYSE symbol*]
SWN .... Sworn   (ROG)
SWNAA...... Southwestern Naturalist [*United States*] [*A publication*]
SWNCC...... State, War, Navy Coordinating Committee
SWND .... Social Workers for Nuclear Disarmament   (EA)
SWNJ .... Southwest New Jersey Consortium for Health Information Services [*Library network*]
SWNS........ Sprawozdanie z Prac Naukowych Wydzialu Nauk Spolecznych Pan [*A publication*]
SWO .... Senior Watch Officer [*Navy*]   (NVT)
SWO .... Shallow Resources, Inc. [*Vancouver Stock Exchange symbol*]
SWO .... Solid Waste Office [*Later, Office of Solid Waste Management Programs*] [*Environmental Protection Agency*]
SWO .... Southwestern Oregon Community College, Coos Bay, OR [*OCLC symbol*]   (OCLC)
SWO .... Squadron Wireless Officer [*Navy*] [*British*]
SWO .... Squarewave Oscillator
SWO .... Staff Watch Officer   (NVT)
SWO .... Staff Weather Officer
SWO .... Station Warrant Officer [*Air Force*] [*British*]
SWO .... Stillwater [*Oklahoma*] [*Airport symbol*]   (OAG)
SWO .... Stop Work Order
SWO .... Stud Welding Outfit
SWO .... Support Work Order   (AAG)
SWO .... Surface Warfare Officer [*Navy*]   (NVT)
SW/O .... Switchover
SWOB .... Salaries, Wages, Overhead, and Benefits   (NASA)
SWOB .... Ship Waste Off-Loading Barge [*Navy*]   (CAAL)
SWOC .... Special Weapons Operation Center [*Army*]   (AABC)
SWOC .... Steel Workers Organizing Committee [*Became United Steelworkers of America*]
SWOC .... Subject Word out of Context [*Data processing*]   (DIT)
SWOD .... Special Weapons Ordnance Devices
SWOG .... Special Weapons Overflight Guide   (AFM)
SWOP........ Service Weapons Operational Procedures   (MCD)
SWOP........ Special Weapons Ordnance Publication [*Navy*]   (NVT)
SWOP........ Specifications for Web Offset Publications [*Printing technology*]
SWOP........ Stop Without Pay
SWOP........ Structural Weight Optimization Program [*NASA*]   (KSC)
SWOPS ..... Single Well Oil Production Ship [*British*]
SWOPSI ..... Stanford Workshop on Political and Social Issues [*Stanford University*]
SWORD ..... Separated, Widowed, or Divorced [*New York City association*]
SWORD ..... Shallow Water Oceanographic Research Data [*System*] [*Naval Ordnance Laboratory and Naval Oceanographic Office*]
SWORDS.... Standard Work Ordering and Reporting Data System [*Army*]
SWORL ..... Southwestern Ohio Rural Libraries [*Library network*]
SwOrM....... Regionsjukhuset, Medicinska Biblioteket [*Regional Hospital, Medical Library*], Orebro, Sweden [*Library symbol*] [*Library of Congress*]   (LCLS)
SWOS .... Surface Warfare Officer's School [*Navy*]   (NVT)
SWOSCOLCOM ... Surface Warfare Officer's School Command [*Navy*]   (NVT)
SWOT........ Strengths, Weaknesses, Opportunities, Threats [*Analysis for organizations*]
SWOV........ Switchover   (MSA)
SWP .... Safe Working Pressure
SWP .... Salt-Water Pump   (MSA)
SWP .... Science Working Panel [*NASA*]
SWP .... Sector Working Party [*British*]
SWP .... Semi-Tech Microelectronics, Inc. [*Toronto Stock Exchange symbol*]
SWP .... Service Water Pump [*Nuclear energy*]   (NRCH)
SWP .... Shock Wave Profile
SWP .... Short Wavelength Prime [*Camera for spectra*]
SWP .... Socialist Workers' Party [*London, England*]   (PPW)
SWP .... Society of Wireless Pioneers
SWP .... Society for Women in Plastics [*Sterling Heights, MI*]   (EA)
SWP .... Soil-Test Water Probe
SWP .... Solid Waste Packaging   (NRCH)
SWP .... Solid Waste Processing [*Nuclear energy*]   (NRCH)
SWP .... Southwest Pacific
SWP .... Space, Weight, and Power
SWP .... Special Weapons Project [*Military*]
SWP .... Special Working Party [*Military*]
SWP .... Standby Warning Panel   (MCD)

SWP .... Stiftung Wissenschaft und Politik [*Foundation for Science and Politics*] [*Ebenhausen, West Germany*] [*Information service*]   (EISS)
SWP .... Submersible Water Pump
SWP .... Summer Work Program
SWP .... Supply Working Party of Official Committee on Armistice Terms and Civil Administration [*World War II*]
SWP .... Surface Warfare Plan [*Navy*]   (CAAL)
SWP .... Surface Wave Phenomena
SWP .... Survey of Western Palestine [*C. R. Conder et al*] [*A publication*]   (BJA)
SWP .... Swamp   (ADA)
SWP .... Swamp Creek [*Montana*] [*Seismograph station code, US Geological Survey*] [*Closed*]   (SEIS)
SWP .... Sweep
SWPA........ Southwest Pacific Area [*World War II*]
SWPA........ Southwestern Power Administration [*Department of Energy*]
SWPA........ Southwestern Psychological Association   (MCD)
SWPA........ Spotweld Pattern [*Tool*]   (AAG)
SWPA........ Submersible Wastewater Pump Association [*Chicago, IL*]   (EA)
SWPA........ Surplus War Property Administration [*Terminated, 1944*]
SW Pacific ... South West Pacific [*A publication*]
SWPB........ Surplus War Property Board [*Terminated, 1945*]
SWPC........ Smaller War Plants Corporation [*World War II*]
SWPC........ Southwest Pacific Command [*Navy*]
SWPCP ...... Prince Albert National Park, Parks Canada [*Parc National Prince Albert, Parcs Canada*] Waskesiu Lakes, Saskatchewan [*Library symbol*] [*National Library of Canada*]   (NLC)
SWPF .... Southwest Pacific Force [*Later, Southwest Pacific Command*] [*Navy*]
SWPJ .... Study of Western Palestine: Jerusalem [*C. Warren and C. R. Conder*] [*A publication*]   (BJA)
SWPM .... Survey of Western Palestine: Memoirs [*C. R. Conder*] [*A publication*]   (BJA)
SW Pol Sci Q ... Southwestern Political Science Quarterly   (DLA)
SWPP .... Service Water Pressurization Pump [*Nuclear energy*]   (IEEE)
SWPP .... Southwest Power Pool [*Regional power council*]   (NRCH)
SWPPD ...... Society for Women in Philosophy, Pacific Division   (EA)
SWP(S) ...... Solid Waste Processing (System)   (NRCH)
SWPSA ..... Southwestern Peanut Shellers Association
SWPSD ..... Society for Women in Philosophy, Southwest Division   (EA)
SWPSP....... Survey of Western Palestine: Special Papers [*A publication*]   (BJA)
SWPT .... Service Weapons Test   (NVT)
SWR .... Serum Wassermann Reaction [*Clinical chemistry*]
SWR .... Service Water Reservoir [*Nuclear energy*]   (NRCH)
SwR........... Sewanee Review [*A publication*]
SWR .... Short Wavelength Radiation   (KSC)
SWR .... Shortwave Ratio   (DEN)
SWR .... Sine Wave Response
SWR .... Siphon Withdrawal Response
SWR .... Sodium-Water Reaction   (NRCH)
SWR .... Sons of the Whiskey Rebellion   (EA)
SWR .... South Western Reporter   (DLA)
SWR .... Southwest Review [*A publication*]
SWR .... Southwestern Railway [*British*]   (ROG)
SWR .... Special Warning Receiver   (MCD)
SWR .... Standing Wave Ratio [*Voltage*] [*Electronics*]
SWR .... Steel Wire Rope
SWR .... Stress Wave Riveter [*Metal forming*]
SWR .... Submarine Water Reactor   (NRCH)
SWR .... Switch Rails
SWRA........ Selected Water Resources Abstracts [*Service of WRSIC*] [*Database*]
SWRB........ Sadler's Wells Royal Ballet [*British*]
SWRB........ Standing Wave Ratio Bridge [*Electronics*]
SW Rep ...... South Western Reporter   (DLA)
SW Repr ..... South Western Reporter   (DLA)
SWRF........ Sine Wave Response Filter [*Program*]
SWRHL...... Southwestern Radiological Health Laboratory [*HEW*]
SWRI .... Southwestern Research Institute [*San Antonio, TX*] [*Research center*]
SWRJ .... Split Wing Ramjet
SWRL .... Southwest Regional Laboratory for Educational Research and Development
SWRLSS... Southwest Regional Library Service System [*Library network*]
SWRM .... Standing Wave Ratio Meter [*Electronics*]
SWRMPAC ... Southwestern Regional Manpower Advisory Committee [*Terminated, 1974*] [*Department of Labor*]   (EGAO)
SWRN........ Southwestern [*Meteorology*]   (FAAC)
SWROM ..... Standing Wave Read-Only Memory [*Data processing*]
SWROSS.... Southwest Regional Office for Spanish Speaking   (EA)
SWRP .... Satellite Wildlife Research Project
SWRP .... Sectionalized Work Requirements Package   (MCD)
SWRPRS .... Sodium-Water Reaction Pressure Relief Subsystem [*Nuclear energy*]   (NRCH)
SWRSIC ..... Southern Water Resources Scientific Information Center [*Raleigh, NC*]
SWS .... Saturn Workshop [*NASA*]
SWS .... Seam Welding System

SWS .... Service Water System [*Nuclear energy*]   (NRCH)
SWS .... Service-Wide Supply
SWS .... Shallow Water SONAR
SWS .... Shift Word, Substituting
SWS .... Shock Wave Sensor   (RDA)
SWS .... Single White Silk-Covered [*Wire insulation*]
SWS .... Slow-Wave Sleep
SWS .... Sniper Weapon Sight   (INF)
SWS .... Sociologists for Women in Society   (EA)
SWS .... Solar Wind Spectrometer
SWS .... Solid Waste System   (NRCH)
SWS .... Southwest Writers Series [*A publication*]
SWS .... Southwestern Studies [*University of Texas, El Paso*] [*A publication*]
SWS .... Space Weapon Systems [*Air Force*]
SWS .... Special Weapon Systems [*Military*]
SWS .... Standard Weapon Station [*Nuclear arms control*]
SWS .... Static Water Supply   (ADA)
SWS .... Still Water Surface
SWS .... Strategic Weapon System [*Military*]   (CAAL)
SWS .... Swansea [*Wales*] [*Airport symbol*]   (OAG)
SWS .... Switch Scan   (MCD)
SWS .... Switch Stand
SWS .... Systolic Wall Stress [*Cardiology*]
SWSA .... Southern Wood Seasoning Association
SWSD .... Special Weapons Supply Depot
SWSE .... Southeast Regional Library, Weyburn, Saskatchewan [*Library symbol*] [*National Library of Canada*]   (NLC)
SWSF .... Society for a World Service Federation
SWSG .... Security Window Screen and Guard
SWSI .... Stanley Well Service [*NASDAQ symbol*]   (NQ)
SWSJ .... Son of WSFA Journal [*A publication*]
SwSK .... Kungliga Tekniska Hoegskolan [*Royal Institute of Technology*], Stockholm, Sweden [*Library symbol*] [*Library of Congress*]   (LCLS)
SwSKB .... Kungliga Biblioteket, Bibliotheca Regia Holmiensis, Stockholm, Sweden [*Library symbol*] [*Library of Congress*]   (LCLS)
SwSKM ...... Kungliga Karolinska Mediko-Kirurgiska Institutes, Stockholm, Sweden [*Library symbol*] [*Library of Congress*]   (LCLS)
SwSL .... Latinamerika-Institutet, Stockholm, Sweden [*Library symbol*] [*Library of Congress*]   (LCLS)
SWSM .... Special Weapons Supply Memorandum [*Army*]   (AABC)
SW Social Sci Q ... Southwestern Social Science Quarterly [*A publication*]
SWSR .... Solid Waste Shipping Room   (NRCH)
SWST .... Service Water Storage Tank [*Nuclear energy*]   (IEEE)
SWST .... Society of Wood Science and Technology   (EA)
SW St (UTEP) ... Southwestern Studies (University of Texas, El Paso) [*A publication*]
SwSU .... Stockholms Universitetsbibliotheket, Stockholm, Sweden [*Library symbol*] [*Library of Congress*]   (LCLS)
SWSVC ...... Souris Valley Regional Care Center, Weyburn, Saskatchewan [*Library symbol*] [*National Library of Canada*]   (NLC)
SWSWTU ... Sheffield Wool Shear Workers' Trade Union [*British*]
SWT .... Search-while-Track   (CAAL)
SWT .... Seward, NE [*Location identifier*] [*FAA*]   (FAAL)
SWT .... Shortwave Transmitter
SWT .... Single-Weight [*Paper*]
SWT .... Special Weapons Test
SWT .... Spiral Wrap Tubing
SWT .... Spotweld Template   (MCD)
SWT .... Supersonic Wind Tunnel   (MCD)
SWT .... Sweat
SWT .... Swept Frequency Transform   (CAAL)
SWT .... Swift Aire Lines, Inc. [*San Luis Obispo, CA*] [*FAA designator*]   (FAAC)
SWT .... Switch Ties
SWTA .... System Work Team   (MCD)
SWTA .... Special Weapons Training Allowance
SWTC .... Special Weapon Technical Command [*Navy*]   (MCD)
SWTI .... Special Weapons Technical Instructions [*Army*]   (AABC)
SWTL .... Surface Wave Transmission Line
SWTN .... Sprawozdania Wroclawskiego Towarzystwa Naukowego [*A publication*]
SWTN .... Swanton Corp. [*NASDAQ symbol*]   (NQ)
SWTR .... Southern California Water Co. [*NASDAQ symbol*]   (NQ)
Sw & Tr ...... Swabey and Tristram's Probate and Divorce Reports [*164 English Reprint*]   (DLA)
SWTS .... Secondary Waste Treatment System [*Nuclear energy*]   (NRCH)
SWTTEU ... Special Weapons Test and Tactical Evaluation Unit
SWTZ .... Switzerland
SWU .... Idaho Falls, ID [*Location identifier*] [*FAA*]   (FAAL)
SWU .... Sagami Women's University [*UTLAS symbol*]
SWU .... Separation Work Unit [*Measure of enrichment of atomic reactivity*]
SWU .... Separative Work Unit [*Measure of uranium enrichment capability*]
SWU .... Slovenian Women's Union   (EA)
SW U L Rev ... Southwestern University Law Review [*A publication*]
SwUmU ...... Umea Universitetsbibliotek, Umea, Sweden [*Library symbol*] [*Library of Congress*]   (LCLS)
SWUS .... Southwest United States

SWUSL ...... Southwestern University School of Law   (DLA)
SwUU .... Universitet i Uppsala [*University of Uppsala*], Uppsala, Sweden [*Library symbol*] [*Library of Congress*]   (LCLS)
SWV .... Suave Shoe Corp. [*NYSE symbol*]
SWV .... Swan View [*Australia*] [*Seismograph station code, US Geological Survey*]   (SEIS)
SWV .... Swivel   (AAG)
SWVA .... Scottish War Veterans of America   (EA)
SWVB .... Social Work Vocational Bureau   (EA)
SWVL .... Swivel   (MSA)
SWW .... Severe Weather Warning   (KSC)
SWW .... Sweetwater, TX [*Location identifier*] [*FAA*]   (FAAL)
SWW .... Winthrop College, Rock Hill, SC [*OCLC symbol*]   (OCLC)
SWWA .... South-West Water Authority [*British*]
SWWBDS ... Software Work Breakdown Structure   (MCD)
SWWF .... Speed-Welding Wire Feeder
SWWIAH ... Society of World War I Aero Historians
SWWU .... Singapore Wood Workers' Union
SWX .... Southwest Gas Corp. [*NYSE symbol*]
SWXO .... Staff Weather Officer [*NASA*]   (KSC)
SWY .... Albemarle, NC [*Location identifier*] [*FAA*]   (FAAL)
SWY .... Stopway
SWY .... Stornaway Resources Corp. [*Vancouver Stock Exchange symbol*]
SWY .... Swiss Yiddish   (BJA)
SWZ .... Smyrna, TN [*Location identifier*] [*FAA*]   (FAAL)
SWZ .... Special Watch Zone [*Navy*]   (NVT)
SWZ .... Swaziland [*Three-letter standard code*]   (CNC)
SX .... Greece [*Aircraft nationality and registration mark*]   (FAAC)
SX .... Pia Societas Sancti Francisci Xaverii pro Exteris Missionibus [*St. Francis Xavier Foreign Mission Society*] [*Xaverian Missionary Fathers*] [*Roman Catholic religious order*]
SX .... Sacks
SX .... Sigma Xi [*Society*]
SX .... Simplex [*Transmission direction*]   (CET)
SX .... Solvent Extraction   (DEN)
sx .... South West Africa [*Namibia*] [*MARC country of publication code*] [*Library of Congress*]   (LCCP)
SX .... Stability Index [*Aviation*]   (FAAC)
SX .... Sterling Philippines Airways, Inc. [*ICAO designator*]   (FAAC)
SX .... Sussex [*County in England*]
SX .... SXT Resources Ltd. [*Vancouver Stock Exchange symbol*]
SX .... Union of Soviet Socialist Republics [*Later, FC*] [*License plate code assigned to foreign diplomats in the US*]
SX-1980 ...... Model number used by U.S. Pioneer Electronic Corp. [*Name is derived from "S" in "stereo amplifier" and "X" in "TX tuner"*]
SXA .... Stored Index to Address
SXAD .... Sioux Army Depot
SXAPS ...... Soft X-Ray Appearance Potential Spectrometer [*or Spectroscopy*] [*Air Force*]
SXB .... Strasbourg [*France*] [*Airport symbol*]   (OAG)
SXBT .... Shipboard Expendable Bathythermograph [*System*] [*Naval Oceanographic Office*]
SXBT .... Surface Expendable Bathythermograph [*Marine science*]   (MSC)
SXC .... Saint Xavier College [*Chicago, IL*]
SXC .... Santa Catalina, CA [*Location identifier*] [*FAA*]   (FAAL)
SXCO .... Switchco, Inc. [*NASDAQ symbol*]   (NQ)
SXD .... Springfield, VT [*Location identifier*] [*FAA*]   (FAAL)
SXE .... Sale [*Australia*] [*Airport symbol*]   (OAG)
SXE .... Soft X-Ray Experiment [*Also, SXX*]
SXE .... Spencar Explorations Ltd. [*Vancouver Stock Exchange symbol*]
SXEW .... Solvent Extraction and Electrowinning [*Metallurgy*]
SXF .... Berlin [*East Germany*] [*Airport symbol*]   (OAG)
SXF .... Solvent Extraction Feed   (NRCH)
SXG .... Senanga [*Zambia*] [*Airport symbol*]   (OAG)
SXH .... Sehulea [*Papua New Guinea*] [*Airport symbol*]   (OAG)
SXI .... Standex International Corp. [*NYSE symbol*]
SXI .... Synex International, Inc. [*Vancouver Stock Exchange symbol*]
SXIS .... Scattered X-Ray Internal Standard [*for surface analysis*]
SXL .... Sexless [*Connector*]
SXL .... Short-Arc Xenon Lamp
SXL .... Summersville, WV [*Location identifier*] [*FAA*]   (FAAL)
SXM .... St. Maarten [*Netherlands Antilles*] [*Airport symbol*]
SXM .... Sphinx Mining Inc. [*Vancouver Stock Exchange symbol*]
SXML .... San Xavier Mining Laboratory [*University of Arizona*] [*Research center*]   (RCD)
SXN .... Sao Jose Do Xingu [*Brazil*] [*Airport symbol*]   (OAG)
SXN .... Section   (MDG)
SXNP .... Saxton Products [*NASDAQ symbol*]   (NQ)
SXO .... Senior Experimental Officer [*Also, SEO, SExO*] [*Ministry of Agriculture, Fisheries, and Food*] [*British*]
SXP .... Sheldon Point [*Alaska*] [*Airport symbol*]   (OAG)
SXP .... Sunnyvale Public Library, Sunnyvale, CA [*OCLC symbol*]   (OCLC)
SXQ .... Soldotna, AK [*Location identifier*] [*FAA*]   (FAAL)
SXR .... Soft X-Ray Region
SXR .... Srinagar [*India*] [*Airport symbol*]   (OAG)
SXRF .... Synchrotron X-Ray Fluorescence [*Spectrometry*]

SXS .... Sigma Xi Society
SXS .... Stellar X-Ray Spectra
SxS .... Step-by-Step Switching System [*Telecommunications*]
SXSKA ...... Sakura X-Rei Shashin Kenkyu [*A publication*]
SXT .... Sextant   (NASA)
SXT .... Sexton Summit, OR [*Location identifier*] [*FAA*]   (FAAL)
SXT .... Sextuple   (MSA)
SXT .... Stable X-Ray Transmitter
SXTF .... Satellite X-Ray Test Facility
SXTN .... Sextant   (MSA)
SXX .... Secolul XX [*A publication*]
SXX .... Soft X-Ray Experiment [*Also, SXE*]
SXY .... Sidney [*New York*] [*Airport symbol*]   (OAG)
SY .... Air Alsace [*France*] [*ICAO designator*]   (FAAC)
SY .... School Year   (AABC)
SY .... Security
SY .... Sefer Yezirah   (BJA)
SY .... Seychelles
SY .... Shipyard
SY .... Shoulder Yaw   (MCD)
SY .... Sloppy [*Track condition*] [*Thoroughbred racing*]
SY .... Southern Yiddish   (BJA)
SY .... Square Yard
SY .... Staff Years   (OICC)
SY .... Steam Yacht   (ROG)
SY .... Supply
SY .... Surrey [*County in England*]
SY .... Survey
SY .... Sustainer Yaw   (AAG)
Sy .... Symmachus   (BJA)
SY .... Symposium [*A publication*]
Sy .... Symptoms [*Medicine*]
SY .... Synchronized   (MDG)
SY .... Syphilis [*Medicine*]
sy .... Syria [*MARC country of publication code*] [*Library of Congress*]   (LCCP)
SY .... Syria [*or Syrian Arab Republic*] [*Two-letter standard code*]   (CNC)
Sy .... Syria. Revue d'Art Oriental et d'Archeologie [*A publication*]
SYA .... Save Your Afterdeck [*Bowdlerized version*]
SYA .... Shemya Island [*Alaska*] [*Airport symbol*]   (OAG)
SYB .... Seal Bay [*Alaska*] [*Airport symbol*]   (OAG)
SYB .... Syracuse University, Syracuse, NY [*OCLC symbol*]   (OCLC)
SYBEAUXARTS ... Syndicat des Beaux Arts Africains [*Union of African Fine Arts*]
SyBU .... Symbolae Biblicae Upsalienses [*A publication*]
SYC .... Seychelles [*Three-letter standard code*]   (CNC)
SYC .... Sycamore   (AAG)
SYC .... Synco Development [*Vancouver Stock Exchange symbol*]
SYCATE ..... Symptom-Cause-Test
SYCLOPS ... SYFA Concurrent Logic Operating System
SYCOM ...... Synchronous Communications [*Satellite*] [*GSFC*]
SYCOSPARE ... Shipyard Checkout Spare
SYCOT ...... Shipyard Checkout Test
SYCP .... Syncom Corporation [*NASDAQ symbol*]   (NQ)
SYD .... Casper, WY [*Location identifier*] [*FAA*]   (FAAL)
SYD .... Scheer Energy Development [*Vancouver Stock Exchange symbol*]
SYD .... Scotland Yard
SYD .... Shipyard
SYD .... South Yemen Dinar   (BJA)
SYD .... [*Release*] Subject Your Discretion   (FAAC)
SYD .... Sum of the Year's Digits [*Statistics*]
SYD .... Sydney [*Australia*] [*Airport symbol*]   (OAG)
SYD .... Sydney [*Australia*] [*Seismograph station code, US Geological Survey*] [*Closed*]   (SEIS)
SYD .... Sydney [*Australia*]
Syd App ..... Sydney Appeals [*Australia*]   (DLA)
SYDHARB ... Sydney Harbour [*Measurement of water*] [*Australia*]   (ADA)
SYDIA .... System Developer Interface Activity [*Data processing*]
Syd Jaycee ... Sydney Jaycee [*A publication*]
Syd Jewish News ... Sydney Jewish News [*A publication*]
Syd Law R ... Sydney Law Review [*A publication*]
Syd LR .... Sydney Law Review [*A publication*]
Syd L Rev ... Sydney Law Review [*A publication*]
SYDMF ...... Scheer Energy Development Corp. [*NASDAQ symbol*]   (NQ)
Syd Morning Her ... Sydney Morning Herald [*A publication*]
Syd Morning Herald ... Sydney Morning Herald [*A publication*]
Sydney GCN ... Sydney Gay Community News [*A publication*]
Sydney Law R ... Sydney Law Review [*A publication*]
Sydney Law Rev ... Sydney Law Review [*A publication*]
Sydney L Rev ... Sydney Law Review [*A publication*]
Sydney Q Mag ... Sydney Quarterly Magazine [*A publication*]
Sydney Univ Med J ... Sydney University. Medical Journal [*A publication*]
Sydney Univ Sch Civ Eng Res Rep ... Sydney University. School of Civil Engineering. Research Report [*A publication*]
Sydney Water Bd J ... Sydney Water Board. Journal [*A publication*]
Sydowia Ann Mycol ... Sydowia. Annales Mycologici [*A publication*]
Sydowia Ann Mycolog Beih ... Sydowia. Annales Mycologici. Beihefte [*A publication*]
Syd Stud .... Sydney Studies in English [*A publication*]

Sydsven Medicinhist ... Sydsvenska Medicinhistoriska Saellskapets Arsskrift [*A publication*]
Sydsvenska Ortnamns-Sallsk Arsskr ... Sydsvenska Ortnamns-Sallskapets Arsskrift [*A publication*]
Syd Univ Ag Economics Res Bul ... University of Sydney. Department of Agricultural Economics. Research Bulletin [*A publication*]
Syd Univ Civ Engng Schl Res Rep ... University of Sydney. School of Civil Engineering. Research Report [*A publication*]
Syd Univ Dep Agric Econ Mimeo Rep ... University of Sydney. Department of Agricultural Economics. Mimeographed Report [*A publication*]
Syd Univ Gaz ... Sydney University. Gazette [*A publication*]
Syd Univ Med J ... Sydney University. Medical Journal [*A publication*]
Syd Univ Post Grad Comm Med Bul ... University of Sydney. Postgraduate Committee in Medicine. Bulletin [*A publication*]
Syd Univ Post Grad Comm Med Oration ... University of Sydney. Postgraduate Committee in Medicine. Annual Postgraduate Oration [*A publication*]
Syd Univ Sch Agric Rep ... University of Sydney. School of Agriculture. Report [*A publication*]
Syd Wat Bd J ... Sydney Water Board. Journal [*A publication*]
Syd Water Bd J ... Sydney Water Board. Journal [*A publication*]
Syd Water Board J ... Sydney Water Board. Journal [*A publication*]
SYE .... Sa'Dah [*Yemen Arab Republic*] [*Airport symbol*]   (OAG)
SYEP .... Summer Youth Employment Program [*Department of Labor*]
SYEP .... Symmetrica Disubstituted Ethoxy Propane [*Organic chemistry*]   (MCD)
SYES .... Syesis [*A publication*]
SYF .... St. Francis, KS [*Location identifier*] [*FAA*]   (FAAL)
SYFA .... System for Application [*Data processing*]
SYG .... Arcola, TX [*Location identifier*] [*FAA*]   (FAAL)
SYG .... Secretary-General   (NATG)
SYG .... Synergy International [*Vancouver Stock Exchange symbol*]
SYGA .... Systems Gauge [*Tool*]   (AAG)
SYH .... Scottish & York Holdings Ltd. [*Toronto Stock Exchange symbol*]
SYH .... See You Home [*Teen slang*]
Syh .... Syrohexapla   (BJA)
SYHA .... Scottish Youth Hostels Association
SYI .... Shelbyville, TN [*Location identifier*] [*FAA*]   (FAAL)
Sy J Int L ... Syracuse Journal of International Law and Commerce [*A publication*]
SYK .... Stykkisholmur [*Iceland*] [*Airport symbol*]   (OAG)
SYKE .... Sykes Datatronics [*NASDAQ symbol*]   (NQ)
SYL .... San Miguel, CA [*Location identifier*] [*FAA*]   (FAAL)
SYL .... Somali Youth League [*Political Party*]
SYL .... Spartacus Youth League   (EA)
Syl .... [*The*] Syllabi   (DLA)
SYL .... Syllable   (ADA)
Syl .... Syllogos. Journal de la Societe Philologique Grecque de Constantinople [*A publication*]
SYLL .... Syllable
SYLL .... Syllogeus [*A publication*]
SYLP .... Support Your Local Police
Sy LR .... Syracuse Law Review [*A publication*]
Sylvatrop Philipp For Res J ... Sylvatrop. The Philippine Forest Research Journal [*A publication*]
SYM .... Salesian Youth Movement   (EA)
SYM .... Secondary Yield Measurement
SYM .... Seymour Resources [*Vancouver Stock Exchange symbol*]
SYM .... Simao [*China*] [*Airport symbol*]   (OAG)
SYM .... Simmons Aviation [*Negaunee, MI*] [*FAA designator*]   (FAAC)
SYM .... Symbiont
SYM .... Symbol [*or Symbolic*]   (AAG)
Sym .... Symmachus' Greek Translation of the Bible [*A publication*]   (BJA)
sym .... Symmetrical [*Also, s*] [*Chemistry*]
SYM .... Symmetry
SYM .... Symphony
Sym .... Symphony Recording Co. [*Record label*]
Sym .... Symposium [*A publication*]
SYM .... Syms Corp. [*NYSE symbol*]
SYM .... System   (MDG)
SYMAN ..... Symbol Manipulation [*Data processing*]
SYM/ANNOT ... Symbology Annotation   (MCD)
SYMAP .... Synagraphic Mapping System [*Computer-made maps*]
SYMB .... Symbol
SYMBA ..... Symbioses [*A publication*]
SYMBAL .... Symbolic Algebraic Language [*Data processing*]
SYMBAS .... Symbolization All Series   (ADA)
SYMBOLANG ... Symbolic Manipulation Language [*Data processing*]   (CSR)
SymbOsl .... Symbolae Osloenses [*A publication*]
Symb Oslo ... Symbolae Osloenses [*A publication*]
Symb Philol Danielsson ... Symbolae Philologicae [*O. A.*] Danielsson Octogenario Dicatae [*Uppsala*] [*A publication*]   (OCD)
Sym Code ... Syms' Code of English Law [*1870*]   (DLA)
SYMDEB ... Symbolic Debugger [*Data processing*]
Syme .... Syme's Scotch Justiciary Reports [*1826-30*]   (DLA)
SYMED ...... Synthetic Metals [*A publication*]

SYMEVETOPHARSA ... Syndicat des Medecins, Veterinaires, Pharmaciens, et Sages Femmes Africains du Mali [*Union of African Doctors, Pharmacists, Midwives, and Veterinarians of the Mali Federation*]

Symf.......... Symfoni & Artist [*Record label*] [*Sweden*]

SYMK .... Sym-Tek Systems [*NASDAQ symbol*]   (NQ)

SYMM .... Symmetrical   (MSA)

SYMMTRAC ... Sylvania Multimode Tracking [*Aerospace*]   (MCD)

Sym News ... Symphony News [*A publication*]

Symp.......... Symposium [*of Xenophon*] [*Classical studies*]   (OCD)

SYMP .... Symposium   (MSA)

Symp.......... Symposium [*of Lucian*] [*Classical studies*]   (OCD)

Symp.......... Symposium [*of Plato*] [*Classical studies*]   (OCD)

Symp Abnorm Subsurf Pressure Proc ... Symposium on Abnormal Subsurface Pressure. Proceedings [*A publication*]

SYMPAC .... Symbolic Program for Automatic Control

Symp Angiol Sanitoriana ... Symposia Angiologica Sanitoriana [*A publication*]

sympat....... Sympathetic [*Neurology*]

Symp Biol Hung ... Symposia Biologica Hungarica [*A publication*]

Symp Br Soc Parasitol ... Symposia. British Society for Parasitology [*A publication*]

Symp Cell Biol ... Symposia for Cell Biology [*Japan*] [*A publication*]

Symp Coal Manag Tech Pap ... Symposium on Coal Management Techniques. Papers [*A publication*]

Symp Coal Mine Drain Res Pap ... Symposium on Coal Mine Drainage Research. Papers [*A publication*]

Symp Coal Prep Pap ... Symposium on Coal Preparation. Papers [*A publication*]

Symp Coal Util Pap ... Symposium on Coal Utilization. Papers [*A publication*]

Symp Ecol Res Humid Trop Vegtn ... Symposium on Ecological Research in Humid Tropics Vegetation [*A publication*]

Symp Eng Geol Soils Eng Proc ... Symposium on Engineering Geology and Soils Engineering. Proceedings [*A publication*]

Symp Faraday Soc ... Symposia. Faraday Society [*A publication*]

Symp Foods ... Symposium of Foods [*A publication*]

Symp Freq Control Proc ... Symposium on Frequency Control. Proceedings [*A publication*]

Symp Fundam Cancer Res Collect Pap ... Symposium on Fundamental Cancer Research. Collections of Papers [*A publication*]

Symp Genet Biol Ital ... Symposia Genetica et Biologica Italica [*A publication*]

Symp Genet Breed Wheat Proc ... Symposium on Genetics and Breeding of Wheat. Proceedings [*A publication*]

SYMPH....... Symphony   (ADA)

Symp Int Soc Cell Biol ... Symposia. International Society for Cell Biology [*A publication*]

Symp Int Union Biol Sci Proc ... Symposia. International Union of Biological Sciences. Proceedings [*A publication*]

Symp Maize Prod Southeast Asia ... Symposium on Maize Production in Southeast Asia [*A publication*]

Symp Med Hoechst ... Symposia Medica Hoechst [*A publication*]

Symp Mine Prep Plant Refuse Disposal Pap ... Symposium on Mine and Preparation Plant Refuse Disposal. Papers [*A publication*]

Symp Oral Sens Percept ... Symposium on Oral Sensation and Perception [*A publication*]

Symposium ... Symposium: a Quarterly Journal in Modern Foreign Literatures [*A publication*]

Symposum Jun Bar ... Symposium. Association de Jeune Barreau de Montreal   (DLA)

Symp Particleboard Proc ... Symposium on Particleboard. Proceedings [*A publication*]

Symp Pharmacol Ther Toxicol Group ... Symposium. Pharmacology, Therapeutics, and Toxicology Group. International Association for Dental Research [*A publication*]

Symp Priv Invest Abroad ... Symposium. Private Investors Abroad   (DLA)

Symp Regul Enzyme Act Synth Norm Neoplast Tissues Proc ... Symposium on Regulation of Enzyme Activity and Syntheses in Normal and Neoplastic Tissues. Proceedings [*A publication*]

Symp R Entomol Soc Lond ... Symposia. Royal Entomological Society of London [*A publication*]

Symp Ser Australas Inst Min Metall ... Australasian Institute of Mining and Metallurgy. Symposia Series [*A publication*]

Symp Ser Australas Inst Min Metall ... Symposia Series. Australasian Institute of Mining and Metallurgy [*A publication*]

Symp Ser Immunobiol Stand ... Symposia Series in Immunobiological Standardization [*A publication*]

Symp Ser Inst Fuel (London) ... Symposium Series. Institute of Fuel (London) [*A publication*]

Symp Soc Dev Biol ... Symposia. Society for Developmental Biology [*A publication*]

Symp Soc Exp Biol ... Symposia. Society for Experimental Biology [*A publication*]

Symp Soc Gen Microbiol ... Symposium. Society for General Microbiology [*A publication*]

Symp Soc Study Dev Growth ... Symposium. Society for the Study of Development and Growth [*A publication*]

Symp Soc Study Hum Biol ... Symposia. Society for the Study of Human Biology [*A publication*]

Symp Soc Study Inborn Errors Metab ... Symposium. Society for the Study of Inborn Errors of Metabolism [*A publication*]

Symp Surf Min Reclam Pap ... Symposium on Surface Mining and Reclamation. Papers [*A publication*]

Symp Swed Nutr Found ... Symposia. Swedish Nutrition Foundation [*A publication*]

sympt......... Symptom [*Medicine*]

Symp Theor Phys Math ... Symposia on Theoretical Physics and Mathematics [*United States*] [*A publication*]

Symp Turbul Liq Proc ... Symposium on Turbulence in Liquids. Proceedings [*A publication*]

Symp Underground Min Pap ... Symposium on Underground Mining. Papers [*A publication*]

Symp Zool Soc Lond ... Symposia. Zoological Society of London [*A publication*]

SYMRO ...... System Management Research Operation   (DIT)

SYMS .... Secondary Yield Measurement System

SYMWAR ... System for Estimating Wartime Attrition and Replacement Requirements   (AABC)

SYN............ Stanton, MN [*Location identifier*] [*FAA*]   (FAAL)

SYN............ Synagogue

SYN............ Synaptec, A Knowledge Engineering Corp. [*Vancouver Stock Exchange symbol*]

SYN............ Synchronous   (AAG)

SYN............ Synchronous Idle [*Transmission control character*] [*Data processing*]

SYN............ Syndicate   (ROG)

SYN............ Synod

SYN............ Synonym

Syn............ Synopsis   (DLA)

syn............ Synovial [*Fluid*] [*Medicine*]

syn............ Synovitis [*Medicine*]

SYN............ Syntex Corp. [*NYSE symbol*]

SYN............ Syntex Corp., Palo Alto, CA [*OCLC symbol*]   (OCLC)

Syn............ Syntheses [*A publication*]

SYN............ Synthesizer

SYN............ Synthetic   (AAG)

SYNAC ...... Synthesis of Aircraft   (MCD)

SYNAPSE ... CUEA Synthesis and Publication Segment [*Marine science*]   (MSC)

SYNBAPS ... Synthetic Bathymetric Profiling System [*Naval Oceanographic Office*]

SYNC .... Synchromechanism

SYNC .... Synchronize   (AAG)

sync .... Synchrony

SYNCD ...... Synchronized   (AAG)

SYNCELL .... Synthetic Cell [*Biological research*]

SYNCG ...... Synchronizing   (AAG)

SYNCH ...... Synchronize

SYNCH ...... Synchronous Transmission [*Data processing*]   (TSSD)

SYNCOM ... Synchronous-Orbiting Communications Satellite [*GSFC*]

Syn Commun ... Synthetic Communications [*A publication*]

SYNCR ...... Synchronizer   (AAG)

SYNCRO .... Synchromesh [*Automotive engineering*]

SYNCRUDE ... Synthetic Crude

SYNCS .... Synchronous   (AAG)

SYND .... Syndicate

synd .... Syndrome [*Medicine*]

SYNDARC ... Standard Format for Exchange of MAPMOPP Data among Data Centers   (MSC)

SYNDETS ... Synthetic Detergents

SYNE......... Syntech International [*NASDAQ symbol*]   (NQ)

SYNED .... Synerjy [*A publication*]

SYNESCI ... Syndicat National des Enseignants du Second Degre de Cote d'Ivoire

SYNFRQ..... Synthesizer Frequency

SYNFUELS ... Synthetic Fuels

SYNG .... Synergetics International [*NASDAQ symbol*]   (NQ)

SYNG .... Synergy. Syncrude Canada [*A publication*]

Syn Hist L ... Synthese Historical Library [*A publication*]

Syn Inorg Met-Org Chem ... Synthesis in Inorganic and Metal-Organic Chemistry [*Later, Synthesis and Reactivity in Inorganic and Metalorganic Chemistry*] [*A publication*]

SYNMAS .... Synchronous Missile Alarm System

SYNON .... Synonym   (ROG)

SYNOP .... Synopsis   (AABC)

Synopsis R ... Synopsis Revue [*A publication*]

Synpt .... Synoptic [*or Synoptist*]   (BJA)

Syn Reac In ... Synthesis and Reactivity in Inorganic and Metalorganic Chemistry [*A publication*]

Syn Reactiv Inorg Metal Org C ... Synthesis and Reactivity in Inorganic and Metalorganic Chemistry [*A publication*]

SYNROC .... Synthetic Rock [*For storage of nuclear waste*]

SYNS.......... Synopsis   (MSA)

SYNSCP..... Synchroscope   (KSC)

SYNSEM .... Syntax and Semantics   (IEEE)

Syn Ser ...... Synopsis Series of the United States Treasury Decisions   (DLA)

SYNSPADE ... Symposium on the Numerical Solution of Partial Differential Equations [*Book title, Academic Press*]

SYNTAC .... Synthetic Tactics

SYNTEEDISETO ... Syndicat des Travailleurs de l'Energie Electrique et de Distribution d'Eau du Togo [*Union of Electrical and Water Distribution Workers of Togo*]
SYNTH .... Synthesizer
SYNTH .... Synthetic
Synth Commun ... Synthetic Communications [*A publication*]
Synth Fuels ... Synthetic Fuels [*A publication*]
Synth Fuels Update ... Synthetic Fuels Update [*A publication*]
Synth Libr ... Synthese Library [*A publication*]
Synth Met ... Synthetic Metals [*Switzerland*] [*A publication*]
Synth Methods Org Chem Yearb ... Synthetic Methods of Organic Chemistry Yearbook [*A publication*]
Synth Pipeline Gas Symp Proc ... Synthetic Pipeline Gas Symposium. Proceedings [*A publication*]
Synth React Inorg Metorg Chem ... Synthesis and Reactivity in Inorganic and Metalorganic Chemistry [*A publication*]
Synth Rubber ... Synthetic Rubber [*A publication*]
SYNTI .... Synchro Tie
SYNTIRT .... Syndicat des Travailleurs des Industries Reunies du Togo [*Union of Workers of United Industries of Togo*]
SYNTOL ..... Syntagmatic Organization Language [*Data processing*]
SYNTRAN ... Syntax Translation [*Data processing*]   (DIT)
SYNZYMES ... Synthetic Enzymes
SYO .... Sayre, OK [*Location identifier*] [*FAA*]   (FAAL)
SYO .... Synalloy Corp. [*American Stock Exchange symbol*]
SYO .... Syowa [*Ongul*] [*Antarctica*] [*Seismograph station code, US Geological Survey*]   (SEIS)
SYO .... Syowa Base [*Antarctica*] [*Geomagnetic observatory code*]
SYP .... Parkland Regional Library, Yorkton, Saskatchewan [*Library symbol*] [*National Library of Canada*]   (NLC)
SYP .... Santa Ynez Peak [*California*] [*Seismograph station code, US Geological Survey*]   (SEIS)
SYP .... Suomen Yksityisyrittaejaein Puoluejaerjesto [*Finnish Private Entrepreneurs' Party*]   (PPE)
Syp .... Syropalaestinum [*BJA*]
SYPH .... Syphilis   (DSUE)
syr .... Sirop [*Syrup*] [*Pharmacy*]
SYR .... Smyrna [*Washington*] [*Seismograph station code, US Geological Survey*]   (SEIS)
SYR .... South Yorkshire Railway [*British*]   (ROG)
SYR .... Syracuse [*New York*] [*Airport symbol*]
SYR .... Syria [*or Syrian Arab Republic*] [*Three-letter standard code*]   (CNC)
Syr .... Syria. Revue d'Art Oriental et d'Archeologie [*A publication*]
syr .... Syriac [*MARC language code*] [*Library of Congress*]   (LCCP)
SYR .... Syrian [*Language, etc.*]   (ROG)
SYR .... Syringe [*Medicine*]
SYR .... Syrupus [*Syrup*] [*Pharmacy*]
SYRA .... Syracuse Supply [*NASDAQ symbol*]   (NQ)
Syrac Law R ... Syracuse Law Review [*A publication*]
Syracuse Int'l L & Com ... Syracuse Journal of International Law and Commerce [*A publication*]
Syracuse J Int'l L ... Syracuse Journal of International Law   (DLA)
Syracuse L Rev ... Syracuse Law Review [*A publication*]
Syr D .... De Syria Dea [*of Lucian*] [*Classical studies*]   (OCD)
SyrH .... Hexaplaric Syriac   (BJA)
Syrian J Stomatol ... Syrian Journal of Stomatology [*A publication*]
Syr J Intl L & Com ... Syracuse Journal of International Law and Commerce [*A publication*]
SYRP .... Summer Youth Recreation Program
SYRUCL ..... Syracuse University College of Law   (DLA)
SyrW .... Syriac Version in Walton's Polyglot   (BJA)
SYS .... ISI Systems [*American Stock Exchange symbol*]
SYS .... See Your Service   (FAAC)
SYS .... Sobeys Stores Ltd. [*Toronto Stock Exchange symbol*]
SYS .... Somerset, PA [*Location identifier*] [*FAA*]   (FAAL)
SYS .... Sweet Yet Simple [*Data processing*]
SYS .... System   (AFM)
SYSAD ...... Systems Adviser
SYSCAP ..... System of Circuit Analysis Program
SYSCOM .... System Communications
SYSCOM .... Systems Command [*Navy*]
SYSCON .... Systems Control   (AABC)
SYSEC .... System Synthesizer and Evaluation Center
SYSG .... Systematics General Corp. [*NASDAQ symbol*]   (NQ)
SYSGEN ..... Systems Generator [*or Generation*] [*Data processing*]
SYSIN .... System Input [*Data processing*]   (MDG)
SYSLIB ...... System Library [*Data processing*]   (MDG)
SYSLOG ..... System Log [*Data processing*]
SYSM .... System Industries [*NASDAQ symbol*]   (NQ)
SYSOP ...... System Operator [*Computer networking*]
SYSOUT ..... System Output [*Data processing*]
SYSP .... Sixth-Year Specialist Program [*Library science*]
SYSPLLTM ... System Purchase of Long Lead Time Material
SYSPM ...... System Performance Measure   (MCD)
SYSPOP ..... System Programed Operators [*Data processing*]   (MDG)
Sys Proced ... Systems and Procedures [*A publication*]
SYSRES ..... System Residence [*Data processing*]
SYST .... System
SYST .... Systematics, Inc. [*NASDAQ symbol*]   (NQ)
syst .... Systemic [*Medicine*]

Syst .... Systems [*A publication*]
syst .... Systolic [*Cardiology*]
Syst Assoc Publ ... Systematics Association. Publication [*A publication*]
Syst Assoc Spec Vol ... Systematics Association. Special Volume [*A publication*]
Syst Ass Spec Vol ... Systematics Association. Special Volume [*A publication*]
Syst Bot ..... Systematic Botany [*A publication*]
Syst-Comput-Controls ... Systems-Computers-Controls [*A publication*]
Syst & Control ... Systems and Control [*A publication*]
Syst and Control Lett ... Systems and Control Letters [*A publication*]
Systematics Assoc Pub ... Systematics Association. Publication [*A publication*]
Systems & Proc J ... Systems and Procedures Journal [*A publication*]
Systems Sci ... Systems Science [*A publication*]
SYSTEP ..... Systems Test and Evaluation Plan   (AABC)
Syst Int ...... Systems International [*A publication*]
Syst Logiques ... Systemes Logiques [*A publication*]
SYSTO .... System Staff Office [*or Officer*]
Syst Objectives Solutions ... Systems, Objectives, Solutions [*A publication*]
SYSTRAN ... Systems Analysis Translator [*Data processing*]
Syst Sci ...... Systems Science [*A publication*]
Syst Technol ... Systems Technology [*A publication*]
Syst Theory Res ... Systems Theory Research [*A publication*]
Syst Zool .... Systematic Zoology [*A publication*]
SYSVER ..... System Specification Verification   (IEEE)
SYT .... Sweet Young Thing [*An attractive girl*] [*Slang*]
SYTA .... Sustained-Yield Tropical Agroecosystem
SYU .... Sudanese Youth Union
SYU .... Syuhurei [*South Korea*] [*Seismograph station code, US Geological Survey*] [*Closed*]   (SEIS)
SYUS .... Specialized Youth Units [*Canada*]
SYV .... Saynor Varah, Inc. [*Toronto Stock Exchange symbol*]
SYV .... Society for Young Victims [*Newport, RI*]   (EA)
SYV .... Sylvester, GA [*Location identifier*] [*FAA*]   (FAAL)
SYV .... Syva Research Library, Palo Alto, CA [*OCLC symbol*]   (OCLC)
Syvrem Med ... Syvremenna Meditsina [*A publication*]
SYVV .... Sowthistle Yellow Vein Virus
SYW .... Skyway Resources Ltd. [*Vancouver Stock Exchange symbol*]
SYY .... Stornoway [*Scotland*] [*Airport symbol*]   (OAG)
SYY .... Sysco Corp. [*NYSE symbol*]
SYZ .... Shelbyville, IL [*Location identifier*] [*FAA*]   (FAAL)
SYZ .... Shiraz [*Iran*] [*Airport symbol*]   (OAG)
SZ .... Aerolineas de El Salvador [*ICAO designator*]   (FAAC)
SZ .... Sceptre Investment Counsel [*Toronto Stock Exchange symbol*]
sz .... Schizophrenia [*Medicine*]
Sz .... Schweizerische Landesbibliothek [*Swiss National Library*], Bern, Switzerland [*Library symbol*] [*Library of Congress*]   (LCLS)
SZ .... Schweizerische Zeitschrift fuer Volkswirtschaft und Statistik [*A publication*]
SZ .... Seizure [*Telecommunications*]   (TEL)
sz .... Seizure [*Medicine*]
SZ .... Sekspirovskij Zbornik [*A publication*]
SZ .... Sha'arei Zedek   (BJA)
SZ .... Shigaku Zasshi [*A publication*]
SZ .... Size   (MDG)
SZ .... Sovremennye Zapiski [*A publication*]
SZ .... Splash Zone
SZ .... Stimmen der Zeit [*A publication*]
SZ .... Streptozocin [*An antibiotic*]
SZ .... Surface Zero [*Navy*]   (NVT)
SZ .... Swaziland [*Two-letter standard code*]   (CNC)
sz .... Switzerland [*MARC country of publication code*] [*Library of Congress*]   (LCCP)
SZA .... Solar Zenith Angle [*Geophysics*]
SZA .... Soyo [*Angola*] [*Airport symbol*]   (OAG)
Szakszerv Szle ... Szakszervezeti Szemle [*A publication*]
Szamki Koezlem ... Szamki Koezlemenyek [*A publication*]
SZB .... Silver-Zinc Battery
SZB .... Sintered Zinc Battery
SzBaL .... Lonza Aktiengesellschaft, Zentralbibliothek, Basel, Switzerland [*Library symbol*] [*Library of Congress*]   (LCLS)
SzBaM .... Museum fur Volkerkunde und Schweizerisches Museum fur Volkskunde, Basel, Switzerland [*Library symbol*] [*Library of Congress*]   (LCLS)
SzBaU .... Universitat Basel, Basel, Switzerland [*Library symbol*] [*Library of Congress*]   (LCLS)
SzBaU-IO ... Institut fur Organische Chemie der Universitat Basel, Basel, Switzerland [*Library symbol*] [*Library of Congress*]   (LCLS)
SZC .... Silver-Zinc Cell
SZC .... Studia Zrodloznawcze. Commentationes [*A publication*]
SZD .... St. George, SC [*Location identifier*] [*FAA*]   (FAAL)
SZDKA .... Sovetskoe Zdravookhranenie Kirgizii [*A publication*]
SzDL .... Studien zur Deutschen Literatur [*A publication*]
SZE .... Szeged [*Hungary*] [*Seismograph station code, US Geological Survey*] [*Closed*]   (SEIS)
SZEC .... Silver-Zinc Electrochemical Cell
SZECC .... Silver-Zinc Electrochemical Cell
SzEP .... Studien zur Englischen Philologie [*A publication*]

SZG............ Salzburg [*Austria*] [*Airport symbol*]   (OAG)
SZG............ Schweizerische Zeitschrift fuer Geschichte [*A publication*]
SZG............ Soviet Zone Germany   (NATG)
SzGB.......... Bibliotheque Battelle, Centre de Recherche, Geneve, Switzerland [*Library symbol*] [*Library of Congress*]   (LCLS)
SzGBNU..... Bibliotheque des Nations Unies, Geneve, Switzerland [*Library symbol*] [*Library of Congress*]   (LCLS)
SzGE.......... Ecole de Chimie, Geneva, Switzerland [*Library symbol*] [*Library of Congress*]   (LCLS)
SzGPAr...... Archives Jean Piaget, Geneve, Switzerland [*Library symbol*] [*Library of Congress*]   (LCLS)
SzGSI......... Societe Generale pour l'Industrie, Geneve, Switzerland [*Library symbol*] [*Library of Congress*]   (LCLS)
SZI.............. Seattle, WA [*Location identifier*] [*FAA*]   (FAAL)
Szigma Mat-Koezgazdasagi Folyoirat ... Szigma. Matematikai-Koezgazdasagi Folyoirat [*A publication*]
SZJ............. Atlanta, GA [*Location identifier*] [*FAA*]   (FAAL)
SZK............ Roanoke, VA [*Location identifier*] [*FAA*]   (FAAL)
SZK............ Skukuza [*South Africa*] [*Airport symbol*]   (OAG)
Szk Gl Gospod Wiejsk Akad Roln Warszawie Zesz Nauk Ogrod ... Szkola Glowna Gospodarstwa Wiejskiego - Akademia Rolnicza w Warszawie. Zeszyty Naukowe. Ogrodnictwo [*A publication*]
Szk Gl Gospod Wiejsk Akd Roln Warszawie Zesz Nauk Weter ... Szkola Glowna Gospodarstwa Wiejskiego - Akademia Rolnicza w Warszawie. Zeszyty Naukowe. Weterynaria [*A publication*]
SZKKB....... Shimizu Kensetsu Kenkyusho-Ho [*A publication*]
Szklo Ceram ... Szklo i Ceramika [*A publication*]
SZL............. Knob Noster, MO [*Location identifier*] [*FAA*]   (FAAL)
SzL............. Schriften zur Literatur [*A publication*]
SzLaCU..... Bibliotheque Cantonal et Universitaire de Lausanne, Lausanne, Switzerland [*Library symbol*] [*Library of Congress*]   (LCLS)
SzLaS........ Station Federale d'Essais Agricoles, Lausanne, Switzerland [*Library symbol*] [*Library of Congress*]   (LCLS)
SZLGD....... Sozialgerichtsbarkeit [*A publication*]
SZM............ Stereo Zoom Microscope
SZM............ Synthetic Zeolite Molecule
SZN............ Santa Barbara, CA [*Location identifier*] [*FAA*]   (FAAL)
SzNU......... Sbornik za Narodni Umotvorenija [*A publication*]
SZO............ Student Zionist Organization [*Defunct*]   (EA)
SZOG......... Soviet Zone of Occupation of Germany   (NATG)
Szolesz Boraszat ... Szoleszet es Boraszat [*A publication*]
SZOR......... Sintered Zinc Oxide Resistor
SZOT......... Szakszervezetek Orszagos Tanacsa [*National Trade Union Council*] [*Hungary*]
SZP............ Santa Paula, CA [*Location identifier*] [*FAA*]   (FAAL)
SZP............ Surf Zone Process
SZP............ Synchro Zeroing Procedure
SZPAA....... Schweizerische Zeitschrift fuer Psychologie und Ihre Anwendungen [*A publication*]
SZPMA....... Sozial- und Praeventivmedizin [*A publication*]
SZR............ Sintered Zinc Resistor
SZR............ Stargazer Resources Ltd. [*Vancouver Stock Exchange symbol*]
SZR............ University of South Carolina, Regional Campus Processing Center, Columbia, SC [*OCLC symbol*]   (OCLC)
SZS............ Srpska Zemljoradnicka Stranka [*Serbian Agrarian Party*] [*Yugoslav*]   (PPE)
SZS............ Staatliche Zentrale fuer Strahlenschutz Berlin [*East Germany*]
SZS............ Stewart Island [*New Zealand*] [*Airport symbol*]   (OAG)
SZSB......... Silver-Zinc Secondary [*or Storage*] Battery
SzStg........ Stadtbibliothek Vadiana, St. Gallen, Switzerland [*Library symbol*] [*Library of Congress*]   (LCLS)
SZT............ Sandpoint, ID [*Location identifier*] [*FAA*]   (FAAL)
SzT............ Schriften zur Theaterwissenschaft [*A publication*]
SZutNu....... Sifre Zuta on Numbers   (BJA)
SZVR......... Silicon Zener Voltage Regulator
SZY............ Selmer, TN [*Location identifier*] [*FAA*]   (FAAL)
SZZ............ Szczecin [*Poland*] [*Airport symbol*]   (OAG)
SzZ............. Zentralbibliothek Zurich, Zurich, Switzerland [*Library symbol*] [*Library of Congress*]   (LCLS)
SzZE......... Eidgenoessische Technische Hochschule, Zurich, Switzerland [*Library symbol*] [*Library of Congress*]   (LCLS)
SzZU......... Universitat Zurich, Universitatsspital-Bibliothek, Kantonsspital, Zurich, Switzerland [*Library symbol*] [*Library of Congress*]   (LCLS)

T

T	Absolute Temperature [*Symbol*] [*IUPAC*]
T	Air Temperature Correction
T	American Telephone & Telegraph Co. [*NYSE symbol*] [*Wall Street slang name: "Telephone"*]
t-------	Antarctic [*MARC geographic area code*] [*Library of Congress*] (LCCP)
t	Celsius Temperature [*Symbol*] [*IUPAC*]
T	Cleared Through for Landing and Takeoff [*Aviation*] (FAAC)
T	Internal Transmittance [*Symbol*] [*IUPAC*]
T	Kinetic Energy [*Symbol*] [*IUPAC*]
T	Meridian Angle
t	Metric Ton [*or Tonne*] [*Symbol*]
T	Military Sealift Command Ship [*When precedes vessel classification*] [*Navy symbol*]
T	Octodecimo [*Book from 12-1/2 to 15 centimeters in height*] [*Bibliography*]
T	Ribothymidine [*One-letter symbol; see Thd*]
T	Shape Descriptor [*T-bar and T-square, for example. The shape resembles the letter for which it is named*]
T	Table
T	Tablespoon [*Measure*]
T	Tablet-Shaped [*As in "T-grains"*] [*Photography*]
T	Tabulated [*or Charted*] LORAN [*Long-Range Aid to Navigation*] Reading
T	Tace [*Be Silent*]
T	Tackle [*Football*]
T	Tactical Organization
T	Tactual
T	Taken
T	Takeoff [*Aviation*] (FAAC)
T	Tala [*Monetary unit in Western Samoa*]
T	Talon [*Heel of the Bow*] [*Music*]
T	Tamoxifen [*Also, TAM*] [*Antineoplastic drug*]
T	Tan (FAAC)
T	Tango [*Phonetic alphabet*] [*International*] (DSUE)
T	Tanhuma (BJA)
T	Tank [*Trains*] [*British*]
T	Tanna (BJA)
T	Taper
T	Tappan's Ohio Common Pleas Reports (DLA)
T	Tare [*Phonetic alphabet*] [*World War II*] (DSUE)
T	Target
T	Tasto [*Touch, Key, Fingerboard*] [*Music*]
T	Taxes (DLA)
T	Teacher
T	Tear [*Phonetic alphabet*] [*World War II*]
t	Teaspoon [*Measure*]
T	Teatar [*Sofia*] [*A publication*]
T	Teatr [*A publication*]
T	Technical [*or Technician*]
T	Tee [*Piping joint, etc.*] [*Technical drawings*]
T	Teeth [*Technical drawings*]
T	Teich [*Pond*] [*German military*]
T	Telefunken [*Record label*] [*Germany, etc.*]
T	Telegram (BJA)
T	Telegraph (ROG)
T	Telegrapher [*Navy*]
T	Telephone
T	Telephone Trunk Call [*British*] (ROG)
T	Teletype
T	Temperance [*i.e., entitled to a daily rum ration but voluntarily not drawing it and receiving money instead*] [*See also G, UA*] [*Navy*] [*British*]
T	Temperature
T	Tempo
T	Temporal
T	Temporary
T	Tempore [*In the Time of*] [*Latin*]
T	Tendre [*Tender*] [*Music*]
T	Tenero [*Tender*]
T	Tennessee State Library and Archives, Nashville, TN [*Library symbol*] [*Library of Congress*] (LCLS)
T	Tenor
T	Tenor [*Genotype of Phlox paniculata*]
T	Tense
T	Tension
T	Tensor
T	Tentative Target
T	Ter [*Three Times*] [*Pharmacy*]
T	Tera [*A prefix meaning multiplied by 10¹²*] [*SI symbol*]
T	Teracycle (BUR)
T	Term [*Medicine*]
T	Terminal
T	Terminal Area Chart [*Followed by identification*] [*Aviation*]
T	Termination
T	Terminator [*Genetics*]
T	Terrain
T	Territory
t	Tertiary [*Also, tert*] [*Chemistry*]
T	Tertiary
T	Tesla [*Symbol*] [*SI unit of flux density*]
T	Test (MSA)
T	Test Equipment (NG)
T	Test Reactor
T	Test Set
T	Testament (ROG)
T	Tetracycline [*Also, TC, TE, Tet*] [*Antibiotic compound*]
T	Teuthonista [*A publication*]
T	Texana [*A publication*]
T	Thaler [*or Talari*] [*Monetary unit*] [*Ethiopia*]
T	Than
T	That
T	Theatres [*Public-performance tariff class*] [*British*]
T	Theft
T	Theophylline [*Pharmacology*]
T	Thermodynamic Temperature [*Symbol*] [*IUPAC*]
T	Thermometer
T	Thermoplastic [*Also, TP*] [*Plastics technology*] (MSA)
T	Thickness
T	Thief
T	Thioguanine [*Also, TG*] [*Antineoplastic drug*]
T	Thiopental [*An anesthetic*]
T	Third Word Designator [*Data processing*]
T	Thoracic [*Anatomy*]
T	Thread
T	Threonine [*One-letter symbol; see Thr*]
T	Thromboxane [*Also, TA, Tx, TX*] [*Biochemistry*]
T	Thunderstorm [*Meteorology*]
T	Thymine [*Also, Thy*] [*Biochemistry*]
T	Thymus [*Medicine*]
T	Thymus Derived [*Hematology*]
T	Thyroid [*Medicine*]
T	Tidal Gas [*Respiration*] [*Medicine*]
T	Tide Rips [*Navigation*]
T	Tie [*Sports*]
T	Tied
T	Tier [*Psychology*]
T	Tiler [*Freemasonry*]
T	Tilic Subgroup [*Ilmenite, titanite, perofskite, rutile*] [*CIPW classification*] [*Geology*]
T	Time [*A publication*]
T	Time
t	Time [*Symbol*] [*IUPAC*]
T	Time Consumed in Playing Game [*Baseball*]
T-	Time Prior to Launch [*Usually followed by a number*] [*NASA*] (KSC)
T	Time-Reversal [*Atomic physics*]
t	Time in Seconds [*Aerospace*]
T	Time Trial
T	Timekeeper [*Sports*]
T	Tip [*Switchboard plug*] [*Telecommunications*] (TEL)

T .... Tithing [*Geographical division*] [*British*]
T .... Title [*Bibliography*]
T .... Tobacco Tax Ruling, Internal Revenue Bureau [*United States*] (DLA)
T .... Toc [*Phonetic alphabet*] [*Pre-World War II*] (DSUE)
T .... Tocopherol [*Biochemistry*]
T .... Toe
T .... Toilet (MSA)
T .... Toll
T .... Tommy [*Phonetic alphabet*] [*Royal Navy*] [*World War I*] (DSUE)
T .... Tomus [*Volume*]
T .... Ton
T .... Tonnage [*Shipping*]
t .... Tonne [*Metric*]
T .... Tooth
3T .... Top
t .... Top [*or Truth*] (Quark) [*Atomic physics*]
T .... Top Secret
T .... Topical (ADA)
T .... Toronto Stock Exchange
T .... Torpedo [*Obsolete*] [*Navy*] [*British*] (ROG)
T .... Torpedoman [*Navy*] [*British*]
T .... Torque
T .... Tosefta (BJA)
T .... Total
T .... Tourist [*Rate*] [*Value of the English pound*]
T .... Toward [*Altitude difference*]
T .... Town
T .... Township
T .... Trace of Precipitation [*Less than 0.005 inch of rain or 0.05 inch of snow*]
T .... Tracer [*Ammunition*] (NATG)
T .... Traded
T .... Traditio [*A publication*]
T .... Traditional (BJA)
T .... Trafalgar [*On army list*] [*British*] (ROG)
T .... Traffic Cases (DLA)
T .... Traffic Headquarters
T .... Trainer [*Designation for all US military aircraft*]
T .... Training (FAAC)
t .... Trans [*Chemical conformation*]
T .... Transcription
T .... Transferred [*Navy*]
T .... Transformation Rule [*Linguistics*]
T .... Transformer
T .... Transfusion [*Medicine*]
T .... Transit
T .... Transition
T .... Transitive
T .... Translated (ROG)
T .... Translation
T .... Translocation
T .... Transmit [*or Transmitting*]
T .... Transmitter
T .... Transpiration [*Botany*]
T .... Transport (NATG)
t .... Transport Number [*Symbol*] [*Electrochemistry*]
T .... Transvaal Provincial Division Reports [*South Africa*] (DLA)
T .... Transverse Tubule [*Muscle neurobiology*]
T .... Tread [*Stair details*] [*Technical drawings*]
T .... Treasurer
T .... Treasury [*As in T-Bill, T-Bond, T-Note*]
T .... Treated
T .... Treatment
T .... Treble [*Music*] (ROG)
T .... Triangle
T .... Trillion [*10¹²*]
T .... Trillo [*Trill*] [*Music*]
T .... Trimethoprim [*Also, TMP*] [*Antibacterial compound*]
T .... Trinitas [*The Trinity*]
T .... Triode
T .... Triple
T .... Tritium [*Also, H₃*] [*Radioisotope of hydrogen*]
t .... Triton [*A nuclear particle*]
T .... Triton Industries [*Toronto Stock Exchange symbol*]
T .... Tropical [*Load line mark, or air mass*]
T .... Trotter
T .... Troy [*A system of weights for precious metals*]
T .... Truce
T .... True [*Direction*]
T .... Truss (AAG)
T .... Tuesday
T .... Tufa [*Quality of the bottom*] [*Nautical charts*]
T .... Tug [*Navy*]
T .... Tumor [*Oncology*]
T .... Tun [*Unit of liquid capacity*]
T .... Turbocharged [*Automotive engineering*]
T .... Turin [*A publication*]
T .... Turkish
T .... Turn [*or Turning*]

T .... Turner [*Navy rating*] [*British*]
T .... Tutti [*Sing or Play Together*] [*Music*]
T .... Twentyfourmo [*Book up to 15 centimeters in height*]
T .... Twin Screw [*Shipping*]
T .... Typed [*Manuscript descriptions*]
T .... Typhlosole [*Biology*]
T .... Wrong Tense of Verb [*Used in correcting manuscripts, etc.*]
T-0 .... Time Zero (MCD)
T-1 .... Carrier which identifies the all-digital communications links (TSSD)
T₁ .... Tricuspid First Heart Sound [*Cardiology*]
T₂ .... Diiodothyronine [*Endocrinology*]
T2 .... Time of Flight to Intercept [*Military*] (CAAL)
T₂ .... Tricuspid Second Heart Sound [*Cardiology*]
T-3 .... Tocotrienol [*Biochemistry*]
T₃ .... Triiodothyronine [*Also, TITh*] [*Endocrinology*]
3T .... Triple Throw [*Switch*]
T₄ .... Thyroxine [*Also, Thx, Ty*] [*An amino acid*] [*Endocrinology*]
5T .... Mauritania [*Aircraft nationality and registration mark*] (FAAC)
T/5 .... Technician Fifth Grade [*Army*]
7T .... Algeria [*Aircraft nationality and registration mark*] (FAAC)
T (Bird) ..... Thunderbird [*Automobile*] (DSUE)
T (Colds).... Toxic Colds [*Medicine*]
T (Count) ... Terminal Count [*Flight-readiness count*] (MCD)
T (Day) .... Transition Day [*Based on the expected transition from a two-front to a one-front war*] [*World War II*]
T (Day) .... Truce Day
Ta .... Ta'anith (BJA)
TA .... Table of Allowances (MCD)
TA .... Tabled Agreement [*in labor relations*]
TA .... Tablet (ADA)
TA .... TACAN [*Tactical Air Navigation*] Approach (FAAC)
TA .... Tactical Air Missile
TA .... Tactical Aircraft
T/A .... Tactical Airlift [*Tactical Air Command*]
TA .... Tailhook Association (EA)
TA .... Talanta [*A publication*]
TA .... Talmudical Academy (BJA)
TA .... Talmudische Archaeologie [*A publication*] (BJA)
TA .... Tanabe Seiyaku Co. Ltd. [*Japan*] [*Research code symbol*]
Ta .... Tank
TA .... Tank Army (MCD)
TA .... Tank Tainers
TA .... Tanker [*Shipping*]
Ta .... Tantalum [*Chemical element*]
TA .... Tape Adapter
TA .... Tape Advance (AAG)
TA .... Tape Armored [*Telecommunications*] (TEL)
TA .... Target (DEN)
TA .... Target Acquisition (MCD)
TA .... Target Aircraft (MUGU)
TA .... Target Area (AFM)
TA .... Targeting Agent [*Medicine*]
TA .... Tariff Act [*1930*]
TA .... Tartana [*Ship's rigging*] (ROG)
TA .... Task Analysis
TA .... Task Assignment (AAG)
TA .... Tax Agent
TA .... Tax Amortization [*Plan*]
TA .... Tea Association of the USA [*New York, NY*] (EA)
TA .... Teaching Assistant [*in a university*]
TA .... Technical Advisor (MCD)
TA .... Technical Analysis (NG)
TA .... Technical Assessor
TA .... Technical Assistance [*or Assistant*]
TA .... Technology Assessment
TA .... Technonet Asia (EA)
TA .... Tel Aviv [*Israel*] (BJA)
TA .... Telegraphic Address
TA .... Telephone Apparatus [*JETDS nomenclature*] [*Military*] (CET)
TA .... Telescope Assembly (KSC)
TA .... Tell-Amarna [*Egypt*] (BJA)
TA .... Tell Asmar [*Iraq*] (BJA)
TA .... Telluride Association (EA)
TA .... Temperature, Axillary
TA .... Temple Autobiographies [*A publication*]
TA .... Temporal Arteritis [*Medicine*]
TA .... Tension by Applanation [*Ophthalmology*]
TA .... Tension Arterielle [*Blood Pressure*] [*Medicine*]
TA .... Tenuazonic Acid [*Biochemistry*]
TA .... Teologinen Aikakauskirja [*Helsinki*] [*A publication*] (BJA)
TA .... Terephthalic Acid [*Also, TPA*] [*Organic chemistry*]
TA .... Terminal Adapter [*Telecommunications*]
T of A .... Terms of Agreement (NATG)
TA .... Terrain Avoidance [*Helicopter*]
TA .... Terrarium Association (EA)
TA .... Territorial Army
TA .... Test Access [*Telecommunications*] (TEL)
TA .... Test Accessory (AAG)
TA .... Test Article (NASA)
TA .... Testantibus Actis [*As the Records Show*] [*Latin*]

TA............ Theater Annual [*A publication*]
TA............ Theatre Authority   (EA)
TA............ Therapeutic Abortion [*Medicine*]
TA............ Thermal Activation [*Physics*]
TA............ Thermal Analysis
TA............ Thermophilic Actinomyces [*Microbiology*]
TA............ Third Attack [*Men's lacrosse position, until 1933*]
TA............ Threat Analysis   (MCD)
TA............ Threat Axis [*Military*]   (NVT)
TA............ Thromboxane [*Also, T, Tx, TX*] [*Biochemistry*]
TA............ Thromboxane A [*Also, TxA, TXA*] [*Biochemistry*]
TA............ Thunderbirds of America   (EA)
TA............ Tibialis Anterior [*A muscle*]
TA............ Time Actual   (NASA)
T & A......... Time and Allowance
TA............ Time and Attendance
T & A......... Time and Attendance   (AFM)
TA............ Tippers Anonymous [*Cochitvate, MA*]   (EA)
TA............ Tithe Annuity
TA............ Titratable Acid [*Clinical chemistry*]
TA............ Titration Alkalinity [*Oceanography*]
TA............ Tnu'at 'Aliyah   (BJA)
TA............ Tobacco Associates [*Washington, DC*]   (EA)
T & A......... Tonsillectomy and Adenoidectomy [*or Tonsils and Adenoids*] [*Medicine*]
TA............ Tool Available
T & A......... Tops and Accessories [*Show business slang*] [*Bowdlerized version*]
TA............ Torah Atmosphere   (BJA)
TA............ Total Aboard [*Aviation*]   (FAAC)
TA............ Total Adenine [*Nucleotide pool*] [*Medicine*]
TA............ Total Alkaloids [*Medicine*]
TA............ Total Audience [*Television ratings*]
TA............ Toxin-Antitoxin [*Also, TAT*] [*Immunology*]
TA............ Track Accelerator [*Missile simulator*]
T/A........... Trade Acceptance [*Business and trade*]
TA............ Trade Agreements Act [*of US*]
TA............ Trade Association
TA............ Trading As
TA............ Traduction Automatique [*A publication*]
TA............ Traffic Agent [*or Auditor*]
T/A........... Traffic Analysis [*National Security Agency*]
TA............ Trained Aide [*Medicine*]
T/A........... Training As
TA............ Transactional Analysis [*System of psychotherapy developed by Eric Berne, MD*]
TA............ Transalta Resources Corp. [*Toronto Stock Exchange symbol*]
TA............ Transamerica Corp. [*NYSE symbol*]
T/A........... Transfer of Accountability
TA............ Transfer Agent [*Business and trade*]
TA............ Transfer Aisle   (NRCH)
TA............ Transient Alert   (MCD)
TA............ Transit Authority
TA............ Transition Agreement
TA............ Transition Altitude
TA............ Transition Area [*For chart use only*] [*Aviation*]
TA............ Transmission Authenticator [*Telecommunications*]   (TEL)
TA............ Transplantation Antigen [*Medicine*]
TA............ Transportation Agent
TA............ Transportation Alternatives [*An organization*]   (EA)
TA............ Transportation Authorization   (AAG)
TA............ Transverse Acoustic
TA............ Travel Allowance
TA............ Travel [*or Trip*] Authorization   (MCD)
TA............ Traveler's Advisory [*Weather information*]
TA............ Triacetin [*Antifungal compound*] [*Organic chemistry*]
TA............ Tricuspid Atresia [*Cardiology*]
TA............ Trierisches Archiv [*A publication*]
TA............ Triple Antigen [*Medicine*]
TA............ Triplex Annealed
TA............ Trophoblast Antigen [*Immunochemistry*]
TA............ True Altitude [*Height*] [*Navigation*]
TA............ True Anomaly
TA............ Trunnion Angle   (KSC)
TA............ Trustee under Agreement   (DLA)
TA............ Truth in Advertising [*An association*] [*Defunct*]   (EA)
TA............ Tuberculin, Alkaline [*Medicine*]
TA............ Tubular Atrophy [*Nephrology*]
T/A........... Turboalternator
TA............ Turbulence Amplifier
TA............ Turkish Army   (NATG)
T/A........... Turnaround   (NASA)
T & A......... Turnbull & Asser [*Men's fashions*]
TA............ Type Americain [*World War I troop train in France made according to US specifications*]
TA............ Type Approval
TA............ Type Availability
TA............ VEB Fahlberg-List [*East Germany*] [*Research code symbol*]
TA1........... Trophoblast Antigen One [*Immunochemistry*]
TAA........... Tactical Air Army   (NATG)
TAA........... Tactical Army Automation   (MCD)

TAA........... Tactical Automation Appraisal   (MCD)
TAA........... Taiwanese Association of America   (EA)
TAA........... Tamburitza Association of America   (EA)
TAA........... Tannic Acid Agar [*Culture media*]
TAA........... Technical Assistance Administration [*United Nations*]
TAA........... Technical Assistance Agreement [*NASA*]   (NASA)
TAA........... Technology Assessment Annex   (MCD)
TAA........... Telephone Artifacts Association   (EA)
TAA........... Television Appliance Association
TAA........... Terre Adelie [*Antarctica*] [*Seismograph station code, US Geological Survey*] [*Closed*]   (SEIS)
TAA........... Territorial Army Association [*British*]
TAA........... Tertiary-Amyl Alcohol [*Organic chemistry*]
TAA........... Texas Armadillo Association [*Commercial firm*]   (EA)
TAA........... Thioacetamide [*Organic chemistry*]
TAA........... Thoracic Aortic Aneurysm [*Cardiology*]
TAA........... Three-Axis Accelerometer
TAA........... Tobacconists Association of America [*Annandale, VA*]   (EA)
TAA........... Total Army Analysis   (AABC)
TAA........... Trade Adjustment Act
TAA........... Trade Adjustment Assistance [*Department of Commerce*]
TAA........... Trade Agreements Act [*of US*]
TAA........... Trans-American Airline
TAA........... Trans-Australia Airlines [*Melbourne*]   (ADA)
TAA........... Transcript of Absentee's Account
TAA........... Transferable Account Area [*Business and trade*]
TAA........... Transient Absorption Anisotropy [*Physics*]
TAA........... Transit Advertising Association [*Washington, DC*]   (EA)
TAA........... Transportation Association of America   (EA)
TAA........... Triamcinolone Acetonide [*Synthetic steroidal drug*]
TAA........... Tumor-Associated Antigen [*Immunology*]
TAA........... Turbine Alternator Assembly
TAA........... Turkish-American Associations
TAAA......... Teen-Age Assembly of America [*Honolulu, HI*]   (EA)
TAAA......... Thoracoabdominal Aortic Aneurysm [*Cardiology*]
TAAA......... Travelers Aid Association of America [*Formerly, TAISSA*] [*Arlington Heights, IL*]   (EA)
TAABS...... [*The*] Army Automated Budget System
TAAC........ Target Area Advisory Council   (OICC)
TAAC........ Technology Assessment Advisory Council   (EGAO)
TAAC........ Trade Adjustment Assistance Center [*Department of Commerce*]
TAAC........ Training Ammunition Authorization Committee   (MCD)
TAACOM... Theater Army Area Command   (AABC)
TAAD........ Task Assignment and Directive   (MCD)
TAAD........ Terrain Avoidance Accessory Device
TAADC...... Theater Army Air Defense Command   (AABC)
TAADCOM ... Theater Army Air Defense Command   (AABC)
TAADS...... [*The*] Army Authorization Document System
TAAF........ Test, Analyze, and Fix Program [*Navy*]   (MCD)
TAAF........ Thromboplastic Activity of Amniotic Fluid [*Medicine*]
TAAFFEE ... Tactical Air Against First and Following Enemy Echelons   (MCD)
TAAG........ Technical Analysis and Advisory Group [*Navy*]   (MCD)
TAAGA...... Transactions. American Association of Genitourinary Surgeons [*A publication*]
TAALODS ... [*The*] Army Automated Logistic Data System
TAALS...... [*The*] American Association of Language Specialists [*Washington, DC*]   (EA)
TAALS...... Tactical Army Aircraft Landing Systems
TAAM........ Tomahawk Air Field Attack Missile   (MCD)
TAAM........ Transportation Army Aviation Maintenance
Ta'an...... Ta'anith   (BJA)
TAAN........ Transworld Advertising Agency Network [*Englewood, CO*]   (EA)
TAANA...... [*The*] American Association of Nurse Attorneys [*Baltimore, MD*]   (EA)
TAAOA...... Transactions. American Academy of Ophthalmology and Oto-Laryngology [*A publication*]
TAAP........ Three-Axis Antenna Positioner
TAAP........ Trade Adjustment Assistance Program [*Department of Commerce*]
TAAP........ Transient Analysis Array Program
TAAPA...... Transactions. Association of American Physicians [*A publication*]
TAAR........ Target Area Analysis-RADAR
TAARS...... [*The*] Army Ammunition Reporting System   (AABC)
TAARSAN ... Trans-Australia Airlines Reservations System Automatic Network   (ADA)
TAAS........ Tactical Air Armament Study   (MCD)
TAAS........ Thorotrast-Associated Angiosarcoma [*Oncology*]
TAAS........ Three-Axis Attitude Sensor   (IEEE)
TAAS........ Traffic Account Analysis System [*Military*] [*British*]
TAASC...... [*The*] Association of American Sword Collectors   (EA)
TAASP...... [*The*] Association for the Anthropological Study of Play
TAB.......... Airborne Tanker, Boom   (NVT)
TAB.......... Tabella [*Tablet*] [*Pharmacy*]
TAB.......... Table
TAB.......... Tabloncillo [*Race of maize*]
TAB.......... Tabriz [*Iran*] [*Seismograph station code, US Geological Survey*]   (SEIS)

TAB .... Tabular Language [*Data processing*] (IEEE)
TAB .... Tabulate (AAG)
TAB .... Tactical Air Base (AFM)
TAB .... Tamper Attempt Board
TAB .... Tandy Brands, Inc. [*American Stock Exchange symbol*]
TAB .... Tape Automated Bonding [*Integrated circuit technology*]
TAB .... Target Acquisition Battalion
TAB .... Target Acquisition Battery (MCD)
TAB .... Tax Anticipation Bill
TAB .... Technical Abstract Bulletin [*ASTIA*] [*A publication*]
TAB .... Technical Activities Board (MCD)
TAB .... Technical Assistance Board [*United Nations*]
TAB .... Technology Assessment Board (EGAO)
TAB .... Telecommunications Advisory Board
TAB .... Testing, Adjusting, and Balancing [*Heating and cooling technology*]
TAB .... Tetraaminobiphenyl [*Organic chemistry*]
TAB .... Thiolacetoxybenzanilide [*Organic chemistry*]
TAB .... Title Announcement Bulletin
TAB .... Tobago [*Trinidad and Tobago*] [*Airport symbol*] (OAG)
TAB .... Total Abstinence Brotherhood
TAB .... Traffic Audit Bureau [*New York, NY*] (EA)
TAB .... Training Aid Bulletins [*Navy*]
TAB .... Transatlantic Broadcasting Company [*In TV series "W.E.B."*]
TAB .... Transports Aeriens du Benin [*Cotonou, Benin*]
TAB .... Typhoid, Paratyphoid A and B [*Vaccine*]
TABA .... [*The*] American Book Award [*Later, ABA*]
TABA .... Transcaribe [*Airline*] [*Colombian*]
TABA .... Transportes Aereos da Bacia Amazonica [*Airline*] [*Brazil*]
TABAMLN ... Tampa Bay Medical Library Network [*Library network*]
TABBSS .... Tactical Bare Base Support Study [*Air Force*]
TABC .... Total Aerobic Bacteria Counts
TABCASS ... Tactical Air Beacon Command and Surveillance System (MCD)
TAB-CD ..... Tabulating Card
TABEL .... Tabella [*Tablet*] [*Pharmacy*] (ROG)
TABL .... Tropical Atlantic Biological Laboratory
TableR .... La Table Ronde [*Paris*] [*A publication*]
TABP .... Tetraaminobenzophenone [*Organic chemistry*]
TABPM ...... Transportation Authorized in Accordance with BUPERS Manual, Article _____
TabR .... La Table Ronde [*Paris*] [*A publication*]
TABS .... Tables [*Publishing*]
TABS .... Tabulator Stops (AAG)
TABS .... Tactical Airborne Beacon System (AFM)
TABS .... Tangential Bomb Suspension (MCD)
TABS .... Technical and Business Service
TABS .... Telephone Area Billing System
TABS .... Terminal Access to Batch Service [*Data processing*] (BUR)
TABS .... Theater Air Base Survivability [*Air Force*]
TABS .... Time Analysis and Billing System (BUR)
TABS .... Total Automatic Banking System [*Trademark of Diebold, Inc.*]
TABS .... Transatlantic Book Service [*British*]
TABSIM ..... Tabulator Simulator
TABSOL .... Tabular Systems-Oriented Language [*General Electric Co.*] [*British*]
TABSTONE ... Target and Background Signal-to-Noise Evaluation (MUGU)
TABU .... Typical Army Ball-Up [*Slang for a military muddle*]
Tabulae Biol ... Tabulae Biologicae [*A publication*]
TABV .... Theater Air Base Vulnerability [*Air Force*] (AFM)
TAB VEE .... Theater Air Base Vulnerability [*Air Force*]
TABWAG .... Tank Battle War Game
TABWDS .... Tactical Air Base Weather Dissemination System [*Air Force*]
TABWE ...... Tactical Air Base Weather Element [*Air Force*]
TABWS ..... Tactical Airborne Weather Stations (MCD)
TABWX ..... Tactical Air Base Weather
TAC .... [*The*] Alien Critic [*A publication*]
TAC .... [*The*] Architects Collaborative [*Design firm*]
TAC .... [*The*] Athletics Congress [*Track*] [*An association*]
TAC .... Austin Community College, Austin, TX [*OCLC symbol*] (OCLC)
Tac .... Tacitus [*First century AD*] [*Classical studies*] (OCD)
TAC .... Tacloban [*Philippines*] [*Airport symbol*] (OAG)
TAC .... Tacon [*Flamenco dance term*]
TAC .... Tactical (AAG)
TAC .... Tactical Air Command [*Air Force*]
TAC .... Tactical Air Controller (NVT)
TAC .... Tactical Assignment Console
TAC .... Tactical Coordinator (NATG)
TAC .... Tacubaya [*Mexico*] [*Later, TEO*] [*Geomagnetic observatory code*]
TAC .... Tacubaya [*Mexico*] [*Seismograph station code, US Geological Survey*] (SEIS)
TAC .... Tamoxifen, Adriamycin, Cyclophosphamide [*Antineoplastic drug regimen*]
TAC .... Tandycrafts, Inc. [*NYSE symbol*]
TAC .... Target Acquisition Center [*Army*]
TAC .... Target Acquisition Console [*Military*] (CAAL)
TAC .... Tax Court of the United States Reports [*A publication*]
TAC .... Team Activity Chart
TAC .... Technical Advisory Center [*National Bureau of Standards*]
TAC .... Technical Advisory Committee
TAC .... Technical Applications Center [*Air Force*]

TAC .... Technical Area Coordinator
TAC .... Technical Assignment Control (NRCH)
TAC .... Technical Assistance Center [*State University College at Plattsburgh*] [*Research center*] (RCD)
TAC .... Technical Assistance Center [*Telecommunications*]
TAC .... Technical Assistance Committee [*of the Economic and Social Council of the United Nations*]
TAC .... Technical Assistance Contract (NRCH)
TAC .... Technology Application Center [*University of New Mexico*] [*Albuquerque, NM*]
TAC .... Teleconference Association of Canada [*Toronto, ON*] [*Information service*] (TSSD)
TAC .... Telemetry and Command (MCD)
TAC .... TELENET Access Controller
TAC .... Television Advisory Committee [*British*] (DEN)
TAC .... Temperature Altitude Chamber
TAC .... Terminal Access Controller [*Advanced Research Projects Agency Network*] [*DoD*]
TAC .... Terminal Area Chart [*FAA*] (FAAC)
TAC .... Terrain Analysis Center [*Army*] (RDA)
TAC .... Test Access Control [*Telecommunications*] (TEL)
TAC .... Test Advisory Committee (MUGU)
TAC .... Thai Airways Company Ltd. [*Later, Thai Airways International*]
TAC .... Time Action Calendar [*Management*]
TAC .... Time-to-Amplitude Converter
TAC .... Time at Completion (MCD)
TAC .... Total Alkaloids of Cinchona [*Medicine*]
TAC .... Total Allowable Catch [*Fishing regulation proposed by EEC*]
TAC .... Total Average Cost (KSC)
TAC .... Tracking Accuracy Control
TAC .... Trade Agreements Committee [*An interagency committee of the executive branch of US government*]
TAC .... Traders and Contacts
TAC .... Trades Advisory Council [*British*]
TAC .... Training Alarm Controller
TAC .... Trans-Aminocrotonic Acid [*Also, TACA*] [*Organic chemistry*]
TAC .... TRANSAC [*Transistorized Automatic Computer*] Assembler Compiler
TAC .... Transformer Analog Computer
TAC .... Transistor-Assisted Circuit (ADA)
TAC .... Transistorized Automatic Control
TAC .... Translations Activities Committee [*Special Libraries Association*]
TAC .... Translator, Assembler, Compiler
TAC .... Transonic Aerodynamic Characteristics
TAC .... Transportation Account Code (AFM)
TAC .... Transportes, Aduanas, y Consignaciones, SA [*Shipping company*] [*Barcelona, Spain*]
TAC .... Trapped Air Cushion
TAC .... Travelcraft Ambassadors Club (EA)
TAC .... Trialkoxycitrate [*Organic chemistry*]
TAC .... Triallyl Cyanurate [*Organic chemistry*]
TAC .... Triamcinolone Cream [*Anti-inflammatory steroid*]
TAC .... Trouble Analysis Chart
TAC .... True Airspeed Computer
TAC .... Turboalternator Compressor
TACA .... [*The*] Association of Comedy Artists (EA)
TAC(A) ...... Tactical Air Coordinator (Airborne)
TACA .... Tactical Airborne Controller Aircraft [*Military*] (CAAL)
TACA .... Telecoms Authorities Cryptographic Algorithm [*Bell Telephone encryption chip*]
TACA .... Test of Adult College Aptitude
TACA .... Trans-Aminocrotonic Acid [*Also, TAC*] [*Organic chemistry*]
TACA .... Tucker Automobile Club of America (EA)
TACAC ...... Theater Army Civil Affairs Command (AABC)
TACAD ...... Tactical Advisory [*Military*] (CAAL)
TACAD ...... Traffic Alert and Collision Avoidance Detection [*Aviation*]
TACADE .... Teachers' Advisory Council on Alcohol and Drug Education [*British*]
TACADS .... Tactical Automated Data Processing System
TAC/AFSC ... Tactical Air Command/Air Force Systems Command
TACAID ..... Tactical Airborne Information Document (NVT)
TACAIR ...... Tactical Air [*Military*] (AABC)
TACAN ...... Tactical Air Navigation [*System*]
TACAN-DME ... Tactical Air Navigation Distance Measuring Equipment
TACAP ...... Tactical Air Command Aircraft Profiler Capability [*Air Force*]
TACAV ...... Linea Aerea TACA de Venezuela
TACAV ...... Tactical Aviation Model
TACC .... [*The*] Australian Comic Collector [*A publication*]
TACC .... Tactical Air Command Center [*Air Force*] (NVT)
TACC .... Tactical Air Control Center
TACC .... Tactical Air Coordination Center [*Military*] (CAAL)
TACC .... Thorotrast-Associated Cholangiocarcinoma [*Oncology*]
TACC .... Time Averaged Clutter Coherent
TACCAR .... Time Averaged Clutter Coherent Airborne RADAR
TACCO ..... Tactical Control Officer [*Army*] (AABC)
TACCO ..... Tactical Coordinator (MCD)
TACCOM .... Tactical Communications (MCD)
TACCOPS ... Tactical Air Control Center Operations (NVT)
TACCP ...... Tactical Command Post [*Army*]
TACCS .... Tactical Air Command Control System (MCD)

TACCS....... Tactical Army Combat [*Service Support*] Computer System [*Army*]
TACCTA .... Tactical Commander's Terrain Analysis [*Military*]　(AABC)
TAC-D....... Tactical Deception　(MCD)
TACDA....... [*The*] American Civil Defense Association　(EA)
TACDACS ... Target Acquisition and Data Collection System
TAC D & E ... Tactical Development and Evaluation [*Military*]　(CAAL)
TACDEN .... Tactical Data Entry Unit [*Army*]
TACDEW.... Tactical Advanced Combat Direction and Electronic Warfare　(MCD)
TAC-E....... Tactical Emergency [*Army*]
TACE......... Talos Conversion Equipment　(MCD)
TACE......... Tri-para-anisylchloroethylene [*Estrogen*]
TACED ...... Tank Appended Crew Evaluation Device　(MCD)
TACELIS.... Tactical Automated Communications Emitter　(MCD)
TACELIS.... Tactical Communications Emitter Location and Identification System [*Army*]　(MCD)
TACEST..... Tactical Test [*Military*]　(NVT)
TACEVAL... Tactical Evaluation　(MCD)
TACFAX..... Tactical Digital Facsimile Equipment　(MCD)
TACFDC .... Tactical Fire Direction Center [*Army*]　(AABC)
TACFIRE.... Tactical Fire
TACFIRE.... Tactical Fire Control System [*of ADSAF*]
TACFO...... TASAMS [*The Army Supply and Maintenance System*] Coordination Field Office　(AABC)
TACG .... Tactical Air Control Group [*Military*]
TACGP...... Tactical Air Control Group [*Military*]
TACGRU .... Tactical Air Control Group [*Military*]　(NVT)
TACH .... Athens Community Hospital, Athens, TN [*Library symbol*] [*Library of Congress*]　(LCLS)
TACH .... Tachometer　(AAG)
TACHO...... Tachometer　(DSUE)
TACI.......... Test Access Control Interface [*Telecommunications*]　(TEL)
TACINTEL ... Tactical Intelligence Information Exchange System　(NVT)
TACIT........ Technical Advisory Committee on Inland Transport
TACIT........ Time-Authenticated Cryptographic Identity Transmission [*Military*]
TACJAM .... Tactical Jamming
TACL......... Tactical Air Command Letter [*Air Force*]
TACL......... Tank-Automotive Concepts Laboratory [*Army*]　(RDA)
TACL......... Theater Authorized Consumption List [*Army*]　(AABC)
TACL......... Time and Cycle Log [*NASA*]　(KSC)
TACLAND ... Tactical Instrument Landing　(MCD)
TACLO ...... Tactical Air Command Liaison Officer [*Air Force*]　(FAAC)
TACLOG .... Tactical-Logistical [*Army*]　(AABC)
TACM........ Tactical Air Command Manual [*Air Force*]
TACM........ Transit Air Cargo Manifest
TACMAN.... Tactical Manuals [*Aircraft*]　(MCD)
TACMAR.... Tactical Multifunction Array RADAR [*Air Force*]
TACMIS ..... Tactical Management Information System [*Army*]　(RDA)
TACMS ...... Tactical Missile System [*Provisional*] [*Army*]　(RDA)
TACNAV .... Tactical Navigation System
TACNAVMOD ... Tactical/Navigational Modernization [*Navy*]
TACNOTE ... Tactical Notice　(NVT)
TACO .... Good Taco Corp. [*NASDAQ symbol*]　(NQ)
TACO .... Tactical Coordinator　(NG)
TACO .... Tamoxifen, Adriamycin, Cyclophosphamide, Oncovin [*Vincristine*] [*Antineoplastic drug regimen*]
TACO .... Test and Checkout Operations [*NASA*]　(NASA)
TACOC ...... Tactical Air Control Operation Center
TACODA .... Target Coordinate Data　(IEEE)
TACOL ...... Thinned Aperture Computed Lens　(IEEE)
TACOM ...... Tactical Area Communications System　(MCD)
TACOM ..... Tactical Communications　(AFM)
TACOM ..... Tank-Automotive Command [*Army*]　(MCD)
TACOMA.... Take Charge and Move Out [*Military*]
TACOMM... Tactical Communications　(AABC)
TACOMPLAN ... Tactical Communications Plan [*NATO*]
TACOMSAT .. Tactical Communications Satellite [*Also, TACSAT*] [*DoD*]
TACON ...... Tactical Control [*Military*]　(CAAL)
TACOR...... Threat Assessment and Control Receiver [*Air Force*]
TACOS....... Tactical Air Combat Simulation　(NATG)
TACOS...... Tactical Airborne Countermeasures or Strike [*Air Force*]
TACOS...... Tactical Communications System
TACOS...... Tool for Automatic Conversion of Operational Software
TACOS...... Travel Agents Computer Society [*Cambridge, MA*]　(EA)
TACOSS .... Tactical Container Shelter System [*Rockwell International Corp.*]
TACP......... Tactical Air Command Pamphlet [*Air Force*]
TACP......... Tactical Air Command Post [*Air Force*]　(MCD)
TACP......... Tactical Air Control Party [*Air Force*]
TACP......... Technical Analysis of Cost Proposals [*DoD*]
TACPACS .. Tactical Packet Switching System [*Army*]　(RDA)
TACPOL..... Tactical Procedure Oriented Language [*Data processing*]　(CSR)
TACPOL..... Tactile Procedure-Oriented Language　(CSR)
TACR .... TACAN [*Tactical Air Navigation*] Collocated with VOR [*Very-High-Frequency Omnidirectional Range*]　(FAAC)
TACR .... Tactical Air Command Regulation [*Air Force*]
TAC/R........ Tactical Reconnaissance
TACR .... Time and Cycle Record [*NASA*]　(KSC)

TACRAC .... Tactical Warfare Research Advisory Committee [*Military*]　(RDA)
TACRAPS ... Tactical Range Prediction System
TACREACT ... Tactical Reconnaissance Reaction Aircraft　(MCD)
TAC RISE... Tactical Reconnaissance Intelligence System Enhancement [*Air Force*]
TACRON .... Tactical Air Control Squadron [*Air Force*]
TACRON .... Tactical Air Control Squadron [*Navy*] [*British*]
TACRV .... Tracked Air-Cushion Research Vehicle [*DoD*]
TACS .... Tactical Air Control System [*Air Force*]
TACS .... Technical Assignment Control System　(NRCH)
TACS .... Test Assembly Conditioning Station　(NRCH)
TACS .... Theater Area Communications Systems [*Military*]
TACS .... Thruster Attitude Control System [*NASA*]
TACSAT.... Tactical Communications Satellite [*Also, TACOMSAT*] [*DoD*]
TACSATCOM ... Tactical Satellite Communications
TACSI .... Tactical Air Control System Improvements [*Air Force*]　(MCD)
TACSS .... Tactical Schoolship [*Navy*]　(NVT)
TACS/TADS ... Tactical Air Control System/Tactical Air Defense System
TACSYR.... Tactical Communications Systems Requirements　(MCD)
Tact............ Tactica [*of Arrian*] [*Classical studies*]　(OCD)
TAC T........ Tactical Transport [*Aircraft*]
TACT......... Terminal Activated Channel Test
TACT......... Transact International [*NASDAQ symbol*]　(NQ)
TACT......... Transactional Analysis Control Technique [*Training program*] [*American Airlines*]
TACT......... Transistor and Component Tester
TACT......... Transonic Aircraft Technology [*Program*] [*NASA and Air Force*]
TACT......... Truth about Civil Turmoil
TAC/TADS ... Tactical Air Control/Tactical Air Defense System [*Military*]　(CAAL)
TACTAN..... Tactical Air Control and Navigation
TACTAS.... Tactical Towed Array SONAR [*Formerly, ETAS*] [*Navy*]
TACTASS ... Tactical Tone and Acoustic Surveillance System [*Military*]　(CAAL)
TACTEC..... Tactical Technology Center [*Battelle Memorial Institute*] [*Columbus, OH*] [*Information service*]　(MCD)
TACTEC..... Totally Advanced Communications Technology
TACTIC...... Technical Advisory Committee to Influence Congress [*Federation of American Scientists*]
TACTICS ... Technical Assistance Consortium to Improve College Services [*Defunct*]　(EA)
TACTL....... Tactical　(AAG)
TACTLASS ... Tactical Towed Array Surveillance System [*Military*]　(MCD)
TAC T MR ... Tactical Transport Medium Range [*Aircraft*]
TACTRUST ... [*The*] Athletics Congress/USA Trust Fund
TACTS .... Tactical Aircrew Combat Training System　(NVT)
TACTS/ACMI ... Tactical Aircrew Combat Training System/Air Combat Maneuvering Instrumentation　(MCD)
TAC T SR ... Tactical Transport Short Range [*Aircraft*]
TAC/USA... [*The*] Athletics Congress/USA　(EA)
TACV .... Tracked Air-Cushion Vehicle [*High-speed ground transportation*]
TACVA....... Tactical Vulnerability Assessment [*Military*]　(MCD)
TACVA/CEWIS ... Tactical Communications Vulnerability Assessment of Combat Electronics Warfare Intelligence System　(MCD)
TACWE ...... Tactical Weather System　(MCD)
TAD .... Air Traffic Control Tower, Approach Control, and Departure Control Facility [*Aviation*]　(FAAC)
TAD .... Airborne Tanker, Drogue　(NVT)
TAD .... [*The*] Armchair Detective [*A publication*]
TAD .... Tactical Action Display [*SAGE*]
TAD .... Tactical Air Defense　(MCD)
TAD .... Tactical Air Direction
TAD .... Tactical Atomic Demolition [*Munitions*] [*Obsolete*] [*Military*]　(NG)
TAD .... Tadotu [*Japan*] [*Seismograph station code, US Geological Survey*] [*Closed*]　(SEIS)
TAD .... Target Acquisition Data
TAD .... Target Activation Date　(AAG)
TAD .... Target Area Designator [*Air Force*]
TAD .... Task Assignment Directive　(KSC)
TAD .... Task Assignment Drawing　(MCD)
T Ad .... Tax Advisor [*A publication*]
TAD .... Technical Acceptance Date　(AAG)
TAD .... Technical Analysis Division [*National Bureau of Standards*]
TAD .... Technical Approach Demonstration
TAD .... Technical Approval Demonstration　(AAG)
TAD .... Technology Area Description　(MCD)
TAD .... Telecommunications Automation Directorate [*Army*]　(RDA)
TAD .... Telemetry Analog to Digital [*Information converter*]
TAD .... Telephone Answering Device
TAD .... Television Advertising Duty
TAD .... Temporary Additional Duty [*Navy*]
TAD .... Temporary Attached Duty
TAD .... Terminal Address Designator
TAD .... Test and Development　(MCD)
TAD .... Thermal Analysis Data
TAD .... Thioguanine, ara-C, Daunomycin [*Daunorubicin*] [*Antineoplastic drug regimen*]

TAD .... Thioguanine, ara-C, Daunorubicin [*Antineoplastic drug regimen*]
TAD .... Thomas Aloysius Dorgan [*Satirical cartoonist*]
TAD .... Throw Away Detector [*Space shuttle*] [*NASA*]
TAD .... Thrust-Augmented Delta [*NASA*]
TAD .... Time Available for Delivery (CET)
TAD .... Tobyhanna Army Depot, Library, Tobyhanna, PA [*OCLC symbol*] (OCLC)
TAD .... Tooele Army Depot [*Utah*]
TAD .... Top Assembly Drawing
TAD .... Toward Affective Development [*Educational tool*]
TAD .... Trade and Development Board
TAD .... Traffic Accident Data [*Project*] [*National Safety Council*]
TAD .... Training Aids Division [*Navy*]
TAD .... Traitement Automatique des Donnees [*Automatic Data Processing*] [*French*]
TAD .... Transaction Application Drive [*Computer Technology, Inc.*]
TAD .... Traveling Around Drunk
TAD .... Trinidad [*Colorado*] [*Airport symbol*] [*Obsolete*] (OAG)
TAD .... Trio Archean Developments [*Vancouver Stock Exchange symbol*]
TAD .... Turk Arkeoloji Dergisi [*Ankara*] [*A publication*]
TADAR ...... Tactical Area Defense Alerting RADAR (MCD)
TADARS .... Target Acquisition/Designation Aerial Reconnaissance System (MCD)
TADAS ..... Tactical Air Defense Alerting System [*Army*]
TADC .... Tactical Air Direction Center
TADC .... Training and Distribution Center [*Navy*]
TADD .... Tangential Abrasive Dehulling Device [*for grains*]
TADD .... Target Alert Data Display Set (MCD)
TADD .... Termite and Ant Detection Dog [*In TADD Services Corp.*]
TADD .... Truckers Against Drunk Drivers [*Shreveport, LA*] (EA)
TADDS .... Target Alert Data Display Set (RDA)
TADE .... Tetraaminodiphenylether [*Organic chemistry*]
TADF .... Thermally Activated Delayed Fluorescence [*Analytical chemistry*]
TADF .... Thomas A. Dooley Foundation [*Later, Dooley Foundation/Intermed-USA*]
TADGC ...... Tactical Air Designation Grid System [*Tactical Air Command*]
TADIC .... Telemetry Analog-Digital Information Converter
TADIL .... Tactical Data Information Link [*Tactical Air Command*]
TADILS ..... Tactical Automatic Data Information Links (MCD)
TADIXS ..... Tactical Data Information Exchange Subsystem
TAD J .... Technical Aid to the Disabled Journal [*A publication*]
TADJET ..... Transport Air Drop and Jettison Test [*Air Force, Army*]
TADLR .... Tooling Automated Direct Labor Reporting (MCD)
TADM .... Tactical Atomic Demolition Munitions [*Obsolete*] [*Military*] (AABC)
TADO .... Tactical Airlift Duty Officer (AFM)
TADOR ...... Table Data Organization and Reductions
TADP .... Tactical Air Direction Post [*Military*]
TAD/P .... Terminal Area Distribution Processing
TADP .... Toronto Anti-Draft Programme [*Defunct*] (EA)
TA3DPT ..... Twitchell-Allen Three-Dimensional Personality Test [*Psychology*]
TADR .... Tabulated Drawing (MSA)
TADR .... Test Answer Document Reader
TADREPS .. Tactical Data Replay System (NVT)
TADRS .... Target Acquisition/Designation Reconnaissance System (MCD)
TADS .... Tactical Air Defense Systems (RDA)
TADS .... Tactical Automatic Digital Switch
TADS .... Target Acquisition and Designation System (MCD)
TADS .... Target and Activity Display System [*Military*]
TADS .... Technical Assistance Data
TADS .... Teletypewriter Automatic Dispatch System
TADS .... Thermal Analysis Data Station
TADS .... Tracking and Display System
TADS .... Type [*Command*] Automated Data System [*Navy*]
TADSO ...... Tactical Digital Systems Office [*Navy*] (MCD)
TADS/PNVS ... Tactical Air Direction System/Pilot Night Vision System [*Army*] (MCD)
TADS/PNVS ... Target Acquisition Designation System/Pilot Night Vision System (RDA)
TADSS .... Tactical Automatic Digital Switching System
TADSYS .... Turbine Automated Design System
TADYL .... Tom Dooley Youth League [*Defunct*]
TadzhSSR ... Tadzhik Soviet Socialist Republic
Tadzik Gos Univ Trudy Meh-Mat Fak ... Tadzikskii Gosudarstvennyi Universitet Imeni V. I. Lenina. Trudy Mehaniko-Matematiceskogo Fakulteta [*A publication*]
Tadzik Gos Univ Ucen Zap ... Tadzikskii Gosudarstvennyi Universitet Imeni V. I. Lenina. Ucenye Zapiski. Trudy Fiziko-Matematiceskogo Fakulteta. Serija Matematiceskaja [*A publication*]
Tadzik S-h Inst Trudy ... Tadzikskii Sel'skohozjaistvennyi Institut i Tadzikskii Gosudarstvennyi Universitet. Trudy [*A publication*]
TAE .... Tactical Aeromed Evacuation (CINC)
TAE .... Taegu [*South Korea*] [*Seismograph station code, US Geological Survey*] [*Closed*] (SEIS)
TAE .... Tannic Acid Equivalent [*Analytical chemistry*]

TAE .... Test and Evaluation (MCD)
TAE .... Textes Arameens d'Egypte [*A publication*] (BJA)
TAE .... Transantarctic Expedition (ADA)
TAE .... Transcatheter Arterial Embolization [*Medicine*]
TAE .... Transoceanic Airborne Environment
TAEA .... Tangipahoa & Eastern [*AAR code*]
TAEAS .... Tactical ASW [*Antisubmarine Warfare*] Environmental Acoustic Support [*Navy*] (CAAL)
TAeB .... Tuebinger Aegyptologische Beitraege [*A publication*]
TAEC .... Thailand Atomic Energy Commission for Peace
TAEC .... Turkish Atomic Energy Commission
TAED .... Tetraacetylethylenediamine [*Laundry bleaching agent*]
TAEDA Newsl ... TAEDA [*Technology Assessment of Energy Development in Appalachia*] Newsletter [*United States*] [*A publication*]
TAEDP .... Total Army Equipment Distribution Program (AABC)
TAEDS .... Total Army Equipment Distribution System (MCD)
TAEG .... Training Analysis and Evaluation Group [*Navy*]
Taehan Chikkwa Uisa Hyophoe Chi ... Taehan Chikkwa Uisa Hyophoe Chi [*Journal of the Korean Dental Association*] [*A publication*]
TAEM .... Terminal Area Energy Management [*NASA*] (NASA)
TAEMS .... Transportable Automated Electromagnetic Measurement System (MCD)
TAEO .... Test Article Engineering Order (MCD)
TAER .... Time, Azimuth, Elevation, and Range [*Aerospace*]
TAERS ...... [*The*] Army Equipment Record System [*Later, TAMMS*]
TAES .... Tactical Aeromedical Evacuation System
TAES .... Texas Agricultural Experiment Station [*Texas A & M University*] [*Research center*] (RCD)
TAETGM .... Test and Evaluation Task Group Manager (MCD)
TAF .... Aerodrome Forecast [*Aviation*] (FAAC)
TAF .... Arnold Engineering Development Center, Arnold Air Force Station, TN [*OCLC symbol*] (OCLC)
TAF .... [*The*] Asia Foundation (EA)
TAF .... Oran-Tafaraoui [*Algeria*] [*Airport symbol*] (OAG)
TAF .... Stores Ship [*Military Sea Transportation Service*] (CINC)
TAF .... Tactical Air Force
TAF .... Tactical Area Files [*Military*] (CAAL)
TAF .... Taforalt [*Morocco*] [*Seismograph station code, US Geological Survey*] (SEIS)
TAF .... Task Analysis Form
TAF .... Technology Access Fund [*Chrysler Corp.*]
TAF .... Terminal Aerodrome Forecast [*Also, TAFOR*]
TAF .... Test, Analyze, Fix (MCD)
TAF .... Third Air Force
TAF .... Top of Active Fuel [*Nuclear energy*] (NRCH)
TAF .... Toxoid-Antitoxin Floccules [*Immunology*]
TAF .... Traditional Acupuncture Foundation [*Columbia, MD*] (EA)
TAF .... Training Analysis and Feedback (MCD)
TAF .... Transaction Facility
TAF .... Trim after Forming (MSA)
TAF .... Tumor-Angiogenesis Factor [*Medicine*]
TAF .... Turkish Air Force (NATG)
TAFAD ...... Task Force Air Defense (MUGU)
TAFB .... Travis Air Force Base [*California*]
TAFB .... Tyndall Air Force Base [*Florida*]
TAFCSD .... Total Active Federal Commissioned Service to Date
TAFDS ...... Tactical Airfield Fuel Dispensing System (NG)
TAFEQ ...... TAFE [*New South Wales Department of Technical and Further Education*] Quarterly [*A publication*]
TAFFE .... Tactical Air Against First and Follow-On Eschelon (MCD)
Taffie .... Technologically Advanced Family [*Lifestyle classification*]
TAFFS .... [*The*] Army Functional Files System
TAFFTS ..... [*The*] Army Functional Files Test System (MCD)
TAFG .... Two-Axis Free Gyro (AAG)
TAFHQ ...... Tactical Air Force Headquarters
TAFI .... Technical Association of the Fur Industry
TAFI .... Turnaround Fault Isolation [*Aviation*]
TAFIES ...... Tactical Air Forces Intelligence Exploitation System
TAFIIS .... Tactical Air Force Integrated Information Systems (MCD)
TAFIN .... Tactical Air Force Initiative (MCD)
TAFMM ...... Tactical Air Force Maintenance Management (MCD)
TAFMSD .... Total Active Federal Military Service to Date
TAFNORNOR ... Allied Tactical Air Force, Northern Norway [*NATO*]
TAFO .... Theater Accounting and Finance Office [*Military*] (AFM)
TAFOR ...... Terminal Aerodrome Forecast [*Also, TAF*]
TAFROC .... Tactical Air Force Required Operational Capability (MCD)
TAFS .... Stores Ship
TAFS .... Training Aid Feasibility Studies (AAG)
TAFSA ...... Transactions. American Fisheries Society [*A publication*]
TAFSD ...... Technical Report. AFWAL-TR (United States. Air Force Wright Aeronautical Laboratories) [*A publication*]
TAFSEA ..... Technical Applications for Southeast Asia [*Air Force*]
TAFSEG ..... Tactical Air Force Systems Engineering Group (MCD)
TAFSONOR ... Allied Tactical Air Force, South Norway [*NATO*] (NATG)
TAFSUS ..... Turkish American Friendship Society of the United States (EA)
TAFT .... Technical Assistance Field Team (MCD)
TAFUBAR ... Things Are Fouled Up Beyond All Recognition [*Military slang*] [*Bowdlerized version*]
TAFX .... Tapping Fixture
TAFY .... American Theatre Arts for Youth (EA)
TAG .... [*The*] Acronym Generator [*An RCA computer program*]

TAG............ [*The*] Acrylonitrile Group [*Washington, DC*]   (EA)
TAG............ [*The*] Adjutant General [*Army*]
TAG............ Airborne Tanker, General   (NVT)
TAG............ American Group of CPA Firms   (EA)
TAG............ [*The*] Association for the Gifted [*Council for Exceptional Children*]
TAG............ [*The*] Attorneys Group   (EA)
TAG............ [*The*] Audiotex Group [*Princeton, NJ*] [*Telecommunications service*]   (TSSD)
TAG............ Orion Air, Inc. [*Chapel Hill, NC*] [*FAA designator*]   (FAAC)
TAG............ Tactical Airlift Group   (MCD)
TAG............ Tactical Analysis Group [*Military*]   (CAAL)
tag............ Tagalog [*MARC language code*] [*Library of Congress*]   (LCCP)
TAG............ Tagbilaran [*Philippines*] [*Army*]   (OAG)
Tag............ Tagoro [*A publication*]
TAG............ Target Attitude Group [*Advertising*]
TAG............ Tavern and Guild Association [*Division of Homophile Effort for Legal Protection*]   (EA)
TAG............ Taxi Air Group, Inc.
TAG............ Technical Air-to-Ground   (NASA)
TAG............ Technical Art Group
TAG............ Technical Assessment Group [*Navy*]
TAG............ Technical Assistance Group [*NASA*]   (KSC)
TAG............ Technical Assistance Group [*An association*]   (EA)
TAG............ Technical Assistance Guides   (OICC)
TAG............ Technician Affiliate Group [*of American Chemical Society*]
TAG............ Telecomputer Applications Group
TAG............ Telemetry System Analysis Group
TAG............ Tennessee, Alabama & Georgia Railway Co. [*AAR code*]
TAG............ Terminal Applications Group, Inc.
TAG............ Terminating and Grounding
TAG............ Test Analysis Guide
TAG............ Test Assembly Grapple [*Nuclear energy*]   (NRCH)
TAG............ Test Automation Growth
TAG............ Texas A & M University at Galveston, Galveston, TX [*OCLC symbol*]   (OCLC)
TAG............ Tijdschrift Aardrijkskundig Genootschap [*A publication*]
TAG............ Time Arrive Guarantee   (AAG)
TAG............ Time Automated Grid
TAG............ Training Aids Guide [*Navy*]
TAG............ Trans-Atlantic Geotraverse [*Project*] [*National Oceanic and Atmospheric Administration*]
TAG............ Transient Analysis Generator
TAG............ Transport Air Group [*Joint Army, Navy, and Marine Corps*]
TAG............ Trauma Action Group   (EA)
TAG............ Triacylglycerol [*Food technology*]
TAGA .... Technical Association of the Graphic Arts [*Rochester, NY*]   (EA)
TAGA .... Telegraphist Air Gunner's Association [*Navy*] [*British*]
TAGA .... Trace Atmospheric Gas Analyser [*Instrument*]
TAGA .... Travel Agents Guild of America   (EA)
TAGAMET .... Antagonist Cimetidine [*Ulcer medicine manufactured by SmithKline Beckman Corp.*]
TAGBDUSA ... [*The*] Adjutant General's Board, United States Army
Tagber Dt Akad Landw-Wiss Berl ... Tagungsberichte. Deutsche Akademie der Landwirtschaftswissenschaften zu Berlin [*A publication*]
TAGC .... Tripped Automatic Gain Control
TAGCEN ... [*The*] Adjutant General Center [*Army*]   (AABC)
TAGER ...... [*The*] Association for Graduate Education and Research
TAGEX ...... Travel at Government Expense [*Aviation*]   (FAAC)
TAGIU .... Tracking and Ground Instrumentation Unit [*NASA*]
TAGLA ...... Tropical Agriculture [*A publication*]
TAGM........ Range Instrumentation Ship
TAGM........ Table and Art Glassware Manufacturers [*Pittsburgh, PA*]   (EA)
Tag Muellerei-Technol Ber ... Tagung ueber die Muellerei-Technologie. Bericht [*A publication*]
TAGO .... [*The*] Adjutant General's Office [*Army*]
TAGO .... Tago, Inc. [*NASDAQ symbol*]   (NQ)
TAGRDCUSA ... [*The*] Adjutant General's Research and Development Command, United States Army
TAGS .... FBM [*Fleet Ballistic Missile*] Support Ship
TAGS .... Tactical Aircraft Guidance System [*Air Force*]
TAGS .... Teledyne Airborne Geophysical Services
TAGS .... Text and Graphic System [*Savoy Software Science Ltd.*] [*Software package*]
TAGS .... Theater Air-Ground Warfare Simulation   (MCD)
TAGSRWC ... [*The*] Andy Griffith Show Rerun Watchers Club   (EA)
TAGSUSA ... [*The*] Adjutant General's School [*United States*], Army
TAGUA ...... Transactions. American Geophysical Union [*A publication*]
Tagungsber Ges Inn Med DDR ... Tagungsbericht der Gesellschaft fuer Innere Medizin der DDR [*A publication*]
TAH .... [*The*] American Hispanist [*A publication*]
TAH .... Hospital Ship
Tah .... Taehti [*Record label*] [*Finland*]
TAH .... Tahiti [*Society Islands*] [*Seismograph station code, US Geological Survey*] [*Closed*]   (SEIS)
TAH .... Tanna Island [*Vanuatu*] [*Airport symbol*]   (OAG)
TAH .... Tell Abu Huwam   (BJA)
TAH .... Total Abdominal Hysterectomy [*Medicine*]
TAH .... Total Artificial Heart

TAHA............ Tapered Aperture Horn Antenna
TAHCD ...... Taehan Ankwa Hakhoe Chapchi [*A publication*]
TAHOE ...... TOW Against Helicopter Operational Equipment   (RDA)
TAHOP ...... Tank/Attack Helicopter Operational Performance   (MCD)
TAHQ .... Theater Army Headquarters
TAI............ T. A. Informations [*A publication*]
TAI............ Tainan [*Republic of China*] [*Seismograph station code, US Geological Survey*]   (SEIS)
TAI............ Taiz [*Yemen Arab Republic*] [*Airport symbol*]   (OAG)
TAI............ Target Area of Interest [*Army intelligence matrix*]   (INF)
TAI............ Temps Atomique International [*International Atomic Time*] [*Telecommunications*]   (TEL)
TAI............ Thai Airways International   (MCD)
TAI............ Time-to-Autoignition [*NASA*]   (KSC)
TAI............ Total Active Inventory   (MCD)
TAI............ Total Aircraft Inventory
TAI............ Traditionally Administered Instruction   (BUR)
TAI............ Transamerica Income Shares, Inc. [*NYSE symbol*]
TAI............ Transports Aeriens Intercontinentaux [*Privately owned French airline*]
TAI............ Turnaround Index [*Data processing*]
TAI............ Tuskegee Airmen, Incorporated   (EA)
TAIC .... Technical Air Intelligence Center [*Navy*]
TAIC .... Tokyo Atomic Industrial Consortium
TAIC .... Triallylisocyanurate [*Organic chemistry*]
TAICH .... Technical Assistance Information Clearing House [*of ACVAFS*] [*Information service*]   (EA)
TAID .... Thrust-Augmented Improved Delta [*Launch vehicle*] [*NASA*]
TAID .... Thunderbird American Indian Dancers   (EA)
TAIDB........ Tank Automative Integrated Database   (MCD)
TAIDET ..... Triple Axis Inertial Drift Erection Test
TAIDHS ..... Tactical Air Intelligence Data Handling System   (NATG)
TAik .... Teologinen Aikakauskirja. Teologisk Tidskrift [*Helsinki*] [*A publication*]
Taikomoji Branduoline Fiz ... Taikomoji Branduoline Fizika [*A publication*]
TAILRATS ... Tail RADAR Acquisition and Tracking System   (MCD)
TAILS .... Tactical Automatic Landing System [*Aviation*]   (NG)
TAINS........ TERCOM [*Terrain Contour Mapping*]-Assisted Inertial Navigation System   (MCD)
TAIP .... Terminal Area Impact Point   (MUGU)
TAIR .... Terminal Area Instrumentation RADAR   (MCD)
TAIR .... Test Assembly Inspection Record [*NASA*]   (NASA)
TAIRCG..... Tactical Air Control Group [*Military*]   (AFIT)
TAIS .... Tactical Air Intelligence System   (MCD)
TAISSA ...... Travelers Aid - International Social Service of America [*Later, split into ISS/AB and TAAA*]
Tait............ Tait's Edinburgh Magazine [*A publication*]
Tait............ Tait's Index to Morison's Dictionary [*Scotland*]   (DLA)
Tait............ Tait's Index to Scotch Session Cases [*1823*]   (DLA)
Tait............ Tait's Manuscript Decisions, Scotch Session Cases   (DLA)
TAIU .... Technical Aircraft Instrument Unit [*Navy*]
Taiwan Agr Res J ... Taiwan Agricultural Research Journal [*A publication*]
Taiwan Environ Sanit ... Taiwan Environmental Sanitation [*A publication*]
Taiwan Fish Res Inst Fish Cult Rep ... Taiwan. Fisheries Research Institute. Fish Culture. Report [*A publication*]
Taiwan Fish Res Inst Lab Biol Rep ... Taiwan. Fisheries Research Institute. Laboratory of Biology. Report [*A publication*]
Taiwan Fish Res Inst Lab Fish Biol Rep ... Taiwan. Fisheries Research Institute. Laboratory of Fishery Biology. Report [*A publication*]
Taiwan J Vet Med Anim Husb ... Taiwan Journal of Veterinary Medicine and Animal Husbandry [*A publication*]
Taiwan Sugar Exp Stn Annu Rep ... Taiwan. Sugar Experiment Station. Annual Report [*A publication*]
Taiwan Sugar Exp Stn Res Rep ... Taiwan. Sugar Experiment Station. Research Report [*A publication*]
Taiwan Sugar Res Inst Annu Rep ... Taiwan. Sugar Research Institute. Annual Report [*A publication*]
Taiw Svy .... Monthly Economic Survey. Taiwan [*A publication*]
TAJ............ Tadji [*Papua New Guinea*] [*Airport symbol*]   (OAG)
taj .... Tajik [*MARC language code*] [*Library of Congress*]   (LCCP)
TAJ............ Tanegashima [*Ryukyu Islands*] [*Seismograph station code, US Geological Survey*]   (SEIS)
TAJ............ Thermal Arc Jet
TAJ............ Turbulent Air Jet
TAJAG .... [*The*] Assistant Judge Advocate General [*Army*]   (AABC)
TAK .... Cargo Ship [*Military Sea Transportation Service*]   (CINC)
TAK .... Takaka [*New Zealand*] [*Seismograph station code, US Geological Survey*] [*Closed*]   (SEIS)
TAK .... Takamatsu [*Japan*] [*Airport symbol*]   (OAG)
TAK .... Taken
TAK .... Tonan Ajia Kenkyu [*Southeast Asia Studies*] [*A publication*]
TAK .... Trainer Appraisal Kit
TAK .... Transparent Armor Kit
TAKC .... Taking Care. Newsletter of the Center for Consumer Health Education [*A publication*]
TAKC .... Theological Associate, King's College [*London*]
TAKIS........ Tutmonda Asocio pri Kibernetiko, Informatiko, kaj Sistemiko [*World Association of Cybernetics, Computer Science, and System Theory*]   (EA-IO)
TAKIT........ Teaching Aids Kit [*Red Cross Youth*]

TAKR.........	Vehicle Cargo Ship
TAKRX	Fast Sealift Ship
TAKV.........	Cargo Ship and Aircraft Ferry [*Military Sea Transportation Service*] (CINC)
TAKX.........	Maritime Prepositioning Ship
TAL	[*The*] Apocryphal Literature: A Brief Introduction [*1945*] [*A publication*] (BJA)
Tal	Cases Tempore Talbot, English Chancery (DLA)
TAL	Tailor (MSA)
TAL	Talara [*Peru*] [*Seismograph station code, US Geological Survey*] (SEIS)
Tal	Talbot's Cases in Equity [*1734-38*] (DLA)
Tal	Talcorp Ltd. [*Toronto Stock Exchange symbol*]
Tal	Taliesin [*England*] [*A publication*]
Tal	Talis [*Such*] [*Pharmacy*]
Tal	Talisman [*A publication*]
TAL	Talladega College, Talladega, AL [*OCLC symbol*] (OCLC)
TAL	Talley Industries, Inc. [*NYSE symbol*]
TAL	Talmud
TAL	Tanana [*Alaska*] [*Airport symbol*] (OAG)
TAL	Target Acquisition Laboratory
TAL	Technische Akademie der Luftwaffe [*Germany*] (MCD)
TAL	TEPI [*Technical Equipment Planning Information*] Approved Letter
TAL	Terminal Application Language
TAL	Tetraalkyllead [*Organic chemistry*]
TAL	Training Aids Library [*Navy*]
TAL	Transalpine [*Pipeline*] [*Western Europe*]
TAL	Transatlantic Landing
TAL	Transocean Air Lines
TAL	Transporter Air Lock (NRCH)
TALA.........	Teacher Author League of America [*Formerly, TALNY*] (EA)
TALA.........	Textile Association of Los Angeles [*Los Angeles, CA*] (EA)
TALAFIT	Tank, Laying, Aiming, and Firing Trainer (MCD)
TALAR.......	Tactical Approach and Landing RADAR [*NASA*]
TALAR.......	Talos Activity Report (MCD)
Talb...........	Cases Tempore Talbot, English Chancery (DLA)
Talb...........	Talbot's Cases in Equity [*1734-38*] (DLA)
TALBE.......	Talk and Listen Beacon [*Radio*]
TALC.........	Tactical Airlift Center (AFM)
TALC.........	Take-a-Look-See (MCD)
TALC.........	Tank-Automotive Logistics Command [*Army*]
TALCM.......	Tactical Air-Launched Cruise Missile (MCD)
TALDT........	Total Administrative and Logistics Downtime (MCD)
TALF	Take a Look Foundation (EA)
TALFF	Total Allowable Level of Foreign Fishing
TALIA	Transactions. Association of Life Insurance Medical Directors of America [*A publication*]
TALISSI.....	Tactical Light Shot Simulation (MCD)
TALK.........	Titles Alphabetically Listed by Keyword (KSC)
T-ALL.........	T-Cell Acute Lymphoblastic Leukemia [*Oncology*]
Tallin Polueteh Inst Toim ...	Tallinna Polutehnilise Instituudi Toimetised [*A publication*]
Tall Timbers Res Stn Misc Publ ...	Tall Timbers Research Station. Miscellaneous Publication [*A publication*]
TALM	Thredbo Accelerated Learning Method (ADA)
TALMIS......	Technology-Assisted Learning Market Information Services [*Educational Programming Systems, Inc.*]
TALMS.......	Tunable Atomic Line Molecular Spectroscopy
TALNY	Teacher Author League of New York [*Later, TALA*] (EA)
TALO.........	Tactical Air Liaison Officer [*Air Force*]
TALO.........	Time after Lift-Off
TALOG	Theater Army Logistical Command
TALON	South Central Regional Medical Library Program [*Library network*]
TALON	Tactical Air-Land Operations (MCD)
TALONS.....	Tactical Airborne LORAN Navigation System [*Model*] (MCD)
TALOP	Terminology, Administrative, Logistical, and Operational Procedures [*Military*]
TAL QUAL ...	Talis Qualis [*Such As It Is*] [*Latin*] (ROG)
TALR	Law Reports of the District Court of Tel Aviv [*A publication*] (BJA)
TALS	[*The*] American Lupus Society [*Torrance, CA*] (EA)
TALS	[*The*] Army Language School
TALS	Barge Cargo Ship
TALS	Transport Approach and Landing Simulator
TALT	Tracking Altitude (MCD)
TALTC........	Test Access Line Termination Circuit [*Telecommunications*] (TEL)
TALTT	Thrust Augmented Long Tank Thor (MCD)
TALUS	Transportation and Land Use Study [*Michigan*]
TAm	[*The*] Americas: A Quarterly Review of Inter-American Cultural History [*A publication*]
TAM	[*The*] Associated Missions (EA)
TAM	Tactical Air Missile
TAM	Tactical Air Mission [*Air Force*]
TAM	Tamanrasset [*Algeria*] [*Geomagnetic observatory code*]
TAM	Tamanrasset [*Algeria*] [*Seismograph station code, US Geological Survey*] (SEIS)
TAM	Tamara Resources, Inc. [*Vancouver Stock Exchange symbol*]
Tam...........	Tamid (BJA)
TAM	Tamil [*Language, etc.*] (ROG)
tam...........	Tamil [*MARC language code*] [*Library of Congress*] (LCCP)
Tam	Tamlyn's English Rolls Court Reports [*48 English Reprint*] (DLA)
TAM	Tamoxifen [*Also, T*] [*Antineoplastic drug*]
TAM	Tampico [*Mexico*] [*Airport symbol*] (OAG)
TAM	Tangent Approximating Manifold
TAM	Target Acquisition Model [*Military*]
TAM	Target Activated Munition [*Air-delivered land mines*]
TaM	Tarybine Mokykla [*A publication*]
TAM	Technical Acknowledgment Message [*Aviation*]
TAM	Technical Ammunition
TAM	Technical Area Manager
TAM	Techniques of Alcohol Management [*Campaign, sponsored in part by the National Licensed Beverage Association, to prevent drunk driving*]
TAM	Telecommunications Access Method
TAM	Telephone Answering Machine (IEEE)
TAM	Television Audience Measurement
TAM	Terminal Access Method
TAM	Test Access Multiplexer [*Telecommunications*] (TEL)
TAM	Texas A & M University
TAM	Theatre Arts Magazine [*A publication*]
TAM	Theatre Arts Monthly [*A publication*]
TAM	Thermal Analytical Model [*Apollo*] [*NASA*]
TAM	Throw Away Maintenance
TAM	Time and Materials (MCD)
TAM	Tituli Asiae Minoris [*Vienna*] [*A publication*] (OCD)
TAM	Total Active Motion [*Orthopedics*]
TAM	Toxoid-Antitoxin Mixture [*Immunology*]
TAM	Trajectory Application Method (MCD)
TAM	Transparent Anatomical Manikin [*An exhibit at the Chicago Museum of Science and Industry*]
TAM	Triangle Amplitude Modulation
TAM	Tubos de Acero de Mexico, SA [*American Stock Exchange symbol*]
TAM	Tumor-Associated Macrophages [*Immunology*]
TAM	Twentieth Anniversary Mobilization (EA)
TAM	Type-Approval Model
TAMA	Technical Assistance and Manufacturing Agreement
TAMA	Training Aids Management Agency [*Army*] (AABC)
TAMAC	Three-Axis Manual Attitude Controller
Tamarack R ...	Tamarack Review [*A publication*]
Tamb.........	Tambyah's Reports [*Ceylon*] (DLA)
TamC.........	Tamil Culture [*A publication*]
TAMC........	Tripler Army Medical Center (AABC)
TAMCO	Training Aid for MOBIDIC Console Operations
TAME	Tactical Air-to-Air Mission Evaluation (MCD)
TAME	Tactical Missile Encounter [*Air Force*] (KSC)
TAME	Tertiary-Amyl Methyl Ether [*Gasoline additive*]
TAME	Tosyl-L-arginine Methyl Ester [*Also, TosArgOMe*] [*Biochemical analysis*]
T Am Fish S ...	Transactions. American Fisheries Society [*A publication*]
T Am Geophy ...	Transactions. American Geophysical Union [*A publication*]
TAMI	Tanks and Mechanized Infantry Experiment (MCD)
TAMI	Tip Air Mass Injection [*Helicopter*]
Tamil Nadu J Coop ...	Tamil Nadu Journal of Co-operation [*A publication*]
TAMIRAD ...	Tactical Mid-Range Air Defense Program [*Army*] (AABC)
TAMIS.......	Telemetric Automated Microbial Identification System
TAMIS.......	Training Ammunition Management Information System (MCD)
Tamkang J Math ...	Tamkang Journal of Mathematics [*Taipei*] [*A publication*]
TamkR	Tamkang Review [*A publication*]
Taml..........	Tamlyn's English Rolls Court Reports [*48 English Reprint*] (DLA)
TAML	Taunton Municipal Lighting Plant [*Nuclear energy*] (NRCH)
Taml Ev......	Tamlyn's Evidence in Chancery [*2nd ed.*] [*1846*] (DLA)
Taml TY	Tamlyn's Terms of Years [*1825*] (DLA)
Tamlyn......	Tamlyn's English Rolls Court Reports [*48 English Reprint*] (DLA)
Tamlyn Ch ...	Tamlyn's English Rolls Court Reports [*48 English Reprint*] (DLA)
Tamlyn (Eng) ...	Tamlyn's English Rolls Court Reports (DLA)
TAMM	Tetrakis(acetoxymercuri)methane [*Organic chemistry*]
T Am Math S ...	Transactions. American Mathematical Society [*A publication*]
T Am Micros ...	Transactions. American Microscopical Society [*A publication*]
TAMMS......	[*The*] Army Maintenance Management System [*Formerly, TAERS*] (AABC)
T Am Nucl S ...	Transactions. American Nuclear Society [*A publication*]
TAMO........	Tooling Advance Material Order (MCD)
TAMO.........	Training Aids Management Office [*Army*] (AABC)
TAMOS......	Terminal Automatic Monitoring System
TAMP	Tactical Armament Master Plan (MCD)
TAMP	Tampering [*FBI standardized term*]
TAMP	Thai Army Munitions Plant (MCD)
TAMP	Thailand Ammunition Manufacturing Plant (CINC)
TAMPD......	TAPPI [*Technical Association of the Pulp and Paper Industry*] Annual Meeting. Proceedings [*United States*] [*A publication*]

TAMPER .... Tables for Approximation of Midpoints for Exponential Regression (MCD)

T Am Phil S ... Transactions. American Philosophical Society [*A publication*]

TAMPS .... Teaming Analysis Model Personnel Selector (MCD)

TamR .... Tamarack Review [*Toronto*] [*A publication*]

TAMR .... Teen Association of Model Railroading (EA)

TAMS .... Tactical Avionics Maintenance Simulation (KSC)

TAMS .... Tandem Accelerator Mass Spectrometry

TAMS .... Token and Medal Society (EA)

TAMS .... Total Active Military Service (AFM)

TAMS .... Training Ammunition Management Study [*Army*] (MCD)

TAMSA ...... Transactions. American Microscopical Society [*A publication*]

TAMSA ...... Transportes Aereos Mexicano, Sociedad Anonima

T Am S Art ... Transactions. American Society for Artificial Internal Organs [*A publication*]

TAMSJ .... TAMS [*Token and Medal Society*] Journal [*A publication*]

TAMT .... [*The*] American Mime Theatre (EA)

TAMTA .... Transactions. American Mathematical Society [*A publication*]

TAMU .... Texas A & M University

TAN .... Tactical Air Navigational Aid (FAAC)

TAN .... Tananarive [*Madagascar*] [*Geomagnetic observatory code*]

TAN .... Tananarive [*Madagascar*] [*Seismograph station code, US Geological Survey*] (SEIS)

TAN .... Tandem (AAG)

TAN .... Tandy Corp. [*NYSE symbol*]

Tan .... Taney's United States Circuit Court Reports (DLA)

TAN .... Tangent [*Mathematics*]

TAN .... Tanglewood Consolidated Resources, Inc. [*Toronto Stock Exchange symbol*]

Tan .... Tanhuma (BJA)

TAN .... Tanned (MSA)

TAN .... Task Authorization Notice

TAN .... Taunton, MA [*Location identifier*] [*FAA*] (FAAL)

TAN .... Tax Anticipation Note

TAN .... Technische Arbeitsnorm

TAN .... Teletype Alert Network (NVT)

TAN .... Test Area North [*AEC*]

TAN .... Thiazolylazonaphthol [*An indicator*] [*Chemistry*]

TAN .... Title Analytic [*Bibliography*]

TAN .... Total Adenine Nucleotide [*Medicine*]

TAN .... Total Ammonia Nitrogen

TAN .... Trainable Adaptive Network

TAN .... Transall-Normen (MCD)

TAN .... Transonic Aerodynamic Nozzle

TAN .... Transportes Aereos Nacionales, SA [*TAN Airlines*]

TAN .... Twilight All Night

TANAA .... Transactions. American Neurological Association [*A publication*]

TANC .... Total Absorption Nuclear Cascade

TANCAV ..... Tactical Navigation and Collision Avoidance [*Military*] (CAAL)

T Anc Monum ... Ancient Monuments Society. Transactions [*A publication*]

TAND .... Tandem (FAAC)

TANDA ...... Time and Attendance Report (FAAC)

TANDEM .... Tibi Aderit Numen Divinum, Expecta Modo [*God Will Help Thee - Only Wait*] [*Latin*] [*Motto of Elisabeth Ernestine Antonie, Duchess of Saxony (1681-1766)*]

TANDOC .... Tanzania National Documentation Centre [*National Central Library*] [*Dar Es Salaam, Tanzania*] [*Information service*] (EISS)

TANE .... Transportes Aereos Nacionales Ecuatorianas [*Airline*] [*Ecuadorean*]

TANESCO ... Tanzania Electric Supply Company

Taney .... Taney's United States Circuit Court Reports (DLA)

TANEYCOMO ... Taney County, MO [*A lake at Branson, MO*]

Taney's CC Dec ... Taney's United States Circuit Court Reports (DLA)

Taney's Dec (USCC) ... Taney's United States Circuit Court Reports (DLA)

TANG .... Tangential (AAG)

TANH .... Tangent, Hyperbolic

Tanh .... Tanhuma (BJA)

TANJUG ..... Telegrafska Agencija Nove Jugoslavije [*Press agency*] [*Yugoslavia*]

TANKBAT ... Tank Battalion [*Army*]

Tank Bulk Marit Manage ... Tanker and Bulker Maritime Management [*England*] [*A publication*]

Tanker Bulk Carr ... Tanker and Bulk Carrier [*A publication*]

Tanker Bulker Int ... Tanker and Bulker International [*England*] [*A publication*]

TANKEX ..... Tank Field Exercise (NVT)

Tan LR .... Tanganyika Territory Law Reports (DLA)

Tann .... Tanner's Reports [*13-17 Utah*] (DLA)

Tann .... Tanner's Reports [*8-14 Indiana*] (DLA)

TANN .... Taqrimiut Nipingat News [*Salluit, Quebec*] [*A publication*]

Tanner ...... Tanner's Reports [*13-17 Utah*] (DLA)

Tanner ...... Tanner's Reports [*8-14 Indiana*] (DLA)

TANO .... Tano Corp. [*NASDAQ symbol*] (NQ)

TANO .... Triacetoneamine Nitroxide [*Organic chemistry*]

TANREM ..... Tactical Nuclear Weapons Requirements Methodology

TANS .... Tactical Air Navigation System [*Helicopter*]

TANS .... Tax Anticipation Notes

TANS .... Terminal Area Navigation System

TANS .... Territorial Army Nursing Service [*British*]

TA-NS .... Total Abstinence - No Smoking [*On social invitations*]

TANSA .... Transactions. American Nuclear Society [*A publication*]

TANSTAAFL ... There Ain't No Such Thing As a Free Lunch [*Principle of economics indicating that one cannot get something for nothing*] [*See also TINSTAAFL*]

TANT .... Tennant Co. [*NASDAQ symbol*] (NQ)

TANU .... Tanganyika African National Union [*Political party*]

Tanulmanyok MTA Szamitastechn Automat Kutato Int Budapest ... Tanulmanyok. MTA Szamitastechnikai es Automatizalasi Kutato Intezet Budapest [*A publication*]

TANWERE ... Tactical Nuclear Weapons Requirements (CINC)

TANY .... Typographers Association of New York [*New York, NY*] (EA)

TAN-ZAM ... Tanzania-Zambia [*Railway*]

Tanzania Miner Resour Power Annu Rep Geol Surv Div ... Tanzania. Ministry of Industries. Mineral Resources and Power. Annual Report of the Geological Survey Division [*A publication*]

Tanzania Rec Geol Surv Tanganyika ... Tanzania. Records of the Geological Survey of Tanganyika [*A publication*]

Tanzania Silvic Res Note ... Tanzania Silviculture Research Note [*A publication*]

Tanzania Silvic Res Stn Tech Note (New Ser) ... Tanzania. Silviculture Research Station. Technical Note (New Series) [*A publication*]

TAO .... Hammond, LA [*Location identifier*] [*FAA*] (FAAL)

TAO .... Oiler

TAO .... Qingdao [*China*] [*Airport symbol*] (OAG)

TAO .... TACAN [*Tactical Air Navigation*] Only (FAAC)

TAO .... Tactical Action Observer [*Military*] (CAAL)

TAO .... Tactical Action Officer [*Navy*] (NVT)

TAO .... Tactical Air Observation [*or Observer*] (NATG)

TAO .... Tactical Air Officer (NVT)

TAO .... Tactical Air Operations

TAO .... Technical Analysis Office (MCD)

TAO .... Technical Assistance Operations [*United Nations*]

TAO .... Technical Assistance Order (KSC)

TAO .... Technology Applications Office [*NASA*]

TAO .... Technology Assistance Officer [*Small Business Administration*]

TAO .... Telephone Area Office [*British*]

TAO .... Terrain Avoidance Override (MCD)

TAO .... Test Analysis Outline

TAO .... Thromboangitis Obliterans [*Cardiology*]

TAO .... Time and Altitude Over [*Aviation*] (FAAC)

TAO .... Tokyo Astronomical Observatory

TAO .... Total Acid Output [*Clinical chemistry*]

TAO .... Transportation Applications Office [*Jet Propulsion Laboratory, NASA*]

TAO .... Troleandomycin [*Formerly, Triacetyloleandomycin*] [*Antibacterial compound*]

TAOBBATED ... [*The*] Adventures of Buckaroo Banzai across the Eighth Dimension [*1984 movie title*]

TAOC .... [*The*] Army Operations Center

TAOC .... Tactical Air Operations Center

TAOC .... Train Axis Optical Cube

TAOCC ...... Tactical Air Operations Control Center (NATG)

TAOG .... Gasoline Tanker [*Military Sea Transportation Service*] (CINC)

TAOI .... Tactical Area of Interest

TAOO .... Tactical Air Operations Officer [*Tactical Air Command*]

TAOR .... Tactical Area of Responsibility [*Military*] (AFM)

TAOS .... Thrust-Assisted Orbiter Shuttle [*NASA*]

TAOS .... Travel Allowance on Separation [*Military*]

TA/OSD ..... Task Analysis/Operational Sequence Diagram

TAOT .... Transport Oiler Ship

TAP .... Amarillo Public Library, Amarillo, TX [*OCLC symbol*] (OCLC)

TAP .... Onitap Resources, Inc. [*Toronto Stock Exchange symbol*]

TAP .... Table of Authorized Personnel (NATG)

TAP .... Tackled Attempting to Pass [*Football*]

TAP .... Tactical Action Programs

TAP .... Tactical Armament Plan (MCD)

TAP .... Taipei [*Taiwan*] [*Later, LNP*] [*Geomagnetic observatory code*]

TAP .... Taipei [*Taihoku*] [*Taiwan*] [*Seismograph station code, US Geological Survey*] (SEIS)

TAP .... Tapachula [*Mexico*] [*Airport symbol*] (OAG)

TAP .... Tapestry (ADA)

Tap .... Tappan's Ohio Common Pleas Reports (DLA)

TAP .... Target Aim Points

TAP .... Target Analysis and Planning [*Computer system*] [*Military*]

TAP .... Target Assignment Panel

TAP .... Task Area Plan

TAP .... Teacher's Aide Program

TAP .... Technical Achievement Plan [*NASA*] (NASA)

TAP .... Technical Action Panel [*Department of Agriculture*]

TAP .... Technical Action Program (OICC)

TAP .... Technical Advisory Panel [*United Nations*]

TAP .... Technical Area Plan [*Navy*] (MCD)

TAP .... Technical Assistance Program

TAP .... Technical Assistance Project (EA)

TAP .... Technological Adjustment Pay

TAP .... Technological American Party (EA)

TAP .... Technology Adaptation Program [*Massachusetts Institute of Technology*] [*Research center*] (RCD)

TAP .... Technology Applications Program [*NASA*] [*University of Kentucky*] [*Lexington, KY*]
TAP .... Telemetry Acceptance Pattern   (KSC)
TAP .... Telemetry Antenna Pedestal
TAP .... Temporal Analysis of Products [*System developed by Monsanto Chemical Co.*]
TAP .... Tension by Applanation [*Ophthalmology*]
TAP .... Terminal Access Processor
TAP .... Terminal Applications Package   (IEEE)
TAP .... Terrestrial Auxiliary Power
TAP .... Test Assistance Program [*Sperry UNIVAC*]
TAP .... Theater of All Possibilities [*International touring company of actor-authors*]
TAP .... Thermal Analysis Program
TAP .... Thermosiphoning Air Pan
TAP .... Thermoviscoelastic Analysis Program   (MCD)
TAP .... Thesaurus at Play [*Acronym is trademark for word game*]
TAP .... Thiol Alkaline Phosphatase [*An enzyme*]
TAP .... Three-Axis Package
TAP .... Tibetan Aid Project [*Berkeley, CA*]   (EA)
TAP .... Time-Sharing Assembly Program [*Data processing*]   (DIT)
TAP .... Total Action Against Poverty [*A federal government program*]
TAP .... Total Air Pressure   (NASA)
TAP .... Toxicological Agent Protective Item   (MCD)
TAP .... Tracking Alarms Processor [*Space Flight Operations Facility, NASA*]
TAP .... Trajectory Analysis Program   (MCD)
TAP .... Trans-Alaska Pipeline
TAP .... Transaction Application Program [*Data processing*]
TAP .... Transcription Activating Protein [*Biochemistry*]
TAP .... Transferable Assets Program
TAP .... Transponder Access Program [*Satellite Business Systems*] [*McLean, VA*] [*Telecommunications*]   (TSSD)
TAP .... Transport Ship [*Military Sea Transportation Service*]   (CINC)
TAP .... Transportes Aereos Portugueses, SARL [*Portuguese Air Transport*]
TAP .... Trend Analysis Program [*American Council of Life Insurance*] [*Washington, DC*] [*Information service*]   (EISS)
TAP .... Triaminopyrimidine [*Organic chemistry*]
TAP .... Trickle Ammonia Process [*for drying grain feedstuffs*]
TAP .... Trimethylaminoethylpiperazine [*Organic chemistry*]
TAP .... Truck Assembly Plants
TAP .... Trustee, Administration, and Physician's Institute [*Seminar*]
TAP .... Tunis-Afrique Presse [*Press agency*] [*Tunisia*]
TAPA .... (Tetranitrofluorylideneaminooxy)propionic Acid
TAPA .... Three-Dimensional Antenna Pattern Analyzer [*Air Force*]
TAPA .... Transactions and Proceedings. American Philological Association [*A publication*]
TAPA .... Turkish American Physicians Association [*Syosset, NY*]   (EA)
TAPAC .... Tape Automatic Positioning and Control
TAPAC .... Transportation Allocations, Priorities, and Controls Committee
TAPAK .... Tape-Pack
TAPAT .... Tape Programed Automatic Tester
TAPATS ...... Threat Artillery Preparation Against Thermal Sights   (MCD)
TAPCC .... Technology and Pollution Control Committee [*Environmental Protection Agency*]
TAPCHAN ... Tapered Channel [*Wave power technology*]
TAPCO .... Thompson Products, Inc. [*Later, Thompson Ramo Woolridge, Inc.*]
TAP-D .... Test of Articulation Performance - Diagnostic
TAPE .... Tactical Air Power Evaluation [*Air Force*]
TAPE .... Tape Automatic Preparation Equipment
TAPE .... Target Profile Examination Technique [*RADAR analysis concept*] [*Air Force*]
TAPE .... Technical Advisory Panel for Electronics [*Air Force*]
TAPE .... Television Audience Program Evaluation
TAPE .... Tentative Annual Planning Estimate   (NVT)
TAPE .... Timed Access to Pertinent Excerpts
TAPE .... Total Application of Prerecorded Evidence
TAPE .... Totally Automated Programing Equipment
TAPER .... [*The*] Army Plan for Equipment Records
TAPER .... Temporary Appointment Pending Establishment of a Register [*Civil Service*]
TAPER .... Theater Army Personnel   (MCD)
TAPER .... Turbulent Air Pilot Environment Research [*NASA-FAA project*]
TAPFOR ..... [*The*] Army Portion of Force Status and Identify Report [*Force Status Report*]   (AABC)
TAPH .... Toluic Acid Phenylhydrazide [*Organic chemistry*]
TAPhA .... Transactions and Proceedings. American Philological Association [*A publication*]
TAPIT .... Tactical Photographic Image Transmission
TAPITS ...... Tactical Airborne Processing, Interpretation, and Transmission System [*Military*]
TAPITS ...... Tactical Photographic Image Transmission System
TAPLINE .... Trans-Alaska Pipeline
TAPLINE .... Trans-Arabian Pipeline
Tap Man ..... Tapping on the Writ of Mandamus [*1848*]   (DLA)
TAPO .... Termination Accountable Property Officer
Tapp .... Tappan's Ohio Common Pleas Reports   (DLA)
TAPP .... Tumor Acquisition, Processing, and Preservation [*Oncology*]
TAPP .... Two-Axis Pneumatic Pickup   (IEEE)

Tappan .... Tappan's Ohio Common Pleas Reports   (DLA)
Tappan (Ohio) ... Tappan's Ohio Common Pleas Reports   (DLA)
Tappan's Ohio Rep ... Tappan's Ohio Common Pleas Reports   (DLA)
Tappan's R ... Tappan's Ohio Common Pleas Reports   (DLA)
TAPPI .... Technical Association of the Pulp and Paper Industry [*Atlanta, GA*]   (EA)
TAPPI Alkaline Pulping Conf Prepr ... TAPPI [*Technical Association of the Pulp and Paper Industry*] Alkaline Pulping Conference Preprint [*A publication*]
TAPPI Annu Meet Prepr ... TAPPI [*Technical Association of the Pulp and Paper Industry*] Annual Meeting. Preprint [*A publication*]
TAPPI Annu Meet Proc ... TAPPI [*Technical Association of the Pulp and Paper Industry*] Annual Meeting. Proceedings [*A publication*]
TAPPI Bibl ... TAPPI [*Technical Association of the Pulp and Paper Industry*] Bibliography of Pulp and Paper Manufacture [*A publication*]
TAPPI For Biol Wood Chem Conf Conf Pap ... TAPPI [*Technical Association of the Pulp and Paper Industry*] Forest Biology Wood Chemistry Conference. Conference Papers [*A publication*]
TAPPI Monogr Ser ... TAPPI [*Technical Association of the Pulp and Paper Industry*] Monograph Series [*A publication*]
Tapping ..... Tapping on the Writ of Mandamus   (DLA)
TAPPI Papermakers Conf Pap ... TAPPI [*Technical Association of the Pulp and Paper Industry*] Papermakers Conference. Papers [*A publication*]
TAPPI Special Rept ... TAPPI [*Technical Association of the Pulp and Paper Industry*] Special Reports [*A publication*]
TAPPI Spec Tech Assoc Publ ... TAPPI [*Technical Association of the Pulp and Paper Industry*] Special Technical Association. Publication [*A publication*]
Tapp M & Ch ... Tapp on Maintenance and Champerty [*1861*]   (DLA)
TAPPS .... [*The*] Automated Procurement Planning System
TAPR .... Toxic Altitude Propulsion Research   (MCD)
TAPRE .... Tracking in an Active and Passive RADAR Environment
TAPS .... Tactical Area Positioning System
TAPS .... Tactical Protective Structures   (MCD)
TAPS .... Tarapur Atomic Power Station [*India*]
TAPS .... Teachers Audio Placement System
TAPS .... Telemetry Antenna Positions System [*Military*]   (CAAL)
TAPS .... TERCOM [*Terrain Contour Mapping*] Aircraft Positioning Systems [*Air Force*]
TAPS .... Terminal Application Program System [*Data processing*]
TAPS .... Terminal Area Positive Separation [*FAA*]
TAP-S .... Test of Articulation Performance - Screen
TAPS .... Time Analysis of Program Status
TAPS .... Trajectory Accuracy Prediction System [*Air Force*]
TAPS .... Trans-Alaska Pipeline System
TAPS .... Transactions. American Philosophical Society [*A publication*]
TAPS .... Tris(hydroxymethyl)methylamino Propanesulfonic Acid
TAPS .... Turboalternator Power System   (IEEE)
TAPSC .... Trans-Atlantic Passenger Steamship Conference [*Later, IPSA*]   (EA)
TAPU .... Tanganyika African Postal Union
TAPVC .... Total Anomalous Pulmonary Venous Connection [*Cardiology*]
TAPVR .... Total Anomalous Pulmonary Venous Return [*Cardiology*]
TAQ .... Transient Airman Quarters [*Air Force*]   (AFM)
TAQK .... Taqralik [*A publication*]
TAQO .... Tawow. Canadian Indian Cultural Magazine [*A publication*]
TAQT .... Task Assignment Queue Table   (MCD)
TAQTD .... Task Assignment Queue Table Display   (MCD)
TAQTU .... Task Assignment Queue Table Update   (MCD)
TAR .... Tactical Air Reconnaissance   (AFM)
TAR .... Tactical Air Request   (NVT)
TAR .... Tactical Aircraft Recovery   (CINC)
tar .... Tadzhik Soviet Socialist Republic [*MARC country of publication code*] [*Library of Congress*]   (LCCP)
TAR .... Tara Exploration & Development Co. Ltd. [*Toronto Stock Exchange symbol*]
TAR .... Taranto [*Italy*] [*Seismograph station code, US Geological Survey*]   (SEIS)
TAR .... Target
tar .... Tatar [*MARC language code*] [*Library of Congress*]   (LCCP)
TAR .... Technical Action Request [*Army*]   (AABC)
TAR .... Technical Analysis Request [*NASA*]   (KSC)
TAR .... Technical Assistance Request   (NRCH)
TAR .... Terminal Address Register
TAR .... Terminal Area Surveillance RADAR
TAR .... Terrain Avoidance RADAR
TAR .... Test Action Requirement   (NASA)
TAR .... Test Agency Report   (NASA)
TAR .... Test Analysis Report
TAr .... Theater Arts [*A publication*]
TAR .... Threat Avoidance Receiver   (MCD)
TAR .... Thrombocytopenia with Absent Radii [*Medicine*]
TAR .... Thrust-Augmented Rocket [*NASA*]
TAR .... Total Assets Reporting   (MCD)
TAR .... Towed Array RADAR
TAR .... Track Address Register
TAR .... Training and Administration of the Reserve
TAR .... Trajectory Analysis Room [*NASA*]   (KSC)

TAR .... Transportes Aereos Regionais [*Airline*] [*Brazil*]
TAR .... Triannual Review   (NATG)
TAR .... Truck and Rail
TAR .... Turnaround Ratio
TA/RA .... Technical Availability/Restricted Availability [*Navy*]   (NVT)
TARA .... Total Articular Replacement Arthroplasty [*Orthopedics*]
TARA .... Truck-Frame and Axle Repair Association [*Brooklyn, NY*]   (EA)
TARABS .... Tactical Air Reconnaissance and Aerial Battlefield Surveillance System
TARADCOM ... Tank-Automotive Research and Development Command [*Army*]
TARAF .... Taurus Resources CI A [*NASDAQ symbol*]   (NQ)
TARAN .... Tactical Attack RADAR and Navigation
TARAN .... Test and Repair [*or Replace*] as Necessary
Tarb .... Tarbiz. Jerusalem   (BJA)
Tar Bak Orm Gen Mud Yay ... Tarim Bakanligi. Orman Genel Mudurlugu Yayinlarindan [*A publication*]
TARC .... [*The*] Army Research Council
TARC .... Cable Ship
TARC .... Tactical Air Reconnaissance Center [*Shaw Air Force Base*]
TARC .... Television Allocation Research Committee [*or Council*]
TARC .... Theater Army Replacement Command
TARC .... Through Axis Rotational Control   (MCD)
TARC .... Total Available Residual Chlorine [*Water quality*]
TARC .... Toxics Testing and Assessment Research Committee [*Terminated, 1984*] [*Environmental Protection Agency*]   (EGAO)
TARC .... TransAtlantic Resources [*NASDAQ symbol*]   (NQ)
TARCAP .... Target Combat Air Patrol [*Navy*]
TARCOG .... Top of Alabama Regional Council of Governments
TARCOM .... Tank-Automotive Materiel Readiness Command [*Army*]
TARCOMSA ... Tank-Automotive Materiel Readiness Command, Selfridge Activity   (MCD)
TArDC .... Arlington Development Center, Arlington, TN [*Library symbol*] [*Library of Congress*]   (LCLS)
TARDIS ...... Time and Relative Dimensions in Space [*Acronym is name of spaceship in British TV series "Dr. Who"*]
TARE .... Telegraphic Automatic Relay [*or Routing*] Equipment   (NG)
TARE .... Telemetry Automatic Reduction Equipment
TARE .... Transistor Analysis Recording Equipment
TAREWS .... Tactical Air Reconnaissance and Electronic Warfare Support   (MCD)
TAREX .... Target Exploitation [*Military*]   (AABC)
TARF .... Tracking and Reporting Format [*Military*]   (CAAL)
TARFU .... Things Are Really Fouled Up [*Military slang*] [*Bowdlerized version*]
TARFX .... Tracking and Reporting Format Extended [*Military*]   (CAAL)
Targ........... Targum   (BJA)
TARGET ..... Team to Advance Research for Gas Energy Transformation [*Group of US gas and gas-electric companies*]
TARGET ..... Thermal Advanced Reactor, Gas-Cooled, Exploiting Thorium
TARGET ..... Transportability Analysis Reports Generator [*Military*]   (MCD)
TARGET ..... Transportation Accident Research Graduate Education and Training
TargJer ...... [*The*] Jerusalem Targum of the Pentateuch   (BJA)
TargJon ..... Targum Jonathan   (BJA)
TargOnk..... Targum Onkelos   (BJA)
TargYer...... Targum Yerusahlmi   (BJA)
TARIC .... Texas American Resources [*NASDAQ symbol*]   (NQ)
TARIF .... Telegraphic Automatic Routing in the Field   (MCD)
TarI............ Tarleton Term Reports [*A publication*]
TARL .... Training Aids Research Laboratory [*Air Force*]   (MCD)
TARLOCS ... Target Locating System [*Military*]   (MCD)
Tarl Term R ... Tarleton Term Reports [*A publication*]
TARMAC .... Tar Macadam
TARMAC .... Terminal Area RADAR/Moving Aircraft   (KSC)
TARMOCS .. [*The*] Army Operations Center System
TArnA .... ARO, Inc., AEDC Library, Arnold Air Force Station, TN [*Library symbol*] [*Library of Congress*]   (LCLS)
TARND ...... Turnaround   (FAAC)
TARO .... Territorial Army Reserve of Officers [*British*]
TAROF ...... Taro-Vit Industries Ltd. [*NASDAQ symbol*]   (NQ)
TAROM ...... Transporturi Aeriene Romane [*Romanian Air Transport*]
TAROT .... [*The*] Associated Readers of Tarot International   (EA)
TARP .... Tactical Airborne Reconnaissance Pod
TARP .... Tactical Airborne Recording Package
TARP .... Tarpaulin   (AAG)
TARP .... Test and Repair Processor [*Data processing*]
TARP .... Total Army Requirements Program
TARP .... Transient Acoustic Radiation Program
TARP .... Typical Airland Resupply Profile   (MCD)
TARPAC .... Television and Radio Political Action Committee [*National Association of Broadcasters*]
TARPS .... Tactical Aerial Reconnaissance Pod System   (MCD)
TARPTOLA ... Theologiae Apud Remonstrantes Professorem, Tyrannidis Osorem, Limburgium Amstelodamensem [*Pseudonym used by John Locke*]
TARS.......... Tactical Air Reconnaissance School [*Air Force*]
TARS.......... Tactical Air Research and Survey Office [*Air Force*]
TARS.......... Technical Assistance Recruitment Service [*United Nations*]
TARS.......... Teen Age Republicans

TARS.......... Terminal Automated RADAR Services [*Aviation*]   (FAAC)
TARS.......... Terrain Analog RADAR Simulator
TARS.......... Terrain Avoidance RADAR System   (MCD)
TARS.......... Theater Army Replacement System   (AABC)
TARS.......... Three-Axis Reference System [*Used in reference to Titan missile*]
TARS.......... Training and Administrative Reserves [*on permanent active duty*]
TARS.......... Transportation Aircraft Rebuild Shops [*National Guard*]   (MCD)
TARS.......... Turnaround Ranging Station [*Telecommunications*]   (TEL)
TARS-75..... Tactical Reconnaissance and Surveillance - 1975 [*Army*]
TARSA .... Transportes Aereos Ranquettes, Sociedad Anonima [*Argentina*]
Tarsad Szle ... Tarsadalmi Szemle [*A publication*]
Tarsadtud Kozl ... Tarsadalomtudomanyi Kozlemenyek [*A publication*]
TARSCC .... Three-Axis Reference System Checkout Console [*Used in reference to Titan missile*]
TARSD .... Tropical Agriculture Research Series [*A publication*]
TARSLL...... Tender and Repair Ship Load List [*Navy*]   (NG)
TARS OCUL ... Tarsis Oculorum [*To the Eyelids*] [*Pharmacy*]
TART.......... Tactical Antiradiation Tracker [*Military*]   (CAAL)
TART.......... Tartarum [*Tartar*] [*Pharmacy*]   (ROG)
TART.......... Tartrate
TART.......... Task Analysis Reduction Technique [*Navy*]
TART.......... Theodore Army Terminal
TART.......... Transonic Armament Technology   (MCD)
TART.......... Twin Accelerator Ring Transfer   (IEEE)
TARTA .... Tactical RADAR Target Analysis [*Military*]   (CAAL)
TARTC....... Theater Army Replacement and Training Command
TArts .... Theater Arts [*A publication*]
Tartu Riikl UI Toimetised ... Tartu Riikliku Uelikooli Toimetised [*A publication*]
TARU Research Note ... New South Wales. Traffic Accident Research Unit. TARU Research Note [*A publication*]
TARVAN..... Truck and Rail Van
TAS .... [*The*] Air Surgeon [*Army*]
TAS .... [*The*] Army Staff
TAS .... Tactical Advisory Service [*Department of Commerce*]
TAS .... Tactical Air Support [*Tactical Air Command*]
TAS .... Tactical Area Switching
TAS .... Tactical Automated System   (MCD)
TAS .... Tactical Automatic Switch   (AABC)
TAS .... Taiwanese-American Society   (EA)
TAS .... Tallow Alkyl Sulfate [*Surfactant*]
TAS .... Tampa Southern Railroad [*AAR code*]
TAS .... Taos, NM [*Location identifier*] [*FAA*]   (FAAL)
TAS .... Tape Alteration Subroutine
TAS .... Target Acquisition System
TAS .... Tashkent [*USSR*] [*Airport symbol*]   (OAG)
TAS .... Tashkent [*USSR*] [*Seismograph station code, US Geological Survey*]   (SEIS)
TAS .... Tasmania
TAS .... Tasu Resources Ltd. [*Vancouver Stock Exchange symbol*]
TAS .... Tax Administration System [*Internal Revenue Service*]
TAS .... Technical Advisory Services [*Army*]   (RDA)
TAS .... Telecommunications Authority Singapore   (TEL)
TAS .... Telemetry Antenna Subsystem   (NASA)
TAS .... Telephone Answering Service [*or System*]
TAS .... Telephone Area Staff [*British*]
TAS .... Temperature-Actuated Switch   (IEEE)
TAS .... Terminal Access System   (MCD)
TAS .... Terminal Address Selector
TAS .... Test Access Selector [*Telecommunications*]   (TEL)
TAS .... Test Answer Sheets
TAS .... Test Article Specification   (NASA)
TAS .... Test and Set [*Data processing*]
TAS .... Texture Analysis System [*Image analysis for biochemistry*]
TAS .... Theatre Arts Society [*British*]
TAS .... Three-Axis Stabilization   (AAG)
TAS .... Time Air Speed   (NATG)
TAS .... Torpedo and Antisubmarine [*Obsolete*] [*Navy*] [*British*]
TAS .... Towed Array SONAR
TAS .... Tracking Adjunct System [*I-HAWK*]   (MCD)
TAS .... Tracking Antenna System
TAS .... Traffic Analysis Survey   (MCD)
TAS .... Training Aids Section [*Navy*]
TAS .... Transportes Aereos Salvador [*Brazil*]
TAS .... Transverse Air Spring
TAS .... Troop Airlift Squadron   (CINC)
TAS .... True Airspeed
TAS .... Tychon's Assembler   (MCD)
TASA .... [*The*] Aircraft Service Association
TASA .... [*The*] Antique Stove Association   (EA)
TASA .... [*The*] Assistant Secretary of the Army
TASA .... Task and Skill Analysis   (AABC)
TASA .... Technical Advisory Service for Attorneys
TASA .... Television Audio Support Activity [*Army*]
TASA .... Test Area Support Assembly
TASA .... Tumor-Associated Surface Antigen [*Immunology*]
TASAE .... Training and Audio-Visual Support Activity - Europe   (MCD)

T ASAE ...... Transactions. ASAE [*American Society of Agricultural Engineers*] [*A publication*]
TASAG .... TACOM [*Tank Automotive Command*] Scientific Advisory Group [*DoD*] (EGAO)
TASAMS .... [*The*] Army Supply and Maintenance System (AABC)
TASAP .... [*The*] Army Scientific Advisory Panel
Tas Arch .... Tasmanian Architect [*A publication*]
Tas Architect ... Tasmanian Architect [*A publication*]
TASB .... Texas Archaeological Society. Bulletin [*A publication*]
Tas Bldg App R ... Tasmanian Building Appeal Reports [*A publication*]
TASC .... [*The*] Analytic Sciences Corporation
TASC .... Tabular Sequence Control
TASC .... Tactical Air Support Center (CINC)
TASC .... Target Area Sequential Correlator (MCD)
TASC .... Technical Activity Steering Committee [*Nuclear energy*] (NRCH)
TASC .... Tehran Area Support Center [*Military*] (MCD)
TASC .... Telecommunication Alarm Surveillance and Control [*AT & T*]
TASC .... Terminal Area Sequencing and Control
TASC .... Test Anxiety Scale for Children [*Psychology*]
TASC .... Total Absorption Shower Cascade
TASC .... Total Avionic Support Capability
TASC .... Training Aids Support Center [*Army*]
TASC .... Training and Audiovisual Support Center [*Army*]
TASC .... Treatment Alternatives to Street Crime [*Antidrug program*]
TASC .... True Airspeed Computer
TASCC .... Tactical Air Support Coordination Center (MCD)
TASCC .... Test Access Signaling Conversion Circuit [*Telecommunications*] (TEL)
TASCOM .... Theater Army Support Command [*Terminated, 1975*] [*West Germany*] (AABC)
TASCOM(S) ... Theater Army Support Command (Supply)
TASCON .... Television Automatic Sequence Control
TASD .... Tactical Action Situation Display
TASD .... Terminal Railway, Alabama State Docks [*AAR code*]
TASDA .... [*The*] American Safe Deposit Association [*Greenwood, IN*] (EA)
TASDA .... Tactical Airborne SONAR Decision Aid
TASDC .... Tank-Automotive Systems Development Center [*Army*]
Tas Dep Agric Bull ... Bulletin. Department of Agriculture. Tasmania [*A publication*]
Tas Div Bul ... Institution of Engineers of Australia. Tasmania Division. Bulletin [*A publication*]
TASE .... Tactical Air Support Element (AABC)
TASE .... Tactical Support Equipment
Tas Ed .... Tasmanian Education [*A publication*]
Tas Ed Gaz ... Tasmanian Education Gazette [*A publication*]
Tas Ed Rec ... Educational Record. Tasmania Education Department [*A publication*]
Tas Educ ..... Tasmanian Education [*A publication*]
TASER .... Teleactive Shock Electronic Repulsion [*Nonlethal weapon*]
TASER .... Tom Swift and His Electric Rifle [*Electronic "stun gun"*]
TASES .... Tactical Airborne Signal Exploitation System (MCD)
TASF .... Tactical Air Strike Force [*Air Force*]
Tas Fish ..... Tasmanian Fisheries Research [*A publication*]
TASFMA .... Target Acquisition Systems Force Mix Analysis [*Military*]
Tas Fruitgrower and Farmer ... Tasmanian Fruitgrower and Farmer [*A publication*]
TASFUIRA ... Things Are So Fouled Up It's Really Amazing [*Military slang*] [*Bowdlerized version*]
TASG .... Tactical Air Support Group [*Air Force*] (AFIT)
Tas Geol Surv Geol Atlas 1 Mile Ser ... Tasmanian Geological Survey. Geological Atlas. 1 Mile Series [*A publication*]
Tas Govt Gaz ... Tasmanian Government Gazette [*A publication*]
TASH .... [*The*] Association for the Severely Handicapped [*Later, TASH: the Association for Persons with Severe Handicaps*] [*Seattle, WA*] (EA)
Tas Hist Research Assoc Papers & Proc ... Tasmanian Historical Research Association. Papers and Proceedings [*A publication*]
Tas Hotel R ... Tasmanian Hotel Review [*A publication*]
TASI .... Time Assignment Speech Interpolation [*Timesharing technique*] [*Telecommunications*]
TASI .... Transactional Analysis Systems Institute
Tas Ind .... Tasmanian Industry [*A publication*]
TASIS .... [*The*] American School in Switzerland
TASJ .... Transactions. Asiatic Society of Japan [*A publication*]
Tas J Ag ..... Tasmanian Journal of Agriculture [*A publication*]
Tas J Agric ... Tasmanian Journal of Agriculture [*A publication*]
Tas J Ed ..... Tasmanian Journal of Education [*A publication*]
TASK .... Temporary Assigned Skeleton [*Data processing*]
Taskent Gos Ped Inst Ucen Zap ... Taskentskii Gosudarstvennyi Pedagogiceskii Institut Imeni Nizami. Ucenye Zapiski [*A publication*]
Taskent Gos Univ Buharsk Ped Inst Naucn Trudy ... Taskentskii Gosudarstvennyi Universitet. Buharskii Pedagogiceskii Institut. Naucnye Trudy [*A publication*]
Taskent Gos Univ Naucn Trudy ... Taskentskii Gosudarstvennyi Universitet Imeni V. I. Lenina. Naucnyi Trudy [*A publication*]
Taskent Gos Univ Sb Naucn Trudov ... Taskentskii Gosudarstvennyi Universitet. Sbornik Naucnyh Trudov [*A publication*]

Taskent Inst Inz Zeleznodoroz Transporta Trudy ... Taskentskii Institut Inzenerov Zeleznodoroznogo Transporta Trudy [*A publication*]
Taskent Inst Narod Hoz Naucn Zap Mat v Prilozen ... Taskentskii Institut Narodnogo Hozjaistva. Naucnye Zapiski. Matematika v Prilozenijah [*A publication*]
Taskent Politehn Inst Naucn Trudy ... Taskentskii Politehniceskii Institut. Naucnye Trudy. Novaja Serija [*A publication*]
Taskent Politehn Inst Naucn Trudy NS ... Taskentskii Politehniceskii Institut. Naucnye Trudy. Novaja Serija [*A publication*]
TASKFLOT ... Task Flotilla
TASKFORNON ... Allied Task Force, North Norway [*NATO*] (NATG)
TASL .... Theater Authorized Stockage List [*Military*] (AABC)
Tas Lab & Ind Bul ... Tasmania. Department of Labour and Industry. Bulletin [*A publication*]
Tas LR .... Tasmanian Law Reports [*A publication*]
Tas L Rev ... University of Tasmania. Law Review [*A publication*]
TASM .... Tactical Air-to-Surface Missile (NATG)
TASM .... Tasmania (ROG)
Tasm .... Tasmanian State Reports [*A publication*]
TASM .... Tomahawk Antiship Missile (MCD)
TASM .... Trialkylstannylmaleate [*Organic chemistry*]
Tasmania Build J ... Tasmanian Building Journal [*A publication*]
Tasmania Dep Agric Annu Rep ... Tasmania. Department of Agriculture. Annual Report [*A publication*]
Tasmania Dep Mines Geol Surv Bull ... Tasmania. Department of Mines. Geological Survey. Bulletin [*A publication*]
Tasmania Dep Mines Geol Surv Rec ... Tasmania. Department of Mines. Geological Survey. Record [*A publication*]
Tasmania Dep Mines Geol Surv Rep ... Tasmania. Department of Mines. Geological Survey. Report [*A publication*]
Tasmania Dep Mines Tech Rep ... Tasmania. Department of Mines. Technical Report [*A publication*]
Tasmania Dep Mines Underground Water Supply Pap ... Tasmania. Department of Mines. Underground Water Supply Paper [*A publication*]
Tasmania For Comm Bull ... Tasmania. Forestry Commission. Bulletin [*A publication*]
Tasmania Geol Surv Bull ... Tasmania. Geological Survey. Bulletin [*A publication*]
Tasmania Geol Surv Explanatory Rep ... Tasmania. Geological Survey. Explanatory Report [*A publication*]
Tasmania Geol Surv Rec ... Tasmania. Geological Survey. Record [*A publication*]
Tasmania Geol Surv Rep ... Tasmania. Geological Survey. Report [*A publication*]
Tasmania Geol Surv Underground Water Supply Pap ... Tasmania. Geological Survey. Underground Water Supply Paper [*A publication*]
Tasmania Inland Fish Comm Rep ... Tasmania. Inland Fisheries Commission. Report [*A publication*]
Tasmania LR ... University of Tasmania. Law Review (DLA)
Tasmania Mines Dep Bull ... Tasmania. Department of Mines. Bulletin [*A publication*]
Tasmanian Dep Agric Insect Pest Surv ... Tasmanian Department of Agriculture. Insect Pest Survey [*A publication*]
Tasmanian Fis Res ... Tasmanian Fisheries Research [*A publication*]
Tasmanian J Agr ... Tasmanian Journal of Agriculture [*A publication*]
Tasmanian J Agric ... Tasmanian Journal of Agriculture [*A publication*]
Tasmanian U L Rev ... Tasmanian University Law Review [*A publication*]
Tasmanian Univ L Rev ... Tasmanian University Law Review [*A publication*]
Tasm Dep Agric Bull ... Tasmania. Department of Agriculture. Bulletin [*A publication*]
Tasm Dep Agric Res Bull ... Tasmania. Department of Agriculture. Research Bulletin [*A publication*]
TASME .... Tosyl-L-arginyl Sarcosine Methyl Ester [*Biochemistry*]
Tasm Fmr ... Tasmanian Farmer [*A publication*]
Tasm Fruitgr Fmr ... Tasmanian Fruitgrower and Farmer [*A publication*]
Tasm Fruitgow Fmr ... Tasmanian Fruitgrower and Farmer [*A publication*]
Tasm Geol Surv Bull ... Tasmania. Geological Survey. Bulletin [*A publication*]
Tasm Geol Surv Geol Atlas 1 Mile Ser ... Tasmania. Geological Survey. Geological Atlas: 1 Mile Series [*A publication*]
Tasm Geol Surv Undergr Wat Supply Pap ... Tasmania. Geological Survey. Underground Water Supply Paper [*A publication*]
TASMGS .... Tomahawk Antiship Missile Guidance Set (MCD)
Tasm Hist Res Ass Pap Proc ... Tasmanian Historical Research Association. Papers and Proceedings [*A publication*]
Tasm J Agr ... Tasmanian Journal of Agriculture [*A publication*]
Tasm J Agric ... Tasmanian Journal of Agriculture [*A publication*]
Tasm LR ..... Tasmania Law Reports [*Australia*] (DLA)
Tasm Nat ... Tasmanian Naturalist [*A publication*]
TASMO ...... Tactical Air Support for Maritime Operations [*Navy*] (NVT)
TASMOL .... Tactical Aircraft Support Model (MCD)
Tas Motor Trade & Transport J ... Tasmanian Motor Trade and Transport Journal [*A publication*]
Tasm SR ..... Tasmanian State Reports [*A publication*]
Tasm Stat ... Tasmanian Statutes [*Australia*] (DLA)
Tasm Stat R ... Tasmanian Statutory Rules, with Tables [*Australia*] (DLA)
Tasm St R ... Tasmanian State Reports [*A publication*]
Tasm UL Rev ... Tasmanian University. Law Review [*A publication*]

Tasm Univ Law Rev ... University of Tasmania. Law Review [*A publication*]
Tas Nat...... Tasmanian Naturalist [*A publication*]
Tas News ... Tasmanian Motor News [*A publication*]
Tas News ... Tasmanian News Reports [*A publication*]
Tas Nurse ... Tasmanian Nurse [*A publication*]
TASO .... Television Allocations Study Organization [*Defunct*]
TASO .... Terminal Area Security Officer [*Military*]   (AABC)
TASO .... Training Aids Service Office [*Army*]   (AABC)
TASOS ...... Towed Array SONAR System
TASP.......... [*The*] Army Studies Program   (AABC)
TASP .... Target Antisubmarine Patrol   (NVT)
TASP .... Telemetry Analysis and Simulation Program [*Spacecraft*]
　　　　　[*NASA*]
TASP .... Tentative Acceptance Sampling Procedure [*Army*]
TASP .... Texas Archaeological Society. Papers [*A publication*]
TASP .... Toll Alternatives Studies Program
　　　　　[*Telecommunications*]   (TEL)
TAS-PAC ... Total Analysis System for Production, Accounting, and Control
　　　　　[*Data processing*]
TASPR .... Technical and Schedule Performance Report [*NASA*]   (NASA)
TASQ .... Tactical Airlift Squadron
Tas R .... Tasmanian Reports [*A publication*]
Tas R .... Tasmanian State Reports [*A publication*]
TASR .... Terminal Area Surveillance RADAR
TASR .... Torque Arm Speed Reducer
TASRA ...... Thermal Activation-Strain Rate Analysis
TASROCO ... Tactical Aerial Surveillance and Reconnaissance Operational
　　　　　Capability Objectives [*1995*]   (MCD)
TASS.......... [*The*] Army Study System
TASS.......... Tactical Air Support Section
TASS.......... Tactical Air Support Squadron [*Military*]
TASS.......... Tactical Avionics System Simulator [*Army*]   (MCD)
TASS.......... Tactical Signal Simulator [*Canadian Astronautics Ltd. RADAR
　　　　　threat simulation system*]
TASS.......... Technical Assembly System
TASS.......... Telegraphnoye Agentstvo Sovyetskovo Soyuza [*Telegraph
　　　　　Agency of the Soviet Union*] [*News agency*]
TASS.......... Terminal Application Support System   (MCD)
TASS.......... Terrain Analyst's Synthesizer Station [*Army*]   (RDA)
TASS.......... Towed Acoustic Surveillance System [*Marine science*]   (MSC)
TASS.......... Towed Array SONAR System
TASS.......... Towed Array Surveillance System [*Navy*]   (CAAL)
TASS.......... Trouble Analysis System or Subsystem
　　　　　[*Telecommunications*]   (TEL)
TASSA .... [*The*] Army Signal Supply Agency
TASSC .... [*The*] American Specialty Surety Council [*Later, ASA*]   (EA)
TASSEL ..... Three-Astronaut Space System Experimental
　　　　　Laboratory   (MCD)
TASSI......... Tactical Airborne SIGINT Support Improvement Acquisition
　　　　　Plan   (MCD)
TASSO ...... Tactical Special Security Office [*Army*]   (AABC)
TASSO ...... Transatlantic Air Safety Service Organization
TASSO .... Two-Arm Spectrometer Solenoid   (MCD)
TASSq .... Tactical Air Support Squadron [*Military*]   (AFM)
Tas S R ...... Tasmanian State Reports [*A publication*]
TASSRAP .. Towed Array Surveillance Range Prediction   (MCD)
TASST .... Tentative Airworthiness Standards for Supersonic Transports
TAST.......... Tactical Assault Supply Transport   (MCD)
TAST .... Test Article Signal Translator   (MCD)
TAST.......... Thermoacoustic Sensing Technique   (IEEE)
TASTA .... [*The*] Administrative Support Theaters Army
TASTE........ Thermal Accelerated Short Time Evaporator [*Facetious term
　　　　　used in orange juice industry*]
Tas Teach ... Tasmanian Teacher [*A publication*]
Tas Teacher ... Tasmanian Teacher [*A publication*]
Tas Trader ... Tasmanian Trader and Successful Independent [*A publication*]
Tas Tramp ... Tasmanian Tramp [*A publication*]
Tas Univ Gaz ... University of Tasmania. Gazette [*A publication*]
Tas Univ Law R ... University of Tasmania. Law Review [*A publication*]
Tas Univ Law Rev ... University of Tasmania. Law Review [*A publication*]
Tas Univ L Rev ... Tasmanian University Law Review [*A publication*]
Tas Univ L Rev ... University of Tasmania. Law Review [*A publication*]
Tasw Lang Hist ... Taswell-Langmead's English Constitutional History [*10th
　　　　　ed.*] [*1946*]   (DLA)
TASWM...... Test ASW [*Antisubmarine Warfare*] Missile [*Navy*]   (CAAL)
TAT .... [*The*] Absolute Truth [*In Julian Barnes' novel "Staring at the
　　　　　Sun"*]
TAT .... [*The*] Associated Turtles   (EA)
TAT .... Tactical Armament Turret   (NG)
T & AT .... Tank and Antitank [*Artillery and ammunition*]   (NATG)
TAT .... Target Aircraft Transmitter
TAT .... Task Assignment Table   (MCD)
TAT .... Tateyama [*Japan*] [*Seismograph station code, US Geological
　　　　　Survey*]   (SEIS)
TAT .... Tatry/Poprad [*Czechoslovakia*] [*Airport symbol*]   (OAG)
TAT .... Technical Acceptance Team   (AAG)
TAT .... Technical Approval Team
TAT .... Technical Assistance Team [*Air Force*]   (AFM)
TAT .... Technical Assistance and Training
TAT .... Technology Application Team [*NASA*]
TAT .... Television Awareness Training

TAT .... Tensile Adhesion Test [*for coatings*]
TAT .... Terrorist Action Team [*Military*]   (MCD)
TAT .... Tetanus Antitoxin [*Medicine*]
TAT .... Thematic Apperception Test [*Psychology*]
TAT .... Thinned Aperture Telescope
TAT .... Thromboplastin Activation Test [*Clinical chemistry*]
TAT .... Thrust-Augmented Thor [*NASA*]
TAT .... To Accompany Troops
TAT .... Tochas Affen Tish [*In television production company name
　　　　　"TAT Productions." Words are Yiddish and translate
　　　　　figuratively as "Let's Be Honest"*]
TAT .... Torpedo Attack Teacher [*Navy*]
TAT .... Total Air Temperature   (NASA)
TAT .... Total Aircraft Time   (MCD)
TAT .... Touraine Air Transport [*Private airline*] [*French*]
TAT .... Toxin-Antitoxin [*Also, TA*] [*Immunology*]
TAT .... Trace Acceptance Tester
TAT .... Training and Technology
TAT .... Trans Atlantic Resources, Inc. [*Vancouver Stock Exchange
　　　　　symbol*]
TAT .... Transatlantic Telephone [*Cable*]
TAT .... Transcontinental Air Transport
TAT .... Transportes Aeroside Timor [*Portuguese Timor*]
TAT .... Triamterene [*Diuretic*]
TAT .... True Air Temperature   (AFM)
TAT .... Turnaround Time [*Navy*]
TAT .... Two-Axis Tracking
TAT .... Type-Approval Test
TAT .... Tyrosine Aminotransferase [*An enzyme*]
Tatabanyai Szenbanyak Musz Kozgazdasagi Kozl ... Tatabanyai
　　　　　Szenbanyak Muszaki Kozgazdasagi Kozlemenyei
　　　　　[*Hungary*] [*A publication*]
TATAC .... Temporary Air Transport Advisory Committee [*NATO*]   (NATG)
Tata Inst Fund Res Lectures on Math and Phys ... Tata Institute of
　　　　　Fundamental Research. Lectures on Mathematics and
　　　　　Physics [*A publication*]
Tata Inst Fund Res Studies in Math ... Tata Institute of Fundamental
　　　　　Research. Studies in Mathematics [*A publication*]
TATAWS .... Tank, Antitank, and Assault Weapons Study [*or System*]
　　　　　[*Army*]
TATB .... Theater Air Transportation Board
TATB .... Triaminotrinitrobenzene [*Organic chemistry*]
TATC......... Tactical Air Traffic Control   (NVT)
TATC......... Terminal Air Traffic Control
TATC......... Transatlantic Telephone Cable   (IEEE)
TATCA ...... Trialkoxytricarballylate [*Organic chemistry*]
TATCE ...... Terminal Air Traffic Control Element
TATCF ...... Terminal Air Traffic Control Facility
TATCO ...... Tactical Automatic Telephone Central Office [*Military*]
TATCS ...... Terminal Air Traffic Control System
TATD .... Task Assignment Table Display   (MCD)
TATDL....... Tabulated Assembly Technical Data List
TATE .... Ashton-Tate [*NASDAQ symbol*]   (NQ)
TATE .... Tank Arrangement Thermal Efficiency [*Computer
　　　　　program*]   (KSC)
TATEJ .... Tasmanian Association for the Teaching of English. Journal [*A
　　　　　publication*]
TATER....... Talos-Terrier-Recruit [*Flight-test vehicle*]
Tate's Dig .. Tate's Digest of Laws [*Virginia*]   (DLA)
TATG......... Tuned Anode Tuned Grid   (DEN)
TATHS ...... Tool and Trades History Society   (EA-IO)
TATO.......... Taipei [*Taiwan*] [*Seismograph station code, US Geological
　　　　　Survey*]   (SEIS)
TATP .... Two-Axis Tracking Pedestal
TATr.......... Tyrosine Aminotransferase Regulator
TATRC .... Type-Approval Test Review Committee
TATS .... Tactical Aerial Targets Squadron   (MCD)
TATS .... Tactical Armament Turret System
TATS .... Tactical Transmission System Summary   (KSC)
TATS .... Target Acquisition and Track System   (MUGU)
TATS .... Technical Assistance and Training Survey [*Department of
　　　　　Labor*]   (OICC)
TATS .... Test and Training Satellite [*Also, TETR, TTS*] [*NASA*]
TATSA .... Transportation Aircraft Test and Support Activity [*Military*]
Tatsuta Tech Rev ... Tatsuta Technical Review [*A publication*]
TATTE .... Talos [*Missile*] Tactical Test Equipment
TATU .... Technical Advanced Training for Units   (MCD)
TAU .... Fort Meade, MD [*Location identifier*] [*FAA*]   (FAAL)
TAU .... Tasmania University [*Tasmania*] [*Seismograph station code,
　　　　　US Geological Survey*]   (SEIS)
Tau .... Taurus [*Constellation*]
TAU .... Technical Advisory Unit   (OICC)
TAU .... Tel Aviv University [*Israel*]
TAU .... Temporary Authorization [*Personnel*]   (OICC)
TAU .... Test Access Unit [*Telecommunications*]   (TEL)
TAU .... Thousand Astronomical Units [*NASA*]
TAU .... Transalta Utilities Corp. [*Toronto Stock Exchange symbol*]
TAU .... Trunk Access Unit
TAU .... Twin Agent Unit [*Fire fighting*]   (NVT)
TAUCH....... Tauchnitz [*Bibliography*]   (ROG)
TAUF .... Test Assembly Unloading Fixture [*Nuclear energy*]   (NRCH)

Taun.......... Taunton's English Common Pleas Reports   (DLA)
TAUN .... Technical Assistance of the United Nations
Taunt (Eng) ... Taunton's English Common Pleas Reports [*127, 129 English Reprint*]   (DLA)
Taur........... Taurus [*Constellation*]
TAUS......... Tobacco Association of United States [*Raleigh, NC*]   (EA)
TAUSA ...... Trans-Atlantic Universities Speech Association
Taut .... Taunton's English Common Pleas Reports   (DLA)
TAUT......... Tautology   (ADA)
TAV .... Tau [*American Samoa*] [*Airport symbol*]   (OAG)
TAV .... Tavern   (ROG)
TAV .... Tavurvur [*New Britain*] [*Seismograph station code, US Geological Survey*]   (SEIS)
TAV .... Technical Assistance Visit   (MCD)
TAV .... Technical Availability [*Navy*]   (NG)
TAV .... Tender Availability [*Navy*]
TAV .... Test and Validation   (KSC)
TAV .... Transatmospheric Vehicle [*Proposed futuristic plane capable of flying at hypersonic speeds*]
TAVC .... Total Active Vitamin C [*Nutrition*]
TAVE......... Average Temperature   (NRCH)
TAVE......... Thor-Agena Vibration Experiment [*NASA*]
TAVET........ Temperature Acceleration Vibration Environmental Tester
TAVIP........ Tahun Vivere Pericoloso [*The Year of Living Dangerously*] [*President Sukarno's national policy in 1964*] [*Indonesia*]
T & AVR..... Territorial and Army Volunteer Reserve [*British*]
TAVS......... Turbine Area Ventilation System [*Nuclear energy*]   (NRCH)
TAW .... Tactical Air Wing
TAW .... Tactical Assault Weapon
TAW .... Tawu [*Republic of China*] [*Seismograph station code, US Geological Survey*]   (SEIS)
TAW .... Tennessee Wesleyan College, Athens, TN [*Library symbol*] [*Library of Congress*]   (LCLS)
TAW .... Thrust-Augmented Wing [*NASA*]   (MCD)
TAW .... [*The*] Toledo, Angola & Western Railway Co. [*AAR code*]
TAW .... Troop Airlift Wing   (CINC)
TAW .... Twice a Week [*Advertising frequency*]
TAWACS.... Tactical Airborne Warning and Control System   (AFM)
TAWAR ..... Tactical All Weather Attack Requirements [*Air Force*]   (MCD)
TAWC .... Tactical Air Warfare Center [*Air Force*]
TAWC .... Tactical Armored Weapons Carrier   (MCD)
TAWCS ..... Tactical Air Weapons Control System
TAWDS ..... Target Acquisition Weapon Delivery System [*Air Force*]   (MCD)
TAWDS ..... Terminal Area Weapon Delivery Simulator   (MCD)
TAWG .... Tactical Air Warfare Group
TAWG........ Target Acquisition Working Group [*Air Force*]
TAWOG..... Travel Arrangements without Government Expense   (FAAC)
TAWS........ Tactical Area Weather Sensor   (MCD)
TAWS........ Tactical Automatic Weather Station [*Buoy*]   (MSC)
TAWS........ Tactical Warfare Center [*Army*]   (AABC)
TAWS........ Technical Analysis Work Sheet   (AAG)
TAWS........ Terrain Analyst Work Station [*Army*]   (RDA)
TAWS........ Total Airborne Weapon Systems   (MUGU)
TAWS........ Total Armament Weapons System   (MUGU)
TAWU........ Transport and Allied Workers' Union [*Rhodesia, Nyasaland, and Kenya*]
TAX .... Madison, WI [*Location identifier*] [*FAA*]   (FAAL)
TAX .... Tactical Air Exercise   (CINC)
Tax .... Taxandria [*A publication*]
TAX .... Taxiing [*Aviation*]
TAX .... Training Assessment Exercise
Tax ABC.... Canada Tax Appeal Board Cases   (DLA)
Tax Ad....... Tax Advisor [*A publication*]
Tax Adm'rs News ... Tax Administrators News   (DLA)
Tax in Aust ... Taxation in Australia [*A publication*]
Tax Cas...... Tax Cases   (DLA)
Tax Coun Q ... Tax Counselor's Quarterly [*A publication*]
Tax Ct Mem Dec ... Tax Court Memorandum Decisions [*Commerce Clearing House*]   (DLA)
Tax Ct Rep ... Tax Court Reporter [*Commerce Clearing House*]   (DLA)
Tax Ct Rep Dec ... Tax Court Reported Decisions [*Prentice-Hall, Inc.*]   (DLA)
Tax Ct Rep & Mem Dec (P-H) ... Tax Court Reported and Memorandum Decisions [*Prentice-Hall, Inc.*]   (DLA)
Taxes .... Tax Magazine   (DLA)
TAXIR........ Taxonomic Information Retrieval [*Data processing*]   (DIT)
Tax Law ..... Tax Lawyer [*A publication*]
Tax Law R ... Tax Law Review [*A publication*]
Tax Law Rep ... Tax Law Reporter   (DLA)
TAXLE........ Tandem Cantilevered Axle
Tax LR........ Tax Law Reporter   (DLA)
Tax L Rep... Tax Law Reporter   (DLA)
Tax L Rev... Tax Law Review [*A publication*]
Tax Mag..... Tax Magazine   (DLA)
Tax Management Int'l ... Tax Management International Journal [*A publication*]
Tax Mgmt (BNA) ... Tax Management [*Bureau of National Affairs*]   (DLA)
Tax Mngm't ... Tax Management [*Bureau of National Affairs*]   (DLA)
Tax Mo (Manila) ... Tax Monthly (Manila) [*A publication*]
TAXN......... Taxation   (ROG)
Taxn in Aust ... Taxation in Australia [*A publication*]
TAXON....... Taxonomy

Taxpayers Bul ... Taxpayers' Bulletin [*A publication*]
Tax Pl Int.... Tax Planning International   (DLA)
Tax Pl Rev ... Tax Planning Review   (DLA)
Tax R........ Tax Review [*A publication*]
Tax R........ Taxation Reports [*England*]   (DLA)
Tax & Rev... Taxation and Revenue   (DLA)
t-ay---........ Antarctica [*MARC geographic area code*] [*Library of Congress*]   (LCCP)
TAY .... Taylor, FL [*Location identifier*] [*FAA*]   (FAAL)
Tay .... Taylor's North Carolina Reports [*1 North Carolina*] [*1798-1802*]   (DLA)
Tay .... Taylor's Supreme Court Reports [*1847-48*] [*Bengal, India*]   (DLA)
Tay .... Taylor's Upper Canada King's Bench Reports [*1823-1827*]   (DLA)
Tay & B...... Taylor and Bell's Bengal Reports [*India*]   (DLA)
Tay Bk R.... Taylor's Book of Rights [*1833*]   (DLA)
TAYD......... Taylor Devices, Inc. [*NASDAQ symbol*]   (NQ)
Tay Ev .... Taylor on Evidence [*12th ed.*] [*1931*]   (DLA)
Tay Glos.... Taylor's Law Glossary [*2nd ed.*] [*1823*]   (DLA)
Tay J L....... [*J. L.*] Taylor's Reports [*1 North Carolina*]   (DLA)
Tayl Civil Law ... Taylor on Civil Law   (DLA)
Tayl Corp ... Taylor on Private Corporations   (DLA)
Tayl Ev ...... Taylor on Evidence   (DLA)
Tayl Gloss ... Taylor's Law Glossary   (DLA)
Tayl Hist Gav ... [*Silas*] Taylor's History of Gavelkind   (DLA)
Tayl Landl & Ten ... Taylor's Landlord and Tenant   (DLA)
Tayl Med Jur ... Taylor's Medical Jurisprudence   (DLA)
Tayl NC ..... Taylor's North Carolina Reports [*1 North Carolina*]   (DLA)
Taylor......... Taylor's Customary Laws of Rembau [*1903-28*] [*Malaya*]   (DLA)
Taylor......... Taylor's North Carolina Reports [*1 North Carolina*]   (DLA)
Taylor......... Taylor's North Carolina Term Reports [*4 North Carolina*]   (DLA)
Taylor......... Taylor's Reports [*Bengal, India*]   (DLA)
Taylor......... Taylor's Upper Canada King's Bench Reports   (DLA)
Taylor KB (Can) ... Taylor's Upper Canada King's Bench Reports   (DLA)
Taylor (Malaya) ... Taylor's Customary Laws of Rembau [*1903-28*] [*Malaya*]   (DLA)
Taylor Soc Bul ... Taylor Society. Bulletin [*A publication*]
Taylor UC ... Taylor's Upper Canada King's Bench Reports   (DLA)
Tayl Priv Corp ... Taylor on Private Corporations   (DLA)
Tayl St....... Taylor's Revised Statutes [*Wisconsin*]   (DLA)
Tay L & T... Taylor's Landlord and Tenant   (DLA)
Tay Med Jur ... Taylor's Medical Jurisprudence [*12th ed.*] [*1966*]   (DLA)
Tay NC ...... Taylor's North Carolina Reports [*1 North Carolina*]   (DLA)
Tay Poi...... Taylor on Poisons [*3rd ed.*] [*1875*]   (DLA)
Tay Rep..... Taylor's North Carolina Reports [*1 North Carolina*]   (DLA)
Tay Tit....... Taylor on Tithe Commutation [*1876*]   (DLA)
Tay UC ...... Taylor's Upper Canada King's Bench Reports [*1 vol.*] [*1823-27*]   (DLA)
TAZ .... Tactical Alert Zone   (NATG)
TAZ .... Taylorville, IL [*Location identifier*] [*FAA*]   (FAAL)
TAZ .... Theater Administrative Zone [*Military*]
TAZ .... Triazolam [*Tranquilizer*]
TAZARA...... Tanzania-Zambia Railway
TAzerbPI.... Trudy Azerbajdzanskogo Gosudarstvennogo Pedagogiceskogo Instituta [*A publication*]
Tb.............. Body Temperature [*Medicine*]
TB.............. Tabulation Block   (MSA)
TB.............. Tail Back [*Football*]
TB.............. Talk Back [*NASA*]   (KSC)
TB.............. Talmud Bavli   (BJA)
TB.............. Tangential Bracket
TB.............. Tank Battalion [*Army*]
TB.............. Tapes for the Blind [*An association*] [*Downey Lions Club*] [*Downey, CA*] [*Defunct*]   (EA)
TB.............. Tariff Bureau
T & B .... Taylor and Bell's Calcutta Supreme Court Reports [*India*]   (DLA)
TB.............. Technical Bulletin
TB.............. Telegraph Bureau
TB.............. Temple Biographies [*A publication*]
TB.............. Tempo Brasileiro [*A publication*]
TB.............. Temporary Buoy [*Nautical charts*]
Tb.............. TeraBIT [*Binary Digit*] [*10¹² BITs*]
TB.............. Terabyte [*10¹² bytes*]
Tb.............. Terbium [*Chemical element*]
TB.............. Terminal Base   (MCD)
TB.............. Terminal Block
TB.............. Terminal Board
TB.............. Test Bed   (MCD)
TB.............. Test Bulletin
TB.............. Theologische Blaetter [*Leipzig*] [*A publication*]
TB.............. Thermobarometer
TB.............. Thoroughbred
TB.............. Thrill Book [*A publication*]
TB.............. Thromboxane B [*Also, TxB, TXB*] [*Biochemistry*]
T/B............ Thunderbird [*Automobile*]
TB.............. Thymol Blue [*An indicator*]
TB.............. Tile Base [*Technical drawings*]
T/B............ Tile Block [*Technical drawings*]

TB	Time-Bandwidth
TB	Time Base
TB	Time Duration of Burn (MCD)
TB	Times at Bat [Baseball]
Tb	Tobit [Old Testament book] [Roman Catholic canon]
TB	Toggle Buffer (MCD)
TB	Toluidine Blue [Organic chemistry]
TB	Tone Burst
T & B	Top and Bottom [Technical drawings]
TB	Top Boy [British] (DSUE)
TB	Torch Bible Commentaries [A publication] (BJA)
TB	Torch Brazing
TB	Torpedo Boat [Navy symbol] [Obsolete]
TB	Torpedo Bomber [or Bombing]
TB	Total Bases
TB	Total Blank [Entertainment slang for poor show town]
TB	Total Body [Nuclear energy] (NRCH)
TB	Total Bouts [Boxing]
TB	Total Burn
TB	Tracer Bullet
TB	Tracheal-Bronchiolar [Region] [Medicine]
TB	Tracheobronchitis [Medicine]
TB	Tractor Biplane
TB	Traffic Bureau
TB	Training Back [Main parachute]
TB	Tranquility Base [Moon landing site]
TB	Transfer Building
TB	Transmitter-Blocker (DEN)
TB	Trapezoid Body [Audiometry]
TB	Travelair [Cargo] BV [Netherlands] [ICAO designator] (FAAC)
TB	Treasury Bill
TB	Treasury Board Secretariat [Canada]
TB	Trial Balance [Bookkeeping]
TB	Trial Balloon
TB	Triple-Braided (CET)
TB	Troop Basis
T & B	Truck and Bus
TB	True Bearing [Navigation]
TB	True Blue [A fluorescent dye]
TB	Tryptone Broth [Culture medium]
TB	Tubercle Bacillus [Bacteriology]
TB	Tuberculosis (AABC)
TB	Tumor-Bearing [Animal]
TB	Tundra Biome [Ecological biogeographic study]
TB	Turbine Building (NRCH)
T & B	Turn-and-Bank Indicators
T and B	Turned and Bored
TB	Tvorba [A publication]
TB	Twin Branch Railroad Co. [AAR code]
TB	Twirly Birds [An association] (EA)
TB	Two Beauts [Slang] [Australian] (DSUE)
TB	Tyndale Bulletin [A publication]
TBA	[The] Bettmann Archive [A publication]
TBA	Tabibuga [Papua New Guinea] [Airport symbol] (OAG)
TBA	Tables of Basic Allowances [Previously, Basic Tables of Commissioning Allowances] [Navy]
TBA	Task Budget Allocation (MCD)
TBA	Taurine Bibliophiles of America (EA)
TBA	Television Bureau of Advertising
TBA	Terminal Board Assembly (MSA)
TBA	Tertiary Butyl Acetate [Organic chemistry]
TBA	Tertiary Butyl Alcohol [Gasoline additive]
TBA	Test of Basic Assumptions [Psychology]
TBA	Test Bed Aircraft
TBA	Test Boring Association [Jamesburg, NJ] (EA)
TBA	Thiobarbituric Acid [Organic chemistry]
TBA	Tires, Batteries, and Accessories
TBA	To Be Activated
TBA	To Be Added (AAG)
TBA	To Be Announced
TBA	To Be Assigned
TBA	To Be Avoided [Slang]
TBA	Torsional Braid Analysis [Instrumentation]
TBA	Towed Buoy Antenna
TBA	Tributylamine [Organic chemistry]
TBA	Trichlorobenzoic Acid [Herbicide] [Organic chemistry]
TBAB	Theosophical Book Association for the Blind [Ojai, CA] (EA)
TBAC/FLM	Treasury Board Advisory Committee on Federal Land Management [Canada]
TBAH	Tetrabutylammonium Hydroxide [Organic chemistry]
TBAI	Temporary Base Activation Instruction (AAG)
TBAM	Tone Burst Amplitude Modulation
TBAN	To Be Announced [Army] (AABC)
TBAP	Tetrabutylammoniumperchlorate [Photovoltaic energy systems]
TBARA	Trakehner Breed Association and Registry of America [Defunct] (EA)
TBAS	[The] Band Appreciation Society [Cheltenham, Gloucestershire, England] (EA-IO)
TBAT	Tow/Bushmaster Armored Turret [Military]

TBAWRBA	Travel by Military Aircraft, Military and/or Naval Water Carrier, Commercial Rail and/or Bus Is Authorized [Army] (AABC)
TBAX	Tube Axial
TBAZFCA	Toledo Bird Association, Zebra Finch Club of America (EA)
TBB	Columbus, MS [Location identifier] [FAA] (FAAL)
TBB	Die Tempel von Babylon und Borsippa [A publication] (BJA)
TBB	Temporal Bone Banks [Otology] (EA)
TBB	Tenor, Baritone, Bass
T & BB	Top and Bottom Bolt [Technical drawings]
TBB	Transbronchial Biopsy [Medicine]
TB & B	Tuberculosis and Brucellosis [Medicine] (ADA)
TBBA	Terephthalyl Bis(butylaniline) [Organic chemistry]
TBBF	Top Baseband Frequency
TBBFA	Trudy Buryatskogo Instituta Estestvennykh Nauk. Buryatskii Filial, Sibirskoe Otdelenie, Akademiya Nauk SSSR [A publication]
TBBM	Total Body Bone Mineral
TBBPA	Tetrabromobisphenol-A [Organic chemistry]
TBBSA	Transactions. British Bryological Society [A publication]
TBC	Belmont College, Nashville, TN [OCLC symbol] (OCLC)
TBC	Confederation College of Applied Arts and Technology [UTLAS symbol]
TBC	Taiwan Base Command (CINC)
TBC	Tanker and Bulk Carrier
TBC	Tasty Baking Company [American Stock Exchange symbol]
TBC	Technology & Business Communications, Inc. [Sudbury, MA] [Information service] (EISS)
TBC	Television Briefing Console
TBC	Tembec Inc. [Toronto Stock Exchange symbol]
TBC	Thermal Barrier Coating (RDA)
TBC	Thyroxine-Binding Capacity [Biochemistry]
TBC	Time Base Corrector [Videotape recording element] [Early processing device]
TBC	To Be Cooked [Food]
TBC	Token Bus Controller [Motorola, Inc.]
TBC	Torch Bible Commentaries [New York/London] [A publication] (BJA)
TBC	Torrey Botanical Club (EA)
TBC	Toss Bomb Computer
TBC	Total Body Calcium
TBC	Trinidad Base Command [World War II]
TBC	Trunk Block Connector
TBC	Tuba City, AZ [Location identifier] [FAA] (FAAL)
TBC	Tubercle Bacillus [Bacteriology]
TBC	Tuberculosis
TBCA	Test Boring Contractors Association [Later, TBA] (EA)
TBCA	Transportation Brokers Conference of America [Oak Forest, IL] (EA)
TBCC	TBC Corporation [NASDAQ symbol] (NQ)
TBCC	Tom Baker Cancer Centre [University of Calgary] [Formerly, Southern Alberta Cancer Centre] [Research center] (RCD)
TBCCW	Turbine-Building Closed Cooling Water [Nuclear energy] (NRCH)
TBCR	Times British Colonies Review [London] [A publication]
TBD	Tactical Battle Drill [Army] (INF)
TBD	Target Bearing Designator [Navy]
TBD	Terminal Bomber Defense [Army] (AABC)
TBD	Thibodaux, LA [Location identifier] [FAA] (FAAL)
TBD	Thousand Barrels Daily
TBD	To Be Declassified (AAG)
TBD	To Be Defined
TBD	To Be Designated (MCD)
TBD	To Be Determined (AFM)
TBD	To Be Developed (NASA)
TBD	To Be Disbanded
TBD	To Be Done (AAG)
TBD	Too Badly Decomposed
TBD	Torpedo-Boat Destroyer [Obsolete]
TBD	Troubleshooting Block Diagram
TBD	Twin Boundary Diffusion
TBDF	Transborder Data Flows [Also, TDF] [Telecommunications]
TBDL	To Be Designated Later (CINC)
TBDMIM	Tertiary-Butyldimethylsilylimidazole [Organic chemistry]
TBDS	Test Base Dispatch Service (AAG)
TBD/TDA	Too Badly Decomposed/Technician Destroyed Animal [Laboratory testing]
TBE	European Federation of Tile and Brick Manufacturers
TBE	Federation Europeenne des Fabricants de Tuiles et de Briques [European Association of Brick and Tile Manufacturers] (EA-IO)
TBE	Tetrabromoethane [Microscopy]
TBE	Thread Both Ends (MSA)
TBE	Tiber Energy Corp. [Toronto Stock Exchange symbol]
TBE	Tick-Borne Encephalitis
TBE	Time Base Error
TBE	To Be Evaluated (NASA)
TBE	To Be Expended (AAG)
TBE	Tobe, CO [Location identifier] [FAA] (FAAL)
TBE	Toronto Board of Education, Professional Library [UTLAS symbol]

TBE	....	Total Body Ergometer
TBE	....	Transmitter Buffer Empty [*Data processing*]
TBE	....	Tuberculin Bacillen Emulsion [*Medicine*]
TBEA	....	Truck Body and Equipment Association [*Bethesda, MD*] (EA)
TBEM	....	Terminal-Based Electronic Mail
TBeP	....	Polk County High School, Benton, TN [*Library symbol*] [*Library of Congress*] (LCLS)
TBEP	....	Tri(butoxyethyl) Phosphate [*Organic chemistry*]
TBESI	....	Turbine-Building Exhaust System Isolation [*Nuclear energy*] (NRCH)
TBEX	....	Tube Expander
TBF	....	Tabiteuea North [*Kiribati*] [*Airport symbol*] (OAG)
TBF	....	Tail Bomb Fuse (KSC)
TBF	....	Test de Bon Fonctionnement [*Spacelab*] (MCD)
TBF	....	Testicular Blood Flow [*Physiology*]
TBF	....	Tie Bus Fault
TBF	....	Time between Failures [*Quality control*] (AFIT)
TBF	....	Torpedo Bomber Fighter (NATG)
TBF	....	Total Body Fat
TBF	....	Tour Basing Fare [*Air travel term*]
TBF	....	Tributyl Phosphate [*Organic chemistry*]
TBF	....	Two-Body Force
TBFC	....	Teresa Brewer Fan Club (EA)
TBFC	....	Tony Booth Fan Club [*Sulphur Springs, TX*] (EA)
TBFG	....	Tom Baker Friendship Group [*Ashford, Middlesex, England*] (EA-IO)
TBFX	....	Tube Fixture [*Tool*] (AAG)
TBG	....	Tabubil [*Papua New Guinea*] [*Airport symbol*] (OAG)
TBG	....	Testosterone-Binding Globulin [*Endocrinology*]
TBG	....	Teubners Bibliotheca Scriptorum Graecorum et Romanorum (BJA)
TBG	....	Thyroxine-Binding Globulin [*Biochemistry*]
TBG	....	Thyssen-Bornemisza Group NV [*Netherlands*]
TBG	....	Tubing (MSA)
TBGAA	......	Travel by Government Automobile Authorized
TBGP	....	Tactical Bomb Group [*Air Force*]
TBGP	....	Total Blood Granulocyte Pool [*Hematology*]
TBGTA	......	Travel by Government Transportation Authorized [*Military*] (AABC)
TBGU	....	Trudy Belorusskogo Gosudarstvennogo Universiteta [*A publication*]
TBH	....	Tablas [*Philippines*] [*Airport symbol*] (OAG)
TBH	....	Technical Benzene Hexachloride [*Organic chemistry*]
TBH	....	Test Bed Harness (MCD)
TBH	....	Test Bench Harness (NG)
TBH	....	Trinidad [*Brigand Hill*] [*Trinidad-Tobago*] [*Seismograph station code, US Geological Survey*] (SEIS)
TBHP	....	Tertiary-Butyl Hydroperoxide [*Organic chemistry*]
TBHP	....	Trihydroxybutyrophenone [*Antioxidant*] [*Organic chemistry*]
TBHQ	....	Tertiary-Butylhydroquinone [*Also, MTBHQ*] [*Organic chemistry*]
TBI	....	Target Bearing Indicator [*Military*]
TBI	....	Telecom Broadcasting, Incorporated [*Oceanside, CA*] [*Telecommunications service*] (TSSD)
TBI	....	Test Bed Installation (MCD)
TBI	....	Test Bench Installation (NG)
TBI	....	Threaded Blind Insert
TBI	....	Throttle Body Fuel Injection [*Auto mechanics*]
TBI	....	Through-Bulkhead Initiator [*Military*] (MCD)
TBI	....	Time, Bulb, Instantaneous [*Initials on certain Kodak cameras*]
TBI	....	Time between Inspection
TBI	....	To Be Inactivated
TBI	....	Total Body Irradiation [*Medicine*]
TBI	....	Trinity Bible Institute, Ellendale, ND [*OCLC symbol*] (OCLC)
TBI	....	Tromboni [*Trombones*]
TBI	....	Tubuai [*Tubuai Islands*] [*Seismograph station code, US Geological Survey*] (SEIS)
TbIG	....	Terbium Iron Garnet (IEEE)
TBII	....	Thyrotropin-Binding Inhibitor Immunoglobulin
Tbilis Gos Univ Inst Prikl Mat Tr	...	Tbilisskii Gosudarstvennyi Universitet. Institut Prikladnoi Matematiki. Trudy [*A publication*]
Tbilisis Univ Sromebi	...	Stalinis Sacheolobis Tbilisis Universitatis Sromebi [*A publication*]
Tbiliss Gos Univ Inst Prikl Mat Trudy	...	Tbilisskii Gosudarstvennyi Universitet. Institut Prikladnoi Matematiki. Trudy [*A publication*]
TBJ	....	Turbulent Bounded Jet
TBJT	....	Turbojet (FAAC)
TBK	....	TEFLON Bonding Kit
TBK	....	Total Body Potassium [*Clinical chemistry*]
TBK	....	Toyo Bungaku Kenkyu [*Studies on Oriental Literature*] [*A publication*]
T/BKL	....	Turn Buckle [*Automotive engineering*]
TBKZA	......	Trudy Instituta Botaniki. Akademiya Nauk Kazakhskoi SSR [*A publication*]
TBL	....	Tabele [*Papua New Guinea*] [*Seismograph station code, US Geological Survey*] (SEIS)
TBL	....	Table
TBL	....	Tactical Bomb Line (NVT)
TBL	....	[*The*] Tamarind Book of Lithography
TBL	....	Terminal Ballistics Laboratory [*Army*]
TBL	....	Thin Base Laminate
TBL	....	Thomas Branigan Memorial Library, Las Cruces, NM [*OCLC symbol*] (OCLC)
TBL	....	Through Back of Loop [*Knitting*]
TBL	....	Through Bill of Lading
TBL	....	Tombill Mines Ltd. [*Toronto Stock Exchange symbol*]
TBL	....	Trouble [*Telecommunications*] (TEL)
TBL	....	True Blood Loss
TBL	....	Turbulent Boundary Layer
TBLC	....	Term Birth, Living Child [*Medicine*]
T/BLK	....	Terminal Block [*Automotive engineering*]
TBLN	....	Tracheobronchial Lymph Node [*Anatomy*]
TBLR	....	Tumbler (MSA)
TBLS	....	Trail Blazer Library System [*Library network*]
TBLSP	....	Tablespoon
TBM	....	School of Aerospace Medicine, Brooks AFB, TX [*OCLC symbol*] (OCLC)
TBM	....	Tactical Ballistic Missile [*Military*] (CAAL)
TBM	....	Tax Board Memorandum [*Internal Revenue Bulletin*] [*United States*] (DLA)
TBM	....	Tell Beit Mirsim (BJA)
TBM	....	Temporary Bench Mark
TBM	....	TeraBIT [*Binary Digit*] Memory [*Data processing*]
TBM	....	Theater Battle Model (MCD)
TBM	....	Tone Burst Modulation
TB & M	......	Tracewell, Bowers, and Mitchell's United States Comptroller's Decisions (DLA)
TBM	....	Tuberculous Meningitis [*Medicine*]
TBM	....	Tubular Basement Membrane
TBMA	....	Textile Bag Manufacturers Association [*Northbrook, IL*] (EA)
TBMAA	.....	Travel by Military Aircraft Authorized
TBMAC	....	Tributylmethylammonium Chloride [*Organic chemistry*]
TBMC	.....	Test Bed Mode Control
TBMD	.....	Terminal Ballistic Missile Defense [*Army*] (AABC)
TBMO	.....	Test Base Material Operation (AAG)
T B Mon	.....	T. B. Monroe's Kentucky Supreme Court Reports [*17-23 Kentucky*] [*1824-28*] (DLA)
T B Mon (KY)	...	T. B. Monroe's Kentucky Reports [*17-23 Kentucky*] (DLA)
TBMS	....	Text-Based Management Systems [*Data processing*]
TBMT	....	Transmitter Buffer Empty [*Data processing*]
TBMX	....	Tactical Ballistic Missile Experiment
TBN	....	Fort Leonard Wood [*Missouri*] [*Airport symbol*] (OAG)
TBN	....	Tertiary-Butylnaphthalene [*Organic chemistry*]
TBN	....	Titratable Base Number [*Analytical chemistry*]
TBN	....	To Be Negotiated (NASA)
TBN	....	To Be Nominated
TBN	....	Total Base Number [*Automotive engineering*]
TBN	....	Traveling Businesswomen's Network (EA)
TBN	....	Trinity Broadcasting Network [*Cable-television system*]
TBNAA	....	Treated but Not Admitted [*Medicine*]
TBNAA	....	Total Body Neutron Activation Analysis
TBNHL	....	Tippecanoe Battleground National Historical Landmark (EA)
TBNNA	....	Trudy. Bashkirskii Nauchno-Issledovatel'skii Institut po Pererabotke Nefti [*A publication*]
TBO	....	Tabora [*Tanzania*] [*Airport symbol*] (OAG)
TBO	....	Thermal Bakeout
TBO	....	Time between Overhauls [*of engine, or other equipment*]
TBO	....	Transactions by Others
TBOA	....	Tuna Boat Owners' Association [*Defunct*] (EA)
t-Boc	....	Butoxycarbonyl [*or t-BOC*] [*Biochemistry*]
t-BOC	....	tert-Butyloxycarbonyl [*Also, t-Boc*] [*Organic chemistry*]
TBOI	....	Tentative Basis of Issue [*Army*] (AABC)
TBOIP	....	Tentative Basis of Issue Plan [*Army*] (AABC)
TBoIMH	......	Western Mental Health Institute, Boliver, TN [*Library symbol*] [*Library of Congress*] (LCLS)
TBP	....	Tab Products Co. [*American Stock Exchange symbol*]
TbP	....	Tampa Blue Print Co., Tampa, FL [*Library symbol*] [*Library of Congress*] (LCLS)
TBP	....	Tau Beta Pi Association
TBP	....	Tetraphenylboron [*Analytical chemistry*]
TBP	....	Thiobisdichlorophenol [*Pharmacology*]
TBP	....	Thyroxine-Binding Protein [*Biochemistry*]
TBP	....	Timing Belt Pulley
TBP	....	To Be Planned (MCD)
TBP	....	To Be Provided (NASA)
TBP	....	Trainable Bow Propeller
TBP	....	Tributyl Phosphate [*Organic chemistry*]
TBP	....	Tributyl Phosphine [*Organic chemistry*]
TBP	....	Trigonal Bipyramidal [*Geometry of molecular structure*]
TBP	....	True Boiling Point
TBP	....	Tumbes [*Peru*] [*Airport symbol*] (OAG)
TBP	....	Turk Birligi Partisi [*Turkish Union Party*] [*Turkish Cypriot*] (PPE)
TBP	....	Twisted Bonded Pair
TBP	....	Two-Body Problem
TBPA	....	Tetrabromophthalic Anhydride [*Flame retardant*] [*Organic chemistry*]
TBPA	....	Textile Bag and Packaging Association [*Chicago, IL*] (EA)
TBPA	....	Thyroxine-Binding Prealbumin [*Biochemistry*]
TBPA	....	Transatlantic Brides and Parents Association
TBPC	....	Text-Books of Physical Chemistry [*A publication*]

TBPI .... Thigh Brachial Pressure Index

TBPS .... Tert-Butylbicyclophosphorothionate [*Biochemistry*]

TBQ .... Addison, TX [*Location identifier*] [*FAA*]   (FAAL)

TBR .... Advisory Tax Board Recommendation [*Internal Revenue Bureau*] [*United States*]   (DLA)

TBR .... New York Times Book Review [*A publication*]

TBR .... Statesboro, GA [*Location identifier*] [*FAA*]   (FAAL)

TBR .... T-Bar, Inc. [*American Stock Exchange symbol*]

TBR .... Table Base Register

TBR .... Table Rock [*New York*] [*Seismograph station code, US Geological Survey*]   (SEIS)

TBR .... Test of Behavioral Rigidity [*Psychology*]

TBR .... Three Banks Review [*A publication*]

TBR .... Tilt Board Reach [*Test*] [*Occupational therapy*]

TBR .... Torpedo Bomber Reconnaissance Aircraft [*Navy*]

TBR .... Training Base Review   (MCD)

TBR .... Trickle Bed Reactor [*Chemical engineering*]

TBR .... Tumor-Bearing Rabbit Serum [*Immunology*]

TBR .... Turbo Resources Ltd. [*Toronto Stock Exchange symbol*]

TBRC .... Top-Blown Rotary Converter [*Nonferrous metallurgy*]

TBRD .... Taxation Board of Review Decisions [*A publication*]

TBRD .... Taxation Board of Review Decisions, New Series [*Australia*]   (DLA)

TBRD (NS) ... Taxation Board of Review Decisions (New Series) [*A publication*]

TBRI .... Technical Book Review Index

TBriH .... Bristol Memorial Hospital, Bristol, TN [*Library symbol*] [*Library of Congress*]   (LCLS)

TBriK .... King College, Bristol, TN [*Library symbol*] [*Library of Congress*]   (LCLS)

T Br Mycol ... Transactions. British Mycological Society [*A publication*]

TBroH .... Haywood Park General Hospital, Brownsville, TN [*Library symbol*] [*Library of Congress*]   (LCLS)

TBS .... Sir Thomas Beecham Society   (EA)

TBS .... Tablespoon

TBS .... Tactical Bomb Squadron [*Air Force*]

TBS .... Talk-between-Ships [*which are tactically maneuvering; also, the VHF radio equipment used for this purpose*]

TBS .... Tape and Buffer System [*Data processing*]

TBS .... Task Breakdown Structure (NASA)

TBS .... Tbilisi [*USSR*] [*Airport symbol*]   (OAG)

TBS .... Temple, Barker & Sloane, Inc. [*Lexington, MA*] [*Telecommunications service*]   (TSSD)

TBS .... Tertiary Butylphenyl Salicylate [*Food packaging*]

TBS .... Test Bench Set   (MCD)

TBS .... Tetrapropylene Alkylbenzenesulfonate [*Surfactant*] [*Organic chemistry*]

TBS .... Text-Books of Science [*A publication*]

TBS .... Tired Bureaucrat Syndrome

TBS .... To Be Selected   (KSC)

TBS .... To Be Specified   (NASA)

TBS .... To Be Superseded   (NASA)

TBS .... To Be Supplied   (KSC)

TBS .... Tokyo Broadcasting System

TB & S .... Top, Bottom, and Sides [*Lumber*]

TBS .... Toronto Baptist Seminary

TBS .... Toronto Board of Education, Secondary Schools [*UTLAS symbol*]

TBS .... Total Body Solute [*Biochemistry*]

TBS .... Total Body Surface [*Medicine*]

TBS .... Training and Battle Simulation [*SAGE*]

TBS .... Translator Bail Switch

TBS .... Treasury Board Secretariat [*Canada*]

TBS .... Tribromosalicylanilide [*or Tribromsalan*] [*Organic chemistry*]

TBS .... TRIS-Buffered Saline [*Solution*]

TBS .... Turbine Bypass System [*Nuclear energy*]   (NRCH)

TBS .... Turner Broadcasting System [*Cable-television system*]

TBS .... Turner Broadcasting System, Inc. [*American Stock Exchange symbol*]

TBSA .... Total Body Surface Area [*Medicine*]

TBSA .... Tris- [*Tris(hydroxymethyl)aminomethane*] Buffered Saline Azide [*Culture media*]

TBSCCW .... Turbine Building Secondary Closed Cooling Water [*Nuclear energy*]   (NRCH)

TBSG .... Test Base Support Group   (AAG)

TBSIC .... Turner Broadcasting [*NASDAQ symbol*]   (NQ)

TBSM .... Tributylstannylmaleate [*Organic chemistry*]

TBSP .... Tablespoon

TBSV .... Time between Scheduled Visits   (MCD)

TBSV .... Tomato Bushy Stunt Virus

TBT .... Mid American Baptist Theological Seminary, Memphis, TN [*OCLC symbol*]   (OCLC)

TBT .... Tabatinga [*Brazil*] [*Airport symbol*]   (OAG)

TBT .... Taburiente [*Canary Islands*] [*Seismograph station code, US Geological Survey*]   (SEIS)

TBT .... Target Bearing Transmitter

TBT .... Terminal Ballistic Track

TBT .... Tetrabutyl Titanate [*Organic chemistry*]

TBT .... Thallium Beam Tube

TBT .... Tilt Board Tip [*Test*] [*Occupational therapy*]

TBT .... Trends in Biotechnology [*A publication*]

TBT .... Tributylin [*Organic radical*]

TBTF .... Tributyltin Fluoride [*Antimicrobial agent*]

TBTI .... Telebyte Technology [*NASDAQ symbol*]   (NQ)

TBTO .... Tributyltin Oxide [*Organic chemistry*]

TBTP .... Tributyl Trithiophosphate [*Defoliant*] [*Organic chemistry*]

TBTU .... Tributylthiourea [*Organic chemistry*]

TBU .... Terminal Buffer Unit [*Telecommunications*]   (TEL)

TBU .... Test Before Using   (MCD)

TBU .... Time Base Unit

TBU .... Tongatapu [*Tonga Island*] [*Airport symbol*]   (OAG)

TBurNII ...... Trudy Burjatskogo Komplesnogo Naucno-Issledovatel'skogo Instituta [*A publication*]

TBV .... Thermal Bypass Valve

TBV .... Total Blood Volume [*Physiology*]

TBV .... Trabecular Bone Volume

TBV .... Tubercle Bacillus Vaccine [*Medicine*]

TBV .... Turbine Building Ventilation [*Nuclear energy*]   (NRCH)

TBW .... Tampa Bay-Ruskin, FL [*Location identifier*] [*FAA*]   (FAAL)

TBW .... That Bloody Woman [*Nickname given to British Prime Minister Margaret Thatcher*]

TBW .... Titanium Butt Weld

TBW .... To Be Withheld

TBW .... Tobacco Bud Worm [*Agronomy*]

TBW .... Total Bandwidth

TBW .... Total Body Water [*Man*]

TBW .... Total Body Weight [*Medicine*]

TBW .... Tracking Band Width   (MCD)

TBWCA ...... Texas Barbed Wire Collectors Association   (EA)

TBWEP ...... Trial Boll Weevil Eradication Program [*Department of Agriculture*]

TBWG .... Tactical Bomb Wing [*Air Force*]

TBWO .... Tuned Backward Wave Oscillator

TBY .... Oxford, CT [*Location identifier*] [*FAA*]   (FAAL)

TBY .... Terrace Bay Resources [*Vancouver Stock Exchange symbol*]

TBZ .... Istanbul [*Trabzon*] [*Turkey*] [*Seismograph station code, US Geological Survey*]   (SEIS)

TBZ .... Tabriz [*Iran*] [*Airport symbol*]   (OAG)

TBZ .... Tetrabenazine [*Tranquilizer*]

TBZ .... Thiabendazole [*or Thiazolyl*] Benzimidazole [*Pesticide*]

TC .... 13 Coins Restaurants Ltd. [*Vancouver Stock Exchange symbol*]

TC .... Air Tanzania [*ICAO designator*]   (FAAC)

TC .... All India Reporter, Travancore-Cochin [*1950-57*]   (DLA)

TC .... Chattanooga-Hamilton County Bicentennial Library, Chattanooga, TN [*Library symbol*] [*Library of Congress*]   (LCLS)

TC .... Chronicle (Toowoomba) [*A publication*]

TC .... Cold Leg Temperature [*Nuclear energy*]   (NRCH)

Tc .... Core Temperature [*Medicine*]

TC .... [*The*] Courier [*Code name for Robert W. Owen, participant in the Iran-Contra affair during the Reagan Administration*]

TC .... Order of the Trinity Cross [*Trinidad and Tobago*]

TC .... Reports of English Tax Cases   (DLA)

TC .... T-Carrier [*Telecommunications*]   (TEL)

TC .... Tablettes Cappadociennes [*Paris*] [*A publication*]   (BJA)

TC .... Tabulating Card   (AAG)

TC .... Tactical Command   (NATG)

TC .... Tactical Computer   (IEEE)

T/C .... Tactical Coordinator   (NVT)

TC .... Tactile Communicator [*Device which aids the deaf by translating certain sounds into coded vibrations*]

TC .... Tail Clamp

TC .... Talk[*ing*] Club

TC .... Tamil Culture [*A publication*]

TC .... Tank Car

TC .... Tank Commander   (RDA)

TC .... Tank Company [*Military*]   (MCD)

TC .... Tank Corps

TC .... Tantalum Capacitor   (IEEE)

TC .... Tape Command

TC .... Tape Core

TC .... Target Cell [*Immunology*]

TC .... Target Control   (MCD)

TC .... Tariff Circular

TC .... Tariff Commission [*Later, International Trade Commission*]

TC .... Tax Cases [*Legal*] [*British*]

TC .... Tax Council   (EA)

TC .... Tax Court [*of the United States*] [*Also, TCUS*] [*Later, United States Tax Court*]

TC .... Taxpayers' Committee   (EA)

TC .... Tea Council of the United States of America [*New York, NY*]   (EA)

TC .... Teacher's Certificate [*British*]

TC .... Teachers College

TC .... Teardown Compliance

Tc .... Technetium [*Chemical element*]

TC .... Technical Characteristics   (AABC)

TC .... Technical Circular

TC .... Technical College

TC .... Technical Committee

TC .... Technical Communication

TC	Technical Control (MSA)	
TC	Technicolor (KSC)	
T & C	Technology and Culture [*A publication*]	
TC	Tekakwitha Conference National Center [*Ministry for American Indians and Eskimos*] (EA)	
T/C	Telecine	
TC	Telecommunications	
TC	Telecommunications Counselor [*Voice & Data Resources, Inc.*] [*New York, NY*] [*Information service*] (EISS)	
TC	[*The*] Telex Corporation [*NYSE symbol*]	
TC	Temperament Comparator [*Psychology*]	
TC	Temperature Capability	
TC	Temperature Change [*Refrigeration*]	
TC	Temperature Coefficient	
TC	Temperature Compensating (MSA)	
TC	Temperature Control	
TC	Temperature Controller [*Nuclear energy*] (NRCH)	
TC	Temple Classics [*A publication*]	
TC	Temporary Constable	
TC	Temporary Correction	
TC	Tennessee Central Railway Co. [*AAR code*]	
TC	Tennis Club	
TC	Teracycle	
TC	Terminal Computer (BUR)	
TC	Terminal Concentrator	
TC	Terminal Congestion [*Telecommunications*] (TEL)	
TC	Terminal Controller	
T/C	Termination Check [*NASA*] (NASA)	
T & C	Terms and Conditions	
TC	Terra Cotta [*Technical drawings*]	
TC	Terrain Clearance [*Military*] (NG)	
TC	Terrain Correlation (MCD)	
TC	Test Chief	
TC	Test Collection [*Educational Testing Service*] [*Information service*] (EISS)	
TC	Test Conductor (AAG)	
TC	Test Console	
TC	Test Controller	
TC	Test Coordinator	
TC	Testing Complete (CAAL)	
TC	Tetracycline [*Also, TE, Tet*] [*Antibiotic compound*]	
TC	Tetrahedral Cubic [*Metallography*]	
TC	Texas Central Railroad	
TC	Theory of Computation Series [*Elsevier Book Series*] [*A publication*]	
TC	Therapeutic Concentration [*Pharmacology*]	
TC	Thermal Conductivity	
TC	Thermal Control (KSC)	
TC	Thermal Cutting [*Welding*]	
TC	Thermocouple	
TC	Thermocurrent (IEEE)	
TC	Thinking Cap [*Layman's term for neocortex*]	
TC	Thomas C. Calvin [*Character in TV series "Magnum, P.I."*]	
T & C	Thompson and Cook's New York Supreme Court Reports (DLA)	
TC	Thoracic Cage [*Medicine*]	
TC	Thread Cutting (MSA)	
TC	Throat Culture [*Clinical chemistry*]	
TC	Thrust Chamber [*Air Force, NASA*]	
TC	Tical [*Monetary unit in Thailand*]	
TC	Tidal Constants Data Base [*Marine science*] (MSC)	
TC	Tie Connector (MCD)	
TC	Tierce [*Unit of measurement*]	
T/C	Till Counterbalanced	
T/C	Till Countermanded	
TC	Tilt Covered [*Truck*]	
T & C	Time and Charges [*Telecommunications*] (TEL)	
T/C	Time Charter [*Shipping*]	
TC	Time Check	
TC	Time to Circular (MCD)	
TC	Time Clock	
TC	Time Closing (MSA)	
TC	Time Compensation	
TC	Time to Computation	
TC	Time Constant (MSA)	
TC	Timing Channel	
TC	Timing Cover Gasket [*Automotive engineering*]	
TC	Tinned Copper	
TC	Tissue Culture [*Microbiology*]	
TC	To Contain [*Pipet calibration*]	
TC	Tobramycin-Clindamycin [*Antimicrobial regime*]	
TC	Togoland Congress [*Political party*] [*Ghanaian*]	
TC	Toilet Case (MSA)	
TC	Toll Center [*Telecommunications*]	
TC	Toll Completing [*Telecommunications*]	
TC	Toluene-Cellosolve [*Scintillation solvent*]	
TC	Top Cat [*Cartoon character*]	
TC	Top Center [*Valve position*]	
TC	Top Chord	
TC	Top of Column	
TC	Top Contact [*Valve*] (DEN)	
TC	Topographic Center [*Defense Mapping Agency*]	
TC	Total Capacity [*Lung*]	
TC	Total Chances	
TC	Total Cholesterol [*Medicine*]	
TC	Total Colonoscopy [*Proctoscopy*]	
TC	Total Cost	
TC	Touring Club	
TC	Town Clerk [*or Councillor*]	
TC	Traceability Code (NASA)	
TC	Track Circuit	
TC	Track Commander [*Army*] (INF)	
TC	Tracking Camera	
TC	Tracking Console	
TC	Trade Cases [*Commerce Clearing House*] (DLA)	
TC	Traffic Collision	
TC	Traffic Commissioner [*or Consultant*]	
TC	Traffic Controller (CAAL)	
TC	Training Center	
TC	Training Chest [*Emergency parachute*]	
TC	Training Circular [*Military*]	
TC	Training Command (AAG)	
TC	Transaction Code [*Military*]	
TC	Transceiver Code [*Navy*]	
TC	Transcobalamin [*Biochemistry*]	
TC	Transcutaneous	
TC	Transfer Canal (NRCH)	
TC	Transfer Clerk [*Deltiology*]	
TC	Transistorized Carrier	
TC	Transit Canal (NVT)	
TC	Translation Controller	
TC	Transmission Controller	
TC	Transpersonal Consciousness [*Parapsychology*]	
TC	Transponder Component (MCD)	
TC	Transport Canada	
TC	Transport Cargo (NATG)	
TC	Transport Combine [*Combined Transport*] [*French*] [*Business and trade*]	
TC	Transport and Communications [*Department of Employment*] [*British*]	
TC	Transportation Corps	
TC	Transporte Combinado [*Combined Transport*] [*Spanish*] [*Business and trade*]	
TC	Transporto Combinato [*Combined Transport*] [*Italy*] [*Business and trade*]	
TC	Travellers Cheque [*British*] (ADA)	
TC	Tre Corde [*With three strings, or release the soft pedal*] [*Music*]	
TC	Treasury Circular	
T/C	Treatment Charge [*Metallurgy*]	
TC	Trial Counsel	
TC	Tribology Centre [*British*]	
TC	Tricycle Club [*British*]	
TC	Triennial Cycle (BJA)	
TC	Trierische Chronik [*A publication*]	
TC	Trilateral Commission (EA)	
TC	Trim Coil (AAG)	
TC	[*Order of the*] Trinity Cross [*Trinidad and Tobago*]	
TC	Trip Coil	
TC	Triple Certificated (ADA)	
TC	Triplet Connection [*An association*] [*Stockton, CA*] (EA)	
TC	Triton Corporation [*An association*] (EA)	
TC	Troop Carrier [*Air Force*]	
TC	Tropical Continental [*American air mass*]	
TC	Tropical Cyclone (ADA)	
TC	Truck Commander [*Military*] (INF)	
T/C	True or Complement	
TC	True Course	
TC	Trunk Control	
TC	Trusteeship Council [*of the United Nations*]	
TC	Tubocurarine [*Muscle relaxant*]	
TC	Turf Course [*Horse racing*]	
TC	Turkey [*Aircraft nationality and registration mark*] (FAAC)	
tc	Turks and Caicos Islands [*MARC country of publication code*] [*Library of Congress*] (LCCP)	
TC	Turks and Caicos Islands [*Two-letter standard code*] (CNC)	
TC	Turn-Cock (ROG)	
T & C	Turn and Cough [*Medicine*]	
TC	Turnip Crinkle Virus	
TC	Turret Captain [*Navy*]	
TC	Twentieth Century [*A publication*]	
TC	[*The*] Twentieth Century New Testament [*A publication*] (BJA)	
TC	Two Cycle [*Mechanics*]	
TC	Tworczosc [*A publication*]	
TC	Type Certificate	
TC	Type Classification	
TC	Type and Crossmatch [*of blood*]	
TC	United States Tax Court Cases (DLA)	
T4C	Technology for Children [*Vocational program*]	
TCA	Adventist Network of Georgia, Cumberland Elementary Library, Collegedale, TN [*OCLC symbol*] (OCLC)	
TCA	Tactical Combat Aircraft (IEEE)	
TCA	Tactical Communications Area	

TCA............ Tanner's Council of America [Later, LIA]   (EA)
TCA............ Tanzer 22 Class Association   (EA)
TCA............ Tattoo Club of America
TCA............ TEAC Corporation of America [Montebello, CA] [Hardware
              manufacturer]
TCA............ Teach Cable Assembly [Robot technology]
TCA............ Teaching Curriculum Association [A generic term; not the
              name of a specific organization]
TCA............ Technical Change Analysis   (MCD)
TCA............ Technical Contract Administrator
TCA............ Technical Cooperation Administration [Transferred to Foreign
              Operations Administration, 1953]
TCA............ Tele-Communications Association [Santa Ana, CA]   (EA)
TCA............ Telemetering Control Assembly   (AAG)
TCA............ Telephone Consultants of America [Bergenfield, NJ]
              [Telecommunications]   (TSSD)
TCA............ Television Critics Association [Pittsburgh, PA]   (EA)
TCA............ Tempelhof Central Airport [West Berlin]
TCA............ Temperature Control Assembly   (KSC)
TCA............ Temperature-Controlled Animal
TCA............ Tennant Creek [Australia] [Airport symbol]   (OAG)
TCA............ Terminal Cancer [Medicine]
TCA............ Terminal Communication Adapter
TCA............ Terminal Control Area [Aviation]   (AFM)
TCA............ Tetracyanoanthracene [Organic chemistry]
TCA............ Textile Converters Association [New York, NY]   (EA)
TCA............ Theater Commander's Approval [Military]
TCA............ Therapeutic Communities of America [Providence, RI]   (EA)
TCA............ Thermal Critical Assembly [Nuclear energy]
TCA............ Thermocentrifugometric Analysis [Analytical chemistry]
TCA............ Thermochimica Acta [A publication]
TCA............ Thiocarbanilide [Organic chemistry]
TCA............ Thistle Class Association   (EA)
TCA............ Thoroughbred Club of America   (EA)
TCA............ Thrust Chamber Assembly [Missile technology]
TCA............ Thyrocalcitonin [Also, CT, TCT] [Endocrinology]
TCA............ Tiger Cat Association [Defunct]   (EA)
TCA............ Tile Council of America [Princeton, NJ]   (EA)
TCA............ Tilt-Up Concrete Association [Skokie, IL]   (EA)
TCA............ Time of Closest Approach [Aerospace]
TCA............ Tissue Culture Association   (EA)
TCA............ Tithe Commutation Act [British]
TCA............ To Come Again [in a given number of days] [Medicine]
TCa .... Total Calcium [Clinical chemistry]
TCA............ Trace Contamination Analysis
TCA............ Track Continuity Area   (NATG)
TCA............ Track Crossing Angle
TCA............ Traffic Control Area [Aviation]
TCA............ Trailer Coach Association [Later, Manufactured Housing
              Institute]   (EA)
TCA............ Train Collectors Association   (EA)
TCA............ Trans-Canada Airlines
TCA............ Translation Controller Assembly   (NASA)
TCA............ Tricarboxylic Acid [Cycle] [Biochemistry]
TCA............ Trichloroacetate [Organic chemistry]
TCA............ Trichloroacetic Acid [Also, TCAA] [Organic chemistry]
TCA............ Trichloroanisole [Organic chemistry]
TCA............ Tricyclic Antidepressant [Medicine]
TCA............ Turbulent Contacting Absorber
TCA............ Turks and Caicos Islands [Three-letter standard code]   (CNC)
TCA............ Two Crashes Apiece [Humorous interpretation for TCA, Trans-
              Canada Airlines]
TCA............ Two Hundred Contemporary Authors [A publication]
TCA............ Typographic Communications Association [Commercial
              firm]   (EA)
TCAA .... Tile Contractors' Association of America [Alexandria,
              VA]   (EA)
TCAA .... Trichloroacetic Acid [Also, TCA] [Organic chemistry]
TCAAP .... Twin Cities Army Ammunition Plant   (AABC)
TCAAS ...... Transactions. Connecticut Academy of Arts and Sciences [A
              publication]
TCAB .... Temperature of Cabin   (MCD)
TCAB .... Tetrachloroazobenzene [Organic chemistry]
TCABG ...... Triple Coronary Artery Bypass Graft [Cardiology]
TCAC .... Technical Control and Analysis Center
TC ACCIS ... Transportation Coordination Automated Command and
              Control Information System
TCAC-D ..... Technical Control and Analysis Center - Division
TCAF .... TEFLON-Coated Aluminum Foil
TCAI .... Tutorial Computer-Assisted Instruction   (IEEE)
TCAL .... Total Calorimeter   (KSC)
TCAM .... Telecommunications Access Method [IBM Corp.] [Data
              processing]
TCA Man .... TCA [Tissue Culture Association] Manual [A publication]
TCaMH ...... Smith County Memorial Hospital, Carthage, TN [Library
              symbol] [Library of Congress]   (LCLS)
TCAOB ...... Tetrachloroazoxybenzene [Organic chemistry]
TCAP .... Tactical Channel Assignment Panel [Military radio]
T/CAP .... Thermal Capacitor   (MCD)
TCAP .... Tricyanoaminopropene [Organic chemistry]

TCAP......... Trimethylcetylammonium Pentachlorphenate [Organic
              chemistry]
TCAPE .... Truck Computer Analysis of Performance and Economy
TCaS .... Smith County High School Library, Carthage, TN [Library
              symbol] [Library of Congress]   (LCLS)
TCAS .... T-Carrier Administration System [Minicomputer] [Bell System]
TCAS .... Technical Control and Analysis System   (MCD)
T-CAS .... Threat Alert and Collision Avoidance System [Electronic
              warning system for US aircraft]
TCAS .... Traffic Alert and Collision Avoidance System
TCASNY .... Turkish Cypriot Aid Society of New York   (EA)
TCAT......... Tape-Controlled Automatic Testing
TCAT......... TCA Cable TV, Inc. [NASDAQ symbol]   (NQ)
TCAT......... Test Coverage Analysis Tool   (IEEE)
TCATA ...... Textile Care Allied Trades Association [Formerly, LACATA,
              LCATA] [Upper Montclair, NJ]   (EA)
TCATA ...... TRADOC Combined Arms Test Activity [Army]   (MCD)
TCAus........ Twentieth Century (Australia) [A publication]
TCAX........ Trans Continental Air Transport [Air carrier designation
              symbol]
TCB............ [The] College Board [An association]   (EA)
TCB............ [The] Conference Board [Formerly, National Industrial
              Conference Board]   (EA)
TCB............ Fort Worth, TX [Location identifier] [FAA]   (FAAL)
TCB............ Take Care of Business [Slang]
TCB............ Taking Care of Business [Brand name of Alberto-Culver Co.]
TCB............ Tantalum Carbon Bond
TCB............ Task Control Block [Data processing]
TCB............ Task Force for Community Broadcasting   (EA)
TCB............ Taylor-Carlisle Bookseller [ACCORD] [UTLAS symbol]
TCB............ Technical Coordinator Bulletin [NASA]   (KSC)
TCB............ TEN Private Cable Systems, Inc. [Vancouver Stock Exchange
              symbol]
TCB............ Tent City Bravo [Area near Tan Son Nhut Air Base, formerly
              site of USAR headquarters]
TCB............ Tetrachlorobiphenyl [Organic chemistry]
TCB............ Texas Commerce Bancshares, Inc. [NYSE symbol]
TCB............ Thermal Compression Bond
TCB............ Time Correlation Buffer   (MCD)
TCB............ Title Certificate Book   (DLA)
TCB............ Trans-Continental Freight Bureau, Chicago IL [STAC]
TCB............ Transfer Control Block
TCB............ Treasure Cay [Bahamas] [Airport symbol]   (OAG)
TCB............ Tulare County Free Library System, Visalia, CA [OCLC
              symbol]   (OCLC)
TCB............ Tumor Cell Burden [Oncology]
TCBA .... Tesla Coil Builders Association   (EA)
T-CBA .... Transfluxor, Constant Board Assembly   (AAG)
TCBC .... Trichlorobenzyl Chloride [Organic chemistry]
TCBC .... Twin Cities Biomedical Consortium [Library network]
TCBCS ...... Blue Cross and Blue Shield of Tennessee, Chattanooga, TN
              [Library symbol] [Library of Congress]   (LCLS)
TCBE......... Thermocompression Bonding Equipment
TCBEFC .... TCB [Taking Care of Business] for Elvis Fan Club [Gastonia,
              NC]   (EA)
TCBHHA .... [The] Church of the Brethren Homes and Hospitals
              Association   (EA)
TCBI .... Television Center for Business and Industry
TCBM .... Transcontinental Ballistic Missile [Air Force]
TCBO .... Trichlorobutylene Oxide [Organic chemistry]
TCBS .... Thiosulfate-Citrate-Bile Salt Sucrose [Growth medium]
TCBS .... Transactions. Cambridge Bibliographical Society [A
              publication]
TCBV .... Temperature Coefficient of Breakdown Voltage
TCC............ [The] Cesarean Connection   (EA)
TCC............ [The] Cola Clan [Later, Coca-Cola Collectors Club
              International]   (EA)
TCC............ [The] Computer Company [Richmond, VA] [Information
              service]   (EISS)
TCC............ [The] Conservative Caucus [An association]   (EA)
TCC............ [The] Curwood Collector [A publication]   (EA)
TCC............ New Mexico Institute of Mining and Technology Computer
              Center [Socorro, NM] [Research center]   (RCD)
TCC............ T-Cell Clone [Cytology]
TCC............ Tactical Command Control   (MCD)
TCC............ Tactical Communications Center
TCC............ Tactical Control Center [Military]
TCC............ Tactical Control Computer   (AAG)
TCC............ Tactical Control Console   (NATG)
TCC............ Tagliabue Closed Cup [Analytical chemistry]
TCC............ Tara Collectors Club [Jonesboro, GA]   (EA)
TCC............ Task Control Character   (CMD)
TCC............ Teachers College of Connecticut
TCC............ Technical Computing Center   (IEEE)
TCC............ Technical Control Center
TCC............ Technology Commercialization Center [Minority Business
              Development Administration]
TCC............ Telecommunications Center   (CET)
TCC............ Telecommunications Consumer Coalition   (EA)
TCC............ Telecommunications Coordinating Committee [Department of
              State]

TCC...........	Teleconcepts in Communications, Inc. [*New York, NY*] [*Telecommunications*] (TSSD)
TCC...........	TeleConcepts Corporation [*American Stock Exchange symbol*]
TCC...........	Television Control Center
TCC...........	Temperature Coefficient of Capacitance
TCC...........	Temperature Control Circuit
TCC...........	Temporary Council Committee [*NATO*]
TCC...........	Terminal Control Corridor [*Aviation*]
TCC...........	Test Conductor Console (AAG)
TCC...........	Test Control Center
TCC...........	Test Controller Computer (MCD)
TCC...........	Test Controller Console (KSC)
TCC...........	Test Coordinating Center [*Army*]
TCC...........	Test Coordinator Console (CAAL)
TCC...........	Tetrachlorocatechol [*Organic chemistry*]
TCC...........	Theater Communications Center (MCD)
TCC...........	Theater Communications Command (MCD)
TCC...........	Thermal Control Coating
TCC...........	Therofor Catalytic Cracking
TCC...........	Thiokol Chemical Corporation [*Later, Thiokol Corp.*] (AAG)
TCC...........	Third Continental Congress [*Tulsa, OK*] (EA)
TCC...........	Thromboplastic Cell Component [*Hematology*]
TCC...........	Through-Connected Circuit [*Telecommunications*] (TEL)
TCC...........	Time Compression Coding
TCC...........	Toroidal Combustion Chamber
TCC...........	Torque Converter Clutch [*Automotive engineering*]
TCC...........	Tracking Computer Controls (MCD)
TCC...........	Tracking and Control Center
TCC...........	Traffic Control Center
TCC...........	Transcontinental Corps [*Amateur radio*]
TCC...........	Transfer Channel Control (IEEE)
TCC...........	Transient Combustion Chamber [*Analysis*] (MCD)
TCC...........	Transitional Cell Carcinoma
TCC...........	Transmission Control Character [*Telecommunications*] (TEL)
TCC...........	Transmit Carry and Clear
TCC...........	Transport Control Center [*Air Force*]
TCC...........	Transportation Commodity Classification Code
TCC...........	Transportation Control Card
TCC...........	Transportation Control Center
TCC...........	Transportation Control Committee [*Navy*]
TCC...........	Travel Classification Code
TCC...........	Travel Correction Calculator (MSA)
TCC...........	Travelers' Century Club (EA)
TCC...........	Triactor Resources Corporation [*Vancouver Stock Exchange symbol*]
TCC...........	Trichlorocarbanilide [*Organic chemistry*]
TCC...........	Triclocarban [*Pharmacology*]
TCC...........	Trilobita-Crustacea-Chelicerata [*Evolution history*]
TCC...........	Triple Cotton-Covered [*Wire insulation*]
TCC...........	Troop Carrier Command [*World War II*]
TCC...........	Tucumcari, NM [*Location identifier*] [*FAA*] (FAAL)
TCC...........	Turbine Close Coupled (MSA)
TCC...........	Turnbull Canyon [*California*] [*Seismograph station code, US Geological Survey*] [*Closed*] (SEIS)
TCCA........	Teachers' Committee on Central America (EA)
TCCA........	Textile Color Card Association of the US [*Later, CAUS*]
TCCA........	Thermometer Collectors Club of America (EA)
TCCA........	Tin Container Collectors Association (EA)
TCCA........	Trichloroisocyanuric Acid [*Organic chemistry*]
TCCB........	Test and County Cricket Board [*British*]
TCCBL.......	Tons of Cubic Capacity Bale Space [*Shipping*] [*British*]
TCC/CT......	Telecommunications/Communications Terminal (MCD)
TCCDC......	Chattem Drug and Chemical Co., Chattanooga, TN [*Library symbol*] [*Library of Congress*] (LCLS)
TCCF........	Tactical Communications Control Facility [*Air Force*] (MCD)
TCCFU.......	Typical Coastal Command Foul Up [*RAF slang*] [*World War II*]
TCCH........	Tracer Control Chassis
TCCM........	Thermal Control Coating Material
TC/CMS.....	Technical Data/Configuration Management System (MCD)
TCCO........	Technical Communications [*NASDAQ symbol*] (NQ)
TCCO........	Temperature-Compensated Crystal Oscillator (MCD)
T & CCP	Telecommunications and Command and Control Program [*Air Force*] (AFIT)
TCCPSWG ...	Tactical Command and Control Procedures Standardization Working Group [*Army*] (AABC)
TCCRAEF ...	[*The*] Conservative Caucus Research, Analysis, and Education Foundation (EA)
TCCS........	Technical Committee on Communications Satellites
TCCS........	Tide Communication Control Ship (NATG)
TCCS........	Trace Contaminant Control System
TCCT........	Tactical Communications Control Terminal (MCD)
TCD..........	Chad [*Three-letter standard code*] (CNC)
TCD..........	Target Center Display
TCD..........	Task Completion Date (AAG)
TCD..........	Technical Contracts Department
TCD..........	Telemetry and Command Data (KSC)
TCD..........	Tentative Classification of Damage
TCD..........	Tentative Classification of Defects (NG)
TCD..........	Tentative Classification of Documents
TCD..........	Terminal Countdown Demonstration
TCD..........	Test Completion Date (NASA)

TCD..........	Test Control Document (MCD)
TCD..........	Test Control Drawings (MCD)
TCD..........	Thermal Conductivity Detector [*Analytical instrumentation*]
TCD..........	Thermochemical Deposition
TCD..........	Three-Channel Decoder
TCD..........	Thyratron Core Driver
TCD..........	Time Compliance Directive [*Air Force*] (MCD)
TCD..........	Time Correlation Data
T & CD......	Timing and Countdown [*NASA*] (NASA)
TCD..........	Tor-Cal Resources [*Toronto Stock Exchange symbol*]
TCD..........	Total Cost Approach to Distribution
TCD..........	Tour Completion Date
TCD..........	TOXLINE Chemical Dictionary [*A publication*]
TCD..........	Transistor Chopper Driver
TCD..........	Transistor-Controlled Delay (MCD)
TCD..........	Transportability Clearance Diagram (MCD)
TCD..........	Trinity College, Dublin [*Ireland*]
TCD..........	Tumor Control Dose [*Oncology*]
TCD₅₀........	Tissue Culture Dose, 50% Infectivity
TC & DB.....	Turn, Cough, and Deep Breathe [*Medicine*]
TCDC........	Taurochenodeoxycholate [*Biochemistry*]
TCDC........	Technical Cooperation among Developing Countries [*United Nations*]
TCDC/INRES ...	Information Referral System for Technical Co-operation among Developing Countries [*United Nations Development Programme*] [*New York, NY*] [*Information service*] (EISS)
TCDD........	Tetrachlorodibenzodioxin [*Organic chemistry*]
TCDF........	Temporary Container Discharge Facility
TCDF........	Tetrachlorodibenzofuran [*Organic chemistry*]
TCDF........	TIN [*Taxpayer Identification Number*] Control Number/DLN [*Document Locator Number*] File [*IRS*]
TCDMS......	Telecommunication/Data Management System
TCDS........	Tryptamine Chemical Delivery System [*Pharmacology*]
TCE..........	20th Century Energy [*Vancouver Stock Exchange symbol*]
TCE..........	Talker Commission Error (MUGU)
TCE..........	Tax Counseling for the Elderly [*Internal Revenue Service*]
TCE..........	Teachers' Centers Exchange (EA)
TCE..........	Telemetry Checkout Equipment (KSC)
TCE..........	Telephone Company Engineered [*Telecommunications*] (TEL)
TCE..........	Temperature Coefficient of Expansion
TCE..........	Terminal Control Element (CAAL)
TCE..........	Terminal Cretaceous Event [*Geology*]
TCE..........	Terrace (ROG)
TCE..........	Tetrachloroethylene [*Also, P*] [*Organic chemistry*]
TCE..........	Thermal Canister Experiment [*Space shuttle*] [*NASA*]
TCE..........	Tons of Coal Equivalent
TCE..........	Total Composite Error
TCE..........	Trans-Colorado Airlines, Inc. [*Gunnison, CO*] [*FAA designator*] (FAAC)
TCE..........	Transportation-Communication Employees Union [*Later, BRAC*]
TCE..........	Trichloroethanol [*Organic chemistry*]
TCE..........	Trichloroethylene [*Also, TRI*] [*Organic chemistry*]
TCE..........	Tubular Carbon Electrode
TCE..........	Tulcea [*Romania*] [*Airport symbol*] (OAG)
TCEA........	Theoretical Chemical Engineering Abstracts [*A publication*]
TCEA........	Training Center for Experimental Aerodynamics [*NATO*]
TCEA........	Trichloroethane [*Organic chemistry*]
TCEBA.......	Tribune. CEBEDEAU [*Centre Belge d'Etude et de Documentation des Eaux et de l'Air*] [*A publication*]
TCEC........	Erlanger Medical Center, Medical Library, Chattanooga, TN [*Library symbol*] [*Library of Congress*] (LCLS)
TCEC-N	Erlanger Medical Center, Nursing School, Chattanooga, TN [*Library symbol*] [*Library of Congress*] (LCLS)
TCEC-P	Erlanger Medical Center, I. C., Thompson's Children's Pediatric Library, Chattanooga, TN [*Library symbol*] [*Library of Congress*] (LCLS)
TCED........	Thrust Control Exploratory Development (KSC)
TCEO........	Theatre Committee for Eugene O'Neill (EA)
TCEP........	Tris(chloroethyl)phosphite [*Organic chemistry*]
TCEP........	Tris(cyanoethoxy)propane [*Organic chemistry*]
TCES........	Transcutaneous Cranial Electrical Stimulation [*Medicine*]
TCESOM.....	Trichlorethylene-Extracted Soybean Oil Meal
TCET........	Transcerebral Electrotherapy
TCF..........	[*The*] Children's Foundation [*Washington, DC*] (EA)
TCF..........	[*The*] Compassionate Friends [*Oak Brook, IL*] (EA)
TCF..........	Tactical Control Flight
TCF..........	Technical Control Facility [*or Function*]
TCF..........	Temporary Chaplain to the Forces [*British*]
TCF..........	Test Control Fixture (MCD)
TCF..........	Time Correction Factor (ADA)
TCF..........	Toulx Ste. Croix [*France*] [*Seismograph station code, US Geological Survey*] (SEIS)
TCF..........	Tres Cher Frere [*Dear Brother*] [*French*] [*Freemasonry*] (ROG)
TCF..........	Trillion Cubic Feet
TCF..........	Troop Carrier Forces
TCF..........	Tunable Control Frequency
TCF..........	Twentieth Century Fiction [*A publication*]
TCF..........	Twentieth Century Fund (EA)
TCFB........	Trans-Continental Freight Bureau

TCFC......... Tommy Cash Fan Club [*Belchertown, MA*]   (EA)
TCFIC....... Textile, Clothing, and Footwear Industries Committee [*British*]
TCFM........ Temperature Control Flux Monitor [*NASA*]
TCFNO....... [*The*] Common Fund for Nonprofit Organizations [*Ford Foundation*]
TCFS......... Turkish Cypriot Federated State
TCFU......... Tumor Colony-Forming Unit [*Oncology*]
TCG............ [*The*] Crimson Group [*Cambridge, MA*] [*Telecommunications*]   (TSSD)
TCG............ Technical Coordination Group   (MCD)
TCG............ Telecommunications Consulting Group, Inc. [*Washington, DC*]   (TSSD)
TCG............ Telecommunications Group [*Range Commanders Council*] [*NASA*]
TCG............ Territorial College of Guam
TCG............ Test Call Generator [*Telecommunications*]   (TEL)
TCG............ Theatre Communications Group
TCG............ Time Code Generator
TCG............ Time-Compensated Gain [*Cardiology*]
TCG............ Time Controlled Gain   (AAG)
TCG............ Tooling Coordination Group   (AAG)
TCG............ Trans Canada Glass Ltd. [*Toronto Stock Exchange symbol*] [*Vancouver Stock Exchange symbol*]
TCG............ Transponder Control Group
TCG............ Tritocerebral Commissure, Giant [*Zoology*]
TCG............ Tucson, Cornelia & Gila Bend Railroad Co. [*AAR code*]
TCG............ Tune-Controlled Gain
TCGCB...... Transactions. Caribbean Geological Conference [*A publication*]
TCGE........ Tool and Cutter Grinding Equipment   (MCD)
TCGE-G..... Technika Hronika (Greece) [*A publication*]
TCGF......... T-Cell Growth Factor [*Biochemistry*] [*See also IL-2*]
TCGF......... Thymus Cell Growth Factor [*Cytology*]
TCGH......... Downtown General Hospital, Chattanooga, TN [*Library symbol*] [*Library of Congress*]   (LCLS)
TCGp......... Tactical Control Group [*Air Force*]   (AFM)
TCGS......... Terak Corporation [*NASDAQ symbol*]   (NQ)
TCGT......... Georgia-Tennessee Regional Health Commission, Chattanooga, TN [*Library symbol*] [*Library of Congress*]   (LCLS)
TCGT......... Tool and Cutter Grinding Tool   (MCD)
TCGU......... Texaco Continuous Grease Unit
TCH............ Chattanooga-Hamilton County Bicentennial Library, Chattanooga, TX [*OCLC symbol*]   (OCLC)
TCH............ Tchibanga [*Gabon*] [*Airport symbol*]   (OAG)
TCH............ Tchimkent [*USSR*] [*Seismograph station code, US Geological Survey*] [*Closed*]   (SEIS)
TCH............ Tchoupitoulas [*Virus*]
TCH............ TechAmerica Group, Inc. [*American Stock Exchange symbol*]
TCh............ Temoignage Chretien [*A publication*]
TCH............ Temporary Construction Hole [*Technical drawings*]
TCH............ Tetrachlorohydroquinone [*Organic chemistry*]
TCH............ Thiocarbohydrazide [*Organic chemistry*]
TCH............ Threshold Crossing Height [*Aviation*]   (FAAC)
TCH............ Trans-Canada Highway
TCH............ Transfer in Channel
TCH............ Trust Chamber [*NASA*]   (KSC)
TCH............ Turn, Cough, Hyperventilate [*Medicine*]
TCHCB...... Chattanooga-Hamilton County Bicentennial Library, Chattanooga, TN [*Library symbol*] [*Library of Congress*]   (LCLS)
TCHD........ Threshold Crossing Height Downwind [*Aviation*]   (FAAC)
TCHEP....... Technical Committee on High Energy Physics [*of the Federal Council for Science and Technology*]
TCHHC...... Ti Ch'iu Hua Hsueh [*A publication*]
TCHHW..... Tropic Higher High Water [*Tides*]
TCHHWI..... Tropic Higher High-Water Interval [*Tides*]
TCHLW..... Tropic Higher Low Water [*Tides*]
TCHMA...... Technika v Chemii [*A publication*]
TCHNG...... Teaching
TChO......... Olin Corp., D. B. Beene Technical Information Center, Charleston, TN [*Library symbol*] [*Library of Congress*]   (LCLS)
TCHR......... Teacher
TCHT......... Tanned-Cell Hemagglutination Test [*Immunology*]
TCHU........ Threshold Crossing Height Upwind [*Aviation*]   (FAAC)
TCI............. Tall Clubs International [*Denver, CO*]   (EA)
TCI............. Technical Critical Item   (NASA)
TCI............. Technology Catalysts, Incorporated [*Falls Church, VA*] [*Information service*]   (EISS)
TCI............. Technology Communications, Incorporated
TCI............. Technology Concepts, Incorporated [*Sudbury, MA*] [*Telecommunications*]   (TSSD)
TCI............. Tele-Communications, Incorporated [*Brookpark, OH*]   (TSSD)
TCI............. Teleconferencing Systems International, Inc. [*Elk Grove Village, IL*] [*Telecommunications*]   (TSSD)
TCI............. Telemetry Components Information   (KSC)
TCI............. Telephone Collectors International [*San Antonio, TX*]   (EA)
TCI............. Temperature Control Instrument
TCI............. Temporary Customs Impost [*British*]
TCI............. Tenerife [*Canary Islands*] [*Airport symbol*]   (OAG)

TCI............. Terrain Clearance Indicator
TCI............. Test Control Instruction   (KSC)
TCI............. Theoretical Chemistry Institute [*University of Wisconsin - Madison*] [*Research center*]   (RCD)
TCI............. Thimble Collectors International   (EA)
TCI............. Time Change Item   (MCD)
TCI............. To Come In [*to hospital*] [*Medicine*]
TCI............. Total Cerebral Ischemia
TCI............. Traffic Clubs International   (EA)
TCI............. Transient Cerebral Ischemia [*Medicine*]
TCI............. Transportation Clubs International [*Orlando, FL*]   (EA)
TCI............. Travel Consultants, Incorporated
TCI............. Trunk Cut-In
TCI............. Twentieth Century Interpretations [*A publication*]
TCIC.......... Technical Committee on Industrial Classification [*Office of Management and Budget*]   (EGAO)
TCID.......... Terminal Computer Identification   (KSC)
TCID.......... Test Configuration Identifier   (NASA)
TCID.......... Tissue Culture Infectious [*or Infective*] Dose
Tc-IDA....... Technetium Iminodiacetic Acid [*Clinical chemistry*]
TCII........... Technology for Communications International [*NASDAQ symbol*]   (NQ)
TCIR.......... Technical Command Informal Reports [*Army*]   (MCD)
TCIS.......... TELEX Computer Inquiry Service
TCJ............ Tactical Communications Jamming [*Military*]   (CAAL)
TCJ............ Tarrant County Junior College, Hurst, TX [*OCLC symbol*]   (OCLC)
TCJ............ Thermocouple Junction
TCJ............ Town and Country Journal [*A publication*]
T & CJ....... Town and Country Journal [*A publication*]
TCJ............ Turbulent Confined Jet
TCJCC....... Trades Councils' Joint Consultative Committee [*British*]
TCK........... TEC, Inc. [*American Stock Exchange symbol*]
TCK........... Thermochemical-Kinetic
TCK........... Tilletia controversa Kuehn [*Wheat fungus*]
TCK........... Track   (AAG)
TCK........... Two-Cavity Klystron
TCKHA...... Ti Chih Ko Hsueh [*A publication*]
TCL............ Takeoff Cruise Landing [*Aviation*]
TCL............ Telecommunication Laboratories [*Taiwan*]
TCL............ Terminal Command Language [*Applied Digital Data Systems*]
TCL............ Terminal Control Language
TCL............ Textes Cuneiformes. Departement des Antiquites Orientales. Musee du Louvre [*A publication*]   (BJA)
TCL............ Thin Charcoal Layer
TCL............ Time and Cycle Log [*NASA*]   (KSC)
TCL............ Toll Circuit Layout [*Telecommunications*]   (TEL)
TCL............ Tool Control List [*Military*]   (AFIT)
TCL............ Transcon, Inc. [*NYSE symbol*]
TCL............ Transfer Chemical LASER   (IEEE)
TCL............ Transistor Contact Land
TCL............ Transistor Coupled Logic
TCL............ Transport Canada Library, Ottawa [*UTLAS symbol*]
TCL............ Transportable Calibration Laboratory
TCL............ Trap Control Line
TCL............ Trinity College, London
TCL............ Troposcatter Communications Link
TCL............ Tulane Computer Laboratory [*Tulane University*] [*Research center*]   (RCD)
TCL............ Tuscaloosa [*Alabama*] [*Airport symbol*]   (OAG)
TCL............ Tusculum College, Greenville, TN [*OCLC symbol*] [*Inactive*]   (OCLC)
TCL............ Twentieth Century Literature [*A publication*]
TCIA.......... Austin Peay State University, Clarksville, TN [*Library symbol*] [*Library of Congress*]   (LCLS)
TCLAS...... Type Classification   (AABC)
TCLBRP.... Tank Cannon Launched Beam Rider Projectile   (MCD)
TCLBS....... Tropical Constant-Level Balloon System [*Meteorology*]
TCLC......... Travaux. Cercle Linguistique de Copenhague [*A publication*]
TCLC......... Tri-State College Library Cooperative [*Rosemont College Library*] [*Rosemont, PA*] [*Library network*]
TCLC......... Twentieth-Century Literary Criticism [*A publication*]
TC/LD........ Thermocouple/Lead Detector   (NRCH)
TCIe.......... Cleveland Public Library, Cleveland, TN [*Library symbol*] [*Library of Congress*]   (LCLS)
TCLE......... Thermal Coefficient of Linear Expansion [*Rocket motor stress*]
TCIeB........ Bradley Memorial Hospital, Cleveland, TN [*Library symbol*] [*Library of Congress*]   (LCLS)
TCIeC........ Cleveland State Community College, Cleveland, TN [*Library symbol*] [*Library of Congress*]   (LCLS)
TCIeL........ Lee College, Cleveland, TN [*Library symbol*] [*Library of Congress*]   (LCLS)
TCIH.......... Clarksville Memorial Hospital, Clarksville, TN [*Library symbol*] [*Library of Congress*]   (LCLS)
TCLHW...... Tropic Lower High Water [*Tides*]
TCLL.......... T-Cell Chronic Lymphocytic Leukemia [*Oncology*]
TCLLW...... Tropic Lower Low Water [*Tides*]
TCLLWI...... Tropic Lower Low-Water Interval [*Tides*]
TCLNA...... Tall Cedars of Lebanon of North America   (EA)
TCLP......... Toxicity Characteristic Leaching Procedure [*Environmental Protection Agency*]

TCLP .... Travaux. Cercle Linguistique de Prague [*A publication*]
TCLP .... Type Classification, Limited Procurement
TCLR .... Toll Circuit Layout Record [*Telecommunications*]   (TEL)
TCLSC .... Theater COMSEC [*Communications Security*] Logistic Support Center [*Army*]   (AABC)
TCLSC-E ... Theater COMSEC Logistics Support Center - Europe   (MCD)
TCM .... Tacoma, WA [*Location identifier*] [*FAA*]   (FAAL)
TCM .... Tactical Cruise Missile   (MCD)
TCM .... Tax Court Memorandum Decisions [*Commerce Clearing House or Prentice-Hall, Inc.*]   (DLA)
TCM .... Teaching Career Month
TCM .... Technical Committee Minutes [*Military*]   (AFIT)
TCM .... Technical Coordination Meeting   (MCD)
TCM .... Telecommunications Monitor
TCM .... Teledyne Continental Motors [*Muskegon, MI*] [*FAA designator*]   (FAAC)
TCM .... Telemetry Code Modulation
TC & M ...... Telemetry Control and Monitoring
TCM .... Telephone Channel Monitor
TCM .... Temperature Control Model
TCM .... Teratogenesis, Carcinogenesis, and Mutagenesis [*A publication*]
TCM .... Terminal-to-Computer Multiplexer
TCM .... Termination of Centralized Management   (MCD)
TCM .... Terrain Clearance Measurement
TCM .... Terrestrial Carbon Model [*Earth science*]
TCM .... Test Call Module [*Telecommunications*]   (TEL)
TCM .... Tetrachloromercurate [*Inorganic chemistry*]
TCM .... Theater Combat Model   (NATG)
TCM .... Thermal Conduction Module [*IBM Corp.*]
TCM .... Thermoplastic Cellular Molding [*Plastics technology*]
TCM .... Tissue Culture Medium
TCM .... Torpedo Countermeasures   (NVT)
TCM .... Total Downtime for Corrective Unscheduled Maintenance [*Quality control*]   (MCD)
TCM .... Trajectory Correction Maneuver
TCM .... Transcutaneous [*Oxygen*] Monitoring [*Medicine*]
TCM .... Transfluxor Constants Matrix   (AAG)
TCM .... Truck Components Marketing [*Eaton Corp.*]
TCM .... Tucuman [*Argentina*] [*Seismograph station code, US Geological Survey*] [*Closed*]   (SEIS)
TCM .... Twentieth Century Monthly [*A publication*]
TCM .... Twin-Cartridge Machine
TCMA .... Tabulating Card Manufacturers Association [*Later, IOSA*]   (EA)
TCMA .... Textile Chemical Manufacturers Association [*Later, IOSA*]   (EA)
TCMA .... Third Class Mail Association [*Formerly, ATCMU*] [*Washington, DC*]   (EA)
TCMA .... Tooling Component Manufacturers Association [*Westminster, CA*]   (EA)
TCM/A .... Toxic Chemical Munitions/Agents   (MCD)
TCMB .... Turkiye Cumhuriyet Merkez Bankasi [*The Central Bank of the Republic of Turkey*]
TCM (CCH) ... Tax Court Memorandum Decisions [*Commerce Clearing House*]   (DLA)
TCMD .... Transportation Control and Movement Document
TC Memo ... Tax Court Memorandum Decisions [*Commerce Clearing House or Prentice-Hall, Inc.*]   (DLA)
TCMF .... Touch Calling Multifrequency   (IEEE)
TCMH .... Memorial Hospital, Chattanooga, TN [*Library symbol*] [*Library of Congress*]   (LCLS)
TCMI .... Moccasin Bend Mental Health Institute, Chattanooga, TN [*Library symbol*] [*Library of Congress*]   (LCLS)
T C MITS .... [*The*] Common Man in the Street [*The average man*] [*See also MITS*]
TCMP .... Taxpayer Compliance Measurement Program [*IRS*]
TCM (P-H) ... Tax Court Memorandum Decisions [*Prentice-Hall, Inc.*]   (DLA)
TCMS .... Technical Control and Management Subsystem   (MCD)
TCMS .... Toll Centering and Metropolitan Sectoring [*AT & T*] [*Telecommunications*]   (TEL)
TCMUA ..... Telecommunications [*English Translation*] [*A publication*]
TCN .... Carson-Newman College, Jefferson City, TN [*OCLC symbol*]   (OCLC)
TCN .... Telecommunications Cooperative Network [*New York, NY*] [*Telecommunications*] [*Information service*]   (EA)
TCN .... Teleconference Network [*University of Nebraska Medical Center*] [*Omaha, NE*] [*Telecommunications*]   (TSSD)
TCN .... Territorial Command Net
TCN .... Test Change Notice   (MCD)
TCN .... Texcan Technology Corp. [*Vancouver Stock Exchange symbol*]
TCN .... Toconce [*Chile*] [*Seismograph station code, US Geological Survey*]   (SEIS)
TCN .... Tracing Change Notice
TCN .... Trade Commission of Norway   (EA)
TCN .... Trans Continental Airlines [*Ypsilanti, MI*] [*FAA designator*]   (FAAC)
TCN .... Transportation Control Number [*Air Force*]   (AFM)
TCNA .... Tube Council of North America [*Formerly, MTPC, MTPCNA*]   (EA)
TCNB .... Tetracyanobenzene [*Organic chemistry*]

TC-NBT ...... Thiocarbamyl-nitro-blue Tetrazolium [*Organic chemistry*]
TCNCO ...... Test Control Noncommissioned Officer   (AFM)
TCNE .... Tetracyanoethylene [*Organic chemistry*]
TCNJ .... Trust Co. of New Jersey [*NASDAQ symbol*]   (NQ)
TCNM .... Trimethylcyclopropenyl(nitrophenyl)malononitrile [*Organic chemistry*]
TCNQ .... Tetracyanoquinodimethane [*Organic chemistry*]
TCNRS .... Transactions. Canadian Numismatic Research Society [*A publication*]
TCNSB .... Technos [*A publication*]
TCNT .... Transpiration-Cooled Nose Tip
TCNTL .... Transcontinental   (FAAC)
TCO .... Tactical Combat Operations
TCO .... Tactical Control Officer [*Army*]
TCO .... Taken Care Of   (MCD)
TCO .... Technical Checkout [*Nuclear*]   (MCD)
TCO .... Technical Contracting Office [*Navy*]
TCO .... Telecommunications Certifying Officer [*Air Force*]   (AFIT)
TCO .... Telemetry and Command Subsystem [*Deep Space Instrumentation Facility, NASA*]
TCO .... Terminal Control Office [*or Officer*]
TCO .... Termination Contracting Officers
T & C/O ..... Test and Checkout [*NASA*]   (KSC)
TCO .... Test Control Officer
TCO .... Thrust Cutoff   (NVT)
TCO .... Tillamook County Library, Tillamook, OR [*OCLC symbol*]   (OCLC)
TCO .... Time and Charges, Operate
TCO .... Tjaenstemaennens Centralorganisation [*Central Organization of Salaried Employees*] [*Sweden*]
TCO .... Tool Change Order   (MCD)
TCO .... Trans Canada Options [*Stock exchange network of VSE, TSE, and MSE*]
TCO .... Trans-Canada Resources Ltd. [*Toronto Stock Exchange symbol*]
TCO .... Transparent Conductive Oxide [*Photovoltaic energy systems*]
TCO .... Transportation Company [*Army*]
TCO .... Transportation Control Officer [*Air Force*]   (AFM)
TCO .... Trunk Cutoff
TCO .... Tumaco [*Colombia*] [*Airport symbol*]   (OAG)
TCOBS .... Type Classification - Obsolete   (MCD)
TCOC .... Transverse Cylindrical Orthomorphic Chart
TCollSM .... Southern Missionary College, Collegedale, TN [*Library symbol*] [*Library of Congress*]   (LCLS)
TCOM .... Terminal Communications   (FAAC)
TCOM .... Tethered Communications, Inc. [*Westinghouse subsidiary*]
TCOMA ..... Tele-Communications, Inc. Cl A [*NASDAQ symbol*]   (NQ)
TCOMB ..... Tele-Communications, Inc. Cl B [*NASDAQ symbol*]   (NQ)
TCOMP ..... Tape Compare Processor [*Data processing*]
T/COMP ..... Trimmed Complete [*Automotive engineering*]
TCOMW ..... Tele-Communications, Inc. Wts [*NASDAQ symbol*]   (NQ)
T/CONT ..... Throttle Control [*Automotive engineering*]
T/CONV .... Torque Converter [*Automotive engineering*]
TCoo .... Putnam County Public Library, Cookeville, TN [*Library symbol*] [*Library of Congress*]   (LCLS)
TCooH .... Cookeville General Hospital, Stephen Farr Health Sciences Library, Cookeville, TN [*Library symbol*] [*Library of Congress*]   (LCLS)
TCooP .... Tennessee Technological University, Cookeville, TN [*Library symbol*] [*Library of Congress*]   (LCLS)
TCOP .... Test and Checkout Plan [*NASA*]   (KSC)
TCOR .... Chrysler Town and Country Owners Registry   (EA)
TCOR .... Tandon Corporation [*NASDAQ symbol*]   (NQ)
TCORA ...... Teacher's College Record [*A publication*]
TCOS .... Trunk Class of Service [*Telecommunications*]   (TEL)
T-COUNT ... Terminal Count [*Flight readiness count*]   (MCD)
TCovH .... Tipton County Hospital, Covington, TN [*Library symbol*] [*Library of Congress*]   (LCLS)
TCP .... Tactical Control Panel   (MCD)
TCP .... Tactical Cryptologic Program [*DoD*]
TCP .... Tape Conversion Program [*Data processing*]   (MDG)
TCP .... Task Change Proposal   (AAG)
TCP .... Task Control Program
TCP .... Teachers College Press
TCP .... Technical Change Proposal
TCP .... Technical Coordination Program [*Military*]   (AFIT)
TCP .... Technical Cost Proposal   (AAG)
TCP .... Technology Coordinating Paper
TCP .... Telemetry and Command Processor Assembly [*Deep Space Instrumentation Facility, NASA*]
TCP .... Temple Cyclopaedic Primers [*A publication*]
TCP .... Temporary Change Procedure   (AAG)
TCP .... Terminal Control Program
TCP .... Test Change Proposal   (CAAL)
TCP .... Test and Checkout Procedure [*NASA*]   (KSC)
TCP .... Test Control Package   (NASA)
TCP .... Tetrachlorobiphenyl [*Organic chemistry*]
TCP .... Tetrachlorophenol [*Organic chemistry*]
TCP .... Tetracyanoplatinate [*Inorganic chemistry*]
TCP .... Tetracyanopyrazine [*Organic chemistry*]
TCP .... Thrust Chamber Pressure   (IEEE)

TCP .... Time, Cost, and Performance
TCP .... Time Limited Correlation Processing
TCP .... Timing and Control Panel
TCP .... Tocopilla [Chile] [Seismograph station code, US Geological Survey] [Closed] (SEIS)
TCP .... Torpedo Certification Program [Military] (CAAL)
TC + P ...... Total Colonoscopy + Polypectomy [Proctoscopy]
TCP .... Traffic Control Post
TCP .... Trainer Change Proposal [Military] (AFIT)
TCP .... Training Controller Panel
TCP .... Transmission Control Program
TCP .... Transmission Control Protocol [Advanced Research Projects Agency Network] [DoD]
TCP .... Transparent Conducting Polymers [Photovoltaic energy systems]
TCP .... Tricalcium Phosphate [Inorganic chemistry]
TCP .... Trichlorophenol [Organic chemistry]
TCP .... (Trichlorophenoxy)acetic Acid [Also known as 2,4,5-T] [Herbicide]
TCP .... Trichloropropane [Organic chemistry]
TCP .... Tricresyl Phosphate [Organic chemistry]
TCP .... Tropical Canine Pancytopenia (RDA)
TCP .... Trust Chamber Pressure [Missile technology] (KSC)
TCPA.......... Tetrachlorophthalic Anhydride [Flame retardant] [Organic chemistry]
TCPA.......... Time to Closest Point of Approach [Navigation]
TCPA.......... Trichlorophenylacetic Acid [Herbicide] [Organic chemistry]
TCPAM ...... Tentative CNO [Chief of Naval Operations] Program Analysis Memorandum (NVT)
TCPC .... Tab Card Punch Control
TCPH.......... Toluoyl Chloride Phenylhydrazine [Drug for sheep]
TCPI .... "To Complete" Performance Index (MCD)
TCPI .... Transportation Club of the Petroleum Industry (EA)
TCPLA .... Town and Country Planning [A publication]
TCPO .... Third-Class Post Office
TCPP.......... (Tetrachlorophenyl)pyrrole [Organic chemistry]
TCPPA .... (Trichlorophenoxy)propionic Acid [Plant hormone] [Herbicide]
TCPTF .... Target Cost Plus Target Fee
TCpY.......... Transcarpathian Yiddish (BJA)
TCQ .... Tacna [Peru] [Airport symbol] (OAG)
TCQ .... Tax Counselor's Quarterly [A publication]
TCQ .... Trichlorobenzoquinoneimine [Reagent]
TCQC .... Tank Crew Qualification Course [Army]
TCQM........ [The] Chief Quartermaster [Military]
TCR .... Central Air Transport, Inc. [Nashville, TN] [FAA designator] (FAAC)
TCR .... T-Cell Receptor [Immunology]
TCR .... Tab Card Reader
TCR .... Tantalum-Controlled Rectifier
TCR .... Tape Cassette Recorder
TCR .... Teacher's College Record [A publication]
TCR .... Technical Change Request
TCR .... Technical Characteristics Review
TCR .... Technical Compliance Record
TCR .... Telemetry Compression Routine
TCR .... Temperature Coefficient of Resistance
TCR .... Temperature Control Reference
TCR .... Tentative Cancellation Request
TCR .... Terrain Clearance RADAR
TCR .... Test Compare Results (MCD)
TCR .... Test Condition Requirements [Army]
TCR .... Test Conductor (MCD)
TCR .... Test Constraints Review (MCD)
TCR .... Tetrachlororesourcinol [Organic chemistry]
TCR .... Thalamocortical Relay [Neurology]
TCR .... Thermal Concept Review (NASA)
TCR .... Thermochemical Recuperator [Proposed heat recovery system]
TCR .... Tie Control Relay (MCD)
TCR .... Time Code Reader
TCR .... Time Critical Requirements (MCD)
TCR .... Tonecraft Realty, Inc. [Toronto Stock Exchange symbol]
TCR .... Tool Completion Report
TCR .... Tooling Change Request
TCR .... Total Contractual Requirements (MCD)
TCR .... Total Control Racing [Road-racing game] [Ideal Toy Corp.]
TCr .... Total Creatine [Pool]
TCR .... Tracer (AAG)
TCR .... Traffic Control RADAR
TCR .... Training/Conversion/Replacement (MCD)
TCR .... Trammell Crow Real Estate Investment [NYSE symbol]
TCR .... Transceiver (AABC)
TCR .... Transfer Control Register
TCR .... Transit Commission Reports [New York] (DLA)
TCR .... Transmittal Control Record [Data processing]
TCR .... Transportation Corps Release
TCR .... Travaux. Centre de Recherche sur le Proche-Orient et la Grece Antiques. Universite de Sciences Humaines de Strasbourg [A publication] (BJA)
TCR .... Two-Color Radiometer

TCrA .... Art Circle Public Library, Crossville, TN [Library symbol] [Library of Congress] (LCLS)
TCRC .... Time and Cycle Record Card [NASA] (KSC)
TCRD .... Telecredit, Inc. [NASDAQ symbol] (NQ)
TCRD .... Test and Checkout Requirements Document [NASA] (KSC)
TCRE......... Temperature-Compensated Reference Element
TCREC ...... Transportation Research Command [Army] (MCD)
T Crit .... Texto Critico [A publication]
TCRJ .... Thermocouple Reference Junction
TCRM........ Thermochemical Remanent Magnetization
TCRMG ..... Tripartite Commission for the Restitution of Monetary Gold (EA-IO)
TCRN .... Temporary Chaplain to the Royal Navy [British]
TCRPA ...... Trans-Continental Railroad Passenger Association [Defunct] (EA)
TCRPC ...... Tri-County Regional Planning Commission [Lansing, MI] [Information service] (EISS)
TCRSD ...... Test and Checkout Requirements Specification Documentation [NASA] (NASA)
TCS .... [The] Classification Society (EA)
TCS .... [The] Coastal Society (EA)
TCS .... [The] Computer Store [NASDAQ symbol] (NQ)
TCS .... [The] Constant Society (EA)
TCS .... [The] Cousteau Society (EA)
TCS .... [The] Cybele Society [Spokane, WA] (EA)
TCS .... Tactical Computer System [Army] (MCD)
TCS .... Tactical Control Squadron
TCS .... Tanking Control System (AAG)
TCS .... Target Control System
TCS .... Target Cost System
TCS .... Teacher Characteristics Schedule
TCS .... Technical Change Summary (MCD)
TCS .... Technical Countdown Sequences (KSC)
TCS .... Telecommunications Control System [Toshiba Corp.] [Data processing]
TCS .... Telecommunications System
TCS .... Teleconference System [Memorial University of Newfoundland] [St. John's, NF] [Telecommunications] (TSSD)
TCS .... Telemetry and Command Station [Aerospace] (MCD)
TCS .... Telephone Conference Summary (NRCH)
TCS .... Television Camera System
TCS .... Television Control Set
TCS .... Temperature Control Subsystem (KSC)
TCS .... Temporary Change of Station
TCS .... Temporary Conditioning Station [Nuclear energy] (NRCH)
TCS .... Temporary Correction Sheet (MCD)
TCS .... Terminal Communications Subsystem
TCS .... Terminal Computer System (BUR)
TCS .... Terminal Control System [Hewlett-Packard Co.]
TCS .... Terminal Countdown Sequencer [or Sequences] [NASA] (KSC)
TCS .... Ternary Compound Semiconductor
TCS .... Test Control Supervisor (NASA)
TCS .... Test Control System (NASA)
TCS .... Texas Centennial Society (EA)
TCS .... Texts from Cuneiform Sources [A publication] (BJA)
TCS .... Thermal Conditioning System (KSC)
TCS .... Thermal Control System [or Subsystem]
TCS .... Thermally Stimulated Charge [Analytical chemistry]
TCS .... Timing Cover and Seal Set [Automotive engineering]
TCS .... Tin Can Sailors (EA)
TCS .... Tool Clearance Slip (AAG)
TCS .... Total Communication Systems [Pittsburgh, PA] [Telecommunications service] (TSSD)
TCS .... Trac Resources, Inc. [Vancouver Stock Exchange symbol]
TCS .... Tracheal Cellular Score [Medicine]
TCS .... Traffic Control Satellite
TCS .... Traffic Control Station
TCS .... Traffic Control System [Army]
TCS .... Transaction Control System [Hitachi Ltd.]
TCS .... Transducer Calibration System
TCS .... Transfer Carry Subtract
TCS .... Transmission Controlled Spark (MCD)
TCS .... Transportable Communications System
TCS .... Transportation and Communications Service [of GSA] [Abolished, 1972]
TCS .... Transportation Concepts & Services [Metuchen, NJ] [Software manufacturer]
TCS .... Transportation Consulting & Service Corp., Chicago IL [STAC]
TCS .... Trichlorosilane [Inorganic chemistry]
TCS .... Trim Control System
TCS .... Troop Carrier Squadron [Military] (CINC)
TCS .... Troposcatter Communications System
TCS .... Truth Or Consequences, NM [Location identifier] [FAA] (FAAL)
TCS .... Tube Cooling Supply
TCS .... Turbine Control System [Nuclear energy] (NRCH)
TCS .... Two-Photon Coherent States (MCD)
TCSA .... Tetrachlorosalicylanilide [Organic chemistry]
TCSC .... Time-Critical Shipment Committee [Washington, DC] (EA)
TCSC .... Trainer Control and Simulation Computer

TCSCLC..... Two-Carrier Space-Charge-Limited Current
TCSD .... Telemetry and Communications Systems Division [*Apollo*] [*NASA*]
T C Ser Soil Conserv Auth VIC ... T C Series. Soil Conservation Authority. Victoria [*A publication*]
T C Ser Soil Conserv Auth Vict ... T C Series. Soil Conservation Authority. Victoria [*A publication*]
TCSL.......... Tri-County Savings & Loan Association [*NASDAQ symbol*]   (NQ)
TCSM......... Transactions. Colonial Society of Massachusetts [*A publication*]
TCSMC ...... Transportation Corps Supply Maintenance Command [*Army*]
TCSP.......... Tactical Communications Satellite Program [*DoD*]   (MCD)
TCSP.......... Tandem Cross-Section Program [*Bell System*]
TCSP.......... Test Checkout Support Plan   (KSC)
TCSPr .... Second Presbyterian Church Library, Chattanooga, TN [*Library symbol*] [*Library of Congress*]   (LCLS)
TCSq.......... Troop Carrier Squadron [*Air Force*]   (AFM)
TCSR.......... Tri-Comp Sensors [*NASDAQ symbol*]   (NQ)
TCSR.......... Typographic Council for Spelling Reform   (EA)
TCSS.......... Tactical Control Surveillance System
TCSS.......... Tri-Cone Support Structure [*NASA*]
TCSSS .... Thermal Control Subsystem Segment [*NASA*]   (NASA)
TCST.......... Chattanooga State Technical Community College, Chattanooga, TN [*Library symbol*] [*Library of Congress*]   (LCLS)
TC STD ...... Type Classification - Standard   (MCD)
TCT .... Tactical Computer Terminal [*Army*]   (MCD)
TCT .... Takotna [*Alaska*] [*Airport symbol*]   (OAG)
TCT .... Takotna, AK [*Location identifier*] [*FAA*]   (FAAL)
T Ct .... Tax Court of the United States, Reports   (DLA)
TCT .... Telemetry-Computer Translator [*Bell Laboratories*]
TCT .... Tennessee Temple Schools, Chattanooga, TN [*Library symbol*] [*Library of Congress*]   (LCLS)
TCT .... Tennessee Temple University, Chattanooga, TN [*OCLC symbol*]   (OCLC)
TCT .... Terracotta Tile [*Classified advertising*]   (ADA)
TCT .... Texas City Terminal Railway Co. [*AAR code*]
TCT .... Thyrocalcitonin [*Also, CT, TCA*] [*Endocrinology*]
TCT .... Time Code Translator
TCT .... Tin Can Tourists of the World   (EA)
TCT .... Toll Connecting Trunk [*Telecommunications*]   (TEL)
TCT .... Tool Change Time
TCT .... Total Composite Tolerance
TCT .... Traffic Control Transponder
TCT .... Translator and Code Treatment Frame   (IEEE)
TCT .... Tricentrol Ltd. [*NYSE symbol*] [*Toronto Stock Exchange symbol*]
TCT .... True Centerline Tested
TCT .... Two-Component TOKAMAK
TCTA......... Teaching Certificate for Teachers of Art [*British*]
T & CTB...... Thames and Chilterns Tourist Board [*British*]
TCTC .... Transportation Corps Technical Committee [*Army*]
TCTFE........ Trichlorotrifluoroethane [*Organic chemistry*]
TCTI .... Time Compliance Technical Instruction   (NASA)
TCTL .... Tactical   (AAG)
TCTL .... Tectel, Inc. [*NASDAQ symbol*]   (NQ)
TCTM .... Aircraft Time Compliance Technical Manuals
T Ct Mem ... Tax Court of the United States, Memorandum   (DLA)
TCTNB ...... Trichlorotrinitrobenzene [*Organic chemistry*]
TCTO .... Time Compliance Technical Order   (AAG)
TCTP......... Tetrachlorothiophene [*Organic chemistry*]
TCTS......... Tank Crew Turret Simulator   (MCD)
TCTS......... Trans-Canada Telephone System   (MCD)
TCTU......... Turkish Confederation of Trade Unions
TCTV......... Telemedia Communication Television [*Cable-television system*]
TCTV......... Today's Child, Tomorrow's Victim [*Book title*]
TCTVA .... Tennessee Valley Authority, Technical Library, Chattanooga, TN [*Library symbol*] [*Library of Congress*]   (LCLS)
TCTY......... Twin City Barge, Inc. [*NASDAQ symbol*]   (NQ)
TCU.......... Tactical Control Unit   (MCD)
TCU.......... Taichung [*Taityu*] [*Republic of China*] [*Seismograph station code, US Geological Survey*]   (SEIS)
TCU.......... Tape Control Unit
TCU.......... Tecumseh, MI [*Location identifier*] [*FAA*]   (FAAL)
TCU.......... Teletype Communications Unit   (NVT)
TCU.......... Teletypewriter Control Unit   (CET)
TCU.......... Temperature Control Unit
TCU.......... Tentative Clean Up   (MCD)
TCU.......... Terminal Cluster Unit
TCU.......... Terminal Control Unit   (MCD)
TCU.......... Test Computer Unit
TCU.......... Test of Concept Utilization [*Psychometrics*]
TCU.......... Test Control Unit
TCU.......... Texas Christian University
TCU.......... Thermal Control Unit
TCU.......... Threshold Control Unit   (CET)
TCU.......... Thrust Control Unit
TCU.......... Time Change Unit   (MCD)
TCU.......... Timing Control Unit

TCU............ Topping Control Unit   (AAG)
TCU............ Torpedo Control Unit
TCU............ Towering Cumulus [*Meteorology*]
TCU............ Transmission Control Unit
TCU............ Transportation-Communication Employees Union [*Later, BRAC*]
TCU............ Transportation, Communications, and Utilities
TCU............ Tri-College University Library Consortium [*Library network*]
TCU............ Turbine Control Unit
TCU............ University of Tennessee at Chattanooga, Chattanooga, TN [*Library symbol*] [*Library of Congress*]   (LCLS)
TCUA .... [*The*] Committee to Unite America   (EA)
TCUA .... Time-Critical, Unspecified Area
TCUCC...... Texas Christian University Computer Center [*Fort Worth, TX*] [*Research center*]   (RCD)
TCUL .... Tap Changing Under Load   (MSA)
TC(UN) ...... Trusteeship Council of the United Nations
TCUS .... Tax Court of the United States [*Also, TC*] [*Later, United States Tax Court*]
TCUSA ...... Trans Am Club USA   (EA)
TCV .... Tank Cleaning Vessel   (ADA)
TCV .... Temperature Coefficient of Voltage
TCV .... Temperature Control Valve   (AAG)
TCV .... Terminal-Configured Vehicle [*NASA*]
TCV .... Thoracic Cage Volume [*Medicine*]
TCV .... Thrust Chamber Valve   (MCD)
TCV .... Thrust Control Valve
TCV .... Total Containment Vessel   (CAAL)
TCV .... Tracked Combat Vehicle   (MCD)
TCV .... Troop Carrying Vehicle
TCV .... Turbine Control Valves [*Nuclear energy*]   (NRCH)
TCV .... Turnip Crinkle Virus
TCV .... Twentieth Century Views [*A publication*]
TCVA .... Terminal-Configured Vehicles and Avionics [*Program*] [*NASA*]
TCVC .... Tape Control via Console
TCVR........ Transceiver   (CET)
TCW.......... Time Code Word
TCW .... Tinned Copper Weld
TCW .... Tocumwal [*Australia*] [*Airport symbol*]   (OAG)
TCW .... Track Confirmation Word [*Data processing*]
TCW .... Triple-Crown Resources [*Vancouver Stock Exchange symbol*]
TCW .... Troop Carrier Wing [*Military*]   (CINC)
TCWA........ Transactions. Cumberland and Westmorland Antiquarian and Archaeological Society [*A publication*]
TCWC .... Texas Cooperative Wildlife Collections [*Texas A & M University*] [*Research center*]   (RCD)
TCWG .... Telecommunication Working Group
TCWg........ Troop Carrier Wing [*Air Force*]   (AFM)
T-CW & IB ... Trans-Continental Weighing and Inspection Bureau
TCWSA ..... T'ai-Wan Huan Ching Wei Sheng [*A publication*]
TCX .... Transfer of Control Cancellation Message [*Aviation*]
TCXO .... Temperature-Compensated Crystal Oscillator
TCYC .... Tropical Cyclone   (FAAC)
TCZD......... Temperature-Compensated Zener Diode
TD.............. Area Training Director [*Red Cross*]
TD.............. Chad [*Two-letter standard code*]   (CNC)
Td.............. T-Cell, Delayed Type [*Immunology*]
TD.............. Table of Distribution [*Military*]
TD.............. Tabular Data   (BUR)
TD.............. Tactical Division [*Air Force*]
TD.............. Tank Destroyer [*Military*]
TD.............. Tank Division   (MCD)
TD.............. Tape Degausser
TD.............. Tardive Dyskinesia [*Medicine*]
TD.............. Target Designator   (MCD)
TD.............. Target Discrimination
TD.............. Target Drone
TD.............. Task Description   (AAG)
TD.............. Task Directive   (AAG)
TD.............. Teacher's Diploma [*British*]
TD.............. Teachta Dala [*Member of Parliament*] [*Ireland*]
TD.............. Technical Data
TD.............. Technical Demonstration   (AAG)
TD.............. Technical Design   (AAG)
TD.............. Technical Direction [*or Directive*]
TD.............. Technical Director [*Television*]
TD.............. Technical Division
TD.............. Technological Dependence
TD.............. Technology Document   (KSC)
TD.............. Telegraph Department
TD.............. Telemetry Data
TD.............. Telephone Department
TD.............. Telephone Directory
T/D............ Temperature Datum   (NG)
TD.............. Temperature Differential   (MSA)
TD.............. Temporarily Discontinued [*Fog signal*]
TD.............. Temporary Disability
TD.............. Temporary Duty
TD.............. Ter in Die [*Three Times a Day*] [*Pharmacy*]
TD.............. Terminal Device [*of a prosthesis*]
TD.............. Terminal Digit [*Telecommunications*]   (TEL)

TD...............	Terminal Display (BUR)
TD...............	Terminal Distributor (KSC)
T (for) D	Termination for Default (MCD)
TD...............	Territorial Decoration [*Military*] [*British*]
TD...............	Test Data
TD...............	Test Design Specification (IEEE)
TD...............	Test Directive (AAG)
TD...............	Test Director
TD...............	Test Distributor [*Telecommunications*] (TEL)
TD...............	Test Drawing (MCD)
TD...............	Testing and Development Division [*Coast Guard*]
TD...............	Testing Device (MSA)
TD...............	Tetanus and Diphtheria [*Toxoids*] [*Medicine*]
Td...............	Tetrahedral [*Molecular geometry*]
TD...............	Theatre Documentation [*A publication*]
TD...............	Theology Digest [*St. Mary's, KS*] [*A publication*]
TD...............	Theoretical Density (NRCH)
TD...............	Therapy [*or Treatment*] Discontinued [*Medicine*]
TD...............	Thermal Desorption [*from surfaces*]
TD...............	Thermodilution
TD...............	Third Defense [*Men's lacrosse position, until 1933*]
TD...............	Thor-Delta [*Satellite*]
TD...............	Thoracic Duct [*Anatomy*]
TD...............	Thoria Dispersed [*Nickel*]
TD...............	Threat Determination (MCD)
TD...............	Threshold Detection
TD...............	Threshold Dose [*Medicine*]
TD...............	Thymus Dependent [*Cells*] [*Hematology*]
TD...............	Tied
TD...............	Tilbury Docks (ROG)
TD...............	Tile Drain [*Technical drawings*]
TD...............	Time Delay
TD...............	Time of Departure
TD...............	Time Deposit [*Banking*]
TD...............	Time Difference
TD...............	Timed Disintegration [*Pharmacy*]
TD...............	Timing Device
TD...............	Tinned
TD...............	To Deliver [*Pipet calibration*]
TD...............	Tod [*Unit of weight*]
TD...............	Tolerance Detector
TD...............	Tons per Day
TD...............	Tool Design
TD...............	Tool Disposition
TD...............	Tool Drawing (MCD)
TD...............	Top Down
TD...............	Topographic Draftsman [*Navy*]
TD...............	Toronto Dominion Bank [*Toronto Stock Exchange symbol*] [*Vancouver Stock Exchange symbol*]
TD...............	Torpedo Dive Bomber Aircraft
T and D	[*Jayne*] Torvill and [*Christopher*] Dean [*British ice dancers*]
TD...............	Total Damage [*Meteorology*]
TD...............	Total Denier [*Textile technology*]
TD...............	Total Depth
TD...............	Total Disability [*Medicine*]
TD...............	Total Dose [*of radiation*]
TD...............	Touchdown [*Football*]
T/D.............	Touchdown [*NASA*] (NASA)
TD...............	Track Data
TD...............	Track Display
TD...............	Track Dog [*Dog show term*]
TD...............	Tractor-Drawn
TD...............	Trade Dispute (OICC)
TD...............	Tradesman [*Navy rating*] [*British*]
TD...............	TRADEVMAN [*Training Devices Man*] [*Navy rating*]
TD...............	Traffic Decisions [*Interstate Commerce Commission*]
TD...............	Traffic Department [*Scotland Yard*]
TD...............	Traffic Director
TD...............	Training Detachment
TD...............	Training Developments
TD...............	Training Device (MCD)
TD...............	Training of Documentalists
TD...............	Trajectory Diagram [*Army*] (MCD)
TD...............	Transfer Dolly [*Bottom-loading transfer cask*] [*Nuclear energy*] (NRCH)
TD...............	Transform Domain
TD...............	Transient Detector
T & D	Transmission and Distribution
TD...............	Transmit Data (IEEE)
T-D.............	Transmitter-Distributor
TD...............	Transportation Department
TD...............	Transportation and Docking (MCD)
TD...............	Transporte Aereo de Cargo SA [*Venezuela*] [*ICAO designator*] (FAAC)
T & D	Transposition and Docking [*NASA*] (KSC)
TD...............	Transverse Diameter [*Of heart*] [*Anatomy*]
TD...............	Transverse Direction
TD...............	Transverse Division [*Cytology*]
TD...............	Treasury Decision [*In references to rulings*]
TD...............	Treasury Department
TD...............	Treatment Day

T/D.............	Treatment Discontinued [*Medicine*]
TD...............	Trinidad and Tobago
TD...............	Tropical Depression [*Meteorology*]
TD...............	Tropical Deterioration Committee Reports [*of NDRC*] [*World War II*]
TD...............	Truck Driving Program [*Association of Independent Colleges and Schools specialization code*]
TD...............	True Depth [*Diamond drilling*]
TD...............	Trust Deed
TD...............	Tuberoinfundibular Dopaminergic [*Neurons*] [*Neurology*]
TD...............	Tunnel Diode
TD...............	Turbine Direct
TD...............	Turbine Drive [*or Driven*]
TD...............	Turntable Desk (DEN)
TD...............	Typographic Draftsman [*Navy*]
TD1.............	TRADEVMAN [*Training Devices Man*], First Class [*Navy rating*]
TD2.............	TRADEVMAN [*Training Devices Man*], Second Class [*Navy rating*]
TD3.............	TRADEVMAN [*Training Devices Man*], Third Class [*Navy rating*]
TDA...........	American Train Dispatchers Association
TDA...........	[*The*] Disposables Association
TDA...........	Table of Distribution and Allowances [*Military*] (AABC)
TDA...........	Table of Distribution-Augmentation [*Military*]
TDA...........	Tactical Development Agent [*Military*] (CAAL)
TDA...........	Target Docking Adapter [*NASA*] (KSC)
TDA...........	Tax Deferred Annuity
TDA...........	Taxpayer Delinquent Account [*IRS*]
TDA...........	Technical Directing Agency
TDA...........	Telecommunications Dealers Association [*Formerly, Telephone Retailers Association*] [*Cincinnati, OH*] (EA)
TDA...........	Telemetric Data Analyzer
TDA...........	Test Development Activity [*Army*]
TDA...........	Test Development Agent (CAAL)
TDA...........	Tetradecenyl Acetate [*Organic chemistry*]
TDA...........	Textile Distributors Association [*New York, NY*] (EA)
TDA...........	Thermal Depolarization Analysis
TDA...........	Thermodifferential Analysis
TDA...........	Time Delay Amplifier
TDA...........	Titanium Development Association [*Dayton, OH*] (EA)
TDA...........	Today (FAAC)
TDA...........	Toll Dial Assistance [*Telecommunications*] (TEL)
TDA...........	Toluenediamine [*Organic chemistry*]
TDA...........	Torpedo Danger Area (NVT)
TDA...........	Total Dissolved Arsenic
T & DA	Tracking and Data Acquisition (CET)
TDA...........	Tracking and Data Acquisition
TDA...........	Tracking Data Analysis
TDA...........	Training Development Advisors (MCD)
TDA...........	Transport Distribution Analysis
TDA...........	Transportation Development Agency [*British*]
TDA...........	Trigger Distribution Amplifier [*Aviation*] (FAAC)
TDA...........	Tuning Device Assembly
TDA...........	Tunnel-Diode Amplifier
TDA...........	Tyrosine-D-Arginine [*Biochemistry*]
TDAA	Airman Apprentice, TRADEVMAN [*Training Devices Man*], Striker [*Navy rating*]
TDA/AE	Tracking and Data Acquisition/Advanced Engineering
TDaB	William Jennings Bryan University, Dayton, TN [*Library symbol*] [*Library of Congress*] (LCLS)
TDA Bull....	Timber Development Association. Bulletin [*A publication*]
TDAC	Tropical Deterioration Administrative Committee [*of NDRC*] [*World War II*]
TDAE........	Tactics Development and Evaluation [*Military*] (MCD)
TDAE........	Test Design and Evaluation (MCD)
TDAFP.......	Turbine-Driven Auxiliary Feed Pump [*Nuclear energy*] (NRCH)
TDAFWP	Turbine-Driven Auxiliary Feedwater Pump [*Nuclear energy*] (NRCH)
TDAIR........	Taxpayer Delinquent Account Information Record [*IRS*]
TDAL..........	Tetradecenal [*Biochemistry*]
TDAMM.......	Training Device Acquisition Management Model (MCD)
TDAMTB ...	Tables of Distribution and Allowances Mobilization Troop Basis [*Army*] (AABC)
TDAN	Airman, TRADEVMAN [*Training Devices Man*], Striker [*Navy rating*]
TDANA	Time-Domain Automatic Network Analyzer [*National Bureau of Standards*]
TDARA	Threat Determination and Resource Allocation (MCD)
TDAS..........	Thermal Decomposition Analytical System [*For study of incineration*]
TDAS..........	Thermocouple Data Acquisition System
TDAS..........	Thickness Data Acquisition System [*Southwest Research Institute*]
TDAS..........	Tracking and Data Acquisition System
TDAS..........	Traffic Data Administration System [*Bell System*]
TDAS..........	Tunnel-Diode Amplifier System
TDAT........	Third National Corp. [*NASDAQ symbol*] (NQ)
TDAZA	Tautsaimnieciba Derigie Augi [*A publication*]
TDB	Technical Directive Board
TDB	Temporary Disability Benefits [*Insurance*]
TDB	Terminological Data Bank

TDB .... Terrestrial Dust Belt
TDB .... Test Documentation Booklet [*Navy*] (CAAL)
TDB .... Tetebedi [*Papua New Guinea*] [*Airport symbol*] (OAG)
TDB .... Top Drawing Breakdown (AAG)
TDB .... Total Disability Benefit (DLA)
TDB .... Toxicology Data Bank [*National Library of Medicine*] [*Bethesda, MD*] [*Information service*] (EISS)
TDB .... Toxicology Data Bank [*Database*] [*Department of Energy*] [*Oak Ridge, TN*] (EISS)
TDB .... Trade Development Bank [*International banking concern*]
TDB .... Trade and Development Board [*United Nations Conference on Trade and Development*]
TDB .... Turbine-Driven Blower
TdbE .... Tanna di-be Eliahu (BJA)
TDBP .... Tris(dibromopropyl) Phosphate [*Also, TDBPP, Tris, Tris-BP*] [*Flame retardant, mutagen*]
TDBPP .... Tris(dibromopropyl) Phosphate [*Also, TDBP, Tris, Tris-BP*] [*Flame retardant, mutagen*]
TDC .... Chief TRADEVMAN [*Training Devices Man*] [*Navy rating*]
TDC .... Dallas Christian College, Dallas, TX [*OCLC symbol*] (OCLC)
TDC .... [*The*] Developing Child [*A publication*]
TDC .... [*The*] Discovery Channel [*Television*]
TDC .... Tactical Data Converter
TDC .... Tactical Digital Computer (MCD)
TDC .... Tactical Document Copier (MCD)
TDC .... Taiwan Defense Command (MCD)
TDC .... Tank Destroyer Center [*Army*]
TDC .... Target Data Collection
TDC .... Tarif Douanier Commun [*Common Customs Tariff*]
TDC .... Taurodeoxycholate [*or Taurodeoxycholic*] Acid [*Biochemistry*]
TDC .... Technical Data Center [*Department of Labor*] [*Washington, DC*] [*Information service*] (EISS)
TDC .... Technical Development Center
TDC .... Technical Development Contractor
TDC .... Technical Directive Compliance (MCD)
TDC .... Technical Document Center
TDC .... Technical Document Change (MCD)
TDC .... TEFLON Dielectric Capacitor
TDC .... Teledyne Canada Ltd. [*Toronto Stock Exchange symbol*]
TDC .... Temperature Density Computer
TDC .... Temporary Detective Constable [*Scotland Yard*]
TDC .... Terminal Data Corporation [*Woodland Hills, CA*] [*Information service*] (EISS)
TDC .... Termination Design Change
TDC .... Test Director Console
TDC .... Thermal Diffusion Chamber
TDC .... Thermal Diffusion Coefficient (NRCH)
TDC .... Through Deck Cruisers [*British*]
TDC .... Time Data Card (AAG)
TDC .... Time Delay Closing
TDC .... Time Distribution Card (AAG)
TDC .... Time-Domain Coding
TDC .... Tooling Design Change
TDC .... Top Dead Center
TDC .... Torpedo Data Computer [*Navy*] (NVT)
TDC .... Total Design Concept [*Sarcastic reference to a completely coordinated wardrobe, decorating scheme, etc.*] [*Slang*]
TDC .... Total Distributed Control [*Data processing*]
TDC .... Track Data Central
TDC .... Training Device Center
T & DC ...... Training and Distribution Center [*Navy*]
TDC .... Transferable Development Credit
TDC .... Transportation Development Center [*Cambridge, MA*] [*Department of Transportation*] [*Formerly, NASA Electronic Research Center*]
TDC .... Transportation Development Centre [*Transport Canada*] [*Research center*] (RCD)
TDC .... Transportation Development Centre Library [*UTLAS symbol*]
TDC .... Treasury Department Circular (DLA)
TDC .... Trinidad [*Colorado*] [*Seismograph station code, US Geological Survey*] [*Closed*] (SEIS)
TDC .... Tube Deflection Coil
TDC .... Type Directors Club [*New York, NY*] (EA)
TDCC .... Tactical Data Communications Center
TDCC .... Transportation Data Coordinating Committee [*Later, TDCC - The Electronic Data Interchange Association*] [*Washington, DC*]
TDCE .... Technical Direction Contract Effort
TDCF .... Technical Directive Compliance Form (NVT)
TDCK .... Technisch Documentatie Centrum voor der Krijgsmacht [*Netherland Armed Services Technical Documentation and Information Center*] (MCD)
TDCM .... Master Chief TRADEVMAN [*Training Devices Man*] [*Navy rating*]
TDCM .... Transistor Driver Core Memory
TDCN .... Technical Data Change Notice (MCD)
TDCN .... Time Delay Compression Network
TDCO .... Test Director Console Operator [*Navy*] (CAAL)
TDCO .... Thermal Dilution Cardiac Output
TDCO .... Torpedo Data Computer Operator [*Navy*]
TDCR .... Technical Data Change Request [*NASA*] (KSC)

TDCR .... Technical Data Contract Requirement (MCD)
TDCR .... Test Deficiency Change Request [*Nuclear energy*] (NRCH)
TDCS .... Senior Chief TRADEVMAN [*Training Devices Man*] [*Navy rating*]
TDCS .... Tape Data Control Sheet [*Data processing*]
TDCS .... Target Detection-Conversion Sensor
TDCS .... Time-Division Circuit Switching [*Telecommunications*]
TDCS .... Traffic Data Collection System (MCD)
TDCSP .... Tactical Defense Communications Satellite Program (MCD)
TDCT .... Time-Domain Coding Technique
TDCT .... Tunnel-Diode Charge Transformer
TDCTL .... Tunnel-Diode Charge-Transformer Logic
TDCU .... Target Data Control Unit (AAG)
TDCU .... Target Designator Control Unit (MCD)
TDCU .... Threat Display Control Unit (MCD)
TDCU .... Tinned Copper
TDD .... Target Detecting Device
TDD .... Task Description Document (NASA)
TDD .... Teardown Deficiency (MCD)
TDD .... Technical Data Digest [*Air Force*]
TDD .... Technical Documents Division [*Naval Air Systems Command*]
TDD .... Telecommunications Device for the Deaf
TDD .... Telemetry Data Digitizer
TDD .... Telephone Device for the Deaf
TDD .... Test Definition Document
TDD .... Test Design Description (NRCH)
TDD .... Test Development Director
TDD .... Tetradecadiene [*Organic chemistry*]
TDD .... Thedford, NE [*Location identifier*] [*FAA*] (FAAL)
TDD .... Thoracic Duct Drainage [*Medicine*]
TDD .... Three D Departments, Inc. [*American Stock Exchange symbol*]
TDD .... Treasury Department Decision (AFIT)
TDD .... Trinidad [*Bolivia*] [*Airport symbol*] (OAG)
TDD .... Tuberculous Diseases Diploma [*British*]
TDDA .... Tetradecadienyl Acetate [*Biochemistry*]
TDDL .... Time-Division Data Link [*Radio*]
TDDM .... Time Division Digital Multiplexer (MCD)
TDDM .... Training Device Development Management [*Model*] (MCD)
TDDO .... Time Delay Dropout [*Relay*] (AAG)
TDDR .... Technical Data Department Report [*NASA*] (KSC)
TDDS .... Tactical Data Display System (MCD)
TDDS .... Teacher Development in Desegregating Schools [*Office of Education*]
TDDS .... Television Data Display System (KSC)
TDE .... Tactical Deception Element (NVT)
TDE .... Tactics Development Evaluation (MCD)
TDE .... Technical Data Engineer (MCD)
TDE .... Technical Data Evaluation
TDE .... Testing Difficulty Estimator
TDE .... Tetrachlorodiphenylethane [*Also, DDD*] [*Insecticide*]
TDE .... Toluene-Dioxane-Ethanol [*Scintillation solvent*]
TDE .... Total Data Entry
TDE .... Total Differential Equation
TDE .... Total Digestible Energy [*Nutrition*]
TDE .... Trans-Dominion Energy [*Toronto Stock Exchange symbol*]
TD & E ...... Transposition, Docking, and Ejection [*NASA*] (KSC)
TDE .... Triethylene Glycol Diglycidyl Ether [*Medicine*]
TDE .... Two-Dimensional Equilibrium
TDEC .... Technical Development Evaluation Center
TDEC .... Technical Division and Engineering Center [*FAA*] (MCD)
TDEC .... Telephone Line Digital Error Checking
TDECC .... Tactical Display Engagement Control Console [*Military*] (RDA)
TDED .... Istanbul Universitesi Edegiyat Fakultesi Turk Dili ve Edebiyati Dergisi [*A publication*]
TDEFWP .... Turbine-Driven Emergency Feedwater Pump [*Nuclear energy*] (NRCH)
TDEL .... Time Delay (FAAC)
TDEP .... Tracking Data Editing Program [*NASA*]
TDES .... [*The*] Duke Ellington Society (EA)
TDF .... Tactical Digital Facsimile (MCD)
TDF .... Tape Data Family
TDF .... Target Development Facility [*Proposed, 1986, for fusion research*]
TDF .... Task Deletion Form (NRCH)
TDF .... Telediffusion de France [*Broadcasting agency*] [*French*]
TDF .... Temporary Detention Facility
TDF .... Testis-Determining Factor [*Genetics*]
TDF .... Theatre Development Fund (EA)
TDF .... Thin Dielectric Film
TDF .... Time-Domain Filter
TDF .... Time Dose Fractionation Factor [*Roentgenology*]
TDF .... Transborder Data Flows [*Also, TBDF*] [*Telecommunications*]
TDF .... Trial-Dependent-Forgetting [*Process*] [*Psychology*]
TDF .... Trim and Drill Fixture (MCD)
TDF .... Trunk Distribution Frame (DEN)
TDF .... Two Degrees of Freedom
TDFCHB ..... Telemetry Data Format Control Handbook (KSC)
TDFS .... Terminal Digit Fitting System (AABC)
TDG .... Tactical Development Group [*Military*] (CAAL)
TDG .... Tactical Drone Group (MCD)

TD & G........ Tall, Dark, and Gruesome [*Slang*]
TDG............ Talladega, AL [*Location identifier*] [*FAA*]　(FAAL)
TDG............ Tandag [*Philippines*] [*Airport symbol*]　(OAG)
TDG............ Technical Design Guide
TDG............ Telemetry Data Generation
TDG............ Test Data Generator　(BUR)
TDG............ Test Display Generator
TDG............ Test Documentation Group
TDG............ Tetradecanylglutarate [*Biochemistry*]
TDG............ Textile Designers Guild [*New York, NY*]　(EA)
TDG............ Thiodigalactoside [*Organic chemistry*]
TDG............ Time Delay Generator
TDG............ Top-Down Greedy
TDG............ Trading
TDGS......... Twist Drill Gauge
TDGS .... Test Data Generation Section [*Social Security Administration*]
TD & H........ Tall, Dark, and Handsome [*Slang*]
TDH............ Terre des Hommes [*An international organization*]
TDH............ Total Dynamic Head [*Aerospace*]　(AAG)
TDH............ Tracking Data Handling
TDH............ Transport Disengaging Height [*Fluidized beds of particles*]
TDHGA....... Travel of Dependents and Household Goods Authorized　(AABC)
TDHL......... Transdihydrolisuride [*Biochemistry*]
TDHS......... Tape Data Handling System
TDHYA ...... Tohoku Daigaku Hisuiyoeki Kagaku Kenkyusho Hokoku [*A publication*]
TDI .... TACAN [*Tactical Air Navigation*] Distance Indicator
TDI .... Target Data Inventory　(AFM)
TDI .... Target Doppler Indicator [*RADAR*]
TDI .... Task Description Item　(MCD)
TDI .... Taxpayer Delinquent Investigation [*IRS*]
TDI .... Teardown Inspection
TDI .... Telecommunications Data Interface
TDI .... Telecommunications for the Deaf, Incorporated [*Silver Spring, MD*]　(EA)
TDI .... Teletec Development, Incorporated [*Vancouver Stock Exchange symbol*]
TDI .... Temporary Disability Insurance [*Unemployment*]
TDI .... Test Data Interpolation
TDI .... Textile Dye Institute [*Later, American Dye Manufacturers Institute*]
TDI .... Therapy Dogs International [*Hillside, NJ*]　(EA)
TDI .... Time Delay and Integration　(MCD)
TDI .... Toluene [*or Tolylene*] Diisocyanate [*Organic chemistry*]
TDI .... Tool and Die Institute　(KSC)
T & DI .... Tool and Die Institute　(EA)
TDI .... Total Domestic Incomes [*Department of Employment*] [*British*]
TDI .... Training Developments Institute [*Army*]
TDI .... TSH [*Thyroid-Stimulating Hormone*] Displacing Immunoglobulin [*Endocrinology*]
TDI .... Turbine Disk Integrity [*Nuclear energy*]　(NRCH)
TDI .... Twin Disc, Inc. [*NYSE symbol*]
TDI .... Tymnet DTS, Incorporated [*San Jose, CA*] [*Telecommunications*]　(TSSD)
TDIC.......... Target Data Input Computer
TDIC.......... Total Dissolved Inorganic Carbon [*Environmental chemistry*]
TDIL.......... Target Detection, Identification, and Location
TDINF........ Taxpayer Delinquency Investigation Notice File [*IRS*]
TDIO.......... Timing Data Input-Output
TDIP .... Total Disability Income Provisions [*Military*]　(AABC)
TDIPR........ Test Design In-Process Review　(MCD)
TDIS .... Technical Data Impact Summary　(MCD)
TDIS .... Terminal Data Input System　(MCD)
TDIS .... Thai Development Information Service　(EA-IO)
TDIS .... Time Distance [*Military*]　(AABC)
TDIS .... Training Development Information System [*Army*]
TDIS .... Travel Document and Issuance System [*US passport*] [*Department of State*]
TDISTR ...... Tape Distributor　(MSA)
TDIU.......... Target Data Input Unit
TDJ............ Dallas County Community College District, Dallas, TX [*OCLC symbol*]　(OCLC)
TDJ............ Tadjoura [*Djibouti*] [*Airport symbol*]　(OAG)
TDJ............ Tadjoura [*Djibouti*] [*Seismograph station code, US Geological Survey*]　(SEIS)
TDJKA....... Tokyo Daigaku Jishin Kenkyusho Iho [*A publication*]
TDK .... TDK Corp. [*NYSE symbol*]
TDK .... Tokyo Denki Kagaku [*Tokyo Electronics and Chemical Co.*] [*Initialism is now name of recording tape manufacturer and brand name of its products*]
TDK .... Toyo Daigaku Kiyo [*Bulletin. Department of Liberal Arts. Tokyo University*] [*A publication*]
TDKIB .... Tokai Daigaku Kiyo Kogakubu [*A publication*]
TDKP......... Turkish Revolutionary Communist Party　(PD)
TDL .... David Lipscomb College, Nashville, TN [*OCLC symbol*]　(OCLC)
TDL .... Tactical Data Link
TDL .... Tandil [*Argentina*] [*Airport symbol*]　(OAG)
TDL .... Tapped Delay Line
TDL .... Target Development Laboratory [*Eglin AFB*]　(AAG)
TDL .... Task-Directed Learning

TDL .... Technical Data Laboratory [*National Weather Service*]
TDL .... Technical Document List
TDL .... Test Description Log　(MCD)
TDL .... Test and Diagnostic Language　(MCD)
TDL .... Thoracic Duct Lymphocyte [*Immunochemistry*]
TDL .... Threshold Damage Level
TDL .... Threshold Detection Level
TDL .... Thymus-Dependent Lymphocyte [*Hematology*]
TDL .... Transaction Definition Language
TDL .... Transformation Definition Language [*Data processing*]　(IBMDP)
TDL .... Translation Definition Language
TDL .... Tunable Diode LASER [*Also, SDL*]
TDL .... Tunnel-Diode Logic
TDLAS ...... Tunable Diode LASER Absorption Spectrometry
TDLCA ...... Thoracic Duct Lining Cells Antigen [*Immunology*]
TDLOA ...... Training Device Letter of Agreement
TDLR........ Terminal Descent and Landing RADAR
TDLR........ Training Device Letter Requirement
TDLS .... Topographic Data Library System
TDLU .... Terminal Duct Lobular Unit [*Of mammary gland*]
TDM .... Mount Alvernia Friary, Wappingers Falls, NY [*OCLC symbol*] [*Inactive*]　(OCLC)
TDM .... Tandem
TDM .... Tandem Resources [*Vancouver Stock Exchange symbol*]
TDM .... Tank Destroyer Armed with Missiles　(INF)
TDM .... Task Description Memo　(MCD)
TDM .... Technical Division Manager
TDM .... Telecommunications Data-Link Monitor　(CET)
TDM .... Telemetric Data Monitor
TDM .... Template Descriptor Memory
TDM .... Ternary Delta Modulation
TDM .... Test Data Memorandum　(AAG)
TDM .... Test Development Manager [*Military*]　(CAAL)
TDM .... Therapeutic Drug Monitoring
TDM .... Thermal Diffusion Method
TDM .... Thermodynamic Molding
TDM .... Time-Division Multiplexing [*Communications*]
TDM .... Time Duration Modulation　(DEN)
TDM .... Tire Degradation Monitor　(MCD)
TDM .... Tool Design Manual　(MCD)
TDM .... Torpedo Detection Modification [*SONAR*]
TDM .... Total Dissolvable Manganese [*Chemistry*]
TDM .... Trehalose Dimycolate [*Biochemistry*]
TDM .... Trouble Detection and Monitoring
TDM .... Tunnel-Diode Mixer
TDMA .... Tape Direct Memory Access
TDMA .... Time-Division [*or Time-Domain*] Multiple Access [*Computer control system*]
TDMA .... Trophy Dealers and Manufacturers Association [*Formed by a merger of Trophy Dealers of America and AAMA*] [*Fresno, CA*]　(EA)
TDMAC ...... Tridodecylmethylammonium Chloride [*Organic chemistry*]
TDMC........ Technical Data Management Center [*Department of Energy*] [*Oak Ridge, TN*] [*Information service*]　(EISS)
TDMD........ Time-Division Multiplex Device [*Radio*]
TDME .... Test, Diagnostic, and Measurement Equipment　(MCD)
TDMG........ Telegraph and Data Message Generator　(MCD)
TDMM ...... International Union of Tool, Die, and Mold Makers
TDMO........ Technical Data Management Office [*Navy*]
TDMOD...... Therapeutic Drug Monitoring [*A publication*]
TDMP .... Technical Data Management Program [*Navy*]
TDMR........ Technical Division Memo Report [*Army*] [*World War II*]
TDMRA ...... Texas Delaine-Merino Record Association [*Later, TDSA*]　(EA)
TDMS .... Telegraph Distortion Measuring System
TDMS .... Telemetry Data Monitor Set
TDMS .... Time-Division Multiplex System [*Radio*]　(MCD)
TDMS .... Time-Shared/Data Management System
TDMS .... Transmission Distortion Measuring Set
TDMTB...... Tables of Distribution Mobilization Troop Basis [*Army*]　(AABC)
TDM-VDMA ... Time-Division Multiplex - Variable Destination Multiple Access [*Telecommunications*]　(TEL)
TDN............ Target Doppler Nullifier [*RADAR*]
TDN............ Total Digestible Nutrients
TDN............ Touchdown [*Aviation*]　(FAAC)
TDN............ Travel as Directed Is Necessary in the Military Service　(MUGU)
TDNCA ...... Texas Date Nail Collectors Association　(EA)
TDNLA ...... Trudy Universiteta Druzhby Narodov [*A publication*]
TDNS........ Total Data Network System
TDNT......... Theological Dictionary of the New Testament [*A publication*]　(BJA)
TDO............ Technical Development Objective
TDO............ Technical Directives Ordnance　(NG)
TDO............ Technical Divisions Office [*Jet Propulsion Laboratory, NASA*]
TDO............ Telegraph Delivery Order
TDO............ Time Delay Opening
TDO............ Toledo, WA [*Location identifier*] [*FAA*]　(FAAL)
TDO............ Tornado
TDO............ Training Development Office [*Army*]
TDO............ Training Development Officer [*British*]
TDO............ Treasury Department Order　(DLA)

TDO............ Tuesday Downtown Operators and Observers [*An association*] (EA)
TDOA .... Time Delay of Arrival (MCD)
TDOA .... Time Deposit, Open Account
TDOA/DD .. Time Difference of Arrival and Differential Doppler (MCD)
TDOD .... Training and Development Organizations Directory [*A publication*]
TDOL........ Tetradecanol [*Organic chemistry*]
TDOP......... Truck Design Optimization Project [*Railroads*]
TDOS......... Tape Disk Operating System [*Data processing*]
TDOT........ Thorndike Dimensions of Temperament [*Psychology*]
TDP .... Tank Development Program [*Military*]
TDP .... Target Data Processor (NVT)
TDP .... Target Director Post [*RADAR*]
TDP .... Technical Data Package
TDP .... Technical Development Plan
TDP .... Technical Documentation for Provisioning [*Military*] (AFIT)
TDP .... Teledata Processing
TDP .... Temperature Density Plotter
TDP .... Temperature and Dew Point (KSC)
TDP .... Temporary Detention of Pay
TDP .... Test Design Plan [*Army*]
TDP .... Thermal Death-Point
TDP .... Thermistor Detector Package
TDP .... Thiamine Diphosphate [*Also, DPT, TPP*] [*Biochemistry*]
TDP .... Thiodiphenol [*Organic chemistry*]
TDP .... Thymidine Diphosphate [*Biochemistry*]
TDP .... Total Development Plan
TDP .... Touchdown Protection [*Military*] (MCD)
TDP .... Tracking Data Processor
TDP .... Tracking and Display Processor (CAAL)
TDP .... Trade and Development Program [*US International Development Cooperation Agency*]
TDP .... Traffic Data Processing
TDP .... Traffic Demand Predictor [*Aviation*]
TDP .... Trainee Discharge Program [*Army*]
TDP .... Trim and Drain Pump [*Navy*] (CAAL)
TDPA .... Textile Data Processing Association [*Later, ATMI*] (EA)
TDPA .... Thiodipropionic Acid [*Organic chemistry*]
TDPAC ...... Time Differential Perturbed Angular Correlation [*Physics*]
TDPB......... Tactical Display Plotting Board
TDPF......... Tail Damping Power Factor [*Aviation*]
TDPFO........ Temporary Duty Pending Further Orders [*Military*]
TDPJ .... Truck Discharge Point Jet (NATG)
TDPL .... Technical Data Package List (AABC)
TDPL .... Top-Down Parsing Language
TDPM........ Truck Discharge Point Mogas (NATG)
TDPP......... Traffic Data Processing Program (MCD)
TDPRha...... Thymidine Diphosphorhamnose [*Biochemistry*]
TDPS......... Tracking Data Processor System (MCD)
TDPSK ...... Time Differential Phase-Shift Keying
TDPU......... Telemetry Data Processing Unit (CAAL)
TDQP......... Trimethyldihydroquinoline Polymer [*Organic chemistry*]
TDR .... Drama Review [*Formerly, Tulane Drama Review*] [*A publication*]
TDR .... Tail Damping Ratio [*Aviation*]
TDR .... Talos Discrepancy Report (MCD)
TDR .... Tape Data Register
TDR .... Target Detection and Recognition (MCD)
TDR .... Target Discrimination RADAR (IEEE)
TDR .... Teardown Deficiency Report
TDR .... Technical Data Relay (IEEE)
TDR .... Technical Data Report
TDR .... Technical Data Requests
TDR .... Technical Deficiency Report
TDR .... Technical Design Review (NASA)
TDR .... Technical Development Requirement
TDR .... Technical Directive Records (NG)
TDR .... Technical Documentary Report
TDR .... Temperature Depth Recorder
TDR .... Temporarily Disconnected at Subscriber's Request [*Telecommunications*] (TEL)
TDR .... Tender [*Navy*] (NVT)
TDR .... Terminal Digit Requested [*Telecommunications*] (TEL)
TDR .... Test Data Recorder
TDR .... Test Data Report (AAG)
TDR .... Test Deficiency Report [*Nuclear energy*] (NRCH)
TD/R .... Test Disable/Reset (AAG)
TDR .... Test Discrepancy Report (MCD)
TDR .... Thailand Development Report [*Bangkok*] [*A publication*]
TDR .... Threat Detection RADAR [*Military*] (CAAL)
TDR .... Time Delay Relay
TDR .... Time-Domain Reflectometry
TDR .... Todoroki [*Japan*] [*Seismograph station code, US Geological Survey*] [*Closed*] (SEIS)
TDR .... Tone Dial Receiver
TDR .... Tool Design Request (KSC)
TDR .... Torque-Differential Receiver (MUGU)
TDR .... Track Data Request (CAAL)
TDR .... Tracking and Data Relay [*NASA*]

TDR .... Training Device Requirement [*Army*] (AABC)
TDR .... Transferable Development Rights [*Community planning*]
TDR .... Transistorized Digital Readout
TDR .... Transmit Data Register [*Data processing*] (MDG)
TDR .... Transnational Data and Communicative Report [*A publication*] (TSSD)
TDR .... Trap Designator Register
TDR .... Treasury Deposit Receipt
TDR .... Tropical Disease Research [*WHO*]
TDR .... Tudor Corp. Ltd. [*Toronto Stock Exchange symbol*]
TDRC .... Total Diet Research Center [*Public Health Service*]
TDRE......... Tracking and Data Relay Experiment [*Telecommunications*] (TEL)
TDRF......... Target Doppler Reference Frequency
TDRL .... Temporary Disability Retired List [*Military*]
T/DRLY...... Time Delay Relay
TDRM........ Time-Domain Reflectometry Microcomputer
TDRRB........ Technical Data Requirement Review Board
TDRRC ...... Training Device Requirements Review Committee [*Army*]
TDRS......... Telemetering Data Recording Set (CAAL)
TDRS......... Tracking and Data Relay Satellite [*NASA*]
TDRS......... Traffic Data Recording System [*Bell System*]
TDRS......... Transnational Data Reporting Service, Inc. [*Springfield, VA*] [*Telecommunications service*] (TSSD)
TDRSS ...... Tracking and Data Relay Satellite System [*NASA*]
TDRTC ...... Tank Destroyer Replacement Training Center
TDS............ Tactical Data System
TDS............ Tactical Display System (CAAL)
TDS............ Tape Data Selector
TDS............ Tape Decal System
TDS............ Target Data Sheet (MCD)
TDS............ Target Designation System [*Navy*]
TDS............ Technical Data System (KSC)
TDS............ Technical Database Services, Inc. [*New York, NY*] [*Information service*] (EISS)
TDS............ Technical Directive System (MCD)
TDS............ Technology Demonstration Satellite [*NASA*] (NASA)
TDS............ Teleflora Delivery Service (EA)
TDS............ Telemetry Decommutation System
TDS............ Telephone & Data Systems, Inc. [*American Stock Exchange symbol*]
TDS............ Temperature-Depth-Salinity [*Oceanography*]
TDS............ Temporary Duty Station [*Air Force*] (AFM)
TDS............ Ter in Die Sumendum [*To Be Taken Three Times a Day*] [*Pharmacy*]
TDS............ Test Data Sheet (KSC)
TDS............ Test Data System (NASA)
TDS............ Thermal Degradation Sample [*Apollo*]
TDS............ Thermal Desorption Spectroscopy
TDS............ Time Delay Switch
TDS............ Time, Distance, Speed
TDS............ Time Distribution System (MCD)
TDS............ Time-Division Switching [*Telecommunications*]
TDS............ Time-Domain Spectroscopy (IEEE)
TDS............ Tool Data Sheet (MCD)
TDS............ Tool Design Service (MCD)
TDS............ Tool Design Study (MCD)
TDS............ Torpedo Destruction System
TDS............ Total Dissolved Solids
TDS............ Track Data Simulator
TDS............ Track Data Storage
TDS............ Tracking and Data System [*NASA*]
T & DS........ Tracking and Data System [*NASA*]
TDS............ Training Developments Study
TDS............ Training Directors Seminar [*LIMRA*]
TDS............ [*Annual*] Training Duty Status [*Navy Reserve*]
TDS............ Transaction Distribution System
TDS............ Transaction Driven System [*Honeywell, Inc.*]
TDS............ Transistor Display and Data-Handling System [*Data processing*] (MDG)
TDS............ Translation and Docking Simulator [*Navy*] (KSC)
TDS............ Trap Designator Set
TDS............ Trash Disposal System
TDS............ Traverse des Sioux Library System, Mankato MN [*OCLC symbol*] (OCLC)
TDS............ [*US*] Treasury Daily Statement
TDS............ Trusco Data Systems [*Atlanta, GA*] [*Software manufacturer*]
TDS............ Tunnel Destruct System
TDSA......... Technical Data Status Accounting (MCD)
TDSA......... Telegraph and Data Signals Analyzer (MCD)
TD & SA...... Telephone, Data, and Special Audio (NASA)
TDSA......... TRADEVMAN [*Training Devices Man*], Seaman Apprentice [*Navy rating*]
TDSC .... Tesdata Systems Corporation [*NASDAQ symbol*] (NQ)
TDSCC........ Tidbinbilla Deep Space Communications Complex
TDSDT ...... Tactical Data System Development Testbed
TDSIC .... Theatre/Drama, and Speech Information Center (EISS)
TDSKB ...... Reports. Research Institute for Strength and Fracture of Materials. Tohoku University [*A publication*]

TDSMO	Tactical Data Systems Management Office [*Army*] [*Fort Leavenworth*] (MCD)
TDSN..........	TRADEVMAN [*Training Devices Man*], Seaman [*Navy rating*]
TDSQB.......	Time Delay Squib [*Navy*]
TDST..........	Track Data Storage (MSA)
TDT	Tactical Data Terminal (MCD)
TDT	Target Designation Transmitter
TDT	Target Docking Trainer [*NASA*] (KSC)
TDT	Tavil-Dara [*USSR*] [*Seismograph station code, US Geological Survey*] [*Closed*] (SEIS)
TDT	Terminal Deoxynucleotidyl Transferase [*An enzyme*]
TDT	Test Direction Team
TDT	Test Dwell Time
TDT	Thermal Death Time [*Bacteriological testing*]
TDT	Thiodiethanethiol [*Organic chemistry*]
TDT	This Day Tonight (ADA)
TDT	Tidioute, PA [*Location identifier*] [*FAA*] (FAAL)
TDT	Tone Decay Test [*Audiometry*]
TDT	Toronto Dance Theatre
TDT	Translation and Docking Trainer
TDT	Transonic Dynamic Tunnel [*NASA*]
TDT	Tunnel-Diode Transducer
TDT and CU ...	Target Designation Transmitter and Control Unit
TDT/FC......	Tank Destroyer Tactical and Firing Center
TDTG..........	True Date-Time Group
TDTL..........	Tunnel-Diode Transistor Logic
TDTS.........	Tactical Data Transfer System (NATG)
TDU	Tactical Deception Unit (NVT)
TDU	Tactical Display Unit (NVT)
TDU	Target Detection Unit
TDU	Teamsters for a Democratic Union (EA)
TDU	Threat Display Unit (MCD)
TDU	Time Display Unit (NASA)
TDU	Tondu [*British depot code*]
TDU	Towed Unit [*Aerial Target*] (CAAL)
TDU	Tracking Display Unit
TDU	Trigger Delay Unit
TDU	Tropendienstunfaehig [*Unfit for service in tropics*] [*German military - World War II*]
TDUKA.......	Tokyo Daigaku Uchu Koku Kenkyusho Hokoku [*A publication*]
TDUM........	Tape Dump and Utility Monitor [*Data processing*]
TDUP.........	Technical Data Usage Program
TDV	Technology Development Vehicle (IEEE)
TDV	Terminal Delivered Vehicle [*Army*]
TDV	Touchdown Velocity [*Aviation*]
TDV	Tumbleweed Diagnostic Vehicle
TDVA.........	37th Division Veterans Association (EA)
TDW	Amarillo, TX [*Location identifier*] [*FAA*] (FAAL)
TDW	Tidewater, Inc. [*NYSE symbol*]
TDW	Tons Deadweight
TDW	Trunk Destination Words (CET)
TDWO........	Test and Development Work Order
TDWT	Transonic Dynamic Wind Tunnel [*NASA*] (KSC)
TDWU	Transport and Dock Workers' Union [*India*]
TDX	Thermal Demand Transmitter (MSA)
TDX	Time-Division Exchange
TDX	Timken-Detroit Axle [*Later, TKR*] [*NYSE symbol*]
TDX	Torque-Differential Transmitter (MUGU)
TDX	Tridex Corp. [*American Stock Exchange symbol*]
TDY	Teledyne, Inc. [*NYSE symbol*]
TDY	Temporary Duty
TDY	Trading Bay, AK [*Location identifier*] [*FAA*] (FAAL)
TDYKA	Tokushima Daigaku Yakugaku Kenkyu Nempo [*A publication*]
TDYN........	Thermodynetics, Inc. [*NASDAQ symbol*] (NQ)
TDZ	Thioridazine [*Tranquilizer*]
TDZ	Toledo, OH [*Location identifier*] [*FAA*] (FAAL)
TDZ	Torpedo Danger Zone (NVT)
TDZ	Touchdown Zone [*Aviation*] (FAAC)
TDZ	Tridel Enterprises [*Toronto Stock Exchange symbol*]
TDZL	Touchdown Zone Lights [*Aviation*] (FAAC)
TE..............	Air New Zealand [*International*] [*New Zealand*] [*ICAO designator*] (FAAC)
TE..............	Journal of Transportation Engineering [*A publication*]
TE..............	Light Temporarily Extinguished [*Navigation*]
TE..............	Table of Equipment [*Army*]
T/E	Tactical Emergency [*Army*]
TE..............	Tageseinfluesse [*Weather factors, a gunnery term*] [*German military - World War II*]
TE..............	Talmudic Encyclopedia [*A publication*] (BJA)
TE..............	Tamper Evident
TE..............	Tangent Elevation (MSA)
TE..............	Task Element
TE..............	Teacher Education [*A publication*]
TE..............	Teacher of Electrotherapy [*British*]
Te..............	Teatr [*Moscow*] [*A publication*]
TE..............	Technical Engineer
TE..............	Technical Exchange
TE..............	Technician [*Communications*] [*Navy rating*]
TE..............	Technological Engineer [*A publication*]
TE..............	TECO Energy, Inc. [*NYSE symbol*]

TE..............	Telecom Eireann [*Dublin, Ireland*] [*Telecommunications service*] (TSSD)
TE..............	Telegram
TE..............	Teleman [*Navy rating*] [*British*]
TE..............	Teller of the Exchequer [*British*] (ROG)
Te	Tellurium [*Chemical element*]
TE..............	Temperature Element [*Nuclear energy*] (NRCH)
Te	Tempo [*A publication*]
TE..............	Tenants by the Entirety [*Real estate*]
TE..............	Tension Equalizer [*Electrical*] Wave
TE..............	Teologia Espiritual [*A publication*]
TE..............	Terminal Equipment
TE..............	Terminal Exchange (MCD)
TE..............	Tertiary Entrance (ADA)
TE..............	Test and Engineering (MCD)
TE..............	Test Equipment
T & E..........	Test and Evaluation [*Navy*] (NG)
TE..............	Test Exception [*Nuclear energy*] (NRCH)
TE..............	Test Explicit
TE..............	Tetlit Tribune [*Fort McPherson*] [*A publication*]
TE..............	Tetracycline [*Also, TC, Tet*] [*Antibiotic compound*]
TE..............	Text Editor [*Data processing*]
TE..............	Theatre in Education (EA)
TE..............	Theistic Evolutionist
TE..............	Theological Educator [*A publication*]
TE..............	Theological Examination
TE..............	Thermactor Emission [*Automotive engineering*]
TE..............	Thermal Efficiency
TE..............	Thermal Element (KSC)
TE..............	Thermal Expansion Load (NRCH)
TE..............	Thermoelectric
TE..............	Threat Evaluation (NVT)
TE..............	Thromboembolic [*Medicine*]
TE..............	Throughput Efficiency (CAAL)
TE..............	Thunder Engines Corp. [*Vancouver Stock Exchange symbol*]
TE..............	Tiger's Eye [*A publication*]
TE..............	Tight End [*Football*]
Te	Tigre (BJA)
TE..............	Time to Echo [*Medicine*]
TE..............	Time Error in Psychophysical Judgments [*Psychology*]
T & E..........	Time and Events (AAG)
T/E	Time Expired (ADA)
TE..............	Timing Electronics (KSC)
TE..............	Tocopherol Equivalent [*Nutrition*]
TE..............	Today's Education [*A publication*]
TE..............	Toluene-Ethanol [*Scintillation solvent*]
TE..............	Topographical Engineer
TE..............	Tornisterempfaenger [*Pack-type portable receiver*] [*German military - World War II*]
TE..............	Total Expenditure
TE..............	Totally Enclosed (MSA)
TE..............	Tracheoesophageal [*Also, TOE*] [*Medicine*]
TE..............	Tracking Enhancement (MCD)
TE..............	Traction Engine [*British*]
TE..............	Trade Expenses [*Business and trade*]
TE..............	Trailing Edge
T & E..........	Training and Education
TE..............	Training Equipment
TE..............	Training and Evaluation (OICC)
TE..............	Trajectory Engineer
TE..............	Transequatorial [*Scatter*]
TE..............	Transient Eddy
TE..............	Transient Event [*Nuclear energy*] (NRCH)
TE..............	Transitional Engineering (MCD)
TE..............	Transport Empty
T/E	Transporter-Erector [*NASA*] (KSC)
TE..............	Transposable Element [*Genetics*]
TE..............	Transverse Electric [*or Electrostatic*] [*Wave propagation mode*]
TE..............	Travaux. Musee d'Etat de l'Ermitage [*A publication*]
T & E..........	Travel and Entertainment [*Internal Revenue*]
TE..............	Trial and Error
TE..............	Tuning Eye
TE..............	Turbine Electric Drive
TE..............	Twin Engine
TE..............	Type Equipment (MCD)
TE2.............	That's Entertainment, Part 2 [*Initialism is shortened form of movie title*]
TEA	Task Equipment Analysis
Tea	Tea Boards of Kenya, Uganda, and Tanganyika. Journal [*A publication*]
TEA	Technical Engineers Association (EA)
TEA	Technical Exchange Agreement
TEA	Tegra Ent Inc. [*Vancouver Stock Exchange symbol*]
TEA	Temporary Employment Assistance
TEA	Test Equipment Accessory (MCD)
TEA	Test Equipment Analysis
TEA	Test and Evaluation Agency
TEA	Tetraethylammonium [*Organic chemistry*]
TEA	Textile Export Association of the US (EA)
TEA	Thai Exiles Association (CINC)

TEA .... Theatre Equipment Association [*Formed by a merger of TEDA and TESMA*] [*New York, NY*] (EA)
TEA .... Thermal Energy Analysis [*or Analyzer*]
TEA .... Thiazoylethylamine [*Organic chemistry*]
TEA .... Tiselius Electrophoresis Apparatus
TEA .... Titanic Enthusiasts of America [*Later, THS*] (EA)
TEA .... Trade Expansion Act [*1962*]
TEA .... Training Effectiveness Analysis
TEA .... Transferred Electron Amplifier
TEA .... Transversely Excited Atmospheric [*LASER*] (RDA)
TEA .... Treasury Enforcement Agent
TEA .... Triethanolamine [*Organic chemistry*]
TEA .... Triethylaluminum [*Organic chemistry*]
TEA .... Triethylamine [*Organic chemistry*]
TEA .... Triethylammonium [*Organic chemistry*]
TEA .... Tunnel-Emission Amplifier (IEEE)
TEAAC ...... Trade Expansion Act Advisory Committee [*Inactive*] (EGAO)
TEAB .... Tetraethylammonium Bromide [*Organic chemistry*]
TEAC .... Test and Evaluation Advisory Council [*Military*] (CAAL)
TEAC .... Tetraethylammonium Chloride [*Organic chemistry*]
TEAC .... Tokyo Electro Acoustical Company [*Acronym is now name of electronics company and brand name of its products*]
TEAC .... Turbine Engine Analysis Check (AABC)
TEACH ...... Teacher Equity and Choice Act [*Proposed*]
TEACH ...... Training and Education Activities Clearing House [*Military*]
Teach Aids News ... Teaching Aids News [*A publication*]
Teach Coll Rec ... Teacher's College Record [*A publication*]
Teach Col R ... Teacher's College Record [*A publication*]
Teach Deaf ... Teacher of the Deaf [*A publication*]
Teach Educ ... Teacher Education [*A publication*]
Teach Eng ... Teaching of English [*A publication*]
Teach Engl ... Teaching of English [*A publication*]
Teach Engl Deaf ... Teaching English to the Deaf [*A publication*]
Teacher Ed ... Teacher Education in New Countries [*A publication*]
Teacher Librn ... Teacher-Librarian [*A publication*]
Teachers J ... Teachers' Journal [*A publication*]
Teach Excep Child ... Teaching Exceptional Children [*A publication*]
Teach Feedback ... Teacher Feedback [*A publication*]
Teach Guild NSW Proc ... Teachers Guild of New South Wales. Proceedings [*A publication*]
Teach Hist ... Teaching History [*A publication*]
Teaching Polit Sci ... Teaching Political Science [*A publication*]
Teach J ...... Teachers' Journal [*A publication*]
Teach J and Abst ... Teachers' Journal and Abstract [*A publication*]
Teach J Spec Educ ... Teachers' Journal of Special Education [*A publication*]
Teach J Vic ... Teachers' Journal (Victorian Teachers Union) [*A publication*]
Teach Lib... Teacher-Librarian [*A publication*]
Teach Math ... Teaching Mathematics [*A publication*]
Teach Phil ... Teaching Philosophy [*A publication*]
Teach Pol S ... Teaching Political Science [*A publication*]
Teach Pol Sci ... Teaching Political Science [*A publication*]
Teach Socio ... Teaching Sociology [*A publication*]
Teach Sociol ... Teaching Sociology [*A publication*]
Tea & Coff ... Tea and Coffee Trade Journal [*A publication*]
TEAD .... Tooele Army Depot [*Utah*] (AABC)
TEAE .... Tigers East/Alpines East (EA)
TEAE .... Triethylaminoethyl [*Organic chemistry*]
Tea East Afr ... Tea in East Africa [*A publication*]
TEA-ER ..... Traffic Executives Association, Eastern Railroads
TEAF .... Total Environmental Action Foundation (EA)
TEAF .... Triethylammonium Formate [*Organic chemistry*]
TEAHA ...... Trans-East African Highway Authority (EA)
TEAL .... Tactics, Equipment, and Logistics Conference [*between US, Great Britain, Australia, and Canada*] [*Developed "duck" designations for Mallard and Gander military communications systems*]
TEAL .... Tasman Empire Airways Limited [*Australia*] (ADA)
TEAL .... Transversely Excited Atmospheric LASER (RDA)
Tea Lib ...... Teacher-Librarian [*A publication*]
TEALS .... Triethanolamine Lauryl Sulfate [*Organic chemistry*]
TEAM .... [*The*] European-Atlantic Movement
TEAM .... [*The*] Evangelical Alliance Mission (EA)
TEAM .... Teacher Education and Media [*Project*]
TEAM .... Teamster Economic Action Mobilization
TEAM .... Technical Engineer-Architect Management (MCD)
TEAM ...... Technique for Evaluation and Analysis of Maintainability
TEAM .... Technology Evaluation and Acquisition Method
TEAM .... Teleterminals Expandable Added Memory
TEAM .... Terminology Evaluation and Acquisition Method
TEAM .... Test and Evaluation of Air Mobility
TEAM .... Test, Evaluation, Analysis, and Modeling [*Army*] (RDA)
TEAM .... Top European Advertising Media
TEAM .... Torpedo Evasive Maneuvering (MCD)
TEAM .... Total Exposure Assessment Monitoring [*Environmental chemistry*]
TEAM .... Training and Education in Adoption Methods [*Conference sponsored by the North American Council on Adoptable Children*]
TEAM .... Training/Employment of Automotive Mechanics [*Project*]
TEAM .... Training in Expanded Auxiliary Management

TEAM .... Trend Evaluation and Monitoring [*Congressional Clearinghouse on the Future*] (EA)
TEAM .... Truck Expense Analysis and Management [*Data processing*]
TEAM-A ..... Theological Education Association of Mid-America
TEAM A ...... Theological Education Association of Mid-America, Library Section [*Library network*]
TEAMMATE ... Total Electronic Advanced Microprocessing Maneuvers and Tactics Equipment [*A game*]
TEAMS ...... Technical Evaluation & Management Systems, Inc. [*Dallas, TX*] [*Software manufacturer*]
TEAMS ...... Test Evaluation and Monitoring System
TEAMS ...... Tests of Engineering Aptitude, Mathematics, and Science
TEAMS ...... Trend and Error Analysis Methodology System (MCD)
TEAM-UP ... Test, Evaluation, Analysis, and Management Uniformity Plan [*or Procedure*] [*Army*]
TEAP .... Tetraethylammonium Perchlorate [*Organic chemistry*]
TEAP .... Trajectory Error Analysis Program [*NASA*]
TEAP .... Transversely Excited Atmospheric Pressure
TEAP .... Triethylammonium Phosphate [*Organic chemistry*]
TEAPA ...... Technikas Apskats [*A publication*]
TEAPA ...... Triethanolamine Phosphoric Acid [*Organic chemistry*]
Tea Q .... Tea Quarterly [*A publication*]
TEAR .... [*The*] Evangelical Alliance Relief [*of The TEAR Fund*] (EA)
TEAR .... Time, Elevation, Azimuth, Range (MCD)
Tea Res Assoc Annu Sci Rep ... Tea Research Association. Annual Scientific Report [*A publication*]
Tea Res Inst Ceylon Annu Rep ... Tea Research Institute of Ceylon. Annual Report [*A publication*]
Tea Res Inst Sri Lanka Tech Rep ... Tea Research Institute of Sri Lanka. Technical Report [*A publication*]
Tea Res J ... Tea Research Journal [*A publication*]
TEARR .... Times, Elevations, Azimuths, Ranges, and Range Rates [*Aerospace*]
TEARS .... [*The*] Exeter Abstract Reference System [*Exeter University*] [*Information service*] (EISS)
TEAS .... Threat Evaluation and Action Selection [*Civilian defense program*]
TEAS .... Twayne's English Author Series [*A publication*]
TEASE ...... Tracking Errors and Simulation Evaluation [*RADAR*]
TEASER .... Tunable Electron Amplifier for Stimulated Emission of Radiation (MCD)
teasp .... Teaspoonful
TEA-TOW... Training Effectiveness Analysis - Tube-Launched Optically Tracked Wire-Guided (MCD)
TEB .... Tax-Exempt Bond
TEB .... Teterboro, NJ [*Location identifier*] [*FAA*] (FAAL)
TEB .... Textile Economics Bureau
TEB .... Tone Encoded Burst
TEB .... Triethylbenzene [*Organic chemistry*]
TEB .... Triethylborane [*Organic chemistry*]
TEB .... Tropical Experiment Board [*of World Meteorological Organization and International Council on Scientific Unions*]
TEB .... Turk Ekonomi Bankasi AS [*Turkey*]
TEBAC ...... Triethylbenylammonium Chloride [*Organic chemistry*]
TEBDA .... Truck Equipment and Body Distributor Association [*Later, NTEA*] (EA)
TeBG .... Testosterone-Estradiol Binding Globulin [*Endocrinology*]
TEBOL....... Terminal Business-Oriented Language
TEBUTATE ... Tertiary Butyl Acetate [*Organic chemistry*] [*USAN*]
TEC .... Blacksburg, VA [*Location identifier*] [*FAA*] (FAAL)
TEC .... [*The*] Electrification Council [*Washington, DC*] (EA)
TEC .... [*The*] Entertainment Channel [*Pay-television network*] [*Obsolete*]
TEC .... Tactical Electromagnetic Coordinator (IEEE)
TEC .... Tactical Exercise Controller [*Marine Corps*] (MCD)
TEC .... Target Engagement Console
TEC .... Target Entry Console
TEC .... Tarif Exterieur Commun [*Common External Tariff*] [*for EEC countries*]
TEC .... Technical
TEC .... Technical Education Center
TEC .... Technical Escort Center [*Army*] (RDA)
Tec .... Technischord [*Record label*]
TEC .... Technological Excellence Commission
TEC .... Technology for Energy Corporation (NRCH)
TEC .... Tele-Engineering Corporation [*Framingham, MA*] [*Telecommunications*] (TSSD)
TEC .... Telemetry and Command
TEC .... Telephone Engineering Center [*Telecommunications*] (TEL)
TEC .... Temporary Engineering Change (AAG)
TEC .... Temporary Extended Compensation [*Labor*]
TEC .... Ternary Eutectic Chloride [*Fire extinguishing agent*]
TEC .... Test Equipment Center (NASA)
TEC .... Test Equipment Committee (AAG)
T & EC .... Test and Evaluation Command [*Army*]
TEC .... Thermal End Cover
TEC .... Thermal Energy Converter (RDA)
TEC .... Thermal Expansion Coefficient
TEC .... Tlemcen [*Algeria*] [*Seismograph station code, US Geological Survey*] (SEIS)

TEC .... Ton Equivalent of Coal
TEC .... Total Electric Content
TEC .... Total Eosinophil Count [*Hematology*]
TEC .... Total Estimated Cost
TEC .... Tower En-Route Control [*Aviation*]   (FAAC)
TEC .... Track Entry Console   (MCD)
TEC .... Tract Evaluation Computer   (NATG)
TEC .... Training Evaluation and Control
TEC .... Training Exercise Coordinator [*Military*]   (NVT)
TEC .... Training Extension Course [*Army*]
TEC .... Transearth Coast [*AEC*]
TEC .... Transient Early Curvature [*Orthopedics*]
TEC .... Transient Erythroblastopenia of Childhood [*Hematology*]
TEC .... Transport Environment Circulation [*A publication*]
T & EC .... Trauma and Emergency Center [*Medicine*]
TEC .... Tripartite Engineering Committee [*Allied German Occupation Forces*]
TEC .... Triple Erasure Correction
TEC .... Tropical Experiment Council [*of World Meteorological Organization and International Council on Scientific Unions*]
TECA .... Technical Evaluation and Countermeasures Assignment
TECA .... Temporary Emergency Court of Appeals
TECA .... Totally Enclosed - Closed-Air Circuit
TECA .... Tower En-Route Control Area [*Aviation*]   (FAAC)
TECAD ..... Technical Advisory [*Military*]   (CAAL)
TECADS ..... Techniques to Counter Air Defense Suppression   (MCD)
Tec Agr ...... Tecnica Agricola [*A publication*]
Tec Agric (Catania) ... Tecnica Agricola (Catania) [*A publication*]
TECC .... Technology Education for Children Council [*California, PA*]   (EA)
TECC .... Texas Education Computer Cooperative [*Houston*] [*Information service*]   (EISS)
TECCE ...... Tactical Exploitation Collection and Coordination Element   (MCD)
TECE .... Teleprinter Error Correction Equipment
TECED ...... Techniques de l'Energie [*A publication*]
TECG .... Test and Evaluation Coordinating Group [*Military*]   (CAAL)
TECH .... Teach Each Customer How [*Tire repair training seminar*] [*Technical Rubber Co.*]
TECH .... Technical   (AAG)
TECH .... Technician
TECH .... Technique
TECH .... Technological Education Clearinghouse
TECH .... Technology   (AAG)
Tech .... Technology [*A publication*]
TECH .... Techtran Industries, Inc. [*NASDAQ symbol*]   (NQ)
Tech Abstr Bull ... Technical Abstract Bulletin [*A publication*]
TECHAD .... Technical Advisor [*Navy*]
Tech Adv Shikoku Agric ... Technical Advances in Shikoku Agriculture [*A publication*]
Tech Agri ... Technique Agricole [*France*] [*A publication*]
Tech Appl Pet ... Techniques et Applications du Petrole [*France*] [*A publication*]
Tech Apskats ... Technikas Apskats [*United States*] [*A publication*]
Tech Assn Pa ... Technical Association Papers [*A publication*]
TECHAV ..... Technical Availability [*Navy*]   (NVT)
Tech Bau.... Technik am Bau [*West Germany*] [*A publication*]
Tech Ber Heinrich-Hertz Inst (Berlin-Charlottenburg) ... Technischer Bericht. Heinrich-Hertz Institut (Berlin-Charlottenburg) [*A publication*]
Tech Ber Sticht Nederl Graan-Cent ... Technisch Bericht. Stichting Nederlands Graan-Centrum [*A publication*]
Tech Bibliogr Birmingham Public Lib ... Technical Bibliographies. Birmingham Public Libraries [*A publication*]
Tech Bibliogr Ser Birmingham Cent Lib ... Technical Bibliographies Series. Birmingham Central Libraries [*A publication*]
Tech Biochem Biophys Morphol ... Techniques of Biochemical and Biophysical Morphology [*A publication*]
Tech Bull Agric Res Inst (Cyprus) ... Technical Bulletin. Agricultural Research Institute (Cyprus) [*A publication*]
Tech Bull Amersham Buchler ... Technisches Bulletin - Amerisham Buchler [*A publication*]
Tech Bull Anim Ind Agric Branch NT ... Technical Bulletin. Animal Industry and Agricultural Branch. Department of the Northern Territory [*A publication*]
Tech Bull Anim Ind Agric Br NT ... Technical Bulletin. Animal Industry and Agriculture Branch. Northern Territory [*A publication*]
Tech Bull Ariz Agr Exp Sta ... Technical Bulletin. Arizona Agricultural Experiment Station [*A publication*]
Tech Bull Ariz Agric Exp Stn ... Technical Bulletin. Arizona Agricultural Experiment Station [*A publication*]
Tech Bull Banana Res Adv Comm ... Technical Bulletin. Banana Research Advisory Committee [*A publication*]
Tech Bull Can Inland Waters Dir ... Technical Bulletin. Canada Inland Waters Directorate [*A publication*]
Tech Bull Colo Agric Exp Stn ... Technical Bulletin. Colorado Agricultural Experiment Station [*A publication*]
Tech Bull Colo State Univ Agr Exp Sta ... Technical Bulletin. Colorado State University. Agricultural Experiment Station [*A publication*]

Tech Bull Commonwealth Inst Biol Contr ... Technical Bulletin. Commonwealth Institute of Biological Control [*A publication*]
Tech Bull Commonw Inst Biol Control ... Technical Bulletin. Commonwealth Institute of Biological Control [*A publication*]
Tech Bull Cyprus Agr Res Inst ... Technical Bulletin. Cyprus Agricultural Research Institute [*A publication*]
Tech Bull Dep Agric NSW ... New South Wales. Department of Agriculture. Technical Bulletin [*A publication*]
Tech Bull Dep Agric Vict ... Technical Bulletin. Department of Agriculture. Victoria [*A publication*]
Tech Bull Dep Agric West Aust ... Technical Bulletin. Department of Agriculture. Western Australia [*A publication*]
Tech Bull Exp For Taiwan Univ ... Technical Bulletin. Experimental Forest. National Taiwan University [*A publication*]
Tech Bull Fac Agric Kagawa Univ ... Technical Bulletin. Faculty of Agriculture. Kagawa University [*A publication*]
Tech Bull Fac Agr Kagawa Univ ... Technical Bulletin. Faculty of Agriculture. Kagawa University [*A publication*]
Tech Bull Fac Hort Chiba Univ ... Technical Bulletin. Faculty of Horticulture. Chiba University [*A publication*]
Tech Bull Fac Hortic Chiba Univ ... Technical Bulletin. Faculty of Horticulture. Chiba University [*A publication*]
Tech Bull Fla Agric Exp Stn ... Technical Bulletin. Florida Agricultural Experiment Station [*A publication*]
Tech Bull GA Agr Exp Sta ... Technical Bulletin. Georgia Agricultural Experiment Stations. University of Georgia. College of Agriculture [*A publication*]
Tech Bull Gt Brit Min Agr Fish Food ... Technical Bulletin. Great Britain Ministry of Agiculture, Fisheries, and Food [*A publication*]
Tech Bull Harper Adams Agr Coll ... Technical Bulletin. Harper Adams Agricultural College [*A publication*]
Tech Bull Hawaii Agric Exp Stn ... Technical Bulletin. Hawaii Agricultural Experiment Station [*A publication*]
Tech Bull Inst Ld Wat Mgmt Res ... Technical Bulletin. Institute for Land and Water Management Research [*A publication*]
Tech Bull Kagawa Agr Coll ... Technical Bulletin. Kagawa Agricultural College [*A publication*]
Tech Bull Kans Agr Exp Sta ... Technical Bulletin. Kansas Agricultural Experiment Station [*A publication*]
Tech Bull Kans Agric Exp Stn ... Technical Bulletin. Kansas Agricultural Experiment Station [*A publication*]
Tech Bull Land Resour Div Dir Overseas Surv ... Technical Bulletin. Land Resources Division. Directorate of Overseas Surveys [*A publication*]
Tech Bull Mich State Univ Agr Exp Sta ... Technical Bulletin. Michigan State University. Agricultural Experiment Station [*A publication*]
Tech Bull Minist Agric E Niger ... Technical Bulletin. Ministry of Agriculture of Eastern Nigeria [*A publication*]
Tech Bull Minist Agric Fish Fd ... Technical Bulletin. Ministry of Agriculture, Fisheries, and Food [*A publication*]
Tech Bull Minn Agric Exp Sta ... Technical Bulletin. University of Minnesota. Agricultural Experiment Station [*A publication*]
Tech Bull Miss Agr Exp Sta ... Technical Bulletin. Mississippi Agricultural Experiment Station [*A publication*]
Tech Bull Miss Agric For Exp Stn ... Technical Bulletin. Mississippi Agricultural and Forestry Experiment Station [*A publication*]
Tech Bull Miyagi Prefect Agr Exp Sta ... Technical Bulletin. Miyagi Prefectural Agricultural Experiment Station [*A publication*]
Tech Bull Mont Agr Exp Sta ... Technical Bulletin. Montana Agricultural Experiment Station [*A publication*]
Tech Bull NC Agr Exp Sta ... Technical Bulletin. North Carolina Agricultural Experiment Station [*A publication*]
Tech Bull NC Agric Exp Sta ... Technical Bulletin. North Carolina Agricultural Experiment Station [*A publication*]
Tech Bull N Carol Agric Exp Stn ... Technical Bulletin. North Carolina Agricultural Experiment Station [*A publication*]
Tech Bull N Carol St Coll Agric Exp Stn ... Technical Bulletin. North Carolina State College. Agricultural Experiment Station [*A publication*]
Tech Bull Okla State Univ Agr Exp Sta ... Technical Bulletin. Oklahoma State University. Agricultural Experiment Station [*A publication*]
Tech Bull Ore Agric Exp Stn ... Technical Bulletin. Oregon Agricultural Experiment Station [*A publication*]
Tech Bull Oreg State Coll Agr Exp Sta ... Technical Bulletin. Oregon State College. Agricultural Experiment Station [*A publication*]
Tech Bull Regist Med Technol ... Technical Bulletin. Registry of Medical Technologists [*A publication*]
Tech Bull Rhodesia Agric J ... Technical Bulletin. Rhodesia Agricultural Journal [*A publication*]
Tech Bull S Dak Agr Exp Sta ... Technical Bulletin. South Dakota Agricultural Experiment Station [*A publication*]
Tech Bull Sulphur Inst ... Technical Bulletin. Sulphur Institute [*A publication*]
Tech Bull Taiwan Agric Res Inst ... Technical Bulletin. Taiwan Agricultural Research Institute [*A publication*]
Tech Bull Taiwan Fertil Co ... Technical Bulletin. Taiwan Fertilizer Company [*A publication*]
Tech Bull Tex Eng Exp Stn ... Technical Bulletin. Texas Engineering Experiment Station [*A publication*]

Tech Bull Univ Maine Life Sci Agric Exp Stn ... Technical Bulletin. University of Maine. Life Sciences and Agriculture Experiment Station [*A publication*]

Tech Bull Univ Minn Agr Exp Sta ... Technical Bulletin. University of Minnesota. Agricultural Experiment Station [*A publication*]

Tech Bull Univ Nev Agr Exp Sta ... Technical Bulletin. University of Nevada. Agricultural Experiment Station [*A publication*]

Tech Bull Univ Philippines Coll Agr ... Technical Bulletin. University of the Philippines. College of Agriculture [*A publication*]

Tech Bull USDA ... Technical Bulletin. United States Department of Agriculture [*A publication*]

Tech Bull US Dep Agric ... Technical Bulletin. United States Department of Agriculture [*A publication*]

Tech Bull US Dep Agric Agric Res Serv ... Technical Bulletin. United States Department of Agriculture. Agricultural Research Service [*A publication*]

Tech Bull US For Serv ... Technical Bulletin. United States Forest Service [*A publication*]

Tech Bull VA Agr Exp Sta ... Technical Bulletin. Virginia Agricultural Experiment Station [*A publication*]

Tech Bull Vic Ctry Rd Bd ... Technical Bulletin. Victoria Country Roads Board [*A publication*]

Tech Bull Wash Agr Exp Sta ... Technical Bulletin. Washington Agricultural Experiment Station [*A publication*]

Tech Bull Wash Agric Exp Stn ... Technical Bulletin. Washington Agricultural Experiment Station [*A publication*]

Tech Bull Wash State Univ Coll Agric Res Cent ... Technical Bulletin. Washington State University. College of Agriculture. Research Center [*A publication*]

Tech CEM ... Techniques CEM [*Compagnie Electro-Mecanique*] [*A publication*]

Tech Chem (Prague) ... Technika v Chemii (Prague) [*A publication*]

Tech Chron ... Technika Chronika [*A publication*]

Tech Circ Maurit Sug Ind Res Inst ... Technical Circular. Mauritius Sugar Industry Research Institute [*A publication*]

Tech Commun ... Technical Communications [*A publication*]

Tech Commun Bur Sugar Exp Stn Queensl ... Technical Communication. Bureau of Sugar Experiment Stations. Queensland [*A publication*]

Tech Commun Bur Sug Exp Stns QD ... Technical Communication. Bureau of Sugar Experiment Stations. Queensland [*A publication*]

Tech Commun Central Inform Libr Edit Sect CSIRO ... Technical Communication. Central Information, Library, and Editorial Section. Commonwealth Scientific and Industrial Research Organisation [*A publication*]

Tech Commun CILES CSIRO ... Technical Communication. Central Information, Library, and Editorial Section. Commonwealth Scientific and Industrial Research Organisation [*A publication*]

Tech Commun CSIRO (Aust) ... Technical Communication. Minerals Research Laboratories. Commonwealth Scientific and Industrial Research Organisation (Australia) [*A publication*]

Tech Commun CSIRO Div Mineral ... Australia. Commonwealth Scientific and Industrial Research Organisation. Division of Mineralogy. Technical Communication [*A publication*]

Tech Commun CSIRO Div Miner Chem ... Australia. Commonwealth Scientific and Industrial Research Organisation. Division of Mineral Chemistry. Technical Communication [*A publication*]

Tech Commun CSIRO Inst Earth Resour ... CSIRO [*Commonwealth Scientific and Industrial Research Organisation*] Institute of Earth Resources. Technical Communication [*A publication*]

Tech Commun CSIRO Miner Res Lab ... CSIRO [*Commonwealth Scientific and Industrial Research Organisation*] Minerals Research Laboratories. Technical Communication [*A publication*]

Tech Commun Dept Agr Tech Serv Repub S Afr ... Technical Communication. Department of Agricultural Technical Services. Republic of South Africa [*A publication*]

Tech Commun Div Miner Chem CSIRO ... Technical Communication. Division of Mineral Chemistry. Commonwealth Scientific and Industrial Research Organisation [*A publication*]

Tech Commun Div Miner CSIRO ... Technical Communication. Division of Mineralogy. Commonwealth Scientific and Industrial Research Organisation [*A publication*]

Tech Commun For Bur (Oxf) ... Technical Communication. Commonwealth Forestry Bureau (Oxford) [*A publication*]

Tech Commun Miner Res Lab CSIRO ... Technical Communication. Minerals Research Laboratories. Commonwealth Scientific and Industrial Research Organisation [*A publication*]

Tech Commun R Sch Mines ... Technical Communications. Royal School of Mines [*A publication*]

Tech Commun S Afr Dep Agric Tech Serv ... Technical Communications. South Africa Department of Agricultural Technical Services [*A publication*]

Tech Commun Woodld Ecol Unit CSIRO ... Technical Communication. Woodland Ecology Unit. Commonwealth Scientific and Industrial Research Organisation [*A publication*]

Tech & Cult ... Technology and Culture [*A publication*]

Tech & Culture ... Technology and Culture [*A publication*]

Tech Cybern USSR ... Technical Cybernetics USSR [*A publication*]

TECHDATA ... Technical Data [*DoD*]

Tech Data Digest ... Technical Data Digest [*United States*] [*A publication*]

Tech Dig .... Technical Digest [*A publication*]

Tech Doc FAO Plant Prot Comm Southeast Asia Pac Reg ... Technical Document. Food and Agriculture Organization of the United Nations. Plant Protection Committee for the South East Asia and Pacific Region [*A publication*]

Tech Eau .... Technique de l'Eau et de l'Assainissement [*A publication*]

Tech Econ Stud Inst Geol Geophys Ser I ... Technical and Economical Studies. Institute of Geology and Geophysics. Series I. Mineralogy-Petrology [*A publication*]

Tech Educ ... Technical Education [*A publication*]

Tech Educ Abstr ... Technical Education Abstracts [*A publication*]

Tech Educ Yrbk ... Technician Education Yearbook [*A publication*]

Tech Electron Son Telev ... Techniques Electroniques Son Television [*A publication*]

Tech Energ ... Techniques de l'Energie [*France*] [*A publication*]

Tech Energ (Paris) ... Techniques de l'Energie (Paris) [*A publication*]

TECHEVAL ... Technical Evaluation [*Navy*]   (NG)

Tech Forum Soc Vac Coaters ... Technical Forum. Society of Vacuum Coaters [*A publication*]

Tech Gem ... Technische Gemeinschaft [*A publication*]

Tech Gemeindebl ... Technisches Gemeindeblatt [*West Germany*] [*A publication*]

Tech Gids Ziekenhuis Instelling ... Technische Gids voor Ziekenhuis en Instelling [*A publication*]

TECHGL ..... Technological

Tech Gospod Morsk ... Technika i Gospodarka Morska [*Poland*] [*A publication*]

Tech Heute ... Technik Heute [*German Federal Republic*] [*A publication*]

Tech Hochsch Leipzig Wiss Z ... Technische Hochschule Leipzig. Wissenschaftliche Zeitschrift [*A publication*]

Tech Hogesch Delft Afd Werktuigbouwkd (Rep) WTHD ... Technische Hogeschool Delft. Afdeling der Werktuigbouwkunde (Report) WTHD [*A publication*]

Tech-Index Plasmaphys Forsch Fusionreakt ... Technik-Index ueber Plasmaphysikalische Forschung und Fusionsreaktoren [*West Germany*] [*A publication*]

Tech Inf GRW ... Technische Information GRW [*Geraete- und Regler Werke*] [*East Germany*] [*A publication*]

TECHINFO ... Technical Information [*DoD*]

Tech Info Service ... Technical Information Service [*A publication*]

TECHINT .... Technical Intelligence [*Spy satellites, etc.*]

Tech Jahrb ... Technica Jahrbuch [*A publication*]

Tech J Ankara Nucl Res Cent ... Technical Journal. Ankara Nuclear Research Center [*A publication*]

Tech J Ankara Nucl Res Train Cent ... Technical Journal. Ankara Nuclear Research and Training Center [*A publication*]

Tech J Jap Broadcast Corp ... Technical Journal. Japan Broadcasting Corporation [*A publication*]

Tech J Jpn Broadcast Corp ... Technical Journal. Japan Broadcasting Corporation [*A publication*]

Tech Knih ... Technicka Knihovna [*A publication*]

Tech Knihovna ... Technicka Knihovna [*A publication*]

Tech Kurir ... Technikai Kurir [*Hungary*] [*A publication*]

TECHL .... Technical

Tech Lab Cent Res Inst Electr Power Ind Rep ... Technical Laboratory. Central Research Institute of Electrical Power Industry. Report [*Japan*] [*A publication*]

Tech Landwirt ... Technik und Landwirtschaft. Landtechnischer Ratgeber [*A publication*]

Tech Lotnicza Astronaut ... Technika Lotnicza i Astronautyczna [*Poland*] [*A publication*]

Tech Manpower ... Technical Manpower [*A publication*]

Tech Mem Calif Inst Technol Jet Propul Lab ... Technical Memorandum. California Institute of Technology. Jet Propulsion Laboratory [*A publication*]

Tech Memo Daresbury Lab ... Technical Memorandum. Daresbury Laboratory [*A publication*]

Tech Memo Daresbury Nucl Phys Lab ... Technical Memorandum. Daresbury Nuclear Physics Laboratory [*A publication*]

Tech Memo Div Appl Geomech CSIRO ... Technical Memorandum. Division of Applied Geomechanics. Commonwealth Scientific and Industrial Research Organisation [*A publication*]

Tech Memo Div Land Use Res CSIRO ... Technical Memorandum. Division of Land Use Research. Commonwealth Scientific and Industrial Research Organisation [*A publication*]

Tech Memo Div Wildl Res CSIRO ... Technical Memorandum. Division of Wildlife Research. Commonwealth Scientific and Industrial Research Organisation [*A publication*]

Tech Memo Jet Propul Lab Calif Inst Technol ... Technical Memorandum. Jet Propulsion Laboratory. California Institute of Technology [*A publication*]

Tech Mess ATM ... Technisches Messen ATM [*Archiv fuer Technisches Messen*] [*A publication*]

Tech Methods Polym Eval ... Techniques and Methods of Polymer Evaluation [*A publication*]

Tech Meun ... Technique Meuniere [*A publication*]

Tech Mitt ... Technische Mitteilungen [*A publication*]

Tech Mitt AEG-Telefunken ... Technische Mitteilungen AEG- [*Allgemeine Elektrizitaets-Gesellschaft*] Telefunken [*A publication*]

Tech Mitteil Krupp Forschungsber ... Technische Mitteilungen Krupp. Forschungsberichte [*A publication*]

Tech Mitteil Krupp Werksber ... Technische Mitteilungen Krupp. Werksberichte [*A publication*]

Tech Mitt (Essen) ... Technische Mitteilungen (Essen) [*A publication*]

Tech Mitt Krupp ... Technische Mitteilungen Krupp [*West Germany*] [*A publication*]

Tech Mitt Krupp Forschungsber ... Technische Mitteilungen Krupp. Forschungsberichte [*A publication*]

Tech Mitt Krupp Werksber ... Technische Mitteilungen Krupp. Werksberichte [*A publication*]

Tech Mitt PTT ... Technische Mitteilungen PTT [*A publication*]

Tech Mitt RFZ ... Technische Mitteilungen. RFZ [*Rundfunk- und Fernsehtechnisches Zentralamt*] [*A publication*]

Tech Mod... Technique Moderne [*A publication*]

TECHMOD ... Technology Modernization Program [*DoD*]

Tech Motoryzacyjna ... Technika Motoryzacyjna [*A publication*]

TECHN ...... Technical

TECHN ...... Technician

TECHN ...... Technology

Techn Dict ... Crabb's Technological Dictionary (DLA)

Tech Newslett For Prod Res Inst (Ghana) ... Technical Newsletter. Forest Products Research Institute (Kumasi, Ghana) [*A publication*]

Technical J ... Technical Journal [*A publication*]

Technic Int ... Technic International [*West Germany*] [*A publication*]

Technmcs ... Technometrics [*A publication*]

TECHNOL ... Technologic

Technol...... Technology [*A publication*]

Technol Conserv ... Technology and Conservation [*A publication*]

Technol Cul ... Technology and Culture [*A publication*]

Technol Dev Rep EPS (Can Environ Prot Serv) ... Technology Development Report EPS (Canada Environmental Protection Service) [*A publication*]

Technol For ... Technological Forecasting and Social Change [*A publication*]

Technol Forecast ... Technological Forecasting [*Later, Technological Forecasting and Social Change*] [*A publication*]

Technol Forecasting ... Technological Forecasting [*Later, Technological Forecasting and Social Change*] [*United States*] [*A publication*]

Technol Forecasting Soc Change ... Technological Forecasting and Social Change [*A publication*]

Technol Index Plasmaphys Res Fusion React ... Technology Index for Plasmaphysics Research and Fusion Reactors [*West Germany*] [*A publication*]

Technol Inf (Sapporo) ... Technology and Information (Sapporo) [*A publication*]

Technol Ireland ... Technology Ireland [*A publication*]

Technol J Natl Sci Dev Board (Philip) ... Technology Journal. National Science Development Board (Philippines) [*A publication*]

Technol-Nachr Manage Inf ... Technologie-Nachrichten. Management-Informationen [*West Germany*] [*A publication*]

Technol-Nachr Programm-Inf ... Technologie-Nachrichten Programm-Informationen [*West Germany*] [*A publication*]

Technol-Nachr Sonderdienst-Programme ... Technologie-Nachrichten Sonderdienst-Programme [*German Federal Republic*] [*A publication*]

Technol News ... Technology News. Bureau of Mines [*United States*] [*A publication*]

Technol News Bur Mines ... Technology News. Bureau of Mines [*United States*] [*A publication*]

Technolog Pap Div Forest Prod CSIRO ... Technological Paper. Division of Forest Products. Commonwealth Scientific and Industrial Research Organisation [*A publication*]

Technol Pap Div Forest Prod CSIRO ... Technological Paper. Division of Forest Products. Commonwealth Scientific and Industrial Research Organisation [*A publication*]

Technol Pap Forest Prod Lab Div Appl Chem CSIRO ... Technological Paper. Forest Products Laboratory. Division of Applied Chemistry. Commonwealth Scientific and Industrial Research Organisation [*A publication*]

Technol Pap Forest Prod Lab Div Bldg Res CSIRO ... Technological Paper. Forest Products Laboratory. Division of Building Research. Commonwealth Scientific and Industrial Research Organisation [*A publication*]

Technol Pap For Prod Lab Div Appl Chem CSIRO ... Technological Paper. Forest Products Laboratory. Division of Applied Chemistry. Commonwealth Scientific and Industrial Research Organisation [*A publication*]

Technol Pap For Prod Lab Div Build Res CSIRO ... Technological Paper. Forest Products Laboratory. Division of Building Research. Commonwealth Scientific and Industrial Research Organisation [*A publication*]

Technol R .. Technology Review [*Boston*] [*A publication*]

Technol Rep Iwate Univ ... Technology Reports. Iwate University [*A publication*]

Technol Rep Kansai Univ ... Technology Reports. Kansai University [*A publication*]

Technol Rep Kyushu Univ ... Technology Reports. Kyushu University [*A publication*]

Technol Rep Osaka Univ ... Technology Reports. Osaka University [*A publication*]

Technol Rep Seikei Univ ... Technology Reports. Seikei University [*A publication*]

Technol Rep Tohoku Univ ... Technology Reports. Tohoku University [*Sendaik, Japan*] [*A publication*]

Technol Rep Tohoku Univ (Jpn) ... Technology Reports. Tohoku University (Japan) [*A publication*]

Technol Rep Yamaguchi Univ ... Technology Reports. Yamaguchi University [*A publication*]

Technol Respir ... Technologie Respiratoire [*A publication*]

Technol Rev ... Technology Review [*A publication*]

Technol Rev Chonnam Natl Univ ... Technological Review. Chonnam National University [*Republic of Korea*] [*A publication*]

Technol Soc ... Technology and Society [*A publication*]

Technol (Syd) ... Technology (Sydney) [*A publication*]

Technomet ... Technometrics [*A publication*]

Technop..... Technopaegnion [*of Ausonius*] [*Classical studies*] (OCD)

Tech Note Aust Def Stand Lab ... Technical Note. Australia Defence Standards Laboratories [*A publication*]

Tech Note Brick Manuf Assoc NSW ... Technical Note. Brick Manufacturers Association of New South Wales [*A publication*]

Tech Note Brick Mf Assoc NSW ... Technical Note. Brick Manufacturers Association of New South Wales [*A publication*]

Tech Note Charles Kolling Res Lab ... Technical Note. Charles Kolling Research Laboratory. Department of Mechanical Engineering. University of Sydney [*A publication*]

Tech Note Def Stand Lab Aust ... Australia. Defence Standards Laboratories. Technical Note [*A publication*]

Tech Note Dep For Res (Nigeria) ... Technical Note. Department of Forest Research (Nigeria) [*A publication*]

Tech Note E Afr Agric For Res Organ ... Technical Note. East African Agriculture and Forestry Research Organization [*A publication*]

Tech Note For Dep (Brit Solomon Islands Protect) ... Technical Note. Forestry Department (British Solomon Islands Protectorate) [*A publication*]

Tech Note For Dep (Kenya) ... Technical Note. Forest Department (Nairobi, Kenya) [*A publication*]

Tech Note For Dep (Uganda) ... Technical Note. Forest Department (Uganda) [*A publication*]

Tech Note For Prod Res Ind Dev Comm (Philipp) ... Technical Note. Forest Products Research and Industries Development Commission (Philippines) [*A publication*]

Tech Note For Prod Res Inst (Ghana) ... Technical Note. Forest Products Research Institute (Ghana) [*A publication*]

Tech Note For Timb Bur ... Technical Note. Bureau of Forestry and Timber [*A publication*]

Tech Note Harbour Tech Res Inst Minist Transp (Jpn) ... Technical Note. Port and Harbour Technical Research Institute. Ministry of Transportation (Japan) [*A publication*]

Tech Note Mater Res Lab Aust ... Australia. Materials Research Laboratories. Technical Note [*A publication*]

Tech Note Oji Inst For Tree Impr ... Technical Note. Oji Institute for Forest Tree Improvement [*A publication*]

Tech Note Quetico-Sup Wild Res Cent ... Technical Note. Quetico-Superior Wilderness Research Center [*A publication*]

Tech Note Res Inst Ind Saf ... Technical Note. Research Institute of Industrial Safety [*A publication*]

Tech Notes Clay Prod ... Technical Notes on Clay Products [*Brick Development Research Institute*] [*A publication*]

Tech Notes For Comm NSW ... Technical Notes. Forestry Commission of New South Wales [*A publication*]

Tech Notes NSW For Comm Div Wood Technol ... New South Wales. Forestry Commission. Division of Wood Technology. Technical Notes [*A publication*]

Tech Note Sol Energy Stud CSIRO ... Technical Note. Solar Energy Studies. Commonwealth Scientific and Industrial Research Organisation [*A publication*]

Tech Notes Rubber Ind ... Technical Notes for the Rubber Industry [*A publication*]

TECHNQ .... Technique

TECHOPEVAL ... Technical Operational Evaluation

Tech Pap Agric Exp Stn (P Rico) ... Technical Paper. Agricultural Experiment Station (Puerto Rico) [*A publication*]

Tech Pap Amer Pulpw Ass ... Technical Papers. American Pulpwood Association [*A publication*]

Tech Pap Anim Res Lab CSIRO ... Technical Paper. Animal Research Laboratories. Commonwealth Scientific and Industrial Research Organisation [*A publication*]

Tech Pap (Aust) CSIRO Div Mineragraphic Invest ... Technical Paper. (Australia) Commonwealth Scientific and Industrial Research Organisation. Division of Mineragraphic Investigation [*A publication*]

Tech Pap Aust Water Resour Coun ... Technical Paper. Australian Water Resources Council [*A publication*]

Tech Pap Aust Wat Resour Coun ... Technical Paper. Australian Water Resources Council [*A publication*]

Tech Pap Canad Pulp Pap Ass ... Technical Paper. Canadian Pulp and Paper Association [*A publication*]
Tech Pap Dep For QD ... Technical Paper. Department of Forestry. Queensland [*A publication*]
Tech Pap Dep For Queensl ... Technical Paper. Department of Forestry. Queensland [*A publication*]
Tech Pap Div Appl Chem CSIRO ... Technical Paper. Division of Applied Chemistry. Commonwealth Scientific and Industrial Research Organisation [*A publication*]
Tech Pap Div Appl Geomech CSIRO ... Technical Paper. Division of Applied Geomechanics. Commonwealth Scientific and Industrial Research Organisation [*A publication*]
Tech Pap Div Appl Miner CSIRO ... Technical Paper. Division of Applied Mineralogy. Commonwealth Scientific and Industrial Research Organisation [*A publication*]
Tech Pap Div Appl Org Chem CSIRO ... Technical Paper. Division of Applied Organic Chemistry. Commonwealth Scientific and Industrial Research Organisation [*A publication*]
Tech Pap Div Atmosph Phys CSIRO ... Technical Paper. Division of Atmospheric Physics. Commonwealth Scientific and Industrial Research Organisation [*A publication*]
Tech Pap Div Atmos Phys CSIRO ... Technical Paper. Division of Atmospheric Physics. Commonwealth Scientific and Industrial Research Organisation [*A publication*]
Tech Pap Div Bldg Res CSIRO ... Technical Paper. Division of Building Research. Commonwealth Scientific and Industrial Research Organisation [*A publication*]
Tech Pap Div Build Res CSIRO ... Technical Paper. Division of Building Research. Commonwealth Scientific and Industrial Research Organisation [*A publication*]
Tech Pap Div Chem Technol CSIRO ... Technical Paper. Division of Chemical Technology. Commonwealth Scientific and Industrial Research Organisation [*A publication*]
Tech Pap Div Ent CSIRO ... Technical Paper. Division of Entomology. Commonwealth Scientific and Industrial Research Organisation [*A publication*]
Tech Pap Div Fd Preserv CSIRO ... Technical Paper. Division of Food Preservation. Commonwealth Scientific and Industrial Research Organisation [*A publication*]
Tech Pap Div Fd Res CSIRO ... Technical Paper. Division of Food Research. Commonwealth Scientific and Industrial Research Organisation [*A publication*]
Tech Pap Div Fd Res CSIRO Aust ... Technical Paper. Division of Food Research. Commonwealth Scientific and Industrial Research Organisation. Australia [*A publication*]
Tech Pap Div Fish Oceanogr CSIRO ... Technical Paper. Division of Fisheries and Oceanography. Commonwealth Scientific and Industrial Research Organisation [*A publication*]
Tech Pap Div Food Res CSIRO ... Technical Paper. Division of Food Research. Commonwealth Scientific and Industrial Research Organisation [*A publication*]
Tech Pap Div Land Resour Manage CSIRO ... Technical Paper. Division of Land Resources Management. Commonwealth Scientific and Industrial Research Organisation [*A publication*]
Tech Pap Div Land Use Res CSIRO ... Technical Paper. Division of Land Use Research. Commonwealth Scientific and Industrial Research Organisation [*A publication*]
Tech Pap Div Ld Res CSIRO ... Technical Paper. Division of Land Research. Commonwealth Scientific and Industrial Research Organisation [*A publication*]
Tech Pap Div Ld Res Reg Surv CSIRO (Aust) ... Technical Papers. Division of Land Research and Regional Survey. Commonwealth Scientific and Industrial Research Organisation (Australia) [*A publication*]
Tech Pap Div Ld Use Res CSIRO ... Technical Paper. Division of Land Use Research. Commonwealth Scientific and Industrial Research Organisation [*A publication*]
Tech Pap Div Math Stat CSIRO ... Technical Paper. Division of Mathematics and Statistics. Commonwealth Scientific and Industrial Research Organisation [*A publication*]
Tech Pap Div Math Statist CSIRO ... Technical Paper. Division of Mathematical Statistics. Commonwealth Scientific and Industrial Research Organisation [*A publication*]
Tech Pap Div Mat Statist CSIRO ... Technical Paper. Division of Mathematical Statistics. Commonwealth Scientific and Industrial Research Organisation [*A publication*]
Tech Pap Div Meteorol Phys CSIRO ... Technical Paper. Division of Meteorological Physics. Commonwealth Scientific and Industrial Research Organisation [*A publication*]
Tech Pap Div Met Phys CSIRO ... Technical Paper. Division of Meteorological Physics. Commonwealth Scientific and Industrial Research Organisation [*A publication*]
Tech Pap Div Plant Ind CSIRO ... Technical Paper. Division of Plant Industry. Commonwealth Scientific and Industrial Research Organisation [*A publication*]
Tech Pap Div Pl Ind CSIRO ... Technical Paper. Division of Plant Industry. Commonwealth Scientific and Industrial Research Organisation [*A publication*]
Tech Pap Div Pl Ind CSIRO (Aust) ... Technical Papers. Division of Plant Industry. Commonwealth Scientific and Industrial Research Organisation (Australia) [*A publication*]

Tech Pap Div Soil Mechanics CSIRO ... Technical Paper. Division of Soil Mechanics. Commonwealth Scientific and Industrial Research Organisation [*A publication*]
Tech Pap Div Soils CSIRO ... Technical Paper. Division of Soils. Commonwealth Scientific and Industrial Research Organisation [*A publication*]
Tech Pap Div Tech Conf Soc Plast Eng ... Technical Papers. Divisional Technical Conference. Society of Plastics Engineers [*A publication*]
Tech Pap Div Trop Agron CSIRO ... Technical Paper. Division of Tropical Agronomy. Commonwealth Scientific and Industrial Research Organisation [*A publication*]
Tech Pap Div Trop Crops Pastures CSIRO ... Technical Paper. Division of Tropical Crops and Pastures. Commonwealth Scientific and Industrial Research Organisation [*A publication*]
Tech Pap Div Trop Pastures CSIRO ... Technical Paper. Division of Tropical Pastures. Commonwealth Scientific and Industrial Research Organisation [*A publication*]
Tech Pap Div Wildl Res CSIRO ... Technical Paper. Division of Wildlife Research. Commonwealth Scientific and Industrial Research Organisation [*A publication*]
Tech Pap For Comm NSW ... Technical Paper. Forestry Commission of New South Wales [*A publication*]
Tech Pap For Res Inst NZ For Serv ... Technical Paper. Forest Research Institute. New Zealand Forest Service [*A publication*]
Tech Pap Hydrol ... Technical Papers in Hydrology [*A publication*]
Tech Pap Intersoc Energy Convers Eng Conf ... Technical Papers. Intersociety Energy Conversion Engineering Conference [*A publication*]
Tech Pap Natl Meas Lab CSIRO ... Technical Paper. National Measurement Laboratory. Commonwealth Scientific and Industrial Research Organisation [*A publication*]
Tech Pap Natn Stand Lab CSIRO ... Technical Paper. National Standards Laboratory. Commonwealth Scientific and Industrial Research Organisation [*A publication*]
Tech Pap NY State Dep Environ Conserv ... Technical Paper. New York State Department of Environmental Conservation [*A publication*]
Tech Pap SME Ser EE ... Technical Paper. Society of Manufacturing Engineers. Series EE (Electrical Engineering) [*A publication*]
Tech Pap Soc Manuf Eng Ser AD ... Technical Paper. Society of Manufacturing Engineers. Series AD (Assembly Division) [*A publication*]
Tech Pap Soc Manuf Eng Ser EE ... Technical Paper. Society of Manufacturing Engineers. Series EE (Electrical Engineering) [*A publication*]
Tech Pap Soc Manuf Eng Ser EM ... Technical Paper. Society of Manufacturing Engineers. Series EM (Engineering Materials) [*A publication*]
Tech Pap Soc Manuf Eng Ser FC ... Technical Paper. Society of Manufacturing Engineers. Series FC (Finishing and Coating) [*A publication*]
Tech Pap Soc Manuf Eng Ser IQ ... Technical Paper. Society of Manufacturing Engineers. Series IQ (Inspection and Quality) [*A publication*]
Tech Pap Soc Manuf Eng Ser MF ... Technical Paper. Society of Manufacturing Engineers. Series MF (Material Forming) [*A publication*]
Tech Pap Soc Manuf Eng Ser MR ... Technical Paper. Society of Manufacturing Engineers. Series MR (Material Removal) [*A publication*]
Tech Pap Univ PR Agr Exp Sta ... Technical Paper. University of Puerto Rico. Agricultural Experiment Station [*A publication*]
Tech Pet ..... Techniques du Petrole [*France*] [*A publication*]
Tech Phot ... Technical Photography [*A publication*]
Tech-Phys Monogr ... Technisch-Physikalische Monographien [*A publication*]
Tech Phys Ser ... Techniques of Physics Series [*A publication*]
Tech Poszukiwan ... Technika Poszukiwan [*A publication*]
Tech Poszukiwan Geol ... Technika Poszukiwan Geologicznych [*A publication*]
Tech Pr ...... Technika Prace [*Czechoslovakia*] [*A publication*]
Tech Prat Agr ... Technique et Pratique Agricoles [*A publication*]
Tech Prepr Am Soc Lubr Eng ... Technical Preprints. American Society of Lubrication Engineers [*A publication*]
Tech Prog Rep US Bur Mines ... Technical Progress Report. United States Bureau of Mines [*A publication*]
Tech Progr Rep Hawaii Agr Exp Sta ... Technical Progress Report. Hawaii Agricultural Experiment Station. University of Hawaii [*A publication*]
Tech Publ Aust Soc Dairy Technol ... Australian Society of Dairy Technology. Technical Publication [*A publication*]
Tech Publ Div Wood Technol For Comm NSW ... Technical Publication. Division of Wood Technology. Forestry Commission of New South Wales [*A publication*]
Tech Publ NY St Coll For ... Technical Publication. New York State University. College of Forestry [*A publication*]
Tech Publs ... Technical Publications [*A publication*]
Tech Publs Aust Soc Dairy Technol ... Technical Publications. Australian Society of Dairy Technology [*A publication*]

Tech Publs Dep Agric Vict ... Technical Publications. Department of Agriculture. Victoria [*A publication*]

Tech Publs Div Wood Technol NSW For Comm ... Technical Publications. Division of Wood Technology. New South Wales Forestry Commission [*A publication*]

Tech Publs NSW For Comm Div Wood Technol ... Technical Publications. New South Wales Forestry Commission. Division of Wood Technology [*A publication*]

Tech Publ State Univ Coll For Syracuse Univ ... Technical Publication. State University College of Forestry. Syracuse University [*A publication*]

Tech Q .... Technology Quarterly and Proceedings of the Society of Arts [*A publication*]

Tech Quart Master Brew Ass Amer ... Technical Quarterly. Master Brewers Association of America [*A publication*]

Tech R........ Technology Review [*A publication*]

Tech Radia & Telew ... Technika Radia i Telewizji [*A publication*]

Tech Rdsch (Bern) ... Technische Rundschau (Bern) [*Switzerland*] [*A publication*]

Tech Refrig Air Cond ... Technics of Refrigeration and Air Conditioning [*A publication*]

Tech Release Amer Pulpw Ass ... Technical Release. American Pulpwood Association [*A publication*]

TECHREP... Technical Representative [*Military*]

Tech Rep AFAPL TR Air Force Aero Propul Lab (US) ... Technical Report. AFAPL-TR. Air Force Aero Propulsion Laboratory (United States) [*A publication*]

Tech Rep AFFDL TR Air Force Flight Dyn Lab (US) ... Technical Report. AFFDL-TR. Air Force Flight Dynamics Laboratory (United States) [*A publication*]

Tech Rep AFML TR Air Force Mater Lab (US) ... Technical Report. AFML-TR. Air Force Materials Laboratory (United States) [*A publication*]

Tech Rep AFWAL-TR US Air Force Wright Aeronaut Lab ... Technical Report. AFWAL-TR. United States Air Force Wright Aeronautical Laboratories [*A publication*]

Tech Rep Agric Eng Res Stn Min Agric For Ser F ... Technical Report. Agricultural Engineering Research Station. Ministry of Agriculture and Forestry. Series F. General [*Japan*] [*A publication*]

Tech Rep Agric Ld Serv Minist Agric Fish Fd ... Technical Report. Agricultural Land Service. Ministry of Agriculture, Fisheries, and Food [*A publication*]

Tech Rep Air Pollut Yokohama-Kawasaki Ind Area ... Technical Report on Air Pollution in Yokohama-Kawasaki Industrial Area [*Japan*] [*A publication*]

Tech Rep Aust Weapons Res Establ ... Australia. Weapons Research Establishment. Technical Report [*A publication*]

Tech Rep Bur Met ... Technical Report. Bureau of Meteorology [*A publication*]

Tech Rep Bur Meteorol ... Technical Report. Bureau of Meteorology [*A publication*]

Tech Rep Cent Res Inst Electr Power Ind ... Technical Report. Central Research Institute of Electric Power Industry [*Japan*] [*A publication*]

Tech Rep Constr Eng Res Lab ... Technical Report. Construction Engineering Research Laboratory [*United States*] [*A publication*]

Tech Rep Dep Mines Tas ... Technical Report. Department of Mines. Tasmania [*A publication*]

Tech Rep Desert Locust Control Organ East Afr ... Technical Report. Desert Locust Control Organization for Eastern Africa [*A publication*]

Tech Rep Div Appl Geomech CSIRO ... Technical Report. Division of Applied Geomechanics. Commonwealth Scientific and Industrial Research Organisation [*A publication*]

Tech Rep Div Mech Eng CSIRO ... Technical Report. Division of Mechanical Engineering. Commonwealth Scientific and Industrial Research Organisation [*A publication*]

Tech Rep Div Mech Engng CSIRO ... Technical Report. Division of Mechanical Engineering. Commonwealth Scientific and Industrial Research Organisation [*A publication*]

Tech Rep Div Soil Mech CSIRO ... Technical Report. Division of Soil Mechanics. Commonwealth Scientific and Industrial Research Organisation [*A publication*]

Tech Rep Eng Res Inst Kyoto Univ ... Technical Reports. Engineering Research Institute. Kyoto University [*A publication*]

Tech Rep Fac For Univ Toronto ... Technical Report. Faculty of Forestry. University of Toronto [*A publication*]

Tech Rep Grassld Res Inst ... Technical Report. Grassland Research Institute [*A publication*]

Tech Rep Inst Atom Energy Kyoto Univ ... Technical Reports. Institute of Atomic Energy. Kyoto University [*A publication*]

Tech Rep Inst Printed Circuits ... Technical Report. Institute of Printed Circuits [*A publication*]

Tech Rep ISSP (Inst Solid State Phys) Ser A ... Technical Report. ISSP (Institute for Solid State Physics). Series A [*A publication*]

Tech Rep Jet Propul Lab Calif Inst Technol ... Technical Report. Jet Propulsion Laboratory. California Institute of Technology [*A publication*]

Tech Rep Kansai Univ ... Technology Reports. Kansai University [*A publication*]

Tech Rep Natl Space Dev Agency Jpn ... Technical Report. National Space Development Agency of Japan [*A publication*]

Tech Rep Nisshin Steel Co Ltd ... Technical Report of the Nisshin Steel Company Limited [*Japan*] [*A publication*]

Tech Reports Osaka Univ ... Technology Reports. Osaka University [*A publication*]

Tech Rep Reg Res Sta (Samaru) ... Technical Report. Regional Research Station (Samaru) [*A publication*]

Tech Repr Graver Water Cond Co ... Technical Reprint. Graver Water Conditioning Company [*A publication*]

Tech Rep Sch For Resour NC St Univ ... Technical Report. School of Forest Resources. North Carolina State University [*A publication*]

Tech Rep Ser ARL/TR Aust Radiat Lab ... Australia. Australian Radiation Laboratory. Technical Report Series ARL/TR [*A publication*]

Tech Rep Ser Int Atom Energy Ag ... Technical Reports Series. International Atomic Energy Agency [*A publication*]

Tech Rep Ser Victoria Dep Agric ... Victoria. Department of Agriculture. Technical Report Series [*A publication*]

Tech Rep Soil Res Inst Ghana Acad Sci ... Technical Report. Soil Research Institute. Ghana Academy of Sciences [*A publication*]

Tech Rep Syst ASM ... Technical Report System. American Society for Metals [*A publication*]

Tech Rep Tasmania Dep Mines ... Tasmania. Department of Mines. Technical Report [*A publication*]

Tech Rep Tasm Dep Mines ... Technical Report. Tasmania Department of Mines [*A publication*]

Tech Rep Tex For Serv ... Technical Report. Texas Forest Service [*A publication*]

Tech Rep Toyo Kohan Co Ltd ... Technical Reports of Toyo Kohan Company Limited [*Japan*] [*A publication*]

Tech Rep Univ Tex Austin Cent Res Water Resour ... Technical Report. University of Texas at Austin. Center for Research in Water Resources [*A publication*]

Tech Rep US Army Eng Waterw Exp Stn ... Technical Report. US Army Engineer Waterways Experiment Station [*A publication*]

Tech Rep Water Resour Res Cent Hawaii Univ ... Technical Report. Hawaii University. Water Resource Research Center [*A publication*]

Tech Rep Yale Sch For ... Technical Report. Yale University. School of Forestry [*A publication*]

Tech Res Cent Finland Electr and Nucl Technol Publ ... Technical Research Centre of Finland. Electrical and Nuclear Technology Publication [*A publication*]

Tech Res Cent Finland Mater and Process Technol Publ ... Technical Research Centre of Finland. Materials and Processing Technology Publication [*A publication*]

Tech Res Cent Finl Build Technol Community Dev Publ ... Technical Research Centre of Finland. Building Technology and Community Development Publication [*A publication*]

Tech Res Cent Finl Electr Nucl Technol Publ ... Technical Research Centre of Finland. Electrical and Nuclear Technology Publication [*A publication*]

Tech Res Cent Finl Gen Div Publ ... Technical Research Centre of Finland. General Division Publication [*A publication*]

Tech Res Cent Finl Mater Process Technol Publ ... Technical Research Centre of Finland. Materials and Processing Technology Publication [*A publication*]

Tech Rev Mitsubishi Heavy-Ind (Jpn Ed) ... Technical Review. Mitsubishi Heavy-Industries (Japanese Edition) [*A publication*]

Tech Rev Sumitomo Heavy Ind Ltd ... Technical Review. Sumitomo Heavy Industries Limited [*A publication*]

Tech Routiere ... Technique Routiere [*Belgium*] [*A publication*]

Tech Rundsch ... Technische Rundschau [*A publication*]

Tech Rundsch Sulzer ... Technische Rundschau Sulzer [*Switzerland*] [*A publication*]

TECHSAT ... Technology Satellite (MCD)

Tech Sci Aeronaut Spat ... Technique et Science Aeronautiques et Spatiales [*France*] [*A publication*]

Tech Sci Munic ... Techniques et Sciences Municipales [*France*] [*A publication*]

Tech Sci Munic Eau ... Techniques et Sciences Municipales/l'Eau [*A publication*]

Tech Ser Fla Dep Nat Resour Mar Res Lab ... Technical Series. Florida Department of Natural Resources. Marine Research Laboratory [*A publication*]

Tech Skoda ... Technika Skoda [*A publication*]

Tech Smarownicza ... Technika Smarownicza [*A publication*]

Tech Smarownicza Trybol ... Technika Smarownicza. Trybologia [*A publication*]

Tech Soc Pacific Coast Tr ... Technical Society of the Pacific Coast. Transactions [*A publication*]

Tech Stud Common Exp Bldg Stn ... Technical Study. Commonwealth Experimental Building Station [*A publication*]

Tech Stud Commonw Exp Bldg Stn ... Technical Studies. Commonwealth Experimental Building Station [*A publication*]

TECHSVS ... Technical Services [*Army*]

TECHTAF... Technical Training Air Force

Tech Teach ... Technical Teacher [*A publication*]

Tech Timber Guide ... Technical Timber Guide [*A publication*]
Tech Timb Guide ... Technical Timber Guide [*A publication*]
Tech Times ... Technology Transfer Times [*A publication*]
TECHTNG ... Technical Training   (NVT)
TECHTRA ... Air Technical Training [*Navy*]
Tech Trav... Techniques des Travaux [*Belgium*] [*A publication*]
Tech Trav (Liege) ... Technique des Travaux (Liege) [*A publication*]
Tech Ueberwach ... Technische Ueberwachung [*Technological Supervising*]
    [*A publication*]
Tech Umweltschutz ... Technik und Umweltschutz [*East Germany*] [*A
    publication*]
Tech Univ Muenchen Jahrb ... Technische Universitaet Muenchen. Jahrbuch
    [*A publication*]
Tech W...... Technical World [*Chicago*] [*A publication*]
Tech W...... Technology Week [*A publication*]
Tech-Wiss Abh Osram-Ges ... Technisch-Wissenschaftliche Abhandlungen
    der Osram-Gesellschaft [*A publication*]
Tech Wk..... Technology Week [*A publication*]
Tech Wlok ... Technik Wlokienniczy [*A publication*]
Tech World ... Technical World Magazine [*A publication*]
Tech Zentralbl ... Technisches Zentralblatt [*A publication*]
Tech Zukunft ... Techniken der Zukunft [*A publication*]
Tec Ind (Madrid) ... Tecnica Industrial (Madrid) [*A publication*]
Tec Ital ... Tecnica Italiana [*A publication*]
TECK........ Technodyne, Inc. [*NASDAQ symbol*]   (NQ)
TECL......... Test Equipment Configuration Log [*NASA*]   (KSC)
TECM......... Test Equipment Commodity Manager
Tec Metal... Tecnica Metalurgica [*Spain*] [*A publication*]
Tec Met (Barcelona) ... Tecnica Metalurgica (Barcelona) [*A publication*]
Tec Mit K F ... Technische Mitteilungen Krupp. Forschungsberichte [*A
    publication*]
Tec Mit K W ... Technische Mitteilungen Krupp. Werksberichte [*A
    publication*]
TECMOD.... Technology Modernization   (MCD)
Tec Molit ... Tecnica Molitoria [*A publication*]
TECN......... Technalysis Corp. [*NASDAQ symbol*]   (NQ)
TEC-NACS ... Teachers Educational Council - National Association
    Cosmetology Schools
Tecnica Lisb ... Tecnica. Rivista de Engenharia (Lisboa) [*A publication*]
Tecn Ital..... Tecnica Italiana [*A publication*]
Tecnol Aliment ... Tecnologia Alimentaria [*A publication*]
TECO .... Tesco American Corp. [*NASDAQ symbol*]   (NQ)
TECO .... Trinity Engineering Company [*Huxley, IA*] [*Telecommunications
    service*]   (TSSD)
TECO .... Turbine Engine Checkout
TECOM ...... Test and Evaluation Command [*Army*]
TECOMAP ... Technical Conference of the Observation and Measurement of
    Atmospheric Pollution [*Helsinki, 1973*]
TECP......... Training Equipment Checkout Procedure
TECPD .... TAPPI [*Technical Association of the Pulp and Paper Industry*]
    Environmental Conference. Proceedings [*A publication*]
Tec Pecuar Mex ... Tecnica Pecuaria en Mexico [*A publication*]
Tec Pecu Mex ... Tecnica Pecuaria en Mexico [*A publication*]
TECR......... Technical Reason [*Aviation*]
TECR......... Technical Requirement   (AABC)
Tec R......... Technology Review [*A publication*]
TECR......... Test Equipment Change Requirement   (NATG)
TECRAS..... Technical Reconnaissance and Surveillance   (MCD)
Tec Regul & Mando Autom ... Tecnica de la Regulacion y Mando Automatico
    [*A publication*]
TECS......... Television Confirming Sensor   (MCD)
TECS......... Total Environmental Control System [*Army*]   (RDA)
TECS......... Treasury Enforcement Communications System [*Customs
    Service*]
TECSTAR .. Technical Missions, Structures and Career Development
Tectonophys ... Tectonophysics [*A publication*]
TECTRA..... Technology Transfer Data Bank [*California State University*]
    [*Sacramento*] [*Information service*]   (EISS)
TECU......... Tecumseh Products Co. [*NASDAQ symbol*]   (NQ)
TECU......... Thermoelectric Environmental Control Unit
TECU......... Transportation Employees' Canadian Union
TED .... International Association for Training and Education in
    Distribution
TED .... Tasks of Emotional Development Test [*Psychology*]
TeD............ Te Deum [*Music*]
TED .... Teacher Education Division [*Council for Exceptional Children*]
TED .... Teal Industries Ltd. [*Vancouver Stock Exchange symbol*]
TeD............ Telefunken-Decca [*Video disk system*]
TED .... Tenders Electronic Daily [*Office for Official Publications of the
    European Communities*] [*Database*] [*Luxembourg*]
TED .... Terminal Editor   (ADA)
TED .... Test Engineering Division [*Navy*]
TED .... Test Engineering Documentation   (MCD)
TED .... Test, Evaluation, and Development   (MUGU)
TED .... Test and Evaluation Division [*National Weather Service*]
T Ed .... Theological Educator [*A publication*]
TED .... Thermionic Emission Detector [*For gas chromatography*]
TED .... Thermoelectric Device
TED .... Thisted [*Denmark*] [*Airport symbol*]   (OAG)
TED .... Thomas Edmund Dewey [*Republican candidate for President,
    1948*]

TED .... Threshold Erythema Dose [*Medicine*]
TED .... Threshold Extension Demodulator
TED .... Thromboembolic Disease [*Medicine*]
TED .... Toledo Edison Co. [*NYSE symbol*]
TED .... Total Energy Detector
TED .... Trace Element Doping
TED .... Tracking Error Detector   (MCD)
TED .... Trailing Edge Down   (MCD)
TED .... Training Equipment Development
TED .... Traitement Electronique des Donnees [*Electronic Data
    Processing - EDP*] [*French*]
TED .... Transfer Effective Date [*Military*]   (AFM)
TED .... Transferred Electron Device [*Air Force*]
TED .... Translation Error Detector   (DIT)
TED .... Trawling Efficiency Device [*Tool attached to shrimp boats in
    the Gulf of Mexico which allows the endangered Kemp's
    ridley turtle to escape the shrimp nets*]
TED .... Troop Exercise Director   (CINC)
TED .... True Economic Depreciation
TED .... Trunk Encryption Device [*Telecommunications*]   (TEL)
TED .... Turbine Electric Drive
TED .... Turbine Engine Division [*Air Force*]
TED .... Turtle Exclusion Device [*Tool attached to shrimp boats in the
    Gulf of Mexico which allows the endangered Kemp's ridley
    turtle to escape the shrimp nets*]
TEDA .... Theatre Equipment Dealers Association [*Later, TEA*]   (EA)
TEDA .... Triethylenediamine [*Organic chemistry*]
TEDAR .... Telemetered Data Reduction   (AAG)
TEDC .... Technical Education Center
TEDC......... Tellurium Diethyldithiocarbamate [*Organic chemistry*]
TEDDS .... Tactical Environmental Dissemination and Display
    System   (MCD)
TEDE .... Temperature-Enhanced Displacement Effect
TEDES .... Telemetry Data Evaluation System
TEDGA .... Technical Digest [*A publication*]
TEDL .... Transferred-Electron-Device Logic   (MSA)
TEDMA .... Triethylene Dimethacrylate [*Organic chemistry*]
TEDP .... Tetraethyl Dithionopyrophosphate [*Organic chemistry*]
TEDPAS ..... Technical Data Package Automated System
TEDS .... Tactical Expendable Drone System   (MCD)
TEDS .... Target Effluent Detection System   (MCD)
TEDS .... Teleteach Expanded Delivery System [*US Air Force*] [*Wright-
    Patterson AFB, OH*] [*Telecommunications*]   (TSSD)
TEDSCO .... Test Equipment Documentation Scheduling Committee
TEE .... Tape Editing Equipment
TEE .... Tbessa [*Algeria*] [*Airport symbol*]   (OAG)
TEE .... Teeples Ranch [*Montana*] [*Seismograph station code, US
    Geological Survey*] [*Closed*]   (SEIS)
TEE .... Teeshin Resources Ltd. [*Vancouver Stock Exchange symbol*]
TEE .... Terminal Effects and Experimentation   (MCD)
TEE .... Test Equipment Engineering   (AAG)
TEE .... Torpedo Experimental Establishment [*British*]
TEE .... Total Effective Exposure [*Advertising*]
TEE .... Trans-Europ-Express [*Continental high-speed train*]
TEE .... Transesophageal Echocardiography
TEE .... Triaxial Earth Ellipsoid
TEEF .... Tax-Exempt Equity Fund
TEEL .... Temporary Expedient Equipment List [*Army*]   (AABC)
TEEM .... Trans-Europ-Express-Marchandises [*Continental high-speed
    train*]
TEES .... Texas Engineering Experiment Station [*Texas A & M
    University*] [*Research center*]
TEESS....... Tank Engine Exhaust Smoke System   (MCD)
TEES Tech Bull ... TEES [*Texas Engineering Experiment Station*] Technical
    Bulletin [*A publication*]
TEF .... [*The*] Environmental Fund [*Later, PEB*]   (EA)
TEF............ Tear Efficiency Factor [*Textiles*]
Tef............ Tefillin   (BJA)
TEF............ Telfer [*Australia*] [*Airport symbol*]   (OAG)
TEF............ Temperance Education Foundation [*Defunct*]   (EA)
TEF............ Tunable Etalon Filter
TEFA .... Total Essential Fatty Acid [*of foodstuffs*]
TEFA .... Total Esterified Fatty Acid
TEFAP....... Temporary Emergency Food Assistance Program [*Department
    of Agriculture*]
TEFC .... Totally Enclosed - Fan Cooled
TEFL.......... Teaching English as a Foreign Language
TEFLON ..... Tetrafluoroethylene Resin [*Du Pont*]
TEFL/TESL Newsl ... TEFL [*Teaching English as a Foreign Language*]/TESL
    [*Teaching English as a Second Language*] Newsletter [*A
    publication*]
TEFO .... Technological Forecasting and Social Change [*A publication*]
TEFORS ..... Technological Forecasting and Simulation for Program
    Selection   (MCD)
TEFRA........ Tax Equity and Fiscal Responsibility Act [*1982*]
TEG .... Tactical Employment Guide [*Military*]   (CAAL)
TEG .... Templar Mining [*Vancouver Stock Exchange symbol*]
TEG .... Test Element Group
TEG .... Tetraethylene Glycol [*Organic chemistry*]
TEG .... Thermoelectric Generator
TEG .... Thromboelastogram [*Medicine*]

TEG .... Top Edge Gilt [*Bookbinding*]
TEG .... Triethylene Glycol [*Organic chemistry*]
TEGAS ...... Test Generation and Simulation
TEGAS ...... Time Generation and Simulation [*Telecommunications*]   (TEL)
TEGDN ...... Triethylene Glycol Dinitrate [*An explosive*]
TEGG .... Thermogrip Electric Glue Gun
TEGMA ...... Terminal Elevator Grain Merchants Association   (EA)
TEGMA ...... Triethylene Glycol Dimethacrylate [*Organic chemistry*]   (MCD)
TEGO .... Taylor's Encyclopedia of Government Officials [*A publication*]
TEGTA .... Technische Gemeinschaft [*A publication*]
TEGWAR .... [*The*] Exciting Game Without Any Rules [*Card game*]
TEH .... Blare Lake, AK [*Location identifier*] [*FAA*]   (FAAL)
Teh .... Tehillim   (BJA)
TEH .... Tehran [*Iran*] [*Geomagnetic observatory code*]
TEH .... Tehran [*Iran*] [*Seismograph station code, US Geological Survey*]   (SEIS)
TEH .... Tehua [*Race of maize*]
TEH .... Topics in Environmental Health [*Elsevier Book Series*] [*A publication*]
TEH .... Twin-Engined Helicopter   (MCD)
Teh Fiz ...... Tehnicka Fizika [*A publication*]
Teh Hronika ... Tehnika Hronika [*A publication*]
TEHP .... Thermoelectric Heat Pump   (MCD)
Teh Tootmine ... Tehnika ja Tootmine [*Estonian SSR*] [*A publication*]
TEI .... Tax Executives Institute   (EA)
TEI .... Technical Engineering Item   (MCD)
TE & I .... Technology Evaluation and Integration   (MCD)
TEI .... Telecommunications Engineering, Incorporated [*Dallas, TX*]   (TSSD)
TEI .... Temporary Engineering Instruction [*Navy*]   (NG)
TEI .... Texas International Co. [*NYSE symbol*] [*Toronto Stock Exchange symbol*]
TEI .... Thorne Ecological Institute   (EA)
TEI .... Trait Evaluation Index [*Psychology*]
TEI .... Transearth Injection [*AEC*]
TEI .... Transfer on Error Indication
TEI .... Trucking Employers, Incorporated [*Later, TMI*]
TEIC .... Tissue Equivalent Ionization Chamber
TEICA .... Transactions. Engineering Institute of Canada [*A publication*]
TEIGA .... Teishin Igaku [*A publication*]
Teilhard Rev ... Teilhard Review [*London*] [*A publication*]
Teiss .... Teissler's Court of Appeal, Parish of Orleans, Reports [*1903-17*]   (DLA)
Teissler ...... Teissler's Court of Appeal, Parish of Orleans, Reports [*1903-17*]   (DLA)
TEJ .... Emmanuel School of Religion, Johnson City, TN [*OCLC symbol*]   (OCLC)
TEJ .... Transverse Expansion Joint [*Technical drawings*]
TEJA .... Tutmonda Esperantista Jurnalista Asocio [*World Association of Esperanto Journalists - WAEJ*]   (EA-IO)
TEJAC .... Trade Effluent Joint Advisory Committee [*British*]
TEJIA .... Transport Engineer [*A publication*]
TEJO .... Tutmonda Esperantista Junulara Organizo [*World Organization of Young Esperantists*]   (EA-IO)
TEJPA .... Tejipar [*A publication*]
TEK .... Teck Corp. [*Toronto Stock Exchange symbol*] [*Vancouver Stock Exchange symbol*]
TEK .... Teekin [*Tonga*] [*Seismograph station code, US Geological Survey*]   (SEIS)
TEK .... Tektronix, Inc. [*NYSE symbol*]
TEK .... Test Equipment Kit
TeK........... Text und Kontext [*A publication*]
TEK .... Truppenentgiftungskompanie [*Personnel decontamination company*] [*German military - World War II*]
Tek Aikak... Teknillinen Aikakauslehti [*A publication*]
Tek Bul Petkim Petrokimya A S Arastirma Mudurlugu ... Teknik Bulten. Petkim Petrokimya A. S. Arastirma Mudurlugu [*A publication*]
Tek Forum ... Teknisk Forum [*Finland*] [*A publication*]
TEKHA .... Teoreticheskaya i Eksperimental'naya Khimiya [*A publication*]
Tekh Dokl Gidrol ... Tekhnicheskie Doklady po Gidrologii [*A publication*]
Tekh Estetika ... Tekhnicheskaya Estetika [*USSR*] [*A publication*]
Tekh Inf Sov Nar Khoz Kuibyshev Ekon Adm Raiona ... Tekhnicheskaya Informatsiya. Sovet Nardnogo Khozyaistva Kuibyshevskogo Ekonomicheskogo Administrativnogo Raiona [*A publication*]
Tekh Kibern ... Tekhnicheskaya Kibernetika [*A publication*]
Tekh Kino i Telev ... Tekhnika Kino i Televideniya [*A publication*]
Tekh Kino Telev ... Tekhnika Kino i Televideniya [*A publication*]
Tekh Mis'l ... Tekhnicheska Mis'l [*A publication*]
Tekh Misul ... Tekhnicheska Misul [*Bulgaria*] [*A publication*]
Tekhnol Legk Splavov ... Tekhnologiya Legkikh Splavov [*A publication*]
Tekhnol Neorg Veshchestv ... Tekhnologiya Neorganicheskikh Veshchestv [*A publication*]
Tekhnol Organ Proizvod ... Tekhnologiya i Organizatsiya Proizvodstva [*A publication*]
Tekhnol Proizvod Sukhikh Diagn Pitatel'nykh Sred ... Tekhnologiya Proizvodstva Sukhikh Diagnosticheskikh Pitatel'nykh Sred [*A publication*]
Tek Hoegsk Handl ... Tekniska Hoegskolan Handlingar [*A publication*]

Tek Hogsk Helsingfors Vetensk Publ ... Tekniska Hoegskolan i Helsingfors Vetenskapliga Publikationer [*A publication*]
Tekh Sel'Khoz ... Tekhnika v Sel'skom Khozyaistve [*A publication*]
Tekh Usloviya Metody Opred Vrednykh Veshchestv Vozdukhe ... Tekhnicheskie Usloviya na Metody Opredeleniya Vrednykh Veshchestv v Vozdukhe [*A publication*]
Tekh Vooruzhenie ... Tekhnika i Vooruzhenie [*USSR*] [*A publication*]
Tekh Vozdushn Flota ... Tekhnika Vozdushnogo Flota [*A publication*]
Tekh Zhelezn Dorog ... Tekhnika Zheleznykh Dorog [*A publication*]
Tek Inf........ Teknisk Information [*Sweden*] [*A publication*]
TEKKA ...... Tekkokai [*A publication*]
Tek Kem Aikak ... Teknillisen Kemian Aikakauslehti [*Finland*] [*A publication*]
Tek Medd... Tekniska Meddelanden [*Sweden*] [*A publication*]
Tekn Forsknstift Skogsarb ... Teknik Forskningsstiftelsen Skogsarbeten [*A publication*]
TEKSA ...... Tekhnika (Sofia) [*A publication*]
TEKSIF....... Turkiye Tekstil ve Orme Sanayii Iscileri Sendikalari Federasyonu [*National Federation of Textile Unions*] [*Turkey*]
Tekstil Prom ... Tekstil'naya Promyshlennost [*A publication*]
Tekst Prom (Sofia) ... Tekstilna Promishlennost (Sofia) [*A publication*]
Tekst Prom-st ... Tekstil'naya Promyshlennost [*A publication*]
TEKTA ...... Tekstil [*A publication*]
Tek Tidskr ... Teknisk Tidskrift [*A publication*]
Tek Tidsskr Text Beklaedning ... Teknisk Tidsskrift for Textil og Beklaedning [*A publication*]
Tektonika Sib ... Tektonika Sibiri [*A publication*]
Tek Ukebl ... Teknisk Ukeblad [*A publication*]
Tek Vetensk Forsk ... Teknisk Vetenskaplig Forskning [*Sweden*] [*A publication*]
Tek Yay Kavak Arast Enst (Izmit) ... Teknik Yayinlar. Kavakcihk Arastirma Enstitusu (Izmit, Turkey) [*A publication*]
TEL............ Task Execution Language
TEL............ Taxpayers Education Lobby   (EA)
TEL............ TeleCom Corp. [*NYSE symbol*]
TEL............ Telecommunications   (FAAC)
TEL............ Telegram
TEL............ Telegraph
TEL............ Telemetry   (KSC)
TEL............ Telephone   (AAG)
TEL............ Telescope   (AAG)
Tel .... Telescopium [*Constellation*]
TEL............ Teletypewriter [*Telecommunications*]   (NOAA)
TEL............ Tell City, IN [*Location identifier*] [*FAA*]   (FAAL)
tel .... Telugu [*MARC language code*] [*Library of Congress*]   (LCCP)
TEL............ Terex Equipment Limited
TEL............ Tetraethyllead [*Organic chemistry*]
TEL............ Thomas Edward Lawrence [*Lawrence of Arabia*] [*British archaeologist, soldier, and writer, 1888-1935*]
TEL............ Training Equipment List
TEL............ Transporter-Erector-Launcher [*Air Force*]
Telan .... Telenoticiosa Americana [*Press agency*] [*Argentina*]
TELATS ..... Tactical Electronic Locating and Targeting System   (MCD)
Tel-Aviv Univ Stud L ... Tel-Aviv University Studies in Law [*Tel-Aviv, Israel*]   (DLA)
TELB .... Telephone Booth
TELC .... Teleglobe Canada
TELCAM .... Telecommunication Equipment Low-Cost Acquisition Method [*Navy*]
TELCO .... Telephone Operating Company [*Also, TELOP*]
TELCOM .... Telecommunications   (NASA)
Telcom Rep ... Telcom Report [*A publication*]
TELCON..... Telephone Conference [*or Conversation*]   (AAG)
TELD .... Test of Early Language Development
TELE .... Telecom Plus International, Inc. [*NASDAQ symbol*]   (NQ)
TELE .... Telegram
TELE .... Telegraph
TELE .... Telephone
Tele .... Telescopium [*Constellation*]
TELE .... Television   (ADA)
TELEC .... Teleglobe Canada
TELEC........ Thermoelectronic LASER Energy Converter
TELECAMRA ... Television Camera   (MDG)
TELECAR... Telemetry Carrier Acquisition and Recovery   (MCD)
TELECAST ... Television Broadcasting   (CET)
TELECOM ... Telecommunications   (AFM)
Telecom..... Telecommunications [*A publication*]
Telecom Aust Res Q ... Telecom Australia Research Quarterly [*A publication*]
Telecom J ... Telecommunication Journal of Australia [*A publication*]
Telecom J Aust ... Telecommunication Journal of Australia [*A publication*]
Telecomm ... Telecommunications [*A publication*]
Telecomm J ... Telecommunication Journal [*A publication*]
Telecomm J Aust ... Telecommunication Journal of Australia [*A publication*]
Telecomms ... Telecommunications [*International Edition*] [*A publication*]
Telecommun J ... Telecommunication Journal [*A publication*]
Telecommun J Aust ... Telecommunication Journal of Australia [*A publication*]
Telecommun J (Engl Ed) ... Telecommunication Journal (English Edition) [*A publication*]

Telecommun Radio Eng ... Telecommunications and Radio Engineering [*A publication*]
Telecommun Radio Eng (USSR) Part 2 ... Telecommunications and Radio Engineering (USSR). Part 2. Radio Engineering [*A publication*]
TELECON ... Telephone [*or Teletype*] Conference [*or Conversation*] (AFM)
TELECONV ... Telephone Conversation
TELEDAC... Telemetric Data Converter
TELEDAQ... Television Data Acquisition System (MCD)
TELEDIS .... Teletypewriter Distribution (NATG)
Tele (Engl Ed) ... Tele (English Edition) [*A publication*]
TELEFLORA ... Telegraph Florists Delivery Service
Telefon Rep ... Telefon Report [*A publication*]
Telef Rep ... Telefon Report [*A publication*]
Telefunken-Ztg ... Telefunken-Zeitung [*West Germany*] [*A publication*]
TELEG........ Telegram
TELEG........ Telegraph
Telegr & Telef ... Telegraaf en Telefoon [*A publication*]
TELEMAN ... Telephone Management System
Telem Ant ... Telemetry Antenna
TELENET... TELENET Communications Corp. [*GTE*] (TEL)
TELEPAK... Telemetering Package
TELEPH...... Telephone
Teleph Eng & Manage ... Telephone Engineer and Management [*A publication*]
Telephone ... Telephone Engineer and Management [*A publication*]
TELER ...... Telecommunications Requirements (MCD)
TELERAN... Television and RADAR Navigation System (MUGU)
TELESAT... Telecommunications Satellite
TELESUN... Telecommunications Software User's Network [*Telesun Corp.*] [*Salt Lake City, UT*] (TSSD)
Tele (Swed Ed) ... Tele (Swedish Edition) [*A publication*]
TELETECH ... National Telecommunications & Technology Fund, Inc. [*New York, NY*] (TSSD)
Tele-Tech & Electronic Ind ... Tele-Tech and Electronic Industries [*A publication*]
TELETYPE ... Teletypewriter [*Telecommunications*]
Televerket ... National Swedish Telecommunications Administration [*Stockholm*] [*Information service*] (EISS)
Television (JR Telev Soc) ... Television (Journal of the Royal Television Society) [*A publication*]
TELEX........ Automatic Teletypewriter Exchange Service [*of Western Union*]
TELF.......... Tamil Eelam Liberation Front [*Sri Lankan*] (PPW)
TELFAD ..... Telephone Executive Leader for a Day [*New England Telephone Co. program for high school students*]
TELG.......... Telegram
Telhan Patrica Oilseeds J ... Telhan Patrica/Oilseeds Journal [*A publication*]
TELIDON.... [*A*] television terminal-based interactive information retrieval system
TELINT....... Telemetry Intelligence
TELIST....... Telegraphist (DSUE)
TELL........... Teleci, Inc. of Texas [*NASDAQ symbol*] (NQ)
TELL-A-GRAF ... [*A*] programing language [*1978*] (CSR)
Tellus Ser A ... Tellus. Series A. Dynamic Meteorology and Oceanography [*A publication*]
TELM.......... Telegram (ROG)
TELMTR...... Telemotor
TELNET...... Georgia Telecommunications Network [*Georgia Hospital Association*] [*Atlanta, GA*] [*Telecommunications*] (TSSD)
TELO .... Tamil Eelam Liberation Organization [*Sri Lankan*]
Tel Off .... Telegraph Office
TELOP........ Telephone Operating Co. [*Also, TELCO*]
TELOPS ...... Telemetry Online Processing System [*Data processing*]
TELOZ......... TEL Offshore Trust UBI [*NASDAQ symbol*] (NQ)
TELPAK....... Telephone Package
TelQ .... Tel Quel [*A publication*]
TELR .... Teleram Communications [*NASDAQ symbol*] (NQ)
Tel Rad E R ... Telecommunications and Radio Engineering (USSR) [*A publication*]
TELRY .... Telegraph Reply (FAAC)
TELS .... Turbine Engine Loads Simulator
TELSAM..... Telephone Service Attitude Measurement [*Telephone interviews*] [*AT & T*]
TELSCAR... Transmit Electronically Location Shippers' Car Advice Reports
TELSCOM ... Telemetry-Surveillance-Communications
TELSCPD... Telescoped
TELSIM ..... Teletypewriter Simulation
TELSUN ..... Television Series for United Nations [*A foundation formed to produce, and telecast on a commercial basis, dramatized descriptions of UN activities*]
TEL SUR .... Telephone Survey (MUGU)
TEL-SYS.... Telephone System
TELTA .... Tethered Lighter-than-Air (KSC)
TELUQ .... Tele-Universite (University of Quebec) [*Quebec, PQ*] [*Telecommunications*] (TSSD)
TELUS .... Telemetric Universal Sensor
TELV .... TeleVideo Systems [*NASDAQ symbol*] (NQ)
Tel Vaani .... Telugu Vaani [*Hyderabad*] [*A publication*]
TEM............ Memphis University School, Hyde Library, Memphis, TN [*OCLC symbol*] (OCLC)
TeM............ O Tempo e o Modo [*A publication*]

TEM........... Officers for Temporary Service [*Navy*] [*British*] (ROG)
TEM........... Roswell Park Memorial Institute [*Research code symbol*]
TEM........... Target Engagement Message (NVT)
TEM........... Target Evaluation Maintenance (MCD)
TEM........... Technical Error Message [*Aviation*]
TE & M .... Telephone Engineer & Management [*Harcourt Brace Jovanovich Publications, Inc.*] [*Geneva, IL*] [*Information service*] [*A publication*]
TEM........... Temiskaming & Northern Ontario Railway [*AAR code*]
tem............ Temne [*MARC language code*] [*Library of Congress*] (LCCP)
TEM........... Temora [*Australia*] [*Airport symbol*] (OAG)
TEM........... Temperature (DEN)
TEM........... Tempered (DEN)
Tem............ [*The*] Templar [*1788-79*] [*London*] (DLA)
TEM........... Template (DEN)
TEM........... Tempo [*Music*]
Tem............ Tempo [*Record label*] [*Germany*]
Tem............ Tempore [*In the Time Of*] [*Latin*] (DLA)
TEM........... Temuco [*Chile*] [*Seismograph station code, US Geological Survey*] [*Closed*] (SEIS)
TeM............ Tennessee Microfilms, Nashville, TN [*Library symbol*] [*Library of Congress*] (LCLS)
TEM........... Terramar Resource [*Toronto Stock Exchange symbol*] [*Vancouver Stock Exchange symbol*]
TEM........... Thermoelectric Module
TEM........... Transmission Electron Microscope [*or Microscopy*]
TEM........... Transverse Electromagnetic [*Wave*] [*Radio*]
TEM........... Triethylenemelamine [*Organic chemistry*]
TEM........... Typical Egg Mass
TEMA .... Telecommunication Engineering and Manufacturing Association [*British*]
TEMA .... Test of Early Mathematics Ability
TEMA .... Trace Elements in Man and Animals [*An international symposium*]
TEMA .... Training, Education, and Mutual Assistance in the Marine Sciences [*IOC working committee*] (MSC)
TEMA .... Tubular Exchanger Manufacturers Association [*Tarrytown, NY*] (EA)
TEMAC .... Temporary Active Duty
TEMAC ...... Turbine Engine Monitoring and Control [*ASMAP Electronics Ltd.*] [*Software package*]
TEMACDIFOT ... Temporary Active Duty in a Flying Status Involving Operational or Training Flights [*Navy*]
TEMACDIFOTINS ... Temporary Active Duty under Instruction in a Flying Status Involving Operational or Training Flights [*Navy*]
TEMACDU ... Temporary Active Duty [*Navy*]
TEMACINS ... Temporary Active Duty under Instruction [*Navy*]
TEMADD .... Temporary Additional Duty [*Navy*]
TEMADDCON ... Temporary Additional Duty in Connection with [*Specified activity*] [*Navy*]
TEMADDINS ... Temporary Additional Duty under Instruction [*Navy*]
TEMARS .... Transportation Environmental Measurement and Recording System (MCD)
Temas Odontol ... Temas Odontologicos [*A publication*]
Temas Socs ... Temas Sociales [*A publication*]
Temat Sb Inst Fiziol Biofiz Rast Akad Nauk Tadzh SSR ... Tematicheskii Sbornik. Institut Fiziologii i Biofiziki Rastenii. Akademiya Nauk Tadzhikskoi SSR [*A publication*]
Temat Sb Nauc Trud Alma-Atin Semipalatin Zoovet Inst ... Tematicheskii Sbornik Nauchnykh Trudov Alma-Atinskogo i Semipalatinskogo Zooveterinarnykh Institutov [*A publication*]
Temat Sb Otd Fiziol Biofiz Rast Akad Nauk Tadzh SSR ... Tematicheskii Sbornik Otdel Fiziologii i Biofiziki Rastenii Akademiya Nauk Tadzhikskoi SSR [*A publication*]
TEMAW...... Tactical Effectiveness of Minefields in Antiarmor Warfare Systems [*Army*] (INF)
TEMC .... Temcohome Health Care [*NASDAQ symbol*] (NQ)
TEMC .... Test and Evaluation Management Course (MCD)
TEMDIFOT ... Temporary Duty in a Flying Status Involving Operational or Training Flights [*Navy*]
TEMDIFOTINS ... Temporary Duty under Instruction in a Flying Status Involving Operational or Training Flights [*Navy*]
TEMDU...... Temporary Duty [*Navy*]
TEMDUCON ... Temporary Duty in Connection With [*Specified activity*] [*Navy*]
TEMDUINS ... Temporary Duty under Instruction [*Navy*]
TEMEC...... Translational Electromagnetic Environment Chamber (MCD)
TEMED....... Tetramethylethylenediamine [*Also, TMED, TMEDA*] [*Organic chemistry*]
TEMFLY ..... Temporary Duty Involving Flying [*Navy*]
TEMFLYINS ... Temporary Duty Involving Flying under Instruction [*Navy*]
TEMINS...... Temporary Duty under Instruction [*Navy*]
TEMIS....... Targets Engineering Management Information System [*Navy*]
TEMO......... Test and Evaluation Management Office [*Army*] (RDA)
TEMOD ...... Test, Measurement, and Diagnostic Equipment Modernization [*Military*] (RDA)
TEMP .... Electrical Resistance Temperature (MCD)
TEMP .... Taxation Employment Number [*Canada*]
TEMP .... Technique for Econometric Modeling Program (BUR)
TEMP .... Temp-Stik Corp. [*NASDAQ symbol*] (NQ)

TEMP .... Temperance (ADA)
TEMP .... Temperature (AAG)
TEMP .... Tempered (AAG)
TEMP .... Template (AAG)
TEMP .... Tempo [*Music*]
TEMP .... Temporal
TEMP .... Temporary
Temp........ Temporary Light [*Navigation signal*]
TEMP .... Temporary Worker
TEMP .... Test Evaluation Master Plan (MCD)
TEMP .... Texas Educational Microwave Project
TEMP .... Total Energy Management Professionals [*Defunct*] (EA)
Temp Bar .... Temple Bar [*A publication*]
TEMP DEXT ... Tempus Dextra [*Right Temple*] [*Medicine*]
Temp Emer Ct App ... Temporary Emergency Court of Appeals [*United States*] (DLA)
TEMPER..... Technological, Economic, Military, and Political Evaluation Routine [*Computer-based simulation model*]
TEMPER..... Tent, Extendable, Modular, Personnel [*DoD*]
Temp Geo II ... Cases in Chancery Tempore George II [*England*] (DLA)
TEMPISTORS ... Temperature Compensating Resistors (NATG)
TEMPL .... Template [*Engineering*]
Temple Dent Rev ... Temple Dental Review [*A publication*]
Temple Law ... Temple Law Quarterly [*A publication*]
Temple L Quart ... Temple Law Quarterly [*A publication*]
Temple & M ... Temple and Mew's English Crown Cases (DLA)
Temple & M (Eng) ... Temple and Mew's English Crown Cases (DLA)
Templ L Q... Temple Law Quarterly [*A publication*]
Temp & M ... Temple and Mew's English Crown Cases [*1848-51*] (DLA)
TEMPO...... Tactical Electromagnetic Project Office [*Military*] (CAAL)
TEMPO...... Technical Electronic Management Planning Organization
TEMPO...... Technical Military Planning Operation (AAG)
TEMPO...... Technique for Extreme Point Optimization (BUR)
TEMPO...... Temporary (AAG)
TEMPO...... Time and Effort Measurement through Periodic Observation (MCD)
TEMPO...... Total Evaluation of Management and Production Output
TEMPOS .... Timed Environment Multipartitioned Operating System
TEMP PRIM ... Tempo Primo [*Original Tempo*] [*Music*]
TEMPROX ... Temporary Duty Will Cover Approximately [*Navy*]
TEMPS...... Transportable Electromagnetic Pulse Simulator (RDA)
TEMPSAL ... Temperature Salinity Data [*Oceanography*] (MCD)
TEMP SINIST ... Tempori Sinistro [*To the Left Temple*] [*Pharmacy*] (ADA)
Temps Mod ... Temps Modernes [*A publication*]
Temp Univ LQ ... Temple University. Law Quarterly (DLA)
Temp Wood ... Manitoba Reports Tempore Wood [*Canada*] (DLA)
TEMPY...... Temporary
TEMS .... Test Equipment Maintenance Set
TEMS .... Thermal Elastic Model Study
TEMS .... Toyota Electronically Modulated Suspension [*Automotive engineering*]
TEMS .... Transport Environment Monitoring System (MCD)
TEMS .... Turbine Engine Monitoring System
TEMSEPRAD ... Temporary Duty Connection, Separation Processing. Upon Completion and When Directed Detach; Proceed Home for Release from Active Duty in Accordance with Instructions [*Navy*]
TEMSS....... Total Emergency Medical Services System
TEMWAIT... Temporary Duty Awaiting [*Specified event*] [*Navy*]
TEN .... Canarias [*Formerly, Tenerife*] [*Spain*] [*Geomagnetic observatory code*]
TEN .... Tee-Comm Electronics [*Toronto Stock Exchange symbol*]
ten............. Tenacious [*Quality of the bottom*] [*Nautical charts*]
TEN .... Tenerife [*Canary Islands*] [*Seismograph station code, US Geological Survey*] (SEIS)
TEN .... Tennessee (ROG)
TEN .... Tennessee Airways [*Alcoa, TN*] [*FAA designator*] (FAAC)
TEN .... Tenor
TEN .... Tenuto [*Held, Sustained*] [*Music*]
TEN .... Total Enteral Nutrition
TEN .... Total Excreted [*or Excretory*] Nitrogen
TEN .... Toxic Epidermal Necrolysis [*Medicine*]
Tenakh...... Torah, Veni'im, Ketubim (BJA)
Ten App ..... Tennessee Appeals Reports (DLA)
TENCA...... Traffic Engineering and Control [*England*] [*A publication*]
TENCAP..... Tactical Exploitation of National Space Capabilities
Ten Cas..... Shannon's Tennessee Cases (DLA)
Ten Cas...... Thompson's Unreported Tennessee Cases (DLA)
TENCY...... Tenancy (ROG)
Tendances Conjonct ... Tendances de la Conjoncture [*A publication*]
Tendances Polit Act Dom ... Tendances et Politiques Actuelles dans le Domaine de l'Habitation de la Construction et de la Planification [*A publication*]
TENEMT..... Tenement (ROG)
TENES .... Teaching English to the Non-English Speaking
TEng .... Teaching English [*A publication*]
TENG .... Technical Engineers Association
TENN........ Tennessee (AAG)
TENN........ Tennessee Natural Resources [*NASDAQ symbol*] (NQ)
TENN.......... Tennessee Railway Co. [*AAR code*]

Tenn........... Tennessee Supreme Court Reports (DLA)
Tenn Admin Comp ... Official Compilation of the Rules and Regulations of the State of Tennessee (DLA)
Tenn Admin Reg ... Tennessee Administrative Register (DLA)
Tenn Ag Exp ... Tennessee. Agricultural Experiment Station. Publications [*A publication*]
Tenn Agr Exp Sta ... Tennessee. Agricultural Experiment Station [*A publication*]
Tenn Agric Exp Stn Annu Rep ... Tennessee. Agricultural Experiment Station. Annual Report [*A publication*]
Tenn Agric Exp Stn Bull ... Tennessee. Agricultural Experiment Station. Bulletin [*A publication*]
Tenn Agric Exp Stn Farm Econ Bull ... Tennessee. Agricultural Experiment Station. Farm Economics Bulletin [*A publication*]
Tenn Apiculture ... Tennessee Apiculture [*A publication*]
Tenn App ... Tennessee Civil Appeals Reports (DLA)
Tenn App Bull ... Tennessee Appellate Bulletin (DLA)
Tenn Appeals ... Tennessee Appeals Reports (DLA)
Tenn App R ... Tennessee Appeals Reports (DLA)
Tenn Bar J ... Tennessee Bar Journal [*A publication*]
Tenn Cas ... Shannon's Unreported Tennessee Cases [*1847-1894*] (DLA)
Tenn Cas (Shannon) ... [*R. T.*] Shannon's Tennessee Cases (DLA)
Tenn Cas (Shannon) ... Thompson's Unreported Tennessee Cases [*1847-69*] (DLA)
Tenn CCA ... Tennessee Court of Civil Appeals (DLA)
Tenn CCA (Higgins) ... Higgins' Tennessee Court of Civil Appeals Reports (DLA)
Tenn Ch ..... Cooper's Tennessee Chancery Reports [*1878*] (DLA)
Tenn Ch A ... Tennessee Chancery Appeals (DLA)
Tenn Chancery ... Tennessee Chancery Reports - Cooper (DLA)
Tenn Chancery App ... Tennessee Chancery Appeals Reports Wright (DLA)
Tenn Ch App ... Tennessee Chancery Appeals [*Wright*] (DLA)
Tenn Ch App Dec ... Tennessee Chancery Appeals Decisions [*1895-1907*] (DLA)
Tenn Ch Ap Reps ... Wright's Tennessee Chancery Appeals Reports (DLA)
Tenn Ch R ... Tennessee Chancery Reports - Cooper (DLA)
Tenn Civ A ... Tennessee Civil Appeals (DLA)
Tenn Civ App ... Tennessee Civil Appeals (DLA)
Tenn Code Ann ... Tennessee Code, Annotated (DLA)
Tenn Conservationist ... Tennessee Conservationist [*A publication*]
Tenn Cr App ... Tennessee Criminal Appeals (DLA)
Tenn Crim App ... Tennessee Criminal Appeals Reports (DLA)
Tenn Dep Conserv Div Geol Bull ... Tennessee. Department of Conservation. Division of Geology. Bulletin [*A publication*]
Tenn Dept Labor Ann Rept ... Tennessee. Department of Labor. Annual Report [*A publication*]
Tenn Div Geol Bull ... Tennessee. Division of Geology. Bulletin [*A publication*]
Tenn Div Geol Environ Geol Ser ... Tennessee. Division of Geology. Environmental Geology Series [*A publication*]
Tenn Div Geol Inf Circ ... Tennessee. Division of Geology. Information Circular [*A publication*]
Tenn Div Geol Inform Circ ... Tennessee. Division of Geology. Information Circular [*A publication*]
Tenn Eng ... Tennessee Engineer [*A publication*]
Tennessee Acad Sci Jour ... Tennessee Academy of Science. Journal [*A publication*]
Tennessee Div Geology Geol Map ... Tennessee. Division of Geology. Geologic Map [*A publication*]
Tennessee Div Geology Rept Inv ... Tennessee. Division of Geology. Report of Investigations [*A publication*]
Tennessee R ... Tennessee Reports (DLA)
Tennessee Rep ... Tennessee Reports (DLA)
Tenn Farm & Home Sci ... Tennessee Farm and Home Science [*A publication*]
Tenn Farm Home Sci Progr Rep ... Tennessee Farm and Home Science. Progress Report. University of Tennessee. Agricultural Experiment Station [*A publication*]
Tenn Folk S ... Tennessee Folklore Society. Bulletin [*A publication*]
Tenn G S Res Tenn B ... Tennessee State Geological Survey. Resources of Tennessee. Bulletin [*A publication*]
Tenn His M ... Tennessee Historical Magazine [*A publication*]
Tenn Hist Mag ... Tennessee Magazine of History [*A publication*]
Tenn Hist Q ... Tennessee Historical Quarterly [*A publication*]
Tenn Law Rev ... Tennessee Law Review [*A publication*]
Tenn Leg Rep ... Tennessee Legal Reporter (DLA)
Tenn Libn .. Tennessee Librarian [*A publication*]
Tenn Librn ... Tennessee Librarian [*A publication*]
Tenn L R... Tennessee Law Review [*A publication*]
Tenn L Rev ... Tennessee Law Review [*A publication*]
Tenn Mag... Tennessee Magazine [*A publication*]
Tenn Priv Acts ... Private Acts of the State of Tennessee (DLA)
Tenn Pub Acts ... Public Acts of the State of Tennessee (DLA)
Tenn R........ Tennessee Reports (DLA)
Tenn Rep ... Tennessee Reports (DLA)
Tenn St Bd Health B Rp ... Tennessee State Board of Health. Bulletin. Report [*A publication*]
Tenn Surv Bus ... Tennessee Survey of Business [*A publication*]
TENN-TOM... Tennessee-Tombigbee [*Proposed waterway*]
Tenn Univ Eng Exp Sta Bull ... Tennessee University. Engineering Experiment Station. Bulletin [*A publication*]

Tenn Val Auth Chem Eng Bul ... Tennessee Valley Authority. Chemical Engineering Bulletin [*A publication*]
Tenn Val Auth Natl Fert Dev Cent Bull Y ... Tennessee Valley Authority. National Fertilizer Development Center. Bulletin Y [*A publication*]
Tenn Valley Perspect ... Tennessee Valley Perspective [*A publication*]
Tenn Wildl ... Tennessee Wildlife [*A publication*]
TENOC......... Ten-Year Oceanographic Program [*Navy*]
TENR......... Technically Enhanced Naturally Radioactive   (NRCH)
TENRAP..... Technically Enhanced Naturally Radioactive Product   (NRCH)
TENS......... Tensile
TENS......... Tension   (AAG)
TENS......... Transcutaneous Electrical Nerve Stimulation [*Also, TES, TNS*] [*A method of pain control*] [*Medicine*]
Tensai Kenkyu Hokoku Suppl ... Tensai Kenkyu Hokoku. Supplement [*Japan*] [*A publication*]
TENSEGRITY ... Tensional Integrity [*Construction principle named by Buckminster Fuller*]
Tenside..... Tenside-Detergents [*A publication*]
Tenside-Deterg ... Tenside-Detergents [*A publication*]
TENT......... Tenant   (ROG)
TENT......... Tenement   (ROG)
TENT......... Tentative   (AAG)
TENV......... Totally Enclosed - Nonventilated
TEO............ Technical Electronic Office [*Data General Corp.*]
TEO............ Telephone Equipment Order [*Telecommunications*]   (TEL)
TEO............ Teoloyucan [*Mexico*] [*Geomagnetic observatory code*]
TEO............ Terapo [*Papua New Guinea*] [*Airport symbol*]   (OAG)
TEO............ Terato Resources [*Toronto Stock Exchange symbol*] [*Vancouver Stock Exchange symbol*]
TEO............ Test Equipment Operator
TEO............ Total Extractable Organic [*Analytical chemistry*]
T & EO...... Training and Evaluation Outline
TEO............ Transferred Electron Oscillator
TEO............ Transmittal Engineering Order
TEOA......... Test and Evaluation Objectives Annex   (MCD)
TEOA......... Triethanolamine [*Organic chemistry*]
TEOC......... Texas Eagle Oil Company [*NASDAQ symbol*]   (NQ)
TEOF......... Triethyl Orthoformate [*Organic chemistry*]
Teolisuuden Keskuslab Tied ... Teolisuuden Keskuslaboratorion Tiedonantoja [*A publication*]
Teollis Tiedottaa ... Teollisuuslitto Tiedottaa [*A publication*]
Teol Vida.... Teologia y Vida [*A publication*]
TEOM......... Tapered Element Oscillating Microbalance
TEOM......... Transformer Environment Overcurrent Monitor   (IEEE)
Teor Ehksp Khim ... Teoreticheskaya i Ehksperimental'naya Khimiya [*A publication*]
Teor Ehlektrotekh ... Teoreticheskaya Ehlektrotekhnika [*A publication*]
Teor & Eksp Khim ... Teoreticheskaya i Eksperimental'naya Khimiya [*A publication*]
Teoret Mat Fiz ... Teoreticeskaja i Matematiceskaja Fizika [*A publication*]
Teoret i Prikladna Meh ... Teoreticna i Prikladna Mehanika [*A publication*]
Teoret Prikl Mat ... Teoreticna i Prikladna Matematika [*A publication*]
Teoret i Prikl Mekh ... Belorusskii Politekhnicheski Institut. Teoreticheskaya i Prikladnaya Mekhanika [*A publication*]
Teoret i Priloz Meh ... Teoreticna i Prilozna Mehanika [*A publication*]
Teor Funkcii Funkcional Anal i Prilozen ... Teorija Funkcii. Funkcional'nyi Analiz i Ih Prilozenija [*A publication*]
Teor i Mat Fiz ... Teoreticheskaya i Matematicheskaya Fizika [*A publication*]
Teor Mat Fiz ... Teoreticheskaya i Matematicheskaya Fizika [*A publication*]
Teor Metod ... Teorie a Metoda [*A publication*]
Teor Osn Khim Tekhnol ... Teoreticheskie Osnovy Khimicheskoi Tekhnologii [*A publication*]
Teor Prakt Fiz Kul't ... Teoriya i Praktika Fizicheskoi Kul'tury [*A publication*]
Teor Prakt Metall ... Teoriya i Praktika Metallurgii (Chelyabinsk) [*USSR*] [*A publication*]
Teor Prakt Podgot Koksovaniya Uglei ... Teoriya i Praktika Podgotovki i Koksovaniya Uglei [*A publication*]
Teor Prakt Szhiganiya Gaza ... Teoriya i Praktika Szhiganiya Gaza [*USSR*] [*A publication*]
Teor Prakt Vopr Mikrobiol Epidemiol ... Teoreticheskie i Prakticheskie Voprosy Mikrobiologii i Epidemiologii [*A publication*]
Teor Prakt Vopr Mikrobiol Epidemiol Resp Mezhved Sb ... Teoreticheskie i Prakticheskie Voprosy Mikrobiologii i Epidemiologii Respublikanskii Mezhvedomstvennyi Sbornik [*A publication*]
Teor Prakt Vopr Vaktsinno Syvorot Dela ... Teoreticheskie i Prakticheskie Voprosy Vaktsinno Syvorotochnogo Dela [*A publication*]
Teor Prilozh Mekh ... Teoretichna i Prilozhna Mekhanika [*A publication*]
Teor Primen Meh ... Jugoslovensko Drustvo za Mehaniku. Teorijska i Primenjena Mehanika [*A publication*]
TEORS .... Transient Electro-Optic Raman Scattering [*Physics*]
Teor Verojatn Mat Stat ... Teoriya Verojatnostej i Matematicheskaya Statistika [*A publication*]
Teor Verojatnost i Mat Statist ... Teorija Verojatnostei i Matematicheskaya Statistika [*A publication*]
Teor Veroya ... Teoriya Veroyatnostei i Ee Primeneniya [*A publication*]
Teor Veroyatn Primen ... Teoriya Veroyatnostei i Ee Primeneniya [*A publication*]
Teor Veroyat Primen ... Teoriya Veroyatnostei i Ee Primeneniya [*USSR*] [*A publication*]

TEOS......... Tetraethyl Orthosilicate [*Organic chemistry*]   (NASA)
TEOSS ...... Tactical Emitter Operational Support System   (MCD)
TEOTA ...... [*The*] Eyes of the Army   (AAG)
TEP .... Table Editing Process
TEP .... Tactical ELINT Processor   (MCD)
TEP .... Tape Edit Processor [*Data processing*]
TEP .... Tau Epsilon Phi [*Fraternity*]
TEP .... Technical Education Program   (OICC)
TEP .... Technical Evaluation Panel   (NASA)
TEP .... Tepecintle [*Race of maize*]
TEP .... Teptep [*Papua New Guinea*] [*Airport symbol*]   (OAG)
TEP .... Terminal Error Program
TEP .... Territory Enterprises Proprietary
TEP .... Test and Evaluation Plan [*Military*]   (CAAL)
TEP .... Thermal Enzyme Probe
TEP .... Token Economy Program [*Psychiatry*]
TEP .... Tons Equivalent of Petroleum [*Fuel measure*]
TEP .... Total Extractable Protein [*Food technology*]
TEP .... Toxicant Extraction Procedure
TEP .... Trace Element Pattern   (KSC)
TEP .... Tracheo-Esophageal Puncture [*Medicine*]
TEP .... Transmitter Experiment Package
TEP .... Transparent Electrophotography [*Proposed archival storage medium*]
TEP .... Triethyl-Phosphine [*Organic chemistry*]
TEP .... Tube Evaluation Program
TEP .... Tucson Electric Power Co. [*NYSE symbol*]
TEP .... Turbine Extreme Pressure   (MCD)
TEP .... Turkiye Emekci Partisi [*Workers' Party of Turkey*]   (PPW)
TEP .... Tyrone Energy Park   (NRCH)
TEPA......... Roswell Park Memorial Institute [*Research code symbol*]
TEPA......... Tetraethylenepentamine [*Organic chemistry*]
TEPA......... Triethylenephosphoramide [*Also, APO*] [*Organic chemistry*]
TEPAC....... Tube Engineering Panel Advisory Council [*Washington, DC*]   (EA)
TEPC......... Test and Evaluation Planning Committee [*Military*]   (CAAL)
TEPCO....... Tokyo Electric Power Company
TEPD......... Trademark Examining Procedure Directives [*A publication*]
TEPG......... Test Evaluation Planning Group   (MCD)
TEPG......... Thermionic Electrical Power Generator   (IEEE)
TEPI.......... Technical Equipment Planning Information
TEPI.......... Terminal Phase Intercept
TEPI.......... Training Equipment Planning Information [*Military*]   (AFM)
TEPI.......... Triadal Equated Personality Inventory [*Psychology*]
TEPIAC ...... Thermophysical and Electronic Properties Information Analysis Center [*Purdue University*]
TEPIC........ Tris(epoxypropyl)isocyanurate [*Organic chemistry*]
TEPID........ Tepidus [*Lukewarm*] [*Pharmacy*]   (ROG)
TEPIGEN.... Television Picture Generator   (MCD)
Teploehnerg ... Teploehnergetika [*A publication*]
Teploenergetika Akad Nauk SSSR Energ Inst ... Teploenergetika Akademiya Nauk SSSR. Energeticheskii Institut [*A publication*]
Teplofiz Kharakt Veshchestv ... Teplofizicheskie Kharakteristiki Veshchestv [*USSR*] [*A publication*]
Teplofiz Optim Tepl Protsessov ... Teplofizika i Optimizatsiya Teplovykh Protsessov [*A publication*]
Teplofiz Svoistva Veshchestv ... Teplofizicheskie Svoistva Veshchestv [*A publication*]
Teplofiz Svoistva Veshchestv Mater ... Teplofizicheskie Svoistva Veshchestv i Materialov [*A publication*]
Teplofiz Teplotekh ... Teplofizika i Teplotekhnika [*A publication*]
Teplofiz Vys Temp ... Teplofizika Vysokikh Temperatur [*A publication*]
Teplotekh Probl Pryamogo Preobraz Energ ... Teplotekhnicheskie Problemy Pryamogo Preobrazovaniya Energii [*Ukrainian SSR*] [*A publication*]
TEPOS .... Test Program Operating System
TEPP .... Tetraethyl Pyrophosphate [*Insecticide*] [*Pharmacology*]
TEPPS .... Technique for Establishing Personnel Performance Standards [*Navy*]
TEPR......... Training Equipment Progress Report
TEPRSSC... Technical Electronic Product Radiation Safety Standards Committee   (MCD)
TEPS .... National Commission on Teacher Education and Professional Standards [*Defunct*]
TEPSA....... Trans European Policy Studies Association   (EA)
TEQ .... Turner Equity Investors, Inc. [*American Stock Exchange symbol*]
TER .... Tau Epsilon Rho [*Fraternity*]
TeR............ Te Reo [*A publication*]
TER .... Technical Evaluation Report [*Nuclear energy*]   (NRCH)
TER .... Teradyne, Inc. [*NYSE symbol*]
TER .... Terceira [*Azores*] [*Airport symbol*]   (OAG)
TER .... Tere [*Rub*] [*Pharmacy*]
Ter............. Terence [*Second century BC*] [*Classical studies*]   (OCD)
ter.............. Tereno [*MARC language code*] [*Library of Congress*]   (LCCP)
TER .... Terra Mines Ltd. [*Toronto Stock Exchange symbol*] [*Vancouver Stock Exchange symbol*]
TER .... Terrace
TER .... Terranova [*Guatemala*] [*Seismograph station code, US Geological Survey*]   (SEIS)

TER .... Terrazzo
TER .... Territory
Ter .... Terry's Delaware Reports　(DLA)
TER .... Tertiary　(KSC)
Ter .... Terumot　(BJA)
TER .... Test Effectiveness Ratio [Data processing]
TER .... Test Equipment Readiness [NASA]　(NASA)
TER .... Test Evaluation Report [NASA]　(KSC)
TER .... Thermal Enhancement Ratio
TE-R .... Thermostable E-Rosetting [Cells] [Medicine]
TER .... Time Estimating Relationship　(NASA)
TER .... Time and Event Recorder
TER .... Total Endoplasmic Reticulum [Cytology]
TER .... Total External Reflection
TE/R .... Trailing Edge Radius　(MSA)
TER .... Training Equipment Requirements Plan
TER .... Transcapillary Escape Rate
TER .... Transmission Equivalent Resistance　(IEEE)
TER .... Triple Ejection Rack　(NVT)
TERA .... Terminal Effects Research and Analysis Group [New Mexico
　　　　　　　Institute of Mining and Technology] [Research
　　　　　　　center]　(RCD)
TERA .... Terramar Corp. [NASDAQ symbol]　(NQ)
TERA .... Test of Early Reading Ability
TERA .... Tradable Emission Reduction Assessments [Environmental
　　　　　　　Protection Agency]
TERAC .... Tactical Electromagnetic Readiness Advisory Council　(MCD)
Ter Arkh..... Terapevticheskii Arkhiv [A publication]
TERAS .... Tactical Energy Requirements and Supply System　(MCD)
TERAT....... Teratology　(ROG)
Teratogenesis Carcinog Mutagen ... Teratogenesis, Carcinogenesis, and
　　　　　　　Mutagenesis [A publication]
TERB .... Terrazzo Base
TERC .... Technical Education Research Centers, Inc. [Cambridge, MA]
　　　　　　　[Research center]
TERCOM .... Terrain Contour Mapping　(MCD)
TERCOM .... Terrain Contour Matching [Navigation system] [Air Force]
TERCOM .... Terrain Correlation Method
TERD .... Turbine Electric Reduction Drive
TEREBINTH ... Terebinthinae Oleum [Oil of Turpentine]
　　　　　　　[Pharmacology]　(ROG)
TEREC .... Tactical Electronic Reconnaissance [Aircraft]
TERENVSVC ... Terrestrial Environmental Services [Army]　(AABC)
TERF .... Trudeau Early Retirement Fund [Defunct] [Established 1982 by
　　　　　　　Canadians who hoped that the money would persuade
　　　　　　　their prime minister to retire from office]
TERG......... Training Equipment Requirements Guide　(KSC)
TERI .... Torpedo Effective Range Indicator
TERL .... Test Equipment Readiness List [NASA]　(NASA)
TERLS .... Thumba Equatorial Launching Station [Indian rocket station]
TERM .... Temporary Equipment Recovery Mission　(CINC)
Term .... Term Reports [North Carolina] [1816-18]　(DLA)
Term .... Term Reports, English King's Bench [Durnford and East's
　　　　　　　Reports]　(DLA)
TERM .... Terminal　(AAG)
TERM .... Terminal Data Corp. [NASDAQ symbol]　(NQ)
TERM .... Terminate　(AFM)
TERM .... Terminology
TERM .... Termite　(ADA)
Termeloeszoevet Tanacsadoja ... Termeloeszoevetkezetek Tanacsadoja [A
　　　　　　　publication]
Termes de la Ley ... Terms of the Common Laws and Statutes Expounded
　　　　　　　and Explained by John Rastell [1685]　(DLA)
Termeszettud Koezloeny ... Termeszettudomanyi Koezloeny [A publication]
TERMIA...... Association Internationale de Terminologie [International
　　　　　　　Association of Terminology]　(EA-IO)
TERMINACTRAORD ... Directed to Request Termination of Inactive Duty
　　　　　　　Training Orders [Navy]
TERMINON ... Termination　(ROG)
TERMINOQ ... Banque de Terminologie de Quebec [Terminology Bank of
　　　　　　　Quebec] [Information service]
Term de la L ... Les Termes de la Ley [Terms of the Law] [A law French
　　　　　　　dictionary]　(DLA)
TERMN....... Termination
Term NC .... Taylor's North Carolina Term Reports　(DLA)
TERMNET ... International Network for Terminology [INFOTERM]
Term Obrab Fiz Met ... Termicheskaya Obrabotka i Fizika Metallov [A
　　　　　　　publication]
Termoprochn Mater Konstr Elem ... Termoprochnost Materialov i
　　　　　　　Konstruktivnykh Elementov [USSR] [A publication]
Termotecnica Suppl ... Termotecnica. Supplemento [Italy] [A publication]
Term R .... Term Reports, English King's Bench [Durnford and East's
　　　　　　　Reports]　(DLA)
Term Rep ... Term Reports, English King's Bench [Durnford and East's
　　　　　　　Reports] [England]　(DLA)
Term Rep (NC) ... Taylor's North Carolina Term Reports [4 North
　　　　　　　Carolina]　(DLA)
TERMS....... Terminal Management System　(AABC)
TERMTRAN ... Terminal Translator　(KSC)
TERO.......... Tribal Employment Rights Office

Ter Ortop Stomatol ... Terapevticheskaya i Ortopedicheskaya
　　　　　　　Stomatologiva [A publication]
TERP .... Terminal Equipment Replacement Program [Electronic
　　　　　　　communications system] [Department of State]
TERP .... Terminal Instrument Procedure [Aviation]
TERP .... Terrain Elevation Retrieval Program　(IEEE)
TERPACIS ... Trust Territory of the Pacific Islands
TERPE....... Tactical Electronic Reconnaissance Processing and Evaluation
　　　　　　　[Air Force]　(MCD)
TERPES ..... Tactical Electronic Reconnaissance Processing and Evaluation
　　　　　　　System　(MCD)
TERPS....... Terminal Instrument Procedures
TERPS....... Terminal Planning System [Military]
TERR........ Terrace
Terr .... Terrell's Reports [38-71 Texas]　(DLA)
TERR........ Territory　(AFM)
Terr .... Terrorist [Slang term used by whites in Zimbabwe to refer to a
　　　　　　　black nationalist guerrilla]
TERRA ...... Terricide-Escape by Rethinking, Research, Action [An
　　　　　　　association]
Terra Amer ... Terra America [A publication]
TERRAP ..... TERRAP [Territorial Apprehensiveness] Programs
　　　　　　　[Commercial firm] [Menlo Park, CA]　(EA)
Terra Trent ... Terra Trentina [A publication]
Terre Maroc ... Terre Marocaine [A publication]
TERRES ..... Territorial Residents
Terre Vie Rev Ecol Appl ... Terre et la Vie. Revue d'Ecologie Appliquee [A
　　　　　　　publication]
TERRHICO ... Territorial Rhine Coordination [NATO]　(NATG)
Territ......... Territorian [A publication]
TERRIT...... Territory
Terr L .... Territories Law [Northwest Territories]　(DLA)
Terr L (Can) ... Territories Law Reports [1885-1907] [Canada]　(DLA)
Terr LJ ...... Territory Law Journal [A publication]
Terr LR ...... Territories Law Reports [1885-1907] [Canada]　(DLA)
Terr Magn ... Terrestrial Magnetism and Atmospheric Electricity [A
　　　　　　　publication]
Terr & Walk ... Terrell and Walker's Reports [38-51 Texas]　(DLA)
TERS........ Tactical Electronic Reconnaissance System　(IEEE)
TerS .... Terra Santa [Jerusalem]　(BJA)
TER SIM .... Tere Simul [Rub Together] [Latin]　(ADA)
TERSSE ..... Total Earth Resources System for the Shuttle Era [NASA]
TERT .... Tertiary [Period, era, or system] [Geology]
tert .... Tertiary [Also, t] [Chemistry]
TERT .... Tertius [Third] [Latin]
Tert .... Tertullian [160-240AD] [Classical studies]　(OCD)
TERT .... Tracking/Erosion Resistance Tester
Tertiary Res Spec Pap ... Tertiary Research Special Papers [A publication]
TERTM...... Thermal Expansion Resin Transfer Molding
TERU......... Teruletrendezes [Hungary] [A publication]
Teruv......... Teruvenkatachariar's Railway Cases [India]　(DLA)
TES .... [The] Engineers School　(MCD)
TES .... Tactical Environment Simulator [Navy]　(MCD)
TES .... Target Engagement Simulator [Military]　(MCD)
TES .... Technical Engagement Simulation
TES .... Technical Enquiry Service [British]
TES .... Telemetry Evaluation Station
TES .... Temporary Employment Subsidy [British]
TES .... Terminal Encounter System
TeS........... Terre Sainte　(BJA)
TES .... Territorial Experiment Stations Division [of ARS, Department of
　　　　　　　Agriculture]
TES .... Tertiary Entrance Score　(ADA)
Tes .... Tesaur [A publication]
TES .... Test Squadron [Air Force]
TES .... Text Editing System
TES .... Thermal Energy Storage
TES .... Thin Elastic Shell
TES .... Thymic Epithelial Supernatant [Endocrinology]
TES .... Tidal Electric Station
TES .... Time Encoded Speech [Telecommunications]　(TEL)
TES .... Times Educational Supplement [A publication]
TES .... Training Equipment Summary　(MCD)
TES .... Transcutaneous Electrical Stimulation [Also, TENS, TNS] [A
　　　　　　　method of pain control] [Medicine]
TES .... Transmural Electrical Stimulation
TES .... Transportable Earth Station [British]
TES .... Tris(hydroxymethyl)methylaminoethanesulfonic Acid [A buffer]
TES .... Tungsten Electron Snatcher
TES .... Twelve English Statesmen [A publication]
TESA......... Television and Electronics Service Association
TESAC....... Temperature-Salinity-Currents [Oceanography]　(EISS)
TESDA....... Tenside [Later, Tenside-Detergents] [A publication]
TESE......... Tactical Exercise Simulator and Evaluator　(NVT)
TE(S)FC..... Totally-Enclosed (Separately) Fan-Cooled [Reactor]　(DEN)
TESG......... Target Echo Signature Generator [SONAR]
TESG......... Tijdschrift voor Economische en Sociale Geografie [A
　　　　　　　publication]
TESG-A...... Tijdschrift voor Economische en Sociale Geografie
　　　　　　　[Netherlands] [A publication]
TESI .... Thermal Energy Storage [NASDAQ symbol]　(NQ)

TESI .... Transfer of Electrostatic Images [*Electrophotography*]
TESICO ...... Threshold Electron Secondary Ion Coincidence [*Spectroscopy*]
TESL .... Teaching English as a Second Language
TESLAC ..... Testolactone [*Antineoplastic drug*]
Tesla Electron Q Rev Czech Electron Telecommun ... Tesla Electronics. Quarterly Review of Czechoslovak Electronics and Telecommunications [*A publication*]
TESM .... Triethylstannylmaleate [*Organic chemistry*]
TESMA ...... Theatre Equipment and Supply Manufacturers Association [*Later, TEA*] (EA)
TESOL .... Teachers of English to Speakers of Other Languages
TESOLQ ..... TESOL [*Teachers of English to Speakers of Other Languages*] Quarterly [*A publication*]
TESOL Quart ... TESOL [*Teachers of English to Speakers of Other Languages*] Quarterly [*A publication*]
TESP .... Telephone Specialists [*NASDAQ symbol*] (NQ)
TESR .... Tactical Environment Satellite Readout (MCD)
TESR .... Test Equipment Status Report
TESR .... Time of Sunrise
TESRP .... Test and Evaluation Support Resource Plan (MCD)
TESS .... Tactical Electromagnetic Systems Study (IEEE)
TESS .... Tactical and Environmental Support System [*Military*] (CAAL)
TESS .... Temporary Employment Subsidy Scheme [*Department of Employment*] [*British*]
TESS .... Time of Sunset
TEST .... Teen-Age Employment Skills Training, Inc.
TEST .... Testament
Test .... Testamentary (DLA)
TEST .... Testator (ADA)
TEST .... Testimonial (ADA)
TEST .... Thesaurus of Engineering and Scientific Terms [*A publication*]
TEST .... Track Evaluation System [*Canadian National Railways*]
TEST .... Transamerica Electronic Scoring Technique [*Credit risk evaluation*]
TEST .... Two Element Synthesis Telescope (ADA)
TestAbr ...... Testament of Abraham [*Pseudepigrapha*] (BJA)
TestAsh ..... Testament of Asher [*Pseudepigrapha*] (BJA)
TestBen ..... Testament of Benjamin [*Pseudepigrapha*] (BJA)
TESTCOMDNA ... Test Command Defense Nuclear Agency (AABC)
Test Eng Manage ... Test Engineering and Management [*A publication*]
TESTFAC ... Test Facility
Test Instrum Controls ... Testing, Instruments, and Controls [*Australia*] [*A publication*]
TestIss .... Testament of Issachar [*Pseudepigrapha*] (BJA)
TestJos ...... Testament of Joseph [*Pseudepigrapha*] (BJA)
TestJud ...... Testament of Judah [*Pseudepigrapha*] (BJA)
TestLevi ..... Testament of Levi [*Pseudepigrapha*] (BJA)
Test Memor Timb Res Developm Ass ... Test Memorandum. Timber Research and Development Association [*A publication*]
TestNaph ... Testament of Naphtali [*Pseudepigrapha*] (BJA)
TESTO .... Testigo [*Witness*] [*Latin*] (ADA)
TESTOR ..... Testator (ROG)
Test Polym ... Testing of Polymers [*A publication*]
TESTRAN ... Test Translator [*Data processing*]
Test Rec Timb Res Developm Ass ... Test Record. Timber Research and Development Association [*A publication*]
TestReub ... Testament of Reuben [*Pseudepigrapha*] (BJA)
TESTRIX .... Testatrix (ROG)
TESTS .... Technical-Engineering-Science Training for Secretaries
TESTS .... Test Squadron (MCD)
TestSim ...... Testament of Simeon [*Pseudepigrapha*] (BJA)
TESTT .... Testament
TestXII .... Testaments of the Twelve Patriarchs [*Pseudepigrapha*] (BJA)
TESTY .... Testamentary (ROG)
TestZeb ...... Testament of Zebulun [*Pseudepigrapha*] (BJA)
TET .... East Tennessee State University, Johnson City, TN [*OCLC symbol*] (OCLC)
TeT .... Taal en Tongval [*Antwerpen*] [*A publication*]
TET .... Teacher Effectiveness Training [*A course of study*]
TET .... Teacher of Electrotherapy [*British*]
TET .... Technical Evaluation Team (MCD)
TET .... Telescope and Electron Telescope
TET .... Test Equipment Team (AAG)
TET .... Test Equipment Tool (AAG)
TET .... Test Evaluation Team [*NASA*] (KSC)
Tet .... Tetanus [*Medicine*]
TET .... Tete [*Mozambique*] [*Airport symbol*] (OAG)
TET .... Tete [*Mozambique*] [*Seismograph station code, US Geological Survey*] (SEIS)
TET .... Tetrachloride [*Chemistry*] (AAG)
Tet .... Tetracycline [*Also, TC, TE*] [*Antibiotic compound*]
TET .... Tetrahedron (FAAC)
Tet .... Tetralogy [*Medicine*]
Tet .... Tetrode [*Electronics*]
TET .... Texas Eastern Corp. [*Formerly, Texas Eastern Transmission Corp.*] [*NYSE symbol*] [*Toronto Stock Exchange symbol*]
TET .... Thermionic Emission Technique
TET .... Thermometric Enthalpy Titration [*Analytical chemistry*]
TET .... Titanium Elevon Track
TET .... Total Elapsed Time (KSC)
TET .... Transistor Evaluation Test

TET .... Transportable Electronic Tower (MCD)
TET .... Troop Evaluation Tests [*Army*]
TET .... Turbine Entry Temperature [*Aviation*]
TET .... Turbo-Electric Tanker
TETA .... Test Equipment Technical Adviser
TETA .... Travelers Emergency Transportation Association [*Sought to pool transportation of salesmen traveling similar routes*] [*World War II*]
TETA .... Triethylenetetramine [*Organic chemistry*]
TETAM ...... Tactical Effectiveness Testing of Antitank Missiles [*DoD*]
TETD .... Tetraethylthiuram Disulfide [*Also, TTD*] [*Organic chemistry*]
TETF .... Terminal Equipment Test Facility [*Army*] (RDA)
TETFLEYNE ... Tetrafluorethylene [*Organic chemistry*]
Tethys Suppl ... Tethys. Supplement [*A publication*]
TETM .... Thermal Effects Tests Model
TETOC .... Council for Technical Education and Training for Overseas Countries [*British*]
TETR .... Test and Training Satellite [*Also, TATS, TTS*] [*NASA*]
TETR .... Tetragonal
TETRA ...... Terminal Tracking Telescope
TETRAC ..... Tension Truss Antenna Concept
Tetrahedr L ... Tetrahedron Letters [*A publication*]
Tetrahedron Lett ... Tetrahedron Letters [*A publication*]
Tetrahedron Suppl ... Tetrahedron. Supplement [*A publication*]
TETROON ... Tetrahedral Balloon [*Meteorology*]
TEU .... Te Anau [*New Zealand*] [*Airport symbol*] (OAG)
TEU .... Technical Escort Unit [*Army*] (AABC)
TeU .... Tekst en Uitleg (BJA)
TEU .... Telemetry Equipment Unit
TEU .... Temple University, Philadelphia, PA [*OCLC symbol*] (OCLC)
TEU .... Test of Economic Understanding
TEU .... Tetraethyl Urea [*Organic chemistry*]
TEU .... Transducer Excitation Unit
TEU .... Twenty-Foot Equivalent Unit [*Used to compare capacity of containerships*]
Teubner Studienskr ... Teubner Studienskripten [*A publication*]
TEUC .... Temporary Extended Unemployment Compensation [*Labor*]
TEUN .... Trust for Education on the United Nations (EA)
Teut .... Teuthonista [*A publication*]
TEUT .... Teuton
TEV .... Talipes Equinovarus [*Anatomy*]
T Ev .... Taylor on Evidence [*12th ed.*] [*1931*] (DLA)
TEV .... Thermoelectric Voltage
TEV .... Thermostatic Expansion Valve [*Refrigeration*]
TEV .... Time Expanded Video
TEV .... Today's English Version [*of the Bible*]
TeV .... Trillion Electron Volts
TEV .... Turbo-Electric Vessel
TEV .... Victoria College, Victoria, TX [*OCLC symbol*] (OCLC)
TEVA .... Tennessee Virginia Energy Corp. [*NASDAQ symbol*] (NQ)
TEVA .... Tutmonda Esperantista Vegetara Asocio [*World Esperantist Vegetarian Association - WEVA*] (EA-IO)
TEVIY .... Teva Pharmaceutical [*NASDAQ symbol*] (NQ)
TEVROC ..... Tailored Exhaust Velocity Rocket
TEW .... Tactical Early Warning
TEW .... Tactical Electronic Warfare [*Aircraft*] (NATG)
TEW .... Total Equivalent Weight
TE/W .... Tractive Effort to Weight Ratio (MCD)
TEWA .... Target Evaluation and Weapon Assignment (MCD)
TEWA .... Threat Evaluation and Weapons Assignment (NVT)
TEWC .... Totally-Enclosed Water-Cooled [*Reactor*] (DEN)
TEWDS .... Tactical Electronic Warfare Deception System (MCD)
TEWG .... Test and Evaluation Work Group [*Military*] (CAAL)
TEWGp ...... Tactical Electronic Warfare Group [*Air Force*] (AFM)
TEWP .... Williams [*T. E.*] Pharmaceuticals, Inc. [*NASDAQ symbol*] (NQ)
TEWS .... Tactical Effectiveness of Weapons Systems [*Army*] (AABC)
TEWS .... Tactical Electronic Warfare Support (MCD)
TEWS .... Threat Evaluation and Weapon Selection [*Military*] (CAAL)
TEWT .... Tactical Exercise without Troops [*British*]
TEW Tech Ber ... TEW [*Technische Edelstahlwerke*] Technische Berichte [*Later, Thyssen Edelstahl Technische Berichte*] [*A publication*]
TEX .... Air Texana [*Beaumont, TX*] [*FAA designator*] (FAAC)
TEX .... Automatic Teleprinter Exchange Service [*of Western Union Corp.*]
TEX .... TELEX
tex .... Tex [*Formerly, den*] [*Linear density*] [*SI unit*]
TEX .... Texas (AAG)
TEX .... Texas Air Corp. [*American Stock Exchange symbol*]
TEX .... Texas Airlines, Inc. [*Galveston, TX*] [*FAA designator*] (FAAC)
Tex .... Texas Supreme Court Reports (DLA)
TEX .... Textile (AABC)
TEX .... Transaction Exception Code [*Military*] (AFIT)
TEX .... Tumbling Explorer [*Aerospace*]
TEX .... University of Texas at Tyler, Tyler, TX [*OCLC symbol*] (OCLC)
Tex A Civ ... White and Wilson's [*or Willson's*] Civil Cases, Texas Court of Appeals (DLA)
Tex A Civ Cas ... White and Wilson's [*or Willson's*] Civil Cases, Texas Court of Appeals (DLA)
Tex A Civ Cas (Wilson) ... Texas Court of Appeal Civil Cases [*Wilson*] [*or Willson*] (DLA)

TEXACO .... Texas Company
Tex Admin Code ... Texas Administrative Code (DLA)
Tex Ag Exp ... Texas. Agricultural Experiment Station. Publications [*A publication*]
Tex Agric Exp Stn Bull ... Texas. Agricultural Experiment Station. Bulletin [*A publication*]
Tex Agric Exp Stn Leafl ... Texas. Agricultural Experiment Station. Leaflet [*A publication*]
Tex Agric Exp Stn Misc Publ ... Texas. Agricultural Experiment Station. Miscellaneous Publication [*A publication*]
Tex Agric Exp Stn Prog Rep ... Texas. Agricultural Experiment Station. Progress Report [*A publication*]
Tex Agric Exp Stn Tech Monogr ... Texas. Agricultural Experiment Station. Technical Monograph [*A publication*]
Tex Agric Ext Serv Fish Dis Diagn Lab ... Texas. Agricultural Extension Service. Fish Disease Diagnostic Laboratory [*A publication*]
Tex Agric Prog ... Texas Agricultural Progress [*A publication*]
Tex Agr Progr ... Texas Agricultural Progress [*A publication*]
Tex A & M Univ Dep Civ Eng Rep ... Texas A & M University. Department of Civil Engineering. Report [*A publication*]
Tex A M Univ Oceanogr Stud ... Texas A & M University. Oceanographic Studies [*A publication*]
Tex A & M Univ Syst Tex Agric Ext Serv Fish Dis Diagn Lab ... Texas A & M University System. Texas Agricultural Extension Service. Fish Disease Diagnostic Laboratory [*A publication*]
Tex A M Univ Syst Tex Agric Ext Serv Fish Dis Diagn Lab FDDL ... Texas A & M University System. Texas Agricultural Extension Service. Fish Disease Diagnostic Laboratory. FDDL [*A publication*]
Tex A & M Univ Tex Eng Exp Stn Tech Bull ... Texas A & M University. Texas Engineering Experiment Station. Technical Bulletin [*A publication*]
Tex App ..... Texas Civil Appeals Cases (DLA)
Tex App ..... Texas Court of Appeals Reports [*Criminal Cases*] (DLA)
Tex App Civ Cas (Wilson) ... White and Wilson's [*or Willson's*] Civil Cases, Texas Court of Appeals (DLA)
TEXAS .... Tactical Exchange Automation System (MCD)
Texas Acad of Sci Trans ... Texas Academy of Sciences. Transactions [*A publication*]
Texas Archeol Paleont Soc Bull ... Texas Archeological and Paleontological Society. Bulletin [*A publication*]
Texas BJ .... Texas Bar Journal [*A publication*]
Texas Board of Water Engineers Bull ... Texas. Board of Water Engineers. Bulletin [*A publication*]
Texas Bus Rev ... Texas Business Review [*A publication*]
Texas Civ ... Texas Civil Appeals Reports (DLA)
Texas Civ App ... Texas Civil Appeals Reports (DLA)
Texas Cour Rec Med ... Texas Courier Record of Medicine [*A publication*]
Texas Cr App ... Texas Court of Appeals Reports (DLA)
Texas Crim ... Texas Criminal Reports (DLA)
Texas Crim App ... Texas Criminal Appeals Reports (DLA)
Texas Crim Rep ... Texas Criminal Reports (DLA)
Texas Cr Rep ... Texas Criminal Reports (DLA)
Texas Ct App ... Texas Court of Appeals Reports (DLA)
Texas Ct of App ... Texas Court of Appeals Reports (DLA)
Texas Ct App Civ Cas ... Texas Civil Cases (DLA)
Texas Ct Rep ... Texas Court Reporter [*1900-1908*] (DLA)
Texas Dig ... Texas Digest (DLA)
Texas Eng Expt Sta Research Rept ... Texas. Engineering Experiment Station. Research Report [*A publication*]
Texas Internat L Forum ... Texas International Law Forum [*A publication*]
Texas Internat LJ ... Texas International Law Journal [*A publication*]
Texas Int'l LF ... Texas International Law Forum [*A publication*]
Texas Int'l LJ ... Texas International Law Journal [*A publication*]
Texas Jour Sci ... Texas Journal of Science [*A publication*]
Texas L Rev ... Texas Law Review [*A publication*]
Texas Memorial Mus Pearce-Sellards Ser ... Texas Memorial Museum. Pearce-Sellards Series [*A publication*]
Texas Mo ... Texas Monthly [*A publication*]
Texas Nurs ... Texas Nursing [*A publication*]
Texas Oil Jour ... Texas Oil Journal [*A publication*]
Texas Petroleum Research Comm Bull ... Texas Petroleum Research Committee. Bulletin [*A publication*]
Texas R ...... Texas Reports (DLA)
Texas Rep ... Texas Reports (DLA)
Texas South UL Rev ... Texas Southern University. Law Review [*A publication*]
Texas Tech L Rev ... Texas Tech Law Review [*A publication*]
Texas Univ Austin Bur Econ Geology Geol Circ ... Texas University at Austin. Bureau of Economic Geology. Geological Circular [*A publication*]
Texas Univ Austin Bur Econ Geology Geol Quad Map ... University of Texas at Austin. Bureau of Economic Geology. Geologic Quadrangle Map [*A publication*]
Texas Univ Austin Bur Econ Geology Guidebook ... Texas University at Austin. Bureau of Economic Geology. Guidebook [*A publication*]
Texas Univ Austin Bur Econ Geology Rept Inv ... Iniversity of Texas at Austin. Bureau of Economic Geology. Report of Investigations [*A publication*]

Texas Univ Pub Bur Econ Geology Mineral Res Circ Rept Inv ... Texas University. Publication. Bureau of Economic Geology. Mineral Resource Circular. Report of Investigations [*A publication*]
Texas Water Devel Board Rept ... Texas. Water Development Board. Report [*A publication*]
Tex B J .... Texas Bar Journal [*A publication*]
Tex Board Water Eng Chem Compos Tex Surf Waters ... Texas. Board of Water Engineers. Chemical Composition of Texas Surface Waters [*A publication*]
Tex Bus Corp Act Ann ... Texas Business Corporation Act, Annotated (DLA)
Tex Bus Exec ... Texas Business Executive [*A publication*]
Tex Busin Rev ... Texas Business Review [*A publication*]
Tex Bus R... Texas Business Review [*A publication*]
Tex Bus Rev ... Texas Business Review [*A publication*]
TEXC......... Texas Central Railroad Co. [*AAR code*]
Tex Civ App ... Texas Civil Appeals Reports (DLA)
Tex Civ Cas ... Texas Court of Appeals Decisions, Civil Cases [*White and Wilson*] [*or Willson*] [*1876-92*] (DLA)
Tex Civ Rep ... Texas Civil Appeals Reports (DLA)
Tex Code Ann ... Texas Codes, Annotated (DLA)
Tex Code Crim Proc Ann ... Texas Code of Criminal Procedure, Annotated (DLA)
Tex Cr .... Texas Criminal (DLA)
Tex Cr App ... Texas Criminal Appeals Reports (DLA)
Tex Crim .... Texas Criminal Reports (DLA)
Tex Crim Rep ... Texas Criminal Reports (DLA)
Tex Cr R... Texas Criminal Appeals Reports (DLA)
Tex Cr Rpts ... Texas Criminal Reports (DLA)
Tex Ct App ... Texas Court of Appeals Reports (DLA)
Tex Ct App Civ ... Texas Civil Cases (DLA)
Tex Ct App Dec Civ ... Texas Civil Cases (DLA)
Tex Ct App R ... Texas Court of Appeals Reports (DLA)
Tex Ct Rep ... Texas Court Reporter (DLA)
TEXDEALAM ... Textile Dealers Association of America (EA)
Tex Dec...... Texas Decisions (DLA)
Tex Dent J ... Texas Dental Journal [*A publication*]
Tex Dig Op Att'y Gen ... Digest of Opinions of the Attorney General of Texas (DLA)
Tex Elec Code Ann ... Texas Election Code, Annotated (DLA)
Tex Energy ... Texas Energy [*A publication*]
Tex Energy Miner Resour ... Texas Energy and Mineral Resources [*A publication*]
TEXF .... TGIF Texas, Inc. [*NASDAQ symbol*] (NQ)
Tex For Pap ... Texas Forestry Paper [*A publication*]
Tex Gen Laws ... General and Special Laws of the State of Texas (DLA)
Tex G S Rp Prog ... Texas. Geological Survey. Report of Progress [*A publication*]
Tex His Q ... Texas State Historical Association Quarterly [*A publication*]
Tex Hist Assoc Q ... Texas State Historical Association Quarterly [*A publication*]
Tex Hosp.... Texas Hospitals [*A publication*]
Tex Hospitals ... Texas Hospitals [*A publication*]
Tex Ins Code Ann ... Texas Insurance Code, Annotated (DLA)
Tex Inst...... Texas Institutes [*A publication*]
Tex Int L Forum ... Texas International Law Forum [*A publication*]
Tex Int L J ... Texas International Law Journal [*A publication*]
TEXIW .... Texas International Wts [*NASDAQ symbol*] (NQ)
Tex J .... Texas Journal [*A publication*]
Tex J Pharm ... Texas Journal of Pharmacy [*A publication*]
Tex J Sci .... Texas Journal of Science [*A publication*]
Tex J Sci Spec Publ ... Texas Journal of Science. Special Publication [*A publication*]
Tex Jur...... Texas Jurisprudence (DLA)
Tex Jur 2d ... Texas Jurisprudence [*2nd ed.*] (DLA)
Tex Law & Leg ... Texas Law and Legislation (DLA)
Tex Law Rev ... Texas Law Review [*A publication*]
TexLex .... Texas Lexicon [*Slang*]
Tex Lib .... Texas Libraries [*A publication*]
Tex Lib J .... Texas Library Journal [*A publication*]
Tex Libr...... Texas Libraries [*A publication*]
Tex LJ .... Texas Law Journal (DLA)
Tex L R .... Texas Law Review [*A publication*]
Tex L Rep... Texas Law Reporter [*1882-84*] (DLA)
Tex L Rev ... Texas Law Review [*A publication*]
Tex Med ..... Texas Medicine [*A publication*]
Tex Mem Mus Misc Pap ... Texas Memorial Museum. Miscellaneous Papers [*A publication*]
TEX MEX.... Texas Mexican Railway Co.
TexMex ...... Texas and Mexico [*Refers to fashion, food, language, or lifestyle that has characteristics of these two regions*]
Tex Mo ...... Texas Monthly [*A publication*]
Tex Nurs ..... Texas Nursing [*A publication*]
Tex Outl ..... Texas Outlook [*A publication*]
TEXP .... Time Exposure [*Photography*]
Tex Parks Wildl ... Texas Parks Wildlife [*A publication*]
Tex Pharm ... Texas Pharmacy [*A publication*]
Tex Q......... Texas Quarterly [*A publication*]
Tex Rep Bio ... Texas Reports on Biology and Medicine [*A publication*]
Tex Rep Biol Med ... Texas Reports on Biology and Medicine [*A publication*]
Tex Res ...... Textile Research [*A publication*]

Tex Res J ... Textile Research Journal [*A publication*]
Tex Rev ...... Texas Review [*A publication*]
Tex Rev Civ Stat Ann (Vernon) ... Texas Revised Civil Statutes, Annotated Vernon (DLA)
TEXS .... Tactical Explosive System [*Military*] (RDA)
Tex S .... Texas Supreme Court Reports, Supplement (DLA)
Tex S Ct ..... Texas Supreme Court Reporter (DLA)
Tex Sess Law Serv ... Texas Session Law Service [*Vernon*] (DLA)
Tex So Intra L Rev ... Texas Southern Intramural Law Review (DLA)
Tex So U L Rev ... Texas Southern University. Law Review [*A publication*]
Tex Stat Ann ... Texas Statutes, Annotated (DLA)
Tex State Hist Assoc Quar ... Texas State Historical Association. Quarterly [*A publication*]
Tex State J Med ... Texas State Journal of Medicine [*A publication*]
Tex St Lit ... Texas Studies in Literature and Language [*A publication*]
Tex Stud Lit & Lang ... Texas Studies in Literature and Language [*A publication*]
Tex SUL Rev ... Texas Southern University. Law Review [*A publication*]
Tex Supp ... Texas Supplement (DLA)
Tex Suppl ... Texas Supplement (DLA)
TEXT ...... Texas Experimental TOKAMAK [*Atomic physics*]
TEXT .... Textile
TEXTA .... Technical Extracts of Traffic [*National Security Agency*] [*A publication*]
Text Asia .... Textile Asia [*A publication*]
Tex Tax-Gen Ann ... Texas Tax-General, Annotated (DLA)
Text Beklaedning ... Textil og Beklaedning [*A publication*]
Text Bull .... Textile Bulletin [*A publication*]
Text Bull .... Textiles Bulletin [*A publication*]
Text Chem Color ... Textile Chemist and Colorist [*A publication*]
Text Chim ... Textiles Chimiques [*A publication*]
Text Color ... Textile Colorist [*A publication*]
Text Color Converter ... Textile Colorist and Converter [*A publication*]
Tex Tech L Rev ... Texas Tech Law Review [*A publication*]
TexteM .... Texte Metzler [*A publication*]
Textes et Doc (Bruxelles) ... Textes et Documents (Bruxelles) [*A publication*]
Tex-Text .... Tex-Textilis [*A publication*]
Text Faerberei Ztg ... Textil und Faerberei-Zeitung [*A publication*]
Text Faserstofftech ... Textil und Faserstofftechnik [*A publication*]
Text Forsch ... Textil-Forschung [*A publication*]
Text Hist .... Textile History [*A publication*]
Text I Ind ... Textile Institute and Industry [*A publication*]
Textile Ind ... Textile Industries [*A publication*]
Textile Inst Ind ... Textile Institute and Industry [*A publication*]
Textile J Aust ... Textile Journal of Australia [*A publication*]
Textile Progr ... Textile Progress [*A publication*]
Textile Res J ... Textile Research Journal [*A publication*]
Textile Technol Dig ... Textile Technology Digest [*A publication*]
Textil Rep ... America's Textiles Reporter Bulletin [*A publication*]
Textilvered ... Textilveredelung [*A publication*]
Textil-W ..... Textil-Wirtschaft [*A publication*]
Textil Wld .. Textile World Buyer's Guide/Fact File [*A publication*]
Text Ind ...... Textile Industries [*A publication*]
Text Ind (Munich) ... Textil-Industrie (Munich) [*A publication*]
Text Ind Sthn Afr ... Textile Industries Southern Africa [*A publication*]
Text Ind (Zurich) ... Textil-Industrie (Zurich) [*A publication*]
Text Inst Ind ... Textile Institute and Industry [*A publication*]
TEXTIR .... Text Indexing and Retrieval [*Data processing*]
Text J Aust ... Textile Journal of Australia [*A publication*]
Text Mag .... Textile Magazine [*A publication*]
Text Mfr .... Textile Manufacturer [*A publication*]
Text Mon .... Textile Month [*A publication*]
Text-Prax ... Textil-Praxis [*Later, Textil Praxis International*] [*A publication*]
Text Prax Int ... Textil Praxis International [*A publication*]
Text Prog ... Textile Progress [*A publication*]
Text Q .... Textile Quarterly [*A publication*]
Tex Transp Res ... Texas Transportation Researcher [*A publication*]
Text Rec ..... Textile Recorder [*A publication*]
TEXT REC ... Textus Receptus [*The Received Text*] [*Latin*]
Text Rent ... Textile Rental [*A publication*]
Text Res J ... Textile Research Journal [*A publication*]
Text Tech Dig ... Textile Technology Digest [*A publication*]
Texture Cryst Solids ... Texture of Crystalline Solids [*A publication*]
Textures and Microstruct ... Textures and Microstructures [*A publication*]
Text Wkly ... Textile Weekly [*A publication*]
Text World ... Textile World [*A publication*]
Text World J ... Textile World Journal [*A publication*]
Text World R ... Textile World Record [*A publication*]
Tex Univ B Min S B ... Texas University. Bulletin. Mineral Survey Bulletin [*A publication*]
Tex Univ Bur Econ Geol Geol Circ ... Texas University. Bureau of Economic Geology. Geological Circular [*A publication*]
Tex Univ Bur Econ Geol Miner Resour Circ ... Texas University. Bureau of Economic Geology. Mineral Resource Circular [*A publication*]
Tex Univ Bur Econ Geol Publ ... Texas University. Bureau of Economic Geology. Publication [*A publication*]
Tex Univ Bur Econ Geol Rep Invest ... Texas University. Bureau of Economic Geology. Report of Investigations [*A publication*]
Tex Univ Bur Econ Geol Res Note ... Texas University. Bureau of Economic Geology. Research Note [*A publication*]

Tex Univ Cent Res Water Resour Tech Rep ... Texas University. Center for Research in Water Resources. Technical Report [*A publication*]
Tex Unrep Cas ... Posey's Unreported Cases [*Texas*] (DLA)
TE (XVIII) ... Textos y Estudios del Siglo XVIII [*A publication*]
Tex Water Comm Circ ... Texas. Water Commission. Circular [*A publication*]
Tex Water Comm Mem Rep ... Texas. Water Commission. Memorandum Report [*A publication*]
Tex Water Dev Board Rep ... Texas. Water Development Board. Report [*A publication*]
TEY .... Thingeyri [*Iceland*] [*Airport symbol*] (OAG)
TeZ .... Texte und Zeichen [*A publication*]
TEZ .... Tezpur [*India*] [*Airport symbol*] (OAG)
Tez Doklad Nauch Konf Zootech Sek ... Tezisy Dokladov Nauchnoi Konferentsii. Zootekhnicheskaya Sektsiya [*A publication*]
TEZG .... Tribological Experiments in Zero Gravity
TF .... [*The*] FORUM [*Foundation of Research for Understanding Man*] [*Santa Fe, NM*] (EA)
TF .... Iceland [*Aircraft nationality and registration mark*] (FAAC)
TF .... Tabulating Form (AAG)
TF .... Tactical Fighter (AFM)
TF .... Tactile Fremitus [*Medicine*]
TF .... Taeria Foundation [*Carrizozo, NM*] (EA)
Tf .... Tafel (BJA)
TF .... Tallulah Falls Railway Co. [*AAR code*]
TF .... Tank Farm (NATG)
TF .... Tape Feed
TF .... Target File (MCD)
TF .... Task Force
TF .... Tax Foundation
TF .... Tayu Fellowship (EA)
TF .... Teaching Fellow
TF .... Tear Fund [*An association*] (EA)
TF .... Teased Fibers [*Neurology*]
TF .... Technical File (MCD)
TF .... Technological Forecasting
TF .... Telegram for Delivery by Telephone
TF .... Telegraph Form (ROG)
TF .... Telephone (NATG)
TF .... Temperature Factor
TF .... Temporary Fix (AAG)
TF .... Terminal Frame (NATG)
TF .... Terrain-Following [*Helicopter*]
TF .... Territorial Force [*Military*] [*British*]
TF .... Test Facility [*NASA*] (NASA)
TF .... Test Fixture (KSC)
TF .... Test Flight [*Air Force*]
TF .... Test Frame [*Telecommunications*] (TEL)
TF .... Tetralogy of Fallot [*Cardiology*]
TF .... Text-Fiche
TF .... THEOS [*They Help Each Other Spiritually*] Foundation [*Pittsburgh, PA*] (EA)
TF .... Thin Film
TF .... Thoreau Fellowship (EA)
TF .... Thread Forming (MSA)
TF .... Thymidine Factor [*Endocrinology*]
TF .... Thymol Flocculation [*Clinical chemistry*]
TF .... Tibet Fund (EA)
T & F .... Ticknor & Fields [*Publisher*]
TF .... Tile Floor [*Technical drawings*]
TF .... Till Forbidden [*i.e., repeat until forbidden to do so*] [*Advertising*]
TF .... Time Factor (CAAL)
T/F .... Time of Fail (MSA)
TF .... Time Frame
TF .... Time to Function
TF .... To Fill
TF .... To Follow
TF .... Tolkien Fellowships (EA)
TF .... Tolstoy Foundation (EA)
TF .... Toroidal Field (MCD)
TF .... Torpedo Fighter Aircraft [*Navy*]
TF .... Total Forfeiture [*of all pay and allowances*] [*Army*] (AABC)
TF .... Toxicology Forum (EA)
TF .... Tracking Filter
TF .... Trainer Fighter
TF .... Training Film [*Military*]
TF .... TransAfrica Forum (EA)
TF .... Transcription Factor [*Genetics*]
TF .... Transfer Factor [*Immunochemistry*]
TF .... Transfer Fee [*Banking*]
TF .... Transfer Function (AAG)
T/F .... Transfer of Function [*Military*] (AFM)
TF .... Transferrin [*Also, TRF*] [*Biochemistry*]
TF .... Transformation [*A publication*]
TF .... Transformers [*JETDS nomenclature*] [*Military*] (CET)
TF .... Transmitter Frequency
TF .... Transportation Factor (MCD)
TF .... Travail Force [*Penal Servitude*] [*French*]
TF .... Trench Feet [*or Fever*]
TF .... Trichloroethylene Finishing

TF	Triple Frequency
TF	Triple Fronted [*Classified advertising*] (ADA)
TF	Tropical Fresh Water [*Vessel load line mark*]
TF	Trunk Frame [*Telecommunications*] (TEL)
TF	Trust Fund
TF	Tuberculin Filtrate [*Medicine*]
TF	Turbofan [*Engine*]
TF	Twentieth Century-Fox Film Corp. [*NYSE symbol*]
TF	Twins Foundation [*Providence, RI*] (EA)
TF	Type of Foundation [*IRS*]
TF1	Channel One [*French television station*]
TFA	[*The*] Ferroalloys Association [*Washington, DC*] (EA)
TFA	Target Factor Analysis [*Statistical technique*]
TFA	Task Force A
TFA	Tie Fabrics Association [*Defunct*] (EA)
TFA	Top Farmers of America Association (EA)
TFA	Total Fatty Acids
TFA	Transfer Function Analyzer
TFA	Transistor Feedback Amplifier
TFA	Transverse Fascicular Area [*Neuroanatomy*]
TFA	Transverse Film Attenuator
TFA	Trifluoroacetic [*or Trifluoroacetyl*] Acid [*Organic chemistry*]
TFA	Trifluoroacetic Anhydride [*Organic chemistry*]
TFA	Tube Failure Alarm
TFA	Two-Way Finite Automata
TFA	United States Trout Farmers Association
TFAA	Track and Field Athletes of America
TFAA	Trifluoroacetic Anhydride [*Organic chemistry*]
TFAG	Tropical Forest Action Group (EA)
TFAI	Territoire Francaise des Afars et des Issas [*French Territory of the Afars and Issas*]
TFAI	Trifluoroacetylimidazole [*Organic chemistry*]
TFAIP	Task Force on Alternatives in Print (EA)
TFANP	Task Force Against Nuclear Pollution (EA)
TFAR	Tentative Findings and Recommendations
TFA/USA	Track and Field Association of the United States of America [*Formerly, USTFF, USTCA*] (EA)
TFB	Taft Broadcasting Co. [*NYSE symbol*]
TFB	Testing Facilities Branch [*Social Security Administration*]
TFB	Thin-Film Barrier
TFBA	Textile Fibers and By-Products Association
TFBPA	Textile Fibers and By-Products Association [*Charlotte, NC*] (EA)
TFC	[*The*] Felician College [*Chicago, IL*]
TFC	[*The*] Freedom Council (EA)
TFC	Tactical Fire Control (MCD)
TFC	Tactical Flag Commander (MCD)
TFC	Tactical Flight Control
TFC	Tactical Fusion Center (MCD)
TFC	Tank Fire Control
TFC	Tantalum Foil Capacitor
TFC	Terminal Flight Control (NATG)
TFC	Territorial Fund Campaign [*Red Cross*]
TFC	Thin-Film Capacitor
TFC	Thin-Film Cell
TFC	Thin-Film Circuit
TFC	Time from Cutoff [*NASA*] (NASA)
TFC	Time of First Call [*Navy*]
TFC	Toccoa Falls College [*Georgia*]
TFC	Top Flight Club [*Northwest Airlines' club for frequent flyers*] (EA)
TFC	Torpedo Fire Control
TFC	Total Fixed Cost
TFC	Total Fuel Consumption (KSC)
TFC	Traffic
TFC	Traffic Control (NG)
TFC	Transcapital Financial Corp. [*NYSE symbol*]
TFC	Transfer Function Computer
TFC	Transfer Function, Cumulative
TFC	Transistorized Frequency Converter
TFC	Transmission Fault Control [*Telecommunications*] (TEL)
TFC	Transport for Christ International [*An association*] (EA)
TFC	Transportation Facilitation Center [*Department of Transportation*]
TFC	Trifluoromethyldichlorocarbanilide [*Organic chemistry*]
TFC	Trigonometric Function Computer
TFC	Trilon Financial Corporation [*Toronto Stock Exchange symbol*] [*Vancouver Stock Exchange symbol*]
TFC	Trustees for Conservation [*Defunct*] (EA)
TFC	Turret Fire Control
TFC	United States Overseas Tax Fairness Committee (EA)
TFCA	[*The*] Federation of Commodity Associations (EA-IO)
TFCA	Thin-Film Cell Array
TF-CAS	Time Frequency Collision Avoidance System
TFCB	Thanks for Coming By [*Exxon slogan*]
TFCC	Tactical Flag Command Center [*Navy*]
TFCC	Tank Fire Combat Computer
TFCC	Triangular Fibrocartilage Complex [*Anatomy*]
TFCF	Twenty-First Century Foundation [*New York, NY*] (EA)
TFCG	Thin Film Crystal Growth
TFCNN	Task Force Commander, North Norway [*NATO*] (NATG)

TFCOS	Task Force on Children Out of School (EA)
TFCP	Technical Facility Change Procedure (AAG)
TFCS	Tank Fire Control System
TFCS	Task Force for Child Survival [*Atlanta, GA*] (EA)
TFCS	Torpedo Fire Control System
TFCS	Treasury Financial Communication System
TFCS	Triplex Flight Control System [*or Subsystem*] [*NASA*] (NASA)
TFCSD	Total Federal Commissioned Service Date
TFCX	TOKAMAK [*Toroidal Kamera Magnetic*] Fusion Core Experiment [*Plasma physics*]
TFD	Tactical Fighter Dispenser (MCD)
TFD	Target-to-Film Distance [*X-Ray machine*] [*Navy*]
TFD	Television Feasibility Demonstration [*NASA*] (KSC)
TFD	Terrain-Following Display
TFD	Test Flow Diagram (MCD)
TFD	Thin-Film Distillation
TFD	Time Frequency Digitizer (MCD)
TF/D	Time-Frequency Dissemination (IEEE)
TFD	Total Frequency Deviation (AAG)
TFD	Tube Flood and Drain
TFD	Tube Form Die (MCD)
TFDA	Textile Fabric Distributors Association [*Later, TDA*] (EA)
TFDM	Tactical Fighter Dispensing Munition (AFM)
TFDM	Technical Feasibility Demonstration Model
TFDOP	Total Field Detection Only Processor (CAAL)
TFDRL	Trustees of the Franklin Delano Roosevelt Library [*Abolished, 1958*] [*Library is now operated by the General Services Administration*]
TFDS	Tactical Ferret Display System
TFDS	Tactical Flag Data System (NG)
TFDS	Troms Fylkes Dampskipsselskap [*Shipping line*] [*Norway*]
TFDU	Thin Film Deposition Unit
TFE	Orlando, FL [*Location identifier*] [*FAA*] (FAAL)
TFE	Terminal Flight Evaluation
TFE	Terrain-Following Evaluator
TFE	Tetrafluoroethylene [*Organic chemistry*]
TFE	Thermionic Fuel Element
TFE	Thin-Film Electrode [*Electrochemistry*]
TFE	Time from Event [*NASA*] (KSC)
TFE	Total Fly-By Energy
TFE	Trainer Flight Equipment (MCD)
TFE	Transform Fault Effect [*Geology*]
TFE	Transportation Feasibility Estimator
TFE	Trifluoroethanol [*Organic chemistry*]
TFE	Turbofan Engine
TFE	Two-Fraction Fast Exchange [*Biophysics*]
TFECB	Task Force on Emphysema and Chronic Bronchitis [*Public Health Service and National Lung Association*] (EA)
TFECS	Theater Force Evaluation by Combat Simulation (MCD)
TFEDSA	Tetrafluoroethanedisulfonic Acid [*Organic chemistry*]
TFEL	Thin-Film Electroluminescence
TFEO	Tetrafluoroethylene-Epoxide [*Organic chemistry*]
TFEO	Tetrafluoroethylene Oxide [*Organic chemistry*]
TFER	Transfer
TFEWJ	Task Force on Equality of Women in Judaism (EA)
TFF	Fletcher School of Law and Diplomacy, Tufts University, Medford, MA [*OCLC symbol*] (OCLC)
TFF	Tactical Fighter Force (ADA)
TFF	Tefe [*Brazil*] [*Airport symbol*] (OAG)
TFF	Terrain-Following Flight
TFF	Time of Free Fall [*NASA*] (KSC)
TFF	Total Feedwater Flow
TFF	Transverse Flow Fan
TFF	Tuning Fork Filter
TFF	Turbine Flow Function
TFFASF	Temporaries Food for All Seasons Foundation [*Washington, DC*] (EA)
TFFC	Task Force on Families in Crisis (EA)
TFFC	Texas Federal Financial Corporation [*NASDAQ symbol*] (NQ)
TFFE	Terrain-Following Flight Evaluator
TFG	[*The*] Fashion Group [*New York, NY*] (EA)
TFG	[*The*] Futures Group [*Commercial firm*] (EA)
TFG	Tentative Fiscal Guidance (MCD)
TFG	Tentative Force Guidance (NG)
TFG	Terminal Facilities Guide [*DoD*]
TFG	Test File Generator [*Data processing*]
TFG	Textile Foremen's Guild
TFG	Transmit Format Generator
TFG	Typefounding (ADA)
TFGM	Tentative Fiscal Guidance Memorandum [*Military*] (AFIT)
TFGP	Tactical Fighter Group [*Air Force*]
TFH	Thick-Film Hybrid
TFH	Touch for Health Foundation [*Pasadena, CA*] (EA)
TFH	Transfer Function Hazard
TFH	Transit Financial Holdings [*Toronto Stock Exchange symbol*]
TFH	Tufts University, Health Sciences Library, Boston, MA [*OCLC symbol*] (OCLC)
TFI	[*The*] Fertilizer Institute [*Formed by a merger of Agricultural Nitrogen Institute and NPFI*] [*Washington, DC*] (EA)
TFI	Table Fashion Institute (EA)
TFI	Tax Foundation, Incorporated

TFI............. Textile Foundation, Incorporated
TFI............. Theatre for Ideas [*An association*]   (EA)
TFI............. Time from Ignition [*Apollo*] [*NASA*]
TFI............. True Fibrous Involution [*Medicine*]
TFI........ Tufi [*Papua New Guinea*] [*Airport symbol*]   (OAG)
TFIB........ Thin-Film Interface Barrier
TFIC .... Times Fiber Communications [*NASDAQ symbol*]   (NQ)
TFI-I .... Thin Film Ignition [*Automotive engineering*]
TFIM........ Tool Fabrication Instruction Manual   (MCD)
TFIN........ TecFin Corp. [*NASDAQ symbol*]   (NQ)
TFIS .... Theft from Interstate Shipment [*FBI standardized term*]
TfK .... Tidskrift foer Konstvetinskap [*A publication*]
TFKVA ...... Teplofizicheskie Kharakteristiki Veshchestv [*A publication*]
TFL........ Tail-Flick Latency
TFL........ Taiwan Federation of Labor [*Nationalist China*]
TFL........ Tanganyika Federation of Labor
TFL........ Telemetry Format Load   (MCD)
TFL........ Tensor Fascia Lata [*Anatomy*]
TFL........ Through Flow Line
TFL........ Time to Failure Location
TFL........ Time from Launch [*NASA*]
TFL........ Transient Fault Locator
TFLC .... Tulane Factors of Liberalism-Conservatism [*Psychology*]
TFLX .... Termiflex Corp. [*NASDAQ symbol*]   (NQ)
TFM........ Tactical Flight Management   (MCD)
TFM........ Tape File Management
TFM........ Teaching Family Model [*Psychology*]
TFM........ Telefomin [*Papua New Guinea*] [*Airport symbol*]   (OAG)
TFM........ Terminal Forecast Manual
TFM........ Testicular Feminization [*Endocrinology*]
TFM........ Textes Francais Modernes [*A publication*]
TFM........ Thin-Film Microelectronics
TFM........ Transmit Frame Memory
TFM........ Transmitter Frequency Multiplier
TFM........ Transportation Financial Management [*Army*]
TFM........ Trifluoromethylnitrophenol [*Organic chemistry*]
TFM........ Turbine Flow Meter   (KSC)
TFM........ Two-Fluid Manometer
TFMA........ Technical Facility Modification Authorization   (AAG)
TFME........ Thin-Film Mercury Electrode [*Electrochemistry*]
TFMRA ...... Top Fuel Motorcycle Riders Association [*Teaneck, NJ*]   (EA)
TFMS .... Tactical Frequency Management System   (MCD)
TFMS .... Text and File Management System
TFMS .... Trunk and Facilities Maintenance System [*Telecommunications*]   (TEL)
TFMSA...... Trifluoromethanesulfonic Acid [*Organic chemistry*]
TFN .... Till Further Notice
TFN .... Total Fecal Nitrogen
TFN .... Track File Number   (CAAL)
TFNA.......... Tennis Foundation of North America [*North Palm Beach, FL*]   (EA)
TFNG........ Thirty-Five New Guys [*Group of new astronauts*] [*NASA*]
TFNS .... Territorial Force Nursing Service
TFO .... Telemedicine for Ontario [*Toronto, ON*] [*Telecommunications*]   (TSSD)
TFO .... Tiffany Resources, Inc. [*Vancouver Stock Exchange symbol*]
TFO .... Tonto Forest Array [*Arizona*] [*Seismograph station code, US Geological Survey*] [*Closed*]   (SEIS)
TFO .... Transactions for Others
TFO .... Tuning Fork Oscillator
TFOL .... Tape File Octal Load
TFONY ...... Telefonos de Mexico [*NASDAQ symbol*]   (NQ)
TFOPS....... Task Force Operations [*Navy*]   (NVT)
TFORMR .... Transformer
TFOS .... Total Federal Officer Service [*Military*]   (AABC)
TFOTB....... [*The*] Friends of Tom Baker [*Stanford, CA*]   (EA)
TFOUT ...... Thin-Film Oxygen Uptake Test
TFOV........ Total Field of View   (MCD)
TFP............. [*The*] Friends Program [*Pensacola, FL*]   (EA)
TFP............. Teachers Freedom Party   (EA)
TFP............. Temporary Forfeiture of Pay
TFP............. Test Facility Program [*NASA*]   (KSC)
TFP............. Total Factor Productivity [*Economics*]
TFP............. Total Finish Positions [*Horse racing*]
TFP............. Tradition, Family, and Property [*In association name American TFP*]   (EA)
TFP............. Trans-Fiberoptic-Photographic [*Electron microscopy*]
TFP............. Travaux. Faculte de Philosophie et Lettres. Universite Catholique de Louvain [*A publication*]   (BJA)
TFP............. Trees for People [*An association*]   (EA)
TFP............. Trifluoperazine [*Also, Trifluoroperazine*] [*Organic chemistry*]
TFP............. Trifluoroperazine [*Also, Trifluoperazine*] [*Organic chemistry*]
TFPA .... Tubular Finishers and Processors Association [*Houston, TX*]   (EA)
TFPC .... Thin-Film Photovoltaic Cell
TFPCA ...... Thin-Film Photovoltaic Cell Array
TFPECTS ... Thin-Film Personal Communications and Telemetry System   (MCD)
TFPIA .... Textile Fiber Products Identification Act [*1960*]
TFPL.......... Texas Forest Products Laboratory
TFPL.......... Training Film Production Laboratory [*Military*]

TFR............. Pueblo, CO [*Location identifier*] [*FAA*]   (FAAL)
TFR............. Tape-to-File Recorder
TFR............. Television Film Recorder
TFR............. Terrain-Following RADAR
TFR............. Territorial Force Reserve [*British*]
TFR............. Test Failure Report   (CAAL)
TFR............. Theoretical Final Route [*Telecommunications*]   (TEL)
TFR............. Thin-Film Resist
TFR............. TOKAMAK [*Toroidal Kamera Magnetic*] at Fontenay-aux-Roses
T/FR.......... Top of Frame   (AAG)
TFR............. Total Fertility Rate [*Medicine*]
TFR............. Total Final Reports
TFR............. Trafalgar Resources, Inc. [*Vancouver Stock Exchange symbol*]
TFR............. Transaction Formatting Routines
TFR............. Transfer
TFR............. Transfer Function Response
TFR............. Traveler/Failure Report [*Deep Space Instrumentation Facility, NASA*]
TFR............. Trouble and Failure Report
TFR............. Tubular Flow Reactor
TFR............. Tunable Frequency Range
TFR/CAR ... Trouble and Failure Report/Corrective Action Report
TFRCD ...... Traffic Received   (FAAC)
TFRD .... Test Facilities Requirements Document
TFS............. Tactical Fighter Squadron [*Air Force*]
TFS............. Tape File Supervisor
TFS............. Tbilisi [*USSR*] [*Geomagnetic observatory code*]
TFS............. Telemetry Format Selection   (NASA)
TFS............. Tenerife-Reinasofia [*Canary Islands*] [*Airport symbol*]   (OAG)
TFS............. Tennessee Folklore Society   (EA)
TFS............. Terrain-Following System
TFS............. Testicular Feminization Syndrome [*Endocrinology*]
TFS............. Thrombus-Free Surface [*Hematology*]
TFS............. Time and Frequency Standard
TFS............. Tin-Free Steel
TFS............. Traffic Flow Security [*Telecommunications*]   (TEL)
TFS............. Traffic Forecasting System [*Telecommunications*]   (TEL)
TFS............. Transport Ferry Service [*English Channel*]
TFS............. Transverse Feed System
TFS............. Trim Fuel System   (MCD)
TFS............. Trunk Forecasting System [*Telecommunications*]   (TEL)
TFS............. Tunable Frequency Source
TFS............. Turbine First Stage [*Nuclear energy*]   (NRCH)
TFS............. Turbine Flow Sensor
TFS............. Type Finish Specification   (MCD)
TFSA........ Thin-Film Spreading Agent [*For enhanced oil recovery*]
TFSB........ Tennessee Folklore Society. Bulletin [*A publication*]
TFSC........ [*From the Latin for*] Franciscan Tertiaries of the Holy Cross
TFSC........ Turkish Federated State of Cyprus
TFSO........ Tonto Forest Seismological Observatory [*Arizona*]
TFSP........ Task Force on Service to the Public [*Canada*]
TFSP........ Texas Folklore Society. Publications [*A publication*]
TFSQ........ Tactical Fighter Squadron [*Air Force*]
TFSS........ Technical Facilities Subsystem [*Space Flight Operations Facility, NASA*]
TFST........ Thin Films Science and Technology [*Elsevier Book Series*] [*A publication*]
TFT............. Tabular Firing Table [*Military*]   (AABC)
TFT............. Technical Feasibility Testing [*Army*]
TF & T .... Theatre, Film, and Television Biographies Master Index [*A publication*]
TFT............. Thermal Fatigue Test
TFT............. Thin-Film Field-Effect Transistor
TFT............. Thin-Film Technique
TFT............. Thin-Film Technology
TFT............. Thin-Film Transducer
TFT............. Thin-Film Transistor
TFT............. Threshold Failure Temperatures
TFT............. Tight Fingertip [*Medicine*]
TFT............. Trifluorothymidine [*Pharmacology*]
TF/TA........ Terrain Following/Terrain Avoidance   (MCD)
TFTB........ Taping for the Blind [*Houston, TX*]   (EA)
TF/TG .... Task Force/Task Group
TFTP .... Task Force on Teaching as a Profession [*Washington, DC*]   (EA)
TFTP .... Television Facility Test Position [*Telecommunications*]   (TEL)
TFTR .... TOKAMAK [*Toroidal Kamera Magnetic*] Fusion Test Reactor [*Princeton, NJ*]
TFTS .... Tactical Fighter Training Squadron [*Air Force*]   (MCD)
TFTS .... TOW [*Tube-Launched Optically Tracked Wire-Guided*] Field Test Set   (MCD)
TFTTA........ Teplofizika i Teplotekhnika [*A publication*]
TFTW .... Tactical Fighter Training Wing [*Air Force*]   (MCD)
TFU............. Telecommunications Flying Unit [*British*]
TFU............. Test Facility Utilization [*NASA*]   (NASA)
TFU............. Theoretical First Unit [*Economics*]
TFV............. Twin Falls Victory [*Tracking ship*] [*NASA*]
TFW........... Tactical Fighter Wing [*Air Force*]
TFW........... Tethered Free-Floating Worker
TFW........... Thermoplastic Fan Wheel

TFW............ Tropical Fresh Water
TFW............ Tufts University, Medford, MA [*OCLC symbol*]   (OCLC)
TFW............ Turbulent Far Wake
TFWBKEL ... Theologische Forschung Wissenschaftliche Beitraege zur
                Kirchlichevangelischen Lehre [*A publication*]
TFWC .... Tactical Fighter Weapons Center   (AFM)
TFWG........ Tactical Fighter Wing [*Air Force*]
TFWRR...... Task Force on Women's Rights and Responsibilities [*National
                Council on Family Relations*]   (EA)
TFWS .... Tactical Fighter Weapon School [*Air Force*]   (MCD)
TFWS .... Task Force on Women in Sports [*of NOW*]   (EA)
TFX............ Tactical Fighter Experimental [*Air Force*]
TFX............ Teleflex, Inc. [*American Stock Exchange symbol*]
TFX............ Thymic Factor X [*Endocrinology*]
TFX............ Tri-Service Fighter, Experimental   (MCD)
TFX-N.......... Tactical Fighter Experimental - Navy
TFX-O .... Tactical Fighter Experimental - Offensive
TFX-R.......... Tactical Fighter Experimental - Reconnaissance
TFY............ Target Fiscal Year   (MCD)
TFYQA ...... Think for Yourself and Question Authority [*Term coined by Dr.
                Timothy Leary*]
TFZ............ Tail Fuze   (MSA)
TFZ............ Traffic Zone   (FAAC)
TFZ............ Trifluroperazine [*Tranquilizer*]
TFZ............ Tropospheric Frontal Zone
Tg .... Glass Transition
TG .... Guatemala [*Aircraft nationality and registration mark*]   (FAAC)
TG .... Positioning Devices [*JETDS nomenclature*] [*Military*]   (CET)
TG .... Tail Gear
TG .... Tangent Group [*An association*] [*Hollywood, CA*]   (EA)
TG .... Tape Gauge
TG .... Target Gate   (CAAL)
TG .... Task Group
TG .... Task Guidance
TG .... Technology Gap
TG .... Telegram
TG .... Telegraph
TG .... Teleilaet Ghassul   (BJA)
TG .... Temporary Gentleman [*British slang term for officer for
                duration of the war*] [*World War I*]
TG .... Terminal Guidance
TG .... Terminator Group
TG .... Test Group
TG .... Test Guaranteed
TG .... Thai Airways International [*ICAO designator*]   (FAAC)
TG .... Theologie und Glaube [*A publication*]
TG .... Therapeutic Gazette [*Philadelphia*] [*A publication*]
TG .... Thermogravimetry
TG .... Thioglucose [*Biochemistry*]
TG .... Thioglycolate [*Biochemistry*]
TG .... Thioguanine [*Also, T*] [*Antineoplastic drug*]
TG .... Third Generation [*An association*]   (EA)
TG .... Thoracic Ganglion [*Neuroanatomy*]
TG .... Thromboglobulin [*Clinical chemistry*]
TG .... Thyroglobulin [*Also, Thg*] [*Endocrinology*]
TG .... Tijdschrift voor Geschiedenis. Land en Volkenkunde [*A
                publication*]
TG .... Timing Gate   (AAG)
tg .... Togo [*MARC country of publication code*] [*Library of
                Congress*]   (LCCP)
TG .... Togo [*Two-letter standard code*]   (CNC)
TG .... Toho Gakuho [*A publication*]
TG .... Tollgate [*Maps and charts*]
T & G .... Tongue and Groove [*Lumber*]
TG .... Torpedo Group
T & G .... Touch and Go [*Landings*] [*Aviation*]   (MCD)
TG .... Track Geometry [*In TG-01, an Austrian built subway inspection
                car*]
TG .... Tracking and Guidance
TG .... Traders Group Ltd. [*Toronto Stock Exchange symbol*]
                [*Vancouver Stock Exchange symbol*]
TG .... Traffic Guidance [*Aviation*]
T-G .... Transformational-Generative [*Linguistics*]
TG .... Transglutaminase [*An enzyme*]
TG .... Transmissible Gastroenteritis [*Virus*]
TG .... Triglyceride [*Biochemistry*]
TG .... Tropical Gulf [*American air mass*]
TG .... Tuned Grid   (KSC)
TG .... Turbine Generator   (NRCH)
TG .... Turbogenerator
TG .... TV Guide [*A publication*]
TG .... Tying Goals [*Sports*]
TG .... Type Genus
T & G .... Tyrwhitt and Granger's English Exchequer Reports [*1835-
                36*]   (DLA)
T2G............ Technician, Second Grade [*Military*]
TGA............ Antibody Thyroglobulin [*Immunology*]
TGA............ [*The*] Glutamate Association - United States [*Atlanta,
                GA*]   (EA)
TGA............ Taurocholate-Gelatin Agar [*Microbiology*]
T/GA .... Temperature Gauge [*Automotive engineering*]

TGA............ Thermogravimetric [*or Thermogravimetry*] Analysis
                [*Instrumentation*]
TGA............ Thioglycolic Acid [*Organic chemistry*]
TGA............ Toilet Goods Association [*Later, CTFA*]   (EA)
TGA............ Tolmetin Glycine Amide [*Biochemistry*]
TGA............ Total Glycoalkaloids [*Analytical biochemistry*]
TGA............ Trace Gas Analysis
TGA............ Transient Global Amnesia [*Medicine*]
TGA............ Transposition of Great Arteries [*Cardiology*]
TGA............ Triglycollamic Acid [*Organic chemistry*]
TGA............ Tuebinger Germanistische Arbeiten [*A publication*]
T-GAM ...... Training - Guided Air Missile   (MUGU)
TGANA ...... Tsitologiya i Genetika [*A publication*]
TGAOTU ... [*The*] Great Architect of the Universe [*Freemasonry*]
TGARQ...... Telegraphic Approval Requested   (NOAA)
TGAS .... TACAN [*Tactical Air Navigation*] Guidance Augmentation
                System [*Military*]   (CAAL)
TGAS .... Trace Gas Acquisition System
TG-ATS...... Theatre Guild-American Theatre Society   (EA)
TGaV .... Volunteer State Community College, Learning Resources
                Center, Gallatin, TN [*Library symbol*] [*Library of
                Congress*]   (LCLS)
TGB............ Tongued, Grooved, and Beaded [*Lumber*]
TGB............ Torpedo Gunboat   (ROG)
TGB............ Turbine Generator Building   (NRCH)
TGBL.......... Through Government Bill of Lading   (AABC)
TGC............ [*The*] Grantsmanship Center [*Los Angeles, CA*]   (EA)
TGC............ Teleglobe Canada
TGC............ Theater Ground Command [*Military*]
TGC............ Thermocouple Gauge Control
TGC............ Throttle Governor Control
TGC............ Tomato Genetics Cooperative
TGC............ Total Gas-Phase Carbon [*Environmental chemistry*]
TGC............ Tougaloo College, Tougaloo, MS [*OCLC symbol*]   (OCLC)
TGC............ Transfer Gear Case   (MCD)
TGC............ Transmit Gain Control   (MSA)
TGC............ Travel Group Charter [*Airline fare*]
TGC............ Trenton, TN [*Location identifier*] [*FAA*]   (FAAL)
TGCA .... Texas Gun Collectors Association
TGCA .... Transportable Group Control Approach   (NG)
TGCGA ..... Transactions. Gulf Coast Association of Geologic Societies [*A
                publication*]
TGCO........ Transidyne General Corporation [*NASDAQ symbol*]   (NQ)
TGCS .... Transportable Ground Communications Station
TGD............ Task Group Delta   (MCD)
TGD............ Technical Guidance Directions
TGD............ Titograd [*Yugoslavia*] [*Airport symbol*]   (OAG)
TGD............ Trajectory and Guidance Data
TGDR .... Tokyo Gailkokugo Daigaku Ronshu [*Area and Cultural Studies*]
                [*A publication*]
TGE............ Transmissible Gastroenteritis [*Virus*]
TGE............ Traverse Gravimeter Experiment   (KSC)
TGE............ Trialkoxyglyceryl Ether [*Organic chemistry*]
TGE............ Tryptone Glucose Extract [*Cell growth medium*]
TGE............ Tuskegee, AL [*Location identifier*] [*FAA*]   (FAAL)
TGEEP........ Terminal Guidance Environmental Effects Program   (MCD)
TGegw ...... Theologie der Gegenwart [*A publication*]
TGEOD...... Technika Poszukiwan Geologicznych [*A publication*]
TGEP.......... Turbine Generator Emergency Power [*Nuclear
                energy*]   (NRCH)
TGET.......... Target Ground Elapsed Time
TGF............ Therapeutic Gain Factor [*Medicine*]
TGF............ Through Group Filter [*Telecommunications*]   (TEL)
TGF............ Tijdschrift voor Geschiedenis en Folklore [*A publication*]
TGF............ Tragicorum Graecorum Fragmenta [*A publication*]   (OCD)
TGF............ Transforming Growth Factor
TGF............ Transonic Gasdynamics Facility [*Air Force*]
TGF............ Treasury Guard Force
TGF............ Triglycine Fluoberyllate [*Ferroelectrics*]
TGF............ Tumor Growth Factor [*Oncology*]
TGFA.......... Triglyceride Fatty Acid [*Biochemistry*]
TGG............ Kuala Trengganu [*Malaysia*] [*Airport symbol*]   (OAG)
TGG............ Temporary Geographic Grid
TGG............ Third Generation Gyro   (MCD)
TGG............ Turkey Gamma G [*Immunology*]
TGGL-B...... Travaux Geographique de Liege (Belgium) [*A publication*]
TGH............ Tongoa [*Vanuatu*] [*Airport symbol*]   (OAG)
TGI............ Tactics Guide Issued   (CAAL)
TGI............ Taghi Ghambar [*Iran*] [*Seismograph station code, US
                Geological Survey*]   (SEIS)
TGI............ Tangier, VA [*Location identifier*] [*FAA*]   (FAAL)
TGI............ Target Group Index [*British Market Research Bureau Ltd.*]
                [*London*]
TGI............ Target Intensifier
TGI............ Textbuch zur Geschichte Israels [*A publication*]   (BJA)
TGI............ TGI Friday's [*NYSE symbol*]
TGI............ Tingo Maria [*Peru*] [*Airport symbol*]   (OAG)
TGI............ Tournament Golf International
TGIC.......... Tobacco Growers' Information Committee   (EA)
TGIC.......... Triglycidyl Isocyanurate [*Organic chemistry*]
TGID.......... Trunk Group Identification [*Telecommunications*]   (TEL)

TGIF .... Terminal Guidance Indirect Fire   (MCD)
TGIF .... Thank God It's Friday [*Meaning work-week is nearly over*]
TGIF .... Toe Goes in First [*As in "You're so dumb you have 'TGIF' on your shoes!"*]
TGIF-OTMWDUM ... Thank God It's Friday - Only Two More Work Days Until Monday [*Pentagon saying*]
TGIS .... Thank God It's Summer
TGJ............ Tiga [*Loyalty Islands*] [*Airport symbol*]   (OAG)
TGKHA........ Takenaka Gijutsu Kenkyu Hokoku [*A publication*]
TGKZA .... Trudy Instituta Geologicheskikh Nauk. Akademiya Nauk Kazakhskoi SSR [*A publication*]
TGL .... Tagula [*Papua New Guinea*] [*Airport symbol*]   (OAG)
TGL .... Tangent Oil & Gas [*Vancouver Stock Exchange symbol*]
TGL .... Task Group Leader
TGL .... Temperature Gradient Lamp [*Spectroscopy*]
TGL .... Thin Glass Laminate
TGL .... Toggle   (AAG)
TGL .... Touch and Go Landings [*Aviation*]
TGL .... Treasury Gold License   (MCD)
TGL .... Triangular Guide Line
TGL .... Triglyceride Lipase [*Clinical chemistry*]
TGL .... Triglycerides [*Clinical chemistry*]
TGLC........ Total Gate Leakage Current
TGLM .... Task Group Lung Model [*ICRP*]
TG-LORAN ... Traffic-Guidance Long-Range Aid to Navigation   (DEN)
TGLS.......... Tongueless
TGLV.......... Tijdschrift voor Geschiedenis. Land en Volkenkunde [*A publication*]
TGLVQ ...... Terminal Guidance for Lunar Vehicles [*Aerospace*]   (AAG)
TGM .... Task Group Manager   (CAAL)
TGM .... Telegram   (ROG)
TGM .... Theatre Guild Magazine [*A publication*]
TGM .... Tirgu Mures [*Romania*] [*Airport symbol*]   (OAG)
TGM .... Torpedo Gunner's Mate [*Obsolete*] [*Navy*] [*British*]
TGM .... Total Gaseous Mercury [*Environmental chemistry*]
TGM .... Training Guided Missile [*Air Force*]
TGM .... Trunk Group Multiplexer [*Telecommunications*]   (TEL)
TGM .... Turbine Generator Management
TGMA .... Tone Generator and Master Alarm   (KSC)
TGMEA ...... Tropical and Geographical Medicine [*A publication*]
TGN............ Anchorage, AK [*Location identifier*] [*FAA*]   (FAAL)
TGN............ Tournigan Mining [*Vancouver Stock Exchange symbol*]
TGN............ Trigeminal Neuralgia [*Medicine*]
TGN............ Trunk Group Number [*Telecommunications*]   (TEL)
TGNR .... Tactics Guide Not Required   (CAAL)
TGNXF .... Tournigan Mining Explorations Ltd. [*NASDAQ symbol*]   (NQ)
TGO............ Time to Go [*Apollo*] [*NASA*]
TGO............ Togo [*Three-letter standard code*]   (CNC)
TGO............ Tongliao [*China*] [*Airport symbol*]   (OAG)
TGO............ Tuned Grid Oscillator
TGOPS...... Task Group Operations [*Navy*]   (NVT)
TGorPI........ Trudy Gorijskogo Gosudarstvennogo Pedagogiceskogo Instituta [*A publication*]
TGP .... Tasmanian Government Publications [*A publication*]
TGP .... Technigen Platinum Corp. [*Vancouver Stock Exchange symbol*]
TGP .... Theft of Government Property [*FBI standardized term*]
TGP .... Timothy Grass Pollen [*Immunology*]
TGP .... Tobacco Glycoprotein [*Biochemistry*]
TGP .... Tone Generator Panel
TGP .... Transcontinental Gas Pipe Line Corp. [*NYSE symbol*]
TGPIA .... Trudy Gruzinskii Politekhnicheskii Institut Imeni V. I. Lenina [*A publication*]
TGPSG........ Tactical Global Positioning System Guidance   (MCD)
TGPWU ...... Transport, General and Port Workers' Union [*Aden*]
TGR .... Tiger International, Inc. [*Formerly, FLY*] [*NYSE symbol*]
TGR .... Tohoku Gakuin Daigaku Ronshu [*North Japan College Review: Essays and Studies in English Language and Literature*] [*A publication*]
TGR .... Touggourt [*Algeria*] [*Airport symbol*]   (OAG)
TGRLSS ..... Two-Gas Regenerative Lift Support System
TGrT.......... Tusculum College, Greeneville, TN [*Library symbol*] [*Library of Congress*]   (LCLS)
TGS .... Gulf States Utilities Co., Beaumont, TX [*OCLC symbol*]   (OCLC)
TGS .... Target Generating System
TGS .... Taxiing Guidance System [*Aviation*]
TGS .... Telemetry Ground Station
TGS .... Telemetry Ground System   (NASA)
TGS .... Telemetry Guidance System [*From computer game "Hacker II"*]
TGS .... Terminal Guidance Sensor [*or System*]
TGS .... Thermogravimetric [*or Thermogravimetry*] System [*Instrumentation*]
TGS .... Tide Gauge System
TGS .... Traite de Grammaire Syriaque [*A publication*]   (BJA)
TGS .... Translator Generator System   (IEEE)
TGS .... Transportable Ground Station
TGS .... Triglycine Sulfate [*Ferroelectrics*]
TGS .... Turbine Generator System [*Nuclear energy*]   (NRCH)
TGS .... Turkish General Staff   (NATG)
TGSE.......... Telemetry Ground Support Equipment [*NASA*]   (KSC)

TGSE......... Test Ground Support Equipment
TGSG .... Transactions. Gaelic Society of Glasgow [*A publication*]
TGSI .... Transactions. Gaelic Society of Inverness [*A publication*]
TGSM........ Terminally Guided Submissile   (MCD)
TGSM........ Terminally Guided Submunitions   (MCD)
TGSR......... Triglyceride Secretion Rate [*Physiology*]
TGSS .... Terminal Guidance Sensor System
TGSS .... Turbine Gland Sealing System [*Nuclear energy*]   (NRCH)
TGSS/UGS ... Tactical Ground Sensor System/Unattended Ground Sensor   (MCD)
TGT .... Tail Gate
TGT .... Tanga [*Tanzania*] [*Airport symbol*]   (OAG)
TGT .... Target   (AAG)
TGT .... Tenneco, Inc. [*Formerly, Tennessee Gas Transmission Co.*] [*NYSE symbol*] [*Toronto Stock Exchange symbol*]
TGT .... Thermocouple Gauge Tube
TGT .... Thromboplastin Generation Test [*Hematology*]
TGT .... True Ground Track   (MCD)
TGT .... Turbine Gas Temperature   (NATG)
TGU .... Technical Guidance Unit   (NVT)
TGU .... Tegucigalpa [*Honduras*] [*Airport symbol*]   (OAG)
TGU .... Triglycidylurazol [*Antineoplastic drug*]
TGUBA ...... Bulletin. Tokyo Gakugei University [*A publication*]
TGUOS...... Transactions. Glasgow University Oriental Society [*A publication*]
TGURG...... Telegraphic Authority Requested   (NOAA)
TGV .... Targovishte [*Bulgaria*] [*Airport symbol*]   (OAG)
TGV .... Train a Grande Vitesse [*High-Speed Train*] [*Also called Tres Grande Vitesse*] [*French*]
TGV .... Transposition of the Great Vessels [*Cardiology*]
TGV .... Tres Grande Vitesse [*Also called Train a Grande Vitesse*] [*Very Great Speed*] [*French high-speed train*]
TGV .... Turbine Governor Valve [*Nuclear energy*]   (NRCH)
TGV .... Two Gentlemen of Verona [*Shakespearean work*]
TGW .... Terminally Guided Warhead
TGW .... Theologie der Gegenwart [*A publication*]
TGWU........ Transport and General Workers' Union [*British*]
TGX .... Tube-Generated X-Ray
TGZ .... Tuxtla Gutierrez [*Mexico*] [*Airport symbol*]   (OAG)
Th.............. C. H. Boehringer Sohn, Ingelheim [*Germany*] [*Research code symbol*]
TH.............. Harriman Public Library, Harriman, TN [*Library symbol*] [*Library of Congress*]   (LCLS)
TH.............. Hot Leg Temperature [*Nuclear energy*]   (NRCH)
TH.............. Reports of the Witwatersrand High Court [*Transvaal, South Africa*]   (DLA)
Th.............. T-Cell, Helper Type [*Immunology*]
T-H .... Taft-Hartley [*Act*]
TH.............. Tally Ho [*Air Force*]
TH.............. Teacher of Hydrotherapy [*British*]
TH.............. Teaching History [*A publication*]
TH.............. Technische Hochschule
TH.............. Teki Historyczne [*A publication*]
TH.............. Telegraph Apparatus [*JETDS nomenclature*] [*Military*]   (CET)
TH.............. Tell Halaf   (BJA)
TH.............. Temporary Hold
TH.............. Terrain Height   (MCD)
TH.............. Territory of Hawaii [*to 1959*]
T & H .... Test and Handling [*Equipment*]   (NG)
TH.............. Thai Airways Co. Ltd. [*Later, TG*] [*ICAO designator*]   (FAAC)
th.............. Thailand [*MARC country of publication code*] [*Library of Congress*]   (LCCP)
TH.............. Thailand [*Two-letter standard code*]   (CNC)
TH.............. Theatre   (ROG)
TH.............. Their Highnesses   (ADA)
th.............. Thenardite [*CIPW classification*] [*Geology*]
Th.............. Theodotion   (BJA)
Th.............. Theogonia [*of Hesiod*] [*Classical studies*]   (OCD)
Th.............. Theologia [*A publication*]
TH.............. Theology
Th.............. Theology [*A publication*]
TH.............. Theraplix [*France*] [*Research code symbol*]
TH.............. Thermal
T/H .... Thermal and Hydraulic [*Nuclear energy*]   (NRCH)
Th.............. Thessalonians [*New Testament book*]   (BJA)
Th.............. Thick [*Automotive engineering*]
Th.............. Things [*A publication*]
Th.............. Thionine [*Organic chemistry*]
Th.............. Thiopental [*An anesthetic*]
TH.............. Thoracic Surgery
Th.............. Thorium [*Chemical element*]
Th.............. Thought [*A publication*]
TH.............. Through-Hole [*Data processing*]
TH.............. Thunder
TH.............. Thursday
TH.............. Thyroid Hormone [*Thyroxine*] [*Endocrinology*]
TH.............. Today's Health [*A publication*]
TH.............. Toilet-Paper Holder
TH.............. Toluene-Hyamine [*Scintillation solvent*]
TH.............. Total Hysterectomy [*Medicine*]
TH.............. Town Hall   (ROG)

TH............... Tracing-Hold
T-H............. Transhydro (AABC)
TH............... Transmission Header [*Data processing*] (IBMDP)
TH............... Transponder-Hopping
T/H............. Transportation and Handling [*Army*]
TH............... True Heading
TH............... Trust House [*British*]
TH............... Two Hands
TH............... Tyrosine Hydroxylase [*An enzyme*]
ThA .... Associate in Theology (ADA)
THA .... Taft-Hartley Act
T-HA........... Terminal High Altitude
THA .... Tetrahydroaminoacridine [*Pharmacology*]
tha.............. Thai [*MARC language code*] [*Library of Congress*] (LCCP)
THA .... Thailand [*Three-letter standard code*] (CNC)
THA .... Thames Ontario Library Service Board [*UTLAS symbol*]
ThA .... Theatre Annual [*A publication*]
ThA .... Thoracic Aorta [*Medicine*]
THA .... Thorcheron Hunter Association (EA)
THA .... Total Hip Arthroplasty [*Orthopedics*]
THA .... Tower Hill School, Wilmington, DE [*OCLC symbol*] (OCLC)
THA .... Treasury Historical Association (EA)
THA .... Tullahoma, TN [*Location identifier*] [*FAA*] (FAAL)
THA .... Turk Haberler Ajansi [*Press agency*] [*Turkey*]
THAA.......... Tourist House Association of America [*Greentown, PA*] (EA)
THAB......... Tetrahexylammonium Benzoate [*Organic chemistry*]
THABTS..... Thereabouts
Thac Cr Cas ... Thacher's Criminal Cases [*1823-42*] [*Massachusetts*] (DLA)
Thach Cr..... Thacher's Criminal Cases [*Massachusetts*] (DLA)
Thacher Cr ... Thacher's Criminal Cases [*Massachusetts*] (DLA)
Thacher Cr Cas ... Thacher's Criminal Cases [*Massachusetts*] (DLA)
Thacher Crim Cas (Mass) ... Thacher's Criminal Cases [*Massachusetts*] (DLA)
THAE.......... Transcatheter Hepatic Artery Embolization [*Medicine*]
THAI .... Thai Airways International
Thai J Agric Sci ... Thai Journal of Agricultural Science [*A publication*]
Thai J Dev Adm ... Thai Journal of Development Administration [*Bangkok*] [*A publication*]
Thai J Nurs ... Thai Journal of Nursing [*A publication*]
Thailand Dep Miner Resour Ground Water Bull ... Thailand. Department of Mineral Resources. Ground Water Bulletin [*A publication*]
Thailand Dep Miner Resour Rep Invest ... Thailand. Department of Mineral Resources. Report of Investigation [*A publication*]
Thail Plant Prot Serv Tech Bull ... Thailand Plant Protection Service. Technical Bulletin [*A publication*]
Thai Natl Sci Pap Fauna Ser ... Thai National Scientific Papers. Fauna Series [*A publication*]
Thai Nurses Assoc J ... Thai Nurses Association Journal [*A publication*]
Thai Sci Bull ... Thai Science Bulletin [*A publication*]
Thal............ Thalassemia [*Medicine*]
Thalassia Jugosl ... Thalassia Jugoslavica [*A publication*]
THAM......... Tris(hydroxymethyl)aminomethane [*Also, TRIS*] [*Biochemical analysis*]
THAMA ...... Toxic and Hazardous Materials Agency [*Army*] (RDA)
ThanaCAP ... Thana [*The Greek word for death*] and CAP [*Consumer Action Panel*] [*An association*]
THAP......... Tactical High-Altitude Penetration (MCD)
THAQ .... Tetrahydroanthraquinone [*Organic chemistry*]
Tharandter Forstl Jahrb ... Tharandter Forstliches Jahrbuch [*A publication*]
THARIES.... Total Hip Articular Replacement with Internal Eccentric Shells [*Orthopedics*]
THarol....... Lincoln Memorial University, Harrogate, TN [*Library symbol*] [*Library of Congress*] (LCLS)
THART ...... Theodore Army Terminal
ThArts........ Theatre Arts [*A publication*]
ThAS.......... Tumbleweed High-Altitude Samples (MUGU)
ThAT .... Theologie des Alten Testaments [*A publication*] (BJA)
THAT......... Theologisches Handwoerterbuch zum Alten Testament [*A publication*] (BJA)
THAT......... Twenty-Four-Hour Automatic Teller [*Trademark for self-service banking display panel*]
Th Aust ..... Theatre Australia [*A publication*]
THAWS ...... Tactical Homing and Warning System
Thayer....... Thayer's Reports [*18 Oregon*] (DLA)
Thayer Prelim Treatise Ev ... Thayer's Preliminary Treatise on Evidence (DLA)
THB .... Thaba Tseka [*Lesotho*] [*Airport symbol*] (OAG)
Th B........... Theologiae Baccalaureas [*Bachelor of Theology*]
ThB............ Theologische Blaetter [*A publication*]
ThB............ Theologische Buecherei. Neudrucke und Berichte aus dem 20 Jahrhundert [*Munich*] [*A publication*] (BJA)
THB .... Third-Harmonic Band
THB .... Today's Housing Briefs [*A publication*]
THB .... [*The*] Toronto, Hamilton & Buffalo Railway Co. [*AAR code*]
TH & B .... [*The*] Toronto, Hamilton & Buffalo Railway Co. [*Nickname: To Hell and Back*]
THB .... Trierer Heimatbuch [*A publication*]
THBF......... Total Hepatic Blood Flow
THBF......... Traditional Hi-Bye Function [*Army*]

Thbilis Sahelmc Univ Gamoqeneb Math Inst Srom ... Thbilisis Sahelmcipho Universiteti Gamoqenebithi Mathematikis Instituti. Sromebi [*A publication*]
Thbilis Univ Srom ... Thbilisis Universitetis. Phizika-Mathematikisa de Sabunebismetqvelo Mecnierebani. Sromebi [*A publication*]
Thbilis Univ Srom A ... Thbilisis Universitetis Sromebi. A. Phizika-Mathematikisa de Sabunebismetqvelo Mecnierebani [*A publication*]
THbl .... Trierische Heimatblaetter [*A publication*]
ThBNL........ National Library, Bangkok, Thailand [*Library symbol*] [*Library of Congress*] (LCLS)
THBP......... Tetrahydrobenzopyrene [*Organic chemistry*]
Th Br .... Thesaurus Brevium [*2 eds.*] [*1661, 1687*] (DLA)
THBR......... Thoroughbred Half-Bred Registry (EA)
THBR......... Thyroid Hormone Binding Ratio [*Clinical chemistry*]
THBY......... Thereby
Th C .... Candidate of Theology
THC........... Houston Community College System, Learning Resource Center, Houston, TX [*OCLC symbol*] (OCLC)
THC........... Hydraulic Company [*NYSE symbol*]
THC........... Target Homing Correlator
THC........... Tchien [*Liberia*] [*Airport symbol*] (OAG)
TH & C .... Terpin Hydrate and Codeine [*Medicine*]
THC........... Tetrahydrocannabinol [*Active principle of marijuana*]
THC........... Tetrahydrocortisol
THC........... Thermal Converter (MSA)
THC........... Thiocarbanidin [*Pharmacology*]
Th & C .... Thompson and Cook's New York Supreme Court Reports [*1873-75*] (DLA)
THC........... Thrust Hand Controller [*NASA*] (KSC)
THC........... Total Hydrocarbon
THC........... Translation Hand Controller [*NASA*]
THC........... Tridont Health Care [*Toronto Stock Exchange symbol*]
THC........... Tube Humidity Control
T & HCA ...... Towboat and Harbor Carriers Association of New York and New Jersey [*New York, NY*] (EA)
THCA .... Trihydroxycholestanoic Acid [*Biochemistry*]
THCA .... Trihydroxycoprostanic Acid [*Biochemistry*]
Th CC .... Thacher's Criminal Cases [*1823-42*] [*Massachusetts*] (DLA)
THCC .... Tube Heating and Cooling Control
Th C Const Law ... Thomas' Leading Cases on Constitutional Law (DLA)
THCF......... Thompson-Huston Company of France
THCF......... Topics in Health Care Financing [*A publication*]
THCN .... Tetrahydrocorynantheine [*Biochemistry*]
THCO .... [*The*] Hammond Corporation [*NASDAQ symbol*] (NQ)
THCS .... Temperature of Hot-Channel Sodium [*Nuclear energy*] (NRCH)
ThD .... Doctor of Thinkology [*Honorary degree awarded the scarecrow by the wizard in 1939 film "The Wizard of Oz"*]
Thd............ Ribothymidine [*Also, T*] [*A nucleoside*]
THD........... Testicular Hypothermia Device [*Medicine*]
Th D........... Theologiae Doctor [*Doctor of Theology*]
ThD........... Theology Digest [*St. Mary's, KS*] [*A publication*]
THD .... Third Canadian General Investment Trust Ltd. [*Toronto Stock Exchange symbol*]
THD .... Thread (AAG)
THD .... Thunderhead (FAAC)
THD .... Total Harmonic Distortion [*Electronics*]
THD .... Tube Heat Dissipator
THD .... University of Houston, Downtown College, Houston, TX [*OCLC symbol*] (OCLC)
THDA .... Telluraheptadecanoic Acid [*Organic chemistry*]
THDC .... Technical Handbook Distribution Code (MCD)
THDI.......... Thread Die
ThDig .... Theology Digest [*St. Mary's, KS*] [*A publication*]
ThDip .... Diploma in Theology (ADA)
THDNK...... Threaded Neck
THDOC...... Tetrahydrodeoxy Corticosterone [*Biochemistry*]
THDPC...... Threadpiece
THDr.......... Doctor of Theology
THDR........ Thunander Corp. [*NASDAQ symbol*] (NQ)
THDR........ Thunder (FAAC)
THDS .... Time Homogenous Data Set (MCD)
THE .... [*The*] Hudson Bay Mines Ltd. [*Toronto Stock Exchange symbol*]
THE .... T & H Resources [*Formerly, Hudson Bay Mines Ltd.*] [*Toronto Stock Exchange symbol*]
THE .... Tape-Handling Equipment
THE .... Technical Help to Exporters [*An association*]
THE .... Teresina [*Brazil*] [*Airport symbol*] (OAG)
THE .... Tetrahydrocortisone [*Endocrinology*]
ThE........... Theologische Existenz Heute [*Munich*] [*A publication*] (BJA)
THE .... Thomas Hewett Edward Cat [*In TV series "T.H.E. Cat"*]
THE .... Transhepatic Embolization [*Medicine*]
THE .... Transportable Helicopter Enclosure (RDA)
THE .... Tube Heat Exchanger
THEA .... Theata [*A publication*]
THEAT ...... Theatrical
Theat C ..... Theatre Crafts [*A publication*]
Theat J ...... Theatre Journal [*A publication*]

Theat Q ...... Theatre Quarterly [*A publication*]
Theatre Arts M ... Theatre Arts Magazine [*A publication*]
Theatre J .... Theatre Journal [*A publication*]
Theatre M ... Theatre Magazine [*A publication*]
Theatre Notebk ... Theatre Notebook [*A publication*]
Theatre Pol ... Theatre en Pologne - Theatre in Poland [*A publication*]
Theatre Q ... Theatre Quarterly [*A publication*]
Theatre Res Int ... Theatre Research International [*A publication*]
Theatre S ... Theatre Studies [*A publication*]
Theatre S ... Theatre Survey [*A publication*]
Theat Res I ... Theatre Research International [*A publication*]
Theat Stud ... Theatre Studies [*A publication*]
Theb .... Thebais [*of Statius*] [*Classical studies*] (OCD)
THEBES ..... [*The*] Electronic Banking Economics Society [*New York, NY*] (EA)
THECC .... Truck and Heavy Equipment Claims Council [*St. Louis, MO*] (EA)
Th Ed .... Theological Education [*A publication*]
THEED ...... Tetrahydroxyethylethylenediamine [*Organic chemistry*]
THEIC .... Tris(hydroxyethyl)isocyanurate [*Organic chemistry*]
Thel .... Theloall's Le Digest des Briefs [*2 eds.*] [*1579, 1687*] (DLA)
Them .... American Themis [*New York*] (DLA)
Them .... La Themis (DLA)
Them .... Themelios [*A publication*]
Them .... Themistocles [*of Plutarch*] [*Classical studies*] (OCD)
THEN .... Those Hags Encourage Neuterism [*Organization opposed to NOW (National Organization for Women)*]
THEO .... Theology
THEO .... Theophylline [*Pharmacology*]
THEO .... Theoretical
Theobald ... Theobald on Wills [*11 eds.*] [*1876-1954*] (DLA)
Theoc .... Theocritus [*Third century BC*] [*Classical studies*] (OCD)
Theod .... Theodotion (BJA)
Theo Ecl ..... Theological Eclectic [*A publication*]
Theog .... Theogonia [*of Hesiod*] [*Classical studies*] (OCD)
Theokr .... Theokratia [*Leiden/Cologne*] [*A publication*]
THEOL .... Theological
Theol .... Theology [*London*] [*A publication*]
TheolArb .... Theologische Arbeiten [*A publication*] (BJA)
Theol Dgst ... Theology Digest [*A publication*]
Theo & Lit J ... Theological and Literary Journal [*A publication*]
THEOLOG ... Theology Student (DSUE)
Theol Phil .... Theologie und Philosophie [*A publication*]
Theol Quart-schrift ... Theologischer Quartalschrift [*A publication*]
Theol R .... Theologische Revue [*A publication*]
Theol & Rel Ind ... Theological and Religious Index [*A publication*]
Theol Stds ... Theological Studies [*A publication*]
Theol Today ... Theology Today [*A publication*]
Theol Via .... Theologia Viatorum [*A publication*]
Theom L ..... Theomonistic Licensee
Theo Mo ..... Theological Monthly [*A publication*]
Theophr ..... Theophrastus [*Third century BC*] [*Classical studies*] (OCD)
Theopomp ... Theopompus Historicus [*Fourth century BC*] [*Classical studies*] (OCD)
Theo Pr & S ... Theobald's Principal and Surety [*1832*] (DLA)
Theo R .... Theological Review [*A publication*]
THEOR ...... Theorem (ROG)
THEOR ...... Theoretical (AAG)
Theor A Gen ... Theoretical and Applied Genetics [*A publication*]
Theor Appl Genet ... Theoretical and Applied Genetics [*A publication*]
Theor Appl Mech (Sofia) ... Theoretical and Applied Mechanics (Sofia) [*A publication*]
Theor Chem ... Theoretical Chemistry [*A publication*]
Theor Chem Adv Perspect ... Theoretical Chemistry. Advances and Perspectives [*A publication*]
Theor Chem Engng Abstr ... Theoretical Chemical Engineering Abstracts [*A publication*]
Theor Chim ... Theoretica Chimica Acta [*A publication*]
Theor Chim Acta ... Theoretica Chimica Acta [*A publication*]
Theor Comput Sci ... Theoretical Computer Science [*A publication*]
Theor Decis ... Theory and Decision [*A publication*]
Theo Repos ... Theological Repository [*A publication*]
Theoret Appl Genet ... Theoretical and Applied Genetics [*A publication*]
Theoret Chim Acta ... Theoretica Chimica Acta [*A publication*]
Theoret Comput Sci ... Theoretical Computer Science [*A publication*]
Theoret Linguist ... Theoretical Linguistics [*A publication*]
Theoret and Math Phys ... Theoretical and Mathematical Physics [*A publication*]
Theoret Population Biol ... Theoretical Population Biology [*A publication*]
Theor Exp Biol ... Theoretical and Experimental Biology [*A publication*]
Theor Exp Chem ... Theoretical and Experimental Chemistry [*A publication*]
Theor Exp Methoden Regelunstech ... Theoretische und Experimentelle Methoden der Regelungstechnik [*A publication*]
Theor Found Chem Eng ... Theoretical Foundations of Chemical Engineering [*A publication*]
Theorie et Polit ... Theorie et Politique [*A publication*]
Theor Klin Med Einzeldarstell ... Theoretische und Klinische Medizin in Einzeldarstellungen [*West Germany*] [*A publication*]
Theor Math ... Theoretical and Mathematical Physics [*A publication*]
Theor Math Phys ... Theoretical and Mathematical Physics [*A publication*]
Theor Pop B ... Theoretical Population Biology [*A publication*]

Theor Popul Biol ... Theoretical Population Biology [*A publication*]
Theor Probability Appl ... Theory of Probability and Its Applications [*A publication*]
Theor Theor ... Theoria to Theory [*A publication*]
Theory Exp Exobiol ... Theory and Experiment in Exobiology [*A publication*]
Theory Probab Appl ... Theory of Probability and Its Applications [*A publication*]
Theory Probability and Math Statist ... Theory of Probability and Mathematical Statistics [*A publication*]
Theory Probab Math Statist ... Theory of Probability and Mathematical Statistics [*A publication*]
Theory and Soc ... Theory and Society [*A publication*]
THEOS .... Theosophy
THEOS .... They Help Each Other Spiritually [*Motto of THEOS Foundation*]
Theosophy in Aust ... Theosophy in Australia [*A publication*]
Theos Q ..... Theosophical Quarterly [*A publication*]
THEOS R ..... Theosophical Review [*A publication*] (ROG)
Theo Wills ... Theobald on Wills [*13th ed.*] [*1971*] (DLA)
THer .... Ladies Hermitage Association, Hermitage, TN [*Library symbol*] [*Library of Congress*] (LCLS)
THER .... Therapeutic
Ther .... Theriaca [*of Nicander*] [*Classical studies*] (OCD)
THERAP ..... Therapeutic
Therapeutic Ed ... Therapeutic Education [*A publication*]
Therap Gegenw ... Therapie der Gegenwart [*A publication*]
Therap Halbmonatsh ... Therapeutische Halbmonatshefte [*A publication*]
Therap Monatsh Vet-Med ... Therapeutische Monatshefte fuer Veterinaermedizin [*A publication*]
Ther Drug Monit ... Therapeutic Drug Monitoring [*A publication*]
The Rep ..... [*The*] Reporter, Phi Alpha Delta (DLA)
The Rep ..... [*The*] Reports, Coke's English King's Bench (DLA)
Ther Gaz .... Therapeutic Gazette [*A publication*]
Ther Ggw ... Therapie der Gegenwart [*A publication*]
Ther Hung ... Therapia Hungarica [*A publication*]
THERM ...... Thermal (DEN)
THERM ...... Thermometer (AAG)
THERM ...... Thermostat (DEN)
THERMA .... Transfer of Heat Reduced Magnetically
Therm Abstr ... Thermal Abstracts [*A publication*]
Therm Eng ... Thermal Engineering [*A publication*]
Therm Engng ... Thermal Engineering [*A publication*]
Therm Engr ... Thermal Engineering [*A publication*]
THERMISTOR ... Thermal Resistor
Therm Nucl Power ... Thermal and Nuclear Power [*Japan*] [*A publication*]
THERMO .... Thermal and Hydrodynamic Experiment Research Module in Orbit (MCD)
THERMO .... Thermostat (AAG)
Thermoc Act ... Thermochimica Acta [*A publication*]
Thermochim Acta ... Thermochimica Acta [*A publication*]
THERMODYN ... Thermodynamics (AAG)
Therm Power Conf Proc ... Thermal Power Conference. Proceedings [*United States*] [*A publication*]
THerP .... [*The*] Papers of Andrew Jackson, Hermitage, TN [*Library symbol*] [*Library of Congress*] (LCLS)
THERP .... Technique for Human Error Rate Prediction
Ther Probl Today ... Therapeutic Problems of Today [*A publication*]
Ther Recreation J ... Therapeutic Recreation Journal [*A publication*]
Ther Recr J ... Therapeutic Recreation Journal [*A publication*]
Ther Sem Hop ... Therapeutique. Semaine des Hopitaux [*A publication*]
Ther Umsch ... Therapeutische Umschau [*A publication*]
Thes .... Thesaurus [*A publication*]
Thes .... Theseus [*of Plutarch*] [*Classical studies*] (OCD)
THES .... Thesis (ADA)
Thes .... Thessalonians [*New Testament book*]
THES .... Times Higher Education Supplement [*A publication*]
Thes Brev .. Thesaurus Brevium (DLA)
Theses Cathol Med Coll ... Theses. Catholic Medical College [*A publication*]
Theses Cathol Med Coll (Seoul) ... Theses. Catholic Medical College (Seoul) [*A publication*]
Theses Collect Chonnam Univ Chonnam Univ ... Theses Collection of Chonnam University. Chonnam University [*A publication*]
Theses Collect Kyungnam Ind Jr Coll ... Theses Collection. Kyungnam Industrial Junior College [*Republic of Korea*] [*A publication*]
Theses Collect Kyungnam Univ ... Theses Collection. Kyungnam University [*Republic of Korea*] [*A publication*]
Theses Collect Yeungnam Univ ... Theses Collection. Yeungnam University [*Republic of Korea*] [*A publication*]
Theses Collect Yeungnam Univ Nat Sci ... Theses Collection. Yeungnam University. Natural Sciences [*Republic of Korea*] [*A publication*]
Thesis Theo Cassettes ... Thesis Theological Cassettes [*A publication*]
THESLA ..... Tennessee Health Science Library Association [*Library network*]
Thesm .... Thesmophoriazusae [*of Aristophanes*] [*Classical studies*] (OCD)
Thess .... Thessalonians [*New Testament book*]
THETA .... [*The*] Handicapped and Elderly Travelers Association [*Commercial firm*] [*San Francisco, CA*] (EA)
THETA .... Teenage Health Education Teaching Assistants [*National Foundation for the Prevention of Oral Disease*]

T Heth .... Text der Hethiter [*A publication*]
ThExNF ...... Theologische Existenz Heute. Neue Folge [*A publication*]   (BJA)
THF .... Freelance Research Service, Houston, TX [*OCLC symbol*]   (OCLC)
THF .... Target Height Finding   (MCD)
THF .... Tetrahydrofluorenone [*Organic chemistry*]
THF .... Tetrahydrofolate [*Biochemistry*]
THF .... Tetrahydrofuran [*Organic chemistry*]
ThF .... Theologische Forschung [*Hamburg*] [*A publication*]
THF .... Thermal Hysteresis Factor
THF .... Thymic Humoral Factor [*Endocrinology*]
THF .... Thymic Hypocalcemic Factor [*Biochemistry*]
THF .... Tian Hua Fen [*Chinese herbal medicine*]
THF .... Tremendously High Frequency [*Telecommunications*]   (TEL)
THF .... Trust Houses Forte Ltd. [*Hotel empire*]
THFA .... Tetrahydrofolic Acid [*Biochemistry*]
THFA .... Tetrahydrofurfuryl Alcohol [*Organic chemistry*]
THFA .... Three-Conductor, Heat and Flame Resistant, Armor Cable
THFM .... Therefrom
THFOR ...... Therefor [*Legal*] [*British*]   (ROG)
THFR .... Thetford Corp. [*NASDAQ symbol*]   (NQ)
THFR .... Three-Conductor, Heat and Flame Resistant, Radio Cable
THFROM .... Therefrom [*Legal*] [*British*]   (ROG)
THG .... Thangool [*Australia*] [*Airport symbol*]   (OAG)
ThG .... Theologie der Gegenwart [*A publication*]
ThG .... Theologie und Glaube [*A publication*]
THG .... Third-Harmonic Generation [*Physics*]
THG .... Thomson, GA [*Location identifier*] [*FAA*]   (FAAL)
Thg .... Thyroglobulin [*Also, TG*] [*Endocrinology*]
THGA .... Thread Gauge
THGA .... Trihydroxyglutamic Acid [*Organic chemistry*]
THGA .... Trihydroxyglutaric Acid [*Organic chemistry*]
TH GAZ ..... Therapeutic Gazette [*Philadelphia*] [*A publication*]   (ROG)
THGEA .... Therapie der Gegenwart [*A publication*]
THGG .... Transportable Horizontal Gravity Gradiometer
THHF .... Tetrahydrohomofolate [*Organic chemistry*]
ThHK .... Theologischer Hand-Kommentar zum Neuen Testament [*A publication*]   (BJA)
THHP .... Target Health Hazard Program [*Occupational Safety and Health Administration*]
THHP .... Tung-Hai Hsueh-Pao [*Tunghai Journal*] [*A publication*]
THI .... Telehop, Incorporated [*Fresno, CA*] [*Telecommunications*]   (TSSD)
THI .... Temperature-Humidity Index
THi .... Tennessee Historical Society, Nashville, TN [*Library symbol*] [*Library of Congress*]   (LCLS)
THI .... Terre Haute [*Indiana*] [*Seismograph station code, US Geological Survey*]   (SEIS)
THI .... Texas Heart Institute [*University of Texas*] [*Research center*]   (RCD)
THI .... Theodor Herzl Institute   (EA)
THI .... Time Handed In [*Navy*]
THI .... Travelers Health Institute [*Later, ITHI*]
THI .... Trihydroxyindol [*Organic chemistry*]
THIEF .... [*The*] Human-Initiated Equipment Failures
Thiemig-Taschenb ... Thiemig-Taschenbuecher [*A publication*]
Thieraerzt Mitth (Carlsruhe) ... Thieraerztliche Mittheilungen (Carlsruhe) [*A publication*]
Thiermed Rundschau ... Thiermedicinische Rundschau [*A publication*]
Thin Sol Fi ... Thin Solid Films [*A publication*]
THIO .... Thiopental [*An anesthetic*]
THioTEPA ... Triethylenethiophosphoramide [*Also, TSPA*] [*Antineoplastic drug*]
THIP .... Tetrahydroisooxazolopyridineol [*Organic chemistry*]
THIR .... Temperature-Humidity Infrared Radiometer
Third World Q ... Third World Quarterly [*A publication*]
Thirties Soc Jnl ... Thirties Society. Journal [*A publication*]
Thirty-3 ...... 33 Magazine [*A publication*]
Thirty-Three/33 Mag Met Prod Ind ... Thirty-Three/33. Magazine of the Metals Producing Industry [*A publication*]
THIS .... [*The*] Hospitality and Information Service [*For diplomatic residents and families in Washington, DC*]
ThisMag ..... This Magazine [*A publication*]
This Mag ... This Magazine Is about Schools [*Later, This Magazine: Education, Culture, Politics*] [*A publication*]
THJ .... Laurel, MS [*Location identifier*] [*FAA*]   (FAAL)
ThJ .... Theologische Jahrbuecher [*A publication*]
THJCS .... Tsing Hua Journal of Chinese Studies [*A publication*]
THJUA .... Thalassia Jugoslavica [*A publication*]
THK .... Thackeray Corp. [*NYSE symbol*]
THK .... Thick   (AAG)
THKF .... Thick Film   (MSA)
THKNS .... Thickness
THKR .... Thicker   (MSA)
THKSA .... Taiki Hoshano Kansoku Seiseki [*A publication*]
Th L .... Licentiate in Theology
'tHL .... 'T Heiling Land [*Nijmegen*] [*A publication*]   (BJA)
THL .... Tachilek [*Burma*] [*Airport symbol*]   (OAG)
THL .... Tally-Ho Exploration Limited [*Vancouver Stock Exchange symbol*]

ThL .... Theologisches Literaturblatt [*Leipzig*] [*A publication*]
THL .... Thermoluminescence [*Also, TL*]
THL .... Thule [*Denmark*] [*Geomagnetic observatory code*]
THL .... Transhybrid Loss [*Telecommunications*]   (TEL)
THL .... Tuned Hybrid Lattice
THL .... University of Houston, Law Library, Main, Houston, TX [*OCLC symbol*]   (OCLC)
ThLB .... Theologisches Literaturblatt [*A publication*]
ThlBer .... Theologischer Literaturbericht [*A publication*]   (BJA)
ThLBl .... Theologisches Literaturblatt [*Leipzig*] [*A publication*]
THLD .... Threshold
Th Lit .... Theologische Literaturzeitung [*A publication*]
ThLL .... Thesaurus Linguae Latinae [*A publication*]
THLR .... Thaler [*Numismatics*]
THLRA .... Taft-Hartley Labor Relations Act   (OICC)
THLS .... Turret Head Limit Switch
ThLZ .... Theologische Literaturzeitung [*A publication*]
THM .... Tapia House Movement [*Trinidadian and Tobagan*]   (PPW)
THM .... Textos Hispanicos Modernos [*A publication*]
Th M .... Theologiae Magister [*Master of Theology*]
THM .... Therm   (MSA)
Thm .... Thomist [*A publication*]
THM .... Thompson Falls, MT [*Location identifier*] [*FAA*]   (FAAL)
THM .... Thomson Newspapers Ltd. [*Toronto Stock Exchange symbol*]
THM .... Tien Hsia Monthly [*A publication*]
THM .... Traveling Heater Method
THM .... Trihalomethane[*s*] [*Organic chemistry*]
THM .... TRIS, HEPES, Mannitol [*A buffer*]
THM .... Trotting Horse Museum   (EA)
THM .... University of Tennessee at Martin, Martin, TN [*OCLC symbol*]   (OCLC)
THMA .... Trailer Hitch Manufacturers Association [*Washington, DC*]   (EA)
THMD .... Thermedics, Inc. [*NASDAQ symbol*]   (NQ)
THMFP .... Trihalomethane Formation Potential [*Environmental chemistry*]
THMF-TS-TGSE ... Teachers Have More Fun - They Should - They Get Stewed Enough [*Slogan*] [*Bowdlerized version*]
THMP .... Tetrahydromethanopterin [*Biochemistry*]
THMP .... Thermal Industries [*NASDAQ symbol*]   (NQ)
THMS .... Thermistor [*Electronics*]
Th M S .... Thomas Mann-Studien [*A publication*]
THMZ .... Three Hundred Mile Zone
THN .... Thin   (FAAC)
THN .... Trihydroxynaphthalene [*Organic chemistry*]
THN .... Trollhattan [*Sweden*] [*Airport symbol*]   (OAG)
THNR .... Thinner [*Freight*]
THNR T .... Thinner Than [*Freight*]
THO .... Thor Industries, Inc. [*NYSE symbol*]
THO .... Thorco Gold Finders, Inc. [*Toronto Stock Exchange symbol*]
THO .... Thorshofn [*Iceland*] [*Airport symbol*]   (OAG)
THO .... Though
THO .... Thursdays Only [*British railroad term*]
THO .... Tonto Hills Observatory [*Arizona*] [*Seismograph station code, US Geological Survey*] [*Closed*]   (SEIS)
THOF .... Thereof
Thol Ed ...... Theological Educator [*A publication*]
Thom .... Thomas' Reports [*1 Wyoming*]   (DLA)
Thom .... Thomist [*A publication*]
Thom .... Thomson's Nova Scotia Reports   (DLA)
Thomas ..... Thomas' Reports [*1 Wyoming*]   (DLA)
Thomas Mortg ... Thomas on Mortgages   (DLA)
Thomas Negl ... Thomas on Negligence   (DLA)
THOMCAT ... Thomas Register Catalog File [*A publication*]
Thom Co Lit ... Thomas' Edition of Coke upon Littleton   (DLA)
Thom Co Litt ... Thomas' Edition of Coke upon Littleton   (DLA)
Thom Const L ... Thomas' Leading Cases on Constitutional Law   (DLA)
Thom Dec ... Thomson's Nova Scotia Reports [*1834-52*]   (DLA)
Thom & Fr ... Thomas and Franklin's Chancery Reports [*1 Maryland*]   (DLA)
THOMIS ..... Total Hospital Operating and Medical Information System
Thom LC .... Thomas' Leading Cases on Constitutional Law   (DLA)
Thom N Sc ... Thomson's Nova Scotia Reports [*1834-51, 1856-59*] [*Canada*]   (DLA)
Thomp & C ... Thompson and Cook's New York Supreme Court Reports   (DLA)
Thomp Cal ... Thompson's Reports [*39, 40 California*]   (DLA)
Thomp Cit ... Thompson's Ohio Citations   (DLA)
Thomp & Cook ... Thompson and Cook's New York Supreme Court Reports   (DLA)
Thomp Corp ... Thompson's Commentaries on Law of Private Corporations   (DLA)
Thomp Dig ... Thompson's Digest of Laws [*Florida*]   (DLA)
Thomp Liab Stockh ... Thompson on Liability of Stockholders   (DLA)
Thomp NB Cas ... Thompson's National Bank Cases   (DLA)
Thomp Neg ... Thompson's Cases on Negligence   (DLA)
Thomp Pat ... Thompson on Patent Laws of All Countries [*13th ed.*] [*1905*]   (DLA)
Thomps Cas ... Thompson's Tennessee Cases   (DLA)
Thompson ... Thompson's Reports [*39, 40 California*]   (DLA)
Thompson's Fla Dig ... Thompson's Digest of Laws [*Florida*]   (DLA)
Thompson Unrep (PA) ... Thompson's Unreported Cases [*Pennsylvania*]   (DLA)

Thompson Yates and Johnston Lab Rep ... Thompson, Yates, and Johnston Laboratories Reports [*A publication*]
Thompson Yates Lab Rep ... Thompson-Yates Laboratories Reports [*A publication*]
Thomp & St Code ... Thompson and Steger's Code [*Tennessee*] (DLA)
Thomp Tenn Cas ... Thompson's Unreported Tennessee Cases (DLA)
Thomp Trials ... Thompson on Trials (DLA)
Thom Rep ... Thomson's Nova Scotia Reports (DLA)
Thom Sel Dec ... Thomson's Nova Scotia Select Decisions (DLA)
Thomson's Process Chem Eng ... Thomson's Process and Chemical Engineering [*Australia*] [*A publication*]
Thom Un Jur ... Thomas' Universal Jurisprudence [*2nd ed.*] [*1829*] (DLA)
THON .... Thereon
THOPS ...... Tape Handling Operational System [*Data processing*] (IEEE)
THOR .... Tape-Handling Optional Routines [*Honeywell, Inc.*]
THOR .... Thor Industries [*NASDAQ symbol*] (NQ)
Thor .... Thorington's Reports [*107 Alabama*] (DLA)
THOR .... Thought Organizer [*Computer program produced by Fastware, Inc.*]
THOR .... Transistorized High-Speed Operations Recorder
THOR .... Tsing Hua Open-Pool Reactor [*Formosa*]
THORAC .... Thoraci [*To the Throat*] [*Pharmacy*]
Thorac Cardiovasc Surg ... Thoracic and Cardiovascular Surgeon [*A publication*]
THORAD .... Thor-Agena D [*Rocket*] [*NASA*]
Thoraxchir Vask Chir ... Thoraxchirurgie - Vaskulaere Chirurgie [*A publication*]
Thorn .... Thornton's Notes of Ecclesiastical and Maritime Cases [*1841-50*] (DLA)
Thornt & Bl Bldg & Loan Ass'ns ... Thornton and Blackledge's Law Relating to Building and Loan Associations (DLA)
Thornton Gifts ... Thornton on Gifts and Advancements (DLA)
Thoro .... Thoroughfare [*Maps and charts*]
THORP ...... Thermal Oxide Reprocessing Plant [*Nuclear energy*]
Thorpe .... Thorpe's Annual Reports [*52 Louisiana*] (DLA)
THORS .... Thermal-Hydraulic Out-of-Reactor Safety Facility [*Department of Energy*]
THOT .... Thought
Thoth Res ... Thoth Research Journal [*A publication*]
THOU .... Thousand (AFM)
THP .... Terminal Handling Processor
TH & P .... Terre Haute & Peoria Railroad [*Nickname: Take Hold and Push*]
THP .... Tetrahydropalmatine [*Organic chemistry*]
THP .... Tetrahydropapaveroline [*Biochemistry*]
thp .... Tetrahydropyranyl [*As substituent on nucleoside*] [*Biochemistry*]
THP .... Tetrakis(hydroxymethyl)phosphonium [*Organic chemistry*]
THP .... Thermopolis, WY [*Location identifier*] [*FAA*] (FAAL)
THP .... Through Hole Probe
THP .... Thrust Horsepower [*Jet engines*]
T & HP .... Transportation and Handling Procedure
THP .... Triangle Home Products, Inc. [*American Stock Exchange symbol*]
THP .... Trihydroxypropane [*Organic chemistry*]
THP .... Tris(hydroxymethyl)phosphine [*Organic chemistry*]
THPA .... Tetrahydrophthalic Anhydride [*Organic chemistry*]
THPC .... Tetrakis(hydroxymethyl)phosphonium Chloride [*Flame retardant*]
THPDX .... Tetrahydropyranyldoxorubicin [*Antineoplastic drug*]
THPF .... Total Hepatic Plasma Flow [*Physiology*]
THPFB .... Treated Hard-Pressed Fiberboard [*Technical drawings*]
Th & Ph ...... Theologie und Philosophie [*A publication*]
THPO .... Tris(hydroxymethyl)phosphine Oxide [*Organic chemistry*]
Th P Q .... Theologisch-Praktische Quartalschrift [*A publication*]
THPR .... Thermal Profiles [*NASDAQ symbol*] (NQ)
T & H Prac ... Troubat and Haly's Pennsylvania Practice (DLA)
ThPract ...... Theologie en Practijk [*Rotterdam*] [*A publication*] (BJA)
ThPrM .... Theologisch-Praktische Monatsschrift [*A publication*] (BJA)
Th Pr Ma St ... Theory of Probability and Mathematical Statistics [*A publication*]
Th Prob Ap ... Theory of Probability and Its Applications [*A publication*]
ThPrQSchr ... Theologisch-Praktische Quartalschrift [*Linz, Austria*] [*A publication*]
THPS .... Tetrakis(hydroxymethyl)phosphonium Sulfate [*Flame retardant*] [*Organic chemistry*]
THQ .... Tennessee Historical Quarterly [*A publication*]
THQ .... Tetrahydroxyquinone [*Chemical indicator*]
THQ .... Theater Headquarters [*Military*]
ThQ .... Theologische Quartalschrift [*A publication*]
THQ .... Troop Headquarters
ThQ .... Tuebinger Theologische Quartalschrift [*A publication*]
ThQR .... Theological Quarterly Review [*A publication*]
THR .... Target Heart Rate [*Exercise*] (INF)
THR .... Tehran [*Iran*] [*Airport symbol*] (OAG)
ThR .... Theatre Research [*A publication*]
THR .... Their (ROG)
THR .... Their Royal Highnesses [*British*] (ROG)
ThR .... Theological Review [*Princeton, NJ*] [*A publication*]
ThR .... Theologische Revue [*A publication*]
ThR .... Theologische Rundschau [*A publication*]

THR .... There (ROG)
THR .... Thor Energy Resources, Inc. [*American Stock Exchange symbol*]
Thr .... Threni (BJA)
Thr .... Threonine [*Also, T*] [*An amino acid*]
THR .... Threshold
THR .... Through (ADA)
THR .... Throughput Rate
THR .... Thrust (AAG)
THR .... Total Hip Replacement [*Medicine*]
THR .... Total Hydrocarbon Reforming [*Hydrogen production*]
THR .... Transmittal Header Record [*Data processing*]
THR .... Transmitter Holding Register
THR .... Travaux d'Humanisme et Renaissance [*A publication*]
THRA .... Theratech Corp. [*NASDAQ symbol*] (NQ)
THRABTS ..... Thereabouts [*Legal*] [*British*] (ROG)
THRAP .... Tasmanian Historical Research Association. Papers and Proceedings [*A publication*] (ADA)
THRAR .... Thereafter [*Legal*] [*British*] (ROG)
THRAT .... Thereat [*Legal*] [*British*] (ROG)
THRB .... Theodore Roosevelt Birthplace National Historic Site
THRD .... Thread
Th Rdschau ... Theologische Rundschau [*A publication*]
Three Bank ... Three Banks Review [*A publication*]
Three Banks R ... Three Banks Review [*A publication*]
Three R Int ... Three R International [*West Germany*] [*A publication*]
TH Rep Eindhoven Univ Technol Dep Electr Eng ... TH-Report-Eindhoven University of Technology. Department of Electrical Engineering [*A publication*]
ThRev .... Theologische Revue [*A publication*]
THRFTR ...... Thereafter (FAAC)
THR-HR ...... Tydskrif vir Hedendaagse Romeins-Hollandse Reg (DLA)
THRIC .... Treasure Hunter Research and Information Center [*Patterson, LA*] (EA)
THRILLO .... Transfer to Higher Rated Job in Lieu of Layoff (MCD)
THRIN .... Therein
THRINAR ..... Thereinafter [*Legal*] [*British*] (ROG)
THRINBEFE ... Thereinbefore [*Legal*] [*British*] (ROG)
Thring J St Com ... Thring on Joint Stock Companies [*5th ed.*] [*1889*] (DLA)
Thring LD ... Thring on the Land Drainage Act [*1862*] (DLA)
Th Ri Po ... Three Rivers Poetry Journal [*A publication*]
THRM .... Thermal (AAG)
THRMST .... Thermostat
THRMSTC ... Thermostatic (MSA)
ThRNF .... Theologische Rundschau. Neue Folge [*Tuebingen*] [*A publication*]
THRO .... Theodore Roosevelt National Memorial Park
THRO .... Through
THROF .... Thereof
Thromb Diat ... Thrombosis et Diathesis Haemorrhagica [*A publication*]
Thromb Diath Haemorrh ... Thrombosis et Diathesis Haemorrhagica [*A publication*]
Thromb Haemost ... Thrombosis and Haemostasis [*A publication*]
Thromb Haemostas ... Thrombosis and Haemostasis [*A publication*]
Thromb Res ... Thrombosis Research [*A publication*]
THRON .... Thereon [*Legal*] [*British*] (ROG)
Throop Pub Off ... Throop's Treatise on Public Officers (DLA)
THROT .... Throttle (AAG)
THROUT ..... Thereout [*Legal*] [*British*] (ROG)
THRP .... Therapist
THRPY .... Therapy
Th Rsch ...... Theologische Rundschau [*A publication*]
THRSHL ..... Thrust Shell
THRSUM .... Threat Summary Message (MCD)
THRT .... Threat [*or Threatening*] [*FBI standardized term*]
THRT .... Throat
THRU .... I am connecting you to another switchboard [*Telecommunications*] (FAAC)
ThRu .... Theologische Rundschau [*A publication*]
THRU .... Through (AAG)
THRU .... Thrust [*A publication*]
THRU .... Toxic Hazards Research Unit [*NASA*] (KSC)
THRUPON ... Thereupon [*Legal*] [*British*] (ROG)
THRUSH ..... Technological Hierarchy for the Removal of Undesirables and the Subjugation of Humanity [*Fictitious organization in "The Man from UNCLE" television series*]
THRUT .... Throughout (FAAC)
Th Rv .... Theologische Revue [*A publication*]
THS .... [*The*] Hydrographic Society (EA-IO)
THS .... St. Thomas, PA [*Location identifier*] [*FAA*] (FAAL)
THS .... Target Homing System
THS .... Tenement House Smell [*British*] (ROG)
THS Tetrahydro-11-Deoxycortisol
THS .... Textes pour l'Histoire Sacree [*A publication*]
THS .... Textile History Society [*Defunct*] (EA)
THS .... Theatre Historical Society (EA)
ThS .... Theatre Survey [*A publication*]
ThS .... Theological Studies [*A publication*]
ThS .... Theologische Studien und Kritiken [*A publication*]
THS .... Thermostat Switch
THS .... Three-Stage Least Squares [*Econometrics*]

THS .... Times Health Supplement [*London*] [*A publication*]
THS .... Titanic Historical Society [*Formerly, TEA*]   (EA)
THS .... Tourist Hospitality Service [*British*]
THS .... Transparent Hull Submersible [*Navy*]
THS .... Tube Heating Supply
THSA......... Thomas Hardy Society of America   (EA)
THSA......... Traveling Hat Salesmen's Association [*Defunct*]   (EA)
THSAM...... Topographie Historique de la Syrie Antique et Medievale [*A publication*]   (BJA)
THSC .... Transactions. Honourable Society of Cymmrodorion [*A publication*]
THSD........ Thousand   (FAAC)
THSI .... Thermal Systems [*NASDAQ symbol*]   (NQ)
ThSK .... Theologische Studien und Kritiken [*Hamburg/Berlin*] [*A publication*]
THSP.......... Thermal Spraying [*Welding*]
THSRB ...... Tufts Health Science Review [*A publication*]
ThSt .... Theological Studies [*A publication*]
ThSt .... Theologische Studien [*A publication*]   (BJA)
ThStKr .... Theologische Studien und Kritiken [*Hamburg/Berlin*] [*A publication*]
ThSzemle ... Theologiai Szemle [*Budapest*] [*A publication*]   (BJA)
THT .... Papeete [*Orstom*] [*Society Islands*] [*Seismograph station code, US Geological Survey*]   (SEIS)
THT .... Teacher of Hydrotherapy [*British*]
THT .... Tetrahydrothiophene [*Organic chemistry*]
Tht............. Theaetetus [*of Plato*] [*Classical studies*]   (OCD)
ThT............ Theologisch Tijdschrift [*A publication*]
Th T .... Theology Today [*A publication*]
THT .... Thrust Resources, Inc. [*Vancouver Stock Exchange symbol*]
THT .... Total Homing Time
THTA......... Thread Tap
THTAD ...... Thiemig-Taschenbuecher [*A publication*]
THTD........ Too Hard to Do   (CAAL)
THTF......... Thermal Hydraulic Test Facility   (NRCH)
THTH........ Too Hot to Handle
THTMS...... Tetramethylthiuram Monosulfide [*Also, TMTD*] [*Organic chemistry*]
THTN......... Threaten   (FAAC)
THTO......... Thereto
THTO......... Threading Tool   (AAG)
Th Today.... Theology Today [*A publication*]
THTR......... Theater   (AFM)
THTR......... Thorium High-Temperature Reactor [*Germany*]
THU .... Thule [*Greenland*] [*Seismograph station code, US Geological Survey*] [*Closed*]   (SEIS)
THU .... Thunder Explorations [*Vancouver Stock Exchange symbol*]
THU .... Thursday   (AFM)
Thuc.......... De Thucydide [*of Dionysius Halicarnassensis*] [*Classical studies*]   (OCD)
THUC .... Thucydides [*Greek historian, c. 460-400BC*] [*Classical studies*]   (ROG)
THUD .... Thorium, Uranium, Deuterium
THUDD...... Thermal Uplink Data Display [*Data processing*]
ThuGI .... Theologie und Glaube [*A publication*]
Thule Int Symp ... Thule International Symposia [*A publication*]
THUMB....... Tiny Humans Underground Military Bureau [*Government organization in TV cartoon series "Tom of T.H.U.M.B."*]
THUMS....... Texaco, Humble, Union, Mobil, and Shell [*Petroleum companies*]
THURS ...... Thursday
THUT......... Thyroid Hormone Uptake Test [*Clinical chemistry*]
THV........... Terminal Homing Vehicle
ThV............ Theologia Viatorum. Jahrbuch der Kirchlichen Hochschule [*Berlin*] [*A publication*]
THV .... Thoracic Vertebra [*Medicine*]
THV .... Tool Handling Vehicle   (MCD)
THV .... Total Heart Volume [*Physiology*]
THV .... York, PA [*Location identifier*] [*FAA*]   (FAAL)
ThViat .... Theologia Viatorum. Jahrbuch der Kirchlichen Hochschule [*Berlin*] [*A publication*]
ThW........... Theologisches Woerterbuch zum Neuen Testament [*A publication*]   (BJA)
THW .... Therewith [*Legal*] [*British*]   (ROG)
THW .... Torsion Head Wattmeter
ThWAT...... Theologisches Woerterbuch zum Alten Testament [*A publication*]   (BJA)
ThWB .... Theologisches Woerterbuch zum Neuen Testament [*A publication*]   (BJA)
ThWBNT .... Theologisches Woerterbuch zum Neuen Testament [*A publication*]   (BJA)
THWITH...... Therewith [*Legal*] [*British*]   (ROG)
THWM .... Trinity High-Water Mark
ThWNT....... Theologisches Woerterbuch zum Neuen Testament [*A publication*]   (BJA)
THWR........ Thrower
THWT .... Throwout [*Mechanical engineering*]
THX .... Thor Explorations [*Vancouver Stock Exchange symbol*]
THX .... Three Rivers, TX [*Location identifier*] [*FAA*]   (FAAL)
THX .... Thyroxine [*Also, T, Ty*] [*An amino acid*] [*Endocrinology*]

THX .... Tomlinson-Holman Cross-Over [*Motion picture theater sound system*]
THX .... Total Hypophysectomy [*Medicine*]
THY .... Thomas Hardy Yearbook [*A publication*]
Thy .... Thymine [*Also, T*] [*Biochemistry*]
THY .... Thymocyte [*Clinical chemistry*]
THY .... Turk Hava Yollari AO [*Turkish Airlines, Inc.*]
THYB........ Tai Hei Yo Bashi [*Bridge over the Great Ocean*] [*Japan*] [*An association*]   (EA)
THYMD...... Thymus [*A publication*]
THYMOTRO ... Thyratron Motor Control [*Electronics*]   (MCD)
THYMOTROL ... Thyratron Motor Control [*Electronics*]
THYP........ Total Hydroxyproline [*Clinical chemistry*]
THYR......... Thyristor [*Electronics*]
Thyssen Edelstahl Tech Ber ... Thyssen Edelstahl Technische Berichte [*A publication*]
Thyssen Forsch Ber Forsch Betr ... Thyssen Forschung. Berichte aus Forschung und Betrieb [*A publication*]
Thyssen Tech Ber ... Thyssen Technische Berichte [*A publication*]
THZ .... Tahoua [*Niger*] [*Airport symbol*]   (OAG)
THz .... Terahertz
ThZ........... Theologische Zeitschrift [*A publication*]
TI .... Costa Rica [*Aircraft nationality and registration mark*]   (FAAC)
TI .... Table Indicator [*Data processing*]
TI .... Tamarind Institute [*New Mexico*]   (EA)
TI .... Tamiment Institute   (EA)
TI .... Tape Inverter
TI .... Target Identification
TI .... Target Indicator
TI .... Target Intelligence   (MCD)
TI .... Tariff Item
TI .... Teardown Inspection
ti .... Technical Indexes Ltd. [*Bracknell, Berks., England*] [*Information service*]   (EISS)
TI .... Technical Information   (CINC)
TI .... Technical Inspection
TI .... Technical Institute
TI .... Technical Instruction [*or Instructor*]
TI .... Technical Integration [*NASA*]   (NASA)
TI .... Technical Intelligence
TI .... Technical Interchange   (KSC)
TI .... Temperature Indicator
Ti .... Temperature of Injectate
TI .... Temporary Instruction [*Nuclear energy*]   (NRCH)
TI .... Teresian Institute [*Coral Gables, FL*]   (EA)
TI .... Terminal Interface
TI .... Terminal Island [*San Pedro*] [*Navy base*]
TI .... Termination Instruction
TI .... Test Implicit
TI .... Test Index   (CAAL)
TI .... Test Instruction   (MCD)
TI .... Test Instrumentation
TI .... Texas Instruments, Inc.
TI .... Textile Institute [*South African*]   (EA-IO)
TI .... Thalassemia Intermedia [*Hematology*]
TI .... Think Ink [*An association*]   (EA)
TI .... Thread Institute [*Washington, DC*]   (EA)
TI .... Thursday Island [*Australia*]   (ADA)
TI .... Thymidine-Labeling Index [*Biochemical analysis*]
TI .... Thymus Independent [*Cells*] [*Hematology*]
TI .... TI Travel International, Inc. [*Vancouver Stock Exchange symbol*]
TI .... Tie In   (MCD)
TI .... Tiferet Israel   (BJA)
TI .... TII Industries, Inc. [*American Stock Exchange symbol*]
Ti .... Timaeus [*of Plato*] [*Classical studies*]   (OCD)
TI .... Timarit Pjooreknisfelags Islendinga 1957 [*A publication*]
TI .... Time Index
TI .... Time Interval   (IEEE)
TI .... Tippers International [*An association*] [*Wausau, WI*]   (EA)
Ti .... Titanium [*Chemical element*]
TI .... Title [*Online database field identifier*] [*Data processing*]
Ti .... Title Information [*Publishing*]
Ti .... Titus [*New Testament book*]
TI .... Toastmasters International
TI .... Tobacco Institute [*Washington, DC*]   (EA)
TI .... Together, Incorporated [*An association*] [*Tulsa, OK*]   (EA)
TI .... Tonic Immobility [*Neurophysiology*]
T/I .... Torque/Inertia
TI .... Total Immersion [*Language study*]
T/I .... TPFDD Interface
TI .... Track Identity
TI .... Track Initiator
TI .... Trade and Industry Index [*Information Access Corp.*] [*Information service*]   (EISS)
TI .... Traditional Instruction
TI .... Traffic Identification
TI .... Training Instructor
TI .... Training Integrator [*or Integration*]   (MCD)
TI .... Trajectory Integration   (CAAL)

TI .... Transaction Interpretation (MCD)
TI .... Transfer Impedance (IEEE)
TI .... Transfrigoroute International (EA)
TI .... Transillumination
TI .... Transmission Identification (NG)
TI .... Transportation Institute [*Washington, DC*] (EA)
TI .... Transportes Aereos Internacionales, SA [*TAISA*] [*Peru*] [*ICAO designator*] (FAAC)
TI .... Treasure Island [*San Francisco Bay*] [*Navy base*]
TI .... Treasury Instruction (ADA)
TI .... Trial Installation (MCD)
TI .... Tricuspid Insufficiency [*Cardiology*]
TI .... Troop Information
TI .... Trypsin Inhibitor [*Food technology*]
Ti .... Tumor-inducing [*Plasmids*] [*Plant cytology*]
TI .... Tungsten Institute [*Defunct*] (EA)
TI .... Tuning Indicator (DEN)
ti .... Tunisia [*MARC country of publication code*] [*Library of Congress*] (LCCP)
TI .... Type Item [*Military*]
T2000I........ Transport 2000 International (EA-IO)
TIA.............. [*The*] International Alliance, an Association of Executive and Professional Women [*Baltimore, MD*] (EA)
TIA.............. Tactical Identification and Acquisition [*Navy*] (NG)
TIA.............. Taian [*Republic of China*] [*Seismograph station code, US Geological Survey*] (SEIS)
TIA.............. Task Item Authorization (MCD)
TIA.............. Tax Institute of America [*Later, NTA-TIA*] (EA)
TIA.............. Taxation in Australia [*A publication*]
TIA.............. Teacher Investigator Awards
TIA.............. Test Interface Assembly
TIA.............. Tiaprofenic Acid
TIA.............. Tilapia International Association (EA-IO)
TIA.............. Tirana [*Albania*] [*Airport symbol*] (OAG)
TIA.............. Trans International Airlines
TIA.............. Transient Ischemic Attack [*Medicine*]
TIA.............. Transimpedance Amplifier [*Instrumentation*]
TIA.............. Transportation Intelligence Agency (AAG)
TIA.............. Travel Industry Association of America [*Formed by a merger of NATO and Discover America*] [*Washington, DC*] (EA)
TIA.............. Treaties and Other International Acts
TIA.............. Trend Impact Analysis [*The Futures Group, Inc.*] [*Glastonbury, CT*] [*Information service*] (EISS)
TIA.............. Trends, Indicators, and Analyses [*on the Southeast Asia war*] [*Classified Air Force document*]
TIA.............. Tri-Basin Resources [*Vancouver Stock Exchange symbol*]
TIA.............. Tricot Institute of America [*Defunct*] (EA)
TIA.............. Trouser Institute of America [*Absorbed by NOSA*] (EA)
TIA.............. Trypsin Inhibitor Activity [*Food technology*]
TIA.............. Tumor-Induced Angiogenesis [*Immunology*]
TIA.............. Typographers International Association [*Washington, DC*] (EA)
TIAA .... Task Identification and Analysis (MCD)
TIAA .... Teachers Insurance and Annuity Association (EA)
TIAA .... Timber Importers Association of America
TIAC.......... Technical Information Advisory Committee [*AEC*]
TIAC.......... Technical Information Analysis Centers
TIAC.......... Techniques and Instrumentation in Analytical Chemistry [*Elsevier Book Series*] [*A publication*]
TIAC.......... Texas Instruments Automatic Computer
TIAC.......... Travel [*later, Tourism*] Industry Association of Canada
TIAFT .... [*The*] International Association of Forensic Toxicologists (EA-IO)
TIAH .... Totally Implantable Artificial Heart
TIARA........ Tactical Intelligence and Related Activity
TIARA........ Target Illumination and Recovery Aid
TIARA........ Telephone Installation and Requisition Application (MCD)
TIAS .... Target Identification and Acquisition System
TIAS .... Treaties and Other International Acts Series [*Department of State*]
TIAVSC ...... [*The*] International Assets Valuation Standards Committee (EA-IO)
TIAX .... Trans International Airlines [*Air carrier designation symbol*]
TIB.............. Technical Information Base (MCD)
TIB.............. Technical Information Bulletin [*Cincinnati, OH*] (AAG)
TIB.............. Technical Information Bureau [*British*]
TIB.............. Technische Informationsbibliothek [*Technical Information Library*] [*Germany*]
TIB.............. Temporary Importation Bond (MCD)
TIB.............. This I Believe Test [*Education*]
Tib.............. Tiberius [*of Suetonius*] [*Classical studies*] (OCD)
tib.............. Tibetan [*MARC language code*] [*Library of Congress*] (LCCP)
Tib.............. Tibullus [*First century BC*] [*Classical studies*] (OCD)
TIB.............. Tourist Information Brussels [*Belgium*]
TIB.............. Training Improvement Board [*Military*] (CAAL)
TIB.............. Triisopropylbenzene [*Organic chemistry*]
TIB.............. Trimmed in Bunkers [*Shipping*]
TIBA .... Triiodobenzoic Acid [*Plant growth regulator*]
TIBA .... Triisobutylaluminum [*Organic chemistry*]
TIBA .... Triisobutylamine [*Organic chemistry*]
TIBC .... Total Iron-Binding Capacity [*Hematology*]

Tibetan R ... Tibetan Review [*New Delhi*] [*A publication*]
Tibet J........ Tibet Journal [*Dharmasala*] [*A publication*]
Tibet Soc B ... Tibet Society Bulletin [*United States*] [*A publication*]
TIB and FIB ... Tibia and Fibula (DSUE)
TIBOE........ Transmitting Information by Optical Electronics (KSC)
T I Br Geog ... Transactions. Institute of British Geographers [*A publication*]
TIBS .... Trends in Biochemical Sciences [*A publication*]
TIBTPG ...... Texas Instruments Bourdon Tube Pressure Gauge
TIC .... [*The*] Interchurch Center (EA)
TIC .... Tactical Intelligence Concepts (MCD)
TIC .... Tactical Intercom Systems (MCD)
TIC .... Taken into Consideration
TIC .... Tantalum-Niobium International Study Center [*Formerly, Tantalum Producers International Study Center*] (EA)
TIC .... Tantalum Producers International Study Center [*Later, Tantalum-Niobium International Study Center*] (EA-IO)
TIC .... Tape Identification Card
TIC .... Tape Intersystem Connection [*Data processing*]
TIC .... Target Integration Center (MCD)
TIC .... Target Intercept Computer
TIC .... Teacher in Charge (ADA)
TIC .... Teacher Information Center (EA)
TIC .... Technical Information Capability
TIC .... Technical Information Center [*Department of Energy*]
TIC .... Technical Institute Council (EA)
TIC .... Technical Instructors Course [*Air Force*] (AFM)
TIC .... Technical Intelligence Center [*Navy*]
TIC .... Technical Interface Concepts (RDA)
TIC .... Technicon Integrator/Calculator
TIC .... Technology and Innovation Council [*Information Industry Association*]
TIC .... Telecommunications Information Center [*George Washington University*] [*Washington, DC*] [*Information service*] (EISS)
TIC .... Telemetry Instruction Conference (KSC)
TIC .... Telemetry Instrumentation Controller
TIC .... Temperature Indicator Controller [*Aerospace*]
TIC .... Terminal Identification Code
TIC .... Thai Information Center (EA)
TIC .... Thermostatic Ignition Control [*Automotive engineering*]
TIC .... Time Interval Counter
TIC .... Tinak [*Marshall Islands*] [*Airport symbol*] (OAG)
TIC .... Tool Issue Center [*Military*] (AFIT)
TIC .... Total Ion Chromatography
TIC .... Total Ion Current [*Spectroscopy*]
TIC .... Total Item Change (NASA)
TIC .... Toumodi [*Ivory Coast*] [*Seismograph station code, US Geological Survey*] (SEIS)
TIC .... Trade Information Committee [*Department of State*] (EA)
TIC .... Transaction Identification Code [*Military*] (AFIT)
TIC .... Transducer Information Center (MCD)
TIC .... Transfer-In Channel (CMD)
TIC .... Transport Industries Committee [*Trades Union Congress*] [*British*]
TIC .... Transvaal Indian Congress [*South African*] (PD)
TIC .... Travel Information Center [*An association*] (EA)
TIC .... [*The*] Travelers Corporation [*NYSE symbol*]
TIC .... Troops-in-Contact
TIC .... Trypsin Inhibitory Capacity [*Biochemistry*]
TIC .... Tuned Integrated Circuit
TICA.......... [*The*] International Cat Association (EA)
TICA.......... Tactical Intercom Assembly [*Ground Communications Facility, NASA*]
TICA.......... Technical Information Center Administration [*Conference*]
TICA.......... Timpanogos Cave National Monument
TICACE...... Technical Intelligence Center Allied Command Europe [*NATO*] (NATG)
TICAF........ [*The*] Industrial College of the Armed Forces [*Later, UND*]
TICC.......... Technical Industrial Cooperation Contract
TICC.......... Technical Intelligence Coordination Center [*NATO*] (NATG)
TICCIH ...... [*The*] International Committee for the Conservation of the Industrial Heritage (EA)
TICCIT .... Time-Shared Interactive Computer-Controlled Information Television [*System*] [*Mitre Corp.*] [*Brigham Young University*] [*1971*]
TICE .... Time Integral Cost Effectiveness
TICER........ Temporary International Council for Educational Reconstruction (DLA)
TICF .... Transient Installation Confinement Facility [*Military*] (AABC)
Tichb Tr ..... Report of the Tichborne Trial [*London*] (DLA)
T I Chem En ... Transactions. Institution of Chemical Engineers and the Chemical Engineer [*A publication*]
TICI .... TIC International Corp. [*NASDAQ symbol*] (NQ)
TICL .... Topics in Culture Learning [*A publication*]
TICLER....... Technical Input Checklist/Evaluation Report (MCD)
TICM .... Test Interface and Control Module (MCD)
TICM .... Thermal Imaging Common Modules
TICM .... Trust Investment Committee Memorandum (DLA)
TICO.......... Transactions. International Congress of Orientalists [*A publication*] (BJA)
TICODS...... Time Compression Display System (NVT)

TICOJ........ Transactions. International Conference of Orientalists in Japan [*A publication*]
TICOM....... Texas Institute for Computational Mechanics [*University of Texas at Austin*] [*Research center*]　(RCD)
TICOS .... Truncated Icosahedra [*Crystallography*]
TICP.......... Theater Inventory Control Point [*Military*]　(AABC)
TICP.......... Travaux. Institut Catholique de Paris [*A publication*]　(BJA)
TICS.......... Teacher Interactive Computer System　(IEEE)
TICS.......... Telecommunication Information Control System
TICS.......... Turret Interaction Crew Simulator　(MCD)
TICT.......... Tactical Intelligence Collection Team [*Military*]　(AFM)
TICTAC...... Time Compression Tactical Communications
TICUS........ Tidal Current System
TICWAN..... Trailerable Intracoastal Waterway Aids to Navigation [*Boat*]
TID .... Tactical Information Display
TID .... Tactical Intrusion Detectors　(MCD)
TID .... Target Identification Device [*Military*]　(CAAL)
TID .... Technical Information Division [*Romar Consultants, Inc.*] [*Philadelphia, PA*] [*Information service*]　(EISS)
TID .... Technology Information Division [*Department of Energy, Mines, and Resources*] [*Ottawa, ON*]　(EISS)
TID .... Ter in Die [*Three Times a Day*] [*Pharmacy*]
TID .... Test Identify　(CAAL)
TID .... Thermal Imaging Devices　(MCD)
TID .... Thermionic Ionization Detector [*Instrumentation*]
TID .... Ticket Information Data
TID .... Total Integrated Dose [*Nuclear energy*]　(NRCH)
TID .... Touch Information Display
TID .... Traitement Integre des Donnees [*Integrated Data Processing - IDP*] [*French*]
TID .... Traveling Ionospheric Disturbance
TID .... Trifluoromethyl(iodophenyl)deazirine [*Biochemistry*]
TID .... Turn-In Document [*DoD*]
TIDA.......... 30th Infantry Division Association　(EA)
TIDAR........ Texas Instruments Digital Analog Readout
TIDAR........ Time Delay Array RADAR
Tidd........... Tidd's Costs　(DLA)
Tidd........... Tidd's Practice　(DLA)
TIDDAC...... Time in Deadband Digital Attitude Control
Tidd App.... Appendix to Tidd's Practice　(DLA)
Tid Dok ..... Tidskrift foer Dokumentation [*A publication*]
Tidd Pr ...... Tidd's Practice　(DLA)
Tidd Prac ... Tidd's Practice　(DLA)
Tidd's Pract ... Tidd's Practice　(DLA)
TIDE .... Tactical International Data Exchange　(NG)
TIDE .... Tide West Oil Co. [*NASDAQ symbol*]　(NQ)
TIDE .... Timer Demodulator
TIDES........ Time-Division Electronics Switching System　(KSC)
TIDF .... Trunk Intermediate Distribution Frame [*Telecommunications*]　(TEL)
TIDMA....... Tape Interface Direct Memory Access
TIDOC .... Technical Information Documentation Center [*Advisory Group for Aerospace Research and Development*]　(NATG)
TIDOS .... Table and Item Documentation System
TIDP-TE .... Technical Interface Design Plan - Test Edition　(RDA)
TIDS .... Tactical Information Distribution Systems [*Army*]　(RDA)
Tidsk Dokum ... Tidskrift foer Dokumentation [*A publication*]
Tidskr Dok ... Tidskrift foer Dokumentation [*A publication*]
Tidskr Hushallningssaellsk Skogsvardsstyr Gaevleborgs Laen ... Tidskrift foer Hushallningssaellskapet och Skogsvardsstyrelsen i Gaevleborgs Laen [*A publication*]
Tidskr Lantmaen Andelsfolk ... Tidskrift foer Lantmaen och Andelsfolk [*A publication*]
Tidskr Mil Halsov ... Tidskrift i Militar Halsovard [*Sweden*] [*A publication*]
Tidskr Sjukvardspedagog ... Tidskrift foer Sjukvardspedagoger [*A publication*]
Tidskr Skogbruk ... Tidsskrift foer Skogbruk [*A publication*]
Tidskr Sver Sjukskot ... Tidskrift foer Sveriges Sjukskoterskor [*A publication*]
Tidskr Sver Skogvardsforb ... Tidskrift Sveriges Skogsvardsforbund [*A publication*]
Tidskr Varme- Vent- Sanitetstek ... Tidskrift foer Varme-, Ventilations-, och Sanitetsteknik [*Sweden*] [*A publication*]
Tids Samfun ... Tidsskrift foer Samfunnsforskning [*A publication*]
Tidssk Kjemi Bergves Metall ... Tidsskrift foer Kjemi. Bergvesen og Metallurgi [*A publication*]
Tidsskr Kemi ... Tidsskrift foer Kemi [*A publication*]
Tidsskr Kemi Farm Ter ... Tidsskrift foer Kemi. Farmaci og Terapi [*A publication*]
Tidsskr Kjemi Bergves ... Tidsskrift foer Kjemi og Bergvesen [*A publication*]
Tidsskr Kjemi Bergvesen Met ... Tidsskrift foer Kjemi. Bergvesen og Metallurgi [*A publication*]
Tidsskr Landokon ... Tidsskrift foer Landokonomi [*A publication*]
Tidsskr Nor Laegeforen ... Tidsskrift foer den Norske Laegeforening [*A publication*]
Tidsskr Norske Landbruk ... Tidsskrift foer det Norske Landbruk [*A publication*]
Tidsskr Planteavl ... Tidsskrift foer Planteavl [*A publication*]
Tidsskr Plavl ... Tidsskrift foer Planteavl [*A publication*]
Tidsskr Skogbr ... Tidsskrift foer Skogbruk [*A publication*]
Tidsskr Skogbruk ... Tidsskrift foer Skogbruk [*A publication*]

Tidsskr Textiltek ... Tidsskrift foer Textilteknik [*A publication*]
TIDY .... Teletypewriter Integrated Display　(NVT)
TIDY .... Track Identity
TIE............. [*The*] Information Exchange on Young Adult Chronic Patients　(EA)
TIE............. [*The*] Institute of Ecology [*Defunct*]
TIE............. Target Identification Equipment　(MCD)
TIE............. Technical Idea Exchange　(MCD)
TIE............. Technical Information Exchange [*National Bureau of Standards*]
TIE............. Technical Integration and Evaluation [*Apollo*] [*NASA*]
TIE............. Technology Information Exchange [*of Public Technology, Inc.*]　(EISS)
TIE............. Temporary/Intermittent Employee
TIE............. Terminal Interface Equipment
TIE............. Texas Information Exchange
TIE............. Texas Israel Exchange [*A trade and research venture*]
TIE............. Tie Communications [*American Stock Exchange symbol*]
TIE............. Tientsin [*Republic of China*] [*Seismograph station code, US Geological Survey*]　(SEIS)
TIE............. Time Interval Error [*Telecommunications*]　(TEL)
TIE............. Tippi [*Ethiopia*] [*Airport symbol*]　(OAG)
TIE............. Toyota Industrial Equipment
TIE............. Training Instrumentation Evaluation　(MCD)
TIE............. Transient Ischemic Episode [*Medicine*]
TIE............. Travel Industry for the Environment
TI & E........ Troop Information and Education
TIED.......... Troop Information and Education Division
Tiedeman Real Prop ... Tiedeman on Real Property　(DLA)
Tied Lim Police Power ... Tiedeman's Treatise on the Limitations of Police Power in the United States　(DLA)
Tied Metsateho ... Tiedotus Metsateho [*A publication*]
Tied Mun Corp ... Tiedeman's Treatise on Municipal Corporations　(DLA)
Tied Valt Tekn Tutkimusl ... Tiedotus. Valtion Teknillinen Tutkimuslaitos [*A publication*]
Tied Valt Tek Tutkimuskeskus Poltto Voiteluainelab ... Tiedonanto-Valtion Teknillinen Tutkimuskeskus, Poltto-, ja Voiteluainelaboratorio [*Finland*] [*A publication*]
TIEED........ Transactions. Institute of Electronics and Communication Engineers of Japan. Section E. English [*A publication*]
TIEG .... Teen International Entomology Group [*Later, YES*]　(EA)
TIEO .... Toyota Industrial Engine Operations [*Torrance, CA*]
TIER .... Tierce [*Unit of measurement*]　(ROG)
TIER .... Tierco Group, Inc. [*NASDAQ symbol*]　(NQ)
Tieraerztl Prax ... Tieraerztliche Praxis [*A publication*]
Tieraerztl Rundsch ... Tieraerztliche Rundschau [*A publication*]
Tieraerztl Umsch ... Tieraerztliche Umschau [*A publication*]
Tierernaehr Fuetter ... Tierernaehrung und Fuetterung [*A publication*]
Tierphysiol Tierernaehr Futtermittelk ... Tierphysiologie, Tierernaehrung, und Futtermittelkunde [*A publication*]
TIERS........ Title I Evaluation and Reporting System [*Department of Education*]
TIES .... Tactical Information Exchange System [*Navy*]　(MCD)
TIES .... Technological Information Exchange System [*UNIDO*]
TIES .... Textbook Information and Exchange Service [*Regional clearinghouses for used textbooks*]
TIES .... Theater Information and Engagement System [*Military*]　(MCD)
TIES .... Total Information for Educational Systems [*Saint Paul, MN*]　(BUR)
TIES .... Total Integrated Engineering System
TIES .... Translators' and Interpreters' Educational Society [*Stanford, CA*]　(EA)
TIES .... Transmission and Information Exchange System
Tiet Julk Helsingin Tek Korkeakoulu ... Tieteellisia Julkaisuja. Helsingin Teknillinen Korkeakoulu [*A publication*]
TIEtn .... Trudy Instituta Etnografii Imeni N. N. Miklucho Maklaja. Akademija Nauk SSSR [*A publication*]
TIEYACP.... [*The*] Information Exchange on Young Adult Chronic Patients [*New York, NY*]　(EA)
TIF............. [*The*] International Foundation [*State University of New York*] [*Brooklyn*]　(EA)
TIF............. Taif [*Saudi Arabia*] [*Airport symbol*]　(OAG)
TIF............. Tape Inventory File　(IEEE)
TIF............. Target Intelligence File　(CINC)
TIF............. Task Initiation Force　(NRCH)
TIF............. Task Initiation Form　(NRCH)
TIF............. Tax Increment Financing
TIF............. Taxpayer Information File [*IRS*]
TIF............. Technical Information File
TIF............. Telephone Interference Factor　(DEN)
TIF............. Terminal Independent Format
TIF............. Thin Iron Film
TIF............. Tiflis [*Tbilisi*] [*USSR*] [*Seismograph station code, US Geological Survey*]　(SEIS)
TIF............. Tilapia International Foundation　(EA)
TIF............. Transport International par Fer [*International Transport of Goods by Railway*]
TIF............. True Involute Form
TIF............. Tumor-Inducing Factor [*Oncology*]
TIF............. Tumor-Infiltrating Lymphocyte [*Immunotherapy*]
TIF............. Tumor Inhibitory Factor [*Oncology*]

TIFF............ Tag Image File Format [*Data processing*]
Tiff............. Tiffany's Reports [*28-39 New York Court of Appeals*] (DLA)
TIFF........... Tokyo International Film Festival
Tiffany....... Tiffany's Reports [*28-39 New York Court of Appeals*] (DLA)
Tiffany Landlord & Ten ... Tiffany on Landlord and Tenant (DLA)
Tiffany Landl & T ... Tiffany on Landlord and Tenant (DLA)
Tiffany Real Prop ... Tiffany on Real Property (DLA)
TIFI............. Titus Foods, Incorporated [*NASDAQ symbol*] (NQ)
TIFO .... Technical Inspection Field Office, Office of the Inspector
                General
TIFR........... Total Improved Frequency Response
TIFS........... Total In-Flight Simulation [*or Simulator*] [*Air Force*]
TIG .... [*The*] Inspector General [*Army*]
TIG .... Target Image Generator
TIG .... Taxicab Industry Group [*New York, NY*] (EA)
TIG .... Telegram Identification Group [*Telecommunications*] (TEL)
TIG .... Teletype Input Generator
TIG .... Tetanus Immune Globulin [*Immunology*]
tig .... Tigre [*MARC language code*] [*Library of Congress*] (LCCP)
TIG .... Time in Grade [*Air Force*]
TIG .... Time of Ignition
TIG .... Tungsten-Inert-Gas [*Underwater welding*]
TIGC.......... Topics in Inorganic and General Chemistry [*Elsevier Book
                Series*] [*A publication*]
TIGER........ Total Information Gathering and Executive Reporting
                [*International Computers Ltd.*]
TIGER........ Traveling Industrial Gaseous Emission Research [*Vehicle*]
                [*Exxon Corp.*]
TIGER........ Treasury Investors Growth Receipt
TIG(H)........ Tetanus Immune Globulin (Human) [*Immunology*]
TIGN.......... Time of Ignition
TIGR.......... Transmission Integrated Rotor
TIGR.......... Treasury Investment Growth Receipts [*Merrill Lynch & Co.*]
TIGR.......... Turbine-Integrated Geared Rotor
Ti Gracch .. Tiberius Gracchus [*of Plutarch*] [*Classical studies*] (OCD)
TIGRB........ Technische Information GRW [*Geraete- und Regler Werke*] [*A
                publication*]
TIGRIS ...... Televised Images of Gaseous Region in Interplanetary Space
TIGS.......... Terminal Independent Graphics System
TIGS.......... Transactions. Inverness Gaelic Society [*A publication*]
TIGT.......... Turbine Inlet Gas Temperature [*Aviation*]
TIGZD........ Teikyo Igaku Zasshi
TIH............. Technical Information Handbook
TIH............. Their Imperial Highnesses
TIH............. Tikehau [*French Polynesia*] [*Airport symbol*] (OAG)
TIH............. Toromont Industries Ltd. [*Toronto Stock Exchange symbol*]
TIH............. Total Installed Horsepower
TIH............. Trunk Interface Handler
Tihanyi Biol Kutatointezetenek Evkoen ... Tihanyi Biologiai
                Kutatointezetenek Evkoenyve [*A publication*]
TIHP .... Total Installed Horsepower
TII.............. European Association for the Transfer of Technologies,
                Innovation, and Industrial Information [*Kirchberg,
                Luxembourg*] [*Information service*] (EISS)
TII.............. Talos Integration Investigation
TII.............. Texas Instruments, Incorporated
TII.............. Texas Instruments, Incorporated, IS and S Library, Dallas, TX
                [*OCLC symbol*] (OCLC)
TII.............. Thomas Industries, Incorporated [*NYSE symbol*]
TII.............. Tiffin, OH [*Location identifier*] [*FAA*] (FAAL)
TII.............. Tooling Inspection Instrumentation (NASA)
TII.............. Trusteeship Institute, Incorporated (EA)
TIIAL .... [*The*] International Institute of Applied Linguistics
TIIC........... Technical Industrial Intelligence Committee [*US Military
                Government, Germany*]
TIID .... Technical Industrial Intelligence Division [*Allied Board set up to
                send experts into Germany to ferret out Germany's war-
                developed scientific secrets*] [*Post-World War II*]
TIIF........... Tactical Image Interpretation Facility
TIIPS .... Technically Improved Interference Prediction System (IEEE)
TIJ .... Tijuana [*Mexico*] [*Airport symbol*] (OAG)
TIJa........... Trudy Instituta Jazykoznanija [*A publication*]
Tijd............ Onze Tijd [*A publication*]
Tijd Ec Soc ... Tijdschrift voor Economische en Sociale Geografie [*A
                publication*]
Tijd Filos.... Tijdschrift voor Filosofie [*A publication*]
Tijd Kindergeneeskd ... Tijdschrift voor Kindergeneeskunde [*A publication*]
Tijd Logop Audiol ... Tijdschrift voor Logopedie en Audiologie [*A
                publication*]
Tijd Psych ... Tijdschrift voor Psychiatrie [*A publication*]
Tijdschr Diergeneeskd ... Tijdschrift voor Diergeneeskunde [*A publication*]
Tijdschr Diergeneeskd Q Engl Issue ... Tijdschrift voor Diergeneeskunde.
                Quarterly English Issue [*A publication*]
Tijdschr Econ Soc Geogr ... Tijdschrift voor Economische en Sociale
                Geografie [*A publication*]
Tijdschr Ent ... Tijdschrift voor Entomologie [*A publication*]
Tijdschr Entomol ... Tijdschrift voor Entomologie [*A publication*]
Tijdschr Filosof ... Tijdschrift voor Filosofie [*A publication*]
Tijdschr Gastro-Enterol ... Tijdschrift voor Gastro-Enterologie [*A
                publication*]
Tijdschr Geneeskd ... Tijdschrift voor Geneeskunde [*A publication*]

Tijdschrift Taal & Lett ... Tijdschrift voor Taal en Letteren [*A publication*]
Tijdschr Ind Taal- Land- en Volkenkunde ... Tijdschrift voor Indische Taal-,
                Land-, en Volkenkunde [*A publication*]
Tijdschr Kindergeneeskd ... Tijdschrift voor Kindergeneeskunde [*A
                publication*]
Tijdschr Lev Talen ... Tijdschrift voor Levende Talen [*A publication*]
Tijdschr Ned Elektron- & Radiogenoot ... Tijdschrift van het Nederlands
                Elektronica- en Radiogenootschap [*A publication*]
Tijdschr Ned Heidemaatsch ... Tijdschrift der Nederlandsche
                Heidemaatschappij [*A publication*]
Tijdschr Ned TL ... Tijdschrift voor Nederlandsche Taal- en Letterkunde [*A
                publication*]
Tijdschr Oppervlakte Tech Metal ... Tijdschrift voor Oppervlakte
                Technieken van Metalen [*A publication*]
Tijdschr Plantenz ... Tijdschrift voor Plantenziekten [*A publication*]
Tijdschr Plantenziekten ... Tijdschrift voor Plantenziekten [*A publication*]
Tijdschr Polit ... Tijdschrift voor Politicologie [*Netherlands*] [*A publication*]
Tijdschr Primaire Energ ... Tijdschrift Primaire Energie [*Belgium*] [*A
                publication*]
Tijdschr Soc Geneeskd ... Tijdschrift voor Sociale Geneeskunde [*A
                publication*]
Tijdschr Stud Verlichting ... Tijdschrift voor Studie. Verlichting [*A
                publication*]
Tijdschr Veeartsenijk ... Tijdschrift voor Veeartsenijkunde [*A publication*]
Tijdschr Veeartsenijk en Veeteelt ... Tijdschrift voor Veeartsenijkunde en
                Veeteelt [*A publication*]
Tijdschr Ziekenverpl ... Tijdschrift voor Ziekenverpleging [*A publication*]
Tijds Econ ... Tijdschrift voor Economie [*A publication*]
Tijds Soc Wetensch ... Tijdschrift voor Sociale Wetenschappen [*A
                publication*]
TIK .... Oklahoma City, OK [*Location identifier*] [*FAA*] (FAAL)
TIK .... Target Indicator Kit
TIK .... Tiara Enterprises Ltd. [*Vancouver Stock Exchange symbol*]
TIK .... Tiksi [*USSR*] [*Seismograph station code, US Geological
                Survey*] (SEIS)
TIK .... Tixie [*USSR*] [*Geomagnetic observatory code*]
TIKP .... Turkiye Isci Koylu Partisi [*Worker-Peasant Party of
                Turkey*] (PD)
TIL .... Technical Information and Library Service
TIL .... Temperature Indicating Label
TIL .... Temporary Instructor Lieutenant [*Navy*] [*British*]
TIL .... Tilco Aviation Co., Inc. [*Baton Rouge, LA*] [*FAA
                designator*] (FAAC)
Til .... Tilskueren [*A publication*]
TIL .... Travaux. Institut de Linguistique [*A publication*]
TIL .... Tree Island Steel Co. Ltd. [*Toronto Stock Exchange symbol*]
                [*Vancouver Stock Exchange symbol*]
T-i-L .... Truth-in-Lending [*Act*] [*1968*]
TIL .... Tumor Infiltrating Lymphocyte [*Oncology*]
TIL .... Until (FAAC)
TILA .... Truth-in-Lending Act [*1968*]
TILAS........ Travaux. Institut d'Etudes Latino-Americaines. Universite de
                Strasbourg [*A publication*]
TILE........... Color Tile, Inc. [*NASDAQ symbol*] (NQ)
TILF........... Tactical Integrity Loss Factor
TILL .... Total Initial Lamp Lumens
Tillman....... Tillman's Reports [*68, 69, 71, 73, 75 Alabama*] (DLA)
TILLO .... Transfer in Lieu of Layoff (MCD)
Till & Yates App ... Tillinghast and Yates on Appeals (DLA)
TILMC........ Tobacco Industry Labor/Management Committee (EA)
TILO .... Technical Industrial Liaison Office
TILRA .... Tribal Indian Land Rights Association (EA)
TILS........... Tactical Instrument Landing System
Til & Sh Pr ... Tillinghast and Shearman's New York Practice (DLA)
TILSRA....... Truth-in-Lending Simplification and Reform Act [*1980*]
Tils St L...... Tilsley on Stamp Laws [*3rd ed.*] [*1871*] (DLA)
TILT........... Taxpayer Inquiry Lookup Table [*IRS*]
TILT........... Transmission Intercept and Landing Terminated (MCD)
TIM .... Table Input to Memory
TIM .... Tangential Inlet Manifold
TIM .... Target Intelligence Material (MCD)
TIM .... Technical Information Manual
TIM .... Technical Information on Microfilm [*British*] (DIT)
TIM .... TEFLON Insulation Material
TIM .... Tembagapura [*Indonesia*] [*Airport symbol*] (OAG)
TIM .... Temperature Indicator Monitor
TIM .... Test Instrumented Missile [*Army*]
TIM .... Test Interface Module (CAAL)
TIM .... Test Item Malfunction (MCD)
TIM .... Texas Instruments, Inc., Central Library Services, Dallas, TX
                [*OCLC symbol*] (OCLC)
TIM .... Thailand Independence Movement [*Communist-directed
                activity outside Thailand*] [*Merged with TPF*]
TIM .... Ticket Issue Machines
TIM .... Time Indicator, Miniature (MUGU)
TIM .... Time Interval Measurement
TIM .... Time Interval Meter
TIM .... Time Meter (AAG)
Tim .... Timely [*Record label*]
TIM .... Timisoara [*Romania*] [*Seismograph station code, US
                Geological Survey*] (SEIS)

TIM .... Timminco Ltd. [*Toronto Stock Exchange symbol*]
Tim .... Timoleon [*of Plutarch*] [*Classical studies*]   (OCD)
Tim .... Timon of Athens [*Shakespearean work*]
Tim .... Timothy [*New Testament book*]
TIM .... Titanium Mesh [*Medicine*]
TIM .... Topic Indexing Matrix
TIM .... Total Ion Scanning Mode [*Spectroscopy*]
TIM .... Track Imitation   (MSA)
TIM .... Track Initiator Monitor   (CAAL)
TIM .... Tracking Information Memorandum
TIM .... Tracking Instruction Manual
TIM .... Tracking Instrument Mount   (MUGU)
TIM .... Transient Intermodulation [*Distortion*]
TIM .... Transistor Information Microfile
TIM .... Trigger Inverter Module
TIM .... Triose Phosphate Isomerase [*An enzyme*]
TIMA .... Technical Illustrators Management Association [*Later, IG*]
TIMA .... Thermal Insulation Manufacturers Association [*Mt. Kisco, NY*]   (EA)
TIMA .... Truth in Mileage Act of 1986
TIMAR .... Near-Term Improvement in Materiel Asset Reporting [*Military*]   (AABC)
Timarit Verkfraedingafelags Is ... Timarit Verkfraedingafelags Islands [*A publication*]
TIMATION ... Time Location System [*Navy*]
TIMB .... Timballes [*Kettle drum*]
TIMB .... Timber   (ADA)
TIMB .... Timberland Industries [*NASDAQ symbol*]   (NQ)
Timb Bull Europe FAO ... Timber Bulletin for Europe. Food and Agricultural Organization [*A publication*]
Timber Dev Assoc Inf Bull A/IB ... Timber Development Association. Information Bulletin A/IB [*A publication*]
Timber Dev Assoc Inf Bull B/IB ... Timber Development Association. Information Bulletin B/IB [*A publication*]
Timber Dev Assoc Inf Bull G/IB ... Timber Development Association. Information Bulletin G/IB [*A publication*]
Timber Supp Rev ... Timber Supply Review [*A publication*]
Timber Technol ... Timber Technology [*A publication*]
Timb Grower ... Timber Grower [*A publication*]
Timb Leafl For Dep (Brit Solomon Islands Protect) ... Timber Leaflet. Forestry Department (British Solomon Islands Protectorate) [*A publication*]
Timb Leafl For Dep (Kenya) ... Timber Leaflet. Forest Department (Nairobi, Kenya) [*A publication*]
Timb Leafl For Dep (Uganda) ... Timber Leaflet. Forest Department (Uganda) [*A publication*]
Timb & Plyw Ann ... Timber and Plywood Annual [*A publication*]
Timb Pres Assoc Aust ... Timber Preservers' Association of Australia. Pamphlet [*A publication*]
Timb Tr J ... Timber Trades Journal [*A publication*]
TIME .... Technique for Information Management and Employment
TIME .... Time Energy Systems [*NASDAQ symbol*]   (NQ)
TIMEA .... Transactions. Institute of Marine Engineeers [*A publication*]
Time (Can) ... Time (Canada) [*A publication*]
Times Ednl Supp ... Times Educational Supplement [*A publication*]
Times Educ Supp ... Times Educational Supplement [*A publication*]
Times Higher Ed Supp ... Times Higher Education Supplement [*A publication*]
Times Ind A ... Times of India Annual [*Bombay*] [*A publication*]
Times L ...... Times Literary Supplement [*A publication*]
Times L (Eng) ... Times Law Reports [*England*]   (DLA)
Times Lit Supp ... Times Literary Supplement [*A publication*]
Times Lit Suppl ... Times Literary Supplement [*A publication*]
Times LR.... Times Law Reports [*England*]   (DLA)
Times LR.... Times Law Reports [*Ceylon*]   (DLA)
Times L Rep ... Times Law Reports [*England*]   (DLA)
Times L Rep ... Times Law Reports [*Ceylon*]   (DLA)
Times Rev Ind ... Times Review of Industry [*A publication*]
Times R Ind & Tech ... Times Review of Industry and Technology [*A publication*]
Times Sci Rev ... Times Science Review [*A publication*]
TIMFA .... Transactions. Institute of Metal Finishing [*A publication*]
TIMI .... Technical Information Maintenance Instruction
TIMI .... Thrombolysis in Myocardial Infarction (Study) [*Medicine*]
TIMIG .... Time in Grade [*Army*]
TIMINT .... Time Interval   (AABC)
Timisoara Inst Politeh Traian Vuia Bul Stiint Teh Ser Chim ... Timisoara. Institutul Politehnic "Traian Vuia." Buletinul Stiintific si Tehnic. Seria Chimie [*A publication*]
Timisoara Med ... Timisoara Medicala [*Romania*] [*A publication*]
TIMIX .... [*The*] International Microcomputer Information Exchange [*Austin, TX*]   (EA)
TiMixE .... TI-MIX [*Texas Instruments Mini/Microcomputer Information Exchange*] Europe   (EA)
TIMM .... Thermionic Integrated Micromodule
TIMM .... Timberline Minerals [*NASDAQ symbol*]   (NQ)
TIMMS .... Total Integrated Manpower Management System
TIMP .... Texas Instructional Media Project [*Education*]
TIMP .... Timpani [*Kettle drum*]
TIMP .... Tissue Inhibitor of Metalloproteinases [*Biochemistry*]
TIMS .... [*The*] Institute of Management Sciences [*Providence, RI*]   (EA)

TIMS .... [*The*] International Molinological Society   (EA)
TIMS .... Tactical Incapacitating Munitions System   (MCD)
TIMS .... Technology Integration of Missile Subsystems   (MCD)
TIMS .... Telephone Information and Management Systems   (ADA)
TIMS .... Thermal Infrared Multispectral Scanner [*Airborne instrument for geological applications*]
TIMS .... Thermal Ionization Mass Spectrometry
TIMS .... Time Sharing Resources, Inc. [*NASDAQ symbol*]   (NQ)
TIMS .... Transmission Impairment Measuring Set [*Telecommunications*]   (TEL)
TIN .... Taro Industries Ltd. [*Toronto Stock Exchange symbol*]
TIN .... Task Implementation Notice
TIN .... Taxpayer Identification Number [*IRS*]
TIN .... Temperature Independent [*Ferrite computer memory core*]
TIN .... Temple-Inland, Inc. [*NYSE symbol*]
TIN .... Temporary Identification Number
TIN .... Temporary Instruction Notice
TIN .... Ter in Nocte [*Three Times a Night*] [*Pharmacy*]
TIN .... Tindouf [*Algeria*] [*Airport symbol*]   (OAG)
TIN .... Tinemaha [*California*] [*Seismograph station code, US Geological Survey*]   (SEIS)
TIN .... Transaction Identification Number   (AFM)
TIN .... Tubulointerstitial Nephritis [*Nephrology*]
TINA .... There Is No Alternative [*Nickname given to British Prime Minister Margaret Thatcher because she so often uses this phrase to defend her government's economic policies*]
TINC .... Tincture   (ADA)
TINCT .... Tinctura [*Tincture*] [*Pharmacy*]
TINDECO ... Tin Decorating Company
TINDX .... Texas Instruments, Inc. Index Access Method
TI-NET .... Transparent Intelligent Network
TINET .... Travel Industry Network, Inc. [*Winter Springs, FL*] [*Telecommunications*]   (TSSD)
TINFO .... Tieteellisen Informoinnin Neuvosto [*Finnish Council for Scientific Information and Research Libraries*] [*Helsinki*] [*Information service*]   (EISS)
TIN/FS ...... Taxpayer Identification Number/File Source [*IRS*]
Tingo Maria Peru Est Exp Agric Bol ... Tingo Maria Peru Estacion Experimental Agricola. Boletin [*A publication*]
Tin Int........ Tin International [*A publication*]
Tin Intern ... Tin International [*A publication*]
Tink .... Two Incomes, No Kids [*Lifestyle classification*]
TINKER ...... Timber Information Keyword Retrieval [*Timber Research and Development Association*] [*Information service*] [*High Wycombe, Bucks., England*]   (EISS)
TINNER ...... Tea and Dinner [*Slang*] [*British*]   (DSUE)
TINOP .... Transponder Inoperative [*Aviation*]   (FAAC)
Tin Print Box Mkr ... Tin-Printer and Box Maker [*A publication*]
TINR .... Target Identification Navigation RADAR
TINS .... Thermal Imaging Night Sight
TINS .... Transinertial Navigation System
TINS .... Trends in Neurosciences [*A publication*]
Tinsley .... Tinsley's Magazine [*A publication*]
TINSTAAFL ... There Is No Such Thing as a Free Lunch [*Principle of economics indicating that one cannot get something for nothing*] [*See also TANSTAAFL*]
TINSY........ Treasure Island Naval Shipyard [*San Francisco Bay*]
TINT .... Target Intercept Timer   (MCD)
TINTM .... Triisononyl Trimellitate [*Organic chemistry*]
TINTS .... Tactical Intelligence Transfer System
TINTS .... Turret Integrated Night Thermal Sight
Tin Uses ..... Tin and Its Uses [*A publication*]
Tinw .... Tinwald's Reports, Scotch Court of Session   (DLA)
TIO .... Target Indication Officer [*Navy*]
TIO .... Technical Information Office
TIO .... Technology Integration Office [*Army*]   (RDA)
TIO .... Television Information Office [*National Association of Broadcasters*] [*New York, NY*]   (EA)
TIO .... Test Input/Output [*Data processing*]
TIO .... Time Interval Optimization   (IEEE)
TIO .... Tiouine [*Morocco*] [*Seismograph station code, US Geological Survey*]   (SEIS)
TIO .... Transistorized Image Orthicon
TIO .... Troop Information Officer
TIOC .... Terminal Input/Output Coordinator [*Data processing*]   (IBMDP)
TIOC .... Triumph International Owners Club   (EA)
TIOF .... [*The*] International Osprey Foundation   (EA)
TIOH .... [*The*] Institute of Heraldry [*Military*]
TIOKA .... Trudy Instituta Okeanologii. Akademiya Nauk SSSR [*A publication*]
TIOLR .... Texas Instruments Online Reporting System [*Data processing*]
TIOM .... Terminal Input/Output Module [*Data processing*]
TIOS .... Tactical Integrated Ocean Surveillance [*Military*]   (CAAL)
TIOT .... Task Input/Output Table [*Data processing*]   (BUR)
TIOTM .... Triisooctyl Trimellitate [*Organic chemistry*]
TIOWQ .... Terminal Input/Output Wait Queue [*Data processing*]
TIP .... [*The*] Information Partnership [*London, England*] [*Information service*]   (EISS)
TIP .... Tactile Information Presentation [*Biotechnology*]
TIP .... Target Identification Point   (NATG)

TIP............. Target Impact Point
TIP............. Target Industries Program [*Occupational Safety and Health Administration*]
TIP............. Target Input Panel
TIP............. Target Intelligence Package   (MCD)
TIP............. Task Initiation and Prediction
TIP............. Tax-Based Incomes Policy
TIP............. Taxpayer Information Processing [*IRS*]
TIP............. Teachers Instructional Plan
TIP............. Technical Improvement Program
TIP............. Technical Information Panel [*AEC*]
TIP............. Technical Information Pilot [*A publication*] [*Obsolete*]
TIP............. Technical Information Pool
TIP............. Technical Information Processing   (IEEE)
TIP............. Technical Information Program
TIP............. Technical Information Project [*MIT*]
TIP............. TELENET Interface Processor
TIP............. Telephone Information Processing   (MCD)
TIP............. Teletype Input Processing
TIP............. Terminal Impact Prediction
TIP............. Terminal Interface Package [*Data processing*]
TIP............. Terminal Interface [*Message*] Processor [*Data processing*] [*DoD*]
TIP............. Tests in Print [*A publication*]
TIP............. Theory into Practice [*A publication*]
TIP............. Thrust Inlet Pressure   (MCD)
TIP............. Tiburon Petroleum [*Vancouver Stock Exchange symbol*]
TIP............. Tilt Isolation Platform
TIP............. To Insure Promptness
TIP............. Total Information Processing   (BUR)
TIP............. Total Isomerization Process [*Petroleum refining*]
TIP............. Toxic Integration Program [*Environmental Protection Agency*]
TIP............. Toxicology Information Program [*National Library of Medicine*] [*Bethesda, MD*]
TIP............. Track Initiation and Prediction [*RADAR*]
TIP............. Tracking Impact Prediction [*of satellites*]
TIP............. Trans-Israel Pipeline
TIP............. Transaction Interface Package [*Sperry UNIVAC*] [*Data processing*]
TIP............. Transaction Interface Processor
TIP............. Transient [*or Traveling*] In-Core Probe [*Nuclear energy*]   (NRCH)
TIP............. Transit Improvement Program [*Satellite*]   (MCD)
TIP............. Translation Inhibitory Protein
TIP............. Transponder Interrogator Processor
TIP............. Transport Individuel Publique [*Also known as PROCOTIP*] [*French auto cooperative*]
TIP............. Transportation Improvement Program
TIP............. Traveling In-Core Probe   (IEEE)
TIP............. Traversing In-Core Probe [*Nuclear energy*]   (NRCH)
TIP............. Tripoli [*Libya*] [*Airport symbol*]   (OAG)
TIP............. Troop Information Program
TIP............. Truth in Press [*An association*]   (EA)
TIP............. Tumor-Inducing Principle [*Plant cytology*]
TIP............. Tumor Inhibitory Principle [*Oncology*]
TIP............. Turbine Inlet Pressure   (MSA)
TIP............. Turn In a Pusher [*Organization combating drug traffic*]
TIP............. Until Past [*Followed by place*]   (FAAC)
TIPA.......... Triisopropanolamine [*Organic chemistry*]
TIPACS...... Texas Instruments Planning and Control System
TIPAT........ Technical Information on Patents [*Swiss Intellectual Property Office*] [*Bern*] [*Information service*]   (EISS)
TIPC.......... Texas Instruments Pressure Controller
TIPCC........ TI [*Texas Instruments*] Programmable Calculator Club [*Largo, FL*]   (EA)
TIPE.......... Transponder, Interrogator, Pinger, and Echo Sounder
TIPGA........ Trudy Instituta Prikladnoi Geofiziki [*A publication*]
TIPI........... Tactical Information Processing and Interpretation [*Military*]   (AFM)
TIPI........... Transportable Automated Intelligence Processing and Interpretation System   (MCD)
TIPIC......... Turkish Investment Promotion and Information Center [*Subdivision of the Union of Chambers of Commerce, Industry, and Commodity Exchanges of Turkey*]
TIPITEF..... Tactical Information Processing and Interpretation Total Environment Facility   (MCD)
TIPL.......... Tactical Imagery Processing Laboratory [*Army*]   (MCD)
TIPL.......... Tactical Information Processing Laboratory [*Army*]   (MCD)
TIPL.......... Teach Information Processing Language
TIPMG........ [*The*] International Project Management Group, Inc. [*Glyndon, MD*] [*Telecommunications*]   (TSSD)
TIPP.......... Time Phasing Program [*NASA*]   (KSC)
TIPP.......... Tipperary [*County in Ireland*]
TIPPS........ Tetraiodophenolphthalein Sodium [*Pharmacology*]
TIPPS........ Total In-House Publication Production System   (MCD)
TIPR.......... Tactics Inspection Procedures Report
TIPR.......... Tipperary Corp. [*NASDAQ symbol*]   (NQ)
TIPRE........ Tactical Inertial Performance Requirements   (MCD)
TIPRO........ Texas Independent Producers and Royalty Owners Association [*Austin, TX*]   (EA)

TIPRO Rep ... TIPRO [*Texas Independent Producers and Royalty Owners Association*] Reporter [*A publication*]
TIPS.......... [*The*] Italia Philatelic Society   (EA)
TIPS.......... Tactical Information about Perilous Situations [*New York City Fire Department program*]
TIPS.......... Tactical Information Processing System [*Military*]   (CAAL)
TIPS.......... Tactical Intelligence Processing System
TIPS.......... Teaching Individual Protective Strategies and Teaching Individual Positive Solutions [*In association name TIPS Program*]   (EA)
TIPS.......... Teaching Information Processing System
TIPS.......... Technical Information Periodicals Service [*General Electric Co.*]
TIPS.......... Technical Information Processing System [*Rockwell International Corp.*] [*Downey, CA*]   (AFM)
TIPS.......... Technical Information for Product Safety [*Consumer Product Safety Commission*]   (EISS)
TIPS.......... Technical Information and Product Service
TIPS.......... Techniques in Product Selection [*National Association of Manufacturers*]
TIPS.......... Telemetry Impact Prediction System [*Air Force*]
TIPS.......... Telemetry Integrated Processing System [*Air Force*]
TIPS.......... Terminal Information Processing System [*Aviation*]   (FAAC)
TIPS.......... Test Information Processing System [*Air Force*]
TIPS.......... Text Information Processing System
TIPS.......... Textile Industry Product Safety [*A publication*]
Tips.......... Tiny Income, Parents Supporting [*Lifestyle classification*]
TIPS.......... Total Information Processing System [*Veterans Administration*]
TIPS.......... Total Integrated Pneumatic System   (MCD)
TIPS.......... Transistorized Inverter Power Supply
TIPS.......... Transportation Induced Pollution Surveillance [*Marine science*]   (MSC)
TIPS.......... Trends in Pharmacological Sciences [*A publication*]
TIPS.......... Truevision Image Paint Software [*AT & T*] [*Computer graphics*]
TIPSY........ Task Input Parameter Synthesizer
TIP/TAP..... Target Input Panel and Target Assign Panel
TIPTOP...... Tape Input - Tape Output [*Honeywell, Inc.*] [*Data processing*]
TIP TOP .... Tax Information Plan and Total Owed Purchase Accounting
TIQ .... Paris, TN [*Location identifier*] [*FAA*]   (FAAL)
TIQ .... Task Input Queue [*Data processing*]   (IBMDP)
TIQ .... Tetrahydroisoquinoline [*Biochemistry*]
TIQ .... Tinian [*Mariana Islands*] [*Airport symbol*]   (OAG)
TI/QC........ Technical Inspection/Quality Control   (MCD)
TIQRC....... Toxicology Information Query Response Center [*National Library of Medicine*]
TIR............. Target Illuminating RADAR [*Air Force*]
TIR............. Target Indication Room [*Navy*]
TIR............. Target Industries [*Industry segments which have been selected by the US Department of Commerce for special trade promotion emphasis*]
TIR............. Target Instruction Register
TIR............. Technical Information Release
TIR............. Technical Information Report   (IEEE)
TIR............. Technical Intelligence Report
TIR............. Terminal Imaging RADAR [*Military*]   (RDA)
TIR............. Terminal Innervation Ratio [*Psychiatry*]
TIR............. Test Incidence and Reporting System
tir............. Tigrina [*MARC language code*] [*Library of Congress*]   (LCCP)
TIR............. Time in Rate
TIR............. Tirana [*Albania*] [*Seismograph station code, US Geological Survey*]   (SEIS)
TIR............. Tirupati [*India*] [*Airport symbol*]   (OAG)
TIR............. Tooling Investigation Report
TIR............. Total Immunoreaction [*Immunochemistry*]
TIR............. Total Indicated Runout
TIR............. Total Indicator Reading
TIR............. Total Internal Reflecting
TIR............. Total Item Record   (MCD)
TIR............. Transaction Item Report [*Navy*]   (NG)
TIR............. Transport International Routier [*International Transport of Goods by Road*]
TIRA .... Thrift Institutions Restructuring Act [*1982*]
TIRACS ...... Telecommanded Inertially Referenced Attitude Control System   (MCD)
TIRAS........ Technical Information Retrieval and Analysis System   (CAAL)
TIRB .... Transportation Insurance Rating Bureau [*Later, AAIS*]   (EA)
TIRC .... T Tauri Infrared Companion [*Object believed to be first planet sighted that is not in our solar system*]
TIRC .... Tobacco Industry Research Committee [*Later, Council for Tobacco Research, USA*]   (EA)
TIRC .... Toxicology Information Research Center [*Department of Energy*] [*Oak Ridge National Laboratory*] [*Oak Ridge, TN*]
TIRE .... One Liberty Firestone [*NASDAQ symbol*]   (NQ)
TIRE .... Tank Infrared Elbow [*Night vision device*] [*Army*]   (RDA)
TIRE .... Tires as Imaginative Recreation Equipment
TIREC........ TIROS [*Television Infrared Observation Satellite*] Ice Reconnaissance [*NASA*]
Tire Rev..... Tire Review [*A publication*]
Tire Sci Technol ... Tire Science and Technology [*A publication*]
TIRH .... Theoretical Indoor Relative Humidity

TIRIS .... Traversing Infrared Inspection System (MCD)
TIRJa.......... Trudy Instituto Russkogo Jazyka [*A publication*]
TIRKS........ Trunks Integrated Record Keeping System [*Bell System*]
TIRM.......... Transparent Infrared Material
TIRMMS ..... Technical Information Reports for Music-Media Specialists [*Music Library Association publication series*]
TIROD .... Test Instruction Record of Discussion (MCD)
T Iron St I ... Transactions. Iron and Steel Institute of Japan [*A publication*]
TIROS........ Television and Infrared Observation Satellite [*NASA*]
TIRP .... Total Internal Reflection Prism
TIRPF .... Total Integrated Radial Peaking Factor (IEEE)
TIRR .... [*The*] Institute for Rehabilitation and Research [*Houston, TX*]
TIRR .... Tactics Inspection Results Report
TIRR .... Tierra Energy Corp. [*NASDAQ symbol*] (NQ)
TIRS .... Tactical Information Recording System [*Military*] (CAAL)
TIRS .... Thermal Infrared Scanner (RDA)
TIRS .... Travaux. Institut de Recherches Sahariennes [*A publication*]
TIRT .... Total Internal Reflection Technique
TIRU .... Service du Traitement Industriel des Residus Urbains [*France*]
TIRZC .... Tidelands Royalty CI B [*NASDAQ symbol*] (NQ)
TIS .... [*The*] Infantry School [*Army*]
TIS .... Tactical Intelligence Squadron (MCD)
TIS .... Taft Information System [*Provides information on private foundations*] (EISS)
TIS .... Target Identification Software [*Military*] (CAAL)
TIS .... Target Information Sheet [*Air Force*]
TIS .... Target Information System
TIS .... Technical Information Section [*Navy*]
TIS .... Technical Information Service [*American Institute of Aeronautics and Astronautics*] [*New York, NY*] (EISS)
TIS .... Technical Information Service [*Caribbean Industrial Research Institute*] [*Trinidad*] [*Information service*] (EISS)
TIS .... Technical Information Services [*Acurex Corp.*] [*Mountain View, CA*] (EISS)
TIS .... Technical Information Systems [*Department of Agriculture*]
TIS .... Technical Interface Specification (NATG)
TIS .... Technical Research Centre of Finland, Espoo, Finland [*OCLC symbol*] (OCLC)
TIS .... Technology, Information, and Society
TIS .... Technology Information System [*Lawrence Livermore National Laboratory*] [*University of California*] [*Livermore, CA*] (EISS)
TIS .... Telemetry Input System
TIS .... Temperature Indicating Switch
TIS .... Terminal Interface Subsystem [*Telecommunications*] (TEL)
TIS .... Test Information Sheet (MCD)
TIS .... Test Instrumentation System
TIS .... Test Interface Summary (MCD)
TIS .... Tetracycline-Induced Steatosis [*Medicine*]
TIS .... Tetrahydroisoquinoline Sulfonamide [*A drug*]
TIS .... Theater Intelligence Section [*Navy*]
TIS .... Thermal Imaging Scanner
TIS .... Thermal Insulation System
TIS .... Thursday Island [*Australia*] [*Airport symbol*] (OAG)
TIS .... Time Resources Corp. [*Vancouver Stock Exchange symbol*]
TIS .... Time in Service (FAAC)
TIS .... Tissue (ADA)
TIS .... Tobacco Inspection Service [*Philippines*]
TIS .... Tops in Science Fiction [*A publication*]
TIS .... Total Information System [*Data processing*]
TIS .... Tracking and Injection Station
TIS .... Tracking Instrumentation Subsystem (MCD)
TIS .... Traffic Information System
TIS .... Transponder Interrogation SONAR
TIS .... Travel Information Service [*A division of Moss Regional Resource and Information Center for Disabled Individuals*] [*Philadelphia, PA*] (EA)
TIS .... Travelers Information Service [*Oracle Corp.*] [*New Fairfield, CT*] [*Information service*] (EISS)
TIS .... Triskaidekaphobia Illuminatus Society (EA)
TIS .... Trypsin-Insoluble Segment [*Cytochemistry*]
TIS .... Tumor in Situ [*Oncology*]
TISA .... Technical Information Support Activities [*Army*]
TISA .... Technique for Interactive Systems Analysis (NVT)
TISA .... Troop Issue Subsistence Activity [*Military*] (AABC)
TISA .... Troop Issue Support Agency (MCD)
TISAL........ Tactical Instrument Steep Approach and Landing System (MCD)
TISAP........ Technical Information Support Activities Project [*Army*] (DIT)
TISAP........ Totalized Interface Subroutine and Post Processor [*Data processing*] (BUR)
TISC .... Technology Integration Steering Committee [*Army*] (RDA)
TISC .... Tire Industry Safety Council [*Washington, DC*] (EA)
TISCA .... Technical Information System for Carrier Aviation [*Navy*] (MCD)
TISCO .... TISCO [*Tata Iron & Steel Company*] Technical Journal [*A publication*]
TISEO........ Target Identification System, Electro-Optical [*Air Force*]
TISL.......... Telecommunications and Information Systems Laboratory [*University of Kansas*] [*Research center*] (RCD)
TISO .... Troop Issue Subsistence Officer [*Military*] (AABC)

TISP .... Technical Information Support Personnel [*Department of Labor*]
TISS .... Troop Issue Support System [*Army*]
Tissue Anti ... Tissue Antigens [*A publication*]
TISTHR ...... Tool Inspection Small Tools Historical Record (MCD)
Tit.............. Divus Titus [*of Suetonius*] [*Classical studies*] (OCD)
TIT .... Technician-in-Training (ADA)
TIT .... Terminal Interface Table (MCD)
TIT .... Test Item Taker
TIT .... Thermal Inactivation Time
TIT .... Thermoisolation Technique
Tit.............. Titan [*Record label*]
TIT .... Title [*Bibliography*]
Tit.............. Titus [*New Testament book*]
Tit.............. Titus Andronicus [*Shakespearean work*]
TIT .... Total Insertion Time
TIT .... Treponema Immobilization Test [*Clinical chemistry*]
TIT .... Turbine Inlet Temperature
TIT .... Turbine Interstage Temperature
TITC .... Traction-Immune Track Circuits [*Railway signals system*] [*British*]
TITE .... Tijuana & Tecate Railway Co. [*Later, TTR*] [*AAR code*]
TI Tech Inf Ind ... TI. Technical Information for Industry [*South Africa*] [*A publication*]
TITh............ Triiodothyronine [*Also, T_3*] [*Endocrinology*]
TIT J Lif ...... TIT [*Tower International Technomedical*] Journal of Life Sciences [*A publication*]
TIT J Life Sci ... TIT [*Tower International Technomedical*] Journal of Life Sciences [*A publication*]
TITL............ Tijdschrift van het Institut voor Toegepaste Linguistiek Leuven [*A publication*]
titr .... Titrate [*Analytical chemistry*]
TI/TTR........ Target Illumination/Target Tracking RADAR (MCD)
TITUS........ Textile Information Treatment Users' Service [*French Textile Institute*] [*Bibliographic database*] [*Information service*] (EISS)
TIU .... Tape Identification Unit
TIU .... Target Indication Unit [*Navy*]
TIU .... Technical Information Unit (ADA)
TIU .... Telecommunications International Union [*Hamden, CT*] [*Independent labor union*] (EA)
TIU .... Terminal Interface Unit [*Bell System*]
TIU .... Timaru [*New Zealand*] [*Airport symbol*] (OAG)
TIU .... Time Isolation Unit
TIU .... Toxicologically Insignificant Usage
TIU .... Trigger Inverter Unit
TIU .... Trypsin Inhibitory Unit [*Food analysis*]
TIUC .... Textile Information Users Council [*Greensboro, NC*] (EA)
TIUV .... Total Intrauterine Volume [*Gynecology*]
TIV .... Target Intensifier Vidicon
TIV .... Time in View
TIV .... Tivat [*Yugoslavia*] [*Airport symbol*] (OAG)
TIV .... Tiverton Petroleums Ltd. [*Toronto Stock Exchange symbol*]
TIV .... Tivoli Music Hall [*London*] (DSUE)
TIW .... Tacoma, WA [*Location identifier*] [*FAA*] (FAAL)
TIW .... Tamarind Institute Workshop [*Graphic arts school*] [*New Mexico*]
TIW .... TEFLON-Insulated Wire
tiw .... Three Times a Week [*Pharmacology*]
TIWG .... Test Integration Working Group
TIWSS .... Theater Integrated Warfare Scenarios Study
TIX............. Timeplex, Inc. [*NYSE symbol*]
TIX............. Titusville, FL [*Location identifier*] [*FAA*] (FAAL)
TIXA .... Thioxanthone [*Organic chemistry*]
TIXI........... Turret Integrated Xenon Illuminator
TIY............. Tidjikja [*Mauritania*] [*Airport symbol*] (OAG)
TIZ............. Tari [*Papua New Guinea*] [*Airport symbol*] (OAG)
TJ .... Air Traffic GmbH [*ICAO designator*] (FAAC)
TJ .... Cameroun [*Aircraft nationality and registration mark*] (FAAC)
TJ .... East Germany [*License plate code assigned to foreign diplomats in the US*]
TJ .... Talk Jockey [*Radio*]
TJ .... Talmud Jerushalmi (BJA)
TJ .... Targum Jonathan (BJA)
TJ .... Technical Journal (MCD)
TJ .... Telephone Jack (DEN)
TJ .... Temperature Junction (MCD)
TJ .... Terajoule [*SI unit of energy*]
TJ .... Test Jack (DEN)
TJ .... Theatre Journal [*A publication*]
TJ .... Thermal Junction (KSC)
TJ .... Tijuana [*Mexico*]
TJ .... Today's Japan [*A publication*]
TJ .... Tolkien Journal [*A publication*]
TJ .... Tomato Juice
TJ .... Trajectory (AABC)
TJ .... Trans-Jordan (BJA)
TJ .... Triceps Jerk
TJ .... Turbojet
TJA............. Tarija [*Bolivia*] [*Airport symbol*] (OAG)
TJA............. Telecommunication Journal of Australia [*A publication*]

TJA............ Trial Judge Advocate [*Army*]
TJA............ Turbojet Aircraft
TJADC .... Theater Joint Air Defense Command [*Military*] (AABC)
TJAETDS ... Turbine and Jet Aircraft Engine Type Designation System
TJAG......... [*The*] Judge Advocate General [*Army*]
TJAGC ...... [*The*] Judge Advocate General's Corps [*Army*]
TJaGH .... Jackson-Madison County General Hospital, Learning Center, Jackson, TN [*Library symbol*] [*Library of Congress*] (LCLS)
TJAGSA ..... [*The*] Judge Advocate General's School, Army
TJak .... Trudy Instituta Jazyka, Literatury, i Istorii [*A publication*]
TJaL .... Lane College, Jackson, TN [*Library symbol*] [*Library of Congress*] (LCLS)
TJaLam...... Lambuth College, Jackson, TN [*Library symbol*] [*Library of Congress*] (LCLS)
TJaLaw ...... Tennessee State Law Library, Jackson, TN [*Library symbol*] [*Library of Congress*] (LCLS)
T Jap I Met ... Transactions. Japan Institute of Metals [*A publication*]
TJAS .... Tom Jones Appreciation Society [*Huddersfield, Yorkshire, England*] (EA-IO)
TJaU .... Union University, Jackson, TN [*Library symbol*] [*Library of Congress*] (LCLS)
TJB............ Theologischer Jahresbericht [*A publication*]
TJB............ Tijuana Brass [*Musical group*]
TJB............ Tilting Journal Bearing
TJB............ Time-Sharing Job Control Block [*Data processing*] (IBMDP)
TJB............ Trench Junction Box
T J Br Cer... Transactions and Journal. British Ceramic Society [*A publication*]
TJC............ Temple Junior College [*Texas*]
TJC............ Thornton Junior College [*Illinois*]
TJC............ Trajectory Chart
TJC............ Trinidad [*Colorado*] [*Seismograph station code, US Geological Survey*] (SEIS)
TJC............ Tyler Junior College [*Texas*]
TJC............ Vanderbilt University Library, Nashville, TN [*OCLC symbol*] (OCLC)
TJCO.......... Trus Joist Corporation [*NASDAQ symbol*] (NQ)
TJD............ Trajectory Diagram
TJE............ Trojan Energy Corp. [*Vancouver Stock Exchange symbol*]
TJE............ Turbojet Engine
TJefC......... Carson-Newman College, Jefferson City, TN [*Library symbol*] [*Library of Congress*] (LCLS)
TJEMD .... Tokai Journal of Experimental and Clinical Medicine [*A publication*]
TJETS .... Thomas Jefferson Equal Tax Society (EA)
TJF............ Time-to-Jitter Flag
TJFS.......... T. J.'s Fans of Soul [*Tom Jones fan club*] (EA)
TJG............ Travel Journalists Guild [*New York, NY*] (EA)
TJHC .... Theology. Journal of Historic Christianity [*A publication*]
TJHPA........ T'u Jang Hsueh Pao [*A publication*]
TJI .... Tabak Journal International [*A publication*]
TJI .... Tex Johnston, Incorporated
TJI .... Trus-Joist I-Beam
TJID........... Terminal Job Identification (BUR)
TJIDA .... Tokyo Jikeikai Ika Daigaku Zasshi [*A publication*]
TJISRF .... Thomas Jefferson Institute for the Study of Religious Freedom [*Fredericksburg, VA*] (EA)
TJIZA .... Tokyo Joshi Ika Daigaku Zasshi [*A publication*]
TJM........... Tower Jettison Motor
TJM........... Vanderbilt Medical Center, Nashville, TN [*OCLC symbol*] (OCLC)
T Jo .... T. Jones' English King's Bench Reports [*84 English Reprint*] (DLA)
TJOC.......... Theater Joint Operations Center [*Military*]
TJoE.......... Emmanuel School of Religion, Johnson City, TN [*Library symbol*] [*Library of Congress*] (LCLS)
TJoMC .... Johnson City Medical Center Hospital, Learning Resources Center, Johnson City, TN [*Library symbol*] [*Library of Congress*] (LCLS)
T Jones ..... T. Jones' English King's Bench Reports [*84 English Reprint*] (DLA)
T Jones (Eng) ... T. Jones' English King's Bench Reports [*84 English Reprint*] (DLA)
TJoS.......... East Tennessee State University, Johnson City, TN [*Library symbol*] [*Library of Congress*] (LCLS)
TJoS-M ...... East Tennessee State University, Medical Library, Johnson City, TN [*Library symbol*] [*Library of Congress*] (LCLS)
TJoV.......... United States Veterans Administration Center, Johnson City, TN [*Library symbol*] [*Library of Congress*] (LCLS)
TJP............ Tactical Jamming Pod [*Military*] (CAAL)
TJP............ Turbojet Propulsion
TJPDA........ Turkish Journal of Pediatrics [*A publication*]
TJPOI........ Twisted Jute Packing and Oakum Institute [*Defunct*] (EA)
TJQ............ Tanjung Pandan [*Indonesia*] [*Airport symbol*] (OAG)
TJQ............ Thoreau Journal Quarterly [*A publication*]
TJR............ Tactical Jammer [*Military*] (CAAL)
TJR............ Tajee Resources Ltd. [*Vancouver Stock Exchange symbol*]
TJR............ Tenri Journal of Religion [*A publication*]
TJR............ Trunk and Junction Routing [*Telecommunications*] (TEL)
TJRC .... Thomas Jefferson Research Center [*Pasadena, CA*] (EA)

TJS............ Tactical Jamming System
TJS............ Tenajon Silver [*Vancouver Stock Exchange symbol*]
TJS............ Terminal Junction System
TJS............ Transverse Junction Stripe (MCD)
TJT............ Tactical Jamming Transmitter [*Navy*]
TJT............ Tough Jeans Territory [*Sears, Roebuck & Co. advertising slogan*]
TJTA .... Taylor-Johnson Temperament Analysis [*Psychology*]
TJTC .... Targeted Jobs Tax Credits [*Federal program*]
TJTCC....... Targeted Jobs Tax Credit Coalition (EA)
TJW .... North Haven, ME [*Location identifier*] [*FAA*] (FAAL)
TJY .... Tulsa, OK [*Location identifier*] [*FAA*] (FAAL)
Tk .... Milli Kutuphane [*National Library*], Ankara, Turkey [*Library symbol*] [*Library of Congress*] (LCLS)
Tk .... T-Cell, Killer Type [*Immunology*]
TK............. Tank (AAG)
TK............. Tanker
TK............. Tekawennake. Six Nations. New Credit Reporter [*A publication*]
TK............. Tetzugaku-Kenkyu [*Tokyo*] [*A publication*]
TK............. Text und Kritik [*A publication*]
TK............. Thick (ROG)
TK............. Through Knee [*Medicine*]
TK............. Thymidine Kinase [*An enzyme*]
TK............. To Kum [*i.e., To Come*] [*Publishing*]
TK............. Tokelau Islands [*Two-letter standard code*] (CNC)
TK............. Tool Kits [*JETDS nomenclature*] [*Military*] (CET)
TK............. Torath Kohanim (BJA)
TK............. Track
TK............. Transducer Kit (MCD)
TK............. Truck (AAG)
TK............. Trunk Equipment [*Telecommunications*] (TEL)
TK............. Turk Hava Yollari AO [*Turkish Airlines, Inc.*] [*ICAO designator*] (FAAC)
TK............. Tuskegee R. R. [*AAR code*]
TKA .... Talkeetna, AK [*Location identifier*] [*FAA*] (FAAL)
TKA .... Tanaka [*New Britain*] [*Seismograph station code, US Geological Survey*] (SEIS)
TKA .... Terminator Kit Assembly [*Robot*]
TKA .... Thermokinetic Analysis
TKA .... Tonka Corp. [*NYSE symbol*]
TKA .... Toy Knights of America (EA)
TKA .... Trudy Kierskoi Dukhovnoi Akademii [*A publication*]
TKAM........ Knoxville Academy of Medicine, Knoxville, TN [*Library symbol*] [*Library of Congress*] (LCLS)
TKar .... Trudy Karel'skogo Filiala. Akademii Nauk SSSR [*A publication*]
TKB .... Kingsville, TX [*Location identifier*] [*FAA*] (FAAL)
TKBN......... Tank Battalion [*Marine Corps*]
TKBRAS.... Transactions. Korean Branch. Royal Asiatic Society [*A publication*]
TKCS .... Knoxville City Schools, Knoxville, TN [*Library symbol*] [*Library of Congress*] (LCLS)
TKD .... Takada [*Japan*] [*Seismograph station code, US Geological Survey*] (SEIS)
TKD .... Tokodynamometer
TKD .... Top Kit Drawing
TKDE......... Tetrakis(dimethylamino)ethylene [*Organic chemistry*]
TKE .... Tau Kappa Epsilon [*Fraternity*] [*Pronounced "Teke"*]
TKE .... Tenakee [*Alaska*] [*Airport symbol*] (OAG)
TKE .... Tenakee Springs, AK [*Location identifier*] [*FAA*] (FAAL)
TKE .... Total Kinetic Energy
TKE .... Track Angle Error
TKE .... Turbulent Kinetic Energy
TKEBH ...... East Tennessee Baptist Hospital, Knoxville, TN [*Library symbol*] [*Library of Congress*] (LCLS)
TKETHi ..... East Tennessee Historical Society, Knoxville, TN [*Library symbol*] [*Library of Congress*] (LCLS)
TKFN........ Telkwa Foundation Newsletter [*Telkwa, British Columbia*] [*A publication*]
TKFSM....... Fort Sanders Regional Medical Center, Knoxville, TN [*Library symbol*] [*Library of Congress*] (LCLS)
TKG.......... Bandar Lampung [*Indonesia*] [*Airport symbol*] (OAG)
TKG.......... Tanking (AAG)
TKG.......... Tokodynagraph
TKG.......... Tongkang [*Ship's rigging*] (ROG)
TKGA .... [*The*] Knitting Guild of America (EA)
TKGJA .... Taisei Kensetsu Gijutsu Kenkyusho-Ho [*A publication*]
TKGS .... Church of Jesus Christ of Latter-Day Saints, Genealogical Society Library, Knoxville Branch, Knoxville, TN [*Library symbol*] [*Library of Congress*] (LCLS)
TKH.......... Tikhaya Bay [*USSR*] [*Later, HIS*] [*Geomagnetic observatory code*]
TKi........... Kingsport Public Library, Kingsport, TN [*Library symbol*] [*Library of Congress*] (LCLS)
TKI .... McKinney, TX [*Location identifier*] [*FAA*] (FAAL)
TKI .... Trial Kit Installation (CAAL)
TKIF .... Training Name and Address Key Index File [*IRS*]
TKiH.......... Holston Valley Community Hospital, Health Science Library, Kingsport, TN [*Library symbol*] [*Library of Congress*] (LCLS)

TKimJ .... Johnson Bible College, Knoxville, TN [*Library symbol*] [*Library of Congress*] (LCLS)
TKIOY .... Tokio Marine & Fire Insurance Co. ADR [*NASDAQ symbol*] (NQ)
Tk J .... Tamkang Journal [*A publication*]
TKJ............. Tok, AK [*Location identifier*] [*FAA*] (FAAL)
TKK .... Token Kenkyu Kai [*An association*] (EA)
TKK .... Toyo Kogyo Co. [*Auto manufacturer*]
TKK .... Truk [*Caroline Islands*] [*Airport symbol*] (OAG)
TKKSA ...... Trudy Khar'kovskogo Sel'skokhozyaistvennogo Instituta [*A publication*]
TKKTA ...... Trudy po Khimii i Khimicheskoi Tekhnologii [*A publication*]
TKKTFSLB ... [*The*] Kandy-Kolored Tangerine-Flake Streamline Baby [*Title of book by Tom Wolfe*]
TKL .... Knoxville-Knox County Public Library, Knoxville, TN [*OCLC symbol*] (OCLC)
TKL .... Public Library of Knoxville and Knox County, Knoxville, TN [*Library symbol*] [*Library of Congress*] (LCLS)
TKL .... Tackle [*Mechanical engineering*]
TKL .... Taku Lodge, AK [*Location identifier*] [*FAA*] (FAAL)
TKL .... Tanker Oil & Gas [*Vancouver Stock Exchange symbol*]
TKL .... Tokelau Islands [*Three-letter standard code*] (CNC)
TKLaw....... Tennessee State Law Library, Knoxville, TN [*Library symbol*] [*Library of Congress*] (LCLS)
TKLMI .... Lakeshore Mental Health Institute, Staff Library, Knoxville, TN [*Library symbol*] [*Library of Congress*] (LCLS)
TKLN......... Toklan Oil Corp. [*NASDAQ symbol*] (NQ)
TKM .... Takamatsu [*Japan*] [*Seismograph station code, US Geological Survey*] (SEIS)
TKM .... TRIS, Potassium Chloride, Magnesium Chloride [*A buffer*]
TKMEB...... Theoretische und Klinische Medizin in Einzeldarstellungen [*A publication*]
TKN .... Tek-Net International Ltd. (Canada) [*Vancouver Stock Exchange symbol*]
TKN .... Tokuno Shima [*Japan*] [*Airport symbol*] (OAG)
TKN .... Total Kjeldahl Nitrogen [*Organic analysis*]
TKN.......... University of Tennessee, Knoxville, TN [*OCLC symbol*] (OCLC)
TKNGMP.... Tijdschrift van het Koninklijk Nederlandsch Genootschap voor Munt en Penningkunde [*A publication*]
TKO........... Mankato, KS [*Location identifier*] [*FAA*] (FAAL)
TKO........... Taseko Mines Ltd. [*Vancouver Stock Exchange symbol*]
TKO........... Technical Knockout [*Boxing*]
TKO........... Technische Kontrollorganisation
TKO........... To Keep Open [*Medicine*]
TKOF......... Takeoff [*Aviation*]
TKP........... Takapoto Island [*French Polynesia*] [*Airport symbol*] (OAG)
TKP........... Theta Kappa Phi [*Fraternity*]
TKP........... Ton-Kilometer Performed
TKP........... Trans Korea Pipeline
TKP........... Turkiye Komunist Partisi
TKPH......... Park West Hospital, Knoxville, TN [*Library symbol*] [*Library of Congress*] (LCLS)
TKP-ML...... People's Revolutionary Union - Marxist-Leninist [*Turkey*] (PD)
TKQ.......... Kigoma [*Tanzania*] [*Airport symbol*] (OAG)
TkR.......... [*Telephone*] Talker
TkR.......... Tamkang Review [*A publication*]
TKR .... Tanker (AAG)
TKR .... Terrestrial Kilometric Radiation [*NASA*]
TKR .... [*The*] Timken Co. [*Formerly, TDX*] [*NYSE symbol*]
TKR .... Total Knee Replacement [*Medicine*]
tkr.............. Turkmen Soviet Socialist Republic [*MARC country of publication code*] [*Library of Congress*] (LCCP)
TKrasPI...... Trudy Krasnodarskogo Gosudarstvennogo Pedagogiceskogo Instituta [*A publication*]
TKS .... Knoxville City School, Knoxville, TN [*OCLC symbol*] (OCLC)
TKS .... Tamavack Resources, Inc. [*Vancouver Stock Exchange symbol*]
TKS .... Thanks (ADA)
TKS .... Tokushima [*Japan*] [*Airport symbol*] (OAG)
TKS .... Tokushima [*Japan*] [*Seismograph station code, US Geological Survey*] (SEIS)
TKSBB ...... Tektonika Sibiri [*A publication*]
TK-SC .... Tennessee State Supreme Court Law Library, Knoxville, TN [*Library symbol*] [*Library of Congress*] [*Obsolete*] (LCLS)
TKSGA....... Trudy Koordinatsionnykh Soveshchanyi po Gidrotekhnike [*A publication*]
TKSGB....... Tektonika i Stratigrafiya [*A publication*]
TKSMC ...... Saint Mary's Medical Center, Medical Library, Knoxville, TN [*Library symbol*] [*Library of Congress*] (LCLS)
TKSMC-N ... Saint Mary's Medical Center, Nursing School Library, Knoxville, TN [*Library symbol*] [*Library of Congress*] (LCLS)
TKST.......... Tukisiviksat [*A publication*]
TK SUP ...... Track Supervisor (CAAL)
TKT .... Tashkent [*USSR*] [*Geomagnetic observatory code*]
TKT .... Ticker Tape Resources Ltd. [*Vancouver Stock Exchange symbol*]
TKT .... Ticket
TKTF .... Tanker Task Force
TKTRANSR ... Tank Transporter (AABC)
TKTS......... Thermodynamic Kelvin Temperature Scale

TKTU......... Thymidine Kinase (Activity) Transforming Unit [*Biochemistry*]
TKTVA ...... Tennessee Valley Authority, Knoxville, TN [*Library symbol*] [*Library of Congress*] (LCLS)
TKU .... Takayasuyama [*Japan*] [*Seismograph station code, US Geological Survey*] (SEIS)
TKU .... Turku [*Finland*] [*Airport symbol*] (OAG)
TKUAA ...... Trudy Kuibyshevskii Aviatsionnyi Institut [*A publication*]
TKutPI .... Trudy Kutaisskogo Gosudarstvennogo Pedagogiceskogo Instituta [*A publication*]
TKV .... Tatakoto [*French Polynesia*] [*Airport symbol*] (OAG)
TKW .... Thermal Kilowatts
TKX .... Kennett, MO [*Location identifier*] [*FAA*] (FAAL)
TKY .... Takayama [*Japan*] [*Seismograph station code, US Geological Survey*] (SEIS)
TKZRA ...... Taika Zairyo [*A publication*]
TL.............. Central African Republic [*Aircraft nationality and registration mark*] (FAAC)
TL.............. Lira [*Monetary unit in Turkey*]
TL.............. Reports of the Witwatersrand High Court [*Transvaal, South Africa*] (DLA)
TL.............. Tackline [*British naval signaling*]
T/L .... Tactical Landing
TL.............. Tail-Lift [*of trucks and vans*]
T/L .... Talk/Listen (NASA)
TL.............. Tank Lease (ADA)
TL.............. Tape Library (BUR)
TL.............. Target Language
TL.............. Task Leader (NRCH)
T/L .... Task List (KSC)
TL.............. Team Leader (AABC)
TL.............. Technical Letter
TL.............. Technical Library
TL.............. Telegraphist-Lieutenant [*Navy*] [*British*]
T-L............. Tennessee State Law Library, Nashville, TN [*Library symbol*] [*Library of Congress*] (LCLS)
TL.............. Termes de la Ley [*Terms of the Law*] [*Law French dictionary*] (DLA)
TL.............. Terminal Limen
TL.............. Test Laboratory (AFM)
TL.............. Test Link
TL.............. Test Load
TL.............. Test Log (IEEE)
TL.............. Testolactone [*Biochemistry*]
TL.............. Texas League [*Baseball*]
Tl............... Thallium [*Chemical element*]
TL.............. Theologisches Literaturblatt [*Leipzig*] [*A publication*]
TL.............. Theoretical Linguistics [*Berlin*] [*A publication*]
TL.............. Therapeutic Level [*Medicine*]
TL.............. Thermoluminescence [*Also, THL*]
TL.............. Thoreau Lyceum (EA)
T & L .... Thrift & Loans [*Industrial loan company*]
TL.............. Throws Left-Handed [*Baseball*]
TL.............. Thrust Level (NASA)
TL.............. Thrust Line
TL.............. Thymic Lymphoma [*Medicine*]
TL.............. Thymus-Derived Lymphocyte [*Hematology*]
TL.............. Thymus Leukemia [*Hematology*]
TL.............. Ticket of Leave (ADA)
TL.............. Tie Line [*Communication channel*]
TL.............. Time, Inc. [*NYSE symbol*]
TL.............. Time to Launch [*Navy*] (CAAL)
TL.............. Time Lengths
T-L............. Time-Life Books [*Publisher*]
TL.............. Time Limit
T/L .... Time Loan [*Banking*]
TL.............. Timeline (MCD)
TL.............. Title List
tl................ Tokelau Islands [*MARC country of publication code*] [*Library of Congress*] (LCCP)
TL.............. Ton Load
TL.............. Tools [*JETDS nomenclature*] [*Military*] (CET)
TL.............. Torpedo Lieutenant [*Navy*] [*British*]
TL.............. Torus Longitudinalis [*Anatomy*]
TL.............. Total
TL.............. Total Length
TL.............. Total Lipids [*Clinical chemistry*]
TL.............. Total Load [*Engineering*]
TL.............. Total Loss
TL.............. Total Luminescence [*Spectroscopy*]
TL.............. Tower of London
TL.............. Tracker Lock [*NASA*] (KSC)
TL.............. Trade-Last
T/L .... Training Literature
TL.............. Trans Mediterranean Airlines [*Lebanon*] [*ICAO designator*] (FAAC)
TL.............. Transaction Language
TL.............. Transaction Listing (AFM)
TL.............. Transfer Line [*Manufacturing technology*]
TL.............. Transient Load (MCD)
TL.............. Translocation Defect [*Medicine*]
TL.............. Transmission Level [*or Line*]

TL	Transmittal Letter (AAG)
TL	Transmitter Location
TL	Transport Loaded
T/L	Transporter/Launcher [NASA] (KSC)
T/L	Transporter/Loader (MCD)
TL	Trial
TL	Triple-Layer [Pharmacy]
TL	Triple Lindy [Dance step]
TL	Truck Lock (NRCH)
TL	Truckload
TL	Trybuna Literacka [A publication]
TL	Tubal Ligation [Medicine]
TL	Turkish Lira (BJA)
T²L	Transistor-Transistor Logic [Also, TTL]
TLA	A-A-A Air Enterprises, Inc. [Omaha, NE] [FAA designator] (FAAC)
TLA	Teller [Alaska] [Airport symbol] (OAG)
TLA	Teller, AK [Location identifier] [FAA] (FAAL)
TLA	Temporary Lodging Allowance [Military]
TLA	Terminal Low Altitude
TLA	Textile Labor Association [India]
TLA	Theatre Library Association (EA)
TLA	Time Line Analysis
TLa	Transition Layer
TLA	Translumbar Aortogram [Medicine]
TLA	Transmission Line Adapter [or Assembly]
TLA	Transportation Lawyers Association (EA)
TLA	Travel and Living Allowance [Military] (AABC)
TLA	Trunk Line Association
TLAB	Tellabs [NASDAQ symbol] (NQ)
TLAB	Translation Lookaside Buffer [Data processing] (CMD)
TLAC	Top Loading Air Cleaner (MCD)
TLACV	Track-Laying Air-Cushion Vehicle
TLAM	Tomahawk Land Attack Missile (MCD)
TLAM	Tony Lama Co. [NASDAQ symbol] (NQ)
TLAM-N	Tomahawk Land Attack Missile - Nuclear (MCD)
TLAP	Prace Komisji Jezykowej Polskiej Akademii Umiejetnosci. Travaux de la Commission Linguistique de l'Academie Polonaise des Sciences et des Lettres [A publication]
TLAS	Tactical Logical and Air Simulation
TLAT	TOW [Tube-Launched Optically Tracked Wire-Guided] Light Antitank Battalion (MCD)
TLB	Temporary Lighted Buoy [Maps and charts]
TLB	Texas-Louisiana Freight Bureau, St. Louis MO [STAC]
TLB	Theologisches Literaturblatt [A publication]
TLB	Time-Life Books
TLB	Tractor/Loader/Backhoe
TLB	Translation Lookaside Buffer [Data processing] (BUR)
TLBAA	Texas Longhorn Breeders Association of America (EA)
TL/BBC	Tax Limitation/Balanced Budget Coalition (EA)
TLBI	Theologisches Literaturblatt [A publication]
TLBR	Tactical LASER Beam Recorder (MCD)
TLC	[The] Learning Channel [Cable-television system]
TLC	Lee College, Cleveland, TN [OCLC symbol] (OCLC)
TLC	T Lymphocyte Clones [Immunology]
TLC	Tactical Leadership Course [Army] (INF)
TLC	Tangent Latitude Computer
TLC	Tank Landing Craft [Army] [British]
TLC	Task Level Controller
TLC	Tele-Link Communications, Inc. [Miami, FL] [Telecommunications service] (TSSD)
TLC	Telecommand (NASA)
TLC	Television Licensing Center (EA)
TLC	Tender Loving Care
TLC	Texas Lutheran College
TLC	Textile Laundry Council [Moorestown ,NJ] (EA)
TLC	Thin-Layer Chromatography [Analytical chemistry]
TLC	Tillicum Gold Mines [Vancouver Stock Exchange symbol]
TLC	Time-Lapse Cinematography
TLC	Time Line Controller
TLC	Tom's Love Connection [Ft. Smith, AR] [Tom Jones fan club] (EA)
TLC	Total Load Control (MCD)
TLC	Total Lung Capacity [Physiology]
TLC	Total Lung Compliance [Medicine]
TLC	Touch and Learn Computer
TLC	Transient Late Curvature [Orthopedics]
TLC	Translunar Coast [Aerospace]
TLC	Tri-County Library Council, Inc. [Library network]
TLC	Trilateral Commission [International study group]
TLC	Type and Learn Concept [Minolta Corp. office system]
TLCA	Tangent Latitude Computer Amplifier
TLCC	Thin-Line Communications Connectivity
TLC(C)	Trades and Labour Congress of Canada [1883-1956]
TLCE	Transmission Line Conditioning Equipment (MCD)
TLCF	Tactical Link Control Facility [Military] (CAAL)
TLCI	Tea Leaf Club International (EA)
TLCI	Tender-Loving Care Health Care Services [NASDAQ symbol] (NQ)
TLC/IR	Thin-Layer Chromatography/Infrared [Analytical chemistry]
TLCK	Tosyllysine Chloromethyl Ketone [Biochemistry]
T-LCL	T-Cell Lymphosarcoma Cell Leukemia [Oncology]
TLCO	Teleco Oilfield Service [NASDAQ symbol] (NQ)
TLCPC	Trunk Line-Central Passenger Committee
TLCR	Telecrafter Corp. [NASDAQ symbol] (NQ)
TLCT	Total Life Cycle Time
TL-CTR	Trunk Line-Central Territory Railroad Tariff Bureau
TLD	[The] Living Daylights [A publication]
TLD	Technical Logistics Data [Army] (AABC)
TLD	Thermoluminescent Device
TLD	Thermoluminescent Dosimeter [or Dosimetry]
TLD	Tiled [Classified advertising] (ADA)
TLD	Traffic Loading Device (CAAL)
TLDC	Taiwan Land Development Corporation
TLDF	Thomas Legal Defense Fund (EA)
TLDI	Technical Logistics Data and Information [Army] (AABC)
TLDIP	Technical Logistics Data Information Program
TLE	[The] Learning Exchange (EA)
TLE	Target Location Error (AABC)
TLE	Technical Liaison Engineer
TLE	Temperature-Limited Emission
TLE	Thin-Layer Electrophoresis [Analytical chemistry]
TLE	Thin Leading Edge
TLE	Total Erickson Resources Ltd. [Vancouver Stock Exchange symbol]
TLE	Total Lipid Extract [Biochemistry]
TLE	Toward Liberal Education [In book title]
TLE	Tower Lighting Equipment
TLE	Tracking Light Electronics (KSC)
TLE	Traffic Law Enforcement
TLE	Transferline Heat Exchanger [Chemical engineering]
TLE	Tulear [Madagascar] [Airport symbol] (OAG)
TLebC	Cumberland College of Tennessee, Lebanon, TN [Library symbol] [Library of Congress] (LCLS)
TLEICS	Treasury Law Enforcement Information and Communications System
TLEPA	Trudy Laboratorii Elektromagnitnykh Polei Radiochastot Instituta Gigieny Truda i Professional'nykh Zabolevanii Akademii Meditsinskikh Nauk SSSR [A publication]
T Letterkd ...	Tydskrif vir Letterkunde [A publication]
TLF	Temporary Loading Facilities (MCD)
TLF	Terminal Launch Facility
TLF	Textes Litteraires Francais [A publication]
TLF	Time Line Form
TLF	Trunk Link Frame [Telecommunications] (TEL)
TLFB	Texas-Louisiana Freight Bureau
TLFN	Tunison Laboratory of Fish Nutrition [Department of the Interior]
TLG	Tail Landing Gear
TLG	Talgar [Also, AAB] [Alma-Ata] [USSR] [Seismograph station code, US Geological Survey] (SEIS)
TLG	Telegraph (AAG)
TLG	Tentative Logistics Guidance (MCD)
TLG	Thin-Layer Gel [Filtration] [Analytical chemistry]
TLG	Tilting
TLGB	Tube-Launched Guided Projectiles (MCD)
TLH	Tallahassee [Florida] [Airport symbol] (OAG)
TLI	T-Logic, Incorporated [Princeton, NJ] [Information service] (EISS)
TLI	Telephone Line Interface (IEEE)
TLI	Theoretical Lethality Index (MCD)
TLI	Thymidine-Labeling Index [Oncology]
TLI	Time-Life International
tli	Tlingit [MARC language code] [Library of Congress] (LCCP)
TLI	Tolitoli [Indonesia] [Airport symbol] (OAG)
TLI	Total Lymphoid Irradiation
TLI	Translunar Injection [Aerospace]
TLI	True Life Institute [Altadena, CA] (EA)
TLIB	Tape Library [National Center for Atmospheric Research]
TLIB	Transportation Library [National Academy of Sciences] [Washington, DC] [Information service] (EISS)
TLIEF	Thin-Layer Isoelectric Focusing [Analytical chemistry]
TLIG	Tasmanian Legal Information Guide [A publication]
TLJ	Laredo Junior College, Laredo, TX [OCLC symbol] (OCLC)
TLJ	Tatalina [Alaska] [Airport symbol] (OAG)
TLJ	Tatalina, AK [Location identifier] [FAA] (FAAL)
TLJ	Travancore Law Journal [India] (DLA)
TLK	New York, NY [Location identifier] [FAA] (FAAL)
TLK	Talkeetna Mountains [Alaska] [Seismograph station code, US Geological Survey] (SEIS)
TLK	Talking [Telecommunications] (TEL)
TLK	Test Link (IEEE)
TLK	University of Tennessee, Law Library, Knoxville, TN [OCLC symbol] (OCLC)
T-LL	T-Cell Lymphoblastic Lymphoma [Oncology]
TLL	Tallinn [USSR] [Airport symbol] (OAG)
TLL	Tank Lighter
TLL	Television LASER Link
TLL	Tender Load List
TLL	Threshold Lactose Load [Clinical chemistry]
TLL	Tololo Astronomical Observatory [Chile] [Seismograph station code, US Geological Survey] (SEIS)

TLL............ Tom's Look of Love [Chicago, IL] [Tom Jones fan club]   (EA)
TLL............ Travaux de Linguistique et de Litterature [Strasbourg] [A publication]
TLLD .... Total Load
TLLM........ Temperature and Liquid Level Monitor   (NRCH)
TLLS .... Travaux de Linguistique et de Litterature (Strasbourg) [A publication]
TLLW........ Tank Lighter (Medium Tank-Well Type)
TLM........... Technical Liaison Memo
TLM........... Telemeter [or Telemetry]   (AAG)
TLM........... Tilimsen [Algeria] [Airport symbol]   (OAG)
TLM........... Toledo-Lucas County Public Library, Toledo, OH [OCLC symbol]   (OCLC)
TLM........... Tolmezzo [Italy] [Seismograph station code, US Geological Survey]   (SEIS)
TLM........... Transmission Line Method [Photovoltaic energy systems]
TLM........... Transmitted Light Microscope
TLM........... Trillium Telephone Systems, Inc. [Toronto Stock Exchange symbol]
TLM........... Tube-Launched Missile   (MCD)
TLMB .... Telemetry Data Buffer
TLMG........ Telemetering   (AAG)
TLMI......... Tag and Label Manufacturers Institute [Glenview, IL]   (EA)
TLMS .... Tape Library Management System
TLMT....... Telemation, Inc. [NASDAQ symbol]   (NQ)
TLMY .... Telemetry   (MSA)
TLN .... Talang [Sumatra] [Seismograph station code, US Geological Survey] [Closed]   (SEIS)
TLN .... Title plus Last Name
TLN .... Torque-Limiting Nut
TLN .... Toulon/Hyeres [France] [Airport symbol]   (OAG)
TLN .... Transmittal Locator Number [Data processing]
TLN .... Trunk Line Network
TLO .... [The] Last One [A microcomputer program manufactured by DJ-AI]
TLO .... [The] Lifestyles Organization [Buena Park, CA]   (EA)
TLO .... Technical Liaison Office [Military]
TLO .... Terminal Learning Objective
TLO .... Tol [Papua New Guinea] [Airport symbol]   (OAG)
TLO .... Toledo [Spain] [Seismograph station code, US Geological Survey]   (SEIS)
TLO .... Total Loss Only
TLO .... Tracking Local Oscillator
TLO .... Training Liaison Officer [Ministry of Agriculture, Fisheries, and Food] [British]
TLOBS ...... Tailored List of Base Spares [Military]   (AFIT)
TLOCC ...... Tomlinson Oil [NASDAQ symbol]   (NQ)
TLOP......... [The] Language of Poetry [A publication]
TLOS .... Tailored List of Spares [Military]   (AFIT)
TLOS........ Troop List for Operations and Supply
TLO(S)...... Turbine Lube Oil (System) [Nuclear energy]   (NRCH)
TLOST....... Turbine Lube Oil Storage Tank [Nuclear energy]   (NRCH)
TLP........... Tabular List of Parts   (AAG)
T/LP.......... Tail Lamp [Automotive engineering]
TLP........... Tapered Link Pin
TLP........... Target Letter Position [Psychology]
TLP........... Telegraph Line Pair   (BUR)
TLP........... Telephone Line Patch
TLP........... Tension-Leg Platform [Oil exploration]
TLP........... Term-Limit Pricing [Agreement] [Price Commission]
TLP........... Threshold Learning Process   (IEEE)
TLP........... Top Load Pad   (NRCH)
TLP........... Top Load Plane [Nuclear energy]   (NRCH)
TLP........... Torpedo Landplane [Navy]
TLP........... Total Language Processor [Data processing]   (IEEE)
TLP........... Total Loss of Pay [Court-martial sentence] [Military]
TLP........... Transient Lunar Phenomena
TLP........... Transmission Level Point [Telecommunications]
TLP........... Travaux Linguistiques de Prague [A publication]
TLP........... Trouble Location Problem   (AAG)
TLP........... Truck Loading Point   (NATG)
0TLP......... Zero Transmission Level Point   (IEEE)
TLPC......... Tailpiece
TLPJ......... Trial Lawyers for Public Justice   (EA)
TLPR........ Terrestrial Low-Power Reactor
TLQ .... Temple Law Quarterly [A publication]
TLR........... Tailor
TLR........... Tally Resources [Vancouver Stock Exchange symbol]
TLR........... Tanganyika Law Reports [1921-52]   (DLA)
TLR........... Tanzania Gazette Law Reports   (DLA)
TLR........... Tape Loop Recorder
TLR........... Tasmanian Law Reports [A publication]
TLR........... Telerate, Inc. [NYSE symbol]
TLR........... Teller
TLR........... Tiler [Freemasonry]
TLR........... Tiller   (MSA)
TLR........... Times Law Reports [1884-1952] [England]   (DLA)
TLR........... Toll Line Release
TLR........... Tool Liaison Request   (AAG)
TLR........... Top Level Requirements [Navy]
TLR........... Topped Long Resid [Petroleum technology]

TLR........... Trailer   (AAG)
TLR........... Travancore Law Reports [India]   (DLA)
TLR........... Triangulation-Listening-Ranging [SONAR]
TLR........... Tulane Law Review [A publication]
TLR........... Tulare, CA [Location identifier] [FAA]   (FAAL)
TLR........... Twin Lens Reflex [Camera]   (MCD)
TLRG........ Target List Review Group   (CINC)
TLRMTD.... Trailer Mounted
TLRNC ...... Tolerance   (FAAC)
TLRP........ Track Last Reference Position
TLR (R)...... Tanganyika Law Reports [Revised] [1921-52]   (DLA)
TLR/S........ Total Logistic Readiness/Sustainability Analysis [Military]
TLRS .... Transportable LASER Ranging Station [for measurement of earth movement]
TLRT .... Telerent Leasing Corp. [NASDAQ symbol]   (NQ)
TLRV .... Tracked Levitated Research Vehicle
TLS........... Laredo State University, Laredo, TX [OCLC symbol]   (OCLC)
TLS........... Tactical Landing System
TLS........... Talasea [New Britain] [Seismograph station code, US Geological Survey]   (SEIS)
TLS........... Tank LASER Sight   (MCD)
TLS........... Tape Librarian System
TLS........... Target Location System
TLS........... Technical Library Service   (EISS)
TLS........... Telecommunication Liaison Staff   (IEEE)
TLS........... Telemetry Listing Submodule
TLS........... Telescope   (KSC)
TLS........... Terminal Landing System   (KSC)
TLS........... Territorial Long Service Medal [Military] [British]
TLS........... Testing the Limits for Sex [Psychology]
TLS........... Theater Level Scenario [Military]
TLS........... Throttle Lever Setting   (KSC)
TLS........... Time Limited Signal
TLS........... Time Line Sheet
TLS........... Times Literary Supplement [London] [A publication]
TLS........... Top Level Side   (MCD)
TLS........... Top Level Specification [Military]   (CAAL)
TLS........... Total Library System [OCLC]
TLS........... Total Logic Solution
TLS........... Total Luminescence Spectroscopy
TLS........... Toulouse [France] [Airport symbol]   (OAG)
TLS........... Training Launch Station   (MCD)
TLS........... Typed Letter Signed
TLSA .... Torso Limb Suit Assembly   (MCD)
TLSA .... Transparent Line Sharing Adapter
TLSAP....... Wydawnictwa Slaskie Polskiej Akademii Umiejetnosci. Prace Jezykowe. Publications Silesiennes. Academie Polonaise des Sciences et des Lettres. Travaux Linguistiques [A publication]
TLSC........ Target Logistics Support Costs
TLSC........ TLS Company [NASDAQ symbol]   (NQ)
TLSCP....... Telescope   (MSA)
TLSD........ Torque-Limiting Screwdriver
TLSFT .... Tailshaft
TLSG........ Turret Lathe Stop Gauge
TLSGT....... Tactical Landing System Guidance Techniques   (MCD)
TLSO........ Thoracolumbosacral Orthosis [Medicine]
TLSP........ Telecommunications Specialists [NASDAQ symbol]   (NQ)
TLSP........ Transponder Location by Surface Positioning [RADAR]
TLSS .... Technical Library Services Section
TLT........... LeTourneau College, Longview, TX [OCLC symbol]   (OCLC)
TLT........... Teleprinter Load Tables   (KSC)
TLT........... Telstar Resource Corp. [Vancouver Stock Exchange symbol]
TLT........... Transportable Link Terminal [AMC]
TLT........... Travancore Law Times [India]   (DLA)
TLT........... Tuluksak [Alaska] [Airport symbol]   (OAG)
TLT........... Tuluksak, AK [Location identifier] [FAA]   (FAAL)
TLTA .... Thin Line Towed Array [Navy]   (CAAL)
TLTA .... Two-Loop Test Apparatus   (NRCH)
TLTB .... Trunk Line Tariff Bureau
TLTC .... Ta-Lu Tsa-Chih [Continent Magazine] [Taiwan] [A publication]
TLTK .... Teletek, Inc. [NASDAQ symbol]   (NQ)
TLTK .... Tool Truck
TLTM .... Third Level Thermal Margin [Nuclear energy]   (NRCH)
TLTP .... Too Long to Print [Strip marking] [Aviation]   (FAAC)
TLTP .... Trunk Line Test Panel [Telecommunications]   (TEL)
TLTR .... Translator   (AFM)
TLTS .... Tracking Loop Test Set
TLU .... Table Look Up [Data processing]
TLU .... Terminal Logic Unit [Telecommunications]   (TEL)
TLU .... Threshold Logic Unit
TLU .... Time of Last Update
TLU .... Tolu [Colombia] [Airport symbol]   (OAG)
TLU .... Transportable LASER Unit
TLU .... Tropical Livestock Unit [Ratio of livestock to humans]
TLV........... Talemon Investments Ltd. [Vancouver Stock Exchange symbol]
TLV........... Target Launch Vehicle [NASA]
TLV........... Tel Aviv-Yafo [Israel] [Airport symbol]   (OAG)
TLV........... Threshold Limit Value [Industrial hygiene]
TLV........... Total Lung Volume [Physiology]

TLV............ Track Levitated Vehicle [*Department of Transportation*]
TLv............ Transition Level
TLV............ Transporter - Loader Vehicle [*NASA*]   (NASA)
TLV............ Two-Lung Ventilation [*Medicine*]
TLW.......... [*The*] Lighted Way [*An association*]   (EA)
TLW.......... Test Load Wire
TLWD........ Tail Wind   (FAAC)
TLWM....... Trinity Low-Water Mark
TLWS........ Terrier Land Weapon System
T Lwyr........ Tax Lawyer [*A publication*]
TLX.......... TELEX [*Automated Teletypewriter Exchange Service*] [*Western Union Corp.*]
TLX............ Trans-Lux Corp. [*American Stock Exchange symbol*]
TLX............ Tri-Line Expressways [*Toronto Stock Exchange symbol*]
TLX............ Trophoblast/Lymphocyte Cross-Reactive (Antigens) [*Immunochemistry*]
TLXN.......... Telxon Corp. [*NASDAQ symbol*]   (NQ)
TLY............ Tally
TLZ............ Target Launch Zone
TLZ............ Theologische Literaturzeitung [*A publication*]
TLZ............ Titanium-Lead-Zinc
TLZ............ Transfer on Less than Zero
TM............ Linhas Aereas de Mocambique [*LAM*] [*Mozambique*] [*ICAO designator*]   (FAAC)
TM............ [*The*] Maccabees   (EA)
TM............ Memphis-Shelby County Public Library and Information Center, Memphis, TN [*Library symbol*] [*Library of Congress*]   (LCLS)
TM............ National Income Tax Magazine   (DLA)
TM............ T-Cell Marker [*Biochemistry*]
TM............ Tactical Manager [*Military*]   (CAAL)
TM............ Tactical Missile [*Air Force*]
TM............ Tactical Monitor
TM............ Tailor-Made   (DSUE)
TM............ Talking Machine
TM............ Tangent Mechanism
TM............ Tape Mark [*Data processing*]   (BUR)
TM............ Tape Module   (DEN)
TM............ Target Mechanism   (MCD)
TM............ Taurine Mustard [*Antineoplastic drug*]
TM............ Tax Magazine   (DLA)
TM............ Tax Management   (DLA)
TM............ Tax Memo   (DLA)
TM............ Tax Module [*IRS*]
TM............ Team   (AABC)
TM............ Team Member
TM............ Technical Manager
TM............ Technical Manual
TM............ Technical Memorandum
TM............ Technical Minutes
TM............ Technical Monograph
TM............ Tectorial Membrane [*of the cochlea*] [*Ear anatomy*]
TM............ Tele-Metropole, Inc. [*Toronto Stock Exchange symbol*]
TM............ Telegramme Multiple [*Telegram with Multiple Addresses*] [*French*]   (ROG)
TM............ Telemetry
TM............ Temperature, Mean
TM............ Temperature Meter
TM............ Temperature Monitor   (NRCH)
TM............ Temple Magazine [*A publication*]   (ROG)
TM............ Temple of Man [*Venice, CA*]   (EA)
T & M........ Temple and Mew's English Criminal Appeal Cases   (DLA)
T & M........ Temple and Mew's English Crown Cases [*1848-51*]   (DLA)
TM............ Temporomandibular [*Anatomy*]
TMS............ Temps Modernes [*A publication*]
TM............ Tennessee Musician [*A publication*]
TM............ Tenu'at Ha-Moshavim   (BJA)
TM............ Test Manual
TM............ Test Mode
TM............ Test Model [*NASA*]
T & M........ Test and Monitor   (CAAL)
TM............ Texas Mexican Railway Co. [*AAR code*]
TM............ Textus Minores [*A publication*]
TM............ Thalassemia Major [*Hematology*]
TM............ Thames Measurement [*Formula for rating yachts*] [*British*]
TM............ Theatre Magazine [*A publication*]
TM............ Their Majesties
TM............ Thematic Mapper [*Satellite technology*]
TM............ Thermal Mapper
TM............ Thompson Medical Co., Inc. [*NYSE symbol*]
Tm............ Thulium [*Chemical element*]
Tm............ Time [*A publication*]
TM............ Time Management   (MCD)
T & M........ Time and Materials
TM............ Time, Mission
TM............ Time Modulation
TM............ Time Monitor
TM............ Time Motion Technique
TM............ Timing of Movements [*Physiology*]
Tm............ Timothy [*New Testament book*]
TM............ Titanium Chloride [*Inorganic chemistry*]

TM............ Tlalocan: A Journal of Source Materials on the Native Cultures of Mexico [*A publication*]
TM............ Tobramycin [*An antibiotic*]
TM............ Ton-Miles
TM............ Tone Modulation
TM............ Tons per Minute
TM............ Top Man
TM............ Top Management
TM............ Torpedoman's Mate [*Navy rating*]
T/M............ Torque Meter   (NG)
TM............ Torque Motor
TM............ Tour du Monde [*World Tour*] [*French*]   (BJA)
TM............ Track Monitor   (CAAL)
TM............ Tractor Monoplane
TM............ Trade Mission
TM............ Trademark
TM............ Traffic Manager
TM............ Traffic Model   (NASA)
TM............ Trager's Medium [*Chemically defined culture medium*]
TM............ Train Master
TM............ Training Manual [*Military*]
TM............ Training Missions [*Air Force*]
TM............ Trainmaster [*Railroading*]
TM............ Transcendental Meditation
TM............ Transfer Memorandum
TM............ "Transitional" Mucosa [*Oncology*]
TM............ Transmedullary [*Anatomy*]
TM............ Transmetatarsal [*Anatomy*]
TM............ Transmission Matrix   (IEEE)
TM............ Transmittal Memorandum   (MCD)
TM............ Transport Mechanism [*Physiology*]
TM............ Transverse Magnetic
TM............ Travelwriter Marketletter [*New York, NY*] [*Information service*]   (EISS)
TM............ Trench Mortar
TM............ Trombone, Muted
TM............ Tropical Maritime
TM............ Tropical Medicine
TM............ Tropomyosin [*Biochemistry*]
TM............ True Mean
TM............ True Motion [*RADAR*]   (DEN)
TM............ Tuberal Magnocellular [*Nuclei, neuroanatomy*]
TM............ Tunicamycin [*Biochemistry*]
TM............ Tuning Meter   (DEN)
TM............ Turkiyat Mecmuasi [*A publication*]
TM............ Twisting Moment
TM............ Tygodnik Morski [*A publication*]
TM............ Tympanic Membrane [*Anatomy*]
TM1............ Torpedoman's Mate, First Class [*Navy rating*]
T/M²............ Metric Tons per Square Meter
TM2............ Torpedoman's Mate, Second Class [*Navy rating*]
T/M³............ Metric Tons per Cubic Meter
TM3............ Torpedoman's Mate, Third Class [*Navy rating*]
TMA .... Memphis Academy of Arts, Memphis, TN [*Library symbol*] [*Library of Congress*]   (LCLS)
TMA .... Memphis State University, Memphis, TN [*OCLC symbol*]   (OCLC)
TMA .... [*The*] Money Advocate [*A publication*]
TMA .... Taiwan Maintenance Agency [*Military*]   (AABC)
TMA .... Target Motion Analyzer
TMA .... Telecommunications Managers Association [*Orpington, England*]   (TSSD)
TMA .... Temperature Monitoring Apparatus
TMA .... Tennis Manufacturers Association [*North Palm Beach, FL*]   (EA)
TMA .... Terminal Control Area [*Aviation*]   (FAAC)
TMA .... Terminal Maneuvering Area [*Aviation*]
TMA .... Tetramethylammonium [*Organic chemistry*]
TMA .... Theatrical Mutual Association   (EA)
TMA .... Thermomagnetic Analysis [*Analytical chemistry*]
TMA .... Thermomechanical Analysis [*or Analyzer*]
TMA .... Thiomalic Acid [*Organic chemistry*]
TMA .... Thomas More Association   (EA)
TMA .... Thrombotic Microangiopathy [*Nephrology*]
TMA .... Thyroid Microsomal Antibody [*Immunology*]
TMA .... Tifton, GA [*Location identifier*] [*FAA*]   (FAAL)
TMA .... Tile Manufacturers Association   (EA)
TMA .... Time-Modulated Antenna
TMA .... Tobacco Mechanics' Association [*A union*] [*British*]
TMA .... Tobacco Merchants Association of the United States [*New York, NY*]   (EA)
TMA .... Toiletry Merchandisers Association [*Later, NASM*]   (EA)
TMA .... Tooling and Manufacturing Association [*Park Ridge, IL*]   (EA)
TMA .... Top Management Abstracts [*A publication*]
TMA .... Torpedo Main Assembly
TMA .... Total Maintenance Actions   (MCD)
TMA .... Total Materiel Assets [*Military*]
TMA .... Toy Manufacturers of America [*New York, NY*]   (EA)
TMA .... Traffic Management Agency   (CINC)
TMA .... Trailer Manufacturers Association [*Formerly, BTMA, OIA*] [*Later, NAMPS*]   (EA)

TMA	Trans-Mediterranean Airways (BJA)
TMA	Trans Mo Airlines [*Jefferson City, MO*] [*FAA designator*] (FAAC)
TMA	Transmetatarsal Amputation [*Medicine*]
TMA	Transport Museum Association (EA)
TMA	Transportation Management Association
TMA	Trimac Ltd. [*Toronto Stock Exchange symbol*] [*Vancouver Stock Exchange symbol*]
TMA	Trimellitic Anhydride [*Chemistry*]
TMA	Trimethylaluminum [*Organic chemistry*]
TMA	Trimethylamine [*Organic chemistry*]
TMA	Trimethylammonium [*Organic chemistry*]
TMaab	Thyroid Microsomal Autoantibody [*Immunology*]
TMAB	Telecommunications Managers Association - Belgium [*Brussels*] (TSSD)
TMAB	Temporary Missile Assembly Building (AAG)
TMAB	Tetramethylammonium Borohydride [*Organic chemistry*]
TMA BITS ...	TMA [*Tobacco Merchants Association*] Bibliographic Index to the Tobacco Scene [*Database*]
TMAC	Agrico Chemical Co., Memphis, TN [*Library symbol*] [*Library of Congress*] (LCLS)
TMAC	Telecommunication Management and Control [*AT & T*]
TMACS	Tone Multiplex Apollo Command System [*NASA*] (KSC)
TMACS	Training Management Control System [*Army*] (INF)
TMAD	Tank Main Armament Development (MCD)
TMAD	Target Marker Air Droppable (MCD)
TMAD	Target Marker and Dispenser (MCD)
TMadH	Nashville Memorial Hospital, Madison, TN [*Library symbol*] [*Library of Congress*] (LCLS)
TMadM	Madison Academy, Madison College, TN [*Library symbol*] [*Library of Congress*] (LCLS)
TMAE	Tetrakis(dimethylamino)ethylene [*Organic chemistry*]
TMAG	Travel More Advantageous to the Government (AAG)
TMAGD	Tennessee Magazine [*A publication*]
TMAH	Tetramethylammonium Hydroxide [*Organic chemistry*]
TMAI	Tetramethylammonium Iodide [*Organic chemistry*]
TMAIC	Trimethallyl Isocyanurate [*Organic chemistry*]
TMAO	Trimethylamine Oxide [*Organic chemistry*]
TMAO	Troop Movement Action Officer
TMAO	Troop Movement Assignment Order
TMAP	Temporary Mortgage Assistance Payments Program [*HUD*]
TMARS	Technical Manual Audit and Requirement Reporting System (MCD)
TMaryB	Blount Memorial Hospital, Medical Library, Maryville, TN [*Library symbol*] [*Library of Congress*] (LCLS)
TMaryC	Maryville College, Maryville, TN [*Library symbol*] [*Library of Congress*] (LCLS)
TMAS	Tank Main Armament Systems (RDA)
TMAS	Taylor Manifest Anxiety State [*Psychology*]
TMaU	University of Tennessee at Martin, Martin, TN [*Library symbol*] [*Library of Congress*] (LCLS)
TMAX	Maximum Time [*Telecommunications*] (TEL)
TMB	David W. Taylor Model Basin [*Also, DATMOBAS, DTMB*] [*Later, DTNSRDC, NSRDC*]
TMB	Miami, FL [*Location identifier*] [*FAA*] (FAAL)
TMB	Tambrands, Inc. [*NYSE symbol*]
TMB	Task Maintenance Burden
TMB	Tetramethylbenzidine [*Organic chemistry*]
TMB	Textes Mathematiques Babyloniens [*A publication*] (BJA)
TMB	Thimble
TMB	Tide-Measuring Buoy
TMB	Time Maintenance Began [*Military*] (AFIT)
TMB	Transportation Management Bulletin [*NASA*] (NASA)
TMB	Trimethoxyboroxine [*Organic chemistry*]
TMB	Trimethylbenzene [*Organic chemistry*]
TMB	Tumble (MSA)
TMB	University of Texas, Medical Branch Library, Galveston, TX [*OCLC symbol*] (OCLC)
TMBA	Brooks Art Gallery, Memphis, TN [*Library symbol*] [*Library of Congress*] (LCLS)
TMBA	Tetramethylene-bis-Acetamide [*Biochemistry*]
TMBA	Trimethylbenzanthracene [*Carcinogen*]
TMBAC	Trimethylbenzylammonium Chloride [*Also, BTM*] [*Organic chemistry*]
TMBC	Buckeye Cellulose Corp., Technical Division Library, Memphis, TN [*Library symbol*] [*Library of Congress*] (LCLS)
TMBDA	Tetramethylbutanediamine [*Organic chemistry*]
TMBDB	Thermal Margin beyond Design Basis [*Nuclear energy*] (NRCH)
TMBH	Baptist Memorial Hospital, Memphis, TN [*Library symbol*] [*Library of Congress*] (LCLS)
TMBH-N	Baptist Memorial Hospital, School of Nursing, Memphis, TN [*Library symbol*] [*Library of Congress*] (LCLS)
TMBL	Buckman Laboratories, Inc., Memphis, TN [*Library symbol*] [*Library of Congress*] (LCLS)
TMBL	Tacoma Municipal Belt Line Railway [*AAR code*]
TMBO	Team Management by Objectives [*Management technique*] (ADA)
TMBP	(Tetramethylbutyl)phenol [*Organic chemistry*]
TMBR	Timber (AAG)
TMBR	Tom Brown, Inc. [*NASDAQ symbol*] (NQ)

TM Bull	Trade Mark Bulletin, New Series (DLA)
TMC	Chief Torpedoman's Mate [*Navy rating*]
TMC	Houston Academy of Medicine for Texas Medical Center, Houston, TX [*OCLC symbol*] (OCLC)
TMC	Indo-Pacific International [*Tamuning, GU*] [*FAA designator*] (FAAC)
TMC	[*The*] Maintenance Council of the American Trucking Associations (EA)
TMC	[*The*] Movie Channel [*Cable-television system*]
TMC	Table Mountain [*California*] [*Seismograph station code, US Geological Survey*] [*Closed*] (SEIS)
TMC	Tactical Medical Center
TMC	Tambolaka [*Indonesia*] [*Airport symbol*] (OAG)
TMC	Tape Management Catalog
TMC	Telamarketing Communications, Inc. [*Louisville, KY*] [*Telecommunications*] (TSSD)
TMC	Telecommunications Management Corporation [*Dedham, MA*] (TSSD)
TMC	Telecommunications Marketing Corporation [*Bay Shore, NY*] (TSSD)
TMC	Temporary Minor Change (MCD)
TMC	Terrestrial Microcosm Chamber [*For environmental studies*]
TMC	Test, Monitor, and Control [*Aviation*]
TMC	Test Monitoring Console (NASA)
TMC	Thermal Micrometeoroid Cover (MCD)
TMC	Thick Molding Compound [*Plastics technology*]
TM-C	Thomas Micro-Catalogs
TMC	Three-Mode Control (AAG)
TMC	Thrust Magnitude Control (KSC)
TMC	[*The*] Times Mirror Company [*NYSE symbol*]
TMC	Titan Missile Contractor (AAG)
TMC	Tool Management Culture
TMC	Total Market Coverage [*Advertising*]
TMC	Transition Metal Chemistry [*A publication*]
TMC	Transmedia Enterprises, Inc. [*Vancouver Stock Exchange symbol*]
TMC	Transmission Maintenance Center [*Telecommunications*] (TEL)
TMC	Transport Movement Control [*Military*] (AFM)
TMC	Transportation Materiel Command [*AMC - Mobility*]
TMC	Triple Molecular Collision
TMC	Tube Moisture Control
TMCA	Thrust Management Control Analysis
TMCA	Titanium Metals Corporation of America
TMCA	Toxic Materials Control Activity [*General Motors Corp.*]
TMCBC	Christian Brothers College, Memphis, TN [*Library symbol*] [*Library of Congress*] (LCLS)
TMCC	Chapman Chemical Co., Memphis, TN [*Library symbol*] [*Library of Congress*] (LCLS)
TMCC	Theater Movement Control Center [*Military*] (AABC)
TMCC	Time-Multiplexer Communications Channels
TMCDT	Trimethylcyclododecatriene [*Organic chemistry*]
TMCF	Campbell Foundation, Memphis, TN [*Library symbol*] [*Library of Congress*] (LCLS)
TMCH	City of Memphis Hospital, Memphis, TN [*Library symbol*] [*Library of Congress*] (LCLS)
TMCHD	Transition Metal Chemistry [*A publication*]
TMCI	Telemetering Control Indicator
TMckB	Bethel College, McKenzie, TN [*Library symbol*] [*Library of Congress*] (LCLS)
TMckB-C ...	Cumberland Presbyterian Theological Seminary, Bethel College, McKenzie, TN [*Library symbol*] [*Library of Congress*] (LCLS)
TMCL	Target Map Coordinate Locator [*Military*]
TMCM	Master Chief Torpedoman's Mate [*Navy rating*]
TMCOMP ...	Telemetry Computation
TMCOT	Tetramethylcyclooctatetraene [*Organic chemistry*]
TMCP	Trimethylcyclopentanone [*Organic chemistry*]
TMCR	Technical Manual Contract Requirement
TMCRL	Tailored Master Cross Reference List (AABC)
TMCS	Memphis City Schools Professional Library, Memphis, TN [*Library symbol*] [*Library of Congress*] (LCLS)
TMCS	Senior Chief Torpedoman's Mate [*Navy rating*]
TMCS	Tactical Maintenance Control System
TMCS	Toshiba Minicomputer Complex System
TMCS	Trimethylchlorosilane [*Organic chemistry*]
TMD	Meharry Medical College, Nashville, TN [*OCLC symbol*] (OCLC)
TMD	Tactical Mission Data [*Military*] (AFM)
TMD	Tactical Munitions Dispenser (MCD)
TMD	Telemetered Data (AAG)
TMD	Temperature of Maximum Density
TMD	Tetramethyldioxetane [*Organic chemistry*]
TMD	Theoretical Maximum Density
TMD	Timed (MSA)
TMD	Toluene-Methanol-Dioxane [*Scintillation solvent*]
TMD	Transient Mass Distribution Code (NRCH)
TMDA	Telemedia Class A SV [*Toronto Stock Exchange symbol*]
TMDA	Training Media Distributors' Association (EA)
TMDAG	This Mode of Transportation has been Determined to be More Advantageous to the Government

TMDC......... Technical Manual Data Cards [*DoD*]   (MCD)
TMDC......... TIME-DC, Inc. [*NASDAQ symbol*]   (NQ)
TMDC......... Transportation Movement Document Control   (MCD)
TM & DE..... Test, Measuring, and Diagnostic Equipment [*Later, TMDE*] [*Army*]   (AABC)
TMDE........ Test, Measuring, and Diagnostic Equipment [*Formerly, TM & DE*] [*Army*]   (AABC)
TMDESG.... Test, Management, and Diagnostic Equipment Support Group [*Army*]   (MCD)
TMDI .... Transponder Miss Distance Indicator
TMDI .... Trimethylhexamethylene Diisocyanate [*Organic chemistry*]
TMDI .... United States Defense Industrial Plant Equipment Center, Memphis, TN [*Library symbol*] [*Library of Congress*]   (LCLS)
TMDL .... Technical Manual Data List [*DoD*]
TMDL .... Total Maximum Daily Load [*Environmental Protection Agency*]
TMDO .... Training Management Development Office [*Army*]
TMDP .... Technetium Methylene Diphosphonate [*Organic chemistry*]
TMDR .... Technical Manual Data Record [*DoD*]   (MCD)
TMDS .... Test, Measurement, and Diagnostic Systems [*Army*]   (RDA)
TMDS .... Tetramethyldisilazane [*Organic chemistry*]
TMDT .... Total Mean Downtime
TMDT .... Trace Metals Detection Technique
TMDT .... Trimethyldodecatetraene [*Organic chemistry*]
TME........... Eastwood Hospital, Memphis, TN [*Library symbol*] [*Library of Congress*]   (LCLS)
TME........... Tame [*Colombia*] [*Airport symbol*]   (OAG)
TME........... Teacher of Medical Electricity [*British*]
TME........... Termex Resources, Inc. [*Vancouver Stock Exchange symbol*]
TME........... Test Maintenance Equipment [*Data processing*]
TME........... Test Marketing Exemption [*Environmental Protection Agency*]
TME........... Test and Measurement Equipment   (MCD)
TME........... Tetramethylethylene [*Organic chemistry*]
TME........... Theatre Mask Ensemble
TME........... Thermal Marrow Expansion [*Roentgenology*]
TME........... Thermal/Mechanical Enzyme [*Fermentation*]
TME........... Thrust Monopropellant Engine
TME........... Torpedoman's Mate, Electrical [*Navy rating*]
TME........... Total Market Estimates [*ADA*]
TME........... Total Metabolizable Energy [*Nutrition*]
TME........... Transmissible Mink Encephalopathy
TME........... Transmural Enteritis [*Medicine*]
TME........... Trimethylolethane [*Organic chemistry*]
TMEA .... Typewriter Manufacturers Export Association [*Defunct*]
TMECO ..... Time of the Main Engine Cutoff   (MCD)
TMED .... Tetramethylethylenediamine [*Also, TEMED, TMEDA*] [*Organic chemistry*]
TMED .... Trimedyne, Inc. [*NASDAQ symbol*]   (NQ)
TMEDA...... Tetramethylethylenediamine [*Also, TEMED, TMED*] [*Organic chemistry*]
TMEDA...... Trimethylenediamine [*Organic chemistry*]
TME/FH ..... Total Maintenance Effort per Flight Hour [*Navy*]   (NG)
TMEL........ Tender Master Equipment List
TMEL........ Trimethylethyllead [*Organic chemistry*]
TM-ENG ..... Technical Manual - Engineering [*Marine Corps*]
TMeP......... Trimethylpsoralen [*Photochemotherapeutic compound*]
TMES .... Tactical Missile Electrical Simulator [*Obsolete*]
TMETN...... Trimethylolethane Trinitrate [*Organic chemistry*]
TMEV .... Theiler's Murine Encephalitis Virus
TMEXF ...... Terra Mines Ltd. [*NASDAQ symbol*]   (NQ)
TMF........... Technical Transmitter Holding Future   (MCD)
TMF........... Telemetry Module Facility
TMF........... Test Mode Fail [*Apollo*] [*NASA*]
TMF........... Time Marker Frequency
TMF........... Transaction Monitoring Facility [*Tandem Computers*]
TMF........... Transfer Mold Forming   (MCD)
TMF........... Transporter Maintenance Facility [*NASA*]   (NASA)
TMF........... Trunk Maintenance Files [*Telecommunications*]   (TEL)
TMFL........ Time of Flight   (MSA)
TMFZA ...... Teoreticheskaya i Matematicheskaya Fizika [*A publication*]
TMG .... Goodwyn Institute, Memphis, TN [*Library symbol*] [*Library of Congress*]   (LCLS)
TMG .... Tactical Missile Group [*Air Force*]
TMG .... Tetramethylguanidine [*Organic chemistry*]
TMG .... Thermal Meteoroid [*or Micrometeoroid*] Garment [*NASA*]   (KSC)
TMG .... Thermomagnetometry [*Analytical chemistry*]
TMG .... Thiomethylgalactoside [*Organic chemistry*]
TMG .... Time Mark Generator
TMG .... Timing
TMG .... Tomanggong [*Malaysia*] [*Airport symbol*]   (OAG)
TMG .... Track Made Good [*Aviation*]
TMG .... Trimethylguanosine [*Biochemistry*]
TMGC........ W. R. Grace & Co., Agricultural Chemicals Group, Memphis, TN [*Library symbol*] [*Library of Congress*]   (LCLS)
TMGD........ Timing Devices   (MSA)
TMGE .... Thermomagnetic-Galvanic Effect
TMGG........ Goldsmith Civic Garden Center, Memphis, TN [*Library symbol*] [*Library of Congress*]   (LCLS)
TMGRS ...... Trace Material Generation Rate Simulator

TMGS......... Church of Jesus Christ of Latter-Day Saints, Genealogical Society Library, Memphis Branch, Memphis, TN [*Library symbol*] [*Library of Congress*]   (LCLS)
TMGS......... Terrestrial Magnetic Guidance System [*Aerospace*]   (AAG)
TMH .... Harding Graduate School of Religion, Memphis, TN [*Library symbol*] [*Library of Congress*]   (LCLS)
TMH .... Tanahmerah [*Indonesia*] [*Airport symbol*]   (OAG)
TMH .... Texte und Materialien der Frau Professor Hilprecht Collection of Babylonian Antiquities im Eigentum der Universitaet Jena   (BJA)
TMH .... Tons per Man-Hour
TMH .... Trainable Mentally Handicapped
TMH .... Trolley Mounted Hoist   (NRCH)
TMHA .... Memphis Housing Authority, Memphis, TN [*Library symbol*] [*Library of Congress*]   (LCLS)
TMHA .... [*The*] Military Housing Association
TMHB .... Harland Bartholomew & Associates, Memphis, TN [*Library symbol*] [*Library of Congress*]   (LCLS)
TMHI .... Holiday Inns of America, Memphis, TN [*Library symbol*] [*Library of Congress*]   (LCLS)
TMHI-U....... Holiday Inn University, Olive Branch, MS [*Library symbol*] [*Library of Congress*]   (LCLS)
TMHL .... Triplet Metastable Helium Level
TMI .... International Harvester Co., Memphis, TN [*Library symbol*] [*Library of Congress*]   (LCLS)
TMI .... [*The*] Media Institute   (EA)
TMI .... Midwestern State University, George Moffett Library, Wichita Falls, TX [*OCLC symbol*]   (OCLC)
TMI .... [*The*] Monroe Institute [*Faber, VA*]   (EA)
TMI .... [*The*] Mortgage Index, Inc. [*Remote Computing Corp.*] [*Information service*]   (EISS)
TMI .... Taylor Mountain [*Idaho*] [*Seismograph station code, US Geological Survey*]   (SEIS)
TMI .... Team, Incorporated [*American Stock Exchange symbol*]
TMI .... Technical Manual Index [*Navy*]
TMI .... Teen Missions International [*Merritt Island, FL*]   (EA)
TMI .... Telecommunications Management, Incorporated [*Oakbrook, IL*] [*Telecommunications*]   (TSSD)
TmI .... Telematics International [*Palo Alto, CA*] [*Telecommunications service*]   (TSSD)
TMI .... Thornicroft's Mounted Infantry [*Military*] [*British*]   (ROG)
TMI .... Three Mile Island [*Pennsylvania*] [*Site of nuclear reactor accident, 1979*]
TMI .... Tolyl(mono)isocyanate [*Organic chemistry*]
TMI .... Tool Manufacturing Instruction   (AAG)
TMI .... Tracking Merit Interception
TMI .... Trans-Mars Injection [*Aerospace*]
TMI .... Transaction Management, Incorporated [*Lexington, MA*] [*Hardware manufacturer*]
TMI .... Transmural Myocardial Infarction [*Cardiology*]
TMI .... Travel Managers International   (EA)
TMI .... Trucking Management, Incorporated [*An association*] [*Washington, DC*]   (EA)
TMI .... Tumlingtar [*Nepal*] [*Airport symbol*]   (OAG)
TMI .... Tune-Up Manufacturers Institute [*Formerly, IMI*] [*Teaneck, NJ*]   (EA)
TMIA .... Three Mile Island Alert [*An association*]   (EA)
TMIC .... Thomas Marketing Information Center [*Thomas Publishing Co.*] [*New York, NY*] [*Information service*]   (EISS)
TMIC .... Toxic Materials Information Center [*Oak Ridge National Laboratory*]   (EISS)
TMICP .... Topographic Map Inventory Control Point [*Army*]   (AABC)
TMIEB .... Trudy Moskovskii Institut Elektronnogo Mashinostroeniya [*A publication*]
TMIF......... Tumor-Cell Migratory Inhibition Factor [*Immunology*]
TMIG .... [*The*] Marketing Information Guide [*A publication*]
TMIG .... Time in Grade [*Navy*]
TMiiM .... Milligan College, Milligan College, TN [*Library symbol*] [*Library of Congress*]   (LCLS)
TMIMIS ...... Technical Manual Integrated Management Information Systems [*DoD*]
TMIN .... Minimum Time [*Telecommunications*]   (TEL)
TMiNA .... United States Naval Air Station Library, Millington, TN [*Library symbol*] [*Library of Congress*]   (LCLS)
TMiNH .... United States Naval Hospital, Millington, TN [*Library symbol*] [*Library of Congress*]   (LCLS)
TMINS .... Technical Manual Identification Numbering System   (MCD)
TMINS .... Three Mile Island Nuclear Station   (NRCH)
TMIP.......... Training Management Instruction Packet
TMIS.......... Tank Management Information System   (MCD)
TMIS.......... Technical Meetings Information Service
TMIS.......... Total Management Information System
TMIU .... Teletype Modulator Interface Units   (MCD)
TMJ .... Temporomandibular Joint [*Medicine*]
TMJ .... Trade-Marks Journal [*A publication*]
TMJS.......... Temporomandibular Joint Syndrome [*Medicine*]
TMK .... Kimberly-Clark Corp., Memphis, TN [*Library symbol*] [*Library of Congress*]   (LCLS)
TMK .... Timiskaming [*Quebec*] [*Seismograph station code, US Geological Survey*] [*Closed*]   (SEIS)

TMK	Tiravita Munnerrat Kalam
TMK	Tomahawk Airways, Inc. [Alcoa, TN] [FAA designator] (FAAC)
TMK	Tomsk [USSR] [Geomagnetic observatory code]
TMK	Tonnage Mark [Found on each side of the ship aft]
TMK	Torchmark Corp. [NYSE symbol]
TMK	Transistor Mounting Kit
TMK	Trumark Resource Corp. [Vancouver Stock Exchange symbol]
TMKFA	Technische Mitteilungen Krupp. Forschungsberichte [A publication]
TMKT	Technology Marketing [NASDAQ symbol] (NQ)
TMKWA	Technische Mitteilungen Krupp. Werksberichte [A publication]
TML	Lakeside Hospital, Memphis, TN [Library symbol] [Library of Congress] (LCLS)
TML	Tamale [Ghana] [Airport symbol] (OAG)
TML	Tandem Matching Loss [Telecommunications] (TEL)
TML	Technical Manual List (MCD)
TML	Terminal (AABC)
TML	Terrestrial Microwave Link
TML	Tetramethyl Lead (MCD)
TML	Tetramethyllead [Organic chemistry]
TML	Texas Tech University, School of Medicine at Lubbock, Library of the Health Science, Lubbock, TX [OCLC symbol] (OCLC)
TML	Thermomechanical Loading
TML	Three-Mile Limit
TML	Titanium Metallurgical Laboratory (MCD)
TMLBC	Le Bonheur Children's Medical Center, Health Sciences Library, Memphis, TN [Library symbol] [Library of Congress] (LCLS)
TMLE	Transient-Mode Liquid Epitaxy
TMLG	Memphis Light, Gas, and Water Division Library, Memphis, TN [Library symbol] [Library of Congress] (LCLS)
TMLO	LeMoyne-Owen College, Memphis, TN [Library symbol] [Library of Congress] (LCLS)
TM/LP	Thermal Margin/Low Pressure (NRCH)
TMM	Memphis State University, Memphis, TN [Library symbol] [Library of Congress] (LCLS)
TMM	Tamatave [Madagascar] [Airport symbol] (OAG)
TMM	Tank Master Mechanic (MCD)
TMM	Tax Management Memorandum [Bureau of National Affairs] (DLA)
TMM	Technologico De Monterrey [Mexico] [Seismograph station code, US Geological Survey] (SEIS)
TMM	Test Message Monitor
TMM	Thermal Mathematical Model
TMM	Too Many Metaphors [Used in correcting manuscripts, etc.]
TMM	Trimethylenemethane [Organic chemistry]
TMM	Trimethylolmelamine [Organic chemistry]
TMMAB	Mid-America Baptist Theological Seminary, Memphis, TN [Library symbol] [Library of Congress] (LCLS)
TMM-B	Memphis State University, Bureau of Business Research Library, Memphis, TN [Library symbol] [Library of Congress] (LCLS)
TMMB	Truck Mixer Manufacturers Bureau [Silver Spring, MD] (EA)
TMMBC	Mid-South Bible College, Memphis, TN [Library symbol] [Library of Congress] (LCLS)
TMMC	Tetramethylammonium Manganese Chloride [Organic chemistry]
TMMC	Theater Materiel Management Center [Military] (AABC)
TMMD	Tactical Moving Mad Display (MCD)
TMM-E	Memphis State University, Engineering Library, Memphis, TN [Library symbol] [Library of Congress] (LCLS)
TMMEE	Memphis Eye and Ear Hospital, Memphis, TN [Library symbol] [Library of Congress] (LCLS)
TMMG	Teacher of Massage and Medical Gymnastics [British]
TMMH	Methodist Hospital, Stratton Medical Library, Memphis, TN [Library symbol] [Library of Congress] (LCLS)
TMMH-P	Methodist Hospital, Pathology Library, Memphis, TN [Library symbol] [Library of Congress] (LCLS)
TMM-L	Memphis State University, School of Law, Memphis, TN [Library symbol] [Library of Congress] (LCLS)
TMMM	Textes et Monuments Figures Relatifs aux Mysteres de Mithra [A publication] (BJA)
TMMP	Technical Manual Management Program [Navy] (NVT)
TMM-SH	Memphis State University, Speech and Hearing Center, Memphis, TN [Library symbol] [Library of Congress] (LCLS)
TMMT	Technical Manual Management Team [DoD]
TMN	Charlotte Amalie, St. Thomas, VI [Location identifier] [FAA] (FAAL)
TMN	Memphis and Shelby County Public Library and Information Center, Memphis, TN [OCLC symbol] (OCLC)
TMN	National Cotton Council of America, Memphis, TN [Library symbol] [Library of Congress] (LCLS)
TMN	Tamana [Kiribati] [Airport symbol] (OAG)
TMN	Technical and Management Note (IEEE)
TMN	Timber Mountain [Nevada] [Seismograph station code, US Geological Survey] (SEIS)
TMN	Transmission (AFM)
TMN	Trigeminal Mesencephalic Nucleus [Neuroanatomy]
TMNP	[The] Mystery Readers Newsletter [A publication]

TMo	O Tempo e o Modo [A publication]
TMO	Targets Management Office [MIRCOM] (RDA)
TMO	Telegraph Money Order
TMO	Thermo Electron Corp. [NYSE symbol]
TMO	Tool Manufacturing Order [NASA] (NASA)
TMO	Tooling Manufacturing Outline
TMO	Total Materiel Objective [Military]
TMO	Traffic Management Office [or Officer] [Air Force] (AFM)
TMO	Trans MO Airlines [Jefferson City, MO] [FAA designator] (FAAC)
TMO	Transportation Movements Office [or Officer]
TMO	Treminco Resources Ltd. [Vancouver Stock Exchange symbol]
TMO	Tumeremo [Venezuela] [Airport symbol] (OAG)
TMOD	TMDE [Test, Measuring, and Diagnostic Equipment] Modernization [Army] (RDA)
TMOR	Technical Manual Ordtask Requirement (MCD)
TMorM	Morristown College, Morristown, TN [Library symbol] [Library of Congress] (LCLS)
TMorNII	Trudy Mordovskogo Nauchno-Issledovatel'skogo Instituta Jazyka, Literatury, Istorii, i Ekonomiki [A publication]
TMorNR	Nolichucky Regional Library Center, Morristown, TN [Library symbol] [Library of Congress] (LCLS)
TMOS	Thermosetting (MSA)
T-MOS	Trench-Metal Oxide Silicon [Transistor]
TMOTFSM	[The] Master of the Free School, Margate [Pseudonym used by Zachariah Cozens]
TMP	[The] Madison Project (EA)
TMP	[The] Management Processor (MCD)
TMP	Tampere [Finland] [Airport symbol] (OAG)
TMP	Target Materials Program [DoD]
TMP	Technical Manual Parts [Army] (AABC)
TMP	Technical Manual Plan [DoD]
TMP	Teleprinter Message Pool
TMP	Temazepam [Tranquilizer]
TMP	Temperature (BUR)
Tmp	[The] Tempest [Shakespearean work]
TMP	Terminal Monitor Program [Data processing] (BUR)
TMP	Terminal Panel (NASA)
TMP	Test Maintenance Panel [Data processing]
TMP	Test Methods and Procedures
TMP	Theodolite Measuring Point (MUGU)
TMP	Thermal Mass Penalty (KSC)
TMP	Thermal Modeling Program
TMP	Thermomechanical Processing
TMP	Thermomechanical Pulps
TMP	Thermomicrophotometry
TMP	Thymidine Monophosphate [Biochemistry]
TMP	Thymolphthalein Monophosphate [Biochemistry]
TMP	Times Mirror Press
TMP	Total Milk Proteinate [Trademark of New Zealand Milk Products, Inc.]
TMP	Traditional Medical Practice
TMP	Trans Mountain Pipe Line Co. Ltd. [Toronto Stock Exchange symbol] [Vancouver Stock Exchange symbol]
TMP	Transistor Mounting Pad
TMP	Transmembrane Potential [Biochemistry]
TMP	Transportable Measurement Package (MCD)
TMP	Transportation Motor Pool [Military] (AABC)
TMP	Transversely Magnetized Plasma
TMP	Trimetaphosphate [Organic chemistry]
TMP	Trimethoprim [Also, T] [Antibacterial compound]
TMP	Trimethyl Phosphate [Organic chemistry]
TMP	Trimethylolpropane [Organic chemistry]
TMPA	Transocean Marine Paint Association [Rotterdam, Netherlands] (EA-IO)
TMPA	Trimethylphosphoramide [Organic chemistry]
TMPC	Memphis Planning Commission, Memphis, TN [Library symbol] [Library of Congress] (LCLS)
TMPD	Tempered (MSA)
TMPD	Tetramethyl-para-phenylenediamine [Analytical chemistry]
TMPD	Trimethylpentanediol [Organic chemistry]
TMPI	Plough, Inc., Memphis, TN [Library symbol] [Library of Congress] (LCLS)
TMPI	Target Material Production Instruction [Air Force]
TMPL	Templeton Energy [NASDAQ symbol] (NQ)
TMPN	Tetramethylpiperidinol N-oxyl [Organic chemistry]
TMPO	Total Materiel Procurement Objective [Military]
TMPO	Traffic Management and Proceedings Office [CONUS] (MCD)
TMPRG	Tempering
TMPRLY	Temporarily (MDG)
TMPROC	Telemetry Processing
TMPRY	Temporary (AFM)
TMPS	Temperature Monitoring Power Supply
TMPS	Test Maintenance Panel Subassembly [Data processing]
TMPS	Theater Mission Planning System [Military] (CAAL)
TMPS	Tracking Modifier Power Supply
TMPS	Trans-Mississippi Philatelic Society (EA)
TMPT	Tactical Marine Petroleum Terminal (MCD)
TMPTA	Trimethylolpropane Triacrylate [Organic chemistry]
TMPTMA	Trimethylol Propane Trimethacrylate [Organic chemistry]

TMPV .... Torque Motor Pilot Valve (NASA)
TMR .... Tactical Microwave Radio
TMR .... Tactical Missile Receiver
TMR .... Tamanrasset [*Algeria*] [*Airport symbol*] (OAG)
TMR .... Tandem Mirror Reactor (MCD)
TMR .... Technical Memorandum Report
TMR .... Technology Management Review [*Military*] (AFIT)
TMR .... Telemanagement Resources, Inc. [*Charlotte, NC*]
         [*Telecommunications*] (TSSD)
TMR .... Tetramethylrhodamine [*Fluorescent dye*]
TMR .... Thermistor Micropower Resistor
TMR .... Timber Management Research [*Department of Agriculture*]
TMR .... Time Meter Reading
TMR .... Timer (AAG)
TMR .... Tomakomai [*Japan*] [*Seismograph station code, US Geological
         Survey*] (SEIS)
TMR .... Topical Magnetic Resonance [*Medical diagnostic technique*]
TMR .... Total Materiel Requirement [*Military*] (AABC)
TMR .... Trade-Mark Reporter [*A publication*]
TMR .... Trainable Mentally Retarded
TMR .... Transportation Movements Release (AABC)
TMR .... Triple Modular Redundancy [*Data processing*]
TMR .... True Money Rate
TMRAO ..... Table Mountain Radio Astronomy Observatory
TMRBM ..... Transportable Medium-Range Ballistic Missile
TMRC .... Technical Maintenance Repair Center (MCD)
TMRC .... Theoretical Maximum Residue Contribution [*to acceptable
         daily intake*] [*Environmental Protection Agency*]
TMRD .... Transportation Movement Requirements Data (MCD)
TM Rec ...... Trade Mark Record [*United States*] (DLA)
TM Rep ...... Trade-Mark Reporter [*A publication*]
TMRI .... RAMCON, Inc., Environmental Engineering Library, Memphis,
         TN [*Library symbol*] [*Library of Congress*] (LCLS)
TMRI .... Tetramethylrhodamine Isothiocyanate [*Analytical
         biochemistry*]
TMRK .... Trade Marks [*Canada Systems Group*] [*Ottawa, ON*]
         [*Information service*] (EISS)
TMRKH ...... Tromura. Tromsoe Museum Rapportserie. Kulturhistorie [*A
         publication*]
TMRN .... [*The*] Mystery Readers Newsletter [*A publication*]
TMRNV ...... Tromura. Tromsoe Museum Rapportserie. Naturvitenskap [*A
         publication*]
TMRP .... Technology Mobilization and Reemployment Program
         [*Department of Labor*]
TMRS .... Traffic Measuring and Recording System
         [*Telecommunications*] (TEL)
TMRVDP .... Terminal-Modified RADAR Video Data Processor [*Noise
         control*]
TMS .... [*The*] Magnolia Society [*Hammond, LA*] (EA)
TMS .... [*The*] Manufacturing System [*Burroughs Machines Ltd.*]
         [*Software package*]
TMS .... [*The*] Masonry Society (EA)
TMS .... [*The*] Metallurgical Society [*Later, TMS-AIME*] (EA)
TMS .... Sao Tome Island [*Sao Tome Islands*] [*Airport symbol*] (OAG)
TMS .... Siena College, Memphis, TN [*Library symbol*] [*Library of
         Congress*] (LCLS)
TMS .... Southern Missionary College, Collegedale, TN [*OCLC
         symbol*] (OCLC)
TMS .... Tactical Missile Squadron [*Air Force*]
TMS .... Tape Management System (MCD)
TMS .... Target Marking System
TMS .... Target Materials Squadron (MCD)
TMS .... Technisonic [*Record label*]
TMS .... Technological Market Segmentation
TMS .... Telecommunications Message Switcher
TMS .... Telemetry Modulation System
TMS .... Telemetry Multiplex System
TMS .... Temperature Management Station
TMS .... Temperature Measurement Society
TMS .... Temsco Helicopters, Inc. [*Ketchikan, AK*] [*FAA
         designator*] (FAAC)
TMS .... Tesla Memorial Society (EA)
TMS .... Test Monitor System
TMS .... Test and Monitoring Station
TMS .... Tetramethoxysilane [*Organic chemistry*]
TMS .... Tetramethylsilane [*Organic chemistry*]
TMS .... Thallium Myocardial Scintigraphy [*Cardiology*]
TMS .... Thematic Mapper Simulator [*for aerial photography*]
TMS .... Thermomechanical System [*Instrumentation*]
TMS .... Thrust Measuring System
TMS .... Tight Model Series (MCD)
TMS .... Time and Motion Study (NG)
TMS .... Time Multiplexed Switching [*Telecommunications*]
TMS .... Time-Shared Monitor System [*Data processing*] (IEEE)
TMS .... Times Square Energy Resource Ltd. [*Vancouver Stock
         Exchange symbol*]
TMS .... Tissu Musculaire Specifique [*Medicine*] [*France*]
TMS .... Tlalocan: A Journal of Source Materials on the Native Cultures
         of Mexico [*A publication*]
TMS .... Tomisaki [*Mera*] [*Japan*] [*Seismograph station code, US
         Geological Survey*] [*Closed*] (SEIS)

TMS .... Top Management Simulation [*Game*]
TMS .... TOW Missile System (RDA)
TMS .... Toyota Motor Sales, Inc.
TMS .... Trademark Section, Official Gazette [*Federal government*]
TMS .... Trademark Society (EA)
TMS .... Traffic Measurement System
TMS .... Trainee Management System (MCD)
TMS .... Training Material Support
TMS .... Training Media Services
TMS .... [*The*] Tramway Museum Society [*British*]
TMS .... Transaction Management System (BUR)
TMS .... Transmatic Money Service
TMS .... Transmission Measuring Set [*Bell Laboratories*]
TMS .... Transport Management Survey (MCD)
TMS .... Transportation Management School [*Navy*]
TMS .... Transportation Management Services [*Salt Lake City, UT*]
         [*Software manufacturer*]
TMS .... Treasury Management Services [*British*]
TMS .... Trimethylsilyl [*Organic chemistry*]
TMS .... Turbine Management Station
TMS .... Turbulence Measuring System
TMS .... Type, Model, and Series
TMSA .... Technical Marketing Society of America [*Long Beach,
         CA*] (EA)
TMSA .... Telecommunications Marketing/Sales Association
         [*Defunct*] (EA)
TMSA .... Thomas More Society of America (EA)
TMSAA ..... Transactions. Metallurgical Society of AIME [*American Institute
         of Mining, Metallurgical, and Petroleum Engineers*] [*A
         publication*]
TMS-AIME ... [*The*] Metallurgical Society (EA)
TMSAN ...... Trimethylsilylacetonitrile [*Organic chemistry*]
TMSB .... Memphis and Shelby County Bar Association, Memphis, TN
         [*Library symbol*] [*Library of Congress*] (LCLS)
TMSC .... Southwestern at Memphis, Memphis, TN [*Library symbol*]
         [*Library of Congress*] (LCLS)
TMSC .... Talcott Mountain Science Center for Student Involvement, Inc.
         [*Avon, CT*] [*Telecommunications service*] (TSSD)
TMSCH ...... Memphis and Shelby County Health Department, Memphis, TN
         [*Library symbol*] [*Library of Congress*] (LCLS)
TMSCI .... Trimethylsilyl Chloride [*Organic chemistry*]
TMSCN ...... Trimethylsilylcyanide [*Organic chemistry*]
TMSCS ...... Memphis and Shelby County Safety Council, Memphis, TN
         [*Library symbol*] [*Library of Congress*] (LCLS)
TMSD .... Total Military Service to Date
TMSD .... Training Material Support Detachment [*Army*]
TMSDEA .... Trimethylsilyldiethylamine [*Organic chemistry*]
TMSIM ...... (Trimethylsilyl)imidazole [*Also, TSIM*] [*Organic chemistry*]
TMSM .... Shiloh Military Trail Library, Memphis, TN [*Library symbol*]
         [*Library of Congress*] (LCLS)
TMSM .... Trimethylstannylmaleate [*Organic chemistry*]
TMSMC ...... Semmes-Murphey Clinic, Memphis, TN [*Library symbol*]
         [*Library of Congress*] (LCLS)
TMSO .... Southern College of Optometry, Memphis, TN [*Library symbol*]
         [*Library of Congress*] (LCLS)
TMSR .... Technical Manual Status Report (MCD)
TMSS .... Shelby State Community College, Memphis, TN [*Library
         symbol*] [*Library of Congress*] (LCLS)
TMSS .... Technical Manual Specifications and Standards
         [*Military*] (AFIT)
TMSS .... Technical Munitions Safety Study [*Air Force*]
TMSS .... Tecmar Music Synthesis System
TMSS .... Towanda-Monroeton Shippers Lifeline, Inc. [*AAR code*]
TMStF .... Saint Francis Hospital, Medical Library, Memphis, TN [*Library
         symbol*] [*Library of Congress*] (LCLS)
TMStJ .... Saint Jude Children's Research Hospital, Memphis, TN [*Library
         symbol*] [*Library of Congress*] (LCLS)
TMStJo ...... Saint Joseph Hospital, Memphis, TN [*Library symbol*] [*Library
         of Congress*] (LCLS)
TMSVCS .... TOW [*Tube-Launched Optically Tracked Wire-Guided*] Missile
         Sight Video Camera System (MCD)
TMT .... Tactical Marine Terminal (MCD)
TMT .... Talcott Mountain [*Connecticut*] [*Seismograph station code, US
         Geological Survey*] [*Closed*] (SEIS)
TMT .... Temperature (MDG)
TMT .... Terminal Monitor Program [*Data processing*] (MDG)
TMT .... Testing Methods and Techniques [*Telecommunications*] (TEL)
TMT .... Tetramethylthiourea [*Also, TMTU*] [*Organic chemistry*]
TMT .... Thermal Measurement Treatment
TMT .... Thermomechanical Treatment
TMT .... Tire Management Terminal [*Automotive engineering*]
TMT .... Total Maintenance Time (MCD)
TMT .... TOW [*Tube-Launched Optically Tracked Wire-Guided*] Missile
         Transporter (MCD)
TMT .... Trans Midwest Airlines, Inc. [*Columbus, GA*] [*FAA
         designator*] (FAAC)
TMT .... Transmit (FAAC)
TMT .... Transonic Model Tunnel [*NASA*]
TMT .... Transportation Motor Transport [*Military*] (AABC)
TMT .... Treatment [*Medicine*]
TMT .... Troy Mineral & Tech [*Vancouver Stock Exchange symbol*]

TMT............	Turret Maintenance Trainer (MCD)
TMTBL........	Transmittable (FAAC)
TMTC.........	Thru-Mode [*or Tri-Mode*] Tape Converter
TMTD.........	Tetramethylthiuram Disulfide [*Also, THTMS, TMTDS*] [*Organic chemistry*]
TMTD.........	Transmitted (FAAC)
TMTDS........	Tetramethylthiuram Disulfide [*Also, TMTD, THTMS*] [*Organic chemistry*]
TMTF..........	Tile, Marble, and Terrazzo Finishers and Shopmen International Union
TMTG.........	Transmitting (FAAC)
TMTI..........	State Technical Institute at Memphis, Memphis, TN [*Library symbol*] [*Library of Congress*] (LCLS)
TMTN.........	Transmission (FAAC)
TMTNO.......	No Transmitting Capability (FAAC)
TMTP.........	Tennessee Psychiatric Hospital and Institute, Memphis, TN [*Library symbol*] [*Library of Congress*] (LCLS)
TMTR.........	Thermistor (AAG)
TMTR.........	Transmitter
TMTS.........	Memphis Theological Seminary of the Cumberland Presbyterian Church, Memphis, TN [*Library symbol*] [*Library of Congress*] (LCLS)
TMTS.........	Transmits (FAAC)
TMTSF........	Tetramethyltetraselenafulvene [*Organic chemistry*]
TMTU.........	Tetramethylthiourea [*Also, TMT*] [*Organic chemistry*]
TMTX.........	Temtex Industries [*NASDAQ symbol*] (NQ)
TMU...........	Groton, CT [*Location identifier*] [*FAA*] (FAAL)
TMU...........	Tactical Mobile Unit [*Police*]
TMU...........	Temperature Measurement Unit (NASA)
TMU...........	Temuco [*Chile*] [*Seismograph station code, US Geological Survey*] (SEIS)
TMU...........	Test Maintenance Unit [*Data processing*]
TMU...........	Tetramethylurea [*Organic chemistry*]
TMU...........	Thermal-Mechanical Unit
TMU...........	Time Measurement Unit [*Basic MTM unit*]
TMU...........	Transmission Message Unit
TMU...........	Turret Mock-Up (MCD)
TMUP.........	Union Planters National Bank, Memphis, TN [*Library symbol*] [*Library of Congress*] (LCLS)
TMurH........	Highland Rim Regional Library Center, Murfreesboro, TN [*Library symbol*] [*Library of Congress*] (LCLS)
TMurS........	Middle Tennessee State University, Murfreesboro, TN [*Library symbol*] [*Library of Congress*] (LCLS)
TMUS.........	Temporarily Mounted User Set [*Data processing*] (ADA)
TMUS.........	Toy Manufacturers of the United States
TMUSAE.....	United States Army Engineers Library, Memphis, TN [*Library symbol*] [*Library of Congress*] (LCLS)
TMUSDC.....	United States Department of Commerce, Memphis, TN [*Library symbol*] [*Library of Congress*] (LCLS)
TMV...........	Tanker Motor Vessel
TMV...........	Texas A & M University, Medical Sciences Library, College Station, TX [*OCLC symbol*] (OCLC)
TMV...........	Tobacco Mosaic Virus
TMV...........	Todd Memorial Volumes [*A publication*]
TMV...........	Torpedoman's Mate, Aviation [*Navy rating*]
TMV...........	True Mean Value
TMV...........	United States Veterans Administration Hospital, Memphis, TN [*Library symbol*] [*Library of Congress*] (LCLS)
TMVP.........	Tobacco Mosaic Virus Protein
TMVS.........	Times Mirror Videotex Services, Inc. [*Information service*] [*Inactive*] (EISS)
TMW..........	Tactical Missile Wing [*Air Force*]
TMW..........	Tamworth [*Australia*] [*Airport symbol*] (OAG)
TMW..........	Thermal Megawatt [*Also, Mwt*]
TMW..........	Tomorrow (FAAC)
TMW..........	Toyota Motor Workers' Union
TMW..........	Transverse Magnetic Wave [*Radio*]
TMWR........	Technical Manual Work Requirement (MCD)
TMX..........	Tandem Mirror Experiment [*Atomic fusion*]
TMX..........	Telemeter Transmitter
TMXDI........	Tetramethylxylene Diisocyanate [*Organic chemistry*]
TMXO........	Tactical Miniature Crystal Oscillator
TMXRT.......	Three-Mirror X-Ray Telescope [*NASA*]
TMZ..........	Houston, TX [*Location identifier*] [*FAA*] (FAAL)
TN.............	Congo (Brazzaville) [*Aircraft nationality and registration mark*] (FAAC)
TN.............	Public Library of Nashville and Davidson County, Nashville, TN [*Library symbol*] [*Library of Congress*] (LCLS)
TN.............	Stewardsman [*Nonrated enlisted man*] [*Navy*]
TN.............	Tagesarbeitsnormen [*Workday Standards*] [*German*]
T/N............	Tar and Nicotine [*In cigarettes*]
TN.............	Tariff Number
TN.............	Taunton [*British depot code*]
TN.............	Team Nursing
TN.............	Technical Note
TN.............	Technology Needs (MCD)
TN.............	Telephone (NATG)
TN.............	Telephone Number
TN.............	Tell en-Nasbeh (BJA)
TN.............	Temperature Normal [*Medicine*]
TN.............	Temple Name (BJA)

TN.............	Tennessee [*Postal code*]
TN.............	Tennessee Reports (DLA)
TN.............	Terminal Node
TN.............	Test Narrative (CAAL)
TN.............	Test Negative [*Clinical chemistry*]
TN.............	Test Number (AAG)
TN.............	Texas & Northern Railway Co. [*AAR code*]
TN.............	Theatre Notebook [*A publication*]
TN.............	Thermonuclear
TN.............	Tin
tn.............	Titanite [*CIPW classification*] [*Geology*]
TN.............	Title News [*A publication*]
TN.............	Ton
TN.............	Tone (MSA)
TN.............	Top of the News [*A publication*]
TN.............	Total Nitrogen [*Analytical chemistry*]
TN.............	Town
TN.............	Track Number
TN.............	Trade Name (DEN)
TN.............	Train (AAG)
TN.............	Trans-Australia Airlines [*ICAO designator*] (FAAC)
TN.............	Transfer on Negative
TN.............	Translator's Note
TN.............	Transport
TN.............	Transportation
TN.............	Transverse Nerve [*Neuroanatomy*]
TN.............	Travel News [*A publication*]
TN.............	Triafol
TN.............	Troponin [*Biochemistry*]
T/N............	True Name
TN.............	True Negative [*Medicine*]
TN.............	True North
Tn.............	Tukulti-Ninurta (BJA)
TN.............	Tuning Units [*JETDS nomenclature*] [*Military*] (CET)
TN.............	Tunisia [*Two-letter standard code*] (CNC)
TN.............	Twelfth Night [*Shakespearean work*]
TN.............	Twisted Nematic [*Telecommunications*] (TEL)
TN²............	[*The*] News Is the News [*Television comedy program*]
TNA...........	Jinan [*China*] [*Airport symbol*] (OAG)
TNA...........	[*The*] National Alliance of Professional and Executive Women's Networks [*Later, TIA*] (EA)
TNA...........	[*The*] National Archives [*of the United States*]
TNA...........	Telocator Network of America [*Washington, DC*] (EA)
TN A..........	Tennessee Appeals Reports (DLA)
TNA...........	Tetranitroadamantane [*Explosive*] [*Organic chemistry*]
TNA...........	Tetranitroaniline [*Organic chemistry*]
TNA...........	Thomas Nelson - Australia [*Publisher*]
TNA...........	Tidsskrift foer Norron Arkeologi [*A publication*]
Tna...........	Tigrinya (BJA)
TNA...........	Time of Nearest Approach
TNA...........	Tin City [*Alaska*] [*Seismograph station code, US Geological Survey*] (SEIS)
TNA...........	Total Nucleic Acid
TNA...........	Trans National Airlines [*South San Francisco, CA*] [*FAA designator*] (FAAC)
TNA...........	Transient Network Analyzer (IEEE)
TNA...........	Trinitroaniline [*Organic chemistry*]
TNA...........	Tropicana Resources Ltd. [*Vancouver Stock Exchange symbol*]
TNAE.........	United States Army Engineer District, Nashville, Nashville, TN [*Library symbol*] [*Library of Congress*] (LCLS)
TNAEA.......	Teplovye Napryazheniya v Elementakh Konstruksii [*A publication*]
TNAF.........	Training Name and Address File [*IRS*]
TNAM........	Theater Network Analysis Model [*Europe*] (MCD)
TNAN........	Texas Numismatic Association. News [*A publication*]
TNB..........	[*The*] New Brood
TNB..........	Tanabu [*Japan*] [*Seismograph station code, US Geological Survey*] [*Closed*] (SEIS)
TNB..........	Technical News Bulletin [*National Bureau of Standards*]
TNB..........	Technion News Bulletin [*Haifa*] [*A publication*] (BJA)
TNB..........	Thio(nitro)benzoic Acid [*Analytical biochemistry*]
TNB..........	Thomas & Betts Corp. [*NYSE symbol*]
TNB..........	Trinitrobenzene [*Explosive*]
TNBA.........	Tri-normal-butylamine [*Organic chemistry*]
TNBe.........	Belmont College, Nashville, TN [*Library symbol*] [*Library of Congress*] (LCLS)
TNBH.........	Baptist Hospital, Medical Library, Nashville, TN [*Library symbol*] [*Library of Congress*] (LCLS)
TNBMD......	Bureau of Mines. Technology News [*United States*] [*A publication*]
TNBS.........	Trinitrobenzenesulfonic Acid [*Biochemistry*]
TNBT.........	American Baptist Theological Seminary, Nashville, TN [*Library symbol*] [*Library of Congress*] (LCLS)
TNBT.........	Tetranitro Blue Tetrazolium [*A dye*] [*Organic chemistry*]
TNC..........	Country Music Foundation Library and Media Center, Nashville, TN [*Library symbol*] [*Library of Congress*] (LCLS)
TNC..........	[*The*] National Crossbowmen [*An association*] (EA)
TNC..........	[*The*] Nature Conservancy [*Arlington, VA*] [*An association*]
TNC..........	Tail Number Change [*Air Force*] (AFIT)

TNC............ Tekniska Nomenklaturcentralen [*Swedish Center for Technical Terminology*] [*Stockholm, Sweden*] [*Information service*] (EISS)
TNC............ Terminal Network Controller
TNC............ Texas Nuclear Corporation (KSC)
TNC............ Theater Naval Commander
TNC............ Thymic Nurse Cell [*Cytology*]
TNC............ Tide Net Controller (NATG)
TNC............ Tin City [*Alaska*] [*Airport symbol*] (OAG)
TNC............ Tin City, AK [*Location identifier*] [*FAA*] (FAAL)
TNC............ Too Numerous to Count
TNC............ Track Navigation Computer
TNC............ Track No Conversion
TNC............ Trans-National Communications, Inc.
TNC............ Transnational Corporation
TNC............ Transport Network Controller
TNC............ Trevecca Nazarene College [*Tennessee*]
TNC............ Trinitrocellulose [*Organic chemistry*]
TNC............ Trionics Technology Ltd. [*Vancouver Stock Exchange symbol*]
TNC............ Tripartite Naval Commission [*Allied German Occupation Forces*]
TnC .... Troponin C [*Biochemistry*]
TNCA .... Thionaphthenecarboxylic Acid [*Organic chemistry*]
TNCC .... Tripartite Nuclear Cross-Sections Committee [*British, Canadian, and US*]
TNCD .... Ten Nation Committee on Disarmament [*Defunct, 1960*]
TNCL .... Tail Number Configuration List [*Navy*] (NG)
TN Cr........ Tennessee Criminal Appeals Reports (DLA)
TNCSS...... Temporary National Commission on Supplies and Shortages [*Initiated 1974*]
TND .... Technodyne, Inc. [*American Stock Exchange symbol*]
TND............ Tinned
TND .... Todwind Development Corp. [*Vancouver Stock Exchange symbol*]
TND .... Trade Names Dictionary [*A publication*]
TND............ Turned (AAG)
TNDC .... Disciples of Christ Historical Society, Nashville, TN [*Library symbol*] [*Library of Congress*] (LCLS)
TNDC .... Thai National Documentation Center (EISS)
TNDCY...... Tendency (FAAC)
TNDM........ Tandem Computers [*NASDAQ symbol*] (NQ)
TNDNA...... Tokyo Nogyo Daigaku Nogaku Shuho [*A publication*]
TNDP......... Tetranitrodiphenyl [*Organic chemistry*]
TNDS......... Tactical Navigational Display System
TNDS......... Total Network Data System [*Bell System*]
TNDSA...... Trends [*A publication*]
TNDZR...... Tenderizer
TNE ... Tanegashima [*Japan*] [*Airport symbol*] (OAG)
TNE .... Terra Nova Energy [*Vancouver Stock Exchange symbol*]
TNE .... TRIS, Sodium Chloride, EDTA [*A buffer*]
TNEC......... Temporary National Economic Committee [*Congressional committee which studied the American economic system*] [*World War II*]
TNEF .... Trinitroethyl Formal [*An explosive*]
TNEL .... Nelson [*Thomas*], Inc. [*NASDAQ symbol*] (NQ)
TNEOC...... Trinitroethyl Orthocarbonate [*An explosive*]
TNEOF...... Trinitroethyl Orthoformate [*An explosive*]
TNET......... American Telnet Corp. [*NASDAQ symbol*] (NQ)
TNF .... Fisk University, Nashville, TN [*Library symbol*] [*Library of Congress*] (LCLS)
TNF .... Tactical Nuclear Force (MCD)
TNF .... Theater Nuclear Forces
TNF .... Thin Nickel Film
TNF .... Third Normal Form [*Databases*]
TNF .... Timing Negative Film
TNF .... Trainfire
TNF .... Transfer on No Overflow
TNF .... Trinitrofluorenone [*Organic chemistry*]
TNF .... Tumor Necrosis Factor [*Antineoplastic drug*]
TNFB.......... Free-Will Baptist Bible College, Nashville, TN [*Library symbol*] [*Library of Congress*] (LCLS)
TNFS .... Theater Nuclear Forces Survivability (MCD)
TNFSS....... Theater Nuclear Forces Survivability and Security (MCD)
TNG............ [*The*] Newspaper Guild [*Formerly, ANG*]
TNG............ Tanger [*Morocco*] [*Airport symbol*] (OAG)
TNG............ Tangerang [*Java*] [*Seismograph station code, US Geological Survey*] (SEIS)
TNG............ Tangerang [*Java*] [*Geomagnetic observatory code*]
TNG............ Tongue (MSA)
TNG............ Training (AAG)
TNG............ Transdermal Nitroglycerine Patch [*Pharmacology*]
TNG............ Tungco Resources Corp. [*Vancouver Stock Exchange symbol*]
TNGANCH .. Training Anchorage [*Navy*] (NVT)
TNGE .... Tonnage [*Shipping*]
TNGLIT ...... Training Literature
TNGSUP..... Training Support [*Navy*] (NVT)
TNGSVCS ... Training Services [*Navy*] (NVT)
TNGT......... Tonight (FAAC)
TNH .... Tampa-Hillsborough County Public Library, Tampa, FL [*OCLC symbol*] (OCLC)

TNH .... Tienshui [*Republic of China*] [*Seismograph station code, US Geological Survey*] (SEIS)
TNHCA....... Hospital Corp. of America, Research/Information Services, Nashville, TN [*Library symbol*] [*Library of Congress*] (LCLS)
TNHCA...... Taehan Naekwa Hakhoe Chapchi [*A publication*]
TNHQ .... Theater Navy Headquarters
TNI .... [*The*] Networking Institute [*Commercial firm*] [*West Newton, MA*] (EA)
TNI .... Peipeinimaru, TT [*Location identifier*] [*FAA*] (FAAL)
TNI .... Thin Nickel Iron
TNI .... Total Nodal Irradiation [*Oncology*]
TNI .... Traffic Noise Index [*Department of Transportation*]
TnI............. Troponin I [*Biochemistry*]
TNIA........... [*The*] Network Incorporated of America [*Milwaukee, WI*] [*Information service*] (EISS)
TNIF .... Thin Nickel Iron Film
TNizam ...... Trudy Instituta Literatury i Jazyka Imeni Nizami [*A publication*]
TNJ............ Joint University Libraries, Nashville, TN [*Library symbol*] [*Library of Congress*] (LCLS)
TNJ............ Tanjung Pinang [*Indonesia*] [*Airport symbol*] (OAG)
TNJ-L .... Joint University Libraries, Vanderbilt School of Law, Nashville, TN [*Library symbol*] [*Library of Congress*] (LCLS)
TNJ-M .... Joint University Libraries, Vanderbilt Medical Center, Nashville, TN [*Library symbol*] [*Library of Congress*] (LCLS)
TNJ-P .... Joint University Libraries, George Peabody College for Teachers, Nashville, TN [*Library symbol*] [*Library of Congress*] (LCLS)
TNJ-R .... Joint University Libraries, Vanderbilt School of Religion, Nashville, TN [*Library symbol*] [*Library of Congress*] (LCLS)
TNJ-S .... Joint University Libraries, Scarritt College for Christian Workers, Nashville, TN [*Library symbol*] [*Library of Congress*] (LCLS)
TNK .... Tank (AAG)
TNK .... Tinkers Knob [*California*] [*Seismograph station code, US Geological Survey*] (SEIS)
TNK .... Tunkwa Copper Mining [*Vancouver Stock Exchange symbol*]
TNK .... Tununak [*Alaska*] [*Airport symbol*] (OAG)
TNK .... [*The*] Two Noble Kinsmen [*Shakespearean work*]
TNKPB .... Trudy Nauchno-Issledovatel'skogo Instituta Kraevoi Patologii [*Alma-Ata*] [*A publication*]
TNKR.......... Tanker (FAAC)
TNKUL .... Towarzystwo Naukowe Katolickiego Univwersytet Lubelskiego [*A publication*]
TNKULWP ... Towarzystwo Naukowe Katolickiego Uniwersytetu Lubelskiego. Wyklady i Przemowienia [*Lublin*] [*A publication*]
TNL .... David Lipscomb College, Nashville, TN [*Library symbol*] [*Library of Congress*] (LCLS)
TNL .... Technical Newsletter
TNL .... Technitrol, Inc. [*American Stock Exchange symbol*]
TN L............ Tennessee Law Review [*A publication*]
TNL .... Terminal Net Loss
TNL .... Times Newspapers Limited [*British*]
TNL .... Tunnel (MSA)
TNLDIO ...... Tunnel Diode [*Electronics*]
TNLG.......... Technology, Inc. [*NASDAQ symbol*] (NQ)
TNLR.......... Railroad Tunnel [*Board on Geographic Names*]
TN LR .... Tennessee Law Review [*A publication*]
TNLS .... Trans-National Leasing [*NASDAQ symbol*] (NQ)
TNM .... Meharry Medical College, Nashville, TN [*Library symbol*] [*Library of Congress*] (LCLS)
TNM .... Tashota-Nipigon Mines [*Vancouver Stock Exchange symbol*]
TNM .... Tetranitromethane [*Organic chemistry*]
TNM .... Texas-New Mexico Railway Co. [*AAR code*]
TNM .... Topical Nitrogen Mustard [*Dermatology*]
TNM .... Tumor classification system derived from symbols: T for Primary Tumor; N for Regional Lymph Node Metastasis; M for Remote Metastasis [*Medicine*]
TNM .... Tumor-Nodal-Metastasis [*Oncology system*]
TNMH........ Metro General Hospital, Nashville, TN [*Library symbol*] [*Library of Congress*] (LCLS)
TNMPH....... Methodist Publishing House Library, Nashville, TN [*Library symbol*] [*Library of Congress*] (LCLS)
TNMR......... Tritium Nuclear Magnetic Resonance [*Spectrometry*]
TNN .... [*The*] Nashville Network [*Cable-television system*]
TNN .... Nashville Public Library, Nashville, TN [*OCLC symbol*] (OCLC)
TNN .... Tainan [*Taiwan*] [*Airport symbol*] (OAG)
TNN .... Tanana [*Alaska*] [*Seismograph station code, US Geological Survey*] (SEIS)
TNN .... TermNet News [*A publication*]
TNNIA .... Trudy Groznenskogo Neftyanogo Nauchno-Issledovatel'skogo Instituta [*A publication*]
TNO............ Nederlaendsche Centrale Organisatie voor Toegepast Natuurwetenschappelijk Onderzoek [*Netherlands Institute for Applied Scientific Research*]
TNO............ Tamarindo [*Costa Rica*] [*Airport symbol*] (OAG)
TNO............ Tenore Oil & Gas [*Vancouver Stock Exchange symbol*]
TNO............ Texas & New Orleans R. R. [*AAR code*]
TNO............ Torino [*Italy*] [*Seismograph station code, US Geological Survey*] (SEIS)

TNOC .... Threads No Couplings
TNOP......... Total Network Operations Plan [*Telecommunications*]   (TEL)
TNO Proj .... TNO [*Toegepast-Natuurwetenschappelijk Onderzoek*] Project [*A publication*]
TNOR......... Temiskaming & Northern Ontario Railway
TNOSA....... Tunnels et Ouvrages Souterrains [*A publication*]
TNP .... Thailand National Police   (CINC)
TNP .... Theatre National Populaire [*France*]
TNP .... TNP Enterprises, Inc. [*NYSE symbol*]
TNP .... Tonopah [*Nevada*] [*Seismograph station code, US Geological Survey*]   (SEIS)
TNP .... Trinitrophenol [*or Trinitrophenyl*] [*Organic chemistry*]
TNP .... Trojan Nuclear Plant   (NRCH)
TNP .... Twenty Nine Palms [*California*] [*Airport symbol*]   (OAG)
TNP .... Twentynine Palms, CA [*Location identifier*] [*FAA*]   (FAAL)
TNPA......... Tri-normal-propylamine [*Organic chemistry*]
TNPF......... Tidewater Nicaragua Project Foundation [*Hampton, VA*]   (EA)
TNPG......... [*The*] Nuclear Power Group [*British*]
TNPH......... Tennessee Department of Public Health, Nashville, TN [*Library symbol*] [*Library of Congress*]   (LCLS)
TNPK......... Turnpike
TNP-KLH.... Trinitrophenyl Keyhole Limpet Hemocyanin [*Immunology*]
Tn Plann Rev ... Town Planning Review [*A publication*]
TNPO......... Terminal Navy Post Office   (AFM)
TNPP......... Planned Parenthood of Nashville, Nashville, TN [*Library symbol*] [*Library of Congress*]   (LCLS)
TNPP......... Tris(nonylphenyl) Phosphite [*Organic chemistry*]
TNPWS...... Tasmania National Parks and Wildlife Service [*Australia*]
TNPZOW .... Towarzystwo Niesienia Pomocy Zydom Ofiarom Wojny [*A publication*]   (BJA)
TNR .... Antananarivo [*Madagascar*] [*Airport symbol*]   (OAG)
TNR .... [*The*] New Repertory
TNR .... [*The*] New Republic [*A publication*]
TNR .... Non-RADAR Transfer of Control Message [*Communications*]   (FAAC)
TNR .... Tanzania Notes and Records [*A publication*]
TNR .... Thinner
TNR .... Titan Resources [*Vancouver Stock Exchange symbol*]
TNR .... Tone Not Relevant
TNR .... Tonic Neck Reflex [*Physiology*]
TNR .... Trainer   (AAG)
TNR .... Transit Nuclear Radiation
TNRE .... Transit Nuclear Radiation Effect
TNRIS....... Texas Natural Resources Information System [*Austin*] [*Information service*]   (EISS)
TNRIS....... Transportation Noise Research Information Service [*Department of Transportation*]
TNRY........ Tannery
TNS .... [*The*] Names Society   (EA)
TNS .... [*The*] National Switchboard [*Phoenix, AZ*] [*Telecommunications*]   (TSSD)
TNS .... [*The*] New Salesmanship [*Book by Steve Salerno*]
TNS .... [*The*] Next Step [*Physics*]
TNS .... Tank Nitrogen Supply   (AAG)
TNS .... Tanos Petroleum Corp. [*Vancouver Stock Exchange symbol*]
TNS .... Taunus [*Federal Republic of Germany*] [*Seismograph station code, US Geological Survey*]   (SEIS)
TNS .... Tennessee State Library and Archives, Nashville, TN [*OCLC symbol*]   (OCLC)
TNS .... Thermal Night Site
TNS .... Toluidinylnaphthalene Sulfonate [*Organic chemistry*]
TNS .... Toronto Normal School
TNS .... Transaction Network Service [*AT & T*]
TNS .... Transcutaneous Nerve Stimulation [*Also, TENS, TES*] [*A method of pain control*] [*Medicine*]
TNS .... Triple Nine Society   (EA)
TNS .... Tunable Noise Source
TNSA........ [*The*] National Spiritual Alliance of the United States of America
TNSA........ Technical Nuclear Safety   (MCD)
TNSB........ Southern Baptist Convention Historical Commission, Nashville, TN [*Library symbol*] [*Library of Congress*]   (LCLS)
TNSDUNSPHI ... [*The*] National Society to Discourage Use of the Name Smith for Purposes of Hypothetical Illustration
TNSI .... [*A*] Text-Book of North-Semitic Inscriptions [*A publication*]   (BJA)
TNSKA....... Tohoku Nogyo Shikenjo Kenkyu Hokoku [*A publication*]
TNSL........ Tensile
TNSL........ Tinsley Laboratories, Inc. [*NASDAQ symbol*]   (NQ)
TNSN........ Tension   (MSA)
TNSP........ Transportation   (CINC)
TNStT....... Saint Thomas Hospital, Health Sciences Library, Nashville, TN [*Library symbol*] [*Library of Congress*]   (LCLS)
TNSX........ Taniisix. Aleutian Regional School District [*A publication*]
TNT .... Miami, FL [*Location identifier*] [*FAA*]   (FAAL)
TNT .... Teleconference Network of Texas [*University of Texas*] [*San Antonio*] [*Telecommunications*]   (TSSD)
TNT .... Tinto Gold Corp. [*Vancouver Stock Exchange symbol*]
TNT .... Titles Now Troublesome [*School books*] [*American Library Association*]
TNT .... TNT Tariff Agents Inc., New York NY [*STAC*]

TNT .... Tobramycin-Nafcillin-Ticarcillin [*Antibiotic combination*]
TNT .... Toronto [*Ontario*] [*Seismograph station code, US Geological Survey*] [*Closed*]   (SEIS)
TNT .... Towarzystwo Naukowe w Toruniu [*A publication*]
TNT .... Transient Nuclear Test
TNT .... Transnational Terrorism   (ADA)
TNT .... Trim, Neat, and Terrific [*Slang*]
TNT .... Trinitrotoluene [*Explosive*]
TnT .... Troponin T [*Biochemistry*]
TNTC......... Too Numerous to Count [*Microbiology*]
TNTC......... Tyndale New Testament Commentary [*A publication*]   (BJA)
TNTDL....... Tabulated Numerical Technical Data List
TNT-FF...... Towarzystwo Naukowe w Toruniu. Prace Wydziau Filologiczno-Filosoficznego [*A publication*]
TNTHA...... Tennessee Hospital Association, Nashville, TN [*Library symbol*] [*Library of Congress*]   (LCLS)
TNTL........ Tijdschrift voor Nederlandsche Taal- en Letterkunde [*Leiden*] [*A publication*]
TNTN........ Trevecca Nazarene College, Nashville, TN [*Library symbol*] [*Library of Congress*]   (LCLS)
TNTU........ University of Tennessee, Nashville, TN [*Library symbol*] [*Library of Congress*]   (LCLS)
TNTV........ Tentative   (AFM)
TNU .... Newton, IA [*Location identifier*] [*FAA*]   (FAAL)
tnu............ Tennessee [*MARC country of publication code*] [*Library of Congress*]   (LCCP)
TNU .... Upper Room Devotional Library and Museum, Nashville, TN [*Library symbol*] [*Library of Congress*]   (LCLS)
TNUK .... Thomas Nelson - United Kingdom [*Publisher*]
TNUM........ United Methodist Publishing House, Nashville, TN [*Library symbol*] [*Library of Congress*]   (LCLS)
TNV .... Navasota, TX [*Location identifier*] [*FAA*]   (FAAL)
TNV .... Tobacco Necrosis Virus
TNV .... Total Net Value
TNV .... Trinova Corp. [*NYSE symbol*]
TNVS........ Thermal Night Vision System
TNW .... Tactical Nuclear Warfare   (MCD)
TNW .... Tactical Nuclear Weapon
TNW .... Theater Nuclear Weapon
TNW .... Towarzystwo Naukowe Warszawskie [*A publication*]
TNX .... Thanks [*Communications operator's procedural remark*]
TNX .... Tonopah, NV [*Location identifier*] [*FAA*]   (FAAL)
TNX .... Trinitroxylene [*Organic chemistry*]
TNY .... Tenney Engineering, Inc. [*American Stock Exchange symbol*]
TNY .... Trans New York [*New York, NY*] [*FAA designator*]   (FAAC)
TNY .... Trinity University, Library, San Antonio, TX [*OCLC symbol*]   (OCLC)
T NY Ac Sci ... Transactions. New York Academy of Sciences [*A publication*]
TNYTI........ [*The*] New York Times Index
TNZ .... Tarata [*New Zealand*] [*Seismograph station code, US Geological Survey*]   (SEIS)
TNZ .... Thermoneutral Zone
TNZ .... Transfer on Nonzero
TNZ .... Tranzonic Companies [*American Stock Exchange symbol*]
TO .... Games Taken Out [*Baseball*]
TO .... [*The*] Medina Aviation Co. [*ICAO designator*]   (FAAC)
TO .... Oak Ridge Public Library, Oak Ridge, TN [*Library symbol*] [*Library of Congress*]   (LCLS)
TO .... People's Republic of South Yemen [*Aircraft nationality and registration mark*]   (FAAC)
TO .... Table of Organization
TO .... Tactical Observer
TO .... Tactical Officer [*Military*]   (RDA)
TO .... Take One [*A publication*]
T/O............ Take Over   (MCD)
T & O .... Taken and Offered [*Sporting*] [*British*]
TO .... Takeoff [*Aviation*]
TO .... Tandem Outlet
T/O............ Target of Opportunity
TO .... Targum Onkelos   (BJA)
TO .... Task Order   (MCD)
TO .... Tech/Ops, Inc. [*American Stock Exchange symbol*]
TO .... Technical Observer
TO .... Technical Officer [*Military*] [*British*]
TO .... Technical Order
TO .... Telegraph Office
TO .... Telephone Office
TO .... Telephone Order [*Medicine*]
TO .... Tell el-Obed   (BJA)
TO .... Temperature, Oral [*Medicine*]
TO .... Test Operation   (AAG)
T & O .... Test and Operation [*NASA*]   (KSC)
TO .... Test Outline   (CAAL)
TO .... Theater of Operations [*Military*]
TO .... Theiler's Original [*Strain of mouse encephalitis virus*]
TO .... Ticked Off [*Slang*]
T-O .... Time of Launch [*NASA*]   (KSC)
TO .... Time Opening
TO .... Time-Out
TO .... Tinctura Opii [*Tincture of Opium*]
TO .... Tobacco Observer [*A publication*]

to .... Tonga [*MARC country of publication code*] [*Library of Congress*] (LCCP)
TO .... Tonga [*Two-letter standard code*] (CNC)
TO .... Tonnage Opening
TO .... Tool Order
TO .... Tops Order (MCD)
TO .... Toronto
TO .... Torpedo Officer [*Obsolete*] [*Navy*] [*British*]
TO .... Township
TO .... Traditional Orthography [*Writing system*]
TO .... Traffic Officer
T & O .... Training and Operations [*Military*]
TO .... Transfer Order
TO .... Transistor Outline (IEEE)
TO .... Transmitter Oscillator
TO .... Transportation Officer
TO .... Transverse Optic
TO .... Travel Order
TO .... Treasury Order [*British*] (ROG)
TO .... Troy Ounce
TO .... Tuberculin Ober [*Supernatant portion*] [*Medicine*]
TO .... Tuberculin Old [*or Original*] [*Also, OT*] [*Medicine*]
TO .... Tuesdays Only [*British railroad term*]
TO .... [*A*] Turn Over [*A prospective customer who cannot be sold by one clerk and is turned over to another*] [*Merchandising slang*]
T/O .... Turned Out [*for Examination*] [*Tea trade*] (ROG)
TO .... Turnout (AAG)
TO .... Turnover [*Number*] [*With reference to enzyme activity*]
TO .... Type of Organization Code [*IRS*]
TOA .... Table of Allowances
TOA .... Table of Organization and Allowance
TOA .... Terms of Agreement [*Army*] (AABC)
TOA .... Theatre Owners of America [*Later, NATO*] (EA)
TOA .... Thermal Optical Analysis
TOA .... Time of Arrival (AFM)
TOA .... Time Out of Area (MCD)
TOA .... Tolsona [*Alaska*] [*Seismograph station code, US Geological Survey*] (SEIS)
TOA .... Torrance, CA [*Location identifier*] [*FAA*] (FAAL)
TOA .... Total Obligational Authority
TOA .... Toyota Owners Association (EA)
TOA .... Trade-Off Analysis [*Military*]
TOA .... Transportation Operating Agencies (AFM)
TOA .... Transportation Operations Authority (MCD)
TOA .... Trim on Assembly (MCD)
TOA .... Tubo-Ovarian Abscess [*Medicine*]
TOAC .... Tool Accessory (AAG)
TOAD .... Take Off and Die [*Surfers' slang for a very dangerous wave*]
TOAD .... Tobyhanna Army Depot [*Pennsylvania*] (AABC)
TOAD .... Towed Optical Assessment Device [*Marine science*] (MSC)
TOADS ...... Terminal-Oriented Administrative Data System
TOAL .... Test of Adolescent Language
TOAL .... Total Ordnance Alteration Application List [*Navy*]
TOAMAC ... [*The*] Optimum Army Materiel Command (RDA)
TOAP .... Prace Komisji Orientalistycznej Polskiej Akademii Umiejetnosci. Travaux de la Commission Orientaliste de l'Academie Polonaise des Sciences et des Lettres [*A publication*]
TOAP .... Thioguanine, Oncovin [*Vincristine*], ara-C, Prednisone [*Antineoplastic drug regimen*]
TOB .... Takeoff Boost [*Aviation*]
TOB .... Telemetry Output Buffer [*Data processing*]
TOB .... Tobacco (ADA)
Tob .... Tobacco Branch, Internal Revenue Bureau [*United States*] (DLA)
TOB .... Tobias [*Old Testament book*] [*Douay version*]
TOB .... Tobit [*Old Testament book*] [*Roman Catholic canon*] (ROG)
TOB .... Toboggan
TOB .... Tobruk [*Libya*] [*Airport symbol*] (OAG)
TOB .... Tow Bar (MCD)
TOB .... Tube over Bar [*Suspension*] (MCD)
TOBA .... Theater Owners Booking Association [*Vaudeville*]
TOBA .... Thoroughbred Owners and Breeders Association (EA)
TOBA .... Tough on Black Actors [*Facetious translation of acronym for Theater Owners Booking Association*]
Tob Abstracts ... Tobacco Abstracts [*A publication*]
Tobacco J ... Tobacco Journal [*A publication*]
Tobey .... Tobey's Reports [*9, 10 Rhode Island*] (DLA)
TOBI .... Test of Basic Information [*Education*]
TOBI .... Toxicity Bibliography [*MEDLARS*]
Tob Int (NY) ... Tobacco International (New York) [*A publication*]
Tob Leaf ... Tobacco Leaf [*A publication*]
Tob Res ..... Tobacco Research [*A publication*]
Tob Res Board Rhod Bull ... Tobacco Research Board of Rhodesia. Bulletin [*A publication*]
Tob Res Counc Res Pap ... Tobacco Research Council. Research Paper [*England*] [*A publication*]
TobRV .... Tobacco Ring Spot Virus
TOBS .... Telemetering Ocean Bottom Seismometer [*Marine science*] (MSC)

Tob Sci ...... Tobacco Science [*A publication*]
TOBWE ...... Tactical Observing Weather Element [*Air Force*]
TOC .... [*The*] Operations Council of the American Trucking Associations (EA)
TOC .... Table of Coincidences [*Telecommunications*] (TEL)
TOC .... Table of Contents
TOC .... Tactical Operations Center [*Military*]
TOC .... Tagliabue Open Cup [*Analytical chemistry*]
TOC .... Tanker Operational Circular
TOC .... Task Order Contract
TOC .... Task-Oriented Costing [*Telecommunications*] (TEL)
TOC .... Technical Order Compliance
TOC .... Television Operating Center
TOC .... Test of Cure [*Medicine*]
TOC .... Test Operations Center [*NASA*] (NASA)
TOC .... Test Operations Change [*NASA*] (NASA)
TOC .... Theater of Operations Command [*Military*]
TOC .... Timber Operators Council [*Formed by a merger of Lumbermen's Industrial Relations Council, Oregon Coast Operators, Plywood and Door Manufacturers Industrial Committee, and Willamette Valley Lumber Operators Association*] [*Tigard, OR*] (EA)
TOC .... Time of Correlation (MCD)
TOC .... Time Optimal Control (MCD)
TOC .... Timing Operation Center
TOC .... Tinctura Opii Camphorata [*Paregoric Elixir*] [*Pharmacy*] (ROG)
TOC .... To Be Continued, Circuit Time Permitting (FAAC)
TOC .... Toccoa, GA [*Location identifier*] [*FAA*] (FAAL)
TOC .... Tocklai [*India*] [*Seismograph station code, US Geological Survey*] (SEIS)
TOC .... Tooling Order Change
TOC .... Top of Climb [*Aviation*]
TOC .... Total Organic Carbon
TOC .... Traditional Organized Crime
TOC .... Transfer of Control
TOC .... Turn-On Command (KSC)
TOCAP ...... Terminal Oriented Control Applications Program
TOCC .... Technical and Operations Control Center [*INTELSAT*]
TOCC .... Transfer of Control Card
TOC/CP ..... Tactical Operations Center/Command Post [*Military*]
TOCCWE ... Tactical Operations Control Center Weather Element [*Air Force*]
TOC/ECP ... Technical Order Compliance/Engineering Change Proposal [*Military*] (AFIT)
TOCED .... Table of Contents Editor Processor [*Data processing*]
Tocklai Exp Stn Advis Bull ... Tocklai Experimental Station. Advisory Bulletin [*A publication*]
Tocklai Exp Stn Advis Leafl ... Tocklai Experimental Station. Advisory Leaflet [*A publication*]
TOCI .... Total Organic Chlorine [*Analytical chemistry*]
TOCM .... Tocom, Inc. [*NASDAQ symbol*] (NQ)
TOCM .... Trust Officers Committee Minutes (DLA)
TOCN .... Technical Order Change Notice [*Air Force*] (MCD)
Tocn i Nadezn Kibernet Sistem ... Tocnost i Nadeznost Kiberneticeskih Sistem [*A publication*]
TOCP .... Tri-ortho-cresyl Phosphate [*Organic chemistry*]
TOCS .... Oriental Ceramic Society. Transactions [*A publication*]
TOCS .... Terminal Operations Control System
TOCS .... Terminal-Oriented Computer System
TOCS .... Textile Operational Control System [*Data processing*]
TOCS .... Tool Order Control System (MCD)
TOD .... Technical Objective Directive [*or Document*] [*Air Force*] (MCD)
TOD .... Technical Operations Department
TOD .... Test Operations Directorate (RDA)
TOD .... Theater-Oriented Depot [*Military*]
TOD .... Time of Day
TOD .... Time of Delivery
TOD .... Time of Departure (NVT)
TOD .... Time of Despatch [*British*]
TOD .... Tioman [*Malaysia*] [*Airport symbol*] (OAG)
TOD .... Todd Shipyards Corp. [*NYSE symbol*]
TOD .... Total Oxygen Demand [*Analytical chemistry*]
TOD .... Tourist-Oriented-Directional [*Traffic sign*]
TOD .... Trade-Off Determination [*Military*] (AABC)
TOD .... Turnover Device
TODA .... Takeoff Distance Available [*Aviation*] (FAAC)
TODA .... Third-Octave Digital Analyzer
Toda Educ ... Today's Education [*A publication*]
TODARS ...... Terminal Oriented Data Analysis and Retrieval System [*National Bureau of Standards*]
TODAS ...... Towed Oceanographic Data Acquisition System [*Marine science*] (MSC)
TODAS ...... Typewriter-Oriented Documentation-Aid System
Today's Ed ... Today's Education [*A publication*]
Todays Educ ... Today's Education [*A publication*]
Today's Fmkr ... Today's Filmmaker [*A publication*]
Today's Sec ... Today's Secretary [*A publication*]
Today Technol ... Today Technology [*A publication*]
Today & Tomorrow Educ ... Today and Tomorrow in Education [*A publication*]
TODC .... Technical Order Distribution Code [*Air Force*]

TODC .... Theater-Oriented Depot Complex [*Military*] (AABC)

Tod Cath Teach ... Today's Catholic Teacher [*A publication*]

TODD-AO ... Todd-American Optical Co. [*Wide-screen system used by producer Michael Todd and the American Optical Co.*]

TODES .... Transcript of Data Extraction System (MCD)

Tod Parish ... Today's Parish [*A publication*]

TODrL .... Trudy Otdela Drevnerusskoj Literatury [*A publication*]

TODS .... Test-Oriented Disk System (IEEE)

TODS .... Transactions on Database Systems

TODT .... Tool Detail (AAG)

TOE .... Epidermatophyton

TO & E .... Tables of Organization and Equipment [*Military*] (AAG)

TOE .... Talker Omission Error (MUGU)

TOE .... Term of Enlistment [*Military*]

TOE .... Texas, Oklahoma & Eastern Railroad Co. [*AAR code*]

TOE .... Theory of Everything [*Cosmology*]

TOE .... Thread One End (MSA)

TOE .... Time of Entry (MCD)

TOE .... Time of Event [*Military*] (CAAL)

TOE .... Tons of Oil Equivalent

TOE .... Tony, Oscar, Emmy [*Refers to actors who have won these three major awards, for stage, film, and television work, respectively*]

TOE .... Top of Edge (AAG)

TOE .... Total Operating Expense

TOE .... Tozeur [*Tunisia*] [*Airport symbol*] (OAG)

TOE .... Tracheoesophageal [*Also, TE*] [*Medicine*]

TOE .... Trainborne Operational Equipment

TOE .... Tryout Employment [*Job Training and Partnership Act*] (OICC)

TOE .... United States Energy Research and Development Administration, Technical Information, Oak Ridge, TN [*Library symbol*] [*Library of Congress*] (LCLS)

TOEFL .... Teaching of English as a Foreign Language

TOEFL .... Test of English as a Foreign Language

TOEL .... Time Only Emitter Location System (MCD)

TOELA .... Toute l'Electronique [*A publication*]

TOEMTB .... Tables of Organization and Equipment Mobilization Troop Basis [*Army*] (AABC)

TOES .... Test of Enquiry Skills (ADA)

TOES .... Trade-Off Evaluation System

TOF .... Beverly, MA [*Location identifier*] [*FAA*] (FAAL)

TOF .... Tales of the Frightened [*A publication*]

TOF .... Test Operations Facility (MCD)

TOF .... Tetralogy of Fallot [*Cardiology*]

TOF .... Time of Filing

TOF .... Time of Fire [*Military*] (CAAL)

TOF .... Time of Flight

TOF .... To Order From

TOF .... Tofutti Brands, Inc. [*American Stock Exchange symbol*]

TOF .... Tone Off [*Telecommunications*] (TEL)

TOF .... Top of Form [*Data processing*]

TOF .... Transfer of Function (MCD)

TOFA .... Tall Oil Fatty Acids [*Organic chemistry*]

TOFABS .... Time-of-Flight Aerosol Beam Spectrometry

TOFC .... Tony Orlando Fan Club [*Allentown, PA*] (EA)

TOFC .... Trailer on Flatcar [*Railroad*]

TOFCN .... Technical Order Field Change Notice [*Air Force*] (MCD)

TOFDC .... Total Operational Flying Duty Credit [*Military*] (AABC)

TOFI .... Time-of-Flight Isochronous Spectrometer

TOFL .... Takeoff Field Length [*Aviation*]

TOFM .... Tooling Form (AAG)

TOFMS .... Time-of-Flight Mass Spectrometer

TOFS .... Time-of-Flight Spectrometer [*or Spectroscopy*]

TOFU .... Tofu Time, Inc. [*NASDAQ symbol*] (NQ)

TOG .... Skyway of Ocala [*Ocala, FL*] [*FAA designator*] (FAAC)

TOG .... Takeoff Gross [*Weight*] [*Aviation*]

TOG .... Target-Observer-Gun [*Method*] [*Army*]

TOG .... Target Opportunity Generator (KSC)

TOG .... Temagami Oil & Gas Ltd. [*Toronto Stock Exchange symbol*]

TOG .... Togane [*Japan*] [*Seismograph station code, US Geological Survey*] [*Closed*] (SEIS)

TOG .... Together

TOG .... Toggle

TOG .... Togiak [*Alaska*] [*Airport symbol*] (OAG)

TOG .... Togiak Village, AK [*Location identifier*] [*FAA*] (FAAL)

TOG .... Top of Grade (MCD)

TOG .... Toronto Game [*Simulation game*]

TOGA .... Tooling Gauge (AAG)

TOGA .... Tropical Oceans and Global Atmosphere [*UNESCO*]

Tog Cand ... Oratio in Senatu in Toga Candida [*of Cicero*] [*Classical studies*] (OCD)

TOGI .... Target Oil & Gas, Incorporated [*NASDAQ symbol*] (NQ)

TOGI .... Trans-Oceanic Geophysical Investigations [*Marine science*] (MSC)

TOGR .... Together (ROG)

TOGW .... Takeoff Gross Weight [*Aviation*]

TOH .... Natchitoches, LA [*Location identifier*] [*FAA*] (FAAL)

TOH .... Oak Ridge Hospital, Oak Ridge, TN [*Library symbol*] [*Library of Congress*] (LCLS)

TOH .... Time Overhead (NVT)

Toh .... Tohoroth [*or Toharoth*] (BJA)

TOH .... Tyrosine Hydroxylase [*An enzyme*]

T & OHI ...... Truck & Off-Highway Industries [*A publication*]

Toh J Ex Me ... Tohoku Journal of Experimental Medicine [*A publication*]

TOHM .... Terohmmeter (IEEE)

Toho .... Tohoroth [*or Toharoth*] (BJA)

Tohoku Agr Res ... Tohoku Agricultural Research [*A publication*]

Tohoku Geophys J Sci Rep Tohoku Univ Fifth Ser ... Tohoku Geophysical Journal. Science Reports of the Tohoku University. Fifth Series [*A publication*]

Tohoku Imp Univ Technol Rep ... Tohoku Imperial University Technology Reports [*Japan*] [*A publication*]

Tohoku J Agric Res ... Tohoku Journal of Agricultural Research [*A publication*]

Tohoku J Agr Res ... Tohoku Journal of Agricultural Research [*A publication*]

Tohoku J Exp Med ... Tohoku Journal of Experimental Medicine [*A publication*]

Tohoku Math J ... Tohoku Mathematical Journal [*A publication*]

Tohoku Med J ... Tohoku Medical Journal [*A publication*]

Tohoku Psychol Folia ... Tohoku Psychologica Folia [*A publication*]

Tohoku Univ Sci Rep Ser 2 ... Tohoku University. Science Reports. Series 2. Geology [*A publication*]

Tohoku Univ Sci Rep Ser 3 ... Tohoku University. Science Reports. Series 3. Mineralogy, Petrology, and Economic Geology [*A publication*]

Tohoku Univ Sci Rep Ser 5 ... Tohoku University. Science Reports. Series 5 [*A publication*]

Tohoku Univ Sci Repts Geology ... Tohoku University. Science Reports. Geology [*A publication*]

TOHP .... Takeoff Horsepower [*Aviation*]

TOI .... Target of Interest [*Military*] (CAAL)

TOI .... Technical Operation Instruction (KSC)

TOI .... Technical Operations, Incorporated (MCD)

TOI .... Term of Induction [*Military*]

TOI .... Time of Intercept [*Military*] (CAAL)

TOI .... Troy, AL [*Location identifier*] [*FAA*] (FAAL)

TOID .... Technical Order Identification (MCD)

TOIL .... Time Off in Lieu

Toim Eesti NSV Tead Akad Fuus Mat ... Toimetised. Eesti NSV Teaduste Akadeemia. Fuusika. Matemaatika [*A publication*]

TOJ .... Track on Jamming

To Jo .... [*Sir*] Thomas Jones' English King's Bench Reports [*1667-84*] (DLA)

TOK .... Thrust Okay [*NASA*] (KSC)

TOK .... Tokheim Corp. [*NYSE symbol*]

TOK .... Tokyo [*Japan*] [*Later, KAK*] [*Geomagnetic observatory code*]

TOK .... Tokyo [*Japan*] [*Seismograph station code, US Geological Survey*] (SEIS)

TOK .... Torokina [*Papua New Guinea*] [*Airport symbol*] (OAG)

Tokai J Exp Clin Med ... Tokai Journal of Experimental and Clinical Medicine [*Japan*] [*A publication*]

Tokai-Kinki Natl Agric Exp Stn Res Prog Rep ... Tokai-Kinki National Agricultural Experiment Station. Research Progress Report [*A publication*]

Tokai Technol J ... Tokai Technological Journal [*Japan*] [*A publication*]

TOKAMAK ... Toroidal Kamera Magnetic [*Thermonuclear-fusion system*] [*Acronym formed from the Russian*]

Tokoginecol Prac ... Toko-Ginecologia Practica [*A publication*]

Toko-Ginecol Pract ... Toko-Ginecologia Practica [*A publication*]

TOKSA .... Tokushuko [*A publication*]

Tokushima J Exp Med ... Tokushima Journal of Experimental Medicine [*A publication*]

Tokyo Astron Bull ... Tokyo Astronomical Bulletin [*A publication*]

Tokyo Astron Bull Ser II ... Tokyo Astronomical Bulletin. Series II [*A publication*]

Tokyo Astron Obs Rep ... Tokyo Astronomical Observatory. Report [*A publication*]

Tokyo Bk Dev Centre Newsl ... Tokyo Book Development Centre. Newsletter [*A publication*]

Tokyo Inst Technol Bull ... Tokyo Institute of Technology. Bulletin [*A publication*]

Tokyo Jikeika Med J ... Tokyo Jikeika Medical Journal [*A publication*]

Tokyo J Math ... Tokyo Journal of Mathematics [*A publication*]

Tokyo J Med Sci ... Tokyo Journal of Medical Sciences [*A publication*]

Tokyo Kyoiku Daigaku Sci Rep Sec C ... Tokyo Kyoiku Daigaku. Science Reports. Section C. Geology, Mineralogy, and Geography [*A publication*]

Tokyo Metrop Isot Cent Annu Rep ... Tokyo Metropolitan Isotope Centre. Annual Report [*A publication*]

Tokyo Metrop Res Inst Environ Prot Annu Rep Engl Transl ... Tokyo Metropolitan Research Institute for Environmental Protection. Annual Report. English Translation [*A publication*]

Tokyo Metrop Univ Geogr Rep ... Tokyo Metropolitan University. Geographical Reports [*A publication*]

Tokyo Natl Sci Mus Bull ... Tokyo National Science Museum. Bulletin [*A publication*]

Tokyo Tanabe Q ... Tokyo Tanabe Quarterly [*A publication*]

Tokyo Univ Coll Gen Educ Sci Pap ... Tokyo University. College of General Education. Scientific Papers [*A publication*]

Tokyo Univ Earthquake Research Inst Bull ... Tokyo University. Earthquake Research Institute. Bulletin [*A publication*]

Tokyo Univ Faculty Sci Jour ... Tokyo University. Faculty of Science. Journal [*A publication*]
TOL .... Test-Oriented Language [*Data processing*]
TOL .... Toledo [*Spain*] [*Geomagnetic observatory code*]
TOL .... Toledo [*Spain*] [*Seismograph station code, US Geological Survey*] (SEIS)
TOL .... Toledo [*Ohio*] [*Airport symbol*] (OAG)
TOL .... Tolerance (AAG)
TOL .... Toll Brothers, Inc. [*NYSE symbol*]
TOL .... Tower of London
TOL .... University of Toledo, Toledo, OH [*OCLC symbol*] (OCLC)
TOLA .... Takeoff and Landing Analysis [*Air Force*]
TOLA .... Test of Learning Ability (ADA)
TOLA .... Theatre of Latin America (EA)
TOLAR ...... Terminal On-Line Availability Reporting
TOLCAT .... Takeoff and Landing Critical Atmosphere Turbulence [*Aviation*] (MCD)
TOLD .... Telecoms On-Line Data System [*Telecommunications*] (TEL)
TOLD .... Test of Language Development [*Education*]
Toledo L Rev ... University of Toledo. Law Review [*A publication*]
Toledo Mus N ... Toledo. Museum of Art. Museum News [*A publication*]
Toledo Univ Inst Silicate Research Inf Circ ... Toledo University. Institute of Silicate Research. Information Circular [*A publication*]
TOLEYIS .... Turkiye Otel, Lokanta ve Eglence Yerleri Isci Sendikalari Federasyonu [*National Federation of Hotel, Restaurant, and Amusement Places Workers' Unions*] [*Turkey*]
TOLIP .... Trajectory Optimization and Linearized Pitch [*Computer program*]
Toller .... Toller on Executors (DLA)
Tol LR .... University of Toledo. Law Review [*A publication*]
TOLM .... Toledo Mining [*NASDAQ symbol*] (NQ)
TOLO .... Tool and Operation Liaison Order (AAG)
TOLO .... Tooling Layout (AAG)
TOLR .... Toll Restricted [*Telecommunications*] (TEL)
TOLR .... Transmitting Objective Loudness Rating [*of telephone connections*] (IEEE)
To LR .... University of Toledo. Law Review [*A publication*]
Tolst Div ..... Tolstoy on Divorce and Matrimonial Causes (DLA)
TOLT .... Towing Light (AAG)
TOLTEP ..... Teleprocessing On-Line Test Executive Program [*IBM Corp.*]
TOLTS .... Total On-Line Testing System [*Honeywell, Inc.*]
Tolva .... Tolva. Revista del Trigo. Harina y del Pan [*A publication*]
Tolvmandsbl ... Tolvmandsbladet [*A publication*]
TOM .... GMT [*Greenwich Mean Time*] of Orbital Midnight
TOM .... [*The*] Old Man
TOM .... Technical Operations Manager [*Navy*]
TOM .... Texas College of Osteopathic Medicine, Fort Worth, TX [*OCLC symbol*] (OCLC)
TOM .... Thompson-Lundmark Gold Mines Ltd. [*Toronto Stock Exchange symbol*]
TOM .... Tombouctou [*Mali*] [*Airport symbol*] (OAG)
TOM .... Tomie [*Japan*] [*Seismograph station code, US Geological Survey*] [*Closed*] (SEIS)
TOM .... Toronto, Ottawa, Montreal [*Derogatory reference to people in these cities; used by other Canadians who think people living in these cities "run things"*]
TOM .... Tracking Operation Memorandum [*Obsolete*]
TOM .... Translator Octal Mnemonic
TOM .... Typical Ocean Model [*Oceanography*]
TOMA .... Technical Order Management Agency [*Military*] (AFIT)
TOMA .... Test of Mathematical Abilities
TOMA .... Turn Off My Addiction [*Proposed clinic*]
TOMARA .... Texas Outlaw Midget Automobile Racing Association [*Car racing*]
TOMB .... Technical Organizational Memory Bank (RDA)
TOMCAT .... Telemetry On-Line Monitoring Compression and Transmission
TOMCAT .... Teleoperator for Operations, Maintenance, and Construction Using Advanced Technology
TOMCAT .... Theater of Operations Missile Continuous-Wave Antitank Weapon
TOMH .... Regional Mental Health Center of Oak Ridge, Oak Ridge, TN [*Library symbol*] [*Library of Congress*] (LCLS)
Tomkins & J Mod Rom Law ... Tomkins and Jencken's Compendium of the Modern Roman Law (DLA)
Toml .... Tomlins' Election Cases [*1689-1795*] (DLA)
Toml Cas ..... Tomlins' Election Cases [*1689-1795*] (DLA)
Tomlins ..... Tomlins' Law Dictionary (DLA)
Toml Law Dict ... Tomlins' Law Dictionary (DLA)
Toml LD ...... Tomlins' Law Dictionary [*4th ed.*] [*1835*] (DLA)
Toml Supp Br ... Tomlins' Supplement to Brown's Parliamentary Cases (DLA)
TOMM .... Time-Oriented Metropolitan Model (MCD)
TOMMS ...... Terminal Operations and Movements Management System (MCD)
TOMR .... Tomorrow (ROG)
TOMS .... Torus Oxygen Monitoring System (IEEE)
TOMS .... Total Ozone Mapping Spectrometer (MCD)
TOMS .... Total Ozone Mapping System [*Meteorology*]
TOMS .... Transactions on Mathematical Software
TOMSI .... Transfer of Master Scheduled Item

Tomsk Gos Univ Ucen Zap ... Tomskii Gosudarstvennyi Universitet Imeni V. V. Kuibyseva. Ucenye Zapiski [*A publication*]
TOMSS ...... Theater of Operations Medical Support System [*Military*] (MCD)
TOMT .... Target Organizational Maintenance Trainer (MCD)
TOMUS ...... [*The*] On-line Multi-User System [*Carlyle Systems, Inc.*] [*Berkeley, CA*] [*Information service*] (EISS)
TON .... Tone On [*Telecommunications*] (TEL)
TON .... Tonga [*Three-letter standard code*] (CNC)
TON .... Tongariro [*New Zealand*] [*Seismograph station code, US Geological Survey*] [*Closed*] (SEIS)
TON .... Tonic [*Permanently Strengthening*] [*Pharmacy*] (ROG)
TON .... Tonopah Resources, Inc. [*Vancouver Stock Exchange symbol*]
TON .... Top of the News [*A publication*]
TON .... Tyrone, PA [*Location identifier*] [*FAA*] (FAAL)
TONAC .... Technical Order Notification and Completion System (AAG)
TON/FT² ...... Tons per Square Foot
TONGA .... Trudy Nauchno-Issledovatel'skogo Instituta Onkologii Gruzinskoi SSR [*A publication*]
TONI .... Test of Nonverbal Intelligence
Tonind-Ztg Keram Rundsch ... Tonindustrie-Zeitung und Keramische Rundschau [*A publication*]
TONL .... Union Carbide Nuclear Co., Oak Ridge National Laboratories, Oak Ridge, TN [*Library symbol*] [*Library of Congress*] (LCLS)
TONLAR ..... Tone-Operated Net Loss Adjuster Receiving
TONL-B ...... Union Carbide Nuclear Co., Oak Ridge National Laboratories, Biology Library, Oak Ridge, TN [*Library symbol*] [*Library of Congress*] (LCLS)
TONL-T ...... Union Carbide Nuclear Co., Oak Ridge National Laboratories, Thermal-Nuclear Library, Oak Ridge, TN [*Library symbol*] [*Library of Congress*] (LCLS)
TONL-Y ...... Union Carbide Nuclear Co., Oak Ridge National Laboratories, Y-12 Technical Library, Oak Ridge, TN [*Library symbol*] [*Library of Congress*] (LCLS)
TONN .... Tonnage [*Shipping*]
Tono .... Tono [*Record label*] [*Denmark*]
TONT .... Tonto National Monument
TONT .... Toronto Native Times [*A publication*]
TOO .... 2001 Resource Industries Ltd. [*Vancouver Stock Exchange symbol*]
TOO .... La Tour de l'Orle d'Or [*A publication*]
TOO .... Target of Opportunity [*Military*] (CAAL)
TOO .... Test Operations Orders
TOO .... Time of Origin [*Communications*]
TOO .... Toolangi [*Australia*] [*Seismograph station code, US Geological Survey*] (SEIS)
TOO .... Toolangi [*Australia*] [*Geomagnetic observatory code*]
TOOIS .... Transactions on Office Information Systems [*A publication*]
TOOL .... Teams of Our Lady [*See also END*] (EA-IO)
TOOL .... Test-Oriented Operated Language [*Programing language*] [*Data processing*]
Tool Die J ... Tool and Die Journal [*A publication*]
Tool Eng .... Tool Engineer [*A publication*]
Tool Mfg Eng ... Tool and Manufacturing Engineer [*A publication*]
Tool & Mfg Eng ... Tool and Manufacturing Engineer [*A publication*]
Tool and Prod ... Tooling and Production [*A publication*]
Tool Prod ... Tooling and Production [*A publication*]
TOOS .... Torque Overload Switch (NRCH)
TOOT .... 202 Data Systems [*NASDAQ symbol*] (NQ)
TOOTJFC .... [*The*] One and Only Tom Jones Fan Club [*Sayville, NY*] (EA)
TOP .... [*The*] Opportunity Prospector [*A publication*]
TOP .... [*The*] Option Process [*HUD*]
TOP .... Tactical Operations Plot [*Military*] (CAAL)
TOP .... Target Occulting Processor (MCD)
TOP .... Targeted Outreach Program [*Department of Labor*]
TOP .... Tax-Offset Pension [*Account*]
TOP .... Teacher Organizing Project (EA)
TOP .... Technical, Office, and Professional Department [*UAW*]
TOP .... Technical and Office Protocol [*Data communications standards*]
TOP .... Technical Operating Procedure
TOP .... Temple Opportunity Program [*Temple University*] (EA)
TOP .... Temporarily Out of Print
TOP .... Tertiary Operation
TOP .... Test and Operations Plan
TOP .... Test Outline Plan [*Army*] (AABC)
TOP .... Topeka [*Kansas*] [*Airport symbol*] (OAG)
TOP .... Topeka, KS [*Location identifier*] [*FAA*] (FAAL)
Top .... Topic [*Record label*] [*Great Britain*]
Top .... Topica [*of Aristotle*] [*Classical studies*] (OCD)
Top .... Topica [*of Cicero*] [*Classical studies*] (OCD)
top .... Topical
TOP .... Topology
TOP .... Topolovo [*USSR*] [*Seismograph station code, US Geological Survey*] (SEIS)
TOP .... Toponimic [*An antigen*]
TOP .... Torque Oil Pressure [*Air Force*]
TOP .... Total Obscuring Power [*Smoke cloud*]
TOP .... Trade Opportunities Program [*Departments of State and Commerce*]

TOP .... Training Operation Plan [*Military*]   (CAAL)
TOP .... Transient Overpower Accident [*Physics*]
TOP .... Transovarial Passage [*Virology*]
TOP .... Transverse Optical Pumping   (MCD)
TOP .... Turn Out Perfection [*US Air Force Southern Command's acronym for the Zero Defects Program*]
TOP .... Turn Over, Please [*Correspondence*]   (ROG)
TOPA......... Tooling Pattern
Top Antibiot Chem ... Topics in Antibiotic Chemistry [*A publication*]
Top Appl Phys ... Topics in Applied Physics [*A publication*]
Top Astrophys Space Phys ... Topics in Astrophysics and Space Physics [*A publication*]
Top Bioelectrochem Bioenerg ... Topics in Bioelectrochemistry and Bioenergetics [*A publication*]
TOPCAP..... Total Objective Plan for Career Airmen Personnel [*Air Force*]   (AFM)
Top Clin Nurs ... Topics in Clinical Nursing [*A publication*]
Top Curr Chem ... Topics in Current Chemistry [*A publication*]
Top Curr Phys ... Topics in Current Physics [*A publication*]
Top Emerg Med ... Topics in Emergency Medicine [*A publication*]
Top Enzyme Ferment Biotechnol ... Topics in Enzyme and Fermentation Biotechnology [*A publication*]
TOPES .... Telephone Office Planning and Engineering System [*Telecommunications*]   (TEL)
TOPEX .... Topographic Experiment [*Proposed oceanographic satellite*]
TOPF......... Transplant Organ Procurement Foundation   (EA)
TOPG .... Topping   (MSA)
TOPHAT..... Terrier Operation Proof High-Altitude Target   (MUGU)
Top Health Care Financ ... Topics in Health Care Financing [*A publication*]
Top Horm Chem ... Topics in Hormone Chemistry [*A publication*]
T Ophth Soc ... Transactions. Ophthalmological Societies of the United Kingdom [*A publication*]
Top Hum Genet ... Topics in Human Genetics [*A publication*]
TOPIC .... [*The*] Objective Personnel Inventory - Civilian [*Air Force*]
TOPIC .... Time-Ordered Programer Integrated Circuit [*NASA*]
TOPICS ..... Total On-Line Program and Information Control System [*Japan*]
TOPICS ..... Traffic Operations to Increase Capacity and Safety [*Department of Transportation*]
TOPICS ..... Transcripts of Parlibs Information Classification System [*Queensland Parliamentary Library*] [*A publication*]
Topics Current Phys ... Topics in Current Physics [*A publication*]
TOPLAS ..... Transactions on Programing Languages and Systems   (MCD)
Top Lipid Chem ... Topics in Lipid Chemistry [*A publication*]
Top Manage Abstr ... Top Management Abstracts [*A publication*]
Top Math Phys ... Topics in Mathematical Physics [*A publication*]
Top Med Chem ... Topics in Medicinal Chemistry [*A publication*]
Top News... Top of the News [*A publication*]
T of OPNS ... Theater of Operations [*Military*]
TOPNS .... Theater of Operations [*Military*]
TOPO .... Test Operations and Policy Office [*TECOM*]   (RDA)
TOPO .... Topography   (AFM)
TOPO .... Tri-n-Octyl Phosphine Oxide [*Organic chemistry*]
TOPO .... Trioctylphosphine Oxide [*Organic chemistry*]
TOPOCOM ... Topographic Command [*Army*]
TOPOENGR ... Topographical Engineer
TOPOG....... Topography
Topology Proc ... Topology Proceedings [*A publication*]
TOPO-MIBK ... Trioctylphosphorine Oxide/Methyl Isobutyl Keton [*Solvent mixture*]
TOPOSS..... Tests of Perception of Scientists and Self   (ADA)
TOPP.......... [*The*] Organization of Plastics Processors [*Delray Beach, FL*]   (EA)
TOPP.......... Terminal-Operated Production Program   (BUR)
TOPPER ..... Toy Press Publishers, Editors, and Reporters
Top Phosphorus Chem ... Topics in Phosphorus Chemistry [*A publication*]
Top Photosynth ... Topics in Photosynthesis [*A publication*]
Top Probl Psychiatry Neurol ... Topical Problems in Psychiatry and Neurology [*A publication*]
Top Probl Psychother ... Topical Problems of Psychotherapy [*A publication*]
TOPR......... Taiwan Open Pool Reactor
TOPRA .... Tooling and Production [*A publication*]
TOPREP ..... Total Objective Plan for Reserve Personnel [*Air Force*]   (AFM)
TOPS.......... [*The*] Operational PERT System
TOPS.......... Tactical Optical Projection System   (NVT)
TOPS.......... Tailored Owner Protection System [*Automotive optional warranty*]
TOPS.......... Take Off Pounds Sensibly [*Milwaukee, WI*]   (EA)
TOPS.......... Telemetry On-Line Processing System [*Data processing*]
TOPS.......... Telephone Order Personalities and Smiles [*Organization of chief telephone operators*]
TOPS.......... Telephone Order Processing System
TOPS.......... Telephone Order Purchasing System   (MCD)
TOPS.......... Teleregister Omni Processing and Switching [*Data processing*]
TOPS.......... Teletype Optical Projection System   (IEEE)
TOPS.......... Terminal Oriented Planning System   (MCD)
TOPS.......... Test Operations Procedures [*Army*]   (RDA)
TOPS.......... Tested Overhead Projection Series [*Education*]
TOPS.......... Testing and Operating System
TOPS.......... Thermal Noise Optical Optimization Communication System [*NASA*]

TOPS.......... Thermoelectric Outer Planet Spacecraft [*NASA*]
TOPS.......... Time-Sharing Operating System
TOPS.......... Total Operations Processing System [*Data processing*]
TOPS.......... Traffic Operator Position System [*Telecommunications*]   (TEL)
TOPS.......... Training Opportunities Schemes [*Department of Employment*] [*British*]
TOPS.......... Transcendental Network [*Centram Systems West, Inc.*] [*Berkeley, CA*] [*Telecommunications*]   (TSSD)
TOPS.......... Transistorized Operational Phone System   (MCD)
TOPS.......... Transportation Operational Personal Property System [*Army*]
TOPS.......... Truck Ordering and Pricing System
TOPS.......... United States Travelers' Overseas Personalized Service [*Also known as USTOPS*]
TOPSA .... Topsy's International CI A [*NASDAQ symbol*]   (NQ)
TOPSEC.... Top Secret [*Security classification*]
TOPSEP ..... Targeting/Optimization for Solar Electric Propulsion [*NASA*]
TOPSI........ Topside Sounder, Ionosphere [*NASA*]
TOPSTAR .. [*The*] Officer Personnel System, The Army Reserve   (AABC)
Top Stereochem ... Topics in Stereochemistry [*A publication*]
Top Sulfur Chem ... Topics in Sulfur Chemistry [*A publication*]
TOPSY .... Test Operations Planning System
TOPSY .... Thermally Operated Plasma System
TOPTS .... Test-Oriented Paper-Tape System [*Data processing*]   (IEEE)
TOPV........ Trivalent Oral Poliomyelitis Vaccine [*Medicine*]
TOR .... Tactical Operational Requirement [*Military*]   (CAAL)
TOR .... Tactical Operations Room [*Air Force*]
TOR .... Tall Oil Rosin [*Organic chemistry*]
TOR .... Technical Operating Report
TOR .... Technical Operations Research   (KSC)
TOR .... Technical Override
TOR .... Telegraph on Radio [*Telecommunications*]   (TEL)
TOR .... Tentative Operational Requirement
TOR .... Terms of Reference [*Army*]   (AABC)
TOR .... Test Operation Report   (KSC)
TOR .... Third Order Regular of St. Francis [*Roman Catholic men's religious order*]
TOR .... Time of Receipt [*Military*]   (AABC)
TOR .... Time of Reception [*Communications*]
TOR .... Torhsen Energy Corp. [*Vancouver Stock Exchange symbol*]
TOR .... Torishima [*Japan*] [*Seismograph station code, US Geological Survey*] [*Closed*]   (SEIS)
TOR .... Toronto   (ROG)
TOR .... Toronto Airways Ltd. [*Markom, ON*] [*FAA designator*]   (FAAC)
TOR .... Torque   (AAG)
TOR .... Torrance [*California*]
Tor .... Torre [*A publication*]
TOR .... Torrington, WY [*Location identifier*] [*FAA*]   (FAAL)
TOR .... Totalizing Relay
TOR .... Traffic on Request [*Aviation*]   (FAAC)
TOR .... Turn-On Rate   (CAAL)
TORA .... Takeoff Run Available [*Aviation*]   (FAAC)
TORAC...... Torpedo Acquisition
TORAH....... Tough Orthodox Rabbis and Hassidim [*An association*]
TORC .... Test of Reading Comprehension
TORC .... Traffic Overload Reroute Control
TORCH...... Toxoplasma, Other [*Viruses*], Rubella, Cytomegaloviruses, Herpes [*Virus*]
TOREA .... Toshiba Review [*A publication*]
TOREADOR ... Torero-Matador [*Said to have been coined by Georges Bizet for opera "Carmen"*]
TORF......... Time of Retrofire [*NASA*]   (KSC)
Torf Promst ... Torfyanaya Promyshlennost [*A publication*]
Tori Bull Ornithol Soc Jpn ... Tori. Bulletin of the Ornithological Society of Japan [*A publication*]
Torino Univ Ist Geol Pub ... Torino Universita. Istituto Geologico. Pubblicazioni [*A publication*]
TORM........ Torquemeter
TORNL .... Torsional
Toronto U Faculty L Rev ... Toronto University. Faculty Law Review [*Canada*]   (DLA)
Toronto Univ Dep Mech Eng Tech Publ Ser ... Toronto University. Department of Mechanical Engineering. Technical Publication Series [*A publication*]
Toronto Univ Inst Aerosp Stud UTIAS Rep ... Toronto University. Institute for Aerospace Studies. UTIAS Report [*A publication*]
Toronto Univ Inst Aerosp Stud UTIAS Rev ... Toronto University. Institute for Aerospace Studies. UTIAS Review [*A publication*]
Toronto Univ Inst Aerosp Stud UTIAS Tech Note ... Toronto University. Institute for Aerospace Studies. UTIAS Technical Note [*A publication*]
Toronto Univ Studies G S ... Toronto University Studies. Geological Series [*A publication*]
TORP........ Torpedo   (AABC)
TORP.......... Total Ossicular Replacement Prosthesis
TORPA ...... Torfyanaya Promyshlennost [*A publication*]
TORPCM... Torpedo Countermeasures and Deception
TORPEX .... Torpedo Exercise   (NVT)
TORPRON ... Torpedo Squadron
TORQ .... Torque [*Automotive engineering*]
TORQUE .... Tests of Reasonable Quantitative Understanding of the Environment [*Education*]

TORR.......... Torricelli [*Unit of pressure*]
Torrey Bot Club Bull ... Torrey Botanical Club Bulletin [*A publication*]
Torry Res Stn Aberdeen Scotl Annu Rep ... Torry Research Station. Aberdeen, Scotland. Annual Report [*A publication*]
Torry Res Stn Annu Rep Handl Preserv Fish Fish Prod ... Torry Research Station. Annual Report on the Handling and Preservation of Fish and Fish Products [*A publication*]
TORS......... Time-Ordered Reporting System   (MCD)
TORS......... Torsion [*Automotive engineering*]
TORS......... Trade Opportunity Referral Service [*Department of Agriculture*] [*Washington, DC*] [*Information service*]   (EISS)
TOS............ Tactical Offense Subsystem
TOS............ Tactical Operations System [*ADSAF*]
TOS.......... Taken Out of Service [*Telecommunications*]   (TEL)
TOS.......... Tape Operating System [*IBM Corp.*] [*Data processing*]
TOS.......... Technical Operational Support
TOS.......... Technical Orders   (MCD)
TOS.......... Temporarily Out of Service   (DEN)
TOS.......... Temporarily Out of Stock [*Business and trade*]
TOS.......... Term of Service
TOS.......... Terminal-Oriented Software [*Data processing*]   (IEEE)
TOS.......... Terminal-Oriented System [*Data processing*]   (IEEE)
TOS.......... Test Operating System
TOS.......... Texas Ornithological Society. Bulletin [*A publication*]
TOS.......... Thermally and Oxidatively Stable
TOS.......... Thoracic Outlet Syndrome [*Medicine*]
TOS.......... Time-Ordered System   (MCD)
TOS.......... Time-on-Station [*Military*]   (INF)
TOS............ TIROS [*Television Infrared Observation Satellite*] Operational Satellite [*NASA*]
TOS............ Top of Stack [*Data processing*]
TOS............ Top of Steel [*Flooring*]   (AAG)
TOS............ Torque Overload Switch [*Nuclear energy*]   (NRCH)
Tos............ Tosafoth   (BJA)
TOS............ Tosco Corp. [*NYSE symbol*]
TOS............ Tosco Corp., Los Angeles, CA [*OCLC symbol*]   (OCLC)
Tos............ Tosefta   (BJA)
tos............ Tosyl [*As substituent on nucleoside*] [*Biochemistry*]
Tos............ Tosyl [*Also, Ts*] [*Organic chemistry*]
TOS............ Tramiel Operating System [*Atari, Inc.*]
TOS............ Transfer Orbit Stage [*Satellite booster*]
TOS............ Tromso [*Norway*] [*Airport symbol*]   (OAG)
TOS............ Turkiye Ogretmenler Sendikasi
TOS............ Type of Shipment
TOS2......... Tactical Operations System Operable Segment   (MCD)
Tosaf.......... Tosafoth   (BJA)
TosArgOMe ... Tosylarginine Methyl Ester [*Also, TAME*] [*Biochemistry*]
TOSBAC .... Toshiba Scientific and Business Automatic Computer [*Toshiba Corp.*]
TOSC .... Tactical Ocean Surveillance Coordinator [*Military*]   (CAAL)
TOSC .... To Other Service Center [*IRS*]
TOSC .... Touch-Operated Selector Control
TOSCA...... Total On-Line Searching and Cataloging Activities [*Information service*]
TOSCA...... Toxic Substances Control Act [*1976*]
TOSD .... Telephone Operations and Standards Division [*Rural Electrification Administration*] [*Telecommunications*]   (TEL)
TOSD .... Third Order of Saint Dominic   (EA-IO)
TOSE .... Tooling Samples
Tosef.......... Tosefta   (BJA)
Toseph........ Tosephta   (BJA)
TOSF.......... Tertiary of Third Order of St. Francis [*Later, SFO*] [*Roman Catholic religious order*]
TOSHIBA ... Tokyo Shibaura Electric Co. [*Computer manufacturer*] [*Japan*]
Toshiba Rev ... Toshiba Review [*Japan*] [*A publication*]
Toshiba Rev (Int Ed) ... Toshiba Review (International Edition) [*A publication*]
Tosh-Kai .... Toshokan-Kai [*A publication*]
Tosh Kenk ... Toshokan Kenkyu [*A publication*]
Tosh Zass ... Toshokan Zasshi [*A publication*]
TOSL .... Terminal-Oriented Service Language
TOSMIC ..... Toluenesulfonylmethyl Isocyanide [*or Tosylmethylisocyanide*] [*Organic chemistry*]
TOSMIC ..... Tosylmethyl Isocyanide [*Organic chemistry*]
TOS/OITDS ... Tactical Operations System/Operations and Intelligence Tactical Data Systems [*Military*]   (RDA)
TOSPDR..... Technical Order System Publication Deficiency Report [*Military*]   (AFIT)
TosPheCH₂Cl ... Tosylphenylalanine Chloromethyl Ketone [*Biochemistry*]
TOSR.......... Technical Order Status Report   (MCD)
TOSR.......... Thermally and Oxidatively Stable Resin
TOSS......... Tactical Operational Scoring System   (MCD)
TOSS......... Tactical Operations Support System   (MCD)
TOSS......... Television Ordnance Scoring System   (MCD)
TOSS......... Terminal-Oriented Support System
TOSS......... Test Operation Support Segment
TOSS......... TIROS [*Television Infrared Observation Satellite*] Operational Satellite System [*NASA*]
TOS-S .... Transfer Orbit Stage - Shortened Version [*Space technology*]

TOSS......... Transient and/or Steady State   (NRCH)
TOSS......... Turbine-Operated Suspension System [*NASA*]
TOSSA .... Transient or Steady-State Analysis [*Data processing*]
Tosyl .... Tolylsulfonyl [*Organic chemistry*]
TOT .... Denver, CO [*Location identifier*] [*FAA*]   (FAAL)
T/OT .... Table of Organization (Tentative)
TOT .... Takeoff Trim [*Aviation*]   (MCD)
TOT .... Tales of Tomorrow [*A publication*]
TOT .... Task Oriented Training   (MCD)
TOT .... Texas Opera Theatre
TOT .... Theatrum Orbis Terrarum [*Dutch firm*]
TOT .... Time of Takeoff [*Air Force*]   (AFIT)
TOT .... Time on Tape [*Military*]
TOT .... Time over Target [*Air support*]
TOT .... Time on Target [*Artillery support*]
TOT .... Time on Track
TOT .... Time of Transmission [*Communications*]
TOT .... Time of Travel   (MCD)
TOT .... Tincture of Time [*Medical slang for treatment of problems that are better left alone*]
TOT .... Tip-of-Tongue Phenomenon [*Medicine*]
TOT .... Total   (AAG)
TOT .... Totem Industries [*Vancouver Stock Exchange symbol*]
Tot............. Tothill's English Chancery Reports   (DLA)
Tot............. Tothill's Transactions in Chancery [*21 English Reprint*]   (DLA)
TOT .... Tottori [*Japan*] [*Seismograph station code, US Geological Survey*]   (SEIS)
TOT .... Trade-Off and Technology
TOT .... Transfer of Technology [*Telecommunications*]   (TEL)
TOT .... Transovarial Transmission [*Virology*]
TOT .... Transportation Office Will Furnish the Necessary Transportation [*Military*]
TOT .... Turbine Outlet Temperature   (NG)
TOT .... Turn-On Time
TOTE......... Teleprocessing On-Line Test Executive [*Data processing*]   (IBMDP)
TOTE......... Test-Operator-Test-Exit [*Unit*] [*Psychology*]
TOTE......... Time Out to Enjoy [*An association*] [*Oak Park, IL*]   (EA)
TOTEM....... Theater Operations and Tactical Evaluation Model
TOTES....... Time-Ordered Techniques Experiment System
TOTFORF... Total Forfeiture [*of all pay and allowances*] [*Army*]   (AABC)
TOTH.......... Toth Aluminum Corp. [*NASDAQ symbol*]   (NQ)
Tothill (Eng) ... Tothills English Chancery Reports   (DLA)
Tothill (Eng) ... Tothill's Transactions in Chancery [*21 English Reprint*]   (DLA)
TOTJ.......... Training on the Job
TOTLZ......... Totalize
TOTM......... Totalmed Associates [*NASDAQ symbol*]   (NQ)
TOTM......... Trioctyl Trimellitate [*Chemistry*]
TOTO.......... Tongue of the Ocean [*Area of the Bahama Islands*] [*Navy*]
TOTO.......... Totable Tornado Observatory [*National Oceanic and Atmospheric Administration*]
TOTP......... Tooling Template
TOTP......... Triorthotolylphosphate [*Organic chemistry*]
TOTPAR..... Total Pain Relief [*Medicine*]
TOTR......... Test Observation and Training Room [*Military*]   (CAAL)
TOTRAD..... Tape Output Test Rack Autonetics Diode
TOTS......... Total Operating Traffic System [*Bell System*]
TOTS......... Turn Off Television Saturday [*of Action for Children's Television organization*]
TOU............ Neah Bay, WA [*Location identifier*] [*FAA*]   (FAAL)
TOU............ Oak Ridge Associated Universities, Oak Ridge, TN [*Library symbol*] [*Library of Congress*]   (LCLS)
TOU............ Time of Use [*Utility rates*]
TOU............ Touho [*New Caledonia*] [*Airport symbol*]   (OAG)
TOU............ Trace Operate Unit
Touch........ Sheppard's Touchstone   (DLA)
Toull........... Toullier's Droit Civil Francais   (DLA)
TOUR......... Tourist Class Passengers [*Shipping*] [*British*]
Tourg Dig... Tourgee's North Carolina Digest   (DLA)
Tourism Aust ... Tourism Australia [*A publication*]
Tourism Intell Q ... Tourism Intelligence Quarterly [*A publication*]
TOURN...... Tournament
TOUS......... Test on Understanding Science
TOUS......... Transmission Oscillator Ultrasonic Spectrometer
Toute Electron ... Toute l'Electronique [*A publication*]
TOV............ El Indio, TX [*Location identifier*] [*FAA*]   (FAAL)
TOV............ El Tocuyo [*Venezuela*] [*Seismograph station code, US Geological Survey*]   (SEIS)
TOV............ Telemetering Oscillator Voltage
TOV............ Time out of View
TOV............ Tooele Valley Railway Co. [*AAR code*]
Tov............ Tovaris [*A publication*]
TOVA .... [*The*] Other Victims of Alcoholism [*New York, NY*]   (EA)
TOVALOP ... Tanker Owners Voluntary Agreement on Liability for Oil Pollution
Tovar Poshir Polit Nauk Znan Ukr SSR ... Tovaristvo dlya Poshirennya Politichnikh i Naukovikh Znan Ukrains'koi SSR [*A publication*]
TOVC .... Top of Overcast [*Aviation*]   (FAAC)
TOVD .... Transistor-Operated Voltage Divider

TOVR.......... Turnover (NVT)
TOVS.......... TIROS [*Television Infrared Observation Satellite*] Operational Vertical Sounder [*NASA*]
TOW .... Cooperstown, ND [*Location identifier*] [*FAA*] (FAAL)
TOW .... Takeoff Weight [*Aviation*]
TOW .... Tales of Wonder [*A publication*]
TOW .... Tank and Orbiter Weight (MCD)
TOW .... Towards (ROG)
TOW .... Tube-Launched, Optically Tracked, Wire-Guided [*Weapon*]
TOWA....... Terrain and Obstacle Warning and Avoidance
TOW CAP... TOW [*Tube-Launched, Optically-Tracked, Wire Guided (Weapon)*] Cover Artillery Protection
TOWER ...... Testing Orientation and Work Evaluation for Rehabilitation
Tower Hamlets Local Trade Dev ... Tower Hamlets Local Trade Development [*A publication*]
TO WHD ..... Two Wheeled [*Freight*]
TOWL........ Test of Written Language
Town & Country Plan ... Town and Country Planning [*A publication*]
Town Plan Inst J ... Town Planning Institute Journal [*A publication*]
Town Planning R ... Town Planning Review [*United Kingdom*] [*A publication*]
Town Plann Inst J ... Town Planning Institute Journal [*A publication*]
Town Plann Q ... Town Planning Quarterly [*New Zealand*] [*A publication*]
Town Plann Rev ... Town Planning Review [*A publication*]
Town Plan R ... Town Planning Review [*A publication*]
Townsh Pl ... Townshend's Pleading (DLA)
Townsh Sland & L ... Townshend on Slander and Libel (DLA)
Town Sl & Lib ... Townshend on Slander and Libel (DLA)
Town St Tr ... Townsend's Modern State Trials [*1850*] (DLA)
Townsville Nat ... Townsville Naturalist [*A publication*]
TOWPROS ... TOW [*Tube-Launched Optically Tracked Wire-Guided*] Protective Shelters (MCD)
TOWRS ...... Towermarc SBI [*NASDAQ symbol*] (NQ)
TOX .... Total Oxidants
TOX .... Toxicology
Tox Appl Ph ... Toxicology and Applied Pharmacology [*A publication*]
TOXBACK ... TOXLINE Back-File
TOXBIB ...... Toxicity Bibliography [*MEDLARS*]
TOXIA .... Toxicon [*A publication*]
Toxic Hazard Waste Disposal ... Toxic and Hazardous Waste Disposal [*A publication*]
TOXICOL ... Toxicology
Toxicol Annu ... Toxicology Annual [*A publication*]
Toxicol Appl Pharmacol ... Toxicology and Applied Pharmacology [*A publication*]
Toxicol Appl Pharmacol Suppl ... Toxicology and Applied Pharmacology. Supplement [*A publication*]
Toxicol Environ Chem Rev ... Toxicological and Environmental Chemistry Reviews [*A publication*]
Toxicol Eur Res ... Toxicological European Research [*A publication*]
Toxicol Lett ... Toxicology Letters [*A publication*]
TOXICON... Toxicology Information Conversational On-Line Network [*National Library of Medicine*] [*Later, TOXLINE*]
Toxic Subst J ... Toxic Substances Journal [*A publication*]
TOXLINE.... Toxicology On-Line [*National Library of Medicine*] [*Bethesda, MD*] [*Bibliographic database*]
TOXNET..... Toxicology Data Network [*National Library of Medicine*] [*Bethesda, MD*] [*Information service*] (EISS)
TOXREP..... Toxic Incident Report
TOXREPT... Toxic Incident Report (MUGU)
TOXT........ Toxteth (ROG)
TOY .... Toyama [*Japan*] [*Seismograph station code, US Geological Survey*] (SEIS)
TOY .... Toys R Us, Inc. [*NYSE symbol*]
TOY .... Troy, IL [*Location identifier*] [*FAA*] (FAAL)
TOYCOM ... [*A*] programing language [*1971*] (CSR)
TOYM........ Ten Outstanding Young Men of America [*Jaycees' program*]
Toyo Bunka Kenkyu Kiyo ... Toyo Bunka Kenkyushu Kiyo [*A publication*]
Toyo Junior Coll Food Technol Toyo Inst Food Technol Res Rep ... Toyo Junior College of Food Technology and Toyo Institute of Food Technology. Research Report [*Japan*] [*A publication*]
Toyota Eng ... Toyota Engineering [*Japan*] [*A publication*]
TOYOY...... Toyota Motor Co. ADR [*NASDAQ symbol*] (NQ)
TOZ .... Harvard University, Tozzer Library, Cambridge, MA [*OCLC symbol*] (OCLC)
TOZ .... Touba [*Ivory Coast*] [*Airport symbol*] (OAG)
TOZ .... Towarzystwo Ochrony Zdrowia [*A publication*] (BJA)
TP.............. Palestinian Talmud (BJA)
TP.............. [*The*] Prosperos [*El Monte, CA*] (EA)
T-P .... Tabloncillo Perla [*Race of maize*]
TP.............. Tail-Pinch Stress
TP.............. Tank Parliament [*British*]
TP.............. Tank Piercing [*Ammunition*] [*Military*]
TP.............. Tape (BUR)
TP.............. Target Point
TP.............. Target Population
TP.............. Target Practice [*Military*]
TP.............. Tax Planning (DLA)
TP.............. Taxpayer
TP.............. Teaching Practice
TP.............. Technical Pamphlet

TP.............. Technical Paper
TP.............. Technical Performance (MCD)
TP.............. Technical Problem
TP.............. Technical Proposal
TP.............. Technical Publication
TP.............. Technographic Publication
TP.............. Technology Parameter
TP.............. Technophility Index [*Mining technology*]
TP.............. Telemetry Processor
TP.............. Telephone (CET)
TP.............. Teleprensa [*Press agency*] [*Colombia*]
TP.............. Teleprinter
TP.............. Teleprocessing [*Data processing*] (MCD)
TP.............. Temperature and Pressure [*Medicine*]
TP.............. Temperature Probe (AAG)
T + P........ Temperature and Pulse [*Medicine*]
TP.............. Tempo Presente [*A publication*]
TP.............. Tempo Primo [*Original Tempo*] [*Music*]
TP.............. Temporary Patient [*British*]
TP.............. Tempore Paschale [*At Easter Time*] [*Latin*]
TP.............. Tensile Properties (MCD)
TP.............. Tentative Pamphlet
TP.............. Term Pass (AAG)
TP.............. Terminal Phalanx [*Anatomy*]
TP.............. Terminal Point (NATG)
TP.............. Terminal Pole [*Telecommunications*] (TEL)
TP.............. Terminal Processor
TP.............. Terrestrial Plants
TP.............. Territorial Party [*Northern Marianas*] (PPW)
TP.............. Terzo Programma [*Roma*] [*A publication*]
T/P .... Test Panel (AAG)
TP.............. Test Plan
TP.............. Test Point
TP.............. Test Port (KSC)
TP.............. Test Position
TP.............. Test Positive [*Clinical chemistry*]
TP.............. Test Pressure (NRCH)
TP.............. Test Procedure (NATG)
TP.............. Testosterone Propionate [*Endocrinology*]
TP.............. [*The*] Texas & Pacific Railway Co. [*Absorbed into Missouri Pacific System*] [*AAR code*]
T and P .... [*The*] Texas & Pacific Railway Co. [*Absorbed into Missouri Pacific System*]
TP.............. Text Processor
T and P .... Theft and Pilferage
TP.............. Thermoplastic [*Also, T*] [*Plastics technology*]
TP.............. Thermosphere Probe
TP.............. Thiamphenicol [*Antimicrobial compound*]
TP.............. Thiopental [*An anesthetic*]
T/P .... Third Party (ADA)
TP.............. Thomas Power [*"Tay Pay"*] O'Connor [*Irish journalist and politician, 1848-1929*]
TP.............. Thought Patterns [*A publication*]
TP.............. Thrombocytopenic Purpura [*Medicine*]
TP.............. Thrombophlebitis [*Medicine*]
TP.............. Throttle Positioner
TP.............. Thymic Polypeptide [*Endocrinology*]
TP.............. Thymopentin [*Biochemistry*]
TP.............. Thymopoietin
TP.............. Thymus Protein
TP.............. Tibialis Posterior [*Anatomy*]
TP.............. Tie Plate [*Technical drawings*]
TP.............. Tie Point
TP.............. Tijdschrift voor Philosophie [*A publication*]
T-P .... Timbre Poste [*Postage Stamp*] [*French*]
TP.............. Time to Perigee (MCD)
TP.............. Time Pulse
TP.............. Timing Point (AFM)
TP.............. Timpano [*Music*]
TP.............. Tin Plate
TP.............. Title Page [*Bibliography*]
TP.............. To Pay (ADA)
TP.............. Toilet Paper [*Slang*] [*To be "TP'd" is to have your yard covertly decorated with unrolled toilet paper*]
TP.............. Toll Point [*Telecommunications*] (TEL)
TP.............. Toll Prefix [*Telecommunications*] (TEL)
TP.............. Top
TP.............. Top Priority
TP.............. Topics in Photosynthesis [*Elsevier Book Series*] [*A publication*]
TP.............. Torpedo Part of Beam (MSA)
TP.............. Total Parts
TP.............. Total Phosphorus [*Analytical chemistry*]
TP.............. Total Points
TP.............. Total Power
TP.............. Total Pressure
TP.............. Total Production [*or Product*] [*Ecology*]
TP.............. Total Protein
TP.............. Totally Positive
TP.............. Touchdowns Passing [*Football*]
TP.............. T'oung Pao [*A publication*]
TP.............. Township

TP .... Toxic Pregnancy [*Gynecology*]
TP .... Tracking Program (MUGU)
TP .... Trade Protection Service [*or Society*] [*British*]
TP .... Traffic Post
TP .... Training Period [*Military*] (AFM)
TP .... Transaction Processing
TP .... Transannular Patch [*Cardiology*]
TP .... Transfer on Positive
TP .... Transforming Principle [*Bacteriology*]
TP .... Transition Period (NASA)
TP .... Transition Plans (MCD)
TP .... Translucent Paper (ADA)
TP .... Transport Pack
TP .... Transport Pilot
TP .... Transport Protein [*Superseded by SC, Secretory Component*] [*Immunology*]
TP .... Transportation Priority (AFM)
TP .... Transporter
TP .... Transportes Aereos Portugueses [*ICAO designator*] (FAAC)
TP .... Transvaal Province [*Republic of South Africa*]
TP .... Transvaal Supreme Court Reports [*South Africa*] (DLA)
TP .... Travaux Forces a Perpetuite [*Penal Servitude for Life*] [*French*]
TP .... Travaux Publics [*Public Works*] [*French*]
TP .... Travers Pensions [*Formerly, Naval Knights of Windsor*] [*Military*] [*British*] (ROG)
TP .... Treaty Port
TP .... Tree Project [*An association*] [*New York, NY*] (EA)
TP .... Treponema pallidum [*A spirochete*] [*Clinical chemistry*]
TP .... Trigonometrischer Punkt [*Triangulation Point*] [*German military - World War II*]
TP .... Triple Play [*Baseball*]
TP .... Triple Pole [*Switch*]
TP .... Troop
TP .... Troop Program [*Military*] (AABC)
TP .... Tropical Pacific [*American air mass*]
TP .... True Position
TP .... True Positive [*Medicine*]
TP .... True Profile [*Technical drawings*]
TP .... Trumpet
TP .... Tryptophan Pyrrolase [*Same as TPO*] [*An enzyme*]
TP .... Tuberculin Precipitation [*Medicine*]
TP .... Tuned Plate (DEN)
TP .... Turboprop (AAG)
TP .... Turbopump (AAG)
T & P .... Turner and Phillips' English Chancery Reports (DLA)
TP .... Turning Point
TPA .... Austin Peay State University, Clarksville, TN [*OCLC symbol*] (OCLC)
TPA .... Taildragger Pilots Association (EA)
TPA .... Tala Pozo [*Argentina*] [*Seismograph station code, US Geological Survey*] [*Closed*] (SEIS)
TPA .... Tampa Air Center [*Tampa, FL*] [*FAA designator*] (FAAC)
TPA .... Tampa/St. Petersburg/Clearwater [*Florida*] [*Airport symbol*]
TPA .... Tantalum Producers Association [*Cleveland, OH*] (EA)
TPA .... Tape Pulse Amplifier
TPA .... Target Position Analyzer [*Military*] (CAAL)
TPA .... Tariff Programs and Appraisals [*Canada Customs*]
TPA .... TASS [*Towed Array SONAR System*] Probability Area (NVT)
TPA .... Technical Practice Aid (ADA)
TPA .... Technical Publications Agent (MCD)
TPA .... Technical Publications Announcement
TPA .... Telemetry Power Amplifier
TPA .... Telepanel, Inc. [*Vancouver Stock Exchange symbol*]
TPA .... Telephone Pioneers of America [*New York, NY*] (EA)
TPA .... Tennis Professionals Association [*Canada*]
TPA .... Terephthalic Acid [*Also, TA*] [*Organic chemistry*]
TPA .... Test Plans and Analysis
TPA .... Test Preparation Area (KSC)
TPA .... Test Project Agreement (NG)
TPA .... Tetradecanoylphorbolacetate [*Also, PMA, PTA*] [*Organic chemistry*]
TPA .... Tetrapropylammonium [*Chemical radical*]
TPA .... Texture Profile Analysis [*Food technology*]
TPA .... Theta Phi Alpha [*Sorority*]
TPA .... Timber Producers Association of Michigan and Wisconsin [*Tomahawk, WI*] (EA)
TPA .... Tissue Plasminogen Activator [*Anticlotting agent*]
TPA .... Tissue Polypeptide Antigen [*Immunochemistry*]
TPA .... Toll Pulse Accepter [*Telecommunications*] (TEL)
TPA .... Tons per Annum (ADA)
TPA .... T'oung Pao. Archives [*A publication*]
TPA .... Tournament Players Association (EA)
TPA .... Track Production Area [*Air Force*]
TPA .... Traffic Pattern Altitude [*Aviation*]
TPA .... Training Problem Analysis (MCD)
TPA .... Trans-Pacific Airlines Ltd.
TPA .... Transfer of Pay Account [*Military*]
TPA .... Transient Program Area
TPA .... Transmission Products Association [*Tarrytown, NY*] (EA)
TPA .... TransPacific Asbestos [*Vancouver Stock Exchange symbol*]

TPA .... Travel by Personal Auto Authorized [*Military*]
TPA .... Trim Power Assembly
TPA .... Triphenylamine [*Organic chemistry*]
TPA .... Tunable Parametric Amplifier
TPA .... Turboprop Aircraft
TPA .... Turbopump Assembly (KSC)
TPA .... Type of Professional Activity
TPAA .... Travelers Protective Association of America (EA)
TPAC .... Technology Policy and Assessment Center [*Georgia Institute of Technology*] [*Research center*] (RCD)
TPAC .... Telescope Precision Angle Counter
TP-AD .... Technical Publications - Administration [*Naval Facilities Engineering Command Publications*]
TPAD .... Trunnion Pin Attachment Device [*NASA*]
TPAM .... Teleprocessing Access Method
TPAM .... Three-Phase Aquatic Microcosms [*Technique for study of waters*]
TPAMF .... Transpacific Asbestos Capital Shares [*NASDAQ symbol*] (NQ)
TPAOH .... Tetrapropylammonium Hydroxide [*Organic chemistry*]
TPAP .... Time-Phased-Action Plan [*DoD*]
TPAPA .... Transactions and Proceedings. American Philological Association [*A publication*]
TPAPOABITCOS ... [*The*] Precentor and Prebendary of Alton Borealis in the Church of Sarum [*Pseudonym used by Arthur Ashley Sykes*]
TPAR .... Tactical Penetration Aids Rocket
TPARR .... TRADOC Program Analysis and Resource Review [*Military*] (MCD)
TPAT .... Test Point Algorithm Technique (MCD)
TPAX .... Tampax, Inc. [*NASDAQ symbol*] (NQ)
TPB .... Nebraska Library Commission, Lincoln, NE [*OCLC symbol*] (OCLC)
TPB .... Tape Playback BIT [*Binary Digit*] [*Data processing*]
TPB .... Tennessee Philological Bulletin [*A publication*]
TPB .... Tetraphenylbutadiene [*Organic chemistry*]
TPB .... Tetraphenylbutane [*Organic chemistry*]
TpB .... Trypan Blue [*Biological stain*]
TPB .... Tryptone Phosphate Broth
T(PBEIST) ... Transport - Planning Board European Inland Surface Transport (NATG)
TPBF .... Total Pulmonary Blood Flow [*Physiology*]
TPBK .... Tape Block
T(PBOS) ..... Transport - Planning Board Ocean Shipping (NATG)
TPBS .... Tetrapropylenbenzenesulfonate [*Organic chemistry*]
TPBT .... Technical Papers for the Bible Translator [*A publication*] (BJA)
TPBVP .... Two-Point Boundary Value Problem
TPC .... Nebraska Library Commission, Lincoln, NE [*OCLC symbol*] (OCLC)
TPC .... Tactical Pilotage Chart
TPC .... Tangential Period Correction
TPC .... Technical Prime Contractor
TPC .... Technical Progress Committee [*British*]
TPC .... Technical Protein Colloid
TPC .... Telecommunications Planning Committee [*Civil Defense*]
TPC .... Telemetry Preprocessing Computer (MCD)
TPC .... Telephone Pickup Coil
TPC .... Territorial Production Complex [*Russian*]
TPC .... Test Point Controller
TPC .... Texas Petroleum Corporation [*Vancouver Stock Exchange symbol*]
TPC .... Thermafor Pyrolytic Cracking [*A chemical process developed by Surface Combustion*]
TP & C .... Thermal Protection and Control (NASA)
TPC .... Thermally Protected Composite
TPC .... Thromboplastic Plasma Component [*Factor VIII*] [*Also, AHF, AHG, PTF*] [*Hematology*]
TPC .... Thymolphthalein complexone [*Analytical reagent*]
TPC .... Time Polarity Control
TPC .... Time Projection Chamber [*High-energy physics*]
TPC .... Tons per Centimeter
TPC .... Topical Pulmonary Chemotherapy [*Medicine*]
TPC .... Topographic Center [*Defense Mapping Agency*]
TPC .... Total Package Contract
TPC .... Total Plasma Cholesterol [*Clinical chemistry*]
TPC .... Total Program Costs (KSC)
TPC .... Tournament Players Championship
TPC .... Trade Policy Committee [*Advisory to President*] [*Abolished, 1963*]
TPC .... Trade Practices Cases [*A publication*]
TPC .... Training Plans Conference
TPC .... Trans-Pacific Freight Conference of Japan/Korea Agent, San Francisco CA [*STAC*]
TPC .... Transistor Photo Control
TPC .... Transport Plane Commander
TPC .... Transvascular Protein Clearance [*Medicine*]
TPC .... Travaux Publics Canada [*Public Works Canada - PWC*]
TPC .... Travel by Privately-Owned Conveyance Permitted for Convenience [*Military*] (AFM)
TPC .... Treated Paper Copier [*Reprography*]
TPC .... Tricalcium Phosphate Ceramic [*Inorganic chemistry*]
TPC .... Triple Paper-Covered [*Wire insulation*] (DEN)

TPC .... Triple-Product Convolver [*Acousto-optic technology*]   (RDA)
TPC .... Turbopump Control
TPC .... Turns per Centimeter [*Yarn*]
TPC .... Twentynine Palms [*California*] [*Seismograph station code, US Geological Survey*]   (SEIS)
TPC .... Twisted Pair Cable
TPCA .... Test Procedure Change Authorization   (NATG)
TPCB .... [*The*] Personal Computer Book
TPCC .... TPC Communications [*NASDAQ symbol*]   (NQ)
TPCCA ...... Topics in Current Chemistry [*A publication*]
TPCD .... Trade Practices Commission. Decisions and Determinations [*A publication*]
TPCDD .... Trade Practices Commission. Decisions and Determinations [*A publication*]
TPCF .... Treponema pallidum Complement Fixation [*Clinical chemistry*]
TPCK .... Tosylamidophenylethyl Chloromethyl Ketone [*Organic chemistry*]
TPCN .... Task Plan Change Notice   (MCD)
TPCO .... Teleprinter Coordinator
TPCP .... Trainer Power Control Panel
TPCR .... Task Plan Change Request   (MCD)
TPCS .... Torquay Pottery Collectors' Society   (EA)
TPCU .... Thermal Preconditioning Unit
TPCV .... Turbine Power Control Valve
TPD .... Five Associated University Libraries, Rochester, NY [*OCLC symbol*]   (OCLC)
TPD .... South African Law Reports, Transvaal Provincial Division [*South Africa*]   (DLA)
T/PD .... Table of Personnel Distribution   (NATG)
TPD .... Tape Playback Discriminator
TPD .... Tapped   (MSA)
TPD .... Temperature Programed Desorption [*Catalysis*]
TPD .... Terminal Protective Device   (MSA)
TPD .... Test Plasma Produced by Discharge   (MCD)
TPD .... Test Point Data
TPD .... Test Procedure Deviation [*Nuclear energy*]   (NRCH)
TPD .... Test Procedure Drawing [*NASA*]   (KSC)
TPD .... Theophylline, Proxyphylline, and Dyphylline [*Antineoplastic drug regimen*]
TPD .... Thermoplastic Photoconductor Device
TPD .... Time Pulse Distributor   (MCD)
TPD .... Tons per Day
TPD .... Torque Proportioning Differential [*Automotive engineering*]
TPD .... Tournament Players Division of the Professional Golfers Association of America [*Later, TPA*]
TPD .... Training Programs Directorate [*Army*]
TPD .... Tumor-Producing Dose [*Virology*]
TPDB .... Tape Deblock
TPDLRI ...... Textile Printers and Dyers Labor Relations Institute [*Wayne, NJ*]   (EA)
TPDS .... Tape Playback Discriminator System
TPDS-T ..... Target Practice Discarding Sabot-Tracer [*Projectile*]   (MCD)
TPDT .... Triple-Pole, Double-Throw [*Switch*]
TPE .... Five Associated University Libraries, Rochester, NY [*OCLC symbol*]   (OCLC)
TPE .... T-Pulse Effectiveness [*Neurology*]
TPE .... Tactical Performance Evaluation
TPE .... Taipei [*Taiwan*] [*Airport symbol*]   (OAG)
TPE .... Technology, People, Environment [*National Science Foundation project*]
TPE .... Test Planning and Evaluation
TP & E .... Test Planning and Evaluation   (MCD)
TPE .... Test Project Engineer   (NASA)
TPE .... Thermoplastic Elastomer [*Plastics technology*]
TPE .... Threshold Photoelectron [*Spectroscopy*]
TPE .... Total Potential Energy
TPE .... Transaction Processing Executive   (MCD)
TPE .... Transport Planning and Economics [*British*]
TPE .... Triple Crown Electronics, Inc. [*Toronto Stock Exchange symbol*]
TPE .... Turbopropeller Engine
TPEA .... Television Program Export Association   (EA)
TPED .... Trade and Professional Exhibits Directory [*Later, TSPED*] [*A publication*]
T-PEES ..... Triplane Elevated Evaluation System [*Army*]   (RDA)
TPer .... Tetradi Perevodcika [*A publication*]
TPESP .... Technical Panel on the Earth Satellite Program
TPET .... Terrapet Energy Corp. [*NASDAQ symbol*]   (NQ)
TPEX .... TPEX Exploration [*NASDAQ symbol*]   (NQ)
TPEY .... Tellurite-Polymyxin-Egg Yolk [*Agar*] [*Microbiology*]
TPF .... Tactical Patrol Force [*Police*]
TPF .... Tampa, FL [*Location identifier*] [*FAA*]   (FAAL)
TPF .... Telemetry Processing Facility   (MCD)
TPF .... Temporary Program File [*Data processing*]
TPF .... Terminal Phase Finalization [*or Finish*] [*NASA*]   (KSC)
TPF .... Tetraphenylfuran [*Organic chemistry*]
TPF .... Thai Patriotic Front [*Communist-directed activity outside Thailand*] [*Merged with TIM*]
TPF .... Theoretical Point of Fog   (MSA)
TPF .... Time Prism Filter [*Telecommunications*]   (TEL)
TPF .... Total Peaking Factor [*Nuclear energy*]   (NRCH)

TPF .... Trainer Parts Fabrication   (AAG)
TPF .... Transfer Phase Final   (MCD)
TPF .... Tri-Pacific Resources Ltd. [*Vancouver Stock Exchange symbol*]
TPF .... Tug Processing Facility [*NASA*]   (NASA)
TPF .... Two-Phase Flow
TPFC .... [*The*] Platters Fan Club [*Las Vegas, NV*]   (EA)
TPF & C .... Towers, Perrin, Forster & Crosby [*Compensation and actuarial consulting company*]
TPFDD ...... Time-Phased Force Deployment Data [*Military*]   (AABC)
TPFDL .... Time-Phased Force Deployment List [*Military*]   (AFM)
TPFI .... Terminal Pin Fault Insertion
TPFP .... Transkei People's Freedom Party [*South Africa*]   (PPW)
TPFW .... Thermoplastic Fan Wheel
TPFW .... Three-Phase Full Wave
TPG .... Tapping
TPG .... Technology Planning Guide [*Military*]   (AFIT)
TPG .... Telecommunication Program Generator
TPG .... Teletype Preamble Generator
TPG .... Thermionic Power Generator
TPG .... Timing Pulse Generator
TPG .... Topping   (FAAC)
TPG .... Town Planning and Local Government Guide [*A publication*]
TPG .... Triphenylguanidine [*Organic chemistry*]
TPG .... Trypticase, Peptone, Glucose
TPGC .... Temperature Programed Gas Chromatography
TPGS .... Tocopherol Polyethylene Glycol Succinate [*Organic chemistry*]
TPH .... Theosophical Publishing House
TPH .... Thromboembolic Pulmonary Hypertension [*Medicine*]
TPh. .... Tijdschrift voor Philosophie [*A publication*]
TPH .... Tonopah [*Nevada*] [*Seismograph station code, US Geological Survey*]   (SEIS)
TPH .... Tonopah, NV [*Location identifier*] [*FAA*]   (FAAL)
TPH .... Tons per Hour
TPH .... Total Possessed Hours   (MCD)
TPH .... Trumph Resources Corp. [*Vancouver Stock Exchange symbol*]
TPH .... University of Texas, Health Science Center at Houston, School Public Health, Houston, TX [*OCLC symbol*]   (OCLC)
TPHA .... Treponema Pallidum Hemagglutination
TPHA .... Truman Philatelic and Historical Association   (EA)
TPHASAP... Telephone as Soon as Possible   (NOAA)
TPHAT .... Telephone at [*Followed by time*]   (NOAA)
TPHAYC.... Telephone at Your Convenience   (NOAA)
TPHC .... Time-to-Pulse Height Converter
TPhl .... Turfan Pahlavi   (BJA)
TPHO .... Telephotograph
TPhS .... Transactions. Philological Society [*A publication*]
TPhS .... Transactions. Philosophical Society [*London and Strassburg*] [*A publication*]
TPHSG ...... Troop Housing [*Army*]   (AABC)
TPHW .... Three-Phase Half Wave
TPI............ [*The*] Progress Interview
TPI............ Tape Phase Inverter
TPI............ Tape-Position Indicator   (DEN)
TPI............ Tapini [*Papua New Guinea*] [*Airport symbol*]   (OAG)
TPI............ Target Position Indicator
TPI............ Task Parameter Interpretation
TPI............ Tax Planning Ideas   (DLA)
TPI............ Tax and Price Index [*British*]
TPI............ Taxpayer Inquiry [*IRS*]
TPI............ Teatro Popolare Italiano [*Italian theatrical troupe*]
TPI............ Technical Proficiency Inspection
TPI............ Teeth per Inch [*of cog wheels*]
TPI............ Tennessee Polytechnic Institute
TPI............ Terminal Phase Ignition [*NASA*]
TPI............ Terminal Phase Initiate [*NASA*]   (KSC)
TPI............ Terminal Phase Insertion [*NASA*]
TPI............ Test Program Instruction   (MCD)
TPI............ Thermal Protection Investigation
TPI............ Threads per Inch
TPI............ Timing Pulse Idler
TPI............ Tire Pressure Indicating System   (MCD)
TPI............ Tons per Inch
TPI............ Total Positive Income [*IRS*]
TPI............ Totally and Permanently Incapacitated   (ADA)
T & PI........ Totally and Permanently Incapacitated   (ADA)
TPI............ Tracks per Inch [*Magnetic storage devices*] [*Data processing*]
TPI............ TRADOC Procurement Instruction   (MCD)
TPI............ Training Plan Information   (MCD)
TPI............ Transmission Performance Index [*Telecommunications*]   (TEL)
TPI............ Treponema pallidum Immobilization [*or Immobilizing*] [*Clinical chemistry*]
TPI............ Trim Position Indicator
TPI............ Triosephosphate Isomerase [*An enzyme*]
TPI............ Triphosphoinositide [*Biochemistry*]
TPI............ Truss Plate Institute [*Madison, WI*]   (EA)
TPI............ Tuned Port Fuel Injection
TPI............ Turns per Inch
TPIA .... Treponema pallidum Immune Adherence [*Clinical chemistry*]
TPIM .... Tool Process Instruction Manual   (MCD)

TPIRA .... Trudy Gosudarstvennyi Institut po Proektirovaniyu i Issledovatel'skim Rabotam v Neftedobyvayushchei Promyshlennosti [*A publication*]
TPI Rep Trop Prod Inst ... TPI Report. Tropical Products Institute [*A publication*]
TPIS .... Tire Pressure Indicating System (MCD)
TPIX .... Telepictures Corp. [*NASDAQ symbol*] (NQ)
TPJ .... Tangkuban-Prahu [*Java*] [*Seismograph station code, US Geological Survey*] [*Closed*] (SEIS)
TPJ .... Tennessee Poetry Journal [*A publication*]
TPJSL .... Transactions and Proceedings. Japan Society (London) [*A publication*]
TPK .... Test of Practical Knowledge
TPK .... Tulare Free Public Library, Tulare, CA [*OCLC symbol*] (OCLC)
TPK .... Turnpike
TPK .... Turns per Knot [*Navy*] (CAAL)
TPKE .... Turnpike (MCD)
TPKrR .... Theologicka Priloha (Krestanske Revue) [*A publication*] (BJA)
TPL .... Table Producing Language [*1971*] [*Data processing*] (EISS)
TPL .... Tabular Parts List
TPL .... Target Position Location (MCD)
TPL .... Technical Publications Library (MCD)
TPL .... Temple [*Texas*] [*Airport symbol*] (OAG)
TPL .... Temple, TX [*Location identifier*] [*FAA*] (FAAL)
TPL .... Terminal per Line [*Telecommunications*]
TPL .... Terminal Processing Language
TPND .... Test Parts List
TPL .... Test Plan (CAAL)
TPL .... Test Plan Log (MCD)
TPL .... Test Point Logic
TPL .... Texas Pacific Land Trust [*NYSE symbol*]
TPL .... Tocopilla [*Chile*] [*Seismograph station code, US Geological Survey*] (SEIS)
TPL .... Toll Pole Line [*Telecommunications*] (TEL)
TPL .... Topsail [*Ship's rigging*] (ROG)
TPL .... Toronto Public Library [*UTLAS symbol*]
TPL .... Training Parts List (AAG)
TPL .... Transistorized Portable Laboratory
TPL .... Trap Processing Line
TPL .... Triple (MSA)
TPL .... Triumph Petroleums Limited [*Vancouver Stock Exchange symbol*]
TPL .... Troop Program List [*Army*]
TPL .... Tropicalized (MSA)
TPL .... Trust for Public Land [*An association*] (EA)
TPL .... Tunable Pulsed LASER
TPL .... Turns per Layer
TPLA .... [*The*] Product Liability Alliance [*Washington, DC*] (EA)
TPLA .... Triphenyllead Acetate [*Organic chemistry*]
TPLA .... Turkish People's Liberation Army (PD)
TPLAF .... Thai People's Liberation Armed Forces [*Thailand*]
TPLD .... Test Planning Liaison Drawing (AAG)
TPLF .... Tigre People's Liberation Front [*Ethiopian*] (PD)
TP & LGG .. Town Planning and Local Government Guide [*A publication*]
TPLGG ...... Town Planning and Local Government Guide [*A publication*]
TPLP .... Tobacco Products Liability Project [*An association*] [*Boston, MA*] (EA)
TPLP .... Turkish People's Liberation Party (PD)
TPLP/F ...... Turkish People's Liberation Party/Front (PD)
TPLPZ .... Teeco Properties [*NASDAQ symbol*] (NQ)
TPLQ-A ..... Town Planning and Quarterly [*New Zealand*] [*A publication*]
TPLR-A ..... Town Planning Review [*United Kingdom*] [*A publication*]
TPLS .... Terminal Position Location System
TPLS .... Texas Panhandle Library System [*Library network*]
TPLS .... Tunable Pulsed LASER System
T/PLT .... Tapping Plate [*Automotive engineering*]
TPLW .... Triple Wall
TPM .... Tape Preventive Maintenance
TPM .... Tape Processing Machine
TPM .... Technical Performance Measurement
TPM .... Technical Performance Module (MCD)
TPM .... Telemetry Processor Module
TPM .... Tepoztlan [*Mexico*] [*Seismograph station code, US Geological Survey*] (SEIS)
TPM .... Terminal Phase Maneuver (MCD)
TPM .... Terminal Phase Midcourse (MCD)
TPM .... Test Planning Manager [*NASA*] (KSC)
TPM .... Theoretical Platers per Meter [*Chromatography*]
TPM .... Thermal Power Monitor [*Nuclear energy*] (NRCH)
TPM .... Timber Products Manufacturers [*Spokane, WA*] (EA)
TPM .... Title Page Mutilated
TPM .... Tons per Minute
TPM .... Tons per Month
TPM .... Total Downtime for Preventive Scheduled Maintenance [*Quality control*] (MCD)
TPM .... Total Particulate Matter [*The "tar" of cigar and cigarette smoke*]
TPM .... Total Passive Motion
TPM .... Total Population Management [*Department of Agriculture*]
TPM .... Tours par Minute [*Revolutions per Minute*] [*French*]
TPM .... Transfer Phase Midcourse (MCD)

TPM .... Transmission and Processing Model
TPM .... Trigger Pricing Mechanism
TPM .... Triplate Module
TPMA .... Thermodynamic Properties of Metals and Alloys (KSC)
TPMA .... Timber Products Manufacturers Association [*Later, TPM*]
TPMF .... Tax Practitioner Master File [*IRS*]
TPMG .... [*The*] Provost Marshal General [*Army*]
TPMGA ..... Teoriya i Praktika Metallurgii [*A publication*]
TPMM .... Teleprocessing Multiplexer Module
TP-MO .... Technical Publications - Maintenance Operation [*Naval Facilities Engineering Command Publications*]
TPMP .... Tender Production Management Program
TPMP .... Texas Pacific-Missouri Pacific Terminal [*Railroad of New Orleans*] [*AAR code*]
TPN .... Pan American University, Library, Edinburg, TX [*OCLC symbol*] (OCLC)
TPN .... Sandoz Pharmaceuticals [*Research code symbol*]
TPN .... Tapini [*Papua New Guinea*] [*Seismograph station code, US Geological Survey*] [*Closed*] (SEIS)
TPN .... Tetrachlorophthalodinitrile [*Organic chemistry*]
TPN .... Thalamic Projection Neurons [*Neurology*]
TPN .... Total Parenteral Nutrition
TPN .... Total Petroleum (North America) Ltd. [*American Stock Exchange symbol*] [*Toronto Stock Exchange symbol*]
TPN .... Triphosphopyridine Nucleotide [*See NADP*] [*Biochemistry*]
TP & N .... Triple Pole and Neutral [*Switch*]
TPND .... Theft, Pilferage, and Nondelivery [*Business and trade*]
TP & ND ..... Theft, Pilferage, and Nondelivery [*Business and trade*] (ADA)
TPNEG ...... Travel Will Be Performed at No Expense to the Government [*Military*]
TPNG .... Territory of Papua and New Guinea
TPNG .... Topping (AAG)
TPNH .... Triphosphopyridine Nucleotide (Reduced) [*See NADPH*] [*Biochemistry*]
TPNL .... Townsend Plan National Lobby [*Hyattsville, MD*] (EA)
T/PNL .... Trim Panel [*Automotive engineering*]
TPNO .... Tree Planters' Notes [*A publication*]
TPNS .... Teleprocessing Network Simulator
TPO .... Sandoz Pharmaceuticals [*Research code symbol*]
TPO .... Tanalian Point, AK [*Location identifier*] [*FAA*] (FAAL)
TPO .... Tank Pressurizing Orifice (KSC)
TPO .... Technical Planning Office
TPO .... Technology Planning Objectives (MCD)
TPO .... Telecommunications Program Objective [*Army*] (AABC)
TPO .... Temperature Programed Oxidation [*For surface analysis*]
Tpo .... Tempo [*Record label*] [*Germany*]
TPO .... TEMPO Enterprises, Inc. [*American Stock Exchange symbol*]
TPO .... Tentative Program Objectives [*Navy*]
TPO .... Test Program Outline [*Military*]
TPO .... Thermoplastic Olefinic [*Elastomer*]
TPO .... Thyroid Peroxidase [*An enzyme*]
TPO .... Track Production Officer [*NATO Air Defense Ground Environment*] (NATG)
TPO .... Transportation Packaging Order (AFM)
TPO .... Traveling Post Office
TPO .... Tryptophan Oxygenase [*Same as TP*] [*An enzyme*]
TPO .... Tuned Plate Oscillator
TPOD .... Test Plan of the Day
TPOM .... Tentative Program Objectives Memorandum [*Military*] (CAAL)
TPOM .... Tube Propagation d'Ondes Magnetron
TPorH .... Highland Hospital, Portland, TN [*Library symbol*] [*Library of Congress*] (LCLS)
TPOS .... Track Position
TPow .... Tygodnik Powszechny [*A publication*]
TPP .... Tarapoto [*Peru*] [*Airport symbol*] (OAG)
TPP .... Technical Performance Parameter (MCD)
TPP .... Technology Program Plan [*Military*] (AFIT)
TPP .... Telephony Preprocessor [*Telecommunications*] (TEL)
TPP .... Teletype Page Printer
TPP .... Test Point Pace (KSC)
TPP .... Test Program Plan (MCD)
TPP .... Tetraphenylporphine [*Organic chemistry*]
TPP .... Tetraphenylporphyrin [*Biochemistry*]
TPP .... Textured Peanut Protein [*Food industry*]
TPP .... Thermal Power Plant (CINC)
TPP .... Thermal Protection Panel
TPP .... Thermally Protected Plastic
TPP .... Thiamine Pyrophosphate [*Also, DPT, TDP*] [*Biochemistry*]
TP & P .... Time, Place, and Person
TPP .... Toledo Progressive Party [*Belizean*] (PPW)
TPP .... Total Package Procurement [*Government contracting*]
TPP .... Total Program Planning/Procurement
TPP .... Trained Profile Panel [*Sensory testing*]
TPP .... Trans-Pluto Probe
TPP .... Transducer Power Programer
TP & P .... Transients, Patients, and Prisoners [*Military*]
TPP .... Transients, Patients, and Prisoners [*Military*]
TPP .... Transport Policies and Programme [*British*]
TPP .... Tri-Power Petroleum [*Toronto Stock Exchange symbol*] [*Vancouver Stock Exchange symbol*]

TPP............ Trinidad [*Pointe-A-Pierre*] [*Trinidad-Tobago*] [*Seismograph station code, US Geological Survey*]   (SEIS)
TPP............ Triphenyl Phosphite [*Organic chemistry*]
TPP............ Tripolyphosphate [*Food industry*]
TPP............ True Path Party [*Turkey*]
TPP............ Two-Phase Principle
TPPC.......... Total Package Procurement Concept [*Government contracting*]
TPPC.......... Trans-Pacific Passenger Conference [*Later, PCC*]   (EA)
TPPD.......... Technical Program Planning Division [*Air Force*]   (MCD)
TPPEP........ Turkey Point Performance Enforcement Program [*Nuclear energy*]   (NRCH)
TPPGM....... Tentative Planning and Programing Guidance Memorandum [*Navy*]   (NVT)
TPPIS......... Treasury Payroll/Personnel Information System
TP-PL......... Technical Publications - Planning [*Naval Facilities Engineering Command Publications*]
TPPN.......... Total Peripheral Parenteral Nutrition
TPPS.......... Tape Post-Processing System
TPPS.......... Tetraphenylporphinesulfonate [*Reagent*]
TP-PU......... Technical Publications - Public Utilities [*Naval Facilities Engineering Command Publications*]
TPQ............ AMIGOS Bibliographic Council, Dallas, TX [*OCLC symbol*]   (OCLC)
TPQ............ Government of Quebec [*Canada*] [*FAA designator*]   (FAAC)
TPQ............ Tepic [*Mexico*] [*Airport symbol*]
T P Q .... Theologisch-Praktische Quartalschrift [*A publication*]
TPQI........... Teacher-Pupil Question Inventory
TPQS.......... Theologische Praktische Quartalschrift [*A publication*]
TPR............ AMIGOS Bibliographic Council, Dallas, TX [*OCLC symbol*]   (OCLC)
TPR............ Tamper-Protected Recording [*3M Co.*]
TPR............ Tape Programed Row [*Data scanner*]
TPR............ Taper   (MSA)
TPR............ Team Power Rating [*Hockey*]
TPR............ Technical Progress Report
TPR............ Technical Proposal Requirement   (MCD)
TPR............ Teleprinter   (AAG)
TPR............ Telescopic Photographic Recorder
TPR............ Temperature Profile Recorder   (AAG)
TPR............ Temperature Programed Reduction [*For analysis of surfaces*]
TPR............ Temperature, Pulse, Respiration [*Medicine*]
TPr............ Tempo Presente [*A publication*]
TPR............ Terrain Profile Recorder
TPR............ Test Performance Recorder
TPR............ Test Phase Report
TPR............ Test Problem Report [*NASA*]   (NASA)
TPR............ Test Procedure Record   (NATG)
TPR............ Thermoplastic Rubber
TPR............ Three Penny Review [*A publication*]
TPR............ Total Peripheral Resistance
TPR............ Total Pulmonary Resistance [*Cardiology*]
TPR............ Trained Personnel Requirements [*Air Force*]
TPR............ Transmitter Power Rating
TPR............ Trapped Pressure Ratio [*Gas analysis*]
TPR............ Trooper
TPRC.......... Thermophysical Properties Research Center [*DoD*]
TPRG.......... Technology Performance Requirements Guideline
TPRI........... Teacher-Pupil Relationship Inventory
TPRI........... Total Peripheral Resistance Index
TPRL.......... Thermophysical Properties Research Laboratory [*Purdue University*] [*Research center*]   (RCD)
TPRRD ...... Technik-Index ueber Plasmaphysikalische Forschung und Fusionsreaktoren [*A publication*]
TPRS.......... Temperature-Programed Reaction Spectroscopy
TPRS.......... Trade Practices Reporting Service [*A publication*]
TPRSL....... Transactions and Proceedings. Royal Society of Literature [*A publication*]
TPRU.......... Technical Processing and Reporting Unit   (CAAL)
TPRU.......... Tropical Pesticides Research Unit [*Later, Centre for Overseas Pest Research*] [*British*]
TPRV .... Transient Peak Reverse Voltage
TPrzPI .... Trudy Przeval'skogo Pedagogiceskogo Instituta [*A publication*]
TPS .... Bibliographic Center for Research, Denver, CO [*OCLC symbol*]   (OCLC)
TPS .... [*The*] Pope Speaks [*A publication*]
TPS .... Tandem Propeller Submarine
TPS .... Tangent Plane System   (MUGU)
TPS .... Tank Pressure Sensing   (AAG)
TPS .... Tape Plotting System
TPS .... Tape Processing System   (CMD)
TPS .... Tape Punch Subassembly
TPS .... Task Parameter Synthesizer
TPS .... Technical Publishing Society [*Later, STC*]
TPS .... Technology Policy Statement [*1982*] [*Indian*]
TPS .... Telecommunications Programing System
TPS .... Telemation Program Services
TPS .... Telemetry Processing System [*Space Flight Operations Facility, NASA*]
TPS .... Terminal Performance Specification
TPS .... Terminal Polling System

TPS .... Terminals per Station [*Telecommunications*]
TPS .... Test Pilot School [*Navy*]
TPS .... Test Plotting System
TPS .... Test Point Selector
TPS .... Test Preparation Sheet   (AAG)
TPS .... Test Procedure Specification [*NASA*]   (KSC)
TPS .... Test Program Set   (MCD)
TPS .... Theologie Pastorale et Spiritualite [*A publication*]
TPS .... Thermal Protection System [*or Subsystem*]
TPS .... Thermoplastic Storage
TPS .... Threat Platform Simulator [*Military*]   (CAAL)
TPS .... Throttle Position Sensor [*Automotive engineering*]
TPS .... Total Parameter Space [*Statistics*]
TPS .... Total Product Support
TPS .... TPA of America [*American Stock Exchange symbol*]
TPS .... Trail Pilot Sensor
TPS .... Tramp Power Supply
TPS .... Transaction Processing System
TPS .... Transactions. Philological Society [*London*] [*A publication*]
TPS .... Transduodenal Pancreatic Sphincteroplasty
TPS .... Translunar Propulsion Stage [*Aerospace*]   (AAG)
TPS .... Trapani [*Italy*] [*Airport symbol*]   (OAG)
TPS .... Tree Pruning System
TPS .... Tube Pin Straightener
TPS .... Tumor Polysaccharidal Substance [*Oncology*]
TPS .... Turkey Point Station [*Nuclear energy*]   (NRCH)
TPS .... Turner Program Services [*Broadcasting*]
TPS .... Tuvalu Philatelic Society   (EA)
TPSB......... Telemetry Processing System Buffer [*Space Flight Operations Facility, NASA*]
TPSC......... Test Planning and Status Checker [*Data processing*]
TPSC......... Trade Policy Staff Committee [*Federal interagency group*]
TPSE......... (Tritylphenyl)sulfonylethanol [*Organic chemistry*]
TPSF......... Telephonie sans Fil [*Wireless Telephony*]
TPSF......... Terminal Profile Security File [*IRS*]
TPSFA....... Tohoku Psychologica Folia [*A publication*]
TPSI.......... Torque Pressure in Pounds per Square Inch
TPSL......... Tyoevaeen ja Pienviljelijaein Sosialidemokraattinen Liitto [*Social Democratic League of Workers and Smallholders*] [*Finland*]   (PPE)
TPSM .... Tepatshimuwin. Journal d'Information des Attikamekes et des Montagnais [*A publication*]
TPSN......... Transposition   (AAG)
TPSN........ Troop Program Sequence Number
TPSO......... Triphenylstibine Oxide [*Organic chemistry*]
TPSP......... Tape Punch Subassembly Panel
TPSRS....... Theologie Pastorale et Spiritualite. Recherches et Syntheses [*A publication*]
TPSS......... Thermal Protection System Selection
TPST......... Training and Personnel Systems Technology   (MCD)
TPST......... Triple-Pole, Single-Throw [*Switch*]
TPSTe....... Triisopropylbenzenesulfonyl Tetrazolide [*Organic chemistry*]
TPT............ Air Transport Corp. [*Detroit, MI*] [*FAA designator*]   (FAAC)
TPT............ Bibliographic Center for Research, Denver, CO [*OCLC symbol*]   (OCLC)
TPT............ Tail Pipe Temperature   (NG)
TPT............ Tappet [*Mechanical engineering*]
TPT............ Tappit Resources [*Vancouver Stock Exchange symbol*]
TPT............ Target Practice [*Ammunition*] with Tracer
TPT............ Teleprinter Planning Table
TPT............ Temporary Part Time [*Personnel*]   (MCD)
TPT............ Test Pilot Training
TPT............ Tetraisopropyl Titanate [*Organic chemistry*]
TPT............ Time to Peak Tension
TPT............ Time Priority Table
TPT............ Tiputa [*Tuamotu Archipelago*] [*Seismograph station code, US Geological Survey*]   (SEIS)
TPT............ Total Pressure Transducer
TPT............ Totul pentru Tara [*"All for the Fatherland"*] [*Romanian*]   (PPE)
TPT............ Training Proficiency Test [*Army*]   (INF)
TPT............ Transonic Pressure Tunnel [*NASA*]
TPT............ Transport
TPT............ Trenton-Princeton Traction Co. [*Absorbed into Consolidated Rail Corp.*] [*AAR code*]
TPT............ Trumpet
TPT............ Typhoid-Paratyphoid [*Medicine*]
TPTA......... Thiophosphoryl Triamide [*Fertilizer technology*]
TPTA......... Tin Triphenyl [*or Triphenyltin*] Acetate [*Organic chemistry*]
TPTC......... Triphenyltin Chloride [*Organic chemistry*]
TPTD......... Test Pilot Training Division
TPTD......... Transported
TPTE......... (Tritylphenyl)thioethanol [*Organic chemistry*]
TPTG......... Tuned Plate Tuned Grid [*Electronic tube*]
TPTH......... Triphenyltin Hydroxide [*Organic chemistry*]
TPTOL....... True Position Tolerance   (MSA)
TPTR......... Topps and Trousers [*NASDAQ symbol*]   (NQ)
TPTR......... Transporter
TPTR......... Trumpeter
TPTRL....... Time-Phased Transportation Requirements List [*Military*]   (AABC)
TPTS......... Two-Phase Thermosyphon [*Heat exchanger*]

TPTX .... Thyroparathyroidectomized [*Medicine*]
TPTZ .... Triphenyltetrazolium Chloride [*Also, RT, TTC*] [*Chemical indicator*]
TPTZ .... Tris(pyridyl)-s-triazine [*Analytical chemistry*]
TPU .... Capitol Consortium Network, Washington, DC [*OCLC symbol*] (OCLC)
TPU .... Tape Preparation Unit
TPU .... Tarn Pure Technology Corp. [*Vancouver Stock Exchange symbol*]
TPU .... Task Processing Unit
TPU .... Telecommunications Processing Unit
TPU .... Thermoplastic Urethane [*Plastics technology*]
TPU .... Troop Program Unit [*Army*] (AABC)
TPU .... Trunk Processing Unit [*Bell System*]
TPU .... Turbopower Unit
TPUC .... Telephone Pickup Coil
TPUG .... Toronto PET Users Group [*Canada*]
TP/UMF ..... Total Package/Unit Materiel Fielding [*Army*] (RDA)
TPUN .... Test Procedure Update Notice (NASA)
TPUS .... Transportation and Public Utilities Service [*Later, part of Transportation and Communication Service, GSA*]
TPV .... Capitol Consortium Network, Washington, DC [*OCLC symbol*] (OCLC)
TPV .... Thermophotovoltaic
TPV .... Thermoplastic Vulcanizate [*Plastics technology*]
TPV .... Tonopah [*Nevada*] [*Seismograph station code, US Geological Survey*] [*Closed*] (SEIS)
TPV .... Transverse Pallial Vein
TPV .... Triple Polio Vaccine [*Medicine*]
TPW .... Tenth-Power Width
TPW .... Title Page Wanting
TPW .... Toledo, Peoria & Western Railroad Co. [*AAR code*]
TP & W ..... Toledo, Peoria & Western Railroad Co.
TPW .... Tons per Week
TPW .... True Polar Wandering [*Geophysics*]
TPWBH ...... Tax Paid Wine Bottling House
TPWG .... Test Planning Working Group [*Military*]
TPWIC .... Theater Prisoner of War Information Center
TPWU .... Tanganyika Plantation Workers Union
TPWU .... Tea Plantation Workers' Union [*Kenya*]
TPX .... Total Pancreatectomy [*Medicine*]
TPX .... Transponder (KSC)
TPY .... FEDLINK [*Federal Library and Information Network*], Washington, DC [*OCLC symbol*] (OCLC)
TPY .... Tapestry (ADA)
TPY .... Tons per Year
TPY .... Trans-Provincial Airlines Ltd. [*Prince Rupert, BC*] [*FAA designator*] (FAAC)
TPZ .... FEDLINK [*Federal Library and Information Network*], Washington, DC [*OCLC symbol*] (OCLC)
TPZ .... Thioperazine [*or Thioproperazine*] [*Tranquilizer*]
TQ .... Tale Quale [*Of Conditions on Arrival*] [*Latin*]
TQ .... Texas Quarterly [*A publication*]
TQ .... Theatre Quarterly [*A publication*]
TQ .... Theologische Quartalschrift [*Tuebingen*] [*A publication*]
TQ .... Thought Quality [*Psychology*]
TQ .... Three-Quarter Midget [*Horse racing*]
TQ .... Tocopherolquinone [*Vitamin E*] [*Biochemistry*]
TQ .... Toronto Quarterly [*A publication*]
TQ .... Trans Oceanic Airways Ltd. [*Great Britain*] [*ICAO designator*] (FAAC)
TQ .... Transition Quarter
TQ .... Tri-Quarterly [*A publication*]
TQ-3 .... Tocotrienolquinone [*Biochemistry*]
TQA .... Abilene, TX [*Location identifier*] [*FAA*] (FAAL)
TQA .... ILLINET [*Illinois Library Information Network*], Springfield, IL [*OCLC symbol*] (OCLC)
TQAGA ...... Technique Agricole [*A publication*]
TQB .... ILLINET [*Illinois Library Information Network*], Springfield, IL [*OCLC symbol*] (OCLC)
TQC .... Indiana Cooperative Library Services Authority, Indianapolis, IN [*OCLC symbol*] (OCLC)
TQC .... Technical Quality Control [*Telecommunications*] (TEL)
TQC .... Time, Quality, Cost
TQC .... Total Quality Control
TQCA .... Textile Quality Control Association [*Atlanta, GA*] (EA)
TQCM .... Thermoelectric Quartz Crystal Microbalance
TQD .... Indiana Cooperative Library Services Authority, Indianapolis, IN [*OCLC symbol*] (OCLC)
TQD .... Ter Quaterve in Die [*Three or Four Times a Day*] [*Pharmacy*]
TQE .... Michigan Library Consortium, Detroit, MI [*OCLC symbol*] (OCLC)
TQE .... Technical Quality Evaluation [*Polaris*]
TQE .... Tekamah, NE [*Location identifier*] [*FAA*] (FAAL)
TQE .... Timer Queue Element
TQF .... Michigan Library Consortium, Detroit, MI [*OCLC symbol*] (OCLC)
TQF .... Threshold Quality Factor
TQG .... MIDLNET [*Midwest Regional Library Network*], St. Louis, MO [*OCLC symbol*] (OCLC)

TQH .... MIDLNET [*Midwest Regional Library Network*], St. Louis, MO [*OCLC symbol*] (OCLC)
TQH .... Tahlequah, OK [*Location identifier*] [*FAA*] (FAAL)
TQI .... MINITEX [*Minnesota Interlibrary Teletype Exchange*], Minneapolis, MN [*OCLC symbol*] (OCLC)
TQI .... Training Quality Index [*Military*] (CAAL)
TQJ .... MINITEX [*Minnesota Interlibrary Teletype Exchange*], Minneapolis, MN [*OCLC symbol*] (OCLC)
TQK .... NELINET [*New England Library Information Network*], Newton, MA [*OCLC symbol*] (OCLC)
TQL .... NELINET [*New England Library Information Network*], Newton, MA [*OCLC symbol*] (OCLC)
TQM .... OCLC [*Online Computer Library Center*] Western Services Center, Claremont, CA [*OCLC symbol*] (OCLC)
TQM .... Transport Quartermaster
TQMG .... [*The*] Quartermaster General [*Army*]
TQMS .... Technical Quartermaster Sergeant
TQMS .... Triple Quadrupole Mass Spectrometer
TQN .... OCLC [*Online Computer Library Center*] Western Services Center, Claremont, CA [*OCLC symbol*] (OCLC)
TQO .... OHIONET, Columbus, OH [*OCLC symbol*] (OCLC)
TQP .... OHIONET, Columbus, OH [*OCLC symbol*] (OCLC)
TQP .... Transistor Qualification Program
TQQ .... Pennsylvania Area Library Network, Philadelphia, PA [*OCLC symbol*] (OCLC)
TQR .... Pennsylvania Area Library Network, Philadelphia, PA [*OCLC symbol*] (OCLC)
TQR .... Saginaw, MI [*Location identifier*] [*FAA*] (FAAL)
TQR .... Tenquille Resources Ltd. [*Vancouver Stock Exchange symbol*]
TQS .... Pittsburgh Regional Library Center, Pittsburgh, PA [*OCLC symbol*] (OCLC)
TQS .... Theologische Quartalschrift [*A publication*]
TQS .... Tres Esquinas [*Colombia*] [*Airport symbol*] (OAG)
TQT .... Pittsburgh Regional Library Center, Pittsburgh, PA [*OCLC symbol*] (OCLC)
TQT .... Transistor Qualification Test
TQTP .... Transistor Qualification Test Program
TQU .... Southeastern Library Network, Atlanta, GA [*OCLC symbol*] (OCLC)
TQV .... Southeastern Library Network, Atlanta, GA [*OCLC symbol*] (OCLC)
TQW .... Pittsburgh, PA [*Location identifier*] [*FAA*] (FAAL)
TQW .... State University of New York, OCLC [*Online Computer Library Center*], Albany, NY [*OCLC symbol*] (OCLC)
TQX .... State University of New York, OCLC [*Online Computer Library Center*], Albany, NY [*OCLC symbol*] (OCLC)
TQY .... Tanquery Resources Ltd. [*Vancouver Stock Exchange symbol*]
TQY .... Wisconsin Library Consortium, Madison, WI [*OCLC symbol*] (OCLC)
TQZ .... Wisconsin Library Consortium, Madison, WI [*OCLC symbol*] (OCLC)
TR .... Caines' Term Reports [*New York*] (DLA)
TR .... Gabon [*Aircraft nationality and registration mark*] (FAAC)
TR .... Stewardsman Recruit [*Navy*]
TR .... Table Ronde [*A publication*]
TR .... Tactical Reconnaissance (NATG)
TR .... Talyllyn Railway [*Wales*]
TR .... Tank Regiment (MCD)
TR .... Tape Reader
TR .... Tape Recorder
TR .... Tape Register
TR .... Tape Resident
TR .... Tare (ROG)
TR .... Target Recognition (AFM)
TR .... Tariff Reform
TR .... Taxation Reports [*England*] (DLA)
TR .... Teaching and Research [*Medicine*]
TR .... Team Recorder [*Sports*]
TR .... Tear [*Deltiology*]
TR .... Technical Readiness
TR .... Technical Regulation
TR .... Technical Report
TR .... Technical Representative
TR .... Technical Requirement (MCD)
TR .... Technical Review (NRCH)
TR .... Technology Review [*A publication*]
TR .... Telegraphe Restant [*Telegram to Be Called for at a Telegraph Office*] [*French*] (ROG)
TR .... Tell-Rimah (BJA)
TR .... Temperature Range
TR .... Temperature Recorder
TR .... Temperature, Rectal [*Medicine*]
TR .... Temporary Resident
TR .... Tempore Regis [*In the Time of the King*] [*Latin*]
TR .... Terbium [*Chemical element*] [*Symbol is Tb*] (ROG)
TR .... Term Reports [*Legal*] [*British*]
TR .... Term Reports, English King's Bench [*Durnford and East's Reports*] [*England*] (DLA)
TR .... Terminal Ready [*Data processing*]
TR .... Terminal Rendezvous
TR .... Terminal Repeat [*Genetics*]

TR............... Terminalischer Reiz [*Terminal Stimulus*] [*German*] [*Psychology*]
TR............... Terms of Reference
TR............... Test Regulation   (MCD)
TR............... Test Report
TR............... Test Request
TR............... Test-Retest
TR............... Test Routine   (AAG)
TR............... Test Run
T & R .... Testing and Regulating Department [*Especially, in a wire communications maintenance division*]
TR............... Textus Receptus   (BJA)
TR............... Theatre Research [*A publication*]
TR............... Theatre Royal   (ROG)
TR............... Thematic Resource Nomination [*National Register of Historic Places*]
TR............... Theodore [*Teddy*] Roosevelt
TR............... Theologische Revue [*Muenster*] [*A publication*]
TR............... Theologische Rundschau [*A publication*]
TR............... Therapeutic Radiology
TR............... Thioredoxin [*Biochemistry*]
TR............... Thioredoxin Reductase [*An enzyme*]
TR............... Threat Reaction [*Military*]   (CAAL)
TR............... Throws Right-Handed [*Baseball*]
TR............... Thrust Reverser   (MCD)
TR............... Time Rate [*Payment system*]
TR............... Time Record   (MCD)
TR............... Time to Repetition [*Medicine*]
TR............... Time to Retrofire
TR............... Time-to-Retrograde [*NASA*]   (KSC)
T/R............. Time of Rise   (MSA)
TR............... Timed-Release [*Pharmacy*]
TR............... Tinctura [*Tincture*] [*Pharmacy*]
TR............... Tirailleur Regiments [*Military*]
TR............... Tobacco Reporter [*A publication*]
TR............... Tone Relevant
TR............... Tons Registered [*Shipping*]
TR............... Tool Resistant [*Rating for safes*]
TR............... Toothed Ring [*Technical drawings*]
TR............... Tootsie Roll Industries, Inc. [*NYSE symbol*]
TR............... Topical Report [*Nuclear energy*]   (NRCH)
TR............... Torpedo Reconnaissance Aircraft [*Navy*]
TR............... Torque Synchro Receiver   (MUGU)
TR............... Total Regulation
TR............... Total Revenue
TR............... Touchdowns Running [*Football*]
TR............... Towel Rack   (MSA)
TR............... Tower
TR............... Trace
TR............... Tracer
TR............... Track
TR............... Tracking RADAR
TR............... Tract
TR............... Trade
TR............... Traffic Route [*Telecommunications*]   (TEL)
TR............... Tragedy
TR............... Trailer   (AAG)
TR............... Train   (ADA)
TR............... Trainer   (AAG)
TR............... Training   (ROG)
TR............... Training Regulations [*Military*]
TR............... Training Requirements
TR............... Tramway   (ROG)
TR............... Transaction
TR............... Transaction Record
TR............... Transatlantic Review [*A publication*]
TR............... Transbrasil SA Linhas Aereas [*Brazil*] [*ICAO designator*]   (FAAC)
T/R............. Transceiver
TR............... Transcontinental Resources [*Vancouver Stock Exchange symbol*]
Tr................ Transcript   (DLA)
TR............... Transducers [*JETDS nomenclature*] [*Military*]   (CET)
TR............... Transfer   (DEN)
TR............... Transfer Register
TR............... Transfer Reset
TR............... Transformation Ratio
TR............... Transformer   (DEN)
T-R............. Transformer-Rectifier
TR............... Transfusion Reaction [*Medicine*]
TR............... Transfusion Receptors [*Oncology*]
TR............... Transient Response   (IEEE)
TR............... Transitive
TR............... Translate [*or Translation, or Translator*]
TR............... Translation Register
TR............... Transmission Report [*Telecommunications*]   (TEL)
T-R............. Transmit-Receive
TR............... Transmitter
TR............... Transom   (MSA)
TR............... Transport
TR............... Transportation [*or Travel*] Request [*Military*]

TR............... Transpose
TR............... Transverse   (DEN)
T/R............. Travel Request
TR............... Travel Required [*Civil Service*]
TR............... Trawler
TR............... Treasurer
TR............... Treasury Receipt
TR............... Treatise   (ROG)
TR............... Treaty   (ROG)
TR............... Treble [*Knitting*]
TR............... Treble [*Music*]
TR............... Trial   (ROG)
TR............... Trial Report
TR............... Tributary   (ROG)
TR............... Tricuspid Regurgitation [*Cardiology*]
TR............... Trigonal [*Molecular geometry*]
TR............... Trillo [*Trill*] [*Music*]
tr................ Trinidad and Tobago [*MARC country of publication code*] [*Library of Congress*]   (LCCP)
TR............... Trip Report
TR............... Triple Screw [*Shipping*]
Tr................ Tristia [*of Ovid*] [*Classical studies*]   (OCD)
Tr................ Tristram's Consistory Judgments [*England*]   (DLA)
TR............... Tritium Ratio [*Measure of tritium activity*] [*AEC*]
TR............... Tritium Recovery [*Nuclear energy*]   (NRCH)
Tr................ Trityl [*Organic chemistry*]
tr................ Trityl [*As substituent on nucleoside*] [*Biochemistry*]
Tr................ Trivium [*A publication*]
TR............... Troop
TR............... Trouble Report
TR............... Trough   (ADA)
TR............... Troupe   (ROG)
TR............... Truck
TR............... True   (FAAC)
TR............... Trumpet
TR............... Trunnion [*Pivot*]
TR............... Truro [*British depot code*]
TR............... Truss   (MSA)
TR............... Trust
T/R............. Trust Receipt [*Banking*]
TR............... Trustee
TR............... Tubercular Rueckstand [*Medicine*]
TR............... Tuberculin Residue [*Medicine*]
TR............... Tunnel Rectifier
TR............... Turbine Rate   (NVT)
TR............... Turkey [*Two-letter standard code*]   (CNC)
TR............... Turkish Reactor
TR............... Turnaround Requirements   (MCD)
T & R .... Turner and Russell's English Chancery Reports [*1822-25*]   (DLA)
Tr................ Y Traethodydd [*A publication*]
1TR............. One Turn Right [*Dance terminology*]
Tra.............. Epistulae ad Traianum [*of Pliny the Younger*] [*Classical studies*]   (OCD)
TRA .... La Tuyere a Reverse Aval [*Concorde*]
TRA .... RADAR Transfer of Control Message [*Communications*]   (FAAC)
TRA .... Tackle Representatives Association [*Later, TRA, Int'l*]   (EA)
TRA .... Taiwan Railway Administration
TRA .... Tandem Rotary Activator
TRA .... Tape Recorder Amplifier
TRA .... Taramajima [*Japan*] [*Airport symbol*]   (OAG)
TRA .... Tax Reform Act [*1984*]
TRA .... Technical Risk Assessment   (MCD)
TRA .... Television/Radio Age [*A publication*]
TRA .... Temporary Restricted Area [*USSR*]   (NATG)
TRA .... Terrain-Related Accident [*Aviation*]
TRA .... Test Requirement Analysis   (CAAL)
TRA .... Textile Refinishers Association   (EA)
TRA .... Theodore Roosevelt Association   (EA)
TRA .... Thoroughbred Racing Association
TRA .... Thrace Requirements Analysis [*Military*]
TRA .... Tinctura [*Tincture*] [*Pharmacy*]   (ROG)
TRA .... Tire and Rim Association [*Akron, OH*]   (EA)
TRA .... Tracan Oil & Gas [*Vancouver Stock Exchange symbol*]
TRA .... Trade Readjustment Allowance [*or Assistance*]
TRA .... Trade Recovery Act
TRA .... Trade Relations Association   (EA)
TrA.............. Traduction Automatique [*The Hague*] [*A publication*]
TRA .... Training
TRA .... Training Readjustment Allowance   (OICC)
TRA .... Training Requirements Analysis [*NASA*]   (NASA)
TRA .... Transracial Adoption
TRA .... Travnik [*Yugoslavia*] [*Seismograph station code, US Geological Survey*] [*Closed*]   (SEIS)
TrA.............. Triangulum Australe [*Constellation*]
TRA .... Triaxial Recording Accelerometer
TRA .... Triumph Register of America   (EA)
TRA .... Tubular Reactor Assembly   (NRCH)
TRA .... Turnaround Requirements Analysis [*NASA*]   (NASA)

TRA .... United States Army TRADOC, Institute for Military Assistance, Library, Fort Bragg, NC [*OCLC symbol*] (OCLC)

TRAA......... Towing and Recovery Association of America [*Winter Park, FL*] (EA)

TRAAC...... Transit Research and Attitude Control [*Navy satellite*]

TRAACS..... Transit Research and Attitude Control Satellite [*Navy*] (IEEE)

TRAB......... Triaminobenzene [*Organic chemistry*]

Trabajos Estadist ... Trabajos de Estadistica [*A publication*]

Trabajos Estadist Investigacion Oper ... Trabajos de Estadistica y de Investigacion Operativa [*A publication*]

Trab Antropol Etnol ... Trabalhos de Antropologia e Etnologia [*A publication*]

Trab Cent Bot Junta Invest Ultramar ... Trabalhos. Centro de Botanica. Junta de Investigacoes do Ultramar [*A publication*]

Trab Compostelanos Biol ... Trabajos Compostelanos de Biologia [*A publication*]

Trab 5 Cong Med Latino-Am ... Trabajos Presentados al Quinto Congreso Medico Latino-Americano [*A publication*]

TrabEsta .... Trabajos de Estadistica [*A publication*]

Trab Estac Agric Exp Leon ... Trabajos. Estacion Agricola Experimental de Leon [*A publication*]

Trab Estadistica ... Trabajos de Estadistica y de Investigacion [*A publication*]

Trab Geol... Trabajos de Geologia [*A publication*]

Trab Geol (Oviedo Univ Fac Cienc) ... Trabajos de Geologia (Oviedo Universidad. Facultad de Ciencias) [*A publication*]

Trab Inst Cajal Invest Biol ... Trabajos. Instituto Cajal de Investigaciones Biologicas [*A publication*]

Trab Inst Econ Prod Ganad Ebro ... Trabajos. Instituto de Economia y Producciones Ganaderas del Ebro [*A publication*]

Trab Inst Esp Entomol ... Trabajos. Instituto Espanol de Entomologia [*A publication*]

Trab Inst Esp Oceanogr ... Trabajos. Instituto Espanol de Oceanografia [*A publication*]

Trab Inst Oceanogr Univ Recife ... Trabalhos. Instituto Oceanografico. Universidade do Recife [*A publication*]

Trab Investigacao 79 ... Trabalhos de Investigacao 79 [*A publication*]

Trab Investigacao 80 ... Trabalhos de Investigacao 80 [*A publication*]

Trab Oceanogr Univ Fed Pernambuco ... Trabalhos Oceanograficos. Universidade Federal de Pernambuco [*A publication*]

TRABOT..... Terrier RADAR and Beacon Orientation Test (MUGU)

Trab Pesqui Inst Nutr Univ Bras ... Trabalhos e Pesquisas. Instituto de Nutricao. Universidade do Brasil [*A publication*]

TRAC .... Tandem Razor and Cartridge [*Gillette Co.*]

TRAC .... Target Research Analysis Center (CINC)

TRAC .... Tax Reform Action Coalition (EA)

TRAC .... Technical Reports Announcement Checklist

TRAC .... Telecommunications Research and Action Center [*Washington, DC*] [*Information service*] [*Telecommunications*] (TSSD)

TRAC .... Telescoping Rotor Aircraft Concept (MCD)

TRAC .... Texas Reconfigurable Array Computer

TRAC .... Text Reckoning and Compiling [*Data processing*]

TRAC .... Thermally Regenerative Alloy Cell

TRAC .... Tracer (AABC)

TRAC .... Tractor (AAG)

TRAC .... Trade Reform Action Coalition [*Washington, DC*] (EA)

TRAC .... Transaction Reporting and Control System (MCD)

TRAC .... Transient Radiation Analysis by Computer (KSC)

TRAC .... Transient Reactor Analysis Code (NRCH)

TRAC .... Transportation Account Code (AFM)

TrAC .... Trends in Analytical Chemistry [*A publication*]

TRACAB..... Terminal RADAR Approach Control Cab [*Aviation*] (FAAC)

TRACAD .... Training for [*US Military Academy*] Cadets (NVT)

TRACALS ... Traffic Control Approach and Landing System [*Aviation electronics*]

TRACAP..... Transient Circuit Analysis Program [*Data processing*]

TRACC....... Target Review and Adjustment for Continuous Control (MCD)

TRACDR..... Tractor-Drawn

TRACE .... Tactical Readiness and Checkout Equipment

TRACE .... Tactical Resources and Combat Effectiveness Model (MCD)

TRACE .... Tape-Controlled Recording Automatic Checkout Equipment [*Component of automatic pilot*] [*Aviation*]

TRACE .... Task Reporting and Current Evaluation

TRACE .... Taxiing and Routing of Aircraft Coordinating Equipment (MCD)

TRACE .... Taxiway Routing and Coordination Equipment [*Aviation*]

TRACE .... Technical Report Analysis, Condensation, Evaluation

TRACE .... Teleprocessing Recording for Analysis by the Customer (IEEE)

TRACE .... Test Equipment for Rapid Automatic Checkout and Evaluation [*Pan American Airways*]

TRACE .... Time-Shared Routines for Analysis, Classification, and Evaluation (DIT)

TRACE .... Tolls Recording and Computing Equipment (IEEE)

TRACE .... Toronto Region Aggregation of Computer Enthusiasts [*Canada*]

TRACE .... Total Resource Allocation Cost Estimating (RDA)

TRACE .... Total Risk Assessing Cost Estimate [*Army*] (RDA)

TRACE .... Trace Remote Atmospheric Chemical Evaluation [*National Center for Atmospheric Research*]

TRACE .... Track Retrieve and Account for Configuration of Equipment (MCD)

TRACE .... Tracking and Communications, Extraterrestrial

TRACE .... Traffic Routing and Control Equipment (MCD)

TRACE .... Trane Air Conditioning Economics [*The Trane Co.*]

TRACE .... Transistor Radio Automatic Circuit Evaluator

TRACE .... Transportable Automated Control Environment

Trace & M ... Tracewell and Mitchell's United States Comptroller's Decisions (DLA)

TRACEN..... Training Center

TRACE-P ... Total Risk Assessing Cost Estimate - Production [*Army*] (RDA)

TRACERS ... Teleprocessed Record and Card Entry Reporting System (MCD)

TRACES..... Technology in Retrospect and Critical Events in Science [*IITRI*]

Trace Subst Environ Health ... Trace Substances in Environmental Health [*A publication*]

Trace Subst Environ Health Proc Univ Mo Annu Conf ... Trace Substances in Environmental Health. Proceedings. University of Missouri. Annual Conference [*A publication*]

TRACEX..... Amphibious Tractor Exercise [*Navy*] (NVT)

Tracey Evidence ... Tracey's Cases on Evidence (DLA)

TRACH...... Trachea [*or Tracheotomy*] [*Medicine*]

Trach.......... Trachiniae [*of Sophocles*] [*Classical studies*] (OCD)

TRACHY..... Tracheotomy (DSUE)

TRACINFO ... Tracer, Number as Indicated. Furnish Information Immediately or Advise

TRACIS ...... Traffic Records Criminal Justice Information System (OICC)

TRACKEX ... Tracking Exercise [*Navy*] (NVT)

Track Field Q Rev ... Track and Field Quarterly Review [*A publication*]

TRACOMDLANT ... Training Command, Atlantic Fleet [*Navy*]

TRACOMDPAC ... Training Command, Pacific Fleet [*Navy*]

TRACOMDSUBPAC ... Training Command, Submarines, Pacific Fleet [*Navy*]

TRACOMDWESTCOAST ... Training Command, West Coast [*Navy*]

TRACOMP ... Tracking Comparison

TRACON .... Terminal RADAR Control [*FAA*]

TRACS .... Tool Record Accountability System [*NASA*] (NASA)

TRACS .... Travel Accounting Control System [*Citicorp Diners Club*]

TRACS .... Triangulation Ranging and Crossfix System [*Military*] (CAAL)

tract .... Traction

Tracts Math Nat Sci ... Tracts in Mathematics and Natural Science [*A publication*]

TRACY .... Technical Reports Automated Cataloging - Yes [*National Oceanic and Atmospheric Administration*]

TRAD......... Terminal RADAR [*Aviation*] (FAAC)

Trad .... Traditio [*A publication*]

TRAD......... Tradition

TRADA .... Timber Research and Development Association [*High Wycombe, Bucks., England*]

TRADAC .... Trajectory Determination and Acquisition Computation

TRADAD .... Trace to Destination and Advise

TRADCOM ... Transportation Corps Research and Development Command [*Army*]

Trad Dep Exploit Util Bois Univ Laval ... Traduction. Departement d'Exploitation et Utilisation des Bois. Universite Laval [*A publication*]

TRADE .... Tracking RADAR Angle Deception Equipment (NG)

TRADE .... Training Devices (RDA)

Trade Cas ... Trade Cases [*Commerce Clearing House*] (DLA)

Trade and Commer ... Trade and Commerce [*A publication*]

Trade D ...... Trade Digest [*A publication*]

Trade Dig ... Trade Digest [*A publication*]

Trade Ind ... Trade and Industry [*A publication*]

Trademark Bull ... Bulletin. United States Trademark Association Series (DLA)

Trademark Bull (NS) ... Trademark Bulletin. United States Trademark Association [*New Series*] [*New York*] (DLA)

Trade-Mark Rep ... Trade-Mark Reporter [*A publication*]

Trademark Rptr ... Trademark Reporter [*A publication*]

Trade Mks J ... Trade Marks Journal [*A publication*]

Trade News N ... Trade News North [*A publication*]

Trade R ...... Trade Review. Swedish Chamber of Commerce for Australia [*A publication*]

TRADER..... Training Devices Requirements Office [*TRADOC*] (MCD)

TRADER..... Transient Radiation Effects Recorder (MCD)

Trade Reg Rep ... Trade Regulation Reporter [*Commerce Clearing House*] (DLA)

Trade Reg Rev ... Trade Regulation Review (DLA)

TRADES..... TRADOC Data Evaluation Study (MCD)

Trades Union D ... Trades Union Digest [*A publication*]

TRADET..... Training Detachment [*Navy*]

TRADEVCO ... Trading & Development Bank Ltd. [*Liberia*]

TRADEVMAN ... Training Devices Man [*Navy rating*]

TRADEX..... Target Resolution and Discrimination Experiment [*ARPA*]

TRADEX..... Trade Data Element Exchange

TRADIC..... Transistorized Airborne Digital Computer [*Air Force*]

TRADIS ...... Tape Repeating Automatic Data Integration System

Traditional Kent Bldgs ... Traditional Kent Buildings [*A publication*]

Trad Mus.... Traditional Music [*A publication*]

TRADOC .... Training and Doctrine Command [*Army*]

TRADSTAT ... World Trade Statistics Database [*Electronic Data Systems Ltd.*] [*Harrow, Middlesex, England*] [*Information service*] (EISS)

TRAE.......... Transport Airlift Estimator [*Air Force*]

TRAEX .... Training and Experience [*Military*] (AFM)

TRAF .... Traffic

TRAFCO..... Television, Radio and Film Communications [*of the Methodist Church*]

TRAFF........ Traffic (ROG)

Traff Cas ..... Railway, Canal, and Road Traffic Cases (DLA)

Traff Engng Control ... Traffic Engineering and Control [*A publication*]

TRAFFIC .... Trade Records Analysis of Flora and Fauna in Commerce [*An association*]

Traffic Dig Rev ... Traffic Digest and Review [*A publication*]

Traffic Eng ... Traffic Engineering [*A publication*]

Traffic Eng Contr ... Traffic Engineering and Control [*A publication*]

Traffic Eng & Control ... Traffic Engineering and Control [*A publication*]

Traffic Manage ... Traffic Management [*A publication*]

Traffic Q..... Traffic Quarterly [*A publication*]

Traffic Qly ... Traffic Quarterly [*A publication*]

Traffic Saf ... Traffic Safety [*A publication*]

Traffic Saf Res Rev ... Traffic Safety Research Review [*A publication*]

TRAFOLPERS ... Transfer Following Enlisted Personnel

TRAG .... Traffic Responsive Advance Green [*Control strategy*]

TRAG .... Tragedy

Trag............ Tragoedopodagra [*of Lucian*] [*Classical studies*] (OCD)

TRAGB .... Trudy po Radiatsionnoi Gigiene. Leningradskii Nauchno-Issledovatel'skii Institut Radiatsionnoi Gigieny [*A publication*]

TRAI .... Tackle Representatives Association International [*Later, TSSAA*] (EA)

TRAIB......... Trudy Astrofizicheskogo Instituta. Akademiya Nauk Kazakhskoi SSR [*A publication*]

TRAIF .... Torso Restraint Assembly with Integrated Flotation

TRAIN.......... Telerail Automated Information Network [*Association of American Railroads*]

TRAIN........ To Restore American Independence Now [*An association*]

train........... Training

Train Agric Rural Dev ... Training for Agriculture and Rural Development [*A publication*]

TRAINBASEFOR ... Training Base Force, Pacific Fleet [*Navy*]

TRAINCON ... Training Conference (MCD)

Train Dev Aust ... Training and Development in Australia [*A publication*]

Train & Devel J ... Training and Development Journal [*A publication*]

Train Dev J ... Training and Development Journal [*A publication*]

TRAINDIV... Training Division [*Canadian Navy*]

TRAINLANT ... Training Atlantic Fleet [*Navy*]

TRAINPACHQ ... Training Group Pacific Headquarters [*Canadian Navy*]

TRAINRON ... Training Squadron [*Later, SERRON*] [*Navy*]

Train Sch B ... Training School Bulletin [*A publication*]

TRA INT'L ... Tackle Representatives Association International [*Later, TSSAA*] (EA)

TRAIS......... Transportation Research Activities Information Service [*Department of Transportation*]

Traite du Mar ... Pothier's Traite du Contrat de Mariage (DLA)

Trait Surf ... Traitements de Surface [*A publication*]

Trait Therm ... Traitement Thermique [*A publication*]

TRAJ .... Trajectory (AAG)

Tr Akad Nauk Gruz SSR Inst Sist Upr ... Trudy. Akademii Nauk Gruzinskoi SSR. Institut Sistem Upravleniya [*A publication*]

Tr Akad Nauk Kaz SSR Inst Mikrobiol Virusol ... Trudy. Akademiia Nauk Kazakhskoi SSR. Institut Mikrobiologii i Virusologii [*A publication*]

Tr Akad Nauk Latv SSR Inst Mikrobiol ... Trudy. Akademii Nauk Latviiskoi SSR. Institut Mikrobiologii [*A publication*]

Tr Akad Nauk Litov SSR Inst Biol ... Trudy. Akademii Nauk Litovskoi SSR. Institut Biologii [*A publication*]

Tr Akad Nauk Lit SSR Ser V ... Trudy. Akademii Nauk Litovskoi SSR. Seriya V [*A publication*]

Tr Akad Nauk Lit SSR Ser V Biol Nauki ... Trudy. Akademii Nauk Litovskoi SSR. Seriya V. Biologicheskie Nauki [*A publication*]

Tr Akad Nauk SSSR Inst Biol Vnutr Vod ... Trudy. Akademiia Nauk SSSR Institut Biologii Vnutrennikh Vod [*A publication*]

Tr Akad Nauk SSSR Karel Fil ... Trudy. Akademii Nauk SSSR. Karel'skii Filial [*A publication*]

Tr Akad Nauk Tadzh SSR ... Trudy. Akademii Nauk Tadzhikskoi SSR [*A publication*]

Tr Akad Nauk Turkm SSR ... Trudy. Akademii Nauk Turkmenskoi SSR [*A publication*]

Trak Sel'khozmashiny ... Traktory i Sel'khozmashiny [*USSR*] [*A publication*]

Trakt Landmasch ... Traktor und die Landmaschine [*A publication*]

TRAK TROL ... Trackless Trolley [*Freight*]

Trakt Sel'khozmash ... Traktory i Sel'khozmashiny [*A publication*]

TRALA........ Truck Renting and Leasing Association [*Washington, DC*] (EA)

TRALANT... Fleet Training Command, Atlantic [*Navy*]

TRALINET ... TRADOC Library Information Network (MCD)

Tr Alma-At Med Inst ... Trudy Alma-Atinskogo Meditsinskogo Instituta [*A publication*]

Tr Alma At Nauchno Issled Proektn Inst Stroit Mater ... Trudy Alma-Atinskogo Nauchno-Issledovatel'skogo i Proektnogo Instituta Stroitel'nykh Materialov [*A publication*]

Tr Alma-At Zoovet Inst ... Trudy Alma-Atinskogo Zooveterinarnogo Instituta [*A publication*]

Tr Altai Gorno Metall Nauchno Issled Inst Akad Nauk Kaz SSR ... Trudy Altaiskogo Gorno-Metallurgicheskogo Nauchno-Issledovatel'skogo Instituta Akademiya Nauk Kazakhskoi SSR [*A publication*]

TRAM .... Target Recognition Attack Multisensor [*DoD*]

TRAM .... Tensioned Replacement Alongside Method (MCD)

TRAM .... Test Reliability and Maintenance Program [*Navy*] (NVT)

TRAM .... Tracking RADAR Automatic Monitoring (AFM)

TRAM .... Training Readiness Analysis Monitor (MCD)

Tr Am Ass Genito-Urin Surg ... Transactions. American Association of Genito-Urinary Surgeons [*A publication*]

Tr Am Fish Soc ... Transactions. American Fisheries Society [*A publication*]

TRAMID ..... Training for [*US Naval Academy/Naval Reserve Officers Training Corps*] Midshipmen (NVT)

TRAMIS...... TRADOC [*Training and Doctrine Command*] Management Information System [*Army*]

TRAMOD.... Training Requirements Analysis Model (MCD)

TRAMP...... Temperature Regulation and Monitor Panel

TRAMP...... Test Retrieval and Memory Print [*Data processing*]

TRAMP....... Time-Shared Relational Associative Memory Program [*Data processing*] (IEEE)

TRAMPCO ... Thioguanine, Rubidomycin [*Daunorubicin*], ara-C, Methotrexate, Prednisolone, Cyclophosphamide, Oncovin [*Vincristine*] [*Antineoplastic drug regimen*]

TRAMPCOL ... Thioguanine, Rubidomycin [*Daunorubicin*], ara-C, Methotrexate, Prednisolone, Cyclophosphamide, Oncovin [*Vincristine*], L-Asparaginase [*Antineoplastic drug regimen*]

TRAMPL.... TRADOC Master Priority List (MCD)

TRAMPS ... Temperature Regulator and Missile Power Supply

TRAMPS ... Traffic Measure and Path Search [*Telecommunications*] (TEL)

Tr Am Soc Trop Med ... Transactions. American Society of Tropical Medicine [*A publication*]

Tr Amur Skh Opytn Stn ... Trudy Amurskoi Sel'skokhozyaistvennoi Opytnoi Stantsii [*A publication*]

TRAN.......... Transformer

TRAN.......... Transient (AABC)

TRAN.......... Transit

TRAN.......... Transmit

TRAN.......... Transport

TRANA .... Transfusion [*Philadelphia*] [*A publication*]

TRANC .... Transient Center [*Marine Corps*]

TRAND .... Tone Reproduction and Neutral Determination [*Chart*] [*Printing technology*]

TRANDIR.... Translation Director (IEEE)

TRANET ..... Tracking [*or Transit*] Network [*Navy*]

TRANET ..... Transnational Network for Appropriate/Alternative Technologies

Tranq .... De Tranquillitate Animi [*of Seneca the Younger*] [*Classical studies*] (OCD)

TRANQ....... Tranquillo [*Quietly*] [*Music*] (ROG)

TRANS .... Telemetry Redundancy Analyzer System

TRANS .... Transaction

TRANS .... Transcript (ADA)

TRANS ...... Transfer (AAG)

TRANS ...... Transformer (AFM)

TRANS ...... Transient (AFIT)

TRANS ...... Transistor (ADA)

TRANS ...... Transition (ROG)

TRANS ...... Transitive

TRANS ...... Transitory

TRANS ...... Translation

Trans.......... Translator (DLA)

TRANS ...... Transmission

TRANS ...... Transmittance (AAG)

TRANS ...... Transparent (MSA)

TRANS ...... Transport [*or Transportation*] (AAG)

TRANS ...... Transpose [*Proofreading*]

TRANS ...... Transverse

TRANSA..... Transaction (MSA)

Trans AACE ... Transactions. American Association of Cost Engineers [*A publication*]

TRANSAC ... Transistorized Automatic Computer

Trans Acad Sci St Louis ... Transactions. Academy of Science of St. Louis [*A publication*]

Transact Roy Soc Canada ... Transactions. Royal Society of Canada [*A publication*]

Trans Act Soc Aust & NZ ... Transactions. Actuarial Society of Australia and New Zealand [*A publication*]

Trans AIChE ... Transactions. AIChE [*American Institute of Chemical Engineers*] [*A publication*]

Trans All-India Inst Ment Health ... Transactions. All-India Institute of Mental Health [*A publication*]

Trans Am Acad Ophthalmol Oto-Laryngol ... Transactions. American Academy of Ophthalmology and Oto-Laryngology [*A publication*]

Trans Am Assoc Genito-Urin Surg ... Transactions. American Association of Genito-Urinary Surgeons [*A publication*]

Trans Am Assoc Obstet Gynecol ... Transactions. American Association of Obstetricians and Gynecologists [*A publication*]

Trans Am Assoc Obstet Gynecol Abdom Surg ... Transactions. American Association of Obstetricians, Gynecologists, and Abdominal Surgeons [*A publication*]

Trans Am Broncho-Esophagol Assoc ... Transactions. American Broncho-Esophagological Association [*A publication*]

Trans Am Clin Climatol Assoc ... Transactions. American Clinical and Climatological Association [*A publication*]

Trans Am Crystallogr Assoc ... Transactions. American Crystallographic Association [*A publication*]

Trans Am Electroch Soc ... Transactions. American Electrochemical Society [*A publication*]

Trans Am Entomol Soc (Phila) ... Transactions. American Entomological Society (Philadelphia) [*A publication*]

Trans Am Ent Soc ... Transactions. American Entomological Society [*A publication*]

Trans Amer Ass Cereal Chem ... Transactions. American Association of Cereal Chemists [*A publication*]

Trans Amer Foundrymen's Soc ... Transactions. American Foundrymen's Society [*A publication*]

Trans Amer Geophys Union ... Transactions. American Geophysical Union [*A publication*]

Trans Amer Math Soc ... Transactions. American Mathematical Society [*A publication*]

Trans Amer Microscop Soc ... Transactions. American Microscopical Society [*A publication*]

Trans Amer Nucl Soc ... Transactions. American Nuclear Society [*A publication*]

Trans Am Fisheries Soc ... Transactions. American Fisheries Society [*A publication*]

Trans Am Fish Soc ... Transactions. American Fisheries Society [*A publication*]

Trans Am Geophys Union ... Transactions. American Geophysical Union [*A publication*]

Trans Am Inst Chem Eng ... Transactions. American Institute of Chemical Engineers [*A publication*]

Trans Am Inst Electr Eng ... Transactions. American Institute of Electrical Engineers [*A publication*]

Trans Am Inst Electr Eng Part 1 ... Transactions. American Institute of Electrical Engineers. Part 1. Communication and Electronics [*A publication*]

Trans Am Inst Electr Eng Part 2 ... Transactions. American Institute of Electrical Engineers. Part 2. Applications and Industry [*A publication*]

Trans Am Inst Electr Eng Part 3 ... Transactions. American Institute of Electrical Engineers. Part 3. Power Apparatus and Systems [*A publication*]

Trans Am Inst Min Eng ... Transactions. American Institute of Mining Engineers [*A publication*]

Trans Am Inst Min Metall Eng ... Transactions. American Institute of Mining and Metallurgical Engineers [*A publication*]

Trans Am Inst Min Metall Pet Eng ... Transactions. American Institute of Mining, Metallurgical, and Petroleum Engineers [*A publication*]

Trans Am Math Soc ... Transactions. American Mathematical Society [*A publication*]

Trans Am Microsc Soc ... Transactions. American Microscopical Society [*A publication*]

Trans Am Neurol Assoc ... Transactions. American Neurological Association [*A publication*]

Trans Am Nucl Soc ... Transactions. American Nuclear Society [*A publication*]

Trans Am Nucl Soc Suppl ... Transactions. American Nuclear Society. Supplement [*A publication*]

Trans Am Ophthalmol Soc ... Transactions. American Ophthalmological Society [*A publication*]

Trans Am Otol Soc ... Transactions. American Otological Society [*A publication*]

Trans Am Philos Soc ... Transactions. American Philosophical Society [*A publication*]

Trans Am Soc Agric Eng (Gen Ed) ... Transactions. American Society of Agricultural Engineers (General Edition) [*A publication*]

Trans Am Soc Agric Engrs Gen Edn ... Transactions. American Society of Agricultural Engineers. General Edition [*A publication*]

Trans Am Soc Artif Intern Organs ... Transactions. American Society for Artificial Internal Organs [*A publication*]

Trans Am Soc Heat Air-Cond Eng ... Transactions. American Society of Heating and Air-Conditioning Engineers [*A publication*]

Trans Am Soc Met ... Transactions. American Society for Metals [*A publication*]

Trans Am Soc Ophthalmol Otolaryngol Allergy ... Transactions. American Society of Ophthalmologic and Otolaryngologic Allergy [*A publication*]

Trans Am Soc Steel Treat ... Transactions. American Society for Steel Treating [*A publication*]

Trans Am Ther Soc ... Transactions. American Therapeutic Society [*A publication*]

Trans Ann Anthracite Conf Lehigh Univ ... Transactions. Annual Anthracite Conference of Lehigh University [*A publication*]

Trans Annu Conf Can Nucl Soc ... Transactions. Annual Conference. Canadian Nuclear Society [*A publication*]

Trans Annu Meet Allen O Whipple Surg Soc ... Transactions. Annual Meeting. Allen O. Whipple Surgical Society [*A publication*]

Trans Annu Tech Conf Am Soc Qual Control ... Transactions. Annual Technical Conference. American Society for Quality Control [*A publication*]

Trans Annu Tech Conf ASQC ... Transactions. Annual Technical Conference. American Society for Quality Control [*A publication*]

Trans Annu Tech Conf Soc Vac Coaters ... Transactions. Annual Technical Conference. Society of Vacuum Coaters [*A publication*]

Trans Ap .... Transcript Appeals [*New York*] [*1867-68*]   (DLA)

Trans App ... Transcript Appeals [*New York*]   (DLA)

Trans Appeal R ... New York Transcript Appeals Reports   (DLA)

Trans Architect Inst Jpn ... Transactions. Architectural Institute of Japan [*A publication*]

Trans ASAE ... Transactions. ASAE [*American Society of Agricultural Engineers*] [*A publication*]

Trans ASME J Appl Mech ... Transactions. American Society of Mechanical Engineers. Journal of Applied Mechanics [*A publication*]

Trans ASME J Biomech Eng ... Transactions. ASME [*American Society of Mechanical Engineers*] Journal of Biomechanical Engineering [*A publication*]

Trans ASME J Biomech Engng ... Transactions. American Society of Mechanical Engineers. Journal of Biomechanical Engineering [*A publication*]

Trans ASME J Dyn Syst Meas & Control ... Transactions. American Society of Mechanical Engineers. Journal of Dynamic Systems Measurement and Control [*A publication*]

Trans ASME J Energy Resour Technol ... Transactions. American Society of Mechanical Engineers. Journal of Energy Resources Technology [*A publication*]

Trans ASME J Eng Ind ... Transactions. ASME [*American Society of Mechanical Engineers*] Journal of Engineering for Industry [*A publication*]

Trans ASME J Engng Ind ... Transactions. American Society of Mechanical Engineers. Journal of Engineering for Industry [*A publication*]

Trans ASME J Engng Mater & Technol ... Transactions. American Society of Mechanical Engineers. Journal of Engineering Materials and Technology [*A publication*]

Trans ASME J Engng Power ... Transactions. American Society of Mechanical Engineers. Journal of Engineering for Power [*A publication*]

Trans ASME J Fluids Engng ... Transactions. American Society of Mechanical Engineers. Journal of Fluids Engineering [*A publication*]

Trans ASME J Heat Transfer ... Transactions. American Society of Mechanical Engineers. Journal of Heat Transfer [*A publication*]

Trans ASME J Lubr Technol ... Transactions. American Society of Mechanical Engineers. Journal of Lubrication Technology [*A publication*]

Trans ASME J Mech Des ... Transactions. American Society of Mechanical Engineers. Journal of Mechanical Design [*A publication*]

Trans ASME J Pressure Vessel Technol ... Transactions. American Society of Mechanical Engineers. Journal of Pressure Vessel Technology [*A publication*]

Trans ASME J Sol Energy Engng ... Transactions. American Society of Mechanical Engineers. Journal of Solar Energy Engineering [*A publication*]

Trans ASME Ser A ... Transactions. ASME [*American Society of Mechanical Engineers*] Series A. Journal of Engineering for Power [*A publication*]

Trans ASME Ser A J Eng Power ... Transactions. ASME [*American Society of Mechanical Engineers*] Series A. Journal of Engineering for Power [*A publication*]

Trans ASME Ser B ... Transactions. ASME [*American Society of Mechanical Engineers*] Series B. Journal of Engineering for Industry [*A publication*]

Trans ASME Ser C ... Transactions. ASME [*American Society of Mechanical Engineers*] Series C. Journal of Heat Transfer [*A publication*]

Trans ASME Ser E ... Transactions. ASME [*American Society of Mechanical Engineers*] Series E. Journal of Applied Mechanics [*A publication*]

Trans ASME Ser E J Appl Mech ... Transactions. ASME [*American Society of Mechanical Engineers*] Series E. Journal of Applied Mechanics [*A publication*]

Trans ASME Ser F ... Transactions. ASME [*American Society of Mechanical Engineers*] Series F. Journal of Lubrication Technology [*A publication*]

Trans ASME Ser F J Lubr Technol ... Transactions. ASME [*American Society of Mechanical Engineers*] Series F. Journal of Lubrication Technology [*A publication*]

Trans ASME Ser G ... Transactions. ASME [*American Society of Mechanical Engineers*] Series G. Journal of Dynamic Systems Measurement and Control [*A publication*]

Trans ASME Ser GJ Dynamic Systems ... Transactions. ASME [*American Society of Mechanical Engineers*] Series G. Journal of Dynamic Systems. Measurement and Control [*A publication*]

Trans ASME Ser H ... Transactions. ASME [*American Society of Mechanical Engineers*] Series H. Journal of Engineering Materials and Technology [*A publication*]

Trans ASME Ser I ... Transactions. ASME [*American Society of Mechanical Engineers*] Series I. Journal of Fluids Engineering [*A publication*]

Trans Assoc Am Physicians ... Transactions. Association of American Physicians [*A publication*]

Trans Assoc Life Ins Med Dir Am ... Transactions. Association of Life Insurance Medical Directors of America [*A publication*]

Transatl R ... Transatlantic Review [*A publication*]

Trans B'ham Warwks Arch Soc ... Transactions. Birmingham and Warwickshire Archaeological Society [*A publication*]

Trans Biochem Soc ... Transactions. Biochemical Society [*A publication*]

Trans Birmingham Warwickshire Archaeol Soc ... Transactions. Birmingham and Warwickshire Archaeological Society [*A publication*]

Trans Bose Res Inst (Calcutta) ... Transactions. Bose Research Institute (Calcutta) [*A publication*]

Trans Bot Soc Edinb ... Transactions and Proceedings. Botanical Society of Edinburgh [*A publication*]

Trans Br Bryol Soc ... Transactions. British Bryological Society [*A publication*]

Trans Br Ceram Soc ... Transactions. British Ceramic Society [*A publication*]

Trans Bristol Gloucestershire Archaeol Soc ... Transactions. Bristol and Gloucestershire Archaeological Society [*A publication*]

Trans Bristol Gloucestershire Arch Soc ... Transactions. Bristol and Gloucestershire Archaeological Society [*A publication*]

Trans Br Mycol Soc ... Transactions. British Mycological Society [*A publication*]

Trans Br Soc Hist Pharm ... Transactions. British Society for the History of Pharmacy [*A publication*]

Transc A .... Transcript Appeals [*New York*] (DLA)

Trans Can Inst Mining Soc NS ... Transactions. Canadian Institute of Mining and Metallurgy and Mining Society of Nova Scotia [*A publication*]

Trans Can Inst Min Metall ... Transactions. Canadian Institute of Mining and Metallurgy and Mining Society of Nova Scotia [*A publication*]

Trans Can Nucl Soc ... Transactions. Canadian Nuclear Society [*A publication*]

Trans Can Soc Mech Eng ... Transactions. Canadian Society for Mechanical Engineers [*A publication*]

Trans Can Soc Mech Engrs ... Transactions. Canadian Society of Mechanical Engineers [*A publication*]

Trans Cardiff Nat Soc ... Transactions. Cardiff Naturalists Society [*A publication*]

Trans Cave Res Group GB ... Transactions. Cave Research Group of Great Britain [*A publication*]

TRANSCEIVER ... Transmitter-Receiver (NATG)

Trans Ceylon Coll ... Transactions. Ceylon College of Physicians [*A publication*]

Trans Chalmers Univ Technol (Gothenburg) ... Transactions. Chalmers University of Technology (Gothenburg) [*Sweden*] [*A publication*]

Trans Chin Assoc Adv Sci ... Transactions. Chinese Association for the Advancement of Science [*A publication*]

Trans Citrus Eng Conf ... Transactions. Citrus Engineering Conference [*A publication*]

Trans Coll Med S Afr ... Transactions. College of Medicine of South Africa [*A publication*]

Trans Coll Physicians Philadelphia ... Transactions. College of Physicians of Philadelphia [*A publication*]

TRANSCOM ... Transportable Communications

TRANSCON ... Transcontinental (MCD)

Trans Conf Cold Inj ... Transactions. Conference on Cold Injury [*A publication*]

Trans Conf Glaucoma ... Transactions. Conference on Glaucoma [*A publication*]

Trans Conf Group Processes ... Transactions. Conference on Group Processes [*A publication*]

Trans Conf Group Soc Adm Hist ... Transactions. Conference Group for Social and Administrative History [*A publication*]

Trans Conf Neuropharmacol ... Transactions. Conference on Neuropharmacology [*A publication*]

Trans Conf Physiol Prematurity ... Transactions. Conference on Physiology of Prematurity [*A publication*]

Trans Conf Polysaccharides Biol ... Transactions. Conference on Polysaccharides in Biology [*A publication*]

Trans Conn Acad Arts Sci ... Transactions. Connecticut Academy of Arts and Sciences [*A publication*]

TRANSCR ... Transcribed

Transcr A ... Transcript Appeals [*New York*] (DLA)

TRANSCRON ... Transcription (ROG)

Transcult Psychiat Res ... Transcultural Psychiatric Research Review [*A publication*]

TRANSDEC ... SONAR Transducer Test and Evaluation Center, Naval Electronics Laboratory [*San Diego, CA*] [*Navy*]

TRANSDEF ... Transducer Evaluation Facility

TRANSDIV ... Transport Division [*Navy*]

Transducer Technol ... Transducer Technology [*A publication*]

Trans Dumfries Galloway Nat Hist Antiq Soc ... Transactions. Dumfriesshire and Galloway Natural History and Antiquarian Society [*A publication*]

Trans Dumfriesshire Galloway Natur Hist Ant Soc ... Transactions. Dumfriesshire and Galloway Natural History and Antiquarian Society [*A publication*]

Trans Dynam Dev ... Transactions. Dynamics of Development [*A publication*]

Trans East Lothian Antiq Field Nat Soc ... Transactions. East Lothian Antiquarian and Field Naturalists Society [*A publication*]

TRANSEC ... Transmission Security [*Communications*]

Trans Econ & Oper Anal ... Transport Economics and Operational Analysis [*A publication*]

Trans Edinburgh Geol Soc ... Transactions. Edinburgh Geological Society [*A publication*]

Trans Electrochem Soc ... Transactions. Electrochemical Society [*A publication*]

Trans Electr Supply Auth Eng Inst NZ ... Transactions. Electric Supply Authority Engineers' Institute of New Zealand, Inc. [*A publication*]

Trans Electr Supply Eng Inst ... Transactions. Annual Conference. Electric Supply Authority Engineers' Institute of New Zealand, Inc.

Trans E Lothian Antiq Fld Natur Soc ... Transactions. East Lothian Antiquarian and Field Naturalists' Society [*A publication*]

Trans Eng Inst Can ... Transactions. Engineering Institute of Canada [*A publication*]

Trans Essex Arch Soc ... Transactions. Essex Archaeological Society [*A publication*]

Trans Eur Orthod Soc ... Transactions. European Orthodontic Society [*A publication*]

TRANSF ..... Transferred

TRANSF ..... Transformer (AAG)

Trans Fac Hortic Chiba Univ ... Transactions. Faculty of Horticulture. Chiba University [*A publication*]

Trans Farady Soc ... Transactions. Faraday Society [*A publication*]

TRANSFAX ... Facsimile Transmission [*Telecommunications*]

TRANSFD ... Transferred (ROG)

Trans Fed-Prov Wildl Conf ... Transactions. Federal-Provincial Wildlife Conference [*A publication*]

TRANSFIG ... Transfiguration

TRANSFLTNG ... Transitional Flight Training (NVT)

TRANSFORM ... Trade-Off Analysis - Systems/Force Mix Analysis [*Military*]

Transform (Papeterie) ... Transformation (Supplement to La Papeterie) [*A publication*]

Trans Geol Soc Glasg ... Transactions. Geological Society of Glasgow [*A publication*]

Trans Geol Soc S Afr ... Transactions. Geological Society of South Africa [*A publication*]

Trans Geotherm Resour Counc ... Transactions. Geothermal Resources Council [*United States*] [*A publication*]

Trans Glasgow Univ Orient Soc ... Transactions. Glasgow University Oriental Society [*A publication*]

Trans Greenwich Lewisham Antiq Soc ... Transactions. Greenwich and Lewisham Antiquarian Society [*A publication*]

TRANSGRPPHIBFOR ... Transportation Group Amphibious Forces [*Navy*]

TRANSGRPSOPAC ... Transport Group, South Pacific Force [*Navy*]

Trans Gulf Coast Ass Geol Soc ... Transactions. Gulf Coast Association of Geological Societies [*A publication*]

Trans Gulf Coast Assoc Geol Soc ... Transactions. Gulf Coast Association of Geological Societies [*A publication*]

Trans Hertfordshire Nat Hist Soc Field Club ... Transactions. Hertfordshire Natural History Society and Field Club [*A publication*]

Trans Highl Agric Soc Scotl ... Transactions. Highland and Agricultural Society of Scotland [*A publication*]

Trans Hist Soc Ghana ... Transactions. Historical Society of Ghana [*A publication*]

Trans Hist Soc Lancashire Cheshire ... Transactions. Historic Society of Lancashire and Cheshire [*A publication*]

Trans Hunter Archaeol Soc ... Transactions. Hunter Archaeological Society [*A publication*]

Trans ILA ... Transactions. International Law Association [*1873-1924*] (DLA)

Trans Ill State Acad Sci ... Transactions. Illinois State Academy of Science [*A publication*]

Trans Ill State Hortic Soc Ill Fruit Counc ... Transactions. Illinois State Horticultural Society and the Illinois Fruit Council [*A publication*]

Trans Ill St Hort Soc ... Transactions. Illinois State Horticultural Society [*A publication*]

Trans Illum Eng Soc ... Transactions. Illuminating Engineering Society [*A publication*]

TRANSIM ... Transit Simplified Receiver [*Satellite navigation system*]

Trans Indiana Acad Ophthalmol Otolaryngol ... Transactions. Indiana Academy of Ophthalmology and Otolaryngology [*A publication*]

Trans Indian Ceram Soc ... Transactions. Indian Ceramic Society [*A publication*]

Trans Indian Inst Met ... Transactions. Indian Institute of Metals [*A publication*]

Trans Indian Inst Metals ... Transactions. Indian Institute of Metals [*A publication*]

Trans Indian Soc Desert Technol Univ Cent Desert Stud ... Transactions. Indian Society of Desert Technology and University Centre of Desert Studies [*A publication*]

Trans Ind Inst Chem Eng ... Transactions. Indian Institute of Chemical Engineers [*India*] [*A publication*]

Trans Inst Act Aust & NZ ... Transactions. Institute of Actuaries of Australia and New Zealand [*A publication*]

Trans Inst Brit Geogr ... Transactions. Institute of British Geographers [*A publication*]

Trans Inst Chem Eng ... Transactions. Institution of Chemical Engineers [*A publication*]

Trans Inst Chem Engrs ... Transactions. Institution of Chemical Engineers [*A publication*]

Trans Inst Civ Eng Ir ... Transactions. Institution of Civil Engineers of Ireland [*A publication*]

Trans Inst Electr Eng Jpn ... Transactions. Institute of Electrical Engineers of Japan [*A publication*]

Trans Inst Electr Eng Jpn B ... Transactions. Institute of Electrical Engineers of Japan. Part B [*A publication*]

Trans Inst Electr Eng Jpn C ... Transactions. Institute of Electrical Engineers of Japan. Part C [*A publication*]

Trans Inst Electr Eng Jpn Part A ... Transactions. Institute of Electrical Engineers of Japan. Part A [*A publication*]

Trans Inst Electron & Commun Eng Jap A ... Transactions. Institute of Electronics and Communication Engineers of Japan. Part A [*A publication*]

Trans Inst Electron Commun Eng Jap Sect J Part D ... Transactions. Institute of Electronics and Communication Engineers of Japan. Section J [*Japanese*] Part D [*A publication*]

Trans Inst Electron Commun Eng Jpn Part B ... Transactions. Institute of Electronics and Communication Engineers of Japan. Part B [*A publication*]

Trans Inst Electron and Commun Eng Jpn Part B ... Transactions. Institute of Electronics and Communication Engineers of Japan. Part B [*A publication*]

Trans Inst Electron and Commun Eng Jpn Part C ... Transactions. Institute of Electronics and Communication Engineers of Japan. Part C [*A publication*]

Trans Inst Eng Aust Civ Eng ... Transactions. Institute of Engineers. Australia. Civil Engineering [*A publication*]

Trans Inst Eng Aust Electr Eng ... Transactions. Institute of Engineers. Australia. Electrical Engineering [*A publication*]

Trans Inst Eng Aust Mech Eng ... Transactions. Institute of Engineers. Australia. Mechanical Engineering [*A publication*]

Trans Inst Engrs (Aust) Civ Engng ... Transactions. Institution of Engineers (Australia). Civil Engineering [*A publication*]

Trans Inst Engrs (Aust) Mech Engng ... Transactions. Institution of Engineers (Australia). Mechanical Engineering [*A publication*]

Trans Inst Eng Shipbuilders Scot ... Transactions. Institution of Engineers and Shipbuilders in Scotland [*A publication*]

Trans Inst Gas Eng ... Transactions. Institution of Gas Engineers [*England*] [*A publication*]

Trans Inst Mar Eng ... Transactions. Institute of Marine Engineers [*A publication*]

Trans Inst Mar Eng Conf Pap ... Transactions. Institute of Marine Engineers. Conference Papers [*A publication*]

Trans Inst Mar Engrs ... Transactions. Institute of Marine Engineers [*A publication*]

Trans Inst Mar Eng Ser C ... Transactions. Institute of Marine Engineers. Series C [*A publication*]

Trans Inst Mar Eng Tech Meet Pap ... Transactions. Institute of Marine Engineers. Technical Meeting Papers [*A publication*]

Trans Inst Marine Eng ... Transactions. Institute of Marine Engineers [*A publication*]

Trans Inst Meas & Control ... Transactions. Institute of Measurement and Control [*A publication*]

Trans Inst Meas Control ... Transactions. Institute of Measurement and Control [*A publication*]

Trans Inst Met Finish ... Transactions. Institute of Metal Finishing [*A publication*]

Trans Inst Mining Met Sect A ... Transactions. Institution of Mining and Metallurgy. Section A [*A publication*]

Trans Inst Mining Met Sect B ... Transactions. Institution of Mining and Metallurgy. Section B [*A publication*]

Trans Inst Mining Met Sect C ... Transactions. Institution of Mining and Metallurgy. Section C [*A publication*]

Trans Inst Min Metall ... Transactions. Institution of Mining and Metallurgy [*A publication*]

Trans Inst Min Metall Sec C ... Transactions. Institution of Mining and Metallurgy. Section C [*United Kingdom*] [*A publication*]

Trans Inst Min Metall Sect B Appl Earth Sci ... Transactions. Institute of Mining and Metallurgy. Section B. Applied Earth Science [*United Kingdom*] [*A publication*]

Trans Instn Chem Engrs ... Transactions. Institution of Chemical Engineers [*A publication*]

Trans Instn E Shipb Scot ... Transactions. Institution of Engineers and Shipbuilders in Scotland [*A publication*]

Trans Instn Min Metall ... Transactions. Institution of Mining and Metallurgy [*A publication*]

Trans Inst Plast Ind ... Transactions. Institute of the Plastics Industry [*A publication*]

Trans Inst Weld (London) ... Transactions. Institute of Welding (London) [*A publication*]

Trans Int Assoc Math and Comput Simulation ... Transactions. International Association for Mathematics and Computers in Simulation [*A publication*]

Trans Int Conf Oral Surg ... Transactions. International Conference on Oral Surgery [*A publication*]

Trans Int Conf Or Ja ... Transactions. International Conference of Orientalists in Japan [*A publication*]

Trans Int Conf Soil Sci ... Transactions. International Conference of Soil Science [*A publication*]

Trans Int Congr Agric Engng ... Transactions. International Congress for Agricultural Engineering [*A publication*]

Trans Int Congr Soil Sci ... Transactions. International Congress of Soil Science [*A publication*]

Trans Int Soc Geotherm Eng ... Transactions. International Society for Geothermal Engineering [*A publication*]

Trans Iowa State Hortic Soc ... Transactions. Iowa State Horticultural Society [*A publication*]

Trans Iron Steel Inst Jap ... Transactions. Iron and Steel Institute of Japan [*A publication*]

Trans Iron Steel Inst Jpn ... Transactions. Iron and Steel Institute of Japan [*A publication*]

TRANSIS.... Transportation Safety Information System [*Department of Transportation*] (EISS)

TRANSISTOR ... Transfer Resistor

TRANSITEX ... Transit Exercise (NVT)

Transition Met Chem ... Transition Metal Chemistry [*A publication*]

Transit J..... Transit Journal [*A publication*]

Transit L Rev ... Transit Law Review (DLA)

Transit Met Chem (Weinheim Ger) ... Transition Metal Chemistry (Weinheim, Germany) [*A publication*]

Trans Japan Soc Civ Engrs ... Transactions. Japan Society of Civil Engineers [*A publication*]

Trans Japan Soc Compos Mater ... Transactions. Japan Society for Composite Materials [*A publication*]

Trans Japan Soc Mech Engrs Ser B ... Transactions. Japan Society of Mechanical Engineers. Series B [*A publication*]

Trans Japan Soc Mech Engrs Ser C ... Transactions. Japan Society of Mechanical Engineers. Series C [*A publication*]

Trans Jap Inst Met ... Transactions. Japan Institute of Metals [*A publication*]

Trans Jap Inst Metals ... Transactions. Japan Institute of Metals [*A publication*]

Trans Jap Soc Aeronaut Space Sci ... Transactions. Japan Society for Aeronautical and Space Sciences [*A publication*]

Trans Jap Soc Mech Eng ... Transactions. Japan Society of Mechanical Engineers [*A publication*]

Trans Jap Weld Soc ... Transactions. Japan Welding Society [*A publication*]

Trans J Br Ceram Soc ... Transactions and Journal. British Ceramic Society [*A publication*]

Trans and J Br Ceram Soc ... Transactions and Journal. British Ceramic Society [*A publication*]

Trans J Brit Ceram Soc ... Transactions and Journal. British Ceramic Society [*A publication*]

Trans J Plast Inst ... Transactions and Journal. Plastics Institute [*England*] [*A publication*]

Trans Jpn Inst Met ... Transactions. Japan Institute of Metals [*A publication*]

Trans Jpn Inst Met Suppl ... Transactions. Japan Institute of Metals. Supplement [*A publication*]

Trans Jpn Pathol Soc ... Transactions. Japanese Pathological Society [*A publication*]

Trans Jpn Soc Civ Eng ... Transactions. Japan Society of Civil Engineers [*A publication*]

Trans Jpn Soc Irrig Drain Reclam Eng ... Transactions. Japanese Society of Irrigation Drainage and Reclamation Engineering [*A publication*]

Trans Jpn Soc Mech Eng Ser B ... Transactions. Japan Society of Mechanical Engineers. Series B [*A publication*]

Trans Jt Mtg Comm Int Soc Soil Sci ... Transactions. Joint Meeting of Commissions. International Society of Soil Science [*A publication*]

Trans JWRI ... Transactions. JWRI [*Japanese Welding Research Institute*] [*A publication*]

Trans K Acad Sci ... Transactions. Kentucky Academy of Science [*A publication*]

Trans Kans Acad Sci ... Transactions. Kansas Academy of Science [*A publication*]

Trans Kansai Ent Soc ... Transactions. Kansai Entomological Society [*A publication*]

Transkei Dev Rev ... Transkei Development Review [*A publication*]

Trans Koll Geneeskd S-Afr ... Transaksies. Kollege van Geneeskunde van Suid-Afrika [*A publication*]

Trans Korean Soc Mech Eng ... Transactions. Korean Society of Mechanical Engineers [*Republic of Korea*] [*A publication*]

Trans KY Acad Sci ... Transactions. Kentucky Academy of Science [*A publication*]

TRANSL ..... Translation   (AAG)

TRANSLANG ... Translator Language [*Data processing*]

TRANSLANT ... Transports, Atlantic Fleet [*Navy*]

TRANSLANTEX ... Transatlantic Training Exercise   (MCD)

Translat ..... Translation   (BJA)

Transl Beltone Inst Hear Res ... Translations. Beltone Institute for Hearing Research [*A publication*]

Transl Commonw Sci Industr Res Organ (Aust) ... Translation. Commonwealth Scientific and Industrial Research Organisation (CSIRO) (Australia) [*A publication*]

Transl Dep Fish For (Can) ... Translation. Department of Fisheries and Forestry (Ottawa, Canada) [*A publication*]

Trans Leeds Geol Assoc ... Transactions. Leeds Geological Association [*A publication*]

Trans Leicestershire Archaeol Hist Soc ... Transactions. Leicestershire Archaeological and Historical Society [*A publication*]

Transl Fac For Univ BC ... Translation. Faculty of Forestry. University of British Columbia [*A publication*]

Transl For Comm (Lond) ... Translation. Forestry Commission (London) [*A publication*]

Trans Lich S Staffs Arch Hist Soc ... Transactions. Lichfield and South Staffordshire Archaeological and Historical Society [*A publication*]

Trans Linn Soc Lond ... Transactions. Linnean Society of London [*A publication*]

Trans Linn Soc NY ... Transactions. Linnaean Society of New York [*A publication*]

TRANSLIT ... Transliteration

Trans Liverpool Eng Soc ... Transactions. Liverpool Engineering Society [*A publication*]

TRANSLOC ... Trade-Off Analysis Systems/Force Mix   (MCD)

TRANSLOC ... Transportable LORAN-C   (MCD)

Trans London M'sex Arch ... Transactions. London and Middlesex Archaeological Society [*A publication*]

Transl Reg-Index ... Translations Register-Index [*A publication*]

Transl Russ Game Rep ... Translations of Russian Game Reports [*A publication*]

Transl Soviet Agr US Joint Publ Res Serv ... Translations on Soviet Agriculture. US Joint Publications Research Service [*A publication*]

Transl US For Prod Lab (Madison) ... Translation. US Forest Products Laboratory (Madison) [*A publication*]

TRANSM .... Transmission   (AFM)

TRANSMAN ... Enlisted Transfer Manual [*Military*]

Trans Manchester Assoc Eng ... Transactions. Manchester Association of Engineers [*A publication*]

Trans Mass Hort Soc ... Transactions. Massachusetts Horticultural Society [*A publication*]

Trans Math Monographs ... Translations of Mathematical Monographs. American Mathematical Society [*A publication*]

Transm & Distrib ... Transmission and Distribution [*A publication*]

Transm Distrib ... Transmission and Distribution [*A publication*]

Trans Med Soc Lond ... Transactions. Medical Society of London [*A publication*]

Trans Med Soc London ... Transactions. Medical Society of London [*A publication*]

Trans Meet Commns II & IV Int Soc Soil Sci ... Transactions. Meeting of Commissions II and IV. International Society of Soil Science [*A publication*]

Trans Metall Soc AIME (Am Inst Min Metall Pet Eng) ... Transactions. Metallurgical Society of AIME (American Institute of Mining, Metallurgical, and Petroleum Engineers) [*A publication*]

Trans Mining Geol Met Inst India ... Transactions of the Mining, Geological, and Metallurgical Institute of India [*A publication*]

Trans Min Metall Alumni Assoc ... Transactions. Mining and Metallurgical Alumni Association [*Japan*] [*A publication*]

Trans Min Metall Assoc (Kyoto) ... Transactions. Mining and Metallurgical Association (Kyoto) [*A publication*]

TRANSMO ... Transportation Model [*Military*]

Trans MO Acad Sci ... Transactions. Missouri Academy of Science [*A publication*]

Trans MO Acad Scie ... Transactions. Missouri Academy of Science [*A publication*]

TRANSMON ... Transmission   (ROG)

Trans Morris C Res Counc ... Transactions. Morris County Research Council [*A publication*]

Trans Moscow Math Soc ... Transactions. Moscow Mathematical Society [*A publication*]

TRANSMTG ... Transmitting

Trans Mycol Soc Jap ... Transactions. Mycological Society of Japan [*A publication*]

Trans Mycol Soc Japan ... Transactions. Mycological Society of Japan [*A publication*]

Trans Mycol Soc Jpn ... Transactions. Mycological Society of Japan [*A publication*]

Trans N Amer Wildlife Conf ... Transactions. North American Wildlife and Natural Resources Conference [*A publication*]

Trans N Am Wildl Nat Resour Conf ... Transactions. North American Wildlife and Natural Resources Conference [*A publication*]

Trans Nat Hist Northumberl Durham Newcastle Upon Tyne ... Transactions. Natural History Society of Northumberland Durham and Newcastle Upon Tyne [*A publication*]

Trans Nat Hist Soc Northumberl Durham Newcastle-Upon-Tyne ... Transactions. Natural History Society of Northumberland, Durham, and Newcastle-Upon-Tyne [*Later, Natural History Society of Northumbria. Transactions*] [*A publication*]

Trans Nat Hist Soc Northumbria ... Transactions. Natural History Society of Northumbria [*A publication*]

Transnat'l ... Transnational   (DLA)

Trans Natl Inst Sci India ... Transactions. National Institute of Sciences. India [*A publication*]

Transnat'l Rep ... Transnational Reporter   (DLA)

Trans Natl Res Inst Met (Tokyo) ... Transactions. National Research Institute for Metals (Tokyo) [*A publication*]

Trans Natl Saf Congr ... Transactions. National Safety Congress [*United States*] [*A publication*]

Trans Nat Res Inst Metals (Tokyo) ... Transactions. National Research Institute for Metals (Tokyo) [*A publication*]

Trans Nat Vac Symp ... Transactions. National Vacuum Symposium [*A publication*]

Trans Nebr Acad Sci ... Transactions. Nebraska Academy of Sciences [*A publication*]

Trans N E Cst Instn Engrs Shipbldrs ... Transactions. North East Coast Institution of Engineers and Shipbuilders [*A publication*]

Trans Newbury Dist Fld Club ... Transactions. Newbury District Field Club [*A publication*]

Trans Newcomen Soc Study His Eng Technol ... Transactions. Newcomen Society for the Study of the History of Engineering and Technology [*A publication*]

Trans New Engl Obstet Gynecol Soc ... Transactions. New England Obstetrical and Gynecological Society [*United States*] [*A publication*]

Trans New Orleans Acad Ophthalmol ... Transactions. New Orleans Academy of Ophthalmology [*A publication*]

Trans New York Acad Sci Ser II ... Transactions. New York Academy of Sciences. Series II [*A publication*]

Trans NJ Obstet Gynecol Soc ... Transactions. New Jersey Obstetrical and Gynecological Society [*A publication*]

Trans North Am Wildl Conf ... Transactions. North American Wildlife Conference [*A publication*]

Trans Northeast Sect Wildl Soc ... Transactions of the Northeast Section. Wildlife Society [*A publication*]

Trans NY Acad Sci ... Transactions. New York Academy of Sciences [*A publication*]

Trans NZ Inst Eng ... Transactions. New Zealand Institution of Engineers [*A publication*]

Trans Ophthalmol Soc Aust ... Transactions. Ophthalmological Society of Australia [*A publication*]

Trans Ophthalmol Soc NZ ... Transactions. Ophthalmological Society of New Zealand [*A publication*]

Trans Ophthalmol Soc UK ... Transactions. Ophthalmological Societies of the United Kingdom [*A publication*]

Trans Ophthal Soc Aust ... Transactions. Ophthalmological Society of Australia [*A publication*]

TRANSP ..... Transparency   (AAG)

TRANSP ..... Transportation

Transp ..... Transporter [*A publication*]

Trans PA Acad Ophthalmol Otolaryngol ... Transactions. Pennsylvania Academy of Ophthalmology and Otolaryngology [*A publication*]

TRANSPAC ... Thermal Structure Monitoring Program in the Pacific [*Marine science*]   (MSC)

Trans-Pac ... Trans-Pacific [*A publication*]

TRANSPAC ... Transpacific

Trans Pac Coast Obstet Gynecol Soc ... Transactions. Pacific Coast Obstetrical and Gynecological Society [*United States*] [*A publication*]

Trans Pac Coast Oto-Ophthalmol Soc ... Transactions. Pacific Coast Oto-Ophthalmological Society [*A publication*]

Trans Pac Coast Oto-Ophthalmol Soc Annu Meet ... Transactions. Pacific Coast Oto-Ophthalmological Society. Annual Meeting [*United States*] [*A publication*]

Trans Papers L Brit G ... Institute of British Geographers. Liverpool. Transactions and Papers [*A publication*]

Transp Aust ... Transport Australia [*A publication*]

Trans Peirce Soc ... Transactions. Charles S. Peirce Society [*A publication*]

Transp Eng ... Transportation Engineering [*A publication*]

Transp Eng J ASCE ... Transportation Engineering Journal. ASCE [*American Society of Civil Engineers*] [*A publication*]

Transp Engng ... Transportation Engineering [*Formerly, Traffic Engineering*] [*A publication*]

Transp Engng J Proc ASCE ... Transportation Engineering Journal. Proceedings of the American Society of Civil Engineers [*A publication*]

Transp Engr ... Transport Engineer [*A publication*]

Trans Peninsula Hortic Soc ... Transactions. Peninsula Horticultural Society [*A publication*]

Transp En J ... Transportation Engineering Journal. ASCE [*American Society of Civil Engineers*] [*A publication*]
TRANSPHIBLANT ... Transports, Amphibious Force, Atlantic Fleet [*Navy*]
TRANSPHIBPAC ... Transports, Amphibious Force, Pacific Fleet [*Navy*]
Trans Philol Soc ... Transactions. Philological Society [*A publication*]
Trans Phil Soc ... Transactions. Philological Society [*A publication*]
Transp His ... Transportation History [*A publication*]
Transp Hist ... Transport History [*A publication*]
TRANSPIRE ... Transpiration-Cooled Stacked Platelet Injection (MCD)
Transp J ..... Transport Journal [*A publication*]
Transp J ..... Transportation Journal [*A publication*]
Transp J of Aust ... Transport Journal of Australia [*A publication*]
Transp Khranenie Nefti Nefteprod ... Transport i Khranenie Nefti i Nefteproduktov [*USSR*] [*A publication*]
transpl .... Transplant
TRANSPLAN ... Transaction Network Service Planning Model [*Telecommunications*] (TEL)
Transplan P ... Transplantation Proceedings [*A publication*]
Transplan R ... Transplantation Reviews [*A publication*]
Transplant ... Transplantation [*A publication*]
Transplant Bull ... Transplantation Bulletin [*A publication*]
Transplant Clin Immunol ... Transplantation and Clinical Immunology [*A publication*]
Transplant Immunol Clin ... Transplantation et Immunologie Clinique [*A publication*]
Transplant Proc ... Transplantation Proceedings [*A publication*]
Transplant Proc Suppl ... Transplantation Proceedings. Supplement [*A publication*]
Transplant Rev ... Transplantation Reviews [*A publication*]
Transp L J ... Transportation Law Journal [*A publication*]
Transp-Med Vesti ... Transportno-Meditsinski Vesti [*A publication*]
Transportat ... Transportation [*A publication*]
Transportation Plann Tech ... Transportation Planning and Technology [*London*] [*A publication*]
Transportation Q ... Transportation Quarterly [*A publication*]
Transportation Res ... Transportation Research [*A publication*]
Transportation Res Part A ... Transportation Research. Part A. General [*A publication*]
Transportation Res Part B ... Transportation Research. Part B. Methodological [*A publication*]
Transport D ... Transport Digest [*A publication*]
Transport Theory Statist Phys ... Transport Theory and Statistical Physics [*A publication*]
Trans Powder Metall Assoc India ... Transactions. Powder Metallurgy Association of India [*A publication*]
Transp Plann Technol ... Transportation Planning and Technology [*A publication*]
Transp Policy Decision Making ... Transport Policy and Decision Making [*A publication*]
Transp Q .... Transportation Quarterly [*A publication*]
Transp Res ... Transportation Research [*A publication*]
Transp Res Board Spec Rep ... Transportation Research Board. Special Report [*A publication*]
Transp Res Board Transp Res Rec ... Transportation Research Board. Transportation Research Record [*A publication*]
Transp Res News ... Transportation Research News [*A publication*]
Transp Res Part A ... Transportation Research Part A. General [*A publication*]
Transp Res Part A Gen ... Transportation Research. Part A. General [*England*] [*A publication*]
Transp Res Part B ... Transportation Research Part B. Methodological [*A publication*]
Transp Res Rec ... Transportation Research Record [*United States*] [*A publication*]
Trans Princeton Conf Cerebrovasc Dis ... Transactions. Princeton Conference on Cerebrovascular Diseases [*A publication*]
Transp Road Res Lab (GB) TRRL Rep ... Transport and Road Research Laboratory (Great Britain). TRRL Report [*A publication*]
Trans Proc Birmingham Arch Soc ... Transactions and Proceedings. Birmingham Archaeological Society [*A publication*]
Trans Proc Bot Soc Edinb ... Transactions and Proceedings. Botanical Society of Edinburgh [*A publication*]
Trans Proc Geol Soc S Afr ... Transactions and Proceedings. Geological Society of South Africa [*A publication*]
Trans Proc Palaeontol Soc Jap ... Transactions and Proceedings. Palaeontological Society of Japan [*A publication*]
Trans Proc Palaeontol Soc Japan New Ser ... Transactions and Proceedings. Palaeontological Society of Japan. New Series [*A publication*]
Trans Proc Palaeontol Soc Jpn New Ser ... Transactions and Proceedings. Palaeontological Society of Japan. New Series [*A publication*]
Trans Proc Perthshire Soc Natur Sci ... Transactions and Proceedings. Perthshire Society of Natural Science [*A publication*]
Transp Sci ... Transportation Science [*A publication*]
Transp Stroit ... Transportnoe Stroitel'stvo [*USSR*] [*A publication*]
Transp Theo ... Transport Theory and Statistical Physics [*A publication*]
Transp Theory Stat Phys ... Transport Theory and Statistical Physics [*A publication*]
Transp Th St P ... Transport Theory and Statistical Physics [*A publication*]
Transp Traffic ... Transport and Traffic [*A publication*]

Trans Q Am Soc Met ... Transactions Quarterly. American Society for Metals [*A publication*]
Trans R ...... Transatlantic Review [*A publication*]
Trans Radnorshire Soc ... Transactions. Radnorshire Society [*A publication*]
Trans R Can Inst ... Transactions. Royal Canadian Institute [*A publication*]
Trans R Entomol Soc Lond ... Transactions. Royal Entomological Society of London [*A publication*]
Trans R Ent Soc Lond ... Transactions. Royal Entomological Society of London [*A publication*]
Trans Res Abstr ... Transportation Research Abstracts [*A publication*]
Trans R Geol Soc (Corn) ... Transactions. Royal Geological Society (Cornwall) [*A publication*]
Trans R Highl Agric Soc Scotl ... Transactions. Royal Highland and Agricultural Society of Scotland [*A publication*]
Trans Rhod Sci Assoc ... Transactions. Rhodesia Scientific Association [*A publication*]
Trans RINA ... Transactions. Royal Institutions of Naval Architects [*London*] [*A publication*]
Trans R Instn Naval Archit ... Quarterly Transactions. Royal Institution of Naval Architects [*London*] [*A publication*]
TRANSRON ... Transport Squadron [*Navy*]
Trans Roy Inst Technol (Stockholm) ... Transactions. Royal Institute of Technology (Stockholm) [*A publication*]
Trans Roy Soc Canada ... Transactions. Royal Society of Canada [*A publication*]
Trans Roy Soc NZ Bot ... Transactions. Royal Society of New Zealand. Botany [*A publication*]
Trans Roy Soc S Aust ... Royal Society of South Australia. Transactions [*A publication*]
Trans Roy Soc South Africa ... Transactions. Royal Society of South Africa [*A publication*]
Trans R Sch Dent (Stockh Umea) ... Transactions. Royal Schools of Dentistry (Stockholm and Umea) [*A publication*]
Trans R Soc Can ... Transactions. Royal Society of Canada [*A publication*]
Trans R Soc Can Sect 3 ... Transactions. Royal Society of Canada. Section 3. Chemical, Mathematical, and Physical Sciences [*A publication*]
Trans R Soc Can Sect 4 ... Transaction. Royal Society of Canada. Section 4. Geological Sciences Including Mineralogy [*A publication*]
Trans R Soc Edinb ... Transactions. Royal Society of Edinburgh [*A publication*]
Trans R Soc NZ ... Transactions. Royal Society of New Zealand [*A publication*]
Trans R Soc NZ Biol Sci ... Transactions. Royal Society of New Zealand. Biological Science [*A publication*]
Trans R Soc NZ Bot ... Transactions. Royal Society of New Zealand. Botany [*A publication*]
Trans R Soc NZ Earth Sci ... Transactions. Royal Society of New Zealand. Earth Science [*A publication*]
Trans R Soc NZ Gen ... Transactions. Royal Society of New Zealand. General [*A publication*]
Trans R Soc NZ Geol ... Transactions. Royal Society of New Zealand. Geology [*A publication*]
Trans R Soc NZ Zool ... Transactions. Royal Society of New Zealand. Zoology [*A publication*]
Trans R Soc S Afr ... Transactions. Royal Society of South Africa [*A publication*]
Trans R Soc S Aust ... Transactions. Royal Society of South Australia [*A publication*]
Trans R Soc South Aust ... Transactions. Royal Society of South Australia [*A publication*]
Trans R Soc Trop Med Hyg ... Transactions. Royal Society of Tropical Medicine and Hygiene [*A publication*]
Trans SAEST ... Transactions. SAEST [*Society for Advancement of Electrochemical Science and Technology*] [*A publication*]
Trans S Afr Inst Civ Eng ... Transactions. South African Institution of Civil Engineers [*A publication*]
Trans S Afr Inst Elec Eng ... Transactions. South African Institute of Electrical Engineers [*A publication*]
Trans San Diego Soc Nat Hist ... Transactions. San Diego Society of Natural History [*A publication*]
TransSBA ... Transactions. Society of Biblical Archaeology [*London*] [*A publication*] (BJA)
Trans Sci Soc China ... Transactions. Science Society of China [*A publication*]
Trans SHASE ... Transactions. Society of Heating, Air Conditioning, and Sanitary Engineers [*Japan*] [*A publication*]
Trans SHASE Japan ... Transactions. SHASE [*Society of Heating, Air Conditioning, and Sanitary Engineers*] (Japan) [*A publication*]
Trans Shikoku Entomol Soc ... Transactions. Shikoku Entomological Society [*A publication*]
Trans Shikoku Ent Soc ... Transactions. Shikoku Entomological Society [*A publication*]
Trans Shropshire Archaeol Soc ... Transactions. Shropshire Archaeological Society [*A publication*]
Trans Soc Adv Electrochem Sci Technol ... Transactions. Society for Advancement of Electrochemical Science and Technology [*A publication*]
Trans Soc Br Entomol ... Transactions. Society for British Entomology [*A publication*]

Trans Soc Heat Air Cond Sanit Eng Jpn ... Transactions. Society of Heating, Air Conditioning, and Sanitary Engineers of Japan [*A publication*]

Trans Soc Instr Control Eng ... Transactions. Society of Instrument and Control Engineers [*Japan*] [*A publication*]

Trans Soc Instrum Control Eng ... Transactions. Society of Instrument and Control Engineers [*A publication*]

Trans Soc Instrum & Control Engrs (Japan) ... Transactions. Society of Instrument and Control Engineers (Japan) [*A publication*]

Trans Soc Instrum Technol ... Transactions. Society of Instrument Technology [*England*] [*A publication*]

Trans Soc Min Eng AIME ... Transactions. Society of Mining Engineers. AIME [*American Institute of Mining, Metallurgical, and Petroleum Engineers*] [*A publication*]

Trans Soc Min Engrs AIME ... Transactions. Society of Mining Engineers. AIME [*American Institute of Mining, Metallurgical, and Petroleum Engineers*] [*A publication*]

Trans Soc Motion Pict Eng ... Transactions. Society of Motion Picture Engineers [*A publication*]

Trans Soc Occup Med ... Transactions. Society of Occupational Medicine [*A publication*]

Trans Soc Pathol Jpn ... Transactiones Societatis Pathologicae Japonicae [*Japan*] [*A publication*]

Trans Soc Pet Eng AIME ... Transactions. Society of Petroleum Engineers of AIME [*American Institute of Mining, Metallurgical, and Petroleum Engineers*] [*A publication*]

Trans Soc Rheol ... Transactions. Society of Rheology [*A publication*]

Trans Southwest Fed Geol Soc ... Transactions. Southwestern Federation of Geological Societies [*A publication*]

Trans SPWLA Annu Log Symp ... Transactions. SPWLA [*Society of Professional Well Log Analysts*] Annual Logging Symposium [*A publication*]

Trans St John's Hosp Dermatol Soc ... Transactions. St. John's Hospital Dermatological Society [*A publication*]

Trans Stud Coll Physicians Phila ... Transactions and Studies. College of Physicians of Philadelphia [*A publication*]

Trans Suffolk Natur Soc ... Transactions. Suffolk Naturalists' Society [*A publication*]

Trans Tech Sect Can Pulp and Pap Assoc ... Transactions. Technical Section. Canadian Pulp and Paper Association [*A publication*]

Trans Tech Sect Can Pulp Pap Assoc ... Transactions. Technical Section. Canadian Pulp and Paper Association [*A publication*]

Trans Thoroton Soc Nottinghamshire ... Transaction. Thoroton Society of Nottinghamshire [*A publication*]

Trans Thoroton Soc Notts ... Transactions. Thoroton Society of Nottinghamshire [*A publication*]

Transtl ... Transitional   (DLA)

Trans Tottori Soc Agric Sci ... Transactions. Tottori Society of Agricultural Sciences [*A publication*]

Trans Tottori Soc Agr Sci ... Transactions. Tottori Society of Agricultural Science [*A publication*]

Trans Udgivet Dan Ing ... Transactions. Udgivet af Dansk Ingenioeren [*Denmark*] [*A publication*]

Trans Univ Cent Desert Stud (Jodhpur India) ... Transactions. University Centre of Desert Studies (Jodhpur, India) [*A publication*]

Trans Utah Acad Sci ... Transactions. Utah Academy of Sciences [*A publication*]

TRANSV ... Transvaal [*South Africa*]   (ROG)

TRANSV ... Transverse   (AAG)

Transvaal Agric J ... Transvaal Agricultural Journal [*A publication*]

Transvaal Mus Bull ... Transvaal Museum. Bulletin [*A publication*]

Transvaal Mus Mem ... Transvaal Museum. Memoirs [*A publication*]

Transvaal Mus Rep ... Transvaal Museum. Report [*A publication*]

Transvaal Nat Conserv Div Annu Rep ... Transvaal Nature Conservation Division. Annual Report [*A publication*]

Trans Wis Acad Sci ... Transactions. Wisconsin Academy of Sciences, Arts, and Letters [*A publication*]

Trans Wis Acad Sci Arts Lett ... Transactions. Wisconsin Academy of Sciences, Arts, and Letters [*A publication*]

Trans & Wit ... Transvaal and Witswatersrand Reports   (DLA)

Trans Woolhope Naturalists ... Transactions. Woolhope Naturalists' Field Club [*A publication*]

Trans Worcestershire Archaeol Soc 3 Ser ... Transactions. Worcestershire Archaeological Society. Series 3 [*A publication*]

Trans Worcs Arch Soc ... Transaction. Worcestershire Archaeological Society [*A publication*]

Trans Worcs Arc Soc ... Transactions. Worcestershire Archaeological Society [*A publication*]

Trans World Energy Conf ... Transactions. World Energy Conference [*A publication*]

Transylvania J Med ... Transylvania Journal of Medicine [*A publication*]

Trans Zimbabwe Sci Assoc ... Transactions. Zimbabwe Scientific Association [*A publication*]

Trans Zimb Sci Assoc ... Transactions. Zimbabwe Scientific Association [*A publication*]

Trans Zool Soc Lond ... Transactions. Zoological Society of London [*A publication*]

Tran USA ... Transportation USA [*A publication*]

TRAP ... Tank, Racks, Adapters, Pylons [*Military*]

TRAP ... Tape Recorder Action Plan [*Committee*] [*NASA/Air Force*]

TRAP ... Tartrate Resistant Acid Phosphatase [*An enzyme*]

TRAP ... Terminal Radiation Airborne Program [*Air Force*]

TRAP ... Thioguanine, Rubidomycin [*Daunorubicin*], Cytosine arabinoside [*ara-C*], Prednisone [*Antineoplastic drug regimen*]

TRAP ... Time Response Approximation

TRAP ... Tracker Analysis Program   (MCD)

TRAP ... Trapezoid   (MSA)

TRAP ... Treasury Relief Aid Project

TRAP ... Tyrosine-Rich Amelogenin Polypeptide [*Biochemistry of dental enamel*]

TRAPAC ... Fleet Training Command, Pacific [*Navy*]

TRAPATT ... Trapped Plasma Avalanche Triggered Transit [*Bell Laboratories*]

TRAPP ... Training and Retention as Permanent Party [*Army*]   (AABC)

Tr App ... Transcript Appeals [*New York*] [*1867-68*]   (DLA)

TRAPS ... Tactical Rapid Access Processing System   (KSC)

TRAPS ... Transportable Reliable Acoustic Path SONAR   (MCD)

TRAPS ... Troop Reaction and Posture Sequence   (MCD)

TRAPV ... Trap on Overflow BIT [*Binary Digit*] Set [*Data processing*]

TRAQA ... Traffic Quarterly [*A publication*]

TRAR ... Total Radiation Absolute Radiometer [*NASA*]

Tr Arkhang Lesotekh Inst ... Trudy Arkhangel'skogo Lesotekhnicheskogo Instituta [*A publication*]

Tr Arkt Antarkt Nauchno-Issled Inst ... Trudy Arkticheskogo i Antarkticheskogo Nauchno-Issledovatel'skogo Instituta [*A publication*]

Tr Arm Nauchno Issled Inst Vinograd Vinodel Plodovod ... Trudy Armyanskogo Nauchno-Isseldovatel'skogo Instituta Vinogradarstva. Vinodeliya i Plodovodstva

Tr Arm Nauchno-Issled Inst Zhivotnovod Vet ... Trudy Armyanskogo Nauchno-Issledovatel'skogo Instituta Zhivotnovodstva i Veterinarii [*A publication*]

Tr Arm Nauchno-Issled Vet Inst ... Trudy Armyanskogo Nauchno-Issledovatel'skogo Veterinarnogo Instituta [*A publication*]

Tr Arm Protivochumn Stn ... Trudy Armyanskoi Protivochumnoi Stantsii [*A publication*]

TRARON ... Training Squadron

TRAS ... Training Requirements Analysis System [*Army*]

TRASA ... Traktory i Sel'khozmashiny [*A publication*]

TRASANA ... TRADOC [*Training and Doctrine Command*] Systems Analysis Activity [*Army*]

Trasfus Sangue ... Trasfusione del Sangue [*A publication*]

TRASH ... Trash Remover and Satellite Hauler [*Proposed device to remove orbiting space debris*]

TRASH ... Tsunami Research Advisory System of Hawaii

Tr Ashkhab Nauchno Issled Inst Epidemiol Gig ... Trudy Ashkhabadskogo Nauchno-Issledovatel'skogo Instituta Epidemiologii i Gigieny [*A publication*]

TRASOP ... Tax Reduction Act Stock Ownership Plan

TRASSO ... TRADOC Systems Staff Officer [*Army*]

TRASTA ... Training Station [*Navy*]

Tr Astrakh Gos Med Inst ... Trudy Astrakhanskogo Gosudarstvennogo Meditinskogo Instituta [*A publication*]

Tr Astrakh Gos Zapov ... Trudy Astrakhanskogo Gosudarstvennogo Zapovednika [*A publication*]

Tr Astrofiz Inst Akad Nauk Kaz SSR ... Trudy Astrofizicheskogo Instituta. Akademiya Nauk Kazakhskoi SSR [*Kazakh SSR*] [*A publication*]

TRAT ... Torpedo Readiness Assistance Team

TRAT ... Triacetylhexahydrotriazine [*Organic chemistry*]

TRATE ... Trace Test and Evaluation

TRATEL ... Tracking through Telemetry [*Air Force*]

Tr Atl Nauchno-Issled Inst Ryb Khoz Okeanogr ... Trudy Atlanticheskii Nauchno-Issledovatel'skii Institut Rybnogo Khozyaistva i Okeanografii [*USSR*] [*A publication*]

Tratt ... Trattenuto [*Music*]

Tratt Met ... Trattamenti dei Metalli [*A publication*]

Tr At Zoovet Inst ... Trudy Alma-Atinskogo Instituta [*A publication*]

TRAU ... Tanganyika Railway African Union

TrAu ... Triangulum Australe [*Constellation*]

TRAV ... Training Availability [*Navy*]   (NVT)

TRAV ... Travancore [*India*]   (ROG)

Trav ... Travel [*A publication*]

Trav ... Travel Holiday [*A publication*]

Trav ... Travelling [*A publication*]

TRAV ... Travels

TRAV ... Traverse   (AABC)

TRAVA ... Travaux [*A publication*]

Travailleur Can ... Travailleur Canadien [*A publication*]

Trav Alphabet ... Travail de l'Alphabetisation [*A publication*]

Trav Assoc H Capitant ... Travaux. Association Henri Capitant [*A publication*]

Travaux du Com Franc de Droit Internat Prive ... Travaux. Comite Francais de Droit International Prive [*Paris, France*]   (DLA)

Travaux et Conf Univ Libre de Brux ... Travaux et Conferences. Universite Libre de Bruxelles. Faculte de Droit [*Brussels, Belgium*]   (DLA)

Travaux Sem Anal Convexe ... Travaux. Seminaire d'Analyse Convexe [*A publication*]

TRAVC ... Travail Canada [*Labour Canada - LC*]

TRAVCHAR ... Cost Travel Chargeable
Trav Chim Aliment Hyg ... Travaux de Chimie Alimentaire et d'Hygiene [*A publication*]
Trav-Cochin ... Indian Law Reports, Kerala Series   (DLA)
Trav Communaux ... Travaux Communaux [*France*] [*A publication*]
Trav Doc ORSTOM ... Travaux et Documents. ORSTOM [*Office de la Recherche Scientifique et Technique d'Outre-Mer*] [*A publication*]
TRAVEL ..... Transportable Vertical Erectable Launcher
Trav/Holiday ... Travel/Holiday [*A publication*]
Trav Hum ... Travail Humain [*A publication*]
Trav Humain ... Travail Humain [*A publication*]
Trav Inst Franc Et Andines ... Travaux. Institut Francais d'Etudes Andines [*A publication*]
Trav Inst Geol Anthropol Prehist Fac Sci Poitiers ... Travaux. Institut de Geologie et d'Anthropologie Prehistorique. Faculte des Sciences de Poitiers [*A publication*]
Trav Inst L ... Travaux. Institut de Linguistique de Lund [*A publication*]
Trav Inst Rech Sahar ... Travaux. Institut de Recherches Sahariennes [*A publication*]
Trav Inst Sci Cherifien Fac Sci Rabat Ser Gen ... Travaux. Institut Scientifique Cherifien et Faculte des Sciences de Rabat. Serie Generale [*A publication*]
Trav Inst Sci Cherifien Fac Sci Ser Zool ... Travaux. Institut Scientifique Cherifien et Faculte des Sciences. Serie Zoologie [*A publication*]
Trav Inst Sci Cherifien Ser Bot ... Travaux. Institut Scientifique Cherifien. Serie Botanique [*A publication*]
Trav Inst Sci Cherifien Ser Bot Biol Veg ... Travaux. Institut Scientifique Cherifien. Serie Botanique et Biologique Vegetale [*A publication*]
Trav Inst Sci Cherifien Ser Geol Geogr Phys ... Travaux. Institut Scientifique Cherifien. Serie Geologie et Geographie Physique [*A publication*]
Trav Inst Sci Cherifien Ser Sci Phys ... Travaux. Institut Scientifique Cherifien. Serie Sciences Physiques [*A publication*]
Trav Inst Sci Cherifien Ser Zool ... Travaux. Institut Scientifique Cherifien. Serie Zoologique [*A publication*]
Trav Inst Speleo "Emile Racovitza" ... Travaux. Institut de Speleologie "Emile Racovitza" [*A publication*]
TRAVIS ...... Traffic Retrieval Analysis Validation and Information System [*Telecommunications*]   (TEL)
Trav Jeunes Sci ... Travaux des Jeunes Scientifiques [*A publication*]
Trav et Jours ... Travaux et Jours [*A publication*]
Trav Lab Anthropol Prehist Ethnol Pays Mediterr Occid ... Travaux. Laboratoire d'Anthropologie de Prehistoire et d'Ethnologie des Pays de la Mediterranee Occidentale [*A publication*]
Trav Lab For Toulouse ... Travaux. Laboratoire Forestier de Toulouse [*A publication*]
Trav Lab For Toulouse Tome I Artic Divers ... Travaux. Laboratoire Forestier de Toulouse. Tome I. Articles Divers [*A publication*]
Trav Lab For Toulouse Tome II Etud Dendrol ... Travaux. Laboratoire Forestier de Toulouse. Tome II. Etudes Dendrologiques [*A publication*]
Trav Lab For Toulouse Tome V Geogr For Monde ... Travaux. Laboratoire Forestier de Toulouse. Tome V. Geographie Forestier du Monde [*A publication*]
Trav Lab For Univ Toulouse ... Travaux. Laboratoire Forestier. Universite de Toulouse [*A publication*]
Trav Lab Geol Fac Sci Grenoble ... Travaux. Laboratoire de Geologie. Faculte des Sciences de Grenoble [*A publication*]
Trav Lab Geol Fac Sci Grenoble Mem ... Travaux. Laboratoire de Geologie. Faculte des Sciences de Grenoble. Memoires [*A publication*]
Trav Lab Hydrogeol Geochim Fac Sci Univ Bordeaux ... Travaux. Laboratoire d'Hydrogeologie Geochimie. Faculte des Sciences Universite de Bordeaux [*A publication*]
Trav Lab Matiere Med Pharm Galenique Fac Pharm (Paris) ... Travaux. Laboratoires de Matiere Medicale et de Pharmacie Galenique. Faculte de Pharmacie (Paris) [*A publication*]
Trav Lab Microbiol Fac Pharm Nancy ... Travaux. Laboratoire de Microbiologie. Faculte de Pharmacie de Nancy [*A publication*]
Trav LJ .... Travancore Law Journal [*India*]   (DLA)
Trav LR ...... Travancore Law Reports [*India*]   (DLA)
Trav LT .... Travancore Law Times [*India*]   (DLA)
Trav Met Deform ... Travail des Metaux par Deformation [*A publication*]
Trav et Meth ... Travail et Methodes [*A publication*]
Trav Mus Hist Nat "Grigore Antipa" ... Travaux. Museum d'Histoire Naturelle "Grigore Antipa" [*A publication*]
TRAVNEC ... Subject Travel Was Necessary at This Time and Time Consumed in Administrative Channels Prevented Written Orders Being Issue
Trav Pech Que ... Travaux sur les Pecheries du Quebec [*A publication*]
Trav Peint ... Travaux de Peinture [*A publication*]
Trav Quebec ... Travail Quebec [*A publication*]
Trav et Rech ... Travaux et Recherches [*A publication*]

Trav Rech Haut Comite Et Inform Alcool ... Travaux et Recherches. Haut Comite d'Etude et d'Information sur l'Alcoolisme [*A publication*]
Trav Sect Scient Tech Inst Fr Pondichery ... Travaux. Section Scientifique et Technique. Institut Francais de Pondichery [*A publication*]
Trav Sect Sci Tech Inst Franc Pondichery ... Travaux. Section Scientifique et Technique. Institut Francais de Pondichery [*A publication*]
Trav Sect Sci Tech Inst Fr Pondichery ... Travaux. Section Scientifique et Technique. Institut Francais de Pondichery [*A publication*]
Trav Secur ... Travail et Securite [*A publication*]
Trav et Soc ... Travail et Societe [*A publication*]
Trav Soc Bot Geneve ... Travaux. Societe Botanique de Geneve [*A publication*]
Trav Soc Pharm Montp ... Travaux. Societe de Pharmacie de Montpellier [*A publication*]
Trav Soc Pharm Montpellier ... Travaux. Societe de Pharmacie de Montpellier [*France*] [*A publication*]
Trav Soc Sci Lettres Wroclaw ... Travaux. Societe des Sciences et des Lettres de Wroclaw [*A publication*]
Trav Sta Rech Groenendaal ... Travaux. Station de Recherches des Eaux et Forets. Groenendaal-Hoeilaart [*A publication*]
Tr Avtom Svarke Flyusom ... Trudy po Avtomaticheskoi Svarke pod Flyusom [*A publication*]
TRAWL .... Tape Read and Write Library
T Ray .... [*Sir*] T. Raymond's English King's Bench Reports [*83 English Reprint*] [*1660-84*]   (DLA)
Tray Lat Max ... Trayner's Latin Maxims and Phrases, Etc.   (DLA)
T Raym .... [*Sir*] T. Raymond's English King's Bench Reports [*83 English Reprint*]   (DLA)
T Raym (Eng) ... [*Sir*] T. Raymond's English King's Bench Reports [*83 English Reprint*]   (DLA)
Tr Azerb Inst Nefti Khim ... Trudy Azerbaidzhanskogo Instituta Nefti i Khimii [*A publication*]
Tr Azerb Nauchno Issled Inst Buren Neft Gazov Skvazhin ... Trudy Azerbaidzhanskogo Nauchno-Issledovatel'skogo Instituta po Bureniyu Neftyanykh i Gazovykh Skvazhin [*A publication*]
Tr Azerb Nauchno-Issled Inst Energ ... Trudy Azerbaidzhanskogo Nauchno-Issledovatel'skogo Instituta Energetiki [*A publication*]
Tr Azerb Nauchno-Issled Inst Gig Tr Prof Zabol ... Trudy Azerbaidzhanskogo Nauchno-Issledovatel'skogo Instituta Gigieny Truda i Professional'nykh Zabolevaniya [*A publication*]
Tr Azerb Nauchno-Issled Inst Lesn Khoz Agrolesomelior ... Trudy Azerbaidzhanskogo Nauchno-Issledovatel'skogo Instituta Lesnogo Khozyaistva i Agrolesomelioratsii [*A publication*]
Tr Azerb Nauchno-Issled Inst Med Parazitol Trop Med ... Trudy Azerbaidzhanskogo Nauchno-Issledovatel'skogo Instituta Meditsinskoi Parazitologii i Trophicheskoi Meditsiny [*A publication*]
Tr Azerb Nauchno Issled Vet Inst ... Trudy Azerbaidzhanskogo Nauchno-Issledovatel'skogo Veterinarnogo Instituta [*A publication*]
Tr Azerb Neft Nauchno Issled Inst ... Trudy Azerbaidzhanskogo Neftyanogo Nauchno-Issledovatel'skogo Instituta [*A publication*]
TRB .... Signature for Washington correspondent's column in "New Republic" magazine [*Said to have been derived by reversing the initialism for Brooklyn Rapid Transit: BRT*]
TRB .... Tactical Review Board [*Military*]   (CAAL)
TRB .... Tapered Roller Bearing
TRB .... Tax Review Board [*Canada*]
TRB .... Technical Reference Branch [*Department of Transportation*]   (EISS)
TRB .... Technical Review Board [*NASA*]   (KSC)
TRB .... Tennyson Research Bulletin [*A publication*]
TRB .... Test Requirement Bulletins [*NASA*]   (KSC)
TRB .... Test Review Board [*NASA*]   (NASA)
TRB .... Tom Robinson Band
TRB .... Torpedo Recovery Boat
TRB .... Trabaccolo [*Small coasting vessel of the Adriatic*]
TRB .... Transportation Research Board [*Formerly, HRB*]   (EA)
TRB .... Trapped Radiation Belt
TRB .... Treble
TRB .... [*The*] Tribune Co. [*NYSE symbol*]
TRB .... Troop Basis   (MUGU)
TRB .... Turbo [*Colombia*] [*Airport symbol*]   (OAG)
TRB .... United States Army TRADOC, Engineering School Library and Learning Resource Center, Fort Belvoir, VA [*OCLC symbol*]   (OCLC)
Tr Baik Limnol Stn Akad Nauk SSSR Vost Sib Fil ... Trudy Baikal'skoi Limnologicheskoi Stantsii. Akademiya Nauk SSSR Vostochno-Sibirskii Filial [*A publication*]
Tr Bakinsk Nauchno-Issled Inst Travmatol Ortop ... Trudy Bakinskogo Nauchno-Issledovatel'skogo Instituta Travmatologii Ortopedii [*A publication*]
Tr Bakinskogo Nauchno Issled Inst Travmatol Ortop ... Trudy Bakinskogo Nauchno-Issledovatel'skogo Instituta Travmatologii Ortopedii [*A publication*]

Tr Balt Nauchno Issled Inst Rybn Khoz ... Trudy Baltiiskogo Nauchno-Issledovatel'skogo Instituta Rybnogo Khozyaistva [*A publication*]

Tr Bashk Gos Zapov ... Trudy Bashkirskogo Gosudarstvennogo Zapovednika [*A publication*]

Tr Bashk Nauchno-Issled Inst Pererab Nefti ... Trudy Bashkirskii Nauchno-Issledovatel'skii Institut po Pererabotke Nefti [*USSR*] [*A publication*]

Tr Bashk S-kh Inst ... Trudy Bashkirskogo Sel'skokhozyaistvennogo Instituta [*A publication*]

Tr Batum Bot Sada Akad Nauk Gruz SSR ... Trudy Batumskogo Botanicheskogo Sada Akademii Nauk Gruzinskoi SSR [*A publication*]

Tr Belgorod Gos Skh Opytn Stn ... Trudy Belgorodskoi Gosudarstvennoi Sel'skokhozyaistvennoi Opytnoi Stantsii [*A publication*]

Tr Belgorod Tekhnol Inst Stroit ... Trudy Belgorodskogo Tekhnologicheskogo Instituta Stroitel'nyhmaterialov [*A publication*]

Tr Belomorsk Biol Stn Mosk Gos Univ ... Trudy Belomorskoi Biologicheskoi Stantsii Moskovskogo Gosudarstvennogo Universiteta [*A publication*]

Tr Beloruss Nauchno-Issled Inst Melior Vodn Khoz ... Trudy Belorusskogo Nauchno-Issledovatel'skogo Instituta Melioratsii i Vodnogo Khozyaistva [*A publication*]

Tr Beloruss Nauchno Issled Inst Pochvoved ... Trudy Belorusskii Nauchno-Issledovatel'skii Institut Pochvovedenii [*A publication*]

Tr Beloruss Nauchno Issled Inst Promsti Prodovol Tovarov ... Trudy Belorusskii Nauchno-Issledovatel'skii Institut Promyshlennosti Prodovol'stvennykh Tovarov [*A publication*]

Tr Beloruss Nauchno Issled Inst Rybn Khoz ... Trudy Belorusskogo Nauchno-Issledovatel'skogo Instituta Rybnogo Khozyaistva [*A publication*]

Tr Beloruss Nauchno Issled Inst Zhivotnovod ... Trudy Belorusskii Nauchno-Issledovatel'skii Institut Zhivotnovodstva [*A publication*]

Tr Beloruss Naucno-Issled Inst Pishch Prom-Sti ... Trudy Belorusskogo Nauchno-Issledovatel'skogo Instituta Pishchevoi Promyshlennosti [*A publication*]

Tr Beloruss Sel'skokhoz Akad ... Trudy Belorusskoi Sel'skokhozyaistvennoi Akademii [*A publication*]

Tr Beloruss Skh Akad ... Trudy Belorusskoi Sel'skokhozyaistvennoi Akademii [*A publication*]

Tr Berdyanskii Opytn Neftemaslozavod ... Trudy Berdyanskii Opytnyi Neftemaslozavod [*A publication*]

TRBF .... Total Renal Blood Flow [*Medicine*]

Tr Biogeokhim Lab Akad Nauk SSSR ... Trudy Biogeokhimicheskoi Laboratorii. Akademiya Nauk SSSR [*A publication*]

Tr Biol Inst Akad Nauk SSSR Sib Otd ... Trudy Biologicheskogo Instituta. Akademiya Nauk SSSR. Sibirskoe Otdelenie [*A publication*]

Tr Biol Inst Zapadno-Sib Fil Akad Nauk SSSR ... Trudy Biologicheskogo Instituta Zapadno-Sibirskogo Filiala Akademii Nauk SSSR [*A publication*]

Tr Biol Nauchno Issled Inst Biol Stn Permsk Gos Univ ... Trudy Biologicheskogo Nauchno-Issledovatel'skogo Instituta i Biologicheskoi Stantsii pri Permskom Gosudarstvennom Universitete [*A publication*]

Tr Biol Nauchno Issled Inst Molotov Gos Univ ... Trudy Biologicheskogo Nauchno-Issledovatel'skogo Instituta pri Molotovskom Gosudarstvennom Universitete [*A publication*]

Tr Biol Pochv Inst Dalnevost Nauchn Tsentr Akad Nauk SSSR ... Trudy Biologo-Pochvennogo Instituta. Dal'nevostochnyi Nauchnyi Tsentr. Akademiya Nauk SSSR [*A publication*]

Tr Biol Stn Borok Akad Nauk SSSR ... Trudy Biologicheskoi Stantsii "Borok." Akademiya Nauk SSSR [*A publication*]

TRBL .... Trouble   (FAAC)

Tr Blagoveshch Gos Med Inst ... Trudy Blagoveshchenskogo Gosudarstvennogo Meditsinskogo Instituta [*A publication*]

Tr Blagoveshch Skh Inst ... Trudy Blagoveshchenskogo Sel'skokhozyaistvennogo Instituta [*A publication*]

TRBN .... Trombone [*Music*]

Tr Bot Inst Akad Nauk SSSR ... Trudy Botanicheskogo Instituta. Akademii Nauk SSSR [*A publication*]

Tr Bot Inst Akad Nauk SSSR Ser 4 ... Trudy Botanicheskogo Instituta. Akademii Nauk SSSR. Seriya 4 [*A publication*]

Tr Bot Inst Akad Nauk SSSR Ser 5 ... Trudy Botanicheskogo Instituta. Akademiya Nauk SSSR. Seriya 5. Rastitel'noe Syr'ye [*A publication*]

Tr Bot Inst Akad Nauk SSSR Ser 6 ... Trudy Botanicheskogo Instituta. Akademiya Nauk SSSR. Seriya 6. Introduktsiya Rastenii i Zelenoe [*A publication*]

Tr Bot Inst Akad Nauk Tadzhikskoi SSR ... Trudy Botanicheskogo Instituta. Akademiya Nauk Tadzhikskoi SSR [*A publication*]

Tr Bot Inst Akad Nauk Tadzh SSR ... Trudy Botanicheskogo Instituta. Akademiya Nauk Tadzhikskoi SSR [*A publication*]

Tr Bot Inst V L Komarova Akad Nauk SSSR Ser VII ... Trudy Botanicheskogo Instituta Imeni V. L. Komarova. Akademiya Nauk SSSR. Seriya VII [*A publication*]

Tr Bot Sada Akad Nauk Ukr SSR ... Trudy Botanicheskogo Sada Akademii Nauk Ukrainskoi SSR [*A publication*]

Tr Bot Sada Tashk Akad Nauk Uzb SSR ... Trudy Botanicheskogo Sada v Tashkente. Akademii Nauk Uzbekskoi SSR [*A publication*]

Tr Bot Sada Tashkente Akad Nauk Uzb SSR ... Trudy Botanicheskogo Sada v Tashkente. Akademii Nauk Uzbekskoi SSR [*A publication*]

Tr Bot Sada Zapadn-Sib Fil Akad Nauk SSSR ... Trudy Botanicheskogo Sada Zapadno-Sibirskogo Filiala. Akademii Nauk SSSR [*A publication*]

Tr Bot Sadov Akad Nauk Kaz SSR ... Trudy Botanicheskikh Sadov. Akademii Nauk Kazakhskoi SSR [*A publication*]

TRBP .... Trainable Retractable Bow Propeller

Tr Briansk Lesokhoz Inst ... Trudy Brianskogo Lesokhozyaistvennogo Instituta [*A publication*]

TRBU .... Treasury Bulletin

Tr Buryat-Mong Nauchno-Issled Vet Opytn Stn ... Trudy Buryat-Mongol'skoi Nauchno-Issledovatel'skoi Veterinarnoi Opytnoi Stantsii [*A publication*]

Tr Buryat Mong Zoovet Inst ... Trudy Buryat-Mongol'skogo Zooveterinarnogo Instituta [*A publication*]

Tr Buryat S-kh Inst ... Trudy Buryatskogo Sel'skokhozyaistvennogo Instituta [*A publication*]

TRC .... [*The*] Radiochemical Centre [*British*]

TRC .... [*The*] Ranchero Club   (EA)

TRC .... [*The*] Revitalization Corps [*Hartford, CT*]   (EA)

TRC .... Tanned Red Cell [*Clinical chemistry*]

TRC .... Tape Reader Calibrator

TRC .... Tape Reader Control

TRC .... Tape Record Coordinator [*Data processing*]

TRC .... Tape Relay Center   (NATG)

TRC .... Taylor Ranch [*California*] [*Seismograph station code, US Geological Survey*]   (SEIS)

TrC .... Tayloreed Corporation, Rochester, NY [*Library symbol*] [*Library of Congress*]   (LCLS)

TRC .... Technical Repair Center [*Air Force*]   (AFIT)

TRC .... Technical Research Center   (MCD)

TRC .... Technical Resources Center [*Syracuse University*] [*Research center*]

TRC .... Technical Review Committee [*International Atomic Energy Agency*]   (NRCH)

TRC .... Technology Reports Centre [*British*]

TRC .... Technology Resource Center [*Makati, Metro Manila, Philippines*] [*Information service*]   (EISS)

TRC .... Tejon Ranch Co. [*American Stock Exchange symbol*]

TRC .... Telemetry and Remote Control   (IEEE)

TRC .... Temperature Recording Controller

TRC .... Teryl Resources Corporation [*Vancouver Stock Exchange symbol*]

TRC .... Test Readiness Certificate   (AAG)

TRC .... Thermal Regenerative Cracking [*Hydrocarbon pyrolysis process*]

TRC .... Thermodynamics Research Center [*Texas A & M University*] [*College Station, TX*]

TRC .... Thrombosis Research Center [*Temple University*] [*Research center*]   (RCD)

TRC .... Tierce [*Unit of measurement*]

TRC .... Tithe Rent-Charge

TRC .... Topic [*Record label*] [*Great Britain*]

TRC .... Toroidal Propellant Container

TRC .... Torreon [*Mexico*] [*Airport symbol*]   (OAG)

TRC .... Total Residual Chlorine [*Environmental chemistry*]

TRC .... Total Ridge Count [*Anthropology*]

TRC .... Tough Rubber-Sheathed Cable

TRC .... Tracking, RADAR-Input, and Correlation

TRC .... Trade Relations Council of the United States [*Washington, DC*]   (EA)

TRC .... Traffic Records Committee [*National Safety Council*] [*Chicago, IL*]   (EA)

TRC .... Transcaribbean   (MCD)

TRC .... Transmit/Receive Control Unit

TRC .... Transportation Research Center [*Ohio*]

TRC .... Transverse Redundancy Check [*Data processing*]   (IBMDP)

TRC .... Travelers Research Center [*Oceanography*]

TRC .... Tricon International Airlines [*Dallas, TX*] [*FAA designator*]   (FAAC)

TRC .... Triumph Roadster Club   (EA)

TRC .... Trona Railway Company [*AAR code*]

TRC .... Type Requisition Code

TRC .... United States Army TRADOC, Fort Leavenworth Post Library, Commander, General Staff, Fort Leavenworth, KS [*OCLC symbol*]   (OCLC)

TRCA .... Tricycle Racing Club of America

TRC-AS ..... Transmit/Receive Control Unit-Asynchronous Start/Stop

TRCC .... T-Carrier Restoration Control Center [*Bell System*]

TRCC .... Theodore Roosevelt Centennial Commission [*Government agency*] [*Terminated, 1959*]

TRCC .... TRC Companies, Inc. [*NASDAQ symbol*]   (NQ)

TRCCC .... Tracking RADAR Central Control Console [*BMEWS*]

TRCE .... Tactical Radio Communications Equipment

TRCE .... Terrace [*Classified advertising*]   (ADA)

TRCE .... Thermionic Reactor Critical Experiment [*NASA*]

TRCE .... Trace

Tr Ch .... Transactions of the High Court of Chancery [*Tothill's Reports*] (DLA)
Tr Chelyab Gos Pedagog Inst ... Trudy Chelyabinskii Gosudarstvennyi Pedagogicheskii Institut [*A publication*]
Tr Chelyab Inst Mekh Elektrif Selsk Khoz ... Trudy Chelyabinskogo Instituta Mekhanizatsii i Elektrifikatsii Sel'skogo Khozyaistva [*A publication*]
Tr Chelyab Politekh Inst ... Trudy Chelyabinskii Politekhnicheskii Institut [*USSR*] [*A publication*]
Tr Chernomorsk Biol Stan Varna ... Trudove na Chernomorskata Biologichna Stantsiya v Varna [*A publication*]
TRCHI .... Tanned Red Cell Hemagglutination Inhibition Test [*Immunology*]
TRCO .... Technical Representative of the Contracting Officer   (MCD)
TRCO .... Trade and Commerce [*A publication*]
TRCO .... Transportation Research Command [*Army*]   (KSC)
TRCO .... Trico Products [*NASDAQ symbol*]   (NQ)
TRCONS .... Theater Rate Consolidation Data File [*Military*]
Tr Consist J ... Tristram's Consistory Judgments [*1872-90*] [*England*]   (DLA)
TRCP.......... Tape Recorder Control Panel   (MCD)
TRCR.......... Tracer   (MSA)
TRCR.......... Tractor
TRCR.......... Trail Riders of the Canadian Rockies   (EA)
TRCS.......... Tactical Radio Communications System
TRCS.......... Techniques for Determining RADAR Cross Section [*Air Force*]
TRC-SC...... Transmit/Receive Control Unit-Synchronous Character
TRC-SF...... Transmit/Receive Control Unit-Synchronous Framing
TRCVR .... Transceiver   (CET)
TRD .... Registry of Tissue Reactions to Drugs   (EA)
TRD .... Test Requirements Document [*NASA*]   (AAG)
TRD .... Thread   (AAG)
TRD .... Toyota Racing Development [*Toyota Motor Corp.*]
TRD .... Transferred   (ROG)
TRD .... Trapped Radiation Detector
TRD .... Tread
TRD .... Trivandrum [*India*] [*Geomagnetic observatory code*]
TRD .... Trivandrum [*India*] [*Seismograph station code, US Geological Survey*]   (SEIS)
TRD .... Trondheim [*Norway*] [*Airport symbol*]   (OAG)
TRD .... Trouble Reporting Desk [*NASA*]   (KSC)
TRD .... Troudor Resources, Inc. [*Vancouver Stock Exchange symbol*]
TRD .... Try Repeating Dose [*Medicine*]
TRD .... Turbine Reduction Drive
TRD .... United States Army TRADOC, Fort Dix Post Library, Fort Dix, NJ [*OCLC symbol*]   (OCLC)
Tr Dagest Gos Pedagog Inst Estestv-Geogr Fak ... Trudy Dagestanskogo Gosudarstvennogo Pedagogicheskogo Instituta Estestvenno-Geograficheskii Fakul'tet [*A publication*]
Tr Dagest S-kh Inst ... Trudy Dagestanskogo Sel'skokhozyaistvennogo Instituta [*A publication*]
Tr Dalnevost Fil Akad Nauk SSSR Ser Geol ... Trudy Dal'nevostochnogo Filiala Akademii Nauk SSSR. Seriya Geologicheskaya [*A publication*]
Tr Dalnevost Fil Akad Nauk SSSR Ser Khim ... Trudy Dal'nevostochnogo Filiala Akademii Nauk SSSR. Seriya Khimicheskaya [*A publication*]
Tr Dalnevost Geol Razved Tresta ... Trudy Dal'nevostochnogo Geologo-Razvedochnogo Tresta [*A publication*]
Tr Dalnevost Gos Univ ... Trudy Dal'nevostochnogo Gosudarstvennogo Universiteta [*A publication*]
Tr Dalnevost Gos Univ Ser 4 ... Trudy Dal'nevostochnogo Gosudarstvennogo Universiteta. Seriya 4. Lesnye Nauki [*A publication*]
Tr Dalnevost Gos Univ Ser 5 ... Trudy Dal'nevostochnogo Gosudarstvennogo Universiteta. Seriya 5. Sel'skoe Khozyaistvo [*A publication*]
Tr Dalnevost Gos Univ Ser 7 ... Trudy Dal'nevostochnogo Gosudarstvennogo Universiteta. Seriya 7. Fizika i Khimiya [*A publication*]
Tr Dalnevost Gos Univ Ser 8 ... Trudy Dal'nevostochnogo Gosudarstvennogo Universiteta. Seriya 8. Biologiya [*A publication*]
Tr Dalnevost Gos Univ Ser 11 ... Trudy Dal'nevostochnogo Gosudarstvennogo Universiteta. Seriya 11. Geologiya [*A publication*]
Tr Dalnevost Gos Univ Ser 12 ... Trudy Dal'nevostochnogo Gosudarstvennogo Universiteta. Seriya 12. Gornoe Delo [*A publication*]
Tr Dalnevost Gos Univ Ser 13 ... Trudy Dal'nevostochnogo Gosudarstvennogo Universiteta. Seriya 13. Tekhnika [*A publication*]
Tr Dalnevost Gos Univ Ser 15 ... Trudy Dal'nevostochnogo Gosudarstvennogo Universiteta. Seriya 15. Matematika [*A publication*]
Tr Dalnevost Kraev Nauchno Issled Inst ... Trudy Dal'nevostochnogo Kraevogo Nauchno-Issledovatel'skogo Instituta [*A publication*]
Tr Dalnevost Nauchno Issled Gidrometeorol Inst ... Trudy Dal'nevostochnogo Nauchno-Issledovatel'skogo Gidrometeorologicheskogo Instituta [*A publication*]

Tr Dalnevost Nauchno Issled Vet Inst ... Trudy Dal'nevostochnogo Nauchno-Issledovatel'skogo Veterinarnogo Instituta [*A publication*]
Tr Dalnevost Politekh Inst ... Trudy Dal'nevostochnogo Politekhnicheskogo Instituta [*A publication*]
Tr Dalnevost Tekh Inst Rybn Promsti Khoz ... Trudy Dal'nevostochnogo Tekhnicheskogo Instituta Rybnoi Promyshlennosti i Khozyaistva [*A publication*]
Tr Darvinsk Gos Zapov ... Trudy Darvinskogo Gosudarstvennogo Zapovednika [*A publication*]
TRDC .... Tourism Reference and Data Centre [*Department of Regional and Industrial Expansion*] [*Information service*] [*Ottawa, ON*]   (EISS)
TRDC .... Transport Research and Development Command [*Army*]   (MCD)
TRDE......... Transparent Rotating Disk Electrode [*Electrochemistry*]
TRDG .... Trading
TRDI .... Trim Die   (AAG)
TRDIA........ Transmission and Distribution [*A publication*]
Tr Din Raz ... Trudy po Dinamike Razvitiya [*A publication*]
TRDJSDOPII ... [*The*] Reverend Doctor Jonathan Swift, Dean of Patrick's in Ireland [*Pseudonym used by Jonathan Swift*]
TRDL .... Tactical Reconnaissance Data Link   (MCD)
TR & DL...... Tung Research and Development League [*Defunct*]   (EA)
TRDM......... Tactical Reconnaissance Data Marking
Tr Dnepropetr Inst Inzh Zheleznodorozhn Transp ... Trudy Dnepropetrovskogo Instituta Inzhenerov Zheleznodorozhnogo Transporta [*A publication*]
Tr Dnepropetr Khim Tekhnol Inst ... Trudy Dnepropetrovskogo Khimiko-Tekhnologicheskogo Instituta [*A publication*]
Tr Dnepropetr S-kh Inst ... Trudy Dnepropetrovskogo Sel'skokhozyaistvennogo Instituta [*A publication*]
Tr Donbasskaya Nauchno Issled Lab ... Trudy. Donbasskaya Nauchno-Issledovatel'skaya Laboratoriya [*A publication*]
Tr Donetsk Gos Med Inst ... Trudy Donetskogo Gosudarstvennogo Meditsinskogo Instituta [*A publication*]
Tr Donetsk Ind Inst ... Trudy Donetskogo Industrial'nogo Instituta [*Ukrainian SSR*] [*A publication*]
Tr Donetsk Politekh Inst Ser Fiz Mat ... Trudy Donetskogo Politekhnicheskogo Instituta. Seriya Fiziko-Matematicheskaya [*A publication*]
Tr Donetsk Politekh Inst Ser Khim Tekhnol ... Trudy Donetskogo Politekhnicheskogo Instituta. Seriya Khimiko-Tekhnologicheskaya [*A publication*]
Tr Donetsk Politekh Inst Ser Metall ... Trudy Donetskogo Politekhnicheskogo Instituta. Seriya Metallurgicheskaya [*A publication*]
TRDS......... Towards   (ROG)
TRDT......... Trim and Drill Template   (MCD)
TRDT......... Triple Rotating Directional Transmission [*Military*]   (CAAL)
TRDTO .... Tracking RADAR Data Takeoff
TRE .... Tempore Regis Edwardi [*In the Time of King Edward*] [*Latin*]   (DLA)
TRE .... Terratech Resources, Inc. [*Toronto Stock Exchange symbol*]
TRE .... Tidal Regenerator Engine
TRE .... Timing Read Error
TRE .... Tiree Island [*Scotland*] [*Airport symbol*]   (OAG)
TRE .... Total Rare Earths   (NRCH)
TRE .... Total Resource Effectiveness Index [*Environmental Protection Agency*]
TRE .... Training Equipment   (KSC)
TRE .... Training Readiness Evaluation   (MCD)
TRE .... Training-Related Expenses [*Work Incentive Program*]
TRE .... Transient Radiation Effects
TRE .... Treasury
TRE .... Trent University [*UTLAS symbol*]
TRE .... Trente [*Italy*] [*Seismograph station code, US Geological Survey*] [*Closed*]   (SEIS)
TRE .... True Radiation Emittance
TRE .... United States Army TRADOC, Fort Eustis Post Library and Translation School Library, Fort Eustis, VA [*OCLC symbol*]   (OCLC)
TREA......... [*The*] Retired Enlisted Association   (EA)
Tread .... Treadway's South Carolina Constitutional Reports   (DLA)
Tread .... Treadway's South Carolina Law Reports [*1812-16*]   (DLA)
TREAD .... Troop Recognition and Detection   (MCD)
Tread Const ... Treadway's South Carolina Constitutional Reports   (DLA)
Treadway Const (SC) ... Treadway's South Carolina Constitutional Reports   (DLA)
TREAS ...... Treasurer
TREAS ...... Treasury   (ROG)
Treas Dec ... Treasury Decisions under Customs and Other Laws [*United States*]   (DLA)
Treas Dec Int Rev ... Treasury Decisions under Internal Revenue Laws   (DLA)
Treas Regs ... United States Treasury Regulations   (DLA)
TREAT....... Transient Radiation Effects Automated Tabulation
TREAT....... Transient Reactor Test Facility
TREAT....... Treatment   (AAG)
TREAT....... Trouble Report Evaluation and Analysis Tool   (MCD)
Treatise Mater Sci Technol ... Treatise on Materials Science and Technology [*A publication*]

Treatises Sect Med Sci Pol Acad Sci ... Treatises of the Section of Medical Sciences. Polish Academy of Sciences [*A publication*]
TREB .... Treble (ROG)
TREC .... Tracking RADAR Electronic Component (AFM)
TREC .... Transistor Radiation Effects Compilation [*Program*] (MCD)
TREC .... Treco [*NASDAQ symbol*] (NQ)
TRECOM ... Transportation Research and Engineering Command (MUGU)
TRECOMS ... Treasury Computer Systems (ADA)
TRED .... TDA [*Taxpayer Delinquent Account*] Report Edit Data [*IRS*]
TRED .... Transmitting and Receiving Equipment Development (MCD)
Tred .... Tredgold's Cape Colony Reports (DLA)
TREDS .... TRADOC Educational Data System
TREDS-NRI ... TRADOC [*Training and Doctrine Command*] Educational Data System - Nonresident Instruction [*Army*]
TREE .... Transient Radiation Effects on Electronics
TREE .... Trustee
TREELS ..... Time-Resolved Electron Energy-Loss Spectroscopy
Tree Plant Notes ... Tree Planters' Notes [*A publication*]
Tree Plant Notes US For Serv ... Tree Planter's Notes. United States Forest Service [*A publication*]
Tree-Ring Bull ... Tree-Ring Bulletin [*A publication*]
TREES .... Time-Resolved Europium Excitation Spectroscopy
TREES .... Transient Radiation Effects on Electronic Systems [*Air Force*] (MCD)
Trees Mag ... Trees Magazine [*A publication*]
Trees S Afr ... Trees in South Africa [*A publication*]
TREET .... [*A*] programing language (CSR)
T Regswet ... Tydskrif vir Regswetenskap [*A publication*]
Trehern ...... British and Colonial Prize Cases (DLA)
TREKA .... Technical Reports. Engineering Research Institute. Kyoto University [*A publication*]
TREKZINE ... Trek Magazine [*Generic term for a publication of interest to fans of the television program "Star Trek"*]
TREL .... Transitron Electronic Corp. [*NASDAQ symbol*] (NQ)
TREM .... Tape Reader Emulator Module
Trem .... Tremaine's Pleas of the Crown [*England*] (DLA)
TREM .... Tremolando [*Trembling*] [*Music*]
Trem PC ..... Tremaine's Pleas of the Crown [*England*] (DLA)
tren .... Tris(aminoethyl)amine [*Organic chemistry*]
TREND .... Trade-Offs for Lifting Reentry Vehicle Evaluation and Nominal Design
TREND .... Transportation Research News [*A publication*]
TREND .... Tropical Environmental Data
Trend Eng ... Trend in Engineering [*A publication*]
Trend Eng Univ Wash ... Trends in Engineering. University of Washington [*A publication*]
Trend Prognosticke Inf ... Trend Prognosticke Informace [*A publication*]
Trends Biochem Sci ... Trends in Biochemical Sciences [*A publication*]
Trends Biochem Sci (Pers Ed) ... Trends in Biochemical Sciences (Personal Edition) [*Netherlands*] [*A publication*]
Trends Biochem Sci (Ref Ed) ... Trends in Biochemical Sciences (Reference Edition) [*Netherlands*] [*A publication*]
Trends Ed ... Trends in Education [*A publication*]
Trends in Ed ... Trends in Education [*A publication*]
Trends Educ ... Trends in Education [*A publication*]
Trends Fluoresc ... Trends in Fluorescence [*A publication*]
Trends Haematol ... Trends in Haematology [*A publication*]
Trends Neurosci ... Trends in Neurosciences [*Netherlands*] [*A publication*]
Tr Energ Inst Im I G Es'mana Akad Nauk Azerb SSR ... Trudy Energeticheskogo Instituta Imeni I. G. Es'mana. Akademiya Nauk Azerbaidzhanskoi SSR [*Azerbaidzhan SSR*] [*A publication*]
TR (Eng) .... Term Reports [*99-101 English Reprint*] (DLA)
TRENS .... Transcutaneous Random Electrical Nerve Stimulator [*Medicine*]
Trent LJ ..... Trent Law Journal (DLA)
Tr Entom Soc London ... Transactions. Entomological Society of London [*A publication*]
Trep .... Treponema [*Microbiology*]
Tr Erevan Med Inst ... Trudy Erevanskogo Meditsinskogo Instituta [*A publication*]
Tr Erevan Zoovet Inst ... Trudy Erevanskogo Zooveterinarnogo Instituta [*A publication*]
TRES .... Thermally Regenerative Electrochemical System [*Power source*]
TRES .... Time Resolved Emission Spectra
TRESI .... Target Resolution Extraction of Statistical Invariances
TRESNET ... Trent Resource Sharing Network [*Ontario Library Service Trent*] [*Richmond Hill, ON*] [*Telecommunications*] (TSSD)
Tr Estestvennonauchn Inst Permsk Gos Univ ... Trudy Estestvennonauchnogo Instituta pri Permskom Gosudarstvennom Universitete [*A publication*]
Tr Estestv Inst Permsk Gos Univ Radiospektrosk ... Trudy Estestvennonauchnogo Instituta pri Permskom Gosudarstvennom Universitete Imeni A. M. Gor'kogo Radiospektroskopiy [*A publication*]
TRev .... Theologische Revue [*A publication*]
Trev Tax Suc ... Trevor's Taxes on Succession [*4th ed.*] [*1881*] (DLA)
TRF .... T Cell Replacing Factor [*Biochemistry*]
TRF .... Tank Range-Finder
TRF .... Tariff

TRF .... Technical Reference File
TRF .... Technical Replacement Factor
TRF .... Terminal Renal Failure [*Medicine*]
TRF .... Test Tube and Ring-Shaped Forms [*AIDS cytology*]
TRF .... Thermal Radiation at Microwave Frequencies
TRF .... Thymus-Cell Replacing Factor [*Immunology*]
TRF .... Thyrotrophin-Releasing Factor [*Later, TRH*] [*Endocrinology*]
TRF .... Tragicorum Romanorum Fragmenta [*A publication*] (OCD)
TRF .... Transfer (AABC)
TRF .... Transferrin [*Also, TF*] [*Biochemistry*]
TRF .... Transportation Research Forum (EA)
TRF .... Transportation Research Foundation
TRF .... Tuna Research Foundation [*Washington, DC*] (EA)
TRF .... Tuned Radio Frequency
TRF .... Turf Research Foundation [*Defunct*] (EA)
TRF .... United States Army TRADOC, Fort McClellan, Fort McClellan, AL [*OCLC symbol*] (OCLC)
TRFA .... Triple Revolving Fund Account (AABC)
TRFB .... Tariff Board [*Canada*]
TRFC .... Tanya Roberts Fan Club [*Daly City, CA*] (EA)
TRFC .... Traffic (MSA)
TRFCS .... Temperature Rate Flight Control System
Tr Ferg Politekh Inst ... Trudy Ferganskogo Politekhnicheskogo Instituta [*A publication*]
Tr (Fifteenth) Internat Cong Hyg and Demog ... Transactions. Fifteenth International Congress on Hygiene and Demography [*A publication*]
Tr Fiz Inst Akad Nauk SSSR ... Trudy Fizicheskogo Instituta Imeni P. N. Lebedeva. Akademiya Nauk SSSR [*A publication*]
Tr Fiz Inst Im Lebedeva ... Trudy Ordena Lenina Fizicheskogo Instituta Imeni P. N. Lebedeva [*A publication*]
Tr Fiz Inst Im P N Lebedeva Akad Nauk SSSR ... Trudy Fizicheskogo Instituta Imeni P. N. Lebedeva. Akademiya Nauk SSSR [*USSR*] [*A publication*]
Tr Fiziol Biokhim Rast ... Trudy po Fiziologii i Biokhimii Rastenii [*Estonian SSR*] [*A publication*]
Tr Fiziol Lab Akad Nauk SSSR ... Trudy Fiziologicheskoi Laboratorii. Akademii Nauk SSSR [*A publication*]
Tr Fiziol Patol Zhen ... Trudy Fiziologicheskoi Patologii Zhenshchiny [*A publication*]
Tr Fiz Mosk Gorn Inst ... Trudy po Fizike. Moskovskii Gornyi Institut [*A publication*]
Tr Fiz Poluprovodn ... Trudy po Fizike Poluprovodnikov [*A publication*]
Tr Fiz Tekh Inst Akad Nauk Turkm SSR ... Trudy Fiziko-Tekhnicheskogo Instituta. Akademiya Nauk Turkmenskoi SSR [*A publication*]
Tr Frunz Politekh Inst ... Trudy Frunzenskogo Politekhnicheskogo Instituta [*A publication*]
TRFS .... Trace Fuselage Station (MCD)
TRG .... [*The*] Record Group [*Funded by N. V. Philips*]
TRG .... T-Cell Rearranging Gene [*Genetics*]
TRG .... Tactical Reconnaissance Group
TRG .... Tauranga [*New Zealand*] [*Airport symbol*] (OAG)
TRG .... Technical Research Group, Inc. (MCD)
TRG .... Telecommunications Research Group [*Culver City, CA*] [*Telecommunications*] (TSSD)
TRG .... Tijdschrift voor Rechtsgeschiedenis [*A publication*]
TRG .... Track-Rich Grains[*s*] [*Cosmic-ray path in meteorites*]
TRG .... Trailing (AAG)
TRG .... Training
T/R & G ...... Transmit, Receive, and Guard (MSA)
TRG .... [*The*] Triangle Corp. [*American Stock Exchange symbol*]
TRG .... Trilogy Resource Corp. [*Toronto Stock Exchange symbol*]
TRG .... Triton Research Group (EA)
TRG .... Trudeau, R. G., Bloomfield Hills MI [*STAC*]
TRG .... Tuned Rotor Gyro (MCD)
TRG .... United States Army TRADOC, Fort Benning Post and Infantry School Library, Fort Benning, GA [*OCLC symbol*] (OCLC)
TRGA .... Trust Co. of Georgia [*NASDAQ symbol*] (NQ)
Tr Gelmintol Lab ... Trudy Gel'mintologicheskoi Laboratorii [*A publication*]
Tr Gel'mintol Lab Akad Nauk SSSR ... Trudy Gel'mintologicheskaya Laboratoriya. Akademiya Nauk SSSR [*A publication*]
Tr Geofiz Inst Akad Nauk SSSR ... Trudy Geofizicheskogo Instituta. Akademiya Nauk SSSR [*A publication*]
Tr Geol Bulg Ser Geokhm Mineral Petrogr ... Trudove Vurkhu Geologiyata na Bulgariya. Seriya Geokhimaya Mineralogiya i Petrografiya [*A publication*]
Tr Geol Bulg Ser Inzh Geol Khidrogeol ... Trudove Vurkhu Geologiyata na Bulgariya. Seriya Inzhenerna Geologiya i Khidrogeologiya [*A publication*]
Tr Geol Bulg Ser Paleonto ... Trudove Vurkhu Geologiyata na Bulgariya. Seriya Paleontologiya [*A publication*]
Tr Geol Inst Akad Nauk Gruz SSR ... Trudy Geologicheskogo Instituta. Akademiya Nauk Gruzinskoi SSR [*A publication*]
Tr Geol Inst Akad Nauk Gruz SSR Geol Ser ... Trudy Geologicheskogo Instituta. Akademiya Nauk Gruzinskoi SSR. Geologicheskaya Seriya [*A publication*]
Tr Geom Semin ... Trudy Geometricheskogo Seminara [*A publication*]
TrgGpRM ... Training Group, Royal Marines [*British*]
TRGH .... Trough [*Freight*]

Tr Gidrometeorol Nauchno-Issled Tsentr SSSR ... Trudy Gidrometeorologicheskii Nauchno-Issledovatel'skii Tsentr SSSR [*A publication*]

Tr Gidrometeorol Nauchno-Issled Tsentr SSSR ... Trudy Gidrometeorologicheskii Nauchno-Issledovatel'skii Tsentral'nogo SSSR [*A publication*]

Tr "Giprotsement" ... Trudy "Giprotsement" [*A publication*]

TRGL .... Toreador Royalty Corp. [*NASDAQ symbol*]   (NQ)

TRGLA .... Triangle [*English Edition*] [*A publication*]

TrGlasgUOrS ... Transactions. Glasgow University Oriental Society [*Hertford, England*] [*A publication*]

Tr Glav Bot Sada ... Trudy Glavnogo Botanicheskogo Sada [*A publication*]

Tr Glavgeologii (Gl Upr Geol Okhr Nedr) Uzb SSR ... Trudy Glavgeologii (Glavnoe Upravlenie Geologii i Okhrany Nedr) Uzbekskoi SSR [*A publication*]

TRGLB .... Triangle [*A publication*]

Tr Gl Bot Sada ... Trudy Glavnogo Botanicheskogo Sada [*A publication*]

Tr Gl Bot Sada Akad Nauk SSSR ... Trudy Glavnogo Botanicheskogo Sada. Akademiya Nauk SSSR [*A publication*]

Tr Gl Geofiz Obs ... Trudy Glavnoi Geofizicheskoi Observatorii [*USSR*] [*A publication*]

Tr Golovn Nauchno-Issled Inst Tsem Mashinostr ... Trudy Golovnoi Nauchno-Issledovatel'skii Institut Tsementnogo Mashinostroeniya [*A publication*]

Tr Goriiskogo Gos Pedagog Inst ... Trudy Goriiskogo Gosudarstvennogo Pedagogicheskogo Instituta [*A publication*]

Tr Gor'k Gos Med Inst ... Trudy Gor'kovskogo Gosudarstvennogo Meditsinskogo Instituta [*A publication*]

Tr Gork Gos Pedagog Inst ... Trudy Gor'kovskogo Gosudarstvennogo Pedagogicheskogo Instituta [*A publication*]

Tr Gork Inst Inzh Vodn Transp ... Trudy Gor'kovskogo Instituta Inzhenerov Vodnogo Transporta [*A publication*]

Tr Gork Inzh Stroit Inst ... Trudy Gor'kovskogo Inzhenero-Stroitel'nogo Instituta [*A publication*]

Tr Gork Nauchno Issled Pediatr Inst ... Trudy Gor'kovskogo Nauchno-Issledovatel'skogo Pediatricheskogo Instituta [*A publication*]

Tr Gor'k Nauchno-Issled Vet Opytn Stn ... Trudy Gor'kovskoi Nauchno-Issledovatel'skoi Veterinarnoi Opytnoi Stantsii [*A publication*]

Tr Gork Politekh Inst ... Trudy Gor'kovskogo Politekhnicheskogo Instituta [*A publication*]

Tr Gor'k S-kh Inst ... Trudy Gor'kovskogo Sel'skokhozyaistvennogo Instituta [*A publication*]

Tr Gorno Geol Inst Akad Nauk SSSR Ural Fil ... Trudy Gorno-Geologicheskogo Instituta. Akademiya Nauk SSSR. Ural'skii Filial [*A publication*]

Tr Gorno Geol Inst Akad Nauk SSSR Zapadno Sib Fil ... Trudy Gorno-Geologicheskogo Instituta Akademiya Nauk SSSR Zapadno-Sibirskii Filial [*A publication*]

Tr Gos Astron Inst Im Shternberga ... Trudy Gosudarstvennogo Astronomicheskogo Instituta Imeni P. K. Shternberga [*A publication*]

Tr Gos Astron Inst Mosk Gos Univ ... Trudy Gosudarstvennogo Astronomicheskogo Instituta Moskovskii Gosudarstvennyi Universitet [*A publication*]

Tr Gos Dorozhn Proektno Izyskatel'skii Nauchno Issled Inst ... Trudy Gosudarstvennyi Dorozhnyi Proektno-Izyskatel'skii i Nauchno-Issledovatel'skii Institut [*A publication*]

Tr Gos Gidrol Inst ... Trudy Gosudarstvennogo Gidrologicheskogo Instituta [*A publication*]

Tr Gos Inst Prikl Khim ... Trudy Gosudarstvennyi Institut Prikladnoi Khimii [*A publication*]

Tr Gos Inst Proekt Issled Rab Neftedobyvayushchei Prom-sti ... Trudy Gosudarstvennyi Institut po Proektirovaniyu i Issledovatel'skim Rabotam v Neftedobyvayushchei Promyshlennosti [*USSR*] [*A publication*]

Tr Gos Inst Usoversh Vrachei I M Lenina ... Trudy Gosudarstvennogo Instituta Usovershenstvovaniya Vrachei I. M. Lenina [*A publication*]

Tr Gos Issled Elektrokeram Inst ... Trudy Gosudarstvennogo Issledovatel'skogo Elektrokeramicheskogo Instituta [*USSR*] [*A publication*]

Tr Gos Issled Keram Inst ... Trudy Gosudarstvennogo Issledovatel'skogo Keramicheskogo Instituta [*A publication*]

Tr Gos Makeev Nauchno-Issled Inst Bezop Rab Gorn Prom-sti ... Trudy Gosudarstvennyi Makeevski Nauchno-Issledovatel'skii Institut po Bezopasnosti Rabot v Gornoi Promyshlennosti [*Ukrainian SSR*] [*A publication*]

Tr Gos Nauchno Eksp Inst Grazhdanskikh Prom Inzh Sooruzh ... Trudy Gosudarstvennogo Nauchno-Eksperimental'nogo Instituta Grazhdanskikh Promyshlennykh i Inzhenernykh Sooruzhenii [*A publication*]

Tr Gos Nauchno Issled Inst Gornokhim Syr ... Trudy Gosudarstvennogo Nauchno-Issledovatel'skogo Instituta Gornokhimicheskogo Syr'ya [*A publication*]

Tr Gos Nauchno-Issled Inst Gornokhim Syr'ya ... Trudy Gosudarstvennogo Nauchno-Issledovatel'skogo Instituta Gornokhimicheskogo Syr'ya [*USSR*] [*A publication*]

Tr Gos Nauchno-Issled Inst Prom Sanit Ochistke Gazov ... Trudy Gosudarstvennogo Nauchno-Issledovatel'skogo Instituta po Promyshlennoi i Sanitarnoi Ochistke Gazov [*USSR*] [*A publication*]

Tr Gos Nauchno Issled Inst Psikhiatrii ... Trudy Gosudarstvennogo Nauchno-Issledovatel'skogo Instituta Psikhiatrii [*A publication*]

Tr Gos Nauchno-Issled Inst Stroit Keram ... Trudy Gosudarstvennyi Nauchno-Issledovatel'skii Institut Stroitel'noi Keramiki [*USSR*] [*A publication*]

Tr Gos Nauchno-Issled Inst Ukha Gorla Nosa ... Trudy Gosudarstvennogo Nauchno-Issledovatel'skogo Instituta Ukha Gorla i Nosa [*A publication*]

Tr Gos Nauchno-Issled Proekt Inst Splavov Obrab Tsvet Met ... Trudy Gosudarstvennyi Nauchno-Issledovatel'skii i Proektnyi Institut Splavov i Obrabotki Tsvetnykh Metallov [*USSR*] [*A publication*]

Tr Gos Nauchno Issled Proektn Inst "Gipromorneft" ... Trudy Gosudarstvennogo Nauchno-Issledovatel'skogo i Proektnogo Instituta "Gipromorneft" [*A publication*]

Tr Gos Nauchno-Issled Proektn Inst Splavov Obrab Tsvetn Met ... Trudy Gosudarstvennyj Nauchno-Issledovatel'skij i Proektnyj Institut Splavov i Obrabotki Tsvetnykh Metallov [*A publication*]

Tr Gos Nauchno-Kontrol'n Inst Vet Prep ... Trudy Gosudarstvennogo Nauchno-Kontrol'nogo Instituta Veterinarnykh Preparatov [*A publication*]

Tr Gos Opt Inst ... Trudy Gosudarstvennogo Opticheskogo Instituta [*USSR*] [*A publication*]

Tr Gos Proektno Konstr Nauchno Issled Inst Morsk Transp ... Trudy Gosudarstvennyi Proektno-Konstruktorskii i Nauchno-Issledovatel'skii Institut Morskogo Transporta [*A publication*]

Tr Gos Soyuzn Nauchno Issled Trakt Inst ... Trudy Gosudarstvennyi Soyuznyi-Nauchno-Issledovatel'skii Traktornyi Institut [*A publication*]

Tr Gos Tsentr Nauchno Issled Inst Tekhnol Organ Proizvod ... Trudy Gosudarstvennyi Tsentral'yni Nauchno-Issledovatel'skii Institut Tekhnologii i Organizatsii Proizvodstva [*A publication*]

Tr Gos Vses Dorozhn Nauchno Issled Inst ... Trudy Gosudarstvennyi Vsesoyuznyi Dorozhnyi Nauchno-Issledovatel'skii Institut [*A publication*]

Tr Gos Vses Inst Proekt Nauchno-Issled Rab Giprotsement ... Trudy Gosudarstvennogo Vsesoyuznogo Instituta po Proektirovaniyu i Nauchno-Issledovatel'skim Rabotam "Giprotsement" [*A publication*]

Tr Gos Vses Inst Proekt Nauchno-Issled Rab Tsem Promsti ... Trudy Gosudarstvennogo Vsesoyuznyi Instituta po Proektirovaniyu i Nauchno-Issledovatel'skim Rabotam v Tsementnoi Promyshlennosti [*A publication*]

Tr Gos Vses Proektn Nauchno-Issled Inst Tsem Prom-sti ... Trudy Gosudarstvennyi Vsesoyuznyi Proektnyi i Nauchno-Issledovatel'skii Institut Tsementnoi Promyshlennosti [*USSR*] [*A publication*]

TRGP .... Tactical Reconnaissance Group [*Air Force*]

Tr Gruz Nauchno-Issled Inst Energ ... Trudy Gruzinskogo Nauchno-Issledovatel'skogo Instituta Energetiki [*Georgian SSR*] [*A publication*]

Tr Gruz Nauchno-Issled Inst Gidrotekh Melior ... Trudy Gruzinskogo Nauchno-Issledovatel'skogo Instituta Gidrotekhniki i Melioratsii [*A publication*]

Tr Gruz Politekh Inst ... Trudy Gruzinskogo Politekhnicheskogo Instituta [*Georgian SSR*] [*A publication*]

Tr Gruz S-kh Inst ... Trudy Gruzinskogo Sel'skokhozyaistvennogo Instituta [*A publication*]

TRGT .... Target   (AAG)

TRH .... Technical Reference Handbook

TRH .... Test Requirements Handbook   (MUGU)

TRH .... Their Royal Highnesses

TRH .... Thyrotrophin-Releasing Hormone [*Formerly, TRF*] [*Endocrinology*]

TRH .... Truss Head [*Engineering*]

TRH .... United States Army TRADOC, Fort Benjamin Harrison Library System, Fort Benjamin Harrison, IN [*OCLC symbol*]   (OCLC)

TRHAZCON ... Training Hazardous Condition   (MCD)

Tr & H Pr ... Troubat and Haly's Pennsylvania Practice   (DLA)

TRHS .... Transactions. Royal Historical Society [*A publication*]

TRHUA .... Travail Humain [*A publication*]

TRI .... Bristol, TN [*Location identifier*] [*FAA*]   (FAAL)

TRI .... [*The*] Refractories Institute [*Pittsburgh, PA*]   (EA)

TRI .... Tactical Reconnaissance/Intelligence [*Air Force*]   (AFM)

TRI .... Technical Report Instruction   (AAG)

TRI .... Technical Research Institute [*Japan*]

TRI .... Telecomputer Research, Incorporated [*Bala Cynwyd, PA*] [*Information service*] [*Telecommunications*]   (TSSD)

TRI .... Textile Research Institute [*Princeton, NJ*]   (EA)

TRI .... Time-Reversal Invariance [*Physics*]

TRI .... Tin Research Institute [*Columbus, OH*]   (EA)

TRI .... Tire Retreading Institute   (EA)

TRI.............	Torsion Reaction Integrating
TRI.............	Total Response Index [*Psychology*]
TRI.............	Transaction Routing Index
TRI.............	Translation Research Institute (EA)
TR-I............	Translations Register - Index (MCD)
TRI.............	Transpacific Resources, Incorporated [*Formerly, TransPacific Asbestos, Inc.*] [*Toronto Stock Exchange symbol*]
TRI.............	Transponder Receiver Isolation
TRI.............	Transportation Research Institute [*Carnegie-Mellon University*]
TRI.............	Tri-City Airport [*Tennessee*] [*Airport symbol*] (OAG)
TRI.............	Tri-College Library, Moorhead, MN [*OCLC symbol*] (OCLC)
TRI.............	Tri-State Airlines, Inc. [*White Lake, NY*] [*FAA designator*] (FAAC)
TRI.............	Triangle Industries, Inc. [*NYSE symbol*]
Tri..............	Triangulation
Tri..............	Triangulum [*Constellation*]
TRI.............	Triassic [*Period, era, or system*] [*Geology*]
Tri..............	Tribuna [*A publication*]
TRI.............	Trichloroethylene [*Anesthesiology*]
TRI.............	Tricycle (AAG)
TRI.............	Trieste [*Grotta Gigante*] [*Italy*] [*Seismograph station code, US Geological Survey*] (SEIS)
TRI.............	Triode (AAG)
TRI.............	Tropical Research Institute [*Smithsonian Institution*]
TRI.............	Tuboreticular Inclusions [*Hematology*]
TRIA	Telemetry Range Instrumentation Aircraft
TRIA	Temperature Removable Instrument Assembly (NRCH)
TRIA	Triacontanol [*Plant growth regulator*]
Tria............	Triangulum [*Constellation*]
TRIAC	Test Resources Improvement Advisory Council [*Military*]
TRIAC	Triiodothyroacetic Acid [*Endocrinology*]
TRIAC	Triode Alternating Current Semiconductor Switch
TRIAD.........	Target Resolving Information Augmentation Device (MCD)
TRIAL	Technique to Retrieve Information from Abstracts of Literature [*Data processing*]
TRIB	Tire Retread Information Bureau [*Pebble Beach, CA*] (EA)
TRIB	Transfer Rate of Information BITs [*Binary Digits*] [*Dial telephone network*] [*American National Standards Institute*]
TRIB	Tribal
TRIB	Tribulation (DSUE)
Trib	Tribunale [*Ordinary court of First Instance*] [*Italy*] (DLA)
TRIB	Tribunus [*Latin*] (OCD)
TRIB	Tributary
TRIB	Tribute (ADA)
Trib Admin ...	Tribunaux Administratifs [*French*] (DLA)
Trib Arb Mixtes ...	Tribunaux Arbitraux Mixtes [*French*] (DLA)
Trib CEBEDEAU ...	Tribune. CEBEDEAU [*Centre Belge d'Etude et de Documentation des Eaux et de l'Air*] [*A publication*]
Trib Con.....	Tribunal des Conflits [*French*] (DLA)
TRIBE.........	Teaching and Research in Bicultural Education [*Indian organization in Maine*]
TriBeCa......	Triangle Below Canal Street [*Artists' colony in New York City*] [*See also NoHo, SoHo, SoSo*]
TRIBF	Tri-Basin Resources [*NASDAQ symbol*] (NQ)
Trib Farm (Curitiba) ...	Tribuna Farmaceutica (Curitiba) [*A publication*]
Tri Bish	Trial of the Seven Bishops (DLA)
Trib Mus.....	Tribune Musical [*A publication*]
Trib Odontol ...	Tribuna Odontologica [*A publication*]
Tribol Int	Tribology International [*A publication*]
Tribol Lubrificazione ...	Tribologia e Lubrificazione [*A publication*]
Tribologia & Lubr ...	Tribologia e Lubrificazione [*A publication*]
Tribology Int ...	Tribology International [*A publication*]
TRIB POT	Tribunicia Potestas [*Latin*] (OCD)
Tribuna Postale ...	Tribuna Postale e delle Telecomunicazioni [*A publication*]
TRIC..........	Trachoma-Inclusion Conjunctivitis [*Ophthalmology*]
TRIC..........	Tracking RADAR Input and Correlation (MSA)
TRIC..........	Transaction Identification Code [*Military*] (AFIT)
TRIC..........	Transit Research Information Center [*Office of Transportation Management*]
TRIC..........	Tri-Chem, Inc. [*NASDAQ symbol*] (NQ)
TRIC..........	Tricks for Research in Cancer
TRICAP.......	Triple Capability [*Army*]
TRICC	Tariff Rules of the Interstate Commerce Commission
TRICE........	Transistorized Realtime Incremental Computer
Trich..........	Trichomonas [*A protozoan*] [*Medicine*]
TRICI.........	Trichinopoli Cigar (DSUE)
TRICINE	Tris(hydroxymethyl)methylglycine [*Biochemical analysis*]
TRICL........	Triclinic
TRICS........	Threat Reactive Integrated Combat System
TRICS........	Trajectory Incremental Correction System (MCD)
TRID	Track Identity
TRID	Triduum [*Three Days*] [*Latin*] (ADA)
TRIDAC	Three-Dimensional Analog Computer [*British*] (MCD)
TRIDENT	South Atlantic Cooperative Investigation Phase [*Marine science*] (MSC)
TRIDO	Table Ronde Internationale pour le Developpement de l'Orientation [*International Round Table for the Advancement of Counselling - IRTAC*] [*London, England*] (EA-IO)
TRIDOP	Tridoppler

Tri E of Cov ...	Trial of the Earl of Coventry (DLA)
Trier Archiv ...	Trierisches Archiv [*A publication*]
TriererThZ ...	Trierer Theologische Zeitschrift [*Trier*] [*A publication*]
TriererZ......	Trierer Zeitschrift fuer Geschichte und Kunst des Trierer Landes und Seiner Nachbargebiete [*A publication*]
Trierer Z Gesch Kunst ...	Trierer Zeitschrift fuer Geschichte und Kunst des Trierer Landes und Seiner Nachbargebiete [*A publication*]
TrierThZ.....	Trierer Theologische Zeitschrift [*Trier*] [*A publication*]
TRIFED/USA ...	Triathlon Federation/USA (EA)
TRIFLIC......	Trifluoromethanesulfonic [*Organic chemistry*]
TRIG..........	Triangulation (AABC)
TRIG..........	Trigger (AAG)
trig	Triglycerides [*Clinical chemistry*]
TRIG..........	Trigonometry
TRIGA	Training Reactor, Isotopes General Atomic
TRIGA	Traitement Industrial des Gadoues [*French company*]
TRIGLYME ...	Triethylene Glycol Dimethyl Ether [*Organic chemistry*]
TRIGON......	Trigonometry (ROG)
TRILF	Trilogy Ltd. [*NASDAQ symbol*] (NQ)
TRIM..........	Tailored Retrieval and Information Management
TRIM..........	Targets, Receivers, Impacts, and Methods
TRIM..........	Tax Reform Immediately (EA)
TRIM..........	Tax Reform Information Materials
TRIM..........	Technical Requirements Identification Matrix (MCD)
TRIM..........	Technique for Report and Index Management [*University of California, Riverside*] [*Information service*] [*No longer available*] (EISS)
TRIM..........	Test of Reasoning in Mathematics (ADA)
TRIM..........	Test Rules for Inventory Management
TRIM..........	Thin Region Integral Method
TRIM..........	Timely Responsive Integrated Multiuse System (MCD)
TRIM..........	Trails, Roads, and Interdiction Missions [*or Multisensor*] [*Navy*]
TRIM..........	Training Relation and Instruction Mission [*Military*] [*Vietnam, France, United States*]
TRIM..........	Training Requirements and Information Management System [*Navy*]
TRIM..........	Transformation of Imagery [*Data processing*] [*NASA*]
TRI-M........	Tri-M Music Honor Society (EA)
TRIM..........	Trimmer [*Mining engineering*]
Trim Econ ...	Trimestre Economico [*A publication*]
Trimes Econ ...	Trimestre Economico [*A publication*]
TRIMET......	Trimethylolethane [*Organic chemistry*]
TRIMIS	Tri-Service Medical Information Systems [*Military*]
TRIMM	Triple Missile Mount (MCD)
TRIMMS	Telecom Canada Remote Interface Monitoring and Management System
TRIMMS	Total Refinement and Integration of Maintenance Management Systems [*Army*]
TRIMS	Training Requirements and Information Management System (MCD)
TRIMS	Transportation Integrated Management System [*Air Force*]
TRIN	Trans-Industries [*NASDAQ symbol*] (NQ)
TRIN	Trans International Airlines
TRIN	Trinity
Trin............	Trinity Term (DLA)
TRINCO......	Trincomalee [*Sri Lanka port city*] (DSUE)
Tr Indiana Med Soc ...	Transactions. Indiana State Medical Society [*A publication*]
TRI Newsl...	Textile Research Institute. Newletter [*A publication*]
Trinidad LR ...	Trinidad Law Reports (DLA)
Trinkwasser-Verord ...	Trinkwasser-Verordnung [*A publication*]
Tr Inst Biol Akad Nauk Latv SSR ...	Trudy Institut Biologii. Akademiya Nauk Latviiskoi SSR [*A publication*]
Tr Inst Biol Akad Nauk SSSR Ural Fil ...	Trudy Instituta Biologii. Akademiya Nauk SSSR. Ural'skii Filial [*USSR*] [*A publication*]
Tr Inst Biol Bashk Univ ...	Trudy Instituta Biologii Bashkirskogo Universiteta [*A publication*]
Tr Inst Biol Ural Fil Akad Nauk SSSR ...	Trudy Instituta Biologii Ural'skogo Filiala. Akademii Nauk SSSR [*A publication*]
Tr Inst Biol Vnutr Vod Akad Nauk SSSR ...	Trudy Instituta Biologii Vnutrennikh Vod. Akademii Nauk SSSR [*A publication*]
Tr Inst Biol Yakutsk Fil Sib Otd Akad Nauk SSSR ...	Trudy Instituta Biologii Yakutskii Filial Sibirskogo Otdeleniya. Akademii Nauk SSSR [*A publication*]
Tr Inst Bot Akad Nauk Azerb SSR ...	Trudy Instituta Botaniki. Akademiya Nauk Azerbaidzhanskoi SSR [*A publication*]
Tr Inst Bot Akad Nauk Kazakh SSR ...	Trudy Instituta Botaniki. Akademiya Nauk Kazakhskoi SSR [*A publication*]
Tr Inst Ehkol Rast Zhivotn ...	Trudy Instituta Ehkologii Rastenij i Zhivotnykh [*A publication*]
Tr Inst Ehlektrokhim Akad Nauk SSSR Ural Fil ...	Trudy Instituta Ehlektrokhimii. Akademiya Nauk SSSR. Ural'skij Filial [*A publication*]
Tr Inst Ehlektrokhim Ural Nauch Tsentr Akad Nauk SSSR ...	Trudy Instituta Ehlektrokhimii. Ural'skij Nauchnyj Tsentr. Akademiya Nauk SSSR [*A publication*]
Tr Inst Ekol Rast Zhivotn ...	Trudy Instituta Ekologii Rasteni i Zhivotnykh [*USSR*] [*A publication*]
Tr Inst Ekol Rast Zhivotn Ural Fil Akad Nauk SSSR ...	Trudy Instituta Ekologii Rastenii i Zhivotnykh Ural'skogo Filiala. Akademii Nauk SSSR [*A publication*]

Tr Inst Ekol Rast Zhivotn Ural Nauchn Tsentr Akad Nauk SSSR ... Trudy Instituta Ekologii Rastenii i Zhivotnykh. Ural'skii Nauchnyi Tsentr. Akademiya Nauk SSSR [*USSR*] [*A publication*]

Tr Inst Eksper Biol Akad Nauk Eston SSR ... Trudy Instituta Eksperimental'noi Biologii. Akademiya Nauk Estonskoi SSR [*A publication*]

Tr Inst Eksp Klin Khir Gematol ... Trudy Instituta Eksperimental'noi i Klinicheskoi Khirurgii i Gematologii [*A publication*]

Tr Inst Eksp Klin Med Akad Nauk Latv SSR ... Trudy Instituta Eksperimental'noi i Klinicheskoi Meditsiny Akademii Nauk Latviiskoi SSR [*A publication*]

Tr Inst Eksp Klin Onkol Akad Med Nauk SSSR ... Trudy Instituta Eksperimental'noi i Klinicheskoi Onkologii. Akademiya Meditsinskikh Nauk SSSR [*USSR*] [*A publication*]

Tr Inst Eksp Med Akad Med Nauk SSR ... Trudy Instituta Eksperimental'noi Meditsiny. Akademii Meditsinskikh Nauk SSR [*A publication*]

Tr Inst Eksp Med Akad Nauk Latv SSR ... Trudy Instituta Eksperimental'noi Meditsiny. Akademii Nauk Latviiskoi SSR [*A publication*]

Tr Inst Eksp Meteorol ... Trudy Institut Eksperimental'noi Meteorologii [*USSR*] [*A publication*]

Tr Inst Elektrokhim Ural Nauchn Tsentr Akad Nauk SSSR ... Trudy Instituta Elektrokhimii. Ural'skii Nauchnyi Tsentr. Akademiya Nauk SSSR [*USSR*] [*A publication*]

Tr Inst Energ Akad Nauk BSSR ... Trudy Instituta Energetiki. Akademiya Nauk Belorusskoi SSR [*Belorussian SSR*] [*A publication*]

Tr Inst Fiz Akad Nauk Azerb SSR ... Trudy Instituta Fiziki. Akademiya Nauk Azerbaidzhanskoi SSR [*Azerbaidzhan SSR*] [*A publication*]

Tr Inst Fiz Akad Nauk Est SSR ... Trudy Instituta Fiziki. Akademii Nauk Estonskoi SSR [*A publication*]

Tr Inst Fiz Akad Nauk Gruz SSR ... Trudy Instituta Fiziki. Akademiya Nauk Gruzinskoi SSR [*Georgian SSR*] [*A publication*]

Tr Inst Fiz Astron Akad Nauk Ehst SSR ... Trudy Instituta Fiziki i Astronomii. Akademiya Nauk Ehstonskoj SSR [*A publication*]

Tr Inst Fiziol Akad Nauk Gruz SSR ... Trudy Instituta Fiziologii. Akademiya Nauk Gruzinskoi SSR [*Georgian SSR*] [*A publication*]

Tr Inst Fiziol Akad Nauk Kaz SSR ... Trudy Instituta Fiziologii. Akademiya Nauk Kazakhskoi SSR [*A publication*]

Tr Inst Fiziol Akad Nauk SSSR ... Trudy Instituta Fiziologii. Akademii Nauk SSSR [*A publication*]

Tr Inst Fiziol Im I P Pavlova Akad Nauk SSSR ... Trudy Instituta Fiziologii Imeni I. P. Pavlova Akademii Nauk SSSR [*A publication*]

Tr Inst Fiziol Im I P Pavlova Akad SSSR ... Trudy Instituta Fiziologii Imeni I. P. Pavlova. Akademii Nauk SSSR [*A publication*]

Tr Inst Fiziol Rast Im K A Timiryazeva ... Trudy Instituta Fiziologii Rastenii Imeni K. A. Timiryazeva [*A publication*]

Tr Inst Fiz Met Ural Nauchn Tsent Akad SSSR ... Trudy Instituta Fiziki Metallov Ural'skogo Nauchnogo Tsentra. Akademiya Nauk SSSR [*USSR*] [*A publication*]

Tr Inst Fiz Vys Ehnerg ... Trudy Instituta Fiziki Vysokikh Ehnergij [*A publication*]

Tr Inst Fiz Vys Energ Akad Nauk Kaz SSR ... Trudy Instituta Fiziki Vysokikh Energii. Akademiya Nauk Kazakhskoi SSR [*Kazakh SSR*] [*A publication*]

Tr Inst Fiz Zemli Akad Nauk SSSR ... Trudy Instituta Fiziki Zemli. Akademiya Nauk SSSR [*USSR*] [*A publication*]

Tr Inst Genet Akad Nauk SSSR ... Trudy Instituta Genetiki. Akademii Nauk SSSR [*A publication*]

Tr Inst Genet Sel Akad Nauk Az SSR ... Trudy Instituta Genetiki i Selektsii. Akademii Nauk Azerbaidzhanskoi SSR [*A publication*]

Tr Inst Geofiz Akad Nauk Gruz SSR ... Trudy Instituta Geofiziki. Akademiya Nauk Gruzinskoi SSR [*Georgian SSR*] [*A publication*]

Tr Inst Geogr Akad Nauk SSSR ... Trudy Instituta Geografii. Akademii Nauk SSSR [*A publication*]

Tr Inst Geol Akad Nauk Est SSR ... Trudy Instituta Geologii. Akademiya Nauk Estonskoi SSR [*Estonian SSR*] [*A publication*]

Tr Inst Geol Geofiz Akad Nauk SSSR Sib Otd ... Trudy Instituta Geologii i Geofiziki. Akademiya Nauk SSSR. Sibirskoe Otdelenie [*USSR*] [*A publication*]

Tr Inst Geol Korisnikh Koplain Akad Nauk Ukr RSR ... Trudy Institut Geologii Kori Korisnikh Koplain. Akademiya Nauk Ukrains'koi RSR [*Ukrainian SSR*] [*A publication*]

Tr Inst Geol Nauk Akad Nauk Kaz SSR ... Trudy Instituta Geologicheskikh Nauk. Akademiya Nauk Kazakhskoi SSR [*Kazakh SSR*] [*A publication*]

Tr Inst Goryuch Iskop (Moscow) ... Trudy Instituta Goryuchikh Iskopaemykh (Moscow) [*A publication*]

Tr Inst Istor Estestvozn Tekh Akad Nauk SSSR ... Trudy Instituta Istorii Estestvoznaniya i Tekhniki Akademiya Nauk SSSR [*USSR*] [*A publication*]

Tr Inst Khig Okhr Tr Prof Zabol ... Trudove na Instituta po Khigiena. Okhrana na Truda i Profesionalni Zabolyavaniya [*A publication*]

Tr Inst Khim Akad Nauk SSSR Ural Fil ... Trudy Instituta Khimii. Akademiya Nauk SSSR Ural'skii Filial [*USSR*] [*A publication*]

Tr Inst Khim Akad Nauk Turkm SSR ... Trudy Instituta Khimii. Akademiya Nauk Turkmenskoi SSR [*A publication*]

Tr Inst Khim Akad Nauk Uzb SSR ... Trudy Instituta Khimii. Akademiya Nauk Uzbekskoi SSR [*A publication*]

Tr Inst Khim Metall Akad Nauk SSSR Ural Fil ... Trudy Instituta Khimii i Metallurgii Akademiya Nauk SSSR. Ural'skii Filial [*A publication*]

Tr Inst Khim Nauk Akad Nauk Kaz SSR ... Trudy Instituta Khimicheskikh Nauk. Akademiya Nauk Kazakhskoi SSR [*A publication*]

Tr Inst Khim Nefti Prir Solei Akad Nauk Kaz SSR ... Trudy Instituta Khimii Nefti i Prirodnykh Solei. Akademiya Nauk Kazakhskoi SSR [*A publication*]

Tr Inst Khim Ural Nauchn Tsentr Akad Nauk SSSR ... Trudy Instituta Khimii. Ural'skii Nauchnyi Tsentr. Akademiya Nauk SSSR [*A publication*]

Tr Inst Klin Eksp Kardiol ... Trudy Instituta Klinicheskoi i Eksperimental'noi Kardiologii [*A publication*]

Tr Inst Klin Eksp Kardiol Akad Nauk Gruz SSR ... Trudy Instituta Klinicheskoi i Eksperimental'noi Kardiologii. Akademiya Nauk Gruzinskoi SSR [*A publication*]

Tr Inst Klin Eksp Khir Akad Nauk Kaz SSR ... Trudy Instituta Klinicheskoi i Eksperimental'noi Khirurgii. Akademii Nauk Kazakhskoi SSR [*A publication*]

Tr Inst Klin Eksp Nevrol Gruz SSR ... Trudy Instituta Klinicheskoi i Eksperimental'noi Nevrologii Gruzinskoi SSR [*A publication*]

Tr Inst Kom Stand Mer Izmer Prib Sov Minist SSSR ... Trudy Institutov Komiteta Standartov. Mer i Izmeritel'nykh Priborov pri Sovete Ministrov SSSR [*A publication*]

Tr Inst Kraev Eksp Med Akad Nauk Uzb SSR ... Trudy Instituta Kraevoi Eksperimental'noi Meditsiny. Akademiya Nauk Uzbekskoi SSR [*A publication*]

Tr Inst Kraev Med Akad Nauk Kirg SSR ... Trudy Instituta Kraevoi Meditsiny. Akademii Nauk Kirgizskoi SSR [*A publication*]

Tr Inst Kraev Patol Akad Nauk Kaz SSR ... Trudy Instituta Kraevoi Patologii. Akademii Nauk Kazakhskoi SSR [*A publication*]

Tr Inst Kristallogr Akad Nauk SSSR ... Trudy Instituta Kristallografii. Akademiya Nauk SSSR [*A publication*]

Tr Inst Lesa Akad Nauk Gruzin SSR ... Trudy Instituta Lesa. Akademiya Nauk Gruzinskoi SSR [*A publication*]

Tr Inst Lesa Akad Nauk Gruz SSR ... Trudy Instituta Lesa. Akademii Nauk Gruzinskoi SSR [*A publication*]

Tr Inst Lesa Akad Nauk SSSR ... Trudy Instituta Lesa. Akademii Nauk SSSR [*A publication*]

Tr Inst Lesa Drev Akad Nauk SSSR Sib Otd ... Trudy Instituta Lesa i Drevesiny. Akademiya Nauk SSSR. Sibirskoe Otdelenie [*A publication*]

Tr Inst Lesokhoz Probl Khim Drev Akad Nauk Latv SSR ... Trudy Instituta Lesokhozyaistvennykh Problem i Khimii Drevesiny. Akademiya Nauk Latviiskoi SSR [*Latvian SSR*] [*A publication*]

Tr Inst Malyarii Med Parazitol ... Trudy Instituta Malyarii i Meditsinskoi Parazitologii [*A publication*]

Tr Inst Mat Mekh Akad Nauk Az SSR ... Trudy Instituta Matematiki i Mekhaniki. Akademii Nauk Azerbajdzhanskoj SSR [*A publication*]

Tr Inst Merzlotoved Akad Nauk SSSR ... Trudy Instituta Merzlotovedeniya. Akademiya Nauk SSSR [*A publication*]

Tr Inst Metall Akad Nauk SSSR ... Trudy Instituta Metallurgii. Akademiya Nauk SSSR [*A publication*]

Tr Inst Metall Akad Nauk SSSR Ural Nauchn Tsentr ... Trudy Instituta Metallurgii. Akademiya Nauk SSSR Ural'skii Nauchnyi Tsentr [*A publication*]

Tr Inst Metall Im A A Baikova Akad Nauk SSSR ... Trudy Instituta Metallurgii Imeni A. A. Baikova. Akademiya Nauk SSSR [*USSR*] [*A publication*]

Tr Inst Metall Obogashch Akad Nauk Kaz SSR ... Trudy Instituta Metallurgii i Obogashcheniya. Akademiya Nauk Kazakhskoi SSR [*A publication*]

Tr Inst Metallofiz Metall Akad Nauk SSSR Ural Fil ... Trudy Instituta Metallofiziki Metallurgii. Akademiya Nauk SSSR Ural'skii Filial [*A publication*]

Tr Inst Metall (Sverdlovsk) ... Trudy Instituta Metallurgii (Sverdlovsk) [*A publication*]

Tr Inst Met (Leningrad) ... Trudy Instituta Metallov (Leningrad) [*A publication*]

Tr Inst Mikrobiol Akad Nauk Latv SSR ... Trudy Instituta Mikrobiologii. Akademii Nauk Latviiskoi SSR [*A publication*]

Tr Inst Mikrobiol Akad Nauk SSSR ... Trudy Instituta Mikrobiologii. Akademii Nauk SSSR [*A publication*]

Tr Inst Mikrobiol Virusol Akad Nauk Kaz SSR ... Trudy Instituta Mikrobiologii i Virusologii. Akademii Nauk Kazakhskoi SSR [*A publication*]

Tr Inst Morfol Zhivotn Akad Nauk SSSR ... Trudy Instituta Morfologii Zhivotnykh. Akademii Nauk SSSR [*A publication*]

Tr Inst Mosk Inst Tonkoi Khim Tekhnol ... Trudy Instituta. Moskovskii Institut Tonkoi Khimicheskoi Tekhnologii [*A publication*]

Tr Inst Nefti Akad Nauk Az SSR ... Trudy Instituta Nefti Akademiya Nauk Azerbaidzhanskoi SSR [*A publication*]

Tr Inst Nefti Akad Nauk Kaz SSR ... Trudy Instituta Nefti. Akademiya Nauk Kazakhoskoi SSR [*A publication*]

Tr Inst Norm Patol Fiziol Akad Med Nauk SSSR ... Trudy Instituta Normal'noi i Patologicheskoi Fiziologii. Akademii Meditsinskikh Nauk SSSR [*A publication*]

Tr Inst Obogashch Tverd Goryuch Iskop ... Trudy Instituta Obogashcheniya Tverdykh Goryuchikh Iskopaemykh [*USSR*] [*A publication*]

Tr Inst Okeanol Akad Nauk SSSR ... Trudy Instituta Okeanologii. Akademii Nauk SSSR [*A publication*]

Tr Inst Org Katal Elektrokhim Akad Nauk Kaz SSR ... Trudy Instituta Organicheskogo Kataliza i Elektrokhimii. Akademiya Nauk Kazakhskoi SSR [*Kazakh SSR*] [*A publication*]

Tr Inst Pastera ... Trudy Instituta Imeni Pastera [*A publication*]

Tr Inst Pochvoved Agrokhim Akad Nauk Az SSR ... Trudy Instituta Pochvovedeniya i Agrokhimii. Akademii Nauk Azerbaidzhanskoi SSR [*A publication*]

Tr Inst Pochvoved Akad Nauk Gruz SSR ... Trudy Instituta Pochvovedeniya. Akademii Nauk Gruzinskoi SSR [*A publication*]

Tr Inst Pochvoved Akad Nauk Kaz SSR ... Trudy Instituta Pochvovedeniya. Akademii Nauk Kazakhskoi SSR [*A publication*]

Tr Inst Polevod Akad Nauk Gruz SSR ... Trudy Instituta Polevodstva. Akademii Nauk Gruzinskoi SSR [*A publication*]

Tr Inst Polio Virusn Entsefalitov Akad Med Nauk SSSR ... Trudy Instituta Poliomielita i Virusnykh Entsefalitov Akademii Meditsinskikh Nauk SSSR [*A publication*]

Tr Inst Prikl Geofiz ... Trudy Instituta Prikladnoi Geofiziki [*USSR*] [*A publication*]

Tr Inst Proektn Nauchno-Issled Inst Ural Promstroiniiproekt ... Trudy Instituta. Proektnyi i Nauchno-Issledovatel'skii Institut Ural'skii Promstroiniiproekt [*A publication*]

Tr Inst Razrab Neft Gazov Mestorozhd Akad Nauk Az SSR ... Trudy Instituta Razrabotki Neftyanykh i Gazovykh Mestorozhdenii. Akademiya Nauk Azerbaidzhanskoi SSR [*A publication*]

Tr Inst Sadovod Vinograd Vinodel Gruz SSR ... Trudy Instituta Sadovodstva Vinogradarstva i Vinodeliya Gruzinskoi SSR [*A publication*]

Tr Inst Sadovod Vinograd Vinodel Tiflis ... Trudy Instituta Sadovodstva. Vinogradarstva i Vinodeliya. Tiflis [*A publication*]

Tr Inst Sel Semenovod Khlop (Tashkent) ... Trudy Instituta Selektsii i Semenovodstva Khlopchatnika (Tashkent) [*A publication*]

Tr Inst Sist Upr Akad Nauk Gruz SSR ... Trudy Institut Sistem Upravleniya. Akademiya Nauk Gruzinskoj SSR [*A publication*]

Tr Inst Stroit Dela Akad Nauk Gruz SSR ... Trudy Instituta Stroitel'nogo Dela Akademiya Nauk Gruzinskoi SSR [*A publication*]

Tr Inst Teor Astron ... Trudy Instituta Teoreticeskoi Astronomii [*USSR*] [*A publication*]

Tr Inst Teor Geofiz Akad Nauk SSSR ... Trudy Instituta Teoreticheskoi Geofiziki. Akademiya Nauk SSSR [*A publication*]

Tr Inst Torfa Akad Nauk B SSR ... Trudy Instituta Torfa. Akademiya Nauk Belorusskoi SSR [*A publication*]

Tr Inst Vinograd Vinodel Akad Nauk Arm SSR ... Trudy Instituta Vinogradarstva i Vinodeliya. Akademii Nauk Armyanskoi SSR [*A publication*]

Tr Inst Vinograd Vinodel Akad Nauk Gruz SSR ... Trudy Instituta Vinogradarstva i Vinodeliya. Akademii Nauk Gruzinskoi SSR [*A publication*]

Tr Inst Vses Nauchno-Issled Inst Tsellyul Bum Prom-sti ... Trudy Instituta. Vsesoyuznyi Nauchno-Issledovatel'skii Institut Tsellyulozno-Bumazhnoi Promyshlennosti [*USSR*] [*A publication*]

Tr Inst Vulkanol Akad Nauk SSSR Sib Otd ... Trudy Instituta Vulkanologii. Akademiya Nauk SSSR. Sibirskoe Otdelenie [*A publication*]

Tr Inst Vyssh Nervn Deya Akad Nauk SSSR Fiziol ... Trudy Instituta Vysshei Nervnoi Deyatel'nosti Akademii Nauk SSSR. Seriya Fiziologicheskaya [*A publication*]

Tr Inst Vyssh Nervn Deyat Akad Nauk SSSR Ser Fiziol ... Trudy Instituta Vysshei Nervnoi Deyatel'nosti Akademii Nauk SSSR. Seriya Fiziologicheskaya [*A publication*]

Tr Inst Vyssh Nervn Deyat Ser Fiziol ... Trudy Instituta Vysshei Nervnoi Deyatel'nosti. Seriya Fiziologicheskaya [*A publication*]

Tr Inst Vyssh Nervn Deyat Ser Patofiziol ... Trudy Instituta Vysshei Nervnoi Deyatel'nosti. Seriya Patofiziologicheskaya [*A publication*]

Tr Inst Yad Fiz Akad Nauk Kaz SSR ... Trudy Instituta Yadernoi Fiziki. Akademii Nauk Kazakhskoi SSR [*A publication*]

Tr Inst Zasch Rast (Tiflis) ... Trudy Instituta Zashchity Rastenii (Tiflis) [*Georgian SSR*] [*A publication*]

Tr Inst Zashch Rast Akad Nauk Gruz SSR ... Trudy Instituta Zashchity Rastenii Akademii Nauk Gruzinskoi SSR [*A publication*]

Tr Inst Zashch Rast (Tiflis) ... Trudy Instituta Zashchity Rastenii (Tiflis) [*A publication*]

Tr Inst Zemled Akad Nauk Azerb SSR ... Trudy Instituta Zemledeliya. Akademii Nauk Azerbaidzhanskoi SSR [*A publication*]

Tr Inst Zemled Kaz Fil Akad Nauk SSSR ... Trudy Instituta Zemledeliya Kazakhskogo Filiala. Akademii Nauk SSSR [*A publication*]

Tr Inst Zemled (Leningrad) Razdel 3 ... Trudy Instituta Zemledeliya (Leningrad). Razdel 3. Pochvovedenie [*A publication*]

Tr Inst Zhivotnovod Akad Nauk Turkm SSR ... Trudy Instituta Zhivotnovodstva. Akademii Nauk Turkmenskoi SSR [*A publication*]

Tr Inst Zhivotnovod Dagest Fili Akad Nauk SSSR ... Trudy Instituta Zhivotnovodstva Dagestanskogo Filiala Akademii Nauk SSSR [*A publication*]

Tr Inst Zhivotnovod Minist Skh Uzb SSR ... Trudy Instituta Zhivotnovodstva Ministerstvo Sel'skokhozyaistva Uzbekistanskoi SSR [*A publication*]

Tr Inst Zool Akad Nauk Az SSR ... Trudy Instituta Zoologii. Akademii Nauk Azerbaidzhanskoi SSR [*A publication*]

Tr Inst Zool Akad Nauk Gruz SSR ... Trudy Instituta Zoologii. Akademii Nauk Gruzinskoi SSR [*A publication*]

Tr Inst Zool Akad Nauk Kazakh SSR ... Trudy Instituta Zoologii. Akademiya Nauk Kazakhskoi SSR [*A publication*]

Tr Inst Zool Akad Nauk Kaz SSR ... Trudy Instituta Zoologii. Akademii Nauk Kazakhskoi SSR [*A publication*]

Tr Inst Zool Akad Nauk Ukr SSR ... Trudy Instituta Zoologii. Akademii Nauk Ukrainskoi SSR [*A publication*]

Tr Inst Zool Biol (Kiev) ... Trudy Instytutu Zoolohiyi ta Biolohiyi (Kiev) [*A publication*]

Tr Inst Zool Parazitol Akad Nauk Uzb SSR ... Trudy Instituta Zoologii i Parazitologii. Akademii Nauk Uzbekskoi SSR [*A publication*]

Tr Inst Zool Parazitol Akad Tadzh SSR ... Trudy Instituta Zoologii i Parazitologii. Akademiya Nauk Tadzhikskoi SSR [*A publication*]

Tr Inst Zool Parazitol Kirg Fil Akad Nauk SSR ... Trudy Instituta Zoologii i Parazitologii Kirgizskogo Filiala. Akademii Nauk SSR [*A publication*]

Trin Tob For ... Trinidad and Tobago Forester [*A publication*]

Trint T .... Trinity Term [*England*]   (DLA)

TRIOS .... Thermionic Reactor for Installed Oceanic Service   (KSC)

Trip .... All India Reporter, Tripura   (DLA)

TRIP .... [*The*] Road Information Program [*Washington, DC*]   (EA)

TRIP .... Tartar Reliability Improvement Plan [*Military*]

TRIP .... Technical Reports Indexing Project   (KSC)

TRIP .... Test Requirement Implementation Plan   (CAAL)

TRIP .... Thunderstorm Research International Project [*Meteorology*]

TRIP .... Transformation and Identification Program [*Commercial & Industrial Development Bureau*] [*Software package*]

TRIP .... Transformation-Induced Plasticity [*Steel*]

TRIP .... Triplicate   (AABC)

Trip .... Tripolitania [*Libya*]   (BJA)

TRipLH .... Lauderdale County Hospital, Ripley, TN [*Library symbol*] [*Library of Congress*]   (LCLS)

TRIPLTEE ... True Temperature Tunnel [*Acronym pronounced, "Triple T"*]

TRIPOD ...... Transit Injector Polaris Derived   (AAG)

TRIPOLD .... Transit Injector Polaris Derived

Tripp .... Tripp's Reports [*5, 6 Dakota*]   (DLA)

TRIPS .... Transformation-Induced Plasticity (Steel)

TRIPS .... Transportation Planning Suite [*MVA Systematica*] [*Software package*]

TRIPS .... Triplets [*Slang*]   (DSUE)

TriQ .... Tri-Quarterly [*A publication*]

Tri-Quar ..... Tri-Quarterly [*A publication*]

Tr Irkutsk Nauchno Issled Inst Epidemiol Mikrobiol ... Trudy Irkutsk Nauchno-Issledovatel'skogo Instituta Epidemiologii i Mikrobiologii [*A publication*]

Tr Irkutsk Politekh Inst ... Trudy Irkutskogo Politekhnicheskogo Instituta [*USSR*] [*A publication*]

TRIS .... Transportation Research Information Services [*National Academy of Sciences*] [*Washington, DC*] [*Bibliographic database*]

Tris .... Tris(2,3-dibromopropyl)phosphate [*Also, TDBP, TDBPP, Tris-BP*] [*Flame retardant, mutagen*]

TRIS .... Tris(hydroxymethyl)aminomethane [*Also, THAM*] [*Biochemical analysis*]

Tris .... Trito-Isaiah   (BJA)

TRISAFE .... Triple Redundancy Incorporating Self-Adaptive Failure Exclusion   (MCD)

TRISAT ...... Target Recognition through Integral Spectrum Analysis Techniques   (MCD)

Tris-BP .... Tris(2,3-dibromopropyl)phosphate [*Also, TDBP, TDBPP, Tris*] [*Flame retardant, mutagen*]

TRISECT .... Total Reconnaissance Intelligence System Evaluation and Comparison Technique   (MCD)

TRISNET .... Transportation Research Information Services Network [*Department of Transportation*] [*Library network*]

Tris Pr Pr ... Tristram's Probate Practice [*25th ed.*] [*1978*]   (DLA)

Trist .... Supplement to 4 Swabey and Tristram's Probate and Divorce Reports [*England*]   (DLA)

TRIST .... Traveling Image Storage Tube   (MCD)

Trist .... Tristram's Consistory Judgments [*England*]   (DLA)

Tri State Med J (Greensburo NC) ... Tri-State Medical Journal (Greensburo, North Carolina) [*A publication*]

Tri State Med J (Shreveport LA) ... Tri-State Medical Journal (Shreveport, Louisiana) [*A publication*]

Tristram ..... Tristram's Consistory Judgments [*1872-90*]   (DLA)

Tristram ..... Tristram's Probate Practice [*25th ed.*] [*1978*]   (DLA)

Tristram ..... Tristram's Supplement to 4 Swabey and Tristram   (DLA)

TRISYLL ..... Trisyllable   (ROG)

TRIT .... Tritura [*Triturate*] [*Pharmacy*]

TRITAC ...... DIFAR Triangular Tactic   (NVT)

TRITAC ...... Joint Tactical Communications Program [*DoD*]

TRITC .... Tetramethyl Rhodamine Isothiocyanate [*Organic chemistry*]

TRIUMF ...... Tri-University-Meson Facility [*Nuclear research facility at the University of British Columbia*]

TRIUN .... Department of Trusteeship and Information from Non-Self-Governing Territories of the United Nations

Tr Ivanov Med Inst ... Trudy Ivanovskogo Meditsinskogo Instituta [*A publication*]

TRIX .... Total Rate Imaging with X-Rays

Tr Izhevsk Med Inst ... Trudy Izhevskogo Meditsinskogo Instituta [*A publication*]

TRJ .... Tarija [*Bolivia*] [*Seismograph station code, US Geological Survey*]   (SEIS)

TRJ .... Thermocouple Reference Junction

TRJ .... United States Army TRADOC, Fort Jackson, Fort Jackson, SC [*OCLC symbol*]   (OCLC)

Tr Japan Path Soc ... Transactions. Japanese Pathological Society [*A publication*]

TRJaVUZ .... Trudy Kafedry Russkogo Jazyka Vuzov Vostocnoj Sibiri i Dal'nego Vostoka [*A publication*]

Tr Judge J ... Trial Judges' Journal   (DLA)

TRJWD .... Transactions. JWRI [*Japanese Welding Research Institute*] [*A publication*]

TRK .... Roche Products Ltd. [*Great Britain*] [*Research code symbol*]

TRK .... Tank Range-Finder Kit

TRK .... Tarakan [*Indonesia*] [*Airport symbol*]   (OAG)

TRK .... Track   (AAG)

TRK .... Truck   (AAG)

TRK .... Truckee, CA [*Location identifier*] [*FAA*]   (FAAL)

TRK .... Trunk   (AAG)

TRK .... United States Army TRADOC, Fort Knox, Library Service Center, RSL Section, Fort Knox, KY [*OCLC symbol*]   (OCLC)

TRKA .... Trak Auto Corp. [*NASDAQ symbol*]   (NQ)

Tr Kafedry Avtomob Trakt Vses Zaochn Mashinostroit Inst ... Trudy Kafedry Avtomobili i Traktory. Vsesoyuznyi Zaochnyi Mashinostroitel'nyi Institut [*A publication*]

Tr Kafedry Gosp Khir Lech Fak Sarat Med Inst ... Trudy Kafedry Gospital'noi Khirugii i Lechebnogo Fakul'teta Saratovskogo Meditsinskogo Instituta [*A publication*]

Tr Kafedry Kozhnykh Vener Bolezn Tashk ... Trudy Kafedry Kozhnykh i Venericheskikh Boleznei Tashkentskii Meditsinskii Institut [*A publication*]

Tr Kafedry Kozhnykh Vener Bolezn Tashk Med Inst ... Trudy Kafedry Kozhnykh i Venericheskikh Boleznei Tashkentskii Meditsinskii Institut [*A publication*]

Tr Kafedry Norm Anat Sarat Gos Med Inst ... Trudy Kafedry Normal'noi Anatomii Saratovskogo Gosudarstvennogo Meditsinskogo Instituta [*A publication*]

Tr Kafedry Oper Khir Topogr Anat Tbilis Gos Med Inst ... Trudy Kafedry Operativnoi Khirurgii i Topograficheskoi Anatomii Tbilisskogo Gosudarstvennogo Meditsinskogo Instituta [*A publication*]

Tr Kalinin Gos Med Inst ... Trudy Kalininskogo Gosudarstvennogo Meditsinskogo Instituta [*A publication*]

Tr Kaliningr Nauchno Issled Vet Stn ... Trudy Kaliningradskoi Nauchno-Issledovatel'skoi Veterinarnoi Stantsii [*A publication*]

Tr Kaliningr Tekh Inst Rybn Promsti Khoz ... Trudy Kaliningradskogo Tekhnicheskogo Instituta Rybnoi Promyshlennosti i Khozyaistva [*A publication*]

Tr Kalinin Politekh Inst ... Trudy Kalininskii Politekhnicheskii Institut [*USSR*] [*A publication*]

Tr Kalinin Torf Inst ... Trudy Kalininskogo Torfyanogo Instituta [*A publication*]

Tr Kaluzhskoi Gos Obl Skh Opytn Stn ... Trudy Kaluzhskoi Gosudarstvennoi Oblastnoi Sel'skokhozyaistvennoi Opytnoi Stantsii [*A publication*]

Tr Kamenetsk Podolsk Skh Inst ... Trudy Kamenetsk-Podolskogo Sel'skokhozyaistvennogo Instituta [*A publication*]

Tr Kandalakshskogo Gos Zapov ... Trudy Kandalakshskogo Gosudarstvennogo Zapovednika [*A publication*]

Tr Kansas Acad Sc ... Transactions. Kansas Academy of Science [*A publication*]

Tr Karagandin Bot Sada ... Trudy Karagandinskogo Botanicheskogo Sada [*A publication*]

Tr Karel Fil Akad Nauk SSSR ... Trudy Karel'skogo Filiala. Akademii Nauk SSSR [*A publication*]

Tr Karel Otd Gos Nauchno Issled Inst Ozern Rechn Rybn Khoz ... Trudy Karel'skogo Otdeleniya Gosudarstvennogo Nauchno-Issledovatel'skogo Instituta Ozernogo i Rechnogo Rybnogo Khozyaistva [*A publication*]

Tr Kasp Nauchno Issled Inst Rybn Khoz ... Trudy Kaspiiskii Nauchno-Issledovatel'skii Institut Rybnogo Khozyaistva [*A publication*]

Tr Kaunas Gos Med Inst ... Trudy Kaunasskogo Gosudarstvennogo Meditsinskogo Instituta [*A publication*]

Tr Kavk Inst Miner Syrya ... Trudy Kavkazskogo Instituta Mineral'nogo Syr'ya [*A publication*]

Tr Kazan Aviats Inst ... Trudy KAI. Kazanskij Ordena Trudovogo Krasnogo Znameni Aviatsionnyj Institut Imeni A. N. Tupoleva [*A publication*]

Tr Kazan Aviats Inst Ser Khim ... Trudy Kazanskogo Aviatsionogo Instituta. Seriya Khimicheskaya [*A publication*]

Tr Kazan Fil Akad Nauk SSSR Ser Geol Nauk ... Trudy Kazanskogo Filiala Akademii Nauk SSSR. Seriya Geologicheskikh Nauk [*A publication*]

Tr Kazan Fil Akad Nauk SSSR Ser Khim Nauk ... Trudy Kazanskogo Filiala Akademii Nauk SSSR. Seriya Khimicheskikh Nauk [*A publication*]

Tr Kazan Gor Astron Obs ... Trudy Kazanskoi Gorodskoi Astronomicheskoi Observatorii [*A publication*]

Tr Kazan Inst Usoversh Vrachei Im V I Lenina ... Trudy Kazanskogo Instituta Usovershenstvovaniya Vrachei Imeni V. I. Lenina [*A publication*]

Tr Kazan Med Inst ... Trudy Kazanskogo Meditsinskogo Instituta [*A publication*]

Tr Kazan Nauchno-Inst Onkol Radiol ... Trudy Kazanskogo Nauchno-Issledovatel'skogo Instituta Onkologii i Radiologii [*A publication*]

Tr Kazan Nauchno-Issled Inst Onkol Radiol ... Trudy Kazanskogo Nauchno-Issledovatel'skogo Instituta Onkologii i Radiologii [*A publication*]

Tr Kazan Nauchno-Issled Inst Travmatol Ortop ... Trudy Kazanskogo Nauchno-Issledovatel'skogo Instituta Travmatologii i Ortopedii [*A publication*]

Tr Kazan Nauchno Issled Vet Inst ... Trudy Kazanskogo Nauchno-Issledovatel'skogo Veterinarnogo Instituta [*A publication*]

Tr Kazan S-kh Inst ... Trudy Kazanskogo Sel'skokhozyaistvennogo Instituta [*A publication*]

Tr Kaz Fil Akad Stroit Arkhit SSSR ... Trudy Kazakhskogo Filiala Akademiya Stroitel'stva i Arkhitektury SSSR [*A publication*]

Tr Kaz Gos Pedagog Inst ... Trudy Kazanskii Gosudarstvennyi Pedagogicheskii Institut [*A publication*]

Tr Kaz Gos Skh Inst ... Trudy Kazakhskogo Gosudarstvennogo Sel'skokhozyaistvennogo Instituta [*A publication*]

Tr Kaz Nauchno-Issled Gidrometeorol Inst ... Trudy Kazakhskogo Nauchno-Issledovatel'skogo Gidrometeorologicheskogo Instituta [*A publication*]

Tr Kaz Nauchno-Issled Inst Lesn Khoz ... Trudy Kazakhskogo Nauchno-Issledovatel'skogo Instituta Lesnogo Khozyaistva [*A publication*]

Tr Kaz Nauchno-Issled Inst Lesn Khoz Agrolesomelior ... Trudy Kazakhskogo Nauchno-Issledovatel'skogo Instituta Lesnogo Khozyaistva i Agrolesomelioratsii [*A publication*]

Tr Kaz Nauchno Issled Inst Miner Syrya ... Trudy Kazakhskogo Nauchno-Issledovatel'skogo Instituta Mineral'nogo Syr'ya [*A publication*]

Tr Kaz Nauchno-Issled Inst Onkol Radiol ... Trudy Kazakhskogo Nauchno-Issledovatel'skogo Instituta Onkologii i Radiologii [*A publication*]

Tr Kaz Nauchno-Issled Inst Tuberk ... Trudy Kazakhskogo Nauchno-Issledovatel'skogo Instituta Tuberkuleza [*A publication*]

Tr Kaz Nauchno Issled Inst Vodn Khoz ... Trudy Kazakhskogo Nauchno-Issledovatel'skogo Instituta Vodnogo Khozyaistva [*A publication*]

Tr Kaz Nauchno Issled Inst Zashch Rast ... Trudy Kazakhskogo Nauchno-Issledovatel'skogo Instituta Zashchity Rastenii [*A publication*]

Tr Kaz Nauchno-Issled Vet Inst ... Trudy Kazakhskogo Nauchno-Issledovatel'skogo Veterinarnogo Instituta [*A publication*]

Tr Kaz Opytn Stn Pchelovod ... Trudy Kazakhskoi Opytnoi Stantsii Pchelovodstva [*A publication*]

Tr Kaz Politekh Inst ... Trudy Kazakhskogo Politekhnicheskogo Instituta [*Kazakh SSR*] [*A publication*]

Tr Kaz S-kh Inst ... Trudy Kazakhskogo Sel'skokhozyaistvennogo Instituta [*A publication*]

Tr Kaz S-kh Inst Ser Agron ... Trudy Kazakhskogo Sel'skokhozyaistvennogo Instituta. Seriya Agronomii [*A publication*]

TRKD .... Tracked

TRKDR .... Truck-Drawn

Tr Kemer Obl Gos S-kh Opytn Stn ... Trudy Kemerovskoi Oblastnoi Gosudarstvennoi Sel'skokhozyaistvennoi Opytnoi Stantsii [*A publication*]

TRKG .... Tracking   (AAG)

TrKH .... Die Transkriptionen des Hieronymus in Seinem Kommentarwerken [*A publication*]   (BJA)

Tr Khabar Inst Inzh Zheleznodorozhn Transp ... Trudy Khabarovskogo Instituta Inzhenerov Zheleznodorozhnogo Transporta [*A publication*]

Tr Khabar Med Inst ... Trudy Khabarovskogo Meditsinskogo Instituta [*A publication*]

Tr Khabar Politekh Inst ... Trudy Khabarobskogo Politekhnicheskogo Instituta [*A publication*]

Tr Khark Avtomob Dorozhnogo Instituta ... Trudy Khar'kovskogo Avtomobil'no-Dorozhnogo Instituta [*A publication*]

Tr Khark Gos Farm Inst ... Trudy Khar'kovskogo Gosudarstvennogo Farmatsevticheskogo Instituta [*A publication*]

Tr Khar'k Gos Med Inst ... Trudy Khar'kovskii Gosudarstvennyi Meditsinskii Institut [*A publication*]

Tr Khark Inst Gorn Mashinostr Avtom Vychisl Tekh ... Trudy Khar'kovskogo Instituta Gornogo Mashinostroeniya. Avtomatiki i Vychislitel'noi Tekhniki [*A publication*]

Tr Khark Inst Inzh Zheleznodorozhn Transp ... Trudy Khar'kovskogo Instituta Inzhenerov Zheleznodorozhnogo Transporta [*A publication*]

Tr Khark Inzh Ekon Inst ... Trudy Khar'kovskogo Inzhenerno-Ekonomicheskogo Instituta [*A publication*]

Tr Khark Khim Tekhnol Inst ... Trudy Khar'kovskogo Khimiko-Tekhnologicheskogo Instituta [*A publication*]

Tr Khar'k Med Inst ... Trudy Khar'kovskogo Meditsinskogo Instituta [*A publication*]

Tr Khark Nauchno Issled Khim Farm Inst ... Trudy Khar'kovskogo Nauchno-Issledovatel'skogo Khimiko-Farmatsevticheskogo Instituta [*A publication*]

Tr Khar'kov Med Inst ... Trudy Khar'kovskogo Meditsinskogo Instituta [*A publication*]

Tr Khark Politekh Inst ... Trudy Khar'kovskogo Politekhnicheskogo Instituta [*A publication*]

Tr Khar'k S-kh Inst ... Trudy Khar'kovskogo Sel'skokhozyaistvennogo Instituta [*A publication*]

TRKHD .... Truck Head

Tr Khim Inst Im L Ya Karpova ... Trudy Khimicheskogo Instituta Imeni L. Ya. Karpova [*A publication*]

Tr Khim Khim Tekhnol ... Trudy po Khimii i Khimicheskoi Tekhnologii [*A publication*]

Tr Khim-Metall Inst Akad Nauk Kaz SSR ... Trudy Khimiko-Metallurgicheskogo Instituta. Akademiya Nauk Kazakhskoj SSR [*A publication*]

Tr Khim Metall Inst Akad Nauk SSSR Sib Otd ... Trudy Khimiko-Metallurgicheskogo Instituta. Akademiya Nauk SSSR. Sibirskoe Otdelenie [*A publication*]

Tr Khim Prir Soedin ... Trudy po Khimii Prirodnykh Soedinenii [*A publication*]

Tr Kiev Vet Inst ... Trudy Kievskogo Veterinarnogo Instituta [*A publication*]

Tr Kirg Gos Med Inst ... Trudy Kirgizskogo Gosudarstvennogo Meditsinskogo Instituta [*A publication*]

Tr Kirg Gos Univ Ser Fiz Nauk ... Trudy Kirgizskogo Gosudarstvennogo Universiteta. Seriya Fizicheskikh Nauk [*A publication*]

Tr Kirgiz Nauch Issled Inst Zemled ... Trudy Kirgizskogo Nauchno-Issledovatel'skogo Instituta Zemledeliya [*A publication*]

Tr Kirg Nauchno-Issled Inst Onkol Radiol ... Trudy Kirgizskogo Nauchno-Issledovatel'skoi Instituta Onkologii i Radiologii [*A publication*]

Tr Kirg Nauchno-Issled Inst Pochvoved ... Trudy Kirgizskogo Nauchno-Issledovatel'skogo Instituta Pochvovedeniya [*A publication*]

Tr Kirg Nauchno Issled Inst Zemled ... Trudy Kirgizskogo Nauchno-Issledovatel'skogo Instituta Zemledeliya [*A publication*]

Tr Kirg Nauchno-Issled Inst Zhivotnovod ... Trudy Kirgizskogo Nauchno-Issledovatel'skogo Instituta Zhivotnovodstva [*A publication*]

Tr Kirg Nauchno-Issled Inst Zhivotnovod Vet ... Trudy Kirgizskogo Nauchno-Issledovatel'skogo Instituta Zhivotnovodstva i Veterinarii [*A publication*]

Tr Kirg Opytno-Sel Stn Sakh Svekle ... Trudy Kirgizskoi Opytno-Selektsionnoi Stantsii po Sakharnoi Svekle [*A publication*]

Tr Kirg Opytn Stn Khlopkovod ... Trudy Kirgizskoi Opytnoi Stantsii Khlopkovodstva [*A publication*]

Tr Kirg S-kh Inst ... Trudy Kirgizskogo Sel'skokhozyaistvennogo Instituta [*A publication*]

Tr Kirg Skh Inst Ser Agron ... Trudy Kirgizskogo Sel'skokhozyaistvennogo Seriya Agronomii [*A publication*]

Tr Kirg Univ Ser Biol Nauk ... Trudy Kirgizskogo Universiteta Seriya Biologicheskikh Nauk [*A publication*]

Tr Kirov S-kh Inst ... Trudy Kirovskogo Sel'skokhozyaistvennogo Instituta [*A publication*]

Tr Kishinev Gos Med Inst ... Trudy Kishinevskogo Gosudarstvennogo Meditsinskogo Instituta [*A publication*]

Tr Kishinev Politekh Inst ... Trudy Kishinevskii Politekhnicheskii Institut [*A publication*]

Tr Kishinev S-kh Inst ... Trudy Kishinevskogo Sel'skokhozyaistvennogo Instituta [*A publication*]

Tr Kishinev S-kh Inst Im M V Frunze ... Trudy Kishinevskii Sel'skokhozyaistvennyi Institut Imeni M. V. Frunze [*USSR*] [*A publication*]

Tr Klin Nervn Bolezn Mosk Obl Nauchno-Issled Klin Inst ... Trudy Kliniki Nervnykh Boleznei Moskovskogo Oblastnogo Nauchno-Issledovatel'skogo Klinicheskogo Instituta [*A publication*]

Tr Klin Otd Nauchno Issled Inst Gig Tr Profzabol ... Trudy Klinicheskogo Otdeleniya Nauchno-Issledovatel'skogo Instituta Gigieny Truda i Profzabolevanii [*A publication*]

TRKMTD .... Truck-Mounted (AABC)

Tr Kolomenskogo Fil Vses Zaochn Politekh Inst ... Trudy Kolomenskogo Filiala Vsesoyuznogo Zaochnogo Politekhnicheskogo Instituta [*A publication*]

Tr Kom Anal Khim Akad Nauk SSSR ... Trudy Komissii po Analiticheskoi Khimii. Akademiya Nauk SSSR [*USSR*] [*A publication*]

Tr Kom Borbe s Korroz Met Akad Nauk SSSR ... Trudy Komissii po Bor'be s Korroziei Metallov. Akademiya Nauk SSSR [*A publication*]

Tr Komi Fil Akad Nauk SSSR ... Trudy Komi Filiala. Akademii Nauk SSSR [*A publication*]

Tr Kom Irrig Akad Nauk SSSR ... Trudy Komissii po Irrigatsii. Akademiya Nauk SSSR [*A publication*]

Tr Kom Okhr Prir Ural Fil Akad Nauk SSSR ... Trudy Komissii po Okhrane Prirody Ural'skogo Filiala. Akademii Nauk SSSR [*A publication*]

Tr Kom Pirom Vses Nauchno Issled Inst Metrol ... Trudy Komissii po Pirometrii. Vsesoyuznyi Nauchno-Issledovatel'skii Institut Metrologii [*A publication*]

Tr Kompleksn Eksped Dnepropetr Univ ... Trudy Kompleksnoi Ekspeditsii Dnepropetrovskogo Universiteta [*A publication*]

Tr Kom Spektros Akad Nauk SSSR ... Trudy Komissii po Spektroskopii. Akademiya Nauk SSSR [*USSR*] [*A publication*]

Tr Koord Soveshch Gidrotekh ... Trudy Koordinatsionnykh Soveshchanyi po Gidrotekhnike [*A publication*]

TRKR .... Tracker

Tr Krasnodar Fil Vses Neftegazov Nauchno Issled Inst ... Trudy Krasnodarskii Filial Vsesoyuznogo Neftegazovogo Nauchno-Issledovatel'nogo Instituta [*A publication*]

Tr Krasnodar Gos Pedagog Inst ... Trudy Krasnodarskogo Gosudarstvennogo Pedagogicheskogo Instituta [*A publication*]

Tr Krasnodar Inst Pishch Promsti ... Trudy Krasnodarskogo Instituta Pishchevoi Promyshlennosti [*A publication*]

Tr Krasnodar Nauchno-Issled Inst Pishch Promsti ... Trudy Krasnodarskogo Nauchno-Issledovatel'skogo Instituta Pischevoi Promyshlennosti [*A publication*]

Tr Krasnodar Nauchno-Issled Inst Selsk Khoz ... Trudy Krasnodarskogo Nauchno-Issledovatel'skogo Instituta Sel'skogog Khozyaistva [*A publication*]

Tr Krasnoyarsk Med Inst ... Trudy Krasnoyarskogo Meditsinskogo Instituta [*A publication*]

Tr Krasnoyarsk S-kh Inst ... Trudy Krasnoyarskogo Sel'skokhozyaistvennogo Instituta [*A publication*]

Tr Krym Gos Med Inst Im I V Stalina ... Trudy Krymskogo Gosudarstvennogo Meditsinskogo Instituta Imeni I. V. Stalina [*A publication*]

Tr Krym Gos Skh Opytn Stn ... Trudy Krymskoi Gosudarstvennoi Sel'skokhozyaistvennoi Opytnoi Stantsii [*A publication*]

Tr Krym Gosud Sel'skokhoz Opyt Sta ... Trudy Krymskoi Gosudarstvennoi Sel'skokhozyaistvennoi Opytnoi Stantsii [*A publication*]

Tr Krym Obl Gos Skh Opytn Stn ... Trudy Krymskoi Oblastnoi Gosudarstvennoi Sel'skokhozyaistvennoi Opytnoi Stantsii [*A publication*]

Tr Krym Skh Inst ... Trudy Krymskogo Sel'skokhozyaistvennogo Instituta [*A publication*]

Tr Krym S-kh Inst Im M I Kalinina ... Trudy Krymskogo Sel'skokhozyaistvennogo Instituta Imeni M. I. Kalinina [*A publication*]

TRKUA .... Technology Reports. Kansai University [*A publication*]

Tr Kuban Otd Vses Ova Genet Sel ... Trudy Kubanskoe Otdelenie Vsesoyuznogo Obshchestva Genetikovi Selektsionerov [*A publication*]

Tr Kuban S-kh Inst ... Trudy Kubanskogo Sel'skokhozyaistvennogo Instituta [*A publication*]

Tr Kuibyshev Aviats Inst ... Trudy Kuibyshevskii Aviatsionnyi Institut [*USSR*] [*A publication*]

Tr Kuibyshev Gos Nauchno-Issled Inst Neft Prom-sti ... Trudy Kuibyshevskii Gosudarstvennyi Nauchno-Issledovatel'skii Institut Neftyanoi Promyshlennosti [*USSR*] [*A publication*]

Tr Kuibyshev Inzh-Stroit Inst ... Trudy Kuibyshevskii Inzhenerno-Stroitel'nyi Institut [*A publication*]

Tr Kuibyshev Med Inst ... Trudy Kuibyshevskii Meditsinskii Instituta [*A publication*]

Tr Kuibyshev Nauchno-Issled Inst Neft Promsti ... Trudy Kuibyshevskii Nauchno-Issledovatel'skii Institut Neftyanoi Promyshlennosti [*A publication*]

Tr Kuibyshev S-kh Inst ... Trudy Kuibyshevskogo Sel'skokhozyaistvennogo Instituta [*A publication*]

Tr Kurgan Mashinostroit Inst ... Trudy Kurganskogo Mashinostroitel'nogo Instituta [*A publication*]

Tr Kurortol ... Trudy po Kurortologii [*A publication*]

Tr Kursk Med Inst ... Trudy Kurskogo Meditsinskogo Instituta [*A publication*]

Tr Kutais Skh Inst ... Trudy Kutaisskogo Sel'skokhozyaistvennogo Instituta [*A publication*]

TRKWHL .... Trick Wheel

TRL .... Tariff Reform League [*British*] (ROG)

TRL .... Terrell, TX [*Location identifier*] [*FAA*] (FAAL)

TRL .... Test Readiness List [*NASA*] (NASA)

TRL .... Thermodynamics Research Laboratory (MCD)

TRL .... Tool Room Lathe

TRL .... Trail (MCD)

TRL .... Training Research Laboratory [*Army Research Institute for the Behavioral and Social Sciences*] (RDA)

TRL .... Transistor Resistor Logic

trl .... Translator [*MARC relator code*] [*Library of Congress*]

TRL .... Transuranium Research Laboratory [*AEC*]

TRL .... Trial (ROG)

TRL .... Trillo [*Trill*] [*Music*] (ROG)

TRL .... Trunk Register Link [*Telecommunications*] (TEL)

TRL .... United States Department of Transportation, Library, Washington, DC [*OCLC symbol*] (OCLC)

TRLA .... Trans Louisiana Gas [*NASDAQ symbol*] (NQ)

Trla .... Triola [*Record label*] [*Finland*]

TRLA .... Truck Renting and Leasing Association (EA)

Tr Lab Biokhim Fiziol Zhivotn Inst Biol Akad Nauk Latv SSR ... Trudy Laboratorii Biokhimii i Fiziologii Zhivotnykh Instituta Biologii. Akademiya Nauk Latviiskoi SSR [*A publication*]

Tr Lab Eksp Biol Mosk Zooparka ... Trudy Laboratorii Eksperimental'noi Biologii Moskovskogo Zooparka [*A publication*]

Tr Lab Evol Ekol Fiziol Akad Nauk SSSR Inst Fiziol Rast ... Trudy Laboratorii Evolyutsionnoi i Ekologicheskoi Fiziologii. Akademiya Nauk SSSR. Institut Fiziologii Rastenii [*A publication*]

Tr Lab Fiziol Zhivotn Inst Biol Akad Nauk Lit SSR ... Trudy Laboratorii Fiziologii Zhivotnykh Instituta Biologii Akademii Nauk Litovskoi SSR [*A publication*]

Tr Lab Geol Dokembr Akad Nauk SSSR ... Trudy Laboratorii Geologii Dokembriya Akademii Nauk SSSR [*A publication*]

Tr Lab Geol Uglya Akad Nauk SSSR ... Trudy Laboratorii Geologii Uglya Akademiya Nauk SSSR [*A publication*]

Tr Lab Gidrogeol Probl Akad Nauk SSSR ... Trudy Laboratorii Gidrogeologicheskikh Problem. Akademia Nauk SSSR [*USSR*] [*A publication*]

Tr Lab Izuch Belka Akad Nauk SSSR ... Trudy Laboratorii po Izucheniyu Belka Akademiya Nauk SSSR [*A publication*]

Tr Latviiskogo Nauchno-Issled Inst Zhivotnovod Vet ... Trudy Latviiskogo Nauchno-Issledovatel'skogo Instituta Zhivotnovodstva i Veterinarii [*A publication*]

Tr Latv Inst Eksp Klin Med Akad Med Nauk SSSR ... Trudy Latviiskogo Instituta Eksperimental'noi i Klinicheskoi Meditsiny Akademii Meditsinskikh Nauk SSSR [*A publication*]

Tr Latv Nauchno Issled Inst Gidrotekh Melior ... Trudy Latviiskogo Nauchno-Issledovatel'skogo Instituta Gidrotekhniki i Melioratsii [*A publication*]

Tr Latv Sel'kh Akad ... Trudy Latviiskaia Sel'skokhoziaistvennaia Akademiia [*A publication*]

Tr Latv S-kh Akad ... Trudy Latviiskoi Sel'skokhozyaistvennoi Akademii [*A publication*]

Tr Law Guide ... Trial Lawyer's Guide [*A publication*]

Tr Law Q .... Trial Lawyer's Quarterly [*A publication*]

TRLB .... Temporarily Replaced by Lighted Buoy Showing Same Characteristic [*Maps and charts*]

Tr Legochn Patol Inst Eksp Klin Med Est SSR ... Trudy po Legochnoi Patologii Institut Eksperimental'noi i Klinicheskoi Meditsiny Estonskoi SSR [*A publication*]

Tr Leningrad Tekhnol Inst Tsellyul-Bumazh Prom ... Trudy Leningradskogo Tekhnologicheskogo Instituta Tsellyulozno-Bumazhnoi Promyshlennosti [*A publication*]

Tr Leningr Geol Upr ... Trudy Leningradskogo Geologicheskogo Upravleniya [*A publication*]

Tr Leningr Gidrometeorol Inst ... Trudy Leningradskii Gidrometeorologicheskii Institut [*A publication*]

Tr Leningr Gos Nauchno Issled Inst Travmatol Ortop ... Trudy Leningradskogo Gosudarstvennogo Nauchno-Issledovatel'skogo Instituta Travmatologii i Ortopedii [*A publication*]

Tr Leningr Ind Inst ... Trudy Leningradskii Industrial'nogo Instituta [*A publication*]

Tr Leningr Inst Epidemiol Mikrobiol ... Trudy Leningradskogo Instituta Epidemiologii i Mikrobiologii [*A publication*]

Tr Leningr Inst Inzh Kommunal'n Stroit ... Trudy Leningradskii Institut Inzhenerow Kommunal'nogo Stroitel'stva [*A publication*]

Tr Leningr Inst Kinoinzh ... Trudy Leningradskogo Instituta Kinoinzhenerov [*A publication*]

Tr Leningr Inst Tochn Mekh Opt ... Trudy Leningradskii Institut Tochnoi Mekhaniki i Optiki [*A publication*]

Tr Leningr Inst Usoversh Vrachei ... Trudy Leningradskogo Instituta Usovershenstvovaniya Vrachei [*A publication*]

Tr Leningr Inst Vodn Transp ... Trudy Leningradskogo Instituta Vodnogo Transporta [*A publication*]

Tr Leningr Inzh Ekon Inst ... Trudy Leningradskogo Inzhenerno-Ekonomicheskogo Instituta [*A publication*]

Tr Leningr Khim-Farm Inst ... Trudy Leningradskogo Khimiko-Farmatsevticheskogo Instituta [*A publication*]

Tr Leningr Khim Tekhnol Inst ... Trudy Leningradskogo Khimiko-Tekhnologicheskogo Instituta [*A publication*]

Tr Leningr Korablestroit Inst ... Trudy Leningradskogo Korablestroitel'nogo Instituta [*A publication*]

Tr Leningr Korablestroit'nogo Inst ... Trudy Leningradskogo Korablestroitel'nogo Instituta [*USSR*] [*A publication*]

Tr Leningr Lesotekh Akad ... Trudy Leningradskoi Lesotekhnicheskoi Akademii [*A publication*]

Tr Leningr Med Inst ... Trudy Leningradskogo Meditsinskogo Instituta [*A publication*]

Tr Leningr Met Zavod ... Trudy Leningradskii Metallicheskii Zavod [*A publication*]

Tr Leningr Nauchno-Issled Inst Antibiot ... Trudy Leningradskogo Nauchno-Issledovatel'skogo Instituta Antibiotiki [*A publication*]

Tr Leningr Nauchno-Issled Inst Epidemiol Mikrobiol ... Trudy Leningradskogo Nauchno-Issledovatel'skogo Instituta Epidemiologii i Mikrobiologii [*A publication*]

Tr Leningr Nauchno Issled Inst Neirokhir ... Trudy Leningradskogo Nauchno-Issledovatel'skogo Instituta Neirokhirurgii [*A publication*]

Tr Leningr Nauchno-Issled Konstr Inst Khim Mashinostr ... Trudy Leningradskii Nauchno-Issledovatel'skii i Konstruktorskii Institut Khimicheskogo Mashinostroeniya [*USSR*] [*A publication*]

Tr Leningr Nauchno Issled Psikhonevrol Inst ... Trudy Leningradskogo Nauchno-Issledovatel'skogo Psikhonevrologisheskogo Instituta [*A publication*]

Tr Leningr Nauchno Ova Patologoanat ... Trudy Leningradskogo Nauchnogo Obshchestva Patologoanatomov [*A publication*]

Tr Leningr O-va Estestvoispyt ... Trudy Leningradskogo Obshchestva Estestvoispytatelei [*A publication*]

Tr Leningr Pediatr Med Inst ... Trudy Leningradskogo Pediatricheskogo Meditsinskogo Instituta [*A publication*]

Tr Leningr Politekh Inst ... Trudy Leningradskogo Politekhnicheskogo Instituta Imeni M. I. Kalinina [*A publication*]

Tr Leningr Politekh Inst Im M I Kalinina ... Trudy Leningradskogo Politekhnicheskogo Instituta Imeni M. I. Kalinina [*USSR*] [*A publication*]

Tr Leningr Sanit-Gig Med Inst ... Trudy Leningradskogo Sanitarno-Gigienicheskogo Meditsinskogo Instituta [*A publication*]

Tr Leningr Tekhnol Inst Kholod Prom-St' ... Trudy Leningradskogo Tekhnologicheskogo Instituta Kholodil'noi Promyshlennosti [*A publication*]

Tr Leningr Tekhnol Inst Pishch Prom-sti ... Trudy Leningradskogo Tekhnologicheskogo Instituta Pishchevoi Promyshlennosti [*A publication*]

Tr Leningr Teknol Inst ... Trudy Leningradskogo Tekhnologicheskogo Instituta [*USSR*] [*A publication*]

TRLFSW ..... Tactical Range Landing Force Support Weapon

TRLGA .... Translog [*A publication*]

Tr Limnol Inst Sib Otd Akad Nauk SSSR ... Trudy Limnologicheskogo Instituta Siberskogo Otdeleniya. Akademii Nauk SSSR [*A publication*]

Tr Litov Nauchno Issled Geologorazves Inst ... Trudy Litovskogo Nauchno-Issledovatel'skogo Geologorazvedochnogo Instituta [*A publication*]

Tr Litov Nauchno Issled Inst Lesn Khoz ... Trudy Litovskogo Nauchno-Issledovatel'skogo Instituta Lesnogo Khozyaistva [*A publication*]

Tr Litov Nauchno Issled Inst Vet ... Trudy Litovskogo Nauchno-Issledovatel'skogo Instituta Veterinarii [*A publication*]

TRLP .... Transport Landplane [*Navy*]

TRLR .... Trailer

Tr LR .... Trinidad Law Reports (DLA)

TRLS .... Thousand Trails, Inc. [*NASDAQ symbol*] (NQ)

TRLU .... TISEO RADAR Logic Unit [*Air Force*] (MCD)

Tr Lugansk S-kh Inst ... Trudy Luganskogo Sel'skokhozyaistvennoi Instituta [*A publication*]

TRLY .... Trolley

TRM .... Task Response Module [*Office furniture*]

TRM .... Tay River Petroleum [*Vancouver Stock Exchange symbol*]

TRM .... Terminal Response Monitor

TRM .... Test Request Message [*Data processing*]

TRM .... Test Requirements Manual

TRM .... Test Responsibility Matrix (MCD)

TRM .... Theater Rates Model [*Military*]

TRM .... Thermal, CA [*Location identifier*] [*FAA*] (FAAL)

TRM .... Thermal Remanent Magnetization (IEEE)

TRM .... Thermal Resistance Measurement

TRM .... Thermoremanence

TRM .... Thermoremanent Magnetism [*or Magnetization*]

TRM .... Thickness Readout Module

TRM .... Time Ratio Modulation

TRM .... Time Release Mechanism [*Martin-Baker seat system*] [*Aviation*] (NG)

TRM .... Totally Reflective Mirror

Tr M .... Traditional Music [*A publication*]

TRM .... TRADOC Resources Management (MCD)

TRM .... TRADOC [*Training and Doctrine Command*] Review of Manpower

TRM .... Turner [*Maine*] [*Seismograph station code, US Geological Survey*] (SEIS)

TRM .... United States Army TRADOC, Fort Monroe Post Library and Headquarters Technical Library, Fort Monroe, VA [*OCLC symbol*] (OCLC)

Tr Magadan Zon Nauchno Issled Inst Selsk Khoz Sev Vostoka ... Trudy Magadanskogo Zonal'nogo Nauchno-Issledovatel'skogo Instituta Sel'skogo Khozyaistva Severo-Vostoka [*A publication*]

TRMAP .... Theater Rate Mapping Data File [*Military*]

Tr Mater Donetsk Nauchno Issled Inst Fiziol Tr ... Trudy i Materialy. Donetskii Nauchno-Issledovatel'skii Institut Fiziologii Truda [*A publication*]

Tr Mater Leningr Inst Organ Okhr Tr ... Trudy i Materialy. Leningradskii Institut Organizatsii i Okhrany Truda [*A publication*]

Tr Mat Inst Akad Nauk SSSR ... Trudy Matematicheskogo Instituta Akademiya Nauk SSSR [*A publication*]

TRMC .... Time-Resolved Microwave Conductivity [*Physical chemistry*]

TRMD .... Trimmed

TRME .... Theater Readiness Monitoring Equipment   (MCD)

TRMEA ...... Trattamenti dei Metalli [*A publication*]

Tr Med and Phys Soc Bombay ... Transactions. Medical and Physical Society of Bombay [*A publication*]

Tr Metrol Inst SSSR ... Trudy Metrologicheskih Institutov SSSR [*A publication*]

Tr Mezhdunar Simp Tsitoekol ... Trudy Mezhdunarodnogo Simpoziuma po Tsitoekologii [*A publication*]

TRMF .... Test Report Management Forms   (MCD)

TRMF .... Theater Readiness Monitoring Facility [*Missile testing*]

TRMF .... Theodore Roethke Memorial Foundation   (EA)

Tr MFTI Ser "Obshch Mol Fiz" ... Trudy Moskovskogo Fiziko-Tekhnicheskogo Instituta. Seriya "Obshchaya i Molekulyarnaya Fizika" [*A publication*]

TRMG .... Trimming

TRMI .... Tubular Rivet and Machine Institute [*Formerly, TSRC*] [*Tarrytown, NY*]   (EA)

Tr Mineral Inst Akad Nauk SSSR ... Trudy Mineralogicheskogo Instituta Akademiya Nauk SSSR [*A publication*]

Tr Mineral Muz Akad Nauk SSSR ... Trudy Mineralogicheskogo Muzeya. Akademiya Nauk SSSR [*USSR*] [*A publication*]

Tr Minniya Nauchnoizsled Proekto Konstr Inst ... Trudove na Minniya Nauchnoizsledovatelski i Proektno Konstruktorski Institut [*A publication*]

TRML .... Terminal   (AFM)

TRML .... Tropical Research Medical Laboratory [*Army*]

Tr Moldav Nauch Issled Inst Orosh Zemled Ovoshchev ... Trudy Moldavskogo Nauchno-Issledovatel'skogo Instituta Oroshaemogo Zemledeliya i Ovoshchevodstva [*A publication*]

Tr Mold Nauchno Issled Inst Gig Epidemiol ... Trudy Moldavskii Nauchno-Issledovatel'skii Institut Gigieny i Epidemiologii [*A publication*]

Tr Mold Nauchno Issled Inst Oroshaemogo Zemled Ovoshchevod ... Trudy Moldavskogo Nauchno-Issledovatel'skogo Instituta Oroshaemogo Zemledeliya i Ovoshchevodstva [*A publication*]

Tr Mold Nauchno-Issled Inst Orosh Zemled Ovoshchevod ... Trudy Moldavskogo Nauchno-Issledovatel'skogo Instituta Oroshaemogo Zemledeliya i Ovoshchevodstva [*A publication*]

Tr Mold Nauchno Issled Inst Pishch Promsti ... Trudy Moldavskogo Nauchno-Issledovatel'skogo Instituta Pishchevoi Promyshlennosti [*A publication*]

Tr Mold Nauchno Issled Inst Tuberk ... Trudy Moldavskogo Nauchno-Issledovatel'nogo Instituta Tuberkuleza [*A publication*]

Tr Mold Nauchno Issled Inst Zhivotnovod Vet ... Trudy Moldavskii Nauchno-Issledovatel'skii Institut Zhivotnovodstva i Veterinarii [*A publication*]

Tr Molotov Gos Med Inst ... Trudy Molotovskogo Gosudarstvennogo Meditsinskogo Instituta [*A publication*]

Tr Mord Gos Zapovednika Im PG Smirovicha ... Trudy Mordovskogo Gosudarstvennogo Zapovednika Imeni P. G. Smirovicha [*A publication*]

Tr Morsk Biol Stn Stalin ... Trudove na Morskata Biologichna Stantsiya v Stalin [*A publication*]

Tr Morsk Gidrofiz Inst Akad Nauk Ukr SSR ... Trudy Morskogo Gidrofizicheskogo Instituta. Akademiya Nauk Ukrainskoj SSR [*A publication*]

Tr Mosk Aviats Inst Im S Ordzhonikidze Sb Statei ... Trudy Moskovskij Aviatsionnyj Institut Imeni S. Ordzhonikidze Sbornik Statei [*USSR*] [*A publication*]

Tr Mosk Aviats Tekhnol Inst ... Trudy Moskovskij Aviatsionnyj Tekhnologicheskij Institut [*A publication*]

Tr Mosk Ehnerg Inst ... Trudy Moskovskogo Ordena Lenina Ehnergiticheskogo Instituta [*A publication*]

Tr Mosk Energ Inst ... Trudy Moskovskogo Energeticheskogo Instituta [*USSR*] [*A publication*]

Tr Mosk Energ Inst Fiz ... Trudy Moskovskogo Energeticheskogo Instituta Fizika [*USSR*] [*A publication*]

Tr Mosk Fiz Tekh Inst Ser "Obshch Mol Fiz" ... Trudy Moskovskogo Fiziko-Tekhnicheskogo Instituta. Seriya "Obshchaya i Molekulyarnaya Fizika" [*A publication*]

Tr Mosk Gor Nauchno Issled Inst Skoroi Pomoshchi ... Trudy Moskovskogo Gorodskogo Nauchno-Issledovatel'skogo Instituta Skoroi Promoshchi [*A publication*]

Tr Mosk Inst Elektron Mashinostr ... Trudy Moskovskii Institut Elektronnogo Mashinostroeniya [*USSR*] [*A publication*]

Tr Mosk Inst Inzh Gor Stroit ... Trudy Moskovskogo Instituta Inzhenerov Gorodskogo Stroitel'stva [*A publication*]

Tr Mosk Inst Inzh Zheleznodorozhn Transp ... Trudy Moskovskogo Instituta Inzhenerov Zheleznodorozhnogo Transporta [*A publication*]

Tr Mosk Inst Khim Mashinostr ... Trudy Moskovskogo Instituta Khimicheskogo Mashinostroeniya [*A publication*]

Tr Mosk Inst Nar Khoz ... Trudy Moskovskogo Instituta Narodnogo Khozyaistva [*A publication*]

Tr Mosk Inst Neftekhim Gazov Prom-sti Im I M Gubkina ... Trudy Moskovskii Institut Neftekhimicheskoi i Gazovoi Promyshlennosti Imeni I. M. Gubkina [*USSR*] [*A publication*]

Tr Mosk Inst Neftekhim Gaz Promsti ... Trudy Moskovskii Institut Neftekhimicheskoi i Gazovoi Promyshlennosti [*A publication*]

Tr Mosk Inst Radiotekh Elektron Avtom ... Trudy Moskovskogo Instituta Radiotekhniki, Elektroniki, i Avtomatiki [*A publication*]

Tr Mosk Inst Tonkoi Khim Tekhnol ... Trudy Moskovskogo Instituta Tonkoi Khimicheskoi Tekhnologii [*A publication*]

Tr Mosk Khim-Tekhnol Inst ... Trudy Moskovskogo Khimiko-Tekhnologicheskogo Instituta Imeni D. I. Mendeleeva [*A publication*]

Tr Mosk Mat O-va ... Trudy Moskovskogo Matematicheskogo Obshchestva [*A publication*]

Tr Mosk Med Stomatol Inst ... Trudy Moskovskogo Meditsinskogo Stomatologichesko Instituta [*A publication*]

Tr Mosk Nauchno-Issled Inst Epidemiol Mikrobiol ... Trudy Moskovskogo Nauchno-Issledovatel'skogo Instituta Epidemiologii i Mikrobiologii [*A publication*]

Tr Mosk Nauchno-Issled Inst Psikhiatr ... Trudy Moskovskogo Nauchno-Issledovatel'skogo Instituta Psikhiatrii [*A publication*]

Tr Mosk Nauchno-Issled Inst Ukha Gorla Nosa ... Trudy Moskovskogo Nauchno-Issledovatel'skogo Instituta Ukha Gorla i Nosa [*A publication*]

Tr Mosk Nauchno Issled Inst Virusn Prep ... Trudy Moskovskii Nauchno-Issledovatel'skii Institut Virusnykh Preparatov [*A publication*]

Tr Mosk Neft Inst ... Trudy Moskovskii Neftyanoi Institut [*A publication*]

Tr Mosk Obl Nauchno Issled Klin Inst Prakt Nevropatol ... Trudy Moskovskogo Oblastnogo Nauchno-Issledovatel'skogo Klinicheskogo Instituta Prakticheskoi Nevropatologii [*A publication*]

Tr Mosk O-va Ispyt Prir ... Trudy Moskovskogo Obshchestva Ispytatelei Prirody [*USSR*] [*A publication*]

Tr Mosk O-va Ispyt Prir Otd Biol ... Trudy Moskovskogo Obshchestva Ispytatelei Prirody. Otdel Biologicheskii [*USSR*] [*A publication*]

Tr Mosk Radiotekh Elektron Avtomat ... Trudy Moskovskogo Instituta Radiotekhniki, Elektroniki, i Avtomatiki [*USSR*] [*A publication*]

Tr Mosk Tekh Inst Rybn Prom-sti Khoz ... Trudy Moskovskogo Tekhnologicheskogo Instituta Rybnoi Promyshlennosti i Khozyaistva [*USSR*] [*A publication*]

Tr Mosk Tekhnol Inst Myasn Molochn Promsti ... Trudy. Moskovskii Tekhnologicheskii Institut Myasnoi i Molochnoi Promyshlennosti [*A publication*]

Tr Mosk Tekhnol Inst Myasn Molochn Prom-sti ... Trudy Moskovskogo Tekhnologicheskogo Instituta Myasnoi Molochnoi Promyshlennosti [*A publication*]

Tr Mosk Tekhnol Inst Pishch Promsti ... Trudy. Moskovskii Tekhnologicheskii Institut Pishchevoi Promyshlennosti [*A publication*]

Tr Mosk Torf Inst ... Trudy Moskovskogo Torfyanogo Instituta [*A publication*]

Tr Mosk Vet Akad ... Trudy Moskovskoi Veterinarnoi Akademii [*A publication*]

Tr Mosk Vyssh Tekh Uchil ... Trudy Moskovskogo Vysshego Tekhnicheskogo Uchilishcha [*USSR*] [*A publication*]

TRMR .... Trimmer [*Mining engineering*]

TRMS .... Technical Requirements Management System

TRMS .... Test Resource Management System [*TECOM*]   (RDA)

TRMT .... Terminate   (FAAC)

TRMT .... Treatment   (AFM)

Tr Murm Biol Stn ... Trudy Murmanskoi Biologicheskoi Stantsii [*A publication*]

Tr Murm Morsk Biol Stn ... Trudy Murmanskogo Morskogo Biologicheskogo Instituta [*A publication*]

TRMW .... Triangle Microwave [*NASDAQ symbol*]   (NQ)

TRN .... OCLC [*Online Computer Library Center*] Training Symbol, Columbus, OH [*OCLC symbol*]   (OCLC)

TRN .... Technical Research Note   (IEEE)

TRN .... Temporary Record Number

TRN .... Teriton Resources Ltd. [*Vancouver Stock Exchange symbol*]

TRN .... Trade Name   (MSA)

TRN .... Train   (FAAC)

TRN .... Transfer   (DEN)

TRN .... Transmit   (BUR)

TRN .... Trinidad [*Trinidad-Tobago*] [*Seismograph station code, US Geological Survey*]   (SEIS)

TRN .... Trinity Industries, Inc. [*NYSE symbol*]

TRN .... Turin [*Italy*] [*Airport symbol*]   (OAG)

tRNA .... Ribonucleic Acid, Transfer [*Replaces sRNA*] [*Biochemistry, genetics*]

TRNA .... Topolino Register of North America   (EA)

Tr Nakhich Kompleksn Zon Opytn Stn ... Trudy Nakhichevanskoi Kompleksnoi Zonal'noi Opytnoi Stantsii [*A publication*]

Tr Nauch Issled Inst Klopkovod (Tashkent) ... Trudy Nauchno-Issledovatel'skii Institut po Khlopkovodstvu (Tashkent) [*A publication*]

Tr Nauchn Korresp Inst Stroit Dela Akad Nauk Gruz SSR ... Trudy Nauchnykh Korrespondentov Instituta Stroitel'nogo Dela. Akademiya Nauk Gruzinskoi SSR [*A publication*]

Tr Nauchno-Issled Gidrometerol Inst (Alma-Ata) ... Trudy Nauchno-Issledovatel'skogo Gidrometeorologicheskogo Instituta (Alma-Ata) [*Kazakh SSR*] [*A publication*]

Tr Nauchno-Issled Inst Betona Zhelezobetona ... Trudy Nauchno-Issledovatel'skogo Instituta Betona i Zhelezobetona [*USSR*] [*A publication*]

Tr Nauchno-Issled Inst Biol Khar'k Gos Univ ... Trudy Nauchno-Issledovatel'skogo Instituta Biologii Khar'kovskogo Gosudarstvennogo Universiteta [*A publication*]

Tr Nauchno-Issled Inst Dobyche Pererab Slantsev ... Trudy Nauchno-Issledovatel'skogo Instituta po Dobyche i Pererabotke Slantsev [*USSR*] [*A publication*]

Tr Nauchno-Issled Inst Eksp Klin Ter Gruz SSR ... Trudy Nauchno-Issledovatel'skogo Instituta Eksperimental'noi i Klinicheskoi Terapii Gruzinskoi SSR [*A publication*]

Tr Nauchno-Issled Inst Epidemiol Mikrobiol ... Trudy Nauchno-Issledovatel'skogo Instituta Epidemiologii i Mikrobiologii [*A publication*]

Tr Nauchno Issled Inst Fiziol ... Trudy Nauchno-Issledovatel'skogo Instituta Fiziologii [*A publication*]

Tr Nauchno-Issled Inst Fiziol Patol Zhen ... Trudy Nauchno-Issledovatel'skogo Instituta Fiziologii i Patologii Zhenshchiny [*A publication*]

Tr Nauchno-Issled Inst Geol Arktiki ... Trudy Nauchno-Issledovatel'skogo Instituta Geologii Arktiki [*USSR*] [*A publication*]

Tr Nauchno-Issled Inst Geol Mineral ... Trudy Nauchno-Issledovatel'skogo Instituta Geologii i Mineralogii [*A publication*]

Tr Nauchno Issled Inst Gig Vodn Transp ... Trudy Nauchno-Issledovatel'skogo Instituta Gigieny Vodnoi Transportatsii [*A publication*]

Tr Nauchno Issled Inst Kabeln Prom ... Trudy Nauchno-Issledovatel'skogo Instituta Kabel'noi Promyshlennosti [*A publication*]

Tr Nauchno Issled Inst Kamnya Silik ... Trudy Nauchno-Issledovatel'skogo Instituta Kamnya i Silikatov [*A publication*]

Tr Nauchno-Issled Inst Kartofel'nogo Khoz ... Trudy Nauchno-Issledovatel'skogo Instituta Kartofel'nogo Khozyaistva [*A publication*]

Tr Nauchno Issled Inst Klin Eksp Khir ... Trudy Nauchno-Issledovatel'skogo Instituta Klinicheskoi i Eksperimental'noi Khirurgii [*A publication*]

Tr Nauchno-Issled Inst Kraev Patol (Alma-Ata) ... Trudy Nauchno-Issledovatel'skogo Instituta Kraevoi Patologii (Alma-Ata) [*A publication*]

Tr Nauchno-Issled Inst Med Parazitol Trop Med Gruz SSR ... Trudy Nauchno-Issledovatel'skogo Instituta Meditsinskoi Parazitologii i Tropicheskoi Meditsiny Gruzinskoi SSR [*A publication*]

Tr Nauchno Issled Inst Mestnoi Topl Promsti ... Trudy Nauchno-Issledovatel'skogo Instituta Mestnoi i Toplivnoi Promyshlennosti [*A publication*]

Tr Nauchno Issled Inst Minist Radiotekh Promsti SSSR ... Trudy Nauchno-Issledovatel'skogo Instituta. Ministerstvo Radiotekhnicheskoi Promyshlennosti SSSR [*A publication*]

Tr Nauchno Issled Inst Neftekhim Proizvod ... Trudy Nauchno-Issledovatel'skii Institut Neftekhimicheskikh Proizvodstv [*A publication*]

Tr Nauchno-Issled Inst Okhr Tr Prof Zabol ... Trudy Nauchno-Issledovatel'skogo Instituta Okhrany Truda i Professional'nykh Zabolevanii [*A publication*]

Tr Nauchno Issled Inst Onkol Gruz SSR ... Trudy Nauchno-Issledovatel'skogo Instituta Onkologii Gruzinskoi SSR [*A publication*]

Tr Nauchno Issled Inst Onkol (Tiflis) ... Trudy Nauchno-Issledovatel'skii Institut Onkologii (Tiflis) [*A publication*]

Tr Nauchno Issled Inst Osnovnoi Khim ... Trudy Nauchno-Issledovatel'skogo Instituta Osnovnoi Khimii [*A publication*]

Tr Nauchno Issled Inst Pishch Promsti ... Trudy Nauchno-Issledovatel'skogo Instituta Pishchevoi Promyshlennosti [*A publication*]

Tr Nauchno Issled Inst Pochvoved Agrokhim Melior Tiflis ... Trudy Nauchno-Issledovatel'skogo Instituta Pochvovedeniya. Agrokhimii i Melioratsii. Tiflis [*A publication*]

Tr Nauchno-Issled Inst Pochvoved Agrokhim Yerevan ... Trudy Nauchno-Issledovatel'skogo Instituta Pochvovedeniya i Agrokhimii. Yerevan [*A publication*]

Tr Nauchno-Issled Inst Profil Pnevmokoniozov ... Trudy Nauchno-Issledovatel'skogo Instituta Profilaktiki i Pnevmokoniozov [*A publication*]

Tr Nauchno-Issled Inst Rentgenol Radiol Onkol Az SSR ... Trudy Nauchno-Issledovatel'skogo Instituta Rentgenologii Radiologii i Onkologii Azerbaidzhanskoi SSR [*A publication*]

Tr Nauchno-Issled Inst Sel'sk Khoz Krainego Sev ... Trudy Nauchno Issledovatel'skogo Instituta Sel'skogo Khozyaistva Krainego Severa [*A publication*]

Tr Nauchno-Issled Inst Sin Spirtov Org Prod ... Trudy Nauchno-Issledovatel'skii Institut Sinteticheskikh Spirtov i Organicheskikh Produktov [*A publication*]

Tr Nauchno-Issled Inst Slantsev ... Trudy Nauchno-Issledovatel'skogo Instituta Slantsev [*USSR*] [*A publication*]

Tr Nauchno Issled Inst Teploenerg Priborostr ... Trudy Nauchno-Issledovatel'skii Institut Teploenergeticheskogo Priborostroeniya [*A publication*]

Tr Nauchno Issled Inst Transp Khraneniyu Nefti Nefteprod ... Trudy Nauchno-Issledovatel'skii Institut po Transportu i Khraneniyu Nefti i Nefteproduktov [*A publication*]

Tr Nauchno-Issled Inst Tuberk ... Trudy Nauchno-Issledovatel'skogo Instituta Tuberkuleza [*A publication*]

Tr Nauchno-Issled Inst Udobr Insektofungits ... Trudy Nauchno-Issledovatel'skii Institut po Udobreniyam i Insektofungitsidam [*USSR*] [*A publication*]

Tr Nauchno Issled Inst Virusol Mikrobiol Gig ... Trudy Nauchno-Issledovatel'skogo Instituta Virusologii Mikrobiologii Gigieny [*A publication*]

Tr Nauchno Issled Inst Zashch Rast Uzb SSR ... Trudy Nauchno-Issledovatel'skogo Instituta Zashchity Rastenii Uzbekskoi SSR [*A publication*]

Tr Nauchno Issled Inst Zhivotnovod (Tashkent) ... Trudy Nauchno-Issledovatel'skogo Instituta Zhivotnovodstva (Tashkent) [*A publication*]

Tr Nauchno Issled Khim Inst Mosk Univ ... Trudy Nauchno-Issledovatel'skogo Khimicheskogo Instituta. Moskovskii Universitet [*A publication*]

Tr Nauchno Issled Konstr Inst Mekh Rybn Prom-sti ... Trudy Nauchno-Issledovatel'skogo i Konstruktorskogo Instituta Mekhanizatsii Rybnoi Promyshlennosti [*A publication*]

Tr Nauchno Issled Lab Geol Zarub Stran ... Trudy Nauchno-Issledovatel'skaya Laboratoriya Geologii Zarubezhnykh Stran [*A publication*]

Tr Nauchno Issled Protivochumn Inst Kavk Zakavk ... Trudy Nauchno-Issledovatel'skogo Protivochumnogo Instituta Kavkaza i Zakavkaz'ya [*A publication*]

Tr Nauchno Issled Sel'sk Khoz Krainego Sev ... Trudy Nauchno-Issledovatel'skogo Instituta Sel'skogo Khozyaistva Krainego Severa [*A publication*]

Tr Nauchnoizsled Inst Epidemio Mikrobiol ... Trudove na Nauchnoizsledovatelskiya Instituta po Epidemiologiya i Mikrobiologiya [*A publication*]

Tr Nauchnoizsled Inst Okhr Tr Prof Zabol ... Trudove na Nauchnoizsledovatelskiya Instituta po Okhrana na Truda i Profesionalnite Zabolyavaniya [*A publication*]

Tr Nauchnoizsled Inst Stroit Mater (Sofia) ... Trudove na Nauchnoizsledovatelskiya Instituta po Stroitelni Materiali (Sofia) [*A publication*]

Tr Nauchnoizsled Inst Vodosnabdyavane Kanaliz Sanit Tekh ... Trudove na Nauchnoizsledovatelskiya Institut po Vodosnabdyavane. Kanalizatsiya i Sanitarna Tekhnika [*Bulgaria*] [*A publication*]

Tr Nauchnoizsled Inst Vodosnabyavane Kanaliz Sanit Tekh ... Trudove na Nauchnoizsledovatelskiya Institut po Vodosnabyavane Kanalizatsiya i Sanitarna Tekhnika [*A publication*]

Tr Nauchnoizsled Khim Farm Inst ... Trudove na Nauchnoizsledovatelskiya Khimiko-Farmatsevtichen Institut [*A publication*]

Tr Nauchnoizsled Proektokonstr Tekhnol Inst Tekst Promst ... Trudove na Nauchnoizsledovatelskiya. Proektokonstruktorski i Tekhnologicheski Institut po Tekstilna Promishlenost [*A publication*]

Tr Nauchno Khim Farm Inst ... Trudy Nauchnogo Khimiko Farmatsevtecheskogo Instituta [*A publication*]

Tr Nauchno Proizvod Konf Agron Buryat Zoovet Inst ... Trudy Nauchno-Proizvodstvennoi Konferentsii po Agronomii. Buryatskii Zooveterinarnyi Institut [*A publication*]

Tr Nauchno-Tekh Konf Leningr Elek-Tekh Inst Svyazi ... Trudy Nauchno-Tekhnicheskoi Konferentsii Leningradskogo Elektro-Tekhnicheskogo Instituta Svyazi [*USSR*] [*A publication*]

Tr Nauchno Tekh Ova Chern Metall ... Trudy Nauchno-Tekhnicheskogo Obshchestva Chernoi Metallurgii [*A publication*]

TRNBKL ..... Turnbuckle [*Aerospace*] (AAG)

TRNCAP ..... Training Capability [*Military*]

TRN CRD .... Turn Coordination (MSA)

TRND .... Turned (MSA)

TRNE .... Trainee (AABC)

TRNF .... Theologische Rundschau. Neue Folge [*A publication*]

TRNFR. .... Transfer (KSC)

TRNG .... Training

TRNGA .... Traffic Engineering [*United States*] [*A publication*]

TRNGL .... Triangle (MSA)

TRNGR .... Turning Gear

Tr NII Metrol Vyssh Uchebn Zaved ... Trudy NII [*Nauchno-Issledovatel'skogo Instituta*] Metrologii Vysshikh Uchebnykh Zavedeniy [*USSR*] [*A publication*]

Tr Nikitsk Bot Sada ... Trudy Nikitskogo Botanicheskogo Sada [*A publication*]

Tr Nikolaev Korablestroit Inst ... Trudy Nikolaevskogo Korablestroitel'nogo Instituta [*A publication*]

TRNJA .... Transportation Journal [*A publication*]

TRNO .... Terrano Corp. [*NASDAQ symbol*]   (NQ)
Tr Norilsk Vech Ind Inst ... Trudy Noril'skogo Vechernego Industrial'nogo Instituta [*A publication*]
Tr Nov Appar Metod ... Trudy po Novoi Apparature i Metodikam [*A publication*]
Tr Novocherkassk Politekh Inst ... Trudy Novocherkasskogo Politekhnicheskogo Instituta [*USSR*] [*A publication*]
Tr Novocherk Inzh Melior Inst ... Trudy Novocherkasskogo Inzhenerno-Meliorativnogo Instituta [*A publication*]
Tr Novocherk Politekh Inst ... Trudy Novocherkasskogo Politekhnicheskogo Instituta [*A publication*]
Tr Novocherk Vet Inst ... Trudy Novocherkasskogo Veterinarnogo Instituta [*A publication*]
Tr Novocherk Zootekh Vet Inst ... Trudy Novocherkasskogo Zootekhnichesko-Veterinarnogo Instituta [*A publication*]
Tr Novokuz Gos Inst Usoversh Vrachei ... Trudy Novokuznetskogo Gosudarstvennogo Instituta Usovershenstvovaniya Vrachei [*A publication*]
Tr Novokuz Gos Pedagog Inst ... Trudy Novokuznetskogo Gosudarstvennogo Pedagogicheskogo Instituta [*A publication*]
Tr Novosib Gos Med Inst ... Trudy Novosibirskogo Gosudarstvennogo Meditsinskogo Instituta [*A publication*]
Tr Novosib Inst Inzh Zheleznodorozhn Transp ... Trudy Novosibirskogo Instituta Inzhenerov Zheleznodorozhnogo Transporta [*A publication*]
T & RNP ...... Transportation and Recruiting Naval Personnel [*Budget appropriation title*]
TRNPS .... Transpose   (MSA)
TRNR .... Trainer   (AAG)
TRNS .... Transition   (AABC)
TRNS .... Transmation, Inc. [*NASDAQ symbol*]   (NQ)
TRNSMT .... Transmitter
TRNSN .... Transition   (MSA)
TRNSP .... Transport [*or Transportation*]   (AFM)
TRNSPN ..... Transportation   (KSC)
TRNSPR ..... Transporter   (KSC)
TRNT .... Transnet Corp. [*NASDAQ symbol*]   (NQ)
TRNTBL .... Turntable   (MSA)
TR (NY) ...... Caines' Term Reports [*New York*]   (DLA)
TRO .... Taree [*Australia*] [*Airport symbol*]   (OAG)
TRO .... Tarron Resources Ltd. [*Vancouver Stock Exchange symbol*]
TRO .... Tax Reduction Option
TRO .... Technical Records Office [*or Officer*] [*British*]
TRO .... Technical Reviewing Office   (AFM)
TRO .... Temporary Restraining Order
TRO .... Terminal Release Order [*Military*]   (AFIT)
TRO .... Test Requirements Outline
TRO .... Transportation Officer
TRO .... Trico Industries, Inc. [*NYSE symbol*]
Tro. .... Troades [*of Euripides*] [*Classical studies*]   (OCD)
Tro. .... Troilus and Cressida [*Shakespearean work*]
TRO .... Tromsoe [*Norway*] [*Geomagnetic observatory code*]
TRO .... Tromsoe [*Norway*] [*Seismograph station code, US Geological Survey*]   (SEIS)
TRO .... Tropical [*Broadcasting antenna*]
TRO .... Truck Route Order [*Army*]   (AABC)
TRO .... United States Army TRADOC, Fort Sill Post Library, Fort Sill, OK [*OCLC symbol*]   (OCLC)
TROA .... [*The*] Retired Officers Association
TROANO .... [*Don Juan*] De Tro y Ortolano [*Acronym identifies manuscript discovered in library of Don Juan De Tro y Ortolano in 1866*]
TROB .... Twenty-First Century Robotics [*NASDAQ symbol*]   (NQ)
TROC .... Trocadero [*London*]   (DSUE)
TROC .... Trochiscus [*Lozenges*] [*Pharmacy*]   (ROG)
TROCA ...... Tangible Reinforcement Operant Conditioning Audiometry
TROCH ...... Trochiscus [*Lozenge*] [*Pharmacy*]
Tr Odess Gidrometeorol Inst ... Trudy Odesskogo Gidrometeorologicheskogo Instituta [*A publication*]
Tr Odess Nauchno-Issled Inst Epidemiol Mikrobiol ... Trudy Odesskogo Nauchno-Issledovatel'skogo Instituta Epidemiologii i Mikrobiologii [*A publication*]
Tr Odess S-kh Inst ... Trudy Odesskogo Sel'skokhozyaistvennogo Instituta [*A publication*]
TRODI .... Touchdown Rate of Descent Indicator [*Aviation*]
TROF .... Trough [*Meteorology*]   (FAAC)
TROL .... Tapeless Rotorless On-Line Cryptographic Equipment   (NATG)
Trol .... Troland [*Unit of light intensity at the retina*]
TROLAMINE ... Triethanolamine [*Organic chemistry*] [*USAN*]
TROLL .... [*A*] programing language [*1966*]   (CSR)
TROM .... Trombone
T Rom .... Trubuna Romaniei [*A publication*]
TROMB ...... Tromba [*Trumpet*] [*Music*]   (ROG)
TROMB ...... Trombone
TROMEX .... Tropical Meteorology Experiment [*National Science Foundation*]
TROMP .... Trompette [*Trumpets*] [*Music*]

Tr Omsk Gos Nauchno-Issled Inst Epidemiol Mikrobiol Gig ... Trudy Omskogo Gosudarstvennogo Nauchno-Issledovatel'skogo Instituta Epidemiologii Mikrobiologii i Gigieny [*A publication*]
Tr Omsk Inst Molochn Khoz Omsk Zon Stn Molochn Khoz ... Trudy Omskogo Instituta Molochnogo Khozyaistva i Omskoi Zonal'noi Stantsii po Molochnomu Khozyaistvu [*A publication*]
Tr Omsk Med Inst Im M I Kalinina ... Trudy Omskogo Meditsinskogo Instituta Imeni M. I. Kalinina [*A publication*]
Tromse Mus Skr ... Tromsoe Museum. Skrifter [*A publication*]
TRON .... Trion, Inc. [*NASDAQ symbol*]   (NQ)
TROO .... Transponder On-Off
TROP .... Tropical
TROP .... Tropopause [*Meteorology*]   (FAAC)
Trop Abstr ... Tropical Abstracts [*A publication*]
TROPAG .... Tropical Agriculture [*Royal Tropical Institute*] [*Bibliographic database*] [*The Netherlands*]
Trop Agr .... Tropical Agriculture [*A publication*]
Trop Agr (Ceylon) ... Tropical Agriculturist (Ceylon) [*A publication*]
Trop Agric ... Tropical Agriculture [*A publication*]
Trop Agric (Colombo) ... Tropical Agriculturist (Colombo) [*A publication*]
Trop Agri (Ceylon) ... Tropical Agriculturist (Ceylon) [*A publication*]
Trop Agric Res Ser (Japan) ... Tropical Agriculture Research Series (Japan) [*A publication*]
Trop Agricst Mag Ceylon Agric Soc ... Tropical Agriculturist and Magazine. Ceylon Agricultural Society [*A publication*]
Trop Agron Tech Memo Aust CSIRO Div Trop Crops Pastures ... Australia. Commonwealth Scientific and Industrial Research Organisation. Division of Tropical Crops and Pastures. Tropical Agronomy. Technical Memorandum [*A publication*]
Trop Anim Health Prod ... Tropical Animal Health and Production [*A publication*]
Trop Anim Prod ... Tropical Animal Production [*Dominican Republic*] [*A publication*]
TROPB .... Tropenlandwirt [*A publication*]
Trop Build Res Notes Div Build Res CSIRO ... Tropical Building Research Notes. Division of Building Research. Commonwealth Scientific and Industrial Research Organisation [*A publication*]
Trop Dis Bull ... Tropical Diseases Bulletin [*A publication*]
Trop Doct ... Tropical Doctor [*A publication*]
Trop Ecol ... Tropical Ecology [*A publication*]
Tropenlandwirt (Germany FR) ... Tropenlandwirtschaft (Germany, Federal Republic) [*A publication*]
Tropenmed P ... Tropenmedizin und Parasitologie [*A publication*]
Tropenmed Parasitol ... Tropenmedizin und Parasitologie [*A publication*]
TROPEX ..... Tropical Experiment [*Proposed by BOMEX*]
Trop For Notes ... Tropical Forest Notes [*A publication*]
Trop Geogr Med ... Tropical and Geographical Medicine [*A publication*]
Trop Geo Me ... Tropical and Geographical Medicine [*A publication*]
Trop Grassl ... Tropical Grasslands [*A publication*]
Trop Grasslands ... Tropical Grasslands [*A publication*]
Trop Grasslds ... Tropical Grasslands [*A publication*]
Tropical Ag ... Tropical Agriculturist [*A publication*]
TROPICS .... Tour Operators Integrated Computer System [*Airline ticket system*]
Trop Man ... Tropical Man [*Leiden*] [*A publication*]
Trop Med ... Tropical Medicine [*A publication*]
Trop Med Hyg News ... Tropical Medicine and Hygiene News [*A publication*]
TROPO .... Tropospheric
Trop Pest Bull ... Tropical Pest Bulletin [*A publication*]
Trop Pestic Res Inst Annu Rep ... Tropical Pesticides Research Institute. Annual Report [*A publication*]
Trop Pestic Res Inst Misc Rep ... Tropical Pesticides Research Institute. Miscellaneous Report [*A publication*]
Trop Prod Inst Crop Prod Dig ... Tropical Products Institute. Crop and Product Digest [*A publication*]
Trop Prod Inst Rep ... Tropical Products Institute. Report [*A publication*]
TROPRAN ... Tropical Regional Analysis [*National Weather Service*]
Trop Sci ..... Tropical Science [*A publication*]
Trop Sci Cent Occas Pap (San Jose Costa Rica) ... Tropical Science Center. Occasional Paper (San Jose, Costa Rica) [*A publication*]
Trop Stored Prod Inf ... Tropical Stored Products Information [*A publication*]
Trop Stored Prod Inform ... Tropical Stored Products Information [*A publication*]
Trop Subtrop Pflwelt ... Tropische und Subtropische Pflanzenwelt [*A publication*]
Trop Vet Bull ... Tropical Veterinary Bulletin [*A publication*]
Trop Woods ... Tropical Woods [*A publication*]
Trop Woods Yale Univ Sch For ... Tropical Woods. Yale University School of Forestry [*A publication*]
Tr Opytn Stn Plodovod Akad Nauk Gruz SSR ... Trudy Opytnoi Stantsii Plodovodstva. Akademii Nauk Gruzinskoi SSR [*A publication*]
Tr Orenb Gos Med Inst ... Trudy Orenburgskogo Gosudarstvennogo Meditsinskogo Instituta [*A publication*]

Tr Orenb Nauchno Issled Inst Molochno Myasn Skotovod ... Trudy Orenburgskii Nauchno-Issledovatel'skii Instituta Molochno-Myasnogo Skotovodstva [*A publication*]

Tr Orenb Obl Otd Vseross-Nauchn O-va Ter ... Trudy Orenburgskogo Oblastnogo Otdeleniya Vserossiiskogonauchnogo Obshchestva Terapevtov [*A publication*]

Tr Orenb Otd Vses Fiziol Ova ... Trudy Orenburgskogo Otdeleniya Vsesoyuznogo Fiziologicheskogo Obshchestva [*A publication*]

Tr Orenb Skh Inst ... Trudy Orenburgskogo Sel'skokhozyaistvennogo Instituta [*A publication*]

TROS......... Tape Resident Operating System [*Data processing*]   (IEEE)

TROS......... Transformer Read Only Storage

TROSA....... Tropical Science [*A publication*]

TROSCOM ... Troop Support Command [*Formerly, MECOM*] [*Army*]

Tr Otd Fiziol Biofiz Rast Akad Nauk Tadzh SSR ... Trudy Otdel Fiziologii i Biofiziki Rastenii. Akademiya Nauk Tadzhikskoi SSR [*A publication*]

Tr Otd Geol Buryat Fil Sib Otd Akad Nauk SSSR ... Trudy Otdela Geologii. Buryatskii Filial. Sibirskoe Otdelenie. Akademiya Nauk SSSR [*A publication*]

Tr Otd Gorn Dela Metall Akad Nauk Kirg SSR ... Trudy Otdela Gornogo Dela i Metallurgii. Akademiya Nauk Kirgizskoi SSR [*A publication*]

Tr Otd Pochvoved Akad Nauk Kirg SSR ... Trudy Otdela Pochvovedeniya. Akademiya Nauk Kirgizskoi SSR [*A publication*]

Tr Otd Pochvoved Dagest Fil Akad Nauk SSSR ... Trudy Otdela Pochvovedeniya Dagestanskogo Filiala. Akademii Nauk SSSR [*A publication*]

TROTTS ..... Theater Realignment of Traffic Transportation Support   (MCD)

TROU .... Tround International, Inc. [*NASDAQ symbol*]   (NQ)

Troub & H Prac ... Troubat and Haly's Pennsylvania Practice   (DLA)

Troub Lim Partn ... Troubat on Limited Partnership   (DLA)

TROV.......... Tethered Remotely Operational Vehicle [*Marine science*]   (MSC)

Tr O-va Fiziol Azerb ... Trudy Obshchestva Fiziologov Azerbaidzhana [*A publication*]

Trow D & Cr ... Trower's Debtor and Creditor [*1860*]   (DLA)

Trow Eq ..... Trower's Manual of the Prevalance of Equity [*1876*]   (DLA)

T Roy Ent S ... Transactions. Royal Entomological Society of London [*A publication*]

T Roy Soc C ... Transactions. Royal Society of Canada [*A publication*]

TRP .... Maryland State Police [*Pikesville, MD*] [*FAA designator*]   (FAAC)

TRP .... Table of Replaceable Parts

TRP .... Tamper Resistant Packaging [*Food and Drug Administration*]

TRP .... Tangible Research Property [*Business*]

TRP .... Target Reference Point   (AABC)

TRP .... Target Reporting Parameters   (MCD)

TRP .... Technical Requirements Package   (MCD)

TRP .... Television Remote Pickup

TRP .... Terminal Rendezvous Phase

TRP .... Threat Recognition Processor [*Navy*]   (MCD)

TRP .... Thunderstorm Research Project [*Environmental Science Services Administration*]

TRP .... Time to Repair Part

TRP .... Timing Release Pin

TRP .... Trade Pattern   (MSA)

TRP .... Traffic Regulation Point

TRP .... Trainable Retractable Propeller

TRP .... Training Review Panel   (CAAL)

TRP .... TransCanada Pipelines Ltd. [*NYSE symbol*] [*Toronto Stock Exchange symbol*] [*Vancouver Stock Exchange symbol*]

TrP .... Transpatent [*German*]   (DLA)

TRP .... Transportation Proceedings [*A publication*]

TRP .... Tree Point, AK [*Location identifier*] [*FAA*]   (FAAL)

TRP .... Tricommand Review Panel [*Military*]   (AFIT)

TRP .... Tripped

TRP .... Troop   (AFM)

TRP .... Trujillo [*Peru*] [*Seismograph station code, US Geological Survey*]   (SEIS)

Trp .... Tryptophan [*Also, W*] [*An amino acid*]

TRP .... Tubular Reabsorption [*or Resorption*] of Phosphate

TRPA......... Tryptophan-Rich Prealbumin [*Biochemistry*]

Tr Paleontol Inst Akad Nauk SSSR ... Trudy Paleontologicheskogo Instituta. Akademiya Nauk SSSR [*A publication*]

Tr Path Soc London ... Transactions. Pathological Society of London [*A publication*]

TRPB......... Thoroughbred Racing Protective Bureau

TRPC......... Tradicion. Revista Peruana de Cultura [*A publication*]

TRPCAR..... Troop Carrier [*Military*]   (CINC)

TRPCAR(M) ... Troop Carrier (Medium)   (CINC)

TRPCL .... Tropical   (FAAC)

TRPCO .... Tropical Continental [*American air mass*]   (FAAC)

Tr Permsk Farm Inst ... Trudy Permskogo Farmatseuticheskogo Instituta [*A publication*]

Tr Permsk Gos Med Inst ... Trudy Permskii Gosudarstvennyi Meditsinskii Institut [*A publication*]

Tr Permsk Gos Nauchno-Issled Proektn Inst Neft Prom-sti ... Trudy Permskij Gosudarstvennyj Nauchno-Issledovatel'skij i Proektnyj Institut Neftyanoj Promyshlennosti [*A publication*]

Tr Permsk Gos Skh Inst ... Trudy Permskogo Gosudarstvennogo Sel'skokhozyaistvennogo Instituta [*A publication*]

Tr Permsk Nauchno Issled Inst Vaktsin Syvorotok ... Trudy Permskogo Nauchno-Issledovatel'skogo Instituta Vaktsin i Syvorotok [*A publication*]

Tr Permsk S-kh Inst ... Trudy Permskogo Sel'skokhozyaistvennogo Instituta [*A publication*]

Tr Perv Mosk Med Inst Im I M Sechenova ... Trudy Pervogo Moskovskogo Meditsinskogo Instituta Imeni I. M. Sechenova [*A publication*]

Tr 1 Pervogo Mosk Med Inst ... Trudy 1 Pervogo Moskovskogo Meditsinskogo Instituta [*USSR*] [*A publication*]

Tr Pervogo Mosk Pedagog Inst ... Trudy Pervogo Moskovskogo Pedagogicheskogo Instituta [*A publication*]

Tr Petergof Estest Nauchn Inst ... Trudy Petergofskogo Estestvenno-Nauchnogo Instituta [*A publication*]

Tr Petrogr Inst Akad Nauk SSSR ... Trudy Petrograficheskogo Instituta. Akademiya Nauk SSSR [*A publication*]

TRPGDA..... Tripropylene Glycol Diacrylate [*Organic chemistry*]

TRPL .... Terneplate [*Materials*]

TRPLA........ Transplantation [*A publication*]

Tr Plodoovoshchn Inst ... Trudy Plodoovoshchnogo Instituta [*A publication*]

Tr Plodovoshchn Inst Im I V Michurina ... Trudy Plodovoshchnogo Instituta Imeni I. V. Michurina [*A publication*]

Tr Plodovo-Yagodnogo Inst Im Akad R R Shredera ... Trudy Plodovo-Yagodnogo Instituta Imeni Akademika R. R. Shredera [*A publication*]

TRPLYR...... Trapping Layer   (FAAC)

Trp-mRNA ... Ribonucleic Acid, Messenger - Tryptophan Constitutive [*Biochemistry, genetics*]

TRPN......... Transportation

TRPO......... Track Reference Printout

Tr Poch Inst V V Dokuchaeva Akad Nauk SSSR ... Trudy Pochvennogo Instituta Imeni V. V. Dokuchaeva. Akademiya Nauk SSSR [*A publication*]

Tr Pochv Inst Im V V Dokuchaeva Akad Nauk SSSR ... Trudy Pochvennogo Instituta Imeni V. V. Dokuchaeva. Akademii Nauk SSSR [*A publication*]

Tr Polyar Nauchno-Issled Proekt Inst Morsk Ryb Khoz Okeanogr ... Trudy Polyarnyi Nauchno-Issledovatel'skii i Proektnyi Institut Morskogo Rybnogo Khozyaistva i Okeanografii [*USSR*] [*A publication*]

TRPPA........ Transplantation Proceedings [*A publication*]

Tr Prik Bot Genet Sel Ser 10 ... Trudy po Prikladnoi Botanike. Genetike i Selektsii. Seriya 10. Dendrologiya i Dekorativnoe Sadovodstvo [*A publication*]

Tr Prikl Bot Genet Sel ... Trudy po Prikladnoi Botanike. Genetike i Selektsii [*USSR*] [*A publication*]

Tr Prikl Bot Genet Selek ... Trudy po Prikladnoi Botanike. Genetike i Selektsii [*A publication*]

Tr Prikl Bot Genet Sel Ser 1 ... Trudy po Prikladnoi Botanike. Genetike i Selektsii. Seriya 1. Sistematika, Geografia, i Ekologia Rastenii [*A publication*]

Tr Prikl Bot Genet Sel Ser 2 ... Trudy po Prikladnoi Botanike. Genetike i Selektsii. Seriya 2. Genetika, Selektsiya, i Tsitologiya Rastenii [*A publication*]

Tr Prikl Bot Genet Sel Ser 3 ... Trudy po Prikladnoi Botanike. Genetike i Selektsii. Seriya 3. Fiziologiya, Biokhimiya, i Anatomiya Rastenii [*A publication*]

Tr Prikl Bot Genet Sel Ser 4 ... Trudy po Prikladnoi Botanike. Genetike i Selektsii. Seriya 4. Semenovedenie i Semennoi Kontrol [*A publication*]

Tr Prikl Bot Genet Sel Ser 5 ... Trudy po Prikladnoi Botanike. Genetike i Selektsii. Seriya 5. Zernovye Kul'tury [*A publication*]

Tr Prikl Bot Genet Sel Ser 13 ... Trudy po Prikladnoi Botanike. Genetike i Selektsii. Seriya 13. Regeraty i Bibliografia [*A publication*]

Tr Prikl Bot Genet Sel Ser 14 ... Trudy po Prikladnoi Botanike. Genetike i Selektsii. Seriya 14. Osvoenie Pustyn [*A publication*]

Tr Prikl Bot Genet Sel Ser 15 ... Trudy po Prikladnoi Botanike. Genetike i Selektsii. Seriya 15. Severnoe (Pripolyarnoe) Zemledelie [*A publication*]

Tr Prikl Bot Genet Sel Ser A ... Trudy po Prikladnoi Botanike. Genetike i Selektsii. Seriya A. Sotsialisticheskoe [*A publication*]

Tr Primorsk S-kh Inst ... Trudy Primorskogo Sel'skokhozyaistvennogo Instituta [*A publication*]

Tr Probl Temat Soveshch Akad Nauk SSSR Zool Inst ... Trudy Problemnykh i Tematicheskikh Soveshchanii. Akademiya Nauk SSSR. Zoologicheskii Institut [*A publication*]

Tr Proizvod Nauchno-Issled Inst Inzh Izyskaniyam Stroit ... Trudy Proizvodstvennyi i Nauchno-Issledovatel'skii Institut po Inzhenernym Izyskaniyam v Stroitel'stve [*A publication*]

TRPS......... Temperature Regulating Power Supply

TRPS......... Troops

TRPSC .... Triple Screw

Tr Pskov Obl Gos Skh Opytn Stn ... Trudy Pskovskoi Oblastnoi Gosudarstvennoi Sel'skokhozyaistvennoi Opytnoi Stantsii [*A publication*]

TRPT .... Time to Reach Peak Tension
Tr Pushkin Nauchno-Issled Lab Razvedeniya S-kh Zhivotn ... Trudy
          Pushkinskoi Nauchno-Issledovatel'skoi Laboratorii
          Razvedeniya Sel'skokhozyaistvennykh Zhivotnykh [*A
          publication*]
TRPX .... TRP Energy Sensors [*NASDAQ symbol*]   (NQ)
TRQ .... Task Ready Queue
TRQ .... Torque   (AAG)
TRQ .... Total Requirements   (AAG)
TRQ .... United States Army TRADOC, Fort Ord, CDEC Library, Fort
          Ord, CA [*OCLC symbol*]   (OCLC)
TRQUD ...... Transportation Quarterly [*A publication*]
TRR .... [*The*] Research Ranch [*An association*]   (EA)
TRR .... [*The*] Rohmer Review [*A publication*]
TRR .... Tactical Range Recorder [*Navy*]
TRR .... Tactical Reaction Reconnaissance
TRR .... Tape Read Register
TRR .... Target Ranging RADAR
TRR .... Tarraleah [*Tasmania*] [*Seismograph station code, US
          Geological Survey*]   (SEIS)
TRR .... Teaching and Research Reactor
TRR .... Test Readiness Review [*NASA*]   (NASA)
TRR .... Test and Research Reactor   (NRCH)
TRR .... Tethered RADAR Reflector
TRR .... Thailand Research Reactor
TRR .... Theoretical Research Report
TRR .... Topical Report Request   (NRCH)
TRR .... Topical Reports Review   (NRCH)
TRR .... Tracor, Inc. [*NYSE symbol*]
TRR .... Trade Regulation Reporter   (DLA)
TRR .... Trader Resource Corp. [*Vancouver Stock Exchange symbol*]
TRR .... Transfer Relay Rack   (CAAL)
TRR .... United States Army TRADOC, Fort Rucker Post Library and
          Aviation School Library, Fort Rucker, AL [*OCLC
          symbol*]   (OCLC)
TRRA .... Tera Corp. [*NASDAQ symbol*]   (NQ)
TRRA .... Terminal Railroad Association of St. Louis [*AAR code*]
TRRA .... Tilt Rotor Research Aircraft
Tr Radiat Gig Leningr Nauchno-Issled Inst Radiats Gig ... Trudy po
          Radiatsionnoi Gigiene. Leningradskii Nauchno-
          Issledovatel'skii Institut Radiatsionnoi Gigieny [*USSR*] [*A
          publication*]
Tr Radiats Gig ... Trudy po Radiatsionnoi Gigiene [*A publication*]
Tr Radiats Gig Leningr Nauchno-Issled Inst Radiats Gig ... Trudy po
          Radiatsionnoj Gigiene. Leningradskij Nauchno-
          Issledovatel'skij Institut Radiatsionnoj Gigieny [*A
          publication*]
Tr Radievogo Inst Akad Nauk SSSR ... Trudy Radievogo Instituta
          Akademiya Nauk SSSR [*A publication*]
Tr Radiotekh Inst ... Trudy Radiotekhnicheskogo Instituta [*USSR*] [*A
          publication*]
Tr Radiotekh Inst Akad Nauk SSSR ... Trudy Radiotekhnicheskogo Instituta.
          Akademiya Nauk SSSR [*A publication*]
TRRAPS ..... Transportable Reliable Acoustic Path Sonobuoy   (NVT)
TRRB .... Test Readiness Review Board [*NASA*]
TRRB .... Transportation Research Board. Special Report [*United
          States*] [*A publication*]
TRRC .... Test Resources Review Committee [*DoD*]
TRRC .... Textile Resource and Research Center   (EA)
TRRE .... Transportation Research Record [*A publication*]
TRREB .... Transportation Research [*A publication*]
TRRED .... Transportation Research Record [*A publication*]
Tr Resp Inst Epidemiol Mikrobiol ... Trudove na Respublikanskiya Instituta
          po Epidemiologiya i Mikrobiologiya [*A publication*]
Tr Resp Opytn Stn Kartofeln Ovoshchn Khoz Kaz SSR ... Trudy
          Respublikanskoi Opytnoi Stantsii Kartofel'nogo i
          Ovoshchnogo Khozyaistva. Kazakhskaya SSR [*A
          publication*]
Tr Resp Ova Ftiziatrov Nauchno Issled Inst Tuberk Kaz SSR ... Trudy
          Respublikanskogo Obshchestva Ftiziatrov Nauchno-
          Issledovatel'skogo Instituta Tuberkuleza Kazakhskoi SSR
          [*A publication*]
Tr Resp Stn Zashch Rast ... Trudy Respublikanskoi Stantsii Zashchity
          Rastenii [*A publication*]
TRRF .... [*The*] Refrigeration Research Foundation [*Bethesda, MD*]   (EA)
TRRF .... Training Review File [*IRS*]
TRRG .... Tax Reform Research Group   (EA)
TRRIA .... Translations Register-Index [*A publication*]
Tr Rizh Inst Inzh Grazhdanskoi Aviats ... Trudy Rizhskogo Instituta
          Inzhenerov Grazhdanskoi Aviatsii [*A publication*]
TRRL .... Tooling Rejection and Rework Laboratory
TRRL .... Transport and Road Research Laboratory [*Departments of the
          Environment and Transport*] [*Crowthorne, Berks.,
          England*] [*Information service*]   (EISS)
TRRL Lab Rep ... TRRL [*Transport and Road Research Laboratory*]
          Laboratory Report [*A publication*]
TRRL Rep ... TRRL [*Transport and Road Research Laboratory*] Report [*A
          publication*]
TRRL Suppl Rep ... TRRL [*Transport and Road Research Laboratory*]
          Supplementary Report [*A publication*]
TRRN .... Terrain   (FAAC)

TRRO .... Triton Group Ltd. [*NASDAQ symbol*]   (NQ)
Tr Rostov na Donu Inst Inzh Zheleznodorozhn Transp ... Trudy
          Rostovskogo-na-Donu Instituta Inzhenerov
          Zheleznodorozhnogo Transporta [*A publication*]
Tr Roy Soc Edinb ... Transactions. Royal Society of Edinburgh [*A
          publication*]
TRRR .... Trilateral Range and Range Rate System
TRR of ST L ... Terminal Railroad Association of St. Louis
TRRT .... Test Results Review Team [*Nuclear energy*]   (NRCH)
Tr Ryazan Med Inst ... Trudy Ryazanskogo Meditsinskogo Instituta [*A
          publication*]
Tr Ryazan Radiotekh Inst ... Trudy Ryazanskogo Radiotekhnicheskogo
          Instituta [*USSR*] [*A publication*]
TRS .... Tactical RADAR System
TRS .... Tactical Radio Set
TRS .... Tactical Reconnaissance Squadron [*Air Force*]
TRS .... Tape Recorder Subsystem
TRS .... Target Range Servo
TRS .... Technical Repair Standards
TRS .... Technical Requirements Specification   (MCD)
TRS .... Technical Research Ship
TRS .... Teleoperator Retrieval System [*NASA*]
TRS .... Terrestrial Radio System
TRS .... Test Requirement Specification   (MCD)
TRS .... Test Requirements Summary   (MUGU)
TRS .... Test Research Service [*Defunct*]   (EA)
TRS .... Test Research Station
TRS .... Test Response Spectrum   (IEEE)
TRS .... Tetrahedral Research Satellite
TRS .... Textes Religieux Sumeriens du Louvre [*A publication*]   (BJA)
TRS .... Theatre Recording Society   (EA)
TRS .... Theologische Rundschau [*A publication*]
TRS .... Thermal Reactor Safety   (NRCH)
TRS .... Third Readiness State   (AAG)
TRS .... Thorson Aviation, Inc. [*Aberdeen, SD*] [*FAA
          designator*]   (FAAC)
TRS .... Threat Reaction System
TRS .... Ticket Reservation Systems, Inc.
TRS .... Time Reference System   (MCD)
TRS .... Time Resolved Spectrometry
TRS .... Toll Room Switch [*Telecommunications*]   (TEL)
TRS .... Top Right Side   (MCD)
TRS .... Torry Research Station [*British*]
TRS .... Total Reduced Sulfur [*Environmental chemistry*]
TRS .... Total Reducing Sugars [*Food science*]
TRS .... Tough Rubber-Sheathed [*Cable*]   (DEN)
TRS .... Traceability and Reporting System
TRS .... Training Reservation System   (MCD)
TRS .... Transfer   (ADA)
TRS .... Transportable Relay Station
TRS .... Transpose   (ROG)
TRS .... Transverse Rupture Strength [*Ceramic technology*]
TRS .... Treasure Island Resources [*Vancouver Stock Exchange
          symbol*]
TRS .... Tree-Ring Society   (EA)
TRS .... Trieste [*Italy*] [*Airport symbol*]   (OAG)
TRS .... Trieste [*Campo Marzio*] [*Italy*] [*Seismograph station code, US
          Geological Survey*] [*Closed*]   (SEIS)
TRS .... Tropical Revolving Storm [*Meteorology*]
TRS .... Troubleshooting Record Sheet [*NASA*]   (NASA)
TRS .... Truss [*Shipping*]
TRS .... Trustees
TRS .... Tuboreticular Structure [*Cytology*]
TRS .... Tug Rotational System [*NASA*]   (NASA)
TRS .... United States Department of Transportation, Transportation
          System Center, Cambridge, MA [*OCLC symbol*]   (OCLC)
TRSA .... Terminal RADAR Service Area   (FAAC)
TRSA .... Textile Rental Services Association of America [*Hallandale,
          FL*]   (EA)
TRSAA ...... Transaction. Royal Society of South Africa [*A publication*]
Tr Sakhalin Obl Stn Zashch Rast ... Trudy Sakhalinskaya Oblastnaya
          Stantsiya Zashchity Rastenii [*A publication*]
Tr Samark Gos Univ ... Trudy Samarkandskogo Gosudarstvennogo
          Universiteta [*A publication*]
Tr Sarat Med Inst ... Trudy Saratovskogo Meditsinskogo Instituta [*A
          publication*]
Tr Sarat Otd Vses Nauchno Issled Inst Ozern Rechn Rybn Khoz ... Trudy
          Saratovskogo Otdeleniya Vsesoyuznogo Nauchno-
          Issledovatel'skogo Instituta Ozernogo i Rechnogo Rybn
          Khoz [*A publication*]
Tr Sarat Ova Estestvoispyt Lyubit Estestvozn ... Trudy Saratovskogo
          Obshchestva Estestvoispytatelei i Lyubitelei
          Estestvoznaniya [*A publication*]
Tr Sarat S-kh Inst ... Trudy Saratovskogo Sel'skokhozyaistvennogo Instituta
          [*A publication*]
Tr Sarat Zootekh Vet Inst ... Trudy Saratovskogo Zootekhnicheskogo
          Veterinarnogo Instituta [*A publication*]
Tr Sary Chelekskogo Gos Zap ... Trudy Sary Chelekskogo
          Gosudarstvennogo Zapovednikia [*A publication*]
TRSB .... Time Reference Scanning Beam [*Aviation*]
TRSBG .... Transcribing   (MSA)

TRSBR .... Transcriber (MSA)
TR/SBS ...... Teleoperator Retrieval/Skylab Boost System
[*Aerospace*] (MCD)
TRSC .... Transactions. Royal Society of Canada [*A publication*]
TRSC .... Triad Systems Corporation [*NASDAQ symbol*] (NQ)
TRSCA .... Transactions. Royal Society of Canada [*A publication*]
TRSCB .... Transcribe (MSA)
TRSCB .... Transportation Science [*A publication*]
TRSD .... Test Requirements/Specification Document (MCD)
TRSD .... Total Radiance Spectral Distribution
TRSD .... Total Rated Service Date [*Air Force*] (AFM)
TRSD .... Transferred
TRSD .... Transposed
Tr Sekt Astrobot Akad Nauk Kazakh SSR ... Trudy Sektora Astrobotaniki. Akademiya Nauk Kazakhskoi SSR [*A publication*]
Tr Sekt Astrobot Akad Nauk Kaz SSR ... Trudy Sektora Astrobotaniki. Akademiya Nauk Kazakhskoi SSR [*A publication*]
Tr Sekt Fiziol Akad Nauk Az SSR ... Trudy Sektora Fiziologii. Akademiya Nauk Azerbaidzhanskoi SSR [*A publication*]
Tr Sel Agrotekh Zashch Rast ... Trudy po Selektsii Agrotekhnike i Zashchite Rastenii [*A publication*]
Tr Semipalat Med Inst ... Trudy Semipalatinskogo Meditsinskogo Instituta [*A publication*]
Tr Semipalat Zoovet Inst ... Trudy Semipalatinskogo Zooveterinarnogo Instituta [*A publication*]
Tr Ser .... Treaty Series (DLA)
Tr Sess Kom Opred Absol Vozrasta Geol Form Akad Nauk SSSR ... Trudy Sessii Komissii po Opredeleniyu Absolyutnogo Vozrasta Geologicheskikh Formatsii. Akademiya Nauk SSSR [*A publication*]
Tr Sevansk Gidrobiol Stn ... Trudy Sevanskoi Gidrobiologicheskoi Stantsii [*A publication*]
Tr Sevastop Biol Stn Akad Nauk Ukr SSR ... Trudy Sevastopol'skoi Biologicheskoi Stantsii. Akademii Nauk Ukrainskoi SSR [*A publication*]
Tr Sevastop Biol Stn Im A D Kovalenskogo Akad Nauk Ukr SSR ... Trudy Sevastopol'skoi Biologicheskoi Stantsii Imeni A. D. Kovalenskogo Akademii Nauk Ukrainskoi SSR [*A publication*]
Tr Severokavkazskogo Gornometall Inst ... Trudy Severokavkazskogo Gornometallurgicheskogo Instituta [*USSR*] [*A publication*]
Tr Sev Kavk Gornometall Inst ... Trudy Severo-Kavkazskogo Gornometallurgicheskogo Instituta [*A publication*]
Tr Sev-Oset Med Inst ... Trudy Severo-Osetinskogo Meditsinskogo Instituta [*A publication*]
Tr Sev-Oset S-kh Inst ... Trudy Severo-Osetinskogo Sel'skokhozyaistvennogo Instituta [*A publication*]
Tr Sev Vost Kompleksn Inst Dalnevost Tsentr Akad Nauk SSSR ... Trudy Severo-Vostochnogo Kompleksnogo Instituta. Dal'nevostochnyi Tsentr. Akademiya Nauk SSSR [*A publication*]
Tr Sev Zapadn Zaochn Politekh Inst ... Trudy. Severo-Zapadnyi Zaochnyi Politekhnicheskii Institut [*A publication*]
TRSF .... Torque-Regulated Speed Follower
TRSG .... Third Reich Study Group [*Germany Philatelic Society*] (EA)
TRSG .... Track RADAR Simulation Group [*Military*] (CAAL)
TRSH .... Trim Shell
Tr Sib Fiz Tekh Inst Tomsk Gos Univ ... Trudy Sibirskogo Fiziko-Tekhnicheskogo Instituta pri Tomskom Gosudarstvennom Universitete [*USSR*] [*A publication*]
Tr Sib Lesotekh Inst ... Trudy Sibirskogo Lesotekhnicheskogo Instituta [*A publication*]
Tr Sib Nauch-Issled Inst Zhivotn ... Trudy Sibirskogo Nauchno-Issledovatel'skogo Instituta Zhivotnovodstva [*A publication*]
Tr Sib Nauchno-Issled Inst Energ ... Trudy Sibirskogo Nauchno-Issledovatel'skogo Instituta Energetiki [*USSR*] [*A publication*]
Tr Sib Nauchno-Issled Inst Geol Geofiz Miner Syr'ya ... Trudy Sibirskogo Nauchno-Issledovatel'skogo Instituta Geologii, Geofiziki, i Mineral'nogo Syr'ya [*A publication*]
Tr Sib Otd Gos Nauchno-Issled Inst Ozern Rechn Rybn Khoz ... Trudy Sibirskogo Otdela Gosudarstvennogo Nauchno-Issledovatel'skogo Instituta Ozernogo i Rechnogo Rybnogo Khozyaistva [*A publication*]
Tr Sib Tekhnol Inst ... Trudy Sibirskogo Tekhnologicheskogo Instituta [*A publication*]
Tr Sikhote-Alinsk Gos Zapov ... Trudy Sikhote-Alinskogo Gosudarstvennogo Zapovednika [*A publication*]
Tr Skh Samarkanskogo Inst ... Trudy Sel'skokhozyaistvennogo Samarkanskogo Instituta [*A publication*]
TRSL .... Toms River Signal Laboratory [*Army*] (MCD)
TRSL .... Transactions. Royal Society of Literature [*A publication*]
Tr Smolensk Gos Med Inst ... Trudy Smolenskogo Gosudarstvennogo Meditsinskogo Instituta [*A publication*]
Tr Smolensk Nauchno Issled Vet Stn ... Trudy Smolenskoi Nauchno-Issledovatel'skoi Veterinarnoi Stantsii [*A publication*]
TRSN .... Torsion (MSA)
TRSN .... Transition (FAAC)
TRSOC .... Trademark Society, Inc.

Tr Soc Trop Med and Hyg (London) ... Transactions. Society of Tropical Medicine and Hygiene (London) [*A publication*]
Tr Solyanoi Lab Vses Inst Galurgii Akad Nauk SSSR ... Trudy Solyanoi Laboratorii. Vsesoyuznyi Institut Galurgii. Akademiya Nauk SSSR [*A publication*]
Tr Sov Antarkt Eksped ... Trudy Sovetskoi Antarkticheskoi Ekspeditsii [*USSR*] [*A publication*]
Tr Soveshch Ikhtiol Kom Akad Nauk SSSR ... Trudy Soveshchanii Ikhtiologicheskoi Komissii. Akademii Nauk SSSR [*A publication*]
Tr Soveshch Morfogen Rast ... Trudy Soveshchanii po Morfogenezu Rastenii [*A publication*]
Tr Soveshch Poliploidiya Selek Akad Nauk SSSR ... Trudy Soveshchaniya. Poliploidiya i Selektsiya. Akademiya Nauk SSSR [*A publication*]
Tr Sovmestnaya Sov Mong Nauchno Issled Geol Eksped ... Trudy Sovmestnaya Sovetsko-Mongol'skaya Nauchno-Issledovatel'skaya Geologicheskaya Ekspeditsiya [*A publication*]
Tr Sov Sekts Mezhdunar Assots Pochvovedov ... Trudy Sovetskoi Sektsii Mezhdunarodnoi Assotsiatsii Pochvovedov [*A publication*]
Tr Soyuzn Geologopoisk Kontora ... Trudy Soyuznaya Geologopoiskovaya Kontora [*A publication*]
Tr Soyuznogo Nauchno-Issled Inst Priborostr ... Trudy Soyuznogo Nauchno-Issledovatel'skogo Instituta Priborostroeniya [*USSR*] [*A publication*]
Tr Soyuzn Trest Razved Burovykh Rab ... Trudy Soyuznyi Trest Razvedochno-Burovykh Rabot [*A publication*]
TRSP .... Total Radiance Spectral Polarization
TRSP .... Transport Seaplane [*Navy*]
TRSq .... Tactical Reconnaissance Squadron [*Air Force*] (AFM)
TRSR .... Taxi and Runway Surveillance RADAR
Tr Sredneaziat Gos Univ ... Trudy Sredneaziatskogo Gosudarstvennogo Universiteta [*A publication*]
Tr Sredneaziat Gos Univ Ser 6 ... Trudy Sredneaziatskogo Gosudarstvennogo Universiteta. Seriya 6. Khimiya [*A publication*]
Tr Sredneaziat Gos Univ Ser 11 ... Trudy Sredneaziatskogo Gosudarstvennogo Universiteta. Seriya 11. Tekhnika [*A publication*]
Tr Sredneaziat Gos Univ Ser 13 ... Trudy Sredneaziatskogo Gosudarstvennogo Universiteta. Seriya 13. Varia [*A publication*]
Tr Sredneaziat Gos Univ Ser 7a ... Trudy Sredneaziatskogo Gosudarstvennogo Universiteta. Seriya 7-a. Geologiya [*A publication*]
Tr Sredneaziat Gos Univ Ser 7d ... Trudy Sredneaziatskogo Gosudarstvennogo Universiteta. Seriya 7-d. Pochvovedenie [*A publication*]
Tr Sredneaziat Nauchno Issled Gidrometeorol Institut ... Trudy Sredneaziat Nauchno-Issledovatel'skii Gidrometeorologicheskii Institut [*A publication*]
Tr Sredne-Aziat Nauchno-Issled Protivochumn Inst ... Trudy Sredne-Aziatskogo Nauchno-Issledovatel'skogo Protivochumnogo Instituta [*A publication*]
TRSS .... Triple Screw Ship
T Rs S Afr ... Transactions. Royal Society of South Africa [*A publication*]
TRSSCOMM ... Technical Research Ship Special Communications [*System*] [*Pronounced "triss-com"*] [*Navy*]
TRSSGM .... Tactical Range Surface-to-Surface Guided Missile
TRSSM .... Tactical Range Surface-to-Surface Missile
TRST .... Throttle Reset
TRST .... TrustCo Bank Corp. of New York [*NASDAQ symbol*] (NQ)
TRSTA .... Transactions. Royal Society of Tropical Medicine and Hygiene [*A publication*]
Tr Stalinab Astron Obs ... Trudy Stalinabadskoi Astronomicheskoi Observatorii [*A publication*]
Tr Stalinab Gos Med Inst ... Trudy Stalinabadskogo Gosudarstvennogo Meditsinskogo Instituta [*A publication*]
Tr Stalingr S-kh Inst ... Trudy Stalingradskogo Sel'skokhozyaistvennogo Instituta [*A publication*]
Tr Stavrop Kraev Nauchno-Issled Vet Stn ... Trudy Stavropol'skoi Kraevoi Nauchno-Issledovatel'skoi Veterinarnoi Stantsii [*A publication*]
Tr Stavrop Nauchno Issled Inst Selsk Khoz ... Trudy Stavropol'skogo Nauchno-Issledovatel'skogo Instituta Sel'skogo Khozyaistva [*A publication*]
Tr Stavropol Sel'skokhoz Inst ... Trudy Stavropol'skogo Sel'skokhozyaistvennogo Instituta [*A publication*]
Tr Stavrop S-kh Inst ... Trudy Stavropol'skogo Sel'skokhozyaistvennogo Instituta [*A publication*]
Tr Stomatol Lit SSR ... Trudy Stomatologov Litovskoi SSR [*A publication*]
T Rs Trop M ... Transactions. Royal Society of Tropical Medicine and Hygiene [*A publication*]
Tr Stud Nauchno Tekh Ova Mosk Vyssh Tekh Uchil ... Trudy Studencheskogo Nauchno-Tekhnicheskogo Obshchestva. Moskovskoe Vysshe Tekhnicheskoe Uchilishche [*A publication*]
Tr Stud Nauchn Ova Azerb Gos Med Inst ... Trudy Studencheskogo Nauchnogo Obshchestva Azerbaidzhanskii Gosudarstvennyi Meditsinskii Institut [*A publication*]

Tr Stud Nauchn Ova Khark Politekh Inst ... Trudy Studencheskogo Nauchnogo Obshchestva. Khar'kovskii Politekhnicheskii Institut [*A publication*]

Tr Sukhum Bot Sada ... Trudy Sukhumskogo Botanicheskogo Sada [*A publication*]

Tr Sukhum Opytn Stn Efiromaslichn Kult ... Trudy Sukhumskoi Opytnoi Stantsii Efiromaslichnykh Kultur [*A publication*]

TRSV .... Tobacco Ring Spot Virus

Tr Sverdl Gorn Inst ... Trudy Sverdlovskogo Gornogo Instituta [*A publication*]

Tr Sverdl Med Inst ... Trudy Sverdlovskogo Meditsinskogo Instituta [*A publication*]

Tr Sverdl Nauchno Issled Inst Lesn Promsti ... Trudy Sverdlovskii Nauchno-Issledovatel'skii Institut Lesnoi Promyshlennosti [*A publication*]

Tr Sverdl Nauchno Issled Vet Stn ... Trudy Sverdlovskoi Nauchno-Issledovatel'skoi Veterinarnoi Stantsii [*A publication*]

Tr Sverdl Skh Inst ... Trudy Sverdlovskogo Sel'skokhozyaistvennogo Instituta [*A publication*]

TRSY .... Treasury (AABC)

TRT .... San Antonio, TX [*Location identifier*] [*FAA*]   (FAAL)

TRT .... TACFIRE Remote Terminal (MCD)

TRT .... Technical Review Team [*Nuclear energy*]   (NRCH)

TRT .... Television Resource Teachers [*Canada*]

TRT .... Tempo di Restituzione Termica [*Thermal Restitution Test*] [*Italian*] [*Medicine*]

TRT .... Torpedo Rocket Thrown

TRT .... Trademark Registration Treaty

TRT .... Traffic Route Testing [*Telecommunications*]   (TEL)

trt .... Treatment [*Medicine*]

TRT .... Treherbert [*Cardiff*] [*Welsh depot code*]

TRT .... Trent Regional Library System [*UTLAS symbol*]

TRT .... Tretes [*Java*] [*Seismograph station code, US Geological Survey*]   (SEIS)

TRT .... Trim Template (MCD)

TRT .... Trinity Resources Ltd. [*Toronto Stock Exchange symbol*]

Trt .... Trityl [*Biochemistry*]

TRT .... Tuned Receiver Tuner

TRT .... Turkish Radio & Television Corp.

TRT .... Turret (AABC)

TRT .... United States Army TRADOC, Fort Bliss, Fort Bliss, TX [*OCLC symbol*]   (OCLC)

TrT₃ .... Total Reverse Triiodothyronine

Tr Tadzh Astron Obs ... Trudy Tadzhikskoi Astronomicheskoi Observatorii [*A publication*]

Tr Tadzh Gos Med Inst ... Trudy Tadzhikskogo Gosudarstvennogo Meditsinskogo Instituta [*A publication*]

Tr Tadzh Med Inst ... Trudy Tadzhikskogo Meditsinskogo Instituta [*A publication*]

Tr Tadzh Nauchno-Issled Inst Zemled ... Trudy Tadzhikskogo Nauchno-Issledovatel'skogo Instituta Zemledeliya [*A publication*]

Tr Tallin Pedagog Inst ... Trudy Tallinskogo Pedagogicheskogo Instituta [*Estonian SSR*] [*A publication*]

Tr Tallin Politekh Inst ... Trudy Tallinskogo Politekhnicheskogo Instituta [*Estonian SSR*] [*A publication*]

Tr Tallin Politekh Inst Ser A ... Trudy Tallinskogo Politekhnicheskogo Instituta. Seriya A [*Estonian SSR*] [*A publication*]

Tr Tambov Inst Khim Mashinostr ... Trudy Tambovskogo Instituta Khimicheskogo Mashinostroeniya [*USSR*] [*A publication*]

Tr Tashk Farm Inst ... Trudy Tashkentskogo Farmatsevticheskogo Instituta [*A publication*]

Tr Tashk Gos Univ ... Trudy Tashkentskogo Gosudarstvennogo Universiteta Imeni V. I. Lenina [*A publication*]

Tr Tashk Gos Univ Im V I Lenina ... Trudy Tashkentskogo Gosudarstvennogo Universiteta Imeni V. I. Lenina [*USSR*] [*A publication*]

Tr Tashk Inst Inzh Irrig Mekh Selsk Khoz ... Trudy Tashkentskogo Instituta Inzhenerov Irrigatsii i Mekhanizatsii Sel'skogo Khozyaistva [*A publication*]

Tr Tashk Inst Inzh Zh Zheleznodorozhn Transp ... Trudy Tashkentskogo Instituta Inzhenerov Zheleznodorozhnogo Transporta [*A publication*]

Tr Tashk Nauchno Issled Inst Vaktsin Syvorotok ... Trudy Tashkentskogo Nauchno-Issledovatel'skogo Instituta Vaktsin i Syvorotok [*A publication*]

Tr Tashk Politekh Inst ... Trudy Tashkentskogo Politekhnicheskogo Instituta [*A publication*]

Tr Tashk S-kh Inst ... Trudy Tashkentskogo Sel'skokhozyaistvennogo Instituta [*A publication*]

Tr Tatar Gos Nauchno Issled Proektn Inst Neft Promsti ... Trudy Tatarskii Gosudarstvennyi Nauchno-Issledovatel'skii i Proektnyi Institut Neftyanoi Promyshlennosti [*A publication*]

Tr Tatar Nauchno Issled Inst Selsk Khoz ... Trudy Tatarskii Nauchno-Issledovatel'skii Institut Sel'skogo Khozyaistva [*A publication*]

Tr Tatar Neft Nauchno Issled Inst ... Trudy Tatarskii Neftyanoi Nauchno-Issledovatel'skii Inst [*A publication*]

Tr Tatar Otd Gos Nauchno Issled Inst Ozern Rechn Rybn Khoz ... Trudy Tatarskogo Otdeleniya Gosudarstvennogo Nauchno-Issledovatel'skogo Instituta Ozernogo i Rechnogo Rybnogo Khozyaistva [*A publication*]

Tr Tatar Respub Gosud Sel'skokhoz Opyt Sta ... Trudy Tatarskoi Respublikanskoi Gosudarstvennoi Sel'skokhozyaistvennoi Opytnoi Stantsii [*A publication*]

Tr Tbilis Bot Inst Akad Nauk Gruz SSR ... Trudy Tbilisskogo Botanicheskogo Instituta Akademiya Nauk Gruzinskoi SSR [*A publication*]

Tr Tbilis Gos Med Inst ... Trudy Tbilisskogo Gosudarstvennogo Meditsinskogo Instituta [*A publication*]

Tr Tbilis Gos Pedagog Inst ... Trudy Tbilisskogo Gosudarstvennogo Pedagogiceskogo Instituta Imeni A. S. Pushkina [*A publication*]

Tr Tbilis Gos Univ ... Trudy Tbilisskogo Gosudarstvennogo Universiteta [*A publication*]

Tr Tbilis Gos Univ Im Stalina ... Trudy Tbilisskogo Gosudarstvennogo Universiteta Imeni Stalina [*A publication*]

Tr Tbilis Gos Univ Inst Prikl Mat ... Trudy Tbilisskii Gosudarstvennyi Universitet. Institut Prikladnoi Matematiki [*A publication*]

Tr Tbilis Inst Usoversh Vrachei ... Trudy Tbilisskogo Instituta Usovershenstvovaniya Vrachei [*A publication*]

Tr Tbilis Mat Inst ... Trudy Tbilisskogo Ordena Trudovogo Krasnogo Znameni Matematicheskogo Instituta [*A publication*]

Tr Tbilis Nauchno-Issled Gidrometeorol Inst ... Trudy Tbilisskogo Nauchno-Issledovatel'skogo Gidrometeorologicheskogo Instituta [*A publication*]

Tr Tbilissk Bot Inst ... Trudy Tbilisskogo Botanicheskogo Instituta [*A publication*]

TRTC .... Tactical Record Traffic Center (MCD)

TRTD .... Treated (MSA)

Tr Teor Polya ... Trudy po Teorii Polya [*USSR*] [*A publication*]

Tr Ternop Gos Med Inst ... Trudy. Ternopol'skii Gosudarstvennyi Meditsinskii Institut [*A publication*]

TRTF .... Tactical Reconnaissance Task Force (CINC)

TRTF .... Tactical Record Traffic Facsimile (MCD)

TRTF .... Tasking Requirements and Tasking File (MCD)

TRTG .... Tactical RADAR Threat Generator (MCD)

TRTG .... Treating

TRTHB .... Traitement Thermique [*A publication*]

TRTL .... Transistor-Resistor-Transistor Logic (IEEE)

TRTMT .... Treatment (MSA)

Tr Tom Nauchno Issled Inst Kabeln Promsti ... Trudy Tomskogo Nauchno-Issledovatel'skogo Instituta Kabel'noi Promyshlennosti [*A publication*]

Tr Tomsk Gos Univ ... Trudy Tomskogo Gosudarstvennogo Universiteta [*USSR*] [*A publication*]

Tr Tomsk Gos Univ Im V V Kuibysheva ... Trudy Tomskogo Gosudarstvennogo Universiteta Imeni V. V. Kuibysheva [*A publication*]

Tr Tomsk Gos Univ Ser Khim ... Trudy Tomskogo Gosudarstvennogo Universiteta Imeni V. V. Kuibysheva. Seriya Khimicheskaya [*USSR*] [*A publication*]

Tr Tomsk Inst Radioehlektron Ehlektron Tekh ... Trudy Tomskogo Instituta Radioehlektroniki i Ehlektronnoj Tekhniki [*A publication*]

Tr Tomsk Med Inst ... Trudy Tomskogo Meditsinskogo Instituta [*A publication*]

Tr Tomsk Nauchno-Issled Inst Vaksiny Syvorotok ... Trudy Tomskogo Nauchno-Issledovatel'skogo Instituta Vaktsiny i Syvorotok [*A publication*]

TRTP .... Toxicology Research and Testing Program [*National Institutes of Health*]

TRTS .... Tactical Record Traffic System (MCD)

TRTS .... Track RADAR Test Set (MCD)

TRTS .... Triple Redundant Timing Systems (MCD)

Tr Tselinograd Sel'skokhoz Inst ... Trudy Tselinogradskogo Sel'skokhozyaistvennogo Instituta [*A publication*]

Tr Tselinogr Gos Med Inst ... Trudy Tselinogradskii Gosudarstvennyi Meditsinskii Institut [*A publication*]

Tr Tselinogr Med Inst ... Trudy Tselinogradskogo Meditsinskogo Instituta [*A publication*]

Tr Tselinogr S-kh Inst ... Trudy Tselinogradskogo Sel'skokhozyaistvennogo Instituta [*A publication*]

Tr Tsent Aerol Obs ... Trudy Tsentral'noi Aerologicheskoi Observatorii [*USSR*] [*A publication*]

Tr Tsent Nauchno-Issled Gornorazved Inst ... Trudy Tsentral'nyi Nauchno-Issledovatel'skii Gornorazvedochnyi Institut [*USSR*] [*A publication*]

Tr Tsent Nauchno-Issled Inst Tekhnol Mashinostr ... Trudy Tsentral'nyi Nauchno-Issledovatel'skii Institut Tekhnologii i Mashinostroeniya [*USSR*] [*A publication*]

Tr Tsent Nauchno-Issled Proekt-Konst Kotloturbinnogo Inst ... Trudy Tsentral'nogo Nauchno-Issledovatel'skogo i Proektno-Konstruktorskogo Kotloturbinnogo Instituta [*USSR*] [*A publication*]

Tr Tsentr Aerol Obs ... Trudy Tsentral'noi Aerologicheskoi Observatorii [*A publication*]

Tr Tsentr Aptechn Nauchno-Issled Inst ... Trudy Tsentral'nogo Aptechnogo Nauchno-Issledovatel'skogo Instituta [*A publication*]

Tr Tsentr Chernozemn Gos Zapov ... Trudy Tsentral'nogo Chernozemnogo Gosudarstvennogo Zapovednika [*A publication*]

Tr Tsentr Genet Lab I V Michurina ... Trudy Tsentral'noi Genetiki Laboratorii I. V. Michurina [*A publication*]

Tr Tsentr Genet Lab Vses Akad Skh Nauk ... Trudy Tsentral'noi Geneticheskoi Laboratorii. Vsesoyuznaya Akademiya Sel'skokhozyaistvennykh Nauk [*A publication*]

Tr Tsentr Inst Prognozov ... Trudy Tsentral'nogo Instituta Prognozov [*A publication*]

Tr Tsentr Inst Travmatol Ortop ... Trudy Tsentral'nogo Instituta Travmatologii i Ortopedii [*A publication*]

Tr Tsentr Inst Usoversh Vrachei ... Trudy Tsentral'nogo Instituta Usovershenstvovaniya Vrachei [*A publication*]

Tr Tsentr Kaz Geol Upr ... Trudy Tsentral'no-Kazakhstanskogo Geologicheskogo Upravleniya [*A publication*]

Tr Tsentr Kom Vodookhr ... Trudy Tsentral'nogo Komiteta Vodookhraneniya [*A publication*]

Tr Tsentr Nauchno Issled Avtomob Avtomot Inst ... Trudy Tsentral'nyi Nauchno-Issledovatel'skii Avtomobil'nyi i Avtomotornyi Institut [*A publication*]

Tr Tsentr Nauchno-Issled Dezinfekts Inst ... Trudy Tsentral'nogo Nauchno-Issledovatel'skogo Dezinfektsionnogo Instituta [*A publication*]

Tr Tsentr Nauchno Issled Dizein Inst ... Trudy Tsentral'nogo Nauchno-Issledovatel'skogo Dizel'nogo Instituta [*A publication*]

Tr Tsentr Nauchno-Issled Gornorazved Inst ... Trudy Tsentral'nyj Nauchno-Issledovatel'skij Gornorazvedochnyj Institut [*A publication*]

Tr Tsentr Nauchno Issled Inst Faner Mebeli ... Trudy Tsentral'nogo Nauchno-Issledovatel'skogo Instituta Fanery i Mebeli [*A publication*]

Tr Tsentr Nauchno Issled Inst Khim Pishch Sredstv ... Trudy Tsentral'nogo Nauchno-Issledovatel'skogo Instituta Khimii Pishchevykh Sredstv [*A publication*]

Tr Tsentr Nauchno Issled Inst Sakh Promsti Moscow ... Trudy Tsentral'nogo Nauchno-Issledovatel'skogo Instituta Sakharnoi Promyshlennosti Moscow [*A publication*]

Tr Tsentr Nauchno-Issled Inst Spirt Likero-Vodochn Prom-sti ... Trudy Tsentral'nogo Nauchno-Issledovatel'skogo Instituta Spirtovoi i Likero-Vodochnoi Promyshlennosti [*USSR*] [*A publication*]

Tr Tsentr Nauchno Issled Lab Novosib Med Inst ... Trudy Tsentral'noi Nauchno-Issledovatel'skoi Laboratorii Novosibirskogo Meditsinskogo Instituta [*A publication*]

Tr Tsentr Nauchno Issled Morsk Flota ... Trudy Tsentral'nyi Nauchno-Issledovatel'skii Institut Morskogo Flota [*A publication*]

Tr Tsentr Nauchno-Issled Rentgeno-Radiol Inst ... Trudy Tsentral'nogo Nauchno-Issledovatel'skogo Rentgeno-Radiologicheskogo Instituta [*A publication*]

Tr Tsentr Nauchnoizsled Inst Ribovud Varna Bulg Akad Nauk ... Trudove na Tsentralniya Nauchnoizsledovatelski Institut po Ribovudstvo i Ribolov. Varna. Bulgarska Akademiya na Naukite [*A publication*]

Tr Tsentr Sib Bot Sada ... Trudy Tsentral'nogo Sibirskogo Botanicheskogo Sada [*A publication*]

TRTT .... Tactical Record Traffic Terminal [*Army*] (MCD)

TRTTF .... Trinity Resources Ltd. [*NASDAQ symbol*] (NQ)

Tr Tul Gos Skh Opytn Stn ... Trudy Tul'skoi Gosudarstvennoi Sel'skokhozyaistvennoi Opytnoi Stantsii [*A publication*]

Tr Turkm Bot Sada Akad Nauk Turkm SSR ... Trudy Turkmenskogo Botanicheskogo Sada. Akademii Nauk Turkmenskoi SSR [*A publication*]

Tr Turkm Gos Med Inst ... Trudy Turkmenskogo Gosudarstvennogo Meditsinskogo Instituta [*A publication*]

Tr Turkm Nauchno-Issled Inst Kozhynykh Bolezn ... Trudy Turkmenskogo Nauchno-Issledovatel'skogo Instituta Kozhynykh Boleznei [*A publication*]

Tr Turkm Nauchno Issled Trakhomatoznogo Inst ... Trudy Turkmenskogo Nauchno-Issledovatel'skogo Trakhomatoznogo Instituta [*A publication*]

Tr Turkm Politekh Inst ... Trudy Turkmenskogo Politekhnicheskogo Instituta [*A publication*]

Tr Turkm Skh Inst ... Trudy Turkmenskogo Sel'skokhozyaistvennogo Instituta [*A publication*]

Tr Turkm S-Kh Inst Im M Kalinina ... Trudy Turkmenskogo Sel'skokhozyaistvennogo Instituta Imeni M. I. Kalinina [*A publication*]

Tr Turk Nauchno Issled Inst Kozhynykh Bolezn ... Trudy Turkmenskogo Nauchno-Issledovatel'skogo Instituta Kozhynykh Boleznei [*A publication*]

Tr Tuvinskoi Gos Skh Opytn Stn ... Trudy Tuvinskoi Gosudarstvennoi Sel'skokhozyaistvennoi Opytnoi Stantsii [*A publication*]

Tr Tyazan Radiotekh Inst ... Trudy Tyazanskogo Radiotekhnicheskogo Instituta [*A publication*]

Tr Tyumen Ind Inst ... Trudy Tyumenskogo Industrial'nogo Instituta [*A publication*]

Tr Tyumen Otd Vses Nauchn Ova Anat Gistol Embriol ... Trudy Tyumenskogo Otdeleniya Vsesoyuznogo Nauchnogo Obshchestva Anatomov, Gistologov, i Embriologov [*A publication*]

Tr Tyumenskogo Ind Inst ... Trudy Tyumenskogo Industrial'nogo Instituta [*USSR*] [*A publication*]

TRU .... Taurus Resources [*Vancouver Stock Exchange symbol*]

TRU .... Test Replaceable Unit

TRu .... Theologische Rundschau [*Tuebingen*] [*A publication*]

TRU .... Time Release Unit (MCD)

TRU .... Transformer-Rectifier Unit (MCD)

TRU .... Transmit-Receive Unit

TRU .... Transportable Radio Unit [*Military*]

TRU .... Transuranic [*or Transuranium*] [*Chemistry*]

TRU .... Transuranium Processing Plant (NRCH)

TRU .... Truancy [*FBI standardized term*]

Tru .... Trueman's New Brunswick Equity Cases [*1876-93*] (DLA)

TRU .... Trujillo [*Peru*] [*Airport symbol*] (OAG)

TRU .... Truk [*Caroline Islands*] [*Seismograph station code, US Geological Survey*] [*Closed*] (SEIS)

TRU .... Truncated Variant [*Genetics*]

TRU .... United States Army TRADOC, Fort Hood, Fort Hood, TX [*OCLC symbol*] (OCLC)

TRUB .... Temporarily Replaced by Unlighted Buoy [*Maps and charts*]

Trubn Proizvod Urala ... Trubnoe Proizvodstvo Urala [*A publication*]

Truck & Bus Trans ... Truck and Bus Transportation [*A publication*]

Truck & Bus Transp ... Truck and Bus Transportation [*A publication*]

Truck Bus Transpn ... Truck and Bus Transportation [*A publication*]

Truck Off-Highw Ind ... Truck and Off-Highway Industries [*United States*] [*A publication*]

TRUD .... Time Remaining until Dive [*Air Force*]

Trud po Mezhdunar Pravo ... Trudove po Mezhdunarodno Pravo [*Studies on International Law*] [*Sofia, Bulgaria*] (DLA)

Trud Viss Ikonom Inst Karl Marks-Sofia ... Trudove. Vissija Ikonomiceski Institut Karl Marks-Sofija [*A publication*]

Trudy Akad Nauk Litov SSR ... Trudy. Akademii Nauk Litovskoi SSR [*A publication*]

Trudy Akad Nauk Litov SSR Ser A Obsc Nauki ... Trudy Akademii Nauk Litovskoj SSR. Serija A. Obscestvennye Nauki [*A publication*]

Trudy Akad Nauk Litov SSR Ser B ... Trudy. Akademii Nauk Litovskoi SSR. Serija B [*A publication*]

Trudy Altai Politehn Inst ... Trudy Altaiskii Politehniceskii Institut Imeni I. I. Polizunova [*A publication*]

Trudy Altaisk Politehn Inst ... Trudy Altaiskii Politehniceskii Institut Imeni I. I. Polizunova [*A publication*]

Trudy Altaisk Sel'khoz Inst ... Trudy Altaiskogo Sel'skokhozyaistvennogo Instituta [*A publication*]

Trudy Altajsk Politehn Inst ... Trudy Altajskogo Politehniceskogo Instituta [*A publication*]

Trudy Andizhan Ped Inst ... Trudy Andizhanskii Gosudarstvennyi Pedagogicheskii Institut [*A publication*]

Trudy Arhangel Lesotehn Inst ... Trudy Arhangel'skogo Lesotehniceskogo Instituta Imeni V. V. Kuibysheva [*A publication*]

Trudy Arkhangel Lesotekh Inst Im V V Kuibysheva ... Trudy Arkhangel'skogo Ordena Trudovogo Kraskogo Znameni Lesotekhnicheskogo Instituta Imeni V. V. Kuibysheva [*A publication*]

Trudy Armyansk Nauchno-Issled Inst Vinograd Vinodel Plodov ... Trudy Armyanskogo Nauchno-Issledovatel'skogo Instituta Vinogradarstva. Vinodeliya i Plodovodstva [*A publication*]

Trudy Armyansk Nauchno-Issled Inst Zhivot Vet ... Trudy Armyanskogo Nauchno-Issledovatel'skogo Instituta Zhivotnovodstva i Veterinarii [*A publication*]

Trudy Aspirantov Gruzin Sel'-khoz Inst ... Trudy Aspirantov Gruzinskogo Sel'skokhozyaistvennogo Instituta [*A publication*]

Trudy Azerbajdzansk Opytn Sta ... Trudy Azerbajdzanskogo Opytnoj Stancii [*A publication*]

Trudy Azerb Nauchno-Issled Inst Gidrotekh Melior ... Trudy Azerbaidzhanskogo Nauchno-Issledovatel'skogo Instituta Gidrotekhniki i Melioratsii [*A publication*]

Trudy Azerb Nauchno-Issled Inst Zhivot ... Trudy Azerbaidzhanskogo Nauchno-Issledovatel'skogo Instituta Zhivotnovodstva [*A publication*]

Trudy Azerb Vet Inst ... Trudy Azerbaidzhanskogo Nauchno-Issledovatel'skogo Veterinarnogo Instituta [*A publication*]

Trudy Bashkir Nauch Inst Sel Khoz ... Trudy Bashkirskogo Nauchnogo Instituta Sel'skogo Khozyaistva [*A publication*]

Trudy Baskir S-h Inst ... Trudy Bashkirskogo Sel'skokhozjaistvennogo Instituta [*A publication*]

Trudy Belorussk Nauchno-Issled Inst Pochv ... Trudy Belorusskogo Nauchno-Issledovatel'skogo Instituta Pochvovedeniya [*A publication*]

Trudy Belorussk Sel'-khoz Akad ... Trudy Belorusskoi Sel'skokhozyaistvennoi Akademii [*A publication*]

Trudy Biol Inst Sib Otd Akad Nauk SSSR ... Trudy Biologicheskogo Instituta. Sibirskoe Otdelenie. Akademiya Nauk SSSR [*A publication*]

Trudy Bot Inst Akad Nauk SSSR Ser VI ... Trudy Botaniceskij Institut. Akademija Nauk SSSR. Serija VI [*A publication*]

Trudy Burjat Inst Obsc Nauk ... Trudy Burjatskogo Instituta Obscestvennyh Nauk [*A publication*]

Trudy Buryat Mongol Nauchno-Issled Vet Opyt Sta ... Trudy Buryat Mongol'skoi Nauchno-Issledovatel'skoi Veterinarnoi Opytnoi Stantsii [*A publication*]

Trudy Buryatsk Sel'khoz Inst ... Trudy Buryatskogo Sel'skokhozyaistvennogo Instituta [*A publication*]

Trudy CNIIKA ... Trudy Gosudarstvennyi Vsesojuznyi Central'nyi Naucno-Issledovatel'skii Institut Kompleksnoi Avtomatizacii [*A publication*]

Trudy Dagest Nauchno-Issled Inst Sel Khoz ... Trudy Dagestanskogo Nauchno-Issledovatel'skogo Instituta Sel'skogo Khozyaistva [*A publication*]

Trudy Doneck Politehn Inst ... Trudy Doneckogo Politehniceskogo Instituta [*A publication*]

Trudy Don Zonal'Inst Sel'Khoz ... Trudy Donskogo Zonal'nogo Instituta Sel'skogo Khozyaistva [*A publication*]

Trudy Fiz Inst Lebedev ... Trudy Fiziceskogo Instituta Imeni P. N. Lebedeva [*A publication*]

Trudy Frunze Politehn Inst ... Trudy Frunzenskogo Politehniceskogo Instituta [*A publication*]

Trudy Geogr Fak Kirgiz Univ ... Trudy Geograficheskogo Fakul'teta Kirgizskogo Universiteta [*A publication*]

Trudy Geometr Sem ... Trudy Geometriceskogo Seminara [*A publication*]

Trudy Geom Sem Kazan Univ ... Trudy Geometriceskogo Seminara. Kazanskii Universitet [*A publication*]

Trudy G Ermitazh ... Trudy Gosudarstvennogo Ermitazha [*A publication*]

Trudy Glav Geofiz Obs ... Trudy Glavnoi Geofizicheskoi Observatorii Imeni A. I. Voeikova [*A publication*]

Trudy Gor'kov Politehn Inst ... Trudy Gor'kovskogo Politehniceskii Institut [*A publication*]

Trudy Gor'kov Sel'-khoz Inst ... Trudy Gor'kovskogo Sel'skokhozyaistvennogo Instituta [*A publication*]

Trudy Gorsk Sel'-khoz Inst ... Trudy Gorskogo Sel'skokhozyaistvennogo Instituta [*A publication*]

Trudy Gos Gidrol Inst ... Trudy Gosudarstvennogo Gidrologicheskogo Instituta [*A publication*]

Trudy Gruz Nauchno-Issled Pishch Prom ... Trudy Gruzinskii Nauchno-Issledovatel'skii Institut Pishchevoi Promyshlennosti [*A publication*]

Trudy Gruz Sel'-khoz Inst ... Trudy Gruzinskogo Sel'skokhozyaistvennogo Instituta Imeni L. P. Beriya [*A publication*]

Trudy Inst Biol Ural Fil (Sverdlovsk) ... Trudy Instituta Biologii Ural'skii Filial. Akademiya Nauk SSSR (Sverdlovsk) [*A publication*]

Trudy Inst Bot (Alma-Ata) ... Trudy Instituta Botaniki. Akademiya Nauk Kazakhskoi SSR (Alma-Ata) [*A publication*]

Trudy Inst Etnogr ... Trudy Instituta Etnografii [*A publication*]

Trudy Inst Fiziol (Baku) ... Trudy Instituta Fiziologii. Akademiya Nauk Azerbaidzhanskoi SSR (Baku) [*A publication*]

Trudy Inst Fiziol I P Pavlova ... Trudy Instituta Fiziologii Imeni I. P. Pavlova Akademiya Nauk SSSR [*A publication*]

Trudy Inst Genet ... Trudy Instituta Genetiki. Akademiya Nauk SSR [*A publication*]

Trudy Inst Istor Estestvoznan Tehn ... Trudy Instituta Istorii Estestvoznanija i Tehniki [*A publication*]

Trudy Inst Jaz Lit Ist Komi Fil Akad Nauk SSSR ... Trudy Instituta Jazyka, Literatury, i Istorii Komi Filiala Akademii Nauk SSSR [*A publication*]

Trudy Inst Mat i Meh Ural Naucn Centr Akad Nauk SSSR ... Trudy Instituta Matematiki i Mehaniki. Ural'skii Naucnyi Centr. Akademija Nauk SSSR [*A publication*]

Trudy Inst Pochv Agrokhim (Baku) ... Trudy Instituta Pochvovedeniya i Agrokhimii. Akademiya Nauk Azerbaidzhanskoi SSR (Baku) [*A publication*]

Trudy Inst Sistem Upravlenija Akad Nauk Gruzin SSR ... Trudy Instituta Sistem Upravlenija. Akademija Nauk Gruzinskoi SSR [*A publication*]

Trudy Inst Sistem Upravleniya Akad Nauk Gruzin SSR ... Trudy Instituta Sistem Upravleniya. Akademiya Nauk Gruzinskoi SSR [*A publication*]

Trudy Inst Teoret Astronom ... Trudy Instituta Teoreticeskoi Astronomii [*A publication*]

Trudy Inst Zool Parazit Tashkent ... Trudy Instituta Zoologii i Parazitologii. Akademiya Nauk Uzbekskoi SSR. Tashkent [*A publication*]

Trudy Irkutsk Gos Univ ... Trudy Irkutskogo Gosudarstvennogo Universiteta [*A publication*]

Trudy Ist-Kraev Muz Mold ... Trudy Istoriko-Kraevedcheskogo Muzeia Moldavskoi SSR [*A publication*]

Trudy Kabardino-Balkarsk Gos Sel'khoz Opyt Sta ... Trudy Kabardino-Balkarskoi Gosudarstvennoi Sel'skohozyaistvennoi Opytnoi Stantsii [*A publication*]

Trudy Kaf Teorii Funkcii i Funkcional Anal Moskov Gos Univ ... Moskovskii Gosudarstvennyi Universitet. Mehanikomatematiceskii Fakul'tet. Kafedra Teorii Funkcii i Funkcional'nogo Analiza. Trudy [*A publication*]

Trudy Karel' Fil Akad Nauk SSSR ... Trudy Karel'skogo Filiala. Akademii Nauk SSSR [*A publication*]

Trudy Kavkaz Gos Zapov ... Trudy Kavkazskogo Gosudarstvennogo Zapovednika [*A publication*]

Trudy Kazakh Sel'-khoz Inst ... Trudy Kazakhskogo Sel'skokhozyaistvennogo Instituta [*A publication*]

Trudy Kazan Aviacion Inst ... Trudy Kazanskogo Aviacionnogo Instituta. Matematika i Mehanika [*A publication*]

Trudy Kazan Gorod Astronom Observator ... Trudy Kazanskoi Gorodskoi Astronomiceskoi Observatorii [*A publication*]

Trudy Kazan Gos Pedagog Inst ... Trudy Kazanskogo Gosudarstvennogo Pedagogicheskogo Instituta [*A publication*]

Trudy Kazan Sel'-khoz Inst ... Trudy Kazanskogo Sel'skokhozyaistvennogo Instituta [*A publication*]

Trudy Kazan S-h Inst ... Trudy Kazanskogo Sel'skokhozjaistvennogo Instituta [*A publication*]

Trudy Kemerov Gos Sel Khoz Opyt Sta ... Trudy Kemerovskoi Gosudarstvennoi Sel'skokhozyaistvennoi Opytnoi Stantsii [*A publication*]

Trudy Kharkov Opyt Sta Pchelov ... Trudy Khar'kovskaya Opytnaya Stantsiya Pchelovodstva [*A publication*]

Trudy Kharkov Sel'-khoz Inst ... Trudy Khar'kovskogo Sel'skokhozyaistvennogo Instituta [*A publication*]

Trudy Kirgiz Gos Univ Ser Biol Nauk ... Trudy Kirgizskogo Gosudarstvennogo Universiteta. Seriya Biologicheskikh Nauk. Zoologiya-Fiziologiya [*A publication*]

Trudy Kirgiz Gos Univ Ser Mat Nauk ... Trudy Kirgizskogo Gosudarstvennogo Universiteta. Serija Matematiceskih Nauk [*A publication*]

Trudy Kirgiz Nauchno-Issled Inst Zeml ... Trudy Kirgizskogo Nauchno-Issledovatel'skogo Instituta Zemledeliya [*A publication*]

Trudy Kirgiz Sel'-khoz Inst ... Trudy Kirgizskogo Sel'skokhozyaistvennogo Instituta [*A publication*]

Trudy Kishinev Sel'-khoz Inst ... Trudy Kishinevskogo Sel'skokhozyaistvennogo Instituta [*A publication*]

Trudy Kolomen Filiala Vsesojuz Zaocn Politehn Inst ... Trudy Kolomenskogo Filiala Vsesojuznyi Zaocnyi Politehniceskii Institut [*A publication*]

Trudy Kom Analit Khim ... Trudy Komissii po Analiticheskoi Khimii. Akademiya Nauk SSSR [*A publication*]

Trudy Komi Fil Akad Nauk SSSR ... Trudy Komi Filiala. Akademii Nauk SSSR [*A publication*]

Trudy Komi Filiala Akad Nauk SSSR ... Trudy Komi Filiala. Akademii Nauk SSSR [*A publication*]

Trudy Konf Pochv Sib Dal'n Vostoka Akad Nauk SSSR ... Trudy Konferentsiya Pochvovedov Sibiri i Dal'nego Vostoka. Akademiya Nauk SSSR [*A publication*]

Trudy Kuban Sel'-khoz Inst ... Trudy Kubanskogo Sel'skokhozyaistvennogo Instituta [*A publication*]

Trudy (Kujbys Aviac) Inst ... Trudy (Kujbysevskij Aviacionnyj) Institut [*A publication*]

Trudy Latv Sel'-khoz Inst ... Trudy Latviiskogo Sel'skokhozyaistvennogo Instituta [*A publication*]

Trudy Leningrad Tehnolog Inst Holod Promysl ... Trudy Leningradskogo Tehnologicheskogo Instituta Holodil'noi Promyslennosti [*A publication*]

Trudy Leningr Gidromet Inst ... Trudy Leningradskogo Gidrometeorologicheskogo Instituta [*A publication*]

Trudy (Leningr Inst Kul't) ... Trudy (Leningradskii Institut Kul'tury) [*A publication*]

Trudy Leningr Obshch Estest ... Trudy Leningradskogo Obshchestva Estest-voispytatelei [*A publication*]

Trudy Litov Nauchno-Issled Inst Zeml ... Trudy Litovskogo Nauchno-Issledovatel'skogo Instituta Zemledeliya [*A publication*]

Trudy Mat Inst Steklov ... Trudy Matematiceskogo Instituta Imeni V. A. Steklova [*A publication*]

Trudy Metrolog Inst SSSR ... Trudy Metrologiceskih Institutov SSSR [*A publication*]

Trudy Mold Akad Nauk ... Trudy Ob'edinennoi Nauchnoi Sessii. Moldavskii Filial Akademii Nauk SSR [*A publication*]

Trudy Mol Ucen Kirigiz Univ ... Trudy Molodyh Ucenyh Kirigizskogo Universiteta [*A publication*]

Trudy Mosk Ordena Lenina Sel'Khoz Akad ... Trudy Moskovskoi Ordena Lenina Sel'sko-Khozyaistvennoi Akademii Imeni K. A. Timiryazeva [*A publication*]

Trudy Moskov Elektrotehn Inst Svjazi ... Trudy Moskovskogo Elektrotehniceskogo Instituta Svjazi [*A publication*]

Trudy Moskov Inst Inzen Zelezno-doroz Transporta ... Trudy Moskovskogo Instituta Inzenernov Zelezno-doroznogo Transporta [*A publication*]

Trudy Moskov Inst Istoriji ... Trudy Moskovskogo Instituta Istoriji, Filosofiji, i Literatury [*A publication*]

Trudy Moskov Inst Radiotehn Elektron i Avtomat ... Trudy Moskovskogo Instituta Radiotekhniki, Elektroniki, i Avtomatiki [*A publication*]

Trudy Moskov Mat Obsc ... Trudy Moskovskogo Matematiceskogo Obscestva [*A publication*]

Trudy Moskov Orden Lenin Energet Inst ... Trudy Moskovskogo Ordena Lenina Energeticeskogo Instituta [*A publication*]

Trudy Nakhich Kompleks Zonal Opyt Sta ... Trudy Nakhichevanskoi Kompleksnoi Zonal'noi Opytnoi Stantsii [*A publication*]

Trudy Nauch Inst Udobr Insektofung ... Trudy Nauchnogo Instituta po Udobreniyam i Insektofungitsidam Imeni Ya. V. Satoilova [*A publication*]

Trudy Nauchno-Issled Inst Pchelov ... Trudy Nauchno-Issledovatel'skogo Instituta Pchelovodstva [*A publication*]

Trudy Nauchno-Issled Inst Prud Rybn Khoz ... Trudy Nauchno-Issledovatel'skogo Instituta Prudovogo Rybnogo Khozyaistva [*A publication*]

Trudy Nauchno-Issled Inst Sel'Khoz Severn Zaural'ya ... Trudy Nauchno-Issledovatel'skogo Instituta Sel'skogo Khozyaistva Severnogo Zaural'ya [*A publication*]

Trudy Nauc-Issled Inst Sociol Kul't ... Trudy Nauchno-Issledovatel'skogo Instituta Sociologiceskoj Kul'tury [*A publication*]

Trudy Novocherk Inzh-Melior Inst ... Trudy Novocherkasskogo Inzherno-Meliorativnogo Instituta [*A publication*]

Trudy Obshch Estest Imp Kazan Univ ... Trudy Obshchestva Estestvoispytatelei pri Imperatordkom Kazanskom Universitete Kazan [*A publication*]

Trudy Obsh Dietsk Vrach Moskve ... Trudy Obshchestva Dietskikh Vrachei v Moskve [*A publication*]

Trudy Omsk Vyss Skoly Milicii ... Trudy Omskogo Vyssej Skoly Milicii [*A publication*]

Trudy Ped Inst Gruzin SSR Ser Fiz i Mat ... Trudy Pedagogiceskih Institutov Gruzinskoi SSR. Serija Fiziki i Matematiki [*A publication*]

Trudy Prikl Bot Genet Selek ... Trudy po Prikladnoi Botanike. Genetike i Selektsii [*A publication*]

Trudy Przeval'sk Gos Ped Inst ... Trudy Przeval'skogo Gosudarstvennogo Pedagogiceskogo Instituta [*A publication*]

Trudy Radiats Gig Leningr Nauchno-Issled Inst Radiats Gig ... Trudy Radiatsii i Gigieny Leningradskogo Nauchno-Issledovatel'skogo Instituta Radiatsii Gigieny [*A publication*]

Trudy Rjazan Radiotehn Inst ... Trudy Rjazanskogo Radiotehniceskogo Instituta [*A publication*]

Trudy Russk Ent Obshch ... Trudy Russkogo Entomologicheskogo Obshchestva [*A publication*]

Trudy Samarkand Gos Univ ... Trudy Samarkandskogo Gosudarstvennogo Universiteta Imeni Alisera Navoi [*A publication*]

Trudy Samarkand Univ ... Trudy Samarkandskogo Universiteta [*A publication*]

Trudy Saratov Inst Meh S-H ... Trudy Saratovskogo Instituta Mehanizacii Sel'skogo-Hozjaistva [*A publication*]

Trudy Saratov Sel'-khoz Inst ... Trudy Saratovskogo Sel'skokhozyaistvennogo Instituta [*A publication*]

Trudy Saratov Zootekh Vet Inst ... Trudy Saratovskogo Zootekhnicheskogo Veterinarnogo Institut [*A publication*]

Trudy Sem Kraev Zadacam ... Trudy Seminara po Kraevym Zadacam [*A publication*]

Trudy Sem Kraev Zadacham ... Trudy Seminara po Kraevym Zadacham [*A publication*]

Trudy Sem Mat Fiz Nelinien Koleban ... Trudy Seminara po Matematiceskoi Fizike i Nelinienym Kolebanijam [*A publication*]

Trudy Sem Petrovsk ... Trudy Seminara Imeni I. G. Petrovskogo [*A publication*]

Trudy Sem Vektor Tenzor Anal ... Trudy Seminara po Vektornomu i Tenzornomu Analizu s ih Prilozenijami k Geometrii. Mehanike i Fizike [*A publication*]

Trudy Sibirsk Fiz-Tehn Inst ... Trudy Sibirskogo Fiziko-Tehniceskogo Instituta Imeni Akademika V. D. Kuznecova [*A publication*]

Trudy SibNIIE ... Trudy Sibirskii Naucno-Issledovatel'skii Institut Energetiki [*A publication*]

Trudy Solikam Sel'-khoz Opyt Sta ... Trudy Solikamskoi Sel'skokhozyaistvennoi Opytnoi Stantsii [*A publication*]

Trudy Stavropol' Sel'-khoz Inst ... Trudy Stavropol'skogo Sel'skokhozyaistvennogo Instituta [*A publication*]

Trudy Sverdlovsk Sel'-khoz Inst ... Trudy Sverdlovskogo Sel'skokhozyaistvennogo Instituta [*A publication*]

Trudy Tadzhik Nauchno-Issled Inst Sel Khoz ... Trudy Tadzhikskogo Nauchno-Issledovatel'skogo Instituta Sel'skogo Khozyaistva [*A publication*]

Trudy Tadzik Politehn Inst ... Trudy Tadzikskogo Politehniceskogo Instituta [*A publication*]

Trudy Tallinsk Politehn Inst ... Trudy Tallinskogo Politekhniceskogo Instituta [*A publication*]

Trudy Taskent Gos Univ ... Trudy Taskentskogo Gosudarstvennogo Universiteta Imeni V. I. Lenina. Matematika [*A publication*]

Trudy Tatar Nauchno-Issled Inst Sel'Khoz ... Trudy Tatarskii Nauchno-Issledovatel'skii Institut Sel'skogo Khozyaistva [*A publication*]

Trudy Tatar Respub Gos Sel-khoz Opyt Sta ... Trudy Tatarskoi Respublikanskoi Gosudarstvennoi Sel'skokhozyaistvennoi Opytnoi Stantsii [*A publication*]

Trudy Tbilisk Univ Fiz-Mat Estestv Nauki ... Trudy Tbilisskogo Universiteta Fiziko-Matematiceskie i Estestvennye Nauki [*A publication*]

Trudy Tbiliss Mat Inst Razmadze Akad Nauk Gruzin SSR ... Trudy Tbilisskogo Matematiceskogo Instituta Imeni A. M. Razmadze. Akademija Nauk Gruzinskoi SSR [*A publication*]

Trudy Tbiliss Univ ... Trudy Tbilisskogo Universiteta Fiziko-Matematiceskie i Estestvennyi Nauki [*A publication*]

Trudy Tomsk Gos Univ ... Trudy Tomskogo Gosudarstvennogo Universiteta [*A publication*]

Trudy Tomsk Univ ... Trudy Tomskogo Universiteta [*A publication*]

Trudy Tsent Chernoz Gos Zapov ... Trudy Tsentral'nogo Chernozemnogo Gosudarstvennogo Zapovednika [*A publication*]

Trudy Tsent Sib Bot Sada ... Trudy Tsentral'nogo Sibirskogo Botanicheskogo Sada [*A publication*]

Trudy Turkmen Sel'Khoz Inst ... Trudy Turkmenskogo Sel'sko-Khozyaistvennogo Instituta [*A publication*]

Trudy Ufmsk Aviac Inst ... Trudy Ufimskogo Aviacionnogo Instituta [*A publication*]

Trudy Ukr Gidromet Inst ... Trudy Ukrainskogo Gidrometeorologicheskogo Instituta [*A publication*]

Trudy Ul'yanov Sel'khoz Inst ... Trudy Ul'yanovskogo Sel'skokhozyaistvennogo Instituta [*A publication*]

Trudy Univ Druzby Narod ... Trudy Universiteta Druzhby Narodov Imeni Patrisa Lumumby [*A publication*]

Trudy Ural Politehn Inst ... Trudy Ural'skogo Politehniceskogo Instituta [*A publication*]

Trudy Volgogr Opytno-Melior Sta ... Trudy Volgogradskoi Opytno-Meliorativnoi Stantsii [*A publication*]

Trudy Vologod Sel'khoz Inst ... Trudy Vologodskogo Sel'skokhozyaistvennogo Instituta [*A publication*]

Trudy Voronezh Zoovetinst ... Trudy Voronezhskogo Zooveterinarnogo Instituta [*A publication*]

Trudy Vost Kazakh Gos Opyt Sta ... Trudy Vostochno-Kazakhstanskaya Gosudarstvennaya Sel'skokhozyaistvennaya Opytnaya Stantsiya [*A publication*]

Trudy Vost-Sibir Tehnol Inst ... Trudy Vostochno-Sibirskogo Tehnologiceskogo Instituta [*A publication*]

Trudy Vses Aerogeol Tresta ... Trudy Vsesoyuznogo Aerogeologicheskogo Tresta [*A publication*]

Trudy Vses Ent Obshch ... Trudy Vsesoyuznogo Entomologicheskogo Obshchestva [*A publication*]

Trudy Vses Nauchno-Issled Inst Sakharn Svekly Sakhara ... Trudy Vsesoyuznogo Nauchno-Issledovatel'skogo Instituta Sakharnoi Svekly i Sakhara [*A publication*]

Trudy Vses Nauchno-Issled Inst Torf Prom ... Trudy Vsesoyuznogo Nauchno-Issledovatel'skogo Instituta Torfyanoi Promyshlennosti [*A publication*]

Trudy Vses Nauchno-Issled Inst Udobr Agrotekh Agropochv ... Trudy Vsesoyuznogo Nauchno-Issledovatel'skogo Instituta Udobrenii. Agrotekhniki i Agropochvovedeniya [*A publication*]

Trudy Vsesojuz Nauc-Issled Inst Sov Zakon ... Trudy Vsesojuznogo Nauchno-Issledovatel'skogo Instituta Sovetskogo Zakonodatel'stva [*A publication*]

Trudy Vsesojuz Nauc-Issled Inst Sov Zakon ... Trudy Vsesojuznogo Naucno-Issledovatel'skogo Instituta Sovetskogo Zakonodatel'stva [*A publication*]

Trudy Vsesojuz Nauc-Issled Inst Zascity Rast ... Trudy Vsesojuznogo Naucno-Issledovatel'skogo Instituta Zascity Rastenij [*A publication*]

Trudy Vsesojuz Naucno-Issled Inst Elektromeh ... Trudy Vsesojuznogo Naucno-Issledovatel'skogo Instituta Elektromehaniki [*A publication*]

Trudy Vsesojuz Zaocn Energet Inst ... Trudy Vsesojuznogo Zaocnogo Energeticeskogo Instituta [*A publication*]

Trudy Vses Ordena Lenina Inst Eksp Vet ... Trudy Vsesoyuznogo Ordena Lenina Instituta Eksperimental'noi Veterinarii [*A publication*]

Trudy VTI ... Trudy Vsesojuznogo Teplotehniceskogo Instituta [*A publication*]

Trudy Vychisl Tsentra Tartu Gos Univ ... Trudy Vychislitel'nogo Tsentra Tartuskii Gosudarstvennyi Universitet [*A publication*]

Trudy Vycisl Centra Akad Nauk Gruzin SSR ... Trudy Vycislitel'nogo Centra. Akademija Nauk Gruzinskoi SSR [*A publication*]

Trudy Vycisl Centra Tartu Gos Univ ... Trudy Vycislitel'nogo Centra. Tartuskii Gosudarstvennyi Universitet [*A publication*]

Trudy Zool Inst (Leningr) ... Trudy Zoologicheskogo Instituta Akademiya Nauk SSSR (Leningrad) [*A publication*]

True........... Trueman's New Brunswick Reports (DLA)

Trueman Eq Cas ... Trueman's New Brunswick Equity Cases (DLA)

Truem Eq Cas ... Trueman's New Brunswick Equity Cases (DLA)

Tr Ufim Aviats Inst ... Trudy Ufimskogo Aviatsionnogo Instituta [*A publication*]

Tr Ufim Nauchno-Issled Inst Gig Profzabol ... Trudy Ufimskogo Nauchno-Issledovatel'skogo Instituta Gigieny i Profzabolevanii [*A publication*]

Tr Ufim Neft Naucho-Issled Inst ... Trudy Ufimskii Neftyanoi Nauchno-Issledovatel'skii Institut [*A publication*]

TRUFOS..... True Unidentified Flying Objects

TRUGA....... Trudy Ukrainskii Nauchno-Issledovatel'skii Geologo-Razvedochnyi Institut [*A publication*]

TRUK......... Builders Transport [*NASDAQ symbol*] (NQ)

Tr Ukr Gos Nauchno-Issled Inst Prikl Khim ... Trudy Ukrainskogo Gosudarstvennogo Nauchno-Issledovatel'skogo Instituta Prikladnoi Khimii [*A publication*]

Tr Ukr Inst Eksp Endokrinol ... Trudy Ukrainskogo Instituta Eksperimental'noi Endokrinologii [*A publication*]

Tr Ukr Nauch-Issled Gidrometeorol Inst ... Trudy Ukrainskogo Nauchno-Issledovatel'skogo Gidrometeorologicheskogo Instituta [*A publication*]

Tr Ukr Nauchno-Issled Gidrometeorol Inst ... Trudy Ukrainskogo Nauchno-Issledovatel'skogo Gidrometeorologicheskogo Instituta [*Ukrainian SSR*] [*A publication*]

Tr Ukr Nauchno-Issled Inst Lesn Khoz Agrolesomelior ... Trudy Ukrainskogo Nauchno-Issledovatel'skogo Instituta Lesnogo Khozyaistva i Agrolesomelioratsii [*A publication*]

Tr Ukr Nauchno-Issled Inst Prir Gazov ... Trudy Ukrainskii Nauchno-Issledovatel'skii Institut Prirodnykh Gazov [*A publication*]

Tr Ukr Nauchno-Issled Inst Rastenievod Sel Genet ... Trudy Ukrainskogo Nauchno-Issledovatel'skogo Instituta Rastenievodstva Selektsii i Genetiki [*A publication*]

Tr Ukr Nauchno-Issled Inst Spirt Likero Vodochn Promsti ... Trudy Ukrainskii Nauchno-Issledovatel'skii Institut Spirtovoi i Likero-Vodochnoi Promyshlennosti [*A publication*]

Tr Ukr Nauchno-Issled Inst Zernovogo Khoz ... Trudy Ukrainskogo Nauchno-Issledovatel'skogo Instituta Zernovogo Khozyaistva [*A publication*]

Tr Ulyanovsk Politekh Inst ... Trudy Ul'yanovskii Politekhnicheskii Institut [*A publication*]

Tr Ul'yanovsk S-kh Inst ... Trudy Ul'yanovskogo Sel'skokhozyaistvennogo Instituta [*A publication*]

Tr Ul'yanovsk Skh Opytn Stn ... Trudy Ul'yanovskoi Sel'skokhozyaistvennoi Opytnoi Stantsii [*A publication*]

TRUMP....... Target Radiation Ultraviolet Measurement Program   (AAG)

TRUMP....... Technical Review Updated Manuals and Publications   (MCD)

TRUMP....... Teller Register Unit Monitoring Program   (IEEE)

TRUMP....... Threat Reaction Upgrade Modernization   (MCD)

TRUMP....... Total Revision and Upgrading of Maintenance Procedures [*Marine Corps*]

TRUMP....... Tribal Class Update and Modernization Project [*Canadian Navy*]

TRUN.......... Trunnion [*Pivot*]   (KSC)

TRUNANG ... Trunnion Angle   (MCD)

Tr Univ Druzhby Nar ... Trudy Universiteta Druzhby Narodov [*USSR*] [*A publication*]

Tr Univ Druzhby Nar Fiz ... Trudy Universiteta Druzhby Narodov. Fizika [*USSR*] [*A publication*]

Tr Univ Druzhby Nar Im Patrisa Lumumby ... Trudy Universiteta Druzhby Narodov Imeni Patrisa Lumumby [*A publication*]

Tr Univ Druzhby Nar Ser Fiz ... Trudy Universiteta Druzhby Narodov Imeni Patrisa Lumumby. Seriya Fizika [*A publication*]

Tr Upr Geol Okhr Nedr Sov Minist Kirg SSR ... Trudy Upravleniya Geologii i Okhrany Nedr pri Sovete Ministrov Kirgizskoi SSR [*A publication*]

Tru Railw Rep ... Truman's American Railway Reports   (DLA)

Tr Ural Lesotekh Inst ... Trudy Ural'skogo Lesotekhnicheskogo Instituta [*A publication*]

Tr Ural Nauchno-Issled Inst Chern Met ... Trudy Ural'skogo Nauchno-Issledovatel'skogo Instituta Chernykh Metallov [*A publication*]

Tr Ural Nauchno-Issled Inst Sel'sk Khoz ... Trudy Ural'skogo Nauchno-Issledovatel'skogo Instituta Sel'skogo Khozyaistva [*A publication*]

Tr Ural Nauchno-Issled Khim Inst ... Trudy Ural'skogo Nauchno-Issledovatel'skogo Khimicheskogo Instituta [*A publication*]

Tr Ural Nauchno-Issled Proekt Inst Mednoi Prom-sti ... Trudy Ural'skii Nauchno-Issledovatel'skii i Proektnyi Institut Mednoi Promyshlennosti [*USSR*] [*A publication*]

Tr Ural Nauchno-Issled Proektn Inst Mednoi Promsti ... Trudy Ural'skii Nauchno-Issledovatel'skii i Proektnyi Institut Mednoi Promyshlennosti [*A publication*]

Tr Ural Otd Gos Nauchno-Issled Inst Ozern Rechn Rybn Khoz ... Trudy Ural'skogo Otdeleniya. Gosudarstvennyi Nauchno-Issledovatel'skii Institut Ozernogo i Rechnogo Rybnogo Khozyaistva [*A publication*]

Tr Ural Otd Mosk Ova Ispyt Prir ... Trudy Ural'skogo Otdeleniya Moskovskogo Obshchestva Ispytatelei Prirody [*A publication*]

Tr Ural Otd Sib Nauchno-Issled Inst Rybn Khoz ... Trudy Ural'skogo Otdeleniya Sibirskogo Nauchno-Issledovatel'skogo Instituta Rybnogo Khozyaistva [*A publication*]

Tr Ural Politekh Inst ... Trudy Ural'skogo Politekhnicheskogo Instituta Imeni S. M. Kirova [*A publication*]

Tr Ural Politekh Inst Im S M Kirova ... Trudy Ural'skogo Politekhnicheskogo Instituta Imeni S. M. Kirova [*USSR*] [*A publication*]

TRURON .... Truronensis [*Signature of the Bishop of Truro*] [*Latin*]   (ROG)

TRUST .... Transportable Units and Self-Sufficient Teams   (MCD)

TRUST .... Trieste United States Troops

Trust Bull ... Trust Bulletin [*A publication*]

Trust Co Mag ... Trust Companies Magazine [*1904-38*]   (DLA)

Trust Newsl ... Trust Newsletter [*National Trust of Australia*] [*A publication*]

Trust Nletter ... Trust Newsletter [*National Trust of Australia*] [*A publication*]

Trusts & Es ... Trusts and Estates [*A publication*]

Trusts & Est ... Trusts and Estates [*A publication*]

Trust Terr ... Trust Territory Reports   (DLA)

TRUT .... Time Remaining until Transition [*Air Force*]

Tr Uzb Gos Nauchno-Issled Inst Kurortol Fizioter ... Trudy Uzbekskogo Gosudarstvennogo Nauchno-Issledovatel'skogo i Instituta Kurortologii i Fizioterapii [*A publication*]

Tr Uzb Inst Malyarii Med Parazitol ... Trudy Uzbekistanskogo Instituta Malyarii i Meditsinskoi Parazitologii [*A publication*]

Tr Uzb Nauchno-Issled Inst Fizioter Kurortol ... Trudy Uzbekistanskogo Nauchno-Issledovatel'skogo Instituta Fizioterapii i Kurortologii [*A publication*]

Tr Uzb Nauchno-Issled Inst Ortop Travmatol Prot ... Trudy Uzbekistanskogo Nauchno-Issledovatel'skogo Instituta Ortopedii Travmatologii i Protezirovaniya [*A publication*]

Tr Uzb Nauchno-Issled Inst Ortop Travmatol Protez ... Trudy Uzbekistanskogo Nauchno-Issledovatel'skogo Instituta Ortopedii Travmatologii i Protezirovaniya [*A publication*]

Tr Uzb Nauchno-Issled Inst Vet ... Trudy Uzbekskogo Nauchno-Issledovatel'skogo Instituta Veterinarii [*A publication*]

TRV .... Tank Recovery Vehicle [*Army*]   (AABC)

TRV .... Thrust Reduction Valve

TRV .... Timing Relay Valve

TRV .... Tobacco Rattle Virus

TRV .... Torpedo-Recovery Vessel [*Navy*] [*British*]

TRV .... Transient Recovery Voltage   (IEEE)

TRV .... Traverse

TRV .... Treviso [*Italy*] [*Seismograph station code, US Geological Survey*] [*Closed*]   (SEIS)

TRV .... Trivandrum [*India*] [*Airport symbol*]   (OAG)

TRV .... United States Army TRADOC, Fort Lee Post, Logistic Center, Logistic, Quartermaster, Fort Lee, VA [*OCLC symbol*]   (OCLC)

TRVB .... Tables of Redemption Values for US Savings Bonds

TRVEH ...... Tracked Vehicle   (AABC)

Tr Velikoluk S-kh Inst ... Trudy Velikolukskogo Sel'skokhozyaistvennogo Instituta [*A publication*]

Tr Vissh Inst Nar Stop (Varna Bulg) ... Trudove na Visshiya Institut za Narodno Stopanstvo "D. Blagoev" (Varna Bulgaria) [*A publication*]

Tr Vissh Pedagog Inst (Plovdiv) Mat Fiz Khim Biol ... Trudove na Visshiya Pedagogicheski Institut (Plovdiv). Matematika, Fizika, Khimiya, Biologiya [*A publication*]

Tr Vladivost Nauchno Issled Inst Epidemiol Mikrobiol Gig ... Trudy Vladivostokskogo Nauchno-Issledovatel'skogo Instituta Epidemiologii, Mikrobiologii, i Gigieny [*A publication*]

TRVLG .... Traveling   (MSA)

TRVLMT ...... Travel Limit

TRVLR .... Traveler   (MSA)

TRVM .... Transistorized Voltmeter

TRVMF .... TRV Minerals Corp. [*NASDAQ symbol*]   (NQ)

Tr VNIIEI .... Trudy VNIIEI [*Vsesoyuznogo Nauchno-Issledovatel'skogo i Proektno-Tekhnologicheskogo Instituta Elektrougol'nykh Izdelii*] [*A publication*]

Tr VNII Fiz-Tekh Radiotekh Izmer ... Trudy Vsesoyuznyj Nauchno-Issledovatel'skij Institut Fiziko-Tekhnicheskikh i Radiotekhnicheskikh Izmerenij [*A publication*]

Tr Volgogr Gos Nauchno-Issled Proektn Inst Neft Promsti ... Trudy Volgogradskii Gosudarstvennyi Nauchno-Issledovatel'skii i Proektnyi Institut Neftyanoi Promyshlennosti [*A publication*]

Tr Volgogr Med Inst ... Trudy Volgogradskogo Meditsinskogo Instituta [*A publication*]

Tr Volgogr Nauchno-Issled Inst Neft Gazov Promsti ... Trudy Volgogradskii Nauchno-Issledovatel'skii Institut Neftyanoi i Gazovoi Promyshlennosti [*A publication*]

Tr Volgogr Opytno Melior Stn ... Trudy Volgogradskaya Opytno-Meliorativnaya Stantsiya [*A publication*]

Tr Volgogr Otd Gos Nauchno-Issled Inst Ozern Rechn Rybn Khoz ... Trudy Volgogradskogo Otdeleniya Gosudarstvennogo Nauchno-Issledovatel'skogo Instituta Ozernogo i Rechnogo Rybnogo Khozyaistva [*A publication*]

Tr Volgogr S-kh Inst ... Trudy Volgogradskogo Sel'skokhozyaistvennogo Instituta [*A publication*]

Tr Vologod Molochn Inst ... Trudy Vologodskogo Molochnogo Instituta [*A publication*]

Tr Vologod Molochno Khoz Inst ... Trudy Vologodskogo Molochno-Khozyaistvennogo Instituta [*A publication*]

Tr Volzh Kamskogo Gos Zapov ... Trudy Volzhsko-Kamskogo Gosudarstvennogo Zapovednika [*A publication*]

Tr Voronezh Gos Med Inst ... Trudy Voronezhskii Gosudarstvennyi Meditsinskii Institut [*A publication*]

Tr Voronezh Gos Univ ... Trudy Voronezhskogo Gosudarstvennogo Universiteta [*A publication*]

Tr Voronezh Gos Zapov ... Trudy Voronezhskogo Gosudarstvennogo Zapovednika [*A publication*]

Tr Voronezh Khim Tekhnol Inst ... Trudy Voronezhskogo Khimiko-Tekhnologicheskogo Instituta [*A publication*]

Tr Voronezh Med Inst ... Trudy Voronezhskogo Meditsinskogo Instituta [*A publication*]

Tr Voronezh Nauchno Issled Vet Stn ... Trudy Voronezhskoi Nauchno-Issledovatel'skoi Veterinarnoi Stantsii [*A publication*]

Tr Voronezh Stn Zashch Rast ... Trudy Voronezhskogo Stantsii Zashchity Rastenii [*A publication*]

Tr Voronezh Tekhnol Inst ... Trudy Voronezhskogo Tekhnologicheskogo Instituta [*A publication*]

Tr Voronezh Zoovet Inst ... Trudy Voronezhskogo Zooveterinarnogo Instituta [*A publication*]

Tr Voroshilovgr S-kh Inst ... Trudy Voroshilovgradskogo Sel'skokhozyaistvennogo Instituta [*A publication*]

Tr Vost Inst Ogneuporov ... Trudy Vostochnogo Instituta Ogneuporov [*USSR*] [*A publication*]

Tr Vost-Sib Fil Akad Nauk SSSR ... Trudy Vostochno-Sibirskogo Filiala Akademii Nauk SSSR [*A publication*]

Tr Vost Sib Geol Inst Akad Nauk SSSR Sib Otd ... Trudy Vostochno-Sibirskogo Geologicheskogo Instituta. Akademiya Nauk SSSR. Sibirskoe Otdelenie [*A publication*]

Tr Vost Sib Geol Upr ... Trudy Vostochno-Sibirskogo Geologicheskogo Upravleniya [*A publication*]

Tr Vost Sib Tekhnol Inst ... Trudy Vostochno-Sibirskogo Tekhnologicheskogo Instituta [*A publication*]

TRVSA .... Travail et Securite [*A publication*]

Tr Vseross Konf Khir Flebol ... Trudy Vserossiiskoi Konferentsii Khirurgov po Flebologii [*A publication*]

Tr Vseross Nauchno Issled Inst Sakh Svekly Sakhara ... Trudy Vserossiiskogo Nauchno-Issledovatel'skogo Instituta Sakharnoi Svekly i Sakhara [*A publication*]

Tr Vses Elektrotekh Inst ... Trudy Vsesoyuznogo Elektrotekhnicheskogo i Instituta [*A publication*]

Tr Vses Entomol Obshch ... Trudy Vsesoyuznogo Entomologicheskogo Obshchestva [*A publication*]

Tr Vses Entomol O-va ... Trudy Vsesoyuznogo Entomologicheskogo Obshchestva [*A publication*]

Tr Vses Geol Razved Obedin ... Trudy Vsesoyuznogo Geologo-Razvedochnogo Ob'edineniya [*A publication*]

Tr Vses Gidrobiol O-va ... Trudy Vsesoyuznogo Gidrobiologicheskogo Obshchestva [*A publication*]

Tr Vses Inst Eksp Vet ... Trudy Vsesoyuznogo Instituta Eksperimental'noi Veterinarii [*USSR*] [*A publication*]

Tr Vses Inst Gel'mintol ... Trudy Vsesoyuznogo Instituta Gel'mintologii [*A publication*]

Tr Vses Inst Rastenievod ... Trudy Vsesoyuznogo Instituta Rastenievodstva [*A publication*]

Tr Vses Inst Rast Prob Pop Vyssh Rast ... Trudy Vsesoyuznyi Institut Rastenievodstva Problema Populatsii u Vysshikh Rastenii [*A publication*]

Tr Vses Inst Zashch Rast ... Trudy Vsesoyuznogo Instituta Zashchity Rastenii [*A publication*]

Tr Vses Nauch-Isled Inst Zashch Rast ... Trudy Vsesoyuznogo Nauchno-Issledovatel'skogo Instituta Zashchity Rastenii [*A publication*]

Tr Vses Nauch-Issled Inst Lub Kul't ... Trudy Vsesoyuznyi Nauchno-Issledovatel'skii Institut Lubyanykh Kul'ture [*A publication*]

Tr Vses Nauch-Issled Inst Ptitsevod ... Trudy Vsesoyuznogo Nauchno-Issledovatel'skogo Instituta Ptitsevodstva [*A publication*]

Tr Vses Nauch-Issled Inst Zerna Prod Ego Pererab ... Trudy Vsesoyuznyi Nauchno-Issledovatel'skii Institut Zerna i Produktov Ego Pererabotki [*A publication*]

Tr Vses Nauch-Issled Inst Zhivotnovod ... Trudy Vsesoyuznyi Nauchno-Issledovatel'skii Institut Zhivotnovodstva [*A publication*]

Tr Vses Nauchn-Issled Inst Spirt Likero-Vodoch Prom ... Trudy Vsesoyuznogo Nauchno-Issledovatel'skogo Instituta Spirtovoi i Likero-Vodochnoi Promyshlennosti [*USSR*] [*A publication*]

Tr Vses Nauchno-Issled Galurgii ... Trudy Vsesoyuznogo Nauchno-Issledovatel'skogo Instituta Galurgii [*A publication*]

Tr Vses Nauchno-Issled Geol Inst ... Trudy Vsesoyuznogo Nauchno-Issledovatel'skogo Geologicheskogo Instituta [*A publication*]

Tr Vses Nauchno-Issled Geologorazved Neft Inst ... Trudy Vsesoyuznyi Nauchno-Issledovatel'skii Geologorazvedochnyi Neftyanoi Instituta [*A publication*]

Tr Vses Nauchno-Issled Inst Abrazivov Shlifovaniya ... Trudy Vsesoyuznyi Nauchno-Issledovatel'skii Institut Abrazivov i Shlifovaniya [*A publication*]

Tr Vses Nauchno-Issled Inst Antibiot ... Trudy Vsesoyuznogo Nauchno-Issledovatel'skogo Instituta Antibiotikov [*A publication*]

Tr Vses Nauchno-Issled Inst Aviats Mater ... Trudy Vsesoyuznogo Nauchno-Issledovatel'skogo Instituta Aviatsionnykh Materialov [*A publication*]

Tr Vses Nauchno-Issled Inst Burovoi Tekh ... Trudy Vsesoyuznyi Nauchno-Issledovatel'skii Instituta Burovoi Tekhniki [*A publication*]

Tr Vses Nauchno-Issled Inst Efirnomaslichn Kult ... Trudy Vsesoyuznogo Nauchno-Issledovatel'skogo Instituta Efirnomaslichnykh Kul'tur [*A publication*]

Tr Vses Nauchno-Issled Inst Elektromekh ... Trudy Vsesoyuznogo Nauchno-Issledovatel'skogo Instituta Elektromekhaniki [*A publication*]

Tr Vses Nauchno-Issled Inst Elektroterm Oborudovaniya ... Trudy Vsesoyuznogo Nauchno-Issledovatel'skogo Instituta Elektrotermicheskogo Oborudovaniya [*A publication*]

Tr Vses Nauchno-Issled Inst Fermentn Spirt Promsti ... Trudy Vsesoyuznyi Nauchno-Issledovatel'skii Institut Fermentnoi i Spirtovoi Promyshlennosti [*A publication*]

Tr Vses Nauchno-Issled Inst Fiziol Biokhim Pitan Skh Zhivotn ... Trudy Vsesoyuznogo Nauchno-Issledovatel'skogo Instituta Fiziologii, Biokhimii, i Pitaniya Sel'skokhozyaistvennykh Zhivotnykh [*A publication*]

Tr Vses Nauchno-Issled Inst Fiziol Biokhim Skh Zhivotn ... Trudy Vsesoyuznogo Nauchno-Issledovatel'skogo Instituta Fiziologii i Biokhimii Sel'skokhozyaistvennykh Zhivotnykh [*A publication*]

Tr Vses Nauchno-Issled Inst Galurgii ... Trudy Vsesoyuznogo Nauchno-Issledovatel'skogo Instituta Galurgii [*A publication*]

Tr Vses Nauchno-Issled Inst G Gidrotekh Melior ... Trudy Vsesoyuznogo Nauchno-Issledovatel'skogo Instituta Gidrotekhniki i Melioratsii [*A publication*]

Tr Vses Nauchno-Issled Inst Gidrotekh Melior ... Trudy Vsesoyuznogo Nauchno-Issledovatel'skogo Instituta Gidrotekhniki i Melioratsii [*A publication*]

Tr Vses Nauchno-Issled Inst Ikusstv Zhidk Topl Gaza ... Trudy Vsesoiuznogo Nauchno-Issledovatel'skogo Instituta Iskusstvennogo Zhidkogo Topliva i Gaza [*USSR*] [*A publication*]

Tr Vses Nauchno-Issled Inst Khim Pererab Gazov ... Trudy Vsesoyuznogo Nauchno-Issledovatel'skogo Instituta Khimicheskoi Pererabotki Gazov [*A publication*]

Tr Vses Nauchno-Issled Inst Khim Reakt ... Trudy Vsesoyuznogo Nauchno-Issledovatel'skogo Instituta Khimicheskikh Reaktivov [*A publication*]

Tr Vses Nauchno-Issled Inst Khlebopek Promsti ... Trudy Vsesoyuznyi Nauchno-Issledovatel'skii Institut Khlebopekarnoi Promyshlennosti [*A publication*]

Tr Vses Nauchno-Issled Inst Khlopkovod ... Trudy Vsesoyuznogo Nauchno-Issledovatel'skogo Instituta Khlopkovodstva [*A publication*]

Tr Vses Nauchno-Issled Inst Khlopkovod Nov Raionov ... Trudy Vsesoyuznogo Nauchno-Issledovatel'skii Institut Khlopkovodstva Novykh Raionov [*A publication*]

Tr Vses Nauchno-Issled Inst Konservn Ovoshchesush Prom-sti ... Trudy Vsesoyuznogo Nauchno-Issledovatel'skogo Instituta Konservnoi i Ovoshchesushyl'noi Promyshlennosti [*A publication*]

Tr Vses Nauchno-Issled Inst Korml S-Kh Zhivotn ... Trudy Vsesoyuznogo Nauchno-Issledovatel'skogo Instituta Kormleniya Sel'skokhozyaistvennykh Zhivotnykh [*A publication*]

Tr Vses Nauchno-Issled Inst L'na ... Trudy Vsesoyuznogo Nauchno-Issledovatel'skogo Instituta L'na [*A publication*]

Tr Vses Nauchno-Issled Inst Med Instrum Oborudovaniya ... Trudy Vsesoyuznogo Nauchno-Issledovatel'skogo Instituta Meditsinskikh Instrumentov Oborudovaniya [*A publication*]

Tr Vses Nauchno-Issled Inst Med Priborostr ... Trudy Vsesoyuznogo Nauchno-Issledovatel'skogo Instituta Meditsinskikh Priborostroenii [*A publication*]

Tr Vses Nauchno-Issled Inst Molochn Prom-St ... Trudy Vsesoyuznogo Nauchno-Issledovatel'skogo Instituta Molochnoi Promyshlennost [*A publication*]

Tr Vses Nauchno-Issled Inst Morsk Ryb Khoz Okeanogr ... Trudy Vsesoyuznogo Nauchno-Issledovatel'skogo Instituta Morskogo Rybnogo Khozyaistva i Okeanografii [*USSR*] [*A publication*]

Tr Vses Nauchno-Issled Inst Morsk Rybn Khoz Okeanogr ... Trudy Vsesoyuznogo Nauchno-Issledovatel'skogo Instituta Morskogo Rybnogo Khozyaistva i Okeanografii [*A publication*]

Tr Vses Nauchno-Issled Inst Myasn Prom-St ... Trudy Vsesoyuznogo Nauchno-Issledovatel'skogo Instituta Myasnoi Promyshlennost [*A publication*]

Tr Vses Nauchno-Issled Inst Pererab Ispol'z Topl ... Trudy Vsesoyuznogo Nauchno-Issledovatel'skogo Instituta Pererabotki i Ispol'zovaniya Topliva [*USSR*] [*A publication*]

Tr Vses Nauchno-Issled Inst Pererab Nefti ... Trudy Vsesoyuznyj Nauchno-Issledovatel'skij Institut po Pererabotke Nefti [*A publication*]

Tr Vses Nauchno-Issled Inst Pererab Slantsev ... Trudy Vsesoyuznogo Nauchno-Issledovatel'skogo Instituta po Pererabotke Slantsev [*USSR*] [*A publication*]

Tr Vses Nauchno-Issled Inst Podzemn Gazif Uglei ... Trudy Vsesoyuznyi Nauchno-Issledovatel'skii Institut Podzemnoi Gazifikatsii Uglei [*USSR*] [*A publication*]

Tr Vses Nauchno-Issled Inst Prir Gazov ... Trudy Vsesoyuznyi Nauchno-Issledovatel'skii Institut Prirodnykh Gazov [*USSR*] [*A publication*]

Tr Vses Nauchno-Issled Inst Prod Brozheniya ... Trudy Vsesoyuznyi Nauchno-Issledovatel'skii Institut Produktov Brozheniya [*USSR*] [*A publication*]

Tr Vses Nauchno-Issled Inst Prud Rybn Khoz ... Trudy Vsesoyuznogo Nauchno-Issledovatel'skogo Instituta Prudovogo Rybnogo Khozaistva [*A publication*]

Tr Vses Nauchno-Issled Inst Radiat Tekh ... Trudy Vsesoyuznyj Nauchno-Issledovatel'skij Institut Radiatsionnoj Tekhniki [*A publication*]

Tr Vses Nauchno-Issled Inst Spirt Prom-sti ... Trudy Vsesoyuznogo Nauchno-Issledovatel'skogo Instituta Spirtovoi Promyshlennosti [*USSR*] [*A publication*]

Tr Vses Nauchno-Issled Inst Stand Obraztsov Spektr Etalonov ... Trudy Vsesoyuznogo Nauchno-Issledovatel'skogo Instituta Standartnykh Obraztsov i Spektral'nykh Etalonov [*USSR*] [*A publication*]

Tr Vses Nauchno-Issled Inst Torf Prom-sti ... Trudy Vsesoyuznogo Nauchno-Issledovatel'skogo Instituta Torfyanoi Promyshlennosti [*USSR*] [*A publication*]

Tr Vses Nauchno-Issled Inst Udobr Agropochvoved ... Trudy Vsesoyuznogo Nauchno-Issledovatel'skogo Instituta Udobreniya i Agropochvovedeniya [*A publication*]

Tr Vses Nauchno-Issled Inst Vet Sanit ... Trudy Vsesoyuznogo Nauchno-Issledovatel'skogo Instituta Veterinarnoi Sanitarii [*A publication*]

Tr Vses Nauchno-Issled Inst Vet Sanit Ektoparazitol ... Trudy Vsesoyuznogo Nauchno-Issledovatel'skogo Instituta Veterinarnoi Sanitarii i Ektoparazitologii [*A publication*]

Tr Vses Nauchno-Issled Inst Yad Geofiz Geokhim ... Trudy Vsesoyuznyi Nauchno-Issledovatel'skii Institut Yadernoi Geofiziki i Geokhimii [*USSR*] [*A publication*]

Tr Vses Nauchno-Issled Inst Zashch Rast ... Trudy Vsesoyuznogo Nauchno-Issledovatel'skogo Instituta Zashchity Rastenii [*A publication*]

Tr Vses Nauchno-Issled Inst Zerna Prod Pererab ... Trudy Vsesoyuznogo Nauchno-Issledovatel'skogo Instituta Zerna i Produktov Ego Pererabotki [*A publication*]

Tr Vses Nauchno-Issled Inst Zheleznodorozhn Transp ... Trudy Vsesoyuznogo Nauchno-Issledovatel'skogo Instituta Zheleznodorozhnogo Transporta [*A publication*]

Tr Vses Nauchno-Issled Inst Zheleznodorzhn ... Trudy Vsesoyuznogo Nauchno-Issledovatel'skogo Instituta Zheleznodorozhnogo Transporta [*A publication*]

Tr Vses Nauchno-Issled Inst Zhivotn Syr'ya Pushn ... Trudy Vsesoyuznogo Nauchno-Issledovatel'skogo Instituta Zhivotnogo Syr'ya Pushniny [*A publication*]

Tr Vses Nauchno-Issled Inst Zolota Redk Met ... Trudy Vsesoyuznogo Nauchno-Issledovatel'skogo Instituta Zolota i Redkikh Metallov [*USSR*] [*A publication*]

Tr Vses Nauchno-Issled Konstr Inst Avtog Mashinostr ... Trudy Vsesoyuznogo Nauchno-Issledovatel'skogo i Konstruktorskogo Instituta Avtogennogo Mashinostroeniya [*USSR*] [*A publication*]

Tr Vses Neftegazov Nauchno-Issled Inst ... Trudy Vsesoyuznyi Neftegazovyi Nauchno-Issledovatel'skii Institut [*A publication*]

Tr Vses Neft Nauchno-Issled Geologorazved Inst ... Trudy Vsesoyuznogo Neftyanogo Nauchno-Issledovatel'skogo Geologorazvedochnogo Instituta [*USSR*] [*A publication*]

Tr Vses Neft Nauchno-Issled Inst Tekh Bezop ... Trudy Vsesoyuznyi Neftyanoi Nauchno-Issledovatel'skii Institut po Tekhnike Bezopasnosti [*A publication*]

Tr Vses O Genet Sel Kuban Otd ... Trudy Vsesoyuznoe Obshchestvo Genetikov i Selektsionerov. Kubanskoe Otdelenie [*A publication*]

Tr Vses O-va Fiziol Biokhim Farmakol ... Trudy Vsesoyuznogo Obshchestva Fiziologov Biokhimikov i Farmakologov [*A publication*]

Tr Vses S-kh Inst Zaochn Obraz ... Trudy Vsesoyuznogo Sel'skokhozyaistvennogo Instituta Zaochnogo Obrazovaniya [*A publication*]

Tr Vses Teplotekh Nauchno-Issled Inst ... Trudy Vsesoyuznyi Teplotekhnikii Nauchno-Issledovatel'skii Institut [*USSR*] [*A publication*]

Tr VTI .... Trudy VTI [*USSR*] [*A publication*]

TRVV .... Time Radius and Velocity Vector

Tr Vysokogorn Geofiz Inst ... Trudy Vysokogornyj Geofizicheskij Institut [*A publication*]

TRW .... Tactical Reconnaissance Wing [*Air Force*] (MCD)

TRW .... Tarawa [*Kiribati*] [*Airport symbol*] (OAG)

TRW .... Trail Riders of the Wilderness (EA)

TRW .... Trans Western Airlines of Utah [*Logan, UT*] [*FAA designator*] (FAAC)

TRW .... TRW, Inc. [*Formerly, Thompson Ramo Wooldridge, Inc.*] [*NYSE symbol*]

TRW .... United States Army TRADOC, Fort Leonard Wood Post Library, Fort Leonard Wood, MO [*OCLC symbol*] (OCLC)

TRWA .... Trackway

TRWC .... Threat Responsive Weapon Control [*Military*] (CAAL)

TRWG .... Tactical Reconnaissance Wing [*Air Force*]

TRWOA ..... Traffic World [*A publication*]

TRWOV ..... Transit Without Visa

TRX .... Trenton, MO [*Location identifier*] [*FAA*] (FAAL)

TRX .... Tri-State Resources Ltd. [*Vancouver Stock Exchange symbol*]

TRX .... Triplex

TRX .... Two-Region Physics Critical Experiment (NRCH)

TRX .... United States Army TRADOC, Ordnance and Chemical School Library, Aberdeen Proving Ground, MD [*OCLC symbol*] (OCLC)

TRY .... Teens for Retarded Youth [*Program in Fairfax County, Virginia*]

TRY .... Toronto Railway

TRY .... Tororo [*Uganda*] [*Airport symbol*] (OAG)

TRY .... Tri-Arc Energy Ltd. [*Vancouver Stock Exchange symbol*]

TRY .... Troy [*New York*] [*Seismograph station code, US Geological Survey*] (SEIS)

TRY .... Truly (ROG)

TRY .... United States Army TRADOC, TRADOC System Analysis [*TRASANA*], White Sands Range, NM [*OCLC symbol*] (OCLC)

Tr Yakutsk Fil Akad Nauk SSSR Ser Fiz ... Trudy Yakutskogo Filiala. Akademiya Nauk SSSR. Seriya Fizicheskaya [*A publication*]

Tr Yakutsk Fil Akad Nauk SSSR Ser Geol ... Trudy Yakutskogo Filiala Akademii Nauk SSSR. Seriya Geologicheskaya [*A publication*]

Tr Yakutsk Nauchno-Issled Inst Selsk Khoz ... Trudy Yakutskogo Nauchno-Issledovatel'skogo Instituta Sel'skogo Khozyaistva [*A publication*]

Tr Yakutsk Nauchno-Issled Inst Tuberk ... Trudy Yakutskogo Nauchno-Issledovatel'skii Instituta Tuberkuleza [*A publication*]

Tr Yakutsk Otd Sib Nauchno-Issled Inst Rybn Khoz ... Trudy Yakutskogo Otdeleniya Sibirskogo Nauchno-Issledovatel'skogo Instituta Rybnogo Khozyaistva [*A publication*]

Tr Yalt Nauchno-Issled Inst Fiz Metodov Lech Med Klimatol ... Trudy Yaltinskogo Nauchno-Issledovatel'nogo Instituta Fizicheskikh Metodov Lecheniya i Meditsinskoi Klimatologii [*A publication*]

Tr Yarosl Skh Inst ... Trudy Yaroslavskogo Sel'skokhozyaistvennogo Instituta [*A publication*]

Tryb Spold ... Trybuna Spoldzielcza [*A publication*]

TRZ .... Taradale [*New Zealand*] [*Seismograph station code, US Geological Survey*] (SEIS)

TRZ .... Thioridazine [*A drug*]

TRZ .... Tiruchirappalli [*India*] [*Airport symbol*] (OAG)

TrZ .... Trierer Zeitschrift [*A publication*]

TRZ .... United States Army Intelligence Center and School Library, Fort Huachuca, AZ [*OCLC symbol*] (OCLC)

Tr Zakavk Nauchno-Issled Gidrometeorol Inst ... Trudy Zakavkazskogo Nauchno-Issledovatel'skogo Gidrometeorologicheskogo Instituta [*A publication*]

TRZO .... Terrazzo [*Classified advertising*] (ADA)

Tr Zool Inst Akad Nauk SSSR ... Trudy Zoologicheskogo Instituta. Akademii Nauk SSSR [*A publication*]

TS .... Air Benin [*Benin*] [*ICAO designator*] (FAAC)

TS .... Iraq [*Later, BZ*] [*License plate code assigned to foreign diplomats in the US*]

Ts .... Skin Temperature [*Medicine*]

Ts .... T Suppressor [*Cell*] [*Immunology*]

TS .... Tailshaft Survey

TS .... Tangent to Spiral

TS .... Tank Steamer

TS .... Taoist Sanctuary [*Later, DS*] (EA)

TS .... Taper Shank [*Screw*]

TS .... Taper Sided

T/S .... Target Seeker

TS .... Target Strength

TS .... Task Statement (MCD)

TS .... Tasto Solo [*Bass without Accompaniment*] [*Music*]

TS .... Taylor-Schechter Collection. University Library [*Cambridge, England*] (BJA)

TS .... Teacher Survey

TS .... Teachers Section [*Library Education Division*] [*American Library Association*]

TS .... Team Supervisor (FAAC)

T and S .... Technical and Scientific Information [*United Nations Development Program*]

TS .... Technical Secretariat (NATG)

TS .... Technical Specification (MCD)

TS .... Technical Support (NASA)

TS .... Telecommunications System

TS .... Telegraph System (MSA)

TS .... Television, Sound Channel

TS .... Telophase Society [*Commercial firm*] [*San Diego, CA*] (EA)

T-S .... Temperature-Salinity [*Oceanography*]

TS .... Temperature Sensitive

TS .... Temperature Switch

TS .... Template Set-Up (MCD)

TS .... Temporal Stem [*Brain anatomy*]

TS .... Ten Silhouettes [*Psychological testing*]

TS .... Tennyson Society (EA)

TS .... Tensile Strength

TS .... Tensile Stress

TS .... Tentative Specification

TS .... Teratology Society (EA)

TS .... Terminal [*or Greater*] Sensation

TS .... Terminal Service

TS .... Terminal Strip (DEN)

TS .... Terminal Student (OICC)

TS .... Terra Santa [*Jerusalem*] [*A publication*] (BJA)

TS .... Test Items [*JETDS nomenclature*] [*Military*] (CET)

TS .... Test Set (KSC)

TS .... Test Site [*NASA*] (NASA)

TS .... Test Solution [*of a chemical*] [*Medicine*]

TS .... Test Specification (MSA)

T/S .... Test Stand (AAG)

T/S .... Test Station (MCD)

TS .... Test Stimulus

TS .... Test Summary

TS .... Textes Sogdiens. Edites. Traduits et Commentes [*A publication*] (BJA)

TS .... Texts and Studies [*Cambridge*] [*A publication*] (BJA)

TS .... Theater Survey [*A publication*]

TS .... Theatre Studies [*A publication*]

TS .... Theological Studies [*A publication*]

TS .... Theologische Studien [*Utrecht*] [*A publication*] (BJA)

TS .... Theosophical Society

TS .... Thermal Stethoscope [*Medical instrumentation*]

TS .... Thermal Synchrotron [*High-energy physics*]

TS .... Thermosetting [*Plastics technology*]

T/S............	Third Stage [*Aerospace*] (AAG)
TS..............	Thoracic Surgery [*Medicine*]
TS..............	Thoreau Society (EA)
TS..............	Threaded Stud
TS..............	Three Stooges Club (EA)
TS..............	Thunderstorm [*Meteorology*] (FAAC)
TS..............	Thymidylate Synthetase [*An enzyme*]
TS..............	Thymostimulin [*Endocrinology*]
T/S............	Thyroid:Serum [*Radioiodide ratio*]
TS..............	Tibet Society (EA)
TS..............	Tide Surveyor [*British*] (ROG)
TS..............	Tidewater Southern Railway Co. [*AAR code*]
TS..............	Till Sale
TS..............	Time Scheduled (NASA)
TS..............	Time Shack [*NAS operations desk*]
TS..............	Time Sharing [*Data processing*]
TS..............	Time Slot [*Telecommunications*] (TEL)
TS..............	Time Switch (MSA)
TS..............	Timing Selector
TS..............	Timing System (MCD)
TS..............	Tip Speed
TS..............	Tippers
TS..............	Today Show [*Television program*]
TS..............	Today's Speech [*A publication*]
TS..............	Tolkien Society (EA-IO)
TS..............	Toll Switching [*Trunk*] [*Telecommunications*] (TEL)
TS..............	Too Short [*Symbol stamped in shoes which are not actually of the size marked*]
TS..............	Tool Sharpness
TS..............	Tool Steel
TS..............	Tool Storage
TS..............	Tool Strength (ADA)
TS..............	Top Secret
TS..............	Torch Soldering
TS..............	Torpedo Station (MCD)
TS..............	Torstar Corp. [*Toronto Stock Exchange symbol*]
Ts...............	Tosyl [*Also, Tos*] [*Organic chemistry*]
TS..............	Total Solids [*Medicine*]
T and S.......	Touch and Stay
TS..............	Tough Situation [*Bowdlerized version*]
TS..............	Tough Stuff
TS..............	Tourette Syndrome [*Neurology*]
TS..............	Touring Sedan [*As in Olds 98 TS*]
TS..............	Tower Station
ts...............	Tracheosyringeal [*Neuroanatomy of birds*]
TS..............	Tracking Scope
TS..............	Tracking System (AAG)
TS..............	Trade Study (MCD)
TS..............	Trademark Society (EA)
TS..............	Traffic Superintendent [*British*]
TS..............	Training Ship
TS..............	Transaction Services (MCD)
TS..............	Transfer Set
TS..............	Transient Source
TS..............	Transient State (AAG)
TS..............	Transient Synovitis [*Medicine*]
TS..............	Transit Storage
TS..............	Transmission Set
TS..............	Transmittal Sheet [*Military*]
TS..............	Transmitted Shock
TS..............	Transmitter Station
TS..............	Transplantation Society [*Boston, MA*] (EA)
TS..............	Transport Service (ROG)
TS..............	Transport Ship (ROG)
TS..............	Transport and Supply
TS..............	Transsexual [*Medicine*]
T/S............	Transtage [*Upper stage for Titan III C rocket*]
TS..............	Transvaal Supreme Court Reports [*South Africa*] (DLA)
TS..............	Transverse Section [*Medicine*]
TS..............	Transverse System [*Cytology*]
TS..............	Travelling Showmen [*Public-performance tariff class*] [*British*]
TS..............	Treasury Solicitor [*British*]
TS..............	Treatment System [*Nuclear energy*] (NRCH)
TS..............	Tres Sage [*Wisest*] [*Presiding officer in the French rite*] [*Freemasonry*]
TS..............	Tricuspid Stenosis [*Cardiology*]
TS..............	Trinidad Sector [*World War II*]
TS..............	Triple Strength
TS..............	Troubleshoot (MCD)
ts...............	Trucial States [*United Arab Emirates*] [*MARC country of publication code*] [*Library of Congress*] (LCCP)
TS..............	Trust Secretary
TS..............	Tub-Sized [*Paper*]
TS..............	Tube Sheet (MSA)
TS..............	Tuberous Sclerosis [*Medicine*]
TS..............	Tubular [*Tracheal*] Sound
TS..............	Tumor Specific [*Medicine*]
TS..............	Tuning Stability
TS..............	Tunisia [*Aircraft nationality and registration mark*] (FAAC)
ts...............	Turboshaft Engine (IEEE)
T/S............	Turn-In Slip [*Military*]
TS..............	Turner Society (EA-IO)
TS..............	Tutto Solo [*All by Itself*] [*Music*]
TS..............	Twin Screw (ADA)
TS..............	Two-Stage Least Squares [*Statistics*]
T & S.........	Type and Screen
TS..............	Type Specification
TS..............	Typescript
TS..............	United States Treaty Series (DLA)
T²S............	Technology Transfer Society
TSA...........	Aloha Airlines [*Air carrier designation symbol*]
TSA...........	Tablettes Sumeriennes Archaiques [*A publication*] (BJA)
TSA...........	Taipei-Sung Shan [*Taiwan*] [*Airport symbol*] (OAG)
TSA...........	Tamworth Swine Association (EA)
TSA...........	Target Signature Analysis
TSA...........	Target System Alternatives (MCD)
TSA...........	Targhee Sheep Association (EA)
TSA...........	Tariff Schedules of the United States, Annotated
T & SA......	Task and Skill Analysis (AAG)
TSA...........	Tax-Sheltered Annuity
TSA...........	Teater SA. Quarterly for South African Theater [*A publication*]
TSA...........	Technical Supplemental Allowance [*Military*]
TSA...........	Technical Support Activity [*Army*] (RDA)
TSA...........	Technical Support Agent (MCD)
TSA...........	Tele-Systems Associates, Inc. [*Minneapolis, MN*] [*Telecommunications service*] (TSSD)
TSA...........	Telegraph System Analyzer
TSA...........	Test Site Activation [*NASA*] (KSC)
TSA...........	Test Start Approval [*NASA*] (NASA)
TSA...........	Test Support Agent (MCD)
TSA...........	Texas Shrimp Association [*Austin, TX*] (EA)
TSA...........	Textile Salesmen's Association [*New York, NY*] (EA)
TSA...........	Theater Service Area (MCD)
TS in A......	Theosophical Society in America (EA)
TSA...........	Time Series Analysis
TSA...........	Time-Shared Amplifier
TSA...........	Time Slot Access
TSA...........	Time Study Analysis
TSA...........	Tolkien Society of America
TSA...........	Toluenesulfonic Acid [*Organic chemistry*]
TSA...........	Tom Skinner Associates [*New York, NY*] (EA)
TSA...........	Tourette Syndrome Association [*Bayside, NY*] (EA)
TSA...........	Track Subsystem Analyst (MUGU)
TSA...........	Track Supply Association
TSA...........	Training Services Agency [*Department of Employment*] [*British*]
TSA...........	Training Situation Analysis [*Navy*]
TSA...........	Trans America Industries [*Vancouver Stock Exchange symbol*]
TSA...........	Trans Sierra Airline [*Cupertino, CA*] [*FAA designator*] (FAAC)
TSA...........	Transition State Analog
TSA...........	Transportation Service, Army
TSA...........	Transportation Standardization Agency [*DoD*]
TSA...........	Transportation Stores Assignment [*British*]
TSA...........	Tripoli Science Association (EA)
TSA...........	Troop Support Agency [*Army*] (AABC)
TSA...........	Troubleshooting Aid (MCD)
TSA...........	Trypticase Soy Agar [*Cell growth medium*]
TSA...........	Tube Support Assemblies (NRCH)
TSA...........	Tumor-Specific Antigens [*Immunology*]
TSA...........	Turkish Studies Association (EA)
TSA...........	Two-Step Antenna
TSA...........	Type-Specific Antibody [*Immunology*]
TSA...........	University of Texas, Health Science Center at San Antonio, San Antonio, TX [*OCLC symbol*] (OCLC)
TSAA.........	Tobacco Salesmen's Association of America (EA)
TSAA.........	Tuberous Sclerosis Association of America [*Also known as American Tuberous Sclerosis Association and Asociacion de Esclerosis Tuberosa de America*] [*Rockland, MA*] (EA)
TSaab........	Thyroid-Stimulating Autoantibody [*Endocrinology*]
TSAB.........	Theatre-Screen Advertising Bureau [*Defunct*]
TSAb.........	Thyroid-Stimulating Antibodies [*Endocrinology*]
TSABF........	Troop Support Agency Bagger Fund (MCD)
TSAC.........	Target Signature Analysis Center (MCD)
TSAC.........	Testing Accessories (AAG)
TSAC........	Time Slot Assignment Circuit [*Telecommunications*] (TEL)
TSAC.........	Title, Subtitle, and Caption
TSAC........	Topographic Scientific Advisory Committee [*Terminated, 1973*] [*Army*] (EGAO)
TSAC........	Tracking System Analytical Calibration
TSACA.......	Transactions. South African Institution of Civil Engineers [*A publication*]
TSAD.........	Test System Analysis Directorate [*Army*] (MCD)
TSAE.........	Training Support Activity - Europe (MCD)
TSAEA......	Transactions. South African Institute of Electrical Engineers [*A publication*]
TSAF.........	Transportation Service for the Army in the Field (MCD)
TSAF.........	Typical System Acquisition Flow
TSAFA.......	Traffic Safety [*A publication*]
TSAG........	Tracking System Analysis Group [*NASA*]
TSAG........	Trivalent Sodium Antimony Gluconate [*Pharmacology*]

TsAGI......... Tsentralyni Aero-Gidrodinamichescky Institute [*Institute of Aeronautical Research*] [*USSR*]
TSAK.......... Training Support Activity - Korea   (MCD)
TSAM......... [*The*] Skill Alignment Module [*Army*]   (INF)
TSAM........ Time Series Analysis and Modeling [*Software*]
TSAM........ Training Surface-to-Air Missile
TSamU....... Trudy Samarkandskogo Gosudarstvennogo Universiteta Imeni Alisera Navoi [*A publication*]
TSAP......... Time Series Analysis Package
TSAR......... Telemetry System Application Requirements
TSAR......... Throttleable Solid Augmented Rocket   (MCD)
TSAR......... Time Sows and Reaps [*Acronym used in name of Tsar Publishing Co.*]
TSAR......... Timed Scanned Array RADAR
TSAR......... Transmission Security Analysis Report   (AFM)
TSARC...... Test Schedule and Review Committee [*Army*]   (AABC)
TSARCOM ... Troop Support and Aviation Materiel Readiness Command [*Army*]
TSAT......... Tube-Slide Agglutination Test [*Clinical chemistry*]
TSAU......... Time Slot Access Unit [*Telecommunications*]   (TEL)
TSAZ......... Target Seeker-Azimuth
TSB............ [*The*] School Brigade [*Army*]   (INF)
TSB............ Technical Service Bulletin
TSB............ Temporary Stowage Bag   (KSC)
TSB............ Terminal Status Block [*Data processing*]   (IBMDP)
TSB............ Textiles Surveillance Body [*Textile trade agreement*]
TSB............ Theological Studies (Baltimore) [*A publication*]
TSB............ Thoreau Society Bulletin [*A publication*]
TSB............ Thrust Section Blower   (AAG)
TSb............ Tjurkologiceskij Sbornik [*A publication*]
TSB............ Towed SONAR Body
TSB............ Trade Show Bureau [*New Canaan, CT*]   (EA)
TSB............ Transportation Services Branch [*Air Force*]
TSB............ Trustee Savings Bank [*British*]
TSB............ Trypticase Soy Broth [*Cell growth medium*]
TSB............ Tsumeb [*Namibia*] [*Airport symbol*]   (OAG)
TSB............ Twin Sideband
TSB............ Two Complete Science Adventure Books [*A publication*]
TSBA......... Transactions of the Society of Biblical Archaeology [*London*] [*A publication*]   (BJA)
TSBD......... Tracking Servobridge Detector   (MCD)
TS-3 Bibliograf Informacija ... TS-3 Bibliografija Informacija [*A publication*]
TSBMD....... Tellus. Series B. Chemical and Physical Meteorology [*A publication*]
T S Booklet ... Thoreau Society Booklet [*A publication*]
TSBY......... Tuscola & Saginaw Bay Railway Co., Inc. [*AAR code*]
TSC............ Passed a Territorial Army Course in Staff Duties [*British*]
TSC............ Tactical Support Center
TSC............ Tanker Service Committee
TSC............ Tape Station Conversion   (CET)
TSC............ Target Selection Console   (MCD)
TSC............ Tarleton State College [*Later, TSU*] [*Texas*]
TSC............ Technical Subcommittee
TSC............ Technical Support Center   (NRCH)
TSC............ Teleconferencing Systems Canada Ltd. [*Etobicoke, ON*] [*Telecommunications service*]   (TSSD)
TSC............ Teledyne Systems Corporation
TSC............ Telephone Software Connection, Inc.
TSC............ TeleSciences, Inc. [*American Stock Exchange symbol*]
TSC............ Television Scan Converter
TSC............ Terminal Sterilization Chamber
TSC............ Terrestrial Science Center   (MCD)
TSC............ Test Acquisition Module Self Check   (CAAL)
TSC............ Test Set Computer
TSC............ Test Set Connection
TSC............ Test Setup Complete [*NASA*]   (NASA)
TSC............ Test Shipping Cask [*Nuclear energy*]   (NRCH)
TSC............ Test Steering Committee [*Military*]
TSC............ Test Support Controller [*NASA*]   (KSC)
TSC............ Texas Southmost College
TSC............ Thermal Stress Crack [*Plastics*]
TSC............ Thermal Surface Coating
TSC............ Thermally Stimulated Conductivity [*or Currents*]
TSC............ Thiosemicarbazide [*Organic chemistry*]
TSC............ Three-State Control [*Data processing*]
TSC............ Time Sharing Control Task [*Data processing*]   (BUR)
TSC............ Tonic Sol-Fa College [*London*]
TSC............ Top Secret Control   (MCD)
TSC............ Total System Control [*Architecture*]
TSC............ Total System Cost [*Aviation*]
TSC............ Totally Self-Checking
TSC............ Towson State University, Towson, MD [*OCLC symbol*]   (OCLC)
TSC............ Training Support Center [*Army*]   (MCD)
TSC............ Transit Switching Center [*Telecommunications*]   (TEL)
TSC............ Transmitter Start Code [*Bell System*]
TSC............ Transportation Systems Center [*Department of Transportation*]
TSC............ Troop Support Command [*Formerly, MECOM*] [*Army*]
TSC............ Tuscaloosa Oil & Gas [*Vancouver Stock Exchange symbol*]
TSCA......... Target Satellite Controlled Approach   (MUGU)
TSCA......... Textile Supplies and Credit Association   (EA)

TSCA......... Tool Subcontract Authorization   (AAG)
TSCA......... Top Secret Control Agency   (MCD)
TSCA......... Toxic Substances Control Act
TSCA......... Traditional Small Craft Association   (EA)
TSCAP...... Thermally Stimulated Capacitance [*Photovoltaic energy systems*]
TSCAPP..... Toxic Substances Control Act Plant and Production Data [*Environmental Protection Agency*] [*Database*]
TSCATS..... Toxic Substances Control Act Test Submissions [*Environmental Protection Agency*] [*Database*]
TSCC......... Telemetry Standards Coordination Committee
TSCC......... Test Support Control Center [*NASA*]   (KSC)
TSCC......... Top Secret Control Channels [*Military*]
TSCC......... TSC Corporation [*NASDAQ symbol*]   (NQ)
TSCD......... Test Specification and Criteria Document   (MCD)
TSCD......... Tool Specification Control Drawing   (MCD)
TSCDP....... Technical Service Career Development Program
TSCF......... Task Schedule Change Form   (NRCH)
TSCF......... Template Set-Up Check Fixture   (MCD)
TSCF......... Top Secret Cover Folder   (AAG)
TSCGD...... GRS [*Gesellschaft fuer Reaktorsicherheit*] Translations. Safety Codes and Guides [*A publication*]
Tschermaks Mineralog u Petrog Mitt ... Tschermaks Mineralogische und Petrographische Mitteilungen [*A publication*]
Tschermaks Mineral Petrogr Mitt ... Tschermaks Mineralogische und Petrographische Mitteilungen [*A publication*]
TSCHLT..... Test Support Center High-Level Terminal   (CAAL)
Tsch Min Pe ... Tschermaks Mineralogische und Petrographische Mitteilungen [*A publication*]
TSCI.......... Techscience Industries [*NASDAQ symbol*]   (NQ)
TSCIXS...... Tactical Support Center Information Exchange Subsystem
TSCLT........ Transportable Satellite Communications Link Terminal
TSCM........ Taylor Series Correction Method
TSCM........ Technical Surveillance Countermeasures [*Program*] [*Air Force*]
TSCM........ Test Station Configuration Model   (MCD)
TSCN......... Trainer Specification Change Notice   (MCD)
TSCO........ Test Support Coordination Office   (MCD)
TSCO........ Top Secret Control Officer [*Military*]
TSCOM...... TS Communications [*Springfield, IL*] [*Telecommunications*]   (TSSD)
TSCP......... Top Secret Control Proceeding [*Navy*]
TSCP......... Training Simulator Control Panel   (MCD)
TSCPAM..... Tentative Summary CPAM [*Military*]   (CAAL)
TSCRA...... Texas and Southwestern Cattle Raisers Association
TSCS......... Tactical Satellite Communications System [*Air Force*]   (CET)
TSCS......... Tactical Software Control Site [*Missile system evaluation*]   (RDA)
TSCS......... Tennessee Self-Concept Scale [*Psychology*]
TSCS......... Top Secret Control Section [*Navy*]
TSCT......... Transportable Satellite Communications Terminal
TSCVT....... TACSATCOM Single Channel Vehicular Terminal System   (MCD)
TSCVT....... Thomas Self-Concept Values Test [*Psychology*]
TSCW........ Top Secret Codeword   (MCD)
TSD............ Tactical Situation Display
TSD............ TARAN [*Tactical Attack RADAR and Navigation*] System Data
TSD............ Target Skin Distance
TSD............ Tay-Sachs Disease [*Medicine*]
TSD............ Technical Support Directorate
TSD............ Technical Support Document
TSD............ Temperature-Dependent Sex Determination
TSD............ Temperature-Salinity-Density-Depth [*Oceanography*]
TSD............ Tertiary of the Order of St. Dominic [*Roman Catholic religious order*]
TSD............ Test Start Date [*NASA*]   (NASA)
TSD............ Theater Shipping Document
TSD............ Theory of Signal Detection
TSD............ Thermionic Specific Detector [*Analytical instrumentation*]
TSD............ Time-Speed-Distance [*Driving skills*]
TSD............ Torque Screwdriver
TSD............ Total Spectral Density
TSD............ Track Situation Display
TSD............ Traffic Situation [*Status*] Display
TSD............ Transient Signal Detector
TSD............ Triple-Sequence Diffusion
TSD............ United States Army TRADOC, Fort Devens, USAISD, Fort Devens, MA [*OCLC symbol*]   (OCLC)
TSDA......... Theory of Signal Detection Analysis
TSDC......... Tennessee State Data Center [*Tennessee State Planning Office*] [*Nashville*] [*Information service*]   (EISS)
TSDC......... Thermally Stimulated Discharge Current [*Voltage-induced polarization*]
TSDD......... Temperature-Salinity-Density-Depth   (IEEE)
TSDF......... Target System Data File
TSDF......... Treatment, Storage, and Disposal Facility [*Hazardous waste*]
TSDI......... Tactical Situation Display Indicator
TSDK......... Torque Screwdriver Kit
TSDM........ Time-Shared Data Management [*System*] [*Data processing*]   (IEEE)
TS/DMS..... Time-Shared/Data Management System
TSDOS....... Time-Shared Disk Operating System [*Data processing*]   (IEEE)

T/SDPS...... Tube/Sea Differential Pressure Subsystem
TSDS......... Technological Services Delivery System [*UNIDO*]
TSDS......... Two-Speed Destroyer Sweeper [*Military*]
TSDU......... Target System Data Update
TSE .... Memphis, TN [*Location identifier*] [*FAA*]　(FAAL)
TSE .... Tactical Support Element　(AFM)
TSE .... Tactical Support Equipment　(MCD)
TSE .... Target State Estimator　(MCD)
TSE .... Target Support Element　(MCD)
TSE .... Technical Support Effort
TSE .... Tender Support Equipment
TSE .... Terminal Source Editor
TSE .... Test Scoring Equipment
TSE .... Test Set Electrical
TSE .... Test Support Equipment [*NASA*]
TSE .... Testicular Self-Examination
TSE .... Texas South-Eastern Railroad Co. [*AAR code*]
TSE .... Texas Studies in English [*A publication*]
TSE .... Tokyo Stock Exchange [*Japan*]
TSE .... Toronto Stock Exchange [*Toronto, ON*]
TSE .... Total Subsystem Evaluation
TSE .... Transmission Secondary Emission [*Physics*]
TSE .... Transportation Support Equipment　(NASA)
TSE .... Tulane Studies in English [*A publication*]
TSE .... Turboshaft Engine
TSEA......... Training Subsystem Effectiveness Analysis
TSEC......... Taft Sanitary Engineering Center
TSEC......... Telecommunications Security [*Army*]　(AABC)
TSEC......... Terminal Secondary RADAR Beacon [*Aviation*]　(FAAC)
TSEC......... Top Secret　(MCD)
TSEC......... Transierra Explorations Corporation [*NASDAQ symbol*]　(NQ)
TSED......... Training Simulators Engineering Department
TSEE......... Test Support Equipment Evaluation　(MCD)
TSEE......... Thermally Stimulated Exoelectron Emission [*Dosimetry*]
TSEG......... Tactical Satellite Communications Executive Steering Group
TSEG......... Toronto Stock Exchange - Gold
TSEI .... Toronto Stock Exchange - Industrials
TSEI .... Transportation Safety Equipment Institute　(EA)
Tselliul Bum Karton ... Tselliuloza, Bumaga, i Karton [*USSR*] [*A publication*]
TSEM .... Toronto Stock Exchange - Mines
TSEM .... Transmission Secondary Emission Multiplier [*Physics*]
Tsentr Nauchno-Issled Inst Olovyannoi Promsti Nauchny Tr ... Tsentral'nyi Nauchno-Issledovatel'skii Institut Olovyannoi Promyshlennosti. Nauchnye Trudy [*A publication*]
Tsentr Nauchno-Issled Inst Tekhnol Mashinostr Sb ... Tsentral'nyi Nauchno-Issledovatel'skii Institut Tekhnologii i Mashinostroeniya. Sbornik [*A publication*]
Tsentr Ref Med Zh Ser A ... Tsentral'nyi Referativnyi Meditsinskii Zhurnal. Seriya A. Biologiya, Teoreticheskie Problemy Meditsiny [*A publication*]
Tsentr Ref Med Zh Ser B ... Tsentral'nyi Referativnyi Meditsinskii Zhurnal. Seriya B. Vnutrennye Bolezni [*A publication*]
Tsentr Ref Med Zh Ser G ... Tsentral'nyi Referativnyi Meditsinskii Zhurnal. Seriya G. Mikrobiologiya, Gigiena, i Sanitariya [*A publication*]
Tsentr Ref Med Zh Ser V ... Tsentral'nyi Referativnyi Meditsinskii Zhurnal. Seriya V. Khirurgiya [*A publication*]
TSEO......... Toronto Stock Exchange - Oils
TSEQ......... Time Sequenced [*NASA*]　(KSC)
T & SER..... Tilbury & Southend Railway [*British*]　(ROG)
TSES.......... Technical Simulation and Evaluation System
TSES.......... Transportable Satellite Earth Station
TSESG....... Tactical Satellite Executive Steering Group
TSewU .... University of the South, Sewanee, TN [*Library symbol*] [*Library of Congress*]　(LCLS)
TSewU-T.... University of the South, School of Theology, Sewanee, TN [*Library symbol*] [*Library of Congress*]　(LCLS)
TSF............ Tab Sequence Format
TSF............ Tactical Strike Fighter　(MCD)
TSF............ Telephone Service Fitting
TSF............ Ten-Statement FORTRAN [*Data processing*]　(IEEE)
TSF............ Ten Story Fantasy [*A publication*]
TSF............ Terminal Sterilization Facility
TSF............ Tetraselenofulvalene [*Organic chemistry*]
TSF............ Textured Soy Flour
TSF............ Thai Support Foundation　(EA)
TSF............ Theological Student Fellowship. Bulletin [*A publication*]
TSF............ Theological Students Fellowship [*Madison, WI*]　(EA)
TSF............ Thermally Stable Fuel　(MCD)
TSF............ Thin Solid Films　(IEEE)
TSF............ Thrombopoietic Stimulating Factor [*Medicine*]
TSF............ Tower Shielding Facility
TSF............ Track Synthesis Frequency
TSF............ Transverse Shear Force
TSF............ Treasury Security Force [*Department of the Treasury*]
TSF............ Tri-State Flite Services, Inc. [*Dubuque, IA*] [*FAA designator*]　(FAAC)
TSF............ Triceps Skinfold [*Medicine*]
TSF............ Truncation Safety Factor [*In biological systems*]
TSF............ Two-Seater Fighter [*Air Force*] [*British*]
TSFA.......... Two-Step Formal Advertising　(MCD)

TSFC......... Tactical Support Functional Components　(NVT)
TSFC......... Thrust Specific Fuel Consumption
TSFC......... Tom Sneva Fan Club [*Port Hueneme, CA*]　(EA)
TSFET....... Theater Service Forces, European Theater [*World War II*]
TSFO......... Training Set, Fire Observation　(MCD)
TSFO......... Transportation Support Field Office [*Federal disaster planning*]
TSFR......... Transfer　(AFM)
TSFS......... Trunk Servicing Forecasting System [*Telecommunications*]　(TEL)
TSFSOILITU ... [*The*] Search for Signs of Intelligent Life in the Universe [*Lily Tomlin one-woman show written by Jane Wagner*]
TSFSR....... Transcaucasian Soviet Federation Socialist Republic
TSFTA....... Trudy Sibirskogo Fiziko-Tekhnicheskogo Instituta pri Tomskom Gosudarstvennom Universitete [*A publication*]
TSG........... [*The*] Stelle Group [*An association*] [*Quinlan, TX*]　(EA)
TSG........... [*The*] Surgeon General [*Army*]
TSG........... Tanacross, AK [*Location identifier*] [*FAA*]　(FAAL)
TSG........... Technical Specialty Group [*AIAA*]
TSG........... Technical Steering Group　(OICC)
TSG........... Technical Subgroup　(NATG)
TSG........... Technology Support Group
TSG........... Test Signal Generator
TSG........... Test and Switching Gear [*NASA*]　(KSC)
TSG........... Time Signal Generator
TSG........... Timeslot Generator [*Telecommunications*]　(TEL)
TSG........... Timing Systems Group [*NASA*]
TSG........... Tracking Signal Generator
TSG........... Transport Supplement Grant [*British*]
TSG........... Transversely Adjusted Gap　(IEEE)
TSG........... Tri-Service Group [*NATO*]
TSG........... Troubleshooting Guide　(MCD)
TSG........... Truebner's Simplified Grammars [*A publication*]
TSG........... United States Army TRADOC, Fort Gordon, United States Army Signal School and Fort Gordon, Fort Gordon, GA [*OCLC symbol*]　(OCLC)
TSGA......... Three-Conductor, Shipboard, General Use, Armor Cable
TSGAD...... Tri-Service Group on Air Defense [*NATO*]　(NATG)
TSGCEE.... Tri-Service Group on Communications and Electronic Equipment [*NATO*]　(NATG)
TSGF......... T-Suppressor-Cell Growth Factor [*Immunology*]
TSGMS ..... Test Set Guided Missile Set [*or System*]
TSGP......... Test Sequence Generator Program [*European Space Research and Technology Center*]　(NASA)
TSGR......... Thunderstorm with Hail [*Meteorology*]
TSGS......... Time Series Generation System
TSGT......... Technical Sergeant [*Military*]
TSGT(C) .... Technical Sergeant (Commissary) [*Marine Corps*]
TsGw........ Tydskrif vir Geesteswetenskappe [*A publication*]
TSH........... Temperature Switch, High [*Nuclear energy*]　(NRCH)
TSH........... Their Serene Highnesses
TSH........... Thermodynamic Suppression Head
TSH........... Thyroid-Stimulating Hormone [*Thyrotrophin*] [*Also, TTH*] [*Endocrinology*]
TSh........... Torah Shelemah [*A publication*]　(BJA)
TSH........... Tshikapa [*Zaire*] [*Airport symbol*]　(OAG)
TSHIRTS .... [*The*] International Society Handling the Interchange of Remarkable T-Shirts　(EA)
TSHWR ...... Thundershower [*Meteorology*]　(FAAC)
TSI............. Target Signature Investigation
TSI............. Technical Standardization Inspection
TSI............. Technology and Science of Informatics [*A publication*]
TSI............. Telebase Systems, Incorporated [*Narberth, PA*] [*Information service*]　(EISS)
TSI............. Test of Social Insight [*Psychology*]
TSI............. Test Support Instructions [*NASA*]　(KSC)
TSI............. Tests of Social Intelligence [*Psychology*]
TSI............. Theological School Inventory [*Psychology*]
TSI............. Threshold Signal-to-Interference Ratio　(IEEE)
TSI............. Thyroid-Stimulating Immunoglobulin [*Endocrinology*]
TSI............. Time-Significant Item　(MCD)
TSI............. Time Sterile Indicator
TSI............. Timeslot Interchange [*Telecommunications*]　(TEL)
TSI............. Tons per Square Inch　(MCD)
TSI............. Trans-Service Inc., Bala-Cynwyd PA [*STAC*]
TSI............. Transport Studies and Inquiries [*British*]
TSI............. Transportation Safety Institute [*Department of Transportation*]
TSI............. Triad Systems Integration Corp.
TSI............. Triple Sugar-Iron [*Agar*] [*Microbiology*]
tsi .... Tsimshian [*MARC language code*] [*Library of Congress*]　(LCCP)
TSI............. Turbo Sport Intercooler [*Automotive engineering*]
TSI............. Turkish Standards Institution
TSIA.......... Trading Stamp Institute of America　(EA)
TSIA.......... Triple Sugar-Iron Agar [*Microbiology*]
TSIAJ .... This Scherzo Is a Joke [*Used by American composer Charles Edward Ives*]
TSIC.......... Transducer Systems [*NASDAQ symbol*]　(NQ)
TSID .... Track Sector Identification
T/SIG .... Turn Signal [*Automotive engineering*]
TSIGA .... Trudy Sibirskogo Nauchno-Issledovatel'skogo Instituta Geologii, Geofiziki, i Mineral'nogo Syr'ya [*A publication*]

TSII	TSI, Incorporated [*NASDAQ symbol*] (NQ)
TSIL	Time-Significant Item List (AAG)
TSIM	(Trimethylsilyl)imidazole [*Also, TMSIM*] [*Organic chemistry*]
TSIMS	Telemetry Simulation Submodule
TSIN	Total Soluble Inorganic Nitrogen [*Analytical chemistry*]
TSIO	Time-Shared Input/Output [*Data processing*]
TSI-OH	Tube Sheet Inlet and Outlet Head (MSA)
TSIR	Total System Integration Responsibility
Tsirk Shemakh Astrofiz Obs	Tsirkulyar Shemakhinskoi Astrofizicheskoi Observatorii [*Azerbaidzhan SSR*] [*A publication*]
TSIS	Total Specifications Information System
TSIT	Technical Service Intelligence Team
TsIT	Tijdschrift voor Indische Taal-, Land-, en Volkenkunde [*A publication*]
TSITA	Tsitologiya [*A publication*]
Tsititiksiny Sovrem Med	Tsititiksiny e Sovremennoi Meditsine [*A publication*]
Tsitol	Tsitologiya [*A publication*]
Tsitol Genet	Tsitologiya i Genetika [*A publication*]
Tsitol Genet Akad Nauk Ukr SSR	Tsitologiya i Genetika Akademiya Nauk Ukrainsoi SSR [*A publication*]
Tsitologiya Genet	Tsitologiya i Genetika [*A publication*]
TSIU	Telephone System Interface Unit
TSJ	Tsushima [*Japan*] [*Airport symbol*] (OAG)
TSJC	Trinidad State Junior College [*Colorado*]
TSJSNW	Transactions. Samuel Johnson Society of the Northwest [*A publication*]
Ts Jur Foer Finland	Tidskrift Utgiven av Juridiska Foereningen i Finland [*A publication*]
TSK	Computer Task Group, Inc. [*NYSE symbol*]
TSK	Fort Hamilton Post Library, Morale Support Activities, Brooklyn, NY [*OCLC symbol*] (OCLC)
TSK	Theologische Studien und Kritiken [*A publication*]
TSK	Time Shift Keying
TSK	Torque Screwdriver Kit
TSK	Tsukuba - Telemeter [*Japan*] [*Seismograph station code, US Geological Survey*] (SEIS)
TSKT	Test Kit (AAG)
TSKTA	Toyo Shokuhin Kogyo Tanki Daigaku. Toyo Shokuhin Kenkyusho Kenkyu Hokokusho [*A publication*]
TSL	Chicago, IL [*Location identifier*] [*FAA*] (FAAL)
TSL	Tennessee Studies in Literature [*A publication*]
TSL	Test Set Logic
TSL	Test Source Library
TSL	Test Stand Level (AAG)
TSL	Test Support List (CAAL)
TSL	Texas Short Line Railway [*AAR code*]
TSL	Thin Shock Layer
TSL	Torsatron/Stellarator Laboratory [*University of Wisconsin - Madison*] [*Research center*] (RCD)
TSL	Total Service Life [*Telecommunications*] (TEL)
TSL	Travaux. Classe I de Linguistique, de Litterature, et de Philosophie. Societe des Sciences et des Lettres de Lodz [*A publication*]
TSL	Triservice LASER
TSL	Tristate Logic [*Electronics*]
TSL	Troop Safety Line
TSL	Troubleshooting Loop
TSL	Tsaile [*Navajo Community College*] [*Arizona*] [*Seismograph station code, US Geological Survey*] (SEIS)
TSL	Typesetting Lead (MSA)
TSL	United States Army TRADOC, Defense Language Institute, Presidio of Monterey, CA [*OCLC symbol*] (OCLC)
TSLCN	Texas State Library Communication Network [*Library network*]
TSLD	Troubleshooting Logic Diagram (NASA)
TSLI	Time Since Last Inspection (MCD)
Ts LJ	Tulsa Law Journal [*A publication*]
TSLL	Texas Studies in Literature and Language [*A publication*]
TSLS	Two-Stage Least Squares [*Statistics*]
TSM	Methodist Theological School in Ohio, Delaware, OH [*OCLC symbol*] (OCLC)
TSM	Tactical Survey Meter
TSM	Tail Service Mast [*NASA*] (KSC)
TSM	Target Signature Model
TSM	Target-to-Surface-to-Missile Path
TSM	Tentative Standard Method [*of analysis*]
TSM	Terminal Support Module
TSM	Tesoro Sacro-Musical [*A publication*]
TSM	Test Site Manager [*Army*]
TSM	Test Standards Module
TSM	Test Support Manager [*NASA*] (KSC)
TSM	Texte des Spaeten Mittelalters [*A publication*]
TSM	Time Scheduled Maintenance
TSM	Time-Shared Monitor System [*Data processing*] (IEEE)
TSM	Ton Statute Mile (AAG)
TSM	Total Suspended Matter [*Environmental science*]
TSM	Total System Management Concept (MCD)
TSM	Trade Study Management (NASA)
TSM	TRADOC System Manager [*Army*]
TSM	Training and Doctrine Command System Manager (MCD)
TSM	Training Site Manager (MCD)

TSM	Training System Manager (MCD)
TSM	Transportation Systems Management
TSM	Tri-State Motor Transit Co. of Delaware [*American Stock Exchange symbol*]
TSM	Type, Series, and Model (MCD)
TSM	Type-Specific M (Protein) [*Immunology*]
TSMC	Technical Supply Management Code
TSMC	Transportation Supply and Maintenance Command
TSMDA	Test-Section Melt-Down Accident [*Nuclear energy*] (NRCH)
TSMG	Thompson Submachine Gun
TSMNO	Transmitting Capability Out of Service (FAAC)
TSMO	TACSATCOM [*Tactical Satellite Communications*] Management Office
TSMO	TRADOC Systems Management Office [*Military*] (RDA)
TSMOK	Transmitting Capability Returned to Service (FAAC)
TSMT	Transmit
TSMTS	Tri-State Motor Tariff Service
TSN	[*The*] Sports Network [*Huntingdon Valley, PA*] [*Cable-television system*] [*Information service*] (EISS)
TSN	Tailshaft Renewed
TSN	Tan Son Nhut [*Air base*] [*Vietnam*]
TSN	Tape Serial Number [*Data processing*]
TSN	Tecsyn International, Inc. [*Toronto Stock Exchange symbol*]
TSN	Temporary Sort Number [*Data processing*]
TSN	Test Sequence Network (CAAL)
TSN	Thymosin [*A thymus hormone*]
TSN	Tianjin [*China*] [*Airport symbol*] (OAG)
TSN	Time since New [*Navy*] (NG)
TSN	Traffic Safety Now [*An association*] [*Detroit, MI*] (EA)
TSN	Trimethoprim, Sulfamethoxazole, Nystatin [*Antineoplastic drug regimen*]
TSN	Tsingtau [*Republic of China*] [*Seismograph station code, US Geological Survey*] (SEIS)
TSN	United States Army TRADOC, Fort Wadsworth, Chaplains Center Library, Fort Wadsworth, NY [*OCLC symbol*] (OCLC)
TsNAG	Tijdschrift van het Koninglijk Nederlandsch Aardrijkskundig Genootschap [*A publication*]
TSNGA	Trudy. Sredneaziatskii Nauchno-Issledovatel'skii Institut Geologii i Mineral'nogo Syr'ya [*A publication*]
TSNI	(Toluenesulfonyl)nitroimidazole [*Organic chemistry*]
TSNL Index Series	Texas System of Natural Laboratories. Index Series [*A publication*]
TSNT	(Toluenesulfonyl)nitrotriazole [*Organic chemistry*]
TSNT	Transient (FAAC)
TsNTL	Tijdschrift voor Nederlandsche Taal- en Letterkunde [*A publication*]
TSO	Carrollton, OH [*Location identifier*] [*FAA*] (FAAL)
TSo	Fayette County Free Library, Somerville, TN [*Library symbol*] [*Library of Congress*] (LCLS)
TSO	Isles Of Scilly-Tresco [*Airport symbol*] (OAG)
TSO	Table Structure Overview [*NASA*]
TSO	Tactical Surveillance Officer (MCD)
TSO	Technical Service Organization [*A generic term*]
TSO	Technical Specification Order
TSO	Technical Staff Officer
TSO	Technical Standard Order [*FAA*]
TSO	Technical Standing Order (KSC)
TSO	Technical Support Organization [*AEC*]
TSO	Telecommunications Service Order [*Telecommunications*] (TEL)
TSO	Telephone Service Observation [*Telecommunications*] (TEL)
TSO	Terminator Sensor Output
TSO	Tesoro Petroleum Corp. [*NYSE symbol*]
TSO	Test Site Office [*NASA*]
TSO	Test Support Operations [*NASA*] (KSC)
TSO	Thrust Section Observer (AAG)
TSO	Time since Overhaul [*of engine, or other equipment*]
TSO	Time-Sharing Option [*Data processing*]
TSO	Town Suboffice
TSO	Trans Southern Airways [*Florence, SC*] [*FAA designator*] (FAAC)
TSO	Transportation Supply Officer
TSO	Tulsa [*Oklahoma*] [*Seismograph station code, US Geological Survey*] [*Closed*] (SEIS)
TSOA	Technical Standard Order Authorization (MCD)
TSOA	Triumph Sports Owners Association (EA)
T Soc Rheol	Transactions. Society of Rheology [*A publication*]
TSODB	Time Series Oriented Database
TSOET	Tests of Elementary Training [*Military*] [*British*]
TSOL	True Sounds of Liberty [*Musical group*]
TSOP	[*The*] Sound of Philadelphia [*Song*]
TSOP	Tactical Standing Operating Procedure [*Military*]
TSOP	Technical Standard Operating Procedure [*NASA*] (KSC)
TSOR	Tentative Specific Operational Requirement
TSORT	Transmission System Optimum Relief Tool [*Telecommunications*] (TEL)
TSOS	Time-Sharing Operating System [*Data processing*] (IEEE)
TSOSC	Test Set Operational Signal Converter (AAG)
TSP	Teaspoonful (GPO)
TSP	Technical Specification

TSP	Technical Support Package [*NASA*]
TSP	Tehachapi, CA [*Location identifier*] [*FAA*] (FAAL)
TSP	Telemetry Simulation Program
TSP	Telephone Switching Planning (ADA)
TSP	Telesphere International, Inc. [*American Stock Exchange symbol*]
TSP	Temperature-Sensitive Period
TSP	Temporary Standard Practice [*or Procedure*] (AAG)
TSP	Test Site Position [*NASA*] (KSC)
TSP	Test Software Program [*NASA*] (NASA)
TSP	Test Status Panel (MCD)
TSP	Test Support Package
TSP	Test Support Position
TSP	Test Support Program
TSP	Tesuque Peak [*New Mexico*] [*Seismograph station code, US Geological Survey*] (SEIS)
TSP	Textured Soy Protein [*Food industry*]
TSP	Theta Sigma Phi [*Later, Women in Communications*]
TSP	Threat Support Plan (MCD)
TSP	Thrombospondin [*or Thrombin-Sensitive Protein*] [*Hematology*]
TSP	Thyroid-Stimulating Hormone of the Prepituitary Gland [*Endocrinology*]
TSP	Time Sorting Program
TSP	Time and Space Processing (MCD)
TSP	Toronto Sun Publishing Corp. [*Toronto Stock Exchange symbol*]
TSP	Torpedo Seaplane [*Navy*]
TSP	Torpedo Setting Panel [*Military*] (CAAL)
TSP	Total Serum Protein [*Medicine*]
TSP	Total Suspended Particulates
TSP	Total Systems Performance [*MODCOMP*]
TSP	Traffic Service Position [*Telephone*]
TSP	Trans Penn Airlines [*Reedsville, PA*] [*FAA designator*] (FAAC)
TSP	Transshipment Point (AFM)
TSP	Traveling Salesman Problem [*Mathematics*]
TSP	Traveling Scholar Program (EA)
TSP	Trial Shot Point
TSP	Tribal Sovereignty Program [*Later, SGFID*] (EA)
TSP	Trimethylsilyl Propionate [*Organic chemistry*]
TSP	Triple-Super Phosphates
TSP	Triservice Program [*Military*]
TSP	Trisodium Phosphate [*Inorganic chemistry*]
TSP	Tropical Spastic Paraparesis [*Neurology*]
TSP	Tube Support Plate [*Nuclear energy*] (NRCH)
TSP	Tulane Studies in Philosophy [*A publication*]
TSP	Twisted Shielded Pairs [*Cables*] (NASA)
TSP	United States Army TRADOC, Carlisle Barracks, Carlisle Barracks, PA [*OCLC symbol*] (OCLC)
TSPA	Triethylenethiophosphoramide [*Also, THioTEPA*] [*Antineoplastic drug*]
TSPAC	Transpacific (FAAC)
TSPAK	Time Series Package [*Bell System*]
TSPC	Thermal Sciences and Propulsion Center [*Purdue University*] [*Research center*] (RCD)
TSPC	Toxic Substances Priority Committee [*Washington, DC*] [*Environmental Protection Agency*] (EGAO)
TSPEC	Test Specification (MSA)
TSPED	Trade Shows and Professional Exhibits Directory [*Formerly, TPED*] [*A publication*]
TsPhil	Tijdschrift voor Philosophie [*A publication*]
TSPI	Time-Space-Position-Information (MCD)
TSPM	Total Suspended Particulate Matter
TSpMH	South Pittsburg Municipal Hospital, South Pittsburg, TN [*Library symbol*] [*Library of Congress*] (LCLS)
TSPP	Technetium Stannous Pyrophosphate [*Radiochemistry*]
TSPP	Tetrasodium Pyrophosphate [*Inorganic chemistry*]
TSPR	Total Systems Performance Reliability [*or Responsibility*] (MCD)
TSPR	Training System Program Requirements (MCD)
TSPS	Time-Sharing Programing System [*Data processing*] (IEEE)
TSPS	Traffic Service Position System [*Telecommunications*]
TSPSCAP ...	Traffic Service Position System Real-Time Capacity Program [*Telecommunications*] (TEL)
TSP-Z	Trisodium Phosphate - Zephiran [*Clinical chemistry*]
TSQ	Technical Services Quarterly [*A publication*]
TSQ	Time and Super Quick
TSQ	Trade Specialty Qualification (MCD)
TSQ	Triple Stage Quadrupole [*Instrumentation*]
TSQLS	Thundersqualls [*Meteorology*] (FAAC)
TSR	[*The*] Shopper Report [*A publication*]
TSR	Tactical SONAR Range (NVT)
TSR	Tactical Strike and Reconnaissance
TSR	Technical Sales Representative
TSR	Technical Services Representative (MCD)
TSR	Technical Status Review [*NASA*] (NASA)
TSR	Technical Study Report
TSR	Technical Summary Report
TSR	Telecommunications Service Request (CET)
TSR	Temporary Storage Register
TSR	Terminate and Stay Resident [*Data processing*]

TSR	Test Schedule Request
TSR	Test Status Report [*NASA*] (NASA)
TSR	Test Support Requirements (KSC)
TSR	Texas Star Airlines [*Ft. Worth, TX*] [*FAA designator*] (FAAC)
TSR	Thermal Shock Rig [*NRCH*]
TSR	Thermally Stable Resin
TSR	Tile-Shingle Roof [*Technical drawings*]
TSR	Time Sharing Resources, Inc. [*Information service*] (EISS)
TSR	Time Status Register
TSR	Time to Sustained Respirations [*Obstetrics*]
TSR	Timisoara [*Romania*] [*Airport symbol*] (OAG)
TSR	Tokyo Shoko Research Ltd. [*Database producer*] [*Japan*]
TSR	Torpedo-Spotter Reconnaissance [*Obsolete*] [*Military*] [*British*]
TSR	Total Shoulder Replacement [*Medicine*]
TSR	Total Stress Range (NRCH)
TSR	Total System Responsibility
TSR	Towed SONAR Response
TSR	Tower Shielding Reactor
TSR	Trade Study Report
TSR	Trans-Siberian Railway
TSR	Transistor Saturable Reactor
TSR	Transportable Surveillance RADAR (MCD)
TSR	Traveling Stock Reserve
TSR	Tri-Star Resources [*Toronto Stock Exchange symbol*] [*Vancouver Stock Exchange symbol*]
TSR	Tsuruga [*Japan*] [*Seismograph station code, US Geological Survey*] (SEIS)
TSR	Turbine Shaft Rate [*Military*] (CAAL)
TSR	United States Army TRADOC, Redstone Arsenal, USAMMCS [*United States Army Missile and Munitions Center School*] Technical Library, Redstone Arsenal, AL [*OCLC symbol*] (OCLC)
TSRA	Total System Requirements Analysis (NASA)
TSRA	Training Support Requirements Analysis (MCD)
TSRB	Top Salaries Review Board [*British*]
TSRC	Theta-Sensitive Regulatory Cell [*Hypothetical*] [*Hematology*]
TSRC	Tubular and Split Rivet Council [*Later, Tubular Rivet and Machine Institute*] (EA)
TSRE	Tropospheric Scatter Radio Equipment (AAG)
TS-3 Referativnyi Sb ...	TS-3 Referativnyi Sbornik [*A publication*]
TSRI	Technical Skill Reenlistment Incentive
TSRL	Total Support Requirements List (AAG)
TSRLD	TRRL [*Transport and Road Research Laboratory*] Supplementary Report [*A publication*]
TSRLL	Tulane Studies in Romance Languages and Literature [*A publication*]
TSRLM	Tandem Scanning Reflected Light Microscopy
TSRMP	Training System Resource Management Plan [*Army*]
TSRO	Two-Stage Reverse Osmosis [*Chemical engineering*]
TSRP	Technical Support Real Property
TSRP	Toll Service Results Plan [*Bell System*]
TSRS	Training Site Requirements Study [*DoD*]
TSRT	Teacher Situation Reaction Test
TSRTAMAA ...	Tactical Surveillance, Reconnaissance, and Target Acquisition Mission Area Analysis (MCD)
TSRU	Tuberculosis Surveillance Research Unit (EA-IO)
TSRV	Torpedo Ship Ranging Vessel [*Canadian Navy*]
TSRVA	Times Science Review [*A publication*]
TSS	New York [*New York*] E. 34th Street [*Airport symbol*] (OAG)
TSS	[*The*] Safety Society [*Reston, VA*] (EA)
TSS	St. Andrews School, St. Andrews, TN [*Library symbol*] [*Library of Congress*] (LCLS)
TSS	TACFIRE Software Specialist (MCD)
TSS	Tactical Strike System
TSS	Tangential Signal Sensitivity
TSS	Tape Search System
TSS	Target Selector Switch
TSS	Task-State Segment [*Operating system data structure*] [*Data processing*]
TSS	Technical Sales Seminars [*Department of Commerce*]
TSS	Technical Specification Sheet
TSS	Technical Support Services
TSS	Telecommunication Switching System
TSS	Teletype Switching System [*or Subsystem*]
TSS	Temporary Storage Site [*DoD*]
TSS	Tensile Shear Specimen [*Plastics technology*]
TSS	Terminal Security System [*Data processing*]
TSS	Terminal Send Side
TSS	Terminal Support System
TSS	Test Set Simulator
TSS	Thrust Stand System
TSS	Time-Sharing System [*Data processing*]
TSS	Toll Switching System [*Telecommunications*] (TEL)
TSS	Topographic Support System [*Army*] (RDA)
TSS	Toroidal Space Station
TSS	Toroidal Support Submarine
TSS	Total Subscriber Satisfaction [*HBO (Home Box Office) rating system*]
TSS	Total Suspended Solids [*Environmental chemistry*]
TSS	Toxic Shock Syndrome [*Medicine*]
TSS	Training Services [*Job Training and Partnership Act*] (OICC)

TSS .... Training Subsystem   (MCD)
TSS .... Transistor Servo Simulator
TSS .... Transmission Surveillance System [Bell System]
TSS .... Transparent Semiconductor Shutter
TSS .... Tropospheric Scatter System
TSS .... Trunk Servicing System [Bell System]
TSS .... Tsurugisan [Anabuki] [Japan] [Seismograph station code, US
               Geological Survey]   (SEIS)
TSS .... Tug Structural Support [NASA]   (NASA)
TSS .... Turbine Steam Ship
TSS .... Twin-Screw Steamer [Nautical]
TSS .... Typographic Support System   (MCD)
TSS .... United States Army TRADOC, Fort Story, Fort Story, VA
               [OCLC symbol]   (OCLC)
TSSA......... Telemetry Subcarrier Spectrum Analyzer
TSSA......... Test Scorer and Statistical Analyzer [Data processing]
TSSA......... Test Site Support Activity [NASA]
TSSA......... Thunderstorm with Sandstorm [Meteorology]
TSSA......... Trade Show Services Association [Cerritos, CA]   (EA)
TSSA......... Transport Salaried Staff's Association [A union] [British]
TSSAA ...... Tackle and Shooting Sports Agents Association [Arlington
               Heights, IL]   (EA)
TSSC......... Target Selection and Seeking Console
TSSC......... Target System Service Charge   (NG)
TSSC......... Toxic Substances Strategy Committee [Nuclear
               energy]   (NRCH)
TSS-C .... Transmission Surveillance System - Cable
               [Telecommunications]   (TEL)
TS & SCP ... Task, Schedule, and Status Control Plan   (AAG)
TSSCS ...... Tactical Synchronous Satellite Communication System
TSSD......... Telecommunications Systems and Services Directory [A
               publication]
TSSDT .... Thrust Subsystem Design Team [NASA]
TSSE......... Tactical Security Support Equipment [Military]
TSSE......... Toxic Shock Syndrome Exotoxin
TSSI.......... Telephone Support Systems [NASDAQ symbol]   (NQ)
TSSIC........ Tool and Stainless Steel Industry Committee   (EA)
TSSM .... Thruster Subsystem Module [NASA]
TSSM .... Total Ship Simulation Model
TSSNM....... Technologist Section of the Society of Nuclear Medicine [New
               York, NY]   (EA)
TSSP......... Tactical Satellite Signal Processor   (RDA)
TSSPS....... Tsentralniya Suvet na Profesionalnite Suyuzi [Central Council
               of Trade Unions] [Bulgaria]
TSSSP....... Tennessee Study of State Science Policy [National Science
               Foundation]   (EA)
TSSST....... Time-Space-Space-Space-Time [Telecommunications]   (TEL)
TSST......... Toxic Shock Syndrome Toxin [Medicine]
TSSU......... Test Signal Switching Unit   (MCD)
TsSV .... Tijdschrift voor de Studie van de Verlichting [A publication]
TST .... [The] Science Teacher [A publication]
TST .... Tail Stop and Turning [Automotive engineering]
TST .... Telemetry Simulation Terminal
TST .... Television Signal Tracer   (DEN)
TST .... Temperature Sensing Transducer
TST .... Test   (AAG)
TST .... Test Support Table
TST .... Textile Science and Technology [Elsevier Book Series] [A
               publication]
TSt .... Texts and Studies [A publication]   (BJA)
TST .... Thermistor Sterilization Test
TST .... Threshold Setting Tracer
TST .... Time-Sharing Terminals, Inc.
TST .... Time-Space-Time [Digital switching]
               [Telecommunications]   (TEL)
TST .... Total Surface Tested
TST .... Toxic Shock Toxin [Biochemistry]
TST .... Trang [Thailand] [Airport symbol]   (OAG)
TST .... Transaction Step Task
TST .... Transition State Theory [Physical chemistry]
TST .... Transmission Scheme Translator   (MCD)
TST .... Transmission System Test   (MCD)
TST .... Treadmill Stress Testing [Physiology]
TST .... Triceps Skinfold Thickness [Medicine]
TST .... Trilogy Screening Technique
TST .... Twenty Statements Test
TST .... United States Army TRALINET, Systems Center, ATPL-AOT,
               Fort Monroe, VA [OCLC symbol]   (OCLC)
TSTA......... Transmission, Signaling, and Test Access
TSTA......... Tritium Systems Test Assembly   (MCD)
TSTA......... Tumor-Specific Transplantation Antigen [Immunology]
TSTC......... Target Selection and Tracking Console
TSTD......... Total Ship Test Director [Navy]   (CAAL)
TSTE......... Training System Test and Evaluation   (MCD)
TSTEQ ...... Test Equipment
TSTFLT..... Test Set Fault   (AAG)
TSTG......... Testing   (MSA)
TSTIA........ Trudy Sibirskogo Tekhnologicheskogo Instituta [A publication]
TsTK .... Tidsskrift for Teologi og Kirke [Oslo] [A publication]
TSTKA .... Tsuchi To Kiso [A publication]
TStL & KC ... Toledo, St. Louis & Kansas City Railroad

TSTM .... Thunderstorm [Meteorology]   (FAAC)
TSTO......... Test Site Tool Order [NASA]   (AAG)
TSTO......... Testing Tool   (AAG)
TSTP .... Test of Selected Topics in Physics
TSTP .... Thermistor Sterilization Test Program
TSTP .... Total Ship Test Program [Navy]   (CAAL)
TSTP .... Traffic Safety Training Program
TSTPAC..... Transmission and Signaling Test Plan and Analysis Concept
               [Telecommunications]   (TEL)
TSTP/AFS ... Total Ship Test Program/Active Fleet Surface Ships
               [Navy]   (CAAL)
TSTPI .... Tapered Steel Transmission Pole Institute [Chicago, IL]   (EA)
TSTP/SP.... Total Ship Test Program/Ship Production [Navy]   (CAAL)
TSTR......... Tester   (MSA)
TSTR......... Transistor   (AAG)
TSTRC....... Telstar Corporation [NASDAQ symbol]   (NQ)
TSTRZ....... Transistorized   (MSA)
TSTS......... Tail Section Test Stand   (AAG)
TSTS......... Third Stage Test Set [Aerospace]   (MCD)
TSTS......... Thrust Structure Test Stand   (AAG)
TSTS......... Tracking System Test Set   (AAG)
TSU .... Tabiteuea South [Kiribati] [Airport symbol]   (OAG)
TSU .... Tandem Signal Unit [Telecommunications]   (TEL)
TSU .... Tape Search Unit   (CET)
TSU .... Tarleton State University [Formerly, TSC] [Texas]
TSU .... Technical Service Unit
TSU .... Telecommunications Study Unit [American Topical
               Association] [Milwaukee, WI] [Telecommunications]
               [Information service] [An association]   (EA)
TSU .... Telephone Signal Unit [Telecommunications]   (TEL)
TSU .... Telescope Sight Unit   (MCD)
TSU .... Tennessee State University, Nashville, TN [Library symbol]
               [Library of Congress] [OCLC symbol]   (LCLS)
TSU .... Test Signal Unit [Telecommunications]   (TEL)
TSU .... Texas Southern University
TSU .... Thermal Systems Unit   (KSC)
TSU .... This Side Up
TSU .... Time Standard Unit
TSU .... Trans-Species Unlimited [An association] [State College,
               PA]   (EA)
TSU .... Transfer Switch Unit   (AAG)
TSU .... Transportation System Utilization Program [Department of
               Energy]
TSU .... Triple Sugar-Urea Base [Agar] [Microbiology]
TSU .... Tsu [Japan] [Seismograph station code, US Geological
               Survey]   (SEIS)
TSU .... Tsumeb [South-West Africa] [Geomagnetic observatory code]
TSU .... Tulsa-Sapulpa Union Railway Co. [AAR code]
Tsukuba-Daigaku Shakaigaku J ... Tsukuba-Daigaku Shakaigaku Journal [A
               publication]
Tsukuba J Math ... Tsukuba Journal of Mathematics [A publication]
Tsukuba Univ Inst Geosci Annu Rep ... Tsukuba University. Institute of
               Geoscience. Annual Report [A publication]
Tsukumo Earth Sci ... Tsukumo Earth Science [A publication]
TSUS......... Tariff Schedules of the United States
TSUSA ...... Tariff Schedules of the United States, Annotated
TSV .... Taste and Smell in Vertebrates
TSV .... Terminal Stage Vehicle
TSV .... Thru-Sight Video [Army training device]   (INF)
TSV .... Townsville [Australia] [Airport symbol]   (OAG)
TSV .... Turbine Stop Valves [Nuclear energy]   (NRCH)
TSV .... Twin Springs [Nevada] [Seismograph station code, US
               Geological Survey] [Closed]   (SEIS)
Tsvet Metal ... Tsvetnye Metally [A publication]
Tsvetn Met ... Tsvetnye Metally [A publication]
Tsvetn Metall ... Tsvetnaya Metallurgiya [A publication]
Tsvetn Metall Nauchno Tekh Sb ... Tsvetnaya Metallurgiya-Nauchno-
               Tekhnicheskii Sbornik [A publication]
Tsvetn Metall (Ordzhonikidze, USSR) ... Tsvetnaya Metallurgiya
               (Ordzhonikidze, USSR) [A publication]
TSVP......... Tournez s'il Vous Plait [Please Turn Over] [See also PTO]
               [French]
TSVR......... Total Systemic Vascular Resistance
TSVS......... Time Sharing - Virtual System [Data processing]   (MCD)
Tsvtn Metall Nauchno Tekh Byull ... Tsvetnaya Metallurgiya-Nauchno-
               Tekhnicheskii Byulleten [A publication]
TsVUB....... Tijdschrift van de Vrige Universiteit van Brussel [A publication]
TsVV .... Tydskrif vir Volkskunde en Volkstaal [A publication]
TSW .... Prace Wroclawskiego Towarzystwa Naukowego [A publication]
TSW .... Southwestern Baptist Theological Seminary, Fort Worth, TX
               [OCLC symbol]   (OCLC)
TSW .... Technical Scope of Work
TSW .... Temperature Switch   (MSA)
TSW .... Test Software   (MCD)
TSW .... Test Switch
TSW .... Time Switch [Telecommunications]   (TEL)
TSW .... Transfer Switch
TSW .... Transmitting Slide Wire
TSW .... Trau, Schau, Wem [Trust, but Be Careful Whom] [German]
               [Motto of Christian I, Elector of Saxony (1560-91)]
TSW .... Tropical Summer Winter [Vessel load line mark]

tsw .... Tswana [*MARC language code*] [*Library of Congress*] (LCCP)
TSW .... Turbine-Building Service Water [*Nuclear energy*] (NRCH)
TSWE .... Test of Standard Written English
TsWK .... Tydskrif vir Wetenskap en Kuns [*A publication*]
TSWTT .... Test Switch Thrust Termination
TSX .... Telephone Satellite, Experimental
TSX .... Time-Sharing Executive [*Modular Computer Systems*] [*Data processing*]
TSX .... True Seed Exchange [*Later, SSE*] (EA)
TSY .... Tech-Sym Corp. [*American Stock Exchange symbol*]
TSYS .... Total System Services [*NASDAQ symbol*] (NQ)
TSZGK .... Thueringisch-Saechsische Zeitschrift fuer Geschichte und Kunst [*A publication*]
TT .... Chad [*Aircraft nationality and registration mark*] (FAAC)
TT .... Taal en Tongval [*Antwerpen*] [*A publication*]
TT .... TABA [*Transportes Aereos da Bacia Amazonica SA*] [*Brazil*] [*ICAO designator*] (FAAC)
TT .... Tablet Triturate [*Pharmacy*]
TT .... Tactile Tension [*Ophthalmology*]
TT .... Taiga Times '71 [*A publication*]
TT .... Tail-to-Tail [*Polymer structure*]
TT .... Talar Tilt [*Angle of ankle joint*]
TT .... Talith and Tefillin (BJA)
TT .... Talmud Torah (BJA)
TT .... Tanganyika Territory
TT .... Tank Truck [*Freight*]
T & T .... Tanqueray [*Gin*] and Tonic
TT .... Target Towing Aircraft [*Navy*]
TT .... Teacher Training
TT .... Technical Test
TT .... Technical Training (OICC)
TT .... Technical Translation [*A publication*] [*Obsolete*]
TT .... Teetotaler [*Slang*]
TT .... Telegraphic Transfer [*of funds*] [*Banking*]
TT .... Teletype
TT .... Teletypewriter [*Telecommunications*]
TT .... Teletypewriter and Facsimile Apparatus [*JETDS nomenclature*] [*Military*] (CET)
TT .... Tell Taanach (BJA)
TT .... Tempelurkunden aus Tello [*A publication*] (BJA)
TT .... Temperature Transmitter [*Nuclear energy*] (NRCH)
TT .... Temporarily Transferred [*Telecommunications*] (TEL)
TT .... Tendon Transfer [*Surgery*]
TT .... Teologisk Tidsskrift [*A publication*]
T/T .... Terminal Timing (KSC)
tt .... Terminus Technicus (BJA)
TT .... Test Temperature (NRCH)
TT .... Testamentary Trust [*Legal term*]
TT .... Tetanus Toxoid [*Medicine*]
TT .... Tetrathionate [*Nutrient broth*] [*Microbiology*]
TT .... Theologisch Tijdschrift [*A publication*]
TT .... Theology Today [*A publication*]
TT .... Thermal-Tow
TT .... Thermometric Titrimetry
TT .... Thrombin Time [*Hematology*]
TT .... Thrust Termination
TT .... Thymol Turbidity [*Clinical chemistry*]
TT .... Tibial Tubercle [*Anatomy*]
TT .... Ticarcillin and Tobramycin [*Antibacterial mixture*]
TT .... Tidningarnas Telegrambyra [*Press agency*] [*Sweden*]
TT .... Tight Torso [*Women's fashions*]
TT .... Tile Threshold (MSA)
TT .... Tilt Trailers
T & T .... Time and Temperature
T & T .... Time and Tide [*A publication*]
TT .... Time and Tide [*A publication*]
TT .... Timetable
T/T .... Timing and Telemetry
Tt .... Titus [*New Testament book*] (BJA)
TT .... Tobacco Tax Ruling Term (DLA)
TT .... [*The*] Toledo Terminal Railroad Co. [*AAR code*]
TT .... Tooling Template (MCD)
T & T .... Tools and Tillage [*A publication*]
TT .... Torpedo Tube
TT .... Total Task Chaining [*Psychology*]
TT .... Total Temperature (MCD)
TT .... Total Thyroxine [*Endocrinology*]
TT .... Total Time (MSA)
TT .... Totus Tuus [*All Yours*] [*Latin*]
TT .... Tourist Trophy [*Motorcycle racing*] [*British*]
TT .... Townsend Thoreson [*Company running English Channel ferries*]
TT .... Tracking Telescope
TT .... Traffic Tester [*Telecommunications*] (TEL)
TT .... Training Text
TT .... Trans-Texas Airways
TT .... Transaction Terminal (BUR)
TT .... Transit Time [*of blood through heart and lungs*]
TT .... Transonic Tunnel [*NASA*]
TT .... TransTechnology Corp. [*American Stock Exchange symbol*]

TT .... Transthoracic [*Medicine*]
T/T .... Travel/Tourism
TT .... Travel and Tourism Program [*Association of Independent Colleges and Schools specialization code*]
TT .... Tree Test [*Psychology*]
TT .... Tree Tops
TT .... Trees for Tomorrow [*An association*] (EA)
TT .... Tributary Team [*Military*]
TT .... Tricycle and Tail Skid [*Aerospace*] (AAG)
T/T .... Trienoic/Tetraenoic [*Ratio of unsaturated chemicals*]
TT .... Trigesimo-Secundo [*Book from 10 to 12-1/2 centimeters in height*] [*Bibliography*]
TT .... Trinidad and Tobago [*Two-letter standard code*] (CNC)
TT .... Trinity Term
TT .... Troop Test
TT .... Trust Termination
TT .... Trust Territory of the Pacific Islands [*Postal code*]
tt .... Trust Territory of the Pacific Islands [*MARC country of publication code*] [*Library of Congress*] (LCCP)
TT .... Tuberculin Tested [*Milk*]
TT .... Turbine Tanker
TT .... Turbine Trip (IEEE)
TT .... Turntable (ADA)
TT₃ .... Total Triiodothyronine [*Endocrinology*]
TT₄ .... Total Thyroxine [*Endocrinology*]
TT's .... Tripoli Trots [*Term used by entertainers in World War II*]
TTA .... Tan Tan [*Morocco*] [*Airport symbol*]
TTA .... Tatalina [*Alaska*] [*Seismograph station code, US Geological Survey*] (SEIS)
TTA .... Telecommunications and Telephone Association [*Arlington, VA*] [*Telecommunications service*] (TSSD)
TTA .... Test Target Array (AFM)
TTA .... Theatre Television Authority (EA)
TTA .... Thenoyltrifluoroacetone [*Also, TTB*] [*Organic chemistry*]
TTA .... Thermomechanical Test Area [*NASA*] (NASA)
TTA .... Thrust Termination Assembly
TTA .... Time to Apogee (MCD)
TTA .... Tolyltriazole [*Organic chemistry*]
TTA .... Total Tangible Assets [*Business and trade*] (ADA)
TTA .... Total Titratable Acidity [*Analytical chemistry*]
TTA .... Trade and Tourism Alliance (EA)
TTA .... Traffic Trunk Administration [*Telecommunications*] (TEL)
T & TA .... Training and Technical Assistance (OICC)
TTA .... Trans-Texas Airways
TTA .... Transit Time Accelerometer
TTA .... Transtracheal Aspiration [*Medicine*]
TTA .... Travel Time Authorized
TTA .... Travel and Tourism Association (EA)
TTA .... Triplet-Triplet Annihilation [*Spectroscopy*]
TTA .... Tritolylamine [*Organic chemistry*]
TTA .... Turbine-Alternator Assembly (MCD)
TTAB .... Trademark Trial and Appeal Board [*of Patent Office*]
TTAE .... Turk Tarih. Arkeologya ve Etnografya Dergisi [*A publication*]
TTAF .... Technical Training Air Force
TTagPI .... Trudy Taganrogskogo Gosudarstvennogo Pedagogiceskogo Instituta [*A publication*]
TTAP .... Telemetry Technical Analysis Position (MCD)
TTAPS .... [*R. P.*] Turco, [*O. B.*] Toon, [*T. P.*] Ackerman, [*J. B.*] Pollack, and [*Carl*] Sagan [*Authors of a paper on the biological and climatological effects of nuclear war*]
TTAT .... TACFIRE Training Assistance Team (MCD)
TTAT .... Torpedo Tube Acceptance Trials [*Navy*] (NG)
TTAV .... TTAV [*Technical Teachers Association of Victoria*] News [*A publication*]
TTB .... Tanker, Transport, Bomber [*Requirements*] [*Air Force*]
TTB .... Target Triggered Burst
TTB .... Tatuoca [*Brazil*] [*Geomagnetic observatory code*]
TTB .... Teletypewriter Buffer (CET)
TTB .... Tetragonal Tungsten Bronze
TTB .... Time to Blackout
TTB .... Toll Testboard [*Telecommunications*] (TEL)
TTB .... Trifluoro(thienyl)butanedione [*Also, TTA*] [*Organic chemistry*]
TTb .... Trudy Tbilisskogo Pedagogiceskogo Instituta [*A publication*]
TTBB .... First Tenor, Second Tenor, First Bass, and Second Bass [*in all-men choral groups*]
TTBT .... Threshold Test Ban Treaty [*1974*]
TTBWR ...... Twisted Tape Boiling Water Reactor (IEEE)
TTC .... Tape to Card
TTC .... Target Track Central
TTC .... Target Tracking Console (MCD)
TTC .... Tatung [*Republic of China*] [*Seismograph station code, US Geological Survey*] (SEIS)
TTC .... Technical Training Center [*Air Force*]
TTC .... Technical Training Command [*Army Air Forces*] [*World War II*]
TTC .... Telecommunication Training Centre [*Suva, Fiji*] [*Telecommunications*] (TSSD)
TTC .... Telephone Terminal Cables (KSC)
TTC .... Teletypewriter Center [*Military*]
TTC .... Temperature Test Chamber
TTC .... Tender to Contract Policy [*Export Credits Guarantee Department*] [*British*]

TTC	Terminating Toll Center (DEN)	TTF	Transistor Test Fixture
TTC	Test Transfer Cask [*Nuclear energy*] (NRCH)	TTF	Trend Type Forecasts (ADA)
TTC	Tight Tape Contact	TTF	Two/Ten Foundation [*Formerly, TTNF*] [*Watertown, MA*] (EA)
TTC	Time to Circularize (MCD)	TTFA	Thallium Trifluoroacetate [*Organic chemistry*]
TTC	Time to Control	TTFB	Tetrachlorotrifluoromethylbenzimidazole [*Organic chemistry*]
TTC	Tin Telluride Crystal	TTFC	Tactical and Technical Fire Control (MCD)
TTC	Tobacco Tax Council (EA)	TTFD	Thiamine Tetrahydrofurfuryl Disulfide [*Pharmacology*]
TTC	Tobramycin, Ticarcillin, and Cephalothin	TTFN	Ta Ta for Now
TTC	Toro Company [*NYSE symbol*]	TTF & T	Technology Transfer, Fabrication, and Test (RDA)
TTC	Tow Target Cable	TTFT	Tetra(trifluoromethyl)thiophene [*Organic chemistry*]
TTC	Tracking, Telemetry, and Command	TTF-TCNQ ...	Tetrathiafulvene-Tetracyanoquinodimethane [*Organic chemistry*]
TT & C	Tracking, Telemetry, and Command		
TT & C	Tracking, Telemetry, and Control (MCD)	TTFTT	Terminal Tax Filing Time Trauma
TTC	Tracking, Telemetry, and Control [*NASA*] (NASA)	TTFW	Too Tacky for Words [*Slang*]
TTC	Training Technology Centers [*Army*]	TTG	General Trustco of Canada [*Toronto Stock Exchange symbol*]
TTC	Transient Temperature Control	TTG	Gibson General Hospital, Trenton, TN [*Library symbol*] [*Library of Congress*] (LCLS)
TTC	Translation Thrust Control		
TTC	Transportation Test Center [*Department of Transportation*]	TTG	Technical Translation Group (IEEE)
TTC	Treasure Trove Club (EA)	TTG	Test Target Generator
TTC	Triphenyltetrazolium Chloride [*Also, RT, TPTZ*] [*Chemical indicator*]	TTG	Time to Go [*Air Force*]
		TTG	Titograd [*Yugoslavia*] [*Seismograph station code, US Geological Survey*] (SEIS)
TTC	Tropic Test Center [*Army*] (MCD)	TTG	Tobacco Tax Guide [*Internal Revenue Service*]
TTC	Tube Temperature Control	TTG	Travel with Troops Going
TTC	Tunnel Thermal Control (NASA)	TTGA	Tellurite-Taurocholate-Gelatin Agar [*Microbiology*]
TTCA	Thiothiazolidinecarboxylic Acid [*Organic chemistry*]	TTGAC	Travel and Tourism Government Affairs Council [*Washington, DC*] (EA)
T/TCA	Thrust/Translation Control Assembly [*NASA*] (KSC)		
TTCC	[*The*] Technical Cooperation Committee [*Army*] (AABC)	TTGD	Time-to-Go Dial
TTCE	Tooth-to-Tooth Composite Error	TTH	Thyrotrophic Hormone [*Also, TSH*] [*Endocrinology*]
TTCI	Transient Temperature Control Instrument	TTh	Tijdschrift voor Theologie [*Wageningen*] [*A publication*]
TTC & M	Telemetry, Tracking, Command, and Monitoring	TTHA	Triethylenetetraminehexaacetic Acid [*Organic chemistry*]
TTCMA	Turk Tip Cemiyeti Mecmuasi [*A publication*]	TTHE	Thermal Transient Histogram Equivalent (NRCH)
TTCMSC ...	Tonga and Tin Can Mail Study Circle (EA)	TTHM	Total Trihalomethane [*Analytical chemistry*]
TTCO	Toledo Trustcorp [*NASDAQ symbol*] (NQ)	T Th Z	Trierer Theologische Zeitschrift [*A publication*]
TTCP	[*The*] Technical Cooperation Program [*US, UK, Canada, Australia*] [*Research*]	TTI	Tactical Target Illustration (AFM)
		TTI	[*The*] Teachers, Incorporated (EA)
TTCP	Tripartite Technical Cooperation Program [*Military*] (NG)	TTI	Technical Tape, Incorporated [*American Stock Exchange symbol*]
TTCS	Target Tracking and Control System (MCD)	TTI	Technology Transfer Institute [*Santa Monica, CA*] [*Telecommunications*] (TSSD)
TTCS	Toy Train Collectors Society (EA)		
TTCS	Truck Transportable Communications Station	TTI	Teletype Test Instruction (KSC)
TTCU	Teletypewriter Control Unit (AABC)	TTI	Texas Transportation Institute [*Texas A & M University*] [*Research center*]
TTCV	Tracking, Telemetry, Command, and Voice		
TTD	Tank Training Devices (MCD)	TTI	TIE/Telecommunications Canada Ltd. [*Toronto Stock Exchange symbol*]
TTD	Teachers Training Diploma		
TTD	Technical Test Director	TTI	Time to Intercept [*Missiles*] (NG)
TTD	Technical Training Detachment	TTI	Time-Temperature Index
TTD	Temporary Text Delay	TTI	Time Temperature Indicator (IEEE)
TTD	Temporary Travel Document (NATG)	TTI	Training-Testing Intervals
TTD	Tetraethylthiuram Disulfide [*Also, TETD*] [*Organic chemistry*]	TTI	Transthoracic Impedance [*Medicine*]
TTD	Textile Technology Digest [*A publication*]	TTI	Traveling Ticket Inspector
TTD	Things to Do	TTI	Tuck Tummy In [*Slang*]
TTD	Totals to Date (MCD)	TTI	Tulane Tax Institute [*A publication*]
TTD	Transponder Transmitter Detector	TTI	Turner Teleport, Incorporated [*Atlanta, GA*] [*Telecommunications service*] (TSSD)
TTD	Transportation Technical Data [*Army*]		
TTD	Troutdale, OR [*Location identifier*] [*FAA*] (FAAL)	TTIA	Tube Temperature Indication and Alarm
TTDI	Teacher Training in Developing Institutions	TTIC	Test Technology Information Center (MCD)
TTDR	Tracking Telemetry Data Receiver (AAG)	TTIC	Tropical Timber Information Center [*College of Environmental Science and Forestry at Syracuse*] [*Research center*] (RCD)
TTDT	Tactical Test Data Translator (MUGU)		
TTE	Talks to Teachers of English [*A publication*]		
TTE	Technical Training Engineer	TTIF	Training Taxpayer Information File [*IRS*]
TTE	Technical Training Equipment (MCD)	TTIIA	Trudy Tashkentskogo Instituta Inzhenerov Irrigatsii i Mekhanizatsii Sel'skogo Khozyaistva [*A publication*]
TTE	Telephone Terminal Equipment		
TTE	Temporary Test Equipment (AAG)	T Times	These Times [*A publication*]
TTE	Tentative Tables of Equipment	TTIPS	Ticker Tape Information Processing System [*Online stock information service*]
TTE	Ternate [*Indonesia*] [*Airport symbol*] (OAG)		
TTE	Thermal Transient Equipment (NRCH)	TTITS	Thrust Termination Initiator Test Set
TTE	Time to Event [*NASA*] (KSC)	TTJ	Tottori [*Japan*] [*Airport symbol*] (OAG)
T & TE	Tool and Test Equipment (AFIT)	TTK	Turk Tarih Kurumu [*A publication*]
TTE	Total Transportation Expenditure [*Department of Transportation*]	TTK	Two-Tone Keying
		TTK "Belleten" ...	Turk Tarih Kurumu "Belleten" [*A publication*]
TTE	Trailer Test Equipment (AAG)	TTKi	Tidsskrift for Teologi og Kirke [*Oslo*] [*A publication*]
TTE	Trigon Tech, Inc. [*Vancouver Stock Exchange symbol*]	TTKMA	Trudy Tambovskogo Instituta Khimicheskogo Mashinostroeniya [*A publication*]
TTEC	Teletypewriter Technician		
TTEC	Thoratec Laboratories [*NASDAQ symbol*] (NQ)	TTKSA	Tokyo-Toritsu Kogyo Shoreikan Hokoku [*A publication*]
T & TEC	Trinidad & Tobago Electricity Commission	TTL	Tatalina [*Alaska*] [*Seismograph station code, US Geological Survey*] [*Closed*] (SEIS)
TTEES	Trustees		
TTEGDA	Tetraethylene Glycol Diacrylate [*Organic chemistry*]	TTL	Teletype Telling
TTEKA	Tokyo Toritsu Eisei Kenkyusho Kenkyu Hokoku [*A publication*]	TTL	Texas Tech University, School of Law Library, Lubbock, TX [*OCLC symbol*] (OCLC)
TTEL	Tool and Test Equipment List [*NASA*] (NASA)		
TTele	Tatar Tele Hem Adebijaty [*A publication*]	TTL	Theological Translation Library [*A publication*]
TTEM	Tooling Test Equipment Team (AAG)	TTL	Through the Lens [*Trademark of Spiratone, Inc.*]
TTEP	Training and Training Equipment (MCD)	TTL	Title [*Online database field identifier*] [*Data processing*]
TTET	Turbine Transport Evaluation Team [*FAA*] (MUGU)	TTL	To Take Leave
TTF	Tactical Task Force (AFM)	TTL	Torotel, Inc. [*American Stock Exchange symbol*]
TTF	Tanker Task Force (AFM)	TTL	Torrent Resources Limited [*Vancouver Stock Exchange symbol*]
TTF	Test to Failure (NATG)		
TTF	Tetrathiofulvalene [*Organic chemistry*]	TTL	Total Time to Launch [*NASA*] (KSC)
TTF	Time to Failure	TTL	TRADOC Troop List (MCD)
TTF	Time to Fire [*Military*] (CAAL)	TTL	Trail Termination Line (MCD)
TTF	Tone Telegraph Filter	TTL	Transistor-Transistor Logic [*Also, T²L*]
TTF	Training Task Force		
TTF	Transient Time Flowmeter (NRCH)		

TTL............ Tribal Trust Land [*Zimbabwe*]
TTL............ Tribothermoluminescence
TTL............ Turtle Island [*Fiji*] [*Airport symbol*] (OAG)
TTL............ Twin Trapezoidal Links [*Mazda*] [*Automotive engineering*]
TTLC .... Total Threshold Limit Concentration [*Environmental chemistry*]
TTLM........ Through-the-Lens Light Metering (MCD)
TTLM........ Through-the-Lens Metering
TTLR .... Tanganyika Territory Law Reports [*1921-47*] (DLA)
TTLS .... Team Training Launch Station (AAG)
TTL-S .... Transistor-Transistor Logic - Schottky
TTM.......... Tactical Target Materials
TTM.......... Tactical Telemetry
TTM.......... Temperature Test Model
T/TM .... Test and Training Monitor (AAG)
TTM.......... Thermal Test Model
TTM.......... Transit Time Modulation (DEN)
TTM.......... Turtle Mountains [*California*] [*Seismograph station code, US Geological Survey*] (SEIS)
TTM.......... Two-Tone Modulation
TTMA .... Truck Trailer Manufacturers Association [*Alexandria, VA*] (EA)
TTMA .... Tufted Textile Manufacturers Association [*Later, CRI*] (EA)
TTMC .... Tactical Target Materials Catalogue (MCD)
T/TMC ..... Traffic/Traffic Management and Control [*British*]
TTMCFC ... Theater Type Mobilization Corps Force Capabilities
TTMCFO ... Theater Type Mobilization Corps Force Objective
TTMF........ Touch-Tone Multifrequency (CET)
TTMM .... Tergotrochanteral Muscle Motoneuron [*Zoology*]
TTMM .... True Tape Motion Monitor
TTMP .... Tactical Targets Materials Program (AFM)
TTMP .... Transit Time Magnetic Pumping
TTMS .... Telephoto Transmission Measuring Set
TTMTA ..... Tungsram Technische Mitteilungen [*A publication*]
TTN .... Taitung [*Taito*] [*Republic of China*] [*Seismograph station code, US Geological Survey*] (SEIS)
TT/N .... Test Tone to Noise Ratio [*Telecommunications*] (TEL)
TTN .... [*The*] Titan Corp. [*NYSE symbol*]
TTN .... Transient Tachypnea of Newborn [*Gynecology*]
TTN .... Trenton [*New Jersey*] [*Airport symbol*] (OAG)
TTN .... Trenton, NJ [*Location identifier*] [*FAA*] (FAAL)
TTN .... Trevecca Nazarene College, Nashville, TN [*OCLC symbol*] (OCLC)
TTN .... Tumor Site, T-Stage, N-Stage [*Oncology*]
TTNA........ Trinidad and Tobago National Alliance (PPW)
TTNF .... Two/Ten National Foundation [*Later, TTF*] (EA)
TTNG........ Tightening (MSA)
TTNP .... Tactical Telephone Numbering Plan (MCD)
TTNPB....... ((Tetrahydrotetramethylnaphthalenyl)propenyl)benzoic Acid [*Antineoplastic drug*]
TTNS......... TOW Thermal Night Sight [*Night vision device*] [*Army*] (RDA)
TTO .... Telecommunications Technical Officer [*British*]
TTO .... To Take Out [*Medicine*]
TTO .... Total Toxic Organics [*Environmental chemistry*]
TTO .... Traffic Trunk Order [*Telecommunications*] (TEL)
TTO .... Transit Tracers in the Ocean [*Oceanography*]
TTO .... Transmitter Turn-Off
TTO .... Travel and Transportation Order
TTO .... Trinidad and Tobago [*Three-letter standard code*] (CNC)
T Today..... Theology Today [*A publication*]
TTomU .... Trudy Tomskogo Gosudarstvennogo Universiteta [*A publication*]
TTOS.......... Toy Train Operating Society (EA)
TTP........... Tactical Targeting Program (AFM)
TTP........... Tamarind Technical Papers [*A publication*]
TTP........... Tape-to-Print
T & TP ...... Terry and the Pirates [*Pop music group*]
TTP........... Tetilla Peak [*New Mexico*] [*Seismograph station code, US Geological Survey*] (SEIS)
TTP........... Thermistor Test Program
TTP........... Thrombotic Thrombocytopenic Purpura [*Medicine*]
TTP........... Thymidine Triphosphate [*Biochemistry*]
TTP........... Time to Perigee (MCD)
TTP........... Total Taxable Pay
TTP........... Total Temperature Probe (MCD)
TT & P .... Training, Transient and Patient
TTP........... Transverse Thrust Propeller
TTP........... Trudy Tallinskogo Politekhnicheskogo Instituta. Seriya B, XX [*A publication*]
TTP........... Tu-Tahl Petroleum, Inc. [*Vancouver Stock Exchange symbol*]
TTP........... Turn toward Peace [*Later, WWWC*] [*An association*] (EA)
TTPC .... Titanium Toroidal Propellant Container
TTPE .... Total Taxable Pay Earned
TTPES .... Torpedo Tube Pump Ejection System [*Navy*] (CAAL)
TTPFC .... Terry and the Pirates Fan Club (EA)
TTPG........ (Thenoylthio)propionylglycine [*Biochemistry*]
TTPH .... Team Trainer, Pearl Harbor
TTPI.......... Trudy Tbilisskogo Gosudarstvennogo Pedagogiceskogo Instituta [*A publication*]
TTPI.......... Trust Territory of the Pacific Islands
TTQ .... Murphy, NC [*Location identifier*] [*FAA*] (FAAL)
TTQ .... Tuebinger Theologische Quartalschrift [*A publication*]

TTQAP .... Teletherapy Treatment Quality Assurance Program [*Nuclear energy*] (NRCH)
TTQS.......... Tuebinger Theologische Quartalschrift. Stuttgart [*A publication*]
TTR .... Tab-Tronic Recorder (DIT)
TTR .... Tactical Technical Requirements (RDA)
TTR .... Tana Toraja [*Indonesia*] [*Airport symbol*] (OAG)
TTR .... Tape-Reading Tripping Relay
TTR .... Target Track [*or Tracking*] RADAR [*Air Force*]
TTR .... Target Tracking Receiver [*Military*] (CAAL)
TTR .... Tarl Town Reports [*New South Wales*] (DLA)
TTR .... Teletypewriter Translator (CET)
TTR .... Thermal Test Reactor (AAG)
TTR .... Thermal Timing Relay
TTR .... Thermal Transpiration Ratio
TTR .... Thermotolerance Ratio [*Roentgenology*]
TTR .... Tijuana & Tecate Railway Co. [*AAR code*]
TTR .... Time to Repair [*Military*] (CAAL)
TTR .... Time-Temperature Recorder
TTR .... Tonopah Test Range
TTR .... Toshiba Training Reactor [*Japan*] (NRCH)
TTR .... Transient Thermal Radiation
TTR .... Travel with Troops Returning
TTR .... Trust Territory Reports of Pacific Island (DLA)
TTR .... Type-Token Ratio [*Education of the hearing-impaired*]
TTRA .... Tetra Systems, Inc. [*NASDAQ symbol*] (NQ)
TTrA .... Textes et Traitement Automatique [*A publication*]
TTRA........ Travel and Tourism Research Association [*Formed by a merger of Eastern Council for Travel Research and Western Council for Travel Research*] [*Salt Lake City, UT*] (EA)
TTRB .... Timken Tapered Roller Bearing
TTRC .... Transistorized Thyratron Ring Counter
TTRIF .... Trident Resources [*NASDAQ symbol*] (NQ)
TTRSA ...... Twisted Telephone Radio, Shielded, Armored
TTS .... TACFIRE Training System (MCD)
TTS .... Tactical Test Set (MCD)
TTS .... Tank Thermal Site
TTS .... Target Trajectory Sensor
TTS .... Tarleton State University, Dick Smith Library, Stephenville, TX [*OCLC symbol*] (OCLC)
TTS .... Technical Training Squadron (MCD)
TTS .... Tele-Tech Services [*Franklin, NJ*] [*Information service*] [*Telecommunications*] (TSSD)
TTS .... Telecommunications Terminal Systems
TTS .... Telemetry Transmission System
TTS .... Teletype Switching Facilities (FAAC)
TTS .... Teletypesetter
TTS .... Teletypewriter System
TTS .... Temperature Test Set
TTS .... Temporary Threshold Shift
TTS .... Terminal Testing Section [*Social Security Administration*]
TTS .... Terrain Trend System (MCD)
TTS .... Test and Training Satellite [*Also, TATS, TETR*] [*NASA*]
TTS .... Thanks to Scandinavia (EA)
TTS .... [*The*] Theban Tombs Series [*London*] [*A publication*] (BJA)
TTS .... Thermal Transfer Standard
TTS .... Thule Tracking Station (MCD)
TTS .... Thurstone Temperament Schedule [*Psychology*]
TTS .... Tintina Mines Ltd. [*Toronto Stock Exchange symbol*] [*Vancouver Stock Exchange symbol*]
TTS .... Tissue Type Specific [*Antigen*]
TTS .... Tracker Test Set [*Dragon*] (MCD)
TTS .... Transactions. Thoroton Society [*A publication*]
TTS .... Transdermal Therapeutic System [*Medicine*]
TTS .... Transducer Tubing System
TTS .... Transistor-Transistor Logic Schottky Barrier (IEEE)
TTS .... Transmission Test Set (IEEE)
TTS .... Transponder Test Set
TTS .... Transportable Telemetry Set
TTS .... True to Scale
TTS .... Tsaratanana [*Madagascar*] [*Airport symbol*] (OAG)
TTSA .... Tactical Traffic and System Analysis (MCD)
TTSA .... Transition Training Squadron, Atlantic [*Navy*]
TTSC .... TSC, Inc. of California [*NASDAQ symbol*] (NQ)
TTSD .... Telephone Tracking System Directory (MCD)
TTSF .... Test and Timesharing Facility [*Social Security Administration*]
TTSP .... Training Test Support Package [*Army*]
TTSP .... Transition Training Squadron, Pacific [*Navy*]
TTSPB........ Transport Theory and Statistical Physics [*A publication*]
TTSPN ...... Two Terminal Series Parallel Networks
TTSS......... [*The*] Trumpeter Swan Society (EA)
TTSt .... Trierer Theologische Studien [*Trier*] [*A publication*] (BJA)
TTSU .... Tracker Test Set Supplemental Unit (MCD)
TTT .... Tactical Training Team [*Military*] (CAAL)
TTT.......... Taitung [*Taiwan*] [*Airport symbol*] (OAG)
TTT.......... Tallulah, LA [*Location identifier*] [*FAA*] (FAAL)
TTT.......... Tatiko-Tekhnicheskye-Trebovaniya [*Tactical Technical Requirement*] [*for military materiel*] [*USSR*] (RDA)
TTT............ Tetrathiotetracene [*Organic chemistry*]
TTT............ Texas College, Tyler, TX [*OCLC symbol*] (OCLC)
TTT............ Teylers Theologisch Tijdschrift [*A publication*]

TTT............. Thymol Turbidity Test [*Clinical chemistry*]
TTT............. Time to Target (AAG)
TTT............. Time Temperature Transformation
TTT............. Time, Temperature, Turbulence [*Fuel technology*]
TTT............. Time to Turn [*Ship or aircraft*]
TTT............. Tolbutamide Tolerance Test [*Clinical chemistry*]
TTT............. Trade Token Topics [*A publication*]
TTT............. Training of Teacher Trainers
TTT............. Transamerican Trailer Transport
TTT............. Trilateral Tracking Technique
TTT............. Trinidad & Tobago Television Co.
TTT............. True Temperature Tunnel
TTTA......... Teletypewriter Terminal Assembly
TTU........... Tantalus Resources Ltd. [*Vancouver Stock Exchange symbol*]
TTU........... Target Transfer Unit (MCD)
TTU........... Tartu [*Dorpat, Jurjeio*] [*USSR*] [*Seismograph station code, US Geological Survey*] [*Closed*] (SEIS)
TTU........... Tennessee Technical University, Cookville, TN [*OCLC symbol*] (OCLC)
TTU........... Terminal Timing Unit [*NASA*] (KSC)
TTU........... Tetuan [*Morocco*] [*Airport symbol*] (OAG)
TTU........... Thrust Termination Unit (MSA)
TTuGS........ Church of Jesus Christ of Latter-Day Saints, Genealogical Society Library, Tennessee South District Branch, Tullahoma, TN [*Library symbol*] [*Library of Congress*] (LCLS)
TTV .... Teletape Video
TTV .... Tenth Thickness Value [*Nuclear energy*] (NRCH)
TTV .... Territorial Petroleum [*Vancouver Stock Exchange symbol*]
TTV .... Thermal Test Vehicle
TTV .... Tow Test Vehicle [*Aerospace*]
TTVM......... Thermal Transfer Voltmeter
TTVP .... Trentiner Tiroler Volkspartei [*Trentino Tirol People's Party*] [*Italy*] (PPE)
TTW............ Total Temperature and Weight
TTWB .... Turbine Trip with Bypass [*Nuclear energy*] (NRCH)
TTWL .... Twin Tandem Wheel Loading [*Aviation*]
TTX .... Tetrodotoxin [*A poison*] [*Biochemistry*]
TTX .... Thiothixene [*Tranquilizer*]
TTX .... Tultex Corp. [*NYSE symbol*]
TTX .... Tut Enterprises [*Vancouver Stock Exchange symbol*]
TTX .... Tut Enterprises, Inc. [*Toronto Stock Exchange symbol*]
TTY .... Teletype (CAAL)
TTY .... Teletypewriter [*Telecommunications*]
TTY .... Torque-to-Yield [*Automotive engineering*]
TTYA......... Teletypewriter Assembly
TTYD......... Tele-Typewriters for the Deaf [*An association*]
TTYQ/RSS ... Teletypewriter Query-Reply Subsystem (CET)
TTZ............ Tactical-Technical Assignment [*Army*] (RDA)
TTZ............ Titizima [*Bonin Islands*] [*Seismograph station code, US Geological Survey*] [*Closed*] (SEIS)
TTZ............ Transformation Toughened Zirconia [*Metallurgy*]
TTZ............ Treats [*Toronto Stock Exchange symbol*]
TTZ............ Trierer Theologische Zeitschrift [*A publication*]
TTZED........ TIZ. Tonindustrie-Zeitung [*A publication*]
TU............. Ivory Coast [*Aircraft nationality and registration mark*] (FAAC)
TU............. Societe Tunisienne de l'Air [*Tunisia*] [*ICAO designator*]
TU............. Tanking Unit (AAG)
TU............. Tape Unit
TU............. Task Unit
TU............. Taxicrinic Unit [*Data processing*]
TU............. Technical Service Unit [*Military*]
TU............. Technische Ueberwachung [*Technological Supervising*] [*A publication*]
TU............. Technische Universitat [*Technical University*] [*German*]
TU............. Technology Utilization
TU............. Tenebrio Unit [*Endocrinology*]
TU............. Terminal Unit
TU............. Texte und Untersuchungen zur Geschichte der Altchristlichen Literatur [*Berlin*] [*A publication*]
TU............. Thank You [*Communications operator's procedural remark*]
TU............. Thermal Unit
TU............. Thulium [*Chemical element*] [*Symbol is Tm*] (ROG)
TU............. Timing Unit
TU............. Torah Umesorah - National Society for Hebrew Day Schools
TU............. Toxic Unit [*Medicine*]
TU............. Trade Union
TU............. Traffic Unit
TU............. Training Unit [*Army*]
TU............. Transfer Unconditionally
TU............. Transfer Unit (AAG)
TU............. Transmission Unit
TU............. Transport Unit (MCD)
TU............. Transuranium [*Chemistry*]
TU............. Tritium Unit [*Nuclear energy*]
TU............. Trout, Unlimited [*An association*] (EA)
TU............. Tuba
TU............. Tube
Tu............. Tubercle [*Anatomy*] [*Medicine*]
TU............. Tuberculin Unit
TU............. Tudor (ROG)

TU............. Tuesday
TU............. Tuition
TU............. Tulane University [*New Orleans, LA*]
TU............. Tundra Times [*A publication*]
TU............. Tupolev [*Russian aircraft symbol; initialism taken from name of aircraft's designer*]
TU............. Turbidity Unit
tu............. Turkey [*MARC country of publication code*] [*Library of Congress*] (LCCP)
TU............. Turkey [*NATO*] (AFM)
TU............. Type Unique [*French standard troop train, World War I*]
TU............. University of Tennessee, Knoxville, TN [*Library symbol*] [*Library of Congress*] (LCLS)
T₃U........... Triiodothyronine Uptake [*Endocrinology*]
TUA........... AT & T, Americus [*NYSE symbol*]
TUA........... Syndicat International des Travailleurs Unis de l'Automobile, de l'Aerospatiale, et de l'Outillage Agricole d'Amerique [*International Union, United Automobile, Aerospace, and Agricultural Implement Workers of America - UAW*] [*Canada*]
TUA........... Telephone Users Association (EA)
TuA........... Texte und Arbeiten [*Beuron*] [*A publication*] (BJA)
TUA........... Tuai [*New Zealand*] [*Seismograph station code, US Geological Survey*] (SEIS)
TUA........... Tulcan [*Ecuador*] [*Airport symbol*] (OAG)
TUAC OECD ... Trade Union Advisory Committee to the Organization for Economic Cooperation and Development (EA-IO)
TuAF......... Turkish Air Force
T/U/Ag....... Trustee under Agreement (DLA)
TUAL......... Tentative Unit Allowance List [*Air Force*] (AFM)
TUAR......... Turning Arbor
TUB.......... Temporary Unlighted Buoy [*Maps and charts*]
TUB.......... Troop Unit Basis [*Military*]
TUB.......... Tubing (AAG)
TUB.......... Tubingen [*Federal Republic of Germany*] [*Seismograph station code, US Geological Survey*] (SEIS)
TUB.......... Tubuai Island [*Austral Islands*] [*Airport symbol*] (OAG)
TUB.......... Tubular [*Automotive engineering*]
TUB.......... Tulane University. Bulletin [*A publication*]
TUB.......... [*The*] Unborn Book [*A publication*]
TUBA......... John Phillip Tuba Corp. [*NASDAQ symbol*] (NQ)
TUBA......... Tubists Universal Brotherhood Association (EA)
TUBE......... Terminating Unfair Broadcasting Excesses [*Student legal action organization*] (EA)
TUBE......... Trans-Urban Bicentennial Exposition
TUBEA .... Tubercle [*A publication*]
tuberc........ Tuberculosis [*Medicine*]
Tuberc Respir Dis ... Tuberculosis and Respiratory Diseases [*A publication*]
Tuberk Forschungsinst Borstel Jahresber ... Tuberkulose Forschungsinstitut Borstel Jahresbericht [*A publication*]
Tuberk Grenzgeb Einzeldarst ... Tuberkulose und Ihre Grenzgebiete in Einzeldarstellungen [*A publication*]
TUBITAK.... Scientific and Technical Research Council of Turkey [*Ankara*] [*Information service*] (EISS)
TUBLR....... Tubular [*Freight*]
TUBS.......... Tubular Tires [*Cyclist term*] [*British*] (DSUE)
Tubular Struct ... Tubular Structures [*A publication*]
TUC........... Teaching Usefulness Classification [*of a hospital patient*]
TUC........... Technology Utilization Center
TUC........... Telecommunications Users Coalition (EA)
TUC........... Temporary Unemployment Compensation [*Labor*]
TUC........... Time of Useful Consciousness [*Medicine*]
TUC........... Tracer Resources [*Vancouver Stock Exchange symbol*]
TUC........... Trade [*or Trades*] Union Council
TUC........... Trades Union Congress [*British*]
TUC........... Transportation, Utilities, Communications
Tuc........... Tucana [*Constellation*]
TUC........... Tucson [*Arizona*] [*Geomagnetic observatory code*]
TUC........... Tucson [*Arizona*] [*Seismograph station code, US Geological Survey*] (SEIS)
TUC........... Tucuman [*Argentina*] [*Airport symbol*] (OAG)
TUC........... Type Unit Code (CINC)
TUC........... University of Tennessee at Chattanooga, Chattanooga, TN [*OCLC symbol*] (OCLC)
TUCA........ Tilt-Up Concrete Association (EA)
TUCA........ Transient Undercooling Accident [*Nuclear energy*]
TUCA........ Turning Cam [*Tool*] (AAG)
TUCC......... Triangle Universities Computation Center [*Durham, NC*]
TUCE......... Test of Understanding of College Economics
TUCHA....... Type Unit Characteristics
Tu Civ LF ... Tulane Civil Law Forum (DLA)
Tuck.......... Tucker and Clephane's Reports [*21 District of Columbia*] [*1892-93*] (DLA)
TUCK .... Tucker Drilling Co. [*NASDAQ symbol*] (NQ)
Tuck.......... Tucker's New York Surrogate's Court Reports (DLA)
Tuck.......... Tucker's Reports [*156-175 Massachusetts*] (DLA)
Tuck.......... Tucker's Reports [*District of Columbia*] (DLA)
Tuck.......... Tucker's Select Cases [*Newfoundland*] (DLA)
Tuck & C .... Tucker and Clephane's Reports [*21 District of Columbia*] (DLA)

Tuck & Cl ... Tucker and Clephane's Reports [*21 District of Columbia*] [*1892-93*] (DLA)
Tucker .... Tucker's New York Surrogate's Court Reports (DLA)
Tucker's Blackstone ... Tucker's Blackstone's Commentaries (DLA)
Tuck Sel Cas ... Tucker's Select Cases [*1817-28*] [*Newfoundland*] (DLA)
Tuck Sur .... Tucker's Surrogate Reports, City of New York (DLA)
Tuck Surr .... Tucker's Surrogate Reports, City of New York (DLA)
TUCN .... Trades Union Congress of Nigeria
Tucn .... Tucana [*Constellation*]
TUCOPS ..... [*The*] Universal Coterie of Pipe Smokers
TUCOSP .... Tehran Union Catalogue of Scientific Periodicals [*A publication*]
TUCR .... Troop Unit Change Request
TUCSA .... Trade Union Council of South Africa
TUD .... Tambacounda [*Senegal*] [*Airport symbol*] (OAG)
TUD ... Technology Utilization Division [*NASA*] (IEEE)
TUD .... Total Urethral Discharge [*Medicine*]
TUD .... Trudy Universiteta Druzhby Narodov Imeni Patrisa Lumumby [*A publication*]
TUD .... Tugold Resources, Inc. [*Vancouver Stock Exchange symbol*]
TUDC .... Tauroursodeoxycholate [*Biochemistry*]
TUDCA .... Tauroursodeoxycholic Acid [*Biochemistry*]
Tud Cas Merc Law ... Tudor's Leading Cases on Mercantile Law [*3 eds.*] [*1860-84*] (DLA)
Tud Cas RP ... Tudor's Leading Cases on Real Property [*4 eds.*] [*1856-98*] (DLA)
Tud Char Tr ... Tudor's Charitable Trusts [*2nd ed.*] [*1871*] (DLA)
Tud Char Trusts ... Tudor's Charitable Trusts [*2nd ed.*] [*1871*] (DLA)
Tud & Musz Tajek ... Tudomanyos es Muszaki Tajekoztatas [*A publication*]
TUDNL .... Trudy Universiteta Druzhby Narodov Imeni Patrisa Lumumby [*Moscow*] [*A publication*]
Tudom Musz Tajek ... Tudomanyos es Muszaki Tajekoztatas [*A publication*]
Tudor Lead Cas Real Prop ... Tudor's Leading Cases on Real Property (DLA)
Tudor's LCML ... Tudor's Leading Cases on Mercantile Law (DLA)
Tudor's LCRP ... Tudor's Leading Cases on Real Property (DLA)
TUDRIP ...... Tube Plate Drilling Program [*Kongsberg UK*] [*Software package*]
TUDS .... Tunnel Detection System (MCD)
Tud-szerv Tajekoz ... Tudomanyszervezesi Tajekoztato [*A publication*]
TUE .... Tolerance of Unrealistic Experience [*Psychometrics*]
TUE .... Tuesday (AFM)
TUE .... Tupile [*Panama*] [*Airport symbol*] (OAG)
TUE .... University of Tokyo (EDUCATSS) [*UTLAS symbol*]
TUEL .... Trade Union Educational League
Tuerk Ark Derg ... Tuerk Arkeoloji Dergisi [*A publication*]
Tuerk Bitki Koruma Derg ... Tuerkiye Bitki Koruma Dergisi [*A publication*]
Tuerk Ljiyen Tecruebi Biyol Dergisi ... Tuerk Ljiyen ve Tecruebi Biyoloji Dergisi [*A publication*]
Tuerk Tar Derg ... Tuerk Tarih, Arkeologya ve Etnografya Dergisi [*A publication*]
Tuerk Z Hyg Exp Biol ... Tuerkische Zeitschrift fuer Hygiene und Experimentelle Biologie [*A publication*]
TUES .... Tuesday
TUeV Mitt Mitglieder Tech Ueberwach-Ver Bayern ... TUeV [*Technischer Ueberwachungs-Verein*] Mitteilungen fuer die Mitglieder des Technischen Ueberwachungs-Vereins Bayern [*German Federal Republic*] [*A publication*]
TUF .... Tactical Undercover Function [*Chicago police operation*]
TUF .... Thermal Utilization Factor (MCD)
TUF .... Tours [*France*] [*Airport symbol*] (OAG)
TUF .... Trade Union Federation [*British*]
TUF .... Transmitter Underflow
TUFA .... Total Unsaturated Fatty Acid [*of foodstuffs*]
TUFA .... Trans Unsaturated Fatty Acids
TUFCDF ..... Thorium-Uranium Fuel Cycle Development Facility [*Nuclear energy*]
TUFEC .... Thailand-UNESCO Fundamental Education Centre
TUFF-TUG ... Tape Update of Formatted Files-Format Table Tape Updater and Generator [*Data processing*]
TUFI .... This Umbrella Folds Itself [*Trademark for type of umbrella*]
TU-FM .... University of Tennessee Center for the Health Sciences/ Memphis Department of Family Medicine, Memphis, TN [*Library symbol*] [*Library of Congress*] (LCLS)
TUFMIS ...... Tactical Unit Financial Management Information System
TUFPB .... Proceedings. Faculty of Science. Tokai University [*A publication*]
Tufs Folia Med ... Tufs Folia Medica [*A publication*]
Tufts Coll Studies ... Tufts College Studies [*A publication*]
Tufts Dent Outlook ... Tufts Dental Outlook [*A publication*]
Tufts Health Sci Rev ... Tufts Health Science Review [*A publication*]
TUFX .... Turning Fixture
TUG .... Tape Unit Group [*Telecommunications*] (TEL)
TUG .... Telecommunications Users Group [*Montclair, NJ*] [*Telecommunications service*] (TSSD)
TUG .... Teleram Users Group (EA)
TUG .... Total Urinary Gonadotropin [*Clinical chemistry*]
TUG .... Towed Universal Glider
TUG .... TRANSAC [*Transistorized Automatic Computer*] Users Group
TUG .... Tuguegarao [*Philippines*] [*Airport symbol*] (OAG)

TUGAL .... Texte und Untersuchungen zur Geschichte der Altchristlichen Literatur [*A publication*]
TU Gazette ... University of Tasmania. Gazette [*A publication*]
TUH .... Tullahoma, TN [*Location identifier*] [*FAA*] (FAAL)
TU-H .... University of Tennessee Center for the Health Sciences/ Knoxville, Preston Medical Library, Knoxville, TN [*Library symbol*] [*Library of Congress*] (LCLS)
TUHTKP ..... Time Urgent Hard Target Kill Potential (MCD)
TUI .... Green Bay, WI [*Location identifier*] [*FAA*] (FAAL)
TUI .... Tool Usage Instructions (MCD)
TUI .... Trade Union Immunities [*British*]
TUI .... Trade Union International
TUI .... Trypsin Units Inhibited [*Food technology*]
TUI .... Tuition (DSUE)
TUI .... Turaif [*Saudi Arabia*] [*Airport symbol*] (OAG)
TUIAFPW ... Trade Unions International of Agriculture, Forestry, and Plantation Workers [*See also UISTAFP*] [*Prague*] [*Czechoslovak*] (EA-IO)
TUIFU .... [*The*] Ultimate in Foul Ups [*Military slang*] [*Bowdlerized version*]
TUII .... TU International, Incorporated [*NASDAQ symbol*] (NQ)
TUIMWE ..... Trade Unions International of Miners and Workers in Energy [*See also UISMTE*] (EA-IO)
TUIPAE ...... Trade Unions International of Public and Allied Employees [*Berlin*] [*West Germany*] (EA-IO)
TUIR .... Time until in Range
TUITW .... Trade Unions International of Transport Workers (EA-IO)
TUIWC .... Trade Unions International of Workers in Commerce [*Prague, Czechoslovakia*] (EA-IO)
TUJ .... Tubouterine Junction [*Anatomy*]
TUJ .... Tum [*Ethiopia*] [*Airport symbol*] (OAG)
TUK .... Nantucket, MA [*Location identifier*] [*FAA*] (FAAL)
TuK .... Text und Kritik [*A publication*]
TUK .... Tuckahoe Financial Corp. [*Toronto Stock Exchange symbol*]
TUK .... Turbat [*Pakistan*] [*Airport symbol*] (OAG)
tuk .... Turkmen [*MARC language code*] [*Library of Congress*] (LCCP)
TuL .... Tod und Leben nach der Vorstellungen der Babylonier [*A publication*] (BJA)
TUL .... Tula Peak, New Mexico [*Spaceflight Tracking and Data Network*] [*NASA*]
Tu L .... Tulane Law Review [*A publication*]
TUL .... Tulsa [*Oklahoma*] [*Geomagnetic observatory code*]
TUL .... Tulsa [*University of Oklahoma*] [*Oklahoma*] [*Seismograph station code, US Geological Survey*] (SEIS)
TUL .... Tulsa [*Oklahoma*] [*Airport symbol*] (OAG)
TUL .... Tulsa City-County Library System, Tulsa, OK [*OCLC symbol*] (OCLC)
TU-L .... University of Tennessee, Law Library, Knoxville, TN [*Library symbol*] [*Library of Congress*] (LCLS)
TULACS .... Tactical Unit Location and Communication System (MCD)
Tulane Law R ... Tulane Law Review [*A publication*]
Tulane L Rev ... Tulane Law Review [*A publication*]
Tulane St ... Tulane Studies in English [*A publication*]
Tulane Stud Eng ... Tulane Studies in English [*A publication*]
Tulane Stud Geol ... Tulane Studies in Geology [*A publication*]
Tulane Stud Geol Paleontol ... Tulane Studies in Geology and Paleontology [*A publication*]
Tulane Stud Phil ... Tulane Studies in Philosophy [*A publication*]
Tulane Stud Zool ... Tulane Studies in Zoology [*A publication*]
Tulane Stud Zool Bot ... Tulane Studies in Zoology and Botany [*A publication*]
Tulane U Stud Eng ... Tulane University. Studies in English [*A publication*]
TU Law R .... University of Tasmania. Law Review [*A publication*]
TULC .... Trade Union Leadership Council (EA)
TULC .... Tulcum [*Powder*]
TULCC .... Triangle University Library Cooperative Committee [*Library network*]
Tul Civ LF ... Tulane Civil Law Forum (DLA)
TULE .... Transistorized Universal Logic Elements
TULF .... Tamil United Liberation Front [*Sri Lankan*] (PD)
Tul Gos Ped Inst Ucen Zap Mat Kaf ... Tul'skii Gosudarstvennyi Pedagogiceskii Institut Imeni L. N. Tolstogo. Ucenye Zapiski Matematiceskih Kafedr [*A publication*]
Tul L Rev .... Tulane Law Review [*A publication*]
Tu LR .... Tulane Law Review [*A publication*]
TULRA .... Trade Union and Labour Relations Act [*1974 and 1976*] [*British*]
TULSA .... Petroleum Abstracts [*Online*]
Tulsa Geol Soc Dig ... Tulsa Geological Society. Digest [*A publication*]
Tulsa Geol Soc Digest ... Tulsa Geological Society. Digest [*A publication*]
Tulsa L J ... Tulsa Law Journal [*A publication*]
Tulsa Med ... Tulsa Medicine [*A publication*]
Tul Tax Inst ... Tulane Tax Institute [*A publication*]
Tul Tidelands Inst ... Tulane Mineral and Tidelands Law Institute [*A publication*]
TUM .... Technical University in Munich [*West Germany*]
TuM .... Texte und Materialien der Frau Professor Hilprecht Collection of Babylonian Antiquities im Eigentum der Universitaet Jena [*A publication*] (BJA)
TuM .... Torah Umesorah - National Society for Hebrew Day Schools
TUM .... Trades Union Movement

TUM .... Tumut [*Australia*] [*Airport symbol*]   (OAG)
TUM .... Tumwater [*Washington*] [*Seismograph station code, US Geological Survey*]   (SEIS)
TUM .... Tuning Unit Member   (IEEE)
TUM .... University of Tennessee, Center for the Health Sciences, Memphis, TN [*OCLC symbol*]   (OCLC)
TU-M .... University of Tennessee Medical Units, Memphis, TN [*Library symbol*] [*Library of Congress*]   (LCLS)
TUM .... [*The*] Unsatisfied Man [*A publication*]
TUMA .... Tumacacori National Monument
TU-MDC .... University of Tennessee, Downtown Memphis Center, Memphis, TN [*Library symbol*] [*Library of Congress*]   (LCLS)
TUME .... [*The*] Ultimate Musical Experience [*Rock music group*]
TUMEA .... Tunisie Medicale [*A publication*]
Tumor Diagn ... Tumor Diagnostik [*A publication*]
Tumor Diagn Ther ... Tumor Diagnostik und Therapie [*A publication*]
Tumor Res ... Tumor Research [*A publication*]
TU-MS .... University of Tennessee Center for the Health Sciences Library, Stollerman Library, Memphis, TN [*Library symbol*] [*Library of Congress*]   (LCLS)
TUN .... Flint, MI [*Location identifier*] [*FAA*]   (FAAL)
TUN .... Technical University of Nova Scotia [*UTLAS symbol*]
TUN .... Tennessee State University, Downtown Campus, Nashville, TN [*OCLC symbol*]   (OCLC)
TUN .... Transfer Unconditionally
TUN .... Tuning   (AAG)
TUN .... Tunis [*Tunisia*] [*Seismograph station code, US Geological Survey*] [*Closed*]   (SEIS)
TUN .... Tunis [*Tunisia*] [*Airport symbol*]   (OAG)
TUN .... Tunisia [*Three-letter standard code*]   (CNC)
TUN .... Turner Energy & Resources [*Vancouver Stock Exchange symbol*]
TUNA .... Tunable Attribute Display Subsystem   (CAAL)
Tuners JL... Tuners' Journal [*A publication*]
TUNG .... Tungsten   (AAG)
Tungsram Tech Mitt ... Tungsram Technische Mitteilungen [*A publication*]
TUNICAT ... Tunicatae [*Coated*] [*Pharmacy*]
Tunis Agric ... Tunisie Agricole [*A publication*]
TUNISAIR... Societe Tunisienne de l'Air [*Tunisian airline*]
Tunisie Agr ... Tunisie Agricole [*A publication*]
Tunisie Agric Rev Mens Illus ... Tunisie Agricole Revue Mensuelle Illustree [*A publication*]
Tunisie Econ ... Tunisie Economique [*A publication*]
Tunis Med ... Tunisie Medicale [*A publication*]
TUNL .... Triangle Universities Nuclear Laboratory [*Duke University, North Carolina State University, and University of North Carolina at Chapel Hill*] [*Research center*]   (RCD)
TUNL .... Tunnel
Tunnels Ouvrages Souterr ... Tunnels et Ouvrages Souterrains [*A publication*]
Tunnels Tunnell ... Tunnels and Tunnelling [*A publication*]
Tunnlg Technol Newsl ... Tunneling Technology Newsletter [*A publication*]
Tunn Technol Newsl ... Tunneling Technology Newsletter [*United States*] [*A publication*]
TUO .... Taupo [*New Zealand*] [*Airport symbol*]   (OAG)
TUO .... Technology Utilization Office [*NASA*]
TUO .... Teuton Resources Corp. [*Vancouver Stock Exchange symbol*]
TUO .... Tucson Observatory [*Arizona*] [*Seismograph station code, US Geological Survey*]   (SEIS)
TUOC .... Tactical Unit Operations Center   (AFM)
TUP .... Technology Utilization Program [*Defunct*]
TUP .... Telephony User Part [*Telecommunications*]   (TEL)
TUP .... Temple University Press
TUP .... Tovarystvo Ukrainskykh Progresystiv [*Ukrainian Progressive Association*] [*Russian*]   (PPE)
TUP .... Tupelo [*Mississippi*] [*Airport symbol*]   (OAG)
TUP .... Tupik [*USSR*] [*Seismograph station code, US Geological Survey*]   (SEIS)
TUP .... Twin Unit Pack [*for vehicles*]
Tup App..... Tupper's Appeal Reports [*Ontario*]   (DLA)
TUPC......... T. U. P. Charlton's Georgia Reports   (DLA)
T U P Charlt ... T. U. P. Charlton's Georgia Reports   (DLA)
TUPE......... Tanganyika Union of Public Employees
TUPE......... Tupelo National Battlefield
TUPMA...... Trudy Ural'skii Nauchno-Issledovatel'skii i Proektnyi Institut Mednoi Promyshlennosti [*A publication*]
TUPONA .... [*The*] United Provinces of North America [*See also EFISGA*] [*Suggested early name for Canada*]
Tupp......... Tupper's Appeal Reports [*Ontario*]   (DLA)
Tupp......... Tupper's Upper Canada Practice Reports   (DLA)
Tupper ...... Tupper's Appeal Reports [*Ontario*]   (DLA)
Tupper ...... Tupper's Upper Canada Practice Reports   (DLA)
TUPS......... Technical User Performance Specifications [*US Independent Telephone Association*] [*Telecommunications*]   (TEL)
TUR .... American Turners [*An association*]
TUR .... Temporary Unattached Register [*Employment*] [*British*]
TUR .... Traffic Usage Recorder
TUR .... Transurethral Resection [*of prostate gland*]
TUR .... Tucurui [*Brazil*] [*Airport symbol*]   (OAG)

TUR .... Turbat [*USSR*] [*Seismograph station code, US Geological Survey*] [*Closed*]   (SEIS)
TUR .... Turkey [*Three-letter standard code*]   (CNC)
tur.............. Turkish [*MARC language code*] [*Library of Congress*]   (LCCP)
TUR .... Turner Corp. [*American Stock Exchange symbol*]
Tur.............. Turner's Reports [*99-101 Kentucky*]   (DLA)
Tur.............. Turner's Reports [*35-48 Arkansas*]   (DLA)
Tur.............. Turner's Select Pleas of the Forest [*Selden Society Publication, Vol. 13*]   (DLA)
TUR .... Turret   (MSA)
TURB........ Turbine   (AAG)
TURB......... Turbulence
TURBC....... Turbulence   (FAAC)
TURBO ...... Turbocharger [*Automotive engineering*]
TURBOALT ... Turboalternator   (AAG)
TURBOCAT ... Turbine-Powered Catapult
TURBOGEN ... Turbogenerator   (AAG)
Turbomach Int ... Turbomachinery International [*A publication*]
TURBT .... Turbulent   (FAAC)
Turbul Meas Liq Proc Symp ... Turbulence Measurements in Liquids. Proceedings of Symposium [*A publication*]
Turc........... Turcica. Revue d'Etudes Turques [*A publication*]
TURCO....... Turnaround Control [*Navy*]
TURDOK .... Turkish Scientific and Technical Documentation Centre [*Scientific and Technical Research Council of Turkey*] [*Ankara*]
TUREA .... Tumor Research [*A publication*]
TURF.......... Turf Paradise, Inc. [*NASDAQ symbol*]   (NQ)
Turf Cult .... Turf Culture [*A publication*]
TURK......... Turkey
Turk AEC Ankara Nucl Res Cent Tech J ... Turkish Atomic Energy Commission. Ankara Nuclear Research Center. Technical Journal [*A publication*]
Turk Biol Derg ... Turk Biologi Dergisi [*A publication*]
Turk Bull Hyg Exp Biol ... Turkish Bulletin of Hygiene and Experimental Biology [*A publication*]
Turkey Prod ... Turkey Producer [*A publication*]
Turk For Pol Rep ... Turkish Foreign Policy Report [*A publication*]
Turk Gen Kim Kurumu Derg B ... Turkiye Genel Kimyagerler Kurumu Dergisi-B [*A publication*]
Turk Hemsire Derg ... Turk Hemsireler Dergisi [*A publication*]
Turk Hifzissihha Tecr Biol Mecm ... Turk Hifzissihha ve Tecrubi Biologi Mecmuasi [*A publication*]
Turk Hij Deney Biyol Derg ... Turk Hijiyen ve Deneysel Biyoloji Dergisi [*A publication*]
Turk Hij Deneysel Biyol Derg ... Turk Hijiyen ve Deneysel Biyoloji Dergisi [*A publication*]
Turk Hij Tecr Biyol Derg ... Turk Hijiyen ve Tecruby Biyoloji Dergisi [*A publication*]
Turk Jeol Kurumu Bul ... Turkiye Jeoloji Kurumu Bulteni [*A publication*]
Turk Jeomorfologlar Dernegi Yayini ... Turkiye Jeomorfologlar Dernegi. Yayini [*A publication*]
Turk J Nucl Sci ... Turkish Journal of Nuclear Sciences [*A publication*]
Turk J Pediatr ... Turkish Journal of Pediatrics [*A publication*]
Turkmen Gos Univ Ucen Zap ... Turkmenskii Gosudarstvennyi Universitet Imeni A. M. Gor'kogo Ucenye Zapiski [*A publication*]
Turk Mikrobiyol Cemiy Derg ... Turk Mikrobiyoloji Cemiyeti Dergisi [*A publication*]
Turk Miner Res Explor Bull ... Turkey. Mineral Research and Exploration Institute. Bulletin [*A publication*]
Turkm Iskra ... Turkmenskaya Iskra [*USSR*] [*A publication*]
TurkmSSR ... Turkmen Soviet Socialist Republic
Turk Publ Adm Annu ... Turkish Public Administration Annual [*A publication*]
Turk Tip Akad Mecm ... Turkiye Tip Akademisi Mecmuasi [*A publication*]
Turk Tip Cemiy Mecm ... Turkiye Tip Cemiyeti Mecmuasi [*A publication*]
Turk Tip Cem Mecm ... Turkiye Tip Cemiyeti Mecmuasi [*Turkey*] [*A publication*]
Turk Tip Dern Derg ... Turk Tip Dernegi Dergisi [*A publication*]
Turk Tip Encumeni Ars ... Turkiye Tip Encumeni Arsivi [*A publication*]
Turn .... Turner's Reports [*99-101 Kentucky*]   (DLA)
Turn .... Turner's Reports [*35-48 Arkansas*]   (DLA)
Turn .... Turner's Select Pleas of the Forest [*Selden Society Publication, Vol. 13*]   (DLA)
Turn Anglo Sax ... Turner's History of the Anglo Saxon   (DLA)
TURNBKLE ... Turnbuckle[s] [*Freight*]
Turnbull Libr Rec ... Turnbull Library Records [*A publication*]
Turn Ch Pr ... Turner's Practice of the Court of Chancery [*4th ed.*] [*1821*]   (DLA)
Turn Cop.... Turner on Copyright in Designs [*1849*]   (DLA)
Turn & P .... Turner and Phillips' English Chancery Reports   (DLA)
Turn Pat ..... Turner on Patents [*1851*]   (DLA)
Turn & Ph... Turner and Phillips' English Chancery Reports   (DLA)
Turn & R..... Turner and Russell's English Chancery Reports [*37 English Reprint*]   (DLA)
Turn Rec .... Turnbull Library Record [*New Zealand*] [*A publication*]
Turn & R (Eng) ... Turner and Russell's English Chancery Reports [*37 English Reprint*]   (DLA)
Turn & Rus ... Turner and Russell's English Chancery Reports [*37 English Reprint*]   (DLA)

Turn & Russ ... Turner and Russell's English Chancery Reports [*37 English Reprint*] (DLA)
Turon Yliopiston Julk Sar A-II ... Turon Yliopiston Julkaisuja. Sarja A-II [*A publication*]
TURP .... Transurethral Resection of the Prostate [*Medicine*]
TURPS ...... Terrestrial Unattended Reactor Power System
TURQ .... Turquoise [*Jewelry*] (ROG)
Tur & R ...... Turner and Russell's English Chancery Reports [*37 English Reprint*] [*1822-24*] (DLA)
TURRA ...... Turrialba [*Costa Rica*] [*A publication*]
Turrialba .... Turrialba. Revista Interamericana de Ciencias Agricolas [*A publication*]
Tur & Ru ..... Turner and Russell's English Chancery Reports [*37 English Reprint*] [*1822-24*] (DLA)
Tur & Rus ... Turner and Russell's English Chancery Reports [*37 English Reprint*] [*1822-24*] (DLA)
TURS .... Terminal Usage Reporting System [*Data processing*]
Tu & Rus .... Turner and Russell's English Chancery Reports [*1822-24*] (DLA)
TUS .... Tailored Upper Stage (MCD)
TUS .... Treasurer of the United States (AFM)
TUS .... Tucson [*Arizona*] [*Airport symbol*] (OAG)
TUS .... Tugboat Underwriting Syndicate [*Defunct*] (EA)
TUS .... Tuscarora [*New York*] [*Seismograph station code, US Geological Survey*] [*Closed*] (SEIS)
TUS .... Tushaun Resources, Inc. [*Vancouver Stock Exchange symbol*]
TUS .... Tuskegee Institute, Tuskegee, AL [*OCLC symbol*] (OCLC)
TUS .... Tussis [*Cough*] [*Pharmacy*]
TUSA .... Third United States Army [*Terminated, 1973*]
TUSAB ...... [*The*] United States Army Band (AABC)
TUSAC ...... [*The*] United States Army Chorus (AABC)
TUSAFG .... [*The*] United States Air Force Group, American Mission for Aid to Turkey
TUSAS ...... Twayne's United States Authors Series [*A publication*]
TUSC .... Technology Use Studies Center [*Southeastern State College*]
Tusc .... Tusculanae Disputationes [*of Cicero*] [*Classical studies*] (OCD)
TU-SI .... University of Tennessee, Space Institute Library, Tullahoma, TN [*Library symbol*] [*Library of Congress*] (LCLS)
Tuskegee Exp ... Tuskegee Normal and Industrial Institute. Experiment Station. Publications [*A publication*]
TUSLA .... Trudy Ukrainskii Nauchno-Issledovatel'skii Institut Spirtovoi i Likero-Vodochnoi Promyshlennosti [*A publication*]
TUSLOG..... [*The*] United States Logistics Group [*Military*] (AABC)
TUSQA ...... Quarterly Bulletin. Faculty of Science. Tehran University [*A publication*]
TUSSIL...... Tussilago [*Coltsfoot*] [*Pharmacology*] (ROG)
TUSS MOL ... Tussi Molesta [*When the Cough Is Troublesome*] [*Pharmacy*]
Tussock Grassl Mt Lands Inst Annu Rep ... Tussock Grasslands and Mountain Lands Institute. Annual Report [*A publication*]
TUSS URG ... Tussi Urgente [*When the Cough Is Troublesome*] [*Pharmacy*]
TUST .... Texarkana Union Station Trust [*AAR code*]
TUT .... Tafuna, AS [*Location identifier*] [*FAA*] (FAAL)
TUT .... Transistor under Test (IEEE)
TUT .... Travailleurs Unis du Telegraphe [*United Telegraph Workers - UTW*] [*Canada*]
TUT .... Travailleurs Unis des Transports [*United Transportation Union - UTU*] [*Canada*]
TUT .... Tube Template (MCD)
TUT .... Tube under Test (MSA)
TUT .... Tucson - Telemeter [*Arizona*] [*Seismograph station code, US Geological Survey*] [*Closed*] (SEIS)
tut............ Turko-Tataric [*MARC language code*] [*Library of Congress*] (LCCP)
TUT's .... University of St. Thomas, Houston, TX [*OCLC symbol*] (OCLC)
TUT's .... Totally Unified Theories [*Cosmology*]
Tutkimuksia Res Rep ... Tutkimuksia Research Reports [*A publication*]
Tutkimus Tek ... Tutkimus ja Tekniikka [*A publication*]
TUTNB ...... Tunneling Technology Newsletter [*A publication*]
TUTOR ...... [*A*] programing language (CSR)
TUTT .... Tropical Upper Tropospheric Trough [*Meteorology*]
Tutt & C ...... Tuttle and Carpenter's Reports [*52 California*] (DLA)
Tutt & Carp ... Tuttle and Carpenter's Reports [*52 California*] (DLA)
Tuttle .... Tuttle and Carpenter's Reports [*52 California*] (DLA)
Tuttle & Carpenter ... Tuttle and Carpenter's Reports [*52 California*] (DLA)
TUTUB ...... Tunnels and Tunnelling [*A publication*]
TUU .... Huntington, WV [*Location identifier*] [*FAA*] (FAAL)
TUU .... Tabuk [*Saudi Arabia*] [*Airport symbol*] (OAG)
TUUL .... Trade Union Unity League
TUV .... Tucupita [*Venezuela*] [*Airport symbol*] (OAG)
TUV .... Tuvalu [*Three-letter standard code*] (CNC)
TUW .... Trustee under Will (DLA)
TUW .... Tubala [*Panama*] [*Airport symbol*] (OAG)
TUWAH ...... Trade Union Women of African Heritage (EA)
TUWC........ Tactical Utilization Working Committee [*Navy*] (MCD)
TUWR .... Turning Wrench [*Tool*] (AAG)
TUX .... Tuxedo (DSUE)
TUX .... Tuxpeno [*Race of maize*]
TUY .... Tulum [*Mexico*] [*Airport symbol*] [*Obsolete*] (OAG)
TuZ............ Texte und Zeichen [*A publication*]
TUZI .... Tuzigoot National Monument
TV.............. Taff Vale Railway [*Wales*]

TV.............. Target Valve (MCD)
T/V............. Target Vehicle [*Air Force*] (AAG)
TV.............. Target Vulnerability (MCD)
TV.............. Telefunken Variable Microgroove [*Record label*] [*Germany*]
TV.............. Television
TV.............. Television [*A publication*]
TV.............. Television, Vision Channel
TV.............. Terminal Velocity [*Navy*]
TV.............. Test Vehicle
T & V.......... Test and Verify Programs [*Data processing*] (MDG)
TV.............. Tetrazolium Violet [*Also, TZV*]
TV.............. Thames Valley [*England*]
TV.............. Theater of War [*Soviet*] (MCD)
TV.............. Thermal Vacuum
TV.............. Throttle Valve
TV.............. Thrust Vector [*Aerospace*] (NASA)
TV.............. Tidal Volume [*Amount of air that moves in and out of lungs under given conditions*] [*Physiology*]
TV.............. Time Variation of Gain
TV.............. Total Volume
TV.............. Trans America Airlines, Inc. [*ICAO designator*] (FAAC)
TV.............. Transfer Vector
TV.............. Transfer and Void (MCD)
TV.............. Transfer Voucher (AFM)
TV.............. Transport Vehicle
TV.............. Transvestite [*Medicine*]
TV.............. Traverse (IEEE)
TV.............. Treji Varti [*A publication*]
TV.............. Trichomonas vaginalis [*A protozoan*] [*Medicine*]
TV.............. Trip Valve [*Railroad term*]
TV.............. Tube Tester [*JETDS nomenclature*] [*Military*] (CET)
tv.............. Tuvalu [*gn (Gilbert and Ellice Islands*) used in records cataloged before October 1978*] [*MARC country of publication code*] [*Library of Congress*] (LCCP)
TV.............. Tuvalu [*Two-letter standard code*] (CNC)
TV.............. Tzertovnyia Viedomosti [*A publication*]
TVA .... 369th Veterans' Association (EA)
TVA .... Morafenobe [*Madagascar*] [*Airport symbol*] (OAG)
TVA .... Tax on Value Added [*European manufacturing tax*]
TVA .... Taxe a la Valeur Ajoutee [*Value-Added Tax*] [*French*] [*Business and trade*]
TVA .... Television Age [*A publication*]
TvA .... Television Associates Network [*Canada*]
TVA .... Temporary Variance Authority [*or Authorization*] [*NASA*] (AAG)
TVA .... Temporary Voluntary Allowance
TVA .... Tennessee Valley Authority [*Knoxville, TN*] [*Databank originator*]
TVA .... Tennessee Valley Authority, Technical Library, Knoxville, TN [*OCLC symbol*] (OCLC)
TVA .... Textile Veterans Association (EA)
TVA .... Thrust Vector Actuator
TVA .... Thrust Vector Alignment [*Aerospace*] (MCD)
TVA .... Torah Va'Avodah (BJA)
TVA .... Tuned Vertical Array (CAAL)
TVAC .... Thrust Vector Activation Control [*Aerospace*]
TVAC .... Time-Varying Adaptive Correlation
TVA Chem Eng Rept ... Tennessee Valley Authority. Chemical Engineering Report [*A publication*]
Tvaett Ind ... Tvaett Industrin [*A publication*]
TVAR......... Test Variance (NASA)
TV-ARBS.... Television Angle Rate Bombing System (MCD)
Tvarinnictvo Ukr ... Tvarinnictvo Ukraini [*A publication*]
TVAT......... Television Air Trainer
TVA Tech Rept ... Tennessee Valley Authority. Technical Report [*A publication*]
TVB .... Cabol, MO [*Location identifier*] [*FAA*] (FAAL)
TVB .... Television Broadcasters (ADA)
TvB .... Television Bureau of Advertising [*New York, NY*] (EA)
TVB .... Treu und Bestaendig [*Faithful and Steadfast*] [*German*] [*Motto of Johann Georg, Margrave of Brandenburg (1577-1624)*]
TVBN........ Total Volatile Basic Nitrogen [*Food analysis*]
TVBS......... Television Broadcast Satellite [*NASA*]
TVBTA ...... Trudy Vsesoyuznyi Nauchno-Issledovatel'skii Institut Burovoi Tekhniki [*A publication*]
TVC .... Televideo Consultants, Inc. [*Evanston, IL*] [*Telecommunications*] (TSSD)
TVC .... Temperature Valve Control
TVC .... Thermal Vacuum Chamber (NASA)
TVC .... Thermal Voltage Converter
TVC .... Thoracic Vena Cava [*Medicine*]
TVC .... Throttle Valve Control
TVC .... Thrust Vector Control [*Aerospace*]
TVC .... Time-Varying Coefficient
TVC .... Timed Vital Capacity
TVC .... Torsional Vibration Characteristics
TVC .... Total Annual Variable Cost
TVC .... Total Viable Cells [*Microbiology*]
TVC .... Total Volume Capacity [*Physiology*]
TVC .... Traverse City [*Michigan*] [*Airport symbol*] (OAG)
TVC .... Triple Voiding Cystogram [*Medicine*]

TVCA .... Thrust Vector Control Assembly [*Aerospace*]
TVCAM ...... Television Camera and Control Equipment
TVCD .... Thrust Vector Control Driver [*Aerospace*]   (NASA)
TVCL .... Toxic Victims Compensation Legislation
TV Commun ... TV Communications [*A publication*]
TVCS .... Television Communications Subsystem
TVCS .... Thrust Vector Control System [*Aerospace*]   (KSC)
TVCS .... Tyler Vocational Card Sort [*Guidance*]
TVD .... Television Digest [*A publication*]
TVD .... Television Display   (MCD)
TVD .... Thermal Voltaic Detection [*Analytical chemistry*]
TVD .... Toxic Vapor Detector
TVD .... Toxic Vapor Disposal [*NASA*]   (KSC)
TVD .... Transmissable Virus Dementia [*Psychiatry*]
TVD .... Travaux sur Voltaire et le Dix-Huitieme Siecle [*A publication*]
TVD .... True Vertical Depth [*Diamonds*]
TVD .... Tuned Viscoelastic Damper
TVDALV ..... Triple Vessel Disease with Abnormal Left Ventricle [*Cardiology*]
TVDC .... Test Volts, Direct Current
TVDC .... Tidewater Virginia Development Council
TVDP .... Terminal Vector Display Unit
TVDR .... Tag Vector Display Register
TVDY .... Television Deflection Yoke
TVE .... Television Espanola [*Television network*] [*Spain*]
TVE .... Test Vehicle Engine   (AAG)
TVE .... Thermal Vacuum Environment
TVE .... Tricuspid Valve Echophonocardiogram [*Cardiology*]
TVED .... Tuned Viscoelastic Damper
TVEI .... Technical and Vocational Education Initiative [*Manpower Services Commission*] [*British*]
TVEL .... Track Velocity
TVERS .... Television Evaluation and Renewal Standards [*Student legal action organization*]
TVEXPIS .... Television Experiment Interconnecting Station [*NASA*]   (NASA)
TVF .... Tactile Vocal Fremitus [*Medicine*]
TVF .... Tape Velocity Fluctuation
TVF .... Thief River Falls [*Minnesota*] [*Airport symbol*]   (OAG)
TVF .... Tidskrift foer Teknisk-Vettenskaplig Forskning [*A publication*]
TVFA .... Total Volatile Fatty Acid [*of foodstuffs*]
TVFS .... Tactical Vehicle Fleet Simulation   (MCD)
TVFT .... Television Flyback Transformer
TVG .... Tavares & Gulf R. R. [*AAR code*]
TVG .... Threshold Voltage Generator
TVG .... Tijdschrift voor Geschiedenis [*A publication*]
TVG .... Time Variation of Gain
TVG .... Triggered Vacuum Gap
TVG .... TV Guide [*A publication*]
TvG .... Tydskrif vir Geesteswetenskappe [*A publication*]
TVGDHS .... Television Ground Data Handling System [*NASA*]
TVH .... Total Vaginal Hysterectomy [*Gynecology*]
TVI .... Television Interference [*Communications*]
TVI .... Thomasville, GA [*Location identifier*] [*FAA*]   (FAAL)
TVI .... Transient Voltage Indicator
TVI .... Turbo Vapor Injector
TVI .... Tutored Videotape Instruction
TVIC .... Television Input Converter
TVIC .... Television Interference Committee
TVID .... Television Frame Identification Data [*NASA*]
TVIE .... TVI Energy Corp. [*NASDAQ symbol*]   (NQ)
TVIG .... Television and Inertial Guidance
TVIIJ .... Trudy Vojennogo Instituta Inostrannykh Jazykov [*A publication*]
TVIIJa .... Trudy Vojennogo Instituta Inostrannykh Jazykov [*A publication*]
TV Int .... Television International [*A publication*]
TVIS .... Time Video Information Services, Inc.   (EISS)
T-VIS .... Toyota's Variable Induction System [*Automotive engineering*]
TVIS .... Tropical Vegetable Information Service [*Asian Vegetable Research and Development Center*] [*Tainan, Taiwan*] [*Information service*]   (EISS)
TVIS .... Turbine Vibration Indication System   (NG)
TVIST .... Television Information Storage Tube
TVIV .... Taco Viva, Inc. [*NASDAQ symbol*]   (NQ)
TVJ .... Thomas Jefferson University, Philadelphia, PA [*OCLC symbol*]   (OCLC)
TVK .... Target Value Kills   (MCD)
TVK .... Toimihenkilo - ja Virkamiesjarjestojen Keskusliitto [*Confederation of Intellectual and Government Workers*] [*Finland*]
TVKMF ...... Theodore Von Karman Memorial Foundation   (EA)
TVL .... Lake Tahoe [*California*] [*Airport symbol*]   (OAG)
TVL .... Tenth Value Layer
TVL .... Tijdschrift voor Liturgei [*A publication*]
TVL .... Townsville [*Australia*] [*Seismograph station code, US Geological Survey*] [*Closed*]   (SEIS)
TVL .... Transverse Vertical Longitudinal
TVL .... Travel   (AABC)
TvL .... Tydskrif vir Letterkunde [*A publication*]
TVLA .... Taco Villa, Inc. [*NASDAQ symbol*]   (NQ)
TVLADVP... Travel Advance Payment [*TDY*]

TVLALWADV ... Travel Allowance Advance [*in PCS*]
TVLALWS ... Travel Allowance on Separation [*Army*]
Tvl Educ News ... Transvaal Educational News [*A publication*]
TVLF .... Transportable Very-Low-Frequency [*Transmitter*]
TVM........... Tachometer Voltmeter
TVM........... Target Via Missile [*Aviation*]
TVM........... Television Monitor [*Video only*]
TVM........... Thrust Vectoring Motor [*Aerospace*]   (MUGU)
TVM........... Track-Via-Missile
TVM........... Trailer Van Mount
TVM........... Transistorized Voltmeter
TVM........... TRV Minerals [*Vancouver Stock Exchange symbol*]
TVN .... Television News, Inc.
TVN .... Televisora Nacional [*Television network*] [*Venezuela*]
TVN .... Test Verification Network [*NASA*]   (NASA)
TVN .... Total Volatile Nitrogen [*Analytical chemistry*]
TVNZ .... Television, New Zealand
TVO .... Taravao [*Society Islands*] [*Seismograph station code, US Geological Survey*]   (SEIS)
TVO .... Tractor Vaporizing Oil [*Automotive engineering*]
TVOC .... Television Operations Center [*NASA*]   (KSC)
T Volksk Volkstaal ... Tydskrif vir Volkskunde en Volkstaal [*A publication*]
TVOP......... Television Observation Post   (CET)
TVOR......... Terminal VHF [*Very-High Frequency*] Omnidirectional Range
TVOR......... Terminal Visual Omnirange
TVP .... Tamil Vimukhti Peramena [*Political party*] [*Sri Lankan*]   (PPW)
TVP .... Test Verification Program [*NASA*]   (NASA)
TVP .... Textured Vegetable Protein [*Trademark of Archer Daniels Midland Co. for soybean product*]
TVP .... Thermo-Photo-Voltaic
TVP .... Tricuspid Valve Prolapse [*Cardiology*]
TVP .... True Vapor Pressure
TVP .... Victoria Public Library, Victoria, TX [*OCLC symbol*]   (OCLC)
TVPC......... TOW [*Tube-Launched Optically Tracked Wire-Guided*] Vehicle Power Conditioner   (MCD)
TVPED....... Tennessee Valley Perspective [*A publication*]
TVPPA....... Tennessee Valley Public Power Association [*Chattanooga, TN*]   (EA)
TV Q .... Television Quarterly [*A publication*]
TVQ .... Top Visual Quality
TVR .... Temperature Variation of Resistance [*Electricity*]
TVR .... Tennessee Valley Region
TVR .... Thermal Vapor Recompressors [*For evaporators*]
TVR .... Time Variable Reflectivity   (MCD)
TVR .... Trajectory Velocity RADAR   (MCD)
TVR .... Tricuspid Valve Replacement [*Cardiology*]
TVRB......... Tactical Vehicle Review Board [*Army*]   (AABC)
TVRG......... Tijdschrift voor Rechtsgeschiedenis [*A publication*]
TVRI .... Televisi Republik Indonesia [*Television network*]
TVRM .... Television Receiver/Monitor
TVRN......... Tavern
TVRO......... Television Receive Only [*Telecommunications*]
TVRP......... Television Reading Program
TVRS......... Television Video Recording System   (MCD)
TVS .... Tactical Vocoder System
TVS .... Telemetry Video Spectrum
TVS .... Telephone Video System [*NEC America, Inc.*] [*Elk Grove Village, IL*] [*Telecommunications*]   (TSSD)
TVS .... Television Subsystem [*Spacecraft*]
TVS .... Thermal [*or Thermostatic*] Vacuum Switch [*Automotive engineering*]
TVS .... Thrust Vector System [*Aerospace*]
TVS .... Total Volatile Solids [*Analytical chemistry*]
TVS .... Toxic Vapor Suit [*NASA*]   (NASA)
TVS .... Transient Voltage Suppressor
TVS .... Tube-Vehicle System   (MCD)
TVS .... Volunteer State Community College, Gallatin, TN [*OCLC symbol*]   (OCLC)
TVSA......... Thrust Vector Position Servo Amplifier [*Aerospace*]
TVSD......... Time-Varying Spectral Display
TVSG......... Television Signal Generator
TVSM .... Television System Monitor
TVSM .... Time-Varying Sequential Measuring [*Device*]
TVSO........ Television Space Observatory
TV SPOTTS ... Tuneful Viewer's Society for the Preservation of Television Theme Songs
TVSS........ Television Systems Section
TVSSIS ..... Television Subsystem Interconnecting Station [*NASA*]   (NASA)
TVSU......... Television Sight Unit
TVSV......... Thermostatic Vacuum Switching Valve
TVT .... Target Verification Test [*Military*]   (CAAL)
TVT .... Television Terminal   (CMD)
TVT .... Television Trainer/Tapes   (MCD)
TVT .... Television Typewriter
TVT .... Thermal Vacuum Test
TVT .... Tijdschrift voor Theologie [*A publication*]
TVT .... Tiverton, OH [*Location identifier*] [*FAA*]   (FAAL)
TVT .... Tunica Vaginalis Testis [*Anatomy*]
TVTA......... Thermal Vacuum Test Article   (NASA)
TVTK......... Television Technology Corp. [*NASDAQ symbol*]   (NQ)
TV TR .... Television Tower [*Mast*]

TVTV .... Thermostatic Vacuum Transmitting Valve
TVTV .... Top Value Television [Group of 26 young people who photographed the 1972 Democratic convention and presented it on TV]
TVU .... Taveuni [Fiji] [Airport symbol] (OAG)
TVU .... Total Volume Urine [in 24 hours]
TVUB.......... Tijdschrift van de Vrige Universiteit van Brussel [A publication]
TVX .... Target Vehicle Experimental [Air Force]
TVX .... Treasure Valley Exploration [Vancouver Stock Exchange symbol]
TVX .... TVX Mining Corp. [Formerly, Treasure Valley Explorations Ltd.] [Toronto Stock Exchange symbol]
TVXCA .... Travaux Communaux [A publication]
TVY .... Tavoy [Burma] [Airport symbol] (OAG)
TW .... Tactical Warning (MCD)
TW............. Tail Warning [RADAR] (NATG)
TW............. Tail Wind
TW............. Tailwater
TW............. Taiwan [Two-letter standard code] (CNC)
TW............. Tankwagon
TW............. Tap Water [Medicine]
TW............. Tapes and Recording Wires [JETDS nomenclature] [Military] (CET)
TW............. Tapwe [A publication]
TW............. Taxiway [Aviation]
TW............. Teamwork (MSA)
TW............. Technical Works [Air Force] (MCD)
TW............. Temperature Well (MSA)
TW............. Tempered Water
TW............. Temporary Warrant
TW............. Terawatt
TW............. Terre Wallonne [A publication]
TW............. Test Weight
TW............. Textil-Wirtschaft [Textile Industry] [Deutscher Fachverlag GmbH] [Frankfurt Am Main, West Germany] [Information service] (EISS)
TW............. Thermal Wire (KSC)
TW............. Thermit Welding
TW............. Thermoplastic Wire
TW............. Third World [A publication]
T-W .... Three-Wheeler [Type of motorcycle]
TW............. Thrilling Wonder Stories [A publication]
T/W .... Thrust-to-Weight
TW............. Thumbwheel (MCD)
TW............. Tight Wrapped (MSA)
TW............. Tile Wainscot [Technical drawings]
TW............. Time Word
TW............. Torpedo Water
TW............. Total Woman [Title of a 1973 book by Marabel Morgan and of TV seminars based on this book]
TW............. Trail Watcher (CINC)
TW............. Trans World Airlines, Inc. [ICAO designator]
TW............. Transit Working [Telecommunications] (TEL)
TW............. Travel Warrant
TW............. Traveling Wave
TW............. Trow [Ship's rigging] (ROG)
TW............. Tru-Wall Group Ltd. [Toronto Stock Exchange symbol]
TW............. True Watt (MSA)
TW............. Trustee under Will (DLA)
TW............. TW Services [NYSE symbol]
TW............. Twaddell [Specific gravity scale] [Physics]
TW............. Twister (AAG)
Tw............. Tworczosc [A publication]
TW............. Typewriter (AAG)
TW3............ That Was The Week That Was [Also, TWTWTW] [Television program of English origin]
TWA .... Teeny Weeny Airlines [Humorous interpretation for Trans-World Airlines]
TWA .... Textile Waste Association [Later, Textile Fibers and By-Products Association] (EA)
TWA .... Time Weighted Average
TWA .... Tooling Work Authorization
TWA .... Toy Wholesalers Association of America [Moorestown, NJ] (EA)
TWA .... Trailing Wire Antenna [on aircraft]
TWA .... Trans World Airlines, Inc. [NYSE symbol] [Air carrier designation symbol] [Humorously interpreted as "Try Walking Across"]
TWA .... Transaction Work Area
TWA .... Transactions. Wisconsin Academy of Sciences, Arts, and Letters [A publication]
TWA .... Transcontinental & Western Airlines [Later, Trans World Airlines, Inc.]
TWA .... Traveling-Wave Amplifier
TWA .... Trelew [Argentina] [Geomagnetic observatory code]
TWA .... [The] Waferboard Association [Don Mills, ON] (EA)
TWA .... [The] Woman Activist, Inc. (EA)
TW/AA .... Tactical Warning/Attack Assessment
TWAC........ Tactical Weather Analysis Center (MCD)
Twad .... Twaddell [Physics]
TWADL........ Two-Way Air Data Link [Tactical Air Command]

TWAES....... Tactical Warfare Analysis and Evaluation System (MCD)
TWALNDG ... Turnaway Landing [Navy] (NVT)
TWAP........ Thin Wire Analysis Program [Air Force]
TWAR........ Taiwan Acute Respiratory Disease [Pneumonia-causing chlamydia strain named after the ailment that results from it]
TWAS........ Twayne's World Authors Series [A publication]
TWASPIT ... Therapeutic Work Aid Station for Physically Inactive Thinkers (MCD)
TWAT .... Traveling-Wave Amplifier Tube
TWB .... Toowoomba [Australia] [Airport symbol] (OAG)
TWB .... Traveling-Wave Beam [LASER]
TWB .,........ Typewriter Buffer
TWB .... Wayland Baptist College, Plainview, TX [OCLC symbol] (OCLC)
TWBC......... Total White Blood Cells [Medicine]
TWBC......... TransWorld Bancorp [NASDAQ symbol] (NQ)
TWBFA....... Treeing Walker Breeders and Fanciers Association (EA)
TWBNT....... Theologisches Woerterbuch zum Neuen Testament [A publication] (BJA)
TWBS .... Traditional Wooden Boat Society (EA)
TWC .... Suao [Republic of China] [Seismograph station code, US Geological Survey] (SEIS)
TWC .... Tennessee Wesleyan College
TWC .... Texas Wesleyan College
TWC .... Texas Wesleyan College, Fort Worth, TX [OCLC symbol] (OCLC)
TWC .... Texas Western College [Later, UTEP]
TWC .... Theater Weather Central [Military]
TWC .... Three-Way Catalyst [Vehicle exhaust control]
TWC .... Truncated Whitworth Coarse [Thread] (MSA)
TwC .... Twentieth Century [A publication]
TWC .... [The] Weather Channel [Cable TV programing service]
TWCA........ T. W. Cape and Associates [Atlanta, GA] [Telecommunications service] (TSSD)
TWCRT....... Traveling-Wave Cathode-Ray Tube (IEEE)
TWCS........ Test of Work Competency and Stability [Psychology]
TWCS........ Through-Water Communications System [Navy] (CAAL)
TWD .... Hualien [Republic of China] [Seismograph station code, US Geological Survey] (SEIS)
TWD .... Tactical Weapons Delivery
TWD .... Tail Wags Dog [Airspace effects]
TWD .... Thermal Warning Device (MCD)
TWD .... Torpedo Wire Dispenser
TWD .... Toward
TWD .... Twisted Double Shielded (MCD)
TWDD........ Two-Way/Delay Dial [Telecommunications] (TEL)
TWDS........ Tactical Water Distribution System (MCD)
TWE .... Tap Water Enema [Medicine]
TWE .... Textile Waste Exchange [Later, Textile Fibers and By-Products Association]
TWE .... Thumb Wheel Encoder
TWE .... Trans-Western Exploration, Inc. [Toronto Stock Exchange symbol]
TWE .... [The] Washington Establishment
TWEA........ Trading with the Enemy Act
TWEB........ Transcribed Weather Broadcast
TWEC........ Twenty-First Century Envelope [NASDAQ symbol] (NQ)
Twen Cen .. Twentieth Century [A publication]
Twen Ct Lit ... Twentieth Century Literature [A publication]
Twent Cent ... Twentieth Century [A publication]
Twent Cen V ... Twentieth Century Views [A publication]
TWEP .... Terminate with Extreme Prejudice [To kill] [Counterintelligence]
TWERL....... Tropical Wind, Energy Conversion, and Reference Level [National Science Foundation]
TWERLE..... Tropical Wind, Energy Conversion, and Reference Level Experiment [National Science Foundation]
TWEX........ Trans-Western Explorations [NASDAQ symbol] (NQ)
TWF........... Third World Forum (EA-IO)
TWF........... Third World Foundation (EA-IO)
TWF........... Transylvanian World Federation [Sao Paulo, Brazil] (EA-IO)
TWF........... Truncated Whitworth Fine [Thread] (MSA)
TWF........... Twin Falls [Idaho] [Airport symbol] (OAG)
TWF........... Yuli [Republic of China] [Seismograph station code, US Geological Survey] [Closed] (SEIS)
TWF1.......... Yuli [Republic of China] [Seismograph station code, US Geological Survey] (SEIS)
TWFC .... 21st Century Communications, Inc. [NASDAQ symbol]
TWFR .... Twenty-First Century Distributors [NASDAQ symbol] (NQ)
TWG .... Taitung [Republic of China] [Seismograph station code, US Geological Survey] (SEIS)
TWG .... Technical Working Group [of the Conference on the Discontinuance of Nuclear Weapon Tests]
TWG .... Telemetry Working Group
TWG .... Terminally Guided Warhead (MCD)
TWG .... Test Working Group [NASA] (KSC)
TWG .... Transfer Working Group (MCD)
TWGC .... Treatment of War Gas Casualties (MCD)
TWGSS ...... Tank Weapons Gunnery Simulation System (MCD)
TWH .... Catalina Island [California] [Airport symbol] [Obsolete] (OAG)

TWH .... Houston Baptist University, Houston, TX [*OCLC symbol*]   (OCLC)
TWh............ Terawatt Hour   (ADA)
TWH .... Toronto Western Hospital [*UTLAS symbol*]
TWHBEA .... Tennessee Walking Horse Breeders' and Exhibitors' Association   (EA)
TWHBEAA ... Tennessee Walking Horse Breeders' and Exhibitors' Association of America [*Later, TWHBEA*]   (EA)
TWHD........ Tons per Workable Hatch per Day [*Shipping*]
TWHL .... Tail Wheel [*Aviation*]
TWHO .... [*The*] White House Office
TWHTA...... Tennessee Walking Horse Trainers' Association [*Later, Walking Horse Trainers Association*]
TW(I) .... Tail Warning (Indicator) [*RADAR*]   (DEN)
TWI............ Threat Warning Information [*Air Force*]
TWI............ Training with Industry Program [*Army*]   (RDA)
twi .... Twi [*MARC language code*] [*Library of Congress*]   (LCCP)
TWI............ Twilight   (FAAC)
TWI............ [*The*] Welding Institute [*Cambridge, England*] [*Information service*]   (EISS)
TWI............ Wichita, KS [*Location identifier*] [*FAA*]   (FAAL)
TWI............ [*The*] Women's Institute [*Silver Spring, MD*]   (EA)
TWIB .... This Week in Baseball [*Television program*]
TWIC .... Theater Watch Intelligence Center   (NATG)
TWID .... Two-Way/Immediate Dial [*Telecommunications*]   (TEL)
TWIDS .... Threat Warning Information Display System   (MCD)
TWIF.......... Tug of War International Federation
TWIG .... Tandem Wing in Sound Effect   (MCD)
TWIMC ...... To Whom It May Concern
TWIN .... Together Women in Neighborhoods
TWI-N........ Twi-Night [*or Twilight-Night*] [*Doubleheader in baseball*]
TWIRP .... [*The*] Woman Is Requested to Pay [*Some claim that this acronym, originally a designation for certain school dances, evolved into a slang term denoting any male unable to afford a date*]
TWIS .... Technical Writing Improvement Society
TWIS .... Technically Workable Ideal System [*Industrial engineering*]
T Wisc Ac... Transactions. Wisconsin Academy of Sciences, Arts, and Letters [*A publication*]
TWITAS..... Third World Institute of Theatre Arts Studies
TWITW ...... [*The*] Wind in the Willows [*Book by Kenneth Grahame*]
TWIU .... Tobacco Workers International Union [*Later, BCTWIU*]   (EA)
TWIX .... Teletypewriter Message
TWJ .... Tack Welded Joint
TWK .... Hsinying [*Republic of China*] [*Seismograph station code, US Geological Survey*]   (SEIS)
TWK .... Too Well Known
TWK .... Tool Welders Kit
TWK .... Traveling-Wave Klystron
TWK .... Typewriter Keyboard
TWL............ Leased Teletypewriter Service
TWL............ Top Water Level
TWL............ Total Weight Loss   (MCD)
TWL............ Traveling-Wave LASER
TWL............ Tuberculosis Welfare League [*Defunct*]   (EA)
TWL............ Twin Lakes [*California*] [*Seismograph station code, US Geological Survey*]   (SEIS)
TWL............ Twin Wheel Loading [*Aviation*]
TWLA .... Turkish Women's League of America   (EA)
TWLOA ...... Technik Wlokienniczy [*A publication*]
TWLT .... Twilight
TWM.......... Kaohsiung [*Republic of China*] [*Seismograph station code, US Geological Survey*] [*Closed*]   (SEIS)
TWM.......... Tape Wrapping Machine
TWM.......... Traveling-Wave MASER
TWM.......... Two-Way Mirror
TWM1........ Kaohsiung [*Republic of China*] [*Seismograph station code, US Geological Survey*]   (SEIS)
TW-MAE-W ... Third World Movement Against the Exploitation of Women   (EA-IO)
TWMBK..... Traveling-Wave Multiple-Beam Klystron   (MSA)
TWMIP ...... Third World Moving Images Project   (EA)
TWMP .... Track Width Mine Plow   (MCD)
TWMR .... Tungsten Water Moderated Reactor   (KSC)
TWN .... Taiwan [*Three-letter standard code*]   (CNC)
TWN .... Taiwan Fund, Inc. [*American Stock Exchange symbol*]
TWN .... Thomas Wolfe Newsletter [*A publication*]
TWN .... Town   (MCD)
TWN .... Twin Eagles Resources, Inc. [*Vancouver Stock Exchange symbol*]
TWN .... Twin Peaks [*California*] [*Seismograph station code, US Geological Survey*]   (SEIS)
Tw Nat P .... Twiss. Law of Nations in Time of Peace [*2nd ed.*] [*1884*]   (DLA)
Tw Nat W ... Twiss. Law of Nations in Time of War [*2nd ed.*] [*1875*]   (DLA)
TWNG........ Towing
TWNT........ Theologisches Woerterbuch zum Neuen Testament [*A publication*]   (BJA)
TWO .... Meishan [*Republic of China*] [*Seismograph station code, US Geological Survey*]   (SEIS)
TWO .... Neoucom Processing Center, Rootstown, OH [*OCLC symbol*]   (OCLC)

TWO .... Ontario, CA [*Location identifier*] [*FAA*]   (FAAL)
TWO .... This Week Only   (ADA)
TWO .... Tooling Work Order   (MCD)
TWOATAF ... Second Allied Tactical Air Force Central Europe
TWOC .... Taken Without Owner's Consent
TWODS ..... [*The*] World of Dark Shadows [*An association*]   (EA)
T Wolfe New ... Thomas Wolfe Newsletter [*A publication*]
T Wolfe Rev ... Thomas Wolfe Review [*A publication*]
TWOM....... Traveling-Wave Optical MASER
Tworzywa Sztuczne Med ... Tworzywa Sztuczne'w Medycynie [*A publication*]
TWOS........ Tropical Wind Observing Ships [*Marine science*]   (MSC)
TW/OT .... Travel without Troops
Two-Year College Math J ... Two-Year College Mathematics Journal [*A publication*]
Two-Yr Coll Math J ... Two-Year College Mathematics Journal [*A publication*]
TWP........... Task Work Package   (KSC)
TWP........... Technological War Plan
TWP........... Torwood [*Australia*] [*Airport symbol*] [*Obsolete*]   (OAG)
TWP........... Total Wave Pressure
TWP........... Township
TWP........... Traveling-Wave Phototube
TWP........... Trawler Petroleum Explorations Ltd. [*Vancouver Stock Exchange symbol*]
TWP........... Trial Work Period [*Social Security Administration*]   (OICC)
TWP........... Twisted Wire Pair
TWPA .... Traveling-Wave Parametric Amplifier
TWPB .... Total Work Package Budget   (MCD)
TWPL .... Teletypewriter, Private Line
TWPLA ...... Turkish Workers' and Peasants' Liberation Army
TWPP .... Truncated Whitworth, British Standard Pipe (Parallel) [*Thread*]
TWPS .... Traveling-Wave Phase Sifter
TWQ .... Tungshih [*Republic of China*] [*Seismograph station code, US Geological Survey*]   (SEIS)
TWR .... Tape Write Register
TWR .... Threat Warning RADAR
TWR .... Threat Warning Receiver
TWR .... Tool Wear Rate
TWR .... Torpedo Weapons Receiver
TWR .... Total Wrist Replacement [*Medicine*]
TWR .... Tower   (AAG)
TWR .... Trans-World Radio
TWR .... Traveling-Wave Resonator
TWR .... Twin Richfield Oils Ltd. [*Toronto Stock Exchange symbol*]
TWRG......... Towering   (FAAC)
TWRI .... Texas Water Resources Institute [*Texas A & M University*] [*Research center*]   (RCD)
TWRS .... Towers
TWS .... Southwestern at Memphis, Memphis, TN [*OCLC symbol*]   (OCLC)
TWS .... Tactical Warning System   (AAG)
TWS .... Tactical Weapon System   (NG)
TWS .... Tactical Weather Station
TWS .... Tail Warning Set [*or System*] [*Aerospace*]   (MCD)
TWS .... Tartar Weapons System
TWS .... Terrier Weapons System
TWS .... Test of Written Spelling [*Education*]
TWS .... Thermal Wire Stripper
TWS .... Thomas Wolfe Society   (EA)
TWS .... Thrilling Wonder Stories [*A publication*]
TWS .... Track-while-Scan [*Communications*]
TWS .... Truncated Whitworth Special [*Thread*]   (MSA)
TWS .... Tsunami Warning System [*National Oceanic and Atmospheric Administration*]
TWS .... Twin-Wheel Stripper
TWS .... [*The*] Wildlife Society   (EA)
TWSB........ Twin Sideband
TWSC........ Twin Screw
TWSEAS .... Tactical Warfare Simulation, Evaluation, and Analysis System [*Marine Corps*]   (MCD)
TWSO........ Tactical Weapon Systems Operation
TWSP........ Tactical Warfare Simulation Program
TWSR........ Track-while-Scan RADAR
TWSRO ..... Track-while-Scan on Receive Only   (NG)
TWSRS....... Track-while-Scan RADAR Simulator
TWST .... Torus Water Storage Tank   (IEEE)
TWST .... Twistee Freez Corp. [*NASDAQ symbol*]   (NQ)
TWSUA ..... Taiwan Sugar [*A publication*]
TWT........... Sturgis, KY [*Location identifier*] [*FAA*]   (FAAL)
TWT........... Tawi-Tawi [*Philippines*] [*Airport symbol*]   (OAG)
TWT........... Torpedo Water Tube
TWT........... Toy World Test [*Psychology*]
TWT........... Transonic Wind Tunnel [*NASA*]   (AAG)
TWT........... Transworld Corp. [*NYSE symbol*]
TWT........... Travel with Troops
TWT........... Traveling-Wave Tube [*Radio*]
TWT........... Tri-West Resources Ltd. [*Vancouver Stock Exchange symbol*]
TWT........... Tritiated Waste Treatment [*Subsystem*]   (MCD)
TWT........... Two-Way-Traffic-in-Ideas Conference [*of Labor Party*] [*British*]

TWT............ West Texas State University, Canyon, TX [*OCLC symbol*] (OCLC)
TWT............ [*The*] Write Thing [*An association*] (EA)
TWTA........ Traveling-Wave Tube Amplifier [*Radio*]
TWTHF...... Twentieth Century Energy [*NASDAQ symbol*] (NQ)
TWTWTW... That Was The Week That Was [*Also, TW3*] [*Television program of English origin*]
TWU .... Tata Workers' Union [*India*]
TWU .... Tawau [*Malaysia*] [*Airport symbol*] (OAG)
TWU .... Technical Writing Unit [*NASA*]
TWU .... Telecommunications Workers Union [*Canada*]
TWU .... Texas Woman's University
TWU .... Tobacco Workers' Union [*British*]
TWU .... Transport Workers' Union [*British*]
TWU .... Transport Workers' Union of America (EA)
TWU .... University of the South, Sewanee, TN [*OCLC symbol*] (OCLC)
TWUA........ Textile Workers Union of America [*Later, ACTWU*]
TWW.......... Independent Television for Wales and the West of England
TWWP .... Third World Women's Project (EA)
TWWS .... Two-Way/Wink Start [*Telecommunications*] (TEL)
TWX .... Telegraphic Message (MSA)
TWX .... Teletypewriter Exchange Service [*Western Union*] [*Term also used generically for teletypewriter message*]
TWX .... Time Wire Transmission
TWXIL .... TWX Interlibrary Loan Network [*Library network*]
TWY .... Taxiway [*Aviation*] (AAG)
TWY .... Twenty (ADA)
TWYL .... Taxiway-Link [*Aviation*]
TWZ............ Neifu [*Republic of China*] [*Seismograph station code, US Geological Survey*] (SEIS)
TWZO .... Trade Wind Zone Oceanography
TX.............. Nondramatic Literary Works [*US Copyright Office class*]
TX.............. Tax
TX.............. TELEX
TX.............. Terminating Toll Operator [*Telecommunications*] (TEL)
TX.............. Tested Extra (MCD)
TX.............. Texaco, Inc. [*NYSE symbol*]
TX.............. Texas [*Postal code*]
TX.............. Texas Reports (DLA)
Tx .... Texas State Library and Historical Commission, Austin, TX [*Library symbol*] [*Library of Congress*] (LCLS)
TX.............. Thromboxane [*Also, T, TA, Tx*] [*Biochemistry*]
Tx .... Thyroidectomy [*Medicine*]
TX.............. Time to Equipment Reset [*Data processing*] (MDG)
TX.............. Torque Transmitter
TX.............. Traction [*Medicine*]
TX.............. Transformer
TX.............. Translation Hand Controller X-Axis Direction (MCD)
TX.............. Transmitter
Tx .... Transplantation [*Medicine*]
TX.............. Transportes Aereos Nacionales, SA [*Honduras*] [*ICAO designator*] (FAAC)
TX.............. Treatment
TX.............. Treble Cash Ruling [*Business and trade*]
T & X.......... Type and Crossmatch [*Clinical chemistry*]
TXA .... Texas A & M University, College Station, TX [*OCLC symbol*] (OCLC)
TXA .... Texas American Bancshares, Inc. [*NYSE symbol*]
TXA .... Thromboxane A [*Also, TA, TxA*] [*Biochemistry*]
TxAb .... Abilene Public Library, Abilene, TX [*Library symbol*] [*Library of Congress*] (LCLS)
TxAbC....... Abilene Christian University, Abilene, TX [*Library symbol*] [*Library of Congress*] (LCLS)
TxAbH........ Hardin-Simmons University, Abilene, TX [*Library symbol*] [*Library of Congress*] (LCLS)
TxAbM .... McMurry College, Abilene, TX [*Library symbol*] [*Library of Congress*] (LCLS)
TxAl............ Stella Hill Memorial Library, Alto, TX [*Library symbol*] [*Library of Congress*] (LCLS)
TxAlpS .... Sul Ross State University, Alpine, TX [*Library symbol*] [*Library of Congress*] (LCLS)
TxAlvC .... Alvin Junior College, Alvin, TX [*Library symbol*] [*Library of Congress*] (LCLS)
TxAm .... Amarillo Public Library, Amarillo, TX [*Library symbol*] [*Library of Congress*] (LCLS)
TxAmC....... Amarillo College, Amarillo, TX [*Library symbol*] [*Library of Congress*] (LCLS)
TxAmM ...... Mason & Hanger-Silas Mason Co., Inc., Pantex Plant Library, Amarillo, TX [*Library symbol*] [*Library of Congress*] (LCLS)
TxAmSP..... Southwestern Public Service Co., Amarillo, TX [*Library symbol*] [*Library of Congress*] (LCLS)
TxAmV .... United States Veterans Administration Hospital, Amarillo, TX [*Library symbol*] [*Library of Congress*] (LCLS)
TxAng .... Brazoria County Library, Angleton, TX [*Library symbol*] [*Library of Congress*] (LCLS)
TXAPA ...... Toxicology and Applied Pharmacology [*A publication*]
TxArB......... Arlington Baptist Junior College, Arlington, TX [*Library symbol*] [*Library of Congress*] (LCLS)
TxAr-G .... Arlington Public Library, Genealogy Department, Arlington, TX [*Library symbol*] [*Library of Congress*] (LCLS)

TxArJ .... Jet Research Center, Inc., Arlington, TX [*Library symbol*] [*Library of Congress*] (LCLS)
TxArU .... University of Texas at Arlington, Arlington, TX [*Library symbol*] [*Library of Congress*] (LCLS)
TxAtH .... Henderson County Junior College, Athens, TX [*Library symbol*] [*Library of Congress*] (LCLS)
TxAu .... Austin Public Library, Austin, TX [*Library symbol*] [*Library of Congress*] (LCLS)
TxAuA........ Charles E. Stevens American Atheist Library and Archives, Inc., Austin, TX [*Library symbol*] [*Library of Congress*] (LCLS)
TxAu-AT .... Austin Public Library, Austin-Travis County Collection, Austin, TX [*Library symbol*] [*Library of Congress*] (LCLS)
TxAuC........ Concordia Lutheran College, Austin, TX [*Library symbol*] [*Library of Congress*] (LCLS)
TxAuCC ..... Austin Community College, Austin, TX [*Library symbol*] [*Library of Congress*] (LCLS)
TxAuCH ..... Church Historical Society, Austin, TX [*Library symbol*] [*Library of Congress*] (LCLS)
TxAuDR...... Daughters of the Republic of Texas Museum, Austin, TX [*Library symbol*] [*Library of Congress*] (LCLS)
TxAuE .... Episcopal Theological Seminary of the Southwest, Austin, TX [*Library symbol*] [*Library of Congress*] (LCLS)
TxAuEd...... Texas Education Agency, Austin, TX [*Library symbol*] [*Library of Congress*] (LCLS)
TxAuGS ..... Church of Jesus Christ of Latter-Day Saints, Genealogical Society Library, Austin Branch, Austin, TX [*Library symbol*] [*Library of Congress*] (LCLS)
TxAuHi .... Texas State Department of Highways and Public Transportation, Materials and Tests Research Library, Austin, TX [*Library symbol*] [*Library of Congress*] (LCLS)
TxAuHT...... Huston-Tillotson College, Austin, TX [*Library symbol*] [*Library of Congress*] (LCLS)
TxAuL........ Legislative Library Board, Legislative Reference Library, Austin, TX [*Library symbol*] [*Library of Congress*] (LCLS)
TxAuLBJ .... Lyndon B. Johnson School of Public Affairs, Lyndon Baines Johnson Library, Austin, TX [*Library symbol*] [*Library of Congress*] (LCLS)
TxAuM .... Texas Medical Association, Austin, TX [*Library symbol*] [*Library of Congress*] (LCLS)
TxAuMH..... Texas Department of Mental Health and Mental Retardation, Austin, TX [*Library symbol*] [*Library of Congress*] (LCLS)
TxAuP .... Austin Presbyterian Theological Seminary, Austin, TX [*Library symbol*] [*Library of Congress*] (LCLS)
TxAuPW..... Texas Department of Parks and Wildlife, Austin, TX [*Library symbol*] [*Library of Congress*] (LCLS)
TxAuR .... Radian Corp., Austin, TX [*Library symbol*] [*Library of Congress*] (LCLS)
TxAuSE...... Saint Edward's University, Austin, TX [*Library symbol*] [*Library of Congress*] (LCLS)
TxAuSHos ... Austin State Hospital, Austin, TX [*Library symbol*] [*Library of Congress*] (LCLS)
TxAuT .... Tracor, Inc., Technical Library, Austin, TX [*Library symbol*] [*Library of Congress*] (LCLS)
TxAuW .... Texas Water Development Board, Austin, TX [*Library symbol*] [*Library of Congress*] (LCLS)
TXB .... Abilene Public Library, Abilene, TX [*OCLC symbol*] (OCLC)
TXB .... Thromboxane B [*Also, TB, TxB*] [*Biochemistry*]
TxBea......... Tyrrell Public Library, Beaumont, TX [*Library symbol*] [*Library of Congress*] (LCLS)
TxBeaAM ... Beaumont Art Museum, Beaumont, TX [*Library symbol*] [*Library of Congress*] (LCLS)
TxBeaE ...... Beaumont Enterprise & Journal, Beaumont, TX [*Library symbol*] [*Library of Congress*] (LCLS)
TxBeaG ..... Gulf States Utilities Co., Beaumont, TX [*Library symbol*] [*Library of Congress*] (LCLS)
TxBeaL....... Lamar University, Beaumont, TX [*Library symbol*] [*Library of Congress*] (LCLS)
TxBeaMC ... Mobil Chemical Co., Research and Development Laboratory, Beaumont, TX [*Library symbol*] [*Library of Congress*] (LCLS)
TxBeaSE .... Saint Elizabeth Hospital, Health Science Library, Beaumont, TX [*Library symbol*] [*Library of Congress*] (LCLS)
TxBee......... Bee County Public Library, Beeville, TX [*Library symbol*] [*Library of Congress*] (LCLS)
TxBeeC ...... Bee County College, Beeville, TX [*Library symbol*] [*Library of Congress*] (LCLS)
TxBelM...... Mary Hardin-Baylor College, Belton, TX [*Library symbol*] [*Library of Congress*] (LCLS)
TxBHi .... Brownsville Historical Association, Brownsville, TX [*Library symbol*] [*Library of Congress*] (LCLS)
TxBl............ Bellaire City Library, Bellaire, TX [*Library symbol*] [*Library of Congress*] (LCLS)
TXBL .... Taxable
TxBIT .... Texaco, Inc., Bellaire, TX [*Library symbol*] [*Library of Congress*] (LCLS)
TxBor .... Hutchinson County Library, Borger, TX [*Library symbol*] [*Library of Congress*] (LCLS)
TxBorF....... Frank Phillips College, Borger, TX [*Library symbol*] [*Library of Congress*] (LCLS)

Tx-BPH....... Texas Regional Library, Division for the Blind and Physically Handicapped, Austin, TX [*Library symbol*] [*Library of Congress*] (LCLS)

TxBrd........ Brownwood Public Library, Brownwood, TX [*Library symbol*] [*Library of Congress*] (LCLS)

TxBrdH....... Howard Payne College, Brownwood, TX [*Library symbol*] [*Library of Congress*] (LCLS)

TxBreB....... Blinn College, Brenham, TX [*Library symbol*] [*Library of Congress*] (LCLS)

TxBry.......... Bryan Public Library, Bryan, TX [*Library symbol*] [*Library of Congress*] (LCLS)

TxBryA....... Allen Academy, Bryan, TX [*Library symbol*] [*Library of Congress*] (LCLS)

TxBs........... Howard County Library, Big Spring, TX [*Library symbol*] [*Library of Congress*] (LCLS)

TxBS......... Texas Southmost College, Brownsville, TX [*Library symbol*] [*Library of Congress*] (LCLS)

TxBsaA...... Ambassador College, Big Sandy, TX [*Library symbol*] [*Library of Congress*] (LCLS)

TxBsH....... Howard County Junior College, Big Spring, TX [*Library symbol*] [*Library of Congress*] (LCLS)

TxBsV........ United States Veterans Administration Hospital, Big Spring, TX [*Library symbol*] [*Library of Congress*] (LCLS)

TxBUC....... Union Carbide Corp., Chemicals and Plastics Library, Brownsville, TX [*Library symbol*] [*Library of Congress*] (LCLS)

TX Bus Rev ... Texas Business Review [*A publication*]

TxBy.......... Sterling Municipal Library, Baytown, TX [*Library symbol*] [*Library of Congress*] (LCLS)

TxByH....... Humble Oil & Refining Co., Technical Library, Baytown, TX [*Library symbol*] [*Library of Congress*] (LCLS)

TxByH-E.... Humble Oil & Refining Co., Engineering Division Library, Baytown, TX [*Library symbol*] [*Library of Congress*] (LCLS)

TxByL........ Lee College, Baytown, TX [*Library symbol*] [*Library of Congress*] (LCLS)

TXC........... Abilene Christian University, Abilene, TX [*OCLC symbol*] (OCLC)

TXC........... Texaco Canada, Inc. [*American Stock Exchange symbol*] [*Toronto Stock Exchange symbol*] [*Vancouver Stock Exchange symbol*]

TXC........... Thurman, CO [*Location identifier*] [*FAA*] (FAAL)

TxCarP....... Panola College, Carthage, TX [*Library symbol*] [*Library of Congress*] (LCLS)

TxCaW....... West Texas State University, Canyon, TX [*Library symbol*] [*Library of Congress*] (LCLS)

TxCc.......... La Retama Public Library, Corpus Cristi, TX [*Library symbol*] [*Library of Congress*] (LCLS)

TxCcD........ Del Mar College, Corpus Christi, TX [*Library symbol*] [*Library of Congress*] (LCLS)

TxCcGS..... Church of Jesus Christ of Latter-Day Saints, Genealogical Society Library, Corpus Christi Branch, Corpus Christi, TX [*Library symbol*] [*Library of Congress*] (LCLS)

TxCcMST... Art Museum of South Texas, Corpus Christi, TX [*Library symbol*] [*Library of Congress*] (LCLS)

TxCcNHi .... Nueces County Historical Society, La Retama Public Library, Corpus Christi, TX [*Library symbol*] [*Library of Congress*] (LCLS)

TxCcT........ Texas A & I University at Corpus Christi, Corpus Christi, TX [*Library symbol*] [*Library of Congress*] (LCLS)

TxCcU........ University of Corpus Christi, Corpus Christi, TX [*Library symbol*] [*Library of Congress*] [*Obsolete*] (LCLS)

TxCeN........ Northwood Institute of Texas, Cedar Hill, TX [*Library symbol*] [*Library of Congress*] (LCLS)

TX Ci.......... Texas Civil Appeals Reports (DLA)

TxCiC......... Cisco Junior College, Cisco, TX [*Library symbol*] [*Library of Congress*] (LCLS)

TxClaC....... Clarendon College, Clarendon, TX [*Library symbol*] [*Library of Congress*] (LCLS)

TxClcU....... University of Houston at Clear Lake City, Houston, TX [*Library symbol*] [*Library of Congress*] (LCLS)

TxCle......... Cleburne Public Library, Cleburne, TX [*Library symbol*] [*Library of Congress*] (LCLS)

TxCli.......... Nellie Pederson Civic Library, Clifton, TX [*Library symbol*] [*Library of Congress*] (LCLS)

TxClv.......... Cleveland Public [*Charles O. Austin Memorial*] Library, Cleveland, TX [*Library symbol*] [*Library of Congress*] (LCLS)

TxClwC...... Celanese Corp., Clarkwood, TX [*Library symbol*] [*Library of Congress*] (LCLS)

TxCM......... Texas A & M University, College Station, TX [*Library symbol*] [*Library of Congress*] (LCLS)

TxCM-M..... Texas A & M University, Medical Sciences Library, College Station, TX [*Library symbol*] [*Library of Congress*] (LCLS)

TXCO......... [*The*] Exploration Corporation [*NASDAQ symbol*] (NQ)

TxComf...... Comfort Public Library, Comfort, TX [*Library symbol*] [*Library of Congress*] (LCLS)

TxComS..... East Texas State University, Commerce, TX [*Library symbol*] [*Library of Congress*] (LCLS)

TxComS-M ... East Texas State University, Museum, Commerce, TX [*Library symbol*] [*Library of Congress*] (LCLS)

TxCoN........ Navarro Junior College, Corsicana, TX [*Library symbol*] [*Library of Congress*] (LCLS)

TxConM.... Montgomery County Memorial Library, Conroe, TX [*Library symbol*] [*Library of Congress*] (LCLS)

TxCr.......... Crockett Public Library, Crockett, TX [*Library symbol*] [*Library of Congress*] (LCLS)

TX Cr......... Texas Criminal Appeals Reports (DLA)

TxCrMA ..... Mary Allen Junior College, Crockett, TX [*Library symbol*] [*Library of Congress*] (LCLS)

TxCvS........ ARCO Chemical Co., Channelview, TX [*Library symbol*] [*Library of Congress*] (LCLS)

TxCvT........ Texas Butadine & Chemical Corp., Channelview, TX [*Library symbol*] [*Library of Congress*] (LCLS)

TXCYA ...... Toxicology [*A publication*]

TXD........... McMurry College, Abilene, TX [*OCLC symbol*] (OCLC)

TXD........... Telephone Exchange (Digital) [*Telecommunications*] (TEL)

TXD........... Transmit Data [*Data processing*]

TxDa.......... Dallas Public Library, Dallas, TX [*Library symbol*] [*Library of Congress*] (LCLS)

TxDaABC ... AMIGOS Bibliographic Council, Inc., Dallas, TX [*Library symbol*] [*Library of Congress*] (LCLS)

TxDaAC ..... Anderson, Clayton & Co., Foods Division Technical Library, Dallas, TX [*Library symbol*] [*Library of Congress*] (LCLS)

TxDaAR-G ... Atlantic Richfield Co., Geoscience Library, Dallas, TX [*Library symbol*] [*Library of Congress*] (LCLS)

TxDaAR-R ... Atlantic Richfield Co., R and D Library, Dallas, TX [*Library symbol*] [*Library of Congress*] (LCLS)

TxDaAR-T ... Atlantic Richfield Co., Technical Library, Dallas, TX [*Library symbol*] [*Library of Congress*] (LCLS)

TxDaB .... Dallas Baptist College, Dallas, TX [*Library symbol*] [*Library of Congress*] (LCLS)

TxDaBC ..... Bishop College, Dallas, TX [*Library symbol*] [*Library of Congress*] (LCLS)

TxDaBM .... Burgess-Manning co., Dallas, TX [*Library symbol*] [*Library of Congress*] (LCLS)

TxDaBU..... Baylor University in Dallas, Dallas, TX [*Library symbol*] [*Library of Congress*] (LCLS)

TxDaCC ..... Christian College of the Southwest, Dallas, TX [*Library symbol*] [*Library of Congress*] (LCLS)

TxDaCCD... Callier Center for Communication Disorders, Dallas, TX [*Library symbol*] [*Library of Congress*] (LCLS)

TxDaCiA ..... Court of Civil Appeals, Dallas, TX [*Library symbol*] [*Library of Congress*] (LCLS)

TxDaCL...... Core Laboratories, Inc., Dallas, TX [*Library symbol*] [*Library of Congress*] (LCLS)

TxDaCR...... Collins Radio Co., Dallas, TX [*Library symbol*] [*Library of Congress*] (LCLS)

TxDaCS ..... Dallas County Community College System, Dallas, TX [*Library symbol*] [*Library of Congress*] (LCLS)

TxDaDC ..... Dallas Christian College, Dallas, TX [*Library symbol*] [*Library of Congress*] (LCLS)

TxDaDF...... DeGoyler Foundation, Dallas, TX [*Library symbol*] [*Library of Congress*] (LCLS)

TxDaDL...... Dallas County Law Library, Dallas, TX [*Library symbol*] [*Library of Congress*] (LCLS)

TxDaDM .... DeGoyler and MacNaughton Library, Dallas, TX [*Library symbol*] [*Library of Congress*] (LCLS)

TxDaE .... El Centro College, Dallas, TX [*Library symbol*] [*Library of Congress*] (LCLS)

TxDaET ...... East Texas State University, Metroplex Center, Dallas, TX [*Library symbol*] [*Library of Congress*] (LCLS)

TxDaFR...... Federal Reserve Bank of Dallas, Dallas, TX [*Library symbol*] [*Library of Congress*] (LCLS)

TxDaGS ..... Church of Jesus Christ of Latter-Day Saints, Genealogical Society Library, Dallas Branch, Dallas, TX [*Library symbol*] [*Library of Congress*] (LCLS)

TxDaHi .... Dallas Historical Society, Dallas, TX [*Library symbol*] [*Library of Congress*] (LCLS)

TxDaJS ..... Johnson and Swanson, Law Library, Dallas, TX [*Library symbol*] [*Library of Congress*] (LCLS)

TxDaL .... Lone Star Gas Co., Dallas, TX [*Library symbol*] [*Library of Congress*] (LCLS)

TxDaM .... Southern Methodist University, Dallas, TX [*Library symbol*] [*Library of Congress*] (LCLS)

TxDaME ..... Mobil Exploration & Producing Services, Inc., Dallas, TX [*Library symbol*] [*Library of Congress*] (LCLS)

TxDaMF ..... Dallas Museum of Fine Arts, Dallas, TX [*Library symbol*] [*Library of Congress*] (LCLS)

TxDaM-L .... Southern Methodist University, Law Library, Dallas, TX [*Library symbol*] [*Library of Congress*] (LCLS)

TxDaM-P.... Southern Methodist University, Perkins School of Theology, Dallas, TX [*Library symbol*] [*Library of Congress*] (LCLS)

TxDaM-SE ... Southern Methodist University, Science/Engineering Library, Dallas, TX [*Library symbol*] [*Library of Congress*] (LCLS)

TxDaMV ..... Mountain View College, Dallas, TX [*Library symbol*] [*Library of Congress*] (LCLS)

TxDaP .... Dallas Power & Light Co., Dallas, TX [*Library symbol*] [*Library of Congress*] (LCLS)

TxDaPO...... Placid Oil Co. Exploration Library, Dallas, TX [*Library symbol*] [*Library of Congress*] (LCLS)

TxDaPP ...... Planned Parenthood of Northeast Texas, Dallas, TX [*Library symbol*] [*Library of Congress*] (LCLS)

TxDaR ... Richland College, Dallas, TX [*Library symbol*] [*Library of Congress*] (LCLS)

TxDaRI ...... Rockwell International, Collins Radio Group, Technical Information Center, Dallas, TX [*Library symbol*] [*Library of Congress*] (LCLS)

TxDaS .... University of Texas, Health Science Center at Dallas, Dallas, TX [*Library symbol*] [*Library of Congress*] (LCLS)

TxDaSM ..... Mobil Research & Development Corp., Dallas, TX [*Library symbol*] [*Library of Congress*] (LCLS)

TxDaTI-A ... Texas Instruments, Inc., Apparatus Division Library, Dallas, TX [*Library symbol*] [*Library of Congress*] (LCLS)

TxDaTI-C ... Texas Instruments, Inc., Central Research and Engineering Library, Dallas, TX [*Library symbol*] [*Library of Congress*] (LCLS)

TxDaTI-IS ... Texas Instruments, Inc., IS & S Library, Dallas, TX [*Library symbol*] [*Library of Congress*] (LCLS)

TxDaTI-S ... Texas Instruments, Inc., Semiconductor Division, Dallas, TX [*Library symbol*] [*Library of Congress*] (LCLS)

TxDaTI-SS ... Texas Instruments, Inc., Science Services Division, Dallas, TX [*Library symbol*] [*Library of Congress*] (LCLS)

TxDaTS ..... Dallas Theological Seminary and Graduate School, Dallas, TX [*Library symbol*] [*Library of Congress*] (LCLS)

TxDaU .... University of Dallas, Irving, TX [*Library symbol*] [*Library of Congress*] (LCLS)

TxDaUSAF ... United States Army and Air Force Exchange Service, Dallas, TX [*Library symbol*] [*Library of Congress*] (LCLS)

TxDaUSFD ... United States Food and Drug Administration, Dallas, TX [*Library symbol*] [*Library of Congress*] (LCLS)

TxDaVA ..... United States Veterans Administration Hospital, Dallas, TX [*Library symbol*] [*Library of Congress*] (LCLS)

TXDE .... Toluene-Xylene-Dioxane-Ethanol [*Scintillation solvent*]

TxDeni .... Denison Public Library, Denison, TX [*Library symbol*] [*Library of Congress*] (LCLS)

TxDeniG ..... Grayson County College, Denison, TX [*Library symbol*] [*Library of Congress*] (LCLS)

TxDib .... T. L. L. Temple Memorial Library, Diboll, TX [*Library symbol*] [*Library of Congress*] (LCLS)

TxDN .... North Texas State University, Denton, TX [*Library symbol*] [*Library of Congress*] (LCLS)

TxDN-Hi .... North Texas State University, State Historical Collection, Denton, TX [*Library symbol*] [*Library of Congress*] (LCLS)

TxDpS .... Shell Oil Co., Deer Park, TX [*Library symbol*] [*Library of Congress*] (LCLS)

TxDpSC ..... Shell Chemical Co., Deer Park, TX [*Library symbol*] [*Library of Congress*] (LCLS)

TxDunv ...... Duncanville Public Library, Duncanville, TX [*Library symbol*] [*Library of Congress*] (LCLS)

TxDW .... Texas Woman's University, Denton, TX [*Library symbol*] [*Library of Congress*] (LCLS)

TXE .... El Paso Community College, El Paso, TX [*OCLC symbol*] (OCLC)

TxE .... El Paso Public Library, El Paso, TX [*Library symbol*] [*Library of Congress*] (LCLS)

TXE .... Telephone Exchange (Electronics) [*Telecommunications*] (IEEE)

TxEC .... El Paso Community College, El Paso, TX [*Library symbol*] [*Library of Congress*] (LCLS)

TxEdP .... Pan American University, Edinburg, TX [*Library symbol*] [*Library of Congress*] (LCLS)

TxEGS .... Church of Jesus Christ of Latter-Day Saints, Genealogical Society Library, El Paso Branch, El Paso, TX [*Library symbol*] [*Library of Congress*] (LCLS)

TxEHD .... Hotel Dieu Medical-Nursing Educational Media Center, El Paso, TX [*Library symbol*] [*Library of Congress*] (LCLS)

TXEN .... Texas Energies, Inc. [*NASDAQ symbol*] (NQ)

TxENG .... El Paso Natural Gas Co., Technical Information Center, El Paso, TX [*Library symbol*] [*Library of Congress*] (LCLS)

TxEU .... University of Texas at El Paso, El Paso, TX [*Library symbol*] [*Library of Congress*] (LCLS)

TxEWB .... United States Army, William Beaumont General Hospital, Medical and Technical Library, El Paso, TX [*Library symbol*] [*Library of Congress*] (LCLS)

TXF .... Corpus Christi State University, Corpus Christi, TX [*OCLC symbol*] (OCLC)

TxF .... Fort Worth Public Library, Fort Worth, TX [*Library symbol*] [*Library of Congress*] (LCLS)

TXF .... Texfi Industries, Inc. [*NYSE symbol*]

TxFACM .... Amon Carter Museum of Western Art, Fort Worth, TX [*Library symbol*] [*Library of Congress*] (LCLS)

TxFAl .... Alcon Laboratories, Inc., Fort Worth, TX [*Library symbol*] [*Library of Congress*] (LCLS)

TxFbAD ..... United States Army, Air Defense School, Fort Bliss, TX [*Library symbol*] [*Library of Congress*] (LCLS)

TxFBH .... Bell Helicopter Co., Fort Worth, TX [*Library symbol*] [*Library of Congress*] (LCLS)

TxFCB .... Carter & Burgess, Inc., Fort Worth, TX [*Library symbol*] [*Library of Congress*] (LCLS)

TxFCC .... Fort Worth Christian College, Fort Worth, TX [*Library symbol*] [*Library of Congress*] (LCLS)

TxFCO .... Texas College of Osteopathic Medicine, Fort Worth, TX [*Library symbol*] [*Library of Congress*] (LCLS)

TxFF .... Fort Worth Art Museum, Fort Worth, TX [*Library symbol*] [*Library of Congress*] (LCLS)

TxFFAA ...... United States Federal Aviation Administration, Fort Worth, TX [*Library symbol*] [*Library of Congress*] (LCLS)

TxFG .... General Dynamics/Convair Aerospace Division, Fort Worth, TX [*Library symbol*] [*Library of Congress*] (LCLS)

TxFGS .... Church of Jesus Christ of Latter-Day Saints, Genealogical Society Library, Fort Worth Branch, North Richland Hills, Fort Worth, TX [*Library symbol*] [*Library of Congress*] (LCLS)

TxFhH .... Darnell Army Hospital, Medical Library, Fort Hood, TX [*Library symbol*] [*Library of Congress*] (LCLS)

TxFJPS ...... John Peter Smith Hospital, Fort Worth, TX [*Library symbol*] [*Library of Congress*] (LCLS)

TxFK .... Kimbell Art Museum, Fort Worth, TX [*Library symbol*] [*Library of Congress*] (LCLS)

TxFM .... Fort Worth Museum of Science and History, Fort Worth, TX [*Library symbol*] [*Library of Congress*] (LCLS)

TxFNA .... United States National Archives and Record Center, Fort Worth, TX [*Library symbol*] [*Library of Congress*] (LCLS)

TxFNIMH .... National Institute of Mental Health, Clinical Research Center Medical Library, Fort Worth, TX [*Library symbol*] [*Library of Congress*] (LCLS)

TxFrB .... Brazosport Junior College, Freeport, TX [*Library symbol*] [*Library of Congress*] (LCLS)

TxFrD .... Dow Chemical Co., Texas Division, Freeport, TX [*Library symbol*] [*Library of Congress*] (LCLS)

TxFS .... Southwestern Baptist Theological Seminary, Fort Worth, TX [*Library symbol*] [*Library of Congress*] (LCLS)

TxFshBH .... Brooke General Hospital, Medical Library, Fort Sam Houston, TX [*Library symbol*] [*Library of Congress*] (LCLS)

TxFshM ...... Medical Field Service School, Fort Sam Houston, TX [*Library symbol*] [*Library of Congress*] (LCLS)

TxFSJ .... Saint Joseph Hospital, Medical and Nursing Library, Fort Worth, TX [*Library symbol*] [*Library of Congress*] (LCLS)

TxFT .... Tarrant County Junior College, Fort Worth, TX [*Library symbol*] [*Library of Congress*] (LCLS)

TxFTC .... Texas Christian University, Fort Worth, TX [*Library symbol*] [*Library of Congress*] (LCLS)

TxFTE .... Texas Electric Service Co., Fort Worth, TX [*Library symbol*] [*Library of Congress*] (LCLS)

TxFTM .... Terrell's Laboratories Medical Library, Fort Worth, TX [*Library symbol*] [*Library of Congress*] (LCLS)

TxFT-NE ..... Tarrant County Junior College, Northeast Campus, Hurst, TX [*Library symbol*] [*Library of Congress*] (LCLS)

TxFT-S .... Tarrant County Junior College, South Campus, Fort Worth, TX [*Library symbol*] [*Library of Congress*] (LCLS)

TxFTW .... Texas Wesleyan College, Fort Worth, TX [*Library symbol*] [*Library of Congress*] (LCLS)

TXG .... Austin Public Library, Austin, TX [*OCLC symbol*] (OCLC)

TXG .... Taxiing [*Aviation*] (FAAC)

TxGA .... United States Army, Army Engineering District, Office of Administrative Services, Galveston, TX [*Library symbol*] [*Library of Congress*] (LCLS)

TxGaiC ...... Cooke County Junior College, Gainsville, TX [*Library symbol*] [*Library of Congress*] (LCLS)

TxGar .... Nicholson Memorial Library, Garland, TX [*Library symbol*] [*Library of Congress*] (LCLS)

TxGarD ...... Dresser Industries, Inc., Garland, TX [*Library symbol*] [*Library of Congress*] (LCLS)

TxGarV ...... Varo, Inc., Texas Division, Garland, TX [*Library symbol*] [*Library of Congress*] (LCLS)

TxGat .... Gatesville Public Library, Gatesville, TX [*Library symbol*] [*Library of Congress*] (LCLS)

TxGC .... Galveston Community College, Galveston, TX [*Library symbol*] [*Library of Congress*] (LCLS)

TxGeoS ...... Southwestern University, Georgetown, TX [*Library symbol*] [*Library of Congress*] (LCLS)

TxGilGS ...... Church of Jesus Christ of Latter-Day Saints, Genealogical Society Library, Longview Branch, Gilmer, TX [*Library symbol*] [*Library of Congress*] (LCLS)

TxGML .... Texas A & M University, Moody College of Marine Sciences and Maritime Resources, Galveston, TX [*Library symbol*] [*Library of Congress*] (LCLS)

TxGoS .... Spanish Texas Microfilm Center, Goliad, TX [*Library symbol*] [*Library of Congress*] (LCLS)

TxGR .... Rosenberg Library, Galveston, TX [*Library symbol*] [*Library of Congress*] (LCLS)

TxGrp .... Grand Prairie Memorial Library, Grand Prairie, TX [*Library symbol*] [*Library of Congress*] (LCLS)

TxGUSFW ... United States National Marine Fisheries Service, Biological Laboratory, Galveston, TX [*Library symbol*] [*Library of Congress*] (LCLS)

TxH .... Houston Public Library, Houston, TX [*Library symbol*] [*Library of Congress*] (LCLS)

TXH .... Transfer on Index High

TXH .... University of Houston, Houston, TX [*OCLC symbol*] (OCLC)

TxHaJ .... Jarvis Christian College, Hawkins, TX [*Library symbol*] [*Library of Congress*] (LCLS)

TxHAM .... Houston Academy of Medicine for Texas Medical Center, Houston, TX [*Library symbol*] [*Library of Congress*] (LCLS)

TxHAWD .... Arnold, White & Durkee, Houston, TX [*Library symbol*] [*Library of Congress*] (LCLS)

TxHBa .... National Lead Industries, Inc., Baroid Division, Houston, TX [*Library symbol*] [*Library of Congress*] (LCLS)

TxHBB .... Baker, Botts, Shepherd & Coates, Houston, TX [*Library symbol*] [*Library of Congress*] (LCLS)

TxHBC .... Houston Baptist University, Houston, TX [*Library symbol*] [*Library of Congress*] (LCLS)

TxHBec ...... Bechtel Group, Inc., Technical Library, Houston, TX [*Library symbol*] [*Library of Congress*] (LCLS)

TxHBR .... Brown & Root, Inc., Technical Library, Houston, TX [*Library symbol*] [*Library of Congress*] (LCLS)

TxHC .... Houston Community College System, Houston, TX [*Library symbol*] [*Library of Congress*] (LCLS)

TxHCC ...... Continental Carbon Co., Houston, TX [*Library symbol*] [*Library of Congress*] (LCLS)

TxHCG .... Columbia Gulf Transmission Co., Houston, TX [*Library symbol*] [*Library of Congress*] (LCLS)

TxHCI .... Cameron Iron Works, Inc., Houston, TX [*Library symbol*] [*Library of Congress*] (LCLS)

TxHCS .... Community Welfare Planning Association, Social Research Library, Houston, TX [*Library symbol*] [*Library of Congress*] (LCLS)

TxHDC ...... Dow Chemical Co., E and CS Information Center, Houston, TX [*Library symbol*] [*Library of Congress*] (LCLS)

TxHDE .... Dresser Industries, Inc., Lane-Wells Co., Houston, TX [*Library symbol*] [*Library of Congress*] (LCLS)

TxHDom ..... Dominican College, Houston, TX [*Library symbol*] [*Library of Congress*] (LCLS)

TxHe .... Edwards Public Library, Henrietta, TX [*Library symbol*] [*Library of Congress*] (LCLS)

TxHE .... United States Air Force, Base Library, Ellington AFB, Houston, TX [*Library symbol*] [*Library of Congress*] (LCLS)

TxHebO ...... Our Lady of Guadalupe Parish Library, Hebbronville, TX [*Library symbol*] [*Library of Congress*] (LCLS)

TxHE-NA .... United States Air Force, National Aerospace Education Library, Ellington AFB, Houston, TX [*Library symbol*] [*Library of Congress*] (LCLS)

TxHF .... Captain Theodore C. Freeman Memorial Library, Houston, TX [*Library symbol*] [*Library of Congress*] (LCLS)

TxHFE .... Fluor Engineers & Constructors, Fluor Houston Library, Houston, TX [*Library symbol*] [*Library of Congress*] (LCLS)

TxHFO .... Fluor Ocean Services, Engineering Library, Houston, TX [*Library symbol*] [*Library of Congress*] (LCLS)

TxHFR .... Freelance Research Service, Houston, TX [*Library symbol*] [*Library of Congress*] (LCLS)

TxHG .... Gulf Coast Bible College, Houston, TX [*Library symbol*] [*Library of Congress*] (LCLS)

TxHGO .... Gulf Oil Co.-US, Central Reference Library, Houston, TX [*Library symbol*] [*Library of Congress*] (LCLS)

TxHGP .... Gulf Publishing Co., Houston, TX [*Library symbol*] [*Library of Congress*] (LCLS)

TxHGS .... Church of Jesus Christ of Latter-Day Saints, Genealogical Society Library, Houston Branch, Houston, TX [*Library symbol*] [*Library of Congress*] (LCLS)

TxHGS-E .... Church of Jesus Christ of Latter-Day Saints, Genealogical Society Library, Houston East Branch, Houston, TX [*Library symbol*] [*Library of Congress*] (LCLS)

TxHH .... Black, Syvalls & Bryson, Inc., HOMCO Division, Houston, TX [*Library symbol*] [*Library of Congress*] (LCLS)

TxHHC .... Houston Chronicle, Houston, TX [*Library symbol*] [*Library of Congress*] (LCLS)

TxHHG .... Houston-Galveston Area Council Library, Houston, TX [*Library symbol*] [*Library of Congress*] (LCLS)

TxHHH .... Herman Hospital, Houston, TX [*Library symbol*] [*Library of Congress*] (LCLS)

TxHHL .... Houston Lighting & Power Co., Houston, TX [*Library symbol*] [*Library of Congress*] (LCLS)

TxHHO ...... Humble Oil & Refining Co., General Services Library, Houston, TX [*Library symbol*] [*Library of Congress*] (LCLS)

TxHHO-E .... Humble Oil & Refining Co., Marketing Research Library, Houston, TX [*Library symbol*] [*Library of Congress*] (LCLS)

TxHHOM .... Houston Oil and Mineral Corp., Corporate Library, Houston, TX [*Library symbol*] [*Library of Congress*] (LCLS)

TxHHP .... Houston Post, Houston, TX [*Library symbol*] [*Library of Congress*] (LCLS)

TxHHT .... Hughes Tool Co., Houston, TX [*Library symbol*] [*Library of Congress*] (LCLS)

TxHI .... International Business Machines Corp., Corporation Library, Houston, TX [*Library symbol*] [*Library of Congress*] (LCLS)

TXHI .... Texas Hitech, Incorporated [*NASDAQ symbol*] (NQ)

TxHiC .... Hill Junior College, Hillsboro, TX [*Library symbol*] [*Library of Congress*] (LCLS)

TxHIR .... Institute of Religion, Texas Medical Center, Houston, TX [*Library symbol*] [*Library of Congress*] (LCLS)

TXHL .... Texas Health Letter [*A publication*]

TxHLD .... City of Houston Legal Department, Houston, TX [*Library symbol*] [*Library of Congress*] (LCLS)

TxHLJ .... Memorial Baptist Hospital, Lillie Jolly School of Nursing, Houston, TX [*Library symbol*] [*Library of Congress*] (LCLS)

TxHLS .... Lunar Science Institute, Houston, TX [*Library symbol*] [*Library of Congress*] (LCLS)

TxHLT .... Layne Texas Co., Houston, TX [*Library symbol*] [*Library of Congress*] (LCLS)

TxHM .... Museum of Fine Arts, Houston, TX [*Library symbol*] [*Library of Congress*] (LCLS)

TxHMa .... Magcobar Corp., Houston, TX [*Library symbol*] [*Library of Congress*] (LCLS)

TxHMC .... Houston Academy of Medicine, Houston, TX [*Library symbol*] [*Library of Congress*] (LCLS)

TxHMc .... McClelland Engineers, Inc., Houston, TX [*Library symbol*] [*Library of Congress*] (LCLS)

TxHMM ..... Milwhite Co., Houston, TX [*Library symbol*] [*Library of Congress*] (LCLS)

TxHMon ..... Monsanto Co., Houston, TX [*Library symbol*] [*Library of Congress*] (LCLS)

TxHN .... National Association of Corrosion Engineers, Houston, TX [*Library symbol*] [*Library of Congress*] (LCLS)

TxHNASA ... National Aeronautics and Space Administration, Manned Spacecraft Center, Technical Library, Houston, TX [*Library symbol*] [*Library of Congress*] (LCLS)

TxHNH .... North Harris County College, Houston, TX [*Library symbol*] [*Library of Congress*] (LCLS)

TxHP .... Texas Research Institute of Mental Sciences, Houston, TX [*Library symbol*] [*Library of Congress*] (LCLS)

TxHPC .... Pace Company, Houston, TX [*Library symbol*] [*Library of Congress*] (LCLS)

TxHPen ...... Pennzoil Exploration Library, Houston, TX [*Library symbol*] [*Library of Congress*] (LCLS)

TxHPH .... Port of Houston World Trade Center, Houston, TX [*Library symbol*] [*Library of Congress*] (LCLS)

TxHPI .... Prudential Insurance Co. of America, Houston, TX [*Library symbol*] [*Library of Congress*] (LCLS)

TxHPT .... Petro-Tex Chemical Corp., Research Library, Houston, TX [*Library symbol*] [*Library of Congress*] (LCLS)

TxHR .... Rice University, Houston, TX [*Library symbol*] [*Library of Congress*] (LCLS)

TxHRa .... Raymond International, Inc., Houston, TX [*Library symbol*] [*Library of Congress*] (LCLS)

TxHRH .... Roy M. Huffington, Inc., Library, Houston, TX [*Library symbol*] [*Library of Congress*] (LCLS)

TxHRI .... Houston Research Institute, Houston, TX [*Library symbol*] [*Library of Congress*] (LCLS)

TxHSB .... Southern Bible College, Houston, TX [*Library symbol*] [*Library of Congress*] (LCLS)

TxHSD .... Shell Development Co., Bellaire Research Center, Houston, TX [*Library symbol*] [*Library of Congress*] (LCLS)

TxHSDW .... Shell Oil Development Co., Westhollow Research Center Library, Houston, TX [*Library symbol*] [*Library of Congress*] (LCLS)

TxHSJM ..... San Jacinto Museum of History Association, Deer Park, TX [*Library symbol*] [*Library of Congress*] (LCLS)

TxHSOC ..... Standard Oil Company of Texas, Houston, TX [*Library symbol*] [*Library of Congress*] (LCLS)

TxHSOF ..... Shell Oil Co., Information and Library Services Library, Houston, TX [*Library symbol*] [*Library of Congress*] (LCLS)

TxHSOIC .... Shell Oil Co., Information and Computing Services Center Library, Houston, TX [*Library symbol*] [*Library of Congress*] (LCLS)

TxHSP .... Shell Pipe Line Corp., R and D Library, Houston, TX [*Library symbol*] [*Library of Congress*] [*Obsolete*] (LCLS)

TxHSR .... Southwestern Research Institute, Houston, TX [*Library symbol*] [*Library of Congress*] (LCLS)

TxHST .... University of Saint Thomas, Houston, TX [*Library symbol*] [*Library of Congress*] (LCLS)

TxHSTC ..... South Texas Junior College, Houston, TX [*Library symbol*] [*Library of Congress*] (LCLS)

TxHSTL ...... South Texas College of Law, Houston, TX [*Library symbol*] [*Library of Congress*] (LCLS)

TxHSU .... Superior Oil Exploration Library, Houston, TX [*Library symbol*] [*Library of Congress*] (LCLS)

TxHSW .... Schlumberger Well Services, Houston, TX [*Library symbol*] [*Library of Congress*] (LCLS)

TxHTC .... Transcontinental Gas Pipe Line Corp., Houston, TX [*Library symbol*] [*Library of Congress*] (LCLS)

TxHTE .... Texas Eastern Transmission Corp., Houston, TX [*Library symbol*] [*Library of Congress*] (LCLS)

TxHTen ...... Tennessee Gas Transmission Co., Houston, TX [*Library symbol*] [*Library of Congress*] (LCLS)

TxHTexG .... Texas Gas Exploration Co., Houston, TX [*Library symbol*] [*Library of Congress*] (LCLS)

TxHTexO .... Texasgulf Oil & Gas Co., Houston, TX [*Library symbol*] [*Library of Congress*] (LCLS)

TxHTG........ Trunkline Gas Co., Houston, TX [*Library symbol*] [*Library of Congress*] (LCLS)

TxHTGP ..... Tennessee Gas Pipeline Co., Houston, TX [*Library symbol*] [*Library of Congress*] (LCLS)

TxHTGS ..... Texas Gulf Sulphur Co., Inc., Houston, TX [*Library symbol*] [*Library of Congress*] (LCLS)

TxHTI .... Texas Instruments, Inc., Houston, TX [*Library symbol*] [*Library of Congress*] (LCLS)

TxHTide ..... Getty Oil Co., Houston, TX [*Library symbol*] [*Library of Congress*] (LCLS)

TxHTide(Res) ... Getty Oil Co., Exploration and Production Research Library, Houston, TX [*Library symbol*] [*Library of Congress*] (LCLS)

TxHTI-I ...... Texas Instruments, Inc., Industrial Products Division, Houston, TX [*Library symbol*] [*Library of Congress*] (LCLS)

TxHTM .... Texas Manufacturers Association, Houston, TX [*Library symbol*] [*Library of Congress*] (LCLS)

TxHTO........ Tenneco Oil Co., Exploration Research Library, Houston, TX [*Library symbol*] [*Library of Congress*] (LCLS)

TxHTRW..... TRW Systems Group, Houston, TX [*Library symbol*] [*Library of Congress*] (LCLS)

TxHTSU ...... Texas Southern University, Houston, TX [*Library symbol*] [*Library of Congress*] (LCLS)

TxHTu ...... Turner, Collie & Braden, Inc., Houston, TX [*Library symbol*] [*Library of Congress*] (LCLS)

TxHU .... University of Houston, Houston, TX [*Library symbol*] [*Library of Congress*] (LCLS)

TxHUC .... Union Carbide Corp., Houston, TX [*Library symbol*] [*Library of Congress*] (LCLS)

TxHU-D ...... University of Houston, Downtown College, Houston, TX [*Library symbol*] [*Library of Congress*] (LCLS)

TxHU-L....... University of Houston, Law School, Houston, TX [*Library symbol*] [*Library of Congress*] (LCLS)

TxHurT....... Tarrant County Junior College District, Hurst, TX [*Library symbol*] [*Library of Congress*] (LCLS)

TxHUSC ..... United States Department of Commerce, Houston Field Office Library, Houston, TX [*Library symbol*] [*Library of Congress*] (LCLS)

TxHuT .... Sam Houston State University, Huntsville, TX [*Library symbol*] [*Library of Congress*] (LCLS)

TxHUTP...... Union Texas Petroleum Co., Houston, TX [*Library symbol*] [*Library of Congress*] (LCLS)

TxHVA........ United States Veterans Administration Hospital, Houston, TX [*Library symbol*] [*Library of Congress*] (LCLS)

TxHVE........ Vinson, Elkins, Searls, Connally & Smith, Law Library, Houston, TX [*Library symbol*] [*Library of Congress*] (LCLS)

TxHW .... Welex Division, Haliburton Co., Houston, TX [*Library symbol*] [*Library of Congress*] (LCLS)

TxHWB .... World Book Encyclopaedia Science Service, Inc., Houston, TX [*Library symbol*] [*Library of Congress*] (LCLS)

TxHWG...... Western Geophysical Co., Houston, TX [*Library symbol*] [*Library of Congress*] (LCLS)

TxHWH...... Westbury Senior High School, Houston, TX [*Library symbol*] [*Library of Congress*] (LCLS)

TxHWN...... Western Natural Gas Co., Houston, TX [*Library symbol*] [*Library of Congress*] (LCLS)

TXI............. Southwest Texas State University, San Marcos, TX [*OCLC symbol*] (OCLC)

TXI............. Texas Industries, Inc. [*NYSE symbol*]

TXI............. Texas International Airlines, Inc. [*Air carrier designation symbol*]

TXI............. Torex Minerals Ltd. [*Vancouver Stock Exchange symbol*]

TXI............. Transfer with Index Incremented

TxIr............. Irving Municipal Library, Irving, TX [*Library symbol*] [*Library of Congress*] (LCLS)

TxIrS .... Irving Independent School District, Irving, TX [*Library symbol*] [*Library of Congress*] (LCLS)

TXJ............. University of Texas at San Antonio, San Antonio, TX [*OCLC symbol*] (OCLC)

TxJaB........ Baptist Missionary Association Theological Seminary, Jacksonville, TX [*Library symbol*] [*Library of Congress*] (LCLS)

TxJaC........ Jacksonville College, Jacksonville, TX [*Library symbol*] [*Library of Congress*] (LCLS)

TxJaL .... Lon Morris College, Jacksonville, TX [*Library symbol*] [*Library of Congress*] (LCLS)

TXK .... Stephen F. Austin University, Nacogdoches, TX [*OCLC symbol*] (OCLC)

TXK .... Telephone Exchange (Crossbar) [*Telecommunications*] (TEL)

TXK .... Texarkana [*Arkansas*] [*Airport symbol*] (OAG)

TxKeeS ..... Southwestern Union College, Keene, TX [*Library symbol*] [*Library of Congress*] (LCLS)

TxKerS...... Schreiner Institute, Kerrville, TX [*Library symbol*] [*Library of Congress*] (LCLS)

TxKiC .... Central Texas College, Killeen, TX [*Library symbol*] [*Library of Congress*] (LCLS)

TxKilC....... Kilgore College, Kilgore, TX [*Library symbol*] [*Library of Congress*] (LCLS)

TxKT .... Texas A & I University, Kingsville, TX [*Library symbol*] [*Library of Congress*] (LCLS)

TXL............ Berlin [*West Germany*] [*Airport symbol*] (OAG)

TXL............. Lubbock City-County Libraries, Lubbock, TX [*OCLC symbol*] (OCLC)

TxL .... Lubbock City-County Libraries, Lubbock, TX [*Library symbol*] [*Library of Congress*] (LCLS)

TX L............. Texas Law Review [*A publication*]

TXL............. Transfer on Index Low

TxLaH........ United States Air Force, Base Library, Lackland Air Force Base, TX [*Library symbol*] [*Library of Congress*] (LCLS)

TxLaM....... United States Air Force, Wilford Hall Medical Center, Lackland AFB, TX [*Library symbol*] [*Library of Congress*] (LCLS)

TxLapU ...... Upjohn Co., Polymer Chemicals Division Library, La Porte, TX [*Library symbol*] [*Library of Congress*] (LCLS)

TxLar......... Laredo Public Library, Laredo, TX [*Library symbol*] [*Library of Congress*] (LCLS)

TxLarC .... Laredo Junior College, Laredo, TX [*Library symbol*] [*Library of Congress*] (LCLS)

TxLarU .... Laredo State University, Laredo, TX [*Library symbol*] [*Library of Congress*] (LCLS)

TxLC .... Lubbock Christian College, Lubbock, TX [*Library symbol*] [*Library of Congress*] (LCLS)

TxLcD .... Soil and Water Conservation Districts Foundation, Davis Conservation Library, League City, TX [*Library symbol*] [*Library of Congress*] (LCLS)

TxLeS........ South Plains College, Levelland, TX [*Library symbol*] [*Library of Congress*] (LCLS)

TxLib.......... Liberty City Library, Liberty, TX [*Library symbol*] [*Library of Congress*] (LCLS)

TxLivP........ Polk County Enterprise, Livingston, TX [*Library symbol*] [*Library of Congress*] (LCLS)

TX LJ.......... Texas Law Journal (DLA)

TxLjB.......... Brazosport College, Lake Jackson, TX [*Library symbol*] [*Library of Congress*] (LCLS)

TxLMH....... Methodist Hospital, Lubbock, TX [*Library symbol*] [*Library of Congress*] (LCLS)

TxLoL......... LeTourneau College, Longview, TX [*Library symbol*] [*Library of Congress*] (LCLS)

TX LR .... Texas Law Review [*A publication*]

TxLT........... Texas Tech University, Lubbock, TX [*Library symbol*] [*Library of Congress*] (LCLS)

TxLTM........ Texas Tech University, School of Medicine at Lubbock, Lubbock, TX [*Library symbol*] [*Library of Congress*] (LCLS)

TxLufA ...... Angelina College, Lufkin, TX [*Library symbol*] [*Library of Congress*] (LCLS)

TxLufFS ..... Texas Forest Service, Forest Products Laboratory Library, Lufkin, TX [*Library symbol*] [*Library of Congress*] (LCLS)

TxLufK ...... Kurth Memorial Library, Lufkin, TX [*Library symbol*] [*Library of Congress*] (LCLS)

TXM........... Middle Tennessee State University, Murfreesboro, TN [*OCLC symbol*] (OCLC)

Tx-M........... Texas State Medical Library, Austin, TX [*Library symbol*] [*Library of Congress*] (LCLS)

TxMaIC ...... ICI America, Inc., Darco Experimental Laboratory Library, Marshall, TX [*Library symbol*] [*Library of Congress*] (LCLS)

TxMaW....... Wiley College, Marshall, TX [*Library symbol*] [*Library of Congress*] (LCLS)

TxMCa .... McAllen Memorial Library, McAllen, TX [*Library symbol*] [*Library of Congress*] (LCLS)

TxMcaH...... Hidelgo County Library System, McAllen, TX [*Library symbol*] [*Library of Congress*] (LCLS)

TxMcgR ..... North American Rockwell Corp., Solid Rocket Division, McGregor, TX [*Library symbol*] [*Library of Congress*] (LCLS)

TxMck........ McKinney Memorial Public Library, McKinney, TX [*Library symbol*] [*Library of Congress*] (LCLS)

TxMe .... Mesquite Public Library, Mesquite, TX [*Library symbol*] [*Library of Congress*] (LCLS)

TxMeE........ Eastfield College, Mesquite, TX [*Library symbol*] [*Library of Congress*] (LCLS)

TxMM........ Midland County Public Library, Midland, TX [*Library symbol*] [*Library of Congress*] (LCLS)

TXN........... Houston Public Library, Houston, TX [*OCLC symbol*] (OCLC)

TXN .... Taxation

TXN .... Texas Instruments, Inc. [*NYSE symbol*]

TXN .... Texas Northern Oil & Gas [*Vancouver Stock Exchange symbol*]

TXN .... Tunxi [*China*] [*Airport symbol*] (OAG)

TxNacS ...... Stephen F. Austin State University, Nacogdoches, TX [*Library symbol*] [*Library of Congress*] (LCLS)

TXO .... Texico, NM [*Location identifier*] [*FAA*] (FAAL)

TXO .... University of Texas of the Permian Basin, Odessa, TX [*OCLC symbol*] (OCLC)

TxOC.......... Odessa College, Odessa, TX [*Library symbol*] [*Library of Congress*] (LCLS)

TxOE .... Ector County Public Library, Odessa, TX [*Library symbol*] [*Library of Congress*] (LCLS)

TxOEP........ El Paso Products Co., Odessa, TX [*Library symbol*] [*Library of Congress*] (LCLS)

TxOGS .... Church of Jesus Christ of Latter-Day Saints, Genealogical Society Library, Odessa Stake Branch, Odessa, TX [*Library symbol*] [*Library of Congress*] (LCLS)

TXOL .... Texoil, Inc. [*NASDAQ symbol*]   (NQ)
TXON .... Texon Energy Corp. [*NASDAQ symbol*]   (NQ)
TxOr .... Orange Public Library, Orange, TX [*Library symbol*] [*Library of Congress*]   (LCLS)
TXOrD .... E. I. DuPont de Nemours & Co., Sabine River Works, Orange, TX [*Library symbol*] [*Library of Congress*]   (LCLS)
TXP .... El Paso Public Library, El Paso, TX [*OCLC symbol*]   (OCLC)
TxP .... Pasadena Public Library, Pasadena, TX [*Library symbol*] [*Library of Congress*]   (LCLS)
TxPaIMS .... Institute of Marine Science, University of Texas, Port Aransas, TX [*Library symbol*] [*Library of Congress*]   (LCLS)
TxParC .... Paris Junior College, Paris, TX [*Library symbol*] [*Library of Congress*]   (LCLS)
TxPC .... Champion Papers, Inc., Pasadena, TX [*Library symbol*] [*Library of Congress*]   (LCLS)
TxPE .... Ethyl Corp., Pasadena, TX [*Library symbol*] [*Library of Congress*]   (LCLS)
TxPlao .... Plano Public Library, Plano, TX [*Library symbol*] [*Library of Congress*]   (LCLS)
TxPlW .... Wayland Baptist College, Plainview, TX [*Library symbol*] [*Library of Congress*]   (LCLS)
TxPnT .... Texas-United States Chemical Co., Process Engineering Section, R and D Library, Port Neches, TX [*Library symbol*] [*Library of Congress*]   (LCLS)
TxPo .... Gates Memorial Library, Port Arthur, TX [*Library symbol*] [*Library of Congress*]   (LCLS)
TXPRD ...... Tax Period
TxPS .... San Jacinto College, Pasadena, TX [*Library symbol*] [*Library of Congress*]   (LCLS)
TxPT .... Tenneco Chemicals, Inc., Pasadena, TX [*Library symbol*] [*Library of Congress*]   (LCLS)
TxPvC .... Prairie View Agricultural and Mechanical College, Prairie View, TX [*Library symbol*] [*Library of Congress*]   (LCLS)
TXPYR .... Taxpayer
TXQ .... University of Texas, Austin, Law Library, Austin, TX [*OCLC symbol*]   (OCLC)
TXR .... Lamar University, Beaumont, TX [*OCLC symbol*]   (OCLC)
TXR .... Susitna Valley, AK [*Location identifier*] [*FAA*]   (FAAL)
TXR .... Tank Exchange Ratio   (MCD)
TXR .... Triex Resources Ltd. [*Vancouver Stock Exchange symbol*]
TxRaC .... Ranger Junior College, Ranger, TX [*Library symbol*] [*Library of Congress*]   (LCLS)
TXRC .... Texas Export [*AAR code*]
TxReTR ...... Texas Research Foundation, Renner, TX [*Library symbol*] [*Library of Congress*]   (LCLS)
TXRF .... Total-Reflection X-Ray Fluorescence [*Analytical chemistry*]
TxRi .... Richardson Public Library, Richardson, TX [*Library symbol*] [*Library of Congress*]   (LCLS)
TxRiA .... Anderson Clayton Foods [*of Anderson, Clayton & Co.*], Richardson, TX [*Library symbol*] [*Library of Congress*]   (LCLS)
TxRiS .... Sun Oil Co., Richardson, TX [*Library symbol*] [*Library of Congress*]   (LCLS)
TXRX .... Transmitter-Receiver
TXS .... Hardin-Simmons University, Abilene, TX [*OCLC symbol*]   (OCLC)
TXS .... Taxpayer Service [*IRS*]
TXS .... Telephone Exchange (Strowger) [*Telecommunications*]   (TEL)
TxSa .... San Antonio Public Library, San Antonio, TX [*Library symbol*] [*Library of Congress*]   (LCLS)
TxSaBAM ... United States Air Force, School of Aerospace Medicine, Brooks Air Force Base, San Antonio, TX [*Library symbol*] [*Library of Congress*]   (LCLS)
TxSaBHR ... United States Air Force, Human Resources Laboratory Library, Brooks Air Force Base, San Antonio, TX [*Library symbol*] [*Library of Congress*]   (LCLS)
TxSaBM ..... Bexar County Medical Library Association, San Antonio, TX [*Library symbol*] [*Library of Congress*]   (LCLS)
TxSaC .... San Antonio College, San Antonio, TX [*Library symbol*] [*Library of Congress*]   (LCLS)
TxSaGH ...... Robert B. Green Memorial Hospital, San Antonio, TX [*Library symbol*] [*Library of Congress*]   (LCLS)
TxSaGS ..... Church of Jesus Christ of Latter-Day Saints, Genealogical Society Library, San Antonio Branch, San Antonio, TX [*Library symbol*] [*Library of Congress*]   (LCLS)
TxSaI .... Incarnate Word College, San Antonio, TX [*Library symbol*] [*Library of Congress*]   (LCLS)
TxSal .... Tom Green County Library, San Angelo, TX [*Library symbol*] [*Library of Congress*]   (LCLS)
TxSalA .... Angelo State University, San Angelo, TX [*Library symbol*] [*Library of Congress*]   (LCLS)
TxSaO .... Our Lady of the Lake College, San Antonio, TX [*Library symbol*] [*Library of Congress*]   (LCLS)
TxSaOC ..... Oblate College of the Southwest, San Antonio, TX [*Library symbol*] [*Library of Congress*]   (LCLS)
TxSaSFRE ... Southwest Foundation for Research and Education, San Antonio, TX [*Library symbol*] [*Library of Congress*]   (LCLS)
TxSaSM ..... Saint Mary's University, San Antonio, TX [*Library symbol*] [*Library of Congress*]   (LCLS)
TxSaSM-L ... Saint Mary's University, Law Library, San Antonio, TX [*Library symbol*] [*Library of Congress*]   (LCLS)

TxSaSP ...... Saint Philip's College, San Antonio, TX [*Library symbol*] [*Library of Congress*]   (LCLS)
TxSaSR ...... Southwest Research Institute, San Antonio, TX [*Library symbol*] [*Library of Congress*]   (LCLS)
TxSaStJ ..... Saint John's Seminary, San Antonio, TX [*Library symbol*] [*Library of Congress*]   (LCLS)
TxSaT .... Trinity University, San Antonio, TX [*Library symbol*] [*Library of Congress*]   (LCLS)
TxSaT-W .... Trinity University, Whitsett Library Museum, San Antonio, TX [*Library symbol*] [*Library of Congress*]   (LCLS)
TxSaU .... University of Texas at San Antonio, San Antonio, TX [*Library symbol*] [*Library of Congress*]   (LCLS)
TxSaUS ...... United Services Automobile Association, San Antonio, TX [*Library symbol*] [*Library of Congress*]   (LCLS)
TxSaV .... United States Veterans Administration Hospital, San Antonio, TX [*Library symbol*] [*Library of Congress*]   (LCLS)
Tx-SC .... Texas State Law Library, Austin, TX [*Library symbol*] [*Library of Congress*]   (LCLS)
TxSE .... Texas Studies in English [*A publication*]
TxSeTL ..... Texas Lutheran College, Seguin, TX [*Library symbol*] [*Library of Congress*]   (LCLS)
TxShA .... Austin College, Sherman, TX [*Library symbol*] [*Library of Congress*]   (LCLS)
TxShpM ..... United States Air Force, Regional Hospital, Medical Library, Sheppard AFB, TX [*Library symbol*] [*Library of Congress*]   (LCLS)
TxSiW .... Rob and Bessie Welder Wildlife Foundation, Sinton, TX [*Library symbol*] [*Library of Congress*]   (LCLS)
TxSjM .... San Jacinto Museum of History Association, San Jacinto Monument, TX [*Library symbol*] [*Library of Congress*]   (LCLS)
TxSmS .... Southwest Texas State University, San Marcos, TX [*Library symbol*] [*Library of Congress*]   (LCLS)
TxSn .... Scurry County Library, Snyder, TX [*Library symbol*] [*Library of Congress*]   (LCLS)
TxSvT .... Tarleton State University, Stephenville, TX [*Library symbol*] [*Library of Congress*]   (LCLS)
TxSw .... Sweetwater City-County Library, Sweetwater, TX [*Library symbol*] [*Library of Congress*]   (LCLS)
TXT .... Texas Southern University, Houston, TX [*OCLC symbol*]   (OCLC)
TXT .... Text
TXT .... Textron, Inc. [*NYSE symbol*]
TxTA .... American Oil Co. [*Later, Amoco Oil Co.*], Texas City, TX [*Library symbol*] [*Library of Congress*]   (LCLS)
TxTCM .... College of the Mainland, Texas City, TX [*Library symbol*] [*Library of Congress*]   (LCLS)
TxTe .... Texarkana Public Library, Texarkana, TX [*Library symbol*] [*Library of Congress*]   (LCLS)
TxTeC .... Texarkana College, Texarkana, TX [*Library symbol*] [*Library of Congress*]   (LCLS)
TxTeET ...... East Texas State University, Texarkana, TX [*Library symbol*] [*Library of Congress*]   (LCLS)
TxTehW ..... Westminster College, Tehuacana, TX [*Library symbol*] [*Library of Congress*]   (LCLS)
TxTemC ..... Temple Junior College, Temple, TX [*Library symbol*] [*Library of Congress*]   (LCLS)
TxTemH ..... Scott and White Memorial Hospital, Temple, TX [*Library symbol*] [*Library of Congress*]   (LCLS)
TxTerS .... Southwestern Christian College, Terrell, TX [*Library symbol*] [*Library of Congress*]   (LCLS)
TxTeS .... East Texas State University at Texarkana, Texarkana, TX [*Library symbol*] [*Library of Congress*]   (LCLS)
TXTL .... Textile   (MSA)
TXTLE .... Textile
TxTMC .... Monsanto Co., Texas City, TX [*Library symbol*] [*Library of Congress*]   (LCLS)
TXTN .... Textone, Inc. [*NASDAQ symbol*]   (NQ)
TxTUC .... Union Carbide Corp., Chemicals and Plastics Division, Texas City, TX [*Library symbol*] [*Library of Congress*]   (LCLS)
TxTy .... Tyler Carnegie Public Library, Tyler, TX [*Library symbol*] [*Library of Congress*]   (LCLS)
TxTyB .... Butler College, Tyler, TX [*Library symbol*] [*Library of Congress*]   (LCLS)
TxTyC .... Texas Eastern University, Tyler, TX [*Library symbol*] [*Library of Congress*]   (LCLS)
TxTyT .... Texas College, Tyler, TX [*Library symbol*] [*Library of Congress*]   (LCLS)
TXU .... Tabou [*Ivory Coast*] [*Airport symbol*]   (OAG)
txu .... Texas [*MARC country of publication code*] [*Library of Congress*]   (LCCP)
TXU .... Texas Utilities Co. [*NYSE symbol*]
TXU .... Texoro Resources Ltd. [*Vancouver Stock Exchange symbol*]
TxU .... University of Texas, Austin, TX [*Library symbol*] [*Library of Congress*]   (LCLS)
TXU .... University of Texas at El Paso, El Paso, TX [*OCLC symbol*]   (OCLC)
TxU-A .... University of Texas, M. D. Anderson Hospital and Tumor Institute, Houston, TX [*Library symbol*] [*Library of Congress*]   (LCLS)

TxU-B .... University of Texas, Business Administration and Economics Library, Austin, TX [*Library symbol*] [*Library of Congress*] (LCLS)
TxU-D .... University of Texas, School of Dentistry, Houston, TX [*Library symbol*] [*Library of Congress*] (LCLS)
TxU-Da ...... University of Texas at Dallas, Richardson, TX [*Library symbol*] [*Library of Congress*] (LCLS)
TxU-Hu .... Humanities Research Center, University of Texas, Austin, TX [*Library symbol*] [*Library of Congress*] (LCLS)
TxU-J .... University of Texas, Lyndon Baines Johnson Presidential Library, Austin, TX [*Library symbol*] [*Library of Congress*] (LCLS)
TxU-L .... University of Texas, Law Library, Austin, TX [*Library symbol*] [*Library of Congress*] (LCLS)
TxU-M .... University of Texas, Medical School, Galveston, TX [*Library symbol*] [*Library of Congress*] (LCLS)
TxU-O .... University of Texas of the Permian Basin, Odessa, TX [*Library symbol*] [*Library of Congress*] (LCLS)
TxU-PH .... University of Texas, School of Public Health, Houston, TX [*Library symbol*] [*Library of Congress*] (LCLS)
TxU-STM ... University of Texas Medical School at San Antonio, San Antonio, TX [*Library symbol*] [*Library of Congress*] (LCLS)
TxUvS .... Southwest Texas Junior College, Uvalde, TX [*Library symbol*] [*Library of Congress*] (LCLS)
TXV .... Fairfield, CA [*Location identifier*] [*FAA*] (FAAL)
TXV .... University of Houston, Victoria Center, Victoria, TX [*OCLC symbol*] (OCLC)
TxVeC .... Vernon Regional Junior College, Vernon, TX [*Library symbol*] [*Library of Congress*] (LCLS)
TxVi .... Victoria Public Library, Victoria, TX [*Library symbol*] [*Library of Congress*] (LCLS)
TxViC .... Victoria College, Victoria, TX [*Library symbol*] [*Library of Congress*] (LCLS)
TxVidGS .... Church of Jesus Christ of Latter-Day Saints, Genealogical Society Library, Beaumont Branch, Vidor, TX [*Library symbol*] [*Library of Congress*] (LCLS)
TxViHU .... University of Houston, Victoria Center, Victoria, TX [*Library symbol*] [*Library of Congress*] (LCLS)
TXW .... Waco-McLennan County Library, Waco, TX [*OCLC symbol*] (OCLC)
TxW .... Waco-McLennan County Library, Waco, TX [*Library symbol*] [*Library of Congress*] (LCLS)
TxWaS .... Southwestern Assemblies of God College, Waxahachie, TX [*Library symbol*] [*Library of Congress*] (LCLS)
TxWB .... Baylor University, Waco, TX [*Library symbol*] [*Library of Congress*] (LCLS)
TxWB-B ..... Baylor University, Armstrong Browning Library, Waco, TX [*Library symbol*] [*Library of Congress*] (LCLS)
TxWB-L ..... Baylor University, Law School Library, Waco, TX [*Library symbol*] [*Library of Congress*] (LCLS)
TxWB-Mus ... Baylor University, Museum Collection, Waco, TX [*Library symbol*] [*Library of Congress*] (LCLS)
TxWeaC ..... Weatherford College, Weatherford, TX [*Library symbol*] [*Library of Congress*] (LCLS)
TxWeiM ...... Weimar Mercury, Weimar, TX [*Library symbol*] [*Library of Congress*] (LCLS)
TxWFM ...... Masonic Grand Lodge of Texas, Waco, TX [*Library symbol*] [*Library of Congress*] (LCLS)
TxWhaC ..... Wharton County Junior College, Wharton, TX [*Library symbol*] [*Library of Congress*] (LCLS)
TxWhaW ..... Wharton County Library, Wharton, TX [*Library symbol*] [*Library of Congress*] (LCLS)
TxWic .... Kemp Public Library, Wichita Falls, TX [*Library symbol*] [*Library of Congress*] (LCLS)
TxWicM ..... Midwestern State University, Wichita Falls, TX [*Library symbol*] [*Library of Congress*] (LCLS)
TxWM .... McClennan Community College, Waco, TX [*Library symbol*] [*Library of Congress*] (LCLS)
TxWPQ ...... Paul Quinn College, Waco, TX [*Library symbol*] [*Library of Congress*] (LCLS)
TxWV .... United States Veterans Administration Hospital, Waco, TX [*Library symbol*] [*Library of Congress*] (LCLS)
TXX .... Southwestern University, Georgetown, TX [*OCLC symbol*] (OCLC)
TY .... Air Caledonie [*France*] [*ICAO designator*] (FAAC)
TY .... Dahomey [*Aircraft nationality and registration mark*] (FAAC)
TY .... Talmud Yerushalmi (BJA)
TY .... Tax Year
TY .... Tebul [*or Tevul*] Yom (BJA)
Ty .... Temporary
TY .... Territory
TY .... Thank You
Ty .... Thyroxine [*Also, T$_4$, Thx*] [*An amino acid*] [*Endocrinology*]
TY .... Total Yield (AABC)
TY .... Translation Hand Controller Y-Axis Directory (MCD)
TY .... Tri-Continental Corp. [*NYSE symbol*]
TY .... Truly
TY .... Tyler's Quarterly Historical and Genealogical Magazine [*A publication*]
Ty .... Tyndale New Testament Commentaries [*A publication*] (BJA)

TY .... Type
TY .... Typhoid Fever (DSUE)
TYA .... Steele Aviation [*Fresno, CA*] [*FAA designator*] (FAAC)
TYAA .... Textured Yarn Association of America [*Gastonia, NC*] (EA)
Tyazh Mashinostr ... Tyazhelie Mashinostroenie [*A publication*]
TYC .... Teach Yourself by Computer [*In company name, TYC Software*] [*Pittsford, NY*] [*Software manufacturer*]
TYC .... Toby Creek Resources Ltd. [*Vancouver Stock Exchange symbol*]
TYC .... Trinity College, Hartford, CT [*OCLC symbol*] (OCLC)
TYC .... Two-Year[-*Old*] Course [*Horse racing*]
TYC .... Tylerdale Connecting [*AAR code*]
TYCO .... Tylenol and Codeine [*Pharmacy*]
TYCOM .... Type Commander
TYD .... Temporary Duty (MCD)
TyD .... Trabajos y Dias [*A publication*]
tyd .... Type Designer [*MARC relator code*] [*Library of Congress*]
TYDAC .... Typical Digital Automatic Computer
TYDE .... Type Designators (MSA)
TYDS .... Transactions. Yorkshire Dialect Society [*A publication*]
Tydskr Dieetkd Huishoudkd ... Tydskrif vir Dieetkunde en Huishoudkunde [*South Africa*] [*A publication*]
Tydskr Natuurwet ... Tydskrif vir Natuurwetenskappe [*A publication*]
Tydskr Natuurwetenskap ... Tydskrif vir Natuurwetenskappe. Suid-Afrikaanse Akademie vir Wetenskap en Kuns [*A publication*]
Tydskr S-Afr Vet Ver ... Tydskrif van die Suid-Afrikaanse Veterinere Vereniging [*A publication*]
Tydskr Skoon Lug ... Tydskrif vir Skoon Lug [*A publication*]
Tydskr Tandheelkd Ver S-Afr ... Tydskrif van die Tandheelkundige Vereniging van Suid-Afrika [*A publication*]
Tydskr Wet Kuns ... Tydskrif vir Wetenskap en Kuns [*A publication*]
TYE .... Tye Explorations, Inc. [*Vancouver Stock Exchange symbol*]
TYE .... Tyonek, AK [*Location identifier*] [*FAA*] (FAAL)
TYF .... Panama City, FL [*Location identifier*] [*FAA*] (FAAL)
TYF .... Tung Yeun Feng [*Republic of China*] [*Seismograph station code, US Geological Survey*] (SEIS)
TYFSOK ...... Thank You for Shopping Our K-Mart [*or Kresge's*] [*Slogan of K-Mart Corp.*]
TYG .... Temple Youth Group [*Local groups of National Federation of Temple Youth, sometimes called TYG-ers, pronounced "tigers"*]
TYG .... Trypticase, Yeast-Extract, Glucose [*Cell growth medium*]
tyg .... Typographer [*MARC relator code*] [*Library of Congress*]
TygP .... Tygodnik Powszechny [*A publication*]
TYH .... Tihany [*Hungary*] [*Geomagnetic observatory code*]
TYI .... Rocky Mount, NC [*Location identifier*] [*FAA*] (FAAL)
TYK .... Toyooka [*Japan*] [*Seismograph station code, US Geological Survey*] (SEIS)
TYL .... Talara [*Peru*] [*Airport symbol*] (OAG)
TYL .... TANU [*Tanganyika African National Union*] Youth League [*Tanganyika*]
TYL .... Tyler Corp. [*NYSE symbol*]
Tyl .... Tyler's Vermont Supreme Court Reports [*1800-03*] (DLA)
Tyler .... Tyler's Vermont Reports [*1800-03*] (DLA)
Tyler Ej ...... Tyler on Ejectment and Adverse Enjoyment (DLA)
Tyler's .... Tyler's Quarterly Historical and Genealogical Magazine [*A publication*]
Tyler's Quar ... Tyler's Quarterly Historical and Genealogical Magazine [*A publication*]
Tyler Steph Pl ... Tyler's Edition of Stephen on Principles of Pleading (DLA)
TYLN .... Tylan Corp. [*NASDAQ symbol*] (NQ)
TYMNET .... Timeshare, Inc. Network [*Telecommunications*] (TEL)
tymp .... Tympany
TYMV .... Turnip Yellow Mosaic Virus
TYN .... Taiyuan [*China*] [*Seismograph station code, US Geological Survey*] (SEIS)
TYN .... Taiyuan [*China*] [*Airport symbol*] (OAG)
TYN .... Taywin Resources Ltd. [*Vancouver Stock Exchange symbol*]
TYNAA ...... Tydskrif vir Natuurwetenskappe [*A publication*]
TyndHB ...... Tyndale House Bulletin [*Cambridge*] [*A publication*] (BJA)
Tyng .... Tyng's Reports [*2-17 Massachusetts*] (DLA)
TYO .... Tokyo [*Japan*] [*Airport symbol*] (OAG)
TYO .... Two-Year-Old [*Horse racing*] (ROG)
Tyoevaeen Taloudell Tutkimus Katsaus ... Tyoevaeen Taloudellinen Tutkimuslaitos Katsaus [*A publication*]
TYP .... Transitional Year Program [*Brandeis University*] (EA)
TY-P .... Trial Y-Plane
Typ .... Typed (BJA)
TYP .... Typical (AAG)
TYP .... Typography (AAG)
TYP .... [*The*] Youth Project [*Washington, DC*] (EA)
TYPER .... Typographical Error (AAG)
TYPH .... Typhoon
TYPL .... Type-Plate
Typ News ... Typewriting News [*A publication*]
TYPNO .... Teletypewriter Communications Interrupted (FAAC)
TYPO .... Typographical
TYPOE .... Ten Year Plan for Ocean Exploration [*Marine science*] (MSC)
TYPOG .... Typographer [*or Typography*]

TYPOK .... Teletypewriter Communications Resumed   (FAAC)
TYPOUT ..... Typewriter Output
TYPSTG ..... Typesetting   (MSA)
TYPW .... Typewriter   (ADA)
TYPWRT .... Typewriter
TYPWRTR ... Typewriter
TYQ .... Indianapolis, IN [*Location identifier*] [*FAA*]   (FAAL)
TYR .... Tyler [*Texas*] [*Airport symbol*]   (OAG)
TYR .... Tyrone [*County in Ireland*]   (ROG)
Tyr .... Tyrosine [*Also, Y*] [*An amino acid*]
Tyr .... Tyrwhitt and Granger's English Exchequer Reports [*1830-
                 35*]   (DLA)
Tyre Jus Filiz ... Tyre's Jus Filizarii   (DLA)
Tyr & Gr ..... Tyrwhitt and Granger's English Exchequer Reports [*1830-
                 35*]   (DLA)
Tyr Trig ...... Tyranni Triginta [*of Scriptores Historiae Augustae*] [*Classical
                 studies*]   (OCD)
Tyrw .... Tyrwhitt and Granger's English Exchequer Reports [*1830-
                 35*]   (DLA)
Tyrw & G .... Tyrwhitt and Granger's English Exchequer Reports [*1835-
                 36*]   (DLA)
Tyrw & G (Eng) ... Tyrwhitt and Granger's English Exchequer Reports [*1835-
                 36*]   (DLA)
TYRX .... Tyrex Oil Co. [*NASDAQ symbol*]   (NQ)
TYS .... Knoxville [*Tennessee*] [*Airport symbol*]   (OAG)
TYS .... Tensile Yield Strength
TYS .... Tyler Resources, Inc. [*Vancouver Stock Exchange symbol*]
TYS .... Tyseley [*British depot code*]
TYS .... Tyson Valley [*Missouri*] [*Seismograph station code, US
                 Geological Survey*]   (SEIS)
TYSD .... Total Years Service Date
TYSN .... Tyson Foods [*NASDAQ symbol*]   (NQ)
TYT .... Nantucket, MA [*Location identifier*] [*FAA*]   (FAAL)
TYT .... Type Training [*Navy*]   (NVT)
TYTIPT .... Type Training in Port [*Navy*]   (NVT)
Tytler Mil Law ... Tytler on Military Law and Courts-Martial   (DLA)
Tyt Mil L ..... Tytler on Military Law and Courts Martial [*3rd ed.*]
                 [*1812*]   (DLA)
TYU .... Tyuratam [*Satellite launch complex*] [*USSR*]
TYV .... Little Rock, AR [*Location identifier*] [*FAA*]   (FAAL)
TYX .... Tylox Resources Corp. [*Vancouver Stock Exchange symbol*]
TYY .... Abilene, TX [*Location identifier*] [*FAA*]   (FAAL)
TYZ .... Taylor [*Arizona*] [*Airport symbol*] [*Obsolete*]   (OAG)
TZ .... American Trans Air, Inc. [*ICAO designator*]   (FAAC)
TZ .... Der Treue Zionswaechter [*Altona*] [*A publication*]   (BJA)
TZ .... Mali [*Aircraft nationality and registration mark*]   (FAAC)
TZ .... Tactical Zone   (AABC)
tz .... Tanzania [*MARC country of publication code*] [*Library of
                 Congress*]   (LCCP)
TZ .... Theologische Zeitschrift [*A publication*]
TZ .... Tidal Zone
TZ .... Time Zero
TZ .... Transition Zone [*in plant growth*] [*Botany*]
TZ .... Transmitter Zone [*Telecommunications*]   (TEL)
TZ .... Transportation Zone [*Department of Transportation*]
TZ .... Trierer Zeitschrift [*A publication*]
TZ .... Tropical Zodiac
TZ .... [*The*] Twilight Zone [*Television program created by Rod
                 Serling*]
TZ .... United Republic of Tanzania [*Two-letter standard code*]   (CNC)
TZA .... United Republic of Tanzania [*Three-letter standard
                 code*]   (CNC)
TZBas .... Theologische Zeitschrift (Basel) [*A publication*]
TZC .... Trizec Corp. Ltd. [*Toronto Stock Exchange symbol*]
TZD .... True Zenith Distance [*Navigation*]
TZE .... Topaz Exploration Ltd. [*Vancouver Stock Exchange symbol*]
TZE .... Transfer on Zero
TZG .... Thermofit Zap Gun
TZI .... Traditiones. Zbornik Instituta za Slovensko Narodopisje [*A
                 publication*]
TZJ .... Tubular Zippered Jacket
TZKRA ...... Tonindustrie-Zeitung und Keramische Rundschau [*A
                 publication*]
TZM .... Titanium-Zirconium-Molybdenum [*Alloy*]
TZN .... South Andros [*Bahamas*] [*Airport symbol*]   (OAG)
TZN .... Tchaikazan Enterprises, Inc. [*Vancouver Stock Exchange
                 symbol*]
TZP .... Temperate Zone Phase
TZP .... Time Zero Pulse
TZP .... Triazolopyridazine [*Potential antianxiety drug*]
TZ Prakt Metallbearb ... TZ fuer Praktische Metallbearbeitung [*A
                 publication*]
TZTh .... Tuebinger Zeitschrift fuer Theologie [*A publication*]   (BJA)
TZV .... Tetrazolium Violet [*Also, TV*]
TZX .... Trabzon [*Turkey*] [*Airport symbol*]   (OAG)
TZY .... Warsaw, IN [*Location identifier*] [*FAA*]   (FAAL)
TZZ .... Tabubil [*Papua New Guinea*] [*Seismograph station code, US
                 Geological Survey*]   (SEIS)

U

U .... Audio and Power Connectors [*JETDS nomenclature*]
          [*Military*] (CET)
u------ .... Australasia [*MARC geographic area code*] [*Library of
          Congress*] (LCCP)
U .... Benzon [*Denmark*] [*Research code symbol*]
U .... Eased Up [*Horse racing*]
U .... Eaton Laboratories, Inc. [*Research code symbol*]
U .... Electric Tension [*Symbol*] [*IUPAC*]
u .... Group Velocity [*Symbol*] (DEN)
U .... Intensity Unknown [*Meteorology*] (FAAC)
U .... Internal Energy [*Symbol*] [*Thermodynamics*]
U .... Intrinsic Energy [*Symbol*] [*Physics*]
U .... Quartermon Versor [*Symbol of a function*]
          [*Mathematics*] (ROG)
U .... Shape Descriptor [*U-turn, for example. The shape resembles
          the letter for which it is named*]
U .... Thermal Transmittance per Unit of Area [*Heat transmission
          symbol*]
U .... Uafhaengige Parti [*Independent Party*] [*Denmark*] (PPE)
U .... Ubiquinone [*Coenzyme Q*] [*Also, CoQ, Q, UQ*] [*Biochemistry*]
u .... Uebersetzen [*Translate*] [*German*]
U .... Ugly Sky [*Navigation*]
U .... Ugly Threatening Weather [*Meteorology*]
U .... Uhr [*Clock*] [*German*]
U .... Uitgelezen [*A publication*]
U .... Ullage (AAG)
U .... Ultraphon & Supraphon [*Record label*] [*Czechoslovakia*]
U .... Umpire [*Baseball*]
U .... Uncirculated
U .... Unclassified
U .... Uncle
U .... Uncle [*Phonetic alphabet*] [*Royal Navy*] [*World War I*] [*Pre-
          World War II*] [*World War II*] (DSUE)
U .... Und [*And*] [*German*]
U .... Under
U .... Underwater [*Missile launch environment symbol*]
U .... Unemployed Parent [*Aid to Families with Dependent
          Children*] (OICC)
U .... Unified
U .... Uniform
U .... Uniform [*Phonetic alphabet*] [*International*] (DSUE)
U .... Uniformly Labeled [*Also, UL*] [*Compound, with radioisotope*]
U .... Union [*or Unionist*]
U .... Unit
U .... United
U .... Universal
U .... Universal/Unrestricted [*Film certificate*] [*British*]
U .... Universitas [*A publication*]
U .... University
U .... Unknown
U .... Unlimited [*Aviation*] (FAAC)
U .... Unlimited Time [*Broadcasting term*]
U .... Unoccupied
U .... Unpleasant
U .... Unrestricted [*Aviation*] (FAAC)
U .... Unseated Rider [*Horse racing*]
U .... Unsymmetrical
U .... Unter [*Among*] [*German*]
U .... Untreated [*Medicine*]
U .... Unwatched [*With reference to a light*] [*Maps and charts*]
U .... Up [*or Upper*]
U .... Up (quark) [*Atomic physics*]
u .... Upjohn Co. [*Research code symbol*]
U .... Upper (ROG)
U .... Upper Bow [*Music*] (ROG)
U .... Upper-Class Speech [*"Non-U" designates the opposite*]
U .... Uranium [*Chemical element*]
U .... Urban [*District Council*] [*British*]
U .... Urgent
U .... Uridine [*One-letter symbol; see Urd*]
U .... Urinal (ROG)

U .... Urinate [*Medicine*]
U .... Urology [*Medical Officer designation*] [*British*]
U .... Urschrift [*Original, as of a document*] [*German military*]
U .... Uruguay
U .... US Air, Inc. [*NYSE symbol*]
U .... Use
U .... Utah
U .... Utah Reports (DLA)
U .... Utah State Library, Salt Lake City, UT [*Library symbol*] [*Library
          of Congress*] (LCLS)
U .... Utendus [*To Be Used*] [*Pharmacy*]
U .... Utility [*Designation for all US military aircraft*]
U .... You [*Communications*] (FAAC)
U2 .... Popular music group
U² .... Unclassified, Unlimited [*DoD*]
5U .... Niger [*Aircraft nationality and registration mark*] (FAAC)
9U .... Burundi [*Aircraft nationality and registration mark*] (FAAC)
U (Bomb) ... [*A*] theoretical uranium-encased atomic or hydrogen bomb, the
          shell of which would be transformed into deadly
          radioactive dust upon detonation (MUGU)
UA .... Ultra-Audible
UA .... Umbilical Artery [*Anatomy*]
UA .... Unable to Approve Arrival for the Time Specified
          [*Aviation*] (FAAC)
UA .... Unanesthetized [*Physiology*]
UA .... Unauthorized Absence (MUGU)
UA .... Unavailable
UA .... Und Andere [*And Others*] [*German*]
UA .... Under Age [*i.e., entitled neither to a daily rum ration nor money
          instead*] [*See also G, T*] [*Obsolete*] [*Navy*] [*British*]
U/A .... Under Agreement (DLA)
UA .... Underwater Actuator
UA .... Underwater Association for Scientific Research (EA-IO)
U/A .... Underwriting Account [*Business and trade*]
UA .... Uniform Allowance
UA .... Union des Artistes [*Union of Artists*] [*Canada*]
UA .... Union Association [*Major league in baseball, 1884*]
U/A .... Unit of Account [*European Monetary Agreement*]
UA .... Unit Assets [*Army*]
UA .... United Air Lines, Inc. [*ICAO designator*]
ua .... United Arab Republic [*Egypt*] [*MARC country of publication
          code*] [*Library of Congress*] (LCCP)
UA .... United Asia [*A publication*]
UA .... United Association of Journeymen and Apprentices of the
          Plumbing and Pipe Fitting Industry of the United States
          and Canada (OICC)
UA .... Universidad de Antioquia [*Colombia*] [*A publication*]
UA .... University of Alaska
U of A .... University of Alaska
UA .... University of Arizona
U of A .... University of Arkansas
UA .... Unnumbered Acknowledge [*or Acknowledgment*]
          [*Telecommunications*] (IEEE)
UA .... Unstable Angina [*Medicine*]
UA .... Upper Arm
UA .... Ural-Altaische Jahrbuecher [*A publication*]
UA .... Urbanized Area (OICC)
UA .... Uric Acid
UA .... Urinalysis [*Medicine*] (KSC)
UA .... User Area [*Information storage*]
UA .... Usque Ad [*As Far As*] [*Latin*] (ADA)
UA .... Uterine Aspiration [*Medicine*]
UAA .... Undergarment Accessories Association [*New York, NY*] (EA)
UAA .... Union des Avocats Arabes [*Arab Lawyers Union - ALU*] (EA-
          IO)
UAA .... United Action for Animals [*New York, NY*] (EA)
UAA .... United African Appeal (EA)
UAA .... United American and Australasian Film Productions (ADA)
UAA .... United American and Australasian Film Productions
          Proprietary Ltd. (ADA)
UAA .... United Arab Airlines

UAA............ Universitet i Bergen. Arbok. Historisk-Antikvarisk Rekke [*A publication*]
UAA............ University Aviation Association   (EA)
UAA............ Urban Affairs Association [*Formerly, CUIUA*]   (EA)
UAA............ User Action Analyzer
UAA............ Utility Arborist Association   (EA)
UAAF......... United Action Armed Forces [*A publication*]
UAAS .... Ukrainian Academy of Arts and Sciences in the US   (EA)
UAAUSA .... Ukrainian Artists Association in USA   (EA)
UAB............ Underwriters Adjustment Bureau
UAB............ Unemployment Assistance Board
UAB............ University of Alabama in Birmingham
UAB............ University of Alberta Biotron [*University of Alberta*] [*Research center*]   (RCD)
UAB............ Until Advised By [*Aviation*]   (FAAC)
u-ac---........ Ashmore and Cartier Islands [*MARC geographic area code*] [*Library of Congress*]   (LCCP)
UAC............ Unicorp American Corporation [*American Stock Exchange symbol*]
UAC............ Unified Arab Command   (BJA)
UAC............ Uninterrupted Automatic Control
UAC............ Union Army of Commemoration
UAC............ United African Company
UAC............ United Aircraft Corporation [*Later, United Technologies Corp.*]
UAC............ United American Croats
UAC............ Universal Area Code [*Bureau of Census*]
UAC............ Universidad de Antioquia (Colombia) [*A publication*]
UAC............ Universities Advisory Council
UAC............ University of Alberta, Faculty of Library Science, Edmonton, AL, Canada [*OCLC symbol*]   (OCLC)
UAC............ University Analytical Center [*University of Arizona*] [*Research center*]   (RCD)
UAC............ Unusual Appearing Child [*Medicine*]
UAC............ Upper Area Control Center [*Aviation*]
UAC............ Utility Airplane Council [*Defunct*]   (EA)
UAC............ Utility Assemble Compool
UACA .... United American Contractors Association [*Boston, MA*]   (EA)
UACC .... Universal Autograph Collectors Club [*International*]   (EA)
UACC .... Upper Area Control Center [*Aviation*]
UACCDD .... University Affiliated Cincinnati Center for Developmental Disorders [*University of Cincinnati*] [*Research center*]   (RCD)
UACCI........ United Association of Christian Counselors International   (EA)
UACI.......... United Artists Communication, Incorporated [*NASDAQ symbol*]   (NQ)
UACL .... United Aircraft of Canada Limited
UACN .... Unified Automated Communication Network
UACN .... University of Alaska Computer Network [*Fairbanks, AK*] [*Research center*]   (RCD)
UACRL .... United Aircraft Corporation Research Laboratory   (KSC)
UACSC ...... United Aircraft Corporate Systems Center   (KSC)
UACTE .... Universal Automatic Control and Test Equipment
UAD........... Salinas, CA [*Location identifier*] [*FAA*]   (FAAL)
UAD........... Underwater Acoustic Decoupler
UAD........... Undetermined Aerodynamic Disturbance   (MCD)
UAD........... Unit Assembly Drawing
UADC .... Universal Air Data Computer
UADP .... Uniform Automated [*or Automatic*] Data Processing
UADPS....... Uniform Automated [*or Automatic*] Data Processing System
UADPS-ICP ... Uniform Automated [*or Automatic*] Data Processing System for Inventory Control Points [*Navy*]
UADPS/INAS ... Uniform Automated [*or Automatic*] Data Processing System/Industrial Naval Air Station
UADPS-SP ... Uniform Automated [*or Automatic*] Data Processing System for Stock Points [*Navy*]
UADS .... User Attribute Data Set [*Data processing*]   (MDG)
UADW .... Universal Alliance of Diamond Workers [*See also AUOD*] [*Antwerp*] [*Belgium*]   (EA-IO)
UAE........... Unilateral Absence of Excretion [*Medicine*]
UAE........... United Arab Emirates
UAEE......... Union des Associations Europeennes d'Etudiants [*Union of European Student Associations*]
UAegAl...... Urkunden die Aegyptischen Altertums [*A publication*]
UAEI.......... United American Energy, Incorporated [*NASDAQ symbol*]   (NQ)
UA/EM .... University Association for Emergency Medicine [*Lansing, MI*]   (EA)
UAERA .... United States Air Force School of Aerospace Medicine. Technical Report [*A publication*]
UAES......... Utah Agricultural Experiment Station [*Utah State University*] [*Research center*]   (RCD)
UAF .... Ultimate Asbestos Fibril
UAF .... Unit Authorization File
UAF .... University-Affiliated Facility
UAFA......... Union Arab Football Association   (EA)
UAFA......... Union Arabe de Football Association [*Union Arab Football Association*]   (EA-IO)
UAFC .... Universal Air Freight Corporation
UAF-MR ..... University-Affiliated Facility for the Mentally Retarded
UAFRA .... Uniform Aircraft Financial Responsibility Act [*National Conference of Commissioners on Uniform State Laws*]

UAFSC ...... Utilization Air Force Specialty Code
UAFS/T...... Universal Aircraft Flight Simulator/Trainer
UAFUR .... Urgent Amplified Failure of Unsatisfactory Report
UAG........... Untersuchungen zur Altorientalischen Geschichte [*H. Winckler*] [*A publication*]   (BJA)
UAG........... Upper Atmosphere Geophysics   (KSC)
UAG........... USSR. Academy of Science. Proceedings. Geographical Series [*A publication*]
UAGA .... Uniform Anatomical Gift Act [*For organ donation*]
UAH........... Ua Huka [*Marquesas Islands*] [*Airport symbol*]   (OAG)
UAH........... Union of Arab Historians   (EA)
UAH........... University of Alabama in Huntsville
UAHC........ Union of American Hebrew Congregations   (EA)
UAHS........ Ulster Architectural Heritage Society [*Belfast*]
UAI .... Union Academique Internationale [*International Academic Union - IAU*]   (EA-IO)
UAI .... Union des Associations Internationales [*Union of International Associations - UIA*]   (EA-IO)
UAI .... Union Astronomique Internationale [*International Astronomical Union*]
UAI .... Universal Azimuth Indicator
UAI .... Urban Affairs Institute   (EA)
UAI .... Uterine Activity Interval [*Obstetrics*]
UAICC .... Underwater Acoustic Interference Coordinating Committee [*Military*]
UAIDE .... Users of Automatic Information Display Equipment   (EA)
UAIM .... United Andean Indian Mission [*Superseded by Ecuador Concerns Committee*]
UAIMS .... United Aircraft Information Management System
UAIRA .... US Aircraft CI A [*NASDAQ symbol*]   (NQ)
UAJ .... Union of Arab Jurists   (EA-IO)
UAJ .... Ural-Altaische Jahrbuecher [*A publication*]
UAJb .... Ural-Altaische Jahrbuecher [*A publication*]
UAJG......... Union d'Action des Jeunes de Guinee [*Guinean Union of Youth Action*]
UAK........... Narssarssuaq [*Greenland*] [*Airport symbol*]   (OAG)
UAL .... UAL, Inc. [*United Airlines*] [*NYSE symbol*] [*Wall Street slang name: "You All"*]
UAL .... Ukrainian American League   (EA)
UAL .... Unit Area Loading   (AAG)
UAL .... Unit Authorization List
UAL .... Unite Arithmetique et Logique [*Arithmetic and Logic Unit - ALU*] [*French*]
UAL .... United Air Lines, Inc. [*Air carrier designation symbol*]
UAL .... Universal Airline Codes   (MCD)
UAL .... Upper Acceptance Limit
UAL .... Urea-Ammonia Liquor
UAL .... User Adaptive Language
UALE .... Universal Artist League of Esperantists   (EA-IO)
UALE .... Universala Artista Ligo de Esperantistoj [*Universal Artist League of Esperantists*]   (EA-IO)
UALI .... Unit Authorization List Item
UAM........... Und Anderes Mehr [*And So Forth*] [*German*]
UAM........... Underwater-to-Air Missile [*Air Force*]
UAM........... Union Africaine et Malagache [*African and Malagasy Union*] [*Later, Common Afro-Malagasy Organization*]
UAM........... United American Mechanics   (EA)
UAM........... United Asset Management Corp. [*NYSE symbol*]
UAM........... United States Medical Intelligence and Information Agency, Frederick, MD [*OCLC symbol*]   (OCLC)
UAMC .... Utility Assemble Master Compool
UAMCT ..... Union of Automobile, Motorcycle, and Cycle Technology
UAMR........ United Association of Manufacturers' Representatives [*Kansas City, KS*]   (EA)
UAMS......... Ukrainian Academy of Medical Sciences   (EA)
UAMS......... Upper Atmosphere Mass Spectrometer
UAN........... United Animal Nations   (EA-IO)
UAN........... Urea-Ammonium Nitrate [*Fertilizer*]
UAN........... Uric Acid Nitrogen
UANC........ United African National Congress
UANC........ United African National Council [*Zimbabwean*]   (PPW)
UANM........ United African Nationalist Movement   (EA)
UANM........ Universal African Nationalist Movement   (EA)
UAO........... Unconventional Aerial Object
UAO........... Und Andere Orte [*And Elsewhere*] [*German*]
UAO........... Unexplained Aerial Object
UAOD........ United Ancient Order of Druids [*Freemasonry*]   (ROG)
UAP........... Ua Pou [*Marquesas Islands*] [*Airport symbol*]   (OAG)
UAP........... UAP, Inc. [*Toronto Stock Exchange symbol*]
UAP........... Unabhaengige Arbeiterpartei [*Independent Labor Party*] [*West Germany*]   (PPE)
UAP........... Unabhaengige Arbeiterpartei - Deutsche Sozialisten [*Independent Labor Party - German Socialists*] [*West German*]   (PPW)
UAP........... Unidentified Atmospheric Phenomena
UAP........... Union of American Physicians [*Later, UAPD*]   (EA)
UAP........... United Amateur Press   (EA)
UAP........... United Australia Party
UAP........... Universal Availability of Publications [*International Federation of Library Associations*]
UAP........... University-Affiliated Program

UAP .... Unmanned Airborne Position   (MCD)
UAP .... Upper Air Project
UAP .... Upper Arlington Public Library, Upper Arlington, OH [*OCLC symbol*]   (OCLC)
UAP .... Urea-Ammonium Phosphate [*Organic chemistry*]
UAP .... User Area Profile
UAP .... Utility Amphibian Plane [*Navy*]
UAPA .... United Amateur Press Association [*Later, UAP*]   (EA)
UAPD .... Union of American Physicians and Dentists   (EA)
UAQ .... San Juan [*Argentina*] [*Airport symbol*]   (OAG)
UAQUA ...... Urban Affairs Quarterly [*A publication*]
UAR .... Underwater Acoustic Resistance
UAR .... Underwater Angle Receptacle
UAR .... Uniform Airman Record
UAR .... Unit Address Register
UAR .... United Arab Republic [*Egypt and Syria*] [*Obsolete*]
UAR .... Upper Air Route
UAR .... Upper Atmosphere Research
UAR .... Use as Required   (MSA)
UARCO ...... UARCO, Inc. [*Formerly, United Autographic Register Company*]
UAREP .... Universities Associated for Research and Education in Pathology [*Bethesda, MD*]   (EA)
UARI .... University of Alabama Research Institute   (KSC)
UAR Inst Oceanogr Fish Bull ... United Arab Republic. Institute of Oceanography and Fisheries. Bulletin [*A publication*]
UARJ Anim Prod ... United Arab Republic. Journal of Animal Production [*A publication*]
UARJ Bot ... United Arab Republic. Journal of Botany [*A publication*]
UARJ Chem ... United Arab Republic. Journal of Chemistry [*A publication*]
UARJ Geol ... United Arab Republic. Journal of Geology [*A publication*]
UAR J Microbiol ... United Arab Republic. Journal of Microbiology [*A publication*]
UARJ Pharm Sci ... United Arab Republic. Journal of Pharmaceutical Sciences [*A publication*]
UAR J Phys ... United Arab Republic. Journal of Physics [*A publication*]
UARJ Soil Sci ... United Arab Republic. Journal of Soil Science [*A publication*]
UARJ Vet Sci ... United Arab Republic. Journal of Veterinary Science [*A publication*]
UARL .... United Aircraft Research Laboratories
UAR Minist Agric Agrar Reform Tech Bull ... United Arab Republic. Ministry of Agriculture and Agrarian Reform. Technical Bulletin [*A publication*]
UAR Minist Agric Tech Bull ... United Arab Republic. Ministry of Agriculture. Technical Bulletin [*A publication*]
UARRSI ...... Universal Aerial Refueling Receptacle Slipaway Installation   (MCD)
UARS .... Underwater Acoustic Receiving System [*Navy*]   (MCD)
UARS .... Unmanned Arctic Research Submersible
UARS .... Upper Atmosphere Research Satellite   (MCD)
UAR (South Reg) Minist Agric Hydrobiol Dep Notes Mem ... United Arab Republic (Southern Region). Ministry of Agriculture. Hydrobiological Department. Notes and Memoirs [*A publication*]
UART .... Universal Asynchronous Receiver/Transmitter
UAS .... Ulster Archaeological Society [*Belfast*]
UAS .... Uniform Accounting System   (OICC)
UAS .... Union of African States
UAS .... Unit Approval System [*for approval of aircraft materials, parts, and appliances*] [*FAA*]
UAS .... Unit Assets by State [*Army*]
UAS .... United Arab States
UAS .... University Air Squadrons
UAS .... University of Alabama Studies [*A publication*]
UAS .... Unmanned Aerial [*or Aerospace*] Surveillance
UAS .... Unusual Aerial Sighting   (ADA)
UAS .... Upper Atmospheric Sounder
UAS .... Upstream Activating Sequence [*Genetics*]
UAS .... Uralic and Altaic Series. Indiana University. Publications [*A publication*]
UAS (Hebbal) Monogr Ser ... UAS (Hebbal) Monograph Series [*A publication*]
UASS .... Unmanned Aerial Surveillance System   (MCD)
UASSS ...... Underwater Acoustic Sound Source System
u-at--- .... Australia [*MARC geographic area code*] [*Library of Congress*]   (LCCP)
UAT .... Ultraviolet Acquisition Technique
UAT .... Under Armor Tow   (MCD)
UAT .... Underway Acceptance Trials   (MCD)
UAT .... Union Aeromaritime de Transport [*Privately-owned French airline*]
UAT .... Until Advised by the Tower [*Aviation*]   (FAAC)
UAT .... Urban Arts Theatre   (EA)
UAT .... User Acceptance Test   (MCD)
UATE .... Universal Automatic Test Equipment
UATI .... Union de Asociaciones Tecnicas Internacionales [*Union of International Engineering Organizations - UIEO*] [*Spanish*]   (ASF)
UATI .... Union des Associations Techniques Internationales [*Union of International Technical Associations - UITA*]   (EA-IO)

u-at-ne .... New South Wales [*MARC geographic area code*] [*Library of Congress*]   (LCCP)
u-at-no .... Northern Territory [*Australia*] [*MARC geographic area code*] [*Library of Congress*]   (LCCP)
UATP .... Universal Air Travel Plan [*Commercial airlines credit system*]
u-at-qn .... Queensland [*MARC geographic area code*] [*Library of Congress*]   (LCCP)
u-at-sa .... South Australia [*MARC geographic area code*] [*Library of Congress*]   (LCCP)
u-at-tm .... Tasmania [*MARC geographic area code*] [*Library of Congress*]   (LCCP)
u-at-vi .... Victoria [*MARC geographic area code*] [*Library of Congress*]   (LCCP)
u-at-we ...... Western Australia [*MARC geographic area code*] [*Library of Congress*]   (LCCP)
UAU .... Universities Athletics Union [*British*]
UAUM .... Underwater-to-Air-to-Underwater Missile [*Air Force*]
UAUOC ...... United American Ukrainian Organizations Committee   (EA)
UA/USA ..... UNESCO Association/USA   (EA)
UAV .... Ukrainian American Veterans   (EA)
UAV .... University of the Andes [*Merida*] [*Venezuela*] [*Seismograph station code, US Geological Survey*]   (SEIS)
UAV .... Unmanned Aerial Vehicle [*Aircraft*]   (RDA)
UAVA .... Untersuchungen zur Assyriologie und Vorderasiatischen Archaeologie [*A publication*]
UAW .... International Union, United Automobile, Aerospace, and Agricultural Implement Workers of America
UAW-CAP ... United Auto Workers Community Action Program   (EA)
UAWFA ...... United Auto Workers, Family Auxiliary   (EA)
UAWG .... Um Antwort Wird Gebeten [*Please Reply*] [*German*]
UAWIU ...... United Allied Workers International Union   (EA)
UAX .... Unit Automatic Exchange
UAZ .... East Hartford, CT [*Location identifier*] [*FAA*]   (FAAL)
UB .... Ultimobranchial [*Bodies*] [*Medicine*]
UB .... Unaccompanied Baggage   (MCD)
UB .... Underwater Battery [*Navy*]
UB .... Undistributed Budget   (MCD)
UB .... Unemployment Benefits [*Unemployment insurance*]   (OICC)
UB .... Union Bank [*British*]   (ROG)
UB .... Union of Burma Airways [*ICAO designator*]   (FAAC)
UB .... United Benefice
UB .... United Brands Co. [*NYSE symbol*]
UB .... United Brethren in Christ
UB .... United Brotherhood [*Also written VC for secrecy*] [*Fenianism*]   (ROG)
UB .... Upper Bench [*Legal*] [*British*]   (ROG)
UB .... Upper Brace   (MCD)
UB .... Urban Buecher [*A publication*]
UB .... Usage Block   (MSA)
UB .... Utility Bridge   (NASA)
UB .... Uttara Bharati [*A publication*]
UB1 .... University of Connecticut, Stamford Branch, Stamford, CT [*OCLC symbol*]   (OCLC)
UB2 .... University of Connecticut, Hartford Branch, West Hartford, CT [*OCLC symbol*]   (OCLC)
UB3 .... University of Connecticut, Southeastern Branch, Groton, CT [*OCLC symbol*]   (OCLC)
UB4 .... University of Connecticut, MBA Library, Hartford, CT [*OCLC symbol*]   (OCLC)
UBA .... Uberaba [*Brazil*] [*Airport symbol*]   (OAG)
UBA .... Ulan Bator [*Mongolia*] [*Geomagnetic observatory code*]
UBA .... Unblocking Acknowledge [*Telecommunications*]   (TEL)
UBA .... Undenatured Bacterial Antigen
UBA .... Underwater Breathing Apparatus [*Navy*]   (CAAL)
UBA .... Union of Burma Airways
UBA .... United Baltic Appeal   (EA)
UBA .... United Bank for Africa Ltd.
UBA .... United Breweries of America   (EA)
UBA .... Universitet i Bergen. Arbok. Historisk-Antikvarisk Rekke [*A publication*]
UBAEC ...... Union of Burma Atomic Energy Centre
UBAF .... Union des Banques Arabes et Francaises [*Arab bank group*]
UBAK .... United Bancorp of Alaska, Inc. [*NASDAQ symbol*]   (NQ)
U Baltimore L Rev ... University of Baltimore. Law Review [*A publication*]
U Balt L Rev ... University of Baltimore. Law Review [*A publication*]
UBAN .... Union Bancorp, Inc. [*NASDAQ symbol*]   (NQ)
UBARI .... Union of Burma Applied Research Institute
UBAT .... Ultrasonic Bioassay Tank [*Aerospace*]
UBATS ...... Ultrasonic Bioassay Tank System [*Aerospace*]
UBAZ .... United Bancorp of Arizona [*NASDAQ symbol*]   (NQ)
UBB .... Union Bank of Bavaria
UBB .... Universal Building Block
UBBA .... United Boys' Brigades of America [*Later, BGBA*]   (EA)
UBBC .... Unsaturated (Vitamin) B_{12} Binding Capacity
UBBR .... University Bureaus of Business Research
UBC .... Uniform Building Code   (NRCH)
UBC .... United Black Christians   (EA)
UBC .... United Brotherhood of Carpenters and Joiners of America   (OICC)

UBC............ United Business Communications, Inc. [*Atlanta, GA*] [*Telecommunications*] (TSSD)
UBC............ Universal Bibliographic Control
UBC............ Universal Block Channel
UBC............ Universal Buffer Controller
UBC............ University of British Columbia
UBC............ University of British Columbia Library [*UTLAS symbol*]
UBC............ Used Beverage Can
UBcGS....... Church of Jesus Christ of Latter-Day Saints, Genealogical Society Library, Brigham City South Branch, Brigham City, UT [*Library symbol*] [*Library of Congress*] (LCLS)
UBCHEA .... United Board for Christian Higher Education in Asia (EA)
UBcI .... National Indian Training Center, Brigham City, UT [*Library symbol*] [*Library of Congress*] (LCLS)
UBCIO....... University of British Columbia Institute of Oceanography [*Canada*] (MSC)
UBCJ......... United Brotherhood of Carpenters and Joiners of America
UBCL......... Union of Black Clergy and Laity of the Episcopal Church [*Later, Union of Black Episcopalians*] (EA)
UBC Legal N ... University of British Columbia. Legal Notes [*A publication*]
UBC Legal Notes ... University of British Columbia. Legal Notes [*A publication*]
UBCLN....... University of British Columbia. Legal News (DLA)
UBC L Rev ... University of British Columbia. Law Review [*A publication*]
UBCNREP ... University of British Columbia. Programme in Natural Resource Economics. Resources Paper [*A publication*]
UBcT......... Thiokol Chemical Corp., Utah Division, Brigham City, UT [*Library symbol*] [*Library of Congress*] (LCLS)
UBCW .... United Brick and Clay Workers of America [*Later, ABCWIU*] (EA)
UBD........... Bureau of Land Management, Billings, MT [*OCLC symbol*] (OCLC)
UBD........... Utility Binary Dump [*Data processing*]
UBDA........ Uniform Brain Death Act [*National Conference of Commissioners on Uniform State Laws*]
UBDC........ Urban Bikeway Design Collaborative (EA)
UBDd........ You Be Darned [*Bowdlerized version*] (DSUE)
UBDI.......... Underwater Battery Director Indicator
UBDMA ...... United Better Dress Manufacturers Association [*New York, NY*] (EA)
UBE .... Union Bouddhique d'Europe [*Buddhist Union of Europe - BUE*] [*London, England*] (EA-IO)
UBE .... Union of Black Episcopalians [*Formerly, UBCL*] (EA)
UBEA......... United Business Education Association [*Later, NBEA*]
UBEA Forum ... United Business Education Association Forum [*A publication*]
UBEC .... Union of Banana-Exporting Countries [*See also UPEB*] (EA-IO)
UBeGS ...... Church of Jesus Christ of Latter-Day Saints, Genealogical Society Library, Beaver Branch, Beaver, UT [*Library symbol*] [*Library of Congress*] (LCLS)
UBF .... Universal Boss Fitting
UBF .... Universal Buddhist Fellowship (EA)
UBFC........ Underwater Battery Fire Control [*Navy*]
UBFCS ...... Underwater Battery Fire Control System [*Navy*]
UBG........... Newberg, OR [*Location identifier*] [*FAA*] (FAAL)
UBG........... Ultimobranchial Glands [*Endocrinology*]
UBG........... Underground Building [*National Security Agency*]
UBHC........ Unburned Hydrocarbon [*Also, UHC*] [*Fuel technology*]
UBHJ......... University of Birmingham. Historical Journal [*A publication*]
UBHR........ User Block Handling Routine [*Data processing*] (IBMDP)
UBI .... Buin [*Papua New Guinea*] [*Airport symbol*] (OAG)
UBI .... Ultraviolet Blood Irradiation
UBI .... Universal Battlefield Identification
UBIP.......... Ubiquitous Immunopoietic Polypeptide [*Immunochemistry*]
U Birmingham Hist J ... University of Birmingham. Historical Journal [*A publication*]
UBITRON ... Undulating Beam Interaction Electron Tube
UBJ........... Ube [*Japan*] [*Airport symbol*] (OAG)
UBJSA........ Union of Burma. Journal of Science and Technology [*A publication*]
UBK........... Unbleached Kraft [*Pulp and paper processing*]
UBKA .... Universitaetsbibliothek Karlsruhe [*Karlsruhe University Library*] [*Information retrieval*]
UBKHA...... Uspekhi Biologicheskoi Khimii [*A publication*]
UBKR........ United Bankers, Inc. of Texas [*NASDAQ symbol*] (NQ)
UBKS........ United Banks of Colorado [*NASDAQ symbol*] (NQ)
UBL .... Unbleached (MSA)
UBL .... Unblocking [*Telecommunications*] (TEL)
UBLR........ University of Baltimore. Law Review [*A publication*]
UBLSLJ...... University of Botswana, Lesotho, and Swaziland Law Journal (DLA)
UBM .... Ultrasonic Bonding Machine
UBM .... University of Bridgeport, Bridgeport, CT [*OCLC symbol*] (OCLC)
UBN........... United Business Network [*United Business Communications, Inc.*] [*Atlanta, GA*] [*Telecommunications*] (TSSD)
UBO........... Uinta Basin Array [*Utah*] [*Seismograph station code, US Geological Survey*] [*Closed*] (SEIS)
UBO........... Uinta Basin Observatory
UBO........... Unidentified Bright Object
UBO........... US Tobacco Co. [*NYSE symbol*]

UBOA .... United Bus Owners of America [*Washington, DC*] (EA)
U-BOAT-S ... Unterseeboat [*German submarine*]
UBP........... Ubon Ratchathani [*Thailand*] [*Airport symbol*] (OAG)
UBP........... Underwater Battery Plot [*Antisubmarine warfare*]
UBP........... Unit Beat Policing
UBP........... United Bahamian Party (PPW)
UBP........... United Bermuda Party (PPW)
UBP........... Upward Bound Programs [*Department of Labor*]
U-BPH .... Utah State Library Commission, Division of the Blind and Physically Handicapped, Salt Lake City, UT [*Library symbol*] [*Library of Congress*] (LCLS)
UBPLOT ..... Underwater Battery Plotting Room [*Navy*] (NVT)
UB Pr......... Upper Bench Precedents Tempore Car. I (DLA)
UBPVLS ..... Uniform Boiler and Pressure Vessel Laws Society [*Oceanside, NY*] (EA)
UBR........... Uniform Building Regulations (ADA)
UBR........... University of British Columbia Retrospective Conversion [*UTLAS symbol*]
UBR........... Upper Burma Rulings [*India*] (DLA)
UBRF......... Upper Branchial Filament
U Brit Col L Rev ... University of British Columbia. Law Review [*A publication*]
UBS........... Columbus, MS [*Location identifier*] [*FAA*] (FAAL)
UBS........... Uniform Bearing Stress
UBS........... Union Bank of Switzerland
UBS........... Union Broadcasting System [*Fictitious broadcasting organization in film "Network"*]
UBS........... United Bible Societies (EA)
UBS........... United Broadcasting System [*Network in TV series "America 2-Night"*]
UBS........... Universal Builders Supply Co.
UBS........... University of British Columbia, School of Librarianship, Vancouver, BC, Canada [*OCLC symbol*] (OCLC)
UBS........... University of Buffalo. Studies [*A publication*]
UBSA........ United Business Schools Association [*Later, AICS*] (EA)
UBSB........ [*The*] United Bible Societies. Bulletin [*London*] [*A publication*]
UBSF......... United Bank FSB [*NASDAQ symbol*] (NQ)
UBSO........ Uinta Basin Seismological Observatory
UBT........... Ubatuba [*Brazil*] [*Airport symbol*] [*Obsolete*] (OAG)
UBT........... Universal Boattail Thor [*NASA*]
UBT........... Universal Book Tester [*Measures performance of binding*]
UBTA........ Union Bank & Trust [*NASDAQ symbol*] (NQ)
UB/TIB ...... Universitatsbibliothek Hannover und Technische Informationsbibliothek [*University Library of Hannover and Technical Information Library*] [*Hannover, West Germany*] [*Information service*] (EISS)
UBTM........ United Bellows Tankage Module
UBV........... Ultraviolet-Blue-Visual [*Photometric system*]
UBW........... Kuparuk, AK [*Location identifier*] [*FAA*] (FAAL)
UBW........... Unbewusste [*Unconscious Mind*] [*Psychology*]
UBW........... University of Connecticut, Waterbury Branch, Waterbury, CT [*OCLC symbol*] (OCLC)
UBX........... Cuba, MO [*Location identifier*] [*FAA*] (FAAL)
UBZ........... Upper Border Zone [*Geology*]
UBZC .... UBZ Corporation [*NASDAQ symbol*] (NQ)
UBZHA ...... Ukrayinski Biokhimichnyi Zhurnal [*A publication*]
UC .... Linea Aerea del Cobre Ltda. [*Chile*] [*ICAO designator*] (FAAC)
UC .... National Union Catalogue [*A publication*]
UC .... Ulcerative Colitis [*Medicine*]
UC .... Umbilical Cable [*or Connector*]
UC .... Umbilical Cable Unit Cooler [*Aerospace*] (AAG)
UC .... Una Corda [*With one string or with the soft pedal*] [*Music*]
Uc............. Uncanny Stories [*A publication*]
UC .... Uncirculated Coins [*Numismatics*]
U/C .... Unclassified
UC .... Uncut Edges [*Bookbinding*]
U/C .... Under Carriage (MCD)
UC .... Under Charge
UC .... Under Construction
U/C .... Under Conversion (NATG)
U/C .... Under Cover (ADA)
U/C .... Under Current (NASA)
UC .... Underfashion Club [*Formerly, CBWC*] (EA)
UC .... Underwater Communications (MCD)
UC .... Undifferentiated Carcinoma [*Oncology*]
UC .... Unemployment Compensation
UC .... UNESCO [*United Nations Educational, Scientific, and Cultural Organization*] Chronicle [*A publication*]
UC .... Unichannel
UC .... Union Caledonienne [*Caledonian Union*] (PPW)
UC .... Union Camerounaise [*Cameroonese Union*]
UC .... Union Constitutionelle [*Constitutional Union*] [*Moroccan*] (PPW)
UC .... Unit Call [*Also known as CCS*] [*Telecommunications*]
UC .... Unit Chairman
UC .... Unit Clerk
UC .... Unit Cooler
UC .... Unit Cost
UC .... Unit Count (AFIT)

UC .... United Canada Insurance Co.
uc .... United States Miscellaneous Caribbean Islands [*MARC country of publication code*] [*Library of Congress*]   (LCCP)
UC .... University of California
UC .... University College
UC .... University Colleges [*Public-performance tariff class*] [*British*]
UC .... Unoperated Control
UC .... Unsatisfactory Condition   (NASA)
UC .... Untreated Controls [*Medicine*]
UC .... Up Converter
UC .... Uplink Command
UC .... Upper Canada
UC .... Upper Cylinder
UC .... Uppercase [*Typography*]   (ADA)
UC .... Uranium Canada Ltd.
UC .... Urbis Conditae [*From the Foundation of the City; that is, of Rome*] [*Latin*]
UC .... Urea Clearance [*Clinical chemistry*]
U & C .... Urethral and Cervical [*Medicine*]
UC .... Urinary Catheter [*Medicine*]
UC .... Usable Control
UC .... Using Command
U & C .... Usual and Customary
UC .... Usual Health-Care [*Medicine*]
UC .... Utility Car [*British*]
UC .... Utility Cargo
UC .... Utility Corridor
UC .... Utilization Control
UCA............ Under Color Addition [*Printing technology*]
UCA............ Uniform Chart of Accounts [*DoD*]
UCA............ Uniform Companies Act [*A publication*]
UCA............ United Congressional Appeal   (EA)
UCA............ United States Court of Appeals for the District of Columbia, Judges Library, Washington, DC [*OCLC symbol*]   (OCLC)
UCA............ Unitized Component Assembly [*Aerospace*]
UCA............ Units Consistency Analyzer [*Data processing*]
UCA............ Universal Calibration Adapter
UCA............ Upper Control Area   (NATG)
UCA............ Utica [*New York*] [*Airport symbol*]   (OAG)
UCACEP ... United Council of Associations of Civil Employees of Pakistan
UCAM .... United Campuses to Prevent Nuclear War   (EA)
UCAN .... Utilities Conservation Action Now [*Federal Energy Administration*]
UCANF....... United Canso Oil & Gas [*NASDAQ symbol*]   (NQ)
UC App ...... Upper Canada Appeal Reports   (DLA)
UC App (Can) ... Upper Canada Appeal Reports   (DLA)
UC App Rep ... Upper Canada Appeal Reports   (DLA)
UCAR .... United Carolina Bancshares [*NASDAQ symbol*]   (NQ)
UCAR .... University Corporation for Atmospheric Research
UCARCIDE ... Union Carbide Biocide [*Trademark*] [*Union Carbide Corp.*]
UCAS .... Uniform Cost Accounting Standards   (MCD)
UCAS .... Union of Central African States
UCATA....... Uniform Contribution Among Tortfeasors Act [*National Conference of Commissioners on Uniform State Laws*]
UCAVJ ...... Union Continentale Africaine des Villes Jumelees [*Continental African Union of Twin Cities*]
UCB............ Canadian Union Catalogue of Books [*National Library of Canada*] [*Ottawa, ON*] [*Information service*]   (EISS)
UCB............ UCB [*Belgium*] [*Research code symbol*]
UCB............ UCB Chemie [*Germany*] [*Research code symbol*]
UCB............ Unconjugated Bilirubin
UCB............ Union Chimique Belge [*Belgium*]
UCB............ Unit Control Block   (MCD)
UCB............ United Cambridge Mines [*Vancouver Stock Exchange symbol*]
UCB............ Universal Character Buffer
UCB............ University of California, Berkeley
UCB............ University of California, Berkeley School of Library and Information Science, Berkeley, CA [*OCLC symbol*]   (OCLC)
UCBC .... Parti de l'Unite et de la Communaute Belgo-Congolaise [*Political party*]
UCBI.......... United Central Bancshares [*NASDAQ symbol*]   (NQ)
UCBLL ...... Language Laboratory [*University of California, Berkeley*] [*Research center*]   (RCD)
UCBT .... Universal Circuit Board Tester
UCBWM .... United Church Board for World Ministries   (EA)
UCC .... Computing Center [*University of Rochester*] [*Research center*]   (RCD)
UCC .... Uccle [*Belgium*] [*Later, DOU*] [*Geomagnetic observatory code*]
UCC .... Uccle [*Belgium*] [*Seismograph station code, US Geological Survey*]   (SEIS)
UCC .... Umbilical Checkout Cable
UCC .... Unadjusted Contractual Changes
UCC .... Under Cover Cop [*Used in company name, "UCC Co.," a phony "fence" operation staged by New York Police Department, 1973-78*]
UCC .... Uniform Classification Committee [*Chicago, IL*]   (EA)
UCC .... Uniform Classification Committee, Chicago IL [*STAC*]
UCC .... Uniform Code Council [*Dayton, OH*]   (EA)
UCC .... Uniform Commercial Code [*National Conference of Commissioners on Uniform State Laws*]

UCC .... Uniform Credit Code
UCC .... Union Camp Corporation [*NYSE symbol*]
UCC .... Union Carbide Canada Ltd. [*Toronto Stock Exchange symbol*]
UCC .... Union Carbide Corporation   (KSC)
UCC .... United Cancer Council [*Carmel, IN*]   (EA)
UCC .... United Church of Christ
UCC .... Universal Copyright Convention
UCC .... University of California. Chronicle [*A publication*]
UCC .... University College Computer [*London, England*]   (DEN)
UCC .... University College, Cork [*Ireland*]
UCC .... University Computer Center [*University of Minnesota*] [*Research center*]   (RCD)
UCC .... University Computer Center [*Oklahoma State University*] [*Research center*]   (RCD)
UCC .... University Computer Center [*San Diego State University*] [*Research center*]   (RCD)
UCC .... University Computer Center [*North Dakota State University*] [*Research center*]   (RCD)
UCC .... University Computer Center [*New Mexico State University*] [*Research center*]   (RCD)
UCC .... University Computing Company [*International computer bureau*]
UCC .... University of Corpus Christi [*Texas*] [*Closed, 1973*]
UCC .... Upper Control Center   (NATG)
UCC .... Urgent Care Center [*Medicine*]
UCC .... Uruguay Collectors Club   (EA)
UCC .... Utility Control Console
UCC .... Yucca Flat, NV [*Location identifier*] [*FAA*]   (FAAL)
UCCA........ Ukrainian Congress Committee of America   (EA)
UCCA........ Universities Central Council on Admission [*British*]
UCCC........ Computing Center [*University of Cincinnati*] [*Research center*]   (RCD)
UCCC........ Uniform Consumer Credit Code [*National Conference of Commissioners on Uniform State Laws*]
UCCCCWCS ... United Church of Christ Coordinating Center for Women in Church and Society   (EA)
UCCE .... Union des Capitales de la Communaute Europeenne [*Union of Capitals of the European Community*]
UCCE .... Universal Craftsmen Council of Engineers   (EA)
UCC/EMC ... Union Carbide and Carbon/Electric Metallurgical Company   (AAG)
UCCEW...... University of Cape Coast. English Department. Workpapers [*A publication*]
UCCF .... United Campus Christian Fellowship [*Defunct*]
UC Ch .... Upper Canada Chancery Reports [*1849-82*]   (DLA)
UC Cham ... Upper Canada Chambers Reports   (DLA)
UC Chamb ... Upper Canada Chambers Reports [*1846-52*]   (DLA)
UC Cham (Can) ... Upper Canada Chambers Reports [*1846-52*]   (DLA)
UC Chan .... Upper Canada Chancery Reports   (DLA)
UC Ch (Can) ... Upper Canada Chancery Reports   (DLA)
UCC Law Letter ... Uniform Commercial Code Law Letter   (DLA)
UCCL/GC ... United Church Coalition for Lesbian/Gay Concerns   (EA)
UCC-ND ..... Union Carbide Corporation - Nuclear Division   (MCD)
UCCP .... Upper Canada Common Pleas Reports   (DLA)
UCCP (Can) ... Upper Canada Common Pleas Reports   (DLA)
UCCPD...... Upper Canada Common Pleas Division Reports [*Ontario*]   (DLA)
UCCPL .... United Citizens Coastal Protection League   (EA)
UCCR .... Upper Canada Court Records [*Report of Ontario Bureau of Archives*]   (DLA)
UCCRC ...... University of Chicago Cancer Research Center [*Research center*]   (RCD)
UCC Rep Serv ... Uniform Commercial Code Reporting Service   (DLA)
UCCRL....... Union Carbide and Carbon Research Laboratories   (AAG)
UCCRP....... Union College Character Research Project   (EA)
UCCRS .... Underwater Coded Command Release System
UCCS .... Ultrasonic Chemical Cleaning System
UCCS .... Universal Camera Control System
UCCS .... University Classification and Compensation System
UCD............ Unchanged Charge Distribution [*Fission*]
UCD............ Uniform Call Distribution [*Telephone system*]
UCD............ Union de Centro Democratico [*Union of the Democratic Center*] [*Spanish*]   (PPE)
UCD............ United Canadian Shares Ltd. [*Toronto Stock Exchange symbol*]
UCD............ University of California, Davis
UCD............ University College, Dublin [*Ireland*]
UCD............ Urine Collection Device [*NASA*]   (MCD)
UCD............ Usual Childhood Diseases [*Medicine*]
UCDA .... University and College Designers Association   (EA)
UCDC .... Uniado do Centro Democrata Cristao [*Union of the Christian Democratic Center*] [*Portuguese*]   (PPE)
UCDCC ...... Union Centro y Democratica Cristiana de Catalunya [*Union of the Center and Christian Democrats of Catalonia*] [*Spanish*]   (PPE)
UCdE.......... Emery County Library, Castle Dale, UT [*Library symbol*] [*Library of Congress*]   (LCLS)
UCDEC....... Union Chretienne Democrate d'Europe Centrale [*Christian Democratic Union of Central Europe - CDUCE*] [*Rome, Italy*]   (EA-IO)

UCdH .... Emery County High School, Castle Dale, UT [*Library symbol*] [*Library of Congress*] (LCLS)

UCDL .... Union Chretienne Democrate Libanaise [*Lebanese Christian Democratic Union*] (PPW)

UCD L Rev ... UCD [*University of California, Davis*] Law Review [*A publication*]

UCDP .... Uncorrected Data Processor

UCDPE .... University of California (Davis). Publications in English [*A publication*]

UCDS .... Unit Chemical Defense Study (MCD)

UCDWN ...... Until Cleared Down [*Aviation*] (FAAC)

UCDWR ...... University of California Division of War Research

UCE .... UCCEL Corp. [*NYSE symbol*]

UCE .... Unit Checkout Equipment

UCE .... Unit Correction Entry

UCEA .... Uniform Conservation Easement Act [*National Conference of Commissioners on Uniform State Laws*]

UCEA .... Uniform Criminal Extradition Act [*National Conference of Commissioners on Uniform State Laws*]

UCEA .... Union Chimique Elf-Aquitaine [*France*]

UCEA .... University Council for Educational Administration (EA)

UCE & A ..... Upper Canada Error and Appeal Reports [*1846-66*] (DLA)

UCEA .... Used Clothing Exporters Association of America (EA)

UCEC .... Utility Commission Engineers Conference

UCEMT ...... University Consortium in Educational Media and Technology [*Later, UCIDT*]

Ucenyje Zapiski Belorusskogo Gosud Univ ... Ucenyje Zapiski Belorusskogo Gosudarstvennogo Universiteta [*A publication*]

Ucenyje Zapiski Jaroslav ... Ucenyje Zapiski Jaroslavskogo Universiteta [*A publication*]

Ucenyje Zapiski Leningrad ... Ucenyje Zapiski Leningradskogo Gosudarstvennogo. Universiteta [*A publication*]

Ucenyje Zapiski Leningrad Pedag Inst ... Ucenyje Zapiski Leningradskogo Gosudarstvennogo Pedagogiceskogo Instituta [*A publication*]

Ucenyje Zapiski Moskov Gosud Pedag Inst ... Ucenyje Zapiski Moskovskogo Gosudarstvennogo Pedagogiceskogo Instituta Inostraunych Jazykov [*A publication*]

Ucenyje Zapiski Moskva ... Ucenyje Zapiski Moskovskogo Gosudarstvennogo Universiteta Imeni Lononosova [*A publication*]

Ucenyje Zapiski Tomsk ... Ucenyje Zapiski Tomskogo Gosudarstvennogo Universiteta Imeni Kujbyseva. Tomsk [*A publication*]

Ucen Zap (Azerb Gosud Univ) Ser Ist Filos Nauk ... Ucenye Zapiski (Azerbajdzanskij Gosudarstvennyj Universitet) Serija Istoriceskih i Filosofskih Nauk [*A publication*]

Ucen Zap (Azerb Univ) Ser Ist Filos Nauk ... Ucenye Zapiski (Azerbajdzanskij Universitet) Serija Istoriceskih i Filosofskih Nauk [*A publication*]

Ucen Zap CAGI ... Ucenyi Zapiski Central'nogo Aero-Gidrodinamiceskogo Instituta [*A publication*]

Ucen Zap Dal'nevost Univ ... Ucenye Zapiski Dal'nevostocnogo Universiteta [*A publication*]

Ucen Zap Dusan Gos Pedag Inst ... Ucenye Zapiski Dusanbinskogo Gosudarstvennogo Pedagogiceskogo Instituta [*A publication*]

Ucen Zap Erevan Gos Univ Estestv Nauki ... Ucenye Zapiski Erevanskogo Gosudarstvennogo Universiteta. Estestvennye Nauki [*A publication*]

Ucen Zap Hakas Nauc-Issled Inst Jaz Lit Ist ... Ucenye Zapiski Hakasskogo Naucno-Issledovatel'skogo Instituta Jazyka, Literatury, i Istorii [*A publication*]

Ucen Zap Ivanov Univ ... Ucenye Zapiski Ivanovskogo Universitet [*A publication*]

Ucen Zap Kaf Obsc Nauk Leningr Filos ... Ucenye Zapiski Kafedr Obscestvennykh Nauk Vuzov Leningrada Filosofija [*A publication*]

Ucen Zap Kaf Obsc Nauk Vuzov G Leningr Filos ... Ucenye Zapiski Kafedr Obscestvennykh Nauk Vuzov Goroda Leningrada Filosofskih [*A publication*]

Ucen Zap Kaf Obsc Nauk Vuzov G Leningr Probl Nauc Kommunizma ... Ucenye Zapiski Kafedr Obscestvennykh Nauk Vuzov Goroda Leningrada Problemy Naucnogo Kommunizma [*A publication*]

Ucen Zap Kalmyk Nauc-Issled Inst Jaz Lit Ist ... Ucenye Zapiski Kalmykskogo Naucno-Issledovatel'skogo Instituta Jazyka, Literatury, i Istorii [*A publication*]

Ucen Zap Karel Ped Inst Ser Fiz-Mat Nauk ... Ucenye Zapiski. Karel'skii Pedagogiceskii Institut. Serija Fiziko-Matematiceskih Nauk [*A publication*]

Ucen Zap (Kazan Pedag Inst) ... Ucenye Zapiski (Kazanskij Pedagogiceskij Institut) [*A publication*]

Ucen Zap (Latv Univ) ... Ucenye Zapiski (Latvijskogo Universiteta) [*A publication*]

Ucen Zap (Lening Pedag Inst) ... Ucenye Zapiski (Leningradskij Pedagogiceskij Institut) [*A publication*]

Ucen Zap (Moskov Pedag Inst) ... Ucenye Zapiski (Moskovskogo Pedagogiceskogo Instituta) [*A publication*]

Ucen Zap Perm Univ ... Ucenye Zapiski Permskogo Universiteta [*A publication*]

Ucen Zap Statist ... Ucenyi Zapiski po Statistike. Akademija Nauk SSSR. Central'nyi Ekonomiko-Matematiceskii Institut [*A publication*]

Ucen Zap (Vyss Part Skola CK KPSS) ... Ucenye Zapiski (Vyssaja Partijnaja Skola pri CK KPSS) [*A publication*]

UCER .... University Center for Energy Research [*Oklahoma State University*] [*Research center*] (RCD)

UC Err & App ... Upper Canada Error and Appeal Reports [*1846-66*] (DLA)

UC Err & App (Can) ... Upper Canada Error and Appeal Reports [*1846-66*] (DLA)

UCES .... University Center for Environmental Studies [*Virginia Polytechnic Institute and State University*] [*Research center*] (RCD)

U Ceylon LR ... University of Ceylon. Law Review (DLA)

UCF .... Union Culturelle Francais [*French Cultural Union*]

UCF .... Unit Control File [*Air Force*]

UCF .... United Cat Federation (EA)

UCF .... United Companies Financial Corp. [*American Stock Exchange symbol*]

UCF .... United Cooperative Farmers, Inc.

UCF .... Utility Control Facility

UCFA .... Uniform Comparative Fault Act [*National Conference of Commissioners on Uniform State Laws*]

UCFA .... Union pour la Communaute Franco-Africaine [*Union for the Franco-African Community*] [*Niger*]

UCFC .... United Community Funds and Councils of America [*Later, UWA*] (EA)

UCFE .... Unemployment Compensation, Federal Employees

UCFML .... Union des Communistes de France Marxiste-Leniniste [*Marxist-Leninist Union of Communists of France*] (PPW)

UCFRU .... Utah Cooperative Fishery Research Unit [*Utah State University*] [*Research center*] (RCD)

UCG .... Underground Coal Gasification

UCG .... Unidirectional Categorical Grammar

UCG .... University College, Galway [*Ireland*]

UCG .... Urinary Chorionic Gonadotrophin [*Endocrinology*]

UCGA .... University Center in Georgia, Inc. [*Library network*]

UCGF .... Undergraduate Computer Graphics Facility [*Stevens Institute of Technology*] [*Research center*] (RCD)

UCH .... University of Connecticut, Health Center Library, Farmington, CT [*OCLC symbol*] (OCLC)

UCHD .... Usual Childhood Diseases [*Medicine*]

Uchen Zap Azerb Gos Univ Ser Biol Nauk ... Uchenye Zapiski Azerbaidzhanskogo Gosudarstvennogo Universiteta. Seriya Biologicheskikh Nauk [*A publication*]

Uchen Zap Azerb Gos Univ Ser Fiz Mat Nauk ... Uchenye Zapiski Azerbaidzhanskogo Gosudarstvennogo Universiteta. Seriya Fiziko-Matematicheskikh Nauk [*A publication*]

Uchen Zap Dal'nevost Univ ... Uchenye Zapiski Dal'nevostochnogo Universiteta [*A publication*]

Uchen Zap Gor'kov Gos Pedag Inst ... Uchenye Zapiski Gor'kovskogo Gosudarstvennogo Pedagogicheskogo Instituta [*A publication*]

Uchen Zap Gor'kov Gos Univ Ser Biol ... Uchenye Zapiski Gor'kovskogo Gosudarstvennogo Universiteta Imeni N. I. Lobachevskogo. Seriya Biologichevskaya [*A publication*]

Uchen Zap Gor'k Univ Ser Biol ... Uchenye Zapiski Gor'kovskogo Universiteta. Seriya Biologiya [*A publication*]

Uchen Zap Kabardino-Balkar Gos Univ ... Uchenye Zapiski Kabardino-Balkarskogo Gosudarstvennogo Universiteta [*A publication*]

Uchen Zap Kabardino-Balkars Univ ... Uchenye Zapiski Kabardino-Balkarskogo Gosudarstvennogo Universiteta [*A publication*]

Uchen Zap Kazan Gos Univ ... Uchenye Zapiski Kazanskogo Gosudarstvennogo Universiteta [*A publication*]

Uchen Zap Kazan Vet Inst ... Uchenye Zapiski Kazanskogo Veterinarnogo Instituta [*A publication*]

Uchen Zap Kirovabad Ped Inst ... Uchenye Zapiski Kirovabadskii Pedagogicheskii Institut [*A publication*]

Uchen Zap Kishinev Univ ... Uchenye Zapiski Kishinevskii Gosudarstvennyi Universitet [*A publication*]

Uchen Zap Kursk Pedagog Inst ... Uchenye Zapiski Kurskii Gosudarstvennyi Pedagogicheskii Institut [*A publication*]

Uchen Zap Leningr Gos Pedagog Inst Gertsena ... Uchenye Zapiski Leningradskogo Gosudarstvennogo Pedagogicheskogo Instituta Gertsena [*A publication*]

Uchen Zap Mosk Gos Univ ... Uchenye Zapiski Moskovskogo Gosudarstvennogo Universiteta [*A publication*]

Uchen Zap Novgorod Golovn Pedagog Inst ... Uchenye Zapiski Novgorodskogo Golovnogo Pedagogicheskogo Instituta [*A publication*]

Uchen Zap Petrozavodsk Gos Univ ... Uchenye Zapiski Petrozavodskogo Gosudarstvennogo Universiteta [*A publication*]

Uchen Zap Ryazan Gos Pedagog Inst ... Uchenye Zapiski Ryazanskogo Gosudarstvennogo Pedagogicheskii Instituta [*A publication*]

Uchen Zap Sel Khoz Dal'n Vost (Vladivostok) ... Uchenye Zapiski Sel'skogo Khozyaistva Dal'nogo Vostoka (Vladivostok) [*A publication*]

Uchen Zap Tartu Gos Univ ... Uchenye Zapiski Tartuskogo
Gosudarstvennogo Universiteta [*A publication*]
Uchen Zap TSAGI ... Uchenye Zapiski Tsentral'nogo Aero-
Gidrodinamicheskogo Instituta (TSAGI) [*A publication*]
Uchen Zap Ural Univ ... Uchenye Zapiski Ural'skogo Gosudarstvennogo
Universiteta Imeni A. M. Gor'kogo [*A publication*]
Uchen Zap Yaroslav Gos Pedagog Inst ... Uchenye Zapiski Yaroslavskii
Gosudarstvennyi Pedagogicheskii Institut [*A publication*]
Uchet Finan Kolkhoz Sovkhoz ... Uchet i Finansy v Kolkhozakh i
Sovkhozakh [*A publication*]
U Chicago L Rev ... University of Chicago. Law Review [*A publication*]
U Chi L Rec ... University of Chicago. Law School. Record [*A publication*]
U Chi L Rev ... University of Chicago. Law Review [*A publication*]
UCHILS ...... University of Chicago Law School   (DLA)
U Chi L Sch Rec ... University of Chicago. Law School. Record [*A
publication*]
U Chi LS Conf Series ... University of Chicago. Law School. Conference
Series [*A publication*]
U Chi L S Rec ... University of Chicago. Law School. Record [*A publication*]
Uch Tr Gork Gos Med Inst ... Uchenye Trudy Gorkovskogo
Gosudarstvennogo Meditsinskogo Instituta [*A publication*]
Uch Tr Gor'k Med Inst ... Uchenye Trudy Gor'kovskii Meditsinskii Institut [*A
publication*]
Uch Zap Anat Gistol Embriol Resp Sredn Azii Kaz ... Uchenye Zapiski
Anatomov Gistologov i Embriologov Respublik Srednei
Azii i Kazakhstana [*A publication*]
Uch Zap Azerb Gos Inst Usoversh Vrachei ... Uchenye Zapiski
Azerbaidzhanskii Gosudarstvennyi Institut
Usovershenstvovaniya Vrachei [*A publication*]
Uch Zap Azerb Gos Uiv Im S M Kirova ... Uchenye Zapiski Azerbaidzhan-
Gosudarstvennogo Universiteta Imeni S. M. Kirova [*A
publication*]
Uch Zap Azerb Gos Univ ... Uchenye Zapiski Azerbaidzhanskogo
Gosudarstvennogo Universiteta [*A publication*]
Uch Zap Azerb Gos Univ Im S M Kirova ... Uchenye Zapiski
Azerbaidzhanskogo Gosudarstvennogo Universiteta Imeni
S. M. Kirova [*A publication*]
Uch Zap Azerb Gos Univ Ser Biol Nauk ... Uchenye Zapiski
Azerbaidzhanskogo Gosudarstvennogo Universiteta.
Seriya Biologicheskikh Nauk [*A publication*]
Uch Zap Azerb Gos Univ Ser Fiz Mat Nauk ... Uchenye Zapiski
Azerbaidzhanskogo Gosudarstvennogo Universiteta.
Seriya Fiziko-Matematicheskikh Nauk [*A publication*]
Uch Zap Azerb Gos Univ Ser Geol Geogr Nauk ... Uchenye Zapiski
Azerbaidzhanskogo Gosudarstvennogo Universiteta.
Seriya Geologo-Geograficheskikh Nauk [*A publication*]
Uch Zap Azerb Gos Univ Ser Khim Nauk ... Uchenye Zapiski
Azerbaidzhanskogo Gosudarstvennogo Universiteta Imeni
S. M. Kirova. Seriya Khimicheskikh Nauk [*Azerbaidzhan
SSR*] [*A publication*]
Uch Zap Azerb Inst Nefti Khim Ser 9 ... Uchenye Zapiski Azerbajdzhanskij
Institut Nefti i Khimii. Seriya 9 [*A publication*]
Uch Zap Azerb Inst Usoversh Vrachei ... Uchenye Zapiski Azerbaidzhanskii
Institut Usovershenstvovaniya Vrachei [*A publication*]
Uch Zap Azerb Med Inst ... Uchenye Zapiski Azerbaidzhanskogo
Meditsinskogo Instituta [*A publication*]
Uch Zap Azerb Med Inst Klin Med ... Uchenye Zapiski Azerbaidzhanskogo
Meditsinskogo Instituta Klinicheskoi Meditsiny [*A
publication*]
Uch Zap Azerb Politekh Inst ... Uchenye Zapiski Azerbaidzhanskii
Politekhnicheskii Institut [*A publication*]
Uch Zap Azerb Skh Inst ... Uchenye Zapiski Azerbaidzhanskogo
Sel'skokhozyaistvennogo Instituta [*A publication*]
Uch Zap Azerb Skh Inst Ser Agron ... Uchenye Zapiski Azerbaidzhanskogo
Sel'skokhozyaistvennogo Instituta. Seriya Agronomii [*A
publication*]
Uch Zap Azerb S-kh Inst Ser Vet ... Uchenye Zapiski Azerbaidzhanskogo
Sel'skokhozyaistvennogo Instituta. Seriya Veterinarii [*A
publication*]
Uch Zap Azerb Univ Ser Biol Nauk ... Uchenye Zapiski Azerbaidzhanskogo
Universiteta. Seriya Biologicheskoi Nauki [*A publication*]
Uch Zap Bashk Univ ... Uchenye Zapiski Bashkirskogo Universiteta [*A
publication*]
Uch Zap Beloruss Gos Univ ... Uchenye Zapiski Belorusskogo
Gosudarstvennogo Universiteta [*A publication*]
Uch Zap Beloruss Inst Inzh Zheleznodorozhn Transp ... Uchenye Zapiski
Belorusskii Institut Inzhenerov Zheleznodorozhnogo
Transporta [*A publication*]
Uch Zap Bel'tskii Pedagog Inst ... Uchenye Zapiski Bel'tskii Pedagogicheskii
Institut [*A publication*]
Uch Zap Biol Fak Kirg Univ ... Uchenye Zapiski Biologicheskogo Fakul'teta
Kirgizskogo Universiteta [*A publication*]
Uch Zap Biol Fak Osnovn Gos Pedagog Inst ... Uchenye Zapiski
Biologicheskogo Fakul'teta Osnovnogo
Gosudarstvennogo Pedagogicheskogo Instituta [*A
publication*]
Uch Zap Birskogo Gos Pedagog Inst ... Uchenye Zapiski Birskogo
Gosudarstvennogo Pedagogicheskogo Instituta [*A
publication*]
Uch Zap Brst Gos Pedagog Inst ... Uchenye Zapiski Brestskii
Gosudarstvennyi Pedagogicheskii Institut [*A publication*]

Uch Zap Chelyab Gos Pedagog Inst ... Uchenye Zapiski Chelyabinskogo
Gosudarstvennogo Pedagogicheskogo Instituta [*A
publication*]
Uch Zap Chit Gos Pedagog Inst ... Uchenye Zapiski Chitinskii
Gosudarstvennyi Pedagogicheskii Institut [*A publication*]
Uch Zap Dagest Gos Univ ... Uchenye Zapiski Dagestanskogo
Gosudarstvennogo Universiteta [*A publication*]
Uch Zap Dal'nevost Gos Univ ... Uchenye Zapiski Dal'nevostochnyi
Gosudarstvennyi Universitet [*A publication*]
Uch Zap Dushanb Gos Pedagog Inst ... Uchenye Zapiski Dushanbinskii
Gosudarstvennyi Pedagogicheskii Institut [*A publication*]
Uch Zap Erevan Univ ... Uchenye Zapiski Erevanskii Universitet [*A
publication*]
Uch Zap Erevan Univ Estestv Nauk ... Uchenye Zapiski Erevanskogo
Universiteta Estestvennykh Nauk [*A publication*]
Uch Zap Gomel Gos Pedagog Inst ... Uchenye Zapiski Gomel'skii
Gosudarstvennyi Pedagogicheskii Institut [*A publication*]
Uch Zap Gomel Gos Pedagog Inst Im V P Chkalova ... Uchenye Zapiski
Gomel'skogo Gosudarstvennogo Pedagogicheskogo
Instituta Imeni V. P. Chkalova [*A publication*]
Uch Zap Gor'k Gos Med Inst Im S M Kirova ... Uchenye Zapiski
Gor'kovskogo Gosudarstvennogo Meditsinskogo Instituta
Imeni S. M. Kirova [*A publication*]
Uch Zap Gor'k Gos Pedagog Inst ... Uchenye Zapiski Gor'kovskogo
Gosudarstvennogo Pedagogicheskogo Instituta [*A
publication*]
Uch Zap Gor'k Gos Pedagog Inst Im A M Gor'kogo ... Uchenye Zapiski
Gor'kovskogo Gosudarstvennogo Pedagogicheskogo
Instituta Imeni A. M. Gor'kogo [*A publication*]
Uch Zap Gor'k Gos Univ ... Uchenye Zapiski Gor'kovskogo
Gosudarstvennogo Universiteta [*A publication*]
Uch Zap Gor'k Univ ... Uchenye Zapiski Gor'kovskogo Universiteta [*A
publication*]
Uch Zap Gor'k Univ Ser Biol ... Uchenye Zapiski Gor'kovskogo Universiteta.
Seriya Biologiya [*A publication*]
Uch Zap Gorno-Altai Gos Pedagog Inst ... Uchenye Zapiski Gorno-
Altaiskogo Gosudarstvennogo Pedagogicheskogo
Instituta [*A publication*]
Uch Zap Gos Inst Fiz Kul't Im P F Lesgafta ... Uchenye Zapiski
Gosudarstvennogo Instituta Fizicheskoi Kul'tury Imeni P.
F. Lesgafta [*A publication*]
Uch Zap Gos Nauchno-Issled Inst Glazn Bolezn Im Gel'Mgol'Tsa ...
Uchenye Zapiski Gosudarstvennogo Nauchno-
Issledovatel'skogo Instituta Glaznykh Boleznei Imeni
Gel'Mgol'Tsa [*A publication*]
Uch Zap Gos Nauchno-Issled Inst Glaznykh Bolezn ... Uchenye Zapiski
Gosudarstvennogo Nauchno-Issledovatel'skogo Instituta
Glaznykh Boleznei [*A publication*]
Uch Zap Gos Pedagog Inst ... Uchenye Zapiski Gosudarstvennogo
Pedagogicheskogo Instituta Imeni T. G. Shevchenko [*A
publication*]
Uch Zap Gos Pedagog Inst Im T G Shevchenko ... Uchenye Zapiski
Gosudarstvennogo Pedagogicheskogo Instituta Imeni T.
G. Shevchenko [*A publication*]
Uch Zap Imp Yur'ev Univ ... Uchenyya Zapiskik Imperatorskogo Yur'evskago
Universiteta [*A publication*]
Uch Zap Irkutsk Gos Pedagog Inst ... Uchenye Zapiski Irkutskii
Gosudarstvennyi Pedagogicheskii Institut [*A publication*]
Uch Zap Irkutsk Inst Nar Khoz ... Uchenye Zapiski Irkutskii Institut
Narodnogo Khozyaistva [*A publication*]
Uch Zap Ivanov Gos Pedagog Inst ... Uchenye Zapiski Ivanovskogo
Gosudarstvennogo Pedagogicheskogo Instituta [*A
publication*]
Uch Zap Kabard-Balkar Nauchno-Issled Inst ... Uchenye Zapiski
Kabardino-Balkarskogo Nauchno-Issledovatel'skogo
Instituta [*A publication*]
Uch Zap Kabard Gos Pedagog Inst ... Uchenye Zapiski Kabardinskogo
Gosudarstvennogo Pedagogicheskogo Instituta [*A
publication*]
Uch Zap Kalinin Gos Pedagog Inst ... Uchenye Zapiski Kalininskii
Gosudarstvennyi Pedagogicheskii Institut [*A publication*]
Uch Zap Kaliningr Gos Pedagog Inst ... Uchenye Zapiski Kaliningradskogo
Gosudarstvennogo Pedagogicheskogo Instituta [*A
publication*]
Uch Zap Karagand Gos Med Inst ... Uchenye Zapiski Karagandinskii
Gosudarstvennyi Meditsinskii Institut [*A publication*]
Uch Zap Karagand Med Inst ... Uchenye Zapiski Karagandinskogo
Meditsinskogo Instituta [*A publication*]
Uch Zap Karelo Fin Gos Univ Biol Nauki ... Uchenye Zapiski Karelo-
Finskogo Gosudarstvennogo Universiteta Biologicheskie
Nauki [*A publication*]
Uch Zap Karelo Fin Gos Univ Fiz Mat Nauki ... Uchenye Zapiski Karelo-
Finskogo Gosudarstvennogo Universiteta Fiziko
Matematicheskie Nauki [*A publication*]
Uch Zap Karel Pedagog Inst ... Uchenye Zapiski Karel'skogo
Pedagogicheskogo Instituta [*A publication*]
Uch Zap Karsh Gos Pedagog Inst ... Uchenye Zapiski Karshinskii
Gosudarstvennyi Pedagogicheskii Institut [*A publication*]
Uch Zap Kazan Gos Pedagog Inst ... Uchenye Zapiski Kazanskii
Gosudarstvennyi Pedagogicheskii Institut [*A publication*]

Uch Zap Kazan Gos Univ ... Uchenye Zapiski Kazanskii Gosudarstvennyi Universitet [*USSR*] [*A publication*]

Uch Zap Kazan Univ ... Uchenye Zapiski Kazanskogo Universiteta [*A publication*]

Uch Zap Kazan Vet Inst ... Uchenye Zapiski Kazanskogo Veterinarnogo Instituta [*A publication*]

Uch Zap Kazan Yuridicheskogo Inst ... Uchenye Zapiski Kazanskogo Yuridicheskogo Instituta [*A publication*]

Uch Zap Kaz Gos Uiv Im S M Kirova ... Uchenye Zapiski Kazakhskogo Gosudarstvennogo Universiteta Imeni S. M. Kirova [*A publication*]

Uch Zap Kaz Gos Univ ... Uchenye Zapiski Kazakhskii Gosudarstvennyi Universitet [*A publication*]

Uch Zap Kemer Gos Pedagog Inst ... Uchenye Zapiski Kemerovskogo Gosudarstvennogo Pedagogicheskogo Instituta [*A publication*]

Uch Zap Khabar Gos Pedagog Inst ... Uchenye Zapiski Khabarovskogo Gosudarstvennogo Pedagogicheskogo Instituta [*A publication*]

Uch Zap Khabar Gos Pedagog Inst Biol Khim Nauk ... Uchenye Zapiski Khabarovskii Gosudarstvennyi Pedagogicheskii Institut Biologii i Khimicheskikh Nauk [*A publication*]

Uch Zap Khabar Gos Pedagog Inst Ser Biol ... Uchenye Zapiski Khabarovskii Gosudarstvennyi Pedagogicheskii Institut. Seriya Biologiya [*A publication*]

Uch Zap Khabar Gos Pedagog Inst Ser Estestv Nauk ... Uchenye Zapiski Khabarovskii Gosudarstvennyi Pedagogicheskii Institut. Seriya Estestvennykh Nauk [*A publication*]

Uch Zap Khabar Nauchno-Issled Inst Epidemiol Mikrobiol ... Uchenye Zapiski Khabarovskogo Nauchno-Issledovatel'skogo Instituta Epidemiologii i Mikrobiologii [*A publication*]

Uch Zap Khar'k Univ Tr Biol Fak Genet Zool ... Uchenye Zapiski Khar'kovskogo Universiteta Trudy Biologicheskogo Fakul'teta po Genetlike i Zoologii [*A publication*]

Uch Zap Khar'k Univ Tr Nauchno-Issled Inst Biol Biol Fak ... Uchenye Zapiski Khar'kovskogo Universiteta Trudy Nauchno-Issledovatel'skogo Instituta Biologii i Biologicheskogo Fakul'teta [*A publication*]

Uch Zap Kiev Nauchno-Isled Rentgeno Radiol Onkol Inst ... Uchenye Zapiski Kievskogo Nauchno-Issledovatel'skogo Rentgeno Radiologicheskogo i Onkologicheskogo Instituta [*A publication*]

Uch Zap Kirovab Pedagog Inst ... Uchenye Zapiski Kirovabadskii Pedagogicheskii Institut [*A publication*]

Uch Zap Kishinev Gos Univ ... Uchenye Zapiski Kishinevskogo Gosudarstvennogo Universiteta [*A publication*]

Uch Zap Komsomol'skogo-Na-Amure Gos Pedagog Inst ... Uchenye Zapiski Komsomol'skogo-Na-Amure Gosudarstvennogo Pedagogicheskogo Instituta [*A publication*]

Uch Zap Kuibyshev Gos Pedagog Inst ... Uchenye Zapiski Kuibyshevskogo Gosudarstvennogo Pedagogicheskogo Instituta [*A publication*]

Uch Zap Kursk Gos Pedagog Inst ... Uchenye Zapiski Kurskogo Gosudarstvennogo Pedagogicheskogo Instituta [*A publication*]

Uch Zap Latv Gos Univ ... Uchenye Zapiski Latviiskii Gosudarstvennyi Universitet [*A publication*]

Uch Zap Latv Gos Univ ... Uchenye Zapiski Latvijskogo Gosudarstvennogo Universiteta Imeni Petra Stuchki [*A publication*]

Uch Zap Latv Gos Univ Astron ... Uchenye Zapiski Latvijskogo Gosudarstvennogo Universiteta Imeni Petra Stuchki. Astronomiya [*A publication*]

Uch Zap Latv Univ ... Uchenye Zapiski Latviiskogo Universiteta [*A publication*]

Uch Zap Lenigr Gos Univ Ser Fiz Nauk ... Uchenye Zapiski Leningradskogo Gosudarstvennogo Universiteta. Seriya Fizicheskikh Nauk [*A publication*]

Uch Zap Leninab Gos Pedagog Inst ... Uchenye Zapiski Leninabadskogo Gosudarstvennogo Pedagogicheskogo Instituta [*A publication*]

Uch Zap Leningr Gos Im A A Zhdanova Ser Fiz Geol Nauk ... Uchenye Zapiski Leningradskogo Gosudarstvennogo Universiteta Imeni A. A. Zhadanova. Seriya Fizicheskikh i Geologicheskikh Nauk [*USSR*] [*A publication*]

Uch Zap Leningr Gos Inst ... Uchenye Zapiski Leningradskogo Gosudarstvennogo Instituta [*A publication*]

Uch Zap Leningr Gos Pedagog Inst Im A I Gertsena ... Uchenye Zapiski Leningradskogo Gosudarstvennogo Pedagogicheskogo Instituta Imeni A. I. Gertsena [*A publication*]

Uch Zap Leningr Gos Univ Im A A Zhdanova Ser Biol Nauk ... Uchenye Zapiski Leningradskogo Gosudarstvennogo Universiteta Imeni A. A. Zhdanova. Seriya Biologicheskikh Nauk [*USSR*] [*A publication*]

Uch Zap Leningr Gos Univ Im A A Zhdanova Ser Fiz Nauk ... Uchenye Zapiski Leningradskogo Gosudarstvennogo Universiteta Imeni A. A. Zhdanova. Seriya Fizicheskikh Nauk [*USSR*] [*A publication*]

Uch Zap Leningr Gos Univ Ser Biol Nauk ... Uchenye Zapiski Leningradskogo Gosudarstvennogo Universiteta. Seriya Biologicheskikh Nauk [*A publication*]

Uch Zap Leningr Gos Univ Ser Fiz Geol Nauk ... Uchenye Zapiski Leningradskogo Gosudarstvennogo Universiteta. Seriya Fizicheskikh i Geologicheskikh Nauk [*A publication*]

Uch Zap Leningr Gos Univ Ser Geogr Nauk ... Uchenye Zapiski Leningradskogo Gosudarstvennogo Universiteta. Seriya Geograficheskikh Nauk [*A publication*]

Uch Zap Leningr Gos Univ Ser Geol Nauk ... Uchenye Zapiski Leningradskogo Gosudarstvennogo Universiteta. Seriya Geologicheskikh Nauk [*A publication*]

Uch Zap Leningr Gos Univ Ser Khim Nauk ... Uchenye Zapiski Leningradskogo Gosudarstvennogo Universiteta. Seriya Khimicheskikh Nauk [*A publication*]

Uch Zap Leningr Gos Univ Ser Mat Nauk ... Uchenye Zapiski Leningradskogo Gosudarstvennogo Ordena Lenina Universita Imeni A. A. Zhdanova. Seriya Matematicheskikh Nauk [*A publication*]

Uch Zap Leningr Gos Univ Ser Mat Nauk ... Uchenye Zapiski Leningradskogo Gosudarstvennogo Universiteta. Seriya Matematicheskikh Nauk [*A publication*]

Uch Zap Marii Gos Pedagog Inst ... Uchenye Zapiski Mariiskii Gosudarstvennyi Pedagogicheskii Institut [*A publication*]

Uch Zap Michurinsk Gos Pedagog Inst ... Uchenye Zapiski Michurinskii Gosudarstvennyi Pedagogicheskii Institut [*A publication*]

Uch Zap Molotov Gos Univ Im A M Gor'kogo ... Uchenye Zapiski Molotovskogo Gosudarstvennogo Universiteta Imeni A. M. Gor'kogo [*A publication*]

Uch Zap Mord Gos Univ ... Uchenye Zapiski. Mordovskii Gosudarstvennyi Universitet [*A publication*]

Uch Zap Mord Univ ... Uchenye Zapiski Mordovskogo Universiteta [*A publication*]

Uch Zap Mosk Gos Pedagog Inst Im Lenina ... Uchenye Zapiski Moskovskogo Gosudarstvennogo Pedagogicheskogo Instituta Imeni Lenina [*A publication*]

Uch Zap Mosk Gos Univ ... Uchenye Zapiski Moskovskii Gosudarstvennyi Universitet [*USSR*] [*A publication*]

Uch Zap Mosk Inst Tonkoi Khim Tekhnol ... Uchenye Zapiski Moskovskogo Instituta Tonkoi Khimicheskoi Tekhnologii [*A publication*]

Uch Zap Mosk Nauchno-Issled Inst Gig ... Uchenye Zapiski. Moskovskii Nauchno-Issledovatel'skii Institut Gigieny [*A publication*]

Uch Zap Mosk Nauchno-Issled Inst Glaznym Bolezn ... Uchenye Zapiski Moskovskogo Nauchno-Issledovatel'skogo Instituta po Glaznym Boleznam [*A publication*]

Uch Zap Mosk Obl Pedagog Inst ... Uchenye Zapiski Moskovskogo Oblastnogo Pedagogicheskogo Instituta [*A publication*]

Uch Zap Murom Gos Pedagog Inst ... Uchenye Zapiski. Muromskii Gosudarstvennyi Pedagogichskii Institut [*A publication*]

Uch Zap Nauchno-Issled Inst Izuch Lepry ... Uchenye Zapiski Nauchno-Issledovatel'skogo Instituta po Izucheniyu Lepry [*A publication*]

Uch Zap Novgorod Golovn Gos Pedagog Inst ... Uchenye Zapiski Novgorodskii Golovnoi Gosudarstvennyi Pedagogicheskii Institut [*A publication*]

Uch Zap Novgorod Gos Pedagog Inst ... Uchenye Zapiski Novgorodskogo Gosudarstvennogo Pedagogicheskogo Instituta [*A publication*]

Uch Zap Novosib Inst Sov Koop Torg ... Uchenye Zapiski Novosibirskii Institut Sovetskoi Kooperativnoi Torgovli [*A publication*]

Uch Zap Novozybkovskii Gos Pedagog Inst ... Uchenye Zapiski Novozybkovskii Gosudarstvennyi Pedagogicheskii Institut [*A publication*]

Uch Zap Omsk Gos Pedagog Inst ... Uchenye Zapiski Omskogo Gosudarstvennogo Pedagogicheskogo Instituta [*A publication*]

Uch Zap Orenb Gos Pedagog Inst ... Uchenye Zapiski Orenburgskii Gosudarstvennyi Pedagogicheskii Institut [*A publication*]

Uch Zap Orenb Otd Vses Nauchn Ova Anat Gistol Embriol ... Uchenye Zapiski Orenburgskogo Otdela Vsesoyuznogo Nauchnogo Obshchestva Anatomov, Gistologov, i Embriologov [*A publication*]

Uch Zap Orlov Gos Pedagog Inst ... Uchenye Zapiski Orlovskogo Gosudarstvennogo Pedagogicheskogo Instituta [*A publication*]

Uch Zap Osh Gos Pedagog Inst ... Uchenye Zapiski Oshskii Gosudarstvennyi Pedagogicheskii Institut [*A publication*]

Uch Zap Penz Gos Pedagog Inst ... Uchenye Zapiski Penzenskogo Gosudarstvennogo Pedagogicheskogo Instituta [*A publication*]

Uch Zap Penz S-kh Inst ... Uchenye Zapiski Penzenskogo Sel'skokhozyaistvennogo Instituta [*A publication*]

Uch Zap Perm Gos Pedagog Inst ... Uchenye Zapiski Permskii Gosudarstvennyi Pedagogicheskii Institut [*A publication*]

Uch Zap Perm Gos Univ ... Uchenye Zapiski Permskij Gosudarstvennyj Universitet Imeni A. M. Gor'kogo [*A publication*]

Uch Zap Perm Univ Im A M Gor'kogo ... Uchenye Zapiski Permskogo Universiteta Imeni A. M. Gor'kogo [*A publication*]

Uch Zap Petropavlovsk Gos Inst ... Uchenye Zapiski Petropavlovskogo Gosudarstvennogo Instituta [*A publication*]

Uch Zap Petrozavodsk Gos Univ Fiz Mat Nauki ... Uchenye Zapiski Petrozavodskogo Gosudarstvennogo Universiteta Fiziko-Matematicheskie Nauki [*A publication*]

Uch Zap Petrozavodsk Inst ... Uchenye Zapiski Petrozavodskogo Instituta [*A publication*]

Uch Zap Petrozavodsk Univ ... Uchenye Zapiski Petrozavodskogo Universiteta [*A publication*]

Uch Zap Pskov Gos Pedagog Inst ... Uchenye Zapiski Pskovskogo Gosudarstvennogo Pedagogicheskogo Instituta [*A publication*]

Uch Zap Pskov Pedagog Inst Estestv Nauk ... Uchenye Zapiski Pskovskogo Pedagogicheskogo Instituta Estestvennykh Nauk [*A publication*]

Uch Zap Pyatigorsk Farm Inst ... Uchenye Zapiski Pyatigorskii Farmatsevticheskii Institut [*A publication*]

Uch Zap Rostov Na Donu Gos Pedagog Inst Fiz Mat Fak ... Uchenye Zapiski. Rostovskii-Na-Donu Gosudarstvennyi Pedagogicheskii Institut. Fiziko-Matematicheskii Fakul'tet [*A publication*]

Uch Zap Rostov Na Donu Gos Univ ... Uchenye Zapiski Rostovskogo-Na-Donu Gosudarstvennogo Universiteta [*A publication*]

Uch Zap Rostov-Na-Donu Univ Im V M Molotova ... Uchenye Zapiski Rostovskogo-Na-Donu Universiteta Imeni V. M. Molotova [*A publication*]

Uch Zap Ryazan Gos Pedagog Inst ... Uchenye Zapiski Ryazanskogo Gosudarstvennogo Pedagogicheskogo Instituta [*A publication*]

Uch Zap Rybinsk Gos Pedagog Inst ... Uchenye Zapiski Rybinskii Gosudarstvennyi Pedagogicheskii Institut [*A publication*]

Uch Zap Sarat Gos Pedagog Inst ... Uchenye Zapiski Saratovskogo Gosudarstvennogo Pedagogicheskogo Instituta [*A publication*]

Uch Zap Sarat Gos Univ ... Uchenye Zapiski Saratovskogo Gosudarstvennogo Universiteta [*A publication*]

Uch Zap Sev Oset Gos Pedagog Inst ... Uchenye Zapiski Severo-Osetinskii Gosudarstvennyi Pedagogicheskii Institut [*A publication*]

Uch Zap Sev-Oset Gos Pedagog Inst Im K L Khetagurova ... Uchenye Zapiski Severo-Osetinskogo Gosudarstvennogo Pedagogicheskogo Instituta Imeni K. L. Khetagurova [*A publication*]

Uch Zap Smolensk Gos Pedagog Inst ... Uchenye Zapiski Smolenskogo Gosudarstvennogo Pedagogicheskogo Instituta [*A publication*]

Uch Zap Sredneaziat Nauchno-Issled Inst Geol Miner Syr'ya ... Uchenye Zapiski Sredneaziatskii Nauchno-Issledovatel'skii Institut Geologii i Mineral'nogo Syr'ya [*A publication*]

Uch Zap Stavrop Gos Med Inst ... Uchenye Zapiski Stavropol'skogo Gosudarstvennogo Meditsinskogo Instituta [*A publication*]

Uch Zap Sverdl Gos Pedagog Inst ... Uchenye Zapiski Sverdlovskii Gosudarstvennyi Pedagogicheskii Institut [*A publication*]

Uch Zap Tadzh Gos Univ ... Uchenye Zapiski Tadzhikskogo Gosudarstvennogo Universiteta [*A publication*]

Uch Zap Tartu Gos Univ ... Uchenye Zapiski Tartuskogo Gosudarstvennogo Universiteta [*Estonian SSR*] [*A publication*]

Uch Zap Tashk Gos Pedagog Inst ... Uchenye Zapiski Tashkentskogo Gosudarstvennogo Pedagogicheskogo Instituta [*A publication*]

Uch Zap Tashk Vech Pedagog Inst ... Uchenye Zapiski Tashkentskii Vechernii Pedagogicheskii Institut [*A publication*]

Uch Zap Tirasp Gos Pedagog Inst ... Uchenye Zapiski Tiraspol'skii Gosudarstvennyi Pedagogicheskii Institut [*A publication*]

Uch Zap Tomsk Gos Pedagog Inst ... Uchenye Zapiski Tomskogo Gosudarstvennogo Pedagogicheskogo Instituta [*A publication*]

Uch Zap Tomsk Gos Univ ... Uchenye Zapiski Tomskogo Gosudarstvennogo Universiteta [*A publication*]

Uch Zap TsAGI ... Uchenye Zapiski TsAGI [*USSR*] [*A publication*]

Uch Zap Tsentr Nauchno-Issled Inst Olovyannoi Promsti ... Uchenye Zapiski Tsentral'nyi Nauchno-Issledovatel'skii Institut Olovyannoi Promyshlennosti [*A publication*]

Uch Zap Tul Gos Pedagog Inst Fiz Tekh Nauki ... Uchenye Zapiski Tul'skii Gosudarstvennyi Pedagogicheskii Institut. Fiziko-Tekhnicheskie Nauki [*USSR*] [*A publication*]

Uch Zap Turkm Gos Pedagog Inst Ser Estest Nauk ... Uchenye Zapiski Turkmenskii Gosudarstvennyi Pedagogicheskii Institut Seriya Estestvennykh Nauk [*A publication*]

Uch Zap Turkm Gos Univ ... Uchenye Zapiski Turkmenskogo Gosudarstvennogo Universiteta [*A publication*]

Uch Zap Tyumen Gos Pedagog Inst ... Uchenye Zapiski Tyumenskogo Gosudarstvennogo Pedagogicheskogo Instituta [*A publication*]

Uch Zap Udmurt Pedagog Inst ... Uchenye Zapiski Udmurtskogo Pedagogicheskogo Instituta [*A publication*]

Uch Zap Ul'yanovsk Pedagog Inst ... Uchenye Zapiski Ul'yanovskii Pedagogicheskii Institut [*A publication*]

Uch Zap Ural Gos Univ ... Uchenye Zapiski Ural'skogo Gosudarstvennogo Universiteta [*USSR*] [*A publication*]

Uch Zap Ural Gos Univ Im A M Gor'kogo ... Uchenye Zapiski Ural'skogo Gosudarstvennogo Universiteta Imeni A. M. Gor'kogo [*A publication*]

Uch Zap Velikoluk Gos Pedagog Inst ... Uchenye Zapiski. Velikolukskii Gosudarstvennyi Pedagogicheskii Institut [*A publication*]

Uch Zap Vitebsk Gos Pedagog Inst Im S M Kirova ... Uchenye Zapiski Vitebskogo Gosudarstvennogo Pedagogicheskogo Instituta Imeni S. M. Kirova [*A publication*]

Uch Zap Vitebsk Vet Inst ... Uchenye Zapiski Vitebskogo Veterinarnogo Instituta [*A publication*]

Uch Zap Vladimir Gos Pedagog Inst Ser Bot ... Uchenye Zapiski Vladimirskii Gosudarstvennyi Pedagogicheskii Institut. Seriya Botanika [*A publication*]

Uch Zap Vladimir Gos Pedagog Inst Ser Bot ... Uchenye Zapiski Vladimirskogo Gosudarstvennogo Pedagogicheskogo Institut. Seriya Botanika [*A publication*]

Uch Zap Vladimir Gos Pedagog Inst Ser Fiz ... Uchenye Zapiski Vladimirskii Gosudarstvennyi Pedagogicheskii Institut. Seriya Fizika [*A publication*]

Uch Zap Vladimir Gos Pedagog Inst Ser Fiziol Rast ... Uchenye Zapiski Vladimirskii Gosudarstvennyi Pedagogicheskii Institut. Seriya Fiziologiya Rastenii [*A publication*]

Uch Zap Vladimir Gos Pedagog Inst Ser Khim ... Uchenye Zapiski Vladimirskii Gosudarstvennyi Pedagogicheskii Institut. Seriya Khimiya [*A publication*]

Uch Zap Volgogr Gos Pedagog Inst ... Uchenye Zapiski Volgogradskogo Gosudarstvennogo Pedagogicheskogo Instituta [*A publication*]

Uch Zap Vologod Gos Pedagog Inst ... Uchenye Zapiski Vologodskii Gosudarstvennyi Pedagogicheskii Institut [*A publication*]

Uch Zap Vybors Gos Pedagog Inst ... Uchenye Zapiski Vyborskii Gosudarstvennyi Pedagogicheskii Institut [*A publication*]

Uch Zap Yakutsk Gos Univ ... Uchenye Zapiski Yakutskogo Gosudarstvennogo Universiteta [*A publication*]

Uch Zap Yakutsk Inst ... Uchenye Zapiski Yakutskogo Instituta [*A publication*]

Uch Zap Yarosl Gos Pedagog Inst ... Uchenye Zapiski Yaroslavskii Gosudarstvennyi Pedagogicheskii Institut [*A publication*]

Uch Zap Yarosl Tekhnol Inst ... Uchenye Zapiski Yaroslavskogo Tekhnologicheskogo Instituta [*A publication*]

UCI .... Imperial Chemical Industries [*British*]

UCI .... Union Cycliste Internationale [*International Cycling Union*] [*French*] (EA)

UCI .... Unione Coltivatori Italiana [*Farmers Union*] [*Rome, Italy*]

UCI .... Unit Construction Index

UCI .... United Charity Institutions of Jerusalem [*New York, NY*] (EA)

UCI .... University of California at Irvine

UCI .... Urinary Catheter In [*or Input*] [*Medicine*]

UCI .... Utility Card Input

UCIB .... USAFE Command Intelligence Brief (MCD)

UCID .... Independent Democratic Union of Cape Verde (PD)

UCIDT .... University Consortium for Instructional Development and Technology [*Formerly, UCEMT*] (EA)

UCIIM .... Unione Cattolica Italiana Insegnanti Medi

UCIMT .... University Center for Instructional Media and Technology [*University of Connecticut*] [*Research center*] (RCD)

UCIMU .... Unione Costruttori Italiani Macchine Utensili [*Machine Tool Manufacturers Union*] [*Italy*]

UCINA .... Unione Nazionale Cantieri e Industrie Nautiche ed Affini [*Shipyard and Nautical Industries Union*] [*Milan, Italy*]

U Cin L Rev ... University of Cincinnati. Law Review [*A publication*]

UCIP .... Union Catholique Internationale de la Presse [*International Catholic Union of the Press*] (EA-IO)

UCIR .... University Center for International Rehabilitation [*Michigan State University*] [*Research center*] (RCD)

UCIS .... University Center for International Studies [*University of Pittsburgh*] [*Research center*] (EISS)

UCIS .... University Computing and Information Services [*Villanova University*] [*Research center*] (RCD)

UCIS .... Uprange Computer Input System

UCISS .... Union Catholique Internationale de Service Social [*Catholic International Union for Social Service*] (EA-IO)

UCIT .... United Cities Gas Co. [*NASDAQ symbol*] (NQ)

UCJ .... Unsatisfied Claim and Judgment [*State driver insurance*]

UCJG .... Alliance Universelle des Unions Chretiennes de Jeunes Gens [*World Alliance of Young Men's Christian Associations*]

UC Jur .... Upper Canada Jurist (DLA)

UC Jur (Can) ... Upper Canada Jurist (DLA)

UCK .... Union Culturelle Katangaise [*Katangan Cultural Union*]

UCKB .... Upper Canada King's Bench Reports, Old Series [*1831-44*] (DLA)

UCKB (Can) ... Upper Canada King's Bench Reports, Old Series [*1831-44*] (DLA)

UCL .... Ulnar Collateral Ligament [*Anatomy*]

UCL .... Uncomfortable Loudness [*Audiometry*]

UCL .... University of Calgary Library [*UTLAS symbol*]

UCL .... University Catholique de Louvain [*Belgium*] (MCD)

UCL .... University College of London (KSC)

UCL .... University of Connecticut, Law Library, West Hartford, CT [*OCLC symbol*] (OCLC)

UCL .... Unocal Corp. [*NYSE symbol*]

UCL .... Update Control List

UCL .... Upper Confidence Level [*Industrial engineering*] (IEEE)

UCL .... Upper Confidence Limit [*Statistics*]

UCL .... Upper Control Limit [*QCR*]

UCL .... Urea Clearance [*Test*] [*Medicine*]

UCLA .... University of California, Los Angeles [*Databank originator*]
UCLA .... University at the Corner of Lenox Avenue [*Nickname for "The Tree of Life," a Harlem bookstore*]
UCLA-Alaska L Rev ... UCLA [*University of California, Los Angeles*]-Alaska Law Review (DLA)
UCLA Forum Med Sci ... UCLA [*University of California, Los Angeles*] Forum in Medical Sciences [*A publication*]
UCLA Intra L Rev ... UCLA [*University of California, Los Angeles*] Intramural Law Review (DLA)
UCLA J Envt'l L & Pol'y ... UCLA [*University of California, Los Angeles*] Journal of Environmental Law and Policy (DLA)
UCLA Law R ... UCLA [*University of California, Los Angeles*] Law Review
UCLA Law Rev ... University of California at Los Angeles. Law Review (DLA)
UCLA L Rev ... University of California at Los Angeles. Law Review (DLA)
UCLA (Univ Cal Los Angeles)-Alaska Law R ... UCLA (University of California, Los Angeles)-Alaska Law Review [*A publication*]
UCLC .... Utah College Library Council [*Library network*]
UCLEA .... University and College Labor Education Association [*Formerly, ULEA*] (EA)
UCLG .... United Cement, Lime, Gypsum, and Allied Workers International Union [*Formerly, CLGW*] (EA)
UCLJ .... University of California, La Jolla
UCLJ .... Upper Canada Law Journal [*1855-1922*] (DLA)
UCLJ (Can) ... Upper Canada Law Journal (DLA)
UCLJ NS .... Upper Canada Law Journal, New Series (DLA)
UCLJ NS (Can) ... Upper Canada Law Journal, New Series (DLA)
UCLJ OS .... Canada Law Journal, Old Series (DLA)
UCLM .... Unity of Czech Ladies and Men [*Later, CSA*] (EA)
UCLR .... University of Ceylon. Law Review (DLA)
UCLR .... University of Chicago. Law Review [*A publication*]
UCLR .... University of Cincinnati. Law Review [*A publication*]
UCLR .... University of Colorado. Law Review [*A publication*]
UCLRL .... University of California Lawrence Radiation Laboratory
UCLT .... Until Cleared to Land by the Tower [*Aviation*] (FAAC)
UCM .... Can You Come and See Me?
UCM .... Union des Croyants Malagaches [*Malagasy Christian Union*]
UCM .... Universal Christian Movement (EA)
UCM .... Universal Communications Monitor
UCM .... University Christian Movement [*Formerly, NSCF*] [*Defunct*]
UCM .... Unresolved Complex Mixture
UCMJ .... Uniform Code of Military Justice
UCMP .... Union Catalog of Medical Periodicals [*A publication*]
UCMS .... Unit Capability Measurement System (AFM)
UCMS .... United Christian Missionary Society
UCMT .... Unglazed Ceramic Mosaic Tile [*Technical drawings*]
UCN .... Ultracold Neutron
UCN .... Uniform Control Number (NASA)
UCN .... Union Civica Nacional [*National Civic Union*] [*Dominican Republic*] (PPW)
UCNC .... Union Carbide Nuclear Corporation
UCNI .... Unclassified Controlled Nuclear Information [*Department of Energy*]
UCNI .... Unified Communications Navigation Identification
UCNT .... Undifferentiated Carcinoma of Nasopharyngeal Type [*Oncology*]
UCNW .... University College of North Wales
UCNY .... Underfashion Club of New York [*Formerly, CBWC*] (EA)
UCO .... Union Corporation [*NYSE symbol*]
UCO .... Universal Code [*Used for giving transport aircraft meteorological information in wartime*] (NATG)
UCO .... Universal Weather Landing Code
UCO .... Urinary Catheter Out [*or Output*] [*Medicine*]
UCO .... Utility Compiler
UCOD .... University Clearing Office for Developing Countries
U-COFT ..... Unit Conduct of Fire Trainer [*Army*]
UCOIP .... University of Chicago. Oriental Institute. Publications [*A publication*]
UCOL .... Union des Colons du Katanga [*Settlers' Union of Katanga*]
U Colo L Rev ... University of Colorado. Law Review [*A publication*]
U Color L Rev ... University of Colorado. Law Review [*A publication*]
U Colo Stud ... University of Colorado. Studies [*A publication*]
UCON .... Utility Control
UCONN ...... University of Connecticut
UCOP .... University of Cambridge. Oriental Publications [*A publication*]
UCOPOM ... Union Europeenne du Commerce de Gros des Pommes de Terre [*European Union of the Wholesale Potato Trade*] [*Common Market*]
UCOS .... Upper Canada King's Bench Reports, Old Series [*1831-44*] (DLA)
UCOS .... Uprange Computer Output System
UCOSL ...... University of Colorado School of Law (DLA)
UCOWR ..... Universities Council on Water Resources (EA)
UCP .... New Castle, PA [*Location identifier*] [*FAA*] (FAAL)
UCP .... Ubiquitous Crystallization Process [*Photovoltaic energy systems*]
UCP .... Unified Command Plan (AFM)
UCP .... Uninterruptable Computer Power
UCP .... Union Comorienne pour le Progres [*Comorian Union for Progress*] (PD)
UCP .... United Country Party [*Australia*]

UCP .... University of California. Publications in Classical Philology [*A publication*]
UCP .... University of Connecticut, Health Center Library, Processing Center, Farmington, CT [*OCLC symbol*] (OCLC)
UCP .... Update Control Process [*Telecommunications*] (TEL)
UCP .... Urinary C-Peptide [*Urology*]
UCP .... Urinary Coproporphyrin [*Urology*]
UCP .... Utilities Conservation Program [*Navy*] (NG)
UCP .... Utility Control Program
UCPA .... United Cerebral Palsy Associations [*New York, NY*] (EA)
UCPA .... University of California. Publications in Classical Archaeology [*A publication*]
UCPC .... University of Connecticut Paleobotanical Collection
UCPES .... University of California. Publications in English Studies [*A publication*]
UCPF .... United Church Peace Fellowship [*Defunct*] (EA)
UCPFS .... University of California. Publications in Folklore Studies [*A publication*]
UCPh .... Universitas Carolina: Philologica [*A publication*]
UCPL .... University of California. Publications in Linguistics [*A publication*]
UCPM .... University of California. Publications in Music [*A publication*]
UCPMP ...... University of California. Publications in Modern Philology [*A publication*]
UCPMPh .... University of California. Publications in Modern Philology [*A publication*]
UCPN .... Union des Chefs et des Populations du Nord [*Union of Chiefs and Peoples of the North*] [*Togo*]
UCPP .... Urban Crime Prevention Program [*Federal government*]
UCPPh .... University of California. Publications in Classical Philology [*A publication*]
UCPR .... Upper Canada Practice Reports (DLA)
UC Pract .... Upper Canada Practice Reports [*1850-1900*] (DLA)
UC Pr (Can) ... Upper Canada Practice Reports (DLA)
UCPREF ..... United Cerebral Palsy Research and Educational Foundation [*New York, NY*] (EA)
UC Pr R ...... Upper Canada Practice Reports (DLA)
UCPSP .... University of California. Publications in Semitic Philology [*A publication*]
UCPSPh ...... University of California. Publications in Semitic Philology [*A publication*]
UCPT .... Urinary Coproporphyrin Test [*Urology*]
UCPTE .... Union pour la Coordination de la Production et du Transport de l'Electricite [*Union for the Coordination of the Production and Transport of Electric Power - UCPTE*] (EA-IO)
UCQ .... University College Quarterly [*A publication*]
UCQB .... Upper Canada Queen's Bench Reports (DLA)
UC QB OS ... Upper Canada Queen's Bench Reports, Old Series (DLA)
UC QB OS (Can) ... Upper Canada Queen's Bench Reports, Old Series (DLA)
UCR .... Committee on Uniform Crime Records (EA)
UCR .... Unconditioned Reflex [*or Response*] [*Psychometrics*]
UCR .... Under-Color Removal [*Printing technology*]
UCR .... Uniform Crime Reports [*FBI*]
UCR .... Union Centriste et Radicale [*Political party*] [*French*]
UCR .... Union Civica Radical [*Radical Civic Union*] [*Buenos Aires, Argentina*] (PD)
UCR .... Union Confederale des Retraites [*Paris, France*]
UCR .... Unit Card Reader
UCR .... Unit Cost Report [*Military*] (RDA)
UCR .... University of California, Riverside (EISS)
UCR .... University of Ceylon. Review [*A publication*]
UCR .... University of Cincinnati. Law Review [*A publication*]
UCR .... Unsatisfactory Condition Report
UCR .... Upper Canada Reports (DLA)
UCR .... User Control Routine (MCD)
UCR .... Usual, Customary, and Reasonable [*Medicine*]
UCR .... Utah Coal Route [*AAR code*]
UCRC .... Underground Construction Research Council
UCRC .... United Civil Rights Committee
UC Rep ...... Upper Canada Reports (DLA)
UC Rep FM Univ Calif Berkeley Dep Mech Eng ... UC. Report FM. University of California, Berkeley. Department of Mechanical Engineering [*A publication*]
UCRG .... Union des Clubs pour le Renouveau de la Gauche [*Union of Clubs for the Renovation of the Left*] [*French*] (PPE)
UCRI .... Union Carbide Research Institute (KSC)
UCRI .... Union Civica Radical Intransigente [*Left-wing radical political party*] [*Argentina*]
UCRIFER ..... Unione Costruttori e Riparatori Ferrotramviari [*Rolling Stock Manufacturers Union*] [*Florence, Italy*]
UCRL .... University of California Radiation Laboratory (MCD)
UCRL .... University of California Research Laboratory (KSC)
UCRP .... Union Civica Radical del Pueblo [*Moderate radical political party*] [*Argentina*]
UCS .... Canadian Union Catalogue of Serials [*National Library of Canada*] [*Ottawa, ON*] [*Information service*] (EISS)
UCS .... Southern Utah State College, Cedar City, UT [*Library symbol*] [*Library of Congress*] (LCLS)
UCS .... Unbalanced Current Sensing (MCD)

UCS........... Unclosed Contract Status [*Military*] (AFIT)
UCS........... Unconditioned Stimulus [*Psychometrics*]
UCS........... Unconscious [*Medicine*]
UCS........... Underwater Cable System
UCS........... Underwater Communications System
UCS........... Unican Security Systems Ltd. [*Toronto Stock Exchange symbol*]
UCS........... Uniform Chromaticity Scale [*Illuminant*]
UCS........... Uniform Communications System
UCS........... Union of Concerned Scientists
UCS........... Unit of Coastal Sedimentation [*NERC*] [*British*]
UCS........... Unit Cost of Sales
UCS........... Unit-Count System
UCS........... United Community Services
UCS........... United Computing Systems, Inc.
UCS........... United States Army Corps of Engineers, Sacramento, Sacramento, CA [*OCLC symbol*] (OCLC)
UCS........... Universal Call Sequence
UCS........... Universal Camera Site (KSC)
UCS........... Universal Card Scanner [*Data processing*] (DIT)
UCS........... Universal Cargo Sling
UCS........... Universal Character Set [*Data processing*]
UCS........... Universal Classification System
UCS........... Universal Clothing System [*Software package*]
UCS........... Universal Command System (KSC)
UCS........... Universal Communication Systems, Inc. [*American Stock Exchange symbol*]
UCS........... Universal Connector Strip
UCS........... Universal Control System (NASA)
UCS........... University Computer Services [*Ball State University*] [*Research center*] (RCD)
UCS........... University Computing Services [*University of Southern California*] [*Research center*] (RCD)
UCS........... University Computing Services [*State University of New York at Buffalo*] [*Research center*] (RCD)
UCS........... Urine Collection System [*NASA*] (KSC)
UCS........... User Control Store
UCS........... Utilities Control System (KSC)
UCS........... Utility Consulting Services [*Petroleum Information Corp.*] [*Dallas, TX*] [*Information service*] (EISS)
UCSA........ Uniform Controlled Substances Act [*National Conference of Commissioners on Uniform State Laws*]
UCSA........ United Chian Societies of America [*Later, CSA*] (EA)
UCSB........ University of California, Santa Barbara
UCSBS....... Ukrainian Catholic Soyuz of Brotherhoods and Sisterhoods (EA)
UCSC........ University of California, Santa Cruz
UCSC........ University City Science Center [*Philadelphia, PA*] [*Research center*] (RCD)
UCSD........ Universal Communications Switching Device
UCSD........ University of California, San Diego
UCSEL....... University of California Structural Engineering Laboratory (KSC)
UCSF........ University of California, San Francisco
UCSGS...... University of Colorado. Studies. General Series [*A publication*]
UCSJ........ Union of Councils for Soviet Jews (EA)
UCSL........ Union Congolaise des Syndicats Libres [*Congolese Union of Free Syndicates*] [*Leopoldville*]
UCSL........ University of California. Studies in Linguistics [*A publication*]
UCSLL....... University of Colorado. Studies. Series in Language and Literature [*A publication*]
UCSMB...... Union des Carrieres et Scieries de Marbres de Belgique [*Brussels, Belgium*]
UCSMP...... University of California. Studies in Modern Philology [*A publication*]
UCSR........ Ukranian Center for Social Research (EA)
UCSR........ Unionist Committee for Social Reform [*British*]
UCSS........ Universal Communications Switching System (MCD)
UC/SSL...... University of California/Space Sciences Laboratory (KSC)
UCSSLL..... University of Colorado. Studies. Series in Language and Literature [*A publication*]
UCST........ Upper Critical-Solution-Temperature
UCSTR...... Universal Code Synchronous Transmitter Receiver
UCSUR...... University Center for Social and Urban Research [*University of Pittsburgh*] [*Research center*] (RCD)
UCSUS....... Ukrainian Catholic Students of the United States [*Defunct*] (EA)
UCT........... Order of United Commercial Travelers of America (EA)
UCT........... Ultrasonic Computed Tomography [*For examining interiors of solids*]
UCT........... Unchanged Conventional Treatment [*Medicine*]
UCT........... Underwater Construction Team [*Navy*] (NVT)
UCT........... Unite Centrale de Traitement [*Central Processing Unit - CPU*] [*French*]
UCT........... United Cable Television Corp. [*NYSE symbol*]
UCT........... Units Compatibility Test
UCT........... Universal Coordinated Time
UCT........... University of Cape Town [*South Africa*]
UCT........... University of Connecticut [*Storrs*] [*Connecticut*] [*Seismograph station code, US Geological Survey*] (SEIS)
UCT........... Urine Culture Tube [*Clinical chemistry*]

UCTA .... University and College Theatre Association (EA)
UCTA .... Urine Collection/Transfer Assembly [*Apollo*] [*NASA*]
UCTC .... Union Camerounaise des Travailleurs Croyants [*Cameroonese Union of Believing Workers*]
UCTC .... United Counties Bancorp [*NASDAQ symbol*] (NQ)
UCTF......... Union Culturelle et Technique de Langue Francaise [*French-Language Cultural and Technical Union*] (EA)
UCTL........ Up Control [*Aerospace*] (AAG)
UCTS .... United Church Training School
UCTSE ...... University of Cape Town. Studies in English [*A publication*]
UCU........... University of California Union List, Berkeley, CA [*OCLC symbol*] (OCLC)
UCU........... Utilicorp United, Inc. [*NYSE symbol*]
UCV........... Uncontrolled Variable
UCV........... Unimproved Capital Value [*Business and trade*] (ADA)
UCV........... United Confederate Veterans
UCW........... Unit Control Word [*Data processing*] (BUR)
UCW........... United Church Women of the National Council of Churches (EA)
UCW........... University College of Wales
UCW........... University of Connecticut, Storrs, CT [*OCLC symbol*] (OCLC)
UCWA .... United Construction Workers Association (OICC)
UCWE........ Underwater Countermeasures and Weapons Establishment [*British*]
UCWR .... Upon Completion Thereof Will Return To [*Air Force*]
UCX........... Unemployment Compensation, Ex-Servicemen
UCY........... Union City, TN [*Location identifier*] [*FAA*] (FAAL)
UCY........... United Caribbean Youth
UCYM........ United Christian Youth Movement [*Defunct*] (EA)
Uc Zap Adyg Nauc-Issled Inst Jaz Lit Ist ... Ucenye Zapiski Adygejoskogo Naucno-Issledovatel'skogo Instituta Jazyka, Literatury, i Istorii [*A publication*]
Uc Zap (Stavropol Gos Pedag Inst) ... Ucenye Zapiski (Stavropol'skij Gosudarstvennyj Pedagogiceskij Institut) [*A publication*]
UD .... Fast Air Ltda. [*Chile*] [*ICAO designator*] (FAAC)
UD .... Ulnar Deviation [*Medicine*]
UD .... Ultimate Dependability [*Automotive designation*]
UD .... Unable to Approve Departure for the Time Specified [*Aviation*] (FAAC)
UD .... Unavoidable Delay
U/D............. Under Deck (ADA)
UD .... Underground Distribution (MSA)
UD .... Underwater Demolition [*Navy*] (NVT)
UD .... Undesirable Discharge [*Military*]
UD .... Undetected Defect
UD .... Undifferentiated (BJA)
UD .... Unidentifiable (BJA)
UD .... Uniflow Diesel [*Nissan-designed engine*]
UD .... Unit Designation
UD .... Unit Diary
UD .... Unit Director
UD .... Unit Dose [*Medicine*]
UD .... Universal Dipole (DEN)
UD .... University of Denver [*Colorado*]
U of D .... University of Detroit [*Michigan*]
U of D .... University of Dublin [*Ireland*]
UD .... Unlawful Detainer [*Legal term for an eviction proceeding*]
UD .... Unlisted Drugs [*A publication*]
UD .... Unplanned Derating [*Electronics*] (IEEE)
U/D............. Up/Down (KSC)
UD .... Update [*Data processing*] (NASA)
UD .... Upper Deck [*Naval*]
UD .... Urban District
UD .... Urethral Discharge [*Medicine*]
UD .... Uroporphyrinogen Decarboxylase [*Also, UDase*] [*An enzyme*]
UD .... Usable Depth (MCD)
UD .... Usage Data
UD .... Ut Dictum [*As Directed*] [*Latin*]
UD .... Utility Dog [*Dog show term*]
UDA........... Ulster Defence Association
UDA........... Ultrasonic Detergent Action
UDA........... Union for Democratic Action
UDA........... United States Department of the Interior, Alaska Resources, Anchorage, AK [*OCLC symbol*] (OCLC)
UDA........... Universal Detective Association [*Defunct*] (EA)
UDAA .... Unlawfully Driving Away Auto
UDAC........ User Digital Analog Controller
UDAG........ Urban Development Action Grant [*Federal program*]
Udal........... Udal's Fiji Law Reports (DLA)
UDAM....... Universal Digital Avionics Module (MCD)
UDAP .... Universal Digital Autopilot
UDAR .... Universal Digital Adaptive Recognizer (IEEE)
UDAS .... Unified Direct Access System (BUR)
UDAS .... Universal Data Acquisition System
UDase .... Uroporphyrinogen Decarboxylase [*Also, UD*] [*An enzyme*]
UDAT........ Unidata Systems, Inc. [*NASDAQ symbol*] (NQ)
U Dayton L Rev ... University of Dayton. Law Review [*A publication*]
UDB........... Unified Data Base
UDB........... Union Democratique Bretonne - Unvaniezh Demokratel Breizh [*Breton Democratic Union*] [*French*] (PPW)
UDB........... Up-Data Buffer [*Data processing*]

UDC............ National Park Service, National Capital Region, Washington, DC [*OCLC symbol*]   (OCLC)
UDC............ UDC - Universal Development [*NYSE symbol*]
UDC............ Ultrasonic Doppler Cardioscope [*Heartbeat monitor*]
UDC............ Underdeveloped Countries
UDC............ Underwater Decompression Computer [*Navy*]   (CAAL)
UDC............ Uniao Democratica de Cabo Verde [*Democratic Union of Cape Verde*]
UDC............ Union of the Democratic Centre [*Saharan*]   (PPW)
UDC............ Union for Democratic Communications   (EA)
UDC............ Union of Democratic Control [*British*]
UDC............ Union Democratica Cristiana [*Christian Democratic Union*] [*Bolivian*]   (PPW)
UDC............ Union Democratique Centrafricaine [*Central African Democratic Union*]   (PPW)
UDC............ Union Democratique du Centre [*Democratic Union of the Center*] [*Swiss*]   (PPE)
UDC............ Unit Deployment of Containers   (MCD)
UDC............ United Daughters of the Confederacy   (EA)
UDC............ Unity-in-Diversity Council   (EA)
UDC............ Universal Decimal Classification [*Online database field identifier*]
UDC............ Universal Digital Control
UDC............ Universal Disk Controller [*Central Point Software*]
UDC............ University of the District of Columbia
UDC............ Up-Down Counter
UDC............ Upper Dead Center
UDC............ Urban Development Corporation [*New York State agency*]
UDC............ Urban District Council [*British*]
UDC............ Ursodeoxycholate [*Biochemistry*]
UDC............ Ursodeoxycholic Acid
UDC............ User Designation Codes [*Navy*]   (NG)
UDC............ Usual Diseases of Childhood [*Medicine*]
UDCA........ Undesirable Discharge, Trial by Civil Authorities [*Navy*]
UDCA........ Union pour la Defense des Commercants et des Artisans [*Union for the Defense of Traders and Artisans*] [*French*]   (PPE)
UDCA........ Ursodeoxycholic Acid [*Pharmacology*]
UDCCS..... Uniform Data Classification Code Structure [*Navy*]   (NG)
UDCO........ Universal Development [*NASDAQ symbol*]   (NQ)
UDCS........ United Data Collection System   (MCD)
UDCV........ Uniao Democratica de Cabo Verde [*Democratic Union of Cape Verde*]
UDD............ Bermuda Dunes, CA [*Location identifier*] [*FAA*]   (FAAL)
UDD............ Bureau of Land Management, Denver, Denver, CO [*OCLC symbol*]   (OCLC)
UDD............ Uddeholm [*Sweden*] [*Seismograph station code, US Geological Survey*]   (SEIS)
UDD............ Ulster Diploma in Dairying
UDD............ Union Democratique Dahomeene [*Dahomey Democratic Union*]
UDDA........ Uniform Determination of Death Act [*National Conference of Commissioners on Uniform State Laws*]
UDDE........ Undesirable Discharge, Desertion without Trial [*Navy*]
UDDF......... Up and Down Drafts [*Meteorology*]   (FAAC)
UDDIA....... Union Democratique pour la Defense des Interets Africains [*Democratic Union to Defend African Interests*]
UDDL......... Ultrasonic Dispersive Delay Line
UDE............ Underwater Detection Establishment [*British*]   (MCD)
UDE............ Undetermined Etiology
UDE............ Union Douaniere Equatoriale [*Equatorial Customs Union*]
UDE............ United States Fish and Wildlife Service, Region 2, Albuquerque, NM [*OCLC symbol*]   (OCLC)
UDE............ Universal Data Entry
UDEAC....... Union Douaniere et Economique de l'Afrique Centrale [*Central African Customs and Economic Union*]   (EA-IO)
UDEAO....... Union Douaniere des Etats de l'Afrique et l'Ouest [*Customs Union of West African States*] [*Later, CEAO*]
UDEC........ Unitized Digital Electronic Calculator   (MCD)
UDECMA-KMPT ... Parti Democratique Chretien Malgache [*Malagasy Christian Democratic Party*]   (PPW)
UDEFEC..... Union Democratique des Femmes Camerounaises [*Cameroonese Democratic Women's Union*]
UDENAMO ... Uniao Democratica Nacional de Mocambique [*Mozambican National Democratic Union*] [*Later, FRELIMO*]
UDET......... Universal Digital Element Tester   (MCD)
U Det J Urb L ... University of Detroit. Journal of Urban Law [*A publication*]
U Det L J .... University of Detroit. Law Journal [*A publication*]
U Det L Rev ... University of Detroit. Law Review   (DLA)
UDETO....... Union Democratique Togolaise [*Togolese Democratic Union*]
U of Detroit LJ ... University of Detroit. Law Journal [*A publication*]
U Detroit LJ ... University of Detroit. Law Journal [*A publication*]
UDF .... Boise Interagency Fire Center, Boise, ID [*OCLC symbol*]   (OCLC)
UDF .... Federation Guadeloupeenne de l'Union pour la Democratie Francaise [*Guadeloupe Federation of the Union for French Democracy*]   (PPW)
UDF .... UHF [*Ultrahigh Frequency*] Direction Finder   (FAAC)
UDF .... Ulster Defence Force

UDF .... Unducted Fan [*Type of prop engine developed by General Electric Co.*]
UDF .... Union Defence Force [*British*]
UDF .... Union pour la Democratie Francaise [*Union for French Democracy*] [*New Caledonian*]   (PPW)
UDF .... Union pour la Democratie Francaise [*Union for French Democracy*] [*Reunionese*]   (PPW)
UDF .... Union pour la Democratie Francaise [*Union for French Democracy*] [*French*]   (PPW)
UDF .... Union pour la Democratie Francaise [*Union for French Democracy*] [*French Guiana*]   (PPW)
UDF .... Uniroyal, Dunlop, and Firestone [*Alternative translation of South Africa's UDF, United Democratic Front. Translation refers to method of execution consisting of forcing a tire around the victim's body and setting it on fire*]
UDF .... Unit Derating Factor [*Electronics*]   (IEEE)
UDF .... Unit Development Folder   (MCD)
UDF .... United Democratic Front [*Indian*]   (PPW)
UDF .... United Democratic Front [*South African*]   (PPW)
UDF .... Upside-Down Flipper
UDF .... Utility and Data Flow   (NASA)
UDFAA ...... Upholstery and Decorative Fabrics Association of America [*Defunct*]   (EA)
UDFE......... Undesirable Discharge, Fraudulent Enlistment [*Navy*]
UDFMA ...... Upholstery and Drapery Fabric Manufacturers Association [*Later, UFMA*]
UDFT .... Union Democratique des Femmes Tunisiennes [*Democratic Union of Tunisian Women*]
UDG........... National Fisheries Center, Kearneysville, WV [*OCLC symbol*]   (OCLC)
UDG........... Unit Derated Generation [*Electronics*]   (IEEE)
UDH........... National Park Service, Harpers Ferry Center, Harpers Ferry, WV [*OCLC symbol*]   (OCLC)
UDH........... Universal Die Holder
UDH........... Unplanned Derated Hours [*Electronics*]   (IEEE)
UDHS .... Unit Demand History Summary   (AABC)
UDI .... Uberlandia [*Brazil*] [*Airport symbol*]   (OAG)
UDI .... Udine [*Italy*] [*Seismograph station code, US Geological Survey*]   (SEIS)
UDI .... Unilateral Declaration of Independence [*of Southern Rhodesia*]
UDI .... Union Democratica Independiente [*Independent Democratic Union*] [*Chilean*]   (PPW)
UDI .... Union Democratique des Independants [*Democratic Union of Independents*] [*French*]   (PPE)
UDI .... Unique Data Item   (MCD)
UDI .... United States Department of the Interior, Natural Resources Library, Washington, DC [*OCLC symbol*]   (OCLC)
UDI .... Utility Data Institute [*Washington, DC*] [*Information service*]   (EISS)
UDIA......... United Dairy Industry Association [*Rosemont, IL*]   (EA)
UDID......... Unique Data Item Description   (MCD)
U-Dink....... Upper Class - Double Income, No Kids [*Lifestyle classification*]
UDIR......... USAREUR Daily Intelligence Report   (MCD)
UDIT .... Union pour la Defense des Interets du Tchad [*Union for the Defense of Chadian Interests*]
UDITPA ..... Uniform Division of Income for Tax Purposes Act
UDITS........ Universal Digital Test Set
UDJ .... Northern Prairie Wildlife Research Center, Jamestown, ND [*OCLC symbol*]   (OCLC)
UDJM .... Union Democratique de la Jeunesse Marocaine [*Democratic Union of Moroccan Youth*]
UDJV .... Union Democratique de la Jeunesse Voltaique [*Voltaic Democratic Youth Union*]
UDK........... United States Fish and Wildlife Service, Alaska Area Office, Anchorage, AK [*OCLC symbol*]   (OCLC)
UDK........... Upper Deck
UDKKB....... Utsunomiya Daigaku Kyoikugakubu Kiyo, Dai-2-Bu [*A publication*]
UDL .... Bureau of Land Management, Boise District Office, Boise, ID [*OCLC symbol*]   (OCLC)
UDL .... Ultrasonic Delay Line
UDL .... Underwater Data Link   (MCD)
UDL .... Uniform Data Language
UDL .... Uniform Data Link
UDL .... Unit Detail Listings [*Air Force*]
UDL .... Unit Document Listing   (MCD)
UDL .... Universal Development Laboratory [*Computer debugger*] [*Orion Instruments*]
UDL .... Untersuchungen zur Deutschen Literaturgeschichte [*A publication*]
UDL .... Up-Data Link [*Data processing*]
UdLH .... Universidad de la Habana [*A publication*]
UDLP......... United Democratic Labour Party [*Trinidadian and Tobagan*]   (PPW)
UDLP......... United Dominica Labour Party   (PPW)
UDM .... National Mine Health and Safety Academy, Beckley, WV [*OCLC symbol*]   (OCLC)
UDM .... Union Democratique Mauricienne [*Mauritian political party*]
UDM.......... Union Democratique Mauritanienne [*Mauritanian Democratic Union*]   (PD)
UDM .... Universal Drafting Machine Corp.

JDM .... Upright Drilling Machine
JDMA .... United Dance Merchants of America [*Cleveland, OH*] (EA)
JDMH .... Unsymmetrical Dimethylhydrazine [*Rocket fuel base, convulsant poison*]
JDN .... National Park Service, National Register Division, Washington, DC [*OCLC symbol*] (OCLC)
JDN .... Ulcerative Dermal Necrosis [*Medicine*]
JDN .... Underwater Doppler Navigation
JDN .... Uniao Democratica Nacional [*National Democratic Union*] [*Brazil*]
UDN .... Union Democrata Nacional [*National Democratic Union*] [*Salvadoran*] (PPW)
UDN .... Union Democratica Nicaraguense [*Nicaraguan Democratic Union*] (PD)
UDNGA .... Utsonomiya Daigaku Nogakubu Gakujutsu Hokoku [*A publication*]
UDO .... United States Fish and Wildlife Service, Billings, MT [*OCLC symbol*] (OCLC)
Udobr Urozhai ... Udobrenie i Urozhai [*A publication*]
Udobr Urozhai (Kom Khim Nar Khaz SSSR) ... Udobrenie i Urozhai (Komitet po Khimaisatsii Narodnogo Khozyaistva SSSR) [*A publication*]
UDOFT .... Universal Digital Operational Flight Trainer [*Navy*]
UDOP .... UHF [*Ultrahigh Frequency*] Doppler System
UDP .... National Park Service, Denver, Denver, CO [*OCLC symbol*] (OCLC)
UDP .... Ulster Diploma in Poultry Husbandry
UDP .... Uniao Democratica Popular [*Portugal*]
UDP .... Unidad Democratica Popular [*Democratic Popular Unity*] [*Bolivian*] (PPW)
UDP .... Unidad Democratica Popular [*Popular Democratic Unity*] [*Peruvian*] (PPW)
UDP .... Unification du Droit Prive
UDP .... Union pour la Democratie Populaire [*Union for People's Democracy*] [*Senegalese*] (PPW)
UDP .... United Data Processing (BUR)
UDP .... United Democratic Party [*Basotho*] (PPW)
UDP .... United Democratic Party [*Belizean*] (PD)
UDP .... Uridine Diphosphate [*Biochemistry*]
UDPAG ...... Uridine(diphospho)acetylglucosamine [*Biochemistry*]
UDPG .... Uridine Diphosphate Glucose [*Biochemistry*]
UDPGA .... Uridine Diphosphate Glucuronic Acid [*Biochemistry*]
UDPGDH ..... Uridinediphosphoglucose Dehydrogenase [*An enzyme*]
UDPGT ...... Uridine Diphosphate Glucuronosyltransferase [*An enzyme*] [*Biochemistry*]
UDPIA .... Uniform Disclaimer of Property Interests Act [*National Conference of Commissioners on Uniform State Laws*]
UDPK .... United Democratic Party of Kurdistan (BJA)
UDPL .... United Dated Parts List [*Configuration listing*] (MCD)
UDPM .... Union Democratique du Peuple Malien [*Mali People's Democratic Union*] (PPW)
UDPT .... Union Democratique des Populations Togolaises [*Democratic Union of Togolese People*]
UDQ .... Bureau of Land Management, Library, New Orleans, New Orleans, LA [*OCLC symbol*] (OCLC)
UDQ .... University of Denver. Quarterly [*A publication*]
UDR .... Udaipur [*India*] [*Airport symbol*] (OAG)
UDR .... Ulster Defence Regiment [*Military unit*] [*British*]
UDR .... Undersampling Ratio
UDR .... Union pour la Defense de la Republique [*Union for the Defense of the Republic*] [*French*] (PPE)
UDR .... Union pour la Democratie Francaise [*Union for French Democracy*] [*Martiniquais*] (PPW)
UDR .... United States Department of the Interior, Bureau of Reclamation, Denver, CO [*OCLC symbol*] (OCLC)
UDR .... Universal Digital Readout
UDR .... Universal Document Reader (BUR)
UDR .... University of Dayton. Review [*A publication*]
UDR .... Urgent Data Request [*GIDEP*]
UDR .... Usage Data Report
UDR .... Utility Data Reduction
UDRA .... Uniform Divorce Recognition Act [*National Conference of Commissioners on Uniform State Laws*]
UDRA .... United Drag Racers Association (EA)
UDRC .... Utility Data Retrieval Control
UDRI .... University of Dayton Research Institute [*Ohio*]
UDRO .... Utility Data Retrieval Output
UDRP .... Uridine Diribose Phosphate [*Biochemistry*]
UDRPS ...... Ultrasonic Data Recording and Processing System (NRCH)
UDRS .... Universal Driver Rating System [*Harness racing*]
UDRT/RAD ... Union Democratique pour le Respect du Travail - Respect voor Arbeid en Democratie [*Democratic Union for the Respect of Labor*] [*Belgium*] (PPW)
U/DRV .... Underdrive [*Automotive engineering*]
UDS .... Office of Surface Mining Reclamation and Enforcement, Region V, Denver, CO [*OCLC symbol*] (OCLC)
UDS .... Ultraviolet Detector System
UDS .... Unified Data System [*Data processing*]
UDS .... Union Democratique Senegalaise [*Senegalese Democratic Union*]
UDS .... Unit Data System [*Military*]

UDS .... Universal Data Set (CMD)
UDS .... Universal Data System [*Army*]
UDS .... Universal Data Systems [*Hardware manufacturer*]
UDS .... Universal Digital Switch (MCD)
UDS .... Universal Distributed System [*UNIVAC*]
UDS .... Universal Documentation System
UDS .... Unscheduled DNA Synthesis [*Genetics*]
UDS .... Urban Data Service [*International City Management Association*] (EISS)
UDS .... Urban Decision Systems, Inc. [*Los Angeles, CA*] [*Information service*] (EISS)
UDS .... Utility Data Systems [*San Clemente, CA*] [*Information service*] (EISS)
UDS .... Utilization and Disposal Service [*Functions transferred to Property Management and Disposal Service*] [*General Services Administration*]
UDSG .... Union Democratique et Sociale Gabonaise [*Gabonese Democratic and Social Union*]
UDSKD ...... Udenrigspolitiske Skrifter. Serie 15 [*A publication*]
UDSM .... Union des Democrates Sociaux de Madagascar [*Union of Social Democrats of Madagascar*]
UDSM .... Union Departemental de Syndicats du Mungo [*Departmental Union of the Trade Unions of Mungo*] [*Cameroon*]
UDSR .... Union Democratique et Socialiste de la Resistance [*Democratic and Socialist Union of the Resistance*] [*French*] (PPE)
UDSR .... United Duroc Swine Registry (EA)
UDT .... Underdeck Tonnage
UDT .... Underwater Demolition Team [*Navy*]
UDT .... Union of Democratic Thais in the US (EA)
UDT .... United States Fish and Wildlife Service, Science Reference Library, Twin Cities, MN [*OCLC symbol*] (OCLC)
UDT .... United Tire & Rubber Co. Ltd. [*Toronto Stock Exchange symbol*]
UDT .... Universal Data Transcriber [*Navy*]
UDT .... Upgraded Data Terminal (MCD)
UDT .... User Display Terminal
UDT .... Utility Dog Tracker [*Degree of obedience training*]
UDTC .... User-Dependent-Type Code
UDTD .... Updated (MSA)
UDTDET ..... Underwater Demolition Team Detachment [*Navy*] (NVT)
UDT/EOD ... Underwater Demolition Team/Explosive Ordnance Proposal [*Navy*] (MCD)
UDTI .... Universal Digital Transducer Indicator
UDTPHIBSPAC ... Underwater Demolition Teams, Amphibious Forces, Pacific Fleet [*Navy*]
UDTS .... Universal Data Transfer Service [*ITT World Communications, Inc.*] [*Secaucus, NJ*] [*Telecommunications*] (TSSD)
UDTS .... Universal Data Transmission System [*For international access*]
UDTUNIA .... Uniform Disclaimer of Transfers under Nontestamentary Instruments Act [*National Conference of Commissioners on Uniform State Laws*]
UDTX .... Utility Dog and Tracking Excellent [*Degree of obedience training*]
UDU .... National Maritime Museum, San Francisco, CA [*OCLC symbol*] (OCLC)
UDU .... Unabhaengige Demokratische Union [*Independent Democratic Union*] [*Austria*] (PPE)
UDU .... Underwater Demolition Unit
UDUAL .... Union de Universidades de America Latina [*Union of Latin American Universities*] [*Mexico*]
UDucGS ..... Church of Jesus Christ of Latter-Day Saints, Genealogical Society Library, Duchesne Branch, Stake Center, Duchesne, UT [*Library symbol*] [*Library of Congress*] (LCLS)
UDUF .... Undesirable Discharge, Unfitness [*Navy*]
UDUPA ...... Uniform Distribution of Unclaimed Property Act [*National Conference of Commissioners on Uniform State Laws*]
UDURA ...... Udobrenie i Urozhai [*Ministerstvo Sel'skogo Khozyaistva SSSR*] [*A publication*]
UDV .... Union Democratique Voltaique [*Voltaic Democratic Union*] [*Banned, 1974*]
UD-Ve .... Union Democratique pour la Cinquieme Republique [*Democratic Union for the Fifth Republic*] [*French*] (PPE)
UDW .... Ultradeep Water
UDW .... Western Energy and Land Use Team, Fort Collins, CO [*OCLC symbol*] (OCLC)
UDX .... Office of Surface Mining Reclamation and Enforcement, Washington, DC [*OCLC symbol*] (OCLC)
UDX .... Utility Dog Excellent [*Dog show term*] [*Canada*]
UDY .... USGS [*United States Geological Survey*] Water Resources Division, New York District, Albany, NY [*OCLC symbol*] (OCLC)
UDZ .... United States Department of the Interior, Western Archeological Center, Tucson, AZ [*OCLC symbol*] (OCLC)
UE .... Ultrasonic Engineering (MCD)
UE .... Unexpired (ADA)
UE .... Unit Entry
UE .... Unit Equipment [*as authorized to an Air Force unit*]
UE .... Unit Establishment
UE .... Unit Exception (CMD)
UE .... United Air Services [*South Africa*] [*ICAO designator*] (FAAC)

UE .... United Electrical, Radio, and Machine Workers of America
UE .... United Electrical, Radio, and Machine Workers of Canada [See also OUE]
UE .... United Electrodynamics   (AAG)
UE .... United Empire [Canada]
UE .... Unity of Empire [Award] [British]
UE .... Universale Economica [A publication]
UE .... University Extension
UE .... Until Exhausted
UE .... Update and Ephemeria   (MUGU)
UE .... Upper Entrance [Theater]
UE .... Upper Extremity [Medicine]
UE .... Urinary Energy [Nutrition]
UE .... Use of English [A publication]
UE .... User Equipment
UE .... Uterine Epithelium [Medicine]
UEA .... Graphic Arts Union Employers of America   (EA)
UEA .... Ulex europeus Agglutinin [Immunology]
UEA .... Unattended Equipment Area
UEA .... Union Europeenne de l'Ameublement [European Furniture Manufacturers Federation] [Brussels, Belgium]   (EA-IO)
UEA .... Union Europeenne des Aveugles [European Blind Union - EBU]   (EA-IO)
UEA .... United Egg Association   (EA)
UEA .... United Epilepsy Association [Later, EFA]   (EA)
UEA .... United Evangelical Action [A publication]
UEA .... Universal Esperanto Association
UEA .... Universala Esperanto Asocio [Universal Esperanto Association]   (EA-IO)
UEA .... University of East Anglia [England]
UEA .... Uranium Enrichment Associates [Bechtel Corp., Union Carbide Corp., Westinghouse Electric Corp.]
UEAC .... Unit Equipment Aircraft
UEAC .... United European American Club
UEAI .... Ulex Europaeus Agglutinin I
UEAI .... Union Europeenne des Arabisants et des Islamisants [European Union of Arab and Islamic Studies - EUAIS]   (EA-IO)
UEB .... Ultrasonic Epoxy Bonder
UEB .... Unexploded Bomb
UEB .... Union Economique BENELUX
UEB .... Upper Equipment Bay [NASA]   (KSC)
UEBC .... Union Espanola Benefica de California   (EA)
UEC .... Union Electric Company
UEC .... Union des Etudiants Communistes [France]
UEC .... Union Europeenne de la Carrosserie [European Union of Coachbuilders - EUC]
UEC .... Union Europeenne des Experts Comptables Economiques et Financiers [European Union of Public Accountants]
UEC .... Unit Endurance Chamber   (MCD)
UEC .... United Engineering Center
UEC .... Unmanned Equipment Cabinet
UEC .... Urban Elderly Coalition   (EA)
UEC .... Urban Environment Conference   (EA)
UEC .... USS Engineers & Consultants, Inc. [Information service]   (EISS)
UECA .... Underground Engineering Contractors Association [Later, ECA]   (EA)
UECB .... Union Europeenne des Commerces du Betail
UECBV ...... Union Europeenne du Commerce du Betail et de la Viande [European Livestock and Meat Trading Union] [Brussels, Belgium]   (EA-IO)
UECL .... Union Europeenne des Constructeurs de Logements [European Union of Independent Building Contractors]
UECS .... Unified Electronic Computer System [Air Force]
UECU .... Union for Experimenting Colleges and Universities [Formerly, UREHE]   (EA)
UED .... Uranian Electrostatic Discharge [Planetary science]
UEDC .... Union Europeenne Democrate Chretienne [European Christian Democratic Union]
UEDS .... Uniao de Esquerda para a Democracia Socialista [Left Union for Social Democracy] [Portuguese]   (PPE)
UEE .... Queenstown [Australia] [Airport symbol]   (OAG)
UEE .... Unit Essential Equipment   (NATG)
UEEB .... Union des Exploitations Electriques en Belgique
UEEBA ...... Bulletin. Utah Engineering Experiment Station [A publication]
UEEJ .... Union Europeenne des Etudiants Juifs [European Union of Jewish Students - EUJS]   (EA)
UEF .... Uniform Electric Field
UEF .... Union Europeenne des Federalistes
UEF .... Union Europeenne Feminine [European Union of Women]
UEF .... Upper End Fitting [Nuclear energy]   (NRCH)
UEFA .... Union of European Football Associations
UEFJA .... Uniform Enforcement of Foreign Judgments Act [National Conference of Commissioners on Uniform State Laws]
UEI .... Union of Educational Institutions [British]
UEIC .... United East India Company
UEIES .... Uppsala English Institute. Essays and Studies [A publication]

UEIS .... United Engineering Information System
UEITP .... Union Europeenne des Industries de Transformation de Pomme de Terre [European Union of the Potato Processing Industries]
UEJ .... Unattended Expendable Jammer   (MCD)
UEJ .... University of Edinburgh. Journal [A publication]
UEJDC .... Union Europeenne des Jeunes Democrates-Chretiens [European Union of Young Christian Democrats]
UEK .... Elmira, NY [Location identifier] [FAA]   (FAAL)
UEL .... Quelimane [Mozambique] [Airport symbol]   (OAG)
UEL .... Underwater Environmental Laboratory [General Electric Co.]
UEL .... Union Enterprises Limited [Toronto Stock Exchange symbol]
UEL .... United Empire Loyalist
UEL .... Uomini e Libri [A publication]
UEL .... Upper Electrical Limit [Nuclear energy]   (NRCH)
UEL .... Upper Explosive Limit
UEL .... Usage Exception List   (MCD)
UE Law J .... University of the East. Law Journal [Manila, Philippines]   (DLA)
UELF .... Union des Editeurs de Langue Francaise [Brussels, Belgium]   (EA-IO)
UELJ .... UE [University of the East] Law Journal [Manila] [A publication]
UEM .... Union Electrica Madrilena [Spain]
UEM .... Union Europeenne de Malacologie [European Malacological Union]
UEM .... Union Evangelique Mondiale [World Evangelical Fellowship]
UEM .... Unite Electromagnetique [Electromagnetic Unit]
UEM .... Universal Electron Microscope
UEM .... University Extension Manuals [A publication]
UEMC .... Unidentified Endosteal Marrow Cell [Hematology]
UEMO .... Union Europeenne des Medecins Omnipraticiens [European Union of General Practitioners]   (EA)
UEMS .... Union Europeenne de Medecine Sociale [European Association of Social Medicine]
UEMS .... Unione Europea di Medicina Sociale [European Union of Social Medicine - EUSM]   (EA-IO)
UEN .... Unisave Energy Ltd. [Vancouver Stock Exchange symbol]
UENDC ...... Union Europeenne des Negociants Detaillants en Combustibles
UEO .... Kume Jima [Japan] [Airport symbol]   (OAG)
UEO .... Union de l'Europe Occidentale [Western European Union - WEU]   (EA-IO)
UEO .... Unit Emplaning Officer [Military] [British]
UEOA .... Union des Etudiants Ouest Africains [Union of West African Students]
UEP .... Underwater Electric Potential
UEP .... Unequal Error Protection   (IEEE)
UEP .... Uniform External Pressure
UEP .... Union Electric Co. [NYSE symbol]
UEP .... Union Europeenne de Paiements
UEP .... Union Europeenne de Pedopsychiatres [European Union for Child Psychiatry]
UEP .... Unit Evolutionary Period
UEP .... United Egg Producers   (EA)
UEP .... Unplanned Event Pickup [NASA]   (KSC)
UEP .... Unusual End of Program [Data processing]
UEPMD ...... Union Europeenne des Praticiens en Medecine Dentaire [European Union of Dental Medicine Practitioners]   (EA-IO)
UEPR .... Unsatisfactory Equipment Performance Report [Military]   (AABC)
UEPS .... Union Europeenne de la Presse Sportive [European Sports Press Union] [Itterbeek, Belgium]   (EA-IO)
UER .... Union Europeenne de Radiodiffusion [European Broadcasting Union - EBU]   (EA-IO)
UER .... Unique Equipment Register   (NASA)
UER .... Unite d'Enseignement et de Recherche [Units of Teaching and Research] [University of Paris]
UER .... Uniunea Evreilor Romani   (BJA)
UER .... Unplanned Event Record [NASA]   (KSC)
UER .... Unsatisfactory Equipment Report
UER .... Ust-Elegest [USSR] [Seismograph station code, US Geological Survey]   (SEIS)
UERA .... Umbilical Ejection Relay Assembly   (AAG)
UERA .... Uniform Extradition and Rendition Act [National Conference of Commissioners on Uniform State Laws]
UERD .... Underwater Explosives Research Division [Navy]
UERDC ...... Underwater Explosion Research and Development Center [Navy]   (CAAL)
UERE .... Ultrasonic Echo Ranging Equipment
UERG .... Universitywide Energy Research Group [University of California] [Research center]   (RCD)
UERL .... Underwater Explosives Research Laboratory
UERL .... Unplanned Event Record Log [NASA]   (KSC)
UERMWA ... United Electrical, Radio, and Machine Workers of America
UERP .... Unione Europea di Relazioni Pubbliche [European Union of Public Relations - International Service Organization - EURPISO]   (EA-IO)
UERPS ...... Uniform Excess Reporting Procedures [DoD]
UERS .... Unusual Event Recording System [Jet transport]
UERT .... Union Explosivos-Rio Tinto [Spain]
UERT .... Universal Engineer Tractor, Rubber-Tired [Army]

UES .... Snow College, Ephraim, UT [*Library symbol*] [*Library of Congress*] (LCLS)
UES .... Uniform Emission Standard
UES .... UNISA [*University of South Africa*] English Studies [*A publication*]
UES .... Universal Environmental Shelter (KSC)
UES .... University Extension Series [*A publication*]
UES .... Upper Esophageal Sphincter [*Anatomy*]
UES .... Upstream Expression Sequence [*Genetics*]
UES .... Waukesha, WI [*Location identifier*] [*FAA*] (FAAL)
UESA .... Ukrainian Engineers' Society of America (EA)
UESC .... Union Electric Steel Corporation [*NASDAQ symbol*] (NQ)
UESD .... Uniao da Esquerda Socialista Democratica [*Union of the Socialist and Democratic Left*] [*Portuguese*] (PPW)
UESK .... Unit Emergency Supply Kit
UESK .... Unit Essential Spares Kit [*Military*] (AFM)
UESS .... United Education & Software [*NASDAQ symbol*] (NQ)
UET .... Quetta [*Pakistan*] [*Airport symbol*] (OAG)
UET .... Unattended Earth Terminal
UET .... Unit Equipment Table [*Military*]
UET .... United Engineering Trustees
UET .... Universal Emulating Terminal
UET .... Universal Engineer Tractor [*Later, BEST*] [*Army*]
UET .... Ur Excavations: Texts [*London*] [*A publication*] (BJA)
UETA .... Universal Engineer Tractor, Armored [*Army*]
UETRT........ Universal Engineer Tractor, Rubber-Tired [*Army*]
UEW .... United Electrical Workers
UEX .... Underexposed [*Photography*]
UEX .... Ur Excavations [*A publication*] (BJA)
UF .... All Cargo Airlines Ltd. [*Great Britain*] [*ICAO designator*] (FAAC)
UF .... Ugarit-Forschungen [*A publication*]
UF .... Ulster Folklife [*Belfast*] [*A publication*]
UF .... Ultrafilter [*or Ultrafiltration*]
UF .... Ultrafine
UF .... Ultrasonic Frequency (MSA)
UF .... Unavailability Factor [*Electronics*] (IEEE)
UF .... Underground Feeder
UF .... Unemployed Father (OICC)
UF .... Unified Forces [*Military*]
UF .... Union Fidelity Corp. [*NYSE symbol*]
UF .... Union de Fribourg: Institut International des Sciences Sociales et Politiques [*Union de Fribourg: International Institute of Social and Political Sciences*] (EA-IO)
UF .... Unit of Fire (MUGU)
UF .... United Focus [*Later, Omni Learning Institute*] (EA)
UF .... United Force [*Guyanese*] (PD)
UF .... United Foundation
UF .... United Fruit Co. [*NYSE symbol*] [*Later, UB*]
UF .... Uniterra Foundation (EA)
UF .... University of Florida [*Gainesville*]
UF .... Unknown Factor
UF .... Unofficial Funds [*British*]
U & F .... Unterricht und Forschung [*A publication*]
UF .... Upper Air Fallout [*Civil Defense*]
UF .... Urea Formaldehyde
UF .... Used For
UF .... Utility File
UFA .... Ukrainian Fraternal Association [*Formerly, UWA*] (EA)
UFA .... Unesterified Fatty Acid [*Biochemistry*]
UFA .... Uniform Firearms Act
UFA .... Uniformed Firefighters Association
UFA .... Union des Femmes d'Algerie [*Union of Algerian Women*]
UFA .... Union of Flight Attendants (EA)
UFA .... United Families of America [*Washington, DC*] (EA)
UFA .... University Film Association [*Later, UFVA*] (EA)
UFA .... Universum-Film Aktien-Gesellschaft [*German motion picture company*]
UFA .... Unsaturated Fatty Acid [*Organic chemistry*]
UFA .... Until Further Advised
UFA .... Usable Floor Area [*Classified advertising*] (ADA)
UFA .... Use Frequency Analysis
UFAA .... United Food Animal Association (EA)
UFAC .... Unlawful Flight to Avoid Custody
UFAC .... Upholstered Furniture Action Council [*High Point, NC*] (EA)
UFAED ...... Unit Forecast Authorization Equipment Data (AFM)
UFAJ .... University Film Association. Journal [*A publication*]
UFAM .... Universal File Access Method
UFAP .... Union Francaise des Annuaires Professionels [*French Union for Professional Yearbooks*] [*Trappes*] [*Information service*] (EISS)
UFAP .... Universal-Fine Ammonium Perchlorate [*Organic chemistry*] (MCD)
UFAP .... Unlawful Flight to Avoid Prosecution
UFA Rev Union Fed Coop Agric Suisse ... UFA Revue. Union des Federations Cooperatives Agricoles de la Suisse [*A publication*]
UFAS .... Unified Flight Analysis System [*NASA*]
UFAT .... Unlawful Flight to Avoid Testimony
UFAW .... Universities Federation for Animal Welfare [*British*]
UFAWU ...... United Fishermen and Allied Workers' Union [*Canada*]

UFBC .... United Financial Banking Companies [*NASDAQ symbol*] (NQ)
UFBK .... United Federal Bank FSB [*NASDAQ symbol*] (NQ)
UFBS .... Union des Francais de Bon Sens [*Union of Frenchmen of Good Sense*] (PPW)
UFC .... Unidirectional Filamentary Composite
UFC .... Unified Fire Control (MCD)
UFC .... Uniform Freight Classification
UFC .... Union des Facteurs du Canada [*Letter Carriers' Union of Canada - LCUC*]
UFC .... Unit Funded Costs (MCD)
UFC .... United Flight Classification
UFC .... United Free Church [*Scotland*]
UFC .... Universal Flight Computer
UFC .... Universal Foods Corporation [*NYSE symbol*]
UFC .... Universal Frequency Counter
UFC .... Urinary Free Cortisol
UFCA .... Uniform Fraudulent Conveyance Act [*National Conference of Commissioners on Uniform State Laws*]
UFCA .... United Film Carriers Association [*Defunct*] (EA)
UFCA .... Urethane Foam Contractors Association [*Austin, TX*] (EA)
UFCC .... Underwater Fire Control Computer [*Navy*] (CAAL)
UFCC .... Uniform Freight Classification Committee
UFCE .... Union Federaliste des Communautes Ethniques Europeennes [*Federal Union of European Nationalities*]
UFCG .... Underwater Fire Control Group
UFCP.......... Up-Front Control Panel (MCD)
UFCS.......... UF-6 Chemical Feed Station [*Nuclear energy*] (NRCH)
UFCS.......... Underwater Fire Control System
UFCS.......... United Fellowship for Christian Service [*Later, BMMFI*] (EA)
UFCS.......... United Fire & Casualty Co. of Iowa [*NASDAQ symbol*] (NQ)
UFCS.......... Universal Fire Control System
UFCS.......... Up-Front Control Set (MCD)
UFCT.......... United Federation of College Teachers [*AFL-CIO*]
UFCW........ United Food and Commercial Workers International Union
UFCWIU ..... United Food and Commercial Workers International Union (EA)
UFD .... Davis County Library, Farmington, UT [*Library symbol*] [*Library of Congress*] (LCLS)
UFD .... Ultrafast Detection
UFD .... Union des Forces Democratiques [*Union of Democratic Forces*] [*French*] (PPE)
UFD .... United Foods, Inc. [*American Stock Exchange symbol*]
UFD .... Universal Firing Device [*Military*] (AABC)
UFD .... User File Directory (NASA)
UFDC .... United Federation of Doll Clubs (EA)
UFDC .... Universal Flight Director Computer
UFE .... Union des Francais a l'Etranger [*Union of French Citizens Abroad*] (PPW)
UFE .... Union des Groupements Professionnels de l'Industrie de le Feculerie de Pommes de Terre [*Union of Professional Groups of the Potato Starch Industry*]
UFE .... Universal Field Element (MCD)
UFEBB ...... Bulletin. Faculty of Education. Utsunomiya University [*A publication*]
UFEMAT .... Union Europeenne des Federations Nationales des Negociants en Materiaux de Construction [*European Association of National Builders Merchants Associations*] (EA)
UFEMTO .... Union des Femmes du Togo [*Togolese Women's Union*]
UFER.......... Mouvement International pour l'Union Fraternelle entre les Races et les Peuples [*International Movement for Fraternal Union among Races and Peoples*]
UFESA ...... United Fire Equipment Service Association [*Aurora, IL*] (EA)
UFF............ Ufficiale [*Official, Officer*]
UFF............ Ulster Freedom Fighters
UFF............ Union et Fraternite Francaise [*French Union and Fraternity*] (PPE)
UFF............ United Freedom Front (EA)
UF-F .... Universal Flip-Flop [*Data processing*]
UFF............ University Film Foundation (EA)
UFFCS .... IEEE Ultrasonics, Ferroelectrics and Frequency Control Society [*New York, NY*] (EA)
UFFI .... Urea-Formaldehyde Foam Insulation
UFFVA ...... United Fresh Fruit and Vegetable Association (EA)
UFGI.......... United Financial Group [*NASDAQ symbol*] (NQ)
UFH .... Upper Facial Height [*Medicine*]
UFi............ Fillmore City Library, Fillmore, UT [*Library symbol*] [*Library of Congress*] (LCLS)
UFI............ Union des Foires Internationales [*Union of International Fairs*] (EA-IO)
UFI............ Unit Fault Isolation (MCD)
UFI............ Universal Fermi Interaction
UFI............ Usage Frequency Indicator
UFI............ User Friendly Interface
UFIB .... Union Federazioni Italiane Bocce [*Italian lawn bowling, or boccie, organization*]
UFIDA........ Union Financiere Internationale pour le Developpement de l'Afrique [*International Financial Union for the Development of Africa*]
Ufim Aviacion Inst Trudy ... Ufimskii Aviacionnyi Institut Imeni Ordzonikidze. Trudy [*A publication*]

UFIPTE....... Union Franco-Iberique pour la Coordination de la Production et du Transport de l'Electricite [*Franco-Iberian Union for Coordinating the Production and Transmission of Electricity*] (EA-IO)
UFIRS......... Uniform Fire Incident Reporting System [*National Fire Protection Association*]
UFIRS......... Universal Far Infrared Sensor (MCD)
UFIZA....... Ukrainskii Fizicheskii Zhurnal [*A publication*]
UFJC......... United Fund for Jewish Culture [*Defunct*] (EA)
UFKT......... Universitetsforlagets Kronikktjeneste [*A publication*]
U Fla L Rev ... University of Florida. Law Review [*A publication*]
UFLC......... Union Internationale des Femmes Liberales Chretiennes [*International Union of Liberal Christian Women*]
U Florida L Rev ... University of Florida. Law Review [*A publication*]
UFLT .... Uniflite, Inc. [*NASDAQ symbol*] (NQ)
UFM........... Uganda Freedom Movement
UFM........... Union Fleuve de Mano [*Mano River Union - MRU*] (EA-IO)
UFM........... United Financial Management Ltd. [*Toronto Stock Exchange symbol*]
UFM........... University for Man [*Manhattan, KS*]
UFM........... Upper Figure of Merit
UFM........... User to File Manager
UFMA........ United Fur Manufacturers Association [*New York, NY*] (EA)
UFMA........ Upholstered Furniture Manufacturers Association (EA)
UFMA........ Upholstery Fabric Manufacturers Association [*Defunct*] (EA)
UFMCC...... Universal Fellowship of Metropolitan Community Churches (EA)
UFMH....... University of Florida. Monographs. Humanities Series [*A publication*]
UFMOP....... Unintentional Frequency Modulation on Pulse (MCD)
UFMT .... Urban Federation for Music Therapists [*Later, AAMT*] (EA)
UFN .... Union Franco-Nigerienne [*French-Nigerian Union*]
UFN .... Until Further Notice
UFNAA .... Uspekhi Fizicheskikh Nauk [*A publication*]
UFNSHD..... Unfinished
UFO........... Ultralight Flight Organization (EA)
UFO........... Unidentified Flying Object [*"Flying saucers"*]
UFO........... Uniform Field Organization [*DoD*]
UFO........... Unit Families Officer [*Military*] [*British*]
UFO........... Universal Fiber Optic (MCD)
UFO........... Unlimited Freak-Out [*Slang*] (DSUE)
UFO........... Unwanted Falling Objects (MCD)
UFO........... User Friendly Operating System [*UFO Systems, Inc.*]
UFOA .... Union des Femmes de l'Ouest Africain [*West African Women's Union*]
UFOCAT .... UFO [*Unidentified Flying Object*] Catalog [*Center for Unidentified Flying Object Studies*]
UFOIC .... UFO [*Unidentified Flying Object*] Investigation Center [*Australian*] [*Defunct*]
UFOIN .... UFO Investigators Network [*British*]
UFOIRC...... Unidentified Flying Object Information Retrieval Center, Inc. [*Phoenix, AZ*] (EA)
UFOP......... Ultrafast-Opening Parachute (NG)
UFOPIA ..... Unidentified Flying Objects Phenomena Investigations, Australia
UFOR......... UFO [*Unidentified Flying Object*] Research [*Australian*]
UFOS......... Unacceptable Face of Socialism (DSUE)
UFP .... Ultrafine Powder [*Materials processing*]
UFP .... Under Frequency Protector (MCD)
UFP .... Unemployed Full Pay [*Military*] [*British*]
UFP .... United Federal Party [*Northern Rhodesia*]
UFP .... Universal Folded Plate [*Structural system*] (RDA)
UFP .... Utility Facilities Program [*Data processing*] (IBMDP)
UFPA......... University Film Producers Association [*Later, UFA, UFVA*] (EA)
UFPC......... United Federation of Postal Clerks [*Formerly, NFPOC*] [*Later, APWU*] (EA)
UFPO......... Underground Facilities Protective Organization (EA)
UFR .... UF-6 Recovery Room [*Nuclear energy*] (NRCH)
UFR .... Under Frequency Relay
UFR .... Urine Flow Rate
UFRCC....... Uniform Federal Regional Council City
UFRWO ...... United Federation of Russian Workers' Organizations of USA and Canada (EA)
UFS .... Ulster Folklife Society (EA)
UFS .... Ultimate Factor of Safety
UFS .... Under Frequency Sensing (MCD)
UFS .... United Features Syndicate [*Commercial firm*]
UFS .... Unnormalized Floating Subtract
UFSA......... Ukrainian Free Society of America (EA)
UFSB......... University Federal Savings Bank [*NASDAQ symbol*] (NQ)
UFSI-IWA... Universities Field Staff International-Institute of World Affairs [*Formerly, AUFS-IWA*] (EA)
UFSJ .... Unitarian Fellowship for Social Justice
UFSS......... Unified Flexible Spacecraft Simulation
UFST......... Unifast Industries [*NASDAQ symbol*] (NQ)
UFT .... Ultrasonic Frequency Transformer [*or Translator*]
UFT .... United Federation of Teachers [*New York*]
UFT .... United Fly Tyers (EA)
UFTA......... Uniform Fraudulent Transfer Act [*National Conference of Commissioners on Uniform State Laws*]

UFTAA ...... Universal Federation of Travel Agents' Associations [*See also FUAAV*] [*Brussels, Belgium*] (EA-IO)
UFTR .... University of Florida Teaching Reactor
UFU .... Utility Flight Unit [*Navy*]
UFURF....... Universal Furniture [*NASDAQ symbol*] (NQ)
UFV .... Unsymmetrical Free Vibration
UFVA........ University Film and Video Association [*Formerly, UFPA, UFA*] (EA)
UFW .... United Farm Workers of America (EA)
UFW .... United Furniture Workers of America (EA)
UFWA........ United Farm Workers of America
UFWA........ United Furniture Workers of America
UFWDA ..... United Four-Wheel Drive Associations (EA)
UFWOC ..... United Farm Workers Organizing Committee [*Later, UFW*]
UFWU........ United Farm Workers Union
UG .... Radio Frequency Connectors [*JETDS nomenclature*] [*Military*] (CET)
ug .... Uganda [*MARC country of publication code*] [*Library of Congress*] (LCCP)
UG .... Uganda [*Two-letter standard code*] (CNC)
UG .... Uganda Airlines Corp. [*ICAO designator*] (FAAC)
Ug............. Ugaritica [*Paris*] [*A publication*]
UG .... Uncertain Glory: Folklore and the American Revolution [*A publication*]
UG .... Undergarment
UG .... Undergraduate
UG .... Underground [*Technical drawings*]
UG .... Unite Guyanaise [*Guyanese Unity*] (PPW)
UG .... Universal Generalization [*Rule of quantification*] [*Logic*]
UG .... Universal Government
UG .... Upgrading Training [*Job Training and Partnership Act*] (OICC)
UG .... Urban Gorillas [*An association*] (EA)
UG .... Urogenital [*Medicine*]
UG .... US-North Africa (Gibraltar) Convoy [*World War II*]
UG .... Uteroglobin [*Physiology*]
UGA .... Uganda [*Three-letter standard code*] (CNC)
uga .... Ugaritic [*MARC language code*] [*Library of Congress*] (LCCP)
UGA........... Ugashik [*Alaska*] [*Airport symbol*] (OAG)
UGA........... Ugashik, AK [*Location identifier*] [*FAA*] (FAAL)
UGA........... Underwriters Grain Association (EA)
UGA........... United Golfers' Association (EA)
UGA........... Unity Gain Amplifier
UGA........... Urgeschichtlicher Anzeiger [*A publication*]
UGAA........ Untersuchungen zur Geschichte und Altertumskunde Aegyptens [*K. Sethe*] [*A publication*] (BJA)
UGAL .... Union des Groupements d'Achat de l'Alimentation [*Association of Retailer-Owned Wholesalers in Foodstuffs - AROWF*] (EA-IO)
Uganda Dep Agric Annu Rep ... Uganda. Department of Agriculture. Annual Report [*A publication*]
Uganda Dep Agric Mem Res Div Ser II Veg ... Uganda. Department of Agriculture. Memoirs of the Research Division. Series II. Vegetation [*A publication*]
UgandaJ.... Uganda Journal [*A publication*]
Uganda Leg Focus ... Uganda Legal Focus (DLA)
Uganda LF ... Uganda Law Focus (DLA)
Uganda LR ... Uganda Protectorate Law Reports [*1904-51*] (DLA)
Uganda Natl Parks Dir Rep ... Uganda National Parks Director's Report [*A publication*]
UGAPB....... Publication. Utah Geological Association [*A publication*]
UGAS........ Union Gas Systems [*NASDAQ symbol*] (NQ)
UGB........... Pilot Point, AK [*Location identifier*] [*FAA*] (FAAL)
UGB........... Union Giovantu Benadir [*Benadir Youth Union*] [*Somalia*]
UGB........... Union de Guerreros Blancos [*White Warriors' Union*] [*Salvadoran*] (PD)
UGB........... United Gulf Bank [*Middle East*]
UGB........... Unity Gain Bandwidth
UGBW........ Unity Gain Bandwidth
UGC .... Ukrainian Gold Cross [*An association*] (EA)
UGC .... Ultrasonic Grating Constant
UGC .... United Nations Food and Agriculture Organization Intergovernmental Committee [*World Food Program*]
UGC .... Unity Gain Crossover
UGC .... Universal Guided Column
UGC .... University Grants Commission [*India*]
UGC .... University Grants Committee [*British*]
UGC .... Urgench [*USSR*] [*Airport symbol*] (OAG)
UGCAA ...... Union Generale des Cooperatives Agricoles d'Approvisionnement
UGCW .... United Glass and Ceramic Workers of North America
UGD........... United Greenwood [*Vancouver Stock Exchange symbol*]
UGDP .... University Group Diabetes Program [*Study group involving 12 medical schools*] [*Defunct*]
UGE........... Undergraduate Engineering Program [*Air Force*]
UGEAO...... Union Generale des Etudiants d'Afrique Occidentale [*General Union of West African Students*]
UGEC........ Union Generale des Etudiants Congolais [*General Union of Congolese Students*]
UGEED...... Union Generale des Etudiants et Eleves Dahomeens
U Gefl AWG ... Um Gefaellige Antwort Wird Gebeten [*The Favor of an Answer Is Requested*] [*German*]

UGEG .... Union Generale des Etudiants Guineens [*General Union of Guinean Students*]

UGEM .... Union Generale des Etudiants du Maroc [*General Union of Moroccan Students*]

UGEMA ..... Union Generale des Etudiants Musulmans d'Algerie [*General Union of Moslem Students of Algeria*]

UGEN .... University Genetics [*NASDAQ symbol*]   (NQ)

Ugeskr Agron Hortonomer ... Ugeskrift foer Agronomer og Hortonomer [*A publication*]

Ugeskr Laeg ... Ugeskrift foer Laeger [*A publication*]

Ugeskr Landmaend ... Ugeskrift foer Landmaend [*A publication*]

UGET .... Union Generale des Etudiants Tunisiens [*General Union of Tunisian Students*]

Ug F .... Ugarit-Forschungen [*A publication*]

UGF .... Unidentified Growth Factor

UGF .... United Givers Fund

UGF .... Unserviceable Generation Factor [*Military*]

UGF .... US-North Africa (Gibraltar) Convoy-Fast [*World War II*]

UGGI .... Union Geodesique et Geophysique Internationale [*International Union of Geodesy and Geophysics*]

UGH .... Uveitis-Glaucoma-Hyphemia [*Ophthalmology*]

UGHA .... United in Group Harmony Association   (EA)

UGI .... Uganik [*Alaska*] [*Airport symbol*]   (OAG)

UGI .... UGI Corp. [*Formerly, United Gas Improvement Co.*] [*NYSE symbol*]

UGI .... Union Geographique Internationale [*International Geographical Union*]

UGI .... Upper Gastrointestinal [*Medicine*]

UGIB .... Upper Gastrointestinal Bleeding [*Medicine*]

UGIH .... Upper Gastrointestinal Tract Hemorrhage [*Medicine*]

UGIMA ...... Unione Generale degli Industriali Apuani del Marmo ed Affini [*Marble Industry Union*] [*Italy*]

UGJA .... United Galician Jews of America [*Defunct*]   (EA)

UGL .... Uglegorsk [*USSR*] [*Seismograph station code, US Geological Survey*]   (SEIS)

UGL .... Utility General

UGLAA ...... Ugeskrift foer Laeger [*A publication*]

UGLAS ...... Uniform General Ledger Accounting Structure   (NVT)

UGLE .... United Grand Lodge of England [*Masonry*]

UGLE .... Universal Graphics Language Executive   (MCD)

Ug LF .... Uganda Law Focus   (DLA)

UGLI .... Universal Gate for Logic Implementation [*Data processing*]   (MCD)

UGLIAC ..... United Gas Laboratories Internally Programmed Automatic Computer

UGLJ .... University of Ghana. Law Journal   (DLA)

Ug LR .... Uganda Law Reports [*Africa*]   (DLA)

UGLRC ...... Upper Great Lakes Regional Commission [*Department of Commerce*]

UgM .... Ugaritic Manual [*A publication*]   (BJA)

UG/M .... Umdrehungen je Minute [*Revolutions per Minute*] [*German*]

UGM .... Underwater Guided Missile [*DoD*]   (MCD)

UGM .... University of Georgia. Monographs [*A publication*]

UGM .... Urogenital Mesenchyme [*Medicine*]

UGMA .... Uniform Gifts to Minors Act [*National Conference of Commissioners on Uniform State Laws*]

UGML .... Universal Guided Missile Launcher [*Navy*]   (MCD)

UGN .... Waukegan, IL [*Location identifier*] [*FAA*]   (FAAL)

UGNCO ...... Unit Gas Noncommissioned Officer [*Army*] [*World War II*]

UGND .... Underground   (AABC)

UGO .... Uige [*Angola*] [*Airport symbol*] [*Obsolete*]   (OAG)

UGO .... Unit Gas Offices [*Army*] [*World War II*]

UGO .... Unmanned Geophysical Observatory [*National Science Foundation*]

UGOB .... Unigesco Class B [*Toronto Stock Exchange symbol*]

UGOC .... United Greek Orthodox Charities [*Defunct*]   (EA)

Ugol' Ukr .... Ugol' Ukrainy [*A publication*]

UGOT .... Urine Glutamic-Oxaloacetic Transaminase [*An enzyme*]

UGOUA ...... Ugol' Ukrainy [*A publication*]

UGP .... Union des Gaullistes de Progres [*Union of Progressive Gaullists*] [*French*]   (PPE)

UGP .... United Global Petroleum, Inc. [*Vancouver Stock Exchange symbol*]

UGPA .... Undergraduate Grade-Point Average [*Higher education*]

UGPCC ...... Uniform Grocery Product Code Council [*Later, UPCC*]   (EA)

UGPP .... Uridine Diphosphoglucose Pyrophosphorylase [*An enzyme*]

Ug Pr LR .... Uganda Protectorate Law Reports [*Africa*]   (DLA)

UGR .... Ultrasonic Grain Refinement

UGR .... United Gunn Resources [*Vancouver Stock Exchange symbol*]

UGR .... Universal Graphic Recorder [*Raytheon Co.*]

UGRE .... Undergraduate Record Examination [*Education*]

UGRR .... Underground Railroad [*A smuggling system*] [*Criminal slang*]

UGS .... Unattended Ground Sensors

UGS .... Uniaxial Gyrostabilizer

UGS .... Union de la Gauche Socialiste

UGS .... Union Graduate School [*Yellow Springs, Ohio*]

UGS .... Union des Guineens au Senegal [*Union of Guineans in Senegal*]   (PD)

UGS .... Upper Group Stop [*Nuclear energy*]   (NRCH)

UGS .... Upper Guide Structure [*Nuclear energy*]   (NRCH)

UGS .... Urogenital Sinus [*Anatomy*]

UGS .... Urogenital System [*Medicine*]

UGS .... US-North Africa (Gibraltar) Convoy-Slow [*World War II*]

UGSA .... Union Generale des Syndicats Algeriens [*General Federation of Algerian Trade Unions*]

UGSP .... United Galaxy Sanitation Patrol [*In TV series "Quark"*]

UgT .... Ugaritic Textbook [*A publication*]   (BJA)

UGT .... Underground Test   (MCD)

UGT .... Union General de Trabajadores de Espana [*General Union of Spanish Workers*] [*In exile*]

UGT .... United Bible Societies' Greek New Testament [*A publication*]   (BJA)

UGT .... Upgrade Training [*Military*]   (AFM)

UGT .... Upgraded Third-Generation Enroute Software Program [*Data processing*]   (MCD)

UGT .... Urgent

UGT .... Urogenital Tract [*Medicine*]

UGTA .... Union Generale des Travailleurs Algeriens [*General Union of Algerian Workers*]

UGTAN ...... Union Generale des Travailleurs d'Afrique Noire [*General Union of Workers of Black Africa*]

UGTC .... Union Generale des Travailleurs du Cameroun [*General Union of Workers of Cameroon*]

UGTC .... Union Generale des Travailleurs Centrafricains [*General Union of Central African Workers*]

UGTCI .... Union Generale des Travailleurs de la Cote D'Ivoire [*General Union of Workers of the Ivory Coast*]

UGTD .... Uniform Geometrical Theory of Diffraction   (MCD)

UGTD .... Union Generale des Travailleurs du Dahomey [*General Union of Workers of Dahomey*]

UGTG .... Union Generale des Travailleurs de la Guadeloupe   (PD)

UGTK .... Union Generale des Travailleurs du Kamerun [*General Union of Workers of the Cameroon*]

UGTM .... Union Generale des Travailleurs du Maroc [*General Union of Workers of Morocco*]

UGTM .... Union Generale des Travailleurs de Mauritanie [*General Union of Workers of Mauritania*]

UGTP .... Uniao Geral dos Trabalhadores de Portugal [*Labor union*] [*Lisbon, Portugal*]

UGTS .... Union Generale des Travailleurs du Senegal [*General Union of Workers of Senegal*]

UGTT .... Union Generale de Travailleurs Tunisiens [*General Federation of Tunisian Workers*]

UGW .... United Garment Workers of America   (EA)

UH .... Air-Cushion Vehicle built by Universal Hovercraft [*US*] [*Usually used in combination with numerals*]

UH .... Bristow Helicopters Group Ltd. [*Great Britain*] [*ICAO designator*]   (FAAC)

UH .... Ugaritic Handbook [*C. H. Gordon*] [*A publication*]   (BJA)

UH .... Ukrainian Herald [*A publication*]

UH .... Unavailable Hours [*Electronics*]   (IEEE)

UH .... Underhatch

UH .... Unit Head

UH .... Unit Heater [*Technical drawings*]

UH .... United Humanitarians [*Philadelphia, PA*]   (EA)

UH .... Universidad de la Habana [*A publication*]

UH .... University of Hawaii

UH .... Upper Half

UH .... Upper Hemispherical   (MCD)

UH .... US Home Corp. [*NYSE symbol*]

UH .... Utah [*Obsolete*]   (ROG)

UH .... Utility Helicopter   (AABC)

UHA .... Ukrains'ka Halyts'ka Armiia

UHA .... Ultrahigh Altitude

UHA .... Universitets- och Hogskoleambetet [*National Board of Universities and Colleges*] [*Ministry of Education and Cultural Affairs*] [*Stockholm, Sweden*] [*Information service*]   (EISS)

UHA .... Upper Half Assembly

UHAA .... United Horological Association of America [*Later, American Watchmakers Institute*]

UHAB .... Urban Homesteading Assistance Board [*New York, NY*]   (EA)

UHAC .... United Hellenic American Congress   (EA)

U Hart St L ... University of Hartford. Studies in Literature [*A publication*]

U Hawaii L Rev ... University of Hawaii. Law Review   (DLA)

UHC .... Ultimate Holding Company

UHC .... Unburned Hydrocarbon [*Also, UBHC*] [*Fuel technology*]

UHC .... Under Honorable Conditions

UHC .... Unit Hardware Cost   (MCD)

UHC .... University of Houston at Clear Lake City, Houston, TX [*OCLC symbol*]   (OCLC)

UHCC .... University of Houston Coastal Center [*Research center*]   (RCD)

UHCMWIU ... United Hatters, Cap, and Millinery Workers International Union

UHCO .... Universal Holding Corporation [*NASDAQ symbol*]   (NQ)

UHCS .... Ultrahigh Capacity Storage

UHDDS .... Uniform Hospital Discharge Data Set

UHE .... Uherske Hradiste [*Czechoslovakia*] [*Airport symbol*] [*Obsolete*]   (OAG)

UHE .... Ultimate Hour Estimate   (MCD)

UHE .... Ultrahigh Efficiency [*Arc lamp*]

UHE .... Ultrahigh Energy

UHELP .... [*A*] programing language   (CSR)

UHF .... Ulster Historical Foundation   (EA)
UHF .... Ultrahigh-Frequency [*Electricity of radio waves*]
UHF .... United Health Foundations [*Defunct*]
UHF .... Unrestricted Hartree-Fock [*Wave-Function*]
UHFDF .... Ultrahigh-Frequency Direction Finder
UHFF .... Ultrahigh-Frequency Filter
UHFG .... Ultrahigh-Frequency Generator
UHF/HF ..... Ultrahigh-Frequency/High-Frequency   (MCD)
UHFJ .... Ultrahigh-Frequency Jammer
UHFO .... Ultrahigh-Frequency Oscillator
UHFR......... Ultrahigh-Frequency Receiver
UHFS .... Unsteady Heat Flux Sensor
UHG .... Urban History Group [*Defunct*]   (EA)
UHI .... Upper Head Injection   (NRCH)
UHi .... Utah State Historical Society, Salt Lake City, UT [*Library symbol*] [*Library of Congress*]   (LCLS)
UHJA .... United Hungarian Jews of America   (EA)
UHK........... University of Hard Knocks [*West Virginia*] [*"University" founded by Jim Comstock and based on the expression "school of hard knocks"*]
UHL .... User Header Label   (CMD)
UHLCADS ... Ultra-High-Level Container Airdrop System [*Military*]   (MCD)
UHMS........ Ultrasonic Helmet Mounted Sight [*Army*]   (MCD)
UHMS........ Undersea and Hyperbaric Medical Society [*Bethesda, MD*]   (EA)
UHMW .... Ultrahigh Molecular Weight
UHMW-PE ... Ultrahigh Molecular Weight Polyethylene [*Organic chemistry*]
UHP .... Ugaritic-Hebrew Philology [*Rome*] [*M. Dahood*] [*A publication*]   (BJA)
UHP .... Ultra-High Performance [*in UHP Imposer, a product of Opti-Copy, Inc.*]
UHP .... Ultrahigh Power
UHP .... Ultrahigh Purity
UHP .... Undergraduate Helicopter Pilot Training [*Army*]
UHP .... University of Hawaii Press
UHPFB .... Untreated Hard Pressed Fiberboard
UHPS........ Underground Hydro-Pumped Storage [*Room*]
UHPT........ Undergraduate Helicopter Pilot Training   (MCD)
UHQ .... Utah Historical Quarterly [*A publication*]
UHR.......... Ultrahigh Resistance
UHR.......... Ultrahigh Resolution
UHR.......... United Hearne Resources [*Vancouver Stock Exchange symbol*]
UHR.......... Upper Hybrid Resonance [*Spectroscopy*]
UHRA .... United Hunts Racing Association [*Later, NSHA*]
UHRNF ...... United Hearne Resources [*NASDAQ symbol*]   (NQ)
UHS........... Ultimate Heat Sink   (NRCH)
UHS........... Ultrahigh Speed
UHS........... Unit Handling System
UHS........... Unitarian Historical Society [*Later, UUHS*]   (EA)
UHS........... United HIAS Service [*Later, HIAS, Inc.*]   (EA)
UHS........... Universalist Historical Society [*Later, UUHS*]   (EA)
UHSA .... United Halsingian Society of America [*Defunct*]   (EA)
UHSIB .... Universal Health Service Cl B [*NASDAQ symbol*]   (NQ)
UHT .... Ultrahigh Temperature
UHT .... Ultrasonic Hardness Tester
UHT .... Underheat
UHT .... Unit Horizontal Tail
UHT .... United Hebrew Trades of the State of New York   (EA)
UHT .... Universal Hand Tool
UHT .... Universal Health Realty [*NYSE symbol*]
UHT .... Universal Horizontal Tail [*Aviation*]   (NG)
UHTPB .... Unsaturated Hydroxyl-Terminated Polybutadiene [*Organic chemistry*]
UHTREX .... Ultrahigh-Temperature Reactor Experiment
UHTV .... Unmanned Hypersonic Test Vehicle   (MCD)
UHV.......... Ultrahigh Vacuum
UHV.......... Ultrahigh Voltage
UHV.......... Under Hatch Valve
UHVA .... United Hellenic Voters of America   (EA)
UHVC .... Ultrahigh Vacuum Chamber
UHVS .... Ultrahigh Vacuum System
UI.............. Societe de Transport Aerien du Rwanda [*ICAO designator*]   (FAAC)
UI.............. Uj Iras [*A publication*]
U/I............. Under Instructions   (ADA)
UI.............. Underground Injection [*of wastes*]
UI.............. Underwear Institute [*Later, NKMA*]   (EA)
UI.............. Undifferentiated Infiltrating [*Tumor*] [*Oncology*]
UI.............. Unemployment Insurance
UI.............. Unexplained Infertility
U/I............. Unidentified
UI.............. Union-Intersection [*Statistics*]
UI.............. Unit of Issue   (KSC)
UI.............. United Inches
UI.............. United Inns, Inc. [*NYSE symbol*]
ui.............. United Kingdom Miscellaneous Islands [*MARC country of publication code*] [*Library of Congress*]   (LCCP)
UI.............. Universal Instantiation [*Rule of quantification*] [*Logic*]
U of I......... University of Illinois
U of I......... University of Iowa   (OICC)
UI.............. Unreported Income [*IRS*]

UI.............. Uranium Institute   (EA-IO)
UI.............. Urban Institute [*Washington, DC*] [*Research center*]   (EA)
UI.............. Urinary Infection [*Medicine*]
UI.............. USE, Incorporated [*Acronym is now used as organization name*]   (EA)
UI.............. User Interface
UI.............. Ut Infra [*As Below*] [*Latin*]
UIA............ Ukrainian Institute of America   (EA)
UIA............ Ultrasonic Industry Association [*Formed by a merger of Ultrasonic Manufacturers Association and Ultrasonic Industry Council*] [*Jamesburg, NJ*]   (EA)
UIA............ Unemployment Insurance Act [*Canada*]
UIA............ Union of International Associations [*See also UAI*]   (EA-IO)
UIA............ Union Internationale des Architectes [*International Union of Architects*]   (EA-IO)
UIA............ Union Internationale des Avocats [*International Union of Lawyers*]
UIA............ Union Internationale Contre l'Alcoolisme
UIA............ Union Internationale des Syndicats des Industries Alimentaires
UIA............ Unit Identifier Applications   (MCD)
UIA............ United Israel Appeal [*New York, NY*]   (EA)
UIA............ Universidad Iberoamericana, Mexico, DF, Mexico [*OCLC symbol*]   (OCLC)
UIA............ Uranium Institute of America   (EA)
UIA............ Usable Inside Area   (MCD)
UIAA .... Union Internationale des Associations d'Alpinisme [*International Union of Alpine Associations*]
UIAA .... Union Internationale des Associations d'Annonceurs [*International Union of Advertisers Associations*]
UIAA .... Union Internationale des Assureurs Aeronautiques
UIACM ...... Union Internationale des Automobile-Clubs Medicaux [*International Union of Associations of Doctor-Motorists*]
UIAL .... United Italian American League   (EA)
UIALC .... United Italian American Labor Council   (EA)
UIAMS....... Union Internationale d'Action Morale et Sociale [*International Union for Moral and Social Action*]
UIAPME...... Union Internationale de l'Artisanat et des Petites et Moyennes Entreprises [*International Association of Crafts and Small and Medium-Sized Enterprises*]
UIARVEP.... Unione Italiana Agenti Rappresentati Viaggiatori e Piazzisti [*Italian Union of Agents and Travelers*]
UIAT.......... Union Internationale des Syndicats des Industries de l'Alimentation et des Tabacs
UIATF........ United Indians of All Tribes Foundation   (EA)
UIB............ Quibdo [*Colombia*] [*Airport symbol*]   (OAG)
UIB............ Union Internationale des Maitres Boulangers [*International Union of Master Bakers*]
UIB .... Unione Italiana Bancari [*Italian Union of Bank Employees*]
UIBC.......... Unsaturated Iron-Binding Capacity [*Clinical chemistry*]
UIBPIP........ United International Bureau for the Protection of Intellectual Property [*Superseded by WIPO*]
UIBWM...... Trade Unions International of Workers of Building, Wood, and Building Materials Industries
UIC .... Ultraviolet Image Converter
UIC .... Underground Injection Control [*Environmental Protection Agency*]
UIC .... Unemployment Insurance Code   (OICC)
UIC .... Unemployment Insurance Commission [*Canada*]
UIC .... Unidad de Izquierda Comunista [*Unity of the Communist Left*] [*Mexico*]   (PPW)
UIC .... Union of International Conventions
UIC .... Union Internationale des Chemins de Fer [*International Union of Railways*] [*Paris, France*]   (EA-IO)
UIC .... Unit Identification Code [*Army*]   (AABC)
UIC .... United Industrial Corporation [*NYSE symbol*]
UIC .... Upper Information Center [*Aviation*]
UIC .... Urban Information Center [*Milwaukee Urban Observatory*] [*Information service*] [*Ceased operations*]   (EISS)
UIC .... Urinary Immune Complex
UIC .... User Identification Code
UICA.......... Union of Independent Colleges of Art   (EA)
UICA.......... Union Internationale des Constructeurs d'Ascenseurs [*International Union of Elevator Constructors - IUEC*]
UICANY..... United Irish Counties Association of New York   (EA)
UICB.......... Union Internationale des Centres du Batiment [*International Union of Building Centers*]
UICC .... Union Internationale Contre le Cancer [*International Union Against Cancer*]
UICC .... University of Illinois at Chicago Circle
UICC Monogr Ser ... UICC [*Union Internationale Contre le Cancer*] Monograph Series [*A publication*]
UICC Tech Rep Ser ... UICC [*Union Internationale Contre le Cancer*] Technical Report Series [*A publication*]
UICGF .... Union Internationale du Commerce en Gros de la Fleur [*International Union for the Wholesale Flower Trade*]
UICIO .... Unit Identification Code Information Officer   (AABC)
UICM.......... Union Internationale Catholique des Classes Moyennes [*International Catholic Union of the Middle Classes*]

UICN........... Union Internationale pour la Conservation de la Nature et de Ses Ressources [*International Union for Conservation of Nature and Natural Resources*]

UICP.......... Uniform Inventory Control Points System [*Military*]

UICP.......... Union Internationale de la Couverture et Plomberie [*Formerly, International Union of Roofing, Plumbing, Sanitary Installations, and General Gas and Hydraulics*] (EA)

UICPA .... Union Internationale de Chimie Pure et Appliquee [*International Union of Pure and Applied Chemistry*]

UICR.......... Union Internationale des Chauffeurs Routiers (EA-IO)

UICSM....... University of Illinois Committee on School Mathematics

UICT.......... Union Internationale Contre la Tuberculose [*International Union Against Tuberculosis - IUAT*] (EA-IO)

UICWA .... United Infants' and Children's Wear Association [*New York, NY*] (EA)

UID .... Selected Decisions by Umpire for Northern Ireland, Respecting Claims to Benefit (DLA)

UID .... Unemployment Insurance Department

UID .... Usable Inside Depth (MCD)

UIDA.......... Union Internationale des Organisations de Detaillants de la Branche Alimentaire [*International Federation of Grocers' Associations*]

UIDA.......... United Indian Development Association [*Los Angeles, CA*] (EA)

UIDAC........ Unione Italiana Dipendenti Aziende Commerciali ed Affini [*Italian Union of Commerical and Allied Workers*]

UIE .... UNESCO Institute for Education

UIE .... Union Internationale d'Editeurs [*International Publishers Association - IPA*] (EA-IO)

UIE .... Union Internationale d'Electrothermie [*International Union for Electroheat*] (EA-IO)

UIE .... Union Internationale des Etudiants [*International Union of Students - IUS*] (EA-IO)

UIEA.......... Union Internationale des Etudiants en Architecture [*International Union of Students in Architecture*]

UIEC.......... Union Internationale de l'Exploitation Cinematographique [*International Union of Cinematographic Exhibitors*] (EA-IO)

UIEIS .... Union Internationale pour l'Etude des Insectes Sociaux

UIEO.......... Union of International Engineering Organizations

UIEP .... Union Internationale des Entrepreneurs de Peinture

UIES .... Union Internationale d'Education pour la Sante [*International Union of Health Education - IUHE*] (EA-IO)

UIES .... Union Internationale d'Etudes Sociales [*International Union for Social Studies*]

UIEUA .... Upravlenie Yadernymi Energeticheskimi Ustanovkami [*A publication*]

UIF............. Ultraviolet Interference Filter

UIF............. Unfavorable Information File [*Military*]

UIF............. Universal Intermolecular Force

UIF............. USLIFE Income Fund, Inc. [*NYSE symbol*]

UIFA .... Union Internationale des Femmes Architectes [*International Union of Women Architects - IUWA*] (EA-IO)

UIFI............ Union Internationale des Fabricants d'Impermeables

UIFL........... Union Internationale des Federations de Detaillants en Produits Laitiers

uig .... Uigur [*MARC language code*] [*Library of Congress*] (LCCP)

UIG .... Uniglobe International Energy Corp. [*Vancouver Stock Exchange symbol*]

UIG .... User Instruction Group

UIGDC........ Unione Internazionale des Giovani Democratici Cristiana [*International Union of Young Christian Democrats*]

UIGSE .... Union Internationale des Guides et Scouts d'Europe [*International Union of European Guides and Scouts - IUEGS*] (EA-IO)

UIH .... Urban and Industrial Health (KSC)

UIHE.......... Union Internationale de l'Humanisme et de l'Ethique

UIHMSU ..... Union Internationale d'Hygiene et de Medecine Scolaires et Universitaires [*International Union of School and University Health and Medicine - IUSUHM*] (EA-IO)

UIHPS........ Union Internationale d'Histoire et de Philosophie des Sciences

UII............. Universal Identification Interface [*Allen-Bradley Co.*]

UII............. Utila Island [*Honduras*] [*Airport symbol*] [*Obsolete*] (OAG)

UIIG .... Union Internationale de l'Industrie du Gaz [*International Gas Union - IGU*] (EA-IO)

UIII............ Urban Information Interpreters, Incorporated (EISS)

UIIPI .... Unione Italiana Lavoratori Pubblico Impiego [*Public Office Workers Union*] [*Rome, Italy*]

UIJA .... Union Internationale des Journalistes Agricoles [*International Union of Agricultural Journalists*]

UIJDC........ Union Internationale de Jeunesse Democrate Chretienne [*International Union of Young Christian Democrats*]

UIJPLF .... Union Internationale des Journalistes et de la Presse de Langue Francaise [*International Union of French-Language Journalists and Press - IUFLJP*] (EA-IO)

UIJS .... Union Internationale de la Jeunesse Socialiste [*International Union of Socialist Youth*]

UIL............. Quillayute, WA [*Location identifier*] [*FAA*] (FAAL)

UIL............. Unione Italiana del Lavoro [*Italian Union of Labor*]

UIL............. United Illuminating Co. [*NYSE symbol*]

UIL............. UNIVAC Interactive Language [*Data processing*] (IEEE)

UIL............. University of Iowa, School of Library Science, Iowa City, IA [*OCLC symbol*] (OCLC)

UILA .... Unione Italiana Lavoratori Assicurazioni [*Italian Union of Insurance Workers*]

UILAM .... Unione Italiana Lavoratori Albergo e Mensa [*Italian Union of Hotel and Restaurant Workers*]

UILAS........ Unione Italiana Lavoratori Assicurazioni [*Assurance Company Workers Union*] [*Rome, Italy*]

UILC .... Unione Italiana Lavoratori Chimici [*Italian Union of Chemical Workers*]

UILE .... Union Internationale pour la Liberte d'Enseignement [*International Union for the Liberty of Education*]

UIL-GAS.... Unione Italiana Lavoratori Aziende Gas [*Italian Union of Gas Workers*]

UILI............ Union Internationale des Laboratoires Independents (EA-IO)

UILIA .... Unione Italiana Lavoratori Industrie Alimentari [*Italian Union of Food-Processing Workers*]

UILIAS....... Unione Italiana Lavoratori Industrie Alimentari Saccariferi [*Food Workers Union*] [*Rome, Italy*]

UILIC .... Unione Italiana Lavoratori Imposte Consumo [*Italian Union of Food Tax Levy Workers*]

UILL........... University of Illinois. Studies in Language and Literature [*A publication*]

U III LB....... University of Illinois. Law Bulletin (DLA)

U III L Bull.. University of Illinois. Law Bulletin (DLA)

U III L F....... University of Illinois. Law Forum [*A publication*]

U III L Forum ... University of Illinois. Law Forum [*A publication*]

UILM.......... Unione Italiana Lavoratori Metallurgici [*Italian Metalworkers' Union*]

UILPEM...... Unione Italiana Lavoratori Petrolieri e Metanieri [*Italian Union of Oil and Methane Gas Workers*]

UILS .... Unione Italiana Lavoratori Saccariferi [*Italian Union of Sugar Industry Workers*]

UILT .... Unione Italiana Lavoratori delle Terra [*Italian Union of Landworkers*]

UILT .... Unione Italiana Lavoratori Tessili [*Italian Union of Textile Workers*]

UILTATEP ... Unione Italiana Lavoratori Trasporti Ausiliari Traffico e Portuali [*Transport and Associated Workers Union*] [*Rome, Italy*]

UILTRAS .... Unione Italiana Trasporti ed Ausiliari del Traffico [*Italian Union of Transport Workers and Auxiliary Services*]

UILTuCS .... Unione Italiana Lavoratori Turismo Commercio e Servizi [*Tourism industry*] [*Rome, Italy*]

UILU .... University of Illinois, Urbana

UILVECA.... Unione Italiana Lavoratori Vetro, Ceramica, ed Abrasivi [*Italian Union of Glass, Ceramics, and Abrasive Workers*]

UIM............ Quitman, TX [*Location identifier*] [*FAA*] (FAAL)

UIM............ Ufficio Informazioni Militaire [*Office of Military Information*] [*Italian*]

UIM............ Ultra-Intelligent Machine

UIM............ Union of International Motorboating (EA)

UIM............ Union Internationale des Magistrats [*International Association of Judges - IAJ*] (EA-IO)

UIM............ Union Internationale des Metis [*International Union of Individuals of Mixed Parentage*]

UIM............ Union Internationale Monarchiste (EA-IO)

UIM............ Union Internationale Motonautique [*Union of International Motorboating*] (EA-IO)

UIM............ Unione Italiana Marittimi [*Italian Union of Seamen*]

UIMC .... Union Internationale des Services Medicaux des Chemins de Fer [*International Union of Railway Medical Services*]

UIMEC........ Unione Italiana Mezzadri e Coltivatori Diretti [*Land Workers Union*] [*Rome, Italy*]

UIMJ .... Union Internationale des Maisons de Jeunesse [*Service de la FIJC*]

UIMP .... Union Internationale pour la Protection de la Moralite Publique

UIN .... Quincy [*Illinois*] [*Airport symbol*] (OAG)

UIN .... USR Industries, Inc. [*American Stock Exchange symbol*]

UINA .... Uintah Energy Corp. [*NASDAQ symbol*] (NQ)

UINF .... Union Internationale de la Navigation Fluviale [*International Union for Inland Navigation - IUIN*] (EA-IO)

UINL .... Union Internationale du Notariat Latin [*International Union of Latin Notaries*]

UIO .... Quito [*Ecuador*] [*Airport symbol*] (OAG)

UIO .... Union Internationale des Orientalistes [*International Union of Orientalists*]

UIO .... United Infertility Organization (EA)

UIO .... Units in Operation [*Business and trade*]

UIO .... Utility Iterative Operation

UIOD .... User Input/Output Devices [*Data processing*] (RDA)

UIOF.......... Union Internationale des Organismes Familiaux [*International Union of Family Organizations*]

UIOOT .... Union Internationale des Organismes Officiels de Tourisme [*International Union of Official Travel Organizations*]

UIOVD........ Union Internationale des Ouvriers du Vetement pour Dames [*International Ladies' Garment Workers' Union - ILGW*]

U Iowa L Rev ... University of Iowa. Law Review (DLA)

UIP .... Quimper [*France*] [*Airport symbol*] (OAG)

UIP .... Unallowable Items Program [*IRS*]

UIP .... Unfair Industrial Practice
UIP .... Union Internationale d'Associations de Proprietaires de Wagons Particuliers [*International Union of Private Railway Truck Owners' Associations*]   (EA-IO)
UIP .... Union Internationale de Patinage [*International Skating Union - ISU*]   (EA-IO)
UIP .... Union Internationale de Physique Pure et Appliquee [*International Union of Pure and Applied Physics*]
UIP .... Union Internationale des Publicitaires
UIP .... Union Interparlementaire
UIP .... Unione Italiana Pescatori [*Italian Union of Fishermen*]
UIP .... United Ireland Party
UIP .... University of Illinois Press
UIP .... Usable in Place   (MCD)
UIP .... Usual Interstitial Pneumonia [*Medicine*]
UIPA .... United Indian Planners Association [*Defunct*]   (EA)
UIPC .... Union Internationale de la Presse Catholique [*International Catholic Press Union*]
UIPCG .... Union Internationale de la Patisserie, Confiserie, Glacerie [*International Union of Bakers and Confectioners*]
UIPD .... Ulrich's International Periodicals Directory [*A publication*]
UIPE .... Union Internationale de Protection de l'Enfance [*International Union for Child Welfare - IUCW*] [*French*]   (EA)
UIPFB .... Union Internationale de la Propriete Fonciere Batie [*International Union of Landed Property Owners*]
UIPI .... Union Internacional de Proteccion a la Infancia [*International Union for Child Welfare*]
UIPI .... Union Internationale de la Propriete Immobiliere [*International Union of Property Owners*]   (EA-IO)
UIPM .... Union Internationale de la Presse Medicale [*International Union of the Medical Press*]
UIPMB .... Union Internationale de Pentathlon Moderne et Biathlon [*International Modern Pentathlon and Biathlon Union*] [*French*]   (EA)
UIPPA .... Union Internationale de Physique Pure et Appliquee [*International Union of Pure and Applied Physics*]
UIPPI .... Union Internationale pour la Protection de la Propriete Industrielle [*International Union for the Protection of Industrial Property*]
UIPRE .... Union Internationale de la Presse Radiotechnique et Electronique   (EA-IO)
UIPVT .... Union Internationale Contre le Peril Venerien et la Treponematose [*International Union Against the Venereal Diseases and the Treponematoses*]
UIQ .... Upper Inner Quadrant [*Anatomy*]
UIR .... Quirindi [*Australia*] [*Airport symbol*] [*Obsolete*]   (OAG)
UIR .... Union Internationale des Radioecologistes [*International Union of Radioecologists - IUR*]   (EA-IO)
UIR .... Union Internationale des Rembourreurs de l'Amerique du Nord [*Upholsterers' International Union of North America - UIU*] [*Canada*]
UIR .... Unitary Irreducible Representation
UIR .... United International Research, Inc.
UIR .... University Industrial Research
UIR .... Upper Flight Information Region [*Aviation*]   (FAAC)
UIR .... Upper Information Region   (NATG)
UIR .... Urban Intelligence Reports   (CINC)
UIR .... User Instruction Register
UIRC .... Universal Interline Reservations Code
UIRD .... Union Internationale de la Resistance et de la Deportation [*International Union of Resistance and Deportee Movements*]
UIRR .... University-Industry Research Relationship
UIR/Res Newsl ... UIR [*University-Industry Research Program*]/Research Newsletter [*A publication*]
UIS .... Ulster-Irish Society   (EA)
UIS .... Unemployment Insurance Service [*Labor*]
UIS .... Union Internationale de Secours [*International Relief Union*]
UIS .... Union Internationale de Speleologie [*International Union of Speleology - IUS*]   (EA-IO)
UIS .... Unisys Corp. [*NYSE symbol*]
UIS .... Unit Identification System
UIS .... United Information Services, Inc. [*Kansas City, MO*]   (EISS)
UIS .... Universal Isolation Switch
UIS .... Upper Internals Structure [*Nuclear energy*]   (NRCH)
UISA .... United Inventors and Scientists of America   (EA)
UISAE .... Union Internationale des Sciences Anthropologiques et Ethnologiques [*International Union of Anthropological and Ethnological Sciences - IUAES*]   (EA-IO)
UISB .... Union Internationale des Sciences Biologiques [*International Union of Biological Sciences*]
UISC .... Unreported Interstate Shipment of Cigarettes
UISDC .... Unemployment Insurance Service Design Center [*Department of Labor*]
UISE .... Union Internationale de Secours aux Enfants
UISG .... Union Internationale des Superieures Majeures [*International Union of Superiors General*]
UISIF .... Union Internationale des Societes d'Ingenieurs Forestiers [*International Union of Societies of Foresters - IUSF*]   (EA-IO)

UISJM .... Upper Internals Structure Jacking Mechanism [*Nuclear energy*]   (NRCH)
UISM .... Union Internationale des Syndicats des Mineurs [*Miners' Trade Unions International*]
UISMM .... Union Internationale des Syndicats des Industries Metallurgiques et Mecaniques
UISMTE ...... Union Internationale des Syndicats des Mineurs et des Travailleurs de l'Energie [*Trade Unions International of Miners and Workers in Energy - TUIMWE*]   (EA-IO)
UISN .... Union Internationale des Sciences de la Nutrition [*International Union of Nutritional Sciences - IUNS*] [*French*]   (EA)
UISP .... Union Internationale des Societes de la Paix [*International Union of Peace Societies*]
UISP .... Union Internationale des Syndicats de Police [*International Union of Police Syndicates*]   (EA-IO)
UISPI .... Urethane Institute, Society of the Plastics Industry   (EA)
UISPP .... Union Internationale des Sciences Prehistoriques et Protohistoriques [*International Union of Prehistoric and Protohistoric Sciences*]
UISPTT ...... Union Internationale Sportive des Postes, des Telephones, et des Telecommunications [*International Sports Union of Post, Telephone, and Telecommunications Services*]
UISTABP .... Union Internacional de Sindicatos de Trabajadores de la Agricultura, de los Bosques, y de las Plantaciones [*Trade Unions International of Agricultural, Forestry, and Plantation Workers*]
UISTAF ...... Union Internationale des Syndicats des Travailleurs Agricoles et Forestiers et des Organisations des Paysans Travailleurs
UISTAFP .... Union Internationale des Syndicats des Travailleurs de l'Agriculture, des Forets, et des Plantations [*Trade Unions International of Agriculture, Forestry, and Plantation Workers - TUIAFPW*]   (EA-IO)
UISTAV ...... Union Internationale pour la Science, la Technique, et les Applications du Vide [*International Union for Vacuum Science, Technique, and Applications - IUVSTA*]   (EA-IO)
UISTC .... Union Internationale des Syndicats des Travailleurs du Commerce [*Trade Unions International of Workers in Commerce*]
UISTICPS... Union Internationale des Syndicats des Travailleurs des Industries Chimiques du Petrole et Similaires
UIT .... Jaluit [*Marshall Islands*] [*Airport symbol*]   (OAG)
UIT .... Ultraviolet Imaging Telescope
UIT .... Union des Independants de Tananarive [*Union of Independents of Tananarive*]
UIT .... Union Internationale de Tir [*International Shooting Union*]   (EA-IO)
UIT .... Union Internationale des Typographes [*International Typographical Union - ITU*]
UIT .... Unit Impulse Train
UIT .... Unit Investment Trust
UITA .... Union of International Technical Associations [*See also UATI*] [*ICSU*]   (EA-IO)
UITA .... Union Internationale des Travailleurs de l'Alimentation et des Branches Connexes [*International Union of Food and Allied Workers Associations*]
UITAM........ Union Internationale de Mecanique Theorique et Appliquee [*International Union of Theoretical and Applied Mechanics*]
UITBB .... Union Internationale des Syndicats des Travailleurs du Batiment, du Bois, et des Materiaux de Construction [*Trade Unions International of Workers of the Building, Wood, and Building Materials Industries*]
Uitgaben Natuurwet Stud Suriname Ned Antillen ... Uitgaben Natuurwetenschappelijke Studichring voor Suriname en de Nederlander Antillen [*A publication*]
Uitg Natuurwet Studiekring Suriname Ned Antillen ... Uitgaven Natuurwetenschappelijke Studiekring voor Suriname en de Nederlandse Antillen [*A publication*]
Uitg Natuurwet Werkgroep Ned Antillen (Curacao) ... Uitgaven. Natuurwetenschappelijke Werkgroep Nederlandse Antillen (Curacao) [*A publication*]
UITP .... Union Internationale des Transports Publics [*International Union of Public Transport*]   (EA-IO)
UIT Rep ...... UIT [*Ulsan Institute of Technology*] Report [*A publication*]
Uitvoerige Versl Sticht Bosbouwproefstn De Dorschkamp ... Uitvoerige Verslagen van de Stichting Bosbouwproefstation "De Dorschkamp" [*A publication*]
Uitvoer Versl Bosbouwproefsta ... Uitvoerige Verslagen van de Stichting Bosbouwproefstation "De Dorschkamp" [*A publication*]
UIU .... University of Illinois, Urbana, IL [*OCLC symbol*]   (OCLC)
UIU .... Upholsterers' International Union of North America [*Absorbed by USWA*]
UIU .... Upper Iowa University [*Fayette*]
UIUSD .... Union Internationale Universitaire Socialiste et Democratique [*International Union of Social Democratic Teachers*]
UIV .... Union Internationale des Villes et Pouvoirs Locaux [*International Union of Local Authorities*]
UIW .... United Iron Workers
UIW .... Usable Inside Width   (MCD)
UIWU .... United Israel World Union   (EA)

UIWV .... United Indian War Veterans, USA   (EA)
UIZ............. Utica, MI [*Location identifier*] [*FAA*]   (FAAL)
UJ .... Air Lanka [*Sri Lanka*] [*ICAO designator*]   (FAAC)
UJ .... Uganda Journal [*A publication*]
UJ .... Ungarische Jahrbuecher [*A publication*]
UJ .... Union Jack
UJ .... Union Joint   (MSA)
UJ .... Unique Jargon
UJ .... Uniwersytet Jagiellonski [*A publication*]
U de J .... Ursulines of Jesus [*Roman Catholic women's religious order*]
UJA .... United Jewish Appeal [*New York, NY*]   (EA)
UJB............ Umbilical Junction Box
UJB............ United Jersey Banks [*NYSE symbol*]
UJC .... Union de la Jeunesse Congolaise [*Congolese Youth Union*]
UJC .... Union Junior College [*New Jersey*]
UJC .... Urbana Junior College [*Ohio*]
UJC .... Urgency Justification Code [*Military*]   (AFIT)
UJCD.......... Union de la Jeunesse de la Cote d'Ivoire [*Ivory Coast Youth
                Union*]
UJCL .... Universal Job Control Language
UJCML .... Union des Jeunesses Communistes Marxistes-Leninistes
                [*Union of Young Marxist-Leninist Communists*]
                [*French*]   (PPE)
UJCT Rep... UJCT [*Ulsan Junior College of Technology*] Report [*Republic of
                Korea*] [*A publication*]
UJD .... Ultriusque Juris Doctor [*Doctor of Either Law; i.e., Canon Law
                or Civil Law*]
UJDG.......... Union de la Jeunesse Democratique Gabonaise [*Union of
                Democratic Youth of Gabon*]
UJDK.......... Union de la Jeunesse Democratique du Kongo [*Union of
                Democratic Youth of the Congo*]
UJDS.......... Universitetsjubilaeets Danske Samfund [*A publication*]
UJE .... Universal Jewish Encyclopedia [*New York*] [*1939-1943*] [*A
                publication*]   (BJA)
UJEKO .... Union de la Jeunesse Congolaise [*Congolese Youth Union*]
UJF .... Unsatisfied Judgment Fund [*Insurance*]
UJH .... International Union of Journeymen Horseshoers of the United
                States and Canada
UJISLAA .... UNESCO [*United Nations Educational, Scientific, and Cultural
                Organization*] Journal of Information Science,
                Librarianship, and Archives Administration [*A publication*]
UJJ .... Ujjain [*India*] [*Geomagnetic observatory code*]
UJL .... Uninet Japan Limited [*Telecommunications*]
UJNR .... United States - Japan Cooperative Program on Natural
                Resources
U/JNT .... Universal Joint [*Automotive engineering*]
UJS .... Universal Jamming System
UJSP .... United States–Japan Science Program   (MSC)
UJT............. Ultrasonic Journal Tester
UJT............. Unijunction Transistor
UJTS .... United Jewish Teachers Seminary [*Montreal*] [*A
                publication*]   (BJA)
UK .... Air UK Ltd. [*Great Britain*] [*ICAO designator*]   (FAAC)
Uk.............. British Library, London, United Kingdom [*Library symbol*]
                [*Library of Congress*]   (LCLS)
UK .... Pfizer Ltd. [*Great Britain*] [*Research code symbol*]
'Uk............. 'Ukzin   (BJA)
UK .... Unabkoemmlich [*Indispensable, irreplaceable*] [*German
                military - World War II*]
UK .... Union Carbide Corp. [*NYSE symbol*] [*Wall Street slang name:
                "Ukelele"*]
UK .... Union Katangaise [*Katanga Union*]
UK .... Unit Check
UK .... United Kingdom
uk .... United Kingdom [*MARC country of publication code*] [*Library
                of Congress*]   (LCCP)
UK .... University of Kansas
UK .... Unknown [*A publication*]
UK .... Unknown
UK .... Unknown Worlds [*A publication*]
UK .... Urokinase [*An enzyme*]
UKA............ Ulster King-at-Arms
UKA............ United Kingdom Alliance
UkAc .... Accrington Public Library, Accrington, United Kingdom
                [*Library symbol*] [*Library of Congress*]   (LCLS)
UKAC .... United Kingdom Automation Council [*London, England*]
UKADGE .... United Kingdom Air Defense Ground Environment
UKADR....... United Kingdom NATO Air Defense Region   (NATG)
UKAEA....... United Kingdom Atomic Energy Authority [*London, England*]
                [*Databank originator and operator*]
UKaGS .... Church of Jesus Christ of Latter-Day Saints, Genealogical
                Society Library, Kanab Branch, Stake Center, Kanab, UT
                [*Library symbol*] [*Library of Congress*]   (LCLS)
U Kan City L Rev ... University of Kansas City. Law Review [*A publication*]
U Kan LR.... University of Kansas. Law Review   (DLA)
U Kan L Rev ... University of Kansas. Law Review   (DLA)
U of Kansas City L Rev ... University of Kansas City. Law Review [*A
                publication*]
U of Kansas L Rev ... University of Kansas. Law Review   (DLA)
U Kans Publ ... University of Kansas. Publications. Library Series [*A
                publication*]

UKAPC....... United Kingdom Agricultural Production Committee
UKARC....... United Kingdom Agricultural Research Council
UKASE....... University of Kansas Automated Serials
UK At Energy Auth At Weapons Res Establ Lib Bibliogr ... United Kingdom.
                Atomic Energy Authority. Atomic Weapons Research
                Establishment. Library Bibliography [*A publication*]
UK At Energy Auth At Weapons Res Establ Rep Ser NR ... United Kingdom.
                Atomic Energy Authority. Atomic Weapons Research
                Establishment. Report. Series NR [*A publication*]
UK At Energy Auth At Weapons Res Establ Rep Ser O ... United Kingdom.
                Atomic Energy Authority. Atomic Weapons Research
                Establishment. Report. Series O [*A publication*]
UK At Energy Auth At Weapons Res Establ Rep Ser R ... United Kingdom.
                Atomic Energy Authority. Atomic Weapons Research
                Establishment. Report. Series R [*A publication*]
UK At Energy Auth Auth Health Saf Branch Mem ... United Kingdom.
                Atomic Energy Authority. Authority Health and Safety
                Branch. Memorandum [*A publication*]
UK At Energy Auth Auth Health Saf Branch Rep ... United Kingdom. Atomic
                Energy Authority. Authority Health and Safety Branch.
                Report [*A publication*]
UK At Energy Auth Dev Eng Group DEG Rep ... United Kingdom. Atomic
                Energy Authority. Development and Engineering Group.
                DEG Report [*A publication*]
UK At Energy Auth Health Saf Code Auth Code ... United Kingdom. Atomic
                Energy Authority. Health and Safety Code. Authority Code
                [*A publication*]
UK At Energy Auth Radiochem Cent Mem ... United Kingdom. Atomic
                Energy Authority. Radiochemical Centre. Memorandum [*A
                publication*]
UK At Energy Auth Radiochem Cent Rep ... United Kingdom. Atomic
                Energy Authority. Radiochemical Centre. Report [*A
                publication*]
UK At Energy Auth React Group Rep ... United Kingdom. Atomic Energy
                Authority. Reactor Group. Report [*A publication*]
UK At Energy Auth React Group TRG Rep ... United Kingdom. Atomic
                Energy Authority. Reactor Group. TRG Report [*A
                publication*]
UK At Energy Auth Res Group Culham Lab Rep ... United Kingdom. Atomic
                Energy Authority. Research Group. Culham Laboratory.
                Report [*A publication*]
UK At Energy Auth Res Group Culham Lab Transl ... United Kingdom.
                Atomic Energy Authority. Research Group. Culham
                Laboratory. Translation [*A publication*]
UK At Energy Auth Saf Reliab Dir SRD Rep ... United Kingdom. Atomic
                Energy Authority. Safety and Reliability Directorate. SRD
                Report [*A publication*]
UK At Energy Res Establ Anal Method ... United Kingdom. Atomic Energy
                Research Establishment. Analytical Method [*A
                publication*]
UK At Energy Res Establ Bibliogr ... United Kingdom. Atomic Energy
                Research Establishment. Bibliography [*A publication*]
UK At Energy Res Establ Health Phys Med Div Res Prog Rep ... United
                Kingdom. Atomic Energy Research Establishment. Health
                Physics and Medical Division. Research Progress Report
                [*A publication*]
UK At Energy Res Establ Lect ... United Kingdom. Atomic Energy Research
                Establishment. Lectures [*A publication*]
UK At Energy Res Establ Memo ... United Kingdom. Atomic Energy
                Research Establishment. Memorandum [*A publication*]
UK At Energy Res Establ Rep ... United Kingdom. Atomic Energy Research
                Establishment. Report [*A publication*]
UK At Energy Res Establ Transl ... United Kingdom. Atomic Energy
                Research Establishment. Translation [*A publication*]
UkAuI .... Ashton-Under-Lyne Public Library, Ashton-Under-Lyne,
                United Kingdom [*Library symbol*] [*Library of
                Congress*]   (LCLS)
UkB .... Birmingham Public Libraries, Birmingham, United Kingdom
                [*Library symbol*] [*Library of Congress*]   (LCLS)
UKB............ United Kingdom Base [*World War II*]
UKB............ Universal Keyboard [*Data processing*]   (AABC)
UKBC .... United Kingdom Bomber Command   (NATG)
UKBelQU.... Queen's University of Belfast, Belfast, United Kingdom [*Library
                symbol*] [*Library of Congress*]   (LCLS)
UkBl .... Blackpool Central Library, Blackpool, United Kingdom [*Library
                symbol*] [*Library of Congress*]   (LCLS)
UkBlG........ Blackpool Gazette & Herald Ltd., Blackpool, United Kingdom
                [*Library symbol*] [*Library of Congress*]   (LCLS)
UkBoN........ Bolton Evening News, Bolton, United Kingdom [*Library
                symbol*] [*Library of Congress*]   (LCLS)
UkBot......... Burton-On-Trent Public Library, Burton-On-Trent, United
                Kingdom [*Library symbol*] [*Library of Congress*]   (LCLS)
UkBP .... Birmingham Post & Mail Ltd., Birmingham, United Kingdom
                [*Library symbol*] [*Library of Congress*]   (LCLS)
UkBrP......... Bristol Evening Post, Bristol, United Kingdom [*Library symbol*]
                [*Library of Congress*]   (LCLS)
UKBS.......... United Kingdom Base Section [*World War II*]
UkBU.......... Birmingham University, Birmingham, United Kingdom [*Library
                symbol*] [*Library of Congress*]   (LCLS)
UKC............ Ukrainian Gold Cross   (EA)
UKC............ Unit Kind Code [*Military*]   (AFIT)

UKC............ United Kennel Club   (EA)

UKC............ University of Kansas City [*Later, University of Missouri at Kansas City*]

UKC............ University of Kansas City. Review [*A publication*]

UKCBS....... United Kingdom Combat Support Boat   (MCD)

UKCC......... United Kingdom Central Council [*for Nursing, Midwifery, and Health Visiting*]

UKCC......... United Kingdom Commercial Corporation

UkCh.......... Chelmsford Library, Chelmsford, United Kingdom [*Library symbol*] [*Library of Congress*]   (LCLS)

UKCHH...... United Kingdom or Continent (Havre to Hamburg)   (ROG)

UKCICC ..... United Kingdom Commanders-in-Chiefs' Committee

UKCIS .... United Kingdom Chemical Information Service [*University of Nottingham*] [*Nottingham, England*] [*Information broker, databank originator, and host*]

UkCoE....... Essex County Newspapers Ltd., Colchester, United Kingdom [*Library symbol*] [*Library of Congress*]   (LCLS)

UK Cont ..... United Kingdom or Continent [*Shipping*]

UK/Cont (BH) ... United Kingdom or Continent (Bordeaux-Hamburg) [*Shipping*]

UK/Cont (GH) ... United Kingdom or Continent (Gibraltar-Hamburg) [*Shipping*]

UK/Cont (HH) ... United Kingdom or Continent (Havre-Hamburg) [*Shipping*]

UkCov .... Coventry Corp., Coventry, United Kingdom [*Library symbol*] [*Library of Congress*]   (LCLS)

UkCr.......... Croydon Library, Croydon, United Kingdom [*Library symbol*] [*Library of Congress*]   (LCLS)

UKCR .... United Kingdom Communication Region [*Air Force*]   (MCD)

UKCR .... University of Kansas City. Review [*A publication*]

UkCrA .... Croydon Advertiser, Croydon, United Kingdom [*Library symbol*] [*Library of Congress*]   (LCLS)

UkCraT ...... Cranfield Institute of Technology, Cranfield, Bedfordshire, United Kingdom [*Library symbol*] [*Library of Congress*]   (LCLS)

UkCrC....... Coulsdon Library, Croydon, United Kingdom [*Library symbol*] [*Library of Congress*]   (LCLS)

UkCrP .... Purley Library, Croydon, United Kingdom [*Library symbol*] [*Library of Congress*]   (LCLS)

UKCRv ...... University of Kansas City. Review [*A publication*]

UKCS .... United Kingdom Continental Shelf

UkCU.......... Cambridge University, Cambridge, United Kingdom [*Library symbol*] [*Library of Congress*]   (LCLS)

UkCwN...... North Wales Weekly News, Conway, United Kingdom [*Library symbol*] [*Library of Congress*]   (LCLS)

UKD............ Unusual Killing Device [*Counterintelligence*]

UkDo .... Doncaster Public Library, Doncaster, United Kingdom [*Library symbol*] [*Library of Congress*]   (LCLS)

UkDw .... Dewsbury Central Library, Dewsbury, United Kingdom [*Library symbol*] [*Library of Congress*]   (LCLS)

UkE .... Edinburgh Public Library, Edinburgh, United Kingdom [*Library symbol*] [*Library of Congress*]   (LCLS)

UKE............ Uke Resources [*Vancouver Stock Exchange symbol*]

UKE............ Ukelele   (DSUE)

UkEc .... Eccles Public Library, Central Library, Eccles, United Kingdom [*Library symbol*] [*Library of Congress*]   (LCLS)

UkENL....... National Library of Scotland, Edinburgh, United Kingdom [*Library symbol*] [*Library of Congress*]   (LCLS)

UkEPh .... Pharmaceutical Society of Great Britain, Scottish Department, Edinburgh, United Kingdom [*Library symbol*] [*Library of Congress*]   (LCLS)

UkERCP ..... Royal College of Physicians, Edinburgh, United Kingdom [*Library symbol*] [*Library of Congress*]   (LCLS)

UkERCS ..... Royal College of Surgeons, Edinburgh, United Kingdom [*Library symbol*] [*Library of Congress*]   (LCLS)

UkES .... Scottish Central Library, Edinburgh, United Kingdom [*Library symbol*] [*Library of Congress*]   (LCLS)

UkEU .... University of Edinburgh, Edinburgh, United Kingdom [*Library symbol*] [*Library of Congress*]   (LCLS)

UKF .... United Karate Federation   (EA)

UKFO .... United Kingdom for Orders [*Shipping*]

UkGM......... Mitchell Library, Glasgow, United Kingdom [*Library symbol*] [*Library of Congress*]   (LCLS)

UkGO .... George Outram & Co. Ltd., Glasgow, United Kingdom [*Library symbol*] [*Library of Congress*]   (LCLS)

UkGP.......... Royal Faculty of Procurators in Glasgow, Glasgow, United Kingdom [*Library symbol*] [*Library of Congress*]   (LCLS)

UkGU .... University of Glasgow, Glasgow, United Kingdom [*Library symbol*] [*Library of Congress*]   (LCLS)

UKH............ United Keno Hill Mines Ltd. [*Toronto Stock Exchange symbol*]

UkHA.......... Atomic Energy Research Establishment, Didcot, Oxfordshire, United Kingdom [*Library symbol*] [*Library of Congress*]   (LCLS)

UKHAD...... United Kingdom and Havre, Antwerp and Dunkirk [*Shipping*]

UkHe .... Heywood Public Library, Heywood, Lancashire, United Kingdom [*Library symbol*] [*Library of Congress*]   (LCLS)

UKHH .... United Kingdom and Havre-Hamburg [*Shipping*]

UkHu .... Huddersfield Public Libraries, Huddersfield, United Kingdom [*Library symbol*] [*Library of Congress*]   (LCLS)

UKI .... Ukiah [*California*] [*Seismograph station code, US Geological Survey*]   (SEIS)

UKI .... Ukiah, CA [*Location identifier*] [*FAA*]   (FAAL)

UKIAS .... United Kingdom Immigrants Advisory Service

UKIP........... United Kingdom Import Plan

UKIRT........ United Kingdom Infrared Telescope

UKITO .... United Kingdom Information Technology Organization

UK Jt Fire Res Organ Fire Res Tech Pap ... United Kingdom Joint Fire Research Organization. Fire Research Technical Paper [*A publication*]

UkK .... Keighley Central Library, Keighley, United Kingdom [*Library symbol*] [*Library of Congress*]   (LCLS)

UKK .... Urho Kekkonen [*President of Finland*]

UkKi .... Kilmarnock Public Library, Central Library, Dick Institute, Kilmarnock, United Kingdom [*Library symbol*] [*Library of Congress*]   (LCLS)

UkKuK .... Knapp, Drewett & Sons Ltd., Kingston-Upon-Thames, United Kingdom [*Library symbol*] [*Library of Congress*]   (LCLS)

UKL .... Utashik Lake [*Alaska*] [*Seismograph station code, US Geological Survey*]   (SEIS)

UkLA .... Associated Newspapers Ltd., London, United Kingdom [*Library symbol*] [*Library of Congress*]   (LCLS)

UKLA.......... Ukalaha [*Quzinkie High School, Alaska*] [*A publication*]

UkLB .... Beaverbrook Newspapers Ltd., London, United Kingdom [*Library symbol*] [*Library of Congress*]   (LCLS)

UkLBOA ..... British Optical Association, London, United Kingdom [*Library symbol*] [*Library of Congress*]   (LCLS)

UkLC .... Chemical Society, London, United Kingdom [*Library symbol*] [*Library of Congress*]   (LCLS)

UkLCS........ Institute of Commonwealth Studies, London, United Kingdom [*Library symbol*] [*Library of Congress*]   (LCLS)

UkLe........... Leeds City Library, Leeds, United Kingdom [*Library symbol*] [*Library of Congress*]   (LCLS)

UKLF.......... United Kingdom Land Forces [*Military*]

UkLG .... Guildhall Library, Aldermanbury, London, United Kingdom [*Library symbol*] [*Library of Congress*]   (LCLS)

UkLH .... Hampstead Public Libraries, Central Library, London, United Kingdom [*Library symbol*] [*Library of Congress*]   (LCLS)

UkLHu .... A. J. Hurley Ltd., London, United Kingdom [*Library symbol*] [*Library of Congress*]   (LCLS)

UkLi............ Liverpool Public Libraries, Liverpool, United Kingdom [*Library symbol*] [*Library of Congress*]   (LCLS)

UkLin .... City of Lincoln Public Library, Lincoln, United Kingdom [*Library symbol*] [*Library of Congress*]   (LCLS)

UkLIO........ India Office Library and Records, Foreign and Commonwealth Office, London, United Kingdom [*Library symbol*] [*Library of Congress*]   (LCLS)

UkLIP .... IPC Newspapers Ltd., London, United Kingdom [*Library symbol*] [*Library of Congress*]   (LCLS)

UkLiP .... Liverpool Daily Post & Echo Ltd., Liverpool, United Kingdom [*Library symbol*] [*Library of Congress*]   (LCLS)

UkLiU .... University of Liverpool, Liverpool, United Kingdom [*Library symbol*] [*Library of Congress*]   (LCLS)

UkLJ .... Jews' College, London, United Kingdom [*Library symbol*] [*Library of Congress*]   (LCLS)

UkLLA .... Library Association, London, United Kingdom [*Library symbol*] [*Library of Congress*]   (LCLS)

UkLLT .... Lambeth Public Libraries, Tate Central Library, London, United Kingdom [*Library symbol*] [*Library of Congress*]   (LCLS)

UkLMS ...... Morning Star Co-Operative Society, London, United Kingdom [*Library symbol*] [*Library of Congress*]   (LCLS)

UkLNw ...... North West London Press Ltd., London, United Kingdom [*Library symbol*] [*Library of Congress*]   (LCLS)

UkLPh .... Pharmaceutical Society of Great Britain, London, United Kingdom [*Library symbol*] [*Library of Congress*]   (LCLS)

UkLPo .... H. Pordes, Publisher and Bookseller, London, United Kingdom [*Library symbol*] [*Library of Congress*]   (LCLS)

UkLPR....... Public Record Office, London, United Kingdom [*Library symbol*] [*Library of Congress*]   (LCLS)

UkLQ .... Friends Reference Library, London, United Kingdom [*Library symbol*] [*Library of Congress*]   (LCLS)

UKLR.......... University of Kansas. Law Review   (DLA)

UkLRCP ..... Royal College of Physicians, London, United Kingdom [*Library symbol*] [*Library of Congress*]   (LCLS)

UkLRCS ..... Royal College of Surgeons of England, London, United Kingdom [*Library symbol*] [*Library of Congress*]   (LCLS)

UkLRSM.... Royal Society of Medicine, London, United Kingdom [*Library symbol*] [*Library of Congress*]   (LCLS)

UkLS .... Science Museum, London, United Kingdom [*Library symbol*] [*Library of Congress*]   (LCLS)

UkLTh .... Thomasons Ltd., London, United Kingdom [*Library symbol*] [*Library of Congress*]   (LCLS)

UkLU .... University of London, London, United Kingdom [*Library symbol*] [*Library of Congress*]   (LCLS)

UkLuH .... Home Counties Newspapers Ltd., Luton, United Kingdom [*Library symbol*] [*Library of Congress*]   (LCLS)

UkLU-K ...... University of London, Kings College, London, United Kingdom [*Library symbol*] [*Library of Congress*]   (LCLS)

UkLW .... Wellcome Historical Medical Library, London, United Kingdom [*Library symbol*] [*Library of Congress*]   (LCLS)

UkLWa ...... Wandsworth Borough News Co. Ltd., London, United Kingdom [*Library symbol*] [*Library of Congress*]   (LCLS)

UKM .... UK MARC [*United Kingdom Machine-Readable Cataloging*] [*Source file*] [*UTLAS symbol*]

UkMa.......... Manchester Public Libraries, Central Library, Manchester, United Kingdom [*Library symbol*] [*Library of Congress*] (LCLS)

UkMaG....... Guardian Newspapers Ltd., Manchester, United Kingdom [*Library symbol*] [*Library of Congress*] (LCLS)

UK MARC... UK [*British Library*] Machine Readable Catalogue [*Bibliographic database*]

UkMe.......... Public Libraries, Central Library, Merthyr-Tydfil, United Kingdom [*Library symbol*] [*Library of Congress*] (LCLS)

UKMF......... United Kingdom Mobile Force

UkMg .... Margate Public Library, Margate, United Kingdom [*Library symbol*] [*Library of Congress*] (LCLS)

UKMJB....... Ukrainian Mathematical Journal [*English Translation*] [*A publication*]

UKML......... United Knitwear Manufacturers League [*New York, NY*] (EA)

UKMO .... United Kingdom Meteorological Office

UKMRC...... United Kingdom Medical Research Council

UKN........... Unknown (KSC)

UKN........... Waukon, IA [*Location identifier*] [*FAA*] (FAAL)

UK/NL........ United Kingdom/Netherlands (MCD)

UkNr.......... Norwich Public Libraries, Norwich, United Kingdom [*Library symbol*] [*Library of Congress*] (LCLS)

UKNR .... University of Kansas Nuclear Reactor

UkNrE .... Eastern Counties Newspapers Ltd., Norwich, United Kingdom [*Library symbol*] [*Library of Congress*] (LCLS)

UKO........... Unverhofft Kommt Oft [*The Unexpected Often Happens*] [*Motto of Franz, Duke of Pomerania (1577-1620)*]

UKOLUG .... United Kingdom On-Line User Group [*Information service*] (EISS)

UkOxU....... Oxford University, Bodleian Library, Oxford, United Kingdom [*Library symbol*] [*Library of Congress*] (LCLS)

UkOxU-AS ... Oxford University, All Souls College, Oxford, United Kingdom [*Library symbol*] [*Library of Congress*] (LCLS)

UkOxU-N.... Oxford University, Nuffield College, Oxford, United Kingdom [*Library symbol*] [*Library of Congress*] (LCLS)

UkOxU-Rh ... Oxford University, Bodleian Library, Rhodes House, Oxford, United Kingdom [*Library symbol*] [*Library of Congress*] (LCLS)

UkPe .... Sandeman Public Library, Perth, United Kingdom [*Library symbol*] [*Library of Congress*] (LCLS)

UKPHS ...... University of Kansas. Publications. Humanistic Studies [*A publication*]

UKPJA....... Ukrainian Physics Journal [*A publication*]

UKPO .... United Kingdom Post Office [*Telecommunications*] (TEL)

UkPS .... Portsmouth & Sunderland Newspapers Ltd., Portsmouth, Hants, United Kingdom [*Library symbol*] [*Library of Congress*] (LCLS)

UKR........... Ukraine

ukr............. Ukrainian [*MARC language code*] [*Library of Congress*] (LCCP)

UKR........... Uranian Kilometric Radiation [*Planetary science*]

Ukrain Fiz Z ... Ukrainskii Fizicheskii Zhurnal [*A publication*]

Ukrain Geometr Sb ... Ukrainskii Geometriceskii Sbornik [*A publication*]

Ukrain Geom Sb ... Ukrainskii Geometriceskii Sbornik [*A publication*]

Ukrainian Math J ... Ukrainian Mathematical Journal [*A publication*]

Ukrain Mat Z ... Ukrainskii Matematicheskii Zhurnal [*A publication*]

Ukrain Mat Zh ... Akademiya Nauk Ukrainskoi SSR. Institut Matematiki. Ukrainskii Matematicheskii Zhurnal [*A publication*]

Ukrain Phys J ... Ukrainian Physics Journal [*A publication*]

Ukr Biokhim ... Ukrainskii Biokhimicheski Zhurnal [*A publication*]

Ukr Biokhim Zh ... Ukrainskii Biokhimicheskij Zhurnal [*A publication*]

Ukr Biokhim Zh ... Ukrayins'kyi Biokhimichnyi Zhurnal [*A publication*]

Ukr Biokhim Zh (1946-1977) ... Ukrains'kii Biokhimichnii Zhurnal (1946-1977) [*Ukrainian SSR*] [*A publication*]

Ukr Bot Zh ... Ukrayins'kyi Botanichnyi Zhurnal [*A publication*]

Ukr Fiz Zh ... Ukrainskii Fizichni Zhurnal [*A publication*]

Ukr Fiz Zh ... Ukrainskij Fizicheskij Zhurnal [*A publication*]

Ukr Fiz Zh ... Ukrayins'kyi Fizychnyi Zhurnal [*A publication*]

Ukr Fiz Zh (Kiev) ... Ukrayinskoyi Fizichnij Zhurnal (Ukrainian Edition) (Kiev) [*A publication*]

Ukr Geom Sb ... Ukrainskij Geometricheskij Sbornik [*A publication*]

Ukrl .... Ukrajins'kyj Istoryk [*A publication*]

UkRiH........ Richmond Herald Ltd., Richmond, Surrey, United Kingdom [*Library symbol*] [*Library of Congress*] (LCLS)

Ukr Ist Zhurnal ... Ukrainskyi Istorichnyi Zhurnal [*A publication*]

Ukr J Biochem ... Ukrainian Journal of Biochemistry [*A publication*]

UkrK .... Ukrajins'ka Knyha [*A publication*]

Ukr Khim Zh ... Ukrainskii Khimicheskii Zhurnal [*A publication*]

UkrM .... Ukrajins'ka Mova i Literatura v Skoli [*A publication*]

Ukr Math J ... Ukrainian Mathematical Journal [*A publication*]

Ukr Mat Zh ... Ukrainskij Matematicheskij Zhurnal [*A publication*]

Ukr Mov ..... Ukrajins'ke Movoznavstvo [*A publication*]

UkRoS....... G. & A. N. Scott Ltd., Rochdale, United Kingdom [*Library symbol*] [*Library of Congress*] (LCLS)

Ukr Phys J ... Ukrainian Physics Journal [*A publication*]

UkrR.......... Ukrainian Review [*A publication*]

UkrS.......... Ukrajins'kyj Samostijnyk [*A publication*]

UkrSSR...... Ukranian Soviet Socialist Republic

UKS........... United Kingdom Subsatellite

UKSATA .... United Kingdom-South Africa Trade Association

UkSh .... Sheffield City Libraries, Central Library, Sheffield, United Kingdom [*Library symbol*] [*Library of Congress*] (LCLS)

UkShU........ University of Sheffield, Sheffield, United Kingdom [*Library symbol*] [*Library of Congress*] (LCLS)

UkSlO........ Slough Observer Ltd., Slough, United Kingdom [*Library symbol*] [*Library of Congress*] (LCLS)

UkSsB .... John H. Burrows & Sons Ltd., Southend-On-Sea, United Kingdom [*Library symbol*] [*Library of Congress*] (LCLS)

UkSta .... Stamford Public Library and Museum, Stamford, United Kingdom [*Library symbol*] [*Library of Congress*] (LCLS)

UKSTC....... United Kingdom Strike Command (NATG)

UKSTU...... United Kingdom Schmidt Telescope Unit

UkSw........ Swansea Public Library, Swansea, United Kingdom [*Library symbol*] [*Library of Congress*] (LCLS)

UKT........... Quakertown, PA [*Location identifier*] [*FAA*] (FAAL)

UKT........... United Kingdom Tariff

UKTA .... United Kingdom Trade Agency

UKTD .... United Kingdom Treasury Delegation

UKTOTC ... United Kingdom Tariff and Overseas Trade Classification

UKU........... Nuku [*Papua New Guinea*] [*Airport symbol*] (OAG)

UKUSA...... United Kingdom-United States Agreement [*Intelligence*] [*1947*]

UKV........... Underground Keybox Vault (NATG)

UKW......... Ultrakurzwelle [*Ultrashort wave*] [*German*]

UkWE .... Eton College, Windsor, Berks, United Kingdom [*Library symbol*] [*Library of Congress*] (LCLS)

UKWE........ Ultrakurzwellenempfaenger [*Very-High-Frequency Receiver*] [*German*]

UkWg .... County Borough of Wigan Public Libraries, Central Library, Wigan, United Kingdom [*Library symbol*] [*Library of Congress*] (LCLS)

UkWoE....... Express & Star Ltd., Wolverhampton, United Kingdom [*Library symbol*] [*Library of Congress*] (LCLS)

UkWr .... Wrexham Public Library, Wrexham, United Kingdom [*Library symbol*] [*Library of Congress*] (LCLS)

UKY........... United Kingdom Energy [*Vancouver Stock Exchange symbol*]

'Ukz .... 'Ukzin (BJA)

UKZHA...... Ukrainskii Khimicheskii Zhurnal [*A publication*]

UL............. Ugaritic Literature [*C. H. Gordon*] [*A publication*] (BJA)

Ul.............. Ulisse [*A publication*]

UL............. Ulitsa [*Street*]

UL............. Ultralinear

UL............. Ultralow

UL............. Underwriters Laboratories [*Northbrook, IL*] (EA)

UL............. Uniformly Labeled [*Compound, with radioisotope*] [*Also, U*]

UL............. Union Liberal [*Liberal Union*] [*Spanish*] (PPW)

UL............. Union List

UL............. Unionist Liberal [*British*] (ROG)

UL............. Universal League (EA-IO)

UL............. Universal Life [*Insurance*]

UL............. Universala Ligo (EA)

u/l............. Unlimited [*Water depth*]

UL............. Unterlafette [*Bottom carriage*] [*German military - World War II*]

U e L .... Uomini e Libri [*A publication*]

UL............. Up Left [*The rear left portion of a stage*] [*A stage direction*]

UL............. Up Link [*Data processing*]

UL............. Upper Leg

UL............. Upper Level (NRCH)

UL............. Upper Limb [*Upper edge of sun, moon, etc.*] [*Navigation*]

UL............. Upper Limit

UL............. Upper Lobe [*Anatomy*]

U & L .... Upper and Lower (MSA)

UL............. Urban League (MCD)

UL............. Usage List (MSA)

UL............. User Language [*Data processing*] (DIT)

UL............. Utility Lead [*Telecommunications*] (TEL)

ULA .... San Julian [*Argentina*] [*Airport symbol*] (OAG)

ULA .... Ulamona Field Station [*New Britain*] [*Seismograph station code, US Geological Survey*] (SEIS)

ULA .... Uncommitted Logic Array [*Semiconductor technology*]

ULA .... Uniform Laws, Annotated (DLA)

ULA .... Utah State University, Logan, UT [*Library symbol*] [*Library of Congress*] (LCLS)

ULAA........ Ukrainian Library Association of America (EA)

ULAA........ United Latin Americans of America (EA)

ULAE........ Universal Limited Art Editions

ULAEY ...... Union of Latin American Ecumenical Youth (EA)

ULAIDS ..... Universal Locator Airborne Integrated Data System (MCD)

ULAJE....... Union Latino-Americaine des Jeunesses Evangeliques [*Union of Latin American Evangelical Youth*]

ULAJE....... Union Latinoamericana de Juventudes Ecumenicas [*Union of Latin American Ecumenical Youth - ULAEY*] (EA-IO)

ULANG...... User Language [*Data processing*]

ULAPC ...... Union Latino-Americaine de la Presse Catholique

ULAS........ University of Louisville Archaeological Survey [*Research center*] (RCD)

ULASM...... Undersea Multichannel Large-Scale Scattering Meter [*NASA*] (MCD)

ULAST ...... Union Latino Americana de Sociedades de Tisiologia [*Latin American Union of Societies of Phthisiology*]

ULB .... Underwater Locator Beacon (MCD)

ULB .... Universal Logic Block (IEEE)

ULBA.......... Universal Love and Brotherhood Association (EA-IO)
ULB-VUB Inter-Univ High Energ Rep ... ULB-VUB [*Universite Libre de Bruxelles - Vrije Universiteit Brussel*] Inter-University Institute for High Energies. Report [*A publication*]
ULC .... Cache County Public Library, Logan, UT [*Library symbol*] [*Library of Congress*] (LCLS)
ULC .... Philippines Civil Liberties Union (PD)
ULC .... Underwriters' Laboratories of Canada
ULC .... Uniform Loop Clock
ULC .... Union Library Catalogue
ULC .... Union de la Lutte Communiste [*Political party*] [*Burkina Faso*]
ULC .... Unit Ledger Card [*Data processing*]
ULC .... Unit Level Code (AFM)
ULC .... Unit Level Computers [*Army*]
ULC .... Unitary Launch Concept [*or Control*] (AAG)
ULC .... United Labor Congress [*Nigeria*]
ULC .... Universal Life Church
ULC .... Universal Load Cell
ULC .... Universal Logic Circuit
ULC .... Upper Left Center [*The rear left center portion of a stage*] [*A stage direction*]
U & LC .... Uppercase and Lowercase [*i.e., capital and small letters*] [*Typography*]
ULC .... Urban Libraries Council
ULC .... Utah State Library, Salt Lake City, UT [*OCLC symbol*] (OCLC)
ULCA .... Ukrainian Life Cooperative Association
ULCC .... Ulster Loyalist Central Coordinating Committee [*Ireland*]
ULCC .... Ultralarge Crude Carrier [*Oil tanker*]
ULCER ...... Underwater Launch Control Energy Requirements
ULCER ...... Underwater Launch Current and Energy Recorder
ULCHi......... Cache Valley Historical Society, Logan, UT [*Library symbol*] [*Library of Congress*] (LCLS)
ULCJ .... University Law College. Journal. Rajputana University [*India*] (DLA)
ULCM .... United Lutheran Church Men [*Defunct*] (EA)
ULCS......... Unit Level Circuit Switch (CAAL)
ULD .... Ultrasonic Leak Detector
ULD .... Ultrasonic Light Diffraction
ULD .... Unit Load Demand [*Nuclear energy*] (NRCH)
ULD .... Unit Logic Device
ULD .... Upper Level Deck [*Cargo containers*]
ULDEST ..... Ultimate Destination [*Army*] (AABC)
ULDF .... United Left Democratic Front [*Indian*] (PPW)
ULDMI........ Ultraprecise LASER Distance Measuring Instrument
ULDP......... Ulster Loyalist Democratic Party [*Northern Ireland*] (PPW)
ULDS......... Union Liberale-Democratique Suisse [*Liberal Democratic Union of Switzerland*] (PPE)
ULE .... Sule [*Papua New Guinea*] [*Airport symbol*] (OAG)
ULE .... Ultralow Expansion [*Trademark, Corning Glass Works*]
ULE .... Unit Location Equipment (MCD)
ULEA......... University Labor Education Association [*Later, UCLEA*]
ULECA ...... Ultra-Low-Energy Charge Analyzer [*Instrumentation*]
ULECA ...... Ultralow Energy Charge Analyzer [*Instrumentation*]
ULew .... Lewiston Public Library, Lewiston, UT [*Library symbol*] [*Library of Congress*] (LCLS)
ULEWAT .... Ultralow-Energy Wide-Angle Telescope
ULF........... Ultralow Frequency
ULF........... United Labour Front [*Trinidadian and Tobagan*] (PD)
ULF........... University Labour Federation [*British*]
ULF........... Upper Limiting Frequency (ADA)
ULFJ......... Ultralow-Frequency Jammer
ULFO........ Ultralow-Frequency Oscillator
ULG........... Upholstery Leather Group [*Later, Autoleather Guild*] (EA)
ULGS......... Church of Jesus Christ of Latter-Day Saints, Genealogical Society Library, Cache Branch, Logan, UT [*Library symbol*] [*Library of Congress*] (LCLS)
ULH .... Universidad de la Habana [*A publication*]
ULI............. Underwriters Laboratories, Incorporated [*Also, UL*]
ULI............. Union pour la Langue Internationale Ido [*Union for the International Language Ido*]
ULI............. Uniono por la Linguo Internaciona Ido [*International Language Union*] (EA)
ULI............. Universal Logic Implementer
ULI............. Urban Land Institute (EA)
ULI............. Urban Law Institute of Antioch College (EA)
ULIA .... Unattached List, Indian Army
ULIB .... Utility Library [*National Center for Atmospheric Research*]
ULI Lm Rep ... Urban Land Institute. Landmark Report [*A publication*]
ULI Res Rep ... Urban Land Institute. Research Report [*A publication*]
ULIS .... Uniform Law on the International Sale of Goods
ULI Spe Rep ... Urban Land Institute. Special Report [*A publication*]
ULJ............. Bedford, MA [*Location identifier*] [*FAA*] (FAAL)
Ul'janovsk Gos Ped Inst Ucen Zap ... Ul'janovskii Gosudarstvennyi Pedagogiceskii Institut Imeni I. N. Ul'janova. Ucennyi Zapiski [*A publication*]
ULL............. Savoonga, AK [*Location identifier*] [*FAA*] (FAAL)
ULL............. Ullage [*NASA*] (KSC)
ULL............. Unit Local Loading (AAG)
ULL............. Unitarian Laymen's League
ULL............. United States Department of Labor, Washington, DC [*OCLC symbol*] (OCLC)

ULL............. Upper Lip Length [*Medicine*]
ULLOS ...... University of London. London Oriental Series [*A publication*]
ULLS .... Ultrasonic Liquid Level Sensor
ULLV .... Unmanned Lunar Logistics Vehicle [*OMSF*]
ULM........... Meiji University, Maruzen Co. Ltd. [*UTLAS symbol*]
ULM........... Mine Safety and Health Administration, Denver, Denver, CO [*OCLC symbol*] (OCLC)
ULM........... New Ulm [*Minnesota*] [*Airport symbol*] [*Obsolete*] (OAG)
ULM........... New Ulm Flight Service, Inc. [*New Ulm, MN*] [*FAA designator*] (FAAC)
ULM........... Ultramar Capital Corp. [*Toronto Stock Exchange symbol*]
ULM........... Ultrasonic Light Modulator
ULM........... Undersea [*or Underwater*] Long-Range Missile [*Navy*]
ULM........... Union List of Manuscripts [*Canada*] [*A publication*]
ULM........... Universal Line Multiplexer
ULM........... Universal Logic Module
ULMA .... University Laboratory Managers Association [*Later, ALMA*] (EA)
Ulm L Rec ... Ulman's Law Record [*New York*] (DLA)
ULMS .... Undersea [*or Underwater*] Long-Range Missile System [*Redesignated "Trident"*] [*Navy*]
ULMS .... Union List of Montana Serials [*Library network*]
ULN .... Ulan Bator [*Mongolia*] [*Airport symbol*] (OAG)
ULN .... University of Lowell, North Campus, Lowell, MA [*OCLC symbol*] (OCLC)
ULN .... Upper Limits of Normal [*Medicine*]
ULO .... Occupational Safety and Health Administration, Technical Data Center, Washington, DC [*OCLC symbol*] (OCLC)
ULO .... Unilateral Ovariectomy [*Gynecology*]
ULO .... United Labour Organization [*Burma*]
ULO .... Unmanned Launch Operations [*NASA*] (KSC)
ULO .... Unmanned Lunar Orbiter [*NASA*] (MCD)
U Lond I Cl ... University of London. Institute of Classical Studies. Bulletin [*A publication*]
ULOS .... Unliquidated Obligations (MCD)
ULOSSOM ... Union List of Selected Serials of Michigan [*Wayne State University Libraries*] [*Information service*] [*Ceased*] (EISS)
ULOW........ Unmanned Launch Operations - Western Test Range [*NASA*] (KSC)
ULP .... Quilpie [*Australia*] [*Airport symbol*] (OAG)
Ulp............. Ulpiani Fragmenta (DLA)
ULP .... Ulster Petroleums Ltd. [*Toronto Stock Exchange symbol*]
ULP .... Unfair Labor Practice
ULP .... Unleaded Petrol [*British*] (ADA)
ULP .... Utilitaire Logique Processor [*Programing language*] [*Data processing*] (CSR)
ULP .... Utility Landplane [*Navy*]
ULPA........ Uniform Limited Partnership Act [*National Conference of Commissioners on Uniform State Laws*]
ULPA........ United Lightning Protection Association [*Webster, NY*] (EA)
ULPOD ...... Urban Law and Policy [*A publication*]
ULPR .... Ultralow-Pressure Rocket
ULQ .... Tulua [*Colombia*] [*Airport symbol*] (OAG)
ULQ .... Utah Foreign Language Quarterly [*A publication*]
ULR .... Uganda Law Reports (DLA)
ULR .... Uganda Protectorate Law Reports [*1904-51*] (DLA)
ULR .... Ultralinear Rectifier
ULR .... Uniform Law Review (DLA)
ULR .... Union Law Review [*South Africa*] (DLA)
ULR .... United Liberty Resources Ltd. [*Vancouver Stock Exchange symbol*]
ULR .... University Law Review [*United States*] (DLA)
ULR .... University of Leeds. Review [*A publication*]
ULR .... Utah Law Review [*A publication*]
ULR .... Utilities Law Reporter (DLA)
ULRA........ United Lithuanian Relief Fund of America (EA)
ULRED .... UCLA [*University of California, Los Angeles*] Law Review [*A publication*]
ULRF .... Urban Land Research Foundation (EA)
Ulrich's Q ... Ulrich's Quarterly [*A publication*]
ULRSA ...... Union and League of Romanian Societies of America (EA)
ULS .... ULS Capital Corp. [*Toronto Stock Exchange symbol*]
ULS .... Ultimatist Life Society [*Formed by a merger of Alternatives to Abortion Society and Ultimatist Vegetarian Society*] [*Erie, PA*] (EA)
ULS .... Ultrasystems, Inc. [*American Stock Exchange symbol*]
ULS .... Ultraviolet Light Stabilizer
ULS .... Ulysses, KS [*Location identifier*] [*FAA*] (FAAL)
ULS .... Union List of Serials [*A publication*]
ULS .... Unit Level Switchboard (MCD)
ULS .... United Lutheran Society (EA)
ULS .... University Libraries Section [*Association of College and Research Libraries*]
ULS .... University of Lowell, South Campus, Lowell, MA [*OCLC symbol*] (OCLC)
ULS .... Unsecured Loan Stock
ULSA......... Ultralow Sidelobe Antenna [*Air Force*] (MCD)
UL Sci Mag ... UL [*University of Liberia*] Science Magazine [*A publication*]
ULSI.......... Ultralarge-Scale Integration [*of circuits*] [*Semiconductor technology*]

ULSIA........ Uniform Land Security Interest Act [*National Conference of Commissioners on Uniform State Laws*]
ULSP........ Unified Legal Services Program
ULSS......... Underwater LASER Surveying System   (MCD)
ULSSCL..... Union List of Scientific Serials in Canadian Libraries [*A publication*]
Ulster Folk ... Ulster Folklife [*A publication*]
Ulster J Arch ... Ulster Journal of Archaeology [*A publication*]
Ulster Med J ... Ulster Medical Journal [*A publication*]
ULSV........ Unmanned Launch Space Vehicles [*NASA*]   (KSC)
ULT .... Ultimate   (AAG)
ULT .... Ultimate Corp. [*NYSE symbol*]
ULT .... Ultime [*Lastly*] [*Pharmacy*]
ULT .... Ultralow Tar [*Cigarettes*] [*Tobacco industry*]
ULT .... Ultralow Temperature
ULT .... Ultramar [*Toronto Stock Exchange symbol*]
ULT .... Ultramarine [*Philately*]   (ROG)
ULT .... Uniform Low-Frequency Technique
ULT .... Unione per la Lotta alla Tubercolosi [*Union of Anti-Tuberculosis Association Workers*] [*Italy*]
ULT .... United Lodge of Theosophists
ULTA .... Uniform Land Transactions Act [*National Conference of Commissioners on Uniform State Laws*]
ULTB........ Ultra Bancorporation [*NASDAQ symbol*]   (NQ)
ULTC .... Urban Library Trustees Council [*Later, ULC*]   (EA)
ULTK........ Ultrak, Inc. [*NASDAQ symbol*]   (NQ)
ULTO......... Ultimo [*In the Month Preceding the Present*] [*Latin*]
ULT PRAESCR ... Ultimo Praescriptus [*The Last Ordered*] [*Pharmacy*]   (ROG)
ULTR .... Ultrasystems, Inc. [*NASDAQ symbol*]   (NQ)
ULTRA....... Ultramarine [*Philately*]   (ROG)
ULTRA....... Ultrasonics [*A publication*]
ULTRACOM ... Ultraviolet Communications
ULTRAJ..... Ultrajectum [*Utrecht*] [*Imprint*] [*Latin*]   (ROG)
Ultramicrosc ... Ultramicroscopy [*A publication*]
Ultrason ... Ultrasonics [*A publication*]
Ultrason Imaging ... Ultrasonic Imaging [*A publication*]
Ultrason Symp Proc ... Ultrasonics Symposium. Proceedings [*A publication*]
Ultrasound Med & Biol ... Ultrasound in Medicine and Biology [*A publication*]
Ultrasound Med Biol ... Ultrasound in Medicine and Biology [*A publication*]
Ultrastruct Pathol ... Ultrastructural Pathology [*A publication*]
ULTRA-X.... Universal Language for Typographic Reproduction Applications
ULTRD .... Ultramicroscopy [*A publication*]
ULTSIGN.... Ultimate Assignment
ULU .... Gulu [*Uganda*] [*Airport symbol*]   (OAG)
ULV .... Ultralow Volume
ULW .... Unsafe Landing Warning
ULWC........ Ultra-Lightweight Coated [*Paper*]
ULY .... Ulyanovsk [*USSR*] [*Airport symbol*]   (OAG)
Ul'yanovsk Skh Opytn Stn Tr ... Ul'yanovskaya Sel'skokhozyaistvennaya Opytnaya Stantsiya. Trudy [*A publication*]
ULz............ Ukrajins'ke Literaturoznavstvo [*A publication*]
ULZP .... United Labor Zionist Party [*Later, LZA*]   (EA)
UM............. Air Manila, Inc. [*Philippines*] [*ICAO designator*]   (FAAC)
UM............. Salt Lake County Library System, Midvale, UT [*Library symbol*] [*Library of Congress*]   (LCLS)
UM............. Ugaritic Manual [*C. H. Gordon*] [*A publication*]   (BJA)
UM............. Umbilical Mast [*NASA*]   (KSC)
UM............. Umot Me'uhadot [*United Nations*] [*Hebrew*]
UM............. Unable to Maintain [*Aviation*]   (FAAC)
UM............. Unaccompanied Minor [*Airline passenger*]
UM............. Under-Mentioned [*i.e., mentioned later in a document*]
UM............. Underwater Mechanic
UM............. Uninsured Motorists [*Insurance*]
UM............. Unio Mallorquina [*Majorcan Union*]   (PPW)
UM............. Union Movement Party [*British*]
UM............. Unione Maniferro [*Somalia*]
UM............. Unit of Measure   (MCD)
UM............. United Medical Corp. [*American Stock Exchange symbol*]
UM............. Universal Machine Gun   (MCD)
UM............. Universal Monitor   (MCD)
UM............. Universidad de Mexico [*A publication*]
UM............. University of Manitoba [*Canada*]
UM............. University of Massachusetts [*Amherst, MA*]
UM............. University of Miami [*Florida*]
U of M........ University of Michigan
UM............. University Microfilms [*A publication*]
UM............. University of Missouri Press
U/M............ Unmanned   (NASA)
UM............. Unmarried
UM............. Unpopular Magnetic Fields
UM............. Unpriced Material
UM............. Unscheduled Maintenance
UM............. Upper Magazine [*Typography*]
UM............. Upper Motor [*Neurons*] [*Medicine*]
UM............. Useful Method
UM............. User Manual   (MCD)
U & M .... Utilization/Reutilization and Marketing [*DoD*]
UMA .... Ultrasonic Manufacturers Association [*Later, UIA*]   (EA)

UMA .... Union Mathematique Africaine [*African Mathematical Union - AMU*]   (EA)
UMA .... Union Membership Agreement
UMA .... Union Mondiale des Aveugles [*World Blind Union - WBU*]   (EA)
UMA .... Union de Mujeres Americanas [*United Women of the Americas*]
UMA .... United Maritime Administration
UMA .... United Maritime Authority
UMA .... United Methodist Association of Health and Welfare Ministries [*Dayton, OH*]   (EA)
UMA .... Universal Measurement Assembly   (MCD)
UMA .... Universal Measuring Amplifier   (KSC)
UMA .... University of Mid-America [*Consortium of six midwestern universities*]
UMA .... Unscheduled Maintenance Action [*Military*]   (AABC)
UMa........... Ursa Major [*Constellation*]
UMAA......... United Martial Arts Association   (EA)
UMAC........ UMI [*University Microfilms International*] Article Clearinghouse [*Ann Arbor, MI*] [*Information service*]   (EISS)
UMAD........ Umatilla Army Depot [*Oregon*]   (AABC)
UMAH........ Union Mondiale d'Avancee Humaine [*World Union for Human Progress*]
U Maine L Rev ... University of Maine. Law Review   (DLA)
UMaj......... Ursa Major [*Constellation*]
U of Malaya L Rev ... University of Malaya. Law Review [*A publication*]
UMan......... Manti City Library, Manti, UT [*Library symbol*] [*Library of Congress*]   (LCLS)
UMANA ...... Ukrainian Medical Association of North America [*Chicago, IL*]   (EA)
UMANA ...... Uspekhi Matematicheskikh Nauk [*A publication*]
UMAP........ University of Michigan Assembly Program
U Mary L Forum ... University of Maryland Law Forum   (DLA)
UMASS ..... University of Massachusetts [*Amherst, MA*]
UMASS ...... Unlimited Machine Access from Scattered Sites [*Data processing*]
Umb .... Umbelliferyl [*Biochemistry*]
UMB .... Umberatana [*Australia*] [*Seismograph station code, US Geological Survey*]   (SEIS)
UMB .... Umberto's Pasta Enterprises, Inc. [*Vancouver Stock Exchange symbol*]
UMB .... Umbilical   (MCD)
umb .... Umbundu [*MARC language code*] [*Library of Congress*]   (LCCP)
UMB .... Umnak, AK [*Location identifier*] [*FAA*]   (FAAL)
UMB .... Union Mondiale de Billard [*World Billiards Union*]
UMB .... Universal Missile Building   (MCD)
UMBA........ United Mortgage Bankers of America [*Philadelphia, PA*]   (EA)
UMBC........ Umbilical Cord [*Aerospace engineering*]
UMBC........ United Malayan Banking Corporation
UMBC........ University of Maryland, Baltimore County
UMBC Econ R ... UMBC Economic Review [*Kuala Lumpur*] [*A publication*]
UMBL .... Umbilical   (AAG)
UMBP .... University Museum. Bulletin (Philadelphia) [*A publication*]
UMBR .... Unclad-Metal Breeder Reactor
UMBR .... Universal Multiple Bomb Rack   (NG)
UMBS........ University of Michigan Biological Station [*Research center*]   (RCD)
UMBS........ University of Pennsylvania. University Museum. Publications of the Babylonian Section [*A publication*]
UMB V .... Umbilical Vein [*Anatomy*]
UMC .... Ukrainian Museum of Canada [*UTLAS symbol*]
UMC .... Unibus Microchannel
UMC .... Uniform Motion Coupling
UMC .... Uniform Moving Charge
UMC .... Union du Moyen-Congo [*Union of the Middle Congo*]
UMC .... Unit Mail Clerk
UMC .... Unit Mobility Center [*Military*]   (AFIT)
UMC .... United Maritime Council
UMC .... United Methodist Church
UMC .... United Mining Corporation [*Vancouver Stock Exchange symbol*]
UMC .... United Motor Courts
UMC .... Universal Match Corporation
UmC .... Universal Microfilming Corporation, Salt Lake City, UT [*Library symbol*] [*Library of Congress*] [*Obsolete*]   (LCLS)
UMC .... University of Maryland, College Park, MD [*OCLC symbol*]   (OCLC)
UMCA .... United Mining Councils of America [*Hinkley, CA*]   (EA)
UMCA .... Universities Mission to Central Africa [*British*]
UMCA .... Uraba, Medellin & Central Airways, Inc.
UMCAA..... Union Medicale du Canada [*A publication*]
UMCC .... United Maritime Consultative Committee
UMCE........ UMC Electronics [*NASDAQ symbol*]   (NQ)
UMCI .... Universal Money Centers [*NASDAQ symbol*]   (NQ)
UMCJA...... University of Michigan. Medical Center. Journal [*A publication*]
UMCMP..... University of Michigan. Contributions in Modern Philology [*A publication*]
UMCO .... United Michigan Corporation [*NASDAQ symbol*]   (NQ)
UMCOR..... United Methodist Committee on Relief   (EA)
UMCP........ Unit Maintenance Collection Point [*Army*]   (INF)
UMCP........ University of Maryland, College Park

UM/CR ...... Unsatisfactory Material/Condition Report (MCD)
UMCS .... Uniwersytet Marii Curie-Sklodowskiej [*A publication*]
UMD .... Ultrasonic Material Dispersion
UMD .... Unit Manning Document [*DoD*]
UMD .... Unitized Microwave Devices
UMD .... University of Maryland
UMDA .... Uniform Marriage and Divorce Act [*National Conference of Commissioners on Uniform State Laws*]
UMDA .... United Micronesia Development Association
UMDC .... Union Mondiale Democrate Chretienne [*Christian Democratic World Union*]
UMDK .... United Movement for Democracy in Korea [*Later, UMDUK*] (EA)
UMDUK ...... United Movement for Democracy and Unification in Korea [*Woodside, NY*] (EA)
UME .... Umea [*Sweden*] [*Seismograph station code, US Geological Survey*] (SEIS)
UME .... Umea [*Sweden*] [*Airport symbol*] (OAG)
UME .... Uniform Manufacturers Exchange [*New York, NY*] (EA)
UME .... Unit Mission Equipment (AAG)
UME .... Unit Mobility Equipment
UME .... Unit Monthly Equipment (MSA)
UME .... United Ministries in Education (EA)
UME .... University of Maryland, Eastern Shore, Princess Anne, MD [*OCLC symbol*] (OCLC)
UmE .... University Music Editions, New York, NY [*Library symbol*] [*Library of Congress*] (LCLS)
UME .... Unpredictable Main Event
UME .... Urethane Mixing Equipment
UMEA .... Universal Medical Esperanto Association (EA-IO)
UMEA .... Universala Medicina Esperanto Asocio [*Universal Medical Esperanto Association*] (EA-IO)
UMEA Psychol Rep ... UMEA Psychological Reports [*A publication*]
UMEA Psychol Reports ... UMEA Psychological Reports [*A publication*]
UMEB .... United Maritime Executive Board
UMEC .... Union Mondiale des Enseignants Catholiques [*World Union of Catholic Teachers*] [*Rome, Italy*]
UMED .... Unimed, Inc. [*NASDAQ symbol*] (NQ)
UMEJ .... Union Mondiale des Etudiants Juifs [*World Union of Jewish Students - WUJS*] (EA-IO)
UMES .... University of Maryland, Eastern Shore
UmF .... National Cash Register Co., New York, NY [*Library symbol*] [*Library of Congress*] (LCLS)
UMF .... Ultramicrofiche
UMF .... Uniform Magnetic Field
UMF .... University of Maine at Farmington, Farmington, ME [*OCLC symbol*] (OCLC)
UMFC .... United Methodist Free Churches
Umform Tech ... Umform Technik [*A publication*]
UMFP .... Unit Materiel Fielding Point [*Army*] (RDA)
UMFS .... United Mutual Fund Selector [*United Business Service Co.*]
UMG .... Universal Machine Gun (MCD)
UMG .... Universal Matchbox Group Ltd. [*NYSE symbol*]
UMG .... Universal Mercator Grid (NVT)
UMHE .... United Ministries in Higher Education [*Later, UME*] (EA)
UMHK .... Union Miniere du Haut Katanga [*Mining Company of Upper Katanga*]
UMHP .... Union Mondiale des Societes d'Histoire Pharmaceutique [*World Organization of Societies of Pharmaceutical History*]
UMHS .... University of Miami. Hispanic Studies [*A publication*]
UMI .... Udruzena Metalna Industrija [*Belgrade, Yugoslavia*]
UMI .... Ukrainian Music Institute in America
UMI .... Underway Material Inspection [*Navy*] (NVT)
UMI .... Union Mathematique Internationale [*International Mathematical Union - IMU*] (EA-IO)
UMI .... Union Mundial pro Interlingua (EA)
UMI .... Unit Movement Identifier [*Army*] (AABC)
UMI .... University Microfilms International Article Clearinghouse [*UTLAS symbol*]
UMi .... Ursa Minor [*Constellation*]
U Miami L Rev ... University of Miami. Law Review [*A publication*]
UMICH ...... University of Michigan
U Mich Bus R ... University of Michigan. Business Review [*A publication*]
U Mich J Law Reform ... University of Michigan. Journal of Law Reform [*A publication*]
U Mich J L Ref ... University of Michigan. Journal of Law Reform [*A publication*]
UMIFA .... Uniform Management of Institutional Funds Act [*National Conference of Commissioners on Uniform State Laws*]
UMin .... Ursa Minor [*Constellation*]
UMINF .... United Movement of Iranian National Forces (EA)
UMIP .... Uniform Material Issue Priority [*Navy*]
UMIPS .... Uniform Material Issue Priority System [*Navy*] (NG)
UMIS .... Urban Management Information System
U Missouri at KCL Rev ... University of Missouri at Kansas City. Law Review [*A publication*]
UMIST .... University of Manchester Institute of Science and Technology [*British*] [*Databank originator and research institute*]
UMJ .... Ukrainian Mathematical Journal [*A publication*]
UMJL .... Union Mondiale pour un Judaisme Liberal

UMJOA .... Ulster Medical Journal [*A publication*]
UMK .... University of Missouri at Kansas City, Kansas City, MO [*OCLC symbol*] (OCLC)
UMKC .... University of Missouri at Kansas City
UMKCLR ... University of Missouri at Kansas City. Law Review [*A publication*]
UMKC L Rev ... University of Missouri at Kansas City. Law Review [*A publication*]
UML .... Universal Mission Load [*Military*] (AABC)
UML .... University of Missouri, Columbia School of Library and Information Science, Columbia, MO [*OCLC symbol*] (OCLC)
U of MLB ... University of Missouri. Law Bulletin (DLA)
UMLC .... Institute of Estate Planning, University of Miami Law Center (DLA)
UMLC .... Universal Multiline Controller
UMLC .... University of Miami Law Center (DLA)
UMLER ...... Universal Machine Language Equipment Register [*Association of American Railroads*] [*Washington, DC*]
UMLR .... University of Malaya. Law Review [*A publication*]
UMLR .... University of Miami. Law Review [*A publication*]
UMLRB ...... University of Miami. Law Review [*A publication*]
UMLS .... Ukrajins'ka Mova i Literatura v Skoli [*A publication*]
UMM .... Summit, AK [*Location identifier*] [*FAA*] (FAAL)
UMM .... United Merchants & Manufacturers, Inc. [*NYSE symbol*]
UMM .... Universal Measuring Machine
UMM .... University of Manitoba Medical Library [*UTLAS symbol*]
UM-MaP ...... University of Maryland Mathematics Project
UMMC .... Union Metal Manufacturing [*NASDAQ symbol*] (NQ)
UMMH .... Unscheduled Maintenance Manhours (MCD)
UMMIPS .... Uniform Materiel Movement and Issue Priority System [*Military*] (AFM)
UMMJ .... University of Manitoba. Medical Journal [*A publication*]
UMML .... Unione Medicale Mediterranea Latina [*Latin Mediterranean Medical Union - LMMU*] (EA-IO)
UMML .... University of Miami Marine Laboratory [*Florida*]
UMMZ .... University of Michigan Museum of Zoology
UMN .... Monett, MO [*Location identifier*] [*FAA*] (FAAL)
UMN .... Union pour la Majorite Nouvelle [*Union for the New Majority*] [*French*] (PPE)
UMN .... Union des Musiciens Nordiques [*Nordic Musicians' Union - NMU*] (EA-IO)
UMN .... Unsatisfactory Material Notice (MSA)
UMN .... Upper Motor Neuron [*Medicine*]
UMNL .... Upper Motor Neuron Lesion [*Neurology*]
UMNO .... United Malays National Organization [*Political party*] [*Malaysian*]
UMO .... Unconventional Military Operations (MCD)
UMO .... University of Maine, Orono
UMO .... Unmanned Orbital [*NASA*] (NASA)
U MO B Law Ser ... University of Missouri. Bulletin. Law Series (DLA)
U MO Bull L Ser ... University of Missouri. Bulletin. Law Series (DLA)
UMOC .... Ugly Man on Campus [*Contest*]
UMOFC ..... Union Mondiale des Organisations Feminines Catholiques [*World Union of Catholic Women's Organizations*]
U MO-Kansas City L Rev ... University of Missouri at Kansas City. Law Review [*A publication*]
U MO KCL Rev ... University of Missouri at Kansas City. Law Review [*A publication*]
UMOL .... Unmanned Orbital Laboratory
U MO L Bull ... University of Missouri. Law Bulletin (DLA)
UMOS .... U-Grooved Metal Oxide Semiconductors (MCD)
UMoS .... University of Missouri. Studies [*A publication*]
UMOSBESL ... Union Mondiale des Organisations Syndicales sur Base Economique et Sociale Liberale [*World Union of Liberal Trade Union Organizations*]
UMOSEA .... Union Mondiale pour la Sauvegarde de l'Enfance et de l'Adolescence [*World Union for the Safeguard of Youth*]
UMP .... Umpire (DSUE)
UMP .... Uniformly Most Powerful Test [*Statistics*]
UMP .... Union of Moderate Parties [*Vanuatuan*] (PPW)
UMP .... Upper Mantle Project
UMP .... Upper Merion & Plymouth Railroad Co. [*AAR code*]
UMP .... Upward Mobility Program
UMP .... Uridine Monophosphate [*Biochemistry*]
UMPAL ...... University of Minnesota. Pamphlets on American Literature [*A publication*]
UMPAW ...... University of Minnesota. Pamphlets on American Writers [*A publication*]
UMPEAL .... University of Miami. Publications in English and American Literature [*A publication*]
UMpGS ...... Church of Jesus Christ of Latter-Day Saints, Genealogical Society Library, Mount Pleasant Branch, Stake Center, Mount Pleasant, UT [*Library symbol*] [*Library of Congress*] (LCLS)
UMPLL .... University of Michigan. Publications in Language and Literature [*A publication*]
UMPR .... Uniform Military Personnel Record (AFM)
UMPT .... Ultrahigh-Frequency Multi-Platform Transceiver [*Navy*] (MCD)
UMpW .... Wasatch Academy, Mount Pleasant, UT [*Library symbol*] [*Library of Congress*] (LCLS)

UMR .... Ultraviolet Mitogenic Radiation
UMR .... Unimar Co. [*American Stock Exchange symbol*]
UMR .... Unipolar Magnetic Regions
UMR .... Unit Mail Room [*Air Force*]   (AFM)
UMR .... University of Missouri at Rolla
UMR .... University of Missouri at Rolla, Library, Rolla, MO [*OCLC symbol*]   (OCLC)
UMR .... Unsatisfactory Material Reports [*Military*]   (AABC)
UMR .... Upper Maximum Range
UMR .... Usual Marketing Requirement [*Business and trade*]
UMR .... Woomera [*Australia*] [*Airport symbol*]   (OAG)
UMRB .... Upper Mississippi River Basin
UMRCC ..... Upper Mississippi River Conservation Committee   (EA)
UMREL ...... Upper Midwest Regional Educational Laboratory, Inc.
UMR-MEC Conf Energy Resour Proc ... UMR-MEC [*University of Missouri, Rolla - Missouri Energy Council*] Conference on Energy Resources. Proceedings [*A publication*]
UMRR .... University of Missouri Research Reactor
UMS .... Ukrajins'ka Mova v Skoli [*A publication*]
UMS .... Ultrasonic Motion Sensor   (MCD)
UMS .... Undersea Medical Society [*Later, UHMS*]   (EA)
UMS .... Unfederated Malay States
UMS .... United Missionary Society
UMS .... Universal Maintenance Standards
UMS .... Universal Memory System [*Intel Corp.*]
UMS .... Universal Micro Systems [*San Rafael, CA*] [*Software manufacturer*]
UMS .... Universal Military Service
UMS .... University of Maine. Studies [*A publication*]
UMS .... University of Michigan. Studies [*A publication*]
UMS .... University of Missouri at St. Louis, St. Louis, MO [*OCLC symbol*]   (OCLC)
UMS .... University of Missouri. Studies [*A publication*]
UMS .... Unmanned Multifunction Satellite
UMS .... Upstream Modulation Sequence [*Genetics*]
UMSA .... Utah-Manhattan-Sundt & Associates   (AAG)
UMSB .... United Missouri Bancshares [*NASDAQ symbol*]   (NQ)
Umschau ... Umschau in Wissenschaft und Technik [*A publication*]
Umsch Fortschr Wiss Tech ... Umschau ueber die Fortschritte in Wissenschaft und Technik [*A publication*]
Umsch Wiss Tech ... Umschau in Wissenschaft und Technik [*A publication*]
UMSDC ...... Unscheduled Maintenance Sample Data Collection   (MCD)
UMSE .... Unconditional Mean Square Error [*Statistics*]
UMSE .... University of Mississippi. Studies in English [*A publication*]
UMSE .... Unmanned Surveillance Equipment
UMSHS ..... University of Michigan. Studies. Humanistic Series [*A publication*]
UMSN .... Union Mondiale de Ski Nautique [*World Water Ski Union - WWSU*]   (EA-IO)
UMSOA ..... Umi To Sora [*A publication*]
UMSP .... User Maintenance Support Plan   (MCD)
UMSPA ...... Uniform Metric System Procedure Act [*National Conference of Commissioners on Uniform State Laws*]
UMSR .... Universal Movement for Scientific Responsibility [*See also MURS*]   (EA-IO)
UMSSS ...... UDAM [*Universal Digital Avionics Module*] Microprocessor Software Support System   (MCD)
UMT .... Ultrasonic Material Testing
UMT .... Umiat, AK [*Location identifier*] [*FAA*]   (FAAL)
UMT .... Union Marocaine du Travail [*Moroccan Labor Union*]
UMT .... Unit of Medical Time [*Each 4-hour period after 40-hour work week*] [*British*]
UMT .... United Methodist Today [*A publication*]
UMT .... Universal Microwave Trainer
UMT .... Universal Military Training [*Participants known as Umtees*] [*Army*] [*Post World War II*]
UMTA .... Urban Mass Transportation Act [*1964*]
UMTA .... Urban Mass Transportation Administration [*Department of Transportation*]
UMTD .... Using Mails to Defraud
UMTR .... Universal Movement Theater Repertory [*Defunct*]
UMTR .... University of Maryland Teaching Reactor   (NRCH)
UMTRAP .... Uranium Mill Trailings Remedial Action Program [*Department of Energy*]
UMTRI .... University of Michigan Transportation Research Institute [*Research center*]   (RCD)
UMTRIS...... Urban Mass Transportation Research Information Service [*National Academy of Sciences*] [*Washington, DC*] [*Database*]
UMTRI (Univ Mich Transportation Research Inst) ... UMTRI (University Michigan Transportation Research Institute) Research Review [*A publication*]
UMTS .... Universal Military Training Service [*or System*]   (GPO)
UMTSA ...... Universal Military Training and Service Act
UMu........... Murray Public Library, Murray, UT [*Library symbol*] [*Library of Congress*]   (LCLS)
UMU .... Uplink Multiplexer Unit   (MCD)
UMUKY ...... Universal Money Center plc ADR [*NASDAQ symbol*]   (NQ)
UMUS........ Unbleached Muslin
UMVF .... Union Mondiale des Voix Francaises [*World Union of French-Speakers - WUFS*]   (EA-IO)

UMVF .... Unmanned Vertical Flight [*NASA*]   (NASA)
UMW .... Ultramicrowaves
UMW .... Upper Midwest
UMWA....... International Union, United Mine Workers of America   (EA)
Umwelt (Inf Bundesminist Innern) ... Umwelt (Informationen des Bundesministers des Innern zur Umweltplanung und zum Umweltschutz) [*A publication*]
Umwelt-Rep ... Umwelt-Report [*A publication*]
Umweltschutz Gesundheitstech ... Umweltschutz. Gesundheitstechnik [*A publication*]
Umweltschutz - Staedtereinig ... Umweltschutz - Staedtereinigung [*A publication*]
Umwelt Z Biol Stn Wilhelminenberg ... Umwelt Zeitschrift der Biologischen Station. Wilhelminenberg [*A publication*]
UMW J........ United Mine Workers. Journal [*A publication*]
UMWLA...... Umwelt Zeitschrift der Biologischen Station. Wilhelminenberg [*A publication*]
Umw Planungsrecht ... Umwelt- und Planungsrecht [*A publication*]
UMWTA...... Umwelt [*A publication*]
UMx........... University of Mexico [*A publication*]
UMZHA ..... Ukrainskii Matematicheskii Zhurnal [*A publication*]
UN .... Nephi Public Library, Nephi, UT [*Library symbol*] [*Library of Congress*]   (LCLS)
UN .... Unable   (FAAC)
UN .... Unassigned [*Telecommunications*]   (TEL)
UN .... Underworld Nobility [*Used by Walter Winchell to refer to mobsters in television series "The Untouchables"*]
UN .... Unico National [*An association*]   (EA)
UN .... Unified   (AAG)
UN .... Unilever NV [*NYSE symbol*]
UN .... Union   (MSA)
UN .... Union Flag [*Navy*] [*British*]
UN .... Union Nacional [*National Union*] [*Spanish*]   (PPE)
UN .... Union Nationale [*National Union*] [*Political party*] [*Canada*]
UN .... Unit   (AAG)
UN .... United
UN .... United Nations
UN .... University
UN .... Unknown [*Telecommunications*]   (TEL)
UN .... Urea-Nitrogen [*Medicine*]
UNA........... Ukrainian National Association   (EA)
UNA........... Unalaska [*Alaska*] [*Seismograph station code, US Geological Survey*] [*Closed*]   (SEIS)
UNA........... Underwear-Negligee Associates [*Formed by a merger of Lingerie Salesmen Association and Underwear Salesmen Association*] [*New York, NY*]   (EA)
UNA........... Unione Nazionale dell'Avicoltura [*Aviculture Union*] [*Rome, Italy*]
UNA........... United Nations Association
UNA........... United Native Americans [*El Cerrito, CA*]   (EA)
UNA........... United States Naval Academy, Annapolis, MD [*OCLC symbol*]   (OCLC)
UNA........... Universal Night Answering [*Telecommunications*]   (TEL)
UNAAA...... Ukrainian National Aid Association of America   (EA)
UNAAF ...... Unified Action Armed Forces [*Military*]
UNAB .... Unabridged   (ADA)
Unabashed Libn ... Unabashed Librarian [*A publication*]
UNABR ...... Unabridged
UNAC .... United Nations Appeal for Children
UNACC ..... Unaccompanied
UNACOM ... Universal Army Communication System
UNACOMA ... Unione Nazionale Costruttori Macchine Agricole [*Farm Machinery Manufacturers Union*] [*Rome, Italy*]
UNA Commun ... UNA [*Utah Nurses Association*] Communique [*A publication*]
UNADE....... Union Nacional Democratica [*National Democratic Union*] [*Ecuadorean*]   (PPW)
UNADS....... UNIVAC Automated Documentation System [*Data processing*]
UNAEC....... United Nations Atomic Energy Commission [*Superseded by Disarmament Commission, 1952*]
UNAECC .... United Nations Atomic Energy Control Commission
UNAF......... Universities National Antiwar Fund
UNAFEI ..... United Nations Asia and Far East Institute for the Prevention of Crime and Treatment of Offenders
UNAFPA..... Union des Associations des Fabricants de Pates Alimentaires de la Communaute Economique Europeenne [*Union of Organizations of Manufacturers of Pasta Products in the European Economic Community*]
UNAGA ..... Union Agriculture [*A publication*]
UNAH .... Universidad Nacional Autonoma, Tegucigalpa [*Honduras*]
UNAIS .... United Nations Association International Service [*British*]
UNAKI....... Union des Colons Agricoles du Kivu [*Union of Agricultural Settlers of Kivu*] [*Congo - Leopoldville*]
UNALC....... User Network Access Link Control
UNALOT..... Unallotted   (AABC)
UNALTD..... Unaltered   (ROG)
UNAMACE ... Universal Automatic Map Compilation Equipment
UNAMAP.... Users Network for Applied Modeling of Air Pollution [*Set of computer simulation models being developed by Battelle for EPA*]

UNAMI........ Uniao Nacional Africana de Mocambique Independente [*Political party*] [*Mozambican*]

UNAN .... Unanimous

UNANSD .... Unanswered (ROG)

UNA Nursing J ... UNA Nursing Journal [*Royal Victorian College of Nursing*] [*A publication*]

UNA Nurs J ... UNA [*Utah Nurses Association*] Nursing Journal [*A publication*]

UNAP .... Union Nationale Progressite [*National Progressive Union*] [*Burundi*]

UNAPEC .... United Nations Action Program for Economic Cooperation

Un Apic ...... Union Apicole [*A publication*]

UNAPOC .... United National Association of Post Office Craftsmen [*Later, APWU*]

UNAPPD..... Unappointed (ROG)

UNAPV .... Unable to Approve (FAAC)

UNAR .... Unable to Approve Altitude Requested [*Aviation*] (FAAC)

UNAR .... Union Nationale Ruandaise [*Ruanda National Union*]

UNARU....... Union Nationale Africaine du Ruanda-Urundi [*African National Union of Ruanda-Urundi*]

UNASA....... Unasylva [*A publication*]

UNASABEC ... Union Nationale des Syndicats Agricoles Forestiers, des Bois, de l'Elevage, et la Peche du Cameroun [*National Union of Farmers, Fishermen, Forest Guards, and Timber Workers of Cameroon*]

UNASGD .... Unassigned (AABC)

UNASGN .... Unassigned [*Navy*] (NVT)

UNASSD .... Unassembled

UNAT .... Union Nationale des Agriculteurs Tunisiens [*National Union of Tunisian Farmers*]

UNATAC .... Union d'Assistance Technique pour l'Automobile et la Circulation Routiere [*Union of Technical Assistance for Motor Vehicle and Road Traffic*] (EA-IO)

UNATRACAM ... Union des Associations Traditionelles du Cameroun [*Union of Traditional Associations of Cameroon*]

UNATRACO ... Union Nationale des Travailleurs du Congo [*National Union of Workers of the Congo*]

UNATT .... Unattached (ROG)

UNATT .... Unattended (ADA)

UNATTRIB ... Unattributed

UNA-USA... United Nations Association of the United States of America

Unauth .... Unauthorized (DLA)

UNAUTHD ... Unauthorized (AABC)

UNAVBL..... Unavailable (FAAC)

UNAVIC..... United Nations Audiovisual Information Center

UNB............ Fredericton [*New Brunswick*] [*Seismograph station code, US Geological Survey*] (SEIS)

UNB............ Kanab, UT [*Location identifier*] [*FAA*] (FAAL)

UNB............ Unbound (ROG)

UNB............ United Nations Beacon

UNB............ Universal Navigation Beacon

UNB............ University of New Brunswick [*Canada*]

UNB............ University of New Brunswick Library [*UTLAS symbol*]

UNBAL ...... Unbalanced [*Telecommunications*] (TEL)

UNBC .... Union National Corporation [*NASDAQ symbol*] (NQ)

UnBCh .... United Board Chaplain [*Navy*] [*British*]

UNBCL .... University of Nebraska College of Law (DLA)

UNBIS .... United Nations Bibliographic Information System [*United Nations Headquarters*] [*New York, NY*] (EISS)

UNBJ.......... United National Bank of Central Jersey [*NASDAQ symbol*] (NQ)

UNB Law Journal ... University of New Brunswick. Law Journal [*A publication*]

UNB L J ...... University of New Brunswick. Law Journal [*A publication*]

UNBLK .... Unblanking (MSA)

UNBLSJ..... University of New Brunswick. Law School. Journal (DLA)

UNBSA ...... United Nations Bureau of Social Affairs

UNBTAO ... United Nations Bureau of Technical Assistance Operations

UN Bul....... United Nations Bulletin [*A publication*]

UN Bull...... United Nations Bulletin [*A publication*]

UNC............ UNC, Inc. [*Formerly, United Nuclear Corporation*] [*NYSE symbol*]

Unc............. Uncanny Stories [*A publication*]

UNC............ Uncertain (ADA)

UNC............ Uncirculated [*Numismatics*]

UNC............ Unclassified (KSC)

UNC............ Uncle (DSUE)

UNC............ Unified Coarse [*Thread*]

UNC............ Union Nationale Camerounaise [*Cameroon National Union*]

UNC............ United Corporations Ltd. [*Toronto Stock Exchange symbol*]

UNC............ United National Convention [*Ghanaian*] (PPW)

UNC............ United Nations Command

UNC............ United Network Company [*New TV broadcasting network*]

UNC............ United New Conservationists (EA)

UNC............ Universal Navigation Computer

UNC............ University of North Carolina

UNC............ University of Northern Colorado [*Formerly, Colorado State College*] [*Greeley*]

UNC............ Uranyl Nitrate Concentrate [*Nuclear energy*]

UNCA .... United Nations Correspondents Association [*New York, NY*] (EA)

UNCA .... United Neighborhood Centers of America [*Formerly, NFS, NFS & CA*] (EA)

UNCACK.... United Nations Civil Assistance Command, Korea

UNCAFE..... United Nations Commission for Asia and the Far East

UNCAH....... National Union of Authentic Peasants of Honduras (PD)

UNCAST .... United Nations Conference on Applications of Science and Technology [*1963*]

UNCASTD ... United Nations Advisory Committee on the Application of Science and Technology to Development (ASF)

UNCAT....... Uncatalogued (ADA)

UNCC........ Unable to Contact Company Radio (FAAC)

UNCC........ Union Nationale des Cheminots du Cameroun [*National Union of Railway Workers of Cameroon*]

UNCCP...... United Nations Conciliation Commission for Palestine

UNCDF...... United Nations Capital Development Fund

UNCE .... United Nations Commission for Europe

UNCERT.... Uncertainty [*Standard deviation*] [*Data processing*]

UNCF .... United Negro College Fund (EA)

UNCG........ Uncage

UNCHBP ... Center for Housing, Building, and Planning [*United Nations*]

UNCHE...... United Nations Conference on the Human Environment (MSC)

UNCHR....... United Nations High Commissioner for Refugees (DLA)

UN Chron ... United Nations Chronicle [*A publication*]

UNCHS...... United Nations Center for Human Settlements [*Information broker*] [*Kenya*]

UNCI.......... United Nations Committee on Information (EA)

UNCIO....... United Nations Conference on International Organization [*San Francisco, 1945*]

UNCIP .... United Nations Commission for India and Pakistan

UNCITRAL ... United Nations Commission on International Trade Law

UNCIVPOL ... United Nations Civilian Police [*Peace-keeping force in Cyprus*]

UNCIWC ... United Nations Commission for Investigation of War Criminals

UNCLAS .... Unclassified (AABC)

UNCLE ...... United Network Command for Law and Enforcement [*Fictitious intelligence organization in various television series*]

UNCLOS .... United Nations Conference on the Law of the Sea

UNCLP .... Unclamp

UNCM .... User Network Control Machine

UNCMAC ... United Nations Command Military Armistice Commission

UNCN .... United Nations Censorship Network

UNCOA ...... UNESCO [*United Nations Educational, Scientific, and Cultural Organization*] Courier [*A publication*]

UNCOD ...... United Nations Conference on Desertification

UNCOK ...... United Nations Committee on Korea

UNCOL ...... Universal Computer Oriented Language [*Programing language*] [*Data processing*]

uncomp..... Uncomplicated

uncon......... Unconscious

uncond...... Unconditioned

UNCONDL ... Unconditional (ROG)

UNCONFD ... Unconfirmed (ROG)

Unconsol Laws ... Unconsolidated Laws (DLA)

UNCOPUOS ... United Nations Committee on the Peaceful Uses of Outer Space

uncorr .... Uncorrected

Uncov......... Uncover

UNCP .... United Nations Conference of Plenipotentiaries

UNCR .... United Nations Command (Rear)

UNCR .... University of North Carolina. Record. Research in Progress [*A publication*]

UNCRD...... United Nations Center for Regional Development

UNCSCL .... University of North Carolina. Studies in Comparative Literature [*A publication*]

UNCSF ...... United Nations Command Security Force [*Military*] (INF)

UNCSGL .... University of North Carolina. Studies in Germanic Languages and Literatures [*A publication*]

UNCSGLL ... University of North Carolina. Studies in Germanic Languages and Literatures [*A publication*]

UNCSRL..... University of North Carolina. Studies in the Romance Languages and Literatures [*A publication*]

UNCSRLL... University of North Carolina. Studies in the Romance Languages and Literatures [*A publication*]

UNCSTD .... United Nations Conference on Science and Technology for Development [*1979*]

UNCT .... Unctus [*Smeared*] [*Pharmacy*]

UNCT .... Uncut (ROG)

UNCTAD ... United Nations Conference on Trade and Development

UNCTD....... Uncoated

UNCURK ... United Nations Commission for the Unification and Rehabilitation of Korea

UND............ Kunduz [*Afghanistan*] [*Airport symbol*] [*Obsolete*] (OAG)

UND............ Undecaprenol [*Organic chemistry*]

UND............ Under (AAG)

und .... Undetermined [*MARC language code*] [*Library of Congress*] (LCCP)

Und .... Undivided (DLA)

UND............ Union Nationale et Democratique [*National Democratic Union*] [*Monegasque*] (PPW)

UND............ Unit Derating [*Electronics*] (IEEE)

UND............ University of National Defense [*Formerly, Industrial College of the Armed Forces and National War College*]

UND .... University of North Dakota, Grand Forks, ND [*OCLC symbol*] (OCLC)

UND .... University of Notre Dame [*Indiana*] (KSC)

UND .... Urgency of Need Designator (AFM)

UND .... User Need Date (KSC)

UNDA .... Uniform Narcotic Drug Act [*National Conference of Commissioners on Uniform State Laws*]

UNDAT .... United Nations Development Advisory Team

UNDBK .... Undivided Back [*Deltiology*]

UNDC .... Undercurrent

UNDC .... United Nations Disarmament Commission [*Also, DC, DC(UN)*]

UNDCC ...... United Nations Development Cooperation Cycle

Und Child ... Understanding the Child [*A publication*]

Und Ch Pr ... Underhill's Chancery Procedure [*1881*] (DLA)

Und Conv ... Underhill on New Conveyancing [*1925*] (DLA)

UNDED .... Undercurrents [*A publication*]

UNDED .... Undereducated

UNDEF .... Undefined

UNDEL .... Unione Nazionale Dipendenti Enti Locali [*National Union of Local Government Employees*] [*Italy*]

UNDELORDCAN ... Undelivered Orders Cancelled [*Military*]

Undercur ... Undercurrents [*A publication*]

Underground Eng ... Underground Engineering [*A publication*]

Underground Min Symp ... Underground Mining Symposia [*A publication*]

Underground Water Conf Aust Newsl ... Underground Water Conference of Australia. Newsletter [*A publication*]

Undergr Wat Supply Pap (Tasm) ... Underground Water Supply Papers (Tasmania) [*A publication*]

Underhill Ev ... Underhill on Evidence (DLA)

UNDERSD ... Undersigned (ROG)

Undersea Biomed Res ... Undersea Biomedical Research [*A publication*]

Undersea Technol ... Undersea Technology [*A publication*]

UNDERSECNAV ... Under Secretary of the Navy

Under Sign ... Under the Sign of Pisces/Anais Nin and Her Circle [*A publication*]

UNDERSTG ... Understanding (ROG)

UNDERTG ... Undertaking (ROG)

Underwater Inf Bull ... Underwater Information Bulletin [*A publication*]

Underwater J ... Underwater Journal [*A publication*]

Underwater J Inf Bull ... Underwater Journal and Information Bulletin [*A publication*]

Underwater J & Inf Bull ... Underwater Journal and Information Bulletin [*A publication*]

Underwater Nat ... Underwater Naturalist [*A publication*]

Underwater Sci Technol J ... Underwater Science and Technology Journal [*A publication*]

Underw J Inf Bull ... Underwater Journal and Information Bulletin [*A publication*]

Underwriters Lab Stand ... Underwriters Laboratories. Standards [*A publication*]

Underwrit Lab Bull Res ... Underwriters Laboratories. Bulletin of Research [*A publication*]

UNDET .... Undetermined

UNDETM .... Undetermined (AABC)

UNDEX .... Underwater Explosion [*Navy*]

UNDEX .... United Nations Index [*A publication*]

UNDF .... Underfrequency

UNDG .... Undergoing (AABC)

UNDH .... Unit Derated Hours [*Electronics*] (IEEE)

UNDHR .... United Nations Declaration of Human Rights (BJA)

UNDI .... United Nations Document Index

UNDK .... Undock [*NASA*] (KSC)

UNDLD .... Undelivered (FAAC)

UNDLD .... Underload

UNDO .... Ukrainian National Democratic Organization

UNDO .... Union for National Draft Opposition

UN Doc .... United Nations Documents (DLA)

Und-Oder-Nor & Steuerungstech ... Und-Oder-Nor und Steuerungstechnik [*A publication*]

Und-Oder-Nor Steuerungstech ... Und-Oder-Nor und Steuerungstechnik [*A publication*]

UNDOF .... United Nations Disengagement Observer Force [*Damascus, Syria*]

UNDP .... University of Notre Dame Press

Und Part ..... Underhill on Parternship [*10th ed.*] [*1975*] (DLA)

UNDP/FAO Pakistan Nat For Res Train Proj Rep ... UNDP [*United Nations Development Programme*]/FAO [*Food and Agriculture Organization of the United Nations*] Pakistan National Forestry Research and Training Project Report [*A publication*]

UNDRO .... Office of the United Nations Disaster Relief Co-Ordinator (EA-IO)

Und Torts ... Underhill on Torts (DLA)

Und Tr .... Underhill on Trusts and Trustees (DLA)

UNDV .... Undervoltage

UNDW .... Underwater (KSC)

UNDWC ...... Ultrasonically Nebulized Distilled Water Challenge

UNE .... Qacha's Nek [*Lesotho*] [*Airport symbol*] (OAG)

UNE .... Underground Nuclear Explosion

UNE .... United Nations European Headquarters [*Geneva, Switzerland*]

UNE .... Universal Nonlinear Element

UNE .... University of North Dakota, Law Library, Grand Forks, ND [*OCLC symbol*] (OCLC)

UNEA .... Unearth [*A publication*]

UNEASICO ... Union des Etudiants et Anciens des Instituts Sociaux de Congo [*Congolese Union of Students and Former Students of Social Institutes*]

UNEC .... Union Nationale des Etudiants Camerounais [*National Union of Cameroonese Students*]

UNEC .... United Nations Education Conference

UNEC .... Unnecessary (FAAC)

UNECA .... United Nations Economic Commission for Africa (EA)

UNECO .... Union Economique du Congo [*Economic Union of the Congo*] [*Usumbura*]

UNECOLAIT ... Union Europeenne du Commerce Laitier [*European Milk Trade Union*] [*Common Market*]

UN Econ Comm Asia Far East Water Resour Ser ... United Nations Economic Commission for Asia and the Far East. Water Resources Series [*A publication*]

UN Econ Comm Eur Comm Agr Prob Work Party Mech Agr AGRI/WP ... United Nations Economic Commission for Europe. Committee on Agricultural Problems. Working Party on Mechanization of Agriculture AGRI/WP [*A publication*]

UN Econo Comm Asia Far East Miner Resour Develop Ser ... United Nations Economic Commission for Asia and the Far East. Mineral Resources Development Series [*A publication*]

UNEDA .... United Nations Economic Development Administration

UN (Educ Sci Cult Organ) Cour ... UNESCO (United Nations Educational, Scientific, and Cultural Organization) Courier [*A publication*]

UNEEG .... Union Nationale des Eleves et Etudiants de la Guadeloupe [*National Union of Pupils and Students of Guadeloupe*] (PD)

UNEEM ...... Union Nationale des Eleves et Etudiants du Mali [*National Union of Pupils and Students of Mali*] (PD)

UNEF .... Unified Extra Fine [*Thread*]

UNEF .... United Nations Emergency Force [*to separate hostile forces of Israel and Egypt*]

UNEF .... United Nations Environment Fund

UNEGA .... Union Europeenne des Fondeurs et Fabricants de Corps Gras Animaux [*European Union of Animal Fat Producers*] (EA)

UNEM .... Union Nationale des Etudiants du Maroc [*National Union of Moroccan Students*] (PD)

Unempl Ins Rep ... Unemployment Insurance Reports [*Commerce Clearing House*] (DLA)

Unempl Ins Rep (CCH) ... Unemployment Insurance Reports [*Commerce Clearing House*] (DLA)

Unemployment Ins Statis ... Unemployment Insurance Statistics [*A publication*]

Unempl Unit Bull Briefing ... Unemployment Unit Bulletin and Briefing [*A publication*]

UNEP .... United Nations Environment Programme [*Nairobi, Kenya*] (EA-IO)

UNEP .... United Nations Environmental Program [*Nairobi, Kenya*] [*Database originator*]

UNEP/IRS ... United Nations Environmental Program/International Referral System

UNEPPA ..... United Nations Environment Program Participation Act of 1973

UNERG .... United Nations Conference on New and Renewable Sources of Energy [*1981*]

UNESCO .... United Nations Educational, Scientific, and Cultural Organization [*Paris, France*] [*Database originator and operator*] [*Research center*]

UNESCO B Li ... UNESCO [*United Nations Educational, Scientific, and Cultural Organization*] Bulletin for Libraries [*A publication*]

UNESCO Bul Lib ... UNESCO [*United Nations Educational, Scientific, and Cultural Organization*] Bulletin for Libraries [*A publication*]

UNESCO Bull Lib ... UNESCO [*United Nations Educational, Scientific, and Cultural Organization*] Bulletin for Libraries [*A publication*]

UNESCO Cour ... UNESCO [*United Nations Educational, Scientific, and Cultural Organization*] Courier [*A publication*]

UNESCO Inf Circ ... Australian National Advisory Committee for UNESCO [*United Nations Scientific, Educational, and Cultural Organization*]. Information Circular [*A publication*]

UNESCO J Inf Sci Librarianship and Arch Adm ... UNESCO [*United Nations Educational, Scientific, and Cultural Organization*] Journal of Information Science, Librarianship, and Archives Administration [*A publication*]

UNESCO Nat Resour Res ... United Nations Educational, Scientific, and Cultural Organization. Natural Resources Research [*A publication*]

UNESCOR ... United Nations Economic and Social Council Official Record (DLA)

UNESCO Tech Pap Mar Sci ... UNESCO [*United Nations Educational, Scientific, and Cultural Organization*] Technical Papers in Marine Science [*A publication*]

UNESEM .... Union Europeenne des Sources d'Eaux Minerales du Marche Commun [*European Union of Natural Mineral Water Sources of the Common Market*] [*Paris, France*] (EA-IO)

UNESOB .... United Nations Economic and Social Office in Beirut

UNET .... United Energy Technology [*NASDAQ symbol*] (NQ)

UNETAS ..... United Nations Emergency Technical Aid Service

UNETPSA ... United Nations Educational and Training Program for Southern Africa
UNEV .... Unevaluated (MCD)
unev .... Uneven [*Quality of the bottom*] [*Nautical charts*]
U Newark L Rev ... University of Newark. Law Review (DLA)
U New South Wales LJ ... University of New South Wales. Law Journal [*A publication*]
UNEX .... Unexecuted
UNEXPL ..... Unexplained
UNEXPL ..... Unexploded
UNEXPL ..... Unexplored
UNEXSO ...... International Underwater Explorers Society (EA)
UNF .... Unfused (KSC)
UNF .... Unified Fine [*Thread*]
UNF .... Unifirst Corp. [*NYSE symbol*]
UNF .... Union Flights [*Sacramento, CA*] [*FAA designator*] (FAAC)
UNF .... Union Freight R. R. [*AAR code*]
UNF .... United National Front [*Lebanese*] (BJA)
UNF .... Universal National Fine (MCD)
UNF .... University of North Dakota, Medical Library, Grand Forks, ND [*OCLC symbol*] (OCLC)
UNFAO .... United Nations Food and Agriculture Organization
UNFAV .... Unfavorable
UNFB .... United Nations Film Board
UNFC .... Universal Fuels Company [*NASDAQ symbol*] (NQ)
UNFDAC .... United Nations Fund for Drug Abuse Control
UNFF .... United First Federal Savings & Loan [*NASDAQ symbol*] (NQ)
UNFGA .... Unternehmensforschung [*A publication*]
UNFI .... Unfinished
UNFI .... Unifi, Inc. [*NASDAQ symbol*] (NQ)
UNFIN .... Unfinished
UNFKA .... Uspekhi Nauchnoi Fotografii [*A publication*]
UNFO .... Unidentified Nonflying Objects
UNFP .... Union Nationale des Forces Populaires [*National Union of Popular Forces*] [*Political party*] [*Morocco*]
UNFP .... United National Federal Party [*Zimbabwean*] (PPW)
UNFPA .... United Nations Fund for Population Activities [*New York, NY*]
UNFSSTD ... United Nations Financing System for Science and Technology for Development
UNFT .... Union Nationale des Femmes de Tunisie [*National Union of Tunisian Women*]
UNFTP .... Unified Navy Field Test Program (MCD)
UNFURNOTE ... Until Further Notice
UNG .... Kiunga [*Papua New Guinea*] [*Airport symbol*] (OAG)
UNG .... Ungava [*Canada*]
UNG .... Unguentum [*Ointment*] [*Pharmacy*]
UNG .... Union Gas Ltd. [*American Stock Exchange symbol*] [*Delisted*] [*Toronto Stock Exchange symbol*]
UNGA .... United Nations General Assembly (MCD)
UNGAOR .... United Nations General Assembly Official Record (DLA)
UNGEGN .... United Nations Group of Experts on Geographical Names
Ungerer's Bull ... Ungerer's Bulletin [*A publication*]
Un of Gh LJ ... University of Ghana. Law Journal (DLA)
UNGR .... Ungermann-Bass, Inc. [*NASDAQ symbol*] (NQ)
UNGT .... Unguentum [*Ointment*] [*Pharmacy*]
Ung Z Berg Huettenwes Bergbau ... Ungarische Zeitschrift fuer Berg und Huettenwesen. Bergbau [*A publication*]
UNH .... United Homes, Inc. [*Vancouver Stock Exchange symbol*]
UNH .... Uranyl Nitrate Hexahydrate [*Inorganic chemistry*]
UNHC .... United Nations High Commission (BJA)
UNHCC ...... University of New Haven Computer Center [*West Haven, CT*] [*Research center*] (RCD)
UNHCR .... United Nations High Commission [*or Commissioner*] for Refugees [*Geneva, Switzerland*]
UNHJ .... University of Newcastle. Historical Journal [*A publication*]
UNHQ .... United Nations Headquarters (DLA)
UNHRC ...... United Nations Human Rights Commission (BJA)
UNHRD .... Unheard (FAAC)
UNI .... Athens/Albany, OH [*Location identifier*] [*FAA*] (FAAL)
Uni .... Unicorn [*Record label*]
UNI .... Unicorp Canada Corp. [*Toronto Stock Exchange symbol*]
UNI .... Uniform (DSUE)
UNI .... Union Island [*Windward Islands*] [*Airport symbol*] (OAG)
UNI .... Union Nationale des Independants [*National Union of Independents*] [*Monegasque*] (PPE)
UNI .... United News of India Ltd.
UNI .... United States International Airways
UNI .... Unity Railways Co. [*AAR code*]
Uni .... Universe Science Fiction [*A publication*]
UNI .... University (ADA)
UNI .... University of Northern Iowa (OICC)
UNIA .... Universal Negro Improvement Association [*Organization led by Marcus Aurelius Garvey*]
UNIADUSEC ... Union Internationale des Associations de Diplomes Universitaires en Sciences Economiques et Commerciales
UNIAPAC ... Union Internationale Chretienne des Dirigeants d'Entreprise [*International Christian Union of Business Executives*] (EA-IO)
UNIATEC ... Union Internationale des Associations Techniques Cinematographiques [*International Union of Technical Cinematograph Associations - IUTCA*] (EA-IO)

UNIBID .... UNISIST International Centre for Bibliographic Descriptions [*UNESCO*] [*Information service*] [*Paris, France*] (EISS)
UNIBUS ...... Universal Bus [*Digital Equipment Corp.*]
UNIC .... Union Internationale des Cinemas [*International Union of Cinemas*] (EA-IO)
UNIC .... United International Club, Inc.
UNIC .... United Nations Information Centre
UNICA .... Association of Caribbean Universities and Research Institutes (EA)
UNICA .... Union Internationale du Cinema Non Professionnel [*International Union of Amateur Cinema*] (EA-IO)
UNICAP ..... Universidade Catolica de Pernambuco [*Brazil*]
UNICCAP ... Universal Cable Circuit Analysis Program [*Bell System*]
UNICE .... Union des Industries de la Communaute Europeenne [*Union of Industries of the European Community*]
UNICEF ..... United Nations Children's Fund [*Acronym taken from former name: United Nations International Children's Emergency Fund*]
UNICHAL ... Union Internationale des Distributeurs de Chaleur [*International Union of Heat Distributors*] (EA-IO)
UNICIS ...... Unit Concept Indexing System
UNICIV Rep ... UNICIV [*School of Civil Engineering, University of New South Wales*] Report [*A publication*]
UNICO .... Union pour les Interets du Peuple Congolais [*Union for the Interests of the Congolese People*]
UNICO .... Universal Cooperatives [*An association*] (EA)
UNICOCYM ... International Association of Bicycle and Motorcycle Trade and Repair (EA-IO)
UNICOCYM ... Union Internationale du Commerce et de la Reparation du Cycle et du Motocycle [*International Union of Cycle and Motocycle Trade and Repair*]
UNICOL ...... Union des Colons de la Province Orientale [*Union of Settlers in Orientale Province*]
UNICOM ..... Underwater Integration Communication
UNICOM ..... Unidad Informativa Computable [*Computerized Information Unit*] [*Mexico*] [*Information service*] (EISS)
UNICOM ..... Unified Communications [*Radio station*]
UNICOM ..... Universal Components [*Construction*]
UNICOM ..... Universal Integrated Communication System [*Military*]
UNICOMP ... Universal Compiler (IEEE)
UNICON ..... Unidensity Coherent Light Recording (IEEE)
Unicorn J ... Unicorn Journal [*A publication*]
UNICYP ...... United Nations International Force, Cyprus
UNID .... Unidentified (FAAC)
UNIDA .... Unidia [*A publication*]
UNIDAHO ... Union des Independants du Dahomey [*Independents Union of Dahomey*]
UNIDENT ... Unidentified
UNIDF .... United Nations Industrial Development Fund
UNIDO .... United Nations Industrial Development Organization [*Vienna, Austria*] [*Information service*] (EISS)
UNIDROIT ... Institut International pour l'Unification du Droit Prive [*International Institute for the Unification of Private Law*] (EA-IO)
Unidroit Yb ... International Institute for the Unification of Private Law. Yearbook [*Rome, Italy*] (DLA)
UNIEF .... USEUCOM [*United States European Command*] Nuclear Interface Element Fastbreak (MCD)
UNIEP .... Union Internationale des Entrepreneurs de Peinture [*International Union of Master Painters - IUMP*] (EA-IO)
Unif .... Unified (DLA)
UNIF .... Uniflex, Inc. [*NASDAQ symbol*] (NQ)
UNIF .... Uniform (AFM)
UNIF .... Uniformity
UNIFAC ...... Universal Functional Activity Coefficient [*Chemical engineering*]
Unif C Code ... Uniform Commercial Code Law Journal [*A publication*]
UNIFE .... Union des Industries Ferroviaires Europeennes [*Union of European Railway Industries*] (EA)
UNIFET ...... Unipolar Field-Effect Transistor
UNIFIL .... United Nations Interim Force in Lebanon [*Naqoura*]
Unif L Conf ... Proceedings, Uniform Law Conference of Canada (DLA)
UNIFOR ...... Unified Forces [*Military*]
UNIFORCE ... United Defense Force [*Established by the Brussels Treaty*] (NATG)
Uniform City Ct Act ... Uniform City Court Act (DLA)
Uniform Dist Ct Act ... Uniform District Court Act (DLA)
UNI-FREDI ... Universal Flight Range and Endurance Data Indicator
Unif Sys Citation ... Uniform System of Citation (DLA)
UNIGABON ... Union Interprofessionnelle du Gabon [*Inter-Trade Union of Gabon*]
UNILAC ...... Universal Linear Accelerator
unilat .... Unilateral
Uni Ljubljai Teh Fak Acta Tech Ser Chim ... Univerza v Ljubljani Tehniska Fakulteta Acta Technica. Series Chimica [*A publication*]
UNIMA .... Union Internationale de Grands Magasins [*International Union of Department Stores*]
UNIMA .... Union Internationale de la Marionette [*International Puppeteers Union*]

UNIMA........ Unione Nazionale Imprese di Meccanizzazione Agricola [*Agricultural Mechanization Enterprises Union*] [*Rome, Italy*]

UNIMARC .. Universal Machine Readable Cataloging   (ADA)

UNIMA-USA ... American Center of the Union Internationale de la Marionnette [*International Puppeteers Union*]   (EA)

UNIMERC... Universal Numeric Coding System [*Distilling industry*]

UNIMOD..... Unified Modular Plant [*Nuclear energy*]

UNIN.......... Unilife Corp. [*NASDAQ symbol*]   (NQ)

Un Ins Co ... Unemployment Insurance Code   (DLA)

UNIO .... United Nations Information Organization

Union Agric ... Union Agriculture [*A publication*]

Union Burma J Life Sci ... Union of Burma. Journal of Life Sciences [*A publication*]

Union Burma J Sci and Technol ... Union of Burma. Journal of Science and Technology [*A publication*]

Union Burma J Sci Technol ... Union of Burma. Journal of Science and Technology [*A publication*]

Union Carbide Met Rev ... Union Carbide Metals Review [*A publication*]

UNION FLEURS ... Union Internationale du Commerce de Gros en Fleurs [*International Union of the Wholesale Flower Trade*]

Union Int Sci Biol Ser A Gen ... Union Internationale des Sciences Biologiques. Serie A. Generale [*A publication*]

Union Int Sci Biol Ser B (Colloq) ... Union Internationale des Sciences Biologiques. Serie B (Colloques) [*A publication*]

Union Med Can ... Union Medicale du Canada [*A publication*]

Union Med Mexico ... Union Medica de Mexico [*A publication*]

Union Med (Paris) ... Union Medicale (Paris) [*A publication*]

Union Oceanogr Fr ... Union des Oceanographes de France [*France*] [*A publication*]

Union Pac LDB ... Union Pacific Law Department. Bulletin   (DLA)

Union Pharm ... Union Pharmaceutique [*A publication*]

Union Rec ... Union Recorder [*A publication*]

Union S Afr Dep Commer Ind Div Fish Invest Rep ... Union of South Africa. Department of Commerce and Industries. Division of Fisheries. Investigational Report [*A publication*]

Union Soc Fr Hist Nat Bull Trimest ... Union des Societes Francaises d'Histoire Naturelle. Bulletin Trimestriel [*A publication*]

Union S Q R ... Union Seminary. Quarterly Review [*A publication*]

Union Tank Car Co Graver Water Cond Div Tech Repr ... Union Tank Car Company. Graver Water Conditioning Division. Technical Reprint [*A publication*]

Union Univ Q ... Union University Quarterly [*A publication*]

UNIP .... United National Independence Party [*Zambian*]   (PD)

UNIP .... United National Independence Party [*Trinidadian and Tobagan*]   (PPW)

UNIPAC..... Unified Prediction and Analysis Code   (MCD)

UNIPAC..... Unit Packaging

UNIPAC..... Universal Payload Accommodation Capsule

UNIPEDE.... Union Internationale de Producteurs et Distributeurs d'Energie Electrique [*International Union of Producers and Distributors of Electrical Energy*]

UNIPI.......... Unione Industriali Pastai Italiani [*Pasta Manufacturers Union*] [*Rome, Italy*]

UNIPOCONGO ... Union des Populations Rurales du Congo [*Union of Rural People of the Congo*]

UNIPOL ...... Universal Problem-Oriented Language [*Data processing*]   (MCD)

UNIPOL ...... Universal Procedure-Oriented Language

UNIPRO...... Unite et Progres du Burundi [*Unity and Progress of Burundi*]

UNIPRO...... Universal Processor [*Data processing*]

UNIPZ......... United National Independence Party of Zambia

Uni of Q LR ... University of Queensland. Law Review [*A publication*]

UNIQUAC... Universal Quasichemical [*Chemical engineering*]

UNIQUE...... Uniform Inquiry Update Element

UNIR.......... Unemployment Insurance Review [*A publication*]

UNIR.......... Union de Izquierda Revolucionaria [*Union of the Revolutionary Left*] [*Peruvian*]   (PPW)

UNIR.......... Union Nationale pour l'Initiative et la Responsabilite [*National Union for Initiative and Responsibility*] [*French*]   (PPW)

UNIR.......... United-Guardian, Inc. [*NASDAQ symbol*]   (NQ)

UNIRAC..... Union Involved Racketeering [*FBI undercover investigation*]

UNIRAR...... Universal Radio Relay

UNIS .... Ukrainian National Information Service   (EA)

UNIS .... Underwater Television and Inspection System

UNIS .... Unison

UNIS .... United Nations Information Service

UNIS .... United Nations International School

UNISA .... University of South Africa

UNISAP...... UNIVAC Share Assembly Program [*Sperry UNIVAC*] [*Data processing*]   (IEEE)

UNISCAMTA ... Union Territoriale des Syndicats de Cadres, Agents de Maitrise, Techniciens, et Assimiles du Senegal [*Territorial Union of Leaders, Supervising Personnel, and Related Workers of Senegal*]

UNISCAN... United Kingdom and Scandinavia   (NATG)

UNISCO ..... Union des Interets Sociaux Congolais [*Congolese Union of Social Interests*]

UNISIST ..... Universal System for Information in Science and Technology [*UNESCO*] [*Zagreb, Yugoslavia*]

UNISOR...... University Isotope Separator at Oak Ridge

UNISPACE ... United Nations Conference on the Exploration and Peaceful Uses of Outer Space

UNISPEC ... Universal Spectroscopy [*Trademark*] [*Kevex Corp.*]

UNISTAR.... UNIVAC Storage and Retrieval System [*Sperry UNIVAC*] [*Data processing*]

UNISTAR.... User Network for Information Storage, Transfer Acquisition, and Retrieval   (MCD)

UNISTAT.... University Science Statistics Project [*Moshman Associates, Inc.*] [*Information service*]   (EISS)

UNISTOCK ... Union Professionnelle des Stockeurs de Cereales dans la CEE [*Organization of Cereal Storage Firms in the European Economic Community*]

UNISURV G Rep ... UNISURV G Report. School of Surveying. University of New South Wales [*A publication*]

UNISURV Rep ... UNISURV Report. School of Surveying. University of New South Wales [*A publication*]

UNISWEP... Unified Switching Equipment Practice   (MCD)

UNIT .... Unitarian

UNIT .... Universal Numerical Interchange Terminal

UNITA .... Uniao Nacional para a Independencia Total de Angola [*National Union for the Complete Independence of Angola*]

Unit Aborig Messenger ... United Aborigines' Messenger [*A publication*]

Unita R .... Unitarian Review [*A publication*]

UNITAS....... United International Antisubmarine Warfare

Uni-Taschenb ... Uni-Taschenbuecher [*A publication*]

Uni of Tas LR ... University of Tasmania. Law Review [*A publication*]

United Dent Hosp Syd Inst Dent Res Annu Rep ... United Dental Hospital of Sydney. Institute of Dental Research. Annual Report [*A publication*]

United Fresh Fruit Veg Assoc Yearb ... United Fresh Fruit and Vegetable Association. Yearbook [*A publication*]

United Plant Assoc South India Sci Dep Bull ... United Planters' Association of Southern India. Scientific Department. Bulletin [*A publication*]

United Service Q ... United Service Quarterly [*A publication*]

United Serv Rev ... United Services Review [*A publication*]

UNITEL...... Universal Teleservice [*Satellite information service*]

UNITEL...... University Information Technology Corporation [*MIT-Harvard*]

UNITNG...... Unit Training   (NVT)

UNITOPOS ... Unit to Which Ordered Will Operate in an Overseas Area a Contemplated Continuous Period of One Year or More [*Military*]

UNITOR...... United Nations International TOKAMAK Reactor [*Proposed experimental fusion power plant*]

UNITRAC ... Universal Trajector Compiler   (IEEE)

UNITREP.... Unit Status and Identity Report [*DoD*]

UNIUM........ Union Nationale des Intellectuels et Universitaires Malgaches [*National Union of Intellectuals and University People of Madagascar*]

UNIV .... Universal   (AFM)

UNIV .... Universalist

Univ .... Universitas [*A publication*]

UNIV .... University   (AFM)

Univ .... Universo [*A publication*]

UNIVA .... Universitas [*A publication*]

Univ Abidjan Dep Geol Ser Doc ... Universite d'Abidjan. Departement de Geologie. Serie Documentation [*A publication*]

UNIVAC...... Universal Automatic Computer [*Remington Rand Corp.*] [*Early computer*]

Univ Agric Sci (Bangalore) Curr Res ... University of Agricultural Sciences (Bangalore). Current Research [*A publication*]

Univ Agric Sci (Bangalore) Misc Ser ... University of Agricultural Sciences (Bangalore). Miscellaneous Series [*A publication*]

Univ Agric Sci (Bangalore) Res Ser ... University of Agricultural Sciences (Bangalore). Research Series [*A publication*]

Univ Agric Sci (Hebbal Bangalore) Annu Rep ... University of Agricultural Sciences (Hebbal Bangalore). Annual Report [*A publication*]

Univ Agric Sci (Hebbal Bangalore) Ext Ser ... University of Agricultural Sciences (Hebbal Bangalore). Extension Series [*A publication*]

Univ Agric Sci (Hebbal Bangalore) Stn Ser ... University of Agricultural Sciences (Hebbal Bangalore). Station Series [*A publication*]

Univ Agric Sci (Hebbal Bangalore) Tech Ser ... University of Agricultural Sciences (Hebbal Bangalore). Technical Series [*A publication*]

Univ Alaska Inst Mar Sci Rep ... University of Alaska. Institute of Marine Science. Report [*A publication*]

Univ Alberta Agric Bull ... University of Alberta. Agriculture Bulletin [*A publication*]

Univ Alberta Agric For Bull ... University of Alberta. Agriculture and Forestry Bulletin [*A publication*]

Univ Alberta Dep Civ Eng Struct Eng Rep ... University of Alberta. Department of Civil Engineering. Structural Engineering Report [*A publication*]

Univ Alberta Fac Agric Bull ... University of Alberta. Faculty of Agriculture. Bulletins [*A publication*]

Univ Alger Trav Inst Rech Sahariennes ... Universite d'Alger. Travaux. Institut de Recherches Sahariennes [*A publication*]

Univ Allahabad Stud ... University of Allahabad. Studies [*A publication*]

Univ Allahabad Stud Biol Sect ... University of Allahabad. Studies. Biology Section [*A publication*]

Univ Allahabad Stud Bot Sect ... University of Allahabad. Studies. Botany Section [*A publication*]

Univ Allahabad Stud Chem Sect ... University of Allahabad. Studies. Chemistry Section [*A publication*]

Univ Allahabad Stud Math Sect ... University of Allahabad. Studies. Mathematics Section [*A publication*]

Univ Allahabad Stud Phys Sect ... University of Allahabad. Studies. Physics Section [*A publication*]

Univ Allahabad Stud Zool Sect ... University of Allahabad. Studies. Zoology Section [*A publication*]

Univ Ankara Fac Agri Publ ... Universite d'Ankara. Faculte de l'Agriculture. Publications [*A publication*]

Univ Ankara Fac Sci Commun Ser A ... Universite d'Ankara. Faculte des Sciences. Communications. Serie A. Mathematiques, Physique, et Astronomie [*A publication*]

Univ Ankara Fac Sci Commun Ser A2 ... Universite d'Ankara. Faculte des Sciences. Communications. Serie A2. Physique [*A publication*]

Univ Ankara Fac Sci Commun Ser C ... Universite d'Ankara. Faculte des Sciences. Communications. Serie C. Sciences Naturelles [*A publication*]

Univ Ankara Yearb Fac Agric ... University of Ankara. Yearbook. Faculty of Agriculture [*A publication*]

Univ Antioquia ... Universidad de Antioquia [*Colombia*] [*A publication*]

UNIVAR ...... Universal Valve Action Recorder

Univ Ariz Coop Ext Serv Bull ... University of Arizona. Cooperative Extension Service. Bulletin [*A publication*]

Univ Ariz Coop Ext Serv Circ ... University of Arizona. Cooperative Extension Service. Circular [*A publication*]

Univ Ariz Coop Ext Serv Ser P ... University of Arizona. Cooperative Extension Service. Series P [*A publication*]

Univ Arkansas Eng Exp Stn Res Rep Ser ... University of Arkansas. Engineering Experiment Station. Research Report Series [*A publication*]

Univ Austral Chile Fac Cienc Agrar Agro Sur ... Universidad Austral de Chile. Facultad de Ciencias Agrarias. Agro Sur [*A publication*]

Univ Auton Barcelona Col Univ Gerona Secc Cienc An ... Universidad Autonoma de Barcelona. Colegio Universitario de Gerona. Seccion de Ciencias. Anales [*A publication*]

Univ Baghdad Nat Hist Res Cent Annu Rep ... University of Baghdad. Natural History Research Center. Annual Report [*A publication*]

Univ Baghdad Nat Hist Res Cent Publ ... University of Baghdad. Natural History Research Center. Publication [*A publication*]

Univ Bahia Esc Geol Publ Avulsa ... Universidade de Bahia. Escola de Geologia. Publicacao Avulsa [*A publication*]

Univ B Aires Fac Agron Vet Bol Tec Inf ... Universidad de Buenos Aires. Facultad de Agronomia y Veterinaria. Boletin Tecnico Informativo [*A publication*]

Univ BC Res For Annu Rep ... University of British Columbia. Research Forest. Annual Report [*A publication*]

Univ Beograd Publ Elektrotehn Fak Ser Mat Fiz ... Univerzitet u Beogradu. Publikacije Elektrotehnickog Fakulteta. Serija Matematika i Fizika [*A publication*]

Univ Beograd Tehn Fiz ... Univerzitet u Beogradu. Tehnicka Fizika [*A publication*]

Univ Beograd Zb Radova Gradevin Fak ... Univerzitet u Beogradu. Zbornik Radova Gradevinskog Fakulteta u Beogradu [*A publication*]

Univ Bergen Arb (Naturv R) ... Universitetet i Bergen Arbok (Naturvitenskapelig Rekke) [*A publication*]

Univ Bergen Arbok Med Rekke ... Universitetet i Bergen Arbok Medisinsk Rekke [*A publication*]

Univ Bergen Arbok Naturvitensk Rekke ... Universitetet i Bergen Arbok Naturvitenskapelig Rekke [*A publication*]

Univ Bergen Arsmeld ... Universitetet i Bergen Arsmelding [*A publication*]

Univ Bergen Med Avh ... Universitetet i Bergen Medisinske Avhandlinger [*A publication*]

Univ Bergen Skr ... Universitetet i Bergen Skrifter [*A publication*]

Univ Botswana Swaziland Agric Res Div Annu Rep ... University of Botswana, Swaziland. Agricultural Research Division. Annual Report [*A publication*]

Univ Bras Cent Estud Zool Avulso ... Universidade do Brasil. Centro de Estudos Zoologicos Avulso [*A publication*]

Univ Brasov Lucrari Stiint ... Universitatea din Brasov. Lucrari Stiintifice [*A publication*]

Univ of Brit Columbia L Rev ... University of British Columbia. Law Review [*A publication*]

Univ Bruxelles Inst Phys Bull ... Universite de Bruxelles. Institut de Physique. Bulletin [*A publication*]

Univ Buenos Aires Fac Agrom Vet Bol ... Universidad de Buenos Aires. Facultad de Agronomia y Veterinaria. Boletin [*A publication*]

Univ Buenos Aires Inst Anat Publ ... Universidad de Buenos Aires. Instituto de Anatomia. Publicacion [*A publication*]

UNIVC .... Universal Energy Corporation [*NASDAQ symbol*] (NQ)

Univ Calicut Zool Monogr ... University of Calicut. Zoological Monograph [*A publication*]

Univ Calif Agric Ext Serv ... University of California. Agricultural Extension Service [*A publication*]

Univ Calif (Berkeley) Publ Agric Sci ... University of California (Berkeley). Publications in Agricultural Sciences [*A publication*]

Univ Calif (Berkeley) Publ Bot ... University of California (Berkeley). Publications in Botany [*A publication*]

Univ Calif (Berkeley) Publ Eng ... University of California (Berkeley). Publications in Engineering [*A publication*]

Univ Calif (Berkeley) Publ Entomol ... University of California (Berkeley). Publications in Entomology [*A publication*]

Univ Calif (Berkeley) Publ Health ... University of California (Berkeley). Publications in Public Health [*A publication*]

Univ Calif (Berkeley) Publ Pharmacol ... University of California (Berkeley). Publications in Pharmacology [*A publication*]

Univ Calif (Berkely) Publ Pathol ... University of California (Berkeley). Publications in Pathology [*A publication*]

Univ Calif Bull ... University of California. Bulletin [*A publication*]

Univ of Calif Davis L Rev ... University of California at Davis. Law Review [*Davis, California*] (DLA)

Univ Calif Div Agric Sci Bull ... University of California. Division of Agricultural Sciences. Bulletin [*A publication*]

Univ Calif Div Agric Sci Leafl ... University of California. Division of Agricultural Sciences. Leaflet [*A publication*]

Univ Calif Lawrence Livermore Lab Rep ... University of California. Lawrence Livermore Laboratory. Report [*A publication*]

Univ California Los Angeles L Rev ... University of California at Los Angeles. Law Review [*Los Angeles, California*] (DLA)

Univ Calif Publ Bot ... University of California. Publications in Botany [*A publication*]

Univ of Calif Publ in English Ling M Ph ... University of California. Publications in English, Linguistics, Modern Philology [*A publication*]

Univ Calif Publ Entomol ... University of California. Publications in Entomology [*A publication*]

Univ Calif Publ Geol Sci ... University of California. Publications in Geological Sciences [*A publication*]

Univ Calif Publications Zool ... University of California. Publications in Zoology [*A publication*]

Univ Calif Publ Zool ... University of California. Publications in Zoology [*A publication*]

Univ Calif Sea Water Convers Lab Rep ... University of California. Sea Water Conversion Laboratory. Report [*A publication*]

Univ Calif Univ Los Angeles Publ Biol Sci ... University of California. University at Los Angeles. Publications in Biological Sciences [*A publication*]

Univ Calif Univ Los Angeles Publ Math Phys Sci ... University of California. University at Los Angeles. Publications in Mathematical and Physical Sciences [*A publication*]

Univ Calif Water Resour Cent Contrib ... University of California. Water Resources Center. Contribution [*A publication*]

Univ Camb Dep Appl Biol Mem Rev Ser ... University of Cambridge. Department of Applied Biology. Memoirs. Review Series [*A publication*]

Univ Cambridge Dep Eng Rep CUDE/A-Aerodyn ... University of Cambridge. Department of Engineering. Report. CUDE [*Cambridge University Department of Engineering*]/A-Aerodynamics [*A publication*]

Univ Cambridge Dep Eng Rep CUDE/A-Thermo ... University of Cambridge. Department of Engineering. Report. CUDE [*Cambridge University Department of Engineering*]/A-Thermo [*A publication*]

Univ Cambridge Dep Eng Rep CUDE/A-Turbo ... University of Cambridge. Department of Engineering. Report. CUDE [*Cambridge University Department of Engineering*]/A-Turbo [*A publication*]

Univ Cambridge Inst Anim Pathol Rep Dir ... University of Cambridge. Institute of Animal Pathology. Report of the Director [*A publication*]

Univ Canterbury Publ ... University of Canterbury. Publications [*A publication*]

Univ Cathol Louvain Fac Sci Agron Lab Biochim Nutr Publ ... Universite Catholique de Louvain. Faculte des Sciences Agronomiques. Laboratoire de Biochimie de la Nutrition. Publication [*A publication*]

Univ Cathol Louv Inst Agron Mem ... Universite Catholique de Louvain. Institut Agronomique. Memoires [*A publication*]

Univ Cent Desert Stud Trans (Jodhpur India) ... University Centre of Desert Studies. Transactions (Jodhpur, India) [*A publication*]

Univ Cent Venez Inst Mater Modelos Estruct Bol Tec ... Universidad Central de Venezuela. Instituto de Materiales y Modelos Estructurales. Boletin Tecnico [*A publication*]

Univ of Chicago L Rev ... University of Chicago. Law Review [*A publication*]

Univ Chicago Publ ... University of Chicago. Publications [*A publication*]

Univ Chicago Rep ... University of Chicago. Reports [*A publication*]

Univ Chic L ... University of Chicago. Law Review [*A publication*]

Univ Chic M ... University of Chicago. Magazine [*A publication*]

Univ Chic Rec ... University of Chicago. Record [*A publication*]

Univ of Chi Law Rev ... University of Chicago. Law Review [*A publication*]

Univ Chile Dep Prod Agric Publ Misc Agric ... Universidad de Chile. Departamento de Produccion Agricola. Publicaciones Miscelaneas Agricolas [*A publication*]
Univ Chile Fac Agron Dep Sanid Veg Bol Tec ... Universidad de Chile. Facultad de Agronomia. Departamento Sanidad Vegetal. Boletin Tecnico [*A publication*]
Univ Chile Fac Agron Publ Misc Agric ... Universidad de Chile. Facultad de Agronomia. Publicaciones Miscelaneas Agricolas [*A publication*]
Univ Chile Fac Cienc Fis Mat An ... Universidad de Chile. Facultad de Ciencias Fisicas y Matematicas. Anales [*A publication*]
Univ Chile Fac Cienc Fis Mat Inst Geol Publ ... Universidad de Chile. Facultad de Ciencias Fisicas y Matematicas. Instituto de Geologia. Publicacion [*A publication*]
Univ Chile Fac Cienc For Bol Tec ... Universidad de Chile. Facultad de Ciencias Forestales. Boletin Tecnico [*A publication*]
Univ Chile Fac Quim Farm Tesis Quim Farm ... Universidad de Chile. Facultad de Quimica y Farmacia. Tesis de Quimicos Farmaceuticos [*A publication*]
Univ Chile Inst Invest Ensayes Mater Inf Tec ... Universidad de Chile. Instituto de Chile. Instituto de Investigaciones y Ensayes de Materiales. Informe Tecnico [*A publication*]
Univ of Cincinnati L Rev ... University of Cincinnati. Law Review [*A publication*]
Univ Cincin Stud ... University of Cincinnati. Studies [*A publication*]
Univ of Cinc Law Rev ... University of Cincinnati. Law Review [*A publication*]
Univ Coll Dublin Agric Fac Rep ... University College Dublin. Agricultural Faculty. Report [*A publication*]
Univ Coll Dublin Fac Gen Agric Res Rep ... University College of Dublin. Faculty of General Agriculture. Research Report [*A publication*]
Univ Coll Wales (Aberystwyth) Memorandum ... University College of Wales (Aberystwyth). Memorandum [*A publication*]
Univ of Colorado L Rev ... University of Colorado. Law Review [*A publication*]
Univ of Colo Studies ... University of Colorado. Studies [*A publication*]
Univ Colo Stud Ser Anthropol ... University of Colorado. Studies. Series in Anthropology [*A publication*]
Univ Colo Stud Ser Biol ... University of Colorado. Studies. Series in Biology [*A publication*]
Univ Colo Stud Ser Chem Pharm ... University of Colorado. Studies. Series in Chemistry and Pharmacy [*A publication*]
Univ Colo Stud Ser D ... University of Colorado. Studies. Series D. Physical and Biological Sciences [*A publication*]
Univ Colo Stud Ser Earth Sci ... University of Colorado. Studies. Series in Earth Sciences [*A publication*]
Univ Col Stud ... University of Colorado. Studies [*A publication*]
Univ Conn Occas Pap Biol Sci Ser ... University of Connecticut. Occasional Papers. Biological Science Series [*A publication*]
Univ Craiova An Ser 3 ... Universitatea din Craiova. Analele. Seria a/3. Stiinte Agricole [*A publication*]
Univ Craiova An Ser Biol Med Stiinte Agric ... Universitatea din Craiova. Analele. Seria. Biologie, Medicina, Stiinte Agricole [*A publication*]
Univ Craiova An Ser Mat Fiz Chim Electroteh ... Universitatea din Craiova. Analele. Seria. Matematica, Fizica, Chimie, Electrotehnica [*A publication*]
Univ D .... Doctor of the University
Univ Debaters Annual ... University Debaters' Annual [*A publication*]
Univ Del Mar Lab Inf Ser Publ ... University of Delaware. Marine Laboratories. Information Series Publication [*A publication*]
Univ Durham King's Coll Dep Civ Eng Bull ... University of Durham. King's College. Department of Civil Engineering. Bulletin [*A publication*]
Univ Edinb Pfizer Med Monogr ... University of Edinburgh. Pfizer Medical Monographs [*A publication*]
UNIVER ...... Universal Inverter and Register (MCD)
Universe Nat Hist Ser ... Universe Natural History Series [*A publication*]
Universitas (Bogota) ... Universitas Pontificia Universidad Catolica Javeriana (Bogota) [*A publication*]
Universities Q ... Universities Quarterly [*A publication*]
University of Singapore School of Archre Jnl ... University of Singapore. School of Architecture. Journal [*A publication*]
University of Southern Calif School of Archre Yearbook ... University of Southern California. School of Architecture. Yearbook [*A publication*]
Univ Fed Pernambuco Inst Biocienc Publ Avulsa ... Universidade Federal de Pernambuco. Instituto de Biociencias. Publicacao Avulsa [*A publication*]
Univ Fed Pernambuco Inst Micol Publ ... Universidade Federal de Pernambuco. Instituto de Micologia. Publicacao [*A publication*]
Univ Fed Pernambuco Mem Inst Biocienc ... Universidade Federal de Pernambuco. Memorias do Instituto de Biociencias [*A publication*]
Univ Fed Rio De Janeiro Inst Geocienc Geol Bol ... Universidade Federal do Rio De Janeiro. Instituto de Geociencias. Geologia. Boletim [*A publication*]

Univ Fed Rio De J Inst Geocienc Bol Geol ... Universidade Federal do Rio De Janeiro. Instituto de Geociencias. Boletim Geologia [*A publication*]
Univ Fed Rio De J Inst Geocienc Dep Geol Contrib Dida ... Universidade Federal do Rio De Janeiro. Instituto de Geociencias. Departamento de Geologia. Contribuicao Didatica [*A publication*]
Univ Fed Rural Rio Grande Do Sul Dep Zootec Bol Tec ... Universidade Federal Rural do Rio Grande Do Sul. Departamento do Zootecnia. Boletim Tecnico [*A publication*]
Univ Fed Vicosa Bibl Centr Ser Bibliogr Espec ... Universidade Federal de Vicosa. Biblioteca Central. Serie Bibliografias Especializadas [*A publication*]
Univ Fed Vicosa Ser Tec Bol ... Universidade Federal de Vicosa. Serie Tecnica. Boletin [*A publication*]
Univ Ferrara Mem Geopaleontol ... Universita di Ferrara. Memorie Geopaleontologiche [*A publication*]
Univ Fla Agric Ext Serv Circ ... University of Florida. Agricultural Extension Service. Circular [*A publication*]
Univ Fla Coastal Oceanogr Eng Lab Rep UFL COEL TR ... University of Florida. Coastal and Oceanographic Engineering Laboratory. Report. UFL/COEL/TR [*A publication*]
Univ Fla Coop Ext Serv Bull ... University of Florida. Cooperative Extension Service. Bulletin [*A publication*]
Univ Fla Inst Food Agric Sci Annu Res Rep ... University of Florida. Institute of Food and Agricultural Sciences. Annual Research Report [*A publication*]
Univ Fla Inst Food Agri Sci Publ ... University of Florida. Institute of Food and Agricultural Sciences. Publication [*A publication*]
Univ Fla Inst Gerontol Ser ... University of Florida. Institute of Gerontology Series [*A publication*]
Univ Fla Publ Biol Sci Ser ... University of Florida. Publications. Biological Science Series [*A publication*]
Univ Fla Water Resour Res Cent Publ ... University of Florida. Water Resources Research Center. Publication [*A publication*]
Univ of Florida L Rev ... University of Florida. Law Review [*A publication*]
Univ Fl SSM ... University of Florida. Social Sciences Monograph [*A publication*]
Univ For Bois (Sopron) Publ Sci ... Universite Forestiere et du Bois (Sopron). Publications Scientifiques [*A publication*]
Univ Forst Holzwirtsch (Sopron) Wiss Mitt ... Universitaet fuer Forst- und Holzwirtschaft (Sopron). Wissenschaftliche Mitteilungen [*A publication*]
Univ For Timber Ind (Sopron) Sci Publ ... University of Forestry and Timber Industry (Sopron). Scientific Publications [*A publication*]
Univ F Study ... University Film Study Center. Newsletter [*A publication*]
Univ Gaz .... University Gazette [*University of Melbourne*] [*A publication*]
Univ Genova Pubbl Ist Mat ... Universita di Genova. Pubblicazioni dell'Istituto di Matematica [*A publication*]
Univ Geograd Radovi Zavoda za Fiz ... Univerzitet u Geogradu Radovi. Zavoda za Fiziku [*A publication*]
Univ Ghana Agric Irrig Res Stn (Kpong) Annu Rep ... University of Ghana. Agricultural Irrigation Research Station (Kpong). Annual Report [*A publication*]
Univ Ghana Agric Res Stn (Kpong) Annu Rep ... University of Ghana. Agricultural Research Station (Kpong). Annual Report [*A publication*]
Univ of Ghana LJ ... University of Ghana. Law Journal [*London, England*] (DLA)
Univ de Grenoble Annales n s Sci ... Universite de Grenoble. Sciences-Medecine. Annales [*A publication*]
Univ Hawaii Coll Trop Agric Dep Pap ... University of Hawaii. College of Tropical Agriculture. Departmental Paper [*A publication*]
Univ Hawaii Coop Ext Ser Misc Publ ... University of Hawaii. Cooperative Extension Service. Miscellaneous Publication [*A publication*]
Univ Hawaii Hawaii Inst Geophys Bienn Rep ... University of Hawaii. Hawaii Institute of Geophysics. Biennial Report [*A publication*]
Univ Hawaii Hawaii Inst Geophys Rep HIG ... University of Hawaii. Hawaii Institute of Geophysics. Report HIG [*A publication*]
Univ Hawaii Occas Pap ... University of Hawaii. Occasional Papers [*A publication*]
Univ Hawaii Res Publ ... University of Hawaii. Research Publications [*A publication*]
Univ Hisp An Ser Med ... Universidad Hispalense. Anales. Serie Medicina [*A publication*]
Univ H Sch J ... University High School. Journal [*A publication*]
Univ Human Rights ... Universal Human Rights [*A publication*]
Univ Hum Rts ... Universal Human Rights [*A publication*]
Univ IL Law ... University of Illinois. Law Forum [*A publication*]
Univ of Illinois L Forum ... University of Illinois. Law Forum [*A publication*]
Univ Ill L Forum ... University of Illinois. Law Forum [*A publication*]
Univ Ill Urbana-Champaign Water Resour Cent Res Rep ... University of Illinois at Urbana-Champaign. Water Resources Center. Research Report [*A publication*]
Univ Ill Urbana-Champaign Water Resour Cent Spec Rep ... University of Illinois at Urbana-Champaign. Water Resources Center. Special Report [*A publication*]
Univ Indore Res J Sci ... University of Indore. Research Journal. Science [*A publication*]

Univ Ind Santander Bol Geol ... Universidad Industrial de Santander. Boletin de Geologia [*A publication*]

Univ Iowa Monogr Studies in Med ... University of Iowa. Monographs. Studies in Medicine [*A publication*]

Univ Iowa Stud Nat Hist ... University of Iowa. Studies in Natural History [*A publication*]

Univ J Busan Natl Univ ... University Journal. Busan National University [*South Korea*] [*A publication*]

Univ J of Business ... University Journal of Business [*A publication*]

Univ J Nat Sci Ser ... University Journal. Natural Sciences Series. Busan National University [*Republic of Korea*] [*A publication*]

Univ Kansas Sci Bull ... University of Kansas. Science Bulletin [*A publication*]

Univ Kans Mus Nat Hist Misc Publ ... University of Kansas. Museum of Natural History. Miscellaneous Publication [*A publication*]

Univ Kans Mus Nat Hist Monogr ... University of Kansas. Museum of Natural History. Monograph [*A publication*]

Univ Kans Paleontol Contrib Artic ... University of Kansas. Paleontological Contributions. Article [*A publication*]

Univ Kans Paleontol Contrib Pap ... University of Kansas. Paleontological Contributions. Paper [*A publication*]

Univ Kans Primary Rec Psychol Publ ... University of Kansas. Primary Records in Psychology. Publication [*A publication*]

Univ Kans Publ Mus Nat Hist ... University of Kansas. Publications. Museum of Natural History [*A publication*]

Univ Kans Sci Bull ... University of Kansas. Science Bulletin [*A publication*]

Univ Kans Sci Bull Suppl ... University of Kansas. Science Bulletin. Supplement [*A publication*]

Univ KC R ... University of Kansas City. Review [*A publication*]

Univ K Inst Min Miner Res Tech Rep ... University of Kentucky. Institute for Mining and Minerals Research. Technical Report [*A publication*]

Univ Kiril Metodij-Skopje Fac Math ... Universite Kiril et Metodij-Skopje. Faculte des Mathematiques [*A publication*]

Univ KY Coll Agric Coop Ext Ser Rep ... University of Kentucky. College of Agriculture. Cooperative Extension Service. Report [*A publication*]

Univ KY Coop Ext Serv Circ ... University of Kentucky. Cooperative Extension Service. Circular [*A publication*]

Univ KY Coop Ext Serv 4-H ... University of Kentucky. Cooperative Extension Service. 4-H [*A publication*]

Univ KY Coop Ext Serv Leafl ... University of Kentucky. Cooperative Extension Service. Leaflet [*A publication*]

Univ KY Coop Ext Serv Misc ... University of Kentucky. Cooperative Extension Service. Miscellaneous [*A publication*]

Univ KY Eng Exp Stn Bull ... University of Kentucky. Engineering Experiment Station. Bulletin [*A publication*]

Univ KY Inst Min Miner Res Rep IMMR ... University of Kentucky. Institute for Mining and Minerals Research. Report IMMR [*A publication*]

Univ KY Inst Min Miner Res Tech Rep IMMR ... University of Kentucky. Institute for Mining and Minerals Research. Technical Report. IMMR [*A publication*]

Univ KY Publ Anthropol Archaeol ... University of Kentucky. Publications in Anthropology and Archaeology [*A publication*]

Univ Laval Dep Exploit Util Bois Note Rech ... Universite Laval. Departement d'Exploitation et Utilisation des Bois. Note de Recherches [*A publication*]

Univ Laval Dep Exploit Util Bois Note Tech ... Universite Laval. Departement d'Exploitation et Utilisation des Bois. Note Technique [*A publication*]

Univ L Coll J ... University Law College. Journal. Rajputana University [*India*] (DLA)

Univ Lesn Khoz Derevoobrab Prom-Sti (Sopron) Nauchn Publ ... Universitet Lesnogo Khozyaistva i Derevoobrabatyvaoushchei Promyshlennosti (Sopron) Nauchnye Publikatsii [*A publication*]

Univ Libre Bruxelles Inter-Univ Inst High Energ Rep ... Universite Libre de Bruxelles. Inter-University Institute for High Energies. Report [*A publication*]

Univ Liege Fac Sci Appl Coll Publ ... Universite de Liege. Faculte des Sciences Appliques. Collection des Publications [*Belgium*] [*A publication*]

Univ Lisboa Fac Farm Bol ... Universidade de Lisboa. Faculdade de Farmacia. Boletim [*A publication*]

Univ Lisboa Revista Fac Ci A ... Universidade de Lisboa. Revista da Faculdade de Ciencas. 2a Serie A. Ciencias Matematicas [*A publication*]

Univ Liverp Rec ... University of Liverpool. Recorder [*A publication*]

Univ Lond Univ Coll Galton Lab Eugen Lab Mem ... University of London. University College. Galton Laboratory. Eugenics Laboratory. Memoirs [*A publication*]

Univ LR ...... University Law Review (DLA)

Univ L Rev ... University Law Review (DLA)

Univ M........ University Magazine [*Montreal*] [*A publication*]

Univ Madr Fac Vet Publ ... Universidad de Madrid. Facultad de Veterinaria. Publicacion [*A publication*]

Univ Maine Orono Life Sci Agric Exp Stn Annu Rep ... University of Maine at Orono. Life Sciences and Agriculture Experiment Station. Annual Report [*A publication*]

Univ of Maine Studies ... University of Maine. Studies [*A publication*]

Univ of Manila L Gaz ... University of Manila. Law Gazette [*Manila, Philippines*] (DLA)

Univ Maria Curie-Sklodowsk Ann Sect B ... Universitas Maria Curie-Sklodowsk. Annales. Sectio B [*A publication*]

Univ MD Nat Resour Inst Contrib ... University of Maryland. Natural Resources Institute. Contribution [*A publication*]

Univ MD Water Resour Res Cent Tech Rep ... University of Maryland. Water Resources Research Center. Technical Report [*A publication*]

Univ Med Rec (London) ... Universal Medical Record (London) [*A publication*]

Univ Melb Gaz ... University of Melbourne. Gazette [*A publication*]

Univ Melb Sch For Bull ... University of Melbourne. School of Forestry. Bulletin [*A publication*]

Univ Miami Law R ... University of Miami. Law Review [*A publication*]

Univ Miami Law Rev ... University of Miami. Law Review [*A publication*]

Univ of Miami L Rev ... University of Miami. Law Review [*A publication*]

Univ Miami Rosenstiel Sch Mar Atmos Sci Annu Rep ... University of Miami. Rosenstiel School of Marine and Atmospheric Science. Annual Report [*A publication*]

Univ Miami Sea Grant Program Sea Grant Field Guide Ser ... University of Miami. Sea Grant Program. Sea Grant Field Guide Series [*A publication*]

Univ Miami Sea Grant Program Sea Grant Tech Bull ... University of Miami. Sea Grant Program. Sea Grant Technical Bulletin [*A publication*]

Univ Mich Bus Rev ... University of Michigan. Business Review [*A publication*]

Univ Mich Dep Nav Archit Mar Eng Rep ... University of Michigan. Department of Naval Architecture and Marine Engineering. Report [*A publication*]

Univ of Michigan J of Law Reform ... University of Michigan. Journal of Law Reform [*A publication*]

Univ Mich J Law Reform ... University of Michigan. Journal of Law Reform [*A publication*]

Univ Mich Med Bull ... University of Michigan. Medical Bulletin [*A publication*]

Univ Mich Med Cent J ... University of Michigan. Medical Center. Journal [*A publication*]

Univ Mich Mus Anthropol Tech Rep ... University of Michigan. Museum of Anthropology. Technical Reports [*A publication*]

Univ Mich Mus Zool Circ ... University of Michigan. Museum of Zoology. Circular [*A publication*]

Univ Minn Agric Ext Serv Ext Bull ... University of Minnesota. Agricultural Extension Service. Extension Bulletin [*A publication*]

Univ Minn Agric Ext Serv Ext Folder ... University of Minnesota. Agricultural Extension Service. Extension Folder [*A publication*]

Univ Minn Agric Ext Serv Ext Pam ... University of Minnesota. Agricultural Extension Service. Extension Pamphlet [*A publication*]

Univ Minn Agric Ext Serv Misc ... University of Minnesota. Agricultural Extension Service. Miscellaneous Publications [*A publication*]

Univ Minn Agric Ext Serv Misc Publ ... University of Minnesota. Agricultural Extension Service. Miscellaneous Publications [*A publication*]

Univ Minn Agric Ext Serv Spec Rep ... University of Minnesota. Agricultural Extension Service. Special Report [*A publication*]

Univ Minn Med Bull ... University of Minnesota. Medical Bulletin [*A publication*]

Univ of Missouri at Kansas City L Rev ... University of Missouri at Kansas City. Law Review [*A publication*]

Univ Missouri Stud ... University of Missouri. Studies [*A publication*]

Univ MO Bull Eng Exp Stn Ser ... University of Missouri. Bulletin. Engineering Experiment Station Series [*A publication*]

Univ MO Eng Exp Sta Eng Ser Bull ... University of Missouri. Engineering Experiment Station. Engineering Series. Bulletin [*A publication*]

Univ MO Sch Mines Metall Bull Tech Ser ... University of Missouri. School of Mines and Metallurgy. Bulletin. Technical Series [*A publication*]

Univ MO Stud ... University of Missouri. Studies [*A publication*]

Univ of MO Studies ... University of Missouri. Studies [*A publication*]

Univ Mus Bull Univ PA ... University Museum. Bulletin. University of Pennsylvania [*A publication*]

Univ Nac Auton Mex Inst Geol An ... Universidad Nacional Autonoma de Mexico. Instituto de Geologia. Anales [*A publication*]

Univ Nac Auton Mex Inst Geol Bol ... Universidad Nacional Autonoma de Mexico. Instituto de Geologia. Boletin [*A publication*]

Univ Nac Auton Mex Inst Geol Paleontol Mex ... Universidad Nacional Autonoma de Mexico. Instituto de Geologia Paleontologicas Mexicanas [*A publication*]

Univ Nac Auton Mex Inst Geol Rev ... Universidad Nacional Autonoma de Mexico. Instituto de Geologia. Revista [*A publication*]

Univ Nac Cuyo Fac Cien Agrar Bol Tec ... Universidad Nacional de Cuyo. Facultad de Ciencias Agrarias. Boletin Tecnico [*A publication*]

Univ Nac de Cuyo Fac Cienc Agrar Bol de Ext ... Universidad Nacional de Cuyo. Facultad de Ciencias Agrarias. Boletin de Extension [*A publication*]

Univ Nac Cuyo Fac Cienc Fis-Quim Mat Ses Quim Argent ... Universidad Nacional de Cuyo. Facultad de Ciencias Fisico-Quimico Matematicas. Sesiones Quimicas Argentinas [*A publication*]

Univ Nac Cuyo Inst Pet Publ ... Universidad Nacional de Cuyo. Instituto del Petroleo. Publicacion [*A publication*]

Univ Nac Eva Peron Fac Cienc Fisicomat Publ Ser 2 ... Universidad Nacional de Eva Peron. Facultad de Ciencias Fisicomatematicas. Publicaciones. Serie 2. Revista [*A publication*]

Univ Nac La Plata Fac Agron Lab Zool Agric Bol ... Universidad Nacional de La Plata. Facultad de Agronomia. Laboratorio de Zoologia Agricola. Boletin [*A publication*]

Univ Nac La Plata Fac Cienc Nat Mus Ser Tec Didact ... Universidad Nacional de La Plata. Facultad de Ciencias Naturales y Museo. Serie Tecnica y Didactica [*A publication*]

Univ Nac La Plata Notas Mus Bot ... Universidad Nacional de La Plata. Notas del Museo. Botanica [*A publication*]

Univ Nac La Plata Notas Mus Geol ... Universidad Nacional de La Plata. Notas del Museo. Geologia [*A publication*]

Univ Nac La Plata Notas Mus Zool ... Universidad Nacional de La Plata. Notas del Museo. Zoologia [*A publication*]

Univ Nac La Plata Publ Fac Cienc Fisicomat Ser 2 ... Universidad Nacional de La Plata. Publicaciones. Facultad de Ciencias Fisicomatematicas. Serie 2. Revista [*A publication*]

Univ Nac Tucuman Fac Agron Zootec Misc ... Universidad Nacional de Tucuman. Facultad de Agronomia y Zootecnia. Miscelanea [*A publication*]

Univ Nac Tucuman Fac Agron Zootec Publ Espec ... Universidad Nacional de Tucuman. Facultad de Agronomia y Zootecnia. Publicacion Especial [*A publication*]

Univ Nac Tucuman Fac Agron Zootec Ser Didact ... Universidad Nacional de Tucuman. Facultad de Agronomia y Zootecnia. Serie Didactica [*A publication*]

Univ Nac Tucuman Fund Inst Miguel Lillo Misc ... Universidad Nacional de Tucuman. Fundacion e Instituto Miguel Lillo. Miscelanea [*A publication*]

Univ Nac Tucuman Inst Fis Publ ... Universidad Nacional de Tucuman. Instituto de Fisica. Publicacion [*A publication*]

Univ Nac Tucuman Inst Ing Quim Pub ... Universidad Nacional de Tucuman. Instituto de Ingenieria Quimica. Publicacion [*A publication*]

Univ Nac Tucuman Rev Ser A ... Universidad Nacional de Tucuman. Facultad de Ciencias Exactas y Tecnologia. Revista. Serie A. Matematicas y Fisica Teorica [*A publication*]

Univ de Nancy Fac d Lettres Annales de l'Est ... Universite de Nancy. Faculte des Lettres. Annales de l'Est [*A publication*]

Univ Natal Wattle Res Inst Rep ... University of Natal. Wattle Research Institute. Report [*A publication*]

Univ Nebr Coll Agric Home Econ Q ... University of Nebraska. College of Agriculture and Home Economics. Quarterly [*A publication*]

Univ NE Bul ... University of New England. Bulletin [*A publication*]

Univ N Engl Annu Rep ... University of New England. Annual Report [*A publication*]

Univ N Engl Explor Soc Aust Rep ... University of New England. Exploration Society of Australia. Report [*A publication*]

Univ Nev Mackay Sch Mines Geol Min Ser Bull ... University of Nevada. Mackay School of Mines. Geological and Mining Series. Bulletin [*A publication*]

Univ Nev Max C Fleischmann Coll Agric Rep ... University of Nevada. Max C. Fleischmann College of Agriculture. Report [*A publication*]

Univ Nev Max C Fleischmann Coll Agric T Ser ... University of Nevada. Max C. Fleischmann College of Agriculture. T Series [*A publication*]

Univ of New Brunswick LJ ... University of New Brunswick. Law Journal [*A publication*]

Univ Newcastle Upon Tyne Rep Dove Mar Lab Third Ser ... University of Newcastle Upon Tyne. Report of the Dove Marine Laboratory. Third Series [*A publication*]

Univ New Eng Bull ... University of New England. Bulletin [*A publication*]

Univ New South Wales Occas Pap ... University of New South Wales. Occasional Papers [*Australia*] [*A publication*]

Univ NM Bull Biol Ser ... University of New Mexico. Bulletin. Biological Series [*A publication*]

Univ NM Bull Geol Ser ... University of New Mexico. Bulletin. Geological Series [*A publication*]

Univ NM Inst Meteorit Spec Publ ... University of New Mexico. Institute of Meteoritics. Special Publication [*A publication*]

Univ NM Publ Anthropol ... University of New Mexico. Publications in Anthropology [*A publication*]

Univ NM Publ Biol ... University of New Mexico. Publications in Biology [*A publication*]

Univ NM Publ Geol ... University of New Mexico. Publications in Geology [*A publication*]

Univ NM Publ Meteorit ... University of New Mexico. Publications in Meteoritics [*A publication*]

Univ Nottingham Dep Agric Hortic Misc Publ ... University of Nottingham. Department of Agriculture and Horticulture. Miscellaneous Publication [*A publication*]

Univ u Novom Sadu Zb Rad Prirod-Mat Fak ... Univerzitet u Novom Sadu. Zbornik Radova Prirodno-Matematickog Fakulteta [*A publication*]

Univ of NSW LJ ... University of New South Wales. Law Journal [*A publication*]

Univ NSW LJ ... University of New South Wales. Law Journal [*A publication*]

Univ NSW Occas Pap ... University of New South Wales. Occasional Papers [*A publication*]

Univ NSW Q ... University of New South Wales. Quarterly [*A publication*]

Univ Oriente Inst Oceanogr Bol ... Universidad de Oriente. Instituto Oceanografico. Boletin [*A publication*]

Univ Oriente Inst Oceanogr Bol Bibliogr ... Universidad de Oriente. Instituto Oceanografico. Boletin Bibliografico [*A publication*]

Univ Oxford Dept Eng Sci Rep ... University of Oxford. Department of Engineering. Science Reports [*A publication*]

Univ PA Bull Vet Ext Q ... University of Pennsylvania. Bulletin. Veterinary Extension Quarterly [*A publication*]

Univ Palermo Ann Fac Econom Commercio ... Universita di Palermo. Annali della Facolta di Economia e Commercio [*A publication*]

Univ Palermo Ann Fac Econom e Commercio ... Universita di Palermo. Annali della Facolta di Economia e Commercio [*A publication*]

Univ PA Med Bull ... University of Pennsylvania. Medical Bulletin [*A publication*]

Univ of PA Pub Pol Econ ... University of Pennsylvania. Publications in Political Economy [*A publication*]

Univ Penn Law Rev ... University of Pennsylvania. Law Review [*A publication*]

Univ of Pennsylvania L Rev ... University of Pennsylvania. Law Review [*A publication*]

Univ of Pittsburgh L Rev ... University of Pittsburgh. Law Review [*A publication*]

Univ Pontif Bolivariana Publ Trimest ... Universidad Pontificia Bolivariana. Publicacion Trimestral [*A publication*]

Univ Pretoria Publ Ser 2 ... University of Pretoria. Publications. Series 2. Natural Sciences [*A publication*]

Univ Q .... Universalist Quarterly Review [*Boston*] [*A publication*]

Univ Q .... Universities Quarterly [*London*] [*A publication*]

Univ QD Agric Dep Pap ... University of Queensland. Agriculture Department. Papers [*A publication*]

Univ QD Bot Dep Pap ... University of Queensland. Botany Department. Papers [*A publication*]

Univ QD Ent Dep Pap ... University of Queensland. Entomology Department. Papers [*A publication*]

Univ Q Gaz ... University of Queensland. Gazette [*A publication*]

Univ Q Law J ... University of Queensland. Law Journal [*A publication*]

Univ Qld Gaz ... University of Queensland. Gazette [*A publication*]

Univ Qld Law J ... University of Queensland. Law Journal [*A publication*]

Univ Q LJ ... University of Queensland. Law Journal [*A publication*]

Univ Quart ... Universities Quarterly [*A publication*]

Univ of Queensland LJ ... University of Queensland. Law Journal [*A publication*]

Univ Queensl Comput Cent Pap ... University of Queensland. Computer Centre. Papers [*A publication*]

Univ Queensl Great Barrier Reef Comm Heron Isl Res Stn ... University of Queensland. Great Barrier Reef Committee. Heron Island Research Station [*A publication*]

Univ Queensl Pap Dep Bot ... University of Queensland. Papers. Department of Botany [*A publication*]

Univ Queensl Pap Dep Entomol ... University of Queensland. Papers. Department of Entomology [*A publication*]

Univ Queensl Pap Dep Geol ... University of Queensland. Papers. Department of Geology [*A publication*]

Univ Queensl Pap Dep Zool ... University of Queensland. Papers. Department of Zoology [*A publication*]

Univ Queensl Pap Fac Vet Sci ... University of Queensland. Papers. Faculty of Veterinary Science [*A publication*]

Univ R........ Universal Review [*A publication*]

Univ R........ University Review [*A publication*]

Univ Reading Natl Inst Res Dairy Bienn Rev ... University of Reading. National Institute for Research in Dairying. Biennial Reviews [*A publication*]

Univ Reading Natl Inst Res Dairy Rep ... University of Reading. National Institute for Research in Dairying. Report [*A publication*]

Univ Rec..... University Record [*A publication*]

Univ Repub Fac Agron Bol (Montev) ... Universidad de la Republica. Facultad de Agronomia. Boletin (Montevideo) [*A publication*]

Univ Repub Montevideo Fac Agron Bol ... Universidad de la Republica. Montevideo. Facultad de Agronomia. Boletin [*A publication*]

Univ Rhod Fac Med Res Lect Ser ... University of Rhodesia. Faculty of Medicine. Research Lecture Series [*A publication*]

Univ of Richmond L Not ... University of Richmond. Law Notes [*Richmond, Virginia*] (DLA)

Univ of Richmond L Rev ... University of Richmond. Law Review [*A publication*]

Univ RI Mar Publ Ser ... University of Rhode Island. Marine Publication Series [*A publication*]

Univ Rio Grande do Sul Esc Geol Avulso ... Universidade do Rio Grande do Sul. Escola de Geologia. Avulso [*A publication*]

Univ Rochester Lib Bull ... University of Rochester. Library Bulletin [*A publication*]

Univ Rochester Libr Bull ... University of Rochester. Library Bulletin [*A publication*]

Univ Roma Ist Autom Not ... Universita di Roma. Istituto di Automatica. Notiziario [*A publication*]

Univ Roorkee Res J ... University of Roorkee. Research Journal [*A publication*]

Univ Rural Pernambuco Comun Tec ... Universidade Rural de Pernambuco. Comunicado Tecnico [*A publication*]

Univ of San Fernando Valley L Rev ... University of San Fernando Valley. Law Review [*Sepulveda, California*] (DLA)

Univ of San Francisco L Rev ... University of San Francisco. Law Review [*A publication*]

Univ Sao Paulo Fac Filos Cienc Let Bol Bot ... Universidade de Sao Paulo. Faculdade de Filosofia, Ciencias, e Letras. Boletim. Botanica [*A publication*]

Univ Sao Paulo Fac Filos Cienc Let Bol Geol ... Universidade de Sao Paulo. Faculdade de Filosofia, Ciencias, e Letras. Boletim. Geologia [*A publication*]

Univ Sao Paulo Fac Filos Cienc Let Bol Mineral ... Universidade de Sao Paulo. Faculdade de Filosofia, Ciencias, e Letras. Boletim. Mineralogia [*A publication*]

Univ Sao Paulo Fac Filos Cienc Let Bol Quim ... Universidade de Sao Paulo. Faculdade de Filosofia, Ciencias, e Letras. Boletim Quimica [*A publication*]

Univ Sao Paulo Inst Geocienc Astron Bol ... Universidade de Sao Paulo. Instituto de Geociencias e Astronomia. Boletim [*A publication*]

Univ Sao Paulo Inst Geocienc Bol IG ... Universidade de Sao Paulo. Instituto de Geociencias. Boletim IG [*Instituto de Geociencias*] [*A publication*]

Univ Sevilla Publ Ser Med ... Universidad de Sevilla. Publicaciones. Serie Medicina [*A publication*]

Univ South Calif Allan Hancock Found ... University of Southern California. Allan Hancock Foundation [*A publication*]

Univs Q ...... Universities Quarterly [*A publication*]

Univ Strathclyde Annu Rep ... University of Strathclyde. Annual Report [*A publication*]

Univ Strathclyde Res Rep ... University of Strathclyde. Research Report [*A publication*]

Univ Stud ... University Studies in History and Economics [*A publication*]

Univ Stud Hist ... University Studies in History [*A publication*]

Univ Stud Hist Ec ... University Studies in History and Economics [*A publication*]

Univ Studies ... University Studies in History and Economics [*A publication*]

Univ Studies ... University Studies in Western Australian History [*A publication*]

Univ Studies Math ... University Studies in Mathematics [*A publication*]

Univ Studi Trieste Fac Econ Commer Ist Merceol Pubbl ... Universita degli Studi di Trieste. Facolta di Economia e Commercio. Istituto di Merceologia. Pubblicazione [*A publication*]

Univ Studi Trieste Fac Ing Ist Chim App Pubbl ... Universita degli Studi di Trieste. Facolta di Ingegneria. Istituto di Chimica Applicata. Pubblicazioni [*A publication*]

Univ Studi Trieste Fac Sci Ist Chim Pubbl ... Universita degli Studi di Trieste. Facolta di Scienze. Istituto di Chimica. Pubblicazioni [*A publication*]

Univ Studi Trieste Ist Chim Farm Tossicol Pubbl ... Universita degli Studi di Trieste. Istituto di Chimica Farmaceutica e Tossicologica. Pubblicazioni [*A publication*]

Univ Studi Triest Fac di Sci Ist Geol Pubbl ... Universita degli Studi di Trieste. Facolta di Scienze. Istituto di Geologia. Pubblicazioni [*A publication*]

Univ Stud Trieste Fac Farm Ist Chim Farm Tossicol Pubbl ... Universita degli Studi di Trieste. Facolta di Farmacia. Istituto di Chimica, Farmaceutica, e Tossicologica. Pubblicazioni [*A publication*]

Univ Stud Trieste Fac Farm Ist Tec Farm Pubbl ... Universita degli Studi di Trieste. Facolta di Farmacia. Istituto di Tecnica Farmaceutica. Pubblicazioni [*A publication*]

Univ Stud Trieste Ist Tec Farm Pubbl ... Universita degli Studi di Trieste. Istituto di Tecnica Farmaceutica. Pubblicazioni [*A publication*]

Univ Stud Univ Neb ... University Studies. University of Nebraska [*A publication*]

Univ Syd Post Grad Ctee Med Bull ... University of Sydney. Postgraduate Committee in Medicine. Bulletin [*A publication*]

Univ Tas Gaz ... University of Tasmania. Gazette [*A publication*]

Univ Tas LR ... University of Tasmania. Law Review [*A publication*]

Univ of Tasmania L Rev ... University of Tasmania. Law Review [*A publication*]

Univ Tenn Rec ... University of Tennessee. Record [*A publication*]

Univ Tenn Surv Bus ... University of Tennessee. Survey of Business [*A publication*]

Univ Tex Austin Bur Econ Geol Handb ... University of Texas at Austin. Bureau of Economic Geology. Handbook [*A publication*]

Univ Tex Austin Bur Econ Geol Miner Resour Circ ... University of Texas at Austin. Bureau of Economic Geology. Mineral Resource Circular [*A publication*]

Univ Tex Austin Bur Econ Geol Res Note ... University of Texas at Austin. Bureau of Economic Geology. Research Note [*A publication*]

Univ Tex Austin Cent Highw Res Res Rep ... University of Texas at Austin. Center for Highway Research. Research Report [*A publication*]

Univ Tex Austin Cent Res Water Resour Tech Rep ... University of Texas at Austin. Center for Research in Water Resources. Technical Report [*A publication*]

Univ Tex Bull ... University of Texas. Bulletin [*A publication*]

Univ Tex Bur Econ Geol Rep Invest ... University of Texas. Bureau of Economic Geology. Report of Investigations [*A publication*]

Univ TLR .... University of Tasmania. Law Review [*A publication*]

Univ Toledo Law R ... University of Toledo. Law Review [*A publication*]

Univ of Toledo L Rev ... University of Toledo. Law Review [*A publication*]

Univ Toronto Fac For Tech Rep ... University of Toronto. Faculty of Forestry. Technical Report [*A publication*]

Univ of Toronto LJ ... University of Toronto. Law Journal [*A publication*]

Univ Toronto Med J ... University of Toronto. Medical Journal [*A publication*]

Univ Toronto Q ... University of Toronto. Quarterly [*A publication*]

Univ Toronto Stud Biol Ser ... University of Toronto. Studies. Biological Series [*A publication*]

Univ Toronto Stud Geol Ser ... University of Toronto. Studies. Geological Series [*A publication*]

Univ Toronto Stud Pap Chem Lab ... University of Toronto. Studies. Papers from the Chemical Laboratories [*A publication*]

Univ Toronto Stud Pathol Ser ... University of Toronto. Studies. Pathological Series [*A publication*]

Univ Toronto Stud Physiol Ser ... University of Toronto. Studies. Physiological Series [*A publication*]

Univ Toronto Stud Phys Ser ... University of Toronto. Studies. Physics Series [*A publication*]

Univ Tor Q ... University of Toronto. Quarterly [*A publication*]

Univ Tripoli Bull Fac Eng ... University of Tripoli. Bulletin. Faculty of Engineering [*A publication*]

Univ of Tulsa LJ ... University of Tulsa. Law Journal [*Tulsa, Oklahoma*] (DLA)

Univ Udaipur Res J ... University of Udaipur. Research Journal [*A publication*]

Univ Udaipur Res Stud ... University of Udaipur. Research Studies [*A publication*]

Univ Umea Commun Res Unit Proj Rep ... University of Umea. Communication Research Unit. Project Report [*A publication*]

Univ Utah Anthropol Pap ... University of Utah. Anthropological Papers [*A publication*]

Univ Utah Biol Ser ... University of Utah. Biological Series [*A publication*]

Univ V .... University Vision [*A publication*]

Univ WA Ann L Rev ... Annual Law Review. University of Western Australia [*A publication*]

Univ WA Ann L Rev ... University of Western Australia. Annual Law Review [*A publication*]

Univ WA Law Rev ... University of Western Australia. Law Review [*A publication*]

Univ WA L Rev ... University of Western Australia. Law Review [*A publication*]

Univ Warsaw Dep Radiochem Publ ... University of Warsaw. Department of Radiochemistry. Publication [*A publication*]

Univ Wash Coll Fish Tech Rep ... University of Washington. College of Fisheries. Technical Report [*A publication*]

Univ Wash Eng Exp Stn Bull ... University of Washington. Engineering Experiment Station. Bulletin [*A publication*]

Univ Wash Eng Exp Stn Rep ... University of Washington. Engineering Experiment Station. Report [*A publication*]

Univ Wash Eng Exp Stn Tech Note ... University of Washington. Engineering Experiment Station. Technical Note [*A publication*]

Univ Wash Inst For Prod Contrib ... University of Washington. Institute of Forest Products. Contributions [*A publication*]

Univ Wash Publ Biol ... University of Washington. Publications in Biology [*A publication*]

Univ Wash Publ Fish ... University of Washington. Publications in Fisheries [*A publication*]

Univ Wash Publ Oceanogr ... University of Washington. Publications in Oceanography [*A publication*]

Univ Waterloo Biol Ser ... University of Waterloo. Biology Series [*A publication*]

Univ Waterloo Fac Environ Stud Occas Pap ... University of Waterloo. Faculty of Environmental Studies. Occasional Paper [*A publication*]

Univ of West Australia L Rev ... University of Western Australia. Law Review [*A publication*]

Univ Western Australia Law R ... University of Western Australia. Law Review [*A publication*]

Univ Western Ontario Series in Philos Sci ... University of Western Ontario. Series in Philosophy of Science [*A publication*]

Univ West Indies Reg Res Cent Soil Land Use Surv ... University of the West Indies. Regional Research Centre. Soil and Land Use Surveys [*A publication*]

Univ West Ont Ser Philos Sci ... University of Western Ontario. Series in Philosophy in Science [*A publication*]

Univ Windsor R ... University of Windsor. Review [*A publication*]
Univ Wis Coll Agric Life Sci Res Div Bull ... University of Wisconsin. College of Agricultural and Life Sciences. Research Division. Bulletin [*A publication*]
Univ Wis Coll Agric Life Sci Res Div Res Rep ... University of Wisconsin. College of Agricultural and Life Sciences. Research Division. Research Report [*A publication*]
Univ Wis Eng Exp Stn Rep ... University of Wisconsin. Engineering Experiment Station. Report [*A publication*]
Univ Wis-Madison Coll Agric Life Sci Res Div Res Bull ... University of Wisconsin-Madison. College of Agricultural and Life Sciences. Research Division. Research Bulletin [*A publication*]
Univ Wis Sea Grant Coll Tech Rep ... University of Wisconsin. Sea Grant College. Technical Report [*A publication*]
Univ Wis Sea Grant Program Tech Rep ... University of Wisconsin. Sea Grant Program. Technical Report [*A publication*]
Univ Wis Water Resour Cent Eutrophication Inf Prog Lit Rev ... University of Wisconsin. Water Resources Center. Eutrophication Information Program. Literature Review [*A publication*]
Univ Witwatersrand Dep Geogr Environ Stud Occas Pap ... University of the Witwatersrand. Department of Geography and Environmental Studies. Occasional Paper [*A publication*]
Univ of Wyoming Publ ... University of Wyoming. Publications [*A publication*]
Univ Wyo Publ ... University of Wyoming. Publications [*A publication*]
Uniw Adama Mickiewicza Poznaniu Inst Chem Ser Chem ... Uniwersytet Imienia Adama Mickiewicza w Poznaniu. Instytut Chemii. Seria Chemia [*A publication*]
Uniw Adama Mickiewicza Poznaniu Ser Astron ... Uniwersytet Imienia Adama Mickiewicza w Poznaniu. Seria Astronomia [*A publication*]
Uniw Adama Mickiewicza Poznaniu Ser Biol ... Uniwersytet Imienia Adama Mickiewicza w Poznaniu. Seria Biologia [*A publication*]
Uniw Adama Mickiewicza Poznaniu Ser Chem ... Uniwersytet Imienia Adama Mickiewicza w Poznaniu. Seria Chemia [*A publication*]
Uniw Gdanski Wydz Mat Fiz Chem Zesz Nauk Ser Chem ... Uniwersytet Gdanski Wydzial Matematyki, Fizyki, Chemii, Zeszyty Naukowe. Seria Chemia [*A publication*]
Uniw Lodz Acta Univ Lodz Ser 2 ... Uniwersytet Lodzki. Acta Universitatis Lodziensis. Seria 2 [*A publication*]
Uniw Marii Curie-Sklodowskiej Ann Sect AA ... Uniwersytet Marii Curie-Sklodowskiej. Annales. Sectio AA. Physica et Chemia [*A publication*]
Uniw Slaski w Katowicach Prace Naukowe ... Uniwersytet Slaski w Katowicach. Prace Naukowe [*A publication*]
Uniw Slaski w Katowicach Prace Naukowe Prace Mat ... Uniwersytet Slaski w Katowicach. Prace Naukowe. Prace Matematyczne [*A publication*]
Uniw Slaski w Katowicach Prace Nauk-Prace Mat ... Uniwersytet Slaski w Katowicach. Prace Naukowe. Prace Matematyczne [*A publication*]
Unix ... [*An*] operating system developed by Bell Laboratories [*Software*]
UNJBS ... United Nations Joint Board of Strategy
UNJC ... Unified National J Series Coarse [*Thread*]
UNJEF ... Unified National J Series Extra Fine [*Thread*]
UNJF ... Unified National J Series Fine [*Thread*]
UNJS ... Unified National J Series Special [*Thread*]
UN Juridical YB ... United Nations Juridical Year Book (DLA)
UNK ... Unalakleet [*Alaska*] [*Airport symbol*] (OAG)
UNK ... Unknown (AFM)
Unk ... Unknown Worlds [*A publication*]
UNKN ... Unknown
UNKRA ... United Nations Korean Reconstruction Agency
UNK UNK ... Unknown Unknowns [*Design engineering*]
UNKWN ... Unknown
UNL ... United Leader Resources, Inc. [*Vancouver Stock Exchange symbol*]
UNL ... University of Nebraska - Lincoln
UNL ... University of New Brunswick Law Library [*UTLAS symbol*]
UNL ... Unlimited
UNL ... Unloading
UNLA ... Uganda National Liberation Army [*Political party*]
UNLA ... Unione Nazionale per la Lotta Contra l'Analfabatismo [*Union for the Struggle Against Illiteracy*] [*Italy*]
UNLCH ... Unlatch (MCD)
UNLF ... Ugandan National Liberation Front (PD)
UNLGTD ... Unlighted (FAAC)
UNLIM ... Unlimited
UNLIQ ... Unliquidated
UNLIS ... United National Life Insurance Society (EA)
UNLKG ... Unlocking
UNLL ... United Nations League of Lawyers
UNLOS ... United Nations Law of the Sea [*Conference*]
UNLR ... United Nations Law Reports (DLA)
UNLV ... University of Nevada, Las Vegas
UNM ... National University of Mexico [*Mexico*] [*Seismograph station code, US Geological Survey*] [*Closed*] (SEIS)
UNM ... Unified Miniature
UNM ... United Nations Medal

UnM ... University Microfilms International, Ann Arbor, MI [*Library symbol*] [*Library of Congress*] (LCLS)
UNM ... University of Nebraska, Medical Center, Omaha, NE [*OCLC symbol*] (OCLC)
UNM ... Unmarried
UNM ... UNUM Corp. [*NYSE symbol*]
UNMAC ... United Nations Mixed Armistice Commission
UNMC ... United Nations Mediterranean Command (BJA)
UNMC ... United Nations Mediterranean Commission
UNMCB ... Unscheduled Not Mission Capable Both [*Maintenance and supply*] (MCD)
UNMCM ... Unscheduled Not Mission Capable Maintenance (MCD)
UNMD ... Unmanned (KSC)
Un Med Can ... Union Medicale du Canada [*A publication*]
UNMEM ... United Nations Middle East Mission
UNMKD ... Unmarked
UnM-L ... University Microfilms Ltd., Penn, Buckinghamshire, United Kingdom [*Library symbol*] [*Library of Congress*] (LCLS)
UNMO's ... United Nations Military Observers (BJA)
UN Mo Chron ... UN Monthly Chronicle [*A publication*]
UNMOGIP ... United Nations Military Observer Group for India and Pakistan (AABC)
UNMON ... Unable to Monitor (FAAC)
Unm Ox ... Unmuzzled Ox [*A publication*]
UNMSC ... United Nations Military Staff Committee (AABC)
UNMTD ... Unmounted
UNNB ... University National Bank & Trust [*NASDAQ symbol*] (NQ)
UNNE ... Universidad Nacional del Nordeste [*Argentina*]
UNNECY ... Unnecessary (ROG)
UNNEFO ... United Nations of the New Emerging Forces [*Indonesia*]
UNNUS ... Uralic News and Notes from the United States [*A publication*]
UNO ... Unicorn Resources [*Vancouver Stock Exchange symbol*]
UNO ... Unified Nimbus Observatory (MCD)
UNO ... Union Nacional Odriista [*Peruvian political party*]
UNO ... United Nations Observer Corps (BJA)
UNO ... United Nations Organization
UNO ... United Nicaraguan Opposition
UNO ... University of Nebraska at Omaha
UNO ... University of New Orleans [*Louisiana*]
UNO ... Utility Night Observer
UNOBSD ... Unobserved (ROG)
UNOC ... Union Nationale des Ouvriers Congolais [*National Union of Congolese Workers*]
UNOC ... United Nations Operation in the Congo
UNO-CARA-PEN ... Union Internationale pour la Cooperation Culturelle [*International Union for Cultural Co-operation*]
UNODIR ... Unless Otherwise Directed
UNOEOA ... United Nations Office for Emergency Operations in Africa [*New York, NY*] (EA)
Unof ... Unofficial Reports (DLA)
UNOFFL ... Unofficial (FAAC)
UNOG ... United Nations Organization - Geneva
UNOGIL ... United Nations Observer Group in Lebanon
UNOINDC ... Unless Otherwise Indicated
UNOLS ... University National Oceanographic Laboratory System [*National Science Foundation*]
UNOP ... Unopened (ADA)
UNOP ... Unopposed
UNOPAR ... Universal Operator Performance Analyzer and Recorder
UNORDCAN ... Unexecuted Portion of Orders Cancelled
UNOREQ ... Unless Otherwise Requested (NVT)
UNOS ... United Network for Organ Sharing (EA)
U Notr D St ... University of Notre Dame. Studies in the Philosophy of Religion [*A publication*]
UNP ... Union Nacional Paraguaya [*Paraguayan political party*]
UNP ... Union Pacific Corp. [*NYSE symbol*]
UNP ... United National Party [*Sri Lankan*] (PPW)
UNP ... United Nations Philatelists (EA)
UNP ... United Northern Petroleum Corp. [*Vancouver Stock Exchange symbol*]
UNP ... Unpaged
UNP ... Unpostable [*Data processing*]
UNPA ... Unione Nazionale Protexione Antiaeres [*Italy*]
UNPA ... United Nations Participation Act of 1945
UNPA ... United Nations Postal Administration
UNPAC ... Union Pacific Railroad Co.
UNPAD ... Universitas Negeri Padjadjaran [*Indonesia*]
Unpartizan R ... Unpartizan Review [*A publication*]
UNPC ... United Nations Palestine Commission
UNPCC ... United Nations Palestine Conciliation Commission (BJA)
UNPD ... Unpaid (AABC)
UNPERF ... Unperformed [*Music*]
UNPERFD ... Unperformed (ROG)
UNPI ... United Nations Philatelists, Incorporated (EA)
UNPIK ... United Nations Partisan Infantry Korea
UNPOC ... United Nations Peace Observation Commission
Unpop R ... Unpopular Review [*A publication*]
Un Prac News ... Unauthorized Practice News [*A publication*]
UNPS ... Unified Network Planning Study
UNPS ... United Nations Philatelic Society (EA)
UNPS ... Universal Power Supply

UNPUB .... Unpublished
UNPUBD .... Unpublished
UNQ .... Providence, RI [*Location identifier*] [*FAA*]   (FAAL)
UNQTE .... Unquote
UNQUAL .... Unqualified   (AABC)
unr .... Ukrainian Soviet Socialist Republic [*MARC country of publication code*] [*Library of Congress*]   (LCCP)
UNR .... Ukrains'ka Natsional'na Rada
UNR .... Uniao Nacional Republicana [*National Republican Union*] [*Portuguese*]   (PPE)
UNR .... Unicorp Resources Ltd. [*Toronto Stock Exchange symbol*]
UN R .... United Nations Review [*A publication*]
UNRDBL .... Unreadable   (FAAC)
UNREF .... United Nations Refugee Fund
UNREF .... Unreformed   (ROG)
UNREL .... Unreliable
UNREP .... Underway Replenishment [*Military*]
Unrep Cr C .. Bombay Unreported Criminal Cases [*1862-98*] [*India*]   (DLA)
Unrep NY Est TC ... Unreported New York Estate Tax Cases [*Prentice-Hall, Inc.*]   (DLA)
Unrep Wills Cas ... Unreported Wills Cases [*Prentice-Hall, Inc.*]   (DLA)
UN Rev .... United Nations Review [*A publication*]
UNRF .... Uganda National Rescue Front   (PD)
UNRGLTD ... Unregulated
UNRIAA ...... United Nations Reports of International Arbitral Awards   (DLA)
UNRIQ .... UNR Industries, Inc. [*NASDAQ symbol*]   (NQ)
UNRISD ..... United Nations Research Institute for Social Development [*Geneva, Switzerland*]
UNROD ...... United Nations Relief Operation in Dacca
UNRP .... University of Nottingham. Research Publications [*A publication*]
UNRPR .... United Nations Relief for Palestine Refugees
UNRR .... Unable to Approve Route Requested [*Aviation*]   (FAAC)
UNRRA ...... United Nations Relief and Rehabilitation Administration [*"United Nations" in this body's name derives from the wartime alliance of this name, not from any affiliation with the postwar international organization*]
UNRRC .... United Nations Relief and Rehabilitation Conference
UNRS .... Union pour la Nouvelle Republique Senegalaise [*Union for the New Senegalese Republic*] [*Political party*]
UNRSTD ..... Unrestricted   (FAAC)
UNRTD .... United Nations Resources and Transport Division
UNRWA ...... United Nations Relief and Works Agency for Palestine Refugees in the Near East [*Vienna, Austria*]   (PD)
UNRWAPR ... United Nations Relief and Works Agency for Palestine Refugees in the Near East   (DLA)
UNRWAPRNE ... United Nations Relief and Works Agency for Palestine Refugees in the Near East [*Pronounced: "Unwrap me"*]
UNS .... Umnak, AK [*Location identifier*] [*FAA*]   (FAAI \
UNS .... Unified Numbering Systems [*for metals*]   (MCD)
UNS .... Unified Special [*Thread*]
UNS .... Universal Night Sight
UNS .... University of Nebraska. Studies [*A publication*]
UNS .... Unsymmetrical
UNSAC ...... United Nations Scientific Advisory Committee [*ICSU*]
UNSAT .... Unsatisfactory   (AABC)
unsat .... Unsaturated [*Chemistry*]
UNSATFY .. Unsatisfactory
UNSB .... United Bank, a Savings Bank [*NASDAQ symbol*]   (NQ)
UNSBL .... Unseasonable   (FAAC)
UNSC .... United Nations Security Council
UNSC .... United Nations Social Commission
UNSCC ...... United Nations Standards Co-Ordinating Committee
UNSCC ...... University of Nevada System Computing Center [*Research center*]   (RCD)
UNSCCUR ... United Nations Scientific Conference on the Conservation and Utilization of Resources
UNSCEAR ... United Nations Scientific Committee on the Effects of Atomic Radiation
UNSCOB .... United Nations Special Committee on the Balkans [*Greece*]
UNSCOP .... United Nations Special Committee on Palestine
UNSCOR .... United Nations Security Council Official Records   (DLA)
UNSD .... Unsweetened   (ROG)
UNSDD ...... United Nations Social Development Division
UNSDRI ..... United Nations Social Defense Research Institute [*UN/Italy*]
UNSECNAV ... Under Secretary of the Navy
UnSemQR ... Union Seminary. Quarterly Review [*New York*] [*A publication*]
Unser Sozial Dorf ... Unser Sozialistisches Dorf [*A publication*]
Un Serv M ... United Service Magazine [*A publication*]
Un Serv (Phila) ... United Service (Philadelphia) [*A publication*]
UNSF .... United Nations Special Fund
UNSFH .... United Nations Security Forces, Hollandia   (AABC)
UNSG .... United Nations Secretary General
UNSKED .... Unscheduled   (FAAC)
UNSM .... United Nations Service Medal
UNSO .... United Nations Sudano-Sahelian Office
UNSPD .... Underground Space [*A publication*]
UNSS .... United Nations Sales Section [*for UN documents*]
UNST .... Union Nordique pour la Sante et le Travail [*Nordic Union for Health and Work*] [*Koge, Denmark*]   (EA-IO)
UNSTBL ..... Unstable

UNSTD .... Union Nationale des Syndicats des Travailleurs du Dahomey [*National Federation of Workers' Unions of Dahomey*]
UNSTDY ..... Unsteady
UNSTHV ..... Union Nationale des Syndicats des Travailleurs de la Haute Volta [*National Federation of Workers' Unions of the Upper Volta*]
UNSTL .... Unsettle   (FAAC)
UNSU .... United Nations Staff Union   (EA)
UNSU .... United Nations Study Unit [*Philatelic organization*]   (EA)
UNSUB .... Unknown Subject [*FBI*]
UNSUPPR ... Unsuppressed   (MSA)
UNSVC ...... Unserviceable   (AABC)
UNSVM ..... United Nations Service Medal
UNSW .... University of New South Wales [*Australia*]
UNSWLJ ..... University of New South Wales. Law Journal [*A publication*]
UNSYM ...... Unsymmetrical
UN Symp Dev Use Geotherm Resour Abstr ... United Nations Symposium on the Development and Use of Geothermal Resources. Abstracts [*A publication*]
UN Symp Dev Use Geotherm Resour Proc ... United Nations Symposium on the Development and Use of Geothermal Resources. Proceedings [*A publication*]
UnT .... Uncanny Tales [*A publication*]
UNT .... Undergraduate Navigator Training [*Air Force*]   (AFM)
UNT .... Underground Nuclear Test
UNT .... Unit Corp. [*NYSE symbol*]
UNT .... United Tariff Bureau, Inc., New York NY [*STAC*]
UNT .... Unst [*Scotland*] [*Airport symbol*]   (OAG)
UNT .... Untersuchungen zum Neuen Testament [*A publication*]
UNT .... Uppsala Nya Tidning [*A publication*]
UNTA .... Union Nationale des Travailleurs Angolais [*National Union of Angolan Workers*]
UNTA .... United Nations Technical Assistance
UNTAA ...... United Nations Technical Assistance Administration
UNTAF ...... United Nations Technical Assistance Fellowship
UNTAG ...... United Nations Transition Assistance Group
UNTAMEL ... International Association of Metropolitan City Libraries
UNTC .... Unable to Establish Contact   (FAAC)
UNTC .... Union Nationale des Travailleurs Congolais [*National Union of Congolese Workers*]
UNTC .... United Nations Trusteeship Council   (DLA)
UNTCI .... Union Nationale des Travailleurs de Cote d'Ivoire [*National Union of Ivory Coast Workers*]
UNTCOK .... United Nations Temporary Committee on Korea
UNTCOR .... United Nations Trusteeship Council Official Record   (DLA)
UNTD .... University Naval Training Division [*Canada*]
UNTEA ...... Undersea Technology [*A publication*]
UNTEA .... United Nations Temporary Executive Authority [*Supervised transfer of Netherlands New Guinea to Indonesia*]
Unternehm ... Unternehmung. Schweizerische Zeitschrift fuer Betriebswirtschaft [*A publication*]
Unters Angebot Nachfrage Miner Rohst ... Untersuchungen ueber Angebot und Nachfrage Mineralischer Rohstoffe [*A publication*]
UNTFDPP ... United Nations Trust Fund for Development Planning and Projections
UNTFSD .... United Nations Trust Fund for Social Development
UNTG .... United Nations Theatre Group   (EA)
UNTHD ...... Unthreaded
UNTL .... Universal Telephone [*NASDAQ symbol*]   (NQ)
UNTM .... Union Nationale des Travailleurs du Mali [*National Union of Malian Workers*]
UNTN .... Union Nationale des Travailleurs Nigeriens [*National Union of Nigerian Workers*]
UNTP .... Universidad de Tucuman. Publications [*A publication*]
Un Trav Dec ... Unreported Travancore Decisions   (DLA)
UNTS .... Undergraduate Navigator Training System [*Air Force*]
UNTS .... Union Nationale des Travailleurs du Senegal [*National Union of Workers of Senegal*]
UNTS .... United Nations Treaty Series [*Project*] [*University of Washington*]
UNTSO ...... United Nations Truce Supervision Organization [*Works in Middle East between Israel and Arab nations*] [*Jerusalem*]
UNTT .... Union Nationale des Travailleurs du Togo [*National Union of Togolese Workers*]
UNTT .... United Nations Trust Territory
UNTW .... Untwist
UNU .... Juneau, WI [*Location identifier*] [*FAA*]   (FAAL)
UNU .... United Nations University [*Tokyo*]
UNUMO ...... Universal Underwater Mobile [*Robot*]
UNUSBL ..... Unusable
UNUSL .... Unusual   (ROG)
UNV .... State College, PA [*Location identifier*] [*FAA*]   (FAAL)
UNV .... United Nations Volunteers
UNV .... Unitel Video, Inc. [*American Stock Exchange symbol*]
Unverd .... Unverified
UNVS-A ..... Universo [*Italy*] [*A publication*]
UNVXA .... Universal Trading Exchange Cl A [*NASDAQ symbol*]   (NQ)
UNWAL Rev ... University of Western Australia. Law Review [*A publication*]
UN W Bul ... United Nations Weekly Bulletin [*A publication*]

UNWCC...... Unions Nation-Wide Coordinating Council for Oil and Allied Industries (EA)
UNWCC...... United Nations War Crimes Commission [*"United Nations" in this body's name derives from the wartime alliance of this name, not from any affiliation with the postwar international organization*]
UNWG .... United Nations Women's Guild [*New York, NY*] (EA)
UNWLA ..... Ukrainian National Women's League of America (EA)
UNWMG .... Utility Nuclear Waste Management Group (EA)
UN World ... United Nations World [*A publication*]
UNWR .... Unwritten (ROG)
UNWRAP.... United We Resist Additional Packaging [*Student legal action organization*]
UNWRF ..... United Westland Resources [*NASDAQ symbol*] (NQ)
UNWS........ Uniwest Financial Corp. [*NASDAQ symbol*] (NQ)
UNWSA ..... Unterrichtswissenschaft [*A publication*]
UNX.......... Underground Nuclear Explosion
UNX.......... Univex Mining Corp. [*Vancouver Stock Exchange symbol*]
UNY.......... San Antonio, TX [*Location identifier*] [*FAA*] (FAAL)
UNY.......... University of New York (ROG)
UNYB .... United Nations Year Book (DLA)
UNYFA ...... Ukrainian National Youth Federation of America [*Later, Ukrainian Youth Association of America*] (EA)
UNYOM ..... United Nations Yemen Observation Mission
u-nz---........ New Zealand [*MARC geographic area code*] [*Library of Congress*] (LCCP)
UNZ.......... Unzendake [*Japan*] [*Seismograph station code, US Geological Survey*] (SEIS)
UO .... Empresa Aero Uruguay SA [*ICAO designator*] (FAAC)
UO .... Trans-Union [*France*] [*ICAO designator*] [*Obsolete*] (FAAC)
UO .... Ukrainica Occidentalia [*Winnipeg*] [*A publication*]
UO .... Ulm-Oberschwaben [*A publication*]
UO .... Und Oefters [*And Often*] [*German*]
UO .... Undelivered Orders [*Army*] (AABC)
UO .... Union Office (ROG)
UO .... Union Railroad of Oregon [*AAR code*]
UO .... Unit Operator (NRCH)
UO .... University of Oxford (ROG)
UO .... Urinary Output [*Medicine*]
U & O .... Use and Occupancy [*Real estate*]
U/O .... Used On (MSA)
UO .... Weber County Library, Ogden, UT [*Library symbol*] [*Library of Congress*] (LCLS)
UOA.......... United Ostomy Association [*Los Angeles, CA*] (EA)
UOA.......... University of Arizona [*Arizona*] [*Seismograph station code, US Geological Survey*] [*Closed*] (SEIS)
UOA.......... Use of Other Automobiles [*Insurance*]
UOA.......... Used on Assembly
UOBI........ United Oklahoma Bankshares [*NASDAQ symbol*] (NQ)
UOC .... Ultimate Operating Capability
UOC .... Ultimate Operational Configuration (AAG)
UOC .... Unequilibrated Ordinary Chondrites
UOC .... Union de l'Ouest Cameroun [*Union of West Cameroon*]
UOC .... Unit of Choice
UOC .... United Orpington Club [*Formerly, UOCA*] (EA)
UOC .... Universal Output Computer
UOC .... Unusual Occurrence Control
UOC .... Uranium Ore Concentrate
UOC .... Useable on Code (MCD)
UOCA........ United Orpington Club of America [*Later, UOC*] (EA)
UOCB........ Uncrossed Olivocochlear Bundle [*Otology*]
UOCO........ Union Oil Company
UODDL...... User-Oriented Data Display Language [*Data processing*]
UODG........ Underwater Ordnance Development Group
UOE.......... Unit of Error (MCD)
UOEF........ Union de Obreros Estivadores de Filipinos [*Union of Longshoremen of the Philippines*]
UOF.......... Unplanned Outage Factor [*Electronics*] (IEEE)
UOFS........ United States Forest Service, Intermountain Range and Experiment Station Library, Ogden, UT [*Library symbol*] [*Library of Congress*] (LCLS)
UOGC........ United Order of the Golden Cross [*Defunct*] (EA)
UOGF .... Uranium Off-Gas Filter [*Nuclear energy*] (NRCH)
UOGS........ Church of Jesus Christ of Latter-Day Saints, Genealogical Society Library, Ogden Branch, Ogden, UT [*Library symbol*] [*Library of Congress*] (LCLS)
UOH.......... Unplanned Outage Hours [*Electronics*] (IEEE)
UOHC........ Under Other than Honorable Conditions [*Military*]
UOI .... University of Illinois [*Record label*]
UOI .... User On-Line Interaction [*Data processing*]
UOIL........ UNIOIL [*NASDAQ symbol*] (NQ)
UOIW........ United Optical and Instrument Workers of America
UOJC........ Union of Orthodox Jewish Congregations of America (EA)
UOJCA ...... Union of Orthodox Jewish Congregations of America (EA)
UOK.......... University of Oklahoma [*Record label*]
UOL.......... Underwater Object Locator
UOL.......... Utility Octal Load
UOL.......... Utility-Oriented Language (MCD)
UOLS........ Underwater Object Location and Search Operations [*Navy*] (NVT)
U of Omaha Bull ... Night Law School Bulletin. University of Omaha (DLA)

UOMCA...... United Orthodox Ministers and Cantors Association of America and Canada (EA)
UOMS........ Union des Originaires de Mauritanie du Sud [*Union of Natives of South Mauritania*]
UOMS........ Unmanned Orbital Multifunction Satellite
UOO .... Undelivered Orders Outstanding [*Military*] (AFM)
UOP .... Understanding of the Problem (MCD)
UOP .... Unit Operating Procedure (NRCH)
UOP .... University of the Pacific [*Stockton, CA*]
UOP .... Urine Output [*Physiology*]
UOPA .... Uranium Ore Processing Association
UOPDP....... Union Ouvriere et Paysanne pour la Democratie Proletarienne [*Peasant and Worker Union for Proletarian Democracy*] [*French*] (PPE)
UOPH .... Unaccompanied Officer Personnel Housing [*Navy*]
UOQ .... Upper Outer Quadrant [*Anatomy*]
UOr........... Orem City Library, Orem, UT [*Library symbol*] [*Library of Congress*] (LCLS)
UOR.......... Uniform Officer Record
UOR.......... Unplanned Outage Rate [*Electronics*] (IEEE)
UORUSC ... Union of Orthodox Rabbis of the US and Canada (EA)
UOS .... Sewanee, TN [*Location identifier*] [*FAA*] (FAAL)
UOS .... Ultraviolet Ozone Spectrometer (MCD)
UOS .... Undelivered Orders Schedule [*Army*]
UOS .... Underwater Ordnance Station [*Navy*]
UOS .... University of the South [*Record label*]
UOS .... Unless Otherwise Specified (MSA)
UOS .... Unmanned Orbital Satellite
UOSAT ...... University of Surrey Satellite
UOT .... Uncontrollable Overtime
UOT.......... Union, SC [*Location identifier*] [*FAA*] (FAAL)
UOT.......... Upper Outer Tube
UOTASP..... United Order of the Total Abstaining Sons of the Phoenix (ROG)
UOTS .... United Order True Sisters (EA)
UOV.......... Union Ouvriere du Viet-Nam [*Vietnam Labor Union*] [*South Vietnam*]
UOV.......... Units of Variance
UOW.......... Weber State College, Ogden, UT [*Library symbol*] [*Library of Congress*] (LCLS)
UOX.......... Oxford, MS [*Location identifier*] [*FAA*] (FAAL)
UOX.......... University [*Mississippi*] [*Airport symbol*] (OAG)
UP............. Air Foyle Ltd. [*Great Britain*] [*ICAO designator*] (FAAC)
UP............. Journal of Urban Planning and Development [*A publication*]
UP............. Lab. UPSA [*France*] [*Research code symbol*]
UP............. Oregon Short Line R. R. [*of Union Pacific Railroad Co.*] [*AAR code*]
UP............. Oregon-Washington R. R. & Navigation [*of Union Pacific Railroad Co.*] [*AAR code*]
UP............. Provo Public Library, Provo, UT [*Library symbol*] [*Library of Congress*] (LCLS)
UP............. Ultra Presse [*Press agency*] [*Colombia*]
UP............. Umbilical Pin
UP............. Uncertified Patient [*British*]
UP............. Under-Proof [*Of spirituous liquors*] [*Distilling*]
UP............. Under Provisions Of [*Military*]
UP............. Undergraduate Program [*Subject area tests*]
UP............. Unearned Premium [*Insurance*]
UP............. Unemployed Parent [*Work Incentive Program*]
UP............. Union Patriotica [*Patriotic Union*] [*Spanish*] (PPE)
UP............. Union Popular [*Popular Union*] [*Uruguayan*] (PD)
UP............. Union del Pueblo [*Union of the People*] [*Mexico*] (PD)
UP............. Uniprocessor
UP............. Unit Pack
UP............. Unit Price
UP............. United Party [*Papua New Guinean*] (PPW)
UP............. United Party [*Gambian*] (PPW)
UP............. United Presbyterian
UP............. United Press [*Merged with International News Service to form UPI*]
UP............. United Provinces [*India*]
up............. United States Miscellaneous Pacific Islands [*MARC country of publication code*] [*Library of Congress*] (LCCP)
UP............. University Presses [*General term applied to presses of various universities*]
UP............. Uniwersytet Imienia Adama Mickiewicza w Poznaniu [*A publication*]
UP............. Unpostable [*Data processing*]
UP............. Unrotated Projectile [*Rocket*]
UP............. Unsolicited Proposal (MCD)
UP............. Unterrichtspraxis [*A publication*]
UP............. Update [*Online database field identifier*] [*Data processing*]
UP............. Upper (ADA)
UP............. Upper Peninsula [*Michigan*]
UP............. Upper Proof (ROG)
UP............. Ureteropelvic [*Anatomy*]
U/P............ Urine-Plasma Ratio [*Clinical chemistry*]
UP............. Uroporphyrin [*Biochemistry*]
UP............. Urticaria Pigmentosa [*Dermatology*]
UP............. User Program (MCD)
UP............. Utility Path (IEEE)

UP.............. Utility Program   (MCD)
U & P .... Uttering and Publishing
UPA............ Ukrains'ka Povstans'ka Armiia
UPA............ Uncooled Parametric Amplifier
UPA............ Uniao das Populacoes de Angola [*Angolan People's Union*]
UPA............ Union Panamericana [*Pan-American Union*] [*Washington, DC*]
UPA............ Union of Poles in America
UPA............ Union Postale Arabe [*Arab Postal Union*]
UPA............ Unique Product Advantage [*Advertising*]
UPA............ Unitary Pole Approximation
UPA............ United Patternmakers Association
UPA............ United Producers of America [*Motion picture company*]
UPA............ University Photographers Association of America
UPA............ University Press of America
UPA............ Urokinase Plasminogen Activator [*An enzyme*]
UPAA .... University Photographers Association of America   (EA)
UPAC......... Unemployed and Poverty Action Council   (EA)
UPAC .... Unificacion y Progreso [*Unification and Progress*]
               [*Mexico*]   (PPW)
UPAC .... United Parents of Absconded Children [*Defunct*]   (EA)
UPACS....... Universal Performance Assessment and Control System
UPADI .... Union Pan-Americana de Asociaciones de Igenieros [*Pan
               American Federation of Engineering Societies*]
               [*Uruguay*]   (EA-IO)
UPAE......... Union Postal de las Americas y Espana [*Postal Union of the
               Americas and Spain - PUAS*]   (EA-IO)
UPAJ .... Union Panafricaine des Journalistes
UPAL......... Utrechtse Publikaties voor Algemene Literatuurwetenschap [*A
               publication*]
U PA Law Rev ... University of Pennsylvania. Law Review and American Law
               Register [*A publication*]
U PA L Rev ... University of Pennsylvania. Law Review [*A publication*]
UPAM........ United People's Association of Matabeleland
               [*Zimbabwean*]   (PPW)
UPAO .... University Professors for Academic Order   (EA)
UPAP......... Union Pan Africaine des Postes [*Pan African Postal Union -
               PAPU*]   (EA-IO)
UPAP......... Urban Planning Assistance Program
UPARR .... Urban Park and Recreation Recovery
UPAS......... Uniform Performance Assessment System [*Education*]
UPAT......... Union Panafricaine des Telecommunications [*Pan African
               Telecommunications Union - PATU*]   (EA-IO)
UPAT......... University Patents [*NASDAQ symbol*]   (NQ)
UPB .... Brigham Young University, Provo, UT [*Library symbol*] [*Library
               of Congress*]   (LCLS)
UPB .... Union Patriotica Bonairiana [*Bonaire Patriotic Union*]
               [*Netherlands Antillean*]   (PPW)
UPB .... United Press of Bangladesh
UPB .... Universal Patents Bureau [*British*]   (ROG)
UPB .... Universidad Pontificia Bolivariana [*A publication*]
UP/BA .... Unitary Payroll Benefit Accounting   (MCD)
Up Ben Pr.. Upper Bench Precedents Tempore Car. I [*England*]   (DLA)
Up Ben Pre ... Upper Bench Precedents Tempore Car. I   (DLA)
UPB-L........ Brigham Young University, J. Reuben Clark Law Library,
               Provo, UT [*Library symbol*] [*Library of Congress*]   (LCLS)
UPC........... Pennsylvania State University, Commonwealth Campuses,
               University Park, PA [*OCLC symbol*]   (OCLC)
UPC........... Uganda People's Congress [*Suspended*]
UPC........... Underwater Pipe Cutter
UPC........... Uniform Practice Code
UPC........... Uniform Probate Code
UPC........... Union of the Corsican People [*France*]
UPC........... Union des Populations Camerounaises [*Union of Cameroonian
               Peoples*]   (PD)
UPC........... Union pour le Progres Comorien [*Union for Comorian
               Progress*]   (PPW)
UPC........... Union Progressiste Congolaise [*Congolese Progressive Union*]
UPC........... Union del Pueblo Canario [*Union of the Canarian People*]
               [*Spanish*]   (PPE)
UPC........... Unione di u Populu Corsu [*Union of the Corsican People*]
               [*French*]   (PPE)
UPC........... Unit of Packed Cells [*Hemology*]
UPC........... Unit of Processing Capacity
UPC........... Unit Processing Code   (AFM)
UPC........... United Power Company [*British*]
UPC........... United Presbyterian Church
UPC........... Universal Peripheral Controller
UPC........... Universal Product Code [*Grocery industry*]
UPC........... Unpostable Code [*Data processing*]
UPC........... US Plywood - Champion Papers, Inc. [*Later, CHA*] [*NYSE
               symbol*]
UPC........... USPCI, Inc. [*NYSE symbol*]
UPCA .... Uniform Planned Community Act [*National Conference of
               Commissioners on Uniform State Laws*]
UPCC .... Uniform Product Code Council [*Formerly, UGPCC*]   (EA)
UPCHUK .... University Program for the Comprehensive Handling and
               Utilization of Knowledge [*Humorous*]

UPCM......... Union Planters Corporation of Memphis [*NASDAQ
               symbol*]   (NQ)
UPCO .... Union Progressiste Congolaise [*Congolese Progressive Union*]
UPCO .... United Presidential Corporation [*NASDAQ symbol*]   (NQ)
UPCON....... Upgraded Constellation   (MCD)
UPCS .... Universal Philatelic Cover Society
UPD............ Under-Potential Deposition [*of metals on electrodes*]
UPD............ Underpotential Deposition [*Electrochemistry*]
UPD............ Unpaid   (ADA)
UPD............ Urban Planning Directorate [*British*]
UPDA .... United Plastics Distributors Association [*Later, NAPD*]   (EA)
UPDATE..... Unlimited Potential Data through Automation Technology in
               Education   (IEEE)
UPDEA .... Union des Producteurs, Transporteurs, et Distributeurs
               d'Energie Electrique d'Afrique [*Union of Producers,
               Conveyors, and Distributors of Electric Power in Africa -
               UPDEA*]   (EA-IO)
UPDFT....... Updraft   (MSA)
UPDFTS...... Updrafts   (FAAC)
UPDMA ...... United Popular Dress Manufacturers Association [*Later,
               LACA*]   (EA)
UPE .... Unit Proficiency Exercise
UPE .... Unitary Pole Expansion
UPEB......... Union de Paises Exportadores de Banano [*Union of Banana-
               Exporting Countries - UBEC*]   (EA-IO)
UPECO .... Union Progressiste Congolaise [*Congolese Progressive Union*]
UPEN.......... Upper Peninsula Power [*NASDAQ symbol*]   (NQ)
UPEP......... Undergraduate Preparation of Educational Personnel [*Office of
               Education*]
UPEQUA .... Union Progressiste de l'Equateur [*Progressive Union of
               Equateur Province*] [*Congo - Leopoldville*]
UPEU......... Uganda Public Employees' Union
UPF .... Uganda Popular Front   (PD)
UPF .... United Parkinson Foundation [*Chicago, IL*]   (EA)
UPF .... United Patriotic Front   (EA)
UPF .... United People's Front [*Singapore*]   (PPW)
UPF .... Unofficial Personnel Folder
UPFAW....... United Packinghouse Food and Allied Workers [*Later,
               UFCWIU*]   (EA)
UPFD .... United Pesticide Formulators and Distributors Association
               [*College Park, GA*]   (EA)
UPFDA ...... United Pesticide Formulators and Distributors Association
UPFF .... Universal Proutist Farmers Federation   (EA)
UPFM .... Union Progressive des Femmes Marocaines [*Progressive
               Union of Moroccan Women*]
UPG........... Ujung Pandang [*Indonesia*] [*Airport symbol*]   (OAG)
UPG........... Union des Populations de Guinee [*Guinea People's
               Union*]   (PD)
UPG........... Union Progressiste Guineenne [*Guinean Progressive Union*]
UPG........... United Parents under God   (EA)
UPG........... Unpaying Guest [*In a rooming or boarding house*]
UPG........... Upgrade [*Data processing*]
UPGRADE ... University of Pittsburgh Generalized Recording and
               Dissemination Experiment
UPGRADE ... User-Prompted Graphic Data Evaluation [*US Council on
               Environmental Quality*]
UPGS .... Church of Jesus Christ of Latter-Day Saints, Genealogical
               Society Library, Utah Valley Branch, Provo, UT [*Library
               symbol*] [*Library of Congress*]   (LCLS)
UPGS .... Unione Progressista della Gioventu Somala [*Progressive Union
               of Somali Youth*]
UPGWA...... International Union, United Plant Guard Workers of
               America   (EA)
UPH........... Unaccompanied Personnel Housing [*Military*]
UPH........... Underground Pumped Hydro [*Energy storage*]
UPH........... Union Patriotique Hatienne [*Haitian Patriotic Union*]   (EA)
UPHA .... United Professional Horsemen's Association   (EA)
UPHC .... United Party of Haitian Communists
UPHCI .... Undistributed Personal Holding Company Income
UPHD .... Uphold [*Law*]   (ROG)
UPHD .... Upholstered
UPHEWA.... United Presbyterian Health, Education, and Welfare
               Association [*Later, PHEWA*]   (EA)
UPHG .... Upholstering
UPHPISEC ... Union for the Protection of the Human Person by International,
               Social, and Economic Cooperation [*Defunct*]   (EA)
UPI .... Fayetteville/Fort Bragg, NC [*Location identifier*] [*FAA*]   (FAAL)
UPI .... United Press International [*Formed by a merger of United
               Press Associations and International News Service*]
               [*Washington, DC*]   (EA)
UPI .... Upper Plenum Injection [*Nuclear energy*]   (NRCH)
UPI .... Uteroplacental Insufficiency [*Medicine*]
UPIA........... Underwater Photography Instruction Association
               [*Defunct*]   (EA)
UPIA........... Uniform Principal and Income Act [*National Conference of
               Commissioners on Uniform State Laws*]
UPICV .... Uniao dos Povos das Ilhas do Cabo Verde [*Union of the
               Peoples of the Cape Verde Islands*]
UPIGO .... Union Professionnelle Internationale des Gynecologues et
               Obstetriciens [*International Union of Professional
               Gynecologists and Obstetricians*]

UPIN .... United Press International Newspictures
UPIR .... Uniform Photographic Interpretation Report [*Military*]   (AFM)
U Pit Law .... University of Pittsburgh. Law Review [*A publication*]
UPITN .... United Press International Television News
U Pitt L R .... University of Pittsburgh. Law Review [*A publication*]
U of Pitt L Rev ... University of Pittsburgh. Law Review [*A publication*]
UPIU .... United Paperworkers International Union
UPJ .... Underwater Pump Jet
UPJ .... Upjohn Co. [*NYSE symbol*]
UPJ .... Ureteropelvic Junction [*Anatomy*]
UPK .... United Park City Mines Co. [*NYSE symbol*]
UPK .... Upkeep Period [*Navy*]   (NVT)
UPL .... Unidentified Process Loss
UPL .... Unit Personnel List [*Army*]
UPL .... Universal Programing Language [*Data processing*]   (BUR)
UPL .... Universal Publications, London [*British*]
UPL .... Upala [*Costa Rica*] [*Airport symbol*] [*Obsolete*]   (OAG)
UPL .... Uplink
UPL .... Uranium Product Loadout [*Nuclear energy*]   (NRCH)
UPL .... User Programing Language [*Burroughs Corp.*] [*Data processing*]   (IEEE)
UPLAC .... Union des Producteurs de Levure-Aliment de la CEE [*Union of Dried Yeast Producers of the Common Market*]
UPLD .... Upland [*Plateau, highland*] [*Board on Geographic Names*]
UPLF .... Universal Payload Fairing [*NASA*]   (KSC)
UPLG .... Union Populaire pour la Liberation de la Guadeloupe [*Popular Union for the Liberation of Guadeloupe*]   (PD)
UPLI .... United Poets Laureate International   (EA)
UPLR .... Uganda Protectorate Law Reports [*1904-51*]   (DLA)
UPLR .... United Provinces Law Reports [*India*]   (DLA)
U of PLR .... University of Pennsylvania. Law Review [*A publication*]
U of PL Rev ... University of Pennsylvania. Law Review [*A publication*]
UPLT .... United Provinces Law Times [*India*]   (DLA)
UPLV .... Upper Leg Vein [*Anatomy*]
UPM .... Pennsylvania State University, University Park, PA [*OCLC symbol*]   (OCLC)
UPM .... Uganda Patriotic Movement   (PD)
UPM .... Ultrapure Metal
UPM .... Union du Peuple Malgache [*Malagasy People's Union*]
UPM .... Union Progressiste Mauritanienne [*Mauritanian Progressive Union*]
UPM .... Unione Politica Maltese [*Maltese Political Union*]   (PPE)
UPM .... Unit Production Manager [*Filmmaking*]
UPM .... United People's Movement [*St. Vincentian*]   (PPW)
UPM .... United People's Movement [*Antiguan*]   (PPW)
UPM .... Universal Permissive Module   (IEEE)
UPM .... Unreached Peoples Mission [*Boring, OH*]   (EA)
UPMB .... University of Pennsylvania. Museum Bulletin [*A publication*]
UPMFF .... University of Pennsylvania. Monographs in Folklore and Folklife [*A publication*]
UPMI .... Union Progressiste Melanesienne [*Progressive Melanesian Union*] [*New Caledonian*]   (PPW)
UPN .... Union del Pueblo Navarrese [*Union of the Navarrese People*] [*Spanish*]   (PPW)
UPN .... United Party of Nigeria
UPN .... Uruapan [*Mexico*] [*Airport symbol*]   (OAG)
UPNCA .... United Pants and Novelties Contractors Association [*Defunct*]   (EA)
UPNE .... University Press of New England
U P News .... Unauthorized Practice News [*A publication*]
UPNI .... Unionist Party of Northern Ireland
UP (Noth) ... Ueberlieferungsgeschichte des Pentateuch (M. Noth) [*A publication*]   (BJA)
UPNS .... Ukranian Philatelic and Numismatic Society   (EA)
UPO .... Undistorted Power Output
UPO .... Unidentified Paleontological Object
UPO .... Unit Personnel Office [*or Officer*]
UPOS .... Utility Program Operating System   (IEEE)
UPOV .... Union Internationale pour la Protection des Obtentions Vegetales [*International Union for the Protection of New Varieties of Plants*]   (EA-IO)
UPP .... Hawi, HI [*Location identifier*] [*FAA*]   (FAAL)
UPP .... Ultraprecision Parachute   (NG)
UPP .... United Papermakers and Paperworkers [*Later, UPIU*]   (EA)
UPP .... United Peasants' Party [*Poland*]   (PD)
UPP .... United People's Party [*Grenadian*]   (PPW)
UPP .... United People's Party [*Sierra Leone*]
UPP .... United Press of Pakistan
UPP .... United Progressive Party [*Zambia*]
UPP .... United Progressive Party [*Trinidadian and Tobagan*]   (PPW)
UPP .... Universal PROM Programer
UPP .... Upolu Point [*Hawaii*] [*Airport symbol*]   (OAG)
UPP .... Uppsala [*Sweden*] [*Seismograph station code, US Geological Survey*]   (SEIS)
UPP .... Utility Print Punch
UPPA .... United People's Party of Arunachal [*Indian*]   (PPW)
UPPC .... Universal Pin Pack Connector
UPPE .... Ultraviolet Photometric and Polarimetric Explorer
UPPF .... United Presbyterian Peace Fellowship   (EA)
UPPG .... Union des Paysans Pauvres de la Guadeloupe   (PD)

UPPN .... Union Postale des Pays du Nord [*Nordic Postal Union - NPU*]   (EA-IO)
UPPN .... United People's Party of Nigeria
UPPOE ...... University of Pittsburgh Production Organization Exercise [*Simulation game*]
UPPP .... Uvulo-Palato-Pharyngoplasty [*Surgical procedure*] [*Initials are derived from the name of the problem the procedure cures*]
UPPS .... Ultimate Plant Protection System [*Nuclear energy*]   (NRCH)
UPPS .... Unified Pilot Publication System [*American Chemical Society*]
Uppsala Univ G Inst B ... Uppsala University. Geological Institution. Bulletin [*A publication*]
Upps Arsskr ... Uppsala Universitets Arsskrift [*A publication*]
Upps Univ Geol Inst Bull ... Uppsala University. Geological Institution. Bulletin [*A publication*]
UPr .... Ucilisten Pregled [*A publication*]
UPR .... Ultraportable RADAR   (MCD)
UPR .... Ultrasonic Parametric Resonance   (IEEE)
UPR .... Ultraviolet Proton Radiation
UPR .... Uniform Parole Reports [*Law Enforcement Assistance Administration*]
UPR .... Union des Populations Rurales [*Union of Rural People*] [*Lomela-Kasai*]
UPR .... University of Puerto Rico
UPR .... Upper   (AAG)
UPR .... Uranium Production Reactor
UPR .... Urethral Profile at Rest [*Medicine*]
Upravlenie Slozn Sistemami ... Upravlenie Sloznymi Sistemami. Rizskii Politehniceskii Institut [*A publication*]
Uprawa Rosl Nawozenie ... Uprawa Roslin i Nawozenie [*A publication*]
UPR Co ...... Union Pacific Railroad Company [*A publication*]
UPrE .... College of Eastern Utah, Price, UT [*Library symbol*] [*Library of Congress*]   (LCLS)
UPREAL ..... Unit Property Record and Equipment Authorization List
UPREC ...... Upon Receipt
UPREL .... Unit Property Record and Equipment List
UP Res Dig ... UP [*University of the Philippines*] Research Digest [*A publication*]
UPRG .... Unit Personnel Records Group [*Air Force*]   (AFM)
UPRGp .... Unit Personnel Records Group [*Air Force*]   (AFM)
UPrGS .... Church of Jesus Christ of Latter-Day Saints, Genealogical Society Library, Price Branch, Price, UT [*Library symbol*] [*Library of Congress*]   (LCLS)
UPRI .... Up-Right, Inc. [*NASDAQ symbol*]   (NQ)
UPRI .... Uteroplacental Respiratory Insufficiency [*Gynecology*]
UPRICO ...... University of Puerto Rico
Uprochnyayushchaya Term Termomekh Obrab Prokata ... Uprochnyayushchaya Termicheskaya i Termomekhanicheskaya Obrabotka Prokata [*A publication*]
UPROCO .... Union Progressiste du Congo [*Progressive Union of the Congo*] [*Niangara*]
UPRONA .... Union pour le Progres National [*Union for National Progress*] [*Burundi*]   (PPW)
UPRP .... Union des Paysans Ruraux et Progressistes [*Union of Rural and Progressive Farmers*] [*Congo-Kasai*]
UPRR .... Union Pacific Railroad Co.
Upr Sist Mash ... Upravlyayushchie Sistemy i Mashiny [*Ukrainian SSR*] [*A publication*]
Upr Yad Energ Ustanovkami ... Upravlenie Yadernymi Energeticheskimi Ustanovkami [*A publication*]
UPS .... Ultraviolet Photoemission Spectroscopy
UPS .... Uncontested Physical Searches [*CIA term for break-ins*]
UPS .... Under Provisions of Section [*Military*]
UPS .... Underground Press Syndicate [*Later, APS*]   (EA)
UPS .... Underwater Photographic Society   (EA)
UP & S .... Uniform Printing and Supply
UPS .... Uninterruptible Power Supply [*or System*]
UPS .... Union Progressiste Senegalaise [*Senegalese Progressive Union*] [*Political party*]
UPS .... Unit Personnel Section [*Military*]
UPS .... Unit Price Standards   (MCD)
UPS .... Unit Proficiency System   (AAG)
UPS .... United Parcel Service
UPS .... United Peregrine Society   (EA)
UPS .... Universal Polar Stereographic Grid
UPS .... Universal Processing System
UPS .... Universities and Public Schools Battalions [*Military units*] [*British*] [*World War I*]
UPS .... Upright Perigee Stage [*Aerospace*]   (MCD)
UPS .... Urethral Profile under Stress [*Medicine*]
UPS .... Uterine Progesterone System [*Contraceptive device*]
UPSA .... Ukrainian Political Science Association in the US   (EA)
UPSA .... Ukrainian Professional Society of America   (EA)
UPSA .... Uniform Program Salary Administration   (MCD)
Upsala J Med Sci ... Upsala Journal of Medical Sciences [*A publication*]
Upsala J Med Sci Suppl ... Upsala Journal of Medical Sciences. Supplement [*A publication*]
UPSEELL ... University of Pennsylvania. Studies in East European Languages and Literatures [*A publication*]
UPSF .... Universal Proutist Student Federation   (EA)

UPSI .... User Program Sense Indicator

UPSI .... User Program Switch Indicator [*Data processing*]

UPSIS .... United States Political Science Information Service [*University of Pittsburgh*] (EISS)

Ups J Med Sci ... Upsala Journal of Medical Sciences [*A publication*]

Ups J Med Sci Suppl ... Upsala Journal of Medical Sciences. Supplement [*A publication*]

UPSLP .... Upslope (FAAC)

UPSN .... University Peace Studies Network (EA)

UPSR .... Unit Proficiency System Requirements (AAG)

UPSS .... Ukrainska Partiia Samostiinykiv-Sotsiialistiv [*Ukrainian Party of Socialist-Independentists*] [*Russian*] (PPE)

UPSS .... United Postal Stationery Society (EA)

UPSSL .... University of Puget Sound School of Law (DLA)

UPSTAGE ... Upper-Stage Guidance Experiment

UPSTARS .. Universal Propulsion Stabilization, Retardation, and Separation [*Air Force*]

UPSTART ... Universal Parachute Support Tactical and Research Target (NG)

UPSTEP ..... Undergraduated Pre-Service Teacher Education Program [*National Science Foundation*] (EA)

UPSUB .... Submit Draft to a Superior for Approval [*From George Orwell's novel, "1984"*]

UPT .... Undergraduate Pilot Training [*Air Force*]

UP & T .... Unit Personnel and Tonnage Table [*Military*]

UPT .... University Patents, Inc. [*American Stock Exchange symbol*]

UPT .... Urgent Postal Telegram

UPT .... User Process Table

UPTA .... Uniform Perpetuation of Testimony Act [*National Conference of Commissioners on Uniform State Laws*]

UPTA .... United Parent-Teachers Association of Jewish Schools (EA)

UPTA .... University Resident Theatre Association (EA)

UPTC .... Union Panafricaine des Travailleurs Croyants [*Pan-African Union of Believing Workers*]

UPTF .... Upper Plenum Test Facility [*Nuclear energy*] (NRCH)

UPT-H .... Undergraduate Pilot Training - Helicopter [*Air Force*]

UPTLM .... Up-Link Telemetry [*NASA*] (NASA)

UPTP .... Universal Package Test Panel

UPTT .... Unit Personnel and Tonnage Table [*Military*] (AABC)

UPUC .... Unauthorized Publication or Use of Communications

UPUC .... Universal Postal Union Collectors (EA)

UPUC .... Universal Postal Union Convention

UPUP .... Ulster Popular Unionist Party [*Northern Ireland*] (PPW)

UPUP .... Ulster Progressive Unionist Party [*Northern Ireland*] (PPW)

UPUS .... United Public Utility Systems

UPUSA .... UPU [*Universal Postal Union*] Staff Association (EA-IO)

UPV .... Unfired Pressure Vessel

UPV .... Universal Pre-Vent, Inc. [*Vancouver Stock Exchange symbol*]

UPVC .... Unfired Pressure Vessel Code (AAG)

UPVC .... Unplasticized Polyvinyl Chloride

UP Vet .... UP [*University of the Philippines*] Veterinarian [*A publication*]

UPW .... Union of Post Office Workers [*British*]

UPW .... United Port Workers' Union [*Ceylon*]

UPW .... United Presbyterian Women (EA)

UPW .... United Public Workers of America

UPWA .... Union of Polish Women in America (EA)

UPWA .... United Packinghouse Workers of America [*Later, UFCWIU*]

UPWA .... United Polish Women of America (EA)

UPWARD .... Understanding Personal and Racial Dignity [*Navy program*]

UPWD .... Upward (MSA)

UPWF .... Ukrainian Patriarchal World Federation (EA)

UPWT .... Unitary Plan Wind Tunnel (KSC)

UPY .... Union of People's Youth [*Bulgaria*]

UPYF .... Universal Proutist Youth Federation (EA)

UPz .... Urkunden der Ptolemaerzeit [*U. Wilcken*] [*A publication*] (BJA)

UQ .... Fronte dell'Uomo Qualunque; Uomo Qualunque [*Common Man Front*] [*Italy*] (PPE)

UQ .... Ubiquinone [*Also, CoQ, Q, U*] [*Biochemistry*]

UQ .... Ukrainian Quarterly [*A publication*]

UQ .... Ultraquick [*Flashing*] Light [*Navigation signal*]

UQ .... Universities Quarterly [*A publication*]

UQ .... Upper Quadrant [*Anatomy*]

UQ .... Upper Quadrile

UQAM .... Universite du Quebec a Montreal [*Canada*]

UQB .... Universite de Quebec [*UTLAS symbol*]

UQC .... Underwater Telephone [*Navy*] (CAAL)

UQCP .... Uniform Quality Control Program

UQE .... Queen [*Alaska*] [*Airport symbol*] [*Obsolete*] (OAG)

UQGS .... Uniform Quality Grading System [*Tires*]

UQL .... Unacceptable Quality Level

UQLJ .... University of Queensland. Law Journal [*A publication*]

UQOT .... Unquote (FAAC)

UQP .... Universities and the Quest for Peace [*An association*]

UQP .... University of Queensland. Papers [*A publication*]

UQS .... Nuiqsut Village, AK [*Location identifier*] [*FAA*] (FAAL)

Uqs .... 'Uqsin (BJA)

U Qsld P SS ... University of Queensland. Papers. Social Sciences [*A publication*]

UQT .... User Queue Table

U Queens L J ... University of Queensland. Law Journal [*A publication*]

U of Queensl LJ ... University of Queensland. Law Journal [*A publication*]

U Queensl LJ ... University of Queensland. Law Journal [*A publication*]

UQY .... Kansas City, MO [*Location identifier*] [*FAA*] (FAAL)

UR .... AeroSun International, Inc. [*ICAO designator*] (FAAC)

UR .... [*The*] Item Requested Is Under Revision By the Proponent. Copies of Edition Presently in Use Are Not Available [*Advice of supply action code*] [*Army*]

UR .... Lab. J. Uriach & Cia. SA [*Spain*] [*Research code symbol*]

UR .... Lloyd's Universal Register of Shipping [*British*] (ROG)

UR .... Ukrainian Review [*London*] [*A publication*]

UR .... Ullage Rocket (KSC)

UR .... Umjetnost Rijeci [*A publication*]

UR .... Unconditioned Response [*Psychometrics*]

UR .... Under the Rule [*Business and trade*]

U/R .... Underrange (IEEE)

UR .... Underreporter [*IRS*]

UR .... Undulator Radiation [*High-energy physics*]

UR .... Unfinanced Requirement [*Army*] (AABC)

UR .... Unfractionated Reservoir [*Geology*]

UR .... Unfunded Requirement [*Military*] (AFIT)

UR .... Uniao Republicana [*Republican Union*] [*Portuguese*] (PPE)

UR .... Unidentified Remittance [*IRS*]

UR .... Uniform Regulations

UR .... Unit Record [*Data processing*]

UR .... Unit Register

UR .... Unitatis Redintegratio [*Decree on Ecumenism*] [*Vatican II document*]

UR .... University Relations

UR .... University Review [*A publication*]

UR .... University of Rochester [*New York*] (KSC)

UR .... Unprogrammed Requirements (MCD)

UR .... Unreleasable (MCD)

UR .... Unsatisfactory Report

U/R .... Up Range [*NASA*] (KSC)

U/R .... Up Right [*The rear right portion of a stage*] [*A stage direction*]

UR .... Upper Rail

UR .... Upper Respiratory [*Medicine*]

UR .... Upper Right (MCD)

UR .... Uprange

UR .... Uranium (ROG)

UR .... Urban Rat [*Virus*]

UR .... Urinal (MSA)

UR .... Urine

UR .... Urology

UR .... User Requirements [*Nuclear energy*] (NRCH)

ur .... USSR [*Union of Soviet Socialist Republics*] [*MARC country of publication code*] [*Library of Congress*] (LCCP)

UR .... Uti Rogas [*Be It as You Desire*] [*Used by Romans to express assent to a proposition*] [*Latin*]

UR .... Utility Room (MSA)

UR .... Utilization Review

UR .... Your

URA .... United Red Army [*Japan*] (PD)

URA .... United Republicans of America

URA .... Universities Research Association

URA .... Upper Respiratory Allergy [*Medicine*]

Ura .... Uracil [*Biochemistry*]

URA .... Urakawa [*Japan*] [*Seismograph station code, US Geological Survey*] (SEIS)

Ura .... Urania [*Record label*] [*USA, Europe, etc.*]

URA .... Uranium Recycle Acid [*Nuclear energy*] (NRCH)

URA .... Urban Redevelopment Authority

URA .... Urban Renewal Administration [*of HHFA*] [*Terminated*]

URA .... Urine Receptacle Assembly (MCD)

URA .... User Requirements Analysis

URAAA .... Urania [*Poland*] [*A publication*]

URAC .... Union des Republiques de l'Afrique Centrale [*Union of Central African Republics*]

URACTY ..... Your Activity

URAD .... [*Reference*] Your Radio [*Message*] [*Military*]

URAEP .... University of Rochester Atomic Energy Project

URAF .... Unidentified Remittance Amount File [*IRS*]

URAI .... Universities Research Association, Incorporated

Ural Gos Univ Mat Zap ... Ural'skii Gosudarstvennyi Universitet Imeni A. M. Gor'kogo. Ural'skoe Matematiceskoe Obscestvo. Matematiceskie Zapiski [*A publication*]

Ural Politehn Inst Sb ... Urel'skii Politehniceskii Institut Imeni S. M. Kirova. Sbornik [*A publication*]

URAM .... Unrelated Adult Man

Uranium Abstr ... Uranium Abstracts [*A publication*]

URAPA .... Uniform Rendition of Accused Persons Act [*National Conference of Commissioners on Uniform State Laws*]

URARPAA ... Uniform Relocation Assistance and Real Property Acquisition Act [*1970*] (OICC)

URARPAPA ... Uniform Relocation Assistance and Real Property Acquisition Policies Act of 1970

URARRED ... US Army Readiness Command (MCD)

URAS .... Union des Republicains d'Action Sociale [*Union of Republicans of Social Action*] [*French*] (PPE)

URAUZ .... You Are Authorized (FAAC)

URAW .... Unrelated Adult Woman

URB .... Union Regionale de Bamileke [*Regional Union of Bamileke*] [*Cameroon*]
URB .... University of Riyad. Bulletin. Faculty of Arts [*Saudi Arabia*] [*A publication*]
URB .... Unridable Bicycle
URB .... Urban
URB .... Urbana College, Urbana, OH [*OCLC symbol*]   (OCLC)
URB .... Urubupunga [*Brazil*] [*Airport symbol*]   (OAG)
Urb Aff Abstr ... Urban Affairs Abstracts [*A publication*]
Urb Aff Ann R ... Urban Affairs Annual Review [*A publication*]
Urb Aff Q ... Urban Affairs Quarterly [*A publication*]
Urb Aff Quart ... Urban Affairs Quarterly [*A publication*]
Urb Aff Rep ... Urban Affairs Reporter [*Commerce Clearing House*]   (DLA)
Urban Abs ... Urban Abstracts [*A publication*]
Urban Aff Abs ... Urban Affairs Abstracts [*A publication*]
Urban Affairs Q ... Urban Affairs Quarterly [*A publication*]
Urban Anthr ... Urban Anthropology [*A publication*]
Urban Des ... Urban Design [*A publication*]
Urban Design Intl ... Urban Design International [*A publication*]
Urban Des Int ... Urban Design International [*A publication*]
Urban Des Q ... Urban Design Quarterly [*A publication*]
Urban Ecol ... Urban Ecology [*A publication*]
Urban Ed .... Urban Education [*A publication*]
Urban Educ ... Urban Education [*A publication*]
Urban Hist ... Urban History Review [*Revue d'Histoire Urbaine*] [*A publication*]
Urban Hist R ... Urban History Review [*A publication*]
Urban Hist Yearb ... Urban History Yearbook [*A publication*]
URBANICOM ... Association Internationale Urbanisme et Commerce [*International Association for Town Planning and Distribution*]   (EA-IO)
Urban Innov Abroad ... Urban Innovation Abroad [*A publication*]
Urban Inst Policy Res Rep ... Urban Institute. Policy and Research Report [*A publication*]
URBANK .... Urban Development Bank
Urban L Ann ... Urban Law Annual [*A publication*]
Urban Law ... Urban Lawyer [*A publication*]
Urban Lif C ... Urban Life and Culture [*Later, Urban Life*] [*A publication*]
Urban R .... Urban Review [*A publication*]
Urban Rev ... Urban Review [*A publication*]
Urban Soc C ... Urban and Social Change Review [*A publication*]
Urban Stud ... Urban Studies [*A publication*]
Urban Syst ... Urban Systems [*A publication*]
Urb Anthrop ... Urban Anthropology [*A publication*]
Urban Transp Abroad ... Urban Transportation Abroad [*A publication*]
URBCOM ... [*The*] Urban Communications Game
URBE......... Urban Ecology [*Netherlands*] [*A publication*]
URBH .... Urban Health [*A publication*]
URBK .... Union Rheinische Braunkohlen Kraftstoff [*West Germany*]
Urb Law ...... Urban Lawyer [*A publication*]
Urb Law Pol ... Urban Law and Policy [*A publication*]
Urb Life ...... Urban Life [*A publication*]
Urb Life & Cult ... Urban Life and Culture [*Later, Urban Life*] [*A publication*]
URBM........ Ultimate Range Ballistic Missile [*Air Force*]
URBN-A ...... Urbanisme [*France*] [*A publication*]
URBOE .... Ultimatist Religious Bodies on Earth [*An association*]   (EA)
URBPOP..... Urban Population File   (MCD)
URBS-A....... Urban Studies [*United Kingdom*] [*A publication*]
Urb Soc Change R ... Urban and Social Change Review [*A publication*]
Urb Stud ..... Urban Studies [*A publication*]
URC............ Uganda Railways Corporation
URC........... Ultrasonic Resin Cleaner   (NRCH)
URC........... Unit Record Card
URC........... Unit Record Control
URC........... United Reform Church in England and Wales
URC........... Upper Rib Cage [*Anatomy*]
URC........... Ursuline College Library, Pepper Pike, OH [*OCLC symbol*]   (OCLC)
URC........... Urumqi [*China*] [*Airport symbol*]   (OAG)
URC........... Utility Radio Communication
URCC .... University of Rochester Cancer Center [*Research center*]   (RCD)
URCF......... Unidentified Remittance Control File [*IRS*]
URCLK .... Universal Receiver Clock
URCO .... Union des Ressortissants du Congo pour la Defense et la Promotion du Congo [*Union of Congolese for the Defense and Promotion of the Congo*]
URCS .... Uniform Ration Cost System   (MCD)
URD........... New York, NY [*Location identifier*] [*FAA*]   (FAAL)
URD........... Underground Residential Distribution [*Cable*]
URD........... Union Republicana Democratica [*Democratic Republican Union*] [*Puerto Rico, Venezuela*]
URD........... Upper Respiratory Disease [*Medicine*]
urd........... Urdu [*MARC language code*] [*Library of Congress*]   (LCCP)
Urd .... Uridine [*Also, U*] [*A nucleoside*]
URD........... User Requirements Document   (MCD)
URDA .... Uniform Retirement Date Act [*National Conference of Commissioners on Uniform State Laws*]
URDA .... Urban Resources Development Agency   (OICC)
URDIS .... Your Dispatch [*Military*]

Urdmurt i Glazov Ped Inst Ucen Zap ... Urdmurtskogo i Glazovskogo Pedagogiceskogo Instituta Ucenye Zapiski [*A publication*]
Urdmurt Ped Inst Ucen Zap ... Urdmurtskogo Pedagogiceskogo Instituta Ucenye Zapiski [*A publication*]
URDP......... Ukrains'ka Revoliutsiino-Demokratychna Partiia
URE .... Undergraduate Record Examination [*Education*]
URE .... Unintentional Radiation Exploitation   (AFM)
URECD .... Urban Ecology [*A publication*]
UREHE .... Union for Research and Experimentation in Higher Education [*Later, UECU*]
UREKA ...... Unlimited Resources Ensure Keen Answers
UREP......... University Research Expeditions Programs
URESA .... Uniform Reciprocal Enforcement of Support Act
U-REST ..... Universal Range, Endurance, Speed, and Time   (NG)
ureth .... Urethra [*Anatomy*]
Urethane..... Urethane Plastics and Products [*A publication*]
Urethane Plast Prod ... Urethane Plastics and Products [*A publication*]
URETS ...... University Real Estate Trust [*NASDAQ symbol*]   (NQ)
URev.......... University Review [*Dublin*] [*A publication*]
URF .... Ukrainian Research Foundation   (EA)
URF .... Unassigned Reading Frame [*Genetics*]
URF .... Unidentified Reading Frame [*Genetics*]
URF .... Unidentified Remittance File [*IRS*]
URF .... Union des Services Routiers des Chemins de Fer Europeens [*Union of European Railways Road Services*]
URF .... United Religious Front [*Israeli*]   (BJA)
URF .... United Republican Fund
URFDA-NYC ... United Retail Fish Dealers Association of New York City   (EA)
URG........... Underway Replenishment Group [*Military*]
URG........... Unit Review Group [*Nuclear energy*]   (NRCH)
URG........... United Rayore Gas [*Vancouver Stock Exchange symbol*]
URG........... Universal Radio Group
URG........... Urgent   (AFM)
URG........... Urheberrechtsgesetz [*German Copyright Act*]   (DLA)
URG........... Uruguaiana [*Brazil*] [*Airport symbol*]   (OAG)
URGAB ...... Urologe. Ausgabe A [*A publication*]
URGE .... Urgent Care Centers of America [*NASDAQ symbol*]   (NQ)
URGENT..... Universal Relevance Group Enterprise in a National Theater [*Theater workshop*]
URGR .... Underway Replenishment Group [*Military*]
URHB .... Urban Renewal Handbook
URi .... Richmond City Library, Richmond, UT [*Library symbol*] [*Library of Congress*]   (LCLS)
URI .... Union Research Institute, Kowloon, Hong Kong [*Library symbol*] [*Library of Congress*]   (LCLS)
URI .... United Research, Incorporated
URI .... University Research Initiative [*DoD*]   (RDA)
URI .... University of Rhode Island
URI .... Unpublished Research Information [*Conducted by National Science Foundation*]
URI .... Upper Respiratory Infection [*Medicine*]
URI .... Uribe [*Colombia*] [*Airport symbol*] [*Obsolete*]   (OAG)
URICA .... Universal Real-Time Information Control and Administration   (MCD)
URICA .... Using Reading in Creative Activities
U Rich LN... University of Richmond. Law Notes   (DLA)
U Richmond L Rev ... University of Richmond. Law Review [*A publication*]
URifGS ...... Church of Jesus Christ of Latter-Day Saints, Genealogical Society Library, Richfield Branch, Richfield, UT [*Library symbol*] [*Library of Congress*]   (LCLS)
URII .... Ukrainian Research and Information Institute [*Defunct*]   (EA)
URIMA....... University Risk and Insurance Managers Association [*Later, URMIA*]   (EA)
URINA .... Urologia Internationalis [*A publication*]
URINT........ Unintentional Radiation Intelligence   (MCD)
URIPS........ Undersea Radioisotope Power Supply
URIR .... Unified Radioactive Isodromic Regulator
URISA .... Urban and Regional Information Systems Association [*Washington, DC*]
URIZR........ Your Recommendation Is Requested   (FAAC)
URJA .... United Roumanian Jews of America   (EA)
Urk .... Urkunden des Aegyptischen Altertums [*G. Steindorff*] [*Leipzig*] [*A publication*]   (BJA)
URL .... University of Regina Library [*UTLAS symbol*]
URL .... Unrequited Love [*Slang*]
URL .... Unrestricted Line Officer [*Navy*]
URL .... User Requirements Language [*Data processing*]
URLAA .... Urban Land [*A publication*]
URLB........ University of Rochester. Library Bulletin [*A publication*]
URLBB....... Urologe. Ausgabe B [*A publication*]
URLGA .... Urologe [*A publication*]
URLH........ Urban Renewal and Low Income Housing [*A publication*]
URLTR....... [*Reference*] Your Letter [*Military*]
URM .... Uncle Remus Museum
URM .... University Reform Movement [*in Latin America*]
URM .... Unlimited Register Machine
URM .... Urban Renewal Manual
URM .... Uriman [*Venezuela*] [*Airport symbol*]   (OAG)
URMGM ..... [*Reference*] Your Mailgram [*Military*]
URMIA........ University Risk Management and Insurance Association   (EA)

URMIS....... Uniform Retail Meat Identity Standard [*Pronounced "er-miss"*]
UR M-L....... Uniao Revolucionaria, Marxista-Leninista [*Marxist-Leninist Revolutionary Union*] [*Portuguese*] (PPE)
URMSG ...... [*Reference*] Your Message [*Military*]
URN........... Covington/Cincinnati, OH [*Location identifier*] [*FAA*] (FAAL)
URN........... Ultrahigh Radio Navigation (NATG)
URN........... Uniform Random Numerator [*Data processing*]
URN........... Unique Record Number [*Data processing*] (ADA)
URNEA....... Urologiya i Nefrologiya [*A publication*]
URNF........ Unidentified Remittance Name File [*IRS*]
URNG........ Unidad Revolucionaria Nacional Guatemalteca [*Guatemalan National Revolutionary Unity*] (PD)
URO........... United Restitution Organization
URO........... United Rink Operators [*Defunct*] (EA)
URO........... Urology
URO........... Uroporphyrin [*Biochemistry*]
URO........... Uroporphyrinogen [*Clinical medicine*]
URO........... User Readout (MCD)
URO........... Ustredni Rada Odboru [*Central Council of Trade Unions*] [*Czechoslovakia*]
UROBA...... United Russian Orthodox Brotherhood of America (EA)
UROC....... United Railroad Operating Crafts [*Defunct*]
UROEA....... UNESCO Regional Office for Education in Asia and Oceania (DLA)
UROGEN .... Uroporphyrinogen [*Biochemistry*]
UROL......... Urology
UROLA .... UNEP [*United Nations Environmental Programme*] Regional Office for Latin America [*Mexico City, Mexico*] (EA-IO)
Urol Ausg A ... Urologe. Ausgabe A [*A publication*]
Urol Clin North Am ... Urologic Clinics of North America [*A publication*]
Urol i Nefrol ... Urologiya i Nefrologiya [*A publication*]
Urol Int .... Urologia Internationalis [*A publication*]
Urol Intern ... Urologia Internationalis [*A publication*]
Urol Nefrol (Mosk) ... Urologiia i Nefrologiia (Moskva) [*A publication*]
Urol Nephrol Sz ... Urologiai es Nephrologiai Szemle [*Hungary*] [*A publication*]
Urologe ...... Urologe. Ausgabe A [*A publication*]
Urologe A... Urologe. Ausgabe A. Zeitschrift fuer Klinische und Praktische Urologie [*A publication*]
Urologe B... Urologe. Ausgabe B. Organ des Berufverbandes der Deutschen Urologen [*A publication*]
Urol Panam ... Urologia Panamericana [*A publication*]
Urol Pol ..... Urologia Polska [*A publication*]
Urol Radiol ... Urologic Radiology [*A publication*]
Urol Res ..... Urological Research [*A publication*]
Urol Suppl (Treviso) ... Urologia. Supplemento (Treviso) [*A publication*]
Urol Surv.... Urological Survey [*A publication*]
UROP .... Undergraduate Research Opportunities Program [*Pronounced "your-op"*] [*Massachusetts Institute of Technology*]
UROS .... Uroporphyrinogen I Synthase [*An enzyme*]
URP........... Undergraduate Research Participation [*National Science Foundation project*] [*Defunct*] (EA)
URP........... Underreporter Program [*IRS*]
URP........... Unique Radiolytic Product [*Food technology*]
URP........... Unit Record Processor
URP........... United Reef Petroleums Ltd. [*Toronto Stock Exchange symbol*]
URP........... Unmanned Recovery Platform [*Navy*] (NVT)
URP........... Untersuchungen zur Romanischen Philologie [*A publication*]
URP........... Upper-Stage Reusable Payload
URP........... Urban Renewal Project [*HUD*] (OICC)
URPE........ Union for Radical Political Economics (EA)
URPE........ Union des Resistants pour une Europe Unie [*Union of Resistance Veterans for a United Europe*]
URPE........ Union Revolucionaria Popular Ecuatoriana [*Ecuadorean Popular Revolutionary Union*] (PPW)
URPG .... President's Urban and Regional Policy Group [*Terminated, 1978*] (EGAO)
URPP........ Undergraduate Research Participation Program [*Formerly, URP*] (EA)
URPT-A...... Urban and Rural Planning Thought [*India*] [*A publication*]
URQ........... Unsatisfactory Report Questionnaire
URQ........... Upper Right Quadrant [*Medicine*]
URR........... Ultra-Rapid Reader [*Data processing*]
URR........... Union Railroad Co. [*Pittsburgh, PA*] [*AAR code*]
URR........... Unit Readiness Report [*Army*] (AABC)
URR........... United Redford Resources, Inc. [*Vancouver Stock Exchange symbol*]
URR........... Universities Research Reactor [*British*]
URR........... Urrao [*Colombia*] [*Airport symbol*] (OAG)
URR........... Utilization Research Report
URRC .... Urological Rehabilitation and Research Center [*University of Alabama in Birmingham*] [*Research center*] (RCD)
URS........... Ugurusu [*Japan*] [*Seismograph station code, US Geological Survey*] (SEIS)
URS........... Unate Ringe Sum [*Logic expression*] (IEEE)
URS........... UNESCO Relations Staff
URS........... Uniform Reporting System
URS........... Unit Reference Sheet (AABC)
URS........... United Research Service (MCD)
URS........... Universal Reference System

URS .... Universal Regulating System
URS .... University Research Support [*Department of Energy*]
URS .... Update Report System (TEL)
URS .... Urban Resource Systems [*San Francisco, CA*] (EA)
URS .... URS Corp. [*NYSE symbol*]
URS .... Ursinus College, Collegeville, PA [*OCLC symbol*] (OCLC)
URS .... Utilization Reporting System (MCD)
URSA .... Unit Replacement System Analysis [*Military*]
URSA .... United Russia Societies Association [*London*]
URSA .... Urban and Rural Systems Associates
URSER .... [*Reference*] Your Serial [*Military*]
URSI .... Union Radio Scientifique Internationale [*International Union of Radio Science*] [*Also, ISRU*] [*Brussels, Belgium*]
URSNSC .... Union Regionale des Syndicats du Nyong-et-Sanaga
URSP........ Universal RADAR Signal Processor
URSS......... Union des Republiques Socialistes Sovietiques [*Union of Socialist Soviet Republics; USSR*]
URSUA...... Urological Survey [*A publication*]
URSW........ Union Regionale des Syndicats du Wouri [*Regional Union of Wouri Unions*]
URT .... Surat Thani [*Thailand*] [*Airport symbol*] (OAG)
URT .... Unit Recruit Training [*Army*] (AABC)
URT .... Universal RADAR Tracker
URT .... University Research and Training [*Programs*]
URT .... Upper Respiratory Tract [*Medicine*]
URT .... Upright (MSA)
URT .... Utility Radio Transmitter
URTA .... University Resident Theatre Association (EA)
URTEL....... [*Reference*] Your Telegram [*Military*]
URTI .... Universite Radiophonique et Televisuelle Internationale [*International Radio-Television University*]
URTI .... Upper Respiratory Tract Infection [*Medicine*]
URTIA......... Uniform Rights of the Terminally Ill Act [*National Conference of Commissioners on Uniform State Laws*]
URTNA ...... Union des Radio-Televisions Nationales Africaines [*African National Radio-Television Union*]
URTU......... United Road Transport Union [*British*]
URTX......... URI Therm-X, Inc. [*NASDAQ symbol*] (NQ)
URU .... Uruguay
URV .... Undersea Research Vehicle
URW .... Ultrasonic Ring Welder
URW .... United Racquetsports for Women (EA)
URW .... United Rubber, Cork, Linoleum, and Plastic Workers of America (EA)
URWA .... United Railroad Workers of America
URWC .... Urinal Water Closet (MSA)
URY .... Gurayat [*Saudi Arabia*] [*Airport symbol*] (OAG)
URY .... Union Railway of Memphis [*AAR code*]
URY .... Uruguay [*Three-letter standard code*] (CNC)
URZ .... Uroozgan [*Afghanistan*] [*Airport symbol*] [*Obsolete*] (OAG)
US .... Military Airlift Command [*Air Force*] [*ICAO designator*] (FAAC)
US .... Ubi Supra [*In the Place Mentioned Above*] [*Latin*]
US .... Ultrasonic Spectroscopy
US .... Ultrasound
U/S............ Unassorted [*Metal trade*] (ROG)
US .... Uncle Sam
US .... Unconditional Selection
US .... Unconditional Surrender
US .... Unconditioned Stimulus [*Psychometrics*]
US .... Under Secretary
US .... Undersize (AAG)
US .... Underspeed (MSA)
US .... Underwriters' Special Request
U/S............ Unhelpful, Helpless, Useless Persons [*From abbreviation for "unserviceable"*]
U & S .... Unified and Specified [*Command*] (MCD)
US .... Uniform System
US .... Union Settlement Association [*New York, NY*] (EA)
US .... Unit Separator [*Control character*] [*Data processing*]
US .... United Serpents (EA)
US .... United Service
US .... United Sisters [*An association*] [*Garwood, NJ*] (EA)
us .... United States [*MARC country of publication code*] [*Library of Congress*] (LCCP)
US .... United States [*Two-letter standard code*]
US .... United States Supreme Court Reports (DLA)
US .... Universal Service [*News agency*]
US .... Universale Studium [*A publication*]
US .... Unknown Significance
US .... Unlike-Sexed
US .... Unserviceable
U/S............ Unsorted
US .... Up Stage [*Away from audience*] [*A stage direction*]
US .... Update State [*Online database field identifier*]
US .... Upper Stage (MCD)
US .... Uprighting Subsystem [*NASA*] (KSC)
US .... US Supreme Court Reports (GPO)
US .... Useless
US .... Uterine Ditroma
US .... Uusi Suomi [*A publication*]
US1............ United States 1 Worksheets [*A publication*]

J3S .... United Software Systems & Services Corp. [*Los Angeles, CA*] [*Software manufacturer*]

USA .... INFO-DOC [*ACCORD*] [*UTLAS symbol*]

USA .... Liberty All-Star Equity [*NYSE symbol*]

USA .... Ukiyo-E Society of America (EA)

USA .... Ullage Simulation Assembly (MCD)

USA .... Ultrasonic Agitation

USA .... Ultraviolet Spectral Analysis

US of A .... Under Secretary of the Army

USA .... Underwater Society of America (EA)

USA .... Underwriters Service Association

USA .... Unicycling Society of America (EA)

USA .... Union of South Africa

USA .... Union Syndicale de l'Agriculture [*Union of Agricultural Workers*] [*Morocco*]

USA .... United Scenic Artists (EA)

USA .... United Secularists of America (EA)

USA .... United Shareowners of America [*New York, NY*] (EA)

USA .... United Shoppers Association

USA .... United Sidecar Association (EA)

USA .... United Soccer Association [*Later, NASL*]

USA .... United Spoilers of America (EA)

USA .... United States of ACORN [*Publication of the Association of Community Organizations for Reform Now*]

USA .... United States of America [*Three-letter standard code*]

USA .... United States Army

USA .... United States Automobile Association, San Antonio, TX [*OCLC symbol*] (OCLC)

USA .... United Steelworkers of America

USA .... United Students for America [*Defunct*] (EA)

USA .... United Support of Artists [*In USA for Africa, the chorus of American pop stars who recorded "We Are the World" to benefit famine victims in Africa*]

USA .... United Synagogue of America (EA)

USA .... Unity for Safe Airtravel [*Program of Air Line Pilots Association*]

USA .... Universal Subject Access [*Librarianship*]

USA .... Unix Systems Association (EA)

USA .... Unsegmented Storage Analyzer [*Instrumentation*]

USA .... Urban Sanitary Authority [*British*]

USA .... Utility Shareholders Association (EA)

USAA .... United Specialty Agents Alliance [*Also known as USA Alliance*] [*Huntington, WV*] (EA)

USAA .... United States Academy of Arms (EA)

USAA .... United States Arbitration Act (DLA)

USAA .... United States Armor Association (EA)

USAA .... United States Athletes Association (EA)

USAA .... US Armbrust Association (EA)

USAAA .... United States Army Audit Agency

USAAA .... US Amputee Athletic Association (EA)

USAAAVS ... United States Army Agency for Aviation Safety [*Formerly, USAABAAR*] (AABC)

USAAAWR ... United States Army Audit Agency, Washington Region

USAAB .... United States Army Aviation Board

USAABELCTBD ... United States Army Airborne and Electronics Board [*Later, USAAESWBD*]

USA/ABF ... USA Amateur Boxing Federation (EA)

USAABMDA ... United States Army Advanced Ballistic Missile Defense Agency (AABC)

USAABMU ... United States Army Aircraft Base Maintenance Unit (AABC)

USAAC .... United States Army Administration Center [*Obsolete*] (AABC)

USAAC .... United States Army Air Corps

USAACDA ... United States Army Aviation Combat Developments Agency [*CDC*]

USAACEBD ... United States Army Airborne Communications and Electronics Board

USAADAT ... United States Army Alcohol and Drug Abuse Team Training (MCD)

USAADB .... United States Army Air Defense Board

USAADCEN ... United States Army Air Defense Center

USAADCENFB ... United States Army Air Defense Center and Fort Bliss (AABC)

USAADEA ... United States Army Air Defense Engineering Agency [*Formerly, USASADEA*] [*AEC*]

USAADMAC ... United States Army Aeronautical Depot Maintenance Center

USAADS .... United States Army Air Defense School (AABC)

USAADTA ... United States Army Aircraft Development Test Activity

USAADVCOM ... United States Army Advance Command

USAAEFA ... United States Army Aviation Engineering Flight Activity

USAAESWBD ... United States Army Airborne, Electronics, and Special Warfare Board (AABC)

USAAF .... United States Army Air Forces

USAAFIME ... United States Army Air Forces in the Middle East

USAAFINO ... United States Army Aviation Flight Information and Nav-Aids Office (AABC)

USAAFIO ... United States Army Aviation Flight Information Office

USAAFO ... United States Army Avionics Field Office [*Formerly, USASAFO*]

USAAFUK ... United States Army Air Forces in the United Kingdom

USAAGAR ... United States Army Advisor Group O - Army Reserve (AABC)

USAAGDPSC ... United States Army Adjutant General Data Processing Service Center (AABC)

USAAGNG ... United States Army Advisory Group (National Guard) (AABC)

USAAGPC ... United States Army Adjutant General Publications Centers

USAAGS .... United States Army Adjutant General's School (AABC)

USAALS .... United States Army Aviation Logistics School (INF)

USAAMA ... United States Army Advent Management Agency (MUGU)

USAAMC ... United States Army Aeromedical Center

USAAMC ... United States Army Artillery and Missile Center

USAAML .... United States Army Aviation Materiel Laboratories

USAAMR & DL ... United States Army Air Mobility Research and Development Laboratory [*Also, AMR & DL, USAAMRDL*]

USAAMRDL ... United States Army Air Mobility Research and Development Laboratory [*Also, AMR & DL, USAAMR & DL*]

USAAMS ... United States Army Artillery and Missile School [*Later, Field Artillery School*]

USAAPDT ... United States Army Aviation Precision Demonstration Team (AABC)

USAAPSA ... United States Army Ammunition Procurement and Supply Agency

USAARC .... United States Army Antiaircraft Replacement Center

USAARCOM ... United States Army Armament Command

USAARDC ... United States Army Aberdeen Research and Development Center

USAARENBD ... United States Army Armor and Engineer Board (AABC)

USAARL ..... United States Army Aeromedical Research Laboratory [*Ft. Rucker, AL*] (AABC)

USAARMA ... United States Assistant Army Attache

USAARMBD ... United States Army Armor Board

USAARMC ... United States Army Armor Center [*Fort Knox, KY*]

USAARMHRU ... United States Army Armor Human Research Unit [*Fort Knox, KY*] (AABC)

USAARMS ... United States Army Armor School

USAARTYBD ... United States Army Artillery Board

USAARU .... United States Army Aeromedical Research Unit

USAAS ...... United States Army Air Services [*World War II*]

USAASC .... United States Army Air Service Command

USAASCFBH ... United States Army Administrative School Center and Fort Benjamin Harrison (AABC)

USAASD .... United States Army Aeronautical Services Detachment

USAASD-E ... United States Army Aeronautical Services Detachment, Europe (AABC)

USAASD-LA ... United States Army Aeronautical Services Detachment, Latin America (AABC)

USAASD-PAC ... United States Army Aeronautical Services Detachment, Pacific (AABC)

USAASL ..... United States Army Atmospheric Sciences Laboratory (RDA)

USAASO .... United States Army Aeronautical Services Office (AABC)

USAASTA ... United States Army Aviation Systems Test Activity [*Also, AASTA*]

USAATBD ... United States Army Arctic Test Board

USAATC .... United States Army Arctic Test Center

USAATCO ... United States Army Air Traffic Coordinating Officer

USAATMS ... United States Army Air Traffic Management System

USAAVA .... United States Army Audio-Visual Agency (AABC)

USAAVCOM ... United States Army Aviation Materiel Command (AABC)

USAAVLABS ... United States Army Aviation Materiel Laboratories (AABC)

USAAVNBD ... United States Army Aviation Board

USAAVNC ... United States Army Aviation Center [*CONARC*]

USAAVNHRU ... United States Army Aviation Human Research Unit [*Ft. Rucker, AL*] (AABC)

USAAVNS ... United States Army Aviation School [*CONARC*]

USAAVNTA ... United States Army Aviation Test Activity (AABC)

USAAVNTBD ... United States Army Aviation Test Board

USAAVRADCOM ... United States Army Aviation Research and Development Command

USAAVS .... United States Agency for Aviation Safety (MCD)

USAAVSCOM ... United States Army Aviation Systems Command [*Obsolete*] (AABC)

USAB .... United States Air Base (AAG)

USAB .... United States Animal Bank (EA)

USAB .... United States Army, Berlin (AABC)

USABA .... US Association for Blind Athletes

USABAAR ... United States Army Board for Aviation Accident Research [*Later, USAAAVS*]

USABDA .... US Amateur Ballroom Dancers Association (EA)

USABESRL ... United States Behavioral Science Research Laboratory [*Obsolete*] (IEEE)

USABF .... United States Amateur Baseball Federation

USA-BIAC ... United States of America - Business and Industry Advisory Committee to the OECD [*Organisation for Economic Co-operation and Development*] (EA)

USABIOLABS ... United States Army Biological Laboratories (AABC)

USABML ..... United States Army Biomedical Laboratory

USABRL ..... United States Army Ballistic Research Laboratories (AABC)

USABVAPAC ... United States Army Broadcasting and Visual Activities, Pacific

USAC .... Union des Syndicats Autonomes Camerounais [*Federation of Cameroonese Autonomous Unions*]

USAC .... United States Air Corps

USAC .... United States Alpine Club [*Defunct*]

USAC .... United States of America Confederation [*Later, USAC/RC*] (EA)

USAC .... United States Apparel Council [*Morristown, NJ*] (EA)

USAC .... United States Archery Congress [*Madison, WI*] (EA)
USAC .... United States Army Corps (AABC)
USAC .... United States Auto Club (EA)
USAC .... Urban Information Systems Inter-Agency Committee [*HUD*] (EGAO)
USAC .... US Antimony Corporation [*NASDAQ symbol*] (NQ)
USAC .... US Aquaculture Council [*Defunct*] (EA)
USAC .... User Services Advisory Committee [*NERComP*]
USAC .... Utah State Agricultural College
USACA ...... United States Allied Commission Austria
USACA ...... United States Army Civil Affairs [*World War II*]
USACA ...... United States Army Communications Agency
USACAA .... United States Army Concepts Analysis Agency (AABC)
USACAC .... United States Army Combined Arms Center (AABC)
USACAC .... United States Army Continental Army Command [*CONARC*] [*Superseded by FORSCOM*]
USACAF .... United States Army Construction Agency, France
USACAK .... United States Army Construction Agency, Korea
US-ACAN ... United States Advisory Committee on Antarctic Names [*1947-*]
USACARMSCDA ... United States Army Combined Arms Combat Developments Agency
USACAS .... United States Army Civil Affairs School
USACATB ... United States Army Combat Arms Training Board (AABC)
USACBRWOC ... United States Army Chemical, Biological, and Radiological Weapons Orientation Course (AABC)
USACBRWOCAAB ... United States Army Chemical, Biological, and Radiological Weapons Orientation Course Academic Advisory Board (AABC)
USACC ...... United States Army Communications Command (AABC)
USACC ...... US-Arab Chamber of Commerce (EA)
USACC ...... USA Convertible Club (EA)
USACC-A .... United States Army Communications Command - Alaska (AABC)
USACCA .... United States Army Congressional Correspondence Agency (AABC)
USACC-AMC ... United States Army Communications Command - Army Materiel Command (AABC)
USACC COMMAGCY-HSC ... United States Army Communications Command Communications Agency - Health Services Command (AABC)
USACC COMMAGCY-MTMC ... United States Army Communications Command Communications Agency - Military Traffic Management Command (AABC)
USACC COMMAGCY-USACIDC ... United States Army Communications Command Communications Agency - United States Army Criminal Investigation Command (AABC)
USACC-CONUS ... United States Army Communications Command - Continental United States (AABC)
USACC-EUR ... United States Army Communications Command - Europe (AABC)
USACC-FORCES ... United States Army Communications Command - Forces (AABC)
USACCIA ... United States Army Chemical Corps Intelligence Agency
USACCL .... United States Army Coating and Chemical Laboratory (AABC)
USACCO .... United States Army Commercial Communications Office
USACC-PAC ... United States Army Communications Command - Pacific (AABC)
USACC-R/FMD ... United States Army Communications Command Radio and Frequency Management Division
USACCSD ... United States Army Command and Control Support Detachment (AABC)
USACC-SO ... United States Army Communications Command - South (AABC)
USACC-T ... United States Army Communications Command - Thailand (AABC)
USACCTC ... United States Army Chemical Corps Technical Committee
USACC-TRADOC ... United States Army Communications Command - Training and Doctrine Command (AABC)
USACDA .... United States Arms Control and Disarmament Agency
USACDA .... United States Army Catalog Data Agency (AABC)
USACDC .... United States Army Combat Developments Command
USACDCADA ... United States Army Combat Developments Command Air Defense Agency (AABC)
USACDCAGA ... United States Army Combat Developments Command Adjutant General Agency
USACDCARMA ... United States Army Combat Developments Command Armor Agency (AABC)
USACDCARTYA ... United States Army Combat Developments Command Artillery Agency (AABC)
USACDCAVNA ... United States Army Combat Developments Command Aviation Agency (AABC)
USACDCCA ... United States Army Combat Developments Command Combined Arms Agency (AABC)
USACDCCAA ... United States Army Combat Developments Command Civil Affairs Agency (AABC)
USACDCCAG ... United States Army Combat Developments Command Combat Army Group [*Obsolete*] (AABC)
USACDCCARMSA ... United States Army Combat Developments Command Combat Arms Agency
USACDCCBRA ... United States Army Combat Developments Command Chemical-Biological-Radiological Agency (AABC)

USACDCCEA ... United States Army Combat Developments Command Communications-Electronics Agency (AABC)
USACDCCHA ... United States Army Combat Developments Command Chaplain Agency (AABC)
USACDCCOMSG ... United States Army Combat Developments Command Combat Systems Group (AABC)
USACDCCONFG ... United States Army Combat Developments Command Concept and Force Design Group (AABC)
USACDCCSG ... United States Army Combat Developments Command Combat Support Group [*Obsolete*] (AABC)
USACDCCSSG ... United States Army Combat Developments Command Combat Service Support Group [*Obsolete*] (AABC)
USACDCDPFO ... United States Army Combat Developments Command Data Processing Field Office (AABC)
USACDCEA ... United States Army Combat Developments Command Engineer Agency [*Later, USACDCENA*] (AABC)
USACDCEC ... United States Army Combat Developments Command Experimentation Command
USACDCENA ... United States Army Combat Developments Command Engineer Agency [*Formerly, USACDCEA*] (AABC)
USACDCFAA ... United States Army Combat Developments Command Field Artillery Agency (AABC)
USACDCFINA ... United States Army Combat Developments Command Finance Agency (AABC)
USACDCIA ... United States Army Combat Developments Command Infantry Agency [*Later, USACDCINA*] (AABC)
USACDCIAS ... United States Army Combat Developments Command Institute of Advanced Studies [*Obsolete*] (AABC)
USACDCICAS ... United States Army Combat Developments Command Institute of Combined Arms and Support [*Obsolete*] (AABC)
USACDCIDDFO ... United States Army Combat Developments Command Internal Defense and Development Field Office (AABC)
USACDCILC ... United States Army Combat Developments Command Institute of Land Combat [*Obsolete*] (AABC)
USACDCINA ... United States Army Combat Developments Command Infantry Agency [*Formerly, USACDCIA*] (AABC)
USACDCINCSG ... United States Army Combat Developments Command Intelligence and Control Systems Group (AABC)
USACDCINS ... United States Army Combat Developments Command Institute of Nuclear Studies [*Obsolete*] (AABC)
USACDCINTA ... United States Army Combat Developments Command Intelligence Agency (MCD)
USACDCISA ... United States Army Combat Developments Command Institute of Systems Analysis [*Obsolete*] (AABC)
USACDCISS ... United States Army Combat Developments Command Institute of Special Studies [*Obsolete*] (AABC)
USACDCISSO ... United States Army Combat Developments Command Institute of Strategic and Stability Operations [*Obsolete*] (AABC)
USACDCJAA ... United States Army Combat Developments Command Judge Advocate Agency (AABC)
USACDCMA ... United States Army Combat Developments Command Maintenance Agency (AABC)
USACDCMPA ... United States Combat Developments Command Military Police Agency (AABC)
USACDCMSA ... United States Army Combat Developments Command Medical Service Agency (AABC)
USACDCNG ... United States Army Combat Developments Command Nuclear Group
USACDCNUA ... United States Army Combat Developments Command Nuclear Agency (AABC)
USACDCOA ... United States Army Combat Developments Command Ordnance Agency
USACDCPALSG ... United States Army Combat Developments Command Personnel and Logistics Systems Group (AABC)
USACDCPASA ... United States Army Combat Developments Command Personnel and Administrative Services Agency (AABC)
USACDCQA ... United States Army Combat Developments Command Quartermaster Agency
USACDCSA ... United States Army Combat Developments Command Supply Agency [*Later, USACDCSUA*] (AABC)
USACDCSAG ... United States Army Combat Developments Command Systems Analysis Group (AABC)
USACDCSOA ... United States Army Combat Developments Command Special Operations Agency (AABC)
USACDCSSI ... United States Army Combat Developments Command Strategic Studies Institute (AABC)
USACDCSUA ... United States Army Combat Developments Command Supply Agency [*Formerly, USACDCSA*] (AABC)
USACDCSWA ... United States Army Combat Developments Command Special Warfare Agency (AABC)
USACDCSWCAG ... United States Army Combat Developments Command Special Warfare and Civil Affairs Group
USACDCSWG ... United States Army Combat Developments Command Special Warfare Group
USACDCTA ... United States Army Combat Developments Command Transportation Agency (AABC)
USACDEC ... United States Army Combat Developments Experimentation Center

USACE....... United States Army Corps of Engineers [*Merged with General Equipment Command*]
USACEBD ... United States Army Airborne Communications and Electronics Board   (AABC)
USACECDA ... United States Army Communications - Electronics Combat Developments Agency
USACEEIA ... United States Army Communications-Electronics Engineering Installation Agency   (AABC)
USACEEIA-PAC ... United States Army Communications - Electronics Engineering Installation Agency - Pacific   (RDA)
USACEEIA-WH ... United States Army Communications-Electronics Engineering Installation Agency - Western Hemisphere   (AABC)
USACEIBN ... United States Army Communications - Electronics Installation Battalion   (AABC)
USACENCDCSA ... United States Army Corps of Engineers National Civil Defense Computer Support Agency   (AABC)
USACESSEC ... United States Army Computer Systems Support and Evaluation Command
USACGSC ... United States Army Command and General Staff College
USACHB .... United States Army Chaplain Board
USACHS .... United States Army Chaplain School
USACI ...... United States Advisory Commission on Information
USACICD ... United States Army Criminal Investigation Command [*Formerly, USACIDA*]   (AABC)
USACIDA ... United States Army Criminal Investigation Division Agency [*Later, USACICD*]   (AABC)
USACIECA ... United States Advisory Commission on International Educational and Cultural Affairs
USACIL ...... United States Army Criminal Investigation Laboratory   (AABC)
USACIR ...... United States Army Criminal Investigation Repository
USACISO ... United States Army Counterinsurgency Support Office, Okinawa [*Obsolete*]   (AABC)
USACIU ...... United States Army Command Information Unit   (AABC)
USACJE ..... United Synagogue of America Commission on Jewish Education [*New York, NY*]   (EA)
USACMA.... United States Army Club Management Agency   (AABC)
USACMLC ... United States Army Chemical Center [*Later, United States Army Ordnance and Chemical Center and School*]
USACMLCB ... United States Army Chemical Corps Board
USACMLCS ... United States Army Chemical Center and School [*Later, United States Army Ordnance and Chemical Center and School*]   (AABC)
USACMLCSCH ... United States Army Chemical Corps School
USACMLRDL ... United States Army Chemical Research and Development Laboratories
USACMLS ... United States Army Chemical School   (AABC)
USACMR.... United States Army Court of Military Review   (AABC)
USACMS.... United States Army Command Management School
USACOMZEUR ... United States Army Communications Zone, Europe
USACOR .... US Association for the Club of Rome   (EA)
USACPEB ... United States Army Central Physical Evaluation Board   (AABC)
USACRAPAC ... United States Army Command Reconnaissance Activities, Pacific Command
USACRC .... United States Army Crime Records Center   (AABC)
USACRF..... United States Army Counterintelligence Records Facility   (MCD)
USACRREL ... United States Army Cold Regions Research and Engineering Laboratory   (AABC)
USAC/RS... United States Amateur Confederation of Roller Skating [*Formerly, USFARS, USARSA, USAC*]   (EA)
USACS....... United States Army Combat Surveillance Agency   (AAG)
USACS....... United States Army Courier Service   (AABC)
USACSA .... United States Army Combat Surveillance Agency
USACSA .... United States Army Communications Systems Agency   (AABC)
USACSC .... United States Army Computer Systems Command
USACSG .... United States Army CINPAC Support Group
USACSLA ... United States Army Communications Security Logistics Agency   (AABC)
USACSR .... United States Air Corps Specialist Reserve
USACSS .... United States Army Chief of Support Services
USACSS .... United States Army Combat Surveillance School   (AABC)
USACSSAA ... United States Army Computer Systems Selection and Acquisition Agency   (AABC)
USACSSC ... United States Army Computer Systems Support and Evaluation Command   (IEEE)
USACSSEA ... United States Army Computer Systems Support and Evaluation Agency   (AABC)
USACSSEC ... United States Army Computer Systems Support and Evaluation Command
USACSTA ... United States Army Courier Station   (AABC)
USACSTATC ... United States Army Combat Surveillance and Target Acquisition Training Command
USACT....... United States Accident Containment Team [*Government agency in 1985 movie "Warning Sign"*]
USACTA ... US Army Central TMDE Activity   (RDA)
USACTC .... United States Army Clothing and Textile Center
USACTMC ... United States Army Clothing and Textile Materiel Center
USACWL.... United States Army Chemical Warfare Laboratory
USAD .... United States Army Dispensary   (AABC)

USADACS ... United States Army Defense Ammunition Center and School   (AABC)
USADATCOM ... United States Army Data Support Command
USADC....... United States Army Data Support Command
USADC....... United States Army Dental Clinic
USADCJ.... United States Army Depot Command, Japan   (AABC)
USADEG .... United States Army Dependents' Education Group   (AABC)
USADIP...... United States Army Deserter Information Point   (AABC)
USADJ...... United States Army Depot, Japan   (AABC)
USADOFL ... United States Army Diamond Ordnance Fuze Laboratory [*Later, HDL*]
USADP....... Uniform Shipboard Automatic Data Processing
USADPC .... United States Army Data Processing Center
USADPS..... Uniform Automatic Data Processing System [*Navy*]
USADRB .... United States Army Discharge Review Board   (AABC)
USADSC .... United States Army Data Services and Administrative Systems Command
USADTC .... United States Army Armor and Desert Training Center   (AABC)
USAE.......... United States Army Engineer
USAEAGSC ... United States Army, Europe, Adjutant General Support Center   (AABC)
USAEARA ... United States Army Equipment Authorization Review Activity   (AABC)
USAEARC ... United States Army Equipment Authorizations Review Center   (AABC)
USAEB .... United States Army Engineer Board
USAEC....... United States Army Electronics Command [*Obsolete*]
USAEC....... United States Atomic Energy Commission
USAECA .... United States Army Electronics Command Computation Agency [*Obsolete*]
USAECAV ... United States Army Engineer Construction Agency, Vietnam
USAECBDE ... United States Army Engineer Center Brigade   (AABC)
USAECFB ... United States Army Engineer Center and Fort Belvoir   (AABC)
USAECOM ... United States Army Electronics Command [*Obsolete*]
USAECR .... United States Army Engineer Center Regiment   (AABC)
USAEC Rep CONF ... US Atomic Energy Commission. Report. CONF [*A publication*]
USAEC (Rep) GJO ... United States Atomic Energy Commission. (Report) GJO [*A publication*]
USAEC Res Dev Rep AEC-TR ... US Atomic Energy Commission. Research and Development Report. AEC-TR [*A publication*]
USAEC Res Dev Rep ANL ... US Atomic Energy Commission. Research and Development Report. ANL [*A publication*]
USAEC Res Dev Rep BNL ... US Atomic Energy Commission. Research and Development Report. BNL [*A publication*]
USAEC Res Dev Rep COO ... US Atomic Energy Commission. Research and Development Report. COO [*A publication*]
USAEC Res Dev Rep HASL ... US Atomic Energy Commission. Research and Development Report. HASL [*A publication*]
USAEC Res Dev Rep HW ... US Atomic Energy Commission. Research and Development Report. HW [*A publication*]
USAEC Res Dev Rep LAMS (LA) ... US Atomic Energy Commission. Research and Development Report. LAMS (LA) [*A publication*]
USAEC Res Dev Rep LF ... US Atomic Energy Commission. Research and Development Report. LF [*A publication*]
USAEC Res Dev Rep NYO ... US Atomic Energy Commission. Research and Development Report. NYO [*A publication*]
USAEC Res Dev Rep ORINS ... US Atomic Energy Commission. Research and Development Report. ORINS [*A publication*]
USAEC Res Dev Rep ORNL ... US Atomic Energy Commission. Research and Development Report. ORNL [*A publication*]
USAEC Res Dev Rep ORO ... US Atomic Energy Commission. Research and Development Report. ORO [*A publication*]
USAEC Res Dev Rep RLO ... US Atomic Energy Commission. Research and Development Report. RLO [*A publication*]
USAEC Res Dev Rep SCR ... US Atomic Energy Commission. Research and Development Report. SCR [*A publication*]
USAEC Res Dev Rep TID ... US Atomic Energy Commission. Research and Development Report. TID [*A publication*]
USAEC Res Dev Rep UCD ... US Atomic Energy Commission. Research and Development Report. UCD [*A publication*]
USAEC Res Dev Rep UCLA ... US Atomic Energy Commission. Research and Development Report. UCLA [*A publication*]
USAEC Res Dev Rep UCRL ... US Atomic Energy Commission. Research and Development Report. UCRL [*A publication*]
USAEC Res Dev Rep UCSF ... US Atomic Energy Commission. Research and Development Report. UCSF [*A publication*]
USAEC Res Dev Rep UH ... US Atomic Energy Commission. Research and Development Report. UH [*A publication*]
USAEC Res Dev Rep UR ... US Atomic Energy Commission. Research and Development Report. UR [*A publication*]
USAEC Res Dev Rep WT ... US Atomic Energy Commission. Research and Development Report. WT [*A publication*]
USAEC Symp Ser ... US Atomic Energy Commission. Symposium Series [*A publication*]
USAECV(P) ... United States Army Engineer Command, Vietnam (Provisional)
USAED....... United States Army Engineer District
USAEDE..... United States Army Engineer Division, Europe   (AABC)
USAEDH .... United States Army Engineer Division, Huntsville   (AABC)

USAEDLMV ... United States Army Engineer Division, Lower Mississippi Valley (AABC)
USAEDM .... United States Army Engineer Division, Mediterranean (AABC)
USAEDMR ... United States Army Engineer Division, Missouri River (AABC)
USAEDNA ... United States Army Engineer Division, North Atlantic (AABC)
USAEDNC ... United States Army Engineer Division, North Central (AABC)
USAEDNE ... United States Army Engineer Division, New England (AABC)
USAEDNP ... United States Army Engineer Division, North Pacific (AABC)
USAEDOR ... United States Army Engineer Division, Ohio River (AABC)
USAEDPO ... United States Army Engineer Division, Pacific Ocean (AABC)
USAEDSA ... United States Army Engineer Division, South Atlantic (AABC)
USAEDSP ... United States Army Engineer Division, South Pacific (AABC)
USAEDSW ... United States Army Engineer Division, Southwestern (AABC)
USAEEA ..... United States Army Enlistment Eligibility Activity (AABC)
USAEFMA ... United States Army Electronics Command Financial Management Agency [*Obsolete*] (AABC)
USAEGD ... United States Army Engineer, Gulf District
USAEHA .... United States Army Environmental Hygiene Agency (AABC)
USAEHL ..... United States Army Environmental Health Laboratory
USAEIGHT ... Eighth United States Army (CINC)
USAEIS ...... United States Army Electronic Intelligence and Security (AABC)
USAELRO ... United States Army Electronics Logistics Research Office
USAELRU .. United States Army Electronics Research Unit
USAEMA .... United States Army Electronics Materiel Agency [*Formerly, USASSA*]
USAEMAFHPO ... United States Army Electronics Materiel Agency, Fort Huachuca Procurement Office
USAEMAFMPO ... United States Army Electronics Materiel Agency, Fort Monmouth Procurement Office
USAEMAPICO ... United States Army Electronics Materiel Agency, Plant Inventory Control Office
USAEMAWPO ... United States Army Electronics Materiel Agency, Washington Procurement Office
USAEMCA ... United States Army Engineer Mathematical Computation Agency (AABC)
USAEMSA ... United States Army Electronics Materiel Support Agency [*Formerly, USASMSA*]
USAENGCOMEUR ... United States Army Engineer Command, Europe (AABC)
USAENPG ... United States Army Engineer Power Group (RDA)
USAENPG-ED ... United States Army Engineer Power Group Engineering Division
USAEPA ..... United States Army Electronics Command Patent Agency [*Obsolete*] (AABC)
USAEPG ..... United States Army Electronic Proving Ground
USAEPMARA ... United States Army, Europe, Personnel Management and Replacement Activity (AABC)
USAEPOC ... United States Army Engineer Procurement Office, Chicago
USAERA ..... United States Army Electronics Command Logistics Research Agency [*Obsolete*] (AABC)
USAERADCOM ... United States Army Electronics Research and Development Command (RDA)
USAERDA ... United States Army Electronic Research and Development Agency
USAERDAA ... United States Army Electronics Research and Development Activity [*Fort Huachuca, AZ*] (AABC)
USAERDAW ... United States Army Electronics Research and Development Activity, White Sands [*New Mexico*] (AABC)
USAERDL ... United States Army Electronics Research and Development Laboratory [*Formerly, USASRDL*] (MCD)
USAEREC ... United States Army Enlisted Records and Evaluation Center (MCD)
USAERG .... United States Army Engineer Reactor Group (AABC)
USAERLO ... United States Army Electronics Regional Labor Office
US Aerosp Med Res Lab Tech Rep AMRL-TR ... US Aerospace Medical Research Laboratory. Technical Report. AMRL-TR [*A publication*]
US Aerosp Res Lab Rep ... United States. Aerospace Research Laboratories. Reports [*A publication*]
USAES .... United States Army Engineer School
USAES .... United States Association of Evening Students (EA)
USAESC .... United States Army Electronics Support Command (AABC)
USAET & DL (ECOM) ... United States Army Electronics Technology and Devices Laboratory (Electronics Command) (AABC)
USAETL .... United States Army Engineer Topographic Laboratories
USAEU ...... United States Army Exhibit Unit (AABC)
USAEUR ..... United States Army, Europe (MCD)
USAEWES ... United States Army Engineer Waterways Experiment Station
US of AF ..... Under Secretary of the Air Force
USAF .... United States Aikido Federation (EA)
USAF .... United States Air Force [*Washington, DC*]
USAF .... United States Army Forces
USAF .... United Student Aid Fund
USAF .... United Students of America Foundation (EA)
USAF .... US Aquaculture Federation (EA)
USAF .... USA Foundation [*Washington, DC*] (EA)
USAFA .... United States Air Force Academy
USAFA .... USA Finn Association (EA)
USAFABD ... United States Army Field Artillery Board (AABC)
USAFAC .... United States Army Finance and Accounting Center (AABC)

USAFACFS ... United States Army Field Artillery Center and Fort Sill (AABC)
USAFACS ... United States Air Force Air Crew School
USAFADWC ... United States Air Force Air Defense Weapons Center (MCD)
USAF AFHRL ... United States Air Force. Human Resources Laboratory [*A publication*]
USAFAG .... United States Air Force Auditor General
USAFAGOS ... United States Air Force's Air-Ground Operations School
USAF AMRL ... United States Air Force. Aerospace Medical Research Laboratory [*A publication*]
USAFAPC ... United States Air Force Airframe Production Contract
USAFAPS ... United States Air Force Air Police School
USAF ARL ... United States Air Force. Aeromedical Research Laboratory [*A publication*]
USAFAS ..... United States Army Field Artillery School (AABC)
USAFB .... United States Army Field Band (AABC)
USAFBI ...... United States Army Forces in the British Isles
USAFBMD ... United States Air Force Ballistic Missile Division
USAFBMS ... United States Air Force Basic Military School
USAFBS .... United States Air Force Bandsman School (AFM)
USAFBS .... United States Air Force Bombardment School
USAFCBI .... United States Forces, China, Burma, India [*World War II*]
USAFCBIT ... United States Forces, China, Burma, India Theater [*World War II*]
USAFCC .... United States Army Forces in Central Canada [*World War II*]
USAF CMR ... United States Air Force Court of Military Review (AFM)
USAFCO .... United States Air Force, Southern Command (MCD)
USAFCRL ... United States Air Force Cambridge Research Laboratories
USAFD .... United States Air Force Dictionary [*A publication*]
USAFE .... United States Air Force in Europe
USAFEC ..... United States Army Forces in Eastern Canada [*World War II*]
USAFECI .... United States Air Force Extension Course Institute
USAF/EDA ... Society of United States Air Force Flight Surgeons (EA)
USAFEHL ... United States Air Force Environmental Health Laboratory
USAFEL ..... United States Air Force Epidemiological Laboratory (AFM)
USAFESA ... United States Army Facilities Engineering Support Agency (AABC)
USAFESA-ED ... United States Army Facilities Engineering Support Agency Engineering Division
USAFESA-RT ... United States Army Facilities Engineering Support Agency Research and Technology Division
USAFESA-RTD ... United States Army Facilities Engineering Support Agency Research and Technology Division
USAFESA-TS ... United States Army Facilities Engineering Support Agency - Technology Support Division
USAFESA-TSD ... United States Army Facilities Engineering Support Agency - Technology Support Division
USAFETAC ... United States Air Force Environmental Technical Applications Center [*Scott Air Force Base, IL*] (AFM)
USAFETO ... United States Army Forces, European Theater of Operations [*World War II*]
USAFETPS ... United States Air Force Experimental Test Pilot School
USAFEURPCR ... United States Air Force European Postal and Courier Region (AFM)
USAFF .... USA Film Festival (EA)
USAFFE ..... United States Army Forces, Far East [*World War II*]
USAFFGS ... United States Air Force Flexible Gunnery School
USAFFSR ... United States Air Force Flight Safety Research
USAFH .... United States Air Force Hospital
USAFHD ..... United States Air Force Historical Division
USAFHG .... United States Air Force Honor Guard
USAFI .... United States Air Forces Institute
USAFI .... United States Armed Forces Institute
USAFIA ...... United States Army Forces in Australia
USAFIB ...... United States Army Aviation Flight Information Bulletin (FAAC)
USAFIC ...... United States Association of Firearm Instructors and Coaches (EA)
USAFICA ... United States Army Forces in Central Africa [*World War II*]
USAFICPA ... United States Army Forces in Central Pacific Area
USAFIFC ... United States Air Force Instrument Flight Center (AFM)
USAFIK ...... United States Army Forces in Korea
USAFIL ...... United States Army Forces in Liberia [*World War II*]
USAFIME ... United States Armed Forces in Middle East
USAFINCISCOM ... United States Army Finance and Comptroller Information Systems Command (AABC)
USAFINTEL ... United States Air Force Intelligence Publication
USAFINZ ... United States Army Forces in New Zealand
USAFIP(NL) ... United States Army Forces in the Philippines (Northern Luzon) [*World War II*]
USAFISPA ... United States Army Forces in the South Pacific Area
USAFIT ...... United States Air Force Institute of Technology
USAFLANT ... United States Air Forces, Atlantic (AABC)
USAFMC .... United States Association of Former Members of Congress (EA)
USAFMD .... United States Army Frequency Management Directorate (MCD)
USAFMEPCR ... United States Air Force Mideast Postal and Courier Region (AFM)
USAFMEPCS ... United States Air Force Mideast Postal and Courier Service (AFM)
USAFMIDPAC ... United States Army Forces, Middle Pacific [*World War II*] [*See AFMIDPAC*]

USAFMPC ... United States Air Force Military Personnel Center
USAFMTC ... United States Air Force Marksmanship Training Center
USAFMTO ... United States Army Forces, Mediterranean Theater of Operations [*World War II*]
USAF/NRD ... United States Air Force, National Range Division
USAFNS..... United States Air Force Navigation School
USAF Nucl Saf ... USAF [*United States Air Force*] Nuclear Safety [*A publication*]
USAFO...... United States Army Field Office   (RDA)
USAFOB..... USA Federation of Bocce   (EA)
USAFOCA ... United States Army Field Operating Cost Agency   (AABC)
USAFOCS ... United States Air Force Officer Candidate School
USAFOF..... United States Army Flight Operations Facility   (AABC)
USAFOSR ... United States Air Force Office of Scientific Research
USAFP .... Uniformed Services Academy of Family Physicians [*Richmond, VA*]   (EA)
USAFPAC ... United States Air Forces, Pacific
USAFPACPCR ... United States Air Force Pacific Postal and Courier Region
USAFPCS ... United States Air Force Postal and Courier Service
USAFPCS Eur-Me Rgn ... United States Air Force Postal and Courier Service, Europe-Mideast Region   (AFM)
USAFPCS LA Rgn ... United States Air Force Postal and Courier Service, Latin American Region   (AFM)
USAFPCS Pac Rgn ... United States Air Force Postal and Courier Service, Pacific Region   (AFM)
USAFPCS US Rgn ... United States Air Force Postal and Courier Service, United States Region   (AFM)
USAFPDC ... United States Air Force Personnel Development Center
USAFPEB... United States Air Force Physical Evaluation Board   (AFM)
USAFPLREP ... United States Air Force Plant Representative Office
USAFPOA ... United States Army Forces, Pacific Ocean Areas [*World War II*]
USAFPRO ... United States Air Force Plant Representative Office
USAFPS..... United States Air Force Pilot School
USAFR ...... Union of South Africa
USAFR ...... United States Air Force Representative   (AFM)
USAFR ...... United States Air Force Reserve
USAFRD..... United States Air Force Recruiting Detachment
USAFRED ... United States Air Force Forces, Readiness Command
USAFRG..... United States Air Force Recruiting Group
USAFRHL... United States Air Force Radiological Health Laboratory
USAFRO..... United States Air Force Recruiting Office
USAFROTC ... United States Air Force Reserve Officer Training Corps
USAFRR ..... United States Air Force Resident Representative   (MCD)
USAFRS..... United States Air Force Recruiting Service
USAFS ...... United States Army Finance School   (AABC)
USAFSA..... United States Army Forces in South America
USAFSA ..... United States Army Forces, South Atlantic [*World War II*]
USAFSAAS ... United States Air Force School of Applied Aerospace Sciences   (AFM)
USAFSACS ... United States Air Force School of Applied Cryptologic Sciences   (AFM)
USAFSAM ... United States Air Force School of Aerospace Medicine
USAFSAM/ED ... Society of United States Air Force Flight Surgeons [*Brooks AFB, TX*]   (EA)
USAFSAWC ... United States Air Force Special Air Warfare Center   (AFM)
USAFSBSS ... United States Air Force Standard Base Supply System
USAFSC..... United States Army Food Service Center   (AABC)
USAFSE..... United States Air Force Supervisory Examination   (AFM)
USAFSG..... United States Army Field Support Group   (AABC)
USAFSO..... United States Air Forces Southern Command   (AABC)
USAFSOC ... United States Air Force Special Operations Center   (AFM)
USAFSOF ... United States Air Force Special Operations Force   (AFM)
USAFSOS ... United States Air Force Special Operations School   (AFM)
USAFSRA ... United States Air Force Special Reporting Agency
USAFSS..... United States Air Force Security Service [*Later, AFESC*]
USAFSTC ... United States Air Force Special Treatment Center   (AFM)
USAFSTC ... United States Army Foreign Science and Technology Center   (AABC)
USAFSTRIKE ... United States Air Forces Strike Command   (AABC)
USAFTAC ... United States Air Force Technical Applications Center   (MCD)
USAFTALC ... United States Air Force Tactical Airlift Center   (AFM)
USAFTARC ... United States Air Force Tactical Air Reconnaissance Center   (AFM)
USAFTAWC ... United States Air Force Tactical Air Warfare Center   (AFM)
USAFTFWC ... United States Air Force Tactical Fighter Weapons Center   (AFM)
USAFTPS... United States Air Force Test Pilot School   (MCD)
USAFTS..... United States Air Force Technical School
USAF-USPCR ... United States Air Force - United States Postal Courier Region   (AFM)
USAFWPO ... United States Air Force Water Port Liaison Office [*or Officer*]   (AFM)
USAG .... United States Army Garrison   (AABC)
USAG .... United States Army in Greece
USAGEM.... US Atlantic and Gulf Ports/Eastern Mediterranean and North African Freight Conference   (EA)
USAGETA ... United States Army General Equipment Test Activity   (AABC)
USAGF ...... United States Army Ground Forces   (MUGU)
USAGG ...... United States Army Group, American Mission for Aid to Greece
USAGIMRADA ... United States Army Geodesy Intelligence and Mapping Research and Development Agency   (AABC)

USAGMPC ... United States Army General Materiel and Parts Center   (AABC)
USAGPC .... United States Adjutant General Publications Center
US Agric .... United States Department of Agriculture. Publications [*A publication*]
US Agric Mark Serv AMS Series ... United States. Agriculture Marketing Service. AMS Series [*A publication*]
US Agric Res Serv ARS-NC ... US Agricultural Research Service. ARS-NC [*A publication*]
US Agric Res Serv ARS-NE ... US Agricultural Research Service. ARS-NE [*A publication*]
US Agric Res Serv ARS-S ... US Agricultural Research Service. ARS-S [*A publication*]
US Agric Res Serv ARS-W ... US Agricultural Research Service. ARS-W [*A publication*]
US Agric Res Serv CA ... US Agricultural Research Service. CA [*A publication*]
US Agric Res Serv East Reg Res Lab Publ ... United States. Agricultural Research Service. Eastern Regional Research Laboratory. Publication [*A publication*]
US Agric Res Serv Mark Res Rep ... US Agricultural Research Service. Marketing Research Report [*A publication*]
US Agric Res Serv North Cent Reg Rep ... United States. Agricultural Research Service. North Central Region. Report [*A publication*]
US Agric Res Serv Northeast Reg Rep ARS NE ... US Agricultural Research Service. Northeastern Region Report. ARS-NE [*A publication*]
US Agric Res Serv South Reg Rep ... US Agricultural Research Service. Southern Region Report [*A publication*]
US Agr Marketing Serv ... United States Agricultural Marketing Service [*A publication*]
US Agr Res Serv ... United States Agricultural Research Service [*A publication*]
USAGSC .... United States Army General Supplies Commodity Center
USAH .... United States Army Hospital
USAHA...... United States Animal Health Association   (EA)
USAHAC ... United States Army Headquarters Area Command
USAHC ...... United States Army Health Clinic   (AABC)
USAHEL..... United States Army Human Engineering Laboratories   (AABC)
USAHOME ... United States Army Homes [*Prefabricated houses, shipped overseas*]
USAHS ...... United States Army Hospital Ship
USAHSC .... United States Army Health Service Command
USAHSDSA ... United States Army Health Services Data Systems Agency   (AABC)
USAHTN..... United States Army Hometown News Center   (AABC)
USAI........... US-Asia Institute   (EA)
USAIA .... United States Army Institute of Administration   (AABC)
USAIB .... United States Army Infantry Board
USAIC .... United States Army Infantry Center
USAIC .... United States Army Intelligence Command
USAICA...... United States Army Interagency Communications Agency   (AABC)
USAICS..... United States Army Intelligence Center and School   (AABC)
USAID .... United States Agency for International Development [*Also, AID*]
USAIDR ..... United States Army Institute of Dental Research   (AABC)
USAIDSC ... United States Army Information and Data Systems Command
USAIDSCOM ... United States Army Information and Data Systems Command   (AABC)
USAIG .... United States Aircraft Insurance Group
USAIGC ..... United States Association of Independent Gymnastic Clubs [*Wilmington, DE*]   (EA)
USAIIA .... United States Army Imagery Interpretation Agency   (AABC)
USAIIC .... United States Army Imagery Interpretation Center   (AABC)
USAILC ...... United States Army International Logistics Center
USAILCOM ... United States Army International Logistics Command   (AABC)
USAILG ...... United States Army International Logistics Group   (AABC)
USAIMA ..... United States Army Institute for Military Assistance   (AABC)
USAIMC ..... United States Army Inventory Management Center   (AABC)
USAIMS ..... United States Army Institute for Military Systems   (AABC)
USAINFHRU ... United States Army Infantry Human Research Unit [*Ft. Benning, GA*]   (AABC)
USAINSB ... United States Army Intelligence Security Board
USAINSBD ... United States Army Intelligence and Security Board   (MCD)
USAINSCOM ... United States Army Intelligence and Security Command
USAINTA ... United States Army Intelligence Agency   (AABC)
USAINTB ... United States Army Intelligence Board
USAINTC ... United States Army Intelligence Center
USAINTCA ... United States Army Intelligence Corps Agency
USAINTELMDA ... United States Army Intelligence Materiel Developments Agency   (AABC)
USAINTS.... United States Army Intelligence School
USAIPSG ... United States Army Industrial and Personnel Security Group
USAIRA ...... United States Air Attache
USAIRC...... United States Army Ionizing Radiation Center
US Air Force Aeronaut Syst Div Tech Note ... United States Air Force. Aeronautical Systems. Division Technical Note [*A publication*]

US Air Force Aeronaut Syst Div Tech Note ... US Air Force. Aeronautical Systems. Division Technical Note [*A publication*]
US Air Force Aeronaut Syst Div Tech Rep ... US Air Force. Aeronautical Systems. Division Technical Report [*A publication*]
US Air Force Cambridge Res Lab Instrum Pap ... United States Air Force. Cambridge Research Laboratories. Instrumentation Papers [*A publication*]
US Air Force Cambridge Res Lab Phy Sci Res Pap ... United States Air Force. Cambridge Research Laboratories. Physical Sciences Research Papers [*A publication*]
US Air Force Hum Resour Lab Tech Rep AFHRL-TR ... United States Air Force. Human Resources Laboratory. Technical Report AFHRL-TR [*A publication*]
US Air Force Hum Resour Lab Tech Rep AFHRL-TR ... US Air Force. Human Resources Laboratory. Technical Report AFHRL-TR [*A publication*]
US Air Force Syst Command Res Technol Div Tech Doc Rep ASD ... United States Air Force. Systems Command Research and Technology Division. Technical Documentary Report. ASD [*A publication*]
US Air Force Tech Doc Rep ... United States Air Force. Technical Documentary Report [*A publication*]
US Air Force Tech Doc Rep AFSWC-TDR ... US Air Force. Technical Documentary Report. AFSWC-TDR [*A publication*]
US Air Force Tech Doc Rep AMRL-TDR ... US Air Force. Technical Documentary Report. AMRL-TDR [*A publication*]
US Air Force Tech Doc Rep ARL-TDR ... US Air Force. Technical Documentary Report. ARL-TDR [*A publication*]
US Air Force Tech Doc Rep ASD-TDR ... US Air Force. Technical Documentary Report. ASD-TDR [*A publication*]
US Air Force Tech Doc Rep RTD-TDR ... US Air Force. Technical Documentary Report. RTD-TDR [*A publication*]
US Air Force Tech Doc Rep SEG-TDR ... US Air Force. Technical Documentary Report. SEG-TDR [*A publication*]
US Air Force WADC Tech Rep ... United States Air Force. Wright Air Development Center. Technical Report [*A publication*]
US Air Force Weapons Lab Tech Rep AFWL-TR ... United States Air Force. Weapons Laboratory Technical Report AFWL-TR [*A publication*]
US Air Force Weapons Lab Tech Rep AFWL-TR ... US Air Force. Weapons Laboratory. Technical Report AFWL-TR [*A publication*]
US Air Force Wright Air Dev Cent Tech Notes ... US Air Force. Wright Air Development Center. Technical Notes [*A publication*]
US Air Force Wright Air Dev Cent Tech Rep ... US Air Force. Wright Air Development Center. Technical Report [*A publication*]
USAIRLO.... United States Air Liaison Officer (CINC)
USAIRMILCOMUN ... United States Air Force Representative, UN Military Staff Committee
USAIRR...... United States Army Investigative Records Repository (AABC)
USAIS .... United States Army Infantry School
USAISR...... United States Army Institute of Surgical Research [*Ft. Sam Houston, TX*] (AABC)
USAITAC ... United States Army Intelligence and Threat Analysis Center (AABC)
USAITAD ... United States Army Intelligence Threat Analysis Detachment
USAITFG.... United States Army Intelligence Threats and Forecasts Group (AABC)
USAJAPA... United States Amateur Jai Alai Players Association (EA)
USAJFKCENMA ... United States Army John Fitzgerald Kennedy Center for Military Assistance (AABC)
USAJFKCENSPWAR ... United States Army John Fitzgerald Kennedy Center for Special Warfare [*Airborne*] (AABC)
USAJHGSOWA ... United States Army Joint Household Goods Shipping Office of the Armed Forces
USAJSC..... United States Army Joint Support Command (AABC)
USAKORSCOM ... United States Army Korea Support Command (AABC)
USALA .... United States Amateur Lacrosse Association
USALAPA ... United States Army Los Angeles Procurement Agency (AABC)
USALC .... United States Army Logistics Center
USALCA..... United States Army Logistic Control Activity (AABC)
USALCJ..... United States Army Logistics Center, Japan (AABC)
USALDC .... United States Army Logistics Data Center
USALDJ ..... United States Army Logistics Depot, Japan
USALDRHRU ... United States Army Leadership Human Research Unit [*Presidio of Monterey, CA*]
USALDSRA ... United States Army Logistics Doctrine, Systems and Readiness Agency [*New Cumberland Army Depot, Harrisburg, PA*] (AABC)
USALEA..... United States Army Logistics Evaluation Agency (AABC)
USALGPM ... United States Army Liaison Group, Project Michigan
USALMC.... United States Army Logistics Management Center
USALOGC .. United States Army Logistics Center (AABC)
USALS .... United States Army Language School
USALSA .... United States Army Legal Services Agency (AABC)
USALWL .... United States Army Limited War Laboratory (AABC)
USAM........ Unified Space Applications Mission (MCD)
USAM........ Union des Syndicats Autonomes de Madagascar [*Federation of Malagasy Autonomous Unions*]
USAM........ Unique Sequential Access Method
USAM........ United States Army Mothers Organization, National (EA)
USAMAA.... United States Army Memorial Affairs Agency (AABC)

USAMANRRDC ... United States Army Manpower Resources Research and Development Center (AABC)
USAMAPLA ... United States Army Military Assistance Program Logistics Agency
USAMB ...... United States Army Maintenance Board (AABC)
USAMBRDL ... United States Army Medical Bioengineering Research and Development Laboratory [*Fort Detrick, MD*] (AABC)
USAMBRL ... United States Army Medical Biomechanical Research Laboratory [*Walter Reed Army Medical Center*] (AABC)
USAMC...... United States Army Materiel Command
USAMC...... United States Army Medical Corps
USAMC...... United States Army Missile Command [*Obsolete*]
USAMC...... United States Army Mobility Command [*Later, Troop Support Command*]
USAMC...... United States Army Munitions Command [*Later, Armaments Command*]
USAMCALMSA ... United States Army Materiel Command Automated Logistics Management Systems Agency (AABC)
USAMCC ... United States Army Metrology and Calibration Center (AABC)
USAMCFG ... United States Army Medical Center, Fort Gordon (AABC)
USAMCFO ... United States Army Materiel Command Field Office (RDA)
USAMCFSA ... United States Army Materiel Command Field Safety Agency (AABC)
USAMC-IRO ... United States Army Materiel Command Inventory Research Office
USAMCI & SA ... United States Army Materiel Command Installations and Service Agency (AABC)
USAMC-ITC ... United States Army Materiel Command Intern Training Center
USAMCLDC ... United States Army Materiel Command Logistics Data Center
USAMCLSSA ... United States Army Materiel Command Logistic Systems Support Agency (AABC)
USAMCSFO ... United States Army Materiel Command Surety Field Office
USAMD ...... United States Army Missile Detachment (AABC)
USAMDAR ... United States Army Medical Depot Activity, Ryukyu Islands (AABC)
USAMDPC ... United States Army Maintenance Data Processing Center
USAMEAF ... United States Army Middle East Air Forces [*World War II*]
USAMEC.... United States Army Mobility Equipment Command [*Obsolete*]
USAMECOM ... United States Army Mobility Equipment Command [*Obsolete*] (AABC)
USAMEDCOMERU ... United States Army Medical Command, Europe (AABC)
USAMEDDBD ... United States Army Medical Department Board (RDA)
USAMEDLAB ... United States Army Medical Laboratory
USAMEDS ... United States Army Medical Service
USAMEDSVS ... United States Army Medical Service Veterinary School (AABC)
USAMEDTC ... United States Army Medical Training Center [*Ft. Sam Houston, TX*] (AABC)
USAMEERU ... United States Army Medical Environmental Engineering Research Unit
USAMEOS ... United States Army Medical Equipment and Optical School (AABC)
USAMERCC ... United States Army Middle East Regional Communications Command
USAMERDC ... United States Army Mobility Equipment Research and Development Center (AABC)
USAMERDL ... United States Army Medical Equipment Research and Development Laboratory (AABC)
USAMETA ... United States Army Management Engineering Training Agency (AABC)
USAMFSS ... United States Army Medical Field Service School (AABC)
USAMGIK ... United States Army Military Government in Korea
USAMHRC ... United States Army Military History Research Collection (AABC)
USAMICOM ... United States Army Missile Command [*Obsolete*] (AABC)
USAMIDA... United States Army Major Item Data Agency (AABC)
USAMIIA .... United States Army Medical Intelligence and Information Agency (AABC)
USAML...... United States Army Medical Laboratory (AABC)
USAMMA ... United States Army Medical Materiel Agency (AABC)
USAMMAE ... United States Army Materiel Management Agency, Europe
USAMMAPAC ... United States Army Medical Materiel Agency, Pacific (AABC)
USAMMC ... United States Army Maintenance Management Center (AABC)
USAMMCS ... United States Army Missile and Munitions Center School (AABC)
USA-MMDA ... US Army Medical Materiel Development Activity (RDA)
USAMMT ... United States Army Military Mail Terminal
USAMN ...... United States Army Mothers, National (EA)
USAMOAMA ... United States Army Medical Optical and Maintenance Activity
USAMOCOM ... United States Army Mobility Command [*Later, Troop Support Command*]
USAMOMA ... United States Army Medical Optical and Maintenance Agency (AABC)
USAMP ...... United States Army Mine Planter
USAMPHIBFOR ... United States Amphibious Forces (AABC)
USAMPS .... United States Army Military Police School (AABC)

USAMPTAO ... United States Army Military Personnel and Transportation Assistance Office (AABC)

USAMRAA ... United States Army Medical Research Acquisition Agency

USAMRDC ... United States Army Medical Research and Development Command [Washington, DC] (AABC)

USAMRICD ... United States Army Medical Research Institute for Chemical Defense [Aberdeen Proving Ground, MD] (RDA)

USAMRIID ... United States Army Medical Research Institute of Infectious Diseases [Fort Detrick, MD] (AABC)

USAMRL ... United States Army Medical Research Laboratory [Ft. Knox, KY] (AABC)

USAMRN.... United States Army Medical Research and Nutrition (MCD)

USAMRNL ... United States Army Medical Research and Nutrition Laboratory [Denver, CO] (AABC)

USAMRU.... United States Army Medical Research Unit [Malaysia, Panama] (AABC)

USAMRU-E ... United States Army Medical Research Unit - Europe (INF)

USAMS ...... United States Army Management School

USAMSAA ... United States Army Materiel Systems Analysis Agency

USAMSMADHS ... United States Army Medical Service Meat and Dairy Hygiene School

USAMSSA ... United States Army Management Systems Support Agency

USAM & TTC ... United States Army Mechanical and Technical Training Center [Also called MECHTECH]

USAMTU.... United States Army Marksmanship Training Unit

USAMU ...... United States Army Marksmanship Unit [Fort Benning, GA]

USAMU ...... United States Army Medical Unit

USAMUCOM ... United States Army Munitions Command [Later, Armaments Command]

USAMUFD ... United States Army Medical Unit, Fort Detrick [Maryland] (AABC)

USAMV ...... United States Association of Museum Volunteers [Later, AAMV] (EA)

USAN .... United States Adopted Name [Drugs]

USANA...... United States Army Nuclear Agency (AABC)

USANAFBA ... United States Army, Navy, and Air Force Bandsmen's Association [Defunct]

USANAVEUR ... United States Navy, Europe

USANC....... United States Army Nurse Corps

USANCA .... US Army Nuclear and Chemical Agency (RDA)

USANCG.... United States Army Nuclear Cratering Group (AABC)

USANCSG ... United States Army Nuclear and Chemical Surety Group [Formerly, USANWSG]

USANDL..... United States Army Nuclear Defense Laboratory (AABC)

USANF ...... United States Auxiliary Naval Force

U San Fernando Valley L Rev ... University of San Fernando Valley. Law Review (DLA)

U San Fernando VL Rev ... University of San Fernando Valley. Law Review (DLA)

U San Francisco L Rev ... University of San Francisco. Law Review [A publication]

U San Fran L Rev ... University of San Francisco. Law Review [A publication]

USANG...... United States Army National Guard

USanGS ..... Church of Jesus Christ of Latter-Day Saints, Genealogical Society Library, Santaquin Stake Branch, Santaquin, UT [Library symbol] [Library of Congress] (LCLS)

USANIBC ... United States Army Northern Ireland Base Command [World War II]

USANIF ...... United States Army Northern Ireland Force [World War II]

USA-NLABS ... United States Army Natick Laboratories

USANP....... United South African National Party

USANWCG ... United States Army Nuclear Weapon Coordination Group

USANWSG ... United States Army Nuclear Weapon Surety Group [Later, USANCSG]

USANWTC ... United States Army Northern Warfare Training Center (AABC)

USAOAC .... United States Army Ordnance Ammunition Command [Merged with Munitions Command, which later became Armaments Command]

USAOCBRL ... United States Army Ordnance Corps Ballistic Research Laboratory

USAOCCCL ... United States Army Ordnance Corps Coating and Chemical Laboratory

USAOCCS ... United States Army Ordnance-Chemical Center and School

USAOCDPS ... United States Army Ordnance Corps Development and Proof Services

USAOC & S ... United States Army Ordnance Center and School [Later, United States Army Ordnance and Chemical Center and School] (AABC)

USAOD....... United States Army Ordnance District

USAOEC .... United States Army Officer Evaluation Center

USAOGMS ... United States Army Ordnance Guided Missile School

USAOMC ... United States Army Ordnance Missile Command [Later, Missile Command]

USAOMSA ... United States Army Ordnance Missile Support Agency (AAG)

USAORDCORPS ... United States Army Ordnance Corps

USAORP .... United States Army Oversea Research Program

USAORRF ... United States Army Ordnance Rocket Research Facility

USAOSA .... United States Army Overseas Supply Agency (CINC)

USAOSANO ... United States Army Overseas Supply Agency, New Orleans

USAOSANY ... United States Army Overseas Supply Agency, New York

USAOSASF ... United States Army Overseas Supply Agency, San Francisco

USAOSREPLSTA ... United States Army Oversea Replacement Station

USAOSWAC ... United States Army Ordnance Special Weapons-Ammunition Command

USAOWC ... United States Army Ordnance Weapons Command [Merged with Missile Command]

USAP.......... United States Antarctic Program [National Science Foundation]

US Ap........ United States Appeals Reports (DLA)

USAPA....... United States Army Photographic Agency [Obsolete]

USAPACDA ... United States Army Personnel and Administration Combat Developments Activity (AABC)

USAPAE..... United States Army Procurement Agency, Europe (AABC)

USAPATACE ... United States Army Publications and Training Aids Center, Europe

USAPAV..... United States Army Procurement Agency, Vietnam

USAPC....... United States Army Petroleum Center

USAPC....... United States Army Pictorial Center

USAPCC .... United States Army Personnel Coordination Center

USAPDA .... United States Army Physical Disability Agency

USAPDC .... United States Army Property Disposal Center [Merged with Defense Logistics Services Center]

USAPDCE ... United States Army Petroleum Distribution Command, Europe (AABC)

USAPDSC ... United States Army Personnel Data Support Center (AABC)

USAPDSK ... United States Army Petroleum Distribution System, Korea (AABC)

USAPEB..... United States Army Physical Evaluation Board (AABC)

USAPEQUA ... United States Army Productions Equipment Agency

USAPERSCEN ... United States Army Personnel Center

USAPG....... United States Army Participation Group (AABC)

USAPHC..... United States Army Primary Helicopter Center (AABC)

USAPHS..... United States Army Primary Helicopter School

USAPIA..... United States Army Personnel Information Activity (AABC)

USAPIC...... United States Army Photointerpretation Center

USAPO....... United States Antarctic Projects Office

USAPO....... USA Plowing Organization [Versailles, OH] (EA)

USAPOP..... United States Army Port Operations, Pusan (AABC)

US App...... United States Appeals Reports (DLA)

US App DC ... United States Court of Appeals for District of Columbia (DLA)

USAPRC .... United States Army Physical Review Council (AABC)

USAPRDC ... United States Army Polar Research and Development Center

USAPRO .... United States Army Personnel Research Office

USAPSG .... United States Army Personnel Security Group (AABC)

USAPT .... United States Army Parachute Team

USAPWA.... United Stone and Allied Products Workers of America [Later, USWA] (EA)

USAQMC ... United States Army Quartermaster Corps [Merged with Supply and Maintenance Command]

USAQMCENFL ... United States Army Quartermaster Center and Fort Lee (AABC)

USAQMS.... United States Army Quartermaster School

USAQMTC ... United States Army Quartermaster Training Command

USAR .... Uniform Systems of Accounts and Reports for Certified Air Carriers [Civil Aeronautics Board]

USAR .... United States Aeronautical Reserve

USAR .... United States Army Reserve

USARA....... United States Army Air Racing Association [Formerly, PRPA] (EA)

USARA....... US Army Ranger Association (EA)

USARACS ... United States Army Alaska Communications Center

USARADBD ... United States Army Air Defense Board

USARADCOM ... United States Army Air Defense Command

USARADSCH ... United States Army Air Defense School

USARADSCH ... United States Army Research and Development School (AAG)

USARAE..... United States Army Reserve Affairs, Europe (AABC)

USARAL..... United States Army, Alaska

USARB....... United States Army Retraining Brigade (AABC)

USARBCO ... United States Army Base Command, Okinawa (AABC)

USARC....... United States Army Reserve Center (AABC)

USARCARIB ... United States Army, Caribbean

USARCC .... United States Association of Roller Canary Culturists (EA)

USA-RCEC ... USA-Republic of China Economic Council (EA)

USARCEN ... United States Army Records Center

USARCPC ... United States Army Reserve Components Personnel Center (AABC)

USARCS .... United States Army Claims Service (AABC)

USARctBad ... United States Army Recruiter Badge [Military decoration] (AABC)

USARDA .... United States Army Regional Dental Activity (AABC)

USARDAISA ... United States Army Research, Development, and Acquisition Information Systems Agency (AABC)

USARDL..... United States Army Research and Development Laboratories

USARDORAG ... United States Army Research and Development Operational Research Advisory Group (AABC)

USARDSG-GE ... United States Army Research, Development, and Standardization Group - Germany (RDA)

USAREC .... United States Army Recruiting Command (AABC)

USARECSTA ... United States Army Reception Station

USARENBD ... United States Army Armor and Engineer Board (RDA)

USAREPG ... United States Army Electronic Proving Ground

USARET-RSGSTA ... United States Army Returnee - Reassignment Station

USAREUR ... United States Army, Europe
USAREURAGLO ... United States Army, Europe, Adjutant General Liaison Office (AABC)
USAREURCSTC ... United States Army, Europe, Combat Support Training Center (AABC)
USAREURORDCOM ... United States Army European Ordnance Command
USARF .... United States Army Reserve Forces
USARFA ..... United States of America Rugby Fives Association (EA)
USARFANT ... United States Army Forces, Antilles
USARFEO ... United States Army Frequency Engineering Office (MCD)
USARFT ..... United States Army Forces, Taiwan
USARFU ..... United States of America Rugby Football Union (EA)
US Argonne Nat Lab Biol Med Res Div Semiannu Rep ... United States Argonne National Laboratory. Biological and Medical Research Division. Semiannual Report [*A publication*]
US Argonne Natl Lab Rep ... US Argonne National Laboratory. Report [*A publication*]
USARHAW ... United States Army, Hawaii
USARIA ...... United States Army Rock Island Arsenal
USARIBSS ... United States Army Research Institute for the Behavioral and Social Sciences (AABC)
USARIEM ... United States Army Research Institute of Environmental Medicine [*Natick, MA*] (AABC)
USARIS ...... United States Army Information School
USARJ .... United States Army, Japan
USARK .... United States Army, Korea (MCD)
USARLANT ... United States Army Forces, Atlantic (AABC)
USARLT ...... United States Army Reserve Losses Tally
USARMA .... United States Army Attache
USARMCOM ... United States Army Armament Command
US Armed Forces Food Container Inst Libr Bull ... United States Armed Forces Food and Container Institute. Library Bulletin [*A publication*]
US Armed Forces Food Container Inst Libr Bull ... US Armed Forces. Food and Container Institute. Library Bulletin [*A publication*]
US Armed Forces Med J ... US Armed Forces Medical Journal [*A publication*]
USARMIS ... United States Army Mission
USARMLO ... United States Army Liaison Officer
USARMY .... Uncle Sam Ain't Released Me Yet
US Army Armament Res Dev Command Tech Rep ... US Army. Armament Research and Development Command. Technical Report [*A publication*]
US Army Behav Sci Res Lab Tech Res Note ... US Army. Behavioral Science Research Laboratory. Technical Research Note [*A publication*]
US Army Behav Syst Res Lab Tech Res Note ... United States Army. Behavior and Systems Research Laboratory. Technical Research Note [*A publication*]
US Army Behav Syst Res Lab Tech Res Rep ... United States Army. Behavior and Systems Research Laboratory. Technical Research Report [*A publication*]
US Army BESRL ... United States Army. Behavior and Systems Research Laboratory [*A publication*]
US Army Coastal Eng Res Cent Misc Pap ... United States Army. Coastal Engineering Research Center. Miscellaneous Paper [*A publication*]
US Army Coastal Eng Res Cent Tech Memo ... US Army. Coastal Engineering Research Center. Technical Memorandum [*A publication*]
US Army Corps Eng Cold Reg Res Eng Lab Res Rep ... United States Army Corps of Engineers. Cold Regions Research and Engineering Laboratory. Hanover, New Hampshire. Research Report [*A publication*]
US Army Corps Eng Cold Reg Res Eng Lab Tech Rep ... United States Army Corps of Engineers. Cold Regions Research and Engineering Laboratory. Hanover, New Hampshire. Technical Report [*A publication*]
US Army Corps of Engineers Comm Tidal Hydraulics Rept ... United States Army Corps of Engineers. Committee on Tidal Hydraulics. Report [*A publication*]
US Army Corps Engineers Waterways Expt Sta Misc Paper ... United States Army Corps of Engineers. Waterways Experiment Station. Miscellaneous Paper [*A publication*]
US Army Corps Engineers Waterways Expt Sta Tech Rept ... United States Army Corps of Engineers. Waterways Experiment Station. Technical Report [*A publication*]
US Army Diamond Ordnance Fuze Lab Tech Rep ... United States Army. Diamond Ordnance Fuze Laboratories. Technical Report [*A publication*]
US Army Diamond Ordnance Fuze Lab Tech Rep ... US Army. Diamond Ordnance Fuze Laboratories. Technical Report [*A publication*]
US Army Eng Waterw Exp Stn Tech Rep ... US Army Engineers. Waterways Experiment Station. Technical Report [*A publication*]
US Army Med Res Lab Rep ... United States Army. Medical Research Laboratory. Report [*A publication*]
US Army Natick Lab Tech Rep Microbiol Ser ... US Army. Natick Laboratories. Technical Report. Microbiology Series [*A publication*]
USARO .... United States Army Research Office

USA-ROCEC ... USA-Republic of China Economic Council [*Crystal Lake, IL*] (EA)
USAROD .... United States Army Research Office (Durham)
USAROTC ... United States Army Reserve Officer Training Corps
USAROTCR ... United States Army Reserve Officers' Training Corps Region (AABC)
USARP .... United States Antarctic Research Program [*National Science Foundation*]
USARPA .... United States Army Radio Propagation Agency (AABC)
USARPAC ... United States Army, Pacific
USARPACINTS ... United States Army Pacific Intelligence School (AABC)
USARR .... United States Army Readiness Regions (AABC)
USARRACL ... United States Army Reserve Report Activity Control List
USARRADCOM ... United States Army Armament Research and Development Command (RDA)
USARRED ... United States Army Forces, Readiness Command
USARS .... US Army Regimental System (INF)
USARSA .... United States Amateur Roller Skating Association [*Later, USAC/RS*] (EA)
USARSCV ... United States Army Support Command, Vietnam [*Obsolete*]
USARSG .... United States Army Standardization Group
USARSO .... United States Army Forces, Southern Command
USARSO-PR ... United States Army Forces, Southern Command - Puerto Rico (AABC)
USARSOUTHCOM ... United States Army Forces, Southern Command
USARSSO ... United States Army Safeguard Systems Office
USARSTRIKE ... United States Army Forces Strike Command (AABC)
USARSUPTHAI ... United States Army Support, Thailand (AABC)
USART .... Universal Synchronous/Asynchronous Receiver and Transmitter [*Data processing*]
USARTL .... United States Army Research and Technical Labs (MCD)
USARTLS ... United States Army Reserve Troop List by State
USARUCU ... United States Army Reserve Unit Commander Unit
USARV .... United States Army Vietnam [*Obsolete*]
USARYIS ... United States Army, Ryukyu Islands
USAS .... United States Air Service
USAS .... United States of America Standard (IEEE)
USAS .... United States Antarctic Service [*1939-41*] [*Navy*]
USAS .... US Aquatic Sports (EA)
USASA .... United States Army Security Agency
USASAALA ... United States Army Security Assistance Agency, Latin America (AABC)
USASAC .... United States Army Security Assistance Center
USASAC .... US Army Security Affairs Command (RDA)
USASACDA ... United States Army Security Agency Combat Development Activity (AABC)
USASACDSA ... United States Army Security Agency Command Data Systems Activity (AABC)
USASADEA ... United States Army Signal Air Defense Engineering Agency [*Later, USAADEA*]
USASAE ..... United States Army Security Agency, Europe (AABC)
USASAFLOG ... United States Army Safeguard Logistics Command
USASAFO ... United States Army Signal Avionics Field Office [*Later, USAAFO*]
USASAFS ... United States Army Security Agency Field Station
USASAFSCOM ... United States Army Safeguard System Command (AABC)
USASAPAC ... United States Army Security Agency, Pacific (AABC)
USASASA ... United States Army Security Agency Systems Activity (AABC)
USASASA ... United States Army Small Arms Systems Agency
USASASSA ... United States Army Security Agency Signal Security Activity (AABC)
USASATCOMA ... United States Army Satellite Communications Agency (AABC)
USASATC & S ... United States Army Security Agency Training Center and School (AABC)
USASATEC ... United States Army Security Agency Test and Evaluation Center (AABC)
USASATSA ... United States Army Signal Aviation Test Support Activity
USASC .... United States Army Safety Center
USASC .... United States Army Signal Corps [*Merged with Communications and Electronics Command*]
USASC .... United States Army Subsistence Center
USASC .... United States Army Support Center
USASCA .... United States Army Safeguard Communications Agency (RDA)
USASCAF ... United States Army Service Center for the Armed Forces (AABC)
USASCC .... United States Army Strategic Communications Command
USASC & FG ... United States Army Signal Center and Fort Gordon (AABC)
USASCH .... United States Army Support Command, Hawaii (AABC)
USASCHEUR ... United States Army School, Europe [*Obsolete*] (AABC)
USASCII ..... United States of America Standard Code for Information Interchange
USASCOCR ... United States of America Standard Character Set for Optical Character Recognition [*Data processing*]
USASCR .... United States Army Support Center, Richmond (AABC)
USASCS .... United States Army Signal Center and School
USASCSA ... United States Army Signal Communications Security Agency
USASCSOCR ... United States of America Standard Character Set for Optical Character Recognition [*Data processing*]
USASCV .... United States Army Support Command, Vietnam [*Obsolete*]

USASD....... United States Army Student Detachment (AABC)
USASEA..... United States Army Signal Engineering Agency
USASESA ... United States Army Signal Equipment Support Agency (MCD)
USASESS ... United States Army Southeastern Signal School (AABC)
USASETAF ... United States Army Southern European Task Force
USASEUR ... United States Army School, Europe [*Obsolete*]
USASEXC ... United States Armed Services Exploitation Center (AABC)
USASF....... United States Army Special Forces (CINC)
USASFG..... United States Army Special Forces Group
USASFGV ... United States Army Special Forces Group, Vietnam
USASFV..... United States Army Special Forces, Vietnam [*Obsolete*]
USASG(Aus) ... United States Army Standardization Group
    (Australia) (AABC)
USASG(Ca) ... United States Army Standardization Group (Canada) (AABC)
USASG(UK) ... United States Army Standardization Group (United
    Kingdom) (AABC)
USASGV .... United States Army Support Group, Vietnam [*Obsolete*]
USASI .... United States of America Standards Institute [*Formerly, ASA*]
    [*Later, ANSI*]
USASIGC ... United States Army Signal Corps [*Merged with
    Communications and Electronics Command*]
USASIGS ... United States Army Signal School (AABC)
USASIMSA .. United States Army Signal Materiel Support Agency [*Later,
    USAEMSA*]
USASIS...... United States Army Strategic Intelligence School
USASMA.... United States Army Sergeant Major Academy (AABC)
USASMC.... United States Army Supply and Maintenance Command
USASMCOM ... United States Army Supply and Maintenance
    Command (MUGU)
USASMSA ... United States Army Signal Materiel Support Agency [*Later,
    USAEMSA*]
USASOPAC ... United States Army Support Office, Pacific (AABC)
USASOS .... United States Army Services of Supply
USASPSAE ... United States Army Special Services Agency, Europe (AABC)
USASPTAP ... United States Army Support Activity, Philadelphia (AABC)
USASPTC ... United States Army Support Center (AABC)
USASPTCC ... United States Army Support Command, Chicago
USASPTCM ... United States Army Support Center, Memphis (AABC)
USASPTCP ... United States Army Support Center, Philadelphia (AABC)
USASPTCR ... United States Army Support Center, Richmond (AABC)
USASRDL ... United States Army Signal Research and Development
    Laboratory [*Later, USAERDL*]
USASRU .... United States Army Surgical Research Unit (AABC)
USASSA .... United States Army Signal Supply Agency [*Later, USAEC*]
USASSAFMPO ... United States Army Signal Supply Agency, Fort
    Monmouth Procurement Office
USASSAMRO ... United States Army Signal Supply Agency, Midwestern
    Regional Office
USASSAUSAEPGPO ... United States Army Signal Supply Agency, United
    States Army Electronic Proving Ground Procurement
    Office
USASSAWPO ... United States Army Signal Supply Agency, Washington
    Procurement Office
USASSAWRO ... United States Army Signal Supply Agency, Western
    Regional Office
USASSC & FBH ... United States Army Soldier Support Center and Fort
    Benjamin Harrison (AABC)
USASSD .... United States Army Special Security Detachment
USASSG .... United States Army Special Security Group (AABC)
USASTAF .. United States Army Southern European Task Force
USASTAF .. United States Army Strategic Air Forces in the Pacific
USASTC .... United States Army Signal Training Center [*Fort Gordon, GA*]
USASTCFM ... United States Army Signal Training Command and Fort
    Monmouth
USASTRATCOM ... United States Army Strategic Communications
    Command [*Later, USACC*] (AABC)
USASTRATCOM-A ... United States Army Strategic Communications
    Command - Alaska (AABC)
USASTRATCOM-CONUS ... United States Army Strategic Communications
    Command - Continental United States (AABC)
USASTRATCOM-EUR ... United States Army Strategic Communications
    Command - Europe (AABC)
USASTRATCOM-PAC ... United States Army Strategic Communications
    Command - Pacific (AABC)
USASTRATCOM-SIGGP-T ... United States Army Strategic
    Communications Command Signal Group -
    Thailand (AABC)
USASTRATCOM-SO ... United States Army Strategic Communications
    Command - South (AABC)
USASTRATCOM-V ... United States Army Strategic Communications
    Command - Vietnam [*Obsolete*] (AABC)
USASUPCOM-CRB ... United States Army Support Command - Cam Ranh
    Bay [*Obsolete*] (AABC)
USASUPCOM-QN ... United States Army Support Command - Qui Nhon
    [*Obsolete*] (AABC)
USASUPCOM-SGN ... United States Army Support Command - Saigon
    [*Obsolete*] (AABC)
USASWL .... United States Army Signals Warfare Laboratory
USASWS.... United States Army Special Warfare School
USAT......... United States Army Transport
USATAC .... United States Army Terrain Analysis Center (MCD)

USATAC .... United States Army Training Center, Engineer [*Fort Leonard
    Wood, MO*]
USATACOM ... United States Army Tank-Automotive Command [*Obsolete*]
USATAFO ... United States Army Transportation Aviation Field Office
USATATSA ... United States Army Transportation Aircraft Test and Support
    Activity
USATA(WH) ... United States Army Transportation Agency (White
    House) (AABC)
USATB .... United States Army Training Board
USATC....... United States Army Topographic Command
USATC....... United States Army Training Center
USATC....... United States Army Transportation Center and School
USATC....... United States Assault Training Center [*World War II*]
USATCA .... United States Army Terminal Command, Atlantic
USATCAD ... United States Army Training Center, Air Defense
USATCARMOR ... United States Army Training Center, Armor [*Ft. Knox, KY*]
USATCBASIC ... United States Army Training Center, Basic
USATCD .... United States Army Training Center, Air Defense
USATCEFLW ... United States Army Training Center, Engineer, Fort Leonard
    Wood [*Missouri*] (AABC)
USATCENGR ... United States Army Training Center, Engineer
USATCEUR ... United States Army Terminal Command, Europe (AABC)
USATC FA ... United States Army Training Center, Field Artillery [*Ft. Sill,
    OK*] (AABC)
USATCFE ... United States Army Transportation Center and Fort
    Eustis (AABC)
USATCFLW ... United States Army Training Center and Fort Leonard
    Wood (AABC)
USATCG .... United States Army Terminal Command, Gulf (AABC)
USATCINF ... United States Army Training Center, Infantry
USATCO .... Universal Satellite Corporation [*New York, NY*]
    [*Telecommunications*] (TSSD)
USATCO .... US Air Traffic Controllers Organization [*Defunct*] (EA)
USATCP..... United States Army Terminal Command, Pacific
USATCRTSA ... United States Army Transportation Corps Road Test
    Support Activity
USATDA .... United States Army Training Device Agency
USATDGL ... United States Army Terminal Detachment, Great
    Lakes (AABC)
USATEA..... United States Army Transportation Engineering
    Agency (AABC)
USATEC..... United States Army Test and Evaluation Command [*Obsolete*]
USATECOM ... United States Army Test and Evaluation Command
    [*Obsolete*]
USATHAMA ... United States Army Toxic and Hazardous Materials
    Agency (RDA)
USATIA ...... United States Army Transportation Intelligence Agency
USATL .... United States Army Technical Library (DIT)
USATLA ..... USA Toy Library Association [*Glenview, IL*] (EA)
USATMACE ... United States Army Traffic Management Agency, Central
    Europe (AABC)
USATMC.... United States Army Transportation Materiel Command
USATMC.... United States Army Troop Medical Clinic (AABC)
US Atom Energy Commn Pub ... US Atomic Energy Commission.
    Publication [*A publication*]
US Atomic Energy Comm Map Prelim Map ... United States Atomic Energy
    Commission. Map. Preliminary Map [*A publication*]
US Atomic Energy Comm Rept ... US Atomic Energy Commission. Report [*A
    publication*]
USATOPOCOM ... United States Army Topographic Command (AABC)
USATOWA ... US Amateur Tug of War Association (EA)
USATRADOC ... United States Army Training and Doctrine Command
USATRASANA ... United States Army TRADOC Systems Analysis
    Activity (AABC)
USATRC..... United States Army Transportation Research Command
USATRECOM ... United States Army Transportation Research and
    Engineering Command
USATREOG ... United States Army Transportation Environmental
    Operations Group (AABC)
USATRFSTA ... United States Army Transfer Station
USATRML ... United States Army Tropical Research Medical Laboratory
USATROSCOM ... United States Army Troop Support Command
USATSA..... United States Army Technical Support Activity (AABC)
USATSC .... United States Army Terrestrial Sciences Center (AABC)
USATSC .... United States Army Training Support Center
USATSCH ... United States Army Transportation School
USATT .... Union des Syndicats Autonomes des Travailleurs Tchadiens
    [*Federation of Autonomous Workers Unions of Chad*]
USATTAY ... United States Army Transportation Test Activity, Yuma
    [*Arizona*] (AABC)
USATTB..... United States Army Transportation Terminal, Brooklyn
USATTC..... United States Army Transportation Training Command
USATTC..... United States Army Tropic Test Center (AABC)
USATTCA ... United States Army Transportation Terminal Command,
    Atlantic
USATTCARC ... United States Army Transportation Terminal Command,
    Arctic
USATTCG ... United States Army Transportation Terminal Command, Gulf
USATTCP ... United States Army Transportation Terminal Command, Pacific
USATTU..... United States Army Transportation Terminal Unit (AABC)
USATUC .... United States Army Terminal Unit, Canaveral (AABC)

USAV .... United Savings Life Insurance [*NASDAQ symbol*]   (NQ)
US Av .... United States Aviation Reports   (DLA)
USAVETS ... United States Army Veterinary School
US Aviation Rep ... United States Aviation Reports   (DLA)
US Avi Rep ... United States Aviation Reports   (DLA)
US Av R...... United States Aviation Reports   (DLA)
USAW......... Underwater Security Advance Warnings [*Navy*]
USAWC....... United States Army War College
USAWC....... United States Army Weapons Command [*Later, Armaments Command*]
USAWECOM ... United States Army Weapons Command [*Later, Armaments Command*]
USAWES.... United States Army Waterways Experiment Station   (AABC)
USAWF ...... United States Amateur Wrestling Foundation
USAWOA ... United States Army Warrant Officers Association   (EA)
USB............. Unified S-Band   (MCD)
USB............. United States Bases [*British*] [*World War II*]
USB............. Universal Serials and Book Exchange, Inc. [*ACCORD*] [*UTLAS symbol*]
USB............. Upflow Sludge Blanket [*Reactor, wastewater treatment*]
USB............. Upper Sideband
USB............. Upper Surface Blown [*Jet flap*] [*Aviation*]
USB............. US Bass [*An association*] [*Mesa, AZ*]   (EA)
USBA .... Union Syndicale des Bases Americaines [*Union of American Base Workers*] [*Morocco*]
USBA .... United States Badminton Association [*Formerly, ABA*]   (EA)
USBA .... United States Bartenders Association [*Tarzana, CA*]   (EA)
USBA .... United States Brewers Association [*Defunct*]   (EA)
USBA .... US Base Association   (EA)
USBA .... US Biathlon Association   (EA)
USBA .... US Boomerang Association   (EA)
US Banker ... United States Banker [*A publication*]
USBATU..... United States - Brazil Aviation Training Unit
USBBC....... United States Beef Breeds Council   (EA)
USBBS .... United States Bureau of Biological Survey [*Terminated, 1940; later, Fish and Wildlife Service*]
USBC .... United States Bureau of the Census   (OICC)
USBC .... US Bancorp [*NASDAQ symbol*]   (NQ)
USBCA....... United States Braille Chess Association   (EA)
USBCJ .... US Business Committee on Jamaica   (EA)
USBE.......... Unified S-Band Equipment
USBE.......... Universal Serials and Book Exchange, Inc. [*Acronym now used as official name of association*] [*Washington, DC*]   (EA)
US Beach Erosion Board Bull Tech Memo Tech Rept ... United States Beach Erosion Board. Bulletin. Technical Memorandum. Technical Report [*A publication*]
USBEP .... United States Bureau of Engraving and Printing
USBER .... United States Mission, Berlin
USBF.......... United States Baseball Federation
USBF.......... United States Brewers Foundation [*Later, USBA*]
USBF.......... United States Bureau of Fisheries [*Terminated*]
USBF.......... US Bobsled and Skeleton Federation   (EA)
USBFA........ US Bass Fishing Association [*Later, USB*]   (EA)
USBFDC..... United States Bureau of Foreign and Domestic Commerce
USBG .... United States Bartenders Guild [*Later, USBA*]   (EA)
USBG .... United States Botanic Garden
USBGA........ United States Blind Golfer's Association   (EA)
USBGN....... United States Bureau on Geographical Names [*Terminated, 1947; later, Board on Geographical Names*]
USBIA .... United States Bureau of Insular Affairs
USBIA .... Uspekhi Sovremennoi Biologii [*A publication*]
USBJA........ United States Barrel Jumping Association   (EA)
USBL.......... United States Bureau of Lighthouses
USBL.......... Usable   (FAAC)
USBLM....... United States Bureau of Land Management [*Department of the Interior*]
USBLS .... United States Bureau of Labor Statistics
USBM......... United States Bureau of Mines
USBMG ..... United States Berlin Mission in Germany
USBN .... United States Bureau of Navigation
USBNP .... United States Bureau of Navy Personnel [*Terminated*]
USBP.......... United States Border Patrol [*Department of the Treasury*]
USBPA .... United States Bicycle Polo Association
USBPR .... United States Bureau of Public Roads
USBR.......... United States Bureau of Reclamation [*Department of the Interior*]
USBRO....... United States Base Requirements Overseas   (AABC)
USBS.......... Unified S-Band System [*Radio*]
USBS.......... United States Bureau of Standards
USBSA....... United States Beet Sugar Association   (EA)
USBSA....... United States Board Sailing Association   (EA)
USBTA .... United States Board of Tax Appeals [*Later, the Tax Court of the United States*]
US Bur Am Ethnology Bull ... US Bureau of American Ethnology. Bulletin [*A publication*]
US Bur Commer Fish Rep Cal Year ... US Bureau of Commercial Fisheries. Report for the Calendar Year [*A publication*]
US Bureau Sport Fish Wildl Invest Fish Control ... US Bureau of Sport Fisheries and Wildlife. Investigations in Fish Control [*A publication*]

USBurEducBul ... United States Bureau of Education. Bulletins [*A publication*]
USBurEducCirc ... United States Bureau of Education. Circulars [*A publication*]
US Bur Mines Bull ... United States Bureau of Mines. Bulletin [*A publication*]
US Bur Mines Inf Circ ... US Bureau of Mines. Information Circular [*A publication*]
US Bur Mines Inform Circ ... United States Bureau of Mines. Information Circular [*A publication*]
US Bur Mines Miner Yearb ... United States Bureau of Mines. Minerals Yearbook [*A publication*]
US Bur Mines New Publ ... United States Bureau of Mines. New Publications. Monthly List [*A publication*]
US Bur Mines Rep Invest ... United States Bureau of Mines. Report of Investigations [*A publication*]
US Bur Mines Rept Inv ... US Bureau of Mines. Report of Investigations [*A publication*]
US Bur Mines Tech Pa ... United States Bureau of Mines. Technical Paper [*A publication*]
US Bur Mines Tech Prog Rep ... United States Bureau of Mines. Technical Progress Report [*A publication*]
US Bur Reclam Div Des Dams Br Rep ... United States Department of the Interior. Bureau of Reclamation. Division of Design. Denver, Colorado. Dams Branch Report [*A publication*]
US Bur Reclam Eng Monogr ... United States Department of the Interior. Bureau of Reclamation, Denver, Colorado. Engineering Monographs [*A publication*]
US Bur Reclam Res Rep ... United States Department of the Interior. Bureau of Reclamation. Research Report [*A publication*]
US Bur Reclam Tech Rec Des Constr ... United States Department of the Interior. Bureau of Reclamation. Technical Record of Design and Construction (Dams and Powerplants) [*A publication*]
US Bur Soils B ... US Bureau of Soils. Bulletin [*A publication*]
US Bur Sport Fish Wildl Invest Fish Control ... United States Bureau of Sport Fisheries and Wildlife. Investigations in Fish Control [*A publication*]
US Bur Sport Fish Wildl Resour Publ ... United States Bureau of Sport Fisheries and Wildlife. Resource Publication [*A publication*]
US Bur Sport Fish Wildl Resour Publ ... US Bureau of Sport Fisheries and Wildlife. Resource Publication [*A publication*]
US Bur Sport Fish Wildl Res Rep ... US Bureau of Sport Fisheries and Wildlife. Research Report [*A publication*]
US Bur Sport Fish Wildl Tech Pap ... US Bureau of Sport Fisheries and Wildlife. Technical Papers [*A publication*]
USBWA ...... United States Basketball Writers Association
USC............. Ultrasonic Storage Cell
USC............. Under Separate Cover
USC............. Union of Sephardic Congregations   (EA)
USC............. Union Sociale Camerounaise [*Cameroonese Social Union*]
USC............. Unitarian Service Committee [*Later, UUSC*] [*Post-World War II*]
USC............. United Satellite Communications [*Cable TV programing service*]
USC............. United Service Club [*Charter jet service to Europe for servicemen and dependents*]
USC............. United States Catalog [*A bibliographic publication*]
USC............. United States Citizen
USC............. United States Code [*Law*]
USC............. United States of Colombia
USC............. United States Congress
USC............. United States Custom Service, Washington, DC [*OCLC symbol*]   (OCLC)
USC............. United States Customs
USC............. United Strasser Club
USC............. United Survival Clubs   (EA)
USC............. Universal Specimen Chamber
USC............. University of Santa Clara [*California*]
USC............. University Scholarships of Canada
USC............. University of South Carolina
USC............. University of Southern California [*Los Angeles*] [*Seismograph station code, US Geological Survey*]   (SEIS)
USC............. University of Southern California
USC............. University Statistics Center [*New Mexico State University*] [*Research center*]   (RCD)
USC............. Up Stage Center [*Away from audience*] [*A stage direction*]
USC............. User Service Center   (MCD)
USC............. User Support Center   (MCD)
USC............. USLICO Corporation [*NYSE symbol*]
USCA .... Under Secretary for Civil Aviation
USCA .... Uniformed Services Contingency Act
USCA .... United States Canoe Association   (EA)
USCA .... United States Code Annotated [*Law*] [*Based on official USC*]
USCA .... United States Copper Association [*Later, American Bureau of Metal Statistics*]   (EA)
USCA .... United States Courts of Appeals
USCA .... United States Croquet Association   (EA)
USCA .... United States Curling Association [*Formerly, USMCA*]   (EA)
USCA App ... United States Code, Annotated, Appendix   (DLA)
USCAB....... United States Congressional Advisory Board   (EA)

USCAC ...... United States Continental Army Command [*Superseded by FORSCOM*]

USCAD .... University of Southern California. Abstracts of Dissertations [*A publication*]

USCAL .... University of Southern California, Aeronautical Laboratory   (MCD)

US Cal Sch L Tax Inst ... University of Southern California School of Law Tax Institute   (DLA)

USCAM ...... United States Civil Aviation Mission   (AFM)

US & Can Av ... United States and Canadian Aviation Reports [*A publication*]

USCANS ..... Unified S-Band Communication and Navigation System [*NASA*]

USCANW .... US Committee Against Nuclear War   (EA)

USCAPP .... Advanced Professional Programs, University of Southern California Law Center   (DLA)

USC App .... United States Code Appendix   (DLA)

USCAR .... United States Civil Administration, Ryukyu Islands

US Cath ...... United States Catholic [*A publication*]

US Cath M ... United States Catholic Magazine [*A publication*]

US Cath S ... United States Catholic Historical Society. Historical Records and Studies [*A publication*]

US & C Avi Rep ... United States and Canadian Aviation Reports [*A publication*]

US & C Av R ... United States and Canadian Aviation Reports [*A publication*]

USCB .... United States Customs Bonded

USCBRA .... United States CB Radio Association   (EA)

USCC .... Union des Syndicats Croyants du Cameroun [*Federation of Cameroonese Believers' Unions*]

USCC .... United States Calorimetry Conference

USCC .... United States Camaro Club   (EA)

USCC .... United States Cancellation Club

USCC .... United States Catholic Conference [*Formerly, NCWC*]

USCC .... United States Cellular Corporation [*Park Ridge, IL*] [*Telecommunications*]   (TSSD)

USCC .... United States Chamber of Commerce

USCC .... United States Circuit Court

USCC .... United States Citizens' Congress [*Defunct*]

USCC .... United States Commerical Company [*World War II*]

USCC .... United States Cotton Commission

USCC .... United States Court of Claims [*Abolished, 1982*]

USCC .... United States Criminal Code

USCC .... United States Criminal Court

USCC .... United States Customs Court [*Later, United States Court of International Trade*]

USCC .... United Student Christian Council in United States

USCC .... US Capital Corporation [*NASDAQ symbol*]   (NQ)

USCCA ...... United States Circuit Court of Appeals

USCCA ...... United States Circuit Court of Appeals Reports   (DLA)

USCCCA .... United States Cross Country Coaches Association   (EA)

USCCEC .... United States Committee for Care of European Children [*Post-World War II*]

USCCHO .... United States Conference of City Health Officers   (EA)

USCCHSO ... United States Conference of City Human Service Officials [*Washington, DC*]   (EA)

USCCPA .... United States Court of Customs and Patent Appeals [*Abolished, 1982*]

USCCSA .... US Corporate Council on South Africa   (EA)

USCDC ...... United States Civil Defense Council   (EA)

USCEC ...... University of Southern California, Engineering Center   (MCD)

USCEF .... US-China Education Foundation   (EA)

USCEFI ...... United Social, Cultural, and Educational Foundation of India

USCEI .... United States–China Educational Institute   (EA)

USCENTCOM ... United States Central Command

US Cert Den ... Certiorari Denied by United States Supreme Court   (DLA)

US Cert Dis ... Certiorari Dismissed by United States Supreme Court   (DLA)

USCESS ..... US Cultural Exchange and Sports Society   (EA)

USCF .... United States Chess Federation   (EA)

USCF .... United States Churchill Foundation [*Later, Winston Churchill Foundation*]

USCF .... United States Cycling Federation [*Formerly, ABLA*]   (EA)

USCFSTI AD Rep ... United States. Clearinghouse for Federal Scientific and Technical Information. AD Reports [*A publication*]

USCFSTI PB Rep ... United States. Clearinghouse for Federal Scientific and Technical Information. PB Report [*A publication*]

USC & G ..... United States Coast and Geodetic Survey [*Later, National Ocean Survey*]   (MUGU)

USCG .... United States Coast Guard

USCG .... United States Consul General

USCGA ...... United States Coast Guard Academy [*New London, CT*]

USCGA ...... United States Coast Guard Auxiliary

USCGAD .... United States Coast Guard Air Detachment

USC-GARP ... United States Committee for the Global Atmospheric Research Program [*Defunct*]   (EA)

USCGAS .... United States Coast Guard Air Station

USCGASB ... United States Coast Guard Aircraft and Supply Base

USCGAUX ... United States Coast Guard Auxiliary   (EA)

USCGB .... United States Coast Guard Base

USCG-B .... United States Coast Guard Office of Boating Safety

USCGC ...... United States Coast Guard Cutter

USCG-C ..... United States Coast Guard Office of Chief of Staff

USCGD ...... United States Coast Guard Depot

USC Govt'l Rev ... University of South Carolina. Governmental Review   (DLA)

USCGR .... United States Coast Guard Reserve

USCGRC .... United States Coast Guard Receiving Center

USCGR(T) ... United States Coast Guard, Reserve (Temporary)

USCGR(W) ... United States Coast Guard, Reserve (Women)

USCGS .... United States Coast and Geodetic Survey [*Later, National Ocean Survey*]

USC & GS ... United States Coast and Geodetic Survey [*Later, National Ocean Survey*]

USCGSCF ... United States Coast Guard Shore Communication Facilities

USCGTS .... United States Coast Guard Training Station

US Chil Bur Pub ... United States Children's Bureau. Publications [*A publication*]

US China Bus R ... US-China Business Review [*Washington, DC*] [*A publication*]

USCHS ...... United States Capitol Historical Society   (EA)

USCHS ...... United States Catholic Historical Society   (EA)

USCI .... United Satellite Communications Incorporated

USCIA .... United States Customs Inspectors' Association Port of New York   (EA)

USCIAA ...... United States Committee of the International Association of Art   (EA)

USCIB .... United States Communications Intelligence Board [*Later, National Security Agency*]

USCIB .... United States Council for International Business [*New York, NY*]   (EA)

USCIB/IC ... United States Communications Intelligence Board Intelligence Committee [*Obsolete*]

USCICC ..... United States Council of the International Chamber of Commerce [*Later, USCIB*]   (EA)

USCICSW ... United States Committee of the International Council on Social Welfare [*Washington, DC*]   (EA)

USCIDFC ... US Committee on Irrigation, Drainage, and Flood Control [*Later, US/ICID*]   (EA)

USCIIC .... United States Civilian Internee Information Center [*Army*]   (AABC)

USCIIC(Br) ... United States Civilian Internee Information Center (Branch) [*Army*]   (AABC)

USCINCAFRED ... United States Commander-in-Chief, Air Force Forces, Readiness Command

USCINCARRED ... United States Commander-in-Chief, Army Forces, Readiness Command

USCINCCENT ... Commander in Chief, United States Central Command

USCINCEMEAFSA ... United States Commander-in-Chief, Middle East, Africa South of the Sahara, and Southern Asia [*Military*]   (AABC)

USCINCEUR ... United States Commander-in-Chief, Europe

USCINCLANT ... Commander in Chief, United States Atlantic Command

USCINCPAC ... Commander in Chief, United States Pacific Command

USCINCRED ... United States Commander-in-Chief, Readiness Command

USCINCREDCOM ... Commander-in-Chief, US Readiness Command   (MCD)

USCINCSO ... United States Commander-in-Chief, Southern Command   (AFM)

US Cir Ct Rep DC ... Hayward and Hazelton's United States Circuit Court Reports [*District of Columbia*]   (DLA)

USCISCO ... United States Counterinsurgency Support Office

USCJE .... United Synagogue Commission on Jewish Education [*Later, USACJE*]   (EA)

USCL .... United Society for Christian Literature [*British*]

USCL .... United States Coalition for Life [*Export, PA*]   (EA)

USCLA .... United States Club Lacrosse Association   (EA)

USCM .... Unit Simulated Combat Mission   (AAG)

USCM .... United States Conference of Mayors   (EA)

USCM .... United States Council of Mayors   (OICC)

USCM .... Usibelli Coal Miner [*Usibelli, AK*] [*A publication*]

USCMA ...... United States Catholic Mission Association   (EA)

USCMA ...... United States Cheese Makers Association [*Madison, WI*]   (EA)

USCMA ...... United States Court of Military Appeals

USCMA ...... United States Crutch Manufacturers Association   (EA)

USCMA Adv Op ... United States Court of Military Appeals, Advance Opinions   (DLA)

USCMC ...... United States Catholic Mission Council   (EA)

USCMH ...... United States Commission of Maritime History [*Marine science*]   (MSC)

USCMI .... United States Commission on Mathematical Instruction

USCO .... United States Committee for the Oceans   (EA)

USCOA ...... Uniformed Services Contingency Option Act

US Coast and Geod Survey Pub ... US Coast and Geodetic Survey. Publication [*A publication*]

US Coast Geod Surv Magnetograms Hourly Values MHV ... US Department of Commerce. Coast and Geodetic Survey. Magnetograms and Hourly Values MHV [*A publication*]

USCOB .... United States Commander, Berlin

US Code Cong & Ad News ... United States Code Congressional and Administrative News   (DLA)

USCOLD .... United States Committee on Large Dams [*of the International Commission on Large Dams*]   (EA)

USCOMEAST ... United States Commander, Eastern Atlantic   (MCD)

USCOMEASTLANT ... United States Commander, Naval Forces, Eastern Atlantic   (NATG)

US Comp St ... United States Compiled Statutes   (DLA)

USCOMSUBGRUEASTLANT ... United States Commander, Submarines Group, Eastern Atlantic   (NATG)
USCONARC ... United States Continental Army Command [*Superseded by FORSCOM*]
US Cond Rep ... Peters' Condensed United States Reports   (DLA)
US Cong .... United States Congress [*A publication*]
US Const ... United States Constitution   (DLA)
US Consum Marketing Serv C & MS ... US Consumer and Marketing Service. C & MS [*A publication*]
USCP .... United States Capitol Police
USCPFA ..... United States - China Peoples Friendship Association   (EA)
USCPSHHM ... United States Committee to Promote Studies of the History of the Habsburg Monarchy   (EA)
USCR .... United States Committee for Refugees   (EA)
USCRA ...... United States Citizens' Rights Association   (EA)
USCS .... United States Coast Survey
USCS .... United States Code Service   (DLA)
USCS .... United States Commercial Standard
USCS .... United States Conciliation Service [*Functions transferred to Federal Mediation and Conciliation Service, 1947*]
USCS .... United States Customary System [*System of units used in the US*]
USCS .... United States Customs Service   (MCD)
USCS .... Universal Ship Cancellation Society [*Later, MPS*]   (EA)
USCS .... Urine Sampling and Collection System [*NASA*]
USCS .... US Commercial Service [*International Trade Administration*]
USCSB ...... United States Communications Security Board
USCSC ...... United States Chefs Ski Club   (EA)
USCSC ...... United States Civil Service Commission [*Later, MSPB*]
USCSC ...... United States Collegiate Sports Council
USCSC ...... United States Cuban Sugar Council [*Defunct*]   (EA)
USCSCV ... US Committee for Scientific Cooperation with Vietnam   (EA)
USCSE ...... United States Civil Service Examination
USC-SFI .... United States Committee - Sports for Israel   (EA)
USCSRA ... United States Cane Sugar Refiners' Association [*Washington, DC*]   (EA)
USCSSB .... United States Cap Screw Service Bureau [*Later, Cap Screw and Special Threaded Products Bureau*]   (EA)
USCT .... Union des Syndicats Confederes du Togo [*Federation of Confederated Unions of Togo*]
USCT .... United States Colored Troops [*Civil War*]
USCTA ...... United States Combined Training Association
US Ct Cl .... United States Court of Claims   (DLA)
US-CUES ... US Campaign for the University of El Salvador   (EA)
USCUN ...... United States Committee for the United Nations [*Later, UNA-USA*]
USCV .... Union Scientifique Continentale de Verre [*European Union for the Scientific Study of Glass - EUSSG*]   (EA-IO)
USCWC ...... United States Chemical Warfare Committee
USCWCC ... United States Conference for the World Council of Churches   (EA)
USCWF ...... US Council for World Freedom   (EA)
USC-WHO ... United States Committee for the World Health Organization   (EA)
USD .... Ultimate Strength Design   (IEEE)
USD .... Ultrasonic Separation Detector
USD .... Uniao Social Democratico [*Social Democratic Union*] [*Portuguese*]   (PPE)
USD .... Unified School District
USD .... United States Dispensatory [*Pharmacology*]
USD .... United States Diving, Inc.   (EA)
USD .... United States Dollars
USD .... University Science Development [*National Science Foundation*]
USD .... University of South Dakota
USD .... University of South Dakota, Vermillion, SD [*OCLC symbol*]   (OCLC)
USD .... Uranium Series Dating
USDA .... Uniform Simultaneous Death Act [*National Conference of Commissioners on Uniform State Laws*]
USDA .... United Square Dancers of America   (EA)
USDA .... United States Department of Agriculture [*Washington, DC*] [*Database originator*]
USDA .... United States Disarmament Administration [*Transferred to US Arms Control and Disarmament Agency, 1961*]
USDA .... United States Duffers' Association   (EA)
USDA .... US Darting Association   (EA)
USDA .... US Disc Sports Association [*West Hampton Beach, NY*]   (EA)
USDA Agr Econ Rep ... US Department of Agriculture. Agricultural Economic Report [*A publication*]
USDA Agr Handb ... United States. Department of Agriculture. Agricultural Handbook [*A publication*]
USDA Bur Biol Surv Bull ... US Department of Agriculture. Bureau of Biological Survey. Bulletin [*A publication*]
USDA Fert ... US Department of Agriculture. Fertilizer Supply [*A publication*]
USDA For Ser Res Pap PSW US Pac Southwest For Range Exp Stn ... USDA [*United States Department of Agriculture*] Forest Service. Research Paper PSW-United States. Pacific Southwest Forest and Range Experiment Station [*A publication*]

USDA For Serv Gen Tech Rep NC US North Cent For Exp Stn ... USDA [*United States Department of Agriculture*] Forest Service. General Technical Report NC-United States. North Central Forest Experiment Station [*A publication*]
USDA For Serv Gen Tech Rep PSW US Pac Southwest For Exp Stn ... USDA [*United States Department of Agriculture*] Forest Service. General Technical Report PSW-United States. Pacific Southwest Forest and Range Experiment Station [*A publication*]
USDA For Serv Res Note FPL US For Prod Lab ... USDA [*United States Department of Agriculture*] Forest Service. Research Note FPL-United States. Forest Products Laboratory [*A publication*]
USDA For Serv Res Note PSW US Pac Southwest For Range Exp St ... USDA [*United States Department of Agriculture*] Forest Service. Research Note PSW-United States. Pacific Southwest Forest and Range Experiment Station [*A publication*]
USDA For Serv Res Note SE US Southeast For Exp Stn ... USDA [*United States Department of Agriculture*] Forest Service. Research Note SE-United States. Southeastern Forest Experiment Station [*A publication*]
USDA For Serv Res Pap NC US North Cent For Exp Stn ... USDA [*United States Department of Agriculture*] Forest Service. Research Paper NC-United States. North Central Forest Experiment Station [*A publication*]
USDA For Serv Res Pap RM US Rocky Mt For Range Exp Stn ... USDA [*United States Department of Agriculture*] Forest Service. Research Paper RM-United States. Rocky Mountain Forest and Range Experiment Station [*A publication*]
USDAO ...... United States Defense Attache Office [*or Officer*]   (AABC)
USDA PA .... United States Department of Agriculture. PA (Program Aid) [*A publication*]
USDA Prod Res Rep ... United States Department of Agriculture. Production Research Report [*A publication*]
USDA RDD ... USDA Regional Document Delivery [*Library network*]
USDASL ..... USDA [*United States Department of Agriculture*] Sedimentation Laboratory [*Research center*]   (RCD)
USDAW ...... Union of Ship Distributive and Allied Workers [*British*]
USDB .... United States Disciplinary Barracks
USDC .... Underwater Search, Detection, Classification   (AAG)
USDC .... United States Defense Committee   (EA)
USDC .... United States Department of Commerce
USDC .... United States District of Columbia   (DLA)
USDC .... United States District Court
USDC .... US Design Corporation [*NASDAQ symbol*]   (NQ)
USDCFO ... United States Defense Communication Field Office   (NATG)
USDC Haw ... United States District Court, District of Hawaii   (DLA)
USDC Haw ... United States District Court, District of Hawaii, Reports   (DLA)
USDC Hawaii ... United States District Court, District of Hawaii   (DLA)
USDC Hawaii ... United States District Court, District of Hawaii, Reports   (DLA)
USDD .... United States Department of Defense
USDE .... United States Department of Education
USDE .... United States Department of Energy   (MCD)
USDELIADB ... United States Delegation, Inter-American Defense Board   (AABC)
US Dep Agric Agric Handb ... US Department of Agriculture. Agriculture Handbook [*A publication*]
US Dep Agric Agric Inf Bull ... US Department of Agriculture. Agriculture Information Bulletin [*A publication*]
US Dep Agric Agric Monogr ... United States Department of Agriculture. Agriculture Monograph [*A publication*]
US Dep Agric Agric Res Serv ... United States Department of Agriculture. Agricultural Research Service [*A publication*]
US Dep Agric Agric Res Serv ARS (Ser) ... United States Department of Agriculture. Agricultural Research Service ARS (Series) [*A publication*]
US Dep Agric Agric Res Serv Rep ... United States Department of Agriculture. Agricultural Research Service. Report [*A publication*]
US Dep Agric Agric Res Serv Stat Bull ... United States Department of Agriculture. Agricultural Research Service. Statistical Bulletin [*A publication*]
US Dep Agric ARS ... United States Department of Agriculture. Agricultural Research Service [*A publication*]
US Dep Agric Bull ... United States Department of Agriculture. Bulletin [*A publication*]
US Dep Agric Circ ... US Department of Agriculture. Circular [*A publication*]
US Dep Agric Conserv Res Rep ... US Department of Agriculture. Conservation Research Report [*A publication*]
US Dep Agric Farmers' Bull ... US Department of Agriculture. Farmers' Bulletin [*A publication*]
US Dep Agric For Serv For Prod Lab Rep ... United States Department of Agriculture. Forest Service. Forest Products Laboratory. Report [*A publication*]
US Dep Agric Home Econ Res Rep ... United States Department of Agriculture. Home Economics Research Report [*A publication*]
US Dep Agric Home Gard Bull ... US Department of Agriculture. Home and Garden Bulletin [*A publication*]

US Dep Agric Index-Cat Med Vet Zool Spec Publ ... United States Department of Agriculture. Index-Catalogue of Medical and Veterinary Zoology. Special Publication [*A publication*]

US Dep Agric Index-Cat Med Vet Zool Suppl ... United States Department of Agriculture. Index-Catalogue of Medical and Veterinary Zoology. Supplement [*A publication*]

US Dep Agric Leafl ... US Department of Agriculture. Leaflet [*A publication*]

US Dep Agric Mark Res Rep ... United States Department of Agriculture. Marketing Research Report [*A publication*]

US Dep Agric Misc Publ ... US Department of Agriculture. Miscellaneous Publications [*A publication*]

US Dep Agric Northeast For Stn Stn Pap ... United States Department of Agriculture. Northeastern Forest Experiment Station. Station Paper [*A publication*]

US Dep Agric Prod Res Rep ... US Department of Agriculture. Production Research Report [*A publication*]

US Dep Agric Res Serv Mark Res Rep ... United States Department of Agriculture. Agricultural Research Service. Marketing Research Report [*A publication*]

US Dep Agric Soil Conserv Ser Soil Surv ... United States Department of Agriculture. Soil Conservation Service. Soil Survey [*A publication*]

US Dep Agric Soil Conserv Serv Soil Surv Invest Rep ... US Department of Agriculture. Soil Conservation Service. Soil Survey Investigation Report [*A publication*]

US Dep Agric Soil Surv ... United States Department of Agriculture. Soil Survey [*A publication*]

US Dep Agric Stat Bull ... US Department of Agriculture. Statistical Bulletin [*A publication*]

US Dep Agric Tech Bull ... US Department of Agriculture. Technical Bulletin [*A publication*]

US Dep Agric Util Res Rep ... United States Department of Agriculture. Utilization Research Report [*A publication*]

US Dep Agric Yearb Agric ... US Department of Agriculture. Yearbook of Agriculture [*A publication*]

US Dep Commer Natl Bur Stand Tech Note ... US Department of Commerce. National Bureau of Standards. Technical Note [*A publication*]

US Dep Commer Natl Mar Fish Serv Circ ... US Department of Commerce. National Marine Fisheries Service. Circular [*A publication*]

US Dep Commer Natl Mar Fish Serv Spec Sci Rep Fish ... US Department of Commerce. National Marine Fisheries Service. Special Scientific Report. Fisheries [*A publication*]

US Dep Commer Off Tech Serv AD ... United States. Department of Commerce. Office of Technical Services. AD [*A publication*]

US Dep Commer Off Tech Serv PB Rep ... United States. Department of Commerce. Office of Technical Services. PB Report [*A publication*]

US Dep Energy Bartlesville Energy Technol Cent Pet Prod Surv ... US Department of Energy. Bartlesville Energy Technology Center. Petroleum Product Surveys [*A publication*]

US Dep Energy Bartlesville Energy Technol Cent Publ ... US Department of Energy. Bartlesville Energy Technology Center. Publications [*A publication*]

US Dep Health Educ Welfare Annu Rep ... US Department of Health, Education, and Welfare [*Later, US Department of Health and Human Services*] Annual Report [*A publication*]

US Dep Health Educ Welfare DHEW Publ (FDA) ... United States Department of Health, Education, and Welfare. DHEW [*Department of Health, Education, and Welfare*] Publication. (FDA) [*Food and Drug Administration*] [*A publication*]

US Dep Health Educ Welfare DHEW Publ (NIH) ... US Department of Health, Education, and Welfare [*Later, US Department of Health and Human Services*] DHEW Publication (NIH) [*A publication*]

US Dep Health Educ Welfare Health Serv Adm Publ HSA ... United States Department of Health, Education, and Welfare. Health Services Administration. Publication HSA [*Health Services Administration*] [*A publication*]

US Dep Health Educ Welfare Natl Inst Occup Saf Health ... United States Department of Health, Education, and Welfare. National Institute for Occupational Safety and Health [*A publication*]

US Dep Inter Bur Mines New Publ ... United States Department of the Interior. Bureau of Mines. New Publications [*A publication*]

US Dep Inter Conserv Yearb ... US Department of the Interior. Conservation Yearbook [*A publication*]

US Dep Inter Fish Wildl Res Rep ... United States Department of the Interior. Fish and Wildlife Service. Research Report [*A publication*]

US Dep Inter MESA Inf Rep ... US Department of the Interior. Mining Enforcement and Safety Administration. Informational Report [*A publication*]

US Dep Inter Off Libr Serv Bibliogr Ser ... United States Department of the Interior. Office of Library Services. Bibliography Series [*A publication*]

US Dep State Bur Public Aff Backgr Notes ... United States. Department of State. Bureau of Public Affairs. Background Notes [*A publication*]

US Dept Agriculture Tech Bull Yearbook ... United States Department of Agriculture. Technical Bulletin. Yearbook [*A publication*]

US Dept HEW Publ ... US Department of Health, Education, and Welfare [*Later, US Department of Health and Human Services*] Publications [*A publication*]

US Dept HHS Publ ... US Department of Health and Human Services. Publications [*A publication*]

US Dept Int ... United States Department of Interior   (DLA)

US Dep Transp (Rep) DOT/TST ... US Department of Transportation (Report). DOT/TST [*A publication*]

US des AL ... Union Syndicale des Artistes Lyriques [*French*]   (ROG)

USDESEA ... United States Dependent Schools, European Area [*Army*]

USDF......... United States Dressage Federation   (EA)

USDFRC...... US Dairy Forage Research Center [*Research center*]   (RCD)

USDGA...... United States Durum Growers Association   (EA)

USDH .... United States Direct Hire [*Military*]

USDHE & W ... United States Department of Health, Education, and Welfare

USDHUD .... United States Department of Housing and Urban Development

USDI .... United States Department of the Interior

US Dig....... United States Digest   (DLA)

USDISBad ... United States Distinguished International Shooter Badge [*Military decoration*]   (AABC)

US Dist Ct Haw ... United States District Court for the District of Hawaii   (DLA)

USDJ.......... United States Department of Justice

USDJ.......... United States District Judge

USDL.......... United States Department of Labor

USDLGI...... United States Defense Liaison Group, Indonesia [*Army*]   (AABC)

USDO .... United States Disbursing Officer

USDOC ...... United States Department of Commerce

USDOCO.... United States Documents Officer   (AFM)

USDOCOLANDSOUTHEAST ... United States Document Office, Allied Land Forces, Southeastern Europe   (AABC)

USDOD...... United States Department of Defense

USDOE....... United States Department of Energy

USDOI .... United States Department of the Interior   (MCD)

USDOT....... United States Department of Transportation   (MCD)

USD(P)....... Undersecretary of Defense for Policy   (MCD)

US Dp Agr B ... US Department of Agriculture. Bulletin [*A publication*]

US Dp Int ... US Department of the Interior. Publication [*A publication*]

USDR .... United States Divorce Reform [*Kenwood, CA*]   (EA)

USDRE .... Office of the Under Secretary of Defense for Research and Engineering

USDS .... United States Department of State

USDSA....... United States Deaf Skiers Association   (EA)

USDSEA..... United States Dependent Schools, European Area [*Army*]   (AABC)

USDT.......... United States Department of Transportation

USDT.......... United States Department of the Treasury

USDTA ...... United States Dental Tennis Association   (EA)

USDTP .... Ukrainska Sotsial Demokraticheskaia Truda Partiia [*Ukrainian Social Democratic Labor Party*] [*Russian*]   (PPE)

USE .... Encyclopedia of United States Reports   (DLA)

USE .... Underground Service Entrance

USE .... Undersea Scientific Expedition

USE .... Unified S-Band Equipment

USE .... Unit Support Equipment

USE .... United States Economic Problems [*British*] [*World War II*]

USE .... United States Embassy

USE .... United States Envelope Co.

USE .... UNIVAC Scientific Exchange [*Later, UI, USE, Inc.*]

USE .... University of South Dakota, Law Library, Vermillion, SD [*OCLC symbol*]   (OCLC)

USE .... University Space Experiments

USE .... Unmanned Surveillance Equipment

USE .... US English [*An association*]   (EA)

USE .... Wauseon, OH [*Location identifier*] [*FAA*]   (FAAL)

USEA .... Undersea   (AABC)

USEASA.... United States Eastern Amateur Ski Association [*Later, ESA*]

USEC .... United States Endurance Cup [*Car racing*]

USEC .... United States Mission to European Communities

USEC .... United System of Electronic Computers   (IEEE)

USEC .... United System of Electronic Services   (MCD)

USEC .... Universal Security Instruments, Inc. [*NASDAQ symbol*]   (NQ)

USECC....... United States Employees' Compensation Commission [*Functions transferred to Federal Security Agency, 1946*]

USECOM.... United States Army Electronics Command [*Obsolete*]

US Econ Res Serv Foreign Agric Econ Rep ... US Economic Research Service. Foreign Agricultural Economic Report [*A publication*]

USEE.......... United States Exploring Expedition [*1838-42*] [*Navy*]

USEEM....... United States Establishment and Enterprise Microdata Base [*Brookings Institution*]

USEES .... United States Naval Engineering Experiment Station [*Annapolis, MD*]

USEFP........ United States Educational Foundation in Pakistan

USEG .... US Energy Corp. [*NASDAQ symbol*]   (NQ)

US Egg .... United States Egg and Poultry Magazine [*A publication*]
USEI .... United States Society of Esperanto Instructors [*Later, AATE*]
USELMCENTO ... United States Element Central Treaty Organization (AFM)
USEMA ...... [*The*] United States Electronic Mail Association
USEMB .... United States Embassy (MCD)
US Energy Res Dev Adm (Rep) CONF ... United States Energy Research and Development Administration (Report) CONF [*A publication*]
US Energy Res Dev Adm (Rep) GJO ... US Energy Research and Development Administration (Report) GJO [*Grand Junction Office*] [*A publication*]
US Environ Prot Agency Munic Constr Div Rep ... United States Environmental Protection Agency. Municipal Construction Division. Report [*A publication*]
US Environ Prot Agency Natl Environ Res Cent Ecol Res Ser ... US Environmental Protection Agency. National Environmental Research Center. Ecological Research Series [*A publication*]
US Environ Prot Agency Off Air Qual Plann Stand Tech Rep ... US Environmental Protection Agency. Office of Air Quality Planning and Standards. Technical Report [*A publication*]
US Environ Prot Agency Off Pestic Programs Rep ... United States Environmental Protection Agency. Office of Pesticide Programs. Report [*A publication*]
US Environ Prot Agency Off Radiat Programs EPA ... US Environmental Protection Agency. Office of Radiation Programs. EPA [*A publication*]
US Environ Prot Agency Off Radiat Programs EPA-ORP ... US Environmental Protection Agency. Office of Radiation Programs. EPA-ORP [*A publication*]
US Environ Prot Agency Off Radiat Programs Tech Rep ... United States Environmental Protection Agency. Office of Radiation Programs. Technical Report [*A publication*]
US Environ Prot Agency Off Radiat Programs Tech Rep ORP-SID ... US Environmental Protection Agency. Office of Radiation Programs. Technical Reports ORP-SID [*A publication*]
US Environ Prot Agency Off Res Dev Rep EPA ... United States Environmental Protection Agency. Office of Research and Development. Report. EPA [*A publication*]
US Environ Prot Agency Publ AP Ser ... US Environmental Protection Agency. Publication. AP Series [*A publication*]
USEO .... United States Engineer Office
USEORD .... Use Order [*Navy*] (NVT)
USEP .... United States Escapee Program
USEP .... Urban Slum Employment Program (OICC)
USEPA .... United States Environmental Protection Agency
US EPA Ecol Res ... US Environmental Protection Agency. Ecological Research [*A publication*]
US EPA Envir Health Res ... US Environmental Protection Agency. Environmental Health Effects Research [*A publication*]
US EPA Envir Monit ... United States Environmental Protection Agency. Environmental Monitoring [*A publication*]
US EPA Envir Prot Technol ... US Environmental Protection Agency. Environmental Protection Technology [*A publication*]
US EPA Socioecon Studies ... United States Environmental Protection Agency. Socioeconomic Environmental Studies [*A publication*]
USER .... Ultra-Small Electronics Research [*DoD*]
USERC .... United States Environment and Resources Council (EA)
USERDA ..... United States Energy Research and Development Administration [*Superseded by Department of Energy, 1977*]
USERIA ...... Ultrasensitive Enzymatic Radioimmunoassay [*Clinical chemistry*]
USERID ...... User Identification [*Data processing*]
USER INC ... Urban Scientific and Educational Research, Incorporated (EA)
USERS .... Uniform Socio-Economic Reporting System [*Financial reporting system for voluntary health and welfare organizations*]
U Serv M ... United Service Magazine [*A publication*]
USES .... United States Employment Service [*Department of Labor*]
USES .... US Energy Search [*NASDAQ symbol*] (NQ)
USESF .... United States Exchange Stabilization Fund
US-ESRIC ... US-El Salvador Research and Information Center (EA)
USESSA ..... United States Environmental Science Services Administration (AABC)
USET .... United South and Eastern Tribes [*An association*] [*Nashville, TN*] (EA)
USET .... United States Equestrian Team
USEUCOM ... United States European Command
USEX .... US Exploration Corp. [*NASDAQ symbol*] (NQ)
USF .... Lommen Health Science Library, University of South Dakota, Vermillion, SD [*OCLC symbol*] (OCLC)
USF .... Und So Fort [*And So Forth*] [*German*]
USF .... Uniaxial Stress Field
USF .... United Scleroderma Foundation [*Watsonville, CA*] (EA)
USF .... United Socialist Front [*Thai*] (PD)
USF .... United States Fleet
USF .... United States Forces (CINC)
USF .... University of San Francisco [*California*]
USF .... University of Santa Fe [*A publication*]

USF .... USACafes [*American Stock Exchange symbol*]
USFA .... United Sports Fans of America (EA)
USFA .... United States Fencing Association [*Formerly, AFLA*] (EA)
USFA .... United States Forces in Austria
USFA .... United States Fuel Administration [*Terminated*]
USFA .... US Farmers Association (EA)
USFADTC ... United States Fleet Air Defense Training Center
USFAIRWINGMED ... United States Fleet Air Wing, Mediterranean (NATG)
US Farm .... US Farm News [*A publication*]
USFARS .... United States Federation of Amateur Roller Skaters [*Later, USAC-RS*] (EA)
USFBI .... United States Forces, British Isles [*World War II*]
USFC .... United States Foil Company
USFCC ...... United States Fire Companies Conference [*Defunct*] (EA)
USFCC ...... US Federation for Culture Collections (EA)
USFCF ...... USF Constellation Foundation (EA)
USFCT .... United States Forces, China Theater
US Fed Railroad Adm Rep ... US Federal Railroad Administration. Report [*A publication*]
USFET .... United States Forces, European Theater [*American headquarters for occupation of Germany after SHAEF was dissolved*] [*World War II*]
USFF .... United States Flag Foundation (EA)
USFFL .... United States Flag Football League [*Sanibel, FL*] (EA)
USF & G ... United States Fidelity & Guaranty Co.
USFGC ...... United States Feed Grains Council (EA)
USFHA .... United States Field Hockey Association (EA)
USFI .... Unione Sindacale Ferrovieri Italiani [*National Union of Italian Railway Workers*]
USFIA .... United States Forces in Australia
USFIP .... United States Forces in the Philippines
USFIS .... United States Foundation for International Scouting [*Irving, TX*] (EA)
USFISC ...... United States Foreign Intelligence Surveillance Court
US Fish and Wildlife Service Fishery Bull ... US Fish and Wildlife Service. Fishery Bulletin [*A publication*]
US Fish Wildl Serv Bur Commer Fish Fish Leafl ... US Fish and Wildlife Service. Bureau of Commercial Fisheries. Fishery Leaflet [*A publication*]
US Fish Wildl Serv Bur Commer Fish Stat Dig ... US Fish and Wildlife Service. Bureau of Commercial Fisheries. Statistical Digest [*A publication*]
US Fish Wildl Serv Bur Sport Fish Wildl EGL ... US Fish and Wildlife Service. Bureau of Sport Fisheries and Wildlife. EGL [*A publication*]
US Fish Wildl Serv Circ ... US Fish and Wildlife Service. Circular [*A publication*]
US Fish Wildl Serv Fish Distrib Rep ... US Fish and Wildlife Service. Fish Distribution Report [*A publication*]
US Fish Wildl Serv Invest Fish Control ... US Fish and Wildlife Service. Investigations in Fish Control [*A publication*]
US Fish Wildl Serv N Am Fauna ... US Fish and Wildlife Service. North American Fauna [*A publication*]
US Fish Wildl Serv Resour Publ ... US Fish and Wildlife Service. Resource Publication [*A publication*]
US Fish Wildl Serv Res Rep ... US Fish and Wildlife Service. Research Report [*A publication*]
US Fish Wildl Serv Spec Sci Rep Fish ... US Fish and Wildlife Service. Special Scientific Report. Fisheries [*A publication*]
US Fish Wildl Serv Spec Sci Rep Wildl ... US Fish and Wildlife Service. Special Scientific Report. Wildlife [*A publication*]
US Fish Wildl Serv Tech Pap ... US Fish and Wildlife Service. Technical Papers [*A publication*]
US Fish Wildl Serv Wildl Res Rep ... US Fish and Wildlife Service. Wildlife Research Report [*A publication*]
US Fish Wild Serv Fish Bull ... US Fish and Wildlife Service. Fishery Bulletin [*A publication*]
USFJ .... United States Forces, Japan (CINC)
USFK .... United States Forces, Korea
USFL .... United States Football League
USFLQ .... USF Language Quarterly [*A publication*]
USFLR .... University of San Francisco. Law Review [*A publication*]
USF L Rev ... University of San Francisco. Law Review [*A publication*]
USFMG ...... United States Fastener Manufacturing Group (EA)
USFMIA ...... United States Fishmeal Importers Association [*Defunct*] (EA)
USFOA .... United States Forces, Occupation Austria [*World War II*]
USFOA .... Uspekhi Fotoniki [*A publication*]
US Food Drug Adm DHEW Publ ... United States Food and Drug Administration. DHEW [*Department of Health, Education, and Welfare*] Publication [*A publication*]
USFOR .... United States Forces
USFORAZ ... United States Forces in Azores
US Forest Serv Agr Hdb ... United States Forest Service. Agriculture Handbooks [*A publication*]
US Forest Serv Res Note ... US Forest Service. Research Notes [*A publication*]
US Forest Serv Res Paper ... US Forest Service. Research Papers [*A publication*]
US For Prod Lab Res Note FPL ... United States Forest Products Laboratory. Research Note FPL [*A publication*]

US For Prod Lab Tech Notes ... United States Forest Products Laboratory. Technical Notes [*A publication*]

US For Serv AIB ... US Forest Service. AIB [*A publication*]

US For Serv Div State Priv For North Reg Rep ... US Forest Service. Division of State and Private Forestry. Northern Region Report [*A publication*]

US For Serv For Pest Leafl ... US Forest Service. Forest Pest Leaflet [*A publication*]

US For Serv For Prod Lab Annu Rep ... US Forest Service. Forest Products Laboratory. Annual Report [*A publication*]

US For Serv For Prod Lab Gen Tech Rep FPL ... United States Forest Service. Forest Products Laboratory. General Technical Report FPL [*A publication*]

US For Serv For Resour Rep ... United States Forest Service. Forest Resource Report [*A publication*]

US For Serv For Res What's New West ... US Forest Service. Forestry Research. What's New in the West [*A publication*]

US For Serv Gen Tech Rep INT ... US Forest Service. General Technical Report. INT [*A publication*]

US For Serv Gen Tech Rep NC ... US Forest Service. General Technical Report. NC [*A publication*]

US For Serv Gen Tech Rep NE ... US Forest Service. General Technical Report. NE [*A publication*]

US For Serv Gen Tech Rep PNW ... US Forest Service. General Technical Report. PNW [*A publication*]

US For Serv Gen Tech Rep PSW ... US Forest Service. General Technical Report. PSW [*A publication*]

US For Serv Gen Tech Rep RM ... US Forest Service. General Technical Report. RM [*A publication*]

US For Serv Gen Tech Rep SE ... US Forest Service. General Technical Report. SE [*A publication*]

US For Serv Gen Tech Rep SO ... US Forest Service. General Technical Report. SO [*A publication*]

US For Serv Northeast For Exp Stn Ann Rep ... United States Forest Service. Northeastern Forest Experiment Station. Annual Report [*A publication*]

US For Serv Northeast For Exp Stn Annu Rep ... US Forest Service. Northeastern Forest Experiment Station. Annual Report [*A publication*]

US For Serv Northeast For Exp Stn Stn Pap ... United States Forest Service. Northeastern Forest Experiment Station. Station Paper [*A publication*]

US For Serv North Reg For Environ Prot ... US Forest Service. Northern Region. Forest Environmental Protection [*A publication*]

US For Serv Pac Northwest For Range Experiment Stn Res Notes ... United States Forest Service. Pacific Northwest Forest and Range Experiment Station. Research Notes [*A publication*]

US For Serv Pac Northwest For Range Exp Stn Ann Rep ... United States Forest Service. Pacific Northwest Forest and Range Experiment Station. Annual Report [*A publication*]

US For Serv Pac Northwest For Range Exp Stn Annu Rep ... US Forest Service. Pacific Northwest Forest and Range Experiment Station. Annual Report [*A publication*]

US For Serv Pac Northwest For Range Exp Stn Res Pap ... United States Forest Service. Pacific Northwest Forest and Range Experiment Station. Research Paper [*A publication*]

US For Serv Pac Northwest For Range Exp Stn Res Prog ... US Forest Service. Pacific Northwest Forest and Range Experiment Station. Research Progress [*A publication*]

US For Serv Pac Southwest For Range Exp Stn Misc Pap ... United States Forest Service. Pacific Southwest Forest and Range Experiment Station. Miscellaneous Paper [*A publication*]

US For Serv Res Note FPL ... US Forest Service. Research Note. FPL [*A publication*]

US For Serv Res Note Inst Trop For ... United States Forest Service. Research Note. Institute of Tropical Forestry [*A publication*]

US For Serv Res Note INT ... US Forest Service. Research Note. INT [*A publication*]

US For Serv Res Note Intermt For Range Exp Sta ... United States Forest Service. Research Note. Intermountain Forest and Range Experiment Station [*A publication*]

US For Serv Res Note ITF ... US Forest Service. Research Note. ITF [*A publication*]

US For Serv Res Note NC ... US Forest Service. Research Note. NC [*A publication*]

US For Serv Res Note NE ... US Forest Service. Research Note. NE [*A publication*]

US For Serv Res Note Nth Cent For Exp Sta ... United States Forest Service. Research Note. North Central Forest Experiment Station [*A publication*]

US For Serv Res Note Ntheast For Exp Sta ... United States Forest Service. Research Note. Northeastern Forest Experiment Station [*A publication*]

US For Serv Res Note Nth For Exp Sta ... United States Forest Service. Research Note. Northern Forest Experiment Station [*A publication*]

US For Serv Res Note Pacif Nthwest For Range Exp Sta ... United States Forest Service. Research Note. Pacific Northwest Forest and Range Experiment Station [*A publication*]

US For Serv Res Note Pacif Sthwest For Range Exp Sta ... US Forest Service. Research Note. Pacific Southwest Forest and Range Experiment Station [*A publication*]

US For Serv Res Note PNW ... US Forest Service. Research Note. PNW [*A publication*]

US For Serv Res Note PSW ... US Forest Service. Research Note. PSW [*A publication*]

US For Serv Res Note RM ... US Forest Service. Research Note. RM [*A publication*]

US For Serv Res Note Rocky Mt For Range Exp Sta ... US Forest Service. Research Note. Rocky Mountain Forest and Range Experiment Station [*A publication*]

US For Serv Res Note SE ... US Forest Service. Research Note. SE [*A publication*]

US For Serv Res Note SO ... US Forest Service. Research Note. SO [*A publication*]

US For Serv Res Note Stheast For Exp Sta ... US Forest Service. Research Note. Southeastern Forest Experiment Station [*A publication*]

US For Serv Res Note Sth For Exp Sta ... United States Forest Service. Research Note. Southern Forest Experiment Station [*A publication*]

US For Serv Res Note US For Prod Lab (Madison) ... US Forest Service. Research Note. US Forest Products Laboratory (Madison, Wisconsin) [*A publication*]

US For Serv Resour Bull INT ... US Forest Service. Resource Bulletin. INT [*A publication*]

US For Serv Resour Bull NC ... US Forest Service. Resource Bulletin. NC [*A publication*]

US For Serv Resour Bull NE ... US Forest Service. Resource Bulletin. NE [*A publication*]

US For Serv Resour Bull PNW ... US Forest Service. Resource Bulletin. PNW [*A publication*]

US For Serv Resour Bull PSW ... US Forest Service. Resource Bulletin. PSW [*A publication*]

US For Serv Resour Bull SE ... US Forest Service. Resource Bulletin. SE [*A publication*]

US For Serv Resour Bull SO ... US Forest Service. Resource Bulletin. SO [*A publication*]

US For Serv Resource Bull Intermt For Range Exp Sta ... United States Forest Service. Resource Bulletin. Intermountain Forest and Range Experiment Station [*A publication*]

US For Serv Resource Bull Nth Cent For Exp Sta ... US Forest Service. Resource Bulletin. North Central Forest Experiment Station [*A publication*]

US For Serv Resource Bull Ntheast For Exp Sta ... US Forest Service. Resource Bulletin. Northeastern Forest Experiment Station [*A publication*]

US For Serv Resource Bull Nth For Exp Sta ... US Forest Service. Resource Bulletin. Northern Forest Experiment Station [*A publication*]

US For Serv Resource Bull Pacif Nthwest For Range Exp Sta ... United States Forest Service. Pacific Northwest Forest and Range Experiment Station. Resource Bulletin [*A publication*]

US For Serv Resource Bull Pacif Sthwest For Range Exp Sta ... US Forest Service. Resource Bulletin. Pacific Southwest Forest and Range Experiment Station [*A publication*]

US For Serv Resource Bull Stheast For Exp Sta ... US Forest Service. Resource Bulletin. Southeastern Forest Experiment Station [*A publication*]

US For Serv Resource Bull Sth For Exp Sta ... US Forest Service. Resource Bulletin. Southern Forest Experiment Station [*A publication*]

US For Serv Res Pap FPL ... US Forest Service. Research Paper. FPL [*A publication*]

US For Serv Res Pap Inst Trop For ... US Forest Service. Research Paper. Institute of Tropical Forestry [*A publication*]

US For Serv Res Pap INT ... US Forest Service. Research Paper. INT [*A publication*]

US For Serv Res Pap Intermt For Range Exp Sta ... US Forest Service. Research Paper. Intermountain Forest and Range Experiment Station [*A publication*]

US For Serv Res Pap ITF ... US Forest Service. Research Paper. ITF [*A publication*]

US For Serv Res Pap NC ... US Forest Service. Research Paper. NC [*A publication*]

US For Serv Res Pap NE ... US Forest Service. Research Paper. NE [*A publication*]

US For Serv Res Pap Nth Cent For Exp Sta ... US Forest Service. Research Paper. North Central Forest Experiment Station [*A publication*]

US For Serv Res Pap Ntheast For Exp Sta ... US Forest Service. Research Paper. Northeastern Forest Experiment Station [*A publication*]

US For Serv Res Pap Nth For Exp Sta ... United States Forest Service. Research Paper. Northern Forest Experiment Station [*A publication*]

US For Serv Res Pap Pacif Nthwest For Range Exp Sta ... US Forest Service. Research Paper. Pacific Northwest Forest and Range Experiment Station [*A publication*]

US For Serv Res Pap Pacif Sthwest For Range Exp Sta ... US Forest Service. Research Paper. Pacific Southwest Forest and Range Experiment Station [*A publication*]

US For Serv Res Pap PNW ... US Forest Service. Research Paper. PNW [*A publication*]

US For Serv Res Pap PSW ... US Forest Service. Research Paper. PSW [*A publication*]

US For Serv Res Pap RM ... US Forest Service. Research Paper. RM [*A publication*]

US For Serv Res Pap Rocky Mt For Range Exp Sta ... United States Forest Service. Research Paper. Rocky Mountain Forest and Range Experiment Station [*A publication*]

US For Serv Res Pap SE ... US Forest Service. Research Paper. SE [*A publication*]

US For Serv Res Pap SO ... US Forest Service. Research Paper. SO [*A publication*]

US For Serv Res Pap Stheast For Exp Sta ... US Forest Service. Research Paper. Southeastern Forest Experiment Station [*A publication*]

US For Serv Res Pap Sth For Exp Sta ... US Forest Service. Research Paper. Southern Forest Experiment Station [*A publication*]

US For Serv Res Pap US For Prod Lab (Madison) ... United States Forest Service. Research Paper. United States Forest Products Laboratory (Madison, Wisconsin) [*A publication*]

US For Serv Res Pap WO ... US Forest Service. Research Paper. WO [*A publication*]

US For Serv Rocky Mount For Range Exp Stn For Sur Release ... United States Forest Service. Rocky Mountain Forest and Range Experiment Station. Forest Survey Release [*A publication*]

US For Serv Rocky Mount For Range Exp Stn Res Notes ... United States Forest Service. Rocky Mountain Forest and Range Experiment Station. Research Notes [*A publication*]

US For Serv Southeast For Exp Stn Stn Pap ... United States Forest Service. Southeastern Forest Experiment Station. Station Paper [*A publication*]

US For Serv South For Exp Stn Annu Rep ... US Forest Service. Southern Forest Experiment Station. Annual Report [*A publication*]

US For Serv South For Exp Stn For Surv Release ... United States Forest Service. Southern Forest Experiment Station. Forest Survey Release [*A publication*]

US For Serv Tech Bull ... US Forest Service. Technical Bulletin [*A publication*]

US For Serv Tree Plant Notes ... US Forest Service. Tree Planters' Notes [*A publication*]

USFP .... Union Socialiste des Forces Populaires [*Socialist Union of Popular Forces*] [*Rabbat, Morocco*]   (PPW)

USFP .... United States Federation of Pelota   (EA)

USFP .... United States Forces, Police

USFR .... United States Fleet Reserve

USFS .... United States Foreign Service [*Department of State*]

USFS .... United States Forest Service

USFS .... United States Frequency Standard

USFSA .... United States Figure Skating Association   (EA)

USFSS .... United States Fleet SONAR School

USFTA .... United States Floor Tennis Association [*Defunct*]   (EA)

USFU .... Unglazed Structural Facing Units [*Technical drawings*]

USFV .... United States Forces, Vietnam

USFVL Rev ... University of San Fernando Valley. Law Review   (DLA)

USFWS .... United States Fish and Wildlife Service [*Department of the Interior*]

USFWSWRR ... United States. Fish and Wildlife Service. Wildlife Research Report [*A publication*]

USG .... Ultrasonic Space Grating

USG .... Ultrasonography

USG .... Underwater Systems Group [*Range Commanders Council*] [*NASA*]

USG .... Union of Superiors General   (EA)

USG .... United States Gauge

USG .... United States Government

USG .... US Gypsum Co. [*NYSE symbol*] [*Wall Street slang name: "Gyp"*]

USG .... USG Corp. [*NYSE symbol*]

USGA .... Ulysses S. Grant Association

USGA .... United States Golf Association   (EA)

USGA .... US Green Alliance

USGC .... US Geodynamics Committee [*National Academy of Sciences*]   (EA)

USGCC/A ... United States Group Control Council/Austria [*World War II*]

USGCC/G ... United States Group Control Council/Germany [*World War II*]

USGCLR .... United States-German Committee on Learning and Remembrance   (EA)

USGCM ...... United States Government Correspondence Manual

US Geog G S Rocky Mtn Reg (Powell) ... United States Geographical and Geological Survey of the Rocky Mountain Region (Powell) [*A publication*]

US Geol S Bul ... United States Geological Survey. Bulletin [*A publication*]

US Geol S Professional Pa ... United States Geological Survey. Professional Paper [*A publication*]

US Geol Surv Annu Rep ... United States Geological Survey. Annual Report [*A publication*]

US Geol Surv Bull ... United States Geological Survey. Bulletin [*A publication*]

US Geol Surv Circ ... United States Geological Survey. Circular [*A publication*]

US Geol Surv Coal Invest Map ... US Geological Survey. Coal Investigations Map [*A publication*]

US Geol Survey Bull ... United States Geological Survey. Bulletin [*A publication*]

US Geol Survey Circ ... US Geological Survey. Circular [*A publication*]

US Geol Survey Coal Inv Map ... US Geological Survey. Coal Investigations Map [*A publication*]

US Geol Survey Geol Quad Map ... United States Geological Survey. Geological Quadrangle Map [*A publication*]

US Geol Survey Geol Quadrangle Map ... US Geological Survey. Geologic Quadrangle Map [*A publication*]

US Geol Survey Geophys Inv Map ... US Geological Survey. Geophysical Investigations Map [*A publication*]

US Geol Survey Hydrol Inv Atlas ... US Geological Survey. Hydrologic Investigations Atlas [*A publication*]

US Geol Survey Index Geol Mapping US ... US Geological Survey. Index to Geologic Mapping in the United States [*A publication*]

US Geol Survey Mineral Inv Field Studies Map ... US Geological Survey. Mineral Investigations Field Studies Map [*A publication*]

US Geol Survey Mineral Inv Res Map ... US Geological Survey. Mineral Investigations Resource Map [*A publication*]

US Geol Survey Misc Geol Inv Map ... United States Geological Survey. Miscellaneous Geologic Investigations Map [*A publication*]

US Geol Survey Oil and Gas Inv Chart ... US Geological Survey. Oil and Gas Investigations Chart [*A publication*]

US Geol Survey Oil and Gas Inv Map ... United States Geological Survey. Oil and Gas Investigations Map [*A publication*]

US Geol Survey Prof Paper ... US Geological Survey. Professional Paper [*A publication*]

US Geol Survey Water-Supply Paper ... United States Geological Survey. Water-Supply Paper [*A publication*]

US Geol Surv Geol Quadrangle Map ... US Geological Survey. Geologic Quadrangle Map [*A publication*]

US Geol Surv Geophys Invest Map ... United States Geological Survey. Geophysical Investigations Map [*A publication*]

US Geol Surv Hydrol Invest Atlas ... US Geological Survey. Hydrologic Investigations Atlas [*A publication*]

US Geol Surv Miner Invest Field Stud Map ... United States Department of the Interior. Geological Survey. Mineral Investigations Field Studies Map [*A publication*]

US Geol Surv Misc Field Stud Map ... US Geological Survey. Miscellaneous Field Studies Map [*A publication*]

US Geol Surv Misc Geol Invest Map ... United States Geological Survey. Miscellaneous Geologic Investigations Map [*A publication*]

US Geol Surv Oil Gas Invest Chart ... US Geological Survey. Oil and Gas Investigations Chart [*A publication*]

US Geol Surv Oil Gas Invest Map ... US Geological Survey. Oil and Gas Investigations Map [*A publication*]

US Geol Surv Open-File Rep ... US Geological Survey. Open-File Report [*A publication*]

US Geol Surv Prof Pap ... United States Geological Survey. Professional Paper [*A publication*]

US Geol Surv Trace Elem Memo Rep ... United States Geological Survey. Trace Elements Memorandum Report [*A publication*]

US Geol Surv Water-Resour Invest ... US Geological Survey. Water-Resources Investigations [*A publication*]

US Geol Surv Water-Supply Pap ... US Geological Survey. Water-Supply Paper [*A publication*]

USGF .... United States Gymnastics Federation   (EA)

US G Geog S Terr (Hayden) ... United States Geological and Geographies Survey of the Territories (Hayden) [*A publication*]

USGLI .... United States Government Life Insurance

USGM .... United States Government Manual [*A publication*]   (OICC)

US Gov Res Dev Rep ... US Government Research and Development Reports [*A publication*]

US Gov Res Rep ... US Government Research Reports [*A publication*]

US Govt Paper Spec Std ... US Government Paper. Specification Standards [*A publication*]

USGPM .... United States Government Purchasing Mission [*World War II*]

USGPO .... United States Government Printing Office

USGR .... United States Government Report   (IEEE)

USGRA ...... United States Government Report Announcements   (EISS)

USGRDR ... United States Government Research and Development Reports [*Later, GRA*]

USGRDR-I ... United States Government Research and Development Reports Index [*Later, GRI*]

USGRR .... United States Government Research Reports [*National Bureau of Standards publication*]

USGS .... United States Geological Survey [*Reston, VA*] [*Databank originator*]

USGSA .... United States Grass Ski Association   (EA)

USGSA .... United States Gymnastic Safety Association

USGS An Rp PPB W-S P Mon Min Res G Atlas Top Atlas ... United States Geological Survey. Annual Report. Professional Paper. Bulletin. Water-Supply Paper Monograph. Mineral Resources Geology Atlas [*A publication*]

USGSB...... United States Geological Survey. Bulletin [*A publication*]

USGSC...... United States Geological Survey. Circular [*A publication*]

USGSPP.... United States Geological Survey. Professional Paper [*A publication*]

USGS Terr ... United States Geological Survey of the Territories [*A publication*]

USGW .... Under-Surface Guided Weapon   (MCD)

US Gym Fed Gym News ... United States Gymnastic Federation. Gymnastic News [*A publication*]

U SH........... Shilling [*Monetary unit in Uganda*]

USH............ Ushuaia [*Argentina*] [*Airport symbol*]   (OAG)

USH............ USLIFE Corp. [*NYSE symbol*]

USHA .... United States Handball Association   (EA)

USHA .... United States Housing Authority [*Functions transferred to Public Housing Commissioner, 1947*]

USHB .... Uniformed Services Health Benefits

USHBP .... Uniformed Services Health Benefits Program

USHC .... United States Housing Corporation [*Terminated, 1952*]

USHC .... US Health Care Systems [*NASDAQ symbol*]   (NQ)

USHCA ...... US Horse Cavalry Association   (EA)

USHCC ...... US Hispanic Chamber of Commerce   (EA)

USHDA....... United States Highland Dancing Association   (EA)

USHDI .... United States Historical Documents Institute

USHE.......... Upstream Heat Exchanger   (AAG)

USHG .... United States Home Guard

USHGA...... United States Hang Gliding Association   (EA)

USHGA...... United States Hop Growers Association

USHI .... US Health, Incorporated [*NASDAQ symbol*]   (NQ)

USHIGEO ... United States National Committee for the History of Geology   (EA)

USHL.......... United States Hockey League

USHL.......... United States Hydrograph Laboratory

USHL.......... United States Hygienic Laboratory

USHMAC... United States Health Manpower Advisory Council

USHMC ..... US Holocaust Memorial Council   (EA)

USHO .... United States Hydrographic Office [*Later, Naval Oceanographic Office*]

USHP......... United States Helium Plant [*Amarillo, TX*]

USHSLA..... US Hide, Skin, and Leather Association [*Formed by a merger of AAHSLM and National Hide Association*] [*Washington, DC*]   (EA)

USHTA .... United States Handicap Tennis Association   (EA)

USHWA ...... United States Harness Writers' Association

USHWC...... US Helsinki Watch Committee   (EA)

US Hydrog Office Pub ... US Hydrographic Office. Publication [*A publication*]

USI .... Mabaruma [*Guyana*] [*Airport symbol*]   (OAG)

USI .... Ultraviolet Spectroheliographic Instrument

USI .... United Schools International   (EA-IO)

USI .... United Sons of Israel   (EA)

USI .... United States Information Agency, Washington, DC [*OCLC symbol*]   (OCLC)

USI .... United States Investor [*A publication*]

USI .... Universal Software Interface [*MRI Systems Corp.*]

USI .... Unlawful Sexual Intercourse

USI .... Unresolved Safety Issues [*Nuclear energy*]   (NRCH)

USI .... Update Software Identity   (MCD)

USI .... User Software Integration Subsystem [*Space Flight Operations Facility, NASA*]

USI .... User/System Interface

USIA.......... United States Information Agency [*Formerly called BECA, it later became known as ICA or USICA, then again as USIA*]

USIAC .... United States Inter-American Council [*Later, COA*]   (EA)

USIAEA...... United States Mission to the International Atomic Energy Agency

USIB.......... United States Intelligence Board [*Later, NFIB*] [*National Security Council*]

US-IBP Anal Ecosyst Program Interbiome Abstr ... US-IBP [*International Biological Program*] Analyses of Ecosystems Program. Interbiome Abstracts [*A publication*]

US-IBP Ecosyst Anal Stud Abstr ... US-IBP [*International Biological Program*] Ecosystem Analysis Studies Abstracts [*A publication*]

US-IBP Synth Ser ... US-IBP [*International Biological Program*] Synthesis Series [*A publication*]

USIC.......... Undersea Instrument Chamber [*Marine science*]   (MSC)

USIC.......... United States Industrial Council   (EA)

USIC.......... United States Information Center [*Department of State*]   (MCD)

USICA .... United States International Communication Agency [*Also, ICA*] [*Formerly called BECA and USIA, it later became known again as USIA*]

USICC .... United States Industrial Chemical Company   (KSC)

USICC Rep ... United States Interstate Commerce Commission Reports   (DLA)

USICCVR ... United States Interstate Commerce Commission Valuation Reports   (DLA)

USICID .... United States National Committee, International Commission on Irrigation and Drainage

US/ICID ..... US Committee on Irrigation and Drainage [*Formerly, USCIDFC*]   (EA)

US/ICOMOS ... United States National Committee for the International Council of Monuments and Sites   (EA)

USIDF........ United States Icelandic Defense Forces   (MCD)

USIFA........ US International Fireball Association   (EA)

USIHR .... United States Institute of Human Rights   (EA)

USIITA........ United States Indian International Travel Agency, Inc.

USILA........ United States Intercollegiate Lacrosse Association

USIMCA..... United States International Moth Class Association   (EA)

Usine Nouv ... Usine Nouvelle [*A publication*]

Usine Nouv Ed Suppl ... Usine Nouvelle. Edition Supplementaire [*France*] [*A publication*]

Usine Nouv Suppl ... Usine Nouvelle. Edition Supplementaire [*A publication*]

USINOA...... United States Immigration and Naturalization Officers' Association   (EA)

US Inst Text Res Bull ... United States Institute for Textile Research. Bulletin [*A publication*]

USINT........ United States Interests Section [*Foreign Service*]

US Interdep Comm Atmos Sci Rep ... US Interdepartmental Committee for Atmospheric Sciences. Report [*A publication*]

USIO.......... United States Industrial Outlook [*A publication*]

USIO.......... Unlimited Sequential Input/Output

USIP.......... United Solomon Islands Party   (PPW)

USIP .... University of Stockholm Institute of Physics

USIPC .... Uniformed Services Identification and Privilege Card   (AFM)

USIPU........ United States Inter-Parliamentary Union   (EA)

USIRB........ United States Internal Revenue Bonded

USIS.......... Ultraviolet Stratospheric Imaging Spectrometer   (MCD)

USIS.......... United States Information Service [*Name used abroad for USIA offices*]

USISA .... United States International Sailing Association

USISA .... United States International Skating Association

USISCA...... US Islands 17 Class Association [*Defunct*]   (EA)

USISL........ United States Information Service Library   (DIT)

USISSA...... US International Speed Skating Association   (EA)

USIT .... Unit Share Investment Trust

USIT .... United States. International Trade Commission [*A publication*]

USITA........ United States Independent Telephone Association [*Washington, DC*]   (EA)

USITA........ United States International Tempest Association   (EA)

USITC........ United States International Trade Commission

USITT........ United States Institute for Theatre Technology

USIU.......... United States International University [*San Diego, CA*]

USJ............ United States Jaycees [*Tulsa, OK*]   (EA)

USJ............ United States Judo   (EA)

USJAC .... US-Japan Culture Center   (EA)

US JAYCEE ... United States Junior Chamber of Commerce [*Later, United States Jaycees*]   (EA)

USJB .... Union Saint-Jean-Baptiste   (EA)

USJCA .... United States Joint Communication Agency   (NATG)

USJCC .... United States Junior Chamber of Commerce [*Later, United States Jaycees*]   (EA)

USJCIRPTE ... United States - Japan Committee on Industry Related Policies and Their Trade Effects [*Acronym pronounced "use-jay-krip-tee"*]

USJCS .... United States Joint Chiefs of Staff   (NATG)

USJF .... United States Judo Federation

USJF .... US Justice Foundation   (EA)

USJNRP .... United States/Japan Natural Resources Panel

US Joint Publ Res Serv Transl E Eur Agr Forest Food Ind ... United States. Joint Publication Research Service. Translations on East European Agriculture, Forestry, and Food Industries [*A publication*]

USJPRS ..... United States Joint Publications Research Service

US-JTC ..... United States - Japan Trade Council   (EA)

USJTF .... United States Joint Task Force   (AABC)

US Jur .... United States Jurist   (DLA)

USJUWTF ... United States Joint Unconventional Warfare Task Force   (AABC)

USK........... Ultrasonic Kit

USK........... United States Forces, Korea

USKA .... United States Kart Association [*Defunct*]   (EA)

USKBA...... United Strictly Kosher Butchers Association

USKBTC ... United States Kerry Blue Terrier Club   (EA)

USKEC .... US-Korea Economic Council [*Formerly, KACIA*]   (EA)

USKF......... United States Korfball Federation [*Portland, OR*]   (EA)

USKHA....... Uspekhi Khimii [*A publication*]

Uskor Mosk Inzh-Fiz Inst Sb Statei ... Uskoriteli. Moskovskii Inzherno-Fizicheskii Institut. Sbornik Statei [*USSR*] [*A publication*]

USl .... Salt Lake City Public Library, Salt Lake City, UT [*Library symbol*] [*Library of Congress*]   (LCLS)

USL .... Underwater Sound Laboratory [*New London, CT*] [*Navy*]

USL .... Unemployed Supernumerary List [*Military*] [*British*]

USL .... Unique Suppliers List

USL .... United Satellites Limited [*London, England*] [*Telecommunications*]   (TSSD)

USL .... United Soccer League (EA)
USL .... United States Legation
USL .... Up Stage Left [Away from audience] [A stage direction]
USL .... US Leasing International, Inc. [NYSE symbol]
USL .... Useless Loop [Australia] [Airport symbol] (OAG)
USL .... Usual (ROG)
USLA .... United States Committee for Justice to Latin American Political Prisoners [Defunct] (EA)
USLA .... United States Lifesaving Association [Formerly, NSLSA] (EA)
USLA .... United States Luge Association (EA)
US Land Off ... United States General Land Office [A publication]
USLANT ..... United States Atlantic Subarea [NATO]
US Law Ed ... United States Supreme Court Reports, Lawyers' Edition (DLA)
US Law Int ... United States Law Intelligencer and Review [Providence and Philadelphia] (DLA)
US Law Jour ... United States Law Journal (DLA)
US Law Mag ... United States Law Magazine (DLA)
US Law R ... United States Law Review [A publication]
USIC .... Church of Jesus Christ of Latter-Day Saints, Historian's Office, Salt Lake City, UT [Library symbol] [Library of Congress] (LCLS)
USLC .... United States Locals Collectors (EA)
USLCA .... United States Lacrosse Coaches' Association
USLCMBA ... United States Letter Carriers Mutual Benefit Association (EA)
USID .... Daughters of Utah Pioneers Museum Library, Salt Lake City, UT [Library symbol] [Library of Congress] (LCLS)
USLD .... Ultrasonic Link Detector
USLD .... Union des Syndicats Libres du Dahomey [Federation of Free Unions of Dahomey]
USLDMA .... United States Lanolin and Derivative Manufacturers Association [Newark, NJ] (EA)
USLE .... Universal Soil Loss Equation [Agricultural engineering]
USL Ed .... Lawyers' Edition, United States Supreme Court Reports (DLA)
USL Ed 2d ... Lawyers' Edition, United States Supreme Court Reports, Second Series (DLA)
USIGS .... Church of Jesus Christ of Latter-Day Saints, Genealogical Society Library, Salt Lake City, UT [Library symbol] [Library of Congress] (LCLS)
USL & H...... United States Longshoremen and Harborworkers Act
US Lit Gaz ... United States Literary Gazette [A publication]
USLJ .... United States Law Journal [New Haven and New York] (DLA)
USIL .... Latter-Day Saints Museum, Salt Lake City, UT [Library symbol] [Library of Congress] (LCLS)
USLL .... Utah Studies in Literature and Linguistics [A publication]
USL Mag .... United States Law Magazine (DLA)
USLO.......... United States Liaison Office [or Officer]
USLO.......... University Students for Law and Order
USIOr .... Oregon Short Line Law Department, Salt Lake City, UT [Library symbol] [Library of Congress] [Obsolete] (LCLS)
USLO SACA ... United States Liaison Officer to Supreme Allied Commander, Atlantic (MUGU)
USIP .... Pioneer Memorial Museum, Salt Lake City, UT [Library symbol] [Library of Congress] (LCLS)
USLP .... United States Labor Party
USL Rev ..... United States Law Review [A publication]
USLS.......... United States Lake Survey [Marine science] (MSC)
USLS.......... United States Lighthouse Society (EA)
USLSA .... United States League of Savings Associations [Later, USLSI]
USLSA .... United States Livestock Sanitary Association [Later, United States Animal Health Association] (EA)
USLSI........ United States League of Savings Institutions [Chicago, IL] (EA)
USLSO ...... United States Logistics Support Office (AFM)
USIStM....... College of Saint Mary-of-the-Wasatch, Salt Lake City, UT [Library symbol] [Library of Congress] [Obsolete] (LCLS)
USIT .... Utah Technical College at Salt Lake, Salt Lake City, UT [Library symbol] [Library of Congress] (LCLS)
USLTA ...... United States Lawn Tennis Association [Later, USTA] (EA)
USLTC ...... United States Lakeland Terrier Club (EA)
USLW .... United States Law Week [Bureau of National Affairs] (DLA)
USIW .... Westminster College, Salt Lake City, UT [Library symbol] [Library of Congress] (LCLS)
USM .... Underwater-to-Surface Missile [Air Force]
USM .... Uniform Staffing Methodologies [DoD]
USM .... Union des Syndicats de Monaco [Union of Monaco Trade Unions]
USM .... United Service Magazine [A publication]
USM .... United States Mail
USM .... United States Marine
USM .... United States Mint
USM .... United States Minutemen [Defunct] (EA)
USM .... United States Representative to the Military Committee Memorandum [NATO] (NATG)
USM .... Unlisted Securities Market [London Stock Exchange]
USM .... Unsaponifiable Matter [Organic analytical chemistry]
USM .... Unscheduled Maintenance
UsM .... US Microfilm Corp., Jacksonville, FL [Library symbol] [Library of Congress] (LCLS)
USMA........ Union Special Corp. [NASDAQ symbol] (NQ)
USMA........ United States Maritime Administration
USMA........ United States Metric Association

USMA........ United States Military Academy
USMA........ United States Military Attache
USMA........ United States Monopoly Association [For legal reasons, only the initialism is used by the group; it is never officially spelled out] (EA)
USMAC ...... United States Marine Air Corps
USMAC ...... United States Military Assistance Command
USMACSV ... United States Military Assistance Command, South Vietnam [Obsolete]
USMACTHAI ... United States Military Assistance Command, Thailand [Obsolete] (AFM)
USMACV.... United States Military Assistance Command, Vietnam [Obsolete]
USMAG ...... United States Military Advisory Group
USMAPS .... United States Military Academy Preparatory School
USMAPU.... United States Military Academy Preparatory Unit
USMARC.... Advisory Committee for the US Meat Animal Research Center [Terminated, 1977] (EGAO)
USMATS .... United States Military Air Transport Service [Later, Military Airlift Command]
USMB........ United States Marine Barracks
USMBHA... US-Mexico Border Health Association [El Paso, TX] (EA)
USMBP...... US-Mexico Border Program (EA)
USMC........ United States Marine Corps
USMC........ United States Maritime Commission [Functions transferred to Department of Commerce, 1950]
USMC........ United States Maritime Committee [Defunct] (EA)
USMCA ..... United States Men's Curling Association [Later, USCA] (EA)
USMCA ..... US Mariner Class Association (EA)
USMCAM ... United States Military Community Activity, Mannheim
USMCAS.... United States Marine Corps Air Station
USMCB ...... United States Marine Corps Base (MCD)
USMCC ..... United States Mint - Carson City (ROG)
USMCCCA ... US Marine Corps Combat Correspondents Association [San Diego, CA] (EA)
USMCEB.... United States Military Communications Electronics Board (NVT)
USMCP ..... United States Military Construction Program (CINC)
USMCR ..... United States Marine Corps Reserve
USMCR(AF) ... United States Marine Corps Reserve (Aviation Fleet)
USMCR(AO) ... United States Marine Corps Reserve (Aviation, Organized)
USMCR(AV) ... United States Marine Corps Reserve (Aviation, Volunteer)
USMCR(F) ... United States Marine Corps Reserve (Fleet)
USMCR(LS) ... United States Marine Corps Reserve (Limited Service)
USMCR(NAV) ... United States Marine Corps Reserve (Naval Aviators)
USMCR(NAVO) ... United States Marine Corps Reserve (Graduate Aviation Cadets, Volunteer)
USMCR(NAVT) ... United States Marine Corps Reserve (Aviation Specialist Transport Pilot, Volunteer)
USMCR(O) ... United States Marine Corps Reserve (Organized)
USMCRTC ... United States Marine Corps Reserve Training Center
USMCR(V) ... United States Marine Corps Reserve (Volunteer)
USMCR(VS) ... United States Marine Corps Reserve (Volunteer Specialists)
USMCR(W) ... United States Marine Corps Reserve (Women)
USMCSS.... United States Marine Corps Selective Service Selectee
USMCSSV ... United States Marine Corps Selective Service Volunteer
USMC(W) ... United States Marine Corps (Women)
USMCWR... United States Marine Corps Women's Reserve
USMECBL ... United States Mission to the European Communities in Belgium and Luxembourg
US Med ...... US Medicine [A publication]
USMEF....... United States Meat Export Federation [Denver, CO] (EA)
USMEMILCOMUN ... United States Members, United Nations Military Staff Committee
USMEOUN ... United States Mission to the European Office of the United Nations
USMEPC.... United States Military Enlistment Processing Command
USMES....... Unified Science and Mathematics for Elementary Schools [National Science Foundation]
USMG........ United States Medical Graduate
USMH........ United States Marine Hospital
USMHS...... United States Marine Hospital Service
USMI .... Universal Software Market Identifier [Technique Learning] [Dobbs Ferry, NY] [Information service] (EISS)
USMI .... US Mineral & Royalty [NASDAQ symbol] (NQ)
USMIAEAA ... United States Mission to the International Atomic Energy Agency in Austria
USMICC.... United States Military Information Control Committee (AFM)
USMID....... Ultrasensitive Microwave Infrared Detector
USMILADREP ... United States Military Advisor's Representative (CINC)
USMILADREPSMPO ... United States Military Advisor's Representative, Southeast Asia Treaty Organization, Military Planning Office (CINC)
USMILATTACHE ... United States Military Attache
USMILCOMUN ... United States Delegation, United Nations Military Staff Committee
USMILLIAS ... United States Military Liaison Office
USMILTAG ... United States Military Technical Advisory Group (AFM)
USMITT...... United States Masters International Track Team [Defunct] (EA)
USMKA .... Uspekhi Mikrobiologii [A publication]

USMLMCINCGSFG ... United States Military Liaison Mission to Commander-in-Chief, Group Soviet Forces, Germany (AABC)

USMLS....... United States Museum Librarian Society (EA)

USMM .... Union Socialiste des Musulmans Mauritaniens [*Socialist Union of Mauritanian Moslems*]

USMM .... United States Merchant Marine

USMMA...... United States Merchant Marine Academy

USMMCC.... United States Merchant Marine Cadet Corps

USMMVETS WW2 ... US Merchant Marine Veterans of World War II (EA)

USMNAM .... United States Military North African Mission [*World War II*]

US Month Law Mag ... United States Monthly Law Magazine (DLA)

USMP......... United States Mallard Project [*Army*]

USMPA ...... United States Modern Pentathlon Association (EA)

USMPBA .... United States Modern Pentathlon and Biathlon Association [*Later, USMPA*] (EA)

USMPTC .... United States Modern Pentathlon Training Center (AABC)

USMR .... US Mutual Financial Corp. [*NASDAQ symbol*] (NQ)

USMS......... Unattended Sensor Monitoring System

USMS......... United States Maritime Service

USMS......... United States Marshall Service [*Department of Justice*]

USMS......... United States Mint - San Francisco (ROG)

USMSGS.... United States Maritime Service Graduate Station

USMSMI..... United States Military Supply Mission to India (AFM)

USMSOS.... United States Maritime Service Officers School

USMSR ..... United States Military Specification Requirements (MCD)

USMSSB .... United States Machine Screw Service Bureau [*Defunct*] (EA)

USMSTS .... United States Maritime Service Training School

USMSTS .... United States Maritime Service Training Ship

USMSTS .... United States Maritime Service Training Station

USMT .... United States Military Transport

USMTM ...... United States Military Training Mission (MCD)

USMTMSA ... United States Military Training Mission to Saudi Arabia

USMWR...... United States Mission Weekly Report [*Military*]

USMX........ US Minerals & Explorations [*NASDAQ symbol*] (NQ)

USN........... Ultrasonic Nebulizer

USN........... Under Secretary of the Navy

USN........... Union des Scolaires Nigeriens [*Union of Nigerian Scholars*]

USN........... United States Navy

USNA .... United States National Army

USNA .... United States Naval Academy [*Annapolis, MD*]

USNA .... United States Naval Aircraft

USNAAA .... United States Naval Academy Alumni Association

USNAAA .... United States Naval Academy Athletic Association

USNA ANNA ... United States Naval Academy, Annapolis [*Maryland*]

USNAAS .... United States Naval Auxiliary Air Station

USNAB....... United States Naval Advanced Base [*World War II*]

USNAB....... United States Naval Amphibious Base

USNAC....... United States Naval Administrative Command

USNAC....... United States Naval Air Corps

USNACC .... United States Naval Member of the Allied Control Commission [*Germany*]

USNADC .... United States Naval Air Development Center

USNA-EPRD ... United States Naval Academy Energy-Environment Study Group and Development Team

USNA-EW ... United States Naval Academy Division of Engineering and Weapons

USNAF .... United States Naval Avionics Facility

USNAHALO ... United States NATO Hawk Liaison Office [*Missiles*] (NATG)

USN AMI .... United States Navy Aerospace Medical Institute [*A publication*]

USNAMTC ... United States Naval Air Missile Test Center

USNARS .... United States National Archives and Records Service (DIT)

USNAS....... United States Naval Air Service

USNAS....... United States Naval Air Station

USNASA Conf Publ ... United States National Aeronautics and Space Administration. Conference Publication [*A publication*]

US Nat Bur Stand ... US National Bureau of Standards [*A publication*]

USNATC .... United States Naval Air Training Center

US Natl Aeronaut Space Admin Spec Publ ... US National Aeronautics and Space Administration. Special Publication [*A publication*]

US Natl Bur Stand Handb ... US National Bureau of Standards. Handbook [*A publication*]

US Natl Bur Stand J Res ... United States National Bureau of Standards. Journal of Research [*A publication*]

US Natl Bur Stand J Res Sec A ... US National Bureau of Standards. Journal of Research. Section A [*A publication*]

US Natl Fert Dev Cent Bull Y ... United States National Fertilizer Development Center. Bulletin Y [*A publication*]

US Natl Ind Pollut Control Counc Publ ... US National Industrial Pollution Control Council. Publications [*A publication*]

US Natl Inst Health Publ ... US National Institutes of Health. Publication [*A publication*]

US Natl Lab (Oak Ridge Tenn) Rev ... United States National Laboratory (Oak Ridge, Tennessee). Review [*A publication*]

US Natl Mar Fish Serv Curr Fish Stat ... US National Marine Fisheries Service. Current Fisheries Statistics [*A publication*]

US Natl Mar Fish Serv Fish Bull ... US National Marine Fisheries Service. Fishery Bulletin [*A publication*]

US Natl Mar Fish Serv Fish Facts ... US National Marine Fisheries Service. Fishery Facts [*A publication*]

US Natl Mar Fish Serv Mar Fish Rev ... US National Marine Fisheries Service. Marine Fisheries Review [*A publication*]

US Natl Mar Fish Serv Rep Natl Mar Fish Serv ... US National Marine Fisheries Service. Report of the National Marine Fisheries Service [*A publication*]

US Natl Mar Fish Serv Stat Dig ... US National Marine Fisheries Service. Statistical Digest [*A publication*]

US Natl Mus Bull ... US National Museum. Bulletin [*A publication*]

US Natl Mus Bull Proc ... United States National Museum. Bulletin. Proceedings [*A publication*]

US Natl Oceanic Atmos Adm Environ Data Serv Tech Memo ... United States. National Oceanic and Atmospheric Administration. Environmental Data Service. Technical Memorandum [*A publication*]

US Natl Oceanic Atmos Adm Key Oceanogr Rec Doc ... US National Oceanic and Atmospheric Administration. Key to Oceanographic Records Documentation [*A publication*]

US Natl Oceanog Data Center Pub ... US National Oceanographic Data Center. Publication [*A publication*]

US Natl Park Serv Ecol Serv Bull ... US National Park Service. Ecological Services Bulletin [*A publication*]

US Natl Park Serv Fauna Natl Parks US Fauna Ser ... US National Park Service. Fauna of the National Parks of the United States. Fauna Series [*A publication*]

US Natl Park Service Nat History Handb Ser ... US National Park Service. Natural History Handbook Series [*A publication*]

US Natl Park Serv Natl Cap Reg Sci Rep ... US National Park Service. National Capitol Region Scientific Report [*A publication*]

US Natl Park Serv Occas Pap ... US National Park Service. Occasional Paper [*A publication*]

US Natl Park Serv Sci Monogr Ser ... US National Park Service. Scientific Monograph Series [*A publication*]

US Natl Sci Found Res Appl Natl Needs Rep ... United States National Science Foundation. Research Applied to National Needs. Report [*A publication*]

US Nat Mus Bull ... United States National Museum. Bulletin [*A publication*]

US Nat Mus Rept ... United States National Museum. Reports [*A publication*]

USNATO .... United States Mission to the North Atlantic Treaty Organization (NATG)

USNATRA ... United States Naval Training

US Nav Aerosp Med Inst (Pensacola) Monogr ... US Naval Aerospace Medical Institute (Pensacola). Monograph [*A publication*]

US Nav Aerosp Med Inst (Pensacola) NAMI ... US Naval Aerospace Medical Institute (Pensacola). NAMI [*A publication*]

US Nav Aerosp Med Res Lab (Pensacola) NAMRL ... US Naval Aerospace Medical Research Laboratory (Pensacola). NAMRL [*A publication*]

US Nav Aerosp Med Res Lab (Pensacola) Spec Rep ... US Naval Aerospace Medical Research Laboratory (Pensacola). Special Report [*A publication*]

US Nav Air Dev Cent NADC ... US Naval Air Development Center. NADC [*A publication*]

US Naval Med Bull ... United States Naval Medical Bulletin [*A publication*]

US Naval Ordnance Test Sta NAVORD Report ... United States. Naval Ordnance Test Station. NAVORD Report [*A publication*]

US Naval Res Lab Shock Vib Bull ... United States Naval Research Laboratories. Shock and Vibration Bulletin [*A publication*]

US Naval Submar Med Cent Rep ... US Naval Submarine Medical Center. Report [*A publication*]

US Nav Civ Eng Lab Tech Rep ... United States Department of the Navy. Naval Civil Engineering Laboratory. Port Hueneme, California. Technical Report [*A publication*]

USNAVEUR ... United States Naval Forces Europe (MCD)

US Nav Inst Proc ... US Naval Institute. Proceedings [*A publication*]

US Nav Med Res Lab Rep ... US Naval Medical Research Laboratory. Report [*A publication*]

US Nav Oceanogr Off Spec Publ ... US Naval Oceanographic Office. Special Publication [*A publication*]

US Nav Postgrad Sch Tech Rep/Res Paper ... United States Naval Postgraduate School. Technical Report/Research Paper [*A publication*]

USNAVPRO ... United States Navy Plan Representative Office

US Nav Sch Aviat Med Monogr ... US Naval School of Aviation Medicine. Monograph [*A publication*]

US Nav Sch Aviat Med Res Rep ... US Naval School of Aviation Medicine. Research Report [*A publication*]

US Nav Ship Eng Cent Ship Struct Com Rep ... United States Department of the Navy. Naval Ship Engineering Center. Ship Structure Committee. Report [*A publication*]

US Nav Ship Res Dev Cent Rep ... United States Naval Ship Research and Development Center. Report [*A publication*]

USNAVSO ... United States Navy Forces Southern Command (AFM)

USNAVSOUTHCOM ... United States Navy Southern Command

US Nav Submar Med Cent Memo Rep ... US Naval Submarine Medical Center. Memorandum Report [*A publication*]

US Nav Submar Med Cent Rep ... United States Naval Submarine Medical Center Report [*A publication*]

US Nav Submar Med Res Lab Memo Rep ... United States Naval Submarine Medical Research Laboratory. Memorandum Report [*A publication*]

US Nav Submar Med Res Lab Rep ... US Naval Submarine Medical Research Laboratory. Report [*A publication*]
USNAVSUPACT ... United States Naval Supply Activity   (CINC)
USNAVWEASERV ... United States Naval Weather Service
US Navy Electronics Lab Rept ... United States Navy Electronics Laboratory Report [*A publication*]
US Navy Med ... US Navy Medicine [*A publication*]
USNAVYMILCOMUN ... United States Naval Representative, United Nations Military Staff Committee
USNB .... United States Naval Base   (MUGU)
USNC .... United States National Commission for UNESCO [*of the Department of State*]
USNC .... United States National Committee [*IEC*]
USNCB...... United States National Central Bureau
USNCB....... United States Naval Construction Battalion [*SEABEES*] [*BUDOCKS; later, FEC, NFEC*]
USNC/CIE ... US National Committee of the International Commission on Illumination   (EA)
USNCEREL ... United States Naval Civil Engineering Research and Evaluation Laboratory
USNCFID ... United States National Committee for Federation Internationale de Documentation
USNC/IBP ... United States National Committee for the International Biological Program [*Defunct*]   (EA)
USNCIEC ... United States National Committee of the International Electrotechnical Commission
USNC-IGY ... United States National Committee for the International Geophysical Year
USNCIPS ... US National Committee of the International Peat Society   (EA)
USNCPNM ... United States National Committee for the Preservation of Nubian Monuments [*Defunct*]   (EA)
USNCSCOR ... US National Committee for the Scientific Committee on Oceanic Research   (EA)
USNCSM & FE ... United States National Council on Soil Mechanics and Foundation Engineering
USNC-STR ... United States National Committee for Solar-Terrestrial Research   (MCD)
USNC/TAM ... United States National Committee on Theoretical and Applied Mechanics
USNC/UPSI ... United States National Committee/International Union of Radio Science   (MCD)
USNC-URSI ... United States National Committee for the International Union of Radio Science   (EA)
USNCWEC ... United States National Committee of the World Energy Conference [*Later, Member Committee of the United States, World Energy Conference*]   (EA)
USNDC...... United States Nuclear Data Committee
USNDD....... United States Naval Drydocks
USNEDS .... United States Navy Experimental Diving Station
USNEL ...... United States Naval Electronics Laboratory
USNELM ... United States Naval Forces, Eastern Atlantic and Mediterranean   (MCD)
US News .... United States News and World Report [*A publication*]
US News .... US News and World Report [*A publication*]
US News World Rep ... US News and World Report [*A publication*]
USNFCLC ... US National Federation of Christian Life Communities   (EA)
USNFEC..... US National Fruit Export Council [*Defunct*]   (EA)
USNFPN..... US Nuclear Free Pacific Network   (EA)
USNFR .... United States Naval Fleet Reserve
USNG .... United States National Guard
USNH .... United States Naval Hospital
USNH .... United States, North of Cape Hatteras [*Shipping*]
USNHO...... United States Navy Hydrographic Office [*Later, NOO*]   (NATG)
USNI .... United States Naval Institute [*Annapolis, MD*]
USN-I .... United States Regular Navy - Inductee
USN-I-CB... United States Regular Navy - Inductee - Construction Battalion
USNIP .... United States Naval Institute. Proceedings [*A publication*]
USN(I)(SA) ... United States Navy (Inductee) (Special Assignment)
USNL .... United States Navy League
USNLO....... United States Naval Liaison Officer
USNM .... United States National Museum [*Smithsonian Institution*]
USNMATOEROF ... United States Mission to the North Atlantic Treaty Organization and European Regional Organizations in France
USNMDL ... United States Navy Mine Defense Laboratory   (MUGU)
USNMF....... United States Naval Missile Facility
USNMR ...... United States National Military Representative
USNMSC.... United States Navy Medical Service Corps
USNMTC.... United States Naval Missile Test Center [*Point Mugu, CA*]   (AAG)
USNO .... United Sabah National Organization [*Malaysian*]   (PPW)
USNO .... United States Naval Observatory
USNOA....... United States Norton Owners' Association   (EA)
USNOBSY ... United States Naval Operating Bases System
USNOF....... United States NOTAM Office   (FAAC)
USNOO ...... United States Naval Oceanographic Office [*Marine science*]   (MSC)
US (Noth)... Ueberlieferungsgeschichtliche Studien (M. Noth) [*A publication*]   (BJA)
USNOTS .... United States Naval Ordnance Test Station
USNP......... United States Naval Prison

USNP......... United States Newspaper Program [*National Foundation on the Arts and the Humanities*] [*Washington, DC*] [*Information service*]   (EISS)
USNPG....... United States Naval Proving Ground
USNPGS ... United States Naval Postgraduate School   (MUGU)
USNPS ...... United States Naval Postgraduate School
USNR .... United States Naval Reserve
USNR .... United States Navy Regulations
USNRB ...... United States Naval Repair Base
USNRC ...... United States Nuclear Regulatory Commission   (NRCH)
USNRDL.... United States Naval Radiological Defense Laboratory
USNRDL.... United States Navy Research and Development Laboratory
USN(Ret) ... United States Navy (Retired)
USNRF ...... United States Naval Reserve Force
USNRL ...... United States Naval Research Laboratory
USNRM ...... United States Merchant Marine Reserve
USNRM1 ... United States Merchant Marine Reserve Seagoing
USNRM2 ... United States Merchant Marine Reserve Coastal Defense
USNRO ...... United States Organized Naval Reserve
USNRO1.... United States Organized Naval Reserve Seagoing
USNRO2.... United States Organized Naval Reserve Aviation
USNRS...... United States Navy Recruiting Station
USNR & SL ... United States Navy Radio and Sound Laboratory [*San Diego, CA*]
USNRSV.... United States Naval Reserve, Selective Volunteer
USNRTC ... United States Naval Reserve Training Center
USNRV ...... United States Naval Reserve, Volunteer
USNR(W) ... United States Naval Reserve (Women's Reserve)
USNS .... United States Naval Ship [*Civilian manned*]
USNS .... United States Naval Station
USNS .... Universal Stabilized Night Sight
USNSA ...... United States National Student Association [*Later, USSA*]
USNSC...... United States Naval Safety Code
USNSISSMFE ... US National Society for the International Society of Soil Mechanics and Foundation Engineering   (EA)
USNSMC.... United States Naval Submarine Medical Center
USNSMSES ... United States Navy Ship Missile System Engineering Station
USNSO...... United States Navy Southern Command
USNSPS..... United States National Stockpile Purchase Specification [*for metals*]
USN-SV...... United States Regular Navy Selective Volunteer
USNTC ...... United States Naval Training Center
USNTDC ... United States Naval Training Device Center
USNTI........ United States Navy Travel Instructions
US NTIS AD Rep ... United States National Technical Information Service. AD Report [*A publication*]
USNTPS..... United States Naval Test Pilot School
USNTS ...... United States Naval Training School
USNUSL.... United States Navy Underwater Sound Laboratory [*BUSHIPS; later, ESC, NESC*]
USNWC..... United States Naval War College
USNWR ...... US News and World Report [*A publication*]
USO........... Under Secretary of the Navy's Office
USO........... Unidentified Submarine Object
USO........... Unit Security Officer   (AAG)
USO........... United Service Organizations [*of the Board of Governors*] [*Washington, DC*]   (EA)
USO........... United Siscoe Mines, Inc. [*Toronto Stock Exchange symbol*]
USO........... Universal Service Order [*Bell System*]   (TEL)
USO........... Unmanned Seismological Observatory
USO........... US Office - UTLAS Corp. [*UTLAS symbol*]
USOA .... Uniform System of Accounts [*Telecommunications*]   (TEL)
USOA .... United States Olympic Association [*Later, USOC*]
USOA .... United States Othello Association   (EA)
USOA .... United States Overseas Airlines
US Oak Ridge Natl Lab Radiat Shield Inf Cent Rep ... United States Oak Ridge National Laboratory. Radiation Shielding Information Center. Report [*A publication*]
USOAS...... United States Mission to the Organization of American States
USO-ASPCC ... United Service Organizations - All Service Postal Chess Club   (EA)
USOC .... Uniform Service Order Code [*Bell System*]   (TEL)
USOC .... United States Olympic Committee   (EA)
USOCA ...... United States Office of Consumer Affairs
USOCA ...... US Out of Central America   (EA)
U So Cal Tax Inst ... University of Southern California Tax Institute   (DLA)
U So Carol ... University of South Carolina. Business and Economic Review [*A publication*]
USOCDC ... US Overseas Cooperative Development Committee   (EA)
USO-CLAT ... US Relations Office of CLAT [*Central Latinoamericana de Trabajadores*]   (EA)
USOE .... United States Office of Education [*Later, USDE*]
USOECD .... United States Mission to the Organization for Economic Cooperation and Development
USOF......... United States Orienteering Federation   (EA)
USOFA .... Under Secretary of the Army
USOFAF.... Under Secretary of the Air Force
US Office Ed Bul ... United States Office of Education. Bulletin [*A publication*]
US Office Ed Circ ... United States Office of Education. Circulars [*A publication*]

US Office Ed Pub ... United States Office of Education. Publications [*A publication*]

US Office Ed Voc Div Bul ... United States Office of Education. Vocational Division Bulletin [*A publication*]

US Office Saline Water Research and Devel Progress Rept ... United States. Office of Saline Water Research and Development. Progress Report [*A publication*]

US Off Libr Serv Bibliogr Ser ... US Office of Library Service. Bibliography Series [*A publication*]

US Off Nav Res Rep ACR ... United States Office of Naval Research Report ACR [*A publication*]

US Off Pub Roads B ... US Office of Public Roads. Bulletin [*A publication*]

USOID .... United States Oversea Internal Defense [*Army*]   (AABC)

USOL .... US Oil Co. [*NASDAQ symbol*]   (NQ)

USOLTA ..... Uniform Simplification of Land Transfers Act [*National Conference of Commissioners on Uniform State Laws*]

USOM .... United States Operations Mission

USOMC .... United States Ordnance Missile Command

USONIA ...... United States of North America [*Name of a cooperative community in Pleasantville, NY designed by Frank Lloyd Wright*]

USONR .... United States Office of Naval Research

USOPA .... United States Ordnance Producers Association [*Washington, DC*] [*Inactive*]   (EA)

USOVA .... United States Outdoor Volleyball Association   (EA)

USp .... Springville City Library, Springville, UT [*Library symbol*] [*Library of Congress*]   (LCLS)

USP .... Ultrasensitive Position   (AFM)

USP .... Under the Sign of Pisces [*A publication*]

USP .... Underwater Sound Projection

USP .... Uniform Specification Program   (AAG)

USP .... Unique Selling Point

USP .... Unique Selling Proposition [*Advertising*]

USP .... Unit Stream Power [*Hydrology*]

USP .... Unit Support Plan   (MCD)

USP .... United Socialist Party [*Tongsa Dang*] [*South Korean*]   (PPW)

USP .... United States Patent

USP .... United States Penitentiary

USP .... United States Pharmacopeia [*Following name of a substance, signifies substance meets standards set by USP*]

USP .... United States Pharmacopeial Convention [*Rockville, MD*]   (EA)

USP .... United States Postal Service Library, Washington, DC [*OCLC symbol*]   (OCLC)

USP .... United States Property

USP .... Universal Signal Processor

USP .... Upper Sequential Permissive [*Nuclear energy*]   (NRCH)

USP .... Upper Solution Point

USP .... Urban Studies Project

USP .... US Precious Metals, Inc. [*Vancouver Stock Exchange symbol*]

USP .... Usage Sensitive Pricing [*Telecommunications*]

USP .... Utility Seaplane [*Navy, Coast Guard*]

USP .... Utility Summary Program

USPA .... Uniform Single Publication Act [*National Conference of Commissioners on Uniform State Laws*]

USPA .... Uniformed Services Pay Act

USPA .... United States Parachute Association   (EA)

USPA .... United States Passport Agency [*Department of State*]

USPA .... United States Polo Association   (EA)

USPA .... United States Potters' Association [*East Liverpool, OH*]   (EA)

USPA .... US Patents Alert [*Derwent, Inc.*] [*Database*]

USPA .... US Psychotronics Association   (EA)

US Pacific RR Expl ... US War Department. Pacific Railroad Explorations [*A publication*]

USPAK .... US-Pakistan Economic Council   (EA)

US Pap Maker ... United States Paper Maker [*A publication*]

US Pat Q .... United States Patent Quarterly   (DLA)

US Pat Quar ... United States Patent Quarterly   (DLA)

US Pat Quart ... United States Patent Quarterly   (DLA)

Usp Biol Khim ... Uspekhi Biologicheskoi Khimii [*USSR*] [*A publication*]

USPC .... Union des Syndicats Professionels du Cameroun [*Federation of Professional Trade Unions of Cameroon*]

USPC .... United States Parole Commission [*Formerly, United States Parole Board*]

USPC .... United States Pony Clubs   (EA)

USPC .... United States Procurement Committee

USPC .... United States Purchasing Commission

USPC .... US Peace Council   (EA)

USPC .... US Playing Card Corp. [*NASDAQ symbol*]   (NQ)

USPCA .... United States Police Canine Association   (EA)

USPCF .... US Professional Cycling Federation   (EA)

USPCS .... United States Philatelic Classics Society   (EA)

USPCU .... US Postal Chess Union   (EA)

USPD .... Unabhaengige Sozialdemokratische Partei Deutschlands [*Independent Social Democratic Party of Germany*]   (PPE)

USPD .... US Publicity Director [*A publication*]

USPDCA ..... United States Professional Diving Coaches Association [*Boca Raton, FL*]   (EA)

USPDI .... United States Professional Development Institute [*Silver Spring, MD*]

USPDLTR ... [*Reference*] Your Speedletter [*Military*]

USP & DO ... United States Property and Disbursing Officer

USPDO ...... United States Property and Disbursing Officer

USPEC ...... United States Paper Exporters Council [*New York, NY*]   (EA)

Uspehi Fiz Nauk ... Akademija Nauk SSSR. Uspehi Fiziceskih Nauk [*A publication*]

Uspehi Mat Nauk ... Akademija Nauk SSSR i Moskovskoe Matematiceskoe Obscestvo. Uspehi Matematiceskih Nauk [*A publication*]

Uspekhi Fiz Nauk ... Uspekhi Fiziceskih Nauk [*A publication*]

Uspekhi Mat Nauk ... Uspekhi Matematiceskih Nauk [*A publication*]

USPEPA ..... United States Poultry and Egg Producers Association   (EA)

USPF .... US Powerlifting Federation   (EA)

Usp Fiziol Nauk ... Uspekhi Fiziologicheskikh Nauk [*A publication*]

Usp Fiz Nau ... Uspekhi Fizicheskikh Nauk [*A publication*]

Usp Fiz Nauk ... Uspekhi Fizicheskii Nauk [*A publication*]

USPFO .... United States Property and Fiscal Officer

Usp Foton ... Uspekhi Fotoniki [*A publication*]

Usp Fotoniki ... Uspekhi Fotoniki [*A publication*]

US/PFUN ... United States People for the United Nations [*Defunct*]   (EA)

USPG .... Uniform System of Accounts Prescribed for Natural Gas Companies

USPG .... United Society for the Propagation of the Gospel [*London, England*]   (EA-IO)

USpGS .... Church of Jesus Christ of Latter-Day Saints, Genealogical Society Library, Springville Branch, Springville, UT [*Library symbol*] [*Library of Congress*]   (LCLS)

USPh .... United States Pharmacopoeia

USPHS .... United States Postal History Society [*Defunct*]   (EA)

USPHS .... United States Public Health Service

USPHSR ..... United States Public Health Service Reserve

USPIRG ..... US Public Interest Research Group   (EA)

Usp Kh .... Uspekhi Khimii [*A publication*]

Usp Khim ... Uspekhi Khimii [*A publication*]

Usp Khim Fosfororg Seraorg Soedin ... Uspekhi Khimii Fosfororganicheskikh i Seraorganicheskikh Soedinenii [*A publication*]

Usp Khim Tekhnol Polim ... Uspekhi Khimii i Tekhnologii Polimerov [*A publication*]

USPL .... Uniform System of Accounts, Public Utilities, and Licensees [*Federal Power Commission*]

USPL .... Unpriced Spare Parts List

USPLS .... United States Public-Land Surveys

USPLTA ..... United States Professional Lawn Tennis Association [*Later, USPTA*]   (EA)

Usp Mat Nauk ... Uspekhi Matematicheskikh Nauk [*A publication*]

USPMF .... US Patent Model Foundation [*Washington, DC*]   (EA)

Usp Mikrobiol ... Uspekhi Mikrobiologii [*A publication*]

Usp Nauchn Fotogr ... Uspekhi Nauchnoj Fotografii [*A publication*]

USPO .... United Sabah People's Organization [*Pertubuhan Rakyat Sabah Bersatu*] [*Malaysian*]   (PPW)

USPO .... United States Patent Office [*Department of Commerce*]

USPO .... United States Post Office [*Later, United States Postal Service*]

USPP .... United States Pacifist Party   (EA)

USPP .... United States Park Police [*Department of the Interior*]

USPP .... University Science Policy Planning [*Program*] [*National Science Foundation*]

USPPA ...... United States Pulp Producers Association [*Later, API*]   (EA)

USPPS .... US Possessions Philatelic Society   (EA)

USPQ .... United States Patents Quarterly

USPS .... United States Postal Service

USPS .... United States Power Squadrons   (EA)

USPSA .... US Practical Shooting Association   (EA)

USPSD .... United States Political Science Documents [*University of Pittsburgh*] [*Pittsburgh, PA*] [*Bibliographic database*] [*Information service*]   (EISS)

USPSDA ..... United States Private Security and Detective Association   (EA)

USPSF .... United States Pigeon Shooting Federation [*Defunct*]   (EA)

Usp Sovrem Biol ... Uspekhi Sovremennoi Biologii [*A publication*]

Usp Sovrem Genet ... Uspekhi Sovremennoj Genetiki [*A publication*]

USPT .... United Societies of Physiotherapists [*Syosset, NY*]   (EA)

USPTA .... United States Paddle Tennis Association   (EA)

USPTA .... United States Physical Therapy Association [*Arlington Heights, IL*]   (EA)

USPTA .... United States Pony Trotting Association   (EA)

USPTA .... United States Professional Tennis Association   (EA)

USPTO .... United States Patent and Trademark Office

USPTS .... USP Real Estate Investment Trust [*NASDAQ symbol*]   (NQ)

US Public Health Serv Public Health Monogr ... United States Public Health Service. Public Health Monograph [*A publication*]

US Public Health Serv Radiol Health Data Rep ... US Public Health Service. Radiological Health Data and Reports [*A publication*]

USPWIC ..... United States Prisoner of War Information Center [*Army*]   (AABC)

USPWIC(Br) ... United States Prisoner of War Information Center (Branch) [*Army*]   (AABC)

USQ .... United States Quarterly Book Review [*A publication*]

US Q Bk R ... United States Quarterly Book Review [*A publication*]

USQBL .... United States Quarterly Book List [*A publication*]

USQBR .... United States Quarterly Book Review [*A publication*]

USQR .... Union Seminary. Quarterly Review [*A publication*]

US Quartermaster Food Container Inst Armed Forces Libr Bull ... US Quartermaster Food and Container Institute for the Armed Forces. Library Bulletin [*A publication*]
USR .... Ukrainska Partiia Sotsialistov Revolyutsionerov [*Ukrainian Socialist Revolutionary Party*] [*Russian*]   (PPE)
USR .... Ultrasonic Radiation
USR .... Under Speed Relay   (MCD)
USR .... Union Seminary. Review [*A publication*]
USR .... United States [*Supreme Court*] Reports
USR .... United States Reserves
USR .... Up Stage Right [*Away from audience*] [*A stage direction*]
USR .... US Shoe Corp. [*NYSE symbol*]
USR .... User Service Request
USR .... User Service Routine [*Digital Equipment Corp.*]
USR .... User Status Reporting   (MCD)
USR .... Usher of the Scarlet Rod   (ROG)
USRA .... United Sportsman Racers Association   (EA)
USRA .... United States Racquetball Association   (EA)
USRA .... United States Railway Association [*In 1974, superseded United States Railroad Administration, which had been absorbed by the Department of Transportation in 1939*]
USRA .... United States Revolver Association   (EA)
USRA .... United States Rowing Association [*Formerly, NAAO*]   (EA)
USRA .... United Street Rod Association   (EA)
USRA .... Universities Space Research Association
USRAC ...... US Repeating Arms Company
USRAD .... United States Fleet Shore Radio Station
USR-Borotbists ... Ukrainska Partiia Sotsialistov Revolyutsionerov-Borotbists [*Ukrainian Socialist Revolutionary Party-Fighters*] [*Russian*]   (PPE)
USRCPAC ... United States Reserve Components and Personnel Administration Center
USRCS .... United States Revenue Cutter Service
USRCSI ..... United States Red Cedar Shingle Industry
USRD .... Underwater Sound Reference Detachment [*Navy*]
USRDA .... US Recommended Daily Allowance [*Nutrition*]
USREC .... United States Environment and Resources Council [*Marine science*]   (MSC)
USREDA ..... United States Rice Export Development Association [*Later, RCMD*]
USREDCOM ... United States Readiness Command
US Reg .... United States Register [*Philadelphia*]   (DLA)
US Reh Den ... Rehearing Denied by United States Supreme Court   (DLA)
US Reh Dis ... Rehearing Dismissed by United States Supreme Court   (DLA)
US Rep .... United States Reports   (DLA)
US Rep (L Ed) ... United States Supreme Court Reports, Lawyers' Edition   (DLA)
USREPMC ... United States Representative to the Military Committee [*NATO*]   (NATG)
USREPMILCOMLO ... United States Representative to the Military Committee Liaison Office [*NATO*]   (NATG)
USREPMILCOMUN ... United States Representative, United Nations Military Staff Committee
USREPOF ... United States Navy Reporting Office [*or Officer*]
US Res Developm Rep ... United States Government Research and Development Reports [*A publication*]
US Rev St ... United States Revised Statutes   (DLA)
USRL .... Underwater Sound Reference Laboratory [*Navy*]
USRM .... United States Revenue Marine
USRNMC .... United States Representative to NATO Military Committee   (AABC)
USRO .... Ultrasmall Structures Research Office [*University of Michigan*] [*Research center*]   (RCD)
USRO .... United States Mission to NATO and European Regional Organizations
USRO .... United States Navy Routing Office
USRP .... United States Refugee Program
USRPA .... United States Racing Pigeon Association [*Defunct*]   (EA)
USRRC .... United States Road Racing Championship
USRR Lab Bd Dec ... Decisions of the United States Railroad Labor Board   (DLA)
USRS .... United States Reclamation Service
USRS .... United States Revised Statutes
USRS .... United States Robotics Society   (CSR)
USRS .... United States Rocket Society   (EA)
USRSA .... United States Racquet Stringers Association [*Del Mar, CA*]   (EA)
USRSG ...... United States Representative, Standing Group [*Military*]   (AABC)
USRT .... Universal Synchronous Receiver/Transmitter
USRTA .... United States Recreational Tennis Association   (EA)
USS .... Ultrasound Scanning
USS .... Ultraviolet Scanning Spectrometer
US of S .... Under Secretary of State
USS .... Underwater Sound Source
USS .... Unified S-Band System [*Radio*]
USS .... Union Syndicale Suisse [*Swiss Federation of Trade Unions*]
USS .... United Scholarship Service [*Later, NCAIAE, NCAIE*]
USS .... United Seamen's Service [*New York, NY*]   (EA)
USS .... United States Naval Vessel
USS .... United States Sellers [*Standard threads*]   (DEN)

USS .... United States Senate
USS .... United States Ship
USS .... United States Standard
USS .... United States Steamer
USS .... United States Swimming, Inc.   (EA)
USS .... United Swedish Societies   (EA)
USS .... Universities Superannuation Scheme
USS .... US Steel Canada, Inc. [*Toronto Stock Exchange symbol*]
USS .... US Steel Corp. [*Also, USSC*] [*Later, USX Corp.*]
USS .... USAF [*United States Air Force*] Security Service
USS .... Usage Sensitive Service [*Telecommunications*]
USS .... User Support System   (MCD)
USS .... Utility Support Structure   (MCD)
USSA .... Underground Security Storage Association [*Defunct*]
USSA .... Union Suisse des Syndicats Autonomes [*Swiss Association of Autonomous Unions*]
USSA .... United Saw Service Association   (EA)
USSA .... United States Salvage Association [*New York, NY*]   (EA)
USSA .... United States Security Authority [*for NATO affairs*]
USSA .... United States Ski Association   (EA)
USSA .... United States Snowshoe Association   (EA)
USSA .... United States Sports Academy   (EA)
USSA .... United States Standard Atmosphere   (KSC)
USSA .... United States Student Assembly
USSA .... United States Student Association [*Formerly, USNSA*]   (EA)
USSA .... United States Swimming Association   (EA)
USSA .... United Sugar Samplers' Association [*Defunct*]
USSA .... US Sidewinder Association   (EA)
USSA .... US Soling Association [*Chicago, IL*]   (EA)
USSAC ...... United States Army Ambulance Service Association [*Defunct*]   (EA)
USSAC ...... United States Security Authority for CENTO Affairs   (AABC)
USSAF .... United States Strategic Air Force [*Later, Strategic Air Command*]
USSAF .... US Sports Acrobatic Federation   (EA)
USSAFE ..... United States Strategic Air Forces in Europe
USSAH ...... United States Soldiers' and Airmen's Home   (AABC)
USSALEP ... United States - South Africa Leader Exchange Program
USSAS ...... United States Security Authority for SEATO Affairs   (AABC)
USSB .... United States Satellite Broadcasting Co., Inc. [*Minneapolis, MN*] [*Telecommunications*]   (TSSD)
USSB .... United States Shipping Board [*Terminated, 1933*]
USSB .... United States Shipping Board Decisions   (DLA)
USSBA .... United States Seniors Bowling Association [*Later, Seniors Division of the American Bowling Congress*]   (EA)
USSBB .... United States Shipping Board Bureau Decisions   (DLA)
USSBD .... United States Savings Bonds Division [*Department of the Treasury*]
USSBF .... United States Skibob Federation   (EA)
USSBIA ...... United States Stone and Bead Importers Association   (EA)
USSBL .... United States Stickball League   (EA)
USSBS .... United States Strategic Bombing Survey
USSC .... United States Servas Committee   (EA)
USSC .... United States Strike Command [*Military combined Tactical Air Command and Strategic Army Command Force*]
USSC .... United States Supreme Court
USSC .... US Steel Corporation [*Also, USS*] [*Later, USX Corp.*]   (MCD)
USSC .... US Surgical Corporation [*NASDAQ symbol*]   (NQ)
USSCA ...... US Ski Coaches Association   (EA)
US-SCAN ... United States Special Committee on Antarctic Names [*1943-47*]
USSC Rep ... United States Supreme Court Reports   (DLA)
USSCT .... United States Supreme Court
USSDP .... Uniformed Services Savings Deposits Program   (AABC)
USSE .... Ultrasonic Soldering Equipment
USSEA ...... United States Scientific Export Association
USSEA ...... United States Space Education Association   (EA)
USSECMILCOMUN ... [*The*] Secretary, United States Delegation United Nations Staff Committee
US Seed Rep ... United States Seed Reporter [*A publication*]
USSEF .... United States Ski Educational Foundation
US Serv M ... United States Service Magazine [*A publication*]
USSES .... US Sheep Experiment Station [*University of Idaho*] [*Research center*]   (RCD)
USSF .... United States Soccer Federation [*Formerly, USSFA*]   (EA)
USSF .... United States Softball Federation
USSF .... United States Special Forces
USSF .... United States Steel Foundation
USSF .... United States Surfing Federation   (EA)
USSF .... United States Swimming Foundation   (EA)
USSFA ...... United States Soccer Football Association [*Later, USSF*]   (EA)
USSFFA .... United Soft Serve and Fast Food Association   (EA)
USSF(P) .... United States Special Forces (Provisional)   (CINC)
USSG .... United States Standard Gauge
USSG .... United States Storekeeper-Gauger
USSGA ...... United States Seniors Golf Association [*Defunct*]   (EA)
USSGA ...... Uspekhi Sovremennoi Genetiki [*A publication*]
USSGREP ... United States Standing Group Representative [*NATO*]   (AABC)
USSH .... United States Soldiers' Home
US Ship Struct Com Rep ... United States Ship Structure Committee Report [*A publication*]

USSI.......... Ultrasonic Soldering Iron
USSI.......... United States Strategic Institute   (MCD)
USSIA........ United States Shellac Importers Association [*Islip, NY*]   (EA)
USSID....... United States Signal Intelligence Directive   (AABC)
US-SIOP.... United States Single Integrated Operational Plan   (NATG)
USSIS......... United States Signals Intellignce System   (MCD)
USSLL........ United States Savings and Loan League [*Later, USLSI*]   (EA)
USSMA...... US Spanish Merchants Association   (EA)
US Soil Conserv Service Sedimentation Bull (TP) ... United States Soil
                Conservation Service. Sedimentation Bulletin (Technical
                Publication) [*A publication*]
US Soil Conserv Serv Soil Surv ... US Soil Conservation Service. Soil Survey
                [*A publication*]
USSOUTHCOM ... United States Southern Command [*Air Force*]
USSP.......... User Systems Support Plan
USSPA........ United States Student Press Association [*Superseded by CPS*]
USSPC........ US Student Pugwash Committee [*Later, ISP, Student Pugwash
                (USA)*]   (EA)
USSPEI....... Union des Syndicats des Services Publics Europeens et
                Internationaux [*European and International Public
                Services Union*]   (EA-IO)
USSPG........ United States Senate Press Photographers Gallery   (EA)
USSPG........ US Sweetener Producers Group   (EA)
USSPPG...... United States Senate Press Photographers Gallery
                [*Washington, DC*]   (EA)
USSR.......... State Music Trust [*Record label*] [*Soviet Union*]
USSR.......... Union of Soviet Socialist Republics [*See also SSSR, CCCP*]
USSRA........ United States Squash Racquets Association   (EA)
USSR Comp Info B ... USSR. Union of Composers. Information Bulletin [*A
                publication*]
USSR Computational Math and Math Phys ... USSR Computational
                Mathematics and Mathematical Physics [*A publication*]
USSR Comput Math Math Phys ... USSR Computational Mathematics and
                Mathematical Physics [*A publication*]
USSR Comput Math and Math Phys ... USSR Computational Mathematics
                and Mathematical Physics [*A publication*]
USSRM........ State Music Trust [*78 RPM*] [*Record label*] [*Soviet Union*]
USSRN........ Under Secretary of State for the Royal Navy [*British*]
USSS.......... Undersea Surveillance System   (MCD)
USSS.......... United States Secret Service
USSS.......... United States Steamship
USSS.......... Unmanned Sensing Satellite System
USSSA........ United States Slo-Pitch Softball Association   (EA)
USSSA........ United States Snowshoe Association   (EA)
USSSI......... United Stamp Society for Shut-Ins   (EA)
USSSI......... United States Synchronized Swimming, Incorporated   (EA)
USSSMA...... US Shake and Shingle Manufacturers Association   (EA)
USSSO........ United States Sending State Office [*Navy*]
USSSS........ US Shelter Corp. [*NASDAQ symbol*]   (NQ)
USSS/UD..... United States Secret Service Uniformed Division
USSTAF....... United States Strategic Air Force [*Later, Strategic Air
                Command*]
USSTAFE...... United States Strategic Tactical Air Force, Europe
US Stat........ United States Statutes at Large   (DLA)
US St at L.... United States Statutes at Large   (DLA)
USSTRICOM ... United States Strike Command [*Military combined Tactical
                Air Command and Strategic Army Command Force*]
USSTS......... United States Student Travel Service   (EA)
US St Tr...... United States State Trials [*Wharton*]   (DLA)
US Sup Ct ... United States Supreme Court Reporter   (DLA)
US Sup Ct (L Ed) ... United States Supreme Court Reports, Lawyers'
                Edition   (DLA)
US Sup Ct R ... United States Supreme Court Reporter [*West*]   (DLA)
US Sup Ct Rep ... United States Supreme Court Reporter   (DLA)
US Sup Ct Reps ... Supreme Court Reporter   (DLA)
USSWA........ United States Ski Writers Association
UST............ Ultrasonic Test
UST............ Ultrasonic Transducer [*Crystal*] [*Used in measuring human
                cardiac output*]
UST............ Unblocked Serial Telemetry   (MCD)
UST............ Underground Storage Tank [*Environmental Protection
                Agency*]
UST............ Undersea Technology
UST............ Uniform Specification Tree
UST............ Union Senegalaise du Travail [*Senegalese Labor Union*]
UST............ Union Socialiste Tchadienne [*Chadian Socialist Union*]
UST............ United States Time
UST............ United States Treaties and Other International
                Agreements   (DLA)
UST............ University of Saint Thomas [*Texas*]
UST............ Ustilago [*A fungus*]
UST............ Ustus [*Burnt*] [*Pharmacy*]
USTA.......... Union des Syndicats des Travailleurs Algeriens [*Federation of
                Unions of Algerian Workers*]
USTA.......... United States Telephone Association [*Washington, DC*]   (EA)
USTA.......... United States Tennis Association [*Formerly, USLTA*]
USTA.......... United States Trademark Association   (EA)
USTA.......... United States Trotting Association [*Governing body of US
                harness racing*]
USTA.......... United States Twirling Association
USTA.......... Unlisted Securities Trading Act [*1936*]

USTA.......... US Tornado Association   (EA)
USTA.......... US Triathlon Association   (EA)
USTA.......... US Trivia Association   (EA)
USTAF........ United States/Thai Forces
US Tariff Comm Rep ... United States Tariff Commission. Reports [*A
                publication*]
US Tariff Comm TC Publ ... United States Tariff Commission. TC Publication
                [*A publication*]
Ustav Jad Fyz Cesk Akad Ved Rep ... Ustav Jaderne Fyziky Ceskoslovenska
                Akademia Ved. Report [*A publication*]
Ustav Vedeckotech Inf Sb UVTI Genet Slechteni ... Ustav
                Vedeckotechnickych Informaci. Sbornik UVTI. Genetika a
                Slechteni [*A publication*]
Ustav Vedeckotech Inf Sb UVTI Melior ... Ustav Vedeckotechnickych
                Informaci. Sbornik UVTI. Rada. Meliorace [*A publication*]
Ustav Vedeckotech Inf Zemed ... Ustav Vedeckotechnickych Informaci pro
                Zemedelstvi [*A publication*]
Ustav Vedeckotech Inf Zemed Sb UVTIZ Melior ... Ustav
                Vedeckotechnickych Informaci pro Zemedelstvi. Sbornik
                UVTIZ. Rada. Meliorace [*A publication*]
Ustav Vedeckotech Inf Zemed Stud Inf Ochr Rostl ... Ustav
                Vedeckotechnickych Informaci pro Zemedelstvi Studijni
                Informace Ochrana Rostlin [*A publication*]
Ustav Vyzk Vyuziti Paliv Monogr ... Ustav pro Vyzkum a Vyuziti Paliv
                Monografie [*A publication*]
US Tax Cas ... United States Tax Cases [*Commerce Clearing House*]   (DLA)
US Tax Rpt ... United States Tax Report [*A publication*]
USTB.......... United States Travel Bureau
USTB.......... UST Corp. [*NASDAQ symbol*]   (NQ)
USTC......... United States Tariff Commission [*Later, ITC*]
USTC......... United States Tax Cases [*Commerce Clearing House*]   (DLA)
USTC......... United States Testing Company, Inc.
USTC......... United States Tourist Council   (EA)
USTC......... United States Transportation Commission [*Proposed
                commission to consolidate CAB, ICC, and FMC*]
USTC......... US Trust Corporation [*NASDAQ symbol*]   (NQ)
USTCA....... United States Track Coaches Association [*Later, TFA/USA*]
USTCTBA ... United States Tennis Court and Track Builders Association
                [*Charlottesville, VA*]   (EA)
USTD......... Union des Syndicats des Travailleurs du Dahomey [*Federation
                of Workers' Unions of Dahomey*]
USTD......... United States Treasury Department
USTD......... United States Treaty Development   (DLA)
USTDA....... United States Truck Drivers Association
USTDC....... United States Forces, Taiwan Defense Command   (CINC)
USTDC....... US Travel Data Center   (EA)
US TEL....... US Telephone, Inc. [*Dallas, TX*] [*Telecommunications*]   (TSSD)
USTES........ United States Training and Employment Service [*Abolished,
                1971*] [*Department of Labor*]
USTF.......... United States Tuna Foundation [*Washington, DC*]   (EA)
USTFA........ United States Trout Farmers Association   (EA)
USTFF......... United States Track and Field Federation [*Later, TFA/USA*]
USTFFA....... United States Touch and Flag Football Association   (EA)
UStG.......... Umsatzteuergesetz [*German Turnover Tax Act*]   (DLA)
USTG.......... Union Syndicale des Travailleurs de Guinee [*Guinean
                Federation of Workers*]
UStgD........ Dixie College, St. George, UT [*Library symbol*] [*Library of
                Congress*]   (LCLS)
UStgGS...... Church of Jesus Christ of Latter-Day Saints, Genealogical
                Society Library, St. George Branch, St. George, UT
                [*Library symbol*] [*Library of Congress*]   (LCLS)
UStgW........ Washington County Library, St. George, UT [*Library symbol*]
                [*Library of Congress*]   (LCLS)
USTHF........ US Team Handball Federation   (EA)
USTIIC........ United States Technical Industrial Intelligence
                Committee   (MCD)
USTJ.......... United States Tobacco Journal [*A publication*]
USTL.......... US Telephone, Inc. [*NASDAQ symbol*]   (NQ)
USTOA........ United States Tour Operators Association [*New York,
                NY*]   (EA)
USTOL........ Ultrashort Takeoff and Landing [*Aviation*]   (MCD)
USTOPS...... United States Travelers' Overseas Personalized Service [*Also
                known as TOPS*]
USTR.......... United States Trade Representative [*Formerly, SRTN*]
                [*Executive Office of the President*]
USTR.......... United Stationers, Inc. [*NASDAQ symbol*]   (NQ)
USTRA........ United States Touring Riders Association   (EA)
USTRC........ United States Transportation Research Command [*Army*]
US Treas Dept ... United States Treasury Department   (DLA)
US Treas Reg ... United States Treasury Regulations   (DLA)
US Treaty Ser ... United States Treaty Series   (DLA)
USTS.......... Union Syndicale des Travailleurs du Soudan [*Federation of
                Sudanese Workers*] [*Mali*]
USTS.......... United States Time Standard [*National Bureau of Standards*]
USTS.......... United States Travel Service [*Replaced by United States Travel
                and Tourism Administration*] [*Department of Commerce*]
USTSA........ United States Targhee Sheep Association   (EA)
USTSA........ US Telecommunications Suppliers Association [*Chicago, IL*]
                [*Telecommunications*]   (EA)
USTTA........ United States Table Tennis Association   (EA)

USTTA .... United States Travel and Tourism Administration [*Formerly, US Travel Service*] [*Department of Commerce*]
USTTI .... US Telecommunications Training Institute [*Washington, DC*] [*Telecommunications*] (TSSD)
USTU .... Ultrasonic Test Unit
USTU .... US Taxpayers Union (EA)
USTV .... Universal Subscription Television
USTV .... Unmanned Supersonic Test Vehicle (MCD)
USTVA .... United States Tennessee Valley Authority
Ust Ved Inf MZLVH Rostl Vyroba ... Ustav Vedeckotechnickych Informaci. Ministerstva Zemedelstvi. Lesniho a Vodnlho Hospodarstvi. Rostlinna Vyroba [*A publication*]
Ust Ved Inf MZLVH Stud Inf Pudoz ... Ustav Vedeckotechnickych Informaci. MZLVH [*Ministerstva Zemedelstvi. Lesniho a Vodnlho Hospodarstvi*] Studijni Informace Pudoznalstvi a Meliorace [*A publication*]
Ust Ved Inf MZ Rostl Vyroba ... Ustav Vedeckotechnickych Informaci. Ministerstva Zemedelstvi. Rostlinna Vyroba [*A publication*]
Ust Ved Inf MZVZ Rostl Vyroba ... Ustav Vedeckotechnickych Informaci. Ministerstva Zemedelstvi a Vyzivy. Rostlinna Vyroba [*A publication*]
USTWA ...... US Tennis Writers Association [*Formerly, LTWA*] (EA)
USTZD ...... Unsensitized
USU .... Uniformed Services University of the Health Sciences Library, Bethesda, MD [*OCLC symbol*] (OCLC)
USU .... Usually
USUB .... Unglazed Structural Unit Base [*Technical drawings*]
USUCA ...... United Steel Workers' Union of Central Africa [*Rhodesia and Nyasaland*]
USUG .... US Sugar Corp. [*NASDAQ symbol*] (NQ)
USUHS ...... Uniformed Services University of the Health Sciences [*DoD*] [*Bethesda, MD*] (EGAO)
US/UK .... United States/United Kingdom
USUMS ..... Utah State University. Monograph Series [*A publication*]
USUN .... United States United Nations Delegation (CINC)
USURP .... Usurpandus [*To Be Used*] [*Pharmacy*]
USUSA ...... United Societies of the United States of America (EA)
USV .... United States Volunteers [*Civil War*]
USV .... Unmanned Strike Vehicle
USVAAD .... United States Veteran's Administration Administrator's Decisions (DLA)
USVAC ...... United States Veterans' Assistance Center (OICC)
USVB .... United States Veterans Bureau
USVBA .... United States Volleyball Association (EA)
USVBA .... US Venetian Blind Association (EA)
USVBDD .... United States Veterans Bureau Director's Decisions (DLA)
USVC .... United Services Life Insurance [*NASDAQ symbol*] (NQ)
US Veterans Adm (W) Dep Med Surg Bull Prosthet Res ... United States. Veterans Administration (Washington, DC). Department of Medicine and Surgery. Bulletin of Prosthetics Research [*A publication*]
US Veterans Bureau Med Bull ... United States Veterans Bureau. Medical Bulletin [*A publication*]
USVH .... United States Veterans Hospital
USVMD ...... Urine Specimen Volume Measuring Device
USVMS ...... Urine Sample Volume Measurement System (MCD)
USVR .... US Vacation Resorts [*NASDAQ symbol*] (NQ)
USVT .... Universal Stray Voltage Tester
USW .... Ultrashort Wave
USW .... Ultrasonic Welding
USW .... Und So Weiter [*And So Forth*] [*German*]
USW .... Under Secretary of War [*Obsolete*]
USW .... Undersea Warfare
USW .... US West, Inc. [*NYSE symbol*]
USW .... US Wheat Associates (EA)
USWA .... American Association for the Study of the United States in World Affairs (EA)
USWA .... United Shoe Workers of America [*Later, ACTWU*] (EA)
USWA .... United States Wayfarer Association (EA)
USWA .... United Steelworkers of America
USWAB ..... United States Warehouse Act Bonded
USWACC ... United States Women's Army Corps Center
USWACS ... United States Women's Army Corps School
USWAP ..... United South West Africa Party [*Political party*] [*Namibian*]
USWAP ..... United Steel Workers' Association of the Philippines
US (War Dp) Chief Eng An Rp ... United States (War Department). Chief of Engineers. Annual Report [*A publication*]
US Waterw Exp Stn Contract Rep ... United States Waterways Experiment Station. Contract Report [*A publication*]
US Waterw Exp Stn Misc Pap ... United States Waterways Experiment Station. Miscellaneous Paper [*A publication*]
US Waterw Exp Stn Res Rep ... United States Waterways Experiment Station. Research Report [*A publication*]
US Waterw Exp Stn Tech Rep ... United States Waterways Experiment Station. Technical Report [*A publication*]
US Waterw Exp Stn Vicksburg Miss Tech Rep ... United States Waterways Experiment Station. Vicksburg, Mississippi. Technical Report [*A publication*]
USWB .... United States Weather Bureau [*Later, National Weather Service*]
USWBC ...... United States War Ballot Commission [*World War II*]

USWCA ...... United States Women's Curling Association (EA)
USWF .... United States Wrestling Federation (EA)
USWF .... US Weightlifting Federation (EA)
USWGA ...... United States Wholesale Grocers' Association [*Later, NAWGA*] (EA)
USWI .... United States West Indies
USWISOMWAGMOHOTM ... United Single Women in Search of Men Who Aren't Gay, Married, or Hung-Up on Their Mothers [*Fictitious association*]
USWLA ...... United States Women's Lacrosse Association (EA)
US Women's Bur Bul ... United States Women's Bureau. Bulletin [*A publication*]
USWP .... United States Water Polo [*An association*] (EA)
USWSRA .... United States Women's Squash Racquets Association (EA)
USWSSB .... United States Wood Screw Service Bureau [*Defunct*] (EA)
USWTCA .... United States Women's Track Coaches Association (EA)
USWV .... United Spanish War Veterans (EA)
USX .... Ultrasoft X-Ray
USX .... US Steel Corp. [*Formerly, USS, USSC*]
USXFS .... Ultrasoft X-Ray Fluoescence [*Spectroscopy*]
USXRS .... Ultrasoft X-Ray Spectroscopy
USY .... United Synagogue Youth
USY .... US Pay-Tel, Inc. [*Vancouver Stock Exchange symbol*]
USYC .... United States Youth Council
USYEC .... US Yugoslav Economic Council [*Washington, DC*] (EA)
USYRU ...... United States Yacht Racing Union (EA)
USYSA ...... United States Youth Soccer Association (EA)
USZI .... United States Zone of the Interior
UT .... Conference Internationale pour l'Unite Technique des Chemins de Fer
UT .... Tooele Public Library, Tooele, UT [*Library symbol*] [*Library of Congress*] (LCLS)
UT .... Ugaritic Text [*A publication*]
UT .... Ultrasonic Test
UT .... Ultrathin
UT .... Umbilical Tower [*Aerospace*]
UT .... Uncontrolled Term [*Online database field identifier*]
U/T .... Under Trust (DLA)
UT .... Underway Trials [*Shipbuilding*]
UT .... Unemployed Time [*Military*] [*British*]
UT .... Unexpired Term [*Real estate*] [*British*] (ROG)
UT .... Union Terminal Railway Co. [*AAR code*]
UT .... Union de Transports Aeriens [*France*] [*ICAO designator*] (FAAC)
UT .... Unit (MCD)
UT .... Unit Tester (NASA)
UT .... United Telecommunications, Inc. [*NYSE symbol*]
UT .... United Territory
UT .... United Together [*An association*] [*Lawrence, KS*] (EA)
UT .... Universal Time [*Astronomy*]
UT .... Universal Torpedo (MCD)
UT .... Universal Trainer
UT .... Universal Turret (MCD)
U of T .... University of Toronto [*Ontario*]
UT .... University of Toronto [*Ontario*]
UT .... University of Tulsa [*Oklahoma*]
UT .... Unspecified Temperature
UT .... Untested
U/T .... Untrained
UT .... Up Through [*Parapsychology*]
UT .... Up Time
UT .... Upper Torso
UT .... Urinary Tract [*Medicine*]
UT .... User Test
UT .... User's Terminal (MCD)
UT .... Utah [*Postal code*]
Ut. .... Utah Reports (DLA)
UT .... Utah Territory [*Prior to statehood*]
UT .... Utendum [*To Be Used*] [*Pharmacy*] (ROG)
UT .... Utilitiesman [*Navy rating*]
UT .... Utility (BUR)
UT .... Utility Boat
UT .... Utility Player
UT1 .... Utilitiesman, First Class [*Navy rating*]
UT2 .... Utilitiesman, Second Class [*Navy rating*]
UT3 .... Utilitiesman, Third Class [*Navy rating*]
UTA .... Ultrasonic Thermal Action
UTA .... Union de Transports Aeriens [*Air Transport Union*] [*Private airline*] [*Paris, France*]
UTA .... Unit Training Assembly [*Military*] (AABC)
UTA .... United Technologies Automotive
UTA .... United Typothetae of America [*Later, Printing Industries of America*]
UTA .... Upper Terminal Area (NATG)
UTA .... Urban Transportation Administration [*HUD*]
UTA .... User Transfer Address
UTAC .... Union Tunisienne de l'Artisanat et du Commerce [*Tunisian Union of Artisans and Merchants*]
UTACV ...... Urban Tracked Air-Cushion Vehicle [*Transit*] [*Department of Transportation*]
UTAD .... Utah Army Depot (AABC)

UTAH.......... Utah Railway Co. [*AAR code*]
UTAH.......... Utah Shale Land & Mining [*NASDAQ symbol*]   (NQ)
Utah.......... Utah Supreme Court Reports   (DLA)
Utah Acad Sci Proc ... Utah Academy of Sciences, Arts, and Letters. Proceedings [*A publication*]
Utah Ac Sc Tr ... Utah Academy of Sciences. Transactions [*A publication*]
Utah Admin Bull ... State of Utah Bulletin   (DLA)
Utah Admin R ... Administrative Rules of Utah   (DLA)
Utah Ag Exp ... Utah. Agricultural Experiment Station. Publications [*A publication*]
Utah Agric Exp Stn Bull ... Utah. Agricultural Experiment Station. Bulletin [*A publication*]
Utah Agric Exp Stn Circ ... Utah. Agricultural Experiment Station. Circular [*A publication*]
Utah Agric Exp Stn Res Rep ... Utah. Agricultural Experiment Station. Research Report [*A publication*]
Utah Agric Exp Stn Spec Rep ... Utah. Agricultural Experiment Station. Special Report [*A publication*]
Utah Agric Exp Stn Utah Resour Ser ... Utah. Agricultural Experiment Station. Utah Resources Series [*A publication*]
Utah Bar Bull ... Utah Bar Bulletin [*A publication*]
Utah B Bull ... Utah Bar Bulletin [*A publication*]
Utah Code Ann ... Utah Code, Annotated   (DLA)
Utah 2d ...... Utah Reports, Second Series   (DLA)
Utah Dep Nat Resour Tech Publ ... Utah. Department of Natural Resources. Technical Publication [*A publication*]
Utah Dep Nat Resour Water Cir ... Utah. Department of Natural Resources. Water Circular [*A publication*]
Utah Dept Nat Resources Tech Pub ... Utah. Department of Natural Resources. Division of Water Rights. Technical Publication [*A publication*]
Utah Div Water Resources Coop Inv Rept ... Utah. Division of Water Resources. Cooperative Investigations Report [*A publication*]
Utah Eng Exp Stn Bull ... Utah. Engineering Experiment Station. Bulletin [*A publication*]
Utah Farm Home Sci ... Utah Farm and Home Science [*A publication*]
Utah Geol... Utah Geology [*A publication*]
Utah Geol Assoc Publ ... Utah Geological Association. Publication [*A publication*]
Utah Geol and Mineralog Survey Bull ... Utah. Geological and Mineralogical Survey. Bulletin [*A publication*]
Utah Geol and Mineralog Survey Circ ... Utah. Geological and Mineralogical Survey. Circular [*A publication*]
Utah Geol and Mineralog Survey Quart Rev ... Utah. Geological and Mineralogical Survey. Quarterly Review [*A publication*]
Utah Geol and Mineralog Survey Spec Studies ... Utah. Geological and Mineralogical Survey. Special Studies [*A publication*]
Utah Geol and Mineralog Survey Water Resources Bull ... Utah. Geological and Mineralogical Survey. Water Resources Bulletin [*A publication*]
Utah Geol Mineral Surv Bull ... Utah. Geological and Mineralogical Survey. Bulletin [*A publication*]
Utah Geol Mineral Surv Circ ... Utah. Geological and Mineralogical Survey. Circular [*A publication*]
Utah Geol Mineral Surv Spec Stud ... Utah. Geological and Mineralogical Survey. Special Studies [*A publication*]
Utah Geol Mineral Surv Water Resour Bull ... Utah. Geological and Mineralogical Survey. Water Resources Bulletin [*A publication*]
Utah Geol Miner Surv Circ ... Utah. Geological and Mineralogical Survey. Circular [*A publication*]
Utah Geol Miner Surv Q Rev ... Utah. Geological and Mineralogical Survey. Quarterly Review [*A publication*]
Utah Geol Miner Surv Surv Notes ... Utah. Geological and Mineralogical Survey. Survey Notes [*A publication*]
Utah Geol Soc Guidebook to Geology of Utah ... Utah Geological Society. Guidebook to the Geology of Utah [*A publication*]
Utah Hist Q ... Utah Historical Quarterly [*A publication*]
Utah Hist Quar ... Utah Historical Quarterly [*A publication*]
Utah Hist Quart ... Utah Historical Quarterly [*A publication*]
Utah IC Bull ... Utah Industrial Commission. Bulletin   (DLA)
Utah Lib ..... Utah Libraries [*A publication*]
Utah Lib Assn Newsl ... Utah Library Association. Newsletter [*A publication*]
Utah Libr.... Utah Libraries [*A publication*]
Utah L Rev ... Utah Law Review [*A publication*]
Utah M .... Utah Genealogical and Historical Magazine [*A publication*]
Utah Med Bull ... Utah Medical Bulletin [*A publication*]
Utah PUC ... Utah Public Utilities Commission Report   (DLA)
Utah R .... Utah Reports   (DLA)
Utah Resour Ser Utah Agr Exp Sta ... Utah Resources Series. Utah Agricultural Experiment Station [*A publication*]
Utah Sci ..... Utah Science [*A publication*]
Utah State Engineer Bienn Rept Tech Pub ... Utah State Engineer. Biennial Report. Technical Publications [*A publication*]
Utah State Engineer Inf Bull ... Utah State Engineer. Information Bulletin [*A publication*]
Utah State Eng Off Basic Data Rep ... Utah. State Engineer's Office. Basic Data Report [*A publication*]
Utah State Eng Tech Publ ... Utah State Engineer. Technical Publication [*A publication*]

Utah State Med J ... Utah State Medical Journal [*A publication*]
Utah State Univ Agric Exp Stn Bull ... Utah State University. Agricultural Experiment Station. Bulletin [*A publication*]
Utah Univ Anthropol Papers Bull ... Utah University. Anthropological Papers. Bulletin [*A publication*]
Utah Univ Eng Exp Stn Tech Pap ... Utah University. Engineering Experiment Station. Technical Paper [*A publication*]
Utah Univ Eng Expt Sta Bull ... Utah University. Engineering Experiment Station. Bulletin [*A publication*]
UTAP.......... Unified Transportation Assistance Program [*Proposed*]
UTAP.......... Urban Transportation Assistance Program [*Canada*]
UTAS.......... Underwater Target-Activated Sensor   (MCD)
U Tasmania L Rev ... University of Tasmania. Law Review [*A publication*]
U Tasm L Rev ... University of Tasmania. Law Review [*A publication*]
UTASN....... University of Texas at Austin School of Nursing
UT/AT .... Underway Trial/Acceptance Trial [*Navy*]   (NVT)
UTATA .... Uniform Testamentary Additions to Trusts Act [*National Conference of Commissioners on Uniform State Laws*]
UTB .... Muttaburra [*Australia*] [*Airport symbol*]   (OAG)
UTB .... Uni Taschenbuecher GmbH [*German publishers cooperative*]
UTB .... United Tariff Bureau
UTB .... University of Toronto Library, Brieflisted Records [*UTLAS symbol*]
UTB .... Utilitiesman, Boilerman [*Navy rating*]
UTBC .... Union Trust Bancorp [*NASDAQ symbol*]   (NQ)
UT BJ .... Utah Bar Journal [*A publication*]
UTBN.......... Utah Bancorp [*NASDAQ symbol*]   (NQ)
UTC........... Uncle Tom's Cabin [*Title of book by Harriet Beecher Stowe*]
UTC........... Underwater Training Centre [*British*]
UTC........... Union de Trabajadores Campesinos [*Agricultural Workers' Union*] [*Salvadoran*]   (PD)
UTC........... Union des Travailleurs Congolais [*Union of Congolese Workers*] [*Leopoldville*]
UTC........... Unit Time Coding
UTC........... Unit Training Center [*Military*]
UTC........... Unit Type Code   (AFM)
UTC........... United Canso Oil & Gas Ltd. [*Toronto Stock Exchange symbol*]
UTC........... United States Tax Court, Library, Washington, DC [*OCLC symbol*]   (OCLC)
UTC........... United Technologies Corporation [*East Hartford, CT*] [*Information service*]   (EISS)
UTC........... Universal Test Console   (KSC)
UTC........... Universal Time Code
UTC........... Universal Time Coordinated [*The universal time emitted by coordinated radio stations*]
UTC........... University Teachers Certificate
UTC........... University Training Corps [*British*]
UTC........... Urban Technology Conference
UTC........... Urban Training Center
UTC........... Utilities Telecommunications Council [*Washington, DC*]   (EA)
UTC........... Utilitiesman, Chief [*Navy rating*]
UTCA .... Constructionman Apprentice, Utilitiesman, Striker [*Navy rating*]
UTCA .... Utica Bankshares Corp. [*NASDAQ symbol*]   (NQ)
UTCAA....... Uncle Tom Cobley and All [*Refers to everyone*] [*Slang*] [*British*]   (DSUE)
UTCC .... University of Tennessee at Knoxville Computer Center [*Research center*]   (RCD)
UTCEU .... Universidad de Tucuman. Cuadernos de Extension Universitaria [*A publication*]
UTCL.......... Union des Travailleurs Communistes Libertaires [*Union of Libertarian Communist Workers*] [*French*]   (PPW)
UTCLK .... Universal Transmitter Clock
UTCM......... Utilitiesman, Master Chief [*Navy rating*]
UTCN......... Constructionman, Utilitiesman, Striker [*Navy rating*]
UTCPTT ..... Union Internationale des Organismes Touristiques et Culturels des Postes et des Telecommunications [*International Union of Tourist and Cultural Associations in the Postal and Telecommunications Services*]
UTCS .... Urasenke Tea Ceremony Society   (EA)
UTCS .... Urban Traffic Control System
UTCS .... Utilitiesman, Senior Chief [*Navy rating*]
UTCT......... Undermanned Tank Crew Test [*Military*]   (MCD)
UTD........... Undetermined
UTD........... United
UTD........... Universal Transfer Device
UTD........... University of Texas at Dallas   (MCD)
UTD........... Uranium-Thorium Dating
UTD........... User Terminal and Display Subsystem [*Space Flight Operations Facility, NASA*]
UTDC .... Urban Transportation Development Corporation [*Canada*]
UTDEMS .... University of Tulsa. Department of English. Monograph Series [*A publication*]
UT DICT ..... Ut Dictum [*As Directed*] [*Latin*]
UTE .... Chandler, AZ [*Location identifier*] [*FAA*]   (FAAL)
UTE .... Underwater Tracking Equipment   (MCD)
UTE .... Union Technique de l'Electricite [*France*]
UTE .... Universal Test Equipment
UTE .... Utilization of Theoretical Energy
UTEC......... Universal Test Equipment Compiler   (KSC)

U Tech Umweltmag ... U das Technische Umweltmagazin [*West Germany*] [*A publication*]
UTEELRAD ... Utilization of Enemy Electromagnetic Radiation (MSA)
UTEL .... United Telecontrol Electronics, Inc. [*NASDAQ symbol*] (NQ)
UTEND .... Utendus [*To Be Used*] [*Pharmacy*]
UTEP .... University of Texas at El Paso
UTES .... Unit Training Equipment Site [*Military*] (AABC)
UTET .... Unione Tipografico-Editrice Torinese [*Publisher*] [*Italy*]
UTF .... Underwater Tank Facility
UTF .... Underwater Test Facility [*GE*]
UTF .... Valparaiso [*Chile*] [*Seismograph station code, US Geological Survey*] (SEIS)
U T Fac L Rev ... University of Toronto. Faculty of Law. Review [*A publication*]
UT Faculty LR ... Faculty of Law Review, University of Toronto [*A publication*]
UTFO .... Untouchable Force [*Recording artists*]
UTFS .... University of Toronto. French Series [*A publication*]
UTG .... University of Toronto Library, Government Documents [*UTLAS symbol*]
UTGA .... United Tobacco Growers Association (EA)
UTGT .... Under Thirty Group for Transit [*Defunct*] (EA)
UTH .... Udon Thani [*Thailand*] [*Airport symbol*] (OAG)
UTH .... Upper Turret Half
UTHS .... University of Texas. Hispanic Studies [*A publication*]
UTI .... International Universal Time [*Telecommunications*] (TEL)
UTI .... Union Telegraphique Internationale (MSC)
UTI .... Universal Trident Industries Ltd. [*Vancouver Stock Exchange symbol*]
UTI .... Urinary Tract Infection [*Medicine*]
UTIA .... University of Toronto, Institute of Aerophysics (MCD)
UTIAS .... University of Toronto, Institute for Aerospace Studies [*Research center*] (MCD)
UTIC .... USAREUR Tactical Intelligence Center (MCD)
UTICI .... Union Technique des Ingenieurs Conseils [*French*]
UTIL .... Utility [*or Utilization*] (AFM)
Utilitas Math ... Utilitas Mathematica [*A publication*]
Util L Rep ... Utilities Law Reporter [*Commerce Clearing House*] (DLA)
UTILN .... Utilitarian (AAG)
UT INF .... Ut Infra [*As Below*] [*Latin*] (ADA)
UTIPS .... Upgraded Tactical Information Processing System [*Data processing*]
UTIRS .... United Tiberias Institutions Relief Society [*New York, NY*] (EA)
UTJ .... Uterotubal Junction [*Medicine*]
UTK .... Utirik [*Marshall Islands*] [*Airport symbol*] (OAG)
UTL .... Unit Transmission Loss
UTL .... UNITIL Corp. [*American Stock Exchange symbol*]
UTL .... Universal Transporter Loader (MCD)
UTL .... University of Toledo, College of Law, Toledo, OH [*OCLC symbol*] (OCLC)
UTL .... University of Toronto Library [*UTLAS symbol*]
UTL .... Up Telecommunications Switch
UTL .... User Trailer Label (CMD)
UTLAS .... UTLAS International Canada [*Formerly, University of Toronto Library Automation System*] [*Library network*]
UTLC .... University of Tennessee College of Law (DLA)
UTLC .... UTL Corporation [*NASDAQ symbol*] (NQ)
UTLD .... Utah Test of Language Development [*Education*]
UTLJ .... University of Toronto. Law Journal [*A publication*]
UTLM .... Up Telemetry (MCD)
UT LR .... Utah Law Review [*A publication*]
UTLY .... Utility (BUR)
UTM .... Union des Travailleurs de Mauritanie [*Union of Workers of Mauritania*]
UTM .... Union des Travailleurs de Mayotte [*Comoran*] (PD)
UTM .... Universal Test Message
UTM .... Universal Testing Machine
UTM .... Universal Transverse Mercator [*Cartography*]
UTMA .... Uniform Transfers to Minors Act [*National Conference of Commissioners on Uniform State Laws*]
UTMCI .... Union des Travailleurs de la Moyenne Cote d'Ivoire [*Union of Middle Ivory Coast Workers*]
UTMD .... Utah Medical Products [*NASDAQ symbol*] (NQ)
UTML .... Utility Motor Launch
UTN .... Upington [*South Africa*] [*Airport symbol*] (OAG)
UTN .... Utensil (MSA)
UTNOTREQ ... Utilization of Government Facilities Not Required as It Is Considered Such Utilization Would Adversely Affect Performance of Assigned Temporary Duty
UTNRS .... Underwater Terrain Navigation and Reconnaissance Simulator (MCD)
UTO .... Indian Mountain, AK [*Location identifier*] [*FAA*] (FAAL)
UTO .... United Telephone Organizations
UTO .... United Towns Organisation [*See also FMVJ*] (EA-IO)
UTO .... Utopia Creek [*Alaska*] [*Airport symbol*] (OAG)
UTOA .... United Truck Owners of America (EA)
UTOC .... United Technologies Online Catalog [*United Technologies Corp.*] [*East Hartford, CT*] [*Information service*] (EISS)
UTOCO ...... Utah Oil Company
UTOG .... Unitog Co. [*NASDAQ symbol*] (NQ)
UTOL .... Universal Translator Oriented Language
UTOLCL ..... University of Toledo College of Law (DLA)

U Toledo Intra LR ... University of Toledo. Intramural Law Review (DLA)
U Toledo L Rev ... University of Toledo. Law Review [*A publication*]
U Tol Law ... University of Toledo. Law Review [*A publication*]
U Tol L Rev ... University of Toledo. Law Review [*A publication*]
Utopian E ... Utopian Eyes [*A publication*]
U Tor Law J ... University of Toronto. Law Journal [*A publication*]
U Tor L Rev ... University of Toronto. School of Law. Review (DLA)
U Toronto Fac L Rev ... University of Toronto. Faculty Law Review [*A publication*]
U Toronto Faculty L Rev ... University of Toronto. Faculty of Law. Review [*A publication*]
U Toronto L J ... University of Toronto. Law Journal [*A publication*]
U Toronto Q ... University of Toronto. Quarterly [*A publication*]
UTP .... Unified Test Plan
UTP .... Unit Territory Plan
UTP .... Unit Test Plan
UTP .... United Teaching Profession (MCD)
UTP .... Universal Tape Processor
UTP .... Universal Test Point (CAAL)
UTP .... Unlisted Trading Privileges
UTP .... Upper Trip Point
UTP .... Upper Turning Point
UTP .... Uridine Triphosphatase [*An enzyme*]
UTP .... Uridine Triphosphate [*Biochemistry*]
UTP .... User Test Program [*Army*]
UTP .... Utah Power & Light Co. [*NYSE symbol*]
UTP .... Utapao [*Thailand*] [*Airport symbol*] [*Obsolete*] (OAG)
UTP .... Utility Tape Processor
UTPA .... Uniform Trustees' Powers Act [*National Conference of Commissioners on Uniform State Laws*]
UTPase ..... Uridine Triphosphatase [*An enzyme*]
UTPL .... Urban Transportation Planning Laboratory [*University of Pennsylvania*] [*Research center*] (RCD)
UTPLF .... Universita di Torino. Pubblicazioni della Facolta di Lettere e Filosofia [*A publication*]
UTPS .... UMTA [*Urban Mass Transit Administration*] Transportation Planning System
UTQ .... Hinesville, GA [*Location identifier*] [*FAA*] (FAAL)
UTQ .... University of Toronto. Quarterly [*A publication*]
UTQA .... Uutuqtwa. Bristol Bay High School [*A publication*]
UTQG .... Uniform Tire Quality Grade
UTR .... Underwater Tracking Range
UTR .... Union Transportation [*AAR code*]
UTR .... Unitrode Corp. [*NYSE symbol*]
UT R .... University of Tampa. Review [*A publication*]
UTR .... University of Toronto, Thomas Fisher Rare Book Library [*UTLAS symbol*]
UTR .... University Training Reactor
UTR .... Unprogramed Transfer Register
UTR .... Up Time Ratio
UTR .... Urticarial Transfusion Reaction [*Medicine*]
UTRA .... Upper Torso Restraint Assembly
UTRAO .... Radio Astronomy Observatory [*University of Texas at Austin*] [*Research center*] (RCD)
Utredn Norsk Tretekn Inst ... Utredning. Norsk Treteknisk Institutt [*A publication*]
UTREP .... University of Tennessee Rehabilitation Engineering Program
UTRF .... Update Training File [*IRS*]
UTRK .... US Truck Lines [*NASDAQ symbol*] (NQ)
Utr Micropaleontol Bull ... Utrecht Micropaleontological Bulletins [*A publication*]
Utr Micropaleontol Bull Spec Publ ... Utrecht Micropaleontological Bulletins. Special Publication [*A publication*]
UTROAA .... Units to Round Out the Active Army
UTRON .... Utility Squadron [*Navy*]
UTRONFWDAREA ... Utility Squadron, Forward Area [*Navy*]
UTRP .... Underwater Tactical Range, Pacific
UTRR .... University of Teheran Research Reactor
UTRTD .... Untreated
UTS .... Huntsville, TX [*Location identifier*] [*FAA*] (FAAL)
UTS .... Ullrich-Turner Syndrome [*Genetics*]
UTS .... Ultimate Tensile Strength [*or Stress*]
UTS .... Umbilical Test Set
UTS .... Underwater Telephone System
UTS .... Unified Transfer System [*Computer to translate Russian to English*]
UTS .... Union Theological Seminary
UTS .... Union des Travailleurs du Senegal [*Senegalese Workers Union*]
UTS .... Unit Training Standard
UTS .... Unit Trouble Shooting
UTS .... United Theological Seminary, Dayton, OH [*OCLC symbol*] (OCLC)
UTS .... Universal Terminal System [*Sperry UNIVAC*] [*Data processing*]
UTS .... Universal Test Station
UTS .... Universal Thrust Stand
UTS .... Universal Time Sharing [*Data processing*] (IEEE)
UTS .... Universal Time Standards (NG)
UTS .... University Tutorial Series [*A publication*]
UTS .... Unmanned Teleoperator Spacecraft (MCD)
UTS .... Update Transaction System (TEL)

UTS .... Urine-Transfer System [Apollo] [NASA]
UTS .... Utsunomiya [Japan] [Seismograph station code, US Geological Survey] (SEIS)
UTSCB .... Utah Science [A publication]
U of T School of LR ... School of Law. Review. Toronto University [Canada] (DLA)
UTSE .... United Transport Service Employees [Later, BRAC] (EA)
UTSE .... University of Texas. Studies in English [A publication]
UTS-FO ...... Union Territoriale des Syndicats - Force Ouvrieres [Territorial Federation of Trade Unions - Workers' Force] [French Somaliland]
UTSH .... University of Tennessee. Studies in the Humanities [A publication]
UTSI .... University of Tennessee Space Institute
UTSL .... University of Texas School of Law (DLA)
UTSMS ...... University of Texas Southwestern Medical School
UT SUP ...... Ut Supra [As Above] [Latin]
UT SUPR .... Ut Supra [As Above] [Latin]
UTSV .... Union Theological Seminary in Virginia
UTT .... Umtata [South Africa] [Airport symbol] (OAG)
UTT .... Utility Tactical Transport (MCD)
UTT .... Uttering [FBI standardized term]
UTTA .... United Thoroughbred Trainers of America (EA)
UTTAS .... Utility Tactical Transport Aircraft System [Helicopter] [Military]
UTTBA .... Bulletin. International Union Against Tuberculosis [A publication]
UTTC .... Universal Tape-to-Tape Converter
UTTR .... Utah Test and Training Range [Air Force]
UTTS .... Union Territoriale du Senegal des Travailleurs [Senegalese Workers Union]
UTTS .... Universal Target Tracking Station (MCD)
UTU .... Ultrasonic Test Unit
UTU .... Underway Training Unit
UTU .... United Transportation Union
UTU .... Ustupo [Panama] [Airport symbol] (OAG)
utu .... Utah [MARC country of publication code] [Library of Congress] (LCCP)
UTUC .... Uganda Trades' Union Congress
UTUC .... United Trades Union Congress [India]
UTV .... Uncompensated Temperature Variation (TEL)
UTV .... Underwater Television
UTV .... Universal Test Vehicle [Military]
UTVI .... United Television, Incorporated [NASDAQ symbol] (NQ)
UTVS .... Ucebni Texty Vysokych Skol [A publication]
UTW .... Under the Wing [Aircraft]
UTW .... United Telegraph Workers (EA)
UTW .... Utilitiesman, Water and Sanitation [Navy rating]
UTWA .... United Textile Workers of America (EA)
UTWG .... Utility Wing [Navy] (MUGU)
UTWING ..... Utility Wing [Navy]
UTWINGSERVLANT ... Utility Wing, Service Force, Atlantic [Navy]
UTWINGSERVPAC ... Utility Wing, Service Force, Pacific [Navy]
UTX .... Jupiter, FL [Location identifier] [FAA] (FAAL)
UTX .... United Technologies Corp. [NYSE symbol]
UTY .... Utility Air, Inc. [Moberly, MO] [FAA designator] (FAAC)
UU .... Reunion Air Service [France] [ICAO designator] (FAAC)
UU .... Uglies Unlimited [An association] [Tulsa, OK] (EA)
UU .... Ulster Unionist Party
UU .... Ultimate User
UU .... Unicorns Unanimous [An association] (EA)
UU .... Union University [Tennessee]
UU .... University of Utah, Salt Lake City, UT [Library symbol] [Library of Congress] (LCLS)
UU .... Urine Urobilinogen [Clinical chemistry]
UU .... User Unit (MCD)
UUA .... Southern Utah State College, Cedar City, UT [OCLC symbol] (OCLC)
UUA .... Unitarian Universalist Association
UUA .... UNIVAC Users Association [Later, AUUA]
UUA .... Uppsala Universitets Arsskrift [A publication]
UUARC .... United Ukrainian American Relief Committee (EA)
UUA/WO .... Unitarian Universalist Association of Churches - Washington Office [Washington, DC] (EA)
UUA/WOSC ... Unitarian Universalist Association - Washington Office for Social Concern [Later, UUA/WO] (EA)
UUB .... Brigham Young University, School of Library and Information Science, Provo, UT [OCLC symbol] (OCLC)
UUBCWG ... Unitarian Universalist Black Concerns Working Group [Boston, MA] (EA)
UUC .... Salt Lake County Library System, Salt Lake City, UT [OCLC symbol] (OCLC)
UUC .... United University Club [British]
UUCA .... United Underwear Contractors Association [Defunct] (EA)
UUCF .... Unitarian Universalist Christian Fellowship (EA)
UUD .... Logan Public Library, Logan, UT [OCLC symbol] (OCLC)
UUE .... University of Utah, Eccles Health Science Library, Salt Lake City, UT [OCLC symbol] (OCLC)
UUE .... Use until Exhausted
UUEW .... United Unions for Employees and Workers [Lebanon]
UUFSJ .... Unitarian Universalist Fellowship for Social Justice (EA)
UUGS .... Unitarian and Universalist Genealogical Society (EA)

UUHS .... Unitarian Universalist Historical Society (EA)
UUIP .... Uppsala University Institute of Physics [Sweden]
UUK .... Kuparuk, AK [Location identifier] [FAA] (FAAL)
UU-L .... University of Utah, Law Library, Salt Lake City, UT [Library symbol] [Library of Congress] (LCLS)
UULGC .... Unitarian Universalist Lesbian Gay Caucus [Boston, MA] (EA)
UUM .... Underwater-to-Underwater Missile [Air Force]
UU-M .... University of Utah, Library of Medical Sciences, Salt Lake City, UT [Library symbol] [Library of Congress] (LCLS)
UUM .... University of Utah, Salt Lake City, UT [OCLC symbol] (OCLC)
UUMA .... Unitarian Universalist Ministers Association (EA)
UUMN .... Unitarian-Universalist Musicians' Network (EA)
UUMPS ...... Unitarian Universalist Ministers' Partners Society (EA)
UUN .... Urinary Urea Nitrogen [Clinical medicine]
UUO .... Weber State College, Ogden, UT [OCLC symbol] (OCLC)
UUP .... Salt Lake City Public Library, Salt Lake City, UT [OCLC symbol] (OCLC)
UUR .... Under Usual Reserves
UURWAW... United Union of Roofers, Waterproofers, and Allied Workers [Formerly, RDWW] (EA)
UUS .... Utah State University, Logan, UT [OCLC symbol] (OCLC)
UUSAE .... Unitarian Universalist Society for Alcohol Education [Boston, MA] (EA)
UUSC .... Unitarian Universalist Service Committee (EA)
UUSS .... University of Utah Seismograph Stations [Research center] (RCD)
UUT .... Unit under Test
UUU .... Manumu [Papua New Guinea] [Airport symbol] (OAG)
UUUC .... United Ulster Unionist Coalition
UUUP .... United Ulster Unionist Party [Northern Ireland] (PPW)
UUW .... Westminster College, Salt Lake City, UT [OCLC symbol] (OCLC)
UUWF .... Unitarian Universalist Women's Federation (EA)
UUZ .... Utah State Library, Processing Center, Salt Lake City, UT [OCLC symbol] (OCLC)
UV .... Ultraviolet [Electromagnetic spectrum range]
UV .... Ultravisible
UV .... Umbilical Vein [Medicine]
UV .... Under Voltage
UV .... Underwater Vehicle
UV .... Universal Aviation, Inc. [ICAO designator] (FAAC)
uv .... Upper Volta [MARC country of publication code] [Library of Congress] (LCCP)
UV .... Urinary Volume [Physiology]
UV .... Uterine Vein [Anatomy]
UV .... Uterine Volume
UV .... Utility Value [Psychology]
UVA .... Ultraviolet Light, Long Wave
UVA .... Uvalde Aero Service [Uvalde, TX] [FAA designator] (FAAC)
UVA .... Uvalde, TX [Location identifier] [FAA] (FAAL)
UVAL .... Ultraviolet Argon LASER
UVAN .... Ukrainian Academy of Arts and Sciences of Canada
UVAR .... University of Virginia Reactor
UVAS .... Unmanned Vehicle for Aerial Surveillance (MCD)
UVASER.... Ultraviolet Amplification by Stimulated Emission of Radiation
UV-B.......... Ultraviolet Band
UVBF .... Umbilical Vein Blood Flow
UVBK .... United Virginia Bankshares, Inc. [NASDAQ symbol] (NQ)
UVC........... Pennsylvania State University, Capitol Campus, Middletown, PA [OCLC symbol] (OCLC)
UVC........... Ultrahigh Vacuum Chamber
UVC........... Ultraviolet Communications System
UVC........... Uniform Vehicle Code
UVC........... Union Valley Corporation [American Stock Exchange symbol]
UVCA .... Uniform Vehicle Code Annotated
UVCB .... Unknown or Variable Composition, Complex Reaction Products, and Biological Materials [Chemical Abstracts Services]
UVD........... Ultrasonic Vapor Degresser
UVD........... Ultraviolet Detector
UVD........... Undervoltage Device
UVD........... Unintegrated Viral DNA [Deoxyribonucleic Acid] [Pathology]
UVDC .... Urban Vehicle Design Competition
UVE .... Ouvea [Loyalty Islands] [Airport symbol] (OAG)
UV-EPROMS ... Ultraviolet-Erasable Programable Read-Only Memories [Data processing]
UVF .... St. Lucia [West Indies] Hewanorra Airport [Airport symbol] (OAG)
UVF .... Ulster Volunteer Force
UVF .... Ultraviolet Filter
UVF .... Ultraviolet Floodlight (AAG)
UVF .... Unmanned Vertical Flight [NASA] (NASA)
UVFLT .... Ultraviolet Floodlight
UVGS .... Church of Jesus Christ of Latter-Day Saints, Genealogical Society Library, Uintah Basin Branch, Vernal, UT [Library symbol] [Library of Congress] (LCLS)
UVH........... Univentricular Heart [Cardiology]
UVI .... Ultraviolet Irradiation
UVI .... Uvira [Zaire] [Seismograph station code, US Geological Survey] [Closed] (SEIS)
UVIC.......... University of Victoria [British Columbia]

UVIL	Ultraviolet Inspection Light
UVIL	Ultraviolet Ion LASER
UVIRSG	Ultraviolet Infrared Scene Generator
UVL	New Valley [*Egypt*] [*Airport symbol*] (OAG)
UVL	Ultraviolet Lamp
UVL	Ultraviolet LASER
UVL	Ultraviolet Light
UVL	Untersuchungen zur Vergleichenden Literatur [*Hamburg*] [*A publication*]
UVLI	Ustav Vedeckych Lekarskych Informaci [*Institute for Medical Information*] [*Czechoslovakia*] [*Database operator*] [*Information service*] (EISS)
UVLS	Ultraviolet Light Stabilizer
UVM	Ultraviolet Meter
UVM	Universitas Viridis Montis [*University of the Green Mountains; i.e., University of Vermont*]
UVM	University of Virginia. Magazine [*A publication*]
UVMag	University of Virginia. Magazine [*A publication*]
UVMC	United Voluntary Motor Corps (EA)
UVN	Unionville [*Nevada*] [*Seismograph station code, US Geological Survey*] [*Closed*] (SEIS)
UVNO	Ultraviolet Nitric-Oxide Experiment
UVO	Uvol [*Papua New Guinea*] [*Airport symbol*] (OAG)
UVOL	Universal Voltronics [*NASDAQ symbol*] (NQ)
UVP	Ultra-Violet Products, Inc. [*San Gabriel, CA*] [*Hardware manufacturer*]
UVP	Ultrahigh Vacuum Pump
UVP	Ultraviolet Photometry
UVP	Unified Vocational Preparation [*Manpower Services Commission*] [*British*]
UVPJU	Uganda Vernacular, Primary and Junior Secondary Teachers' Union
UVPROM	Ultraviolet Programable Read Only Memory
UVPS	Ultrahigh Vacuum Pumping Station
UVR	Ultraviolet Radiation
UVR	Ultraviolet Radiometer (MCD)
UVR	Ultraviolet Receiver
UVR	Ultraviolet Rocket
UVR	Under Voltage Relay
UVR	University of Virginia Reactor
UVR	User Visible Resources
UVS	Ultraviolet Spectrometer
UVS	Under Voltage Sensing (MCD)
UVS	United Voluntary Services (EA)
UVS	Unmanned Vehicle System
UVSC	Ultraviolet Solar Constant
UVSC	Uranium Ventilation Scrubber Cell [*Nuclear energy*] (NRCH)
UVSP	Ultraviolet Spectral Photometer
UV Spectrom Group Bull	UV Spectrometry Group. Bulletin [*A publication*]
UVT	Ultraviolet Transmission
UVT	Ultraviolet Tube
UVT	Universal Voltage Tester
UVT	Usable Vector Table
UVTEI	Ustredi Vedeckych, Technickych, a Ekonomickych Informaci [*Central Office of Scientific, Technical, and Economic Information*] [*Prague, Czechoslovakia*] [*Information service*] (EISS)
UVV	Universal Leaf Tobacco Co., Inc. [*NYSE symbol*]
UVV	Upward Vertical Velocity [*Meteorology*] (FAAC)
UV-VIS	Ultraviolet/Visible [*Spectroscopy*]
UVVO	United Vietnam Veterans Organization (EA)
UVX	Univar Corp. [*Formerly, VWR United Corp.*] [*NYSE symbol*]
UW	Service des Transports Publics Aeriens [*Portugal*] [*ICAO designator*] (FAAC)
UW	Ultimate Weapon (AAG)
UW	Ultrasonic Wave
UW	Unconventional Warfare [*Army*]
U/W	Under Will (DLA)
UW	Underwater
UW	Underwater Weapons [*British*]
U/W	Underway (NVT)
U/W	Underwriter
UW	United Way (OICC)
UW	United Weldors International Union
UW	University of Washington [*State*]
U of W	University of Washington [*State*]
U of W	University of Windsor [*Ontario*]
UW	University of Wisconsin (MCD)
UW	Untere Winkelgruppe [*Angles up to 45°*] [*German military - World War II*]
UW	Uppity Women [*An association*] (EA)
UW	Upset Welding
UW	Us Wurk [*A publication*]
UW	Usable Width (MCD)
U/W	Used With
UW	Utility Water (AAG)
UWA	Ukrainian Workingmen's Association [*Later, UFA*] (EA)
UWA	United Way of America [*Alexandria, VA*] (EA)
UWA	United Weighers Association [*New York, NY*] (EA)
UWA	United Women of the Americas (EA)
UWA	User Working Area

UWA	Uwajima [*Japan*] [*Seismograph station code, US Geological Survey*] (SEIS)
UWA	Ware, MA [*Location identifier*] [*FAA*] (FAAL)
UWAGE	Union Women's Alliance to Gain Equality (EA)
UWAL	Underwater Wide-Angle Lens
UWAL	University of Washington Aeronautical Laboratory (MCD)
UWALR	University of Western Australia. Law Review [*A publication*]
UWAL Rev	University of Western Australia. Law Review [*A publication*]
UWARC	United Whiteruthenian [*Byelorussian*] American Relief Committee (EA)
U Wash L Rev	University of Washington. Law Review (DLA)
UWASIS	United Way of America Services Identification System
UWAT	User Written Application Test [*Data processing*]
UWATU	Underway Training Unit
UW Austl L Rev	University of Western Australia. Law Review [*A publication*]
UWAVM	Underwater Antivehicle Mine (MCD)
UWBBR	University of Wisconsin - Madison Bureau of Business Research [*Research center*] (RCD)
UWBS	Uniform Work Breakdown Structure
UWC	Ulster Workers' Council
UWC	Underwater Communications [*Navy*] (CAAL)
UWC	Universal Water Charts [*Air Force*]
UWC	Universal Winding Company (MCD)
UWC	Widener College, Chester, PA [*OCLC symbol*] (OCLC)
UWCCPGR	University of Washington. Contributions. Cloud Physics Group. Collections from Reprints [*A publication*]
UWCETG	University of Washington. Contributions. Energy Transfer Group. Collections from Reprints [*A publication*]
UWCS	Underwater Weapons Control System
UWCSS	Universal Weapon Control Stabilization System
UWD	UWD [*Umweltschutz-Dienst*] Informationsdienst fuer Umweltfragen [*A publication*]
UWDD	Undersea Warfare Development Division [*Navy*] (MCD)
UWE	University Women of Europe (EA)
UWE	Uwekahuna [*Hawaii*] [*Seismograph station code, US Geological Survey*] (SEIS)
UWEN	United Western Energy [*NASDAQ symbol*] (NQ)
U West Aust Ann L Rev	University of Western Australia. Annual Law Review [*A publication*]
U of West Aust L Rev	University of Western Australia. Law Review [*A publication*]
U Western Aust Ann L Rev	University of Western Australia. Annual Law Review [*A publication*]
U Western Aust L Rev	University of Western Australia. Law Review [*A publication*]
U Western Ont L Rev	University of Western Ontario. Law Review [*A publication*]
U West LA L Rev	University of West Los Angeles. Law Review [*A publication*]
U West Los Angeles L Rev	University of West Los Angeles. Law Review [*A publication*]
UWF	United World Federalists [*Later, World Federalists Association*] (EA)
UWF	University of West Florida [*Pensacola*]
UWFC	Underwater Fire Control [*Navy*] (CAAL)
UWFCS	Underwater Fire Control System
UWFPC	Union Wallisienne et Futunienne pour la Caledonie [*Wallisian and Futunian Union for Caledonia*] (PPW)
UWG	Gesetz Gegen den Unlauteren Wettbewerb [*German Law Against Unfair Competition*] (DLA)
UWGB	University of Wisconsin at Green Bay
UWH	Underwater Habitat
UW-HF	Upset Welding-High Frequency
UWI	Dalton, GA [*Location identifier*] [*FAA*] (FAAL)
UWI	United Way International [*Alexandria, VA*] (EA)
UWI	United Westburne Industries Ltd. [*Toronto Stock Exchange symbol*]
UWI	University of the West Indies [*Jamaica*]
UW-I	Upset Welding-Induction
UWINDS	Upper Winds (FAAC)
U Windsor L Rev	University of Windsor. Law Review (DLA)
UWL	New Castle, IN [*Location identifier*] [*FAA*] (FAAL)
UWL	Underwater Launch
UWL	University of Winnipeg Library [*UTLAS symbol*]
UWL	Utowana Lake [*New York*] [*Seismograph station code, US Geological Survey*] (SEIS)
UWLA L Rev	University of West Los Angeles. Law Review [*A publication*]
UWLA Rev	University of West Los Angeles. School of Law. Law Review (DLA)
UWM	Uniform Wave Motion
UWM	United World Mission
UWM	University of Wisconsin at Milwaukee
UWM	University of Wisconsin at Milwaukee [*Wisconsin*] [*Seismograph station code, US Geological Survey*] (SEIS)
UWMAK	University of Wisconsin TOKAMAK
UWNE	Brotherhood of Utility Workers of New England (EA)
UWNR	University of Wisconsin - Madison Nuclear Reactor Laboratory [*Research center*] (RCD)
UWO	University of Western Ontario (MCD)

UWO .... University of Western Ontario Library [*UTLAS symbol*]
UWO .... University of Western Ontario, School of Library and Information Science, London, ON, Canada [*OCLC symbol*] (OCLC)
UWOA .... Unclassified without Attachment
UWOA .... Unconventional Warfare Operations Area [*Army*] (AABC)
UWOL Rev ... University of Western Ontario. Law Review [*A publication*]
UW Ont L Rev ... University of Western Ontario. Law Review [*A publication*]
UWOPGS .. University of Warwick. Occasional Papers in German Studies [*A publication*]
UWO (Univ West Ont) Med J ... UWO (University of Western Ontario) Medical Journal [*A publication*]
UWP .... United Workers' Party [*St. Lucian*] (PPW)
UWP .... United Workers' Party [*Hungary*] (PPW)
UWP .... Up with People (EA)
UWPC .... United World Press Cooperative [*Later, The Peoples Media Cooperative*] (EA)
UWPLL .... University of Washington. Publications in Language and Literature [*A publication*]
UWR .... Underwater Range (MUGU)
UWR .... United Water Resources, Inc. [*NYSE symbol*]
UWR .... University of Windsor. Review [*A publication*]
UWRC .... Urban Wildlife Research Center (EA)
UWRR .... University of Wyoming Research Reactor
U/Wrs .... Underwriters (DLA)
UWS .... Undersea Weapon System
UWS .... Unmanned Weather Station
UWSAMBS ... United Women's Societies of the Adoration of the Most Blessed Sacrament (EA)
UWSDDMS ... Underwater Weapons System Design Disclosure Management Systems (KSC)
UWSRD ...... Underwater Weapons Systems Reliability Data (KSC)
UWST .... United Western Corp. [*NASDAQ symbol*] (NQ)
UWT .... Underwater Telephone
UWT .... Uniform Wave Train
UWT .... Unit Weight (MSA)
UWTCA ...... Umschau in Wissenschaft und Technik [*A publication*]
UWTM .... Underwater Team (MSA)
UWTR .... Underwater (AABC)
UWTR .... University of Washington Training Reactor
UWU .... Los Angeles, CA [*Location identifier*] [*FAA*] (FAAL)
UWU .... Utility Workers Union of America
UWUA .... Utility Workers Union of America (EA)
UWW .... University without Walls [*Twenty-one-university consortium*]
UWWR .... Unpublished Scholarly Writings on World Religions (BJA)
UX .... Lotus Airways [*Egypt*] [*ICAO designator*] (FAAC)
UXAA .... Unexploded Antiaircraft [*Shell*]
UXAPB .... Unexploded Antipersonnel Bomb
UXB .... Unexploded Bomb
UXGB .... Unexploded Gas Bomb
UXIB .... Unexploded Incendiary Bomb
UXM .... Universal Extension Mechanism (KSC)
UXO .... Unexploded Ordnance
UXOI .... Unexploded Ordnance Incident
UXP .... Union Exploration Partners Ltd. [*NYSE symbol*]
UXPM .... Unexploded Parachuted Mine
UXTGM ...... Unexploded Type G Mine
UXW .... South Bend, IN [*Location identifier*] [*FAA*] (FAAL)
UY .... Cameroon Airlines [*ICAO designator*] (FAAC)
UY .... Unit Years [*Electronics*] (IEEE)
UY .... Universal Youth
uy .... Uruguay [*MARC country of publication code*] [*Library of Congress*] (LCCP)
UY .... Uruguay [*Two-letter standard code*] (CNC)
UYA .... University Year for ACTION [*Refers to federal program, ACTION, which is not an acronym*]
UYF .... London, OH [*Location identifier*] [*FAA*] (FAAL)
UYL .... Nyala [*Sudan*] [*Airport symbol*] (OAG)
UYLNA .... Ukrainian Youth League of North America [*Defunct*] (EA)
UYN .... Yulin [*China*] [*Airport symbol*] (OAG)
UZ .... Uhrzuender [*Clockwork fuze*] [*German military - World War II*]
UZ .... United Aviation Services SA [*Great Britain*] [*ICAO designator*] (FAAC)
UZ .... Upper Zone [*Geology*]
UZ .... Ustredna Zidov [*Slovakia*] [*A publication*]
U Zambia LB ... University of Zambia. Law Bulletin (DLA)
UZAstPI....... Ucenye Zapiski Astrachanskogo Gosudarstvennogo Pedagogiceskogo Instituta [*A publication*]
UZAzPI....... Ucenye Zapiski Pedagogiceskogo Instituta Jazykov Imeni M. F. Achundova. Serija Filologiceskaja [*A publication*]
UZAzU....... Ucenye Zapiski Azerbaidzhanskii Gosudarstvennyi Universitet [*Baku*] [*A publication*]
UZAzU........ Ucenye Zapiski Azerbajdzanskogo Gosudarstvennogo Universiteta Imeni S. M. Kirova. Jazyk i Literatura [*A publication*]
uzb .... Uzbek [*MARC language code*] [*Library of Congress*] (LCCP)
UZBasU....... Ucenye Zapiski Baskirskogo Gosudarstvennogo Universiteta. Serija Filologiceskich Nauk [*A publication*]
Uzb Biol Zh ... Uzbekskii Biologiceskii Zhurnal [*A publication*]
Uzbek Biol Zh ... Uzbekskii Biologiceskii Zhurnal [*A publication*]
Uzbek Geol Zh ... Uzbekskiy Geologiceskiy Zhurnal [*A publication*]

Uzbek Iztim Fanlar ... Uzbekiztonda Iztimoii Fanlar [*A publication*]
Uzbek Khim Zh ... Uzbekskii Khimicheskii Zhurnal [*A publication*]
Uzb Khim Zh ... Uzbekskii Khimicheskii Zhurnal [*A publication*]
UZBurPI ..... Ucenye Zapiski Burjatskogo Gosudarstvennogo Pedagogiceskogo Instituta Imeni Dorzi Banzarova. Istoriko-Filologiceskaja Serija. Ulan-Ude [*A publication*]
UZBZA .... Uzbekskii Biologiceskii Zhurnal [*A publication*]
UZCerepPI ... Ucenye Zapiski Cerepoveckogo Gosudarstvennogo Pedagogiceskogo Instituta [*A publication*]
UZChabPI ... Ucenye Zapiski Chabarovskogo Gosudarstvennogo Pedagogiceskogo Instituta [*A publication*]
UZChakNII ... Ucenye Zapiski Chakasskogo Naucno-Issledovatel'skogo Instituta Jazyka, Literatury, i Istorii [*A publication*]
UZCharU.... Ucenye Zapiski Charkovskogo Universiteta Imeni A. M. Gorkogo. Trudy Filologiceskogo Fakult'teta [*A publication*]
UZCIngPI ... Ucenye Zapiski Ceceno-Ingusskogo Pedagogiceskogo Instituta. Serija Filolo Giceskaja [*A publication*]
UZCuvNII ... Ucenye Zapiski Naucno-Issledovatel'skogo Instituta Jazyka, Literatury, Istorii, i Ekonomiki Pri Sovete Ministrov Cuvasskoj ASSR [*A publication*]
UZDag....... Ucenye Zapiski Dagestanskogo Filiala Akademii Nauk SSSR. Serija Filologiceskaja [*A publication*]
UZDagU ..... Ucenye Zapiski Dagestanskogo Gosudarstvennogo Universiteta. Serija Filologiceskaja [*A publication*]
UZDalU ...... Ucenye Zapiski Dal'nevostocnogo Universiteta. Serija Filologiceskaja [*A publication*]
UZDusPI ...... Ucenye Zapiski Dusanbinskogo Gosudarstvennogo Pedagogiceskogo Instituta Imeni T. G. Seveenko Filologiceskaja Serija [*A publication*]
UZEIPI........ Ucenye Zapiski Elabuzskogo Gosudarstvennogo Pedagogiceskogo Instituta. Serija Istorii i Filologii [*A publication*]
UZEnPI....... Ucenye Zapiski Enisejskogo Gosudarstvennogo Pedagogiceskogo Instituta. Kafedra Russkogo Jazyka [*A publication*]
UZErevU .... Ucenye Zapiski Erevanskogo Gosudarstvennogo Universiteta. Serija Filologiceskich Nauk [*A publication*]
UZGIYa ...... Ucenye Zapiski Gor'kovskii Pedagogiceskii Institut Inostrannykh Yazykov [*Gor'kii*] [*A publication*]
UZGorPI..... Ucenye Zapiski Gor'kovskogo Gosudarstvennogo Pedagogiceskogo Instituta Imeni M. Gor'kogo. Serija Filologiceskaja [*A publication*]
UZGorPIIJa ... Ucenye Zapiski Gor'kovskogo Pedagogiceskogo Instituta Inostrannych Jazykov [*A publication*]
UZGorU...... Ucenye Zapiski Gor'kovskogo Universiteta Imeni N. I. Lobacevskogo. Serija Istoriko-Filologiceskaja [*A publication*]
UZGPI........ Ucenye Zapiski Gor'kovskii Gosudarstvennyi Pedagogiceskii Institut [*Gor'kii*] [*A publication*]
UZGurPI..... Ucenye Zapiski Gur'evskogo Gosudarstvennogo Pedagogiceskogo Instituta. Serija Istoriko-Filologiceskaja [*A publication*]
UZGZA .... Uzbekskii Geologiceskii Zhurnal [*A publication*]
UZH .... Uzhgorod [*Unuar*] [*USSR*] [*Seismograph station code, US Geological Survey*] (SEIS)
UZII .... Ucenye Zapiski Instituta Istorii [*A publication*]
UZIMach .... Ucenye Zapiski Instituta Istorii, Jazyka, i Literatury Imeni G. Cadasy. Serija Filologiceskaja. Machackala [*A publication*]
UZIMO........ Ucenye Zapiski Institut Mezdunarodnych Otnosenij [*A publication*]
UZIPI .... Ucenye Zapiski Irkutskii Pedagogiceskii Institut [*Irkutsk*] [*A publication*]
UZIrkutPI ... Ucenye Zapiski Irkutskogo Gosudarstvennogo Pedagogiceskogo Instituta Inostrannych Jazykov [*A publication*]
UZISL .... Ucenye Zapiski Instituta Slavjanovedenija [*A publication*]
UZIV .... Ucenye Zapiski Instituta Vostokovedenija. Akademija Nauk SSSR [*A publication*]
UZIVAz....... Ucenye Zapiski Instituta Vostokovedenija. Akademii Nauk Azerbajdzanskoj SSSR [*A publication*]
UZK .... Indianapolis, IN [*Location identifier*] [*FAA*] (FAAL)
UZKa .... Ucenye Zapiski Kalininskii Gosudarstvennyi Pedagogiceskii Institut [*Kalinin*] [*A publication*]
UZKalinPI... Ucenye Zapiski Kalininskogo Pedagogiceskogo Instituta Imeni M. I. Kalinina. Serija Filologiceskaja [*A publication*]
UZKAIPI ..... Ucenye Zapiski Kaluzskogo Gosudarstvennogo Pedagogiceskogo Instituta [*A publication*]
UZKaragPI ... Ucenye Zapiski Karagandinskogo Pedagogiceskogo Instituta. Filologiceskie Nauki [*A publication*]
UZKareIPI ... Ucenye Zapiski Karel'skogo Pedagogiceskogo Instituta [*A publication*]
UZKarPI ..... Ucenye Zapiski Karsinskogo Gosudarstvennogo Pedagogiceskogo Instituta. Filologiceskaja Serija [*A publication*]
UZKazanU ... Ucenye Zapiski Kazanskogo Universiteta Imeni V. I. Ul'janova'lenina [*A publication*]
UZKBI........ Ucenye Zapiski Kabardino-Balkarskij Naucno-Issledovatel'skij Institut pri Sovete Ministrov Kbassr [*A publication*]

UZKemPI ... Ucenye Zapiski Kemerovskogo Gosudarstvennogo Pedagogiceskogo Instituta [*A publication*]

UZKGPI ...... Ucenye Zapiski Kujbysevskogo Gosudarstvennogo Pedagogiceskogo Instituta Imeni V. V. Kujbyseva [*A publication*]

UZKi .... Ucenye Zapiski Kishinevskii Universitet [*Kishinev*] [*A publication*]

UZKirovPI ... Ucenye Zapiski Kirovabadskogo Pedagogiceskogo Instituta [*A publication*]

UZKisU .... Ucenye Zapiski Kisinevskogo Gosudarstvennogo Universiteta [*A publication*]

UZKokPI .... Ucenye Zapiski Kokandskogo Pedagogiceskogo Instituta Imeni Mukimi. Serija Filologiceskaja [*A publication*]

UZKolPI ..... Ucenye Zapiski Kolomenskogo Gosudarstvennogo Pedagogiceskogo Instituta Istoriko-Filologiceskij Fakul'tet. Kafedry Russkogo Jazyka [*A publication*]

UZKomPI ... Ucenye Zapiski Komi Gosudarstvennogo Pedagogiceskogo Instituta. Kafedra Russkogo Jazyka [*A publication*]

UZKr .... Ucenye Zapiski Krasnodarskii Pedagogicheskii Institut [*Krasnodar*] [*A publication*]

UZKujPI ..... Ucenye Zapiski Kujbysevskogo Gosudarstvennogo Pedagogiceskogo Instituta Imeni V. V. Kujbyseva [*A publication*]

UZKVA .... Uchenye Zapiski Kazanskogo Veterinarnogo Instituta [*A publication*]

UZKZA .... Uzbekskii Khimicheskii Zhurnal [*A publication*]

UZLa .... Ucenye Zapiski Latviiskii Gosudarstvennyi Universitet [*Riga*] [*A publication*]

UZLenPI ..... Ucenye Zapiski Leningradskogo Pedagogiceskogo Instituta Imeni S. M. Kirova [*A publication*]

UZLPedI ..... Ucenye Zapiski Leningradskogo Pedagogiceskogo Instituta Imeni A. I. Gercena [*A publication*]

UZLPI .... Ucenye Zapiski Leningradskogo Pedagogiceskogo Instituta Imeni A. I. Gercena [*A publication*]

UZLU .... Ucenye Zapiski Leningradskogo Gosudarstvennogo Ordena Lenina Universiteta Imeni A. A. Zdanova [*A publication*]

UZLU .... Ucenye Zapiski Leningradskogo Universiteta [*A publication*]

UZLU-FN .... Ucenye Zapiski Leningradskogo Universiteta. Serija Filologiceskikh Nauk [*A publication*]

UZL'vovU ... Ucenye Zapiski l'Vovskogo Gosudarstvennogo Universiteta [*A publication*]

UZMagPI ..... Ucenye Zapiski Magnitorskogo Gosudarstvennogo Pedagogiceskogo Instituta [*A publication*]

UZMIK .... Ucenye Zapiski Moskovskii Gosudarstvennyi Institut Kul'tury [*Moscow*] [*A publication*]

UZMKrup ... Ucenye Zapiski Moskovskogo Oblastnogo Pedagogiceskogo Instituta Imeni N. K. Krupskoj [*A publication*]

UZMOPI ..... Ucenye Zapiski Moskovskii Oblastnoi Pedagogicheskii Institut Imeni N. K. Krupskoi [*Moscow*] [*A publication*]

UZMorU ..... Ucenye Zapiski Mordovskogo Universiteta. Serija Filologiceskich Nauk [*A publication*]

UZMPedI .... Ucenye Zapiski Moskovskogo Gosudarstvennogo Pedagogiceskogo Instituta [*A publication*]

UZMPI .... Ucenye Zapiski Moskovskii Gosudarstvennyi Pedagogicheskii Institut Imeni Lenina [*Moscow*] [*A publication*]

UZMPI .... Ucenye Zapiski Moskovskogo Gosudarstvennogo Pedagogiceskogo Instituta Imeni Potemkina [*A publication*]

UZMPIIJa ... Ucenye Zapiski Moskovskogo Gosudarstvennogo Pedagogiceskogo Instituta Inostrannych Jazykov [*A publication*]

UZMPIIYa .... Ucenye Zapiski I-I Moskovskii Pedagogicheskii Institut Inostrannykh Yazykov [*Moscow*] [*A publication*]

UZMU .... Ucenye Zapiski Moskovskogo Universiteta [*A publication*]

UZNovPI ..... Ucenye Zapiski Novgorodskogo Gosudarstvennogo Pedagogicesko Instituta. Kafedra Russkogo Jazyka [*A publication*]

UZOrenPI ... Ucenye Zapiski Orenburgskogo Gosudarstvennogo Pedagogiceskogo Instituta Imeni V. P. Ckalova [*A publication*]

UZPe .... Ucenye Zapiski Penzenskii Pedagogicheskii Institut [*Penza*] [*A publication*]

UZPer .... Ucenye Zapiski Permskii Universitet [*Perm'*] [*A publication*]

UZPerm ...... Ucenye Zapiski Permskogo Gosudarstvennogo Universiteta Imeni A. M. Gor'kogo [*A publication*]

UZPs .... Ucenye Zapiski Pskovskii Pedagogicheskii Institut [*Pskov*] [*A publication*]

UZPU .... Ucenye Zapiski Petrozavodskogo Universiteta. Filologiceskie Nauk [*A publication*]

uzr .... Uzbek Soviet Socialist Republic [*MARC country of publication code*] [*Library of Congress*]   (LCCP)

UZRA .... United Zionist Revisionists of America [*Later, Herut - USA*]   (EA)

UZRjazPI .... Ucenye Zapiski Rjazanskogo Gosudarstvennogo Pedagogiceskogo Instituta [*A publication*]

UZRovPI ..... Ucenye Zapiski Rovenskogo Gosudarstvennogo Pedagogiceskogo Instituta. Filologiceskij Fakul'tet [*A publication*]

UZSachPI ... Ucenye Zapiski Sachtinskogo Gosudarstvennogo Pedagogiceskogo Instituta [*A publication*]

UZSarPedI ... Ucenye Zapiski Saratovskogo Gosudarstvennogo Pedagogiceskogo Instituta [*A publication*]

UZSGU .... Ucenye Zapiski Saratovskogo Gosudarstvennogo Universiteta [*A publication*]

UZSmolPI .. Ucenye Zapiski Smolenskogo Gosudarstvennogo Pedagogiceskogo Instituta [*A publication*]

UZSterPI .... Ucenye Zapiski Sterlitamakskogo Gosudarstvennogo Pedagogiceskogo Instituta. Serija Filologiceskaja [*A publication*]

UZTar .... Ucenye Zapiski Tartusskii Universitet [*Tartu*] [*A publication*]

UZTarU ...... Ucenye Zapiski Tartuskogo Gosudarstvennogo Universiteta [*A publication*]

UZTasPIIn ... Ucenye Zapiski Taskentskogo Pedagogiceskogo Instituta Inostrannych Jazykov [*A publication*]

UZTasPINiz ... Ucenye Zapiski Taskentskogo Pedagogiceskogo Instituta Imeni Nizami [*A publication*]

UZTFA .... Uchenye Zapiski Tul'skii Gosudarstvennyi Pedagogicheskii Institut. Fiziko-Tekhnicheskie Nauki [*A publication*]

UZTI .... Ucenye Zapiski Tikhookeanskogo Instituta [*A publication*]

UZTjPI .... Ucenye Zapiski Tjumenskogo Pedagogiceskogo Instituta. Kafedra Russkogo Jazyka [*A publication*]

UZTomU .... Ucenye Zapiski Tomskogo Universiteta Imeni V. V. Kujbyseva [*A publication*]

UZToU .... Ucenye Zapiski Tomskii Universitet [*Tomsk*] [*A publication*]

UZTPI .... Ucenye Zapiski Tomskii Gosudarstvennyj Pedagogiceskij Institut [*A publication*]

UZTuvNII .... Ucenye Zapiski Tuvinskogo Naucno-Issledovatel'skogo Instituta Jazyka, Literatury, i Istorii [*A publication*]

UZU .... Curuzu Cuatia [*Argentina*] [*Airport symbol*]   (OAG)

UZUIPI .... Ucenye Zapiski Ul'janovskogo Gosudarstvennogo Pedagogiceskogo Instituta Imeni I. N. Ul'janova [*A publication*]

UZUPI .... Ucenye Zapiski Ural'skogo Pedagogiceskogo i Ucitel'skogo Instituta Imeni Puskina [*A publication*]

UZUzPI .... Ucenye Zapiski Uzbekskogo Respublikanskogo Pedagogiceskogo Instituta. Kafedra Russkogo Jazyka i Literatury [*A publication*]

UZVinPI ...... Ucenye Zapiski Vinnickogo Gosudarstvennogo Pedagogiceskogo Instituta. Kafedra Russkogo Jazyka i Literatury [*A publication*]

UZVolPI ...... Ucenye Zapiski Vologodskogo Gosudarstvennogo Pedagogiceskogo Instituta [*A publication*]

UZW .... Und Zwar [*That Is*] [*German*]

V

V .... Abstracted Valuation Decisions (DLA)
V .... Deflection of the Vertical
V .... Electric Potential [*Symbol*] [*IUPAC*]
V .... Electromotive Force [*Symbol*] [*See also E, EMF*] [*Electrochemistry*] (DEN)
V .... Five [*Roman numeral*]
V .... Five Dollars [*Slang*]
V .... Five-Year Sentence [*Criminal slang*]
V .... Fixed-Wing Aircraft [*Navy symbol*]
V .... Frequency [*Spectroscopy*]
V .... Irving Bank Corp. [*NYSE symbol*]
V .... Potential Difference [*Symbol*]
V .... Potential Energy [*Symbol*] [*IUPAC*]
V .... Ranger-Parachutist [*Army skill qualification identifier*] (INF)
V .... [*A*] Safe [*Criminal slang*]
V .... Sanol Arzneimittel Dr. Schwarz [*Germany*] [*Research code symbol*]
V .... Shape Descriptor [*V-sign, for example. The shape resembles the letter for which it is named.*]
v .... Specific Volume [*Symbol*] [*IUPAC*]
V .... Staff Transport [*When V is the first of two letters in a military aircraft designation*]
V .... Unusual Visibility
V .... Vacated [*Same case vacated*] [*Used in Shepard's Citations*] (DLA)
V .... Vacuum (AAG)
V .... Vagabond
V .... Vale (ROG)
V .... Valencia [*A publication*]
V .... Valine [*One-letter symbol; see Val*]
V .... Valley (ROG)
V .... Value
V .... Valve
V .... Van
V .... Vanadium [*Chemical element*]
V .... Vancouver Stock Exchange
V .... Vapor
V .... Variable
V .... Variable Region [*Immunochemistry*]
V .... Variant [*Genetics*]
V .... Variation
V .... Variety [*A publication*]
V .... Variety Theatres and Shows [*Public-performance tariff class*] [*British*]
V .... Varnish (AAG)
V .... Varnish-Treated [*Insulation*] (MSA)
V .... Vatican City
V .... Vector [*Mathematics*]
V .... Veen, Publishers [*Holland*]
V .... Vehicles (MCD)
V .... Vein
V .... Vel [*Or*] [*Pharmacy*]
V .... Velocity
V .... Vendor (AAG)
V .... Venerable
V .... Venereology [*Medical Officer designation*] [*British*]
V .... Venous [*Medicine*]
V .... Venstre [*Liberal Party*] [*Norway*] (PPE)
V .... Venstre (Liberale Parti) [*Liberal Party*] [*Denmark*] (PPE)
V .... Vent
V .... Ventilator
V .... Ventral
V .... Ventur [*Quality of carburetor barrel*] [*Automotive engineering*]
V .... Venturi [*Automotive engineering*]
V .... Venue
V .... Verapamil [*A coronary vasodilator*]
V .... Verb
V .... Verbal
V .... Verbo [*A publication*]
V .... Vergeltung [*Retaliation*] [*German*]
V .... Vermessung [*Survey*] [*German military*]

V .... Vermont Reports (DLA)
V .... Verse
V .... Versicle
V .... Versiculo [*In Such a Way*] [*Latin*] (ROG)
V .... Version
V .... Verso
V .... Versus [*Against*]
V .... Vert [*Heraldry*]
V .... Verte [*Turn Over*]
V .... Vertex
V .... Vertical in Line [*Aircraft engine*]
V .... Very
V .... Vespers
V .... Veto (OICC)
V .... Via [*By Way Of*] [*Latin*] (ADA)
V .... Vibrio [*Microbiology*]
V .... Vic [*Phonetic alphabet*] [*Pre-World War II*] (DSUE)
V .... Vicar [*or Vicarage*]
V .... Vice [*In a position or title*]
v .... Vicinal [*Also, vic*] [*Chemistry*]
V .... Victor [*Phonetic alphabet*] [*World War II*] [*International*] (DSUE)
V .... Victoria
V .... Victory [*As in "the V campaign" in Europe, during World War II*]
V .... Village
V .... Vinblastine [*See VBL*]
V .... Vincristine [*Also, LCR, O, V, VCR*] [*Antineoplastic drug*]
V .... Vinegar [*Phonetic alphabet*] [*Royal Navy*] [*World War I*] (DSUE)
V .... Violet
V .... Violin [*Music*]
V .... Virgin
V .... Virginia Reports (DLA)
V .... Virus
V .... Viscosity
V .... Viscount [*or Viscountess*]
V .... Vise Break Distance [*Stress test for steel*]
V .... Visibility
V .... Vision
V .... Visit
V .... Visiting Practice Only [*Chiropody*] [*British*]
V .... Visual
V .... Visual Acuity [*Also, VA*] [*Ophthalmology*]
V .... Visual Magnitude [*When followed by a two-digit number*]
V .... Vixisti [*You Lived*] [*Latin*]
V .... Vixit [*He Lived*] [*Latin*]
V .... Vocative
V .... Voce [*Voice*] [*Latin*]
V .... Voice
V .... Voice Data [*NASA*]
V .... Void [*Decision or finding held invalid for reasons given*] [*Used in Shepard's Citations*] (DLA)
V .... Volcano (ROG)
V .... Volt [*Symbol*] [*SI unit of electric potential difference*]
V .... Voltage
V .... Voltare [*Turn Over*] [*Latin*] (ROG)
V .... Volti [*Turn Over*] [*Music*]
V .... Voltmeter
V .... Volts
V .... Volume [*Bibliography*]
V .... Volume [*Symbol*] [*IUPAC*]
V .... Volunteer [*US Naval Reserve*]
V .... Von [*Of, From*] [*German*]
V .... VOR [*Very-High-Frequency Omnidirectional Range*] Federal Airway [*Followed by identification*]
V .... Vous [*You*] [*French*] (ROG)
V .... Vowel
V .... VTOL [*Vertical Takeoff and Landing*] [*or STOL - Short Takeoff and Landing*] [*when V is the second or only letter in a military aircraft designation*]

V	Vulgate [*Latin translation of the Bible*] [*A publication*] (BJA)
V	Wrong Verb Form [*Used in correcting manuscripts, etc.*]
V₁	Takeoff Decision Speed [*Aviation*]
V-1	Vergeltungswaffe 1 [*Pilotless flying bomb employed by the Germans*] [*World War II*]
V₂	Takeoff Safety Speed [*Aviation*]
V-2	Vergeltungswaffe 2 [*Rocket bomb employed by the Germans*] [*World War II*]
5V	Togo [*Aircraft nationality and registration mark*] (FAAC)
6V	Senegal [*Aircraft nationality and registration mark*] (FAAC)
9V	Singapore [*Aircraft nationality and registration mark*] (FAAC)
V (Bomb)	Vergeltungswaffe Bomb [*German "vengeance weapon"*]
VA	Alveolar Ventilation
VA	Attack Squadron [*Symbol*] (MCD)
VA	End of Work [*Morse telephony*] (FAAC)
VA	Gilmer's Virginia Reports (DLA)
VA	University of Virginia, Charlottesville, VA [*OCLC symbol*] (OCLC)
VA	Vacuum Aspiration [*Medicine*]
Va	Valid [*Decision or finding held valid for reasons given*] [*Used in Shepard's Citations*] (DLA)
VA	Valium Anonymous (EA)
V and A	Valuable and Attractive [*A marking used by RAF on such supplies as watches and cameras*] [*British*]
VA	Value Analysis
VA	Variable Annuity
Va	Vasari [*A publication*]
VA	Vatican City [*Two-letter standard code*] (CNC)
VA	Vehicle Analyst (MCD)
VA	Vehicular Accident [*British police*]
VA	Velocity at Apogee (MCD)
VA	Venezolana Internacional [*Venezuela*] [*ICAO designator*] (FAAC)
VA	Ventral Area [*Anatomy*]
VA	Ventricular Aneurysm [*Cardiology*]
VA	Ventricular Arrhythmia [*Cardiology*]
VA	Verb Active
VA	Verbal Adjective
VA	VERLORT [*Very-Long-Range Tracking*] Azimuth [*NASA*]
VA	Vermiculite Association [*Atlanta, GA*] (EA)
VA	Verpflegungsausgabestelle [*Rations distributing point*] [*German military - World War II*]
VA	Vertebral Artery [*Anatomy*]
VA	Vesicular-Arbuscular [*Mycorrhiza*] [*Botany*]
VA	Veterans Administration
V-A	Vibroacoustic (NASA)
VA	Vicar Apostolic
VA	Vice Admiral [*Also, VADM, VADML*]
VA	Vickers-Armstrong Gun
V-A	Vickers-Armstrong Ltd.
VA	Victims Anonymous [*Northridge, CA*] (EA)
V & A	Victoria and Albert Museum [*London, England*]
VA	Victoria and Albert Order [*British*]
VA	Video Amplifier
V/A	Video/Analog (NASA)
VA	Vincent's Angina [*Medicine*]
VA	Viola [*Music*]
VA	Virginia [*Postal code*]
VA	Virginia Reports (DLA)
VA	Virginia Supreme Court Reports (DLA)
VA	Virtual Address
VA	Virus-Antibody [*Immunology*]
VA	Visual Acuity [*Also, V*] [*Ophthalmology*]
VA	Visual Aid
VA	Visual Approach [*Aviation*] (FAAC)
VA	Visual Arts [*US Copyright Office class*]
VA	Visual Training Aid Specialist [*Navy*]
VA	Vita Apollonii [*of Philostratus*] [*Classical studies*] (OCD)
VA	Vital Area (NRCH)
VA	Voice of America
V-A	Volt-Ampere (AAG)
VA	Voltaire Alternative
VA	Voluntary Aid (ADA)
VA	Volunteer Artillery [*Military*] [*British*] (ROG)
V of A	Volunteers of America (EA)
VA	Vorausabteilung [*Advance detachment*] [*German military - World War II*]
VA	Vorderasiatische Abteilung der Staatlichen Museen zu Berlin [*A publication*]
VA	Vorderasien (BJA)
VA	Vote America [*Washington, DC*] (EA)
VA	Votre Altesse [*Your Highness*] [*French*]
V/A	Voucher Attached [*Banking*]
VA	Vulnerable Area (NATG)
VAA	Vaasa [*Finland*] [*Airport symbol*] (OAG)
VAA	Vegetarian Association of America (EA)
VAA	Vehicle Assembly Area (MCD)
VAA	Verhandelingen der Koninklijke Akademie van Wetenschappen te Amsterdam [*A publication*]
VAA	Vietnamese American Association
VAA	Voice Access Arrangement

VAAC	Vanadyl Acetylacetonate [*Organic chemistry*]
VA Acts	Acts of the General Assembly, Commonwealth of Virginia (DLA)
VA Ag Dept	Virginia. Department of Agriculture and Immigration. Publications [*A publication*]
VA Ag Exp	Virginia Polytechnic Institute. Agricultural Experiment Station. Publications [*A publication*]
VA Agric Exp Stn Bull	Virginia. Agricultural Experiment Station. Bulletin [*A publication*]
VA Agric Exp Stn Tech Bull	Virginia. Agricultural Experiment Station. Technical Bulletin [*A publication*]
VAALY	Vaal Reefs Explorations [*NASDAQ symbol*] (NQ)
VAAP	USSR Copyright Agency [*Acronym is based on Russian name*]
VAAP	Volunteer Army Ammunition Plant (AABC)
VA App	Virginia Appeals (DLA)
VAAR	Vinyl Alcohol Acetate Resin [*NASA*] (KSC)
VAAS	Vermont Academy of Arts and Sciences
VAAUS	Venezuelan American Association of the United States (EA)
VAB	Van Allen Belts
VAB	Variable Action Button (NVT)
VAB	Vehicle Assembly Building [*NASA*] (AFM)
VAB	Vertical Axis Bearing
VAB	Vinblastine, Actinomycin D, Bleomycin [*Antineoplastic drug regimen*]
VAB	Voice Answer Back
VAB	Vorderasiatische Bibliothek [*H. Winckler and A. Jeremias*] [*Leipzig*] [*A publication*] (BJA)
VABA	Value Added by Advertising
VA Bar News	Virginia Bar News (DLA)
VABBA	Vestsi Akademii Navuk BSSR. Seryya Biyalagichnykh Navuk [*A publication*]
VABD	Van Allen Belt Dosimeter
VABF	Variety Artistes' Benevolent Fund [*British*] (ROG)
VABF	Virginia Beach Federal Savings & Loan [*NASDAQ symbol*] (NQ)
VABFA	Vestsi Akademii Navuk BSSR. Seryya Fizika-Tekhnichnykh Navuk [*A publication*]
VABM	Vertical Angle Bench Mark
VABPF	Vice Admiral British Pacific Fleet
VABR	Vehicle Assembly Building Repeater [*NASA*] (KSC)
VAC	Alternating Current Volts
VAC	Fifth Amphibious Corps
VAC	Vacancy (ADA)
VAC	Vacant (AFM)
VAC	Vacate
VAC	Vacation
VAC	Vaccination [*Medicine*]
VAC	Vacuum (AABC)
VAC	Value-Added Carrier [*Telecommunications*]
VAC	Variable Air Capacitor
VAC	Variance at Completion (MCD)
VAC	Vector Analog Computer
VAC	Vehicle Assembly and Checkout [*NASA*] (NASA)
VAC	Verified Audit Circulation [*Newspaper auditing firm*]
VAC	Vermont American Corporation [*American Stock Exchange symbol*]
VAC	Vertical Air Current
VAC	Veterans Administration Center
VAC	Veterans Affairs Canada [*See also AACC*]
VAC	Vice-Admiralty Court [*British*]
VAC	Victor Analog Computer [*Data processing*]
VAC	Video Amplifier Chain
VAC	Vidicon Alignment Coil
VAC	Vincristine, Actinomycin D, Cyclophosphamide [*Antineoplastic drug regimen*]
VAC	Vincristine, Adriamycin, Cyclophosphamide [*Also, VACY*] [*Antineoplastic drug regimen*]
VAC	Virus Capsid Antigen [*Immunochemistry*]
VAC	Visual Aid Console
VAC	Vital Area Center (CAAL)
VAC	Volt-Ampere Characteristics [*Microwave emission*]
VAC	Volts Alternating Current
VAC	Voluntary Action Center
VAC	Volunteer Adviser Corps (EA)
VACAB	Veterans Administration Contract Appeals Board
VACAPES	Virginia Capes [*Navy*] (CAAL)
VA Cas	Virginia Cases [*Brockenbrough and Holmes*] (DLA)
VA Cas	Virginia Criminal Cases [*3-4 Virginia*] [*1789-1826*] (DLA)
VA Cavalcade	Virginia Cavalcade [*A publication*]
vacc	Vaccinate
VACC	Value-Added Common Carrier [*Telecommunications*]
VAcC	Visual Acuity with Spectacle Correction
VACCI	Vaccine [*Medicine*]
VACCJ	VACC [*Victorian Automobile Chamber of Commerce*] Journal [*A publication*]
VAcCL	Visual Acuity with Contact Lens Correction
VACF	Vietnamese-American Children's Fund [*Defunct*] (EA)
VA Ch Dec	Wythe's Virginia Chancery Reports [*1788-99*] (DLA)
VACM	Vector Averaging Current Meter [*Marine science*] (MSC)
VACM	Vincristine, Adriamycin, Cyclophosphamide, Methotrexate [*Antineoplastic drug regimen*]

VA Col Dec ... Virginia Colonial Decisions [*Randolph and Barrandall*] (DLA)
VACR .... Visual Aircraft Recognition (MCD)
VACRS ...... Vocational Assistance Commission for Retired Servicemen (CINC)
VACSAT .... Vaccine Satellite Program (MCD)
VACT .... Alternating Current Test Volts (MSA)
VACTERL ... Vertebral, Anal, Cardiac, Tracheosophageal, Renal, and Limb [*Defects*]
VACTL ...... Vertical Assembly Component Test Laboratory
VACU .... Virtual Access Control Unit
VACUA ...... Vacuum [*A publication*]
VACURG .... Veterans Administration Cooperative Urological Research Group
Vacuum Chem ... Vacuum Chemistry [*Japan*] [*A publication*]
Vacuum R ... Vacuum Review [*A publication*]
VACW .... Alternating Current Working Volts (MSA)
VACY .... Vincristine, Adriamycin, Cyclophosphamide [*Also, VAC*] [*Antineoplastic drug regimen*]
VAD .... Vacuum Arc Degassing [*Metal technology*]
VAD .... Val d'Or Explorations [*Vancouver Stock Exchange symbol*]
VAD .... Valdosta, GA [*Location identifier*] [*FAA*] (FAAL)
VAD .... Value-Added Dealer [*Business and trade*]
VAD .... Vapor Axial Deposition [*Optical fiber technology*]
VAD .... Velocity-Azimuth Display
VAD .... Ventricle-Assist Device [*Cardiology*]
VAD .... Ventricular Assist Device [*Medicine*]
VAD .... Vereinigte Arbeitnehmerpartei Deutschland [*United Employees' Party of Germany*] [*West Germany*] (PPW)
VAD .... Veterans' Affairs Decisions, Appealed Pension and Civil Service Retirement Cases [*United States*] (DLA)
VAD .... Voltmeter Analog-to-Digital Converter
VAD .... Voluntary Aid Detachment [*British World War I nursing unit*]
VAD .... Vulcan Air Defense (MCD)
VADA .... VFR [*Visual Flight Rules*] Arrival Delay Advisory [*Aviation*] (FAAC)
VADAC ...... Voice Analyzer Data Converter
VADC .... Video Analog to Digital Converter
VADC .... Voice Analyzer and Data Converter (MCD)
VADE .... Vandenberg Automatic Data Equipment [*Air Force*]
VADE .... Vandenberg Automatic Data Evaluation [*Air Force*]
VADE .... Versatile Automatic Data Exchange (MCD)
VA Dec .... Virginia Decisions (DLA)
VA Dent J ... Virginia Dental Journal [*A publication*]
VA Dept Highways Div Tests Geol Yearbook ... Virginia. Department of Highways. Divison of Tests. Geological Yearbook [*A publication*]
VA Dept Labor and Industry Ann Rept ... Virginia. Department of Labor and Industry. Annual Report [*A publication*]
VADER .... Vacuum Arc Double-Electrode Remelting [*Metallurgy*]
VADF .... Vietnamese Air Defense Force (MCD)
VADIC .... Vincristine, Adriamycin, DIC [*Dacarbazine*] [*Antineoplastic drug regimen*]
VADIS .... Voice and Data Integrated System [*Telecommunications*] (TEL)
VA Div Geology Bull Reprint Ser ... Virginia. Division of Geology. Bulletin. Reprint Series [*A publication*]
VA Div Mineral Res Bull Inf Circ Mineral Res Circ ... Virginia. Division of Mineral Resources. Bulletin. Information Circular. Mineral Resources Circular [*A publication*]
VA Div Miner Resour Bull ... Virginia. Division of Mineral Resources. Bulletin [*A publication*]
VA Div Miner Resour Inf Cir ... Virginia. Division of Mineral Resources. Information Circular [*A publication*]
VA Div Miner Resour Miner Resour Rep ... Virginia. Division of Mineral Resources. Mineral Resources Report [*A publication*]
VA Div Miner Resour Rep Invest ... Virginia. Division of Mineral Resources. Report of Investigations [*A publication*]
VADM .... Vice Admiral [*Also, VA, VADML*]
VADML ...... Vice Admiral [*Also, VA, VADM*] (FAAC)
VADMS ...... Voice-Analog-Digital Manual Switch (MCD)
VADS .... Value Added and Data Services
VADS .... Vendor Automated Data System (MCD)
VADS .... Veterans Assistance Discharge System (MCD)
VADS .... Visual-Aural Digit Span Test
VADS .... Vulcan Air Defense Systems (MCD)
VAE .... Vinyl Acetate - Ethylene [*Organic chemistry*]
VAE .... Votre Altesse Electorale [*Your Electoral Highness*] [*French*]
VAEP .... Variable, Attributes, Error Propagation (IEEE)
Vaerml Bergsmannafoeren Ann ... Vaermlaendska Bergsmannafoereningens Annaler [*A publication*]
VAES .... Voice-Activated Encoding System
VAEVC ...... Vinyl Acetate - Ethylene - Vinyl Chloride [*Organic chemistry*]
Vaextskyddsanst-Notiser ... Vaextskyddsanstalt-Notiser [*A publication*]
VAF .... Valence [*France*] [*Airport symbol*] (OAG)
VAF .... Vendor Approval Form
VAF .... Vietnamese Air Force (MCD)
VA Farm Econ VA Polytech Inst Agr Ext Serv ... Virginia Farm Economics. Virginia Polytechnic Institute. Agricultural Extension Service [*A publication*]
VAFB .... Vandenberg Air Force Base [*California*]

VA Fish Lab Educ Ser ... Virginia Fisheries Laboratory. Educational Series [*A publication*]
VAG .... Vagabond (DSUE)
VAG .... Vaginal [*Medicine*]
VAG .... Vaginitis [*Medicine*]
VAG .... Vagrancy [*FBI standardized term*]
VAG .... Vancouver Art Gallery [*Canada*]
VAG .... Varginha [*Brazil*] [*Airport symbol*] (OAG)
Vaga .... Vagabond [*A publication*]
VAGA .... Vagabond Hotels [*NASDAQ symbol*] (NQ)
VAGA .... Visual Artists and Galleries Association (EA)
VA Geol Surv Circ ... Virginia Geological Survey. Circular [*A publication*]
VA Geol Survey Bull ... Virginia Geological Survey. Bulletin [*A publication*]
VA Geol Surv Repr Ser ... Virginia Geological Survey. Reprint Series [*A publication*]
VAGO .... Vanderbilt Gold Corp. [*NASDAQ symbol*] (NQ)
VA G S ...... Virginia Geological Survey [*A publication*]
VA GSB ..... Virginia Geological Survey. Bulletin [*A publication*]
VAH .... Heavy Attack Squadron (MCD)
VAH .... Vaihoa [*Tuamotu Archipelago*] [*Seismograph station code, US Geological Survey*] (SEIS)
VAH .... Vertical Array Hydrophone
VAH .... Veterans Administration Hospital [*Later, VAMC*]
VAH .... Virilizing Adrenal Hyperplasia [*Medicine*]
VA Hist Soc Coll ... Virginia Historical Society. Collections [*A publication*]
VAHR .... Veterans Administration Hospital Representative [*Red Cross*]
VAHS .... Virus-Associated Hemophagocytic Syndrome [*Medicine*]
VAI .... Vanimo [*Papua New Guinea*] [*Airport symbol*] (OAG)
VAI .... Vassar Attitude Inventory [*Education*]
VAI .... Ventilation Air Intake [*Hovercraft*]
VA & I .... Verb Active and Intransitive (ROG)
VAI .... Video Arts International, Inc.
VAI .... Video-Assisted Instruction
VAI .... Visual Alignment Indicators [*Tire maintenance*]
VAI .... Vorticity Area Index [*Meteorology*]
VA IC Ops ... Virginia Industrial Commission Opinions (DLA)
VAIL .... Vail Associates [*NASDAQ symbol*] (NQ)
VA Inst Mar Sci ... Virginia Institute of Marine Science [*A publication*]
VA Inst Mar Sci Spec Sci Rep ... Virginia Institute of Marine Science. Special Scientific Report [*A publication*]
Vaizey .... Vaizey's Law of Settlements [*1887*] (DLA)
VAJ .... Vajont [*Belluno*] [*Italy*] [*Seismograph station code, US Geological Survey*] (SEIS)
VA J Ed ...... Virginia Journal of Education [*A publication*]
VA J Educ ... Virginia Journal of Education [*A publication*]
VA J Int L ... Virginia Journal of International Law [*A publication*]
VA J Nat Resour Law ... Virginia Journal of Natural Resources Law [*A publication*]
VA Jour Sci ... Virginia Journal of Science [*A publication*]
VA J Sci ..... Virginia Journal of Science [*A publication*]
VAK .... Chevak [*Alaska*] [*Airport symbol*] (OAG)
VAK .... Vertical Assembly Kit (NASA)
Vakbl Biol ... Vakblad voor Biologen [*A publication*]
Vak Inf .... Vakuum Information [*A publication*]
VAKT .... Visual, Association, Kinesthetic, Tactile [*With reference to reading*]
VAKT .... Visual-Auditory-Kinesthetic-Tactual
VAKTA .... Vakuum-Technik [*A publication*]
Vak-Tech ... Vakuum-Technik [*A publication*]
Vak-Technik ... Vakuum-Technik [*A publication*]
VAL .... Light Attack Aircraft [*Symbol*] (MCD)
VAL .... Plattsburgh, NY [*Location identifier*] [*FAA*] (FAAL)
VAL .... University of Virginia, Law Library, Charlottesville, VA [*OCLC symbol*] (OCLC)
VAL .... Valentia [*Ireland*] [*Seismograph station code, US Geological Survey*] (SEIS)
VAL .... Valentia [*Ireland*] [*Geomagnetic observatory code*]
VAL .... Valid [*or Validation*] (KSC)
Val .... Valine [*Also, V*] [*An amino acid*]
Val .... Valley (MSA)
Val .... [*A*] Valley Girl
VAL .... Valspar Corp. [*American Stock Exchange symbol*]
VAL .... Valuation
VAL .... Value
VAL .... Value Investment Corp. [*Toronto Stock Exchange symbol*]
VAL .... Valve
VAL .... Variable Angle Launcher
VAL .... Vehicle Authorization List [*Military*] (AFM)
VAL .... Vertical Assault Lift
VAL .... Vicarm Arm Language
VAL .... Vieques Air Link [*Caribbean airline*]
VA L .... Virginia Law Review [*A publication*]
VAL .... Visual Approach and Landing Chart [*Aviation*]
VAL .... Vortex Arc LASER
VAL .... Vulnerability Assessment Laboratory [*White Sands Missile Range, NM*] [*Military*] (RDA)
Valachica ... Acta Valachica Studii si Materiale de Istorie a Culturii [*A publication*]
VA Law J ... Virginia Law Journal [*Richmond*] (DLA)
VA Law R ... Virginia Law Review [*A publication*]
VA Law Rev ... Virginia Law Review [*A publication*]

VALB......... Veterans of the Abraham Lincoln Brigade
VALCO....... Volta Aluminum Company Ltd.
Val Com ..... Valen's Commentaries (DLA)
VALD.......... Valued (ROG)
VA L Dig ..... Virginia Law Digest (DLA)
VALDN....... Validation
VALE.......... [*The*] Valley Railroad Co. [*AAR code*]
Vale Evesham Hist Soc Res Pap ... Vale of Evesham Historical Society. Research Papers [*A publication*]
VALF.......... Valley Forge Corp. [*NASDAQ symbol*] (NQ)
VALI........... Validate (AABC)
VA Lib Bul ... Virginia Library Bulletin [*A publication*]
VA Libn...... Virginia Librarian [*A publication*]
VA LJ......... Virginia Law Journal (DLA)
VALL.......... Vortex Arc LASER Light
Vallalatvez -szerv ... Vallalatvezetes-Vallalatszervezes [*A publication*]
VALM......... Valmont Industries [*NASDAQ symbol*] (NQ)
VALN......... Vallen Corp. [*NASDAQ symbol*] (NQ)
VALN......... Valuation
VALN......... Victorian Adult Literacy News [*A publication*]
VALNET ..... Veterans Administration Library Network [*Veterans Administration*] [*Washington, DC*]
VALOR .... Veterans Administration Libraries Online Resources
VALP .... Valex Petroleum, Inc. [*NASDAQ symbol*] (NQ)
VALP .... Vortex Arc LASER Pump
Valparaiso Univ L Rev ... Valparaiso University. Law Review [*A publication*]
VALPO........ Valparaiso (DSUE)
VA L Reg .... Virginia Law Register (DLA)
VA L Reg NS ... Virginia Law Register, New Series (DLA)
Val Rep...... Valuation Reports, Interstate Commerce Commission (DLA)
Val Rep ICC ... Valuation Reports, Interstate Commerce Commission (DLA)
VA L Rev .... Virginia Law Review [*A publication*]
VALS.......... Value and Life-Style [*Patterns*] [*System to classify consumers*]
Valsa.......... Valsalva [*A publication*]
VALSAS..... Variable Length Word Symbolic Assembly System (IEEE)
VALT .... Valtek, Inc. [*NASDAQ symbol*] (NQ)
VALT .... VTOL [*Vertical Takeoff and Landing*] Approach and Landing Technology [*Program*]
Valt Maatalouskoetoiminnan Julk ... Valtion Maatalouskoetoiminnan Julkaisuja [*A publication*]
VALT(S)..... Vulnerability and Lethality Test (System) (MCD)
Valt Tek Tutkimuskeskus Reaktorilab Tied ... Valtion Teknillinen Tutkimuskeskus. Reaktorilaboratorio. Tiedonanto [*A publication*]
Valt Tek Tutkimuslaitos Julk ... Valtion Teknillinen Tutkimuslaitos. Julkaisu [*A publication*]
Valt Tek Tutkimuslaitos Tiedotus Sar II ... Valtion Teknillinen Tutkimuslaitos. Tiedotus. Sarja II. Metalli [*A publication*]
Valt Tek Tutkimuslaitos Tiedotus Sar I Puu ... Valtion Teknillinen Tutkimuslaitos. Tiedotus. Sarja I. Puu [*A publication*]
Valt Tek Tutkimuslaitos Tiedotus Sar IV ... Valtion Teknillinen Tutkimuslaitos. Tiedotus. Sarja IV. Kemia [*A publication*]
Valt Tek Tutkimuslaitos Tied Sar 2 ... Valtion Teknillinen Tutkimuslaitos. Tiedotus. Sarja 2. Metalli [*A publication*]
Valt Tek Tutkimuslaitos Tied Sar 3 ... Valtion Teknillinen Tutkimuslaitos. Tiedotus. Sarja 3. Rakennus [*A publication*]
VALU.......... Value Lines, Inc. [*NASDAQ symbol*] (NQ)
VALUE .... Validated Aircraft Logistics Utilization Evaluation [*Navy*]
VALUE .... Visible Achievement Liberates Unemployment [*DoD project for disadvantaged youth*]
Value Eng ... Value Engineering [*A publication*]
Value Line ... Value Line Investment Survey [*A publication*]
Val U L Rev .... Valparaiso University. Law Review [*A publication*]
VALUON .... Valuation
Valvo Tech Inf Ind ... Valvo Technische Informationen fuer die Industrie [*A publication*]
VA L Wk Dicta Comp ... Virginia Law Weekly Dicta Compilation (DLA)
VAM .... Medium Attack Aircraft [*Navy symbol*] (NVT)
VAM .... University of Virginia, C. Moore Health Sciences Library, Charlottesville, VA [*OCLC symbol*] (OCLC)
VAM .... Vacuum-Assisted Molding [*Automotive technology*]
VAM .... Value Aluminizing Machine
VAM .... Vamos [*Greece*] [*Seismograph station code, US Geological Survey*] (SEIS)
VAM .... Vector Airborne Magnetometer (IEEE)
VAM .... Vehiculos Automotores Mexicanos [*Commercial firm*]
VAM .... Vending and Affixing Machine
VAM .... Vesicular Arbuscular Mycorrhizae [*Agriculture*]
VAM .... Veterans Administration Matters [*FBI standardized term*]
VAM .... Vinyl Acetate Monomer [*Organic chemistry*]
VA M .... Virginia Magazine of History and Biography [*A publication*]
VAM .... Virtual Access Method
VAM .... Visual Approach Monitor [*Aviation*]
VAM .... Vogel's Approximation Method
VAM .... Voltammeter
VA Mag Hist ... Virginia Magazine of History and Biography [*A publication*]
VA Mag Hist Biog ... Virginia Magazine of History and Biography [*A publication*]
VA Mag Hist Biogr ... Virginia Magazine of History and Biography [*A publication*]
VAMC........ Veterans Administration Medical Center [*Formerly, VAH*]

VAMCO...... Village & Marketing Corporation [*Jamaica*]
VAMD........ Virginia & Maryland Railroad [*AAR code*]
VA Med ..... Virginia Medical [*A publication*]
VA Med Mon ... Virginia Medical Monthly [*Later, Virginia Medical*] [*A publication*]
VAMFO...... Variable-Angle Monochromatic Fringe Observation [*Film thickness determination*]
VA Miner.... Virginia Minerals [*A publication*]
VAMIS....... Virginia Medical Information System [*Library network*]
VAMOS ..... Verified Additional Military Occupational Specialty
VAMOSC... Visibility and Management of Operating and Support Costs [*Army*]
VAMP .... Value Analysis of Management Practices (MCD)
VAMP .... Vandenberg Atlas Modification Program [*Air Force*] (MCD)
VAMP .... Variable [*or Visual*] Anamorphic Motion Picture [*Training device to provide realistic environment during simulated flight training*] (MCD)
VAMP .... Vector Arithmetic Multiprocessor [*Data processing*] (IEEE)
VAMP .... Vietnam Ammunition Program (AFM)
VAMP .... Vincristine, Actinomycin, Methotrexate, Prednisone [*Antineoplastic drug regimen*]
VAMP .... Vincristine Amethopterin [*Antitumor agent*]
VAMP .... Vincristine, Amethopterin [*Methotrexate*], Mercaptopurine, Prednisone [*Antineoplastic drug regimen*]
VAMP .... Visual-Acoustic-Magnetic Pressure (IEEE)
VAMP .... Visual-Acoustic-Magnetic Program [*NOO*]
VAMROC.... Veterans Administration Medical and Regional Office Center
VAMS........ Vernon's Annotated Missouri Statutes (DLA)
VAMS........ Victor Airspeed Measuring System (MCD)
VAMSI....... Visual Approach Multiple Slope Indicator [*Aviation*]
VAMT .... Vertical Assault Medium Transport (MCD)
VAN........... Northern Virginia Community College, Springfield, VA [*OCLC symbol*] (OCLC)
VAN........... Value-Added Network [*Data processing*] [*Telecommunications*]
VAN........... Van [*Turkey*] [*Airport symbol*] (OAG)
VAN........... Vance, SC [*Location identifier*] [*FAA*] (FAAL)
VAN........... Vandeno [*Race of maize*]
Van............ Vanguard [*Record label*]
Van............ Vanguard Science Fiction [*A publication*]
VAN........... Vanguard Tracking Station [*NASA*] (NASA)
VAN........... Vanier College [*UTLAS symbol*]
VAN........... Vannovskaya [*USSR*] [*Seismograph station code, US Geological Survey*] (SEIS)
VAN........... Vanwin Resources Corp. [*Vancouver Stock Exchange symbol*]
VAN........... Variable Area Nozzle
VAN........... Vestnik Akademiji Nauk SSSR [*A publication*]
VAN........... Voluntary Action News [*A publication*]
VAN........... Vorlaeufige Arbeitsnormen
VANB .... Vesci Akademii Navuk BSSR [*A publication*]
Vancoram Rev ... Vancoram Review [*A publication*]
Vand.......... De Bello Vandalico [*of Procopius*] [*Classical studies*] (OCD)
VAND .... Vacuum-Air-Nitrogen Distribution
VAND .... Van Den Bergh [*Liver function test*]
VAND .... Van Dusen Air, Inc. [*NASDAQ symbol*] (NQ)
Vanderbilt J Transnat'l L ... Vanderbilt Journal of Transnational Law [*A publication*]
Vanderbilt LR ... Vanderbilt Law Review (DLA)
Vanderbilt Univ Abs Theses Bull ... Vanderbilt University. Abstracts of Theses. Bulletin [*A publication*]
Vander Law ... Vanderbilt Law Review [*A publication*]
Vanderstr... Vanderstraaten's Reports [*1869-71*] [*Ceylon*] (DLA)
Vanderstraaten ... Vanderstraaten's Decisions in Appeal, Supreme Court [*1869-71*] [*Sri L.*] (DLA)
Vand Int ..... Vanderbilt International [*A publication*]
Vand J Trans L ... Vanderbilt Journal of Transnational Law [*A publication*]
Vand L Rev ... Vanderbilt Law Review [*A publication*]
VAND UNIV Q ... Vanderbilt University Quarterly [*Tennessee*] [*A publication*] (ROG)
VANFIS ...... Visible and Near-Visible Frequency Intercept System [*Navy*]
Van Fleet Coll Attack ... Van Fleet on Collateral Attack (DLA)
Van K .... Van Koughnet's Reports [*15-21 Upper Canada Common Pleas*] [*1864-71*] (DLA)
Van K & H... Upper Canada Common Pleas Reports [*1864-71*] (DLA)
Van L......... Vander Linden's Practice [*Cape Colony*] (DLA)
Van N .... Van Ness' Prize Cases, United States District Court, District of New York (DLA)
VAN N .... Van Norden Magazine [*New York*] [*A publication*] (ROG)
Van Ness Prize Cas ... Van Ness' Prize Cases, United States District Court, District of New York (DLA)
VANS .... Value Added Network Service [*Data processing*] [*Telecommunications*]
VANS .... Van Schaack & Co. [*NASDAQ symbol*] (NQ)
VANS .... Vehicle Austere Night Sight [*Army*] (MCD)
VAN SSSR ... Vestnik Akademiji Nauk SSSR [*A publication*]
VA Num..... Virginia Numismatist [*A publication*]
VA Nurse.... Virginia Nurse [*A publication*]
VA Nurse Q ... Virginia Nurse Quarterly [*Later, Virginia Nurse*] [*A publication*]
VANUSL.... Vanderbilt University School of Law (DLA)
VANWACE ... Vulnerability Analysis of Nuclear Weapons in Allied Command, Europe [*Army*] (AABC)

VANZ......... Vanzetti Systems, Inc. [*NASDAQ symbol*]   (NQ)
Van Zee Ld ... Van Zee tot Land [*A publication*]
VAO............ Veterans Administration Office
VAO............ Voting Assistance Officer
VAOKN....... Visual Acuity by Optokinetic Nystagmus
VAOR .... VHF [*Very-High-Frequency*] Aural Omnirange
VAP .... Photographic Squadron (Heavy) [*Navy symbol*]   (NVT)
VAP .... Vaginal Acid Phosphatase [*An enzyme*]
VAP .... Vaporization [*or Vaporizer*]   (KSC)
VAP .... Vehicle Antenna Position [*NASA*]
VAP .... Velocity Analysis Program
VAP .... Vertical Axis Pivots
VAP .... Veteran Air Pilots
VAP .... Voluntary Assistance Program
VAPA......... Video Alliance for the Performing Arts   (EA)
VAPC .... Veterans Administration Prosthetics Center [*Later, VAREC*]
VAP-Cyclo ... Vincristine, Adriamycin, Prednisolone, Cyclophosphamide [*Antineoplastic drug regimen*]
VAPH......... Visual Acuity with Pin Hole
VAPHD ...... Virchows Archiv. Abteilung A. Pathological Anatomy and Histology [*A publication*]
VAPI........... Visual Approach Path Indicator [*Aviation*]
VAPO .... Vaporizing Oil
VA Polytech Inst Bull Eng Expt Sta Ser ... Virginia Polytechnic Institute. Bulletin. Engineering Experiment Station Series [*A publication*]
VA Polytech Inst Eng Ext Ser Cir ... Virginia Polytechnic Institute. Engineering Extension Series Circular [*A publication*]
VA Polytech Inst Res Div Bull ... Virginia Polytechnic Institute. Research Division. Bulletin [*A publication*]
VA Polytech Inst Res Div Wood Res Wood Constr Lab Bull ... Virginia Polytechnic Institute. Research Division. Wood Research and Wood Construction Laboratory [*Blacksburg*]. Bulletin [*A publication*]
VA Polytech Inst State Univ VA Water Resour Res Cent Bull ... Virginia Polytechnic Institute and State University. Virginia Water Resources Research Center. Bulletin [*A publication*]
VA Polytech Inst State Univ Water Resour Res Cent Bull ... Virginia Polytechnic Institute and State University. Water Resources Research Center. Bulletin [*A publication*]
VAPR......... Veterans Administration Procurement [*or Purchase*] Regulations
VAPS......... V/STOL [*Vertical/Short Takeoff and Landing*] Approach System   (MCD)
VAPS......... Volume, Article [*or Chapter*], Paragraph, Sentence [*Numbers*] [*Indexing*]
VAQ............ Visiting Airmen's Quarters [*Air Force*]
VA Q R....... Virginia Quarterly Review [*A publication*]
VA R .... Gilmer's Virginia Reports   (DLA)
VAR............ Reactive Volt-Ampere
VAR .... Vacuum Arc Remelting [*Steel alloy*]
VAR .... Validation Analysis Report [*Social Security Administration*]
VAR .... Value-Added Reseller [*Business and trade*]
VAR .... Value-Added Retailer [*Business and trade*]
VAR .... VANAIR, Inc. [*Gasport, NY*] [*FAA designator*]   (FAAC)
VAR .... Varanasi [*India*] [*Seismograph station code, US Geological Survey*]   (SEIS)
VAR .... Variable   (AFM)
Var............. Variae [*of Cassiodorus*] [*Classical studies*]   (OCD)
VAR .... Varian Associates [*NYSE symbol*]
VAR .... Variance Analysis Report   (MCD)
VAR .... Variant [*Numismatics*]
VAR .... Variation
VAR .... Variegated
var .... Varietas [*Variety*] [*Biology*]
VAR .... Variety [*A publication*]
VAR .... Variety
VAR .... Various
VAR .... Varitech Resources [*Vancouver Stock Exchange symbol*]
VAR .... Varna [*Bulgaria*] [*Airport symbol*]   (OAG)
Var............. Varsity [*Record label*]
VAR .... Vendor Approval Request   (AAG)
VAR .... Verification Analysis Report   (NASA)
VAR .... Vertical Acceleration Ramp
VAR .... Vertical Air Rocket   (NATG)
VAR .... Veterans Administration Regulations
VAR .... Video-Audio Range [*Radio*]
VAR .... Vintage Austin Register   (EA-IO)
VAR .... Visual-Aural Range [*Radio*]
VAR .... Volt-Ampere Reactive
VAR .... Voltage in Acceptable Range   (MCD)
VAR .... Voltage Adjusting Rheostat
VAR .... Voluntary Auto Restraints [*Import quotas on automobiles*]
VAR .... Volunteer Air Reserve [*Air Force*]
VAR .... Votre Altesse Royale [*Your Royal Highness*] [*French*]
VAR .... Vrij Anti-Revolutionaire Partij [*Free Anti-Revolutionary Party*] [*The Netherlands*]   (PPE)
VARA .... Vereiniging van Arbeiders Radio Amateurs
VARAD....... Varying Radiation   (IEEE)
VA R Ann ... Virginia Reports, Annotated   (DLA)
Vara Palsd ... Vara Palsdjur [*A publication*]

VARC .... Variable Axis Rotor Control System [*Telecommunications*]   (TEL)
VARC .... Virginia Associated Research Campus [*Later, Continuous Electron Beam Accelerator Facility*] [*Research center*]   (RCD)
VARC .... Virginia Associated Research Center
vard............ Varied [*Quality of the bottom*] [*Nautical charts*]
VAREC .... Veterans Administration Rehabilitation Engineering Center [*Formerly, VAPC*]
VA Rep Anno ... Virginia Reports, Annotated   (DLA)
VARES .... Vega Aircraft RADAR Enhancing System [*FAA*]
VARGUS .... Variable Generator of Unfamiliar Stimuli [*Computer program*]
VARHM ...... Var-Hour Meter [*Electricity*]
Vari............ Variegation [*A publication*]
VARI........... Varityper
VARIA .... Variamento [*In a Varied Style*] [*Music*]   (ROG)
Varian Instrum Appl ... Varian Instrument Applications [*A publication*]
VARICAP .... Variable Capacitor
VARIG .... Viacao Aerea Rio-Grandense [*Brazilian airline*]   (FAAC)
Varilna Teh ... Varilna Tehnika [*A publication*]
VARION .... Variation   (ROG)
Various Publ Ser ... Various Publications Series [*Aarhus*] [*A publication*]
VARISTOR ... Variable Resistor
VARITRAN ... Variable-Voltage Transformer   (IEEE)
VAR LECT ... Varia Lectio [*Different Reading*] [*Latin*]   (ROG)
VARM......... Varmeter [*Engineering*]
VARN .... Variation   (FAAC)
VARN .... Varnish
var nov ...... Varietas Nova [*New Variety*] [*Biology*]
VARO .... Veterans Administration Regional Office   (AFM)
VARP......... Vietnam Asset Reconciliation Procedure [*Military*]   (AABC)
VARPC ...... Veterans Administration Records Processing Center
VARR .... Variable Range Reflector   (IEEE)
VARR .... Visual-Aural Radio Range   (MSA)
VARS......... Various   (ROG)
VARS......... Vertical Azimuth Reference System   (NATG)
Var Sci Inst Rebois Tunis ... Varietes Scientifiques. Institut de Reboisement de Tunis [*A publication*]
VARSITY .... University [*British*]   (ROG)
VART .... Volunteer Air Reserve Training [*Air Force*]
VARTA Spez Rep ... VARTA Spezial Report [*West Germany*] [*A publication*]
VARTU .... Volunteer Air Reserve Training Unit [*Air Force*]
VARVS .... Variable Acuity Remote Viewing System   (MCD)
VAS .... Sivas [*Turkey*] [*Airport symbol*]   (OAG)
VAS .... Value Added Service [*Telecommunications*]   (TEL)
VAS .... Vassijaure [*Sweden*] [*Seismograph station code, US Geological Survey*] [*Closed*]   (SEIS)
VAS .... Vector Addition System
VAS .... Venomological Artifact Society   (EA)
VAS .... Vesicle Attachment Sites [*Neurology*]
VAS .... Vibration Analysis System
VAS .... Visible Atmospheric Sounder   (MCD)
VAS .... VISSR Atmospheric Sounder [*NASA*]
VAS .... Visual Analog [*Pain*] Scale
VAS .... Visual Analysis System [*Military*]
VAS .... Visual Attack System
VAS .... Visual Augmentation System
VAS .... Vorderasiatische Schriftdenkmaeler der Koeniglichen [*or Staatlichen*] Museen zu Berlin [*A publication*]
VAS .... Vortex Advisory System [*FAA*]
Vasa Suppl ... Vasa Supplementum [*A publication*]
VA SBA ...... Virginia State Bar Association, Reports   (DLA)
VASC .... Vascular
VASC .... Verbal Auditory Screen for Children
VAsC.......... Visual Acuity without Spectacle Correction [*Unaided*]
VASCA .... Vacation and Senior Citizens Association [*Formed by a merger of Vacations for the Aging and New York Association of Senior Centers*] [*New York, NY*]   (EA)
VASCAR .... Visual Average Speed Computer and Recorder [*Speed trap*]
Vasc Dis..... Vascular Diseases [*A publication*]
Vasc Surg ... Vascular Surgery [*A publication*]
VASD .... Veroeffentlichungen der Deutschen Akademie fuer Sprache und Dichtung [*A publication*]
VaSd .... Vorderasiatische Schriftdenkmaeler der Koeniglichen [*or Staatlichen*] Museen zu Berlin [*A publication*]
Vasenlisten ... Vasenlisten zur Griechischen Heldensage [*A publication*]   (OCD)
VASI........... Visual Approach Slope Indicator [*Aviation*]
VASI........... Volunteer Ambulance School of Instruction [*Military*] [*British*]   (ROG)
VASIM....... Voltage and Synchro Interface Module
VASIS........ Visual Approach Slope Indicator System [*Aviation*]
VASOG....... Veterans Administration Surgical Oncology Group
VASP......... Variable Automatic Synthesis Program [*NASA*]
VASP......... Viacao Aerea Sao Paulo, SA [*Brazilian airline*]
VASRD .... Veterans Administration Schedule for Rating Disabilities   (AABC)
VASS......... Visual Analysis Subsystem [*Military*]
VASS.......... Visually Activated Switch System   (MCD)
Vassar Bros Inst Tr ... Vassar Brothers Institute. Transactions [*A publication*]

VASSEL ..... Validation of ASW [*Antisubmarine Warfare*] Subsystem Effectiveness Levels [*Navy*]   (CAAL)
VASSS .... Van Alen Simplified Scoring System [*Tennis*]
VAST .... Versatile Automatic Specification Tester
VAST .... Versatile Avionics Shop Test [*or Tester*] [*NASA*]
VA State Lib Bull ... Virginia State Library Bulletin [*A publication*]
Vasterbotten ... Vasterbottens Lans Hambygdsforenings Arsbok [*A publication*]
Vastergotlands Fornminnesforen Tidskr ... Vastergotlands Fornminnesforenings Tidskrift [*A publication*]
Vastmanlands Fornminnesforen Arsskr ... Vastmanlands Fornminnesforenings Arsskrift [*A publication*]
VASTT .... Variable Speed Towed Target   (RDA)
VASTT .... Versatile Aerial Simulation Tow Target   (MCD)
Vasuti Tud Kut Intez Evk ... Vasuti Tudomanyos Kutato Intezet Evkoenyve [*Hungary*] [*A publication*]
VAS VITR ... Vas Vitreum [*A Glass Vessel*] [*Pharmacy*]
VAT .... Vacuum Arc Thrustor Program   (MCD)
VAT .... Value-Added Tax
VAT .... Variable Area Turbine
VAT .... Variant Antigenic Type [*Genetics, immunology*]
VAT .... Varity Corp. [*NYSE symbol*] [*Toronto Stock Exchange symbol*] [*Vancouver Stock Exchange symbol*]
VAT .... VAT. Victorian Association of Teachers [*A publication*]
VAT .... Vatican
VAT .... Vatican City [*Three-letter standard code*]   (CNC)
VAT .... Vatomandry [*Madagascar*] [*Airport symbol*]   (OAG)
VAT .... Ventricular Activation Time [*Cardiology*]
VAT .... Vibration Acceptance Test
VAT .... Vibroacoustic Test   (NASA)
VAT .... Virtual Address Translation
VAT .... Visual Acquisition Technique
VAT .... Visual Action Time
VAT .... Visual Apperception Test [*Psychology*]
VAT .... Vitro Assistance Team
VAT .... Vocational Apperception Test [*Psychology*]
VAT .... Voice-Activated Typewriter
VAT .... Volt-Ampere Tester
VAT .... Voltage Amplifier Tube
VAT .... Vulnerability Analysis Team   (MCD)
VATA .... Vibroacoustic Test Article   (NASA)
VatBA .... Biblioteca Apostolica Vaticana, Vatican City, Vatican City [*Library symbol*] [*Library of Congress*]   (LCLS)
VATE .... Versatile Automatic Test Equipment [*Computers*]
V-ATE .... Vertical Anisotropic Etch [*Raytheon Co.*]
VA Teach ... Virginia Teacher [*A publication*]
VATEJ .... Victorian Association for the Teaching of English. Journal [*A publication*]
VATER .... Vascular Tracheoesophageal-Limb-Reduction [*Endocrinology*]
VATER .... Vertebral, Anal, Tracheal, Esophageal, Renal
VATF .... Vibration and Acoustic Test Facility   (NASA)
VAtf .... Visual Acuity with Trial Frame
VATISJ .... VATIS [*Victorian Association of Teachers in Independent Schools*] Journal [*A publication*]
VATLIT .... Very Advanced Technology Light Twin   (MCD)
VATLS .... Visual Airborne Target Locator System
VATR .... Variable Aperture Target Recognition   (MCD)
VA Truck Exp ... Virginia Truck Experiment Station. Publications [*A publication*]
VATS .... Vehicle Anti-Theft System [*General Motors Corp.*]
VATS .... Vehicle Automatic Test System
VATS .... Vernon's Annotated Texas Statutes   (DLA)
VATS .... Vertical-Lift Airfield for Tactical Support   (NVT)
VATS .... Video-Augmented Tracking System   (MCD)
VATS/SNAP ... Video-Augmented Tracking System/Single Seat Night Attack Program   (MCD)
Vatt .... Vattel's Law of Nations   (DLA)
Vattel .... Vattel's Law of Nations   (DLA)
Vattel Law Nat ... Vattel's Law of Nations   (DLA)
VA/TVTA ... Vibroacoustic/Thermal/Vacuum Test Article   (NASA)
VAU .... Vertical Accelerometer Unit
VAU .... Vertical Arithmetic Unit
vau .... Virginia [*MARC country of publication code*] [*Library of Congress*]   (LCCP)
VAU .... Volume Accumulator Unit
VAU .... Volunteer Air Units
VAUB .... Vehicle Authorization Utilization Board [*Military*]
VAUD .... Vaudeville
Vaug .... Vaughan's English Common Pleas Reports [*124 ER*]   (DLA)
Vaugh .... Vaughan's English Common Pleas Reports [*124 ER*]   (DLA)
Vaughan .... Vaughan's English Common Pleas Reports [*124 ER*]   (DLA)
Vaughan (Eng) ... Vaughan's English Common Pleas Reports [*124 ER*]   (DLA)
VA Univ Ph Soc B Sc S ... Virginia University. Philosophical Society. Bulletin. Scientific Series [*A publication*]
VAUX .... Vauxhall [*Automobile*]   (DSUE)
Vaux .... Vaux's Recorder's Decisions [*1841-45*] [*Philadelphia, PA*]   (DLA)
Vaux (PA) ... Vaux's Recorder's Decisions [*1841-45*] [*Philadelphia, PA*]   (DLA)

Vaux Rec Dec ... Vaux's Recorder's Decisions [*1841-45*] [*Philadelphia, PA*]   (DLA)
VAV .... Variable Air Volume
VAV .... Vava'u [*Tonga Island*] [*Airport symbol*]   (OAG)
VAV .... Veroeffentlichungen zum Archiv fuer Voelkerkunde [*A publication*]
VAVP .... Variable Angle, Variable Pitch
VAVS .... Veterans Administration Voluntary Service
VAW .... Carrier Airborne Early Warning Squadron [*Navy symbol*]   (NVT)
VAW .... Valley Airways, Inc. [*McAllen, TX*] [*FAA designator*]   (FAAC)
VAW .... Vertical Arc Welder
VA Water Resour Res Cent Bull ... Virginia Water Resources Research Center. Bulletin [*A publication*]
VA Wildl .... Virginia Wildlife [*A publication*]
VAWT .... Vertical Axis Wind Turbine [*Power generator*] [*See also VAWTG*]
VAWTG ...... Vertical Axis Wind Turbine Generator [*Also, VAWT*]
VAX .... Alexandria Public Library, Alexandria, VA [*OCLC symbol*]   (OCLC)
VAX .... Heavy Attack Aircraft, Experimental
VAX .... Trademark of Digital Equipment Corp.
VAX .... Virtual Address Extension [*Data processing*]
Vaxt-Nar-Nytt ... Vaxt-Narings-Nytt [*A publication*]
Vaxtodling Inst Vaxtodlingslara Lantbrukshogsk ... Vaextodling. Institutionen foer Vaextodlingslara. Lantbrukshoegskolan [*A publication*]
Vaxtskyddsnotiser Sver Lantbruksuniver ... Vaxtskyddsnotiser. Sveriges Lantbruksuniversitet [*A publication*]
VAY .... Valandovo [*Yugoslavia*] [*Seismograph station code, US Geological Survey*]   (SEIS)
Vayr .... Vayikra Rabba   (BJA)
Vazduhoplovni Glas ... Vazduhoplovni Glasnik [*Yugoslavia*] [*A publication*]
VB .... Bombing Plane [*Navy symbol*]
VB .... Bretagne Air Services [*France*] [*ICAO designator*]   (FAAC)
VB .... Dive Bomber Squadron [*Navy symbol*]
VB .... Valence Bond   (DEN)
VB .... Valve Box
VB .... Vanity Bar [*Classified advertising*]   (ADA)
VB .... Vapor Barrier [*Boots*] [*Army*]   (INF)
VB .... Ventrobasal Complex [*Brain anatomy*]
VB .... Verb
VB .... Vertical Beam [*of light*]
VB .... Vertical Bomb [*Air Force*]
V & B .... Vesey and Beames' English Chancery Reports [*1812-14*]   (DLA)
VB .... Viable Birth [*Medicine*]
VB .... Vibration   (AAG)
VB .... Victoria Bitter   (ADA)
VB .... Vir Bonus [*A Good Man*] [*Latin*]
vb .... Virgin Islands, British [*MARC country of publication code*] [*Library of Congress*]   (LCCP)
VB .... Viven and Bassiere [*Rifle grenade*]
VB .... Voelkischer Beobachter [*A publication*]
VB .... Voice Band [*Telecommunications*]
VB .... Voice Bank [*Telecommunications*]   (TEL)
VB .... Voks Bulletin [*A publication*]
VB .... Volunteer Battalion [*Military*]
VB .... Vorgeschobener Beobachter [*Forward Observer*] [*German military*]
VB .... Vulgate Bible
VBA .... Vegetarian Brotherhood of America [*Defunct*]   (EA)
VBA .... Vibrating Beam Accelerometer [*Inertial sensor*]   (IEEE)
VBAA .... Vanilla Bean Association of America [*Long Island City, NY*]   (EA)
VBAC .... Vaginal Birth After Caesarean [*Obstetrics*]
VBAP .... Vincristine, BCNU [*Carmustine*], Adriamycin, Prednisone [*Antineoplastic drug regimen*]
VBAS .... Von Braun Astronomical Society [*Formerly, RCAA*]   (EA)
VB (B) .... Voelkischer Beobachter (Berlin) [*A publication*]
vbb .... Volgens Bygaande Brief [*According to Accompanying Letter*] [*Afrikaans*]
VBC .... Bridgewater College, Bridgewater, VA [*OCLC symbol*]   (OCLC)
VBC .... Venetian Blind Council [*Formerly, VBI*]
VBC .... Vinylbenzyl Chloride [*Organic chemistry*]
VBC .... Vogel-Bonner Citrate [*Growth medium*]
VBCS .... Victorian Bing Crosby Society [*South Melbourne, Vic., Australia*]   (EA-IO)
VBD .... Vector-Borne Disease
VBD .... Vertebrobasilar Dolichoectasia [*Medicine*]
VBD .... Voice Band Data   (KSC)
VBD .... Volta Bureau for the Deaf
VBDMA ...... Vinylbenzyldimethylamine [*Organic chemistry*]
VBE .... Vibrating Plate Extractor [*Chemical engineering*]
VBelGrN .... Vesci Akademii Navuk Belaruskaj SSR. Seryja Gramadskich Navuk [*A publication*]
VBF .... Bomber-Fighter Squadron [*Navy symbol*]
VBF .... Bombing-Fighting Aircraft [*Navy symbol*]
VBF .... Vibrated Fluid Bed [*Chemical engineering*]
VBF .... Vibratory Bowl Feeder
VBG .... Lompoc, CA [*Location identifier*] [*FAA*]   (FAAL)

VBGQ .... Vacuum Brazed - Gas Quenched
VBI .... Venetian Blind Institute [*Later, VBC*]   (EA)
VBI .... Vertical Blanking Interval [*Telecommunications*]
VBI .... Video Bible Institute [*Defunct*]   (EA)
VBI .... Vital Bus Inverter [*Data processing*]   (IEEE)
V-BIG .... Ventricular Bigeminy [*Medicine*]
VBJ .... Vacuum Bell Jar
VBKTPS ..... Vierteljahrschrift fuer Bibelkunde, Talmudische, und Patristische Studien [*A publication*]
VBL .... BOCES [*Boards of Cooperative Educational Services*], Monroe 1, Penfield, NY [*OCLC symbol*]   (OCLC)
VBL .... Vector Biology Laboratory [*University of Notre Dame*] [*Research center*]   (RCD)
VBL .... Verbal
VBL .... Vinblastine [*Velban, Vincaleukoblastine*] [*Also, V, Ve, VLB*] [*Antineoplastic drug*]
VBL .... Voyager Biological Laboratory [*NASA*]
VBM .... BOCES [*Boards of Cooperative Educational Services*], Monroe 2, Orleans, Spencerport, NY [*OCLC symbol*]   (OCLC)
VBM .... Vincristine, Bleomycin, Methotrexate [*Antineoplastic drug regimen*]
VBMA .... Vacuum Bag Manufacturers Association [*Jericho, NY*]   (EA)
VBMR .... Ventilation Barrier Machine Room [*Nuclear energy*]   (NRCH)
VB (Mu) ..... Voelkischer Beobachter (Muenich) [*A publication*]
VBMWMO ... Vintage BMW Motorcycle Owners   (EA)
VBN .... Verbal Noun
VBN .... Veterans Bedside Network [*Formerly, BNVHRTVG*] [*Entertainers association*] [*New York, NY*]   (EA)
VBN .... Victorian Bar News [*A publication*]
VBND .... Velo-Bind, Inc. [*NASDAQ symbol*]   (NQ)
VBO .... Oswego County BOCES [*Boards of Cooperative Educational Services*], Mexico, NY [*OCLC symbol*]   (OCLC)
VBO .... Veterans Benefits Office
VBOB .... Veterans of the Battle of the Bulge   (EA)
VBOMP .... Virtual Base Organization and Maintenance Processor
VBOS .... Veronal-Buffered Oxalated Saline
VBot .... Verstreute Boghazkoei-Texte [*A. Goetze*] [*A publication*]   (BJA)
VBP .... Vacuum Backing Pump
VBP .... Virtual Block Processor
VBP .... Vortex Breakdown Position
VBPF .... Variable Bandpass Filter
VBQ .... Visvabharati Quarterly [*A publication*]
VBR .... Vacuum Bottoms Recycle [*Petroleum refining*]
VBR .... Ventricle Brain Ratio [*Medicine*]
VBR .... Vinyl Bromide [*Organic chemistry*]
VBR .... Virginia Blue Ridge Railway [*AAR code*]
VBS .... Vacation Bible Schools [*An association*] [*Formerly, WADVBS*]   (EA)
VBS .... Variable Ballast System
VBS .... Veronal-Buffered Saline
VBSFA .... Vestsi Akademii Navuk BSSR. Seryya Fizika-Matematychnykh Navuk [*A publication*]
VBSKA .... Vestsi Akademii Navuk BSSR. Seryya Khimichnykh Navuk [*A publication*]
VBT .... Bombing, Torpedo Plane [*Navy symbol*]
VBT .... Valence-Bond Theory [*Physical chemistry*]
VBTPS .... Vierteljahrschrift fuer Bibelkunde, Talmudische, und Patristische Studien [*A publication*]
VBU .... Vibrating Bag Unloader
VBULE .... Vestibule [*Classified advertising*]   (ADA)
VBV .... Vanuabalavu [*Fiji*] [*Airport symbol*]   (OAG)
VBW .... Bridgewater, VA [*Location identifier*] [*FAA*]   (FAAL)
VBW .... Video Bandwidth
VBW .... Vortraege der Bibliothek Warburg [*A publication*]
VBWR .... Vallecitos Boiling Water Reactor
VBY .... Visby [*Sweden*] [*Airport symbol*]   (OAG)
VC .... Circular Velocity
VC .... Color Vision [*Ophthalmology*]
VC .... Composite Aircraft Squadron [*Navy symbol*]
VC .... Creditreform Databank [*Verband der Vereine Creditreform eV*] [*Neuss, West Germany*] [*Information service*]   (EISS)
VC .... Cruise Speed [*Aviation*]
VC .... St. Vincent and the Grenadines [*Two-letter standard code*]   (CNC)
VC .... Vacuolated Cell
VC .... Valuable Cargo
VC .... Valuation Clause
VC .... Vaporizer Concentrate   (NRCH)
VC .... Variable Capacitor   (DEN)
VC .... Variable Charge
VC .... Varnished Cambric [*Insulation*]
VC .... Vasoconstrictor [*Medicine*]
VC .... Vatel Club [*New York, NY*]   (EA)
vc .... Vatican City [*MARC country of publication code*] [*Library of Congress*]   (LCCP)
VC .... Vector Character   (NASA)
V/C .... Vector Control   (KSC)
Vc .... Vecuronium [*A muscle relaxant*]
VC .... Vehicular Communications   (MCD)
VC .... Velocity Character   (MCD)

VC .... Velocity Compounded
VC .... Velocity Counter   (KSC)
VC .... Vena Cava [*Anatomy*]
VC .... Vendor Call   (MCD)
VC .... Vendor Code   (MCD)
VC .... Vendor Contact
VC .... Venereal Case [*Medical slang*]
VC .... Ventilated Containers
VC .... Ventilatory Capacity [*Physiology*]
VC .... Ventricular Complex [*Cardiology*]
VC .... Ventricular Coupling [*Cardiology*]
VC .... Verb-Consonant [*Education of the hearing-impaired*]
VC .... Verbi Causa [*For Example*] [*Latin*]
VC .... Verification Condition
VC .... Vernair Transport Services [*Great Britain*] [*ICAO designator*]   (FAAC)
VC .... Vernal Conjunctivitis [*Ophthalmology*]
VC .... Versatility Code
VC .... Vertical Curve
VC .... Veterinary Corps
VC .... Vicar Choral
VC .... Vice Chairman [*or Chairwoman or Chairperson*]
VC .... Vice Chancellor
VC .... Vice-Chancellor's Courts [*England*]   (DLA)
VC .... Vice Commodore [*Navy*]   (NVT)
VC .... Vice Consul
VC .... Victoria Cross [*British*]
VC .... Video Channel [*Auckland, NZ*]
VC .... Video Correlator
VC .... Videodisc Controller
VC .... Vietcong [*Vietnamese Communists*]
VC .... Vigilance Committee
VC .... Vigiliae Christianae [*A publication*]
VC .... Village of Childhelp [*Beaumont, CA*]   (EA)
VC .... Vinyl Chloride [*Organic chemistry*]
VC .... Violoncello [*Music*]
VC .... Vir Clarissimus [*A Most Illustrious Man*] [*Latin*]
VC .... Virginia Cavalcade [*A publication*]
VC .... Virginia Central Railway [*AAR code*]
VC .... Virtual Circuit
VC .... Visiting Committee [*British*]
VC .... Vista Chemical [*NYSE symbol*]
VC .... Visual Capacity [*Acuity*]
VC .... Visual Cortex
VC .... Visum Cultum [*Seen Cultivated*] [*Botany*]   (ROG)
VC .... Vital Capacity
VC .... Vitreous Carbon
VC .... Vitrified Clay [*Technical drawings*]
VC .... Vocal Cord
VC .... Voice Ciphony   (CET)
VC .... Voice Coil
VC .... Volt-Coulomb   (DEN)
VC .... Voltage Comparator [*or Compensator*]   (DEN)
VC .... Volume of Compartment [*Technical drawings*]
VC .... Volume Control   (DEN)
VC .... Voluntary Closing [*Prosthesis*] [*Medicine*]
VC .... Volunteer Consultant [*Red Cross*]
VC .... Volunteer Corps
VC .... Voters for Choice   (EA)
VC .... Voyage Charter
VC .... Vuelta de Correo [*Return Mail*] [*Spanish*]
VC's .... Vocal Chords [*Musical slang*]
VCA .... Valve Control Amplifier   (MDG)
VCA .... Vancomycin-Colistin-Anisomycin [*Growth-inhibiting mixture*] [*Microbiology*]
VCA .... Vehicle Checkout Area
VCA .... Venture Clubs of the Americas [*Philadelphia, PA*]   (EA)
VCA .... Vestnik Ceske Akademie Ved a Umeni [*A publication*]
VCA .... Vestnik Ceskoslovenske Akademie Ved [*A publication*]
VCA .... Veteran Corps of Artillery, State of New York Constituting the Military Society of the War of 1812   (EA)
VCA .... Viewdata Corporation of America, Inc. [*Miami Beach, FL*] [*Telecommunications*]   (TSSD)
VCA .... Vinchina [*Argentina*] [*Seismograph station code, US Geological Survey*]   (SEIS)
VCA .... Viral Capsid Antibody [*Hematology*]
VCA .... Viral Capsular Antigen [*Immunology*]
VCA .... Virtual City Associates Ltd. [*London, England*] [*Telecommunications*]   (TSSD)
VCA .... Visual Course Adapter   (MUGU)
VCA .... Vitrified China Association [*Defunct*]
VC of A ...... Vizsla Club of America
VCA .... Voice Connecting Arrangement [*Telecommunications*]   (TEL)
VCA .... Voltage Control of Amplification
VCAD .... Vertical Contact Analog Display
VC Adm ..... Victoria Reports, Admiralty   (DLA)
VCAM .... Volunteer Committees of Art Museums   (EA)
VCAP .... Vincristine, Cyclophosphamide, Adriamycin, Prednisone [*Antineoplastic drug regimen*]
VCAS .... Vice-Chief of the Air Staff [*British*]
VCASS .... Visually Coupled Airborne Systems Simulator   (IEEE)

VCB............ CBNU Learning Resources Center, Virginia Beach, VA [*OCLC symbol*] (OCLC)
VCB............ Construction Battalion [*USNR classification*]
VCB............ Vertical Location of the Center of Buoyancy
VCB............ Visual Control Board
VCC............ Vancouver Community College Library [*UTLAS symbol*]
VCC............ Variable Ceramic Capacitor
VCC............ Variable Characteristic Car (ADA)
VCC............ Variable Command Count (MCD)
VCC............ Vasoconstrictor Center [*Physiology*]
VCC............ Vehicle Crew Chief [*NASA*] (KSC)
VCC............ Verification Code Counter (MCD)
VCC............ Vermilion Community College, Ely, MN [*OCLC symbol*] (OCLC)
VCC............ Versatile Corporation [*Toronto Stock Exchange symbol*]
VCC............ Vertical Centering Control
VCC............ Vice-Chancellor's Courts (DLA)
VCC............ Video Coaxial Connector
VCC............ Video Compact Cassette [*Video recorder*] [*Philips*]
VCC............ Vietcong Captured
VCC............ Virginia Community College System
VCC............ Viscous-Damped Converter Clutch [*Automotive engineering*]
VCC............ Visual Communications Congress
VCC............ Vogelback Computing Center [*Northwestern University*] [*Research center*] (RCD)
VCC............ Voice Control Center [*NASA*] (KSC)
VCC............ Voltage Coefficient of Capacitance
VCC............ Voltage-Controlled Capacitor
VCC............ Voluntary Census Committee (EA)
VCC............ Volunteer Cadet Corps [*British*]
VCC............ Vuilleumier Cycle Cooler
VCCA......... Vintage Chevrolet Club of America (EA)
VCCC......... Vuilleumier Cycle Cryogenic Cooler
VCCS......... Visually Coupled Control System (MCD)
VCCS......... Voltage-Controlled Current Source [*Electronics*]
VCCUS...... Venezuelan Chamber of Commerce of the United States
VCD............ Vapor Compression Distillation
VCD............ Variable-Capacitance Diode
VCD............ Vernier Engine Cutoff [*Aerospace*]
VCD............ Vibrational Circular Dichroism [*Spectrometry*]
VCD............ Visiting Card (BJA)
VCD............ Voltage Crossing Detector
VCDS......... Vice-Chief of Defence Staff [*British*]
VCDS(P & L) ... Vice Chief of Defence Staff Personnel and Logistics [*British*] (RDA)
VCE............ Vapor Compression Evaporation
VCE............ Variable Cycle Engine (MCD)
VCE............ Vehicle Condition Evaluation (MCD)
VCE............ Venice [*Italy*] [*Airport symbol*] (OAG)
VCE............ Vertical Centrifugal
VCE............ Vice
Vcela Morav ... Vcela Moravska [*A publication*]
VC Eq........ Victoria Reports, Equity (DLA)
VCF............ Vapor Chamber Fin
VCF............ Variable Crystal Filter (DEN)
Vcf............ Velocity of Circumferential Fiber Shortening [*Cardiology*]
VCF............ Verified Circulation Figure [*Periodical publishing*]
VCF............ Visual Comfort Factor
VCF............ Voltage Controlled Filter
VCF............ Voltage-Controlled Frequency (IEEE)
VCFUSA..... Vietnamese Catholic Federation in the USA (EA)
VCG............ Vapor Crystal Growth [*Materials processing*]
VCG............ Vectorcardiogram [*Medicine*]
VCG............ Vehicle Control Group
VCG............ Verification Condition Generator
VCG............ Vertical Location of the Center of Gravity
VCG............ Vice-Consul General [*British*] (ROG)
VCG............ Video Command Generator (MCD)
VCG............ Voltage-Controlled Generator
VCGS........ Vapor Crystal Growth System [*Materials processing*]
VCGS........ Vice Chief of the General Staff [*in the field*] [*Military*] [*British*] (RDA)
VCH............ Veterinary Convalescent Hospital
VCH............ Vichadero [*Uruguay*] [*Airport symbol*] [*Obsolete*] (OAG)
VCH............ Victoria County History [*Classical studies*] (OCD)
VCH............ Video Concert Hall
VCHO......... Vicar Choral
VCHP......... Variable Conductance Heat Pipe
VChr.......... Vigiliae Christianae [*A publication*]
V Christ...... Vetera Christianorum [*A publication*]
VCI............. Variety Clubs International [*New York, NY*] (EA)
VCI............. Velocity Change Indicator (NASA)
VCI............. Vibration Control Index
VCI............. Vietcong Infrastructure
VCI............. Visual Comfort Index
VCI............. Volatile Corrosion Inhibitor (KSC)
VCID.......... Very Close in Defense
VCIGS........ Vice-Chief of the Imperial General Staff [*British*]
VCIM......... Varnished Cambric Insulation Material
VCINS........ Vietcong Infrastructure Neutralization System
VCIP.......... Veterans Cost-of-Instruction Program [*Higher Education Act*]
V-CITE....... Vertical-Cargo Integration Test Equipment (MCD)

VC-K.......... Eli Lilly & Co. [*Canada*] [*Research code symbol*]
VCK............ Video Camera Kit
VCK............ Vietcong Killed
VC KIA(BC) ... Vietcong Killed in Action (Body Count)
VC KIA(POSS) ... Vietcong Killed in Action (Possible)
VCL............ Vehicle Checkout Laboratory
VCL............ Vertical Center Line
VCL............ Voice Communications Laboratory
VCL............ Voluntary College Letter [*British*]
VCLE.......... Versicle
VCLF.......... Vertical Cask-Lifting Fixture [*Nuclear energy*] (NRCH)
VCLLO........ Violoncello [*Music*]
VCLO......... Voltage-Controlled Local Oscillator
VCM.......... Vacuum (AAG)
VCM.......... Ventilation Control Module [*NASA*]
VCM.......... Veracruz [*Mexico*] [*Seismograph station code, US Geological Survey*] (SEIS)
VCM.......... Vertical Current Meter
VCM.......... Vertical Cutter Motion
VCM.......... Vibrating Coil Magnetometer
VCM.......... Victoria College of Music [*London*] (ROG)
VCM.......... Viking Continuation Mission [*NASA*]
VCM.......... Vinyl Chloride Monomer [*Organic chemistry*]
VCM.......... Visual Countermeasure
VCM.......... Volatile Condensable Material
VCM.......... Voltage-Controlled Multivibrator
VCM.......... Voorhees College, Denmark, SC [*OCLC symbol*] (OCLC)
VCMA........ Vacuum Cleaner Manufacturers Association [*Cleveland, OH*] (EA)
VCN............ Christopher Newport College, Newport News, VA [*OCLC symbol*] (OCLC)
VCN............ Millville, NJ [*Location identifier*] [*FAA*] (FAAL)
VCN............ Vancomycin-Colistin-Nystatin [*Growth-inhibiting mixture*] [*Microbiology*]
VCN............ Vendor Contract Notice
VCN............ Vibrio cholerae Neuraminidase [*An enzyme*]
VCN............ Vinyl Cyanide [*Organic chemistry*]
VCN............ Visual Communications Network, Inc. [*Cambridge, MA*]
VCN............ Vulcan Resources [*Vancouver Stock Exchange symbol*]
VCNM........ Vice Chief of Naval Material Command
VCNO........ Vice Chief of Naval Operations
VCNS........ Vice-Chief of the Naval Staff [*British*]
VCNTY....... Vicinity (AFM)
VC/NVA..... Vietcong/North Vietnamese Army
VCO........... Glendale, AZ [*Location identifier*] [*FAA*] (FAAL)
VCO........... Variable Cycle Operation
VCO........... Vehicle Control Officer [*Air Force*] (AFM)
VCO........... Verbal Concrete Object
VCO........... Verbit & Company, Consultants to Management [*Bala Cynwyd, PA*] [*Telecommunications*] (TSSD)
VCO........... Vertical Control Operator [*Military*]
VCO........... Voice Controlled Oscillator [*Telecommunications*] (TEL)
VCO........... Voltage-Controlled Oscillator
VCOA........ Volkswagen Convertible Owners of America (EA)
VCoA......... Volvo Club of America (EA)
VCOFGWBS ... Vietnamese Cross of Gallantry with Bronze Star (AABC)
VCOFGWGS ... Vietnamese Cross of Gallantry with Gold Star (AABC)
VCOFGWP ... Vietnamese Cross of Gallantry with Palm (AABC)
VCOFGWSS ... Vietnamese Cross of Gallantry with Silver Star (AABC)
VCOFS....... Vice Chief of Staff
VCOI.......... Veterans Cost-of-Instruction
VCOP......... Variable Control Oil Pressure (MSA)
VCOS......... Vice-Chiefs of Staff [*British*]
VCOT......... VFR [*Visual Flight Rules*] Conditions on Top [*Aviation*] (FAAC)
VCOV......... Volunteer Consultant for Office of Volunteers [*Red Cross*]
VCP........... Sao Paulo [*Brazil*] Viracopos Airport [*Airport symbol*] (OAG)
VCP........... Vehicle Check Point [*Military*]
VCP........... Vehicle Collecting Point
VCP........... Velocity Control Programer
VCP........... Verdan Checkout Panel
VCP........... Veterinary Creolin-Pearson
VCP........... Video Cassette Player
VCP........... Virus Cancer Program [*National Cancer Institute*]
VCP........... Voluntary Cooperation Program [*World Meteorological Organization*] [*United Nations*]
VCPA......... Virginia-Carolina Peanut Association (EA)
VCPA......... Virginia Crab Packers Association [*Defunct*] (EA)
VCPM........ Video-Enhanced Contrast Polarization Microscopy
VCPOR....... Vanguardia Comunista del Partido Obrero Revolucionario [*Bolivian*] (PPW)
VCPS......... Velocity Control Propulsion Subsystem [*NASA*]
VC PW....... Vietcong Prisoner of War
VCR........... Vacuum Contact Relay
VCR........... Valclair Resources Ltd. [*Vancouver Stock Exchange symbol*]
VCR........... Variable Compression Ratio
VCR........... Vasoconstrictive [*Physiology*]
VCR........... Video Cassette Recorder
VCR........... Vincristine [*Also, LCR, O, V*] [*Antineoplastic drug*]
VCR........... Visual Control Room
VCR........... Viva Cristo Rey [*Long Live Christ the King*] [*Spanish*]
VCR........... Vocal Character Recognition

VCR .... Voltage Coefficient of Resistance
VCRAS .... Office of Vice Chancellor for Research and Advanced Study [*University of Alaska*] [*Research center*]   (RCD)
VCRE .... Vari-Care, Inc. [*NASDAQ symbol*]   (NQ)
VC Rep ...... Vice-Chancellor's Reports [*English, Canadian*]   (DLA)
VCRT .... Variable Contrast Resolution Test [*Optics*]
VCS .... Cruiser-Scouting Aircraft Squadron [*Navy symbol*]
VCS .... Vacuum Control Switch
VCS .... Validation Control System
VCS .... Vane Control System   (MCD)
VCS .... Vapor Coating System
VCS .... Vapor Cooling System
VCS .... Variable Correlation Synchronization
VCS .... Vasoconstrictor Substance [*Physiology*]
VCS .... Vehicular Communications System
VCS .... Velocity Cutoff System   (KSC)
VCS .... Ventilation Control System [*NASA*]   (KSC)
VCS .... Verbal Communication Scales [*Educational testing*]
VCS .... Vernier Control System
VCS .... Veterans Canteen Service [*Veterans Administration*]
VCS .... Veterinary Cancer Society [*Madison, WI*]   (EA)
VC of S .... Vice Chief of Staff
VCS .... Vice Chief of Staff
VCS .... Video Cassette System
VCS .... Video Clutter Suppression   (CAAL)
VCS .... Video Communications System
VCS .... Video Computer System [*Atari, Inc.*]
VCS .... Video Contrast Seeker
VCS .... Vietcong Suspect
VCS .... Viking Change Status [*NASA*]
VCS .... Virginia & Carolina Southern R. R. [*AAR code*]
VCS .... Visual Call Sign [*Communications*]
VCS .... Visually Coupled System   (IEEE)
VCS .... Voice Control Switch [*NASA*]
VCS .... Voice System [*Ground Communications Facility, NASA*]
VCS .... Voltage Calibration Set
VCS .... Voltage-Current-Sequence   (MCD)
VCSA .... Vice Chief of Staff, Army [*Formerly, VC of SA*]
VC of SA .... Vice Chief of Staff, Army [*Later, VCSA*]   (AABC)
VC/SAF ..... Vice Chief of Staff, Air Force
VCSAV ...... Vestnik Ceskoslovenske Akademie Ved [*A publication*]
VCS Bul .... VCS [*Victorian Computer Society*] Bulletin [*A publication*]
VCSFO .... Veterans Canteen Service Field Office [*Veterans Administration*]
VCSL .... Voice Call Signs List
VCSP .... Voice Call Signs Plan
VCSR .... Voltage-Controlled Shift Register
VCSS .... Value Creation Study Society   (CINC)
VCT .... St. Vincent and the Grenadines [*Three-letter standard code*]   (CNC)
VCT .... Vector [*A publication*]
VCT .... Venous Clotting Time [*Clinical chemistry*]
VCT .... Victoria [*Texas*] [*Airport symbol*]   (OAG)
VCT .... Vidicon Camera Tube
VCT .... Vitrified Clay Tile [*Technical drawings*]
VCT .... Voice Code Translation   (BUR)
VCT .... Voltage Control Transfer
VCT .... Voltage Curve Tracer
VCT .... Volume Control Tank [*Nuclear energy*]   (NRCH)
VCTA General J ... Victorian Commercial Teachers' Association. General Journal [*A publication*]
VCTCA ...... Virtual Channel to Channel Adapter
VCTD .... Vendor Contract Technical Data
VCTR .... Vector   (NASA)
VCTR .... Vector Graphic, Inc. [*NASDAQ symbol*]   (NQ)
VCTS .... Variable Cockpit Training System   (MCD)
VCTY .... Vicinity   (NVT)
VCU .... Video Control Unit   (MCD)
VCU .... Videocystourethrography [*Medicine*]
VCU .... Virginia Commonwealth University
VCU .... Voiding Cystourethrogram [*Medicine*]
VCU .... Voltage Control Unit
VCUG .... Vesicoureterogram [*Urology*]
VCV .... Clinch Valley College of the University of Virginia, Wise, VA [*OCLC symbol*]   (OCLC)
VCV .... Vacuum Check Valve
VCV .... Vacuum Control Valve
VCV .... Victorville, CA [*Location identifier*] [*FAA*]   (FAAL)
VCVS .... Voltage-Controlled Voltage Source
VCXO .... Voltage-Controlled Crystal Oscillator
VCY .... Valley City, ND [*Location identifier*] [*FAA*]   (FAAL)
VCY .... Ventura County Railway Co. [*Army*]
VCZ .... Vinylcarbazole [*Organic chemistry*]
VD .... Double Vibrations [*Cycles*]
VD .... Leo Pharm. Products [*Denmark*] [*Research code symbol*]
VD .... Photographic Squadron [*Navy symbol*]
VD .... Valuation Decisions   (DLA)
VD .... Vandyke [*Graphics*]
VD .... Vapor Density
VD .... Various Dates [*Bibliography*]
VD .... Vault Door   (AAG)

VD .... Venereal Disease
VD .... Ventilating Deadlight [*Technical drawings*]
VD .... Ventricular Dilator [*Neuron*] [*Medicine*]
VD .... Verbal Discrimination [*Psychology*]
VD .... Verbum Domini [*Rome*] [*A publication*]   (BJA)
VD .... Vertical Drive
VD .... Viceroy-Designate [*British*]
VD .... Victoria Docks [*British*]   (ROG)
VD .... Victorian Decoration [*British*]
VD .... Video Decoder
VD .... Video Disk   (BUR)
VD .... Violent Defectives [*British*]
VD .... Virtual Data
VD .... Visiting Dignitary
V/D .... Voice/Data   (BUR)
VD .... Void   (AAG)
VD .... Voltage Detector
VD .... Voltage Drop   (MSA)
VD .... Volume Deleted
VD .... Volume of Distribution
VD .... Volunteer Decoration [*British*]
VDA .... Valve Drive Amplifier
VDA .... Variable Depth ASDIC   (NATG)
VDA .... Vendor Data Article
VDA .... Versatile Drone Autopilot   (MCD)
VDA .... Vertical Danger Angle [*Navigation*]
V & DA .... Video and Data Acquisition   (MCD)
VDA .... Video Dimension Analysis [*Sports medicine*]
VDA .... Video Distribution Amplifier
VDA .... Visual Discriminatory Acuity
VDA .... Volksbund fuer das Deutschtum im Ausland [*NAZI Germany*]
VDAC .... Vaginal Delivery after Caesarean [*Obstetrics*]
VDAC .... Vendor Data Article Control
VDAC .... Voltage-Dependent, Anion-Selective Channels [*In the membrane of a mitochondrion*]
VDA/D .... Video Display Adapter with Digital Enhancement [*AT & T*]
VDAM .... Virtual Data Access Method   (IEEE)
VDAS .... Vibration Data Acquisition System   (KSC)
VDAS .... Voltage-Dependent, Anion-Selective [*Proteins*] [*Biochemistry*]
VDASD .... Veroeffentlichungen der Deutschen Akademie fuer Sprache und Dichtung [*A publication*]
VDB .... Brooklyn College, Brooklyn, NY [*OCLC symbol*]   (OCLC)
VdB .... Van Den Bergh [*Liver function test*]
VDB .... Vector Data Buffer
VDB .... Very Dear Brother [*Freemasonry*]
VDB .... Victor D. Brenner [*Designer's mark, when appearing on US coins*]
VDB .... Video Display Board
VDB .... Vrijzinnige-Democratische Bond [*Radical Democratic League*] [*The Netherlands*]   (PPE)
VDC .... Van Dorn Company [*NYSE symbol*]
VDC .... Vanadocene Dichloride [*Antineoplastic drug*]
VDC .... Variable Diode Circuit
VDC .... Vasodilator Center [*Physiology*]
VDC .... Vendor Data Control   (MCD)
VDC .... Ventilation Duct Chase [*Nuclear energy*]   (NRCH)
VDC .... Venture Development Corporation [*Natick, MA*] [*Telecommunications*]   (TSSD)
VDC .... Victoria Diego Resource Corporation [*Vancouver Stock Exchange symbol*]
VDC .... Video-Documentary Clearinghouse   (EA)
VDC .... Voltage to Digital Converter
VDC .... Voltage Doubler Circuit
VDC .... Volts Direct Current
VDC .... Volunteer Defense Corps
VDC .... Volunteer Development Corps   (EA)
VDCP .... Video Data Collection Program
VDCT .... Direct-Current Test Volts
VDCU .... Videograph Display Control Unit
VDCW .... Direct-Current Working Volts
VDD .... Version Description Document   (KSC)
VDD .... Video Detector Diode
VDD .... Visual Display Data
VDD .... Voice Digital Display
VDDAS .... Vehicles Detector Data Acquisition System   (ADA)
VDDI .... Voyager Data Detailed Index [*NASA*]   (KSC)
VDDL .... Voyager Data Distribution List [*NASA*]   (KSC)
VDDP .... Video Digital Data Processing
VDDR .... Vitamin D-Dependent Rickets [*Medicine*]
VDDS .... Voyager Data Description Standards [*NASA*]   (KSC)
VDE .... Vacuum Deposition Equipment
VDE .... Valverde [*Canary Islands*] [*Airport symbol*]   (OAG)
VDE .... Variable Displacement Engine
VDE .... Variable Display Equipment
VDE .... Verband Deutsche Elektrotechniker [*Telecommunications*] [*German*]   (TEL)
VDEFA .... VDE [*Verband Deutscher Elektrotechniker*] Fachberichte [*A publication*]
VDE Fachber ... VDE [*Verband Deutscher Elektrotechniker*] Fachberichte [*A publication*]

VDEh .... Verein Deutscher Eisenhuttenleute [*German Iron and Steel Engineers Association*] [*Dusseldorf, West Germany*] [*Information service*]   (EISS)
VDEL .... Variable Delivery
VDEL .... Venereal Disease Experimental Laboratory
VDEO .... Video Station, Inc. [*NASDAQ symbol*]   (NQ)
VDET .... Voltage Detector   (IEEE)
VDETS .... Voice Data Entry Terminal System
VDEV .... "V" Device [*Military decoration*]   (AABC)
VDEW (Ver Dtsch Elektrizitaetswerke) Informationsdienst ... VDEW (Vereinigung Deutscher Elektrizitaetswerke) Informationsdienst (German Federal Republic) [*A publication*]
VDF .... Very-High-Frequency Direction-Finding
VDF .... Vibration Damping Fastener
VDF .... Video Frequency
VDF .... Vinylidene Fluoride [*Organic chemistry*]
VDF .... Vorkaempfer Deutscher Freiheit. Series [*Munich*] [*A publication*]
VDFAN .... Vestnik Dal'nevostochnogo Filiala Akademii Nauk SSSR [*A publication*]
VDFG .... Variable Diode Function Generator
VDG .... Royal Inniskilling Dragoon Guards [*Military unit*] [*British*]
VDG .... Vehicle Data Guide
VDG .... Venereal Disease Gonorrhea
VDG .... Vertical and Direction Gyro
VDG .... Vertical Display Generator   (NG)
VDG .... Video Display Generator
VdgB .... Vereinigung der Gegenseitigen Bauernhilfe [*Mutual Farmers' Aid Society*] [*Germany*]
VdGSA .... Viola da Gamba Society of America   (EA)
VdGSA .... Viola da Gamba Society of America. Journal [*A publication*]
VDH .... Valvular Disease of the Heart [*Medicine*]
VDH .... Van Der Hout Associates Ltd. [*Toronto Stock Exchange symbol*]
VDI .... Vat Dye Institute [*Later, American Dye Manufacturers Institute*]   (EA)
VDI .... Verein Deutscher Ingenieure [*Society of German Engineers*]
VDI .... Vertical Direction Indicator   (CAAL)
VDI .... Vertical Display Indicator   (NG)
VDI .... Vestnik Drevnei Istorii [*A publication*]
VDI .... Vidalia, GA [*Location identifier*] [*FAA*]   (FAAL)
VDI .... Video Display Input
VDI .... Video Display Interface
VDI .... Virtual Device Interface [*Computer technology*]
VDI .... Visual Display Input
VDI .... Voluntary Data Inquiry
VDI Ber .... VDI [*Verein Deutscher Ingenieure*] Berichte [*A publication*]
VDIEO .... Vendor Data Information Engineering Order   (MCD)
VDIFA .... VDI [*Verein Deutscher Ingenieure*] Forschungsheft [*A publication*]
VDI Forschungsh ... VDI [*Verein Deutscher Ingenieure*] Forschungsheft [*A publication*]
VDIG .... Vertical Display Indicator Group
VDI-N .... VDI-Nachrichten [*VDI-Verlag GmbH*] [*Database*]
VDI Nachr ... Verein Deutscher Ingenieure. Nachrichten [*A publication*]
VDISK .... Virtual Disk [*Data processing*]
VDI Z .... VDI [*Verein Deutscher Ingenieure*] Zeitschrift [*A publication*]
VDI Z Fortschr Ber Reihe 5 ... VDI [*Verein Deutscher Ingenieure*] Zeitschriften. Fortschritt-Berichte. Reihe 5. Grund- und Werkstoffe [*A publication*]
VDJ .... Variable-Diversity-Joining [*Genetics*]
VDK .... Vicinal Diketone [*Organic chemistry*]
VDL .... Van Diemen's Land [*Former name of Tasmania*]
VDL .... Variable Delay Line
VDL .... Vasodepressor Lipid [*Physiology*]
VDL .... Ventilating Deadlight
VDL .... Video Data Link   (NVT)
VDL .... Vienna Definition Language [*1960*] [*Data processing*]   (CSR)
VDL .... Voice Direct Line
VDLF .... Variable Depth Launch Facility   (AAG)
VDM .... Variable Direction Microphone
VDM .... Varian Data Machines
VDM .... Vasodepressor Material [*Physiology*]
VDM .... Vector Dominance Model [*Physics*]
VDM .... Vector Drawn Map
VDM .... Vehicle Deadlined for Maintenance   (AFM)
VDM .... Verbi Dei Minister [*Minister, or Preacher, of the Word of God*] [*Latin*]
VDM .... Vibration Damping Mount
VDM .... Video Delta Modulation
VDM .... Viedma [*Argentina*] [*Airport symbol*]   (OAG)
VDMA .... Verband Deutscher Maschinen- und Anlagenbau eV [*German Machine Construction Union*] [*Frankfurt, West Germany*]
VDME .... Vibrating Dropping Mercury Electrode [*Electrochemistry*]
VDMIE .... Verbum Domini Manet in Eternum [*The Word of the Lord Endureth Forever*] [*Latin*]
VDMOS ...... Vertical Double Diffused Metal Oxide Semiconductor   (MCD)
VDMS .... Video Delta Modulation System
VDMS .... Vocal Data Management System
VDN .... Varudeklarationsnamnden [*Labeling system*] [*Sweden*]

VDN .... Vedron Ltd. [*Toronto Stock Exchange symbol*]
VdN .... Voix des Notres [*Record label*] [*France*]
VDNAA .... VDI [*Verein Deutscher Ingenieure*] Nachrichten [*A publication*]
VDNCOA .... Veterans Division of the Non-Commissioned Officers Association of the USA   (EA)
VDNH .... VD [*Venereal Disease*] National Hotline [*Palo Alto, CA*]   (EA)
VDO .... Le Group Videotron SV [*Toronto Stock Exchange symbol*]
VD/OS .... Vacuum Distillation/Overflow Sampler   (NRCH)
VDP .... Vacuum Diffusion Pump
VDP .... Vehicle Deadlined for Parts
VDP .... Verenigde Democratische Partijen [*United Democratic Parties*] [*Surinamese*]   (PPW)
VDP .... Vertical Data Processing
VDP .... Vertical Dipole   (MCD)
VDP .... Vibration Diagnostic Program
VDP .... Vibration-Dissociation Process
VDP .... Video Data Processor
VDP .... Videodisc Player [*RCA Corp.*]
VDP .... Vincristine, Daunorubicin, Prednisone [*Antineoplastic drug regimen*]
VDP .... Visual Descent Point [*Aviation*]   (FAAC)
VDP .... Volunteer Reservists in Drill Pay Status [*Navy*]
VDP .... Von Deutscher Poeterey [*A publication*]
VDPh .... Verhandlung der Versammlung Deutscher Philologen [*A publication*]
VDPI .... Vehicle Direction and Position Indicator
VDPI .... Voyager Data Processing Instructions [*NASA*]   (KSC)
VDPS .... Voice Data Processor System
VDQ .... Visual Display of Quality
VDQS .... Vins Delimites de Qualite Superieure [*Designation on French wine labels*]
VDR .... Validated Data Record
VDR .... Variable Deposit Requirement [*Business and trade*]   (ADA)
VDR .... Variable Diameter Rotor
VDR .... Vehicle Deselect Request [*NASA*]   (KSC)
VDR .... Vendor Data Request
VDR .... Venous Diameter Ratio [*Cancer detection*]
VDR .... Video Disc Recorder
VDR .... Voice & Data Resources, Inc. [*New York, NY*] [*Information service*] [*Telecommunications*]   (TSSD)
VDR .... Voice Digitization Rate
VDR .... Voltage-Dependent Resistor   (DEN)
VDRA .... Voice and Data Recording Auxiliary [*NASA*]   (KSC)
VDRG .... Vendor Data Release Group   (MCD)
VDRL .... Venereal Disease Research Laboratory
VDRT .... Venereal Disease Reference Test [*of Harris*]
VDRY .... Vacu-Dry Co. [*NASDAQ symbol*]   (NQ)
VDS .... Vadso [*Norway*] [*Airport symbol*]   (OAG)
VDS .... Vapor Deposited Silica [*Optical fiber technology*]
VDS .... Vapor Detection System
VDS .... Variable Depth SONAR
VDS .... Vasodilator Substance [*Physiology*]
VDS .... Vehicle Description Summary [*General Motors Corp.*]
VDS .... Vehicle Dynamics Simulator [*NASA*]   (NASA)
VDS .... Velocita di Sedimentazione [*Sedimentation Rate*] [*Medicine*]
VDS .... Vendor Data Service
VDS .... Vendor Direct Shipment
VDS .... Venereal Disease Syphilis
VDS .... Veroeffentlichungen der Deutschen Schillergesellschaft [*A publication*]
VDS .... Vertical Display System [*Navy*]
VDS .... Video Digitizer System   (MCD)
VDS .... Video Display System
VDS .... Vindesine [*Also, E*] [*Antineoplastic drug*]
VDS .... Viola d'Amore Society   (EA)
VDS .... Visual Docking Simulator
VDS .... Voice Data Switch
VDSA .... Veut Dieu Saint Amour [*Knights Templar*] [*Freemasonry*]
VDSM .... Internationaler Verband der Stadt-, Sport-, und Mehrzweckhallen [*International Federation of City, Sport, and Multi-Purpose Halls*]   (EA-IO)
VDSS .... Variable Depth SONAR System
VDSS .... Volume of Distribution at Steady State
VDT .... Varactor Diode Test
VDT .... Variable Deflection Thruster [*Helicopter*]
VDT .... Variable Density Tunnel
VDT .... Variable Depth Transducer [*Navy*]   (NVT)
VDT .... Variable Differential Transformer
VDT .... Vehicle Data Table   (MCD)
VDT .... Video Data Terminal [*Data processing*]
VDT .... Video [*or Visual*] Display Terminal [*Data processing*]
VDT .... Visual Display Terminal
VDTA .... Vacuum Dealers Trade Association [*Des Moines, IA*]   (EA)
VDTJ .... Voprosy Dialektologii Tjurkskich Jazykov [*A publication*]
VDTT .... Very Difficult to Test [*Audiology*]
VDU .... Refugio, TX [*Location identifier*] [*FAA*]   (FAAL)
VdU .... Verband der Unabhaengigen [*League of Independents*] [*Dissolved, 1956*] [*Austria*]   (PPE)
VDU .... Video Display Unit [*Data processing*]
VDU .... Visual Display Unit
VDV .... Vacuum Differential Valve [*Automotive engineering*]

VDV .... Vojski Drzavne Varnosti [*Yugoslavia*]

VDV .... Vozdushno-Desantnye Voiska [*Airborne Troops*] [*An autonomous command*] [*USSR*]

VD-VF .... Vacuum Distillation - Vapor Filtration

VDW .... Venus Departure Window [*NASA*]

VDW .... Very Deep Water

VDX .... Vandorex Energy [*Vancouver Stock Exchange symbol*]

VDYK .... Van Dyk Research Corp. [*NASDAQ symbol*]   (NQ)

VDZ .... Valdez [*Alaska*] [*Airport symbol*]   (OAG)

VE .... AVENSA Aerovias Venezolanas SA [*Venezuela*] [*ICAO designator*]   (FAAC)

Ve .... Biblioteca Nacional, Caracas, Venezuela [*Library symbol*] [*Library of Congress*]   (LCLS)

VE .... Vaginal Epithelium [*Endocrinology*]

VE .... Vaginal Examination [*Medicine*]

VE .... Value Effectiveness

VE .... Value Engineering

VE .... Varicose Eczema [*Medicine*]

VE .... Vehicle Experimental   (MCD)

Ve .... Velban [*See VBL*]

VE .... Velocity Equipment   (MCD)

VE .... Velocity Error

ve .... Venezuela [*MARC country of publication code*] [*Library of Congress*]   (LCCP)

VE .... Venezuela [*Two-letter standard code*]   (CNC)

VE .... Ventilating Equipment   (MSA)

VE .... Verbal Emotional (Stimuli) [*Psychology*]

V-E .... VERLORT [*Very-Long-Range Tracking*] Elevation [*NASA*]

VE .... Vermont Music Educators News [*A publication*]

VE .... Vernal Equinox

VE .... Vernier Engine [*as a modifier*]   (AAG)

VE .... Vesicular Exanthema [*Virus*]

VE .... Vestnik Evropy [*A publication*]

VE .... Veuve [*Widow*] [*French*]   (ROG)

VE .... Victory in Europe [*as in VE-Day*]

V & E .... Vinethene and Ether

VE .... Visalia Electric Railroad Co. [*AAR code*]

VE .... Visual Efficiency

VE .... Vocational Education   (OICC)

VE .... Voltage Efficiency [*Electrochemistry*]

VE .... Volume Ejection [*Medicine*]

VE .... Voluntary Effort [*A cost containment program established by AHA, AMA, and FAH*]

VE .... Votre Eminence [*Your Eminence*] [*French*]

VE .... Vox Evangelica [*A publication*]

V-E (Day) ... Victory in Europe Day [*World War II*]

VEA .... Value Engineering Audit

VEA .... Vehicle Engineering Analysis

VEA .... Veliger Escape Aperture

VEA .... Veterans Educational Assistance [*Act*]

VEA .... Viral Envelope Antigens [*Immunology*]

VEA .... Vocational Education Act [*1963*]

VEAB Ert.... VEAB Ertesitoe [*Hungary*] [*A publication*]

VEAMCOP ... Viking Error Analysis Monte Carlo Program [*Data processing*]

VEAP .... Veterans Educational Assistance Program [*DoD*]

Veazey .... Veazey's Reports [*36-44 Vermont*]   (DLA)

VEB .... Variable Elevation Beam [*RADAR*]

VE & B ...... Vehicle Energy and Biotechnology   (MCD)

VEB .... Ventricular Ectopic Beats [*Cardiology*]

VEB .... Venus Entry Body [*NASA*]

Ve & B ...... Vesey and Beames' English Chancery Reports   (DLA)

VEB .... Vocational Education Board   (OICC)

VEBA.......... Vereinigte Elektrizitaets und Bergwerks, AG [*Holding company*] [*Germany*]

VEBA.......... Voluntary Employee Benefit Association [*Type of trust established by a company, a union, or both to provide members with various insurance benefits*]

VEBR .... Visual Evoked Brain Response

VEB Verlag Tech Mon Tech Rev ... VEB Verlag Technik. Monthly Technical Review [*A publication*]

VEBW .... Vacuum Electron Beam Welder

VEC .... Vacation Exchange Club   (EA)

VEC .... Value Engineering Change

VEC .... Variable Energy Cyclotron   (IEEE)

VEC .... Vector   (KSC)

VEC .... Vector Control   (MUGU)

VEC .... Venice, LA [*Location identifier*] [*FAA*]   (FAAL)

VEC .... Vertical Electrical Chase [*Nuclear energy*]   (NRCH)

VeC .... Vertice (Coimbra) [*A publication*]

VEC .... Vibration Exciter Control

VEC .... Voice Equivalent Channel   (MCD)

VeCAL......... Archivo del Libertador, Caracas, Venezuela [*Library symbol*] [*Library of Congress*]   (LCLS)

VECAS .... Vertical Escape Collision Avoidance System [*Aviation*]

VECC .... Value Engineering Control Committee [*Military*]

VECHCC .... Voluntary Effort to Contain Health Care Costs   (EA)

VECI .... Vehicular Equipment Complement Index   (IEEE)

VECO .... Vernier Engine Cutoff [*NASA*]

VECOS....... Vehicle Checkout Set

VECP......... Value Engineering Change Proposals [*Navy*]

VECP......... Visually Evoked Cortical Potential [*Neurophysiology*]

VECR.......... Vendor Engineering Change Request [*DoD*]

VECS......... Vocational Education Curriculum Specialists   (OICC)

Vect......... De Vectigalibus [*of Xenophon*] [*Classical studies*]   (OCD)

V-ECT .... Ventricular Ectopy

VECTAC ..... Vectored Attack [*Navy*]   (NVT)

VECTAR..... Value, Expertise, Client, Time, Attorney, Result [*Lawyer evaluation method*]

VECTRAN ... [*A*] programing language   (CSR)

VED .... Vacuum Energy Diverter

VED .... Ventricular Ectopic Depolarization

VED .... Viscoelastic Damper

VED .... Volumetric Energy Density [*of fuels*]

VEDAR....... Visible Energy Detection and Ranging

Veda Tech Mladezi ... Veda a Technika Mladezi [*Czechoslovakia*] [*A publication*]

Veda Tech SSSR ... Veda a Technika v SSSR [*A publication*]

Veda Vyzk Potravin Prum ... Veda a Vyzkum v Potravinarskem Prumyslu [*A publication*]

Veda Vyzk Prum Sklarskem ... Veda a Vyzkum v Prumyslu Sklarskem [*A publication*]

Veda Vyzk Prum Text ... Veda a Vyzkum v Prumyslu Textilnim [*A publication*]

Vedeckovyzk Uhelny Ustav Sb Vyzk Pr ... Vedeckovyzkumny Uhelny Ustav Sbornik Vyzkumnych Praci [*Czechoslovakia*] [*A publication*]

Ved Kes ..... Vedanta Kesari [*Madras*] [*A publication*]

VeDo .... Verbum Domino [*A publication*]

Ved Prace Ustr Vyzk Ustavu Rost Vyr (Praha) ... Vedecke Prace Ustredniho Vyzkumneho Ustavu Rostlinne Vyroby (Praha) [*A publication*]

Ved Prace Vyskum Ust Lesn Hosp Zvolen ... Vedecke Prace Vyskumny Ustav Lesneho Hospodarstva v Zvolene [*A publication*]

Ved Prace Vysk Ustavu Kukurice Trnave ... Vedecke Prace Vyskumneho Ustavu Kukurice v Trnave [*A publication*]

Ved Prace Vysk Ustavu Rastlinnej Vyr ... Vedecke Prace Vyskumneho Ustavu Rastlinnej Vyroby [*A publication*]

Ved Prace Vysk Ustavu Zavlahov Hospod Bratislave ... Vedecke Prace Vyskumneho Ustavu Zavlahoveho Hospodarstva v Bratislave [*A publication*]

Ved Prace Vysk Ustavu Zivoc Nitre ... Vedecke Prace Vyskumneho Ustavu Zivocisnej Vyroby v Nitre [*A publication*]

Ved Prace Vyzkum Ust Melior ... Vedecke Prace Vyzkumneho Ustavu Zemedelsko-Lesnickych Melioraci CSAZV [*Ceskoslovenska Akademie Zemedelskych Ved*] v Praze [*A publication*]

Ved Pr Cesk Zemed Muz ... Vedecke Prace Ceskoslovenskeho Zemedelskeho Muzea [*A publication*]

Ved Pr Lab Podoznalectva Bratisl ... Vedecke Prace Laboratoria Podoznalectva v Bratislave [*A publication*]

Ved Pr Ustavu Zelinarskeho Olomouci ... Vedecke Prace Ustavu Zelinarskeho v Olomouci [*A publication*]

Ved Pr Ustr Vyzk Ust Rostl Vyroby Praze-Ruzyni ... Vedecke Prace Ustredniho Vyzkumneho Ustavu Rostlinne Vyroby v Praze-Ruzyni [*A publication*]

Ved Pr VSCHK (Slatinany) ... Vedecke Prace VSCHK [*Vyzkumna Stanice pro Chov Koni*] (Slatinany) [*A publication*]

Ved Pr Vysk Ustavu Chov Hydiny Ivanka Dunaji ... Vedecke Prace Vyskumneho Ustavu pro Chov Hydiny v Ivanka pri Dunaji [*A publication*]

Ved Pr Vysk Ustavu Chov Skotu Caz Rapotine ... Vedecke Prace Vyskumneho Ustavu pro Chov Skotu Caz v Rapotine [*A publication*]

Ved Pr Vysk Ustavu Kukurice Trnave ... Vedecke Prace Vyskumneho Ustavu Kukurice v Trnave [*A publication*]

Ved Pr Vysk Ustavu Lesn Hospod Zvolene ... Vedecke Prace Vyskumneho Ustavu Lesneho Hospodarstva Vo Zvolene [*A publication*]

Ved Pr Vysk Ustavu Luk Pasienkov Banskej Bystrici ... Vedecke Prace Vyskumneho Ustavu Luk a Pasienkov v Banskej Bystrici [*A publication*]

Ved Pr Vysk Ustavu Ovciar Trencine ... Vedecke Prace Vyskumneho Ustavu Ovciarskeho v Trencine [*A publication*]

Ved Pr Vysk Ustavu Podoznalectva Vyz Rastlin Bratisl ... Vedecke Prace Vyskumneho Ustavu Podoznalectva a Vyzivy Rastlin v Bratislave [*A publication*]

Ved Pr Vysk Ustavu Rastlinnej Vyroby Piestanoch ... Vedecke Prace Vyskumneho Ustavu Rastlinnej Vyroby v Piestanoch [*A publication*]

Ved Pr Vysk Ustavu Zavlahoveho Hospod Bratisl ... Vedecke Prace Vyskumneho Ustavu Zavlahoveho Hospodarstva v Bratislave [*A publication*]

Ved Pr Vysk Ustavu Zivocisnej Vyroby Nitre ... Vedecke Prace Vyskumneho Ustavu Zivocisnej Vyroby v Nitre [*A publication*]

Ved Pr Vysk Ust Rastl Vyroby Piestanoch ... Vedecke Prace Vyskumneho Ustavu Rastlinnej Vyroby Piestanoch [*A publication*]

Ved Pr Vysk Ust Rastl Vyroby Praze-Ruzyni ... Vedecke Prace Ustredniho Vyskumneho Ustavu Rastlinnej Vyroby CSAZV [*Ceskoslovenska Akademie Zemedelskych Ved*] v Praze-Ruzyni [*A publication*]

Ved Pr Vyzk Stanice Chov Koni Slatinany ... Vedecke Prace Vyzkumna Stanice pro Chov Koni Slatinany [*A publication*]

Ved Pr Vyzk Ustavu Bramborarskeho Havlickove Brode ... Vedecke Prace Vyzkumneho Ustavu Bramborarskeho v Havlickove Brode [*A publication*]

Ved Pr Vyzk Ustavu Chov Prasat Kostelci Nad Orlice ... Vedecke Prace Vyzkumneho Ustavu pro Chov Prasat v Kostelci Nad Orlice [*A publication*]

Ved Pr Vyzk Ustavu Chov Skotu Caz Rapotine ... Vedecke Prace Vyzkumneho Ustavu pro Chov Skotu Caz v Rapotine [*A publication*]

Ved Pr Vyzk Ustavu Krmivarskeho Czaz Brne ... Vedecke Prace Vyzkumneho Ustavu Krmivarskeho Czaz v Brne [*A publication*]

Ved Pr Vyzk Ustavu Melior Praze Zbraslavi ... Vedecke Prace Vyzkumneho Ustavu Melioraci v Praze or Zbraslavi [*A publication*]

Ved Pr Vyzk Ustavu Obilnarskeho Kromerizi ... Vedecke Prace Vyzkumneho Ustavu Obilnarskeho v Kromerizi [*A publication*]

Ved Pr Vyzk Ustavu Okrasneho Zahradnictvi Pruhonicich ... Vedecke Prace Vyzkumneho Ustavu Okrasneho Zahradnictvi v Pruhonicich [*A publication*]

Ved Pr Vyzk Ustavu Ovilnarskeho Kromerizi ... Vedecke Prace Vyzkumneho Ustavu Ovilnarskeho v Kromerizi [*A publication*]

Ved Pr Vyzk Ustavu Rostl Vyroby Praze-Ruzyni ... Vedecke Prace Vyzkkumnych Ustavu Rostlinne Vyroby v Praze-Ruzyni [*A publication*]

Ved Pr Vyzk Ustavu Vet CSAZV Brne ... Vedecke Prace Vyzkumneho Ustavu Veterinarni CSAZV v Brne [*A publication*]

Ved Pr Vyzk Ustavu Vet Lek Brne ... Vedecke Prace Vyzkumneho Ustavu Veterinarniho Lekarstvi v Brne [*Czechoslovakia*] [*A publication*]

Ved Pr Vyzk Ustavu Zavlahoveho Hospod Bratislave ... Vedecke Prace Vyzkumneho Ustavu Zavlahoveho Hospodarstva v Bratislave [*A publication*]

VEDR......... Value Engineering Design Review
VEDS......... Vehicle Emergency Detection System [*NASA*] (KSC)
VEDS......... Vocational Education Data System
VEE .... Vagina, Ectocervix, and Endocervix [*Cytopathology*]
VEE .... Veeco Instruments, Inc. [*NYSE symbol*]
VEE .... Venetie [*Alaska*] [*Airport symbol*] (OAG)
VEE .... Venezuelan Equine Encephalomyelitis [*Virus*]
VEE .... Veterinary Equine Encephalomyelitis (RDA)
Veeartsenijk Blad Nederl-Indie ... Veeartsenijkundige Bladen voor Nederlandsch-Indie [*A publication*]
VEECO....... Vacuum Electronics Engineering Company (MCD)
VEEG......... Vector Electroencephalograph
VEEGA....... Venus-Earth-Earth-Gravity-Assist [*Spacecraft trajectory*]
VEEI .... Vehicle Electrical Engine Interface [*NASA*] (NASA)
VEEP......... Vice President
VEER......... Variable Emergence Electronically Rotated (MCD)
VEESS....... Vehicle Engine Exhaust Smoke System [*Army*] (RDA)
Veeteelt Zuivelber ... Veeteelt- en Zuivelberichten [*A publication*]
VEF .... Variable Electronic Filter
VEF .... Viscoelastic Fiber
VEF .... Viscoelastic Flow
VEF .... Vision Educational Foundation [*Memphis, TN*] (EA)
VEF .... Visually Evoked Field [*Neurophysiology*]
VEFCA....... Value Engineering Functional Cost Analysis
VEFCO....... Vertient Functional Checkout (IEEE)
VEF Inf Bul ... VEF [*Victorian Employers' Federation*] Information Bulletin [*A publication*]
VEG........... Maikwak [*Guyana*] [*Airport symbol*] (OAG)
VEG........... Value Engineering Guideline
Veg............. Vega [*Record label*] [*France*]
VEG........... Vegetable [*or Vegetation*] (KSC)
VEGA .... Vega Biotechnologies [*NASDAQ symbol*] (NQ)
VEGA .... Venera [*Venus*] and Gallei [*Halley*] [*Russian spacecraft*]
Veg Crops Ser Calif Univ Dept Veg Crops ... Vegetable Crops Series. California University. Department of Vegetable Crops [*A publication*]
Vegetarian Mo ... Vegetarian Monthly [*A publication*]
Veg Ex........ Vegetable Exchange [*Dietetics*]
Veg Grower ... Vegetable Grower [*A publication*]
Veg Grow News ... Vegetable Growers News [*A publication*]
VEGIL......... Vehicle Equipment and Government-Furnished Infrared Locator
VEGL......... Value Engineering Guideline
Veg Situat TVS US Dep Agric Econ Res Serv ... Vegetable Situation. United States Department of Agriculture. Economic Research [*A publication*]
Veg Times ... Vegetarian Times [*A publication*]
Vegyip Kut Intez Kozl ... Vegyipari Kutato Intezetek Kozlemenyei [*A publication*]
VEH .... Emory and Henry College, Emory, VA [*OCLC symbol*] (OCLC)
VEH .... Valence Effective Hamiltonian [*Physical chemistry*]
VEH .... Vehicle (AFM)
VEH .... Veterinary Evacuation Hospital
VEHID........ Vehicle Identification (MCD)
VEH PT...... Vehicle Part[*s*] [*Freight*]
Veh Syst Dyn ... Vehicle System Dynamics [*A publication*]
VEI............. Value Engineered Indicator (NG)

VEI............. Value Engineering Incentive
VEI............. Volcanic Explosivity Index [*Measure of amounts of gas and ash that reach the atmosphere*]
VEIS .... Vocational Education Information System
VEITA .... Vietnam Era Veterans Inter-Tribal Association (EA)
VEK .... Veterana Esperantista Klubo [*Esperantist Club of Veterans - ECV*] (EA-IO)
VEL............ Vehicle Emissions and Fuel Economy Laboratory [*Texas A & M University*] [*Research center*] (RCD)
Vel............. Vela [*Constellation*]
VEL............ Vellum
VEL............ Velocity (AFM)
Vel............. Veltro' [*A publication*]
VEL............ Vernal [*Utah*] [*Airport symbol*] (OAG)
VEL............ Virginia Electric & Power Co. [*NYSE symbol*]
VELARC .... Vertical Ejection Launch Aero-Reaction Control (MCD)
VELCF........ Velcro Industries NV [*NASDAQ symbol*] (NQ)
VELCOR...... Velocity Correction
VELCRO..... Velour and Crochet [*Interlocking nylon tapes - one with tiny loops, the other with tiny hooks - invented as a reusable fastener by George de Mestral*]
VELF .... Velocity Filter (IEEE)
VELG......... Velocity Gain (AAG)
VELKDDR ... Vereinigte Evangelisch-Lutherische Kirche in der Deutschen Demokratischen Republik [*United Evangelical-Lutheran Church of the German Democratic Republic*] [*Berlin, East Germany*]
Vell Pat...... Velleius Paterculus [*First century AD*] [*Classical studies*] (OCD)
Vel Lt Trap ... Velvet Light Trap [*A publication*]
VELOC .... Velocity
VELXF .... Velvet Explorations Co. Ltd. [*NASDAQ symbol*] (NQ)
VEM .... Eastern Mennonite College, Harrisonburg, VA [*OCLC symbol*] (OCLC)
VEM........... Value Engineering Model (NG)
VEM........... Vasoexcitor Material [*Physiology*]
VEM........... Vendor Engineering Memorandum (MCD)
Vema Res Ser ... Vema Research Series [*A publication*]
VEMASID.... Vehicle Magnetic Signature Duplicator (MCD)
VEMS .... Vehicle and Equipment Maintenance System [*Software*]
VEN .... Hawaiian Sky Tours [*Honolulu, HI*] [*FAA designator*] (FAAC)
VEN .... Variable Exhaust Nozzle
VEN .... [*The*] Vendo Co. [*NYSE symbol*]
Ven .... Vendome [*Record label*] [*France*]
VEN .... Venerable
VEN .... Venetian [*Freight*]
VEN .... Venezuela [*Three-letter standard code*] (CNC)
VEN .... Venice [*Italy*] [*Seismograph station code, US Geological Survey*] [*Closed*] (SEIS)
VEN .... Venite [*95th Psalm*]
VEN .... Venture Gold Corp. [*Vancouver Stock Exchange symbol*]
VEN .... Venture Science Fiction [*A publication*]
Ven............ Venus and Adonis [*Shakespearean work*]
Vend.......... Vending Times International Buyers Guide and Directory [*A publication*]
VEND .... Vendor (KSC)
VEND .... Venerated
VENET .... Venetian (ROG)
VEN EX...... Venditione Exponas [*Writ of Execution for Sheriff to Sell Goods*] [*Latin*] (ROG)
VENEZ .... Venezuela
Venez Dir Geol Bol Geol ... Venezuela. Direccion de Geologia. Boletin de Geologia [*A publication*]
Venez Dir Geol Bol Geol Publ Esp ... Venezuela. Direccion de Geologia. Boletin de Geologia. Publicacion Especial [*A publication*]
Venez Inst Nac Nutr Publ ... Venezuela. Instituto Nacional de Nutricion. Publicacion [*A publication*]
Venez Min Minas Hidrocarburos Dir Geol Bol Geol ... Venezuela. Ministerio de Minas e Hidrocarburos. Direccion de Geologia. Boletin de Geologia [*A publication*]
Venez Univ Cent Esc Geol Minas Lab Petrogr Geoquimica Inf ... Venezuela. Universidad Central. Escuela de Geologia y Minas. Laboratorio de Petrografia y Geoquimica. Informe [*A publication*]
VEN FA...... Venire Facias [*Writ to Sheriff to Summon Jury*] [*Latin*] (ROG)
Vengarskaya Farmakoter ... Vengarskaya Farmakoterapiya [*A publication*]
Veng Zh Gorn Dela Metall Gorn Delo ... Vengerskii Zhurnal Gornogo Dela i Metallurgii. Gornoe Delo [*A publication*]
VenPK .... Venizelikon Phileleftheron Komma [*Venizelist Liberal Party*] [*Greek*] (PPE)
VENR......... Veneer
VENT......... Ventilation (AFM)
VENT......... Ventricular [*Cardiology*]
VENT......... Ventriloquist
Vent.......... Ventris' English Common Pleas Reports [*86 ER*] (DLA)
Vent.......... Ventris' English King's Bench Reports (DLA)
Vent (Eng) ... Ventris' English Common Pleas Reports [*86 ER*] (DLA)
Vent (Eng) ... Ventris' English King's Bench Reports (DLA)
Vent Ochistka Vozdukha ... Ventilyatsiya i Ochistka Vozdukha [*A publication*]
ventr.......... Ventral

Ventr .... Ventris' English Common Pleas Reports [*86 ER*]   (DLA)
ventric....... Ventricular
VENTS .... Ventilators
VENUS .... Valuable and Effective Network Utility Services   (BUR)
VENUS .... Vulcain Experimental Nuclear Study [*Nuclear reactor*] [*Belgium*]
Venus Jpn J Malacol ... Venus: The Japanese Journal of Malacology [*A publication*]
VEO .... Value Engineering Organization
VEO .... Veronex Resources Ltd. [*Vancouver Stock Exchange symbol*]
VEOFA .... Vestnik Oftal'mologii [*A publication*]
VEOS .... Versatile Electro-Optical System   (MCD)
VEOXF .... Veronex Resources Ltd. [*NASDAQ symbol*]   (NQ)
VEP .... Value Engineering Program
VEP .... Value Engineering Proposal [*Army*]   (RDA)
VEP .... Vector Equilibrium Principle [*Crystallography*]
VEP .... Vertical Extrusion Press
VEP .... Veterans Education Project [*Washington, DC*]   (EA)
VEP .... Visually Evoked Potential [*Neurophysiology*]
VEP .... Vocational Exploration Program [*Office of Youth Programs*]
VEP .... Voter Education Project [*An association*]
VEPA .... Vocational Education Planning Areas   (OICC)
VEPCO .... Virginia Electric & Power Company
VEPG......... Value Engineering Program Guideline
VEPIS .... Vocational Education Program Information System
VEPL .... Vendor Engineering Procurement Liaison   (MCD)
VEPM .... Value Engineering Program Manager [*Military*]   (AABC)
VEPR .... Value Engineering Program Requirements   (NG)
VEQ .... Visiting Enlisted Quarters [*Army*]   (AABC)
VEQUD .... Veterinary Quarterly [*A publication*]
VER .... Boonville, MO [*Location identifier*] [*FAA*]   (FAAL)
VER .... Veracruz [*Mexico*] [*Airport symbol*]   (OAG)
VER .... Verandah [*Classified advertising*]   (ADA)
VER .... Verapamil [*A coronary vasodilator*]
VeR .... Verbum (Rio De Janeiro) [*A publication*]
VER .... Verein [*Association*] [*German*]
VER .... Verge   (ROG)
VER .... Verify   (AFM)
VER .... Verit Industries [*American Stock Exchange symbol*]
VER .... Vermifuge [*Destroying Worms*] [*Pharmacy*]   (ROG)
VER .... Vermilion   (ROG)
VER .... Vermillion Resources [*Vancouver Stock Exchange symbol*]
VER .... Vermont   (ROG)
Ver .... Vermont Reports   (DLA)
VER .... Vernier [*Engine*]   (AAG)
Ver .... Verri [*A publication*]
VER .... Verse
VER .... Version   (ROG)
Ver............. Versty [*A publication*]
VER .... Vert [*Heraldry*]
VER .... Vertical   (KSC)
VER .... Vertical Earth Rate
VER .... Veterans Employment Representative [*Department of Labor*]
VER .... Visual Evoked Response
VER .... Voluntary Export Restraints
VERA........ Variable Eddington Radiation Approximation   (MCD)
VERA........ Versatile Experimental Reactor Assembly   (DEN)
VERA........ Veterans' Employment and Readjustment Act of 1972
VERA........ Vision Electric Recording Apparatus [*BBC*]
VERAS .... Vehicle Experimental de Recherches Aerothermodynamique et Structurale [*Glider*] [*France*]
VERB......... Verbatim   (MSA)
VERB......... Verbessert [*Improved*] [*German*]
VERB......... Victor Electrowriter Remote Blackboard [*Educational device of Victor Comptometer Corp.*]
Verb C........ Verbum Caro [*A publication*]
VERB ET LIT ... Verbatim et Literatim [*Word for Word, An Exact Copy*] [*Latin*]   (ROG)
Ver Bibl Landes NRW Mitt ... Verband der Bibliotheken des Landes Nordrhein-Westfalen Mitteilungsblatt [*A publication*]
Verb Sap.... Verbum Sapienti Sat Est [*A Word to the Wise Is Sufficient*] [*Latin*]
VERC......... Vacation Eligibility and Request Card [*Military*]
VERC......... Vehicle Effectiveness Remaining Converter
VERDAN..... Versatile Differential Analyzer
Ver Destill Ztg ... Vereinigte Destillateur-Zeitungen [*A publication*]
VERDIN ..... Antijam Modem, Very-Low Frequency   (CAAL)
VERDT .... Verdict   (ROG)
Ver Dtsch Ing Z ... Verein Deutscher Ingenieure. Zeitschrift [*A publication*]
Ver Dtsch Ing Z Fortschr Ber Reihe 5 ... Verein Deutscher Ingenieure. Zeitschriften. Fortschritt-Berichte. Reihe 5. Grund- und Werkstoffe [*A publication*]
Vereinigung Schweizer Petroleum-Geologen u Ingenieure Bull ... Vereinigung Schweizerischer Petroleum-Geologen und Ingenieure. Bulletin [*A publication*]
Vereinte Nationen ... Zeitschrift fuer die Vereinten Nationen und Ihre Sonderorganisationen [*A publication*]
Ver Erdk Dresden Mitt ... Verein fuer Erdkunde zu Dresden. Mitteilungen [*A publication*]
Ver Erdk Leipzig Mitt ... Verein fuer Erdkunde zu Leipzig. Mitteilungen [*A publication*]

Ver Exploit Proefzuivelboerderij Hoorn Versl ... Vereniging tot Exploitatie eener Proefzuivelboerderij te Hoorn. Verslag [*A publication*]
Verfahrenstech ... Verfahrenstechnik International [*A publication*]
Verfass Recht Uebersee ... Verfassung und Recht in Uebersee [*A publication*]
Verfassung u -Wirklichkeit ... Verfassung und Verfassungswirklichkeit [*A publication*]
VerfGH .... Verfassungsgerichtshof [*Provincial Constitutional Court*] [*German*]   (DLA)
Verfinst TNO Circ ... Verfinstituut TNO [*Nederlands Centrale Organisatie voor Toegepast - Natuurwetenschappelijk Onderzoek*] Circulaire [*A publication*]
Ver Freunde Naturg Mecklenberg Arch ... Verein der Freunde der Naturgeschichte in Mecklenberg. Archiv [*A publication*]
Ver Freunden Erdk Leipzig Jber ... Verein von Freunden der Erdkunde zu Leipzig. Jahresbericht [*A publication*]
Verg .... Vergil [*First century BC*] [*Classical studies*]   (OCD)
Ver f d Gesch Berlins Schr ... Verein fuer die Geschichte Berlins. Schriften [*A publication*]
Ver f Gesch Dresdens Mitt ... Verein fuer Geschichte Dresdens. Mitteilungen [*A publication*]
VERGL .... Vergleische [*Compare*] [*German*]   (ROG)
Verh Anat Ges ... Verhandlungen der Anatomischen Gesellschaft [*A publication*]
Verhandl Deutsch Path Gesellsch ... Verhandlungen der Deutschen Pathologischen Gesellschaft [*A publication*]
Verhandl Deutsch Zool Gesellsch ... Verhandlungen der Deutschen Zoologischen Gesellschaft [*A publication*]
Verhandl DPG ... Verhandlungen der Deutschen Physikalischen Gesellschaft [*Stuttgart*] [*A publication*]
Verhandl Geol Bundesanstalt ... Verhandlungen der Geologischen Bundesanstalt [*A publication*]
Verhandl Gesellsch Deutsch Naturf u Aerzte ... Verhandlungen der Gesellschaft Deutscher Naturforscher und Aerzte [*A publication*]
Verhandl Naturw Ver Hamburg ... Verhandlungen des Naturwissenschaftlichen Vereins in Hamburg [*A publication*]
Verhandl Naturw Ver Karlsruhe ... Verhandlungen des Naturwissenschaftlichen Vereins in Karlsruhe [*A publication*]
Verhandl Schweiz Naturf Gesellsch ... Verhandlungen der Schweizerischen Naturforschenden Gesellschaft [*A publication*]
Verhandlungsber Kolloid-Ges ... Verhandlungsberichte der Kolloid-Gesellschaft [*A publication*]
VerhBer Dt Zool Ges ... Verhandlungsbericht. Deutsche Zoologische Gesellschaft [*A publication*]
Verh Bot Ver Prov Brandenb ... Verhandlungen des Botanischen Vereins der Provinz Brandenburg [*A publication*]
Verh Dt Ges Angew Ent ... Verhandlungen. Deutsche Gesellschaft fuer Angewandte Entomologie [*A publication*]
Verh Dtsch Ges Exp Med ... Verhandlungen der Deutschen Gesellschaft fuer Experimentelle Medizin [*A publication*]
Verh Dtsch Ges Inn Med ... Verhandlungen der Deutschen Gesellschaft fuer Innere Medizin [*A publication*]
Verh Dtsch Ges Kreislaufforsch ... Verhandlungen der Deutschen Gesellschaft fuer Kreislaufforschung [*A publication*]
Verh Dtsch Ges Pathol ... Verhandlungen der Deutschen Gesellschaft fuer Pathologie [*A publication*]
Verh Dtsch Ges Rheumatol ... Verhandlungen der Deutschen Gesellschaft fuer Rheumatologie [*A publication*]
Verh Dtsch Phys Ges ... Verhandlungen der Deutschen Physikalischen Gesellschaft [*A publication*]
Verh Dtsch Zool Ges ... Verhandlungen der Deutschen Zoologischen Gesellschaft [*A publication*]
Verh Dt Zool Ges Bonn ... Verhandlungen der Deutschen Zoologischen Gesellschaft in Bonn [*Rhein*] [*A publication*]
Verh Dt Zool Ges Erlangen ... Verhandlungen der Deutschen Zoologischen Gesellschaft in Erlangen [*A publication*]
Verh Dt Zool Ges Frankfurt ... Verhandlungen der Deutschen Zoologischen Gesellschaft in Frankfurt [*A publication*]
Verh Dt Zool Ges Jena ... Verhandlungen der Deutschen Zoologischen Gesellschaft in Jena [*A publication*]
Verh Dt Zool Ges (Kiel) ... Verhandlungen. Deutsche Zoologische Gesellschaft (Kiel) [*A publication*]
Verh Dt Zool Ges (Tuebingen) ... Verhandlungen. Deutsche Zoologische Gesellschaft (Tuebingen) [*A publication*]
Verh Dt Zool Ges (Wien) ... Verhandlungen. Deutsche Zoologische Gesellschaft (Wien) [*A publication*]
Verh Dt Zool Ges (Wilhelmshaven) ... Verhandlungen. Deutsche Zoologische Gesellschaft (Wilhelmshaven) [*A publication*]
Verh Geol Bundesanst ... Verhandlungen der Geologischen Bundesanstalt [*A publication*]
Verh Geol Bundesanst Bundeslaenderser ... Verhandlungen. Geologische Bundesanstalt Bundeslaenderserie [*A publication*]
Verh Ges Dsch Naturfrsch Aerzte ... Verhandlungen der Gesellschaft Deutscher Naturforscher und Aerzte [*A publication*]
Verh Inst Praev Geneeskd ... Verhandelingen. Instituut voor Praeventieve Geneeskunde [*A publication*]

Verh Int Psychother Kongr ... Verhandlungen des Internationalen Psychotherapie Kongresses [*A publication*]
Verh Int Ver Theor Angew Limnol ... Verhandlungen der Internationalen Vereinigung fuer Theoretische und Angewandte Limnologie [*A publication*]
Ver Hist ...... Verae Historiae [*of Lucian*] [*Classical studies*]   (OCD)
Verh K Acad Geneeskd Belg ... Verhandelingen. Koninklijke Academie voor Geneeskunde van Belgie [*A publication*]
Verh K Acad Wet Lett & Schone Kunsten Belg ... Verhandelingen. Koninklijke Academie voor Wetenschappen. Letteren en Schone Kunsten van Belgie [*A publication*]
Verh K Acad Wet Lett Schone Kunsten Belg Kl Wet ... Verhandelingen. Koninklijke Academie voor Wetenschappen. Letteren en Schone Kunsten van Belgie. Klasse der Wetenschappen [*A publication*]
Verh K Acad Wet Lett en Schone Kunsten Belg Kl Wet ... Verhandelingen van de Koninklijke Academie voor Wetenschappen. Letteren en Schone Kunsten van Belgie. Klasse der Wetenschappen [*A publication*]
Verh K Akad Wet Amsterdam Afd Natuurkd ... Verhandelingen. Koninklijke Akademie van Wetenschappen te Amsterdam. Afdeeling Natuurkunde [*A publication*]
Verh K Ned Akad Wet Afd Natuurkd Reeks 1 ... Verhandelingen. Koninklijke Nederlandse Akademie van Wetenschappen. Afdeling Natuurkunde. Reeks 1 [*A publication*]
Verh K Ned Akad Wet Afd Natuurkd Reeks 2 ... Verhandelingen. Koninklijke Nederlandse Akademie van Wetenschappen. Afdeling Natuurkunde. Reeks 2 [*A publication*]
Verh K Ned Akad Wet Afd Natuurkd Tweede Reeks ... Verhandelingen. Koninklijke Nederlandse Akademie van Wetenschappen. Afdeling Natuurkunde. Tweede Reeks [*A publication*]
Verh K Ned Akad Wetensch Afd Natuurk Reeks 1 ... Verhandelingen. Koninklijke Nederlandse Akademie van Wetenschappen. Afdeling Natuurkunde. Reeks 1 [*Netherlands*] [*A publication*]
Verh K Ned Akad Wetensch Afd Natuurk Reeks 2 ... Verhandelingen. Koninklijke Nederlandse Akademie van Wetenschappen. Afdeling Natuurkunde. Reeks 2 [*Netherlands*] [*A publication*]
Verh K Ned Geol Mijnbouwkd Genoot ... Verhandelingen. Koninklijke Nederlands Geologisch Mijnbouwkundig Genootschap [*A publication*]
Verh K Ned Geol Mijnbouwkd Genoot Geol Ser ... Verhandelingen. Koninklijke Nederlandse Geologisch Mijnbouwkundig Genootschap. Geologische Serie [*A publication*]
Verh K Ned Geol Mijnbouwkd Genoot Mijnbouwkd Ser ... Verhandelingen. Koninklijke Nederlandse Geologisch Mijnbouwkundig Genootschap. Mijnbouwkundige Serie [*A publication*]
Verh Konink Acad Wetensch Belgie ... Verhandelingen. Koninklijke Academie voor Wetenschappen. Letteren en Schone Kunsten van Belgie [*A publication*]
Verh Kon Nederl Ak Wetensch Afd Lett ... Verhandelingen. Koninklijke Nederlandse Akademie van Wetenschappen. Afdeeling Letterkunde [*A publication*]
Verh K Vlaam Acad Geneesk Belg ... Verhandelingen. Koninklijke Vlaamse Academie voor Geneeskunde van Belgie [*Belgium*] [*A publication*]
Verh K Vlaam Acad Wetensch Belg Kl Wetensch ... Verhandelingen. Koninklijke Vlaamse Academie voor Wetenschappen, Letteren, en Schone Kunsten van Belgie. Klasse der Wetenschappen [*Belgium*] [*A publication*]
Verh Naturforsch Ges Basel ... Verhandlungen der Naturforschenden Gesellschaft in Basel [*A publication*]
Verh Naturforsch Ver Bruenn ... Verhandlungen des Naturforschenden Vereins in Bruenn [*A publication*]
Verh Natur-Med Ver Heidelb ... Verhandlungen des Naturhistorisch-Medizinischen Vereins du Heidelberg [*A publication*]
Verh Ornithol Ges Bayern ... Verhandlungen der Ornithologischen Gesellschaft in Bayern [*A publication*]
Verh Phys-Med Ges Wuerzburg ... Verhandlungen der Physikalisch-Medizinischen Gesellschaft in Wuerzburg [*A publication*]
Verh Rijksinst Natuurbeheer ... Verhandelingen. Rijksinstituut voor Natuurbeheer [*A publication*]
Verh Schweiz Naturforsch Ges ... Verhandlungen der Schweizerischen Naturforschenden Gesellschaft [*A publication*]
Verh Schweiz Naturforsch Ges Wiss Teil ... Verhandlungen der Schweizerischen Naturforschenden Gesellschaft. Wissenschaftlicher Teil [*A publication*]
Verh Ver Schweiz Physiol ... Verhandlungen des Vereins der Schweizer Physiologen [*A publication*]
Verh Zool-Bot Ges Wien ... Verhandlungen der Zoologisch-Botanischen Gesellschaft in Wien [*A publication*]
VERIC .... Vocational Education Resources Information Center
VERIF .... Verification   (MSA)
VeritCarit ... Veritatem in Caritate. Orgaan van de Protestanse Theologische Faculteit te Brussel [*A publication*]   (BJA)
Verkehrsmed Grenzgeb ... Verkehrsmedizin und Ihre Grenzgebiete [*A publication*]
Verkehrsmed Ihre Grenzgeb ... Verkehrsmedizin und Ihre Grenzgebiete [*German Democratic Republic*] [*A publication*]
VerkF .... Verkuendigung und Forschung [*Munich*] [*A publication*]

Verksamheten Stift Rasforadl Skogstrad ... Verksamheten. Stiftelsen foer Rasforadling av Skogstrad [*A publication*]
VERLORT ... Very-Long-Range Tracking [*NASA*]
VERM .... Vermilion   (ROG)
VERM .... Vermont
Verm .... Vermont Reports   (DLA)
Vermess-Inf ... Vermessungs-Informationen [*A publication*]
Verm Nox Weeds Destr Board Leafl ... Leaflet. Vermin and Noxious Weeds Destruction Board [*Victoria*] [*A publication*]
Verm Nox Weeds Destrn Bd Melb Surv ... Vermin and Noxious Weeds Destruction Board. Melbourne. Survey [*A publication*]
Vermont Geol Survey Bull ... Vermont. Geological Survey. Bulletin [*A publication*]
Vermont Lib ... Vermont Libraries [*A publication*]
Vermont L Rev ... Vermont Law Review [*A publication*]
Vermont R ... Vermont Reports   (DLA)
Vermont Rep ... Vermont Reports   (DLA)
Vermt .... Vermont Reports   (DLA)
VERN .... Vernacular   (ADA)
VERN .... Vernier [*Engineering*]
Vern .... Vernon's English Chancery Reports [*23 ER*]   (DLA)
Vernacular Architect ... Vernacular Architecture [*A publication*]
Vernacular Archre ... Vernacular Architecture [*A publication*]
VERNAV ..... Vertical Navigation System
Vern (Eng) ... Vernon's English Chancery Reports [*23 ER*]   (DLA)
VERNITRAC ... Vernier Tracking by Automatic Correlation [*Aerospace*]
Vernon's Ann CCP ... Vernon's Annotated Texas Code of Criminal Procedure   (DLA)
Vernon's Ann Civ St ... Vernon's Annotated Texas Civil Statutes   (DLA)
Vernon's Ann PC ... Vernon's Annotated Texas Penal Code   (DLA)
Vern & S ..... Vernon and Scriven's Irish King's Bench Reports [*1786-88*]   (DLA)
Vern & Sc ... Vernon and Scriven's Irish King's Bench Reports [*1786-88*]   (DLA)
Vern & Scr ... Vernon and Scriven's Irish King's Bench Reports [*1786-88*]   (DLA)
Vern & Scriv ... Vernon and Scriven's Irish King's Bench Reports [*1786-88*]   (DLA)
Vern & S (Ir) ... Vernon and Scriven's Irish King's Bench Reports [*1786-88*]   (DLA)
Veroeff Bundesanst Alp Landwirtsch Admont ... Veroeffentlichungen der Bundesanstalt fuer Alpine Landwirtsch in Admont [*A publication*]
Veroeff Dtsch Geod Komm Reihe A ... Veroeffentlichungen der Deutschen Geodaetisken Kommission. Bayerischen Akademie der Wissenschaften. Reihe A [*West Germany*] [*A publication*]
Veroeffentlich Schweizer Gesellsch Medizin Naturwissensch ... Veroeffentlichungen. Schweizerische Gesellschaft fuer Geschichte der Medizin und der Naturwissenschaft [*A publication*]
Veroeffentl J-Vet-Ber Beamt Tieraerzte Preuss ... Veroeffentlichungen aus den Jahres-Veterinaer-Berichten der Beamteten Tieraerzte Preussens [*A publication*]
Veroeffentl Leibniz-Archivs ... Veroeffentlichungen, Leibniz-Archivs [*A publication*]
Veroeff Geobot Inst Eidg Tech Hochsch Stift Ruebel Zuer ... Veroeffentlichungen des Geobotanischen Instituts der Eidgenoessischen Technische Hochschule Stiftung Ruebel in Zuerich [*A publication*]
Veroeff Geobot Inst Eidg Tech Hochsch Stift Ruebel Zuerich ... Veroeffentlichungen des Geobotanischen Instituts der Eidgenoessischen Technische Hochschule Stiftung Ruebel in Zuerich [*A publication*]
Veroeff Geobot Inst Ruebel ... Veroeffentlichungen des Geobotanischen Institut Ruebel [*A publication*]
Veroeff Inst Meeresforsch Bremerhaven ... Veroeffentlichungen des Instituts fuer Meeresforschung in Bremerhaven [*A publication*]
Veroeff Inst Meeresforsch Bremerhaven Suppl ... Veroeffentlichungen des Instituts fuer Meeresforschung in Bremerhaven. Supplement [*A publication*]
Veroeff Kaiser Wilhelm Inst Silikatforsch Berlin Dahlem ... Veroeffentlichungen. Kaiser-Wilhelm-Institut fuer Silikatforschung in Berlin-Dahlem [*A publication*]
Veroeff Meteorol Dienstes DDR ... Veroeffentlichungen des Meteorologischen Dienstes der Deutschen Demokratischen Republik [*A publication*]
Veroeff Meterol Hydrol Dienstes DDR ... Veroeffentlichungen des Meteorologischen und Hydrologischen Dienstes der Deutschen Demokratischen Republik [*A publication*]
Veroeff Morphol Pathol ... Veroeffentlichungen aus der Morphologischen Pathologie [*A publication*]
Veroeff Naturh Mus (Wien) ... Veroeffentlichungen. Naturhistorischer Museum (Wien) [*A publication*]
Veroeff Naturschutz Landschaftspflege Baden Wuerttemb ... Veroeffentlichungen fuer Naturschutz und Landschaftspflege in Baden- Wuerttemberg [*A publication*]

Veroeff Naturschutz Landschaftspflege Baden-Wuerttemb Beih ... Veroeffentlichungen fuer Naturschutz und Landschaftspflege in Baden-Wuerttemberg. Beihefte [*A publication*]

Veroeff Pathol ... Veroeffentlichungen aus der Pathologie [*A publication*]

Veroeff Reichsgesundheitsamts ... Veroeffentlichungen. Reichsgesundheitsamts [*A publication*]

Veroeff Ueberseemus (Bremen) Reihe A ... Veroeffentlichungen. Ueberseemuseum (Bremen). Reihe A [*A publication*]

Veroeff Wiss Photo Lab (Wolfen) ... Veroeffentlichungen. Wissenschaftliches Photo-Laboratorien (Wolfen) [*A publication*]

Veroeff Wiss Zent Lab Photogr Abt AGFA ... Veroeffentlichungen. Wissenschaftliches Zentral Laboratoriums der Photographischen Abteilung AGFA [*A publication*]

Veroeff Zentralinst Phys Erde ... Veroeffentlichungen des Zentralinstituts Physik der Erde [*Czechoslovakia*] [*A publication*]

Veroeff Zool Staatssamml (Muench) ... Veroeffentlichungen der Zoologischen Staatssammlung (Muenchen) [*A publication*]

Veroeff Zool StSamml (Muench) ... Veroeffentlichungen der Zoologischen Staatssammlung (Muenchen) [*A publication*]

Veroff Inst Agrarmet Univ (Leipzig) ... Veroeffentlichungen des Instituts fuer Agrarmeteorologie und des Agrarmeteorologischen Observatoriums der Karl Marx-Universitaet (Leipzig) [*A publication*]

Veroff Land-Hauswirtsch Auswertungs-Informationsdienst ... Veroeffentlichungen. Land- und Hauswirtschaftlicher Auswertungs- und Informationsdienst [*A publication*]

VERP .... Vertical Effective Radiated Power (MCD)

Verpack Chemiebetr ... Verpackung im Chemiebetrich [*A publication*]

Verpack-Rundsch ... Verpackungs-Rundschau [*A publication*]

Verr .... In Verrem [*of Cicero*] [*Classical studies*] (OCD)

Ver Rep ...... Vermont Reports (DLA)

Verres Refract ... Verres et Refractaires [*A publication*]

Verre Text Plast Renf ... Verre Textile, Plastiques Renforces [*France*] [*A publication*]

Verrigtinge Kongr S-Afr Genet Ver ... Verrigtinge van die Kongres van dis Suid-Afrikaanse Genetiese Vereniging [*A publication*]

VERS .... Versed Sine (KSC)

VERS .... Version (ROG)

Ver Schweizer Petroleum-Geologen u Ingenieure Bull ... Vereinigung Schweizerischer Petroleum-Geologen und Ingenieure. Bulletin [*A publication*]

Ver Schweiz Pet-Geol Ing Bull ... Vereinigung Schweizerischer Petroleum-Geologen und Ingenieure. Bulletin [*A publication*]

Vers Landbouwkd Onderz ... Verslagen van Landbouwkundige Onderzoekingen [*A publication*]

Versl Interprov Proeven Proefstn Akkerbouw Lelystad (Neth) ... Verslagen van Interprovinciale Proeven. Proefstation voor de Akkerbouw Lelystad (Netherlands) [*A publication*]

Versl Interprov Proeven Proefstn Akkerbouw (Wageningen) ... Verslagen van Interprovinciale Proeven. Proefstation voor de Akkerbouw (Wageningen) [*A publication*]

Versl Landbouwkd Onderz A ... Verslagen van Landbouwkundige Onderzoekingen A. Rijkslandbouwproefstation en Bodemkundig Instituut te Groningen [*A publication*]

Versl Landbouwkd Onderz (Agric Res Rep) ... Verslagen van Landbouwkundige Onderzoekingen (Agricultural Research Reports) [*A publication*]

Versl Landbouwkd Onderz B ... Verslagen van Landbouwkundige Onderzoekingen B. Bodemikundig Instituut te Groningen [*A publication*]

Versl Landbouwkd Onderz Rijkslandbouwproefstn ... Verslagen van Landbouwkundige Onderzoekingen der Rijkslandbouwproefstations [*A publication*]

Versl Landbouwk Onderz ... Verslagen van Landbouwkundige Onderzoekingen [*A publication*]

Versl Landbouwk Onderz Cent Lanbouwpubl Landbouwdoc ... Verslagen van Landbouwkundige Onderzoekingen. Centrum voor Landbouwpublikatien en Landbouwdocumentatie [*A publication*]

Versl Landbouwk Onderz Ned ... Verslagen van het Landbouwkundig Onderzoek in Nederland [*A publication*]

Versl Meded Kon Vl Ak Taal & Letterk ... Verslagen en Mededeelingen. Koninklijke Vlaamse Akademie voor Taal- en Letterkunde [*A publication*]

Versl Meded K Vlaam Acad Taal Lett ... Verslagen en Mededelingen van de Koninklijke Vlaamse Academie voor Taalen Letterkunde [*A publication*]

Versl Meded Rijkslandbouwconsul Westelijk Drenthe ... Verslagen en Mededelingen van het Rijkslandbouwconsulentschap Westelijk Drenthe [*A publication*]

Versl Tien-Jarenplan Graanonderzoek Sticht Nederl Graan-Cent ... Verslagen. Tien-Jarenplan voor Graanonderzoek. Stichting Nederlands Graan-Centrum [*A publication*]

VERSO .... Reverso [*Left-Hand Page of Open Book*] (ROG)

VERST .... Versatile

Verstaendliche Wiss ... Verstaendliche Wissenschaft [*A publication*]

Versuchsgrubenges Quartalsh ... Versuchsgrubengesellschaft Quartalshefte [*West Germany*] [*A publication*]

VERT .... Venture Evaluation and Review Technique

Vert .... Vermont Reports (DLA)

VERT .... Vertebrate

VERT .... Vertical (MCD)

Vert .... Vertical Lights [*Navigation signal*]

VERT .... Vertical Polarization (AFM)

VERTAR ..... Versatile Test Analysis RADAR (MCD)

Vertebr Hung ... Vertebrata Hungarica [*A publication*]

Vertebr Palasiat ... Vertebrata Palasiatica [*A publication*]

Vert File Ind ... Vertical File Index [*A publication*]

Ver f Thuer Gesch u Alt Ztsch ... Verein fuer Thueringische Geschichte und Altertumskunde. Zeitschrift [*A publication*]

VERTIJET ... Vertical Takeoff and Landing Jet [*Aircraft*]

VERTOL ...... Vertical Takeoff and Landing [*Also, VTOL*]

VERTREP ... Vertical Replenishment [*Navy*] (NVT)

Ver Vaterl Naturk Wuerttemberg Jahresh ... Verein fuer Vaterlaendische Naturkunde in Wuerttemberg. Jahreshefte [*A publication*]

Verwarm Vent ... Verwarming en Ventilatie [*A publication*]

VerwGH ...... Verwaltungsgerichtshof [*District Administrative Court of Appeal*] [*German*] (DLA)

VERY .... Vanderbilt Energy Corp. [*NASDAQ symbol*] (NQ)

Verzam Overdruk Plantenziektenk Dienst (Wageningen) ... Verzamelde Overdrukken. Plantenziektenkundige Dienst (Wageningen) [*A publication*]

Verzekerings-Arch ... Verzekerings-Archief [*A publication*]

VES .... Vacuum Evaporator System

VES .... Variable Elasticity of Substitution [*Industrial production*]

VES .... Vehicle Ecological System (AAG)

VES .... Vehicle Engagement Simulator (MCD)

VES .... Versailles, OH [*Location identifier*] [*FAA*] (FAAL)

Ves .... Vesey, Senior's, English Chancery Reports (DLA)

VES .... Vesica [*Bladder*] [*Latin*] (ADA)

VES .... Vesicula [*Blister*] [*Latin*] (ADA)

VES .... Vespere [*In the Evening*] [*Latin*] (ADA)

VES .... Vessel (AABC)

VES .... Vestaur Securities, Inc. [*NYSE symbol*]

VES .... Veterans Employment Service [*Later, VETS*] [*of USES*]

VES .... Victorian Era Series [*A publication*]

VES .... Vieques Air Link, Inc. [*Vieques, PR*] [*FAA designator*] (FAAC)

VES .... Visual Effects Simulator (MCD)

VES .... Visual Efficiency Scale

VES .... Vulcan Engagement Simulator (MCD)

Ves Akad Nauk Kirg SSR ... Vestnik Akademii Nauk Kirgizskoi SSR [*A publication*]

Ves & B ..... Vesey and Beames' English Chancery Reports [*35 ER*] (DLA)

Ves & Bea .. Vesey and Beames' English Chancery Reports [*35 ER*] (DLA)

Ves & Beam ... Vesey and Beames' English Chancery Reports [*35 ER*] (DLA)

Ves & B (Eng) ... Vesey and Beames' English Chancery Reports [*35 ER*] (DLA)

VESC .... Vehicle Equipment Safety Commission

VESCA(S) ... Vessels and Cargo

Vesci Akad Navuk BSSR Ser Fiz-Mat Navuk ... Vesci Akademii Navuk BSSR. Seryja Fizika-Matematycnyh Navuk [*A publication*]

VESE .... Value Engineering Staff Engineer

VESG .... Vocational Education Services Grant (OICC)

VESI .... Victor Educational Services Institute [*Educational division of Victor Comptometer Corp.*]

VESIAC ...... Vela Seismic Information Analysis Center [*University of Michigan*]

Vesic .... Vesicula [*A Blister*] [*Medicine*]

vesic .... Vesicular

Ves Jr .... Vesey, Junior's, English Chancery Reports [*30-34 ER*] (DLA)

Ves Jr (Eng) ... Vesey, Junior's, English Chancery Reports [*30-34 ER*] (DLA)

Ves Jr Suppl ... Supplement to Vesey, Junior's, English Chancery Reports, by Hovenden [*34 English Reprint*] (DLA)

Ves Jun ...... Vesey, Junior's, English Chancery Reports [*30-34 ER*] (DLA)

Ves Jun Supp ... Supplement to Vesey, Junior's, English Chancery Reports, by Hovenden [*34 English Reprint*] (DLA)

Ves Jun Supp (Eng) ... Supplement to Vesey, Junior's, English Chancery Reports, by Hovenden [*34 English Reprint*] (DLA)

Vesn Zavod Geol Geofiz Istraz NR Srb ... Vesnik Zavod za Geoloska i Geofizicka Istrazivanja NR Srbije [*A publication*]

Vesn Zavod Geol Geofiz Istraz Ser A ... Vesnik Zavod za Geoloska i Geofizicka Istrazivanja Serija A. Geologija [*A publication*]

Vesn Zavod Geol Geofiz Istraz Ser C ... Vesnik Zavod za Geoloska i Geofizicka Istrazivanja Serija C. Priminjena Geofizika [*A publication*]

VESO .... Vocalization of the Egyptian Syllabic Orthography [*W. F. Albright*] [*A publication*] (BJA)

VESP .... Value Engineering Supplier Program

Vesp .... Vespae [*Wasps*] [*of Aristophanes*] [*Classical studies*] (OCD)

VESP .... Vesper [*Evening*] [*Pharmacy*]

VESPER ..... Vehicle Sizing and Performance (MCD)

VESR .... Vallecitos Experimental Superheat Reactor

VESR .... Value Engineering Study Request (MCD)

VESS .... Vehicle Exhaust Smoke System (MCD)

VESS .... Visual Environment Simulation System (MCD)

Ves Sen ..... Vesey, Senior's, English Chancery Reports [*27, 28 ER*] (DLA)

Ves Sen Supp ... Supplement to Vesey, Senior's, English Chancery Reports [*28 English Reprint*] (DLA)

Ves Sr .... Vesey, Senior's, English Chancery Reports [*27, 28 ER*] (DLA)

Ves Sr (Eng) ... Vesey, Senior's, English Chancery Reports [*27, 28 ER*] (DLA)
Ves Sr Supp ... Supplement to Vesey, Senior's, English Chancery Reports [*28 English Reprint*] [*1747-56*] (DLA)
Ves Sr Supp (Eng) ... Supplement to Vesey, Senior's, English Chancery Reports [*28 English Reprint*] (DLA)
Ves Supp ... Supplement to Vesey, Junior's, English Chancery Reports, by Hovenden [*34 English Reprint*] [*1789-1817*] (DLA)
VEST .... Vestibule (MSA)
VEST .... Vestry [*Ecclesiastical*] (ROG)
VEST .... Volunteer Engineers, Scientists, and Technicians [*An association*]
Vest Akad Nauk SSSR ... Vestnik Akademii Nauk SSSR [*A publication*]
Vest Ces Akad Zemed ... Vestnik Ceskoslovenske Akademie Zemedelske [*A publication*]
Vest Csl Spol Zool ... Vestnik Ceskoslovenske Spolecnosti Zoologicke [*A publication*]
Vest Dal'nevost Fil Akad Nauk SSSR ... Vestnik Dal'nevostochnogo Filiala Akademii Nauk SSSR [*A publication*]
Vest Gos Muz Gruz ... Vestnik Gosudarstvennogo Muzeja Gruzii Imeni Akademika S. N. Dzhanashia [*A publication*]
Vest Inst Pchelovodstva ... Vestnik Institut Pchelovodstva [*A publication*]
Vest Ist Mirov Kul't ... Vestnik Istorii Mirovoi Kul'tury [*A publication*]
Vest Khar'k Univ Radiofiz Elektron ... Vestnik Khar'kovskogo Universiteta. Radiofizika, Elektronika [*USSR*] [*A publication*]
Vest Latv PSR Akad ... Vestis Latvijas Pasomju Socialistikas Republikas Zinatu Akademija [*Riga, USSR*] [*A publication*]
Vest Leningr Gos Univ Ser Biol ... Vestnik Leningradskogo Gosudarstvennogo Universiteta. Seriya Biologii [*A publication*]
Vest Leningr Inst ... Vestnik Leningradskogo Instituta [*A publication*]
Vest Mikrobiol Epidemiol Parazitol ... Vestnik Mikrobiologii, Epidemiologii, i Parazitologii [*A publication*]
Vest Mosk Gos Univ Ser VI ... Vestnik Moskovskogo Gosudarstvennogo Universiteta. Seriya VI [*A publication*]
Vest Mosk Inst Biol Pochv ... Vestnik Moskovskogo Instituta. Seriya Biologiya, Pochvovedenie [*A publication*]
Vest Mosk Inst Geogr ... Vestnik Moskovskogo Instituta Geografii [*A publication*]
Vest Mosk Univ Ser Biol Pochv Geol Geogr ... Vestnik Moskovskogo Universiteta. Seriya Biologii, Pochvovedeniya, Geologii, Geografii [*A publication*]
Vest Mosk Univ Ser 15 Vychisl Mat Kibern ... Vestnik Moskovskogo Universiteta. Seriya 15. Vychislitel'naya Matematika i Kibernetika [*USSR*] [*A publication*]
Vestn Akad Med Nauk SSSR ... Vestnik Akademii Meditsinskikh Nauk SSSR [*A publication*]
Vestn Akad Nauk Belorussk SSR Ser Obsc Nauk ... Vestnik Akademii Nauk Belorusskoj SSR Serija Obscestvennyh Nauk [*A publication*]
Vestn Akad Nauk Kazah SSR ... Vestnik Akademii Nauk Kazahskoj SSR [*A publication*]
Vestn Akad Nauk Kazakh SSR ... Vestnik Akademiya Nauk Kazakhskoi SSR [*A publication*]
Vestn Akad Nauk Kaz SSR ... Vestnik Akademii Nauk Kazakhskoi SSR [*A publication*]
Vestn Akad Nauk SSSR ... Vestnik Akademii Nauk SSSR [*A publication*]
Vest Nauchno-Issled Inst Pchel ... Vestnik Nauchno-Issledovatel'skii Institut Pchelovodstva [*A publication*]
Vestn Beloruss Gos Univ Ser 1 ... Vestnik Belorusskogo Gosudarstvennogo Universiteta. Seriya 1. Matematika, Fizika, Mekhanika [*A publication*]
Vestn Beloruss Gos Univ Ser 2 Biol Khim Geol Geogr ... Vestnik Belorusskogo Gosudarstvennogo Universiteta. Seriya 2. Biologiya, Khimiya, Geologiya, Geografiya [*A publication*]
Vestn Beloruss Univ ... Vestnik Belorusskogo Universiteta [*A publication*]
Vestn Cesk Akad Zemed ... Vestnik Ceskoslovenske Akademie Zemedelske [*A publication*]
Vestn Cesk Akad Zemed Ved ... Vestnik Ceskoslovenske Akademie Zemedelskych Ved [*A publication*]
Vestn Ceskoslov Akad Zemed Ved ... Vestnik Ceskoslovenske Akademie Zemedelskych Ved [*A publication*]
Vestn Cesk Spol Zool ... Vestnik Ceskoslovenske Spolecnosti Zoologicke [*A publication*]
Vestn Chkal Otd Vses Khim O-va Im D I Mendeleeva ... Vestnik Chkalovckogo Otdeleniya Vsesoyuznogo Khimicheskogo Obshchestva Imeni D. I. Mendeleeva [*A publication*]
Vestn Dermatol Venerol ... Vestnik Dermatologii i Venerologii [*A publication*]
Vestn Drevn Ist ... Vestnik Drevnei Istorii [*A publication*]
Vestn Elektroprom-sti ... Vestnik Elektropromyshlennosti [*USSR*] [*A publication*]
Vestn Gos Muz Gruz ... Vestnik Gosudarstvennogo Muzeja Gruzii [*A publication*]
Vestn Gosud Muz Gruzii ... Vestnik Gosudarstvennogo Muzeja Gruzii Imeni Akademika S. N. Dzhanashia [*A publication*]
Vestnik Akad Nauk Kazah SSR ... Vestnik Akademii Nauk Kazahskoi SSR [*A publication*]
Vestnik Akad Nauk Kazakh SSR ... Vestnik Akademii Nauk Kazahskoi SSR [*A publication*]
Vestnik Akad Nauk SSSR ... Vestnik Akademiji Nauk SSSR [*A publication*]

Vestnik Beloruss Gos Univ Ser I ... Vestnik Belorusskogo Gosudarstvennogo Universiteta Imeni V. I. Lenina. Naucnyi Zurnal. Serija I. Matematika, Fizika, Mehanika [*A publication*]
Vestnik Har'kov Gos Univ ... Vestnik Har'kovskogo Gosudarstvennogo Universiteta [*A publication*]
Vestnik Har'kov Politehn Inst ... Vestnik Har'kovskogo Politehniceskogo Instituta [*A publication*]
Vestnik Karakalpak Fil Akad Nauk UzSSR ... Akademija Nauk UzSSR. Karakalpakskii Filial. Vestnik [*A publication*]
Vestnik K Ceske Spolec Nauk v Praze Trida Mat Prirod ... Vestnik Kralovske Ceske Spolecnosti Nauk v Praze Trida Matematicko Prirodovedecka [*A publication*]
Vestnik Leningrad Univ Fiz Him ... Vestnik Leningradskogo Universiteta. Fizika i Himija [*A publication*]
Vestnik Leningrad Univ Math ... Vestnik Leningrad University. Mathematics [*A publication*]
Vestnik Leningrad Univ Mat Meh Astronom ... Vestnik Leningradskogo Universiteta. Matematika, Mehanika, Astronomija [*A publication*]
Vestnik Leningrad Univ Ser Fiz Khim ... Vestnik Leningradskogo Universiteta. Serija Fiziki i Khimii [*A publication*]
Vestnik Leningr Gosud Univ ... Vestnik Leningradskogo Gosudarstvennogo Universiteta [*A publication*]
Vestnik L'vov Politehn Inst ... Vestnik L'vovskogo Politehniceskogo Instituta [*A publication*]
Vestnik Mikrobiol i Epidemiol ... Vestnik Mikrobiologii i Epidemiologii [*A publication*]
Vestnik Mikrobiol Epidemiol i Parazitol ... Vestnik Mikrobiologii, Epidemiologii, i Parazitologii [*A publication*]
Vestnik Moskov Univ Ser III Fiz Astronom ... Vestnik Moskovskogo Universiteta. Serija III. Fizika, Astronomija [*A publication*]
Vestnik Moskov Univ Ser I Mat Meh ... Vestnik Moskovskogo Universiteta. Serija I. Matematika, Mehanika [*A publication*]
Vestnik Moskov Univ Ser XV Vycisl Mat Kibernet ... Vestnik Moskovskogo Universiteta. Serija XV. Vycislitel'naja Matematika i Kibernetika [*A publication*]
Vestnik Mosk Univ Ser Khim ... Vestnik Moskovskogo Universiteta. Seriya II. Khimiya [*A publication*]
Vestnik Obsh Vet (S Peterburg) ... Vestnik Obshchestvennoi Veterinarii (S. Peterburg) [*A publication*]
Vestnik Rentg i Radiol ... Vestnik Rentgenologii i Radiologii [*A publication*]
Vestnik Sovrem Vet ... Vestnik Sovremennoi Veterinarii [*A publication*]
Vestn Inzh Tekh ... Vestnik Inzhenerov i Tekhnikov [*USSR*] [*A publication*]
Vestn Jaroslav Univ ... Vestnik Jaroslavskogo Universiteta [*A publication*]
Vestn Kabard Balkar Nauc-Issled Inst ... Vestnik Kabardino-Balkarskogo Naucno-Issledovatel'skogo Instituta [*A publication*]
Vestn Karakalp Fil Akad ... Vestnik Karakalpakskogo Filiala Akademii Nauk Uzbekskoj SSR [*A publication*]
Vestn Karakalp Fil Akad Nauk Uzb SSR ... Vestnik Karakalpakskogo Filiala Akademii Nauk Uzbekskoi SSR [*A publication*]
Vestn Khar'k Politekh Inst ... Vestnik Khar'kovskogo Politekhnicheskogo Instituta [*Ukrainian SSR*] [*A publication*]
Vestn Khar'k Univ Astron ... Vestnik Khar'kovskogo Universiteta. Astronomiya [*Ukrainian SSR*] [*A publication*]
Vestn Khar'k Univ Geol Geogr ... Vestnik Khar'kovskogo Universiteta. Geologiya i Geografiya [*Ukrainian SSR*] [*A publication*]
Vestn Khar'k Univ Ser Biol ... Vestnik Khar'kovskogo Universiteta. Seriya Biologicheskaya [*A publication*]
Vestn Khar'k Univ Ser Geol ... Vestnik Khar'kovskogo Universiteta. Seriya Geologicheskaya [*Ukrainian SSR*] [*A publication*]
Vestn Khar'k Univ Ser Khim ... Vestnik Khar'kovskogo Universiteta. Seriya Khimicheskaya [*A publication*]
Vestn Khar'k Univ Vopr Ehlektrokhim ... Vestnik Khar'kovskogo Universiteta. Voprosy Ehlektrokhimii [*A publication*]
Vestn Khir ... Vestnik Khirurgii Imeni I. I. Grekova [*A publication*]
Vestn Khir Im I I Grekova ... Vestnik Khirurgii Imeni I. I. Grekova [*A publication*]
Vestn Kiev Politekh Inst Ser Mashinostr ... Vestnik Kievskogo Politekhnicheskogo Instituta. Seriya Mashinostroeniya [*A publication*]
Vestn Kiev Politekh Inst Ser Teploenerg ... Vestnik Kievskogo Politekhnicheskogo Instituta. Seriya Teploenergetiki [*A publication*]
Vestn Kral Ceske Spol Nauk Trida Mat Prirodoved ... Vestnik Kralovske Ceske Spolecnosti Nauk Trida Matematicko Prirodovedecka [*A publication*]
Vestn La Upr Metallopromsti ... Vestnik Lavnogo Upravleniya Metallopromyshlennosti [*A publication*]
Vestn Leningrad Univ Ser Biol ... Vestnik Leningradskogo Universiteta. Seriya Biologii [*A publication*]
Vestn Leningr Univ ... Vestnik Leningradskogo Universiteta [*A publication*]
Vestn Leningr Univ Biol ... Vestnik Leningradskogo Universiteta. Biologiya [*A publication*]
Vestn Leningr Univ Fiz & Khim ... Vestnik Leningradskogo Universiteta. Fizika i Khimiya [*A publication*]
Vestn Leningr Univ Geol Geogr ... Vestnik Leningradskogo Universiteta. Geologiya, Geografiya [*A publication*]
Vestn Leningr Univ Ist Jaz Lit ... Vestnik Leningradskogo Universiteta. Istorija, Jazyka, i Literatury [*A publication*]

Vestn Leningr Univ Mat Mekh Astron ... Vestnik Leningradskogo Universiteta. Matematika, Mekhanika, Astronomiya [*A publication*]

Vestn Leningr Univ Ser Ekon Filos Pravo ... Vestnik Leningradskogo Universiteta. Serija Ekonomiki, Filosofii, i Pravo [*A publication*]

Vestn Leningr Univ Ser Fiz Khim ... Vestnik Leningradskogo Universiteta. Seriya Fizikii i Khimii [*USSR*] [*A publication*]

Vestn Leningr Univ Ser Geol Geogr ... Vestnik Leningradskogo Universiteta. Seriya Geologii i Geografii [*USSR*] [*A publication*]

Vestn Leningr Univ Ser Mat Fiz Khim ... Vestnik Leningradskogo Universiteta. Seriya Matematiki, Fiziki, i Khimii [*A publication*]

Vestn Leningr Univ Ser Mat Mekh & Astron ... Vestnik Leningradskogo Universiteta. Seriya Matematika, Mekhanika, i Astronomiya [*A publication*]

Vestn Lening Univ Ser Biol Geogr Geol ... Vestnik Leningradskogo Universiteta. Seriya Biologii, Geografii, i Geologii [*A publication*]

Vestn L'viv Derzh Univ Ser Fiz ... Vestnik L'vivs'kogo Derzhavnogo Universitetu. Seriya Fizichna [*Ukrainian SSR*] [*A publication*]

Vestn Mashinostr ... Vestnik Mashinostroeniya [*A publication*]

Vestn Metallopromsti ... Vestnik Metallopromyshlennosti [*A publication*]

Vestn Minist Zdrav ... Vestnik Ministerstva Zdravotnictvi [*Czechoslovakia*] [*A publication*]

Vestn Moskovskogo Univ Fiz-Astron ... Vestnik Moskovskogo Universiteta. Seriya Fizika-Astronomiya [*A publication*]

Vestn Moskovskogo Univ Khim ... Vestnik Moskovskogo Universiteta. Seriya Khimiya [*A publication*]

Vestn Moskov Univ Ser 6 ... Vestnik Moskovskogo Universiteta. Seriya 6 [*A publication*]

Vestn Moskov Univ Ser Ekon ... Vestnik Moskovskogo Universiteta. Serija Ekonomika [*A publication*]

Vestn Moskov Univ Ser Filos ... Vestnik Moskovskogo Universiteta. Serija Filosofija [*A publication*]

Vestn Moskov Univ Ser Geogr ... Vestnik Moskovskogo Universiteta. Serija Geografija [*A publication*]

Vestn Moskov Univ Ser Ist ... Vestnik Moskovskogo Universiteta. Serija Istorija [*A publication*]

Vestn Moskov Univ Ser Pravo ... Vestnik Moskovskogo Universiteta. Serija Pravo [*A publication*]

Vestn Moskov Univ Teorija Nauc Kommunizma ... Vestnik Moskovskogo Universiteta Teorija Naucnogo Kommunizma [*A publication*]

Vestn Mosk Univ ... Vestnik Moskovskogo Universiteta [*A publication*]

Vestn Mosk Univ Biol Pochvoved ... Vestnik Moskovskogo Universiteta. Biologiya, Pochvovedenie [*A publication*]

Vestn Mosk Univ Fiz Astron ... Vestnik Moskovskogo Universiteta. Fizika, Astronomiya [*A publication*]

Vestn Mosk Univ Geogr ... Vestnik Moskovskogo Universiteta Geografiya [*A publication*]

Vestn Mosk Univ Geol ... Vestnik Moskovskogo Universiteta. Geologiya [*A publication*]

Vestn Mosk Univ Khim ... Vestnik Moskovskogo Universiteta Khimiya [*A publication*]

Vestn Mosk Univ Mat Mekh ... Vestnik Moskovskogo Universiteta. Matematika, Mekhanika [*A publication*]

Vestn Mosk Univ Ser 16 Biol ... Vestnik Moskovskogo Universiteta. Seriya 16. Biologiya [*A publication*]

Vestn Mosk Univ Ser Biol Pochvoved Geol Geogr ... Vestnik Moskovskogo Universiteta. Seriya Biologii, Pochvovedeniya, Geologii, Geografii [*A publication*]

Vestn Mosk Univ Ser Fiz-Mat Estestv Nauk ... Vestnik Moskovskogo Universiteta Seriya Fiziko-Matematicheskikh i Estestvennykh Nauk [*USSR*] [*A publication*]

Vestn Mosk Univ Ser 5 Geogr ... Vestnik Moskovskogo Universiteta. Seriya 5. Geografiya [*A publication*]

Vestn Mosk Univ Ser 4 Geol ... Vestnik Moskovskogo Universiteta. Seriya 4. Geologiya [*A publication*]

Vestn Mosk Univ Ser I ... Vestnik Moskovskogo Universiteta. Seriya I. Matematika, Mekhanika [*A publication*]

Vestn Mosk Univ Ser II ... Vestnik Moskovskogo Universiteta. Nauchnyj Zhurnal. Seriya II. Khimiya [*A publication*]

Vestn Mosk Univ Ser III ... Vestnik Moskovskogo Universiteta. Seriya III. Fizika, Astronomiya [*A publication*]

Vestn Mosk Univ Ser III Fiz Astron ... Vestnik Moskovskogo Universiteta. Seriya III. Fizika, Astronomiya [*A publication*]

Vestn Mosk Univ Ser II Khim ... Vestnik Moskovskogo Universiteta. Seriya II. Khimiya [*A publication*]

Vestn Mosk Univ Ser I Mat Mekh ... Vestnik Moskovskogo Universiteta. Seriya I. Matematika, Mekhanika [*A publication*]

Vestn Mosk Univ Ser Mat Mekh Astron Fiz Khim ... Vestnik Moskovskogo Universiteta Seriya Matematiki, Mekhaniki, Astronomii, Fiziki, Khimii [*A publication*]

Vestn Mosk Univ Ser 17 Pochvoved ... Vestnik Moskovskogo Universiteta. Seriya 17. Pochvovedenie [*A publication*]

Vestn Mosk Univ Ser V Geogr ... Vestnik Moskovskogo Universiteta. Seriya V. Geografiya [*A publication*]

Vestn Mosk Univ Ser VI Biol Pochvoved ... Vestnik Moskovskogo Universiteta. Seriya VI. Biologiya, Pochvovedenie [*A publication*]

Vestn Mosk Univ Ser 15 Vychisl Mat Kibern ... Vestnik Moskovskogo Universiteta. Seriya 15. Vychislitel'naya Matematika i Kibernetika [*A publication*]

Vestn Nauchn Inf Zabaik Fil Geogr Ova SSSR ... Vestnik Nauchnoi Informatsii Zabaikal'skogo Filiala Geograficheskogo Obshchestva SSSR [*A publication*]

Vestn Nauchno-Issled Inst Gidrobiol (Dnepropetr) ... Vestnik Nauchno-Issledovatel'skogo Instituta Gidrobiologii (Dnepropetrovski) [*A publication*]

Vestn Obsc Nauk (Akad Nauk Arm SSR) ... Vestnik Obscestvennyh Nauk. (Akademija Nauk Armjanskoj SSR) [*A publication*]

Vestn Oftal'mol ... Vestnik Oftal'mologii [*A publication*]

Vestn ORL ... Vestnik Oto-Rino-Laringologii [*A publication*]

Vestn Otorinolaringol ... Vestnik Otorinolaringologii [*A publication*]

Vestn Rentgenol Radiol ... Vestnik Rentgenologii i Radiologii [*A publication*]

Vestn Respub Inst Okhr Prir Estestvennonauchn Muz Titograde ... Vestnik Respublikanskogo Instituta za Okhranu Prirodyi Estestvennonauchnogo Muzeya v Titograde [*A publication*]

Vestn Sel'skokhoz Nauki (Alma-Ata) ... Vestnik Sel'skokhozyaistvennoi Nauki (Alma-Ata) [*A publication*]

Vestn Sel'skokhoz Nauki (Moscow) ... Vestnik Sel'skokhozyaistvennoi Nauki (Moscow) [*A publication*]

Vestn S-kh Nauki (Alma-Ata) ... Vestnik Sel'skokhozyaistvennoi Nauki (Alma-Ata) [*Kazakh SSR*] [*A publication*]

Vestn S-kh Nauki (Mosc) ... Vestnik Sel'skokhozyaistvennoi Nauki (Moscow) [*A publication*]

Vestn Slov Kem Drus ... Vestnik Slovenskega Kemijskega Drustva [*A publication*]

Vestn Statis ... Vestnik Statistiki [*A publication*]

Vestn Statist ... Vestnik Statistiki [*A publication*]

Vestn Stud Nauchn Ova Kazan Gos Univ Estestv Nauki ... Vestnik Studencheskogo Nauchnogo Obshchestva Kazanskii Gosudarstvennyi Universitet Estestvennye Nauki [*A publication*]

Vestn Tbilis Bot Sada Akad Nauk Gruz SSR ... Vestnik Tbilisskogo Botanicheskogo Sada Akademii Nauk Gruzinskoi SSR [*A publication*]

Vestn USSR Acad Med Sci ... Vestnik. USSR Academy of Medical Science [*A publication*]

Vestn Ustred Ustavu Geol ... Vestnik Ustredniho Ustavu Geologickeho [*A publication*]

Vestn Vyssh Shk ... Vestnik Vysshej Shkoly [*A publication*]

Vestn Vyzk Ustavu Zemed ... Vestnik Vyzkumnych Ustavu Zemedelskych [*A publication*]

Vestn Zapadno Sib Geol Upr ... Vestnik Zapadno-Sibirskogo Geologicheskogo Upravleniya [*A publication*]

Vestn Zapadno Sib i Novosib Geol Upr ... Vestnik Zapadno-Sibirskogo i Novosibirskogo Geologicheskikh Upravlenii [*A publication*]

Vestn Zashch Rast ... Vestnik Zashchity Rastenii [*A publication*]

Vestn Zool ... Vestnik Zoologii [*A publication*]

Vestn Zool Zool Rec ... Vestnik Zoologii/Zoological Record [*A publication*]

Vest Oftal (Kiev) ... Vestnik Oftal'mologii (Kiev) [*A publication*]

Vest Oftal (Mosk) ... Vestnik Oftal'mologii (Moskva) [*A publication*]

Vest Oto-rino-lar ... Vestnik Otorinolaringologii [*A publication*]

Vest Sel'-khoz Nauki (Alma-Ata) Minist Sel Khoz Kazakh SSR ... Vestnik Sel'skokhozyaistvennoi Nauki (Alma-Ata). Ministerstvo Sel'skogo Khozyaistva Kazakhskoi SSR [*A publication*]

Vestsi Akad Navuk BSSR Khim Navuk ... Vestsi Akademii Navuk Belaruskai SSR. Khimichnykh Navuk [*A publication*]

Vestsi Akad Navuk BSSR Ser ... Vestsi Akademii Navuk Belaruskai SSR. Seriya [*A publication*]

Vestsi Akad Navuk BSSR Ser Biyal Navuk ... Vestsi Akademii Navuk Belaruskai SSR. Seryya Biyalagichnykh Navuk [*A publication*]

Vestsi Akad Navuk BSSR Ser Fiz-Ehnerg Navuk ... Vestsi Akademii Navuk BSSR. Seryya Fizika-Ehnergetychnykh Navuk [*A publication*]

Vestsi Akad Navuk BSSR Ser Fiz-Mat Navuk ... Vestsi Akademii Navuk BSSR. Seryya Fizika-Matematychnykh Navuk [*A publication*]

Vestsi Akad Navuk BSSR Ser Fiz-Tekh Navuk ... Vestsi Akademii Navuk BSSR. Seryya Fizika-Tekhnichnykh Navuk [*A publication*]

Vestsi Akad Navuk BSSR Ser Gramadskikh Navuk ... Vestsi Akademii Navuk BSSR. Seryya Gramadskikh Navuk [*Belorussian SSR*] [*A publication*]

Vestsi Akad Navuk BSSR Ser Khim ... Vestsi Akademii Navuk BSSR Seriya Khimicheskikh [*USSR*] [*A publication*]

Vestsi Akad Navuk BSSR Ser Khim Navuk ... Vestsi Akademii Navuk Belaruskai SSR. Seryya Khimichnykh Navuk [*A publication*]

Vestsi Akad Navuk BSSR Ser Sel'skagas Navuk ... Vestsi Akademii Navuk Belaruskai SSR. Seryya Sel'skagaspadar Navuk [*A publication*]

Vestsi Belarus Akad Navuk Ser Biyal Navuk ... Vestsi Belaruskaya Akademiya Navuk. Seryya Biyalagichnykh Navuk [*A publication*]

Vestsyi Akad Navuk BSSR Ser Fyiz-Ehnerg Navuk ... Vestsyi Akadehmyiyi Navuk BSSR. Seryya Fyizyika-Ehnergetychnykh Navuk [*A publication*]
Vestsyi Akad Navuk BSSR Ser Fyiz-Mat Navuk ... Vestsyi Akadehmyiyi Navuk BSSR. Seryya Fyizyika-Matehmatychnykh Navuk [*A publication*]
Vestsyi Akad Navuk BSSR Ser Fyiz-Tehkh Navuk ... Vestsyi Akadehmyiyi Navuk BSSR. Seryya Fyizyika-Tehkhnyichnykh Navuk [*A publication*]
Vestsyi Akad Navuk BSSR Ser Khyim Navuk ... Vestsyi Akadehmyiyi Navuk BSSR. Seryya Khyimyichnykh Navuk [*A publication*]
Vest Ustred Ust Geol ... Vestnik Ustredniho Ustavu Geologickeho [*A publication*]
VES UR ...... Vesica Urinaria [*Urinary Bladder*]
VESV......... Vesicular Exanthema Swine Virus
Veszpremi Vegyip Egy Tud Ulesszakanak Eloadasai ... Veszpremi Vegyipari Egyetem Tudomanyos Ulesszakanak Eloadasai [*Hungary*] [*A publication*]
Veszprem Megyei Muz Koezlem ... Veszprem Megyei Muzeumok Koezlemenyei [*A publication*]
VET .... Value Engineering Training
VET .... Vehicle Elapsed Time   (MCD)
VET .... Verbal Test
V & ET ...... Verification and Evaluation Tests   (MCD)
VET .... Versatile Engine Tester
VET .... Vestigial Testes [*Anatomy*]
VET .... Veteran   (AFM)
VET .... Veterans Administration, Somerville, NJ [*OCLC symbol*]   (OCLC)
Vet............. Veterinaria [*A publication*]
VET .... Veterinary   (AFM)
VET .... Vibrational Energy Transfer [*LASER*]   (MCD)
VET .... Video Editing Terminal [*Data processing*]
VET .... Vidicon Electron Tube
VET .... Vocational Educational and Training
Vet Anesth ... Veterinary Anesthesia [*A publication*]
Vet Annu.... Veterinary Annual [*A publication*]
Vet Arh...... Veterinarski Arhiv [*A publication*]
Vet Bull ...... Veterinary Bulletin [*A publication*]
Vet Bull (London) ... Veterinary Bulletin (London) [*A publication*]
Vet Bull (Weybridge Eng) ... Veterinary Bulletin (Weybridge, England) [*A publication*]
Vet Cas (Kosice) ... Veterinarsky Casopis (Kosice) [*A publication*]
VetChr .... Vetera Christianorum [*A publication*]
Vet Clin North Am ... Veterinary Clinics of North America [*A publication*]
Vet Clin North Am (Large Anim Pract) ... Veterinary Clinics of North America (Large Animal Practice) [*A publication*]
Vet Clin North Am (Small Anim Pract) ... Veterinary Clinics of North America (Small Animal Practice) [*A publication*]
VETDOC .... Veterinary Literature Documentation [*Derwent Publications Ltd.*] [*Bibliographic database*] [*London, England*]
Vetensk Publ Tek Hoegsk Helsingfors ... Vetenskapliga Publikationer. Tekniska Hoegskolan i Helsingfors [*A publication*]
Vetensk Soc i Lund Arsbok ... Vetenskaps-Societeten i Lund Arsbok [*A publication*]
Ve Tes........ Vetus Testamentum [*A publication*]
Vet Espan ... Veterinaria Espanola [*A publication*]
VETF .... Value Engineering Task Force
Vet Glas ..... Veterinarski Glasnik [*A publication*]
Vet Hist ...... Veterinary History Bulletin. Veterinary History Society [*A publication*]
Vet Hum Toxicol ... Veterinary and Human Toxicology [*A publication*]
Vet Immunol Immunopathol ... Veterinary Immunology and Immunopathology [*A publication*]
Vet Insp Annu Inst Vet Insp NSW ... Veterinary Inspector Annual. Institute of Veterinary Inspectors of New South Wales [*A publication*]
Vet Ital........ Veterinaria Italiana [*A publication*]
Vet J........... Veterinary Journal [*A publication*]
Vet J and Ann Comp Path ... Veterinary Journal and Annals of Comparative Pathology [*A publication*]
Vet J (Bratislava) ... Veterinary Journal (Bratislava) [*A publication*]
Vet Mag..... Veterinary Magazine [*A publication*]
Vet MB .... Bachelor of Veterinary Medicine
Vet Med ..... Veterinarni Medicina [*A publication*]
Vet Med ..... Veterinary Medicine [*A publication*]
Vet Med ..... Veterinary Medicine and Small Animal Clinician [*A publication*]
Vet Med Nauki ... Veterinarno Meditsinski Nauki [*A publication*]
Vet Med Nauki (Sofia) ... Veterinarno Meditsinski Nauki (Sofia) [*A publication*]
Vet Med (Prague) ... Veterinarni Medicina (Prague) [*A publication*]
Vet Med (Praha) ... Veterinarni Medicina (Praha) [*A publication*]
Vet Med/SAC ... Veterinary Medicine and Small Animal Clinician [*A publication*]
Vet Med Sci ... Veterinary Medical Science [*A publication*]
Vet Med & Small Anim Clin ... Veterinary Medicine and Small Animal Clinician [*A publication*]
Vet Med Small Anim Clin ... Veterinary Medicine and Small Animal Clinician [*A publication*]
Vet Microbiol ... Veterinary Microbiology [*Netherlands*] [*A publication*]
VETMIS...... Vertical Technical Management Information System   (MCD)
Vet Na B ..... Old Natura Brevium   (DLA)

Vet News.... Veterinary News [*A publication*]
Vet Obozr.... Veterinarnoe Obozrienie [*A publication*]
Vet Parasitol ... Veterinary Parasitology [*A publication*]
Vet Path ..... Veterinary Pathology [*A publication*]
Vet Pathol ... Veterinary Pathology [*A publication*]
Vet Pathol (Suppl) ... Veterinary Pathology. Supplement [*A publication*]
Vet QQJ Vet Sci ... Veterinary Quarterly. Quarterly Journal of Veterinary Science [*A publication*]
Vet Rec ...... Veterinary Record [*A publication*]
Vet Resp Mezhved Temat Nauchn Sb ... Veterinariya Respublikanskii Mezhvedomstvennyi Tematicheskii Nauchnyi Sbornik [*A publication*]
Vet Resp Mizhvid Temat Nauk Zb ... Veterinariya Respublikanskyu Mizhvidomchyi Tematychnyi Naukovyi Zbirnyk [*A publication*]
Vetro Silic ... Vetro e Silicati [*A publication*]
VETS......... Vehicle Electrical Test System   (ADA)
VETS......... Vertical Engine Test Stand
VETS......... Veterans' Employment and Training Service [*Department of Labor*]
Vet Sb (Bratislava) ... Veterinarsky Sbornik (Bratislava) [*A publication*]
Vet Sbirka ... Veterinarna Sbirka [*A publication*]
Vet Sbir (Sof) ... Veterinarna Sbirka (Sofia) [*A publication*]
Vet Sb (Sofia) ... Veterinarna Sbirka (Sofia) [*A publication*]
VetSci .... Veterinary Science
Vet Sci Commun ... Veterinary Science Communications [*A publication*]
Vet Stars.... Vets Stars and Stripes for Peace [*A publication*]
Vet Surg..... Veterinary Surgery [*A publication*]
Vett Cens... De Veterum Censura [*of Dionysius Halicarnassensis*] [*Classical studies*]   (OCD)
Vet Test ..... Vetus Testamentum [*A publication*]
Vet Toxicol ... Veterinary Toxicology [*A publication*]
Vet Urug ... Veterinaria Uruguay [*A publication*]
Vetus Test ... Vetus Testamentum [*A publication*]
Vet World... Veterinary World [*A publication*]
Vet Zh (Bratislava) ... Veterinarnyi Zhurnal (Bratislava) [*A publication*]
VEV .... Barakoma [*Solomon Islands*] [*Airport symbol*]   (OAG)
VEV .... Vernier Engine Vibration [*Aerospace*]
VEV .... Vietnam Era Veterans   (OICC)
VEV .... Vlaams Economisch Verbond
VEV .... Voice-Excited VOCODER
VEVERP ..... Vietnam Era Veteran Recruitment Program
VEWAA ..... Vocational Evaluation and Work Adjustment Association [*Alexandria, VA*]   (EA)
VEWS........ Very Early Warning System
VEWU........ Vietnam Educational Workers' Union [*North Vietnam*]
VEX .... Tioga, ND [*Location identifier*] [*FAA*]   (FAAL)
VEY .... Vestmannaeyjar [*Iceland*] [*Airport symbol*]   (OAG)
Vez .... Vezey's [*or Vesey's*] English Chancery Reports   (DLA)
Vezelinst TNO Delft VI Pam ... Vezelinstituut TNO [*Nederlands Centrale Organisatie voor Toegepast-Natuurwetenschappelijk Onderzoek*] Delft VI Pamflet [*A publication*]
Vezetestud ... Vezetestudomany [*A publication*]
VF.............. British Air Ferries Ltd.   (FAAC)
VF.............. De Vrije Fries [*A publication*]
VF.............. Fighter Plane [*Navy symbol*]
VF.............. Fighter Squadron [*Navy symbol*]
VF.............. Flaps-Down Speed [*Aviation*]
VF.............. Value Foundation   (EA)
VF.............. Vaporizer Feed [*Nuclear energy*]   (NRCH)
VF.............. Variable Frequency   (MSA)
VF.............. Vector Field
VF.............. Velocity Failure
VF.............. Ventricular Fibrillation [*Also, VFIB*] [*Cardiology*]
VF.............. Verification of Function
VF.............. Verkuendigung und Forschung [*Munich*] [*A publication*]
VF.............. Vertical File
VF.............. Vertical Flight   (NASA)
VF.............. Very Fair
VF.............. Very Fine [*Condition*] [*Antiquarian book trade, numismatics, etc.*]
VF.............. Vicarius Foraneus [*Vicar-Forane*] [*Latin*]
VF.............. Video Frequency
VF.............. View Factor
VF.............. Viewfinder [*Photography*]
VF.............. Vilagirodalmi Figyelo [*A publication*]
VF.............. Vinylferrocene [*Organic chemistry*]
VF.............. Vision Foundation [*Watertown, MA*]   (EA)
VF.............. Vision Frequency
VF.............. Visual Field
VF.............. Visual Flight [*Aviation*]   (FAAC)
VF.............. Vocal Fremitus
VF.............. Voice Frequency [*Communications*]
V/F............ Voltage to Frequency [*Converter*] [*Data processing*]
VF.............. Voprosy Filologii [*A publication*]
VF.............. Voprosy Filosofii [*A publication*]
VF.............. Vulcanized Fiber
VFA........... Variation Flow Analysis
VFA........... Victoria Falls [*Zimbabwe*] [*Airport symbol*]   (OAG)
VFA........... Video Free America   (EA)
VFA........... Video Frequency Amplifier

VFA .... Videotape Facilities Association [*Hollywood, CA*] (EA)
VFA .... Visual Flight Attachment [*Aviation*] (RDA)
VFA .... Volatile Fatty Acid [*Organic chemistry*]
VFA .... Volunteer Fire Alarm (TEL)
VFAS/TL ... Vertical Force Accounting System/Troop List (MCD)
VF AW .... Fighter Squadron - All Weather [*Navy symbol*] (MCD)
VFAX .... Heavier-than-Air Fighter/Attack/Experimental [*Aircraft*]
VFB .... Fighter Bombing Plane [*Navy symbol*]
VFB .... Vertical Format Buffer
VFB .... Vierteljahrschrift fuer Bibelkunde, Talmudische, und
                    Patristische Studien [*A publication*]
VFBK .... Vermont Federal Bank FSB [*NASDAQ symbol*] (NQ)
VFC .... Ferrum College, Ferrum, VA [*OCLC symbol*] (OCLC)
VFC .... Variable File Channel
VFC .... Variable Frequency Control
VFC .... Vertical Format Control
VFC .... Very Fine Cognac
VFC .... VF Corporation [*NYSE symbol*]
VFC .... Video Frequency Carrier [*or Channel*] (CET)
VFC .... Visual Field Control [*Aviation*]
VFC .... Voice Frequency Carrier [*or Channel*]
VFC .... Volatile Flavor Compound
VFC .... Voltage to Frequency Converter
VFC .... Volunteer Field Consultant [*Red Cross*]
VFCS .... Vehicle Flight Control System
VFCT .... Voice Frequency Carrier [*or Channel*] Telegraph [*or Teletype*]
VFCTT ...... Voice Frequency Carrier Teletype (MSA)
VFD .... Vacuum Fluorescent Display [*Data processing*]
VFD .... Value for Duty [*Business and trade*]
VFD .... Volunteer Fire Department
VFDBA ...... VFDB [*Vereinigung zur Foerderung des Deutschen
                    Brandschutzes*] Zeitschrift [*A publication*]
VFDB (Ver Foerd Dtch Brandschutzes) Z ... VFDB (Vereinigung zur
                    Foerderung des Deutschen Brandschutzes eV) Zeitschrift
                    [*A publication*]
VFDB Z ...... Vereinigung zur Foerderung des Deutschen Brandschutzes.
                    Zeitschrift [*A publication*]
VFDF .... Very Fast Death Factor
VFDM .... Vsemirnaia Federatsiia Demokraticheskoi Molodezhi [*World
                    Federation of Democratic Youth*]
VFDMIS ..... Vertical Force Development Management Information Systems
VFDR .... Variable-Flow Directed Rocket
VFED .... Valley Federal Savings & Loan [*NASDAQ symbol*] (NQ)
VFER .... Veterans Federal Employment Representative [*Civil Service
                    Commission*]
VFF .... Valence Force Field
VFF .... Voice Frequency Filter
VFFM .... Vestlandets Forstlige Forsoksstasjon. Meddelelse [*A
                    publication*]
VFFT .... Voice Frequency Facility Terminal
                    [*Telecommunications*] (TEL)
VFG .... Valley Fig Growers (EA)
VFG .... Visual Flight Guide [*A publication*]
VFH .... Vacuum Film Handling
VFH .... Vertical Flow Horizontal
VFHG .... Versammlungen der Freunde des Humanistischen
                    Gymnasiums [*A publication*]
VFHS .... Valley Forge Historical Society (EA)
VFHT .... Vacuum Film Handling Technique
VFI .... Verification Flight Instrumentation (NASA)
VFI .... Vinyl Fabrics Institute [*Later, Chemical Fabrics and Film
                    Association*] (EA)
VFI .... Visual Field Information [*Aviation*]
VFI .... Vocational Foundation, Incorporated [*An association*] [*New
                    York, NY*] (EA)
VFIB .... Ventricular Fibrillation [*Also, VF*] [*Cardiology*]
VFil .... Voprosy Filologii [*A publication*]
VFL .... Lemoyne College, Syracuse, NY [*OCLC symbol*] (OCLC)
VFL .... Variable Field Length (MCD)
VFL .... Variable Focal Length
VFL .... Variable Focal-Length Lens
VFL .... Victorian Football League [*Australia*] [*Receives television
                    coverage in the US through the Entertainment and Sports
                    Programming Network*]
VFL .... Voice Frequency Line [*Telecommunications*] (TEL)
VFLA .... Volume Folding and Limiting Amplifier
VFLC .... Video Fluorometric Detection Liquid Chromatograph
VFLT .... Visual Flight [*Aviation*] (FAAC)
VF(M) .... Fighter Plane (Two-Engine) [*Navy symbol*]
VFM .... Vacuum Forming Machine
VFM .... Vendor-Furnished Material (MCD)
VFM .... Vertical Flight Maneuver
VFMED ...... Variable Format Message Entry Device [*Data
                    processing*] (MCD)
VF(N) .... Night Fighter Squadrons [*Navy symbol*]
VFN .... Verticillium Wilt, Fusarium Wilt, Nematode Resistance [*Tomato
                    culture*]
VFO .... Vandenberg Field Office [*Air Force*] (MCD)
VFO .... Vaporized Fuel Oil [*Process*]
VFO .... Variable Frequency Oscillator
VFO .... Viking Flight Operations [*NASA*]

VFON .... Volunteer Flight Officers Network
VFOX .... Vicon Fiber Optics Corp. [*NASDAQ symbol*] (NQ)
VFP .... Fighter Squadron, Photo [*Navy symbol*] (MCD)
VFP .... Vacuum Flash Pyrolysis
VFP .... Vacuum Fore Pump
VFP .... Variable-Factor Programing
VFP .... Variance Frequency Processor (MCD)
VFP .... Veterans for Peace (EA)
VFP .... Volunteers for Peace (EA)
VFP .... Vsemirnaja Federacija Profsojuzov [*World Federation of Trade
                    Unions*]
VFPR .... Via Flight Planned Route [*Aviation*] (FAAC)
VFR .... Vehicle Flight Readiness (KSC)
VFR .... Vehicle Force Ratio (MCD)
VFR .... Verein fuer Raumschiffahrt [*Society for Space Travel*]
                    [*Germany*]
VFR .... Visiting Friends and Relatives [*Airlines*]
VFR .... Visual Flight Rules [*Aviation*]
VFR .... Volunteer Field Representative [*Red Cross*]
VFRA .... Volume Footwear Retailers of America [*Later, FRA*]
VFRCTS .... Visual Flight Rules Control Tower Simulator [*Aviation*] (MCD)
VFRSA ...... VFR [*Visual Flight Rules*] Restrictions Still Apply
                    [*Aviation*] (FAAC)
VFS .... Vapor Feed System
VFS .... Variable Frequency Synthesizer [*Ariel Corp.*] [*Data processing*]
VFS .... Ventilated Flight Suit
VFSC .... Vermont Financial Services [*NASDAQ symbol*] (NQ)
VFSL .... Virginia First Savings & Loan [*NASDAQ symbol*] (NQ)
VFSS .... Voice Frequency Signaling System
VFSSMCQ ... Victorian Federation of State Schools Mothers Clubs.
                    Quarterly Review [*A publication*]
VFSW .... Variable Frequency Sine Wave
VFSW .... Vierteljahrsschrift fuer Sozial- und Wirtschaftsgeschichte [*A
                    publication*]
VFT .... Vacuum Form Tool (MCD)
VFT .... Vacuum Friction Test
VFT .... Velocity False Target [*Military*] (CAAL)
VFT .... Ventricular Fibrillation Threshold [*Cardiology*]
VFT .... Verification Flight Test
VFT .... Vertical Flight Test (MCD)
VFT .... Viking Flight Team [*NASA*]
VFT .... Voice Frequency Telegraphy (NATG)
VFT .... Voice Frequency Terminal
VFTG .... Voice Frequency Telegraphy
VFU .... Van Wert, OH [*Location identifier*] [*FAA*] (FAAL)
VFU .... Vertical Format Unit (BUR)
VFU .... Vocabulary File Utility
VFUNDW .... Voluntary Fund for the United Nations Decade for
                    Women (EA)
VFV .... Venus Flyby Vehicle [*NASA*]
VFVC .... Vacuum Freezing, Vapor Compression [*Desalination*]
VFW .... Variable/Fixed Wavelength [*Electronics*]
VFW .... Verwaltungsamt fuer Wirtschaft [*Executive Committee for
                    Economics*] [*Germany*]
VFW .... Veterans of Foreign Wars of the USA (EA)
VFW .... Veterans of Future Wars [*Facetious organization formed by
                    Princeton students in 1930's*]
VFY .... Verify (AFM)
VG .... British Virgin Islands [*Two-letter standard code*] (CNC)
VG .... Central Caraibes SA [*Haiti*] [*ICAO designator*] (FAAC)
VG .... Grundriss der Vergleichenden Grammatik der Semitischen
                    Sprachen [*A publication*] (BJA)
VG .... Light Transport Plane [*Single-engine*] [*Navy symbol*]
VG .... Validity Generalization Testing (OICC)
VG .... Valuer-General (ADA)
VG .... Variable Geometry [*Refers to an aircraft that is capable of
                    altering the sweep of the wings while in flight*] (NATG)
VG .... Velocity Gravity
VG .... Ventricular Gallop [*Cardiology*]
VG .... Verbi Gratia [*For Example*] [*Latin*]
V & G .... Vergangenheit und Gegenwart [*A publication*]
VG .... Vertical Grain
V-G .... Vertical Gust (MCD)
VG .... Vertical Gyro (MCD)
VG .... Very Good [*Condition*] [*Antiquarian book trade, numismatics,
                    etc.*]
VG .... Vibration Greatness
VG .... Vicarius Generalis [*Vicar-General*] [*Latin*]
VG .... Vice Grand [*Freemasonry*] (ROG)
VG .... Vinylguaiacol [*Biochemistry*]
VG .... Vocational Guidance (ADA)
VG .... Voice Grade [*Telecommunications*] (TEL)
VG .... Volksgrenadier [*Title given to infantry divisions with
                    distinguished combat records*] [*Germany*] [*World War II*]
VG .... Voltage Gain
VG .... Votre Grace [*Your Grace*] [*French*]
VG .... Votre Grandeur [*Your Highness*] [*French*]
Vg .... Vulgate [*Latin translation of the Bible*] (BJA)
VGA .... Vapor Generation Accessory [*Instrumentation*]
VGA .... Variable Gain Amplifier
VGA .... Vertical Gyro Alignment

VGA............ Very General Algorithm (KSC)
VGA............ Vijayawada [India] [Airport symbol] (OAG)
VGA............ Virginia Air Cargo, Inc. [Charlottesville, VA] [FAA designator] (FAAC)
VGAA......... Vegetable Growers Association of America [Defunct] (EA)
VGAM........ Vector Graphics Access Method
VGB........... British Virgin Islands [Three-letter standard code] (CNC)
VGBD......... Virtual Grain Boundary Dislocation
VGC........... Variable Gas Capacitor
VGC........... Velocity Gate Capture [Military] (CAAL)
VGC........... Verdstone Gold Corporation [Vancouver Stock Exchange symbol]
VGC........... Very Good Condition [Doll collecting]
VGC........... Vesterheim Genealogical Center (EA)
VGC........... Video Graphics Controller [Apple Computer, Inc.]
VGC........... Viscosity Gravity Constant
VGC........... Visual Graphics Corporation [American Stock Exchange symbol]
VGCA......... Voice Gate Circuit Adaptors [Data processing] (MCD)
VGCH........ Vent Gas Collection Header [Nuclear energy] (NRCH)
VGCI......... Veta Grande Companies [NASDAQ symbol] (NQ)
VGCL .... Vietnam General Confederation of Labor
VGDIP .... Very God-Damned Important Person
VGE........... Visual Gross Error
VGF........... Escort Fighter Squadron [Navy symbol]
VGF........... Vaccinia Growth Factor [Biochemistry]
VGF........... Virus Growth Factor [Biochemistry]
VGFTU ...... Vietnam General Federation of Trade Unions [North Vietnam]
VGH........... Vancouver General Hospital
VGH........... Velocity, Normal Gravity, and Height
VGH........... Verwaltungsgerichtshof [District Administrative Court of Appeal] [German] (DLA)
VGH........... Very Good Health [Medicine]
VGH........... Veterinary General Hospital
VGI .... Variable Geometry Inlet
VGI .... Vertical Gyro Indicator
VGIEMTP ... Veroeffentlichungen des Grabmann Instituts zur Erforschung der Mittelalterlichen Theologie und Philosophie [A publication]
VGJ .... Vorgeschichtliches Jahrbuch [A publication]
VGLI.......... Veterans Group Life Insurance
VGLIS .... Video Guidance, Landing, and Imaging System [NASA]
VGLKV ...... Vierteljahrsschrift fuer Geschichte und Landeskunde Vorarlbergs [A publication]
VGLL .... Valstybine Grozines Literaturos Leidykla [A publication]
V/GLLD ..... Vehicular/Ground LASER Locator Designator (MCD)
VGM .... George Mason University, Fairfax, VA [OCLC symbol] (OCLC)
VGM .... Ventriculogram [A roentgenogram]
VGM .... Vestgron Mines Ltd. [Toronto Stock Exchange symbol] [Vancouver Stock Exchange symbol]
VGM .... Vice Grand Master (BJA)
VGM .... Villa Grajales [Mexico] [Seismograph station code, US Geological Survey] [Closed] (SEIS)
VGML .... Vegetarian Meal [Airline notation]
VGMU........ Vulcan Gunner Monitor Unit (MCD)
VGN........... Variable Geometry Nozzle
VGN........... Virginian Railway
VGN........... Virginian Railway Co. [AAR code]
VGO........... Vacuum Gas Oil [Petroleum technology]
VGO........... Vereinigte Gruenen Oesterreich [United Green Party of Austria] [Vienna]
VGO........... Vicar General's Office [British] (ROG)
VGO........... Vigo [Spain] [Airport symbol] (OAG)
VGOR .... Vehicle Ground Operation Requirements [NASA] (NASA)
VGP........... Vehicle Ground Point [NASA] (NASA)
VGP........... Victorian Government Publications [A publication]
VGP........... Virtual Geomagnetic Pole [Geophysics]
VGPI.......... Visual Glide Path Indicator
VGPI.......... Visual Ground Position Indicator (NATG)
VGPO .... Velocity Gate Pulloff [Military] (CAAL)
VGR........... Variable Geometry Rotor
VGS........... Escort-Scouting Squadron [Navy symbol]
VGS........... Variable Geometry Structure
VGS........... Variable-Grade Gravity Sewer
VGS........... Vehicle Generating System
VGS........... Velocity Gate Stealer [Military] (CAAL)
VGSI .... Visual Guidance System [Aviation] (FAAC)
VGSI .... Visual Glide Slope Indicator
VGT........... Las Vegas [Nevada] North Terminal [Airport symbol] (OAG)
VGT........... Las Vegas, NV [Location identifier] [FAA] (FAAL)
VGT........... Vehicle Ground Test [NASA] (NASA)
VGTE......... Vulcan Gunner Tracking Evaluation (MCD)
VGTSA .... Voprosy Gigieny Truda v Slantsevoi Promyshlennosti Estonskoi SSR [A publication]
VGU........... Des Moines, IA [Location identifier] [FAA] (FAAL)
VGV........... Vacuum Gate Valve
VG & VF .... Vicar General and Vicar Foreign [British] (ROG)
VGVT......... Vertical Ground Vibration Test (MCD)
VGW.......... Variable Geometry Wing [Aircraft]
VGWA .... Variable Geometry Wing Aircraft (AAG)
VGWO .... Velocity Gate Walkoff [Military] (CAAL)

VH .... Air Volta [Upper Volta] [ICAO designator] (FAAC)
VH .... Ambulance Plane [Navy symbol]
VH .... Australia [Aircraft nationality and registration mark] (FAAC)
VH .... Rescue Squadrons [Navy symbol]
VH .... Vacuum Housing
VH .... Vaginal Hysterectomy [Gynecology]
VH .... Varia Historia [of Aelianus] [Classical studies] (OCD)
V/H .... Velocity/Height
VH .... Vent Hole [Technical drawings]
VH .... Vermont History [A publication]
VH .... Very Heavy [Cosmic ray nuclei]
VH .... Very High
VH .... Veterans Hospital
VH .... Vickers Hardness Number [Also, HV, VHN] (AAG)
VH .... Vir Honestus [A Worthy Man] [Latin]
VH .... Viral Hepatitis [Medicine]
V/H .... Vulnerability/Hardness [Refers to a weapon system's weakness and capabilities in withstanding adverse operating environments]
VH-1 .... Video Hits One [Cable-television system] [Companion to MTV]
VHA........... Van Houten Associates [Information service] (EISS)
VHA........... Variable Housing Allowance (MCD)
VHA........... Very High Altitude
VHA........... Very High Aluminum [Rock composition]
VHA........... Voluntary Hospitals of America [An association] [Cable-television system] (EA)
VHAA......... Very High Altitude Abort [NASA] (KSC)
VHB........... Buffalo and Erie County Public Library, Buffalo, NY [OCLC symbol] (OCLC)
VHB........... Very Heavy Bombardment [Air Force]
VHBW........ Very-High-Speed Black and White [Photography]
VHC........... Hollins College, Hollins College, VA [OCLC symbol] (OCLC)
VHC........... Saurimo [Angola] [Airport symbol] (OAG)
VHC........... Vertical Hold Control
VHC........... Very Highly Commended
VHD........... Valvular Heart Disease
VHD........... Video High Density [Television]
VHDL......... Very-High Density Lipoprotein [Biochemistry]
VHDV .... Very High Dollar Value
VHE........... Very-High Energy
VHE........... Volatile Human Effluents
VH Eq Dr .... Van Heythuysen's Equity Draftsman [2nd ed.] [1828] (DLA)
VHF........... Vacuum Hydrogen Furnace
VHF........... Very-High-Frequency [Electronics]
VHF........... Visual Half-Field
VHF/AM ..... Very-High-Frequency, Amplitude Modulated (NASA)
VHF/DF ..... Very-High-Frequency Direction-Finding
VHFF .... Very-High-Frequency Filter
VHF-FM ..... Very-High-Frequency, Frequency Modulated (NOAA)
VHFG......... Very-High-Frequency Generator
VHFI .... Very-High-Frequency Indeed [Ultrahigh frequency] [British]
VHFJ .... Very-High-Frequency Jammer
VHFO......... Very-High-Frequency Oscillator
VHFOR ...... Very-High-Frequency Omnirange (AFM)
VHFR......... Very-High-Frequency Receiver
VHFS......... Videnskabernes Selskabs Historisk-Filologiske Skrifter [A publication]
VHFT......... Very-High-Frequency Termination
VHI .... Valhi, Incorporated [NYSE symbol]
VHis.......... Vida Hispanica [A publication]
VHIS.......... Vietnam Head Injury Study
VHJ........... Victorian Historical Journal [A publication]
VHLA......... Viceroy Homes Class A SV [Toronto Stock Exchange symbol]
VHLH......... Very Heavy Lift Helicopter
VHM .... Victorian Historical Magazine [A publication]
VHM .... Virtual Hardware Monitor [Data processing] (IEEE)
VHM .... Visitation Nuns [Roman Catholic religious order]
VHM .... Vista Hermosa [Mexico] [Seismograph station code, US Geological Survey] [Closed] (SEIS)
VHMCP ...... Voluntary Home Mortgage Credit Program [of HHFA] [Terminated]
VHN........... Van Horn, TX [Location identifier] [FAA] (FAAL)
VHN........... Vickers Hardness Number [Also, HV, VH]
VHO........... Very High Output
VHO........... Vila Coutinho [Mozambique] [Airport symbol] [Obsolete] (OAG)
VHO........... Vista Hermosa [Mexico] [Seismograph station code, US Geological Survey] (SEIS)
VHO........... Volatile Halogenated Organic [Analytical chemistry]
VHOC......... Volatile Halogenated Organic Compound [Environmental chemistry]
VHOL......... Very-High-Order Language
VHP .... County of Henrico Public Library, Richmond, VA [OCLC symbol] (OCLC)
VHP .... Variable Horsepower
VHP .... Very High Performance
VHP .... Very-High Polarization [Raw sugar grade]
VHP .... Very High Pressure
VHP .... Vooruitstrewende Hervormings Partij [Progressive Reform Party] [Surinamese] (PPW)
VHPA.......... Vietnam Helicopter Pilots Association [Phoenix, AZ] (EA)

VHR .... Very-Highly Repeated [*Genetics*]
VHR .... Video-to-Hardcopy Recorder
VHRR .... Very High Resolution Radiometer [*NASA*]
VHRTG .... Veterans' Hospital Radio and Television Guild   (EA)
VHS .... Hampden-Sydney College, Hampden-Sydney, VA [*OCLC symbol*]   (OCLC)
VHS .... Honorary Surgeon to the Viceroy of India
VHS .... Versatile High Speed [*Copier*]
VHS .... Very High Speed [*Copier*]
VHS .... Victorian House of Studies
VHS .... Video Home System
VHS .... Viral Hemorrhagic Septicemia [*Medicine*]
VHS-C .... Video Home System - Compact
VHSI .... Very-High-Speed Integrated [*Electronics*]
VHSIC .... Very-High-Speed Integrated Circuit [*Electronics*]
VHST .... Very-High-Speed Transit
VHT .... VMS Hotel Investment Trust [*American Stock Exchange symbol*]
VHTR .... Very-High-Temperature Reactor
V/HUD .... Vertical/Heads-Up Display [*Aviation*]   (MCD)
VHUP .... Veterinary Hospital of the University of Pennsylvania
VHVNB .... Verhandlungen des Historischen Vereines von Niederbayern [*A publication*]
VHVOR .... Verhandlungen des Historischen Vereines von Oberpfalz und Regensburg [*A publication*]
VHY .... Vess, Henry, Kansas City MO [*STAC*]
VI .... Congregation of the Incarnate Word and the Blessed Sacrament [*Roman Catholic women's religious order*]
VI .... Inertial Velocity
VI .... Societe de Travail Aerien [*Algeria*] [*ICAO designator*]   (FAAC)
VI .... Vaginal Irrigation [*Medicine*]
VI .... Valley Industries, Inc. [*NYSE symbol*]
VI .... Value Included Entry [*Business and trade*]
VI .... Vancouver Island
VI .... Variable Interval [*Reinforcement schedule*]
VI .... Vasoinhibitory [*Medicine*]
VI .... Vector International [*Pittsburgh, PA*]   (EA)
VI .... Vegetation Index
VI .... Vendor Item   (AAG)
VI .... Vent Isolation [*Nuclear energy*]   (NRCH)
VI .... Verb Intransitive
VI .... Vermiculite Institute [*Defunct*]
VI .... Vertical Interval [*Mapmaking*]
VI .... Veterinary Inspector   (ADA)
VI .... Vial
Vi .... Viator [*A publication*]
VI .... Vibration Institute   (EA)
VI .... Video Integrator
VI .... Vinegar Institute [*Atlanta, GA*]   (EA)
VI .... Violet
VI .... Virgin Islands Reports   (DLA)
VI .... Virgin Islands of the US [*Two-letter standard code*]   (CNC)
VI .... Virgin Islands of the US [*Postal code*]
vi .... Virgin Islands of the US [*MARC country of publication code*] [*Library of Congress*]   (LCCP)
Vi .... Virginia State Library, Richmond, VA [*Library symbol*] [*Library of Congress*]   (LCLS)
VI .... Virgo Intacta [*Medicine*]
Vi .... Virulence [*Antigen*] [*Immunology*]
VI .... Viscosity Improver [*Element in multigrade engine oil*]
VI .... Viscosity Index
VI .... Visual Impairment
VI .... Visual Inspection
V & I .... Voix et Images. Etudes Quebecoises [*A publication*]
VI .... Volume Indicator [*Radio equipment*]
VI .... Voluntary Indefinite [*Status*] [*Army*]   (INF)
VI .... Volunteers for Israel   (EA)
VI .... Voprosy Istorii [*A publication*]
VIA .... Arlington County Department of Libraries, Arlington, VA [*OCLC symbol*]   (OCLC)
VIA .... Valorisation de l'Innovation dans l'Ameublement [*Committee to Promote Innovation in Furniture Design*] [*France*]
VIA .... Viacom International, Inc. [*NYSE symbol*]
VIA .... Viaduct
VIA .... Video Image Analysis
VIA .... Videotex Industry Association [*Rosslyn, VA*] [*Telecommunications*] [*Information service*]   (EA)
VIA .... Virus Inactivating Agency [*Medicine*]
VIA .... Virus Infection Associated Antigen [*Immunology*]
VIA .... Vision Institute of America [*Later, VSP*]   (EA)
VIA .... Vocational Interests and Vocational Aptitudes [*Psychology*]
VIA .... Volunteers in Asia [*Stanford, CA*]   (EA)
ViAb .... Washington County Public Library, Abingdon, VA [*Library symbol*] [*Library of Congress*]   (LCLS)
VIABLE .... Vertical Installation Automated Baseline [*Army*]
ViAc .... Eastern Shore Public Library, Accomac, VA [*Library symbol*] [*Library of Congress*]   (LCLS)
VIAFF .... Vancouver International Amateur Film Festival [*Canada*]
ViAI .... Alexandria Library, Alexandria, VA [*Library symbol*] [*Library of Congress*]   (LCLS)

ViAIA .... United States Army Material Command Headquarters, Technical Library, Alexandria, VA [*Library symbol*] [*Library of Congress*]   (LCLS)
ViAIbS .... Southside Virginia Community College, Christanna Campus, Alberta, VA [*Library symbol*] [*Library of Congress*]   (LCLS)
ViAID .... Defense Technical Information Center, Cameron Station, Alexandria, VA [*Library symbol*] [*Library of Congress*]   (LCLS)
ViAIDL .... Defense Logistics Agency, Cameron Station, Alexandria, VA [*Library symbol*] [*Library of Congress*]   (LCLS)
ViAIP .... Jacob Simpson Payton Library, Alexandria, VA [*Library symbol*] [*Library of Congress*]   (LCLS)
ViAITh .... Protestant Episcopal Theological Seminary in Virginia, Alexandria, VA [*Library symbol*] [*Library of Congress*]   (LCLS)
ViAnGS ...... Church of Jesus Christ of Latter-Day Saints, Genealogical Society Library, Annandale Branch, Annandale, VA [*Library symbol*] [*Library of Congress*]   (LCLS)
ViAnN .... Northern Virginia Community College, Annandale, VA [*Library symbol*] [*Library of Congress*]   (LCLS)
VIAP .... Vanuatu Independent Alliance Party   (PPW)
ViAr .... Arlington County Department of Libraries, Arlington, VA [*Library symbol*] [*Library of Congress*]   (LCLS)
ViAr-A .... Arlington County Department of Libraries, Aurora Hills Branch, Arlington, VA [*Library symbol*] [*Library of Congress*]   (LCLS)
ViArAL .... Center for Applied Linguistics, Arlington, VA [*Library symbol*] [*Library of Congress*]   (LCLS)
ViAr-Ch ..... Arlington County Department of Libraries, Cherrydale Branch, Arlington, VA [*Library symbol*] [*Library of Congress*]   (LCLS)
ViAr-Cl ...... Arlington County Department of Libraries, Clarendon Branch, Arlington, VA [*Library symbol*] [*Library of Congress*]   (LCLS)
ViAr-F .... Arlington County Department of Libraries, Fairlington Branch, Arlington, VA [*Library symbol*] [*Library of Congress*]   (LCLS)
ViAr-G .... Arlington County Department of Libraries, Glencarlyn Branch, Arlington, VA [*Library symbol*] [*Library of Congress*]   (LCLS)
ViArHD ...... United States Historical Documents Institute, Inc., Arlington, VA [*Library symbol*] [*Library of Congress*]   (LCLS)
ViArM .... Marymount College, Arlington, VA [*Library symbol*] [*Library of Congress*]   (LCLS)
ViArNG ...... National Graduate University, Arlington, VA [*Library symbol*] [*Library of Congress*]   (LCLS)
ViAr-W .... Arlington County Department of Libraries, Westover Branch, Arlington, VA [*Library symbol*] [*Library of Congress*]   (LCLS)
VIAS .... Voice Interference Analysis Set
VIASA .... Venezolana Internacional de Aviacion, Sociedad Anonima [*Venezuelan airline*]
ViAsM .... Mobil Chemical Co., Industrial Chemicals Division, Ashland, VA [*Library symbol*] [*Library of Congress*]   (LCLS)
ViAsR .... Randolph-Macon College, Ashland, VA [*Library symbol*] [*Library of Congress*]   (LCLS)
Viata Med... Viata Medicala. Revista a Unuinii Societatelor de Stiinte Medicale din Republica Socialista [*Romania*] [*A publication*]
Viata Med (Buchar) ... Viata Medicala (Bucharest) [*A publication*]
Viata Med (Medii Sanit) ... Viata Medicala. Revista de Informare Profesionala se Stiintifica a Cadrelor (Medii Sanitare) [*A publication*]
Viator Med ... Viator. Medieval and Renaissance Studies [*A publication*]
VIB .... Vanilla Information Bureau [*New York, NY*]   (EA)
VIB .... Veal Infusion Broth [*Immunology*]
VIB .... Vertical Integration Building
VIB .... Vibraphone [*Music*]
VIB .... Vibrate   (AAG)
VIB .... Vitamin Information Bureau [*Commercial firm*] [*Chicago, IL*]   (EA)
VIBG .... Vibrating   (AAG)
VIBGYOR ... Violet, Indigo, Blue, Green, Yellow, Orange, Red [*Mnemonic for the colors of the spectrum*]
VIBI .... Virgini Immaculatae Bavaria Immaculata [*To the Immaculate Virgin Immaculate Bavaria*] [*Latin*] [*Motto of the Order of St. George of Bavaria*]
VIBJ .... Virgin Islands Bar Journal [*A publication*]
ViBlbV .... Virginia Polytechnic Institute and State University, Blacksburg, VA [*Library symbol*] [*Library of Congress*]   (LCLS)
ViBluC .... Bluefield College, Bluefield, VA [*Library symbol*] [*Library of Congress*]   (LCLS)
VIBN .... Vibration   (AAG)
Vi-BPH .... Virginia State Library for the Visually and Physically Handicapped, Richmond, VA [*Library symbol*] [*Library of Congress*]   (LCLS)
VIBR .... Vibration
VIBRA .... Vehicle Inelastic Bending Response Analysis [*Computer program*]

VIBRAM ..... Vitale Bramani [*Inventor of rubber soles for boots used in mountain climbing*]
ViBrC .... Bridgewater College, Bridgewater, VA [*Library symbol*] [*Library of Congress*] (LCLS)
VIBROT ...... Vibrational-Rotational [*Spectra*] [*Data processing*]
ViBS .... Sullins College, Bristol, VA [*Library symbol*] [*Library of Congress*] (LCLS)
VIBS .... Vocabulatory, Information, Block Design, Similarities [*Psychology*]
Vib Spectra Struct ... Vibrational Spectra and Structure [*A publication*]
ViBV .... Virginia Intermont College, Bristol, VA [*Library symbol*] [*Library of Congress*] (LCLS)
ViC .... McIntire Public Library, Charlottesville, VA [*Library symbol*] [*Library of Congress*] (LCLS)
VIC .... University of Victoria Library [*UTLAS symbol*]
VIC .... Value Incentive Clause [*General Services Administration*]
VIC .... Vapor Injection Curing [*Plastics technology*]
VIC .... Variable Instruction Computer
VIC .... Varnish Insulating Compound
VIC .... Vasoinhibitory Center [*Physiology*]
VIC .... Vehicle Intercommunications System (MCD)
VIC .... Very Important Cargo
VIC .... Very Important Contributors [*Political*]
VIC .... Very Important Customer
VIC .... Veterinary Investigation Centre [*Ministry of Agriculture, Fisheries, and Food*] [*British*]
VIC .... Vicar [*or Vicarage*]
VIC .... Vices [*Times*] [*Pharmacy*]
vic .... Vicinal [*Also, v*] [*Chemistry*]
VIC .... Vicinity (AABC)
Vic .... Victor [*Record label*]
VIC .... Victoria [*State in Australia*]
VIC .... Victoria [*British Columbia*] [*Geomagnetic observatory code*]
VIC .... Victoria [*British Columbia*] [*Seismograph station code, US Geological Survey*] (SEIS)
VIC .... Vienna International Centre [*United Nations*]
VIC .... Viking Integrated Change [*NASA*]
VIC .... Virgin Islands Corporation [*Intended to promote VI economic development, dissolved 1966*] [*Department of the Interior*]
VIC .... Virginia Intermont College
VIC .... Virginia State Library, Richmond, VA [*OCLC symbol*] (OCLC)
VIC .... Virtual Interaction Controller
VIC .... Visibility of Intransit Cargo
VIC .... Visitor Information Center [*Kennedy Space Center*]
VIC .... Vortex in Cell
VICA .... Video Corporation of America [*NASDAQ symbol*] (NQ)
VICA .... Vocational Industrial Clubs of America
ViCAF .... United States Army, Foreign Science and Technical Center, Charlottesville, VA [*Library symbol*] [*Library of Congress*] (LCLS)
ViCAHi .... Abermarle County Historical Society, Charlottesville, VA [*Library symbol*] [*Library of Congress*] (LCLS)
VIC and ALB ... Victoria and Albert Museum [*London*] (DSUE)
VICAM .... Virtual Integrated Communications Access Method [*Sperry UNIVAC*]
VICANA ...... Vietnamese Cultural Association of North America (EA)
VICAP .... Violent Criminal Apprehension Program [*Proposed federal program*]
VICAR .... Video Image Communication and Retrieval
Vic Assn Teach Eng J ... Victorian Association for the Teaching of English. Journal [*A publication*]
Vicat .... Vicat's Vocabularium Juris Utriusque ex Variis Ante Editis (DLA)
Vicat Voc Jur ... Vicat's Vocabularium Juris Utriusque ex Variis Ante Editis (DLA)
Vic Bar News ... Victorian Bar News [*A publication*]
VIC C .... Victoria Cross (DSUE)
Vic CC .... County Court Reports (Victoria) [*A publication*]
Vic Chamber of Manufactures Econ Serv ... Victorian Chamber of Manufactures. Economic Service [*A publication*]
Vic Chap News ... Victorian Chapter Newsletter [*Australian College of Education*] [*A publication*]
Vic Comm Teach Assn General J ... Victorian Commercial Teachers' Association. General Journal [*A publication*]
Vic Conf Soc Welfare Proc ... Victorian Conference of Social Welfare. Proceedings [*A publication*]
Vic Creditman ... Victorian Creditman [*A publication*]
Vic Dairyfarmer ... Victorian Dairyfarmer [*A publication*]
Vic Dep Agric Tech Bull ... Victoria. Department of Agriculture. Technical Bulletin [*A publication*]
VICE .... Vast Integrated Communications Environment [*Carnegie Mellon University*] [*Pittsburgh, PA*]
Vic Ed Gaz ... Education Gazette and Teachers Aid (Victoria) [*A publication*]
Vic Elec Contractor ... Victorian Electrical Contractor [*A publication*]
Vic Employers' Federation AR ... Victorian Employers' Federation. Annual Report [*A publication*]
Vicenza Econ ... Vicenza Economica [*A publication*]
VICF .... Victoria Financial Corp. [*NASDAQ symbol*] (NQ)
Vic For Comm Bull ... Victoria. Forests Commission. Bulletin [*A publication*]
VICGEN ...... Vicar General's Office [*British*]

Vic Geogr J ... Victorian Geographical Journal [*A publication*]
Vic Govt Gaz ... Victorian Government Gazette [*A publication*]
Vic Hist Mag ... Victorian Historical Magazine [*A publication*]
Vic Hortic Dig ... Victorian Horticultural Digest [*A publication*]
ViChT .... John Tyler Community College, Chester, VA [*Library symbol*] [*Library of Congress*] (LCLS)
VICI .... Vantage Information Consultants, Incorporated [*Information service*] (EISS)
VICI .... Velocity Indicating Coherent Integrator
VICI .... Video Console Indexing
VICI .... Voice Input Child Identicant [*Pronounced "Vicki"*] [*Young robot in television show "Small Wonder"*]
VICI .... Voice Input Code Identifier (MCD)
Vic Inst Coll News ... Victoria Institute of Colleges. Newsletter [*A publication*]
VICK .... Vicksburg National Military Park
Vic Legal Exec ... Victorian Legal Executive [*A publication*]
ViCIR .... Robbins Mills, Inc., Clarksville, VA [*Library symbol*] [*Library of Congress*] (LCLS)
Vic LSAJ ...... Victorian LSA [*Limbless Soldiers' Association*] Journal [*A publication*]
VicN .... Victorian Naturalist [*A publication*]
Vic Nat ...... Victorian Naturalist [*A publication*]
Vic Naturalist ... Victorian Naturalist [*A publication*]
VIC News ... Victoria Institute of Colleges. Newsletter [*A publication*]
VICO .... Virginia International Company
VICO .... Volkswagen Insurance Company
ViCoC .... Castle Hill Museum, Cobham, VA [*Library symbol*] [*Library of Congress*] (LCLS)
VICOED ...... Visual Communications Education
VICOM .... Visual Communications Management
VICON .... Visual Confirmation [*of voice takeoff clearing system*] [*Aviation*]
VICORE ...... Visual Conceptual Reading
ViCou .... Walter Cecil Rawls Library and Museum, Courtland, VA [*Library symbol*] [*Library of Congress*] (LCLS)
ViCovI .... Industrial Rayon Corp., Covington, VA [*Library symbol*] [*Library of Congress*] (LCLS)
ViCovW ...... West Virginia Pulp & Paper Co., Covington, VA [*Library symbol*] [*Library of Congress*] (LCLS)
ViCP .... Piedmont Virginia Community College, Learning Resources Center, Charlottesville, VA [*Library symbol*] [*Library of Congress*] (LCLS)
Vic Parl Deb ... Victorian Parliamentary Debates [*A publication*]
Vic Parl Parl Deb ... Victoria. Parliament. Parliamentary Debates [*A publication*]
Vic Poultry J ... Victorian Poultry Journal [*A publication*]
VICR .... Victor Technologies [*NASDAQ symbol*] (NQ)
ViCRA .... National Radio Astronomy Observatory, Charlottesville, VA [*Library symbol*] [*Library of Congress*] (LCLS)
Vic Railways Newsletter ... Victorian Railways Newsletter [*A publication*]
Vic Resour ... Victoria's Resources [*A publication*]
Vic Resources ... Victoria's Resources [*A publication*]
Vic Rev ...... Victorian Review [*A publication*]
VICS .... Verbal Interaction Category System [*Student teacher test*]
VICS .... Vocational Information through Computer Systems [*Philadelphia School District*] [*Pennsylvania*] [*Information service*] (EISS)
Vic Stat Pub ... Victorian Statistics Publications [*A publication*]
ViCT .... Institute of Textile Technology, Charlottesville, VA [*Library symbol*] [*Library of Congress*] (LCLS)
VICT .... Victoria Bankshares [*NASDAQ symbol*] (NQ)
Vict .... Victorian Reports [*A publication*]
Vict Cancer News ... Victorian Cancer News [*A publication*]
Vict Dairyfmr ... Victorian Dairyfarmer [*A publication*]
Vic Teachers J ... Victorian Teachers Journal [*A publication*]
Vic Teach J ... Victorian Teachers Journal [*A publication*]
Vict For Comm Bull ... Victoria. Forests Commission. Bulletin [*A publication*]
Vict For Comm For Tech Pap ... Victoria. Forests Commission. Forestry Technical Paper [*A publication*]
Vict For Comm Misc Publ ... Victoria. Forests Commission. Miscellaneous Publication [*A publication*]
Vict Geogr J ... Victorian Geographical Journal [*A publication*]
Vict Geol Surv Bull ... Victoria. Geological Survey. Bulletin [*A publication*]
Vict Geol Surv Mem ... Victoria. Geological Survey. Memoirs [*A publication*]
Vict Hist Mag ... Victorian Historical Magazine [*A publication*]
Vict Hort Dig ... Victorian Horticultural Digest [*A publication*]
Vict LJ .... Victorian Law Journal [*A publication*]
Vict LR ...... Victorian Law Reports [*A publication*]
Vict LR Min ... Victorian Mining Law Reports [*Aus.*] (DLA)
Vict LT ...... Victorian Law Times [*A publication*]
Vict Nat ...... Victorian Naturalist [*A publication*]
Vict Naturalist ... Victorian Naturalist [*A publication*]
Vict Newsl ... Victorian Newsletter [*A publication*]
Victoria Country Roads Board Eng Note ... Victoria. Country Roads Board. Engineering Note [*A publication*]
Victoria Country Roads Board Tech Bull ... Victoria. Country Roads Board. Technical Bulletin [*A publication*]
Victoria Dep Agric Res Proj Ser ... Victoria. Department of Agriculture. Research Project Series [*A publication*]

Victoria Dep Agric Tech Bull ... Victoria. Department of Agriculture. Technical Bulletin [*A publication*]

Victoria Dep Agric Tech Rep Ser ... Victoria. Department of Agriculture. Technical Report Series [*A publication*]

Victoria Fish Wildl Dep Fish Contrib ... Victoria. Fisheries and Wildlife Department. Fisheries Contribution [*Australia*] [*A publication*]

Victoria Fish Wildl Dep Wildl Contrib ... Victoria. Fisheries and Wildlife Department. Wildlife Contribution [*A publication*]

Victoria Geol Bull ... Victoria. Geological Survey. Bulletin [*A publication*]

Victoria Geol Surv Mem ... Victoria. Geological Survey. Memoirs [*A publication*]

Victoria Inst Tr ... Victoria Institute or Philosophical Society of Great Britain. Journal of the Transactions [*A publication*]

Victoria Inst (Trinidad) Pr ... Victoria Institute (Trinidad). Proceedings [*A publication*]

Victoria Mines Dep Annu Rep ... Victoria. Mines Department. Annual Report [*A publication*]

Victoria Mines Dep Groundwater Invest Program Rep ... Victoria. Mines Department. Groundwater Investigation Program. Report [*Australia*] [*A publication*]

Victoria Minist Conserv Environ Stud Program Proj Rep ... Victoria. Ministry for Conservation. Environmental Studies Program. Project Report [*A publication*]

Victorian Entomol ... Victorian Entomologist [*A publication*]

Victorian Hist J ... Victorian Historical Journal [*A publication*]

Victorian Hist Mag ... Victorian Historical Magazine [*A publication*]

Victorian Nat ... Victorian Naturalist [*A publication*]

Victorian Natl Parks Assoc J ... Victorian National Parks Association. Journal [*A publication*]

Victorian Railw ... Victorian Railways [*A publication*]

Victorian Stud ... Victorian Studies [*A publication*]

Victoria's Resour ... Victoria's Resources [*A publication*]

Victoria State Rivers Water Supply Comm Annu Rep ... Victoria. State Rivers and Water Supply Commission. Annual Report [*A publication*]

Victoria Univ Antarct Data Ser ... Victoria University of Wellington. Antarctic Data Series [*New Zealand*] [*A publication*]

Vict Poet .... Victorian Poetry [*A publication*]

Vict Poetry ... Victorian Poetry [*A publication*]

Vict Rep ..... Victorian Reports [*A publication*]

Vict Rep (Adm) ... Victorian Reports, Admiralty [*Aus.*] (DLA)

Vict Rep (Austr) ... Victorian Reports [*Australian*] [*A publication*]

Vict Rep (Eq) ... Victorian Reports [*Equity*] [*A publication*]

Vict Rep (Law) ... Victorian Reports [*Law*] [*A publication*]

Vict Res ..... Victoria's Resources [*A publication*]

Vict Resour ... Victoria's Resources [*A publication*]

Vict Rev ..... Victorian Review [*A publication*]

Vict Soil Conserv Auth TC ... Victoria. Soil Conservation Authority. TC Report [*A publication*]

Vict Soil Conserv Auth TC Rep ... Victoria. Soil Conservation Authority. TC Report [*A publication*]

Vict Stat ..... Victorian Statutes [*General Public Acts*] [*Aus.*] (DLA)

Vict Stat R Regs & B ... Victorian Statutory Rules, Regulations, and By-Laws [*Aus.*] (DLA)

Vict St Tr .... Victorian State Trials [*Aus.*] (DLA)

Vict Stud .... Victorian Studies [*A publication*]

Vict U C L Rev ... Victoria University. College Law Review [*A publication*]

Vict UL Rev ... Victoria University. Law Review (DLA)

Vict U of Wellington L Rev ... Victoria University of Wellington. Law Review [*A publication*]

Vict U Well L Rev ... Victoria University of Wellington. Law Review [*A publication*]

Vict Vet Proc ... Australian Veterinary Association. Victorian Division. Annual General Meeting. Proceedings [*A publication*]

Vict Vet Proc ... Australian Veterinary Association. Victorian Division. Victorian Veterinary Proceedings [*A publication*]

Vic Veg Grower ... Victorian Vegetable Grower [*A publication*]

Vic Vet Proc ... Victorian Veterinary Proceedings [*A publication*]

ViCVH .... Virginia Highway Research Council, Charlottesville, VA [*Library symbol*] [*Library of Congress*] (LCLS)

Vic Yrbk ..... Victoria Yearbook [*A publication*]

ViD .... Danville Public Library, Danville, VA [*Library symbol*] [*Library of Congress*] (LCLS)

VID .... Vide [*or Videte*] [*See*] [*Latin*]

VID .... Video (AAG)

VID .... Video Image Display Assembly [*Space Flight Operations Facility, NASA*]

Vid .... Vidian's Exact Pleader [*1684*] (DLA)

VID .... Vidin [*Bulgaria*] [*Airport symbol*] (OAG)

VID .... Vienna Institute for Development (EA-IO)

VID .... Virtual Image Display (MCD)

VID .... Visual Identification (CAAL)

VID .... Volunteers for International Development [*Later, Peaceworkers*] (EA)

VID .... Vspomogatel'nye Istorichiskie Distsipliny [*A publication*]

ViDA .... Averette College, Danville, VA [*Library symbol*] [*Library of Congress*] (LCLS)

VIDA .... Ventricular Impulse Detector and Alarm [*Cardiology*]

Vida Agr ..... Vida Agricola [*A publication*]

VIDAC .... Visual Information Display and Control

VidaL .... Vida Literaria [*A publication*]

Vida Med .... Vida Medica [*A publication*]

VIDAMP ..... Video Amplifier

VIDAP .... Vibration Data Accuracy Program

VIDAR .... Velocity Integration, Detection, and Ranging (NG)

VIDAS .... Video Image Digitiser and Storage System [*Sirton Computer*] [*London, England*]

VIDAT .... Visual Data Acquisition

ViDC .... Danville Community College, Danville, VA [*Library symbol*] [*Library of Congress*] (LCLS)

VIDC .... Video Connection of America [*NASDAQ symbol*] (NQ)

VIDC .... Virgin Islands Department of Commerce (EA)

VIDD .... Vehicle Intrusion Detection Device

VIDEM .... Vietnam Demonstration [*FBI security file*]

Videnskabs-Selsk Christiana Forh ... Videnskabs-Selskabet i Christiania. Forhandlingar [*A publication*]

Vidensk Medd Dan Naturhist Foren ... Videnskabelige Meddelelser fra Dansk Naturhistorisk Forening [*A publication*]

Vidensk Medd Dan Naturhist Foren Khobenhavn ... Videnskabelige Meddelelser fra Dansk Naturhistorisk Forening i Khobenhavn [*A publication*]

Video .... Video-Tronics [*A publication*]

VIDEO .... Visual Data Entry On-Line [*Data processing*]

Video Syst ... Video Systems [*A publication*]

Vide Tech-Appl ... Vide. Technique-Applications [*France*] [*A publication*]

VIDF .... Vertical Side of Intermediate Distribution Frame [*Telecommunications*] (TEL)

VIDF .... Video Frequency (IEEE)

VIDI .... Visual Input Detection Instrumentation (MCD)

VIDPI .... Visually Impaired Data Processors International [*Washington, DC*] (EA)

ViDR .... Dan River Mills Co., Danville, VA [*Library symbol*] [*Library of Congress*] (LCLS)

ViDS .... Stratford College, Danville, VA [*Library symbol*] [*Library of Congress*] (LCLS)

VIDS .... Vertical Instruments Display System (MCD)

VIDSL .... Veroeffentlichungen des Instituts fuer Deutsche Sprache und Literatur der Deutschen Akademie der Wissenschaften zu Berlin [*A publication*]

VIDS/MAF ... Visual Information Display System/Maintenance Action Form (NVT)

VIDV .... Veroeffentlichungen des Instituts fuer Deutsche Volkskunde. Deutschen Akademie der Wissenschaften zu Berlin [*A publication*]

Vidya B .... Vidya. Section B. Sciences [*A publication*]

Vidya Bhar ... Vidya Bharati [*Bangalore*] [*A publication*]

VIE .... Vibration Isolation Equipment (RDA)

VIE .... Vienna [*Austria*] [*Airport symbol*] (OAG)

VIE .... Vienna [*Wien-Hohewarte*] [*Austria*] [*Seismograph station code, US Geological Survey*] (SEIS)

vie .... Vietnamese [*MARC language code*] [*Library of Congress*] (LCCP)

VIE .... Vigilance, Initiative, Excellence [*Aerospace Defense Command's acronym for the Zero Defects Program*]

VIE .... Villeneuve Resources [*Vancouver Stock Exchange symbol*]

VIE .... Volunteers in Education

Vie Agric et Rurale ... Vie Agricole et Rurale [*A publication*]

Vie Econ (Berne) ... Vie Economique (Berne) [*A publication*]

ViEIM .... Merck & Co., Inc., Stonewall Process Development Library, Elkton, VA [*Library symbol*] [*Library of Congress*] (LCLS)

Vie Med ...... Vie Medicale [*A publication*]

Vie Med Can Fr ... Vie Medicale au Canada Francais [*A publication*]

Vie Milie A ... Vie et Milieu. Serie A. Biologie Marine [*A publication*]

Vie Milie B ... Vie et Milieu. Serie B. Oceanographie [*A publication*]

Vie Milie C ... Vie et Milieu. Serie C. Biologie Terrestre [*A publication*]

Vie Milieu Ser A ... Vie et Milieu. Serie A. Biologie Marine [*France*] [*A publication*]

Vie Milieu Ser A Biol Mar ... Vie et Milieu. Serie A. Biologie Marine [*A publication*]

Vie Milieu Ser B Oceanogr ... Vie et Milieu. Serie B. Oceanographie [*A publication*]

Vie Milieu Ser C Biol Terr ... Vie et Milieu. Serie C. Biologie Terrestre [*A publication*]

ViEmoE ...... Emory and Henry College, Emory, VA [*Library symbol*] [*Library of Congress*] (LCLS)

ViEmP .... Greenville County Library, Emporia, VA [*Library symbol*] [*Library of Congress*] (LCLS)

Vie Mus ...... Vie Musicale [*A publication*]

Vie Mus Belge ... Vie Musicale Belge [*A publication*]

Vien .... Viennola [*Record label*] [*Austria*]

Vienna Circle Coll ... Vienna Circle Collection [*A publication*]

VIEO .... Vendor's Item Engineering Order

VIER Bul ..... Victorian Institute of Educational Research. Bulletin [*A publication*]

VIER Bull .... Victorian Institute of Educational Research. Bulletin [*A publication*]

VIERS .... Virgin Islands Ecological Research Station

Vierteljahresschr Gerichtl Med Oeff Sanitaetswes ... Vierteljahresschrift fuer Gerichtliche Medizin und Oeffentliches Sanitaetswesen [*A publication*]

Vierteljahresschr Prakt Pharm ... Vierteljahresschrift fuer Praktische Pharmazie [*A publication*]

Vierteljahrsschr Naturforsch Ges Zuer ... Vierteljahrsschrift der Naturforschenden Gesellschaft in Zuerich [*A publication*]

Vierteljahrsschr Naturforsch Ges (Zuerich) ... Vierteljahrsschrift Naturforschende Gesellschaft (Zuerich) [*A publication*]

Vierteljahrsschr f Wiss Philos ... Vierteljahrsschrift fuer Wissenschaftliche Philosophie und Soziologie [*A publication*]

Viert Naturf Ges Zuerich ... Vierteljahrschrift der Naturforschenden Gesellschaft in Zuerich [*A publication*]

Vier Zeitg ... Vierteljahrshefte fuer Zeitgeschichte [*A publication*]

Vie Sci Econ ... Vie et Sciences Economiques [*A publication*]

Vie et Sciences Econs ... Vie et Sciences Economiques [*A publication*]

Vie Soc ... Vie Sociale [*A publication*]

Viet Stud .... Vietnamese Studies [*Hanoi*] [*A publication*]

VIEW .... Visible, Informative, Emotionally Appealing, Workable [*Package evaluation in marketing*]

VIEW .... Vital Information for Education and Work   (OICC)

Vie Wallonne ... La Vie Wallonne. Revue Mensuelle Illustree [*A publication*]

View Bot ..... View from the Bottom [*A publication*]

Vieweg Tracts Pure Appl Phys ... Vieweg Tracts in Pure and Applied Physics [*A publication*]

Viewpoints Biol ... Viewpoints in Biology [*A publication*]

Viewpoint Ser Aust Conserv Fdn ... Viewpoint Series. Australian Conservation Foundation [*A publication*]

Viewpoints Teach & Learn ... Viewpoints in Teaching and Learning [*A publication*]

VIEWS .... Vibration Indicator Early Warning System   (MCD)

Views & R ... Views and Reviews [*A publication*]

ViF .... Fairfax County Public Library, Fairfax, VA [*Library symbol*] [*Library of Congress*]   (LCLS)

VIF .... Vale International Airlines, Inc. [*Nashville, TN*] [*FAA designator*]   (FAAC)

VIF .... Variance Inflation Factor [*Statistics*]

VIF .... Vertical Infrared Fuze   (CAAL)

VIF .... Video Information [*Winslow Associates*] [*Information service*] [*No longer available*]   (EISS)

VIF .... Virus-Induced Interferon [*Cell biology*]

VIF .... Visual Image Formula [*of psychotherapist Joseph Bird's self-help theory*]

ViFarL .... Longwood College, Farmville, VA [*Library symbol*] [*Library of Congress*]   (LCLS)

ViFbE .... United States Army Engineer School, Fort Belvoir, VA [*Library symbol*] [*Library of Congress*]   (LCLS)

ViFbEM ...... United States Army, Engineer Museum, Fort Belvoir, VA [*Library symbol*] [*Library of Congress*]   (LCLS)

ViF-BPH .... Fairfax County Public Library, Services for the Blind and Physically Handicapped, Alexandria, VA [*Library symbol*] [*Library of Congress*]   (LCLS)

VIFC .... VTOL [*Vertical Takeoff and Landing*] Integrated Flight Control

ViFeAM ...... United States Army, Air Mobility Research and Development Laboratory, Fort Eustis, VA [*Library symbol*] [*Library of Congress*]   (LCLS)

ViFeAT ...... United States Army Transportation School, Fort Eustis, VA [*Library symbol*] [*Library of Congress*]   (LCLS)

ViFerF .... Ferrum College, Ferrum, VA [*Library symbol*] [*Library of Congress*]   (LCLS)

VIFF .... Vectoring in Forward Flight   (MCD)

ViFGM .... George Mason College [*Later, George Mason University*], Fairfax, VA [*Library symbol*] [*Library of Congress*]   (LCLS)

VIFI .... Voyager Information Flow Instructions [*NASA*]   (KSC)

ViFIL .... United States Army Logistics Management Center, Fort Lee, VA [*Library symbol*] [*Library of Congress*]   (LCLS)

ViFIQ .... Quartermaster Technical Library, Fort Lee, VA [*Library symbol*] [*Library of Congress*]   (LCLS)

ViFmTD ..... United States Army, Training and Doctrine Command Library, Fort Monroe, VA [*Library symbol*] [*Library of Congress*]   (LCLS)

ViFmTS ..... United States Army Tralinet Systems Center, Fort Monroe, VA [*Library symbol*] [*Library of Congress*]   (LCLS)

ViFmUS ..... United States Army Field Forces Library, Fort Monroe, VA [*Library symbol*] [*Library of Congress*]   (LCLS)

ViFmyA ..... United States Army, Fort Meyer Post Library, Fort Meyer, VA [*Library symbol*] [*Library of Congress*]   (LCLS)

ViFraC .... Camp Manufacturing Co., Franklin, VA [*Library symbol*] [*Library of Congress*]   (LCLS)

ViFraPC ..... Paul D. Camp Community College, Franklin, VA [*Library symbol*] [*Library of Congress*]   (LCLS)

ViFre .... Central Rappahannock Regional Library, Fredericksburg, VA [*Library symbol*] [*Library of Congress*]   (LCLS)

ViFreJM ..... James Monroe Memorial Foundation, Fredericksburg, VA [*Library symbol*] [*Library of Congress*]   (LCLS)

ViFreM .... Mary Washington College of the University of Virginia, Fredericksburg, VA [*Library symbol*] [*Library of Congress*]   (LCLS)

ViFroA .... American Viscose Co., Front Royal, VA [*Library symbol*] [*Library of Congress*]   (LCLS)

VIFSC .... VTOL [*Vertical Takeoff and Landing*] Integrated Flight System Control

VIG .... Vaccinia Immune Globulin [*Medicine*]

VIG .... Video Image Generator

VIG .... Video Integrating Group

VIG .... Vigil   (ROG)

VIG .... Vigilant Identification   (MCD)

VIG .... Vignette   (ADA)

VIG .... Vigoroso [*With Vigor*] [*Music*]   (ROG)

VIGB .... Variable Inlet Guide Blades   (MCD)

Vig C .... Vigiliae Christianae [*A publication*]

Vig Chr .... Vigiliae Christianae [*A publication*]

ViGcS .... Scott County Library, Gate City, VA [*Library symbol*] [*Library of Congress*]   (LCLS)

VIGIL .... Vertical Indicating Gyro Internally Lighted   (MCD)

VIGORN ...... Vigorniensis [*Signature of the Bishops of Worcester*] [*Latin*]   (ROG)

ViGpD .... Deepsea Ventures, Inc., Gloucester Point, VA [*Library symbol*] [*Library of Congress*]   (LCLS)

ViGpM .... Virginia Institute of Marine Science, Gloucester Point, VA [*Library symbol*] [*Library of Congress*]   (LCLS)

VIGS .... Vertical Impact Guidance System [*Army*]   (MCD)

VIGS .... Video Disc Gunnery Simulator [*Army*]   (INF)

VIGS .... Visual Glide Slope

VIH .... Rolla/Vichy, MO [*Location identifier*] [*FAA*]   (FAAL)

VIH .... Velocity Impact Hardening

ViHa .... Charles H. Taylor Memorial Library, Hampton, VA [*Library symbol*] [*Library of Congress*]   (LCLS)

ViHaI .... Hampton Institute, Hampton, VA [*Library symbol*] [*Library of Congress*]   (LCLS)

ViHal .... Halifax County-South Boston Regional Library, Halifax, VA [*Library symbol*] [*Library of Congress*]   (LCLS)

ViHaNASA ... National Aeronautics and Space Administration, Langley Research Center, Hampton, VA [*Library symbol*] [*Library of Congress*]   (LCLS)

ViHar .... Rockingham Public Library, Harrisonburg, VA [*Library symbol*] [*Library of Congress*]   (LCLS)

ViHarEM .... Eastern Mennonite College, Harrisonburg, VA [*Library symbol*] [*Library of Congress*]   (LCLS)

ViHarT .... James Madison University, Harrisonburg, VA [*Library symbol*] [*Library of Congress*]   (LCLS)

ViHaT .... Thomas Nelson Community College, Hampton, VA [*Library symbol*] [*Library of Congress*]   (LCLS)

ViHaV .... United States Veterans Administration Center, Medical Library, Hampton, VA [*Library symbol*] [*Library of Congress*]   (LCLS)

ViHdsC .... Hampden-Sydney College, Hampden-Sydney, VA [*Library symbol*] [*Library of Congress*]   (LCLS)

ViHi .... Virginia Historical Society, Richmond, VA [*Library symbol*] [*Library of Congress*]   (LCLS)

ViHo .... Hollins College, Hollins College, VA [*Library symbol*] [*Library of Congress*]   (LCLS)

ViHop .... Appomattox Regional Library, Hopewell, VA [*Library symbol*] [*Library of Congress*]   (LCLS)

ViHopA .... Allied Corp., Hopewell, VA [*Library symbol*] [*Library of Congress*]   (LCLS)

ViHopAT .... American Tobacco Co., Department of Research and Development, Hopewell, VA [*Library symbol*] [*Library of Congress*]   (LCLS)

ViHopHC .... Hercules Powder Co. [*Later, Hercules, Inc.*], Cellulose Products Division, Hopewell, VA [*Library symbol*] [*Library of Congress*]   (LCLS)

ViHopHV .... Hercules Powder Co. [*Later, Hercules, Inc.*], Virginia Cellulose Division, Hopewell, VA [*Library symbol*] [*Library of Congress*]   (LCLS)

VII .... Vacuum-Impregnated Inductor

VII .... Vicon Industries, Incorporated [*American Stock Exchange symbol*]

VII .... Viscosity Index Improver

VIIS .... Virgin Islands National Park

Viitor Soc ... Viitorul Social [*A publication*]

VIJ .... Vera Institute of Justice [*New York, NY*]   (EA)

VIJ .... Virgin Gorda [*British Virgin Islands*] [*Airport symbol*]   (OAG)

VIJ .... Vishveshvaranand Indological Journal [*A publication*]

VIK .... Kavik River, AK [*Location identifier*] [*FAA*]   (FAAL)

VIK .... Vik [*Iceland*] [*Seismograph station code, US Geological Survey*] [*Closed*]   (SEIS)

VIK .... Viking International Air Freight, Inc. [*Minneapolis, MN*] [*FAA designator*]   (FAAC)

Vik .... Viking. Norsk Arkeologisk Selskap [*A publication*]

VIKA .... Viking Air Lines

ViKeS .... Southside Virginia Community College, John H. Daniel Campus, Keysville, VA [*Library symbol*] [*Library of Congress*]   (LCLS)

VIKG .... Viking Freight Systems [*NASDAQ symbol*]   (NQ)

Viking Fund Publ Anthropol ... Viking Fund Publication in Anthropology [*A publication*]

VIK Mitt ...... VIK [*Vereinigung Industrielle Kraftwirtschaft*] Mitteilungen [*A publication*]

Vikram Quart Res J Vikram University ... Vikram. Quarterly Research Journal of Vikram University [*A publication*]

VIL .... Dakhla [*Mauritania*] [*Airport symbol*]   (OAG)

ViL .... Jones Memorial Library, Lynchburg, VA [*Library symbol*] [*Library of Congress*]   (LCLS)

VIL .... University of Victoria Law Library [*UTLAS symbol*]

VIL	Vendor Item List (AAG)
VIL	Vertical Injection Logic [Data processing]
VIL	Very Important Ladies
VIL	Very Important Launch (MUGU)
VIL	Villa Mercy [Maryland] [Seismograph station code, US Geological Survey] [Closed] (SEIS)
VIL	Village
Vi-L	Virginia State Law Library, Richmond, VA [Library symbol] [Library of Congress] (LCLS)
VIL	Vivisection Investigation League [New York, NY] (EA)
ViLanAF	United States Air Force, Langley Air Force Base Library, Langley AFB, VA [Library symbol] [Library of Congress] (LCLS)
Vilas	Vilas' Criminal Reports [1-5 New York] (DLA)
ViLaw	Brunswick-Greensville Regional Library, Lawrenceville, VA [Library symbol] [Library of Congress] (LCLS)
ViLawS	Saint Paul's College, Lawrenceville, VA [Library symbol] [Library of Congress] (LCLS)
Vil & Br	Vilas and Bryant's Edition of the Wisconsin Reports (DLA)
ViLBW	Babcock & Wilcox Co., Lynchburg, VA [Library symbol] [Library of Congress] (LCLS)
ViLC	Lynchburg College, Lynchburg, VA [Library symbol] [Library of Congress] (LCLS)
ViLCV	Central Virginia Community College, Lynchburg, VA [Library symbol] [Library of Congress] (LCLS)
V I Lenin Sakharth Politekh Inst Samecn Srom	V. I. Leninis Sahelobis Sromis Citheli Drosis Ordenosani Sakharthvelos Politekhnikuri Instituti. Samecniero Sromebi [A publication]
VILIOR	Vladimir Ilyich Lenin, Initiator of the October Revolution [Given name popular in Russia after the Bolshevik Revolution]
VILL	Village
Vill	Villandry Festival [Record label] [France]
Villanova L Rev	Villanova Law Review [A publication]
Vill L Rev	Villanova Law Review [A publication]
ViLoGH	Gunston Hall Plantation Library, Lorton, VA [Library symbol] [Library of Congress] (LCLS)
VILP	Vector Impedance Locus Plotter
ViLRM	Randolph-Macon Woman's College, Lynchburg, VA [Library symbol] [Library of Congress] (LCLS)
ViLuV	Virginia Oak Tannery, Luray, VA [Library symbol] [Library of Congress] (LCLS)
Vil V	Village Voice [A publication]
ViLx	Botetourt-Rockbridge Regional Library, Lexington, VA [Library symbol] [Library of Congress] (LCLS)
ViLxV	Virginia Military Institute, Lexington, VA [Library symbol] [Library of Congress] (LCLS)
ViLxW	Washington and Lee University, Lexington, VA [Library symbol] [Library of Congress] (LCLS)
ViLxW-L	Washington and Lee University, Law Library, Lexington, VA [Library symbol] [Library of Congress] (LCLS)
VIM	CDC 6000 Series users organization [Abbreviation is derived from the Roman numerals for 6 and thousand]
VIM	Vacuum Induction Melting [Metallurgy]
VIM	Vendor Initial Measurement
VIM	Vertical Improved Mail [Mail-delivery system for large buildings in which all tenants pick up their mail from lockboxes in a central mailroom]
VIM	Vibration Isolation Module
VIM	Vinyl Insulation Material
VIM	Vocational Instructional Materials Section [American Vocational Association] (EA)
VIM	Voice Input Module [Cascade Graphics Development Ltd.] [Software package]
ViMan	Ruffner-Carnegie Public Library, Manassas, VA [Library symbol] [Library of Congress] [Obsolete] (LCLS)
ViManCo	Prince William County Public Library, Manassas, VA [Library symbol] [Library of Congress] (LCLS)
ViMarC	Marion Junior College, Marion, VA [Library symbol] [Library of Congress] (LCLS)
ViMat	Mathews Memorial Library, Mathews, VA [Library symbol] [Library of Congress] (LCLS)
VIMBA	Veroeffentlichungen des Instituts fuer Meeresforschung in Bremerhaven [A publication]
ViMcC	Central Intelligence Agency, McLean, VA [Library symbol] [Library of Congress] (LCLS)
ViMelE	Eastern Shore Community College, Learning Resources Center, Melfa, VA [Library symbol] [Library of Congress] (LCLS)
VIMEX	Visit Mexico [Airline fares]
VIMHEX	Venezuela International Meteorological and Hydrological Experiment [Colorado State University project]
ViMidL	Lord Fairfax Community College, Learning Resources Center, Middletown, VA [Library symbol] [Library of Congress] (LCLS)
ViMiN	Notre Dame Institute, Middleburg, VA [Library symbol] [Library of Congress] (LCLS)
ViMiNS	National Sporting Library, Inc., Middleburg, VA [Library symbol] [Library of Congress] (LCLS)
VIMP	Vertical Impulse
VIMS	Vehicle Integrated Management System

VIMS	Virginia Institute of Marine Science [College of William and Mary] [Research center]
VIMTPG	Virtual Interactive Machine Test Program Generator
ViMtvL	Mount Vernon Ladies' Association of the Union, Mount Vernon, VA [Library symbol] [Library of Congress] (LCLS)
VIMVAR	Vacuum Induction Melt, Vacuum Arc Remelt
ViMvD	E. I. DuPont de Nemours & Co., Martinsville, VA [Library symbol] [Library of Congress] (LCLS)
VIN	Miami, FL [Location identifier] [FAA] (FAAL)
ViN	Norfolk Public Library, Norfolk, VA [Library symbol] [Library of Congress] (LCLS)
VIN	Vehicle Identification Number
VIN	Vendor Identification Number (MCD)
Vin	Vinduet [A publication]
VIN	Vineyard [California] [Seismograph station code, US Geological Survey] [Closed] (SEIS)
VIN	Vintage Enterprises, Inc. [American Stock Exchange symbol]
VIN	Vinum [Wine] [Pharmacy] (ROG)
VIN	Voltage Input (TEL)
Vin Abr	Supplement to Viner's Abridgment of Law and Equity [England] (DLA)
Vin Abr (Eng)	Viner's Abridgment of Law and Equity [1741-53] [England] (DLA)
Vina Q	Vina Quarterly [A publication]
ViNarC	Celanese Corp., Narrows, VA [Library symbol] [Library of Congress] (LCLS)
Vinar Obz	Vinarsky Obzor [A publication]
ViNC	Chrysler Art Museum, Jean Outland Chrysler Library, Norfolk, VA [Library symbol] [Library of Congress] (LCLS)
Vin Comm	Viner's Abridgment [or Commentaries] (DLA)
VIND	Vicarious Interpolations Not Desired
VIND	Vindication (ROG)
VIndJ	Vishveshvaranand Indological Journal [A publication]
ViNE	Eastern Virginia Medical School, Norfolk, VA [Library symbol] [Library of Congress] (LCLS)
ViNe	Newport News Public Library, Newport News, VA [Library symbol] [Library of Congress] (LCLS)
ViNeC	Christopher Newport College, Newport News, VA [Library symbol] [Library of Congress] (LCLS)
ViNeM	Mariners' Museum, Newport News, VA [Library symbol] [Library of Congress] (LCLS)
ViNeN	Newport News Shipbuilding & Dry Dock Co., Newport News, VA [Library symbol] [Library of Congress] (LCLS)
Viner Abr	Viner's Abridgment of Law and Equity [1741-53] (DLA)
VINES	Virtual Networking Software [Banyan Systems]
ViNeV	Virginia Associated Research Center, Newport News, VA [Library symbol] [Library of Congress] (LCLS)
VINFA	Volunteers in the National Forests Act of 1972
Vingt Siecle Feder	Vingtieme Siecle Federaliste [A publication]
Vinifera Wine Grow J	Vinifera Wine Growers Journal [A publication]
Vini Ital	Vini d'Italia [A publication]
VINITI	Vsesoyuznyy Institut Nauchnoi i Tekhnicheskoy Informatsii [All-Union Institute of Scientific and Technical Information] [USSR]
ViNM	Norfolk County Medical Society, Inc., Norfolk, VA [Library symbol] [Library of Congress] (LCLS)
ViNMoN	Monsanto Chemical Co., Norfolk, VA [Library symbol] [Library of Congress] (LCLS)
Vinn ad Inst	Vinnius' Commentary on the Institutes of Justinian (DLA)
ViNO	Old Dominion University, Norfolk, VA [Library symbol] [Library of Congress] (LCLS)
Vinodel Vinograd SSSR	Vinodelie i Vinogradarstvo SSSR [A publication]
Vinograd Plodovod (Budapest)	Vinogradarstvo i Plodovodstvo (Budapest) [A publication]
Vinograd Vinar (Budapest)	Vinogradarstvo i Vinarstvo (Budapest) [A publication]
Vinograd Vinorobstvo	Vinogradarstvo i Vinorobstvo [A publication]
ViNott	Nottoway County Library, Nottoway, VA [Library symbol] [Library of Congress] (LCLS)
ViNR	F. S. Royster Guano Co., Norfolk, VA [Library symbol] [Library of Congress] (LCLS)
ViNS	Norfolk State College, Norfolk, VA [Library symbol] [Library of Congress] (LCLS)
VINS	Velocity Inertia Navigation System
ViNSC	United States Armed Forces Staff College, Norfolk, VA [Library symbol] [Library of Congress] (LCLS)
Vin Supp	Supplement to Viner's Abridgment of Law and Equity (DLA)
ViNT	Norfolk Testing Laboratories, Norfolk, VA [Library symbol] [Library of Congress] (LCLS)
VINT	Video Integrate (NVT)
VInt	Vie Intellectuelle [A publication] (BJA)
ViNWe	Virginia Wesleyan College, Norfolk, VA [Library symbol] [Library of Congress] (LCLS)
Vinyls Polym	Vinyls and Polymers [Japan] [A publication]
VIO	Heavy [Used to qualify interference or static reports] [Telecommunications] (FAAC)
VIO	Veroeffentlichungen des Instituts fuer Orientforschung. Deutsche Akademie der Wissenschaften zu Berlin [A publication]
VIO	Very Important Object

VIO .... Veterinary Investigation Officer [*Ministry of Agriculture, Fisheries, and Food*] [*British*]
VIO .... Video Input/Output
VIO .... Violet   (AAG)
VIO .... Violino [*Violin*] [*Music*]   (ROG)
VIO .... Virtual Input/Output [*Data processing*]   (IBMDP)
VIO .... Visual Intercept Officer [*Navy*]
VIOC .... Variable Input-Output Code
VIODAWB ... Deutsche Akademie der Wissenschaften zu Berlin. Institut fuer Orientforschung. Veroeffentlichungen [*A publication*]
VIOL .... Viola [*Music*]   (ROG)
VIOLE .... Violone [*Double Bass*] [*Music*]   (ROG)
VIOLENT .... Viewers Intent on Listing Violent Episodes on Nationwide Television [*Student legal action organization*]
VIOLO .... Violino [*Violin*] [*Music*]   (ROG)
ViOr .... Orange County Public Library, Orange, VA [*Library symbol*] [*Library of Congress*]   (LCLS)
VIP .... Value Improving Products
VIP .... Value in Performance
VIP .... Variable Incentive Pay [*Military*]   (NVT)
VIP .... Variable Individual Protection [*Insurance*]
VIP .... Variable Inductance Pickup
VIP .... Variable Information Processing [*Naval Ordnance Laboratory*] [*Information retrieval*]
VIP .... Variable Input Phototypesetter
VIP .... Vasoactive Inhibitory Principle [*Biochemistry*]
VIP .... Vasoactive Intestinal Peptide [*Biochemistry*]
VIP .... Vasoactive Intestinal Polypeptide [*Oncology*]
VIP .... Vector Instruction Processor
VIP .... Vermont Information Processes, Inc. [*Middlebury, VT*] [*Information service*]   (EISS)
VIP .... Versatile Information Processor [*Data processing*]
VIP .... Very Important Passenger
VIP .... Very Important Person
VIP .... Very Important Poor
VIP .... Very Important Pregnancy [*In book title, "VIP Program"*]
VIP .... Vice President   (AAG)
VIP .... Video Inertial Pointing [*System*] [*NASA*]
VIP .... Video Integrator and Processor
VIP .... Viewers in Profile [*A. C. Nielsen Co. reports for television industry*]
VIP .... Virgil Partch [*Cartoonist*]
VIP .... Vision Information Program   (EISS)
VIP .... Visit-Investigate-Purchase [*Department of Commerce program*]
VIP .... Visitor Information Publications   (EA)
VIP .... Visual Identification Point   (AFM)
VIP .... Visual Image Projection
VIP .... Visual Information Projection
VIP .... Visual Input [*System*] [*AT & T*]
VIP .... Visual Integrated Presentation [*Aviation*]   (FAAC)
VIP .... Voice Integrated Presentations [*Telecommunications*]   (RDA)
VIP .... Voix et Images du Pays [*University of Quebec*] [*A publication*]
VIP .... Volume Inverse Pricing [*Business and trade*]
VIP .... Vulcan Packaging, Inc. [*Toronto Stock Exchange symbol*]
VIP .... Vulcanized Interlinked Polyethylene [*Union Carbide Corp.*]
VIPA .... Volunteers in the Parks Act of 1969
ViPe .... Vita e Pensiero [*Milan*] [*A publication*]
VIPER .... Video Processing and Electronic Reduction   (IEEE)
ViPet .... Petersburg Public Library, Petersburg, VA [*Library symbol*] [*Library of Congress*]   (LCLS)
ViPetA .... Allied Chemical Corp., Fibers Division, Technical Center Library, Petersburg, VA [*Library symbol*] [*Library of Congress*]   (LCLS)
ViPetS .... Virginia State College, Petersburg, VA [*Library symbol*] [*Library of Congress*]   (LCLS)
VIPI .... Very Important Person Indeed
VIPI .... Volunteers in Probation, Incorporated [*Later, VIP Division of National Council on Crime and Delinquency*] [*An association*]   (EA)
VIPID .... Visual Information Processing Interface Device   (MCD)
VIPLF .... Vulcan Industrial Packaging Limited [*NASDAQ symbol*]   (NQ)
ViPo .... Portsmouth Public Library, Portsmouth, VA [*Library symbol*] [*Library of Congress*]   (LCLS)
ViPoN .... Norfolk Naval Hospital, Portsmouth, VA [*Library symbol*] [*Library of Congress*]   (LCLS)
ViPoVC ...... Virginia Chemicals, Inc., Portsmouth, VA [*Library symbol*] [*Library of Congress*]   (LCLS)
ViPoVS ...... Virginia Smelting Co., Portsmouth, VA [*Library symbol*] [*Library of Congress*]   (LCLS)
VIPP .... Variable Information Processing Package
VIPP .... Venda Independent People's Party   (PPW)
ViPrA .... American Cyanamid Co., Pigments Division, Piney River, VA [*Library symbol*] [*Library of Congress*]   (LCLS)
VIPRA .... Vest Individual Protective Reflective Adjustable [*System*] [*Military*]   (INF)
VIPS .... Variable Item Processing System
VIPS .... Versatile Isotope Power System   (MCD)
VIPS .... Veterans in Public Service Act
VIPS .... Video Image Processing System

VIPS .... Voice Information Processing Station [*UNISYS Corp.*] [*Telecommunications service*]   (TSSD)
VIPS .... Voice Interruption Priority System
ViPur .... Purcellville Library, Purcellville, VA [*Library symbol*] [*Library of Congress*]   (LCLS)
VIQ .... Neillsville, WI [*Location identifier*] [*FAA*]   (FAAL)
ViQM .... United States Marine Corps Schools, Quantico, VA [*Library symbol*] [*Library of Congress*]   (LCLS)
ViQM-E ...... United States Marine Corps Schools, Educational Center, Quantico, VA [*Library symbol*] [*Library of Congress*]   (LCLS)
VIR .... A. H. Robins Co., Richmond, VA [*OCLC symbol*]   (OCLC)
VIR .... Point Barrow, AK [*Location identifier*] [*FAA*]   (FAAL)
ViR .... Richmond Public Library, Richmond, VA [*Library symbol*] [*Library of Congress*]   (LCLS)
VIR .... Si Vires Permittant [*If the Strength Will Bear It*] [*Pharmacy*]   (ROG)
VIR .... Variable Interest Rate
VIR .... Vendor Information Request
VIR .... Vendor Item Release
VIR .... Vertical Interval Reference [*Automatic color adjustment*] [*Television*]
ViR .... Viata Romaneasca [*Bucharest*] [*A publication*]
VIR .... Virco Manufacturing Corp. [*American Stock Exchange symbol*]
VIR .... Virgin Islands of the US [*Three-letter standard code*]   (CNC)
Vir .... Virginia Cases [*Brockenbrough and Holmes*]   (DLA)
Vir .... Virgin's Reports [*52-60 Maine*]   (DLA)
Vir .... Virgo [*Constellation*]
VIR .... Viridis [*Green*] [*Pharmacy*]
Vir .... Virittaja. Kotikielen Seuran Aikakauslehti [*Helsinki*] [*A publication*]
Vir .... Virittaja. Revue de Kotikielen Seura [*A publication*]
VIR .... Virology
VIR .... Virtuoso [*A publication*]
VIR .... Virulent
VIR .... Visible [*or Visual*] and Infrared Radiometer [*NASA*]
VIR .... Vulcanized India Rubber
ViRa .... Radford College, Radford, VA [*Library symbol*] [*Library of Congress*]   (LCLS)
ViRA .... Richmond Academy of Medicine, Richmond, VA [*Library symbol*] [*Library of Congress*]   (LCLS)
VIRA .... Vehicular Infrared Alarm   (MCD)
VIRA .... Video Review Award
VIRA .... Viratek, Inc. [*NASDAQ symbol*]   (NQ)
VIRA .... Voprosy Istorii Religii i Ateizma. Sbornik Statei [*Moscow*] [*A publication*]
Vira-A .... Vidarabine [*Also, ara-A*] [*Biochemistry*]
VIRAD .... Virtual RADAR Defense [*Army*]   (MCD)
ViRaP .... Radford Public Library, Radford, VA [*Library symbol*] [*Library of Congress*]   (LCLS)
ViRAV .... Atlantic Varnish & Paint Co., Richmond, VA [*Library symbol*] [*Library of Congress*]   (LCLS)
ViRC .... Museum of the Confederacy, Richmond, VA [*Library symbol*] [*Library of Congress*]   (LCLS)
Virc Arch A ... Virchows Archiv. A. Pathological Anatomy and Histology [*A publication*]
Virc Arch B ... Virchows Archiv. B. Cell Pathology [*A publication*]
ViRCC .... [*The*] Computer Co., Richmond, VA [*Library symbol*] [*Library of Congress*]   (LCLS)
Virchows Arch Abt A ... Virchows Archiv. Abteilung A. Pathologische Anatomie [*A publication*]
Virchows Arch Abt A Pathol Anat ... Virchows Archiv. Abteilung A. Pathologische Anatomie [*A publication*]
Virchows Arch Abt B ... Virchows Archiv. Abteilung B. Zellpathologie [*A publication*]
Virchows Arch Abt B Zellpathol ... Virchows Archiv. Abteilung B. Zellpathologie [*A publication*]
Virchows Arch A Pathol Anat Histol ... Virchows Archiv. A. Pathological Anatomy and Histology [*A publication*]
Virchows Arch B Cell Pathol ... Virchows Archiv. B. Cell Pathology [*A publication*]
Virchows Arch Path Anat ... Virchows Archiv fuer Pathologische Anatomie [*A publication*]
Virchows Arch Pathol Anat Physiol Klin Med ... Virchows Archiv fuer Pathologische Anatomie und Physiologie und fuer Klinische Medizin [*A publication*]
ViRCU .... Virginia Commonwealth University, Richmond, VA [*Library symbol*] [*Library of Congress*]   (LCLS)
ViRCU-A .... Virginia Commonwealth University, Academic Division, Richmond, VA [*Library symbol*] [*Library of Congress*]   (LCLS)
ViRCU-H .... Virginia Commonwealth University, Health Sciences Division, Richmond, VA [*Library symbol*] [*Library of Congress*]   (LCLS)
ViREP .... Virginia Electric & Power Co., Richmond, VA [*Library symbol*] [*Library of Congress*]   (LCLS)
ViREx .... Experiment, Inc., Richmond, VA [*Library symbol*] [*Library of Congress*]   (LCLS)
ViRFR .... Federal Reserve Bank of Richmond, Richmond, VA [*Library symbol*] [*Library of Congress*]   (LCLS)

ViRG......... Richmond Guano Co., Richmond, VA [*Library symbol*] [*Library of Congress*] (LCLS)

VIRG.......... Virgin

Virg .... Virgin's Reports [*52-60 Maine*] (DLA)

Virg .... Virgo [*Constellation*]

Virg Cas .... Virginia Cases [*by Brockenbrough and Holmes*] (DLA)

Virgin .... Virgin's Reports [*52-60 Maine*] (DLA)

Virginia Div Mineral Rsources Rept Inv ... Virginia. Division of Mineral Resources. Report of Investigations [*A publication*]

Virginia Jour Sci ... Virginia Journal of Science [*A publication*]

Virginia J Sci ... Virginia Journal of Science [*A publication*]

Virginia Med Month ... Virginia Medical Monthly [*Later, Virginia Medical*] [*A publication*]

Virginia Polytech Inst Research Div Bull ... Virginia Polytechnic Institute. Research Division. Bulletin [*A publication*]

Virginia Polytech Inst Research Div Mon ... Virginia Polytechnic Institute. Research Division. Monograph [*A publication*]

Virginia Q R ... Virginia Quarterly Review [*A publication*]

Virg J Int'l L ... Virginia Journal of International Law [*A publication*]

Virg LJ........ Virginia Law Journal [*Richmond*] (DLA)

ViRGS .... Church of Jesus Christ of Latter-Day Saints, Genealogical Society Library, Richmond Stake Branch, Richmond, VA [*Library symbol*] [*Library of Congress*] (LCLS)

ViRHC .... Henrico County Public Library, Richmond, VA [*Library symbol*] [*Library of Congress*] (LCLS)

Vir LJ.......... Virginia Law Journal (DLA)

VIRM .... Variable-Interest-Rate Mortgage

ViRMu .... Virginia Museum of Fine Arts, Richmond, VA [*Library symbol*] [*Library of Congress*] (LCLS)

VIRNS........ Velocity Inertia RADAR Navigation System

ViRo .... Roanoke Public Library, Roanoke, VA [*Library symbol*] [*Library of Congress*] (LCLS)

ViRoA .... American Viscose Co., Roanoke, VA [*Library symbol*] [*Library of Congress*] (LCLS)

Virol .... Virology [*A publication*]

Virol Abstr ... Virology Abstracts [*A publication*]

Virol Monogr ... Virology Monographs [*A publication*]

ViRoNW...... Norfolk & Western Railway Co., Roanoke, VA [*Library symbol*] [*Library of Congress*] (LCLS)

ViRoV .... Virginia Western Community College, Brown Library, Roanoke, VA [*Library symbol*] [*Library of Congress*] (LCLS)

ViRPM .... Philip Morris Research Center, Richmond, VA [*Library symbol*] [*Library of Congress*] (LCLS)

ViRPol .... W. P. Poythress Co., Richmond, VA [*Library symbol*] [*Library of Congress*] (LCLS)

Vir Q R........ Virginia Quarterly Review [*A publication*]

ViRR .... Reynolds Metals Co., Richmond, VA [*Library symbol*] [*Library of Congress*] (LCLS)

VIRR .... Visible [*or Visual*] and Infrared Radiometer [*NASA*]

ViRRC .... J. Sargeant Reynolds Community College, Downtown Campus, Richmond, VA [*Library symbol*] [*Library of Congress*] (LCLS)

ViRR-E .... Reynolds Metals Co., Executive Office Library, Richmond, VA [*Library symbol*] [*Library of Congress*] (LCLS)

VIR & Regs ... Virgin Islands Rules and Regulations (DLA)

ViRRob....... A. H. Robins Co., Richmond, VA [*Library symbol*] [*Library of Congress*] (LCLS)

ViRR-P .... Reynolds Metals Co., Packaging Research Division, Richmond, VA [*Library symbol*] [*Library of Congress*] (LCLS)

ViRR-T........ Reynolds Metals Co., Technical Information Services Library, Richmond, VA [*Library symbol*] [*Library of Congress*] (LCLS)

VIRS .... Veroeffentlichungen des Instituts fuer Romanische Sprachwissenschaft. Deutsche Akademie der Wissenschaften zu Berlin [*A publication*]

Virt .... De Virtutibus [*of Philo*] (BJA)

ViRU .... University of Richmond, Richmond, VA [*Library symbol*] [*Library of Congress*] (LCLS)

ViRUCA...... United States Circuit Court of Appeals, Fourth Circuit, Richmond, VA [*Library symbol*] [*Library of Congress*] (LCLS)

ViRUT........ Union Theological Seminary, Richmond, VA [*Library symbol*] [*Library of Congress*] (LCLS)

ViRUV........ United Virginia Bankshares, Inc., Richmond, VA [*Library symbol*] [*Library of Congress*] (LCLS)

ViRV .... United States Veterans Administration Hospital, Richmond, VA [*Library symbol*] [*Library of Congress*] (LCLS)

ViRVal .... Valentine Museum, Richmond, VA [*Library symbol*] [*Library of Congress*] (LCLS)

ViRVB......... Virginia Baptist Historical Society, University of Richmond, Richmond, VA [*Library symbol*] [*Library of Congress*] (LCLS)

ViRVI .... Virginia Institute for Scientific Research, Richmond, VA [*Library symbol*] [*Library of Congress*] (LCLS)

ViRVM .... Valentine Meat Juice Co., Richmond, VA [*Library symbol*] [*Library of Congress*] (LCLS)

ViRVU .... Virginia Union University, Richmond, VA [*Library symbol*] [*Library of Congress*] (LCLS)

VIS .... Minority Vendor Information Service [*National Minority Supplier Development Council, Inc.*] (EISS)

VIS .... Vector Instruction Set [*Data processing*]

VIS .... Vegetarian Information Service (EA)

VIS .... Verification Information System (NASA)

VIS .... Veroeffentlichungen des Instituts fuer Slawistik. Deutschen Akademie zu Berlin [*A publication*]

VIS .... Veterinary Investigation Service [*Ministry of Agriculture, Fisheries, and Food*] [*British*]

VIS .... Vibration Isolation System

VIS .... Videotex Information System [*Radio Shack*] [*Fort Worth, TX*] [*Information service*] (EISS)

VIS .... Vietnamese Information Service

VIS .... Virtual Information Storage (BUR)

VIS .... Visalia [*California*] [*Airport symbol*] (OAG)

VIS .... Viscosity

VIS .... Viscount [*or Viscountess*]

VIS .... Viscount Resources [*Vancouver Stock Exchange symbol*]

VIS .... Vishakhapatnam [*Andhra, Waltair*] [*India*] [*Seismograph station code, US Geological Survey*] (SEIS)

VIS .... Visible [*or Visibility*] (AFM)

VIS .... Visitor (ROG)

VIS .... Vista

VIS .... Visual

VIS .... Visual Imagery System [*NASA*]

VIS .... Visual Information Storage

VIS .... Visual Information System

VIS .... Visual Instrumentation Subsystem

VIS .... Visual Spectrophotometry

VIS .... VNR [*Van Nostrand Reinhold*] Information Services [*Van Nostrand Reinhold Co., Inc.*] [*New York, NY*] (EISS)

VIS .... Voice Intercom Subsystem (MCD)

VIs .... Voprosy Istorii [*Moscow*] [*A publication*]

ViSa........... Salem Public Library, Salem, VA [*Library symbol*] [*Library of Congress*] (LCLS)

VISA.......... Ventricular Inhibiting Synchronous with Atrium [*Cardiac pacemaker*] [*Trademark*]

Vis Aids News ... Visual Aids News [*A publication*]

Vis Aids Rev ... Visual Aids Review [*A publication*]

VISAR........ Velocity Interferometer System for Any Reflector (MCD)

ViSaRC .... Roanoke College, Salem, VA [*Library symbol*] [*Library of Congress*] (LCLS)

ViSaV .... United States Veterans Administration Hospital, Salem, VA [*Library symbol*] [*Library of Congress*] (LCLS)

Visbl Lang ... Visible Language [*A publication*]

VISC.......... Video Disc

visc........... Visceral

VISC.......... Viscosity (AAG)

VISC.......... Viscount [*or Viscountess*]

VISC.......... Visual Electronics [*NASDAQ symbol*] (NQ)

VISC.......... Vitreous Infusion Suction Cutter [*Ophthalmology*]

VISCA Rev Visayas State Coll Agric ... VISCA Review. Visayas State College of Agriculture [*A publication*]

VISCO .... Visual Systems Corporation

VISCOM..... Visual Communications

VISCT........ Viscount [*or Viscountess*]

Vis Educ..... Visual Education [*A publication*]

Vish Indo J ... Vishveshvaranand Indological Journal [*Hoshiarpur*] [*A publication*]

VISI .... Volar Intercalated Segment Instability [*Orthopedics*]

Visible Lang ... Visible Language [*A publication*]

VISID.......... Visual Identification (MSA)

Vis Ind....... Vision Index [*A publication*]

Visindafelag Isl Rit ... Visindafelag Islendinga Rit [*A publication*]

VISION .... Volunteers in Service to India's Oppressed and Neglected (EA)

Vision Res ... Vision Research [*A publication*]

VISIT .... Vehicle Internal Systems Investigative Team [*UFO study group*]

VISI .... Veroeffentlichungen des Instituts fuer Slawistik. Deutsche Akademie der Wissenschaften zu Berlin [*A publication*]

VIS LAB....... Visibility Laboratory [*University of California, San Diego*] [*Research center*] (RCD)

VISMOD ..... Visual Modifications [*Program*] [*Army*] (RDA)

VISMR........ Viscometer [*Engineering*]

Visn Akad Nauk Ukr RSR ... Visnyk Akademiyi Nauk Ukrayins'koyi RSR [*A publication*]

Visnik Kiiv Univ Ser Mat Meh ... Visnik Kiivs'kogo Universitetu. Serija Matematiki ta Mehaniki [*A publication*]

Visnik Kiiv Univ Ser Mat Mekh ... Visnik Kiivs'kogo Universitetu. Seriya Matematiki ta Mekhaniki [*A publication*]

Visnik L'viv Derz Univ Ser Meh-Mat ... Visnik L'vivs'kogo Ordena Lenina Derzavogo Universitetu Imeni Ivana Franka. Serija Mehaniko-Matematicna [*A publication*]

Visnik L'viv Politehn Inst ... Visnik L'vivs'kogo Politehnicnogo Institutu [*A publication*]

Visn Kharkiv Univ Astron ... Visnik Kharkivs'kogo Universitetu. Astronomiya [*Ukrainian SSR*] [*A publication*]

Visn Kharkiv Univ Radiofiz ... Visnik Kharkivs'kogo Universitetu. Radiofizika [*Ukrainian SSR*] [*A publication*]

Visn Kharkiv Univ Radiofiz Elektron ... Visnik Kharkivs'kogo Universitetu. Radiofizika i Elektronika [*Ukrainian SSR*] [*A publication*]

Visn Kiiv Politekh Inst Ser Khim Mashinobuduv Tekhnol ... Visnik Kiivs'kogo Politekhnichnogo Institutu. Seriya Khimichnogo Mashinobuduvannya ta Tekhnologii [*Ukrainian SSR*] [*A publication*]

Visn Kiiv Univ Ser Astron ... Visnik Kiivs'kogo Universitetu. Seriya Astronomii [*Ukrainian SSR*] [*A publication*]

Visn Kiiv Univ Ser Biol ... Visnik Kiivs'kogo Universitetu. Seriya Biologii [*Ukrainian SSR*] [*A publication*]

Visn Kiiv Univ Ser Fiz ... Visnik Kiivs'kogo Universitetu. Seriya Fiziki [*A publication*]

Visn Kiiv Univ Ser Fiz Khim ... Visnik Kiivs'kogo Universitetu. Seriya Fiziki ta Khimii [*Ukrainian SSR*] [*A publication*]

Visn Kiiv Univ Ser Khim ... Visnik Kiivs'kogo Universitetu. Seriya Khimii [*Ukrainian SSR*] [*A publication*]

Visn Kiyiv Univ Ser Fiz ... Visnik Kiyivs'kogo Universitetu. Seriya Fizika [*Ukrainian SSR*] [*A publication*]

Visn Kyyiv Univ Ser Biol ... Visnyk Kyyivs'koho Universytetu. Seriya Biolohiyi [*A publication*]

Visn L'viv Derzh Univ Ser Biol ... Visnik L'vivs'kogo Derzhavnogo Universitetu. Seriya Biologichna [*A publication*]

Visn L'viv Derzh Univ Ser Fiz ... Visnik L'vivs'kii Derzhavnii Universitet Imeni Ivana Franka. Seriya Fizichna [*Ukrainian SSR*] [*A publication*]

Visn L'viv Derzh Univ Ser Fiz ... Visnik L'vivs'kogo Derzhavnogo Universitetu. Seriya Fizichna [*A publication*]

Visn L'viv Derzh Univ Ser Geol ... Visnik L'vivs'kogo Derzhavnogo Universitetu. Seriya Geologichna [*A publication*]

Visn L'viv Derzh Univ Ser Khim ... Visnik L'vivs'kogo Derzhavnogo Universitetu Imeni Ivana Franka. Seriya Khimichna [*Ukrainian SSR*] [*A publication*]

Visn L'viv Derzh Univ Ser Khim ... Visnik L'vivs'kogo Derzhavnogo Universitetu. Seriya Khimichna [*A publication*]

Visn L'viv Univ Ser Biol Heohr ... Visnyk L'vivs'koho Universytetu. Seriya Biolohiyi, Heohrafiyi, ta Heolohiyi [*A publication*]

Visn L'viv Univ Ser Biol Heohr Heol ... Visnyk L'vivs'koho Universytetu. Seriya Biolohiyi, Heohrafiyi, ta Heolohiyi [*A publication*]

Visn Sil-hospod Nauky ... Visnyk Sil's'ko-hospodars'koyi Nauky [*A publication*]

Visn Sil's'kohospod Nauki ... Visnyk Sil'skohospodars'koi Nauki [*A publication*]

Visn Sil's'kohospod Nauky ... Visnyk Sil's'kohospodarskoyi Nauky [*A publication*]

Visn Tsentr Resp Bot Sad Akad Nauk Ukr RSR ... Visnik Tsentral'nii Respublikans'kii Botanichnii Sad Akademiya Nauk Ukrains'koi RSR [*A publication*]

VISPAC ...... Videotex Information Service Providers Association of Canada [*Defunct*] (EISS)

ViSpN .... National Technical Information Service, Springfield, VA [*Library symbol*] [*Library of Congress*] (LCLS)

VISR .... Virginia Institute for Scientific Research [*University of Richmond*] [*Research center*] (MCD)

VISRF .... Viscount Resources [*NASDAQ symbol*] (NQ)

VISSI .... Visindafelag Islendinga. Societas Scientiarum Islandica [*A publication*]

VISSR .... Visible [*or Visual*] and Infrared Spin Scan Radiometer [*NASA*]

ViSt .... Staunton Public Library, Staunton, VA [*Library symbol*] [*Library of Congress*] (LCLS)

VIST .... Vista Resources, Inc. [*NASDAQ symbol*] (NQ)

VISTA .... Variable Interlace System for Television Applications

VISTA .... Verbal Information Storage and Text Analysis [*in FORTRAN computer language*]

VISTA .... Very Intelligent Surveillance and Target Acquisition [*Army*] (RDA)

VISTA .... Videodisc Interpersonal Skills Training and Assessment (INF)

VISTA .... Viewing Instantly Security Transactions Automatically [*Wall Street*]

VISTA .... Visual Information for Satellite Telemetry Analysis

VISTA .... Visually Impaired Secretarial/Transcribers Association [*Indianapolis, IN*] (EA)

VISTA .... Volunteers in Service to America [*Washington, DC*] (EA)

Vistas Astron ... Vistas in Astronomy [*A publication*]

Vistas Astronaut ... Vistas in Astronautics [*A publication*]

Vistas Volunt ... Vistas for Volunteers [*A publication*]

ViSte .... Sterling Public Library, Sterling, VA [*Library symbol*] [*Library of Congress*] (LCLS)

Visti Akad Nauk Ukr RSR ... Visti Akademii Nauk Ukrains'koi RSR [*A publication*]

ViStM .... Mary Baldwin College, Staunton, VA [*Library symbol*] [*Library of Congress*] (LCLS)

VISTRAC .... Visual Target Reconnaissance and Acquisition (MCD)

ViStrR .... Robert E. Lee Memorial Association, Stratford Hall, Stratford, VA [*Library symbol*] [*Library of Congress*] (LCLS)

Visual Aids R ... Visual Aids Review [*A publication*]

Visual Ed .... Visual Education [*A publication*]

Visual Med ... Visual Medicine [*A publication*]

Visual Sonic Med ... Visual Sonic Medicine [*A publication*]

ViSwC .... Sweet Briar College, Sweet Briar, VA [*Library symbol*] [*Library of Congress*] (LCLS)

VIT .... Roanoke, VA [*Location identifier*] [*FAA*] (FAAL)

VIT .... Variable Impedance Tube

VIT .... Very Important Traveler

VIT .... Vibration Isolation Table

VIT .... Victoria Resources [*Vancouver Stock Exchange symbol*]

VIT .... Vineyard [*Telemeter*] [*California*] [*Seismograph station code, US Geological Survey*] [*Closed*] (SEIS)

Vit .... Vita [*of Josephus*] [*Classical studies*] (OCD)

Vit .... Vitae Parallelae [*of Plutarch*] [*Classical studies*] (OCD)

VIT .... Vital

VIT .... Vitamin

Vit .... Vitellius [*of Suetonius*] [*Classical studies*] (OCD)

VIT .... Vitoria [*Spain*] [*Airport symbol*] (OAG)

VIT .... Vitreous (AAG)

Vita .... Vita. Revue Bimensuelle. Confederation de l'Alimentation Belge [*A publication*]

VITA .... VMEbus International Trade Association [*Formed by a merger of VMEbus Manufacturers Group and VMEbus Users Group*] [*Scottsdale, AZ*] (EA)

VITA .... Volunteer Income Tax Assistance [*Internal Revenue Service*]

VITA .... Volunteers in Technical Assistance [*Arlington, VA*] [*Telecommunications*] (EA)

Vita Hum .... Vita Humana [*A publication*]

Vita Int .... Vita International [*A publication*]

Vita Ital .... Vita Italiana [*A publication*]

VITAL .... Variably Initialized Translator for Algorithmic Languages [*Data processing*]

VITAL .... VAST [*Versatile Avionics Shop Test*] Interface Test Application Language

VITAL .... Virtual Image Takeoff and Landing [*Simulator*] (MCD)

Vital C .... Vital Christianity [*A publication*]

Vital Health Stat 1 ... Vital and Health Statistics. Series 1. Programs and Collection Procedures [*Unied States*] [*A publication*]

Vital Health Stat 2 ... Vital and Health Statistics. Series 2. Data Evaluation and Methods Research [*United States*] [*A publication*]

Vital Health Stat 3 ... Vital and Health Statistics. Series 3. Analytical Studies [*United States*] [*A publication*]

Vital Health Stat 4 ... Vital and Health Statistics. Series 4. Documents and Committee Reports [*United States*] [*A publication*]

Vital Health Stat 10 ... Vital and Health Statistics. Series 10. Data from the National Health Survey [*United States*] [*A publication*]

Vital Health Stat 11 ... Vital and Health Statistics. Series 11. Data from the National Health Survey [*United States*] [*A publication*]

Vital Health Stat 13 ... Vital and Health Statistics. Series 13. Data from the National Health Survey [*United States*] [*A publication*]

Vital Health Stat 14 ... Vital and Health Statistics. Series 14. Data on National Health Resources [*United States*] [*A publication*]

Vital Health Stat 20 ... Vital and Health Statistics. Series 20. Data from the National Vital Statistics System [*United States*] [*A publication*]

Vital Health Stat 21 ... Vital and Health Statistics. Series 21. Data from the National Vital Statistics System [*United States*] [*A publication*]

Vital Health Stat 23 ... Vital and Health Statistics. Series 23. Data from the National Survey of Family Growth [*United States*] [*A publication*]

Vital Health Statist Ser 2 Data Evaluation Methods Res ... Vital and Health Statistics. Series 2. Data Evaluation and Methods Research [*A publication*]

Vital Speeches ... Vital Speeches of the Day [*A publication*]

Vital Speeches Day ... Vital Speeches of the Day [*A publication*]

Vitalstoffe ... Vitalstoffe Zivilisationskrankheiten [*A publication*]

Vitalst Zivilisationskr ... Vitalstoffe Zivilisationskrankheiten [*A publication*]

Vita Luc ...... Vita Lucani [*of Suetonius*] [*Classical studies*] (OCD)

Vitam D Dig ... Vitamin D Digest [*A publication*]

Vitam Eksp Klin ... Vitaminy v Eksperimente i Klinike [*A publication*]

Vitam Horm ... Vitamins and Hormones [*A publication*]

Vita Mon ..... Vita Monastica [*A publication*]

Vitam Resur Ikh Ispol'z ... Vitaminnye Resursy i Ikh Ispol'zovanie [*A publication*]

Vitams Horm ... Vitamins and Hormones [*A publication*]

VITAP .... Viking Targeting Analysis Program [*NASA*]

VITAS .... Visual Target Acquisition System [*Navy*] (MCD)

Vit Auct ...... Vitarum Auctio [*of Lucian*] [*Classical studies*] (OCD)

VITEK .... Life Technology (MCD)

Vitel .... Vitellus [*Yolk*] [*Pharmacy*]

Vitic Arboric ... Viticulture, Arboriculture [*A publication*]

Vitic Enol (Budapest) ... Viticulture and Enology (Budapest) [*A publication*]

VITIS-VEA ... VITIS-Viticulture and Enology Abstracts [*International Food Information Service*] [*Frankfurt, West Germany*] [*Information service*] (EISS)

Viti-Vinic (Budapest) ... Viti-Viniculture (Budapest) [*A publication*]

VITL .... Vitality Unlimited [*NASDAQ symbol*] (NQ)

Vit Ov Sol ... Vitello Ovi Solutus [*Dissolved in Yolk of Egg*] [*Pharmacy*]

VITR .... Vitramon, Inc. [*NASDAQ symbol*] (NQ)

VITR .... Vitreum [*Glass*] [*Latin*] (ADA)

Vitr .... Vitruvius [*First century BC*] [*Classical studies*] (OCD)

VITRAN ...... Vibration Transient Analysis (MCD)

VITS .... Vertical Interval Test Signal (IEEE)

VITT .... Vehicle Integration Test Team (MCD)

ViU .... University of Virginia, Charlottesville, VA [*Library symbol*] [*Library of Congress*] (LCLS)

VIU .... Vehicle in Use

VIU .... Video Interface Unit (MCD)

ViU .... Voice Intercommunications Unit
ViU .... Voice Interface Unit [Telecommunications]   (TEL)
ViU-ES .... University of Virginia, School of General Studies, Eastern Shore Branch, Wallops Island, VA [Library symbol] [Library of Congress]   (LCLS)
ViU-H......... University of Virginia Medical Center, Health Sciences Library, Charlottesville, VA [Library symbol] [Library of Congress]   (LCLS)
ViU-L......... University of Virginia, Law Library, Charlottesville, VA [Library symbol] [Library of Congress]   (LCLS)
ViU-Mu...... University of Virginia, Music Library, Charlottesville, VA [Library symbol] [Library of Congress]   (LCLS)
ViURAM ..... Video Interface Unit Random Access Memory
ViU-ST .... University of Virginia, Science/Technology Information Center, Charlottesville, VA [Library symbol] [Library of Congress]   (LCLS)
VIV............. Variable Inlet Vanes   (NRCH)
VIV............. Vivace [Lively] [Music]
Viv............. Vivarium [A publication]
VIV............. Vivian, LA [Location identifier] [FAA]   (FAAL)
VIV............. Vivid-Inventive-Vital [Spring fashions]
VIV............. Vivigani [Papua New Guinea] [Airport symbol]   (OAG)
VIV............. Vlaamse Ingenieurs-Vereiniging
VIVA........... Victory in Vietnam Association
VIVA........... Virgin Islands Visitors Association
VIVA........... Visually Impaired Veterans of America [Washington, DC]   (EA)
VIVA........... Voices in Vital America
ViVb........... Department of Public Libraries and Information, City of Virginia Beach, Reference Department, Virginia Beach, VA [Library symbol] [Library of Congress]   (LCLS)
ViVbGS ...... Church of Jesus Christ of Latter-Day Saints, Genealogical Society Library, Norfolk Virginia Stake Branch, Virginia Beach, VA [Library symbol] [Library of Congress]   (LCLS)
ViVbRE....... Association for Research and Enlightenment, Virginia Beach, VA [Library symbol] [Library of Congress]   (LCLS)
VIVED........ Virtual Visual Environment Display [Helmet equipped with liquid crystal display screens viewed through wide-angle lenses] [NASA]
VIVI .... Vivienda [Mexico] [A publication]
VIVI .... Vivigen, Inc. [NASDAQ symbol]   (NQ)
ViW........... College of William and Mary, Williamsburg, VA [Library symbol] [Library of Congress]   (LCLS)
ViWaR .... Rappahannock Community College, North Campus, Warsaw, VA [Library symbol] [Library of Congress]   (LCLS)
ViWarUS .... United States Army, Post Library, Vint Hill Farms Station, Warrenton, VA [Library symbol] [Library of Congress]   (LCLS)
ViWb .... Waynesboro Public Library, Waynesboro, VA [Library symbol] [Library of Congress]   (LCLS)
ViWbD........ E. I. DuPont de Nemours & Co., Benger Laboratory, Waynesboro, VA [Library symbol] [Library of Congress]   (LCLS)
ViWbF .... Fairfax Hall Junior College, Waynesboro, VA [Library symbol] [Library of Congress]   (LCLS)
ViWC .... Colonial Williamsburg, Inc., Williamsburg, VA [Library symbol] [Library of Congress]   (LCLS)
ViWI........... Institute of Early American History and Culture, Williamsburg, VA [Library symbol] [Library of Congress]   (LCLS)
ViWiN .... United States National Aeronautics and Space Administration, Technical Library, Wallops Island, VA [Library symbol] [Library of Congress]   (LCLS)
ViWisC ...... Clinch Valley College of the University of Virginia, Wise, VA [Library symbol] [Library of Congress]   (LCLS)
ViW-L .... College of William and Mary, Law School, Williamsburg, VA [Library symbol] [Library of Congress]   (LCLS)
ViWn .... Handley Library, Winchester, VA [Library symbol] [Library of Congress]   (LCLS)
ViWnS .... Shenandoah College and Conservatory of Music, Winchester, VA [Library symbol] [Library of Congress]   (LCLS)
ViWyC .... Wytheville Community College, Wytheville, VA [Library symbol] [Library of Congress]   (LCLS)
VIX............. Vitoria [Brazil] [Airport symbol]   (OAG)
VIX............. Vixit [He Lived] [Latin]
VIY............. Nashville, TN [Location identifier] [FAA]   (FAAL)
ViYNW....... United States Naval Weapons Station, Yorktown, VA [Library symbol] [Library of Congress]   (LCLS)
VIZ............. Videlicet [Namely] [Latin]
VIZ............. Vizianagram [India] [Seismograph station code, US Geological Survey]   (SEIS)
Vizgazdalkodasi Tud Kut Intez Tanulmanyok Kut Eredmenyek ... Vizgazdalkodasi Tudomanyos Kutato Intezet Tanulmanyok es Kutatasi Eredmenyek [A publication]
Vizugyi Kozl ... Vizugyi Kozlemenyek [A publication]
Vizugyi Kozlem ... Vizugyi Kozlemenyek [A publication]
VizV.......... Vizantijskij Vremenik [A publication]
VJ .... Sempati Air Transport P.T. [Indonesia] [ICAO designator]   (FAAC)
VJ .... Utility Plane [Navy symbol]
VJ .... Vacuum-Jacketed   (KSC)
VJ .... Vassar Journal of Undergraduate Studies [A publication]
VJ .... Ventriculojugular [Medicine]

VJ............... Video Jockey [Television version of disc jockey; originated on all-rock-music cable station MTV]
VJ............... Visiting Judges [British]
VJ............... Voprosy Jazykoznanija [Lvov] [A publication]
V-J (Day).... Victory over Japan [Japanese surrender, World War II, 14 August 1945]
VJA........... Adelphi University, Garden City, NY [OCLC symbol]   (OCLC)
VJa .... Voprosy Jazykoznanija [Moscow] [A publication]
VJaL.......... Voprosy Jazyka i Literatury [A publication]
VJB........... Verdan Junction Box
Vjber .... Vierteljahresberichte [A publication]
VJC .... Vallejo Junior College [California]
VJC .... Vermont Junior College
VJC .... Virginia Junior College [Minnesota] [Later, Mesabi Community College]
Vjesn Bibliot Hrv ... Vjesnik Bibliotekara Hrvatske [A publication]
Vjhber Probl Entwickliaend ... Vierteljahresberichte Probleme der Entwicklungslaender [A publication]
Vjh Wirtsch-Forsch ... Vierteljahreshefte zur Wirtschaftsforschung [A publication]
Vjh Zeitgesch ... Vierteljahreshefte fuer Zeitgeschichte [A publication]
VJJ .... Johnson & Johnson Dental Products Co., Science Information Center, East Windsor, NJ [OCLC symbol]   (OCLC)
VJLB.......... Veterans Jewish Legion. Bulletin [A publication]
VJMC .... Vintage Japanese Motorcycle Club   (EA)
VJOD......... Vereinigung Juedischer Organisationen Deutschlands zur Wahrung der Rechte der Juden des Ostens [A publication]
Vjschr Naturf Ges (Zuerich) ... Vierteljahrsschrift. Naturforschende Gesellschaft (Zuerich) [A publication]
Vjschr Soz- und Wirtschaftsgesch ... Vierteljahrsschrift fuer Sozial- und Wirtschaftsgeschichte [A publication]
VJWPh .... Vierteljahrsschrift fuer Wissenschaftliche Philosophie [A publication]
VK .... Airbus Industrie [France] [ICAO designator]   (FAAC)
VK .... Vedanta Kesari [Mylapore] [A publication]
VK .... Ventral Wall, Kidney [Anatomy]
VK .... Vertical Keel
VK .... Voelkische Kultur [A publication]
VKA........... Vienna-Kobenzl [Austria] [Seismograph station code, US Geological Survey]   (SEIS)
VKA........... Volatile Keying Assembly   (AFM)
VKAW........ Verhandelingen der Koninklijke Akademie van Wetenschappen [A publication]
VKC........... Canisius College, Buffalo, NY [OCLC symbol]   (OCLC)
VKCSN....... Vestnik Kralovske Ceske Spolecnosti Nauk [A publication]
VKE .... Von Karman Equation
VKF .... Von Karman Facility
VKF .... Voprosy Klassicekoj Filologii [A publication]
VKH........... Vogt-Koyanagi-Harada [Syndrome] [Ophthalmology]
VKI .... Von Karman Institute   (NATG)
VKIFD........ Von Karman Institute for Fluid Dynamics
VKL .... Verhandelingen. Koninklijke Akademie van Wetenschappen. Letterkunde [Elsevier Book Series] [A publication]
VKN........... Barre-Montpelier, VT [Location identifier] [FAA]   (FAAL)
VKN........... Verhandelingen. Koninklijke Akademie van Wetenschappen. Natuurkunde [Elsevier Book Series] [A publication]
VKNA .... Verhandelingen. Koninklijke Nederlandse Akademie van Wetenschappen. Afdeling Letterkunde [A publication]
VKNAL ...... Verhandelingen. Koninklijke Nederlandse Akademie van Wetenschappen. Afdeling Letterkunde [A publication]
VKNAW ..... Verhandelingen. Koninklijke Nederlandse Akademie van Wetenschappen [A publication]
VKO........... Moscow [USSR] Vnukovo Airport [Airport symbol]   (OAG)
VKR........... Volkstum und Kultur der Romanen [A publication]
VKR........... Voprosy Kul'tury Reci [A publication]
VKS........... Vicksburg, MS [Location identifier] [FAA]   (FAAL)
VKT .... Vehicle Kit Test
VKyjU........ Visnyk Kyjiv'koho Universytetu [A publication]
VL .... Deutsche Vierteljahrsschrift fuer Literaturwissenschaft und Geistesgeschichte [A publication]
VL .... Eagleair Ltd. [Arnarflug hf] [Iceland] [ICAO designator]   (FAAC)
VL .... Value Line Investment Survey
V-L .... Van Langenhoven [Rifle]
VL .... Vandalia Line [Railroad]
V/L .... Vapor-to-Liquid
VL .... Vapor Return Line
VL .... Varia Lectio [Variant Reading]
VL .... Vario-Losser [Electronics]
VL .... Velar Lobe
VL .... Ventralis Lateralis [Brain anatomy]
VL .... Vereinigte Linke [United Left] [West Germany]   (PPW)
VL .... Vertical Ladder [Technical drawings]
VL .... Vertical Landing   (MCD)
VL .... Vetenskaps-Societeten i Lund [A publication]
VL .... Vice Lieutenant [British]
VL .... Vide Locum [See the Place Indicated] [Latin]
VL .... Videlicet [Namely] [Latin]
VL .... Video Logic   (IEEE)
V & L.......... Vie et Langage [A publication]
VL............... View Loss

VL............. Viking Lander [*NASA*]
VL............. Ville
VL............. Violation of Lawful [*Order*] [*Military*]
VL............. Violin [*Music*]   (ROG)
VL............. Vision, Left Eye
VL............. Visual Laydown
VL............. Voprosy Literatury [*A publication*]
VL............. Vraie Lumiere [*True Light*] [*French*] [*Freemasonry*]   (ROG)
VL............. Vulgar Latin
VLA .... Vachel Lindsay Association   (EA)
VLA .... Valhalla Energy Corp. [*Vancouver Stock Exchange symbol*]
VLA .... Vandalia, IL [*Location identifier*] [*FAA*]   (FAAL)
VLA .... Vertical Landing Aid [*Military*]   (CAAL)
VLA .... Vertical Launch ASROC [*Antisubmarine Rocket*]
VLA .... Vertical Line Array
VLA .... Very Large Array [*Radioscope*]
VLA .... Very Late Activation Antigen [*Immunology*]
VLA .... Very Low Altitude
VLA .... Veterans' Land Act [*Canada*]
VLA .... Video Logarithmic Amplifier
VLa .... Vie et Langage [*A publication*]
VLA .... Viola [*Music*]
VLA .... Visual Landing Aid
VLA .... Vladivostok [*USSR*] [*Seismograph station code, US Geological Survey*]   (SEIS)
VLA .... Vladivostok [*USSR*] [*Geomagnetic observatory code*]
VLA .... Voice of Liberty Association   (EA)
VLA .... Volume Limiting Amplifier
VLA .... Volunteer Lawyers for the Arts   (EA)
Vlaams Diergeneeskd Tijdschr ... Vlaams Diergeneeskundig Tijdschrift [*A publication*]
Vlaams Diergeneesk Tijdschr ... Vlaams Diergeneeskundig Tijdschrift [*A publication*]
VLAB........ Vipont Laboratories [*NASDAQ symbol*]   (NQ)
VLAC........ Vertical Lift Aircraft Council   (EA)
VLAD........ Vertical Line Array DIFAR   (MCD)
VLADD ...... Visual Low-Angle Drogue Delivery   (AFM)
Vladimir Gos Ped Inst Ucen Zap ... Vladimirskii Gosudarstvennyi Pedagogiceskii Institut Imeni P. I. Lebedeva-Poljanskogo. Ucenyi Zapiski [*A publication*]
Vladimir Vecer Politehn Inst Sb Naucn Trudov ... Vladimirskii Vecernyi Politehniceskii Institut. Sbornik Naucnyh Trudov [*A publication*]
VLAM........ Variable Level Access Method [*Data processing*]
VLAM........ Vlamertinghe [*City in Flanders*] [*Army*] [*World War I*]   (DSUE)
V Lang....... Visible Language [*A publication*]
VLAP........ Vietnam Laboratory Assistance Program [*Naval Oceanographic Office*]
VLAPA ...... Vietnam Laboratory Assistance Program, Army   (RDA)
VLAR........ VFR [*Visual Flight Rules*] Low-Altitude High-Speed Routes [*Aviation*]   (FAAC)
VLAT .... Very Large Array Telescope [*NASA*]
VLATME..... Very-Lighweight Air Traffic Management Equipment   (MCD)
VLB .... Glider [*Special*] [*Navy symbol*]
VLB .... Vacuum Lens Blank
VLB .... Very Long Baseline
VLB .... Verzeichnis Lieferbarer Buecher [*List of Deliverable Books, i.e., books in print*] [*Germany*]
VLB .... Vincaleukoblastine [*Also, V, VBL, Ve*] [*Antineoplastic drug*]
VLB .... Visual LASER Beam
VLBA........ Very Long Baseline Array
VLBI......... Very Long Baseline Interferometer [*or Interferometry*]
VLBI......... Viking Lander Biological Instrument [*NASA*]
VLBR........ Very Low Birth Rate
VLC .... Longwood College, Farmville, VA [*OCLC symbol*]   (OCLC)
VLC .... Valencia [*Spain*] [*Airport symbol*]   (OAG)
VLC .... Viking Lander Capsule [*NASA*]
VLC .... Violoncello [*Music*]
VLC .... Vital Load Center   (MSA)
VLCC........ Very Large Cargo [*or Crude*] Carrier [*Oil tanker*]
VLCD........ Very-Low Calorie Diet
VLCE........ Visible LASER Communication Experiment
VLCF........ Vectored Lift Cannon Fighter   (MCD)
VLCF........ Victoria League for Commonwealth Fellowship [*British*]
VLCHV ...... Very-Low-Cost Harassment Vehicle   (MCD)
VLCR........ Variable Light Cavity Resonance
VLCS........ Voltage-Logic-Current-Switching [*Electronics*]
VLCTY....... Velocity   (FAAC)
VLD .... Vacuum Leak Detector
VLD .... Valdez [*Alaska*] [*Seismograph station code, US Geological Survey*] [*Closed*]   (SEIS)
VLD .... Valdosta [*Georgia*] [*Airport symbol*]   (OAG)
VLD .... Vendor List of Drawings
VLD .... Victorian Licensing Decisions [*A publication*]
VLD .... Village and Local Development
VLD .... Visual Laydown Delivery   (AFM)
VLD .... Vulnerability/Lethality Division [*Ballistic Research Laboratory*]   (RDA)
VLDBS ...... Very-Large Data Base System
VLDF........ Very-Long Delay Fuze [*Military*]   (CAAL)
VLDL .... Very Low Density Lipoprotein [*Biochemistry*]

VLDTN ...... Validation   (AAG)
VLE.......... Landing-Gear-Extended Speed [*Aviation*]
VLE.......... V & L Enterprises [*ACCORD*] [*UTLAS symbol*]
VLE.......... Valle, AZ [*Location identifier*] [*FAA*]   (FAAL)
VLE.......... Vapor-Liquid Equilibrium
VLE.......... Victorian Legal Executive [*A publication*]
VLE.......... Violone [*Violins*] [*Music*]
VLEASS .... Visible Light Emission
VLEASS .... Very Long Endurance Acoustic Submarine Simulator
VLED........ Visible Light-Emitting Diodes
V Lenin Fiz ... Vestnik Leningradskogo Universiteta. Seriya Fiziki i Khimii [*A publication*]
V Lenin Mek ... Vestnik Leningradskogo Universiteta. Seriya Matematiki Mekhaniki [*A publication*]
VLenU .... Vestnik Leningradskogo Gosudarstvennogo Universiteta [*A publication*]
VLF........... Variable Length Field
VLF........... Vectored Lift Fighter   (MCD)
VLF........... Vertical Launch Facility
VLF........... Very-Low Fluence [*Physics*]
VLF........... Very-Low-Frequency [*Electronics*]
VLFJ.......... Very-Low-Frequency Jammer [*Electronics*]
VLFR.......... Very-Low-Frequency Receiver [*Electronics*]
VLFS.......... Variable Low-Frequency Standard
VLG........... Vertical Load Gun
VLG........... Villa Gesell [*Argentina*] [*Airport symbol*]   (OAG)
VLG........... Village   (MCD)
VLG........... Visible Light Generator
VLG........... Vlaamse Gids [*A publication*]
VLGE.......... Village Super Market [*NASDAQ symbol*]   (NQ)
VLH........... Very Large Herbivores
VLH........... Very Lightly Hinged [*Philately*]
VLH........... Volatile Liquid Hydrocarbon
VLI............ Port Vila [*Vanuata*] [*Airport symbol*]   (OAG)
VLI............ Variable Life Insurance
VLI............ Very-Low Inertia
VLI............ Video Load Impedance
VLIB.......... Valodas un Literaturas Instituta Biletens [*A publication*]
VLID.......... Valid Logic Systems [*NASDAQ symbol*]   (NQ)
VLIR.......... Valodas un Literaturas Instituta Raksti [*A publication*]
VLIS.......... Viking Lander Imaging System [*NASA*]
VLIS.......... Viking Library System [*Library network*]
VLIS.......... VLI Corp. [*NASDAQ symbol*]   (NQ)
VLit.......... Voprosy Literatury [*A publication*]
Vliyanie Rab Sred Svoistva Mater ... Vliyanie Rabochikh Sred na Svoistva Materialov [*A publication*]
VLJ.......... Val Joyeux [*France*] [*Later, CLF*] [*Geomagnetic observatory code*]
VLJaTas..... Voprosy Literaturovedenija i Jazykoznanija (Taskent) [*A publication*]
VLL........... Amigo Airways [*Harlingen, TX*] [*FAA designator*]   (FAAC)
VLL........... Valladolid [*Spain*] [*Airport symbol*]   (OAG)
VLLO......... Violoncello [*Music*]
VLM........... Variable Length Multiply
VLM........... Visceral Larval Migrans [*Medicine*]
VLM........... Vortex Lattice Method
VLMTRC .... Volumetric
VLN........... Training Glider [*Navy symbol*]
VLN........... Valencia [*Venezuela*] [*Airport symbol*]   (OAG)
VLN........... Vanua-Lava [*Sola*] [*New Hebrides*] [*Seismograph station code, US Geological Survey*]   (SEIS)
VLN .... Very Low Nitrogen [*Fuel technology*]
VLN .... Villebon Resources Ltd. [*Vancouver Stock Exchange symbol*]
VLN .... Violin [*Music*]
VLNT......... Violent   (FAAC)
VLO .... Valero Energy Corp. [*NYSE symbol*]
VLO .... Vertical Lockout
VLON........ Verwaltungslexikon [*NOMOS Datapool*] [*Database*]
VLP.......... Valero Natural Gas Partner [*NYSE symbol*]
VLP.......... Valparaiso [*Chile*] [*Seismograph station code, US Geological Survey*]   (SEIS)
VLP.......... Vaporizing Liquid Plenum
VLP.......... Vasopressin-Like Peptide [*Biochemistry*]
VLP.......... Vertical Landing Point   (AFM)
VLP.......... Vertical Long Period
VLP.......... Video Long Player [*Video disk system*] [*Philips/MCA*]
VLP.......... Virus-Like Particle
VLPE........ Very Long Period Experiment [*Geophysics*]
VLPP........ Very Low Pressure Pyrolysis
VLPS........ Vandenberg Launch Processing System [*Aerospace*]   (MCD)
VLR.......... Randolph-Macon Woman's College, Lynchburg, VA [*OCLC symbol*]   (OCLC)
VLR .... Transport Glider [*Navy symbol*]
VLR .... Valar Resources Ltd. [*Vancouver Stock Exchange symbol*]
VLR .... Vanderbilt Law Review [*A publication*]
VLR .... Very Long Range
VLR .... Very Low Range
VLR .... Victorian Law Reports [*A publication*]
VLR .... Violation of Law of Road [*Traffic offense charge*]
VLR .... Voluntary Loss Rate [*of Air Force officers resigning before retirement*]

VLR (Adm) ... Victorian Law Reports (Admiralty) [*A publication*]
VLR (E) ...... Victorian Law Reports (Equity) [*A publication*]
VLR (Eq) .... Victorian Law Reports (*Equity*) [*A publication*]
VLR (IP & M) ... Victorian Law Reports (Insolvency, Probate, and Matrimonial) [*A publication*]
VLR (L) .... Victorian Law Reports (Law) [*A publication*]
VLR (M)...... Victorian Law Reports (Mining) [*A publication*]
VLR (P & M) ... Victorian Law Reports (Probate and Matrimonial) [*A publication*]
VLRSN .... Violation of Lawful Regulation Issued by the Secretary of the Navy
VLS .... Vacuum Loading System
VLS .... Valesdir [*Vanuata*] [*Airport symbol*]   (OAG)
VLS .... Valsamata [*Kephallenia*] [*Greece*] [*Seismograph station code, US Geological Survey*]   (SEIS)
VLS .... Valstieciu Liaudininku Sajunga [*Peasant Populist Union*] [*Lithuanian*]   (PPE)
VLS .... Vandenberg Launch Site [*Aerospace*]   (MCD)
VLS .... Vapor-Liquid-Solid
VLS .... Vertical Launch System [*Military*]
VLS .... Vertical Liquid Spring
VLS .... Very Long Shot [*A photograph or motion picture sequence taken from a considerable distance*]
VLS .... Very Low Speed
VLS .... Viking Lander System [*NASA*]   (KSC)
VLS .... Village Voice. Literary Supplement [*A publication*]
VLS .... Virtual Linkage System [*or Subsystem*]
VLS .... Visible Light Sensors   (MCD)
VLS .... Visual Lunacy Society   (EA)
VLS .... Voice Literary Supplement [*A publication*]
VLS .... Volume Loadability Speed   (IEEE)
VLSI .... Very-Large-Scale Integration [*of circuits*] [*Electronics*]
VLSI .... VLSI Technology, Inc. [*NASDAQ symbol*]   (NQ)
VLSIC........ Very-Large-Scale Integrated Circuit [*Electronics*]
VLSM .... Vertical Launched Standard Missile   (MCD)
VLSW .... Virtual Line Switch
VLT........... Vault Explorations, Inc. [*Vancouver Stock Exchange symbol*]
VLT........... Vehicle Licensing and Traffic [*British*]
VLT........... Victorian Law Times [*A publication*]
VLT........... Video Layout Terminal [*Data processing*]
VLT........... Volute
VLTG........ Voltage   (AAG)
VLTT .... Vehicular Leger Toot Terrain [*Light All-Terrain Vehicle*] [*French*]   (MCD)
VLU .... Vacuum Lifting Unit
VLU .... Vestnik Leningradskogo Gosudarstvennogo Universiteta [*A publication*]
VLU .... Vestnik Leningradskogo Universiteta. Seriya Istorii, Jazyka, i Literatury [*A publication*]
VLU .... Video Logic Unit   (MCD)
VLU .... Worldwide Value Fund [*NYSE symbol*]
VLUist .... Vestnik Leningradskogo Gosudarstvennogo Universiteta [*A publication*]
VLV .... Valdivia [*Chile*] [*Seismograph station code, US Geological Survey*]   (SEIS)
VLV .... Valera [*Venezuela*] [*Airport symbol*]   (OAG)
VLV .... Valve   (AAG)
VLV .... Velvet Exploration Co. [*Vancouver Stock Exchange symbol*]
VLV .... Very-Low Volume
VLV .... Visna Lentivirus
VLvivU....... Visnyk L'vivs'koho Derzavnoho Universytetu [*A publication*]
VLVM........ Vlastivedny Vestnik Moravsky [*A publication*]
v-LVN........ Ventral Lateral Ventricular Nerve [*Anatomy*]
VLVS........ Voltage-Logic-Voltage-Switching [*Electronics*]
VLW......... Village Level Workers [*India*]
VLW......... Washington and Lee University, Lexington, VA [*OCLC symbol*]   (OCLC)
VLY .... Valley   (MCD)
VLY .... Valley Oil & Gas [*Vancouver Stock Exchange symbol*]
VLZ.......... Valdez [*Alaska*] [*Seismograph station code, US Geological Survey*]   (SEIS)
VM............. Abacus Air [*West Germany*] [*ICAO designator*]   (FAAC)
VM............. V-Mail Specialists [*Navy*]
VM............. Validation Material [*Social Security Administration*]
VM............. Vasomotor [*Physiology*]
VM............. Vastus Medialis [*A muscle*]
VM............. Vector Message
VM............. Velocity Meter
VM............. Velocity Modulation
VM............. Ventilation Management
VM............. Verslagen en Mededeelingen [*A publication*]
VM............. Vertical Magnet
VM............. Vestibular Membrane [*Medicine*]
VM............. Victory Medal [*British*]
VM............. Vietminh   (CINC)
vm .... Vietnam [*MARC country of publication code*] [*Library of Congress*]   (LCCP)
VM............. Vir Magnificus [*A Great Man*] [*Latin*]
VM............. Viral Myocarditis [*Medicine*]
VM............. Virgin and Martyr [*Church calendars*]
V & M....... Virgin and Martyr [*Church calendars*]

VM............. Virtual Machine [*Data processing*]
VM............. Virtual Memory [*Data processing*]   (MCD)
VM............. Voennoe Ministerstvo [*Ministry of War*] [1950-53; *merged into the Ministry of Defense*] [*Russian*]
VM............. Voice Modulation
VM............. Volatile Matter
VM............. Volksmarine
VM............. Voltmeter
V/m........... Volts per Meter [*Also, VPM*]
V/M........... Volts per Mil   (DEN)
VM............. Vorigen Monats [*Last Month*] [*German*]
VM............. Votre Majeste [*Your Majesty*] [*French*]
VM............. Voyager Mars [*NASA*]
VMA .... Marine Attack Squadron [*Navy symbol*]   (NVT)
VMA .... Valid Memory Address [*Data processing*]
VMA .... Valve Manufacturers Association of America [*Washington, DC*]   (EA)
VMA .... Vanillylmandelic Acid [*Also, HMMA*] [*Biochemistry*]
VMA .... Vehicle Maintenance Area
VMA .... Vero Monmouth Airlines [*Vero Beach, FL*] [*FAA designator*]   (FAAC)
VMA .... Virtual Machine Assist [*IBM Corp.*]
VMA .... Virtual Memory Allocation
VMA .... Visual Maneuverability Aids   (MCD)
VMAAI....... Violin Makers Association of Arizona International [*Tucson, AZ*]   (EA)
VMA(AW)... Marine Attack Squadron (All-Weather) [*Navy symbol*]   (NVT)
VMAP....... Video Map Equipment
VMAPS...... Virtual Memory Array Processing System
VMarJa...... Voprosy Marijskogo Jazykoznanija [*A publication*]
VMAVA .... Verdun-Meuse-Argonne Veterans Association   (EA)
VMAW .... Verslagen en Mededeelingen. Koninklijke Akademie van Wetenschappen [*A publication*]
VMAX........ Maximum Velocity
VMB .... Marine Medium and Heavy Patrol Bomber Squadron [*Land-based and seaplane*] [*Navy symbol*]
VMB .... Mary Baldwin College, Staunton, VA [*OCLC symbol*]   (OCLC)
VMB .... Vandringar Med Boeker [*A publication*]
VMB .... Vermont Motor Rate Bureau Inc., Barre VT [*STAC*]
VMBC........ Vintage Motor Bike Club   (EA)
VMBF .... Marine Fighter Bomber Squadron [*Navy symbol*]
VMBLOK.... Virtual Machine Control Block [*Data processing*]   (IBMDP)
VMC .... James Madison University, Harrisonburg, VA [*OCLC symbol*]   (OCLC)
VMC .... Variable Message Cycle
VMC .... Variable Mica Capacitor
VMC .... Vasomotor Center [*Physiology*]
VMC .... Velocity Minimum Control   (AAG)
VMC .... Veritable Master of Crewelwork
VMC .... Vertical Motion Compensation   (CAAL)
VMC .... Viet Montagnard Cong
VMC .... Villa Madonna College [*Kentucky*]
VMC .... Villa Maria College [*Pennsylvania*]
VMC .... Ville Marie [*Quebec*] [*Seismograph station code, US Geological Survey*] [*Closed*]   (SEIS)
VMC .... Virginia Medical College
VMC .... Visual Meteorological Conditions [*Aviation*]
VMC .... Void Metallic Composite
VMC .... Vulcan Materials Company [*NYSE symbol*]
VMCB......... Virtual Machine Control Block
VMCCA ...... Veteran Motor Car Club of America   (EA)
VMCF .... Virtual Machine Communication Facility
VMCJ .... Marine Composite Reconnaissance [*Photo*] Squadron [*Navy symbol*]
VMCM .... Vector-Measuring Current Meter [*Instrumentation*]
VM/CMS .... Virtual Machine/Conversational Monitor System [*Data processing*]
VMCP......... Vincristine, Melphalan, Cyclophosphamide, Prednisone [*Antineoplastic drug regimen*]
VMCP......... Vincristine, Melphalen, Cyclophosphamide, Prednisone [*Antineoplastic drug regimen*]
VMCR....... Volunteer Marine Corps Reserve
VMD .... Doctor of Veterinary Medicine
VMD .... Marine Photographic Squadron [*Navy symbol*]
VMD .... Vertical Magnetic Dipole   (IEEE)
VMD .... Volume Median Diameter [*Particle size*]
VMDF .... Vertical Side of Main Distribution Frame [*Telecommunications*]   (TEL)
VMDP......... Veterinary Medical Data Program [*Association of Veterinary Medical Data Program Participants*] [*Ithaca, NY*] [*Information service*]   (EISS)
VME........... British Columbia Ministry of Education [*UTLAS symbol*]
VME........... Villa Mercedes [*Argentina*] [*Airport symbol*]   (OAG)
VME........... Vinyl Methyl Ether [*Organic chemistry*]
VME........... Virtual Machine Environment [*International Computers Ltd.*]
VME........... Volvo, Michigan, Euclid [*In company name VME Americas, Inc.*]
VMEC........ Vehicle Mounted Explosive Container   (MCD)
VMF.......... Marine Fighter Squadron [*Navy symbol*]
VMF.......... Vacuum Melting Furnace
VMF.......... Vertical Maintenance Facility   (NASA)

VMFA .... Marine Fighter Attack Squadron [*Navy symbol*] (NVT)
VMFAT ...... Marine Fighter Attack Training Squadron [*Navy symbol*] (NVT)
VMF(AW) ... Marine Fighter Squadron (All-Weather) [*Navy symbol*] (NVT)
VMFI .... Voltage Monitor and Fault Indicating
VMF(N) ...... Marine Night Fighter Squadron [*Navy symbol*]
VMG .... Video Mapping Group
VMG .... Video Mixer Group
VMGR .... Marine Aerial Refueler/Transport Squadron [*Navy symbol*] (NVT)
VMGSE ...... Vehicle Measuring Ground Support Equipment (KSC)
VMH .... Misericordia Hospital, Medical Library, Bronx, NY [*OCLC symbol*] (OCLC)
VMH .... Ventral Medial Hypothalamus [*Anatomy*]
VMH .... Victoria Medal of Honour
VMHB .... Virginia Magazine of History and Biography [*A publication*]
VMHI .... Victorian Military History Institute (EA)
VMI .... Developmental Test of Visual-Motor Integration [*Beery & Buktenica*]
VMI .... Variable Moment of Inertia [*Nuclear physics*]
VMI .... Vibration Measurement Integrator
VMI .... Videodisc-Mouse Interface
VMI .... Virginia Military Institute
VMI .... Virginia Military Institute, Lexington, VA [*OCLC symbol*] (OCLC)
VMI .... Visual Maneuvering Indicator (MCD)
VMI .... Voicemail International, Incorporated [*Santa Clara, CA*] [*Telecommunications*] (TSSD)
VMIA .... Vinyl Metal Industry Association [*Defunct*] (EA)
VMIC .... Vermont Maple Industry Council [*Burlington, VT*] (EA)
VMID .... Virtual Machine Identifier
VMIG .... View-Master International Group [*NASDAQ symbol*] (NQ)
VMII 1986 ... Vertical Markets Information Index 1986 [*Amidon/Litman Associates*] [*A publication*]
V/mil .... Volts per Mil
VMIRL .... VMI Research Laboratories [*Virginia Military Institute*] [*Research center*] (RCD)
VMJ .... Marine Utility Squadron [*Navy symbol*]
VMJ .... Vertical Multijunction [*Solar cell*]
VMK .... Vita-Metall-Keramik [*German dental material for crowns and bridgework*]
VMKA .... Verslagen en Mededeelingen. Koninklijke Akademie voor Nederlandse Taal- en Letterkunde [*A publication*]
VMKT .... Victory Markets [*NASDAQ symbol*] (NQ)
VMKVA ...... Verslagen en Mededeelingen. Koninklijke Vlaamse Akademie voor Taal- en Letterkunde [*A publication*]
VML .... Marine Glider Squadron [*Navy symbol*]
VML .... Mohawk Valley Library Association, Schenectady County Public Library, Schenectady, NY [*OCLC symbol*] (OCLC)
VML .... Valley Migrant League (EA)
VMLH .... Ventromedial and Lateral Hypothalami [*Neuroanatomy*]
VMLI .... Veterans Mortgage Life Insurance
VMM .... Vacuum Melting Module
V & MM ...... Vandalism and Malicious Mischief [*Insurance*]
VMM .... Vehicle Model Movement
VMM .... Vertical Milling Machine
VMM .... Video Map Module
VMM .... Virtual Machine Monitor [*Data processing*] (IEEE)
VMM .... Volunteer Missionary Movement (EA-IO)
VMMC .... Veterans Memorial Medical Center [*Philippines*]
VMMMA ..... Vestnik Moskovskogo Universiteta. Seriya 1. Matematika, Mekhanika [*A publication*]
VMMPS ...... Vehicle Management and Mission Planning System [*NASA*]
VMN .... Ventromedial Nucleus [*Brain anatomy*]
VMO .... Marine Observation Squadron [*Navy symbol*]
VMO .... Maximum Operating Speed (MCD)
VMO .... Vastus Medialis Obliquus [*Muscle*]
VMO .... Velocity-Modulated Oscillator
VMO .... Very Massive Object [*Astronomy*]
VMO .... Visiting Medical Officer (ADA)
VMO(AS) ... Marine Observation Squadron (Artillery Spotting) [*Navy symbol*]
VMOGA ..... Vestnik Moskovskogo Universiteta. Seriya 5. Geografiya [*A publication*]
VMOS .... V-Groove Metal-Oxide Semiconductor (MCD)
VMOS .... Virtual Memory Operating System [*Sperry UNIVAC*] [*Data processing*] (IEEE)
V Mosk Fiz ... Vestnik Moskovskogo Universiteta. Seriya Fiziki i Astronomii [*A publication*]
V Mosk Mekh ... Vestnik Moskovskogo Universiteta. Seriya Matematiki i Mekhaniki [*A publication*]
V Mosk U Kh ... Vestnik Moskovskogo Universiteta. Seriya Khimiya [*A publication*]
VMOW .... Vice Minister of War (MCD)
VMP .... Value as Marine Policy
VMP .... Variable Major Protein [*Genetics*]
VM & P ...... Varnish Makers' and Painters' Naphtha
VMP .... Vertically Moored Platform [*Offshore drilling*]
VMPA .... Vancouver Museums and Planetarium Association [*Canada*]
VMPP .... Vincristine, Melphalan, Prednisone, Procarbazine [*Antineoplastic drug regimen*]
VMR .... Marine Transport Squadron [*Navy symbol*]

VMR .... Variance to Mean Rate
VMR .... Vasomotor Rhinitis [*Medicine*]
VMR .... Violation Monitor and Remover [*Bell System*]
VMR .... Volumetric Mixing Ratio
VMRB .... Vereinigte Metallwerke Ranshofen-Berndorf [*AG*]
VMRC .... Virginia Mason Research Center [*Virginia Mason Hospital and Mason Clinic*] [*Research center*] (RCD)
VMRI .... Veterinary Medical Research Institute [*Iowa State University*] [*Research center*] (RCD)
VMRO .... Vnatresna Makedonska Revolucionerna Organizacija [*Internal Macedonian Revolutionary Organization (Known popularly among English-speaking nations as the IMRO)*] [*Yugoslav*] (PPE)
VMRO .... Vutreshna Makidoniski Revoliutsionna Organizatsiia [*Internal Macedonian Revolutionary Organization*] [*Bulgarian*] (PPE)
VMRO(U) ... Vnatresna Makedonska Revolucionerna Organizacija (Udruzena) [*Internal Macedonian Revolutionary Organization (United)*] [*Yugoslav*] (PPE)
VMRR .... Vendor Material Review Report [*NASA*] (KSC)
VMRS .... Vessel Movement Reporting System
VMS .... Valve Mounting System
VMS .... Variable Mass System
VMS .... Vehicle Monitoring System (RDA)
VMS .... Velocity Measurement System
VMS .... Vertical Motion Simulator [*NASA*]
VMS .... Vibration Measuring System
VMS .... Video Modulation System
VMS .... Video Movie System [*For video recording tapes*]
VMS .... Videofile Microwave System
VMS .... Viewfinder-Metering System (KSC)
VMS .... Virtual Memory Operating System [*Data processing*]
VMS .... Visual Motion Simulator (MCD)
VMS .... Voice Messaging System [*Telecommunications*]
VMSB .... Marine Scout Bombing Squadron [*Navy symbol*]
VMSEA ...... Vehicle Monitoring System Electronics Assembly (RDA)
VMSP .... Volunteer Management Support Program [*ACTION*]
VMT .... Validate Master Tape
VMT .... Variable Microcycle Timing
VMT .... Variable Mu Tube [*Electronics*]
VMT .... Vehicle-Miles Traveled
VMT .... Velocity Modulated Transistor [*Solid-state physics*]
VMT .... Velocity-Modulated Tube
VMT .... Very Many Thanks
VMT .... Video Matrix Terminal
VMT .... Virtual Memory Technique [*Data processing*] (MDG)
VMT .... Von Mises Theory
VMTB .... Marine Torpedo Bomber Squadron [*Navy symbol*]
VMTSS .... Virtual Machine Time-Sharing System [*Data processing*] (IEEE)
VMU .... Baimuru [*Papua New Guinea*] [*Airport symbol*] (OAG)
VMU .... Vestnik Moskovskogo Gosudarstvennogo Universiteta [*A publication*]
VMUBA ..... Vestnik Moskovskogo Universiteta. Seriya 6. Biologiya, Pochvovedenie [*A publication*]
VMUFA ...... Vestnik Moskovskogo Universiteta. Seriya 3. Fizika, Astronomiya [*A publication*]
VMUGA ..... Vestnik Moskovskogo Universiteta. Seriya 4. Geologiya [*A publication*]
VMUist ...... Vestnik Moskovskogo Gosudarstvennogo Universiteta [*A publication*]
VMUKA ..... Vestnik Moskovskogo Universiteta. Seriya 2. Khimiya [*A publication*]
VMUZh ...... Vestnik Moskovskogo Universiteta. Zhurnalistika [*A publication*]
VMVBORG ... Verslagen en Mededeelingen van de Vereeniging tot Beoefening van Overijsselsch Recht en Geschiedenis [*A publication*]
VMVOVR .... Verslagen en Mededeelingen van de Vereeniging tot Uitgaaf van der Bronnen van het Oud-Vaderlandsche Recht [*A publication*]
VMW .... Mary Washington College, Fredericksburg, VA [*OCLC symbol*] (OCLC)
V Mw .... Vierteljahrsschrift fuer Musikwissenschaft [*A publication*]
VMWWI ..... Victory Medal World War I [*British*]
VMWWII .... Victory Medal World War II [*British*]
VMXI .... VMX, Incorporated [*NASDAQ symbol*] (NQ)
VMY .... York College of the City University of New York, Jamaica, NY [*OCLC symbol*] (OCLC)
VN .... Hang Khong Vietnam [*Vietnam*] [*ICAO designator*] (FAAC)
VN .... Training Plane [*Navy symbol*]
VN .... Van Ness' Prize Cases [*United States*] (DLA)
VN .... (Vanillyl)nonanamide [*Biochemistry*]
VN .... Vegetative Nucleus [*Botany*]
VN .... Ventral Nerve [*Neuroanatomy*]
VN .... Ventral Nozzle
VN .... Verb Neuter
VN .... Verbal Noun
VN .... Verify Number If No Answer [*Telecommunications*] (TEL)
VN .... Victorian Newsletter [*A publication*]
VN .... Vietnam [*Two-letter standard code*] (CNC)

vn .... Vietnam, North [*vm (Vietnam) used in records cataloged after January 1978*] [*MARC country of publication code*] [*Library of Congress*] (LCCP)

VN .... VietNow [*Oregon, IL*] (EA)

VN .... Violin [*Music*]

VN .... Visiting Nurse

VN .... Vladimir Nabokov [*In book title, "VN: The Life and Art of Vladimir Nabokov"*]

VN .... Vocational Nurse

VN .... Vomeronasal [*Anatomy*]

VN .... Von Neumann [*Procedure*] [*Statistics*]

VN .... Vulnerability Number

VNA............ Air Viet-Nam

VNA............ Jetstream International Airlines [*Latrobe, PA*] [*FAA designator*] (FAAC)

VNA............ Mercy Hospital, Library, Watertown, NY [*OCLC symbol*] (OCLC)

VNA............ Vienna, GA [*Location identifier*] [*FAA*] (FAAL)

VNA............ Vietnam News Agency

VNA............ Visiting Nurse Association

VNAA.......... Visiting Nurse Associations of America [*Denver, CO*] (EA)

VNAF.......... Vietnam Air Force

VNAF.......... Vietnam Armed Forces

VNAF I & M ... Vietnam Air Force Improvement and Modernization Program

VNAV.......... Vertical Navigation Mode (IEEE)

VNB .... Wadhams Hall Seminary College, Library, Ogdensburg, NY [*OCLC symbol*] (OCLC)

VNBP.......... Valley National Bancorp of Passaic [*NASDAQ symbol*] (NQ)

VNC............ North Country Reference and Research Resources Council, Union List of Serials, Canton, NY [*OCLC symbol*] (OCLC)

VNC............ Variable Neutralizing Capacitor

VNC............ Venice, FL [*Location identifier*] [*FAA*] (FAAL)

VNC............ Ventral Nerve Cord [*Neuroanatomy*]

VNC............ Voice Numerical Control

VNC............ Votes National Committee (EA)

VNCCI......... Volunteer - The National Center [*Arlington, VA*] (EA)

VNCCI......... Volunteer: the National Center for Citizen Involvement [*Formerly, NCVA, NICOV*] [*Later, VNC*] (EA)

VNCP .... Valley National Corporation of Arizona [*NASDAQ symbol*] (NQ)

VNCS .... Vietnam Christian Service [*Defunct*] (EA)

VND............ Jefferson Community College, Library, Watertown, NY [*OCLC symbol*] (OCLC)

VND............ Vanda [*Antarctica*] [*Seismograph station code, US Geological Survey*] (SEIS)

VND............ Vprasanja Nasih Dni [*A publication*]

VNE............ Ogdensburg Public Library, Ogdensburg, NY [*OCLC symbol*] (OCLC)

VNE............ Velocity Never to Exceed

VNE............ Verbal Nonemotional (Stimuli) [*Psychology*]

VNESE .... Vietnamese

Vnesn Torg ... Vnesnjaja Torgovlja [*A publication*]

VNETF........ Vietnam Expediting Task Force [*Military*]

VNF .... Paul Smiths College, Library, Paul Smiths, NY [*OCLC symbol*] (OCLC)

VNF .... Vietnam Foundation (EA)

VNFH.......... Vjesnik Narodnog Fronta Hrvatske [*A publication*]

VNG............ Ventral Surface, Nephridial Gland [*Anatomy*]

VNG............ W. Alton Jones Cell Science Center Library, Lake Placid, NY [*OCLC symbol*] (OCLC)

VNHP.......... Vermont Natural Heritage Program [*Montpelier, VT*] [*Information service*] (EISS)

VNI .... Violini [*Violins*] [*Music*]

VNIC........... Voltage Negative Immittance Converter

VNIIMP .... Vsesoiuznyi Nauchno-Issledovatel'skii Institut Miasnoi Promyshlennosti [*All-Union Scientific Research Institute of the Meat Industry*]

Vnitr Lek .... Vnitrni Lekarstvi [*A publication*]

VNL .... Bogalusa, LA [*Location identifier*] [*FAA*] (FAAL)

VNL .... Variable Neodymium LASER

VNL .... Via Net Loss [*Telecommunications*]

VNL .... Victorian Newsletter [*A publication*]

VNLF .... Via Net Loss Factor (TEL)

VNM .... Tijdschrift van de Vereeniging voor Nederlandse Muziekgeschiedenis [*A publication*]

VNM .... Vietnam [*Three-letter standard code*] (CNC)

VNMC......... Vietnam Marine Corps

VNN............ Eastern Virginia Medical Authority, Norfolk, VA [*OCLC symbol*] (OCLC)

VNN............ Mount Vernon, IL [*Location identifier*] [*FAA*] (FAAL)

VNN............ Vacant National Number [*Telecommunications*] (TEL)

VNN............ Vietnam Navy

VNO............ Value Not Obtained

VNO............ Vilnius [*USSR*] [*Airport symbol*] (OAG)

VNO............ Vital National Objective (AAG)

VNO............ Vomeronasal Organ [*Anatomy*]

VNO............ Vornado, Inc. [*NYSE symbol*]

VNP .... Venda National Party (PPW)

VNP .... Van Nostrand Reinhold [*Publishers*]

VNR............ Variable Navigation Ratio

VNR............ VFR [*Visual Flight Rules*] Not Recommended [*Pilot brief*] [*Aviation*] (FAAC)

VNR............ Video News Release [*A news release in the form of video tape*]

VNR............ Vietnam Reactor

VNRS.......... Vietnamese National Railway System (CINC)

VNS............ Norfolk State College, Norfolk, VA [*OCLC symbol*] (OCLC)

VNS............ Vagus Nerve Stimulation [*Physiology*]

VNS............ Varanasi [*India*] [*Airport symbol*] (OAG)

VNS............ Vasomotor Nervous System [*Physiology*]

VNS............ Ventral Nervous System [*Neuroanatomy*]

VNS............ Very North Shore [*Women's Wear Daily*]

VNS............ Visiting Nurse Service

VNS............ Vladimir Nabokov Society (EA)

VnSc .... Florence Williams Public Library, Christiansted, St. Croix, VI [*Library symbol*] [*Library of Congress*] (LCLS)

VNSF.......... Vietnamese Special Forces (CINC)

VNSL.......... Variable Nozzle Slow Landing (MCD)

VNSP.......... Vacant Nozzle Shield Plug (NRCH)

VnSt .... Saint Thomas Public Library, Charlotte Amalie, VI [*Library symbol*] [*Library of Congress*] (LCLS)

VnStC .... College of the Virgin Islands, St. Thomas, VI [*Library symbol*] [*Library of Congress*] (LCLS)

VNT .... Ventora Resources [*Vancouver Stock Exchange symbol*]

VNTRF........ Ventora Resources Ltd. [*NASDAQ symbol*] (NQ)

VNU............ Verenigde Nederlandse Uitgeversbedrijven [*Publishing group*] [*Netherlands*]

VNV............ Vlaamsch Nationaal Verbond [*Flemish National League*] [*Dissolved*] [*Belgium*] (PPE)

VNVO .... Verbal-Nonverbal Operation [*Psychometrics*]

VNW........... Van Wert, OH [*Location identifier*] [*FAA*] (FAAL)

VNXL.......... Vane Axial

VNY............ Van Nuys, CA [*Location identifier*] [*FAA*] (FAAL)

VO.............. Battleship Observation Squadron [*Navy symbol*]

Vo.............. Initial Velocity

VO.............. Observation Plane [*Navy symbol*]

VO .... [*The*] Seagram Co. Ltd. [*NYSE symbol*] [*Toronto Stock Exchange symbol*] [*Vancouver Stock Exchange symbol*]

VO .... Valve Oscillator (DEN)

VO .... Varying Order [*British*]

VO .... Vehicle Operations [*NASA*] (NASA)

VO .... Verb-Object [*Education of the hearing-impaired*]

VO .... Verbal Orders

VO .... Verbindungsoffizier [*Liaison Officer*] [*German military - World War II*]

VO .... Vernehmungsoffizier [*Interrogation Officer*] [*German military - World War II*]

VO .... Verpflegungsoffizier [*Mess Officer*] [*German military - World War II*]

VO .... Verso

VO .... Very Old [*Wines and spirits*]

VO .... Vesnjani Orbriji [*Kyjiv*] [*A publication*]

VO .... Veterinary Officer [*British*]

VO .... Victorian Order [*British*] (ROG)

VO .... Viking Orbiter [*NASA*]

VO .... Violation of [*Local*] Ordinance

VO .... Violino [*Violin*] [*Music*] (ROG)

VO .... Visa Office [*Department of State*]

VO .... Vocal (AAG)

VO .... Voice (AAG)

VO .... Voice Over [*Commentary read over a program*] [*Television*]

Vo .... Voices [*A publication*]

VO .... Volatile Oil

VO .... Volcanic Origin (AAG)

VO .... Volt (ROG)

VO .... Volume

VO .... Voluntary Opening [*Prosthesis*] [*Medicine*]

VO .... Von Oben [*From the Top*] [*German*]

VO .... Voucher (MCD)

VO of A....... Vasa Order of America (EA)

VOA............ Vibrational Optical Activity [*Spectroscopy*]

VOA............ Voice of America

VOA............ Volkswagen of America

VOA............ Volunteers of America [*Metairie, LA*] (EA)

VO-AG......... Vocational Agriculture [*Education*]

VOAR.......... St. John's, NF [*AM radio station call letters*]

VOARS .... Velocity over Altitude Ratio Sensor (MCD)

VOB............ Vacuum Optical Bench

VOB............ Volume over Bark [*Forestry*]

VOBANC .... Voice Band Compression (CET)

VOC............ Observation Spotter Squadron [*Navy symbol*]

VOC............ Onondaga Community College, Syracuse, NY [*OCLC symbol*] (OCLC)

VOC............ Variable Oil Capacitor

VOC............ Variable Output Circuit (DEN)

VOC............ Vehicle Observer Corps [*Road Haulage Association*] [*British*]

VOC............ Vehicle Out of Commission [*Army*] (AFIT)

VOC............ Verbal Orders of the Commander

VOC............ Vincent Owners Club (EA)

VOC............ Virago Owners Club (EA)

VOC............ Vocabulary [*Linguistics*]

VOC............ Vocal (ADA)

VOC........... Vocational
VOC........... Vocative
VOC........... Voice of Calvary [An association]
VOC........... Voice-Operated Coder
VOC........... Voice Order Circuit (CET)
VOC........... Volatile Organic Compounds [Environmental chemistry]
VOC........... Volunteer Officer Candidate [Army]
VOCA........ Victims of Crime Act of 1984
VOCA........ Voice of China and Asia Missionary Society (EA)
VOCA........ Voice Communications Assembly [Ground Communications Facility, NASA]
VOCA........ Voice Output Communications Aid
VOCA........ Voltmeter Calibrator
VOCA........ Volunteers in Overseas Cooperative Assistance [Washington, DC] (EA)
VOCAB...... Vocabulary
VOCAL...... Vessel Ordnance Allowance List
VOCAL...... Victims of Child Abuse Laws (EA)
VOCAL...... Victims of Crime and Leniency [Montgomery, AL] (EA)
Voc Aspect Ed ... Vocational Aspect of Education [A publication]
VOCAT...... Vocative [Grammar] (ROG)
Vocat Guid ... Vocational Guidance Quarterly [A publication]
Vocational Aspect ... Vocational Aspect of Education [A publication]
VOC-ED ..... Vocational Education (OICC)
Voc Educ ... Vocational Education [A publication]
Voc Educ M ... Vocational Education Magazine [A publication]
VOCG....... Verbal Order Commanding General
Voc Guid Q ... Vocational Guidance Quarterly [A publication]
VOCM .... St. John's, NF [AM radio station call letters]
VOCM .... Vehicle Out of Commission for Maintenance [Military]
VOCM-FM ... St. John's, NF [FM radio station call letters]
VOCNA ..... Velocette Owners Club of North America (EA)
VOCO....... Verbal Order Commanding Officer
VOCODER ... Voice Coder
VOCOM..... Voice Communications
VOCP....... Vehicle Out of Commission for Parts [Military]
VocRehab ... Vocational Rehabilitation (OICC)
VOCS....... Verbal Orders of the Chief of Staff
VOCS........ Voice Operated Computer Systems [St. Louis Park, MN] [Software manufacturer]
VOD........... Old Dominion University, Norfolk, VA [OCLC symbol] (OCLC)
VOD........... Vacuum Oxygen Decarburization [Stainless-steel processing]
VOD........... Velocity of Detonation (IEEE)
VOD........... Veno-Occlusive Disease [of the liver]
VOD........... Vertical On-Board Delivery [Navy] (NVT)
VOD........... Via Omnidirect (FAAC)
VOD........... Vision, Right Eye
VODACOM ... Voice Data Communications
VODARO .... Vertical Ozone Distribution from the Absorption and Radiation of Ozone (AAG)
VODAS...... Voice-Operated Device Antising (CET)
VODAT...... Voice-Operated Device for Automatic Transmission
VODC........ Viking Orbiter Design Change [NASA]
VODER...... Voice Coder
VODER...... Voice-Operated Demonstrator
VODK........ [The] Voice of Democratic Kampuchea [Radio station of the Red Khmers] (PD)
Vodn Hospod ... Vodni Hospodarstvi [A publication]
Vodn Hospod Rada B ... Vodni Hospodarstvi. Rada B [A publication]
Vodni Hospod A ... Vodni Hospodarstvi. Rada A [Czechoslovakia] [A publication]
Vodni Hospod Rada B ... Vodni Hospodarstvi. Rada B [A publication]
Vodn Resur ... Vodnye Resursy [USSR] [A publication]
Vodohospod Cas ... Vodohospodarsky Casopis [A publication]
Vodopodgot Ochistka Prom Stokov ... Vodopodgotovka i Ochistka Promyshlennykh Stokov [A publication]
Vodorosli Griby Sib Dal'nego Vostoka ... Vodorosli i Griby Sibiri i Dal'nego Vostoka [A publication]
Vodosnabzh Kanaliz Gidrotekh Sooruzh ... Vodosnabzhenie Kanalizatsiya Gidrotekhnicheskie Sooruzheniya [A publication]
Vodosnabzh Sanit Tekh ... Vodosnabzhenie i Sanitarnaya Tekhnika [A publication]
Vodos Sanit Tekhn ... Vodosnabzhenie i Sanitarnaya Tekhnika [A publication]
VODP .... Verbal Orders by Direction of the President
VOE........... Venus Orbit Ejection [NASA] (MCD)
VOE........... Visual Order Error
VOE........... Vocational Office Education [NASA employment program]
VOEC .... Vegetable Oil Export Corporation (EA)
VOECRN .... Vietnamese Organization to Exterminate Communists and Restore the Nation (EA)
Voedingsmiddelen Technol ... Voedingsmiddelen Technologie [A publication]
VOEI......... Veroeffentlichungen des Osteuropa-Instituts [A publication]
Voen Khim ... Voennaya Khimiya [A publication]
Voen Med Delo ... Voenno Meditsinsko Delo [A publication]
Voen-Med Zh ... Voenno-Meditsinskii Zhurnal [A publication]
Voenna Tekh ... Voenna Tekhnika [Bulgaria] [A publication]
Voenno-Ist Zhurnal ... Voenno-Istoricheskii Zhurnal [A publication]
Voenno-Med Zh ... Voenno-Meditsinskii Zhurnal [A publication]

Voenno Med Zhurnal (Leningrad) ... Voenno-Meditsinskii Zhurnal (Leningrad) [A publication]
Voenno-Med Zhurnal (S Peterburg) ... Voenno-Meditsinskii Zhurnal (S. Peterburg) [A publication]
Voen Sanit Delo ... Voenno-Sanitarnoe Delo [A publication]
Voen Vest ... Voennyi Vestnik [USSR] [A publication]
Voen Znaniya ... Voennye Znaniya [USSR] [A publication]
Voet Com ad Pand ... Voet's Commentarius ad Pandectas (DLA)
VOF........... Covington, GA [Location identifier] [FAA] (FAAL)
VOF........... Observation Fighter Squadron [Navy symbol]
VOF........... Variable Operating Frequency (NATG)
VOF........... Vsesoiuznoe Obshchestvo Filatelistov [or Fizioterapistov]
VOG........... Observation Plane Squadron [Navy symbol]
VOG........... Vanguard Operations Group
VOG........... Vectoroculogram
VOG........... Vessel Off-Gas [Nuclear energy] (NRCH)
Vog........... Vogue [Record label] [France]
VOG........... Volgograd [USSR] [Airport symbol] (OAG)
VOGAA ...... Voice-Operated Gain-Adjusting Amplifier [NASA]
VOGAD ...... Voice-Operated Gain-Adjusting Device [NASA]
VOGIN........ Nederlandse Vereniging van Gebruikers van Online Informatie-Systemen [Netherlands Association of Users of Online Information Systems] [Amsterdam] (EISS)
Vog Liv...... Vogue Living [A publication]
VOGOV ...... Verbal Orders of the Governor
VOGT .... Vogart Crafts Corp. [NASDAQ symbol] (NQ)
VOH........... Vohemar [Madagascar] [Airport symbol] (OAG)
VOHCA...... Veterans Omnibus Health Care Act of 1976
VOI........... Vehicle Ordnance Installation
VOI........... Video Output Impedance
VOI........... Vocational Opinion Index (OICC)
VOI........... Voinjama [Liberia] [Airport symbol] (OAG)
VOIB......... Veroeffentlichungen der Abteilung fuer Slavische Sprachen und Literaturen des Osteuropa-Instituts [Slavisches Seminar] an der Freien Universitaet Berlin [A publication]
VOICE .... Victims of Incest Can Emerge (EA)
Voice........ Village Voice [A publication]
VOICE .... Vocabulary of Intelligence Concept Expressions
VOICE .... Voice of Informed Community Expression
VOICE .... Volunteer Oil Industry Communications Effort [Program] [Phillips Petroleum Co.]
VOIR......... Venus Orbiting and Imaging RADAR [NASA]
VOIS......... Visual Observation Instrumentation Subsystem [Lunar space program]
VOIS......... Visual Observation Integration Subsystem (AAG)
Voith Forsch Konstr ... Voith Forschung und Konstruktion [A publication]
Voith Res & Constr ... Voith Research and Construction [A publication]
VOIZD .... Voice of Z-39 [A publication]
Vojen Zdrav Listy ... Vojenske Zdravotnicke Listy [A publication]
Vojnoekon Pregl ... Vojnoekonomski Pregled [Yugoslavia] [A publication]
Vojnosanit Pregl ... Vojnosanitetski Pregled [A publication]
VOK........... Camp Douglas, WI [Location identifier] [FAA] (FAAL)
VOKS .... Soviet Union Society for Cultural Relations with Foreign Countries. Weekly News Bulletin [A publication]
VOKS .... Vsesoiuznoe Obshchestvo Kul'turnoi Sviazi s Zagranitsei [All-Union Society for Cultural Relations with Foreign Countries] [USSR] [Initialism also used as title of periodical]
VOL........... Variable Orientation Launcher (AAG)
Vol........... Volans [Constellation]
VOL........... Volante [Lightly and Rapidly] [Music] (ROG)
VOL........... Volatilis [Volatile] [Pharmacy]
Vol........... Volcanic [Quality of the bottom] [Nautical charts]
VOL........... Volcano [Maps and charts]
VOL........... Volume
VOL........... Voluntary [or Volunteer] (AFM)
VOLA........ Volume, American Stock Exchange [Selection symbol]
VOLAD...... Voice of the Lakes [A publication]
VOLAG...... Voluntary Agency [Generic term for a charitable organization]
VOLAR ...... Volunteer Army [Project, absorbed by MVA, 1972]
Vol Ash ...... Volcanic Ash [Quality of the bottom] [Nautical charts]
VOLC........ Volcanics [Lithology]
VOLC .... Volcano
Volcani Inst Agric Res Div For Ilanot Leafl ... Volcani Institute of Agricultural Research. Division of Forestry. Ilanot Leaflet [A publication]
Volcani Inst Agric Res Div Sci Publ Pam ... Volcani Institute of Agricultural Research. Division of Scientific Publications. Pamphlet [A publication]
Volcanol Bull Jpn Meterol Agency ... Volcanological Meteorological Bulletin. Japan Meteorology Agency [A publication]
Volcanol Soc Jap Bull ... Volcanological Society of Japan. Bulletin [A publication]
VOLCAS .... Voice-Operated Loss Control and Suppressor
VOLCOM..... Value of Life Committee [Brighton, MA] (EA)
Vol Effort Q ... Voluntary Effort Quarterly [A publication]
VOLERE ..... Voluntary/Legal/Regulatory (IEEE)
Vol Feeding Mgt ... Volume Feeding Management [A publication]
Volgograd Gos Ped Inst Ucen Zap ... Volgogradskogo Gosudarstvennogo Pedagogiceskogo Instituta Imeni A. S. Serafimovica Ucenye Zapiski [A publication]

VOLIR......... Volumetric Indicating RADAR
VOLKS....... Volkswagen [*Automobile*]   (DSUE)
Volksmus... Volksmusik. Zeitschrift fuer das Musikalische Laienschaffen [*A publication*]
Volkstum Landschaft ... Volkstum und Landschaft. Heimatblaetter der Muensterlaendische Tageszeitung [*A publication*]
Volleyball Mag ... Volleyball Magazine [*A publication*]
Volleyball Tech J ... Volleyball Technical Journal [*A publication*]
VOLMET .... Meteorological Information for Aircraft in Flight [*Aviation code*]   (FAAC)
Voln........... Volans [*Constellation*]
VOLN......... Volume, New York Stock Exchange [*Selection symbol*]
Vologod Gos Ped Inst Ucen Zap ... Vologodskii Gosudarstvennyi Pedagogiceskii Institut. Ucenye Zapiski [*A publication*]
Vologod I Cerepovec Gos Ped Inst Ucen Zap ... Vologodskii Gosudarstvennyi Pedagogiceskii Institut. Cerepoveckii Gosudarstvennyi Pedagogiceskii Institut. Ucenye Zapiski [*A publication*]
Vo LR......... Villanova Law Review [*A publication*]
VOLRA .... Volta Review [*A publication*]
VOLS........ Voluntary Overseas Libraries Service
VOLSCAN ... Volumetric Scanning RADAR
VOLT....... Volt Information Sciences [*NASDAQ symbol*]   (NQ)
VOLT....... Volume, Toronto Stock Exchange [*Selection symbol*]
VOLTAN..... Voltage Amperage Normalizer
Volta R .... Volta Review [*A publication*]
Volt Electr Trade Mon ... Volt. Electrical Trade Monthly [*Japan*] [*A publication*]
Volunt Action ... Voluntary Action [*A publication*]
Volunt Action Leadersh ... Voluntary Action Leadership [*A publication*]
Volunt Adm ... Volunteer Administration [*A publication*]
Volunt Forum Abs ... Voluntary Forum Abstracts [*A publication*]
Volunt Housing ... Voluntary Housing [*A publication*]
Volunt Leader ... Volunteer Leader [*A publication*]
VOLV......... Volvendus [*To Be Rolled*] [*Pharmacy*]   (ADA)
VOLVEND... Volvendus [*To Be Rolled*] [*Pharmacy*]
VOLY......... Voluntary   (ROG)
Volz Mat Sb ... Volzskii Matematiceskii Sbornik [*A publication*]
VOM .... Nux Vomica Strychnia [*Strychnine-producing plant*] [*Pharmacy*]   (ROG)
VOM .... Volt-Ohm Meter
VOM .... Volt-Ohm-Milliammeter
VOMI .... Volksdeutsche Mittelstelle [*NAZI Germany*]
VOM URG... Vomitione Urgente [*The Vomiting Being Troublesome*] [*Pharmacy*]   (ROG)
VON........... Avon, CO [*Location identifier*] [*FAA*]   (FAAL)
VON........... Vestnik Otdelenija Obscestvennych Nauk. Akademija Nauk Gruzinskoj SSR [*A publication*]
VON........... Victorian Order of Nurses
Von H Const Hist ... Von Holst's Constitutional History of the United States   (DLA)
Von Ihr Str for L ... Von Ihring's Struggle for Law   (DLA)
VONJY .... Elan Populaire pour l'Unite Nationale [*Popular Impulse for National Unity*] [*Malagasy*]   (PPW)
Von Roll Mitt ... Von Roll Mitteilungen [*A publication*]
VONS .... Committee for the Defense of Persons Unjustly Persecuted [*Czechoslovak*]   (PD)
Voorlichting Onderz ... Voorlichting en Onderzoek [*A publication*]
VOP........... Valued as in Original Policy [*Insurance*]
VOP........... Vertical Ozone Profile
VOP........... Very Old Pale [*Designation on brandy labels*]
VOP........... Viral Oncology Program [*National Cancer Institute*]
VOPA .... Verbal Order Purchase Agreement
VOPAN...... Voice Pitch Analysis [*Consumer Response Corp.*]
VOPB......... Voice of the People of Burma [*Radio station of the Burma Communist Party*]   (PD)
Vop Bot Akad Nauk Litov SSR Inst Bot ... Voprosy Botaniki. Akademiya Nauk Litovskoi SSR. Institut Botaniki [*A publication*]
Vop Erozii Povysh Prod Sklon Zemel' Moldavii ... Voprosy Erozii i Povysheniya Produktivnosti Sklonovykh Zemel' Moldavii [*A publication*]
Vop Fil....... Voprosy Filosofii [*A publication*]
Vop Genez Krypnomashtabn Kartir Pochv Kazan Univ ... Voprosy Genezisa i Krypnomashtabnoi Kartirovanii Pochv Kazanskii Universitet [*A publication*]
Vop Geogr Mordovsk ASSR ... Voprosy Geografii Mordovskoi ASSR [*A publication*]
VopIst .... Voprosy Istorii [*A publication*]
Vop Med Kh ... Voprosy Meditsinskoi Khimii [*A publication*]
Vop Mikrobiol Akad Nauk Armyan SSR ... Voprosy Mikrobiologii. Akademiya Nauk Armyanskoi SSR [*A publication*]
VOPNAV .... Vice Chief of Naval Operations
VOPO .... Volkspolizei [*Also, VP*]
VOPP......... Veterinary Medicine, Optometry, Podiatry, and Pharmacy [*HEW program*]
Vop Pitan ... Voprosy Pitaniya [*A publication*]
Vop Psikhol ... Voprosy Psikhologii [*A publication*]
VOPR......... Voice-Operated Relay
Vopr Antropol ... Voprosy Antropologii [*A publication*]

Vopr At Nauki Tekh Ser Fiz Plazmy Probl Upr Termodad Reakts ... Voprosy Atomnoi Nauki i Tekhniki. Seriya Fizika Plazmy i Problemy Upravlyaemykh Termodadernykh Reaktsii [*Ukrainian SSR*] [*A publication*]
Vopr At Nauki Tekh Ser Fiz Vys Energ At Yadra ... Voprosy Atomnoi Nauki i Tekhniki. Seriya Fizika Vysokikh Energii i Atomnogo Yadra [*Ukrainian SSR*] [*A publication*]
Vopr At Nauki Tekh Ser Obshch Yad Fiz ... Voprosy Atomnoi Nauki i Tekhniki. Seriya Obshchaya i Yadernaya Fizika [*Ukrainian SSR*] [*A publication*]
Vopr Bezopasn Ugol'n Shakhtakh ... Voprosy Bezopasnosti v Ugol'nykh Shakhtakh [*A publication*]
Vopr Biokhim Mozga ... Voprosy Biokhimii Mozga [*A publication*]
Vopr Biokhim Nervn Myshechnoi Sist ... Voprosy Biokhimii Nervnoi i Myshechnoi Sistem [*Georgian SSR*] [*A publication*]
Vopr Biokhim Nervn Sist ... Voprosy Biokhimii Nervnoi Sistemy [*A publication*]
Vopr Biol .... Voprosy Biologii [*A publication*]
Vopr Bor'by Silikozom Sib ... Voprosy Bor'by s Silikozom v Sibiri [*A publication*]
Vopr Cenoobraz ... Voprosy Cenoobrazovanija [*A publication*]
Vopr Din Prochn ... Voprosy Dinamiki i Prochnosti [*A publication*]
Vopr Din Teor Rasprostr Seism Voln ... Voprosy Dinamicheskoi Teorii Rasprostraneniya Seismicjeskikh Voln [*USSR*] [*A publication*]
Vopr Dozim Zasch Izluch Mosk Inzh Fiz Inst Sb Statei ... Voprosy Dozimetrii i Zaschity ot Izluchenii. Moskovskii Inzhenerno Fizicheskii Institut Sbornik Statei [*USSR*] [*A publication*]
Vopr Dozim Zashch Izluch ... Voprosy Dozimetrii i Zashchity ot Izluchenii [*A publication*]
Vopr Ekol Biotsenol ... Voprosy Ekologii i Biotsenologii [*A publication*]
Vopr Ekon ... Voprosy Ekonomiki [*A publication*]
Vopr Eksp Klin Radiol ... Voprosy Eksperimental'noi i Klinicheskoi Radiologii [*Ukrainian SSR*] [*A publication*]
Vopr Endokrinol Obmena Veshchestv Resp Mezhved Sb ... Voprosy Endokrinologii Obmena Veshchestvennyi Respublikanskoi Mezhvedomstvennyi Sbornik [*A publication*]
Vopr Filos ... Voprosy Filosofii [*A publication*]
Vopr Fiz Gorn Porod ... Voprosy Fiziki Gornykh Porod [*A publication*]
Vopr Fiziol Akad Nauk Azerb SSR Sekt Fiziol ... Voprosy Fiziologii Akademiya Nauk Azerbaidzhanskoi SSR. Sektor Fiziologii [*Azerbaidzhan SSR*] [*A publication*]
Vopr Fiziol Biokhim Kul't Rast ... Voprosy Fiziologii i Biokhimii Kul'turnykh Rastenii [*A publication*]
Vopr Fiziol Biokhim Zool Parazitol ... Voprosy Fiziologii, Biokhimii, Zoologii, i Parazitologii [*A publication*]
Vopr Fiziol Chel Zhivotn ... Voprosy Fiziologii Cheloveka i Zhivotnykh [*A publication*]
Vopr Fiziol Rast Mikrobiol ... Voprosy Fiziologii Rastenii i Mikrobiologii [*A publication*]
Vopr Fiz Tverd Tela ... Voprosy Fiziki Tverdogo Tela [*A publication*]
Vopr Fiz Zasch Reaktorov ... Voprosy Fiziki Zashchity Reaktorov [*USSR*] [*A publication*]
Vopr Fiz Zashch Reakt ... Voprosy Fiziki Zashchity Reaktorov [*A publication*]
Vopr Fotosint ... Voprosy Fotosinteza [*A publication*]
Vopr Gazotermodin Energoustanovok ... Voprosy Gazotermodinamiki Energoustanovok [*Ukrainian SSR*] [*A publication*]
Vopr Gematol Pereliv Krovi Krovozamenitelei ... Voprosy Gematologii Perelivaniya Krovi i Krovozamenitelei [*A publication*]
Vopr Geogr ... Voprosy Geografii [*A publication*]
Vopr Geogr Dal'nego Vostoka ... Voprosy Geografii Dal'nego Vostoka [*A publication*]
Vopr Geogr Kaz ... Voprosy Geografii Kazakhstana [*A publication*]
Vopr Geogr Mordov ASSR ... Voprosy Geografii Mordovskoj ASSR [*A publication*]
Vopr Geokhim Tipomorfizm Miner ... Voprosy Geokhimii i Tipomorfizm Mineralov [*A publication*]
Vopr Geol Buren Neft Gazov Skvazhin ... Voprosy Geologii i Bureniya Neftyanykh i Gazovykh Skvazhin [*A publication*]
Vopr Geol Metod Razved Zolota ... Voprosy Geologii i Metodiki Razvedki Zolota [*A publication*]
Vopr Geol Tadzh ... Voprosy Geologii Tadzhikistana [*A publication*]
Vopr Geol Yuzhn Urala Povolzh'ya ... Voprosy Geologii Yuzhnogo Urala i Povolzh'ya [*A publication*]
Vopr Geomorfol Geol Bashk ... Voprosy Geomorfologii i Geologii Bashkirii [*A publication*]
Vopr Gerontol Geriatr ... Voprosy Gerontologii i Geriatrii [*A publication*]
Vopr Gidrodin Teploobmena Kriog Sist ... Voprosy Gidrodinamiki i Teploobmena v Kriogennykh Sistemakh [*A publication*]
Vopr Gig Pitan ... Voprosy Gigieny Pitaniya [*A publication*]
Vopr Gig Tr Slants Promsti Est SSR ... Voprosy Gigieny Truda v Slantsevoi Promyshlennosti Estonskoi SSR [*A publication*]
Vopr Ikhtiol ... Voprosy Ikhtiologii [*A publication*]
Vopr Immunol ... Voprosy Immunologii [*A publication*]
Vopr Infekts Patol Immunol ... Voprosy Infektsionnoi Patologii i Immunologii [*A publication*]
Vopr Inf Teor Prakt ... Voprosy Informatsionnoi Teorii i Praktiki [*A publication*]
Vopr Introd Rast Zelenogo Stroit ... Voprosy Introduktsii Rastenii i Zelenogo Stroitel'stva [*A publication*]

Vopr Inzh Geol Gruntoved ... Voprosy Inzhenernoi Geologii i Gruntovedeniya [*A publication*]
Vopr Inzh Seismol ... Voprosy Inzhenernoi Seismologii [*USSR*] [*A publication*]
Vopr Issled Ispol'z Pochv Mold ... Voprosy Issledovaniya i Ispol'zovaniya Pochvovedeniya Moldavii [*A publication*]
Vopr Issled Lessovykh Gruntov Osn Fundam ... Voprosy Issledovaniya Lessovykh Gruntov Osnovanii i Fundamentov [*A publication*]
Vopr Ist ...... Voprosy Istorii [*A publication*]
Vopr Ist KPSS ... Voprosy Istorii KPSS [*A publication*]
Vopr Istor Estestvozn Tekh ... Voprosy Istorii Estestvoznaniya i Tekhniki [*A publication*]
Vopr Ist Udm ... Voprosy Istorii Udmurtii [*A publication*]
Vopr Karstoved ... Voprosy Karstovedeniya [*A publication*]
Vopr Khim Biokhim Sist Soderzh Marganets Polifenoly ... Voprosy Khimii i Biokhimii Sistem. Soderzhashchikh Marganets i Polifenoly [*A publication*]
Vopr Khim Khim Tekhnol ... Voprosy Khimii i Khimicheskoj Tekhnologii [*USSR*] [*A publication*]
Vopr Klin Eksp Onkol ... Voprosy Klinicheskoi i Eksperimental'noi Onkologii [*A publication*]
Vopr Klin Eskp Khir ... Voprosy Klinicheskoi i Eksperimental'noi Khirurgii [*A publication*]
Vopr Klin Lech Zlokach Novoobraz ... Voprosy Kliniki i Lecheniya Zlokachestvennykh Novoobrazovanii [*A publication*]
Vopr Kraev Patol Akad Nauk Uzb SSR ... Voprosy Kraevoi Patologii Akademii Nauk Uzbekskoi SSR [*A publication*]
Vopr Kriog Tekh ... Voprosy Kriogennoi Tekhniki [*A publication*]
Vopr Kurortol Fizioter (Frunze) ... Voprosy Kurortologii i Fizioterapii (Frunze) [*A publication*]
Vopr Kurortol Fizioter Lech Fiz Kul't ... Voprosy Kurortologii, Fizioterapii, i Lechebnoi Fizicheskoi Kul'tury [*A publication*]
Vopr Kurortol Revatol ... Voprosy Kurortologii i Revmatologii [*A publication*]
Vopr Leikozol ... Voprosy Leikozologii [*A publication*]
Vopr Lesoved ... Voprosy Lesovedeniya [*A publication*]
Vopr Litol Petrogr ... Voprosy Litologii i Petrografii [*A publication*]
Vopr Magmat Metamorf ... Voprosy Magmatizma i Metamorfizma [*A publication*]
Vopr Magmat Metamorfiz ... Voprosy Magmatizma i Metamorfizma [*USSR*] [*A publication*]
Vopr Magn Gidrodin Akad Nauk Latv SSR Inst Fiz ... Voprosy Magnitnoi Gidrodinamiki. Akademiya Nauk Latviiskoi SSR. Institut Fiziki [*Latvian SSR*] [*A publication*]
Vopr Med Khim ... Voprosy Meditsinskoi Khimii [*A publication*]
Vopr Med Khim Akad Med Nauk SSR ... Voprosy Meditsinskoi Khimii Akademiya Meditsinskikh Nauk SSSR [*A publication*]
Vopr Med Teor Klin Prakt Kurortnogo Lech ... Voprosy Meditsinskoi Teorii Klinicheskoi Praktiki i Kurortnogo Lecheniya [*A publication*]
Vopr Med Virusol ... Voprosy Meditsinskoi Virusologii [*A publication*]
Vopr Mekh ... Voprosy Mekhaniki [*USSR*] [*A publication*]
Vopr Mekh Real'nogo Tverd Tela ... Voprosy Mekhaniki Real'nogo Tverdogo Tela [*A publication*]
Vopr Metalloved Korroz Met ... Voprosy Metallovedeniya i Korrozii Metallov [*A publication*]
Vopr Metod Nauki ... Voprosy Metodologii Nauki [*A publication*]
Vopr Mikrobiol ... Voprosy Mikrobiologii [*A publication*]
Vopr Mikrodozim ... Voprosy Mikrodozimetrii Ministerstvo Vysshego i Srednego Spetsial'nogo Obrazovaniya SSSR [*A publication*]
Vopr Mineral Osad Obraz ... Voprosy Mineralogii Osadochnykh Obrazonanii [*A publication*]
Vopr Neftekhim ... Voprosy Neftekhimii [*A publication*]
Vopr Neirokhir ... Voprosy Neirokhirurgii [*A publication*]
Vopr Obsc Nauk ... Voprosy Obscestvennykh Nauk [*A publication*]
Vopr Obshch Khim Biokhim ... Voprosy Obshchei Khimii i Biokhimii [*A publication*]
Vopr Okhr Materin Det ... Voprosy Okhrany Materinstva i Detstva [*A publication*]
Vopr Onkol ... Voprosy Onkologii [*A publication*]
Vopr Onkol (Leningr) ... Voprosy Onkologii (Leningrad) [*A publication*]
Vopr Org Geokhim Gidrogeol Neftegazonosn Basseinov Uzb ... Voprosy Organicheskoi Geokhimii i Gidrogeologii Neftegazonosnykh Basseinov Uzbekistana [*A publication*]
Voprosy Dinamiki i Procnosti ... Rizskii Politehniceskii Institut. Voprosy Dinamiki i Procnosti [*A publication*]
Voprosy Filos ... Voprosy Filosofii [*A publication*]
Voprosy Informacion Teorii i Praktiki ... Voprosy Informacionnoi Teorii i Praktiki [*A publication*]
Voprosy Istor Estestvoznan i Tehn ... Voprosy Istorii Estestvoznanija i Tehniki [*A publication*]
Voprosy Kibernet (Moscow) ... Voprosy Kibernetiki (Moscow) [*A publication*]
Voprosy Kibernet (Tashkent) ... Voprosy Kibernetiki (Tashkent) [*A publication*]
Voprosy Vychisl i Prikl Mat ... Akademia Nauk Uzbekskoi SSR Trudy Ordena Trudovogo Krasnogo Znameni Instituta Kibernetiki s Vychisl'nym Tsentrom. Voprosy Vychislitel'noi i Prikladnoi Matematiki [*A publication*]

Voprosy Vycisl i Prikl Mat ... Voprosy Vycislitel'noi i Prikladnoi Matematiki [*A publication*]
Vopr Pediatr Ohkr Materin Det ... Voprosy Pediatrii i Ohkrany Materinstva i Detstva [*A publication*]
Vopr Peredachi Inf ... Voprosy Peredachi Informatsii [*Ukrainian SSR*] [*A publication*]
Vopr Pitan ... Voprosy Pitaniya [*A publication*]
Vopr Proekt Sodovykh Zavodov ... Voprosy Proekhitovaniya Sodovykh Zavodov [*A publication*]
Vopr Proizvod Stali ... Voprosy Proizvodstva Stali [*A publication*]
Vopr Proizvod Vaktsin Syvorotok ... Voprosy Proizvodstva Vaktsin i Syvorotok [*A publication*]
Vopr Psikhiat Nevropatol ... Voprosy Psikhiatrii i Nevropatologii [*USSR*] [*A publication*]
Vopr Psikhiatr Nevropatol ... Voprosy Psikhiatrii i Nevropatologii [*A publication*]
Vopr Psikhol ... Voprosy Psikhologii [*A publication*]
Vopr Radiobiol ... Voprosy Radiobiologii [*A publication*]
Vopr Radiobiol Biol Deistviya Tsitostatich Prep ... Voprosy Radiobiologii i Biologicheskogo Deistviya Tsitostaticheskikh Preparatov [*A publication*]
Vopr Radiobiol Biol Dejstv Tsitostatich Prep ... Voprosy Radiobiologii i Biologicheskogo Dejstviya Tsitostaticheskikh Preparatov [*USSR*] [*A publication*]
Vopr Radiobiol Klin Radiol ... Voprosy Radiobiologii i Klinicheskoi Radiologii [*A publication*]
Vopr Radiobiol Sb Tr ... Voprosy Radiobiologii. Sbornik Trudov [*Armenian SSR*] [*A publication*]
Vopr Radioelektron ... Voprosy Radioelektroniki [*A publication*]
Vopr Ratsion Pitan ... Voprosy Ratsional'nogo Pitaniya [*A publication*]
Vopr Razved Geofiz ... Voprosy Razvedochnoi Geofiziki [*A publication*]
Vopr Razvit Gazov Promsti Ukr SSR ... Voprosy Razvitiya Gazovoi Promyshlennosti Ukrainskoi SSR [*A publication*]
Vopr Razvit Licnosti ... Voprosy Razvitija Licnosti [*A publication*]
Vopr Reg Geol Metallog Zabaikal'ya ... Voprosy Regional'noi Geologii i Metallogenii Zabaikal'ya [*A publication*]
Vopr Rentgenol Onkol ... Voprosy Rentgenologii i Onkologii [*A publication*]
Vopr Revm ... Voprosy Revmatizma [*A publication*]
Vopr Rud Geofiz ... Voprosy Rudnoi Geofiziki [*USSR*] [*A publication*]
Vopr Rud Geofiz Minist Geol Okhr Nedr SSSR ... Voprosy Rudnoi Geofiziki. Ministerstvo Geologii i Okhrany Nedr SSSR [*USSR*] [*A publication*]
Vopr Rudn Geofiz ... Voprosy Rudnoi Geofiziki [*A publication*]
Vopr Rudn Radiom ... Voprosy Rudnoi Radiometrii [*A publication*]
Vopr Rudn Transp ... Voprosy Rudichnogo Transporta [*A publication*]
Vopr Sel'sk Lesn Khoz Dal'n Vost ... Voprosy Sel'skogo i Lesnogo Khozyaistva Dal'nego Vostoka [*A publication*]
Vopr Sov Finno-Ugroved ... Voprosy Sovetskogo Finno-Ugrovedenija [*A publication*]
Vopr Strat Takt Marks-Lenin Partij ... Voprosy Strategii i Taktiki Marksistsko-Leninskih Partij [*A publication*]
Vopr Sudebno-Med Ekspert ... Voprosy Sudebno-Meditsinskoi Ekspertizy [*A publication*]
Vopr Tekhnol Obrab Vody Prom Pit'evogo Vodoshnabzh ... Voprosy Tekhnologii Obrabotki Vody Promyshlennogo i Pit'evogo Vodosnabzheniya [*A publication*]
Vopr Tekhnol Tovaroved Izdelii Legk Promsti ... Voprosy Tekhnologii i Tovarovedeniya Izdelii Legkoi Promyshlennosti [*A publication*]
Vopr Tekhnol Ulavlivaniya Pererab Prod Koksovaniya ... Voprosy Tekhnologii Ulavlivaniya i Pererabotki Produktov Koksovaniya [*A publication*]
Vopr Tekh Teplofiz ... Voprosy Tekhnicheskoi Teplofiziki [*Ukrainian SSR*] [*A publication*]
Vopr Teor At Stolknovenii ... Voprosy Teorii Atomnykh Stolknovenii [*USSR*] [*A publication*]
Vopr Teorii Metod Ideol Raboty ... Voprosy Teorii i Metodov Ideologiceskoj Raboty [*A publication*]
Vopr Teor Plazmy ... Voprosy Teorii Plazmy [*A publication*]
Vopr Teplofiz Yad Reakt ... Voprosy Teplofiziki Yadernykh Reaktorov [*USSR*] [*A publication*]
Vopr Vet Virusol ... Voprosy Veterinarnoi Virusologii [*A publication*]
Vopr Virusol ... Voprosy Virusologii [*A publication*]
Vopr Vodn Khoz ... Voprosy Vodnogo Khozyaistva [*A publication*]
Vopr Vychisl Mat Tekh (Tashkent) ... Voprosy Vychislitel'noi Matematiki i Tekhniki (Tashkent) [*A publication*]
VOPSA ...... Voprosy Psikhologii [*A publication*]
VOPT .... Voice of the People of Thailand [*Radio station of the Communist Party of Thailand*] (PD)
Vop Virusol ... Voprosy Virusologii [*A publication*]
VOQ .... Visiting Officers' Quarters [*Military*]
VOR .... Variable Omnirange
VOR .... Vehicle off the Road [*British*]
VOR .... Very-High-Frequency Omnidirectional Range
VOR .... Vestibulo-Ocular Reflex [*Neurology*]
VOR .... Visual Omnirange [*Directional Beacon*] [*Aviation*] (NG)
VOR .... Voice-Operated Relay
VOR .... Vortex Science Fiction [*A publication*]
VORDAC .... VHF [*Very-High-Frequency*] Omnidirectional Range/Distance-Measuring for Air Coverage

VORDME..... VHF [*Very-High-Frequency*] Omnirange - Distance-Measuring Equipment (CET)

VOR/DMET ... VHF [*Very-High-Frequency*] Omnirange/Distance-Measuring Equipment Compatible with TACAN

VOR-FIX..... Vestibuloocular Reflex with Fixation Light [*Ophthalmology*]

VORLA....... Vestnik Oto-Rino-Laringologii [*A publication*]

VORLOC...... VHF [*Very-High-Frequency*] Omnirange Localizer (CET)

VORM........ Vormittags [*In the Morning*] [*German*]

Voronez Gos Univ Trudy Mat Fak ... Voronezskii Gosudarstvennyi Universitet Imeni Leninskogo Komsomola. Trudy Matematiceskogo Fakul'teta [*A publication*]

Voronez Gos Univ Trudy Naucn Issled Inst Mat VGU ... Voronezskii Ordena Lenina Gosudarstvennyi Universitet Imeni Leninskogo Komsomola. Trudy Naucno-Issledovatel'skogo Instituta Matematiki [*A publication*]

Voronez Gos Univ Trudy Sem Funkcional Anal ... Ministerstvo Vyssego Obrazovanija SSSR. Voronezskii Gosudarstvennyi Universitet.Trudy Seminara po Funkcional'nomu Analizu [*A publication*]

Voronez Tehn Inst Trudy ... Voronezskii Tehnologiceskii Institut. Trudy [*A publication*]

VORS .... Vestibulo-Ocular Reflex Suppression [*Ophthalmology*]

Vorsokr...... Fragmente der Vorsokratiker [*A publication*] (OCD)

VORT......... Vorticity (FAAC)

VORTAC .... VHF [*Very-High-Frequency*] Omnirange TACAN

VORTEX..... Venus Orbiter Radiometric Temperature Experiment [*NASA*]

Vortr Gesamtgeb Bot ... Vortraege aus dem Gesamtgebiet der Botanik [*A publication*]

Vortr Pflanzenz Deut Landwirt Ges Pflanzenzuchtabt ... Vortrage fuer Pflanzenzuchter. Deutsche Landwirtschaftliche Gesellschaft Pflanzenzuchtabteilung [*A publication*]

VOS........... Observation Scout Plane [*Navy symbol*]

VOS........... Vehicle Origin Survey [*R. L. Polk & Co.*] [*Detroit, MI*] [*Information service*] (EISS)

VOS........... Vehicle on Stand (MCD)

VOS........... Veterans of Safety [*Chicago, IL*] (EA)

VOS........... Veterinary Orthopaedic Society [*Salt Lake City, UT*] (EA)

VOS........... Viking Orbiter System [*NASA*]

VOS........... Virtual Operating System

VOS........... Visicoder Oscillograph System

VOS........... Vision, Left Eye

VOS........... Vitello Ovi Solutus [*Dissolved in the Yolk of an Egg*] [*Pharmacy*] (ROG)

VOS........... Voice-Operated Switch

VOS........... Voluntary Observing Ships [*Marine science*] (MSC)

Vos........... Voskhod (BJA)

VOS........... Vostok [*USSR*] [*Geomagnetic observatory code*]

VOSA........ Verbal Orders of the Secretary of the Army

VOSAF...... Verbal Orders of the Secretary of the Air Force

VOSC........ VAST [*Versatile Avionics Shop Test*] Operating System Code

VOSH .... Volunteer Optometric Services to Humanity/International [*St. Louis, MO*] (EA)

VOSL........ Variable Operating and Safety Level

VOST........ Volatile Organic Sampling Train [*For air analysis*]

V Ost Geschichtsv ... Veroeffentlichungen des Verbandes Oesterreichischer Geschichts- Vereine [*A publication*]

Vost Neft.... Vostochnaya Neft [*A publication*]

VOT........... Valve Opening Time [*Nuclear energy*] (NRCH)

VOT........... Very Old Tawny [*Wines and spirits*]

VOT........... Vision of Tomorrow [*A publication*]

VOT........... Vocational Office Trainee

VOT........... Voice Onset Time

VOT........... Voplex Corp. [*American Stock Exchange symbol*]

VOT........... VOR [*Very-High-Frequency Omnidirectional Range*] Test Signal (CET)

VOT........... Vorticity (FAAC)

vot .... Votic [*MARC language code*] [*Library of Congress*] (LCCP)

VOTA .... Vibration Open Test Assembly [*Nuclear energy*] (NRCH)

VOTACT..... Validation of Theoretical Automatic Checkout Techniques (MCD)

VOTAG...... Verbal Orders of the Adjutant General

VOTC .... Volume Table of Contents [*Data processing*]

VOTCA ...... Victims of Terrorism Compensation Act

VOTM........ Vacuum-Operated Throttle Modulator [*Automotive engineering*]

VOU........... Voucher (AFM)

VOU........... Vouglans [*France*] [*Seismograph station code, US Geological Survey*] (SEIS)

VOV........... Verband Oeffentlicher Verkehrsbetriebe eV [*Association of Public Transport*] [*Cologne, West Germany*]

VOV........... Very Old Version

VOV........... Video Output Voltage

VOW........... Voice of Women

VOWR........ St. John's, NF [*AM radio station call letters*]

VOX........... Voice-Operated Keying [*Data processing*]

VOX........... Voice Operated Switch

VOX........... Voice-Operated Transmission

VOX POP.... Vox Populi [*Voice of the People*] [*Latin*]

Vox Sang ... Vox Sanguinis [*A publication*]

Vox Sanguin ... Vox Sanguinis [*A publication*]

VoxTh........ Vox Theologica [*Assen*] [*A publication*]

VoxTheol ... Vox Theologica [*Assen*] [*A publication*]

VOY........... Viceroy Resources Corp. [*Toronto Stock Exchange symbol*] [*Vancouver Stock Exchange symbol*]

VOYA .... Voice of Youth Advocates [*A publication*]

Vozes .... Vozes Revista Catolica de Cultura [*A publication*]

Voz Farm (Lima) ... Voz Farmaceutica (Lima) [*A publication*]

Vozr........... Vozrozdenie [*A publication*]

VP.............. All India Reporter, Vindhya Pradesh [*1951-57*] (DLA)

VP.............. Patrol Plane [*Navy symbol*]

VP.............. Patrol Squadron [*Navy symbol*]

VP.............. United Kingdom Colonies and Protectorates [*Aircraft nationality and registration mark*] (FAAC)

VP.............. Vacant Property (ADA)

VP.............. Vacuum Packaged

VP.............. Vacuum Pickup

VP.............. Vacuum Pump

V & P .... Vagotomy and Pyloroplasty [*Medicine*]

VP.............. Validation Plan [*Social Security Administration*]

VP.............. Valve Pit (AAG)

VP.............. Valve Positioner

VP.............. Vanishing Point [*Term in art/drawing*]

VP.............. Vanuaaku Pati [*Political party*] [*New Hebrides*] (PD)

VP.............. Vanuatu Pati (PD)

VP.............. Vapor Pressure

VP.............. Variable Pitch [*as, an aircraft propeller*]

VP.............. Variable Procedure (AAG)

VP.............. Variable Property

VP.............. Variant Pinocytic [*Cell*] [*Medicine*]

VP.............. Variegate Porphyria [*Medicine*]

VP.............. Various Paging [*Bibliography*]

vp .... Various Places [*MARC country of publication code*] [*Library of Congress*] (LCCP)

VP.............. Various Publishers [*Bibliography*]

VP.............. Vasopressin [*Endocrinology*]

VP.............. Vector Processor

VP.............. Velocity Pressure

V & P .... Vendor and Purchaser (ROG)

VP.............. Venereal Pamphlet [*Navy*]

VP.............. Venous Pressure [*Medicine*]

VP.............. Vent-Clearing Pressure [*Nuclear energy*] (NRCH)

VP.............. Vent Pipe [*Technical drawings*]

V-P .... Ventilation-Perfusion Scintigraphy

VP.............. Ventral Pioneer [*Neuron*]

VP.............. Ventriculoperitoneal [*Medicine*]

VP.............. Verb Passive

VP.............. Verb Phrase

VP.............. Verifying Punch (CMD)

VP.............. Verstell Propeller (MCD)

VP.............. Vertical Planning (NG)

VP.............. Vertical Polarization

VP.............. Vest Pocket

VP.............. Viacao Aerea Sao Paulo, SA [*Brazil*] [*ICAO designator*] (FAAC)

VP.............. Vice President

VP.............. Vice-Principal [*British*]

VP.............. Victorian Poetry [*A publication*]

VP.............. Video Processor (NVT)

VP.............. Videoplayer

VP.............. Vietnam Press

VP.............. Vincristine and Prednisone [*Antitumor agent*]

VP.............. Vinylphenol [*Biochemistry*]

VP.............. Vinylpyrrolidinone [*Organic chemistry*]

VP.............. Viral Protein [*Biochemistry, genetics*]

VP.............. Virtual Processor

VP.............. Visa Petition

VP.............. Vita e Pensiero [*A publication*]

V e P .... Vita e Pensiero [*A publication*]

VP.............. Vivre et Penser [*A publication*] (BJA)

VP.............. Voce del Passato [*A publication*]

VP.............. Voges-Proskauer [*Bacteriology*]

VP.............. Void in Part [*Decision or finding held invalid in part for reasons given*] [*Used in Shepard's Citations*] (DLA)

VP.............. Volkspartie [*People's Party*] [*Liechtenstein*] (PPE)

VP.............. Volkspolizei [*Also, VOPO*]

VP.............. Voluntary Patient [*British*]

VP.............. Vorposten [*Outpost*] [*German military*]

VP.............. Vossa Paternidade [*Yours Paternally*] [*Portuguese*]

V & P .... Votes and Proceedings [*A publication*]

VP.............. Voting Pool [*Said of disposition of stocks*]

VP.............. Vulnerable Period [*Physiology*]

VP.............. Vulnerable Point

VP-16-213... Vepeside [*Etoposide*] [*Antineoplastic drug*]

VPA .... Valproic Acid [*Also, DPA*] [*Anticonvulsant compound*]

VPA .... Vascular Permeability Assay [*Clinical chemistry*]

VPA .... Vibration Pickup Amplifier

VPA .... Victorian Planning Appeal Decisions [*A publication*]

VPA .... Videotape Production Association [*New York, NY*] (EA)

VPA .... Volatile Profile Analysis [*Food chemistry*]

VPA .... Vote Profile Analysis

VPAM........ Virtual Partitioned Access Method

VPAP........ Voluntary Petroleum Allocation Program [*Presidential*]

VPARD ...... Veterinary Parasitology [*A publication*]

VPB .... Medium and Heavy Patrol Bomber Squadron [*Land based and seaplane*] [*Navy symbol*]
VPB .... Patrol-Bombing Plane [*Navy symbol*]
VPB .... Vendors per Block
VPB .... Ventricular Premature Beat [*Cardiology*]
VPB .... Vertical Plot Board [*Navy*]
VPBA .... Varipolarization Beacon Antenna
VPBC......... Virginia Poultry Breeders Club   (EA)
VPB(HL).... Patrol Bomber, Four-Engine, Landplane [*Navy symbol*]
VPB(HS) .... Patrol Bomber, Four-Engine, Seaplane [*Navy symbol*]
VPB(ML).... Patrol Bomber, Two-Engine, Landplane [*Navy symbol*]
VPB(MS).... Patrol Bomber, Two-Engine, Seaplane [*Navy symbol*]
VPC .... La Vente par Correspondance [*Mail Order*] [*Business and trade*] [*French*]
VPC .... Vacuum Pump Chamber
VPC .... Vapor Permeation Curing [*Plastics technology*]
VPC .... Vapor-Phase Chromatography
VPC .... Variable Padder Capacitor
VPC .... Ventricular Premature Contraction [*Cardiology*]
VPC .... Video Processor Control   (MCD)
VPC .... Visual Punch Card
VPC .... Voltage Phasing Control   (DEN)
VPC .... Voltage to Pulse Converter
VPC .... Volume Packed Cells
VPC .... Volume-Pulse-Charge
VPC .... Volunteer Program Consultant [*Red Cross*]
VPCA .... Volunteers for Peaceful Change   (EA)
VPCA .... Video Prelaunch Command Amplifier
VPCDS ...... Video Prelaunch Command Data System [*Air Force*]
VPCE......... Vapor Phase Catalytic Exchange   (MCD)
VPCPr .... Vincristine, Prednisone, Vinblastine, Chlorambucil, Procarbazine [*Antineoplastic drug regimen*]
VPD .... Vapor-Phase Deacidification [*of books and documents*]
VPD .... Variation per Day [*Navigation*]
VPD .... Vehicle Performance Data
VPD .... Vehicles per Day [*Military*]   (AFM)
VPD .... Ventricular Premature Depolarization [*Cardiology*]
VPD .... Vertically Polarized Dipole   (MCD)
VPD .... Vierte Partei Deutschlands [*Fourth Party of Germany*] [*West Germany*]   (PPW)
VPD .... Villa Park Dam [*California*] [*Seismograph station code, US Geological Survey*]   (SEIS)
VPD .... Vremennik Puskinskogo Doma [*A publication*]
VPDF......... Vacuum Pump Discharge Filter
VPE .... Vapor-Phase Epitaxy
VPE .... Vehicle Positioning Equipment   (MCD)
VPE .... Video Processing Equipment
VPen.......... Vita e Pensiero [*A publication*]
VPF............ Vacuum Pump Filter
VPF............ Variable Parts Feeder
VPF............ Variable Phase Filter
VPF............ Vascular Permeability-Increasing Factor [*Nephrology*]
VPF............ Vertical Processing Facility   (MCD)
VPF............ Vibratory Pan Feeder
VPF............ Viscoplastic Flow
VPFG......... Variable Phase Function Generator
VPG........... Variable-Rate Pulse Generator
VPGS........ Venous Pressure Gradient Support Stocking
VPGS........ Vice-President of the Geological Society [*British*]
VPH .... Variation per Hour [*Navigation*]
VPH .... Vehicles per Hour [*Traffic*]   (AFM)
VPH .... Veterans of Pearl Harbor   (EA)
VPH .... Volkspolizeihelfer
VPHD......... Vertical Payload Handling Device   (MCD)
VPI............. Vacuum Pressure Impregnation   (IEEE)
VPI............. Valve Position Indicator   (KSC)
VPI............. Vapor-Phase Inhibitor [*Papermaking*]
VPI............. Vendor Parts Index
VPI............. Vertical Point of Intersection [*Transportation*]
VPI............. Vessel Patentcy Index [*Medicine*]
VPI............. VIP Dynasty International Marketing Corp. [*Vancouver Stock Exchange symbol*]
VPI............. Virginia Polytechnic Institute and State University
VPI............. Virginia Polytechnic Institute and State University, Blacksburg, VA [*OCLC symbol*]   (OCLC)
VPI............. Vocational Preference Inventory [*Psychology*]
VPII............ Vita Plus Industries [*NASDAQ symbol*]   (NQ)
VPIMD........ Vilniaus Pedagoginio Instituto Mokslo Darbai [*A publication*]
VPJT.......... Vertical Power Jump Test
VPK .... Valley Airpark, Inc. [*Fort Collins, CO*] [*FAA designator*]   (FAAC)
VPK .... Vehicle per Kilometer   (AABC)
VPK .... Verdi Peak [*California*] [*Seismograph station code, US Geological Survey*]   (SEIS)
VPK .... Vest Pocket Kodak [*Camera*]
VPK .... Volts Peak   (NASA)
VPKA......... Volkspolizeikreisamt
VP(L)......... US Navy Patrol Squadron (Land)   (CINC)
VPL........... Variable Pulse LASER
VPL............ Vendor Parts List   (AAG)
VPL............ Ventral Posterolateral [*Anatomy*]

VPL........... Virginia Beach Public Library System, Virginia Beach, VA [*OCLC symbol*]   (OCLC)
VPL............ Visible Panty Line [*In reference to clothing*]
VPL............ Volunteer Prison League [*Defunct*]   (EA)
VPL............ Vulcano Piano [*Lipari Islands*] [*Seismograph station code, US Geological Survey*]   (SEIS)
VPLCC ...... Vehicle Propellant Loading Control Center
VPLS .... Vice-President of the Linnaean Society [*British*]
VPM ... Vacuum Pumping Module
VPM ... Variation per Minute [*Navigation*]
VPM ... Vascular Permeability Mediator [*Hematology*]
VPM ... Vehicle Project Manager [*NASA*]   (NASA)
VPM ... Vehicles per Mile
VPM ... Velocity Preset Module   (MCD)
VPM ... Vendor Part Modification   (AAG)
VPM ... Versatile Packaging Machine
VPM ... Vertical Panel Mount
VPM ... Vertical Polarization Mode
VPM ... Vibrations per Minute
VPM ... Voix du Peuple Murundi [*Voice of the Murundi People*]
VPM ... Volts per Meter [*Also, V/m*]
VPM ... Volts per Mil
VPM ... Volumes per Million [*Measure of gas contamination*]
VPMA .... Vegetable Parchment Manufacturers Association [*Later, API*]   (EA)
VPMLL ...... Valstybine Politines ir Mokslines Literatu [*A publication*]
VPMOS ...... Verified Primary Military Occupational Specialty
VPMR .... Vanguard Party of the Malagasy Revolution
VPMS .... Virchow-Pirquet Medical Society [*Formed by a merger of Pirquet Society of Clinical Medicine and Rudolph Virchow Society*] [*New York, NY*]   (EA)
VPN .... Vendor Parts Number
VPN .... Vickers Pyramid Number [*Hardness test*]
VPN .... Victorian Periodicals Newsletter [*A publication*]
VPN .... Virtual Page Number
VPN .... Vopnafjordur [*Iceland*] [*Airport symbol*]   (OAG)
VPNL .... Variable Pulse Neodymium LASER
VPO .... Vapor Phase Oxidation [*Chemical processing*]
VPO .... Vapor Pressure Osmometer
VPO .... Vienna Philharmonic Orchestra
VPO .... Viking Project Office [*NASA*]   (KSC)
VPOF......... Vacuum-Processed Oxide Free
VPP .... Vacuum Pickup Pencil
VPP .... Value Payable by Post
VPP .... Variable Pitch Propeller
VPP .... Vertical Pinpoint   (AFM)
VPP .... Vertical Pouch Packager
VPP .... Very Public Person
VPP .... Viral Porcine Pneumonia [*Veterinary medicine*]
V P-P .... Volt Peak-to-Peak   (NASA)
VPPB......... Vendor Provisioning Parts Breakdown   (AAG)
VPPD......... Vice Presidential Protective Division [*US Secret Service*]
VPR .... Valveless Pulse Rocket
VPR .... Vaporize   (MSA)
VPR .... Variable Parameter Regression [*Statistics*]
VPR .... Ventricle Pressure Response [*Cardiology*]
VPR .... Virtual PPI [*Plan-Position Indicator*] Reflectoscope [*RADAR*]
VPR .... Vital Pacific Resources Ltd. [*Vancouver Stock Exchange symbol*]
VPR .... Voluntary Price Reduction   (AABC)
VPRC......... Volume of Packed Red Cells [*Hematology*]
VPRF......... Variable Pulse Repetition Frequency   (IEEE)
VPRGS ...... Vice-President of the Royal Geographical Society [*British*]
VPRI .... Vice-President of the Royal Institute [*British*]
VPR-NMP ... Virtual PPI [*Plan-Position Indicator*] Reflectoscope with Navigational Microfilm Projector [*RADAR*]
VPRON....... US Navy Patrol Squadron   (CINC)
VPRS .... Vice-President of the Royal Society [*British*]
VPRT......... Vector Pressure Ratio Transducer
VPS .... Fort Walton Beach [*Florida*] [*Airport symbol*]   (OAG)
VP(S) .... US Navy Patrol Squadron (Sea-Based)   (CINC)
VPS .... Vacuum Pickup System
VPS .... Vacuum Pipe Still [*Chemical engineering*]
VPS .... Vacuum Pump System
VPS .... Valparaiso, FL [*Location identifier*] [*FAA*]   (FAAL)
VPS .... Vanguard Planning Summary [*Air Force*]
VPS .... Variable Parameter System
VPS .... Variable Power Supply   (MCD)
VPS .... Vatican Philatelic Society   (EA)
VPS .... Vernier Propulsion System [*Aerospace*]
VPS .... Vibrations per Second
VPS .... Vibrator Power Supply
VPS .... Video-Pac Systems Ltd. [*Hollywood, CA*] [*Telecommunications service*]   (TSSD)
VPS .... Vinylpolysilane [*Organic chemistry*]
VPS .... Visual Programs Systems
VPS .... Volcan Poas [*Costa Rica*] [*Seismograph station code, US Geological Survey*]   (SEIS)
VPS .... Voluntary Product Standard [*National Bureau of Standards*]
VPSA......... Vice-President of the Society of Antiquaries [*British*]
VPSB......... Veterans Placement Service Board [*Post-World War II*]

VPSS......... Vector Processing Subsystem
VPSW........ Virtual Program Status Word
VPT .... Patrol Torpedo Plane [*Navy symbol*]
VPT .... Ventral Posterior Thalamic [*Electrode for stimulation*]
VPT .... Vibratron Pressure Transducer
VPT .... Video Pulse Termination
VPT .... Voice plus Telegraph [*Telecommunications*]   (TEL)
VPT .... Volume-Price Trend [*Finance*]
VPTAR ...... Variable Parameter Terrain-Avoidance RADAR
VPTRM...... Viscous Partial Thermoremanent Magnetization [*Geophysics*]
VPU .... Pace University Library, Union List of Serials, New York, NY [*OCLC symbol*]   (OCLC)
VPU .... Vacuum Penetration Unit
VPU .... Vibrator Power Unit   (MSA)
VPUA........ Vibration Pickup Amplifier
VPVCPr..... Vincristine, Prednisone, Vinblastine, Chlorambucil, Procarbazine [*Antineoplastic drug regimen*]
VPW .... Vertically Polarized Wave
VPW .... Vorarbeiten zum Pommerschen Woerterbuch [*A publication*]
VPX .... Pineville, WV [*Location identifier*] [*FAA*]   (FAAL)
VPY .... Vinylpyridine [*Organic chemistry*]
VPZ .... Valparaiso [*Indiana*] [*Airport symbol*]   (OAG)
VPZ .... Valparaiso, IN [*Location identifier*] [*FAA*]   (FAAL)
VPZ .... Virtual Processing Zero
VPZS .... Vice-President of the Zoological Society [*British*]
VQ .... Aermediterranea Linee Aeree Mediterranee SpA [*Italy*] [*ICAO designator*]   (FAAC)
VQ .... Fleet Air Reconnaissance Squadron [*Navy symbol*]   (CINC)
VQ .... United Kingdom Colonies and Protectorates [*Aircraft nationality and registration mark*]   (FAAC)
V/Q .... Ventilation/Perfusion [*Quotient*] [*Medicine*]
VQ .... Vermont Quarterly [*A publication*]
VQ .... Very Quick [*Flashing*] Light [*Navigation signal*]
VQ .... Virtual Quantum
VQ .... Visvabharati Quarterly [*A publication*]
VQ .... Voluntary Quit [*Unemployment insurance*] [*Bureau of Labor Statistics*]   (OICC)
VQA.......... Al Sigl Center Library, Rochester, NY [*OCLC symbol*]   (OCLC)
VQA.......... Vendor Quality Assurance
VQAR .... Vendor Quality Assurance Representative [*Nuclear energy*]   (NRCH)
VQB.......... Bausch & Lomb, Inc., Library, Rochester, NY [*OCLC symbol*]   (OCLC)
VQC.......... Canandaigua Veterans Administration Medical Center Library, Canandaigua, NY [*OCLC symbol*]   (OCLC)
VQC.......... Variable Quartz Capacitor
VQC.......... Vendor Quality Certification
VQD.......... Center for Governmental Research Library, Rochester, NY [*OCLC symbol*]   (OCLC)
VQD.......... Vendor Quality Defect
VQE.......... Colgate-Rochester Divinity School, Library, Rochester, NY [*OCLC symbol*]   (OCLC)
VQE.......... San Antonio, TX [*Location identifier*] [*FAA*]   (FAAL)
VQF.......... Convalescent Hospital for Children, Library, Rochester, NY [*OCLC symbol*]   (OCLC)
VQG.......... Eastman Dental Center, B. G. Bibby Library, Rochester, NY [*OCLC symbol*]   (OCLC)
VQH.......... Eastman Kodak Co., KAD Library, Rochester, NY [*OCLC symbol*]   (OCLC)
VQI .... Eastman Kodak Co., Business Library, Rochester, NY [*OCLC symbol*]   (OCLC)
VQJ .... Eastman Kodak Co., Engineering Division, Library, Rochester, NY [*OCLC symbol*]   (OCLC)
VQK.......... Eastman Kodak Co., Health and Safety Laboratory, Library, Rochester, NY [*OCLC symbol*]   (OCLC)
V Qk Fl ...... Very-Quick Flashing Light
VQL.......... Eastman Kodak Co., Photographic Technology Library, Rochester, NY [*OCLC symbol*]   (OCLC)
VQM.......... Detroit, MI [*Location identifier*] [*FAA*]   (FAAL)
VQM.......... Eastman Kodak Co., Research Laboratories, Library, Rochester, NY [*OCLC symbol*]   (OCLC)
VQMG .... Vice-Quartermaster-General
VQN.......... General Railway Signal Co., Library, Rochester, NY [*OCLC symbol*]   (OCLC)
VQO.......... Genesee Hospital, Stabins Health Science Library, Rochester, NY [*OCLC symbol*]   (OCLC)
VQO.......... Provincetown, MA [*Location identifier*] [*FAA*]   (FAAL)
VQP.......... Highland Hospital, Williams Health Science Library, Rochester, NY [*OCLC symbol*]   (OCLC)
VQQ.......... Mixing Equipment Co., Library, Rochester, NY [*OCLC symbol*]   (OCLC)
VQR.......... Virginia Quarterly Review [*A publication*]
VQS.......... Isla De Vieques, PR [*Location identifier*] [*FAA*]   (FAAL)
VQS.......... Mobil Chemical Co., Plastics Division, Research Library, Macedon, NY [*OCLC symbol*]   (OCLC)
VQS.......... Valve Qualification Study
VQS.......... Vieques [*Puerto Rico*] [*Later, SJG*] [*Geomagnetic observatory code*]
VQS.......... Vieques [*Puerto Rico*] [*Seismograph station code, US Geological Survey*] [*Closed*]   (SEIS)
VQS.......... Vieques [*Puerto Rico*] [*Airport symbol*]   (OAG)

VQT .... Monroe Community College, L. V. Good Library, Rochester, NY [*OCLC symbol*]   (OCLC)
VQT .... Viewers for Quality Television   (EA)
VQU........... Monroe Community Hospital, Medical-Nursing Library, Rochester, NY [*OCLC symbol*]   (OCLC)
VQV........... Monroe County Department of Health, Library, Rochester, NY [*OCLC symbol*]   (OCLC)
VQV........... Vacaville, CA [*Location identifier*] [*FAA*]   (FAAL)
VQW.......... Monroe Development Center, Library, Rochester, NY [*OCLC symbol*]   (OCLC)
VQX........... Park Ridge Hospital, Medical Library, Rochester, NY [*OCLC symbol*]   (OCLC)
VQY........... Pennwalt Corp., Pharmaceutical Division, Library, Rochester, NY [*OCLC symbol*]   (OCLC)
VQZ........... R. T. French Co., Library, Rochester, NY [*OCLC symbol*]   (OCLC)
VQZD .... Vendor Quality Zero Defects
VR.............. Fleet Tactical Support [*Navy symbol*]   (NVT)
VR.............. Transport Plane [*Multiengine*] [*Navy symbol*]
VR.............. Transport Squadron [*Navy symbol*]
VR.............. Transportes Aereos de Cabo Verde [*Portugal*] [*ICAO designator*]   (FAAC)
VR.............. United Kingdom Colonies and Protectorates [*Aircraft nationality and registration mark*]   (FAAC)
VR.............. Vagabonds Removed [*Prison van nickname used during reign of VR, Victoria Regina*] [*British*]   (DSUE)
VR.............. Vale of Rheidol Light Railway [*Wales*]
V of R......... Vale of Rheidol Light Railway [*Wales*]
VR.............. Validation and Recovery
VR.............. Validation Report [*Army*]
VR.............. Valley Resources, Inc. [*American Stock Exchange symbol*]
VR.............. Valtionrautatiet [*Finnish State Railways*]
VR.............. Valuation Reports, Interstate Commerce Commission   (DLA)
VR.............. Valve Replacement [*Cardiology*]
VR.............. Vanguardia Revolucionaria [*Revolutionary Vanguard*] [*Peruvian*]   (PPW)
VR.............. Variable Ratio [*Reinforcement*]
VR.............. Variable Reluctance
VR.............. Variant Reading
VR.............. Veer [*Aviation*]   (FAAC)
VR.............. Vehicle Recovery
VR.............. Velocity, Relative   (MCD)
VR.............. Vendor Rating
VR.............. Venous Return [*Medicine*]
VR.............. Ventilation Rate
VR.............. Ventral Root [*of a spinal nerve*] [*Anatomy*]
VR.............. Ventricular Rate [*Cardiology*]
VR.............. Verb Reflexive
VR.............. Verification Receiver
V-R .... VERLORT [*Very-Long-Range Tracking*] Range [*NASA*]
VR.............. Vermont Reports   (DLA)
VR.............. Vertical Retort
VR.............. Very Respectfully [*Letter closing*]
VR.............. Veterinary and Remount Services [*Military*] [*British*]
VR.............. VFR [*Visual Flight Rules*] Military Training Routes [*Aviation*]   (FAAC)
VR.............. Viata Romaneasca [*Bucharest*] [*A publication*]
V-R .... Vibrational-Rotational [*Chemical kinetics*]
VR.............. Vicar Rural
VR.............. Victoria Regina [*Queen Victoria*]
VR.............. Victorian Reports [*A publication*]
VR.............. Video Recorder   (NASA)
VR.............. Viera i Razum [*A publication*]
VR.............. Villanova Law Review [*A publication*]
VR.............. Vision, Right Eye
VR.............. Visit Request   (AAG)
VR.............. Visor
VR.............. Visual Reconnaissance
VR.............. Visual Resources [*A publication*]
VR.............. Vital Records [*Genealogy*]
VR.............. Vocal Resonance
VR.............. Vocational Rehabilitation
VR.............. Voice of Reason [*An association*]   (EA)
VR.............. Volja Rossii [*A publication*]
VR.............. Voltage Reference   (DEN)
VR.............. Voltage Regulator
VR.............. Voltage Relay
VR.............. Volume Reduction [*Nuclear energy*]   (NRCH)
VR.............. Voluntary Returnees [*Immigration Service*]
VR.............. Volunteer Reserve   (BJA)
VR.............. Vox Romanica [*A publication*]
VR.............. Voyage Repairs [*Navy*]   (NVT)
Vr.............. Vroom's Law Reports [*30-85 New Jersey Law*]   (DLA)
VR.............. Vulcanized Rubber
VR.............. Vulnerability Reduction [*Military*]   (RDA)
VR.............. Webb, A'Beckett, and Williams' Victorian Reports [*1870-72*] [*Australia*]   (DLA)
VRA............ Radford College, Radford, VA [*OCLC symbol*]   (OCLC)
VRA............ Rough-Air [*or Turbulence*] Speed [*Aviation*]
VRA............ Varadero [*Cuba*] [*Airport symbol*]   (OAG)
VRA .... Vertical Reference Attitude

VRA .... Vertical Rising Aircraft
VRA .... Veterans Readjustment Appointment
VRA .... [*The*] Victorian Railways of Australia
VRA .... Viking RADAR Altimeter [*NASA*]
VRA .... Vocational Rehabilitation Act [*1973*]
VRA .... Vocational Rehabilitation Administration [*Became Social and Rehabilitation Service*] [*HEW*]
VRA .... Vocational Rehabilitation Association
VRA .... Voltage Reference Amplifier
VRA .... Voltage Regulator Alarm
VRA .... Voluntary Restraint Arrangement [*Import quotas*]
VRA .... Voluntary Restriction Agreement [*Pact between the US and Japan on automotive imports*]
VRA .... Voting Rights Act [*1965, 1970, 1975*]
Vrach Delo ... Vrachebnoe Delo [*A publication*]
Vrach Gaz .... Vrachebnaia Gazeta [*A publication*]
VRAD .... Vertically Referenced Attitude Display
VR Adm...... Victorian Reports, Admiralty [*Aus.*] (DLA)
VRAH......... Vertical Receiving Array Hydrophone
VRAM........ Variable Random Access Memory [*Data processing*]
VRAM........ Variable Rate Adaptive Multiplexing [*Telecommunications*] (TEL)
VRAM........ Video Random Access Memory
VRAM........ Virtual Random Access Memory [*Data processing*]
Vrashchenie i Prilivnye Deform Zemli ... Vrashchenie i Prilivnye Deformatsii Zemli [*A publication*]
VRASS .... Voice Recognition and Synthesis System [*Aviation*] [*Navy*]
VRB .... Variable
VRB .... Variable Reenlistment Bonus [*Military*] (AABC)
VRB .... Vehicle Retaining Board
VRB .... Vero Beach [*Florida*] [*Airport symbol*] (OAG)
VRB .... Vero Beach, FL [*Location identifier*] [*FAA*] (FAAL)
VRB .... VHF [*Very-High-Frequency*] Recovery Beacon [*NASA*] (KSC)
VRB .... Violet Red Bile [*Microorganism growth medium*]
VRB .... Voice Rotating Beacon
VRB .... Volunteer Reenlistment Bonus
VRBA......... Violet Red Bile Agar [*Microorganism growth medium*]
VRBL......... Variable (FAAC)
VRBM........ Variable Range Ballistic Missile [*DoD*] (MCD)
VRC .... Fleet Tactical Support Squadron Carrier [*Navy symbol*] (CINC)
VRC .... Vampire Research Center (EA)
VRC .... Varco International, Inc. [*NYSE symbol*]
VRC .... Variable Reluctance Cartridge
VRC .... Vehicle Research Corporation
VRC .... Vertical Redundancy Check (BUR)
VRC .... Vibrating Reed Capacitor
VRC .... Virac [*Philippines*] [*Airport symbol*] (OAG)
VRC .... Virginia Commonwealth University, Richmond, VA [*OCLC symbol*] (OCLC)
VRC .... Virtual Redundancy Check [*Data processing*]
VRC .... Viscometer Recorder-Controller
VRC .... Visual Record Computer
VR & C....... Vocational Rehabilitation and Counseling Service [*Veterans Administration*]
VRC .... Volunteer Rifle Corps [*Military*] [*British*] (ROG)
VRCA .... Voice Recording Assembly [*Ground Communications Facility, NASA*]
VRCAMS.... Vehicle-Road Compatibility Analysis and Modification System (RDA)
VRCCC....... Vandenberg Range Communications Control Center [*Air Force*] (MCD)
VRCI.......... Variable Resistive Components Institute [*Evanston, IL*] (EA)
VRCTR ...... Varactor (MSA)
VRD .... Vacuum-Tube Relay Driver
VRD .... Voltage Regulating Diode
VRD .... Volunteer Reserve Decoration [*British*]
VRDDO...... Variable Retention of Diatomic Differential [*Physics*]
VRDEA ...... Vrachebnoe Delo [*A publication*]
VRDS........ Vacuum Residuum Desulfurization [*Petroleum refining*]
VRDX......... Verdix Corp. [*NASDAQ symbol*] (NQ)
VRE .... Vermont Research Corp. [*American Stock Exchange symbol*]
VRE .... Vibrating Reed Electrometer
VR (E)........ Victorian Reports (Equity) [*A publication*]
VRE .... Voltage Regulator-Exciter
VR (E)........ Webb, A'Beckett, and Williams' Victorian Equity Reports [*1870-72*] [*Australia*] (DLA)
Vrednaya Polezn Fauna Bespozvon Mold ... Vrednaya i Poleznaya Fauna Bespozvonochnykh Moldavii [*A publication*]
V/REG .... Voltage Regulator [*Automotive engineering*]
Vremennik Gl Palaty Mer Vesov ... Vremennik Glavnoi Palaty Mer i Vesov [*A publication*]
VR (Eq) ...... Victorian Reports [*Equity*] [*A publication*]
VRES.......... Vicorp Restaurants [*NASDAQ symbol*] (NQ)
V Rev.......... Very Reverend
VRF .... Ferry Squadron [*Navy symbol*] (NVT)
VRF .... Vascular Research Foundation
VRF .... Versatile Repair Facility
VRF .... Vertical Removal Fixture (NASA)
VRF .... Vietnam Refugee Fund [*McLean, VA*] (EA)
VRF .... Visual Recording Facility (MCD)
VRFI .... Voice Reporting Fault Indicator

VRFWS...... Vehicle Rapid Fire Weapon System [*Army*]
VRFWSS .... Vehicle Rapid-Fire Weapons System Successor (IEEE)
VRFY .... Verify (MSA)
VRG .... Visual Reference Gate [*Aviation*] (FAAC)
VRG .... Vocationally Related Annual Goal
VRGC .... Voucher Register and General Control [*Military*] (AABC)
VRGN .... Viragen, Inc. [*NASDAQ symbol*] (NQ)
VRH .... Var-Hour Meter [*Electricity*]
VRH .... Vertical Receiving Hydrophone
VR(HL) .... Transport, Four-Engine, Landplane [*Navy symbol*]
VRHMU ...... Visor Rectical Helmet Mounted Unit [*Navy*] (MCD)
VR(HS) .... Transport, Four-Engine, Seaplane [*Navy symbol*]
VRI............ Varistor [*Telecommunications*] (TEL)
VRI............ Vehicle Research Institute [*Society of Automotive Engineers*]
VRI............ Verbal Response Inventory
VRI............ Veterans Reopened Insurance
VR et I....... Victoria Regina et Imperatrix [*Victoria, Queen and Empress*]
VRI............ Victoria Regina et Imperatrix [*Victoria, Queen and Empress*]
VRI............ Viral Respiratory Infection [*Medicine*]
VRI............ Visual Rule Instrument Landing (AAG)
VRI............ Vrincioaia [*Romania*] [*Seismograph station code, US Geological Survey*] (SEIS)
VRI............ Vulcanized Rubber Installation
VR (IE & M) ... Victorian Reports (Insolvency, Ecclesiastical, and Matrimonial) [*A publication*]
VR (IE & M) ... Webb, A'Beckett, and Williams' Insolvency, Ecclesiastical, and Matrimonial Reports [*1870-72*] [*Victoria, Australia*]
Vrije Univ Brussel Inter-Univ Inst High Energ Rep ... Vrije Universiteit Brussel. Inter-University Institute for High Energies. Report [*A publication*]
VRIS .... Varistor [*Electronics*]
VRIS .... Vietnam Refugee and Information Services
VRISL........ Vancouver Island, BC, Canada (FAAC)
VRJa.......... Voprosy Russkogo Jazykoznanija [*A publication*]
VRK .... Varkaus [*Finland*] [*Airport symbol*] (OAG)
VRK .... Video Recorder Kit
VRL .... Validation Reject Listing (MCD)
VRL .... Vanterra Resources Limited [*Vancouver Stock Exchange symbol*]
VRL .... Vertical Recovery Line [*NASA*] (NASA)
VRL .... Vertical Reference Line [*Technical drawings*]
VRL .... Vibration Research Laboratory [*Stanford University*] (MCD)
VR (L) .... Victorian Reports (Law) [*A publication*]
VRL .... Vila Real [*Portugal*] [*Airport symbol*] (OAG)
VRL .... Virus Reference Laboratory
VR (Law) ..... Victorian Law Reports [*Law*] [*A publication*]
VRLN......... Varlen Corp. [*NASDAQ symbol*] (NQ)
VRLTRY .... Vale of Rheidol Light Railway [*Wales*]
VRLY .... Voltage Relay
VRM .... Randolph-Macon College, Ashland, VA [*OCLC symbol*] (OCLC)
VRM .... Variable Range Marker
VRM .... Variable-Rate Mortgage
VRM .... Variable Reluctance Microphone
VRM .... Vendor Receiving Memo
VRM .... Venus RADAR Mapper [*Planetary exploration*]
VRM .... Viscous Remanant Magnetization
VRM .... Voltage Regulator Module
VR(ML) ...... Transport, Two-Engine, Landplane [*Navy symbol*]
VR(MS) ...... Transport, Two-Engine, Seaplane [*Navy symbol*]
VRMS......... Voltage Root Mean Square
VRN .... Vernier [*Engine*] (AAG)
VRN .... Vernitron Corp. [*American Stock Exchange symbol*]
VRN .... Verona [*Italy*] [*Airport symbol*] (OAG)
VR Newsletter ... Victorian Railways Newsletter [*A publication*]
VRO .... Roanoke College, Salem, VA [*OCLC symbol*] (OCLC)
VRO .... Variable Ratio Oiling
VRO .... Varo, Inc. [*NYSE symbol*]
VRO .... Verified Record Output [*Data processing*]
VRo .... Viata Romaneasca [*A publication*]
VROA .... Verslagen Omtrent's Rijks Oude Archieven [*A publication*]
VROC .... Vertical Rate of Climb [*Aviation*]
VROM........ Vocabulary Read-Only Memory [*Data processing*]
VROOM ..... Vintage Racers of Old Motorcycles (EA)
Vroom .... Vroom's Law Reports (DLA)
Vroom (G D W) ... [*G. D. W.*] Vroom's Law Reports [*36-63 New Jersey*] (DLA)
Vroom (NJ) ... Vroom's Law Reports [*30-85 New Jersey*] (DLA)
Vroom (P D) ... P. D. Vroom's Law Reports [*30-35 New Jersey*] (DLA)
VRP .... Richmond Public Library, Richmond, VA [*OCLC symbol*] (OCLC)
VRP .... Vapor Reheat Process
VRP .... Variable Reluctance Pickup
VRP .... Vector-to-Raster Processor [*Computer graphics terminology*]
VRP .... Ventral Root Potential [*Neurophysiology*]
VRP .... Vestra Reverendissima Paternitas [*Your Very Reverend Paternity*] [*Latin*]
VRP .... Visual Record Printer

VR-PC .... Vanguardia Revolucionaria - Proletario Comunista [*Revolutionary Vanguard - Proletarian Communist*] [*Peruvian*] (PPW)
VRPF .... Voltage-Regulated Plate Filament
VRPS .... Vintage Radio and Phonograph Society (EA)
VRPS .... Voltage-Regulated Power Supply
VRR .... Rochester Regional Research Library Council, Rochester, NY [*OCLC symbol*] (OCLC)
VRR .... Valley Railroad
VRR .... Verification Readiness Review (NASA)
VRR .... Vero Aero [*Vero Beach, FL*] [*FAA designator*] (FAAC)
VRR .... Veterans Reemployment Rights
VRR .... Vibrating Reed Relay
VRR .... Visual Radio Range
VRR .... Visual Rapid Reorder (MCD)
VRRC .... Vehicle Radio Remote Control
VRRI .... Vocational and Rehabilitation Research Institute [*University of Calgary*] [*Research center*] (RCD)
VRS .... Rochester 3R's Union List of Serials, Rochester, NY [*OCLC symbol*] (OCLC)
VRS .... Vacuum Relief System [*Nuclear energy*] (NRCH)
VRS .... Vehicle Registration System [*Army*]
VRS .... Vehicular RADIAC [*Radioactivity Detection, Indication, and Computation*] System
VRS .... Velocity Response Shape (CET)
VRS .... Video Reception System
VRS .... Video Relay System
VRS .... Visual Reference System
VRS .... Visual Response System
VRS .... Vocational Rehabilitation Services
VRS .... Voice Recording Subsystem
VRS .... Volume Reduction and Solidification [*Hazardous waste disposal*]
VRS .... Volunteer Reserve Section
VRS .... Vortex Rate Sensor
VRSA .... Versa Technologies, Inc. [*NASDAQ symbol*] (NQ)
VRSA .... Voice Reporting Signal Assembly
VRSP .... Voltage Regulator Supervisory Panel (MCD)
VRSS .... Voice Reporting Signal System
VRT .... Vacuum Rectifying Tube
VRT .... Variable Reluctance Transducer
VRT .... Vernon, TX [*Location identifier*] [*FAA*] (FAAL)
VRT .... Vertipile, Inc. [*American Stock Exchange symbol*]
VRT .... Visual Recognition Threshold
VRT .... Vocational Rehabilitation Therapist
VRT .... Voltage Reference Tube
VRT .... Voltage Regulator Tube
VRTC .... Vehicle Research and Test Center [*National Highway Traffic Safety Administration*]
V-RTIF .... Vandenberg Real Time Interface (MCD)
VRTMOTN ... Vertical Motion (FAAC)
VRTX .... Vortec Corp. [*NASDAQ symbol*] (NQ)
VRTY .... Variety (MSA)
VRU .... University of Richmond, Richmond, VA [*OCLC symbol*] (OCLC)
VRU .... Velocity Reference Unit
VRU .... Vertical Reference Unit (MCD)
VRU .... Virtual Resource Unit (MCD)
VRU .... Voice Response Unit
VRU .... Voltage Readout Unit
VRU .... Vryburg [*South Africa*] [*Airport symbol*] (OAG)
VRV .... Vacuum Regulator Valve [*Automotive engineering*]
VRV .... Viper Retrovirus
VRX .... Vestor Exploration [*Vancouver Stock Exchange symbol*]
VRX .... Virtual Resource Executive [*Software*] [*NCR Corp.*]
VRY .... Fayetteville/Fort Bragg, NC [*Location identifier*] [*FAA*] (FAAL)
VRY .... Vaeroy [*Norway*] [*Airport symbol*] (OAG)
VRYG .... Varying
VS .... Air Antisubmarine Squadron [*Navy*]
VS .... Intercontinental Airlines Ltd. [*Nigeria*] [*ICAO designator*] (FAAC)
VS .... La Vie Spirituelle [*Paris*] [*A publication*]
VS .... Search Plane [*Navy symbol*]
VS .... Shore-Based Search Squadron [*Navy symbol*]
VS .... Single Vibrations [*Half cycles*]
VS .... Staging Velocity [*NASA*] (NASA)
VS .... Vaccination Scar [*Medicine*]
VS .... Vacuum Switch
VS .... Vaginal Stroma
VS .... Valley & Siletz Railroad Co. [*AAR code*]
VS .... Vapor Seal [*Technical drawings*]
VS .... Vapor Suppression [*Nuclear energy*] (NRCH)
VS .... Variable Speed (IEEE)
VS .... Variable Sweep (IEEE)
VS .... Vectoring Service
VS .... Vegan Society (EA-IO)
VS .... Vehicle Station [*NASA*] (KSC)
VS .... Velocity Search (MCD)
V/S .... Vendor Supplier (MCD)
VS .... Venerable Sage [*Freemasonry*] (ROG)
VS .... Venesection [*Medicine*]

VS .... Venstresocialisterne [*Left Socialists Party*] [*Denmark*] (PPE)
VS .... Vent Stack [*Technical drawings*]
VS .... Ventilation System [*NASA*]
VS .... Ventral Subiculum [*Brain anatomy*]
VS .... Venture Capital/Special Situations [*Business and trade*]
VS .... Verbal Scale
VS .... Verbum Salutis [*Paris*] [*A publication*]
VS .... Vergilian Society (EA)
VS .... Vermont Statutes (DLA)
VS .... Vernacular Society (EA)
V & S .... Vernon and Scriven's Irish King's Bench Reports [*1786-88*] (DLA)
VS .... Verse
VS .... Versus [*Against*] [*Latin*]
VS .... Vertical [*Activity*] Sensor [*Physiology*]
VS .... Vertical Speed [*Aviation*]
VS .... Vertical Stereoscopic [*Photograph*]
VS .... Vertical Stripes [*Navigation markers*]
VS .... Vertical System [*Government arrangement*] (OICC)
VS .... Very Small Inclusions [*Diamond clarity grade*]
VS .... Very Soluble
VS .... Very Superior
VS .... Vesicular Sound [*in auscultation of chest*] [*Medicine*]
VS .... Vesicular Stomatitis [*Also, VSV*] [*Virus*]
V of S .... Veterans of Safety (EA)
VS .... Veterinary Surgeon
VS .... Vibration Seconds
VS .... Victorian Society (EA)
VS .... Victorian Studies [*A publication*]
VS .... Vida Sobrenatural [*A publication*]
VS .... Vide Supra [*See Above*] [*Latin*]
VS .... Videnskabs Selskapet Skrifter [*A publication*]
VS .... Videnskapsselskapets Skrifter. Kristiana [*A publication*]
VS .... Video Selection
vs. .... Vietnam, South [*vm (Vietnam) used in records cataloged after January 1978*] [*MARC country of publication code*] [*Library of Congress*] (LCCP)
VS .... Vieux Style [*Old Style*] [*French*]
VS .... Villas
VS .... Violoncello Society (EA)
VS .... Virgil Society (EA)
VS .... Virtual Storage [*Data processing*]
VS .... Virtual System
VS .... Visceral Sinus
VS .... Visible Supply
VS .... Visual Signaling [*Military*]
VS .... Visual Storage [*Data processing*]
VS .... Visum Siccum [*Seen in a Dried State*] [*Botany*] (ROG)
VS .... Vitae Sophistarum [*of Philostratus*] [*Classical studies*] (OCD)
VS .... Vital Signs [*Medicine*]
VS .... Vivisection
VS .... Vocal Students Practice Aid Records [*Record label*]
VS .... Vocal Synthesis
VS .... Voicespondence Club (EA)
VS .... Volatile Solids [*Environmental science*]
VS .... Voltaire Society (EA)
VS .... Volti Subito [*Turn Over Quickly*] [*Music*]
VS .... Voltmeter Switch (MSA)
VS .... Volumetric Solution
VS .... Voluntary Sterilization
VS .... Votre Seigneurie [*Your Lordship*] [*French*]
VS .... Vulcan Society (EA)
V2S .... V-Groove on Two Sides [*Lumber*]
VSA .... By Visual Reference to the Ground [*Aviation*] (FAAC)
VSA .... Vancouver School of Art
VSA .... Variable Stability Aircraft (NASA)
VSA .... Variant-Specific Surface Antigen [*Genetics, immunology*]
VSA .... Vehicle Security Association [*Lanham, MD*] (EA)
VSA .... Velocity Sensor Antenna
VSA .... Vereinigung Schweizerischer Angestelltenverbande [*Federation of Swiss Employees' Societies*]
VSA .... Verification Site Approval (MCD)
VSA .... Vernier Solo Accumulator [*Aerospace*] (AAG)
VSA .... Vertical Sensor Assembly
VSA .... Very Special Arts [*An association*] [*Washington, DC*] (EA)
VSA .... Vibrating String Accelerometer
VSA .... Victorian Society in America (EA)
VSA .... Videocom Satellite Associates [*Dedham, MA*] [*Telecommunications*] (TSSD)
VSA .... Videographic Systems of America, Inc. [*New York, NY*] [*Information service*] [*Ceased operation*] (EISS)
VSA .... Villahermosa [*Mexico*] [*Airport symbol*] (OAG)
VSA .... Vintage Sailplane Association (EA)
VSA .... Violin Society of America (EA)
VSA .... Violin Society of America. Journal [*A publication*]
VSA .... Viscoelastic Stress Analysis
VSA .... Voltage-Sensitive Amplifier
VSA/1800 ... Volvo Sports America 1800 [*An association*] (EA)
VSAD .... Vacuum Spark Advance Disconnect [*Auto air pollution control device*]
V/SAF .... Vulnerability and Survivability of the Armed Forces (MCD)

VSAL......... Visual Technology [*NASDAQ symbol*] (NQ)
VSAM......... Virtual Sequential Access Method
VSAM......... Virtual Storage Access Method [*Data processing*]
VSAM......... Virtual System Access Method
VSAV......... Vydavtel'stvo Slovenskej Akademie Vied [*A publication*]
VSB.......... Scout-Bombing Plane [*Navy symbol*]
VSB.......... Sweet Briar College Library, Sweet Briar, VA [*OCLC symbol*] (OCLC)
VSB.......... Venae Sectio Brachii [*Bleeding in the Arm*] [*Pharmacy*] (ROG)
VSB.......... Vent and Supply Bay
VSB.......... Vestigial Sideband [*Radio*]
VSB.......... Visible (FAAC)
VSB.......... Volunteer Services for the Blind (EA)
VSB-AM .... Vestigial Sideband - Amplitude Modulation
VSBD-PdA ... Volkssozialistische Bewegung Deutschlands - Partei der Arbeit [*People's Socialist Movement of Germany - Party of Labor*] [*West Germany*] (PD)
VSBF......... Vestigial Sideband Filter
VSBL......... Visible (MSA)
VSBS........ Very Small Business System
VSBY........ Visibility [*Aviation*] (FAAC)
VSBYDR.... Visibility Decreasing Rapidly [*Aviation*] (FAAC)
VSBYIR ..... Visibility Increasing Rapidly [*Aviation*] (FAAC)
VSC......... Valdosta State College [*Georgia*]
VSC......... Variable Speech Control [*Device that permits distortion-free rapid playback of speech recorded on tape*]
VSC......... Variable Speed Chopper
VSC......... Varnville [*South Carolina*] [*Seismograph station code, US Geological Survey*] (SEIS)
VSC......... Vehicle Sectoring Code
VSC......... Vehicle System Control
VSC......... Vendor Shipping Configuration (AAG)
VSC......... Ventral Spinal Cord [*Anatomy*]
VSC......... Vermont State College
VSC......... Vibration Safety Cutoff [*NASA*] (KSC)
VSC......... Vidicon Camera System (MCD)
V-S/C........ Viking Spacecraft [*NASA*]
VSC......... Vincentian Sisters of Charity [*Roman Catholic religious order*]
VSC......... Virginia State College
VSC......... Virginia State College, Petersburg, VA [*OCLC symbol*] (OCLC)
VSC......... Virtual Subscriber Computer
VSC......... Vocations for Social Change [*Employment clearinghouse*] [*Defunct*] (EA)
VSC......... Volatile Sulfur Compound [*Chemistry*]
VSC......... Voltage-Saturated Capacitor
VSC......... Volunteer Staff Corps [*British*] (ROG)
VSCA .... Vacation and Senior Citizens Association (EA)
VSCA .... Vietnamese Senior Citizens Association (EA)
VSCC .... Voltage-Sensitive Calcium Channel [*Physiology*]
VSCCA ...... Vintage Sports Car Club of America (EA)
VSCDF ...... Vatican's Sacred Congregation for the Doctrine of the Faith
VSCE........ Variable Stream Control Engine [*NASA*] (MCD)
VSCF........ Variable Speed Constant Frequency
VSCNY ...... Vedanta Society of the City of New York (EA)
VSD......... Valve Solenoid Driver
VSD......... Variable Slope Delta
VSD......... Variable Speed Drive
VSD......... Vendor's Shipping Document
VSD......... Vendredi, Samedi, Dimanche [*A publication*]
VSD......... Ventricular Septal Defect [*Cardiology*]
VSD......... Versatile Signal Device
VSD......... Vertical Situation Display
VSD......... Video Subcarrier Detector
VSD......... Village Self-Development
VSD......... Virtually Safe Dose [*Toxicology*]
VSDA .... Video Software Dealers Association [*Cherry Hill, NJ*] (EA)
VSD/ADI .... Vertical Situation Display/Attitude Director Indicator (MCD)
VSDM....... Variable Slope Delta Modulation
VSDR........ Vieteljahrsheft zur Statistik des Deutschen Reichs [*Germany*]
VSE......... Steam Explosion in Vessel [*Nuclear energy*] (NRCH)
VSE......... Vancouver Stock Exchange [*Canada*]
VSE......... Vessel (Reactor) Steam Explosion (IEEE)
VSE......... Virtual Storage Extension [*IBM Corp.*] [*Data processing*]
Vse......... Vsesvit [*Kiev*] [*A publication*]
VSEC........ VSE Corporation [*NASDAQ symbol*] (NQ)
VSEPR....... Valence-Shell Electron Pair Repulsion [*Theory of molecular structure*]
Vses Geogr O-vo Izv ... Vsesoyuznoye Geograficheskoye Obshchestvo. Izvestiya [*A publication*]
Vses Nauchno-Issled Geol Inst Tr ... Vsesoyuznyy Nauchno-Issledovatel'skiy Geologicheskiy Institut. Trudy [*A publication*]
Vses Nauchno-Issled Geologorazved Neft Inst Tr ... Vsesoyuznyy Nauchno-Issledovatel'skiy Geologorazvedochnyi Neftyanoy Institut. Trudy [*A publication*]
Vses Nauchn O-vo Neirokhir ... Vsesoyuznoe Nauchnoe Obshchestvo Neirokhirurgii [*A publication*]
Vsesojuz Zaocn Politehn Inst Sb Trudov ... Vsesojuznyi Zaocnyi Politehniceskii Institut. Sbornik Trudov [*A publication*]

Vsesoyunaya Nauchno Metod Konf Vet Patologoanat ... Vsesoyuznaya Nauchno-Metod Konferentsiya Veterinarnykh Patologoanatomov [*A publication*]
Vsesoyuznoe Paleont Obshch Ezhegodnik ... Vsesoyuznoe Paleontologicheskoe Obshchestyo Ezhegodnik [*A publication*]
VSF .... Antisubmarine Fighter Squadron [*Navy*]
VSF .... Springfield [*Vermont*] [*Airport symbol*] (OAG)
VSF .... Springfield, VT [*Location identifier*] [*FAA*] (FAAL)
VSF .... Vestigial Sideband Filter
VSF .... Vitreous Silica Fabric
VSF .... Voice Store and Forward [*Voice messaging*]
VSFP .... Venous Stop-Flow Pressure [*Medicine*]
VSFR........ Vertical Seismic Floor Response (IEEE)
VSG......... Variable Speed Gear (DEN)
VSG......... Variable Surface Glycoprotein [*Physiology*]
VSG......... Variant Surface Glycoprotein [*Biochemistry*]
VSG......... Vernier Step Gauge [*Aerospace*]
VSG......... Versatile Signal [*or Symbol*] Generator
VSG......... Vierteljahrsschrift fuer Sozial- und Wirtschaftsgeschichte [*A publication*]
VSH......... Village Self-Help
VSH......... Vishay Intertechnology, Inc. [*NYSE symbol*]
VSHPS ...... Vernier Solo Hydraulic Power System [*Aerospace*] (AAG)
VSI .... College of Staten Island, St. George Campus Library, Staten Island, NY [*OCLC symbol*] (OCLC)
VSI .... Vendor Shipping Instruction
VSI .... Vertical Signal [*or Situation*] Indicator [*Helicopters*]
VSI .... Vertical Situation Indicator
VSI .... Vertical Speed Indicator [*Aviation*]
VSI .... Very Seriously Ill [*Army*] (AABC)
VSI .... Video Simulation Interface (NASA)
VSI .... Video Sweep Integrator
VSI .... Videoconferencing Systems, Incorporated [*Norcross, GA*] [*Telecommunications service*] (TSSD)
VSI .... Vinyl Siding Institute [*New York, NY*] (EA)
VSI .... Vuesenoria Ilustrisima [*Your Illustrious Ladyship (or Lordship)*] [*Spanish*]
VS Ilma ..... Vossa Senhoria Ilustrissima [*Your Illustrious Lordship*] [*Portuguese*]
VSIP .... Valence State Ionization Potentials [*of atoms*]
VSJW .... Vise Jaw [*Tool*] (AAG)
VSL .... Special Libraries Cataloguing, Inc. [*UTLAS symbol*]
VSL .... Valve Signal Light
VSL .... Variable Safety Level
VSL .... Variable Specification List
VSL .... Ventilation Sampling Line (IEEE)
VSL .... Vermont State Department of Libraries, Montpelier, VT [*OCLC symbol*] (OCLC)
VSL .... Vessel (FAAC)
VSL .... Vetenskaps-Societeten i Lund [*A publication*]
VSL .... Viscous Shock Layer
VSL .... Volume of the Sacred Law [*Freemasonry*]
VSL .... VS Services Limited [*Toronto Stock Exchange symbol*]
VSLA .... Vetenskaps-Societeten i Lund Arsbok [*A publication*]
VSL Bibs .... Research Service Bibliographies. State Library of Victoria [*A publication*]
VSLE .... Very Small Local Exchange [*Telecommunications*] (TEL)
VSLI .... Veterans Special Life Insurance [*Veterans Administration*]
VSIJa......... Voprosy Slavjanskogo Jazykoznanija [*A publication*]
VSIJa (Lvov) ... Voprosy Slavjanskogo Jazykoznanija (Lvov) [*A publication*]
VSIJa (Moskva) ... Voprosy Slavjanskogo Jazykoznanija (Moskva) [*A publication*]
VSLS .... Very Slightly Soluble
VSM .... Vascular Smooth Muscle [*Anatomy*]
VSM .... Vehicle State Monitor
VSM .... Vestigial Sideband Modulation
VSM .... Vibrating Sample Magnetometer
VSM .... Video Switching Matrix (KSC)
VSM .... Vietnam Service Medal [*Military*] (AFM)
VSM .... Virtual Storage Manager (BUR)
VSM .... Virtual Storage Memory [*Data processing*] (MCD)
VSM .... Voice Switch Monitor (MCD)
VSMA .... Vibrating Screen Manufacturers Association [*Stamford, CT*] (EA)
VSMC .... Vascular Smooth Muscle Cell [*Cytology*]
VSMF .... Visual Search Microfilm File [*Trademark*] [*Data processing*]
VSMOS ..... Verified Secondary Military Occupational Specialty
VSMS .... Video Switching Matrix System
VSMS .... Vineland Social Maturity Scale [*Psychology*]
VSN........... Scout-Training Plane [*Navy symbol*]
VSN........... Video Switching Network (MCD)
VSN........... Vision
VSN........... Volume-Sequence-Number [*Data processing*]
VSN(M)....... Training Plane, 2-engine [*Navy symbol*]
VSNS .... Virgil C. Summer Nuclear Station (NRCH)
VSNY........ Vegetarian Society of New York (EA)
VSO........... Scout Observation Plane [*Navy symbol*]
VSO........... Valdosta Southern Railroad [*AAR code*]
VSO........... Verso (BJA)
VSO........... Very Special Old

VSO .... Very Stable Oscillator
VSO .... Very Superior Old [*Designation on brandy labels*]
VSO .... Voluntary Service Overseas [*Military*]
VSOE .... Venice Simplon Orient-Express [*London-to-Venice train*]
VSOP .... Very Superior Old Pale [*Designation on brandy labels. Facetious French translation is "Versez sans Oublier Personne," or "Pour without Forgetting Anyone"*]
VSP .... Vectored Slipstream Principle
VSP .... Vehicle Scheduling Program [*Data processing*]
VSP .... Vehicle Synthesis Program [*Aerospace*]
VSP .... Vertical Speed [*Aviation*]   (FAAC)
VSP .... Video Signal Processor
VSP .... Vikki's Special People [*An association*]   (EA)
VSP .... Virtual Switching Point [*Telecommunications*]   (TEL)
VSP .... Vision Service Plan National [*Formerly, VIA*] [*An association*] [*St. Louis, MO*]   (EA)
V SP .... Visum Spontaneum [*Seen Wild*] [*Botany*]   (ROG)
V SP .... Visum Sporadicum [*Seen Wild*] [*Botany*]   (ROG)
VSPA .... Vacation Spa Resorts [*NASDAQ symbol*]   (NQ)
VSPC .... Virtual Storage Personal Computing [*IBM Corp.*] [*Data processing*]
V/SPD ...... Variable Speed
VSPEP .... Vehicle Sizing and Performance Evaluation Program   (MCD)
VSPP .... Vangiya Sahitya Parisat Patrika [*A publication*]
VSPRITES ... Virtual Sprites [*Amiga computer hardware*]
VSPS .... Vernier Solo Power Supply [*Aerospace*]   (AAG)
VSPX .... Vehicle Scheduling Program Extended [*Data processing*]
VSQ .... Very Special Quality
VSR .... Vacuum Short Resid [*Petroleum technology*]
VSR .... Validation Summary Report
VSR .... Vallecitos Experimental Superheat Reactor   (NRCH)
VSR .... Versar, Inc. [*NYSE symbol*]
VSR .... Vertical Storage and Retrieval Systems
VSR .... Very Short Range
VSR .... Very Short Run [*Printing technology*]
VSR .... Very Special Reserve   (ADA)
VSR .... Vibration Sensitive Relay
VSR .... Vietnam Supply Rate [*Military*]   (MCD)
VSR .... Vincit Sapientia Robur [*Wisdom Overcomes Strength*] [*Latin*] [*Motto of Johann Ernst, Duke of Saxony-Eisenach (1566-1638)*]
VSR .... Visual Security Range   (NATG)
VSR .... Voltage-Sensing Relay
VSRADWS ... Very-Short-Range Air Defense Weapon System   (NATG)
VSRBM .... Very-Short-Range Ballistic Missile
VSRGSR ...... Very-Short-Range Ground Surveillance RADAR   (MCD)
VSS .... V/STOL [*Vertical/Short Takeoff and Landing*] Support Ship
VSS .... Vampire Studies Society   (EA)
VSS .... Vapor Saver System [*Automobile*]
VSS .... Variable Slit Set
VSS .... Variable SONAR System
VSS .... Variable Stability System [*Aviation*]
VSS .... Vassouras [*Brazil*] [*Geomagnetic observatory code*]
VSS .... Vector Scoring System [*Navy*]   (MCD)
VSS .... Vehicle Surveillance System
VSS .... Vehicle System Simulator
VSS .... Velocity Sensor System
VSS .... Verses   (BJA)
VSS .... Versions   (ROG)
VSS .... Vertical Sounding System
VSS .... Vertical Spike Soderberg [*Pot*] [*Aluminum processing*]
VSS .... Vertical Support Structure
VSS .... Vessel Support System   (MCD)
VSS .... Videnskabs Selskapet Skrifter [*A publication*]
VSS .... Video Select Switch   (MCD)
VSS .... Video Signal Simulator   (NATG)
VSS .... Video Storage System [*or Subsystem*]
VSS .... Video Supervisory Signal
VSS .... Virtual Storage System [*SEMIS*]
VSS .... Visual Sensor Set
VSS .... Visual Simulation System
VSS .... Visual Systems Simulator [*FAA*]
VSS .... Vital Signs Stable [*Medicine*]
VSS .... Vocabulary Switching System [*Data processing*]
VSS .... Voice Storage System [*AT & T*]
VSS .... Volatile Suspended Solids [*Environmental science*]
VSS .... Voltage-Sensing Switch
VSS .... Voltage to Substrate and Sources [*Microelectronics*]
VSS .... Voyager Spacecraft Subsystem [*NASA*]
VSSC .... Vedanta Society of Southern California   (EA)
VSSF .... Videnskabs Selskapet Skrifter (Forhandlingar) [*A publication*]
VSSM .... Video Scanner Switch Matrix
VSSP .... Vendor Standard Settlement Program   (AAG)
VSSSN .... Verification Status Social Security Number   (AABC)
VS Suppl .... Vie Spirituelle. Supplement [*A publication*]
VST .... St. Thomas [*Virgin Islands*] [*Seismograph station code, US Geological Survey*]   (SEIS)
VST .... Valve Seat   (MSA)
VST .... Valve Setpoint Tolerance [*Nuclear energy*]   (NRCH)
VST .... Vancouver School of Theology [*University of British Columbia*]
VST .... Vanstates Resources Ltd. [*Vancouver Stock Exchange symbol*]

VST .... Variable Stability Trainer [*Aviation*]
VST .... Vasteras [*Sweden*] [*Airport symbol*]   (OAG)
VST .... Venom Skin Test [*Immunology*]
VST .... Video Scroller Terminal [*Data processing*]
VST .... Video System Test
VST .... Visit   (NVT)
VST .... VMS Short Term Income Trust [*American Stock Exchange symbol*]
VST .... Vocational Skills Training [*Funds*] [*Job Corps*]
VST .... Volume Sensitive Tariff [*Telecommunications*]   (TEL)
VSTA .... Victoria Station [*NASDAQ symbol*]   (NQ)
VSTC .... Vermont State Teachers College
VSTCB .... Vuoto, Scienza, e Tecnologia [*A publication*]
VStil .... Voprosy Stilistiki [*A publication*]
VSTKJ .... Vesientutkimuslaitoksen Julkaisuja [*Publications. Finnish Water Research Institute*] [*A publication*]
VSTM .... Valve Stem   (MSA)
VSTO .... Vertical/Short Takeoff [*and Landing*]   (MCD)
V/STOL ...... Vertical/Short Takeoff and Landing [*Aircraft*]
VSTP .... Visual Satellite Tracking Program
VSTR .... Ventral Striatum [*Neurology*]
VSTR .... Volt Second Transfer Ratio
VSTSP .... Visit Ship in Port [*Navy*]   (NVT)
VSTT .... Variable Speed Tactical Trainer   (MCD)
VSV .... Vacuum Switching Valve
VSV .... Vesicular Stomatitis Virus [*Also, VS*]
VSv .... Vokrug Sveta [*Moscow*] [*A publication*]
VSW .... Variable Sweep Wing
VSW .... Vertrau Schau Wem [*Trust, but Be Careful Whom*] [*German*] [*Motto of Johann Georg, Duke of Wohlau (1552-92)*]
VSW .... Very Short Wave
VSW .... Vierteljahrsschrift fuer Sozial- und Wirtschaftsgeschichte [*A publication*]
VSW .... Vitrified Stoneware
VSW .... Voltage Standing Wave
VSWG .... Vierteljahrsschrift fuer Sozial- und Wirtschaftsgeschichte [*A publication*]
VSWR .... Voltage Standing-Wave Ratio
VSX .... Navy Submarine Attack Airplane - Experimental   (MCD)
VSYNC .... Vertical Synchronous [*Data processing*]
VSystems ... Video Systems [*A publication*]
VT .... Air-Cushion Vehicle built by Vosper Thorneycroft [*England*] [*Usually used in combination with numerals*]
VT .... Air Polynesie [*France*] [*ICAO designator*]   (FAAC)
VT .... India [*Aircraft nationality and registration mark*]   (FAAC)
Vt .... State of Vermont, Department of Libraries, Montpelier, VT [*Library symbol*] [*Library of Congress*]   (LCLS)
VT .... Target-on-Threshold Speed [*Aviation*]
VT .... Torpedo Plane [*Navy symbol*]
VT .... Training Squadron [*Navy symbol*]   (NVT)
VT .... Vacuum Tube [*Electronics*]
VT .... Validation Testing   (MCD)
VT .... Valitocin [*Endocrinology*]
VT .... Vaportight   (MSA)
VT .... Variable Thrust
VT .... Variable Time [*Fuse*] [*Also known as a "proximity fuse"*]
VT .... Variable Transformer
VT .... Variable Transmission   (ADA)
VT .... Vascular Time
VT .... Vat Petroleum [*Vancouver Stock Exchange symbol*]
VT .... Vehicle Theft
VT .... Vehicular Technology   (MCD)
V-T .... Velocity Time   (MUGU)
VT .... Ventricular Tachycardia [*Cardiology*]
VT .... Verb Transitive
VT .... Verfuegungstruppen   (BJA)
VT .... Vermont [*Postal code*]
VT .... Vermont Reports   (DLA)
VT .... Verotoxin [*Biochemistry*]
VT .... Vertical Tabulation [*Data processing*]
VT .... Vertical Tail
VT .... Vetus Testamentum [*A publication*]
VT .... Vetus Testamentum [*The Old Testament*] [*Bible*] [*Latin*]
VT .... Vibration Testing
V-T .... Vibrational-to-Translational [*Energy transfer*]
VT .... Videotape
VT .... Viere i Tzerkov [*A publication*]
VT .... Vision Test [*Ophthalmology*]
VT .... Visual Telegraphy
VT .... Visual Toss
VT .... Vocational-Technical
V & T .... Vodka and Tonic
VT .... Voice Tube [*Technical drawings*]
V & T .... Volume and Tension [*of pulse*]
VTA .... Vacuum-Tube Amplifier
VTA .... Variable Transfer Address
VTA .... Varnished Tube Association
VTA .... Ventral Tegmental Area [*Anatomy*]
VTA .... Vertical Tracking Angle [*of a phonograph cartridge*]
VTA .... Vision Test Apparatus [*Ophthalmology*]
VTAADS ..... Vertical the Army Authorization Document System

VTAC .... Video Timing and Control
VTAC .... VOR [*Very-High-Frequency Omnidirectional Range*] Collocated with TACAN   (FAAC)
V-TACH ...... Ventricular Tachycardia [*Cardiology*]
VT Admin Comp ... Vermont Administrative Procedure Compilation   (DLA)
VT Ag Exp ... Vermont. Agricultural Experiment Station. Publications [*A publication*]
VT Agric Exp Stn Bull ... Vermont. Agricultural Experiment Station. Bulletin [*A publication*]
VTAJX .... Navy Trainer Advanced Jet - Experimental   (MCD)
VTAM .... Virtual Telecommunications [*or Teleprocessing*] Access Method [*IBM Corp.*] [*Data processing*]
VTAM .... Virtual Terminal Access Method
VTAM .... VORTEX [*Varian Omnitask Real-Time Executive*] Telecommunications Access Method
VTAME .... Virtual Telecommunications Access Method Entry
V-TAS .... Vericom Test Application System [*Vericom Ltd.*] [*Software package*]
VTAS .... Visual Target Acquisition System [*Navy*]
VtB .... Fletcher Free Library, Burlington, VT [*Library symbol*] [*Library of Congress*]   (LCLS)
VTB .... Torpedo-Bombing Plane [*Navy symbol*]
VTB .... Velocity Test Barrel
VtB .... Verfahrenstechnische Berichte [*Chemical and Process Engineering Abstracts*] [*A publication*] [*Leverkusen, West Germany*]
VtB .... Verkehrswasserbaubibliothek [*Bundesanstalt fuer Wasserbau*] [*Database*]
VTB .... Vlaamsche Toeristenbond
VTB .... Voltage Time to Breakdown   (DEN)
VT BA .... Vermont Bar Association Reports   (DLA)
VtBC .... Champlain College, Burlington, VT [*Library symbol*] [*Library of Congress*]   (LCLS)
VtBef .... Rockingham Free Public Library, Bellows Falls, VT [*Library symbol*] [*Library of Congress*]   (LCLS)
VtBenn .... Bennington Free Library, Bennington, VT [*Library symbol*] [*Library of Congress*]   (LCLS)
VtBennC .... Bennington College, Bennington, VT [*Library symbol*] [*Library of Congress*]   (LCLS)
VtBennM .... Bennington Museum, Inc., Bennington, VT [*Library symbol*] [*Library of Congress*]   (LCLS)
VtBennP ..... Putnam Memorial Hospital, Medical Library, Bennington, VT [*Library symbol*] [*Library of Congress*]   (LCLS)
VtBFB .... Grand Lodge of Vermont, F & AM Library, Burlington, VT [*Library symbol*] [*Library of Congress*]   (LCLS)
VtBran .... Brandon Free Public Library, Brandon, VT [*Library symbol*] [*Library of Congress*]   (LCLS)
VtBrt .... Brooks Memorial Library, Brattleboro, VT [*Library symbol*] [*Library of Congress*]   (LCLS)
VtBrtS .... School for International Training, Brattleboro, VT [*Library symbol*] [*Library of Congress*]   (LCLS)
VtBT .... Trinity College, Burlington, VT [*Library symbol*] [*Library of Congress*]   (LCLS)
VT Bul .... Vermont. Free Public Library Commission and State Library. Bulletin [*A publication*]
VTC .... Vandenberg Test Center [*Air Force*]
VTC .... Variable Trimmer Capacitor
VTC .... Vehicular Traffic Control
VTC .... Veractor Tuned Microwave Cavity
VTC .... Viable Titanium Composite
VTC .... Vidicon Television Camera
VTC .... Volunteer Training Corps [*An organization for home defense*] [*British*] [*World War I*]
VTC .... Voting Trust Certificates [*A type of stock certificate*]
VTC .... Voting Trust Company
VTCA .... Vintage Thunderbird Club of America   (EA)
VtCasT .... Castleton State College, Castleton, VT [*Library symbol*] [*Library of Congress*]   (LCLS)
VTCC .... Variable Temperature Compensation Capacitor
VTCCHE ..... Tidewater Consortium, Librarians' Networking Committee [*Library network*]
VTCE .... Vehicle Team Combat Exercise [*Army*]   (INF)
VTCS .... Variable Thermal Control Surface
VTCS .... Vehicular Traffic Control System   (IEEE)
VTCS .... Video Telemetering Camera Systems   (AAG)
VTD .... Aircraft (Training) [*Navy symbol*]
VTD .... Variable Time Delay
VTD .... Vertical Tape Display   (KSC)
VTD .... Vision Testing Device [*Ophthalmology*]
VTDC .... Vacuum Tube Development Committee [*Columbia University*]   (MCD)
VTDI .... Variable Threshold Digital Input
VTE .... Variable Thrust Engine
VTE .... Vertical Tube Effects [*Desalination*]
VTE .... Vertical Tube Evaporation [*Desalination*]
VTE .... Vibration Test Equipment
VTE .... Vicarious Trial and Error [*Psychology*]
VTE .... Vientiane [*Laos*] [*Airport symbol*]   (OAG)
VTE .... Viscous Transonic Equation
VTEC .... Verotoxin-Producing Escherichia Coli
V-TECS ...... Vocational Technical Education Consortium of States   (OICC)

VTEK .... Vodavi Technology [*NASDAQ symbol*]   (NQ)
VTERL .... Veterinary Toxicology and Entomology Research Laboratory [*Department of Agriculture*]
VTERM .... Variable Temperature Electrical Resistivity Measurement [*Physics*]
VTES .... Variable Thrust Engine System
VTES .... Vinyltriethoxysilane [*Organic chemistry*]
VTF .... Vacuum Test Furnace
VTF .... Variable Time, Fragmentation [*Military*]   (CAAL)
VTF .... Venezuelan Trust Fund [*Inter-American Development Bank*]
VTF .... Vertical Test Facility [*NASA*]
VTF .... Vertical Test Fixture
VTF .... Vertical Test Flight   (MCD)
VTF .... Vertical Tracking Force [*of a phonograph cartridge*]
VTF .... Voltage Transfer Function
VT Farm & Home Sci ... Vermont Farm and Home Science [*A publication*]
VT Farm Home Sci ... Vermont Farm and Home Science [*A publication*]
VTFDA ...... Ankara Universitesi Veteriner Fakultesi Dergisi [*A publication*]
VTFE .... Vertical Tube Foam Evaporation [*Chemical engineering*]
VTFS .... Visual Technology Flight Simulator   (MCD)
VTFT .... Value Task Force Team
VTG .... Vantage [*Washington*] [*Seismograph station code, US Geological Survey*]   (SEIS)
VTG .... Vitellogenin [*Biochemistry*]
VTG .... Volume Thoracic Gas [*Medicine*]
VTG .... Voting [*Business and trade*]
VT Geol Sur Econ Geol ... Vermont. Geological Survey. Economic Geology [*A publication*]
VT Geol Surv Bull ... Vermont. Geological Survey. Bulletin [*A publication*]
VT Geol Surv Water Resour Dep Environ Geol ... Vermont. Geological Survey. Water Resources Department. Environmental Geology [*A publication*]
VThB .... Vocabulaire de Theologie Biblique [*A publication*]   (BJA)
VtHi .... Vermont Historical Society, Montpelier, VT [*Library symbol*] [*Library of Congress*]   (LCLS)
VT His S ...... Vermont Historical Society. Proceedings [*A publication*]
VT Hist ...... Vermont History [*A publication*]
VtHS .... Vermont Historical Society. Proceedings [*A publication*]
VTI .... Statens Vag- och Trafikinstitut [*Swedish Road and Traffic Research Institute*] [*Linkoping*] [*Information service*]   (EISS)
VTI .... Valparaiso Technical Institute [*Indiana*]
VTI .... Vanguard Technologies International, Inc. [*American Stock Exchange symbol*]
VTI .... Vermont Telecommunications, Incorporated [*Burlington, VT*] [*Telecommunications*]   (TSSD)
VTI .... Video Terminal Interface
VTI .... Vinton, IA [*Location identifier*] [*FAA*]   (FAAL)
VTI .... Volume Thickness Index
VTI .... Voluntary Termination Incentive [*Business and trade*]
VTIP .... Visual Target Identification Point   (AFM)
VTJ .... Johnson State College, Johnson, VT [*OCLC symbol*]   (OCLC)
VtJoT .... Johnson State College, Johnson, VT [*Library symbol*] [*Library of Congress*]   (LCLS)
VTK .... Viatech, Inc. [*American Stock Exchange symbol*]
VTL .... Vacuum-Tube Launcher
VTL .... Variable Threshold Logic
VTL .... Vertical Turret Lathe
VTL .... Video Tape Lecture
VT Lib .... Vermont Libraries [*A publication*]
VTLM .... Vitalmetrics, Inc. [*NASDAQ symbol*]   (NQ)
Vt-LR .... Vermont Legislative Council, Montpelier, VT [*Library symbol*] [*Library of Congress*]   (LCLS)
VTLS .... Virginia Technical Library System [*Virginia Polytechnic Institute and State University Center for Library Automation*] [*Information service*]
VtLyL .... Lyndon State College, Lyndonville, VT [*Library symbol*] [*Library of Congress*]   (LCLS)
VTM .... Vacuum-Tube Module
VTM .... Vehicle Test Meter [*TACOM*] [*Army*]   (RDA)
VTM .... Vehicles to the Mile [*Military*]
VTM .... Versatile Tracking Mount   (MCD)
VTM .... Vibration Test Module   (MCD)
VTM .... Voltage Tunable Magnetron
VtMan .... Mark Skinner Public Library, Manchester, VT [*Library symbol*] [*Library of Congress*]   (LCLS)
VtMarC ...... Marlboro College, Marlboro, VT [*Library symbol*] [*Library of Congress*]   (LCLS)
VTMC .... Viable Titanium Matrix Composite
VTMDA ...... Veterinarni Medicina [*A publication*]
VtMiM .... Middlebury College, Middlebury, VT [*Library symbol*] [*Library of Congress*]   (LCLS)
VtMiS .... Sheldon Art Museum, Middlebury, VT [*Library symbol*] [*Library of Congress*]   (LCLS)
VTMO .... Voltage Tunable Microwave Oscillator
VtMor .... Morristown Centennial Library, Morrisville, VT [*Library symbol*] [*Library of Congress*]   (LCLS)
VTMoV ...... Velvet Tobacco Mottle Virus
VTMRJa ..... Voprosy Teorii i Metodiki Izucenijy Russkogo Jazyka [*A publication*]

VtMS .... Office of the Secretary of State, State Papers Division, Montpelier, VT [*Library symbol*] [*Library of Congress*] (LCLS)

VTMS .... Vinyltrimethylsilane [*Organic chemistry*]

VtN .... Brown Public Library, Northfield, VT [*Library symbol*] [*Library of Congress*] (LCLS)

VT(N) .... Night Torpedo Bomber Squadron [*Navy symbol*]

VTN .... Valentine, NE [*Location identifier*] [*FAA*] (FAAL)

VTN .... Ventral Tegmental Nuclei [*Neuroanatomy*]

VTN .... Verification Test Network (MCD)

VTN .... Video Tape Network [*An association*] (EA)

VTNA.......... VTAM Telecommunications Network Architecture

VTNC .... VTN Corporation [*NASDAQ symbol*] (NQ)

VTNF .... Variable Time Non-Fragmenting [*Military*] (CAAL)

VtNN.......... Norwich University, Northfield, VT [*Library symbol*] [*Library of Congress*] (LCLS)

VTNS......... Voltage Tunable Noise Source

VTO .... Vertical Takeoff

VTO .... Viable Terrestrial Organism

VTO .... Visual Training Officer [*Navy*]

VTO .... Vocational Training Officer [*Navy*]

VTO .... Voltage Tunable Oscillator

VTOC .... Volume Table of Contents [*Data processing*]

VTOGW ..... Vertical Takeoff Gross Weight

VTOHL ...... Vertical Takeoff and Horizontal Landing

VTOL .... Vertical Takeoff and Landing [*Also, VERTOL*] [*Acronym used for a type of aircraft*]

VTop .... Voprosy Toponomastiki [*A publication*]

VTOVL ...... Vertical Takeoff Vertical Landing

VTP .... Valid Target Presentation [*Military*] (CAAL)

VTP .... Vandenberg Test Program [*Air Force*]

VTP .... Vehicle Test Plan [*NASA*] (NASA)

VTP .... Vendor Test Procedure

VTP .... Verification Test Plan [*or Program*] (NASA)

VTP .... VIEWDATA Terminal Program

VTP .... Virtual Terminal Protocol

VTP .... Visual Transmitter Power

VTPA......... Vertical Turbine Pump Association [*Defunct*]

VTPAI....... Victorian Town Planning Appeals Tribunal. Index of Appeals Decisions [*A publication*]

VtPifi .... Free Library, Pittsfield, VT [*Library symbol*] [*Library of Congress*] (LCLS)

VtPlaG....... Goddard College, Plainfield, VT [*Library symbol*] [*Library of Congress*] (LCLS)

VtPom .... Abbott Memorial Library, Pomfret, VT [*Library symbol*] [*Library of Congress*] (LCLS)

VtPouG ...... Green Mountain College, Poultney, VT [*Library symbol*] [*Library of Congress*] (LCLS)

Vt-PR......... Vermont Public Records Library, Montpelier, VT [*Library symbol*] [*Library of Congress*] (LCLS)

VTPR .... Vertical Temperature Profile [*or Profiling*] Radiometer

VTPS......... Vibration Test Plotting System

VtPuW....... Windham College, Putney, VT [*Library symbol*] [*Library of Congress*] (LCLS)

VtQ............ Vermont Quarterly [*A publication*]

VTR .... McGrath, AK [*Location identifier*] [*FAA*] (FAAL)

VTR .... Value of Time Research [*British*]

VTR .... Variable Tandem Repetition [*Genetics*]

VTR .... Vector (FAAC)

VTR .... Vehicle Track Recovery [*Military*]

VTR .... Vehicle Tracking Receiver

VTR .... Vendor Trouble Report

VTR .... Vermont Railway, Inc. [*AAR code*]

VT R .... Vermont Reports (DLA)

VTR .... Vertical Radial (MSA)

VTR .... Vertical Test Range

VTR .... Videotape Recorder [*or Recording*]

VTR .... Vintage Triumph Register (EA)

VTR .... Voltage Transformation Ratio [*Physics*]

VTRAN ...... Vast Translator (KSC)

VtRaStM .... Saint Mary's Seminary, Randolph, VT [*Library symbol*] [*Library of Congress*] (LCLS)

VTRB......... Variable Trim Reentry Body (MCD)

VT Regist Nurse ... Vermont Registered Nurse [*A publication*]

VT Rep ...... Vermont Reports (DLA)

VtRoc .... Rochester Public Library, Rochester, VT [*Library symbol*] [*Library of Congress*] (LCLS)

VTRS......... Videotape Recording System

VTRS......... Videotape Response System

VTRS......... Visual Technology Research Simulator (CAAL)

VTRX......... Ventrex Laboratories, Inc. [*NASDAQ symbol*] (NQ)

VTS .... IEEE Vehicular Technology Society [*New York, NY*] (EA)

VTS .... Vandenberg Tracking Station [*Air Force*]

VTS .... Variable Time Step

VTS .... Variable Tracking Strategy (MCD)

VTS .... Venture Touring Society (EA)

VTS .... Versatile Training Systems (MCD)

VTS .... Vertical Test Sight (MCD)

VTS .... Vertical Test Stand (KSC)

VTS .... Vertical Thrust Stand

VTS .... Vessel Traffic Service [*Harbor RADAR system*] [*Coast Guard*]

VTS .... Vetus Testamentum. Supplementum [*Leiden*] [*A publication*]

VTS .... Vibration Test Specification

VTS .... Vibration Test System

VTS .... Viewfinder Tracking System

VTS .... Virginia Theological Seminary, Alexandria, VA [*OCLC symbol*] (OCLC)

VTS .... Visual Typing System (MCD)

VTS .... Vitosha [*Bulgaria*] [*Seismograph station code, US Geological Survey*] (SEIS)

VTS .... Vocational Training Scheme [*British*]

VTS .... Vocational Training Service

VTS .... Vote Tally System

VTS .... Vulcan Training System (MCD)

VTSE .... Vehicle Team Subcaliber Exercise [*Army*] (INF)

VtShelM ..... Shelburne Museum, Inc., Research Library, Shelburne, VT [*Library symbol*] [*Library of Congress*] (LCLS)

VTSIC........ Vac-Tec Systems, Incorporated [*NASDAQ symbol*] (NQ)

VTSPS....... Vsesoyuznyy Tsentral'nyy Sovet Professional'nykh Soyuzov [*All-Union Central Council of Trade Unions*] [*USSR*]

VT Stat Ann ... Vermont Statutes, Annotated (DLA)

VT St G Rp ... Vermont State Geologist. Report [*A publication*]

VtStjA .... St. Johnsbury Atheneum, St. Johnsbury, VT [*Library symbol*] [*Library of Congress*] (LCLS)

VtStjF .... Fairbanks Museum of Natural Science, St. Johnsbury, VT [*Library symbol*] [*Library of Congress*] (LCLS)

VTSuppl..... Vetus Testamentum. Supplementum [*Leiden*] [*A publication*]

Vt-SWRL .... Vermont Department of Libraries, Southwest Regional Library, Rutland, VT [*Library symbol*] [*Library of Congress*] (LCLS)

VTT .... Vacuum Thermal Testing

VTT .... Vacuum-Tube Transmitter

VTT .... Valtion Teknillinen Tutkimuskeskus [*Technical Research Center of Finland*] [*Espoo*] [*Information service*] (EISS)

VTT .... Variable Threshold Transistor

VTU .... Las Tunas [*Cuba*] [*Airport symbol*] (OAG)

VTU .... Oxnard, CA [*Location identifier*] [*FAA*] (FAAL)

VTU .... University of Vermont, Bailey Library, Burlington, VT [*OCLC symbol*] (OCLC)

VtU .... University of Vermont, Burlington, VT [*Library symbol*] [*Library of Congress*] (LCLS)

vtu .... Vermont [*MARC country of publication code*] [*Library of Congress*] (LCCP)

V + TU ...... Voice plus Teleprinter Unit

VTU .... Volunteer Reserve Training Unit [*Coast Guard*]

VTU .... Volunteer Training Unit

VTU .... Volunteer Training Units (MCD)

VtU-Med .... University of Vermont, College of Medicine, Burlington, VT [*Library symbol*] [*Library of Congress*] (LCLS)

VTU(MMS) ... Volunteer Training Unit (Merchant Marine Safety)

VtU-W .... University of Vermont and State Agricultural College, Wilbur Collection, Burlington, VT [*Library symbol*] [*Library of Congress*] (LCLS)

VTV .... Vacuum Transmitting Valve

VT(V) .... Vacuum-Tube (Voltmeter) (DEN)

VTV .... Value Television [*Television program*]

VTV .... Verification Test Vehicle [*Military*] (CAAL)

VtVe .... Bixby Memorial Free Library, Vergennes, VT [*Library symbol*] [*Library of Congress*] (LCLS)

VTVM .... Vacuum-Tube Voltmeter

VTW .... Variable Transmission Window

VtWeo .... Wilder Memorial Library, Weston, VT [*Library symbol*] [*Library of Congress*] (LCLS)

VtWinoS..... Saint Michael's College, Winooski, VT [*Library symbol*] [*Library of Congress*] (LCLS)

VTX .... Vacuum-Tube Transmitter

VTX .... Ventex Energy [*Vancouver Stock Exchange symbol*]

VTX .... Vertex [*A publication*]

VTX .... Vertex

VTX .... Vortex (AAG)

VTX .... VTX Electronics [*American Stock Exchange symbol*]

VTXTS....... Navy Jet Trainer (MCD)

VTXX......... Vertz Corp. [*NASDAQ symbol*] (NQ)

VTY .... Vatovaky [*Madagascar*] [*Seismograph station code, US Geological Survey*] (SEIS)

VTY .... Virkamiesten ja Tyoentekijaein Yhteisjaerjestoe [*Joint Organization of Civil Servants and Workers*] [*Helsinki, Finland*]

VTZ .... Vishakhapatnam [*India*] [*Airport symbol*] (OAG)

VU .... Societe Air Ivoire [*Ivory Coast*] [*ICAO designator*] (FAAC)

VU .... Utility Squadron [*Navy symbol*] (MCD)

VU .... Validation Unit (AAG)

VU .... Vanity Unit [*Classified advertising*] (ADA)

VU .... Varicose Ulcer [*Medicine*]

VU .... Vaterlaendische Union [*Patriotic Union*] [*Liechtenstein*] (PPE)

VU .... Vehicle Unit (KSC)

VU .... Vehicle Utility (MCD)

VU .... Very Urgent

VU .... Voice Unit [*Signal amplitude measurement*]

VU .... Volume Unit [*Signal amplitude measurement*]

VU .... Von Unten [*From the Bottom*] [*German*]

VUA............ Valorous Unit Award [*Army*]

VUA............ Verbal Underachievers [*Education*]
VUA............ Virtual Unit Address   (BUR)
VUB............ Variational Upper Bound
VUB............ Vrije Universiteit Brussel [*Free University of Brussels*]
                   [*Belgium*] [*Information service*]   (EISS)
VUBT........ Vuebotics Corp. [*NASDAQ symbol*]   (NQ)
VUCC........ Computer Center [*Vanderbilt University*] [*Research
                   center*]   (RCD)
VUCDT...... Ventilation Unit Condensate Drain Tank   (IEEE)
VUCLR...... Victoria University. College Law Review [*A publication*]
VUCS........ Ventilation Umbilical Connector System
VUE............ Upper Hudson Library Federation, Albany, NY [*OCLC
                   symbol*]   (OCLC)
Vues Econ Aquitaine ... Vues sur l'Economie d'Aquitaine [*A publication*]
VuF............. Verkuendigung und Forschung [*A publication*]
VUF .... Vertical Upward Force
VuG........... Vergangenheit und Gegenwart [*A publication*]
VUHZ........ Vyzkumny Ustav Hutnictvi Zeleza, Dobra [*Dobra Iron and Steel
                   Research Institute*] [*Dobra, Czechoslovakia*] [*Information
                   service*]   (EISS)
VUL .... Vulcan [*Taviliu*] [*New Britain*] [*Seismograph station code, US
                   Geological Survey*]   (SEIS)
VUL .... Vulcan Corp. [*American Stock Exchange symbol*]
VUL .... Vulcanize   (AAG)
VUL .... Vulnerary [*Medicine to heal wounds*]   (ROG)
Vul.............. Vulpecula [*Constellation*]
VULBS .... Virginia Union List of Biomedical Serials [*Library network*]
VULC.......... Vulcanize
VULCAN..... [*A*] programing language   (CSR)
VULG......... Vulgar
VULG......... Vulgate [*Version of the Bible*]
Vulkanol Seismol ... Vulkanologiya i Seismologiya [*A publication*]
Vulp........... Vulpecula [*Constellation*]
VULR........ Valparaiso University. Law Review [*A publication*]
VULREP ..... Vulnerability Report [*Navy*]   (NVT)
VULT .... Voprosy Uzbekskogo Jazyka i Literatury [*A publication*]
VUMD........ Vilniaus Valstybinio V. Kapsuko Vardo Universiteto Mokslo
                   Darbai [*A publication*]
VUMS .... Vyzkumny Ustav pro Matematickych Stroju [*Research Institute
                   for Mathematical Machines*] [*Czechoslovakia*]
VUN............ Vunikawai [*Fiji*] [*Seismograph station code, US Geological
                   Survey*]   (SEIS)
VUNC .... Voice of United Nations Command
Vuorit Bergshant ... Vuoriteollisuus/Bergshanteringen [*A publication*]
Vuoto .... Vuoto, Scienza, e Technologia [*A publication*]
Vuoto Sci Tecnol ... Vuoto, Scienza, e Tecnologia [*A publication*]
VUP .... Valledupar [*Colombia*] [*Airport symbol*]   (OAG)
VUP .... Vela Uniform Platform
VUQ........... Dayton, OH [*Location identifier*] [*FAA*]   (FAAL)
VUR .... Vesicoureteral Reflex [*Nephrology*]
VURB-A...... Vie Urbaine [*France*] [*A publication*]
VUS............ Versatile Upper Stage [*NASA*]
VUSH .... Vanderbilt University. Studies in the Humanities [*A publication*]
VUT .... Union Theological Seminary Library, Richmond, VA [*OCLC
                   symbol*]   (OCLC)
Vutr Boles ... Vutreshni Bolesti [*A publication*]
VUTS......... Verification Unit Test Set   (AFM)
VUU........... Virginia Union University
VUU .... Virginia Union University, Richmond, VA [*OCLC
                   symbol*]   (OCLC)
VUV .... Vacuum Ultraviolet
VUW .... Eugene Isle, LA [*Location identifier*] [*FAA*]   (FAAL)
VUWLR...... Victoria University of Wellington. Law Review [*A publication*]
VUWL Rev ... Victoria University of Wellington. Law Review [*A publication*]
VUZ .... Birmingham, AL [*Location identifier*] [*FAA*]   (FAAL)
VV.............. First and Second Violins [*Music*]   (ROG)
VV.............. Nile Valley Aviation Co. [*Egypt*] [*ICAO designator*]   (FAAC)
VV.............. Vaccinia Virus
VV.............. Vacuum Valve
V/V............ Validation/Verification   (CAAL)
VV.............. Veins [*Medicine*]
VV.............. Velocity Vector   (AAG)
VV.............. Velocity-Volume
VV.............. Vent Valve
VV.............. Verbs   (ADA)
V & V .... Verification and Validation [*Data processing*]
VV.............. Verses
V/V............ Vertical Velocity
VV.............. Vestron, Inc. [*NYSE symbol*]
V-V............ Vibrational-to-Vibrational [*Energy transfer*]
VV.............. Vibrio Vulnificus [*A microorganism*]
VV.............. Vice Versa
VV.............. Victims for Victims [*Los Angeles, CA*]   (EA)
VV.............. Vietnam Veterans   (OICC)
VV.............. Village Voice [*A publication*]
VV.............. Violini [*Violins*] [*Music*]
VV.............. Visna Virus
VV.............. Visum Vivum [*Seen Alive*] [*Botany*]   (ROG)
VV.............. Viva Voce [*Spoken Aloud*] [*Latin*]   (ADA)
VV.............. Vizantiiskii Vremenik [*A publication*]
VV.............. Voices [*Music*]

VV.............. Volk und Volkstum [*A publication*]
V/V............ Volume/Volume
V for V .... Volunteers for Vision [*Austin, TX*]   (EA)
VV.............. Vulva and Vagina [*Physiology*]
VVA........... Southern Adirondack Library System, Saratoga Springs, NY
                   [*OCLC symbol*]   (OCLC)
VVa............ Vida Vasca [*A publication*]
VVA........... Vietnam Veterans of America   (EA)
VVAG......... Vietnam Veterans Arts Group   (EA)
VVAOVI...... Vietnam Veterans Agent Orange Victims [*Stamford, CT*]   (EA)
VVAP......... Mouvement Socialiste Occitan - Volem Viure al Pais
                   [*Occitanian Socialist Movement*] [*French*]   (PPW)
VVAW......... Vietnam Veterans Against the War   (EA)
VVB........... Baruch College, New York, NY [*OCLC symbol*]   (OCLC)
VVB........... Mahanoro [*Madagascar*] [*Airport symbol*]   (OAG)
VVBAA ...... Venetian and Vertical Blind Association of America [*Defunct*]
VVC........... Colgate University, Hamilton, NY [*OCLC symbol*]   (OCLC)
VVC........... Variable Vacuum Capacitor
VVC........... Vertical Velocity Console
VVC........... Villavicencio [*Colombia*] [*Airport symbol*]   (OAG)
VVC........... Voltage Variable Capacitor
VVCAA ...... Veteran and Vintage Chevrolet Automobile Association   (ADA)
VVCC .... Viri Clarissimi [*Most Illustrious Men*] [*Latin*]
VVCD .... Voltage Variable Capacitance Diode
VVCEC ...... Voice and Video Control and Editing Components   (MCD)
VVCS .... Vernier Velocity Correction System [*Aerospace*]   (KSC)
VVD........... Downstate Medical Center, SUNY [*State University of New
                   York*], Brooklyn, NY [*OCLC symbol*]   (OCLC)
VVD........... Valid Verifiable Defense [*Stamped on dismissed traffic tickets*]
VVD........... Valverde [*Canary Islands*] [*Seismograph station code, US
                   Geological Survey*]   (SEIS)
VVD........... Voltage Variable Diode
VVDS......... Video Verter Decision Storage
VVE .... Erie Community College-North, Buffalo, NY [*OCLC
                   symbol*]   (OCLC)
VVF........... New York Medical College, New York, NY [*OCLC
                   symbol*]   (OCLC)
VVG........... New York State Institute for Research in Mental Retardation,
                   Staten Island, NY [*OCLC symbol*]   (OCLC)
VVGF......... Vincent Van Gogh Foundation   (EA)
VVH........... Daemen College, Buffalo, NY [*OCLC symbol*]   (OCLC)
VVH........... Very Very Heavy [*Cosmic ray nuclei*]
VVH........... Veterans Vigil of Honor   (EA)
VVHR......... Vibration Velocity per Hour
VVI............ Beth Israel Medical Center, New York, NY [*OCLC
                   symbol*]   (OCLC)
VVI............ Vertical Velocity Indicator   (MCD)
VVI............ Vietnam Veterans, Incorporated   (EA)
VVI............ Vocational Values Inventory [*Guidance in education*]
VVI............ Voltage Variation Indicator
VVIC.......... Vietnam Veterans in Congress Caucus   (EA)
VVIP.......... Very, Very Important Person
VVIR.......... Voice and Vision of the Iranian Revolution [*Iranian television*]
VVIRA........ Vietnam Veterans Institute for Research and Advocacy
                   [*Washington, DC*]   (EA)
VVIS .... Videovision, Inc. [*NASDAQ symbol*]   (NQ)
VVITA........ Vietnam Veterans Inter-Tribal Association   (EA)
VVJ............ John Jay College of Criminal Justice, New York, NY [*OCLC
                   symbol*]   (OCLC)
VVK .... New York Academy of Medicine, New York, NY [*OCLC
                   symbol*]   (OCLC)
VVK .... Vastervik [*Sweden*] [*Airport symbol*]   (OAG)
VVL .... Mount Sinai School of Medicine of the City University of New
                   York, New York, NY [*OCLC symbol*]   (OCLC)
VV LL .... Variae Lectiones [*Variant Readings*] [*Latin*]
VVLP......... Vietnam Veterans Leadership Program [*ACTION*]
VVM .... Memorial Sloan-Kettering Cancer Center, New York, NY
                   [*OCLC symbol*]   (OCLC)
VVM .... Vector Voltmeter
VVM .... Velocity Vector Measurement
VVM .... Vlastivedny Vestnik Moravsky [*A publication*]
VVMC......... Voice and Video Monitoring Component   (MCD)
VVMF......... Vietnam Veterans Memorial Fund   (EA)
VVMS......... Velocity Vector Measurement System
VVN........... Niagara University, Niagara University, NY [*OCLC
                   symbol*]   (OCLC)
VVnW......... Veterans of the Vietnam War   (EA)
VVO........... New York Medical College, Westchester Medical Center,
                   Valhalla, NY [*OCLC symbol*]   (OCLC)
VVO........... Very Very Old [*Designation on brandy labels*]
VVOH........ Vacuum Valve Operating Handle
VVP........... Bard College, Annandale-On-Hudson, NY [*OCLC
                   symbol*]   (OCLC)
VVPP......... Variable Volume Piston Pump
VVQ........... Roosevelt Hospital, Medical Library, New York, NY [*OCLC
                   symbol*]   (OCLC)
VVR .... Rockland Community College, Suffern, NY [*OCLC
                   symbol*]   (OCLC)
VVR........... Variable Voltage Rectifier
VVR .... Vehicle Vapor Recovery [*Automobile*]

VVRI .... Veterinary Virus Research Institute [*New York State Veterinary College*]
VVRM .... Vortex Valve Rocket Motor   (MCD)
VVRS.......... Viscous Vortex Rate Sensor
VVS .... Connellsville, PA [*Location identifier*] [*FAA*]   (FAAL)
VVS .... Sarah Lawrence College, Bronxville, NY [*OCLC symbol*]   (OCLC)
VVS .... Vein Ventures Ltd. [*Vancouver Stock Exchange symbol*]
VVS .... Very Very Slightly Flawed [*Gems*]
VVS .... Very, Very Small Inclusions [*Diamond clarity grade*]
VVS .... Very Very Superior
VVS .... Voenno-Vozdushnye Sily [*Army Air Forces*] [*Part of the MO*] [*USSR*]
VVS .... Voice Verification System
VVSA.......... Velocity Vector Sensor Assembly
VVSO .... Very, Very Superior Old [*Designation on brandy labels*]
VVSOP .... Very, Very Superior Old Pale [*Designation on brandy labels*]
VVSS........... Vertical Volute Spring Suspension [*Technical drawings*]
VVS Tidskr Vaerme Vent Sanit Kyltetek ... VVS. Tidskrift foer Vaerme, Ventilation, Sanitet, och Kylteteknik [*A publication*]
VVS Tidskr Varme Vent Sanit ... VVS. Tidskrift foer Vaerme, Ventilation, Sanitet [*Sweden*] [*A publication*]
VVS-VMF ... Voenno-Vozdushnye Sily - Voenno-Morskogo Flota [*Naval Air Force*] [*USSR*]
VVT .... Teachers College, Columbia University, New York, NY [*OCLC symbol*]   (OCLC)
VVT .... Velocity Variation Tube
VVT .... Visual-Verbal Test [*Psychology*]
VVTBA .... Vaeg- och Vattenbyggaren [*A publication*]
VVTC.......... Vendor-Vendee Technical Committee
VVU .... New York University, Medical Center, New York, NY [*OCLC symbol*]   (OCLC)
VVUU Zpr... VVUU [*Vedeckovyzkumny Uhelny Ustav*] Ostrava-Radvanice Zprava [*A publication*]
VVV .... Ortonville, MN [*Location identifier*] [*FAA*]   (FAAL)
VVV .... Utica College of Syracuse University, Utica, NY [*OCLC symbol*]   (OCLC)
VVW .... Westchester Library System, Yonkers, NY [*OCLC symbol*]   (OCLC)
VVWCA ...... Vintage Volkswagen Club of America   (EA)
VV:WT .... Vaccinia Virus: Wild Type [*Virology*]
VVX .... Nassau Community College, Garden City, NY [*OCLC symbol*]   (OCLC)
VVY .... St. Luke's Hospital, Bolling Medical Library, New York, NY [*OCLC symbol*]   (OCLC)
VVZ .... Medical Library Center of New York, New York, NY [*OCLC symbol*]   (OCLC)
VW.............. Early Warning Squadron [*Symbol*]   (MCD)
VW.............. Transportes Aereos Trafe, SA [*ICAO designator*]   (FAAC)
VW.............. Very Worshipful
VW.............. Vessel Wall
VW.............. Vie Wallonne [*A publication*]
VW.............. View   (MCD)
VW.............. Volkswagen [*German automobile*]
VWA .... Vacuum Window Assembly
VWA .... Vendor Working Authority
VWA .... Verband der Weiblichen Angestellten [*Association of Female Employees*] [*West Germany*]
VWB .... Bronx Community College Library, Bronx, NY [*OCLC symbol*]   (OCLC)
VWC .... Villa Walsh College [*New Jersey*]
VWCA .... Volkswagen Club of America
VWCL........ Volkswagen Caminhoes Limitada [*Brazil*]
VWD .... Vereinigte Wirtschaftsdienste [*Press agency*] [*West Germany*]
VWD .... Video-West Distributors Ltd. [*Vancouver Stock Exchange symbol*]
VWD .... Vinyl Window and Door Institute [*New York, NY*]   (EA)
vWD........... Von Willebrand's Disease [*Medicine*]
VWDU......... Viewing Window Deicing Unit
VWE .... Vanadium Wire Equilibration [*Nuclear energy*]   (NRCH)
VWED........ Vanadium Wire Equilibration Device [*Nuclear energy*]   (NRCH)
VWF........... Vehicle Work Flow
vWf............ Von Willebrand factor [*Also, vWF, VWF*] [*Hematology*]
VWFC........ Very-Wide-Field Camera
VWG .... Vital Wheat Gluten [*Vegetable protein*]
VWGA .... Vinifera Wine Growers Association   (EA)
VWH .... Vale of White Horse [*Hounds*]
VWH .... Vertical Weld Head
VWHA........ Vertical Weld Head Assembly
VWL........... College of William and Mary, Law School, Williamsburg, VA [*OCLC symbol*]   (OCLC)
VWL........... Variable Word Length
VWM.......... College of William and Mary, Williamsburg, VA [*OCLC symbol*]   (OCLC)
VWM.......... Volume-Weighted Mean [*Statistical technique*]
VWMP .... Vietnam Women's Memorial Project [*Minneapolis, MN*]   (EA)
VWN .... Virginia Woolf Newsletter [*A publication*]
VWO .... Valves Wide Open [*Nuclear energy*]   (NRCH)
VWO .... Woolsey, GA [*Location identifier*] [*FAA*]   (FAAL)
VWOA .... Veteran Wireless Operators Association [*Clifton, NJ*]   (EA)
VWOA .... Volkswagen of America

VWP .... Variable Width Pulse
VWP .... Vietnam Workers' Party   (PPW)
VWPI .... Vacuum Wood Preservers Institute   (EA)
VWQ .... Virginia Woolf Quarterly [*A publication*]
VWR .... North Country Reference and Research Resources Council, Canton, NY [*OCLC symbol*]   (OCLC)
VWR .... Volkswirtschaftsrat [*Political Economy Bureau*] [*German*]
VWRRC ...... Virginia Water Resources Research Center [*Virginia Polytechnic Institute and State University*] [*Research center*]   (RCD)
VWRS........ Vibrating Wire Rate Sensor
VWS .... Valdez, AK [*Location identifier*] [*FAA*]   (FAAL)
VWS .... Variable Word Size
VWS .... Virginia Woolf Society   (EA)
VWS .... Voice Warning System
VWSS........ Vertical Wire Sky Screen   (KSC)
VWSWCA.... Volkswagen Split Window Club of America   (EA)
VWTCA ..... Volkswagen Toy Collectors of America   (EA)
VWU .... Chincoteague Island, VA [*Location identifier*] [*FAA*]   (FAAL)
VWV .... Waterville, OH [*Location identifier*] [*FAA*]   (FAAL)
VWW .... Velocity of Wireless Waves
VWWI .... Veterans of World War I of USA   (EA)
VWY .... Visway Transport [*Toronto Stock Exchange symbol*]
VX.............. Air Development Squadron [*Navy*]
VX.............. Experimental Squadron [*Symbol*]   (MCD)
VX.............. Transvalair [*Switzerland*] [*ICAO designator*]   (FAAC)
VX.............. Vanex Resources Ltd. [*Vancouver Stock Exchange symbol*]
VX.............. Vauxhall [*Automobile*] [*British*]
VX.............. Velocity along the X-Axis   (NASA)
VX.............. Vertex [*Medicine*]
VX.............. Vivas, Care [*May You Live, Dear One*] [*Latin*]
VX.............. Voice
VX-1 .... OPTEVFOR Air Test and Evaluation Squadron One, Naval Air Station, Patuxent River, MD   (CAAL)
VX-4 .... OPTEVFOR Air Test and Evaluation Squadron Four, Naval Air Station, Pt. Mugu, CA   (CAAL)
VX-5 .... OPTEVFOR Air Test and Evaluation Squadron Five, Naval Weapons Center, China Lake, CA   (CAAL)
VXA .... Harlem Hospital Center, Health Sciences Library, New York, NY [*OCLC symbol*]   (OCLC)
VXC............ Lichinga [*Mozambique*] [*Airport symbol*]   (OAG)
VXD............ New York University, College of Dentistry Library, New York, NY [*OCLC symbol*]   (OCLC)
VXE .... Elmira College, Elmira, NY [*OCLC symbol*]   (OCLC)
VXE .... Sao Vicente [*Cape Verde Islands*] [*Airport symbol*]   (OAG)
VXF .... State University of New York, College of Environmental Science and Forestry, Syracuse, NY [*OCLC symbol*]   (OCLC)
VXG............ New York Botanical Garden Library, Bronx, NY [*OCLC symbol*]   (OCLC)
VXH .... Herkimer County Community College, Herkimer, NY [*OCLC symbol*]   (OCLC)
VXI............. Iona College, New Rochelle, NY [*OCLC symbol*]   (OCLC)
VXJ............. Jewish Theological Seminary of America, New York, NY [*OCLC symbol*]   (OCLC)
VXL .... Albany Medical College, Schaffer Library of Health Sciences, Albany, NY [*OCLC symbol*]   (OCLC)
VXLB .... Verex Laboratories [*NASDAQ symbol*]   (NQ)
VXM .... General Theological Seminary, St. Mark's Library, New York, NY [*OCLC symbol*]   (OCLC)
VXN .... New York State Department of Health, Albany, NY [*OCLC symbol*]   (OCLC)
VXO............ Houghton College, Houghton, NY [*OCLC symbol*]   (OCLC)
VXO............ Variable Crystal Oscillator
VXO............ Vaxjo [*Sweden*] [*Airport symbol*]   (OAG)
VXP .... State University of New York, College of Optometry, New York, NY [*OCLC symbol*]   (OCLC)
VXR .... Rochester Museum and Science Center, Rochester, NY [*OCLC symbol*]   (OCLC)
VXR .... Vertex Resources Ltd. [*Vancouver Stock Exchange symbol*]
VXT .... Tompkins-Cortland Community College, Dryden, NY [*OCLC symbol*]   (OCLC)
VXU .... Chautauqua-Cattaraugus Library System, Jamestown, NY [*OCLC symbol*]   (OCLC)
VXV .... Hudson Valley Community College, Troy, NY [*OCLC symbol*]   (OCLC)
VXW .... Vassar College, Poughkeepsie, NY [*OCLC symbol*]   (OCLC)
VXX .... Long Island University, C. W. Post Center, Greenvale, NY [*OCLC symbol*]   (OCLC)
VXY .... Centro de Estudios Puertorriquenos, New York, NY [*OCLC symbol*]   (OCLC)
VXZ .... Dowling College, Oakdale, NY [*OCLC symbol*]   (OCLC)
VY.............. Air Belgium [*Belgium*] [*ICAO designator*]   (FAAC)
VY.............. Valley   (ADA)
VY.............. Various Years [*Bibliography*]
VY.............. Velocity along the Y-Axis   (NASA)
VY.............. Very   (ROG)
VY.............. Victualling Yard [*Obsolete*] [*Navy*] [*British*]   (ROG)
VY.............. Vyquest, Inc. [*American Stock Exchange symbol*]
VYA .... Molloy College, Rockville Centre, NY [*OCLC symbol*]   (OCLC)
Vya .... Voprosy Yazykoznaniya [*Moscow*] [*A publication*]

VYB .... St. Barnabas Medical Staff Library, Livingston, NJ [*OCLC symbol*]   (OCLC)
VYB .... Vivian, Younger & Bond Ltd.
VYB .... Vyborg [*USSR*] [*Seismograph station code, US Geological Survey*] [*Closed*]   (SEIS)
VYBN........ Valley Bancorp [*NASDAQ symbol*]   (NQ)
VYC .... Cornell University, Medical College, New York, NY [*OCLC symbol*]   (OCLC)
Vychisl Metody & Program ... Vychislitel'nye Metody i Programmirovanie [*A publication*]
Vychisl Prikl Mat ... Kievskii Gosudarstvennyi Universitet. Mezhvedomstvennyi Nauchnyi Sbornik. Vychislitel'naya i Prikladnaya Matematika [*A publication*]
Vychisl Prikl Mat ... Vychislitel'naya i Prikladnaya Matematika [*A publication*]
Vychisl Seismol ... Vychislitel'naya Seismologiya [*USSR*] [*A publication*]
Vychisl Sist ... Vychislitel'nye Sistemy [*A publication*]
Vychisl Tekhn i Voprosy Kibernet ... Leningradskii Gosudarstvennyi Universitet. Vychislitel'nyi Tsentr. Moskovskii Gosudarstvennyi Universitet. Vychislitel'nyi Tsentr. Vychislitel'naya Tekhnika i Voprosy Kibernetiki [*A publication*]
Vycisl Mat i Vycisl Tehn (Kharkov) ... Vycislitel'naja Matematika i Vycislitel'naja Tehnika (Kharkov) [*A publication*]
Vycisl Prikl Mat (Kiev) ... Vycislitel'naja i Prikladnaja Matematika (Kiev) [*A publication*]
Vycisl Sistemy ... Akademija Nauk SSSR. Sibirskoe Otdelenie. Institut Matematiki. Vycislitel'nye Sistemy. Sbornik Trudov [*A publication*]
Vycisl Tehn v Masinostroen ... Vycislitel'naja Tehnika v Masinostroenii [*A publication*]
Vycisl Tehn i Voprosy Kibernet ... Vycislitel'naja Tehnika i Voprosy Kibernetiki [*A publication*]
VYD .... Capital District Library Council, Troy, NY [*OCLC symbol*]   (OCLC)
VYD .... Vryheid [*South Africa*] [*Airport symbol*]   (OAG)
VYE .... Manhattanville College, Purchase, NY [*OCLC symbol*]   (OCLC)
Vyestsi Akad Navuk BSSR Syer Biyal Navuk ... Vyestsi Akademii Navuk BSSR. Syeryya Biyalagichnykh Navuk [*A publication*]
Vyestsi Akad Navuk BSSR Syer Syel' Skahaspad Navuk ... Vyestsi Akademii Navuk BSSR. Syeryya Syel' Skahaspadarchukh Navuk [*A publication*]
VYF .... Fordham University, Bronx, NY [*OCLC symbol*]   (OCLC)
VYG........... Finger Lakes Library System, Ithaca, NY [*OCLC symbol*]   (OCLC)
VYGS .... Vermont Yankee Generating Station [*Nuclear energy*]   (NRCH)
VYI............. Kahului, HI [*Location identifier*] [*FAA*]   (FAAL)
Vyisn Akad Nauk Ukr RSR ... Vyisnik Akademyiyi Nauk Ukrayins'koyi RSR [*A publication*]
Vyisn Kiyiv Unyiv Ser Astron ... Vyisnik Kiyivs'kogo Unyiversitetu. Seryiya Astronomii [*A publication*]
Vyisn Kiyiv Unyiv Ser Fyiz ... Vyisnik Kiyivs'kogo Unyiversitetu. Seryiya Fyizika [*USSR*] [*A publication*]
Vyisn L'vyiv Derzh Unyiv Ser Fyiz ... Vyisnik L'vyivs'kij Derzhavnij Unyiversitet Imeni I. Franka. Seryiya Fyizichna [*A publication*]
Vyisn Syil'skogospod Nauki ... Vyisnik Syil'skogospodars'koyi Nauki [*A publication*]
VYJ............. Martinsburg, WV [*Location identifier*] [*FAA*]   (FAAL)
VYK .... Christ the King Seminary, East Aurora, NY [*OCLC symbol*]   (OCLC)
VYK .... Colombia, SC [*Location identifier*] [*FAA*]   (FAAL)
VYL .... Lehman College, Bronx, NY [*OCLC symbol*]   (OCLC)
VYM .... United States Merchant Marine Academy, Kings Point, NY [*OCLC symbol*]   (OCLC)
VYN .... Dallas-Fort Worth, TX [*Location identifier*] [*FAA*]   (FAAL)
VYN .... Union Theological Seminary, New York, NY [*OCLC symbol*]   (OCLC)
Vynohrad Vynorobstvo ... Vynohradarstvo i Vynorobstvo [*A publication*]
VYNP......... Vermont Yankee Nuclear Plant   (NRCH)
VYNPS .... Vermont Yankee Nuclear Power Station   (NRCH)
VYQ........... Upstate Medical Center, Syracuse, NY [*OCLC symbol*]   (OCLC)
VYQT........ Vyquest, Inc. [*NASDAQ symbol*]   (NQ)
VYR .... Rome Air Development Center, Griffiss AFB, NY [*OCLC symbol*]   (OCLC)
VYS .... St. Bonaventure University, St. Bonaventure, NY [*OCLC symbol*]   (OCLC)
VYS .... Visceral Yolk Sac [*Embryology*]
Vyskum Pr Odboru Papiera Celulozy ... Vyskumne Prace z Odboru Papiera a Celulozy [*A publication*]
Vysk Ustav Lesn Hospod Zvolene Lesn Stud ... Vyskumny Ustav Lesneho Hospodarstvavo Zvolene Lesnicke Studie [*A publication*]
Vysokomol Soed ... Vysokomolekulyarnye Soedineniya [*A publication*]
Vysokomol Soedin ... Vysokomolekulyarnye Soedineniya [*A publication*]
Vysokomol Soedin Geterotsepnye Vysokomol Soedin ... Vysokomolekulyarnye Soedineniya Geterotsepnye Vysokomolekulyarnye Soedineniya [*USSR*] [*A publication*]
Vysokomol Soedin Ser A ... Vysokomolekulyarnye Soedineniya. Seriya A [*A publication*]
Vysokomol Soedin Ser B ... Vysokomolekulyarnye Soedineniya. Seriya B [*A publication*]

Vysokomol Soedin Vses Khim Ovo ... Vysokomolekulyarnye Soedineniya Vsesoyuznoe Khimicheskoe Obshchestvo [*A publication*]
Vyso Soed A ... Vysokomolekulyarnye Soedineniya. Seriya A [*A publication*]
Vyso Soed B ... Vysokomolekulyarnye Soedineniya. Seriya B [*A publication*]
Vyssh Uchebn Zaved Izv Geol Razved ... Vysshoye Uchebnoye Zavedeniye. Izvestiya Geologiya i Razvedka [*A publication*]
Vys Sk Chem-Technol Praze Sb Oddil Chem Inz ... Vysoka Skola Chemicko-Technologicka v Praze. Sbornik. Oddil. Chemicke Inzenyrstvi [*A publication*]
Vys Soed B ... Vysokomolekulyarnye Soedineniya. Seriya B [*A publication*]
VYT .... Clarkson College of Technology, Potsdam, NY [*OCLC symbol*]   (OCLC)
Vytr Boles ... Vytreshni Bolesti [*A publication*]
VyV .... Verdad y Vida [*Milan*] [*A publication*]
Vyzk Ustav Vodohospodar Pr Stud ... Vyzkumny Ustav Vodohospodarsky. Prace a Studie [*A publication*]
Vyzk Ustav Vodohospod Pr Stud ... Vyzkumny Ustav Vodohospodarsky. Prace a Studie [*A publication*]
Vyz Lidu ..... Vyziva Lidu [*A publication*]
Vyznach Prisnovod Vodor Ukr RSR ... Vyznachnyk Prisnovodnykh Vodorostei Ukrains'koi RSR
Vyz Rodine ... Vyziva v Rodine [*A publication*]
VyzS........... Vyzvol'nyj Sljax [*A publication*]
Vyz Zdravie ... Vyzica a Zdravie [*A publication*]
VZ.............. Nefertiti Aviation [*Egypt*] [*ICAO designator*]   (FAAC)
VZ.............. Varicella-Zoster [*Also, VZV*] [*A virus*]
VZ.............. Velocity along the Z-Axis   (NASA)
VZ.............. Virtual Zero
VZ.............. Vostocnye Zapiski [*A publication*]
VZB .... State University of New York at Stony Brook, Health Sciences Library, Stony Brook, NY [*OCLC symbol*]   (OCLC)
VZC .... Clinton-Essex-Franklin Library, Plattsburgh, NY [*OCLC symbol*]   (OCLC)
VZD .... Vendor Zero Defect
VZE .... Mercy College, Dobbs Ferry, NY [*OCLC symbol*]   (OCLC)
VZF .... St. Francis College, Brooklyn, NY [*OCLC symbol*]   (OCLC)
VZG .... St. Joseph's College Library, Suffolk Campus, Patchogue, NY [*OCLC symbol*]   (OCLC)
VZH .... Hartwick College, Oneonta, NY [*OCLC symbol*]   (OCLC)
VZI .... Stony Brook Institute for Advanced Studies of World Religions, Stony Brook, NY [*OCLC symbol*]   (OCLC)
VZIG .... Varicella-Zoster Immune Globulin
VZJ .... St. John Fisher College, Rochester, NY [*OCLC symbol*]   (OCLC)
VZK .... King's College, Briarcliff Manor, NY [*OCLC symbol*]   (OCLC)
VZL .... Pace University, Law Library, White Plains, NY [*OCLC symbol*]   (OCLC)
VZL .... Vinzolidine [*Antineoplastic drug*]
VZM........... Margaret Woodbury Strong Museum, Rochester, NY [*OCLC symbol*]   (OCLC)
VZM........... Von Zeipel Method
VZN .... College of New Rochelle, New Rochelle, NY [*OCLC symbol*]   (OCLC)
Vznik Pocatky Slov ... Vznik a Pocatky Slovanu. Origine et Debuts des Slaves [*A publication*]
VZO .... Coatesville, PA [*Location identifier*] [*FAA*]   (FAAL)
VZP .... Pace University, New York, NY [*OCLC symbol*]   (OCLC)
VZQ .... Pratt Institute, Brooklyn, NY [*OCLC symbol*]   (OCLC)
VZR .... Roswell Park Memorial Institute, Buffalo, NY [*OCLC symbol*]   (OCLC)
Vzryvnoe Delo Nauchno-Tekh Gorn O-vo Sb ... Vzryvnoe Delo. Nauchno-Tekhnicheskoe Gornoe Obshchestvo Sbornik [*USSR*] [*A publication*]
VZS .... Skidmore College, Saratoga Springs, NY [*OCLC symbol*]   (OCLC)
VZS .... Valdez South [*Alaska*] [*Seismograph station code, US Geological Survey*]   (SEIS)
VZT .... St. Joseph's College, Brooklyn, NY [*OCLC symbol*]   (OCLC)
VZU .... Pace University, Pleasantville, Pleasantville, NY [*OCLC symbol*]   (OCLC)
VZV .... College of Mount Saint Vincent, New York, NY [*OCLC symbol*]   (OCLC)
VZV .... Varicella-Zoster Virus [*Also, VZ*]
VZW .... College of White Plains, White Plains, NY [*OCLC symbol*]   (OCLC)
VZW .... Valdez West [*Alaska*] [*Seismograph station code, US Geological Survey*]   (SEIS)
VZX .... Western New York Library Resources Council, Buffalo, NY [*OCLC symbol*]   (OCLC)
VZY .... Montefiore Hospital, Bronx, NY [*OCLC symbol*]   (OCLC)
VZZ .... International Museum of Photography, Eastman House, Rochester, NY [*OCLC symbol*]   (OCLC)

W

W .... Climatic Data for the World [*A publication*]
W .... Coast Guard Ship [*When precedes vessel classification*] [*Navy symbol*]
W .... Diameter of Driving-Wheel in Inches [*Railroad term*]
W .... Electrical Energy [*Symbol*] (DEN)
w .... Flow Rate [*Heat transmission symbol*]
W .... Indefinite Ceiling [*Meteorology*] (FAAC)
w .... Load per Unit of Length
W .... Requires an Engineer [*Search and rescue symbol that can be stamped in sand or snow*]
W .... Total Load
w------ .... Tropics [*MARC geographic area code*] [*Library of Congress*] (LCCP)
W .... Tryptophan [*One-letter symbol; see Trp*]
W .... Waffle [*Used in correcting manuscripts, etc.*]
W .... Waist (ADA)
W .... Wales
W .... Walk [*Baseball*]
W .... Wall
W .... Wallace Laboratories [*Research code symbol*]
W .... Waltz [*Music*]
W .... Wander AG [*Switzerland*] [*Research code symbol*]
W .... Wanderer Books [*Publisher's imprint*]
W .... Wanting
W .... War
W .... Warden
W .... Wardroom [*Aerospace*]
W .... Warehouse
W .... Warhead [*Nuclear*] (NG)
W .... Warm
W .... Warner-Lambert Pharmaceutical Co. [*Research code symbol*]
W .... Warning [*Railroad signal arm*] [*British*]
W .... Warning Area [*Followed by identification*]
W .... Warrant [*A document entitling holder to purchase a given issue of stock*]
W .... Washington Reports [*1890-1939*] (DLA)
W .... Waste
W .... Watch Time
W .... Water
W .... Water Point [*British Waterways Board sign*]
W .... Water Vapor Content
W .... Waterloo [*Army*] [*British*] (ROG)
W .... Watermeyer's Cape Of Good Hope Supreme Court Reports (DLA)
W .... Watt [*Broadcasting term*]
W .... Watt [*Symbol*] [*SI unit of power*] (GPO)
W .... Watt's Pennsylvania Reports (DLA)
W .... Wave Height Correction
W .... Weather
W .... Weather Aircraft Equipped with Meteorological Gear [*Designation for all US military aircraft*]
W .... Weather Review [*A publication*]
W .... Web
W .... Weber Fraction [*Psychology*]
W .... Wednesday
W .... Week
w .... Weekly
w .... Weekly Dose [*Medicine*]
W .... Weight
W .... Welding Program [*Association of Independent Colleges and Schools specialization code*]
W .... Welsh [*or Welch*]
W .... Wendell's Reports [*1826-41*] [*New York*] (DLA)
W .... Wesleyan
W .... West [*or Western*]
W .... West Point, NY [*Mint mark when appearing on US coins*]
W .... Westerhout [*Astronomy*]
W .... Westinghouse [*as in "Group W"*]
W .... Westvaco Corp. [*NYSE symbol*]
W .... Wet
W .... Wet Dew

W .... Wheaton's Reports [*14-25 United States*] (DLA)
W .... Wheeled [*Vehicles*] (NATG)
W .... Whip
W .... Whiskey [*Phonetic alphabet*] [*International*] (DSUE)
W .... White [*Maps and charts*]
W .... White [*Light, buoy, beacon*]
W .... Whitehorse Star [*A publication*]
W .... Whole [*Response*] [*Medicine*]
W .... Whole Word Designator [*Data processing*]
W .... Whorls and Compounds [*Fingerprint description*]
W .... Wicket
W .... Wide
W .... Widow [*or Widower*]
W .... Width
W .... Wife
W .... Will Advise [*Business and trade*]
w .... Will Factor [*Psychology*]
W .... Wille [*Will Factor*] [*Psychology*]
W .... William [*Phonetic alphabet*] [*Royal Navy*] [*World War I*] [*Pre-World War II*] [*World War II*] (DSUE)
W .... William (King of England) (DLA)
W .... Wilson's [*or Willson's*] Reports [*Texas Civil Cases, Court of Appeals*] (DLA)
W .... Winch
W .... Wind [*In reference to wind velocity*]
W .... Wins [*Sports*]
W .... Winter [*A publication*]
W .... Winter [*Vessel load line mark*]
W .... Wire
W .... Wisconsin Reports (DLA)
W .... With
W/ .... With [*in conjuction with other abbreviations*]
W .... Without Voice Facilities on Range or Radiobeacon Frequency
W .... Witwatersrand Local Division Reports [*South Africa*] (DLA)
W .... Wolfram [*Tungsten*] [*Chemical element*]
W .... Woman (ADA)
W .... Women's Reserve, Unlimited Service [*USNR officer designation*]
W .... Won [*Monetary unit in the Republic of Korea*]
W .... Won [*Sports statistics*]
W .... Wood
w .... Wooden [*Shipping*] (ROG)
W .... Word
w .... Work [*or w*] [*Symbol*] [*IUPAC*]
W .... Work
W .... Workmen's Compensation [*Insurance*]
W .... Worshipful [*Freemasonry*]
W .... Wortkunst [*A publication*]
W .... [*Alfred*] Wotquenne [*When used in identifying C. P. E. Bach's compositions, refers to cataloging of his works by musicologist Wotquenne*]
W .... Wright's Ohio Reports [*1831-34*] (DLA)
W .... Write
W .... Writer Officer [*Navy*] [*British*]
W .... Wrong
W .... Wyoming Reports (DLA)
1/W .... One-Way
1-W .... Selective Service Class [*for Conscientious Objector Performing Alternate Service Contributing to Maintenance of National Health, Safety, or Interest*]
W2 .... William II [*German emperor and king of Prussia, 1888-1918*] (DSUE)
3W .... Three-Wire (MSA)
4W .... Four-Wire
4-W .... Selective Service Class [*for Conscientious Objector Who Has Completed Alternate Service Contributing to National Health, Safety, or Interest*]
W-4 .... Wage Withholding Form [*IRS*]
4W .... Yemen Arab Republic [*Aircraft nationality and registration mark*] (FAAC)

5W .... Western Samoa [*Aircraft nationality and registration mark*]   (FAAC)
6W .... Senegal [*Aircraft nationality and registration mark*]   (FAAC)
3W's .... [*The*] Who, What, or Where Game [*Also, WWW*] [*Television show*]
5W's .... Who, What, When, Where, Why [*Journalism*]
W (Colds)... Whole Colds [*Medicine*]
WA.............. Appleton Public Library, Appleton, WI [*Library symbol*] [*Library of Congress*]   (LCLS)
WA.............. Independent Watchmen's Association
WA.............. Voice of Washington Music [*A publication*]
WA.............. Wabash Railroad Co. [*NYSE symbol*]
WA.............. Wage Record [*Social Security Administration*]   (OICC)
WA.............. Wainscot
WA.............. Walking Association   (EA)
WA.............. War Aims [*British*]
WA.............. Warbirds of America [*Later, WB*] [*An association*]   (EA)
WA.............. Warm Air
W/A............ Warrant of Arrest
Wa .... Warsaw [*A publication*]
WA.............. Washer
WA.............. Washington [*State*] [*Postal code*]
Wa .... Washington Reports   (DLA)
Wa .... Washington State Library, Olympia, WA [*Library symbol*] [*Library of Congress*]   (LCLS)
WA.............. Water Authority [*British*]
WA.............. Watertown Arsenal [*Massachusetts*] [*Army*]
Wa .... Watts' Reports [*1890-1939*]   (DLA)
WA.............. Waveform Analyzer
WA.............. Weapons Assignment   (NVT)
WA.............. Weather Atlas of the United States [*A publication*]
WA.............. Weighted Average
WA.............. Weizmann Israel Archives [*Rehovoth*]   (BJA)
WA.............. Welfare Administration [*Became Social and Rehabilitation Service*] [*HEW*]
WA.............. Wellness Associates [*Mill Valley, CA*]   (EA)
Wa .... Wellsiania [*An association*]   (EA)
WA.............. Weltwirtschaftliches Archiv [*A publication*]
WA.............. West Africa
WA.............. West Africa [*A publication*]
WA.............. Western Air Lines, Inc. [*ICAO designator*]
WA.............. Western Approaches [*to Great Britain and Ireland*] [*Obsolete*]
WA.............. Western Area
WA.............. Western Australia
W of A........ [*The*] Western Railway of Alabama
WA.............. [*The*] Western Railway of Alabama [*AAR code*]
WA.............. Westminster Abbey [*London*]
WA.............. When Awake
WA.............. Wide Angle [*Photography*]
WA.............. Will Adjust   (AABC)
WA.............. Wire Armored [*Cables*]
WA.............. Wire Assembly   (MSA)
WA.............. Wire Association [*Later, Wire Association International*]
WA.............. Wissenschaftliche Annalen [*A publication*]
WA.............. With Answers
WA.............. With Average [*Insurance*]
WA.............. Withholding Agent   (DLA)
WA.............. Wohl Associates [*Bala Cynwyd, PA*] [*Telecommunications*]   (TSSD)
WA.............. Women's Reserve, Aviation Nonflying Duties [*USNR officer designation*]
WA.............. Woolknit Associates [*New York, NY*]   (EA)
WA.............. Woolwich Armstrong Gun
WA.............. Word Add
WA.............. Word After [*Message handling*]
WA.............. Work Assignments   (MCD)
WA.............. Work Authorization   (MCD)
WA.............. Workers Anonymous [*Mythical organization devoted to helping human beings overcome their desire to lead productive lives; created by columnist Arthur Hoppe in satirizing short work week and early retirement schemes*]
WA.............. Workmanship Assurance
WA.............. Workshop Assembly [*Torpedo*]
WA.............. World Archaeology [*A publication*]
WA.............. Wright Aeronautical Corp.   (KSC)
WA.............. Writing Ability
WA1............ Wongan Hills [*Australia*] [*Seismograph station code, US Geological Survey*]   (SEIS)
WA2............ Wagin [*Australia*] [*Seismograph station code, US Geological Survey*]   (SEIS)
WA3............ Talbot Brook [*Australia*] [*Seismograph station code, US Geological Survey*]   (SEIS)
W-4A .... Wage Withholding Form [*Revised version*] [*IRS*]
WaA........... Aberdeen Public Library, Aberdeen, WA [*Library symbol*] [*Library of Congress*]   (LCLS)
WAA........... Wabash Motor Freight Tariff Association, Springfield IL [*STAC*]
WAA........... Wales [*Alaska*] [*Airport symbol*]   (OAG)
WAA........... Wales, AK [*Location identifier*] [*FAA*]   (FAAL)
WAA........... War Assets Administration [*For disposal of US surplus war property*] [*Post-World War II*]
WAA............ Warden's Association of America [*Later, NAAWS*]   (EA)

WAA........... Waris [*Papua New Guinea*] [*Seismograph station code, US Geological Survey*]   (SEIS)
WAA........... Wartime Aircraft Activity   (AFM)
Wa A.......... Washington Appellate Reports   (DLA)
WAA........... Water-Augmented Air Jet
WAA........... Welded Aluminum Alloy
WAA........... Western Amateur Astronomers   (EA)
WAA........... Western Australia Airways   (ADA)
WAA........... Western Awning Association [*Lomita, CA*]   (EA)
WAA........... Wide-Aperture Array   (MCD)
WAA........... Wien Air Alaska [*Air carrier designation symbol*]
WAA........... Women's Action Alliance   (EA)
WAA........... Worker Adjustment Assistance
WAA........... World Aluminum Abstracts [*A publication*]
WAA........... World Aluminum Abstracts [*American Society for Metals*] [*Metals Park, OH*] [*Database*] [*A publication*]   (EISS)
WAA........... World American Airlift   (FAAC)
WAAA........ Walleye Anglers Association of America [*Defunct*]   (EA)
WAAA .... Winston-Salem, NC [*AM radio station call letters*]
WAAAF ..... Women's Auxiliary Australian Air Force
WAABI....... National Women's Association of Allied Beverage Industries [*Washington, DC*]   (EA)
WAAC .... Valdosta, GA [*FM radio station call letters*]
WAAC .... West African Airways Corporation
WAAC .... Women's Army Auxiliary Corps [*Name later changed to WAC*] [*World War II*]
WAAD .... Westinghouse Air Arm Division
WAADS ..... Washington Air Defense Sector [*ADC*]
WAAE .... World Association for Adult Education
WAAF....... Women's Auxiliary Air Force [*Functioned under direct command of RAF*] [*World War II*] [*British*]
WAAF....... Worcester, MA [*FM radio station call letters*]
WAAFB ..... Walker Air Force Base   (AAG)
WAAG .... Galesburg, IL [*FM radio station call letters*]
WaAG....... Grays Harbor College, Aberdeen, WA [*Library symbol*] [*Library of Congress*]   (LCLS)
WAAIC ...... Women's Association of the African Independent Churches
WAAJ .... Water-Augmented Air Jet
WAAK .... Dallas, NC [*AM radio station call letters*]
WAAL .... Binghamton, NY [*FM radio station call letters*]
WaAlVA..... United States Veterans Administration Hospital, American Lake, WA [*Library symbol*] [*Library of Congress*]   (LCLS)
WAAM....... Ann Arbor, MI [*AM radio station call letters*]
WAAM....... Wide-Area Antiarmor Munitions [*Military*]   (MCD)
WAAMA ..... Woman's Auxiliary to the American Medical Association [*Later, AMAA*]   (EA)
WAAMAC... Weight, Alignment, and Mass Center Determination Equipment   (AAG)
WAAMMS ... Women's Auxiliary of the American Merchant Marine [*World War II*]
WaAn .... Anacortes Public Library, Anacortes, WA [*Library symbol*] [*Library of Congress*]   (LCLS)
WA Ann LR ... University of Western Australia. Annual Law Review [*A publication*]
WAAO .... Andalusia, AL [*AM radio station call letters*]
WAAP........ World Association for Animal Production   (EA-IO)
WAAPM..... Wide-Area Antipersonnel Mine [*Military*]
WAAQ .... Big Rapids, MI [*FM radio station call letters*]
WAAR........ Wartime Aircraft Activity Reporting [*System*]
WAAR........ Western Australian Arbitration Reports [*A publication*]
WA Arb R ... Western Australian Arbitration Reports   (DLA)
WA Arb R ... Western Australian Arbitration Reports [*A publication*]
WaArl .... Indian Ridge Treatment Center, Staff Library, Arlington, WA [*Library symbol*] [*Library of Congress*]   (LCLS)
WaArl-R ..... Indian Ridge Treatment Center, Resident Library, Arlington, WA [*Library symbol*] [*Library of Congress*]   (LCLS)
WA Art Gall Bull ... Western Australian Art Gallery. Bulletin [*A publication*]
WAAS........ Warning and Attack Assessment   (MCD)
WAAS........ Wide-Area Active Surveillance [*Military*]   (MCD)
WAAS........ Women's Auxiliary Army Service [*British*]
WAAS........ World Academy of Art and Science   (EA)
WAASC ..... Women's Auxiliary Army Service Corps [*British*]
WAAT........ Wildwood, NJ [*Television station call letters*]
WAATS ...... Weights Analysis for Advanced Transportation Systems [*NASA*]
WaAu .... Auburn Public Library, Auburn, WA [*Library symbol*] [*Library of Congress*]   (LCLS)
WaAuG....... Green River Community College, Auburn, WA [*Library symbol*] [*Library of Congress*]   (LCLS)
WAAV........ Wilmington-Leland, NC [*AM radio station call letters*]
WAAVP ...... World Association for the Advancement of Veterinary Parasitology   (EA-IO)
WAAW....... Murray, KY [*FM radio station call letters*]
WAAX........ Gadsden, AL [*AM radio station call letters*]
WAAY........ Huntsville, AL [*AM radio station call letters*]
WAAY-TV... Huntsville, AL [*Television station call letters*]
WAAZ-FM ... Crestview, FL [*FM radio station call letters*]
WAB .... Aero Industries, Inc. [*Richmond, VA*] [*FAA designator*]   (FAAC)
WAB .... Wabag [*Papua New Guinea*] [*Seismograph station code, US Geological Survey*]   (SEIS)
WAB .... Wabash Railroad System [*AAR code*] [*Obsolete*]

WAB .... Waffenabwurfbehaelter [*Parachute Weapons Container*] [*German military - World War II*]
WAB .... Wage Adjustment Board [*World War II*]
WAB .... Wage Appeals Board [*Department of Labor*]
WAB .... Water-Activated Battery
WAB .... Westamerica Bancorporation [*American Stock Exchange symbol*]
WAB .... Western Actuarial Bureau [*Later, ISO*]   (EA)
WAB .... When Authorized By
WAB .... Wine Advisory Board [*Later, WAG*]   (EA)
WAB .... World Association for Buiatrics   (EA-IO)
WABA .... Aguadilla, PR [*AM radio station call letters*]
WABA .... Women's American Basketball Association   (EA)
WABASH VLY ALSA ... Wabash Valley Area Library Services Authority [*Library network*]
WaBB .... Bellevue Community College, Bellevue, WA [*Library symbol*] [*Library of Congress*]   (LCLS)
WABB........ Mobile, AL [*AM radio station call letters*]
WABB-FM ... Mobile, AL [*FM radio station call letters*]
WABC .... New York, NY [*AM radio station call letters*]
WABCO...... Westinghouse Air Brake Company
WABC-TV ... New York, NY [*Television station call letters*]
WABD........ Fort Campbell, KY [*AM radio station call letters*]
WABD-FM ... Fort Campbell, KY [*FM radio station call letters*]
WABE........ Atlanta, GA [*FM radio station call letters*]
WaBe.......... Bellingham Public Library, Bellingham, WA [*Library symbol*] [*Library of Congress*]   (LCLS)
WABE........ Western Association of Broadcast Engineers [*Canada*]
WaBeCo..... Whatcom County Public Library, Bellingham, WA [*Library symbol*] [*Library of Congress*]   (LCLS)
WABEF....... Western Allenbee Oil & Gas Co. Ltd. [*NASDAQ symbol*]   (NQ)
WaBeSJ ..... Saint Joseph Hospital, Bellingham, WA [*Library symbol*] [*Library of Congress*]   (LCLS)
WaBeSL ..... Saint Luke's Hospital, Bellingham, WA [*Library symbol*] [*Library of Congress*]   (LCLS)
WaBeW ...... Western Washington State College [*Later, WWU*], Bellingham, WA [*Library symbol*] [*Library of Congress*]   (LCLS)
WABF........ Fairhope, AL [*AM radio station call letters*]
WaBfM .... Mission Creek Youth Camp, Staff Library, Belfair, WA [*Library symbol*] [*Library of Congress*]   (LCLS)
WaBfM-R.... Mission Creek Youth Camp, Resident Library, Belfair, WA [*Library symbol*] [*Library of Congress*]   (LCLS)
WABG .... Greenwood, MS [*AM radio station call letters*]
WaBGS....... Church of Jesus Christ of Latter-Day Saints, Genealogical Society Library, Bellevue Branch, Bellevue, WA [*Library symbol*] [*Library of Congress*]   (LCLS)
WABG-TV ... Greenwood, MS [*Television station call letters*]
WABI.......... Bangor, ME [*AM radio station call letters*]
WABI-TV ... Bangor, ME [*Television station call letters*]
WABJ .... Adrian, MI [*AM radio station call letters*]
WABK-FM ... Gardiner, ME [*FM radio station call letters*]
WABL........ Amite, LA [*AM radio station call letters*]
WABLC ...... Wilmington Area Biomedical Libraries [*Library network*]
WABN-FM ... Abingdon, VA [*FM radio station call letters*]
WABO .... Waynesboro, MS [*AM radio station call letters*]
WABO-FM ... Waynesboro, MS [*FM radio station call letters*]
WaBOH ...... Overlake Hospital, Medical Library, Bellevue, WA [*Library symbol*] [*Library of Congress*]   (LCLS)
WaBP .... Puget Sound Power and Light Co., Bellevue, WA [*Library symbol*] [*Library of Congress*]   (LCLS)
Wa-BPH ..... Washington Regional Library for the Blind and Physically Handicapped, Seattle, WA [*Library symbol*] [*Library of Congress*]   (LCLS)
WABQ .... Cleveland, OH [*AM radio station call letters*]
WaBr .... Kitsap Regional Library, Bremerton, WA [*Library symbol*] [*Library of Congress*]   (LCLS)
WABR........ West Asia Blocking Ridge [*Meteorology*]
WABR-FM ... Tifton, GA [*FM radio station call letters*]
WaBrH........ Harrison Memorial Hospital, Bremerton, WA [*Library symbol*] [*Library of Congress*]   (LCLS)
WaBrNP..... United States Navy, Puget Sound Naval Shipyard, Engineering Library, Bremerton, WA [*Library symbol*] [*Library of Congress*]   (LCLS)
WaBrNR ..... United States Navy, Naval Regional Medical Center, Bremerton, WA [*Library symbol*] [*Library of Congress*]   (LCLS)
WaBrNS ..... United States Navy, Naval Submarine Base, Bangor Library, Bremerton, WA [*Library symbol*] [*Library of Congress*]   (LCLS)
WaBrO........ Olympic College, Bremerton, WA [*Library symbol*] [*Library of Congress*]   (LCLS)
WaBrOC..... Olympic Center, Bremerton, WA [*Library symbol*] [*Library of Congress*]   (LCLS)
WABS........ Arlington, VA [*AM radio station call letters*]
WaBS .... Bellevue School District, Instructional Materials Center, Bellevue, WA [*Library symbol*] [*Library of Congress*]   (LCLS)
WABSIH ..... Society for Italic Handwriting, Western American Branch [*Later, WASIH*]   (EA)
WABTOC ... When Authorized by the Oversea Commander [*Military*]

WaBucR ..... Rainier School, Staff Library, Buckley, WA [*Library symbol*] [*Library of Congress*]   (LCLS)
WaBucR-R ... Rainier School, Resident Library, Buckley, WA [*Library symbol*] [*Library of Congress*]   (LCLS)
W A'B & W ... Webb, A'Beckett, and Williams' Reports [*A publication*]
W A'B & W Eq ... Webb, A'Beckett, and Williams' Equity Reports [*A publication*]
W A'B & W IE & M ... Webb, A'Beckett, and Williams' Insolvency, Ecclesiastical, and Matrimonial Reports [*A publication*]
W A'B & W Min ... Webb, A'Beckett, and Williams' Mining Cases [*A publication*]
WABW-TV ... Pelham, GA [*Television station call letters*]
WABX........ Clare, MI [*AM radio station call letters*]
WABY........ Albany, NY [*AM radio station call letters*]
WABZ-FM ... Albemarle, NC [*FM radio station call letters*]
WAC........... Waca [*Ethiopia*] [*Airport symbol*]   (OAG)
WAC........... Wake Analysis and Control   (MCD)
WAC........... War Assets Corporation [*Post-World War II*] [*Succeeded by War Assets Administration*]
WAC........... Weapon Arming Computer   (MCD)
WAC........... Weapons Assignment Console
WAC........... Weber Aircraft Company
WAC........... Wells American Corporation [*American Stock Exchange symbol*]
WAC........... West Africa Command [*World War II*]
WAC........... West Africa Committee   (EA)
WAC........... Western Archeological Center [*Department of the Interior*]
WAC........... Western Athletic Conference
WAC........... Wolfe Angel Committee [*Defunct*]   (EA)
WAC........... Women's Advisory Committee [*Trades Union Congress*] [*British*]
WAC........... Women's Aerobic Circuit [*Exercise regimen at some health spas*]
WAC........... Women's Army Corps [*Formerly, WAAC*] [*Abolished, 1978*]   (GPO)
WAC........... Work Accomplishment Code [*Military*]   (AFIT)
WAC........... Work Activities Center
WAC........... Work Assignment Card   (MCD)
WAC........... Worked All Continents [*Contacted at least one station on all continents*] [*Amateur radio*]
WAC........... Working Alternating Current   (DEN)
WAC........... World Aeronautical Charts [*Air Force*] [*A publication*]
WAC........... World Affairs Center for the United States [*Later, FPA*]
WAC........... World Area Code   (MCD)
WAC........... World Assistance Corps   (EA-IO)
WAC........... Wright Aeronautical Corporation   (MCD)
WAC........... Write Address Counter
WACA .... Walnut Canyon National Monument
WACA .... West African Court of Appeal, Selected Judgments   (DLA)
WACA .... Western Agricultural Chemicals Association [*Sacramento, CA*]   (EA)
WACA .... Winchester Arms Collectors Association   (EA)
WACA .... Women's Apparel Chains Associations [*New York, NY*]   (EA)
WACA .... World Airlines Clubs Association   (EA-IO)
WACA .... World Association of Center Associates   (EA)
WACAAI.... Women's Africa Committee of the African-American Institute   (EA)
WACASC ... West African Consolidated Administrative Service Center [*Foreign Service*]
WACB .... Kittanning, PA [*AM radio station call letters*]
WACB .... Women's Army Classification Battery   (AABC)
WACC .... Arnold, MD [*FM radio station call letters*]
WACC .... Washing Corrosion Control   (MCD)
WACC .... World Association for Christian Communication
WACCM ..... World Association for Chinese Church Music [*Hong Kong, Hong Kong*]   (EA-IO)
WACD .... Alexander City, AL [*AM radio station call letters*]
WACE .... Chicopee, MA [*AM radio station call letters*]
WaCeC....... Centralia College, Centralia, WA [*Library symbol*] [*Library of Congress*]   (LCLS)
WaCeM ...... Maple Lane School, Staff Library, Centralia, WA [*Library symbol*] [*Library of Congress*]   (LCLS)
WaCeW ...... Weyerhaeuser Co., Forestry Research Center, Centralia, WA [*Library symbol*] [*Library of Congress*]   (LCLS)
WACF........ Paris, IL [*FM radio station call letters*]
WACG-FM ... Augusta, GA [*FM radio station call letters*]
WACH .... Wedge Adjustable Cushioned Heel [*Orthopedics*]
WACH .... Worship Arts Clearing House   (EA)
WaChehG ... Green Hill School, Staff Library, Chehalis, WA [*Library symbol*] [*Library of Congress*]   (LCLS)
WaChehYS ... Washington State Twin City Center for Youth Services, Chehalis, WA [*Library symbol*] [*Library of Congress*]   (LCLS)
WaChenE... Eastern Washington State College, Cheney, WA [*Library symbol*] [*Library of Congress*]   (LCLS)
WACK .... Newark, NY [*AM radio station call letters*]
WACK .... Wait before Transmitting Positive Acknowledgment
WaCl .... Asotin County Library, Clarkston, WA [*Library symbol*] [*Library of Congress*]   (LCLS)
WACL......... Waycross, GA [*AM radio station call letters*]

WACL......... Worcester Area Cooperating Libraries [*Worcester, MA*] [*Library network*]
WACL......... World Anti-Communist League [*Seoul, Republic of Korea*] (EA-IO)
WACL-FM ... Waycross, GA [*FM radio station call letters*]
WaClvSC ... Spruce Canyon Correctional Center, Staff Library, Colville, WA [*Library symbol*] [*Library of Congress*] (LCLS)
WaClvSC-R ... Spruce Canyon Correctional Center, Resident Library, Colville, WA [*Library symbol*] [*Library of Congress*] (LCLS)
WACM....... West Springfield, MA [*AM radio station call letters*]
WACM....... Western Association of Circuit Manufacturers
WACN .... Franklin, KY [*AM radio station call letters*]
WACO .... Waco, TX [*AM radio station call letters*]
WACO .... Waterman Marine [*NASDAQ symbol*] (NQ)
WACO .... Written Advice of Contracting Officer [*Military*]
WaCol .... Whitman County Library, Colfax, WA [*Library symbol*] [*Library of Congress*] (LCLS)
WACPAC ... Whimsical Alternative Coalition Political Action Committee (EA)
WACQ .... Tallassee, AL [*AM radio station call letters*]
WACR .... Columbus, MS [*AM radio station call letters*]
WA Craftsman ... Western Australian Craftsman [*A publication*]
WACRAL.... World Association of Christian Radio Amateurs and Listeners (EA-IO)
WACRES.... Women's Army Corps Reserve
WACR-FM ... Columbus, MS [*FM radio station call letters*]
WACRI .... West African Cocoa Research Institution
WACS .... West African College of Surgeons [*See also COAC*] (EA-IO)
WACS .... Wire Automated Check System (MCD)
WACS .... Workshop Attitude Control System (MCD)
WACS .... World Association of Cooks Societies (EA)
WACSM ..... Women's Army Corps Service Medal
WACS-TV ... Dawson, GA [*Television station call letters*]
WACT....... Tuscaloosa, AL [*AM radio station call letters*]
WACT-FM ... Tuscaloosa, AL [*FM radio station call letters*]
WACU .... West African Customs Union
WACV .... Montgomery, AL [*AM radio station call letters*]
WACVA ..... Women's Army Corps-Veterans Association (EA)
WACY 2000 ... World Association for Celebrating the Year 2000
WAD .... Andriamena [*Madagascar*] [*Airport symbol*] (OAG)
WAD .... Waddy Lake Resources [*Toronto Stock Exchange symbol*] [*Vancouver Stock Exchange symbol*]
WAD .... Washington Aqueduct Division [*Army*]
WAD .... Weapon Assignment Display [*Air Force*]
WAD .... William Addison Dwiggins [*American type designer and illustrator, 1880-1956*]
WAD .... Work Authorization and Delegation
WAD .... Work Authorization Document
WAD .... World Association of Detectives [*Cincinnati, OH*] (EA)
WAD .... World Aviation Directory [*A publication*]
WAD .... World Wide Military Command Control System Automated Data Processing
Wa 2d .... Washington State Reports, Second Series (DLA)
WADA .... Shelby, NC [*AM radio station call letters*]
WADA .... Wissenschaftliche Annalen von der Deutschen Akademie [*A publication*]
WADAAA ... Washington District Army Audit Agency (MUGU)
WADB....... Point Pleasant, NJ [*FM radio station call letters*]
WADC .... Parkersburg, WV [*AM radio station call letters*]
WADC .... Western Air Defense Command
WADC .... Wright Air Development Center [*Air Force*]
W ADD....... With Added [*Freight*]
WADD .... Wright Air Development Division [*Air Force*]
Wad Dig ..... Waddilove's Digest of Ecclesiastical Cases [*1849*] (DLA)
WADE........ Wadesboro, NC [*AM radio station call letters*]
WADE........ World Association of Document Examiners (EA)
Wade Am Mining Law ... Wade on American Mining Law (DLA)
Wade Attachm ... Wade on Attachment and Garnishment (DLA)
WA Democrat ... West Australian Democrat [*A publication*]
WADEX ...... Words and Authors Index [*Computer-produced index*]
WADF........ Western Air Defense Force
WADFFU .... Women's Association for the Defense of Four Freedoms for Ukraine (EA)
WADH .... Wadham College [*Oxford University*] (ROG)
WADI .... Corinth, MS [*FM radio station call letters*]
WADJ........ Somerset, PA [*AM radio station call letters*]
WADK .... Newport, RI [*AM radio station call letters*]
WADL........ Mount Clemens, MI [*Television station call letters*]
WADL........ Wiener Arbeiten zur Deutschen Literatur [*A publication*]
Wadley Med Bull ... Wadley Medical Bulletin [*A publication*]
WADM....... Decatur, IN [*AM radio station call letters*]
Wad Mar & Div ... Waddilove on Marriage and Divorce [*1864*] (DLA)
WADO .... New York, NY [*AM radio station call letters*]
WADR........ Remsen, NY [*AM radio station call letters*]
WADR........ Weight Analysis Data Report
WADS....... Ansonia, CT [*AM radio station call letters*]
WADS....... Wide-Angle Display System
WADS....... Wide-Area Data Service [*Data transmission service*]
WAD/SO .... Work Authorization Document/Shop Order (NASA)
Wadsworth Ath Bul ... Wadsworth Atheneum. Bulletin [*A publication*]

WADU .... Norco, LA [*AM radio station call letters*]
W Adv......... Wesleyan Advocate [*A publication*]
WADVBS.... World Association of Daily Vacation Bible Schools [*Later, Vacation Bible Schools*] (EA)
WADX....... Trenton, GA [*AM radio station call letters*]
WADZ....... Americus, GA [*FM radio station call letters*]
WaE......... Everett Public Library, Everett, WA [*Library symbol*] [*Library of Congress*] (LCLS)
WAE .... Weapon Aiming Error
WAE .... When [*or While*] Actually Employed [*Government short jobs*]
WAE .... Wilfred American Educational Corp. [*NYSE symbol*]
WAE .... Wills and Administration of Estates [*Law*]
WAE .... World Association of Estonians (EA)
WaEawC .... Canyon View Group Home, East Wenatchee, WA [*Library symbol*] [*Library of Congress*] (LCLS)
WAEB....... Allentown, PA [*AM radio station call letters*]
WAEB-FM ... Allentown, PA [*FM radio station call letters*]
WAEC....... Atlanta, GA [*AM radio station call letters*]
Wa-Ec .... Washington State Library, Ecology Department, Olympia, WA [*Library symbol*] [*Library of Congress*] (LCLS)
WAEC .... West African Economic Community
WAED .... Huntsville, AL [*FM radio station call letters*]
WAED........ Westinghouse Aerospace Electrical Division
WA Ed Circ ... Education Circular. Western Australian Education Department [*A publication*]
WaEdE .... Edmonds Community College, Edmonds, WA [*Library symbol*] [*Library of Congress*] (LCLS)
WA Educ News ... WA Education News [*Education Department of Western Australia*] [*A publication*]
WaEE .... Everett Community College, Everett, WA [*Library symbol*] [*Library of Congress*] (LCLS)
WaEG .... Everett General Hospital, Medical Library, Everett, WA [*Library symbol*] [*Library of Congress*] (LCLS)
WA Egg Marketing Board Nletter ... Western Australia. Egg Marketing Board. Newsletter [*A publication*]
WaEGS....... Church of Jesus Christ of Latter-Day Saints, Genealogical Society Library, Everett, Washington Stake Branch, Everett, WA [*Library symbol*] [*Library of Congress*] (LCLS)
WAEJ .... World Association of Esperanto Journalists [*See also TEJA*] (EA-IO)
WaEJP........ Washington State Office of Juvenile Parole Services, Everett, WA [*Library symbol*] [*Library of Congress*] (LCLS)
WaEl.......... Ellensburg Public Library, Ellensburg, WA [*Library symbol*] [*Library of Congress*] (LCLS)
WAEL .... Mayaguez, PR [*AM radio station call letters*]
WaElC .... Central Washington State College, Ellensburg, WA [*Library symbol*] [*Library of Congress*] (LCLS)
WAELD...... Wave Electronics [*A publication*]
WA Electr Contract ... WA [*Western Australian*] Electrical Contractor [*A publication*]
WAEL-FM ... Maricao, PR [*FM radio station call letters*]
WAEMA...... Western and English Manufacturers Association [*Denver, CO*] (EA)
WaEp.......... Ephrata Public Library, Ephrata, WA [*Library symbol*] [*Library of Congress*] (LCLS)
WAEP......... World Association for Element Building and Prefabrication (EA-IO)
WAEPA ...... War Agencies Employees Protective Association
WAEPA ...... Worldwide Assurance for Employees of Public Agencies [*Falls Church, VA*] (EA)
WaEPH....... Providence Hospital, Everett, WA [*Library symbol*] [*Library of Congress*] (LCLS)
WaEpS .... Sunrise Group Home, Ephrata, WA [*Library symbol*] [*Library of Congress*] (LCLS)
WAER........ Syracuse, NY [*FM radio station call letters*]
WAER........ World Association for Educational Research [*See also AMSE*] (EA)
Waerme- Stoffuebertrag ... Waerme- und Stoffuebertragung [*A publication*]
Waerme Stoffuebertrag/Thermo Fluid Dyn ... Waerme- und Stoffuebertragung/Thermo and Fluid Dynamics [*A publication*]
Waermetech ... Waermetechnik [*A publication*]
WAERSA.... World Agricultural Economics and Rural Sociology Abstracts [*A publication*]
WAES........ Workshop on Alternative Energy Strategies
WAEV........ Savannah, GA [*FM radio station call letters*]
WAEW....... Crossville, TN [*AM radio station call letters*]
WAEY........ Princeton, WV [*AM radio station call letters*]
WAEY-FM ... Princeton, WV [*FM radio station call letters*]
WaEYS ...... Washington State Center for Youth Services, Everett, WA [*Library symbol*] [*Library of Congress*] (LCLS)
WAEZ-FM ... Milton, WV [*FM radio station call letters*]
WAF .... Wafer (AAG)
Wa-F.......... Washington State Film Library, Olympia, WA [*Library symbol*] [*Library of Congress*] (LCLS)
WAF .... Width across Flats (MSA)
WAF .... Wiring around Frame (MSA)
WAF .... With All Faults [*i.e., to be sold as is*]
WAF .... Woman Activist Fund (EA)
WAF .... Women in the Air Force

WAF .... Women's Aglow Fellowship (EA)
WAF .... Women's Auxiliary Force [*British*] [*World War I*] [*Later, Victory Corps*]
WAF .... Word Address Format
WAF .... Wound Angiogensis Factor [*Biochemistry*]
WAF .... WTC, Inc. [*American Stock Exchange symbol*]
WAFB........ Warren Air Force Base [*Wyoming*] (AAG)
WAFB-TV .. Baton Rouge, LA [*Television station call letters*]
WAFC........ Clewiston, FL [*AM radio station call letters*]
WAFC........ West African Fisheries Commission
WAFC........ Western Area Frequency Coordinator
WAFC-FM .. Clewiston, FL [*FM radio station call letters*]
WAF/CP..... Women and Foundations/Corporate Philanthropy (EA)
WAFE .... Wives of the Armed Forces, Emeritus [*Defunct*] (EA)
WAFF .... Wartime Fuel Factors
WAFF .... West African Frontier Force
WAFFLE.... Wide-Angle Fixed-Field Locating Equipment
WAFF-TV ... Huntsville, AL [*Television station call letters*]
WAFG........ Fort Lauderdale, FL [*FM radio station call letters*]
WAFL .... Milford, DE [*FM radio station call letters*]
W Af LR ..... West African Law Reports (DLA)
WAFLT Forum ... Washington Association of Foreign Language Teachers. Forum [*A publication*]
WAFM .... Amory, MS [*FM radio station call letters*]
WaForC..... Clearwater Correctional Center, Staff Library, Forks, WA [*Library symbol*] [*Library of Congress*] (LCLS)
WaForC-R ... Clearwater Correctional Center, Resident Library, Forks, WA [*Library symbol*] [*Library of Congress*] (LCLS)
WAFP .... Woody Allen's Fall Picture [*Designation reflecting the filmmaker's reluctance to provide information about his movies in advance of their commercial release*] [*See also WASP*]
WAFR........ Durham, NC [*FM radio station call letters*]
W Afr App ... West African Court of Appeal Reports (DLA)
W Afr J Arc ... West African Journal of Archaeology [*A publication*]
WA Fruitgrower ... Western Australian Fruitgrower [*A publication*]
WAFS........ Women's Auxiliary Ferrying Squadron [*Part of Air Transport Command*] [*World War II*]
WAFS .... Women's Auxiliary Fire Service [*British*] [*World War II*]
WaFsWS .... Western State Hospital, Staff Library, Fort Steilacoom, WA [*Library symbol*] [*Library of Congress*] (LCLS)
WAFT .... Valdosta, GA [*FM radio station call letters*]
WaFtl......... United States Army, Fort Lewis Library System, Grandstaff Library, Fort Lewis, WA [*Library symbol*] [*Library of Congress*] (LCLS)
WaFW........ Whatcom Community College, Ferndale, WA [*Library symbol*] [*Library of Congress*] (LCLS)
WAFWA..... Western Association of Fish and Wildlife Agencies (EA)
WaFwS....... Federal Way School District Central Library, Federal Way, WA [*Library symbol*] [*Library of Congress*] (LCLS)
WAG.......... Wagon (MSA)
WAG.......... Walgreen Co. [*NYSE symbol*]
WAG.......... Wanganui [*New Zealand*] [*Airport symbol*] (OAG)
WAG.......... Warfare Analysis Group [*Navy*]
WAG.......... Water-Alternating Gas
WAG.......... Wellsville, Addison & Galeton Railroad Corp. [*AAR code*]
WAG.......... Wiederaufbaugesellschaft fuer die Juedische Bevoelkerung der Bucovina [*A publication*] (BJA)
WAG.......... Wild Aim Guess [*Bowdlerized version*]
WAG.......... Wine Appreciation Guild [*Formerly, WAB*] (EA)
WAG.......... World Area Grid (MCD)
WaGal .... Intermediate School District 113, Instructional Materials Center, Galvin, WA [*Library symbol*] [*Library of Congress*] (LCLS)
WAGA-TV ... Atlanta, GA [*Television station call letters*]
WAGC........ Centre, AL [*AM radio station call letters*]
WaGc .... Grand Coulee Public Library, Grand Coulee, WA [*Library symbol*] [*Library of Congress*] (LCLS)
WAGC........ World Amateur Golf Council (EA)
WAGCOM ... War Game Comparison (MCD)
WAGE .... Leesburg, VA [*AM radio station call letters*]
WAGE .... Union Women's Alliance to Gain Equality (EA)
Wage-Price L & Econ Rev ... Wage-Price Law and Economics Review [*A publication*]
Wage-Pr L ... Wage-Price Law and Economics Review [*A publication*]
WAGF........ Dothan, AL [*AM radio station call letters*]
WAGFEI ..... Women's Action Group on Excision and Infibulation (EA-IO)
WAGG .... Birmingham, AL [*AM radio station call letters*]
WAGG .... Western Australia Government Gazette [*A publication*]
Wagga Hist Soc News ... Wagga Wagga and District Historical Society. Newsletter [*A publication*]
WAGGGS... World Association of Girl Guides and Girl Scouts [*See also AMGE*] (EA-IO)
WaGhP....... Purdy Treatment Center for Women, Gig Harbor, WA [*Library symbol*] [*Library of Congress*] (LCLS)
WAGI-FM ... Gaffney, SC [*FM radio station call letters*]
WAGL........ Lancaster, SC [*AM radio station call letters*]
WAGM-TV ... Presque Isle, ME [*Television station call letters*]
WAGN .... Menominee, MI [*AM radio station call letters*]
Wagner Free Inst Sci Bull Cards ... Wagner Free Institute of Science. Bulletin. Cards [*A publication*]

Wagner Free I Sc Tr ... Wagner Free Institute of Science [*Philadelphia*]. Transactions [*A publication*]
WAGO........ Reading, PA [*AM radio station call letters*]
WA Govt Gaz ... Western Australia Government Gazette [*A publication*]
WAGP........ Beaufort, SC [*FM radio station call letters*]
WAGQ .... Athens, GA [*FM radio station call letters*]
WAGR .... Lumberton, NC [*AM radio station call letters*]
WAGR .... Wald, Arnold, Goldberg, Rushton [*Test*] [*Statistics*]
WAGR .... Windscale Advanced Gas-Cooled Reactor
WAGRO..... Warsaw Ghetto Resistance Organization (EA)
WAGS .... Bishopville, SC [*AM radio station call letters*]
WAGS .... Weighted Agreement Scores
WAGSO..... Wiener Archiv fuer Geschichte des Slawentums und Osteuropas [*A publication*]
Wag St .... Wagner's Missouri Statutes (DLA)
WAGT .... Augusta, GA [*Television station call letters*]
WAGY .... Forest City, NC [*AM radio station call letters*]
WAH.......... Wahluke [*Washington*] [*Seismograph station code, US Geological Survey*] (SEIS)
WAH.......... Womack Army Hospital Medical Library, Fort Bragg, NC [*OCLC symbol*] (OCLC)
WAH.......... Writings on American History [*A publication*]
WAHA .... Wide-Angle High Aperture (MCD)
WAHC .... Oshkosh, WI [*FM radio station call letters*]
WAHC .... West African Health Community (EA)
WAHC .... World Airlines Hobby Club (EA)
WaHi.......... Washington State Historical Society, Tacoma, WA [*Library symbol*] [*Library of Congress*] (LCLS)
WA Hist Soc J ... Western Australian Historical Society. Journal and Proceedings [*A publication*]
WAHO .... World Arabian Horse Organization (EA-IO)
WAHR........ Huntsville, AL [*FM radio station call letters*]
WAHS........ Auburn Heights, MI [*FM radio station call letters*]
WAHSJ....... Western Australian Historical Society Journal [*A publication*] (ADA)
WAHT........ Annville-Cleona, PA [*AM radio station call letters*]
WAHVM..... World Association for the History of Veterinary Medicine (EA-IO)
WAI .... Antsohihy [*Madagascar*] [*Airport symbol*] (OAG)
WAI .... Wairiri [*Glentunnel*] [*New Zealand*] [*Seismograph station code, US Geological Survey*] [*Closed*] (SEIS)
WAI .... Walk Around Inspection
WAI .... Water Absorption Index [*Analytical chemistry*]
WAI .... Water Alcohol Injection (MCD)
WAI .... Wire Association International [*Formerly, Wire Association*] (EA)
WAI .... Work in America Institute
WAIA .... St. Augustine Beach, FL [*AM radio station call letters*]
WAIC .... Springfield, MA [*FM radio station call letters*]
WAICA ...... Women's Auxiliary of the ICA [*International Chiropractors Association*] [*Lander, WY*] (EA)
WAID .... Clarksdale, MS [*FM radio station call letters*]
WAID .... Wage and Information Documents [*IRS*]
WAIF .... Cincinnati, OH [*FM radio station call letters*]
WAIF .... World Adoption International Fund
WAIG .... Western Australia Industrial Gazette (DLA)
WAIG .... Western Australian Industrial Gazette [*A publication*]
WAIHA ...... Warm Autoimmune Hemolytic Anemia [*Medicine*]
WAIJ.......... Grantsville, MD [*FM radio station call letters*]
WAIK .... Galesburg, IL [*AM radio station call letters*]
Waikato Univ Antarct Res Unit Rep ... Waikato University. Antarctic Research Unit. Reports [*A publication*]
WAIL .... Key West, FL [*FM radio station call letters*]
WAIM .... Anderson, SC [*AM radio station call letters*]
WAIN.......... Columbia, KY [*AM radio station call letters*]
WA Ind Gaz ... Western Australian Industrial Gazette [*A publication*]
WA Indus Gaz ... Western Australian Industrial Gazette [*A publication*]
WAIN-FM ... Columbia, KY [*FM radio station call letters*]
WAIOP .... Will Accept, If Offered, the Position of _____ (FAAC)
WAIP .... World Association for Infant Psychiatry [*Later, WAIPAD*] (EA)
WAIPAD ..... World Association for Infant Psychiatry and Allied Disciplines [*Formerly, WAIP*] [*Washington, DC*] (EA)
WAIQ.......... Montgomery, AL [*Television station call letters*]
WAIR .... Winston-Salem, NC [*AM radio station call letters*]
WAIS .... Buchtel, OH [*AM radio station call letters*]
WAIS .... Wechsler Adult Intelligence Scale [*Education*]
WAIS-R ..... Wechsler Adult Intelligence Scale-Revised [*Test*]
WAIT .... Crystal Lake, IL [*AM radio station call letters*]
WAIT .... Western Australia Institute of Technology [*Database originator and operator*] [*South Bentley, WA, Australia*]
Wait Act & Def ... Wait's Actions and Defences (DLA)
Wait Co ..... Wait's New York Annotated Code (DLA)
Wait Dig ..... Wait's New York Digest (DLA)
Wait Pr .... Wait's New York Practice (DLA)
WAITRO ..... World Association of Industrial and Technological Research Organizations
Waits Prac ... Wait's New York Practice (DLA)
Wait St Pap ... Wait's State Papers of the United States (DLA)
Wait Tab Ca ... Wait's New York Table of Cases (DLA)
WAIV-FM ... Jacksonville, FL [*FM radio station call letters*]

WAJ .... Wajima [*Japan*] [*Seismograph station code, US Geological Survey*] (SEIS)
WAJ .... Water-Augmented Jet
WAJ .... World Association of Judges
WAJC .... Indianapolis, IN [*FM radio station call letters*]
WAJCSC .... W. Alton Jones Cell Science Center, Inc. [*Lake Placid, NY*] [*Research center*] (RCD)
WAJE .... West African Journal of Education [*A publication*]
WAJF .... Decatur, AL [*AM radio station call letters*]
WAJI .... Fort Wayne, IN [*FM radio station call letters*]
WAJK .... La Salle, IL [*FM radio station call letters*]
WAJL .... Winter Park, FL [*AM radio station call letters*]
WAJML .... West Africa Journal of Modern Language [*A publication*]
WAJN .... Ashland City, TN [*AM radio station call letters*]
WAJO .... Marion, AL [*AM radio station call letters*]
WAJR .... Morgantown, WV [*AM radio station call letters*]
WAJY .... New Orleans, LA [*FM radio station call letters*]
WAK .... Ankazoabo [*Madagascar*] [*Airport symbol*] (OAG)
WAK .... Wackenhut Corp. [*NYSE symbol*]
WAK .... Wait Acknowledge
wak .... Wakashan [*MARC language code*] [*Library of Congress*] (LCCP)
WAK .... Wake Island [*Three-letter standard code*] (CNC)
WAK .... Wakkanai [*Japan*] [*Seismograph station code, US Geological Survey*] (SEIS)
WAK .... Water Analyzer Kit
WAK .... Wearable Artificial Kidney
WAK .... Write Access Key
WAKA .... Selma, AL [*Television station call letters*]
Wakayama Med Rep ... Wakayama Medical Reports [*A publication*]
WAKC-TV ... Akron, OH [*Television station call letters*]
WAKE .... Valparaiso, IN [*AM radio station call letters*]
Wake Forest Intra L Rev ... Wake Forest Intramural Law Review (DLA)
Wake Forest L Rev ... Wake Forest Law Review [*A publication*]
Wake For L Rev ... Wake Forest Law Review [*A publication*]
Wake For Univ Dev Nations Monogr Ser Ser II Med Behav Sci ... Wake Forest University. Developing Nations Monograph Series. Series II. Medical Behavioral Science [*A publication*]
Wake For Unive Dev Nations Monogr Ser Ser II Med Behav Sci ... Wake Forest University. Developing Nations Monograph Series. Series II. Medical Behavioral Science [*A publication*]
WaKel .... Kelso Public Library, Kelso, WA [*Library symbol*] [*Library of Congress*] (LCLS)
WaKeM ...... Mid-Columbia Regional Library, Kennewick, WA [*Library symbol*] [*Library of Congress*] (LCLS)
WaKenS ..... Saint Thomas Seminary, Kenmore, WA [*Library symbol*] [*Library of Congress*] (LCLS)
WAKG .... Danville, VA [*FM radio station call letters*]
WAKH .... McComb, MS [*FM radio station call letters*]
WAKI .... McMinnville, TN [*AM radio station call letters*]
WaKiN .... Northwest College, Kirkland, WA [*Library symbol*] [*Library of Congress*] (LCLS)
WAKK .... McComb, MS [*AM radio station call letters*]
WAKM .... Franklin, TN [*AM radio station call letters*]
WAKN .... Aiken, SC [*AM radio station call letters*]
WAKO .... Lawrenceville, IL [*AM radio station call letters*]
WAKO-FM ... Lawrenceville, IL [*FM radio station call letters*]
WAKQ .... Paris, TN [*FM radio station call letters*]
WAKR .... Akron, OH [*AM radio station call letters*]
WAKS .... Fuquay Varina, NC [*AM radio station call letters*]
WAKS-FM ... Fuquay Varina, NC [*FM radio station call letters*]
Waksman Inst Microbiol Rutgers Univ Annu Rep ... Waksman Institute of Microbiology. Rutgers University. Annual Report [*A publication*]
WAKW .... Cincinnati, OH [*FM radio station call letters*]
WAKX .... Duluth, MN [*FM radio station call letters*]
WAKY .... Louisville, KY [*AM radio station call letters*]
WAL .... Chincoteague, VA [*Location identifier*] [*FAA*] (FAAL)
WAL .... Lawrence University, Appleton, WI [*Library symbol*] [*Library of Congress*] (LCLS)
wal .... Walamo [*MARC language code*] [*Library of Congress*] (LCCP)
Wal .... Waldorf [*Record label*]
WAL .... Wallace [*Idaho*] [*Seismograph station code, US Geological Survey*] (SEIS)
WAL .... Walloon (ROG)
WAL .... Walsh College, Canton, OH [*OCLC symbol*] (OCLC)
Wa-L .... Washington State Law Library, Olympia, WA [*Library symbol*] [*Library of Congress*] (LCLS)
WAL .... Waterloo Resources, Inc. [*Vancouver Stock Exchange symbol*]
WAL .... Watertown Arsenal Laboratory [*Massachusetts*] [*Army*]
WAL .... We Are Lost [*Army*]
WAL .... [*The*] Weather Almanac [*A publication*]
WAL .... Western Allegheny Railroad Co. [*AAR code*]
WAL .... Western American Literature [*A publication*]
W-AL .... Westinghouse-Astronuclear Laboratories
WAL .... Wide-Angle Lens
WAL .... World Association of Lawyers (EA)
WAL .... Wright Aeronautical Laboratories (MCD)
WALA News ... West African Library Association. News [*A publication*]
WALA-TV ... Mobile, AL [*Television station call letters*]
WALB .... Walbro Corp. [*NASDAQ symbol*] (NQ)

WALB-TV ... Albany, GA [*Television station call letters*]
WALC .... Worldwide Aviation Logistics Conference (RDA)
Wal Ch .... Walker's Michigan Chancery Reports (DLA)
WALD .... Waldbaum, Inc. [*NASDAQ symbol*] (NQ)
Wald .... Walden [*Record label*]
WALD .... Walterboro, SC [*AM radio station call letters*]
WALD-FM ... Walterboro, SC [*FM radio station call letters*]
WALDO ...... Wichita Automatic Linear Data Output
WALDO ...... Winona Tri College University Library Network [*Library network*]
WALE .... Fall River, MA [*AM radio station call letters*]
WALF .... Alfred, NY [*FM radio station call letters*]
Walf Cust ... Wallford's Laws of the Customs [*1846*] (DLA)
Walford's Antiq ... Walford's Antiquarian and Bibliographer [*A publication*]
Walf Part .... Walford's Parties to Actions [*1842*] (DLA)
Walf Railw ... Walford on Railways [*2nd ed.*] [*1846*] (DLA)
WALG .... Albany, GA [*AM radio station call letters*]
WALH .... Mountain City, GA [*AM radio station call letters*]
WALI .... Cumberland, MD [*AM radio station call letters*]
Wal Jr .... [*J. W.*] Wallace's United States Circuit Court Reports (DLA)
WALK .... Patchogue, NY [*AM radio station call letters*]
Walk .... Walker's Michigan Chancery Reports (DLA)
Walk .... Walker's Pennsylvania Reports [*1855-1885*] (DLA)
Walk .... Walker's Reports [*96, 109 Alabama*] (DLA)
Walk .... Walker's Reports [*22-25, 38-51, 72-88 Texas*] [*1-10 Civil Appeals Texas*] (DLA)
Walk .... Walker's Reports [*1 Mississippi*] (DLA)
Walk Am Law ... Walker's American Law (DLA)
Walk Bank L ... Walker's Banking Law [*2nd ed.*] [*1885*] (DLA)
Walk Ch ..... Walker's Michigan Chancery Reports (DLA)
Walk Chanc Rep ... Walker's Michigan Chancery Reports (DLA)
Walk Ch Cas ... Walker's Michigan Chancery Reports (DLA)
Walk Ch Mich ... Walker's Michigan Chancery Reports (DLA)
Walker .... Walker's Michigan Chancery Reports (DLA)
Walker .... Walker's Pennsylvania Reports [*1855-1885*] (DLA)
Walker .... Walker's Reports [*96, 109 Alabama*] (DLA)
Walker .... Walker's Reports [*22-25, 38-51, 72-88 Texas*] [*1-10 Civil Appeals Texas*] (DLA)
Walker .... Walker's Reports [*1 Mississippi*] (DLA)
Walker's Ch R ... Walker's Michigan Chancery Reports (DLA)
Walk Exec ... Walker and Elgood's Executors and Administrators [*6th ed.*] [*1926*] (DLA)
WALK-FM ... Patchogue, NY [*FM radio station call letters*]
Walk La Dig ... Walker's Louisiana Digest (DLA)
Walk (Mic) Ch ... Walker's Michigan Chancery Reports (DLA)
Walk Mich ... Walker's Michigan Chancery Reports (DLA)
Walk Michig Rep ... Walker's Michigan Chancery Reports (DLA)
Walk Miss ... Walker's Reports [*1 Mississippi*] (DLA)
Walk PA ..... Walker's Pennsylvania Reports [*1855-85*] (DLA)
Walk Pat ..... Walker on Patents (DLA)
Walk Tex .... Walker's Reports [*22-25, 38-51, 72-88 Texas*] [*1-10 Civil Appeals Texas*] (DLA)
WALL .... Middletown, NY [*AM radio station call letters*]
Wall .... Wallace's Nova Scotia Reports (DLA)
Wall .... Wallace's Supreme Court Reports [*68-90 United States*] [*1863-74*] (DLA)
Wall .... Wallace's United States Circuit Court Reports (DLA)
WALL .... Wallachian (ROG)
Wall .... Wallis' Irish Chancery Reports (DLA)
Wal by L ..... Wallis' Irish Chancery Reports, by Lyne (DLA)
Wall .... Wallis' Philadelphia Reports [*1855-85*] [*Pennsylvania*] (DLA)
WALL .... Walloon (ROG)
Wallace Jr Rept ... [*J. W.*] Wallace, Junior's, United States Circuit Court Reports (DLA)
Wallaces F ... Wallaces Farmer [*A publication*]
Walla Walla Coll Publ ... Walla Walla College. Publications [*A publication*]
Wall CC ...... Wallace's United States Circuit Court Reports (DLA)
Wallerstein Lab Commun ... Wallerstein Laboratories. Communications [*A publication*]
Wallis .... Wallis' Irish Chancery Reports (DLA)
Wallis (Ir) ... Wallis' Irish Chancery Reports (DLA)
Wallis by L ... Wallis' Irish Chancery Reports, by Lyne [*1776-91*] (DLA)
Wallis by Lyne ... Wallis' Irish Chancery Reports, by Lyne [*1766-91*] (DLA)
Wall Jr .... [*J. W.*] Wallace's United States Circuit Court Reports (DLA)
Wall Jr CC ... [*J. W.*] Wallace's United States Circuit Court Reports (DLA)
Wall Lyn ..... Wallis' Irish Chancery Reports, by Lyne [*1776-91*] (DLA)
Wall Pr .... Wallace's Principles of the Laws of Scotland (DLA)
Wallraf-Richartz Jahr ... Wallraf-Richartz Jahrbuch [*A publication*]
Wall Rep .... Wallace's "The Reporters" (DLA)
Wall Rep .... Wallace's Supreme Court Reports [*68-90 United States*] (DLA)
Wall SC ...... Wallace's Supreme Court Reports [*68-90 United States*] (DLA)
Wall Sen ..... [*J. B.*] Wallace's United States Circuit Court Reports (DLA)
Wall St J ..... Wall Street Journal [*A publication*]
Wall St J East Ed ... Wall Street Journal. Eastern Edition [*A publication*]
Wall St J Midwest Ed ... Wall Street Journal. Midwest Edition [*A publication*]
Wall St Jnl ... Wall Street Journal [*A publication*]
Wall St J Three Star East Ed ... Wall Street Journal. Three Star Eastern Edition [*A publication*]
Wall St R Bk ... Wall Street Review of Books [*A publication*]
Wall Str J ... Wall Street Journal [*A publication*]
Wall St T .... Wall Street Transcript [*A publication*]

WALMS ..... West African Language Monograph Series [*A publication*]
WALO .... Humacao, PR [*AM radio station call letters*]
WaLo .... Longview Public Library, Longview, WA [*Library symbol*] [*Library of Congress*] (LCLS)
WaLoGS ..... Church of Jesus Christ of Latter-Day Saints, Genealogical Society Library, Longview Stake Branch, Longview, WA [*Library symbol*] [*Library of Congress*] (LCLS)
WaLoL .... Lower Columbia College, Longview, WA [*Library symbol*] [*Library of Congress*] (LCLS)
WALOPT .... Weapons Allocation and Desired Ground-Zero Optimizer [*Military*]
WALP .... Corinth, MS [*FM radio station call letters*]
WALP .... Weapons Assignment Linear Program
WALP .... World Association of Law Professors (EA)
Wal Prin ..... Wallace's Principles of the Laws of Scotland (DLA)
Walp Rub .... Walpole's Rubric of Common Law (DLA)
WALR .... University of Western Australia. Law Review [*A publication*]
Wa LR .... Washington Law Review [*A publication*]
WALR .... West African Law Reports [*Gambia, Ghana, and Sierra Leone*] (DLA)
WALR .... Western Australian Law Reports [*A publication*]
WaLrC .... Cedar Creek Youth Camp, Littlerock, WA [*Library symbol*] [*Library of Congress*] (LCLS)
WALR-FM ... Union City, TN [*FM radio station call letters*]
WALRUS .... Water and Land Resources Use Simulation
WALS .... World Association of Law Students (EA)
Walsh .... Walsh's Irish Registry Cases (DLA)
Walsh's R .... Walsh's American Review [*A publication*]
Wal Sr .... [*J. B.*] Wallace's United States Circuit Court Reports (DLA)
WALT .... Meridian, MS [*AM radio station call letters*]
WALT .... West's Automatic Law Terminal
Walter .... Walter's Reports [*14-16 New Mexico*] (DLA)
Walter C ..... Walter's Code (DLA)
Walters J .... Walters Art Gallery [*Baltimore*]. Journal [*A publication*]
Walt H & W ... Walton on Husband and Wife [*Scotland*] (DLA)
Walt Lim ..... Walter's Statute of Limitations [*4th ed.*] (DLA)
Walt Whit R ... Walt Whitman Review [*A publication*]
Wal US Rep ... Wallace's United States Reports (DLA)
WALV .... Cleveland, TN [*FM radio station call letters*]
WALX .... Selma, AL [*FM radio station call letters*]
WALZ .... Machias, ME [*FM radio station call letters*]
WAM .... Ambatondrazaka [*Madagascar*] [*Airport symbol*] (OAG)
WAM .... Appleton Memorial Hospital, Appleton, WI [*Library symbol*] [*Library of Congress*] (LCLS)
WAM .... Walleye Measurements Program
WAM .... Wambrook [*Australia*] [*Seismograph station code, US Geological Survey*] (SEIS)
WAM .... Warburton Minerals [*Vancouver Stock Exchange symbol*]
WAM .... Weight after Melt [*Metallurgy*]
WAM .... Western Associated Modelers (EA)
WAM .... Western Australian Museum [*Perth*]
WAM .... Wide-Area Mine [*Military*] (MCD)
WAM .... Wiltshire Archaeological Magazine [*A publication*]
WAM .... Women in Advertising and Marketing [*Washington, DC*] (EA)
WAM .... Women's Action Movement
WAM .... Words a Minute
WAM .... Worth Analysis Model (IEEE)
wam .... Writer of Accompanying Material [*MARC relator code*] [*Library of Congress*]
WAMA .... Tampa, FL [*AM radio station call letters*]
WAMA .... Weight after Mars Arrival [*NASA*]
WA Manuf ... West Australian Manufacturer [*A publication*]
WA Manufacturer ... West Australian Manufacturer [*A publication*]
WaMaS .... Sno-Isle Regional Library, Marysville, WA [*Library symbol*] [*Library of Congress*] (LCLS)
WAMB .... Donelson, TN [*AM radio station call letters*]
WAMC .... Albany, NY [*FM radio station call letters*]
WAMD .... Aberdeen, MD [*AM radio station call letters*]
WAME .... Charlotte, NC [*AM radio station call letters*]
WaMeH .... Eastern State Hospital, Medical Lake, WA [*Library symbol*] [*Library of Congress*] (LCLS)
WaMeI .... Interlake School, Staff Library, Medical Lake, WA [*Library symbol*] [*Library of Congress*] (LCLS)
WaMeL .... Lakeland Village School, Medical Lake, WA [*Library symbol*] [*Library of Congress*] (LCLS)
WaMeP .... Pine Lodge Correctional Center, Staff Library, Medical Lake, WA [*Library symbol*] [*Library of Congress*] (LCLS)
WaMeP-R ... Pine Lodge Correctional Center, Resident Library, Medical Lake, WA [*Library symbol*] [*Library of Congress*] (LCLS)
WAMF .... Tallahassee, FL [*FM radio station call letters*]
WAMFLEX ... Wave Momentum Flux Experiment [*National Science Foundation*]
WAMG .... Gallatin, TN [*AM radio station call letters*]
WAMH .... Amherst, MA [*FM radio station call letters*]
WAMI .... Opp, AL [*AM radio station call letters*]
WAMI .... Washington, Alaska, Montana, and Idaho [*Program for states without medical schools*]
WAMI-FM ... Opp, AL [*FM radio station call letters*]
WaMiH .... Highline Community College, Midway, WA [*Library symbol*] [*Library of Congress*] (LCLS)

WA Mining & Commercial R ... West Australian Mining and Commercial Review [*A publication*]
WAMIS .... Watershed Management Information System
WAMJ .... South Bend, IN [*AM radio station call letters*]
WAML .... Laurel, MS [*AM radio station call letters*]
WaMl .... Moses Lake Public Library, Moses Lake, WA [*Library symbol*] [*Library of Congress*] (LCLS)
WAML .... Watertown Arsenal Medical Laboratory [*Massachusetts*] [*Army*]
WAML .... Western Association of Map Libraries (EA)
WAML .... Wright Aero Medical Laboratory [*Air Force*]
WaMlB .... Big Bend Community College, Moses Lake, WA [*Library symbol*] [*Library of Congress*] (LCLS)
WaMlGS ..... Church of Jesus Christ of Latter-Day Saints, Genealogical Society Library, Moses Lake Branch, Moses Lake, WA [*Library symbol*] [*Library of Congress*] (LCLS)
WAMM .... Women Against Military Madness (EA)
WAMM .... Woodstock, VA [*AM radio station call letters*]
WAMN .... Green Valley, WV [*AM radio station call letters*]
WAMO .... Pittsburgh, PA [*AM radio station call letters*]
WAMOC ..... Women's Auxiliary to the Military Order of the Cootie (EA)
WAMOD ..... Wave Motion [*A publication*]
WAMO-FM ... Pittsburgh, PA [*FM radio station call letters*]
WaMonR ..... Washington State Reformatory, Monroe, WA [*Library symbol*] [*Library of Congress*] (LCLS)
WaMonT ..... Twin Rivers Correctional Center, Monroe, WA [*Library symbol*] [*Library of Congress*] (LCLS)
WAMOSCOPE ... Wave-Modulated Oscilloscope
WAMP-FM ... Toledo, OH [*FM radio station call letters*]
WAMPUM .. Wage and Manpower Process Utilizing Machine [*Bureau of Indian Affairs*]
WAMQ .... Loretto, PA [*AM radio station call letters*]
WAMR .... Venice, FL [*AM radio station call letters*]
WAMRAC ... World Association of Methodist Radio Amateurs and Clubs
WAMS .... Weapon Aiming and Mode Selector (MCD)
WAMS .... Wilmington, DE [*AM radio station call letters*]
WAMS .... Women's Automotive Maintenance Staff
WAMSTAS ... Wide-Area Mine Seismic Target Acquisition Sensor [*Military*] (MCD)
WAMT .... Titusville, FL [*AM radio station call letters*]
WaMtJF ...... John Fluke Manufacturing Co., Mountlake Terrace, WA [*Library symbol*] [*Library of Congress*] (LCLS)
WAMTMTS ... Western Area, Military Traffic Management and Terminal Service (AABC)
WaMtv .... Mount Vernon Public Library, Mount Vernon, WA [*Library symbol*] [*Library of Congress*] (LCLS)
WaMtvGS ... Church of Jesus Christ of Latter-Day Saints, Genealogical Society Library, Mount Vernon Branch, Mount Vernon, WA [*Library symbol*] [*Library of Congress*] (LCLS)
WaMtvS ..... Skagit Valley College, Mount Vernon, WA [*Library symbol*] [*Library of Congress*] (LCLS)
WAMU .... Washington, DC [*FM radio station call letters*]
WAMU .... Washington Mutual Savings Bank [*NASDAQ symbol*] (NQ)
WAMW .... Washington, IN [*AM radio station call letters*]
WAMX .... Ashland, KY [*FM radio station call letters*]
WAMY .... Amory, MS [*AM radio station call letters*]
WAMY .... World Assembly of Muslim Youth (EA-IO)
WAMZ .... Louisville, KY [*FM radio station call letters*]
WAn .... Antigo Public Library, Antigo, WI [*Library symbol*] [*Library of Congress*] (LCLS)
WAN .... Wang Laboratories, Inc. [*American Stock Exchange symbol*]
WAN .... Wanigan
WAN .... Wanliss Street [*New Britain*] [*Seismograph station code, US Geological Survey*] (SEIS)
WAN .... Wide Area Network
WAN .... Women's Royal Australian Naval Service [*World War II*] (DSUE)
WAN .... Work Authorization Number (NASA)
WANA .... Anniston, AL [*AM radio station call letters*]
WANA .... Woodworking Association of North America (EA)
WANAP ..... Washington [*DC*] National Airport
WaNasY ..... Naselle Youth Camp, Staff Library, Naselle, WA [*Library symbol*] [*Library of Congress*] (LCLS)
WaNasY-R ... Naselle Youth Camp, Resident Library, Naselle, WA [*Library symbol*] [*Library of Congress*] (LCLS)
WA Nat ...... Western Australian Naturalist [*A publication*]
WA Naturalist ... Western Australian Naturalist [*A publication*]
WANB .... Waynesburg, PA [*AM radio station call letters*]
WANB-FM ... Waynesburg, PA [*FM radio station call letters*]
WANC .... Aberdeen, NC [*AM radio station call letters*]
WAND .... Decatur, IL [*Television station call letters*]
WAND .... Women and Development Unit (EA)
WAND .... Women's Action for Nuclear Disarmament (EA)
Wandell ...... Wandell's New York Reports (DLA)
WANE-TV ... Fort Wayne, IN [*Television station call letters*]
WA News ... West Australian News [*A publication*]
WANI .... Richmond, VA [*AM radio station call letters*]
WANL .... Westinghouse-Astronuclear Laboratories
WANM .... Tallahassee, FL [*AM radio station call letters*]
WANN .... Annapolis, MD [*AM radio station call letters*]
WANO .... Pineville, KY [*AM radio station call letters*]

WANS......... Anderson, SC [*AM radio station call letters*]
WANS......... Women's Australian National Service
WANS-FM ... Anderson, SC [*FM radio station call letters*]
WANT........ Richmond, VA [*AM radio station call letters*]
WANT........ Warrant Apprehension Narcotics Team [*Criminal investigation computer program*]
WANV........ Waynesboro, VA [*AM radio station call letters*]
WANV-FM ... Staunton, VA [*FM radio station call letters*]
WANY........ Albany, KY [*AM radio station call letters*]
WANY-FM ... Albany, KY [*FM radio station call letters*]
WAO........... Outagamie County Hospital, Appleton, WI [*Library symbol*] [*Library of Congress*]   (LCLS)
WaO........... Timberland Regional Library, Olympia, WA [*Library symbol*] [*Library of Congress*]   (LCLS)
WAO........... Weapons Assignment Officer [*Air Force*]   (AFM)
WAO........... Women's American ORT   (EA)
WaOAP....... Washington State Office of Adult Probation and Parole, Olympia, WA [*Library symbol*] [*Library of Congress*]   (LCLS)
WaOAr .... State of Washington Department of General Administration, Division of Archives and Records Management, Olympia, WA [*Library symbol*] [*Library of Congress*]   (LCLS)
WaOB........ Washington State Department of Public Assistance, Ben Tidball Memorial Library, Olympia, WA [*Library symbol*] [*Library of Congress*]   (LCLS)
WAOB .... Winamac, IN [*AM radio station call letters*]
WAOC .... St. Augustine, FL [*AM radio station call letters*]
WaOE .... Evergreen State College, Olympia, WA [*Library symbol*] [*Library of Congress*]   (LCLS)
WaOEd...... Washington State Department of Education, Olympia, WA [*Library symbol*] [*Library of Congress*]   (LCLS)
WaOEng.... Washington State Energy Office, Olympia, WA [*Library symbol*] [*Library of Congress*]   (LCLS)
WaOGS ...... Church of Jesus Christ of Latter-Day Saints, Genealogical Society Library, Olympia Branch, Olympia, WA [*Library symbol*] [*Library of Congress*]   (LCLS)
WAOK .... Atlanta, GA [*AM radio station call letters*]
WaOLI .... State of Washington Department of Labor and Industries Libraries, Olympia, WA [*Library symbol*] [*Library of Congress*]   (LCLS)
WaOLN...... Washington Library Network, Olympia, WA [*Library symbol*] [*Library of Congress*]   (LCLS)
WaONR ...... Washington State Department of Natural Resources, Division of Geology and Earth Resources, Olympia, WA [*Library symbol*] [*Library of Congress*]   (LCLS)
WAOR .... Niles, MI [*FM radio station call letters*]
WaOrtS ...... Washington Soldiers' Home, Staff Library, Orting, WA [*Library symbol*] [*Library of Congress*]   (LCLS)
WaOrtS-R ... Washington Soldiers' Home, Resident Library, Orting, WA [*Library symbol*] [*Library of Congress*]   (LCLS)
WAOS .... Austell, GA [*AM radio station call letters*]
WAOS .... Wide-Angle Optical System
WaOSM...... Saint Martin's College, Olympia, WA [*Library symbol*] [*Library of Congress*]   (LCLS)
WaOSP...... Saint Peter's Hospital, Olympia, WA [*Library symbol*] [*Library of Congress*]   (LCLS)
WaOT .... Washington State Department of Transportation, Olympia, WA [*Library symbol*] [*Library of Congress*]   (LCLS)
WaOTC ...... Olympia Technical Community College, Olympia, WA [*Library symbol*] [*Library of Congress*]   (LCLS)
WAOV .... Vincennes, IN [*AM radio station call letters*]
WAOW-TV ... Wausau, WI [*Television station call letters*]
WAP .... Institute of Paper Chemistry, Appleton, WI [*Library symbol*] [*Library of Congress*]   (LCLS)
WAP .... Wandering Atrial Pacemaker [*Cardiology*]
WAP .... Wapentake [*Subdivision of some English shires*]
WAP .... Warner Audio Publishing
W Ap .... Washington Appellate Reports   (DLA)
WAP .... Weak Anthropic Principle [*Term coined by authors John Barrow and Frank Tipler in their book, "The Anthropic Cosmological Principle"*]
WAP .... Weight after Processing [*Metallurgy*]
WAP .... Wide-Angle Panorama [*Photography*] [*NASA*]
WAP .... Wideband Acoustical Processor   (CAAL)
WAP .... Women Against Pornography
WAP .... Women's Action Program [*HEW*]
WAP .... Work Activity Program
WAP .... Work Analysis Program [*Data processing*]   (BUR)
WAP .... Work Assignment Procedure
WaPa.......... Pasco Public Library, Pasco, WA [*Library symbol*] [*Library of Congress*]   (LCLS)
WAPA........ San Juan, PR [*AM radio station call letters*]
WAPA........ Western Area Power Administration [*Department of Energy*]
WAPA........ White American Political Association   (EA)
WaPaAp ..... Washington State Office of Adult Probation and Parole, Pasco, WA [*Library symbol*] [*Library of Congress*]   (LCLS)
WaPaC....... Columbia Basin College, Pasco, WA [*Library symbol*] [*Library of Congress*]   (LCLS)
WaPaGS..... Church of Jesus Christ of Latter-Day Saints, Genealogical Society Library, Pasco Branch, Pasco, WA [*Library symbol*] [*Library of Congress*]   (LCLS)

WA Parent & Cit ... Western Australian Parent and Citizen [*A publication*]
WA Parent & Citizen ... Western Australian Parent and Citizen [*A publication*]
WA Parl Deb ... Western Australia. Parliamentary Debates [*A publication*]
WAPA-TV... San Juan, PR [*Television station call letters*]
WAPC........ Women's Auxiliary Police Corps [*British*] [*World War II*]
WAPCB ...... West African Produce Control Board [*World War II*]
WAPCOS ... Water and Power Development Consultancy Services
WAPD........ Western Air Procurement District
WAPE-FM ... Jacksonville, FL [*FM radio station call letters*]
WAPET....... West Australian Petroleum Proprietary [*Ltd.*]
WAPF .... McComb, MS [*AM radio station call letters*]
WAPG........ Arcadia, FL [*AM radio station call letters*]
WAPG........ High-Endurance Coast Guard Cutter [*Later, WHEC*]   (CINC)
WAPI .... Birmingham, AL [*AM radio station call letters*]
WAPI-FM... Birmingham, AL [*FM radio station call letters*]
WAPL .... Western Aerial Photography Laboratory [*Department of Agriculture*]
WAPL-FM .. Appleton, WI [*FM radio station call letters*]
WaPIP........ Pacific Lutheran University, Parkland, WA [*Library symbol*] [*Library of Congress*]   (LCLS)
WAPME ..... Writers and Artists for Peace in the Middle East   (EA)
WAPN........ Holly Hill, FL [*FM radio station call letters*]
WAPO........ Jasper, TN [*AM radio station call letters*]
WaPoN ...... North Olympic Library System, Port Angeles, WA [*Library symbol*] [*Library of Congress*]   (LCLS)
WaPoP .... Peninsula College, Port Angeles, WA [*Library symbol*] [*Library of Congress*]   (LCLS)
WAPOR ...... World Association for Public Opinion Research
WAPR........ Avon Park, FL [*AM radio station call letters*]
WAPRA ...... Wissenschaftliche Abhandlungen der Physikalisch Technischen Reichsanstalt [*A publication*]
WA Primary Princ ... WA Primary Principal [*West Australian Primary Principals Association*] [*A publication*]
WAPS........ Akron, OH [*FM radio station call letters*]
WaPS .... Washington State University, Pullman, WA [*Library symbol*] [*Library of Congress*]   (LCLS)
WAPS........ Weighted Airman Promotion System [*Air Force*]
WAPS........ Women of the American Press Service [*Accredited American women war correspondents*] [*World War II*]
WAPS........ World Association of Pathology Societies
WaPS-V..... Washington State University, Veterinary Medical Library, Pullman, WA [*Library symbol*] [*Library of Congress*]   (LCLS)
WAPT........ Jackson, MS [*Television station call letters*]
WAPT........ Wild Animal Propagation Trust [*Defunct*]
WAPT........ Work Area Pointer Table [*Data processing*]
WaPuS....... Washington State University, Western Washington Research and Extension Center, Puyallup, WA [*Library symbol*] [*Library of Congress*]   (LCLS)
WAPX-FM ... Clarksville, TN [*FM radio station call letters*]
WAPZ........ Wetumpka, AL [*AM radio station call letters*]
WAQ.......... Antsalova [*Madagascar*] [*Airport symbol*]   (OAG)
WAQE-FM ... Rice Lake, WI [*FM radio station call letters*]
WaQGS ...... Church of Jesus Christ of Latter-Day Saints, Genealogical Society Library, Quincy Branch, Quincy, WA [*Library symbol*] [*Library of Congress*]   (LCLS)
WAQI........ Miami, FL [*AM radio station call letters*]
WAQP........ Saginaw, MI [*Television station call letters*]
WAQT........ Carrollton, AL [*FM radio station call letters*]
WAQX........ Syracuse, NY [*AM radio station call letters*]
WAQX-FM ... Manlius, NY [*FM radio station call letters*]
WAQY........ Springfield, MA [*FM radio station call letters*]
WAR .... Warrant
WAR .... Warrenton Railroad Co. [*AAR code*]
WAR .... Warrior Resources [*Vancouver Stock Exchange symbol*]
WAR .... Warsaw [*Poland*] [*Seismograph station code, US Geological Survey*]   (SEIS)
WAR .... Warwickshire   (ROG)
WAR .... Wassermann Antigen Reaction [*Test for syphilis*] [*Medicine*]
WAR .... We Are Ridiculous [*Antiwar slogan*]
WAR .... Weapon Accuracy and Results [*Model*]   (MCD)
WAR .... West African Regiment [*Military unit*] [*British*]
WAR .... Western Australian Reports [*A publication*]
WAR .... Whiteruthenian American Relief   (EA)
WAR .... Wisconsin Academy. Review [*A publication*]
WAR .... With All Risks [*Insurance*]
WAR .... Work Acquisition Routine
WAR .... Work Authorization Report [*or Request*]   (MCD)
WAR .... World Administrative Radio Conference for Space Communication
WARA........ Attleboro, MA [*AM radio station call letters*]
WARB........ Covington, LA [*AM radio station call letters*]
WARC .... Meadville, PA [*FM radio station call letters*]
War C .... War Cry [*A publication*]
WARC .... Washington Archaeological Research Center [*Washington State University*] [*Research center*]   (RCD)
WARC .... Wharton Applied Research Center [*University of Pennsylvania*] [*Research center*]   (RCD)

WARC .... World Administrative Radio Conference [*Takes place every 20 years*] [*Held in 1979 in Geneva, Switzerland*] [*International Telecommunications Union*]

WARC .... World Alliance of Reformed Churches [*See also ARM*] (EA-IO)

WARC .... World Alliance of Reformed Churches (Presbyterian and Congregational) [*See also ARM*]

WARCAD ... War Department - Civil Affairs Division [*Obsolete*]

WARCAT .... Workload and Resources Correlation Analysis Technique [*Army*]

W Arch ...... Western Architect [*A publication*]

WARC-MAR ... World Administrative Radio Conference for Maritime Mobile Telecommunications

WARCO ...... War Correspondent   (DSUE)

WARC-ST ... World Administrative Radio Conference for Space Telecommunications

WARD .... Pittston, PA [*AM radio station call letters*]

Ward .... Warden's State Reports [*2, 4 Ohio*] (DLA)

WARD .... Wardship

WARDA ...... West African Rice Development Association [*Liberia*]

Ward AW .... Ward's Auto World [*A publication*]

Warden ...... Warden's State Reports [*2, 4 Ohio*] (DLA)

Warden's Law & Bk Bull ... Warden's Weekly Law and Bank Bulletin [*Ohio*] (DLA)

Warden & Smith ... Warden and Smith's State Reports [*3 Ohio*] (DLA)

War Dept BCA ... United States War Department, Decisions of Board of Contract Adjustment   (DLA)

Ward Leg ... Ward on Legacies   (DLA)

WARDS ...... Welfare of Animals Used for Research in Drugs and Therapy

Wards Auto ... Ward's Automotive Reports [*A publication*]

Ward's Bull ... Ward's Bulletin [*A publication*]

Ward & Sm ... Warden and Smith's State Reports [*3 Ohio*] (DLA)

WaRe .... Renton Public Library, Renton, WA [*Library symbol*] [*Library of Congress*] (LCLS)

WARE .... Ware, MA [*AM radio station call letters*]

Ware .... Ware's United States District Court Reports   (DLA)

WARE .... Water Research [*A publication*]

Warehousing Superv Bull ... Warehousing Supervisor's Bulletin [*United States*] [*A publication*]

WARES ...... Workload and Resources Evaluation System [*Navy*]

Ware's CC Rep ... Ware's United States District Court Reports   (DLA)

Ware's Rep ... Ware's United States District Court Reports   (DLA)

WaRetV ..... Washington Veterans' Home, Medical Library, Retsil, WA [*Library symbol*] [*Library of Congress*] (LCLS)

WaRetV-R ... Washington Veterans' Home, Resident Library, Retsil, WA [*Library symbol*] [*Library of Congress*] (LCLS)

WaReVG ..... Valley General Hospital, Renton, WA [*Library symbol*] [*Library of Congress*] (LCLS)

WAREX ...... Warrant Issued for Extradite

WARF .... Jasper, AL [*AM radio station call letters*]

WARF .... Warfare   (AFM)

WARF .... Wartime Active Replacement Factors   (AABC)

WARF .... Weekly Audit Report File [*IRS*]

WARF .... Wide-Aperture Research Facility [*For hurricane detection*]

WARG .... Summit, IL [*FM radio station call letters*]

WARH .... Tuckahoe, VA [*AM radio station call letters*]

WARHD ..... Warhead   (AAG)

WARI .... Abbeville, AL [*AM radio station call letters*]

WaRi .... Richland Public Library, Richland, WA [*Library symbol*] [*Library of Congress*] (LCLS)

WARI .... Wheezing Associated with Respiratory Injections

WaRiAR ..... Atlantic Richfield Hanford Co., Richland, WA [*Library symbol*] [*Library of Congress*] (LCLS)

WaRiB .... Battelle Memorial Institute, Pacific Northwest Laboratory, Richland, WA [*Library symbol*] [*Library of Congress*] (LCLS)

WaRiBN ..... Battelle-Northwest Hospital, Life Science Library, Richland, WA [*Library symbol*] [*Library of Congress*] (LCLS)

WaRiGS ..... Church of Jesus Christ of Latter-Day Saints, Genealogical Society Library, Richland Branch, Richland, WA [*Library symbol*] [*Library of Congress*] (LCLS)

WaRiMC .... Mid-Columbia Mental Health Center, Richland, WA [*Library symbol*] [*Library of Congress*] (LCLS)

WArI-R .... Indian Ridge Treatment Center, Resident Library, Arlington, WA [*Library symbol*] [*Library of Congress*] (LCLS)

WaRit .... Ritzville Public Library, Ritzville, WA [*Library symbol*] [*Library of Congress*] (LCLS)

WARK .... Hagerstown, MD [*AM radio station call letters*]

WARLA ...... Wide-Aperture Radio Location Array

WARLOCE ... Wartime Lines of Communication, Europe   (AABC)

WARLOG .... Wartime Logistics   (AABC)

WARM .... Scranton, PA [*AM radio station call letters*]

WARM .... Weapons Assignment Research Model [*Military*]

WARM .... Wood and Solid Fuel Association of Retailers and Manufacturers   (EA)

WARMA ..... Waerme [*A publication*]

WARMAPS ... Wartime Manpower Planning System

War Med .... War Medicine [*A publication*]

Warmedies ... Warm, Family Comedies [*Television*]

WARM-FM ... Atlanta, GA [*FM radio station call letters*]

WARN .... Warner Electric Brake & Clutch Co. [*NASDAQ symbol*]   (NQ)

WARN .... Women of All Red Nations   (EA)

WARO .... Canonsburg, PA [*AM radio station call letters*]

War Op .... Warwick's Opinions [*City Solicitor of Philadelphia, PA*]   (DLA)

WARP .... Due West, SC [*FM radio station call letters*]

WARP .... Worldwide Ammunition Reporting Program   (NG)

WARP .... Worldwide AUTODIN [*Automatic Digital Information Network*] Restoral Plan   (CET)

WARPAC .... Wartime Repair Parts Consumption   (MCD)

WARPATH ... World Association to Remove Prejudice Against the Handicapped

War Prof Dut ... Warren. Moral, Social, and Professional Duties of Attorneys and Solicitors [*2nd ed.*] [*1851*]   (DLA)

WARR .... Warranty   (MSA)

WARR .... Warrenton, NC [*AM radio station call letters*]

WARR .... Water Resources Research [*A publication*]

WARRAMP ... Wartime Requirements for Ammunition, Materiel, and Personnel

WARRF .... Warrior Research Ltd. [*NASDAQ symbol*]   (NQ)

WARRT ..... Warrant   (ROG)

Wars .... [*The*] Jewish Wars [*of Josephus*] [*A publication*]   (BJA)

WARS .... Warfare Analysis and Research System [*Navy*]

WARS .... Wide-Area Remote Sensors

WARS .... Worldwide Ammunition Reporting System [*Military*]

WARSCAP ... Wartime Support Capability

WARSL .... War Reserve Stockage List   (MCD)

WART .... Wenceslaus Anxiety Representation Taxonomy [*Satirical psychology term*]

Warta Geol ... Warta Geologi [*A publication*]

Warta Geol (Kuala Lumpur) ... Warta Geologi (Kuala Lumpur) [*A publication*]

Warth Code ... West Virginia Code [*1899*]   (DLA)

WARU .... Peru, IN [*AM radio station call letters*]

WARU-FM ... Peru, IN [*FM radio station call letters*]

WARV .... Warwick-East Greenwich, RI [*AM radio station call letters*]

Warv Abst ... Warvelle on Abstracts of Title   (DLA)

Warv El RP ... Warvelle's Elements of Real Property   (DLA)

Warv V & P ... Warvelle's Vendors and Purchasers of Real Property   (DLA)

WARW .... Warwickshire [*County in England*]

WARWICKS ... Warwickshire [*County in England*]

Warwick's Op ... Warwick's Opinions [*City Solicitor of Philadelphia, PA*]   (DLA)

WARWS ..... Warwickshire [*County in England*]

WARX .... Hagerstown, MD [*FM radio station call letters*]

WARY .... Valhalla, NY [*FM radio station call letters*]

WaS .... Seattle Public Library, Seattle, WA [*Library symbol*] [*Library of Congress*] (LCLS)

WAs .... Vaughn Public Library, Ashland, WI [*Library symbol*] [*Library of Congress*] (LCLS)

WAS .... Wadley Southern Railway Co. [*AAR code*] [*Obsolete*]

WAS .... Wallops Station [*Later, WFC*] [*NASA*]

WAS .... War at Sea   (NVT)

WAS .... Ware Resources Ltd. [*Vancouver Stock Exchange symbol*]

WAS .... Warner & Swasey Co., Solon, OH [*OCLC symbol*]   (OCLC)

WAS .... Washington [*District of Columbia*] [*Airport symbol*]   (OAG)

WAS .... Washington [*District of Columbia*] [*Seismograph station code, US Geological Survey*] [*Closed*]   (SEIS)

was .... Washo [*MARC language code*] [*Library of Congress*]   (LCCP)

WAS .... Waynesburg Southern [*AAR code*]

WAS .... Weapons Alert System [*NORAD*]   (MCD)

WAS .... Weekly Arrival Schedule [*Military*]   (AFIT)

WAS .... Wide-Angle Sensor

WAS .... Wideband Antenna System

WAS .... Wiskott-Aldrich Syndrome [*Immunology*]

WAS .... Witchcraft and Sorcery [*A publication*]

WAS .... Women's Addiction Service [*National Institute of Mental Health*]

WAS .... Worcester Archaeological Society. Transactions [*A publication*]

WAS .... Worked All States [*Contacted at least one station in all states*] [*Amateur radio*]

WAS .... World Animal Science [*Elsevier Book Series*] [*A publication*]

WAS .... World Archaeological Society   (EA)

WAS .... World Around Songs [*An association*]   (EA)

WAS .... World Artifex Society   (EA-IO)

WAS .... World Association for Sexology [*Washington, DC*]   (EA)

WASA .... Havre De Grace, MD [*AM radio station call letters*]

WaSA .... Seattle Art Museum, Seattle, WA [*Library symbol*] [*Library of Congress*] (LCLS)

WaSAA ...... Catholic Archdiocese of Seattle, Archives, Seattle, WA [*Library symbol*] [*Library of Congress*] (LCLS)

WaSAB .... Atomic Bomb Casualty Commission, Seattle, WA [*Library symbol*] [*Library of Congress*] (LCLS)

WASAC ...... Working Group of the Army Study Advisory Committee   (AABC)

WASAG ...... Washington Special Action Group [*National Security Council*]

WASAL ...... Wisconsin Academy of Sciences, Arts, and Letters

WASAR ...... Wide Application System Adapter

WASB .... Brockport, NY [*AM radio station call letters*]

WaSB .... Pacific Northwest Bibliographic Center, Seattle, WA [*Library symbol*] [*Library of Congress*] (LCLS)

WaSBa .... Battelle Human Affairs Research Center, Seattle, WA [*Library symbol*] [*Library of Congress*] (LCLS)

WaSBo .... Boeing Co., Commercial Airplane Group, Technical Libraries, Seattle, WA [*Library symbol*] [*Library of Congress*]　(LCLS)

WaSBo-A ... Boeing Co., Aerospace Division, Technical Library, Kent, WA [*Library symbol*] [*Library of Congress*]　(LCLS)

WaSC .... Seattle Central Community College, Seattle, WA [*Library symbol*] [*Library of Congress*]　(LCLS)

WASC .... Spartanburg, SC [*AM radio station call letters*]

WASC .... West Africa Supply Centre [*World War II*]

WASC .... Western Association of Schools and Colleges　(EA)

WASC .... White Anglo-Saxon Catholic

WASCAL.... Wide-Angle Scanning Array Lens Antenna

WascanaR ... Wascana Review [*A publication*]

WaSC-N ..... North Seattle Community College, Seattle, WA [*Library symbol*] [*Library of Congress*]　(LCLS)

WaSCO ...... Children's Orthopedic Hospital and Medical Center, Seattle, WA [*Library symbol*] [*Library of Congress*]　(LCLS)

WASCO...... War Safety Council

WaSC-S ..... South Seattle Community College, Seattle, WA [*Library symbol*] [*Library of Congress*]　(LCLS)

WaSC-Sh ... Shoreline Community College, Seattle, WA [*Library symbol*] [*Library of Congress*] [*Obsolete*]　(LCLS)

WASD........ Wide-Angle Self-Destruct　(MCD)

WASE........ Saint Elizabeth Hospital, Appleton, WI [*Library symbol*] [*Library of Congress*]　(LCLS)

WASEC ...... Warner-Amex Satellite Entertainment Company [*Cable television*]

Waseda Polit Stud ... Waseda Political Studies [*A publication*]

WaSelY ...... Yakima Valley School, Selah, WA [*Library symbol*] [*Library of Congress*]　(LCLS)

WaSF.......... Fircrest School, Staff Library, Seattle, WA [*Library symbol*] [*Library of Congress*]　(LCLS)

WaSFC....... Firland Correctional Center, Staff Library, Seattle, WA [*Library symbol*] [*Library of Congress*]　(LCLS)

WaSFC-R ... Firland Correctional Center, Resident Library, Seattle, WA [*Library symbol*] [*Library of Congress*]　(LCLS)

WaSF-R...... Fircrest School, Resident Library, Seattle, WA [*Library symbol*] [*Library of Congress*]　(LCLS)

WaSFRC .... Federal Records Center, Seattle, WA [*Library symbol*] [*Library of Congress*]　(LCLS)

WASG .... Atmore, AL [*AM radio station call letters*]

WaSG......... Seattle Genealogical Society, Seattle, WA [*Library symbol*] [*Library of Congress*]　(LCLS)

WASGFC.... Western Association of State Game and Fish Commissioners [*Later, Western Association of Fish and Wildlife Agencies*]　(EA)

WaSGH ...... Group Health Cooperative of Puget Sound, Medical Library, Seattle, WA [*Library symbol*] [*Library of Congress*]　(LCLS)

WaSGS....... Church of Jesus Christ of Latter-Day Saints, Genealogical Society Library, Seattle North Branch, Seattle, WA [*Library symbol*] [*Library of Congress*]　(LCLS)

WaSGS....... Good Samaritan Hospital, Seattle, WA [*Library symbol*] [*Library of Congress*]　(LCLS)

WaSh.......... Shelton Public Library, Shelton, WA [*Library symbol*] [*Library of Congress*]　(LCLS)

WaSH .... Virginia Mason Hospital, Medical Library, Seattle, WA [*Library symbol*] [*Library of Congress*]　(LCLS)

WASH........ Washer　(AAG)

WASH........ Washington　(AAG)

WASH........ Washington, DC [*FM radio station call letters*]

Wash .... Washington Reports　(DLA)

Wash .... Washington State Reports　(DLA)

Wash .... Washington Territory Reports　(DLA)

Wash .... Washington's Reports [*1, 2 Virginia*]　(DLA)

Wash .... Washington's Reports [*16-23 Vermont*]　(DLA)

Wash .... Washington's United States Circuit Court Reports　(DLA)

Wash Ac Sc ... Washington Academy of Sciences [*A publication*]

Wash Actions Health ... Washington Actions on Health [*A publication*]

Wash Admin Code ... Washington Administrative Code　(DLA)

Wash Admin Reg ... Washington State Register　(DLA)

Wash Ag Exp ... Washington. Agricultural Experiment Station. Publications [*A publication*]

Wash Agric Exp Stn Bull ... Washington. Agricultural Experiment Station. Bulletin [*A publication*]

Wash Agric Exp Stn Cir ... Washington. Agricultural Experiment Station. Circular [*A publication*]

Wash Agric Exp Stn Stn Circ ... Washington. Agricultural Experiment Stations. Stations Circular [*A publication*]

Wash Agric Exp Stn Tech Bull ... Washington. Agricultural Experiment Station. Technical Bulletin [*A publication*]

Wash App ... Washington Appellate Reports　(DLA)

Washb Easem ... Washburn on Easements and Servitudes　(DLA)

Washb Real Prop ... Washburn on Real Property　(DLA)

Washburn ... Washburn's Reports [*18-23 Vermont*]　(DLA)

Washburn Coll Lab N H B ... Washburn College. Laboratory of Natural History. Bulletin [*A publication*]

Washburn L J ... Washburn Law Journal [*A publication*]

WaShC....... Washington Correction Center, Staff Library, Shelton, WA [*Library symbol*] [*Library of Congress*]　(LCLS)

Wash CC .... Washington's United States Circuit Court Reports　(DLA)

Wash CCR ... Washington's United States Circuit Court Reports　(DLA)

Wash Co ... Washington County Reports [*Pennsylvania*]　(DLA)

Wash Co (PA) ... Washington County Reports [*Pennsylvania*]　(DLA)

Wash Co R ... Washington County Reports [*Pennsylvania*]　(DLA)

Wash Co Repr ... Washington County Reports [*Pennsylvania*]　(DLA)

WaSHCR .... Fred Hutchinson Cancer Research Center, Seattle, WA [*Library symbol*] [*Library of Congress*]　(LCLS)

WaShC-R ... Washington Correction Center, Resident Library, Shelton, WA [*Library symbol*] [*Library of Congress*]　(LCLS)

Wash Cr L ... Washburn on Criminal Law　(DLA)

Wash 2d ..... Washington Reports, Second Series　(DLA)

Wash Dec ... Washington Decisions　(DLA)

Wash Dep Ecol State Water Program Bienn Rep ... Washington. Department of Ecology. State Water Program. Biennial Report [*A publication*]

Wash Dep Ecol Tech Rep ... Washington. Department of Ecology. Technical Report [*A publication*]

Wash Dep Ecol Water Supply Bull ... Washington. Department of Ecology. Water Supply Bulletin [*A publication*]

Wash Dep Fish Annu Rep ... Washington. Department of Fisheries. Annual Report [*A publication*]

Wash Dep Fish Fish Res Pap ... Washington. Department of Fisheries. Fisheries Research Papers [*A publication*]

Wash Dep Fish Res Bull ... Washington. Department of Fisheries. Research Bulletin [*A publication*]

Wash Dep Fish Tech Rep ... Washington. Department of Fisheries. Technical Report [*A publication*]

Wash Dep Water Resour Water Supply Bull ... Washington. Department of Water Resources. Water Supply Bulletin [*A publication*]

Wash Dig.... Washburn's Vermont Digest　(DLA)

Wash Div Geol Earth Resour Geol Map ... Washington. Division of Geology and Earth Resources. Geologic Map [*A publication*]

Wash Div Geol Earth Resour Inf Circ ... Washington. Division of Geology and Earth Resources. Information Circular [*A publication*]

Wash Div Mines Geol Bull ... Washington. Department of Natural Resources. Division of Mines and Geology. Bulletin [*A publication*]

Wash Div Mines Geol Inform Circ ... Washington. Department of Conservation. Division of Mines and Geology. Information Circular [*A publication*]

Wash Div Mines Geol Inform Circ ... Washington. Division of Mines and Geology. Information Circular [*A publication*]

Wash Div Mines Geol Rep Invest ... Washington. Department of Conservation. Division of Mines and Geology. Report of Investigations [*A publication*]

Wash Div Mines Geol Rep Invest ... Washington. Division of Mines and Geology. Report of Investigation [*A publication*]

Wash Geol Earth Resour Div Bull ... Washington. Department of Natural Resources. Geology and Earth Resources Division. Bulletin [*A publication*]

Wash G S ... Washington. Geological Survey [*A publication*]

Wash GSB ... Washington. Geological Survey. Bulletin [*A publication*]

Wash & Haz PEI ... Washburton and Hazard's Reports [*Prince Edward Island, Canada*]　(DLA)

Wash His Q ... Washington Historical Quarterly [*A publication*]

Wash His S ... Washington State Historical Society. Publications [*A publication*]

Wash Hist Q ... Washington Historical Quarterly [*A publication*]

WaSHi .... Seattle Historical Society, Seattle, WA [*Library symbol*] [*Library of Congress*]　(LCLS)

Washington Acad Sci Jour ... Washington Academy of Sciences. Journal [*A publication*]

Washington Dept Water Resources Water Supply Bull ... Washington. Department of Water Resources. Water Supply Bulletin [*A publication*]

Washington Div Mines and Geology Bull ... Washington. Division of Mines and Geology. Bulletin [*A publication*]

Washington Div Mines and Geology Geol Map ... Washington. Division of Mines and Geology. Geologic Map [*A publication*]

Washington Div Mines and Geology Inf Circ ... Washington. Division of Mines and Geology. Information Circular [*A publication*]

Washington and Lee L Rev ... Washington and Lee Law Review [*A publication*]

Washington L Rev ... Washington Law Review [*A publication*]

Washington M ... Washington Monthly [*A publication*]

Washington Univ L Quart ... Washington University. Law Quarterly [*A publication*]

WaShIR ...... ITT Rayonier, Inc., Olympic Research Center, Shelton, WA [*Library symbol*] [*Library of Congress*]　(LCLS)

Wash Jur.... Washington Jurist　(DLA)

Wash Law Re ... Washington Law Review [*A publication*]

Wash Law Rep ... Washington Law Reporter [*District of Columbia*]　(DLA)

Wash & Lee L Rev ... Washington and Lee Law Review [*A publication*]

Wash Legis Serv ... Washington Legislative Service (West)　(DLA)

Wash LR (Dist Col) ... Washington Law Reporter (District of Columbia)　(DLA)

Wash L Rep ... Washington Law Reporter [*District of Columbia*]　(DLA)

Wash L Rev ... Washington Law Review [*A publication*]

Wash M ...... Washington Monthly [*A publication*]

Wash Med Ann ... Washington Medical Annals [*A publication*]

WASHMIC ... Washington Military Industrial Complex

Wash Mon ... Washington Monthly [*A publication*]

Wash News Beat ... Washington News Beat [*A publication*]

Wash Nurse ... Washington Nurse [*A publication*]

WASHO ...... Western Association of State Highway Officials

Wash Post ... Washington Post [*A publication*]

Wash PUR ... Washington Public Utility Commission Reports   (DLA)

Wash Rep ... Washington Report [*A publication*]

Wash Rep Med Health ... Washington Report on Medicine and Health [*A publication*]

Wash Rev Code ... Revised Code of Washington   (DLA)

Wash Rev Code Ann ... Washington Revised Code, Annotated   (DLA)

Wash RP ..... Washburn on Real Property   (DLA)

Wash SBA ... Washington State Bar Association. Proceedings   (DLA)

Wash St ...... Washington State Reports   (DLA)

Wash State Coll Agric Exp Stn Tech Bull ... Washington State College. Washington Agricultural Experiment Station. Institute of Agricultural Sciences. Technical Bulletin [*A publication*]

Wash State Coll Research Studies ... Washington State College. Research Studies [*A publication*]

Wash State Council Highway Research Eng Soils Manual ... Washington State. Council for Highway Research Engineering. Soils Manual [*A publication*]

Wash State Dent J ... Washington State Dental Journal [*A publication*]

Wash State For Prod Inst Bull New Wood Use Ser ... Washington State Forest Products Institute. Bulletins. New Wood-Use Series [*A publication*]

Wash State Inst Technology Bull ... Washington State Institute of Technology. Bulletin [*A publication*]

Wash State Inst Technol Tech Rep ... Washington State Institute of Technology. Technical Report [*A publication*]

Wash State J Nurs ... Washington State Journal of Nursing [*A publication*]

Wash State Univ Agric Exp Stn Tech Bull ... Washington State University. Agricultural Experiment Station. Institute of Agricultural Sciences. Technical Bulletin [*A publication*]

Wash State Univ Coll Agric Res Cent Bull ... Washington State University. College of Agriculture. Research Center. Bulletin [*A publication*]

Wash State Univ Coll Agric Res Cent Tech Bull ... Washington State University. College of Agriculture. Research Center. Technical Bulletin [*A publication*]

Wash State Univ Coll Eng Bull ... Washington State University. College of Engineering. Bulletin [*A publication*]

Wash State Univ Coop Ext Serv Ext Bull ... Washington State University. Cooperative Extension Service. Extension Bulletin [*A publication*]

Wash State Univ Ext Serv EM ... Washington State University. Extension Service. EM [*A publication*]

Wash State Univ Publ Geol Sci ... Washington State University. Publications in Geological Sciences [*A publication*]

Wash State Univ Symp Particleboard Proc ... Washington State University. Symposium on Particleboard. Proceedings [*A publication*]

Wash St G An Rp ... Washington State Geologist. Annual Report [*A publication*]

WASH T ..... Washington Territory   (ROG)

Wash T .... Washington Territory Opinions [*1854-64*]   (DLA)

Wash T .... Washington Territory Reports [*1854-88*]   (DLA)

Wash Ter .... Washington Territory Opinions [*1854-64*]   (DLA)

Wash Ter .... Washington Territory Reports [*1854-88*]   (DLA)

Wash Ter NS ... Allen's Washington Territory Reports, New Series   (DLA)

Wash Terr ... Washington Territory Opinions [*1854-64*]   (DLA)

Wash Terr ... Washington Territory Reports [*1854-88*]   (DLA)

Wash Ty ..... Washington Territory Opinions [*1854-64*]   (DLA)

Wash Ty ..... Washington Territory Reports [*1854-88*]   (DLA)

Wash U L Q ... Washington University. Law Quarterly [*A publication*]

Wash UL Rev ... Washington University. Law Review [*A publication*]

Wash Univ Bull ... Washington University. Bulletin [*A publication*]

Wash Univ Dep Geol Sci Abstr Res ... Washington University. Department of Geological Sciences. Abstracts of Research [*A publication*]

Wash Univ Pub G ... Washington University. Publications in Geology [*A publication*]

Wash Univ St Hum Ser ... Washington University. Studies. Humanistic Series [*A publication*]

Wash Univ St Sci Ser ... Washington University. Studies. Scientific Series [*A publication*]

Wash Univ Stud Lang & Lit ... Washington University. Studies. Language and Literature [*A publication*]

Wash Univ Stud Sci & Tech ... Washington University. Studies. Science and Technology [*A publication*]

Wash Univ Stud Sci & Tech NS ... Washington University. Studies. Science and Technology. New Series [*A publication*]

Wash Univ Stud Social & Philos Sci ... Washington University. Studies. Social and Philosophical Sciences [*A publication*]

Wash Univ Stud Social & Philos Sci NS ... Washington University. Studies. Social and Philosophical Sciences. New Series [*A publication*]

Wash VA .... Washington's Reports [*1, 2 Virginia*]   (DLA)

WASIA .... Women's Armed Services Integration Act of 1948

WaSIF .... International Fisheries Commission, Seattle, WA [*Library symbol*] [*Library of Congress*]   (LCLS)

WASIH .... Western American Society for Italic Handwriting [*Formerly, WABSIH*]   (EA)

WaSK .... King County Medical Society, Seattle, WA [*Library symbol*] [*Library of Congress*]   (LCLS)

WASK .... Lafayette, IN [*AM radio station call letters*]

WaSKC ...... King County Library System, Seattle, WA [*Library symbol*] [*Library of Congress*]   (LCLS)

WASK-FM ... Lafayette, IN [*FM radio station call letters*]

WASL .... Dyersburg, TN [*FM radio station call letters*]

WAsM .... Memorial Medical Center, Health Sciences Library, Ashland, WI [*Library symbol*] [*Library of Congress*]   (LCLS)

WaSM .... Mountaineers, Inc., Seattle, WA [*Library symbol*] [*Library of Congress*]   (LCLS)

WASM .... Saratoga Springs, NY [*FM radio station call letters*]

WASM .... White Anglo-Saxon Male

Wasmann J Biol ... Wasmann Journal of Biology [*A publication*]

WAsN .... Northland College, Ashland, WI [*Library symbol*] [*Library of Congress*]   (LCLS)

WASNA ...... Western Apicultural Society of North America   (EA)

WaSNH .... Northwest Hospital, Effie M. Storey Learning Center, Seattle, WA [*Library symbol*] [*Library of Congress*]   (LCLS)

WaSnqE ..... Echo Glen Children's Center, Staff Library, Snoqualmie, WA [*Library symbol*] [*Library of Congress*]   (LCLS)

WaSnqE-R ... Echo Glen Children's Center, Resident Library, Snoqualmie, WA [*Library symbol*] [*Library of Congress*]   (LCLS)

WASO .... Women's Association for Symphony Orchestras [*Later, AMSO*]   (EA)

WASP .... Brownsville, PA [*AM radio station call letters*]

WASP .... MARINALG International, World Association of Seaweed Processors   (EA)

WaSp .... Spokane Public Library, Spokane, WA [*Library symbol*] [*Library of Congress*]   (LCLS)

WASP .... War Air Service Program [*Department of Commerce*]

WASP .... Water, Air, and Soil Pollution [*A publication*]

WASP .... Water Spectrum [*A publication*]

WASP .... Water and Steam Program [*NASA*]

WASP .... Weather-Atmospheric Sounding Projectile [*Research rocket*]

WASP .... Weightless Analysis Sounding Probe [*NASA*]

WASP .... Westinghouse Advanced Systems Planning Group

WASP .... White Anglo-Saxon Protestant

WASP .... White Appalachian Southern Protestant [*Chicago slang*]

WASP .... White Ashkenazi Sabra with Pull [*Israeli variation on White Anglo-Saxon Protestant*]

WASP .... Wide Antiarmor Minimissile   (MCD)

WASP .... Williams Aerial Systems Platform [*One-man flying platform*]

WASP .... Window Atmosphere Sounding Projectile [*NASA*]

WASP .... Women's Airforce Service Pilots [*World War II*]

WASP .... Woody Allen's Spring Picture [*Designation reflecting the filmmaker's reluctance to provide information about his movies in advance of their commercial release*] [*See also WAFP*]

WASP .... Work Activity Sampling Plan

WASP .... Workshop Analysis and Scheduling Programing

WASP .... World Association of Societies of Pathology   (EA)

WASP .... World Associations for Social Psychiatry [*Santa Barbara, CA*]   (EA)

WASP .... Wrap-Around Simulation Program [*Military*]   (CAAL)

WASPA ...... White Anglo-Saxon Protestant Ambulatory [*Extension of WASP; indicates the necessity of being able-bodied as an additional requirement for success*]

WaSpBM .... United States Bureau of Mines, Mining Research Center, Spokane, WA [*Library symbol*] [*Library of Congress*]   (LCLS)

WaSpBMW ... United States Bureau of Mines, Western Field Operations Center, Spokane, WA [*Library symbol*] [*Library of Congress*]   (LCLS)

WaSPC .... Seattle Pacific College, Seattle, WA [*Library symbol*] [*Library of Congress*]   (LCLS)

WaSpCN .... Center for Nursing Education, Spokane, WA [*Library symbol*] [*Library of Congress*]   (LCLS)

WaSpCo ..... Spokane County Library, Spokane, WA [*Library symbol*] [*Library of Congress*]   (LCLS)

WaSpD .... Deaconess Hospital, School of Nursing, Spokane, WA [*Library symbol*] [*Library of Congress*]   (LCLS)

WaSPe .... Perkins, Coie, Stone, Olsen & Williams, Seattle, WA [*Library symbol*] [*Library of Congress*]   (LCLS)

WaSpG .... Gonzaga University, Spokane, WA [*Library symbol*] [*Library of Congress*]   (LCLS)

WaSpGL ..... Church of Jesus Christ of Latter-Day Saints, Genealogical Society Library, Spokane Branch, Spokane, WA [*Library symbol*] [*Library of Congress*]   (LCLS)

WaSpG-L ... Gonzaga University, Law Library, Spokane, WA [*Library symbol*] [*Library of Congress*]   (LCLS)

WaSpGS .... United States Geological Survey, Spokane, WA [*Library symbol*] [*Library of Congress*]   (LCLS)

WaSpH .... Holy Family Hospital, Spokane, WA [*Library symbol*] [*Library of Congress*]   (LCLS)

WaSPH .... United States Public Health Service Hospital, Medical Service Library, Seattle, WA [*Library symbol*] [*Library of Congress*]   (LCLS)

WaSpHiE .... Eastern Washington State Historical Society, Museum Library, Spokane, WA [*Library symbol*] [*Library of Congress*]   (LCLS)

WaSpIn ...... Intermediate School District 101, Professional Materials Library, Spokane, WA [*Library symbol*] [*Library of Congress*] (LCLS)
WaSpJ .... Jesuit Archives of the Province of Oregon, Spokane, WA [*Library symbol*] [*Library of Congress*] (LCLS)
WaSpJP ..... Washington State Office of Juvenile Parole Services, Spokane, WA [*Library symbol*] [*Library of Congress*] (LCLS)
WaSpJS ..... Jesuit Scholastic Library, Spokane, WA [*Library symbol*] [*Library of Congress*] (LCLS)
WaSPM ...... Providence Hospital, Medical Library and Learning Resource Center, Seattle, WA [*Library symbol*] [*Library of Congress*] (LCLS)
WaSpM ...... Spokane County Medical Library, Spokane, WA [*Library symbol*] [*Library of Congress*] (LCLS)
WaSpMF .... Murphey Favre, Inc., Spokane, WA [*Library symbol*] [*Library of Congress*] (LCLS)
WaSpN .... Fort Wright College, Spokane, WA [*Library symbol*] [*Library of Congress*] (LCLS)
WASP-NN ... White Anglo-Saxon Protestant Native Born of Native Parents
WaSPoD ..... Population Dynamics, Seattle, WA [*Library symbol*] [*Library of Congress*] (LCLS)
Was Polit .... Waseda Political Studies [*A publication*]
WaSpPS ..... Spokane Public Schools, Curriculum Library, Spokane, WA [*Library symbol*] [*Library of Congress*] (LCLS)
WASPRU .... West African Stored Products Research Unit
WaSPS .... Seattle Public Schools, Library Technical Service, Seattle, WA [*Library symbol*] [*Library of Congress*] (LCLS)
WaSpS .... Spokane Community College, Spokane, WA [*Library symbol*] [*Library of Congress*] (LCLS)
WASPS ...... Women's Auxiliary Service Platoon
WaSpSF ..... Spokane Falls Community College, Spokane, WA [*Library symbol*] [*Library of Congress*] (LCLS)
WaSpSH ..... Sacred Heart Medical Center, Spokane, WA [*Library symbol*] [*Library of Congress*] (LCLS)
WaSpSL ..... Saint Luke's Hospital, Spokane, WA [*Library symbol*] [*Library of Congress*] (LCLS)
WaSpSL ..... Spokane County Law Library, Spokane, WA [*Library symbol*] [*Library of Congress*] (LCLS)
WaSpStM ... Saint Michael's Institute, Spokane, WA [*Library symbol*] [*Library of Congress*] (LCLS)
WaSpVA ..... United States Veterans Administration Hospital, Spokane, WA [*Library symbol*] [*Library of Congress*] (LCLS)
WaSpW ...... Whitworth College, Spokane, WA [*Library symbol*] [*Library of Congress*] (LCLS)
WASPWWII ... Women Airforce Service Pilots WWII (EA)
WaSpYS ..... Washington State Center for Youth Services, Spokane, WA [*Library symbol*] [*Library of Congress*] (LCLS)
WASR .... Wolfeboro, NH [*AM radio station call letters*]
WaSS .... Schick's Schadel Hospital, Medical Library, Seattle, WA [*Library symbol*] [*Library of Congress*] (LCLS)
Wass .... Wassermann [*Test for syphilis*]
WASS .... Wavefront Analysis of Spatial Sampling [*Aircraft landing approach*]
WASS .... Wide-Area Active Surveillance System [*Military*] (MCD)
WaSSB .... Washington State Office for the Services for the Blind, Seattle, WA [*Library symbol*] [*Library of Congress*] (LCLS)
Wasser- Energiewirt ... Wasser- und Energiewirtschaft [*A publication*]
Wasser Luft Betr ... Wasser, Luft, und Betrieb [*A publication*]
Wasserwirtsch-Wassertech ... Wasserwirtschaft-Wassertechnik [*A publication*]
Wasserwirt-Wassertech ... Wasserwirtschaft-Wassertechnik [*A publication*]
WaSSh .... Shoreline Community College, Seattle, WA [*Library symbol*] [*Library of Congress*] (LCLS)
WaSSH .... Swedish Hospital Medical Center, Seattle, WA [*Library symbol*] [*Library of Congress*] (LCLS)
W Assn Map Lib Inf Bull ... Western Association of Map Libraries. Information Bulletin [*A publication*]
WASSP ...... Wallingford Storm Sewer Package [*Hydraulics Research*] [*Software package*]
WASSP ...... Wire Arc Seismic Section Profiler
WaSSW ...... Shannon & Wilson, Inc., Seattle, WA [*Library symbol*] [*Library of Congress*] (LCLS)
Wasswirt Wasstech ... Wasserwirtschaft-Wassertechnik [*A publication*]
WAST .... Ashtabula, OH [*AM radio station call letters*]
WASTE ...... Wisdom, Acclaim, and Status through Expenditures [*Fictional government agency in book "Alice in Blunderland"*]
Waste Disposal Water Manage Aust ... Waste Disposal and Water Management in Australia [*A publication*]
Waste Disposal & Water Manage in Aust ... Waste Disposal and Water Management in Australia [*A publication*]
Waste Dispos Water Manage Aust ... Waste Disposal and Water Management in Australia [*A publication*]
Waste Disp Recyc Bull ... Waste Disposal and Recycling Bulletin [*A publication*]
WaSteM ..... McNeil Island Correction Center, Steilacoom, WA [*Library symbol*] [*Library of Congress*] (LCLS)
Waste Mgmt Inf Bull ... Waste Management Information Bulletin [*A publication*]
Waste Mgmt Res ... Waste Management Research [*A publication*]
Wastes Eng ... Wastes Engineering [*A publication*]
Wastes Mgmt ... Wastes Management [*A publication*]

WaSU .... Seattle University, Seattle, WA [*Library symbol*] [*Library of Congress*] (LCLS)
WASU-FM ... Boone, NC [*FM radio station call letters*]
WaSUN .... United Nursing Homes, Seattle, WA [*Library symbol*] [*Library of Congress*] (LCLS)
WaSVA .... United States Veterans Administration Hospital, Seattle, WA [*Library symbol*] [*Library of Congress*] (LCLS)
WASV-TV ... Asheville, NC [*Television station call letters*]
WaSWG ..... West Seattle General Hospital, Seattle, WA [*Library symbol*] [*Library of Congress*] (LCLS)
WASZ .... Ashland-Lineville, AL [*FM radio station call letters*]
WaT .... Tacoma Public Library, Tacoma, WA [*Library symbol*] [*Library of Congress*] (LCLS)
WAT .... University of Waterloo Library [*UTLAS symbol*]
WAT .... Water [*Automotive engineering*]
Wat .... Watermeyer's Cape Of Good Hope Supreme Court Reports [*1857*] [*South Africa*] (DLA)
WAT .... Watertown Free Public Library, Watertown, MA [*OCLC symbol*] (OCLC)
WAT .... Watheroo [*Australia*] [*Seismograph station code, US Geological Survey*] [*Closed*] (SEIS)
WAT .... Watheroo [*Australia*] [*Later, GNA*] [*Geomagnetic observatory code*]
WAT .... Weapons Assignment Technician (AFM)
WAT .... Web Action Time (MCD)
WAT .... Weight, Altitude, and Temperature (IEEE)
WAT .... Wet Anode Tantalum
WAT .... What Acronym's That? [*A publication*]
WAT .... Wideband Adapter Transformer
WAT .... Word Association Test [*Psychology*]
WAT's .... Wide-Angle [*Galilean*] Telescopes
WATA .... Boone, NC [*AM radio station call letters*]
WATA .... Wisconsin Automatic Test Apparatus
WATA .... World Association of Travel Agents (EA-IO)
WaTAC ...... Allenmore Community Hospital, Tacoma, WA [*Library symbol*] [*Library of Congress*] (LCLS)
WaTAH ...... United States Army [*Madigan*] General Hospital, Tacoma, WA [*Library symbol*] [*Library of Congress*] (LCLS)
Wat Aust .... Water in Australia [*A publication*]
WATC .... [*The*] Washington Terminal Company [*AAR code*]
WATC .... Women's Ambulance and Transportation Corps
WaTCC ...... Tacoma Community College, Tacoma, WA [*Library symbol*] [*Library of Congress*] (LCLS)
Wat CGH .... Watermeyer's Cape Of Good Hope Reports [*South Africa*] (DLA)
WaTCH ...... Mary Bridge Children's Health Center, Tacoma, WA [*Library symbol*] [*Library of Congress*] (LCLS)
WATCH ..... Watchers Against Television Commercial Harrassment [*Student legal action organization*]
WATCH ...... World Against Toys Causing Harm
WaTCJ .... Cascadia Juvenile Diagnostic Center, Tacoma, WA [*Library symbol*] [*Library of Congress*] (LCLS)
Wat Con ..... Watkins on Conveyancing [*9th ed.*] [*1845*] (DLA)
Wat Cop ..... Watkins on Copyholds [*6th ed.*] [*1829*] (DLA)
Wat Cr Dig ... Waterman's Criminal Digest [*United States*] (DLA)
WATD .... Brockton, MA [*AM radio station call letters*]
WaTD .... Doctors Hospital, Tacoma, WA [*Library symbol*] [*Library of Congress*] (LCLS)
WATD-FM ... Marshfield, MA [*FM radio station call letters*]
WATDOC ... Water Resources Document Reference Centre [*Canadian Department of Fisheries and the Environment*] [*Ottawa, ON*] [*Database*] (EISS)
WATE .... Knoxville, TN [*Television station call letters*]
WA Teachers J ... Western Australian Teachers' Journal [*A publication*]
WA Teach J ... Western Australian Teachers' Journal [*A publication*]
Water Air and Soil Pollut ... Water, Air, and Soil Pollution [*A publication*]
Water Air Soil Pollut ... Water, Air, and Soil Pollution [*A publication*]
Water Am Inst Chem Eng ... Water. American Institute of Chemical Engineers [*A publication*]
Water A S P ... Water, Air, and Soil Pollution [*A publication*]
Water Biol Syst ... Water in Biological Systems [*A publication*]
Water DROP ... Distribution Register of Organic Pollutants in Water [*See also DROP*] [*Environmental Protection Agency*]
Water Electrolyte Metab Proc Symp ... Water and Electrolyte Metabolism. Proceedings of the Symposium [*A publication*]
Water Eng ... Water and Wastes Engineering [*A publication*]
WATERF .... Waterford [*County in Ireland*] (ROG)
WATERFD ... Waterford [*County in Ireland*]
Water Law Newsl ... Water Law Newsletter [*United States*] [*A publication*]
Water Manage News ... Water Management News [*A publication*]
Water Manage Techn Rep Colorado State Univ ... Colorado State University. Water Management Technical Report [*A publication*]
Watermeyer ... Watermeyer's Cape Of Good Hope Reports [*South Africa*] (DLA)
Water Poll Abstr ... Water Pollution Abstracts [*A publication*]
Water Poll Cont Fed J ... Water Pollution Control Federation. Journal [*A publication*]
Water Poll Control Fed J ... Water Pollution Control Federation. Journal [*A publication*]
Water Pollut Control ... Water Pollution Control [*A publication*]

Water Pollut Control (Don Mills Can) ... Water and Pollution Control (Don Mills, Canada) [*A publication*]

Water Pollut Control (London) ... Water Pollution Control (London) [*A publication*]

Water Pollut Control Res Ser ... Water Pollution Control Research Series [*A publication*]

Water Pollut Res Can ... Water Pollution Research in Canada [*A publication*]

Water Pollut Res (Stevenage) ... Water Pollution Research (Stevenage) [*A publication*]

Water Purif Liquid Wastes Treat ... Water Purification and Liquid Wastes Treatment [*Japan*] [*A publication*]

Water Qual Instrum ... Water Quality Instrumentation [*A publication*]

Water Res ... Water Research [*A publication*]

Water Res Found Aust Annu Rep Balance Sheet ... Water Research Foundation of Australia. Annual Report and Balance Sheet [*A publication*]

Water Res Found Aust Bull ... Water Research Foundation of Australia. Bulletin [*A publication*]

Water Res Found of Aust Newsl ... Water Research Foundation of Australia. Newsletter [*A publication*]

Water Res Found Aust Rep ... Water Research Foundation of Australia. Report [*A publication*]

Water Res News ... Water Research News [*A publication*]

Water Resour ... Water Resources [*A publication*]

Water Resour Bull ... Water Resources Bulletin [*A publication*]

Water Resources Res ... Water Resources Research [*A publication*]

Water Resour Invest ... Water Resources Investigations [*A publication*]

Water Resour Invest US Geol Surv ... Water Resources Investigations. US Geological Survey [*A publication*]

Water Resour Manag Ser ... Water Resource Management Series [*A publication*]

Water Resour Newsl ... Water Resources Newsletter [*A publication*]

Water Resour Rep Ont Minist Environ Water Resour Branch ... Water Resources Report. Ontario Ministry of the Environment. Water Resources Branch [*A publication*]

Water Resour Res ... Water Resources Research [*A publication*]

Water Resour Res Cent VA Polytech Inst State Univ Bull ... Water Resources Research Center. Virginia Polytechnic Institute and State University. Bulletin [*A publication*]

Water Resour Rev Streamflow Ground-Water Cond ... Water Resources Review for Streamflow and Ground-Water Conditions [*United States - Canada*] [*A publication*]

Water Resour Symp ... Water Resources Symposium [*A publication*]

Water Res R ... Water Resources Research [*A publication*]

Water (S Afr) ... Water (South Africa) [*A publication*]

Water and San ... Water and Sanitation [*A publication*]

Water Sanit Eng ... Water and Sanitary Engineer [*A publication*]

Water Sci & Technol ... Water Science and Technology [*A publication*]

Water Serv ... Water Services [*A publication*]

Water & Sewage Works ... Water and Sewage Works [*A publication*]

Water Supply Manage ... Water Supply and Management [*England*] [*A publication*]

Water Supply Pap Geol Surv GB Hydrogeol Rep ... Water Supply Papers. Geological Survey of Great Britain. Hydrogeological Report [*A publication*]

Water Supply Pap US Geol Surv ... Water Supply Paper. United States Geological Survey [*A publication*]

Water Treat Exam ... Water Treatment and Examination [*A publication*]

Water Waste ... Water and Wastes Engineering [*A publication*]

Water & Waste Engng ... Water and Waste Engineering [*A publication*]

Water Wastes Dig ... Water and Wastes Digest [*A publication*]

Water Wastes Eng ... Water and Wastes Engineering [*A publication*]

Water Wastes Eng Ind ... Water and Wastes Engineering/Industrial [*A publication*]

Water Waste Treat ... Water and Waste Treatment [*A publication*]

Water Wastewater Treat Plants Oper Newsl ... Water and Wastewater Treatment Plants Operators' Newsletter [*A publication*]

Water Water Eng ... Water and Water Engineering [*A publication*]

Water (WC and IC Staff Journal) ... Water (Water Conservation and Irrigation Commission Staff Journal) [*A publication*]

Water Well J ... Water Well Journal [*A publication*]

Water Well Jour ... Water Well Journal [*A publication*]

Water Works Eng ... Water Works Engineering [*A publication*]

WATFOR .... Waterloo FORTRAN [*University of Waterloo*] [*Canada*]

WaTFS .... Fort Steilacoom Community College, Tacoma, WA [*Library symbol*] [*Library of Congress*] (LCLS)

WaTG .... Tacoma Branch Genealogical Library, Tacoma, WA [*Library symbol*] [*Library of Congress*] (LCLS)

WaTGH .... Tacoma General Hospital, Pierce County Medical Library, Tacoma, WA [*Library symbol*] [*Library of Congress*] (LCLS)

WaTGS .... Church of Jesus Christ of Latter-Day Saints, Genealogical Society Library, Tacoma Branch, Tacoma, WA [*Library symbol*] [*Library of Congress*] (LCLS)

WATH .... Athens, OH [*AM radio station call letters*]

WATI .... Danville, IN [*FM radio station call letters*]

WaTJP .... Washington State Office of Juvenile Parole Services, Tacoma, WA [*Library symbol*] [*Library of Congress*] (LCLS)

WATK .... Antigo, WI [*AM radio station call letters*]

Watk Con ... Watkins on Conveyancing (DLA)

Watk Conv ... Watkins on Conveyancing (DLA)

Watk Cop ... Watkins on Copyholds (DLA)

Watk Copyh ... Watkins on Copyholds (DLA)

Watk Des ... Watkins on Descents (DLA)

WATL .... Atlanta, GA [*Television station call letters*]

WaTLG .... Lakewood General Hospital and Convalescent Center, Tacoma, WA [*Library symbol*] [*Library of Congress*] (LCLS)

WATN .... Watertown, NY [*AM radio station call letters*]

WATO .... Oak Ridge, TN [*AM radio station call letters*]

WaTO .... Oakridge Group Home, Tacoma, WA [*Library symbol*] [*Library of Congress*] (LCLS)

WATP .... Marion, SC [*AM radio station call letters*]

WaTP .... Pioneer Group Home, Tacoma, WA [*Library symbol*] [*Library of Congress*] (LCLS)

WaTPC .... Pierce County Library, Tacoma, WA [*Library symbol*] [*Library of Congress*] (LCLS)

WaTPG .... Puget Sound General Hospital, Tacoma, WA [*Library symbol*] [*Library of Congress*] (LCLS)

WATPL .... Wartime Traffic Priority List (NATG)

WaTPM .... Pierce County Medical Library, Tacoma, WA [*Library symbol*] [*Library of Congress*] (LCLS)

WatPolAb ... Water Pollution Abstracts [*A publication*]

Wat Pollut Control ... Water Pollution Control [*A publication*]

WaTPS .... Tacoma Public Schools, Professional and Curriculum Library, Tacoma, WA [*Library symbol*] [*Library of Congress*] (LCLS)

Wat Pwr ..... Water Power [*A publication*]

WATR .... Waterbury, CT [*AM radio station call letters*]

WATR .... Waterville [*AAR code*]

WatResAb ... Water Resources Abstracts [*A publication*]

Wat Res Fdn Aust Bull ... Water Research Foundation of Australia. Bulletin [*A publication*]

Wat Res Fdn Rep ... Water Research Foundation of Australia. Report [*A publication*]

Wat Resour Res ... Water Resources Research [*A publication*]

WATS .... Sayre, PA [*AM radio station call letters*]

WATS .... Wide-Area Military Traffic Management and Terminal Service

WATS .... Wide-Area Telecommunications [*formerly, Telephone*] Service [*American Telephone & Telegraph Co. contract billing system*]

WATS .... Women's Auxiliary Training Service

Wats Arb .... Watson on Arbitration (DLA)

Wats Cler Law ... Watson's Clergyman's Law (DLA)

Wats Comp Eq ... Watson's Compendium of Equity (DLA)

Wat Serv .... Water Services [*A publication*]

Wat Set-Off ... Waterman on Set-Off (DLA)

WaTSJ .... Saint Joseph Hospital, Tacoma, WA [*Library symbol*] [*Library of Congress*] (LCLS)

Watson ...... Watson's Compendium of Equity [*2 eds.*] [*1873, 1888*] (DLA)

Watson Eq ... Watson's Compendium of Equity (DLA)

Wats Part ... Watson on Partnership [*2nd ed.*] [*1807*] (DLA)

Wats Sher ... Watson's Office and Duty of Sheriff [*2nd ed.*] [*1848*] (DLA)

WATSTORE ... National Water Data Storage and Retrieval System [*Marine science*] (MSC)

WATT .... Cadillac, MI [*AM radio station call letters*]

WATTec ..... Welding and Testing Technology Energy Conference [*Acronym is used as name of association*]

Wattle Res Inst Univ Natal (S Afr) Rep ... Wattle Research Institute. University of Natal (South Africa). Report [*A publication*]

Watts .... Watts' Pennsylvania Reports [*1832-40*] (DLA)

Watts .... Watts' Reports [*16-24 West Virginia*] (DLA)

Watts (PA) ... Watts' Pennsylvania Reports [*1832-40*] (DLA)

Watts & S ... Watts and Sergeant's Pennsylvania Reports [*1841-45*] (DLA)

Watts & Serg ... Watts and Sergeant's Pennsylvania Reports [*1841-45*] (DLA)

Watts & S (PA) ... Watts and Sergeant's Pennsylvania Reports [*1841-45*] (DLA)

WaTU .... University of Puget Sound, Tacoma, WA [*Library symbol*] [*Library of Congress*] (LCLS)

WATU .... Western Approaches Tactical Unit [*Navy*]

WATV .... Birmingham, AL [*AM radio station call letters*]

Wat Vict ..... Water in Victoria [*A publication*]

WATW .... Ashland, WI [*AM radio station call letters*]

WaTW .... Weyerhaeuser Co., Tacoma, WA [*Library symbol*] [*Library of Congress*] (LCLS)

WATW .... Wood Awning Type Window

Wat Waste Treat ... Water and Waste Treatment [*A publication*]

Wat Wat Engng ... Water and Water Engineering [*A publication*]

WaTWH ...... Western State Hospital, Staff Library, Tacoma, WA [*Library symbol*] [*Library of Congress*] (LCLS)

WaTWH-R ... Western State Hospital, Resident Library, Tacoma, WA [*Library symbol*] [*Library of Congress*] (LCLS)

WaTW-T ..... Weyerhaeuser Co., Technical Center, Tacoma, WA [*Library symbol*] [*Library of Congress*] (LCLS)

WATX-TV ... Arecibo, PR [*Television station call letters*]

WATZ .... Alpena, MI [*AM radio station call letters*]

WATZ-FM ... Alpena, MI [*FM radio station call letters*]

WaU .... University of Washington, Seattle, WA [*Library symbol*] [*Library of Congress*] (LCLS)

WAU .... University of Washington, Seattle, WA [*OCLC symbol*] (OCLC)

wau .... Washington [*MARC country of publication code*] [*Library of Congress*] (LCCP)
WAU .... Weapon Assignment Unit [*Military*] (CAAL)
WAU .... Work Advisory Unit (ADA)
WAUB .... Auburn, NY [*AM radio station call letters*]
WAUC .... Wauchula, FL [*AM radio station call letters*]
WAUD .... Auburn, AL [*AM radio station call letters*]
WaU-D .... University of Washington, Drama Library, Seattle, WA [*Library symbol*] [*Library of Congress*] (LCLS)
WaU-EA ..... University of Washington, East Asia Library, Seattle, WA [*Library symbol*] [*Library of Congress*] (LCLS)
WaU-FE ..... University of Washington, Far Eastern Library, Seattle, WA [*Library symbol*] [*Library of Congress*] [*Obsolete*] (LCLS)
WaU-HS ..... University of Washington, Health Sciences Library, Seattle, WA [*Library symbol*] [*Library of Congress*] (LCLS)
WAUK .... Waukesha, WI [*AM radio station call letters*]
WaU-L .... University of Washington, Law Library, Seattle, WA [*Library symbol*] [*Library of Congress*] (LCLS)
WAU Law R ... University of Western Australia. Law Review [*A publication*]
WAULR ...... Western Australia University. Law Review [*A publication*]
WaU-MC .... University of Washington, Harborview Medical Center Library, Seattle, WA [*Library symbol*] [*Library of Congress*] (LCLS)
WAUN .... Kewaunee, WI [*FM radio station call letters*]
WA Univ Gaz ... University of Western Australia. Gazette [*A publication*]
WA Univ Geog Lab Res Rept ... University of Western Australia. Geography Laboratory. Research Report [*A publication*]
WAUP .... Akron, OH [*FM radio station call letters*]
WAUR .... Aurora, IL [*FM radio station call letters*]
WAUS .... Berrien Springs, MI [*FM radio station call letters*]
WAUS .... World Association of Upper Silesians (EA)
W Aust For Dep Bull ... Western Australia. Forests Department. Bulletin [*A publication*]
W Aust Geol Surv Bull ... Western Australia. Geological Survey. Bulletin [*A publication*]
W Aust Geol Surv 1:250000 Geol Ser ... Western Australia. Geological Survey. 1:250,000 Geological Series [*A publication*]
W Austl ...... Western Australia Reports (DLA)
W Austl Acts ... Western Australia Acts (DLA)
W Austl Ind Gaz ... Western Australia Industrial Gazette (DLA)
W Austl JP ... Western Australia Justice of the Peace (DLA)
W Austl LR ... Western Australia Law Reports (DLA)
W Aust Nat ... Western Australian Naturalist [*A publication*]
WAUXCP .... West Auxiliary Airborne Command Post (MCD)
WaV .... Fort Vancouver Regional Library, Vancouver, WA [*Library symbol*] [*Library of Congress*] (LCLS)
WAV .... Williford Aviation, Inc. [*Atlanta, GA*] [*FAA designator*] (FAAC)
WAV .... Wirtschaftliche Aufbau Vereinigung [*Economic Reconstruction Union*] [*West Germany*] (PPE)
WAVA .... Arlington, VA [*FM radio station call letters*]
WAVA .... World Association of Veteran Athletes [*West Hill, ON*] (EA-IO)
WAVA .... World Association of Veterinary Anatomists [*Ithaca, NY*] (EA)
WAVAW ..... Women Against Violence Against Women (EA)
WAVB .... Lajas, PR [*AM radio station call letters*]
WaVC .... Clark College, Vancouver, WA [*Library symbol*] [*Library of Congress*] (LCLS)
WAVC .... Duluth, MN [*FM radio station call letters*]
WAVE .... Water-Augmented Vehicle
Wave Electron ... Wave Electronics [*A publication*]
WAVES ...... Weight and Value Engineering System [*Data processing*]
WAVES ...... Women Accepted for Volunteer Emergency Service [*US Navy Women's Reserve*] [*World War II and later*]
WAVES ...... Women Appointed Volunteer Emergency Services [*British*] [*World War II*]
WAVE-TV ... Louisville, KY [*Television station call letters*]
WAVF .... Hanahan, SC [*FM radio station call letters*]
WAVFH ...... World Association of Veterinary Food-Hygienists [*See also AMVHA*] (EA-IO)
WAVG .... Louisville, KY [*AM radio station call letters*]
WaVHS .... United States Park Service, Fort Vancouver National Historical Site, Vancouver, WA [*Library symbol*] [*Library of Congress*] (LCLS)
WAVI .... Portsmouth, NH [*AM radio station call letters*]
WAVK .... Marathon, FL [*FM radio station call letters*]
WAVL .... Apollo, PA [*AM radio station call letters*]
WAVM .... Maynard, MA [*FM radio station call letters*]
WaVMH ..... Vancouver Memorial Hospital, Vancouver, WA [*Library symbol*] [*Library of Congress*] (LCLS)
WAVMI .... World Association of Veterinary Microbiologists, Immunologists, and Specialists in Infectious Diseases [*See also AMVMI*] (EA-IO)
WAVO .... Decatur, GA [*AM radio station call letters*]
WAVP .... World Association of Veterinary Pathologists (EA-IO)
WAVPM ...... Women Against Violence in Pornography and Media (EA)
WAVR .... Waverly, NY [*FM radio station call letters*]
WAVR .... Waverly Press, Inc. [*NASDAQ symbol*] (NQ)
WAVS .... Davie, FL [*AM radio station call letters*]
WAVS .... Wide Angle Visual System (MCD)
WaVSB .... Washington State School for the Blind, Vancouver, WA [*Library symbol*] [*Library of Congress*] (LCLS)

WaVSD .... Washington State School for the Deaf, Vancouver, WA [*Library symbol*] [*Library of Congress*] (LCLS)
WaVStJ ...... Saint Joseph Community Hospital, Vancouver, WA [*Library symbol*] [*Library of Congress*] (LCLS)
WAVT-FM ... Pottsville, PA [*FM radio station call letters*]
WAVU .... Albertville, AL [*AM radio station call letters*]
WAVV .... Marco, FL [*FM radio station call letters*]
WaVVA .... United States Veterans Administration Hospital, Vancouver, WA [*Library symbol*] [*Library of Congress*] (LCLS)
WAVW .... Vero Beach, FL [*FM radio station call letters*]
WAVX .... North Muskegon, MI [*FM radio station call letters*]
WAVY-TV ... Portsmouth, VA [*Television station call letters*]
WAVZ .... New Haven, CT [*AM radio station call letters*]
WAW .... University of Washington, School of Librarianship, Seattle, WA [*OCLC symbol*] (OCLC)
WaW .... Walla Walla Public Library, Walla Walla, WA [*Library symbol*] [*Library of Congress*] (LCLS)
WAW .... Ward's Auto World [*A publication*]
WAW .... Warsaw [*Poland*] [*Airport symbol*] (OAG)
WAW .... Waynesburg & Washington Railroad Co. [*Absorbed into Consolidated Rail Corp.*] [*AAR code*]
WAW .... Wings Airways [*Blue Bell, PA*] [*FAA designator*] (FAAC)
WAWA .... West Africa Wins Again [*A reminder that visitors to this region must exercise caution if they wish to avoid bureaucratic harrassment and overcharging*]
WAWA .... West Allis, WI [*AM radio station call letters*]
WAWA .... Woolens and Worsteds of America [*Defunct*] (EA)
WAWB .... Hahira, GA [*AM radio station call letters*]
WaWC .... Walla Walla College, College Place, WA [*Library symbol*] [*Library of Congress*] (LCLS)
WAWC .... West Africa War Council [*World War II*]
WaWeC ...... Central Washington Hospital, Health Sciences Library, Wenatchee, WA [*Library symbol*] [*Library of Congress*] (LCLS)
WaWeN ...... North Central Regional Library, Wenatche, WA [*Library symbol*] [*Library of Congress*] (LCLS)
WaWeW ...... Wenatchee Valley College, Wenatchee, WA [*Library symbol*] [*Library of Congress*] (LCLS)
WaWeYS .... Washington State Center for Youth Services, Wenatchee, WA [*Library symbol*] [*Library of Congress*] (LCLS)
WAWF .... William Allen White Foundation (EA)
WAWF .... World Arm Wrestling Federation [*Scranton, PA*] (EA)
WAWF .... World Association of World Federalists
WAWG .... Where Are We Going?
WaWiS .... Wilbur Public Schools System, Wilbur, WA [*Library symbol*] [*Library of Congress*] (LCLS)
WAWK .... Kendallville, IN [*AM radio station call letters*]
WaWnvGH ... Woodenville Group Home, Woodenville, WA [*Library symbol*] [*Library of Congress*] (LCLS)
WaWP .... Washington State Penitentiary, Walla Walla, WA [*Library symbol*] [*Library of Congress*] (LCLS)
WAWS-TV ... Jacksonville, FL [*Television station call letters*]
WAWV .... Sylacauga, AL [*FM radio station call letters*]
WaWV .... United States Veterans Administration Hospital, Walla Walla, WA [*Library symbol*] [*Library of Congress*] (LCLS)
WaWW .... Whitman College, Walla Walla, WA [*Library symbol*] [*Library of Congress*] (LCLS)
WaWWC ..... Walla Walla Community College, Walla Walla, WA [*Library symbol*] [*Library of Congress*] (LCLS)
WAWZ .... Zarephath, NJ [*FM radio station call letters*]
WAX .... Weapon Assignment and Target Extermination
WAXA .... Anderson, SC [*Television station call letters*]
WAXC .... Berlin, NH [*AM radio station call letters*]
WAXD .... Wide-Angle X-Ray Diffraction
WAXE .... Vero Beach, FL [*AM radio station call letters*]
WAXI .... Rockville, IN [*FM radio station call letters*]
WAXL .... Lancaster, WI [*FM radio station call letters*]
WAXM .... Waxman Industries, Inc. [*NASDAQ symbol*] (NQ)
WAXO .... Lewisburg, TN [*AM radio station call letters*]
WAXS .... Wide-Angle X-Ray Scattering
WAXT .... Alexandria, IN [*FM radio station call letters*]
WAXX .... Eau Claire, WI [*FM radio station call letters*]
WAXY .... Fort Lauderdale, FL [*FM radio station call letters*]
WAXZ .... Georgetown, OH [*FM radio station call letters*]
WAY .... Wayne State College, Wayne, NE [*OCLC symbol*] (OCLC)
WAY .... Waynesburg [*Pennsylvania*] [*Seismograph station code, US Geological Survey*] [*Closed*] (SEIS)
WAY .... Waynesburg, PA [*Location identifier*] [*FAA*] (FAAL)
WAY .... World Assembly of Youth (EA-IO)
WaY .... Yakima Valley Regional Library, Yakima, WA [*Library symbol*] [*Library of Congress*] (LCLS)
WaYacL ...... Larch Mountain Correctional Center, Staff Library, Yacolt, WA [*Library symbol*] [*Library of Congress*] (LCLS)
WaYacL-R ... Larch Mountain Correctional Center, Resident Library, Yacolt, WA [*Library symbol*] [*Library of Congress*] (LCLS)
WAYB .... Waynesboro, VA [*AM radio station call letters*]
WAYC .... Bedford, PA [*AM radio station call letters*]
WAYD .... Ozark, AL [*AM radio station call letters*]
WAYE .... Birmingham, AL [*AM radio station call letters*]

WaYGS....... Church of Jesus Christ of Latter-Day Saints, Genealogical Society Library, Yakima Branch, Yakima, WA [*Library symbol*] [*Library of Congress*]   (LCLS)
WAYI-FM ... Hudson Falls, NY [*FM radio station call letters*]
WaYJP....... Washington State Office of Juvenile Parole Services, Yakima, WA [*Library symbol*] [*Library of Congress*]   (LCLS)
WAYK........ Melbourne, FL [*Television station call letters*]
WAYL........ Minneapolis, MN [*FM radio station call letters*]
WaYM........ Yakima Valley Memorial Hospital, Yakima, WA [*Library symbol*] [*Library of Congress*]   (LCLS)
WAYMCA... World Alliance of Young Men's Christian Associations   (EA-IO)
WaYMHi..... Yakima Valley Museum and Historical Association, Yakima, WA [*Library symbol*] [*Library of Congress*]   (LCLS)
WAYN........ Rockingham, NC [*AM radio station call letters*]
Wayne L Rev ... Wayne Law Review [*A publication*]
WAYR........ Orange Park, FL [*AM radio station call letters*]
WaYSE....... Saint Elizabeth Hospital, Health Sciences Library, Yakima, WA [*Library symbol*] [*Library of Congress*]   (LCLS)
Way Suppl ... Way. Supplement [*A publication*]
WAYT........ Wabash, IN [*AM radio station call letters*]
WAYU........ Lewiston, ME [*FM radio station call letters*]
WAYV........ Atlantic City, NJ [*FM radio station call letters*]
WAYW........ Worcester, MA [*FM radio station call letters*]
WAYX........ Waycross, GA [*AM radio station call letters*]
WAYY........ Chippewa Falls, WI [*AM radio station call letters*]
WaYY .... Yakima Valley College, Yakima, WA [*Library symbol*] [*Library of Congress*]   (LCLS)
WaYYS....... Washington State Center for Youth Services, Yakima, WA [*Library symbol*] [*Library of Congress*]   (LCLS)
WAYZ........ Waynesboro, PA [*AM radio station call letters*]
WAYZ-FM ... Waynesboro, PA [*FM radio station call letters*]
WAZE........ Dawson, GA [*FM radio station call letters*]
WAZF .... Yazoo City, MS [*AM radio station call letters*]
WAZI .... Morristown, TN [*FM radio station call letters*]
WAZL .... Hazelton, PA [*AM radio station call letters*]
WAZR .... Woodstock, VA [*FM radio station call letters*]
WAZS........ Summerville, SC [*AM radio station call letters*]
WAZU........ Springfield, OH [*FM radio station call letters*]
WAZX........ Georgetown, SC [*AM radio station call letters*]
WAZY-FM ... Lafayette, IN [*FM radio station call letters*]
WAZZ........ New Bern, NC [*FM radio station call letters*]
WB............. Wage Board [*Civil Service classification*]
WB............. Wagon Box   (MSA)
W & B .... Walferstan and Bristowe's Election Cases [*1859-65*]   (DLA)
WB............. Wall Box   (ROG)
WB............. Wallboard
WB............. Warbirds of America [*Formerly, WA*]   (EA)
WB............. Warehouse Book
WB............. Wash Basin
WB............. Wash Bucket
WB............. Washable Base   (ADA)
WB............. Waste Book   (ROG)
WB............. Water Ballast [*Shipping*]
WB............. Water Board
W/B............ Water Boiler   (KSC)
WB............. Water Bottle
WB............. Water Box
WB............. Wave-Band   (ADA)
WB............. Waybill [*Business and trade*]
WB............. Weather Bomber [*Air Force*]
WB............. Weather Bureau [*Later, National Weather Service*]   (EA)
WB............. Weatherboard   (ADA)
Wb............. Weber [*Symbol*] [*SI unit of magnetic flux*]
WB............. Wechsler-Bellevue [*Psychological test*]
WB............. Wedge Biopsy [*Medicine*]
WB............. Weekly Boarding
WB............. Weekly Bulletin [*Army*]   (AABC)
W/B............ Weight and Balance
WB............. Weight Bearing
WB............. Weimarer Beitraege [*A publication*]
wb .... West Berlin [*MARC country of publication code*] [*Library of Congress*]   (LCCP)
WB............. Westbound
WB............. Westminster Biographies [*A publication*]
WB............. Wet Bulb [*Thermometer, of a psychrometer*] [*Meteorology*]
WB............. Whale Boat
WB............. Wheelbarrow   (MSA)
WB............. Wheelbase
WB............. Whole Blood
WB............. Whole Body [*Nuclear energy*]   (NRCH)
WB............. Whole Body [*Medicine*]
WB............. Whole Bow [*Music*]   (ROG)
WB............. Wideband [*Radio transmission*]
WB............. Widebeam   (NATG)
WB............. Wiener Blaetter fuer die Freunde der Antike [*A publication*]
WB............. Will Be   (AABC)
WB............. Winchester Word Book [*A publication*]
WB............. Wingback [*Football*]
WB............. Winner's Bitch [*Dog show term*]
W/B............ Wire Bundles   (MCD)
WB............. Wirebar [*Metal industry*]

WB............. Woerterbuch der Aegyptischen Sprache [*A publication*]   (BJA)
WB............. Women's Bureau [*Department of Labor*]
WB............. Wood Base [*Technical drawings*]
WB............. Wood Burning [*Fireplace*] [*Classified advertising*]
WB............. Wool Back [*Knitting*]
WB............. Wool Bureau [*New York, NY*]   (EA)
WB............. Word Before [*Message handling*]
WB............. Work Book
WB............. Workbench   (AAG)
WB............. World Bank
WB............. World Brotherhood
WB............. Worlds Beyond [*A publication*]
WB............. Worldways Canada Ltd. [*Canada*] [*ICAO designator*]   (FAAC)
WB............. Wort und Brauch [*A publication*]
WB............. Write Buffer
W/B............ Writing on Back [*Deltiology*]
WB2............ Warramunga Array [*Australia*] [*Seismograph station code, US Geological Survey*]   (SEIS)
WB3............ Warramunga Array [*Australia*] [*Seismograph station code, US Geological Survey*]   (SEIS)
WB & A...... Washington, Baltimore & Annapolis Railroad [*Nickname: Wobble, Bump, and Amble*]
WBA .... Wax Bean Agglutinin [*Biochemistry*]
WBA .... Weekly Benefit Amount [*Unemployment insurance*]
WBA .... Wideband Amplifier
WBA .... Wire Bundle Assembly   (MCD)
WBA .... Woman's Benefit Association [*Later, NABA*]
WBA .... Works and Building, High Priority [*British*] [*World War II*]
WBA .... World Boxing Association   (EA)
WBA .... Worn by Astronaut [*NASA*]   (KSC)
WBAA........ West Lafayette, IN [*AM radio station call letters*]
WBAB-FM .. Babylon, NY [*FM radio station call letters*]
WBAC .... Cleveland, TN [*AM radio station call letters*]
WBAD........ Leland, MS [*FM radio station call letters*]
WBAF........ Barnesville, GA [*AM radio station call letters*]
WBAG........ Burlington, NC [*AM radio station call letters*]
WBAI.......... New York, NY [*FM radio station call letters*]
WBAI.......... Wesley Bull & Associates, Incorporated [*Seattle, WA*] [*Telecommunications*]   (TSSD)
WBAIS .... Walworth Barbour American International School in Israel   (BJA)
WBAK-TV .. Terre Haute, IN [*Television station call letters*]
WBAL........ Baltimore, MD [*AM radio station call letters*]
WBAL-TV ... Baltimore, MD [*Television station call letters*]
WBAMC ..... William Beaumont Army Medical Center   (AABC)
WBAM-FM ... Montgomery, AL [*FM radio station call letters*]
WBAN........ Weather Bureau, Air Force, Navy [*Manuals*] [*Obsolete*]
WBANA ...... Wild Blueberry Association of North America   (EA)
WBAP........ Fort Worth, TX [*AM radio station call letters*]
WBAQ .... Greenville, MS [*FM radio station call letters*]
WBAR........ Bartow, FL [*AM radio station call letters*]
WBAR........ Wing Bar Lights [*Aviation*]
WBaraC...... Circus World Museum, Baraboo, WI [*Library symbol*] [*Library of Congress*]   (LCLS)
WBaraHi..... Sauk County Historical Society, Baraboo, WI [*Library symbol*] [*Library of Congress*]   (LCLS)
WBAS........ Crescent City, FL [*AM radio station call letters*]
WBAS........ Weather Bureau Airport Station [*Obsolete*]
WBAS........ Woerterbuch der Aegyptischen Sprache [*A publication*]   (BJA)
WBasR .... Randall Consolidated School, Bassett, WI [*Library symbol*] [*Library of Congress*]   (LCLS)
WBAT........ Marion, IN [*AM radio station call letters*]
WBAT........ Wideband Adapter Transformer
WBAU........ Garden City, NY [*FM radio station call letters*]
WBAW........ Barnwell, SC [*AM radio station call letters*]
WBAW-FM ... Barnwell, SC [*FM radio station call letters*]
WBAWS ..... Weather, Briefing, Advisory, and Warning Service   (AABC)
WBAX........ Wilkes-Barre, PA [*AM radio station call letters*]
WBAY-TV... Green Bay, WI [*Television station call letters*]
WBAZ........ Southhold, NY [*FM radio station call letters*]
WBB .... Beloit College, Beloit, WI [*Library symbol*] [*Library of Congress*]   (LCLS)
WBB .... Stebbins [*Alaska*] [*Airport symbol*]   (OAG)
WBB .... Stebbins, AK [*Location identifier*] [*FAA*]   (FAAL)
WBB .... Webb [*Del E.*] Corp. [*NYSE symbol*]
WBBA........ Pittsfield, IL [*AM radio station call letters*]
WBBA........ Western Bird Banding Association   (EA)
WBBA-FM ... Pittsfield, IL [*FM radio station call letters*]
WBBB........ Burlington-Graham, NC [*AM radio station call letters*]
WBBC........ Blackstone, VA [*FM radio station call letters*]
WBBC........ [*The*] Webb Company [*NASDAQ symbol*]   (NQ)
WBBE........ Georgetown, KY [*AM radio station call letters*]
WBBF........ Rochester, NY [*AM radio station call letters*]
WBBG .... Cleveland, OH [*AM radio station call letters*]
WBBH-TV... Fort Myers, FL [*Television station call letters*]
WBBI......... Abingdon, VA [*AM radio station call letters*]
WBBJ-TV... Jackson, TN [*Television station call letters*]
WBBK........ Blakely, GA [*AM radio station call letters*]
WBBK-FM ... Blakely, GA [*FM radio station call letters*]
WBBL......... Richmond, VA [*AM radio station call letters*]
WBBM........ Chicago, IL [*AM radio station call letters*]

WBBM-FM ... Chicago, IL [*FM radio station call letters*]
WBBM-TV ... Chicago, IL [*Television station call letters*]
WBBN........ Taylorsville, MS [*FM radio station call letters*]
WBBO-FM ... Forest City, NC [*FM radio station call letters*]
WBBQ .... Augusta, GA [*AM radio station call letters*]
WBBQ-FM ... Augusta, GA [*FM radio station call letters*]
WBBR........ Travelers Rest, SC [*AM radio station call letters*]
WBBS-TV... West Chicago, IL [*Television station call letters*]
WBBT........ Lyons, GA [*AM radio station call letters*]
WBBW........ Youngstown, OH [*AM radio station call letters*]
WBBX........ Kinston, TN [*AM radio station call letters*]
WBBY-FM ... Westerville, OH [*FM radio station call letters*]
WBBZ........ Ponca City, OK [*AM radio station call letters*]
WBC .... Washington, DC [*Location identifier*] [*FAA*]   (FAAL)
WBC .... Water Binding Capacity [*Also, WHC*] [*Food industry*]
WBC .... Wayland Baptist College [*Texas*]
WBC .... Weather Bureau Central Office [*Obsolete*]
WBC .... Weather Bureau Communications [*Obsolete*]
WBC .... Westbridge Capital Corp. [*American Stock Exchange symbol*]
WBC .... Western Boundary Current [*Marine science*]   (MSC)
WBC .... Westinghouse Broadcasting Company
WBC .... White Blood Cell [*or Corpuscle*] [*Medicine*]
WBC .... White Blood Cell Count [*Medicine*]
WBC .... Wideband Coupler
WBC .... Wien Bridge Circuit [*Physics*]
WBC .... Wilkes-Barre Connecting Railroad [*AAR code*]
WBC .... Wilkes College Library, Wilkes-Barre, PA [*OCLC symbol*]   (OCLC)
WBC .... Wire Bridge Circuit
WBC .... Women's Broadcasting Corporation
WBC .... World Book Congress
WBC .... World Boxing Council [*Mexico City, Mexico*] [*Information service*]   (EISS)
WBC .... World Business Council [*Washington, DC*]   (EA)
WBC .... Wycliffe Bible Commentary [*A publication*]   (BJA)
WBCA .... Welsh Black Cattle Association   (EA)
WBCA .... Women's Basketball Coaches Association   (EA)
WBCA .... Wyandotte Bantam Club of America   (EA)
WBCB........ Levittown-Fairless Hills, PA [*AM radio station call letters*]
WBCCI .... Wally Byam Caravan Club International [*Association of Airstream trailer owners*]
WBCE........ Wickliffe, KY [*AM radio station call letters*]
WBCF........ Florence, AL [*AM radio station call letters*]
WBCG........ Murfreesboro, NC [*FM radio station call letters*]
WBCH .... Hastings, MI [*AM radio station call letters*]
WBCH-FM ... Hastings, MI [*FM radio station call letters*]
WBCI......... Lebanon, IN [*FM radio station call letters*]
WBCK........ Battle Creek, MI [*AM radio station call letters*]
WBCL........ Fort Wayne, IN [*FM radio station call letters*]
WBCM....... Bay City, MI [*AM radio station call letters*]
WBCN........ Boston, MA [*FM radio station call letters*]
WBCO........ Bucyrus, OH [*AM radio station call letters*]
WBCO........ Wallace Barnes Company
WBCO........ Waveguide below Cutoff   (IEEE)
WBCQ........ Bucyrus, OH [*FM radio station call letters*]
WBCR........ Beloit, WI [*FM radio station call letters*]
WBCS........ Milwaukee, WI [*AM radio station call letters*]
WBCS........ Wideband Communications Subsystem
WBCS-FM ... Milwaukee, WI [*FM radio station call letters*]
WBCT........ Whole-Blood Clotting Time [*Hematology*]
WBCT........ Wideband Current Transformer
WBCT-TV... Bridgeport, CT [*Television station call letters*]
WBCU........ Union, SC [*AM radio station call letters*]
WBCV........ Bristol, TN [*AM radio station call letters*]
WBCV........ Wideband Coherent Video   (IEEE)
WBCW........ Jeannette, PA [*AM radio station call letters*]
WBCX........ Gainesville, GA [*FM radio station call letters*]
WBCY........ Charlotte, NC [*FM radio station call letters*]
WBD .... Befandriana [*Madagascar*] [*Airport symbol*]   (OAG)
WBD .... Washboard [*Musical instrument used in some jazz bands*]
WBD .... Wideband Data
WBD .... Wire Bound   (IEEE)
WBD .... Worlds Beyond [*A publication*]
WBDA........ Wideband Data Assembly [*Ground Communications Facility, NASA*]
WBDC .... Huntingburg, IN [*FM radio station call letters*]
WBDDS ...... Weapons Bay Door Drive Subsystem [*Military*]
WBDF........ Wideband Dicke-Fix   (CET)
WBDFX...... Wideband Dicke-Fix   (MSA)
WBDG .... Indianapolis, IN [*FM radio station call letters*]
WBDI .... Wideband Data Interleaver   (MCD)
W & B Dig.. Walter and Bates' Ohio Digest   (DLA)
WBDL........ Wideband Data Line [*or Link*]
WBDNA...... Women Band Directors National Association   (EA)
WBDS........ Wiggins, MS [*Television station call letters*]
WBdSJ .... Saint Joseph's Hospital, Beaver Dam, WI [*Library symbol*] [*Library of Congress*]   (LCLS)
WBDX........ White Bluff, TN [*AM radio station call letters*]
WBDX........ Wideband Data Switch
WBDY........ Bluefield, VA [*AM radio station call letters*]
WBDY-FM ... Bluefield, VA [*FM radio station call letters*]

WBE .... Bealanana [*Madagascar*] [*Airport symbol*]   (OAG)
WBE .... Waterloo County Board of Education, Professional Education Library [*UTLAS symbol*]
WBE .... West Bromwich [*England*] [*Seismograph station code, US Geological Survey*] [*Closed*]   (SEIS)
WBE .... Whole-Body Extract [*Immunology*]
WBE .... Wideband Electronics
WBEA........ Elyria, OH [*FM radio station call letters*]
WBEB........ Athens, KY [*AM radio station call letters*]
WBEC........ Pittsfield, MA [*AM radio station call letters*]
WBEC-FM ... Pittsfield, MA [*FM radio station call letters*]
WBED........ Classic Corp. [*NASDAQ symbol*]   (NQ)
WBEE........ Harvey, IL [*AM radio station call letters*]
WB/EI........ West Britain/East Ireland
WBEJ........ Elizabethton, TN [*AM radio station call letters*]
WBEK........ Cherry Hill, NJ [*FM radio station call letters*]
WBEL........ South Beloit, IL [*AM radio station call letters*]
WBelH........ Holy Family Convent, Benet Lake, WI [*Library symbol*] [*Library of Congress*]   (LCLS)
WBelSB...... Saint Benedict's Abbey, Benet Library, Benet Lake, WI [*Library symbol*] [*Library of Congress*]   (LCLS)
WBEM....... Windber, PA [*AM radio station call letters*]
WBEN....... Buffalo, NY [*AM radio station call letters*]
WBEN-FM ... Buffalo, NY [*FM radio station call letters*]
WBEP........ Wiener Beitraege zur Englischen Philologie [*A publication*]
WBer .... Berlin Public Library, Berlin, WI [*Library symbol*] [*Library of Congress*]   (LCLS)
WBES........ Charleston, WV [*FM radio station call letters*]
WBET........ Brockton, MA [*AM radio station call letters*]
WBEU........ Beaufort, SC [*AM radio station call letters*]
WBEV........ Beaver Dam, WI [*AM radio station call letters*]
WBEX........ Chillicothe, OH [*AM radio station call letters*]
WBEY........ Grasonville, MD [*FM radio station call letters*]
WBEZ........ Chicago, IL [*FM radio station call letters*]
WBF .... Wood Block Floor [*Technical drawings*]
WBF .... Workmen's Benefit Fund of the USA   (EA)
WBF .... World Bridge Federation
WBFA........ Western Bohemian Fraternal Association [*Later, WFLA*]   (EA)
WBFC........ Stanton, KY [*AM radio station call letters*]
WBFD........ Bedford, PA [*AM radio station call letters*]
WBFF........ Baltimore, MD [*Television station call letters*]
WBFG........ Effingham, IL [*FM radio station call letters*]
WBFH........ Bloomfield Hills, MI [*FM radio station call letters*]
WBFJ........ Winston-Salem, NC [*AM radio station call letters*]
WBFL........ Bellows Falls, VT [*FM radio station call letters*]
WBFM........ Seneca, SC [*FM radio station call letters*]
WBFM........ Wideband Frequency Modulation
WBFN........ Quitman, MS [*AM radio station call letters*]
WBFO........ Buffalo, NY [*FM radio station call letters*]
WBFP........ Wood-Burning Fireplace [*Classified advertising*]
WBFS-TV ... Miami, FL [*Television station call letters*]
WBG .... Webbing
WBG .... Wissenschaftliche Buchgesellschaft [*A publication*]
WBGA .... Brunswick, GA [*AM radio station call letters*]
WBGB .... Mount Dora, FL [*AM radio station call letters*]
WBGC .... Chipley, FL [*AM radio station call letters*]
WBGD .... Bricktown, NJ [*FM radio station call letters*]
WBGK .... Milwaukee, WI [*FM radio station call letters*]
WBGL........ Champaign, IL [*FM radio station call letters*]
WBGM....... Tallahassee, FL [*AM radio station call letters*]
WBGM-FM ... Tallahassee, FL [*FM radio station call letters*]
WBGN........ Bowling Green, KY [*AM radio station call letters*]
WBGO........ Newark, NJ [*FM radio station call letters*]
WBGP........ Waterborne Guard Post   (NVT)
WBGR........ Baltimore, MD [*AM radio station call letters*]
WBGT........ Bluffton, IN [*FM radio station call letters*]
WBGT........ Wet Bulb Globe Temperature
WBGT........ Wet Bulb Globe Thermometer
WBGTI........ Wet Bulb Globe Temperature Index   (RDA)
WBGU........ Bowling Green, OH [*FM radio station call letters*]
WBGU-TV ... Bowling Green, OH [*Television station call letters*]
WBGZ........ Alton, IL [*AM radio station call letters*]
WBHB........ Fitzgerald, GA [*AM radio station call letters*]
WBHC........ Hampton, SC [*AM radio station call letters*]
WBHC-FM ... Hampton, SC [*FM radio station call letters*]
WBHF........ Cartersville, GA [*AM radio station call letters*]
WBHI.......... Chicago, IL [*FM radio station call letters*]
WBHM....... Birmingham, AL [*FM radio station call letters*]
WBHN....... Bryson City, NC [*AM radio station call letters*]
WBHO .... Weather Bureau Hurricane Forecast Office [*Obsolete*]
WBHP........ Huntsville, AL [*AM radio station call letters*]
WBHR........ Bellaire, OH [*FM radio station call letters*]
WBHS........ Brunswick, ME [*FM radio station call letters*]
WBHT........ Brownsville, TN [*AM radio station call letters*]
WBI........... Ward Behavior Inventory [*Psychology*]
WBI........... Washington Beverage Insight [*Wells & Associates*] [*Washington, DC*] [*Information service*]   (EISS)
WBI........... Westburne International Industries Ltd. [*American Stock Exchange symbol*] [*Toronto Stock Exchange symbol*]
WBI........... Whiskey Butte [*Idaho*] [*Seismograph station code, US Geological Survey*] [*Closed*]   (SEIS)

WBI............	Will Be Issued
WBI............	Wooden Box Institute [*Defunct*] (EA)
WBIB	Centreville, AL [*AM radio station call letters*]
WBIF	Wideband Intermediate Frequency (MCD)
WBII...........	Washington Business Information, Incorporated [*Arlington, VA*] [*Information service*] (EISS)
WBII...........	Watertown, WI [*FM radio station call letters*]
WBII...........	Whirley Ball International [*NASDAQ symbol*] (NQ)
WBIL..........	Tuskegee, AL [*AM radio station call letters*]
WBIL-FM.....	Tuskegee, AL [*FM radio station call letters*]
WBIM-FM...	Bridgewater, MA [*FM radio station call letters*]
WBIN	Benton, TN [*AM radio station call letters*]
WBIP	Booneville, MS [*AM radio station call letters*]
WBIP-FM...	Booneville, MS [*FM radio station call letters*]
WBIQ.........	Birmingham, AL [*Television station call letters*]
WBIR-TV....	Knoxville, TN [*Television station call letters*]
WBIS	Bristol, CT [*AM radio station call letters*]
WBIT	Adel, GA [*AM radio station call letters*]
WBIU	Denham Springs, LA [*AM radio station call letters*]
WBIW	Bedford, IN [*AM radio station call letters*]
WBIX	Jacksonville Beach, FL [*AM radio station call letters*]
WBIZ	Eau Claire, WI [*FM radio station call letters*]
WBJA	Guayama, PR [*AM radio station call letters*]
WBJB-FM...	Lincroft, NJ [*FM radio station call letters*]
WBJC.........	Baltimore, MD [*FM radio station call letters*]
WBJW	Orlando, FL [*AM radio station call letters*]
WBJW-FM ...	Orlando, FL [*FM radio station call letters*]
WBJZ.........	Olean, NY [*FM radio station call letters*]
WBK	Webb & Knapp (Canada) Ltd. [*Vancouver Stock Exchange symbol*]
WBKB-TV...	Alpena, MI [*Television station call letters*]
WBKC	Painesville, OH [*AM radio station call letters*]
WBKE-FM ...	North Manchester, IN [*FM radio station call letters*]
WBKH.........	Hattiesburg, MS [*AM radio station call letters*]
WBKJ	Kosciusko, MS [*FM radio station call letters*]
WBKL.........	Wiener Beitraege zur Kulturgeschichte und Linguistik [*A publication*]
WBKN	Brookhaven, MS [*FM radio station call letters*]
WBKO	Bowling Green, KY [*Television station call letters*]
WBKR........	Owensboro, KY [*FM radio station call letters*]
WBKT........	Brockport, NY [*FM radio station call letters*]
WBKV........	West Bend, WI [*AM radio station call letters*]
WBKV-FM ...	West Bend, WI [*FM radio station call letters*]
WBKW........	Beckley, WV [*FM radio station call letters*]
WBKY........	Lexington, KY [*FM radio station call letters*]
WBKZ........	Jefferson, GA [*AM radio station call letters*]
WBL	Western Biological Laboratories
WBL............	White Bluff [*Washington*] [*Seismograph station code, US Geological Survey*] (SEIS)
WBL............	Wideband LASER
WBL............	Wideband Limiting (IEEE)
W BI............	[*Sir*] William Blackstone's English King's Bench Reports [*96 English Reprint*] [*1746-80*] (DLA)
WBL............	Women's Basketball League [*Defunct*] (EA)
WBL............	Wood Blocking
WBLA	Elizabethtown, NC [*AM radio station call letters*]
W Bla	[*Sir*] William Blackstone's English King's Bench Reports [*96 English Reprint*] (DLA)
WBLB	Pulaski, VA [*AM radio station call letters*]
WBLC........	Lenoir City, TN [*AM radio station call letters*]
WBLC........	Water-Borne Logistics Craft
WBLD.........	Orchard Lake, MI [*FM radio station call letters*]
WBLE	Batesville, MS [*FM radio station call letters*]
W BI (Eng) ...	[*Sir*] William Blackstone's English King's Bench Reports [*96 English Reprint*] (DLA)
WBLF	Bellefonte, PA [*AM radio station call letters*]
Wbl voor Fiscaal Recht ...	Weekblad voor Fiscaal Recht [*A publication*]
WBLG........	Smiths Grove, KY [*FM radio station call letters*]
WBLI	Patchogue, NY [*FM radio station call letters*]
WBLJ.........	Dalton, GA [*AM radio station call letters*]
WBLK-FM ...	Depew, NY [*FM radio station call letters*]
WBLM.........	Lewiston, ME [*FM radio station call letters*]
WBLO.........	Weak Black Liquor Oxidation [*Papermaking*]
WBLQ........	Erie, PA [*AM radio station call letters*]
WBLR........	Batesburg, SC [*AM radio station call letters*]
WBLS	New York, NY [*FM radio station call letters*]
WBLT	Bedford, VA [*AM radio station call letters*]
WBLU.........	Hinesville, GA [*FM radio station call letters*]
WBLV.........	Twin Lake, MI [*FM radio station call letters*]
WBLW.........	Royston, GA [*FM radio station call letters*]
WBLX.........	Mobile, AL [*FM radio station call letters*]
WBLY.........	Springfield, OH [*AM radio station call letters*]
WBLZ.........	Hamilton, OH [*FM radio station call letters*]
WBM..........	Beloit Memorial Hospital, Beloit, WI [*Library symbol*] [*Library of Congress*] (LCLS)
WBM..........	Wapenamanda [*Papua New Guinea*] [*Airport symbol*] (OAG)
WB M.........	Weber Meter
WBM..........	Woerterbuch der Mythologie [*A publication*] (BJA)
WBM..........	Women's Board of Missions
WBMA	Western Building Material Association [*Olympia, WA*] (EA)

WBMA	Whirlpool Bath Manufacturers Association [*Glen Ellyn, IL*] (EA)
WBMA	Wirebound Box Manufacturers Association [*Wheeling, IL*] (EA)
WBMB	West Branch, MI [*AM radio station call letters*]
WBMC........	McMinnville, TN [*AM radio station call letters*]
WBMC........	Weight before Mars Capture [*NASA*]
WBMCR	Wideband Multichannel Receiver
WBMD........	Baltimore, MD [*AM radio station call letters*]
WBME	Belfast, ME [*AM radio station call letters*]
WBMG........	Walter Bernard and Milton Glaser [*Founders of the magazine-design firm that bears their initials*]
WBMG-TV ...	Birmingham, AL [*Television station call letters*]
WBMI	West Branch, MI [*FM radio station call letters*]
WBMI	Women's Board of Missions of the Interior
WBMK	Knoxville, TN [*AM radio station call letters*]
WBML	Macon, GA [*AM radio station call letters*]
WBMO........	Weather Bureau Meteorological Observation Station [*Obsolete*]
WBMQ........	Savannah, GA [*AM radio station call letters*]
WBMR........	Telford, PA [*FM radio station call letters*]
WBMS	Wilmington, NC [*AM radio station call letters*]
WBMS	World Bureau of Metal Statistics (EA-IO)
WBMT	Boxford, MA [*FM radio station call letters*]
WBMU-FM ...	Asheville, NC [*FM radio station call letters*]
WBMW........	Manassas, VA [*FM radio station call letters*]
WBMX	Oak Park, IL [*AM radio station call letters*]
WBMX-FM ...	Oak Park, IL [*FM radio station call letters*]
WbMyth	Woerterbuch der Mythologie [*A publication*] (BJA)
WBN	Well Behaved Net
WBN	West by North
W Bn	White Beacon
WBN	Wolfenbuetteler Barock-Nachrichten [*A publication*]
WBNA	Louisville, KY [*Television station call letters*]
WBNC	Conway, NH [*AM radio station call letters*]
WBND	Biloxi, MS [*AM radio station call letters*]
WBND	Westbound (FAAC)
W BNDR	With Binder [*Freight*]
WBNE	Benton, PA [*FM radio station call letters*]
WBNG-TV ...	Binghamton, NY [*Television station call letters*]
WBNI	Fort Wayne, IN [*FM radio station call letters*]
WBNJ	Cape May Court House, NJ [*FM radio station call letters*]
WBNL	Boonville, IN [*AM radio station call letters*]
WBNL	Wideband Noise Limiting
WBNL-FM ...	Boonville, IN [*FM radio station call letters*]
WBNO-FM ...	Bryan, OH [*FM radio station call letters*]
WBNP........	Watts Bar Nuclear Plant (NRCH)
WBNP........	Wood Buffalo National Park. Newsletter [*A publication*]
WBNQ........	Bloomington, IL [*FM radio station call letters*]
WBNR........	Beacon, NY [*AM radio station call letters*]
WBNS........	Columbus, OH [*AM radio station call letters*]
WBNS........	Water Boiler Neutron Source [*Reactor*]
WBNS-FM ...	Columbus, OH [*FM radio station call letters*]
WBNS-TV...	Columbus, OH [*Television station call letters*]
WBNT........	Oneida, TN [*AM radio station call letters*]
WBNT-FM ...	Oneida, TN [*FM radio station call letters*]
WBNV........	Wideband Noise Voltage
WB/NWRC ...	Weather Bureau/National Weather Records Center [*Obsolete*] (KSC)
WBNX-TV...	Akron, OH [*Television station call letters*]
WBNY........	Buffalo, NY [*FM radio station call letters*]
WBNZ........	Frankfort, MI [*FM radio station call letters*]
WBO	Beroroha [*Madagascar*] [*Airport symbol*] (OAG)
WBO	Weather Bureau Office [*Later, National Weather Service*]
WBO	Wideband Oscilloscope
WBO	Wideband Overlap
WBO	Wien Bridge Oscillator [*Physics*]
W/BO	With Blowout (MSA)
WBOB	Galax, VA [*AM radio station call letters*]
WBOC-TV ...	Salisbury, MD [*Television station call letters*]
WBOD	Canton, IL [*AM radio station call letters*]
WBOD	Waste Biochemical Oxygen Demand [*Oceanography*]
WBOK	New Orleans, LA [*AM radio station call letters*]
WBOL	Bolivar, TN [*AM radio station call letters*]
WBOP........	Pensacola, FL [*AM radio station call letters*]
WBOR........	Brunswick, ME [*FM radio station call letters*]
W/BOR	White Border [*Deltiology*]
WBOS........	Brookline, MA [*FM radio station call letters*]
WBOW........	Terre Haute, IN [*AM radio station call letters*]
WBOX........	Bogalusa, LA [*AM radio station call letters*]
WBOX-FM ...	Varnado, LA [*FM radio station call letters*]
WBOY-TV ..	Clarksburg, WV [*Television station call letters*]
WBOZ........	Sabana Grande, PR [*AM radio station call letters*]
WBP	Wartime Basic Plan
WBP	Water Bank Program [*Department of Agriculture*]
WBP	Water Binding Potential [*of protein*]
WBP	Weather- and Boil-Proof (IEEE)
WBP	Woodwind World - Brass and Percussion [*A publication*]
WBPA.........	Elkhorn City, KY [*AM radio station call letters*]
WBPK	Flemingsburg, KY [*FM radio station call letters*]
WBPM........	Kingston, NY [*FM radio station call letters*]

WBPTT...... Whole Blood Partial Thromboplastin Time [*Hematology*]
WBPV........ Charlton, MA [*FM radio station call letters*]
WBPZ........ Lock Haven, PA [*AM radio station call letters*]
WBQ.......... Beaver [*Alaska*] [*Airport symbol*]   (OAG)
WBQ.......... Beaver, AK [*Location identifier*] [*FAA*]   (FAAL)
WBQM........ Decatur, AL [*FM radio station call letters*]
WBQN........ Barceloneta, PR [*AM radio station call letters*]
WBR .... Water Boiler Reactor
WBR .... Westbank Resources, Inc. [*Vancouver Stock Exchange
                   symbol*]
WBR .... Whole Body Radiation
WBR .... Wideband Data Recorder
WBR .... Wideband Receiver
WBR .... Word Buffer Register   (MSA)
WBR .... Workbench Rack   (MCD)
WBRA-TV... Roanoke, VA [*Television station call letters*]
WBRB........ Mount Clemens, MI [*AM radio station call letters*]
WBRBN ...... Will Be Reported by NOTAM [*Notice to Airmen*]   (FAAC)
WBRC........ Walter Bagehot Research Council on National
                   Sovereignty   (EA)
WBRC-TV... Birmingham, AL [*Television station call letters*]
WBRD........ Bradenton, FL [*AM radio station call letters*]
WBRD........ Wallboard
WBrE.......... Elmbrook Memorial Hospital, Brookfield, WI [*Library symbol*]
                   [*Library of Congress*]   (LCLS)
WBRE-TV ... Wilkes-Barre, PA [*Television station call letters*]
WBRF........ Galax, VA [*FM radio station call letters*]
WBRG........ Lynchburg, VA [*AM radio station call letters*]
W/BRG....... Wheel Bearing [*Automotive engineering*]
WBRH........ Baton Rouge, LA [*FM radio station call letters*]
WBRH........ Weather Bureau Regional Headquarters [*Obsolete*]   (FAAC)
WBRI.......... Indianapolis, IN [*AM radio station call letters*]
WBrI .... International Foundation of Employee Benefit Plans,
                   Information Center, Brookfield, WI [*Library symbol*]
                   [*Library of Congress*]   (LCLS)
WBRJ .... Marietta, OH [*AM radio station call letters*]
WBRK........ Pittsfield, MA [*AM radio station call letters*]
WBRL........ Berlin, NH [*AM radio station call letters*]
WBRM........ Marion, NC [*AM radio station call letters*]
WBRN........ Big Rapids, MI [*AM radio station call letters*]
WBRN-FM ... Big Rapids, MI [*FM radio station call letters*]
WBro .... Brodhead Memorial Public Library, Brodhead, WI [*Library
                   symbol*] [*Library of Congress*]   (LCLS)
WBRO........ Waynesboro, GA [*AM radio station call letters*]
WBRO........ Weather Bureau Regional Office [*Obsolete*]
W BRO....... Worshipful Brother [*Freemasonry*]
WBRQ........ Cidra, PR [*FM radio station call letters*]
WBRR........ Bradford, PA [*FM radio station call letters*]
WBRR........ Weather Bureau RADAR Remote [*Meteorology*]
WBRS........ Waltham, MA [*FM radio station call letters*]
WBRS........ Wideband Remote Switch   (IEEE)
WBRS........ Wrought Brass   (MSA)
WBRT........ Bardstown, KY [*AM radio station call letters*]
WBRT........ Weather Bureau Radiotheolite [*Meteorology*]
WBRT........ Whole-Blood Recalcification Time [*Hematology*]
WBRU........ Providence, RI [*FM radio station call letters*]
WBRV........ Boonville, NY [*AM radio station call letters*]
WBRW........ Somerville, NJ [*AM radio station call letters*]
WBRX........ Berwick, PA [*AM radio station call letters*]
WBRY........ Woodbury, TN [*AM radio station call letters*]
WBRZ........ Baton Rouge, LA [*Television station call letters*]
WBS .... Wage Board Staff
WB-S......... Wage Board, Supervisor [*Civil Service classification*]
WBS .... Wallace Barnes Steel [*Wallace Barnes Co.*]
WBS .... Washington Bibliographic Service [*Silver Spring, MD*]
                   [*Information service*]   (EISS)
WBS .... Waterloo County Board of Education [*UTLAS symbol*]
WBS .... Weight and Balance System   (MCD)
WBS .... West by South
WBS .... Western Base Section [*England*] [*World War II*]
WBS .... Western Conservative Baptist Theological Seminary, Portland,
                   OR [*OCLC symbol*]   (OCLC)
WBS .... Whole Body Shower
WBS .... Wideband System [*Ground Communications Facility, NASA*]
WBS .... Without Benefit of Salvage
WBS .... Work Breakdown Sheets [*Army*]
WBS .... Work Breakdown Structure [*Army*]
WBS .... Work Breakdown Structure [*Data processing*]
WBSA........ Boaz, AL [*AM radio station call letters*]
WBSA........ Weather Bureau Synoptic and Aviation Reporting Station
                   [*Obsolete*]
WBSA........ Westlands Diversified Bancorp [*NASDAQ symbol*]   (NQ)
WBSB........ Baltimore, MD [*FM radio station call letters*]
WBSC........ Bennettsville, SC [*AM radio station call letters*]
WBSC........ Wideband Signal Conditioner   (NASA)
WBSC........ Work Breakdown Structure Code   (MCD)
WBSCB .... Work Breakdown Structure Control Board [*Army*]   (AABC)
WBSD........ Burlington, WI [*FM radio station call letters*]
WBSF........ Biddeford, ME [*FM radio station call letters*]
WBSH........ Heflin, AL [*AM radio station call letters*]
WBSI .... Western Behavioral Sciences Institute [*La Jolla, CA*]

WBSIGSTA ... Weather Bureau Signal Station [*Obsolete*]
WBSJ .... Ellisville, MS [*FM radio station call letters*]
WBSL .... Sheffield, MA [*FM radio station call letters*]
WBSL .... Wide Beam Special LASER   (MCD)
WBSM .... New Bedford, MA [*AM radio station call letters*]
WBSN-FM ... New Orleans, LA [*FM radio station call letters*]
WBSO .... Clinton, MA [*AM radio station call letters*]
WBSP........ Western Beet Sugar Producers [*Defunct*]
WBSR........ Pensacola, FL [*AM radio station call letters*]
WBST........ Muncie, IN [*FM radio station call letters*]
WBSU........ Brockport, NY [*FM radio station call letters*]
WBSW....... Kankakee, IL [*FM radio station call letters*]
WBT .... Charlotte, NC [*AM radio station call letters*]
WBT .... Wet Bulb Temperature
WBT .... Wichita Board of Trade [*Defunct*]   (EA)
WBT .... Wide-Band Terminal   (MCD)
WBT .... Wideband Transformer [*or Transmitter*]
WBT .... Women in Broadcast Technology [*Berkeley, CA*]   (EA)
WBT .... Wycliffe Bible Translators   (EA)
WBTA........ Batavia, NY [*AM radio station call letters*]
WBTA........ Wisconsin Board of Tax Appeals Decisions   (DLA)
WBTA-CCH Tax Reporter ... Wisconsin Board of Tax Appeals Decisions
                   (Commerce Clearing House)   (DLA)
WBTB........ Beaufort, NC [*AM radio station call letters*]
WBTC........ Uhrichsville, OH [*AM radio station call letters*]
WBTC........ Waterways Bulk Transportation Council   (EA)
WBTD-FM ... Muscle Shoals, AL [*FM radio station call letters*]
WBTE........ Weapon Battery Terminal Equipment [*Air Force*]
WBTE........ Windsor, NC [*AM radio station call letters*]
WBTF........ Attica, NY [*FM radio station call letters*]
WBTG........ Sheffield, AL [*FM radio station call letters*]
WBTH........ Williamson, WV [*AM radio station call letters*]
WBTM........ Danville, VA [*AM radio station call letters*]
WBTM HYDRO ... Weather Bureau Technical Memorandum: Hydrology
                   [*Office of Hydrology*] [*Washington, DC*] [*A publication*]
WBTN........ Bennington, VT [*AM radio station call letters*]
WBTO........ Linton, IN [*AM radio station call letters*]
WBTQ........ Buckhannon, WV [*FM radio station call letters*]
WBTR-FM ... Carrollton, GA [*FM radio station call letters*]
WBTS........ Bridgeport, AL [*AM radio station call letters*]
WBTS........ Waco, Beaumont, Trinity & Sabine Railway Co. [*AAR code*]
WBTS........ Whereabouts   (FAAC)
WBTS........ Wideband Transmission System   (KSC)
WBTU........ Kendallville, IN [*FM radio station call letters*]
WBTV........ Charlotte, NC [*Television station call letters*]
WBTV........ Weather Briefing Television   (AFM)
WBTW....... Florence, SC [*Television station call letters*]
WBTX........ Broadway-Timberville, VA [*AM radio station call letters*]
WBTY........ Homerville, GA [*FM radio station call letters*]
WBU .... Boulder [*Colorado*] [*Airport symbol*]   (OAG)
WBU .... Wilberforce University, Wilberforce, OH [*OCLC
                   symbol*]   (OCLC)
WBU .... World Blind Union   (EA)
WBUC .... Buckhannon, WV [*AM radio station call letters*]
WBUC .... Western Boundary Undercurrent [*Atlantic Ocean*]
WBUD........ Trenton, NJ [*AM radio station call letters*]
WBUF........ Buffalo, NY [*FM radio station call letters*]
WBUL........ Fort Knox, KY [*AM radio station call letters*]
WBUQ........ Bloomsburg, PA [*FM radio station call letters*]
WBUR........ Boston, MA [*FM radio station call letters*]
WBur .... Burlington Public Library, Burlington, WI [*Library symbol*]
                   [*Library of Congress*]   (LCLS)
WBurSFC... Saint Francis College, Burlington, WI [*Library symbol*] [*Library
                   of Congress*] [*Obsolete*]   (LCLS)
WBUS........ Newnan, GA [*FM radio station call letters*]
WBUT........ Butler, PA [*AM radio station call letters*]
WBUX........ Doylestown, PA [*AM radio station call letters*]
WBUZ........ Fredonia, NY [*AM radio station call letters*]
WBV .... Wideband Voltage
WBVCO...... Wideband Voltage-Controlled Oscillator
WBVCXO ... Wideband Voltage-Controlled Crystal Oscillator
WBVE........ Hamilton, OH [*FM radio station call letters*]
WBVM........ Tampa, FL [*FM radio station call letters*]
WBVP........ Beaver Falls, PA [*AM radio station call letters*]
WBVR........ Russellville, KY [*FM radio station call letters*]
WBVS........ Prestonsburg, KY [*FM radio station call letters*]
WBVTR...... Wideband Video Tape Recorder
WBW .... Wilkes-Barre, PA [*Location identifier*] [*FAA*]   (FAAL)
WBW .... Wilson Butte [*Washington*] [*Seismograph station code, US
                   Geological Survey*]   (SEIS)
WBWA........ Washburn, WI [*AM radio station call letters*]
WBWB....... Bloomington, IN [*FM radio station call letters*]
WBWC....... Berea, OH [*FM radio station call letters*]
WBWT....... Wright Brothers Memorial Wind Tunnel [*Massachusetts
                   Institute of Technology*] [*Research center*]   (RCD)
WBX .... Wooden Box   (MSA)
WBXB........ Edenton, NC [*FM radio station call letters*]
WBXL........ Baldwinsville, NY [*FM radio station call letters*]
WBXQ........ Cresson, PA [*FM radio station call letters*]
WBY .... Wimberly Resources [*Vancouver Stock Exchange symbol*]
WBYE........ Calera, AL [*AM radio station call letters*]

WBYG........	Sandwich, IL [*AM radio station call letters*]
WBYO........	Boyertown, PA [*FM radio station call letters*]
WBYQ........	Baltimore, MD [*FM radio station call letters*]
WBYR........	Wethersfield Township, NY [*FM radio station call letters*]
WBYS........	Canton, IL [*AM radio station call letters*]
WBYS-FM ...	Canton, IL [*FM radio station call letters*]
WBYU........	New Orleans, LA [*FM radio station call letters*]
WBYZ........	Baxley, GA [*FM radio station call letters*]
WBZ........	Boston, MA [*AM radio station call letters*]
WBZ........	Works and Building, Low Priority [*British*] [*World War II*]
WBZA........	Glens Falls, NY [*AM radio station call letters*]
WBZB........	Selma, NC [*AM radio station call letters*]
WBZE........	Indian Head, MD [*AM radio station call letters*]
WBZI-FM....	Xenia, OH [*FM radio station call letters*]
WBZK........	York, SC [*AM radio station call letters*]
WBZN........	Wake Forest, NC [*AM radio station call letters*]
WBZQ........	Greenville, NC [*AM radio station call letters*]
WBZT........	Waynesboro, PA [*AM radio station call letters*]
WBZ-TV	Boston, MA [*Television station call letters*]
WBZW........	Powell, TN [*AM radio station call letters*]
WBZY........	New Castle, PA [*FM radio station call letters*]
WBZZ........	Pittsburgh, PA [*AM radio station call letters*]
WC	Cudahy Public Library, Cudahy, WI [*Library symbol*] [*Library of Congress*] (LCLS)
WC	Wage Change
WC	Wages Council [*British*]
W/C	Waiver of Coinsurance
WC	Walkways Center (EA)
WC	Walnut Council (EA)
WC	War Cabinet [*World War II*]
WC	War College
WC	War Communications
WC	Ward Clerk [*Medicine*]
WC	Watch Commanders
WC	Water Closet [*A toilet*]
WC	Water Cock (ROG)
WC	Water Content
WC	Water-Cooled (DEN)
W/C	Watts per Candle [*Electricity*]
W/C	Wave Change
WC	We Care [*An association*] [*Atmore, AL*] (EA)
WC	Weapon Carrier
WC	Weapons Command [*Later, Armaments Command*] [*Army*]
WC	Weapons Control (NVT)
W/C	Weapons Controller
WC	Weather Condition (NRCH)
W/C	Week Commencing (ADA)
WC	Weiman Company, Inc. [*American Stock Exchange symbol*]
WC	Wesleyan Chapel (ROG)
WC	West Central [*Refers especially to London postal district*]
WC	West Coast Airlines, Inc.
WC	Westbeth Corporation [*An association*] (EA)
WC	Western Cedar [*Utility pole*] [*Telecommunications*] (TEL)
WC	Western Central
WC	Western Classification
WC	Western Command
WC	Westminster Commentaries [*Oxford*] [*A publication*] (BJA)
WC	Whale Center (EA)
WC	Wheel Center (MSA)
WC	Wheelchair
WC	White Cell [*Medicine*]
W/C	White Collar [*Worker*]
WC	White Confederacy (EA)
WC	White Count [*Hematology*]
WC	Whooping Cough [*Medicine*]
WC	Width Codes (AAG)
WC	Wien Air Alaska [*ICAO designator*] (FAAC)
WC	Will Call
WC	Wills Club (EA)
WC	Willys Club [*Bowmanstown, PA*] (EA)
WC	Wilshire Club (EA)
W & C	Wilson and Courtenay's Scotch Appeal Cases (DLA)
WC	Wing Commander [*British*]
WC	Wings Club [*New York, NY*] (EA)
W & C	Wire and Cable (NASA)
WC	Wire Chief [*Test clerk*] [*Telecommunications*] (TEL)
WC	Wisconsin Central Railroad
WC	With Corrections [*Publishing*]
WC	Without Charge
WC	Woden's Coven [*An association*] (EA-IO)
WC	Women in Communications (EA)
WC	Women's Reserve, Communications Duties [*USNR officer designation*]
WC	Wood Casing
WC	Word Count [*Data processing*]
WC	Wordsworth Circle [*A publication*]
WC	Work Card (AAG)
WC	Work Center (AFM)
WC	Work Circle (AAG)
WC	Work Control (AAG)
WC	Working Capital

WC	Working Circle [*Technical drawings*]
WC	Workmen's Circle [*An association*] (EA)
WC	Workmen's Compensation
WC	World Concern [*An association*] [*Seattle, WA*] (EA)
WC	World Coordinate
WC	World's Classics [*A publication*]
WC	Write and Compute
WC	Wspolczesnosc [*A publication*]
3WC...........	Third Wave Civilization [*Title of record album by Ian Lloyd*]
WCA...........	Weapon Control Area [*Military*] (CAAL)
WCA...........	Weimaraner Club of America (EA)
WCA...........	West Coast of Africa (ROG)
WCA...........	West Coast Airlines, Inc.
WCA...........	Westair Commuter Airlines [*Santa Rosa, CA*] [*FAA designator*] (FAAC)
WCA...........	Western College Association (EA)
WCA...........	Who Cares, Anyway?
WCA...........	Whole Core Accident [*Nuclear energy*] (NRCH)
WCA...........	Wideband Cassegrain Antenna
WCA...........	Willys Club of America [*Later, WC*] (EA)
WCA...........	Windmill Class Association (EA)
WCA...........	Wine Conference of America [*Washington, DC*] (EA)
WCA...........	Winston S. Churchill Association (EA)
WCA...........	Wisco of Canada Ltd. [*Vancouver Stock Exchange symbol*]
WCA...........	Women's Caucus for Art (EA)
WCA...........	Women's Christian Association
WCA...........	Workmen's Compensation Act
WCA...........	World Campus Afloat [*Cruise ship educational program*] (EA)
WCA...........	World Citizens Assembly (EA)
WCA...........	World Communication Association [*Formerly, CAP*] (EA)
WCA...........	Worst Case Analysis
WCAB	Rutherfordton, NC [*AM radio station call letters*]
WCAB	Working Committee of the Aeronautical Board
WCAC	Sebring, FL [*FM radio station call letters*]
WCAD	San Juan, PR [*FM radio station call letters*]
WCAE........	Gary, IN [*Television station call letters*]
WCAFS	Wideband Cassegrain Antenna Feed System
WCAI.........	Water Conditioning Association International [*Later, Water Quality Association*] (EA)
WCAJ........	Birmingham, AL [*Television station call letters*]
WCAL........	Northfield, MN [*AM radio station call letters*]
WCAL-FM ...	Northfield, MN [*FM radio station call letters*]
WCAM.......	Camden, SC [*AM radio station call letters*]
WCAM.......	Wisconsin Center for Applied Microelectronics [*University of Wisconsin - Madison*] [*Research center*] (RCD)
WCAN	Worldwide Crisis Alerting Network (MCD)
W Can J Ant ...	West Canadian Journal of Anthropology [*A publication*]
WCAO	Baltimore, MD [*AM radio station call letters*]
WCAP.......	Lowell, MA [*AM radio station call letters*]
WCAP.......	Westinghouse Commercial Atomic Power
WCAP.......	World Climate Applications Program [*WMO*] [*ICSU*]
WCAR	Livonia, MI [*AM radio station call letters*]
WCAR	West Coast Formula Atlantic (Racing)
WCAS	Western Casualty & Surety [*NASDAQ symbol*] (NQ)
WCASS	World Conference of Ashkenazi and Sephardi Synagogues
WCAT........	Orange-Athol, MA [*AM radio station call letters*]
WCAT........	Weiss Comprehensive Articulation Test [*Education*]
WCAT........	Wicat Systems, Inc. [*NASDAQ symbol*] (NQ)
WCAU	Philadelphia, PA [*AM radio station call letters*]
WCAU-FM ...	Philadelphia, PA [*FM radio station call letters*]
WCAU-TV ...	Philadelphia, PA [*Television station call letters*]
WCAV	Brockton, MA [*FM radio station call letters*]
WCAW.......	Charleston, WV [*AM radio station call letters*]
WCAX-TV ...	Burlington, VT [*Television station call letters*]
WCAY-TV ...	Nashville, TN [*Television station call letters*]
WCAZ........	Carthage, IL [*AM radio station call letters*]
WCAZ-FM ...	Carthage, IL [*FM radio station call letters*]
WCB...........	War Communications Board [*World War II*]
WCB...........	Warramunga Array [*Australia*] [*Seismograph station code, US Geological Survey*] (SEIS)
WCB...........	Water Control Board
WCB...........	Way Control Block
WCB...........	Weekly Criminal Bulletin [*Canada Law Book*] [*Database*]
WCB...........	Wellington County Board of Education [*UTLAS symbol*]
WCB...........	Will Call Back
WCB...........	William C. Brown Publishers
WCB...........	Workmen's Compensation Board
WCBA	Corning, NY [*AM radio station call letters*]
WCBB.......	Augusta, ME [*Television station call letters*]
WCBC	Cumberland, MD [*AM radio station call letters*]
WCBC	World Candlepin Bowling Council
WCBD-TV ...	Charleston, SC [*Television station call letters*]
WCBD (VIC) ...	Workers Compensation Board Decisions (Victoria) [*A publication*]
WCBD (WA) ...	Workers Compensation Board Decisions (Western Australia) [*A publication*]
WCBE........	Columbus, OH [*FM radio station call letters*]
WCBF........	Seffner, FL [*AM radio station call letters*]
WCBG	Chambersburg, PA [*AM radio station call letters*]
WCBI........	Columbus, MS [*AM radio station call letters*]
WCBI-TV	Columbus, MS [*Television station call letters*]

WCBK-FM ... Martinsville, IN [*FM radio station call letters*]
WCBL........ Benton, KY [*AM radio station call letters*]
WCBL........ World Council of Blind Lions [*Later, ACBL*] [*Washington, DC*] (EA)
WCBL-FM ... Benton, KY [*FM radio station call letters*]
WCBM....... Baltimore, MD [*AM radio station call letters*]
WCBN-FM ... Ann Arbor, MI [*FM radio station call letters*]
WCBQ........ Oxford, NC [*AM radio station call letters*]
WCBR........ Richmond, KY [*AM radio station call letters*]
WCBS........ New York, NY [*AM radio station call letters*]
WCBS-FM ... New York, NY [*FM radio station call letters*]
WCBS-TV .. New York, NY [*Television station call letters*]
WCBSU...... West Coast Base Service Unit [*Navy*]
WCBT........ Roanoke Rapids, NC [*AM radio station call letters*]
WCBU........ Peoria, IL [*FM radio station call letters*]
WCB (VIC) ... Workers Compensation Board Decisions (Victoria) [*A publication*]
WCBW........ Columbia, IL [*FM radio station call letters*]
WCBX........ Eden, NC [*AM radio station call letters*]
WCBY........ Cheboygan, MI [*AM radio station call letters*]
WCBZ........ Bowling Green, KY [*FM radio station call letters*]
WCC.......... Gerard P. Weeg Computing Center [*University of Iowa*] [*Research center*] (RCD)
WCC.......... Wallace Communications Consultants [*Tampa, FL*] [*Telecommunications*] (TSSD)
WCC.......... War Claims Commission [*Abolished, 1954*]
WCC.......... War Cover Club (EA)
WCC.......... Washington's United States Circuit Court Reports (DLA)
WCC.......... Waste Collection Containers
WCC.......... Water-Cooled Copper
WCC.......... Waters Computing Center [*Rose-Hulman Institute of Technology*] [*Research center*] (RCD)
WCC.......... Watson Collectors Club (EA)
WCC.......... Weapon Control Computer (MCD)
WCC.......... Weapon Control Console [*Military*] (CAAL)
WCC.......... Weapons Control Concept (MCD)
WCC.......... Westchester Community College [*New York*]
WCC.......... Westchester Community College, Technical Services, Valhalla, NY [*OCLC symbol*] (OCLC)
WCC.......... Western Canada Concept [*Political Party*] (PPW)
WCC.......... Western Canada Concept Party
WCC.......... Western Carolina College [*Later, WCU*] [*North Carolina*]
WCC.......... Westminster Choir College [*New Jersey*]
WCC.......... Whim Creek Consolidated [*Toronto Stock Exchange symbol*]
WCC.......... Widows Consultation Center [*Defunct*] (EA)
WCC.......... Wildfire Coordinating Committee [*Washington, DC*] (EA)
WCC.......... Wilson Cloud Chamber [*Physics*]
WCC.......... Women of the Church Coalition (EA)
WCC.......... Women's Classical Caucus (EA)
WCC.......... Women's College Coalition (EA)
WCC.......... Women's Consultative Committee [*Ministry of Labour*] [*British*] [*World War II*]
WCC.......... Work Center Code
WCC.......... Work Control Center (AAG)
WCC.......... Workers' Compensation Cases [*A publication*]
WCC.......... Workmen's Circle Call [*A publication*]
WCC.......... Workmen's Compensation Cases [*Legal*] [*British*]
WCC.......... World Cheerleader Council (EA)
WCC.......... World for Christ Crusade (EA)
WCC.......... World Council of Christians (EA)
WCC.......... World Council of Churches
WCC.......... World Council of Clergymen (EA)
WCC.......... World Crafts Council (EA)
WCC.......... Worldwide Collectors Club (EA)
WCCA........ West Coast Crossarm Association [*Defunct*]
WCCA........ Whiteruthenian [*Byelorussian*] Congress Committee of America [*Later, Byelorussian Congress Committee of America*] (EA)
WCCA........ Whooping Crane Conservation Association (EA)
WCCA........ World Court Clubs Association [*Defunct*] (EA)
WCCA........ Worst Case Circuit Analysis
WCCB........ Charlotte, NC [*Television station call letters*]
WCCC........ Hartford, CT [*AM radio station call letters*]
WCCC........ Warwick China Collectors Club (EA)
WCCC........ Wayne County Community College [*Michigan*]
WCCC........ Wisconsin Clinical Cancer Center [*University of Wisconsin*] [*Research center*] (RCD)
WCCC........ World Convention of Churches of Christ (EA)
WCCC-FM ... Hartford, CT [*FM radio station call letters*]
WCC & CRA ... World Championship Cutter and Chariot Racing Association (EA)
WCCE........ Buie's Creek, NC [*FM radio station call letters*]
WCCE........ West Coast Commodity Exchange
WCCE........ World Council of Christian Education [*Later absorbed into Office of Education of World Council of Churches*]
WCCES...... World Council of Comparative Education Societies (EA)
WCCESSA ... World Council of Christian Education and Sunday School Association [*Later, WCCE*] (EA)
WCCF........ Punta Gorda, FL [*AM radio station call letters*]
WCCH........ Holyoke, MA [*FM radio station call letters*]
WCCI........ Savanna, IL [*FM radio station call letters*]

WCCI........ World Council for Curriculum and Instruction (EA)
WCCJ........ Chatom, AL [*FM radio station call letters*]
WCCK........ Erie, PA [*FM radio station call letters*]
WCCK .... Weapons Control Check (NVT)
WCCLS ..... Washington County Cooperative Library Services [*Library network*]
WCCM........ Lawrence, MA [*AM radio station call letters*]
WCCMORS ... West Coast Classified Military Operations Research Symposium
WCCN........ Neillsville, WI [*AM radio station call letters*]
WCCN-FM ... Neillsville, WI [*FM radio station call letters*]
WCC (NZ) ... Workers' Compensation Cases (New Zealand) (DLA)
WCCO........ Minneapolis, MN [*AM radio station call letters*]
W & C Conv ... Wolstenholme and Cherry's Conveyancing Statutes [*13th ed.*] [*1972*] (DLA)
WCCO-TV ... Minneapolis, MN [*Television station call letters*]
WCCP........ Clemson, SC [*AM radio station call letters*]
WCCPPS..... Waste Channel and Containment Pressurization and Penetration System (IEEE)
WCCQ........ Crest Hill, IL [*FM radio station call letters*]
WCCR........ Clarion, PA [*FM radio station call letters*]
WCCR........ Washington's United States Circuit Court Reports (DLA)
WCCRS...... Western Catholic Charismatic Renewal Services [*A publication*]
WCCS........ Homer City, PA [*AM radio station call letters*]
WCCS........ World Chamber of Commerce Service (EA)
WCCSIS..... Westchester County Community Services Information System [*Westchester Library System*] [*Elmsford, NY*] [*Information service*] (EISS)
WCCT-TV ... Columbia, SC [*Television station call letters*]
WCCU........ Urbana, IL [*Television station call letters*]
WCCV........ Cartersville, GA [*FM radio station call letters*]
WCCW........ Traverse City, MI [*AM radio station call letters*]
WCCW-FM ... Traverse City, MI [*FM radio station call letters*]
WCCX........ Waukesha, WI [*FM radio station call letters*]
WCCY........ Houghton, MI [*AM radio station call letters*]
WCCZ........ New Smyrna Beach, FL [*AM radio station call letters*]
WCD.......... We Can Do! [*Arcadia, CA*] (EA)
WCD.......... Weapons Classification Defects [*Navy*] (NG)
WCD.......... Work Center Description (AFM)
WCD.......... Workshop for Cultural Democracy (EA)
WCDB........ Albany, NY [*FM radio station call letters*]
WCDB........ Wing Control During Boost
WCDB........ Work Control Data Base (NASA)
WCDC........ Adams, MA [*Television station call letters*]
WCDC........ West Coast [*Naval Publications*] Distribution Center
WCDE........ Elkins, WV [*FM radio station call letters*]
WCDFMA ... Water Cooler and Drinking Fountain Manufacturers Association
WCDL........ Carbondale, PA [*AM radio station call letters*]
WCDN........ Chardon, OH [*AM radio station call letters*]
WCDO........ War Consumable Distribution Objective (AFM)
WCDO-FM ... Sidney, NY [*FM radio station call letters*]
WCDP........ Sidney, NY [*AM radio station call letters*]
WCDP........ Widows', Children's, and Dependents' Pension [*British*]
WCDP........ World Climate Data Program [*WMO*] [*ICSU*]
WCDQ........ Sanford, ME [*FM radio station call letters*]
W/Cdr .... Wing Commander [*British*]
WCDR-FM ... Cedarville, OH [*FM radio station call letters*]
WCDS .... Glasgow, KY [*AM radio station call letters*]
WCDT........ Winchester, TN [*AM radio station call letters*]
WCDV .... Covington, IN [*FM radio station call letters*]
WCE.......... Weapon Control Equipment
WCE.......... West Coast of England [*Shipping*]
WCE.......... Wiener Canonical Expansion [*Mathematics*]
WCEA........ Newburyport, MA [*AM radio station call letters*]
WCEB........ Corning, NY [*FM radio station call letters*]
WCEC........ Rocky Mount, NC [*AM radio station call letters*]
WCED........ Du Bois, PA [*AM radio station call letters*]
WCEE........ Mount Vernon, IL [*Television station call letters*]
WCEE........ Women's Council on Energy and the Environment (EA)
WCEF........ Ripley, WV [*FM radio station call letters*]
WCEG........ Middleborough, MA [*AM radio station call letters*]
WCEH........ Hawkinsville, GA [*AM radio station call letters*]
WCEH-FM ... Hawkinsville, GA [*FM radio station call letters*]
WCEI........ Easton, MD [*AM radio station call letters*]
WCEI-FM ... Easton, MD [*FM radio station call letters*]
WC & EL..... Workers' Compensation and Employers' Liability [*Insurance*]
WCEM........ Cambridge, MD [*AM radio station call letters*]
WCEMA...... West Coast Electronic Manufacturers' Association [*Later, AEA*]
WCEM-FM ... Cambridge, MD [*FM radio station call letters*]
WCEN........ Mount Pleasant, MI [*AM radio station call letters*]
WCEN-FM ... Mount Pleasant, MI [*FM radio station call letters*]
WCEO-TV ... Mansfield, OH [*Television station call letters*]
WCER........ Huntington, IN [*AM radio station call letters*]
WCES........ Women's Caucus of the Endocrine Society [*University of Texas Medical School*] [*Houston, TX*] (EA)
WCES-TV... Wrens, GA [*Television station call letters*]
WCET........ Cincinnati, OH [*Television station call letters*]
WCEU........ New Smyrna Beach, FL [*Television station call letters*]

WCEU......... World's Christian Endeavor Union
WCEV........ Cicero, IL [AM radio station call letters]
WCEW........ Charleston, SC [FM radio station call letters]
WCEZ........ Columbia, SC [FM radio station call letters]
WCf............ Chippewa Falls Public Library, Chippewa Falls, WI [Library symbol] [Library of Congress] (LCLS)
WCF .... Waste Calcination [or Calcining] Facility [Nuclear energy]
WCF .... Water Conditioning Foundation [Later, Water Quality Association] (EA)
WCF .... White Cathode Follower
WCF .... Winston Churchill Foundation [Formerly, USCF] (EA)
WCF .... Women's Campaign Fund (EA)
WCF .... Workload Control File
WCF .... World Congress of Faiths (EA-IO)
WCF .... World Congress of Flight
WCFA........ Wholesale Commission Florists of America [Later, WF & FSA]
WCFA........ Wildlife Conservation Fund of America (EA)
WCFB........ Tupelo, MS [AM radio station call letters]
WCFBA ..... World Catholic Federation for the Biblical Apostolate (EA-IO)
WCFC-TV... Chicago, IL [Television station call letters]
WCFE-TV... Plattsburgh, NY [Television station call letters]
WCFL........ Chicago, IL [AM radio station call letters]
WCFM........ Williamstown, MA [FM radio station call letters]
WCFN........ Springfield, IL [Television station call letters]
WCfNC....... Northern Wisconsin Colony and Training School, Chippewa Falls, WI [Library symbol] [Library of Congress] (LCLS)
WCFPR...... Washington Center of Foreign Policy Research (MCD)
WCFR........ Springfield, VT [AM radio station call letters]
WCFR........ Washington Citizens for Recycling (EA)
WCFR-FM ... Springfield, VT [FM radio station call letters]
WCFRU ..... Washington Cooperative Fishery Research Unit [University of Washington] [Research center] (RCD)
WCfSJ........ Saint Joseph's Hospital, Chippewa Falls, WI [Library symbol] [Library of Congress] (LCLS)
WCFTB...... West Coast Freight Tariff Bureau
WCFT-TV ... Tuscaloosa, AL [Television station call letters]
WCFW........ Chippewa Falls, WI [FM radio station call letters]
WCFX........ Clare, MI [FM radio station call letters]
WCG.......... Washington Calligraphers Guild (EA)
WCG.......... Water-Cooled Garment
WCG.......... Weapon Control Group [Military] (CAAL)
WCG.......... Women of the Church of God (EA)
WCG.......... Worldwide Church of God
WCGA .... World Computer Graphics Association [Washington, DC] (EA)
WCGB .... Juana Diaz, PR [AM radio station call letters]
WCGC....... Belmont, NC [AM radio station call letters]
WCGL........ Jacksonville, FL [AM radio station call letters]
WCGLJO.... World Congress of Gay and Lesbian Jewish Organizations (EA)
WCGM....... Maryville, TN [AM radio station call letters]
WCGM....... Writable Character Generation Module [Data processing] (BUR)
WCGO........ Chicago Heights, IL [AM radio station call letters]
WCGQ........ Columbus, GA [FM radio station call letters]
WCGR .... Canandaigua, NY [AM radio station call letters]
WCGS .... Wolf Creek Generating Station (NRCH)
WCGTC...... World Council for Gifted and Talented Children (EA)
WCGV .... Milwaukee, WI [Television station call letters]
WCGY-FM ... Lawrence, MA [FM radio station call letters]
WCGZ .... World Confederation of General Zionists [Later, World Confederation of United Zionists] (EA)
WCh .... Chippewa Falls Public Library, Chippewa Falls, WI [Library symbol] [Library of Congress] [Obsolete] (LCLS)
WCH........... Skyline Aviation, Inc. [Winchester, VA] [FAA designator] (FAAC)
WCH........... Weekly Contact Hours
WCH........... West Coast Handling
WCH........... Working Class Hero (EA)
WCH........... Workshop Conferences Hoechst [Elsevier Book Series] [A publication]
WCHA .... Chambersburg, PA [AM radio station call letters]
WCHA .... Wooden Canoe Heritage Association (EA)
WCHB .... Inkster, MI [AM radio station call letters]
WCHC .... Worcester, MA [FM radio station call letters]
WCHE....... West Chester, PA [AM radio station call letters]
WCHEN...... Western Council on Higher Education for Nursing
W'CHESTER ... Winchester [Borough in South England] (ROG)
WCHI......... Chillicothe, OH [AM radio station call letters]
WCHI......... Women's Council for the Histadrut in Israel (EA)
WCHJ......... Brookhaven, MS [AM radio station call letters]
WCHK .... Canton, GA [AM radio station call letters]
WCHK-FM ... Canton, GA [FM radio station call letters]
WCHL........ Chapel Hill, NC [AM radio station call letters]
WCHN .... Norwich, NY [AM radio station call letters]
Wchnbl K K Gesellsch Aerzte Wien ... Wochenblatt der K. K. Gesellschaft der Aerzte in Wien [A publication]
Wchnschr Ges Heilk ... Wochenschrift fuer die Gesamte Heilkunde [A publication]
Wchnschr Tierh u Viehzucht ... Wochenschrift fuer Tierheilkunde und Viehzucht [A publication]
WCHO-FM ... Washington Court House, OH [FM radio station call letters]

WCHP......... Champlain, NY [AM radio station call letters]
WCHQ........ Camuy, PR [AM radio station call letters]
WCHQ-FM ... Camuy, PR [FM radio station call letters]
WCHR .... Trenton, NJ [FM radio station call letters]
WCHR .... Water Chiller
WCHR .... Worldwide Creme Horse Registry (EA)
WCHS .... Charleston, WV [AM radio station call letters]
WCHS-TV ... Charleston, WV [Television station call letters]
WCHT........ Escanaba, MI [AM radio station call letters]
WCHU .... Soddy-Daisy, TN [AM radio station call letters]
WCHV .... Charlottesville, VA [AM radio station call letters]
WCHW-FM ... Bay City, MI [FM radio station call letters]
WCHX .... Lewistown, PA [FM radio station call letters]
WCHY .... Savannah, GA [FM radio station call letters]
WCI .... Warner Communications, Inc. [NYSE symbol]
WCI .... Washington International College, Washington, DC [OCLC symbol] (OCLC)
WCI .... Weapon Control Index [Military] (CAAL)
WCI .... White Cast Iron
WCIA .... Champaign, IL [Television station call letters]
WCIB .... Falmouth, MA [FM radio station call letters]
WCIC........ Pekin, IL [FM radio station call letters]
WCIC........ Watch Check Is Completed (FAAC)
WCIE........ Lakeland, FL [FM radio station call letters]
WCIE........ World Center for Islamic Education (EA)
WCIF......... Melbourne, FL [FM radio station call letters]
WCIG........ Mullins, SC [FM radio station call letters]
WCII .... Louisville, KY [AM radio station call letters]
WCIK .... Bath, NY [FM radio station call letters]
WCIL .... Carbondale, IL [AM radio station call letters]
WCIL-FM... Carbondale, IL [FM radio station call letters]
WCIN........ Cincinnati, OH [AM radio station call letters]
WC & Ins (Eng) ... Workmen's Compensation and Insurance Reports [1912-33] [England] (DLA)
WC & Ins Rep ... Workmen's Compensation and Insurance Reports [1912-33] [England] (DLA)
WC Ins Rep ... Workmen's Compensation and Insurance Reports (DLA)
WCIP .... Weapon Control Indicator Panel [Military] (CAAL)
WCIP .... World Climate Impacts Program [WMO] [ICSU]
WCIP .... World Council of Indigenous Peoples (EA-IO)
WCIQ........ Mount Cheaha State Park, AL [Television station call letters]
WCIR........ Beckley, WV [AM radio station call letters]
WC & IR...... Workmen's Compensation and Insurance Reports [1912-33] [England] (DLA)
WC & I Rep ... Workmen's Compensation and Insurance Reports [England] (DLA)
WCIR-FM ... Beckley, WV [FM radio station call letters]
WCIS......... Wisconsin Career Information System [Information service]
WC-ISA...... Women's Commission of the Iranian Students Association (EA)
WCIT .... Lima, OH [AM radio station call letters]
WCIU......... Workshop Computer Interface Unit (MCD)
WCIU-TV... Chicago, IL [Television station call letters]
WCIV .... Charleston, SC [Television station call letters]
WCIW .... [The] World Community of Al-Islam in the West
WCIX-TV ... Miami, FL [Television station call letters]
WCJ.......... White Cloud Journal of American Indian/Alaska Native Mental Health [A publication]
WCJA........ Western Canadian Journal of Anthropology [A publication]
WCJA........ World Council of Jewish Archives (EA-IO)
WCJB........ Gainesville, FL [Television station call letters]
WCJC........ Madison, IN [FM radio station call letters]
WCJC........ Webster City Junior College [Iowa]
WCJC........ Wharton County Junior College [Texas]
WCJCC ...... World Confederation of Jewish Community Centers (EA)
WCJCS ...... World Conference of Jewish Communal Service [Formerly, ICJCS] [New York, NY] (EA)
WCJE .... World Council on Jewish Education
WCJL .... Marinette, WI [AM radio station call letters]
WCJL-FM... Menominee, MI [FM radio station call letters]
WCJM........ West Point, GA [FM radio station call letters]
WCJO........ Jackson, OH [FM radio station call letters]
WCJU........ Columbia, MS [AM radio station call letters]
WCJV........ Jefferson, OH [FM radio station call letters]
WCJW........ Warsaw, NY [AM radio station call letters]
WCK .... Wilson Creek [Kentucky] [Seismograph station code, US Geological Survey] (SEIS)
WCKA .... Sutton, WV [FM radio station call letters]
WCKB .... Dunn, NC [AM radio station call letters]
WCKC .... Milton, FL [AM radio station call letters]
WCKG .... Elmwood Park, IL [FM radio station call letters]
WCKI........ Greer, SC [AM radio station call letters]
WCKJ........ Augusta, GA [AM radio station call letters]
WCKK .... Oshkosh, WI [FM radio station call letters]
WCKL........ Catskill, NY [AM radio station call letters]
WCKM........ Winnsboro, SC [AM radio station call letters]
WCKN-FM ... Anderson, SC [FM radio station call letters]
WCKO .... Vicksburg, MS [FM radio station call letters]
WCKQ........ Campbellsville, KY [FM radio station call letters]
WCKR .... Hornell, NY [FM radio station call letters]
WCKS .... Cocoa Beach, FL [AM radio station call letters]

WCKV .... Ceredo, WV [*FM radio station call letters*]
WCKW........ Garyville, LA [*AM radio station call letters*]
WCKW-FM ... La Place, LA [*FM radio station call letters*]
WCKX .... London, OH [*FM radio station call letters*]
WCKY .... Cincinnati, OH [*AM radio station call letters*]
WCL .... Washington College of Law, Washington, DC [*OCLC symbol*]   (OCLC)
WCL .... Water Coolant Line   (MCD)
WCL .... Water Coolant Loop   (MCD)
WCL .... WCI Canada Limited [*Toronto Stock Exchange symbol*]
WCL .... Weekly Cost Ledger   (MCD)
WCL .... Western Carolinas League [*Baseball*]
WCL .... White Clip Level [*Video technology*]
WCL .... White Cross League [*British*]
WCL .... Word Control Logic
WCL .... World Confederation of Labour [*See also CMT*] [*Brussels, Belgium*]   (EA-IO)
WCL .... Wright Center of Laboratories
WCLA........ Claxton, GA [*AM radio station call letters*]
WCLA........ West Coast Lumbermen's Association [*Later, WWPA*]   (EA)
WCLA-FM ... Claxton, GA [*FM radio station call letters*]
WCLB........ Camilla, GA [*AM radio station call letters*]
WCLC........ Jamestown, TN [*AM radio station call letters*]
WCLC........ Watch Check List Completed   (FAAC)
WCLC-FM ... Jamestown, TN [*FM radio station call letters*]
WCLD........ Cleveland, MS [*AM radio station call letters*]
WCLD........ Water-Cooled   (AAG)
WCLD-FM ... Cleveland, MS [*FM radio station call letters*]
WCLE........ Cleveland, TN [*AM radio station call letters*]
WCLF........ Clearwater, FL [*Television station call letters*]
WCLG........ Morgantown, WV [*AM radio station call letters*]
WCLH........ Wilkes-Barre, PA [*FM radio station call letters*]
WCLI......... Corning, NY [*AM radio station call letters*]
WCII .... Lakeshore Technical Institute, Educational Resource Center, Cleveland, WI [*Library symbol*] [*Library of Congress*]   (LCLS)
WCLIB........ West Coast Lumber Inspection Bureau [*Portland, OR*]   (EA)
WCLJ .... Workmen's Compensation Law Journal   (DLA)
WCLK........ Atlanta, GA [*FM radio station call letters*]
WCLL-FM... Wesson, MS [*FM radio station call letters*]
WCLN........ Clinton, NC [*AM radio station call letters*]
WCLN-FM ... Clinton, NC [*FM radio station call letters*]
WCLO........ Janesville, WI [*AM radio station call letters*]
WCLP......... Western Center on Law and Poverty   (EA)
WCLP......... Women's Computer Literacy Project [*Commercial firm*] [*San Francisco, CA*]   (EA)
WCLP-TV ... Chatsworth, GA [*Television station call letters*]
WCLR........ Skokie, IL [*FM radio station call letters*]
WCLR........ Workmen's Compensation Law Review   (DLA)
WCLS........ Columbus, GA [*AM radio station call letters*]
WCLT........ Newark, OH [*AM radio station call letters*]
WCLT-FM ... Newark, OH [*FM radio station call letters*]
WCLU........ Covington, KY [*AM radio station call letters*]
WCLV........ Cleveland, OH [*FM radio station call letters*]
WCLW........ Mansfield, OH [*AM radio station call letters*]
WCLW-FM ... Mansfield, OH [*FM radio station call letters*]
WCLX........ Boyne City, MI [*FM radio station call letters*]
WCLY........ Morningside, MD [*FM radio station call letters*]
WCLZ........ Brunswick, ME [*FM radio station call letters*]
WCM .... Warland Creek [*Montana*] [*Seismograph station code, US Geological Survey*] [*Closed*]   (SEIS)
WCM .... Water Control Module   (KSC)
WCM .... Weapon Control Module   (MCD)
WCM .... Welded Cordwood Module
WCM .... Wesleyan Calvinistic Methodists   (ROG)
WCM .... Whole Cow's Milk
WCM .... Winkelmann Countermeasures, Inc. [*Vancouver Stock Exchange symbol*]
WCM .... Wired-Core Matrix
WCM .... Wired-Core Memory
WCM .... Word Combine and Multiplexer
WCM .... Writable Control Memory [*Data processing*]   (BUR)
W/CM² .... Watts per Square Centimeter   (CET)
WCMA........ Corinth, MS [*AM radio station call letters*]
WCMA........ West Coast Mineral Association   (EA)
WCMA........ Wisconsin Cheese Makers' Association [*Madison, WI*]   (EA)
WCMA........ Working Capital Management Account [*Merrill Lynch & Co.*]
WCMB........ Harrisburg, PA [*AM radio station call letters*]
WCMC........ Wildwood, NJ [*AM radio station call letters*]
WCMD........ La Plata, MD [*AM radio station call letters*]
WCME........ Boothbay Harbor, ME [*FM radio station call letters*]
WCMF........ Rochester, NY [*FM radio station call letters*]
WCMG........ Lawrenceburg, TN [*FM radio station call letters*]
WCMH........ Columbus, OH [*Television station call letters*]
WCMI......... Ashland, KY [*AM radio station call letters*]
WCMIA....... West Coast Metal Importers Association [*Los Angeles, CA*]   (EA)
WCMJ .... Cambridge, OH [*FM radio station call letters*]
WCML .... Women's Caucus for the Modern Languages   (EA)
WCML-FM .. Alpena, MI [*FM radio station call letters*]
WCML-TV ... Alpena, MI [*Television station call letters*]

WCMN........ Arecibo, PR [*AM radio station call letters*]
WCMN-FM ... Arecibo, PR [*FM radio station call letters*]
WCMO........ Marietta, OH [*FM radio station call letters*]
WCMP........ Pine City, MN [*AM radio station call letters*]
WCMP-FM ... Pine City, MN [*FM radio station call letters*]
WCMQ........ Miami Springs, FL [*AM radio station call letters*]
WCMQ-FM ... Hialeah, FL [*FM radio station call letters*]
WCMR........ Elkhart, IN [*AM radio station call letters*]
WCMR........ Western Contract Management Region [*Air Force*]
WCMS........ Norfolk, VA [*AM radio station call letters*]
WCMS-FM ... Norfolk, VA [*FM radio station call letters*]
WCMT........ Martin, TN [*AM radio station call letters*]
WCMT-FM ... Martin, TN [*FM radio station call letters*]
WCM-TV ... Appleton, MN [*Television station call letters*]
WCMU-FM ... Mount Pleasant, MI [*FM radio station call letters*]
WCMU-TV ... Mount Pleasant, MI [*Television station call letters*]
WCMV........ Cadillac, MI [*Television station call letters*]
WCMW........ Manistee, MI [*Television station call letters*]
WCMW........ Williamsburg, VA [*FM radio station call letters*]
WCMX........ Leominster, MA [*AM radio station call letters*]
WCMY........ Ottawa, IL [*AM radio station call letters*]
WCN .... Washoe City [*Nevada*] [*Seismograph station code, US Geological Survey*]   (SEIS)
WCN .... Wescan Energy Ltd. [*Vancouver Stock Exchange symbol*]
WCN .... Workload Control Number   (MCD)
WCN .... World Coin News [*A publication*]
WCNA .... Clearwater, SC [*FM radio station call letters*]
WCNB-FM ... Connersville, IN [*FM radio station call letters*]
WCNC .... Elizabeth City, NC [*AM radio station call letters*]
WCND .... Shelbyville, KY [*AM radio station call letters*]
WCNE .... Batavia, OH [*FM radio station call letters*]
WCNF .... Cincinnati, OH [*FM radio station call letters*]
WCNI .... New London, CT [*FM radio station call letters*]
WCNL .... Newport, NH [*AM radio station call letters*]
WCNL-FM ... Newport, NH [*FM radio station call letters*]
WCNN .... North Atlanta, GA [*AM radio station call letters*]
WCNR .... Bloomsburg, PA [*AM radio station call letters*]
WCNS .... Latrobe, PA [*AM radio station call letters*]
WCNU .... Crestview, FL [*AM radio station call letters*]
WCNW .... Fairfield, OH [*AM radio station call letters*]
WCNX .... Middletown, CT [*AM radio station call letters*]
WCNY-FM ... Syracuse, NY [*FM radio station call letters*]
WCNY-TV ... Syracuse, NY [*Television station call letters*]
WCO .... Columbia Helicopters, Inc. [*Lake Charles, LA*] [*FAA designator*]   (FAAC)
WCO .... War Cabinet Office [*World War II*]
WCO .... Weapons Control Officer
WCO .... Western Coordination Office [*Later, WOO*] [*NASA*]
WCO .... Wrather Corporation [*American Stock Exchange symbol*]
WCOA .... Pensacola, FL [*AM radio station call letters*]
W Coast Rep ... West Coast Reporter   (DLA)
WCOD .... Western Canada Outdoors. Combining The Whooper and Defending All Outdoors [*A publication*]
WCOD-FM ... Hyannis, MA [*FM radio station call letters*]
WCOE .... La Porte, IN [*FM radio station call letters*]
WCOF........ Women's Catholic Order of Foresters [*Later, NCSF*]   (EA)
WCOG........ Ridgeland, SC [*AM radio station call letters*]
WCOH .... Newnan, GA [*AM radio station call letters*]
WCoins ...... World Coins [*A publication*]
WCOJ......... Coatesville, PA [*AM radio station call letters*]
WCOK .... Sparta, NC [*AM radio station call letters*]
WCOL .... Columbus, OH [*AM radio station call letters*]
WCOL........ Walker Color, Inc. [*NASDAQ symbol*]   (NQ)
W Comp Pres Docs ... Weekly Compilation of Presidential Documents [*A publication*]
WCON .... Cornelia, GA [*AM radio station call letters*]
WCON-FM ... Cornelia, GA [*FM radio station call letters*]
WCOP .... Warner Robins, GA [*AM radio station call letters*]
WC Ops...... Workmen's Compensation Opinions, United States Department of Commerce   (DLA)
WCOR .... Lebanon, TN [*AM radio station call letters*]
WCOS .... Columbia, SC [*AM radio station call letters*]
WCOS-FM ... Columbia, SC [*FM radio station call letters*]
WCOT .... Wall Coated Open Tubular [*Instrumentation*]
WCOTP ...... World Confederation of Organizations of the Teaching Profession [*Also known as CMOPE*]
WCOU .... Lewiston, ME [*AM radio station call letters*]
WCOV-TV ... Montgomery, AL [*Television station call letters*]
WCOW ...... Sparta, WI [*AM radio station call letters*]
WCOW-FM ... Sparta, WI [*FM radio station call letters*]
WCOX .... Camden, AL [*AM radio station call letters*]
WCOZ .... Paris, KY [*FM radio station call letters*]
WCP .... War Control Planners   (EA)
WCP .... Warner Computer Systems, Inc. [*American Stock Exchange symbol*]
WCP .... Waste Collector Pump   (IEEE)
WCP .... Wayne County Public Library, Wooster, OH [*OCLC symbol*]   (OCLC)
WCP .... Weapon Control Panel [*Aviation*]
WCP .... Weapon Control Processor [*Military*]   (CAAL)
WCP .... Welder Control Panel

WCP	Western Canada Party [*Separatist political party*]
WCP	White Combination Potentiometer
WCP	Wing Chord Plane
WCP	Wing Command Post　(MCD)
WCP	Work Control Plan　(AAG)
WCP	World Climate Program [*WMO*] [*ICSU*]
WCP	World Council of Peace　(NATG)
WCPA	Clearfield, PA [*AM radio station call letters*]
WCPA	World Constitution and Parliament Association　(EA)
WCPAB	War Contracts Price Adjustment Board [*All functions dispersed, 1951*]
WCPB	Salisbury, MD [*Television station call letters*]
WCPC	Houston, MS [*AM radio station call letters*]
WCPC-FM ...	Houston, MS [*FM radio station call letters*]
WCPD	Waterloo Centre for Process Development [*University of Waterloo*] [*Research center*]　(RCD)
WCPE	Raleigh, NC [*FM radio station call letters*]
WCPH	Etowah, TN [*AM radio station call letters*]
WCPH	World Congress of Professional Hypnotists　(EA)
WCPH-FM ...	Etowah, TN [*FM radio station call letters*]
WCPK	Chesapeake, VA [*AM radio station call letters*]
WCPL-FM ...	Pageland, SC [*FM radio station call letters*]
WCPM	Cumberland, KY [*AM radio station call letters*]
WCPMEF	Willa Cather Pioneer Memorial and Educational Foundation　(EA)
WCPN	Cleveland, OH [*FM radio station call letters*]
WCPO-TV ...	Cincinnati, OH [*Television station call letters*]
WCPQ	Havelock, NC [*AM radio station call letters*]
WCPR	Coamo, PR [*AM radio station call letters*]
WCPR	Weston, Clevedon & Portishead Railway [*British*]
WCPS	Tarboro, NC [*AM radio station call letters*]
WCPS	Women's Caucus for Political Science　(EA)
WCPS	World Confederation of Productivity Science　(EA-IO)
WCPT	Alexandria, VA [*AM radio station call letters*]
WCPT	World Confederation for Physical Therapy　(EA)
WCPX-TV ...	Orlando, FL [*Television station call letters*]
WCPZ	Sandusky, OH [*FM radio station call letters*]
WCQR	Blountville, TN [*AM radio station call letters*]
WCQS-FM ...	Asheville, NC [*FM radio station call letters*]
WCQT	Centerville, TN [*FM radio station call letters*]
WCR	Chandalar [*Alaska*] [*Airport symbol*]　(OAG)
WCR	Chandalar Lake, AK [*Location identifier*] [*FAA*]　(FAAL)
WCR	Warm Core Ring [*Oceanography*]
WCR	Water-Cooled Reactor
WCR	Water-Cooled Rod
WCR	Watercooler　(AAG)
WCR	Waterloo and City Railway　(ROG)
WCR	West Coast Review [*A publication*]
WCR	Western Communications Region [*Air Force*]　(MCD)
WCR	Willcrest Resources Ltd. [*Vancouver Stock Exchange symbol*]
WCRL	Wire Contact Relay
WCR	Women's Council of Realtors [*of the National Association of Realtors*] [*Chicago, IL*]　(EA)
WCR	Word Control Register
WCR	Word Count Register
WCR	Workers' Compensation Commission Reports of Cases [*New South Wales, Australia*]　(DLA)
WCR	Workers' Compensation Reports [*New South Wales*] [*A publication*]
WCRA	Effingham, IL [*AM radio station call letters*]
WCRA	Weather Control Research Association [*Later, Weather Modification Association*]
WCRA	Western College Reading Association　(EA)
WCRB	Waltham, MA [*FM radio station call letters*]
WCRB	West Coast Review of Books [*A publication*]
WCRC	Effingham, IL [*FM radio station call letters*]
WCRC	Water Conditioning Research Council [*Later, WQRC*]　(EA)
WCRD	War Consumables Requirements Document [*Military*]　(AFIT)
WCRE	Cheraw, SC [*AM radio station call letters*]
WC Rep	Workmen's Compensation Reports　(DLA)
WCRF	Cleveland, OH [*FM radio station call letters*]
WCRF	Weekly Collection Report File [*IRS*]
WCRH	Williamsport, MD [*AM radio station call letters*]
WCRJ-FM ...	Jacksonville, FL [*FM radio station call letters*]
WCRK	Morristown, TN [*AM radio station call letters*]
WCRL	Oneonta, AL [*AM radio station call letters*]
WCRLA	Western College Reading and Learning Association　(EA)
WCRM	Dundee, IL [*FM radio station call letters*]
WCRN	Tamaqua, PA [*FM radio station call letters*]
WCRNSW ...	Workers' Compensation Commission Reports of Cases (New South Wales, Australia)　(DLA)
WCR (NSW) ...	Workers' Compensation Reports (New South Wales) [*A publication*]
WCRO	Johnstown, PA [*AM radio station call letters*]
WCROS	White Crossover Vote [*Political science*]
WCRP	Guayama, PR [*FM radio station call letters*]
WCRP	World Climate Research Program [*WMO*] [*ICSU*]
WCRP	World Climate Research Programme [*World Meteorological Organization*]
WCRP	World Conference on Religion and Peace [*Geneva, Switzerland*]　(EA-IO)
WCRP/USA ...	World Conference on Religion and Peace, USA Section　(EA)
WCR (Q)	Workers' Compensation Reports (Queensland) [*A publication*]
WCRQ-FM ...	Arab, AL [*FM radio station call letters*]
WCR (Qld) ...	Workers' Compensation Reports (Queensland) [*A publication*]
WCR (Qn) ...	Worker's Compensation Reports (Queensland) [*A publication*]
WCRR	Rural Retreat, VA [*AM radio station call letters*]
WCRS	Greenwood, SC [*AM radio station call letters*]
WC:RS	Women's Caucus: Religious Studies　(EA)
WCRSI	Western Concrete Reinforcing Steel Institute [*Later, CRSI*]　(EA)
WCRT	Birmingham, AL [*AM radio station call letters*]
WCRW	Chicago, IL [*AM radio station call letters*]
WCRX	Chicago, IL [*FM radio station call letters*]
WCRZ	Flint, MI [*FM radio station call letters*]
WCS	Wallace Computer Services, Inc. [*NYSE symbol*]
WCS	Wang Computer System
WCS	Waste Collection System　(MCD)
WCS	Waste Compaction Station [*Nuclear energy*]　(NRCH)
WCS	Weak Calf Syndrome [*Veterinary medicine*]
WCS	Weapon Control Station [*Military*]　(CAAL)
WCS	Weapons Control System
WCS	Wedgwood Collectors Society [*Commercial firm*]　(EA)
WCS	Western Cover Society　(EA)
WCS	Woman Citizen Series [*A publication*]
WCS	Work Control System　(NASA)
WCS	Work Core Storage
WCS	World Council of Synagogues　(EA)
WCS	Writable Control Storage [*Data processing*]
WCSA	West Coast of South America
WCSB	Cleveland, OH [*FM radio station call letters*]
WCSB	Weapon Control Switchboard [*Military*]　(CAAL)
WCSB(G) ...	Weapon Control Switchboard (Gun)
WCSB(M) ...	Weapon Control Switchboard (Missile)
WCSB(UB) ...	Weapon Control Switchboard (Underwater Battery)
WCSC	Charleston, SC [*AM radio station call letters*]
WCSC	Weapon Control System Console
WCSC	Weapons Control System Coordinator　(NVT)
WCSC	West Coast Switching Center [*Jet Propulsion Laboratory, NASA*]
WCSC	World Correctional Service Center [*Chicago, IL*]　(EA)
WCSC-TV ...	Charleston, SC [*Television station call letters*]
WCSE	Myrtle Beach, SC [*AM radio station call letters*]
WCSF	Clifton Park, NY [*FM radio station call letters*]
WCSG	Grand Rapids, MI [*FM radio station call letters*]
WCSH-TV ...	Portland, ME [*Television station call letters*]
WCSI	Columbus, IN [*AM radio station call letters*]
WCSI	World Centre for Scientific Information
WCSJ	Morris, IL [*AM radio station call letters*]
WCSJ-FM ...	Morris, IL [*FM radio station call letters*]
WCSK	Kingsport, TN [*AM radio station call letters*]
WCSL	Cherryville, NC [*AM radio station call letters*]
WCSM	Celina, OH [*AM radio station call letters*]
WCSM	World Congress of Sports Medicine
WCSM-FM ...	Celina, OH [*FM radio station call letters*]
WCSMLL	Western Canadian Studies in Modern Languages and Literature [*A publication*]
WCSO	Signal Mountain, TN [*FM radio station call letters*]
WCSP	Crystal Springs, MS [*AM radio station call letters*]
WCSPA	West Coast Shrimp Producers Association　(EA)
WCSQ	Central Square, NY [*FM radio station call letters*]
WCSR	Hillsdale, MI [*AM radio station call letters*]
WCSRC	Wild Canid Survival and Research Center - Wolf Sanctuary
WCSR-FM ...	Hillsdale, MI [*FM radio station call letters*]
WCSS	Amsterdam, NY [*AM radio station call letters*]
WCSS	Weapons Control Subsystem　(MCD)
WCSS	Weapons Control System Simulator
WCSS	West Coast Sound School [*Navy*]
WCST	Berkeley Springs, WV [*AM radio station call letters*]
WCST-FM ...	Berkeley Springs, WV [*FM radio station call letters*]
WCSU-FM ...	Wilberforce, OH [*FM radio station call letters*]
WCSUICA ...	Women's Coalition to Stop US Intervention in Central America　(EA)
WCSV	Crossville, TN [*AM radio station call letters*]
WCSW	Shell Lake, WI [*AM radio station call letters*]
WCSX	WCS-International [*NASDAQ symbol*]　(NQ)
WCSY	South Haven, MI [*AM radio station call letters*]
WCSY-FM ...	South Haven, MI [*FM radio station call letters*]
WCSZ	Greenville, MS [*Television station call letters*]
WCT	Trinity Memorial Hospital, Cudahy, WI [*Library symbol*] [*Library of Congress*]　(LCLS)
WCT	Waukesha County Institute, Pewaukee, WI [*OCLC symbol*]　(OCLC)
WCT	West Coast Travel [*Oakland, CA*] [*Information service*]　(EISS)
WCT	World Championship Tennis, Inc.
WCT	World Confederation of Teachers [*See also CSME*]　(EA-IO)
WCT	Worthy Chief Templar
WCTA	Alamo, TN [*AM radio station call letters*]
WCTA	World Committee for Trade Action [*See also CMAP*]　(EA-IO)
WCTB	West Country Tourist Board [*British*]
WCTB	Western Carriers Tariff Bureau
WCTC	New Brunswick, NJ [*AM radio station call letters*]

WCTD-FM ... Federalsburg, MD [*FM radio station call letters*]
WCTE........ Cookeville, TN [*Television station call letters*]
WCTF........ Vernon, CT [*AM radio station call letters*]
WCTG .... Woodcutting   (MSA)
WCTI .... Greenville, NC [*Television station call letters*]
WCTL........ Union City, PA [*FM radio station call letters*]
WCTM........ Eaton, OH [*AM radio station call letters*]
WCTN........ Potomac-Cabin John, MD [*AM radio station call letters*]
WCTO .... Smithtown, NY [*FM radio station call letters*]
WCTP........ Wire Chief Test Panel [*Telecommunications*]   (TEL)
WCTR........ Chestertown, MD [*AM radio station call letters*]
WCTR........ WCTU Railway Co. [*AAR code*]
WCTS........ Weapon Cost Test Site [*Military*]   (CAAL)
W Ct SA ..... Union of South Africa Water Courts Decisions   (DLA)
WCTS-FM ... Minneapolis, MN [*FM radio station call letters*]
WCTT........ Corbin, KY [*AM radio station call letters*]
WCTT........ Weapons Crew Training Test [*TCATA*]   (RDA)
WCTT-FM ... Corbin, KY [*FM radio station call letters*]
WCTU........ National Woman's Christian Temperance Union [*Evanston, IL*]   (EA)
WCTU........ Women's Connubial Temperance Union [*Satirical*]
WCTV........ Thomasville, GA [*Television station call letters*]
WCTV........ Wometco Cable TV, Inc. [*NASDAQ symbol*]   (NQ)
WCTW........ New Castle, IN [*AM radio station call letters*]
WCTX........ Palmyra, PA [*FM radio station call letters*]
WCTY........ Norwich, CT [*FM radio station call letters*]
WCu .... Cumberland Public Library, Cumberland, WI [*Library symbol*] [*Library of Congress*]   (LCLS)
WCU.......... Water Cooler Unit   (AAG)
WCU.......... Weapons Control Unit   (MCD)
WCU.......... West Coast University [*Los Angeles, CA*]
WCU.......... Western Carolina University [*North Carolina*] [*Formerly, WCC*]
WCU.......... Western Catholic Union
WCUB .... Two Rivers, WI [*AM radio station call letters*]
WCUC-FM ... Clarion, PA [*FM radio station call letters*]
WCUE........ Cuyahoga Falls, OH [*AM radio station call letters*]
WCUG....... Cuthbert, GA [*AM radio station call letters*]
WCUL........ Culpeper, VA [*FM radio station call letters*]
WCUMBS .. Western Canadian Universities Marine Biological Society
WCUW....... Worcester, MA [*FM radio station call letters*]
WCUZ........ Grand Rapids, MI [*AM radio station call letters*]
WCUZ........ World Confederation of United Zionists [*Formerly, WCGZ*]   (EA)
WCUZ-FM ... Grand Rapids, MI [*FM radio station call letters*]
WCV .... Water Check Valve
WCV .... Winant and Clayton Volunteers [*New York, NY*]   (EA)
WCVA........ Culpeper, VA [*AM radio station call letters*]
WCVB-TV... Boston, MA [*Television station call letters*]
WCVC .... Tallahassee, FL [*AM radio station call letters*]
WCVE-TV... Richmond, VA [*Television station call letters*]
WCVF-FM ... Fredonia, NY [*FM radio station call letters*]
WCVH .... Flemington, NJ [*FM radio station call letters*]
WCVI......... Connellsville, PA [*AM radio station call letters*]
WCVK .... Bowling Green, KY [*FM radio station call letters*]
WCVL........ Crawfordsville, IN [*AM radio station call letters*]
WCVM....... Middlebury, VT [*FM radio station call letters*]
WCVN .... Covington, KY [*Television station call letters*]
WCVO .... Gahanna, OH [*FM radio station call letters*]
WCVP........ Murphy, NC [*AM radio station call letters*]
WCVP-FM ... Robbinsville, NC [*FM radio station call letters*]
WCVR........ Randolph, VT [*AM radio station call letters*]
WCVR-FM ... Randolph, VT [*FM radio station call letters*]
WCVS........ Springfield, IL [*AM radio station call letters*]
WCVT........ Towson, MD [*FM radio station call letters*]
WCVU........ Naples, FL [*FM radio station call letters*]
WCVV........ Belpre, OH [*FM radio station call letters*]
WCVW....... Richmond, VA [*Television station call letters*]
WCVX........ Vineyard Haven, MA [*Television station call letters*]
WCVY........ Coventry, RI [*FM radio station call letters*]
WCVZ........ Zanesville, OH [*FM radio station call letters*]
WCW .... Western College for Women [*Ohio*]
WCW .... Western College for Women, Oxford, OH [*OCLC symbol*] [*Inactive*]   (OCLC)
WCW .... Wood Casement Window [*Technical drawings*]
WCWA....... Toledo, OH [*AM radio station call letters*]
WCWB....... World Council for the Welfare of the Blind [*See also OMPSA*]   (EA-IO)
WCWC ...... Ripon, WI [*AM radio station call letters*]
WCWL....... Stockbridge, MA [*FM radio station call letters*]
WCWN....... William Carlos Williams Newsletter [*A publication*]
WC/WO..... Working Committee on Weather Operations
WCWP....... Brookville, NY [*FM radio station call letters*]
WCWS....... Wooster, OH [*FM radio station call letters*]
WCWT-FM ... Centerville, OH [*FM radio station call letters*]
WCWV....... Summersville, WV [*FM radio station call letters*]
WCXI......... Detroit, MI [*AM radio station call letters*]
WCXL........ Kettering, OH [*FM radio station call letters*]
WCXN .... Claremont, NC [*AM radio station call letters*]
WCXQ .... Moca, PR [*AM radio station call letters*]
WCXR-FM ... Woodbridge, VA [*FM radio station call letters*]
WCXT........ Hart, MI [*FM radio station call letters*]

WCXU .... Caribou, ME [*FM radio station call letters*]
WCY.......... Viking Express, Inc. [*West Chicago, IL*] [*FAA designator*]   (FAAC)
WCY.......... World Communications Year [*1983*]
WCYB-TV... Bristol, VA [*Television station call letters*]
WCYC .... Chicago, IL [*FM radio station call letters*]
WCYJ-FM .. Waynesburg, PA [*FM radio station call letters*]
WCYN .... Cynthiana, KY [*AM radio station call letters*]
WCYN-FM ... Cynthiana, KY [*FM radio station call letters*]
WCYT........ Rochester, NH [*FM radio station call letters*]
WCZE........ Chicago, IL [*AM radio station call letters*]
WCZY........ Detroit, MI [*AM radio station call letters*]
WCZY-FM ... Detroit, MI [*FM radio station call letters*]
WD .... Decisions Won [*Boxing*]
WD .... [*Qualified for*] Deck Watch [*USNR officer classification*]
Wd............ Seaweed [*Quality of the bottom*] [*Nautical charts*]
WD .... Two-Conductor Cables [*JETDS nomenclature*] [*Military*]   (CET)
WD .... Wallerian Degeneration [*Medicine*]
WD .... War Damage
WD .... War Department [*Created, 1789; became Department of the Army, 1947*]
WD .... Ward
WD .... Wardair Canada Ltd. [*ICAO designator*]   (FAAC)
WD .... Warehouse Distributor
WD .... Warranted
WD .... Washington Decisions   (DLA)
WD .... Waste Disposal [*Nuclear energy*]   (NRCH)
WD .... Water Damage   (ADA)
WD .... Water Desurger
WD .... Watt Demand Meter   (MSA)
WD .... Wavelength Dispersive [*Spectrometry*]
WD .... Weapon Description   (MCD)
WD .... Weapon Director [*SAGE*]
WD .... Weapons Data [*Navy*]
WD .... Weather Division [*Air Force*]   (MCD)
WD .... Web Depth
WD .... [*The*] Weekly Dispatch [*A publication*]
WD .... Well Deck
W-D........... Well-Developed [*Medicine*]
WD .... Well Differentiated [*Medicine*]
WD .... West Division   (ROG)
WD .... Wet Dressing
WD .... Wheel Drive [*Engineering*]
WD .... When Directed
WD .... When Discovered
WD .... When Distributed [*Stock exchange term*]
WD .... Whole Depth
WD .... Widow
WD .... Width   (MSA)
W/D........... Width-to-Diameter [*Ratio*]   (KSC)
WD .... Wife's Divorce   (ROG)
WD .... Will Dated [*Genealogy*]   (ROG)
WD .... Wilson's Disease [*Medicine*]
WD .... Wind   (MSA)
WD .... Wind Direction
WD .... Window Detector
WD .... Window Dimension [*Technical drawings*]
WD .... Winner's Dog [*Dog show term*]
WD .... Winter's Digest [*A publication*]
WD .... Wired Discrete   (NASA)
WD .... With Dependents   (MCD)
W/D........... Withdrawal   (DLA)
WD .... Withdrawn   (AFM)
WD .... Wittenberg Door [*A publication*]
W & D .... Wolferstan and Dew's English Election Cases [*1856-58*]   (DLA)
WD .... Woman's Day [*A publication*]
WD .... Wood   (AAG)
WD .... Wood Door [*Technical drawings*]
WD .... Word
Wd............ Word [*A publication*]
WD .... Word Display
WD .... Work [*or Working*] Day   (AFM)
WD .... Work Description   (MCD)
WD .... Work Directive   (MCD)
WD .... Working Distance [*Microscopy*]
WD .... Works Department
Wd............ World [*A publication*]
W & D .... Wort und Dienst [*A publication*]
WD .... Would
WD .... Wrist Disarticulation [*Medicine*]
WD .... Write Data
WD .... Write Direct
WD .... Writers Digest [*A publication*]
WD .... Wrongful Detention [*British*]
2WD........... Two-Wheel Drive [*Automotive engineering*]
W 2d........... Washington State Reports, Second Series   (DLA)
4WD........... Four-Wheel Drive [*Vehicle*]
W-4-D......... Worth Four Dot [*Ophthalmology*]
W4D.......... Worth Four-Dot Test [*Ophthalmology*]
WDA.......... Aram Public Library, Delavan, WI [*Library symbol*] [*Library of Congress*]   (LCLS)

WDA .... Wallcovering Distributors Association [*Chicago, IL*]   (EA)
WDA .... Waste Disposal Authority [*British*]
WDA .... Wave Data Analyzer [*Marine science*]   (MSC)
WDA .... Weapons Defended Area
WDA .... Western District Area [*Air Force*]
WDA .... Wheel Drive Assembly
WDA .... Wildlife Disease Association   (EA)
WDA .... Wilson's Disease Association [*Washington, DC*]   (EA)
WDA .... Withdrawal of Availability [*Military*]   (AFM)
WDA .... World Aquathemes Ltd. [*Vancouver Stock Exchange symbol*]
WDA .... World Dredging Association   (MSC)
WDAC .... Lancaster, PA [*FM radio station call letters*]
WDAD .... Indiana, PA [*AM radio station call letters*]
WDAE .... Tampa, FL [*AM radio station call letters*]
WDAF .... Kansas City, MO [*AM radio station call letters*]
WDAF .... Western Desert Air Force
WDAF-TV ... Kansas City, MO [*Television station call letters*]
WDAHAC ... National Society Women Descendants of the Ancient and
                   Honorable Artillery Company   (EA)
WDAK .... Columbus, GA [*AM radio station call letters*]
WDAL .... Linden, AL [*FM radio station call letters*]
WDALMP ... Warehouse Distributors Association for Leisure and Mobile
                   Products [*Waukegan, IL*]   (EA)
WDAM-TV ... Laurel, MS [*Television station call letters*]
WDAN .... Danville, IL [*AM radio station call letters*]
WDAO .... Dayton, OH [*AM radio station call letters*]
WDAQ .... Danbury, CT [*FM radio station call letters*]
WDar .... Darien Public Library, Darien, WI [*Library symbol*] [*Library of
                   Congress*]   (LCLS)
WDAR .... Darlington, SC [*AM radio station call letters*]
WDAR-FM ... Darlington, SC [*FM radio station call letters*]
WDAS .... Philadelphia, PA [*AM radio station call letters*]
WDAS-FM ... Philadelphia, PA [*FM radio station call letters*]
WDAV .... Davidson, NC [*FM radio station call letters*]
WDAX .... McRae, GA [*AM radio station call letters*]
WDAX-FM ... McRae, GA [*FM radio station call letters*]
WDAY .... Fargo, ND [*AM radio station call letters*]
WDAY-FM ... Fargo, ND [*FM radio station call letters*]
WDAY-TV ... Fargo, ND [*Television station call letters*]
WDAZ-TV ... Devils Lake, ND [*Television station call letters*]
WDB .... Westminster Dictionary of the Bible [*A publication*]   (BJA)
WDB .... Wide Deadband [*NASA*]
WDB .... Wideband [*Radio*]   (MCD)
WDBA .... Du Bois, PA [*FM radio station call letters*]
WDBB .... Tuscaloosa, AL [*Television station call letters*]
WDBC .... Escanaba, MI [*AM radio station call letters*]
WDBD .... Jackson, MS [*Television station call letters*]
WDBF .... Delray Beach, FL [*AM radio station call letters*]
WDBI-FM ... Tawas City, MI [*FM radio station call letters*]
WDBJ .... Roanoke, VA [*Television station call letters*]
WDBK .... Blackwood, NJ [*FM radio station call letters*]
WDBK .... Wordbook   (ROG)
WDBL .... Springfield, TN [*AM radio station call letters*]
WDBL-FM ... Springfield, TN [*FM radio station call letters*]
WDBN .... Medina, OH [*FM radio station call letters*]
WDBN .... Woodbine Petroleum, Inc. [*NASDAQ symbol*]   (NQ)
WDBO .... Orlando, FL [*AM radio station call letters*]
WDBOR ...... Wood Boring
WDBQ .... Dubuque, IA [*AM radio station call letters*]
WDBR .... Springfield, IL [*FM radio station call letters*]
WDBS .... Eatonton, GA [*AM radio station call letters*]
WDBX .... Waterville, ME [*FM radio station call letters*]
WDBY .... Duxbury, MA [*FM radio station call letters*]
WDC .... War Damage Commission [*British*]
WDC .... War Damage Corporation [*World War II*]
WDC .... Washington Document Center
WDC .... Waste Disposal Cask [*Nuclear energy*]   (NRCH)
WDC .... Waste Disposal Code
WDC .... Water Data Center [*Department of Agriculture*] [*Beltsville, MD*]
                   [*Information service*]   (EISS)
WDC .... Weapon Delivery Computer   (MCD)
WDC .... Weapon Direction Computer [*Military*]   (CAAL)
WDC .... Western Defense Command [*Army*]
WDC .... Western Digital Corporation [*American Stock Exchange
                   symbol*]
WDC .... Westinghouse Defense Center
WDC .... Whiskeytown Dam [*California*] [*Seismograph station code, US
                   Geological Survey*]   (SEIS)
WDC .... Wideband Directional Coupler
WDC .... Women's Distance Committee [*Formerly, WODC*]   (EA)
WDC .... Workers' Defence Committee [*Ghanaian*]   (PPW)
WDC .... Workers' Defence Committee [*Poland*]   (PD)
WDC .... Working Direct Current   (DEN)
WDC .... World Data Center [*National Academy of Sciences*] [*Data
                   collection and exchange center*]
WDC .... World Development Corporation
WDC .... World Disarmament Conference   (NATG)
WDC .... World Druze Congress   (EA)
WDC .... Write Data Check   (CMD)
WDC-A .... World Data Center A [*National Academy of Sciences*]
WDCA .... World Diving Coaches Association   (EA)

WDCA-TV ... Washington, DC [*Television station call letters*]
WDCB .... Glen Ellyn, IL [*FM radio station call letters*]
WDC-B .... World Data Center B [*National Academy of Sciences*]
WDCC .... Sanford, NC [*FM radio station call letters*]
WDCE .... Richmond, VA [*FM radio station call letters*]
WDCF .... Dade City, FL [*AM radio station call letters*]
WDCG .... Durham, NC [*FM radio station call letters*]
WDCJ .... Lorton, VA [*FM radio station call letters*]
WDCL .... Western Digital Corporation [*NASDAQ symbol*]   (NQ)
WDCL-FM ... Somerset, KY [*FM radio station call letters*]
WDCMC ..... War Department Classified Message Center [*Obsolete*] [*World
                   War II*]
WDCN .... Nashville, TN [*Television station call letters*]
WDCO .... Western Energy Development Company, Inc. [*NASDAQ
                   symbol*]   (NQ)
WDCO-FM ... Cochran, GA [*FM radio station call letters*]
WDCO-TV ... Cochran, GA [*Television station call letters*]
WDCQ .... Pine Island Centre, FL [*AM radio station call letters*]
WDCR .... Hanover, NH [*AM radio station call letters*]
WDCS .... Scarborough, ME [*FM radio station call letters*]
WDCS .... Weapons Data Correlation System   (MCD)
WDCS .... Women's Division of Christian Service [*of the Board of
                   Missions, The Methodist Church*]
WDCS .... Writable Diagnostic Control Store
WDCSA .... War Department Chief of Staff, US Army [*World War II*]
WDCSM ..... Walt Disney Comic Strip Maker [*Apple computer software*]
WDCT .... Fairfax, VA [*AM radio station call letters*]
WDCT .... Woodcut   (ROG)
WDCU .... Washington, DC [*FM radio station call letters*]
WDCV-FM ... Carlisle, PA [*FM radio station call letters*]
WDCX .... Buffalo, NY [*FM radio station call letters*]
WDD .... Western Development Division [*ARDC*]
WD (2d) ..... Washington Decisions, Second Series   (DLA)
WDDC .... Portage, WI [*FM radio station call letters*]
WDDC .... Well Deck Debarkation Control [*Navy*]   (CAAL)
WDDD .... Marion, IL [*AM radio station call letters*]
WDDD-FM ... Marion, IL [*FM radio station call letters*]
WDDJ .... Paducah, KY [*FM radio station call letters*]
WDDO .... Macon, GA [*AM radio station call letters*]
WDDQ .... Adel, GA [*FM radio station call letters*]
WDDT .... Greenville, MS [*AM radio station call letters*]
WDDY .... Gloucester, VA [*AM radio station call letters*]
WDE .... Weapons Directing Equipment   (NVT)
wde .... Wood-Engraver [*MARC relator code*] [*Library of Congress*]
WDEA .... Ellsworth, ME [*AM radio station call letters*]
WDEB .... Jamestown, TN [*AM radio station call letters*]
WDEB-FM ... Jamestown, TN [*FM radio station call letters*]
WDEC .... Americus, GA [*AM radio station call letters*]
WDEE .... Reed City, MI [*AM radio station call letters*]
WDEF .... Chattanooga, TN [*AM radio station call letters*]
WDEF-FM ... Chattanooga, TN [*FM radio station call letters*]
WDEF-TV ... Chattanooga, TN [*Television station call letters*]
WDEH .... Sweetwater, TN [*AM radio station call letters*]
WDEH-FM ... Sweetwater, TN [*FM radio station call letters*]
WDEK .... De Kalb, IL [*FM radio station call letters*]
WDEL .... Weapons Development Effectiveness Laboratory   (MCD)
WDEL .... Wilmington, DE [*AM radio station call letters*]
WDEM .... Hollywood, FL [*Television station call letters*]
WDEMCO... Walt Disney Educational Media Company
WDEN .... Macon, GA [*AM radio station call letters*]
WDEN-FM ... Macon, GA [*FM radio station call letters*]
WDEPY .... Western Deep Levels ADR [*NASDAQ symbol*]   (NQ)
WDEQ-FM ... De Graff, OH [*FM radio station call letters*]
WDER .... Derry, NH [*AM radio station call letters*]
WDET-FM ... Detroit, MI [*FM radio station call letters*]
WDEV .... Waterbury, VT [*AM radio station call letters*]
WDEX .... Monroe, NC [*AM radio station call letters*]
WDEY .... Lapeer, MI [*AM radio station call letters*]
WDEY-FM ... Lapeer, MI [*FM radio station call letters*]
WDEZ .... Wausau, WI [*FM radio station call letters*]
WDF .... Wall Distribution Frame   (MUGU)
WDF .... Weapon Defense Facility   (AAG)
WDF .... Weather Data Facility
WDF .... Western Desert Force [*World War II*]
WDF .... Wood Door and Frame [*Technical drawings*]
WDF .... Woodruff
WDF .... World Darts Federation   (EA-IO)
WDF .... World Draughts (Checkers) Federation [*See also FMJD*]   (EA-
                   IO)
WDFB .... Junction City, KY [*AM radio station call letters*]
WDFC .... WD-40 Company [*NASDAQ symbol*]   (NQ)
WD/FE .... Water Dispenser/Fire Extinguisher [*Apollo*] [*NASA*]
WDFL .... Cross City, FL [*AM radio station call letters*]
WDFM .... Defiance, OH [*FM radio station call letters*]
WDFP .... World Day for Peace [*Loomis, CA*]   (EA)
WDG .... Enid [*Oklahoma*] [*Airport symbol*]   (OAG)
WDG .... Enid, OK [*Location identifier*] [*FAA*]   (FAAL)
WDG .... Wallace Dam [*Georgia*] [*Seismograph station code, US
                   Geological Survey*]   (SEIS)
WDG .... Weapons Display Generator   (MCD)

WDG.......... Wedgestone Realty Investors Trust [*American Stock Exchange symbol*]
WDG.......... Winding (MSA)
WDG.......... World Diplomatic Guide [*A publication*]
WDGB .... Wuerzburger Diozesangeschichtsblaetter [*A publication*]
WDGC-FM ... Downers Grove, IL [*FM radio station call letters*]
WDGE .... Saranac Lake, NY [*FM radio station call letters*]
WDGF .... War Department Ground Forces [*Obsolete*]
WDGH .... Panama City, FL [*Television station call letters*]
WDGI........ Wholesale Dry Goods Institute [*Later, NATAD*]
WDGO .... War Department General Order [*Obsolete*]
WDGR .... Dahlonega, GA [*AM radio station call letters*]
WDGS .... New Albany, IN [*AM radio station call letters*]
WDGS .... War Department General Staff [*Obsolete*]
WDGY .... Minneapolis, MN [*AM radio station call letters*]
WDH .... Watery Diarrhea, Hypokalemia [*Syndrome*] [*Medicine*]
WDH .... Winchell's Donut House [*NYSE symbol*]
WDH .... Windhoek [*Namibia*] [*Airport symbol*] (OAG)
WDHA .... Watery Diarrhea, Hypokalemia, Achlorhydria [*Medicine*]
WDHA-FM ... Dover, NJ [*FM radio station call letters*]
WDHCB....... War Department Hardship Claims Board [*Obsolete*]
WDHD .... Woodhead [*Daniel*], Inc. [*NASDAQ symbol*] (NQ)
WDHH .... Watery Diarrhea, Hypokalemia, Hypochlorhydria [*Syndrome*] [*Medicine*]
WDHHA...... Watery Diarrhea, Hypochlorhydria, Hypokalemia, and Alkalosis [*Medicine*]
WDHN-TV ... Dothan, AL [*Television station call letters*]
WDHP........ Presque Isle, ME [*FM radio station call letters*]
WDHR........ Pikeville, KY [*FM radio station call letters*]
WDHS .... Gaston, IN [*FM radio station call letters*]
WDHS........ Worldwide Dental Health Service [*Seattle, WA*] (EA)
WDI .... War Department Intelligence [*Obsolete*]
WDI .... Warfarin Dose Index
WDI .... Warhead Detection Indicator (AAG)
WDI .... Weapon Data Index [*Navy*] (MCD)
WDI .... Weapon Delivery Impairment (NVT)
WDI .... Web Depth Index
WDI .... Wind Direction Indicator [*Aviation*] (FAAC)
WDI .... Wood and Iron [*Freight*]
WDIA .... Memphis, TN [*AM radio station call letters*]
WDIC .... Clinchco, VA [*AM radio station call letters*]
WDICC .... War Department Intelligence Collection Committee
WDICPC..... War Department Intelligence Collection Planning Committee
WDIF .... Marion, OH [*FM radio station call letters*]
WDIF .... Women's Democratic International Federation (NATG)
W Dig .... New York Weekly Digest (DLA)
WDIO-TV.... Duluth, MN [*Television station call letters*]
WDIQ .... Dozier, AL [*Television station call letters*]
WDIR .... Wind Direction
WDIV .... Detroit, MI [*Television station call letters*]
WDIX .... Orangeburg, SC [*AM radio station call letters*]
WDIZ .... Orlando, FL [*FM radio station call letters*]
WdJ .... Wissenschaft des Judentums [*A publication*] (BJA)
WDJB .... Windsor, NC [*FM radio station call letters*]
WDJC .... Birmingham, AL [*FM radio station call letters*]
WDJM-FM ... Framingham, MA [*FM radio station call letters*]
WDJO .... Cincinnati, OH [*AM radio station call letters*]
WDJQ .... Alliance, OH [*FM radio station call letters*]
WDJS .... Mount Olive, NC [*AM radio station call letters*]
WDJT-TV .... Milwaukee, WI [*Television station call letters*]
WDJW .... Somers, CT [*FM radio station call letters*]
WDJX .... Louisville, KY [*AM radio station call letters*]
WDJY .... Washington, DC [*FM radio station call letters*]
WDJZ .... Bridgeport, CT [*AM radio station call letters*]
WDKC .... Dunn, NC [*FM radio station call letters*]
WDKD .... Kingstree, SC [*AM radio station call letters*]
WDKM-TV ... Vicksburg, MS [*Television station call letters*]
WDKN .... Dickson, TN [*AM radio station call letters*]
WDKN-FM ... Dickson, TN [*FM radio station call letters*]
WDKT........ Madison, AL [*AM radio station call letters*]
WDKX........ Rochester, NY [*FM radio station call letters*]
WD KY....... United States District Court for the Western District of Kentucky (DLA)
WDKY-TV .. Danville, KY [*Television station call letters*]
WDL .... Warren Library Association and County Division, Warren, PA [*OCLC symbol*] (OCLC)
WDL .... Waveguide Directional Localizer
WDL .... Weapon Data Link (MCD)
WDL .... Weapons Density List (AABC)
WDL .... Well-Differentiated Lymphocytic [*Lymphoma classification*]
WDL .... Westdeutsche Luftwerbung [*Airline*] [*West Germany*]
WDL .... Western Development Laboratories
WDL .... Wien Displacement Law [*Physics*]
WDL .... Wireless Data Link
Wdl .... Wirkung der Literatur [*A publication*]
WDL .... Workers' Defense League (EA)
WD LA .... United States District Court for the Western District of Louisiana (DLA)
WDLA........ Walton, NY [*AM radio station call letters*]
WDLA-FM ... Walton, NY [*FM radio station call letters*]
WDLB......... Marshfield, WI [*AM radio station call letters*]

WDLC........ Port Jervis, NY [*AM radio station call letters*]
WDLI .... Canton, OH [*Television station call letters*]
WDLK .... Dadeville, AL [*AM radio station call letters*]
WDLL .... Well Differentiated Lymphatic Lymphoma [*Oncology*]
WDLL .... Well-Differentiated Lymphocytic Lymphoma
WDLM .... East Moline, IL [*AM radio station call letters*]
WDLP .... Panama City, FL [*AM radio station call letters*]
WDLR .... Delaware, OH [*AM radio station call letters*]
WDLT .... Chickasaw, AL [*FM radio station call letters*]
WDLV .... Pinehurst, NC [*AM radio station call letters*]
WDLW .... Waltham, MA [*AM radio station call letters*]
WDLX .... Washington, NC [*FM radio station call letters*]
WDLY........ Widely (FAAC)
WDM .... Wavelength Division Multiplex
WDM .... Weight after Departure from Mars [*NASA*]
WDMA....... Wholesale Druggists Merchandising Association (EA)
WDMB....... War Department Manpower Board [*Obsolete*]
WDME .... Dover-Foxcroft, ME [*AM radio station call letters*]
WDME-FM... Dover-Foxcroft, ME [*FM radio station call letters*]
WDMET..... Wound Data Munitions Effectiveness Team (MCD)
WDMF .... Weak Disordered Magnetic Field
WDMG....... Douglas, GA [*AM radio station call letters*]
WDMG-FM... Douglas, GA [*FM radio station call letters*]
WD Mich .... United States District Court for the Western District of Michigan (DLA)
WDMJ........ Marquette, MI [*AM radio station call letters*]
WDML .... Wiring Diagram Maintenance List
WD MO...... United States District Court for the Western District of Missouri (DLA)
WDMO....... Weight before Departure from Mars Orbit [*NASA*]
WDMP .... Dodgeville, WI [*AM radio station call letters*]
WDMP-FM ... Dodgeville, WI [*FM radio station call letters*]
WDMS........ Greenville, MS [*FM radio station call letters*]
WDMT........ Cleveland, OH [*FM radio station call letters*]
WDMV........ Pocomoke City, MD [*AM radio station call letters*]
WDN.......... Wooden
WDNA .... Miami, FL [*FM radio station call letters*]
WDNC .... Durham, NC [*AM radio station call letters*]
WDNC .... United States District Court for the Western District of North Carolina (DLA)
WDND .... Wilmington, IL [*FM radio station call letters*]
WDNE........ Elkins, WV [*AM radio station call letters*]
WDNG .... Anniston, AL [*AM radio station call letters*]
WDNH .... Honesdale, PA [*AM radio station call letters*]
WDNH-FM ... Honesdale, PA [*FM radio station call letters*]
WDNL........ Danville, IL [*FM radio station call letters*]
WDNOWRE ... Wooden Ware [*Freight*]
WDNR .... Chester, PA [*FM radio station call letters*]
WDNS .... Bowling Green, KY [*FM radio station call letters*]
WDNT........ Dayton, TN [*AM radio station call letters*]
WDNX .... Olive Hill, TN [*FM radio station call letters*]
WDNY........ Dansville, NY [*AM radio station call letters*]
WDNY........ United States District Court for the Western District of New York (DLA)
WDO.......... Web Depth Order
WdO .... Welt des Orients. Wissenschaftliche Beitraege zur Kunde des Morgenlandes [*Wuppertal/Stuttgart/Goettingen*] [*A publication*]
WDO.......... Widespread Depression Orchestra
WDO.......... Window (MSA)
WDOC .... Prestonsburg, KY [*AM radio station call letters*]
WDOD .... Chattanooga, TN [*AM radio station call letters*]
WDOD-FM ... Chattanooga, TN [*FM radio station call letters*]
WDOE .... Dunkirk, NY [*AM radio station call letters*]
WDOG .... Allendale, SC [*AM radio station call letters*]
WDOH .... Delphos, OH [*FM radio station call letters*]
WDOK .... Cleveland, OH [*FM radio station call letters*]
WD Okla..... United States District Court for the Western District of Oklahoma (DLA)
WDOM........ Providence, RI [*FM radio station call letters*]
WDOPD...... War Department, Operations Division, General Staff [*World War II*]
WDOR .... Sturgeon Bay, WI [*AM radio station call letters*]
WDOR-FM ... Sturgeon Bay, WI [*FM radio station call letters*]
WDOS .... Oneonta, NY [*AM radio station call letters*]
WDOS .... Wooton Desk Owners Society (EA)
WDOT........ Burlington, VT [*AM radio station call letters*]
WDOV........ Dover, DE [*AM radio station call letters*]
WDOW .... Dowagiac, MI [*AM radio station call letters*]
WDOW-FM ... Dowagiac, MI [*FM radio station call letters*]
WDOY-FM ... Fajardo, PR [*FM radio station call letters*]
WDP .... Weapons Direction Program
WDP .... Wenner Difference Potentiometer
WDP .... Women in Data Processing [*San Diego, CA*] (EA)
WDP .... Wood Panel (AAG)
WDP .... Work Distribution Policy (AAG)
WD PA....... United States District Court for the Western District of Pennsylvania (DLA)
WDPA........ Wisconsin Dairy Products Association (EA)
WDPB........ Seaford, DE [*Television station call letters*]

WDPC......... Western Data Processing Center [*University of California, Los Angeles*]

WDPMG-ID ... War Department Provost Marshal General, Investigation Division [*Obsolete*]

WDPR......... Dayton, OH [*FM radio station call letters*]

WDPS......... Dayton, OH [*FM radio station call letters*]

WDQN........ Du Quoin, IL [*AM radio station call letters*]

WDQN-FM ... Du Quoin, IL [*FM radio station call letters*]

WDR .... Wardair International Ltd. [*Toronto Stock Exchange symbol*] [*Vancouver Stock Exchange symbol*]

WDR .... Westdeutscher Rundfunk [*Radio network*] [*West Germany*]

WDR .... Wide Dynamic Range

WDR .... Winder, GA [*Location identifier*] [*FAA*]   (FAAL)

WDR .... Withdrawal

WDR .... Women's Drug Research Project [*of the National Institute on Drug Abuse*] [*University of Michigan*] [*Ann Arbor, MI*]   (EA)

WDR .... Write Drum

WDRB-TV... Louisville, KY [*Television station call letters*]

WDRC .... Hartford, CT [*AM radio station call letters*]

WDRC .... Women's Defence Relief Corps [*British*] [*World War I*]

WDRC-FM ... Hartford, CT [*FM radio station call letters*]

WDRF........ Des Moines, IA [*FM radio station call letters*]

WDRG .... Women's Direct Response Group [*New York, NY*]   (EA)

WDRK........ Greenville, OH [*FM radio station call letters*]

WDRKA ..... Waseda Daigaku Rikogaku Kenkyusho Hokoku [*A publication*]

WDRM-FM ... Decatur, AL [*FM radio station call letters*]

WDROP ...... Water Distribution Register of Organic Pollutants [*National Institutes of Health*]

WDRSA ...... Wood Research [*A publication*]

WDRV........ Statesville, NC [*AM radio station call letters*]

WDRW....... Eldorado, IL [*FM radio station call letters*]

WDS .... Four Winds Aviation Ltd. [*Colorado Springs, CO*] [*FAA designator*]   (FAAC)

WDS .... Washington Document Service [*Washington, DC*] [*Information service*]   (EISS)

WD(S) .... Waste Disposal (System) [*Nuclear energy*]   (NRCH)

WDS .... Wavelength Dispersive Spectrometer

WDS .... Weapon Delivery System

WDS .... Weapons Directing System [*Navy*]

WDS .... Wire Data Service

WDS .... Wood Dye Stain

WDS .... Woodside [*California*] [*Seismograph station code, US Geological Survey*]   (SEIS)

WDS .... Woodward's Ltd. [*Toronto Stock Exchange symbol*] [*Vancouver Stock Exchange symbol*]

WDS .... Word Discrimination Score

WDS .... Wounds

WDSC .... Dillon, SC [*AM radio station call letters*]

WDSD .... Dover, DE [*FM radio station call letters*]

WDSD .... Water Data Sources Directory [*Marine science*]   (MSC)

WDSD .... Wisconsin School for the Deaf, Delavan, WI [*Library symbol*] [*Library of Congress*]   (LCLS)

WDSE-TV... Duluth, MN [*Television station call letters*]

WDSG .... Dyersburg, TN [*AM radio station call letters*]

WDSI......... Worlco Data Systems [*NASDAQ symbol*]   (NQ)

WDSI-TV ... Chattanooga, TN [*Television station call letters*]

WDSL........ Mocksville, NC [*AM radio station call letters*]

WdSL .... Welt der Slaven [*A publication*]

WDSM....... Superior, WI [*AM radio station call letters*]

WDSO .... Chesterton, IN [*FM radio station call letters*]

WDSPR ..... Widespread

WDSPRD.... Widespread [*Meteorology*]   (FAAC)

WDSR........ Lake City, FL [*AM radio station call letters*]

WDSRF...... Windsor Resources [*NASDAQ symbol*]   (NQ)

WDSS .... War Department Special Staff [*Obsolete*]

WDS SATSIM ... Weapon Direction System Satellite Simulation [*Military*]   (CAAL)

WDST........ Woodstock, NY [*FM radio station call letters*]

WD STL .... Wood or Steel [*Freight*]

WD STV..... Wood Stove[*s*] [*Freight*]

WDSU-TV ... New Orleans, LA [*Television station call letters*]

WDSY........ Pittsburgh, PA [*FM radio station call letters*]

WDT .... Warmth Detection Threshold

WDT .... Watch Dog Timer

WDT .... Wear Durability Trial

WDT .... Wedtech Corp. [*American Stock Exchange symbol*]

WDT .... Weight Distribution Table

WDT .... Width

WDT .... Wiedemann Developed Template   (MCD)

WDT .... World Cement Industries [*Vancouver Stock Exchange symbol*]

WDTC........ Western Defense Tactical Command   (AAG)

WD Tenn ... United States District Court for the Western District of Tennessee   (DLA)

WD Tex .... United States District Court for the Western District of Texas   (DLA)

WDTF........ Wetting-Drying and Temperature Fluctuation [*Geochemistry*]

WDTM....... Selmer, TN [*AM radio station call letters*]

WDTN........ Dayton, OH [*Television station call letters*]

WDTR........ Detroit, MI [*FM radio station call letters*]

WDTV........ Weston, WV [*Television station call letters*]

WDTX........ Detroit, MI [*FM radio station call letters*]

WDu .... Durand Free Library, Durand, WI [*Library symbol*] [*Library of Congress*]   (LCLS)

WdU .... Wahlpartei der Unabhaengigen [*Electoral Party of Independents*] [*Austria*]   (PPE)

WDU.......... Water Data Unit

WDU.......... Weapons Director Unit   (MCD)

WDU.......... Window Deicing Unit

WDU.......... Wireless Development Unit

WDU.......... Workers' Defence Union [*British*]

WDUB........ Granville, OH [*FM radio station call letters*]

WDUF........ Duffield, VA [*AM radio station call letters*]

WDUK .... Havana, FM [*FM radio station call letters*]

WDUN .... Gainesville, GA [*AM radio station call letters*]

WDUQ .... Pittsburgh, PA [*FM radio station call letters*]

WDUR........ Durham, NC [*AM radio station call letters*]

WDUV........ Bradenton, FL [*FM radio station call letters*]

WDUX........ Waupaca, WI [*AM radio station call letters*]

WDUX-FM ... Waupaca, WI [*FM radio station call letters*]

WDUZ........ Green Bay, WI [*AM radio station call letters*]

WDUZ-FM ... Green Bay, WI [*FM radio station call letters*]

WDV .... War Department Vehicle [*Obsolete*]

WDV .... Western Diverging Volcanism [*Geology*]

WDV .... Winchester Diversified [*Vancouver Stock Exchange symbol*]

WDVA........ Danville, VA [*AM radio station call letters*]

WD VA....... United States District Court for the Western District of Virginia   (DLA)

WDVE........ Pittsburgh, PA [*FM radio station call letters*]

WDVR........ Ocean City, NJ [*FM radio station call letters*]

WDVT........ Philadelphia, PA [*AM radio station call letters*]

WDW .... Wholesale Dealer in Wines

WDW .... Window

WDW .... Wood and Wire [*Freight*]

WD Wash ... United States District Court for the Western District of Washington   (DLA)

WD Wis ..... United States District Court for the Western District of Wisconsin   (DLA)

WDWN....... Auburn, NY [*FM radio station call letters*]

WDWN....... Well Developed - Well Nourished [*Medicine*]

WDWRK .... Woodwork [*Freight*]

WDWS....... Champaign, IL [*AM radio station call letters*]

WDWS-FM ... Champaign, IL [*FM radio station call letters*]

WDX .... Wavelength Dispersive X-Ray [*Spectrometer*]

WDXB........ Chattanooga, TN [*AM radio station call letters*]

WDXC .... Pound, VA [*FM radio station call letters*]

WDXE........ Lawrenceburg, TN [*AM radio station call letters*]

WDXE-FM ... Lawrenceburg, TN [*FM radio station call letters*]

WDXI......... Jackson, TN [*AM radio station call letters*]

WDXL........ Lexington, TN [*AM radio station call letters*]

WDXN........ Clarksville, TN [*AM radio station call letters*]

WDXR........ Paducah, KY [*AM radio station call letters*]

WDXRF...... Wavelength-Dispersive X-Ray Fluorescence

WDXRS ..... Wavelength Dispersive X-Ray Spectrometry

WDXY........ Sumter, SC [*AM radio station call letters*]

WDXZ........ Mount Pleasant, SC [*FM radio station call letters*]

WDY .... Woody [*California*] [*Seismograph station code, US Geological Survey*] [*Closed*]   (SEIS)

WDY .... Wordy [*Used in correcting manuscripts, etc.*]

WDYL........ Chester, VA [*FM radio station call letters*]

WDYN-FM ... Chattanooga, TN [*FM radio station call letters*]

WDYT........ What Do You Think?

WDYTYCIWSS ... Why Don't You Take Your Change In War Savings Stamps [*Cashier's sign*] [*World War II*]

WDZ .... Decatur, IL [*AM radio station call letters*]

WDZ .... Werner Dahnz Co. [*Toronto Stock Exchange symbol*]

WDZD........ Shallotte, NC [*FM radio station call letters*]

WDZK........ Chester, SC [*AM radio station call letters*]

WDZL........ Miami, FL [*Television station call letters*]

WDZQ........ Decatur, IL [*FM radio station call letters*]

WDZZ-FM ... Flint, MI [*FM radio station call letters*]

WE............. Eau Claire Public Library, Eau Claire, WI [*Library symbol*] [*Library of Congress*]   (LCLS)

WE............. Staff Meteorologist [*AFSC*]

WE............. Wage Earner [*Social Security Administration*]   (OICC)

WE............. War Establishment

WE............. Watch Error [*Navigation*]

WE............. Watchman-Examiner [*A publication*]   (BJA)

WE............. Water Equivalent   (MCD)

We............. Watt Electric

WE............. Weapons Engineering [*Navy*] [*British*]

WE............. Weather Emergency

We .... Weber Number [*IUPAC*]

WE............. Wednesday

W/E........... Week Ending

WE............. Weekend   (ADA)

WE............. Wescap Enterprises Ltd. [*Vancouver Stock Exchange symbol*]

WE............. Western Electric Co.   (AAG)

We............. Western Tithe Cases [*England*]   (DLA)

We............. West's English Chancery Reports   (DLA)

We............. West's Reports, English House of Lords   (DLA)

WE............. White Edges   (ADA)

WE............. Whole Economy [*Department of Employment*] [*British*]
W/e .... Width-to-Length [*Ratio*]   (MDG)
WE............. Winesburg Eagle [*A publication*]
WE............. Wing Elevon   (MCD)
WE............. With Equipment   (AABC)
WEBELOS ... Withholding Exemptions [*Army*]   (AABC)
WE............. Women Educators
WE............. Women Employed [*Chicago, IL*]   (EA)
WE............. Women in Energy   (EA)
WE............. Women Entrepreneurs [*San Francisco, CA*]   (EA)
WE............. Women Exploited [*An association*] [*Wheaton, MD*]   (EA)
WE............. Women's Reserve, Engineering Duties [*USNR officer designation*]
WE............. Work Experience
WE............. World Education, Inc.
WE............. World Evangelism [*An association*]   (EA)
WE............. Write Enable   (IEEE)
W/E............ Writer/Editor   (MCD)
WEa............ East Troy Public Library, East Troy, WI [*Library symbol*] [*Library of Congress*]   (LCLS)
WEA .... Eastern Washington State College, Cheney, WA [*OCLC symbol*]   (OCLC)
WEA .... Royal West of England Academy
WEA .... Wall Effect Amplifier
WEA .... Warner-Eddison Associates, Inc. [*Information service*]   (EISS)
WEA .... Weak Equity Axiom
WEA .... Weather   (AABC)
WEA .... Weatherford, TX [*Location identifier*] [*FAA*]   (FAAL)
WEA .... Wilderness Education Association   (EA)
WEA .... Women Employed Advocates   (EA)
WEA .... Workers' Educational Association
WEAA........ Baltimore, MD [*FM radio station call letters*]
WEAAC..... Western European Airport Authorities Conference   (MCD)
WEAAP ..... Western European Association for Aviation Psychology   (EA)
WEAB........ Adamsville, TN [*AM radio station call letters*]
WEA Bul..... WEA [*Workers Educational Association*] Bulletin [*A publication*]
WEAC........ Gaffney, SC [*AM radio station call letters*]
WEAC........ Winchester Engineering and Analytical Center [*Food and Drug Administration*]
WEAG .... Indianapolis, IN [*FM radio station call letters*]
WEAL .... Greensboro, NC [*AM radio station call letters*]
WEAL .... Women's Equity Action League [*In association name, WEAL Fund*]   (EA)
WEAM .... Columbus, GA [*AM radio station call letters*]
WEA-N ...... Westinghouse Engineers Association National   (EA)
WEAO .... Akron, OH [*Television station call letters*]
WEAPD ..... Western Air Procurement District
WEAQ .... Eau Claire, WI [*AM radio station call letters*]
WEARCON ... Weather Observation and Forecasting Control System
WEARSCHFAC ... Naval Weather Research Facility
WEAR-TV... Pensacola, FL [*Television station call letters*]
WEASERVCOMM ... Weather Service Command [*Navy*]
WEAS-FM ... Savannah, GA [*FM radio station call letters*]
WEAT........ Weathertight
WEAT........ West Palm Beach, FL [*AM radio station call letters*]
WEAT-FM ... West Palm Beach, FL [*FM radio station call letters*]
Weather and Clim ... Weather and Climate [*A publication*]
Weather C & M ... Weather, Crops, and Markets [*A publication*]
Weather Dev Res Bull ... Weather Development and Research Bulletin [*Australia, Commonwealth Bureau of Meteorology*] [*A publication*]
Weather Research Bull ... Weather Research Bulletin [*A publication*]
WEAU-TV... Eau Claire, WI [*Television station call letters*]
WEAV........ Plattsburgh, NY [*AM radio station call letters*]
WEAW....... Evanston, IL [*AM radio station call letters*]
WEAX........ Angola, IN [*FM radio station call letters*]
WEAX........ En Route Weather Forecast [*Navy*]   (NVT)
WEAZ........ Philadelphia, PA [*FM radio station call letters*]
WEB .... Wagner Earth Bridge
WEB .... War Engineering Board
WEB .... Webbing   (AAG)
WEBA........ Women Exploited by Abortion [*Schoolcraft, MI*]   (EA)
WEBA-TV... Allendale, SC [*Television station call letters*]
WEBB........ Baltimore, MD [*AM radio station call letters*]
Webb......... Webb's Reports [*6-20 Kansas*]   (DLA)
Webb......... Webb's Reports [*11-20 Texas Civil Appeals*]   (DLA)
WEBB........ Writer's Electronic Bulletin Board [*Branson, MO*] [*Information service*]   (EISS)
Webb A'B & W ... Webb, A'Beckett, and Williams' Reports [*A publication*]
Webb A'B & W Eq ... Webb, A'Beckett, and Williams' Equity Reports [*A publication*]
Webb A'B & W Eq ... Webb, A'Beckett, and Williams' Victorian Equity Reports [*Australia*]   (DLA)
Webb A'B & W IE & M ... Webb, A'Beckett, and Williams' Insolvency, Ecclesiastical, and Matrimonial Reports [*A publication*]
Webb A'B & W IP & M ... Webb, A'Beckett, and Williams' Insolvency, Probate, and Matrimonial Reports [*A publication*]
Webb A'B & W Min ... Webb, A'Beckett, and Williams' Mining Cases [*A publication*]
Webb & D... Webb and Duval's Reports [*1-3 Texas*]   (DLA)

Webb & Duval ... Webb and Duval's Reports [*1-3 Texas*]   (DLA)
Webbia Racc Scr Bot ... Webbia; Raccolta di Scritti Botanici [*A publication*]
WEBC........ Duluth, MN [*AM radio station call letters*]
WEBE........ Western European Basic Encyclopedia   (MCD)
WEBE........ Westport, CT [*FM radio station call letters*]
WEBELOS ... We'll Be Loyal Scouts [*Boy Scout slogan*]
WEBF........ Olean, NY [*FM radio station call letters*]
WEBG........ Ebensburg, PA [*AM radio station call letters*]
WEBJ .... Brewton, AL [*AM radio station call letters*]
WEBN........ Cincinnati, OH [*FM radio station call letters*]
WEBO........ Owego, NY [*AM radio station call letters*]
Web Pat ..... Webster's New Patent Law [*4th ed.*] [*1854*]   (DLA)
Web Pat Cas ... Webster's Patent Cases [*1601-1855*]   (DLA)
Web PC ...... Webster's Patent Cases [*1601-1855*]   (DLA)
WEBQ........ Harrisburg, IL [*AM radio station call letters*]
WEBQ-FM ... Harrisburg, IL [*FM radio station call letters*]
WEBR........ Buffalo, NY [*AM radio station call letters*]
Web R........ Webster Review [*A publication*]
WEBROCK ... Weather Buoy Rocket
WEBS........ Calhoun, GA [*AM radio station call letters*]
WEBS......... Weapons Effectiveness Buoy System
Webs......... Webster's Patent Cases [*England*]   (DLA)
WEBSEC.... Western Beaufort Sea Ecological Cruise
Webs Pat Cas ... Webster's Patent Cases [*England*]   (DLA)
Webst Dict ... Webster's Dictionary   (DLA)
Webst Dict Unab ... Webster's Unabridged Dictionary   (DLA)
Webster Pat Cas ... Webster's Patent Cases [*1601-1855*]   (DLA)
Webster Pat Cas (Eng) ... Webster's Patent Cases [*England*]   (DLA)
Webster in Sen Doc ... Webster in Senate Documents   (DLA)
Webst Int Dict ... Webster's International Dictionary   (DLA)
Webst New Int D ... Webster's New International Dictionary   (DLA)
WEBT........ Langdale, AL [*FM radio station call letters*]
Web Tr ...... Trial of Professor Webster for Murder   (DLA)
WEBY........ Milton, FL [*AM radio station call letters*]
WEC .... District One Technical Institute, Eau Claire, Eau Claire, WI [*OCLC symbol*]   (OCLC)
WEC .... Eau Claire County Hospital, Eau Claire, WI [*Library symbol*] [*Library of Congress*]   (LCLS)
WEC .... Walking with Eyes Closed [*Equilibrium test*]
WEC .... Warhead Electrical Connector
WEC .... Water Export Control
WEC .... Weapon Engagement Console [*Military*]   (CAAL)
WEC .... Weapon Engagement Controller [*Military*]   (CAAL)
WEC .... Wescal Resources, Inc. [*Vancouver Stock Exchange symbol*]
WEC .... Westinghouse Electric Corporation
WEC .... Whole Earth Catalog [*A publication*]
WEC .... Wind Energy Conversion
WEC .... Wisconsin Energy Corporation [*NYSE symbol*]
WEC .... Women's Emergency Corps [*British*] [*World War I*]
WEC .... World Energy Conference [*See also CME*] [*London, England*]   (EA-IO)
WEC .... World Environment Center [*Formerly, CIEI*]   (EA)
WEC .... Worldwide Evangelization Crusade   (EA)
WECAF ...... Western Central Atlantic Fishery Commission
WECB .... Weapons Evaluation and Control Bureau [*USACDA*]
WECC .... St. Mary's, GA [*AM radio station call letters*]
WECC .... White English Celtic Catholic
WECEN ..... Weather Center [*Air Force*]
WECI .... Richmond, IN [*FM radio station call letters*]
WECK .... Cheektowaga, NY [*AM radio station call letters*]
WECL .... Elkhorn City, KY [*FM radio station call letters*]
WECN .... Naranjito, PR [*Television station call letters*]
WECO .... Wartburg, TN [*AM radio station call letters*]
WECO .... Washington Energy [*NASDAQ symbol*]   (NQ)
WECO .... Western Electric Company   (MCD)
WECO .... Westinghouse Electric Corporation
WECOM ..... Weapons Command [*Later, Armaments Command*] [*Army*]
WECON ..... Weather Controlled Messages   (NVT)
W Econ J ... Western Economic Journal [*A publication*]
WECPNL.... Weighted Equivalent Continuous Perceived Noise Level
WECQ .... Geneva, NY [*FM radio station call letters*]
WECS........ Willimantic, CT [*FM radio station call letters*]
WECS......... Wind Energy Conversion System
WECST ...... Waste Evaporator Condensate Storage Tank [*Nuclear energy*]   (NRCH)
WECT........ Wilmington, NC [*Television station call letters*]
WECV........ Chippewa Valley Museum, Eau Claire, WI [*Library symbol*] [*Library of Congress*]   (LCLS)
WECW........ Elmira, NY [*FM radio station call letters*]
WED .... Walter Elias Disney [*These initials also identify the theme park division of Walt Disney Enterprises*]
WED .... War Emergency Dose   (DEN)
WED .... Weapons Engineering Duty [*Navy*]   (NG)
WED .... Wedau [*Papua New Guinea*] [*Airport symbol*]   (OAG)
WED .... Wedco Technology, Inc. [*American Stock Exchange symbol*]
WED .... Wednesday
WED .... West Delta Resources Ltd. [*Vancouver Stock Exchange symbol*]
WED .... Work Force Effectiveness and Development Group [*Office of Personnel Management*]
WEDA........ Grove City, PA [*FM radio station call letters*]

WEDA......... Western Dredging Association [*Arlington, VA*]   (EA)
WEDAC...... Westinghouse Digital Airborne Computer
WEDC....... Chicago, IL [*AM radio station call letters*]
WEDCOM... Weapon Effects on D-Region Communications [*Computer code*]
WEDE........ Western Development Corp. [*NASDAQ symbol*]   (NQ)
WEDGE..... Waterless Electrical Data Generating Effortless
WEDGE..... Weapon Development Glide Entry
WEDGE..... Western Education Group [*Canada*]
WEDGS..... Wedgestone Realty Investors Trust [*NASDAQ symbol*]   (NQ)
Wedgw Dict Eng Etymology ... Wedgwood's Dictionary of English Etymology   (DLA)
WEDH........ Hartford, CT [*Television station call letters*]
WEDM........ Indianapolis, IN [*FM radio station call letters*]
WEDN........ Norwich, CT [*Television station call letters*]
WEDO .... McKeesport, PA [*AM radio station call letters*]
WEDR........ Miami, FL [*FM radio station call letters*]
WEDS........ Weapons Effect Display System [*AEC*]
WEDT........ Wedtech Corp. [*NASDAQ symbol*]   (NQ)
WEDU........ Tampa, FL [*Television station call letters*]
WEDW........ Bridgeport, CT [*Television station call letters*]
WEDW-FM ... Stamford, CT [*FM radio station call letters*]
WEDY........ New Haven, CT [*Television station call letters*]
WEE .... Western Equine Encephalomyelitis [*Virus*]
WEEA........ Women's Educational Equity Act [*1974*]
WEEB........ Southern Pines, NC [*AM radio station call letters*]
WEEC........ Springfield, OH [*FM radio station call letters*]
WEECN ..... Women's Educational Equity Communications Network [*Defunct*]
WEED........ Rocky Mount, NC [*AM radio station call letters*]
Weed Abstr ... Weed Abstracts [*A publication*]
Weed Res... Weed Research [*A publication*]
Weed Sci.... Weed Science [*A publication*]
WEEE........ Cherry Hill, NJ [*FM radio station call letters*]
WEEF........ Highland Park, IL [*AM radio station call letters*]
WEEF........ Western Electric Educational Fund
WEEI .... Boston, MA [*AM radio station call letters*]
WEEJ......... Port Charlotte, FL [*FM radio station call letters*]
Week Cin LB ... Weekly Cincinnati Law Bulletin   (DLA)
Week Dig ... New York Weekly Digest [*1876-88*]   (DLA)
Week Dig (NY) ... New York Weekly Digest [*1876-88*]   (DLA)
Week-End R ... Australian Week-End Review of Current Books, the Arts, and Entertainments [*A publication*]
Week Jur.... Weekly Jurist [*Bloomington, IL*]   (DLA)
Week Law & Bk Bull ... Weekly Law and Bank Bulletin   (DLA)
Week Law Bull ... Weekly Law Bulletin and Ohio Law Journal   (DLA)
Week Law Gaz ... Weekly Law Gazette [*Ohio*]   (DLA)
Week L Gaz ... Weekly Law Gazette   (DLA)
Week L Mag ... Weekly Law Magazine [*1842-43*]   (DLA)
Week LR..... Weekly Law Reports   (DLA)
Week L Rec ... Weekly Law Record   (DLA)
Week L Record ... Weekly Law Record   (DLA)
Week LR (Eng) ... Weekly Law Reports (England)   (DLA)
Week L Rev ... Weekly Law Review [*San Francisco*]   (DLA)
Weekly Cin Law Bull ... Cincinnati Weekly Law Bulletin   (DLA)
Weekly Compilation Presidential Docum ... Weekly Compilation of Presidential Documents [*A publication*]
Weekly Comp of Pres Doc ... Weekly Compilation of Presidential Documents [*A publication*]
Weekly Law B ... Weekly Law Bulletin [*Ohio*]   (DLA)
Weekly L Bull ... Weekly Law Bulletin [*England*]   (DLA)
Weekly LR ... Weekly Law Reports [*England*]   (DLA)
Weekly NC ... Weekly Notes of Cases [*Pennsylvania*]   (DLA)
Weekly N L ... Weekly News Letter. United States Department of Agriculture [*A publication*]
Weekly Underw ... Weekly Underwriter [*A publication*]
Week No .... New South Wales Weekly Notes [*A publication*]
Week No .... Weekly Notes of Cases [*1874-99*] [*Pennsylvania*]   (DLA)
Week No .... Weekly Notes of Cases (Law Reports) [*England*]   (DLA)
Week No Cas ... Weekly Notes of Cases [*1874-99*] [*Pennsylvania*]   (DLA)
Week No Cas ... Weekly Notes of Cases (Law Reports) [*England*]   (DLA)
Week R ... Weekly Reporter [*1853-1906*]   (DLA)
Week R (Eng) ... Weekly Reporter (England)   (DLA)
Week Rep... Weekly Reporter [*England*]   (DLA)
Week Reptr ... Weekly Reporter [*London*]   (DLA)
Week Reptr ... Weekly Reporter [*Bengal*]   (DLA)
Week Trans Rep ... Weekly Transcript Reports [*New York*]   (DLA)
Week Trans Repts ... Weekly Transcript Reports [*New York*]   (DLA)
WEEK-TV ... Peoria, IL [*Television station call letters*]
WEEM .... Pendleton, IN [*FM radio station call letters*]
WEEN .... Lafayette, TN [*AM radio station call letters*]
WEEP........ Pittsburgh, PA [*AM radio station call letters*]
WEEP........ Women's Educational Equity Program
Weer........... Weerakoon's Appeal Court Reports [*Ceylon*]   (DLA)
WEER........ Welfare Entered Employment Rate [*Job Training and Partnership Act*]   (OICC)
WEEU........ Reading, PA [*AM radio station call letters*]
WEEX........ Easton, PA [*AM radio station call letters*]
WEEZ........ Heidelburg, MS [*FM radio station call letters*]
WEF........... WAND [*Women's Action for Nuclear Disarmament*] Education Fund [*Arlington, MA*]   (EA)

WEF........... War Emergency Formula
WEF........... With Effect From
WEF........... World Education Fellowship   (EA)
WEF........... World Evangelical Fellowship   (EA)
WEFAX...... Weather Facsimile Experiment [*Environmental Science Services Administration*]
WEFC........ Roanoke, VA [*Television station call letters*]
WEFM .... Michigan City, IN [*FM radio station call letters*]
WEFT .... Champaign, IL [*FM radio station call letters*]
WEFT .... Wings, Engines, Fuselage, Tail [*System for identifying aircraft*]
WEG .... Wind Energy Generator
WEGA .... Vega Baja, PR [*AM radio station call letters*]
WEGG .... Rose Hill, NC [*AM radio station call letters*]
WEGL .... Auburn, AL [*FM radio station call letters*]
WEGN .... Evergreen, AL [*AM radio station call letters*]
WEGN-FM ... Evergreen, AL [*FM radio station call letters*]
WEGO .... Concord, NC [*AM radio station call letters*]
WEGP........ Presque Isle, ME [*AM radio station call letters*]
WEGR........ Memphis, TN [*FM radio station call letters*]
WEGS........ Milton, FL [*FM radio station call letters*]
WE-H .... Weapons Employment Handbook [*DASA*]   (MCD)
WEHB........ Grand Rapids, MI [*FM radio station call letters*]
WEHH........ Elmira Heights-Horseheads, NY [*AM radio station call letters*]
Wehrmed Monatsschr ... Wehrmedizinische Monatsschrift [*A publication*]
Wehrtech ... Wehrtechnik [*A publication*]
WEHSA ..... Work-Environment-Health [*A publication*]
WEHT-TV ... Evansville, IN [*Television station call letters*]
WEI........... Immanuel Lutheran College, Eau Claire, WI [*Library symbol*] [*Library of Congress*]   (LCLS)
WEI........... Weapon Effectiveness Index   (MCD)
WEI........... Weipa [*Australia*] [*Airport symbol*]   (OAG)
WEI........... Western European Institute for Wood Preservation [*Brussels, Belgium*]   (EA-IO)
WEI........... Wherehouse Entertainment, Incorporated [*American Stock Exchange symbol*]
WEI........... Women Employed Institute [*A division of Women Employed*] [*Chicago, IL*]   (EA)
WEI........... Wood Energy Institute [*Later, WHA*]   (EA)
WEI........... Work Experience Instructor   (OICC)
WEI........... World Education, Incorporated   (EA)
WEI........... World Environment Institute
Weibulls Arsbok ... Weibulls Arsbok [*A publication*]
WEIC .... Charleston, IL [*AM radio station call letters*]
WEIC-FM ... Charleston, IL [*FM radio station call letters*]
WEIF.......... Moundsville, WV [*AM radio station call letters*]
Weight Med Leg Gaz ... Weightman's Medico-Legal Gazette   (DLA)
Weight M & L ... Weightman's Marriage and Legitimacy [*1871*]   (DLA)
WEI/IEO ..... Western European Institute for Wood Preservation/Institut de l'Europe Occidentale pour l'Impregnation du Bois [*Brussels, Belgium*]   (EA-IO)
WEIM.......... Fitchburg, MA [*AM radio station call letters*]
Weinbau Kellerwirtsch (Budapest) ... Weinbau und Kellerwirtschaft (Budapest) [*A publication*]
Wein-Wiss ... Wein-Wissenschaft [*A publication*]
WEIQ .... Mobile, AL [*Television station call letters*]
Weir........... Weir's Criminal Rulings [*India*]   (DLA)
WEIR .... Weirton, WV [*AM radio station call letters*]
WEIS .... Centre, AL [*AM radio station call letters*]
WEIS .... Weisfields, Inc. [*NASDAQ symbol*]   (NQ)
Weiterbildungszentrum Math Kybernet Rechentech ... Weiterbildungszentrum fuer Mathematische Kybernetik und Rechentechnik [*A publication*]
WEIU .... Charleston, IL [*FM radio station call letters*]
WEIU .... Women's Educational and Industrial Union [*An association*] [*Boston, MA*]   (EA)
WEIU-TV .... Charleston, IL [*Television station call letters*]
WEI/WUV... Weapons Effectiveness Indices/Weighted Unit Values
Weizmann Mem Lect ... Weizmann Memorial Lectures [*A publication*]
WEJ .... Western Economic Journal [*A publication*]
WEJL.......... Scranton, PA [*AM radio station call letters*]
WEJY .... Monroe, MI [*FM radio station call letters*]
WEK .... Wewak [*Papua New Guinea*] [*Seismograph station code, US Geological Survey*]   (SEIS)
WEKC .... Williamsburg, KY [*AM radio station call letters*]
WEKG .... Jackson, KY [*AM radio station call letters*]
WEKH........ Hazard, KY [*FM radio station call letters*]
WEKO .... Cabo Rojo, PR [*AM radio station call letters*]
WEKR........ Fayetteville, TN [*AM radio station call letters*]
WEKS........ Marietta, GA [*AM radio station call letters*]
WEKS-FM ... LaGrange, GA [*FM radio station call letters*]
WEKT-TV ... Pikeville, KY [*Television station call letters*]
WEKU-FM ... Richmond, KY [*FM radio station call letters*]
WEKW-TV ... Keene, NH [*Television station call letters*]
WEKY........ Richmond, KY [*AM radio station call letters*]
WEKZ........ Monroe, WI [*AM radio station call letters*]
WEKZ-FM ... Monroe, WI [*FM radio station call letters*]
WEL........... Luther Hospital, Eau Claire, WI [*Library symbol*] [*Library of Congress*]   (LCLS)
WEI........... Matheson Memorial Library, Elkhorn, WI [*Library symbol*] [*Library of Congress*]   (LCLS)

WEL............ Warren Explorations Limited [*Toronto Stock Exchange symbol*]
WEL............ Weapons Effects Laboratory [*Army*] (RDA)
WEL............ Weapons/Equipment List
WEL............ Welfare
WEL............ Welkom [*South Africa*] [*Airport symbol*] (OAG)
WEL............ Wellesley College, Wellesley, MA [*OCLC symbol*] (OCLC)
WEL............ Wellesley Hospital, Toronto [*UTLAS symbol*]
WEL............ Wellington [*New Zealand*] [*Seismograph station code, US Geological Survey*] (SEIS)
wel............. Welsh [*MARC language code*] [*Library of Congress*] (LCCP)
Wel............ Welsh's Irish Registry Cases (DLA)
WEL............ Welt-Eis-Lehre [*Cosmic Ice Theory*] [*German*]
WELA......... East Liverpool, OH [*FM radio station call letters*]
WELB........ Elba, AL [*AM radio station call letters*]
WELB........ Welbilt Corp. [*NASDAQ symbol*] (NQ)
WELC........ Welch, WV [*AM radio station call letters*]
WEICL........ Walworth County Law Library, Elkhorn, WI [*Library symbol*] [*Library of Congress*] (LCLS)
WELD......... Fisher, WV [*AM radio station call letters*]
Weld Des Fabr ... Welding Design and Fabrication [*A publication*]
Weld Des and Fabr ... Welding Design and Fabrication [*A publication*]
Weld Eng ... Welding Engineer [*A publication*]
Weld Fabrication Design ... Welding Fabrication and Design [*A publication*]
Weld Fabric Design ... Welding Fabrication and Design [*A publication*]
Welding J... Welding Journal [*A publication*]
Weld Int..... Welding International [*United Kingdom*] [*A publication*]
Weld J (London) ... Welding Journal (London) [*A publication*]
Weld J (Miami) ... Welding Journal (Miami) [*A publication*]
Weld J (NY) ... Welding Journal (New York) [*A publication*]
Weld J Res Suppl ... Welding Journal Research. Supplement [*A publication*]
Weld Metal Fabr ... Welding and Metal Fabrication [*A publication*]
Weld Met Fabr ... Welding and Metal Fabrication [*A publication*]
Weld News ... Welding News [*A publication*]
Weld Prod ... Welding Production [*A publication*]
Weld Prod (USSR) ... Welding Production (USSR) [*A publication*]
Weld Res Abroad ... Welding Research Abroad [*A publication*]
Weld Res C ... Welding Research Council. Bulletin [*A publication*]
Weld Res Counc Bull ... Welding Research Council. Bulletin [*A publication*]
Weld Res Counc Prog Rep ... Welding Research Council. Progress Reports [*A publication*]
Weld Res Int ... Welding Research International [*A publication*]
Weld Res (Miami) ... Welding Research (Miami) [*A publication*]
Weld Res (Miami Fla) ... Welding Research (Miami, Florida) [*A publication*]
Weld Res News ... Welding Research News [*A publication*]
Weld Rev.... Welding Review [*A publication*]
Weld Tech ... Welding Technique [*Japan*] [*A publication*]
Weld Wld ... Welding in the World/Le Soudage dans le Monde [*A publication*]
Weld World ... Welding in the World [*A publication*]
Weld World Soudage Monde ... Welding in the World/Le Soudage dans le Monde [*A publication*]
WELE .... Ormond Beach, FL [*AM radio station call letters*]
Welfare L Bull ... Welfare Law Bulletin (DLA)
Welfare L News ... Welfare Law News (DLA)
Welf Eq ...... Welford's Equity Pleadings [*1842*] (DLA)
Welf Focus ... Welfare Focus [*A publication*]
WELI.......... New Haven, CT [*AM radio station call letters*]
WELK........ Elkins, WV [*FM radio station call letters*]
WELL......... Albion, MI [*AM radio station call letters*]
WEIL.......... Lakeland Hospital, Elkhorn, WI [*Library symbol*] [*Library of Congress*] (LCLS)
WEILC........ Lakeland Counseling Center, Elkhorn, WI [*Library symbol*] [*Library of Congress*] (LCLS)
WELL-FM... Marshall, MI [*FM radio station call letters*]
Well High ... Wellbeloved on Highways [*1829*] (DLA)
Well Inventory Ser (Metric Units) Inst Geol Sci ... Well Inventory Series (Metric Units). Institute of Geological Sciences [*A publication*]
Well Serv ... Well Servicing [*A publication*]
Wells Frgo ... Wells Fargo Bank. Business Review [*A publication*]
Wells Repl ... Wells on Replevin (DLA)
Wells' Res Ad ... Wells' Res Adjudicata and Stare Decisis (DLA)
Wellworthy Top ... Wellworthy Topics [*A publication*]
WELM........ Elmira, NY [*AM radio station call letters*]
WELO......... Tupelo, MS [*AM radio station call letters*]
WELP......... Easley, SC [*AM radio station call letters*]
WELQ........ Hertford, NC [*FM radio station call letters*]
WELR......... Roanoke, AL [*AM radio station call letters*]
WELR-FM... Roanoke, AL [*FM radio station call letters*]
WELS........ Kinston, NC [*AM radio station call letters*]
WELS .... Wisconsin Evangelical Lutheran Synod
WELS .... World-Wide Engineering Logistics Support [*Military*]
Welsb H & G ... Welsby, Hurlstone, and Gordon's English Exchequer Reports [*1848-56*] (DLA)
Welsb Hurl & G ... Welsby, Hurlstone, and Gordon's English Exchequer Reports [*1848-56*] (DLA)
Welsby H & G ... Welsby, Hurlstone, and Gordon's English Exchequer Reports [*1848-56*] (DLA)
Welsby H & G (Eng) ... Welsby, Hurlstone, and Gordon's English Exchequer Reports [*1848-56*] (DLA)

Welsh .... Welsh's Irish Case of James Feighny [*1838*] (DLA)
Welsh .... Welsh's Irish Case at Siligo [*1838*] (DLA)
Welsh .... Welsh's Irish Registry Cases (DLA)
Welsh Bee J ... Welsh Bee Journal [*A publication*]
Welsh Beekprs' Ass Q Bull ... Welsh Beekeepers' Association. Quarterly Bulletin [*A publication*]
Welsh Hist Rev ... Welsh History Review [*A publication*]
Welsh H R ... Welsh History Review [*A publication*]
Welsh J Agric ... Welsh Journal of Agriculture [*A publication*]
Welsh Plant Breed Stn (Aberystwyth) Rep ... Welsh Plant Breeding Station (Aberystwyth). Report [*A publication*]
Welsh Plant Breed Stn (Aberystwyth) Tech Bull ... Welsh Plant Breeding Station (Aberystwyth). Technical Bulletin [*A publication*]
Welsh Plant Breed Stn Bull Ser ... Welsh Plant Breeding Station. Bulletin Series [*A publication*]
Welsh Reg Cas ... Welsh's Irish Registry Cases (DLA)
Welt Isl .... Die Welt des Islam [*A publication*]
Weltraumfahrt Raketentech ... Weltraumfahrt und Raketentechnik [*A publication*]
Weltwir Arc ... Weltwirtschaftliches Archiv [*A publication*]
Weltwirt ...... Weltwirtschaft [*A publication*]
Weltwirtschaft Archiv ... Weltwirtschaftliches Archiv [*Kiel*] [*A publication*]
Weltwirtsch Archiv ... Weltwirtschaftliches Archiv [*A publication*]
WELU........ Aguadilla, PR [*Television station call letters*]
WELV........ Ellenville, NY [*AM radio station call letters*]
WELV-FM... Ellenville, NY [*FM radio station call letters*]
WELW........ Willoughby, OH [*AM radio station call letters*]
WELY........ Ely, MN [*AM radio station call letters*]
WELZ......... Belzoni, MS [*AM radio station call letters*]
WEM.......... Welfare of Enlisted Men [*Air Force*]
WEM.......... West Essex Militia [*British*]
WEM.......... Western European Metal Trades Employers Organization (EA)
WeM.......... Western Microfilm Ltd., Edmonton, AB, Canada [*Library symbol*] [*Library of Congress*] (LCLS)
WEM.......... Western Miner [*A publication*]
WEM.......... Wireless and Electrical Mechanic [*British*] (DSUE)
WEM.......... World's Epoch Makers [*A publication*]
WEM.......... Woven Elastic Manufacturers Association [*Later, EFMCNTA*] (MSA)
WEMA .... Western Electronic Manufacturers Association [*Later, AEA*] (EA)
WEMA .... Woven Elastic Manufacturers Association [*Later, EFMCNTA*] (EA)
WEMB....... Erwin, TN [*AM radio station call letters*]
WEMC....... Harrisonburg, VA [*FM radio station call letters*]
WEMD ...... Western Electronics Maintenance Depot
WEMI........ Neenah-Menasha, WI [*FM radio station call letters*]
WEMJ .... Laconia, NH [*AM radio station call letters*]
WEMK .... Ellisville, MS [*AM radio station call letters*]
WEMM....... Huntington, WV [*FM radio station call letters*]
WEMP .... Milwaukee, WI [*AM radio station call letters*]
WEMR .... Welding Equipment Maintenance and Repair [*UAW job classification*]
WEMSB..... Western European Military Supply Board [*NATO*] (NATG)
WEMU....... Ypsilanti, MI [*FM radio station call letters*]
WEN .... Waive Exchange If Necessary
Wen........... Wendell's Reports [*New York*] (DLA)
wen .... Wendic [*MARC language code*] [*Library of Congress*] (LCCP)
WEN .... Wendy's International, Inc. [*NYSE symbol*]
WEN .... Wentworth Institute of Technology, Boston, MA [*OCLC symbol*] (OCLC)
WEN .... Wentworth Public Library [*UTLAS symbol*]
WENA....... Penuelas, PR [*AM radio station call letters*]
WENC .... Whiteville, NC [*AM radio station call letters*]
WEND....... Brandon, FL [*AM radio station call letters*]
Wend......... Wendell's Reports [*1826-41*] [*New York*] (DLA)
Wend Bl .... Wendell's Blackstone (DLA)
Wendel...... Wendell's Reports [*New York*] (DLA)
Wendell...... Wendell's Reports [*1826-41*] [*New York*] (DLA)
Wendell Rep ... Wendell's Reports [*New York*] (DLA)
Wendell's Rep ... Wendell's Reports [*New York*] (DLA)
Wend (NY) ... Wendell's Reports [*1826-41*] [*New York*] (DLA)
Wend R ...... Wendell's Reports [*New York*] (DLA)
Wend Rep ... Wendell's Reports [*New York*] (DLA)
WENDS ...... World Energy Data System [*Department of Energy*] [*Information service*] (EISS)
Wendt .... Wendt's Reports of Cases [*Ceylon*] (DLA)
Wendt Mar Leg ... Wendt's Maritime Legislation [*3rd ed.*] [*1888*] (DLA)
WENE........ Endicott, NY [*AM radio station call letters*]
WENELA..... Witwatersrand Native Labour Association [*Nyasaland*]
WENG .... Englewood, FL [*AM radio station call letters*]
WENH-TV ... Durham, NH [*Television station call letters*]
WENK....... Union City, TN [*AM radio station call letters*]
WENMD ..... Water Engineering and Management [*A publication*]
Wenner-Gren Cent Int Symp Ser ... Wenner-Gren Center. International Symposium Series [*A publication*]
WENN-FM ... Birmingham, AL [*FM radio station call letters*]
WENO .... Chattahoochee, FL [*AM radio station call letters*]
WENOA...... Weekly Notice to Airmen [*FAA*]
WENR........ Englewood, TN [*AM radio station call letters*]
WENS......... Shelbyville, IN [*FM radio station call letters*]

WENS........ World Electroless Nickel Society [*Defunct*]   (EA)
WENT........ Gloversville, NY [*AM radio station call letters*]
WENT........ Wiener Enterprises [*NASDAQ symbol*]   (NQ)
W Ent .... Winch's Book of Entries   (DLA)
Wentworth Mag ... Wentworth Magazine [*A publication*]
WENU........ Hudson Falls, NY [*FM radio station call letters*]
WENY........ Elmira, NY [*AM radio station call letters*]
WENY-TV... Elmira, NY [*Television station call letters*]
WENZ........ Highland Springs, VA [*AM radio station call letters*]
Wenz......... Wenzell's Reports [*60 Minnesota*]   (DLA)
WEO .... War Economic Operation [*World War II*]
WEO .... Warehouse Economy Outlet [*A & P Co.*]
WEO .... Weaco Resources Ltd. [*Vancouver Stock Exchange symbol*]
WEO .... Western Europe and Others [*United Nations*]
WEO .... Where Economy Originates [*A & P Co. marketing slogan, now obsolete*]
WEO .... World Energy Outlook [*International Energy Agency*]
WEOG .... Western European and Others Group [*United Nations*]
WEOK .... Poughkeepsie, NY [*AM radio station call letters*]
WEOL .... Elyria, OH [*AM radio station call letters*]
WEOS........ Water Extraction of Orange Solids [*Citrus processing*]
WEOS-FM ... Geneva, NY [*FM radio station call letters*]
WEOZ........ Saegertown, PA [*FM radio station call letters*]
WEP .... Walker Energy Partners [*American Stock Exchange symbol*]
WEP .... War and Emergency Plan [*DoD*]
WEP .... Waseda Economic Papers [*A publication*]
WEP .... Water Electrolysis Plenum
WEP .... Water Entry Point [*Navy*]   (CAAL)
WEP .... Water-Extended Polyester
WEP .... Weak Equivalence Principle [*Gravity*]
WEP .... Weam [*Papua New Guinea*] [*Airport symbol*]   (OAG)
WEP .... Weapon
WEP .... Weather Processor   (MCD)
WEP .... Wisconsin Experiment Package [*NASA*]   (MCD)
WEP .... Work Experience Program [*Department of Labor*]
WEP .... World Employment Program [*United Nations*]
WEP .... Writing, Editing, and Publishing
WEPA........ Eupora, MS [*AM radio station call letters*]
WEPA........ Welded Electronic Packaging Association
WEPC........ Weapons and Equipment Policy Committee [*British*]   (RDA)
WEPC........ West Chemical Products [*NASDAQ symbol*]   (NQ)
WEPCOSE ... Weapon Control Systems Engineering [*Navy*]   (NG)
WEPEX ..... Weapons Exercise [*Navy*]   (NVT)
WEPG........ South Pittsburg, TN [*AM radio station call letters*]
WEPH........ Weapon Phenomenology   (RDA)
WEPM .... Martinsburg, WV [*AM radio station call letters*]
WEPR .... Greenville, SC [*FM radio station call letters*]
WEPR........ Women Executives in Public Relations [*New York, NY*]   (EA)
WEPREC .... West Pakistan Research and Evaluation Center
WEPS........ Elgin, IL [*FM radio station call letters*]
WEPSO ...... Naval Weapons Services Office [*Also known as NAVWPNSERVO, NWSO*]
WEPTA....... War Excess Profits Tax Act [*1917*]
WEPTAC .... Weapons and Tactics Analysis Center [*Navy*]   (MCD)
WEPTRAEX ... Weapons Training Exercise   (NVT)
WEPTU...... Weapons Reserve Training Units [*Navy*]
WEPZA....... World Export Processing Zones Association   (EA)
WEQ .... Wind Erosion Equation
WEQO .... Whitley City, KY [*AM radio station call letters*]
WEQR........ Goldsboro, NC [*FM radio station call letters*]
WEQX........ Manchester, VT [*FM radio station call letters*]
WEQZ........ Gluckstadt, MS [*FM radio station call letters*]
WER .... Water Electrolysis Rocket
WER .... Webcor Electronics, Inc. [*American Stock Exchange symbol*]
WER .... Week End Review [*A publication*]
WER .... Weight Estimating Relationship   (KSC)
WER .... Werombi [*Australia*] [*Seismograph station code, US Geological Survey*]   (SEIS)
WERA....... Plainfield, NJ [*AM radio station call letters*]
WERA........ Western Eastern Roadracers Association   (EA)
WERA........ Western/English Retailers of America [*Washington, DC*]   (EA)
WERA........ World Energy Research Authority
WERB........ Berlin, CT [*FM radio station call letters*]
WERC........ Birmingham, AL [*AM radio station call letters*]
WERC........ Warehousing Education and Research Council [*Oak Brook, IL*]   (EA)
WERC........ World Environment and Resources Council   (EA-IO)
WERE .... Cleveland, OH [*AM radio station call letters*]
WERG........ Erie, PA [*FM radio station call letters*]
WERH........ Hamilton, AL [*AM radio station call letters*]
WERH-FM ... Hamilton, AL [*FM radio station call letters*]
WERI .... Water and Energy Research Institute of the Western Pacific [*University of Guam*] [*Guam*] [*Research center*]   (RCD)
WERI .... Westerly, RI [*AM radio station call letters*]
WERI-FM.... Westerly, RI [*FM radio station call letters*]
WERK .... Muncie, IN [*AM radio station call letters*]
Werk......... Werk/Archithese [*A publication*]
WERKA ..... Werkstattstechnik [*A publication*]
Werkstatt Betr ... Werkstatt und Betrieb [*A publication*]
Werkstattstech Z Ind Fertigung ... Werkstattstechnik Zeitschrift fuer Industrielle Fertigung [*A publication*]

Werkst Korros ... Werkstoffe und Korrosion [*A publication*]
Werkst u Korrosion ... Werkstoffe und Korrossion (Wernheim) [*A publication*]
WERL .... Eagle River, WI [*AM radio station call letters*]
WERM .... World Encyclopedia of Recorded Music, 1925-55 [*A publication*]
WERN........ Madison, WI [*FM radio station call letters*]
Wernerian N H Soc Mem ... Wernerian Natural History Society. Memoirs [*A publication*]
WERPG ...... Western European Regional Planning Group [*NATO*]   (NATG)
WERR........ Utuado Rosa, PR [*FM radio station call letters*]
WERS........ Boston, MA [*FM radio station call letters*]
WERS........ War Emergency Radio Service
WERS........ Weapons Effect Reporting Station [*Civil defense*]
WERS........ Wing Equipment Repair Squadron
WERT .... Van Wert, OH [*AM radio station call letters*]
WERT .... Women's Economic Round Table   (EA)
WERT-FM ... Van Wert, OH [*FM radio station call letters*]
WERTS....... Writers' Ever-Ready Textual Service [*Rent-A-Script*] [*Satirical*]
WERU-FM ... Blue Hill, ME [*FM radio station call letters*]
WERZ........ Exeter, NH [*FM radio station call letters*]
WES .... Sacred Heart Hospital, Eau Claire, WI [*Library symbol*] [*Library of Congress*]   (LCLS)
WES .... Washington Ethical Society   (EA)
WES .... Water Electrolysis System
WES .... Waterways Experiment Station [*Army Corps of Engineers*] [*Vicksburg, MS*]
WES .... Weapon Engineering Station   (MCD)
WES .... Weapons Effects Systems   (MCD)
WES .... Weather Editing Section [*FAA*]   (FAAC)
WES .... Wes-Martin Aviation [*Red Bluff, CA*] [*FAA designator*]   (FAAC)
WES .... Wesleyan   (ROG)
WES .... Wesleyan [*A publication*]
WES .... West [*or Western*]
WES .... Westbury [*British depot code*]
WES .... Westmills Carpets Ltd. [*Toronto Stock Exchange symbol*]
WES .... Weston [*Massachusetts*] [*Seismograph station code, US Geological Survey*]   (SEIS)
WES .... Weston [*Massachusetts*] [*Geomagnetic observatory code*]
WES .... Westport Public Library, Westport, CT [*OCLC symbol*]   (OCLC)
WES .... Wind Electric System [*Telecommunications*]   (TEL)
WES .... Wisdom of the East Series [*A publication*]
WESA........ Charleroi, PA [*AM radio station call letters*]
WESA........ White Sands National Monument [*New Mexico*]
WESA........ Wind Energy Society of America [*Inactive*]
WESA........ Wind Energy Systems Act of 1980
WESA-FM ... Charleroi, PA [*FM radio station call letters*]
WESB........ Bradford, PA [*AM radio station call letters*]
WESB........ Western Beef [*NASDAQ symbol*]   (NQ)
WESC........ Greenville, SC [*AM radio station call letters*]
WESC........ Weapon Engagement Simulation Component   (MCD)
WESC........ Whole Earth Software Catalog [*A publication*]
WESCAR.... Western Carolines [*Navy*]
WESCARSUBAREA ... Western Carolines Subarea [*Navy*]
WESC-FM ... Greenville, SC [*FM radio station call letters*]
Wes CLJ..... Westmoreland County Law Journal   (DLA)
WESCO ...... Walnut Export Sales Company   (EA)
WESCO...... Westinghouse Corporation
WESCOBASESERVUNIT ... West Coast Base Service Unit [*Navy*]
WESCOM... Weapons System Cost Model
WESCOM... Western Command [*Army*]   (AABC)
WESCON ... Western Electronics Show and Convention [*IEEE*]
WESCON Tech Pap ... WESCON [*Western Electronics Show and Convention*] Technical Papers [*United States*] [*A publication*]
WESCOSOUNDSCOL ... West Coast Sound School [*Navy*]
WESD........ Schofield, WI [*FM radio station call letters*]
WESE........ Baldwyn, MS [*FM radio station call letters*]
WESED ..... Weapons System Evaluation Division [*DoD*]
WESEG ..... Weapons System Evaluation Group [*DoD*]
WESF .... Waste Encapsulation Storage Facility [*Nuclear energy*]   (NRCH)
WESH-TV... Daytona Beach, FL [*Television station call letters*]
WESI .... Strasburg, VA [*FM radio station call letters*]
WESIAC ..... Weapons Effectiveness Systems Industry Advisory Committee   (MCD)
Weskett Ins ... Weskett's Complete Digest of the Theory, Laws, and Practice of Insurance   (DLA)
Wesk Ins .... Weskett's Complete Digest of the Theory, Laws, and Practice of Insurance   (DLA)
WESL .... East St. Louis, IL [*AM radio station call letters*]
Wesley Th J ... Wesleyan Theological Journal [*A publication*]
Wesley W Spink Lect Comp Med ... Wesley W. Spink Lectures on Comparative Medicine [*A publication*]
WESM .... Princess Anne, MD [*FM radio station call letters*]
WESN........ Bloomington, IL [*FM radio station call letters*]
WESO........ Southbridge, MA [*AM radio station call letters*]
WESO........ Weapons Engineering Service Office [*DoD*]
WESOS ...... Water-Extracted Soluble Orange Solids [*Citrus processing*]
WESP .... War and Emergency Support Plan [*DoD*]
W/E & SP ... With Equipment and Spare Parts

WESPAR .... Weapon Evaluation System Photographic Analog Recorder (MCD)

WESPEX .... War and Emergency Support Plan Exercise [*DoD*]

WESPS....... Wespac Investors Trust [*NASDAQ symbol*] (NQ)

WESR......... Onley-Onancock, VA [*AM radio station call letters*]

WESRAC.... Western Research Application Center [*University of Southern California*]

WESREP .... Weapon Engineering Station Representative (MCD)

Wes Res Law Jo ... Western Reserve Law Journal (DLA)

Wes Res Law Jrl ... Western Reserve Law Journal [*Ohio*] (DLA)

WESR-FM ... Onley-Onancock, VA [*FM radio station call letters*]

WESS........ East Stroudsburg, PA [*FM radio station call letters*]

WESS........ Weapons Engagement Scoring System

WESSEAFRON ... Western Sea Frontier [*Navy*]

WEST .... Easton, PA [*AM radio station call letters*]

WEST .... Weapons Effectiveness Simulated Threat (MCD)

WEST .... Weapons Exhaust Study [*Military*] (MCD)

West.......... West Publishing Co. (DLA)

West.......... Westbury's European Arbitration (Reilly) (DLA)

WEST .... Western Educational Society for Telecommunications [*Arizona State University*] [*Tempe, AZ*] [*Defunct*] (EA)

WEST .... Western Energy Supply and Transmission Associates [*Utility antipollution group*]

WEST .... Western Transportation Co. [*Later, WTCO*] [*AAR code*]

West.......... Western's London Tithe Cases [*England*] (DLA)

West.......... Westminster [*Record label*]

West.......... Westmoreland County Law Journal [*Pennsylvania*] (DLA)

West.......... Weston's Reports [*11-14 Vermont*] (DLA)

West.......... West's English Chancery Reports (DLA)

West.......... West's Reports, English House of Lords (DLA)

WEST .... Westworld, Inc. [*NASDAQ symbol*] (NQ)

WEST .... Women's Enlisted Screening Test [*Air Force*]

WESTA....... White Sands Electromagnetic Pulse Systems Test Array [*New Mexico*] (RDA)

WESTAF .... Western Transport Air Force

West Afr Cocoa Res Inst Tech Bull ... West African Cocoa Research Institute. Technical Bulletin [*A publication*]

West African J of Ed ... West African Journal of Education [*A publication*]

West Afr Inst Oil Palm Res Annu Rep ... West African Institute for Oil Palm Research. Annual Report [*A publication*]

West Afr J Archaeol ... West African Journal of Archaeology [*A publication*]

West Afr J Biol Appl Chem ... West African Journal of Biological and Applied Chemistry [*A publication*]

West Afr J Biol Chem ... West African Journal of Biological Chemistry [*A publication*]

West Afr J Pharmacol Drug Res ... West African Journal of Pharmacology and Drug Research [*A publication*]

West Afr Med J ... West African Medical Journal [*A publication*]

West Afr Med J Nigerian Pract ... West African Medical Journal and Nigerian Practitioner [*A publication*]

West Afr Pharm ... West African Pharmacist [*A publication*]

West Am Sc ... West American Scientist [*A publication*]

WESTAR ... Waterways Experiment Station Terrain Analyzer RADAR

WESTAR 6 ... Communications satellite

West Assn Map Libs Inf Bul ... Western Association of Map Libraries. Information Bulletin [*A publication*]

West AULR ... Western Australia University. Law Review [*A publication*]

West Aust Clin Rep ... Western Australian Clinical Reports [*A publication*]

West Aust Conf Australas Inst Min Metall ... Western Australian Conference. Australasian Institute of Mining and Metallurgy [*A publication*]

West Aust Dep Agric Annu Rep ... Western Australia. Department of Agriculture. Annual Report [*A publication*]

West Aust Dep Fish Fauna Rep ... Western Australia. Department of Fisheries and Fauna. Report [*A publication*]

West Aust Dep Fish Wildl Rep ... Western Australia. Department of Fisheries and Wildlife. Report [*A publication*]

West Aust Dep Mines Annu Rep ... Western Australia. Department of Mines. Annual Report [*A publication*]

West Aust Dep Mines Miner Resour West Aust Bull ... Western Australia. Department of Mines. Mineral Resources of Western Australia. Bulletin [*A publication*]

West Aust Dep Mines Min Resour West Aust Bull ... Western Australia. Department of Mines. Mineral Resources of Western Australia. Bulletin [*A publication*]

West Aust Geol Surv Annu Prog Rep ... Western Australia. Geological Survey. Annual Progress Report [*A publication*]

West Aust Geol Surv Annu Rep ... Western Australia. Geological Survey. Annual Report [*A publication*]

West Aust Geol Surv Bull ... Western Australia. Geological Survey. Bulletin [*A publication*]

West Aust Geol Surv 1:250,000 Geol Ser ... Western Australia. Geological Survey. 1:250,000 Geological Series [*A publication*]

West Aust Geol Surv Geol Ser Explan Notes ... Western Australia. Geological Survey. Geological Series. Explanatory Notes [*A publication*]

West Aust Geol Surv Miner Resour Bull ... Western Australia. Geological Survey. Mineral Resources Bulletin [*A publication*]

West Aust Geol Surv Rep ... Western Australia. Geological Survey. Report [*A publication*]

West Aust Inst Technol Gaz ... Western Australian Institute of Technology. Gazette [*A publication*]

West Austl ... Western Australian Reports [*A publication*]

West Aust L Rev ... University of Western Australia. Law Review [*A publication*]

West Aust Mar Res Lab Fish Res Bull ... Western Australian Marine Research Laboratories. Fisheries Research Bulletin [*A publication*]

West Aust Mus Spec Publ ... Western Australian Museum. Special Publication [*A publication*]

West Aust Nat ... Western Australian Naturalist [*A publication*]

West Aust Naturalist ... Western Australian Naturalist [*A publication*]

West Aust Rep Gov Chem Lab ... Western Australia. Government Chemical Laboratories. Report [*A publication*]

West Austr L ... Western Australian Law Reports [*A publication*]

West Aust Sch Mines ... Western Australian School of Mines [*A publication*]

West Aust SWANS ... Western Australia SWANS [*State Wildlife Authority News Service*] [*A publication*]

West Aust Wildl Res Cent Wildl Res Bull ... Western Australia Wildlife Research Centre. Wildlife Research Bulletin [*A publication*]

West Bird Bander ... Western Bird Bander [*A publication*]

West Build ... Western Building [*United States*] [*A publication*]

West Bus.... Western Business [*A publication*]

West Canad J Anthropol ... Western Canadian Journal of Anthropology [*A publication*]

West Can J Anthropol ... Western Canadian Journal of Anthropology [*A publication*]

West Canner Packer ... Western Canner and Packer [*A publication*]

West Ch ..... West's English Chancery Cases [*25 English Reprint*] (DLA)

West Chapter Int Shade Tree Conf Proc ... Western Chapter. International Shade Tree Conference. Proceedings [*A publication*]

West Chem Metall ... Western Chemist and Metallurgist [*A publication*]

West Ch (Eng) ... West's English Chancery Cases [*25 English Reprint*] (DLA)

Westchester Co Hist Soc Publ ... Westchester County Historical Society. Publications [*A publication*]

Westchester Med Bull ... Westchester Medical Bulletin [*New York*] [*A publication*]

West Chy ... West's English Chancery Cases [*25 English Reprint*] (DLA)

West City ... Western City [*A publication*]

West Coast R ... West Coast Review [*A publication*]

West Coast Rep ... West Coast Reporter (DLA)

WESTCOM ... Western Command [*Army*]

WESTCOMMRGN ... Western Communications Region [*Air Force*] (AFM)

West Constr ... Western Construction [*A publication*]

West Contract ... Western Contractor [*A publication*]

West Co Rep ... West Coast Reporter (DLA)

West Crop Farm Manage N Ed ... Western Crops and Farm Management. Northern Edition [*A publication*]

West Crop Farm Manage S Ed ... Western Crops and Farm Management. Southern Edition [*A publication*]

West Drug ... Western Druggist [*A publication*]

Westd Zeit ... Westdeutsche Zeitschrift fuer Geschichte und Kunst [*A publication*] (OCD)

WESTE....... Weapons Effectiveness and System Test Environment [*Air Force*] (AFM)

WESTEC .... Western Metal and Tool Exposition and Conference [*American Society for Metals*] (TSPED)

West Econ Jour ... Western Economic Journal [*A publication*]

West Elec E ... Western Electric Engineer [*A publication*]

Westerm M ... Westermanns Monatshefte [*A publication*]

Westerm Monatsh ... Westermanns Monatshefte [*A publication*]

Western Am Lit ... Western American Literature [*A publication*]

Western Australia Geol Survey Rept ... Western Australia. Geological Survey. Report. Government Printer [*A publication*]

Western Australia Main Roads Dep Tech Bull ... Western Australia. Main Roads Department. Technical Bulletin [*A publication*]

Western EE ... Western Electric Engineer [*A publication*]

Western Electric Eng ... Western Electric Engineer [*A publication*]

Western Eng ... Western Engineering [*A publication*]

Western Hist Q ... Western Historical Quarterly [*A publication*]

Western Hum R ... Western Humanities Review [*A publication*]

Western Hum Rev ... Western Humanities Review [*A publication*]

Western Law Jour ... Western Law Journal (Reprint) [*A publication*]

Western L Rev ... Western Law Review [*Canada*] (DLA)

Western Ont L Rev ... Western Ontario Law Review [*A publication*]

Western Reserve Hist Soc Tracts ... Western Reserve Historical Society. Tracts [*A publication*]

Western Reserve LN ... Western Reserve Law Notes (DLA)

Western Res L Rev ... Western Reserve Law Review [*A publication*]

Western Rv Sc ... Western Review of Science and Industry [*A publication*]

Western Speleol Inst Bull ... Western Speleological Institute. Bulletin [*A publication*]

Western Wash Ag Exp B ... Western Washington Agricultural Experiment Station. Monthly Bulletin [*A publication*]

West Europe Ed ... Western European Education [*A publication*]

West Eur Politics ... West European Politics [*A publication*]

West-Eur Symp Clin Chem ... West-European Symposia on Clinical Chemistry [*A publication*]

West Ext .... West on Extents [*1817*] (DLA)

Westfael Bienenztg ... Westfaelische Bienenzeitung [*A publication*]

West Farmer ... Western Farmer [*A publication*]

Westf Bienenztg ... Westfaelische Bienenzeitung [*A publication*]

West Feed ... Western Feed [*A publication*]

West Feed Seed ... Western Feed and Seed [*A publication*]

West Folk... Western Folklore [*A publication*]

West Folkl ... Western Folklore [*A publication*]

WESTFORNET ... Western Forestry Information Network [*Forest service*] [*Library network*]

West Found Vertebr Zool Occas Pap ... Western Foundation of Vertebrate Zoology. Occasional Papers [*A publication*]

Westfriesch Jb ... Westfriesch Jaarboek [*A publication*]

West HL ..... West's Reports, English House of Lords　(DLA)

West Horse ... Western Horseman [*A publication*]

West HR ..... Western Humanities Review [*A publication*]

West Humanities Rev ... Western Humanities Review [*A publication*]

West Hum R ... Western Humanities Review [*A publication*]

West Ind Bull ... West Indian Bulletin [*A publication*]

West Indian Med J ... West Indian Medical Journal [*A publication*]

Westinghouse Eng ... Westinghouse Engineer [*A publication*]

Westinghouse Engr ... Westinghouse Engineer [*A publication*]

West J Med ... Western Journal of Medicine [*A publication*]

West J Nurs Res ... Western Journal of Nursing Research [*A publication*]

West J Surg Obstet Gynecol ... Western Journal of Surgery. Obstetrics and Gynecology [*A publication*]

West Jur..... Western Jurist [*Des Moines, Iowa*]　(DLA)

Westlake Int Private Law ... Westlake's Private International Law　(DLA)

WESTLANT ... Western Atlantic Area

West Law J ... Western Law Journal [*A publication*]

West Law Jour ... Western Law Journal (Reprint) [*A publication*]

West Law M ... Western Law Monthly [*Ohio*]　(DLA)

West Law Mo ... Western Law Monthly (Reprint) [*Ohio*]　(DLA)

West Law Month ... Western Law Monthly [*Ohio*]　(DLA)

West Law Rev ... Western Law Review [*Canada*]　(DLA)

WestLB ...... Westdeutsche Landesbank [*West German bank*]

West Leg Obs ... Western Legal Observer [*A publication*]

West L Gaz ... Western Law Gazette [*Cincinnati, OH*]　(DLA)

West Lit J... Western Literary Journal [*A publication*]

West Livestock J ... Western Livestock Journal [*A publication*]

West LJ..... Western Law Journal [*A publication*]

West LJ (Ohio) ... Western Law Journal (Ohio) [*A publication*]

West LM..... Western Law Monthly [*Ohio*]　(DLA)

West L Mo ... Western Law Monthly [*Ohio*]　(DLA)

West L Month ... Western Law Monthly [*Ohio*]　(DLA)

West Locker ... Western Locker [*A publication*]

Westl Priv Int Law ... Westlake's Private International Law　(DLA)

West LR ...... Western Law Reporter [*Canada*]　(DLA)

West LR (Can) ... Western Law Reporter [*Canada*]　(DLA)

West L Rev ... Western Law Review　(DLA)

West LT...... Western Law Times [*Canada*]　(DLA)

Westm ...... State of Westminster　(DLA)

West M ...... Western Monthly Magazine [*A publication*]

WESTM...... Westminster [*London*]

Westm........ Westminster Review [*A publication*]

Westm........ Westmoreland County Law Journal [*Pennsylvania*]　(DLA)

West Mach Steel World ... Western Machinery and Steel World [*A publication*]

West Malays Geol Surv Dist Mem ... West Malaysia. Geological Survey. District Memoir [*A publication*]

West Malays Geol Surv Econ Bull ... West Malaysia. Geological Survey. Economic Bulletin [*A publication*]

WESTMD ... Westmorland [*County in England*]

West Med... Western Medicine [*A publication*]

West Met.... Western Metals [*A publication*]

West Metalwork ... Western Metalworking [*A publication*]

Westm Hall Chron ... Westminster Hall Chronicle and Legal Examiner [*1835-36*]　(DLA)

West Miner ... Western Miner [*A publication*]

Westm LJ... Westmoreland County Law Journal　(DLA)

West Mo R ... Western Monthly Review [*A publication*]

Westmore Co LJ (PA) ... Westmoreland County Law Journal [*Pennsylvania*]　(DLA)

Westmoreland ... Westmoreland County Law Journal [*Pennsylvania*]　(DLA)

Westmoreland Co LJ ... Westmoreland County Law Journal [*Pennsylvania*]　(DLA)

Westm Th J ... Westminster Theological Journal [*A publication*]

WESTN ...... Western

WESTNAVELEX ... Naval Electronics Systems Command, Western Division, Mare Island, Vallejo, California

WESTNAVFACENGCOM ... Western Division, Naval Facilities Engineering Command

West New Engl L Rev ... Western New England Law Review [*A publication*]

West Oil Refin ... Western Oil Refining [*A publication*]

West Oil Rep ... Western Oil Reporter [*A publication*]

WESTOMP ... Western Ocean Meeting Point

Weston....... Weston's Reports [*11-14 Vermont*]　(DLA)

West Ont L Rev ... Western Ontario Law Review [*A publication*]

WESTPAC ... Western Pacific [*Military*]　(CINC)

WESTPACBACOM ... Western Pacific Base Command [*Navy*]

WEST PACK ... Western Packaging Exposition　(TSPED)

WESTPACNORTH ... Western Pacific North [*Navy*]　(CINC)

West PA Hist Mag ... Western Pennsylvania Historical Magazine [*A publication*]

West Paint Rev ... Western Paint Review [*A publication*]

West Pak J Agric Res ... West Pakistan Journal of Agricultural Research [*A publication*]

West Penn Hist Mag ... Western Pennsylvania Historical Magazine [*A publication*]

West Pet Refiners Assoc Tech Publ ... Western Petroleum Refiners Association. Technical Publication [*A publication*]

West Plast ... Western Plastics [*A publication*]

WESTPO .... Western Governors Policy Office

West Polit Quart ... Western Political Quarterly [*A publication*]

West Pol Q ... Western Political Quarterly [*A publication*]

Westpr Geschichtsv Ztsch ... Westpreussischer Geschichtsverein. Zeitschrift [*A publication*]

West Pr Int Law ... Westlake's Private International Law [*7th ed.*] [*1925*]　(DLA)

West Pulp Pap ... Western Pulp and Paper [*A publication*]

West R........ Western Reporter　(DLA)

West R........ Western Review [*A publication*]

West Reg Ext Publ Co-op Ext US Dep Ag ... Western Region Extension Publication. Cooperative Extension. United States Department of Agriculture [*A publication*]

West Rep ... Western Reporter　(DLA)

West Reserve Law Rev ... Western Reserve Law Review [*A publication*]

West Res Law Rev ... Western Reserve Law Review [*A publication*]

West Res L Rev ... Western Reserve Law Review [*A publication*]

West Resour Conf ... Western Resources Conference [*A publication*]

West Rev.... Westminster Review [*A publication*]

West Roads ... Western Roads [*A publication*]

West School L Rev ... Western School Law Review　(DLA)

West Scot Agric Coll Res Bull ... West Scotland Agricultural College. Research Bulletin [*A publication*]

West Scot Iron Steel Inst J ... West of Scotland Iron and Steel Institute. Journal [*A publication*]

WESTSEAFRON ... Western Sea Frontier [*Navy*]　(MUGU)

West Shade Tree Conf Proc Annu Meet ... Western Shade Tree Conference. Proceedings of the Annual Meeting [*A publication*]

West Soc Eng J ... Western Society of Engineers. Journal [*A publication*]

West Soc Malacol Annu Rep ... Western Society of Malacologists. Annual Report [*A publication*]

West Soc Malacol Occas Pap ... Western Society of Malacologists. Occasional Paper [*A publication*]

West's Op ... West's Opinions [*City Solicitor of Philadelphia, PA*]　(DLA)

West's Symb ... West's Symboleographie [*Many eds.*] [*1590-1641*]　(DLA)

West States Jew Hist Q ... Western States Jewish Historical Quarterly [*A publication*]

West States Sect Combust Inst Pap ... Western States Section. Combustion Institute. Paper [*A publication*]

West State UL Rev ... Western State University. Law Review [*A publication*]

West St U L Rev ... Western State University. Law Review [*A publication*]

WESTT....... Weapon System Tactical Tester

West Teach ... Western Teacher [*A publication*]

West Texas Geol Soc Pub ... West Texas Geological Society. Publication [*A publication*]

West Tex Today ... Western Texas Today [*A publication*]

West T H .... West's English Chancery Reports Tempore Hardwicke [*1736-39*]　(DLA)

West T Hard ... West's English Chancery Reports Tempore Hardwicke [*1736-39*]　(DLA)

West T Hardw ... West's English Chancery Reports Tempore Hardwicke [*1736-39*]　(DLA)

West Th J... Westminster Theological Journal [*A publication*]

West Ti Cas ... Western's London Tithe Cases [*1535-1822*]　(DLA)

West Tithe Cas ... Western's London Tithe Cases [*England*]　(DLA)

WestTJ....... Westminster Theological Journal [*Philadelphia*] [*A publication*]

West Union Tech Rev ... Western Union Technical Review [*A publication*]

West Va...... West Virginia Reports　(DLA)

West Va Lib ... West Virginia Libraries [*A publication*]

West Va L Rev ... Western Virginia Law Review　(DLA)

West Va Rep ... West Virginia Reports　(DLA)

West Vet .... Western Veterinarian [*A publication*]

West Virginia Geol and Econ Survey Basic Data Rept ... West Virginia. Geological and Economic Survey. Basic Data Report [*A publication*]

West Virginia Geol and Econ Survey Circ ... West Virginia. Geological and Economic Survey. Circular [*A publication*]

West Virginia L Rev ... West Virginia Law Review [*A publication*]

West Week (Can) ... Western Weekly Notes (Canada)　(DLA)

West Week N ... Western Weekly Notes [*Canada*]　(DLA)

West Week N (Can) ... Western Weekly Notes (Canada)　(DLA)

West Week NS ... Western Weekly, New Series [*Canada*]　(DLA)

West Week Rep ... Western Weekly Reports [*Canada*]　(DLA)

West Wildlands ... Western Wildlands [*A publication*]

WESU........ Middletown, CT [*FM radio station call letters*]

WESX........ Salem, MA [*AM radio station call letters*]

WESY........ Leland, MS [*AM radio station call letters*]

WESYP...... Weapons System Plan [*Navy*]　(NG)

WET .... Wagethe [*Indonesia*] [*Airport symbol*]　(OAG)

WET .... Waste, Environment, and Technology [*Matrix*] [*Environmental Protection Agency*]

WET .... Water Exercise Technique [*In book title "The W.E.T. Workout"*]

WET .... Weapons Effectiveness Testing
WET .... Westfort Petroleums [*Toronto Stock Exchange symbol*]
      [*Vancouver Stock Exchange symbol*]
WET .... Wet Environment Trainer [*Navy*]
WET .... Wettzell [*Federal Republic of Germany*] [*Seismograph station code, US Geological Survey*] (SEIS)
WET .... Work Experience and Training
WETA .... War Estate Tax Act [*1917*]
WETAC .... Westinghouse Electronic Tubeless Analog Computer
WETAF .... Weather Task Force
WETA-FM ... Washington, DC [*FM radio station call letters*]
WETARFAC ... Work Element Timer and Recorder for Automatic Computing
WETA-TV ... Washington, DC [*Television station call letters*]
WETB .... Johnson City, TN [*AM radio station call letters*]
Wet Bydraes PU CHO Reeks B Natuurwet ... Wetenskaplike Bydraes van die PU [*Potchefstroomse Universiteit*] vir CHO [*Christelike Hoere Onderwys*]. Reeks B: Natuurwetenskappe [*A publication*]
WETC .... Wendell-Zebulon, NC [*AM radio station call letters*]
WETD .... Alfred, NY [*FM radio station call letters*]
WETG .... Erie, PA [*Television station call letters*]
Weth .... Wethey's Reports [*Canada*] (DLA)
Wethey ...... Wethey's Reports, Upper Canada Queen's Bench (DLA)
Weth UC .... Wethey's Reports, Upper Canada Queen's Bench (DLA)
WE TIP ...... We Turn in Pushers [*Organization combating drug traffic*]
WETK .... Burlington, VT [*Television station call letters*]
WETL .... South Bend, IN [*FM radio station call letters*]
WETM .... Weather Team [*Air Force*] (AFM)
Wet Meded KNNV ... Wetenschappelijke Mededeling KNNV [*Koninklijke Nederlandse Natuurhistorische Vereniging*] [*A publication*]
WETM-TV ... Elmira, NY [*Television station call letters*]
WETN .... Wheaton, IL [*FM radio station call letters*]
WETNETNG ... Wet-Net Training [*Navy*] (NVT)
WETO .... Greenville, TN [*Television station call letters*]
WETP .... Work Experience Training Program (OICC)
WETS .... Johnson City, TN [*FM radio station call letters*]
WETS .... Weapon Effects Training Simulator (MCD)
WETS .... Week-End Training Site [*Military*] (AABC)
Wet Samenleving ... Wetenschap en Samenleving [*A publication*]
WETSU ...... We Eat This Stuff Up [*Army slang, bowdlerized*]
WETT .... Ocean City, MD [*AM radio station call letters*]
WETT .... Wetterau, Inc. [*NASDAQ symbol*] (NQ)
Wett .... Wettstein's Novum Testamentum Graecum [*A publication*] (BJA)
WETV .... Key West, FL [*Television station call letters*]
WETZ .... New Martinsville, WV [*AM radio station call letters*]
WEU .... University of Wisconsin-Eau Claire, Eau Claire, WI [*Library symbol*] [*Library of Congress*] (LCLS)
WEU .... Ward's Engine Update [*A publication*]
WEU .... Western European Union [*Also, WU*] [*See also UEO*] (EA-IO)
WEUC .... Ponce, PR [*AM radio station call letters*]
WEUC-FM ... Ponce, PR [*FM radio station call letters*]
W Europe Educ ... Western European Education [*A publication*]
W Eur Policies ... West European Policies [*A publication*]
W Eur Politics ... West European Politics [*A publication*]
WEUS .... Eustis, FL [*AM radio station call letters*]
WEUZ .... Jersey Shore, PA [*FM radio station call letters*]
WEV .... Western European Vision
WEVA .... Emporia, VA [*AM radio station call letters*]
WEVA .... World Esperantist Vegetarian Association [*See also TEVA*] (EA-IO)
WEVD-FM ... New York, NY [*FM radio station call letters*]
WEVE .... Eveleth, MN [*AM radio station call letters*]
WEVE-FM ... Eveleth, MN [*FM radio station call letters*]
WEVL .... Memphis, TN [*FM radio station call letters*]
WEVO .... Concord, NH [*FM radio station call letters*]
WEVR .... River Falls, WI [*AM radio station call letters*]
WEVR-FM ... River Falls, WI [*FM radio station call letters*]
WEVU .... Naples, FL [*Television station call letters*]
WEVV .... Evansville, IN [*Television station call letters*]
WEVZ .... Cadillac, MI [*FM radio station call letters*]
WEW .... St. Louis, MO [*AM radio station call letters*]
WeW .... Welt und Wort [*A publication*]
WEW .... Western Electronic Week
WEW .... Wewak [*Papua New Guinea*] [*Seismograph station code, US Geological Survey*] [*Closed*] (SEIS)
WEWAS ..... Water Equipment Wholesalers and Suppliers [*Formerly, WEWSA*]
WEWO .... Laurinburg, NC [*AM radio station call letters*]
WEWS .... Cleveland, OH [*Television station call letters*]
WEWSA ..... Water Equipment Wholesalers and Suppliers Association [*Later, WEWAS*] (EA)
WEWZ .... Elwood, IN [*FM radio station call letters*]
WEX .... Wexford [*County in Ireland*] (ROG)
WEX .... Win-Eldrich Mines Ltd. [*Toronto Stock Exchange symbol*]
WEXA .... Eupora, MS [*FM radio station call letters*]
WEXC .... Greenville, PA [*FM radio station call letters*]
WEXF .... Wexford [*County in Ireland*] (ROG)
WEXFD ...... Wexford [*County in Ireland*]
WEXITA ..... Women Executives International Tourism Association [*New York, NY*] (EA)

WEXL .... Royal Oak, MI [*AM radio station call letters*]
WEXT .... Wrist Extension [*Sports medicine*]
WEXY .... Oakland Park, FL [*AM radio station call letters*]
WEY .... West Yellowstone, MT [*Location identifier*] [*FAA*] (FAAL)
WEYE .... Hillsboro, OH [*AM radio station call letters*]
Weyerhauser For Pap ... Weyerhauser Forestry Paper [*A publication*]
WEYI-TV .... Saginaw, MI [*Television station call letters*]
WEYQ .... Marietta, OH [*AM radio station call letters*]
WEYQ .... Marietta, OH [*FM radio station call letters*]
WEYS .... Institute, WV [*FM radio station call letters*]
WEYS .... Weyenberg Shoe Manufacturing [*NASDAQ symbol*] (NQ)
WEYY-FM ... Talladega, AL [*FM radio station call letters*]
WEYZ .... Erie, PA [*AM radio station call letters*]
WEZB .... New Orleans, LA [*FM radio station call letters*]
WEZC .... Charlotte, NC [*FM radio station call letters*]
WEZE .... Boston, MA [*AM radio station call letters*]
WEZF .... Burlington, VT [*FM radio station call letters*]
WEZG-FM ... North Syracuse, NY [*FM radio station call letters*]
WEZI .... Germantown, TN [*FM radio station call letters*]
WEZJ .... Williamsburg, KY [*AM radio station call letters*]
WEZK .... Knoxville, TN [*FM radio station call letters*]
WEZL .... Charleston, SC [*FM radio station call letters*]
WEZN .... Bridgeport, CT [*FM radio station call letters*]
WEZO .... Rochester, NY [*FM radio station call letters*]
WEZQ .... Winfield, AL [*AM radio station call letters*]
WEZR .... Fort Wayne, IN [*AM radio station call letters*]
WEZS .... Richmond, VA [*FM radio station call letters*]
WEZU .... Witterungseinfluesse und Zeitunterschied [*Weather factors and time difference*] [*German military - World War II*]
WEZV .... Fort Wayne, IN [*FM radio station call letters*]
WEZW .... Wauwatosa-Milwaukee, WI [*FM radio station call letters*]
WEZX .... Scranton, PA [*FM radio station call letters*]
WEZY .... Cocoa, FL [*AM radio station call letters*]
WEZY-FM ... Cocoa, FL [*FM radio station call letters*]
WEZZ .... Clanton, AL [*FM radio station call letters*]
WF .... Four-Conductor Cables [*JETDS nomenclature*] [*Military*] (CET)
wf .... Wallis and Futuna [*MARC country of publication code*] [*Library of Congress*] (LCCP)
WF .... Wallis and Futuna [*Two-letter standard code*] (CNC)
WF .... Wash Fountain (AAG)
W & F .... Water and Feed
WF .... Water Filter
WF .... Water Finish [*Paper*]
WF .... Watershed Foundation (EA)
WF .... Wege der Forschung, Darmstadt, Wissenschaftliche Buchgesellschaft [*A publication*]
WF .... Welfare Appointment Full Time [*Chiropody*] [*British*]
WF .... Western Folklore [*A publication*]
WF .... Western Front [*World War I*]
WF .... Westfaelische Forschungen [*A publication*]
WF .... Westfair Foods Ltd. [*Toronto Stock Exchange symbol*]
WF .... White Fathers [*Roman Catholic men's religious order*]
WF .... White Female
WF .... Wideroe's Flyveselskap A/S [*Norway*] [*ICAO designator*] (FAAC)
WF .... Window-Frame
WF .... Wingfold
WF .... Wire Foundation [*An association*] [*Guilford, CT*] (EA)
WF .... Wistar-Furth [*Rat strain*]
WF .... Won on Foul [*Boxing*]
WF .... Word Fluency [*Psychology*]
W/F .... Wow and Flutter
WF .... Write Forward
W/F .... Writing on Face [*Deltiology*]
WF .... Wrong Font [*Typesetting*] [*Proofreader's mark*]
WFA .... War Food Administration [*Determined military, civilian, and foreign requirements for human and animal food, and for food used industrially*] [*World War II*] [*Terminated, 1945*]
WFA .... Weight-for-Age (ADA)
WFA .... Weightlifting Federation of Africa [*Cairo, Egypt*] (EA-IO)
WFA .... Western Fairs Association [*Sacramento, CA*] (EA)
WFA .... Western Falconry Association [*Defunct*] (EA)
WFA .... White Fish Authority [*MAFF*] [*British*]
WFA .... Wide-Frequency Antenna
WFA .... Wire Fabricators Association [*Naperville, IL*] (EA)
WFA .... World Federalists Association (EA)
WFA .... World Footbag Association (EA)
WFA .... World Friendship Association
WFA .... Worlds of Fantasy [*1968-*] [*A publication*]
WFAA-TV ... Dallas, TX [*Television station call letters*]
WFAB .... Juncos, PR [*AM radio station call letters*]
WFAC .... World Federal Authority Committee (EA-IO)
WFAD .... Middlebury, VT [*AM radio station call letters*]
WFAE .... Charlotte, NC [*FM radio station call letters*]
WFAFW ...... World Federation of Agriculture and Food Workers (EA)
WFAH .... Alliance, OH [*AM radio station call letters*]
WFaH .... Hoard Historical Museum, Fort Atkinson, WI [*Library symbol*] [*Library of Congress*] (LCLS)
WFAI .... Fayetteville, NC [*AM radio station call letters*]
WFAL .... Falmouth, MA [*FM radio station call letters*]

WFALW...... Weltbund Freiheitlicher Arbeitnehmerverbande auf Liberaler Wirtschaftsgrundlage [*World Union of Liberal Trade Union Organisations - WULTUO*]   (EA-IO)
WFAM........ Jacksonville, FL [*AM radio station call letters*]
WFAOSB.... World Food and Agricultural Outlook and Situation Board [*Department of Agriculture*]
WFAP......... Women's Funding Assistance Project   (EA)
WFAPS....... World Federation of Associations of Pediatric Surgeons   (EA-IO)
WFAR......... Danbury, CT [*FM radio station call letters*]
WFAS......... White Plains, NY [*AM radio station call letters*]
WFAS-FM ... White Plains, NY [*FM radio station call letters*]
WFAT-TV ... Johnstown, PA [*Television station call letters*]
WFAU......... Augusta, ME [*AM radio station call letters*]
WFAV......... Cordele, GA [*FM radio station call letters*]
WFAW........ Fort Atkinson, WI [*AM radio station call letters*]
WFAW........ World Federation of Agricultural Workers [*See also FMTA*]   (EA-IO)
WFAX......... Falls Church, VA [*AM radio station call letters*]
WFB........... Waferboard Corp. Ltd. [*Toronto Stock Exchange symbol*]
WFB........... Waterways Freight Bureau [*Fairfax, VA*]   (EA)
WFB........... Wide Flange Beam [*Metal industry*]
WFB........... World Fellowship of Buddhists   (EA-IO)
WFBBA....... World Federation of Bergen-Belsen Associations   (EA)
WFBC........ Greenville, SC [*AM radio station call letters*]
WFBC-FM ... Greenville, SC [*FM radio station call letters*]
WFBE......... Flint, MI [*FM radio station call letters*]
WFBF......... Buffalo, NY [*FM radio station call letters*]
WFBG........ Altoona, PA [*AM radio station call letters*]
WFBG-FM ... Altoona, PA [*FM radio station call letters*]
WFBI.......... Wood Fiber Blanket Institute [*Defunct*]
WFBL......... Syracuse, NY [*AM radio station call letters*]
WFBM........ Noblesville, IN [*AM radio station call letters*]
WFBMA...... Woven Fabric Belting Manufacturers Association   (EA)
WFBQ........ Indianapolis, IN [*FM radio station call letters*]
WFBR........ Baltimore, MD [*AM radio station call letters*]
WFBTMA.... World Federation of Baton Twirling and Majorette Associations   (EA)
WFBY......... World Fellowship of Buddhist Youth   (EA-IO)
WFC........... Committee on the World Food Crisis [*Defunct*]   (EA)
WFC........... Wake Forest College [*Later, WFU*] [*North Carolina*]
WFC........... Walleye Filter Changer
WFC........... Wallops Flight Center [*Formerly, WS*] [*NASA*]
WFC........... War Finance Committee
WFC........... Water Facts Consortium [*Defunct*]   (EA)
WFC........... Weld Flange Connection
WFC........... Wells Fargo & Company [*NYSE symbol*]
WFC........... West Florida Coast
WFC........... Western Football Conference
WFC........... Western Forestry Center   (EA)
WFC........... Wide Field Camera
WFC........... Wings Fun Club [*London, England*]   (EA-IO)
WFC........... Wolf First Class [*A philanderer*] [*Slang*]
WFC........... Women's Forage Corps [*British*] [*World War I*]
WFC........... World Food Council   (EA-IO)
WFC........... World Friendship Centre   (EA)
WFC........... Worldwide Fiero Club   (EA)
WFCA........ Ackerman, MS [*FM radio station call letters*]
WFCA........ Western Forestry and Conservation Association   (EA)
WFCB........ Chillicothe, OH [*FM radio station call letters*]
WFCC........ World Federation for Cancer Care   (EA-IO)
WFCC........ World Federation for Culture Collections [*Norwich, Norfolk, England*]   (EA-IO)
WFCC-FM ... Chatman, MA [*FM radio station call letters*]
WFCE........ World Federation of Czechoslovak Exile   (EA)
WFCG........ Franklinton, LA [*AM radio station call letters*]
WFCH........ Charleston, SC [*FM radio station call letters*]
WFCI.......... Franklin, IN [*FM radio station call letters*]
WFCJ......... Miamisburg, OH [*FM radio station call letters*]
WFCL........ Clintonville, WI [*AM radio station call letters*]
WFCLC...... World Federation of Christian Life Communities [*See also FMCVC*]   (EA-IO)
WFCM-FM ... Orangeburg, SC [*FM radio station call letters*]
WFCMV..... Wheeled Fuel-Consuming Motor Vehicle
WFCNLM ... World Federation of the Cossack National Liberation Movement   (EA)
WFCR........ Amherst, MA [*FM radio station call letters*]
WFCS........ New Britain, CT [*FM radio station call letters*]
WFCS........ World's Fair Collectors Society
WFCT........ Fayetteville, NC [*Television station call letters*]
WFCV........ Fort Wayne, IN [*AM radio station call letters*]
WFCY........ World Federation of Catholic Youth
WFCYWG... World Federation of Catholic Young Women and Girls [*Later, WFCY*]
WFD.......... Waveform Distortion [*Telecommunications*]   (TEL)
WFD.......... Westfield Minerals [*Toronto Stock Exchange symbol*] [*Vancouver Stock Exchange symbol*]
WFD.......... Wool Forward [*Knitting*]
WFD.......... World Federation of the Deaf
WFD.......... World Food Day [*October 16*]
WFDA........ Arcadia, FL [*FM radio station call letters*]

WFDA......... World Fast-Draw Association   (EA)
WFDD-FM ... Winston-Salem, NC [*FM radio station call letters*]
WFDF......... Flint, MI [*AM radio station call letters*]
WFDF......... World Flying Disc Federation [*Sundsvall, Sweden*]   (EA-IO)
WFDFI........ World Federation of Development Financing Institutions [*See also FEMIDE*]   (EA-IO)
WFDG......... New Bedford, MA [*Television station call letters*]
WFDR......... Manchester, GA [*AM radio station call letters*]
WFDRHL .... World Federation of Doctors Who Respect Human Life [*Oak Park, IL*]   (EA)
WFDS......... Warm Fog Dispenser System   (MCD)
WFDSA...... World Federation of Direct Selling Associations   (EA)
WFDSC...... World Federation of Dark Shadows Clubs   (EA)
WFDU......... Teaneck, NJ [*FM radio station call letters*]
WFDW........ World Federation of Democratic Women
WFDWRHL ... World Federation of Doctors Who Respect Human Life   (EA-IO)
WFDY......... World Federation of Democratic Youth [*See also FMJD*] [*Budapest, Hungary*]   (EA-IO)
WFe........... Dwight T. Parker Public Library, Fennimore, WI [*Library symbol*] [*Library of Congress*]   (LCLS)
WFE........... With Food Element
WFEA......... Manchester, NH [*AM radio station call letters*]
WFEA......... World Federation of Educational Associations [*Later, WCOTP*]   (EA)
WFEB........ Sylacauga, AL [*AM radio station call letters*]
WFEB........ Worcester Foundation for Experimental Biology
WFEF......... Terre Haute, IN [*FM radio station call letters*]
WFEL......... Towson, MD [*AM radio station call letters*]
WFEM........ Ellwood City, PA [*FM radio station call letters*]
WFEN........ Fenton, MI [*AM radio station call letters*]
WFEO......... World Federation of Engineering Organizations
WF & EQ.... Wave Filters and Equalizers   (MCD)
WFET......... Fort Pierce, FL [*Television station call letters*]
WFEX......... Western Fruit Express
WFEZ......... Meridian, MS [*AM radio station call letters*]
WFF........... Wanderer Forum Foundation   (EA)
WFF........... Well-Formed Formula [*Logic*]
WFF........... Whiting Field [*Milton*] [*Florida*] [*Seismograph station code, US Geological Survey*] [*Closed*]   (SEIS)
WFF........... William Faulkner Foundation [*Defunct*]   (EA)
WFF........... World Friendship Federation
WFFA......... Women's Fashion Fabrics Association [*New York, NY*]   (EA)
WFFF......... Columbia, MS [*AM radio station call letters*]
WFFF-FM... Columbia, MS [*FM radio station call letters*]
WFFG......... Marathon, FL [*AM radio station call letters*]
WFFL......... World Federation of Free Latvians   (EA)
WFFM........ World Federation of Friends of Museums [*See also FMAM*]   (EA-IO)
WF & FSA... Wholesale Florist and Florist Suppliers of America [*Arlington, VA*]   (EA)
WFFTH....... World Federation of Workers in Food, Tobacco, and Hotel Industries [*See also FMATH*]   (EA-IO)
WFFT-TV ... Fort Wayne, IN [*Television station call letters*]
WFFX......... Tuscaloosa, AL [*FM radio station call letters*]
WFG........... Water Fog
WFG........... Waveform Generator
WFGB........ Kingston, NY [*FM radio station call letters*]
WFGC........ Palm Beach, FL [*Television station call letters*]
WFGH........ Fort Gay, WV [*FM radio station call letters*]
WFGL......... Fitchburg, MA [*AM radio station call letters*]
WFGM........ Fairmont, WV [*FM radio station call letters*]
WFGN........ Gaffney, SC [*AM radio station call letters*]
WFGW........ Black Mountain, NC [*AM radio station call letters*]
WFH........... World Federation of Hemophilia   (EA)
WFHAAVSC ... World Federation of Health Agencies for the Advancement of Voluntary Surgical Contraception [*New York, NY*]   (EA)
WFHC........ Henderson, TN [*FM radio station call letters*]
WFHC........ Westside Federal Savings & Loan Association of Seattle [*NASDAQ symbol*]   (NQ)
WFHFF....... World Federation of Hungarian Freedom Fighters   (EA)
WFHG........ Bristol, VA [*AM radio station call letters*]
WFHJ......... World Federation of Hungarian Jews   (EA)
WFHK........ Pell City, AL [*AM radio station call letters*]
WFHL......... Decatur, IL [*Television station call letters*]
WFHM........ Vineland, NJ [*AM radio station call letters*]
WFHR........ Wisconsin Rapids, WI [*AM radio station call letters*]
WFHSLPAC ... Water-Flooded Helical Screw Low-Pressure Air Compressor [*Navy*]   (CAAL)
WFI............ Fianarantsoa [*Madagascar*] [*Airport symbol*]   (OAG)
WFI............ Wheat Flour Institute [*Absorbed by Miller's National Federation*]   (EA)
WFI............ Wishes and Fears Inventory [*Psychology*]
WFI............ Wood Flooring Institute of America [*Later, WSFI*]   (EA)
WFI............ Wood Foundation Institute [*Toledo, IA*]   (EA)
WFI............ World Faiths Insight [*A publication*]
WFI............ World Federation of Investors   (EA-IO)
WFIA......... Louisville, KY [*AM radio station call letters*]
WFIA......... Western Forest Industries Association [*Portland, OR*]   (EA)
WFIC......... Collinsville, VA [*AM radio station call letters*]
WFID......... Rio Piedras, PR [*FM radio station call letters*]

WFIE-TV.... Evansville, IN [*Television station call letters*]
WFIF......... Milford, CT [*AM radio station call letters*]
WFIG......... Sumter, SC [*AM radio station call letters*]
WFIL......... Philadelphia, PA [*AM radio station call letters*]
WFIM........ World Federation of Islamic Missions   (EA-IO)
WFIN........ Findlay, OH [*AM radio station call letters*]
WFIN........ Women and Food Information Network   (EA)
WFIQ........ Florence, AL [*Television station call letters*]
WFIR........ Roanoke, VA [*AM radio station call letters*]
WFIS........ Fountain Inn, SC [*AM radio station call letters*]
WFIS........ World Federation of Iranian Students
WFIT........ Melbourne, FL [*AM radio station call letters*]
WFIU........ Bloomington, IN [*FM radio station call letters*]
WFIV........ Kissimmee, FL [*AM radio station call letters*]
WFIW........ Fairfield, IL [*AM radio station call letters*]
WFIW-FM.. Fairfield, IL [*FM radio station call letters*]
WFIX........ Huntsville, AL [*AM radio station call letters*]
WFJA........ Sanford, NC [*FM radio station call letters*]
WFJJ........ World Federation of Jewish Journalists   (EA-IO)
WFJT........ Inez, KY [*AM radio station call letters*]
WFK......... Frenchville [*Maine*] [*Airport symbol*]   (OAG)
WFKN........ Franklin, KY [*AM radio station call letters*]
WFKX........ Henderson, TN [*FM radio station call letters*]
WFKY........ Frankfort, KY [*AM radio station call letters*]
WFKZ........ Plantation Key, FL [*FM radio station call letters*]
WFL.......... Windflower Mining Limited [*Vancouver Stock Exchange symbol*]
WFL.......... Woman's Freedom League
WFL.......... Work Flow Language [*Data processing*]   (BUR)
WFL.......... World Football League [*Dissolved, 1975*]
WFL.......... Worshipful [*Freemasonry*]   (ROG)
WFL.......... Wredemann-Frang Law
WFLA........ Tampa, FL [*AM radio station call letters*]
WFLA........ Western Fraternal Life Association   (EA)
WFLB........ Fayetteville, NC [*AM radio station call letters*]
WFLC........ Canandaigua, NY [*FM radio station call letters*]
WFLD........ Work/Family Life Database [*Database*]
WFLD-TV... Chicago, IL [*Television station call letters*]
WFLE........ Flemingsburg, KY [*AM radio station call letters*]
WFLI......... Lookout Mountain, TN [*AM radio station call letters*]
WFLI-TV ... Cleveland, TN [*Television station call letters*]
WFLN-FM.. Philadelphia, PA [*FM radio station call letters*]
WFLO........ Farmville, VA [*AM radio station call letters*]
WFLO-FM .. Farmville, VA [*FM radio station call letters*]
WFLQ........ French Lick, IN [*FM radio station call letters*]
WFLR........ Dundee, NY [*AM radio station call letters*]
WFLR-FM... Dundee, NY [*FM radio station call letters*]
WFLRY...... World Federation of Liberal and Radical Youth
WFLS........ Fredericksburg, VA [*AM radio station call letters*]
WFLS-FM... Fredericksburg, VA [*FM radio station call letters*]
WFLT........ Flint, MI [*AM radio station call letters*]
WFLW....... Monticello, KY [*AM radio station call letters*]
WFLX-TV ... West Palm Beach, FL [*Television station call letters*]
WFLY .... Troy, NY [*FM radio station call letters*]
WFLZ........ Thonotosassa, FL [*AM radio station call letters*]
WFM......... Water Flow Meter
WFM......... Waveform Monitor
WFM......... Waveguide Frequency Meter
WFM......... Wells Fargo Mortgage & Equity Trust [*NYSE symbol*]
WFM......... Western Federation of Miners
WFM......... Westford [*Massachusetts*] [*Seismograph station code, US Geological Survey*]   (SEIS)
WFMB .... Springfield, IL [*FM radio station call letters*]
WFMC........ Goldsboro, NC [*AM radio station call letters*]
WFMC........ Welding Filler Material Control   (NRCH)
WFMD .... Frederick, MD [*AM radio station call letters*]
WFME .... Newark, NJ [*FM radio station call letters*]
WFME .... World Federation for Medical Education   (EA)
WFMF........ Baton Rouge, LA [*FM radio station call letters*]
WFMG .... Richmond, IN [*FM radio station call letters*]
WFMH .... Cullman, AL [*AM radio station call letters*]
WFMH .... World Federation for Mental Health [*Alexandria, VA*]   (EA)
WFMH-FM ... Cullman, AL [*FM radio station call letters*]
WFMI........ Winchester, KY [*FM radio station call letters*]
WFMJ........ Youngstown, OH [*AM radio station call letters*]
WFMJ-TV... Youngstown, OH [*Television station call letters*]
WFMK .... East Lansing, MI [*FM radio station call letters*]
WFML........ Vincennes, IN [*FM radio station call letters*]
WFMLTA... World Federation of Modern Language Teachers' Association   (EA)
WFMM....... Harbor Beach, MI [*FM radio station call letters*]
WFMO .... Fairmont, NC [*AM radio station call letters*]
WFMQ .... Lebanon, TN [*FM radio station call letters*]
WFMR .... Menomonee Falls, WI [*FM radio station call letters*]
WFMS .... Indianapolis, IN [*FM radio station call letters*]
WFMT....... Chicago, IL [*FM radio station call letters*]
WFMU .... East Orange, NJ [*FM radio station call letters*]
WFMU .... Weather and Fixed Map Unit [*FAA*]
WFMV .... Blairstown, NJ [*FM radio station call letters*]
WFMW ...... Madisonville, KY [*AM radio station call letters*]
WFMW ...... World Federation of Methodist Women   (EA-IO)

WFMWNAA ... World Federation of Methodist Women, North America Area   (EA)
WFMX .... Statesville, NC [*FM radio station call letters*]
WFMY-TV ... Greensboro, NC [*Television station call letters*]
WFMZ........ Allentown, PA [*FM radio station call letters*]
WFMZ-TV... Allentown, PA [*Television station call letters*]
WFN .... Weapons and Facilities, Navy   (NG)
WFN .... Well-Formed Net
WFN .... Westminster College, New Wilmington, PA [*OCLC symbol*]   (OCLC)
WFN .... World Federation of Neurology [*Winston-Salem, NC*]   (EA)
WFNA........ White Fuming Nitric Acid
WFNC........ Fayetteville, NC [*AM radio station call letters*]
WFNE........ Forsyth, GA [*FM radio station call letters*]
WFNM........ Lancaster, PA [*FM radio station call letters*]
WFNMW .... World Federation of Trade Unions of Non-Manual Workers [*See also FMTNM*]   (EA-IO)
WFNR........ Christiansburg, VA [*AM radio station call letters*]
WFNS........ Women's Forum on National Security [*Defunct*]   (EA)
WFNS........ World Federation of Neurosurgical Societies   (EA)
WFNX........ Lynn, MA [*FM radio station call letters*]
WFNY........ Racine, WI [*FM radio station call letters*]
WFO .... Wide Field Optics
WF/O........ Wife Of [*Genealogy*]
WFOB........ Fostoria, OH [*AM radio station call letters*]
WFOB-FM ... Fostoria, OH [*FM radio station call letters*]
WFOC........ Western Field Operations Center [*Bureau of Mines*]
WFOF........ Covington, IN [*FM radio station call letters*]
WFOF........ Wide Field Optical Filter
WFOG........ Suffolk, VA [*FM radio station call letters*]
WFOM........ Marietta, GA [*AM radio station call letters*]
WFon........ Fond Du Lac Public Library, Fond Du Lac, WI [*Library symbol*] [*Library of Congress*]   (LCLS)
WFON........ Fond Du Lac, WI [*FM radio station call letters*]
WFonM....... Marian College of Fond Du Lac, Fond Du Lac, WI [*Library symbol*] [*Library of Congress*]   (LCLS)
WFonMM ... Mercury Marine, Fond Du Lac, WI [*Library symbol*] [*Library of Congress*]   (LCLS)
WFonSA..... Saint Agnes Hospital, Fond Du Lac, WI [*Library symbol*] [*Library of Congress*]   (LCLS)
WFont .... Fontana Public Library, Fontana, WI [*Library symbol*] [*Library of Congress*]   (LCLS)
WFonU ...... University of Wisconsin-Fond Du Lac, Fond Du Lac, WI [*Library symbol*] [*Library of Congress*]   (LCLS)
WFOR........ Hattiesburg, MS [*AM radio station call letters*]
WFOS........ Chesapeake, VA [*FM radio station call letters*]
WFOT........ World Federation of Occupational Therapists   (EA-IO)
WFOV........ Wide Field of View
WFOX........ Gainesville, GA [*FM radio station call letters*]
WFOY........ St. Augustine, FL [*AM radio station call letters*]
WF & P ...... Wabash, Frisco, and Pacific Association   (EA)
WFP.......... Warm Front [*or Frontal*] Passage [*Meteorology*]   (FAAC)
WFP.......... Wearout Failure Period
WFP.......... Witness for Peace [*An association*]   (EA)
WFP.......... World Federation of Parasitologists   (EA-IO)
WFP.......... World Food Programme [*Rome, Italy*] [*United Nations*]
WFP.......... Worldwide Fast for Peace [*An association*] [*Defunct*]   (EA)
WFPA .... Fort Payne, AL [*AM radio station call letters*]
WFPA .... World Federation for the Protection of Animals [*Also known as FMPA, WTB*] [*Later, WSPA*]
WFPC........ Petersburg, IN [*FM radio station call letters*]
WFPFC....... Worldwide Fair Play for Frogs Committee   (EA)
WFPG........ Atlantic City, NJ [*FM radio station call letters*]
WFPHA....... World Federation of Public Health Associations [*World Health Organization*] [*Washington, DC*]   (EA)
WFPK .... Louisville, KY [*FM radio station call letters*]
WFPL......... Louisville, KY [*FM radio station call letters*]
WFPLCA .... World Federation of Pipe Line Contractors Association [*Dallas, TX*]   (EA)
WFPMM ..... World Federation of Proprietary Medicine Manufacturers
WFPR........ Hammond, LA [*AM radio station call letters*]
WFPS......... Freeport, IL [*FM radio station call letters*]
WFPS......... Wild Flower Preservation Society   (EA)
WFPT .... Frederick, MD [*Television station call letters*]
WFPT .... Welsh Figure Preference Test [*Psychology*]
WFPT .... World Federation for Physical Therapy
WFQX........ Front Royal, VA [*FM radio station call letters*]
WFR.......... Wafer   (MSA)
WFR.......... Wharf Resources [*Toronto Stock Exchange symbol*] [*Vancouver Stock Exchange symbol*]
WFR.......... Wheal and Flare Reaction [*Immunology*]
WFR.......... Wide-Finding RADAR   (MCD)
WFR.......... Worcestershire and Sherwood Foresters Regiment [*Military unit*] [*British*]
WFRA .... Franklin, PA [*AM radio station call letters*]
WFRAF ...... Wharf Resources Ltd. [*NASDAQ symbol*]   (NQ)
WFRB .... Frostburg, MD [*AM radio station call letters*]
WFRBC ...... Washed, Filtered Red Blood Cells [*Hematology*]
WFRB-FM ... Frostburg, MD [*FM radio station call letters*]
WFRC........ Columbus, GA [*FM radio station call letters*]
WFRD......... Hanover, NH [*FM radio station call letters*]

WFRE .... Frederick, MD [*FM radio station call letters*]
WFRJ .... Johnstown, PA [*FM radio station call letters*]
WFRL .... Freeport, IL [*AM radio station call letters*]
WFRM .... Coudersport, PA [*AM radio station call letters*]
WFRM-FM ... Coudersport, PA [*FM radio station call letters*]
WFRN .... Elkhart, IN [*FM radio station call letters*]
WFRO .... Fremont, OH [*AM radio station call letters*]
WFRO-FM ... Fremont, OH [*FM radio station call letters*]
WFRS .... Middle Island, NY [*FM radio station call letters*]
WFRS .... World Federation of Rose Societies   (EA-IO)
WFRV-TV ... Green Bay, WI [*Television station call letters*]
WFRW .... Webster, NY [*FM radio station call letters*]
WFRX .... West Frankfort, IL [*AM radio station call letters*]
WFRX-FM... West Frankfort, IL [*FM radio station call letters*]
WFS .... Waterhouse-Friderichsen Syndrome [*Medicine*]
WFS .... Weapon Fire Simulator   (MCD)
WFS .... Welfare Food Service [*British*]
WFS .... Women for Sobriety [*Quakertown, PA*]   (EA)
WFS .... Wood Furring Strips [*Technical drawings*]
WFS .... Work Function Surface
WFS .... World Fertility Survey [*Program*]
WFS .... World Food Security [*FAO program*] [*United Nations*]
WFS .... World Future Society   (EA)
WFSA .... Wash Frock Salesmen's Association   (EA)
WFSA .... World Federation of Societies of Anaesthesiologists [*Bristol, England*]   (EA-IO)
WFSBP .... World Federation of the Societies of Biological Psychiatry [*Philadelphia, PA*]   (EA)
WFSB-TV ... Hartford, CT [*Television station call letters*]
WFSC .... Franklin, NC [*AM radio station call letters*]
WFSE .... Edinboro, PA [*FM radio station call letters*]
WFSEC ...... World Fellowship of Slavic Evangelical Christians   (EA)
WFSF .... World Futures Studies Federation   (EA)
WFSG .... Panama City, FL [*Television station call letters*]
WFSGI .... World Federation of the Sporting Goods Industry   (EA-IO)
WFSH .... Valparaiso-Niceville, FL [*AM radio station call letters*]
WFSI .... Annapolis, MD [*FM radio station call letters*]
WFSL .... Washington Federal Savings & Loan Association of Seattle [*NASDAQ symbol*]   (NQ)
WFSP .... Kingwood, WV [*AM radio station call letters*]
WFSR .... Harlan, KY [*AM radio station call letters*]
WFSS .... Fayetteville, NC [*FM radio station call letters*]
WFST .... Caribou, ME [*AM radio station call letters*]
WFSt .... Wehrmachtfuehrungsstab [*Armed Forces Operations Staff*] [*German military - World War II*]
WFSU-FM ... Tallahassee, FL [*FM radio station call letters*]
WFSU-TV ... Tallahassee, FL [*Television station call letters*]
WFSW .... World Federation of Scientific Workers [*See also FMTS*] [*ICSU*]   (EA-IO)
WFSY .... Panama City, FL [*FM radio station call letters*]
WFT........... Warm Fluctuating Temperatures
WFT........... West Fraser Timber Co. Ltd. [*Toronto Stock Exchange symbol*] [*Vancouver Stock Exchange symbol*]
WFTA .... Fulton, MS [*FM radio station call letters*]
WFTA .... Winograd Fourier Transform Algorithm   (MCD)
WFTA .... World Federation of Taiwanese Associations   (EA)
WFTC .... Kinston, NC [*AM radio station call letters*]
WFTC .... Western Flying Training Command [*AAFWFTC*]
WFTD .... Women's Flying Training Detachment [*World War II*]
WFTF........... Rutland, VT [*FM radio station call letters*]
WFTG .... London, KY [*AM radio station call letters*]
WFTH .... Richmond, VA [*AM radio station call letters*]
WFTI-FM ... St. Petersburg, FL [*FM radio station call letters*]
WFTJW....... World Federation of Travel Journalists and Writers   (EA)
WFTL .... Fort Lauderdale, FL [*AM radio station call letters*]
WFTM........ Maysville, KY [*AM radio station call letters*]
WFTM-FM ... Maysville, KY [*FM radio station call letters*]
WFTN .... Franklin, NH [*AM radio station call letters*]
WFTN .... Franklin, NH [*FM radio station call letters*]
WFTO .... Fulton, MS [*AM radio station call letters*]
WFTP .... Fort Pierce, FL [*AM radio station call letters*]
WFTP .... Weapons Fly-To Point [*Military*]   (CAAL)
WFTQ .... Worcester, MA [*AM radio station call letters*]
WFTR .... Front Royal, VA [*AM radio station call letters*]
WFTR-FM... Front Royal, VA [*FM radio station call letters*]
WFTS .... Tampa, FL [*Television station call letters*]
WFTS .... Western Fish Toxicology Station [*Environmental Protection Agency*]
W FTTNGS ... With Fittings [*Freight*]
WFTU .... World Federation of Trade Unions [*See also FSM*] [*Prague, Czechoslovakia*]   (EA-IO)
WFTUNMW ... World Federation of Trade Unions of Non-Manual Workers [*Antwerp, Belgium*]
WFTV .... Orlando, FL [*Television station call letters*]
WFTW .... Fort Walton Beach, FL [*AM radio station call letters*]
WFTW-FM ... Fort Walton Beach, FL [*FM radio station call letters*]
WFTX .... Cape Coral, FL [*Television station call letters*]
WFTY .... Washington, DC [*Television station call letters*]
WFU .... Wake Forest University [*North Carolina*]
WFU .... War Frauds Unit

WFUL .... Fulton, KY [*AM radio station call letters*]
WFUL .... West Florida Union List [*Library network*]
WFUM .... Flint, MI [*Television station call letters*]
WFUM-FM ... Flint, MI [*FM radio station call letters*]
WFUN .... Ashtabula, OH [*AM radio station call letters*]
WFUNA .... World Federation of United Nations Associations   (EA)
WFUPA .... World Federation of Ukrainian Patriarchal Associations   (EA)
WFUR .... Grand Rapids, MI [*AM radio station call letters*]
WFUV .... New York, NY [*FM radio station call letters*]
WFUWO ..... World Federation of Ukrainian Women's Organizations   (EA)
WFVA .... Fredericksburg, VA [*AM radio station call letters*]
WFVA-FM ... Fredericksburg, VA [*FM radio station call letters*]
WFVR .... Valdosta, GA [*AM radio station call letters*]
WFW .... Walden Forever Wild [*An association*]   (EA)
WFWA .... Fort Wayne, IN [*Television station call letters*]
WFWC .... Walden Forever Wild Committee   (EA)
WFWL........ Camden, TN [*AM radio station call letters*]
WFWM....... Frostburg, MD [*FM radio station call letters*]
WFXA-FM ... Augusta, GA [*FM radio station call letters*]
WFXC .... Durham, NC [*FM radio station call letters*]
WFXE .... Columbus, GA [*FM radio station call letters*]
WFXI .... Washington, NC [*FM radio station call letters*]
WFXP .... Pensacola, FL [*AM radio station call letters*]
WFXR .... Ravenel, SC [*FM radio station call letters*]
WFXT .... Boston, MA [*Television station call letters*]
WFXW .... Geneva, IL [*AM radio station call letters*]
WFXX .... South Williamsport, PA [*AM radio station call letters*]
WFXX-FM... South Williamsport, PA [*FM radio station call letters*]
WFXY .... Middlesboro, KY [*AM radio station call letters*]
WFXZ .... Pinconning, MI [*AM radio station call letters*]
WFYC .... Alma, MI [*AM radio station call letters*]
WFYC-FM ... Alma, MI [*FM radio station call letters*]
WFYF .... Watertown, NY [*Television station call letters*]
WFYI .... Indianapolis, IN [*Television station call letters*]
WFYN-FM ... Key West, FL [*FM radio station call letters*]
WFY/NIO.... World Federalist Youth - Youth Movement for a New International Order [*Amsterdam, Netherlands*]   (EA-IO)
WFYR .... Chicago, IL [*FM radio station call letters*]
WFY-USA... World Federalist Youth - United States of America [*Later, Action for World Community: World Federalist Youth in the USA*]   (EA)
WFYV .... Atlantic Beach, FL [*FM radio station call letters*]
WFYZ .... Murfreesboro, TN [*Television station call letters*]
WG .... Air Ecosse Ltd. [*Great Britain*] [*ICAO designator*]   (FAAC)
WG .... Riker Laboratories Ltd. [*Great Britain*] [*Research code symbol*]
WG .... Wage Grade [*Federal employee job classification*]
Wg .... Wandlung [*A publication*]
WG .... Wartime Guidance [*Air Force*]   (AFM)
WG .... Waste Gas [*Nuclear energy*]   (NRCH)
WG .... Water Gauge
W/G........... Water Glycol   (KSC)
WG .... Water Resources News-Clipping Service. General Issue. Water Management Service. Department of the Environment [*Ottawa*] [*A publication*]
WG .... Waveguide
WG .... Wedge   (MSA)
WG .... Wegener's Granulomatosis [*Medicine*]
WG .... Weighing   (ROG)
WG .... Weight Guaranteed
WG .... Welsh Guards [*Military unit*] [*British*]
WG .... Welt als Geschichte Zeitschrift fuer Universalgeschichtliche Forschung [*A publication*]
WG .... West German
WG .... Willcox & Gibbs, Inc. [*NYSE symbol*]
WG .... Window Guard   (AAG)
WG .... Wine Gallon
WG .... Wing
WG .... Wire Gauge
W & G .... Wissen und Glauben [*A publication*]
WG .... With Grain
WG .... Women for Guatemala   (EA)
WG .... Working Group   (FAAC)
WG .... World Goodwill   (EA)
WG .... Wright-Giemsa [*A stain*] [*Cytology*]
WG .... Writing [*Law*]   (ROG)
4WG .... Weather Group (4th) [*Washington, DC*] [*Air Force*]
WGA........... Wagga-Wagga [*Australia*] [*Airport symbol*]   (OAG)
WGA........... Waveguide Assembly
WGA........... Weekly Government Abstracts [*National Technical Information Service*]
WGA........... Weighted Guidelines Analysis [*Air Force*]   (MCD)
WGA........... Wells-Gardner Electronics Corp. [*American Stock Exchange symbol*]
WGA........... Western Golf Association   (EA)
WGA........... Western Growers Association   (EA)
WGA........... Wheat Germ Agglutinin [*Biochemistry*]
WGA........... Wild Goose Association   (EA)
WGA........... Women Grocers of America [*Reston, VA*]   (EA)
WGA........... Writers Guild of America
WGAA......... Cedartown, GA [*AM radio station call letters*]
WGAB .... Bloomfield, CT [*AM radio station call letters*]

WGAC .... Augusta, GA [*AM radio station call letters*]
WGAD .... Gadsden, AL [*AM radio station call letters*]
WGAE .... Girard, PA [*FM radio station call letters*]
WGAE .... Writers Guild of America, East   (EA)
WGAE-US ... World Government of the Age of Enlightenment - US [*Formerly, WPEC*]   (EA)
WGAF .... West Germany Air Force
WGAF-FM .. Quitman, GA [*FM radio station call letters*]
WGAI .... Elizabeth City, NC [*AM radio station call letters*]
WGAJ .... Deerfield, MA [*FM radio station call letters*]
WGAL-TV... Lancaster, PA [*Television station call letters*]
WGAN .... Portland, ME [*AM radio station call letters*]
WGAN-FM .. Portland, ME [*FM radio station call letters*]
WGAO .... Franklin, MA [*FM radio station call letters*]
WGAO .... World Guide to Abbreviations of Organizations [*A publication*]
WGAP .... Maryville, TN [*AM radio station call letters*]
WGAQ .... Franklin, IN [*FM radio station call letters*]
WGAR .... Cleveland, OH [*AM radio station call letters*]
WGAR-FM .. Cleveland, OH [*FM radio station call letters*]
WGAS .... Gastonia, NC [*AM radio station call letters*]
WGAT .... Gate City, VA [*AM radio station call letters*]
WGAU .... Athens, GA [*AM radio station call letters*]
WGAW .... Gardner, MA [*AM radio station call letters*]
WGAW .... Writers Guild of America, West   (EA)
WGAY-FM ... Washington, DC [*FM radio station call letters*]
WGB .... Weltgewerkschaftsbund [*World Federation of Trade Unions*]
WGBA .... Green Bay, WI [*Television station call letters*]
WGBB .... Freeport, NY [*AM radio station call letters*]
WGBC .... Waveguide Operating below Cutoff   (IEEE)
WGBE .... Woodbine, GA [*AM radio station call letters*]
WGBF .... Evansville, IN [*AM radio station call letters*]
WGBF-FM ... Henderson, KY [*FM radio station call letters*]
WGBH .... Boston, MA [*FM radio station call letters*]
WGBH-TV ... Boston, MA [*Television station call letters*]
WGBI .... Scranton, PA [*AM radio station call letters*]
WGBI-FM ... Scranton, PA [*FM radio station call letters*]
WGBO-TV ... Joliet, IL [*Television station call letters*]
WGBP-FM ... Green Bay, WI [*FM radio station call letters*]
WGBQ .... Galesburg, IL [*FM radio station call letters*]
WGBR .... Goldsboro, NC [*AM radio station call letters*]
WGBS-TV ... Philadelphia, PA [*Television station call letters*]
WGBW .... Green Bay, WI [*FM radio station call letters*]
WGBX-TV... Boston, MA [*Television station call letters*]
WGBY-TV .. Springfield, MA [*Television station call letters*]
WGBZ .... Gainesville, FL [*Television station call letters*]
WGc .... Genoa City Public Library, Genoa City, WI [*Library symbol*] [*Library of Congress*]   (LCLS)
WGC .... Waste Gas Compressor [*Nuclear energy*]   (NRCH)
WGC .... Waveguide Shutter
WGC .... West Georgia College [*Carollton*]
WGC .... Western Gear Corporation
WGC .... Western Governors Conference
WGC .... Wisconsin Gas Company [*NYSE symbol*]
WGC .... World Games Council   (EA-IO)
WGC .... World Gospel Crusades
WGC .... Worthy Grand Chaplain [*Freemasonry*]
WGC .... Worthy Grand Conductor [*Freemasonry*]   (ROG)
WGCA .... Wisconsin Gift Cheese Association [*Madison, WI*]   (EA)
WGCA-FM ... Quincy, IL [*FM radio station call letters*]
WGCB .... Red Lion, PA [*AM radio station call letters*]
WGCB-FM ... Red Lion, PA [*FM radio station call letters*]
WGCB-TV ... Red Lion, PA [*Television station call letters*]
WGCC-FM ... Batavia, NY [*FM radio station call letters*]
WGCD .... Chester, SC [*AM radio station call letters*]
WG/CDR .... Wing Commander [*British*]   (NATG)
WGCDR ...... Working Group for Community Development Reform   (EA)
WGCF .... Sans Souci, SC [*AM radio station call letters*]
WGCG-TV ... Greenwood, SC [*Television station call letters*]
WGCH .... Greenwich, CT [*AM radio station call letters*]
WGCI .... Chicago, IL [*AM radio station call letters*]
WGCI-FM ... Chicago, IL [*FM radio station call letters*]
WGCL .... Window Glass Cutters League of America [*Later, GBBA*]   (EA)
WGCM .... Gulfport, MS [*FM radio station call letters*]
WGCQ .... Parris Island, SC [*FM radio station call letters*]
WGCR .... Brevard, NC [*AM radio station call letters*]
WGCR .... West Georgia College. Review [*A publication*]
WGCS .... Goshen, IN [*FM radio station call letters*]
WGD .... Working Group Director
WGDA .... Watermelon Growers and Distributors Association
WGDC .... Waveguide Directional Coupler
WGDHP ..... Working Group on Domestic Hunger and Poverty   (EA)
WGDL .... Lares, PR [*AM radio station call letters*]
WGDL .... Waveguide Delay Line
WGDR .... Plainfield, VT [*FM radio station call letters*]
WGDS .... Warm Gas Distribution System
WGDS .... Waste Gas Disposal System [*Nuclear energy*]   (NRCH)
WGDT .... Waste Gas Decay Tank [*Nuclear energy*]   (NRCH)
WGE .... Walgett [*Australia*] [*Airport symbol*]   (OAG)
WGE .... World's Great Explorers [*A publication*]
WGEA .... Geneva, AL [*AM radio station call letters*]
WGEA-FM ... Geneva, AL [*FM radio station call letters*]

WGEC .... Springfield, GA [*FM radio station call letters*]
WGEE .... Green Bay, WI [*AM radio station call letters*]
WGEEIA ..... Western Ground Electronics Engineering Installation Agency   (AAG)
WGEI .... Tuscumbia, AL [*Television station call letters*]
WGEL .... Greenville, IL [*FM radio station call letters*]
WGEM .... Quincy, IL [*AM radio station call letters*]
WGEM-FM ... Quincy, IL [*FM radio station call letters*]
WGEM-TV ... Quincy, IL [*Television station call letters*]
WGEN .... Geneseo, IL [*AM radio station call letters*]
WGEN-FM ... Geneseo, IL [*FM radio station call letters*]
WGER .... Working Group on Extraterrestrial Resources [*Defunct*] [*NASA*]
WGER-FM ... Bay City, MI [*FM radio station call letters*]
WGET .... Gettysburg, PA [*AM radio station call letters*]
WGETS ...... Wayne George Encoder Test Set
WGEV .... Beaver Falls, PA [*FM radio station call letters*]
WGEZ .... Beloit, WI [*AM radio station call letters*]
WGF .... Waveguide Filter
WGF .... Western Goals Foundation   (EA)
WGF .... Wound Glass Fiber
WGFA .... Watseka, IL [*AM radio station call letters*]
WGFA-FM ... Watseka, IL [*FM radio station call letters*]
WGFAR ...... Wenner-Gren Foundation for Anthropological Research   (EA)
WGFB .... Plattsburgh, NY [*FM radio station call letters*]
WGFC .... Floyd, VA [*AM radio station call letters*]
WGFG .... Lake City, SC [*FM radio station call letters*]
WGFM .... Schenectady, NY [*FM radio station call letters*]
WGFN .... South Glens Falls, NY [*AM radio station call letters*]
WGFP .... Webster, MA [*AM radio station call letters*]
WGFR .... Glens Falls, NY [*FM radio station call letters*]
WGFS .... Covington, GA [*AM radio station call letters*]
WGFT .... Youngstown, OH [*AM radio station call letters*]
WGFW .... Morovis, PR [*AM radio station call letters*]
WGG .... Warm Gas Generator
WGG .... Worthy Grand Guardian [*Freemasonry*]
WGG .... Worthy Grand Guide [*Freemasonry*]
WGGA .... Gainesville, GA [*AM radio station call letters*]
WGGB .... Writers' Guild of Great Britain
WGGB-TV ... Springfield, MA [*Television station call letters*]
WGGC .... Glasgow, KY [*AM radio station call letters*]
WGGF .... Lebanon, PA [*Television station call letters*]
WGGG .... Gainesville, FL [*AM radio station call letters*]
WGGG-FM ... Micanopy, FL [*FM radio station call letters*]
WGGH .... Marion, IL [*AM radio station call letters*]
WGGL-FM ... Houghton, MI [*FM radio station call letters*]
WGGM .... Chester, VA [*AM radio station call letters*]
WGGN .... Castalia, OH [*FM radio station call letters*]
WGGN-TV ... Sandusky, OH [*Television station call letters*]
WGGO .... Salamanca, NY [*AM radio station call letters*]
WGGQ .... Waupun, WI [*FM radio station call letters*]
WGGR .... Hibbing, MN [*AM radio station call letters*]
WGGS-TV ... Greenville, SC [*Television station call letters*]
WGGT-TV ... Greensboro, NC [*Television station call letters*]
WGGZ .... Baton Rouge, LA [*FM radio station call letters*]
WGH .... Newport News, VA [*AM radio station call letters*]
WGH .... Worthy Grand Herald [*Freemasonry*]
WGHB .... Farmville, NC [*AM radio station call letters*]
WGHC .... Clayton, GA [*AM radio station call letters*]
WGHN .... Grand Haven, MI [*AM radio station call letters*]
WGHN-FM ... Grand Haven, MI [*FM radio station call letters*]
WGHP-TV ... High Point, NC [*Television station call letters*]
WGHQ .... Kingston, NY [*AM radio station call letters*]
WGHR .... Marietta, GA [*AM radio station call letters*]
WGHS .... Glen Ellyn, IL [*FM radio station call letters*]
WGHT .... Weigh Tronix, Inc. [*NASDAQ symbol*]   (NQ)
WGHW .... Norristown, PA [*AM radio station call letters*]
WGI .... Waveguide Isolator
WGI .... Western Goldfields [*Toronto Stock Exchange symbol*]
WGI .... Word of God Institute   (EA)
WGI .... Work Glove Institute [*Later, WGMA*]   (EA)
WGI .... World Geophysical Interval
WGIA .... Blackshear, GA [*AM radio station call letters*]
WGIB .... Birmingham, AL [*FM radio station call letters*]
WGIC .... Wheat Gluten Industry Council [*Prairie Village, KS*]   (EA)
WGIG-FM ... Brunswick, GA [*FM radio station call letters*]
WGII .... Western Grain International, Incorporated [*NASDAQ symbol*]   (NQ)
WGIL .... Working Group on Internal Instrumentation [*NASA*]
WGIL .... Galesburg, IL [*AM radio station call letters*]
WGIQ .... Louisville, AL [*Television station call letters*]
WGIR .... Manchester, NH [*AM radio station call letters*]
WGIR-FM ... Manchester, NH [*FM radio station call letters*]
WGIT .... Hormigueros, PR [*FM radio station call letters*]
WGIV .... Charlotte, NC [*AM radio station call letters*]
WGJ .... Worm Gear Jack
WGJB .... World's Greatest Jazz Band
WGKA .... Atlanta, GA [*AM radio station call letters*]
WGKR .... Perry, FL [*AM radio station call letters*]
WGKS .... Swainsboro, GA [*FM radio station call letters*]
WGKX .... Memphis, TN [*FM radio station call letters*]

WGKY-FM ... Greenville, KY [*FM radio station call letters*]
WGL .... Fort Wayne, IN [*AM radio station call letters*]
WGL .... Warangal [*India*] [*Seismograph station code, US Geological Survey*]   (SEIS)
WGL .... Warren, Gorham & Lamont, Inc. [*Publisher*]
WGL .... Washington Gas Light Co. [*NYSE symbol*]
WGL .... Waveguide Load
WGL .... Weapons Guidance Laboratory
WGL .... Weighted Guidelines [*DoD*]
WGL .... Western Guidance Laboratory [*Wright Air Development Center*]   (MUGU)
WGL .... Westeuropaeische Gesellschaft fuer Luftfahrtpsychologie [*Western European Association for Aviation Psychology - WEAAP*]   (EA)
WGL .... Wire Glass   (AAG)
WGL .... Wire Grid Lens
WGL .... Wissenschaftliche Gesellschaft fuer Luftschiffahrt [*Scientific Association for Aeronautics*] [*German*]
WGL .... Wueste und Gelobtes Land [*A publication*]   (BJA)
WGLB .... Port Washington, WI [*AM radio station call letters*]
WGLB-FM ... Port Washington, WI [*FM radio station call letters*]
WGLC .... Mendota, IL [*AM radio station call letters*]
WGLC-FM ... Mendota, IL [*FM radio station call letters*]
WGLD .... Greensboro, NC [*AM radio station call letters*]
WGLE .... Lima, OH [*FM radio station call letters*]
WGLF .... Tallahassee, FL [*FM radio station call letters*]
WGLH .... Mebane, NC [*AM radio station call letters*]
WGLI .... Babylon, NY [*AM radio station call letters*]
WGLI .... Warren, Gorham & Lamont, Incorporated   (DLA)
WGLL .... Mercersburg, PA [*FM radio station call letters*]
WGLO .... Pekin, IL [*FM radio station call letters*]
WGLQ .... Escanaba, MI [*FM radio station call letters*]
WGLR .... Lancaster, WI [*AM radio station call letters*]
WGLR .... Wissenschaftliche Gesellschaft fuer Luft- und Raumfahrt [*Scientific Association for Air and Space Travel*] [*German*]
WGLS-FM ... Glassboro, NJ [*FM radio station call letters*]
WGLT .... Normal, IL [*FM radio station call letters*]
WGLU .... Johnstown, PA [*FM radio station call letters*]
WGLW .... Welsh Grand Lodge of Wales [*Freemasonry*]
WGLX .... Galion, OH [*AM radio station call letters*]
WGLY-FM ... Waterbury, VT [*FM radio station call letters*]
WGM .... Waveguide Meter
WGM .... Weighted Guidelines Method [*Navy*]
WGM .... World Gospel Mission   (EA)
WGM .... Worthy Grand Marshal [*or Master*] [*Freemasonry*]
WGMA .... Spindale, NC [*AM radio station call letters*]
WGMA .... Washington Gallery of Modern Art
WGMA .... West Gulf Maritime Association [*Formed by a merger of Brownsville Maritime Association, Galveston Maritime Association, and Houston Maritime Association*] [*Houston, TX*]   (EA)
WGMA .... Wet Ground Mica Association [*Boston, MA*]   (EA)
WGMA .... Work Glove Manufacturers Association [*Chicago, IL*]   (EA)
WGMB .... Georgetown, SC [*FM radio station call letters*]
WGMC .... Greece, NY [*FM radio station call letters*]
WGMC .... West Germanic [*Language, etc.*]
WGMD .... Rehoboth Beach, DE [*FM radio station call letters*]
WGME-TV ... Portland, ME [*Television station call letters*]
WGMF .... Watkins Glen, NY [*AM radio station call letters*]
WGMK .... Donaldsonville, GA [*FM radio station call letters*]
WGML .... Hinesville, GA [*AM radio station call letters*]
WGMM .... Gladwin, MI [*FM radio station call letters*]
WGMO .... Shell Lake, WI [*FM radio station call letters*]
WGMR .... Tyrone, PA [*FM radio station call letters*]
WGMS .... Bethesda, MD [*AM radio station call letters*]
WGMS .... World Glacier Monitoring Service   (EA)
WGMS-FM ... Washington, DC [*FM radio station call letters*]
WGN .... Chicago, IL [*AM radio station call letters*]
WGN .... Wagon
WGN .... World's Greatest Newspaper [*Sometimes used in reference to Chicago Tribune*]
WGNA .... Albany, NY [*FM radio station call letters*]
WGNB .... Seminole, FL [*AM radio station call letters*]
WGNC .... Gastonia, NC [*AM radio station call letters*]
WGNG .... Western Gold 'n Gas Co. [*NASDAQ symbol*]   (NQ)
WGNI .... Wilmington, NC [*FM radio station call letters*]
WGNL .... Waveguide Nitrogen Load
WGNO-TV ... New Orleans, LA [*Television station call letters*]
WGNR .... Grand Rapids, MI [*FM radio station call letters*]
WGNRR .... Women's Global Network on Reproductive Rights [*Formerly, International Contraception, Abortion, and Sterilisation Campaign*]   (EA)
WGNS .... Murfreesboro, TN [*AM radio station call letters*]
WGNT .... Huntington, WV [*AM radio station call letters*]
WGN-TV ..... Chicago, IL [*Television station call letters*]
WGNU .... Granite City, IL [*AM radio station call letters*]
WGNV .... Milladore, WI [*FM radio station call letters*]
WGNX .... Atlanta, GA [*Television station call letters*]
WGNY .... Newburgh, NY [*AM radio station call letters*]
WGNY-FM ... Newburgh, NY [*FM radio station call letters*]
WGNZ .... Christmas, FL [*AM radio station call letters*]

WGO .... Wehrmacht Graeberoffizier [*Armed forces graves registration officer*] [*German military - World War II*]
WGO .... Winnebago Industries, Inc. [*NYSE symbol*]
WGOC .... Kingsport, TN [*AM radio station call letters*]
WGOCC ..... World Government Organization Coordinating Council   (EA)
WGOD .... Charlotte Amalie, VI [*FM radio station call letters*]
WGOG .... Walhalla, SC [*AM radio station call letters*]
WGOH .... Grayson, KY [*AM radio station call letters*]
WGOJ .... Conneaut, OH [*FM radio station call letters*]
WGOK .... Mobile, AL [*AM radio station call letters*]
WGOL .... Lynchburg, VA [*FM radio station call letters*]
WGOM .... Marion, IN [*AM radio station call letters*]
WGOS .... High Point, NC [*AM radio station call letters*]
WGOT .... Merrimack, NH [*Television station call letters*]
WGOV .... Valdosta, GA [*AM radio station call letters*]
WGOW .... Chattanooga, TN [*AM radio station call letters*]
WGP .... Waingapu [*Indonesia*] [*Airport symbol*]   (OAG)
WGP .... Wattle Grove Press
WGp .... Weather Group [*Air Force*]   (AFM)
WGP .... Westgrowth Petroleums Ltd. [*Toronto Stock Exchange symbol*]
WGP .... Wire Grid Polarizer
WGPA .... Bethlehem, PA [*AM radio station call letters*]
WGPC .... Albany, GA [*AM radio station call letters*]
WGPC-FM ... Albany, GA [*FM radio station call letters*]
WGPL .... Bethal Park, PA [*AM radio station call letters*]
WGPMS .... Warehousing Gross Performance Measurement System   (AFM)
WGPR .... Detroit, MI [*FM radio station call letters*]
WGPR-TV ... Detroit, MI [*Television station call letters*]
WGPT .... Oakland, MD [*Television station call letters*]
WGr .... Brown County Library, Green Bay, WI [*Library symbol*] [*Library of Congress*]   (LCLS)
WGR .... Buffalo, NY [*AM radio station call letters*]
WGR .... War Guidance Requirements   (AFM)
WGR .... Water Graphite Reactor Experiment [*Nuclear energy*]
WGR .... Westbridge Resources Ltd. [*Vancouver Stock Exchange symbol*]
WGR .... Women in Government Relations [*McLean, VA*]   (EA)
WGR .... Working Group Report
WGRA .... Cairo, GA [*AM radio station call letters*]
WGrB .... Bellin Memorial Hospital, Green Bay, WI [*Library symbol*] [*Library of Congress*]   (LCLS)
WGRB .... Campbellsville, KY [*Television station call letters*]
WGrBC .... Brown County Hospital, Green Bay, WI [*Library symbol*] [*Library of Congress*]   (LCLS)
WGRC .... Spring Valley, NY [*AM radio station call letters*]
WGRD-FM ... Grand Rapids, MI [*FM radio station call letters*]
WGRE .... Greencastle, IN [*FM radio station call letters*]
WGREPO ..... Western Governors Regional Energy Policy Office
WGRG .... Greensboro, GA [*FM radio station call letters*]
WGRK .... Greensburg, KY [*AM radio station call letters*]
WGRK-FM ... Greensburg, KY [*FM radio station call letters*]
WGRM .... Greenwood, MS [*AM radio station call letters*]
WGRN .... Greenville, IL [*FM radio station call letters*]
WGrN .... Northeastern Wisconsin Technical Institute, Green Bay, WI [*Library symbol*] [*Library of Congress*]   (LCLS)
WGrNM ...... Neville Public Museum, Green Bay, WI [*Library symbol*] [*Library of Congress*]   (LCLS)
WGRO .... Lake City, FL [*AM radio station call letters*]
WGRP .... Greenville, PA [*AM radio station call letters*]
WGRQ .... Colonial Beach, VA [*FM radio station call letters*]
WGRR .... Prichard, AL [*AM radio station call letters*]
WGrSM .... Saint Mary's Hospital, Green Bay, WI [*Library symbol*] [*Library of Congress*]   (LCLS)
WGrSV .... Saint Vincent Hospital, Green Bay, WI [*Library symbol*] [*Library of Congress*]   (LCLS)
WGRT .... Indianapolis, IN [*AM radio station call letters*]
WGrU .... University of Wisconsin-Green Bay, Green Bay, WI [*Library symbol*] [*Library of Congress*]   (LCLS)
WGRV .... Greeneville, TN [*AM radio station call letters*]
WGRX .... Westminster, MD [*FM radio station call letters*]
WGRY .... Grayling, MI [*AM radio station call letters*]
WGRZ-TV ... Buffalo, NY [*Television station call letters*]
WG(S) .... Waste Gas (System) [*Nuclear energy*]   (NRCH)
WGS .... Water Gas Shift [*Chemical reaction*]
WGS .... Water Glycol Service Unit   (MCD)
WGS .... Waterford Generating Station   (NRCH)
WGS .... Waveguide Glide Slope
WGS .... Web Guide System
WGS .... World Geodetic System   (MUGU)
WGS .... World Government Sponsors
WGS .... Worthy Grand Sentinel [*Freemasonry*]
WGSA .... Ephrata, PA [*AM radio station call letters*]
WGSE .... Myrtle Beach, SC [*Television station call letters*]
WGSF .... Arlington, TN [*AM radio station call letters*]
WGSI .... Russell, PA [*FM radio station call letters*]
WGSIM .... Working Group on Satellite Ionospheric Measurements [*NASA*]
WGSJ .... Worm Gear Screw Jack
WGSL .... Greenville, SC [*AM radio station call letters*]
WGSM .... Huntington, NY [*AM radio station call letters*]
WGSN .... North Myrtle Beach, SC [*AM radio station call letters*]

WGSP........ Charlotte, NC [*AM radio station call letters*]
WGSPR ...... Working Group for Space Physics Research
WGSQ .... Cookeville, TN [*FM radio station call letters*]
WGSR........ Millen, GA [*AM radio station call letters*]
WGST........ Atlanta, GA [*AM radio station call letters*]
WGST........ Waste Gas Storage Tank [*Nuclear energy*]   (IEEE)
WGSU .... Geneseo, NY [*FM radio station call letters*]
WGSV........ Guntersville, AL [*AM radio station call letters*]
WGSX .... Bayamon, PR [*AM radio station call letters*]
WGSX .... Bayamon, PR [*FM radio station call letters*]
WGSY........ Phenix City, AL [*FM radio station call letters*]
WGT .... Wayne General and Technical College, Orrville, OH [*OCLC
                 symbol*] [*Inactive*]   (OCLC)
WGT .... Weight
WGTA........ Summerville, GA [*AM radio station call letters*]
WGTA .... Wisconsin General Test Apparatus [*Psychology*]
WGTC .... Bloomington, IN [*AM radio station call letters*]
WG-T-C...... Waveguide-to-Coaxial [*Aerospace*]   (AAG)
WGTC .... Working Group on Tracking and Computation [*NASA*]
WGT/COMB ... Weighter/Combiner   (MCD)
WGTD........ Kenosha, WI [*FM radio station call letters*]
WGTE-FM ... Toledo, OH [*FM radio station call letters*]
WGTE-TV... Toledo, OH [*Television station call letters*]
WGTH........ Richlands, VA [*FM radio station call letters*]
WGTL........ Kannapolis, NC [*AM radio station call letters*]
WGTM........ Wilson, NC [*AM radio station call letters*]
WGTN........ Georgetown, SC [*AM radio station call letters*]
WGTO........ Cypress Gardens, FL [*AM radio station call letters*]
WGTQ .... Sault Ste. Marie, MI [*Television station call letters*]
WGTR........ Miami, FL [*FM radio station call letters*]
WGTS-FM ... Takoma Park, MD [*FM radio station call letters*]
WGTT........ Alabaster, AL [*AM radio station call letters*]
WGTU........ Traverse City, MI [*Television station call letters*]
WGTV........ Athens, GA [*Television station call letters*]
WGTX .... De Funiak Springs, FL [*AM radio station call letters*]
WGTY........ Gettysburg, PA [*FM radio station call letters*]
WGTZ........ Eaton, OH [*FM radio station call letters*]
WGU .... Working Group on Untouchables   (EA)
WGUC .... Cincinnati, OH [*FM radio station call letters*]
WGUD .... Moss Point, MS [*AM radio station call letters*]
WGUD-FM ... Pascagoula, MS [*FM radio station call letters*]
WGUL .... Dunedin, FL [*AM radio station call letters*]
WGUN .... Atlanta, GA [*AM radio station call letters*]
WGUS .... North Augusta, SC [*AM radio station call letters*]
WGUSEASA ... Working Group of US Overseas Educational Advisers in
                 South America   (EA)
WGUS-FM ... Augusta, SC [*FM radio station call letters*]
WGUY .... Brewer, ME [*AM radio station call letters*]
WGUY-FM ... Brewer, ME [*FM radio station call letters*]
WGVA........ Geneva, NY [*AM radio station call letters*]
WGVC .... Grand Rapids, MI [*Television station call letters*]
WGVC-FM ... Allendale, MI [*FM radio station call letters*]
WGVE........ Gary, IN [*FM radio station call letters*]
WGVK .... Kalamazoo, MI [*Television station call letters*]
WGVM........ Greenville, MS [*AM radio station call letters*]
WGVO........ Greenville, OH [*FM radio station call letters*]
WGW .... Wallila Gap [*Washington*] [*Seismograph station code, US
                 Geological Survey*]   (SEIS)
WGW .... Waveguide Window
WGWC ...... Working Group on Weather Communications [*NATO*]   (NATG)
WGWG .... Boiling Springs, NC [*FM radio station call letters*]
WGWP........ Working Group on Weather Plans [*NATO*]   (NATG)
WGXA-TV ... Macon, GA [*Television station call letters*]
WGXM........ Dayton, OH [*FM radio station call letters*]
WGY .... Schenectady, NY [*AM radio station call letters*]
WGYL........ Vero Beach, FL [*FM radio station call letters*]
WGYV........ Greenville, AL [*AM radio station call letters*]
WGZS........ Elloree-Santee, SC [*AM radio station call letters*]
WH .... City-Flug GmbH [*West Germany*] [*ICAO designator*]   (FAAC)
Wh .... Interrogative [*Linguistics*]
WH............ Wage and Hour Cases [*Bureau of National Affairs*]   (DLA)
W & H .... Wage and Hour Division [*Department of Labor*]   (OICC)
WH............ Walking Hinge   (KSC)
WH............ Wall Hydrant   (AAG)
W-H .... Walsh-Healey Act [*Labor*]
WH............ Warhead
W/H............ Warheading Building   (NATG)
WH............. Water Heater
WH............. Watt-Hour
WH............. We Have, Ready with Called Party
                 [*Telecommunications*]   (TEL)
WH............ Wehrmacht-Heer [*Marking on Army vehicles*] [*German military
                 - World War II*]
WH............. Western Hemisphere
WH............. Western Hemlock [*Utility pole*] [*Telecommunications*]   (TEL)
WH............. Wharf
Wh .... Wharton's Pennsylvania Supreme Court Reports [*1835-
                 41*]   (DLA)
Wh .... Wheaton's International Law   (DLA)

Wh .... Wheaton's Reports [*14-25 United States*]   (DLA)
Wh .... Wheeler's New York Criminal Reports [*3 vols.*]   (DLA)
WH............. Wheelhouse   (MSA)
WH............. Where   (AABC)
WH............. Which
WH............. Whispered   (ADA)
WH............. White
WH............. White [*Thoroughbred racing*]
WH............. White Hornet [*Immunology*]
WH............. White House
WH............. Who
WH............. Whore   (DSUE)
WH............. Wings of Hope [*An association*] [*St. Louis, MO*]   (EA)
WH............. Withholding   (AFM)
WH............. Work Hour   (KSC)
WH2........... Whipple Mountains Number 2 [*California*] [*Seismograph
                 station code, US Geological Survey*]   (SEIS)
WHA .... Madison, WI [*AM radio station call letters*]
WHA .... Wahaula [*Hawaii*] [*Seismograph station code, US Geological
                 Survey*]   (SEIS)
WHA .... Walkaloosa Horse Association   (EA)
WHA .... Washington Headquarters Association   (EA)
WHA .... Weld Head Assembly
WHA .... Western Hardwood Association [*Portland, OR*]   (EA)
WHA .... Western History Association
WHA .... Wood Heating Alliance [*Washington, DC*]   (EA)
WHA .... World Hockey Association
WHA .... Wounded by Hostile Action
WHAB........ Acton, MA [*FM radio station call letters*]
WHAB........ Westminster Historical Atlas to the Bible [*A publication*]   (BJA)
WHAC........ World Hemophilia AIDS Center [*Los Angeles, CA*]   (EA)
WHACK...... Warhead Attack Cruise Killer   (MCD)
WHAD .... Delafield, WI [*FM radio station call letters*]
WHAG .... Halfway, MD [*AM radio station call letters*]
WHAG-TV ... Hagerstown, MD [*Television station call letters*]
WHAI .... Greenfield, MA [*AM radio station call letters*]
WHAI .... Walter Hinchman Associates, Incorporated [*Chevy Chase, MD*]
                 [*Telecommunications*]   (TSSD)
WHAI-FM ... Greenfield, MA [*FM radio station call letters*]
WHAJ .... Bluefield, WV [*FM radio station call letters*]
WHAK .... Rogers City, MI [*AM radio station call letters*]
WHAL .... Shelbyville, TN [*AM radio station call letters*]
WHAM....... Rochester, NY [*AM radio station call letters*]
WHAM....... Water Hammer
WHAM....... Wayne Horizontal Acceleration Mechanism
WHAM....... Winning the Hearts and Minds [*of the people*] [*Vietnam
                 pacification program*]
WHAM....... Work Handling and Maintenance [*Navy*]   (NG)
WHAN .... Wellness and Health Activation Networks [*Formed by a merger
                 of Health Activation Network and Wellness Experience
                 Unlimited*] [*Vienna, VA*]   (EA)
WHAP........ Hopewell, VA [*AM radio station call letters*]
WHAP........ When [*or Where*] Applicable
WHAP........ Women's Health and Abortion Project   (EA)
WHAR........ Clarksburg, WV [*AM radio station call letters*]
Whar.......... Wharton's Pennsylvania Supreme Court Reports [*1835-
                 41*]   (DLA)
WHAR........ Whereafter [*Legal*] [*British*]   (ROG)
WHAR........ Wild Horses of America Registry   (EA)
Whar Ag...... Wharton on Agency   (DLA)
Whar Am Cr L ... Wharton's American Criminal Law   (DLA)
Whar Con Law ... Wharton's Conflict of Laws   (DLA)
Whar Conv ... Wharton on Principles of Conveyancing [*1851*]   (DLA)
Whar Cr Ev ... Wharton on Criminal Evidence   (DLA)
Whar Cri Pl ... Wharton's Criminal Pleading and Practice   (DLA)
Whar Cr Law ... Wharton's American Criminal Law   (DLA)
Whar Dig .... Wharton's Pennsylvania Digest   (DLA)
Whar Hom ... Wharton's Law of Homicide   (DLA)
Whar Innk ... Wharton on Innkeepers [*1876*]   (DLA)
Whar Law Dic ... Wharton's Law Lexicon [*14th ed.*] [*1938*]   (DLA)
Whar Leg Max ... Wharton's Legal Maxims [*3rd ed.*] [*1903*]   (DLA)
Whar Neg .... Wharton's Law of Negligence   (DLA)
Whar & St Med Jur ... Wharton and Stille's Medical Jurisprudence   (DLA)
Whar St Tr ... Wharton's United States State Trials   (DLA)
Whart .... Legal Maxims with Observations by George Frederick
                 Wharton   (DLA)
Whart .... Wharton's Pennsylvania Supreme Court Reports [*1835-
                 41*]   (DLA)
Whart Ag.... Wharton on Agency   (DLA)
Whart Am Cr Law ... Wharton's American Criminal Law   (DLA)
Whart Confl Laws ... Wharton's Conflict of Laws   (DLA)
Whart Cr Ev ... Wharton on Criminal Evidence   (DLA)
Whart Crim Law ... Wharton's American Criminal Law   (DLA)
Whart Cr Pl & Prac ... Wharton's Criminal Pleading and Practice   (DLA)
Whart Ev .... Wharton on Evidence in Civil Issues   (DLA)
Whart Hom ... Wharton's Law of Homicide   (DLA)
Whart Homicide ... Wharton's Law of Homicide   (DLA)
Whart Law Dict ... Wharton's Law Dictionary [*or Lexicon*]   (DLA)
Whart Law Lexicon ... Wharton's Law Lexicon   (DLA)
Whart Lex ... Wharton's Law Lexicon   (DLA)

Whart Neg ... Wharton on Negligence   (DLA)
Whartn Mag ... Wharton Magazine [*A publication*]
Wharton ..... Wharton Magazine [*A publication*]
Wharton ..... Wharton's American Criminal Law   (DLA)
Wharton ..... Wharton's Law Lexicon   (DLA)
Wharton ..... Wharton's Pennsylvania Supreme Court Reports [*1835-41*]   (DLA)
Wharton Crim Evidence ... Wharton's Criminal Evidence   (DLA)
Wharton Crim Proc ... Wharton's Criminal Law and Procedure   (DLA)
Wharton Mag ... Wharton Magazine [*A publication*]
Wharton Q ... Wharton Quarterly [*A publication*]
Whart PA.... Wharton's Pennsylvania Supreme Court Reports [*1835-41*]   (DLA)
Whart & S Med Jur ... Wharton and Stille's Medical Jurisprudence   (DLA)
Whart State Tr ... Wharton's United States State Trials   (DLA)
Whart St Tr ... Wharton's United States State Trials   (DLA)
WHAS........ Louisville, KY [*AM radio station call letters*]
WHAS........ Whereas
WHASA ..... White House Army Signal Agency
WHAS-TV... Louisville, KY [*Television station call letters*]
WHAT........ Philadelphia, PA [*AM radio station call letters*]
WHAT........ Winds, Heights, and Temperatures
Whats New Bldg ... What's New in Building [*A publication*]
Whats New in For Res ... What's New in Forest Research [*A publication*]
Whats New Plant Physiol ... What's New in Plant Physiology [*A publication*]
WHATSR.... Whatsoever
WHA-TV .... Madison, WI [*Television station call letters*]
WHAV........ Haverhill, MA [*AM radio station call letters*]
WHAV........ When Available   (KSC)
WHAW....... Weston, WV [*AM radio station call letters*]
WHAZ........ Troy, NY [*AM radio station call letters*]
WHB........... Kansas City, MO [*AM radio station call letters*]
WHB .... [*The*] Wandering Hand Brigade [*Men who are likely to take liberties with women*]
WHB .... Waste Heat Boiler [*Nuclear energy*]   (CAAL)
WHB .... Wiener Humanistische Blaetter [*A publication*]
WHB .... Wire Harness Board   (MCD)
WHBB......... Selma, AL [*AM radio station call letters*]
WHBC........ Canton, OH [*AM radio station call letters*]
WHBC-FM ... Canton, OH [*FM radio station call letters*]
WHBE........ St. Andrews, SC [*AM radio station call letters*]
WHBF........ Rock Island, IL [*AM radio station call letters*]
WHBF-FM ... Rock Island, IL [*FM radio station call letters*]
WHBF-TV ... Rock Island, IL [*Television station call letters*]
WHBG .... Harrisonburg, VA [*AM radio station call letters*]
WHBL .... Sheboygan, WI [*AM radio station call letters*]
WHBL .... World Home Bible League   (EA)
WHBL-TV ... Sheboygan, WI [*Television station call letters*]
WHBMA ..... Wood Hat Block Manufacturers Association   (EA)
WHBN........ Harrodsburg, KY [*AM radio station call letters*]
WHBN-FM ... Harrodsburg, KY [*FM radio station call letters*]
WHBO .... Pinellas Park, FL [*AM radio station call letters*]
WHBQ .... Memphis, TN [*AM radio station call letters*]
WHBQ-TV ... Memphis, TN [*Television station call letters*]
WHBR........ Pensacola, FL [*Television station call letters*]
WHBU........ Anderson, IN [*AM radio station call letters*]
WHBY........ Appleton, WI [*AM radio station call letters*]
WHBY........ Whereby
WHC........... Wages for Housework Committee   (EA)
WHC........... Washington Hospital Center, Washington, DC [*OCLC symbol*]   (OCLC)
WHC........... Water Holding Capacity [*Also, WBC*] [*Food industry*]
WHC........... Watt-Hour Meter with Contact Device
WHC........... Westinghouse Hanford Company   (NRCH)
WHC........... White House Conference
WHC........... Whitehorse [*Yukon Territory*] [*Seismograph station code, US Geological Survey*]   (SEIS)
WHC........... World Hereford Council [*Hereford, England*]   (EA-IO)
WHC........... World Heritage Committee [*See also CPM*]   (EA-IO)
WHCA .... War Hazards Compensation Act
WHCA .... White House Communications Agency   (AABC)
WHCA .... White House Correspondents' Association [*Washington, DC*]   (EA)
WH Cas ...... Wage and Hour Cases [*Bureau of National Affairs*]   (DLA)
WHCB .... Bristol, TN [*FM radio station call letters*]
WHCC .... Waynesville, NC [*AM radio station call letters*]
WHCCY...... White House Conference on Children and Youth   (EA)
WHCDHR ... Wainwright House Center for Development of Human Resources   (EA)
WHCE........ Forest City, NC [*AM radio station call letters*]
WHCE........ Highland Springs, VA [*FM radio station call letters*]
WHCF........ Bangor, ME [*FM radio station call letters*]
WHCF........ White House Conference on Families [*June 5-July 3, 1980*]   (EGAO)
WHcGS ...... Church of Jesus Christ of Latter-Day Saints, Genealogical Society Library, Milwaukee Branch, Hales Corners, WI [*Library symbol*] [*Library of Congress*]   (LCLS)
WH Chron ... Westminster Hall Chronicle and Legal Examiner [*1835-36*]   (DLA)
WHCJ......... Savannah, GA [*AM radio station call letters*]
WHCL-FM ... Clinton, NY [*FM radio station call letters*]

WHCLIS ..... White House Conference on Library and Information Services [*Washington, DC, 1979*]
WHCM....... Sheffield, AL [*AM radio station call letters*]
WHCN....... Hartford, CT [*FM radio station call letters*]
WHCO....... Sparta, IL [*AM radio station call letters*]
WHCO....... Wheeled Coach Industries [*NASDAQ symbol*]   (NQ)
WHCOA..... White House Conference on Aging
WHCOLIS... White House Conference on Libraries and Information Services
Wh Cr Cas ... Wheeler's New York Criminal Cases [*3 vols.*]   (DLA)
WHCR-FM ... New York, NY [*FM radio station call letters*]
Wh Crim Cas ... Wheeler's New York Criminal Cases   (DLA)
WHcS .... Sacred Heart School of Theology, Hales Corners, WI [*Library symbol*] [*Library of Congress*]   (LCLS)
WHCS .... Well History Control System [*Petroleum Information Corp.*] [*Denver, CO*] [*Information service*]   (EISS)
WHCT-TV... Hartford, CT [*Television station call letters*]
WHCU .... Ithaca, NY [*AM radio station call letters*]
WHCU .... Window Heat Control Unit
WHCU-FM ... Ithaca, NY [*FM radio station call letters*]
WHD .... Wage and Hour Division [*Department of Labor*]
WHD .... Warhead
WHD .... Western Hemisphere Defense
WHDB........ Woods Hole Database, Inc. [*Woods Hole, MA*] [*Information service*]   (EISS)
W-HDCS .... Wyeth Laboratories - Human Diploid Cell Strain [*Rabies vaccine*]
WHDG .... Havre De Grace, MD [*FM radio station call letters*]
WHDH .... Boston, MA [*AM radio station call letters*]
WHDL .... Olean, NY [*AM radio station call letters*]
WHDM........ McKenzie, TN [*AM radio station call letters*]
WHDM........ Watt-Hour Demand Meter
WHDQ........ Claremont, NH [*FM radio station call letters*]
WHDS........ Warhead Section [*Military*]   (AABC)
WHE .... Water Hammer Eliminator
WHE .... Wheaton College, Norton, MA [*OCLC symbol*]   (OCLC)
WHE .... Whole Human Embryo [*Type of cell line*]
Wheat........ Wheaton's Reports [*14-25 United States*]   (DLA)
Wheat Board Gaz ... Wheat Board Gazette [*A publication*]
Wheat El Int Law ... Wheaton's Elements of International Law   (DLA)
Wheat Hist Law Nat ... Wheaton's History of the Law of Nations   (DLA)
Wheat Inform Serv ... Wheat Information Service [*A publication*]
Wheat Inf Serv ... Wheat Information Service [*A publication*]
Wheat Int Law ... Wheaton's Elements of International Law [*7th ed.*] [*1944*]   (DLA)
Wheat Int Law ... Wheaton's International Law   (DLA)
Wheaton .... Wheaton's Reports [*14-25 United States*]   (DLA)
Wheat Situation Bur Agr Econ (Aust) ... Wheat Situation. Bureau of Agricultural Economics (Australia) [*A publication*]
Wheat Stud Food Res Inst ... Wheat Studies. Food Research Institute [*A publication*]
WHEB........ Portsmouth, NH [*AM radio station call letters*]
WHEB-FM ... Portsmouth, NH [*FM radio station call letters*]
WHEC......... High-Endurance Coast Guard Cutter [*Formerly, WAPG*]   (CINC)
WHECON ... Wheel Control   (MCD)
WHEC-TV... Rochester, NY [*Television station call letters*]
WHED-TV... Hanover, NH [*Television station call letters*]
WHEE .... Martinsville, VA [*AM radio station call letters*]
WHEE .... Wheel Extended [*A publication*]
Wheel........ Wheeler's New York Criminal Cases   (DLA)
Wheel........ Wheelock's Reports [*32-37 Texas*]   (DLA)
Wheel Br Cas ... Wheeling Bridge Case   (DLA)
Wheel Cr Cas ... Wheeler's New York Criminal Cases   (DLA)
Wheel Cr Ch ... Wheeler's New York Criminal Cases   (DLA)
Wheel Cr Rec ... Wheeler's New York Criminal Recorder [*1 Wheeler's Criminal Cases*]   (DLA)
Wheeler Abr ... Wheeler's Abridgment   (DLA)
Wheeler Am Cr Law ... Wheeler's Abridgment of American Common Law Cases   (DLA)
Wheeler CC ... Wheeler's New York Criminal Cases   (DLA)
Wheeler Cr Cas ... Wheeler's New York Criminal Cases   (DLA)
Wheeler Cr Cases ... Wheeler's New York Criminal Cases   (DLA)
Wheeler Crim Cas ... Wheeler's New York Criminal Cases   (DLA)
Wheeler's Cr Cases ... Wheeler's New York Criminal Cases   (DLA)
Wheel Ext .. Wheel Extended [*A publication*]
Wheel (Tex) ... Wheelock's Reports [*32-37 Texas*]   (DLA)
WHEI......... Tiffin, OH [*FM radio station call letters*]
WHEN........ Syracuse, NY [*AM radio station call letters*]
WHENCESR ... Whencesoever [*Legal*] [*British*]   (ROG)
WHENR ...... Whenever [*Legal*] [*British*]   (ROG)
WHENSR.... Whensoever [*Legal*] [*British*]   (ROG)
WHEO........ Stuart, VA [*AM radio station call letters*]
WHEP........ Foley, AL [*AM radio station call letters*]
WHER........ Hattiesburg, MS [*FM radio station call letters*]
WHER........ Whether [*Legal*] [*British*]   (ROG)
Where to Find Out More about Educ ... Where to Find Out More about Education [*A publication*]
WHERER .... Wherever [*Legal*] [*British*]   (ROG)
WHES........ World Hunger Education Service   (EA)
Whet.......... Whetstone [*A publication*]

WHETS....... Washington Higher Education Telecommunications System [*Washington State University*] [*Pullman*] [*Telecommunications service*] (TSSD)
WHEW........ Fort Myers, FL [*FM radio station call letters*]
WHEZ........ Portage, MI [*AM radio station call letters*]
WHF .... Waveguide Harmonic Filter
WHF .... Wharf
WHF .... Women in Housing and Finance [*Washington, DC*] (EA)
WHF .... Women's Hall of Fame [*Later, NWHF*] (EA)
WHF .... World Heritage Fund [*UNESCO*]
WHFB........ Benton Harbor, MI [*AM radio station call letters*]
WHFB-FM ... Benton Harbor, MI [*FM radio station call letters*]
WHFC........ Bel Air, MD [*FM radio station call letters*]
WHFD........ Archbold, OH [*FM radio station call letters*]
WHFG........ Wharfage
WHFH........ Flossmoor, IL [*FM radio station call letters*]
WHFL........ Havana, FL [*FM radio station call letters*]
WHFM .... Rochester, NY [*FM radio station call letters*]
WHFM .... Wherefrom [*Legal*] [*British*] (ROG)
WHFORE.... Wherefore [*Legal*] [*British*] (ROG)
WHFR........ Dearborn, MI [*FM radio station call letters*]
WHFR........ Wharfinger [*Shipping*] [*British*] (ROG)
WHFS........ Annapolis, MD [*FM radio station call letters*]
WHFT........ Miami, FL [*Television station call letters*]
WHF-USA... World Health Foundation of the United States of America [*Defunct*] [*Geneva, Switzerland*] (EA)
WH & G...... Welsby, Hurlstone, and Gordon's English Exchequer Reports [*1848-56*] (DLA)
WHGB .... Harrisburg, PA [*AM radio station call letters*]
WHGC .... Bennington, VT [*FM radio station call letters*]
WHGE........ Wharfage
WHGM .... Bellwood, PA [*FM radio station call letters*]
WHGS .... Haines City, FL [*FM radio station call letters*]
WHH .... Hartford Memorial Hospital, Hartford, WI [*Library symbol*] [*Library of Congress*] (LCLS)
WHHA........ White House Historical Association (EA)
WHHB........ Holliston, MA [*FM radio station call letters*]
WHHI......... Highland, WI [*AM radio station call letters*]
WHHL......... Watanabe Hereditary Hyperlipidemic [*Rabbits*]
WHHM....... Henderson, TN [*AM radio station call letters*]
WHHO....... Hornell, NY [*AM radio station call letters*]
WHHR........ Hilton Head Island, SC [*AM radio station call letters*]
WHHR-FM ... Hilton Head Island, SC [*FM radio station call letters*]
WHHS........ Havertown, PA [*FM radio station call letters*]
WHHT........ Orangeburg, SC [*AM radio station call letters*]
WHHV........ Hillsville, VA [*AM radio station call letters*]
WHHY........ Montgomery, AL [*AM radio station call letters*]
WHHY-FM ... Montgomery, AL [*FM radio station call letters*]
WHi........... State Historical Society of Wisconsin, Madison, WI [*Library symbol*] [*Library of Congress*] (LCLS)
WHI............ Washington Homes, Incorporated [*American Stock Exchange symbol*]
WHI............ Wave Height Indicator [*Oceanography*]
WHI............ Weekly Hospital Indemnity
WHI............ Western Highway Institute [*San Bruno, CA*] (EA)
WHI............ Whitney [*Hawaii*] [*Seismograph station code, US Geological Survey*] [*Closed*] (SEIS)
WHIA......... Dawson, GA [*AM radio station call letters*]
WHIA......... Woolen Hosiery Institute of America [*Defunct*] (EA)
WHIC......... Hardinsburg, KY [*AM radio station call letters*]
WHIC-FM ... Hardinsburg, KY [*FM radio station call letters*]
Which Word Process and Off Syst ... Which Word Processor and Office System? [*A publication*]
WHIDDA..... Wideband High-Density Data Acquisition (MCD)
WHIE......... Griffin, GA [*AM radio station call letters*]
WHII .... Bay Springs, MS [*AM radio station call letters*]
WHIL-FM... Mobile, AL [*FM radio station call letters*]
WHIM .... Providence, RI [*AM radio station call letters*]
WHIM .... Western Humor and Irony Membership [*An association*]
WHIM .... Wet High-Intensity Magnet [*for mineral processing*]
WHIM .... Women Happy in Minis [*Boise, Idaho, group opposing below-the-knee fashions introduced in 1970*]
WHIMSY..... Western Humor and Irony Membership. Serial Yearbook [*Tempe, Arizona*] [*A publication*]
WHIN.......... Gallatin, TN [*AM radio station call letters*]
WHIN.......... Wherein [*Legal*] [*British*] (ROG)
WHIO......... Dayton, OH [*AM radio station call letters*]
WHIO-FM... Dayton, OH [*FM radio station call letters*]
WHIO-TV.... Dayton, OH [*Television station call letters*]
WHIP .... Mooresville, NC [*AM radio station call letters*]
WHIP .... Walks plus Hits Divided by Innings Pitched [*Baseball*]
WHIP .... Wideband High Intercept Probability
WHIPS........ Widebeam High-Density Pulsed Source (MCD)
WHIQ......... Huntsville, AL [*Television station call letters*]
WHIR......... Danville, KY [*AM radio station call letters*]
WHIS......... Bluefield, WV [*AM radio station call letters*]
WHIS......... Whiskeytown-Shasta-Trinity National Recreation Area
WHIS......... Whistle [*Navigation*]
Whishaw .... Whishaw's Law Dictionary (DLA)
Whish LD ... Whishaw's New Law Dictionary [*1829*] (DLA)
WHISP........ Woods Hole In-Situ Pump [*Marine biology*] [*Instrumentation*]

WHIST........ Worldwide Household Goods Information System for Traffic Management [*Army*] (AABC)
W Hist Q ..... Western Historical Quarterly [*A publication*]
WHIT .... Madison, WI [*AM radio station call letters*]
WHIT .... Whitman Medical Corp. [*NASDAQ symbol*] (NQ)
Whitak Liens ... Whitaker on Liens (DLA)
White......... White's Justiciary Court Reports [*3 vols.*] [*Scotland*] (DLA)
White......... White's Reports [*31-44 Texas Appeals*] (DLA)
White......... White's Reports [*10-15 West Virginia*] (DLA)
White Char ... Whiteford on Charities [*1878*] (DLA)
White & Civ Cas Ct App ... White and Willson's Civil Cases, Texas Court of Appeals (DLA)
White Coll ... White's New Collection of the Laws, Etc., of Great Britain, France, and Spain (DLA)
White New Coll ... White's New Collection of the Laws, Etc. of Great Britain, France, and Spain (DLA)
White's Ann Pen Code ... White's Annotated Penal Code [*Texas*] (DLA)
White's Rep ... White's Reports [*31-44 Texas Appeals*] (DLA)
White's Rep ... White's Reports [*10-15 West Virginia*] (DLA)
White & TL Cas ... White and Tudor's Leading Cases in Equity (DLA)
White & T Lead Cas Eq ... White and Tudor's Leading Cases in Equity [*England*] (DLA)
White & T Lead Cas in Eq (Eng) ... White and Tudor's Leading Cases in Equity [*England*] (DLA)
White & Tud LC ... White and Tudor's Leading Cases in Equity [*9th ed.*] [*1928*] (DLA)
White & Tudor ... White and Tudor's Leading Cases in Equity (DLA)
White & W ... White and Willson's Reports, Civil Cases, Texas Court of Appeals (DLA)
White & W Civ Cas Ct App ... White and Wilson's [*or Willson's*] Civil Cases, Texas Court of Appeals (DLA)
White & W Civil Cases Ct App ... Texas Civil Cases (DLA)
White & Willson ... Texas Civil Cases (DLA)
White W & M ... Whiteley's Weights, Measures, and Weighing Machines [*1879*] (DLA)
White & W (Tex) ... White and Willson's Reports, Civil Cases, Texas Court of Appeals (DLA)
Whit Lien.... Whitaker's Rights of Lien and Stoppage in Transitu [*1812*] (DLA)
Whitman Pat Cas (US) ... Whitman's Patent Cases [*United States*] (DLA)
Whitm BL ... Whitmarsh's Bankrupt Law [*2nd ed.*] [*1817*] (DLA)
Whitm Lib Cas ... Whitman's Massachusetts Libel Cases (DLA)
Whitm Pat Cas ... Whitman's Patent Cases [*United States*] (DLA)
Whitm Pat Law Rev ... Whitman's Patent Law Review [*Washington, DC*] (DLA)
Whitney...... Whitney's Land Laws [*Tennessee*] (DLA)
Whit Pat Cas ... Whitman's Patent Cases [*United States*] (DLA)
Whit Schol ... Whitgift Scholar [*British*]
Whitt .... Whittlesey's Reports [*32-41 Missouri*] (DLA)
Whittier L Rev ... Whittier Law Review [*A publication*]
Whittlesey ... Whittlesey's Reports [*32-41 Missouri*] (DLA)
WHIY .... Moulton, AL [*AM radio station call letters*]
WHIZ .... Zanesville, OH [*AM radio station call letters*]
WHIZ-FM .... Zanesville, OH [*FM radio station call letters*]
WHIZ-TV .... Zanesville, OH [*Television station call letters*]
WHJB .... Greensburg, PA [*AM radio station call letters*]
WHJC......... Matewan, WV [*AM radio station call letters*]
WHJE......... Carmel, IN [*FM radio station call letters*]
WHJJ......... Providence, RI [*AM radio station call letters*]
WHJT......... Clinton, MS [*FM radio station call letters*]
WHK .... Cleveland, OH [*AM radio station call letters*]
WHK .... Whakatane [*New Zealand*] [*Airport symbol*] (OAG)
WHKE........ Kenosha, WI [*Television station call letters*]
WHKP........ Hendersonville, NC [*AM radio station call letters*]
WHKW........ Fayette, AL [*FM radio station call letters*]
WHKY........ Hickory, NC [*AM radio station call letters*]
WHKY-FM ... Hickory, NC [*FM radio station call letters*]
WHKY-TV... Hickory, NC [*Television station call letters*]
WHL .... Watt-Hour Meter with Loss Compensator (MSA)
WHL .... Western Hockey League
WHL .... Wheel (AAG)
WHL .... World Heritage List [*UNESCO*]
WHLA........ La Crosse, WI [*FM radio station call letters*]
WHLA-TV.... La Crosse, WI [*Television station call letters*]
WHLB........ Virginia, MN [*AM radio station call letters*]
WHLB-FM ... Virginia, MN [*FM radio station call letters*]
WHLD........ Niagara Falls, NY [*AM radio station call letters*]
WHLD........ Wheeled
WHLDY....... Western Holdings ADR [*NASDAQ symbol*] (NQ)
WHLF........ South Boston, VA [*AM radio station call letters*]
WHLG........ Jensen Beach, FL [*FM radio station call letters*]
WHLI......... Hempstead, NY [*AM radio station call letters*]
WHLL........ Worcester, MA [*Television station call letters*]
WHLM .... Bloomsburg, PA [*AM radio station call letters*]
WHLM-FM ... Bloomsburg, PA [*FM radio station call letters*]
WHLN........ Harlan, KY [*AM radio station call letters*]
WHLO........ Akron, OH [*AM radio station call letters*]
WHLP........ Centerville, TN [*AM radio station call letters*]
WHLS........ Port Huron, MI [*AM radio station call letters*]
WHLT........ Hattiesburg, MS [*Television station call letters*]
WHLX........ Bethlehem, WV [*FM radio station call letters*]

WHLY .... Leesburg, FL [*FM radio station call letters*]
WHLZ .... Manning, SC [*FM radio station call letters*]
WHM .... Watt-Hour Meter
WHM .... Wild Horse Parks [*Montana*] [*Seismograph station code, US Geological Survey*] [*Closed*]   (SEIS)
WHMA .... Anniston, AL [*AM radio station call letters*]
WHMA .... Women's Home Mission Association
WHMAA .... Wool Hat Manufacturers Association of America   (EA)
WHMA-FM .... Anniston, AL [*FM radio station call letters*]
WH Man ..... Wage and Hour-Reference Manual [*Bureau of National Affairs*]   (DLA)
WHMA-TV ... Anniston, AL [*Television station call letters*]
WHMB-TV ... Indianapolis, IN [*Television station call letters*]
WHMC .... Conway, SC [*Television station call letters*]
WHMC .... Wilford Hall Medical Center [*Air Force*]
WHMC-FM ... Conway, SC [*FM radio station call letters*]
WHMD .... Hammond, LA [*FM radio station call letters*]
WHME .... South Bend, IN [*FM radio station call letters*]
WHME-TV ... South Bend, IN [*Television station call letters*]
WHMH-FM ... Sauk Rapids, MN [*FM radio station call letters*]
WHMI .... Howell, MI [*AM radio station call letters*]
WHMI .... Whitman Mission National Historic Site
WHMI-FM ... Howell, MI [*FM radio station call letters*]
WHMJ .... Thomasville, GA [*FM radio station call letters*]
WHMM .... Washington, DC [*Television station call letters*]
WHMP .... Northampton, MA [*AM radio station call letters*]
WHMP-FM ... Northampton, MA [*FM radio station call letters*]
WHMQ .... Findlay, OH [*FM radio station call letters*]
WHMT .... Humboldt, TN [*AM radio station call letters*]
WHN .... New York, NY [*AM radio station call letters*]
WHN .... Wharton & Northern Railroad Co. [*Absorbed into Consolidated Rail Corp.*] [*AAR code*]
WHN .... Whonnock Industries Ltd. [*Toronto Stock Exchange symbol*] [*Vancouver Stock Exchange symbol*]
WHN .... Women's History Network   (EA)
WHNC .... Henderson, NC [*AM radio station call letters*]
WHND .... Monroe, MI [*AM radio station call letters*]
WHNE .... Cumming, GA [*AM radio station call letters*]
WHNN .... Bay City, MI [*FM radio station call letters*]
WHNPA ...... White House News Photographers Association [*Washington, DC*]   (EA)
WHNR .... Whenever [*Legal*] [*British*]   (ROG)
WHNRC ...... Western Human Nutrition Research Center [*Department of Agriculture*] [*Research center*]   (RCD)
WHNS .... Asheville, NC [*Television station call letters*]
WHNS .... Wartime Host Nation Support
WHNSR ..... Whensoever [*Legal*] [*British*]   (ROG)
WHNT-TV ... Huntsville, AL [*Television station call letters*]
WHNY .... McComb, MS [*AM radio station call letters*]
WHO .... Des Moines, IA [*AM radio station call letters*]
WHO .... War on Hunger Office [*Department of State*]
WHO .... Western Heraldry Organization   (EA)
WHO .... [*The*] White House Office
WHO .... World Health Organization [*The pronunciation "who" is not acceptable*] [*United Nations affiliate*] [*Geneva, Switzerland*] [*Databank originator*]
WHO .... World Housing Organization
WHO .... Wrist-Hand Orthosis [*Medicine*]
WHOA .... Why Have Overages Afterwards [*DoD*]
WHOA .... Wild Horse Organized Assistance [*An association*]   (EA)
WHOAA ...... Walking Horse Owner's Association of America   (EA)
WHOB .... Nashua, NH [*FM radio station call letters*]
WHOC .... Philadelphia, MS [*AM radio station call letters*]
WHOC-A .... WHO [*World Health Organization*] Chronicle [*Switzerland*] [*A publication*]
WHO Chron ... WHO [*World Health Organization*] Chronicle [*A publication*]
WHOD .... Jackson, AL [*AM radio station call letters*]
WHOD-FM ... Jackson, AL [*FM radio station call letters*]
WHOER ...... Whoever [*Legal*] [*British*]   (ROG)
WHOF .... Whereof [*Legal*] [*British*]   (ROG)
WHO Food Addit Ser ... WHO [*World Health Organization*] Food Additives Series [*A publication*]
WHOG .... Fernandina Beach, FL [*AM radio station call letters*]
WHOH .... Cadiz, OH [*FM radio station call letters*]
WHOI .... Peoria, IL [*Television station call letters*]
WHOI .... Woods Hole Oceanographic Institution [*Woods Hole, MA*] [*Research center*]
WHO Int Agency Res Cancer Annu Rep ... World Health Organization International Agency for Research on Cancer. Annual Report [*A publication*]
WHOK-FM ... Lancaster, OH [*FM radio station call letters*]
WHOL .... Allentown, PA [*AM radio station call letters*]
WHOM .... Mount Washington, NH [*FM radio station call letters*]
WHO Monogr Ser ... World Health Organization. Monograph Series [*A publication*]
WHON .... Centerville, IN [*AM radio station call letters*]
WHON .... Whereon [*Legal*] [*British*]   (ROG)
WHO Offset Publ ... WHO [*World Health Organization*] Offset Publication [*A publication*]
WHOO-FM ... Orlando, FL [*FM radio station call letters*]
WHOP .... Hopkinsville, KY [*AM radio station call letters*]

WHO Pestic Residues Ser ... WHO [*World Health Organization*] Pesticide Residues Series [*A publication*]
WHOP-FM ... Hopkinsville, KY [*FM radio station call letters*]
WHO Publ ... WHO [*World Health Organization*] Publications [*A publication*]
WHO Public Health Papers ... World Health Organization. Public Health Papers [*A publication*]
WHOS .... Decatur, AL [*AM radio station call letters*]
WHOSOR ... Whosoever [*Legal*] [*British*]   (ROG)
WHOT .... Campbell, OH [*AM radio station call letters*]
WHO Tech Rep Ser ... World Health Organization. Technical Report Series [*A publication*]
WHO Tech Rep Sers ... World Health Organization. Technical Report Series [*A publication*]
WHOT-FM ... Youngstown, OH [*FM radio station call letters*]
WHO-TV ..... Des Moines, IA [*Television station call letters*]
WHOU .... Houlton, ME [*AM radio station call letters*]
WHOU-FM ... Houlton, ME [*FM radio station call letters*]
WHOV .... Hampton, VA [*FM radio station call letters*]
WHOW .... Clinton, IL [*AM radio station call letters*]
WHOW-FM ... Clinton, IL [*FM radio station call letters*]
WHOY .... Salinas, PR [*AM radio station call letters*]
WHP .... Harrisburg, PA [*AM radio station call letters*]
WHP .... Los Angeles, CA [*Location identifier*] [*FAA*]   (FAAL)
WHP .... Water Horsepower
WHP .... West Hartford Public Library, West Hartford, CT [*OCLC symbol*]   (OCLC)
WHP .... Western Health Plans, Inc. [*American Stock Exchange symbol*]
WHP .... White House Police [*Later, Executive Protective Service*]
WHPA .... Hollidaysburg, PA [*FM radio station call letters*]
WHPB .... Belton, SC [*AM radio station call letters*]
WHPC .... Garden City, NY [*FM radio station call letters*]
WHPC .... Wage and Hour and Public Contracts Division [*Obsolete*] [*Department of Labor*]
WHPCA ...... Walsh-Healey Public Contracts Act [*1936*] [*Labor*]
WHPCD ...... Wage and Hour and Public Contracts Division [*Obsolete*] [*Department of Labor*]
WHPE-FM ... High Point, NC [*FM radio station call letters*]
WHP-FM ...... Harrisburg, PA [*FM radio station call letters*]
WHPH .... Hanover, NJ [*FM radio station call letters*]
WHPI .... Herrin, IL [*AM radio station call letters*]
WHPK-FM ... Chicago, IL [*FM radio station call letters*]
whpl .... Whirlpool
WHPO .... Hoopeston, IL [*FM radio station call letters*]
WHPO .... White House Personnel Office [*Terminated, 1974*]
WHPR .... Highland Park, MI [*FM radio station call letters*]
WHP-TV ...... Harrisburg, PA [*Television station call letters*]
WHPY .... Clayton, NC [*AM radio station call letters*]
WHQ .... War Headquarters   (NATG)
WHQR .... Wilmington, NC [*FM radio station call letters*]
WHQT .... Coral Gables, FL [*FM radio station call letters*]
WHR .... Vail [*Colorado*] [*Airport symbol*]   (OAG)
WHR .... Wage and Hour Reporter [*Bureau of National Affairs*]   (DLA)
WHR .... Waste Heat Removal
W-HR .... Watt-Hour   (AAG)
WHR .... Welsh History Review [*A publication*]
WHR .... Western Hemisphere Reserve
WHR .... Western Humanities Review [*A publication*]
WHR .... Whether
WHR .... Whirlpool Corp. [*NYSE symbol*]
WHR .... William H. Rorer [*Research code symbol*]
WHR .... Women and Health Roundtable [*Washington, DC*]   (EA)
WHR .... Working Heart Rate [*Cardiology*]
WHRA .... Western Historical Research Associates [*Defunct*]   (EA)
WHRABTS ... Whereabouts [*Legal*] [*British*]   (ROG)
WHRAS ...... Whereas [*Legal*] [*British*]   (ROG)
WHRAT ...... Whereat [*Legal*] [*British*]   (ROG)
WHRB .... Cambridge, MA [*AM radio station call letters*]
WHRC .... Washington Home Rule Committee [*Later, SDDC*]   (EA)
WHRC .... World Health Research Center
WHRF .... Bel Air, MD [*AM radio station call letters*]
WHRIN .... Wherein
WHRK .... Memphis, TN [*FM radio station call letters*]
WHRL .... Albany, NY [*FM radio station call letters*]
WHRM .... Wausau, WI [*FM radio station call letters*]
WHR Man ... Wage and Hour Reference Manual [*Bureau of National Affairs*]   (DLA)
WHRM-TV ... Wausau, WI [*Television station call letters*]
WHRO-FM ... Norfolk, VA [*FM radio station call letters*]
WHRO-TV ... Hampton-Norfolk, VA [*Television station call letters*]
WHRP .... Portland, TN [*AM radio station call letters*]
WHRS .... Winchester, KY [*AM radio station call letters*]
WHRT .... Hartselle, AL [*AM radio station call letters*]
WHRU .... Waste Heat Recovery Unit [*Chemical engineering*]
WHRW .... Binghamton, NY [*FM radio station call letters*]
WHRY .... Hurley, WI [*AM radio station call letters*]
WHRZ .... Providence, KY [*FM radio station call letters*]
WHS .... Warehouse   (AABC)
WHS .... Washington Headquarters Services
WHS .... Water Hydraulic Section
WHS .... Weekly Hansard - Senate [*A publication*]
WHS .... Whalsay [*Shetland Islands*] [*Airport symbol*]   (OAG)

WHS .... White Scale
WHS .... William Hunter Society   (EA)
WHS .... Wolf-Hirschorn Syndrome [Medicine]
WHS .... World Health Statistics Data Base [World Health Organization]
　　　　　　　[Geneva, Switzerland] [Information service]   (EISS)
WHSA .... Brule, WI [FM radio station call letters]
WHSB .... Alpena, MI [FM radio station call letters]
WHSC .... Hartsville, SC [AM radio station call letters]
WHSC .... White House Science Council
WHSCH ...... Whitworth Scholar [British]
WHSD .... Hinsdale, IL [FM radio station call letters]
WHSE .... Newark, NJ [Television station call letters]
WHSE .... Warehouse   (AAG)
W/HSE ...... Wheelhouse [Automotive engineering]
WHSH .... Marlborough, MA [Television station call letters]
WHSHS ...... Wilbur Hot Springs Health Sanctuary   (EA)
WHSI .... Portland, ME [Television station call letters]
WHSK .... Kokomo, IN [FM radio station call letters]
WHSLE ...... Wholesale
WHSL-FM ... Wilmington, NC [FM radio station call letters]
WHSM .... Hayward, WI [AM radio station call letters]
WHSM-FM ... Hayward, WI [FM radio station call letters]
WHSMN ...... Warehouseman   (AABC)
WHSN .... Bangor, ME [FM radio station call letters]
WHSNA ...... Welsh Harp Society of North America   (EA)
WHSNG ...... Warehousing
WHSP .... Vineland, NJ [Television station call letters]
WHSR .... White House Situation Room   (MCD)
WHSR-FM ... Winchester, MA [FM radio station call letters]
WHSS .... Hamilton, OH [FM radio station call letters]
WHSS .... White House Signal Support
WHSUPA .... Wharton School, University of Pennsylvania   (DLA)
WHSV .... Weight-Hourly Space Velocity [Fuel technology]
WHSV-TV ... Harrisonburg, VA [Television station call letters]
WHSY .... Hattiesburg, MS [AM radio station call letters]
WHSY-FM ... Hattiesburg, MS [FM radio station call letters]
WHT .... Watt-Hour Demand Meter, Thermal Type   (IEEE)
WHT .... White   (AAG)
WHT .... Whitehall Corp. [NYSE symbol]
WHTA .... Calumet, MI [Television station call letters]
WHTA .... Walking Horse Trainers Association   (EA)
WHTC .... Holland, MI [AM radio station call letters]
WHTF .... Starview, PA [FM radio station call letters]
WHTG .... Eatontown, NJ [AM radio station call letters]
WHTG-FM ... Eatontown, NJ [FM radio station call letters]
WHTH .... Heath, OH [AM radio station call letters]
Wh & TLC ... White and Tudor's Leading Cases in Equity [9 eds.] [1849-
　　　　　　　1928]   (DLA)
WHTL-FM ... Whitehall, WI [FM radio station call letters]
WHTM .... Wisconsin Hydrologic Transport Model
WHTM-TV ... Harrisburg, PA [Television station call letters]
WHTN .... Murfreesboro, TN [Television station call letters]
WHTO .... Whereto [Legal] [British]   (ROG)
WHTT .... Buffalo, NY [AM radio station call letters]
WHTT-FM ... Buffalo, NY [FM radio station call letters]
Wh & Tud ... White and Tudor's Leading Cases in Equity [9th ed.]
　　　　　　　[1928]   (DLA)
WHTX .... Pittsburgh, PA [FM radio station call letters]
WHTZ .... Newark, NJ [FM radio station call letters]
WHU .... Well Head Unit
WHU .... Wild Horse [Utah] [Seismograph station code, US Geological
　　　　　　　Survey]   (SEIS)
WHUB .... Cookeville, TN [AM radio station call letters]
WHUB-FM ... Cookeville, TN [FM radio station call letters]
WHUC .... Hudson, NY [AM radio station call letters]
WHud .... Hudson Public Library, Hudson, WI [Library symbol] [Library of
　　　　　　　Congress]   (LCLS)
WHUD .... Peekskill, NY [FM radio station call letters]
WHudSO .... Hudson Star-Observer, Hudson, WI [Library symbol] [Library
　　　　　　　of Congress]   (LCLS)
WHUG .... Jamestown, NY [FM radio station call letters]
WHUH .... Houghton, MI [FM radio station call letters]
WHUM .... Colonial Heights, VA [AM radio station call letters]
WHUN .... Huntingdon, PA [AM radio station call letters]
WHUR-FM ... Washington, DC [FM radio station call letters]
WHUS .... Storrs, CT [FM radio station call letters]
WHUT .... Anderson, IN [AM radio station call letters]
WHV .... Woodchuck Hepatic Virus
WHV .... Woodchuck Hepatitis Virus
WHVE .... Sarasota, FL [FM radio station call letters]
WHVL .... Hendersonville, NC [AM radio station call letters]
WHVN .... Charlotte, NC [AM radio station call letters]
WHVP .... Wedged Hepatic Venous Pressure
WHVR .... Hanover, PA [AM radio station call letters]
WHVT .... Clyde, OH [FM radio station call letters]
WHVW .... Hyde Park, NY [AM radio station call letters]
WHW .... Women Helping Women [Stoughton, WI]   (EA)
WHWB .... Rutland, VT [AM radio station call letters]
WHWC .... Menomonie, WI [FM radio station call letters]
WHWC-TV ... Menomonie, WI [Television station call letters]
WHWE .... Howe, IN [FM radio station call letters]

WHWH .... Princeton, NJ [AM radio station call letters]
WHWK .... Binghamton, NY [FM radio station call letters]
WHWL .... Marquette, MI [FM radio station call letters]
WHWTCA ... West Highland White Terrier Club of America   (EA)
WHWTH ..... Wherewith [Legal] [British]   (ROG)
WHY .... What Have You? [British]   (ADA)
WHY .... World Hunger Year [An association]   (EA)
WHYC .... Swan Quarter, NC [FM radio station call letters]
WHYD .... Columbus, GA [AM radio station call letters]
WHYDFTFT ... What Have You Done for the Fleet Today? [Navy]
WHYI-FM ... Fort Lauderdale, FL [FM radio station call letters]
WHYL .... Carlisle, PA [AM radio station call letters]
WHYL-FM ... Carlisle, PA [FM radio station call letters]
WHYM .... Pensacola, FL [AM radio station call letters]
WHYN .... Springfield, MA [AM radio station call letters]
WHYP .... North East, PA [AM radio station call letters]
WHYP-FM ... North East, PA [FM radio station call letters]
WHYR .... Saco, ME [FM radio station call letters]
WHYT-FM ... Detroit, MI [FM radio station call letters]
WHYY-FM ... Philadelphia, PA [FM radio station call letters]
WHYY-TV ... Wilmington, DE [Television station call letters]
WHYZ .... Greenville, SC [AM radio station call letters]
WHZI .... Hanceville, AL [AM radio station call letters]
WI .... Oak Harbor, Whidbey Island, Washington [Naval base]
WI .... Walk In   (ADA)
WI .... Wallops Island [Off coast of Virginia]
WI .... Water Injection
W & I .... Weighing and Inspection
WI .... Welding Institute [Cambridge, England] [Database originator
　　　　　　　and operator]   (EA)
WI .... Welt des Islams [A publication]
WI .... West Coast Airlines Ltd. [Ghana] [ICAO designator]   (FAAC)
WI .... West Indies [Formerly, BWI]
WI .... Westerners International   (EA)
WI .... When Issued [Stock exchange term]
WI .... Wiadomosci [A publication]
WI .... Wine Institute   (EA)
WI .... Wire
WI .... Wisconsin [Postal code]
WI .... Within
WI .... Women's Institute [British]
WI .... Women's Reserve, Intelligence Duties [USNR officer
　　　　　　　designation]
WI .... Word Intelligibility
WI .... World Impact [Los Angeles, CA]   (EA)
WI .... Worldwatch Institute   (EA)
WI .... Wrought Iron
WIA .... Manitowoc Public Library, Manitowoc, WI [OCLC
　　　　　　　symbol]   (OCLC)
WIA .... Watusi International Association   (EA)
WIA .... Western Interpreters Association   (EA)
WIA .... Wien-Auhof [Austria] [Geomagnetic observatory code]
WIA .... Women in the Arts Foundation   (EA)
WIA .... Wounded in Action [Military]
WIAA .... Interlochen, MI [FM radio station call letters]
WIAC .... San Juan, PR [AM radio station call letters]
WIAC .... Women's International Art Club
WIAC-FM ... San Juan, PR [FM radio station call letters]
WIACLALS ... West Indian Association for Commonwealth Literature and
　　　　　　　Language Studies [Kingston, Jamaica]   (EA-IO)
WIACO ...... World Insulation and Acoustic Congress Organization
　　　　　　　[Glenview, IL]   (EA)
Wiad Bot .... Wiadomosci Botaniczne [A publication]
Wiad Chem ... Wiadomosci Chemiczne [A publication]
Wiad Ekol ... Wiadomosci Ekologiczne [A publication]
Wiad Elektrotech ... Wiadomosci Elektrotechniczne [A publication]
Wiad Gorn ... Wiadomosci Gornicze [Poland] [A publication]
Wiad Hutn ... Wiadomosci Hutnicze [A publication]
Wiad Inst Melior Uzytkow Zielon (Warsaw) ... Wiadomosci. Instytut
　　　　　　　Melioracji i Uzytkow Zielonych (Warsaw) [A publication]
Wiad Lek .... Wiadomosci Lekarskie [A publication]
Wiad Melior Lakarsk ... Wiadomosci Melioracyjne i Lakarskie [A publication]
Wiad Meteorol Gospod Wodnej ... Wiadomosci Meteorologii i Gospodarki
　　　　　　　Wodnej [A publication]
Wiad Naft ... Wiadomosci Naftowe [A publication]
Wiadom Mat ... Wiadomosci Matematyczne [A publication]
Wiadom Mat 2 ... Roczniki Polskiego Towarzystwa Matematycznego. Seria II.
　　　　　　　Wiadomosci Matematyczne [A publication]
Wiadom Statyst ... Wiadomosci Statystyczne [A publication]
Wiad Parazyt ... Wiadomosci Parazytologiczne [A publication]
Wiad Parazytol ... Wiadomosci Parazytologiczne [A publication]
Wiad Telekomun ... Wiadomosci Telekomunikacyjne [A publication]
Wiad Zielarskie ... Wiadomosci Zielarskie [A publication]
WIAI .... Danville, IL [FM radio station call letters]
WIAL .... Eau Claire, WI [FM radio station call letters]
WIAM .... Williamston, NC [AM radio station call letters]
WIAN .... Indianapolis, IN [FM radio station call letters]
WIAP .... Wartime Individual Augmentation Program [Military]
WIAP .... Westinghouse Industrial Atomic Power   (MCD)
WIAS .... West Indies Associated State

WIAS .... Whiteruthenian Institute of Arts and Science [*Later, BIAS*] (EA)
WIAV .... Cape Charles, VA [*FM radio station call letters*]
WIB............ Lawrence University, Appleton, WI [*OCLC symbol*] (OCLC)
WIB............ Wallcovering Information Bureau [*Springfield, NJ*] (EA)
WIB............ Wartime Information Board [*World War II*] [*Canada*]
WIB............ Weather Information Branch [*Air Force*] (MCD)
WIB............ When Interrupt Block (NASA)
WIB............ When-Issued-Basis [*Business and trade*]
WIBA .... Madison, WI [*AM radio station call letters*]
WIBA-FM ... Madison, WI [*FM radio station call letters*]
WIBB .... Macon, GA [*AM radio station call letters*]
WIBC .... Indianapolis, IN [*AM radio station call letters*]
WIBC .... Women's International Bowling Congress (EA)
WIBC .... World Institute of Black Communications (EA)
WIBFD .... Will Be Forwarded (NOAA)
WIBF-FM .... Jenkintown, PA [*FM radio station call letters*]
WIBG......... Ocean City, NJ [*AM radio station call letters*]
WIBI .... Carlinville, IL [*FM radio station call letters*]
WIBIS .... Will Be Issued (NOAA)
WIBM .... Jackson, MI [*AM radio station call letters*]
WIBN .... Earl Park, IN [*FM radio station call letters*]
WIBQ-FM ... Remsen, NY [*FM radio station call letters*]
WIBR .... Baton Rouge, LA [*AM radio station call letters*]
WIBS .... Charlotte Amalie, VI [*AM radio station call letters*]
WIBU .... Poynette, WI [*AM radio station call letters*]
WIBV .... Belleville, IL [*AM radio station call letters*]
WIBW .... Topeka, KS [*AM radio station call letters*]
WIBW-FM... Topeka, KS [*FM radio station call letters*]
WIBW-TV ... Topeka, KS [*Television station call letters*]
WIBX .... Utica, NY [*AM radio station call letters*]
WIBZ .... Wedgefield, SC [*FM radio station call letters*]
WIC .... Medical College of Wisconsin, Milwaukee, WI [*OCLC symbol*] (OCLC)
WIC .... Warning Information Correlation (MCD)
WIC .... Washington International Center
WIC .... Wax Insulating Compound
WIC .... Wayfarer International Committee (EA-IO)
WIC .... Weighted Ion Concentration [*Air pollution measure*]
WIC .... Wheat Industry Council [*Washington, DC*] (EA)
WIC .... WIC Western International Communications Ltd. [*Toronto Stock Exchange symbol*] [*Vancouver Stock Exchange symbol*]
WIC .... Wick [*Scotland*] [*Airport symbol*] (OAG)
WIC .... WICOR, Inc. [*NYSE symbol*]
WIC .... Windsor Institute of Complementology [*Later, ICS*] (EA)
WIC .... Women in Cable [*Washington, DC*] (EA)
WIC .... Women in Communications
WIC .... Women in Crisis [*New York, NY*] (EA)
WIC .... Women, Infants, and Children [*Supplemental food program*] [*Department of Agriculture*]
WIC .... Women's Interart Center (EA)
WIC .... Worksheet Inspection Card
WIC .... World Institute Council (EA)
WICA .... Judgments of the West Indian Court of Appeal (DLA)
WICA......... While in Control Area [*Aviation*] (FAAC)
WICA......... Wind Cave National Park
WICB......... Ithaca, NY [*FM radio station call letters*]
WICB......... Women in Cell Biology (EA)
WICBE....... World Information Centre for Bilingual Education [*See also CMIEB*] (EA-IO)
WICC......... Bridgeport, CT [*AM radio station call letters*]
WICD......... Champaign, IL [*Television station call letters*]
WICE .... Pawtucket, RI [*AM radio station call letters*]
WICF .... Women's International Cultural Federation [*See also FICF*] (EA-IO)
WICH......... Norwich, CT [*AM radio station call letters*]
WICHE....... Western Interstate Commission for Higher Education
WICI .... Women in Communications, Incorporated
WICK .... Scranton, PA [*AM radio station call letters*]
WICK......... Wicklow [*County in Ireland*] (ROG)
WICK......... Wicklund Petroleum [*NASDAQ symbol*] (NQ)
WICKL....... Wicklow [*County in Ireland*]
WICN......... Worcester, MA [*FM radio station call letters*]
WICO......... Salisbury, MD [*AM radio station call letters*]
WICO......... W. I. Carr Sons & Co. Overseas [*Stockbroker*] [*Hong Kong*]
WICO......... W.I. Carr Overseas [*Exco*]
WICO-FM... Salisbury, MD [*FM radio station call letters*]
WICR......... Indianapolis, IN [*FM radio station call letters*]
WICR......... Wilson's Creek Battlefield National Park
WICS......... Springfield, IL [*Television station call letters*]
WICS......... Women in Community Service [*Alexandria, VA*] (EA)
WICS......... Worldwide Intelligence Communications System (MCD)
WICU-TV... Erie, PA [*Television station call letters*]
WICY......... Malone, NY [*AM radio station call letters*]
WICZ......... While in Control Zone [*Aviation*] (FAAC)
WICZ-TV... Binghamton, NY [*Television station call letters*]
WID .... University of Wisconsin, Madison Library School, Madison, WI [*OCLC symbol*] (OCLC)
WID .... Wean United, Inc. [*NYSE symbol*]
WID .... Weekly Intelligence Digest [*Military*] (CINC)

WID .... West India Dock
WID .... Widow [*or Widower*]
WID .... Width
WID .... Women in Development [*Peace Corps*]
WIDA........ Carolina, PR [*AM radio station call letters*]
WIDA-FM ... Carolina, PR [*FM radio station call letters*]
WIDD .... Elizabethton, TN [*AM radio station call letters*]
WIDE .... Biddeford, ME [*AM radio station call letters*]
WIDE .... Widergren Communications [*NASDAQ symbol*] (NQ)
WIDE .... Wiring Integration Design (IEEE)
WIDETRACK ... Wideband Transmission Relay Acoustic Communications (MCD)
WIDF .... Women's International Democratic Federation [*See also FDIF*] (EA-IO)
WIDG......... St. Ignace, MI [*AM radio station call letters*]
WIDI .... Women in Design International [*Later, DI*] (EA)
WIDJET ..... Waterloo Interactive Direct Job Entry Terminal System [*IBM Corp.*]
WIDL .... Caro, MI [*FM radio station call letters*]
WIDOWAC ... Wing Design Optimization with Aerolastic Constraints [*Computer program*]
WIDR .... Kalamazoo, MI [*FM radio station call letters*]
WIDS .... Russell Springs, KY [*AM radio station call letters*]
WIDS .... Waterborne Intrusion Detection System (MCD)
WIDU .... Fayetteville, NC [*AM radio station call letters*]
WIE............ University of Wisconsin-Superior, Jim Dan Hill Library, Superior, WI [*OCLC symbol*] (OCLC)
WIE............ With Immediate Effect (FAAC)
WIE............ Women's Information Exchange (EA)
WIEB-TV .... Islamorada, FL [*Television station call letters*]
WIEB/WINB ... Western Interstate Energy Board/WINB [*Formerly, WINC*]
WIEC......... Ponce, PR [*Television station call letters*]
WIEC .... World Institute of Ecology and Cancer [*See also IMEC*] (EA-IO)
Wiederbeleb Organersatz Intensivmed ... Wiederbelebung. Organersatz. Intensivmedizin [*A publication*]
WIEL.......... Elizabethtown, KY [*AM radio station call letters*]
Wien Arch Innere Med ... Wiener Archiv fuer Innere Medizin [*A publication*]
Wien Beitr ... Wiener Beitraege zur Englischen Philologie [*A publication*]
Wien Chem Ztg ... Wiener Chemiker Zeitung [*A publication*]
Wien Entom Monatschr ... Wiener Entomologische Monatsschrift [*A publication*]
Wiener Ethnohist Bl ... Wiener Ethnohistorische Blaetter [*A publication*]
Wiener Voelkerk Mitt ... Wiener Voelkerkundliche Mitteilungen [*A publication*]
Wiener Z Kunde Sud ... Wiener Zeitschrift fuer die Kunde Suedasiens und Archiv fuer Indische Philosophie [*Vienna*] [*A publication*]
Wien Geschichtsbl ... Wiener Geschichtsblaetter [*A publication*]
Wien Klin W ... Wiener Klinische Wochenschrift [*A publication*]
Wien Klin Wochenschr ... Wiener Klinische Wochenschrift [*A publication*]
Wien Klin Wochenschr Suppl ... Wiener Klinische Wochenschrift. Supplementum [*A publication*]
Wien Landwirtsch Ztg ... Wiener Landwirtschaftliche Zeitung [*A publication*]
Wien Med Presse ... Wiener Medizinische Presse [*A publication*]
Wien Med Wochenschr ... Wiener Medizinische Wochenschrift [*A publication*]
Wien Med Wochenschr (Beih) ... Wiener Medizinische Wochenschrift (Beihefte) [*A publication*]
Wien Med Wochenschr Suppl ... Wiener Medizinische Wochenschrift. Supplementum [*A publication*]
Wien Med Wschr ... Wiener Medizinische Wochenschrift [*A publication*]
Wien Mitt Photogr Inhalts ... Wiener Mitteilungen Photographischen Inhalts [*A publication*]
Wien Mitt Wasser Abwasser Gewaesser ... Wiener Mitteilungen. Wasser, Abwaesser, Gewaesser [*A publication*]
Wien Naturh Mus Annalen ... Wien Naturhistorischer Museum. Annalen [*A publication*]
Wien Praehist Z ... Wiener Praehistorische Zeitschrift [*Austria*] [*A publication*]
Wien Stud ... Wiener Studien [*A publication*] (OCD)
Wien Tieraerztl Monatsschr ... Wiener Tieraerztliche Monatsschrift [*A publication*]
Wien Tieraerztl Mschr ... Wiener Tieraerztliche Monatsschrift [*A publication*]
Wien Z Inn Med Ihre Grenzgeb ... Wiener Zeitschrift fuer Innere Medizin und Ihre Grenzgebiete [*A publication*]
Wien Z Kunde Sued Ostasiens ... Wiener Zeitschrift fuer die Kunde Sued- und Ostasiens und Archiv fuer Indische Philosophie [*A publication*]
Wien Z Nervenheilk Grenzgeb ... Wiener Zeitschrift fuer Nervenheilkunde und Deren Grenzgebiete [*Austria*] [*A publication*]
WIERD....... Wind Energy Report [*A publication*]
WIEU .... Weekly Intelligence Estimate Update [*Vietnam*]
WIEZ .... Lewistown, PA [*AM radio station call letters*]
WIF............ Mid-Wisconsin Federated Library System, Fond Du Lac, WI [*OCLC symbol*] (OCLC)
WIF............ Water Immersion Facility (KSC)
WIF............ Weapons Integration Facility (MCD)
WIF............ West India Fruit & Steamship [*AAR code*]
WIF............ West Indies Federation
WIF............ Wildfire Resources Ltd. [*Vancouver Stock Exchange symbol*]
WIF............ Women in Film [*Los Angeles, CA*] (EA)

WIF .... Worlds of If [*A publication*]
WIF .... Worldview International Foundation (EA-IO)
WIFC .... Wausau, WI [*FM radio station call letters*]
WIFE .... Connersville, IN [*AM radio station call letters*]
WIFE .... Women Involved in Farm Economics
WIFE .... Women's Independent Film Exchange (EA)
WIFF .... Auburn, IN [*AM radio station call letters*]
WIFF-FM .... Auburn, IN [*FM radio station call letters*]
WIFI .... Kane, PA [*FM radio station call letters*]
WIFM-FM ... Elkin, NC [*FM radio station call letters*]
WIFO .... Wildfowl [*A publication*]
WIFO-FM .... Jesup, GA [*FM radio station call letters*]
WIFP .... Women's Institute for Freedom of the Press (EA)
WIFR-TV .... Freeport, IL [*Television station call letters*]
WIFU .... Western Interprovincial Football Union [*Canada*]
WIFX.......... Jenkins, KY [*AM radio station call letters*]
WIFX-FM ... Jenkins, KY [*FM radio station call letters*]
WIG .... West-Indische Gids [*A publication*]
WIG .... Wiggins Airways [*Norwood, MA*] [*FAA designator*] (FAAC)
WIG .... Wing in Ground
WIG .... Wisconsin State Library, Processing Center, Madison, WI
             [*OCLC symbol*] (OCLC)
WIG .... Wolfram Inert Gas (MCD)
Wig Disc..... Wigram on Discovery [*2nd ed.*] [*1840*] (DLA)
WIGE .... Wax-Impregnated Graphite Electrode
WIGG .... Wiggins, MS [*AM radio station call letters*]
Wight .... Wightwick's English Exchequer Reports [*145 English
             Reprint*] (DLA)
Wight El Cas ... Wight's Scottish Election Cases [*1784-96*] (DLA)
Wightw....... Wightwick's English Exchequer Reports [*145 English
             Reprint*] (DLA)
Wightw (Eng) ... Wightwick's English Exchequer Reports [*145 English
             Reprint*] (DLA)
WIGL .... Atmore, AL [*AM radio station call letters*]
WIGL .... Orangeburg, SC [*FM radio station call letters*]
WIGM .... Medford, WI [*AM radio station call letters*]
Wigm Ev..... Wigmore on Evidence (DLA)
WIGM-FM... Medford, WI [*FM radio station call letters*]
WIGO......... Atlanta, GA [*AM radio station call letters*]
WIGO......... What Is Going On? [*Humorous definition of science*]
WIGORN..... Wigorniensis [*Signature of Bishop of Worcester*]
             [*British*] (ROG)
WIGS .... Gouverneur, NY [*AM radio station call letters*]
WIGS-FM ... Gouverneur, NY [*FM radio station call letters*]
Wig Wills .... Wigmore on Wills (DLA)
WIGY .... Bath, ME [*FM radio station call letters*]
WIH .... State Historical Society of Wisconsin, Madison, WI [*OCLC
             symbol*] (OCLC)
WIHN .... Normal, IL [*FM radio station call letters*]
WIHS .... Middletown, CT [*FM radio station call letters*]
WIHS .... Western Institute for Health Studies (EA)
WIHT-TV .... Ann Arbor, MI [*Television station call letters*]
WII .... Beloit College Library, Beloit, WI [*OCLC symbol*] (OCLC)
WII .... Weatherford International, Incorporated [*American Stock
             Exchange symbol*]
WIIAD .... Winrock International Institute for Agricultural Development
             [*Formerly, CECA, ADC, IADS*] (EA)
WIIB........... Bloomington, IN [*Television station call letters*]
WIII .... Cincinnati, OH [*Television station call letters*]
WIIM-TV .... Iron Mountain, MI [*Television station call letters*]
WIIN .... Atlantic City, NJ [*AM radio station call letters*]
WIIP .... Waters Intelligent Information Processor
WIIQ .... Demopolis, AL [*Television station call letters*]
WIIS........... Key West, FL [*FM radio station call letters*]
WIIU .... Worker's International Industrial Union
WIIW .... Wiener Institut fuer Internationale Wirtschaftsvergleiche
             [*Vienna Institute for Comparative Economic Studies*]
             [*Vienna, Austria*] [*Information service*] (EISS)
WIJ .... Arrowhead Library System, Janesville Public Library,
             Janesville, WI [*OCLC symbol*] (OCLC)
WIJ .... Warburg Institute. Journal [*A publication*]
Wijsig Perspect ... Wijsgerig Perspectief op Maatschappij en Wetenschap [*A
             publication*]
WIK .... Kenosha Public Library, Kenosha, WI [*OCLC symbol*] (OCLC)
WIK .... Wien-Kobenzl [*Austria*] [*Geomagnetic observatory code*]
WIKB.......... Iron River, MI [*AM radio station call letters*]
WIKB-FM .... Iron River, MI [*FM radio station call letters*]
WIKC.......... Bogalusa, LA [*AM radio station call letters*]
WIKE .... Newport, VT [*AM radio station call letters*]
WIKI .... Carrollton, KY [*FM radio station call letters*]
WIKQ .... Greeneville, TN [*FM radio station call letters*]
WIKU .... Pikesville, TN [*FM radio station call letters*]
WIKX .... Immokalee, FL [*FM radio station call letters*]
WIKY .... Evansville, IN [*AM radio station call letters*]
WIKY-FM ... Evansville, IN [*FM radio station call letters*]
WIKZ .... Chambersburg, PA [*FM radio station call letters*]
WIL .... Lakeland College, Sheboygan, WI [*OCLC symbol*] (OCLC)
WIL .... Nairobi-Wilson [*Kenya*] [*Airport symbol*] (OAG)
WIL .... St. Louis, MO [*AM radio station call letters*]
WIL .... Ward Indicator Light
WIL .... White Indicating Light

WIL .... Wilco Mining Co. Ltd. [*Toronto Stock Exchange symbol*]
WIL .... Wilkes [*Antarctica*] [*Seismograph station code, US Geological
             Survey*] [*Closed*] (SEIS)
WIL .... Women in Leadership [*Project*]
WILA .... Danville, VA [*AM radio station call letters*]
WI Law Rev ... Wisconsin Law Review [*A publication*]
Wilberforce ... Wilberforce on Statute Law (DLA)
Wilb Stat .... Wilberforce on Construction and Operation of Statutes
             [*1881*] (DLA)
WILC .... Laurel, MD [*AM radio station call letters*]
WILC .... West Central Illinois Library Cooperative [*Library network*]
Wilc Cond ... Wilcox's Condensed Ohio Reports (Reprint) [*1-7 Ohio*] (DLA)
Wilc Cond Rep ... Wilcox's Condensed Ohio Reports (Reprint) [*1-7
             Ohio*] (DLA)
WILCO .... Western Interstate Library Coordinating Organization
WILCO....... Will Comply [*Used after "Roger"*] [*Radio term*]
Wilcox .... Wilcox's Lackawanna Reports [*Pennsylvania*] (DLA)
Wilcox .... Wilcox's Reports [*10 Ohio*] (DLA)
Wilcox Cond ... Wilcox's Condensed Ohio Reports (DLA)
WILD .... Boston, MA [*AM radio station call letters*]
WILD .... What I Like to Do [*Psychological testing*]
WILD .... Women's Independent Label Distribution Network [*Lansing,
             MI*] (EA)
Wild Barfield Heat-Treat J ... Wild Barfield Heat-Treatment Journal [*A
             publication*]
Wild Barfield J ... Wild Barfield Journal [*A publication*]
Wild Cat ..... Wild Cat Monthly [*A publication*]
Wildenowia Beih ... Wildenowia Beiheft [*A publication*]
Wildfire Stat US Dep Agric For Serv ... Wildfire Statistics. United States
             Department of Agriculture. Forest Service [*A publication*]
Wildl Aust ... Wildlife in Australia [*A publication*]
Wildl Dis..... Wildlife Diseases [*A publication*]
Wildl Dis Assoc Bull ... Wildlife Disease Association. Bulletin [*A publication*]
Wildlife....... Wildlife in Australia [*A publication*]
Wildlife Aust ... Wildlife in Australia [*A publication*]
Wild Life Rev ... Wild Life Review [*A publication*]
Wildl Manage Bull (Ottawa) Ser 1 ... Wildlife Management Bulletin (Ottawa).
             Series 1 [*A publication*]
Wildl Manage Bull (Ottawa) Ser 2 ... Wildlife Management Bulletin (Ottawa).
             Series 2 [*A publication*]
Wildl Monogr .. Wildlife Monographs [*A publication*]
Wildl Rev.... Wildlife Review [*A publication*]
Wildl Rev NZ Wildl Serv ... Wildlife Review. New Zealand Wildlife Service [*A
             publication*]
Wildl Soc Bull ... Wildlife Society. Bulletin [*A publication*]
Wildm Int Law ... Wildman's International Law (DLA)
WILE .... Cambridge, OH [*AM radio station call letters*]
Wiley Lib Newsl ... Wiley-Interscience Librarian's Newsletter [*A publication*]
WIL-FM ...... St. Louis, MO [*FM radio station call letters*]
WILFQ .... Wilson Foods Corp. [*NASDAQ symbol*] (NQ)
Wilhelm-Pieck Univ Rostock Wiss Z Math Naturwiss Reihe ... Wilhelm-
             Pieck-Universitaet Rostock. Wissenschaftliche Zeitschrift.
             Mathematisch-Naturwissenschaftliche Reihe [*A
             publication*]
Wilhelm Roux' Arch ... [*Wilhelm*] Roux' Archiv fuer Entwicklungsmechanik
             der Organismen [*Later, Roux' Archives of Developmental
             Biology*] [*A publication*]
Wilhelm Roux' Arch Dev Biol ... [*Wilhelm*] Roux' Archives of Developmental
             Biology [*A publication*]
Wilhelm Roux' Arch Entwicklungsmech Org ... [*Wilhelm*] Roux' Archiv fuer
             Entwicklungsmechanik der Organismen [*Later, Roux'
             Archives of Developmental Biology*] [*A publication*]
Wilhelm Roux Arch EntwMech Org ... Wilhelm Roux' Archiv fuer
             Entwicklungsmechanik der Organismen [*A publication*]
WILI........... Willimantic, CT [*AM radio station call letters*]
WILI-FM .... Willimatic, CT [*FM radio station call letters*]
WILJ .... West Indian Law Journal [*Jamaica*] (DLA)
WILK .... Wilkes-Barre, PA [*AM radio station call letters*]
Wilk .... Wilkinson, Owen, Paterson, and Murray's New South Wales
             Reports [*1862-65*] (DLA)
Wilk .... Wilkinson. Texas Court of Appeals and Civil Appeals (DLA)
Wilk Funds ... Wilkinson on Public Funds [*1839*] (DLA)
Wilk & Mur ... Wilkinson, Owen, Paterson, and Murray's New South Wales
             Reports [*1862-65*] (DLA)
Wilk & Ow ... Wilkinson, Owen, Paterson, and Murray's New South Wales
             Reports [*1862-65*] (DLA)
Wilk & Pat ... Wilkinson, Owen, Paterson, and Murray's New South Wales
             Reports [*1862-65*] (DLA)
Wilk P & M ... Wilkinson, Paterson, and Murray's New South Wales Reports
             [*1862-65*] (DLA)
Wilk Prec ... Wilkinson on Precedents in Conveyancing [*4th ed.*]
             [*1890*] (DLA)
Wilk Repl.... Wilkinson on Replevin [*1825*] (DLA)
Wilk Ship ... Wilkinson on Shipping [*1843*] (DLA)
WILL.......... Urbana, IL [*AM radio station call letters*]
Will .... Willes' English Common Pleas Reports (DLA)
Will .... William (King of England) (DLA)
Will........... Williams' Massachusetts Reports [*1 Massachusetts*] [*1804-
             05*] (DLA)

Will .... Williams' Vermont Reports [27-29 Vermont]   (DLA)
Will .... Willson's Reports [29-30 Texas Appeals] [1, 2, Texas Civil Appeals]   (DLA)
WILL........... Workshop In Library Leadership [Canada]
WILL........... Workshop Institute for Living-Learning
WILLA .... Wiley [John] & Sons Cl A [NASDAQ symbol]   (NQ)
Will Abr ...... Williams' Abridgment of Cases [1798-1803]   (DLA)
Willamette L J ... Willamette Law Journal [A publication]
Willamette L Rev ... Willamette Law Review [A publication]
Will Ann Reg ... Williams' Annual Register [New York]   (DLA)
Will Auct .... Williams' Auctions [5th ed.] [1829]   (DLA)
WILLB .... Wiley [John] & Sons Cl B [NASDAQ symbol]   (NQ)
Will Bankt ... Williams' Law and Practice of Bankruptcy [19th ed.] [1977]   (DLA)
Will-Bund St Tr ... Willis-Bund's Cases from State Trials   (DLA)
Willc Const ... Willcock's The Office of Constable   (DLA)
Willc Med Pr ... Willcock's Medical Profession [1830]   (DLA)
Willcock Mun Corp ... Willcock's Municipal Corporation   (DLA)
Will Com ..... Williams on Rights of Common [1880]   (DLA)
Will Con Rep ... Texas Civil Cases   (DLA)
Wildenowia Beih ... Wilddenowia Beiheft [A publication]
Will Eq Jur ... Willard's Equity Jurisprudence   (DLA)
Will Eq Pl .... Willis on Equity Pleading [1820]   (DLA)
Willes .... Willes' English Common Pleas Reports [125 English Reprint]   (DLA)
Willes (Eng) ... Willes' English Common Pleas Reports [125 English Reprint]   (DLA)
Will Ex........ Williams on Executors [15th ed.] [1970]   (DLA)
WILL-FM .... Urbana, IL [FM radio station call letters]
William Car ... William Carlos Williams Review [A publication]
William L Hutcheson Mem For Bull ... William L. Hutcheson Memorial Forest Bulletin [A publication]
William and Mary Law R ... William and Mary Law Review [A publication]
William & Mary L Rev ... William and Mary Law Review [A publication]
William Mitchell L Rev ... William Mitchell Law Review [A publication]
William M Q ... William and Mary Quarterly [A publication]
Williams ..... Peere-Williams' English Chancery Reports   (DLA)
Williams ..... Williams' Reports [10-12 Utah]   (DLA)
Williams ..... Williams' Reports [1 Massachusetts]   (DLA)
Williams ..... Williams' Vermont Reports [27-29 Vermont]   (DLA)
Williams & B Adm Jur ... Williams and Bruce's Admiralty Practice [3 eds.] [1869-1902]   (DLA)
Williams B Pr ... Williams' Bankruptcy Practice [17 eds.] [1870-1958]   (DLA)
Williams & Bruce Ad Pr ... Williams and Bruce's Admiralty Practice [3 eds.] [1869-1902]   (DLA)
Williams Common ... Williams on Rights of Common   (DLA)
Williams Ex'rs ... Williams on Executors   (DLA)
Williams Ex'rs R & T Ed ... Williams on Executors, Randolph and Talcott Edition   (DLA)
Williams P ... Peere-Williams' English Chancery Reports [1695-1736]   (DLA)
Williams Pers Prop ... Williams on Personal Property   (DLA)
Williams Real Prop ... Williams on Real Property   (DLA)
Williams Saund ... Williams' Notes to Saunders' Reports   (DLA)
Williams Seis ... Williams on Seisin   (DLA)
William W Story's Rept ... William W. Story's United States Circuit Court Reports   (DLA)
Willis Eq..... Willis on Equity Pleading [1820]   (DLA)
Williston..... Williston on Contracts   (DLA)
Williston..... Williston on Sales   (DLA)
Williston Basin Oil Rev ... Williston Basin Oil Review [A publication]
Will LJ .... Willamette Law Journal [A publication]
Will Mass ... Williams' Reports [1 Massachusetts]   (DLA)
Willm W & D ... Willmore, Wollaston, and Davison's English Queen's Bench Reports   (DLA)
Willm W & H ... Willmore, Wollaston, and Hodges' English Queen's Bench Reports [52 English Reprint] [1838-39]   (DLA)
Will P .... Peere-Williams' English Chancery Reports   (DLA)
Will Per Pr ... [J.] Williams on Personal Property [18th ed.] [1926]   (DLA)
Will Pet Ch ... Williams' Petitions in Chancery [1880]   (DLA)
Will Real Ass ... Williams' Real Assets [1861]   (DLA)
Will Saund ... Williams' Notes to Saunders' Reports [1666-73]   (DLA)
Wills Circ Ev ... Wills on Circumstantial Evidence   (DLA)
Wills Cir Ev ... Wills on Circumstantial Evidence   (DLA)
Will Seis ... Williams on Seisin of the Freehold [1878]   (DLA)
Wills Est Tr ... Wills, Estates, Trusts [Prentice-Hall, Inc.]   (DLA)
Willson....... Willson's Reports, Civil Cases [29-30 Texas Appeals] [1, 2 Texas Court of Appeals]   (DLA)
Wilson Civ Cas Ct App ... White and Willson's Civil Cases, Texas Court of Appeals   (DLA)
Willson's CC ... Texas Civil Cases   (DLA)
Willson Tex Cr Law ... Willson's Revised Penal Code, Code of Criminal Procedure, and Penal Laws of Texas   (DLA)
WILL-TV..... Urbana, IL [Television station call letters]
Will VT........ Williams' Vermont Reports [27-29 Vermont]   (DLA)
Will Woll & D ... Willmore, Wollaston, and Davison's English Queen's Bench Reports [1837]   (DLA)
Will Woll & Dav ... Willmore, Wollaston, and Davison's English Queen's Bench Reports [1837]   (DLA)
Will Woll & H ... Willmore, Wollaston, and Hodges' English Queen's Bench Reports [1838]   (DLA)

Will Woll & Hodg ... Willmore, Wollaston, and Hodges' English Queen's Bench Reports [1838]   (DLA)
WILM......... Wildlife Monographs [A publication]
WILM......... Wilmington, DE [AM radio station call letters]
WILM......... Wilmington Trust [NASDAQ symbol]   (NQ)
Wilm........... Wilmot's Notes and Opinions, King's Bench [97 English Reprint]   (DLA)
Wilm Judg ... Wilmot's Notes and Opinions, King's Bench [97 English Reprint]   (DLA)
Wilm Op ..... Wilmot's Notes and Opinions, King's Bench [97 English Reprint]   (DLA)
Wilmot's Notes ... Wilmot's Notes and Opinions, King's Bench [97 English Reprint] [1757-70]   (DLA)
Wilmot's Notes (Eng) ... Wilmot's Notes and Opinions, King's Bench [97 English Reprint]   (DLA)
Wilm W & D ... Willmore, Wollaston, and Davison's English Queen's Bench Reports   (DLA)
WILN .... Wildlife News [A publication]
WILN .... Wilson [H. J.] Co. [NASDAQ symbol]   (NQ)
WILO .... Frankfort, IN [AM radio station call letters]
WILPF .... Women's International League for Peace and Freedom [See also LIFPL]   (EA-IO)
WILPFNSW Branch Monthly Bulletin ... WILPF [Women's International League for Peace and Freedom]. New South Wales Branch. Monthly Bulletin [A publication]
WILPF-US ... Women's International League for Peace and Freedom, US Section
WILQ .... Williamsport, PA [FM radio station call letters]
Wil Q .... Wilson Quarterly [A publication]
WI LR......... Wisconsin Law Review [A publication]
WILS .... Lansing, MI [AM radio station call letters]
WILS .... Western Illinois Library System [Library network]
Wils .... Wilson English Chancery Reports [1818-19]   (DLA)
Wils .... Wilson's English Common Pleas Reports, 3 [95 English Reprint]   (DLA)
Wils .... Wilson's English King's Bench Reports [95 English Reprint] [1742-74]   (DLA)
WILS .... Wisconsin Interlibrary Loan Service
Wils Ch....... Wilson's English Chancery Reports [37 English Reprint] [1818-19]   (DLA)
Wils Ch (Eng) ... Wilson's English Chancery Reports [37 English Reprint]   (DLA)
Wils & Court ... Wilson and Courtenay's Scotch Appeal Cases   (DLA)
Wils CP .... Wilson's English Common Pleas   (DLA)
Wils (Eng) ... Wilson's English Common Pleas Reports, 3 [95 English Reprint]   (DLA)
Wils Ent...... Wilson's Entries and Pleading [3 Lord Raymond's King's Bench and Common Pleas Reports] [England]   (DLA)
Wils Ex .... Wilson's English Exchequer Reports [159 English Reprint] [1805-17]   (DLA)
Wils Exch ... Wilson's English Exchequer Reports [159 English Reprint]   (DLA)
Wils Exch (Eng) ... Wilson's English Exchequer Reports [159 English Reprint]   (DLA)
WILS-FM ... Lansing, MI [FM radio station call letters]
Wils Ind...... Wilson's Indiana Superior Court Reports   (DLA)
Wils Ind Gloss ... Wilson's Glossary of Indian Terms   (DLA)
Wils KB ...... Sergeant Wilson's English King's Bench Reports [1724-74]   (DLA)
Wils Minn ... Wilson's Reports [48-59 Minnesota]   (DLA)
Wilson........ Wilson Quarterly [A publication]
Wilson........ Wilson's English Chancery Reports   (DLA)
Wilson........ Wilson's English King's Bench and Common Pleas Reports   (DLA)
Wilson........ Wilson's Exchequer in Equity Reports [England]   (DLA)
Wilson........ Wilson's Indiana Superior Court Reports   (DLA)
Wilson........ Wilson's Reports [48-59 Minnesota]   (DLA)
Wilson..... Wilson's Reports [1-3 Oregon]   (DLA)
Wilson B..... Wilson Bulletin [A publication]
Wilson Bull ... Wilson Bulletin [A publication]
Wilson Lib Bul ... Wilson Library Bulletin [A publication]
Wilson Libr Bull ... Wilson Library Bulletin [A publication]
Wilson Q ..... Wilson Quarterly [A publication]
Wilson & Shaw ... Wilson and Shaw's Scottish Appeal Cases   (DLA)
Wilson's R ... Wilson's Indiana Superior Court Reports   (DLA)
Wilson's Rev & Ann St ... Wilson's Revised and Annotated Statutes [Oklahoma]   (DLA)
Wilson Super Ct (Ind) ... Wilson's Indiana Superior Court Reports   (DLA)
Wils Oreg ... Wilson's Reports [1-3 Oregon]   (DLA)
Wils PC .... Wilson's English Privy Council Reports   (DLA)
Wils & S ...... Wilson and Shaw's Scottish Appeal Cases [1825-35]   (DLA)
Wils & Sh ... Wilson and Shaw's Scottish Appeal Cases [1825-35]   (DLA)
Wils & S (Scot) ... Wilson and Shaw's Scottish Appeal Cases [1825-35]   (DLA)
Wils Super (Ind) ... Wilson's Indiana Superior Court Reports   (DLA)
WILS/WLC ... Wisconsin Interlibrary Loan Service - Wisconsin Library Consortium [Library network]
WilTel......... Williams Telecommunications Co. [Tulsa, OK] [Telecommunications service]   (TSSD)
WILTS .... Wiltshire [County in England]
Wilts Beekprs Gaz ... Wiltshire Beekeepers' Gazette [A publication]

Wiltshire Archaeol Natur Hist Mag ... Wiltshire Archaeological and Natural History Magazine [*A publication*]
Wiltshire Arch Mag ... Wiltshire Archaeological Magazine [*Later, Wiltshire Archaeological and Natural History Magazine*] [*A publication*]
Wiltshire Arch Natur Hist Mag ... Wiltshire Archaeological and Natural History Magazine [*A publication*]
WILUCL ...... Willamette University College of Law   (DLA)
WILV .... Baraboo, WI [*FM radio station call letters*]
WILX-TV ...... Onondaga, MI [*Television station call letters*]
WILY .... Centralia, IL [*AM radio station call letters*]
WIM .... Madison Public Library, Madison, WI [*OCLC symbol*]   (OCLC)
WIM .... Waksman Institute of Microbiology [*Rutgers University*] [*Research center*]   (RCD)
WIM .... Washington, Idaho & Montana Railway Co. [*AAR code*]
WIM .... Women in Management [*Chicago, IL*]   (EA)
WIM .... Women in Mining National [*Denver, CO*]   (EA)
WIMA .... Lima, OH [*AM radio station call letters*]
WIMA .... Women's International Motorcycle Association   (EA)
WIMA .... World International Medical Association   (EA)
WIMA .... Writing Instrument Manufacturers Association [*Washington, DC*]   (EA)
WIMC .... Whom It May Concern
WIMEA .... Wiretap, Investigation Monitoring, and Eavesdrop Activities   (MCD)
WIMG .... Trenton, NJ [*AM radio station call letters*]
WIMG .... Women in Municipal Government   (EA)
WIMI .... Ironwood, MI [*FM radio station call letters*]
WIMI .... Watercraft Intensively Managed Items   (AABC)
WIMIS .... Walk-In Management Information System [*Data processing*]
WIMK .... Iron Mountain, MI [*FM radio station call letters*]
WIML .... Wrightsville, GA [*FM radio station call letters*]
WIMM .... Weapons Integrated Materiel Manager [*Military*]
WIMN .... Women in Mining National   (EA)
WIMO .... Winder, GA [*AM radio station call letters*]
WIMP .... WARF [*Wartime Replacement Factors*] Intermediate Materiel Processor [*Military*]
WIMP .... Weakly Interacting Massive Particle [*Astrophysics*]
WIMS .... Michigan City, IN [*AM radio station call letters*]
WIMS .... Wartime Instruction Manual for Merchant Ships [*For deck officers of the United States Merchant Marine; popularly known as the "Convoy Bible"*] [*World War II*]
WIMS .... Waveguide Impedance Measuring Set
WIMS .... Works Information and Management System [*M & E White Consultants Ltd.*] [*Software package*]
WIMS .... Worldwide Integrated Management of Subsistence
WIMSA .... Webster Institute for Mathematics, Science, and Arts [*Webster College*]
WIMT .... Lima, OH [*FM radio station call letters*]
WIMV .... Madison, FL [*FM radio station call letters*]
WIMZ .... Knoxville, TN [*AM radio station call letters*]
WIN .... INELEC Library Project, Menomonie, WI [*OCLC symbol*] [*Inactive*]   (OCLC)
WIN .... Irwin, Australia [*Spaceflight Tracking and Data Network*] [*NASA*]
WIN .... Water-Insoluble Nitrogen [*Analytical chemistry*]
WIN .... Weapon Index Number [*Military*]   (CAAL)
WIN .... Weapons Interception [*Military electronics*]
WIN .... Well Information Network [*Database*]
WIN .... Western Information Network
WIN .... Whip Inflation Now [*Slogan of President Gerald R. Ford's anti-inflation program, 1974*] [*Program discontinued March, 1975*]
WIN .... White-Indian-Negro
Win .... Win Magazine [*A publication*]
Win .... Winch's English Common Pleas Reports [*124 English Reprint*]   (DLA)
WIN .... Windhoek [*Namibia*] [*Seismograph station code, US Geological Survey*]   (SEIS)
WIN .... Windsor Board of Education [*UTLAS symbol*]
Win .... Winer's Unreported Opinions, New York Supreme Court   (DLA)
WIN .... Winn-Dixie Stores, Inc. [*NYSE symbol*]
Win .... Winston's North Carolina Reports [*1863-64*]   (DLA)
Win .... Winter [*A publication*]
WIN .... Winter
WIN .... Winthrop Laboratories [*Research code symbol*]
WIN .... Winton [*Australia*] [*Airport symbol*]   (OAG)
WIN .... Wiswesser Line Notation
WIN .... Women's International Network
WIN .... Work Incentive Program [*Department of Health, Education, and Welfare, Department of Labor*]
WIN .... Workshop in Nonviolence   (EA)
WIN .... WWMCCS Intercomputer Network [*DoD*]
W/IN² .... Watts per Square Inch
WINA .... Charlottesville, VA [*AM radio station call letters*]
WINA .... Webb Institute of Naval Architecture
WINA .... Witton Network Analyzer
WINB .... Western Interstate Nuclear Board   (NRCH)
WINBA .... World International Nail and Beauty Association [*Orange, CA*]   (EA)
WINBAN ..... Windward Islands' Banana Association

WINC .... Western Interstate Nuclear Compact [*Later, WIEB/WINB*]
WINC .... White Incumbent
WINC .... Winchester, VA [*AM radio station call letters*]
WINC .... Worldwide Integrated Communications [*Mohawk Data Sciences Corp.*] [*Parsippany, NJ*] [*Telecommunications*]   (TSSD)
WINC-FM .... Winchester, VA [*FM radio station call letters*]
WINCH .... Winchester [*City in England*]   (ROG)
Winch .... Winch's English Common Pleas Reports [*124 English Reprint*]   (DLA)
Winch (Eng) ... Winch's English Common Pleas Reports [*124 English Reprint*]   (DLA)
WIND .... Chicago, IL [*AM radio station call letters*]
WIND .... Weather Information Network and Display
WIND .... Windsor Life Insurance Co. [*NASDAQ symbol*]   (NQ)
WIND .... Women in Distribution [*Commercial firm*]
WINDAV .... Wind Direction and Velocity Indicator [*Aviation*]
WINDEE ..... Wind Tunnel Data Encoding and Evaluation [*System*] [*Boeing Co.*]
Wind Energy Rep ... Wind Energy Report [*United States*] [*A publication*]
Wind Eng ... Wind Engineering [*England*] [*A publication*]
Wind Engng ... Wind Engineering [*A publication*]
W Indian Dig ... West Indian Digest [*A publication*]
W Indian Med J ... West Indian Medical Journal [*A publication*]
W Indian World ... West Indian World [*A publication*]
Wind Inst Melior Uzytkow Zielonych ... Windomosci Instytutu Melioracji i Uzytkow Zielonych [*A publication*]
Wind O .... Windless Orchard [*A publication*]
Wind Power Dig ... Wind Power Digest [*A publication*]
WINDS .... Weather Information Network and Display System
Windsor ..... Windsor Magazine [*A publication*]
Wind Technol J ... Wind Technology Journal [*A publication*]
WINE .... Brookfield, CT [*AM radio station call letters*]
WINE .... Schagrins, Inc. [*NASDAQ symbol*]   (NQ)
WINE .... Warning and Indications in Europe   (MCD)
WINE .... Webb Institute of Naval Engineering
Win Eq .... Winston's North Carolina Equity Reports   (DLA)
Wine Rev .... Wine Review [*A publication*]
Winfield Words & Phrases ... Winfield's Adjudged Words and Phrases, with Notes   (DLA)
WING .... Dayton, OH [*AM radio station call letters*]
Wing .... Wingate's Maxims   (DLA)
Wing Max ... Wingate's Maxims   (DLA)
WINI .... Murphysboro, IL [*AM radio station call letters*]
WINJ .... Pulaski, TN [*FM radio station call letters*]
WINK .... Fort Myers, FL [*AM radio station call letters*]
WINK .... Warning in Korea   (MCD)
WINK-FM .... Fort Myers, FL [*FM radio station call letters*]
WINKS .... Women in Numerous Kitchens [*World War II*]
WINK-TV .... Fort Myers, FL [*Television station call letters*]
WINM .... Angola, IN [*Television station call letters*]
WINN .... North Vernon, IN [*AM radio station call letters*]
WINNS .... Winn Enterprises [*NASDAQ symbol*]   (NQ)
WINP .... Water Insoluble Nonstarchy Polysaccharide [*Food composition*]
WINQ-FM ... Winchedon, MA [*FM radio station call letters*]
WINR .... Binghamton, NY [*AM radio station call letters*]
WINRA .... Women in the National Rifle Association
WINS .... New York, NY [*AM radio station call letters*]
WINS .... Weapons and Integrated Navigation System   (MCD)
WINS .... Women in National Service [*Name given by Ladies' Home Journal to American housewives and their teen-age daughters, "the greatest reserve strength of America"*] [*World War II*]
WINS .... Women's Industrial and National Service Corps [*World War II*] [*British*]
WINSNAMS ... Wind Indicating Systems for Navigation Aircraft in Missile Support
Winst .... Winston's North Carolina Equity Reports   (DLA)
Winst .... Winston's North Carolina Law Reports   (DLA)
WINSTAN ... Wings, Nonstraight-Taper Analysis   (MCD)
Winst Eq ..... Winston's North Carolina Equity Reports   (DLA)
Winst Eq (NC) ... Winston's North Carolina Equity Reports   (DLA)
Winst L (NC) ... Winston's North Carolina Law Reports   (DLA)
WINT .... Winter   (FAAC)
Wintertag ... Wintertagung [*A publication*]
Winterthur Jb ... Winterthur Jahrbuch [*A publication*]
WINTEX ...... Winter Exercise   (MCD)
Winthr St M ... Winthrop Studies on Major Modern Writers [*A publication*]
WINTON ..... [*Bishop of*] Winchester [*British*]
WINT-TV .... Crossville, TN [*Television station call letters*]
WINU .... Highland, IL [*AM radio station call letters*]
WINW .... Canton, OH [*AM radio station call letters*]
WINX .... Rockville, MD [*AM radio station call letters*]
WINY .... Putnam, CT [*AM radio station call letters*]
WINZ .... Miami, FL [*AM radio station call letters*]
WIO .... Nashotah House, Nashotah, WI [*OCLC symbol*]   (OCLC)
WIO .... Wilcannia [*Australia*] [*Airport symbol*]   (OAG)
WIO .... Women's International ORT
WIOA .... Mayaguez, PR [*FM radio station call letters*]
WIOB .... San Juan, PR [*FM radio station call letters*]

WIOC.......... Ponce, PR [*FM radio station call letters*]
WIOD.......... Miami, FL [*AM radio station call letters*]
WIOE.......... Huntington, IN [*FM radio station call letters*]
WIOF.......... Waterbury, CT [*FM radio station call letters*]
WIOG.......... Bay City, MI [*FM radio station call letters*]
WIOI............ New Boston, OH [*AM radio station call letters*]
WIOK.......... Falmouth, KY [*FM radio station call letters*]
WION.......... Ionia, MI [*AM radio station call letters*]
WIOO.......... Carlisle, PA [*AM radio station call letters*]
WIOQ.......... Philadelphia, PA [*FM radio station call letters*]
WIOS.......... Tawas City, MI [*AM radio station call letters*]
WIOT.......... Toledo, OH [*FM radio station call letters*]
WIOU.......... Kokomo, IN [*AM radio station call letters*]
WIOV.......... Ephrata, PA [*FM radio station call letters*]
WIOZ.......... Southern Pines, NC [*FM radio station call letters*]
WIP............ Philadelphia, PA [*AM radio station call letters*]
WIP............ Ripon College Library, Ripon, WI [*OCLC symbol*]   (OCLC)
WIP............ Wartime Intelligence Plan   (NATG)
WIP............ Weapon Indicator Panel [*Military*]   (CAAL)
WIP............ Weapons Installation Plan [*Navy*]   (NG)
WIP............ Women in Information Processing [*Washington, DC*]   (EA)
WIP............ Women in Production [*New York, NY*]   (EA)
WIP............ Work Incentive Program [*Department of Health, Education, and Welfare; Department of Labor*]   (DLA)
WIP............ Work in Place   (AABC)
WIP............ Work in Progress   (AFM)
WIP............ Work in Progress [*A publication*]
WIPACE ..... Wartime Intelligence Plan, Allied Command Europe   (NATG)
WIPB .... Muncie, IN [*Television station call letters*]
WIPC .... Lake Wales, FL [*AM radio station call letters*]
WIPIS .... Who Is Publishing in Science [*An Institute for Scientific Information publication*] [*Trademark*]
WIPM.......... Work in Process Measurement   (MCD)
WIPM-TV.... Mayaguez, PR [*Television station call letters*]
WIPP .... Waste Isolation Pilot Plant [*Department of Energy*]
WIPR .... San Juan, PR [*AM radio station call letters*]
WIPR-FM.... San Juan, PR [*FM radio station call letters*]
WIPR-TV .... San Juan, PR [*Television station call letters*]
WIPS .... Ticonderoga, NY [*AM radio station call letters*]
WIPS .... Women in Production Service [*A voluntary, semimilitary organization of women employees, primarily at the E. I. du Pont de Nemours & Co., at Richmond, Va.*] [*World War II*]
WIPS .... Word Image Processing System [*Datacopy Corp.*]
WIPTC........ Women's International Professional Tennis Council   (EA-IO)
WIQ .... Appleton Public Library, Appleton, WI [*OCLC symbol*]   (OCLC)
WIQB.......... Ann Arbor, MI [*FM radio station call letters*]
WIQH.......... Concord, MA [*FM radio station call letters*]
WIQI .... Quincy, FL [*FM radio station call letters*]
WIQO-FM.... Covington, VA [*FM radio station call letters*]
WIQQ.......... Leland, MS [*FM radio station call letters*]
WIQR .... Prattville, AL [*AM radio station call letters*]
WIQT .... Horseheads, NY [*AM radio station call letters*]
WIQUD .... Wilson Quarterly [*A publication*]
WIR .... Racine Public Library, Racine, WI [*OCLC symbol*]   (OCLC)
WIR............ Weapons Inspection Report [*Navy*]   (NG)
WIR............ Weekly Intelligence Review
WIR............ Welfare in Review [*A publication*]
WIR............ West India Regiment
WIR............ West Indian Reports   (DLA)
WIR............ Western Intelligence Report [*A publication*]
WIR............ Western Investment Real Estate Trust SBI [*American Stock Exchange symbol*]
WIR............ Wildrose Petroleum Ltd. [*Vancouver Stock Exchange symbol*]
WIR............ Wuerttemberg Israelitische Religionsgemeinschaft [*A publication*]   (BJA)
WIRA .... Fort Pierce, FL [*AM radio station call letters*]
WIRB .... Enterprise, AL [*AM radio station call letters*]
Wirbelsacule Forsch Prax ... Wirbelsacule in Forschung und Praxis [*A publication*]
WIRC.......... Hickory, NC [*AM radio station call letters*]
WIRD .... Lake Placid, NY [*AM radio station call letters*]
WIRDS....... Weather Information Remoting and Display System
WIRE .... Indianapolis, IN [*AM radio station call letters*]
WIRE .... Waseca Inter-Library Resource Exchange [*Library network*]
WIRE .... Weapons Interference Reduction Effort [*Navy*]   (NG)
WIRE .... Wildlife Review. British Columbia Ministry of Environment [*A publication*]
Wire............ Wire [*Draht Fachzeitschrift*] [*A publication*]
WIRE .... Women's International Resource Exchange   (EA)
Wire Ind ..... Wire Industry [*A publication*]
Wire J......... Wire Journal [*A publication*]
Wireless Eng ... Wireless Engineer [*A publication*]
Wirel World ... Wireless World [*A publication*]
WIRES........ Women in Radio and Electrical Service [*World War II*]
Wire and Wire Prod ... Wire and Wire Products [*A publication*]
Wire World Int ... Wire World International [*A publication*]
WIRF .... Women's International Religious Fellowship   (EA)
Wiring Install and Supplies ... Wiring Installations and Supplies [*A publication*]
WIRJ........... Humboldt, TN [*AM radio station call letters*]
WIRK .... West Palm Beach, FL [*AM radio station call letters*]

Wirkerei Strickerei Tech ... Wirkerei und Strickerei Technik [*A publication*]
WIRK-FM .... West Palm Beach, FL [*FM radio station call letters*]
WIRL............ Peoria, IL [*AM radio station call letters*]
WIRO .... Ironton, OH [*AM radio station call letters*]
WIRQ .... Rochester, NY [*FM radio station call letters*]
WIRR .... Virginia-Hibbing, MN [*FM radio station call letters*]
WIRS .... Wage Information Retrieval System [*IRS*]
WIRS .... Western Illinois Regional Studies [*A publication*]
WIRT .... Hibbing, MN [*Television station call letters*]
Wirt .... Wirtschaftsdienst [*A publication*]
WirtBer Lateinam Laender sowie Spanien und Port ... Wirtschaftsbericht ueber die Lateinamerikanischen Laender sowie Spanien und Portugal [*A publication*]
Wirt Futter ... Wirtschaftseigene Futter [*A publication*]
Wirt und Investment ... Wirtschaft und Investment [*A publication*]
Wirtschaft ... Wirtschafts-Blaetter [*A publication*]
Wirtsch-Dienst ... Wirtschaftsdienst [*A publication*]
Wirtsch u Recht ... Wirtschaft und Recht [*A publication*]
Wirtschseig Futter ... Wirtschaftseigene Futter [*A publication*]
Wirtsch Stat ... Wirtschaft und Statistik [*A publication*]
Wirtsch Verwalt ... Wirtschaft und Verwaltung [*German Federal Republic*] [*A publication*]
Wirtsch Wettbewerb ... Wirtschaft und Wettbewerb [*West Germany*] [*A publication*]
Wirtsch Wiss ... Wirtschaft und Wissenschaft [*A publication*]
Wirtsch-Wiss ... Wirtschaftswissenschaft [*A publication*]
Wirt und Sozwiss Inst Mitt ... Wirtschafts- und Sozialwissenschaftliches Institut. Mitteilungen [*A publication*]
Wirtswoche ... Wirtschaftswoche [*A publication*]
WIRV .... Irvine, KY [*AM radio station call letters*]
WIRX .... St. Joseph, MI [*FM radio station call letters*]
WIRY .... Plattsburgh, NY [*AM radio station call letters*]
WIS............ Columbia, SC [*AM radio station call letters*]
WIS............ University of Wisconsin, Stevens Point, Stevens Point, WI [*OCLC symbol*]   (OCLC)
WIS............ Washington Inventory Service
WIS............ Washington Irving Society   (EA)
WIS............ Weather Information Service [*Air Force*]   (MCD)
WIS............ Wedgwood International Seminar   (EA)
WIS............ Wisconsin   (AAG)
WIS............ Wisconsin Power & Light Co. [*American Stock Exchange symbol*]
Wis .... Wisconsin Reports   (DLA)
Wis .... Wisdom [*Old Testament book*] [*Roman Catholic canon*]
WIS............ Women in Sales Association [*Valhalla, NY*]   (EA)
WIS............ Women in Soccer   (EA)
WIS............ World of Islam [*A publication*]
WIS............ Wright Investors' Service [*Bridgeport, CT*] [*Information service*]   (EISS)
WIS............ WWMCCS Information Systems
WISA .... Isabela, PR [*AM radio station call letters*]
WISA .... West Indian Students Association   (EA)
WISA .... West Indies Sugar Association
WISA .... Wholesale Interservice Supply Agreement [*Military*]   (NG)
WISA .... Women's International Surfing Association   (EA)
Wis Acad Sci Arts Lett ... Wisconsin Academy of Sciences, Arts, and Letters [*A publication*]
Wis Acad Sciences Trans ... Wisconsin Academy of Sciences, Arts, and Letters. Transactions [*A publication*]
Wis Acad of Sci Trans ... Wisconsin Academy of Sciences, Arts, and Letters. Transactions [*A publication*]
Wis Admin Code ... Wisconsin Administrative Code   (DLA)
Wis Ag Dept ... Wisconsin. Department of Agriculture. Publications [*A publication*]
Wis Ag Exp ... Wisconsin. Agricultural Experiment Station. Publications [*A publication*]
Wis Agric Exp Stn Bull ... Wisconsin. Agricultural Experiment Station. Bulletin [*A publication*]
Wis Agric Exp Stn Res Bull ... Wisconsin. Agricultural Experiment Station. Research Bulletin [*A publication*]
Wis Agric Exp Stn Res Rep ... Wisconsin. Agricultural Experiment Station. Research Report [*A publication*]
Wis Agric Exp Stn Spec Bull ... Wisconsin. Agricultural Experiment Station. Special Bulletin [*A publication*]
WISA Law Rep ... Western Indian States Agency Law Reports   (DLA)
WISALR...... Western Indian States Agency Law Reports   (DLA)
Wis Alum M ... Wisconsin Alumni Magazine [*A publication*]
WISAP....... Waste Isolation Safety Assessment Program
Wis Arch ... Wisconsin Archaeologist [*A publication*]
WISARD ... Wideband System for Acquiring and Recording Data
Wisb.......... Laws of Wisby [*Maritime law*]   (DLA)
WISB .... Wildlife Society. Bulletin [*A publication*]
WiSB .... Women in Show Business [*North Hollywood, CA*]   (EA)
Wis BA Bull ... Wisconsin State Bar Association. Bulletin   (DLA)
Wis Badger Bee ... Wisconsin's Badger Bee [*A publication*]
Wis Bar Bull ... Wisconsin State Bar Association. Bulletin   (DLA)
Wis B Bulletin ... Wisconsin Bar Bulletin [*A publication*]
Wis Beekeep ... Wisconsin Beekeeping [*A publication*]
Wis BTA ..... Wisconsin Board of Tax Appeals Reports   (DLA)
WISC .... Wechsler Intelligence Scale for Children [*Education*]
WISC .... Wisconsin   (AFM)

Wisc .... Wisconsin Reports   (DLA)
WISC .... Wisconsin Southern Gas Co. [*NASDAQ symbol*]   (NQ)
WISC .... Women's Information and Study Centre
WISCII .... Wang International Standard Code for Information Interchange [*Pronounced "whiskey"*] [*Canada*]
Wisc Lib Bull ... Wisconsin Library Bulletin [*A publication*]
Wis Coll Agric Life Sci Res Div Res Rep ... Wisconsin College of Agricultural and Life Sciences. Research Division. Research Report [*A publication*]
Wis Coll Agric Life Sci Res Div Sci Rep Bull ... Wisconsin College of Agricultural and Life Sciences. Research Division. Science Report Bulletin [*A publication*]
WISCOM .... Wisconsin Information Science and Communications Consortium [*University of Wisconsin - Madison*] [*Research center*]   (RCD)
Wis Conserv Bull ... Wisconsin Conservation Bulletin [*A publication*]
Wis Conserv Dep Tech Bull ... Wisconsin Conservation Department. Technical Bulletin [*A publication*]
Wisconsin Acad Sci Arts and Letters Trans ... Wisconsin Academy of Sciences, Arts, and Letters. Transactions [*A publication*]
Wisconsin Acad Sci Arts Lett Trans ... Wisconsin Academy of Sciences, Arts, and Letters. Transactions [*A publication*]
Wisconsin Agric Exp Stn Bull ... Wisconsin. Agricultural Experiment Station. Bulletin [*A publication*]
Wisconsin L Rev ... Wisconsin Law Review [*A publication*]
Wisconsin Med J ... Wisconsin Medical Journal [*A publication*]
WISC-R ...... Wechsler Intelligence Scale for Children - Revised [*Education*]
Wisc Stud BJ ... Wisconsin Student Bar Journal   (DLA)
WISC-TV .... Madison, WI [*Television station call letters*]
WISD .... Wisdom   (ADA)
WISD .... Wisdom [*Old Testament book*] [*Douay version*]
WISD .... Wisdom of Solomon [*Old Testament book*] [*Apocrypha*]
Wis 2d .... Wisconsin Reports, Second Series   (DLA)
Wis Dep Nat Resour Publ ... Wisconsin. Department of Natural Resources. Publication [*A publication*]
Wis Dep Nat Resour Tech Bull ... Wisconsin. Department of Natural Resources. Technical Bulletin [*A publication*]
Wisd of Sol ... Wisdom of Solomon [*Old Testament book*] [*Apocrypha*]
WISE .... Asheville, NC [*AM radio station call letters*]
WISE .... Wang Intersystem Exchange
WISE .... Warning Indicators System Europe   (MCD)
WISE .... Weapon Installation System Engineering
WISE .... Wholesalers Institutional Service Extension [*Division of National American Wholesale Grocers Association*]
WISE .... Wiser Oil Co. [*NASDAQ symbol*]   (NQ)
WISE .... Women into Science and Engineering [*1984 campaign sponsored by the Equal Opportunities Commission and the Engineering Council*] [*British*]
WISE .... Women's Information Service, Inc.
WISE .... World Information Service on Energy   (EA)
WISE .... World Information Synthesis and Encyclopaedia [*Project of American Association for the Advancement of Science and American Society for Information Science*]
WISE .... World Information Systems Exchange [*Defunct*]   (EA)
Wis Energy Ext Serv Agric-Energy Transp Dig ... Wisconsin. Energy Extension Service. Agricultural-Energy Transportation Digest [*A publication*]
Wis Eng ...... Wisconsin Engineer [*A publication*]
Wis Eng Exp Stn Repr ... Wisconsin. Engineering Experiment Station. Reprint [*A publication*]
Wis Engineer ... Wisconsin Engineer [*A publication*]
WISER .... Western Information System for Energy Resources [*Dataline, Inc.*] [*Database*]
WiseR .... Wiseman Review [*A publication*]
Wis Geol Nat Hist Surv Bull ... Wisconsin. Geological and Natural History Survey. Bulletin [*A publication*]
Wis Geol Survey Bull Inf Circ ... Wisconsin. Geological Survey. Bulletin. Information Circular [*A publication*]
Wis G S ...... Wisconsin. Geological and Natural History Survey [*A publication*]
Wis G S G Wis B ... Wisconsin. Geological Survey. Geology of Wisconsin. Bulletin [*Later, Wisconsin Geological and Natural History Survey*] [*A publication*]
WISH .... World Institute for Scientific Humanism [*Formerly, ISH*]   (EA)
Wis His Col ... Wisconsin State Historical Society. Collections [*A publication*]
Wis His Proc ... Wisconsin Historical Society. Proceedings [*A publication*]
Wis His S Domesday Bk ... Wisconsin State Historical Society. Domesday Book [*A publication*]
Wis Hist Soc Proc ... Wisconsin State Historical Society. Proceedings [*A publication*]
Wis Hort ..... Wisconsin Horticulture [*A publication*]
WISH-TV .... Indianapolis, IN [*Television station call letters*]
Wis IC .... Wisconsin Industrial Commission Workmen's Compensation Reports   (DLA)
Wis J Ed ..... Wisconsin Journal of Education [*A publication*]
WISK .... Americus, GA [*AM radio station call letters*]
WISL .... Shamokin, PA [*AM radio station call letters*]
Wis Legis Serv ... Wisconsin Legislative Service (West)   (DLA)
Wis Leg N ... Wisconsin Legal News [*Milwaukee*]   (DLA)
Wis Lib Bul ... Wisconsin Library Bulletin [*A publication*]
Wis LN .... Wisconsin Legal News [*Milwaukee*]   (DLA)

Wis L Rev ... Wisconsin Law Review [*A publication*]
WISM .... Eau Claire, WI [*AM radio station call letters*]
Wis M .... Wisconsin Magazine of History [*A publication*]
Wis Mag Hist ... Wisconsin Magazine of History [*A publication*]
Wis Med J ... Wisconsin Medical Journal [*A publication*]
Wis M Hist ... Wisconsin Magazine of History [*A publication*]
WISN .... Milwaukee, WI [*AM radio station call letters*]
Wis Nat Resour Bull ... Wisconsin Natural Resources Bulletin [*A publication*]
Wis N H Soc B ... Wisconsin Natural History Society. Bulletin [*A publication*]
WISN-TV ..... Milwaukee, WI [*Television station call letters*]
WISO .... Ponce, PR [*AM radio station call letters*]
WISP .... Kinston, NC [*AM radio station call letters*]
WISP .... Warning Improvement Study Plan   (MCD)
WISP .... Wartime Information Security Program   (MCD)
WISP .... Weaponization of Increased Speed Projectiles   (MCD)
WISP .... Wide-Area Integrated Spectral Photometer [*Military*]   (MCD)
WISP .... Wide-Range Imaging Spectrophotometer [*Naval Oceanographic Office*]
WISP .... Women in Scholarly Publishing [*Bloomington, IN*]   (EA)
Wis Paper Ind Newsl ... Wisconsin Paper Industry. Information Service Newsletter [*A publication*]
Wis Pharm ... Wisconsin Pharmacist [*A publication*]
Wis Pharm Ext Bull ... Wisconsin. Pharmacy Extension Bulletin [*A publication*]
Wis PSC ..... Wisconsin Public Service Commission Reports   (DLA)
Wis PSC Ops ... Wisconsin Public Service Commission Opinions and Decisions   (DLA)
WISR .... Butler, PA [*AM radio station call letters*]
Wis R .... Wisconsin Reports   (DLA)
Wis RC Ops ... Wisconsin Railroad Commission Opinions and Decisions   (DLA)
Wis RCR ..... Wisconsin Railroad Commission Reports   (DLA)
Wis Rep ...... Wisconsin Reports   (DLA)
WISS .... Berlin, WI [*AM radio station call letters*]
WISS .... Weapon Impact Scoring System [*Navy*]   (MCD)
WISS .... Weekly Induction Scheduling System [*Navy*]   (NG)
WISS .... World Institute of Sephardic Studies   (BJA)
WISSA .... Wholesale Interservice Supply Support Agreements [*Military*]
Wiss Abh Dtsch Materialpruefungsanst ... Wissenschaftliche Abhandlungen der Deutschen Materialpruefungsanstalten [*A publication*]
Wiss Abh Phys-Tech Reichsanst ... Wissenschaftliche Abhandlungen der Physikalische-Technischen Reichsanstalt [*West Germany*] [*A publication*]
Wiss Alpenvereinshefte ... Wissenschaftliche Alpenvereinshefte [*A publication*]
Wiss Ann .... Wissenschaftliche Annalen [*A publication*]
Wiss Arch Landwirtsch Abt B ... Wissenschaftliches Archiv fuer Landwirtschaft. Abteilung B. Archiv fuer Tierernaehrung und Teirzucht [*A publication*]
Wis SBA Bull ... Wisconsin State Bar Association. Bulletin   (DLA)
Wiss Beitr Ingenieurhochsch Zwickau ... Wissenschaftliche Beitraege. Ingenieurhochschule Zwickau [*German Democratic Republic*] [*A publication*]
Wiss Beitr Martin Luther Univ (Halle Wittenberg) Reihe M ... Wissenschaftliche Beitrage. Martin Luther Universitaet (Halle Wittenberg). Reihe M [*A publication*]
Wiss Beitr Univ (Halle) ... Wissenschaftliche Beitrage. Martin-Luther-Universitaet (Halle-Wittenberg) [*A publication*]
Wiss Ber AEG-Telefunken ... Wissenschaftliche Berichte AEG-Telefunken [*A publication*]
Wiss Ber HMFA Braunschweig ... Wissenschaftliche Berichte aus der Hochmagnetfeldanlage der Physikalische Institute der Technischen Universitat Braunschweig [*A publication*]
Wiss Dienst Ostmitteleur ... Wissenschaftlicher Dienst fuer Ostmitteleuropa [*A publication*]
Wiss Dienst Sudosteuropa ... Wissenschaftlicher Dienst Suedosteuropa [*A publication*]
Wissenschaftstheorie- Wissenschaft Philos ... Wissenschaftstheorie- Wissenschaft und Philosophie [*A publication*]
Wissenschaftstheor Wiss Philos ... Wissenschaftstheorie- Wissenschaft und Philosophie [*A publication*]
Wissensch Meeresuntersuch ... Wissenschaftliche Meeresuntersuchungen [*A publication*]
Wissensch Sitzungen Stochastik 80 ... Wissenschaftliche Sitzungen zur Stochastik 80 [*A publication*]
Wissensch Taschenbuecher Reihe Math Phys ... Wissenschaftliche Taschenbuecher. Reihe Mathematik/Physik [*A publication*]
Wissensch Taschenbuecher Reihe Texte Stud ... Wissenschaftliche Taschenbuecher. Reihe Texte und Studien [*A publication*]
WISS-FM .... Berlin, WI [*FM radio station call letters*]
Wiss Forschungsber Naturwiss Reihe ... Wissenschaftliche Forschungsberichte. Naturwissenschaftliche Reihe [*A publication*]
Wiss Fortschr ... Wissenschaft und Fortschritt [*A publication*]
Wiss Konf Ges Dtsch Naturforsch Aerzte ... Wissenschaftliche Konferenz der Gesellschaft Deutscher Naturforscher und Aerzte [*A publication*]

Wiss Kult.... Wissenschaft und Kultur [*A publication*]

WisSL......... Wisconsin Studies in Literature [*A publication*]

Wiss Mitt Historiker-Ges DDR ... Wissenschaftliche Mitteilungen Historiker-Gesellschaft der DDR [*A publication*]

Wiss Mitt Pharm Forsch Fortbild Inst Oesterr Apoth Ver ... Wissenschaftliche Mitteilungen. Pharmazeutisches Forschungs- und Fortbildungs Instituts des Oesterreichischen Apotheker-Vereines [*A publication*]

WissMonANT ... Wissenschaftliche Monographien zum Alten und Neuen Testament [*Neukirchen/Vluyn*] [*A publication*]   (BJA)

Wiss Schriftenr Tech Hochsch Karl-Marx-Stadt ... Wissenschaftliche Schriftenreihe der Technischen Hochschule Karl-Marx-Stadt [*A publication*]

Wiss Taschenb ... Wissenschaftliche Taschenbuecher [*A publication*]

Wis Stat ..... Wisconsin Statutes   (DLA)

Wis Stat Ann (West) ... West's Wisconsin Statutes, Annotated   (DLA)

Wis State Cartogr Off Inf Circ ... Wisconsin State Cartographer's Office. Information Circular [*A publication*]

Wiss-Tech Fortschr Landw ... Wissenschaftlich-Technischer Fortschrift fuer die Landwirtschaft [*A publication*]

Wiss-Tech Inf VEB Kombinat Automatisierungsanlagenbau ... Wissenschaftlich-Technische Informationen des VEB Kombinat Automatisierungsanlagenbau [*A publication*]

Wis Stud Contemp Lit ... Wisconsin Studies in Contemporary Literature [*Later, Contemporary Literature*] [*A publication*]

Wiss Umwelt ISU ... Wissenschaft und Umwelt ISU [*Interdisziplinaerer Sonderbereich Umweltschutz*] [*German Federal Republic*] [*A publication*]

WissUnNT ... Wissenschaftliche Untersuchungen zum Neuen Testament [*Tuebingen*] [*A publication*]   (BJA)

Wiss Veroeff Siemens-Werken ... Wissenschaftliche Veroeffentlichungen aus den Siemens-Werken [*A publication*]

Wiss Veroeff Tech Hochsch (Darmstadt) ... Wissenschaftliche Veroeffentlichungen. Technische Hochschule (Darmstadt) [*A publication*]

Wiss Wb ..... Wissenschaft und Weltbild [*A publication*]

Wiss Weis ... Wissenschaft und Weisheit [*A publication*]

Wiss Welt ... Wissenschaft und Weltbild [*A publication*]

Wiss Wirtsch Polit ... Wissenschaft, Wirtschaft, Politik [*A publication*]

Wiss Z ... Wissenschaftliche Zeitschrift [*A publication*]

WissZ .... Wissenschaftliche Zeitung der Humboldt-Universitaet [*A publication*]

Wiss Z Elektrotech ... Wissenschaftliche Zeitschrift der Elektrotechnik [*A publication*]

Wiss Z Ernst Moritz Arndt Univ (Greifswald) Math Natur Reihe ... Wissenschaftliche Zeitschrift. Ernst-Moritz-Arndt-Universitaet (Greifswald). Mathematisch-Naturwissenschaftliche Reihe [*A publication*]

Wiss Z Ernst Moritz Arndt Univ Greifswald Math Naturw Reihe ... Wissenschaftliche Zeitschrift. Ernst-Moritz-Arndt-Universitaet (Greifswald). Mathematisch-Naturwissenschaftliche Reihe [*A publication*]

Wiss Z Ernst-Moritz-Arndt-Univ Greifsw Math Naturwiss Reihe ... Wissenschaftliche Zeitschrift. Ernst-Moritz-Arndt-Universitaet (Greifswald). Mathematisch-Naturwissenschaftliche Reihe [*A publication*]

Wiss Z Friedrich-Schiller-Univ (Jena) Math Naturwiss Reihe ... Wissenschaftliche Zeitschrift. Friedrich-Schiller-Universitaet (Jena): Mathematisch-Naturwissenschaftliche Reihe [*A publication*]

Wiss Z Hochsch Bauwes (Cottbus) ... Wissenschaftliche Zeitschrift. Hochschule fuer Bauwesen (Cottbus) [*A publication*]

Wiss Z Hochsch Bauwes (Leipzig) ... Wissenschaftliche Zeitschrift. Hochschule fuer Bauwesen (Leipzig) [*East Germany*] [*A publication*]

Wiss Z Hochsch Bauw (Leipzig) ... Wissenschaftliche Zeitschrift. Hochschule fuer Bauwesen (Leipzig) [*A publication*]

Wiss Z Hochsch Elektrotech (Ilmenau) ... Wissenschaftliche Zeitschrift. Hochschule fuer Elektrotechnik (Ilmenau) [*A publication*]

Wiss Z Hochsch Landwirtsch Produktionsgenoss Meissen ... Wissenschaftliche Zeitschrift. Hochschule fuer Landwirtschaftliche Produktionsgenossenschaften Meissen [*A publication*]

Wiss Z Hochsch Maschinenbau (Karl Marx-Stadt) ... Wissenschaftliche Zeitschrift. Hochschule fuer Maschinenbau (Karl Marx-Stadt) [*A publication*]

Wiss Z Hochsch Schwermaschinenbau (Magdeburg) ... Wissenschaftliche Zeitschrift. Hochschule fuer Schwermaschinenbau (Magdeburg) [*A publication*]

Wiss Z Hochschule ... Wissenschaftliche Zeitschrift. Hochschule fuer Oekonomie [*Berlin*] [*A publication*]

Wiss Z Hochsch Verkehrswesen (Dresden) ... Wissenschaftliche Zeitschrift. Hochschule fuer Verkehrswesen (Dresden) [*A publication*]

Wiss Z Hochsch Verkehrswesen Friedrich List Dresden ... Wissenschaftliche Zeitschrift der Hochschule fuer Verkehrswesen "Friedrich List" in Dresden. Die Anwendung Mathematischer Methoden im Transport- und Nachrichtenwesen [*A publication*]

Wiss Z Humboldt-Univ (Berl) ... Wissenschaftliche Zeitschrift. Humboldt Universitaet (Berlin) [*A publication*]

Wiss Z Humboldt-Univ (Berlin) Math-Natur Reihe ... Wissenschaftliche Zeitschrift der Humboldt-Universitaet (Berlin). Mathematisch-Naturwissenschaftliche Reihe [*A publication*]

Wiss Z Humboldt Univ Berlin Math Naturwiss Reihe ... Wissenschaftliche Zeitschrift. Humboldt Universitaet zu Berlin. Mathematisch-Naturwissenschaftliche Reihe [*A publication*]

Wiss Z Humboldt Univ Berl Math Naturwiss ... Wissenschaftliche Zeitschrift der Humboldt-Universitaet zu Berlin. Mathematisch-Naturwissenschaftliche Reihe [*A publication*]

Wiss Z Humboldt-Univ (Berl) Math-Naturwiss Reihe ... Wissenschaftliche Zeitschrift der Humboldt-Universitaet (Berlin). Mathematisch-Naturwissenschaftliche Reihe [*A publication*]

Wiss Z Karl-Marx Univ ... Wissenschaftliche Zeitschrift. Karl-Marx-Universitaet [*A publication*]

Wiss Z Karl-Marx-Univ (Leipzig) Math Natur Reihe ... Wissenschaftliche Zeitschrift der Karl-Marx-Universitaet (Leipzig). Mathematisch-Naturwissenschaftliche Reihe [*A publication*]

Wiss Z Karl-Marx-Univ (Leipzig) Math-Naturwiss Reihe ... Wissenschaftliche Zeitschrift. Karl-Marx-Universitaet (Leipzig). Mathematisch-Naturwissenschaftliche Reihe [*A publication*]

Wiss Z Karl-Marx-Univ (Leipz) Math-Naturwiss Reihe ... Wissenschaftliche Zeitschrift. Karl-Marx-Universitaet (Leipzig): Mathematisch-Naturwissenschaftliche Reihe [*A publication*]

Wiss Z Martin Luther Univ ... Wissenschaftliche Zeitschrift der Martin-Luther-Universitaet Halle-Wittenberg. Mathematisch-Naturwissenschaftliche Reihe [*A publication*]

Wiss Z Martin-Luther-Univ Halle-Wittenb ... Wissenschaftliche Zeitschrift der Martin-Luther Universitaet. Halle-Wittenberg [*A publication*]

Wiss Z Martin-Luther-Univ (Halle-Wittenberg) ... Wissenschaftliche Zeitschrift der Martin-Luther-Universitaet (Halle-Wittenberg) [*A publication*]

Wiss Z Martin-Luther-Univ Halle Wittenberg Math Natur Reihe ... Wissenschaftliche Zeitschrift. Martin-Luther-Universitaet (Halle-Wittenberg). Mathematisch-Naturwissenschaftliche Reihe [*A publication*]

Wiss Z Math Naturwiss Reihe Halle Univ ... Wissenschaftliche Zeitschrift. Mathematisch-Naturwissenschaftliche Reihe. Halle Universitaet [*A publication*]

Wiss Z Paedagog Hochsch Karl Liebknecht (Potsdam) ... Wissenschaftliche Zeitschrift. Paedagogische Hochschule Karl Liebknecht (Potsdam) [*East Germany*] [*A publication*]

Wiss Z Tech Hochsch Chem Carl Schorlemmer (Leuna-Merseburg) ... Wissenschaftliche Zeitschrift. Technischen Hochschule fuer Chemie "Carl Schorlemmer" (Leuna-Merseburg) [*A publication*]

Wiss Z Tech Hochsch Chem (Leuna-Merseburg) ... Wissenschaftliche Zeitschrift der Technischen Hochschule fuer Chemie (Leuna-Merseburg) [*A publication*]

Wiss Z Tech Hochsch (Dresden) ... Wissenschaftliche Zeitschrift. Technische Hochschule (Dresden) [*East Germany*] [*A publication*]

Wiss Z Tech Hochsch (Ilmenau) ... Wissenschaftliche Zeitschrift der Technischen Hochschule (Ilmenau) [*A publication*]

Wiss Z Tech Hochsch Karl-Marx-Stadt ... Wissenschaftliche Zeitschrift der Technischen Hochschule Karl-Marx-Stadt [*East Germany*] [*A publication*]

Wiss Z Tech Hochsch (Karl-Marx-Stadt) Sonderh ... Wissenschaftliche Zeitschrift. Technische Hochschule (Karl-Marx-Stadt) Sonderheft [*A publication*]

Wiss Z Tech Hochsch (Leipzig) ... Wissenschaftliche Zeitschrift der Technischen Hochschule (Leipzig) [*A publication*]

Wiss Z Tech Hochsch (Leuna-Merseburg) ... Wissenschaftliche Zeitschrift der Technischen Hochschule fuer Chemie "Carl Schorlemmer" (Leuna-Merseburg) [*A publication*]

Wiss Z Tech Hochsch (Magdeburg) ... Wissenschaftliche Zeitschrift der Technischen Hochschule Otto von Guericke (Magdeburg) [*A publication*]

Wiss Z Tech Hochsch Otto von Guericke (Magdeb) ... Wissenschaftliche Zeitschrift der Technischen Hochschule Otto Von Guericke (Magdeburg) [*A publication*]

Wiss Z Tech Hochsch Otto v Guericke (Magdeburg) ... Wissenschaftliche Zeitschrift der Technischen Hochschule Otto Von Guericke (Magdeburg) [*A publication*]

Wiss Z Tech Hochsch (Otto Von Guericke) ... Wissenschaftliche Zeitschrift. Technischen Hochschule (Otto Von Guericke) [*A publication*]

Wiss Z Techn Hochsch Chem (Leuna-Merseburg) ... Wissenschaftliche Zeitschrift der Technischen Hochschule fuer Chemie (Leuna-Merseburg) [*A publication*]

Wiss Z Techn Hochsch (Ilmenau) ... Wissenschaftliche Zeitschrift. Technischen Hochschule (Ilmenau) [*A publication*]

Wiss Z Techn Hochsch (Karl-Marx-Stadt) ... Wissenschaftliche Zeitschrift. Technischen Hochschule (Karl-Marx-Stadt) [*A publication*]

Wiss Z Techn Hochsch (Leuna-Merseburg) ... Wissenschaftliche Zeitschrift der Technischen Hochschule (Leuna-Merseburg) [*A publication*]

Wiss Z Techn Univ (Dresden) ... Wissenschaftliche Zeitschrift. Technischen Universitaet (Dresden) [*A publication*]

Wiss Z Tech Univ (Dres) ... Wissenschaftliche Zeitschrift der Technischen Universitaet (Dresden) [*A publication*]

Wiss Z Tech Univ (Dresden) ... Wissenschaftliche Zeitschrift der Technischen Universitaet (Dresden) [*A publication*]

Wiss Z Univ Greifswald ... Wissenschaftliche Zeitschrift der Ernst-Moritz-Arndt-Universitaet Greifswald [*A publication*]

Wiss Z Univ (Greifswald) Math-Naturwiss Reihe ... Wissenschaftliche Zeitschrift der Ernst-Moritz-Arndt-Universitaet (Greifswald). Mathematisch-Naturwissenschaftliche Reihe [*A publication*]

Wiss Z Univ (Halle) ... Wissenschaftliche Zeitschrift der Martin-Luther-Universitaet (Halle-Wittenberg) [*A publication*]

Wiss Z Univ (Halle-Wittenberg) Math-Naturwiss Reihe ... Wissenschaftliche Zeitschrift der Martin-Luther-Universitaet (Halle-Wittenberg). Matematisch-Naturwissenschaftliche Reihe [*A publication*]

Wiss Z Univ (Jena) Math-Naturwiss Reihe ... Wissenschaftliche Zeitschrift der Friedrich-Schiller-Universitaet (Jena): Mathematisch-Naturwissenschaftliche Reihe [*A publication*]

Wiss Z Univ (Leipzig) Ges-u Sprachwiss R ... Wissenschaftliche Zeitschrift. Karl-Marx-Universitaet (Leipzig): Gesellschafts- und Sprachwissenschaftliche Reihe [*A publication*]

Wiss Z Univ (Leipzig) Math-Naturwiss Reihe ... Wissenschaftliche Zeitschrift der Karl-Marx-Universitaet (Leipzig). Mathematisch-Naturwissenschaftliche Reihe [*A publication*]

Wiss Z Univ Rostock Ges Sprachwiss Reihe ... Wissenschaftliche Zeitschrift der Universitaet Rostock. Gesellschafts und Sprachwissenschaftliche Reihe [*A publication*]

Wiss Z Univ Rostock Ges- & Sprachwiss Reihe ... Wissenschaftliche Zeitschrift der Universitaet Rostock. Gesellschafts und Sprachwissenschaftliche Reihe [*A publication*]

Wiss Z Univ Rostock Ges-Wiss ... Wissenschaftliche Zeitschrift der Universitaet Rostock. Gesellschafts-Wissenschaftliche Reihe [*A publication*]

Wiss Z Univ Rostock Math-Natur Reihe ... Universitaet Rostock. Wissenschaftliche Zeitschrift. Mathematisch-Naturwissenschaftliche Reihe [*A publication*]

Wiss Z Univ Rostock Math Naturwiss Reihe ... Wissenschaftliche Zeitschrift der Universitaet Rostock. Mathematisch-Naturwissenschaftliche Reihe [*A publication*]

Wiss Z Univ Rostock Reihe Math Naturw ... Wissenschaftliche Zeitschrift der Universitaet Rostock. Reihe Mathematik und Naturwissenschaften [*A publication*]

WIST .... Lobelville, TN [*FM radio station call letters*]

WIST .... Whitaker Index of Schizophrenic Thinking

WIST .... WIST. Wirtschaftswissenschaftliches Studium [*A publication*]

WIS-TV ...... Columbia, SC [*Television station call letters*]

WISU .... Federation of Westinghouse Independent Salaried Unions

WISU .... Terre Haute, IN [*FM radio station call letters*]

Wis U Bul Eng S ... Bulletin. University of Wisconsin. Engineering Series [*A publication*]

Wis Univ Coll Eng Eng Exp Stn Rep ... Wisconsin University. College of Engineering. Engineering Experiment Station. Report [*A publication*]

Wis Univ Dept Meteorology Rept Lakes and Streams Inv Comm ... Wisconsin University. Department of Meteorology. Report to the Lakes and Streams Investigations Committee [*A publication*]

Wis Univ Eng Exp Stn Bull ... Wisconsin University. Engineering Experiment Station. Bulletin [*A publication*]

Wis Univ Geol Nat Hist Surv Spec Rep ... Wisconsin University. Geological and Natural History Survey. Special Report [*A publication*]

Wis Univ Geol Natur Hist Surv Inform Circ ... Wisconsin University. Geological and Natural History Survey. Information Circular [*A publication*]

WIT .... Washington Institute of Technology [*Washington, DC*]

WIT .... Winnebago International Travelers

WIT .... Winnebago-Itasca Travelers (EA)

WIT .... Wiring Interface Tester (MCD)

WIT .... Wisconsin Institute of Technology

WIT .... Witco Corp. [*NYSE symbol*]

WIT .... Witness (AABC)

WIT .... Wittenberg University, Springfield, OH [*OCLC symbol*] (OCLC)

WIT .... Witteveen [*Netherlands*] [*Geomagnetic observatory code*]

WIT .... Witteveen [*Netherlands*] [*Seismograph station code, US Geological Survey*] (SEIS)

WIT .... Women in Telecommunications [*San Francisco, CA*] (EA)

WIT .... Women in Transition [*Philadelphia, PA*] (EA)

WIT .... World Ice Theory [*Hans Horbiger*]

WIT .... World Identification Test (ADA)

WITA .... Knoxville, TN [*AM radio station call letters*]

WITA .... Women in the Army (MCD)

WITA .... Women in the Arts (EA)

WITA .... Women's International Tennis Association [*Miami, FL*] (EA)

WITAN .... Wind-Time Analyzer

WITB-FM .... Salem, WV [*FM radio station call letters*]

WITC .... Cazenovia, NY [*FM radio station call letters*]

WITCH .... Women Incensed over Traditional Coed Hoopla [*Feminist group*]

WITCH .... Women's International Terrorist Conspiracy from Hell [*Feminist group*]

WITF .... Women's International Tennis Federation

WITF-FM .... Harrisburg, PA [*FM radio station call letters*]

WITF-TV .... Harrisburg, PA [*Television station call letters*]

WITG .... Western International Trade Group [*Phoenix, AZ*] (EA)

WITH .... Baltimore, MD [*AM radio station call letters*]

With Corp Cas ... Withrow's American Corporation Cases (DLA)

WITHDRL ... Withdrawal (ROG)

Withrow ..... Withrow's American Corporation Cases (DLA)

Withrow ..... Withrow's Reports [*9-21 Iowa*] (DLA)

WITHT .... Without (ROG)

WITIS .... Weather Integration with Tactical Intelligence System (MCD)

Witkin Cal Summary ... Witkin's Summary of California Law (DLA)

WITL .... Lansing, MI [*AM radio station call letters*]

WITL-FM .... Lansing, MI [*FM radio station call letters*]

WITNED ..... Witnessed

WITNESS ... Wire Installation Tester for Negating Errors by Sequencing and Standardization

WITNETH ... Witnesseth [*Legal*] [*British*] (ROG)

WITNS .... Witness [*Legal*] [*British*] (ROG)

WITN-TV .... Washington, NC [*Television station call letters*]

WITQ .... Block Island, RI [*FM radio station call letters*]

WITR .... Henrietta, NY [*FM radio station call letters*]

WITS .... Sebring, FL [*AM radio station call letters*]

WITS .... Washington Interagency Telecommunications System [*GSA*]

WITS .... Weather Information Telemetry System [*Air Force*] (CET)

WITS .... West Integrated Test Stand [*NASA*]

WITS .... Women in Technical Service [*World War II*]

WITS .... Work Item Tracking System (NRCH)

WITS .... Worldwide Information and Trade System

WITSEC ..... Witness Security Program [*US government program for protection of witnesses whose lives are endangered by their testimony*]

WITSS .... Witnesses [*Legal*] [*British*] (ROG)

WITT .... Tuscola, IL [*FM radio station call letters*]

Witthaus & Becker's Med Jur ... Witthaus and Becker's Medical Jurisprudence (DLA)

Wittheit Bremen Jahrb ... Wittheit zu Bremen. Jahrbuch [*A publication*]

WITU .... Cobleskill, NY [*FM radio station call letters*]

WITV .... Charleston, SC [*Television station call letters*]

WITW .... We Interrupt This Week [*Television program*]

WITX .... Beaver Falls, PA [*FM radio station call letters*]

WITY .... Danville, IL [*AM radio station call letters*]

WITZ .... Jasper, IN [*AM radio station call letters*]

WITZ-FM .... Jasper, IN [*FM radio station call letters*]

WIU .... Warhead Interface Unit (MCD)

WIU .... Water Injection Unit

WIU .... Weather Intelligence Unit [*Army*] (MCD)

WIU .... Western Illinois University [*Macomb*]

WIU .... Western International University, Phoenix, AZ [*OCLC symbol*] (OCLC)

wiu .... Wisconsin [*MARC country of publication code*] [*Library of Congress*] (LCCP)

WIU .... Witu [*Papua New Guinea*] [*Airport symbol*] (OAG)

WIUJ .... St. Thomas, VI [*FM radio station call letters*]

WIUM .... Macomb, IL [*FM radio station call letters*]

WIUM-TV ... Macomb, IL [*Television station call letters*]

WIUP-FM .... Indiana, PA [*FM radio station call letters*]

WIUS .... Macomb, IL [*FM radio station call letters*]

WIUV .... Castleton, VT [*FM radio station call letters*]

Wiv .... [*The*] Merry Wives of Windsor [*Shakespearean work*]

WIV .... Waukesha Public Library, Waukesha, WI [*OCLC symbol*] (OCLC)

WIVA-FM .... Aguadilla, PR [*FM radio station call letters*]

WIVB-TV .... Buffalo, NY [*Television station call letters*]

WIVE .... Ashland, VA [*AM radio station call letters*]

WIVI-FM .... Christiansted, VI [*FM radio station call letters*]

WIVK .... Knoxville, TN [*AM radio station call letters*]

WIVK-FM ... Knoxville, TN [*FM radio station call letters*]

WIVQ .... Cumberland, MD [*Television station call letters*]

WIVV .... Vieques, PR [*AM radio station call letters*]

WIVY-FM .... Jacksonville, FL [*FM radio station call letters*]

WIW .... Marathon County Public Library, Wausau, WI [*OCLC symbol*] (OCLC)

WIW .... Wooded Island [*Washington*] [*Seismograph station code, US Geological Survey*] (SEIS)

WIWHA ...... Western International Walking Horse Association (EA)

WIWO .... Walk In, Walk Out (ADA)

WIWP .... World Institute for World Peace

WIX .... Steenbock Memorial Library, Madison, WI [*OCLC symbol*] (OCLC)

WIX .... Wickes Companies, Inc. [*NYSE symbol*]

WIXC .... Fayetteville, TN [*AM radio station call letters*]

WIXE .... Monroe, NC [*AM radio station call letters*]
WIXI .... Naples Park, FL [*FM radio station call letters*]
WIXK .... New Richmond, WI [*AM radio station call letters*]
WIXK-FM ... New Richmond, WI [*FM radio station call letters*]
WIXL .... Newton, NJ [*FM radio station call letters*]
WIXN .... Dixon, IL [*AM radio station call letters*]
WIXN-FM .... Dixon, IL [*FM radio station call letters*]
WIXQ .... Millersville, PA [*FM radio station call letters*]
WIXR .... Mount Pleasant, SC [*AM radio station call letters*]
WIXT .... Syracuse, NY [*Television station call letters*]
WIXV .... Savannah, GA [*FM radio station call letters*]
WIXX .... Green Bay, WI [*FM radio station call letters*]
WIXY .... East Longmeadow, MA [*AM radio station call letters*]
WIXZ .... McKeesport, PA [*AM radio station call letters*]
WIY .... University of Wisconsin, Primate Research Center, Primate Library, Madison, WI [*OCLC symbol*]   (OCLC)
WIYD .... Palatka, FL [*AM radio station call letters*]
WIYN .... Rome, GA [*AM radio station call letters*]
WIYQ .... Ebensburg, PA [*FM radio station call letters*]
WIYY .... Baltimore, MD [*FM radio station call letters*]
WiZ .... Wiedza i Zycie [*A publication*]
WiZ .... Wort in der Zeit [*A publication*]
WIZB .... Abbeville, AL [*FM radio station call letters*]
WIZD .... Atmore, AL [*FM radio station call letters*]
WIZE .... Springfield, OH [*AM radio station call letters*]
WIZM .... La Crosse, WI [*AM radio station call letters*]
WIZM-FM ... La Crosse, WI [*FM radio station call letters*]
WIZN .... Vergennes, VT [*FM radio station call letters*]
WIZO .... Franklin, TN [*AM radio station call letters*]
WIZO .... Women's International Zionist Organization   (EA)
WIZR .... Johnstown, NY [*AM radio station call letters*]
WIZS .... Henderson, NC [*AM radio station call letters*]
WIZZ .... Streator, IL [*AM radio station call letters*]
WJ .... Joule [*Unit of work*]   (ROG)
WJ .... Nihon Kinkyori Airways [*ICAO designator*]   (FAAC)
WJ .... Wars of the Jews [*of Josephus*] [*A publication*]   (BJA)
WJ .... Water Jacket   (MSA)
WJ .... Watkins-Johnson Co. [*NYSE symbol*]
wj .... West Bank of the Jordan River [*MARC country of publication code*] [*Library of Congress*]   (LCCP)
WJ .... Western Jurist [*United States*]   (DLA)
WJ .... Wiener Jahreshefte [*A publication*]
WJ .... Wolfram-Jahrbuch [*A publication*]
WJ .... Wood Jalousie
WJa .... Janesville Public Library, Janesville, WI [*Library symbol*] [*Library of Congress*]   (LCLS)
WJA .... Women's Jewelry Association [*New York, NY*]   (EA)
WJA .... Woolen Jobbers Association   (EA)
WJA .... World Jazz Association [*Defunct*]   (EA)
WJA .... Wuerzburger Jahrbuecher fuer die Altertumswissenschaft [*A publication*]
WJaB .... Blackhawk Technical Institute, Janesville, WI [*Library symbol*] [*Library of Congress*]   (LCLS)
WJAC .... Johnstown, PA [*AM radio station call letters*]
WJAC-TV ... Johnstown, PA [*Television station call letters*]
WJAD .... Bainbridge, GA [*FM radio station call letters*]
WJAG .... Norfolk, NE [*AM radio station call letters*]
WJAK .... Jackson, TN [*AM radio station call letters*]
WJAL .... Hagerstown, MD [*Television station call letters*]
WJaM .... Mercy Hospital, Janesville, WI [*Library symbol*] [*Library of Congress*]   (LCLS)
WJAM-FM ... Marion, AL [*FM radio station call letters*]
WJAQ .... Marianna, FL [*FM radio station call letters*]
WJaRH ...... Rock County Health Care Center, Janesville, WI [*Library symbol*] [*Library of Congress*]   (LCLS)
WJAR-TV ... Providence, RI [*Television station call letters*]
WJAS .... Pittsburgh, PA [*AM radio station call letters*]
WJAT .... Swainsboro, GA [*AM radio station call letters*]
WJAX .... Jacksonville, FL [*AM radio station call letters*]
WJAY .... Mullins, SC [*AM radio station call letters*]
WJAZ .... Albany, GA [*AM radio station call letters*]
WJB .... Wire Jig Board   (MCD)
WJBB .... Haleyville, AL [*AM radio station call letters*]
WJBB-FM ... Haleyville, AL [*FM radio station call letters*]
WJBC .... Bloomington, IL [*AM radio station call letters*]
WJBD .... Salem, IL [*AM radio station call letters*]
WJBD-FM... Salem, IL [*FM radio station call letters*]
WJBF .... Augusta, GA [*Television station call letters*]
WJBI .... Batesville, MS [*AM radio station call letters*]
WJBK-TV ... Detroit, MI [*Television station call letters*]
WJBM .... Jerseyville, IL [*AM radio station call letters*]
WJBO .... Baton Rouge, LA [*AM radio station call letters*]
WJBQ .... Portland, ME [*AM radio station call letters*]
WJBR .... Wilmington, DE [*FM radio station call letters*]
WJBR-FM... Wilmington, DE [*AM radio station call letters*]
WJBS .... Holly Hill, SC [*AM radio station call letters*]
WJBU .... Port St. Joe, FL [*AM radio station call letters*]
WJBU .... William Jennings Bryan University [*Tennessee*]
WJBX .... Bridgeport, CT [*AM radio station call letters*]
WJBY .... Rainbow City, AL [*AM radio station call letters*]
WJC .... Washington and Jefferson College [*Pennsylvania*]

WJC .... Washington Journalism Center   (EA)
WJC .... William Jewell College [*Missouri*]
WJC .... Wood Junior College [*Mississippi*]
WJC .... Worcester Junior College [*Massachusetts*]
WJC .... World Jewish Congress
WJC .... Worthington Junior College [*Minnesota*] [*Later, Worthington Community College*]
WJCAR....... World Jewish Congress Annual Report [*New York*] [*A publication*]
WJCB .... World Jersey Cattle Bureau
WJCC .... Norfolk, MA [*AM radio station call letters*]
WJCC .... Western Joint Computer Conference
WJCC .... Women's Joint Congressional Committee   (EA)
WJCD .... Seymour, IN [*AM radio station call letters*]
WJCD-FM ... Seymour, IN [*FM radio station call letters*]
WJCH .... Joliet, IL [*AM radio station call letters*]
WJCIB .... World Jewish Congress Information Bulletin [*New York*] [*A publication*]
WJCL .... Savannah, GA [*Television station call letters*]
WJCL-FM... Savannah, GA [*FM radio station call letters*]
WJCM .... Sebring, FL [*AM radio station call letters*]
WJCO .... Jackson, MI [*AM radio station call letters*]
WJCR .... Washington, PA [*FM radio station call letters*]
WJCT .... Jacksonville, FL [*Television station call letters*]
WJCT-FM... Jacksonville, FL [*FM radio station call letters*]
WJCW .... Johnson City, TN [*AM radio station call letters*]
WJD .... Welded Joint Design
WJDA .... Quincy, MA [*AM radio station call letters*]
WJDB .... Thomasville, AL [*AM radio station call letters*]
WJDB-FM... Thomasville, AL [*FM radio station call letters*]
WJDJ .... Burnside, KY [*FM radio station call letters*]
WJDM .... Elizabeth, NJ [*AM radio station call letters*]
WJDQ .... Meridian, MS [*FM radio station call letters*]
WJDR .... Prentiss, MS [*FM radio station call letters*]
WJDW .... Corydon, IN [*AM radio station call letters*]
WJDX .... Jackson, MS [*AM radio station call letters*]
WJDY .... Salisbury, MD [*AM radio station call letters*]
WJDZ .... Levittown, PR [*FM radio station call letters*]
WJE .... Willis, Joyce, McMinnville OR [*STAC*]
WJEA .... Palm City, FL [*AM radio station call letters*]
WJEB .... Gladwin, MI [*AM radio station call letters*]
WJEC .... Welsh Joint Education Committee [*British*]
WJEF .... Lafayette, IN [*FM radio station call letters*]
WJEH .... Gallipolis, OH [*AM radio station call letters*]
WJEJ .... Hagerstown, MD [*AM radio station call letters*]
WJEL .... Indianapolis, IN [*FM radio station call letters*]
WJEM .... Valdosta, GA [*AM radio station call letters*]
WJEP .... Ochlocknee, GA [*AM radio station call letters*]
WJEQ .... Macomb, IL [*FM radio station call letters*]
WJER .... Dover-New Philadelphia, OH [*AM radio station call letters*]
WJER-FM... Dover, OH [*FM radio station call letters*]
WJES .... Johnston, SC [*AM radio station call letters*]
WJET .... Erie, PA [*FM radio station call letters*]
WJET-TV ... Erie, PA [*Television station call letters*]
WJEZ .... Pontiac, IL [*FM radio station call letters*]
WJF .... Lancaster, CA [*Location identifier*] [*FAA*]   (FAAL)
WJF .... Palmdale/Lancaster [*California*] Fox [*Airport symbol*]   (OAG)
WJF .... White Jewish Female [*Classified advertising*]
WJFB .... Lebanon, TN [*Television station call letters*]
WJFC .... Jefferson City, TN [*AM radio station call letters*]
WJFC .... Waylon Jennings Fan Club [*Corpus Christi, TX*]   (EA)
WJFD-FM... New Bedford, MA [*FM radio station call letters*]
WJFI .... Women's Jazz Festival, Incorporated   (EA)
WJFK .... West Yarmouth, MA [*FM radio station call letters*]
WJFL .... Vicksburg, MS [*AM radio station call letters*]
WJFM .... Grand Rapids, MI [*FM radio station call letters*]
WJFR .... Jacksonville, FL [*FM radio station call letters*]
WJFW-TV ... Rhinelander, WI [*Television station call letters*]
WJFX .... Aiken, SC [*AM radio station call letters*]
WJFX-FM ... Aiken, SC [*FM radio station call letters*]
WJGA-FM ... Jackson, GA [*FM radio station call letters*]
WJGF .... Romney, WV [*FM radio station call letters*]
WJGO .... World Jewish Genealogy Organization   (EA)
WJGS-FM ... Houghton Lake, MI [*FM radio station call letters*]
WJh .... Wiener Jahreshefte [*A publication*]
WJHD .... Portsmouth, RI [*FM radio station call letters*]
WJHG-TV ... Panama City, FL [*Television station call letters*]
WJHL-TV.... Johnson City, TN [*Television station call letters*]
WJHO .... Opelika, AL [*AM radio station call letters*]
WJHS .... Columbia City, IN [*FM radio station call letters*]
WJHU-FM... Baltimore, MD [*FM radio station call letters*]
WJIB .... Boston, MA [*FM radio station call letters*]
WJIC .... Salem, NJ [*AM radio station call letters*]
WJIE .... Okolona, KY [*FM radio station call letters*]
WJIF .... Opp, AL [*FM radio station call letters*]
WJIK .... Camp Lejeune, NC [*AM radio station call letters*]
WJIL .... Jacksonville, IL [*AM radio station call letters*]
WJIM .... Lansing, MI [*AM radio station call letters*]
WJIM-FM ... Lansing, MI [*FM radio station call letters*]
WJIM-TV ... Lansing, MI [*Television station call letters*]
WJIR .... Key West, FL [*FM radio station call letters*]

WJIS.......... Bradenton, FL [*FM radio station call letters*]
WJIT.......... New York, NY [*AM radio station call letters*]
WJIV.......... Cherry Valley, NY [*FM radio station call letters*]
WJIW.......... Cazenovia, NY [*AM radio station call letters*]
WJIZ.......... Albany, GA [*FM radio station call letters*]
WJJA.......... Racine, WI [*Television station call letters*]
WJJB.......... Hyde Park, NY [*FM radio station call letters*]
WJJC.......... Commerce, GA [*AM radio station call letters*]
WJJD.......... Chicago, IL [*AM radio station call letters*]
WJJF.......... Hope Valley, RI [*AM radio station call letters*]
WJJH.......... Ashland, WI [*FM radio station call letters*]
WJJJ.......... Christiansburg, VA [*AM radio station call letters*]
WJJK.......... Eau Claire, WI [*AM radio station call letters*]
WJJL.......... Niagara Falls, NY [*AM radio station call letters*]
WJJM.......... Lewisburg, TN [*AM radio station call letters*]
WJJM-FM .... Lewisburg, TN [*FM radio station call letters*]
WJJN.......... Newburgh, IN [*AM radio station call letters*]
WJJQ.......... Tomahawk, WI [*AM radio station call letters*]
WJJQ-FM .... Tomahawk, WI [*FM radio station call letters*]
WJJR.......... Rutland, VT [*FM radio station call letters*]
WJJS.......... Lynchburg, VA [*AM radio station call letters*]
WJJT.......... Jellico, TN [*AM radio station call letters*]
WJJW.......... North Adams, MA [*FM radio station call letters*]
WJJY.......... Brainerd, MN [*AM radio station call letters*]
WJJY-FM .... Brainerd, MN [*FM radio station call letters*]
WJK.......... Wiener Jahrbuch fuer Kunstgeschichte [*A publication*]
WJKA.......... Wilmington, NC [*Television station call letters*]
WJKB.......... Siesta Key, FL [*AM radio station call letters*]
WJKC.......... Christiansted, VI [*FM radio station call letters*]
WJKL.......... Elgin, IL [*FM radio station call letters*]
WJKM.......... Hartsville, TN [*AM radio station call letters*]
WJKS-TV .... Jacksonville, FL [*Television station call letters*]
WJKY.......... Jamestown, KY [*AM radio station call letters*]
WJLA-TV.... Washington, DC [*Television station call letters*]
WJLB.......... Detroit, MI [*FM radio station call letters*]
WJLC.......... Wye Junction Latching Circulator
WJLCER..... Women's Joint Legislative Committee for Equal Rights [*Defunct*] (EA)
WJLC-FM.... South Boston, VA [*FM radio station call letters*]
WJLD.......... Fairfield, AL [*AM radio station call letters*]
WJLE.......... Smithville, TN [*AM radio station call letters*]
WJLE-FM ... Smithville, TN [*FM radio station call letters*]
WJLH.......... Laurel, MS [*Television station call letters*]
WJLK.......... Asbury Park, NJ [*AM radio station call letters*]
WJLK-FM ... Asbury Park, NJ [*FM radio station call letters*]
WJLM.......... Salem, VA [*FM radio station call letters*]
WJLQ.......... Pensacola, FL [*FM radio station call letters*]
WJLS.......... Beckley, WV [*AM radio station call letters*]
WJLT.......... Crozet, VA [*FM radio station call letters*]
WJLW.......... De Pere, WI [*FM radio station call letters*]
WJLY.......... Braddock, PA [*AM radio station call letters*]
WJMA.......... Orange, VA [*AM radio station call letters*]
WJMB.......... Brookhaven, MS [*AM radio station call letters*]
WJMC.......... Rice Lake, WI [*AM radio station call letters*]
WJMC-FM ... Rice Lake, WI [*FM radio station call letters*]
WJMF.......... Smithfield, RI [*FM radio station call letters*]
WJMG.......... Hattiesburg, MS [*FM radio station call letters*]
WJMI.......... Jackson, MS [*FM radio station call letters*]
WJMJ.......... Hartford, CT [*FM radio station call letters*]
WJMK.......... Chicago, IL [*FM radio station call letters*]
WJML.......... Petoskey, MI [*AM radio station call letters*]
WJML-FM ... Petoskey, MI [*FM radio station call letters*]
WJMM.......... Nicholasville, KY [*AM radio station call letters*]
WJMM-FM ... Versailles, KY [*FM radio station call letters*]
WJMN-TV .. Escanaba, MI [*Television station call letters*]
WJMO.......... Cleveland Heights, OH [*AM radio station call letters*]
WJMQ.......... Clintonville, WI [*FM radio station call letters*]
WJMR.......... Fredricktown, OH [*FM radio station call letters*]
WJMS.......... Ironwood, MI [*AM radio station call letters*]
WJMT.......... Merrill, WI [*AM radio station call letters*]
WJMU.......... Decatur, IL [*FM radio station call letters*]
WJMW.......... Athens, AL [*AM radio station call letters*]
WJMX.......... Florence, SC [*AM radio station call letters*]
WJMX-FM ... Florence, SC [*FM radio station call letters*]
WJNC.......... Jacksonville, NC [*AM radio station call letters*]
WJNF.......... Marianna, FL [*Television station call letters*]
WJNL.......... Johnstown, PA [*AM radio station call letters*]
WJNL-FM ... Johnstown, PA [*FM radio station call letters*]
WJNO.......... West Palm Beach, FL [*AM radio station call letters*]
WJNR-FM... Iron Mountain, MI [*FM radio station call letters*]
WJNS-FM... Yazoo City, MS [*FM radio station call letters*]
WJNT .... Pearl, MS [*AM radio station call letters*]
WJNY.......... Watertown, NY [*AM radio station call letters*]
WJNZ.......... Greencastle, IN [*FM radio station call letters*]
W Jo .... [*Sir*] William Jones' English King's Bench Reports [*82 English Reprint*] (DLA)
WJOB.......... Hammond, IN [*AM radio station call letters*]
WJOE .... Marianna, FL [*Television station call letters*]
WJOI .... Detroit, MI [*FM radio station call letters*]
WJOJ-FM... Milford, OH [*FM radio station call letters*]
WJOL .... Joliet, IL [*AM radio station call letters*]

WJON........ St. Cloud, MN [*AM radio station call letters*]
W Jones ..... [*Sir*] William Jones' English King's Bench Reports [*82 English Reprint*] [*1620-41*] (DLA)
W Jones (Eng) ... [*Sir*] William Jones' English King's Bench Reports [*82 English Reprint*] (DLA)
WJOR........ St. Joseph, TN [*AM radio station call letters*]
WJOS........ Elkin, NC [*AM radio station call letters*]
WJOT........ Lake City, SC [*AM radio station call letters*]
WJOY........ Burlington, VT [*AM radio station call letters*]
WJOZ........ Troy, PA [*AM radio station call letters*]
WJP.......... Water Jet Pump
WJPA .... Washington, PA [*AM radio station call letters*]
WJPC .... Chicago, IL [*AM radio station call letters*]
WJPD .... Ishpeming, MI [*AM radio station call letters*]
WJPD-FM ... Ishpeming, MI [*FM radio station call letters*]
WJPJ .... Huntingdon, TN [*AM radio station call letters*]
WJPM-TV ... Florence, SC [*Television station call letters*]
WJPR .... Lynchburg, VA [*Television station call letters*]
WJPT........ Jacksonville, IL [*Television station call letters*]
WJPW .... Rockford, MI [*AM radio station call letters*]
WJPZ-FM ... Syracuse, NY [*FM radio station call letters*]
WJQY .... Fort Lauderdale, FL [*FM radio station call letters*]
WJQZ .... Wellsville, NY [*FM radio station call letters*]
WJR.......... Cypress Fund [*American Stock Exchange symbol*]
WJR.......... Detroit, MI [*AM radio station call letters*]
WJR.......... Wajir [*Kenya*] [*Airport symbol*] (OAG)
WJR.......... Washington Journalism Review [*A publication*]
WJR.......... World Jewish Register [*A publication*] (BJA)
WJRA .... Priceville, AL [*FM radio station call letters*]
WJRC .... Joliet, IL [*AM radio station call letters*]
WJRD .... Tuscaloosa, AL [*AM radio station call letters*]
WJRE .... Kewanee, IL [*FM radio station call letters*]
WJRH .... Easton, PA [*FM radio station call letters*]
WJRI .... Lenoir, NC [*AM radio station call letters*]
WJRL .... Calhoun City, MS [*AM radio station call letters*]
WJRM .... Troy, NC [*AM radio station call letters*]
WJRO .... Glen Burnie, MD [*AM radio station call letters*]
WJRS .... Jamestown, KY [*FM radio station call letters*]
WJRT-TV.... Flint, MI [*Television station call letters*]
WJRZ.......... Manahawkin, NJ [*FM radio station call letters*]
WJS.......... Wife's Judicial Separation [*Legal*] [*British*] (ROG)
WJSA .... Jersey Shore, PA [*AM radio station call letters*]
WJSB .... Crestview, FL [*AM radio station call letters*]
WJSC-FM ... Johnson, VT [*FM radio station call letters*]
WJSK .... Lumberton, NC [*FM radio station call letters*]
WJSL .... Houghton, NY [*FM radio station call letters*]
WJSM .... Martinsburg, PA [*AM radio station call letters*]
WJSM-FM ... Martinsburg, PA [*FM radio station call letters*]
WJSN-FM... Jackson, KY [*FM radio station call letters*]
WJSO .... Jonesboro, TN [*AM radio station call letters*]
WJSP-FM ... Warm Springs, GA [*FM radio station call letters*]
WJSP-TV ... Columbus, GA [*Television station call letters*]
WJSQ-FM ... Athens, TN [*FM radio station call letters*]
WJSR .... Birmingham, AL [*FM radio station call letters*]
WJST .... Port St. Joe, FL [*FM radio station call letters*]
WJSU .... Jackson, MS [*FM radio station call letters*]
WJSUD...... World Journal of Surgery [*A publication*]
WJSU-TV ... Anniston, AL [*Television station call letters*]
WJSV .... Morristown, NJ [*FM radio station call letters*]
WJSY .... Harrisonburg, VA [*FM radio station call letters*]
WJT.......... World Journal Tribune [*Defunct New York City afternoon newspaper*]
WJTB.......... North Ridgeville, OH [*AM radio station call letters*]
WJTC .... Pensacola, FL [*Television station call letters*]
WJTG .... Fort Valley, GA [*FM radio station call letters*]
WJTH .... Calhoun, GA [*AM radio station call letters*]
WJTL .... Lancaster, PA [*FM radio station call letters*]
WJTM........ Frederick, MD [*FM radio station call letters*]
WJTN .... Jamestown, NY [*AM radio station call letters*]
WJTO .... Bath, ME [*AM radio station call letters*]
WJTP.......... Newland, NC [*AM radio station call letters*]
WJTT.......... Red Bank, TN [*FM radio station call letters*]
WJTV .... Jackson, MS [*Television station call letters*]
WJTW........ Joliet, IL [*FM radio station call letters*]
WJTX.......... Urbana, IL [*AM radio station call letters*]
WJTY.......... Lancaster, WI [*FM radio station call letters*]
WJu.......... Juneau Public Library, Juneau, WI [*Library symbol*] [*Library of Congress*] (LCLS)
WJUL.......... Lowell, MA [*FM radio station call letters*]
WJuMe....... Dodge County Mental Health Center, Juneau, WI [*Library symbol*] [*Library of Congress*] (LCLS)
WJUN .... Mexico, PA [*AM radio station call letters*]
WJVL.......... Janesville, WI [*FM radio station call letters*]
WJVM .... Sterling, IL [*FM radio station call letters*]
WJVO .... South Jacksonville, IL [*FM radio station call letters*]
WJVR .... Callahan, FL [*AM radio station call letters*]
WJVS.......... Cincinnati, OH [*FM radio station call letters*]
WJW.......... Cleveland, OH [*AM radio station call letters*]
WJWF........ Columbus, MS [*AM radio station call letters*]
WJWJ-FM ... Beaufort, SC [*FM radio station call letters*]
WJWJ-TV ... Beaufort, SC [*Television station call letters*]

WJWK .... Jamestown, NY [*FM radio station call letters*]
WJWL .... Georgetown, DE [*AM radio station call letters*]
WJWN-TV ... San Sebastian, PR [*Television station call letters*]
WJWS .... South Hill, VA [*AM radio station call letters*]
WJWT .... Jackson, TN [*Television station call letters*]
WJW-TV .... Cleveland, OH [*Television station call letters*]
WJX............ Wajax Ltd. [*Toronto Stock Exchange symbol*]
WJXL .... Jacksonville, AL [*AM radio station call letters*]
WJXN .... Jackson, MS [*AM radio station call letters*]
WJXQ .... Jackson, MI [*FM radio station call letters*]
WJXR .... Macclenny, FL [*FM radio station call letters*]
WJXT .... Jacksonville, FL [*Television station call letters*]
WJXW .... Jacksonville, FL [*AM radio station call letters*]
WJXY .... Conway, SC [*AM radio station call letters*]
WJY............ Westmoreland County Community College, Youngwood, PA
　　　　　　 [*OCLC symbol*] (OCLC)
WJYA .... Buford, GA [*AM radio station call letters*]
WJYE .... Buffalo, NY [*FM radio station call letters*]
WJYF .... Nashville, GA [*FM radio station call letters*]
WJYJ.......... Fredericksburg, VA [*FM radio station call letters*]
WJYL .... Jeffersontown, KY [*FM radio station call letters*]
WJYM......... Bowling Green, OH [*AM radio station call letters*]
WJYO .... Mount Dora, FL [*FM radio station call letters*]
WJYP .... South Charleston, WV [*FM radio station call letters*]
WJYR .... Myrtle Beach, SC [*FM radio station call letters*]
WJYS .... Hammond, IN [*Television station call letters*]
WJYT.......... Quebradillas, PR [*AM radio station call letters*]
WJYW .... Southport, NC [*FM radio station call letters*]
WJYY .... Concord, NH [*FM radio station call letters*]
WJZM .... Clarksville, TN [*AM radio station call letters*]
WJZQ .... Kenosha, WI [*FM radio station call letters*]
WJZ-TV ..... Baltimore, MD [*Television station call letters*]
WJZZ......... Detroit, MI [*FM radio station call letters*]
WK .... Ratioflug Luftfahrtunternehmen GmbH, Frankfurt Am Main
　　　　　　 [*West Germany*] [*ICAO designator*] (FAAC)
wk .... Wake Island [*MARC country of publication code*] [*Library of
　　　　　　 Congress*] (LCCP)
WK .... Wake Island [*Two-letter standard code*] (CNC)
WK .... Warburg-Keilin System [*Cytochrome-cytochrome oxidase
　　　　　　 system*] [*Named for Otto Warburg and D. Keilin*]
WK .... Warehouse Keeper [*British*] (ROG)
WK .... Waylands Korongo [*Tanzania*]
WK .... Weak (FAAC)
WK .... Week (AFM)
WK .... Well-Known
WK .... Wernicke-Korsakoff [*Syndrome*] [*Medicine*]
WK .... Western Alaska [*Airlines*] (OAG)
WK .... Work
Wk .... Wreck [*Nautical charts*]
WKa............ Kaukauna Public Library, Kaukauna, WI [*Library symbol*]
　　　　　　 [*Library of Congress*] (LCLS)
WKA .... Waffenkarren [*Weapons Cart*] [*German military - World War II*]
WKAA .... Ocilla, GA [*FM radio station call letters*]
WKAB-TV .. Montgomery, AL [*Television station call letters*]
WKAC .... Athens, AL [*AM radio station call letters*]
WKACC ..... Work Accomplishment Code [*Navy*] (NG)
WKAD .... Canton, PA [*FM radio station call letters*]
WKAE........ High Springs, FL [*FM radio station call letters*]
WKAI......... Macomb, IL [*FM radio station call letters*]
WKAJ........ Saratoga Springs, NY [*AM radio station call letters*]
WKAK .... Albany, GA [*FM radio station call letters*]
WKAL........ Rome, NY [*AM radio station call letters*]
WKAL-FM ... Rome, NY [*FM radio station call letters*]
WKAM....... Goshen, IN [*AM radio station call letters*]
WKAN .... Kankakee, IL [*AM radio station call letters*]
WKAP........ Allentown, PA [*AM radio station call letters*]
WKAQ .... San Juan, PR [*AM radio station call letters*]
WKAQ-FM ... San Juan, PR [*FM radio station call letters*]
WKAQ-TV ... San Juan, PR [*Television station call letters*]
WKAR........ East Lansing, MI [*AM radio station call letters*]
WKAR-FM ... East Lansing, MI [*FM radio station call letters*]
WKAR-TV... East Lansing, MI [*Television station call letters*]
WKAS........ Ashland, KY [*Television station call letters*]
WKAT........ Miami Beach, FL [*AM radio station call letters*]
WKAV........ Charlottesville, VA [*AM radio station call letters*]
WKAX........ Russellville, AL [*AM radio station call letters*]
WKAY........ Glasgow, KY [*AM radio station call letters*]
WKAZ........ St. Albans, WV [*AM radio station call letters*]
WKB .... Wentzel-Kramers-Brillouin Approximation [*Mathematics*]
WKBA........ Vinton, VA [*AM radio station call letters*]
WKBB........ West Point, MS [*FM radio station call letters*]
WKBC........ North Wilkesboro, NC [*AM radio station call letters*]
WKBC-FM ... North Wilkesboro, NC [*FM radio station call letters*]
WKBD-TV ... Detroit, MI [*Television station call letters*]
WKBH........ Holmen, WI [*AM radio station call letters*]
WKBH........ Trempealeau, WI [*FM radio station call letters*]
WKBI......... St. Marys, PA [*AM radio station call letters*]
WKBI-FM ... St. Mary's, PA [*FM radio station call letters*]
WKBJ......... Milan, TN [*AM radio station call letters*]
WKBJ......... Wentzel-Kramers-Brillouin-Jeffreys [*Approximation or
　　　　　　 Method*] [*Physics*]

WKBK .... Keene, NH [*AM radio station call letters*]
WKBL......... Covington, TN [*AM radio station call letters*]
WKBL-FM ... Covington, TN [*FM radio station call letters*]
WKBN .... Youngstown, OH [*AM radio station call letters*]
WKBN-FM ... Youngstown, OH [*FM radio station call letters*]
WKBN-TV ... Youngstown, OH [*Television station call letters*]
WKBO .... Harrisburg, PA [*AM radio station call letters*]
WKBQ .... Garner, NC [*AM radio station call letters*]
WKBR .... Manchester, NH [*AM radio station call letters*]
WKBS-TV... Altoona, PA [*Television station call letters*]
WKBT........ La Crosse, WI [*Television station call letters*]
WKBV........ Richmond, IN [*AM radio station call letters*]
WKBW-TV ... Buffalo, NY [*Television station call letters*]
WKBX........ Kingsland, GA [*FM radio station call letters*]
WKBY........ Chatham, VA [*AM radio station call letters*]
WKBZ........ Muskegon, MI [*AM radio station call letters*]
WKC .... Walker Ridge [*California*] [*Seismograph station code, US
　　　　　　 Geological Survey*] (SEIS)
WKC .... Westminster Kennel Club (EA)
WKCA .... Owingsville, KY [*FM radio station call letters*]
WKCB .... Hindman, KY [*AM radio station call letters*]
WKCB-FM ... Hindman, KY [*FM radio station call letters*]
WKCC .... Grayson, KY [*FM radio station call letters*]
WKCE .... Harriman, TN [*AM radio station call letters*]
WKCG .... Augusta, ME [*FM radio station call letters*]
WKCH-TV ... Knoxville, TN [*Television station call letters*]
WKCI.......... Hamden, CT [*FM radio station call letters*]
WKCJ......... Lewisburg, WY [*FM radio station call letters*]
WKCK .... Orocavis, PR [*AM radio station call letters*]
WKCL......... Ladson, SC [*FM radio station call letters*]
WKCM........ Hawesville, KY [*AM radio station call letters*]
WKCN .... Dorchester-Brent, SC [*AM radio station call letters*]
WKCO .... Gambier, OH [*FM radio station call letters*]
WKCQ .... Saginaw, MI [*FM radio station call letters*]
WKCR-FM ... New York, NY [*FM radio station call letters*]
WKCS .... Knoxville, TN [*FM radio station call letters*]
WKCT........ Bowling Green, KY [*AM radio station call letters*]
WKCU .... Corinth, MS [*AM radio station call letters*]
WKCW .... Warrenton, VA [*AM radio station call letters*]
WKCX........ Rome, GA [*FM radio station call letters*]
WKCY........ Harrisonburg, VA [*AM radio station call letters*]
WKD .... Weekday
WKDA .... Nashville, TN [*AM radio station call letters*]
WKDAY ..... Weekday
WKDC .... Elmhurst, IL [*AM radio station call letters*]
WKDD .... Akron, OH [*FM radio station call letters*]
WKDE .... Altavista, VA [*AM radio station call letters*]
WKDF......... Nashville, TN [*FM radio station call letters*]
WKDK .... Newberry, SC [*AM radio station call letters*]
WKDM........ New York, NY [*AM radio station call letters*]
WKDN-FM ... Camden, NJ [*FM radio station call letters*]
WKDO .... Liberty, KY [*AM radio station call letters*]
WKDO-FM ... Liberty, KY [*FM radio station call letters*]
WKDQ .... Henderson, KY [*FM radio station call letters*]
WKDR........ Plattsburgh, NY [*AM radio station call letters*]
WKDS .... Kalamazoo, MI [*FM radio station call letters*]
WKDU .... Philadelphia, PA [*FM radio station call letters*]
WKDW........ Staunton, VA [*AM radio station call letters*]
WKDX........ Hamlet, NC [*AM radio station call letters*]
WKDY........ Spartanburg, SC [*AM radio station call letters*]
WKDZ......... Cadiz, KY [*AM radio station call letters*]
WKDZ-FM ... Cadiz, KY [*FM radio station call letters*]
WKE .... Wake [*Wake Island*] [*Seismograph station code, US Geological
　　　　　　 Survey*] [*Closed*] (SEIS)
WKEA-FM ... Scottsboro, AL [*FM radio station call letters*]
WKEB-TV... Marathon, FL [*Television station call letters*]
WKED......... Frankfort, KY [*AM radio station call letters*]
WKEE......... Huntington, WV [*AM radio station call letters*]
WKEE-FM ... Huntington, WV [*FM radio station call letters*]
WKEF......... Dayton, OH [*Television station call letters*]
WKEG......... Washington, PA [*AM radio station call letters*]
WKEI.......... Kewanee, IL [*AM radio station call letters*]
W Kel.......... [*William*] Kelynge's English Chancery Reports [*25 English
　　　　　　 Reprint*] (DLA)
W Kelynge (Eng) ... [*William*] Kelynge's English Chancery Reports [*25
　　　　　　 English Reprint*] (DLA)
WKEM .... Campbellsville, KY [*FM radio station call letters*]
WKEN .... Dover, DE [*AM radio station call letters*]
WKen .... Gilbert M. Simmons Public Library, Kenosha, WI [*Library
　　　　　　 symbol*] [*Library of Congress*] (LCLS)
WKenA....... Armitage Academy Library, Kenosha, WI [*Library symbol*]
　　　　　　 [*Library of Congress*] (LCLS)
WKenC....... Carthage College, Kenosha, WI [*Library symbol*] [*Library of
　　　　　　 Congress*] (LCLS)
WKEND ..... Weekend
WKenG....... Gateway Technical Institute, Kenosha, WI [*Library symbol*]
　　　　　　 [*Library of Congress*] (LCLS)
WKenG-E ... Gateway Technical Institute, Elkhorn Campus, Elkhorn, WI
　　　　　　 [*Library symbol*] [*Library of Congress*] (LCLS)
WKenG-R... Gateway Technical Institute, Racine Campus, Racine, WI
　　　　　　 [*Library symbol*] [*Library of Congress*] (LCLS)

WKenHi ...... Kenosha County Historical Association, Kenosha, WI [*Library symbol*] [*Library of Congress*]   (LCLS)
WKenM ...... Kenosha Memorial Hospital, Kenosha, WI [*Library symbol*] [*Library of Congress*]   (LCLS)
WKenOS .... Old Songs Library, Kenosha, WI [*Library symbol*] [*Library of Congress*]   (LCLS)
WKenSC .... St. Catherine's Hospital, Kenosha, WI [*Library symbol*] [*Library of Congress*]   (LCLS)
WKenSD .... Unified School District Number One, Media Center, Kenosha, WI [*Library symbol*] [*Library of Congress*]   (LCLS)
WKenSD-B ... Unified School District Number One, Mary D. Bradford High School, Kenosha, WI [*Library symbol*] [*Library of Congress*]   (LCLS)
WKenSD-R ... Unified School District Number One, Walter Reuther High School, Kenosha, WI [*Library symbol*] [*Library of Congress*]   (LCLS)
WKenSD-T ... Unified School District Number One, Tremper High School, Kenosha, WI [*Library symbol*] [*Library of Congress*]   (LCLS)
WKenU .... University of Wisconsin-Parkside, Kenosha, WI [*Library symbol*] [*Library of Congress*]   (LCLS)
WKenU-A ... University of Wisconsin-Parkside, Archives and Art Research Center, Kenosha, WI [*Library symbol*] [*Library of Congress*]   (LCLS)
WKEQ .... Burnside, KY [*AM radio station call letters*]
WKER .... Pompton Lakes, NJ [*AM radio station call letters*]
WKES .... St. Petersburg, FL [*FM radio station call letters*]
WKET .... Kettering, OH [*FM radio station call letters*]
WKEU .... Griffin, GA [*AM radio station call letters*]
WKEU-FM ... Griffin, GA [*FM radio station call letters*]
WKEW .... Greensboro, NC [*AM radio station call letters*]
WKEX .... Blacksburg, VA [*AM radio station call letters*]
WKEY .... Covington, VA [*AM radio station call letters*]
WKEZ-FM ... Yorktown, VA [*FM radio station call letters*]
WKF .... Well-Known Factor
WKFB .... Florence, KY [*FM radio station call letters*]
WKFD .... Wickford, RI [*AM radio station call letters*]
WKFE .... Yauco, PR [*AM radio station call letters*]
WKFI .... Wilmington, OH [*AM radio station call letters*]
WKFM .... Fulton, NY [*FM radio station call letters*]
WKFR-FM ... Battle Creek, MI [*FM radio station call letters*]
WKFT .... Fayetteville, NC [*Television station call letters*]
WKFX .... Kaukauna, WI [*FM radio station call letters*]
WKG .... Working   (MSA)
WKGB .... Bowling Green, KY [*Television station call letters*]
WKGC .... Panama City Beach, FL [*AM radio station call letters*]
WKGC-FM ... Panama City, FL [*FM radio station call letters*]
Wkg Girls Newsl ... Working with Girls Newsletter [*A publication*]
WKGI .... New Martinsville, WV [*FM radio station call letters*]
WKGK .... Saltville, VA [*AM radio station call letters*]
WKGL .... Middletown, NY [*FM radio station call letters*]
WKGM .... Smithfield, VA [*AM radio station call letters*]
WKGN .... Knoxville, TN [*AM radio station call letters*]
WKGO .... Cumberland, MD [*FM radio station call letters*]
WKGQ .... Milledgeville, GA [*AM radio station call letters*]
WKGR .... Fort Pierce, FL [*FM radio station call letters*]
WKGW .... Utica, NY [*FM radio station call letters*]
WKGX .... Lenoir; NC [*AM radio station call letters*]
WKHA .... Hazard, KY [*Television station call letters*]
WKHG .... Leitchfield, KY [*FM radio station call letters*]
WKHI .... Ocean City, MD [*FM radio station call letters*]
WKHJ .... Holly Hill, SC [*AM radio station call letters*]
WKHK .... Colonial Heights, VA [*FM radio station call letters*]
WKHM .... Jackson, MI [*AM radio station call letters*]
WKHQ .... Charlevoix, MI [*AM radio station call letters*]
WKHQ-FM ... Charlevoix, MI [*FM radio station call letters*]
WKHR .... Bainbridge, OH [*FM radio station call letters*]
WKHS .... Worton, MD [*FM radio station call letters*]
WKHT .... Manchester, CT [*AM radio station call letters*]
WKHV .... Altavista, VA [*FM radio station call letters*]
WKHX .... Marietta, GA [*FM radio station call letters*]
WKi .... Kiel Public Library, Kiel, WI [*Library symbol*] [*Library of Congress*]   (LCLS)
WKIC .... Hazard, KY [*AM radio station call letters*]
WKID .... Vevay, IN [*FM radio station call letters*]
WKIE .... Richmond, VA [*AM radio station call letters*]
WKIG .... Glennville, GA [*AM radio station call letters*]
WKIG-FM ... Glennville, GA [*FM radio station call letters*]
WKII .... Port Charlotte, FL [*AM radio station call letters*]
WKIJ .... Parrish, AL [*AM radio station call letters*]
WKIK .... Leonardtown, MD [*AM radio station call letters*]
WKIN .... Kingsport, TN [*AM radio station call letters*]
WKIO .... Urbana, IL [*FM radio station call letters*]
WKIP .... Poughkeepsie, NY [*AM radio station call letters*]
WKIQ .... Inverness, FL [*AM radio station call letters*]
WKIR .... Jackson, TN [*AM radio station call letters*]
WKIS .... Orlando, FL [*AM radio station call letters*]
WKIS .... Wilson Knight Interdiscipline Society   (EA)
WKIT .... Hendersonville, NC [*FM radio station call letters*]
WKIX .... Raleigh, NC [*AM radio station call letters*]
WKIZ .... Key West, FL [*AM radio station call letters*]

WKJ .... Wakkanai [*Japan*] [*Airport symbol*]   (OAG)
WKJA .... Belhaven, NC [*FM radio station call letters*]
WKJB .... Mayaguez, PR [*AM radio station call letters*]
WKJB-FM ... Mayaguez, PR [*FM radio station call letters*]
WKJC .... Tawas City, MI [*FM radio station call letters*]
WKJF .... Cadillac, MI [*AM radio station call letters*]
WKJF-FM ... Cadillac, MI [*FM radio station call letters*]
WKJG-TV ... Fort Wayne, IN [*Television station call letters*]
WKJL-TV ... Baltimore, MD [*Television station call letters*]
WKJM .... Monticello, IN [*FM radio station call letters*]
WKJN .... Hammond, LA [*FM radio station call letters*]
WKJQ .... Jefferson City, IN [*FM radio station call letters*]
WKJR .... Muskegon Heights, MI [*AM radio station call letters*]
WKJV .... Campbellsville, KY [*FM radio station call letters*]
WKJX .... Elizabeth City, NC [*FM radio station call letters*]
WKJY .... Hempstead, NY [*FM radio station call letters*]
WKK .... Aleknagik [*Alaska*] [*Airport symbol*]   (OAG)
WKK .... Aleknagik, AK [*Location identifier*] [*FAA*]   (FAAL)
WKKC .... Chicago, IL [*FM radio station call letters*]
WKKD .... Aurora, IL [*AM radio station call letters*]
WKKD-FM ... Aurora, IL [*FM radio station call letters*]
WKKF .... Anderson, IN [*Television station call letters*]
WKKG .... Columbus, IN [*FM radio station call letters*]
WKKI .... Celina, OH [*FM radio station call letters*]
WKKJ .... Chillicothe, OH [*FM radio station call letters*]
WKKL .... West Barnstable, MA [*FM radio station call letters*]
WKKM .... Harrison, MI [*FM radio station call letters*]
WKKN .... Rockford, IL [*AM radio station call letters*]
WKKO .... Toledo, OH [*FM radio station call letters*]
WKKQ .... Nashwauk, MN [*AM radio station call letters*]
WKKS .... Vanceburg, KY [*AM radio station call letters*]
WKKS-FM ... Vanceburg, KY [*FM radio station call letters*]
WKKW .... Clarksburg, WV [*AM radio station call letters*]
WKKW-FM ... Clarksburg, WV [*FM radio station call letters*]
WKKX .... Jerseyville, IL [*FM radio station call letters*]
WKKY .... Moss Point, MS [*FM radio station call letters*]
WKKZ .... Dublin, GA [*FM radio station call letters*]
WKL .... Waikoloa [*Hawaii*] [*Airport symbol*]   (OAG)
WKLA .... Ludington, MI [*AM radio station call letters*]
WKLA-FM ... Ludington, MI [*FM radio station call letters*]
WKLB .... Manchester, KY [*AM radio station call letters*]
WKLB-FM ... Manchester, KY [*FM radio station call letters*]
WKLC-FM ... St. Albans, WV [*FM radio station call letters*]
WKLD .... Oneonta, AL [*FM radio station call letters*]
WKLE .... Lexington, KY [*Television station call letters*]
WKLEERI ... W. K. Lypynsky East European Research Institute   (EA)
WKLF .... Clanton, AL [*AM radio station call letters*]
WKLG .... Rock Harbor, FL [*FM radio station call letters*]
WKLH .... Milwaukee, WI [*FM radio station call letters*]
WKLI .... Albany, NY [*FM radio station call letters*]
WKLJ .... Oxford, MS [*FM radio station call letters*]
WKLK .... Cloquet, MN [*AM radio station call letters*]
WKLK-FM ... Cloquet, MN [*FM radio station call letters*]
WKLM .... Eden, NC [*FM radio station call letters*]
WKLN .... Cullman, AL [*FM radio station call letters*]
WKLO .... Danville, KY [*FM radio station call letters*]
WKLP .... Keyser, WV [*AM radio station call letters*]
WKLQ .... Holland, MI [*FM radio station call letters*]
WKLR .... Toledo, OH [*AM radio station call letters*]
WKLS .... Atlanta, GA [*FM radio station call letters*]
WKLT .... Kalkaska, MI [*AM radio station call letters*]
WKLT-FM ... Kalkaska, MI [*FM radio station call letters*]
WKLU .... Midway, KY [*AM radio station call letters*]
WKLV .... Blackstone, VA [*AM radio station call letters*]
WKLW .... Paintsville, KY [*AM radio station call letters*]
WKLX .... Rochester, NY [*FM radio station call letters*]
WKLY .... Hartwell, GA [*AM radio station call letters*]
WKLY .... Weekly
Wkly Cin Law Bul ... Weekly Cincinnati Law Bulletin [*Ohio*]   (DLA)
Wkly Dig ..... New York Weekly Digest   (DLA)
Wkly Energy Rep ... Weekly Energy Report [*United States*] [*A publication*]
Wkly Law Bul ... Weekly Law Bulletin [*Ohio*]   (DLA)
Wkly Law Gaz ... Weekly Law Gazette [*Ohio*]   (DLA)
Wkly L Bul ... Weekly Law Bulletin [*Ohio*]   (DLA)
Wkly L Gaz ... Weekly Law Gazette [*Ohio*]   (DLA)
Wkly NC ..... Weekly Notes of Cases [*Pennsylvania*]   (DLA)
Wkly Notes Cas ... Weekly Notes of Cases [*Pennsylvania*]   (DLA)
Wkly Notes Cas (PA) ... Weekly Notes of Cases [*Pennsylvania*]   (DLA)
Wkly Rec ..... Weekly Record [*United States*] [*A publication*]
Wkly Rep ..... Weekly Reporter [*London*]   (DLA)
WKLZ .... Port Henry, NY [*FM radio station call letters*]
WKM .... Hwange National Park [*Zimbabwe*] [*Airport symbol*]   (OAG)
WKM .... State University of New York, Agricultural and Technical College, Cobleskill, Cobleskill, NY [*OCLC symbol*]   (OCLC)
WKMA .... Madisonville, KY [*Television station call letters*]
WKMB .... Stirling, NJ [*AM radio station call letters*]
WKMC .... Roaring Spring, PA [*AM radio station call letters*]
WKMD .... Loogootee, IN [*FM radio station call letters*]
WKMF .... Flint, MI [*AM radio station call letters*]
WKMG .... Newberry, SC [*AM radio station call letters*]

WKMI .... Kalamazoo, MI [*AM radio station call letters*]
WKMJ .... Louisville, KY [*Television station call letters*]
WKML .... Lumberton, NC [*FM radio station call letters*]
WKMM .... Kingwood, WV [*FM radio station call letters*]
WKMO .... Hodgenville, KY [*FM radio station call letters*]
WKMQ .... Winnebago, IL [*FM radio station call letters*]
WKMR .... Morehead, KY [*Television station call letters*]
WKMS-FM ... Murray, KY [*FM radio station call letters*]
WKMT .... Kings Mountain, NC [*AM radio station call letters*]
WKMU .... Murray, KY [*Television station call letters*]
WKMX .... Enterprise, AL [*FM radio station call letters*]
WKMY .... Princeton, WV [*FM radio station call letters*]
WKMZ .... Martinsburg, WV [*FM radio station call letters*]
WKN .... Wakunai [*Papua New Guinea*] [*Airport symbol*]   (OAG)
WKN .... Weaken
Wk N .... Weekly Notes of Cases [*Pennsylvania*]   (DLA)
WKNC-FM ... Raleigh, NC [*FM radio station call letters*]
WKND .... Windsor, CT [*AM radio station call letters*]
WKNE .... Keene, NH [*AM radio station call letters*]
WKNE-FM ... Keene, NH [*FM radio station call letters*]
WKNF .... Oak Ridge, TN [*AM radio station call letters*]
WKNF-FM ... Oak Ridge, TN [*FM radio station call letters*]
WKNG .... Tallapoosa, GA [*AM radio station call letters*]
WKNH .... Keene, NH [*FM radio station call letters*]
WKNJ .... Union Township, NJ [*FM radio station call letters*]
WKNL .... Walter Kidde Nuclear Laboratories, Inc.   (MCD)
WKNO-FM ... Memphis, TN [*FM radio station call letters*]
WKNO-TV ... Memphis, TN [*Television station call letters*]
WKNR .... Battle Creek, MI [*AM radio station call letters*]
WKNS .... Kinston, NC [*FM radio station call letters*]
WKNT .... Kent, OH [*AM radio station call letters*]
WKNU .... Brewton, AL [*FM radio station call letters*]
WKNX .... Frankenmuth, MI [*AM radio station call letters*]
WKNY .... Kingston, NY [*AM radio station call letters*]
WKNZ .... Collins, MS [*FM radio station call letters*]
WKOC .... Kankakee, IL [*FM radio station call letters*]
WKOH .... Owensboro, KY [*Television station call letters*]
WKOI .... Richmond, IN [*Television station call letters*]
WKOK .... Sunbury, PA [*AM radio station call letters*]
WKOL .... Amsterdam, NY [*AM radio station call letters*]
WKOM .... Columbia, TN [*FM radio station call letters*]
WKON .... Owenton, KY [*Television station call letters*]
WKOQ .... Lexington, NC [*FM radio station call letters*]
WKOR .... Starkville, MS [*AM radio station call letters*]
WKOR-FM ... Starkville, MS [*FM radio station call letters*]
WKOV .... Wellston, OH [*AM radio station call letters*]
WKOV-FM ... Wellston, OH [*FM radio station call letters*]
WKOW-TV ... Madison, WI [*Television station call letters*]
WKOX .... Framingham, MA [*AM radio station call letters*]
WKOY .... Bluefield, WV [*AM radio station call letters*]
WKOZ .... Kosciusko, MS [*AM radio station call letters*]
WKP .... Wochenschrift fuer Klassische Philologie [*A publication*]
WKPA .... New Kensington, PA [*AM radio station call letters*]
WKPC-TV ... Louisville, KY [*Television station call letters*]
WKPD .... Paducah, KY [*Television station call letters*]
WKPE .... Orleans, MA [*AM radio station call letters*]
WKPE-FM ... Orleans, MA [*FM radio station call letters*]
WKPG .... Port Gibson, MS [*AM radio station call letters*]
WKPI .... Pikeville, KY [*Television station call letters*]
WKPK .... Gaylord, MI [*FM radio station call letters*]
WKPL .... Platteville, WI [*FM radio station call letters*]
WKPO .... Prentiss, MS [*AM radio station call letters*]
WKPQ .... Hornell, NY [*FM radio station call letters*]
WKPR .... Kalamazoo, MI [*AM radio station call letters*]
WKPT .... Kingsport, TN [*AM radio station call letters*]
WKPT-TV ... Kingsport, TN [*Television station call letters*]
WKPV .... Ponce, PR [*Television station call letters*]
WKPX .... Sunrise, FL [*FM radio station call letters*]
WKQA .... Pekin, IL [*FM radio station call letters*]
WKQB .... St. George, SC [*FM radio station call letters*]
WKQD .... Tullahoma, TN [*AM radio station call letters*]
WKQD-FM ... Tullahoma, TN [*FM radio station call letters*]
WKQDR ...... Work Queue Directory
WKQI .... Catlettsburg, KY [*FM radio station call letters*]
WKQQ .... Lexington, KY [*FM radio station call letters*]
WKQS .... Boca Raton, FL [*FM radio station call letters*]
WKQW .... Oil City, PA [*AM radio station call letters*]
WKQX .... Chicago, IL [*FM radio station call letters*]
WKQZ .... Midland, MI [*FM radio station call letters*]
WKR .... Walker's Cay [*Bahamas*] [*Airport symbol*]   (OAG)
WKR .... Whittaker Corp. [*NYSE symbol*]
WKR .... Work Ranch [*California*] [*Seismograph station code, US
                Geological Survey*]   (SEIS)
WKR .... Worker
WKR .... Wrecker   (AAG)
WKRA .... Holly Springs, MS [*AM radio station call letters*]
WKRA-FM ... Holly Springs, MS [*FM radio station call letters*]
WKRB .... Brooklyn, NY [*FM radio station call letters*]
WKRC .... Cincinnati, OH [*AM radio station call letters*]
WKRC-TV ... Cincinnati, OH [*Television station call letters*]
WKRE .... Jamesville, VA [*AM radio station call letters*]

WKRE-FM ... Exmore, VA [*FM radio station call letters*]
WKRG .... Mobile, AL [*AM radio station call letters*]
WKRG-FM ... Mobile, AL [*FM radio station call letters*]
WKRG-TV ... Mobile, AL [*Television station call letters*]
WKRI .... West Warwick, RI [*AM radio station call letters*]
WKRK .... Murphy, NC [*AM radio station call letters*]
WKRL .... Clearwater, FL [*FM radio station call letters*]
WKRM .... Columbia, TN [*AM radio station call letters*]
WKRN-TV .. Nashville, TN [*Television station call letters*]
WKRO .... Cairo, IL [*AM radio station call letters*]
WKRP .... Dallas, GA [*AM radio station call letters*]
WKRQ .... Cincinnati, OH [*FM radio station call letters*]
WKRR .... Asheboro, NC [*FM radio station call letters*]
WKRS .... Waukegan, IL [*AM radio station call letters*]
WKRT .... Cortland, NY [*AM radio station call letters*]
WKRV .... Vandalia, IL [*FM radio station call letters*]
WKRX .... Roxboro, NC [*FM radio station call letters*]
WKRY .... Key West, FL [*FM radio station call letters*]
WKRZ .... Wilkes-Barre, PA [*AM radio station call letters*]
WKRZ-FM ... Wilkes-Barre, PA [*FM radio station call letters*]
WKS .... Works   (MCD)
WKS .... Worksheet File [*Data processing*]
WKS .... Workshop   (AAG)
Wks .... Wrecks [*Nautical charts*]
WKSA .... Wernicke-Korsakoff Syndrome Association [*La Jolla, CA*]   (EA)
WKSA-FM ... Isabela, PR [*FM radio station call letters*]
WKSB .... Williamsport, PA [*FM radio station call letters*]
WKSC .... Kershaw, SC [*AM radio station call letters*]
WKSC .... Western Kentucky State College [*Later, WKSU*]
WKSE .... Niagara Falls, NY [*FM radio station call letters*]
Wks Engng ... Works Engineering [*A publication*]
Wks Engng Fact Serv ... Works Engineering and Factory Services [*A
                publication*]
WKSF .... Asheville, NC [*FM radio station call letters*]
WKSG .... Mount Clemens, MI [*FM radio station call letters*]
WKSH .... Sussex, WI [*AM radio station call letters*]
WKSI .... Greensboro, NC [*FM radio station call letters*]
WKSJ .... Prichard, AL [*AM radio station call letters*]
WKSK .... West Jefferson, NC [*AM radio station call letters*]
WKSL .... Greencastle, PA [*FM radio station call letters*]
Wks Mgmt ... Works Management [*A publication*]
WKSN .... Jamestown, NY [*AM radio station call letters*]
WKSO .... Somerset, KY [*Television station call letters*]
WKSP .... Kingstree, SC [*AM radio station call letters*]
WKSP .... Workshop
WKSQ .... Ellsworth, ME [*FM radio station call letters*]
WKSR .... Pulaski, TN [*AM radio station call letters*]
WKSS .... Hartford-Meriden, CT [*AM radio station call letters*]
WKST .... New Castle, PA [*AM radio station call letters*]
Wk Study ... Work Study [*A publication*]
Wk Study Mgmt Serv ... Work Study and Management Services [*Later,
                Management Services*] [*A publication*]
WKSU .... Western Kentucky State University [*Formerly, WKSC*]
WKSU-FM ... Kent, OH [*FM radio station call letters*]
WKSW .... Urbana, OH [*FM radio station call letters*]
WKSX .... Johnston, SC [*FM radio station call letters*]
WKSY .... Jupiter, FL [*FM radio station call letters*]
WKSZ .... Media, PA [*FM radio station call letters*]
WKT .... Wicket
WKTC .... Newport News, VA [*Television station call letters*]
WKTC .... Tarboro, NC [*FM radio station call letters*]
WKTE .... King, NC [*AM radio station call letters*]
WKTG .... Madisonville, KY [*FM radio station call letters*]
WKTH .... Grand Rapids, MI [*AM radio station call letters*]
WKTI .... Milwaukee, WI [*FM radio station call letters*]
WKTJ .... Farmington, ME [*AM radio station call letters*]
WKTJ-FM ... Farmington, ME [*FM radio station call letters*]
WKTK .... Crystal River, FL [*FM radio station call letters*]
WKTL .... Struthers, OH [*FM radio station call letters*]
WKTM .... Soperton, GA [*FM radio station call letters*]
WKTN .... Kenton, OH [*FM radio station call letters*]
WKTQ .... South Paris, ME [*AM radio station call letters*]
WKTR .... Earlysville, VA [*AM radio station call letters*]
WKTS .... Sheboygan, WI [*AM radio station call letters*]
WKTT .... Cleveland, WI [*FM radio station call letters*]
WKTV .... Utica, NY [*Television station call letters*]
WKTX .... Mercer, PA [*FM radio station call letters*]
WKTY .... La Crosse, WI [*AM radio station call letters*]
WKTZ .... Jacksonville, FL [*AM radio station call letters*]
WKTZ-FM ... Jacksonville, FL [*FM radio station call letters*]
WKU .... Wakaura [*Wakayama Eri*] [*Japan*] [*Seismograph station code,
                US Geological Survey*]   (SEIS)
WKU .... Western Kentucky University [*Formerly, WKSC*] [*Bowling
                Green*]
WKUB .... Blackshear, GA [*FM radio station call letters*]
WKUN .... Monroe, GA [*AM radio station call letters*]
WKUZ .... Wabash, IN [*FM radio station call letters*]
WKVA .... Lewistown, PA [*AM radio station call letters*]
WKVI .... Knox, IN [*AM radio station call letters*]
WKVI-FM ... Knox, IN [*FM radio station call letters*]
WKVL .... Clarksville, TN [*AM radio station call letters*]

WKVM........ San Juan, PR [*AM radio station call letters*]
WKVR-FM ... Huntingdon, PA [*FM radio station call letters*]
WKVT........ Brattleboro, VT [*AM radio station call letters*]
WKVT-FM ... Brattleboro, VT [*FM radio station call letters*]
WKWA........ Mobile, AL [*AM radio station call letters*]
WKWC........ Owensboro, KY [*AM radio station call letters*]
WKWF........ Key West, FL [*AM radio station call letters*]
WKWI........ Kilmarnock, VA [*FM radio station call letters*]
WKWK........ Wheeling, WV [*AM radio station call letters*]
WKWK-FM ... Wheeling, WV [*FM radio station call letters*]
WKWL........ Florala, AL [*AM radio station call letters*]
WKWM....... Kentwood, MI [*AM radio station call letters*]
WKWQ-FM ... Batesburg, SC [*FM radio station call letters*]
WKWSA ..... Wiener Klinische Wochenschrift. Supplementum (Austria) [*A publication*]
WKWX-FM ... Savannah, TN [*FM radio station call letters*]
WKWZ........ Syosset, NY [*FM radio station call letters*]
WKXA........ Brunswick, ME [*AM radio station call letters*]
WKXC........ New Albany, MS [*AM radio station call letters*]
WKXE-FM ... White River Junction, VT [*FM radio station call letters*]
WKXF........ Eminence, KY [*AM radio station call letters*]
WKXG........ Greenwood, MS [*AM radio station call letters*]
WKXI........ Jackson, MS [*AM radio station call letters*]
WKXJ........ Campbellsville, KY [*AM radio station call letters*]
WKXK........ Pana, IL [*FM radio station call letters*]
WKXL........ Concord, NH [*AM radio station call letters*]
WKXL-FM ... Concord, NH [*FM radio station call letters*]
WKXN........ Greenville, AL [*FM radio station call letters*]
WKXO....... Berea, KY [*AM radio station call letters*]
WKXQ........ Rushville, IL [*FM radio station call letters*]
WKXR........ Asheboro, NC [*AM radio station call letters*]
WKXS........ Marion, SC [*FM radio station call letters*]
WKXT........ Sardis, MS [*AM radio station call letters*]
WKXV........ Knoxville, TN [*AM radio station call letters*]
WKXW-FM ... Trenton, NJ [*FM radio station call letters*]
WKXX........ Birmingham, AL [*FM radio station call letters*]
WKXY........ Sarasota, FL [*AM radio station call letters*]
WKXZ........ Norwich, NY [*FM radio station call letters*]
WKY.......... Oklahoma City, OK [*AM radio station call letters*]
WKY.......... Wakayama [*Japan*] [*Seismograph station code, US Geological Survey*] (SEIS)
WKY.......... Wistar-Kyoto [*Rat variety*]
WKYA........ Central City, KY [*FM radio station call letters*]
WKYB........ Hemingway, SC [*AM radio station call letters*]
WKYC-TV ... Cleveland, OH [*Television station call letters*]
WKYD........ Andalusia, AL [*AM radio station call letters*]
WKYD-FM ... Andalusia, AL [*FM radio station call letters*]
WKYE........ Johnstown, PA [*FM radio station call letters*]
WKYG........ Parkersburg, WV [*AM radio station call letters*]
WKYI......... Defiance, OH [*Television station call letters*]
WKYK........ Burnsville, NC [*AM radio station call letters*]
WKYM....... Monticello, KY [*FM radio station call letters*]
WKYN........ St. Mary's, PA [*FM radio station call letters*]
WKYO........ Caro, MI [*AM radio station call letters*]
WKYQ........ Paducah, KY [*FM radio station call letters*]
WKYR........ Burkesville, KY [*AM radio station call letters*]
WKYS........ Washington, DC [*FM radio station call letters*]
WKYT-TV... Lexington, KY [*Television station call letters*]
WKYU-FM ... Bowling Green, KY [*FM radio station call letters*]
WKYU-TV... Bowling Green, KY [*Television station call letters*]
WKYW........ Frankfort, KY [*FM radio station call letters*]
WKYX........ Paducah, KY [*AM radio station call letters*]
WKYY........ Lancaster, KY [*AM radio station call letters*]
WKYZ........ Gray, KY [*AM radio station call letters*]
WKZA........ Kane, PA [*AM radio station call letters*]
WKZB........ Drew, MS [*FM radio station call letters*]
WKZC........ Scottville, MI [*FM radio station call letters*]
WKZD........ Murrayville, GA [*AM radio station call letters*]
WKZE........ Sharon, CT [*AM radio station call letters*]
WKZG........ Keyser, WV [*FM radio station call letters*]
WKZI......... Casey, IL [*AM radio station call letters*]
WKZK........ North Augusta, SC [*AM radio station call letters*]
WKZL........ Winston-Salem, NC [*FM radio station call letters*]
WKZM....... Sarasota, FL [*FM radio station call letters*]
WKZN........ Crozet, VA [*FM radio station call letters*]
WKZO........ Kalamazoo, MI [*AM radio station call letters*]
WKZQ........ Myrtle Beach, SC [*AM radio station call letters*]
WKZQ-FM ... Myrtle Beach, SC [*FM radio station call letters*]
WKZR........ Milledgeville, GA [*AM radio station call letters*]
WKZS........ Auburn, ME [*FM radio station call letters*]
WKZT........ Elizabethtown, KY [*Television station call letters*]
WKZW........ Peoria, IL [*FM radio station call letters*]
WKZX........ Presque Isle, ME [*AM radio station call letters*]
WKZY........ North Fort Myers, FL [*AM radio station call letters*]
WKZZ........ Lynchburg, VA [*FM radio station call letters*]
WL............. Compagnie Aerienne du Languedoc [*France*] [*ICAO designator*] (FAAC)
WL............. Lao Air Lines [*Later, LS*] [*ICAO designator*] (FAAC)
WL............. Wagons-Lits [*Railroad Sleeping or Pullman cars in Europe*] [*French*]
WL............. Waiting List

WL............. Walther League (EA)
WL............. War Legislation [*British*] [*World War II*]
WL............. Warner-Lambert Pharmaceutical Co. [*Research code symbol*]
W & L......... Washington and Lee Law Review [*A publication*]
WL............. Water Line
WL............. Waterload Test [*Clinical chemistry*]
WL............. Wavelength [*Electronics*]
W & L......... Weapon and/or Launcher
WL............. Weapons Laboratory (MCD)
WL............. Wehrmacht-Luftwaffe [*Marking on Air Force vehicles*] [*German military - World War II*]
W & L......... Welshpool & Llanfair Light Railway [*Wales*]
WL............. Western Larch [*Utility pole*] [*Telecommunications*] (TEL)
WL............. Western League [*Baseball*]
WL............. Westminster Library [*A publication*]
WL............. Wheel Locks
WL............. Wheeler Laboratories, Inc. (MCD)
WL............. White Laboratories, Inc. [*Research code symbol*]
WL............. White Leghorn [*Poultry*]
WL............. White Light (MSA)
WL............. Wideband Limiter
WL............. Wiener Library [*London*] (BJA)
WL............. Will (FAAC)
WL............. Wind Load
WL............. Wiring List
W-L............. Wisconsin State Law Library [*Wisconsin State Library*], Madison, WI [*Library symbol*] [*Library of Congress*] (LCLS)
WL............. With Restrictive Language (MCD)
W & L......... Women and Literature [*A publication*]
WL............. Women's Legion [*British*] [*World War I*]
WL............. Women's Liberation (ADA)
WL............. Women's Lobby [*Defunct*] (EA)
WL............. Women's Reserve, Legal Specialist Duties [*USNR officer designation*]
WL............. Wool
WL............. Word Line
WL............. Work Light
WL............. Work Line (MSA)
WL............. Working Level
WL............. Workload (AABC)
WL............. World List of Future International Meetings [*A publication*]
WL............. Worldloppet [*An association*] (EA)
WL............. Wydawnictwo Literackie [*A publication*]
WL............. Wydawnictwo Lodzkie [*A publication*]
WL............. Wyeth Laboratories [*Research code symbol*]
WL0............. Water Line Zero (KSC)
WLA .... Warner-Lambert Co. [*NYSE symbol*]
WLA .... Wescosa Lumber Association [*Defunct*] (EA)
WLA .... Western Lacrosse Association [*Canada*]
WLA .... Western Literature Association (EA)
WLA .... Wire Line Adapter (MCD)
WLA .... Wire Line Antenna
WLA .... Wittsburg Lake [*Arkansas*] [*Seismograph station code, US Geological Survey*] [*Closed*] (SEIS)
WLA .... Women's Land Army [*Part of the United States Crop Corps*] [*World War II*]
WLAB........ Fort Wayne, IN [*FM radio station call letters*]
WLac.......... La Crosse Public Library, La Crosse, WI [*Library symbol*] [*Library of Congress*] (LCLS)
WLAC........ Nashville, TN [*AM radio station call letters*]
WLAC-FM ... Nashville, TN [*FM radio station call letters*]
WLacFW.... United States Fish and Wildlife Service, Fish Control Laboratory, La Crosse, WI [*Library symbol*] [*Library of Congress*] (LCLS)
WLacL........ La Crosse Lutheran Hospital, La Crosse, WI [*Library symbol*] [*Library of Congress*] (LCLS)
WLacSF ..... Saint Francis Hospital, La Crosse, WI [*Library symbol*] [*Library of Congress*] (LCLS)
WLacU .... University of Wisconsin-La Crosse, La Crosse, WI [*Library symbol*] [*Library of Congress*] (LCLS)
WLacVC .... Viterbo College, La Crosse, WI [*Library symbol*] [*Library of Congress*] (LCLS)
WLAD........ Danbury, CT [*AM radio station call letters*]
WLadM....... Mount Senario College, Ladysmith, WI [*Library symbol*] [*Library of Congress*] (LCLS)
WLAE-TV ... New Orleans, LA [*Television station call letters*]
WLAF........ La Follette, TN [*AM radio station call letters*]
WLAG........ La Grange, GA [*AM radio station call letters*]
WLag.......... Lake Geneva Public Library, Lake Geneva, WI [*Library symbol*] [*Library of Congress*] (LCLS)
WLagB ...... Badger Union High School District, Lake Geneva, WI [*Library symbol*] [*Library of Congress*] (LCLS)
WLagF........ Franciscan Education Center, Lake Geneva, WI [*Library symbol*] [*Library of Congress*] (LCLS)
WLagSD ..... Joint School District Number One, Lake Geneva, WI [*Library symbol*] [*Library of Congress*] (LCLS)
WLAJ-TV.... Lansing, MI [*Television station call letters*]
WLAK........ Chicago, IL [*FM radio station call letters*]
WLAN........ Lancaster, PA [*AM radio station call letters*]
WLAN-FM ... Lancaster, PA [*FM radio station call letters*]

WLAP .... Lexington, KY [*AM radio station call letters*]
WLAP-FM .. Lexington, KY [*FM radio station call letters*]
WLAQ........ Rome, GA [*AM radio station call letters*]
WLAR........ Athens, TN [*AM radio station call letters*]
WLAS .... Jacksonville, NC [*AM radio station call letters*]
WLAT .... Conway, SC [*AM radio station call letters*]
WLAU........ Laurel, MS [*AM radio station call letters*]
WLAV........ Grand Rapids, MI [*AM radio station call letters*]
WLAV........ Will Advise (FAAC)
WLAV-FM .. Grand Rapids, MI [*FM radio station call letters*]
WLAW........ Lawrenceville, GA [*AM radio station call letters*]
W Law Bul ... Weekly Law Bulletin [*Ohio*] (DLA)
WLAX .... La Crosse, WI [*Television station call letters*]
WLAY-FM .. Muscle Shoals, AL [*FM radio station call letters*]
WLB .... National War Labor Board [*World War II*]
WLB........... Seagoing Buoy Tender [*Coast Guard*] (NVT)
WLB........... Wallboard (AAG)
WLB........... Weapons Logbook [*Military*] (AABC)
WLB........... Weekly Law Bulletin [*Ohio*] (DLA)
WLB........... Wiener Library Bulletin [*London*] [*A publication*]
WLB........... Wilson Library Bulletin [*A publication*]
WLBA .... Gainesville, GA [*AM radio station call letters*]
WLBB .... Carrollton, GA [*AM radio station call letters*]
WLBC........ Muncie, IN [*AM radio station call letters*]
WLBC-FM ... Muncie, IN [*FM radio station call letters*]
WLBE .... Leesburg, FL [*AM radio station call letters*]
WLBF .... Montgomery, AL [*FM radio station call letters*]
WLBG........ Laurens, SC [*AM radio station call letters*]
WLBH .... Mattoon, IL [*AM radio station call letters*]
WLBH-FM ... Mattoon, IL [*FM radio station call letters*]
WLBJ......... Bowling Green, KY [*AM radio station call letters*]
WLBK .... De Kalb, IL [*AM radio station call letters*]
WLBL .... Auburndale, WI [*AM radio station call letters*]
WLBM-TV ... Meridian, MS [*Television station call letters*]
WLBN........ Lebanon, KY [*AM radio station call letters*]
WLBQ........ Morgantown, KY [*AM radio station call letters*]
WLBR .... Lebanon, PA [*AM radio station call letters*]
WLBS .... Wright Laboratories [*NASDAQ symbol*] (NQ)
WLBT .... Jackson, MS [*Television station call letters*]
WL Bull...... Weekly Law Bulletin [*Ohio*] (DLA)
WL Bull (Ohio) ... Weekly Law Bulletin [*Ohio*] (DLA)
WLBZ-TV ... Bangor, ME [*Television station call letters*]
WLC .... Weapon-Launching Console (MCD)
WLC .... Well Logging Cable
WLC .... Wellco Enterprises, Inc. [*American Stock Exchange symbol*]
WLC .... West London College [*England*]
WLC .... White Light Coronagraph (KSC)
WLC .... Wildcat
WLC .... Wine Label Circle (EA)
WLCA........ Godfrey, IL [*FM radio station call letters*]
WLCAC ...... Watts Labor Community Action Committee [*Los Angeles, CA*]
WLCB .... Buffalo, KY [*AM radio station call letters*]
WLCC........ Luray, VA [*FM radio station call letters*]
WLCC........ Walker-Lybarger Construction Company [*Colorado*]
WLCE .... White Light Coronagraph Experiment (KSC)
WLCK........ Scottsville, KY [*AM radio station call letters*]
WL(CL) ..... War Legislation, Civil Liabilities [*British*] [*World War II*]
WLCM .... Lancaster, SC [*AM radio station call letters*]
WLCN........ Madisonville, KY [*Television station call letters*]
WLCO........ Clyde, OH [*FM radio station call letters*]
WLCQ........ Clarksville, VA [*FM radio station call letters*]
WLCR........ Lawrence Township, NJ [*AM radio station call letters*]
WLCS .... Baton Rouge, LA [*FM radio station call letters*]
WLCSS ...... Workload and Cost Schedule [*Military*] (AABC)
WLCSS ..... Weapon Launch Console Switching Section (MCD)
WLCX........ Farmville, VA [*FM radio station call letters*]
WLCY........ Dayton, TN [*FM radio station call letters*]
WLD .... South African Law Reports, Witwatersrand Local
                 Division (DLA)
WLD .... Weapon Loading Director (NVT)
WLD .... Welded (MSA)
WLD .... Weldotron Corp. [*American Stock Exchange symbol*]
WLD .... West Longitude Date (AABC)
WLD .... Winfield/Arkansas City, KS [*Location identifier*] [*FAA*] (FAAL)
Wld Aerospace Syst ... World Aerospace System [*A publication*]
Wld Aff ...... World Affairs [*A publication*]
Wld Anim Rev ... World Animal Review [*A publication*]
Wld Crops ... World Crops [*A publication*]
Wld Develop ... World Development [*A publication*]
WLDF .... Women's Legal Defense Fund (EA)
Wld Fishg... World Fishing [*A publication*]
Wld For Congr ... World Forestry Congress [*A publication*]
Wld Hlth Org Techn Rep Ser ... World Health Organization. Technical Report
                 Series [*A publication*]
W & L Dig ... Wood and Long's Digest [*Illinois*] (DLA)
WLDM .... Westfield, MA [*AM radio station call letters*]
Wld Marx R ... World Marxist Review [*A publication*]
Wld Med .... World Medicine [*A publication*]
WLDMT ...... Weldment (MSA)
Wld Orchid Conf ... World Orchid Conference [*A publication*]
Wld Polit .... World Politics [*A publication*]

Wld Pollen Spore Flora ... World Pollen and Spore Flora [*A publication*]
Wld P & PDem ... World Pulp and Paper Demand, Supply, and Trade [*A
                 publication*]
WLDR........ Traverse City, MI [*FM radio station call letters*]
WLDR........ Welder (MSA)
WLDR........ Wilderness Experience [*NASDAQ symbol*] (NQ)
Wld Refrig Air Condit ... World Refrigeration and Air Conditioning [*A
                 publication*]
Wld Rev Pest Control ... World Review of Pest Control [*A publication*]
WLDS........ Jacksonville, IL [*AM radio station call letters*]
WLDS........ Weldless
Wld's Pap Trade Rev ... World's Paper Trade Review [*A publication*]
Wld Surv .... World Survey [*A publication*]
Wld Today ... World Today [*A publication*]
Wld Work Rep ... World of Work Report [*A publication*]
WLDY........ Ladysmith, WI [*AM radio station call letters*]
WLDY-FM ... Ladysmith, WI [*FM radio station call letters*]
WLE .... Wheeling & Lake Erie Railway Co. [*NYSE symbol*] [*AAR code*]
WLEA .... Hornell, NY [*AM radio station call letters*]
WLEC .... Sandusky, OH [*AM radio station call letters*]
WLED-TV ... Littleton, NH [*Television station call letters*]
WLEE .... Richmond, VA [*AM radio station call letters*]
WLEF-TV ... Park Falls, WI [*Television station call letters*]
WLEI.......... Hudson, MI [*AM radio station call letters*]
WLEM........ Emporium, PA [*AM radio station call letters*]
WLEN .... Adrian, MI [*FM radio station call letters*]
WLEO........ Ponce, PR [*AM radio station call letters*]
WLER-FM... Butler, PA [*FM radio station call letters*]
WLES .... Lawrenceville, VA [*AM radio station call letters*]
WLET .... Toccoa, GA [*AM radio station call letters*]
WLEV .... Easton, PA [*FM radio station call letters*]
WLEW .... Bad Axe, MI [*AM radio station call letters*]
WLEW-FM ... Bad Axe, MI [*FM radio station call letters*]
WLEX-TV ... Lexington, KY [*Television station call letters*]
WLEY .... Cayey, PR [*AM radio station call letters*]
WLEZ .... Elmira, NY [*FM radio station call letters*]
WLF........... Walferdange [*Belgium*] [*Seismograph station code, US
                 Geological Survey*] (SEIS)
WLF........... Wallis and Futuna [*Three-letter standard code*] (CNC)
WLF........... Washington Legal Foundation (EA)
WLF........... Welfare (AABC)
WLF........... Whole Lithosphere Failure [*Geology*]
WLF........... Williams-Landel-Ferry [*Polymer physics*]
WLF........... Wolf River Resources Ltd. [*Vancouver Stock Exchange
                 symbol*]
WLF........... Women's Law Fund (EA)
WLF........... Word of Life Fellowship (EA)
WLF........... Workload Factor (AFM)
WLF........... World Law Fund (EA)
WLFA .... La Fayette, GA [*AM radio station call letters*]
WLFA .... West Lancashire Field Artillery [*Military unit*] [*British*]
WLFA .... Wildlife Legislative Fund of America (EA)
WLFB .... Wolfeboro Railroad Co., Inc. [*AAR code*]
WLFC .... Findlay, OH [*FM radio station call letters*]
WLFC .... Washington Library Film Circuit [*Library network*]
WLFE .... St. Albans, VT [*FM radio station call letters*]
WLFF .... Cayce, SC [*AM radio station call letters*]
WLFH .... Little Falls, NY [*AM radio station call letters*]
WLFI-TV.... Lafayette, IN [*Television station call letters*]
WLFJ......... Greenville, SC [*FM radio station call letters*]
WLFL-TV... Raleigh, NC [*Television station call letters*]
WLFM........ Appleton, WI [*FM radio station call letters*]
WLFQ .... Crawfordsville, IN [*FM radio station call letters*]
WLFR .... Pomona, NJ [*FM radio station call letters*]
WLFX .... Welding Fixture (AAG)
WLG .... Waldron Ledge [*Hawaii*] [*Seismograph station code, US
                 Geological Survey*] (SEIS)
WLG .... Washington Liaison Group (AFM)
WLG .... Weekly Law Gazette [*Ohio*] (DLA)
WLG .... Wellington [*New Zealand*] [*Airport symbol*] (OAG)
WLG .... Wiener Linguistische Gazette [*A publication*]
WLGA .... Valdosta, GA [*FM radio station call letters*]
WL Gaz ...... Weekly Law Gazette (Reprint) [*Ohio*] (DLA)
WL Gaz (Ohio) ... Weekly Law Gazette (Ohio) (DLA)
WLGC........ Greenup, KY [*AM radio station call letters*]
WLGC-FM ... Greenup, KY [*FM radio station call letters*]
WLGI .... Hemingway, SC [*FM radio station call letters*]
WLGN........ Logan, OH [*AM radio station call letters*]
WLGN-FM ... Logan, OH [*FM radio station call letters*]
WLGY .... Xenia, OH [*AM radio station call letters*]
WLH .... Walaha [*Vanuatu*] [*Airport symbol*] (OAG)
WLH .... Wilhelmshaven [*Federal Republic of Germany*] [*Geomagnetic
                 observatory code*]
WLHE .... Water LASER Heat Exchange
WLHFP ...... Women's Labor History Film Project (EA)
WLHN........ Anderson, IN [*FM radio station call letters*]
WLHN........ Wolohan Lumber Co. [*NASDAQ symbol*] (NQ)
WLHPA...... Wu Li Hsueh Pao [*A publication*]
WLHQ-FM ... Enterprise, AL [*FM radio station call letters*]
WLHS .... West Chester, OH [*FM radio station call letters*]
WLHT .... Grand Rapids, MI [*FM radio station call letters*]

WLI............ Wellesley Island [New York] [Seismograph station code, US Geological Survey] [Closed]   (SEIS)
WLI............ Wilderness Leadership International   (EA)
WLI............ Women's League for Israel   (EA)
WLIB .... New York, NY [AM radio station call letters]
WLIF.......... Baltimore, MD [FM radio station call letters]
WLIG.......... Riverhead, NY [Television station call letters]
WLIH .... Whitneyville, PA [FM radio station call letters]
WLII............ Caguas, PR [Television station call letters]
WLIJ.......... Shelbyville, TN [AM radio station call letters]
WLIK .... Newport, TN [AM radio station call letters]
WLIL........... Lenoir City, TN [AM radio station call letters]
WLIL-FM .... Lenoir City, TN [FM radio station call letters]
WLIM......... Patchoque, NY [AM radio station call letters]
WLIN .... Jackson, MS [FM radio station call letters]
WLIO .... Lima, OH [Television station call letters]
WLIP........... Kenosha, WI [AM radio station call letters]
WLIR.......... Herkimer, NY [AM radio station call letters]
WLIR-FM .... Garden City, NY [FM radio station call letters]
WLIS .... Old Saybrook, CT [AM radio station call letters]
WLIT........... Steubenville, OH [AM radio station call letters]
W Lit............ World Literature Written in English [A publication]
WLIU .... Lincoln University, PA [FM radio station call letters]
WLIV........... Livingston, TN [AM radio station call letters]
WLIW......... Garden City, NY [Television station call letters]
WLIX........... Islip, NY [AM radio station call letters]
WLIZ........... Lake Worth, FL [AM radio station call letters]
WLJ .... Washburn Law Journal [A publication]
WLJ .... Western Law Journal [A publication]
WLJ .... Wyoming Law Journal [A publication]
WLJA......... Ellijay, GA [AM radio station call letters]
WLJA-FM.... Ellijay, GA [FM radio station call letters]
WLJC .... Beattyville, KY [FM radio station call letters]
WLJC-TV ... Beattyville, KY [Television station call letters]
WLJE.......... Valparaiso, IN [FM radio station call letters]
WLJH.......... Petal, MS [AM radio station call letters]
WLJN.......... Elmwood, MI [AM radio station call letters]
WL Jour...... Washburn Law Journal [A publication]
WL Jour...... Western Law Journal [A publication]
WL Jour...... Willamette Law Journal [A publication]
WL Jour...... Wyoming Law Journal [A publication]
WLJS-FM.... Jacksonville, AL [FM radio station call letters]
WLJT-TV.... Lexington, TN [Television station call letters]
WLJY......... Marshfield, WI [FM radio station call letters]
WLK .... Selawik [Alaska] [Airport symbol]   (OAG)
WLK .... Selawik, AK [Location identifier] [FAA]   (FAAL)
wlk .... Wales [MARC country of publication code] [Library of Congress]   (LCCP)
WLK .... Walk
WLK .... Westlake Resources, Inc. [Vancouver Stock Exchange symbol]
WLK .... Wiest Lake [California] [Seismograph station code, US Geological Survey]   (SEIS)
WLKC......... St. Mary's, GA [FM radio station call letters]
WLKE .... Waupun, WI [AM radio station call letters]
WLKF .... Lakeland, FL [AM radio station call letters]
WLKI .... Angola, IN [FM radio station call letters]
WLKK .... Erie, PA [AM radio station call letters]
WLKL.......... Mattoon, IL [FM radio station call letters]
WLKM .... Three Rivers, MI [AM radio station call letters]
WLKM-FM ... Three Rivers, MI [FM radio station call letters]
WLKMY...... Welkom Gold Mining [NASDAQ symbol]   (NQ)
WLKN......... Lincoln, ME [AM radio station call letters]
WLKN-FM ... Lincoln, ME [FM radio station call letters]
WLKQ......... Buford, GA [FM radio station call letters]
WLKR......... Norwalk, OH [AM radio station call letters]
WLKR......... Walker [B. B.] Co. [NASDAQ symbol]   (NQ)
WLKR-FM ... Norwalk, OH [FM radio station call letters]
WLKS......... Walker-Scott Corp. [NASDAQ symbol]   (NQ)
WLKS......... West Liberty, KY [AM radio station call letters]
WLKT......... Lexington, KY [Television station call letters]
WLKW .... Providence, RI [AM radio station call letters]
WLKW-FM ... Providence, RI [FM radio station call letters]
WLKX-FM ... Forest Lake, MN [FM radio station call letters]
WLKY-TV... Louisville, KY [Television station call letters]
WLKZ........ Wolfeboro, NH [FM radio station call letters]
WLL............ Williamstown [Massachusetts] [Seismograph station code, US Geological Survey] [Closed]   (SEIS)
WLLA .... Kalamazoo, MI [Television station call letters]
WLLE......... Raleigh, NC [AM radio station call letters]
WLLG......... Loville, NY [FM radio station call letters]
WLLH .... Lowell, MA [AM radio station call letters]
WLLI............ Joliet, IL [FM radio station call letters]
WLLL.......... Lynchburg, VA [AM radio station call letters]
WLLN .... Lillington, NC [AM radio station call letters]
WLLO .... Williston, FL [FM radio station call letters]
WLLR .... East Moline, IL [FM radio station call letters]
WLLR ..... Washington and Lee Law Review [A publication]
W & LLR ..... Welshpool & Llanfair Light Railway [Wales]
WLLS .... Hartford, KY [AM radio station call letters]
WLLS-FM.... Hartford, KY [FM radio station call letters]
WLLT.......... Fairfield, OH [FM radio station call letters]

WLLV .... Louisville, KY [AM radio station call letters]
WLLX .... Minor Hill, TN [FM radio station call letters]
WLLY .... Wilson, NC [AM radio station call letters]
WLLZ .... Detroit, MI [FM radio station call letters]
WLM.......... Warning Light Monitor
WLM.......... Western Law Monthly [Cleveland, OH]   (DLA)
WLM.......... Western Lumber Manufacturers [An association] [Later, Western Timber Association]   (EA)
WLM.......... Willow Mountain [Alaska] [Seismograph station code, US Geological Survey] [Closed]   (SEIS)
WLM.......... Wire Line MODEMS
WLM.......... Working Level Month
WLMC .... Okeechobee, FL [FM radio station call letters]
WLMH .... Morrow, OH [FM radio station call letters]
WLMJ .... Jackson, OH [AM radio station call letters]
WLMO .... Geneseo, NY [AM radio station call letters]
WLMO .... Worldwide Logistics Management Office [Army]
WLMR .... Vineland, NJ [Television station call letters]
WLMS .... Poughkeepsie, NY [FM radio station call letters]
WLMV .... Vernon Hills, IL [AM radio station call letters]
WLN........... Washington Library Network [Washington State Library] [Olympia, WA] [Library network]
WLN .... Welcome North Mines [Vancouver Stock Exchange symbol]
WLN .... Wellington [British depot code]
WLN .... Western Library Network [Formerly, Washington Library Network] [Library of Congress] [Olympia, WA] [Database]
WLN .... Wired Librarian's Newsletter [A publication]
WLN .... Wiswesser Line Notation [Chemical structure]
WLNA......... Peekskill, NY [AM radio station call letters]
WLNB .... Charleston, SC [AM radio station call letters]
WLNB-FM ... Goose Creek, SC [FM radio station call letters]
WLNC......... Laurinburg, NC [AM radio station call letters]
WLND........ Cortland, OH [AM radio station call letters]
WLNE......... New Bedford, MA [Television station call letters]
WLNG........ Sag Harbor, NY [AM radio station call letters]
WLNG-FM ... Sag Harbor, NY [FM radio station call letters]
WLNH-FM ... Laconia, NH [FM radio station call letters]
WLNK......... Columbus, MS [FM radio station call letters]
WLNR......... Lansing, IL [FM radio station call letters]
WLNS-TV... Lansing, MI [Television station call letters]
WLNV......... Derby, CT [FM radio station call letters]
WLNX......... Lincoln, IL [FM radio station call letters]
WLNZ......... St. Johns, MI [AM radio station call letters]
WLNZ-FM .. St. Johns, MI [FM radio station call letters]
WLO .... Waterloo Railroad Co. [AAR code]
WLO .... Weapons Liaison Officer   (NVT)
WLO .... Wilson [Oklahoma] [Seismograph station code, US Geological Survey]   (SEIS)
WLOB........ Portland, ME [AM radio station call letters]
WLOC........ Munfordville, KY [AM radio station call letters]
WLOC-FM ... Munfordville, KY [FM radio station call letters]
WLOD........ Loudon, TN [AM radio station call letters]
WLOE........ Eden, NC [AM radio station call letters]
WLOG........ Logan, WV [AM radio station call letters]
WLOH........ Lancaster, OH [AM radio station call letters]
WLOI......... La Porte, IN [AM radio station call letters]
WLOK........ Memphis, TN [AM radio station call letters]
WLOL-FM ... Minneapolis, MN [FM radio station call letters]
WLON........ Lincolnton, NC [AM radio station call letters]
WLOO........ Chicago, IL [FM radio station call letters]
WLOP........ Jesup, GA [AM radio station call letters]
WLOQ........ Winter Park, FL [FM radio station call letters]
WLOR........ Thomasville, GA [AM radio station call letters]
WLOS-TV... Asheville, NC [Television station call letters]
WLOT......... Trenton, TN [FM radio station call letters]
WLOU........ Louisville, KY [AM radio station call letters]
WLOV........ Washington, GA [AM radio station call letters]
WLOV-FM ... Washington, GA [FM radio station call letters]
WLOW........ Wicklow [County in Ireland]   (ROG)
WLOX-TV... Biloxi, MS [Television station call letters]
WLP........... Wallops Island, NASA Center   (MCD)
WLP........... White Light Position
WLP........... Women's Law Project   (EA)
WLPA .... Lancaster, PA [AM radio station call letters]
WLPB-TV... Baton Rouge, LA [Television station call letters]
WL/PD .... Warner-Lambert/Parke-Davis [Computer files of chemical and biological data]
WLPE .... Augusta, GA [FM radio station call letters]
WLPF.......... Lake Placid, FL [AM radio station call letters]
WLPF.......... William L. Patterson Foundation   (EA)
WLPH .... Irondale, AL [AM radio station call letters]
WLPJ-FM ... New Port Richey, FL [FM radio station call letters]
WLPM........ Suffolk, VA [AM radio station call letters]
WLPO......... La Salle, IL [AM radio station call letters]
WLPR......... Mobile, AL [FM radio station call letters]
WLPW .... Lake Placid, NY [FM radio station call letters]
WLPZ .... New Carlisle, IN [FM radio station call letters]
WLQ........... Washington University. Law Quarterly [A publication]
WLQE......... Pleasantville, NJ [FM radio station call letters]
WLQF......... Greenfield, MA [Television station call letters]
WLQH........ Chiefland, FL [AM radio station call letters]

WLQI .... Rensselaer, IN [*FM radio station call letters*]
WLQR .... Toledo, OH [*FM radio station call letters*]
WLQY .... Hollywood, FL [*AM radio station call letters*]
WLR .... Washington Law Reporter [*District of Columbia*]   (DLA)
WLR .... Washington Law Review [*A publication*]
WLR .... Water Level Recorder
WLR .... Weapons Locating RADAR   (AABC)
WLR .... Weekly Law Reports [*British*]
WLR .... West London Railway   (ROG)
WLR .... Western Law Reporter [*Canada*]   (DLA)
WLR .... Wilanour Resources Ltd. [*Toronto Stock Exchange symbol*]
WLR .... World Law Review   (DLA)
WLR .... Wrong Length Record [*Data processing*]
WLRA .... Lockport, IL [*FM radio station call letters*]
WLRA .... Wagner Labor Relations Act   (OICC)
WLRA .... World Leisure and Recreation Association [*Formerly, IRA*]   (EA)
WLRB .... Macomb, IL [*AM radio station call letters*]
WLRC .... Walnut, MS [*AM radio station call letters*]
WLRD .... Warning Light Relay Driver
WLRH .... Huntsville, AL [*FM radio station call letters*]
WLRI .... Warner-Lambert Research Institute [*New Jersey*]
WLRM .... Ridgeland, MS [*AM radio station call letters*]
WLRN-FM ... Miami, FL [*FM radio station call letters*]
WLRN-TV ... Miami, FL [*Television station call letters*]
WLRP .... San Sebastian, PR [*AM radio station call letters*]
WLRP .... Wandsworth's Legal Resource Project   (DLA)
WLRQ-FM ... Franklin, TN [*FM radio station call letters*]
WLRS .... Louisville, KY [*FM radio station call letters*]
WLRV .... Lebanon, VA [*AM radio station call letters*]
WLRW .... Champaign, IL [*FM radio station call letters*]
WLRX .... Lincoln, IL [*FM radio station call letters*]
WLRY .... Rochester, NY [*FM radio station call letters*]
WLRZ .... Peru, IL [*FM radio station call letters*]
WLS .... Chicago, IL [*AM radio station call letters*]
WLS .... Livingston-Steuben-Wyoming BOCES [*Boards of Cooperative Educational Services*], Educational Communications Center, Geneseo, NY [*OCLC symbol*]   (OCLC)
WLS .... Wallis Island [*Wallis and Futuna Islands*] [*Airport symbol*]   (OAG)
WLS .... Water Lily Society   (EA)
WLS .... Weighted Least Squares [*Statistics*]
WLS .... Wells
WLS .... Welschbruch [*France*] [*Seismograph station code, US Geological Survey*]   (SEIS)
WLS .... Welsh Language Society   (EA)
WLS .... Westchester Library System [*Library network*]
WLS .... Westchester Public Library [*UTLAS symbol*]
WLS .... Williams Air, Inc. [*Medford Lakes, NJ*] [*FAA designator*]   (FAAC)
WLS .... Winnefox Library System [*Library network*]
WLS .... World Listening Service   (EA)
WLSA .... Louisa, VA [*FM radio station call letters*]
WLSA .... Wage and Labor Standards Administration   (OICC)
WLSB .... Copperhill, TN [*AM radio station call letters*]
WLSC .... Loris, SC [*AM radio station call letters*]
WLSC .... West Liberty State College [*West Virginia*]
WLSD .... Big Stone Gap, VA [*AM radio station call letters*]
WLSD-FM ... Big Stone Gap, VA [*FM radio station call letters*]
WLSE .... Wallace, NC [*AM radio station call letters*]
WLSH .... Lansford, PA [*AM radio station call letters*]
WLSI .... Pikeville, KY [*AM radio station call letters*]
WLSK-FM ... Lebanon, KY [*FM radio station call letters*]
WLSL .... Walseal
WLSM .... Louisville, MS [*AM radio station call letters*]
WLSM-FM ... Louisville, MS [*FM radio station call letters*]
WLSN .... Greenville, OH [*FM radio station call letters*]
WLSO .... Spencer, KY [*AM radio station call letters*]
WLSP .... Carbondale, PA [*FM radio station call letters*]
WLSP .... World List of Scientific Periodicals [*A publication*]   (DIT)
WLSQ .... Montgomery, AL [*AM radio station call letters*]
WLSR .... Lima, OH [*FM radio station call letters*]
WLST .... Marinette, WI [*FM radio station call letters*]
WLS-TV ..... Chicago, IL [*Television station call letters*]
WLSU .... La Crosse, WI [*FM radio station call letters*]
WLSV .... Wellsville, NY [*AM radio station call letters*]
WLSW .... Scottdale, PA [*FM radio station call letters*]
WLT .... Weighing Less Than
WLT .... Western Law Times [*1890-95*]   (DLA)
WLT .... Wire Line Timing
WLT .... World Literature Today [*A publication*]
WLTA .... Clarkesville, GA [*AM radio station call letters*]
WLTAS .... Wingfoot Lighter-Than-Air Society [*Later, Lighter-Than-Air Society*]   (EA)
WLTB .... Birmingham, AL [*FM radio station call letters*]
WLTC .... Gastonia, NC [*AM radio station call letters*]
WLTD .... Lexington, MS [*AM radio station call letters*]
WLTE .... Minneapolis, MN [*FM radio station call letters*]
WLTE .... Warrant Loss to Enlisted Status [*Revocation of appointment*] [*Navy*]
WLTF .... Cleveland, OH [*FM radio station call letters*]

WLTG .... Panama City, FL [*AM radio station call letters*]
WLTH .... Gary, IN [*AM radio station call letters*]
WLTI .... Detroit, MI [*FM radio station call letters*]
WLTJ .... Pittsburgh, PA [*FM radio station call letters*]
WLTK .... Wiltek, Inc. [*NASDAQ symbol*]   (NQ)
WLTL .... La Grange, IL [*FM radio station call letters*]
WLTM .... Franklin, NC [*AM radio station call letters*]
WLTN .... Littleton, NH [*AM radio station call letters*]
WLTP .... Parkersburg, WV [*AM radio station call letters*]
WLTQ .... Milwaukee, WI [*FM radio station call letters*]
WLTR .... Columbia, SC [*FM radio station call letters*]
WLTS-FM ... Slidell, LA [*FM radio station call letters*]
WLTT .... Bethesda, MD [*FM radio station call letters*]
WLTU .... Manitowoc, WI [*FM radio station call letters*]
WLTV .... Miami, FL [*Television station call letters*]
WLTW .... New York, NY [*FM radio station call letters*]
WLTX-TV ... Columbia, SC [*Television station call letters*]
WLTY .... Norfolk, VA [*FM radio station call letters*]
WLTZ .... Columbus, GA [*Television station call letters*]
WLU .... Washington and Lee University [*Virginia*]
WLU .... Wesleyan University, Middletown, CT [*OCLC symbol*]   (OCLC)
WLub .... Wydawnictwo Lubelskie [*A publication*]
WLUC .... Women Life Underwriters Conference [*Washington, DC*]   (EA)
WLUC-TV ... Marquette, MI [*Television station call letters*]
WLUJ .... Petersburg, IL [*FM radio station call letters*]
WLUK-TV ... Green Bay, WI [*Television station call letters*]
WLUL .... Fort Deposit, AL [*AM radio station call letters*]
WLUM-FM ... Milwaukee, WI [*FM radio station call letters*]
WLUN .... Lumberton, MS [*FM radio station call letters*]
WLUP .... Chicago, IL [*FM radio station call letters*]
WLUR .... Lexington, VA [*FM radio station call letters*]
WLUS .... Gainesville, FL [*AM radio station call letters*]
WLUV .... Loves Park, IL [*AM radio station call letters*]
WLUV-FM ... Loves Park, IL [*FM radio station call letters*]
WLUW .... Chicago, IL [*FM radio station call letters*]
WLUX .... Baton Rouge, LA [*AM radio station call letters*]
WLUZ .... Bayamon, PR [*AM radio station call letters*]
WLUZ-TV ... Ponce, PR [*Television station call letters*]
WLVA .... Lynchburg, VA [*AM radio station call letters*]
WLVC .... Fort Kent, ME [*FM radio station call letters*]
WLVE .... Miami Beach, FL [*FM radio station call letters*]
WLVF .... Haines City, FL [*AM radio station call letters*]
WLVG .... Cambridge, MA [*AM radio station call letters*]
WLVH .... Hartford, CT [*FM radio station call letters*]
WLVI-TV .... Cambridge, MA [*Television station call letters*]
WLVJ .... Royal Palm Beach, FL [*AM radio station call letters*]
WLVK .... Statesville, NC [*FM radio station call letters*]
WLVL .... Lockport, NY [*AM radio station call letters*]
WLVN .... Luverne, AL [*AM radio station call letters*]
WLVQ .... Columbus, OH [*FM radio station call letters*]
WLVR .... Bethlehem, PA [*FM radio station call letters*]
WLVS .... Germantown, TN [*AM radio station call letters*]
WLVT-TV ... Allentown, PA [*Television station call letters*]
WLVU .... Dunedin, FL [*AM radio station call letters*]
WLVU-FM ... Holiday, FL [*FM radio station call letters*]
WLVV .... Panama City, FL [*FM radio station call letters*]
WLVW .... Salisbury, MD [*FM radio station call letters*]
WLW .... Cincinnati, OH [*AM radio station call letters*]
WLW .... Weldwood of Canada Ltd. [*Toronto Stock Exchange symbol*]
WLW .... Willows, CA [*Location identifier*] [*FAA*]   (FAAL)
WLW .... Women Library Workers   (EA)
WLWE .... World Literature Written in English [*A publication*]
WLWH .... Workshop Library on World Humor   (EA)
WLWI .... Montgomery, AL [*AM radio station call letters*]
WLWI-FM ... Montgomery, AL [*FM radio station call letters*]
WLWL .... Rockingham, NC [*AM radio station call letters*]
WLWT .... Cincinnati, OH [*Television station call letters*]
WLXG .... Lexington, KY [*AM radio station call letters*]
WLXI-TV .... Greensboro, NC [*Television station call letters*]
WLXN .... Lexington, NC [*AM radio station call letters*]
WLXR .... La Crosse, WI [*AM radio station call letters*]
WLXR-FM... La Crosse, WI [*FM radio station call letters*]
WLXV .... Cumberland, MD [*Television station call letters*]
WLY .... Westerly
WLYC .... Williamsport, PA [*AM radio station call letters*]
WLYF .... Miami, FL [*FM radio station call letters*]
WLYH-TV ... Lancaster, PA [*Television station call letters*]
WLYJ .... Clarksburg, WV [*Television station call letters*]
WLYN .... Lynn, MA [*AM radio station call letters*]
WLYQ .... Norwalk, CT [*FM radio station call letters*]
WLYT .... Haverhill, MA [*FM radio station call letters*]
WLYX .... Memphis, TN [*FM radio station call letters*]
WLYZ .... Nashville, GA [*AM radio station call letters*]
WM .... [*Qualified for*] Engineering Watch [*USNR officer classification*]
WM .... Milwaukee Public Library, Milwaukee, WI [*Library symbol*] [*Library of Congress*]   (LCLS)
WM .... Multiple-Conductor Cables [*JETDS nomenclature*] [*Military*]   (CET)
WM .... Waldenstrom's Macroglobulinemia [*Medicine*]
W & M .... War and Marine
WM .... War Memorial

WM .... Ward Manager [*Medicine*]
WM .... Warming
W & M .... Washburn and Moen [*Wire gauge*]
W/M .... Washing Machine [*Classified advertising*] (ADA)
WM .... Washington Monthly [*A publication*]
WM .... Waste Management   (NASA)
WM .... Water Meter
WM .... Watermark
WM .... Watt Meter
WM .... Wave Meter
WM .... Ways and Means   (DLA)
WM .... Wehrmacht-Marine [*Marking on Navy vehicles*] [*German military - World War II*]
W/M .... Weight or Measurement
WM .... Welding Memorandum
WM .... Westermanns Monatshefte [*A publication*]
WM .... Western Maryland Railway Co. [*NYSE symbol*] [*AAR code*] [*Wall Street slang name: "Wet Mary"*]
WM .... Wheel-Made   (BJA)
WM .... White Male
WM .... White Metal
WM .... Whitten's Medium [*for cell incubation*]
Wm .... William (King of England)   (DLA)
W & M .... William and Mary [*King and Queen of England*]   (ROG)
W & M .... William and Mary Law Review [*A publication*]
W & M .... Wilson & McLane, Inc. [*White Plains, NY*] [*Information service*] (EISS)
W/M .... Wing Main [*Airfield*] (NATG)
WM .... Wire Mesh
WM .... Without Margin
WM .... Women in the Mainstream   (EA)
WM .... Women Marines
W & M .... Woodbury and Minot's United States Circuit Court Reports [*3 vols.*]   (DLA)
WM .... Word Mark   (BUR)
W/M .... Words per Minute   (KSC)
WM .... Work Measurement [*Army*]   (AABC)
WM .... World Meetings [*A publication*]
WM .... World of Music [*London*] [*A publication*]
WM .... Worshipful Master [*Freemasonry*]
W/M² .... Watts per Square Meter
WMA .... Alverno College, Milwaukee, WI [*Library symbol*] [*Library of Congress*]   (LCLS)
WMa .... Madison Public Library, Madison, WI [*Library symbol*] [*Library of Congress*]   (LCLS)
WMA .... Mandritsara [*Madagascar*] [*Airport symbol*]   (OAG)
WMA .... Wallcovering Manufacturers Association [*Springfield, NJ*]   (EA)
WMA .... War Measures Act
WMA .... Washington Metropolitan Area   (AFM)
WMA .... Waste Management Area [*NASA*]
WMA .... Waterbed Manufacturers Association [*Los Angeles, CA*]   (EA)
WMA .... Weather Modification Association
WMA .... Welding Machine Arc
WMA .... Wentworth Military Academy [*Missouri*]
WMA .... West Mesa [*New Mexico*] [*Seismograph station code, US Geological Survey*]   (SEIS)
WMA .... Wheelchair Motorcycle Association   (EA)
WMA .... Wing Main Airfield   (NATG)
WMA .... Women Marines Association   (EA)
WMA .... World Manx Association
WMA .... World Medical Association
WMA .... World Modeling Association   (EA)
WMAA .... Jackson, MS [*Television station call letters*]
WMAA .... World Martial Arts Association   (EA)
WMAA-FM ... Jackson, MS [*FM radio station call letters*]
WMaAR ..... Wisconsin Alumni Research Foundation, Madison, WI [*Library symbol*] [*Library of Congress*]   (LCLS)
WMAB .... Mississippi State, MS [*Television station call letters*]
WMAB .... Weather Modification Advisory Board
WMAB-FM ... Mississippi State, MS [*FM radio station call letters*]
WMaBR ..... Wisconsin Department of Health and Social Services, Bureau of Research, Madison, WI [*Library symbol*] [*Library of Congress*]   (LCLS)
WMaC .... Central Wisconsin Colony, Staff Library, Madison, WI [*Library symbol*] [*Library of Congress*]   (LCLS)
WMAC .... Metter, GA [*AM radio station call letters*]
WMAC .... Waste Management Advisory Council [*British*]
WMaCH ..... Wisconsin Department of Health and Social Services, Community Health Service, Madison, WI [*Library symbol*] [*Library of Congress*]   (LCLS)
WMACS ..... AC Spark Plug Co., Electronics Division, Milwaukee, WI [*Library symbol*] [*Library of Congress*]   (LCLS)
WMaCT ..... Children's Treatment Center, Madison, WI [*Library symbol*] [*Library of Congress*]   (LCLS)
WMAD .... Sun Prairie, WI [*AM radio station call letters*]
WMAD-FM ... Sun Prairie, WI [*FM radio station call letters*]
WMAE-FM ... Booneville, MS [*FM radio station call letters*]
WMAE-TV ... Booneville, MS [*Television station call letters*]
WMAF .... Madison, FL [*AM radio station call letters*]
WMaF .... United States Forest Products Laboratory, Madison, WI [*Library symbol*] [*Library of Congress*]   (LCLS)

WMAFPH ... World Medical Association for Perfect Health [*Also known as United States Association of Physicians*] [*Washington, DC*]   (EA)
WMAG .... High Point, NC [*FM radio station call letters*]
WMaG .... Madison General Hospital, Madison, WI [*Library symbol*] [*Library of Congress*]   (LCLS)
WMaG-N .... Madison General Hospital, School of Nursing, Madison, WI [*Library symbol*] [*Library of Congress*]   (LCLS)
WMaH .... Wisconsin Division of Health Policy and Planning Library, Madison, WI [*Library symbol*] [*Library of Congress*]   (LCLS)
WMAH-FM ... Biloxi, MS [*FM radio station call letters*]
WMAH-TV ... Biloxi, MS [*Television station call letters*]
W Mail .... Western Mail [*A publication*]
W Mail Ann ... Western Mail Annual [*A publication*]
WMaJ .... Jackson Clinic, Madison, WI [*Library symbol*] [*Library of Congress*]   (LCLS)
WMAJ .... State College, PA [*AM radio station call letters*]
WMAK .... Nashville, TN [*AM radio station call letters*]
WMAL .... Washington, DC [*AM radio station call letters*]
WMaLS ..... Wisconsin Division for Library Services, Bureau for Reference and Local Services, Madison, WI [*Library symbol*] [*Library of Congress*]   (LCLS)
WMAM ...... Marinette, WI [*AM radio station call letters*]
WMaM .... Methodist Hospital School of Nursing, Madison, WI [*Library symbol*] [*Library of Congress*]   (LCLS)
WMaMS ..... Mendota Mental Health Institute, Madison, WI [*Library symbol*] [*Library of Congress*]   (LCLS)
WMan .... Manawa Public Library, Manawa, WI [*Library symbol*] [*Library of Congress*]   (LCLS)
WMAN .... Mansfield, OH [*AM radio station call letters*]
WMani .... Manitowoc Public Library, Manitowoc, WI [*Library symbol*] [*Library of Congress*]   (LCLS)
WManiH .... Holy Family Hospital, Manitowoc, WI [*Library symbol*] [*Library of Congress*]   (LCLS)
WManiHN... Holy Family School of Nursing, Manitowoc, WI [*Library symbol*] [*Library of Congress*]   (LCLS)
WMANT..... Wissenschaftliche Monographien zum Alten und Neuen Testament [*A publication*]   (BJA)
WMAO....... Greenwood, MS [*Television station call letters*]
WMAO-FM ... Greenwood, MS [*FM radio station call letters*]
WMAP .... Monroe, NC [*AM radio station call letters*]
WMaPI........ Department of Public Instruction, Division for Library Services, Professional Library, Madison, WI [*Library symbol*] [*Library of Congress*]   (LCLS)
WMaPI-CC ... Department of Public Instruction, Division for Library Services, Cooperative Children's Book Center, Madison, WI [*Library symbol*] [*Library of Congress*]   (LCLS)
WMaPI-PL ... Department of Public Instruction, Division for Library Services, Public Library Services, Madison, WI [*Library symbol*] [*Library of Congress*]   (LCLS)
WMaPI-RL ... Department of Public Instruction, Division for Library Services, Reference and Loan Library, Madison, WI [*Library symbol*] [*Library of Congress*]   (LCLS)
WMaPR ...... Wisconsin Regional Primate Research Center, Madison, WI [*Library symbol*] [*Library of Congress*]   (LCLS)
WMAQ........ Chicago, IL [*AM radio station call letters*]
WMAQ-TV ... Chicago, IL [*Television station call letters*]
WMaR........ Raltech Scientific Services, Inc., Madison, WI [*Library symbol*] [*Library of Congress*]   (LCLS)
WMAR .... Western Marine Electronics Co. [*NASDAQ symbol*]   (NQ)
WMaraS ..... Saint Anthony Friary, Marathon, WI [*Library symbol*] [*Library of Congress*]   (LCLS)
WMarC .... Marshfield Clinic, Marshfield, WI [*Library symbol*] [*Library of Congress*]   (LCLS)
WMARC ..... World Maritime Administrative Radio Conference
WMarSJ ..... Saint Joseph's Hospital, Marshfield, WI [*Library symbol*] [*Library of Congress*]   (LCLS)
WMAR-TV ... Baltimore, MD [*Television station call letters*]
WMarW ...... Wood County Hospital, Marshfield, WI [*Library symbol*] [*Library of Congress*]   (LCLS)
WMAS .... Springfield, MA [*AM radio station call letters*]
WMaS......... Student Association for the Study of Hallucinogens, Madison, WI [*Library symbol*] [*Library of Congress*]   (LCLS)
WMAS-FM ... Springfield, MA [*FM radio station call letters*]
WMaSM ..... Saint Mary's Hospital, Doctors' Library, Madison, WI [*Library symbol*] [*Library of Congress*]   (LCLS)
WMaSM-N ... Saint Mary's Hospital, School of Nursing, Madison, WI [*Library symbol*] [*Library of Congress*]   (LCLS)
WMAT .... Wastemate Corp. [*NASDAQ symbol*]   (NQ)
WMaTC ...... Madison Area Technical College, Madison, WI [*Library symbol*] [*Library of Congress*]   (LCLS)
WMau .... Mauston Public Library, Mauston, WI [*Library symbol*] [*Library of Congress*]   (LCLS)
WMAU .... Women's Martial Arts Union [*Defunct*]   (EA)
WMaUCS ... University of Wisconsin-Center System, Madison, WI [*Library symbol*] [*Library of Congress*]   (LCLS)
WMaUEx .... University of Wisconsin-Extension, Madison, WI [*Library symbol*] [*Library of Congress*]   (LCLS)
WMAU-FM ... Bude, MS [*FM radio station call letters*]
WMAU-TV ... Bude, MS [*Television station call letters*]

WMaVA	United States Veterans Administration Hospital, Madison, WI [*Library symbol*] [*Library of Congress*] (LCLS)
WMAV-FM ...	Oxford, MS [*FM radio station call letters*]
WMAV-TV ...	Oxford, MS [*Television station call letters*]
WMaW	Wisconsin Alumni Research Foundation Institute, Inc., Madison, WI [*Library symbol*] [*Library of Congress*] (LCLS)
WMAW-FM ...	Meridian, MS [*FM radio station call letters*]
WMAW-TV ...	Meridian, MS [*Television station call letters*]
WMAX	Grand Rapids, MI [*AM radio station call letters*]
WMAY	Springfield, IL [*AM radio station call letters*]
WMAZ	Macon, GA [*AM radio station call letters*]
WMAZ-TV ...	Macon, GA [*Television station call letters*]
WMB	Walnut Marketing Board (EA)
WMB	War Mobilization Board
WMB	Warrnambool [*Australia*] [*Airport symbol*] (OAG)
WMB	[*The*] Williams Companies [*NYSE symbol*]
WMB	Williamsburg Technical College, Kingstree, SC [*OCLC symbol*] (OCLC)
WMBA	Ambridge, PA [*AM radio station call letters*]
WMBA	Wire Machinery Builders Association [*Falls Church, VA*] (EA)
WMBB	Panama City, FL [*Television station call letters*]
WMBC	Columbus, MS [*FM radio station call letters*]
WMBC	Wisconsin Baptist State Convention, Milwaukee, WI [*Library symbol*] [*Library of Congress*] (LCLS)
WMBD	Peoria, IL [*AM radio station call letters*]
WMBD-TV ...	Peoria, IL [*Television station call letters*]
WMBE	Chilton, WI [*AM radio station call letters*]
WMBG	Williamsburg, VA [*AM radio station call letters*]
WMBH	Joplin, MO [*AM radio station call letters*]
WMBI	Chicago, IL [*AM radio station call letters*]
WMBI-FM...	Chicago, IL [*FM radio station call letters*]
Wm Bl........	[*William*] Blackstone's English King's Bench Reports [*1746-80*] (DLA)
WMBL	Morehead City, NC [*AM radio station call letters*]
WMBL	Wrightsville Marine Biomedical Laboratory
WMBM	Miami Beach, FL [*AM radio station call letters*]
WMDN-FM ...	Petoskey, MI [*FM radio station call letters*]
WMBO.......	Auburn, NY [*AM radio station call letters*]
WMBR	Cambridge, MA [*FM radio station call letters*]
WMBS	Uniontown, PA [*AM radio station call letters*]
WMBT	Shenandoah, PA [*AM radio station call letters*]
WMBTOPCITBWTNTALI ...	We May Be the Only Phone Company in Town, but We Try Not to Act Like It [*Slogan*]
WMBW	Chattanooga, TN [*FM radio station call letters*]
WMC	Concordia College, Milwaukee, WI [*Library symbol*] [*Library of Congress*] (LCLS)
WMC	Memphis, TN [*AM radio station call letters*]
WMC	War Manpower Commission [*Within the Office of Emergency Management*] [*World War II*]
WMC	Waste Management Compartment [*NASA*] (KSC)
WMC	Weapons and Mobility Command [*Army*]
WMC	Weapons Monitoring Center
WMC	Weapons Monitoring Console
WMC	Western Maryland College [*Westminster*]
WMC	Wilmington College, Wilmington, OH [*OCLC symbol*] (OCLC)
WmC	Windsor Microfilming Company, Windsor, ON, Canada [*Library symbol*] [*Library of Congress*] (LCLS)
WMC	Winnemucca, NV [*Location identifier*] [*FAA*] (FAAL)
WMC	Wisconsin Motor Carriers Association Inc., Madison WI [*STAC*]
WMC	Wool Manufacturers Council [*Boston, MA*] (EA)
WMC	World Meteorological Center [*World Meteorological Organization*]
WMC	World Methodist Council
WMC	World Ministries Commission (EA)
WMC	World Missions to Children [*Later, WMF*] (EA)
WMC	World Muslim Congress (BJA)
WMCA.......	New York, NY [*AM radio station call letters*]
WMCB	Martinsville, IN [*AM radio station call letters*]
WMCC.......	Marion, IN [*Television station call letters*]
WMCCMEC ...	Women's Missionary Council of the Christian Methodist Episcopal Church (EA)
WMCCS	Worldwide Military Command and Control System [*Pronounced "wimex"*] [*DoD*] (MCD)
WMCCSA...	World Masters Cross-Country Ski Association (EA-IO)
WMCD.......	Statesboro, GA [*FM radio station call letters*]
WMC-FM....	Memphis, TN [*FM radio station call letters*]
WMCF-TV ...	Montgomery, AL [*Television station call letters*]
WMCG.......	Milan, GA [*FM radio station call letters*]
WMCG.......	Milwaukee County General Hospital, Milwaukee, WI [*Library symbol*] [*Library of Congress*] (LCLS)
WMCH.......	Church Hill, TN [*AM radio station call letters*]
WMCH.......	Columbia Hospital School of Nursing, Milwaukee, WI [*Library symbol*] [*Library of Congress*] (LCLS)
WMCHi......	Milwaukee County Historical Society, Milwaukee, WI [*Library symbol*] [*Library of Congress*] (LCLS)
WMCI	Brockton, MA [*FM radio station call letters*]
WMCI	World Mail Center, Incorporated [*NASDAQ symbol*] (NQ)
WMCJ	Moncks Corner, SC [*AM radio station call letters*]
WMCL	McLeansboro, IL [*AM radio station call letters*]
WMCL	Wideband Communications Line
WMCL	William Mitchell College of Law [*Minnesota*]
WMCM	Milwaukee County Institutions, Mental Health Centers Libraries, Milwaukee, WI [*Library symbol*] [*Library of Congress*] (LCLS)
WMCM	Rockland, ME [*FM radio station call letters*]
WMCN.......	St. Paul, MN [*FM radio station call letters*]
WMCO.......	New Concord, OH [*FM radio station call letters*]
WMCP	Columbia, TN [*AM radio station call letters*]
WMCP.......	Woman's Medical College of Pennsylvania
WMCQ.......	William and Mary College. Quarterly [*A publication*]
WMCQ-FM ...	Richmond, KY [*FM radio station call letters*]
WMCR.......	Oneida, NY [*AM radio station call letters*]
WMCR-FM ...	Oneida, NY [*FM radio station call letters*]
WMCS	Machias, ME [*AM radio station call letters*]
WMCSC	Cardinal Stritch College, Milwaukee, WI [*Library symbol*] [*Library of Congress*] (LCLS)
WMCT	Mountain City, TN [*AM radio station call letters*]
WMC-TV	Memphis, TN [*Television station call letters*]
WMCU	Miami, FL [*FM radio station call letters*]
WMCW	Harvard, IL [*AM radio station call letters*]
WMCW	World Movement of Christian Workers [*See also MMTC*] [*Brussels, Belgium*] (EA-IO)
WMCX	West Long Branch, NJ [*FM radio station call letters*]
WMD	Digital Equipment Corp., Westminster, Westminster, MA [*OCLC symbol*] (OCLC)
WMD	Doctors Hospital, Milwaukee, WI [*Library symbol*] [*Library of Congress*] (LCLS)
WMD	Mandabe [*Madagascar*] [*Airport symbol*] (OAG)
WMD	Mars Graphic Services, Inc. [*American Stock Exchange symbol*]
WMD	Water Mineral Development [*A publication*]
WMD	Wind Measuring Device
WMDA........	Woodworking Machinery Distributors Association [*King of Prussia, PA*] (EA)
WMDAA	Watch Material Distributors Association of America [*Later, WMJDA*] (EA)
W M Day Studies ...	Romance Studies Presented to William Morton Day [*A publication*]
WMDB.......	Nashville, TN [*AM radio station call letters*]
WMDC.......	Hazlehurst, MS [*AM radio station call letters*]
WMDC-FM ...	Hazlehurst, MS [*FM radio station call letters*]
WMDD.......	Fajardo, PR [*AM radio station call letters*]
WMDe	Deaconess Hospital, Milwaukee, WI [*Library symbol*] [*Library of Congress*] (LCLS)
WMDH.......	New Castle, IN [*FM radio station call letters*]
WMDio	Diocesan Library, Milwaukee, WI [*Library symbol*] [*Library of Congress*] [*Obsolete*] (LCLS)
WMDJ........	Martin, KY [*AM radio station call letters*]
WMDJ-FM ...	Allen, KY [*FM radio station call letters*]
WMDK.......	Peterborough, NH [*FM radio station call letters*]
WMDM-FM ...	Lexington Park, MD [*FM radio station call letters*]
WMDO.......	Wheaton, MD [*AM radio station call letters*]
WMDR.......	Alcoa, TN [*AM radio station call letters*]
WMDR.......	DePaul Rehabilitation Hospital Medical Library, Milwaukee, WI [*Library symbol*] [*Library of Congress*] (LCLS)
WMDT-TV ...	Salisbury, MD [*Television station call letters*]
WME..........	Eaton Corp., Milwaukee, WI [*Library symbol*] [*Library of Congress*] (LCLS)
WMe	Elisha D. Smith Public Library, Menasha, WI [*Library symbol*] [*Library of Congress*] (LCLS)
WME..........	Window Meteoroid Experiment [*NASA*] (KSC)
WME..........	Women and Mathematics Education (EA)
WME..........	Worldwide Marriage Encounter (EA)
WMEA	Portland, ME [*FM radio station call letters*]
WMEA	Welded Modules for Electronic Assemblies [*NASA*]
WMEA-TV ...	Biddeford, ME [*Television station call letters*]
WMEB-FM ...	Orono, ME [*FM radio station call letters*]
WMEB-TV ...	Orono, ME [*Television station call letters*]
WMEC	Medium Endurance Cutter [*Coast Guard*] (NVT)
WMEC	Western Military Electronics Center (KSC)
WMECO	Western Massachusetts Electric Company
WMED	Calais, ME [*FM radio station call letters*]
WMED-TV ...	Calais, ME [*Television station call letters*]
WMEE	Fort Wayne, IN [*FM radio station call letters*]
WMEH	Bangor, ME [*FM radio station call letters*]
WMEJ........	Proctorville, OH [*FM radio station call letters*]
WMEK.......	Chase City, VA [*AM radio station call letters*]
WMEL.......	Melbourne, FL [*AM radio station call letters*]
WMEM.......	Presque Isle, ME [*FM radio station call letters*]
WMEM-TV ...	Presque Isle, ME [*Television station call letters*]
WMen........	Mabel Tainter Memorial Free Library, Menomonie, WI [*Library symbol*] [*Library of Congress*] (LCLS)
WMenM......	Memorial Hospital and Nursing Home, Menomonie, WI [*Library symbol*] [*Library of Congress*] (LCLS)
WMenofH ...	Community Memorial Hospital, Health Science Library, Menomonee Falls, WI [*Library symbol*] [*Library of Congress*] (LCLS)
WMenU	University of Wisconsin-Stout, Menomonie, WI [*Library symbol*] [*Library of Congress*] (LCLS)
WMeq........	Frank L. Weyenberg Library, Mequon, WI [*Library symbol*] [*Library of Congress*] (LCLS)

WMEQ........ Menomonie, WI [*FM radio station call letters*]
WMeqW ..... Wisconsin Lutheran Seminary, Mequon, WI [*Library symbol*] [*Library of Congress*] (LCLS)
WMer.......... T. B. Scott Free Library, Merril, WI [*Library symbol*] [*Library of Congress*] (LCLS)
WMES .... Ashburn, GA [*AM radio station call letters*]
WMET .... Chicago, IL [*FM radio station call letters*]
WMET .... Gaithersburg, MD [*AM radio station call letters*]
WMeU .... University of Wisconsin-Green Bay, Fox Valley Campus, Menasha, WI [*Library symbol*] [*Library of Congress*] (LCLS)
WMEV .... Marion, VA [*AM radio station call letters*]
WMEV .... Marion, VA [*FM radio station call letters*]
WMEW .... Waterville, ME [*FM radio station call letters*]
WMEX .... Boston, MA [*AM radio station call letters*]
WMEZ .... Pensacola, FL [*FM radio station call letters*]
WMF.......... Maude Shunk Public Library, Menomonee Falls, WI [*OCLC symbol*] (OCLC)
WMF.......... Wire Mattress Federation
WMF.......... World Mercy Fund [*Alexandria, VA*] (EA)
WMF.......... World Missions Fellowship (EA)
WMFC .... Monroeville, AL [*AM radio station call letters*]
WMFC-FM ... Monroeville, AL [*FM radio station call letters*]
WMFD .... Wilmington, NC [*AM radio station call letters*]
WMFE-FM ... Orlando, FL [*FM radio station call letters*]
WMFE-TV ... Orlando, FL [*Television station call letters*]
WMFG .... Hibbing, MN [*FM radio station call letters*]
WMFJ......... Daytona Beach, FL [*AM radio station call letters*]
WMFL......... Monticello, FL [*FM radio station call letters*]
WMFM....... Petal, MS [*FM radio station call letters*]
WMFM....... Wisconsin Scottish Rite Bodies AASR, Milwaukee, WI [*Library symbol*] [*Library of Congress*] (LCLS)
WMFO .... Medford, MA [*FM radio station call letters*]
WMFP......... Lawrence, MA [*Television station call letters*]
WMFQ .... Ocala, FL [*FM radio station call letters*]
WMFR .... High Point, NC [*AM radio station call letters*]
WMFT......... Camden, ME [*FM radio station call letters*]
WMG .... Globe-Union, Inc., Milwaukee, WI [*Library symbol*] [*Library of Congress*] (LCLS)
WMG .... Wire Measure Gauge
WMG .... Wire Metallizing Gun
WMGA........ Moultrie, GA [*AM radio station call letters*]
W & M GA... Washburn and Moen Gauge (MSA)
WMGa .... Wisconsin Gas Co., Milwaukee, WI [*Library symbol*] [*Library of Congress*] (LCLS)
WMGB........ Georgetown, KY [*FM radio station call letters*]
WMGC-TV ... Binghamton, NY [*Television station call letters*]
WMGE .... Danville, KY [*FM radio station call letters*]
WMGF .... Shelby, NC [*FM radio station call letters*]
WMGG........ Columbus, OH [*FM radio station call letters*]
WMGI .... Gainesville, FL [*AM radio station call letters*]
WMGI .... Terre Haute, IN [*FM radio station call letters*]
WMGJ .... Gadsden, AL [*AM radio station call letters*]
WMGK........ Philadelphia, PA [*FM radio station call letters*]
WMGM....... Atlantic City, NJ [*FM radio station call letters*]
WMGM-TV ... Wildwood, NJ [*Television station call letters*]
WMGN....... Madison, WI [*FM radio station call letters*]
WMGO........ Canton, MS [*AM radio station call letters*]
WMGP........ Parkersburg, WV [*FM radio station call letters*]
WMGQ........ New Brunswick, NJ [*FM radio station call letters*]
WMGR........ Bainbridge, GA [*AM radio station call letters*]
WMGR........ Worm Gear [*Mechanical engineering*]
WMGS........ Wilkes-Barre, PA [*FM radio station call letters*]
WMGT........ Macon, GA [*Television station call letters*]
WMGV........ Oshkosh, WI [*FM radio station call letters*]
WMGW........ Meadville, PA [*AM radio station call letters*]
WMGX........ Portland, ME [*FM radio station call letters*]
WMGY........ Montgomery, AL [*AM radio station call letters*]
WMGZ........ Farrell, PA [*AM radio station call letters*]
WMGZ-FM ... Sharpsburg, PA [*FM radio station call letters*]
WMH .... Mountain Home [*Arkansas*] [*Airport symbol*] (OAG)
WMH .... Wisconsin Magazine of History [*A publication*]
WMHB........ Waterville, ME [*FM radio station call letters*]
WMHC........ South Hadley, MA [*FM radio station call letters*]
WMHD........ Terre Haute, IN [*FM radio station call letters*]
WMHE......... Toledo, OH [*FM radio station call letters*]
WMHI .... Coleman, FL [*AM radio station call letters*]
WMHK........ Columbia, SC [*FM radio station call letters*]
WMHR........ Syracuse, NY [*FM radio station call letters*]
WMHS .... Miamisburg, OH [*FM radio station call letters*]
WMHS .... Wall-Mounted Handling System [*AEC*]
WMHS .... World Methodist Historical Society (EA)
WMHT......... Schenectady, NY [*Television station call letters*]
WMHT-FM ... Schenectady, NY [*FM radio station call letters*]
WMHU........ Belmont, NC [*Television station call letters*]
WMHW-FM ... Mount Pleasant, MI [*FM radio station call letters*]
WMHY .... World Mental Health Year [*1960*]
WMI........... War Materials, Incorporated
WMI........... Washington Music Institute
WMI........... Waveguide Moisture Indicator

WMI........... Westmin Resources [*Toronto Stock Exchange symbol*] [*Vancouver Stock Exchange symbol*]
WMI........... Wildlife Management Institute (EA)
WMI........... Winthrop Insured Mortgage Investments II [*American Stock Exchange symbol*]
WMI........... World Metal Index [*Sheffield City Libraries*] [*British*] [*Information service*] (EISS)
WMI........... World Meteorological Intervals
WMIA .... Arecibo, PR [*AM radio station call letters*]
WMIA .... Woodworking Machinery Importers Association of America [*Baltimore, MD*] (EA)
WMIB .... Marco Island, FL [*AM radio station call letters*]
WMIB .... Waste Management Information Bureau [*Atomic Energy Authority*] [*British*] [*Information service*] (EISS)
WMIC .... Sandusky, MI [*AM radio station call letters*]
WMIC .... Western Microwave, Inc. [*NASDAQ symbol*] (NQ)
WMID .... Atlantic City, NJ [*AM radio station call letters*]
WMIE .... Cocoa, FL [*FM radio station call letters*]
WMIH .... Gorham, NH [*FM radio station call letters*]
WMIK .... Middlesboro, KY [*AM radio station call letters*]
WMIK-FM ... Middlesboro, KY [*FM radio station call letters*]
WMIL .... Waukesha, WI [*FM radio station call letters*]
WMiltM ...... Milton College, Milton, WI [*Library symbol*] [*Library of Congress*] (LCLS)
WMIM .... Mount Carmel, PA [*AM radio station call letters*]
WMIN .... Maplewood, MN [*AM radio station call letters*]
WMIO .... Cabo Rojo, PR [*FM radio station call letters*]
WMIP .... Weapons Management Improvement Program [*Military*] (AABC)
WMIQ .... Iron Mountain, MI [*AM radio station call letters*]
WMIR.......... Lake Geneva, WI [*AM radio station call letters*]
WMIS .... Natchez, MS [*AM radio station call letters*]
WMIT......... Black Mountain, NC [*FM radio station call letters*]
WMIV .... Fremont, MI [*AM radio station call letters*]
WMIX......... Mount Vernon, IL [*AM radio station call letters*]
WMIX-FM ... Mount Vernon, IL [*FM radio station call letters*]
WMJ .... Johnson Controls, Corporate Information Center, Milwaukee, WI [*Library symbol*] [*Library of Congress*] (LCLS)
WMJA........ Spencer, WI [*FM radio station call letters*]
WMJC........ Birmingham, MI [*FM radio station call letters*]
WMJD........ Grundy, VA [*FM radio station call letters*]
WMJDA...... Watch Material and Jewelry Distributors Association [*Formerly, WMDAA*] (EA)
WMJI .... Cleveland, OH [*FM radio station call letters*]
WMJJ .... Birmingham, AL [*FM radio station call letters*]
WMJK........ Kissimmee, FL [*AM radio station call letters*]
WMJL .... Marion, KY [*AM radio station call letters*]
WMJM........ Cordele, GA [*AM radio station call letters*]
WMJR........ Warrenton, VA [*FM radio station call letters*]
WMJS........ Prince Frederick, MD [*FM radio station call letters*]
WMJV-FM ... Patterson, NY [*FM radio station call letters*]
WMJW........ Nanticoke, PA [*FM radio station call letters*]
WMJX........ Beston, MA [*FM radio station call letters*]
WMJY........ Long Branch, NJ [*FM radio station call letters*]
WMK .... Watermark
W/(M K).... Watts per Meter Kelvin
WMK .... Weis Markets, Inc. [*NYSE symbol*]
W/(M² K)... Watts per Square Meter Kelvin
WMKC........ St. Ignace, MI [*FM radio station call letters*]
WMKG........ Battle Creek, MI [*FM radio station call letters*]
WMKJ........ New Orleans, LA [*AM radio station call letters*]
WMKM........ Houghton Lake, MI [*AM radio station call letters*]
WMKW-TV ... Memphis, TN [*Television station call letters*]
WMKX........ Brookville, PA [*FM radio station call letters*]
WMKY........ Morehead, KY [*FM radio station call letters*]
WML........... Lakeside Laboratories, Milwaukee, WI [*Library symbol*] [*Library of Congress*] (LCLS)
WML........... Malaimbandy [*Madagascar*] [*Airport symbol*] (OAG)
WML........... Westar Mining Limited [*Toronto Stock Exchange symbol*] [*Vancouver Stock Exchange symbol*]
WML........... Willamette Law Journal [*A publication*]
WMLA .... Normal, IL [*AM radio station call letters*]
WMLA-FM ... Le Roy, IL [*FM radio station call letters*]
WMLC........ Monticello, MS [*AM radio station call letters*]
WMLH .... Lutheran Hospital of Milwaukee, Milwaukee, WI [*Library symbol*] [*Library of Congress*] (LCLS)
Wm LJ........ Willamette Law Journal [*A publication*]
WMLM........ St. Louis, MI [*AM radio station call letters*]
WMLN-FM ... Milton, MA [*FM radio station call letters*]
WMLP........ Milton, PA [*AM radio station call letters*]
WMLQ........ Rogers City, MI [*FM radio station call letters*]
WMLR........ Hohenwald, TN [*AM radio station call letters*]
WMLR .... William and Mary Law Review [*A publication*]
W & M L Rev ... William and Mary Law Review [*A publication*]
WMLT........ Dublin, GA [*AM radio station call letters*]
WMLV .... Ironton, OH [*FM radio station call letters*]
WMLW........ Watertown, WI [*FM radio station call letters*]
WMM......... Marquette University, Milwaukee, WI [*Library symbol*] [*Library of Congress*] (LCLS)
WMM......... Wall-Mounted Manipulator [*Nuclear energy*] (NRCH)
Wm & M ... William and Mary (King and Queen of England) (DLA)

WMM.......... William Mitchell College of Law Library, St. Paul, MN [*OCLC symbol*] (OCLC)

WMM.......... Women Make Movies (EA)

WMM.......... World Medical Missions (EA)

WMM.......... World Movement of Mothers [*See also MMM*] (EA-IO)

WMMA .... Orlando, FL [*AM radio station call letters*]

WMMA .... Woodworking Machinery Manufacturers of America [*Philadelphia, PA*] (EA)

Wm Mar Q ... William and Mary Quarterly [*A publication*]

Wm & Mary Q ... William and Mary Quarterly [*A publication*]

Wm & Mary Rev VA L ... William and Mary Review of Virginia Law (DLA)

WMMB .... Melbourne, FL [*AM radio station call letters*]

WMMB .... Milwaukee Blood Center, Inc., Milwaukee, WI [*Library symbol*] [*Library of Congress*] (LCLS)

WMMBC.... Miller Brewing Co., Research Library, Milwaukee, WI [*Library symbol*] [*Library of Congress*] (LCLS)

WMMC ...... Columbia, SC [*FM radio station call letters*]

WMMC ...... Milwaukee Children's Hospital, Milwaukee, WI [*Library symbol*] [*Library of Congress*] (LCLS)

WMMCW.... Medical College of Wisconsin, Medical-Dental Library, Milwaukee, WI [*Library symbol*] [*Library of Congress*] (LCLS)

WMMG ...... Brandenburg, KY [*AM radio station call letters*]

WMMG-FM ... Brandenburg, KY [*FM radio station call letters*]

WMMGIC .... MGIC Investment Corp., Milwaukee, WI [*Library symbol*] [*Library of Congress*] (LCLS)

WMMH ...... Marshall, NC [*AM radio station call letters*]

WMMH ...... Misericordia Hospital, Milwaukee, WI [*Library symbol*] [*Library of Congress*] (LCLS)

WMMI .... Marshall, MI [*AM radio station call letters*]

WMMK ...... Destin, FL [*FM radio station call letters*]

WMM-L ...... Marquette University, School of Law, Milwaukee, WI [*Library symbol*] [*Library of Congress*] (LCLS)

WMML....... Mobile, AL [*AM radio station call letters*]

WMMM ...... Westport, CT [*AM radio station call letters*]

WMMN ...... Fairmont, WV [*AM radio station call letters*]

WMM-N ..... Marquette University, College of Nursing, Milwaukee, WI [*Library symbol*] [*Library of Congress*] (LCLS)

WMMP....... Wood Moulding and Millwork Producers [*Formerly, WWMP, WWMMP*] (EA)

WMMPA ..... Wood Moulding and Millwork Producers Association [*Portland, OR*] (EA)

WMMQ ...... Charlotte, MI [*FM radio station call letters*]

WMMR ...... Philadelphia, PA [*FM radio station call letters*]

WMMRRI .... Wyoming Mining and Mineral Resource Research Institute [*University of Wyoming*] [*Research center*] (RCD)

WMMS ...... Cleveland, OH [*FM radio station call letters*]

WMMS ...... Mount Sinai Hospital, Milwaukee, WI [*Library symbol*] [*Library of Congress*] (LCLS)

WMMt....... Mount Mary College, Milwaukee, WI [*Library symbol*] [*Library of Congress*] (LCLS)

WMMT....... Whitesburg, KY [*FM radio station call letters*]

WMMTA ..... World Minerals and Metals [*A publication*]

WMMus...... Milwaukee Public Museum, Reference Library, Milwaukee, WI [*Library symbol*] [*Library of Congress*] (LCLS)

WMMW....... Meriden, CT [*AM radio station call letters*]

WMMX .... Fairborn, OH [*AM radio station call letters*]

WMMZ....... Ocala, FL [*FM radio station call letters*]

WMN .... Maroantsetra [*Madagascar*] [*Airport symbol*] (OAG)

WMN .... Winnemucca [*Nevada*] [*Seismograph station code, US Geological Survey*] [*Closed*] (SEIS)

WMNA .... Gretna, VA [*AM radio station call letters*]

WMNA-FM ... Gretna, VA [*FM radio station call letters*]

WMNB....... North Adams, MA [*AM radio station call letters*]

WMNB-FM ... North Adams, MA [*FM radio station call letters*]

WMNC .... Morganton, NC [*AM radio station call letters*]

WMNE .... Menomonie, WI [*AM radio station call letters*]

WMNF .... Tampa, FL [*FM radio station call letters*]

WMNG....... Northwest General Hospital, Milwaukee, WI [*Library symbol*] [*Library of Congress*] (LCLS)

WMNI .... Columbus, OH [*AM radio station call letters*]

WMNJ........ Madison, NJ [*FM radio station call letters*]

Wmn Lib .... Women's Liberation [*A publication*]

WMNR .... Monroe, CT [*FM radio station call letters*]

WMNS....... Olean, NY [*AM radio station call letters*]

WMNS....... William B. McGuire Nuclear Station (NRCH)

WMNT .... Manati, PR [*AM radio station call letters*]

WMNX-FM ... Tallahassee, FL [*FM radio station call letters*]

WMNZ .... Montezuma, GA [*AM radio station call letters*]

WMO .... White Mountain [*Alaska*] [*Airport symbol*] (OAG)

WMO .... White Mountain, AK [*Location identifier*] [*FAA*] (FAAL)

WMO .... Wichita Mountains Array [*Oklahoma*] [*Seismograph station code, US Geological Survey*] [*Closed*] (SEIS)

WMO .... Wing Maintenance Officer

WMO .... World Meteorological Organization [*See also OMM*] [*Geneva, Switzerland*] [*United Nations*] (EA-IO)

WMOA....... Marietta, OH [*AM radio station call letters*]

WMOB....... Mobile, AL [*AM radio station call letters*]

WMO Bull... WMO [*World Meteorological Organization*] Bulletin [*A publication*]

WMOC........ Chattanooga, TN [*AM radio station call letters*]

WMOD........ Melbourne, FL [*Television station call letters*]

WMOG........ Brunswick, GA [*AM radio station call letters*]

WMOH........ Hamilton, OH [*AM radio station call letters*]

WMOI......... Monmouth, IL [*FM radio station call letters*]

WMOK....... Metropolis, IL [*AM radio station call letters*]

WMoM....... Monroe Clinic, Monroe, WI [*Library symbol*] [*Library of Congress*] (LCLS)

WMON....... Montgomery, WV [*AM radio station call letters*]

WMOO....... Mobile, AL [*AM radio station call letters*]

WMOP....... Ocala, FL [*AM radio station call letters*]

WMO Publ ... WMO [*World Meteorological Organization*] Publication [*A publication*]

WMOR....... Morehead, KY [*AM radio station call letters*]

WMOR....... Westmoreland Coal [*NASDAQ symbol*] (NQ)

WMO Rep Mar Sci Aff ... World Meteorological Organization. Reports on Marine Science Affairs [*A publication*]

WMOR-FM ... Morehead, KY [*FM radio station call letters*]

WMOS....... Bath, ME [*FM radio station call letters*]

WMoS .... Saint Clare Hospital, Monroe, WI [*Library symbol*] [*Library of Congress*] (LCLS)

WMO Spec Environ Rep ... World Meteorological Organization. Special Environmental Report [*A publication*]

WMOT....... Murfreesboro, TN [*FM radio station call letters*]

WMO Tech Note ... World Meteorological Organization. Technical Note [*A publication*]

WMOU....... Berlin, NH [*FM radio station call letters*]

WMOV....... Ravenswood, WV [*AM radio station call letters*]

WMOX....... Meridian, MS [*AM radio station call letters*]

WMP.......... War and Mobilization Plan [*Air Force documents*]

WMP.......... Waste Management Paper [*British*]

WMP.......... Weapon Monitor Panel (MCD)

WMP.......... Weather Modification Program

WMP.......... Wiener Mapping Procedure

WMP.......... With Much Pleasure [*Meaning, "We accept the invitation"*]

WmP.......... World Microfilms Publications, London, United Kingdom [*Library symbol*] [*Library of Congress*] (LCLS)

WMPA .... Women's Military Pilots Association (EA)

WMPB .... Baltimore, MD [*Television station call letters*]

WMPC....... Lapeer, MI [*AM radio station call letters*]

WMPC....... War Materiel Procurement Capability (AFIT)

WMPCE...... World Meeting Planners Congress and Exposition [*Defunct*] (EA)

WMPCES(P) ... War Manpower Commission Employment Stabilization (Plan) [*Terminated, 1945*]

WMPF........ Charlotte, NC [*AM radio station call letters*]

WMPG....... Gorham, ME [*FM radio station call letters*]

WMPH....... Wilmington, DE [*FM radio station call letters*]

WM & PHF ... Waste Management and Personal Hygiene Facility [*NASA*] (KSC)

WMPI........ Scottsburg, IN [*FM radio station call letters*]

WMPI........ Women of the Motion Picture Industry, International

WMPL........ Hancock, MI [*AM radio station call letters*]

WMPL........ Western Maryland Public Libraries Regional Resource Center [*Library network*]

WMPL........ World Mission Prayer League (EA)

WMPM....... Smithfield, NC [*AM radio station call letters*]

WMPO....... Middleport-Pomeroy, OH [*AM radio station call letters*]

WMPO....... Weather Modification Program Office [*Marine science*] (MSC)

WMPO-FM ... Middleport-Pomeroy, OH [*FM radio station call letters*]

WMPP .... Chicago Heights, IL [*AM radio station call letters*]

WMPR .... Jackson, MS [*FM radio station call letters*]

WMPS .... Millington, TN [*AM radio station call letters*]

WMPT .... Annapolis, MD [*Television station call letters*]

WMPV-TV ... Mobile, AL [*Television station call letters*]

WMPX .... Midland, MI [*AM radio station call letters*]

WMPZ .... Soperton, GA [*AM radio station call letters*]

WMQ .... Quarles & Brady, Law Library, Milwaukee, WI [*Library symbol*] [*Library of Congress*] (LCLS)

WMQ .... Westmount Public Library [*UTLAS symbol*]

WMQ .... William and Mary Quarterly [*A publication*]

W & M Q ... William and Mary Quarterly [*A publication*]

WMQ .... Wulumuchi [*Republic of China*] [*Seismograph station code, US Geological Survey*] (SEIS)

WMQC....... Westover, WV [*FM radio station call letters*]

WMQM ...... Memphis, TN [*AM radio station call letters*]

WMQT .... Ishpeming, MI [*FM radio station call letters*]

WMR.......... Mananara [*Madagascar*] [*Airport symbol*] (OAG)

WMR.......... Reinhart, Boerner, Van Deuren, Norris and Rieselbach, Law Library, Milwaukee, WI [*Library symbol*] [*Library of Congress*] (LCLS)

WMR.......... Wake Measurements RADAR [*Army*] (MCD)

WMR.......... War Maintenance Reserve [*British*]

WMR.......... War Materiel Requirement (AFIT)

WMR.......... Water-Moderated Reactor

WMR.......... Wideband Multichannel Receiver

WMR.......... William and Mary Review of Virginia Law (DLA)

WMR.......... Woomera Missile Range [*Australia*]

WMR.......... World Medical Relief [*Detroit, MI*] (EA)

WMRA....... Harrisonburg, VA [*FM radio station call letters*]

WMRB .... Greenville, SC [*AM radio station call letters*]

WMRC........ Milford, MA [*AM radio station call letters*]

WMRC .... War Minerals Relief Commission [*Department of the Interior*] [*Abolished, 1940*]   (EGAO)
WMRE .... Boston, MA [*AM radio station call letters*]
WMRF-FM ... Lewistown, PA [*FM radio station call letters*]
WMRI .... Marion, IN [*FM radio station call letters*]
WMRK .... Selma, AL [*AM radio station call letters*]
WMRL .... Water Management Research Laboratory [*Department of Agriculture*]
WMRN .... Marion, OH [*AM radio station call letters*]
WMRN-FM ... Marion, OH [*FM radio station call letters*]
WMRO .... Aurora, IL [*AM radio station call letters*]
Wm Rob ..... William Robinson's English Admiralty Reports [*1838-52*]   (DLA)
Wm Rob Adm ... William Robinson's English Admiralty Reports   (DLA)
WMRQ .... Boston, MA [*FM radio station call letters*]
WMRS .... Laconia, NH [*AM radio station call letters*]
WMRS .... White Mountain Research Station [*University of California, Los Angeles*] [*Research center*]   (RCD)
WMRT .... Marietta, OH [*FM radio station call letters*]
WMRV .... Endicott, NY [*FM radio station call letters*]
WMRY .... East St. Louis, IL [*FM radio station call letters*]
WMRZ .... Moline, IL [*AM radio station call letters*]
WMS .... Warehouse Material Stores   (AAG)
WMS .... Waste Management System   (MCD)
WMS .... Water Management Section [*Apollo*] [*NASA*]
WMS .... Weapons Monitoring System
WMS .... Weather Mapping System
WMS .... Wechsler Memory Scale [*Neuropsychological test*]
WMS .... Wesleyan Missionary Society
WMS .... West Middle School [*South Carolina*] [*Seismograph station code, US Geological Survey*]   (SEIS)
WMS .... Whaling Museum Society   (EA)
WMS .... Wilderness Medical Society [*Port Reyes Station, CA*]   (EA)
WMS .... Willem Mengelberg Society   (EA)
WMS .... William Morris Society [*Later, WMS/AB*]   (EA)
WMS .... Wind Measuring System
WMS .... WMS Industries, Inc. [*Formerly, Williams Electronics*] [*NYSE symbol*]
WMS .... Women for a Meaningful Summit [*Washington, DC*]   (EA)
WMS .... Women in the Medical Service [*Army*]
WMS .... Women's Medical Specialist
WMS .... Women's Missionary Society, AME Church   (EA)
WMS .... Work Measurement System [*Postal Service*]
WM & S ...... Work Methods and Standards
WMS .... World Magnetic Survey [*Defunct*]
WMS .... World Mariculture Society   (EA)
WmS .... World Microfilms Division, Oyez Equipment Ltd., London, United Kingdom [*Library symbol*] [*Library of Congress*]   (LCLS)
WMSA .... Massena, NY [*AM radio station call letters*]
WMSA .... Saint Anthony Hospital, Milwaukee, WI [*Library symbol*] [*Library of Congress*]   (LCLS)
WMS/AB .... William Morris Society, American Branch [*Amherst, MA*]   (EA)
Wms Ann Reg ... Williams' Annual Register [*New York*]   (DLA)
Wms Bank ... [*R. V.*] Williams on Bankruptcy [*17 eds.*] [*1870-1958*]   (DLA)
Wms & Bruce ... [*R. G.*] Williams and [*Sir G.*] Bruce's Admiralty Practice [*3 eds.*] [*1865-1902*]   (DLA)
WMSC .... Upper Montclair, NJ [*FM radio station call letters*]
WMSC .... Weather Message Switching Center
WMSC .... White Mountain Scenic Railroad [*AAR code*]
WMSC .... Women's Medical Specialists Corps
WMSE .... Milwaukee School of Engineering, Walter Schroeder Library, Milwaukee, WI [*Library symbol*] [*Library of Congress*]   (LCLS)
WMSE .... Milwaukee, WI [*FM radio station call letters*]
Wms Ex ...... Williams on Executors [*15th ed.*] [*1970*]   (DLA)
Wms Exors ... [*E. V.*] Williams on Executors [*13 eds.*] [*1832-1953*]   (DLA)
Wms Ex'rs ... [*E. V.*] Williams on Executors [*13 eds.*] [*1832-1953*]   (DLA)
Wms Exs .... [*E. V.*] Williams on Executors [*13 eds.*] [*1832-1953*]   (DLA)
WMSF .... Saint Francis Seminary, Milwaukee, WI [*Library symbol*] [*Library of Congress*]   (LCLS)
WMSFH ...... Saint Francis Hospital, Milwaukee, WI [*Library symbol*] [*Library of Congress*]   (LCLS)
WMSFT ...... Wormshaft
WMSG .... Oakland, MD [*AM radio station call letters*]
WMSI .... Jackson, MS [*FM radio station call letters*]
WMSI .... Western Management Science Institute [*University of California*]   (KSC)
WMSI .... Williams Industries [*NASDAQ symbol*]   (NQ)
WMSJ .... Saint Joseph's Hospital, Milwaukee, WI [*Library symbol*] [*Library of Congress*]   (LCLS)
WMSJ .... William Morris Society. Journal [*A publication*]
WMSK .... Morganfield, KY [*AM radio station call letters*]
WMSKF ...... William Morris Society and Kelmscott Fellowship   (EA)
WMSK-FM ... Morganfield, KY [*FM radio station call letters*]
WMSL .... Decatur, AL [*AM radio station call letters*]
WMSL .... Saint Luke's Hospital, Milwaukee, WI [*Library symbol*] [*Library of Congress*]   (LCLS)
WMSL .... Wet Mock Simulated Launch [*NASA*]   (KSC)
WMSL .... Wichita Mountains Seismological Laboratory

WMSM .... Saint Mary's Hospital, Milwaukee, WI [*Library symbol*] [*Library of Congress*]   (LCLS)
Wms Mass ... Williams' Reports [*1 Massachusetts*]   (DLA)
WMSMi ...... Saint Michael Hospital, Milwaukee, WI [*Library symbol*] [*Library of Congress*]   (LCLS)
WMSMN ..... Saint Mary's School of Nursing, Milwaukee, WI [*Library symbol*] [*Library of Congress*]   (LCLS)
Wms Notes ... Williams' Notes to Saunders' Reports [*England*]   (DLA)
WMSN-TV ... Madison, WI [*Television station call letters*]
WMSO .... Collierville, TN [*AM radio station call letters*]
WMSO .... Wichita Mountains Seismological Observatory
WMSP .... Harrisburg, PA [*FM radio station call letters*]
Wms P .... Peere-Williams' English Chancery Reports [*1695-1736*]   (DLA)
Wms Peere ... Peere-Williams' English Chancery Reports   (DLA)
Wms PP ..... [*J.*] Williams on Personal Property [*18 eds.*] [*1848-1926*]   (DLA)
WMSQ .... Havelock, NC [*FM radio station call letters*]
WMSR .... Manchester, TN [*AM radio station call letters*]
W/(M² SR) ... Watts per Square Meter Steradian
WMSR-FM ... Manchester, TN [*FM radio station call letters*]
WMSRG ...... Weather-Modification Statistical Research Groups
Wms RP ..... [*J.*] Williams on Real Property [*24 eds.*] [*1824-1926*]   (DLA)
WMSS .... Middletown, PA [*FM radio station call letters*]
Wms Saund ... [*Sir Edmund*] Saunders' Reports, Edited by Williams [*85 English Reprint*]   (DLA)
Wms Saund (Eng) ... [*Sir Edmund*] Saunders' Reports, Edited by Williams [*85 English Reprint*]   (DLA)
WMST .... Mount Sterling, KY [*AM radio station call letters*]
WMST-FM ... Mount Sterling, KY [*FM radio station call letters*]
WMSU .... Hattiesburg, MS [*FM radio station call letters*]
Wms VT ..... Williams' Vermont Reports [*27-29 Vermont*]   (DLA)
WMSW .... Hatillo, PR [*AM radio station call letters*]
WMSWH ...... Southeastern Wisconsin Health Systems Agency, Health Science Library, Milwaukee, WI [*Library symbol*] [*Library of Congress*]   (LCLS)
WMSY-TV ... Marion, VA [*Television station call letters*]
WMT .... Cedar Rapids, IA [*AM radio station call letters*]
WMT .... Wal-Mart Stores, Inc. [*NYSE symbol*]
WMT .... Waste Monitor Tank   (IEEE)
WMT .... Weighing More Than
WMT .... West Meridian Time
WMT .... Western Motor Tariff Bureau, Los Angeles CA [*STAC*]
WMT .... Wet Metric Ton [*Waste management*]
WMTA .... Central City, KY [*AM radio station call letters*]
WMTB .... Western Motor Tariff Bureau
WMTB-FM ... Emmitsburg, MD [*FM radio station call letters*]
WMTC .... Milwaukee Technical College, Milwaukee, WI [*Library symbol*] [*Library of Congress*]   (LCLS)
WMTC .... Vancleve, KY [*AM radio station call letters*]
WMTC-N .... Milwaukee Area Technical College, North Campus Center Library, Mequon, WI [*Library symbol*] [*Library of Congress*]   (LCLS)
WMTC-S .... Milwaukee Area Technical College, South Campus Center Library, Oak Creek, WI [*Library symbol*] [*Library of Congress*]   (LCLS)
WMTC-W ... Milwaukee Area Technical College, West Campus Center Library, West Allis, WI [*Library symbol*] [*Library of Congress*]   (LCLS)
WMTD .... Hinton, WV [*AM radio station call letters*]
WMTD-FM ... Hinton, WV. [*FM radio station call letters*]
WMTE .... Manistee, MI [*AM radio station call letters*]
WMT-FM ..... Cedar Rapids, IA [*FM radio station call letters*]
WMTG .... Dearborn, MI [*FM radio station call letters*]
WMTH .... Park Ridge, IL [*FM radio station call letters*]
WMTH .... Westmeath [*County in Ireland*]   (ROG)
WMTJ .... Fajardo, PR [*Television station call letters*]
WMTK .... Littleton, NH [*FM radio station call letters*]
WMTL .... Leitchfield, KY [*AM radio station call letters*]
WMTM .... Moultrie, GA [*AM radio station call letters*]
WMTM-FM ... Moultrie, GA [*FM radio station call letters*]
WMTN .... Morristown, TN [*AM radio station call letters*]
WMTR .... Morristown, NJ [*AM radio station call letters*]
WMTR .... Wheeled Mobility Test Rig [*Army*]   (RDA)
WMTS .... Murfreesboro, TN [*AM radio station call letters*]
WMTT .... Willamette Industries [*NASDAQ symbol*]   (NQ)
WMTV .... Madison, WI [*Television station call letters*]
WMTW-TV ... Poland Spring, ME [*Television station call letters*]
WMTY .... Greenwood, SC [*AM radio station call letters*]
WMTZ .... Martinez, GA [*FM radio station call letters*]
WMU .... West Mountain [*Utah*] [*Seismograph station code, US Geological Survey*]   (SEIS)
WMU .... Western Michigan University
WMU .... Woman's Missionary Union   (EA)
WMU .... World Maritime University [*Malmo, Sweden*]
WMUA .... Amherst, MA [*FM radio station call letters*]
WMUB .... Oxford, OH [*FM radio station call letters*]
WMUC-FM ... College Park, MD [*FM radio station call letters*]
WMUF .... Paris, TN [*AM radio station call letters*]
WMUF .... Universal Foods Corp., Technical Information Services, Milwaukee, WI [*Library symbol*] [*Library of Congress*]   (LCLS)

WMUH.......	Allentown, PA [*FM radio station call letters*]
WMUK.......	Kalamazoo, MI [*FM radio station call letters*]
WMUL	Huntington, WV [*FM radio station call letters*]
WMUM.......	Marathon, FL [*FM radio station call letters*]
WMUR-TV ...	Manchester, NH [*Television station call letters*]
WMUS.......	Muskegon, MI [*AM radio station call letters*]
WMUSE......	World Markets for US Exports [*A publication*]
WMUS-FM ...	Muskegon, MI [*FM radio station call letters*]
WMUU.......	Greenville, SC [*AM radio station call letters*]
WMUU-FM ...	Greenville, SC [*FM radio station call letters*]
WMUW.......	Columbus, MS [*FM radio station call letters*]
WMUW.......	University of Wisconsin-Milwaukee, Milwaukee, WI [*Library symbol*] [*Library of Congress*] (LCLS)
WMUZ.......	Detroit, MI [*FM radio station call letters*]
WMV..........	Valuation Research Corp., Milwaukee, WI [*Library symbol*] [*Library of Congress*] (LCLS)
WMV..........	War Munition Volunteers [*British*] [*World War I*]
WMVA.......	Martinsville, VA [*AM radio station call letters*]
WMVA-FM ...	Martinsville, VA [*FM radio station call letters*]
WMVB-FM ...	Millville, NJ [*FM radio station call letters*]
WMVG.......	Milledgeville, GA [*AM radio station call letters*]
WMVI........	Mechanicville, NY [*AM radio station call letters*]
WMVO.......	Mount Vernon, OH [*AM radio station call letters*]
WMVO-FM ...	Mount Vernon, OH [*FM radio station call letters*]
WMVP	Greenfield, WI [*AM radio station call letters*]
WMVP	Paducah, KY [*Television station call letters*]
WMVQ.......	Amsterdam, NY [*FM radio station call letters*]
WMVR.......	Sidney, OH [*AM radio station call letters*]
WMVR-FM ...	Sidney, OH [*FM radio station call letters*]
WMVS	Milwaukee, WI [*Television station call letters*]
WMVT	Milwaukee, WI [*Television station call letters*]
WMVV.......	McDonough, GA [*FM radio station call letters*]
WMVY.......	Tisburg, MA [*FM radio station call letters*]
WMW..........	Whyte & Hirschboeck, Law Library, Milwaukee, WI [*Library symbol*] [*Library of Congress*] (LCLS)
WMW..........	Women's Media Workshop [*Defunct*] (EA)
WMWA	Glenview, IL [*FM radio station call letters*]
WMWC	Gardner, MA [*FM radio station call letters*]
WMWG	Weichselland, Mitteilungen des Westpreussischen Geschichtsvereins [*A publication*]
WMWHL	Wormwheel
WMWM......	Salem, MA [*FM radio station call letters*]
WMWN	[*The*] Weatherford, Mineral Wells & Northwestern Railway Co. [*AAR code*]
WMWOA	Wiener Medizinische Wochenschrift [*A publication*]
WMWV	Conway, NH [*FM radio station call letters*]
WMX..........	Wamena [*Indonesia*] [*Airport symbol*] (OAG)
WMX..........	Waste Management, Inc. [*NYSE symbol*]
WMX..........	Whirlpool, Massage, Exercise [*Medicine*]
WMXJ.......	Pompano Beach, FL [*FM radio station call letters*]
WMXM	Lake Forest, IL [*FM radio station call letters*]
WMXQ.......	Moncks Corner, SC [*FM radio station call letters*]
WMXY	Hogansville, GA [*AM radio station call letters*]
WMY..........	Wakamiya [*Japan*] [*Seismograph station code, US Geological Survey*] [*Closed*] (SEIS)
WMY..........	Weird Mystery [*A publication*]
WMYD	Rice Lake, WI [*AM radio station call letters*]
WMYF	Exeter, NH [*AM radio station call letters*]
WMYG	Braddock, PA [*FM radio station call letters*]
WMYK	Elizabeth City, NC [*FM radio station call letters*]
WMYM	Minocqua, WI [*AM radio station call letters*]
WMYN	Mayodan, NC [*AM radio station call letters*]
WMYQ.......	Newton, MS [*AM radio station call letters*]
WMYQ-FM ...	Newton, MS [*FM radio station call letters*]
WMYR.......	Fort Myers, FL [*AM radio station call letters*]
WMYS	New Bedford, MA [*FM radio station call letters*]
WMYU	Sevierville, TN [*FM radio station call letters*]
WMYX	Milwaukee, WI [*FM radio station call letters*]
WMZK	Traverse City, MI [*FM radio station call letters*]
WMZQ.......	Arlington, VA [*AM radio station call letters*]
WMZQ-FM ...	Washington, DC [*FM radio station call letters*]
WN	Calcutta Weekly Notes (DLA)
WN	George Weston Ltd. [*Toronto Stock Exchange symbol*] [*Vancouver Stock Exchange symbol*]
WN	Neenah Public Library, Neenah, WI [*Library symbol*] [*Library of Congress*] (LCLS)
WN	Nor-Fly A/S [*Norway*] [*ICAO designator*] (FAAC)
WN	Wake Newsletter [*A publication*]
WN	Washington [*Obsolete*] (ROG)
Wn.............	Washington Reports (DLA)
WN	Wawatay News [*Sioux Lookout, Ontario*] [*A publication*]
WN	Weekly Notes [*Legal*] [*British*]
WN	Weekly Notes of English Law Reports (DLA)
W & N	Weidenfeld & Nicolson [*Publisher*]
W/N..........	Weight Note [*Tea trade*] (ROG)
W-N	Well-Nourished [*Medicine*]
WN	White Noise
WN	Wiadomosci Numizmatyczne [*A publication*]
WN	Will Not
WN	Winch (AAG)
WN	Wisconsin [*Obsolete*] (ROG)
WN	Within (ROG)
WN	Work Notice (AAG)
WN	World Neighbors (EA)
WN	Wrong Number [*Telecommunications*] (TEL)
WN	Wynn's International, Inc. [*NYSE symbol*]
WNA..........	Napaskiak [*Alaska*] [*Airport symbol*] (OAG)
WNA..........	Napaskiak, AK [*Location identifier*] [*FAA*] (FAAL)
WNa..........	Nashotah House, Nashotah, WI [*Library symbol*] [*Library of Congress*] (LCLS)
WNA..........	Washington [*DC*] National Airport [*FAA*]
WNA..........	Wedge Nozzle Assembly
WNA..........	Welcome to the North Atlantic [*A publication*]
WNA..........	Winter, North Atlantic [*Vessel load line mark*]
WNAA.......	Greensboro, NC [*FM radio station call letters*]
WNAAA......	Women of the National Agricultural Aviation Association [*Darlington, SC*] (EA)
WNACFWB ...	Woman's National Auxiliary Convention of Free Will Baptists (EA)
WNAC-TV ...	Providence, RI [*Television station call letters*]
WNAE........	Warren, PA [*AM radio station call letters*]
WNAF........	Women's National Aquatic Forum (EA)
WNAH	Nashville, TN [*AM radio station call letters*]
WNAK	Nanticoke, PA [*AM radio station call letters*]
WNAL-TV	Gadsden, AL [*Television station call letters*]
WNAM.......	Neenah-Menasha, WI [*AM radio station call letters*]
WNAP........	Washington [*DC*] National Airport
WNAQ.......	Naugatuck, CT [*AM radio station call letters*]
WNAR.......	Biometric Society, Western North American Region (EA)
WNAS........	New Albany, IN [*FM radio station call letters*]
WNAT........	Natchez, MS [*AM radio station call letters*]
WNAV.......	Annapolis, MD [*FM radio station call letters*]
WNAX.......	Yankton, SD [*AM radio station call letters*]
WNAZ-FM ...	Nashville, TN [*FM radio station call letters*]
WNB	Will Not Be
WNB	Winter Navigation Board
WNBA........	Women's National Basketball Association [*Defunct*] (EA)
WNBA........	Women's National Book Association [*New York, NY*] (EA)
WNBC	New York, NY [*AM radio station call letters*]
WNBC-TV ...	New York, NY [*Television station call letters*]
WNBF........	Binghamton, NY [*AM radio station call letters*]
WNBG	Waynesboro, TN [*AM radio station call letters*]
WNBH........	New Bedford, MA [*AM radio station call letters*]
WNbH........	New Berlin Memorial Hospital, New Berlin, WI [*Library symbol*] [*Library of Congress*] (LCLS)
WNBI........	Park Falls, WI [*AM radio station call letters*]
WNBI-FM ...	Park Falls, WI [*FM radio station call letters*]
WNBK	New London, WI [*FM radio station call letters*]
WNBN	Meridian, MS [*AM radio station call letters*]
WNBR.......	Wildwood, NJ [*FM radio station call letters*]
WNBR.......	Wind Baron Corp. [*NASDAQ symbol*] (NQ)
WNBS........	Murray, KY [*AM radio station call letters*]
WNBT........	Wellsboro, PA [*AM radio station call letters*]
WNBT-FM ...	Wellsboro, PA [*FM radio station call letters*]
WNBY........	Newberry, MI [*AM radio station call letters*]
WNBY-FM ...	Newbury, MI [*FM radio station call letters*]
WNBZ........	Saranac Lake, NY [*AM radio station call letters*]
WNC..........	Naval War College, Newport, RI [*OCLC symbol*] (OCLC)
WNC..........	WAVES National Corporation [*An association*] (EA)
WNC..........	Weak Neutral Current [*Chemistry*]
WNC..........	Weekly Notes of Cases [*1874-99*] [*Pennsylvania*] (DLA)
WNC..........	Wencarro Resources Ltd. [*Vancouver Stock Exchange symbol*]
WNC..........	Wilmington [*North Carolina*] [*Seismograph station code, US Geological Survey*] (SEIS)
WNCA	Siler City, NC [*AM radio station call letters*]
WN (Calc) ...	Calcutta Weekly Notes (DLA)
WN Cas	Weekly Notes of Cases [*1874-99*] [*Pennsylvania*] (DLA)
WN Cas (PA) ...	Weekly Notes of Cases [*Pennsylvania*] (DLA)
WNCB	Duluth, MN [*FM radio station call letters*]
WNCC	Barnesboro, PA [*AM radio station call letters*]
WNCE	Lancaster, PA [*FM radio station call letters*]
WNCI........	Columbus, OH [*FM radio station call letters*]
WNCK	Woonsocket, RI [*FM radio station call letters*]
WNCM.......	Jacksonville, FL [*FM radio station call letters*]
WNCN	New York, NY [*FM radio station call letters*]
WNCO	Ashland, OH [*AM radio station call letters*]
WNCO	Winco Petroleum Corp. [*NASDAQ symbol*] (NQ)
WNCO-FM ...	Ashland, OH [*FM radio station call letters*]
WN Covers (NSW) ...	Weekly Notes Covers (New South Wales) [*A publication*]
WNC (PA) ...	Weekly Notes of Cases [*1874-99*] [*Pennsylvania*] (DLA)
WNCQ........	Watertown, NY [*FM radio station call letters*]
WNCR	St. Pauls, NC [*AM radio station call letters*]
WNCS........	Montpelier, VT [*FM radio station call letters*]
WNCT........	Greenville, NC [*AM radio station call letters*]
WNCT-FM ...	Greenville, NC [*FM radio station call letters*]
WNCT-TV...	Greenville, NC [*Television station call letters*]
WNCX........	Cleveland, OH [*FM radio station call letters*]
WND..........	Wind (KSC)
WND..........	Windham [*New York*] [*Seismograph station code, US Geological Survey*] (SEIS)
WND..........	Wound (MSA)

Wn 2d .... Washington Reports, Second Series   (DLA)
WNDA .... Huntsville, AL [*FM radio station call letters*]
WNDB .... Daytona Beach, FL [*AM radio station call letters*]
WNDC .... Women's National Democratic Club   (EA)
WNDE .... Indianapolis, IN [*AM radio station call letters*]
WNDH .... Napoleon, OH [*FM radio station call letters*]
WNDI .... Sullivan, IN [*AM radio station call letters*]
WNDI-FM ... Sullivan, IN [*FM radio station call letters*]
WNDLS ...... Windlass
WNDN-FM ... Salisbury, NC [*FM radio station call letters*]
WNDO .... Weather Network Duty Officer [*Air Force*]   (AFM)
WNDR .... Syracuse, NY [*AM radio station call letters*]
WNDR .... Winder
WNDS .... Derry, NH [*Television station call letters*]
WNDS .... Windsor Industries [*NASDAQ symbol*]   (NQ)
WNDU .... South Bend, IN [*AM radio station call letters*]
WNDU-FM ... South Bend, IN [*FM radio station call letters*]
WNDU-TV ... South Bend, IN [*Television station call letters*]
WNDY .... Crawfordsville, IN [*FM radio station call letters*]
WNDZ .... Portage, IN [*AM radio station call letters*]
WNE .... Western New England College, Springfield, MA [*OCLC symbol*]   (OCLC)
WNEA .... Newnan, GA [*AM radio station call letters*]
WNEB .... Worcester, MA [*AM radio station call letters*]
WNEC .... Western New England College [*Springfield, MA*]
WNEC-FM ... Henniker, NH [*FM radio station call letters*]
WNED-FM ... Buffalo, NY [*FM radio station call letters*]
WNED-TV ... Buffalo, NY [*Television station call letters*]
WNEG .... Toccoa, GA [*AM radio station call letters*]
WNEG-TV ... Toccoa, GA [*Television station call letters*]
WNEH .... Greenwood, SC [*Television station call letters*]
WNEK-FM ... Springfield, MA [*FM radio station call letters*]
WNEL .... Caguas, PR [*AM radio station call letters*]
WNeIH .... New London Community Hospital, Health Science Library, New London, WI [*Library symbol*] [*Library of Congress*]   (LCLS)
WNEM-TV ... Bay City, MI [*Television station call letters*]
WN (Eng) ... Weekly Notes of English Law Reports   (DLA)
WNEO-TV ... Alliance, OH [*Television station call letters*]
WNEP-TV ... Scranton, PA [*Television station call letters*]
WNEQ-TV ... Buffalo, NY [*Television station call letters*]
WNER .... Live Oak, FL [*AM radio station call letters*]
WNER .... Winner's Corp. [*NASDAQ symbol*]   (NQ)
WNES .... Central City, KY [*AM radio station call letters*]
WNET .... Newark, NJ [*Television station call letters*]
WNEV-TV ... Boston, MA [*Television station call letters*]
WNEW .... New York, NY [*AM radio station call letters*]
WNEW-FM ... New York, NY [*FM radio station call letters*]
WNEX .... Macon, GA [*AM radio station call letters*]
WNEZ .... Aiken, SC [*FM radio station call letters*]
WNF .... Well-Nourished Female [*Medicine*]
WNF .... [*The*] Winfield Railroad Co. [*AAR code*]
WNFA .... Port Huron, MI [*FM radio station call letters*]
WNFGA ...... Woman's National Farm and Garden Association   (EA)
WNFI .... Palatka, FL [*FM radio station call letters*]
WNFL .... Green Bay, WI [*AM radio station call letters*]
WNFM .... Reedsburg, WI [*FM radio station call letters*]
WNFM .... World Nuclear Fuel Market   (NRCH)
WNFO .... Fair Bluff, NC [*AM radio station call letters*]
WNFR .... Winifrede Railroad Co. [*AAR code*]
WNFT .... Jacksonville, FL [*Television station call letters*]
WNG .... Wang Laboratories, Inc., Lowell, MA [*OCLC symbol*]   (OCLC)
WNG .... Warning   (AFM)
WNG .... Weighing
WNG .... Wingst [*Federal Republic of Germany*] [*Geomagnetic observatory code*]
WNGA .... Wholesale Nursery Growers of America   (EA)
WNGC .... Athens, GA [*AM radio station call letters*]
WNGC .... Western Natural Gas [*NASDAQ symbol*]   (NQ)
WNGGA ..... Welsh National Gymanfa Ganu Association   (EA)
WNGO .... Mayfield, KY [*AM radio station call letters*]
WNGS .... West Palm Beach, FL [*FM radio station call letters*]
WNGZ .... Montour Falls, NY [*FM radio station call letters*]
WNH .... Whiteface [*New Hampshire*] [*Seismograph station code, US Geological Survey*]   (SEIS)
WNHC .... New Haven, CT [*AM radio station call letters*]
WNHP .... Washington Natural Heritage Program [*Washington State Department of Natural Resources*] [*Olympia*] [*Information service*]   (EISS)
WNHP .... Wyoming Natural Heritage Program [*Wyoming State Department of Environmental Quality*] [*Cheyenne*] [*Information service*]   (EISS)
WNHS .... Portsmouth, VA [*FM radio station call letters*]
WNHT .... Concord, NH [*Television station call letters*]
WNHU .... West Haven, CT [*FM radio station call letters*]
WNHV .... White River Junction, VT [*AM radio station call letters*]
WNI .... Wang Institute of Graduate Studies, Tyngsboro, MA [*OCLC symbol*]   (OCLC)
WNI .... Women's National Institute [*Defunct*]   (EA)
WNIB .... Chicago, IL [*FM radio station call letters*]
WNIC-FM ... Dearborn, MI [*FM radio station call letters*]

WNIK .... Arecibo, PR [*AM radio station call letters*]
WNIK-FM ... Arecibo, PR [*FM radio station call letters*]
WNIL .... Niles, MI [*AM radio station call letters*]
WNIN .... Evansville, IN [*FM radio station call letters*]
WNIN .... Evansville, IN [*Television station call letters*]
WNINTEL ... Warning Notice: Sensitive Intelligence Sources and Methods Involved   (MCD)
WNIO .... Niles, OH [*AM radio station call letters*]
WNIR .... Kent, OH [*FM radio station call letters*]
WNIS .... Portsmouth, VA [*AM radio station call letters*]
WNIT-TV ... South Bend, IN [*Television station call letters*]
WNIU-FM ... De Kalb, IL [*FM radio station call letters*]
WNIX .... Greenville, MS [*AM radio station call letters*]
WNIZ-FM ... Zion, IL [*FM radio station call letters*]
WNJ .... Whitman Numismatic Journal [*A publication*]
WNJB .... New Brunswick, NJ [*Television station call letters*]
WNJC-FM ... Senatobia, MS [*FM radio station call letters*]
WNJM .... Montclair, NJ [*Television station call letters*]
WNJO .... Seaside Park, NJ [*AM radio station call letters*]
WNJR .... Newark, NJ [*AM radio station call letters*]
WNJS .... Camden, NJ [*Television station call letters*]
WNJT .... Trenton, NJ [*Television station call letters*]
WNJU-TV ... Linden, NJ [*Television station call letters*]
WNJX-TV ... Mayaguez, PR [*Television station call letters*]
WNJY .... Riviera Beach, FL [*FM radio station call letters*]
WNKC .... Kimberly-Clark Corp., Research and Engineering Library, Neenah, WI [*Library symbol*] [*Library of Congress*]   (LCLS)
WNKJ .... Hopkinsville, KY [*FM radio station call letters*]
WNKO .... Newark, OH [*FM radio station call letters*]
WNKS .... Columbus, GA [*FM radio station call letters*]
WNKU .... Highland Heights, KY [*FM radio station call letters*]
WNKV .... St. Johnsbury, VT [*FM radio station call letters*]
WNKY .... Neon, KY [*AM radio station call letters*]
WNKZ .... Madison, TN [*AM radio station call letters*]
WNL .... Nicolet College, Learning Resources Center, Rhinelander, WI [*OCLC symbol*]   (OCLC)
WNL .... Waveguide Nitrogen Load
Wn L .... Wayne Law Review [*A publication*]
WNL .... Within Normal Limits [*Medicine*]
WNLA .... Indianola, MS [*AM radio station call letters*]
WNLA .... Witwatersrand Native Labour Association [*Nyasaland*]
WNLA-FM ... Indianola, MS [*FM radio station call letters*]
WNLB .... Rocky Mount, VA [*AM radio station call letters*]
WNLC .... New London, CT [*AM radio station call letters*]
WNLE .... Fernandina Beach, FL [*FM radio station call letters*]
WNLF .... Charlotte, MI [*AM radio station call letters*]
WNLK .... Norwalk, CT [*AM radio station call letters*]
WNLN .... Western Nigeria Legal Notice   (DLA)
WNLR .... Churchville, VA [*AM radio station call letters*]
Wn LR .... Washington Law Review [*A publication*]
Wn LR .... Wayne Law Review [*A publication*]
WNLR .... Western Nigeria Law Reports   (DLA)
WNLSC ..... Women's National Land Service Corps [*British*] [*World War I*]
WNLT .... Clearwater, FL [*FM radio station call letters*]
WNM .... Washington National Monument
WNM .... Well-Nourished Male [*Medicine*]
WNM .... White Noise Making [*Psychology*]
WNMA .... Washington National Monument Association   (EA)
WNMB .... North Myrtle Beach, SC [*FM radio station call letters*]
WNMC .... Weather Network Management Center [*Air Force*]   (AFM)
WNMC .... Wincom Corporation [*NASDAQ symbol*]   (NQ)
WNMC-FM ... Traverse City, MI [*FM radio station call letters*]
WNMH .... Northfield, MA [*FM radio station call letters*]
WN Misc ... Weekly Notes, Miscellaneous   (DLA)
WNMT .... Garden City, GA [*AM radio station call letters*]
WNMU .... Marquette, MI [*FM radio station call letters*]
WNMU-TV ... Marquette, MI [*Television station call letters*]
WNN .... World News Network [*In Muriel Dobbin's novel "Going Live"*]
WNNC .... Newton, NC [*AM radio station call letters*]
WNNE-TV ... Hartford, VT [*Television station call letters*]
WNNJ .... Newton, NJ [*AM radio station call letters*]
WNNK .... Harrisburg, PA [*FM radio station call letters*]
WNNN .... Canton, NJ [*FM radio station call letters*]
WNNO .... Wisconsin Dells, WI [*AM radio station call letters*]
WNNO-FM ... Wisconsin Dells, WI [*FM radio station call letters*]
WNNR .... Hamden, CT [*AM radio station call letters*]
WNNR Spes Versl ... WNNR [*Suid-Afrikaanse Wetenskaplike en Nywerheidnavorsingsraad*] Spesiale Verslag [*A publication*]
WNNS .... Springfield, IL [*FM radio station call letters*]
WN (NSW) ... Weekly Notes (New South Wales) [*A publication*]
WNNT .... Warsaw, VA [*AM radio station call letters*]
WNNT-FM ... Warsaw, VA [*FM radio station call letters*]
WNO .... Welsh National Opera
WNO .... Wharton & Northern Railroad Co. [*Later, WHN*] [*AAR code*]
WNO .... Wrong Number [*Telecommunications*]   (TEL)
WNOC .... Wake Forest, NC [*AM radio station call letters*]
WNOD .... Jamestown, NY [*Television station call letters*]
WNOE .... New Orleans, LA [*AM radio station call letters*]
WNOE-FM ... New Orleans, LA [*FM radio station call letters*]

WNOG .... Naples, FL [*AM radio station call letters*]
WNOI .... Flora, IL [*FM radio station call letters*]
WNOK .... Columbia, SC [*AM radio station call letters*]
WNOK-FM ... Columbia, SC [*FM radio station call letters*]
WNOL-TV... New Orleans, LA [*Television station call letters*]
WNOO .... Chattanooga, TN [*AM radio station call letters*]
WNOO-FM ... Soddy-Daisy, TN [*FM radio station call letters*]
WNOP .... Newport, KY [*AM radio station call letters*]
WNOR .... Norfolk, VA [*AM radio station call letters*]
WNOS .... New Bern, NC [*AM radio station call letters*]
WNOV .... Milwaukee, WI [*AM radio station call letters*]
WNOW .... Mint Hill, NC [*AM radio station call letters*]
WNOX .... Knoxville, TN [*AM radio station call letters*]
WNP .... Naga [*Phillipines*] [*Airport symbol*]   (OAG)
WNP .... Washington Nuclear Plant   (NRCH)
WNP .... Will Not Proceed
WNP .... Will Not Process
WNP .... Wire Nonpayment
WNPB-TV ... Morgantown, WV [*Television station call letters*]
WNPC .... Newport, TN [*AM radio station call letters*]
WNPC .... Women's National Press Club [*Later, WPC*]   (EA)
WNPE-TV ... Watertown, NY [*Television station call letters*]
WNPI-TV ... Norwood, NY [*Television station call letters*]
WNPL-TV... Naples, FL [*Television station call letters*]
WNPQ .... New Philadelphia, OH [*FM radio station call letters*]
WNPR .... Norwich, CT [*FM radio station call letters*]
WNPT .... Tuscaloosa, AL [*AM radio station call letters*]
WNPV .... Lansdale, PA [*AM radio station call letters*]
WNPW .... Wide, Notched P Wave [*Cardiology*]
WNQM .... Nashville, TN [*AM radio station call letters*]
WNQQ .... Blairsville, PA [*FM radio station call letters*]
WNQV .... Caldwell, OH [*FM radio station call letters*]
WNR .... Weapons Neutron Research Facility [*Los Alamos*]
WNR .... Western NORAD Region
WNR .... Windorah [*Australia*] [*Airport symbol*]   (OAG)
WNR .... Winners Corp. [*NYSE symbol*]
WNR .... World New Religion [*An association*]   (EA)
WNRC .... Dudley, MA [*FM radio station call letters*]
WNRC .... Washington National Records Center [*GSA*]   (AABC)
WNRC .... Women's National Republican Club   (EA)
WNRCEN.... Washington National Records Center [*GSA*]
WNRE .... Circleville, OH [*AM radio station call letters*]
WNRE .... Whiteshell Nuclear Research Establishment [*Atomic Energy of Canada Ltd.*] [*Research center*]
WNRE-FM ... Circleville, OH [*FM radio station call letters*]
WNRG .... Grundy, VA [*AM radio station call letters*]
WNRI .... Woonsocket, RI [*AM radio station call letters*]
WNRK .... Newark, DE [*AM radio station call letters*]
WNRN .... Virginia Beach, VA [*FM radio station call letters*]
WNRR .... Bellevue, OH [*FM radio station call letters*]
WNRS .... Saline, MI [*AM radio station call letters*]
WNRT .... Manati, PR [*FM radio station call letters*]
WNRV .... Narrows-Pearisburg, VA [*AM radio station call letters*]
WNRW .... Winston/Salem, NC [*Television station call letters*]
WNS .... Nawab Shah [*Pakistan*] [*Airport symbol*]   (OAG)
WNS .... Women's News Service
WNS .... Worldwide News Service. Jewish Telegraphic Agency   (BJA)
WNS .... Wren Resources Ltd. [*Vancouver Stock Exchange symbol*]
WNSA .... Woman's National Sabbath Alliance [*Defunct*]
WNSB .... Norfolk, VA [*FM radio station call letters*]
WNSC-FM ... Rock Hill, SC [*FM radio station call letters*]
WNSC-TV ... Rock Hill, SC [*Television station call letters*]
WNSEA ...... Wood Naval Stores Export Association
WNSH .... Beverly, MA [*AM radio station call letters*]
WNSL .... A. W. Wright Nuclear Structure Laboratory [*Yale University*] [*Research center*]   (RCD)
WNSL-FM ... Laurel, MS [*FM radio station call letters*]
WNSN .... South Bend, IN [*FM radio station call letters*]
WNSR .... New York, NY [*FM radio station call letters*]
WNST .... Winston Mills, Inc. [*NASDAQ symbol*]   (NQ)
WNT .... Washington National Corp. [*NYSE symbol*]
WNT .... Waste Neutralization Tank [*Nuclear energy*]   (NRCH)
WNT .... Waste Neutralizer Tank   (IEEE)
WNT .... World News Tonight [*Television program*]
WNTC .... Theda Clark Memorial Hospital, Neenah, WI [*Library symbol*] [*Library of Congress*]   (LCLS)
WNTE .... Mansfield, PA [*FM radio station call letters*]
WNTF .... Western Naval Task Force [*Navy*]
WNTH .... Winnetka, IL [*FM radio station call letters*]
WNTI .... Hackettstown, NJ [*FM radio station call letters*]
WNTL .... Winterhalter, Inc. [*NASDAQ symbol*]   (NQ)
WNTM .... Detroit, MI [*FM radio station call letters*]
WNTN .... Newton, MA [*AM radio station call letters*]
WNTQ .... Syracuse, NY [*FM radio station call letters*]
WNTR .... Silver Spring, MD [*AM radio station call letters*]
Wntr Sldr ... Winter Soldier [*A publication*]
WNTS .... Indianapolis, IN [*AM radio station call letters*]
WNTT .... Tazewell, TN [*AM radio station call letters*]
WNTV .... Greenville, SC [*Television station call letters*]
WNTXD ...... Wentex International, Inc. [*NASDAQ symbol*]   (NQ)
WNTY .... Southington, CT [*AM radio station call letters*]

WNTZ .... Natchez, MS [*Television station call letters*]
WNU .... Western Newspaper Union
WNUB-FM ... Northfield, VT [*FM radio station call letters*]
WNUE........ Fort Walton Beach, FL [*AM radio station call letters*]
WNUR .... Evanston, IL [*FM radio station call letters*]
WNUS .... Belpre, OH [*FM radio station call letters*]
WNUV-TV... Baltimore, MD [*Television station call letters*]
WNUZ .... Talladega, AL [*AM radio station call letters*]
WNV .... Wehrmachtnachrichtenverbindungen [*Armed Forces Signal Communications*] [*German military - World War II*]
WNV .... West Nile Virus
WNVA .... Norton, VA [*AM radio station call letters*]
WNVA-FM ... Norton, VA [*FM radio station call letters*]
WNVC .... Fairfax, VA [*Television station call letters*]
WNVI-FM ... North Vernon, IN [*FM radio station call letters*]
WNVL .... Nicholasville, KY [*AM radio station call letters*]
WNVT .... Goldvein, VA [*Television station call letters*]
WNVZ .... Norfolk, VA [*FM radio station call letters*]
WNW .... Superior Public Library, Superior, WI [*OCLC symbol*]   (OCLC)
WNW .... Wenatchee [*Washington*] [*Seismograph station code, US Geological Survey*]   (SEIS)
WNW .... West-Northwest
WNWC .... Madison, WI [*FM radio station call letters*]
WNWI .... Valparaiso, IN [*AM radio station call letters*]
WNWK .... Newark, NJ [*FM radio station call letters*]
WNWN .... Coldwater, MI [*FM radio station call letters*]
WNWO-TV ... Toledo, OH [*Television station call letters*]
WNWRN ...... West-Northwestern [*Meteorology*]   (FAAC)
WNWS .... South Miami, FL [*AM radio station call letters*]
WNWWD ...... West-Northwestward [*Meteorology*]   (FAAC)
WNXT .... Portsmouth, OH [*AM radio station call letters*]
WNXT-FM ... Portsmouth, OH [*FM radio station call letters*]
WNY .... Washington [*DC*] Naval Yard
WNY .... Wilmington [*New York*] [*Seismograph station code, US Geological Survey*]   (SEIS)
WNY .... Wynyard [*Australia*] [*Airport symbol*]   (OAG)
WNYB-TV... Buffalo, NY [*Television station call letters*]
WNYC .... New York, NY [*AM radio station call letters*]
WNYC-FM ... New York, NY [*FM radio station call letters*]
WNYC-TV ... New York, NY [*Television station call letters*]
WNYE .... New York, NY [*FM radio station call letters*]
WNYE-TV ... New York, NY [*Television station call letters*]
WNYG .... Babylon, NY [*AM radio station call letters*]
WNYHSL .... Western New York Health Science Librarians [*Library network*]
WNYK .... Nyack, NY [*FM radio station call letters*]
WNYLRC .... Western New York Library Resources Council [*Buffalo, NY*] [*Library network*]
WNYM .... New York, NY [*AM radio station call letters*]
WNYNRC .... Western New York Nuclear Research Center Reactor   (NRCH)
WNYR .... Rochester, NY [*AM radio station call letters*]
WNYS .... Buffalo, NY [*AM radio station call letters*]
WNYT .... Albany, NY [*Television station call letters*]
WNYU-FM ... New York, NY [*FM radio station call letters*]
WNYW .... New York, NY [*Television station call letters*]
WNYZ .... Utica, NY [*FM radio station call letters*]
WNZ .... Wairakei [*New Zealand*] [*Seismograph station code, US Geological Survey*]   (SEIS)
WNZE .... Plymouth, IN [*FM radio station call letters*]
WNZK .... Westland, MI [*AM radio station call letters*]
WNZR .... Mount Vernon, OH [*FM radio station call letters*]
WNZT .... Columbia, PA [*AM radio station call letters*]
WO .... Wait Order
WO .... Walk-Over [*British*]   (ROG)
WO .... Walkover
WO .... War Office [*British*]
WO .... War Orientation [*Navy*]
WO .... Warning Order
WO .... Warrant Officer [*Usually in combination with numbers to denote serviceman's grade*] [*Military*]
WO .... Wash Out [*Medicine*]
WO .... Washington Office [*FAA*]   (FAAC)
W/O............ Water-in-Oil
WO .... Water Outlet Gasket [*Automotive engineering*]
WO .... Welsh Office
WO .... Welt des Orients [*A publication*]
WO .... Western Operation
WO .... White Oval [*on Jupiter*]
WO .... Wind Offset
WO .... Wipe Out   (MSA)
WO .... Wireless Operator
WO .... Without   (AFM)
wo .... Wollastonite [*CIPW classification*] [*Geology*]
WO .... Women
WO .... Women Outdoors   (EA)
WO .... Women's Reserve, Ordnance Duties [*USNR officer designation*]
WO .... Work Order
WO .... Working Overseer   (ADA)
WO .... World Airways, Inc. [*ICAO designator*]   (FAAC)
WO .... World of Opera [*A publication*]
W/O............ Write-Off

WO .... Write Only
WO .... Write Out
W/O .... Written Order [*Medicine*]
WO1 .... Warrant Officer One [*Army*]
WOA .... Warrant Officers Association of the United States of America [*Defunct*] (EA)
WOA .... Washington Office on Africa (EA)
WOA .... Weapons Orientation Advanced (AFM)
WOA .... Work Order Authorization (MCD)
WOA .... World Airways, Inc. [*NYSE symbol*]
WOAB .... Ozark, AL [*FM radio station call letters*]
WOAC-TV ... Canton, OH [*Television station call letters*]
WOAD .... Jackson, MS [*AM radio station call letters*]
WOAI .... San Antonio, TX [*AM radio station call letters*]
WOAK .... La Grange, GA [*FM radio station call letters*]
WOAL-FM ... Pippa Passes, KY [*FM radio station call letters*]
WOAP .... Owosso, MI [*AM radio station call letters*]
WOAP-FM ... Owosso, MI [*FM radio station call letters*]
WOAR .... Women Organized Against Rape
WOAS .... Ontonagon, MI [*FM radio station call letters*]
WOAS .... Wave-Off Advisory System [*Aircraft carrier*] [*Navy*]
WOAY .... Oak Hill, WV [*AM radio station call letters*]
WOAY-FM ... Oak Hill, WV [*FM radio station call letters*]
WOAY-TV ... Oak Hill, WV [*Television station call letters*]
WOB .... Washed Overboard [*Shipping*]
WoB .... Wolffenbuetteler Beitraege, Frankfurt [*M.*], Klostermann [*A publication*]
WOB .... Work Order Bin (MCD)
WOBC-FM ... Oberlin, OH [*FM radio station call letters*]
WOBG .... York, PA [*AM radio station call letters*]
WOBL .... Oberlin, OH [*AM radio station call letters*]
WOBM .... Lakewood, NJ [*AM radio station call letters*]
WOBM-FM ... Toms River, NJ [*FM radio station call letters*]
WOBN .... Westerville, OH [*FM radio station call letters*]
W O BNDR ... Without Binder [*Freight*]
WOBO .... Batavia, OH [*FM radio station call letters*]
W/OBO .... Without Blowout (MSA)
WOBO .... World Organization of Building Officials (EA)
WOBR .... Wanchese, NC [*AM radio station call letters*]
WOBR-FM ... Wanchese, NC [*FM radio station call letters*]
WOBS .... New Albany, IN [*AM radio station call letters*]
WOBT .... Rhinelander, WI [*AM radio station call letters*]
WOC .... Davenport, IA [*AM radio station call letters*]
WOC .... Wilshire Oil Company of Texas [*NYSE symbol*]
WOC .... Win Over Communism [*A fund-raising subsidiary of the Unification Church*]
WOC .... Wing Operations Center (CINC)
WOC .... Without Compensation (ADA)
WOC .... Women's Ordination Conference (EA)
WOC .... Wood's Oriental Cases [*Malaya*] (DLA)
WOC .... Work Order Control (MCD)
WOC .... World Oceanographic Center (MSC)
WOCA .... Ocala, FL [*AM radio station call letters*]
WOCA .... World Outside Communist Areas
WOCAR ..... Aviation Warrant Officer Career Course [*Army*]
WOCB .... West Yarmouth, MA [*AM radio station call letters*]
WOccM ...... Memorial Hospital at Oconomowoc, Oconomowoc, WI [*Library symbol*] [*Library of Congress*] (LCLS)
WOccR ...... Redemptionist Seminary, Oconomowoc, WI [*Library symbol*] [*Library of Congress*] (LCLS)
WOCCU ..... World Council of Credit Unions [*Madison, WI*] (EA)
WOCD .... Amsterdam, NY [*Television station call letters*]
WOCE .... World Ocean Circulation Experiment [*World Climate Research Programme*]
WOCG .... Huntsville, AL [*FM radio station call letters*]
Wochbl Papierfabr ... Wochenblatt fuer Papierfabrikation [*A publication*]
Wochenschr Brau ... Wochenschrift fuer Brauerei [*A publication*]
WOCIT .... We Oppose Computers in Tournaments [*A chess players' group, formed in 1983*]
WOCL .... De Land, FL [*FM radio station call letters*]
WOCLS ...... World Ocean and Cruise Liner Society (EA)
WOCMDC ... Warrant Officer Candidate Military Development Course
WOCN .... Miami, FL [*AM radio station call letters*]
WOCO .... Oconto, WI [*AM radio station call letters*]
WOCO .... World of Computers [*NASDAQ symbol*] (NQ)
WOCO .... World Council of Young Men's Service Clubs (EA)
WOCOD ..... World Coal [*A publication*]
WOCO-FM ... Oconto, WI [*FM radio station call letters*]
WOCQ .... Berlin, MD [*FM radio station call letters*]
WOCR .... Olivet, MI [*FM radio station call letters*]
WOCS .... Work Order Control System (MCD)
WOCT .... Albany, GA [*Television station call letters*]
WOCT .... WAC [*Women's Army Corps*] Officer Candidate Test (AABC)
WOCU .... War on Community Ugliness [*Program*] [*Defunct*] (EA)
WOD .... Washington & Old Dominion R. R. [*AAR code*]
WOD .... Wind over Deck (MCD)
WOD .... Without Dependents [*Military*] (AFM)
WOD .... Woodstream Corp. [*American Stock Exchange symbol*]
WODA .... World Dredging Association (EA)
WODADIBOF ... Workshop on the Determination of Anti-Epileptic Drugs in Body Fluids

WODB .... Camden, AL [*FM radio station call letters*]
WODC .... Women's Olympic Distance Committee [*Later, WDC*] (EA)
WODCON ... World Dredging Conference
WODD .... Wave-Off Decision Device (MCD)
WODD .... World Oceanographic Data Display
WODDIN ..... Worldwide On-Line Data and Document Intelligence System
WODECO ... Western Offshore Drilling & Exploration Company
WODED ...... World Development [*A publication*]
WODI .... Brookneal, VA [*AM radio station call letters*]
WODY .... Bassett, VA [*AM radio station call letters*]
WOE .... Warhead Output Evaluation (MCD)
WOE .... Watchdogs on Environment
WOE .... Withdrawal of Enthusiasm [*Airline pilots objection to "Welcome aboard" talks*]
WOE .... Without Enclosure (MCD)
WOE .... Without Equipment
WOE .... Wound of Entry [*Medicine*]
WOEC .... Port Royal, SC [*FM radio station call letters*]
WOEC .... Warrant Officer Entry Course [*Military*] (INF)
WOEC-RC ... Warrant Office Entry Course, Reserve Component [*Army*] (INF)
WOEL-FM ... Elkton, MD [*FM radio station call letters*]
Woelm Publ ... Woelm Publication [*A publication*]
Woerner Adm'n ... Woerner's Treatise on the American Law of Administration (DLA)
Woert Sach ... Woerter und Sachen [*A publication*]
WOES .... Ovid-Elsie, MI [*FM radio station call letters*]
W/OE & SP ... Without Equipment and Spare Parts
WOEZ-FM ... Milton, PA [*FM radio station call letters*]
WOF .... Walk on Floor [*Ataxia*]
WOF .... Warmed-Over Flavor [*Food technology*]
WOF .... Work of Fracture [*Ceramic property*]
WOF .... Worlds of Fantasy [*1950-1954*] [*A publication*]
WOFA .... Westinghouse Optimized Fuel Assembly [*Nuclear energy*] (NRCH)
WOFC .... Western Ohio Film Circuit [*Library network*]
WOFE .... Rockwood, TN [*AM radio station call letters*]
WOFF .... Camilla, GA [*FM radio station call letters*]
WOFF .... Weight of Fuel Flow (MCD)
WOFI .... Wood Office Furniture Institute (EA)
WOFIWU .... World Federation of Industrial Workers' Unions
WOFL .... Orlando, FL [*Television station call letters*]
WOFM .... Moycock, NC [*FM radio station call letters*]
WOFP .... Wearout Failure Period
WOFR .... Washington Court House, OH [*AM radio station call letters*]
WOFS .... Weather Observing and Forecasting System [*Air Force*] (MCD)
W O FTTNGS ... Without Fittings [*Freight*]
WOG .... Water-Oil-Gas (AAG)
WOG .... Weapon Order Generation [*Military*] (CAAL)
WOG .... Werner Oil & Gas Co. [*Vancouver Stock Exchange symbol*]
WOG .... Westernized Oriental Gentleman [*Singapore term for native following Western fashions*] [*Other translations include "Wily Oriental Gentleman" and "Wonderful Oriental Gentleman"*]
WOG .... With Other Goods [*Business and trade*]
WOG .... World Organization of Gastroenterology [*See also OMGE*] (EA-IO)
WOG .... Wrath of God [*Israeli counterterrorist group*]
WOGA .... Western Oil and Gas Association [*Los Angeles, CA*] (EA)
WOGO .... Hallie, WI [*AM radio station call letters*]
WOGS .... We Old Girls Survive [*A teachers' club in Michigan*]
WOGSC ..... World Organisation of General Systems and Cybernetics [*Salford, England*] (EA-IO)
WOGX .... Ocala, FL [*Television station call letters*]
WOH .... War on Hunger [*Program*] (EA)
WOH .... Washington Office on Haiti (EA)
WOH .... Work on Hand [*Insurance*]
WOHC .... Warrant Officer Hospital Corps
WOHE .... World Health [*A publication*]
WOHELO .... Work, Health, Love [*Camp Fire Girls slogan*]
WOHH .... Women's Organization of Hapoel Hamizrachi [*Later, EWA*] (EA)
WOHI .... East Liverpool, OH [*AM radio station call letters*]
WOHMA ..... Waste Oil Heating Manufacturers Association [*Washington, DC*] (EA)
WOHO .... Toledo, OH [*AM radio station call letters*]
WOHP .... Bellefontaine, OH [*AM radio station call letters*]
WOHP .... World Organization for Human Potential [*Philadelphia, PA*] (EA)
WO & HPS ... Wall Oven and Hot Plates [*Classified advertising*] (ADA)
WOHRC .... Women's Occupational Health Resource Center [*Columbia University*] [*New York, NY*] (EA)
WOHS .... Shelby, NC [*AM radio station call letters*]
WOI .... Ames, IA [*AM radio station call letters*]
WOI .... World Opportunities International [*Hollywood, CA*] (EA)
WOIC .... Columbia, SC [*AM radio station call letters*]
WOI-FM ..... Ames, IA [*FM radio station call letters*]
WOIO .... Shaker Heights, OH [*Television station call letters*]
WOIS .... Worn Out in Service [*Military*]
WOI-TV ...... Ames, IA [*Television station call letters*]
WOIV .... De Ruyter, NY [*FM radio station call letters*]

WOIZ.......... Guayanilla, PR [*AM radio station call letters*]
WOJAC ...... World Organization for Jews from Arab Countries   (EA)
WOJB........ Reserve, WI [*FM radio station call letters*]
WOJC........ Willys Overland Jeepster Club   (EA)
WOJD........ World Organization of Jewish Deaf   (EA-IO)
WOJG........ Warrant Officer Junior Grade
WOJO........ Evanston, IL [*FM radio station call letters*]
Wojsk Przegl Tech ... Wojskowy Przeglad Techniczny [*Poland*] [*A publication*]
WOJY........ High Point, NC [*FM radio station call letters*]
WOK.......... Wiener Oeffentlicher Kueche [*Viennese Open Kitchen*] [*Nonprofit temperance restaurant chain*] [*Austria*]
WOK.......... Wonken [*Venezuela*] [*Airport symbol*]   (OAG)
WOKA........ Douglas, GA [*AM radio station call letters*]
WOKA-FM ... Douglas, GA [*FM radio station call letters*]
WOKB........ Winter Garden, FL [*AM radio station call letters*]
WOKC........ Okeechobee, FL [*AM radio station call letters*]
WOKD........ Arcadia, FL [*FM radio station call letters*]
WOKE........ Charleston, SC [*AM radio station call letters*]
WOKG........ Warren, OH [*AM radio station call letters*]
WOKH........ Bardstown, KY [*FM radio station call letters*]
WOKI-FM ... Oak Ridge, TN [*FM radio station call letters*]
WOKJ........ Jackson, MS [*AM radio station call letters*]
WOKK...... Meridian, MS [*FM radio station call letters*]
WOKN........ Goldsboro, NC [*AM radio station call letters*]
WOKO........ Pontiac, IL [*Television station call letters*]
WOKQ........ Dover, NH [*FM radio station call letters*]
WOKR........ Rochester, NY [*Television station call letters*]
W-O-KR..... Willys-Overland-Knight Registry   (EA)
WOKS........ Columbus, GA [*AM radio station call letters*]
WOKT........ Cannonsburg, KY [*AM radio station call letters*]
WOKU-FM ... Greensburg, PA [*FM radio station call letters*]
WOKV........ Jacksonville, FL [*AM radio station call letters*]
WOKW ...... Cortland, NY [*FM radio station call letters*]
WOKX .... High Point, NC [*AM radio station call letters*]
WOKY .... Milwaukee, WI [*AM radio station call letters*]
WOKZ........ Muncie, IN [*FM radio station call letters*]
WOL .... Wainoco Oil Co. [*NYSE symbol*]
WOL .... War-Office Letter [*An order or an instruction*] [*British*]
WOL .... Washington, DC [*AM radio station call letters*]
WOL .... Wedge Opening Load
WOL .... Weird and Occult Library [*A publication*]
WOL .... Wharf Owner's Liability [*Insurance*]
Wol .... Wolcott's Chancery Reports [*7 Delaware*]   (DLA)
Wol .... Wollaston's English Bail Court Reports   (DLA)
wol .... Wolof [*MARC language code*] [*Library of Congress*]   (LCCP)
WOL .... Wolverton [*England*] [*Seismograph station code, US Geological Survey*]   (SEIS)
WOLA........ Barranquitas, PR [*AM radio station call letters*]
WOLA........ Washington Office on Latin America [*An association*]   (EA)
WOLA........ Wolverine Aluminum [*NASDAQ symbol*]   (NQ)
WOLC........ Princess Anne, MD [*FM radio station call letters*]
WOLD........ Marion, VA [*AM radio station call letters*]
WOLD-FM ... Marion, VA [*FM radio station call letters*]
WOLE-TV... Aguadilla, PR [*Television station call letters*]
WOLF .... Committee for Wildlife on the Last Frontier
WOLF .... Wayne Oakland Library Federation [*Library network*]
WOLF .... Work Order Load Forecast   (MCD)
Wolf & B ..... Wolferstan and Bristow's English Election Cases [*1859-65*]   (DLA)
Wolf & D ..... Wolferstan and Dew's English Election Cases [*1856-58*]   (DLA)
Wolf Dr de la Nat ... Wolffius. Droit de la Nature   (DLA)
Wolff Inst ... Wolffius. Institutiones Juris Naturae et Gentium   (DLA)
Wolff Inst Nat ... Wolffius. Institutiones Juris Naturae et Gentium   (DLA)
Wolffius... Wolffius. Institutiones Juris Naturae et Gentium   (DLA)
Wolffius Inst ... Wolffius. Institutiones Juris Naturae et Gentium   (DLA)
WOLF-TV ... Scranton, PA [*Television station call letters*]
Woll .... Wollaston's English Bail Court Reports, Practice Cases [*1840-41*]   (DLA)
Wollen- Leinen-Ind ... Wollen- und Leinen-Industrie [*A publication*]
WOLM........ Lake Mary, FL [*AM radio station call letters*]
WOLO-TV .. Columbia, SC [*Television station call letters*]
WOLR........ Branford, FL [*FM radio station call letters*]
WOLS........ Florence, SC [*AM radio station call letters*]
WOM .... Weapons Output Makeup
WOM .... Wideband Optical Modulation
WOM .... Wireless Operator Mechanic [*British*]   (DSUE)
WOM .... Wise Old Men [*Term used to refer to group of US statesmen including Dean Acheson, Charles Bohlen, Averell Harriman, George Kennan, Robert Lovett, and John McCloy*]
WOM .... Write-Only Memory [*Data processing*]
WOM .... Write Optional Memory   (IEEE)
WOMAA ..... Works Management [*A publication*]
WOMAN ..... World Organization of Mothers of All Nations
Woman Art J ... Woman's Art Journal [*A publication*]
Woman Cit ... Woman Citizen [*A publication*]
Woman Home C ... Woman's Home Companion [*A publication*]
Woman's H C ... Woman's Home Companion [*A publication*]
Woman's J ... Woman's Journal [*A publication*]
WOMC........ Detroit, MI [*FM radio station call letters*]

Women...... Women/Poems [*A publication*]
Women Coach Clin ... Women's Coaching Clinic [*A publication*]
Women of Eur ... Women of Europe [*A publication*]
Women and Hist ... Women and History [*A publication*]
Women Law J ... Women Lawyers' Journal [*A publication*]
Women Lawyers J ... Women Lawyers Journal [*A publication*]
Women Lit ... Women and Literature [*A publication*]
Women & Lit ... Women and Literature [*A publication*]
Women L Jour ... Women Lawyers Journal [*A publication*]
Women L Jour ... Women's Law Journal   (DLA)
Women's Bur Bull ... Women's Bureau Bulletin [*A publication*]
Women's LJ ... Women's Law Journal   (DLA)
Women's Rights L Rep ... Women's Rights Law Reporter [*A publication*]
Women's Rights L Rptr ... Women's Rights Law Reporter [*A publication*]
Women's Studies ... Women's Studies: An Interdisciplinary Journal [*A publication*]
Womens Studs Newsl ... Women's Studies Newsletter [*A publication*]
Women Stud ... Women's Studies: An Interdisciplinary Journal [*A publication*]
Women Stud Abstracts ... Women Studies Abstracts [*A publication*]
Women Wkrs Bull ... Women Workers Bulletin [*A publication*]
WomHealth ... Women and Health [*A publication*]
WOMI .... Owensboro, KY [*AM radio station call letters*]
Wom March ... Women on the March [*New Delhi*] [*A publication*]
Womn Prss ... Women's Press [*A publication*]
Womn Rgts ... Women's Rights Law Reporter [*A publication*]
Womn Sprt ... Womanspirit [*A publication*]
WOMP........ Bellaire, OH [*AM radio station call letters*]
WOMP....... World Order Models Project
WOMP-FM ... Bellaire, OH [*FM radio station call letters*]
WOMPI...... Women of the Motion Picture Industry, International [*Dallas, TX*]   (EA)
WOMR....... Provincetown, MA [*FM radio station call letters*]
WOMT....... Manitowoc, WI [*AM radio station call letters*]
WOMUA ..... World of Music [*A publication*]
WON.......... Wool over Needle [*Knitting*]
WON.......... Work Order Number   (MCD)
WONA .... Winona, MS [*AM radio station call letters*]
WONAAC ... Women's National Abortion Action Coalition [*Defunct*]
WONA-FM ... Winona, MS [*FM radio station call letters*]
WONARD ... Woman's Organization of the National Association of Retail Druggists [*Indianapolis, IN*]   (EA)
WONC .... Naperville, IL [*FM radio station call letters*]
WONCA...... World Organization of National Colleges, Academies, and Academic Associations of General Practitioners/Family Physicians   (EA-IO)
WOND .... Pleasantville, NJ [*AM radio station call letters*]
WONE .... Dayton, OH [*AM radio station call letters*]
WONE-FM ... Akron, OH [*FM radio station call letters*]
WONF........ With Other Natural Flavors [*Food science*]
WONG .... Canton, MS [*AM radio station call letters*]
WONG .... Weight on Nose Gear [*Aviation*]   (MCD)
WONN .... Lakeland, FL [*AM radio station call letters*]
WONO .... Black Mountain, NC [*AM radio station call letters*]
WONQ .... Orlando, FL [*AM radio station call letters*]
WONS .... Pleasure Ridge Park, KY [*AM radio station call letters*]
WONT....... Ontonagon, MI [*FM radio station call letters*]
Wont Land Reg ... Wontner's Land Registry Practice [*12th ed.*] [*1975*]   (DLA)
W Ont L Rev ... Western Ontario Law Review [*A publication*]
WONW ...... Defiance, OH [*AM radio station call letters*]
WONX .... Evanston, IL [*AM radio station call letters*]
WONY .... Oneonta, NY [*FM radio station call letters*]
WOO.......... College of Wooster, Wooster, OH [*OCLC symbol*]   (OCLC)
WOO.......... Waiting on Orders
WOO.......... Warrant Ordnance Officer [*Navy*] [*British*]
WOO.......... Werke ohne Opuszahl [*Works without Opus Number*] [*Music*]
WOO.......... Western Operations Office [*Later, WSO*] [*NASA*]
WOO.......... Woodchopper, AK [*Location identifier*] [*FAA*]   (FAAL)
WOO.......... Woodstock [*Maryland*] [*Seismograph station code, US Geological Survey*] [*Closed*]   (SEIS)
WOO.......... World Oceanographic Organization
WOOB .... Leeds, AL [*AM radio station call letters*]
WOOD .... Grand Rapids, MI [*AM radio station call letters*]
Wood......... Wood on Mercantile Agreements   (DLA)
Wood......... Wood's English Tithe Cases, Exchequer [*4 vols.*]   (DLA)
Wood......... Woods' United States Circuit Court Reports   (DLA)
WOOD .... Woodward & Lothrop [*NASDAQ symbol*]   (NQ)
Woodb & M ... Woodbury and Minot's United States Circuit Court Reports   (DLA)
Woodb & Min (CC) ... Woodbury and Minot's United States Circuit Court Reports, First Circuit   (DLA)
Wood Conv ... Wood on Conveyancing   (DLA)
Wood Decr ... Wood's Tithe Cases [*England*]   (DLA)
Wooddesson Lect ... Wooddesson's Lecture   (DLA)
Woodd Lect ... Wooddesson's Lectures on the Laws of England   (DLA)
Woodf........ Woodfall on Landlord and Tenant [*25 eds.*] [*1802-1958*]   (DLA)
Woodf Cel Tr ... Woodfall's Celebrated Trials   (DLA)
Woodf Landl & T ... Woodfall on Landlord and Tenant [*25 eds.*] [*1802-1958*]   (DLA)
Woodf Landl & Ten ... Woodfall on Landlord and Tenant [*25 eds.*] [*1802-1958*]   (DLA)

Woodf L & T ... Woodfall on Landlord and Tenant [28th ed.] [1978] (DLA)
WOOD-FM ...... Grand Rapids, MI [FM radio station call letters]
Wood H ...... Hutton Wood's Decrees in Tithe Cases [England] (DLA)
Wood Ind ... Wood Industry [A publication]
Wood Inst... Wood's Institutes of English Law (DLA)
Wood Inst Com Law ... Wood's Institutes of the Common Law (DLA)
Wood Landl & Ten ... Wood on Landlord and Tenant (DLA)
Wood Land & T ... Wood on Landlord and Tenant (DLA)
Woodlds Res Index ... Woodlands Research Index. Pulp and Paper Research Institute of Canada [A publication]
Wood Lect ... Wooddesson's Lectures on the Laws of England (DLA)
Wood Lim .. Wood on Limitation of Actions (DLA)
Woodl Pap Pulp Pap Res Inst Can ... Woodlands Papers. Pulp and Paper Research Institute of Canada [A publication]
Woodl Res Note Union Camp Corp ... Woodland Research Notes. Union Camp Corporation [A publication]
Woodl Sect Index Canad Pulp Pap Ass ... Woodlands Section Index. Canadian Pulp and Paper Association [A publication]
Wood & M ... Woodbury and Minot's United States Circuit Court Reports (DLA)
Wood Mag ... Woodwind Magazine [A publication]
Woodman Cr Cas ... Woodman's Reports of Thacher's Criminal Cases [Massachusetts] (DLA)
Wood Mast & Serv ... Wood on Master and Servant (DLA)
WOODMEM ... Leonard Wood Memorial [Also known as American Leprosy Foundation] [Formerly, LWMEL] [Rockville, MD] (EA)
Wood & Minot ... Woodbury and Minot's United States Circuit Court Reports (DLA)
Wood Nuis ... Wood on Nuisances (DLA)
Wood Preserv ... Wood Preserving [A publication]
Wood Preserv (Chicago) ... Wood Preserving (Chicago) [A publication]
Wood Preserv N ... Wood Preserving News [A publication]
Wood Preserv News ... Wood Preserving News [A publication]
Wood Pres Rep For Prod Res Ind Developm Comm (Philippines) ... Wood Preservation Report. Forest Products Research and Industries Development Commission College (Laguna, Philippines) [A publication]
Wood Res... Wood Research [A publication]
Wood Ry Law ... Wood's Law of Railroads (DLA)
Woods... Woods' United States Circuit Court Reports (DLA)
Woods CC ... Woods' United States Circuit Court Reports (DLA)
Wood Sci ... Wood Science [A publication]
Wood Sci Te ... Wood Science and Technology [A publication]
Wood Sci Technol ... Wood Science and Technology [A publication]
Wood's Civ Law ... Wood's Institutes of the Civil Law of England (DLA)
Wood's Dig ... Wood's Digest of Laws [California] (DLA)
Woods Hole Oceanogr Inst Annu Rep ... Woods Hole Oceanographic Institution. Annual Report [A publication]
Woods Ins ... Wood on Fire Insurance (DLA)
Woods Ins ... Wood's Institutes of English Law (DLA)
Wood's R.... Wood's Manitoba Reports [1875-83] (DLA)
Woods St Frauds ... Wood's Treatise on the Statutes of Frauds (DLA)
WOODSTEIN ... [Bob] Woodward and [Carl] Bernstein [Washington Post reporters who uncovered the Watergate story]
Wood Sthn Afr ... Wood Southern Africa [A publication]
Wood Ti Cas ... Wood's Tithe Cases [1650-1798] (DLA)
Wood Tit Cas ... Wood's Tithe Cases [1650-1798] (DLA)
Wood Tr M ... Wood on Trade Marks [1876] (DLA)
Woodw .... Woodward's Decisions [Pennsylvania] (DLA)
Woodw Dec ... Woodward's Decisions [1861-74] [Pennsylvania] (DLA)
Woodw Dec PA ... Woodward's Decisions [1861-74] [Pennsylvania] (DLA)
Woodwkg Ind ... Woodworking Industry [A publication]
Wood & Wood Prod ... Wood and Wood Products [A publication]
Wood Wood Prod ... Wood and Wood Products [A publication]
Wood World ... Woodwind World [Later, Woodwind World - Brass and Percussion] [A publication]
Wood World-Brass ... Woodwind World - Brass and Percussion [A publication]
WOOF .... Dothan, AL [AM radio station call letters]
Woof.......... Well-Off, Over Fifty [Lifestyle classification]
WOOF-FM ... Dothan, AL [FM radio station call letters]
WOOJ........ Lehigh Acres, FL [AM radio station call letters]
WOOJ-FM ... Lehigh Acres, FL [FM radio station call letters]
Wool.......... Woolworth's United States Circuit Court Reports (DLA)
Wool CC.... Woolworth's United States Circuit Court Reports (Miller's Decisions) (DLA)
Woolf Adult ... Woolf on Adulterations [1874] (DLA)
Wool Int...... Woolsey's Introduction to Study of International Law [6th ed.] [1888] (DLA)
Woolr Cert ... Woolrych's Certificates [1826] (DLA)
Woolr Com ... Woolrych's Rights of Common [2nd ed.] [1850] (DLA)
Woolr Cr L ... Woolrych's Criminal Law [1862] (DLA)
Wool Rec.... Wool Record [A publication]
Wool Rec Text World ... Wool Record and Textile World [A publication]
Woolr LW ... Woolrych's Law of Waters [2nd ed.] [1851] (DLA)
Woolr PW ... Woolrych's Party Walls [1845] (DLA)
Woolr Sew ... Woolrych's Sewert [3rd ed.] [1864] (DLA)
Woolr Waters ... Woolrych's Law of Waters (DLA)
Woolr Ways ... Woolrych's Law of Ways [2nd ed.] [1847] (DLA)
Woolr Wind L ... Woolrych's Window Lights [2nd ed.] [1864] (DLA)
Wool Sci Rev ... Wool Science Review [A publication]

Woolsey Polit Science ... Woolsey's Political Science (DLA)
Wools Int L ... Woolsey's Introduction to Study of International Law [6th ed.] [1888] (DLA)
Wools Pol Science ... Woolsey's Political Science (DLA)
Wool Tech ... Wool Technology [A publication]
Wool Tech ... Wool Technology and Sheep Breeding [A publication]
Wool Technol ... Wool Technology [A publication]
Wool Technol ... Wool Technology and Sheep Breeding [A publication]
Wool Technol Sheep Breed ... Wool Technology and Sheep Breeding [A publication]
Wool Technol (Syd) ... Wool Technology (Sydney) [A publication]
Wool Tech & Sheep ... Wool Technology and Sheep Breeding [A publication]
Wool Tech & Sheep Breeding ... Wool Technology and Sheep Breeding [A publication]
Woolw .... Woolworth's Reports [1 Nebraska] (DLA)
Woolw .... Woolworth's United States Circuit Court Reports (DLA)
Woolworth ... Woolworth's United States Circuit Court Reports (DLA)
Woolworth's Cir Ct R ... Woolworth's United States Circuit Court Reports (DLA)
Woolw Rep ... Woolworth's Reports [1 Nebraska] (DLA)
Woolw Rep ... Woolworth's United States Circuit Court Reports (DLA)
WOOMB ..... World Organization of the Ovulation Method - Billings, USA [Later, Families of the Americas Foundation]
WOOO....... Royal Palm Beach, FL [AM radio station call letters]
Woopie....... Well-Off Older Person [Lifestyle classification]
Woo Sok Univ Med J ... Woo Sok University. Medical Journal [A publication]
WOOW .... Greenville, NC [AM radio station call letters]
WOP .... War on Poverty (OICC)
WOP .... Wing Outer Panel [Aviation]
WOP .... Wireless Operator [RAF slang] [World War II]
WOP .... Without Passport [Stamped on papers of turn-of-the-century immigrants who were arriving to work in specific factories or on railroad gangs. A high percentage of these immigrants were Italian, and the designation eventually became a derogatory term for members of that nationality. Alternate theories hold that the term means "Works on Pavement" or that it derived from the Spanish "guapo" through the Sicilian "guappo," a tough, brave man]
WOP .... Without Payment
W/O/P....... Without Penalty
WOP .... Without Personnel
WOP .... Without Preference [Rating]
WOP .... Without Priorities
WOP .... World Oil Project [National Science Foundation] [Massachusetts Institute of Technology] [Cambridge, MA] (EISS)
WOPA........ War Overtime Pay Act of 1943
W O PAR .... Without Partition [Freight]
WOPC .... World Oceanographic Data Processing and Services Center (MSC)
WOPD .... Warrant Officer Professional Development [Military] (MCD)
WOPE........ Without Personnel and Equipment
WOPHA....... Woman Physician [A publication]
WOPI .... Bristol, TN [AM radio station call letters]
WOPOP ..... WOPOP: Working Papers on Photography [A publication]
WOPP........ Opp, AL [AM radio station call letters]
WOPR........ Oak Park, MI [FM radio station call letters]
WOPR........ War Operation Plan Response [Pronounced "whopper"] [Name of NORAD computer in film "WarGames"]
WOPY........ Jacksonville, NC [AM radio station call letters]
WOQ........ Wave Officers' Quarters
WOQI........ Ponce, PR [FM radio station call letters]
WOQT .... Warrant Officer Qualification Test
WOR .... New York, NY [AM radio station call letters]
WOR .... White and Orange [Buoy]
WOR .... White Owners Register (EA)
WOR .... Worcester [Massachusetts] [Seismograph station code, US Geological Survey] [Closed] (SEIS)
WOR .... Work Order Register (MCD)
WOR .... Work Order Release (MCD)
WOR .... Work Outline Retrieval (MCD)
WoR .... World Review [A publication]
Wor........... Worldview [A publication]
WOR .... Worshipful
WOR .... Worthen Banking Corp. [American Stock Exchange symbol]
WORA .... Mayaguez, PR [AM radio station call letters]
WORAM ..... Word-Oriented Random Access Memory [Data processing] (MCD)
WORA-TV ... Mayaguez, PR [Television station call letters]
WORB........ Farmington Hills, MI [FM radio station call letters]
WORBAT.... Wartime Order of Battle (NATG)
WORC .... Washington Operations Research Council (MCD)
WORC .... Worcester, MA [AM radio station call letters]
WORC .... Worcestershire [County in England]
Worcest Dict ... Worcester's Dictionary (DLA)
Worcester ... Worcester's Dictionary of the English Language (DLA)
Worcester Med News ... Worcester Medical News [Massachusetts] [A publication]
Worcester Mus Ann ... Worcester, Massachusetts. Worcester Art Museum. Annual [A publication]

Worcester Mus N Bul ... Worcester, Massachusetts. Worcester Art Museum. News Bulletin and Calendar [*A publication*]
Worc M....... Worcester Magazine [*A publication*]
WORCS...... Worcestershire [*County in England*]
WORCS...... Work Ordering and Reporting Communication System [*Army*]
WORD .... Spartanburg, SC [*AM radio station call letters*]
Wor Dict..... Worcester's Dictionary   (DLA)
Word and Inf Process ... Word and Information Processing [*A publication*]
Word Process Now ... Word Processing Now [*A publication*]
WordsC..... Wordsworth Circle [*A publication*]
Words Elect ... Wordsworth's Law of Elections [*6th ed.*] [*1868*]   (DLA)
Words Elect Cas ... Wordsworth's Election Cases [*England*]   (DLA)
Wordsworth ... Wordsworth Circle [*A publication*]
Word W ...... Word Watching [*A publication*]
WORG-FM .... Orangeburg, SC [*FM radio station call letters*]
WORI ...... World Order Research Institute
WORJ......... Ozark, AL [*FM radio station call letters*]
WORK ...... Barre, VT [*FM radio station call letters*]
WORKD...... Worklife [*A publication*]
Work-Environ-Health ... Work-Environment-Health [*A publication*]
WORKHO ... Workhouse [*British*]   (ROG)
Workmen's Comp L Rep ... Workmen's Compensation Law Reporter [*Commerce Clearing House*]   (DLA)
Workmen's Comp L Rev ... Workmen's Compensation Law Review   (DLA)
Work Pap Aust Arid Zone Res Conf ... Working Papers. Australian Arid Zone Research Conference [*A publication*]
Work Pap Aust Cereal Pasture Plant Breed Conf ... Working Papers. Australian Cereal and Pasture Plant Breeding Conference [*A publication*]
Work Pap Bur Meteorol ... Working Paper. Bureau of Meteorology [*A publication*]
Work Pap Giannini Found Agric Econ Calif Agric Exp Stn ... Working Paper. Giannini Foundation of Agricultural Economics. California Agricultural Experiment Station [*A publication*]
Work Pap Lang Linguist ... Working Papers in Language and Linguistics [*A publication*]
Work Pap Ling (H) ... Working Papers in Linguistics (Honolulu) [*A publication*]
Work Prog ... Work in Progress [*A publication*]
Work Rel Abstr ... Work Related Abstracts [*A publication*]
Works Courts ... Works on Courts and Their Jurisdiction   (DLA)
Works Eng ... Works Engineering [*England*] [*A publication*]
Works Eng Fact Serv ... Works Engineering and Factory Services [*A publication*]
Works Inst Higher Nerv Act Acad Sci USSR Pathophysiol Ser ... Works. Institute of Higher Nervous Activity. Academy of Sciences of the USSR. Pathophysiological Series [*A publication*]
Works Inst Higher Nerv Act Acad Sci USSR Physiol Ser ... Works. Institute of Higher Nervous Activity. Academy of Sciences of the USSR. Physiological Series [*A publication*]
Works Pavlov Inst Physiol Acad Sci USSR ... Works. Pavlov Institute of Physiology. Academy of Sciences of the USSR [*A publication*]
Works and Plant Maint ... Works and Plant Maintenance [*A publication*]
Works Pr .... Works' Practice, Pleading, and Forms   (DLA)
Work Vang ... Workers Vanguard [*A publication*]
Work Wom ... Working Woman [*A publication*]
WORL........ Eatonville, FL [*AM radio station call letters*]
WORLA ...... Worlco, Inc. Cl A [*NASDAQ symbol*]   (NQ)
World .... National Geographic World [*A publication*]
World .... World Magazine [*A publication*]
World Aff.... World Affairs [*A publication*]
World Aff Q ... World Affairs Quarterly [*A publication*]
World Ag.... World Agriculture [*A publication*]
World Agr ... World Agriculture [*A publication*]
World Agric ... World Agriculture [*A publication*]
World Agri Econ & Rural Sociol Abstr ... World Agricultural Economics and Rural Sociology Abstracts [*A publication*]
World Alum Abstr ... World Aluminum Abstracts [*A publication*]
World Anim Rev ... World Animal Review [*A publication*]
World Archa ... World Archaeology [*A publication*]
World Archaeol ... World Archaeology [*A publication*]
World Assn for Adult Ed B ... World Association for Adult Education. Bulletin [*A publication*]
World Bus W ... World Business Weekly [*A publication*]
World Cem Technol ... World Cement Technology [*Later, World Cement*] [*A publication*]
World Conf Earthquake Eng Proc ... World Conference on Earthquake Engineering. Proceedings [*A publication*]
World Constr ... World Construction [*A publication*]
World Dev ... World Development [*Oxford*] [*A publication*]
World Devel ... World Development [*A publication*]
WORLDDIDAC ... World Association of Manufacturers and Distributors of Educational Materials [*Bern, Switzerland*]   (EA-IO)
World Dredging & Mar Const ... World Dredging and Marine Construction [*A publication*]
World Dredging Mar Constr ... World Dredging and Marine Construction [*A publication*]
World Econ ... World Economy [*England*] [*A publication*]
World Educ Rep ... World Education Reports [*A publication*]

World Energy Conf Trans ... World Energy Conference. Transactions [*A publication*]
World Farm ... World Farming [*A publication*]
World Fish Abstr ... World Fisheries Abstracts [*A publication*]
World For Ser Bull ... World Forestry Series. Bulletin [*A publication*]
World Health Organ Chron ... World Health Organization. Chronicle [*A publication*]
World Health Organ Tech Rep Ser ... World Health Organization. Technical Report Series [*A publication*]
World Health Stat Q ... World Health Statistics. Quarterly [*A publication*]
World Health Stat Rep ... World Health Statistics. Report [*A publication*]
World Highw ... World Highways [*A publication*]
World Hosp ... World Hospitals [*A publication*]
World Ir Nurs ... World of Irish Nursing [*A publication*]
World Jnl Trib ... World Journal Tribune [*Defunct New York City afternoon newspaper*] [*A publication*]
World J Surg ... World Journal of Surgery [*A publication*]
World Jus... World Justice [*A publication*]
World List Pub Stds ... Worldwide List of Published Standards [*A publication*]
World Lit T ... World Literature Today [*A publication*]
World Lit Today ... World Literature Today [*A publication*]
World L Rev ... World Law Review   (DLA)
World Marxist R ... World Marxist Review [*A publication*]
World Marx R ... World Marxist Review [*A publication*]
World Med ... World Medicine [*A publication*]
World Med Electron ... World Medical Electronics [*England*] [*A publication*]
World Med Instrum ... World Medical Instrumentation [*England*] [*A publication*]
World Med J ... World Medical Journal [*A publication*]
World Meet Outside US Can ... World Meetings: Outside United States and Canada [*A publication*]
World Meet Outs US Can ... World Meetings: Outside United States and Canada [*A publication*]
World Meet US Can ... World Meetings: United States and Canada [*A publication*]
World Meteorol Organ Bull ... World Meteorological Organization. Bulletin [*A publication*]
World Meteorol Organ Publ ... World Meteorological Organization. Publications [*A publication*]
World Min ... World Mining [*A publication*]
World Miner Met ... World Minerals and Metals [*A publication*]
World Min US Ed ... World Mining. United States Edition [*A publication*]
World Mus ... World of Music [*A publication*]
World Neurol ... World Neurology [*A publication*]
World O...... World Order [*A publication*]
World Obstet Gynecol ... World of Obstetrics and Gynecology [*Japan*] [*A publication*]
World Oil.... World Oil Forecast. Review Issue [*A publication*]
World Outl ... World Outlook [*A publication*]
World Pet... World Petroleum [*A publication*]
World Pet Cong Prepr ... World Petroleum Congress. Preprints [*A publication*]
World Pet Congr Proc ... World Petroleum Congress. Proceedings [*A publication*]
World Petrol ... World Petroleum [*A publication*]
World Pol ... World Politics [*A publication*]
World Poult ... World's Poultry Science Journal [*A publication*]
World Poultry Sci J ... World's Poultry Science Journal [*A publication*]
World Press R ... World Press Review [*A publication*]
World R ...... World Review [*A publication*]
World Refrig ... World Refrigeration [*England*] [*A publication*]
World Rep ... World Report [*A publication*]
World Rev ... World Review [*A publication*]
World Rev Nutr Diet ... World Review of Nutrition and Dietetics [*A publication*]
World Rev Pest Contr ... World Review of Pest Control [*A publication*]
World Rev Pest Control ... World Review of Pest Control [*A publication*]
World R Pest Control ... World Review of Pest Control [*A publication*]
WORLDS.... Western Ohio Regional Library Development System [*Library network*]
World's Butter Rev ... World's Butter Review [*A publication*]
World Sci News ... World Science News [*India*] [*A publication*]
World's Pap Trade Rev ... World's Paper Trade Review [*A publication*]
World's Poultry Cong Conf Papers Sect C ... World's Poultry Congress. Conference Papers. Section C [*A publication*]
World's Poultry Sci J ... World's Poultry Science Journal [*A publication*]
World's Poult Sci J ... World's Poultry Science Journal [*A publication*]
World Steel (Jpn) ... World of Steel (Japan) [*A publication*]
World Surface Coat Abs ... World Surface Coatings Abstracts [*A publication*]
World Surf Coat ... World Surface Coatings Abstracts [*A publication*]
World Surv ... World Survey [*A publication*]
World Text Abstr ... World Textile Abstracts [*A publication*]
World Textile Abs ... World Textile Abstracts [*A publication*]
World Textile Abstr ... World Textile Abstracts [*A publication*]
World Trade LJ ... World Trade Law Journal   (DLA)
Worldwatch Pap ... Worldwatch Paper [*A publication*]
Worldwide List Published Stand ... Worldwide List of Published Standards [*A publication*]
World-Wide MinAbs ... World-Wide Mining Abstracts [*A publication*]

Worldwide Nucl Power ... Worldwide Nuclear Power [*A publication*]
World Yr Bk Ed ... World Year Book of Education [*A publication*]
WORM....... Savannah, TN [*AM radio station call letters*]
WORM....... Write Once, Read Mainly
WORM....... Write Once, Read Mostly [*Data processing*]
WORM-FM ... Savannah, TN [*FM radio station call letters*]
Worm R ...... Wormwood Review [*A publication*]
Worm Runner's Dig ... Worm Runner's Digest [*A publication*]
WORMS ..... World Organization to Restore Male Supremacy   (EA)
WORO .... Corozal, PR [*FM radio station call letters*]
WOROM ..... Write-Only Read-Only Memory [*Data processing*]   (MDG)
WORP........ Word Processing [*Data processing*]
WORQ .... Stonington, CT [*FM radio station call letters*]
Wor R .... World Review [*A publication*]
WORSAMS ... Worldwide Organizational Structure for Army Medical
　　　　　　　　　Support   (AABC)
WORT........ Madison, WI [*FM radio station call letters*]
WORTAC ... Westinghouse Overall RADAR Tester and Calibrator
Worth Jur ... Worthington's Power of Juries [*1825*]   (DLA)
Worth Prec Wills ... Worthington's General Precedent for Wills [*5th ed.*]
　　　　　　　　　[*1852*]   (DLA)
WOR-TV ..... Seacaucus, NJ [*Television station call letters*]
Wort Wahr ... Wort und Wahrheit [*A publication*]
WORV........ Hattiesburg, MS [*AM radio station call letters*]
WORW....... Port Huron, MI [*FM radio station call letters*]
WORX........ Madison, IN [*AM radio station call letters*]
WORZ........ Daytona Beach, FL [*FM radio station call letters*]
WOS.......... Web Offset Section [*Arlington, VA*]   (EA)
WOS.......... Wilson Ornithological Society
WOS.......... Winchester Financial [*Vancouver Stock Exchange symbol*]
WOS.......... Wonders of the Spaceways [*A publication*]
WOS.......... Worcester [*British depot code*]
WOSAC..... Worldwide Synchronization of Atomic Clocks
WOSB........ War Office Selection Board [*British*]
WOSB .... Weather Observation Site Building   (AABC)
WOSC .... Fulton, NY [*AM radio station call letters*]
WOSC ...... Western Oregon State College
WOSD .... Weapons Operational Systems Development [*NORAD*]
WOSE........ Port Clinton, OH [*FM radio station call letters*]
WOSF........ Work Order Status File   (MCD)
WOsh .... Oshkosh Public Library, Oshkosh, WI [*Library symbol*] [*Library
　　　　　　　　　of Congress*]   (LCLS)
WOSH .... Oshkosh, WI [*AM radio station call letters*]
WOshM ...... Mercy Hospital, Nursing Library, Oshkosh, WI [*Library symbol*]
　　　　　　　　　[*Library of Congress*]   (LCLS)
WOshM-M ... Mercy Medical Center, Medical Library, Oshkosh, WI [*Library
　　　　　　　　　symbol*] [*Library of Congress*]   (LCLS)
WOshU....... University of Wisconsin-Oshkosh, Oshkosh, WI [*Library
　　　　　　　　　symbol*] [*Library of Congress*]   (LCLS)
WOSIC ...... Watchmakers of Switzerland Information Center [*New York,
　　　　　　　　　NY*]   (EA)
WOSL........ Women's Overseas Service League   (EA)
WOSM....... Ocean Springs, MS [*FM radio station call letters*]
WOSO .... San Juan, PR [*AM radio station call letters*]
WOSS .... Ossining, NY [*FM radio station call letters*]
WOST........ World's Oldest Socketed Tool [*A copper implement made
　　　　　　　　　around 2500BC and possibly used for digging or
　　　　　　　　　chopping. It was discovered in 1966 at Non Nok Tha,
　　　　　　　　　Thailand, by archeologist Donn Bayard*]
WOST-TV... Block Island, RI [*Television station call letters*]
WOSU .... Columbus, OH [*AM radio station call letters*]
WOSU-FM ... Columbus, OH [*FM radio station call letters*]
WOSUS ...... Wang Office Systems User Society   (CSR)
WOSU-TV ... Columbus, OH [*Television station call letters*]
WOT .... Wide-Open Throttle
WOT .... Worlds of Tomorrow [*A publication*]
WOTB .... Middletown, RI [*FM radio station call letters*]
WOTB........ Welfare of the Blind [*An association*] [*Washington, DC*]   (EA)
WOTC .... Selma, AL [*Television station call letters*]
WOTCU...... Wave-Off and Transition Control Unit
WOTD .... Winamac, IN [*FM radio station call letters*]
WOTF........ Writers of the Future [*Science fiction writing award*]
WOTL .... Toledo, OH [*FM radio station call letters*]
WOTR........ Wolf Trap Farm Park [*National Park Service designation*]
WOTS....... Warrant Officer Training System [*Military*]   (INF)
WOTT........ Watertown, NY [*AM radio station call letters*]
WOTT........ Wolves on the Track [*A group of philanderers looking for girls*]
　　　　　　　　　[*Slang*]
WOTV........ Grand Rapids, MI [*Television station call letters*]
WOU.......... Work Opportunities Unlimited
WOUB .... Athens, OH [*AM radio station call letters*]
WOUB-FM ... Athens, OH [*FM radio station call letters*]
WOUB-TV ... Athens, OH [*Television station call letters*]
WOUC-FM ... Cambridge, OH [*FM radio station call letters*]
WOUC-TV ... Cambridge, OH [*Television station call letters*]
WOUI......... Chicago, IL [*FM radio station call letters*]
WOUR .... Utica, NY [*FM radio station call letters*]
WOV.......... Warren & Ouachita Valley Railway Co. [*AAR code*]
WOVI......... Novi, MI [*FM radio station call letters*]
WOVK .... Wheeling, WV [*FM radio station call letters*]
WOVO .... Glasgow, KY [*FM radio station call letters*]

WOVR-FM ... Versailles, IN [*FM radio station call letters*]
WOVU .... Ocean View, DE [*FM radio station call letters*]
WOVV........ Fort Pierce, FL [*FM radio station call letters*]
WOW .... Omaha, NE [*AM radio station call letters*]
WOW .... Waiting on Weather [*Ocean storms*]
WOW .... War on Waste [*Navy*]
WOW .... War on Words
WOW .... Washington Opportunities for Women
WOW .... Weight-on-Wheels   (NASA)
WOW .... Wider Opportunities for Women [*Washington, DC*]   (EA)
WOW .... Woman Ordnance Worker
WOW .... Women Our Wonders [*Antifeminist men's group*]
WOW .... Women on Wheels   (EA)
WOW .... Women on Wine [*An association*] [*Modesto, CA*]   (EA)
WOW .... Woodmen of the World   (EA)
WOW .... Word on the Way
WOW .... World of Work [*Career-oriented course of study*]
WOW .... Worlds of Wonder [*Electronic toy manufacturer*]
WOW .... Worldwide Equities Ltd. [*Toronto Stock Exchange symbol*]
WOW .... Worn-Out Wolf [*An aging philanderer*] [*Slang*]
WOW .... Worst-on-Worst
Wow .... Wort und Wahrheit [*A publication*]
WOW .... Written Order of Withdrawal [*Banking*]
WoWa........ Wort und Wahrheit [*A publication*]
WOWAR .... Work Order and Work Accomplishment Record
WOWATE... World War II Equivalent [*Three-year and eight-month unit of
　　　　　　　　　time measurement proposed by former Under Secretary
　　　　　　　　　of the Navy R. James Woolsey*]
WOWE....... Rossville, GA [*FM radio station call letters*]
WOW-FM ... Omaha, NE [*FM radio station call letters*]
WOWI........ Norfolk, VA [*FM radio station call letters*]
WOWI .... Women on Words and Images   (EA)
WOWK-TV ... Huntington, WV [*Television station call letters*]
WOWL-TV ... Florence, AL [*Television station call letters*]
WOWN .... Shawano, WI [*FM radio station call letters*]
WOWN ...... Without Winch
WOWO .... Fort Wayne, IN [*AM radio station call letters*]
WOWQ .... DuBois, PA [*FM radio station call letters*]
WOWS....... Wire Obstacle Warning System   (IEEE)
WOWS........ Women Ordnance Workers [*A national voluntary organization*]
　　　　　　　　　[*World War II*]
WOWSER... We Only Want Social Evils Righted [*Said to be the translation
　　　　　　　　　for an Australian acronym describing a prudish reformer*]
WOWT........ Omaha, NE [*Television station call letters*]
WOWW....... Pensacola, FL [*FM radio station call letters*]
WOXO-FM ... Norway, ME [*FM radio station call letters*]
WOXR........ Talladega, AL [*AM radio station call letters*]
WOXY........ Oxford, OH [*FM radio station call letters*]
WOYE-FM ... Mayaguez, PR [*FM radio station call letters*]
WOYK .... York, PA [*AM radio station call letters*]
WOYL........ Oil City, PA [*AM radio station call letters*]
WOZI .... Presque Isle, ME [*FM radio station call letters*]
WOZK .... Ozark, AL [*AM radio station call letters*]
WOZN........ Key West, FL [*FM radio station call letters*]
WOZQ .... Northampton, MA [*FM radio station call letters*]
WOZW........ Monticello, ME [*AM radio station call letters*]
WP............. Empresa de Aviacion Aeronaves de Peru [*ICAO
　　　　　　　　　designator*]   (FAAC)
WP............. Pakistan Law Reports, West Pakistan Series   (DLA)
WP............. Portage Free Public Library, Portage, WI [*Library symbol*]
　　　　　　　　　[*Library of Congress*]   (LCLS)
WP............. Waiting Period   (OICC)
WP............. Waman Puma [*A publication*]
WP............. War Plans
WP............. Warm Pipe [*Nuclear energy*]   (NRCH)
WP............. Warming Pan [*Refers to a clergyman holding a job under a
　　　　　　　　　bond of resignation*] [*Obsolete*] [*Slang*] [*British*]   (DSUE)
WP............. Warsaw Pact   (NATG)
WP............. Washington Post [*A publication*]
WP............. Waste Pipe [*Technical drawings*]
WP............. Wastepaper
WP............. Water Packed
WP............. Water Plane   (MSA)
WP............. Water Point
WP............. Water Propeller   (AAG)
WP............. Water Pump   (AAG)
WP............. Waterproof
WP............. Way-Point
WP............. We the People [*An association*]   (EA)
WP............. Weapons Power
WP............. Weather Permitting
WP............. Weatherproof
WP............. Weekly Premium [*Insurance*]
WP............. Weight Penalty
WP............. Welding Procedure [*Nuclear energy*]   (NRCH)
WP............. Wespercorp [*American Stock Exchange symbol*]
WP............. West Point
WP............. [*The*] Western Pacific Railroad Co. [*AAR code*]
WP............. Western Pine [*Utility pole*] [*Telecommunications*]   (TEL)
WP............. Western Publishing Co. [*NYSE symbol*]
WP............. Wet Process   (MSA)

WP	Wettable Powder
WP	Wheel of Progress (EA)
WP	Whirlpool [Medicine]
WP	White Painted (BJA)
WP	White Paper (ADA)
WP	White Phosphorus [Military]
WP	Wiedza Powszechna [A publication]
WP	Wild Pitch [Baseball]
WP	Will Proceed To
WP	Will Proved [Legal] [British] (ROG)
WP	Winning Pitcher [Baseball]
WP	Wire Payment
WP	Without Prejudice
WP	Wolfe Pack [An association] (EA)
WP	Wood Pattern (MSA)
WP	Woodstock Papers [A publication]
WP	Word Processing [Movement to improve secretarial/clerical function through a managed system of people, procedures, and modern office equipment]
WP	Word Processor (ADA)
WP	Word Punch
WP	Work Package (NASA)
W/P	Work Picture [or Print] [Cinematography]
WP	Work Procedure [Nuclear energy] (NRCH)
WP	Work Program (NATG)
WP	Work in Progress [A publication]
WP	Working Paper
WP	Working Party
WP	Working Point
WP	Working Pressure
WP	World Peacemakers [An association] (EA)
WP	World Petroleum [A publication]
WP	World Politics [A publication]
WP	World Priorities (EA)
WP	Worship
WP	Worthy Patriarch
WP	Wrist Pitch (MCD)
WP	Write Protect
WP	Writers for Peace (EA)
WP3	Working Party Three [A subcommittee of the OECD]
WPA	Wagner-Peyser Act [1933] (OICC)
WPA	Water Pump Assembly
WPA	Western Pine Association [Later, WWPA] (EA)
WPA	Western Psychological Association (MCD)
WPA	Wet-Process Acid [Fertilizer]
WPA	Wheelchair Pilots Association (EA)
WPA	Whiskey Painters of America (EA)
WPA	William Penn Association (EA)
WPA	With Particular Average
WPA	Women's Prison Association [New York, NY] (EA)
WPA	Woody Point [Australia] [Seismograph station code, US Geological Survey] [Closed] (SEIS)
WPA	Work Package Action (MCD)
WPA	Work Package Address (MCD)
WPA	Working People's Alliance [Guyanese] (PD)
WPA	Works Progress Administration [Created, 1935, to operate public works projects for unemployed persons; name changed to Work Projects Administration, 1939; later, absorbed by Federal Works Agency, which was terminated in 1942]
WPA	Workshop of the Players Art [New York City]
WPA	World Parliament Association
WPA	World Pheasant Association (EA-IO)
WPA	World Presbyterian Alliance
WPA	World Psychiatric Association (EA-IO)
WPA	Worst Possible Accident [Nuclear safety]
WPAA	Andover, MA [FM radio station call letters]
WPAB	Ponce, PR [AM radio station call letters]
WPAC	Ogdensburg, NY [FM radio station call letters]
WPAC	Walden Pond Advisory Committee (EA)
WPAC	Working Program Advisory Committee [DoD]
WPAD	Paducah, KY [AM radio station call letters]
WPAFB	Wright-Patterson Air Force Base [Ohio]
WPAG	Ann Arbor, MI [AM radio station call letters]
WPAG-FM	Ann Arbor, MI [FM radio station call letters]
W PA Hist Mag	Western Pennsylvania Historical Magazine [A publication]
WPAJ	Lancaster, SC [FM radio station call letters]
WPAK	Farmville, VA [AM radio station call letters]
W Pakistan J Agr Res	West Pakistan Journal of Agricultural Research [A publication]
WPAL	Charleston, SC [AM radio station call letters]
WPAM	Pottsville, PA [AM radio station call letters]
WPAN	Fort Walton Beach, FL [Television station call letters]
WPAP	Panama City, FL [FM radio station call letters]
WPAQ	Mount Airy, NC [AM radio station call letters]
WPAQ	Westra Preschool Assessment Questionnaire
WPAR	Claremont, NC [AM radio station call letters]
W PAR	With Partition [Freight]
WP/AS	Word Processing/Administrative Support [Extension of Word Processing]
WPAS	Zephyrhills, FL [AM radio station call letters]

WPAT	Paterson, NJ [AM radio station call letters]
WPATC	Western Pennsylvania Advanced Technology Center [University of Pittsburgh, Carnegie-Mellon University] [Research center] (RCD)
WPAT-FM	Paterson, NJ [FM radio station call letters]
WPA-USA	World Pheasant Association of the USA (EA)
WPAWA	World Professional Armwrestling Association (EA)
WPAX	Thomasville, GA [AM radio station call letters]
WPAY	Portsmouth, OH [AM radio station call letters]
WPAY-FM	Portsmouth, OH [FM radio station call letters]
WPAZ	Pottstown, PA [AM radio station call letters]
WPB	Gunboat [Coast Guard] (NVT)
WPB	Port Berge [Madagascar] [Airport symbol] (OAG)
WPB	Wall Plate Box
WPB	War Production Board [World War II]
WPB	Waste Processing Building [Nuclear energy] (NRCH)
WPB	Wastepaper Basket [or Bin]
WPB	Whirlpool Bath [Medicine]
WPB	Wide Pulse Blanking (MCD)
WPB	Wiener Enterprises, Inc. [American Stock Exchange symbol]
WPB	World Peace Brigade (EA)
WPB	Write Printer Binary
WPBA	Atlanta, GA [Television station call letters]
WPBA	Women's Professional Bowlers Association (EA)
WPBA	Women's Professional Billiard Alliance (EA)
WPBB	Romney, WV [FM radio station call letters]
WPBC	Bangor, ME [FM radio station call letters]
WPBC	Western Pacific Base Command [Marianas] [World War II]
WPBCWS	Waste Processing Building Chilled Water System [Nuclear energy] (NRCH)
WPBD	Atlanta, GA [AM radio station call letters]
WPBE	Huntingdon, TN [FM radio station call letters]
WPBEF	West Pakistan Bank Employees' Federation
WPBIC	Walker Problem Behavior Identification Checklist [Education]
WPBK	Whitehall, MI [AM radio station call letters]
WPBL	Women's Professional Basketball League [Defunct] (EA)
WPBN-TV	Traverse City, MI [Television station call letters]
WPBR	Palm Beach, FL [AM radio station call letters]
WPBRL	Warsaw Pact/Ballistic Research Laboratory (MCD)
WPBT	Miami, FL [Television station call letters]
WPBX	Southampton, NY [FM radio station call letters]
WPBY-TV	Huntington, WV [Television station call letters]
WPC	Walter P. Chrysler Club (EA)
WPC	Warsaw Pact Countries (MCD)
WPC	Washington Press Club [Formerly, WNPC]
WPC	Waste Product Costs [Solid waste management]
WPC	Water Pollution Control
WPC	Watts per Candle [Electricity]
WPC	Webster's Patent Cases [1601-1855] (DLA)
WPC	Wedge Power Clamp
WPC	Weldable Printed Circuit
WPC	Wheat Protein Concentrate [Food technology]
WPC	Whey Protein Concentrate [Food technology]
WPC	William Penn College [Oskaloosa, IA]
WPC	William Peterson College of New Jersey
WPC	Wired Program Computer
WPC	Wisconsin Electric Power Company [NYSE symbol]
WPC	Wollaston's English Bail Court Reports, Practice Cases (DLA)
WPC	Woman Police Constable [Scotland Yard]
WPC	Women's Political Caucus
WPC	Wood-Plastic Combination [or Composite]
WPC	Word Processing Center
WPC	Work Package Concept (MCD)
WP + C	Work Planning and Control [Data processing]
WPC	Workers Party of Canada
WPC	World Peace Congress
WPC	World Peace Council [See also CMP] (EA-IO)
WPC	World Petroleum Congress
WPC	World Petroleum Congresses (EA-IO)
WPC	World Planning Chart [Aviation]
WPC	World Pooling Committee (MCD)
WPC	World Power Conference
WPC	World Print Council (EA)
WPC	World Pumpkin Confederation (EA)
WPCA	Water Pollution Control Administration [Department of the Interior]
WPCA	Wool Pullers Council of America (EA)
WPCAA	White Park Cattle Association of America (EA)
WP Cas	Webster's Patent Cases [1601-1855] (DLA)
WP Cas	Wollaston's English Bail Court Reports, Practice Cases (DLA)
WPCB	Western Pennsylvania Christian Broadcasting Co. [A cable TV station]
WPCB-TV	Greensburg, PA [Television station call letters]
WPCC	Clinton, SC [AM radio station call letters]
WPCC	Wilson Pharmaceutical & Chemical Corporation
WPCC	World Paper Currency Collectors (EA)
WPCD	Champaign, IL [FM radio station call letters]
WPCE	Portsmouth, VA [AM radio station call letters]
WPCF	Panama City Beach, FL [AM radio station call letters]
WPCF	Water Pollution Control Federation (EA)
WPCF	Water Pollution Control Federation. Journal [A publication]

WPCF Highlights ... Water Pollution Control Federation. Highlights [*A publication*]
WPCFJ ...... Water Pollution Control Federation. Journal [*A publication*]
WPCH .... Atlanta, GA [*FM radio station call letters*]
WPCHLIJS ... World Philatelic Congress of Holy Land, Israel, and Judaica Societies (EA)
WPCI .... Perry, FL [*FM radio station call letters*]
WPCJ .... Pittsford, MI [*FM radio station call letters*]
WPCM .... Burlington-Graham, NC [*FM radio station call letters*]
WPCN .... Mount Pocono, PA [*AM radio station call letters*]
WPCND ...... Women's Patriotic Conference on National Defense (EA)
WPCO .... Mt. Vernon, IN [*AM radio station call letters*]
WPCQ-TV ... Charlotte, NC [*Television station call letters*]
WPCR .... Water Pollution Control Research [*Environmental Protection Agency*]
WPCR-FM ... Plymouth, NH [*FM radio station call letters*]
WPCS .... Pensacola, FL [*FM radio station call letters*]
WPCSA ..... Welsh Pony and Cob Society of America [*Winchester, VA*] (EA)
WPCV .... Winter Haven, FL [*FM radio station call letters*]
WPCX .... Auburn, NY [*FM radio station call letters*]
WPD .... War Plan Division [*World War II*]
WPD .... Western Procurement Division [*Marine Corps*]
WPD .... Work Package Description [*NASA*] (NASA)
WPD .... World Pharmaceuticals Directory [*A publication*]
WPD .... Write Printer Decimal
WPDA .... Writing Pushdown Acceptor
WPDC .... Elizabethtown, PA [*AM radio station call letters*]
WPDES ...... Waste Pollution Discharge Elimination System (IEEE)
WPDE-TV ... Florence, SC [*Television station call letters*]
WPDH .... Poughkeepsie, NY [*FM radio station call letters*]
WPDM .... Potsdam, NY [*AM radio station call letters*]
WPDQ .... Jacksonville, FL [*AM radio station call letters*]
WPDR .... Portage, WI [*AM radio station call letters*]
WPDS .... Tampa, FL [*FM radio station call letters*]
WPDX .... Word Processing Document Exchange Program
WPDX-FM ... Clarksburg, WV [*FM radio station call letters*]
WPDZ .... Cheraw, SC [*FM radio station call letters*]
WPE .... West Pittston-Exeter Railroad Co. [*AAR code*]
WPE .... Western Pacific Energy [*Vancouver Stock Exchange symbol*]
WPE .... Western Plastics Exposition [*HBJ Expositions and Conferences*] (TSPED)
WPEA .... Exeter, NH [*FM radio station call letters*]
WPEB .... Philadelphia, PA [*FM radio station call letters*]
WPEC .... Weapons Production Engineering Center [*Navy*]
WPEC .... West Palm Beach, FL [*Television station call letters*]
WPEC .... World Plan Executive Council [*Later, WGAE-US*] (EA)
WPEG .... Concord, NC [*FM radio station call letters*]
WPEH .... Louisville, GA [*AM radio station call letters*]
WPEH-FM ... Louisville, GA [*FM radio station call letters*]
WPEL .... Montrose, PA [*AM radio station call letters*]
WPEL-FM ... Montrose, PA [*FM radio station call letters*]
WPEN .... Philadelphia, PA [*AM radio station call letters*]
WPEO .... Peoria, IL [*AM radio station call letters*]
WPEP .... Taunton, MA [*AM radio station call letters*]
WPET .... Greensboro, NC [*AM radio station call letters*]
WPET .... Western Petroleum Corp. [*NASDAQ symbol*] (NQ)
WPeW .... Waukesha County Technical Institute, Pewaukee, WI [*Library symbol*] [*Library of Congress*] (LCLS)
WPEX .... Hampton, VA [*AM radio station call letters*]
WPEZ .... Macon, GA [*FM radio station call letters*]
WPF .... Watcor Purification Systems, Inc. [*Vancouver Stock Exchange symbol*]
WPF .... Weather Profile Facility
WPF .... Weight, Power, Fulcrum
WPF .... Whale Protection Fund (EA)
WPF .... Work Process Flow [*NASA*] (NASA)
WPF .... World Peace Foundation (EA)
WPF .... World Prohibition Federation
WPF .... Worldwide Pen Friends (EA)
WPFA .... Pensacola, FL [*AM radio station call letters*]
WPFA .... William Penn Fraternal Association [*Later, WPA*] (EA)
WPFB .... Middletown, OH [*AM radio station call letters*]
WPFB-FM ... Middletown, OH [*FM radio station call letters*]
WPFC .... Commission for Fisheries Research in the West Pacific
WPFC .... Waterproof Fan Cooled (MSA)
WPFC .... Westbeth Playwrights Feminist Collective [*Defunct*] (EA)
WPFC .... World Press Freedom Committee (EA)
WPFD .... Fairview, TN [*FM radio station call letters*]
WPFDM ...... Working Papers. Fondazione Dalle Molle [*A publication*]
WPFL .... West Pakistan Federation of Labor
WPFL .... Winter Park, FL [*FM radio station call letters*]
WPFL .... Worshipful (ROG)
WPFM .... Panama City, FL [*FM radio station call letters*]
WPFM .... Wiping Form (AAG)
WPFR .... Terre Haute, IN [*AM radio station call letters*]
WPFR-FM ... Terre Haute, IN [*FM radio station call letters*]
WPFTA ...... White Plate Flat Trackers Association (EA)
WPFUL ...... Worshipful
WPFW .... Washington, DC [*FM radio station call letters*]
WPG .... Waterproofing (AAG)

WPG .... Weighted Pair Group
WPG .... West Point Graduate
WPG .... Wiping (MSA)
WPG .... Worcester Polytechnic Institute, Worcester, MA [*OCLC symbol*] (OCLC)
WPG .... Work Package Grouping [*NASA*] (NASA)
WPGA .... Perry, GA [*AM radio station call letters*]
WPGA-FM ... Perry, GA [*FM radio station call letters*]
WPGC .... Morningside, MD [*AM radio station call letters*]
WPGH-TV ... Pittsburgh, PA [*Television station call letters*]
WPGM .... Danville, PA [*AM radio station call letters*]
WPGM-FM ... Danville, PA [*FM radio station call letters*]
WPGO .... Shallotte, NC [*FM radio station call letters*]
WPGR .... Philadelphia, PA [*AM radio station call letters*]
WPGS .... Scottsmour, FL [*AM radio station call letters*]
WPGT .... Group Fore - Women's Pro Golf Tour (EA)
WPGT .... Roanoke Rapids, NC [*FM radio station call letters*]
WPGU .... Urbana, IL [*FM radio station call letters*]
WPGW .... Portland, IN [*AM radio station call letters*]
WPGW-FM ... Portland, IN [*FM radio station call letters*]
W & PH ...... Wage and Purchase Hire
WPH .... West Pit [*Hawaii*] [*Seismograph station code, US Geological Survey*] [*Closed*] (SEIS)
WPH .... William Penn House [*An association*] (EA)
WPHB .... Philipsburg, PA [*AM radio station call letters*]
WPHC .... Waverly, TN [*AM radio station call letters*]
WPHD .... Buffalo, NY [*AM radio station call letters*]
WPHD-FM ... Buffalo, NY [*FM radio station call letters*]
WPHI .... Western Pennsylvania Horological Institute
WPHK .... Blountstown, FL [*FM radio station call letters*]
WPHL-TV ... Philadelphia, PA [*Television station call letters*]
WPHM .... Port Huron, MI [*AM radio station call letters*]
WPHM .... Western Pennsylvania Historical Magazine [*A publication*]
WPHN .... Gaylord, MI [*FM radio station call letters*]
WPHOA ...... Women Public Health Officer's Association [*British*]
WPHP .... Wheeling, WV [*FM radio station call letters*]
WPHS-FM ... Warren, MI [*FM radio station call letters*]
WPHUJ .... Working Papers. Hebrew University of Jerusalem [*A publication*]
WPI .... Wall Paper Institute [*Later, Wallcovering Manufacturers Association*] (EA)
WPI .... Waxed Paper Institute [*Later, FPA*] (EA)
WPI .... Wedding Photographers International [*Santa Monica, CA*] (EA)
WPI .... Western Personality Inventory [*Psychology*]
WPI .... Whey Products Institute [*Later, ADPI*] (EA)
WPI .... Wholesale Price Index [*Economics*]
WPI .... Women and Priests Involved (EA)
WPI .... Women's Peace Initiative (EA)
WPI .... Worcester Polytechnic Institute [*Massachusetts*]
WPI .... Work Progress Indicator [*NASA*] (NASA)
WPI .... World Patents Index [*Derwent Publications Ltd.*] [*Database*]
WPI .... World Press Institute (EA)
WPIC .... Sharon, PA [*AM radio station call letters*]
WPIC .... Western Psychiatric Institute and Clinic [*University of Pittsburgh*] [*Research center*] (RCD)
WPID .... Piedmont, AL [*AM radio station call letters*]
WPIE .... Trumansburg, NY [*AM radio station call letters*]
WPIO .... Titusville, FL [*FM radio station call letters*]
WPIQ .... Brunswick, GA [*FM radio station call letters*]
WPIT .... Pittsburgh, PA [*AM radio station call letters*]
WPIT-FM .... Pittsburgh, PA [*FM radio station call letters*]
WPIX .... New York, NY [*FM radio station call letters*]
WPIX .... New York, NY [*Television station call letters*]
WPJ .... Weakened Plane Joint
WPJC .... Adjuntas, PR [*AM radio station call letters*]
WPJK .... Orangeburg, SC [*AM radio station call letters*]
WPJL .... Raleigh, NC [*AM radio station call letters*]
WPJM .... Greer, SC [*AM radio station call letters*]
WPK .... Air-Lift Associates, Inc. [*Morrisville, NC*] [*FAA designator*] (FAAC)
WPK .... Winpak [*Toronto Stock Exchange symbol*]
WPKE .... Pikeville, KY [*AM radio station call letters*]
WPKN .... Bridgeport, CT [*FM radio station call letters*]
WPKT .... Middlefield, CT [*FM radio station call letters*]
WPKY .... Princeton, KY [*AM radio station call letters*]
WPKY-FM ... Princeton, KY [*FM radio station call letters*]
WPL .... War Plan, Long-Range (CINC)
WPL .... Warren Public Library, Warren, OH [*OCLC symbol*] (OCLC)
WPL .... Waste Pickle Liquor [*Industrial waste*]
WPL .... Wave Propagation Laboratory [*University of Houston*] [*National Oceanic and Atmospheric Administration*] [*Research center*]
WPL .... Winnipeg Public Library [*UTLAS symbol*]
WPL .... Wisconsin Power & Light Co. [*NYSE symbol*]
WPL .... Working Papers in Linguistics [*A publication*]
WPL .... Worshipful
WPL .... Worst Path Loss
WPLA .... Plant City, FL [*AM radio station call letters*]
WPlaU .... University of Wisconsin-Platteville, Platteville, WI [*Library symbol*] [*Library of Congress*] (LCLS)

WPLB .... Greenville, MI [*AM radio station call letters*]
WPLB-FM... Greenville, MI [*FM radio station call letters*]
WPLG .... Miami, FL [*Television station call letters*]
WPLH .... Tifton, GA [*FM radio station call letters*]
WPLJ .... New York, NY [*FM radio station call letters*]
WPLJ .... White Port and Lemon Juice [*Title of both song and drink*]
WPLK .... Rockmart, GA [*AM radio station call letters*]
WPLM .... Plymouth, MA [*AM radio station call letters*]
WPLM-FM ... Plymouth, MA [*FM radio station call letters*]
WPLN .... Nashville, TN [*FM radio station call letters*]
WPLO .... Atlanta, GA [*AM radio station call letters*]
WPLO .... Water Port Liaison Office [*or Officer*] [*Air Force*]   (AFM)
WPLP .... Pinellas Park, FL [*AM radio station call letters*]
WPLR .... New Haven, CT [*FM radio station call letters*]
WPLS .... Western Plains Library System [*Library network*]
WPLS-FM.... Greenville, VT [*FM radio station call letters*]
WPLT .... Plattsburgh, NY [*FM radio station call letters*]
WPLTO .... Western Plateau [*FAA*]   (FAAC)
WPLUH....... Working Papers in Linguistics (University of Hawaii) [*A publication*]
WPLW .... Carnegie, PA [*AM radio station call letters*]
WPLY .... Plymouth, WI [*AM radio station call letters*]
WPlyM....... Mission House Theological Seminary, Plymouth, WI [*Library symbol*] [*Library of Congress*]   (LCLS)
WPLZ .... Petersburg, VA [*AM radio station call letters*]
WPLZ-FM.... Petersburg, VA [*FM radio station call letters*]
WPM........... War Plan, Mid-Range
WPM........... War Planning Memorandum   (NATG)
WPM........... West Point-Pepperell, Inc. [*NYSE symbol*]
WPM........... White Pine [*Michigan*] [*Seismograph station code, US Geological Survey*]   (SEIS)
WPM........... Wipim [*Papua New Guinea*] [*Airport symbol*]   (OAG)
WPM........... Wire-Wound Porous Material
WPM........... Wood Plastic Material
WPM........... Words per Minute
WPM........... Work Package Management   (MCD)
WPM........... World Presbyterian Missions   (EA)
WPM........... Write Program Memory [*Data processing*]
WPM........... Write Protect Memory
WPMA........ Waterproof Paper Manufacturers Association [*Later, API*]
WPMA........ Wildwood, FL [*AM radio station call letters*]
WPMA........ Wood Products Manufacturers Association [*Formerly, WTSB, WTSA*] [*Gardner, MA*]   (EA)
WPMA........ Writing Paper Manufacturers Association [*Later, API*]   (EA)
WPMB........ Vandalia, IL [*AM radio station call letters*]
WPMC........ Waxed Paper Merchandising Council [*Defunct*]
WPMCP...... Work Package Manpower and Cost Plan [*NASA*]   (NASA)
WPME .... Women for Peace in the Middle East   (EA)
WPMH........ Portsmouth, VA [*AM radio station call letters*]
WPMI......... Mobile, AL [*Television station call letters*]
WPMO .... Moss Point, MS [*AM radio station call letters*]
WPMO-FM ... Pascagoula, MS [*FM radio station call letters*]
WPMRR...... Work Package Milestone Progress Report   (MCD)
WPMT .... York, PA [*Television station call letters*]
WPMW .... Mullens, WV [*FM radio station call letters*]
WPN .... Weapon   (AAG)
WPN .... Weapons Procurement, Navy   (NVT)
WPN .... Wolverhampton [*British depot code*]
WPN .... Write Punch [*Data processing*]   (MCD)
WPNA........ World Proof Numismatic Association   (EA)
WPNC......... Plymouth, NC [*AM radio station call letters*]
WPNE......... Green Bay, WI [*Television station call letters*]
WPNE-FM ... Green Bay, WI [*FM radio station call letters*]
WPNF .... Brevard, NC [*AM radio station call letters*]
WPNFPT..... Weapon Fly-to-Point   (NVT)
WPNGL ...... Workpapers in Papua New Guinea Languages [*A publication*]
WPNH........ Plymouth, NH [*AM radio station call letters*]
WPNH-FM ... Plymouth, NH [*FM radio station call letters*]
WPNR-FM ... Utica, NY [*FM radio station call letters*]
WPNSTA.... Weapons Station
WPNTS...... War Plan Naval Transportation Service
WPNX........ Phenix City, AL-Columbus, GA [*AM radio station call letters*]
WPO .... War Plan Orange [*World War II*]
WPO .... Warsaw Pact Organization   (MCD)
WPO .... Washington Post Co. [*American Stock Exchange symbol*]
WPO .... Water for Peace Office [*Department of State*]
WPO .... Water Programs Office [*Environmental Protection Agency*]
WPO .... World Packaging Organization [*See also OME*]   (EA-IO)
WPO .... World Ploughing Organisation [*England*]   (EA-IO)
WPO .... World Ploughing Organization
WPOA........ Western Pacific Orthopaedic Association   (EA)
WPOB........ Plainview, NY [*FM radio station call letters*]
WPOC .... Baltimore, MD [*FM radio station call letters*]
WPOC .... Water and Pollution Control [*A publication*]
WPoCP....... ICA [*International Co-Operative Alliance*] Working Party on Co-Operative Press   (EA-IO)
WPOD .... Water Port of Debarkation   (AFM)
WPOE........ Greenfield, MA [*AM radio station call letters*]
WPOE........ Water Port of Embarkation   (AFM)
WPOG .... Willard Pease Oil & Gas [*NASDAQ symbol*]   (NQ)
WPOK .... Pontiac, IL [*AM radio station call letters*]

W Pol Q ...... Western Political Quarterly [*A publication*]
WPOM........ Riviera Beach, FL [*AM radio station call letters*]
WPON........ Pontiac, MI [*AM radio station call letters*]
WPOP........ Hartford, CT [*AM radio station call letters*]
WPOR......... Portland, ME [*AM radio station call letters*]
WPOR-FM ... Portland, ME [*FM radio station call letters*]
WPOS-FM ... Holland, OH [*FM radio station call letters*]
WPOW........ Miramar, FL [*FM radio station call letters*]
WPP .... Wage Pause Program [*Business and trade*]   (ADA)
WPP .... Washington Promotion Plan [*FAA*]   (FAAC)
WPP .... Waterproof Paper Packing
WPP .... Weapon Position Preparation   (MCD)
WPP .... Weapons Production Program
WPP .... Web Printing Press
WPP .... Weibull Probability Paper [*Statistics*]
WPP .... Windward Passage Patrol [*Navy*]   (NVT)
WPP .... Work Package Plan [*NASA*]   (NASA)
WPP .... World Pen Pals   (EA)
WPPA........ Pottsville, PA [*AM radio station call letters*]
WPPB-TV ... Boca Raton, FL [*Television station call letters*]
WPPC........ Penuelas, PR [*AM radio station call letters*]
WPPC........ Warning Point Photocell
WPPC........ West Penn Power Company
WPPC........ West Point Parents Club   (EA)
WPPDA ..... Welfare and Pension Plans Disclosure Act [*Department of Labor*]
WPPI .... Carrollton, GA [*AM radio station call letters*]
WPPL .... Blue Ridge, GA [*FM radio station call letters*]
WPPM .... Weight Part per Million
WPPO......... Wood Products Purchasing Office [*Defense Construction Supply Center*] [*Defense Supply Agency*]
WPPR......... Barrington, IL [*FM radio station call letters*]
WPPS .... Work Package Planning Sheet [*NASA*]   (NASA)
WPPSI....... Wechsler Preschool and Primary Scale of Intelligence [*Education*]
WPPSS..... Washington Public Power Supply System [*Nicknamed "Whoops"*]
WPPW .... Association of Western Pulp and Paper Workers
WPQ .... Western Political Quarterly [*A publication*]
WPQR........ Welding Procedure Qualification Record [*Nuclear energy*]   (NRCH)
WPQR-FM ... Uniontown, PA [*FM radio station call letters*]
WPR .... Ward Pound Ridge [*New York*] [*Seismograph station code, US Geological Survey*]   (SEIS)
WPR .... Wartime Personnel Requirements   (NATG)
WPR .... Webster's Patent Reports [*England*]   (DLA)
WPR .... White Puerto Rican
WPR .... Widescope Resources Ltd. [*Vancouver Stock Exchange symbol*]
WPR .... Witness Protection and Relocation [*Government agency in film "F/X"*]
WPR .... Woodpecker Repellent [*In company name, WPR Co.*]
WPR .... Working Party on Rationing [*Allied German Occupation Forces*]
WPR .... Working Pressure
WPRA........ Mayaguez, PR [*AM radio station call letters*]
WPRA........ Women's Professional Racquetball Association [*Atlanta, GA*]   (EA)
WPRA........ Women's Professional Rodeo Association   (EA)
WPRB......... Princeton, NJ [*FM radio station call letters*]
WPRC......... Lincoln, IL [*AM radio station call letters*]
WPRE .... Prairie Du Chien, WI [*AM radio station call letters*]
WPRE-FM ... Prairie Du Chien, WI [*FM radio station call letters*]
WPRI .... Wartime Pacific Routing Instructions [*Navy*]
WPRI-TV ... Providence, RI [*Television station call letters*]
WPRJ......... Mount Pleasant, MI [*AM radio station call letters*]
WPRK......... Winter Park, FL [*FM radio station call letters*]
WPRL .... Lorman, MS [*FM radio station call letters*]
WPRL .... Water Pollution Research Laboratory [*British*]
WPRM .... San Juan, PR [*FM radio station call letters*]
WPRN........ Butler, AL [*AM radio station call letters*]
WPRO......... East Providence, RI [*AM radio station call letters*]
WPRO-FM ... Providence, RI [*FM radio station call letters*]
WPRP......... Ponce, PR [*AM radio station call letters*]
WPRQ......... Colonial Heights, TN [*AM radio station call letters*]
WPRR......... Altoona, PA [*FM radio station call letters*]
WPRS......... Paris, IL [*AM radio station call letters*]
WPRS......... Water and Power Resources Service [*Formerly, Bureau of Reclamation*] [*Department of the Interior*] [*Name changed back to Bureau of Reclamation, 1981*]
WPRS......... Wittenborn Psychiatric Rating Scale
WPRT......... Prestonsburg, KY [*AM radio station call letters*]
WPRV-TV ... Fajardo, PR [*Television station call letters*]
WPRW........ Manassas, VA [*AM radio station call letters*]
WPRY......... Perry, FL [*AM radio station call letters*]
WPRZ......... Warrenton, VA [*AM radio station call letters*]
WPS .... International Association of Word Processing Specialists [*Formerly, NAWPS*]   (EA)
WPS .... War Plan, Short-Range
WPS .... War Planning Slate   (CINC)
WPS .... Warner Publisher Services

WPS	Waste Processing System [*Nuclear energy*] (NRCH)
WPS	Water Phase Salt [*of smoked food*]
WPS	Water Pressure Switch
WPS	Water Purification System
WPS	Waterproof Shroud
WPS	Watts per Steradian
WPS	Wave Power Source
WPS	Waveform Processing System
WPS	Weapons Program Section
WPS	Welding Procedure Specification [*Nuclear energy*] (NRCH)
WPS	White Power Structure
WPS	Widowed Persons Service [*An association*] [*Washington, DC*] (EA)
WPS	Wisconsin Public Service Corp. [*NYSE symbol*]
WPS	With Prior Service
WPS	Women in Public Service (EA)
WPS	Word Processing System (BUR)
WPS	Words per Second
WPS	Workstation Publishing Software
WPS	World Photography Society (EA)
WPS	World Politics Simulation
WPS	World Population Society [*Washington, DC*] (EA)
WPS	Worldwide Plug and Socket [*Proposed standard electrical plug for international use*] [*Pronounced "whoops"*]
WPSA	Paul Smiths, NY [*FM radio station call letters*]
WPSA	Welsh Pony Society of America [*Later, WPCSA*] (EA)
WPSA	World Professional Squash Association (EA)
WPSA	World's Poultry Science Association [*See also AVI*] (EA-IO)
WPSC	Pageland, SC [*AM radio station call letters*]
WPSC	Shipping Control War Plan [*Navy*]
WPSD-TV ...	Paducah, KY [*Television station call letters*]
WPSI	Word Processing Society, Incorporated (EA)
WPSI	World Poetry Society Intercontinental (EA)
WPSK	Pulaski, VA [*AM radio station call letters*]
WPSK-FM ...	Pulaski, VA [*FM radio station call letters*]
WPSL	Port St. Lucie, FL [*AM radio station call letters*]
WPSL	Western Primary Standard Laboratory
WPSM	Fort Walton Beach, FL [*FM radio station call letters*]
WPSO	New Port Richey, FL [*AM radio station call letters*]
WPSR	Weekly Performance Status Report (MCD)
WPS-RA	World Pro Skiing-Racers Association [*Defunct*] (EA)
WPST	Trenton, NJ [*FM radio station call letters*]
WPSU	State College, PA [*FM radio station call letters*]
WPSX-TV ...	Clearfield, PA [*Television station call letters*]
WP & T	War Plans and Training
WPT...........	Waypoint (FAAC)
WPT...........	Windfall Profit Tax
WPT...........	With Promotion To (NOAA)
WPT...........	Workers' Party of Turkey
WPTA	Fort Wayne, IN [*Television station call letters*]
WPTA	Wooden Pail and Tub Association
WPTB	Statesboro, GA [*AM radio station call letters*]
WPTB	Wartime Prices and Trade Board
WPTD	Kettering, OH [*Television station call letters*]
WPTF	National Council for a World Peace Tax Fund (EA)
WPTF	Raleigh, NC [*AM radio station call letters*]
WPTF-TV ...	Durham, NC [*Television station call letters*]
WPTI	Wildlife Preservation Trust International (EA)
WPTL	Canton, NC [*AM radio station call letters*]
WPTLC.......	World Peace through Law Center [*Washington, DC*]
WPTM	Roanoke Rapids, NC [*FM radio station call letters*]
WPTN	Cookeville, TN [*AM radio station call letters*]
WPTNG	Weapons Training (NVT)
WPTO.........	Oxford, OH [*Television station call letters*]
WPTR	Albany, NY [*AM radio station call letters*]
WPTRS.......	Wespac Investors Trust II [*NASDAQ symbol*] (NQ)
WPTS-FM ...	Pittsburgh, PA [*FM radio station call letters*]
WPTT-TV ...	Pittsburgh, PA [*Television station call letters*]
WPTV	West Palm Beach, FL [*Television station call letters*]
WPTW	Piqua, OH [*AM radio station call letters*]
WPTW-FM ...	Piqua, OH [*FM radio station call letters*]
WPTX	Lexington Park, MD [*AM radio station call letters*]
WPTY-TV ...	Memphis, TN [*Television station call letters*]
WPTZ	North Pole, NY [*Television station call letters*]
WPU	With Power Unit (NATG)
WPU	Write Punch
WPUB	Camden, SC [*AM radio station call letters*]
WPUB-FM ...	Camden, SC [*FM radio station call letters*]
WPUC........	Waste-Paper Utilization Council [*Defunct*]
W/PUG.......	Word Processing Users' Group
WPUM	Rensselaer, IN [*FM radio station call letters*]
WPUR........	Americus, GA [*FM radio station call letters*]
WPUT........	Brewster, NY [*AM radio station call letters*]
WPVG........	Boonsboro, MD [*AM radio station call letters*]
WPVI-TV ...	Philadelphia, PA [*Television station call letters*]
WPVR........	Roanoke, VA [*FM radio station call letters*]
WPW	Wolff-Parkinson-White [*Syndrome*] [*Cardiology*]
WPWC........	Dumfries-Triangle, VA [*AM radio station call letters*]
WPWM	Wide Pulse Width Modulation
WPWOD	Will Proceed Without Delay
WPWR	World-Wide Plantation Walker Registry (EA)

WPWR-TV ...	Aurora, IL [*Television station call letters*]
WPWT	Philadelphia, PA [*FM radio station call letters*]
WPXC........	Hyannis, MA [*FM radio station call letters*]
WPXE	Starke, FL [*AM radio station call letters*]
WPXE-FM ...	Starke, FL [*FM radio station call letters*]
WPXI	Pittsburgh, PA [*Television station call letters*]
WPXN	Paxton, IL [*FM radio station call letters*]
WPXT	Portland, ME [*Television station call letters*]
WPXY	Rochester, NY [*AM radio station call letters*]
WPXY-FM ...	Rochester, NY [*FM radio station call letters*]
WPXZ	Punxsutawney, PA [*AM radio station call letters*]
WPXZ-FM...	Punxsutawney, PA [*FM radio station call letters*]
WPY	White Pass & Yukon Corp. Ltd. [*Toronto Stock Exchange symbol*] [*Vancouver Stock Exchange symbol*] [*AAR code*]
WPY	World Population Year [*1974*] [*United Nations*]
WPYB........	Benson, NC [*AM radio station call letters*]
WPYEEJS ...	Working Papers in Yiddish and East European Jewish Studies [*A publication*]
WPYK	Dora, AL [*AM radio station call letters*]
WP&YR	White Pass & Yukon Railway [*Nickname: Wait Patiently and You'll Ride*]
WPYX	Albany, NY [*FM radio station call letters*]
WPZ...........	Waipapa Point [*New Zealand*] [*Seismograph station code, US Geological Survey*] [*Closed*] (SEIS)
WPZ...........	Wiener Praehistorische Zeitschrift [*A publication*]
WQ	Bahamas World Airlines Ltd. [*ICAO designator*] (FAAC)
WQ	Science Wonder Quarterly [*A publication*]
WQ	Wonder Stories Quarterly [*A publication*]
WQA...........	Water Quality Association [*Formed by a merger of WCAI and WCF*] [*Lisle, IL*] (EA)
WQA...........	Weld Quality Assurance
WQAA	Luray, VA [*FM radio station call letters*]
WQAB	Philippi, WV [*FM radio station call letters*]
WQAC	Fort Walton Beach, FL [*Television station call letters*]
WQAD-TV ...	Moline, IL [*Television station call letters*]
WQAL	Cleveland, OH [*FM radio station call letters*]
WQAM	Miami, FL [*AM radio station call letters*]
WQAQ	Hamden, CT [*FM radio station call letters*]
WQAZ	Cleveland, MS [*FM radio station call letters*]
WQB...........	Water-Quality Biological [*Survey*] [*Army*] (RDA)
WQBA	Miami, FL [*AM radio station call letters*]
WQBA-FM ...	Miami, FL [*FM radio station call letters*]
WQBC	Vicksburg, MS [*AM radio station call letters*]
WQBE	Charleston, WV [*AM radio station call letters*]
WQBE-FM ...	Charleston, WV [*FM radio station call letters*]
WQBH	Detroit, MI [*AM radio station call letters*]
WQBK	Rensselaer, NY [*AM radio station call letters*]
WQBK-FM ...	Rensselaer, NY [*FM radio station call letters*]
WQBQ	Leesburg, FL [*AM radio station call letters*]
WQBR........	Atlantic Beach, FL [*AM radio station call letters*]
WQBS	San Juan, PR [*AM radio station call letters*]
WQBZ	Fort Valley, GA [*FM radio station call letters*]
WQC...........	Quinsigamond Community College, Worcester, MA [*OCLC symbol*] (OCLC)
WQC...........	Water Quality Certification (NRCH)
WQC...........	Wheat Quality Council (EA)
WQCB	Brewer, ME [*FM radio station call letters*]
WQCC	Charlotte, NC [*AM radio station call letters*]
WQCK	Clinton, LA [*FM radio station call letters*]
WQCM	Halfway, MD [*FM radio station call letters*]
WQCR	Burlington, VT [*FM radio station call letters*]
WQCS	Fort Pierce, FL [*FM radio station call letters*]
WQCT	Bryan, OH [*AM radio station call letters*]
WQCW	Waycross, GA [*FM radio station call letters*]
WQCY	Quincy, IL [*FM radio station call letters*]
WQDE	Albany, GA [*AM radio station call letters*]
WQDK	Ahoskie, NC [*FM radio station call letters*]
WQDQ	Thompson Station, TN [*AM radio station call letters*]
WQDR	Raleigh, NC [*FM radio station call letters*]
WQDW	Kinston, NC [*FM radio station call letters*]
WQDY	Calais, ME [*AM radio station call letters*]
WQDY-FM ...	Calais, ME [*FM radio station call letters*]
WQEC	Quincy, IL [*Television station call letters*]
WQEC/C	Weapons Quality Engineering Center, Crane [*Indiana*]
WQED	Pittsburgh, PA [*Television station call letters*]
WQED-FM ...	Pittsburgh, PA [*FM radio station call letters*]
WQEN	Gadsden, AL [*FM radio station call letters*]
WQEQ	Freeland, PA [*FM radio station call letters*]
WQEX	Pittsburgh, PA [*Television station call letters*]
WQEZ	Fort Myers Beach, FL [*FM radio station call letters*]
WQF	Wider Quaker Fellowship (EA)
WQFL	Rockford, IL [*FM radio station call letters*]
WQFM	Milwaukee, WI [*FM radio station call letters*]
WQFS	Greensboro, NC [*FM radio station call letters*]
WQFX	Gulfport, MS [*AM radio station call letters*]
WQFX-FM ...	Gulfport, MS [*FM radio station call letters*]
WQGL........	Butler, AL [*FM radio station call letters*]
WQGN-FM ...	Groton, CT [*FM radio station call letters*]
WQHJ	Key West, FL [*Television station call letters*]
WQHK	Fort Wayne, IN [*AM radio station call letters*]
WQHL........	Live Oak, FL [*FM radio station call letters*]

WQHQ .... Salisbury, MD [*FM radio station call letters*]
WQHS ...... Cleveland, OH [*Television station call letters*]
WQHT........ Lake Success, NY [*FM radio station call letters*]
WQHY ...... Prestonsburg, KY [*FM radio station call letters*]
WQI .... Water Quality Index
WQI .... Water Quality Instrument
WQIC......... Meridian, MS [*AM radio station call letters*]
WQID......... Biloxi, MS [*FM radio station call letters*]
WQII .... San Juan, PR [*AM radio station call letters*]
WQIK......... Jacksonville, FL [*AM radio station call letters*]
WQIK-FM... Jacksonville, FL [*FM radio station call letters*]
WQIM .... Prattville, AL [*FM radio station call letters*]
WQIN .... Lykens, PA [*AM radio station call letters*]
WQIQ......... Chester, PA [*AM radio station call letters*]
WQIS .... Laurel, MS [*AM radio station call letters*]
WQIS .... Water Quality Insurance Syndicate [*New York, NY*]   (EA)
WQIX......... Horseheads, NY [*FM radio station call letters*]
WQIZ......... St. George, SC [*AM radio station call letters*]
WQJU .... Mifflintown, PA [*FM radio station call letters*]
WQJY .... West Salem, WI [*FM radio station call letters*]
WQKA .... Penn Yan, NY [*AM radio station call letters*]
WQKI......... St. Matthews, SC [*AM radio station call letters*]
WQKK .... Metter, GA [*FM radio station call letters*]
WQKT .... Wooster, OH [*FM radio station call letters*]
WQKX .... Sunbury, PA [*FM radio station call letters*]
WQKY ...... Emporium, PA [*FM radio station call letters*]
WQLA .... La Follette, TN [*FM radio station call letters*]
WQLC........ Poplarville, MS [*FM radio station call letters*]
WQLK........ Richmond, IN [*FM radio station call letters*]
WQLM .... Punta Gorda, FL [*FM radio station call letters*]
WQLN .... Erie, PA [*Television station call letters*]
WQLN-FM ... Erie, PA [*FM radio station call letters*]
WQLR........ Kalamazoo, MI [*FM radio station call letters*]
WQLT .... Florence, AL [*FM radio station call letters*]
WQLX .... Galion, OH [*FM radio station call letters*]
WQLZ-FM ... Cheboygan, MI [*FM radio station call letters*]
WQM .... University of Massachusetts, Medical Center, Worcester, MA [*OCLC symbol*]   (OCLC)
WQM .... Water Quality Management
WQMA....... Marks, MS [*AM radio station call letters*]
WQMC....... Charlottesville, VA [*FM radio station call letters*]
WQMD....... Water Quantity Measuring Device
WQMF .... Jeffersonville, IN [*FM radio station call letters*]
WQMG....... Greensboro, NC [*FM radio station call letters*]
WQML........ York Center, ME [*FM radio station call letters*]
WQMP....... Water Quality Management Project
WQMR....... Skowhegan, ME [*AM radio station call letters*]
WQMT .... Chatsworth, GA [*FM radio station call letters*]
WQMU .... Indiana, PA [*FM radio station call letters*]
WQNA .... Springfield, IL [*FM radio station call letters*]
WQNS .... Waynesville, NC [*FM radio station call letters*]
WQNY ...... Ithaca, NY [*FM radio station call letters*]
WQNZ........ Natchez, MS [*FM radio station call letters*]
WQO.......... Water Quality Office [*Later, OWP*] [*Environmental Protection Agency*]
WQOD........ Youngstown, OH [*FM radio station call letters*]
WQON .... Grayling, MI [*FM radio station call letters*]
WQOW-TV ... Eau Claire, WI [*Television station call letters*]
WQOX .... Memphis, TN [*FM radio station call letters*]
WQPD .... Lake City, FL [*FM radio station call letters*]
WQPM....... Princeton, MN [*AM radio station call letters*]
WQPM-FM ... Princeton, MN [*FM radio station call letters*]
WQPO .... Harrisonburg, VA [*FM radio station call letters*]
WQPT-TV... Moline, IL [*Television station call letters*]
WQQB .... Bowling Green, KY [*Television station call letters*]
WQQK .... Hendersonville, TN [*FM radio station call letters*]
WQQQ .... Easton, PA [*FM radio station call letters*]
WQQW .... Waterbury, CT [*AM radio station call letters*]
WQRA .... Warrenton, VA [*FM radio station call letters*]
WQRC .... Barnstable, MA [*FM radio station call letters*]
WQRC .... Water Quality Research Council   (EA)
WQRF-TV... Rockford, IL [*Television station call letters*]
WQRK .... Bedford, IN [*FM radio station call letters*]
WQRL........ Benton, IL [*FM radio station call letters*]
WQRO .... Huntington, PA [*AM radio station call letters*]
WQRP........ West Carollton, OH [*FM radio station call letters*]
WQRS-FM ... Detroit, MI [*FM radio station call letters*]
WQRX........ Valley Head, AL [*AM radio station call letters*]
WQRZ........ Alpharetta, GA [*AM radio station call letters*]
WQSA .... Sarasota, FL [*AM radio station call letters*]
WQSB .... Albertville, AL [*AM radio station call letters*]
WQSC .... Andrews, SC [*FM radio station call letters*]
WQSF-FM .. Williamsburg, VA [*FM radio station call letters*]
WQSM....... Fayetteville, NC [*FM radio station call letters*]
WQSN .... Kalamazoo, MI [*AM radio station call letters*]
WQSR........ Catonsville, MD [*FM radio station call letters*]
WQST........ Forest, MS [*AM radio station call letters*]
WQST-FM ... Forest, MS [*FM radio station call letters*]
WQSU .... Selinsgrove, PA [*FM radio station call letters*]
WQT .... Water Quench Test
WQTC-FM ... Manitowoc, WI [*FM radio station call letters*]

WQTE........ Adrian, MI [*FM radio station call letters*]
WQTL........ Ottawa, OH [*FM radio station call letters*]
WQTO .... Ponce, PR [*Television station call letters*]
WQTQ .... Hartford, CT [*FM radio station call letters*]
WQTU .... Rome, GA [*FM radio station call letters*]
WQTV........ Boston, MA [*Television station call letters*]
WQTW .... Latrobe, PA [*AM radio station call letters*]
WQTY .... Linton, IN [*FM radio station call letters*]
WQTZ........ Decatur, IN [*FM radio station call letters*]
WQUE-FM ... New Orleans, LA [*FM radio station call letters*]
WQUH .... De Funiak Springs, FL [*FM radio station call letters*]
WQUIS ...... Water Quality Indicator System [*Marine science*]   (MSC)
WQUT........ Johnson City, TN [*FM radio station call letters*]
WQVR........ Southbridge, MA [*FM radio station call letters*]
WQWK ...... State College, PA [*FM radio station call letters*]
WQWM....... Kaukauna, WI [*AM radio station call letters*]
WQWQ ...... Muskegon Heights, MI [*FM radio station call letters*]
WQWT .... Owego, NY [*FM radio station call letters*]
WQXA .... York, PA [*FM radio station call letters*]
WQXB .... Grenada, MS [*FM radio station call letters*]
WQXC .... Otsego, MI [*AM radio station call letters*]
WQXC-FM ... Otsego, MI [*FM radio station call letters*]
WQXE .... Elizabethtown, KY [*FM radio station call letters*]
WQXI .... Atlanta, GA [*AM radio station call letters*]
WQXI-FM ... Smyrna, GA [*FM radio station call letters*]
WQXJ .... Greenwood, SC [*AM radio station call letters*]
WQXK .... Salem, OH [*FM radio station call letters*]
WQXL........ Columbia, SC [*AM radio station call letters*]
WQXM....... Gordon, GA [*AM radio station call letters*]
WQXM-FM ... Gordon, GA [*FM radio station call letters*]
WQXO .... Munising, MI [*AM radio station call letters*]
WQXO-FM ... Munising, MI [*FM radio station call letters*]
WQXR........ New York, NY [*AM radio station call letters*]
WQXR-FM ... New York, NY [*FM radio station call letters*]
WQXX........ Morganton, NC [*FM radio station call letters*]
WQXY-FM ... Baton Rouge, LA [*FM radio station call letters*]
WQXZ........ Taylorsville, NC [*AM radio station call letters*]
WQYK-FM ... St. Petersburg, FL [*FM radio station call letters*]
WQYX........ Clearfield, PA [*FM radio station call letters*]
WQZK-FM .. Keyser, WV [*FM radio station call letters*]
WQZN .... Gardiner, ME [*AM radio station call letters*]
WQZQ .... Lebanon, TN [*AM radio station call letters*]
WQZX........ Greenville, AL [*FM radio station call letters*]
WQZY........ Dublin, GA [*FM radio station call letters*]
WR............. Journal of Water Resources Planning and Management [*A publication*]
WR............. Sutherland's Weekly Report [*India*]   (DLA)
WR............. Wagons-Restaurants [*Railroad dining cars in Europe*] [*French*]
WR............. Wall Receptacle   (MUGU)
WR............. War Reserve   (AABC)
WR............. War Risk
WR............. War Risk Insurance Decisions [*United States*]   (DLA)
WR............. Wardroom [*Navy*]
WR............. Warehouse Receipt [*Often negotiable*]
WR............. Warner-Lambert Pharmaceutical Co. [*Research code symbol*]
WR............. Wartime Report   (MCD)
WR............. Wartime Requirements [*Air Force document*]   (AFM)
W/R........... Was Received
WR............. Washington Report. News and World Report Newsletter [*A publication*]
WR............. Washroom
WR............. Wassermann Reaction [*Test for syphilis*] [*Medicine*]
WR............. Water and Rail [*Transportation*]
W & R......... Water and Rail [*Transportation*]
W/R........... Water/Rock [*Ratio*] [*Geochemistry*]
WR............. Wave Retardation   (DEN)
WR............. Waveguide, Rectangular
WR............. Weapon Radius   (NVT)
WR............. Weapon Range   (NATG)
WR............. Weapons Requirement [*DoD*]
WR............. Wear Resistant
WR............. Weather Resistant   (MSA)
WR............. Weekly Record [*A publication*]
WR............. Weekly Reporter [*England*]   (DLA)
WR............. Weekly Reporter [*Bengal*]   (DLA)
WR............. Weekly Reporter, Cape Provincial Division [*South Africa*]   (DLA)
WR............. Weekly Review [*A publication*]
WR............. Welfare Recipient   (OICC)
W & R......... Welfare and Recreation [*Navy*]
WR............. Wendell's Reports [*1826-41*] [*New York*]   (DLA)
WR............. Western Review [*A publication*]
WR............. West's English Chancery Reports Tempore Hardwicke [*1736-39*]   (DLA)
WR............. Wet Runway [*Aviation*]   (FAAC)
W/R........... White Room [*NASA*]   (KSC)
WR............. Whiteshell Reactor [*Canada*]
WR............. Whole Rock [*Geology*]
WR............. Wide Range [*Nuclear energy*]   (NRCH)
WR............. Wide Receiver [*Football*]
WR............. Willelmus Rex [*King William*]

WR.............	Wilson Repeater (IEEE)
WR.............	Wiping Reflex [*Physiology*]
WR.............	Wire Recorder (DEN)
WR.............	Wire Rope (AAG)
WR.............	Wirral Railway [*British*] (ROG)
WR.............	Wisconsin Reports (DLA)
WR.............	Wiseman Review [*A publication*]
WR.............	Wissenschaftsrat [*Science Council*] [*Germany*]
WR.............	With Rights [*Securities*]
WR.............	Wolf-Raye [*Star classification*]
WR.............	Wolseley Register (EA)
WR.............	Women's Reserve [*Navy*]
WR.............	Women's Roundtable (EA)
WR.............	Word Restoration
WR.............	Work Request (MCD)
WR.............	Work Requirement (CAAL)
WR.............	Working Register
WR.............	Worthington Register (EA)
WR.............	Wrap
WR.............	Wrench (MSA)
Wr.............	Wright [*Blood group*]
Wr.............	Wright's Reports [*37-50 Pennsylvania*] (DLA)
WR.............	Wrist [*Medicine*]
WR.............	Write
WR.............	Writer (MSA)
WR2.........	Warramunga Array [*Australia*] [*Seismograph station code, US Geological Survey*] (SEIS)
WRA	Walter Reed Army Medical Center, Washington, DC [*OCLC symbol*] (OCLC)
WRA	War Relocation Authority [*Within Office of Emergency Management*] [*To provide for the relocation of persons whose removal seemed necessary for national security, and for their maintenance and supervision*] [*World War II*]
WRA	War Reserve Allowance (CINC)
WRA	Warramunga Array [*Australia*] [*Seismograph station code, US Geological Survey*] (SEIS)
WRA	Water Research Association [*British*]
WRA	Water Resources Abstracts [*Database*] [*A publication*]
WRA	Weapons Replaceable [*or Replacement*] Assembly
WRA	Western Railroad Association [*Formerly, AWR*] [*Chicago, IL*] (EA)
WRA	Western Range Association (EA)
WRA	Whiteware Research Association [*Defunct*] (EA)
WRA	Windarra Minerals [*Vancouver Stock Exchange symbol*]
WRA	With the Rule Astigmatism [*Ophthalmology*]
WRA	Women's Rabbinic Alliance [*Later, WSA*] (EA)
WRA	Work Related Abstracts [*A publication*]
WRAA........	Luray, VA [*AM radio station call letters*]
WRAB........	Arab, AL [*AM radio station call letters*]
WRABD	Wilhelm Roux' Archives of Developmental Biology [*A publication*]
WR/ABPR ...	Weekly Record/American Book Publishing Record [*A publication*]
WRac.........	Racine Public Library, Racine, WI [*Library symbol*] [*Library of Congress*] (LCLS)
WRAC	West Union, OH [*FM radio station call letters*]
WRAC	Willow Run Aeronautical Center [*Michigan*] (MCD)
WRAC	Women's Royal Army Corps [*British*]
WRacC	Racine County Institutions Medical Library, Racine, WI [*Library symbol*] [*Library of Congress*] (LCLS)
WRacCL	Racine County Law Library, Racine, WI [*Library symbol*] [*Library of Congress*] (LCLS)
WRacD	DeKoven Foundation for Church Work, Racine, WI [*Library symbol*] [*Library of Congress*] (LCLS)
WRACELD ...	Wounds Received in Action [*Incurred in*] Combat with the Enemy or in Line of Duty [*Army*] (AABC)
WRacGS.....	Girl Scouts of Racine County, Racine, WI [*Library symbol*] [*Library of Congress*] (LCLS)
WRacJ........	S. C. Johnson & Son, Inc., Racine, WI [*Library symbol*] [*Library of Congress*] (LCLS)
WRacSD.....	Racine Unified School District Number One, Racine, WI [*Library symbol*] [*Library of Congress*] (LCLS)
WRacSL	Saint Luke's Memorial Hospital, School of Nursing, Racine, WI [*Library symbol*] [*Library of Congress*] (LCLS)
WRacSM	Saint Mary's Hospital, Racine, WI [*Library symbol*] [*Library of Congress*] (LCLS)
WRacWa	Walker Manufacturing Co., Racine, WI [*Library symbol*] [*Library of Congress*] (LCLS)
WRacWM ...	Wustum Museum of Fine Arts, Racine, WI [*Library symbol*] [*Library of Congress*] (LCLS)
WRacWP	Western Publishing Co., Inc., Racine, WI [*Library symbol*] [*Library of Congress*] (LCLS)
WRacY	Young Radiator Co., Racine, WI [*Library symbol*] [*Library of Congress*] (LCLS)
WRAD........	Radford, VA [*AM radio station call letters*]
WRAF........	Toccoa Falls, GA [*FM radio station call letters*]
WRAF........	Women's Royal Air Force [*British*]
WRAG	Carrollton, AL [*AM radio station call letters*]
WRAI........	San Juan, PR [*AM radio station call letters*]
WRAIN.......	Walter Reed Army Institute of Nursing (AABC)
WRAIR........	Walter Reed Army Institute of Research (MCD)

WRAIS.......	Wide Range Analog Input Subsystem
WRAJ	Anna, IL [*AM radio station call letters*]
WRAJ-FM...	Anna, IL [*FM radio station call letters*]
WRAK.......	Williamsport, PA [*AM radio station call letters*]
WRAL.......	Raleigh, NC [*FM radio station call letters*]
WRALC	Warner Robins Air Logistics Center [*Formerly, WRAMA*] (MCD)
WRAL-TV...	Raleigh, NC [*Television station call letters*]
WRAM	Monmouth, IL [*AM radio station call letters*]
WRAM	Water Resources Assessment Methodology [*Army Corps of Engineers*]
WRAM	Wide-Range Recording and Monitoring [*System*] [*Radiation*]
WRAMA	Warner Robins Air Materiel Area [*Later, WRALC*]
WRAMC	Walter Reed Army Medical Center
WRAN.......	Dover, NJ [*AM radio station call letters*]
WRANG.....	Wrangler (ROG)
WRANS.......	Womens Royal Australian Naval Service
WRAP........	Norfolk, VA [*AM radio station call letters*]
WRAP........	Water Reactor Analysis Program (NRCH)
WRAP........	Weapons Readiness Achievement Program (MUGU)
WRAP........	Weapons Readiness Analysis Program [*Navy*]
WRAP........	Women's Radical Action Project [*Feminist group*]
WRAP........	Woodland Resource Analysis Program [*Tennessee Valley Authority*]
WRAP........	World Risk Analysis Package [*S. J. Rundt & Associates*] [*New York, NY*] [*Information service*] (EISS)
WRAQ	Asheville, NC [*AM radio station call letters*]
WRAR........	Tappahannock, VA [*AM radio station call letters*]
WRAR-FM ...	Tappahannock, VA [*FM radio station call letters*]
WRAS........	Atlanta, GA [*FM radio station call letters*]
WRAS........	Women's Reserve Ambulance Society [*British*] [*World War I*]
WRASPD....	World Rehabilitation Association for the Psycho-Socially Disabled [*New York, NY*] (EA)
WRAT........	Wide-Range Achievement Test
Wrat-R.......	Wide Range Achievement Test-Revised
WRAU-TV...	Peoria, IL [*Television station call letters*]
WRAV.......	Venice, FL [*FM radio station call letters*]
WRAW.......	Reading, PA [*AM radio station call letters*]
WRAX.......	Bedford, PA [*FM radio station call letters*]
WRAY........	Princeton, IN [*AM radio station call letters*]
WRAY-FM ...	Princeton, IN [*FM radio station call letters*]
WRB	Macon/Warner Robins, GA [*Location identifier*] [*FAA*] (FAAL)
WRB	Walter Reed Army Medical Center, Post/Patient Library, Washington, DC [*OCLC symbol*] (OCLC)
WRB	War Refugee Board [*Terminated, 1945*]
WRB	Wardrobe (MSA)
WRB	Warramunga Array [*Australia*] [*Seismograph station code, US Geological Survey*] (SEIS)
WRB	Water Resources Board [*British*]
WRBA........	Homestead, FL [*AM radio station call letters*]
WRBB........	Boston, MA [*FM radio station call letters*]
WRBC.......	Lewiston, ME [*FM radio station call letters*]
WRBC.......	Weather Relay Broadcast Center
WRBD.......	Pompano Beach, FL [*AM radio station call letters*]
WRBE........	Lucedale, MS [*AM radio station call letters*]
WRBI........	Batesville, IN [*FM radio station call letters*]
WRBK.......	Flomaton, AL [*AM radio station call letters*]
WRBL-TV...	Columbus, GA [*Television station call letters*]
WRBN.......	Warner Robins, GA [*AM radio station call letters*]
WRBND	Wire Bound
WRBN-FM ...	Warner Robins, GA [*FM radio station call letters*]
WRBQ........	St. Petersburg, FL [*AM radio station call letters*]
WRBQ-FM ...	Tampa, FL [*FM radio station call letters*]
WRBR.......	Richland, MS [*AM radio station call letters*]
WRBR.......	Wright Brothers National Memorial
WRBS........	Baltimore, MD [*FM radio station call letters*]
WRBT.......	Baton Rouge, LA [*Television station call letters*]
WRBV.......	Fredericksburg, VA [*Television station call letters*]
WRBW.......	Orlando, FL [*Television station call letters*]
WRBZ-FM ...	Rantoul, IL [*FM radio station call letters*]
WRC	War Resources Council [*Terminated*]
WRC	Washed Red Cells [*Medicine*]
WRC	Water Research Centre [*Research center*] [*British*] (IRC)
WRC	Water Resources Center [*University of Illinois*]
WRC	Water Resources Congress (EA)
WRC	Water Resources Council [*Inactive*]
WRC	Water-Retention Coefficient
WRC	Weapons Release Computer [*or Controller*]
WRC	Weather Relay Center
WRC	Welding Research Council
WRC	Well to Right of Course [*Aviation*] (FAAC)
WRC	Wildland Resources Center [*University of California*] [*Research center*] (RCD)
WRC	Wildlife Rehabilitation Council (EA)
WRC	Williams Ranch [*California*] [*Seismograph station code, US Geological Survey*] [*Closed*] (SEIS)
WRC	Women's Relief Corps
WRC	Women's Rights Committee [*American Federation of Teachers*] (EA)
WRC	World Relief Corporation (EA)
WRC	World Romani Congress

WRCA .... Western Red Cedar Association [*New Brighton, MN*]   (EA)
WR Calc ..... Sutherland's Weekly Reporter, Calcutta [*India*]   (DLA)
WRCB........ War Relief Control Board [*President's*]
WRCB-TV... Chattanooga, TN [*Television station call letters*]
WRCC .... Cape Coral, FL [*FM radio station call letters*]
WRCCC..... Wheeler AFB Range Communications Control Center   (MCD)
WRCCHE... Western Regional Consortium, Librarians' Networking Committee [*Library network*]
WRCD .... Dalton, GA [*AM radio station call letters*]
WRCF........ Whale Research and Conservation Fund   (EA)
WRCG .... Columbus, GA [*AM radio station call letters*]
WRCGR...... Women's Reserve of the Coast Guard Reserve
Wr Ch........ Wright's Ohio Reports   (DLA)
WRCH-FM ... New Britain, CT [*FM radio station call letters*]
WRC Inf..... WRC [*Water Research Centre*] Information [*A publication*]
WRCK .... Utica, NY [*FM radio station call letters*]
WRCLA ..... Western Red Cedar Lumber Association [*Portland, OR*]   (EA)
WRCM........ Jacksonville, NC [*FM radio station call letters*]
WRCN-FM ... Riverhead, NY [*FM radio station call letters*]
WRCNS ...... Women's Royal Canadian Naval Service [*World War II*]
WRCO .... Richland Center, WI [*AM radio station call letters*]
WRCO-FM ... Richland Center, WI [*FM radio station call letters*]
WRCP......... Providence, RI [*AM radio station call letters*]
WRCPATT ... World Rabbinic Committee for the Preservation of Ancient Tombs in Tiberias   (EA)
WRCQ .... New Britain, CT [*AM radio station call letters*]
WRCR......... Rushville, IN [*FM radio station call letters*]
WRCR......... Wife's Restitution of Conjugal Rights [*Law suit*] [*British*]   (ROG)
WRCR......... Wisconsin Railroad Commission Reports   (DLA)
WRCR......... Wyoming Resources Corporation [*NASDAQ symbol*]   (NQ)
WRC Research Report ... Water Resources Center. Research Report [*A publication*]
WRCS........ Ahoskie, NC [*AM radio station call letters*]
WRCS........ Weapons Release Computer Set [*or System*]   (MCD)
WRCT......... Pittsburgh, PA [*FM radio station call letters*]
WRC-TV..... Washington, DC [*Television station call letters*]
WRCU-FM ... Hamilton, NY [*FM radio station call letters*]
WRCW........ Canton, OH [*AM radio station call letters*]
WRCZ......... Pittsfield, MA [*FM radio station call letters*]
WRD .... Warden [*Washington*] [*Seismograph station code, US Geological Survey*]   (SEIS)
WRD .... Water Resources Division [*US Geological Survey*]
WRD .... Worm Runner's Digest [*A satirical publication*]
WRDB........ Reedsburg, WI [*AM radio station call letters*]
WRDC .... Boyle, MS [*AM radio station call letters*]
WRDC .... Western Rural Development Center [*Oregon State University*] [*Research center*]   (RCD)
WRDC .... Westinghouse Research and Development Center   (MCD)
WRDG .... Burlington, NC [*Television station call letters*]
WRDI .... We Remember Dean International [*Fullerton, CA*]   (EA)
WRDIR........ Wrong Direction
WRDJ .... Daleville, AL [*AM radio station call letters*]
WRDL .... Ashland, OH [*FM radio station call letters*]
WRDN........ Durand, WI [*AM radio station call letters*]
WRDN-FM ... Durand, WI [*FM radio station call letters*]
WRDO .... Augusta, ME [*AM radio station call letters*]
WRDO-FM ... Augusta, ME [*FM radio station call letters*]
WRDR........ Egg Harbor, NJ [*FM radio station call letters*]
WRDU........ Wilson, NC [*FM radio station call letters*]
WRDV......... Warminster, PA [*FM radio station call letters*]
WRDW........ Augusta, GA [*AM radio station call letters*]
WRDW-FM ... Wrens, GA [*FM radio station call letters*]
WRDW-TV ... Augusta, GA [*Television station call letters*]
WRDX......... Salisbury, NC [*FM radio station call letters*]
WRE .... Washington Real Estate Investment Trust [*American Stock Exchange symbol*]
WRE .... Weapon Research Establishment
WRE .... Whangarei [*New Zealand*] [*Airport symbol*]   (OAG)
WRE .... Winston Resources Ltd. [*Vancouver Stock Exchange symbol*]
WREA........ Dayton, TN [*AM radio station call letters*]
WREC........ Memphis, TN [*AM radio station call letters*]
WRECISS... Weapons Research Establishment Camera Interception Single Shot
WRECS ...... Weapon Radiation Effects on Communications Systems   (MCD)
WRED........ Monroe, GA [*AM radio station call letters*]
WREDAC.... Weapons Research Establishment Digital Automatic Computer
WREE .... College Park, GA [*AM radio station call letters*]
WREE .... Women for Racial and Economic Equality   (EA)
WREF .... Ridgefield Center, CT [*AM radio station call letters*]
WREFC...... We Remember Elvis Fan Club [*Pittsburgh, PA*]   (EA)
W/REG....... Window Regulator [*Automotive engineering*]
WREG-TV... Memphis, TN [*Television station call letters*]
WREI .... Quebradillas, PR [*FM radio station call letters*]
WREI .... Women's Research and Education Institute   (EA)
WREIS........ Wisconsin Real Estate Investment Trust [*NASDAQ symbol*]   (NQ)
WREK........ Atlanta, GA [*FM radio station call letters*]
WREL .... Lexington, VA [*AM radio station call letters*]
WREN......... Topeka, KS [*AM radio station call letters*]

WRENS ...... Women's Royal Naval Service [*Acronym is a phonetic reference to members of this British service branch*] [*Also, WRNS*]
WREO-FM ... Ashtabula, OH [*FM radio station call letters*]
W Rep........ West's English Chancery Reports Tempore Hardwicke [*1736-39*]   (DLA)
WRES .... Cocoa, FL [*Television station call letters*]
WRESAT..... Weapons Research Establishment Satellite [*Australia*]
W Res L Rev ... Western Reserve Law Review [*A publication*]
WREST...... Washington Regional Engineers, Scientists, and Technicians
WREST...... Wide Range Employability Sample Test
WRET-TV ... Spartanburg, SC [*Television station call letters*]
WREU .... Western Railway Employees' Union [*India*]
WREV .... Reidsville, NC [*AM radio station call letters*]
WREX .... Wrexham [*City in Wales*]
WREX-TV ... Rockford, IL [*Television station call letters*]
WREY .... Millville, NJ [*AM radio station call letters*]
WREZ .... Montgomery, AL [*AM radio station call letters*]
WRF........... University of Wisconsin, River Falls, River Falls, WI [*OCLC symbol*]   (OCLC)
WRF........... Weak Radial Field
WRF........... Weibull Reliability Function [*Statistics*]
WRF........... Wheat Ridge Foundation   (EA)
WRF........... World Rehabilitation Fund [*New York, NY*]   (EA)
WRF........... World Research Foundation [*Sherman Oaks, CA*]   (EA)
WRFA........ Largo, FL [*AM radio station call letters*]
W R Far East ... Weekly Review of the Far East [*A publication*]
WRFB........ Stowe, VT [*FM radio station call letters*]
WRFC........ Athens, GA [*AM radio station call letters*]
WRFD........ Columbus-Worthington, OH [*AM radio station call letters*]
WRFE........ Aguada, PR [*FM radio station call letters*]
WRFG........ Atlanta, GA [*FM radio station call letters*]
WRFK-FM ... Richmond, VA [*FM radio station call letters*]
WRFM .... Homestead, FL [*FM radio station call letters*]
WRFN........ Nashville, TN [*FM radio station call letters*]
WRFR........ Franklin, NC [*FM radio station call letters*]
WRFT......... Indianapolis, IN [*FM radio station call letters*]
WRfU.......... University of Wisconsin-River Falls, River Falls, WI [*Library symbol*] [*Library of Congress*]   (LCLS)
WRFW .... River Falls, WI [*FM radio station call letters*]
WRFX .... Kannapolis, NC [*FM radio station call letters*]
WRFY-FM ... Reading, PA [*FM radio station call letters*]
WRG.......... Wearing   (MSA)
WRG.......... White River [*Alaska*] [*Seismograph station code, US Geological Survey*]   (SEIS)
WRG.......... Wire Routing Guide   (MCD)
WRG.......... Wiring
WRG.......... Wrangell [*Alaska*] [*Airport symbol*]   (OAG)
WRG.......... Wrangell, AK [*Location identifier*] [*FAA*]   (FAAL)
WRG.......... Wrong [*Telecommunications*]   (TEL)
WRGA .... Rome, GA [*AM radio station call letters*]
WRGA .... Western River Guides Association   (EA)
WRGB........ Schenectady, NY [*Television station call letters*]
WRGC .... Sylva, NC [*AM radio station call letters*]
WRGE........ Olyphant, PA [*AM radio station call letters*]
WRGH .... Walter Reed General Hospital   (MCD)
WRGI......... Naples, FL [*FM radio station call letters*]
WRGN .... Sweet Valley, PA [*FM radio station call letters*]
WRGR......... Wringer
WRGS .... Rogersville, TN [*AM radio station call letters*]
WRGT-TV... Dayton, OH [*Television station call letters*]
WRh........... Rhinelander Public Library, Rhinelander, WI [*Library symbol*] [*Library of Congress*]   (LCLS)
WRH .... Warnkenhagen [*German Democratic Republic*] [*Geomagnetic observatory code*]
WRH .... William Randolph Hearst [*American newspaper publisher, 1863-1951*]
WRH .... World Radio Handbook
WRHC .... Coral Gables, FL [*AM radio station call letters*]
WRHD........ Riverhead, NY [*AM radio station call letters*]
WRHI .... Rock Hill, SC [*AM radio station call letters*]
WRHL .... Rochelle, IL [*AM radio station call letters*]
WRHL-FM ... Rochelle, IL [*FM radio station call letters*]
WRHN........ Rhinelander, WI [*FM radio station call letters*]
WRHO .... Oneonta, NY [*FM radio station call letters*]
WRHR......... Henrietta, NY [*FM radio station call letters*]
WRHS .... Park Forest, IL [*FM radio station call letters*]
WRHT......... Morehead, NC [*FM radio station call letters*]
WRHU......... Hempstead, NY [*FM radio station call letters*]
WRHX .... Herndon, VA [*AM radio station call letters*]
WRI........... International Water Resources Institute [*George Washington University*] [*Research center*]   (RCD)
WRI........... War Resisters' International
WRI........... War Risks Insurance [*British*]
WRI........... Water Research Institute [*West Virginia University*] [*Research center*]   (RCD)
WRI........... Waterloo Research Institute [*University of Waterloo*] [*Research center*]   (RCD)
WRI........... Weatherstrip Research Institute
WRI........... Weingarten Realty, Incorporated [*NYSE symbol*]

WRI............. Welfare Research, Incorporated [*An association*] [*Albany, NY*] (EA)
WRI............. Wire Reinforcement Institute [*McLean, VA*] (EA)
WRI............. Wire Rope Institute
WRI............. World Research, Incorporated (EA)
WRI............. World Resources Institute (EA)
WRI............. Wrightstown, NJ [*Location identifier*] [*FAA*] (FAAL)
WRIB.......... Providence, RI [*AM radio station call letters*]
WRIC.......... Richlands, VA [*AM radio station call letters*]
WRIE.......... Erie, PA [*AM radio station call letters*]
WRIF.......... Detroit, MI [*FM radio station call letters*]
WRIG.......... Schofield, WI [*AM radio station call letters*]
Wright........ Wright's Ohio Reports [*1831-34*] (DLA)
Wright........ Wright's Reports [*37-50 Pennsylvania*] (DLA)
Wright Ch ... Wright's Ohio Reports [*1831-34*] (DLA)
Wright Cr Cons ... Wright's Criminal Conspiracies [*1873*] (DLA)
Wright NP ... Wright's Ohio Nisi Prius Reports (DLA)
Wright (Ohio C) ... Wright's Ohio Reports (DLA)
Wright R..... Wright's Ohio Reports (DLA)
Wright's Rep ... Wright's Ohio Reports (DLA)
Wright Ten ... Wright on Tenures (DLA)
WRIK.......... Metropolis, IL [*FM radio station call letters*]
WRIN.......... Rensselaer, IN [*AM radio station call letters*]
WRIO.......... Ponce, PR [*FM radio station call letters*]
WRIOT........ Wide Range Interest and Opinion Test
WRIP.......... Rossville, GA [*AM radio station call letters*]
WRipC........ Ripon College, Ripon, WI [*Library symbol*] [*Library of Congress*] (LCLS)
WRIQ.......... Radford, VA [*FM radio station call letters*]
WRI Rep ..... WRI [*Wattle Research Institute*] Report [*A publication*]
WRIS.......... Roanoke, VA [*AM radio station call letters*]
WRISC........ Western Regional Information Service Center [*University of California*] [*Berkeley*] [*Information service*] (EISS)
WRIS Technical Bulletin ... Water Resources Information System. Technical Bulletin [*A publication*]
WRIT.......... Stuart, FL [*FM radio station call letters*]
WRIT.......... Wright [*William E.*] Co. [*NASDAQ symbol*] (NQ)
Writ Cent S ... Writers of the 21st Century. Series [*A publication*]
WRITG........ Writing (ROG)
Writ Ring.... Writers' Ring [*A publication*]
WRIU.......... Kingston, RI [*FM radio station call letters*]
WRIU.......... Write Interface Unit
WRIV.......... Riverhead, NY [*AM radio station call letters*]
WRIX.......... Homeland Park, SC [*AM radio station call letters*]
WRIX-FM.... Honea Path, SC [*FM radio station call letters*]
WRJ............ Wallraf-Richartz-Jahrbuch [*A publication*]
WRJA-FM... Sumter, SC [*FM radio station call letters*]
WRJA-TV ... Sumter, SC [*Television station call letters*]
WRJB.......... Camden, TN [*FM radio station call letters*]
WRJC.......... Mauston, WI [*AM radio station call letters*]
WRJC-FM .. Mauston, WI [*FM radio station call letters*]
WRJH.......... Brandon, MS [*FM radio station call letters*]
WRJM.......... Troy, AL [*FM radio station call letters*]
WRJM-TV... Troy, AL [*Television station call letters*]
WRJN.......... Racine, WI [*AM radio station call letters*]
WRJO.......... Eagle River, WI [*FM radio station call letters*]
WRJQ.......... Tomahawk, WI [*AM radio station call letters*]
WRJR.......... Zion, IL [*AM radio station call letters*]
WRJS.......... Oil City, PA [*FM radio station call letters*]
WRJT.......... Monterey, TN [*FM radio station call letters*]
WRJW.......... Picayune, MS [*AM radio station call letters*]
WRJX.......... Jackson, TN [*FM radio station call letters*]
WRJZ.......... Knoxville, TN [*AM radio station call letters*]
WRK .... Wall & Redekop Corp. [*Toronto Stock Exchange symbol*] [*Vancouver Stock Exchange symbol*]
WRK .... Westdeutsche Rektorenkonferenz [*West German Standing Committee of University Heads*]
WRK .... Work (FAAC)
WRK .... Wrecker
WRKA.......... St. Matthews, KY [*FM radio station call letters*]
WRKB.......... Kannapolis, NC [*AM radio station call letters*]
WRKC .... Wilkes-Barre, PA [*FM radio station call letters*]
WRKD.......... Rockland, ME [*AM radio station call letters*]
WRKF.......... Baton Rouge, LA [*FM radio station call letters*]
WRKG.......... Lorain, OH [*AM radio station call letters*]
WRKI.......... Brookfield, CT [*FM radio station call letters*]
WRKL.......... New City, NY [*AM radio station call letters*]
WRKM.......... Carthage, TN [*AM radio station call letters*]
WRKM-FM ... Carthage, TN [*FM radio station call letters*]
WRKN.......... Brandon, MS [*AM radio station call letters*]
WRKO .... Boston, MA [*AM radio station call letters*]
Wrk Paper ... Working Papers for a New Society [*A publication*]
Wrk Power ... Workers Power [*A publication*]
WRKQ .... Madisonville, TN [*AM radio station call letters*]
WRKR.......... Racine, WI [*AM radio station call letters*]
WRKR-FM .. Racine, WI [*FM radio station call letters*]
WRKS-FM .. New York, NY [*FM radio station call letters*]
WRKT.......... Cocoa Beach, FL [*AM radio station call letters*]
Wrk World ... Workers' World [*A publication*]
WRKX.......... Ottawa, IL [*FM radio station call letters*]
WRKY.......... Steubenville, OH [*FM radio station call letters*]

WRKZ .... Hershey, PA [*FM radio station call letters*]
WRI............. Rice Lake Public Library, Rice Lake, WI [*Library symbol*] [*Library of Congress*] (LCLS)
WRL............. War Resisters League (EA)
WRL............. Wellcome Research Laboratories [*Research center*] [*British*] (IRC)
WRL............. Westinghouse Research Laboratories (KSC)
WRL............. Wien Radiation Law [*Physics*]
WRL............. Willow Run Laboratory [*NASA*] (KSC)
WRL............. Wing Reference Line
WRL............. Worland [*Wyoming*] [*Airport symbol*] (OAG)
WRL............. Worland, WY [*Location identifier*] [*FAA*] (FAAL)
WRLB .... Florence, NJ [*AM radio station call letters*]
WRLC .... Williamsport, PA [*FM radio station call letters*]
WRLD .... Lanett, AL [*AM radio station call letters*]
WRLH-TV ... Richmond, VA [*Television station call letters*]
WRLK-TV... Columbia, SC [*Television station call letters*]
WRLO-FM ... Antigo, WI [*FM radio station call letters*]
WRLR .... Huntingdon, PA [*FM radio station call letters*]
WRLS.......... Working Reference of Livestock Regulatory Establishments, Stations, and Officials [*A publication*]
WRLS-FM .. Hayward, WI [*FM radio station call letters*]
WRLT .... Buffalo, NY [*FM radio station call letters*]
WRLV .... Salyersville, KY [*AM radio station call letters*]
WRLX .... Tuscaloosa, AL [*AM radio station call letters*]
WRLX .... World Airways, Inc. [*Air carrier designation symbol*]
WRM............ War Readiness Materiel [*Air Force*]
WRM............ War Reserve Mobilization (CINC)
WRM............ War Reserve Munitions
WRM............ Warm (FAAC)
WRM............ Warmifontaine [*Belgium*] [*Seismograph station code, US Geological Survey*] (SEIS)
WRM............ Water Removal Mechanism
WRM............ What Really Matters
WR(M)........ Wide Range (Monitor) [*Nuclear energy*] (NRCH)
WRM............ Worcester State College, Worcester, MA [*OCLC symbol*] (OCLC)
WRM............ Working Reference Material (NRCH)
WRMA .... Welded Ring Manufacturers Association [*Defunct*]
WRMB .... Boynton Beach, FL [*FM radio station call letters*]
WRMC-FM ... Middlebury, VT [*FM radio station call letters*]
WRMF .... Palm Beach, FL [*FM radio station call letters*]
WRMF .... World Radio Missionary Fellowship (EA)
WRMFNT.... Warm Front [*Meteorology*] (FAAC)
WRMG.......... Red Bay, AL [*AM radio station call letters*]
WRMH .... Picayune, MS [*FM radio station call letters*]
WRMJ.......... Aledo, IL [*FM radio station call letters*]
WRMN .... Elgin, IL [*AM radio station call letters*]
WRMN .... Wireman (AABC)
WRMR .... Cleveland, OH [*AM radio station call letters*]
WRMR .... War Reserve Materiel Requirement (AFIT)
WRMRATE ... War Readiness Materiel Rating [*Air Force*]
WRMRB...... War Reserve Materiel Requirement Balance (AFIT)
WRMRP...... War Reserve Materiel Requirement Protectable (AFIT)
WRMRS...... War Reserve Materiel Rating System
WRMS .... Beardstown, IL [*AM radio station call letters*]
WRMS .... War Reserve Materiel Stocks
WRMS .... Watts Root-Mean-Square
WRMS-FM ... Beardstown, IL [*FM radio station call letters*]
WRMSTAT ... War Readiness Materiel Status [*Air Force*]
WRMT .... Rocky Mount, NC [*AM radio station call letters*]
WRMU .... Alliance, OH [*FM radio station call letters*]
WRN .... Blue Bell, Inc. [*Greensboro, NC*] [*FAA designator*] (FAAC)
WRN .... Warnaco of Canada Ltd. [*Toronto Stock Exchange symbol*]
WRN .... Warning (MSA)
WRN .... Wool Round Needle [*Knitting*]
WRNA .... China Grove, NC [*AM radio station call letters*]
WRNB .... New Bern, NC [*AM radio station call letters*]
WRNC .... Reidsville, NC [*AM radio station call letters*]
WRNF .... Whitehall, MI [*FM radio station call letters*]
WRNG .... Warning (FAAC)
WRNI .... Wide-Range Neutron Indicator (IEEE)
WRNI .... Wide-Range Nuclear Instrument (IEEE)
WRNJ .... Hackettstown, NJ [*AM radio station call letters*]
WRNL .... Richmond, VA [*AM radio station call letters*]
WRNLR ...... Western Region of Nigeria Law Reports (DLA)
WRNO .... New Orleans, LA [*FM radio station call letters*]
WRNOA...... Washington Reef Net Owners Association (EA)
WRNR .... Martinsburg, WV [*AM radio station call letters*]
WRNS.......... Kinston, NC [*FM radio station call letters*]
WRNS.......... Women's Royal Naval Service [*Also, WRENS*] [*A member is familiarly called a "Wren"*] [*British*]
WRNT.......... Warrant (AABC)
WRNT.......... Warrenton Railroad Co. [*Later, WAR*] [*AAR code*]
WRNWCA... Western Red and Northern White Cedar Association [*Later, WRCA*] (EA)
WRNY.......... Rome, NY [*AM radio station call letters*]
WRO........... ARC [*Agricultural Research Council*] Weed Research Organization [*Research center*] [*British*] (IRC)
WRO........... Rotor-Aids, Inc. [*Abbeville, LA*] [*FAA designator*] (FAAC)
WRO........... War Records Office

WRO .... War Risks Only
WRO .... Water Rights Office [*Bureau of Indian Affairs*]
WRO .... Western Regional Office
WRO .... Wichita Industries, Inc. [*American Stock Exchange symbol*]
WRO .... Work Release Order (MCD)
WRO .... Wroclaw [*Poland*] [*Airport symbol*] (OAG)
WROA .... Gulfport, MS [*AM radio station call letters*]
W Rob .... W. Robinson's English Admiralty Reports [*166 ER*] (DLA)
WROB........ West Point, MS [*AM radio station call letters*]
W Rob Adm ... W. Robinson's English Admiralty Reports [*166 ER*] (DLA)
W Rob Adm (Eng) ... W. Robinson's English Admiralty Reports [*166 ER*] (DLA)
Wrocl Zap Num ... Wroclawskie Zapiski Numizmatyczne [*A publication*]
WROC-TV ... Rochester, NY [*Television station call letters*]
WROD .... Daytona Beach, FL [*AM radio station call letters*]
WROE........ Neenah-Menasha, WI [*FM radio station call letters*]
WROG .... Cumberland, MD [*FM radio station call letters*]
Wr Ohio...... Wright's Ohio Reports (DLA)
WROI .... Rochester, IN [*FM radio station call letters*]
WROK .... Rockford, IL [*AM radio station call letters*]
WROL .... Boston, MA [*AM radio station call letters*]
WROM....... Rome, GA [*AM radio station call letters*]
WRON .... Ronceverte, WV [*AM radio station call letters*]
WRON-FM ... Ronceverte, WV [*FM radio station call letters*]
WROQ .... Charlotte, NC [*FM radio station call letters*]
WROR........ Boston, MA [*FM radio station call letters*]
WROS........ Jacksonville, FL [*AM radio station call letters*]
W Roux A DB ... [*Wilhelm*] Roux' Archives of Developmental Biology [*A publication*]
WROV........ Roanoke, VA [*AM radio station call letters*]
WROW....... Albany, NY [*AM radio station call letters*]
WROW-FM ... Albany, NY [*FM radio station call letters*]
WROX........ Clarksdale, MS [*AM radio station call letters*]
WROY........ Carmi, IL [*AM radio station call letters*]
WROZ-TV... Owensboro, KY [*Television station call letters*]
WRP .... Water Resource Planning
WRP .... Water Resources Publications
WRP .... Weapons Release Programer
WRP .... Wiener Random Process [*Mathematics*]
WRP .... Wildlife Research Project
WRP .... Wing Reference Plan [*Aviation*]
WRP .... Women's Rights Project (EA)
WRP .... Workers' Revolutionary Party [*British*] (PPW)
WRPA........ Water Resources Planning Act [*1965*]
Wr PA....... Wright's Reports [*37-50 Pennsylvania*] (DLA)
WRPC........ San German, PR [*FM radio station call letters*]
WRPC........ Weather Records Processing Centers
WRPG........ Warping
WRPI .... Troy, NY [*FM radio station call letters*]
WRPLS...... Western Regional Public Library System [*Library network*]
WRPM .... Poplarville, MS [*AM radio station call letters*]
WRPN-FM ... Ripon, WI [*FM radio station call letters*]
WRPPD...... Wrapped
WRPQ....... Baraboo, WI [*AM radio station call letters*]
WRPR........ Mahwah, NJ [*FM radio station call letters*]
WRPR........ Wrapper
WRPS........ Rockland, MA [*FM radio station call letters*]
WRPSM...... War Reserve Publication Shipment Memorandum
WRPT .... Peterborough, NH [*AM radio station call letters*]
WRPX....... Hudson, WI [*AM radio station call letters*]
WRPZ....... Paris, KY [*AM radio station call letters*]
WRQ .... Westinghouse Resolver/Quantizer (IEEE)
WRQK .... Canton, OH [*FM radio station call letters*]
WRQN .... Bowling Green, OH [*FM radio station call letters*]
WRQR........ Farmville, NC [*FM radio station call letters*]
WRQT....... Bear Lake, MI [*FM radio station call letters*]
WRQX....... Washington, DC [*FM radio station call letters*]
WRR .... Dallas, TX [*FM radio station call letters*]
WRR .... Warm Run Record
WRR .... Warrington, Inc. [*Toronto Stock Exchange symbol*]
WRR .... Water Resource Region [*Water Resources Council*]
WRR .... Woodmen Rangers and Rangerettes (EA)
WRRA........ Frederiksted, VI [*AM radio station call letters*]
WRRA........ Water Resources Research Act [*1964*]
WRRB........ Syracuse, NY [*AM radio station call letters*]
WRRC........ Lawrenceville, NJ [*FM radio station call letters*]
WRRC........ Massachusetts Water Resources Research Center [*University of Massachusetts*] [*Research center*] (RCD)
WRRC........ Water Resources Research Center [*University of Minnesota of Minneapolis Saint Paul*] [*Research center*] (RCD)
WRRC........ Water Resources Research Center [*University of Arizona*] [*Research center*] (RCD)
WRRC........ Water Resources Research Center [*University of Hawaii*] [*Research center*] (RCD)
WRRC........ Water Resources Research Center [*Indiana University*] [*Research center*] (RCD)
WRRC........ Water Resources Research Center [*Purdue University*] [*Research center*] (RCD)
WRRC........ Western Rail Road Company [*AAR code*]
WRRC........ Western Regional Research Center [*Department of Agriculture*]

WRRC........ Western Regional Resource Center [*University of Oregon*] [*Research center*] (RCD)
WRRC........ Willow Run Research Center [*Air Force*]
WRRC........ Women's Research and Resources Centre Newsletter [*A publication*]
WRRC Report (Washington) ... Water Resources Research Center. Report (Washington) [*A publication*]
WRRF .... Washington, NC [*AM radio station call letters*]
WRRG .... River Grove, IL [*FM radio station call letters*]
WRRH........ Franklin Lakes, NJ [*FM radio station call letters*]
WRRI .... Water Resources Research Institute [*Oregon State University*] [*Research center*] (RCD)
WRRI .... Water Resources Research Institute [*Clemson University*] [*Research center*]
WRRI .... Water Resources Research Institute [*New Mexico State University*] [*Research center*] (RCD)
WRRI Auburn Univ Bull ... WRRI [*Water Resources Research Institute*]. Auburn University. Bulletin [*A publication*]
WRRK .... Manistee, MI [*FM radio station call letters*]
WRRL .... Rainelle, WV [*AM radio station call letters*]
WRRL-FM... Rainelle, WV [*FM radio station call letters*]
WRRM........ Cincinnati, OH [*FM radio station call letters*]
WRRN .... Warren, PA [*FM radio station call letters*]
WRRO........ Warren, OH [*AM radio station call letters*]
WRRR........ Walter Reed Research Reactor
WRRR-FM ... St. Mary's, WV [*FM radio station call letters*]
WRRS........ Wire Relay Radio System
WRRZ........ Clinton, NC [*AM radio station call letters*]
WRS .... Walter Reed Society (EA)
WRS .... War Reserve Stocks (AABC)
WRS .... Warning and Report System (CET)
WRS .... Warsak [*Pakistan*] [*Seismograph station code, US Geological Survey*] (SEIS)
WRS .... Wasabi Resources Ltd. [*Toronto Stock Exchange symbol*] [*Vancouver Stock Exchange symbol*]
WRS .... Washington Representative Services, Inc. [*Information service*] (EISS)
WRS .... Water Recirculation System
WRS .... Water Recovery Subsystem [*NASA*] (KSC)
WRS .... Wave Radiometer System
WRS .... Weapons Recommendation Sheet (MCD)
WRS .... Weather RADAR Set [*or System*]
WRS .... Weather Reconnaissance Squadron [*Air Force*] (CINC)
WRS .... Western Massachusetts Regional Library System, Springfield, MA [*OCLC symbol*] (OCLC)
WRS .... Wide-Range Sensor
WRS .... Word Recognition System
WRS .... Working Transmission Reference System [*Telecommunications*] (TEL)
WRS .... Worse (FAAC)
WRS .... Write Strobe
WRSA........ Decatur, AL [*FM radio station call letters*]
WRSA........ War Reserve Stocks for Allies (MCD)
WRSA........ World Rabbit Science Association (EA-IO)
WRSB........ Weston, MA [*FM radio station call letters*]
WRSC........ State College, PA [*AM radio station call letters*]
WRSD........ Folsom, PA [*FM radio station call letters*]
WRSE-FM ... Elmhurst, IL [*FM radio station call letters*]
WRSFA...... Western Reinforcing Steel Fabricators Association
WRSG........ Binghamton, NY [*AM radio station call letters*]
WRSH........ Rockingham, NC [*FM radio station call letters*]
WRSI .... Greenfield, MA [*FM radio station call letters*]
WRSIC....... Water Resources Scientific Information Center [*US Geological Survey*] [*Reston, VA*] [*Database originator*]
WRSJ........ Bayamon, PR [*AM radio station call letters*]
WRSK........ War Readiness Spares Kit [*Air Force*] (AFM)
WRSL........ Stanford, KY [*AM radio station call letters*]
WRSL-FM .. Stanford, KY [*FM radio station call letters*]
WRSM........ Sumiton, AL [*AM radio station call letters*]
WRSP........ World Register of Scientific Periodicals
WRSP-TV ... Springfield, IL [*Television station call letters*]
WRSq........ Weather Reconnaissance Squadron [*Air Force*] (AFM)
WRSR........ Newport News, VA [*FM radio station call letters*]
WRSR........ Water Reactor Safety Research (NRCH)
WRSS........ San Sebastian, PR [*AM radio station call letters*]
WRST-FM ... Oshkosh, WI [*FM radio station call letters*]
WRSU-FM ... New Brunswick, NJ [*FM radio station call letters*]
WRSV........ Rocky Mount, NC [*FM radio station call letters*]
WRSW....... Warsaw, IN [*AM radio station call letters*]
WRSW-FM ... Warsaw, IN [*FM radio station call letters*]
WRT .... Warrior River Terminal Co. [*AAR code*]
WRT .... Water Round Torpedo (MSA)
WRT .... With Respect To (KSC)
WRT .... Wright Air Lines, Inc. [*Cleveland, OH*] [*FAA designator*] (FAAC)
WRT .... Wright-Hargreaves Mines Ltd. [*Toronto Stock Exchange symbol*]
WRT .... Wrought
WRTA........ Altoona, PA [*AM radio station call letters*]

WRTA........ Western Railroad Traffic Association [*Formed by a merger of Association of Western Railroads and Western Traffic Association*] [*Chicago, IL*] (EA)
WRTB........ Vincennes, IN [*FM radio station call letters*]
WRTB........ Wire Rope Technical Board [*Stevensville, MD*] (EA)
WRTC........ Working Reference Telephone Circuit [*Telecommunications*] (TEL)
WRTC........ [*The*] Writer Corporation [*NASDAQ symbol*] (NQ)
WRTC-FM ... Hartford, CT [*FM radio station call letters*]
WRTE........ Cahokia, IL [*FM radio station call letters*]
WRTH........ Wood River, IL [*AM radio station call letters*]
WRTH........ World Radio TV Handbook [*A publication*]
WRTHG..... Worthing [*City in England*]
WRTI........ Philadelphia, PA [*FM radio station call letters*]
WRTL........ Rantoul, IL [*AM radio station call letters*]
WRTN........ New Rochelle, NY [*FM radio station call letters*]
WRTP........ Chapel Hill, NC [*AM radio station call letters*]
WRTU........ San Juan, PR [*FM radio station call letters*]
WRTV........ Indianapolis, IN [*Television station call letters*]
WRU.......... Water Research Unit [*Department of Agriculture*]
WRU.......... Wave Run-Up
WRU.......... Western Reserve University [*Later, Case Western Reserve University*]
WRU.......... Western Reserve University. Bulletin [*A publication*]
WRU.......... Who Are You? [*Communication*]
WRUC........ Schenectady, NY [*FM radio station call letters*]
WRUF........ Gainesville, FL [*AM radio station call letters*]
WRUF-FM .. Gainesville, FL [*FM radio station call letters*]
WRUL........ Carmi, IL [*FM radio station call letters*]
WRUM........ Rumford, ME [*AM radio station call letters*]
WRUN........ Utica, NY [*AM radio station call letters*]
WRUP........ Marquette, MI [*FM radio station call letters*]
WRUR-FM .. Rochester, NY [*FM radio station call letters*]
WRUS........ Russellville, KY [*AM radio station call letters*]
WRUT........ Rutland, VT [*FM radio station call letters*]
WRUV........ Burlington, VT [*FM radio station call letters*]
WRUW-FM ... Cleveland, OH [*FM radio station call letters*]
WRV.......... Water Relief Valve
WRV.......... Water-Retention Value
WRVA........ Richmond, VA [*AM radio station call letters*]
WRVG........ Georgetown, KY [*FM radio station call letters*]
WRVI........ Virden, IL [*FM radio station call letters*]
WRVK........ Mount Vernon, KY [*AM radio station call letters*]
WRVL........ Lynchburg, VA [*FM radio station call letters*]
WRVM........ Suring, WI [*FM radio station call letters*]
WRVO........ Oswego, NY [*FM radio station call letters*]
WRVQ........ Richmond, VA [*FM radio station call letters*]
WRVR........ Memphis, TN [*AM radio station call letters*]
WRVR-FM .. Memphis, TN [*FM radio station call letters*]
WRVS........ Women's Royal Voluntary Service [*Formerly, WVS*] [*British*]
WRVS-FM ... Elizabeth City, NC [*FM radio station call letters*]
WRVU........ Nashville, TN [*FM radio station call letters*]
WRVW........ Hudson, NY [*FM radio station call letters*]
WRVX........ Mt. Carmel, TN [*AM radio station call letters*]
WR(W)....... War Reserve (Weapon)
WRW.......... Will's Air [*Barnstable, MA*] [*FAA designator*] (FAAC)
WRWA........ Dothan, AL [*FM radio station call letters*]
WRWC........ Rockton, IL [*FM radio station call letters*]
WRWg........ Weather Reconnaissance Wing [*Air Force*] (AFM)
WRWH........ Cleveland, GA [*AM radio station call letters*]
WRWK........ Warwick Railway Co. [*AAR code*]
WRWR-TV ... San Juan, PR [*Television station call letters*]
WRWX........ Sanibel, FL [*FM radio station call letters*]
WRX.......... Western Refrigerator Line Co. [*AAR code*]
WRXB........ St. Petersburg Beach, FL [*AM radio station call letters*]
WRXC........ Shelton, CT [*FM radio station call letters*]
WRXJ........ Jacksonville, FL [*AM radio station call letters*]
WRXK........ Bonita Springs, FL [*FM radio station call letters*]
WRXL........ Richmond, VA [*FM radio station call letters*]
WRXO........ Roxboro, NC [*AM radio station call letters*]
WRXX........ Centralia, IL [*FM radio station call letters*]
WRY.......... Westray [*Scotland*] [*Airport symbol*] (OAG)
WRY.......... Wheeling Railway
WRY.......... World Refugee Year
WRYM........ New Britain, CT [*AM radio station call letters*]
WRZ.......... Western Rift Zone [*Geology*]
WRZK........ Spring Lake, NC [*AM radio station call letters*]
WRZQ-FM ... Greenburg, IN [*FM radio station call letters*]
WS............. Single Conductor Cable [*JETDS nomenclature*] [*Military*] (CET)
WS............. Superior Public Library, Superior, WI [*Library symbol*] [*Library of Congress*] (LCLS)
WS............. Wagner's Missouri Statutes (DLA)
WS............. Wallops Station [*Later, WFC*] [*NASA*]
WS............. War Scale (ADA)
WS............. War Service
WS............. Ware Shoals Railroad Co. [*AAR code*]
WS............. Warm Shop [*Nuclear energy*] (NRCH)
WS............. Warrants [*Stock market*]
WS............. Warthin-Starry [*Silver impregnation stain*]
WS............. Washine Chemical Corp. [*Research code symbol*]

WS............. Waste Stack [*Technical drawings*]
WS............. Waste System
WS............. Water Safety
WS............. Water Soluble
WS............. Water Supply
WS............. Water Surface [*Elevation*]
WS............. Water System
W S............ Watt Second
w/s............ Watt-Seconds
W & S........ Watts and Sergeant's Pennsylvania Reports [*1841-1845*] (DLA)
W/S............ Watts per Steradian (NG)
WS............. Wave Soldering
WS............. Weak Signals [*Radio*]
WS............. Weapon System
WS............. Weapons Specifications (NG)
W/S............ Weapons System
WS............. Weather Service
W/S............ Weather Ship (NATG)
WS............. Weather Squadron (MCD)
WS............. Weather Station
WS............. Weatherstripping (AAG)
WS............. Wedgwood Society (EA)
WS............. Welsh Society (EA)
WS............. Welt der Slaven [*A publication*]
WS............. West Saxon [*Dialect of Old English*] [*Language, etc.*]
WS............. West Semitic (BJA)
ws............. Western Samoa [*MARC country of publication code*] [*Library of Congress*] (LCCP)
WS............. Western Samoa [*Two-letter standard code*] (CNC)
WS............. Western Speech [*A publication*]
WS............. Wet Smoothed (BJA)
WS............. Wetted Surface
WS............. Wheat Straw
W & S........ Whiskey and Soda
WS............. White Sisters [*Missionary Sisters of Our Lady of Africa*] [*Roman Catholic religious order*]
WS............. Wide Shot [*Photography*]
WS............. Wiener Studien [*A publication*]
W-S............ Wigner-Seitz [*Construction cell*] [*Solid state physics*]
WS............. Wilderness Society
WS............. Wildlife Society
WS............. Will Ship (MCD)
WS............. Williams Syndrome [*Medicine*]
WS............. Willow Society (EA)
W & S........ Wilson and Shaw's Scotch Appeal Cases, English House of Lords (DLA)
WS............. Wind Shield (NASA)
WS............. Wind Speed
WS............. Windsonde (KSC)
WS............. Wing Station [*Aviation*]
WS............. Wire Send [*Telecommunications*] (TEL)
WS............. Wireless Set (MCD)
WS............. Wirtschaft und Statistik [*Germany*]
WS............. Wirtschaftsflug Rhein Main GmbH & Co. KG [*West Germany*] [*ICAO designator*] (FAAC)
Ws............. Wisdom (BJA)
W/S............ With Stock [*Business and trade*]
WS............. Withholding Statement (AAG)
WS............. Woerter und Sachen [*A publication*]
W & S........ Woerter und Sachen [*A publication*]
WS............. Women's Services [*Military*] [*British*]
WS............. Women's Size
WS............. Women's Studies: An Interdisciplinary Journal [*A publication*]
WS............. Women's Suffrage (ROG)
WS............. Wonder Stories [*A publication*]
WS............. Woomera Space Centre [*Australia*]
WS............. Word Study [*A publication*]
WS............. Word Sync
WS............. WordStar [*Computer program*]
WS............. Work Stand (MCD)
WS............. Work Statement (AAG)
W/S............ Work Station [*NASA*] (NASA)
WS............. Work Stoppage (AAG)
WS............. Working Space
WS............. Working Storage [*Data processing*] (MDG)
WS............. Worksheet (AAG)
WS............. Worldscale
WS............. Wort und Sinn [*A publication*]
WS............. Worthy Sister (BJA)
WS............. Writer to the Signet [*British*]
WS............. Wrought Steel (MSA)
WSA.......... Wagner Society of America (EA)
WSA.......... War Shipping Administration [*Within Office of Emergency Management*] [*World War II*]
WSA.......... War Supplies Agency (NATG)
WSA.......... Water-Soluble Adjuvant [*Immunology*]
WSA.......... Waveguide Slot Array
WSA.......... Weapons Systems Analysis [*Army*] (AABC)
WSA.......... Web Sling Association [*Jamesburg, NJ*] (EA)
WSA.......... Weed Society of America [*Later, WSSA*] (EA)

WSA	Western Slavonic Association (EA)
WSA	Western Surfing Association (EA)
WSA	Western Surgical Association [*Denver, CO*] (EA)
WSA	Wholesale Stationers' Association [*Des Plaines, IL*] (EA)
WSA	Wilderness Study Area [*Department of the Interior*]
WSA	Winter Soldier Archive (EA)
WSA	Wisconsin Statutes, Annotated (DLA)
WSA	Wolfenbuetteler Studien zur Aufklarung [*A publication*]
WSA	Wolverine Society of America (EA)
WSA	Women Studies Abstracts [*A publication*]
WSA	Women's Student Association (EA)
WSA	Wonder Story Annual [*A publication*]
WSA	Workplace Standards Administration [*Department of Labor*]
WSA	World Sign Associates [*Denver, CO*] (EA)
WSA	Writers' Sodality of America [*Defunct*]
WSAA	Waveguide Slot Array Antenna
WSAA	Western States Angus Association (EA)
WSAAA	Western States Advertising Agencies Association [*Los Angeles, CA*] (EA)
WSAC	Washington State Apple Commission (EA)
WSAC	Water Space Amenity Commission [*British*]
WSAC-FM ...	Fort Knox, KY [*FM radio station call letters*]
WSAD	Weapon System Analysis Division [*Navy*]
WSAE	Spring Arbor, MI [*FM radio station call letters*]
WSAF	Trion, GA [*AM radio station call letters*]
WSAG	Washington Special Action Group [*National Security Council*]
WSAH	World Smoking and Health [*A publication*]
WSAI	Erlanger, KY [*FM radio station call letters*]
WSAJ	Grove City, PA [*AM radio station call letters*]
WSAJ-FM ..	Grove City, PA [*FM radio station call letters*]
WSAK	Sullivan, IL [*FM radio station call letters*]
WSAL	Logansport, IN [*AM radio station call letters*]
WSAL-FM ...	Logansport, IN [*FM radio station call letters*]
WSAM	Saginaw, MI [*AM radio station call letters*]
WSAM	Weapon Systems Acquisition Management [*Navy*] (MCD)
WSAM	Westamerica Bancorp [*NASDAQ symbol*] (NQ)
WSAN	Vieques, PR [*FM radio station call letters*]
WSAO	Senatobia, MS [*AM radio station call letters*]
WSAO	Weapon System Analysis Office [*Navy*] (MCD)
WSAP	Weapon Status and Approval Panel [*Military*] (CAAL)
WSAP	Weapon System Acquisition Process (MCD)
WSAP	Weighted Sensitivity Analysis Program [*Environmental Protection Agency*]
W & S App ...	Wilson and Shaw's Scotch Appeal Cases, English House of Lords (DLA)
WSAQ	Port Huron, MI [*FM radio station call letters*]
WSAR	Fall River, MA [*AM radio station call letters*]
WSAR	Weekly Significant Action Report (AFIT)
WSAS	Weapon System Acceptance Schedule (AAG)
WSASSA	Wholesale School, Art, and Stationery Supplies Association [*Later, WSA*] (EA)
WSAT	Salisbury, NC [*AM radio station call letters*]
WSAT	Weapon Systems Accuracy [*formerly, Acceptance*] Trials [*Navy*] (NG)
WSATO	War Shipping Administration Training Organization [*Terminated*]
WSAU	Wausau Paper Mills [*NASDAQ symbol*] (NQ)
WSAU	Wausau, WI [*AM radio station call letters*]
WSAVA	World Small Animal Veterinary Association [*See also AMVPA*] (EA-IO)
WSAV-TV ...	Savannah, GA [*Television station call letters*]
WSAWD	White Sands Air Weather Detachment [*New Mexico*]
WSA-WGWC ...	World Service Authority of the World Government of World Citizens (EA)
WSAW-TV ...	Wausau, WI [*Television station call letters*]
WSAX	West Saxon [*Dialect of Old English*] [*Language, etc.*]
WSAY	Salem, VA [*AM radio station call letters*]
WSAZ-TV ...	Huntington, WV [*Television station call letters*]
WSB	Atlanta, GA [*AM radio station call letters*]
WSB	Steamboat Bay, AK [*Location identifier*] [*FAA*] (FAAL)
WSB	Wage Stabilization Board [*Terminated, 1953*]
Wsb	Washburn Law Journal [*A publication*]
WSB	Water-Soluble Base
WSB	Wheat-Soya Blend (EA)
WSB	Will Send Boat
WSB	World Scout Bureau (EA)
WSBA	York, PA [*AM radio station call letters*]
WSBA-FM ...	York, PA [*FM radio station call letters*]
WSBB	New Smyrna Beach, FL [*AM radio station call letters*]
WSBC	Chicago, IL [*AM radio station call letters*]
WSbD	Door County Library, Sturgeon Bay, WI [*Library symbol*] [*Library of Congress*] (LCLS)
WSBE-TV ...	Providence, RI [*Television station call letters*]
WSBF-FM ...	Clemson, SC [*FM radio station call letters*]
WSB-FM	Atlanta, GA [*FM radio station call letters*]
WSBG	Stroudsburg, PA [*FM radio station call letters*]
WSBH	Southhampton, NY [*FM radio station call letters*]
WSBI	Static, TN [*AM radio station call letters*]
WSBK-TV ...	Boston, MA [*Television station call letters*]
WSBL	Sanford, NC [*AM radio station call letters*]

WSBM	Florence, AL [*AM radio station call letters*]
WSBN-TV ...	Norton, VA [*Television station call letters*]
WSBP	Saluda, SC [*FM radio station call letters*]
WSBP	Western Society of Business Publications [*Defunct*] (EA)
WSBR	Boca Raton, FL [*AM radio station call letters*]
WSBS	Great Barrington, MA [*AM radio station call letters*]
WSBSA	Weapon System Base Supply Account [*Military*] (AFIT)
WSBT	South Bend, IN [*AM radio station call letters*]
WSBT-TV ...	South Bend, IN [*Television station call letters*]
WSB-TV	Atlanta, GA [*Television station call letters*]
WSBU	St. Bonaventure, NY [*FM radio station call letters*]
WSBU	Wahlenbergia. Scripta Botanica Umensia [*A publication*]
WSBV	South Boston, VA [*AM radio station call letters*]
WSBW	Sturgeon Bay, WI [*FM radio station call letters*]
WSBW	Weddell Sea Bottom Water [*Oceanography*]
WSBY	Salisbury, MD [*AM radio station call letters*]
WSC	Washington Science Center [*Maryland*] [*Seismograph station code, US Geological Survey*] [*Closed*] (SEIS)
WSC	Water Systems Council [*Formerly, NADFPM*] [*Chicago, IL*] (EA)
WSC	Weapon System Computer (MCD)
WSC	Weapon System Console [*Military*] (CAAL)
WSC	Weapon System Contractor
WSC	Weapon System Costing [*Navy*]
WSC	Weber State College [*Utah*]
WSC	Wesco Financial Corp. [*American Stock Exchange symbol*]
WSC	Westair Commuter Airlines [*Santa Rosa, CA*] [*FAA designator*] (FAAC)
WSC	Westech Resources Ltd. [*Vancouver Stock Exchange symbol*]
WSC	Western Sahara Campaign for Human Rights and Humanitarian Relief (EA)
WSC	Western Simulation Council
WSC	Western Snow Conference [*Spokane, WA*] (EA)
WSC	Western Snow Conference. Proceedings [*A publication*]
WSC	White Sisters of Charity of St. Vincent de Paul [*Roman Catholic religious order*]
WSC	Wideband Signal Conditioner (MCD)
WSC	Wildcat Service Corporation [*An association*] [*New York, NY*] (EA)
WSC	Wing Security Control [*Air Force*] (AFM)
WSC	Winona State College [*Later, Winona State University*] [*Minnesota*]
WSC	Winston Spencer Churchill [*1874-1965*] [*British statesman and prime minister*]
WSC	Wisconsin State College [*Later, University of Wisconsin*]
WSC	Working Security Committee [*Navy*]
WSC	World Series Cricket
WSC	World Spanish Congress (EA)
WSC	World Spiritual Council (EA)
WSC	World Straw Conference
WSC	World Survey of Climatology [*Elsevier Book Series*] [*A publication*]
WSC	Wrap-Spring Clutch
WSC	Wright State, Celina Branch, Celina, OH [*OCLC symbol*] (OCLC)
WSC	Writing Services Center
WSCA	World Surface Coatings Abstracts [*Paint Research Association*] [*Database*] [*A publication*] [*Teddington, Middlesex, England*]
WSCB	Springfield, MA [*FM radio station call letters*]
WSCC	Somerset, KY [*FM radio station call letters*]
WSCC	Weapon System Configuration Control [*Navy*] (AAG)
WSCC	Western State College of Colorado [*Gunnison*]
WSCC	Western Systems Coordinating Council [*Regional power council*]
WSCC	Work Station Control Center [*NASA*] (NASA)
WSCCM	Weapon System Configuration Control Manual [*Navy*] (NG)
WSCD-FM ...	Duluth, MN [*FM radio station call letters*]
WSCF	Titusville, FL [*FM radio station call letters*]
WSCF	World Student Christian Federation (EA)
WSCF Books ...	World Student Christian Federation Books [*A publication*]
WSCG	Corinth, NY [*FM radio station call letters*]
WSCH	Aurora-Rising Sun, IN [*FM radio station call letters*]
WSCHP	Wen Shih Che Hsueh-Pao [*Taiwan University*] [*A publication*]
WSCI	Charleston, SC [*FM radio station call letters*]
WSCI	Washington Scientific Industries [*NASDAQ symbol*] (NQ)
WSCL	Salisbury, MD [*FM radio station call letters*]
WSCL	Wisconsin Studies in Contemporary Literature [*Later, Contemporary Literature*] [*A publication*]
WSCM	Cobleskill, NY [*AM radio station call letters*]
WSCMB	Weapon System Configuration Management Board (MCD)
WSCO	Suring, WI [*Television station call letters*]
WSCOC	Wills Sainte Claire Owners Club (EA)
WSCP	Pulaski-Sandy Creek, NY [*AM radio station call letters*]
WSCP	Weapons System Control Point
WSCP-FM ...	Pulaski, NY [*FM radio station call letters*]
WSCQ	West Columbia, SC [*FM radio station call letters*]
WSCR	Scranton, PA [*AM radio station call letters*]
WSCS	Sodus, NY [*FM radio station call letters*]
WSCS	Washington State College. Studies [*A publication*]

WSCS......... Waste Solidification and Compaction Station [*Nuclear energy*] (NRCH)
WSCS........ Weapon System Communications System (AAG)
WSCS....... Wide Sense Cyclo-Stationary [*Communication*]
WSCSR...... Weapons System Contract Status Report [*Navy*] (NG)
WSCV........ Fort Lauderdale, FL [*Television station call letters*]
WSCW....... South Charleston, WV [*AM radio station call letters*]
WSCZ........ Greenwood, SC [*FM radio station call letters*]
WSD .... Sheboygan County Federated Library System, Mead Public Library, Sheboygan, WI [*OCLC symbol*] (OCLC)
WSD .... Warfare Systems Directorate (MCD)
WSD .... Weapon Support Detachment (MCD)
WSD .... Weapon System Development [*Military*] (CAAL)
WSD .... Weapon System Director
WSD .... Weapons System Demonstration (MCD)
WSD .... White Sands, NM [*Location identifier*] [*FAA*] (FAAL)
WSD .... Wind Speed Detector
WSD .... Working Stress Design (NRCH)
WSD .... World Space Directory [*A publication*]
WSD .... World Systems Division [*of Communications Satellite Corp.*] [*Telecommunications*] (TEL)
WSDA........ Water and Sewer Distributors of America [*Arlington, VA*] (EA)
WSDB........ World Studies Data Bank (EISS)
WSDC .... Hartsville, SC [*AM radio station call letters*]
WSDC .... Weapon System Design Criteria (AAG)
WSDC .... Weapons System Designator Code (NVT)
WSDC .... Wisconsin State Data Center [*Wisconsin State Department of Administration*] [*Madison*] [*Information service*] (EISS)
WSDD .... Weapon Status Digital Display
WSDH........ Sandwich, MA [*FM radio station call letters*]
WSDL........ Slidell, LA [*AM radio station call letters*]
WSDL........ Weapons System Development Laboratory
WSDL........ Weapons Systems Data Link (MCD)
WSDM........ Brazil, IN [*AM radio station call letters*]
WSDM........ Weapon System Data Module
WSDM-FM ... Brazil, IN [*FM radio station call letters*]
WSDP........ Plymouth, MI [*FM radio station call letters*]
WSDP........ Weapons System Development Plan
WSDR........ Sterling, IL [*AM radio station call letters*]
WSDS........ Ypsilanti, MI [*AM radio station call letters*]
WSDT........ Soddy-Daisy, TN [*AM radio station call letters*]
WSD/TD.... Weapon System Demonstration Test Directive (AAG)
WSE .... National Weather Service Employees Organization
WSE .... Weapon Support Equipment [*Navy*] (NG)
WSE .... Weapon System Engineering [*Navy*] (NG)
WSE .... Weapons System Evaluator (MCD)
WSE .... Weapons Systems Effectiveness
WSE .... West-Southeast (ROG)
WSE .... Western Allenbee Oil & Gas [*Vancouver Stock Exchange symbol*]
WSE .... Western Society of Engineers
WSE .... Wound, Skin, Enteric [*Isolation*] [*Medicine*]
WSEA........ Georgetown, DE [*FM radio station call letters*]
WSEC........ Washington State Electronics Council
WSEC........ Watt-Second (AAG)
WSEC........ Williamstown, NC [*FM radio station call letters*]
WSECL...... Weapon System Equipment Component List
WSED .... Weapon System Electrical Diagrams
WSEE........ Erie, PA [*Television station call letters*]
WSEES...... Weapon System Electromagnetic Environment Simulator (MCD)
WSEF........ Weapons System Evaluation Facility (MCD)
WSEF........ Weapons Systems Effectiveness Factors
WSEFGT .... Weapons System Evaluation Facility Group Test (MCD)
WSEG........ Weapon System Evaluation Group [*DoD and Air Force*] (MCD)
WSEI........ Olney, IL [*FM radio station call letters*]
WSEIAC ..... Weapon System Effectiveness Industry Advisory Committee
WSEK .... Somerset, KY [*FM radio station call letters*]
WSEL .... Pontotoc, MS [*AM radio station call letters*]
WSEL .... Weapon System Engineering Laboratory
WSEL-FM... Pontotoc, MS [*FM radio station call letters*]
WSEM .... Donalsonville, GA [*AM radio station call letters*]
WSEM .... Weapon System Evaluation Missile [*Air Force*] (AFM)
WSem .... West Semitic (BJA)
WSEN .... Baldwinsville, NY [*AM radio station call letters*]
WSEN-FM ... Baldwinsville, NY [*FM radio station call letters*]
WSEO........ Weather Service Evaluation Officer [*National Weather Service*]
WSEP........ Waste Solidification Engineering Prototype Plant [*Nuclear energy*]
WSEP........ Weapon System Evaluation Program [*Air Force*]
WSER........ Elkton, MD [*AM radio station call letters*]
WSES........ Raleigh, NC [*AM radio station call letters*]
WSES........ Waterford Steam Electric Station [*Nuclear energy*] (NRCH)
WSESA ...... Weapon System and Equipment Support Analysis
WSET .... Weapon System Evaluation Test [*Navy*] (NG)
WSET .... Writers and Scholars Educational Trust (EA-IO)
WSET-TV ... Lynchburg, VA [*Television station call letters*]
WSEV........ Sevierville, TN [*AM radio station call letters*]
WSEX........ Arlington Heights, IL [*FM radio station call letters*]
WSEY........ Sauk City, WI [*FM radio station call letters*]
WSEZ......... Winston-Salem, NC [*FM radio station call letters*]

WSF .... Waste Shipping Facility [*Nuclear energy*] (NRCH)
WSF .... Water/Sand Fillable
WSF .... Water-Soluble Fraction
WSF .... Water Supply Forecast (NOAA)
WSF .... Weapon System File (MCD)
WSF .... Weather Support Force [*Military*] (AFM)
WSF .... Week Second Feet
WSF .... Well-Springs Foundation (EA)
WSF .... Western Sea Frontier [*Navy*]
WSF .... Women for a Secure Future (EA)
WSF .... Women's Sports Foundation (EA)
WSF .... Work Station Facility
WSF .... World Salt Foundation (EA)
WSF .... World Science Fiction (EA)
WSF .... World Scout Foundation (EA-IO)
WSF .... World Sephardi Federation [*See also FSM*] (EA-IO)
WSFA........ Montgomery, AL [*Television station call letters*]
WSFB........ Quitman, GA [*AM radio station call letters*]
WSFC........ Somerset, KY [*AM radio station call letters*]
WSFC........ White Sands Field Center [*New Mexico*]
WSFI......... Wood and Synthetic Flooring Institute [*Hillside, IL*] (EA)
WSFJ......... Newark, OH [*Television station call letters*]
WSFL-FM... New Bern, NC [*FM radio station call letters*]
WSFM .... Harrisburg, PA [*FM radio station call letters*]
WSFO .... Weather Service Forecast Office [*National Weather Service*]
WSFP .... World Showcase Fellowship Program [*Walt Disney World*]
WSFPF ...... Westfort Petroleum Ltd. [*NASDAQ symbol*] (NQ)
WSFP-FM.. Fort Myers, FL [*FM radio station call letters*]
WSFP-TV ... Fort Myers, FL [*Television station call letters*]
WSFS .... World Science Fiction Society (EA)
WSFT .... Thomaston, GA [*AM radio station call letters*]
WSFU-FM ... Union Springs, AL [*FM radio station call letters*]
WSFW .... Seneca Falls, NY [*AM radio station call letters*]
WSFW-FM ... Seneca Falls, NY [*FM radio station call letters*]
WSG .... International Wool Study Group
WSG .... Washington [*Pennsylvania*] [*Airport symbol*] (OAG)
WSG .... Wesleyan Service Guild [*Defunct*] (EA)
WSG .... Winter Study Group
WSG .... Wire Strain Gauge
WSG .... Wired Shelf Group [*Telecommunications*] (TEL)
WSG .... Worthiest Soldier in the Group
WSGA .... Savannah, GA [*AM radio station call letters*]
WSGA .... Water Soluble Gum Association (EA)
WSGA .... Wine and Spirits Guild of America [*Minneapolis, MN*] (EA)
WSGB .... Sutton, WV [*AM radio station call letters*]
WSGC .... Elberton, GA [*AM radio station call letters*]
WSGC .... Williams-Sonoma, Inc. [*NASDAQ symbol*] (NQ)
WSGE........ Dallas, NC [*FM radio station call letters*]
WSGE........ Western Society of Gear Engineers (MCD)
WSGG .... Scottsboro, AL [*AM radio station call letters*]
WSGH .... Lewisville, NC [*AM radio station call letters*]
WSGI......... Springfield, TN [*AM radio station call letters*]
WSGL........ Naples, FL [*FM radio station call letters*]
WSGM .... Staunton, VA [*FM radio station call letters*]
WSGN .... Gadsden, AL [*FM radio station call letters*]
WSGO .... Oswego, NY [*AM radio station call letters*]
WSGO-FM .. Oswego, NY [*FM radio station call letters*]
WSGR-FM ... Port Huron, MI [*FM radio station call letters*]
WSGS .... Hazard, KY [*FM radio station call letters*]
WSGT........ White Sands Ground Terminal (MCD)
WSGW....... Saginaw, MI [*AM radio station call letters*]
WSGY....... Tifton, GA [*FM radio station call letters*]
Wsh .... Washington State Reports (DLA)
WsH.......... William S. Hein & Co., Inc., Buffalo, NY [*Library symbol*] [*Library of Congress*] (LCLS)
WSH .... Wilshire Energy Resources, Inc. [*Toronto Stock Exchange symbol*]
WS and H ... World Smoking and Health [*A publication*]
WSha.......... Bringham Memorial Library, Sharon, WI [*Library symbol*] [*Library of Congress*] (LCLS)
WSHA........ Raleigh, NC [*FM radio station call letters*]
WShawGS ... Church of Jesus Christ of Latter-Day Saints, Genealogical Society Library, Wisconsin East District Branch, Shawano, WI [*Library symbol*] [*Library of Congress*] (LCLS)
WSHC .... Shepherdstown, WV [*FM radio station call letters*]
WSHE .... Fort Lauderdale, FL [*FM radio station call letters*]
WShe .... Mead Public Library, Sheboygan, WI [*Library symbol*] [*Library of Congress*] (LCLS)
WSheL ...... Lakeland College, Sheboygan, WI [*Library symbol*] [*Library of Congress*] (LCLS)
WSheM ..... Sheboygan Memorial Hospital, Sheboygan, WI [*Library symbol*] [*Library of Congress*] (LCLS)
WSheSN .... Saint Nicholas Hospital, Sheboygan, WI [*Library symbol*] [*Library of Congress*] (LCLS)
WSheU....... University of Wisconsin Center-Sheboygan, Sheboygan, WI [*Library symbol*] [*Library of Congress*] (LCLS)
WSHF........ Wives Self-Help Foundation [*Philadelphia, PA*] (EA)
WSHFT....... Wind Shift (FAAC)
WSHG .... Washing (MSA)
WSHGA..... Washington State Holly Growers Association [*Defunct*] (EA)
WSHH....... Pittsburgh, PA [*FM radio station call letters*]

WSHJ .... Southfield, MI [*FM radio station call letters*]
WSHLD ...... Windshield   (AAG)
WSHL-FM ... Easton, MA [*FM radio station call letters*]
WSHN-FM ... Fremont, MI [*FM radio station call letters*]
WSHO .... New Orleans, LA [*AM radio station call letters*]
WSHP .... Shippensburg, PA [*AM radio station call letters*]
WSHR .... Lake Ronkonkoma, NY [*FM radio station call letters*]
WSHR .... Washer   (MSA)
WSHS .... Sheboygan, WI [*FM radio station call letters*]
WSHU .... Fairfield, CT [*FM radio station call letters*]
WSHV .... South Hill, VA [*FM radio station call letters*]
WSHW .... Frankfort, IN [*FM radio station call letters*]
WSHY .... Shelbyville, IL [*AM radio station call letters*]
WSHY-FM ... Shelbyville, IL [*FM radio station call letters*]
WSI .... Wafer-Scale Integration [*Microelectronics*]
WSI .... WaferScale Integration, Inc.
WSI .... Waingapu [*Sumba Island*] [*Seismograph station code, US Geological Survey*]   (SEIS)
WSI .... War Service Indefinite
WSI .... Water Safety Instructor [*Red Cross*]
WSI .... Water Ski Industry Association [*North Palm Beach, FL*]   (EA)
WSI .... Water Solubility Index [*Analytical chemistry*]
WSI .... Weapon System Integration   (MCD)
WSI .... Weather Services International Corp. [*Information service*]   (EISS)
WSI .... Wind Speed Indicator
WSI .... World Synoptic Interval
WSI .... Writers and Scholars International   (EA-IO)
WSIA .... Staten Island, NY [*FM radio station call letters*]
WSIA .... Water Supply Improvement Association [*Formerly, NWSIA*]   (EA)
WSIA .... Weapons Systems Integration Agent   (MCD)
WSIA J .... WSIA [*Water Supply Improvement Association*] Journal [*United States*] [*A publication*]
WSIC .... Statesville, NC [*AM radio station call letters*]
WSIC .... Watchmakers of Switzerland Information Center   (EA)
WSIE .... Edwardsville, IL [*FM radio station call letters*]
WSIF .... Wilkesboro, NC [*FM radio station call letters*]
WSIG .... Mount Jackson, VA [*AM radio station call letters*]
WSI/L .... War Supporting Industries and Logistics   (MCD)
WSIL-TV ... Harrisburg, IL [*Television station call letters*]
WSIM .... Water Separation Index, Modified
WSI Mitt .... WSI [*Wirtschafts- und Sozialwissenschaftliches Institut*] Mitteilungen [*German Federal Republic*] [*A publication*]
WSIP .... Paintsville, KY [*AM radio station call letters*]
WSIP-FM ... Paintsville, KY [*FM radio station call letters*]
WSIR .... White Sands Integrated Range [*New Mexico*]   (AAG)
WSIR .... Winter Haven, FL [*AM radio station call letters*]
WSIT .... Washington State Institute of Technology   (KSC)
WSIT .... Water Safety Instructor Trainer [*Red Cross*]
WSIU .... Carbondale, IL [*FM radio station call letters*]
WSIU-TV ... Carbondale, IL [*Television station call letters*]
WSIV .... East Syracuse, NY [*AM radio station call letters*]
WSIX .... Nashville, TN [*AM radio station call letters*]
WSIX-FM... Nashville, TN [*FM radio station call letters*]
WSIZ .... Ocilla, GA [*AM radio station call letters*]
WSJ .... San Juan, AK [*Location identifier*] [*FAA*]   (FAAL)
WSJ .... Wall Street Journal [*A publication*]
WSJ .... Wiener Slawistisches Jahrbuch [*A publication*]
WSJ .... Worm Screw Jack
WSJ .... WSFA [*Washington Science Fiction Association*] Journal [*A publication*]
WSJA .... Cookeville, TN [*Television station call letters*]
WSJB-FM... Standish, ME [*FM radio station call letters*]
WSJC .... Magee, MS [*AM radio station call letters*]
WSJC-FM ... Magee, MS [*FM radio station call letters*]
WSJHQ....... Western States Jewish Historical Quarterly [*A publication*]
WSJK-TV ... Sneedville, TN [*Television station call letters*]
WSJL .... Cape May, NJ [*FM radio station call letters*]
WSJM........ St. Joseph, MI [*AM radio station call letters*]
WSJN-TV ... San Juan, PR [*Television station call letters*]
W S Jour .... Wallace Stevens Journal [*A publication*]
WSJP .... Murray, KY [*AM radio station call letters*]
WSJR .... Madawaska, ME [*AM radio station call letters*]
WSJS .... Winston-Salem, NC [*AM radio station call letters*]
WSJU .... San Juan, PR [*Television station call letters*]
WSJV-TV ... Elkhart, IN [*Television station call letters*]
WSJW .... Woodruff, SC [*AM radio station call letters*]
WSJY .... Fort Atkinson, WI [*FM radio station call letters*]
WSKA .... Port Huron, MI [*Television station call letters*]
WSKB........ Westfield, MA [*FM radio station call letters*]
WSKE .... Everett, PA [*AM radio station call letters*]
WSKG .... Binghamton, NY [*Television station call letters*]
WSKG-FM ... Binghamton, NY [*FM radio station call letters*]
WSKI .... Montpelier, VT [*AM radio station call letters*]
WSKQ .... Newark, NJ [*AM radio station call letters*]
WSKT......... Knoxville, TN [*AM radio station call letters*]
WSKV......... Stanton, KY [*FM radio station call letters*]
WSKX......... Suffolk, VA [*FM radio station call letters*]
WSKY......... Asheville, NC [*AM radio station call letters*]
WSKZ......... Chattanooga, TN [*FM radio station call letters*]

WSL........... War Services Loan   (ADA)
WSL........... War Substantive Lieutenant [*British*]
WSL........... Warren Spring Laboratory [*British*]
Ws L .... Washington Law Review [*A publication*]
WSL........... Weather Seal   (AAG)
WSL........... Welt der Slaven [*A publication*]
WSL........... Western Savings & Loan Association [*NYSE symbol*]
WSL........... Windscale
W SI A .... Wiener Slawistischer Almanach [*A publication*]
WSlav .... Welt der Slaven [*A publication*]
WSLB .... Ogdensburg, NY [*AM radio station call letters*]
WSLC .... Roanoke, VA [*AM radio station call letters*]
WSLC .... World Shortwave Listeners Club   (EA)
WSLE .... Bremen, GA [*AM radio station call letters*]
WSLF .... Western Somali Liberation Front
WSLG .... Gonzales, LA [*AM radio station call letters*]
WSLI .... Jackson, MS [*AM radio station call letters*]
WSLJb .... Wiener Slawistisches Jahrbuch [*A publication*]
WSLK .... Hyden, KY [*AM radio station call letters*]
WSLM .... Salem, IN [*AM radio station call letters*]
WSLM-FM ... Salem, IN [*FM radio station call letters*]
WSLN .... Delaware, OH [*FM radio station call letters*]
WSLO .... Weapon System Logistics Officer [*Air Force*]   (AFM)
WSLQ .... Roanoke, VA [*FM radio station call letters*]
WSLR .... Akron, OH [*AM radio station call letters*]
WSLR .... Weapon System Logistic Reviews [*Navy*]   (NG)
WSLS-TV ... Roanoke, VA [*Television station call letters*]
WSLT .... Ocean City, NJ [*FM radio station call letters*]
WSLU .... Canton, NY [*FM radio station call letters*]
WSLV .... Ardmore, TN [*AM radio station call letters*]
WSLW .... White Sulphur Springs, WV [*AM radio station call letters*]
WSLX .... New Canaan, CT [*FM radio station call letters*]
WSLY .... York, AL [*FM radio station call letters*]
WSM.......... Nashville, TN [*AM radio station call letters*]
WSM.......... Weapon Support Manager [*Air Force*]
WSM.......... Weapon System Manager [*Air Force*]   (AFM)
WSM.......... Weapon System Manual
WSM.......... West-Mar Resources Ltd. [*Vancouver Stock Exchange symbol*]
WSM.......... Western Samoa [*Three-letter standard code*]   (CNC)
WSM.......... Western Society of Malacologists   (EA)
WSM.......... White Single Male [*Classified advertising*]
WSM.......... Wigner-Seitz Method [*Physics*]
WSM.......... Wiseman [*Alaska*] [*Airport symbol*]   (OAG)
WSM.......... Wiseman, AK [*Location identifier*] [*FAA*]   (FAAL)
WSM.......... Women's Suffrage Movement   (ROG)
WSM.......... Wright State University, Health Sciences Library, Dayton, OH [*OCLC symbol*]   (OCLC)
WSMA....... Marine City, MI [*AM radio station call letters*]
WSMA....... Western States Meat Association [*Formed by a merger of Western States Meat Packers Association and Pacific Coast Meat Association*] [*Oakland, CA*]   (EA)
WSMA....... Window Shade Manufacturers Association   (EA)
WSMAC ..... Weapon System Maintenance Action Center
WSMaT ...... Weapon System Management Team [*Army*]   (RDA)
WSMB .... New Orleans, LA [*AM radio station call letters*]
WSMC .... Weapons System Management Codes [*Navy*]
WSMC .... Western Space and Missile Center [*Air Force*]
WSMC....... Western States Movers Conference
WSMC-FM ... Collegedale, TN [*FM radio station call letters*]
WSMD .... St. Mary's City, MD [*FM radio station call letters*]
WSME .... Sanford, ME [*AM radio station call letters*]
WSMF .... Florence, SC [*Television station call letters*]
WSM-FM ..... Nashville, TN [*FM radio station call letters*]
WSMG .... Greenville, TN [*AM radio station call letters*]
WSMH .... Flint, MI [*Television station call letters*]
WSMI .... Litchfield, IL [*AM radio station call letters*]
WSMI-FM... Litchfield, IL [*FM radio station call letters*]
WSMJ........ Cave City, KY [*AM radio station call letters*]
WSML .... Graham, NC [*AM radio station call letters*]
WSML .... Saltfree Meal [*Airline notation*]
WSMM .... Gatlinburg, TN [*AM radio station call letters*]
WSMN .... Nashua, NH [*AM radio station call letters*]
WSMO........ Weapon System Materiel Officer [*Air Force*]   (AFM)
WSMO........ Weather Service Meteorological Observatory [*or Observations*] [*National Weather Service*]   (NOAA)
WSMP .... Western Steer Mom 'n Pop [*NASDAQ symbol*]   (NQ)
WSMPA..... Western States Meat Association   (EA)
WSMQ .... Bessemer, AL [*AM radio station call letters*]
WSMR .... Raeford, NC [*AM radio station call letters*]
WSMR .... White Sands Missile Range [*New Mexico*]
WSMR-FM ... Dayton, OH [*FM radio station call letters*]
WSMS .... Memphis, TN [*FM radio station call letters*]
WSMT .... Sparta, TN [*AM radio station call letters*]
WSMT .... Weapons System Maintenance Test   (MCD)
WSMTC...... White Sands Missile Test Center [*New Mexico*]
WSMT-FM ... Sparta, TN [*FM radio station call letters*]
WSMTT ...... White Star Mobile Training Teams [*Military*]   (CINC)
WSMU-FM ... Starkville, MS [*FM radio station call letters*]
WSMV .... Nashville, TN [*Television station call letters*]
WSMX .... Winston-Salem, NC [*AM radio station call letters*]
WSMY .... Weldon, NC [*AM radio station call letters*]

WSN .... South Naknek [*Alaska*] [*Airport symbol*]   (OAG)
WSN .... South Naknek, AK [*Location identifier*] [*FAA*]   (FAAL)
WSN .... Spokane County Library, Spokane, WA [*OCLC symbol*] [*Inactive*]   (OCLC)
WSN .... Wallace Stevens Newsletter [*A publication*]
WSN .... Warm Springs [*Nevada*] [*Seismograph station code, US Geological Survey*] [*Closed*]   (SEIS)
WSN .... Water-Soluble Nitrogen [*Analytical chemistry*]
WSN .... Western Co. of North America [*NYSE symbol*]
WSN .... Western Society of Naturalists
WSNA (Mini J) ... Washington State Nurses Association (Mini Journal) [*A publication*]
WSNC .... Winston-Salem, NC [*FM radio station call letters*]
WSND-FM ... Notre Dame, IN [*FM radio station call letters*]
WSNE .... Taunton, MA [*FM radio station call letters*]
WSNG .... Torrington, CT [*AM radio station call letters*]
WSNGT ..... White Sands NASA Ground Terminal   (MCD)
WSNI .... Philadelphia, PA [*FM radio station call letters*]
WSNJ .... Bridgeton, NJ [*AM radio station call letters*]
WSNJ-FM... Bridgeton, NJ [*FM radio station call letters*]
WSNN .... Potsdam, NY [*FM radio station call letters*]
WSNO .... Barre, VT [*AM radio station call letters*]
WSNP .... Water-Soluble Nonstarchy Polysaccharide [*Food composition*]
WSNS .... Chicago, IL [*Television station call letters*]
WSNSCA ... Washable Suits, Novelties, and Sportswear Contractors Association [*New York, NY*]   (EA)
WSNT .... Sandersville, GA [*AM radio station call letters*]
WSNT-FM ... Sandersville, GA [*FM radio station call letters*]
WSNW .... Seneca, SC [*AM radio station call letters*]
WSNX .... Muskegon, MI [*AM radio station call letters*]
WSNX-FM ... Muskegon, MI [*FM radio station call letters*]
WSNY .... Columbus, OH [*FM radio station call letters*]
WSO .... Warrant Stores Officer [*Navy*] [*British*]
WSO .... Washabo [*Suriname*] [*Airport symbol*]   (OAG)
WSO .... Washington Standardization Officers
WSO .... Water Service Operator   (MCD)
WSO .... Watsco, Inc. [*American Stock Exchange symbol*]
WSO .... Weapon System Officer [*Air Force*]   (AFM)
WSO .... Weather Service Office [*National Weather Service*]   (NOAA)
WSO .... Western Support Office [*Formerly, WOO*] [*NASA*]
WSO .... White Sands Operations [*New Mexico*] [*Formerly, White Sands Missile Operations*] [*NASA*]
WSO .... World Simulation Organization
WSOC .... Charlotte, NC [*AM radio station call letters*]
WSOC .... Weapon System Operational Concept   (AAG)
W Soc E J... Western Society of Engineers. Journal [*A publication*]
WSOC-FM ... Charlotte, NC [*FM radio station call letters*]
WSOC-TV ... Charlotte, NC [*Television station call letters*]
WSOE ...... Elon College, NC [*FM radio station call letters*]
WSOEA ...... Wholesale Stationery and Office Equipment Association [*Later, WSA*]   (EA)
WSOF-FM ... Madisonville, KY [*FM radio station call letters*]
WSOK .... Savannah, GA [*AM radio station call letters*]
WSOL .... San German, PR [*AM radio station call letters*]
WSOM .... Salem, OH [*AM radio station call letters*]
WSOM .... Weather Service Operations Manual [*National Weather Service*]   (FAAC)
WSON .... Henderson, KY [*AM radio station call letters*]
WSON .... Worldwide Satellite Observing Network   (MCD)
WSOO .... Sault Ste. Marie, MI [*AM radio station call letters*]
WSOR .... Fort Myers, FL [*FM radio station call letters*]
WSOS .... St. Augustine, FL [*FM radio station call letters*]
WSOT .... Weapon System Operability Test [*Military*]   (CAAL)
WSOU .... South Orange, NJ [*FM radio station call letters*]
WSOY .... Decatur, IL [*AM radio station call letters*]
WSOY .... Werner Soederstroem Osakeyhtio [*Finnish book printer*]
WSOY-FM ... Decatur, IL [*FM radio station call letters*]
W/SP .... Warheads and Special Projects Laboratory [*Picatinny Arsenal*]
WSP .... Washington School of Psychiatry
WSP .... Washington Square Press [*Publisher's imprint*]
WSP .... Water Supply Papers
WSP .... Water Supply Point
WSP .... Weapon Support Processor [*Military*]   (CAAL)
WSP .... Weapon Systems Pouch   (AFM)
WSP .... Weibull Shape Parameter [*Statistics*]
WSP .... West Penn Power Co. [*NYSE symbol*]
WSP .... Wideband Signal Processor
WSP .... Women Strike for Peace   (EA)
WSP .... Work Study Program   (OICC)
WSP .... Working Steam Pressure
WSP .... Workshop   (NATG)
WSP .... Wright State University, Piqua Branch Campus, Piqua, OH [*OCLC symbol*]   (OCLC)
Wsp .... Wspolczesnosc [*Warsaw*] [*A publication*]
WSpa .... Sparta Free Library, Sparta, WI [*Library symbol*] [*Library of Congress*]   (LCLS)
WSPA .... Spartanburg, SC [*AM radio station call letters*]
WSPA .... World Society for the Protection of Animals   (EA)
WSPACS .... Weapon Systems Planning [*or Programing*] and Control System
WSPA-FM ... Spartanburg, SC [*FM radio station call letters*]

WSPA-TV ... Spartanburg, SC [*Television station call letters*]
WSPB .... Sarasota, FL [*AM radio station call letters*]
WSPC .... St. Paul, VA [*AM radio station call letters*]
WSPC .... Weapons System Partnerships Committee [*NATO*]   (NATG)
WSPC .... Weapons System Program Code [*Defense Supply Agency*]
WSPD .... Toledo, OH [*AM radio station call letters*]
WSPD .... Weapon System Planning Document   (NVT)
WSPD .... Weapons System Planning Data [*Navy*]
WSPF .... Hickory, NC [*AM radio station call letters*]
WSPF .... Watergate Special Prosecution Force [*Terminated, 1977*] [*Department of Justice*]
WSPG .... Wall Street Planning Group   (EA)
WSPG .... Weapon System Phasing Group
WSPG .... Weapon System Purchasing Group
WSPG .... White Sands Proving Ground [*New Mexico*] [*Air Force*] [*Obsolete*]
WSPGL ...... Weapon System Program Guide List
WSPI .... Shamokin, PA [*FM radio station call letters*]
WSPK .... Poughkeepsie, NY [*FM radio station call letters*]
WSPL .... La Crosse, WI [*FM radio station call letters*]
WSPN .... Saratoga Springs, NY [*FM radio station call letters*]
WSPO .... Weapon System Project Office [*Air Force*]
WSPOP ...... Weapon System Phase-Out Procedure [*Air Force*]   (AFM)
WSPPD ...... Weapons Systems Personnel Planning Data   (MCD)
WSPQ .... Springville, NY [*AM radio station call letters*]
WSPR .... Springfield, MA [*AM radio station call letters*]
WSPRD ...... Weapons Systems Progress Reporting Data
WSPS .... Concord, NH [*FM radio station call letters*]
WSpS .... Saint Michael's Hospital, Stevens Point, WI [*Library symbol*] [*Library of Congress*]   (LCLS)
WSPS .... Wire Strike Protection System   (MCD)
WSPT .... Stevens Point, WI [*FM radio station call letters*]
WSpU .... University of Wisconsin-Stevens Point, Stevens Point, WI [*Library symbol*] [*Library of Congress*]   (LCLS)
WSPUS ..... World Socialist Party of the United States   (EA)
WSPV .... Buffalo Gap, VA [*FM radio station call letters*]
WSPY .... Plano, IL [*FM radio station call letters*]
WSPZ .... Douglasville, GA [*AM radio station call letters*]
WSQ .... Wake Seeding and Quenching
WSq .... Weather Squadron [*Air Force*]   (AFM)
WSQ .... Wonder Stories Quarterly [*A publication*]
WSQR .... Sycamore, IL [*AM radio station call letters*]
WSQY-TV .. Forrest City, NC [*Television station call letters*]
WSR .... War Service Regulation
WSR .... Warm Springs Repeater [*Nevada*] [*Seismograph station code, US Geological Survey*] [*Closed*]   (SEIS)
WSR .... Warren & Saline River Railroad Co. [*AAR code*]
W/sr .... Watts per Steradian
WSR .... Weak Signal Reception
WSR .... Weapon System Reliability [*Air Force*]   (AFM)
WSR .... Weapon Systems Requirement   (MCD)
WSR .... Weapons Spares Report [*Navy*]
WSR .... Weapons Status Report [*Navy*]   (NG)
WSR .... Weapons System Review   (NVT)
WSR .... Weather Surveillance RADAR
WSR .... Weekly Summary Report
WSR .... Wet Snow on Runway [*Aviation*]   (FAAC)
WSR .... Wild and Scenic Rivers Act
WSR .... Windsor Resources, Inc. [*Vancouver Stock Exchange symbol*]
WSR .... Wire Shift Register
WSR .... Wood-Shingle Roof [*Technical drawings*]
WSR .... World Students Relief
WSRA .... Guayama, PR [*FM radio station call letters*]
WSRA .... Wild and Scenic Rivers Act
WSRB .... Wall Street Review of Books [*A publication*]
WSRB .... Walpole, MA [*FM radio station call letters*]
WSRC .... Durham, NC [*AM radio station call letters*]
WSRD .... Johnstown, NY [*FM radio station call letters*]
WSRE .... Pensacola, FL [*Television station call letters*]
WSRF .... Fort Lauderdale, FL [*AM radio station call letters*]
WSRG .... Elkton, KY [*AM radio station call letters*]
WSRH .... Weather Service Regional Headquarters [*National Weather Service*]   (NOAA)
WSRI .... World Safety Research Institute
WSRK .... Oneonta, NY [*FM radio station call letters*]
WSRL .... Water Supply Research Laboratory [*National Environmental Research Center*]
WSRL .... Wisconsin Survey Research Laboratory [*University of Wisconsin*] [*Research center*]   (RCD)
WSRN-FM ... Swarthmore, PA [*FM radio station call letters*]
WSRO .... Marlboro, MA [*AM radio station call letters*]
WSRO .... Weapon System Replacement Operations   (MCD)
WSRO .... World Sugar Research Organisation   (EA-IO)
WSRP .... Weapons System Requisitioning Procedure   (AABC)
WSRR .... Washington, NJ [*AM radio station call letters*]
WSRR .... West Shore Railroad
WSRS .... Worcester, MA [*FM radio station call letters*]
WSRT .... Weapon System Readiness Test
WSRT .... Weapons System Reliability Test   (CINC)
WSRT .... Westerbork Synthesis Radio Telescope
WSRU .... Slippery Rock, PA [*FM radio station call letters*]

WSRW........	Hillsboro, OH [AM radio station call letters]
WSRW-FM ...	Hillsboro, OH [FM radio station call letters]
WSRZ........	Sarasota, FL [FM radio station call letters]
WSS	Wage Subsidy Scheme (ADA)
WSS	War Savings Staff
WSS	Warfare Systems School [Air Force] (AFM)
WSS	Weapon Support Systems
WSS	Weapon System Specification (AAG)
WSS	Weather Service Specialist [National Weather Service]
WSS	Weekend Stress Syndrome [Psychiatry]
WSS	Winston-Salem Southbound Railway Co. [AAR code]
WSS	Women's Social Services [Salvation Army]
WSS	Work Summarization System (MCD)
WSS	World Ship Society
WSSA........	Morrow, GA [AM radio station call letters]
WSSA........	Weapon System Support Activities (AAG)
WSSA........	Weed Science Society of America
WSSA........	Welsh Secondary Schools Association [British]
WSSA........	White Sands Signal Agency [New Mexico] [Military] (MCD)
WSSA........	Wine and Spirits Shippers Association [Reston, VA] (EA)
WSSA........	World Secret Service Association [Later, WAD] (EA)
WSSBA	Western Single Side Band Association (EA)
WSSB-FM ..	Orangeburg, SC [FM radio station call letters]
WSSC........	Sumter, SC [AM radio station call letters]
WSSC........	Weapon System Support Center (AAG)
WSSC........	Weapon System Support Code [Navy] (NG)
WSSCA	White Sands Signal Corps Agency [New Mexico] [Military] (AAG)
WSSCL	Weapon System Stock Control List (AAG)
WSSD........	Chicago, IL [FM radio station call letters]
WSSD........	Weapon System Support Development (MCD)
WSSF........	Weather Service Support Facility [National Weather Service] (FAAC)
WSSFN	World Society for Stereotactic and Functional Neurosurgery [Houston, TX] (EA)
WSSG	Goldsboro, NC [AM radio station call letters]
WSSG	Weapon System Support Group (MCD)
WSSH........	Lowell, MA [FM radio station call letters]
WSSI	Carthage, MS [AM radio station call letters]
WSSI	Women's Social Service for Israel [New York, NY] (EA)
WSSIB.......	WWMCCS [Worldwide Military Command and Control System] Standard System Information Base (MCD)
WSSI-FM....	Carthage, MS [FM radio station call letters]
WSSJ	Camden, NJ [AM radio station call letters]
WSSL........	Weapon System Stock/Support List [Air Force] (AFIT)
WSSL........	Western Secondary Standards Laboratory
WSSL-FM ..	Gray Court, SC [FM radio station call letters]
WSSM.......	Weapon System Staff Manager [Army] (RDA)
WSSM.......	Weapon System Support Manager (AAG)
WSSN.......	Weston, WV [AM radio station call letters]
WSSO	Starkville, MS [AM radio station call letters]
WSSO	Weapon System Support Officer [Army] (RDA)
WSSP.......	Cocoa Beach, FL [FM radio station call letters]
WSSP.......	Weapon Systems Support Program [Defense Supply Agency]
WSSPM......	Weapons System Support Program Manager (AFIT)
WSSR........	Springfield, IL [AM radio station call letters]
WSSS	Weapon System Storage Site
WSSSFAF ...	Wartime Standard Support System for Foreign Armed Forces (MCD)
WSSSP	Western States Small School Project
WSST	Miami Beach, FL [FM radio station call letters]
WSSU........	Superior, WI [FM radio station call letters]
WSSU........	Weather Service Support Unit [National Weather Service] (FAAC)
WSSW.......	Mackinaw City, MI [FM radio station call letters]
WSSX-FM ...	Charleston, SC [FM radio station call letters]
WSt	D. R. Moon Memorial Library, Stanley, WI [Library symbol] [Library of Congress] (LCLS)
WST	Water Supply Tank
WST	Weapon System Test
WST	Weapon System Trainer [Navy]
WST	Weightlessness Simulation Test
WST	West Co., Inc. [NYSE symbol]
WST	Westerly [Rhode Island] [Airport symbol] (OAG)
WST	Westerly, RI [Location identifier] [FAA] (FAAL)
WST	Western Air Express [Houston, TX] [FAA designator] (FAAC)
WSt	Word Study [A publication]
WST	World Ship Trust
WST	Write Symbol Table
WSTA........	Charlotte Amalie, VI [AM radio station call letters]
WSTA........	Weapon System Task Analysis (AAG)
WSTA........	White Slave Traffic Act
WSTB........	Streetsboro, OH [FM radio station call letters]
WSTC........	Stamford, CT [AM radio station call letters]
WSTC........	Weapon System Total Complex
WSTC........	Weapons System Test Card (MCD)
WSTC........	Willimantic State Teachers College [Connecticut]
WSTCH	Wasatch Range [National Weather Service] (FAAC)
WSTEA......	Weapon System Training Effectiveness Analysis
WSTED	Water Science and Technology [A publication]

WSTE MAT ...	Waste Material [Freight]
WSTF	Cocoa Beach, FL [FM radio station call letters]
WSTF	White Sands Test Facility [New Mexico] [NASA]
WSTH........	Alexander City, AL [AM radio station call letters]
WSTH........	Weapon System Tactical Handbook (MCD)
WSTH-FM ...	Alexander City, AL [FM radio station call letters]
WSTI	Welded Steel Tube Institute [Cleveland, OH] (EA)
WSTJ.........	St. Johnsbury, VT [AM radio station call letters]
WSTL	Weapon System Test Laboratory
WSTL	Whistle (MSA)
WStL & P ...	Wabash, St. Louis & Pacific Railway
WSTM	Western Micro Technology [NASDAQ symbol] (NQ)
WSTM	White Sands Transverse Mercator [Army] (AABC)
WSTM-TV ...	Syracuse, NY [Television station call letters]
WSTN........	Somerville, TN [AM radio station call letters]
WSTN........	Western
WSTN........	Western Preferred Corp. [NASDAQ symbol] (NQ)
WSTO........	Owensboro, KY [FM radio station call letters]
WSTP	Salisbury, NC [AM radio station call letters]
WSTP	Weapon System Test Program
W & StP	Winona & St. Peter Railroad
WSTPN......	Wrist Pin
WSTQ........	Streator, IL [FM radio station call letters]
WSTR........	Sturgis, MI [AM radio station call letters]
WSTR-FM ...	Sturgis, MI [FM radio station call letters]
WSTS	Laurinburg, NC [AM radio station call letters]
WSTS	Weapon System Training Set (AFM)
WSTS	Western States Life Insurance [NASDAQ symbol] (NQ)
WSTS........	World Semiconductor Trade Statistics [Semiconductor Industry Association] [San Jose, CA] [Information service] (EISS)
WSTT	Charlotte Amalie, VI [FM radio station call letters]
WSTU........	Stuart, FL [AM radio station call letters]
W St UL Rev ...	Western State University. Law Review [A publication]
WSTV	Steubenville, OH [AM radio station call letters]
WSTW	Wilmington, DE [FM radio station call letters]
WSTX	Christiansted, VI [AM radio station call letters]
WSTX-FM ...	Christiansted, VI [FM radio station call letters]
WSTZ-FM ..	Vicksburg, MS [FM radio station call letters]
WSU	University of Wisconsin-Superior, Superior, WI [Library symbol] [Library of Congress] (LCLS)
WSU	Washington State University
WSU	Wasu [Papua New Guinea] [Airport symbol] (OAG)
WSU	Water Servicing Unit (NASA)
WSU	Wayne State University [Michigan]
WSU	Windmill Study Unit [American Topical Association] (EA)
WSU	Women on Stamps Unit [American Topical Association] (EA)
WSU	Work Station Utility
WSU	Wright State University, Dayton, OH [OCLC symbol] (OCLC)
WSUA........	Miami, FL [AM radio station call letters]
WSUB........	Groton, CT [AM radio station call letters]
WSUC-FM ...	Cortland, NY [FM radio station call letters]
WSUE........	Sault Ste. Marie, MI [FM radio station call letters]
WSUH........	Oxford, MS [AM radio station call letters]
WSUI	Iowa City, IA [AM radio station call letters]
WSUL	Monticello, NY [FM radio station call letters]
WSUM........	Parma, OH [AM radio station call letters]
WSUN........	St. Petersburg, FL [AM radio station call letters]
WSUOPR.....	Washington State University, Open Pool Reactor
WSUP........	Platteville, WI [FM radio station call letters]
WSUR-TV ...	Ponce, PR [Television station call letters]
WSUS........	Franklin, NJ [FM radio station call letters]
WSUW.......	Whitewater, WI [FM radio station call letters]
WSUX........	Seaford, DE [AM radio station call letters]
WSUX-FM ...	Seaford, DE [FM radio station call letters]
WSUZ........	Palatka, FL [AM radio station call letters]
WSV	Water Solenoid Valve
WSVA........	Harrisonburg, VA [AM radio station call letters]
WSVA........	Wang Software Vendors' Association [Defunct] (EA)
WSVC........	Dunlap, TN [AM radio station call letters]
WSVE........	Green Cove Springs, FL [FM radio station call letters]
WSVH........	Savannah, GA [FM radio station call letters]
WSVL	Shelbyville, IN [FM radio station call letters]
WSVM........	Valdese, NC [AM radio station call letters]
WSVN........	Miami, FL [Television station call letters]
WSVQ........	Harrogate, TN [AM radio station call letters]
WSVS........	Crewe, VA [AM radio station call letters]
WSVS-FM ..	Crewe, VA [FM radio station call letters]
WSVT........	Smyrna, TN [AM radio station call letters]
WSW	Southwest Wisconsin Library System, Fennimore, WI [OCLC symbol] (OCLC)
WSW	Wall Street Week [Television program]
WSW	West-Southwest
WSW	Western Shelf Water [Oceanography]
WSW	White Sidewall [Tires]
WSWA........	Wine and Spirits Wholesalers of America [Washington, DC] (EA)
WSWB........	Scranton, PA [Television station call letters]
WSWG-FM ...	Greenwood, MS [FM radio station call letters]
WSWI	Evansville, IN [AM radio station call letters]
WSWL	Warheads and Special Weapons Laboratory (MCD)

WSWMA..... Water and Sewage Works Manufacturers Association [*Later, WWEMA*] (EA)
WSWMA..... Western States Weights and Measures Association
WSWN....... Belle Glade, FL [*AM radio station call letters*]
WSWN-FM ... Belle Glade, FL [*FM radio station call letters*]
WSWO....... Wilmington, OH [*FM radio station call letters*]
WSWP-TV ... Grandview, WV [*Television station call letters*]
WSWR....... Shelby, OH [*FM radio station call letters*]
WSWRN ..... West-Southwestern [*Meteorology*] (FAAC)
WSWS-TV ... Opelika, AL [*Television station call letters*]
WSWT....... Peoria, IL [*FM radio station call letters*]
WSWV....... Pennington Gap, VA [*AM radio station call letters*]
WSWV-FM ... Pennington Gap, VA [*FM radio station call letters*]
WSWWD .... West-Southwestward [*Meteorology*] (FAAC)
WSX .... Western Air Lines, Inc. [*Later, WAL*] [*NYSE symbol*]
WSY .... Shute Harbour/Whitsunday [*Australia*] [*Airport symbol*] (OAG)
WSYB....... Rutland, VT [*AM radio station call letters*]
WSYC-FM ... Shippensburg, PA [*FM radio station call letters*]
WSYD....... Mount Airy, NC [*AM radio station call letters*]
WSYL .... Sylvania, GA [*AM radio station call letters*]
WSYM-TV ... Lansing, MI [*Television station call letters*]
WSYP......... White Sulphur Springs & Yellowstone Park Railway Co. [*AAR code*]
WSYR....... Syracuse, NY [*AM radio station call letters*]
WSYT....... Syracuse, NY [*Television station call letters*]
WSYY....... Millinocket, ME [*AM radio station call letters*]
WSYY-FM ... Millinocket, ME [*FM radio station call letters*]
WSZ .... Westport [*New Zealand*] [*Airport symbol*] (OAG)
WSZA....... Truk, TT [*AM radio station call letters*]
WSZC....... Truk, TT [*AM radio station call letters*]
WSZD....... Ponape, TT [*AM radio station call letters*]
WT............. Three-Conductor Cables [*JETDS nomenclature*] [*Military*] (CET)
WT............. Waist Tether [*NASA*] (KSC)
W/T .... Walkie-Talkie
WT............. Wall Thickness [*Nuclear energy*] (NRCH)
WT............. War Tax
WT............. Warm Tone [*Photography*]
WT............. Warning Tag (AAG)
WT............. Warrant
WT............. Wartime
WT............. Washington Territory [*Prior to statehood*]
WT............. Washington Territory Reports (DLA)
WT............. Waste Tank
WT............. Watch Time
WT............. Watchdog Timer (MCD)
WT............. Watchdogs of the Treasury (EA)
WT............. Water Tank
WT............. Water Tanker [*British*]
WT............. Water Tender [*Navy*]
WT............. Water Thermometer
WT............. Water-Tube Boiler [*Naval*]
WT............. Watertight
WT............. Waveguide Transmission
WT............. Weapon Test
WT............. Weapon Training (MCD)
WT............. Weapons Technician [*Air Force*] (AFM)
WT............. Weapons Tight [*Weapons will engage only objects identified as hostile*]
WT............. Weight (AAG)
WT............. Weird Tales [*A publication*]
WT............. Weldwood Transportation Ltd. [*AAR code*]
WT............. Wetenschappelijke Tijdingen [*A publication*]
WT............. Whiffle Tree [*Structural test*] (AAG)
WT............. White Pennant [*Navy*] [*British*]
WT............. Wieczory Teatralne [*A publication*]
WT............. Wild Track [*Cinematography*]
WT............. Wild Type [*of a species*] [*Genetics*]
WT............. Will Talk [*Telecommunications*] (TEL)
WT............. William Tell Gunnery Mate
WT............. Wilms' Tumor [*Oncology*]
WT............. Wind Tunnel
WT............. Winterization Test (AAG)
WT............. [*The*] Winter's Tale [*Shakespearean work*]
WT............. Wire Ticket [*NASA*] (NASA)
WT............. Wire Transfer [*Banking*]
WT............. Wireless Telegraphy [*or Telephony*]
WT............. Wireless Transmitter
WT............. Wireless Truck [*British*]
WT............. With Tape
WT............. With Title [*Bibliography*]
WT............. Withholding Tax [*IRS*]
WT............. Without
WT............. Wood Threshold (MSA)
WT............. Word Target [*Psychology*]
WT............. Word Terminal
WT............. Word Type
W/T .... Work Track [*Cinematography*]
WT............. Workshop Trains [*British*]
WT............. World Tobacco [*A publication*]
WT............. Worldteam (EA)

WT............. Written Testimony (BJA)
WT............. Wyoming Territory
WT's .... Working Tools [*Freemasonry*]
WTA .... Tambohorano [*Madagascar*] [*Airport symbol*] (OAG)
WTA .... Washington Technological Association (MCD)
WTA .... Water Transport Association [*Cincinnati, OH*] (EA)
WTA .... Welded Tube Co. of America [*American Stock Exchange symbol*]
WTA .... Western Timber Association [*West Sacramento, CA*] (EA)
WTA .... Window Test Apparatus
WTA .... Wire Traceability and Accountability [*NASA*] (NASA)
WTA .... Women's Tennis Association [*Later, WITA*] (EA)
WTA .... World Teleport Association [*New York, NY*] [*Telecommunications*] (TSSD)
WTA .... World Textile Abstracts [*Shirley Institute*] [*Database*] [*British*]
WTA .... Wyoming Trucking Association, Casper WY [*STAC*]
WTAB....... Tabor City, NC [*AM radio station call letters*]
WTAC....... Flint, MI [*AM radio station call letters*]
WTAD....... Quincy, IL [*AM radio station call letters*]
WTAE....... Pittsburgh, PA [*AM radio station call letters*]
WTAE-TV ... Pittsburgh, PA [*Television station call letters*]
WTAF-TV ... Philadelphia, PA [*Television station call letters*]
WTAG....... Worcester, MA [*AM radio station call letters*]
WTAH....... Oshkosh, WI [*Television station call letters*]
WTAI....... Melbourne, FL [*AM radio station call letters*]
WTAJ-TV ... Altoona, PA [*Television station call letters*]
WTAL....... Tallahassee, FL [*AM radio station call letters*]
WTAM....... Gulfport, MS [*AM radio station call letters*]
WTAN....... Clearwater, FL [*AM radio station call letters*]
WTAO....... Murphysboro, IL [*FM radio station call letters*]
WTAP-TV ... Parkersburg, WV [*Television station call letters*]
WTAQ....... La Grange, IL [*AM radio station call letters*]
WTAR....... Norfolk, VA [*AM radio station call letters*]
WTAS....... Crete, IL [*FM radio station call letters*]
WTAT-TV ... Charleston, SC [*Television station call letters*]
WTAU....... Albany, GA [*Television station call letters*]
WTAW....... College Station, TX [*AM radio station call letters*]
WTAX....... Springfield, IL [*AM radio station call letters*]
W/TAX ...... Withholding Tax (AAG)
WTAY......... Robinson, IL [*AM radio station call letters*]
WTAY-FM ... Robinson, IL [*FM radio station call letters*]
WTAZ....... Morton, IL [*FM radio station call letters*]
WTB .... Wales Tourist Board
WTB .... War Transportation Board [*World War II*]
WTB .... Water-Tube Boiler [*Naval*]
WTB .... Welttierschutzbund [*Also known as WFPA, FMPA*] [*World Federation for the Protection of Animals*]
WTB .... Where's the Beef? [*Slogan created by the Dancer Fitzgerald Sample advertising agency for Wendy's International, Inc.*]
WTB .... Wilderness Trail Bike
WTB .... Willamette Tariff Bureau Inc., Portland OR [*STAC*]
WTB .... Woerterbuch [*Dictionary*] [*German*] (ROG)
WTBB....... Bonifay, FL [*FM radio station call letters*]
WTBC-FM ... Williston, VT [*FM radio station call letters*]
WTBD....... Work to Be Done (ADA)
WTBF....... Troy, AL [*AM radio station call letters*]
WTBG....... Brownsville, TN [*FM radio station call letters*]
WTBH....... Tice, FL [*Television station call letters*]
WTBI .... Pickens, SC [*AM radio station call letters*]
WTBL....... McConnelsville, OH [*FM radio station call letters*]
WTBO....... Cumberland, MD [*AM radio station call letters*]
WTBP......... Parsons, TN [*AM radio station call letters*]
WTBQ....... Warwick, NY [*AM radio station call letters*]
WTBR....... War Trade Board Rulings [*United States*] (DLA)
WTBR-FM ... Pittsfield, MA [*FM radio station call letters*]
WTBS....... Atlanta, GA [*Television station call letters*]
WTB & TS .. Watch Tower Bible and Tract Society
WTBX....... Hibbing, MN [*FM radio station call letters*]
WTBY......... Poughkeepsie, NY [*Television station call letters*]
WTBZ....... Grafton, WV [*AM radio station call letters*]
WTBZ-FM ... Grafton, WV [*FM radio station call letters*]
WTC .... New York [*New York*] Battery Park [*Airport symbol*] (OAG)
WTC .... War Transport Council [*Later, ITWC*] [*World War II*]
WTC .... Water Thermal and Chemical Technology Center [*University of California*] [*Research center*] (RCD)
WTC .... Waterton [*Colorado*] [*Seismograph station code, US Geological Survey*] [*Closed*] (SEIS)
WTC .... Well-Tempered Clavier [*Compositions of J. S. Bach*]
WTC .... Westcoast Transmission Company Ltd. [*NYSE symbol*] [*Toronto Stock Exchange symbol*] [*Vancouver Stock Exchange symbol*]
WTC .... Western Telecommunications Consulting Co. [*Los Angeles, CA*] [*Telecommunications*] (TSSD)
WTC .... Wind Temperature Correction
WTC .... Wire Test Chamber
WTC .... Women's Talent Corps [*Later, CHS*] (EA)
WTC .... Women's Theater Council
WTC........... Workload Transaction Code [*Navy*] (NG)
WTC .... World Trade Center [*New York City*]

WTC .... World Trade Center of New Orleans [*Formed by a merger of International House - World Trade Center and International Trade Market*] [*New Orleans, LA*]   (EA)
WTCA........ Plymouth, IN [*AM radio station call letters*]
WTCA........ Water Terminal Clearance Authority [*Army*]   (AABC)
WTCA........ Welsh Terrier Club of America   (EA)
WTCA........ Wood Truss Council of America [*Chicago, IL*]   (EA)
WTCA........ World Trade Centers Association [*New York, NY*]   (EA)
WTCARES ... Welsh Terrier Club of America Rescue Service   (EA)
WTCB........ Water Tender Construction Battalion [*Navy*]
WTCC........ Springfield, MA [*FM radio station call letters*]
WTCC .... Water Turbine Closed Coupled   (MSA)
WTCG .... Andalusia, AL [*AM radio station call letters*]
WTCH........ Shawano, WI [*AM radio station call letters*]
WTCI .... Chattanooga, TN [*Television station call letters*]
WTCI .... Western Telecommunications, Incorporated [*Englewood, CO*] [*Telecommunications*]
WTCIB....... Women's Travelers Center and Information Bank [*Washington, DC*]   (EA)
WTCJ .... Tell City, IN [*AM radio station call letters*]
WTCK....... World Trade Center Korea
WTCM....... Traverse City, MI [*AM radio station call letters*]
WTCM....... Weld Timer Control Module
WTCM-FM ... Traverse City, MI [*FM radio station call letters*]
WTCN........ Stillwater, MN [*AM radio station call letters*]
WTCO .... Western Transportation Company [*AAR code*]
WTCQ .... Vidalia, GA [*FM radio station call letters*]
WTCR .... Kenova, WV [*AM radio station call letters*]
WTCR-FM ... Huntington, WV [*FM radio station call letters*]
WTCS .... Fairmont, WV [*AM radio station call letters*]
WTCS .... Windshield Temperature Control Systems
WTCT........ Marion, IL [*Television station call letters*]
WTCV .... Weapon and Tracked Combat Vehicle   (MCD)
WTCW....... Whitesburg, KY [*AM radio station call letters*]
WTD .... War Trade Department [*British*] [*World War II*]
WTD .... Water Turbine Direct   (MSA)
WTD .... Watertight Door
WTD .... Whitland [*British depot code*]
WTD .... Wind Tunnel Data
WTD .... World Trade Directory [*A publication*] [*Department of Commerce*]
WTDR....... World Traders Data Report [*A publication*] [*Department of State*]
WTDY .... Madison, WI [*AM radio station call letters*]
WTE .... Waste-to-Energy [*Resource recycling*]
WTE .... Westate Resources, Inc. [*Vancouver Stock Exchange symbol*]
WTE .... World Tapes for Education [*Defunct*]
WTE .... Wotje [*Marshall Islands*] [*Airport symbol*]   (OAG)
WTEB........ New Bern, NC [*FM radio station call letters*]
WTEL .... Philadelphia, PA [*AM radio station call letters*]
WTEL .... Walker Telecommunications Corp. [*NASDAQ symbol*]   (NQ)
WTEN........ Albany, NY [*Television station call letters*]
W & T Eq Ca ... White and Tudor's Leading Cases in Equity [*9 eds.*] [*1849-1928*]   (DLA)
W TER ...... Washington Territory
WTES .... West Tennessee Experiment Station [*University of Tennessee at Knoxville*] [*Research center*]   (RCD)
WTF............ Waste Treatment Facility   (IEEE)
WTF............ Waste Water Treatment Facility [*Nuclear energy*]   (NRCH)
WTF............ Welcome to Finland [*A publication*]
WTF............ Western Task Force [*Navy*]
WTF........... Will to Fire
WTF............ Wisconsin Test Facility [*Navy*]
WTF............ World Taekwondo Federation   (EA-IO)
WTFAA....... Washington Task Force on African Affairs [*Defunct*]   (EA)
WTFDA....... Worldwide TV-FM DX Association [*"DX" is radio term meaning distance*]   (EA)
WTFL........ Kosrae, TT [*AM radio station call letters*]
WTFM........ Kingsport, TN [*FM radio station call letters*]
WTFPA....... Wolf Trap Foundation for the Performing Arts   (EA)
WTG .... Waiting   (MSA)
WTG .... Weighting   (MSA)
WTG .... Wind Tape Generation
WTG .... Wind Turbine Generator
WTG .... Worker Trait Group
WTGA........ Thomaston, GA [*AM radio station call letters*]
WTGA-FM ... Thomaston, GA [*FM radio station call letters*]
WTGC .... Lewisburg, PA [*AM radio station call letters*]
WTGH........ Cayce, SC [*AM radio station call letters*]
WTGL-TV ... Cocoa, FL [*Television station call letters*]
WTGN........ Lima, OH [*FM radio station call letters*]
WTGP........ Greenville, PA [*FM radio station call letters*]
WTGQ .... Cairo, GA [*FM radio station call letters*]
WTGR....... Cleveland, OH [*FM radio station call letters*]
WTGR....... Welcome to Greenland [*A publication*]
WTGS........ Hardeeville, SC [*Television station call letters*]
WTGV-FM ... Sandusky, MI [*FM radio station call letters*]
WTGY....... Charleston, MS [*FM radio station call letters*]
WTHB........ Augusta, GA [*AM radio station call letters*]
WTHE........ Mineola, NY [*AM radio station call letters*]
WTHE .... Workshop Test and Handling Equipment [*Military*]   (CAAL)

WTHG........ Worthington Industries, Inc. [*NASDAQ symbol*]   (NQ)
WTHI .... Terre Haute, IN [*AM radio station call letters*]
WTHI-FM ... Terre Haute, IN [*FM radio station call letters*]
WTHI-TV .... Terre Haute, IN [*Television station call letters*]
W Th J .... Westminster Theological Journal [*A publication*]
WTHM....... Goulds, FL [*FM radio station call letters*]
WTHO-FM ... Thomson, GA [*FM radio station call letters*]
WTHP .... Thomasville, NC [*FM radio station call letters*]
WTHPRF ... Weatherproof   (MSA)
WTHR........ Indianapolis, IN [*Television station call letters*]
WTHR........ Weather
WTHR........ Weatherford [*R. V.*] Co. [*NASDAQ symbol*]   (NQ)
WTHS........ Holland, MI [*FM radio station call letters*]
WTHU .... Thurmont, MD [*AM radio station call letters*]
WTHZ .... Tallahassee, FL [*FM radio station call letters*]
WTI .... Weapons Training Instruction   (MCD)
WTI .... Welcome to Iceland [*A publication*]
WTI .... Work Training in Industry
WTI .... World Trade Institute
WTI .... World Transindex [*International Translations Centre*] [*Bibliographic database*] [*The Netherlands*]
WTIB .... Iuka, MS [*FM radio station call letters*]
WTIC .... Hartford, CT [*AM radio station call letters*]
WTIC-FM ... Hartford, CT [*FM radio station call letters*]
WTIC-TV ... Hartford, CT [*Television station call letters*]
WTIF.......... Tifton, GA [*AM radio station call letters*]
WTIG .... Massillon, OH [*AM radio station call letters*]
WTIK .... Durham, NC [*AM radio station call letters*]
WTIL .... Mayaguez, PR [*AM radio station call letters*]
WTIM......... Taylorville, IL [*AM radio station call letters*]
WTIN .... Ponce, PR [*Television station call letters*]
WTIP .... Charleston, WV [*AM radio station call letters*]
WTIQ .... Manistique, MI [*AM radio station call letters*]
WTIS .... Tampa, FL [*AM radio station call letters*]
WTIU .... Bloomington, IN [*Television station call letters*]
WTIV .... Titusville, PA [*AM radio station call letters*]
WTIW .... Hialeah, FL [*AM radio station call letters*]
WTIX .... New Orleans, LA [*AM radio station call letters*]
WTJ............ Wedge Type Jack
WTJ............ Westminster Theological Journal [*A publication*]
WTJ............ Wrin, T. J., San Francisco CA [*STAC*]
WTJA .... Kosciusko, MS [*FM radio station call letters*]
WTJB .... Columbus, GA [*FM radio station call letters*]
WTJC .... Springfield, OH [*Television station call letters*]
WTJH .... East Point, GA [*AM radio station call letters*]
WTJP......... Gadsden, AL [*Television station call letters*]
WTJR .... Quincy, IL [*Television station call letters*]
WTJS......... Jackson, TN [*AM radio station call letters*]
WTJU .... Charlottesville, VA [*FM radio station call letters*]
WTJY......... Taylorville, IL [*FM radio station call letters*]
WTJZ .... Newport News, VA [*AM radio station call letters*]
WTK .... Noatak [*Alaska*] [*Airport symbol*]   (OAG)
WTK .... Noatak, AK [*Location identifier*] [*FAA*]   (FAAL)
WTKG........ Wyoming, MI [*AM radio station call letters*]
WTKK........ Manassas, VA [*Television station call letters*]
WTKK........ Wen-Tzu Kai-Ko [*A publication*]
WTKL......... Baton Rouge, LA [*AM radio station call letters*]
WTKM .... Hartford, WI [*AM radio station call letters*]
WTKM-FM ... Hartford, WI [*FM radio station call letters*]
WTKN........ Pittsburgh, PA [*AM radio station call letters*]
WTKO........ Ithaca, NY [*AM radio station call letters*]
WTKR-TV... Norfolk, VA [*Television station call letters*]
WTKS........ Bethesda, MD [*FM radio station call letters*]
WTKV......... Valdosta, GA [*Television station call letters*]
WTKX........ Pensacola, FL [*FM radio station call letters*]
WTKY......... Tompkinsville, KY [*AM radio station call letters*]
WTKY-FM ... Tompkinsville, KY [*FM radio station call letters*]
WTL .... Tuntatuliak [*Alaska*] [*Airport symbol*]   (OAG)
WTL .... Western Trunk Line Committee, Chicago IL [*STAC*]
WTL........... Wyle Test Laboratories
WTLB .... Utica, NY [*AM radio station call letters*]
WTLC........ Indianapolis, IN [*FM radio station call letters*]
WTLC........ Western Trunk Line Committee
W & TLC ..... White and Tudor's Leading Cases in Equity [*9 eds.*] [*1849-1928*]   (DLA)
WTLH........ Bainbridge, GA [*Television station call letters*]
WTLI.......... Plover, WI [*AM radio station call letters*]
WTLJ......... Muskegon, MI [*Television station call letters*]
WTLK......... Taylorsville, NC [*AM radio station call letters*]
WTLN......... Apopka, FL [*AM radio station call letters*]
WTLN-FM .. Apopka, FL [*FM radio station call letters*]
WTLO .... Somerset, KY [*AM radio station call letters*]
WTLQ .... Pittston, PA [*FM radio station call letters*]
WTLR .... State College, PA [*FM radio station call letters*]
WTLS .... Tallassee, AL [*AM radio station call letters*]
WTLS .... West Texas Library System [*Library network*]
WTLT......... Easley, SC [*FM radio station call letters*]
WTLV......... Jacksonville, FL [*Television station call letters*]
WTLW........ Lima, OH [*Television station call letters*]
WTM........... Wind Tunnel Memorandum
WTM........... Wind Tunnel Model

WTMA .... Charleston, SC [*AM radio station call letters*]
WTMA .... Wood Tank Manufacturers Association [*Renick, WV*]   (EA)
WTMB .... Tomah, WI [*AM radio station call letters*]
WTMC .... Ocala, FL [*AM radio station call letters*]
WTME .... Auburn, ME [*AM radio station call letters*]
WTMG .... Murfreesboro, TN [*FM radio station call letters*]
WTMI .... Miami, FL [*FM radio station call letters*]
WTMJ .... Milwaukee, WI [*AM radio station call letters*]
WTMJ-TV .. Milwaukee, WI [*Television station call letters*]
WTMP .... Temple Terrace, FL [*AM radio station call letters*]
WTMR .... Camden, NJ [*AM radio station call letters*]
WTMRF ..... Westmount Resources [*NASDAQ symbol*]   (NQ)
WTMS .... Presque Isle, ME [*FM radio station call letters*]
WTMS .... World Trade in Minerals Data Base System [*Data processing*]
WTMT .... Louisville, KY [*AM radio station call letters*]
WTMV .... Lakeland, FL [*Television station call letters*]
WTMX .... New Albany, MS [*FM radio station call letters*]
WTN .... Western Technical Net [*Air Force*]
WTN .... Wind Tunnel Note
WTN .... Witness
WTN .... Wroclawskie Towarzystwo Naukowe [*A publication*]
WTNC .... Thomasville, NC [*AM radio station call letters*]
WTNE .... Trenton, TN [*AM radio station call letters*]
WTNH-TV... New Haven, CT [*Television station call letters*]
WTNJ .... Mount Hope, WV [*FM radio station call letters*]
WTNL .... Reidsville, GA [*AM radio station call letters*]
WTNS .... Coshocton, OH [*AM radio station call letters*]
WTNS-FM .. Coshocton, OH [*FM radio station call letters*]
WTNSTH ..... Witnesseth [*Legal*] [*British*]   (ROG)
WTNT .... Tallahassee, FL [*AM radio station call letters*]
WTNT-FM ... Tallahassee, FL [*FM radio station call letters*]
WTNX .... Lynchburg, TN [*AM radio station call letters*]
WTNY .... Watertown, NY [*AM radio station call letters*]
WTNY-FM ... Watertown, NY [*FM radio station call letters*]
WTNZ .... Clinton, TN [*FM radio station call letters*]
WTO .... Warsaw Treaty Organization
WTO .... Westam Oil Ltd. [*Vancouver Stock Exchange symbol*]
WTO .... WESTPAC [*Western Pacific*] Transportation Office   (CINC)
WTO .... World Tourism Organization
WTO .... Wotho [*Marshall Islands*] [*Airport symbol*]   (OAG)
WTO .... Write-to-Operator [*Data processing*]   (IBMDP)
WTOB .... Winston-Salem, NC [*AM radio station call letters*]
WTOC-TV ... Savannah, GA [*Television station call letters*]
WTOD .... Toledo, OH [*AM radio station call letters*]
WTOE .... Spruce Pine, NC [*AM radio station call letters*]
WTOEW ...... Welcome to Our Elvis World [*Lutherville, MD*]   (EA)
WTOF .... Canton, OH [*AM radio station call letters*]
WTOF-FM ... Canton, OH [*FM radio station call letters*]
WTOG-TV ... St. Petersburg, FL [*Television station call letters*]
WTOH .... Mobile, AL [*AM radio station call letters*]
WTOH .... Western Ohio Railroad Co. [*AAR code*]
WTOJ .... Carthage, NY [*FM radio station call letters*]
WTOK-TV ... Meridian, MS [*Television station call letters*]
WTOL-TV ... Toledo, OH [*Television station call letters*]
WTOM-TV .. Cheboygan, MI [*Television station call letters*]
WTON .... Staunton, VA [*AM radio station call letters*]
WTOO-FM ... Bellefontaine, OH [*FM radio station call letters*]
WTOP .... Washington, DC [*AM radio station call letters*]
WTOQ .... Platteville, WI [*AM radio station call letters*]
WTOR .... Write-to-Operator with Reply [*Data processing*]   (IBMDP)
WTOS .... Skowhegan, ME [*FM radio station call letters*]
WTOS .... Western Test Range Office of Safety [*Air Force*]   (MCD)
WTOT .... Marianna, FL [*AM radio station call letters*]
WToVA .... United States Veterans Administration Hospital, Tomah, WI [*Library symbol*] [*Library of Congress*]   (LCLS)
WTOV-TV... Steubenville, OH [*Television station call letters*]
WTOY .... Roanoke, VA [*AM radio station call letters*]
WTP .... Warrant to Pollute
WTP .... Waste Water Treatment Plant [*Nuclear energy*]
WTP .... Water Treatment Plant   (NRCH)
WTP .... Weapons Testing Program   (AAG)
WTP .... Woitape [*Papua New Guinea*] [*Airport symbol*]   (OAG)
WTP .... World Tape Pals   (EA)
WTPA .... Mechanicsburg, PA [*FM radio station call letters*]
WTPA .... Wheelchair Tennis Players Association   (EA)
WTPBC ...... Wool Textiles Production Board of Control [*British*] [*World War I*]
WTPC .... Elsah, IL [*FM radio station call letters*]
WTPI .... Indianapolis, IN [*FM radio station call letters*]
WTPL-FM ... Tupper Lake, NY [*FM radio station call letters*]
WTPM .... Aguadilla, PR [*FM radio station call letters*]
WTPO .... Conyers, GA [*AM radio station call letters*]
WTPR .... Paris, TN [*AM radio station call letters*]
WTPS .... Hughesville, PA [*AM radio station call letters*]
WTPS-FM ... Muncy, PA [*FM radio station call letters*]
WTQR .... Winston-Salem, NC [*FM radio station call letters*]
WTQX .... Selma, AL [*AM radio station call letters*]
WTR .... Sierra Spring Water Co. [*American Stock Exchange symbol*]
WTR .... Waiter
WTR .... War Tax Resistance [*An association*] [*Defunct*]   (EA)
WTR .... Warstar Resources [*Vancouver Stock Exchange symbol*]

WTR .... Water
WTR .... Water Turnover Rate [*Physiology*]
WTR .... Waterford and Tranmore Railway [*British*]   (ROG)
WTR .... Waters Associates, Milford, MA [*OCLC symbol*]   (OCLC)
WTR .... Waterville [*Colby College*] [*Maine*] [*Seismograph station code, US Geological Survey*]   (SEIS)
WTR .... Weekly Transcript Reports [*New York*]   (DLA)
WTR .... Well to Right [*Aviation*]   (FAAC)
WTR .... Western Test Range [*Formerly, Pacific Missile Range*] [*Air Force*]
WTR .... Westinghouse Test Reactor
WTR .... Winter
WTR .... Work Transfer Record   (KSC)
WTR .... Work Transfer Request
WTR .... Wrightsville & Tennille R. R. [*AAR code*]
WTR .... Writer
WTRA .... Mayaguez, PR [*Television station call letters*]
WTRB .... Ripley, TN [*AM radio station call letters*]
WTRC .... Elkhart, IN [*AM radio station call letters*]
WTRC .... Weapon Test Reports Committee [*AEC-DoD*]
WTRC .... Women's Training and Resources Corporation
WTRE .... Greensburg, IN [*AM radio station call letters*]
WTRF-TV ... Wheeling, WV [*Television station call letters*]
WTRG .... Rocky Mount, NC [*FM radio station call letters*]
WTRI .... Brunswick, MD [*AM radio station call letters*]
WTRJ .... Troy, OH [*AM radio station call letters*]
WTRK .... Philadelphia, PA [*FM radio station call letters*]
WTRL .... Bradenton, FL [*AM radio station call letters*]
WTRM .... Western Test Range Manual [*Air Force*]   (MCD)
WTRM .... Winchester, VA [*FM radio station call letters*]
WTRN .... Tyrone, PA [*AM radio station call letters*]
WTRO .... Dyersburg, TN [*AM radio station call letters*]
WTRP .... La Grange, GA [*AM radio station call letters*]
WTRPRF ..... Waterproof   (MSA)
WTRPRFG ... Waterproofing
WTRQ .... Warsaw, NC [*AM radio station call letters*]
WTRS .... Dunnellon, FL [*AM radio station call letters*]
WTRS .... Waters Instruments [*NASDAQ symbol*]   (NQ)
WTRS-FM ... Dunellon, FL [*FM radio station call letters*]
WTRSYS ... Water System   (MCD)
WTRT .... Florence, AL [*Television station call letters*]
WTRTT .... Watertight   (MSA)
WTRU .... Jupiter, FL [*AM radio station call letters*]
WTRW .... Two Rivers, WI [*AM radio station call letters*]
WTRW-FM ... Mishicot, WI [*FM radio station call letters*]
WTRX .... Flint, MI [*AM radio station call letters*]
WTRY .... Troy, NY [*AM radio station call letters*]
WTRZ .... Winterize   (AAG)
WTRZ-FM ... McMinnville, TN [*FM radio station call letters*]
WTRZN .... Winterization   (AAG)
WTS .... Tsiroanomandidy [*Madagascar*] [*Airport symbol*]   (OAG)
WTS .... War Training Service [*of the Civil Aeronautics Administration*] [*Formerly Civilian Pilot Training*] [*World War II*]
WTS .... Western Tariff Service Inc., Oakland CA [*STAC*]
WTS .... Westminister Theological Seminary, Philadelphia, PA [*OCLC symbol*]   (OCLC)
WTS .... Whale Tumor Story [*Urban folklore term coined by Rodney Dale*]
WTS .... Wind Tunnel Study
WTS .... Wing Tank Structure
WTS .... Winterswijk [*Netherlands*] [*Seismograph station code, US Geological Survey*]   (SEIS)
WTS .... Women's Transport Service [*British*]
WTS .... Women's Transportation Seminar [*Washington, DC*]   (EA)
WTS .... Word Terminal Synchronous
4WTS .... Four-Wire Terminating Set [*Telecommunications*]   (TEL)
WTSA .... Brattleboro, VT [*AM radio station call letters*]
WTSA .... Wood Turners and Shapers Association [*Later, WPMA*]   (EA)
WTSA-FM ... Brattleboro, VT [*FM radio station call letters*]
WTSB .... Lumberton, NC [*AM radio station call letters*]
WTSB .... Wood Turners Service Bureau [*Later, WPMA*]
WTSC .... West Texas State College [*Later, WTSU*]
WTSC .... Wet Tantalum Slug Capacitor   (NASA)
WTSC-FM .. Potsdam, NY [*FM radio station call letters*]
WTSF .... Ashland, KY [*Television station call letters*]
WTSG .... Albany, GA [*Television station call letters*]
WTSI .... Western Tar Sands, Inc. [*NASDAQ symbol*]   (NQ)
WTSJ .... Cincinnati, OH [*AM radio station call letters*]
WTSK .... Tuscaloosa, AL [*AM radio station call letters*]
WTSL .... Hanover, NH [*AM radio station call letters*]
WTSL-FM ... Hanover, NH [*FM radio station call letters*]
WTSN .... Dover, NH [*AM radio station call letters*]
WTSNG ..... Witnessing [*Legal*] [*British*]   (ROG)
WTSO .... Madison, WI [*AM radio station call letters*]
WTSPT .... Waterspout
WTSP-TV ... St. Petersburg, FL [*Television station call letters*]
WTSR .... Trenton, NJ [*FM radio station call letters*]
WTSU .... Troy, AL [*FM radio station call letters*]
WTSU .... West Texas State University [*Formerly, WTSC*]
WTSV .... Claremont, NH [*AM radio station call letters*]
WTSX .... Port Jervis, NY [*FM radio station call letters*]

WTT............ Weapon Tactics Trainer (MCD)
WTT............ Weird Terror Tales [*A publication*]
WTT............ Western Tank Truck Carriers' Conference Inc., Denver CO [*STAC*]
WTT............ Westmount Resources Ltd. [*Toronto Stock Exchange symbol*] [*Vancouver Stock Exchange symbol*]
WTT............ Wind Tunnel Test
WTT............ Working Timetable
WTT............ World Team Tennis [*League*]
WTTB......... Vero Beach, FL [*AM radio station call letters*]
WTTC......... Towanda, PA [*AM radio station call letters*]
WTTC......... Western Technical Training Command [*AAFWTTC*]
WTTC......... World Technology & Trading [*NASDAQ symbol*] (NQ)
WTTC-FM ... Towanda, PA [*FM radio station call letters*]
WTTE......... Columbus, OH [*Television station call letters*]
WTTF......... Tiffin, OH [*AM radio station call letters*]
WTTF......... Welcome to the Faeroes [*A publication*]
WTTF-FM... Tiffin, OH [*FM radio station call letters*]
WTTG......... Washington, DC [*Television station call letters*]
WTTI.......... Dalton, GA [*AM radio station call letters*]
WTTL......... Madisonville, KY [*AM radio station call letters*]
WTTM......... Trenton, NJ [*AM radio station call letters*]
WTTN......... Watertown, WI [*AM radio station call letters*]
WTTO......... Birmingham, AL [*Television station call letters*]
WTTP......... Natick, MA [*AM radio station call letters*]
WTTR......... Westminster, MD [*AM radio station call letters*]
WTTS......... Bloomington, IN [*FM radio station call letters*]
WTTT......... Amherst, MA [*AM radio station call letters*]
WTTU......... Cookeville, TN [*FM radio station call letters*]
WTTV......... Bloomington, IN [*Television station call letters*]
WTTW........ Chicago, IL [*Television station call letters*] [*Letters stand for "Windows to the World"*]
WTTX......... Appomattox, VA [*AM radio station call letters*]
WTTX-FM... Appomattox, VA [*FM radio station call letters*]
WTU........... Washington University, St. Louis, MO [*OCLC symbol*] (OCLC)
WTU........... Weekly TIF [*Taxpayer Information File*] Update [*IRS*]
WTUE......... Dayton, OH [*FM radio station call letters*]
WTUG-FM ... Tuscaloosa, AL [*FM radio station call letters*]
WTUJ......... Ridgeland, MS [*AM radio station call letters*]
WTUL......... New Orleans, LA [*FM radio station call letters*]
WTUN......... Selma, AL [*FM radio station call letters*]
WTUP......... Tupelo, MS [*AM radio station call letters*]
WTURB ...... Water Turbine (MSA)
WTURN....... White Turnout [*Political science*]
WTUV......... Utica, NY [*Television station call letters*]
WTUX......... Indianapolis, IN [*AM radio station call letters*]
WTV........... Water Tank Vessel [*Navy*]
WTVA......... Tupelo, MS [*Television station call letters*]
WTVB......... Coldwater, MI [*AM radio station call letters*]
WTVC......... Chattanooga, TN [*Television station call letters*]
WTVD......... Durham, NC [*Television station call letters*]
WTVE......... Reading, PA [*Television station call letters*]
WTVF......... Nashville, TN [*Television station call letters*]
WTVG......... Toledo, OH [*Television station call letters*]
WTVH......... Syracuse, NY [*Television station call letters*]
WTVJ......... Miami, FL [*Television station call letters*]
WTVK......... Knoxville, TN [*Television station call letters*]
WTVL......... Waterville, ME [*AM radio station call letters*]
WTVM........ Columbus, GA [*Television station call letters*]
WTVN......... Columbus, OH [*AM radio station call letters*]
WTVN-TV... Columbus, OH [*Television station call letters*]
WTVO......... Rockford, IL [*Television station call letters*]
WTVP......... Peoria, IL [*Television station call letters*]
WTVQ-TV... Lexington, KY [*Television station call letters*]
WTVR......... Richmond, VA [*AM radio station call letters*]
WTVR-FM ... Richmond, VA [*FM radio station call letters*]
WTVR-TV... Richmond, VA [*Television station call letters*]
WTVS......... Detroit, MI [*Television station call letters*]
WTVT......... Tampa, FL [*Television station call letters*]
WTVU......... New Haven, CT [*Television station call letters*]
WTVW........ Evansville, IN [*Television station call letters*]
WTVX......... Fort Pierce, FL [*Television station call letters*]
WTVY......... Dothan, AL [*Television station call letters*]
WTVY-FM ... Dothan, AL [*FM radio station call letters*]
WTVZ......... Norfolk, VA [*Television station call letters*]
WTw.......... Joseph Mann Library, Two Rivers, WI [*Library symbol*] [*Library of Congress*] (LCLS)
WTW........... West Thumb [*Wyoming*] [*Seismograph station code, US Geological Survey*] (SEIS)
WTW........... Writers and Their Work [*A publication*]
WTW........... Wroclawskie Towarzystwo Naukowe [*A publication*]
WTWA......... Thomson, GA [*AM radio station call letters*]
WTWA......... World Trade Writers Association [*New York, NY*] (EA)
WTWB......... Auburndale, FL [*AM radio station call letters*]
WTWC......... Tallahassee, FL [*Television station call letters*]
WT (Werkstattstech) Z Ind Fertigung ... WT (Werkstattstechnik). Zeitschrift fuer Industrielle Fertigung [*A publication*]
WTWO......... Terre Haute, IN [*Television station call letters*]
WTWR........ Monroe, MI [*FM radio station call letters*]
WTWS......... New London, CT [*Television station call letters*]
WTWX-FM ... Guntersville, AL [*FM radio station call letters*]

WTWZ......... Clinton, MS [*AM radio station call letters*]
WTX .... West Texas Utilities Co. [*American Stock Exchange symbol*]
WTXI.......... Ripley, MS [*FM radio station call letters*]
WTXL-TV ... Tallahassee, FL [*Television station call letters*]
WTXN......... Lafayette, AL [*AM radio station call letters*]
WTXR......... Chillicothe, IL [*FM radio station call letters*]
WTXX......... Waterbury, CT [*Television station call letters*]
WTXY......... Whiteville, NC [*AM radio station call letters*]
WTY .... Westley Mines Ltd. [*Toronto Stock Exchange symbol*] [*Vancouver Stock Exchange symbol*]
WTYC......... Rock Hill, SC [*AM radio station call letters*]
WTYD......... New London, CT [*FM radio station call letters*]
WTYF......... World Theosophical Youth Federation (EA-IO)
WTYJ......... Fayette, MS [*FM radio station call letters*]
WTYL .... Tylertown, MS [*AM radio station call letters*]
WTYL-FM... Tylertown, MS [*FM radio station call letters*]
WTYM........ Tampa, FL [*AM radio station call letters*]
WTYN......... Tryon, NC [*AM radio station call letters*]
WTYO......... Hammonton, NJ [*AM radio station call letters*]
W Ty R ...... Washington Territory Reports [*1854-88*] (DLA)
WTYS......... Marianna, FL [*AM radio station call letters*]
WTYX......... Jackson, MS [*FM radio station call letters*]
WTZ........... Weird Tales [*1973-*] [*A publication*]
WTZ........... Western Trinity Resource [*Vancouver Stock Exchange symbol*]
WTZ........... Whakatane [*New Zealand*] [*Seismograph station code, US Geological Survey*] (SEIS)
WTZA......... Kingston, NY [*Television station call letters*]
WTZE......... Tazewell, VA [*AM radio station call letters*]
WTZE-FM... Tazewell, VA [*FM radio station call letters*]
WTZH......... Meridian, MS [*Television station call letters*]
WTZIA........ WT. Zeitschrift fuer Industrielle Fertigung [*A publication*]
Wt Z Ind Fe ... Werkstattstechnik Zeitschrift fuer Industrielle Fertigung [*A publication*]
WT Z Ind Fertigung ... WT [*Werkstattstechnik*]. Zeitschrift fuer Industrielle Fertigung [*A publication*]
WTZX......... Sparta, TN [*AM radio station call letters*]
WU............. University of Wisconsin, Madison, WI [*Library symbol*] [*Library of Congress*] (LCLS)
WU............. Weather Underground [*An association*] (EA)
WU............. Weekly Underwriter [*A publication*]
WU............. Wesleyan University
WU............. Western European Union [*Also, WEU*] (NATG)
WU............. Western Union Corp. [*Upper Saddle River, NJ*] [*NYSE symbol*]
WU............. Whitetails Unlimited (EA)
WU............. Window Unit (MSA)
WU............. Work Unit [*Air Force*] (AFM)
w/u............ Work-Up
WU............. Workshop Unit (MSA)
WU............. World Union (EA)
WU-A......... University of Wisconsin, Agricultural Library, Madison, WI [*Library symbol*] [*Library of Congress*] (LCLS)
WUA .... Weapon Utility Analysis
WUA .... Western Underwriters Association [*Later, ISO*]
WUA .... Work Unit Assignment [*Navy*] (NG)
WUAA .... Wartime Unit Aircraft Activity (AFM)
WUAB........ Lorain, OH [*Television station call letters*]
WUAG........ Greensboro, NC [*FM radio station call letters*]
WUAL-FM ... Tuscaloosa, AL [*FM radio station call letters*]
WUAR........ Women United Against Rape
WUAT........ Pikesville, TN [*AM radio station call letters*]
WUBE-FM ... Cincinnati, OH [*FM radio station call letters*]
WUC.......... Western Union Corporation
WUC.......... Work Unit Code
WUC.......... Writers Union of Canada
WUC.......... Wu-han [*Republic of China*] [*Seismograph station code, US Geological Survey*] (SEIS)
WUCF-FM ... Orlando, FL [*FM radio station call letters*]
WUCI-FM ... Binghamton, NY [*FM radio station call letters*]
WUCM....... Work Unit Code Manual
WUCM-TV ... University Center [*Bay City*], MI [*Television station call letters*]
WUCO........ Marysville, OH [*AM radio station call letters*]
WUCOS....... Western European Union Chiefs of Staff (NATG)
WUCPS ..... World Union of Catholic Philosophical Societies (EA)
WUCT........ World Union of Catholic Teachers
WUCWO....... World Union of Catholic Women's Organizations (EA-IO)
WUCX-TV ... Bad Axe, MI [*Television station call letters*]
WuD .... Wort und Dienst. Jahrbuch der Theologischen Schule Bethel [*Bethel Bei Bielefeld*] [*A publication*]
WUDB........ Work Unit Data Bank
WU-DE .... University of Wisconsin, Center for Demography and Ecology, Madison, WI [*Library symbol*] [*Library of Congress*] (LCLS)
WUDO........ Western European Union Defense Organization (NATG)
WUDZ........ Sweet Briar, VA [*FM radio station call letters*]
WU-E.......... University of Wisconsin, Engineering Library, Madison, WI [*Library symbol*] [*Library of Congress*] (LCLS)
WUE .... Water-Use Efficiency [*Agriculture*]
WUE .... Work Unit Engineer
WUEC........ Eau Claire, WI [*FM radio station call letters*]
WUEMI........ Western Union Electronic Mail, Incorporated [*McLean, VA*] [*Telecommunications*] (TSSD)

Wuerttemb Wochenbl Landwirt ... Wuerttembergisches Wochenblatt fuer Landwirtschaft [A publication]
Wuerzburg Geogr Arb ... Wuerzburger Geographische Arbeiten [A publication]
Wuerz Jb.... Wuerzburger Jahrbuecher fuer die Altertumswissenschaft [A publication]
WUEV......... Evansville, IN [FM radio station call letters]
WUEZ......... Sanford, FL [AM radio station call letters]
WUF........... Wattle-Urea-Formaldehyde [Adhesive component]
WUF........... Western United Front [Fijian] (PPW)
WUF........... World Underwater Federation (ASF)
WUF........... World Union of Free Thinkers
WUF........... World University, Miami Learning Resource Center, Miami, FL [OCLC symbol] (OCLC)
WUFE........ Baxley, GA [AM radio station call letters]
WUFEC...... Western European Union Finance and Economic Committee (NATG)
WUFF......... Eastman, GA [AM radio station call letters]
WUFF-FM... Eastman, GA [FM radio station call letters]
WUFK........ Fort Kent, ME [FM radio station call letters]
WUFM........ Lebanon, PA [FM radio station call letters]
WUFN........ Albion, MI [FM radio station call letters]
WUFO........ Amherst, NY [AM radio station call letters]
WUFS........ World Union of French-Speakers [See also UMVF] (EA-IO)
WUFT........ Gainesville, FL [Television station call letters]
WUFT-FM .. Gainesville, FL [FM radio station call letters]
WUFTU...... World Union of Free Trade Unions
WUg.......... Graham Public Library, Union Grove, WI [Library symbol] [Library of Congress] (LCLS)
WUG.......... Wau [Papua New Guinea] [Airport symbol] (OAG)
WuG.......... Wissenschaft und Gegenwart [A publication]
WUGA........ Athens, GA [FM radio station call letters]
WUGN........ Midland, MI [FM radio station call letters]
WUGO........ Grayson, KY [FM radio station call letters]
WUgSC...... Southern Wisconsin Colony and Training School, Medical Library, Union Grove, WI [Library symbol] [Library of Congress] (LCLS)
WUH.......... Wu-han [Republic of China] [Seismograph station code, US Geological Survey] (SEIS)
WUH.......... Wuhan [China] [Airport symbol] (OAG)
Wuhan Univ J Nat Sci ... Wuhan University Journal. Natural Sciences [People's Republic of China] [A publication]
WUHF......... Rochester, NY [Television station call letters]
WUHN....... Pittsfield, MA [AM radio station call letters]
WUHQ-TV ... Battle Creek, MI [Television station call letters]
WUHS........ Urbana, OH [FM radio station call letters]
WUI.......... Western Union International [Division of WUI, Inc.]
WUIS......... Water Use Information System [Westinghouse Hanford Co.] (EISS)
WUIS......... Work Unit Information System [Defense Documentation Center]
WUIV......... Icard Township, NC [AM radio station call letters]
WUJA........ Caguas, PR [Television station call letters]
WUJC........ University Heights, OH [FM radio station call letters]
WUJS........ World Union of Jewish Students
WUKO........ World Union of Karatedo Organizations (EA-IO)
WU-L.......... University of Wisconsin, Law Library, Madison, WI [Library symbol] [Library of Congress] (LCLS)
WUL.......... Washington University, Law Library, St. Louis, MO [OCLC symbol] (OCLC)
WUL.......... Workers Unity League [Canada]
WULA........ Eufaula, AL [AM radio station call letters]
WULA-FM ... Eufaula, AL [FM radio station call letters]
WULC........ West Virginia Union Catalog Interlibrary Loan Network [Library network]
WULDS...... Western Union Long Distance Service [Western Union Telegraph Co.] [Upper Saddle River, NJ] [Telecommunications] (TSSD)
WULF........ Alma, GA [AM radio station call letters]
WULF........ Wulf Oil Corp. [NASDAQ symbol] (NQ)
WULF-FM... Alma, GA [FM radio station call letters]
WU-LT....... University of Wisconsin, Land Tenure Center, Madison, WI [Library symbol] [Library of Congress] (LCLS)
WULTUO.... World Union of Liberal Trade Union Organisations [See also WFALW] (EA-IO)
WULTUO.... World Union of Liberal Trade Union Organizations [See also WFALW]
WU-M........ University of Wisconsin, School of Medicine, Madison, WI [Library symbol] [Library of Congress] (LCLS)
WUM.......... Washington University, School of Medicine, St. Louis, MO [OCLC symbol] (OCLC)
WUM.......... Women's Universal Movement [Defunct] (EA)
WUM.......... Work Unit Manager
WUMB....... Boston, MA [FM radio station call letters]
WUME-FM... Paoli, IN [FM radio station call letters]
WUMF-FM ... Farmington, ME [FM radio station call letters]
WUMP........ White, Urban, Middle Class, Protestant
WUMPS...... Women Umpires [World War II]
WUMS........ Woman's Union Missionary Society of America [Later, UFCS] (EA)
WUMTPT.... World Union of Martyred Towns, Peace Towns (EA-IO)

WUN.......... Wiluna [Australia] [Airport symbol] (OAG)
WUNA........ Aguadilla, PR [AM radio station call letters]
WUNC........ Chapel Hill, NC [FM radio station call letters]
WUNC-TV ... Chapel Hill, NC [Television station call letters]
W Underw ... Weekly Underwriter [A publication]
WUND-TV ... Columbia, NC [Television station call letters]
WUNE-TV... Linville, NC [Television station call letters]
WUNF-TV... Asheville, NC [Television station call letters]
WUNG-TV ... Concord, NC [Television station call letters]
WUNH........ Durham, NH [FM radio station call letters]
WUNI......... Wheeling, WV [AM radio station call letters]
WUNJ-TV... Wilmington, NC [Television station call letters]
WUNL-TV... Winston-Salem, NC [Television station call letters]
WUNM-TV ... Jacksonville, NC [Television station call letters]
WUNN........ Mason, MI [AM radio station call letters]
WUNO........ San Juan, PR [AM radio station call letters]
WUNP-TV... Roanoke Rapids, NC [Television station call letters]
WUNR........ Brookline, MA [AM radio station call letters]
WUNS........ World Union of National Socialists (EA)
WUNT........ Wissenschaftliche Untersuchungen zum Neuen Testament [Tuebingen] [A publication] (BJA)
WUNY........ Utica, NY [FM radio station call letters]
WUOG........ Athens, GA [FM radio station call letters]
WUOL........ Louisville, KY [FM radio station call letters]
WUOM........ Ann Arbor, MI [FM radio station call letters]
WUOSY...... World Union of Organizations for the Safeguard of Youth [Later, UMOSEA]
WUOT........ Knoxville, TN [FM radio station call letters]
WUP.......... Work Unit Plan [Navy] (NG)
WUPA........ Wupatki National Monument
WUPE........ Pittsfield, MA [FM radio station call letters]
WUPI......... Presque Isle, ME [FM radio station call letters]
WUPJ........ World Union for Progressive Judaism (EA)
WUPM........ Ironwood, MI [FM radio station call letters]
WUPO........ World Union of Pythagorean Organizations (EA-IO)
WUPPE....... Wisconsin Ultraviolet Photo-Polarimeter Experiment
WUPR........ Utuado-Rosa, PR [AM radio station call letters]
WUPS........ World Union of Process Servers
WUPW........ Toledo, OH [Television station call letters]
WUPY........ Ishpeming, MI [AM radio station call letters]
WUR.......... World University Roundtable
WUR.......... Wurlitzer Co. [NYSE symbol]
WURB........ Western Utilization Research Branch (MCD)
WURL........ Moody, AL [AM radio station call letters]
WUS.......... Washington University. Studies [A publication]
WUS.......... Woerterbuch der Ugaritischen Sprache [A publication] (BJA)
WUS.......... World University Service [See also EUM] [Geneva, Switzerland] (EA-IO)
WUSA-FM ... Tampa, FL [FM radio station call letters]
WUSA-TV... Washington, DC [Television station call letters]
WUSB........ Stony Brook, NY [FM radio station call letters]
WUSC........ World University Service of Canada [See also EUMC]
WUSC-FM ... Columbia, SC [FM radio station call letters]
WUSCI........ Western Union Space Communications, Incorporated (MCD)
WUSF........ Tampa, FL [FM radio station call letters]
WUSF-TV ... Tampa, FL [Television station call letters]
WUSG........ World Union Saint Gabriel (EA-IO)
WUSI-TV... Olney, IL [Television station call letters]
WUSJ-FM... Elizabethton, TN [FM radio station call letters]
WUSL........ Philadelphia, PA [FM radio station call letters]
WUSL........ Washburn University School of Law (DLA)
WUSL........ Women's United Service League [British]
WUSM........ North Dartmouth, MA [FM radio station call letters]
WUSN........ Chicago, IL [FM radio station call letters]
WUSO........ Springfield, OH [FM radio station call letters]
WUSQ........ Winchester, VA [AM radio station call letters]
WUSQ-FM ... Winchester, VA [FM radio station call letters]
WUSS........ Atlantic City, NJ [AM radio station call letters]
WUST........ Washington, DC [AM radio station call letters]
WUSV........ Schenectady, NY [Television station call letters]
WUSY........ Cleveland, TN [FM radio station call letters]
WUT.......... Warm Up Time
WUT.......... Washburn University of Topeka [Kansas]
WUT.......... Western Union Telegraph Co. [Upper Saddle River, NJ] [NYSE symbol]
WUTA........ Washington University Technology Associates
WUTC........ Chattanooga, TN [FM radio station call letters]
WUTC........ Western Union Telegraph Company [Upper Saddle River, NJ]
WUTELCO ... Western Union Telegraph Company [Upper Saddle River, NJ]
WUTHH...... World Union of Tnuat Haherut Hatzorar (EA-IO)
WUTK........ Knoxville, TN [FM radio station call letters]
WUTM........ Martin, TN [FM radio station call letters]
WUTQ........ Utica-Rome, NY [AM radio station call letters]
WUTR........ Utica, NY [Television station call letters]
WUTS........ Sewanee, TN [FM radio station call letters]
WUTS........ Work Unit Time Standard [Air Force] (AFM)
WUTS........ Work Unit Tracking Subsystem (MCD)
WUTV........ Buffalo, NY [Television station call letters]
WUTZ........ Summertown, TN [FM radio station call letters]
WUU.......... Wau [Sudan] [Airport symbol] (OAG)
WUUA........ World Union for a Universal Alphabet (EA)

WUUN .... Women United for United Nations   (EA)
WUUU .... Rome, NY [*FM radio station call letters*]
WUV .... Weighted Unit Value   (MCD)
WUV .... Wuvulu Island [*Papua New Guinea*] [*Airport symbol*]   (OAG)
WUVA........ Charlottesville, VA [*FM radio station call letters*]
WUVT-FM ... Blacksburg, VA [*FM radio station call letters*]
WUVU........ St. Augustine, FL [*FM radio station call letters*]
WUW......... Welt und Wort [*A publication*]
WUW .... Wu-wei [*Republic of China*] [*Seismograph station code, US Geological Survey*]   (SEIS)
WU-WA ...... University of Wisconsin, Woodman Astronomical Library, Madison, WI [*Library symbol*] [*Library of Congress*]   (LCLS)
WuWahr ..... Wort und Wahrheit [*A publication*]
WuWelt ...... Wissenschaft und Weltbild [*A publication*]
WUWF .... Pensacola, FL [*FM radio station call letters*]
WUWM ...... Milwaukee, WI [*FM radio station call letters*]
WUX .... Western Union Exchange [*Teleprinter*]
WUXA........ Portsmouth, OH [*Television station call letters*]
WV............ Avair Ltd. [*Ireland*] [*ICAO designator*]   (FAAC)
WV............ Diwag [*Germany*] [*Research code symbol*]
WV............ Walking Ventilation   (ADA)
WV............ Wall Vent [*Technical drawings*]
WV............ Water Valve   (ROG)
WV............ Wave   (FAAC)
W/V.......... Weight/Volume [*Concentration*] [*Chemistry*]
WV............ West Virginia [*Postal code*]
Wv............ West Virginia Library Commission, Charleston, WV [*Library symbol*] [*Library of Congress*]   (LCLS)
WV............ West Virginia Reports   (DLA)
WV............ Westminster Version of the Bible [*A publication*]   (BJA)
WV............ Whispered Voice
W/V.......... Wind Vector [*or Velocity*] [*Navigation*]
WV............ Wireless Van [*British*]
WV............ Working Voltage   (MSA)
WV............ World Vision
WV............ World Vision [*A publication*]
WVA .... Alderson-Broaddus College, Philippi, WV [*OCLC symbol*]   (OCLC)
WVA .... War Veterans Administration [*Canada*]
W VA .... West Virginia   (AAG)
W Va .... West Virginia Supreme Court Reports   (DLA)
WVA .... World Veterinary Association [*See also AMV*]   (EA-IO)
W Va Acad Sci Proc ... West Virginia Academy of Sciences. Proceedings [*A publication*]
W Va Acts ... Acts of the Legislature of West Virginia   (DLA)
W Va Ag Dept ... West Virginia. Department of Agriculture. Publications [*A publication*]
W Va Ag Exp ... West Virginia. Agricultural Experiment Station. Publications [*A publication*]
W Va Agric Exp Stn Bull ... West Virginia. Agricultural Experiment Station. Bulletin [*A publication*]
W Va Agric Exp Stn Cir ... West Virginia. Agricultural Experiment Station. Circular [*A publication*]
W Va Agric Exp Stn Circ ... West Virginia. Agricultural Experiment Station. Circular [*A publication*]
W Va Agric Exp Stn Curr Rep ... West Virginia. Agricultural Experiment Station. Current Report [*A publication*]
W Va Agric Exp Stn Misc Publ ... West Virginia. Agricultural Experiment Station. Miscellaneous Publication [*A publication*]
W Va Agric For ... West Virginia Agriculture and Forestry [*A publication*]
W Va Agric For Exp Stn Bull ... West Virginia. Agricultural and Forestry Experiment Station. Bulletin [*A publication*]
WVAB........ Virginia Beach, VA [*AM radio station call letters*]
WVAB........ War Veterans Allowance Board [*Canada*]
WVAC........ Adrian, MI [*FM radio station call letters*]
WvAC .... Concord College, Athens, WV [*Library symbol*] [*Library of Congress*]   (LCLS)
WVAC .... Working Voltage, Alternating Current   (DEN)
W Va Coal Min Inst Proc ... West Virginia Coal Mining Institute. Proceedings [*A publication*]
W Va Code ... West Virginia Code   (DLA)
W Va Crim Just Rev ... West Virginia Criminal Justice Review   (DLA)
W Va Dent J ... West Virginia Dental Journal [*A publication*]
W Va Dep Mines Annu Rep ... West Virginia. Department of Mines. Annual Report [*A publication*]
WVAF........ Charleston, WV [*FM radio station call letters*]
W Va For Notes ... West Virginia Forestry Notes [*A publication*]
W Va Geol Econ Surv Basic Data Rep ... West Virginia. Geological and Economic Survey. Basic Data Report [*A publication*]
W Va Geol Econ Surv Bull ... West Virginia. Geological and Economic Survey. Bulletin [*A publication*]
W Va Geol Econ Surv Circ Ser ... West Virginia. Geological and Economic Survey. Circular Series [*A publication*]
W Va Geol Econ Surv Cir Ser ... West Virginia. Geological and Economic Survey. Circular Series [*A publication*]
W Va Geol Econ Surv Coal Geol Bull ... West Virginia. Geological and Economic Survey. Coal Geology Bulletin [*A publication*]
W Va Geol Econ Surv Environ Geol Bull ... West Virginia. Geological and Economic Survey. Environmental Geology Bulletin [*A publication*]

W Va Geol Econ Surv Miner Resour Ser ... West Virginia. Geological and Economic Survey. Mineral Resources Series [*A publication*]
W Va Geol Econ Surv Newsl ... West Virginia. Geological and Economic Survey. Newsletter [*A publication*]
W Va Geol Econ Surv Rep Archeol Invest ... West Virginia. Geological and Economic Survey. Report of Archeological Investigations [*A publication*]
W Va Geol Econ Surv Rep Invest ... West Virginia. Geological and Economic Survey. Report of Investigations [*A publication*]
W Va Geol Econ Surv River Basin Bull ... West Virginia. Geological and Economic Survey. River Basin Bulletin [*A publication*]
W Va Geol Surv Rep ... West Virginia. Geological Survey. Reports [*A publication*]
W Va Geol Surv Rep Invest ... West Virginia. Geological Survey. Report of Investigations [*A publication*]
W Va G S .... West Virginia. Geological Survey [*A publication*]
WVaH .... West Virginia History [*A publication*]
W Va His.... West Virginia History [*A publication*]
W Va Hist .... West Virginia History. A Quarterly Magazine [*A publication*]
WVAH-TV... Charleston, WV [*Television station call letters*]
WVAL........ Sauk Rapids, MN [*AM radio station call letters*]
W Va Law R ... West Virginia Law Review [*A publication*]
W Va Law Reports ... West Virginia Reports   (DLA)
W Va Lib ... West Virginia Libraries [*A publication*]
W Va Libr ... West Virginia Libraries [*A publication*]
W Va LQ ... West Virginia Law Quarterly   (DLA)
W Va L Rev ... West Virginia Law Review [*A publication*]
WVALSA .... Whitewater Valley Area Library Services Authority [*Library network*]
WVAM .... Altoona, PA [*AM radio station call letters*]
W Va Med J ... West Virginia Medical Journal [*A publication*]
WVAN-TV... Savannah, GA [*Television station call letters*]
W Va PSCR ... West Virginia Public Service Commission Report   (DLA)
W Va PUR... West Virginia Public Utility Commission Reports   (DLA)
WVAQ .... Morgantown, WV [*FM radio station call letters*]
WVAR........ Richwood, WV [*AM radio station call letters*]
Wv-Ar........ West Virginia Department of Archives and History, Charleston, WV [*Library symbol*] [*Library of Congress*]   (LCLS)
W Va Rep ... West Virginia Reports   (DLA)
WVAS........ Montgomery, AL [*FM radio station call letters*]
WVAS........ Wake Vortex Avoidance System [*FAA*]
W Va Univ Agri Exp Stn Bull ... West Virginia University. Agricultural Experiment Station. Bulletin [*A publication*]
W Va Univ Bull Proc Annu Appalachian Gas Meas Short Course ... West Virginia University. Bulletin. Proceedings. Annual Appalachian Gas Measurement Short Course [*A publication*]
W Va Univ Coal Res Bur Sch Mines Tech Rep ... West Virginia University. Coal Research Bureau. School of Mines. Technical Report [*Morgantown, West Virginia*] [*A publication*]
W Va Univ Coal Res Bur Tech Rep ... West Virginia University. Coal Research Bureau. Technical Report [*A publication*]
W Va Univ Eng Exp Sta Tech Bull ... West Virginia University. Engineering Experiment Station. Technical Bulletin [*A publication*]
W Va Univ Eng Exp Stn Bull ... West Virginia University. Engineering Experiment Station. Bulletin [*A publication*]
W Va Univ Eng Exp Stn Res Bull ... West Virginia University. Engineering Experiment Station. Research Bulletin [*A publication*]
W Va Univ Rp Bd Reg ... West Virginia University. Report of the Board of Regents [*A publication*]
W Va U Phil ... West Virginia University. Philological Papers [*A publication*]
WvB........... Beckley-Raleigh County Library, Beckley, WV [*Library symbol*] [*Library of Congress*]   (LCLS)
WVB .... Bethany College, Bethany, WV [*OCLC symbol*]   (OCLC)
WVB .... Walvis Bay [*Namibia*] [*Airport symbol*]   (OAG)
Wv-B .... West Virginia Library Commission, Book Express Unit, Charleston, WV [*Library symbol*] [*Library of Congress*]   (LCLS)
WVBA........ Frankfort, KY [*FM radio station call letters*]
WvBC .... Beckley College, Beckley, WV [*Library symbol*] [*Library of Congress*]   (LCLS)
WVBC........ Bethany, WV [*FM radio station call letters*]
WvBeC .... Bethany College, Bethany, WV [*Library symbol*] [*Library of Congress*]   (LCLS)
WVBF .... Framingham, MA [*FM radio station call letters*]
WVBH........ Key Largo, FL [*FM radio station call letters*]
WvBl.......... Bluefield Public Library, Bluefield, WV [*Library symbol*] [*Library of Congress*]   (LCLS)
WvBIS .... Bluefield State College, Bluefield, WV [*Library symbol*] [*Library of Congress*]   (LCLS)
WVBM .... Springfield, FL [*FM radio station call letters*]
WvBrA........ Appalachian Bible Institute, Bradley, WV [*Library symbol*] [*Library of Congress*]   (LCLS)
WVBR-FM ... Ithaca, NY [*FM radio station call letters*]
WvBri .... Benedum Civic Center Public Library, Bridgeport, WV [*Library symbol*] [*Library of Congress*]   (LCLS)
WVBS........ Burgaw, NC [*AM radio station call letters*]
WVBS-FM ... Burgaw, NC [*FM radio station call letters*]
WVBT .... Virginia Beach, VA [*Television station call letters*]

WvBu.......... Stonewall Jackson Regional Library, Buckhannon, WV [*Library symbol*] [*Library of Congress*] (LCLS)
WVBU-FM ... Lewisburg, PA [*FM radio station call letters*]
WvBuW ...... West Virginia Wesleyan College, Buckhannon, WV [*Library symbol*] [*Library of Congress*] (LCLS)
WvBV .... United States Veterans Administration Hospital, Beckley, WV [*Library symbol*] [*Library of Congress*] (LCLS)
WVBX......... Georgetown, SC [*AM radio station call letters*]
WvC .... Kanawha County Public Library, Charleston, WV [*Library symbol*] [*Library of Congress*] (LCLS)
WvCA......... West Virginia Department of Agriculture, Charleston, WV [*Library symbol*] [*Library of Congress*] (LCLS)
WvCAE...... Appalachian Educational Laboratory, Inc., Charleston, WV [*Library symbol*] [*Library of Congress*] (LCLS)
WVCA-FM ... Gloucester, MA [*FM radio station call letters*]
WvCAP...... West Virginia Air Pollution Control Commission, Charleston, WV [*Library symbol*] [*Library of Congress*] (LCLS)
WVCB........ Shallotte, NC [*AM radio station call letters*]
WvCBHi...... West Virginia Baptist Historical Society Deposit, Department of Archives and History, Charleston, WV [*Library symbol*] [*Library of Congress*] (LCLS)
WVCC .... Linesville, PA [*FM radio station call letters*]
WvCCD ...... West Virginia Department of Civil and Defense Mobilization, Charleston, WV [*Library symbol*] [*Library of Congress*] (LCLS)
WVCF........ Ocoee, FL [*AM radio station call letters*]
WvCFM ..... West Virginia State Fire Marshal's Department, Charleston, WV [*Library symbol*] [*Library of Congress*] (LCLS)
WVCG .... Coral Gables, FL [*AM radio station call letters*]
WvCGH ..... Charleston General Hospital, Charleston, WV [*Library symbol*] [*Library of Congress*] (LCLS)
WVCH........ Chester, PA [*AM radio station call letters*]
WvCH........ West Virginia Department of Health, Charleston, WV [*Library symbol*] [*Library of Congress*] (LCLS)
WvCheC..... Consolidated Gas Supply Corp., Chelyan, WV [*Library symbol*] [*Library of Congress*] (LCLS)
WvCHi........ West Virginia Department of Highways, Charleston, WV [*Library symbol*] [*Library of Congress*] (LCLS)
WvCI......... Bay City, MI [*Television station call letters*]
WvCI .... Clarksburg Public Library, Clarksburg, WV [*Library symbol*] [*Library of Congress*] (LCLS)
WvCIC........ Consolidated Gas Supply Corp., Clarksburg, WV [*Library symbol*] [*Library of Congress*] (LCLS)
WVCM .... Miami, WV [*FM radio station call letters*]
WvCM .... Morris Harvey College, Charleston, WV [*Library symbol*] [*Library of Congress*] (LCLS)
WvCMH...... West Virginia Department of Mental Health, Charleston, WV [*Library symbol*] [*Library of Congress*] (LCLS)
WvCMi ...... West Virginia Department of Mines, Charleston, WV [*Library symbol*] [*Library of Congress*] (LCLS)
WvCNR....... West Virginia Department of Natural Resources, Charleston, WV [*Library symbol*] [*Library of Congress*] (LCLS)
WVCP........ Gallatin, TN [*FM radio station call letters*]
WvCPS....... West Virginia Department of Public Safety, Charleston, WV [*Library symbol*] [*Library of Congress*] (LCLS)
WVCR........ Loudonville, NY [*FM radio station call letters*]
WVCS........ California, PA [*FM radio station call letters*]
WVCT........ Keavy, KY [*FM radio station call letters*]
WvCTS....... West Virginia State Technical Services, Charleston, WV [*Library symbol*] [*Library of Congress*] (LCLS)
WvCVR....... West Virginia Division of Vocational Rehabilitation, Charleston, WV [*Library symbol*] [*Library of Congress*] (LCLS)
WVCX........ Tomah, WI [*FM radio station call letters*]
WVCY........ Milwaukee, WI [*FM radio station call letters*]
WVCY-TV... Milwaukee, WI [*Television station call letters*]
WVD .... Dane County Hospital, Verona, WI [*Library symbol*] [*Library of Congress*] (LCLS)
WVD .... Davis and Elkins College, Elkins, WV [*OCLC symbol*] (OCLC)
WVD .... Waived (AABC)
WVDC .... Working Voltage, Direct Current
WVDOG...... Wissenschaftliche Veroeffentlichungen der Deutschen Orient-Gesellschaft [*A publication*]
WVE .... Water Vapor Electrolysis [*Cell*]
WVE .... Wind Velocity East (MCD)
WVEC-TV... Hampton, VA [*Television station call letters*]
WvED .... Davis and Elkins College, Elkins, WV [*Library symbol*] [*Library of Congress*] (LCLS)
WVEE........ Atlanta, GA [*FM radio station call letters*]
WVEE........ Wheeled Vehicle Experimental Establishment [*British*]
WVEH........ Wheel Vehicle (AABC)
WVEL .... Pekin, IL [*AM radio station call letters*]
WVEM........ Springfield, IL [*FM radio station call letters*]
WVEM........ Water Vapor Electrolysis Module [*NASA*]
WVEN........ Franklin, PA [*FM radio station call letters*]
WVEO........ Aguadilla, PR [*Television station call letters*]
WVEP........ Martinsburg, WV [*FM radio station call letters*]
WVER........ Rutland, VT [*Television station call letters*]
WVEU........ Atlanta, GA [*Television station call letters*]
WVEZ........ Louisville, KY [*FM radio station call letters*]
WVF........... Fairmont State College, Fairmont, WV [*OCLC symbol*] (OCLC)

WvF .... Marion County Public Library, Fairmont, WV [*Library symbol*] [*Library of Congress*] (LCLS)
WVF........... Wave Vector Filter
WVF........... West Virginia Folklore [*A publication*]
WVF........... World Veterans Federation [*See also FMAC*] (EA-IO)
WVF........... World Veterans Fund (EA)
WvFa .... Fayette County Public Library, Fayetteville, WV [*Library symbol*] [*Library of Congress*] (LCLS)
WVFC........ McConnellsburg, PA [*AM radio station call letters*]
WVFF .... Opelika, AL [*Television station call letters*]
WVFJ-FM ... Manchester, GA [*FM radio station call letters*]
WVFL-TV ... Sebring, FL [*Television station call letters*]
WVFM .... Lakeland, FL [*FM radio station call letters*]
WvFMHi ..... Marion County Historical Society, Fairmont, WV [*Library symbol*] [*Library of Congress*] (LCLS)
WvFS......... Fairmont State College, Fairmont, WV [*Library symbol*] [*Library of Congress*] (LCLS)
WVFT .... Roanoke, VA [*Television station call letters*]
WVG .... West Virginia State College/College of Graduate Studies, Institute, WV [*OCLC symbol*] (OCLC)
WVGA .... Valdosta, GA [*Television station call letters*]
WVGB........ Beaufort, SC [*AM radio station call letters*]
WvGbN...... National Radio Astronomy Observatory, Green Bank, WV [*Library symbol*] [*Library of Congress*] (LCLS)
WvGIS .... Glenville State College, Glenville, WV [*Library symbol*] [*Library of Congress*] (LCLS)
WVGN .... Charlotte Amalie, VI [*FM radio station call letters*]
WVGR........ Grand Rapids, MI [*FM radio station call letters*]
WVGS........ Statesboro, GA [*FM radio station call letters*]
WVH .... Marshall University, Huntington, WV [*OCLC symbol*] (OCLC)
WVH .... West Virginia History [*A publication*]
WVHA........ Wirtschaftsverwaltungshauptamt (BJA)
WvHB .... Pearl S. Buck Birthplace Museum, Hillsboro, WV [*Library symbol*] [*Library of Congress*] (LCLS)
WVHF-FM ... Clarksburg, WV [*FM radio station call letters*]
WvHfP .... United States Park Service, Harpers Ferry National Historical Park, Harpers Ferry, WV [*Library symbol*] [*Library of Congress*] (LCLS)
WVHG .... Labelle, FL [*FM radio station call letters*]
WVHI .... Evansville, TN [*AM radio station call letters*]
WVHP........ West Virginia Association for Health, Physical Education, Recreation, and Dance. Journal [*A publication*]
WVHP-FM ... Highland Park, NJ [*FM radio station call letters*]
WVHT........ Elkins, WV [*FM radio station call letters*]
WvHu.......... Cabell-Huntington Public Library [*Western Counties Regional Library*], Huntington, WV [*Library symbol*] [*Library of Congress*] (LCLS)
WvHuB .... Basic Systems, Inc., Huntington, WV [*Library symbol*] [*Library of Congress*] (LCLS)
WvHuE ...... United States Army, Corps of Engineers, Huntington, WV [*Library symbol*] [*Library of Congress*] (LCLS)
WvHuG....... Huntington Galleries, Huntington, WV [*Library symbol*] [*Library of Congress*] (LCLS)
WvHuH ...... Holland-Suco Color Co., Huntington, WV [*Library symbol*] [*Library of Congress*] (LCLS)
WvHuM ..... Marshall University, Huntington, WV [*Library symbol*] [*Library of Congress*] (LCLS)
WvHuV ...... United States Veterans Administration Hospital, Huntington, WV [*Library symbol*] [*Library of Congress*] (LCLS)
WVi............. Viroqua Public Library, Viroqua, WI [*Library symbol*] [*Library of Congress*] (LCLS)
WVI............. Watsonville, CA [*Location identifier*] [*FAA*] (FAAL)
WVI............. Work Values Inventory [*Psychometrics*]
WVIA-FM ... Scranton, PA [*FM radio station call letters*]
WVIA-TV ... Scranton, PA [*Television station call letters*]
WVIC .... East Lansing, MI [*AM radio station call letters*]
WvIC .... West Virginia State College, Institute, WV [*Library symbol*] [*Library of Congress*] (LCLS)
WVIC-FM ... East Lansing, MI [*FM radio station call letters*]
WvICG........ West Virginia College of Graduate Studies, Institute, WV [*Library symbol*] [*Library of Congress*] (LCLS)
WVID .... Anasco, PR [*FM radio station call letters*]
WVII........... Bangor, ME [*Television station call letters*]
WVIJ.......... Port Charlotte, FL [*FM radio station call letters*]
WVIK.......... Rock Island, IL [*FM radio station call letters*]
WVIM-FM ... Coldwater, MS [*FM radio station call letters*]
WVIN .... Bath, NY [*AM radio station call letters*]
WVIN-FM ... Bath, NY [*FM radio station call letters*]
WVIP.......... Mount Kisco, NY [*AM radio station call letters*]
WVIP-FM... Mount Kisco, NY [*FM radio station call letters*]
WVIR-TV ... Charlottesville, VA [*Television station call letters*]
WVIS .... Christiansted, VI [*FM radio station call letters*]
WVIT .... New Britain, CT [*Television station call letters*]
WVIT .... West Virginia Institute of Technology
WVIZ-TV ... Cleveland, OH [*Television station call letters*]
WVJC-FM .. Mount Carmel, IL [*FM radio station call letters*]
WVJP.......... Caguas, PR [*AM radio station call letters*]
WVJP-FM... Caguas, PR [*FM radio station call letters*]
WVJS .... Owensboro, KY [*AM radio station call letters*]
WVJZ.......... Orange, VA [*FM radio station call letters*]

WVK .... Kanawha County Public Library, Charleston, WV [*OCLC symbol*] (OCLC)
WvK .... Keyser-Mineral County Public and Potomac Valley Regional Library, Keyser, WV [*Library symbol*] [*Library of Congress*] (LCLS)
WVK .... Manakara [*Madagascar*] [*Airport symbol*] (OAG)
WVKC .... Galesburg, IL [*FM radio station call letters*]
WvKeFW .... Bureau of Sport Fisheries and Wildlife, Eastern Fish Disease Laboratory, Kearneysville, WV [*Library symbol*] [*Library of Congress*] (LCLS)
WVKO .... Columbus, OH [*AM radio station call letters*]
WvKP .... Potomac State College, Keyser, WV [*Library symbol*] [*Library of Congress*] (LCLS)
WVKR-FM ... Poughkeepsie, NY [*FM radio station call letters*]
WVKV .... Hurricane, WV [*AM radio station call letters*]
WVKY .... Louisa, KY [*AM radio station call letters*]
WVL .... Warfare Vision Laboratory [*Army*]
WVL .... Waterville [*Maine*] [*Airport symbol*] (OAG)
WVL .... Waterville, ME [*Location identifier*] [*FAA*] (FAAL)
WVL .... West Virginia Law Review [*A publication*]
Wv-L .... West Virginia State Law Library, Charleston, WV [*Library symbol*] [*Library of Congress*] (LCLS)
WVLA .... Woodville, MS [*FM radio station call letters*]
WVLB .... Wheeled Vehicle Launched Bridge (MCD)
WVLD .... Valdosta, GA [*AM radio station call letters*]
WvLe .... Greenbrier County Public Library, Lewisburg, WV [*Library symbol*] [*Library of Congress*] (LCLS)
WVLE .... Scottsville, KY [*FM radio station call letters*]
WvLeG .... Greenbrier College, Lewisburg, WV [*Library symbol*] [*Library of Congress*] (LCLS)
WVLG .... Wuerttembergische Vierteljahresschrift fuer Landesgeschichte [*A publication*]
WVLI .... Buena Vista, VA [*FM radio station call letters*]
WVLJ .... Monticello, IL [*FM radio station call letters*]
WVLK .... Lexington, KY [*AM radio station call letters*]
WVLK-FM ... Lexington, KY [*FM radio station call letters*]
WVLN .... Olney, IL [*AM radio station call letters*]
WVLQ .... West Virginia Law Quarterly (DLA)
WVLR .... West Virginia Law Review [*A publication*]
WVLS .... Jackson, MS [*FM radio station call letters*]
Wv-LS .... West Virginia Library Commission, Library Science Department, Charleston, WV [*Library symbol*] [*Library of Congress*] (LCLS)
WVLT .... Vineland, NJ [*FM radio station call letters*]
WVLV .... Lebanon, PA [*AM radio station call letters*]
WVLY .... Water Valley, MS [*AM radio station call letters*]
WvM .... Morgantown Public Library, Morgantown, WV [*Library symbol*] [*Library of Congress*] (LCLS)
WVM .... West Virginia Medical Center, Morgantown, WV [*OCLC symbol*] [*Inactive*] (OCLC)
WVM .... Wiener Voelkerkundliche Mitteilungen [*A publication*]
WvMa .... Martinsburg-Berkeley County Public Library, Martinsburg, WV [*Library symbol*] [*Library of Congress*] (LCLS)
WVMA .... Women's Veterinary Medical Association [*Later, AWV*]
WvMaV ...... United States Veterans Administration Center, Martinsburg, WV [*Library symbol*] [*Library of Congress*] (LCLS)
WvMBM ..... United States Bureau of Mines, Morgantown, WV [*Library symbol*] [*Library of Congress*] (LCLS)
WVMC .... Mansfield, OH [*FM radio station call letters*]
WvMc .... McMechen Public Library, McMechen, WV [*Library symbol*] [*Library of Congress*] (LCLS)
WVMG .... Cochran, GA [*AM radio station call letters*]
WVMG-FM ... Cochran, GA [*FM radio station call letters*]
WVMH-FM ... Mars Hill, NC [*FM radio station call letters*]
WVMI .... Biloxi, MS [*AM radio station call letters*]
WvMIL .... Institute for Labor Studies, Appalachian Center, Morgantown, WV [*Library symbol*] [*Library of Congress*] (LCLS)
WvMNIO ..... United States Public Health Service, National Institute for Occupational Safety and Health, Appalachian Laboratory for Occupational Safety and Health Library, Morgantown, WV (LCLS)
WvMo .... City-County Public Library, Moundsville, WV [*Library symbol*] [*Library of Congress*] (LCLS)
WvMonI ...... West Virginia Institute of Technology, Montgomery, WV [*Library symbol*] [*Library of Congress*] (LCLS)
WVMR .... Frost, WV [*AM radio station call letters*]
WVMT .... Burlington, VT [*AM radio station call letters*]
WVMW-FM ... Scranton, PA [*FM radio station call letters*]
WVN .... Water Vapor Nitrogen [*Nuclear energy*] (NRCH)
WVN .... West Virginia Northern Railroad Co. [*AAR code*]
WVN .... Wind Velocity North (MCD)
WVN .... Woven
WVNA .... Tuscumbia, AL [*AM radio station call letters*]
WVNA-FM ... Tuscumbia, AL [*FM radio station call letters*]
WVNC .... Canton, NY [*FM radio station call letters*]
WVNE .... Leicester, MA [*AM radio station call letters*]
WVNET ...... West Virginia Network for Educational Telecomputing [*Morgantown, WV*] [*Research center*] (RCD)
WVNH .... Salem, NH [*AM radio station call letters*]
WvNiK .... West Virginia University, Kanawha Valley Graduate Center, Nitro, WV [*Library symbol*] [*Library of Congress*] (LCLS)

WvNmM ..... Mobay Chemical Corp., Research Library, New Martinsville, WV [*Library symbol*] [*Library of Congress*] (LCLS)
WVNO-FM ... Mansfield, OH [*FM radio station call letters*]
WVNP .... Wheeling, WV [*FM radio station call letters*]
WVNR .... Poultney, VT [*AM radio station call letters*]
WVNY-TV ... Burlington, VT [*Television station call letters*]
WVOD .... Manteo, NC [*FM radio station call letters*]
WVOE .... Chadbourn, NC [*AM radio station call letters*]
WVOF .... Fairfield, CT [*FM radio station call letters*]
WVOG .... New Orleans, LA [*AM radio station call letters*]
WVOH .... Hazlehurst, GA [*AM radio station call letters*]
WVOH-FM ... Hazlehurst, GA [*FM radio station call letters*]
WVOI .... Toledo, OH [*AM radio station call letters*]
WVOJ .... Jacksonville, FL [*AM radio station call letters*]
WVOK .... Birmingham, AL [*AM radio station call letters*]
WVOL .... Berry Hill, TN [*AM radio station call letters*]
WVOM .... Iuka, MS [*AM radio station call letters*]
WVON .... Cicero, IL [*AM radio station call letters*]
WVOP .... Vidalia, GA [*AM radio station call letters*]
WVOR-FM ... Rochester, NY [*FM radio station call letters*]
WVOS .... Liberty, NY [*AM radio station call letters*]
WVOS-FM ... Liberty, NY [*FM radio station call letters*]
WVOT .... Wilson, NC [*AM radio station call letters*]
WVOV .... Danville, VA [*AM radio station call letters*]
WVOW .... Logan, WV [*AM radio station call letters*]
WVOW-FM ... Logan, WV [*FM radio station call letters*]
WVOX .... New Rochelle, NY [*AM radio station call letters*]
WVOZ .... San Juan, PR [*AM radio station call letters*]
WVOZ-FM ... Carolina, PR [*FM radio station call letters*]
WvP .... Carnegie Library of Parkersburg and Wood County, Parkersburg, WV [*Library symbol*] [*Library of Congress*] (LCLS)
WVP .... Women's Vote Project (EA)
WVPA .... World Veterinary Poultry Association [*See also AMVA*] (EA-IO)
WVPB .... Beckley, WV [*AM radio station call letters*]
WvPC .... Parkersburg Community College, Parkersburg, WV [*Library symbol*] [*Library of Congress*] (LCLS)
WVPE .... Elkhart, IN [*FM radio station call letters*]
WVPG .... Parkersburg, WV [*FM radio station call letters*]
WVPH .... Piscataway, NJ [*FM radio station call letters*]
WvPhA ...... Alderson-Broaddus College, Philippi, WV [*Library symbol*] [*Library of Congress*] (LCLS)
WVPM .... Morgantown, WV [*FM radio station call letters*]
WVPN .... Charleston, WV [*FM radio station call letters*]
WvPO .... Ohio Valley College, Parkersburg, WV [*Library symbol*] [*Library of Congress*] (LCLS)
WVPO .... Stroudsburg, PA [*AM radio station call letters*]
WVPR .... Windsor, VT [*FM radio station call letters*]
WVPS .... Burlington, VT [*FM radio station call letters*]
WVPT .... Staunton, VA [*Television station call letters*]
WVPW .... Buckhannon, WV [*FM radio station call letters*]
Wv-R .... West Virginia Library Commission, Reference Department, WV [*Library symbol*] [*Library of Congress*] (LCLS)
WVR .... West Virginia Reports (DLA)
WVR .... Within Visual Range [*Missile*] (MCD)
WVR .... Women's Volunteer Reserve [*British*] [*World War I*]
WVRC .... Spencer, WV [*AM radio station call letters*]
WVRC .... Wabash Valley Railroad Company [*AAR code*]
WVRD .... Belzoni, MS [*FM radio station call letters*]
WV Rep ..... West Virginia Reports (DLA)
WVRM .... Hazlet, NJ [*FM radio station call letters*]
WVRN .... Richmond, VA [*Television station call letters*]
WVRQ .... Viroqua, WI [*AM radio station call letters*]
WVRQ-FM ... Viroqua, WI [*FM radio station call letters*]
WVRRTC .... West Virginia Rehabilitation Research and Training Center [*West Virginia University*] [*Research center*] (RCD)
WVRT .... Reform, AL [*FM radio station call letters*]
WVRU .... Radford, VA [*FM radio station call letters*]
WVRY .... Waverly, TN [*FM radio station call letters*]
WVS .... Water Vapor Sensor
W-V(S) ...... Women's Reserve, Emergency Duties [*USNR commissioned officer designation*]
WVS .... Women's Voluntary Services [*Coordinated work of women for national service*] [*Later, WRVS*] [*British*] [*World War II*]
WVSA .... Vernon, AL [*AM radio station call letters*]
WvSaC .... Salem College, Salem, WV [*Library symbol*] [*Library of Congress*] (LCLS)
WVSB-TV ... West Point, MS [*Television station call letters*]
WVSC .... Somerset, PA [*AM radio station call letters*]
WVSC .... West Virginia State College
W-V(S) (CEC) ... Women's Reserve, Civil Engineering Corps Duties [*USNR commissioned officer designation*]
WVSC-FM ... Somerset, PA [*FM radio station call letters*]
WvScU .... Union Carbide Corp., South Charleston, WV [*Library symbol*] [*Library of Congress*] (LCLS)
W-V(S) (DC) ... Women's Reserve, Dental Corps Duties [*USNR commissioned officer designation*]
WVSG .... Cornwall, NY [*AM radio station call letters*]
WVSH .... Huntington, IN [*FM radio station call letters*]
WvSh .... Shepherdstown Public Library, Shepherdstown, WV [*Library symbol*] [*Library of Congress*] (LCLS)

W-V(S) (H) ... Women's Reserve, Hospital Corps Duties [*USNR commissioned officer designation*]

WvShS .... Shepherd College, Shepherdstown, WV [*Library symbol*] [*Library of Congress*] (LCLS)

WVSM .... Rainsville, AL [*AM radio station call letters*]

W-V(S) (MC) ... Women's Reserve, Medical Corps Duties [*USNR commissioned officer designation*]

WVSP .... Warrenton, NC [*FM radio station call letters*]

WVSR .... Charleston, WV [*FM radio station call letters*]

WVSS .... Menomonie, WI [*FM radio station call letters*]

W-V(S) (SC) ... Women's Reserve, Supply Corps Duties [*USNR commissioned officer designation*]

WVST .... Petersburg, VA [*FM radio station call letters*]

WVSU-FM ... Birmingham, AL [*FM radio station call letters*]

WVSV .... Stevenson, AL [*FM radio station call letters*]

WVT .... Water Vapor Transmission

WVT .... Watervliet Arsenal [*New York*] [*Army*]

WVT .... West Virginia Institute of Technology, Montgomery, WV [*OCLC symbol*] (OCLC)

WVTA .... Windsor, VT [*Television station call letters*]

WVTB .... St. Johnsbury, VT [*Television station call letters*]

WVTC .... Randolph, VT [*FM radio station call letters*]

WVTF .... Roanoke, VA [*FM radio station call letters*]

WVTF .... Western Visayan Task Force [*World War II*]

WVTH .... Goodman, MS [*FM radio station call letters*]

WVTI .... Melbourne, FL [*FM radio station call letters*]

WVTK .... Wavetek Corp. [*NASDAQ symbol*] (NQ)

WVTM-TV ... Birmingham, AL [*Television station call letters*]

WVTN .... Gatlinburg, TN [*FM radio station call letters*]

WVTR .... Water Vapor Transmission Rate

WVTV .... Milwaukee, WI [*Television station call letters*]

wvu .... West Virginia [*MARC country of publication code*] [*Library of Congress*] (LCCP)

WVU .... West Virginia University

WVU .... West Virginia University Library, Morgantown, WV [*OCLC symbol*] (OCLC)

WvU .... West Virginia University, Morgantown, WV [*Library symbol*] [*Library of Congress*] (LCLS)

WvU-AE ..... West Virginia University, Agricultural Engineering Library, Morgantown, WV [*Library symbol*] [*Library of Congress*] (LCLS)

WVUA-FM ... Tuscaloosa, AL [*FM radio station call letters*]

WVUB .... Vincennes, IN [*FM radio station call letters*]

WVUBPL .... West Virginia University. Bulletin. Philological Studies [*A publication*]

WVUD-FM ... Kettering, OH [*FM radio station call letters*]

WVUE .... New Orleans, LA [*Television station call letters*]

WvU-J .... West Virginia University, School of Journalism, Morgantown, WV [*Library symbol*] [*Library of Congress*] (LCLS)

WvU-L .... West Virginia University, College of Law, Morgantown, WV [*Library symbol*] [*Library of Congress*] (LCLS)

WVUM .... Coral Gables, FL [*FM radio station call letters*]

WvU-M .... West Virginia University, Medical Center, Morgantown, WV [*Library symbol*] [*Library of Congress*] (LCLS)

WvU-Mu ..... West Virginia University, Music Library, Morgantown, WV [*Library symbol*] [*Library of Congress*] (LCLS)

WvU-P .... West Virginia University, Physical Sciences Library, Morgantown, WV [*Library symbol*] [*Library of Congress*] (LCLS)

WVUPP .... West Virginia University. Philological Papers [*A publication*]

WVUR-FM ... Valparaiso, IN [*FM radio station call letters*]

WVUT .... Vincennes, IN [*Television station call letters*]

WVUV .... Leone, AS [*AM radio station call letters*]

WVUV-FM ... Leone, AS [*FM radio station call letters*]

WVUW .... Pittsfield, MA [*Television station call letters*]

WVV .... Whole Virus Vaccine [*Immunology*]

WVVA-TV ... Bluefield, WV [*Television station call letters*]

WVVS .... Valdosta, GA [*FM radio station call letters*]

WVVV .... Blacksburg, VA [*FM radio station call letters*]

WVVW .... St. Marys, WV [*AM radio station call letters*]

WVVX .... Highland Park, IL [*FM radio station call letters*]

WvW .... Ohio County Public Library, Wheeling, WV [*Library symbol*] [*Library of Congress*] (LCLS)

WvWaB ...... Borg-Warner Corp., Borg-Warner Chemicals Technical Center, Washington, WV [*Library symbol*] [*Library of Congress*] (LCLS)

WVWC .... Buckhannon, WV [*FM radio station call letters*]

WVWC .... West Virginia Wesleyan College

WvWC .... Wheeling College, Wheeling, WV [*Library symbol*] [*Library of Congress*] (LCLS)

WvWelW ..... West Liberty State College, West Liberty, WV [*Library symbol*] [*Library of Congress*] (LCLS)

WvWEPA .... United States Environmental Protection Agency, Wheeling Field Office, Wheeling, WV [*Library symbol*] [*Library of Congress*] (LCLS)

WvWH .... Wheeling Hospital, Medical Library, Wheeling, WV [*Library symbol*] [*Library of Congress*] (LCLS)

WVWI .... Charlotte Amalie, VI [*AM radio station call letters*]

WvWO .... Oglebay Institute, Wheeling, WV [*Library symbol*] [*Library of Congress*] (LCLS)

WVWV .... Huntington, WV [*FM radio station call letters*]

WVXU-FM ... Cincinnati, OH [*FM radio station call letters*]

WVYC .... York, PA [*FM radio station call letters*]

WW .... Australian Women's Weekly [*A publication*]

W & W .... De Witt and Weeresinghe's Appeal Court Reports [*Ceylon*] (DLA)

WW .... Journal of Waterway, Port, Coastal, and Ocean Engineering [*A publication*]

W & W .... Wahlstrom & Widstrand [*Publisher*] [*Sweden*]

WW .... Walking Wounded (ADA)

WW .... Wall-to-Wall [*Carpeting*] [*Classified advertising*]

WW .... Wardroom Window [*Aerospace*] (KSC)

WW .... Warehouse Warrant

WW .... Warrant Writer [*Navy*] [*British*]

WW .... Waste Watch [*An association*] (EA)

WW .... Water Waste (NASA)

WW .... Water-White

WW .... Waterside Workers (ADA)

WW .... Waterwall (MSA)

WW .... Waterworks

WW .... Weather Wing (MCD)

WW .... Weather Working

WW .... Weight Watchers [*An association*]

W/W .... Weight/Weight

WW .... Well Water [*Nuclear energy*] (NRCH)

WW .... Westwater Industries Ltd. [*Toronto Stock Exchange symbol*]

W/W .... Wheel Well (MCD)

W & W .... White and Wilson's [*or Willson's*] Civil Cases, Texas Court of Appeals (DLA)

WW .... White Wyandotte [*Poultry*]

WW .... Wholesale Wine [*License*]

WW .... Who's Who [*A publication*]

WW .... Widow [*Genealogy*]

W/W .... Wild Weasel [*Aerospace*]

WW .... Wilderness Watch [*An association*] (EA)

W & W .... Williams & Wilkins [*Publishing company*]

WW .... Winchester & Western Railroad Co. [*AAR code*]

W/W .... Winding to Winding (MSA)

WW .... Winged Warriors [*Formerly, NSC*] (EA)

WW .... Wire Way [*Technical drawings*]

WW .... Wire-Wound

WW .... Wirkendes Wort [*A publication*]

W u W .... Wirtschaft und Wettbewerb [*German*] [*A publication*]

WW .... Wirtschaftswoche-Databank [*Economic Week Data Bank*] [*Society for Public Economics*] [*Dusseldorf, West Germany*] (EISS)

WW .... Wissenschaft und Weisheit [*A publication*]

WW .... With Warrants [*Stock exchange term*]

WW .... Woodwind [*Instrument*] [*Music*]

WW .... Working Woman [*A publication*]

WW .... Working Women, National Association of Officeworkers (EA)

WW .... World War

WW .... Worldwide

Ww .... Wroclaw [*A publication*]

WW .... Wyatt and Webb's Reports [*1861-63*] [*Victoria, Australia*] (DLA)

W & W .... Wyatt and Webb's Victorian Reports [*A publication*]

WW .... Zas Airlines of Egypt [*Egypt*] [*ICAO designator*] (FAAC)

1WW .... Weather Wing (1st) [*California*] [*Air Force*]

2WW .... Weather Wing (2nd) [*New York*] [*Air Force*]

3WW .... Weather Wing (3rd) [*Nebraska*] [*Air Force*]

4WW .... Weather Wing (4th) [*Colorado*] [*Air Force*]

6WW .... Weather Wing (6th) [*Washington, DC*] [*Air Force*]

7WW .... Weather Wing (7th) [*Illinois*] [*Air Force*]

WWA .... Wallcovering Wholesalers Association [*Later, WDA*] (EA)

WWa .... Wauwatosa Public Library, Wauwatosa, WI [*Library symbol*] [*Library of Congress*] (LCLS)

WWA .... Welsh Water Authority

WWA .... Western Writers of America (EA)

WWA .... With the Will Annexed

WWA .... Woolens and Worsteds of America [*Defunct*]

WWA .... World Warning Agency (MCD)

WWA .... World Wide Airlines, Inc.

WWAB .... Lakeland, FL [*AM radio station call letters*]

W & W & A'B ... Wyatt, Webb, and A'Beckett's Reports [*A publication*]

WW & A'B ... Wyatt, Webb, and A'Beckett's Victorian Reports [*A publication*]

WWABCC ... World Wide Avon Bottle Collectors Club (EA)

WW & A'B (E) ... Wyatt, Webb, and A'Beckett's Reports (Equity) [*A publication*]

WW & A'B Eq ... Wyatt, Webb, and A'Beckett's Equity Reports [*1864-69*] [*Victoria, Australia*] (DLA)

W & W & A'B (Eq) ... Wyatt, Webb, and A'Beckett's Reports (Equity) [*A publication*]

WW & A'B (IE & M) ... Wyatt, Webb, and A'Beckett's Reports (Insolvency, Ecclesiastical, and Matrimonial) [*A publication*]

WW & A'B (M) ... Wyatt, Webb, and A'Beckett's Reports (Mining) [*A publication*]

W & W & A'B (Min) ... Wyatt, Webb, and A'Beckett's Reports (Mining) [*A publication*]

WW & A'B Min ... Wyatt, Webb, and A'Beckett's Reports, Mining [*1864-69*] [*Victoria, Australia*] (DLA)
WWABNCP ... Worldwide Airborne Command Post [*Air Force*] (AFM)
WWAC........ Western World Avon Club (EA)
WWAC-TV ... Atlantic City, NJ [*Television station call letters*]
WWal.......... Walworth Memorial Library, Walworth, WI [*Library symbol*] [*Library of Congress*] (LCLS)
WWalPS ..... Walworth Public Schools, Walworth, WI [*Library symbol*] [*Library of Congress*] (LCLS)
WWalSD..... North Walworth School District Number Five, Walworth, WI [*Library symbol*] [*Library of Congress*] (LCLS)
WWAM .... Savannah, GA [*AM radio station call letters*]
WWaMP ..... Milwaukee Psychiatric Hospital, Wauwatosa, WI [*Library symbol*] [*Library of Congress*] (LCLS)
WWAP........ Worldwide Asset Position [*Military*] (AABC)
WWAS........ Williamsport, PA [*AM radio station call letters*]
WWAS........ World-Wide Academy of Scholars [*Defunct*] (EA)
WWaSC...... Saint Camillus Hospital, Wauwatosa, WI [*Library symbol*] [*Library of Congress*] (LCLS)
WWAT....... Chillicothe, OH [*Television station call letters*]
WWat.......... Watertown Free Public Library, Watertown, WI [*Library symbol*] [*Library of Congress*] (LCLS)
WWatf .... Waterford Public Library, Waterford, WI [*Library symbol*] [*Library of Congress*] (LCLS)
WWatfH...... Holy Redeemer College, Waterford, WI [*Library symbol*] [*Library of Congress*] (LCLS)
WWatN....... Northwestern College, Watertown, WI [*Library symbol*] [*Library of Congress*] (LCLS)
WWau .... Waukesha Public Library, Waukesha, WI [*Library symbol*] [*Library of Congress*] (LCLS)
WWauC ...... Carroll College, Waukesha, WI [*Library symbol*] [*Library of Congress*] (LCLS)
WWauH ...... Waukesha Memorial Hospital, Waukesha, WI [*Library symbol*] [*Library of Congress*] (LCLS)
WWauHi ..... Waukesha County Historical Society, Waukesha, WI [*Library symbol*] [*Library of Congress*] (LCLS)
WWaul........ Waukesha County Institution, Waukesha, WI [*Library symbol*] [*Library of Congress*] (LCLS)
WWaupa..... Waupaca Free Public Library, Waupaca, WI [*Library symbol*] [*Library of Congress*] (LCLS)
WWauU ...... University of Wisconsin Center-Waukesha County, Waukesha, WI [*Library symbol*] [*Library of Congress*] (LCLS)
WWAV .... Santa Rosa Beach, FL [*FM radio station call letters*]
WWAY .... Wilmington, NC [*Television station call letters*]
W Ways ...... Word Ways [*A publication*]
WWAZ .... Providence, RI [*AM radio station call letters*]
WWB .... Waterways Freight Bureau, Washington DC [*STAC*]
WWb........... West Bend Public Library, West Bend, WI [*Library symbol*] [*Library of Congress*] (LCLS)
WWB Writers War Board
WWBA........ Walt Whitman Birthplace Association (EA)
WWBA........ Western Wooden Box Association [*Turlock, CA*] (EA)
WWBA-FM ... St. Petersburg, FL [*FM radio station call letters*]
WWBB .... Madison, WV [*AM radio station call letters*]
WWBC........ Cocoa, FL [*AM radio station call letters*]
WWBD........ Bamberg-Denmark, SC [*AM radio station call letters*]
WWBF .... Bartow, FL [*AM radio station call letters*]
WWBF .... Woodrow Wilson Birthplace Foundation (EA)
WWBPU...... World Wide Baraca-Philathea Union (EA)
WWBR .... Harriman, TN [*AM radio station call letters*]
WWBT .... Richmond, VA [*Television station call letters*]
WWbU .... University of Wisconsin Center-Washington County, West Bend, WI [*Library symbol*] [*Library of Congress*] (LCLS)
WWBZ .... Vineland, NJ [*AM radio station call letters*]
WWC .... Citizen's Library, Washington, PA [*OCLC symbol*] (OCLC)
WWC .... Walla Walla College [*Washington*]
WWC .... Warren Wilson College [*North Carolina*]
WWC .... Wavy Walled Cylinder
WWC .... Who's Who in Consulting [*A publication*]
WWC .... William Woods College [*Missouri*]
WWC .... World's Wristwrestling Championship (EA)
WWC .... Woven Wire Cloth
WWCA........ Gary, IN [*AM radio station call letters*]
WWCA........ Women's Welsh Clubs of America (EA)
WWCB........ Corry, PA [*AM radio station call letters*]
WW & CB ... Weekly Weather and Crop Bulletin [*A publication*]
WWCC........ Western Wisconsin Communications Cooperative [*Independence, WI*] [*Telecommunications*] (TSSD)
W & WCC ... White and Wilson's [*or Willson's*] Civil Cases, Texas Court of Appeals (DLA)
WWCCIS.... World-Wide Command and Control Information System (MCD)
WWCH........ Clarion, PA [*AM radio station call letters*]
W & W Civ Cases Court of Appeals ... White and Wilson's [*or Willson's*] Civil Cases, Texas Court of Appeals (DLA)
WWCJ .... Jackson, MS [*FM radio station call letters*]
WWCK........ Flint, MI [*AM radio station call letters*]
WWCK-FM ... Flint, MI [*FM radio station call letters*]
WWCN........ Albany, NY [*AM radio station call letters*]
WWCO .... Waterbury, CT [*AM radio station call letters*]

W & W Con Cases ... White and Wilson's [*or Willson's*] Civil Cases, Texas Court of Appeals (DLA)
W & W Con Rep ... White and Wilson's [*or Willson's*] Civil Cases, Texas Court of Appeals (DLA)
WWCP........ Walking Wounded Collecting Post [*Military*]
WWCP-TV ... Johnstown, PA [*Television station call letters*]
WWCR........ Brentwood, TN [*AM radio station call letters*]
WWCT .... Peoria, IL [*FM radio station call letters*]
WWCTU ...... World's Woman's Christian Temperance Union (EA-IO)
WWCU........ Cullowhee, NC [*FM radio station call letters*]
WWD .... Cape May [*New Jersey*] [*Airport symbol*] (OAG)
WWd........... Kilbourn Public Library, Wisconsin Dells, WI [*Library symbol*] [*Library of Congress*] (LCLS)
WWD .... Weather Working Days [*Construction*]
WWD .... Weird World [*A publication*]
WWD .... Wildwood, NJ [*Location identifier*] [*FAA*] (FAAL)
WW & D ...... Willmore, Wollaston, and Davison's English Queen's Bench Reports [*1837*] (DLA)
WWD .... Windward (KSC)
WWD .... Women's Wear Daily [*A publication*]
WWDB .... Philadelphia, PA [*FM radio station call letters*]
WWDC....... Washington, DC [*AM radio station call letters*]
WWDCFC... World-Wide Dave Clark Fan Club [*Schelluinen, Netherlands*] (EA-IO)
WWDC-FM ... Washington, DC [*FM radio station call letters*]
WWDE-FM ... Hampton, VA [*FM radio station call letters*]
WWdepSN... Saint Norbert College, West De Pere, WI [*Library symbol*] [*Library of Congress*] (LCLS)
WWDJ .... Hackensack, NJ [*AM radio station call letters*]
WWDL-FM ... Scranton, PA [*FM radio station call letters*]
WWDM-FM ... Sumter, SC [*FM radio station call letters*]
WWDMS...... Worldwide Standard Data Management System (MCD)
WWDS........ Muncie, IN [*FM radio station call letters*]
WWDSA ..... Worldwide Digital System Architecture
WWDSHEX ... Weather Working Days Sundays and Holidays Excluded
WWE .... Wide World of Entertainment [*TV program*]
WWe.......... Wissenschaft und Weisheit [*A publication*]
WWE .... Worldwide Energy Corp. [*Toronto Stock Exchange symbol*]
W & W (E)... Wyatt and Webb's Reports (Equity) [*A publication*]
WWea......... West Allis Public Library, West Allis, WI [*Library symbol*] [*Library of Congress*] (LCLS)
WWeaJ .... Janlen Enterprises, West Allis, WI [*Library symbol*] [*Library of Congress*] (LCLS)
WWeaM....... West Allis Memorial Hospital, West Allis, WI [*Library symbol*] [*Library of Congress*] (LCLS)
WWEB .... Wallingford, CT [*FM radio station call letters*]
WWEE .... Collierville, TN [*AM radio station call letters*]
WWEF .... Working Women Education Fund (EA)
WWEL .... London, KY [*FM radio station call letters*]
WWEMA..... Water and Wastewater Equipment Manufacturers Association [*Washington, DC*] (EA)
W & W (Eq)... Wyatt and Webb's Reports (Equity) [*A publication*]
WWES .... Hot Springs, VA [*AM radio station call letters*]
WWEV .... Cumming, GA [*FM radio station call letters*]
WWEZ .... Cincinnati, OH [*FM radio station call letters*]
WWF .... Washington Workshops Foundation (EA)
WWF .... Waterside Workers' Federation of Australia
WWF .... Wire Wrap Fixture
WWF .... Wonder Woman Foundation (EA)
WWF .... World Wildlife Fund [*Gland, Switzerland*]
WWF .... WorldWide Fund for Nature (EA)
WWFC .... Worldwide Fair Play for Frogs Committee
WWFE .... Miami, FL [*AM radio station call letters*]
WWFF .... Marathon, FL [*FM radio station call letters*]
WWFI.......... World Wildlife Fund International (EA-IO)
WWFL........ Clermont, FL [*AM radio station call letters*]
WWFM........ Trenton, NH [*FM radio station call letters*]
WWFR........ Okeechobee, FL [*FM radio station call letters*]
WWFS .... West Wales Field Society [*British*]
WWF-US .... World Wildlife Fund - United States (EA)
WWFX .... Belfast, ME [*FM radio station call letters*]
WWG .... HSIA [*Halogenated Solvent Industry Alliance*] Water Work Group [*Defunct*] (EA)
WWg........... Weather Wing [*Air Force*] (AFM)
WWG .... Wiederwerbgesetz (BJA)
WWGC .... Carrollton, GA [*FM radio station call letters*]
WWGM .... Nashville, TN [*AM radio station call letters*]
WWGN .... Washington, NC [*AM radio station call letters*]
WWGO .... St. Andrews, SC [*AM radio station call letters*]
WWGP .... Sanford, NC [*AM radio station call letters*]
WWGR........ La Follette, TN [*AM radio station call letters*]
WWGS........ Tifton, GA [*AM radio station call letters*]
WWGT .... Westbrook, ME [*AM radio station call letters*]
WWGT-FM ... Portland, ME [*FM radio station call letters*]
WWH .... W. W. Harrington's Reports [*31-39 Delaware*] (DLA)
WW & H ...... Willmore, Wollaston, and Hodges' English Queen's Bench Reports [*1838-39*] (DLA)
W/WH........ With/Warhead [*Nuclear*]
WWH .... Women Working Home [*A publication*]
WW Harr.... W. W. Harrington's Reports [*31-39 Delaware*] (DLA)
WW Harr Del ... W. W. Harrington's Reports [*31-39 Delaware*] (DLA)

WWHB........ Hampton Bays, NY [*FM radio station call letters*]
WWHE........ Woman Who Has Everything
WW & H (Eng) ... Willmore, Wollaston, and Hodges' English Queen's Bench Reports [*1838-39*] (DLA)
WWHI........ Muncie, IN [*FM radio station call letters*]
WWhiwSD ... Whitewater Unified School District, Joint Number One, Whitewater, WI [*Library symbol*] [*Library of Congress*] (LCLS)
WWhiwU .... University of Wisconsin-Whitewater, Whitewater, WI [*Library symbol*] [*Library of Congress*] (LCLS)
WWHL .... Waterwheel
WWHR........ Pompano Beach, FL [*AM radio station call letters*]
WWHS .... Western World Haiku Society (EA)
WWHS-FM ... Hampden-Sydney, VA [*FM radio station call letters*]
WWHY .... Huntington, WV [*AM radio station call letters*]
WWI............ Weight Watchers International [*Commercial firm*] [*Manhasset, NY*] (EA)
WWI............ Whirlwind I
WWI............ Who's Who in Israel [*A publication*]
WWI............ Working Women's Institute [*Formerly, WWUI*] (EA)
WWI............ World War I
WWI AERO ... World War I Aeroplanes [*An association*] (EA)
WWIB .... Ladysmith, WI [*FM radio station call letters*]
WW & IB ..... Western Weighing and Inspection Bureau
WWIC .... Scottsboro, AL [*AM radio station call letters*]
WWiC .... Winnebago County Hospital, Winnebago, WI [*Library symbol*] [*Library of Congress*] (LCLS)
WWICS...... Woodrow Wilson International Center for Scholars (EA)
W & W (IE & M) ... Wyatt and Webb's Reports (Insolvency, Ecclesiastical, and Matrimonial) [*A publication*]
WWIH .... High Point, NC [*AM radio station call letters*]
WWII........... Shiremanstown, PA [*AM radio station call letters*]
WWII........... World War II
WWIIHSLB ... World War II Honorable Service Lapel Button (AFM)
WWIII.......... World War III
WWIIVM ..... World War II Victory Medal
WWiI........... Barrett Memorial Library, Williams Bay, WI [*Library symbol*] [*Library of Congress*] (LCLS)
WWIL.......... Wilmington, NC [*AM radio station call letters*]
WWIMS ...... Worldwide Integrated Management of Subsistence [*Military*] (NVT)
WWIN .... Baltimore, MD [*AM radio station call letters*]
WWIN .... Western Waste Industries [*NASDAQ symbol*] (NQ)
WWIN-FM ... Glen Burnie, MD [*FM radio station call letters*]
WWIO .... Worldwide Inventory Objective (AABC)
WWiP .... Park View Health Center, Winnebago, WI [*Library symbol*] [*Library of Congress*] (LCLS)
WWIS .... Black River Falls, WI [*AM radio station call letters*]
WWiS .... Winnebago State Hospital, Winnebago, WI [*Library symbol*] [*Library of Congress*] (LCLS)
WWIS .... Worldwide Information Services
WWIT .... Canton, NC [*AM radio station call letters*]
WWIT .... Who's Who in the Theatre [*A publication*]
WWITC........ Worldwide Improved Technical Control (MCD)
WWIVM ..... World War I Victory Medal
WWIW .... New Orleans, LA [*AM radio station call letters*]
WWIZ .... Mercer, PA [*FM radio station call letters*]
WWJ........... Detroit, MI [*AM radio station call letters*]
WWJ........... Who's Who in Japan [*A publication*]
WWJB .... Brooksville, FL [*AM radio station call letters*]
WWJC .... Duluth, MN [*AM radio station call letters*]
WWJCC...... Worldwide Joint Coordinator Center [*NATO*] (NATG)
WWJD .... Savannah, GA [*AM radio station call letters*]
WWJM .... New Lexington, OH [*FM radio station call letters*]
WWJO .... St. Cloud, MN [*FM radio station call letters*]
WWJQ .... Holland, MI [*AM radio station call letters*]
WWJR......... Sheboygan, WI [*FM radio station call letters*]
WWJY......... Crown Point, IN [*FM radio station call letters*]
WWJZ........ Mount Holly, NJ [*AM radio station call letters*]
WWK .... Wewak [*Papua New Guinea*] [*Airport symbol*] (OAG)
WWKA........ Orlando, FL [*FM radio station call letters*]
WWKB........ Buffalo, NY [*AM radio station call letters*]
WWKC........ White Wolf-Kern Canyon [*Geological fault*]
WWKF .... Fulton, KY [*FM radio station call letters*]
WWKI .... Kokomo, IN [*FM radio station call letters*]
WWKI-TV .. Kokomo, IN [*Television station call letters*]
WWKM .... Harrison, MI [*AM radio station call letters*]
WWKS........ Beaver Falls, PA [*FM radio station call letters*]
WWKT .... Kingstree, SC [*FM radio station call letters*]
WWKX........ Gallatin, TN [*FM radio station call letters*]
WWKZ........ New Albany, MS [*FM radio station call letters*]
WWL........... New Orleans, LA [*AM radio station call letters*]
W & W (L)... Wyatt and Webb's Reports (Law) [*A publication*]
WWLB .... Bushnell, FL [*AM radio station call letters*]
WWLD .... Pine Castle-Sky Lake, FL [*AM radio station call letters*]
WWLF-TV .. Hazleton, PA [*Television station call letters*]
WWLI .... Providence, RI [*FM radio station call letters*]
WWLIS .... Woodmen of the World Life Insurance Society (EA)
WWLK .... Eddyville, KY [*AM radio station call letters*]
WWLODS ... Wire and Wire-Like Object Detection System [*Helicopter*] (MCD)

WWLP .... Springfield, MA [*Television station call letters*]
WWLR .... Lyndonville, VT [*FM radio station call letters*]
WWLS .... Norman, OK [*AM radio station call letters*]
WWLT .... Bamberg, SC [*FM radio station call letters*]
WWLTM ..... Women Who Love Too Much [*Title of book by Robin Norwood*]
WWL-TV ..... New Orleans, LA [*Television station call letters*]
WWLV .... Daytona Beach, FL [*FM radio station call letters*]
WWLX .... Lexington, AL [*AM radio station call letters*]
WWM......... Weekly Women's Magazine [*Manila*] [*A publication*]
WWM......... Weizsaecker-Williams Method [*Physics*]
WWM......... Welded Wire Matrix
WWM......... Wings West, Inc. [*Santa Monica, CA*] [*FAA designator*] (FAAC)
WWM......... Wire Wrap Machine
WWM......... World-Wide Missions [*Pasadena, CA*] (EA)
WWMCCS ... Worldwide Military Command and Control System [*Pronounced "wimex"*] [*DoD*]
WWMC-FM ... Mifflinburg, PA [*FM radio station call letters*]
WWMD ...... Hagerstown, MD [*FM radio station call letters*]
WWMG ...... New Bern, NC [*AM radio station call letters*]
WWMH ...... Minocqua, WI [*FM radio station call letters*]
WWMJ ...... Ellsworth, ME [*FM radio station call letters*]
WWML ...... Portage, PA [*AM radio station call letters*]
WWML ...... Wood, Wire, and Metal Lathers' International Union [*Later, UBC*]
WWMMP .... Western Wood Moulding and Millwork Producers [*Later, WMMPA*] (EA)
WWMO ...... Reidsville, NC [*FM radio station call letters*]
WWMP ...... Western Wood Moulding Producers [*Later, WMMPA*] (EA)
WWMR ...... Rumford, ME [*FM radio station call letters*]
WWMS ...... Oxford, MS [*FM radio station call letters*]
WWMS ...... Water and Waste Management Subsystem [*NASA*] (KSC)
WWMT ...... Kalamazoo, MI [*Television station call letters*]
WWMX ...... Baltimore, MD [*FM radio station call letters*]
WWN........ Walt Whitman Newsletter [*A publication*]
WWN........ Washington Women's Network (EA)
WWN........ With Winch
WWNC....... Asheville, NC [*AM radio station call letters*]
WWNFF...... Woodrow Wilson National Fellowship Foundation (EA)
WWNH ...... Rochester, NH [*AM radio station call letters*]
WWNK ...... Cincinnati, OH [*AM radio station call letters*]
WWNK-FM ... Cincinnati, OH [*FM radio station call letters*]
WWNO ...... New Orleans, LA [*FM radio station call letters*]
WWNR ...... Beckley, WV [*AM radio station call letters*]
WWNS....... Statesboro, GA [*AM radio station call letters*]
WWNS....... World Wide News Service (BJA)
WWNSS ... Worldwide Network of Standard Seismograph [*Stations*]
WWNT ...... Dothan, AL [*AM radio station call letters*]
WWNW ...... New Wilmington, PA [*FM radio station call letters*]
WWNY-TV ... Carthage, NY [*Television station call letters*]
WW/O .... Widow Of [*Genealogy*]
WWO .... Wing Warrant Officer [*RAF*] [*British*]
WWOC ...... Avalon, NJ [*FM radio station call letters*]
WWOD ...... Lynchburg, VA [*AM radio station call letters*]
WWOJ ...... Avon Park, FL [*FM radio station call letters*]
WWOK ...... Columbia, NC [*FM radio station call letters*]
WWON ...... Woonsocket, RI [*AM radio station call letters*]
WWOO ...... Berryville, VA [*FM radio station call letters*]
WWooH ...... Howard Young Medical Center, Woodruff, WI [*Library symbol*] [*Library of Congress*] (LCLS)
W Work (Lond) ... World's Work (London) [*A publication*]
WWoVA...... United States Veterans Administration Hospital, Wood, WI [*Library symbol*] [*Library of Congress*] (LCLS)
WWOW ...... Conneaut, OH [*AM radio station call letters*]
WWOZ ...... New Orleans, LA [*FM radio station call letters*]
WWP .... Washington Water Power Co. [*NYSE symbol*]
WWP .... Water Wall (Peripheral Jet) (AAG)
WWP .... Weather Wing Pamphlet [*Air Force*] (MCD)
WWP .... Wire Wrap Panels (MCD)
WWP .... Working Water Pressure
WWP .... World Weather Program [*National Science Foundation*]
WWPA....... Western Wood Products Association [*Formed by a merger of WCLA and WPA*] [*Portland, OR*] (EA)
WWPA....... Williamsport, PA [*AM radio station call letters*]
WWPA....... Woven Wire Products Association [*Chicago, IL*] (EA)
WWPB....... Hagerstown, MD [*Television station call letters*]
WWpC .... Central State Hospital, Waupun, WI [*Library symbol*] [*Library of Congress*] (LCLS)
WWPC-TV ... Altoona, PA [*Television station call letters*]
WWPG....... Widows' War Pensions and Gratuities [*British*]
WWPH....... Princeton Junction, NJ [*FM radio station call letters*]
WWPLS..... World Wide Pet Lovers Society (EA)
WWPMU..... World-Wide Prayer and Missionary Union (EA)
W/WPR ..... Windshield Wiper [*Automotive engineering*]
WWPSA..... Western World Pet Supply Association [*South Pasadena, CA*] (EA)
WWPT ...... Westport, CT [*FM radio station call letters*]
WWPV-FM ... Colchester, VT [*FM radio station call letters*]
WWPZ ...... Petoskey, MI [*AM radio station call letters*]
WWQC ...... Quincy, IL [*FM radio station call letters*]
WWQM-FM ... Middleton, WI [*FM radio station call letters*]
WWQQ-FM ... Wilmington, NC [*FM radio station call letters*]

WWr .... McMillan Memorial Library, Wisconsin Rapids, WI [*Library symbol*] [*Library of Congress*] (LCLS)

WWR .... Walt Whitman Review [*A publication*]

WWR .... Washington Western [*AAR code*]

WWR .... Western Warner Oils [*Vancouver Stock Exchange symbol*]

WWR .... Western Weekly Reports [*Canada*] (DLA)

WWR .... Widower [*Genealogy*]

WWR .... Wire-Wound Resistor

WWR .... Wisconsin Rapids, McMillan Library, Wisconsin Rapids, WI [*OCLC symbol*] (OCLC)

WWR .... Woodill Wildfire Registry (EA)

WWR .... Woodward, OK [*Location identifier*] [*FAA*] (FAAL)

WWRC .... Washington, DC [*AM radio station call letters*]

WWRC .... Wyoming Water Research Center [*University of Wyoming*] [*Research center*] (RCD)

WWRD .... Wilson, NC [*Television station call letters*]

WWREC ..... Western Washington Research and Extension Center [*Washington State University*] [*Research center*] (RCD)

WWRF .... Who's Who Resource File [*Minority Business Development Agency*] [*Database*]

WWRJ .... Hollywood, SC [*AM radio station call letters*]

WWRK .... Elberton, GA [*FM radio station call letters*]

WWRL .... New York, NY [*AM radio station call letters*]

WWRM ...... Pinconning, MI [*FM radio station call letters*]

WWR (NS) ... Western Weekly Reports, New Series [*Canada*] (DLA)

WWRS .... Mayville, WI [*AM radio station call letters*]

WWRS .... Wash-Water Recovery System [*in a spacecraft*] [*NASA*]

WWRT .... Algood, TN [*AM radio station call letters*]

WWRW ...... Wisconsin Rapids, WI [*FM radio station call letters*]

WWS .... Water Wall (Side Skegs) (AAG)

WWS .... Water and Waste Subsystem [*Aerospace*] (MCD)

WWs .... Wausau Public Library, Wausau, WI [*Library symbol*] [*Library of Congress*] (LCLS)

WW(S) .... Well Water (System) (NRCH)

WWS .... Western Writers Series [*A publication*]

WWS .... Wind and Watermill Section [*of the Society for the Protection of Ancient Buildings*] (EA)

WWS .... Women's Welfare Service [*Defunct*] (EA)

WWS .... World Weather System

WWS .... World Wide Minerals [*Vancouver Stock Exchange symbol*]

WWSA .... Savannah, GA [*AM radio station call letters*]

WWSA .... Walt Whitman Society of America [*Defunct*] (EA)

WWSB .... Sarasota, FL [*Television station call letters*]

WWSC .... Glens Falls, NY [*AM radio station call letters*]

WWSD .... Quincy, FL [*AM radio station call letters*]

WWSD .... Women's War Savings Division

WWSE .... Jamestown, NY [*FM radio station call letters*]

WWSF .... World-Wide Stroke Foundation [*World Health Organization*] [*Palm Desert, CA*] (EA)

WWSH .... Hazleton, PA [*FM radio station call letters*]

WWSL .... Philadelphia, MS [*FM radio station call letters*]

WWSM ...... Bay Minette, AL [*FM radio station call letters*]

WWsMC .... Marathon Health Care Center, Wausau, WI [*Library symbol*] [*Library of Congress*] (LCLS)

WWSN....... Dayton, OH [*FM radio station call letters*]

WWSN....... Worldwide Seismology Net [*National Bureau of Standards*]

WWSP .... Stevens Point, WI [*FM radio station call letters*]

WWSP .... Worldwide Surveillance Program [*Military*] (NG)

WWSR .... St. Albans, VT [*AM radio station call letters*]

WWSRA .... Western Winter Sports Representatives Association [*Seattle, WA*] (EA)

WWSS .... Lynn Haven, FL [*AM radio station call letters*]

WWSSB ..... World-Wide Software Support Branch (MCD)

WWSSN .... World-Wide Standard Seismograph Network [*Earthquake detection*]

WWSSN ..... Worldwide Standardized Seismograph Network

WWST .... Wooster, OH [*AM radio station call letters*]

WWSU .... Dayton, OH [*FM radio station call letters*]

WWSU .... World Water Ski Union [*See also UMSN*] (EA-IO)

WWSVA .... Worldwide Secure Voice Architecture (MCD)

WWSVCS... World-Wide Secure Voice Communications System (MCD)

WWSVCS... World-Wide Secure Voice Conference System (MCD)

WWsW ...... Wausau Hospitals, Inc., Wausau, WI [*Library symbol*] [*Library of Congress*] (LCLS)

WWSW-FM ... Pittsburgh, PA [*FM radio station call letters*]

WWsWV ..... Wisconsin Valley Library Service, Wausau, WI [*Library symbol*] [*Library of Congress*] (LCLS)

WWT........... Newtok [*Alaska*] [*Airport symbol*] (OAG)

WWT........... Newtok, AK [*Location identifier*] [*FAA*] (FAAL)

WWTCA ..... World War Tank Corps Association (EA)

WWTCIP.... Worldwide Technical Control Improvement Program (MCD)

WWTG....... Stanwood, MI [*AM radio station call letters*]

WWTL .... Marshfield, WI [*Television station call letters*]

WWTM ...... Gladstone, MI [*FM radio station call letters*]

WWTO-TV ... La Salle, IL [*Television station call letters*]

WWTR-FM ... Bethany Beach, DE [*FM radio station call letters*]

WWTS .... Waste Water Treatment System

WWTT .... Worldwide Tapetalk [*An association*] (EA)

WWTV .... Cadillac, MI [*Television station call letters*]

WWTV .... Western-World TV [*NASDAQ symbol*] (NQ)

WWU .... Western Washington University

WWUF .... Waycross, GA [*FM radio station call letters*]

WWUH .... West Hartford, CT [*FM radio station call letters*]

WWUI .... Working Women's United Institute [*Later, WWI*] (EA)

WWUN-FM ... Clarksdale, MS [*FM radio station call letters*]

WWUP-TV ... Sault Ste. Marie, MI [*Television station call letters*]

WWUS .... Big Pine Key, FL [*FM radio station call letters*]

WWV .... Walla Walla Valley Railway Co. [*AAR code*]

WWV .... Wheeling College, Wheeling, WV [*OCLC symbol*] (OCLC)

WWV .... World Wide Time [*National Bureau of Standards call letters*] (MUGU)

WWV .... World Wide Vermiculture [*An association*] (EA)

WWVA .... Wheeling, WV [*AM radio station call letters*]

WWVH .... World Wide Time Hawaii [*National Bureau of Standards call letters*] (MUGU)

W & W Vict ... Wyatt and Webb's Victorian Reports [*1864-69*] [*Australia*] (DLA)

WWVR .... West Terre Haute, IN [*FM radio station call letters*]

WWVR .... Wire-Wound Variable Resistor

WWVU-FM ... Morgantown, WV [*FM radio station call letters*]

WWW .... Who Was Who [*A publication*]

WWW .... [*The*] Who, What, or Where Game [*Also, 3W's*] [*Television show*]

WWW .... Wolverine World Wide, Inc. [*NYSE symbol*]

WWW .... World Weather Watch [*World Meteorological Organization*] [*Databank*] [*Geneva, Switzerland*] (EISS)

WWW .... Worldwide Warranty [*Canon USA, Inc.*]

WWWA ...... Burnettown, SC [*AM radio station call letters*]

WWWB ...... Jasper, AL [*AM radio station call letters*]

WWWC ...... Wilkesboro, NC [*AM radio station call letters*]

WWWC ...... World without War Council (EA)

WWWCR .... World Wide White and Creme Horse Registry (EA)

WWWD ...... Schenectady, NY [*AM radio station call letters*]

WWWE ...... Cleveland, OH [*AM radio station call letters*]

WWWF ...... Fayette, AL [*AM radio station call letters*]

WWWF ...... Worldwide Wrestling Federation

WWWFC.... [*Kitty*] Wells-[*Johnny*] Wright-[*Bobby*] Wright International Fan Club (EA)

WWWG...... Rochester, NY [*AM radio station call letters*]

WWWH ...... Fredricksburg, VA [*FM radio station call letters*]

WWWI .... Widows of World War I (EA)

WWWJ....... Paoli, IN [*AM radio station call letters*]

WWWJ....... Who's Who in World Jewry [*A publication*] (BJA)

WWWL ...... Amherst, VA [*AM radio station call letters*]

WWWM ...... Cleveland, OH [*FM radio station call letters*]

WWWM ...... Williams [*W. W.*] Co. [*NASDAQ symbol*] (NQ)

WWWN ...... Vienna, GA [*AM radio station call letters*]

WWWO ...... Hartford City, IN [*FM radio station call letters*]

WWWP ...... Franklin, VA [*FM radio station call letters*]

WWWQ ...... Fort Myers, FL [*AM radio station call letters*]

WWWR ...... Russellville, AL [*AM radio station call letters*]

WWWS ...... Saginaw, MI [*FM radio station call letters*]

WWWTTUTWTU ... We Won't Write to Them until They Write to Us [*A servicemen's club*]

WWWU ...... Winchester, VA [*FM radio station call letters*]

WWWV ...... Charlottesville, VA [*FM radio station call letters*]

WWWV ...... Women World War Veterans (EA)

WWWW ...... Detroit, MI [*FM radio station call letters*]

WWWX ...... Albemarle, NC [*AM radio station call letters*]

WWWY ...... Columbus, IN [*FM radio station call letters*]

WWWZ ...... Summerville, SC [*FM radio station call letters*]

WWX .... World Wide Exchange [*Commercial firm*] (EA)

WWXL .... Manchester, KY [*AM radio station call letters*]

WWXL-FM ... Manchester, KY [*FM radio station call letters*]

WWY .... West Wyalong [*Australia*] [*Airport symbol*] (OAG)

WWY .... Wrigley [*Wm.*] Jr. Co. [*NYSE symbol*]

WWYN....... McKenzie, TN [*FM radio station call letters*]

WWYO....... Pineville, WV [*AM radio station call letters*]

WWYZ .... Waterbury, CT [*FM radio station call letters*]

WWZ .... Willow Resources Ltd. [*Vancouver Stock Exchange symbol*]

WWZE .... Central City, PA [*FM radio station call letters*]

WWZQ .... Aberdeen, MS [*AM radio station call letters*]

WWZQ-FM ... Aberdeen, MS [*FM radio station call letters*]

WWZU .... Lock Haven, PA [*FM radio station call letters*]

WWZZ .... Sarasota, FL [*AM radio station call letters*]

WX............. American Eagle Airlines, Inc. [*ICAO designator*] (FAAC)

WX............. Wawatay News Extra. Special Issues [*A publication*]

WX............. Wax

WX............. Weather

WX............. Westinghouse Electric Corp. [*NYSE symbol*] [*Wall Street slang name: "Wex"*]

WX............. Wireless [*Communications*]

WX............. Women's Extra [*Size*]

WXAC .... Reading, PA [*FM radio station call letters*]

WXAG .... Athens, GA [*AM radio station call letters*]

WXAL .... Demopolis, AL [*AM radio station call letters*]

WXAM .... Baton Rouge, LA [*AM radio station call letters*]

WXAN........ Ava, IL [*FM radio station call letters*]

WXAX .... Lexington, SC [*AM radio station call letters*]

WxB........... Wax Bite [*Dentistry*]

WXBA........ Brentwood, NY [*FM radio station call letters*]

WXBK........ Albertville, AL [*AM radio station call letters*]

WXBM-FM ... Milton, FL [*FM radio station call letters*]
WXBQ-FM ... Bristol, VA [*FM radio station call letters*]
WXC .... Westinghouse Canada, Inc. [*Toronto Stock Exchange symbol*]
WXCC .... Williamson, WV [*FM radio station call letters*]
WXCE .... Amery, WI [*AM radio station call letters*]
WXCF .... Clifton Forge, VA [*AM radio station call letters*]
WXCF-FM ... Clifton Forge, VA [*FM radio station call letters*]
WXCI .... Danbury, CT [*FM radio station call letters*]
WXCL .... Peoria, IL [*AM radio station call letters*]
WXCM .... Jackson, MI [*AM radio station call letters*]
WXCO .... Wausau, WI [*AM radio station call letters*]
WXCON...... Pilot Reports by Qualified Weather Personnel on Weather
                   Reconnaissance Flights [*Aviation code*]   (FAAC)
WXCR .... Safety Harbor, FL [*FM radio station call letters*]
WXCV........ Homosassa Springs, FL [*FM radio station call letters*]
WXD .... Meteorological RADAR Station [*ITU designation*]   (CET)
WXD .... Waxed
WXD .... Westrex Development Corp. [*Vancouver Stock Exchange
                   symbol*]
WXDR........ Newark, DE [*FM radio station call letters*]
WXDU........ Durham, NC [*FM radio station call letters*]
WXEE .... Welch, WV [*AM radio station call letters*]
WXEK .... State College, PA [*Television station call letters*]
WXEL .... West Palm Beach, FL [*FM radio station call letters*]
WXET .... Woodstock, IL [*FM radio station call letters*]
WXEW .... Yabucoa, PR [*AM radio station call letters*]
WXEX-TV ... Petersburg, VA [*Television station call letters*]
WXEZ .... Babson Park, FL [*AM radio station call letters*]
WXFL .... Tampa, FL [*Television station call letters*]
WXFM .... Mt. Zion, IL [*FM radio station call letters*]
WXG.......... Warning   (MUGU)
WXGA-TV ... Waycross, GA [*Television station call letters*]
WXGC .... Milledgeville, GA [*FM radio station call letters*]
WXGI .... Richmond, VA [*AM radio station call letters*]
WXGR........ Bay St. Louis, MS [*AM radio station call letters*]
WXGT........ Columbus, OH [*FM radio station call letters*]
WXGZ-TV... Appleton, WI [*Television station call letters*]
WXIA-TV ... Atlanta, GA [*Television station call letters*]
WXIC .... Waverly, OH [*AM radio station call letters*]
WXID .... Mayfield, KY [*FM radio station call letters*]
WXIE .... Oakland, MD [*FM radio station call letters*]
WXII-TV...... Winston-Salem, NC [*Television station call letters*]
WXIN .... Indianapolis, IN [*Television station call letters*]
WXIR .... Plainfield, IN [*FM radio station call letters*]
WXIS .... Erwin, TN [*FM radio station call letters*]
WXIT .... Charleston, WV [*AM radio station call letters*]
WXIV-TV ... Greenville, NC [*Television station call letters*]
WXIX-TV .... Newport, KY [*Television station call letters*]
WXIY .... Bay Springs, MS [*FM radio station call letters*]
WXIZ .... Waverly, OH [*FM radio station call letters*]
WXJY .... Nantucket, MA [*FM radio station call letters*]
WXKC .... Erie, PA [*FM radio station call letters*]
WXKE .... Fort Wayne, IN [*FM radio station call letters*]
WXKG .... Livingston, TN [*FM radio station call letters*]
WXKO .... Fort Valley, GA [*AM radio station call letters*]
WXKQ .... Whitesburg, KY [*FM radio station call letters*]
WXKS .... Medford, MA [*AM radio station call letters*]
WXKS-FM ... Medford, MA [*FM radio station call letters*]
WXKW .... Allentown, PA [*AM radio station call letters*]
WXKX .... Parkersburg, WV [*FM radio station call letters*]
WXKY .... Milan, TN [*AM radio station call letters*]
WXL........... Wix, Inc. [*Toronto Stock Exchange symbol*]
WXLA .... Dimondale, MI [*AM radio station call letters*]
WXLC........ Waukegan, IL [*FM radio station call letters*]
WXLI .... Dublin, GA [*AM radio station call letters*]
WXLK .... Roanoke, VA [*FM radio station call letters*]
WXLL .... Decatur, GA [*AM radio station call letters*]
WXLN .... Louisville, KY [*FM radio station call letters*]
WXLO .... Fitchburg, MA [*FM radio station call letters*]
WXLP .... Moline, IL [*FM radio station call letters*]
WXLR .... State College, PA [*FM radio station call letters*]
WXLT .... McComb, MS [*FM radio station call letters*]
WXLV .... Schnecksville, PA [*FM radio station call letters*]
WXLW .... Indianapolis, IN [*AM radio station call letters*]
WXLX .... Blowing Rock, NC [*AM radio station call letters*]
WXLY .... North Charleston, SC [*FM radio station call letters*]
WXM.......... Worcester Art Museum, Worcester, MA [*OCLC
                   symbol*]   (OCLC)
WXMC .... Parsippany-Troy Hills, NJ [*AM radio station call letters*]
WXMI......... Grand Rapids, MI [*Television station call letters*]
WXOK .... Baton Rouge, LA [*AM radio station call letters*]
WXON-TV ... Detroit, MI [*Television station call letters*]
WXOQ .... Selmer, TN [*AM radio station call letters*]
WXOS........ Plantation Key, FL [*FM radio station call letters*]
WXOW-TV ... La Crosse, WI [*Television station call letters*]
WXOX........ Bay City, MI [*AM radio station call letters*]
WXOZ .... Jacksonville, FL [*AM radio station call letters*]
WxP........... Wax Pattern [*Dentistry*]
WXPL .... Fitchburg, MA [*FM radio station call letters*]
WXPN........ Philadelphia, PA [*FM radio station call letters*]
WXPR........ Rhinelander, WI [*FM radio station call letters*]

WXPX .... West Hazleton, PA [*AM radio station call letters*]
WXQK .... Spring City, TN [*FM radio station call letters*]
WXQR .... Jacksonville, NC [*FM radio station call letters*]
WXR .... Radiosonde Station [*ITU designation*]   (CET)
WXR .... Weather RADAR
WXRA........ North Syracuse, NY [*AM radio station call letters*]
WXRC .... Hickory, NC [*FM radio station call letters*]
WXRECCO ... Weather Reconnaissance Flight [*Navy*]   (NVT)
WXRF .... Guayama, PR [*AM radio station call letters*]
WXRI .... Norfolk, VA [*FM radio station call letters*]
WXRK .... New York, NY [*FM radio station call letters*]
WXRL .... Lancaster, NY [*AM radio station call letters*]
WXRO .... Beaver Dam, WI [*FM radio station call letters*]
WXRQ .... Mount Pleasant, TN [*AM radio station call letters*]
WXRS........ Swainsboro, GA [*AM radio station call letters*]
WXRS-FM ... Swainsboro, GA [*FM radio station call letters*]
WXRT .... Chicago, IL [*FM radio station call letters*]
WXRY .... Ridgeland, SC [*FM radio station call letters*]
WXRZ........ Corinth, MS [*FM radio station call letters*]
WXSS .... Memphis, TN [*AM radio station call letters*]
WXTA .... Rockford, IL [*AM radio station call letters*]
WXTC .... Charleston, SC [*FM radio station call letters*]
WXTN .... Lexington, MS [*AM radio station call letters*]
WXTO .... San Juan, PR [*AM radio station call letters*]
WXTQ .... Athens, OH [*FM radio station call letters*]
WXTR-FM ... La Plata, MD [*FM radio station call letters*]
WXTRN ..... Weak External Reference [*Data processing*]   (BUR)
WXTU .... Philadelphia, PA [*FM radio station call letters*]
WXTV .... Paterson, NJ [*Television station call letters*]
WXTX .... Columbus, GA [*Television station call letters*]
WXTY .... Ticonderoga, NY [*FM radio station call letters*]
WXTZ .... Indianapolis, IN [*FM radio station call letters*]
WXUS .... Lafayette, IN [*FM radio station call letters*]
WXVA........ Charles Town, WV [*AM radio station call letters*]
WXVA-FM ... Charles Town, WV [*FM radio station call letters*]
WXVI .... Montgomery, AL [*AM radio station call letters*]
WXVL .... Crossville, TN [*FM radio station call letters*]
WXVQ .... De Land, FL [*AM radio station call letters*]
WXVS .... Waycross, GA [*FM radio station call letters*]
WXVT .... Greenville, MS [*Television station call letters*]
WXVW .... Jeffersonville, IN [*AM radio station call letters*]
WXVX .... Monroeville, PA [*AM radio station call letters*]
WXWY .... Robertsdale, AL [*AM radio station call letters*]
WXXA-TV ... Albany, NY [*Television station call letters*]
WXXI .... Rochester, NY [*Television station call letters*]
WXXI .... Rochester, NY [*FM radio station call letters*]
WXXI-FM ... Rochester, NY [*FM radio station call letters*]
WXXP .... New Kensington, PA [*FM radio station call letters*]
WXXQ........ Freeport, IL [*FM radio station call letters*]
WXXR .... Cullman, AL [*AM radio station call letters*]
WXXV-TV ... Gulfport, MS [*Television station call letters*]
WXXX .... South Burlington, VT [*FM radio station call letters*]
WXYB .... Cadillac, MI [*FM radio station call letters*]
WXYC .... Chapel Hill, NC [*FM radio station call letters*]
WXYQ .... Stevens Point, WI [*AM radio station call letters*]
WXYT .... Detroit, MI [*AM radio station call letters*]
WXYU .... Lynchburg, VA [*AM radio station call letters*]
WXYV .... Baltimore, MD [*FM radio station call letters*]
WXYX .... Bayamon, PR [*FM radio station call letters*]
WXYZ-TV ... Detroit, MI [*Television station call letters*]
WXZE .... Sylvester, GA [*AM radio station call letters*]
WY............. Oman Aviation Services Co. Ltd. [*Oman*] [*ICAO
                   designator*]   (FAAC)
WY............. Washington Yards [*Navy*]
WY............. Way   (ADA)
WY............. Western Yiddish   (BJA)
WY............. Wey [*Unit of weight*]
WY............. Weyerhaeuser Co. [*NYSE symbol*]
WY............. Wherry   (ROG)
WY............. Woman's Year
WY............. Wrist Yaw   (MCD)
WY............. Wyeth Laboratories [*Research code symbol*]
WY............. Wyoming [*Postal code*]
WY............. Wyoming Music Educator News-Letter [*A publication*]
WY............. Wyoming Reports   (DLA)
Wy .... Wyoming State Library, Cheyenne, WY [*Library symbol*]
                   [*Library of Congress*]   (LCLS)
Wy .... Wythe's Virginia Chancery Reports [*1788-99*]   (DLA)
WyA........... Lincoln County Library, Afton Branch, Afton, WY [*Library
                   symbol*] [*Library of Congress*]   (LCLS)
WYA .... Whyalla [*Australia*] [*Airport symbol*]   (OAG)
WYA .... Wyangala [*Australia*] [*Seismograph station code, US
                   Geological Survey*] [*Closed*]   (SEIS)
WyAGS....... Church of Jesus Christ of Latter-Day Saints, Genealogical
                   Society Library, Afton Branch, Afton, WY [*Library symbol*]
                   [*Library of Congress*]   (LCLS)
WYAH-TV ... Portsmouth, VA [*Television station call letters*]
WYAIO .... Will You Accept, If Offered [*the position of*]   (FAAC)
WYAJ .... Sudbury, MA [*FM radio station call letters*]
WYAK........ Surfside Beach-Garden City, SC [*AM radio station call letters*]
WYAK-FM ... Surfside Beach, SC [*FM radio station call letters*]

WYAL......... Scotland Neck, NC [*AM radio station call letters*]

WYAM....... Marion, MS [*AM radio station call letters*]

WYAN-FM ... Upper Sandusky, OH [*FM radio station call letters*]

Wy-Ar......... Wyoming State Archives and Historical Department, Cheyenne, WY [*Library symbol*] [*Library of Congress*] (LCLS)

WYAT......... New Orleans, LA [*AM radio station call letters*]

Wyatt Prac Reg ... Wyatt's Practical Register in Chancery [*1800*] (DLA)

Wyatt Pr R ... Wyatt's Practical Register in Chancery [*1800*] (DLA)

Wyatt & W ... Wyatt and Webb's Reports [*A publication*]

Wyatt W & A'B ... Wyatt, Webb, and A'Beckett's Reports [*Victoria, Australia*] (DLA)

Wyatt W & A'B (Eq) ... Wyatt, Webb, and A'Beckett's Reports (Equity) [*A publication*]

Wyatt W & A'B IE & M ... Wyatt, Webb, and A'Beckett's Reports (Insolvency, Ecclesiastical, and Matrimonial) [*A publication*]

Wyatt W & A'B IP & M ... Wyatt, Webb, and A'Beckett's Victorian Insolvency, Probate, and Matrimonial Reports [*A publication*]

Wyatt W & A'B Min ... Wyatt, Webb, and A'Beckett's Reports (Mining) [*A publication*]

Wyatt & Webb ... Wyatt and Webb's Reports [*A publication*]

Wyatt & W (Eq) ... Wyatt and Webb's Reports (Equity) [*A publication*]

Wyatt & W (IE & M) ... Wyatt and Webb's Reports (Insolvency, Ecclesiastical, and Matrimonial) [*A publication*]

Wyatt & W (IP & M) ... Wyatt and Webb's Reports (Insolvency, Probate, and Matrimonial) [*A publication*]

Wyatt & W Min ... Wyatt and Webb's Victorian Mining Cases [*Australia*] (DLA)

Wyat & W Eq ... Wyatt and Webb's Victorian Equity Reports [*Australia*] (DLA)

WYAV......... Conway, SC [*FM radio station call letters*]

WYAY......... Gainesville, GA [*FM radio station call letters*]

WYBC-FM ... New Haven, CT [*FM radio station call letters*]

WYBE......... Philadelphia, PA [*Television station call letters*]

WYBL......... Western Young Buddhist League (EA)

WYBR......... Belvidere, IL [*FM radio station call letters*]

WYBT......... Blountstown, FL [*AM radio station call letters*]

WyBu.......... Johnson County Library, Buffalo, WY [*Library symbol*] [*Library of Congress*] (LCLS)

WyC........... Laramie County Library System, Cheyenne, WY [*Library symbol*] [*Library of Congress*] (LCLS)

WYC........... Wiley College, Marshall, TX [*OCLC symbol*] [*Inactive*] (OCLC)

WYCA .... Hammond, IN [*FM radio station call letters*]

WyCa.......... Natrona County Public Library, Casper, WY [*Library symbol*] [*Library of Congress*] (LCLS)

WyCaC....... Casper College, Casper, WY [*Library symbol*] [*Library of Congress*] (LCLS)

WyCaCH .... Wyoming State Children's Home, Casper, WY [*Library symbol*] [*Library of Congress*] (LCLS)

WyCaD....... Wyoming School for the Deaf, Casper, WY [*Library symbol*] [*Library of Congress*] (LCLS)

WyCaGS .... Church of Jesus Christ of Latter-Day Saints, Genealogical Society Library, Casper Branch, Casper, WY [*Library symbol*] [*Library of Congress*] (LCLS)

WYCB........ Washington, DC [*AM radio station call letters*]

WYCC .... Chicago, IL [*Television station call letters*]

WyCC......... Laramie County Community College, Cheyenne, WY [*Library symbol*] [*Library of Congress*] (LCLS)

WYCC .... Write Your Congressman Club (EA)

WyCDA ...... Wyoming Department of Agriculture, Cheyenne, WY [*Library symbol*] [*Library of Congress*] (LCLS)

WyCDE....... Wyoming Department of Education, Cheyenne, WY [*Library symbol*] [*Library of Congress*] (LCLS)

WYCE........ Wyoming, MI [*FM radio station call letters*]

WYCF........ World Youth Crusade for Freedom (EA)

WYCFD ...... World Youth Congress on Food and Development (EA-IO)

WyCGF....... Wyoming Game and Fish Commission, Cheyenne, WY [*Library symbol*] [*Library of Congress*] (LCLS)

WyCGS ...... Church of Jesus Christ of Latter-Day Saints, Genealogical Society Library, Cheyenne Branch, Cheyenne, WY [*Library symbol*] [*Library of Congress*] (LCLS)

WyCHD ...... Wyoming Highway Department, Cheyenne, WY [*Library symbol*] [*Library of Congress*] (LCLS)

WyCHS...... Wyoming Department of Health and Social Services, Cheyenne, WY [*Library symbol*] [*Library of Congress*] (LCLS)

WYCM....... Murfreesboro, NC [*AM radio station call letters*]

WyCMS...... Laramie County Medical Society, Cheyenne, WY [*Library symbol*] [*Library of Congress*] (LCLS)

WYCO .... Wausau, WI [*FM radio station call letters*]

WyCoB....... Buffalo Bill Museum, Cody, WY [*Library symbol*] [*Library of Congress*] (LCLS)

WyCoGS .... Church of Jesus Christ of Latter-Day Saints, Genealogical Society Library, Cody Branch, Cody, WY [*Library symbol*] [*Library of Congress*] (LCLS)

WYCQ .... Shelbyville, TN [*FM radio station call letters*]

WYCR........ York-Hanover, PA [*FM radio station call letters*]

WYCS........ Yorktown, VA [*FM radio station call letters*]

WyCSE....... State Engineer's Office, Cheyenne, WY [*Library symbol*] [*Library of Congress*] (LCLS)

WYCV........ Granite Falls, NC [*AM radio station call letters*]

WyCV .... United States Veterans Administration Center, Cheyenne, WY [*Library symbol*] [*Library of Congress*] (LCLS)

Wy-D......... Wyoming State Documents, Cheyenne, WY [*Library symbol*] [*Library of Congress*] (LCLS)

WYDD........ Pittsburgh, PA [*FM radio station call letters*]

WYDE........ Birmingham, AL [*AM radio station call letters*]

Wy Dic .... Wyatt's Dickens' Chancery Reports (DLA)

Wy Dick..... Dickens' English Chancery Reports, by Wyatt (DLA)

WYDK........ Yadkinville, NC [*AM radio station call letters*]

WyDo......... Converse County Library, Douglas, WY [*Library symbol*] [*Library of Congress*] (LCLS)

Wydz Mat Fiz Chem Uniw Poznan Ser Fiz ... Wydzial Matematyki Fizyki i Chemii Uniwersytet Imeni Adama Mickiewicza w Poznaniu Seria Fizyaka [*A publication*]

WYE .... Yengema [*Sierra Leone*] [*Airport symbol*] (OAG)

WYEA........ Sylacauga, AL [*AM radio station call letters*]

Wye Coll Dep Hop Res Annu Rep ... Wye College. Department of Hop Research. Annual Report [*A publication*]

WYED........ Goldsboro, NC [*Television station call letters*]

WYEF........ Yorkshire, NY [*FM radio station call letters*]

WY Energy Ext Serv Update ... Wyoming. Energy Extension Service. Update [*A publication*]

WYEO........ Superior, WI [*Television station call letters*]

WYEP-FM ... Pittsburgh, PA [*FM radio station call letters*]

WYER........ Mount Carmel, IL [*AM radio station call letters*]

WYER-FM ... Mount Carmel, IL [*FM radio station call letters*]

WYES-TV ... New Orleans, LA [*Television station call letters*]

WyEvGS..... Church of Jesus Christ of Latter-Day Saints, Genealogical Society Library, Evanston Branch, Evanston, WY [*Library symbol*] [*Library of Congress*] (LCLS)

WyEvSH ..... Wyoming State Hospital, Evanston, WY [*Library symbol*] [*Library of Congress*] (LCLS)

WYEZ........ Elkhart, IN [*FM radio station call letters*]

WYF........... World Youth Forum [*Defunct*] (EA)

WYFA........ Waynesboro, GA [*FM radio station call letters*]

WYFB......... Gainesville, FL [*FM radio station call letters*]

WYFC........ Ypsilanti, MI [*AM radio station call letters*]

WyFEW ...... United States Air Force, Francis E. Warren Air Force Base, Cheyenne, WY [*Library symbol*] [*Library of Congress*] (LCLS)

WyFEW-I .... United States Air Force Institute of Technology, Detachment 9, Francis E. Warren Air Force Base, Cheyenne, WY [*Library symbol*] [*Library of Congress*] (LCLS)

WYFF-TV ... Greenville, SC [*Television station call letters*]

WYFG........ Gaffney, SC [*FM radio station call letters*]

WYFH........ North Charleston, SC [*FM radio station call letters*]

WYFI......... Norfolk, VA [*FM radio station call letters*]

WYFJ......... Ashland, VA [*FM radio station call letters*]

WYFK .... Columbus, GA [*FM radio station call letters*]

WYFL .... Henderson, NC [*FM radio station call letters*]

WyFiL .... Fort Laramie Historic Site, Fort Laramie, WY [*Library symbol*] [*Library of Congress*] (LCLS)

WYFM .... Sharon, PA [*FM radio station call letters*]

WYFS........ Savannah, GA [*FM radio station call letters*]

WYFX........ Boynton Beach, FL [*AM radio station call letters*]

WYG.......... Wyoming Airlines Ltd. [*Denver, CO*] [*FAA designator*] (FAAC)

WYGC .... Gainesville, FL [*FM radio station call letters*]

WYGINS ..... What You Get Is No Surprise [*Pronounced "wiggins"*] [*Coined by Dave Tarrant, president of Lotus Development Corp.'s graphics products group*]

WYGL........ Selinsgrove, PA [*AM radio station call letters*]

WYGO .... Corbin, KY [*AM radio station call letters*]

WYGO-FM ... Corbin, KY [*FM radio station call letters*]

WYHY........ Lebanon, TN [*FM radio station call letters*]

WYII........... Williamsport, MD [*FM radio station call letters*]

WYIN .... Gary, IN [*Television station call letters*]

WYIS .... Phoenixville, PA [*AM radio station call letters*]

WYJCA....... Wool Yarn Jobbers Credit Association [*Defunct*] (EA)

WYJD .... Brewton, AL [*AM radio station call letters*]

WYJY .... Biddeford, ME [*FM radio station call letters*]

WYKC .... Grenada, MS [*AM radio station call letters*]

WyKc.......... Johnson County Library, Kaycee Branch, Kaycee, WY [*Library symbol*] [*Library of Congress*] (LCLS)

WyKe.......... Lincoln County Library, Kemmerer, WY [*Library symbol*] [*Library of Congress*] (LCLS)

Wykeham Eng Technol Ser ... Wykeham Engineering and Technology Series [*A publication*]

Wykeham Sci Ser ... Wykeham Science Series [*A publication*]

WYKH........ Hopkinsville, KY [*AM radio station call letters*]

WYKK .... Quitman, MS [*FM radio station call letters*]

WYKM .... Rupert, WV [*AM radio station call letters*]

WYKR .... Wells River, VT [*AM radio station call letters*]

WYKS........ Gainesville, FL [*FM radio station call letters*]

WYKX .... Escanaba, MI [*FM radio station call letters*]

WYKZ........ Beaufort, SC [*FM radio station call letters*]

WYL........... Laramie County Library System, Cheyenne, WY [*OCLC symbol*] (OCLC)

WYL........... Wyle Laboratories [*NYSE symbol*]

WyLan........ Fremont County Library, Lander, WY [*Library symbol*] [*Library of Congress*] (LCLS)

WyLanT...... Wyoming State Training School, Lander, WY [*Library symbol*] [*Library of Congress*] (LCLS)
WyLar......... Albany County Public Library, Laramie, WY [*Library symbol*] [*Library of Congress*] (LCLS)
WyLarBM ... United States Bureau of Mines, Laramie Petroleum Research Center, Laramie, WY [*Library symbol*] [*Library of Congress*] (LCLS)
WyLarHN.... Wyoming Health Science Network, University of Wyoming, Laramie, WY [*Library symbol*] [*Library of Congress*] (LCLS)
WyLarSh .... Sherwood Hall, Laramie, WY [*Library symbol*] [*Library of Congress*] (LCLS)
WyLarSM ... Saint Matthew's Cathedral, Laramie, WY [*Library symbol*] [*Library of Congress*] (LCLS)
WYLD......... New Orleans, LA [*AM radio station call letters*]
WYLD-FM ... New Orleans, LA [*FM radio station call letters*]
WY LJ......... Wyoming Law Journal [*A publication*]
WYLO......... Jackson, WI [*AM radio station call letters*]
WyLoGS..... Church of Jesus Christ of Latter-Day Saints, Genealogical Society Library, Lovell Branch, Lovell, WY [*Library symbol*] [*Library of Congress*] (LCLS)
WYLR......... Glens Falls, NY [*FM radio station call letters*]
WYLS......... York, AL [*AM radio station call letters*]
WYLT......... Raleigh, NC [*FM radio station call letters*]
WyLu.......... Niobrara County Library, Lusk, WY [*Library symbol*] [*Library of Congress*] (LCLS)
WYM.......... Wyoming Health Science Network, Laramie, WY [*OCLC symbol*] (OCLC)
Wyman....... Wyman's Reports [*India*] (DLA)
WYMB........ Manning, SC [*AM radio station call letters*]
WYMC........ Mayfield, KY [*AM radio station call letters*]
WYMC-FM ... Wickliffe, KY [*FM radio station call letters*]
WYMG........ Jacksonville, IL [*FM radio station call letters*]
WYMJ-FM ... Beaver Creek, OH [*FM radio station call letters*]
WYMN........ Wyman-Gordon Co. [*NASDAQ symbol*] (NQ)
WYMS........ Milwaukee, WI [*FM radio station call letters*]
WYMT-TV ... Hazard, KY [*Television station call letters*]
WYN........... Walwyn, Inc. [*Toronto Stock Exchange symbol*]
WYN........... Wyndham [*Australia*] [*Airport symbol*]
WYNA........ Tabor City, NC [*FM radio station call letters*]
WYNC........ Yanceyville, NC [*AM radio station call letters*]
WYND........ De Land, FL [*AM radio station call letters*]
WYNE........ Kimberly, WI [*AM radio station call letters*]
WyNe.......... Weston County Public Library, Newcastle, WY [*Library symbol*] [*Library of Congress*] (LCLS)
WYNF........ Tampa, FL [*FM radio station call letters*]
WYNG-FM ... Evansville, IN [*FM radio station call letters*]
WYNI......... Monroeville, AL [*AM radio station call letters*]
WYNK........ Baton Rouge, LA [*AM radio station call letters*]
WYNK-FM ... Baton Rouge, LA [*FM radio station call letters*]
WYNN........ Florence, SC [*AM radio station call letters*]
Wynne Bov ... Wynne's Bovill's Patent Cases (DLA)
WYNO........ Nelsonville, OH [*AM radio station call letters*]
WYNR........ Brunswick, GA [*FM radio station call letters*]
WYNS........ Lehighton, PA [*AM radio station call letters*]
WYNT......... Upper Sandusky, OH [*FM radio station call letters*]
WYNU........ Milan, TN [*FM radio station call letters*]
WYNX........ Smyrna, GA [*AM radio station call letters*]
WYNY........ New York, NY [*FM radio station call letters*]
WYNZ........ Portland, ME [*AM radio station call letters*]
WYNZ-FM ... Westbrook, ME [*FM radio station call letters*]
WYO........... US Aviation [*Riverton, WY*] [*FAA designator*] (FAAC)
WYO........... Wyoming (AAG)
WYO........... Wyoming Array [*Wyoming*] [*Seismograph station code, US Geological Survey*] (SEIS)
Wyo........... Wyoming Reports (DLA)
Wyo Ag Exp ... Wyoming. Agricultural Experiment Station. Publications [*A publication*]
Wyo Agric Exp Stn Bull ... Wyoming. Agricultural Experiment Station. Bulletin [*A publication*]
Wyo Agric Exp Stn Cir ... Wyoming. Agricultural Experiment Station. Circular [*A publication*]
Wyo Agric Exp Stn Res J ... Wyoming. Agricultural Experiment Station. Research Journal [*A publication*]
Wyo Agric Exp Stn Sci Monogr ... Wyoming. Agricultural Experiment Station. Science Monograph [*A publication*]
Wyo Agric Ext Serv Bull ... Wyoming. Agricultural Extension Service. Bulletin [*A publication*]
Wyo Game Fish Comm Bull ... Wyoming. Game and Fish Commission. Bulletin [*A publication*]
Wyo Geol Assoc Earth Sci Bull ... Wyoming Geological Association. Earth Science Bulletin [*A publication*]
Wyo Geol Assoc Guideb Ann Field Conf ... Wyoming Geological Association. Guidebook. Annual Field Conference [*A publication*]
Wyo Geol Survey Bull Rept Inv ... Wyoming. Geological Survey. Bulletin. Report of Investigations [*A publication*]
Wyo Geol Surv Prelim Rep ... Wyoming. Geological Survey. Preliminary Report [*A publication*]
Wyo Geol Surv Rep Invest ... Wyoming. Geological Survey. Report of Investigations [*A publication*]

Wyo G Off B Wyo St G ... Wyoming. Geologist's Office. Bulletin. Wyoming State Geologist [*A publication*]
Wyo His Col ... Wyoming State Historical Department. Proceedings and Collections [*A publication*]
Wyo Issues ... Wyoming Issues [*A publication*]
Wyo Lib Roundup ... Wyoming Library Roundup [*A publication*]
Wyo L J ...... Wyoming Law Journal [*A publication*]
WYOM........ Wyoming (ROG)
Wyom......... Wyoming Reports (DLA)
Wyoming Geol Survey Prelim Rept ... Wyoming. Geological Survey. Preliminary Report [*A publication*]
Wyoming Hist G Soc Pr Pub ... Wyoming Historical and Geological Society. Proceedings and Collections. Publications [*A publication*]
Wyo Nurse ... Wyoming Nurse [*Formerly, Wyoming Nurses Newsletter*] [*A publication*]
Wyo Nurses News ... Wyoming Nurses Newsletter [*Later, Wyoming Nurse*] [*A publication*]
Wyo Range Manage ... Wyoming Range Management [*A publication*]
Wyo Roundup ... Wyoming Roundup [*A publication*]
Wyo Sess Laws ... Session Laws of Wyoming (DLA)
Wyo St G ... Wyoming State Geologist [*A publication*]
WYOU......... Scranton, PA [*Television station call letters*]
WYOU-FM ... Bangor, ME [*FM radio station call letters*]
Wyo Univ Dep Geol Contrib Geol ... Wyoming University. Department of Geology. Contributions to Geology [*A publication*]
Wyo Univ Nat Resour Res Inst Bull ... Wyoming University. Natural Resources Research Institute. Bulletin [*A publication*]
Wyo Univ Nat Resour Res Inst Inf Cir ... Wyoming University. Natural Resources Research Institute. Information Circular [*A publication*]
Wyo Univ Natur Resour Inst Inform Circ ... Wyoming University. Natural Resources Institute. Information Circular [*A publication*]
Wyo Univ Sch Mines B ... Wyoming University. School of Mines. Bulletin [*A publication*]
Wyo Univ Water Resour Res Inst Water Resour Ser ... Wyoming University. Water Resources Research Institute. Water Resources Series [*A publication*]
WYOV........ Norwell, MA [*Television station call letters*]
Wyo Wild Life ... Wyoming Wild Life [*A publication*]
WYPC........ Gallipolis, OH [*FM radio station call letters*]
WyPdS .... Sublette County Library, Pinedale, WY [*Library symbol*] [*Library of Congress*] (LCLS)
WyPN .... Northwest Community College, Powell, WY [*Library symbol*] [*Library of Congress*] (LCLS)
Wy Pr R ..... Wyatt's Practical Register in Chancery [*England*] (DLA)
WYQC .... Charleston, WV [*FM radio station call letters*]
WYR .... Waybo Resources Ltd. [*Vancouver Stock Exchange symbol*]
WYR .... [*The*] West Yorkshire Regiment [*Army*] [*British*]
WYRE......... Annapolis, MD [*AM radio station call letters*]
WyRi.......... Fremont County Library, Riverton Branch, Riverton, WY [*Library symbol*] [*Library of Congress*] (LCLS)
WyRiC .... Central Wyoming Community College, Riverton, WY [*Library symbol*] [*Library of Congress*] (LCLS)
WYRK........ Buffalo, NY [*FM radio station call letters*]
WYRL........ Melbourne, FL [*FM radio station call letters*]
WYRN........ Louisburg, NC [*AM radio station call letters*]
WYRQ........ Little Falls, MN [*FM radio station call letters*]
WYRS........ Stamford, CT [*FM radio station call letters*]
WyRsW....... Western Wyoming College, Rock Springs, WY [*Library symbol*] [*Library of Congress*] (LCLS)
WYRU........ Red Springs, NC [*AM radio station call letters*]
WYRV........ Cedar Bluff, VA [*AM radio station call letters*]
WYRY........ Hinsdale, NH [*FM radio station call letters*]
WYS .... West Yellowstone, MT [*Location identifier*] [*FAA*] (FAAL)
WYS .... Wyandotte Southern Railroad Co. [*AAR code*]
WYSE........ Bainbridge, GA [*AM radio station call letters*]
WYSH........ Clinton, TN [*AM radio station call letters*]
WyShCD .... Wheden Cancer Detection Foundation, Sheridan, WY [*Library symbol*] [*Library of Congress*] (LCLS)
WyShF .... Sheridan County Fulmer Public Library, Sheridan, WY [*Library symbol*] [*Library of Congress*] (LCLS)
WyShGS .... Wyoming Girls' School, Sheridan, WY [*Library symbol*] [*Library of Congress*] (LCLS)
WyShMH.... Northern Wyoming Mental Health Center, Sheridan, WY [*Library symbol*] [*Library of Congress*] (LCLS)
WyShS .... Sheridan College, Sheridan, WY [*Library symbol*] [*Library of Congress*] (LCLS)
WyShV .... United States Veterans Administration Hospital, Sheridan, WY [*Library symbol*] [*Library of Congress*] (LCLS)
WYSIMOLWYG ... What You See Is More or Less What You Get [*Pronounced "wizzy-mole-wig"*]
WYSIWYG ... What You See Is What You Get [*Pronounced "whizziwig"*] [*Indicates that video display on word processor bears a high-quality resemblance to printed page that will result*]
WYSL......... Avon, NY [*AM radio station call letters*]
WYSO........ Yellow Springs, OH [*FM radio station call letters*]
WYSP........ Philadelphia, PA [*FM radio station call letters*]
WYSR........ Franklin, VA [*AM radio station call letters*]
WYSS........ Sault Ste. Marie, MI [*FM radio station call letters*]
WYST........ Baltimore, MD [*AM radio station call letters*]
WYST-FM ... Baltimore, MD [*FM radio station call letters*]

WYSU......... Youngstown, OH [*FM radio station call letters*]
WYT .... Wyandotte Terminal Railroad Co. [*AAR code*]
WYTE........ Whiting, WI [*FM radio station call letters*]
WYTH........ Madison, GA [*AM radio station call letters*]
Wythe........ Wythe's Virginia Chancery Reports [*1788-99*] (DLA)
Wythe Ch (VA) ... Wythe's Virginia Chancery Reports [*1788-99*] (DLA)
Wythes CC ... Wythe's Virginia Chancery Reports [*2nd ed.*] (DLA)
Wythe's R ... Wythe's Virginia Chancery Reports [*2nd ed.*] (DLA)
Wythe's Rep ... Wythe's Virginia Chancery Reports [*2nd ed.*] (DLA)
Wythe (VA)... Wythe's Virginia Chancery Reports [*1788-99*] (DLA)
WyThP....... Wyoming Pioneer Home, Thermopolis, WY [*Library symbol*] [*Library of Congress*] (LCLS)
WYTI .... Rocky Mount, VA [*AM radio station call letters*]
WyTJ......... Wesleyan Theological Journal [*A publication*]
WYTK........ Washington, PA [*FM radio station call letters*]
WYTM .... Fayetteville, TN [*FM radio station call letters*]
WyToE....... Eastern Wyoming College, Torrington, WY [*Library symbol*] [*Library of Congress*] (LCLS)
WyTs .... Washakie County Library, Ten Sleep Branch, Ten Sleep, WY [*Library symbol*] [*Library of Congress*] (LCLS)
WYTV........ Youngstown, OH [*Television station call letters*]
WYTW .... Cadillac, MI [*FM radio station call letters*]
WYTZ........ Chicago, IL [*FM radio station call letters*]
WyU........... University of Wyoming, Laramie, WY [*Library symbol*] [*Library of Congress*] (LCLS)
WYU .... University of Wyoming, Library, Laramie, WY [*OCLC symbol*] (OCLC)
wyu............ Wyoming [*MARC country of publication code*] [*Library of Congress*] (LCCP)
WyU-Ar ...... University of Wyoming, Archive of Contemporary History, Laramie, WY [*Library symbol*] [*Library of Congress*] (LCLS)
WyUp .... Weston County Public Library, Upton Branch, Upton, WY [*Library symbol*] [*Library of Congress*] (LCLS)
WYUR-FM ... Ripon, WI [*FM radio station call letters*]
WYUS........ Milford, DE [*AM radio station call letters*]
WYUT........ Herkimer, NY [*FM radio station call letters*]
WYVE........ Wytheville, VA [*AM radio station call letters*]
Wy & W...... Wyatt and Webb's Victorian Equity Reports [*Australia*] (DLA)
WyWo......... Washakie County Library, Worland, WY [*Library symbol*] [*Library of Congress*] (LCLS)
WyWoI....... Wyoming Industrial Institute, Worland, WY [*Library symbol*] [*Library of Congress*] (LCLS)
WYWY .... Barbourville, KY [*AM radio station call letters*]
WYWY-FM ... Barbourville, KY [*FM radio station call letters*]
WYXC........ Cartersville, GA [*AM radio station call letters*]
WYXI .... Athens, TN [*AM radio station call letters*]
WYXX........ Holland, MI [*FM radio station call letters*]
WYXY........ Cypress Gardens, FL [*AM radio station call letters*]
WYXZ........ Allendale, SC [*AM radio station call letters*]
WYYD......... Amherst, VA [*FM radio station call letters*]
WYYN........ Jackson, MS [*FM radio station call letters*]
WYYY........ Syracuse, NY [*FM radio station call letters*]
WYYZ........ Jasper, GA [*AM radio station call letters*]
WYZ .... Wyoming State Library, Cheyenne, WY [*OCLC symbol*] (OCLC)
WYZB........ Mary Ester, FL [*FM radio station call letters*]
WYZD......... Dobson, NC [*AM radio station call letters*]
WYZE........ Atlanta, GA [*AM radio station call letters*]
Wyz Szkol Ped Krakow Rocznik Nauk-Dydakt Prace Dydakt Mat ... Wyzsza Szkola Pedagogiczna w Krakowie. Rocznik Naukowo-Dydaktyczny. Prace z Dydaktyki Matematyki [*A publication*]
Wyz Szkol Ped Krakow Rocznik Nauk-Dydakt Prace Mat ... Wyzsza Szkola Pedagogiczna w Krakowie. Rocznik Naukowo-Dydaktyczny. Prace Matematyczne [*A publication*]
WYZZ-TV ... Bloomington, IL [*Television station call letters*]
WZ.............. Royal Swazi National Airways Corp. [*Swaziland*] [*ICAO designator*] (FAAC)
WZ.............. War Zone
Wz.............. Warenzeichen [*Trademark*] [*German*]
WZ.............. Westfaelische Zeitschrift [*A publication*]
WZ.............. Wiedza i Zycie [*A publication*]
WZ.............. Wissenschaftliche Zeitschrift [*A publication*]
WZ.............. Wort in der Zeit [*A publication*]
WZAK........ Cleveland, OH [*FM radio station call letters*]
WZAL .... McDonough, GA [*AM radio station call letters*]
WZAM........ Norfolk, VA [*AM radio station call letters*]
WZAP........ Bristol, VA [*AM radio station call letters*]
WZAR........ Ponce, PR [*FM radio station call letters*]
WZAT........ Savannah, GA [*FM radio station call letters*]
WZAZ........ Jacksonville, FL [*AM radio station call letters*]
WZBC........ Newton, MA [*FM radio station call letters*]
WZ (Berlin) ... Wissenschaftliche Zeitschrift der Humboldt-Universitaet (Berlin) [*A publication*]
WZBO......... Edenton, NC [*AM radio station call letters*]
WZBO-FM ... Edenton, NC [*FM radio station call letters*]
WZBQ........ Jasper, AL [*FM radio station call letters*]
WZBR........ Amory, MS [*AM radio station call letters*]
WZBS........ Ponce, PR [*AM radio station call letters*]
WZBT .... Gettysburg, PA [*FM radio station call letters*]

WzD............ Wege zur Dichtung [*A publication*]
WZDM........ Vincennes, IN [*FM radio station call letters*]
WZDQ........ Humboldt, TN [*FM radio station call letters*]
WZDX........ Huntsville, AL [*Television station call letters*]
WZEE......... Madison, WI [*FM radio station call letters*]
WZEL........ Young Harris, GA [*AM radio station call letters*]
WZEMAUG ... Wissenschaftliche Zeitschrift der Ernst-Moritz-Arndt-Universitaet Greifswald: Gesellschafts- und Sprachwissenschaftliche Reihe [*A publication*]
WZEP .... De Funiak Springs, FL [*AM radio station call letters*]
WZEW .... Fairhope, AK [*FM radio station call letters*]
WZE Wiss Z Elektrotech ... WZE. Wissenschaftliche Zeitschrift der Elektrotechnik [*East Germany*] [*A publication*]
WZEZ........ Nashville, TN [*FM radio station call letters*]
WZFL........ Centreville, MS [*AM radio station call letters*]
WZFL........ Centreville, MS [*FM radio station call letters*]
WZFM........ Briarcliff Manor, NY [*FM radio station call letters*]
WZFMA ..... Wissenschaftliche Zeitschrift der Friedrich-Schiller-Universitaet (Jena). Mathematisch-Naturwissenschaftliche Reihe [*A publication*]
WZFSU....... Wissenschaftliche Zeitschrift der Friedrich-Schiller-Universitaet (Jena): Gesellschafts- und Sprachwissenschaftliche Reihe [*A publication*]
WZFSUJ..... Wissenschaftliche Zeitschrift der Friedrich-Schiller-Universitaet (Jena): Gesellschafts- und Sprachwissenschaftliche Reihe [*A publication*]
WZFSUJ GSR ... Wissenschaftliche Zeitschrift der Friedrich-Schiller-Universitaet (Jena): Gesellschafts- und Sprachwissenschaftliche Reihe [*A publication*]
WZFX .... Whiteville, NC [*FM radio station call letters*]
WZG .... Wissenschaftliche Zeitschrift fuer Juedische Geschichte [*A publication*] (BJA)
WZGA .... Rome, GA [*Television station call letters*]
WZGC .... Atlanta, GA [*FM radio station call letters*]
WZGK........ Westdeutsche Zeitschrift fuer Geschichte und Kunst [*A publication*]
WZ Griefswald ... Wissenschaftliche Zeitschrift der Ernst-Moritz-Arndt-Universitaet Greifswald [*A publication*]
WZ (Halle) ... Wissenschaftliche Zeitschrift der Martin-Luther-Universitaet (Halle-Wittenberg) [*A publication*]
WZHMA...... Wissenschaftliche Zeitschrift der Humboldt-Universitaet zu Berlin. Mathematisch-Naturwissenschaftliche Reihe [*A publication*]
WZHU......... Wissenschaftliche Zeitschrift der Humboldt-Universitaet (Berlin): Gesellschafts- und Sprachwissenschaftliche Reihe [*A publication*]
WZHUB ...... Wissenschaftliche Zeitschrift der Humboldt-Universitaet (Berlin): Gesellschafts- und Sprachwissenschaftliche Reihe [*A publication*]
WZI............ Winzen International, Inc. [*Vancouver Stock Exchange symbol*]
WZID......... Manchester, NH [*FM radio station call letters*]
WZIP .... South Daytona, FL [*AM radio station call letters*]
WZIX .... Artesia, MS [*FM radio station call letters*]
WZJ............ Wissenschaftliche Zeitschrift der Friedrich-Schiller-Universitaet (Jena) [*A publication*]
WZ Jena ..... Wissenschaftliche Zeitschrift der Friedrich-Schiller-Universitaet (Jena) [*A publication*]
WZJT......... Wissenschaftliche Zeitschrift fuer Juedische Theologie [*A publication*] (BJA)
WZJTh........ Wissenschaftliche Zeitschrift fuer Juedische Theologie [*A publication*] (BJA)
WZKB .... Wallace, NC [*FM radio station call letters*]
WZKM .... Wiener Zeitschrift fuer die Kunde des Morgenlandes [*A publication*]
WZKMU...... Wissenschaftliche Zeitschrift der Karl-Marx-Universitaet [*Leipzig*] [*A publication*]
WZKMUL ... Wissenschaftliche Zeitschrift der Karl-Marx-Universitaet (Leipzig): Gesellschafts- und Sprachwissenschaftliche Reihe [*A publication*]
WZKO......... Pineville, KY [*FM radio station call letters*]
WZKS......... Jesup, GA [*FM radio station call letters*]
WZKS......... Wiener Zeitschrift fuer die Kunde Suedasiens und Archiv fuer Indische Philosophie [*A publication*]
WZKSO ..... Wiener Zeitschrift fuer die Kunde Sued- und Ostasiens und Archiv fuer Indische Philosophie [*A publication*]
WZKX .... Gulfport, MS [*FM radio station call letters*]
WZKY........ Albemarle, NC [*AM radio station call letters*]
WZKZ........ Corning, NY [*FM radio station call letters*]
WZL............ Wissenschaftliche Zeitschrift der Karl-Marx-Universitaet (Leipzig) [*A publication*]
WZLD-FM .. Cayce, SC [*FM radio station call letters*]
WZLE .... Lorain, OH [*FM radio station call letters*]
WZ (Leipzig) ... Wissenschaftliche Zeitschrift der Karl-Marx-Universitaet (Leipzig) [*A publication*]
WZLI........... Toccoa, GA [*FM radio station call letters*]
WZLQ........ Tupelo, MS [*FM radio station call letters*]
WZLS......... Valdosta, GA [*FM radio station call letters*]
WZLT......... Lexington, TN [*FM radio station call letters*]
WZLX......... Boston, MA [*FM radio station call letters*]
WZLY .... Wellesley, MA [*FM radio station call letters*]
WZMB .... Greenville, NC [*FM radio station call letters*]

WZMG........ Opelika, AL [*AM radio station call letters*]
WZMLU ...... Wissenschaftliche Zeitschrift der Martin-Luther-Universitaet [*A publication*]
WZMLUH.... Wissenschaftliche Zeitschrift der Martin-Luther-Universitaet (Halle-Wittenberg): Gesellschafts- und Sprachwissenschaftliche Reihe [*A publication*]
WZMM....... Wheeling, WV [*FM radio station call letters*]
WZMU .... Wissenschaftliche Zeitschrift der Karl-Marx-Universitaet [*Leipzig*]: Gesellschafts- und Sprachwissenschaftliche Reihe [*A publication*]
WZMX .... Russellville, AL [*FM radio station call letters*]
WZND........ Zeeland, MI [*FM radio station call letters*]
WZNDA ...... Wiener Zeitschrift fuer Nervenheilkunde und Deren Grenzgebiete [*A publication*]
WZNJ .... Demopolis, AL [*FM radio station call letters*]
WZNPS....... William H. Zimmer Nuclear Power Station [*Also, ZPS*]   (NRCH)
WZNS........ Dillon, SC [*FM radio station call letters*]
WZNT .... San Juan, PR [*FM radio station call letters*]
WZNY .... Augusta, GA [*FM radio station call letters*]
WZO .... Wein Zollordnung [*Wine Duty Order*] [*German*]
WZO .... World Zionist Organization
WZOA .... Women's Zionist Organization of America
WZOB .... Fort Payne, AL [*AM radio station call letters*]
WZOE........ Princeton, IL [*AM radio station call letters*]
WZOE-FM ... Princeton, IL [*FM radio station call letters*]
WZOK........ Rockford, IL [*FM radio station call letters*]
WZOL .... Luqillo, PR [*FM radio station call letters*]
WZOM .... Brookport, IL [*AM radio station call letters*]
WZON .... Bangor, ME [*AM radio station call letters*]
WZOO .... Asheboro, NC [*AM radio station call letters*]
WZOQ .... Wapakoneta, OH [*FM radio station call letters*]
WZOR........ Immokalee, FL [*AM radio station call letters*]
WZOT........ Rockmart, GA [*FM radio station call letters*]
WZOU........ Boston, MA [*FM radio station call letters*]
WZOW....... Goshen, IN [*FM radio station call letters*]
WZOZ........ Oneonta, NY [*FM radio station call letters*]
WZPHP .... Wissenschaftliche Zeitschrift der Paedagogischen Hochschule Potsdam: Gesellschafts- und Sprachwissenschaftliche Reihe [*A publication*]
WZPL .... Greenfield, IN [*FM radio station call letters*]
WZPR .... Meadville, PA [*FM radio station call letters*]
WZRB........ Ringgold, GA [*AM radio station call letters*]
WZRC........ Des Plaines, IL [*FM radio station call letters*]
WZRD........ Chicago, IL [*FM radio station call letters*]
WZRK........ Hancock, MI [*FM radio station call letters*]
WZRO........ Farmer City, FL [*FM radio station call letters*]
WZ Rostock ... Wissenschaftliche Zeitschrift der Universitaet Rostock [*A publication*]
WZRQ........ Columbia City, IN [*FM radio station call letters*]
WZRX .... Jackson, MS [*AM radio station call letters*]
WZSH........ South Bristol Township, NY [*FM radio station call letters*]
WZsl .... Wissenschaftliche Zeitschrift der Karl-Marx-Universitaet. Gesellschafts- und Sprachwissenschaftliche Reihe [*Leipzig*] [*A publication*]
WZT............ Wartegg-Zeichentest [*Wartegg Symbol Test*] [*German*] [*Psychology*]
WZTDA ...... Wissenschaftliche Zeitschrift der Technischen Hochschule (Dresden) [*A publication*]
WZTKA ...... Wissenschaftliche Zeitschrift - Technische Hochschule Karl-Marx-Stadt [*A publication*]
WZTN .... Montgomery, AL [*AM radio station call letters*]
WZTT .... Rhinelander, WI [*FM radio station call letters*]
WZTV .... Nashville, TN [*Television station call letters*]
WZTZ .... Elba, AL [*FM radio station call letters*]
WZUB........ Wissenschaftliche Zeitschrift der Humboldt-Universitaet (Berlin): Gesellschafts- und Sprachwissenschaftliche Reihe [*A publication*]
WZUG........ Wissenschaftliche Zeitschrift der Ernst-Moritz-Arndt-Universitaet Greifswald [*A publication*]
WZUH........ Wissenschaftliche Zeitschrift der Martin-Luther-Universitaet (Halle-Wittenberg): Gesellschafts- und Sprachwissenschaftliche Reihe [*A publication*]
WZUHW ..... Wissenschaftliche Zeitschrift der Martin-Luther-Universitaet (Halle-Wittenberg): Gesellschafts- und Sprachwissenschaftliche Reihe [*A publication*]
WZUJ .... Wissenschaftliche Zeitschrift der Friedrich-Schiller-Universitaet (Jena) [*A publication*]
WZUL .... Wissenschaftliche Zeitschrift der Karl-Marx-Universitaet (Leipzig) [*A publication*]
WZUL .... Wissenschaftliche Zeitschrift der Universitaet Leipzig: Gesellschafts- und Sprachwissenschaftliche Reihe [*A publication*]
WZULeipzig ... Wissenschaftliche Zeitschrift der Karl-Marx Universitaet. Gesellschafts- und Sprachwissenschaftliche Reihe (Leipzig) [*A publication*]
WZUR........ Wissenschaftliche Zeitschrift der Universitaet Rostock [*A publication*]
WZUW .... Wissenschaftliche Zeitschrift der Universitaet Wien [*A publication*]
WZV .... Wiener Zeitschrift fuer Volkskunde [*A publication*]
WZVN........ Lowell, IN [*FM radio station call letters*]

WZW........... Worcester Public Library, Worcester, MA [*OCLC symbol*]   (OCLC)
WZWW .... Bellefonte, PA [*FM radio station call letters*]
WZWZ .... Kokomo, IN [*FM radio station call letters*]
WZXI .... Gastonia, NC [*FM radio station call letters*]
WZXK .... Ashland, VA [*Television station call letters*]
WZXM .... Gaylord, MI [*AM radio station call letters*]
WZXM-FM ... Gaylord, MI [*FM radio station call letters*]
WZXY .... Kingsport, TN [*FM radio station call letters*]
WZY .... Nassau [*Bahamas*] [*Airport symbol*]   (OAG)
WZYC-FM ... Newport, NC [*FM radio station call letters*]
WZYP .... Athens, AL [*FM radio station call letters*]
WZYQ......... Frederick, MD [*AM radio station call letters*]
WZYQ-FM ... Braddock Heights, MD [*FM radio station call letters*]
WZYX .... Cowan, TN [*AM radio station call letters*]
WZYZ .... Fairmount, NC [*FM radio station call letters*]
WZZA .... Tuscumbia, AL [*AM radio station call letters*]
WZZD .... Philadelphia, PA [*AM radio station call letters*]
WZZE .... Glen Mills, PA [*FM radio station call letters*]
WZZF-FM ... Hopkinsville, KY [*FM radio station call letters*]
WZZH .... Highlands, NC [*AM radio station call letters*]
WZZK .... Birmingham, AL [*AM radio station call letters*]
WZZK-FM .. Birmingham, AL [*FM radio station call letters*]
WZZM-TV ... Grand Rapids, MI [*Television station call letters*]
WZZO .... Bethlehem, PA [*FM radio station call letters*]
WZZP .... South Bend, IN [*AM radio station call letters*]
WZZQ .... Terre Haute, IN [*FM radio station call letters*]
WZZR .... Mechanicsville, VA [*FM radio station call letters*]
WZZT .... Johnstown, OH [*AM radio station call letters*]
WZZU .... Burlington-Graham, NC [*FM radio station call letters*]
WZZV .... Magee, MS [*Television station call letters*]
WZZW .... Roanoke, VA [*Television station call letters*]
WZZX .... Lineville, AL [*AM radio station call letters*]
WZZY .... Winchester, IN [*FM radio station call letters*]
WZZZ .... West Point, GA [*AM radio station call letters*]

X

X	Amino Acid, Unknown or Other [*Symbol*] [*Biochemistry*]
X	Any Point on a Great Circle
X	Arithmetic mean
X	By [*As in 9 x 12*]
X	Central Drug Research Institute [*India*] [*Research code symbol*]
X	Christus [*or Christ*]
X	Closed at All Times (Except When in Actual Use) [*Ship's fittings classification*]
X	Cross [*As in X-roads*]
X	Crystal Cut [*Symbol*] (DEN)
X	Drill Sergent [*Army skill qualification identifier*] (INF)
X	Ethnikon Agrotikon Komma Xiton [*National Agrarian Party "X"*] (PPE)
X	Ex-Husband [*or Ex-Wife*] [*Slang*]
X	Ex-Interest [*In bond listings of newspapers*]
X	Examination [*Slang*]
X	Exchange
X	Exclusive [*Concession in a circus or carnival*]
X	Exhibitions [*Trade fairs, etc.*] [*Public-performance tariff class*] [*British*]
X	Exophoria Distance [*Ophthalmology*]
X	Experimental [*Military*] (AABC)
X	Explosion [*Military*] (CAAL)
X	Extension (AAG)
X	Extra [*Designation on brandy labels*]
X	Extra [*As in XHVY, or extra-heavy*]
X	Female Chromosome
X	Frost
X	Horizontal Deflection [*Symbol*] (DEN)
X	Intersect (FAAC)
X	Kiss [*Correspondence*]
X	Komma Xiton Ethnikis Antistasseos [*"X" National Resistance Party*] (PPE)
X	Mistake [*or Error*] [*Symbol*]
X	No-Wind Distance between Pressure Pattern Observations
X	Parallactic Angle
X	Persons under Eighteen [*Sixteen in some localities*] Not Admitted [*Movie rating*]
X	Psychological Problem [*Classification system used by doctors on Ellis Island to detain, re-examine, and possibly deny entry to certain immigrants*]
X	Raw Score [*Psychology*]
X	Reactance [*Symbol*] [*IUPAC*] (AAG)
X	Research [*or Experimental*] [*Designation for all US military aircraft*]
X	St. Andrew's Cross
X	Simes [*Italy*] [*Research code symbol*]
X	Strike [*Bowling symbol*]
X	Submersible Craft [*Self-propelled*] [*Navy ship symbol*]
x	Takes [*As in K x B - King Takes Bishop*] [*Chess*]
X	Ten [*Roman numeral*]
X	Times [*Multiplication sign*] [*Mathematics*]
X	Toilet [*Slang*]
X	Transistor [*Symbol*] (DEN)
X	Transmit
X	[*The First*] Unknown Quantity [*Mathematics*] (ROG)
X	US Steel Corp. [*Later, USX Corp.*] [*NYSE symbol*] [*Wall Street slang name: "Steel"*]
X	USX Corp. [*NYSE symbol*]
X	X-Axis
X	X-Ray (KSC)
X	X-Ray [*Phonetic alphabet*] [*Pre-World War II*] [*World War II*] [*International*] (DSUE)
X	X Records [*Division of RCA-Victor*] [*Record label*]
X	Xanthosine [*One-letter symbol; see Xao*]
X	Xerxes [*Phonetic alphabet*] [*Royal Navy*] [*World War I*] (DSUE)
X	Xylem [*Botany*]
x	Xylose [*As substituent on nucleoside*] [*Biochemistry*]
x	Xylose [*One-letter symbol; see Xyl*]
3X	Guinea [*Aircraft nationality and registration mark*] (FAAC)
4X	Israel [*Aircraft nationality and registration mark*] (FAAC)
5X	Uganda [*Aircraft nationality and registration mark*] (FAAC)
X (Cars)	Designation for General Motors front-wheel-drive cars [*Citation, Omega, Phoenix, Skylark*]
X (Hour)	Hour at which shipping evacuation is ordered from major ports [*NATO exercises*] (NATG)
X (Mode)	Extraordinary Mode (MCD)
XA	Aeronautical Radio, Inc. [*ICAO designator*] (FAAC)
XA	Auxiliary Amplifier (AAG)
xa	Christmas Island [*Indian Ocean*] [*MARC country of publication code*] [*Library of Congress*] (LCCP)
XA	Experimental (Air Force)
XA	Extended Architecture [*Data processing*]
XA	Mexico [*Aircraft nationality and registration mark*] (FAAC)
XA	Transmission Adapter (MDG)
Xa	Xanadu [*A publication*]
Xa	Xanthine [*Biochemistry*]
XA	Xanthurenic Acid [*Clinical chemistry*]
XAAM	Experimental Air-to-Air Missile [*Air Force, NASA*]
XACIC	X-Ray Attenuation Coefficient Information Center [*National Bureau of Standards*]
XACT	X Automatic Code Translation (IEEE)
XAD	Experimental and Development
XAFH	X-Band Antenna Feed Horn
XAID	ADI Electronics [*NASDAQ symbol*] (NQ)
XAK	Cargo Ship, Merchant Marine Manned
XAL	Xenon Arc Lamp
XAM	Merchant Ship Converted to a Minesweeper [*Navy symbol*] [*Obsolete*]
Xan	Xanthine [*Biochemistry*]
XANES	X-Ray Absorption Near-Edge Structure [*Spectroscopy*]
xanth	Xanthomatosis
Xao	Xanthosine [*Also, X*] [*A nucleoside*]
XAP	Chapeco [*Brazil*] [*Airport symbol*] (OAG)
XAP	Merchant Transport [*Ship symbol*]
XAPC	Merchant Coastal Transport, Small [*Ship symbol*]
XARM	Cross Arm (AAG)
XAS	Experimental Air Specification Weapons [*Navy*] (NG)
XAS	X-Band Antenna System
XASM	Experimental Air-to-Surface Missile [*Air Force, NASA*]
XAT	X-Ray Analysis Trial
XAV	Auxiliary Seaplane Tender [*Ship symbol*]
XAV	Xavier University, Cincinnati, OH [*OCLC symbol*] (OCLC)
XAY	Camp Atterbury, IN [*Location identifier*] [*FAA*] (FAAL)
xb	Cocos [*Keeling*] Islands [*MARC country of publication code*] [*Library of Congress*] (LCCP)
XB	Crossbar [*Bell System*]
XB	Experimental Bomber (MCD)
XB	Exploding Bridge-Wire
XB	Mexico [*Aircraft nationality and registration mark*] (FAAC)
XBAR	Crossbar
XBASIC	Extension of BASIC [*Data processing*]
XBB	Berne Public Library, Berne, IN [*OCLC symbol*] (OCLC)
XBC	"B" Corporation [*Toronto Stock Exchange symbol*]
XBC	External Block Controller
XBE	Shasta Air, Inc. [*Yreka, CA*] [*FAA designator*] (FAAC)
XBF	Bird Leasing, Inc. [*North Andover, MA*] [*FAA designator*] (FAAC)
XBF	Fort Wayne, IN [*Location identifier*] [*FAA*] (FAAL)
XBG	Bogande [*Upper Volta*] [*Airport symbol*] (OAG)
XBG	National Jet Corp. [*West Mifflin, PA*] [*FAA designator*] (FAAC)
XBH	Northern Airlines [*Vineyard Haven, MA*] [*FAA designator*] (FAAC)
XBIOS	Extended BIOS [*Basic Input/Output System*] [*Operating system*]
XBJ	Valley Airlines [*Frenchville, ME*] [*FAA designator*] (FAAC)
XBK	Bellair Airways [*Houston, TX*] [*FAA designator*] (FAAC)
XBK	Xebeck [*Type of ship*]
XBL	Extension Bell [*Telecommunications*] (TEL)
XBL	Northstar Aviation [*Redding, CA*] [*FAA designator*] (FAAC)
XBLD	Extrabold [*Typography*]

XBM	Extended BASIC Mode [*International Computers Ltd.*]
XBM	State University of New York, College at Brockport, Brockport, NY [*OCLC symbol*] (OCLC)
XBMIA	Report of Investigations. United States Bureau of Mines [*A publication*]
XBN	Biniguni [*Papua New Guinea*] [*Airport symbol*] (OAG)
XBO	Sajen Air, Inc. [*Manchester, NH*] [*FAA designator*] (FAAC)
XBP	Bancshare Portfolio [*Toronto Stock Exchange symbol*]
XBQ	Denver Charters, Inc. [*Englewood, CO*] [*FAA designator*] (FAAC)
XBR	Aero Coach Aviation International, Inc. [*Ft. Lauderdale, FL*] [*FAA designator*] (FAAC)
XBR	Brockville [*Canada*] [*Airport symbol*] (OAG)
XBR	Experimental Breeder Reactor
XBR	Ozark, AL [*Location identifier*] [*FAA*] (FAAL)
XBRA	Cross Bracing (MSA)
XBS	Ace Air Cargo Express, Inc. [*Brook Park, OH*] [*FAA designator*] (FAAC)
XBT	Crossbar Tandem [*Telecommunications*] (TEL)
XBT	Desert Sun Airlines [*Long Beach, CA*] [*FAA designator*] (FAAC)
XBT	Expendable Bathythermograph [*Oceanography*]
XBU	Arcata Flying Service [*McKinleyville, CA*] [*FAA designator*] (FAAC)
XBV	Western Pacific Express, Inc. [*Van Nuys, CA*] [*FAA designator*] (FAAC)
XBW	Waring Aviation, Inc. [*Charlottesville, VA*] [*FAA designator*] (FAAC)
XBX	Air Cargo America, Inc. [*Miami, FL*] [*FAA designator*] (FAAC)
XBY	Cosmopolitan Airlines, Inc. [*Farmingdale, NY*] [*FAA designator*] (FAAC)
XBZ	Chesapeake Transport, Inc. [*Arlington, VA*] [*FAA designator*] (FAAC)
XC	Air Routing International Corp. [*ICAO designator*] (FAAC)
Xc	Capacitive Reactance
XC	Cross-Clamp [*of carotid artery*]
XC	Cross Country [*Also, XCY*]
X-C	Ex-Coupon [*Without the right to coupons, as of a bond*] [*Finance*]
XC	Expendable Case (MCD)
XC	Experimental Cargo Aircraft
xc	Maldives [*MARC country of publication code*] [*Library of Congress*] (LCCP)
XC	Mexico [*Aircraft nationality and registration mark*] (FAAC)
XC	X-Chromosome
XC	Xerox Copy
XCA	Air East of Delaware, Inc. [*Wilmington, DE*] [*FAA designator*] (FAAC)
XCB	Aero Trends, Inc. [*San Jose, CA*] [*FAA designator*] (FAAC)
XCB	Extended Core Barrel [*Drilling technology*]
XCC	Air Vectors Airways, Inc. [*Newburg, NY*] [*FAA designator*] (FAAC)
XCD	Air Associates Ltd. [*Kansas City, MO*] [*FAA designator*] (FAAC)
XCE	Aerotransit [*Danvers, MA*] [*FAA designator*] (FAAC)
XCE	X-Band Cassegrain Experimental
XCF	Air Niagara, Inc. [*Niagara Falls, NY*] [*FAA designator*] (FAAC)
XCG	Atlantic Express, Inc. [*East Farmingdale, NY*] [*FAA designator*] (FAAC)
XCG	Experimental Cargo Glider
XCH	Exchange (AAG)
XCH	Flight East [*North Hollywood, CA*] [*FAA designator*] (FAAC)
XCIT	Excitation (AAG)
XCJ	Eastman Airways [*Farmingdale, NJ*] [*FAA designator*] (FAAC)
XCK	Richland Aviation [*Sidney, MT*] [*FAA designator*] (FAAC)
XCL	Armed Merchant Cruiser [*Navy symbol*]
XCL	Excess Current Liabilities [*Insurance*]
XCL	Excluded from General Declassification Schedule (MCD)
XCL	Green Aero, Inc. [*Flint, MI*] [*FAA designator*] (FAAC)
XCL	X-Cal Resources Limited [*Toronto Stock Exchange symbol*]
XCN	Northern Airways, Inc. [*Grand Forks, ND*] [*FAA designator*] (FAAC)
XCNGR	Exchanger (AAG)
XCO	Cross Connection
XCOM	Exterior Communications [*Military*] (CAAL)
XCONN	Cross Connection
XCORA	Xcor International, Inc. Cl A [*NASDAQ symbol*] (NQ)
XCP	Ex-Coupon [*Without the right to coupons, as of a bond*] [*Finance*]
XCP	Except (FAAC)
XCP	Expendable Current Profiler [*Instrumentation, oceanography*]
XCPT	Except (KSC)
XCR	Little Falls, MN [*Location identifier*] [*FAA*] (FAAL)
XCS	Cape Seppings, AK [*Location identifier*] [*FAA*] (FAAL)
XCS	Cross-Country Skiing
XCS	Ten Call Seconds [*Telecommunications*] (TEL)
XCS	Xerox Computer Services [*Xerox Corp.*]
XCT	X-Band Communications Transponder
XCU	Explosion Collapse, Underground Operations
XC & UC	Exclusive of Covering and Uncovering
XCVR	Transceiver (AAG)

XCY	Cross Country [*Also, XC*]
XD	Crossed [*Telecommunications*] (TEL)
XD	Ex-Directory [*Telecommunications*] (TEL)
X-D	Ex-Dividend [*Without the right to dividend*] [*Stock exchange term*]
X/D	Ex Dividendum [*Without (or Exclusive) of Dividend*] [*Stock exchange*] (ROG)
XD	Examined (ROG)
XD	Executed (ROG)
XD	Executive Development [*Civil Service Commission*]
X & D	Experiment and Development [*Flotilla*] [*Landing Craft*]
XD	Exploratory Development (MCD)
XD	Extra Dense
XDA	X-Band Drive Amplifier
XDC	Xylene-Dioxane-Cellosolve [*Scintillation solvent*]
XDCR	Transducer (AAG)
XDE	Xylene-Dioxane-Ethanol [*Scintillation solvent*]
XDER	Transducer
XDH	Xanthine Dehydrogenase [*An enzyme*]
XDIVU	Naval Experimental Diving Unit
XDM	State University of New York, Agricultural and Technical College at Delhi, Delhi, NY [*OCLC symbol*] (OCLC)
XDM	X-Ray Density Measurement
XDP	X-Ray Density Probe
XDP	X-Ray Diffraction Powder
XDP	Xanthosine Diphosphate [*Biochemistry*]
XDP	Xeroderma Pigmentosum [*Oncology*]
XDPC	X-Ray Diffraction Powder Camera
XDPS	X-Band Diode Phase Shifter
XDR	Crusader (ROG)
XDR	Transducer (AAG)
XDS	X-Ray Diffraction System
XDS	Xerox Data Systems [*Formerly, SDS*]
XDT	Xenon Discharge Tube
XDUCER	Transducer
XDUP	Extended Disk Utilities Program
XDY	Valdosta Moody Air Force Base, GA [*Location identifier*] [*FAA*] (FAAL)
XE	Euro Control [*Belgium*] [*ICAO designator*] (FAAC)
XE	Experimental Engine [*NASA*]
Xe	Xenon [*Chemical element*]
XEBC	XEBEC [*NASDAQ symbol*] (NQ)
XEC	Execute
XECF	Experimental Engine - Cold Flow Configuration [*NERVA*]
XED	Medford, OK [*Location identifier*] [*FAA*] (FAAL)
XEDS	X-Ray Energy Dispersive System [*Microparticle analysis*]
XEF	Xenon Fluoride (MCD)
XEG	X-Ray Emission Gauge
XEG	Xerox Education Group
XEL	Excelsior Life Insurance [*Toronto Stock Exchange symbol*]
XELEDOP...	Transmitting Elementary Dipole with Optional Polarity (MCD)
Xen	De Xenophane [*of Aristotle*] [*Classical studies*] (OCD)
XEN	Xenia, OH [*Location identifier*] [*FAA*] (FAAL)
Xen	Xenophon [*428-354BC*] [*Classical studies*] (OCD)
XEQ	Execute
XER	Xerox Corp., Xerox Library Services, Webster, NY [*OCLC symbol*] (OCLC)
XER	Xerox Reproduction (AAG)
XERB	Experimental Environmental Research Buoy [*Marine science*] (MSC)
XERG	Xonics Electron Radiography [*Medical x-ray imaging equipment*]
XES	X-Ray Emission Spectra
XES	X-Ray Energy Spectrometry
XF	Experimental Fighter
XF	Extended Family [*Unitarian Universalist program*]
XF	Extra Fine
xf	Midway Islands [*MARC country of publication code*] [*Library of Congress*] (LCCP)
XF	Xudozestvennyj Fol'klor [*A publication*]
X15-F	Model number used by Eastman Kodak Co. [*Name is said to have been derived from symbol on magicube (X), product's place in sales line (15), and flip-flash unit that replaced magicube (F)*]
XFA	Cross-Field Acceleration
XFA	X-Ray Fluorescence Absorption
XFC	Extended Function Code
XFC	Transfer Charge [*Telecommunications*] (TEL)
XFC	X-Band Frequency Converter
XFD	Crossfeed (NASA)
XFD	X-Ray Flow Detection
XFER	Transfer (AAG)
XFES	Xerox Family Education Services
XFH	X-Band Feed Horn
XfL	Cross in Front of Left Foot [*Dance terminology*]
XFLT	Expanded Flight Line Tester
XFM	Expeditionary Force Message [*Usually, EFM*] [*Low-rate cable or radio message selected from a list of standard wordings*]
XFM	State University of New York, College at Fredonia, Fredonia, NY [*OCLC symbol*] (OCLC)

XFM	X-Band Ferrite Modulator
XFMR	Transformer (AAG)
XFN	Victoria, TX [Location identifier] [FAA] (FAAL)
XFQH	Xenon-Filled Quartz Helix
XFR	Transfer
XFRMR	Transformer
XFS	Fort Sill, OK [Location identifier] [FAA] (FAAL)
XFS	Xenogenic Fetal Skin [Medicine]
XFT	Xenon Flash Tube
XG	Crossing
XG	IMP Group Ltd. Aviation Services [Canada] [ICAO designator] (FAAC)
XGAM	Experimental Guided Air Missiles
XGDS	Exempt from General Declassification Schedule (MCD)
XGG	Gorom-Gorom [Upper Volta] [Airport symbol] (OAG)
XGP	Xanthogranulomatous Pyelonephritis [Medicine]
XGP	Xerox Graphic Printer [Xerox Corp.]
XGPRT	Xanthine-Guanine Phosphoribosyltransferase [An enzyme]
XGRAPHY	Xylography [Wood engraving] (ROG)
XH	Experimental Helicopter
xh	Niue [MARC country of publication code] [Library of Congress] (LCCP)
XH	Sign-Filled Half-Word Designator [Data processing]
XH	Xerogrammata Hochschulschriften [A publication]
XHAIR	Cross Hair (IEEE)
XHE	Hawaii Express [Los Angeles, CA] [FAA designator] (FAAC)
XHF	Extra-High Frequency (NVT)
XHM	X-Ray Hazard Meter
XHMO	Extended Huckel Molecular Orbit (IEEE)
xho	Xhosa [MARC language code] [Library of Congress] (LCCP)
XHR	Extra-High Reliability
XHS	Indiana Historical Society, Indianapolis, IN [OCLC symbol] (OCLC)
XHST	Exhaust (AAG)
XHV	Extreme High Vacuum
XHVY	Extra Heavy
X-I	Ex-Interest [Without the right to interest] [Finance]
xi	St. Christopher-Nevis-Anguilla [MARC country of publication code] [Library of Congress] (LCCP)
XIA	X-Band Inteferometer Antenna
XIB	IBM Corp., Library Processing Center, White Plains, NY [OCLC symbol] (OCLC)
XIC	Convent of Immaculate Conception Sisters of St. Benedict, Ferdinand, IN [OCLC symbol] (OCLC)
XIC	Transmission Interface Converter
XIC	Xichang [China] [Airport symbol] (OAG)
XICO	Xicor, Inc. [NASDAQ symbol] (NQ)
XICS	Xerox Integrated Composition System [Xerox Corp.] [Computer typesetting system]
XICTMD	Xerox International Center for Training and Management Development [Leesburg, VA]
XID	Exchange Identification
XIDX	Xidex Corp. [NASDAQ symbol] (NQ)
XII	Washington, DC [Location identifier] [FAA] (FAAL)
XII P	Testaments of the Twelve Patriarchs [Apocalyptic book]
XIM	Ithaca College, Ithaca, NY [OCLC symbol] (OCLC)
XIM	X-Ray Intensity Meter
XIMIA	Information Circular. United States Bureau of Mines [A publication]
XIN	Ex-Interest [Without the right to interest] [Finance]
XING	Crossing (MCD)
XINT	Ex-Interest [Without the right to interest] [Finance]
XI/O	Execute Input/Output (DEN)
XIP	Xerox Individualized Publishing
XIRS	Xenon Infrared Searchlight
XIS	Xenon Infrared Searchlight
XIS	X*PRESS Information Services [Golden, CO] (EISS)
XIT	Extra Input Terminal
xj	St. Helena [MARC country of publication code] [Library of Congress] (LCCP)
XJM	Schenectady County Community College, Schenectady, NY [OCLC symbol] (OCLC)
XJN	Milwaukee, WI [Location identifier] [FAA] (FAAL)
XJP	Jasper Public Library, Jasper, IN [OCLC symbol] (OCLC)
xk	St. Lucia [MARC country of publication code] [Library of Congress] (LCCP)
XK	X-Band Klystron
XL	Cross-Reference List
XL	Crystal
XL	Excess Lactate
XL	Execution Language
XL	Extra Large [Size]
xl	St. Pierre and Miquelon [MARC country of publication code] [Library of Congress] (LCCP)
XL	Unmarried Lady [Citizens band radio slang]
XL	Xudozestvennaja Literatura [A publication]
XL	Xylose-Lysine [Agar base] [Microbiology]
XLA	X-Band Limiter Attenuator
XLATION	Translation
XLC	Extra Luxurious Chaparral

XLC	Indiana University, School of Medicine, Medical Education Resources Program, Indianapolis, IN [OCLC symbol] (OCLC)
XLC	Xenon Lamp Collimator
XLD	Experimental LASER Device (MCD)
XLD	Xylose-Lysine-Deoxycholate [Growth medium]
XLDT	Xenon LASER Discharge Tube
XLE	Columbus, GA [Location identifier] [FAA] (FAAL)
XLI	Extra-Low Interstitial [Alloy]
XLISP	Extension of LISP [List Processor] 1.5 [Programing language] (CSR)
XLIST	Execution List (MCD)
XLM	St. Lawrence University, Canton, NY [OCLC symbol] (OCLC)
XLMR	X-Linked Mental Retardation [Genetics]
XLP	X-Linked Lymphoproliferative (Syndrome) [Medicine]
XLPE	Cross-Linked Polyethylene [Organic chemistry] (NRCH)
XLPS	Xenon Lamp Power Supply
XLR	Experimental Liquid Rocket [Air Force, NASA]
XLR	X-Linked, Lymphocyte-Regulated [Genetics]
XLS	St. Louis [Senegal] [Airport symbol] (OAG)
XLS	Xenon Light Source
XLS	Xerox Learning Systems
XLSS	Xenon Light Source System
XLT	Cross-Linked Polyethylene [Organic chemistry]
XLT	Xenon LASER Tube
XLTN	Translation (NASA)
XLTR	Translator (MSA)
XL & UL	Exclusive of Loading and Unloading
XLWB	Extra-Long Wheelbase
XM	Christmas
XM	Expanded Memory
XM	Experimental Missile [Air Force, NASA]
XM	Experimental Model
XM	Research Missile [NATO]
xm	St. Vincent [MARC country of publication code] [Library of Congress] (LCCP)
XMAP	Sweeper Device [Navy symbol]
XMAS	Christmas
XMAS	Extended Mission Apollo Simulation [NASA] (IEEE)
X/MBR	Cross Member [Automotive engineering]
XMC	Borough of Manhattan Community College, New York, NY [OCLC symbol] (OCLC)
XmC	Standard Microfilm Reproductions Ltd., Scarborough, ON, Canada [Library symbol] [Library of Congress] (LCLS)
XMD	Ozark, AL [Location identifier] [FAA] (FAAL)
XME	Medgar Evers College of the City University of New York, Brooklyn, NY [OCLC symbol] (OCLC)
XMFR	Transformer (AAG)
XMG	Mahendranagar [Nepal] [Airport symbol] (OAG)
XMH	Manihi [French Polynesia] [Airport symbol] (OAG)
XMI	Christmas Island [Seismograph station code, US Geological Survey] (SEIS)
XMI	Masasi [Tanzania] [Airport symbol] (OAG)
XMI	Seymour-Moss International Ltd. [Vancouver Stock Exchange symbol]
XMIT	Transmit [or Transmitter]
XML	Miles Laboratories, Inc., Miles Pharmaceutical Division, West Haven, CT [OCLC symbol] (OCLC)
XML	Minlaton [Australia] [Airport symbol] [Obsolete] (OAG)
XMM	State University of New York, Agricultural and Technical College at Morrisville, Morrisville, NY [OCLC symbol] (OCLC)
XMOFA	Bureau of Mines. Open File Report [United States] [A publication]
XMP	Marion Public Library, Marion, IN [OCLC symbol] (OCLC)
XMP	Xanthosine Monophosphate [Biochemistry]
XMR	Cape Canaveral, FL [Location identifier] [FAA] (FAAL)
XMS	Experimental Development Specification [Military] (CAAL)
XMS	X-Band Microwave Source
XMS	Xavier Mission Sisters [Catholic Mission Sisters of St. Francis Xavier] [Roman Catholic religious order]
XMS	Xerox Memory System
XMSN	Transmission (AAG)
XMT	Exempt (NVT)
XMT	Transmit (MSA)
XMT	X-Band Microwave Transmitter
XMTD	Transmitted (MCD)
XMTG	Transmitting
XMTL	Transmittal (IEEE)
XMTPB	Technical Progress Report. United States Bureau of Mines [A publication]
XMTR	Transmitter
XMT-REC	Transmit-Receive (AAG)
XMTR-REC	Transmitter-Receiver
XN	Christian
XN	Ex-New [Without the right to claim any new stocks or shares] [Stock exchange term]
XN	Experimental (Navy)
XNB	X-Band Navigation Beacon
XNC	Nazareth College of Rochester, Rochester, NY [OCLC symbol] (OCLC)

XNIPA......... United States Naval Institute. Proceedings [*A publication*]
XNL .... NELINET [*New England Library Information Network*], Newton, MA [*OCLC symbol*] (OCLC)
XNN............ Xining [*China*] [*Airport symbol*] (OAG)
XNO............ North, SC [*Location identifier*] [*FAA*] (FAAL)
XNOS .... Experimental Network Operating System
XNRX........... Xenerex Corp. [*NASDAQ symbol*] (NQ)
XNTY........... Christianity
XNWRA ...... US News and World Report [*A publication*]
XNX .... Xenex Industries & Resources Ltd. [*Vancouver Stock Exchange symbol*]
XO .... Crystal Oscillator (IEEE)
XO .... Examination Officer (ADA)
XO .... Executive Officer [*Military*]
XO .... Expenditure Order [*Military*] (AABC)
XO .... Experimental Officer [*Also, EO, ExO*] [*Ministry of Agriculture, Fisheries, and Food*] [*British*]
XO .... Extra Old [*Designation on brandy labels*]
XO .... Xanthine Oxidase [*An enzyme*]
XO .... Xylenol Orange [*An indicator*] [*Chemistry*]
XOB............ Xenon Optical Beacon
XOC........... Experimental On-Line Capabilities [*Data processing*]
XOFF........ Transmitter Off (BUR)
XOID.......... Xyloid [*Woody*] (ROG)
XON........... Cross-Office Highway [*Telecommunications*] (TEL)
XON........... Exxon Corp. [*NYSE symbol*]
XON........... Transmitter On (BUR)
XOP........... Extended Operation
XOR........... Exclusive Or [*Gates*] [*Data processing*]
XOS........... Cross-Office Slot [*Telecommunications*] (TEL)
XOS........... Extra Outsize [*Clothing*]
XOS........... Xerox Operating System
XOVR......... Exovir, Inc. [*NASDAQ symbol*] (NQ)
XOW .... Express Order Wire [*Telecommunications*] (TEL)
XOXIA .... Xonics, Inc. Cl A [*NASDAQ symbol*] (NQ)
XP .... Expansionist Party of the United States (EA)
XP .... Express Paid
XP............. Fire Resistive Protected [*Insurance classification*]
xp .... Spratly Islands [*MARC country of publication code*] [*Library of Congress*] (LCCP)
XP............. Xeroderma Pigmentosum [*Genetic disorder*]
XPA .... Pama [*Upper Volta*] [*Airport symbol*] (OAG)
XPA .... X-Band Parametric Amplifier
XPA .... X-Band Passive Array
XPA .... X-Band Planar Array
XPA .... X-Band Power Amplifier
XPAA .... X-Band Planar Array Antenna
XPARS .... External Research Publication and Retrieval System [*Department of State*]
XPC .... Christus
XPC .... Expect (FAAC)
XPD .... Cross-Polarization Discrimination
XPD .... Expedient Demise [*Used as title of novel by Len Deighton*]
XPD .... Expedite (MUGU)
XPDR .... Transponder (MUGU)
XPG .... Converted merchant ships, assigned to antisubmarine patrol or convoy escort [*Navy symbol*]
XPH .... Port Heiden, AK [*Location identifier*] [*FAA*] (FAAL)
XPI .... Cross-Polarization Interference [*in radio transmission*]
XPL............ Explosive (AAG)
XPLOR .... Xerox 9700 Users' Association (EA)
XPLOS .... Explosive (FAAC)
XPLR .... Xplor Energy Corp. [*NASDAQ symbol*] (NQ)
XPLT .... Exploit (MUGU)
XPM............ Expanded Metal [*Heavy gauge*]
XPM............ Xerox Planning Model [*A computerized representation of the Xerox Corp.'s operations*]
XPN .... Expansion (AAG)
XPNDR .... Transponder (AAG)
XPONDER ... Transponder
X-POP .... X-Body Axis Perpendicular to Orbit Plane [*Aerospace*]
XPP .... Express Paid Letter (ROG)
XPP .... Xi Psi Phi [*Fraternity*]
XPPA.......... X-Band Pseudopassive Array
XPPA.......... X-Band Pulsed Power Amplifier
XPR .... Ex-Privileges [*Without the right to privileges*] [*Finance*]
XPS .... X-Band Phase Shifter
XPS .... X-Ray Photoemission Spectroscopy
XPSW .... External Processor Status Word
XPT .... Crosspoint [*Switching element*] (MSA)
XPT .... Export
XPT .... Express Paid Telegraph
XPT .... External Page Table [*Data processing*] (BUR)
XPT .... X-Band Pulse Transmitter
XPU .... West Kuparuk, AK [*Location identifier*] [*FAA*] (FAAL)
XPW .... American Ex-Prisoners of War (EA)
XQ .... Cross-Question [*Transcripts*]
XQ .... Experimental Target Drone [*Air Force, NASA*]
X/Q............. Relative Concentration [*Symbol*] (NRCH)
XQA........... Greenville, ME [*Location identifier*] [*FAA*] (FAAL)
XQH........... Xenon Quartz Helix

XQM .... Queens College, Flushing, NY [*OCLC symbol*] (OCLC)
XQP .... Quepos [*Costa Rica*] [*Airport symbol*] (OAG)
XR. .... Cross Reference (MCD)
XR. .... Ex-Rights [*Without rights*] [*Business and trade*]
XR. .... Examiner (ROG)
XR. .... Export Reactor (NRCH)
XR. .... Extended Range [*Film*] [*Briteline Corp.*]
XR. .... Index Register
XR. .... X: A Quarterly Review [*A publication*]
XR. .... X-Ray
9XR .... Rwanda [*Aircraft nationality and registration mark*] (FAAC)
XRAY .... Colonial X-Ray Corp. [*NASDAQ symbol*] (NQ)
X-Ray Spect ... X-Ray Spectrometry [*A publication*]
X-Ray Spectrom ... X-Ray Spectrometry [*A publication*]
XRB .... X-Band RADAR Beacon
XRC .... Xerox Research Centre of Canada Library [*UTLAS symbol*]
XRCD .... X-Ray Crystal Density
XRD .... X-Ray Diffraction [*or Diffractometer*]
XRDS .... Crossroads
X-REA .... X-Ray Events Analyzer (KSC)
X-REF .... Cross Reference (NG)
XREP .... Auxiliary Report (FAAC)
XRF .... Experimental Reproduction Film (DIT)
XRF .... Explosion Release Factor [*Nuclear energy*] (NRCH)
XRF .... Rockefeller Foundation, Library, New York, NY [*OCLC symbol*] (OCLC)
XRF .... X-Ray Fluorescence [*Spectrometry*]
XRFS .... X-Ray Fluorescence Spectrometer
XRG .... X-Ray Generator [*Instrumentation*]
XRGP .... Extended Range Guided Projectiles (MCD)
XRI............. Xenium Resources, Incorporated [*Vancouver Stock Exchange symbol*]
XRII............ X-Ray Image Intensifier
XRL............. Extended-Range Lance [*Missile*]
XRM .... External Relational Memory
XRM .... Extra Range Multigrade [*Automotive engineering*]
XRM .... X-Ray Microanalyzer (IEEE)
XRN .... RY NT Financial Capital Shares [*Toronto Stock Exchange symbol*]
XROI........... X-Ray Optical Interferometer
XRP .... X-Ray and Photofluorography Technician [*Navy*]
XRP .... X-Ray Polychromator
XRPM .... X-Ray Projection Microscope (IEEE)
XRPRA .... RY II Financial Pr. [*Toronto Stock Exchange symbol*]
XRS .... X-Ray Spectrometry
XRT .... Ex-Rights [*Without Rights*] [*Stock exchange term*]
XRT .... X-Ray Technician [*Navy*]
X-RT .... X-Ray Telescope (MCD)
XRT .... X-Ray Therapy [*or Treatment*]
XRTOW ...... Extended Range TOW (MCD)
X-RTS .... Ex-Rights [*Without Rights*] [*Business and trade*]
XRW .... Fort Campbell, KY [*Location identifier*] [*FAA*] (FAAL)
XRX .... Xerox Corp. [*NYSE symbol*]
XRY .... Jerez De La Frontera [*Spain*] [*Airport symbol*] (OAG)
XRY .... Yakima, WA [*Location identifier*] [*FAA*] (FAAL)
XRYR.......... RY Financial Prior Installment Receipts [*Toronto Stock Exchange symbol*]
XS.............. Atmospherics (FAAC)
XS.............. Christus
XS.............. Cross Section
XS.............. Excess
XS.............. Expenses
XS.............. Extra Strong
XS.............. Extremely Severe [*Rock climbing*]
XS.............. Xerces Society (EA)
XS3............. Excess Three [*Code*]
XS-11 .... Excess Eleven [*1967 group of scientist-astronauts selected by NASA*]
XSA .... Cross-Sectional Area [*Cardiology*]
XSA .... X-Band Satellite Antenna
XSAL........... Xenon Short Arc Lamp
XSB .... Xavier Society for the Blind [*New York, NY*] (EA)
XSC .... South Caicos [*British West Indies*] [*Airport symbol*] (OAG)
XSC .... Southampton Center of Long Island University, Southampton, NY [*OCLC symbol*] (OCLC)
XSD .... Southeast Dubois County, School Corp. Library, Ferdinand, IN [*OCLC symbol*] (OCLC)
XSD .... Tonopah, NV [*Location identifier*] [*FAA*] (FAAL)
XSE .... Sebba [*Upper Volta*] [*Airport symbol*] (OAG)
XSECT ...... Cross Section
XSF .... Springfield, OH [*Location identifier*] [*FAA*] (FAAL)
XSF .... X-Ray Scattering Facility
XSL .... Experimental Space Laboratory
XSM .... Experimental Strategic Missile
XSM .... Experimental Surface Missile
XSM .... X-Ray Stress Measurement
XSOA .... Excess Speed of Advance Authorized [*Navy*] (NVT)
X-SONAD ... Experimental Sonic Azimuth Detector (MCD)
XSP .... Singapore-Seletar [*Singapore*] [*Airport symbol*] (OAG)
XSP .... Xi Sigma Pi [*Fraternity*]
XSPV .... Experimental Solid Propellant Vehicle

XSR .... X-Band Scatterometer RADAR
XSS .... Experimental Space Station [NASA]
XSS .... Xenon Solar Simulator
XST .... Xylem Sap Tension [Botany]
XSTA .... X-Band Satellite Tracking Antenna
XSTD .... Expendable Salinity/Temperature/Depth Probe [Oceanography] (MSC)
XSTD .... X-Band Stripline Tunnel Diode
XSTDA ...... X-Band Stripline Tunnel Diode Amplifier
XSTR .... Extra Strong (MSA)
XSTR .... Transistor (AAG)
XSTT .... Excess Transit Time
XSV .... Expendable Sound Velocimeter [Oceanography] (MSC)
XT .... Christ
XT .... Cross Talk (IEEE)
XT .... Exotropia Near [Ophthalmology]
XT .... Upper Volta [Aircraft nationality and registration mark] (FAAC)
XT .... X-Ray Tube
XTA .... X-Band Tracking Antenna
XTAL .... Crystal
XTALK .... Crosstalk [Telecommunications] (MSA)
XTASI .... Exchange of Technical Apollo Simulation Information [NASA] (IEEE)
XTC .... Exco Technologies [Toronto Stock Exchange symbol]
XTC .... External Transmit Clock
XTE .... X-Ray Timing Explorer
XTEL .... Cross Tell (IEEE)
XTEN .... Xerox Telecommunications Network [Proposed] (TSSD)
XTIAN .... Christian
XTLK .... Cross Talk [Aviation] (FAAC)
XTLO .... Crystal Oscillator
XTM .... Experimental Test Model
XTN .... Christian (ROG)
XTND .... Extend [or Extended]
XTO .... X-Band Triode Oscillator
XTP .... Xanthosine Triphosphate [Biochemistry]
XTPA .... X-Band Tunable Parametric Amplifier
XTR .... X-Ray Transition Radiation
XTR .... XTRA Corp. [NYSE symbol]
XTRA .... Extra (ROG)
XTRM .... Extreme
XTRY .... Extraordinary (ROG)
XTS .... Cross-Tell Simulator (IEEE)
XTWA .... X-Band Traveling Wave Amplifier
XTWM .... X-Band Traveling Wave MASER
XTX .... X-Band Transmitter
XTY .... Christianity
XU .... Cambodia [Aircraft nationality and registration mark] (FAAC)
XU .... Excretory Urogram [Medicine]
XU .... Fire Resistive Unprotected [Insurance classification]
XU .... X Unit [A unit of wavelength]
XU .... Xavier University [Louisiana; Ohio]
XUB .... Circleville, OH [Location identifier] [FAA] (FAAL)
XUG .... Xyvision Users Group [Richmond, VA] (EA)
XUM .... Xenium [Gift] (ROG)
XUS .... Xavier University. Studies [A publication]
XUV .... Extreme Ultraviolet
XV .... Administration de Aeropuertos y Servicios Auxiliares a la Nauegacion Aerea [AASANA] [Bolivia] [ICAO designator] (FAAC)
XV .... Vietnam [Aircraft nationality and registration mark] (FAAC)
XV .... X-Ray Vision
XVA .... X-Ray Vidicon Analysis
XVERS .... Transverse (AAG)
XVII S .... XVIIe Siecle [A publication]
XVN .... Venice, FL [Location identifier] [FAA] (FAAL)
XVP .... Executive Vice President
XVR .... Exchange Voltage Regulator [Telecommunications] (TEL)
XVT .... Rome, NY [Location identifier] [FAA] (FAAL)
XVTR .... Transverter (AAG)
XW .... Ex-Warrants [Without Warrants] [Stock exchange term]
XW .... Experimental Warhead
XW .... Extra Wide [Size]
XW .... Laos [Aircraft nationality and registration mark] (FAAC)
X-WARR ..... Ex-Warrants [Without Warrants] [Business and trade]
XWAVE ...... Extraordinary Wave (IEEE)
X-WAY ...... Expressway
XWB .... Ozark, Ft. Rucker, AL [Location identifier] [FAA] (FAAL)
XWC .... Wabash-Carnegie Public Library, Wabash, IN [OCLC symbol] (OCLC)
XWCC .... Expanded Water Column Characterization [Oceanography] (MSC)
XWS .... Experimental Weapon Specification
XWS .... Experimental Weapon System
XWY .... West Union, IA [Location identifier] [FAA] (FAAL)
XX .... Dos Equis [Beer] [Standard Brands, Inc.]
XX .... Double Excellent
XX .... Feminine Chromosome Pair
XX .... Heavy [Used to qualify weather phenomena such as rain, e.g., heavy rain equals XXRA] [Aviation code] (FAAC)

xx .... No Place [or Unknown] [MARC country of publication code] [Library of Congress] (LCCP)
X-X .... Pitch Axis [Aerospace] (AAG)
XX .... Twenty Committee [British espionage unit named after a "double-cross" operation it conducted during World War II]
XXC .... University of South Dakota, Card Reproduction Project, Vermillion, SD [OCLC symbol] (OCLC)
XXC .... Xerox Canada, Inc. [Toronto Stock Exchange symbol]
XXL .... Extra-Extra Large [Size]
XXS .... Extra-Extra Strong
XXSTR .... Double Extra Strong
XXUS .... Maxxus, Inc. [NASDAQ symbol] (NQ)
XXX .... International Urgency Signal
XXX .... Peru, IN [Location identifier] [FAA] (FAAL)
XXX .... Test Flight Plan [Aviation code] (FAAC)
XXX .... Triple Excellent
XY .... Burma [Aircraft nationality and registration mark] (FAAC)
XY .... Masculine Chromosome Pair
XY .... Spouse [Citizens band radio slang]
XY .... Xylography [Wood engraving] (ROG)
XYA .... X-Y Axis
XYA .... Yandina [Solomon Islands] [Airport symbol] (OAG)
XYAT .... X-Y Axis Table
XYC .... Irvine, KY [Location identifier] [FAA] (FAAL)
XYD .... Daughter [Citizens band radio slang]
XYL .... Ex-Young-Lady [Wife] [Amateur radio slang]
XYL .... Xylocaine [Topical anesthetic]
XYL .... Xylophone [Music]
Xyl .... Xylose [Also, x] [A sugar]
XYLO .... Xylophone [Music] (ADA)
XYM .... Husband [Citizens band radio slang]
XYP .... X-Y Plotter
XYR .... X-Y Recorder
X Yr Dev ..... Ten-Year Device [US Army badge]
XYXXU .... High Plains Genetics Uts [NASDAQ symbol] (NQ)
XYZ .... Examine Your Zipper
XYZ .... Extra Years of Zest [Gerontology]
XZ .... Burma [Aircraft nationality and registration mark] (FAAC)
XZY .... Philadelphia, PA [Location identifier] [FAA] (FAAL)

Y

Y .... Admittance [*Symbol*] [*IUPAC*]
Y .... Alleghany Corp. [*NYSE symbol*]
Y .... Closed at Sea (for High Degree of Emergency Readiness) [*Ship's fittings classification*]
Y .... Doublecross [*i.e., to betray*] [*Criminal slang*]
Y .... Economy-Class Air Traveler
Y .... Except Sixth Form [*For the wearing of schoolgirls' uniforms*] [*British*]
Y .... Late Operating Contact [*Symbol*]   (DEN)
Y .... Male Chromosome
Y .... Pathfinder [*Army skill qualification identifier*]   (INF)
Y .... Planck Function [*Symbol*] [*IUPAC*]
Y .... Prototype [*Designation for all US military aircraft*]
Y .... [*A*] Pyrimidine Nucleoside [*One-letter symbol; see Pyd*]
Y .... Symbol for Upsilon
Y .... Tanker [*Army symbol*]
Y .... Three-Phase Star Connection [*Symbol*]   (DEN)
Y .... Transitional Testing [*Aircraft*]
Y .... Tyrosine [*One-letter symbol; see Tyr*]
Y .... [*The Second*] Unknown Quantity [*Mathematics*]   (ROG)
Y .... Vertical Deflection [*Symbol*]   (DEN)
Y .... Y-Axis
Y .... Yacht   (ADA)
Y .... Yankee [*Phonetic alphabet*] [*International*]   (DSUE)
Y .... Yard [*Measure*]
Y .... Yaw
Y .... Yea [*Vote*]
Y .... Year
Y .... Yeates' Pennsylvania Reports [*1791-1808*]   (DLA)
Y .... Yellow [*Phonetic alphabet*] [*Royal Navy*] [*World War I*]   (DSUE)
Y .... Yen [*Monetary unit in Japan*]
Y .... Yeoman
Y .... Yerushalmi [*Palestinian Talmud*]   (BJA)
Y .... Yield [*Stock market*]
Y .... Yoke [*Phonetic alphabet*] [*World War II*]   (DSUE)
Y .... Yorker [*Phonetic alphabet*] [*Pre-World War II*]   (DSUE)
Y .... Yoshitomi Pharmaceutical Ind. Co. Ltd. [*Japan*] [*Research code symbol*]
Y .... You
Y .... Young Men's [*or Women's*] Christian Association [*Short form of reference, especially to the group's building or specific facility, as "the Y swimming pool"*]
Y .... Young Vic [*British theatrical company*]
Y .... Younger [*or Youngest*]
Y .... Young's Modulus of Elasticity [*Symbol*] [*See also E, YME*]
Y .... Your
Y .... Yttrium [*Preferred form, but see also Yt*] [*Chemical element*]
Y .... Yukon News [*A publication*]
Y .... Yukon Standard Time [*Aviation*]   (FAAC)
4Y .... Selective Service classification suggested by comedian Bob Hope for himself during World War II [*Y stood for "yellow"*]
5Y .... Kenya [*Aircraft nationality and registration mark*]   (FAAC)
6Y .... Jamaica [*Aircraft nationality and registration mark*]   (FAAC)
9Y .... Trinidad and Tobago [*Aircraft nationality and registration mark*]   (FAAC)
Y (Day) ...... June 1, 1944, the deadline for all preparations for the Normandy invasion [*World War II*]
YA .... Afghanistan [*Aircraft nationality and registration mark*]   (FAAC)
YA .... Ash Lighter [*Navy symbol*]
YA .... Yaw Axis
YA .... Yeda-'am. Journal. Hebrew Folklore Society [*Tel-Aviv*] [*A publication*]
YA .... YIVO Annual [*A publication*]
Y/A .... York-Antwerp Rules [*Marine insurance*]
YA .... Young Adult [*Refers to books published for this market*]
YA .... Young Audiences [*An association*]   (EA)
YAA .... Yachtsmen's Association of America   (EA)
YABA .... Yacht Architects and Brokers Association [*Pembroke, MA*]   (EA)
YAC .... Young Adult Council of National Social Welfare Assembly   (EA)

YAC .... Young Astronaut Council   (EA)
YACC .... Young Adult Conservation Corps
YACC .... Young America's Campaign Committee [*Later, FCM*]   (EA)
YACE .... Yukon Alpine Centennial Expedition
Yacht .... Yachting [*A publication*]
YACTOFF .. Yaw Actuator Offset   (KSC)
Yad .... Yadaim   (BJA)
YAD .... Young's Nova Scotia Admiralty Decisions   (DLA)
Yad Energ ... Yadrena Energiya [*A publication*]
Yadernaya Fiz ... Akademiya Nauk SSSR. Yadernaya Fizika [*A publication*]
Yad Fiz .... Yadernaya Fizika [*A publication*]
Yad-Geofiz Issled Geofiz Sb ... Yaderno-Geofizicheskie Issledovaniya, Geofizicheskii Sbornik [*USSR*] [*A publication*]
YADH .... Yeast Alcohol Dehydrogenase [*An enzyme*]
Ya Div Q ..... Yale Divinity Quarterly [*New Haven, CT*] [*A publication*]
Yad Konstanty ... Yadernye Konstanty [*A publication*]
Yad Priborostr ... Yadernoe Priborostroenie [*USSR*] [*A publication*]
Yad Vashem Stud Eur Jew Catastrophe Resist ... Yad Vashem Studies on the European Jewish Catastrophe and Resistance [*A publication*]
YAEC .... Yankee Atomic Electric Company
YAF .... Asbestos Hill [*Canada*] [*Airport symbol*] [*Obsolete*]   (OAG)
YAF .... Yidishe Arbeter Froyen   (BJA)
YAF .... Young Americans for Freedom
YAF .... Young America's Foundation   (EA)
YAF .... Yugoslavian Air Force
YAG............ Fort Frances [*Canada*] [*Airport symbol*]   (OAG)
YAG............ Miscellaneous Auxiliary [*Self-propelled*] [*Navy ship symbol*]
YAG............ Yagi [*Kashiwara*] [*Japan*] [*Seismograph station code, US Geological Survey*] [*Closed*]   (SEIS)
YAG............ Young Actors Guild [*Connellsville, PA*]   (EA)
YAG............ Yttrium-Aluminum Garnet [*LASER technology*]
YAGL .... Yttrium Aluminum Garnet LASER
YAGR .... Ocean RADAR Station Ship [*Navy symbol*] [*Obsolete*]
YAH .... Alfred University, Alfred, NY [*OCLC symbol*]   (OCLC)
YAH .... Yahtse [*Alaska*] [*Seismograph station code, US Geological Survey*]   (SEIS)
YAI .... Young Adult Institute and Workshop [*New York, NY*]   (EA)
YAIC .... Young American Indian Council
YAJ .... Yeda-'am. Journal. Hebrew Folklore Society [*Tel-Aviv*] [*A publication*]
YAJ .... Yorkshire Archaeological Journal [*A publication*]
YAK .... Yakovlev [*Russian aircraft symbol; initialism taken from name of aircraft's designer*]
YAK .... Yakutat [*Alaska*] [*Airport symbol*]   (OAG)
YAK .... Yakutsk [*USSR*] [*Geomagnetic observatory code*]
YAK .... Yakutsk [*USSR*] [*Seismograph station code, US Geological Survey*]   (SEIS)
YAKUA .... Yakuzaigaku [*A publication*]
Yal .... Yalkut Shim'oni   (BJA)
YAL .... Yalta [*USSR*] [*Seismograph station code, US Geological Survey*] [*Closed*]   (SEIS)
YAL .... Yosemite Airlines [*Columbia, CA*] [*FAA designator*]   (FAAC)
YAL .... Yttrium Aluminum LASER
Yale Art Gal Bul ... Yale University. Art Gallery. Bulletin [*A publication*]
Yale Associates Bul ... Yale University. Associates in Fine Arts. Bulletin [*A publication*]
Yale Bicen Pub Contr Miner ... Yale Bicentennial Publications. Contributions to Mineralogy and Petrography [*A publication*]
Yale CISt.... Yale Classical Studies [*A publication*]
Yale Div Q ... Yale Divinity Quarterly [*A publication*]
Yale Forestry Bull ... Yale University. School of Forestry. Bulletin [*A publication*]
Yale French Stud ... Yale French Studies [*A publication*]
Yale Fr St ... Yale French Studies [*A publication*]
Yale Fr Stud ... Yale French Studies [*A publication*]
Yale J Biol ... Yale Journal of Biology and Medicine [*A publication*]
Yale J Biol Med ... Yale Journal of Biology and Medicine [*A publication*]
Yale Law J ... Yale Law Journal [*A publication*]
Yale Lit Mag ... Yale Literary Magazine [*A publication*]
Yale L J ...... Yale Law Journal [*A publication*]

Yale Math Monographs ... Yale Mathematical Monographs [*A publication*]
Yale R .... Yale Review [*A publication*]
Yale Rev ..... Yale Review [*A publication*]
Yale Rev Law & Soc Act'n ... Yale Review of Law and Social Action   (DLA)
Yale Rev of L and Soc Action ... Yale Review of Law and Social
                      Action   (DLA)
Yale Sci ...... Yale Scientific [*A publication*]
Yale Scient Mag ... Yale Scientific Magazine [*A publication*]
Yale Sci Mag ... Yale Scientific Magazine [*A publication*]
Yale Sc Mo ... Yale Scientific Monthly [*A publication*]
Yale Stud World PO ... Yale Studies in World Public Order [*A publication*]
Yale St Wld Pub Ord ... Yale Studies in World Public Order [*A publication*]
Yale U Lib Gaz ... Yale University. Library Gazette [*A publication*]
Yale U Libr ... Yale University. Library Gazette [*A publication*]
Yale Univ Art Gal Bull ... Yale University. Art Gallery. Bulletin [*A publication*]
Yale Univ Lib Gaz ... Yale University. Library. Gazette [*A publication*]
Yale Univ Peabody Mus Nat Hist Annu Rep ... Yale University. Peabody
           Museum of Natural History. Annual Report [*A publication*]
Yale Univ Peabody Mus Nat Hist Bull ... Yale University. Peabody Museum
           of Natural History. Bulletin [*A publication*]
Yale Univ Peabody Mus Nat History Bull ... Yale University. Peabody
           Museum of Natural History. Bulletin [*A publication*]
Yale Univ Sch For Bull ... Yale University. School of Forestry. Bulletin [*A
           publication*]
Yale Univ Sch For Environ Stud Bull ... Yale University. School of Forestry
           and Environmental Studies. Bulletin [*A publication*]
Yalkut Le-sivim Tekhnol U-Minhal Shel Tekst ... Yalkut Le-sivim
           Tekhnologyah U-Minhal Shel Tekstil [*A publication*]
Y Alm .... Yurosholayimer Almanakh [*A publication*]
YalMakh ..... Yalkut Makhiri   (BJA)
YAM .... American Museum of Natural History, New York, NY [*OCLC
           symbol*]   (OCLC)
YAM .... Sault Ste. Marie [*Canada*] [*Airport symbol*]   (OAG)
YAM .... Yamagata [*Japan*] [*Seismograph station code, US Geological
           Survey*]   (SEIS)
Yamaguchi Med ... Yamaguchi Medicine [*Japan*] [*A publication*]
YAN .... Yancey Railroad Co. [*AAR code*]
YAN .... Yangoru [*Papua New Guinea*] [*Seismograph station code, US
           Geological Survey*]   (SEIS)
YANCON .... Yankee Conference [*College sports*]
YANGPAT ... Yangtze Patrol, Asiatic Fleet [*Navy*]
YANK .... Yankee   (ROG)
YANK .... Youth of America Needs to Know
yao .... Yao (Bantu) [*MARC language code*] [*Library of
           Congress*]   (LCCP)
YAO .... Yaounde [*Cameroon*] [*Airport symbol*]   (OAG)
YAP .... Yap [*Caroline Islands*] [*Airport symbol*]   (OAG)
YAP .... Yaw and Pitch
YAP .... Yield Analysis Pattern [*Data processing*]
Yap .... Young Aspiring Professional [*Lifestyle classification*] [*In book
           title "YAP; the Official Young Aspiring Professional's Fast-
           Track Handbook"*]
YAP .... Younger American Playwright [*Slang*]
YAPD .... Young Americans of Polish Descent   (EA)
YAPLO .... Yorkshire Association of Power Loom Overlookers [*A union*]
           [*British*]
Yappie .... Young Artist Professional [*Lifestyle classification*]
YAPRA .... Yadernoe Priborostroenie [*A publication*]
YAR .... Yemen Arab Republic
YAR .... York-Antwerp Rules [*Marine insurance*]
YARA .... Young Americans for Responsible Action
Y-ARD .... Yarrow Admiralty Research Department [*Navy*] [*British*]
Yard R .... Yardbird Reader [*A publication*]
Yarosl Gos Univ Mezhvuz Temat Sb ... Yaroslavskii Gosudarstvennyi
           Universitet. Mezhvuzovskii Tematicheskii Sbornik [*A
           publication*]
YARU .... Yale Arbovirus Research Unit [*Yale University*] [*Research
           center*]   (RCD)
YAS .... Yasodhara Ashram Society   (EA)
YAS .... Yaw Attitude Sensor
YASD .... Young Adult Services Division [*American Library Association*]
YAT .... Attawapiskat [*Canada*] [*Airport symbol*]   (OAG)
YAT .... Yaldymych [*USSR*] [*Seismograph station code, US Geological
           Survey*] [*Closed*]   (SEIS)
Yate-Lee .... Yates-Lee on Bankruptcy [*3rd ed.*] [*1887*]   (DLA)
Yates Sel Cas ... Yates' Select Cases [*1809*] [*New York*]   (DLA)
Yates Sel Cas (NY) ... Yates' Select Cases [*1809*] [*New York*]   (DLA)
YATS .... Youth Attitude Tracking Survey [*Navy*]
YAVIS .... Young, Attractive, Verbal, Intelligent, and Successful
Yawata Tech Rep ... Yawata Technical Report [*A publication*]
YAWF .... Youth Against War and Fascism
Yawnie .... Youngish Anglophone of Westmount and Notre-Dame-De-
           Grace [*Lifestyle classification*] [*Canadian Yuppie
           identified in Keith Harrison's novel "After Six Days"*]
YB .... Yard Bird [*Confined to camp*] [*Military slang*]
YB .... Yearbook
Yb .... Yearbook of Comparative and General Literature [*A
           publication*]
YB .... Yellowknife Bear Resources, Inc. [*Toronto Stock Exchange
           symbol*]
YB .... Yeshiva Benarroch. Tetuan   (BJA)

YB .... YIVO Bleter [*Vilna/New York*] [*A publication*]
YB .... Yorkshire Bulletin of Economic and Social Research [*A
           publication*]
YB .... Ysgrifau Beirniadol [*A publication*]
Yb .... Ytterbium [*Chemical element*]
YBA .... Youth Basketball Association [*Joint program of NBA Players'
           Association and YMCA*]
Yb Agric Coop ... Yearbook of Agricultural Cooperation [*A publication*]
Yb Agric US Dep Agric ... Yearbook of Agriculture. US Department of
           Agriculture [*A publication*]
YB Air & Space L ... Yearbook of Air and Space Law   (DLA)
YB Ames .... Year Book. Ames Foundation   (DLA)
YBBFC .... Younger Brothers Band Fan Club [*Leola, PA*]   (EA)
YBC .... Baie Comeau [*Canada*] [*Airport symbol*]   (OAG)
YBC .... Yale Babylonian Collection   (BJA)
YBCA .... Yearbook of Commercial Arbitration   (DLA)
Yb Calif Avocado Soc ... Yearbook. California Avocado Society [*A
           publication*]
YBD .... Bowdock [*Navy symbol*]
YBDSA .... Yacht Brokers, Designers, and Surveyors Association   (EA-IO)
YBE .... Stewart Aviation Services, Inc. [*FAA designator*]   (FAAC)
YBE .... Uranium City [*Canada*] [*Airport symbol*]   (OAG)
YBE .... York Borough Board of Education, Professional Education
           Library [*UTLAS symbol*]
YB Ed I .... Year Books of Edward I   (DLA)
YB Eur Conv on Human Rights ... Year Book. European Convention on
           Human Rights   (DLA)
YB of the Eur Conv on Human Rights ... Yearbook. European Convention on
           Human Rights [*The Hague, Netherlands*]   (DLA)
YB Europ Conv HR ... Yearbook. European Convention on Human Rights
           [*The Hague, Netherlands*]   (DLA)
YBG .... Saguenay [*Canada*] [*Airport symbol*]   (OAG)
Yb Gloucester Beekprs Ass ... Yearbook. Gloucestershire Bee-Keepers
           Association [*A publication*]
YB Hum Rts ... Yearbook on Human Rights   (DLA)
YBICJ .... Yearbook. International Court of Justice   (DLA)
YB Int'l L Comm'n ... Yearbook. International Law Commission   (DLA)
YB Int'l Org ... Yearbook of International Organizations   (DLA)
YBJ .... Baie Johan Beetz [*Canada*] [*Airport symbol*]   (OAG)
YBK .... Baker Lake [*Canada*] [*Airport symbol*]   (OAG)
YBL .... Campbell River [*Canada*] [*Airport symbol*]   (OAG)
Yb of Leg Stud ... Year Book of Legal Studies [*Madras, India*]   (DLA)
YbLitgSt .... Yearbook of Liturgical Studies [*Notre Dame, IN*] [*A publication*]
YBM .... State University of New York, College at Buffalo, Buffalo, NY
           [*OCLC symbol*]   (OCLC)
YBP .... Years before Present
YBPC .... Young Black Programmers Coalition [*Jackson, MS*]   (EA)
YB P1 Edw II ... Year Books, Part 1, Edward II   (DLA)
YBR .... Brandon [*Canada*] [*Airport symbol*]   (OAG)
YBR .... Sludge Removal Barge [*Navy*]
YBRA .... Yellowstone-Bighorn Research Association   (EA)
Yb R Hort Soc ... Yearbook. Royal Horticulture Society [*A publication*]
YB Rich II ... Bellewe's Les Ans du Roy Richard le Second [*1378-
           1400*]   (DLA)
YBRIF .... Yellowknife Bear Resources, Inc. [*NASDAQ symbol*]   (NQ)
YB (Rolls Ser) ... Year Books, Rolls Series [*1292-1546*]   (DLA)
YB (RS) ..... Year Books, Rolls Series [*1292-1546*]   (DLA)
YB (RS) ..... Year Books, Rolls Series, Edited by Horwood [*1292-
           1307*]   (DLA)
YB (RS) ..... Year Books, Rolls Series, Edited by Horwood and Pike [*1337-
           46*]   (DLA)
Yb R Vet Agric Coll ... Yearbook. Royal Veterinary and Agricultural College
           [*A publication*]
YBSC .... Year Books, Selected Cases   (DLA)
Yb Soc Pol Britain ... Yearbook of Social Policy in Britain [*A publication*]
YB (SS) ...... Year Books, Selden Society [*1307-19*]   (DLA)
YBT .... Yale Oriental Series. Babylonian Texts [*New Haven, CT*] [*A
           publication*]   (BJA)
YBT .... Youssef Ben Tachfine [*Morocco*] [*Seismograph station code,
           US Geological Survey*]   (SEIS)
Yb US Dep Agric ... Yearbook. United States Department of Agriculture [*A
           publication*]
YBV .... Berens River [*Canada*] [*Airport symbol*]   (OAG)
Yb Wld Aff ... Yearbook of World Affairs [*A publication*]
Yb World Aff ... Yearbook of World Affairs [*A publication*]
YBX .... Blanc Sablon [*Canada*] [*Airport symbol*]   (OAG)
Yb Yorks Beekprs Ass ... Yearbook. Yorkshire Bee-keepers Association [*A
           publication*]
YC .... Open Lighter [*Non-self-propelled*] [*Navy symbol*]
YC .... Y-Chromosome
YC .... Yacht Club
YC .... Yale College   (ROG)
YC .... Yankee Conference [*College sports*]
YC .... Yard Craft [*Navy symbol*]
YC .... Yaw Channel
YC .... Yaw Coupling
YC .... Yeomanry Cavalry [*Military*] [*British*]
YC .... Yesterday's Children [*An association*] [*Evanston, IL*]   (EA)
Y & C .... Younge and Collyer's English Chancery Reports [*1841-
           43*]   (DLA)

Y & C .... Younge and Collyer's English Exchequer Equity Reports [*1834-42*] (DLA)
YC .... Youth Clubs [*Public-performance tariff class*] [*British*]
YC .... Youth Conservative [*Political party*] [*British*]
YCA .... Yachting Club of America
YCA .... Yale-China Association (EA)
YCA .... Yield Component Analysis [*Botany*]
YCA .... Young Concert Artists (EA)
YCA .... Young Conservative Alliance of America [*Later, Campus Action Network*] (EA)
YCAP .... Youth Committee Against Poverty
YCB .... Cambridge Bay [*Canada*] [*Airport symbol*] (OAG)
YCB .... Yeast Carbon Base
YCB .... Yellow Creek Bluff [*Alaska*] [*Seismograph station code, US Geological Survey*] (SEIS)
YCC .... Computer Center [*Yale University*] [*Research center*] (RCD)
YCC .... Yearbook of Comparative Criticism [*A publication*]
YCC .... York Centre [*Vancouver Stock Exchange symbol*]
YCC .... Youth Civic Center
YCC .... Youth Conservation Corps (EA)
YCC .... Yuma City-County Public Library, Yuma, AZ [*OCLC symbol*] (OCLC)
YCCA .... National Youth Council on Civic Affairs [*Superseded by CCNYA*] (EA)
YCCA .... Yorkshire Canary Club of America (EA)
Y & CCC .... Younge and Collyer's English Chancery Cases [*62-63 English Reprint*] [*1841-43*] (DLA)
Y & C Ch .... Younge and Collyer's English Chancery Reports [*1841-43*] (DLA)
Y & C Ch Cas ... Younge and Collyer's English Chancery Cases [*62-63 English Reprint*] [*1841-43*] (DLA)
YCCIP .... Youth Community Conservation and Improvement Projects [*Department of Labor*]
YCD .... Fueling Barge [*Navy symbol*] [*Obsolete*]
YCD .... Nanaimo [*Canada*] [*Airport symbol*] (OAG)
YCD .... Youth Correction Division [*Department of Justice*]
YCEE .... Youth Cost per Entered Employment [*Job Training and Partnership Act*] (OICC)
Y & C Ex ..... Younge and Collyer's English Exchequer Equity Reports [*1834-42*] (DLA)
Y & C Exch ... Younge and Collyer's English Exchequer Equity Reports [*1834-42*] (DLA)
YCF .... Car Float [*Non-self-propelled*] [*Navy symbol*]
YCF .... Yankee Critical Facility [*Nuclear energy*]
YCF .... Young Calvinist Federation (EA)
YCF .... Young Conservative Foundation [*Later, CAF*] (EA)
YCF .... Youth Citizenship Fund (EA)
YCG .... Castlegar [*Canada*] [*Airport symbol*] (OAG)
YCGL .... Yearbook of Comparative and General Literature [*A publication*]
YCH .... Chatham [*Canada*] [*Airport symbol*] (OAG)
YCHP .... Yenching Journal of Chinese Studies [*A publication*]
YCI .... Young Communist International [*Dissolved, 1943*]
YCJCYAQFTJB ... Your Curiosity Just Cost You a Quarter for the Jukebox [*Tavern sign*]
YCK .... Open Cargo Lighter [*Navy ship symbol*] [*Obsolete*]
YCL .... Charlo [*Canada*] [*Airport symbol*] (OAG)
YCL .... Yolk Cytoplasmic Layer [*Embryology*]
YCL .... Young Communist League
YCL .... Young Communist League of the United States of America [*New York, NY*] (EA)
YCL .... Youth Counseling League [*New York, NY*] (EA)
YCLA .... Young Circle League of America [*Later, Workmen's Circle*] (EA)
YCLS .... Yale Classical Studies [*A publication*]
YCM .... State University of New York, College at Cortland, Cortland, NY [*OCLC symbol*] (OCLC)
YCM .... YMCA Camp [*Montana*] [*Seismograph station code, US Geological Survey*] [*Closed*] (SEIS)
YCM .... Young Christian Movement [*Formerly, YCW*] [*Defunct*]
YCMD .... Yaw Gimbal Command (KSC)
YCN .... Cochrane [*Canada*] [*Airport symbol*] (OAG)
YCNP .... Yellow Creek Nuclear Plant (NRCH)
YCO .... Coppermine [*Canada*] [*Airport symbol*] (OAG)
Y & Coll ..... Younge and Collyer's English Chancery Reports [*1841-43*] (DLA)
Y & Coll ...... Younge nd Collyer's English Exchequer Equity Reports [*1834-42*] (DLA)
YCOMA ...... Yearbook. Coke Oven Managers' Association [*A publication*]
YCP .... Yaw Coupling Parameter
YCP .... York College of Pennsylvania, York, PA [*OCLC symbol*] (OCLC)
YCP .... Youth Challenge Program
YCR .... Cross Lake [*Canada*] [*Airport symbol*] (OAG)
YCS .... High School Young Christian Students
YCS .... Yale Classical Studies [*A publication*]
YCS .... Yorkshire Celtic Studies [*A publication*]
YCS .... Young Collector Series [*A publication*]
YCS .... Youth Community Service [*ACTION project*]
YCSM .... Young Christian Student Movement
YCSN .... Yukon Conservation Society. Newsletter [*A publication*]

Y C T .... Young Cinema and Theatre [*A publication*]
YCTF .... Younger Chemists Task Force [*American Chemical Society*]
YCTSD ...... Yugoslav Center for Technical and Scientific Documentation [*Belgrade, Yugoslavia*] [*Information service*] (EISS)
YCU .... Youth Clubs United
YCV .... Aircraft Transportation Lighter [*Non-self-propelled*] [*Navy symbol*]
YCW .... Young Christian Workers [*Later, YCM*] (EA)
YCY .... Clyde River [*Canada*] [*Airport symbol*] (OAG)
YCZ .... Yellow Caution Zone [*Runway lighting*] [*Aviation*]
Y & D .... Bureau of Yards and Docks [*Later, NFEC*] [*Navy*]
YD .... Floating Crane [*Non-self-propelled*] [*Navy symbol*]
YD .... Yard [*Navy*]
YD .... Yard [*Measure*]
YD .... Yaw Deviation
YD .... Yemen (Aden) [*Two-letter standard code*] (CNC)
YD .... Yoreh De'ah. Shulhan 'Arukh (BJA)
YD³ .... Cubic Yard
YDA .... Yesterday (FAAC)
YDA .... Young Democrats of America [*Formerly, YDCA*] (EA)
YDAW .... Dawson Public Library, Yukon [*Library symbol*] [*National Library of Canada*] (NLC)
YDAY .... Yesterday [*Business and trade*]
YDB .... Yield Diffusion Bonding
YDB .... Youth Development Bureau [*Department of Health and Human Services*]
YDC .... Yaw Damper Computer
YDC .... Yiddish Dictionary Committee (EA)
YDCA .... Young Democratic Clubs of America [*Later, YDA*] (EA)
YDDPA .... Youth Development and Delinquency Prevention Administration [*Later, Youth Development Bureau*] [*HEW*]
YDF .... Deer Lake [*Canada*] [*Airport symbol*] (OAG)
YDG .... District Degaussing Vessel [*Navy symbol*]
YDI .... Youth Development, Incorporated [*An association*] (EA)
YDKGA .... Yamaguchi Daigaku Kogakubu Kenkyu Hokoku [*A publication*]
YDM .... State University of New York, College of Ceramics at Alfred University, Alfred, NY [*OCLC symbol*] (OCLC)
YDN .... Dauphin [*Canada*] [*Airport symbol*] (OAG)
YDPCK .... Klondike National Historic Site, Parks Canada [*Lieu Historique National Klondike, Parcs Canada*] Dawson City, Yukon [*Library symbol*] [*National Library of Canada*] (NLC)
YDQ .... Dawson Creek [*Canada*] [*Airport symbol*] (OAG)
YDS .... Yards (MCD)
YDS .... Yorkshire Dialect Society. Transactions [*A publication*]
YDSD .... Yards and Docks Supply Depot [*Obsolete*] [*Navy*]
YDSO .... Yards and Docks Supply Office [*Navy*]
YDT .... Diving Tender [*Non-self-propelled*] [*Navy symbol*]
YE .... Lighter, Ammunition [*Navy symbol*]
YE .... Yellow Edges
YE .... Yellow Enzyme [*Biochemistry*]
ye .... Yemen (Sanaa) [*MARC country of publication code*] [*Library of Congress*] (LCCP)
YE .... Yemen (Sanaa) [*Two-letter standard code*] (CNC)
YE .... Yevreyskaya Entsiklopediya [*A publication*] (BJA)
YEA .... Yaw Error Amplifier
YEA .... Year of Energy Action
Yea .... Yeates' Pennsylvania Reports [*1791-1808*] (DLA)
Yearb Agr Co-op ... Yearbook of Agricultural Co-operation [*A publication*]
Yearb Agric US Dep Agric ... Yearbook of Agriculture. US Department of Agriculture [*A publication*]
Yearb Agr USDA ... Yearbook of Agriculture. US Department of Agriculture [*A publication*]
Yearb Am Pulp Pap Mil Supt Assoc ... Yearbook. American Pulp and Paper Mill Superintendents Association [*A publication*]
Yearb Anesth ... Yearbook of Anesthesia [*A publication*]
Yearb Bharat Krishak Samaj ... Yearbook. Bharat Krishak Samaj [*A publication*]
Yearb Bur Miner Resour Geol Geophys ... Yearbook. Bureau of Mineral Resources. Geology and Geophysics [*A publication*]
Yearb Calif Macad Soc ... Yearbook. California Macadamia Society [*A publication*]
Yearb Carnegie Inst Wash ... Yearbook. Carnegie Institute of Washington [*A publication*]
Yearb Child Lit Assoc ... Yearbook. Children's Literature Association [*A publication*]
Yearb Coke Oven Managers' Assoc ... Yearbook. Coke Oven Managers' Association [*England*] [*A publication*]
Yearb Dermatol Syphilol ... Yearbook of Dermatology and Syphilology [*A publication*]
Yearb Drug Ther ... Yearbook of Drug Therapy [*A publication*]
Yearb Endocrinol ... Yearbook of Endocrinology [*A publication*]
Yearb Est Learned Soc Am ... Yearbook. Estonian Learned Society in America [*A publication*]
Yearb Fac Agr Univ Ankara ... Yearbook. Faculty of Agriculture. University of Ankara [*A publication*]
Yearb Gen Surg ... Yearbook of General Surgery [*A publication*]
Yearb Leo Baeck Inst ... Yearbook. Leo Baeck Institute [*A publication*]
Yearb Med ... Yearbook of Medicine [*A publication*]
Yearb Nat Farmers' Ass ... Yearbook. National Farmers' Association [*A publication*]

Yearb Natl Inst Sci India ... Yearbook. National Institute of Sciences of India [*A publication*]
Year Book Carnegie Inst Wash ... Year Book. Carnegie Institution of Washington [*A publication*]
Year Book Indian Natl Sci Acad ... Year Book. Indian National Science Academy [*A publication*]
Year Book Indian Nat Sci Acad ... Year Book. Indian National Science Academy [*A publication*]
Year Book Natl Auricula Primula Soc North Sec ... Year Book. National Auricula and Primula Society. Northern Section [*A publication*]
Year Book Nucl Med ... Year Book of Nuclear Medicine [*United States*] [*A publication*]
Yearb Pap Ind Manage Assoc ... Yearbook. Paper Industry Management Association [*A publication*]
Yearb Pediatr ... Yearbook of Pediatrics [*A publication*]
Yearb P7 Hen VI ... Year Books, Part 7, Henry VI   (DLA)
Yearb Phys Anthropol ... Yearbook of Physical Anthropology [*A publication*]
Yearb R Asiat Soc Bengal ... Yearbook. Royal Asiatic Society of Bengal [*A publication*]
Year Endocrinol ... Year in Endocrinology [*A publication*]
Year Metab ... Year in Metabolism [*A publication*]
Yeates .... Yeates' Pennsylvania Reports [*1791-1808*]   (DLA)
Yeates (PA) ... Yeates' Pennsylvania Reports [*1791-1808*]   (DLA)
Yeb .... Yebamoth   (BJA)
YEC .... Youngest Empty Cell
YEC .... Youth Employment Competency   (OICC)
YedNum ..... Yedi'ot Numismatiyot be-Yisrael. Jerusalem   (BJA)
YEDPA .... Youth Employment and Demonstration Projects Act of 1977
YEDTA .... Youth Employment and Demonstration Training Act [*Department of the Interior*]
YEE .... Yale Economic Essays [*A publication*]
YEER .... Youth Entered Employment Rate [*Job Training and Partnership Act*]   (OICC)
YEG .... Edmonton [*Canada*] [*Airport symbol*]   (OAG)
YEG .... Yeast Extract - Glucose [*Medium*]
YEH .... Yellow Enzyme, Reduced [*Biochemistry*]
YEIS .... Yamaha Energy Induction System
YEK .... Eskimo Point [*Canada*] [*Airport symbol*]   (OAG)
YEL .... Elliot Lake [*Canada*] [*Airport symbol*]   (OAG)
YEL .... Equitable Life Assurance Society of the United States, General Library, New York, NY [*OCLC symbol*]   (OCLC)
YEL .... Yellow   (AAG)
Yel .... Yelverton's English King's Bench Reports [*1603-13*]   (DLA)
YEL .... Young England Library [*A publication*]
YELL .... Yellow Freight Systems of Delaware [*NASDAQ symbol*]   (NQ)
YELL .... Yellowstone National Park
Yellow B R ... Yellow Brick Road [*A publication*]
Yellowstone-Bighorn Research Proj Contr ... Yellowstone-Bighorn Research Project. Contribution [*A publication*]
Yellowstone Libr and Mus Assoc Yellowstone Interpretive Ser ... Yellowstone Library and Museum Association. Yellowstone Interpretive Series [*A publication*]
Yelv .... Yelverton's English King's Bench Reports [*1603-13*]   (DLA)
Yelv (Eng) ... Yelverton's English King's Bench Reports [*1603-13*]   (DLA)
YEM .... Empire State College, Saratoga Springs, NY [*OCLC symbol*] [*Inactive*]   (OCLC)
YEM .... Yemen (Sanaa) [*Three-letter standard code*]   (CNC)
YEMI .... Youngwood Electronic Metals, Incorporated [*NASDAQ symbol*]   (NQ)
YEO .... Yeomanry
YEO .... Yeovil [*British depot code*]
YEO .... Young Entrepreneurs Organization [*Wichita, KS*]   (EA)
YEO .... Youth Employment Officer [*British*]
YEPD .... Yeast Extract - Peptone Dextrose [*Medium*]
YER .... Yeats Eliot Review [*A publication*]
Yer. .... Yerger's Tennessee Supreme Court Reports   (DLA)
YER .... Yerkesik [*Turkey*] [*Seismograph station code, US Geological Survey*]   (SEIS)
Yer. .... Yerushalmi [*Palestinian Talmud*]   (BJA)
Yerg .... Yerger's Tennessee Reports [*9-18 Tennessee*]   (DLA)
Yerg (Tenn) ... Yerger's Tennessee Reports [*9-18 Tennessee*]   (DLA)
YES .... Yearbook of English Studies [*A publication*]
YES .... Years of Extra Savings
YES .... Yeast Extract Sucrose [*Cell growth medium*]
YES .... Yogurt Extra Smooth [*Trademark of the Dannon Co., Inc.*]
YES .... Young Entomologists' Society [*Formerly, TIEG*]   (EA)
YES .... Young Executive Society [*Automotive Warehouse Distributors Association*]
YES .... Youth Education Services [*Summer program*]
YES .... Youth Emergency Service
YES .... Youth Employment Service [*Department of Employment*] [*British*]   (EA)
YES .... Youth Employment Support Volunteers Program [*ACTION*]
YES .... Youth Exhibiting Stamps [*US Postal Service*]
Yessis Rev ... Yessis Review of Soviet Physical Education and Sports [*A publication*]
YEST .... Yesterday   (DSUE)
YESTU .... Yellowstone Reserves Uts [*NASDAQ symbol*]   (NQ)
YESTY .... Yesterday
YET .... Youth Effectiveness Training [*A course of study*]

YETP .... Youth Employment and Training Programs [*Department of Labor*]
Yeung Nam Univ Inst Ind Technol Rep ... Yeung Nam University. Institute of Industrial Technology. Report [*A publication*]
YEV .... Inuvik [*Canada*] [*Airport symbol*]   (OAG)
Yev .... Yevamot   (BJA)
YF .... Covered Lighter [*Self-propelled*] [*Navy symbol*]
YF .... Wife [*Citizens band radio slang*]
YF .... Yawmiyyaet Filastiniyya   (BJA)
YF .... Yerushalmi Fragments [*A publication*]   (BJA)
YF .... Young Filmakers Foundation   (EA)
YFA .... Fort Albany [*Canada*] [*Airport symbol*]   (OAG)
YFB .... Ferryboat or Launch [*Self-propelled*] [*Navy symbol*]
YFB .... [*The*] First Boston Corp., New York, NY [*OCLC symbol*]   (OCLC)
YFB .... Frobisher Bay [*Canada*] [*Airport symbol*]   (OAG)
YFC .... Fredericton [*Canada*] [*Airport symbol*]   (OAG)
YFC .... Yakima Firing Center   (MCD)
YFC .... Young Farmers' Club [*British*]
YFCI .... Youth for Christ International [*See also JPC*]   (EA-IO)
YFC/USA ... Youth for Christ/USA   (EA)
YFD .... Yard Floating Dry Dock [*Non-self-propelled*] [*Navy symbol*]
YFDC .... Youth Film Distribution Center   (EA)
YFE .... Forestville [*Canada*] [*Airport symbol*]   (OAG)
YFEC .... Youth Forum of the European Communities [*See also FJCE*]   (EA-IO)
YFF .... Waltham, MA [*Location identifier*] [*FAA*]   (FAAL)
YFM .... State University of New York, Agricultural and Technical College at Farmingdale, Farmingdale, NY [*OCLC symbol*]   (OCLC)
YFN .... Covered Lighter [*Non-self-propelled*] [*Navy symbol*]
YFNB .... Large Covered Lighter [*Non-self-propelled*] [*Navy symbol*]
YFND .... Dry Dock Companion Craft [*Non-self-propelled*] [*Navy symbol*]
YFNG .... Covered Lighter (Special Purpose) [*Later, YFNX*] [*Navy symbol*]
YFNX .... Lighter (Special Purpose) [*Non-self-propelled*] [*Navy symbol*]
YFO .... Flin Flon [*Manitoba*] [*Airport symbol*]   (OAG)
Y-FOS .... Y-Force Operations Staff [*Army*] [*World War II*]
YFP .... Floating Power Barge [*Non-self-propelled*] [*Navy symbol*]
YFR .... Refrigerated Covered Lighter [*Self-propelled*] [*Navy symbol*]
YFRN .... Refrigerated Covered Lighter [*Non-self-propelled*] [*Navy symbol*]
YFRT .... Covered Lighter (Range Tender) [*Self-propelled*] [*Navy symbol*]
YFS .... Fort Simpson [*Canada*] [*Airport symbol*]   (OAG)
YFS .... Yale French Studies [*A publication*]
YFS .... Young Flying Service [*Harlingen, TX*] [*FAA designator*]   (FAAC)
YFT .... Torpedo Transportation Lighter [*Navy symbol*] [*Obsolete*]
YFTU .... Yugoslavia Federation of Trade Unions
YFU .... Harbor Utility Craft [*Self-propelled*] [*Navy symbol*]
YFU .... Why Have You Forsaken Us? Letter [*Fundraising*]
YFU .... Yard Freight Unit
YFU .... Youth for Understanding
YF/VA .... Young Filmakers/Video Arts [*Also known as Young Filmakers Foundation*]   (EA)
YF(XYL) .... Wife (Ex-Young-Lady) [*Amateur radio slang*]
YG .... Garbage Lighter [*Self-propelled*] [*Navy symbol*]
YG .... Yankee Group [*Boston, MA*] [*Information service*] [*Telecommunications*]   (TSSD)
YG .... Yellow-Green
YG .... Yellow-Green Beacon [*Aviation*]
YGA .... Gagnon [*Canada*] [*Airport symbol*]   (OAG)
YGB .... Gillies Bay [*Canada*] [*Airport symbol*]   (OAG)
YGC .... Yahweh and the Gods of Canaan [*A publication*]   (BJA)
YGF .... General Foods Technical Center, White Plains, NY [*OCLC symbol*]   (OCLC)
YGJ .... Yonago [*Japan*] [*Airport symbol*]   (OAG)
YGK .... Kingston [*Canada*] [*Airport symbol*]   (OAG)
YGKKA ...... Yuki Gosei Kagaku Kyokaishi [*A publication*]
YGKSA ...... Yogyo Kyokai Shi [*A publication*]
YGL .... La Grande [*Canada*] [*Airport symbol*]   (OAG)
YGL .... Yttrium Garnet LASER
YGM .... State University of New York, College at Geneseo, Geneseo, NY [*OCLC symbol*]   (OCLC)
YGM .... Young Grandmother
YGN .... Garbage Lighter [*Non-self-propelled*] [*Navy symbol*]
YGNR .... Yukon Government News Release [*A publication*]
YGO .... Gods Narrows [*Canada*] [*Airport symbol*]   (OAG)
YGP .... Gaspe [*Canada*] [*Airport symbol*]   (OAG)
YGQ .... Geraldton [*Canada*] [*Airport symbol*]   (OAG)
YGR .... Iles De La Madeleine [*Canada*] [*Airport symbol*]   (OAG)
YGS .... Yale Germanic Studies [*A publication*]
YGS .... Young Guard Society [*Annapolis, MD*]   (EA)
YGV .... Havre Saint Pierre [*Canada*] [*Airport symbol*]   (OAG)
YGW .... Great Whale [*Canada*] [*Airport symbol*]   (OAG)
YGX .... Gillam [*Canada*] [*Airport symbol*]   (OAG)
YH .... Lighter, Ambulance [*Navy symbol*] [*Obsolete*]
YH .... RADAR Beacon [*Maps and charts*]
YH .... Youth Hostel
YHA .... Youth Hostels Association
YHB .... House Boat [*Navy symbol*]

YHD .... Dryden [*Canada*] [*Airport symbol*]   (OAG)
YHI .... Holman Island [*Canada*] [*Airport symbol*]   (OAG)
YHJPCK ..... Kluane National Park, Parks Canada [*Parc National Kluane, Parcs Canada*] Haines Junction, Yukon [*Library symbol*] [*National Library of Canada*]   (NLC)
YHK .... Gjoa Haven [*Canada*] [*Airport symbol*]   (OAG)
YHLC .... Salvage Lift Craft, Heavy [*Non-self-propelled*] [*Navy ship symbol*]
YHM .... Hamilton [*Canada*] [*Airport symbol*]   (OAG)
YHM .... Hamilton College, Clinton, NY [*OCLC symbol*]   (OCLC)
YHMAN ...... Yukon Historical and Museums Association. Newsletter [*A publication*]
YHN .... Hornepayne [*Canada*] [*Airport symbol*]   (OAG)
YHPA .... Your Heritage Protection Association   (EA)
YHR .... Harrington Harbour [*Canada*] [*Airport symbol*]   (OAG)
YHS .... Yukuharu Haiku Society [*Superseded by Yuki Teikei Haiku Society*]   (EA)
YHT .... Heating Scow [*Navy symbol*]
YHT .... Young-Helmholtz Theory [*Physics*]
YHWH .... Yahweh [*Old Testament term for God*]
YHY .... Hay River [*Canada*] [*Airport symbol*]   (OAG)
YHZ .... Halifax [*Canada*] [*Airport symbol*]   (OAG)
YI .... Iraq [*Aircraft nationality and registration mark*]   (FAAC)
YI .... Yukon Indian News [*A publication*]
YIB .... Atikokan [*Canada*] [*Airport symbol*]   (OAG)
yid .... Yiddish [*MARC language code*] [*Library of Congress*]   (LCCP)
YIE .... Young Interference Experiment [*Physics*]
YIEPP .... Youth Incentive Entitlement Pilot Projects [*Department of Labor*]
YIF .... St. Augustin [*Canada*] [*Airport symbol*]   (OAG)
YIFMC .... Yearbook. International Folk Music Council [*A publication*]
YIG .... Yttrium Iron Garnet
YIGIB .... Your Improved Group Insurance Benefits
YIH .... Yichang [*China*] [*Airport symbol*]   (OAG)
YIIJS .... Young Israel Institute for Jewish Studies [*Defunct*]   (EA)
YIK .... Ivugivik [*Canada*] [*Airport symbol*]   (OAG)
YIL .... Yellow Indicating Light   (IEEE)
YILAG .... Yidishe Landvirtshaftlekhe Gezelshaft [*A publication*]   (BJA)
YIN .... Niagara County Community College, Sanborn, NY [*OCLC symbol*]   (OCLC)
YIN .... Yingkow [*Republic of China*] [*Seismograph station code, US Geological Survey*]   (SEIS)
YIN .... Yining [*China*] [*Airport symbol*]   (OAG)
YIO .... Pond Inlet [*Canada*] [*Airport symbol*]   (OAG)
YIP .... Willow Run Airport, Detroit, Michigan [*Airport symbol*]
YIP .... Yield Improvement Program
Yip .... Young Indicted Professional [*Lifestyle classification*]
YIP .... Youth International Party [*Members known as "yippies"*]
YIPL .... Youth International Party Line [*Superseded by Technological American Party*]
YIPME .... Youth Institute for Peace in the Middle East   (EA)
YIR .... Yearly Infrastructure Report   (NATG)
YIS .... Yearbook of Italian Studies [*A publication*]
YITB .... Yours in the Bond [*Motto of fraternity Tau Kappa Epsilon*]
Y It S .... Yale Italian Studies [*A publication*]
YIV .... Island Lake [*Canada*] [*Airport symbol*]   (OAG)
YIVO .... Yidisher Visnshaftlekher Institut [*Yiddish Scientific Institute*]
YIVO .... YIVO Annual of Jewish Social Science [*A publication*]
YJ .... RADAR Homing Beacon [*Maps and charts*]
YJ .... Yellow Jacket [*Immunology*]
Y & J .... Younge and Jervis' English Exchequer Reports [*1826-30*]   (DLA)
YJ .... Yuppie Jeep
YJCS .... Yenching Journal of Chinese Studies [*A publication*]
YJF .... Fort Liard [*Canada*] [*Airport symbol*]   (OAG)
YJM .... Fulton-Montgomery Community College, Johnstown, NY [*OCLC symbol*]   (OCLC)
YJS .... Yale Judaica Series [*A publication*]   (BJA)
YJT .... Stephenville [*Canada*] [*Airport symbol*]   (OAG)
YJV .... Yellow Jacket Venom [*Immunology*]
YK .... RADAR Beacon [*Maps and charts*]
YK .... Syria [*Aircraft nationality and registration mark*]   (FAAC)
YK .... Yiddishe Kultur [*A publication*]
YK .... Yom Kippur   (BJA)
YK .... York Antibodies [*Immunology*]
YKA .... Kamloops [*Canada*] [*Airport symbol*]   (OAG)
YKA .... Yellowknife Array [*Northwest Territories*] [*Seismograph station code, US Geological Survey*]   (SEIS)
YKB .... Yapi-Kredi Bank [*Turkey*]
YKC .... Kingsborough Community College of the City University of New York, Brooklyn, NY [*OCLC symbol*]   (OCLC)
YKC .... Yellowknife [*Northwest Territories*] [*Seismograph station code, US Geological Survey*]   (SEIS)
YKC .... Yellowknife [*Northwest Territories*] [*Geomagnetic observatory code*]
ykc .... Yukon Territory [*MARC country of publication code*] [*Library of Congress*]   (LCCP)
YKE .... Yankee Petroleums Ltd. [*Vancouver Stock Exchange symbol*]
YKIGA .... Yokohama Igaku [*A publication*]
YKK .... Yoshida Kogyo K.K. [*Tokyo, Japan*]

YKK .... Yoshido Kogyo Kabushiki-Kaishi [*Yoshida Industries Ltd.*] [*Japan*]
YKKKA ...... Yakugaku Kenkyu [*A publication*]
YKKZA ...... Yakugaku Zasshi [*A publication*]
YKL .... Schefferville [*Canada*] [*Airport symbol*]   (OAG)
YKM .... Corning Museum of Glass, Corning, NY [*OCLC symbol*]   (OCLC)
YKM .... Yaak [*Montana*] [*Seismograph station code, US Geological Survey*]   (SEIS)
YKM .... Yakima [*Washington*] [*Airport symbol*]   (OAG)
YKM .... Young Kibbutz Movement   (EA)
YKN .... Yankton [*South Dakota*] [*Airport symbol*]   (OAG)
YKN .... Yukon [*FAA*]   (FAAC)
YKQ .... Rupert House [*Canada*] [*Airport symbol*]   (OAG)
YKR .... Yukon Revenue Mines [*Vancouver Stock Exchange symbol*]
YKS .... Yakushima [*Japan*] [*Seismograph station code, US Geological Survey*] [*Closed*]   (SEIS)
YKS .... Yorkshire [*County in England*]
YKT .... Yakutat [*Alaska*] [*Seismograph station code, US Geological Survey*] [*Closed*]   (SEIS)
YKU .... Fort George [*Canada*] [*Airport symbol*]   (OAG)
YKU .... Yakutat [*Alaska*] [*Seismograph station code, US Geological Survey*]   (SEIS)
YKUF .... Yiddisher Kultur Farband   (EA)
YKW .... Yom Kippur War   (BJA)
YKX .... Kirkland Lake [*Canada*] [*Airport symbol*]   (OAG)
YKYRA .... Yakubutsu Ryoho [*A publication*]
YKZ .... Toronto [*Canada*] Buttonville Airport [*Airport symbol*]   (OAG)
YL .... Approach Light Lane [*Aviation*]   (FAAC)
YL .... Yad La-Kore. La-Safran ule-Pe'ile Tarbut   (BJA)
YL .... Yawl   (ROG)
YL .... Yellow [*Maps and charts*]
YL .... Young Lady [*Amateur radio slang*]
YL .... Young Life [*An association*]   (EA)
YL .... Youth Liberation Press   (EA)
YLA .... Open Landing Lighter [*Navy symbol*]
YLB .... Lac La Biche [*Canada*] [*Airport symbol*]
YLC .... Clinton Community College, Plattsburgh, NY [*OCLC symbol*]   (OCLC)
YLC .... Young Life Campaign   (EA)
YLD .... Chapleau [*Canada*] [*Airport symbol*]   (OAG)
YLD .... Yield [*In stock listings of newspapers*]
YLDG .... Yielding   (ROG)
YLG .... Yale University. Library. Gazette [*A publication*]
YLG News ... Library Association. Youth Libraries Group News [*A publication*]
YLI .... [*The*] Yorkshire Light Infantry [*Military unit*] [*British*]
YLI .... Young Ladies Institute   (EA)
YLJ .... Meadow Lake [*Canada*] [*Airport symbol*] [*Obsolete*]   (OAG)
YLJ .... Yale Law Journal [*A publication*]
YLL .... Lederle Laboratories, Pearl River, NY [*OCLC symbol*]   (OCLC)
YLL .... Lloydminster [*Canada*] [*Airport symbol*]   (OAG)
YLLC .... Salvage Lift Craft, Light [*Self-propelled*] [*Navy ship symbol*]
YLM .... Yale Literary Magazine [*A publication*]
YLP .... Mingan [*Canada*] [*Airport symbol*] [*Obsolete*]   (OAG)
YLR .... YAG [*Yttrium Aluminum Garnet*] LASER Range-Finder
Y & LR .... York and Lancaster Regiment [*Military unit*] [*British*]
YLR .... York Legal Record [*Pennsylvania*]   (DLA)
YLRL .... Young Ladies Radio League
YLSTN .... Yellowstone [*FAA*]   (FAAC)
YLT .... Yellow Light   (MSA)
YLT .... Yu-Yen-Hsueh Lun-Ts'ung [*Essays in Linguistics*] [*A publication*]
YLW .... Kelowna [*Canada*] [*Airport symbol*]   (OAG)
YLW .... Yellow   (ADA)
YM .... Dredge [*Self-propelled*] [*Navy symbol*]
YM .... Prototype Missile   (NATG)
YM .... Yacht Measurement
YM .... Yawing Moment   (KSC)
YM .... Yearly Meetings [*Quakers*]
YM .... Yeast Extract - Malt Extract [*Medium*]
YM .... Yellow Man
YM .... Yellow Metal
YM .... Young Man [*A publication*]
YM .... Young Men's [*Christian Association*]
YM .... Young Miss Magazine [*A publication*]
YM .... [*Reference*] Your Message
YMA .... Mayo [*Canada*] [*Airport symbol*]   (OAG)
YMA .... Yarn Merchants Association [*Defunct*]   (EA)
YMA .... Young Menswear Association [*New York, NY*]   (EA)
YMB .... Yeast Malt Broth
YMC .... Moore-Cottrell Subscription Agencies, Inc., North Cohocton, NY [*OCLC symbol*]   (OCLC)
YMC .... Your Marketing Consultant [*An electronic publication*]
YMCA .... Young Men's Christian Association
YMCA-USA ... Young Men's Christian Associations of the United States of America [*Chicago, IL*]   (EA)
YMCU .... Young Men's Christian Union
YMD .... Yemen (Aden) [*Three-letter standard code*]   (CNC)
YMD .... [*Reference*] Your Message Date
YME .... Matane [*Canada*] [*Airport symbol*]   (OAG)

YME............ Young's Modulus of Elasticity [*See also E, Y*]
YMF............ Young Musicians Foundation   (EA)
YMFS........ Young Men's Friendly Society [*British*]
YMHA........ Young Men's Hebrew Association [*Later, YM-YWHA*]
YMHSI....... Yedi'ot ha-Makhon le-Heker ha-Shirah ha-'Ivrit. Jerusalem   (BJA)
YMI............ Young Men's Institute   (EA)
YMISIG...... Young Mensa International Special Interest Group [*Defunct*]   (EA)
YML............ Young Men's Lyceum
YMLC......... Salvage Lift Craft, Medium [*Non-self-propelled*] [*Navy ship symbol*]
YMM.......... Fort McMurray [*Canada*] [*Airport symbol*]   (OAG)
YMM.......... Yeast Minimal Medium [*Microorganism growth medium*]
YMM.......... Youngstown and Mahoning County Public Library, Youngstown, OH [*OCLC symbol*]   (OCLC)
YMMY....... Yedi'ot ha-Makhon le-Mada'ei ha-Yahadut. Jerusalem   (BJA)
YMO .... Moosonee [*Canada*] [*Airport symbol*]   (OAG)
YMP........... Motor Mine Planter [*Navy symbol*]
YMP........... Youth Mobility Program   (OICC)
YMPE......... Year's Maximum Pensionable Earnings
YMS .... Auxiliary Motor Minesweeper [*Navy symbol*]
YMS .... Yaw Microwave Sensor
YMS .... Yield Measurement System
YMS .... Yurimaguas [*Peru*] [*Airport symbol*]   (OAG)
YMT........... Chibougamau [*Canada*] [*Airport symbol*]   (OAG)
YMT........... Motor Tug [*Navy symbol*]
YMTM........ Yikal Maya Than (Mexico) [*A publication*]
Y & MV ...... Yazoo & Mississippi Valley Railroad Co.
YMX .... Montreal [*Canada*] Mirabel International Airport [*Airport symbol*]   (OAG)
YM-YWHA ... Young Men's and Young Women's Hebrew Association [*Formed by a merger of YWHA, YMHA, and Clara de Hirsch Residence*] [*New York, NY*]   (EA)
YN .... Net Tender [*Navy symbol*] [*Obsolete*]
YN .... Yellowknifer [*A publication*]
YN .... Yeoman [*Navy rating*]
YN .... Yes-No [*Response prompt*]
YN .... Young Numismatist [*A publication*]
YN .... [*The*] Youngstown & Northern Railroad Co. [*AAR code*]
YN1............ Yeoman, First Class [*Navy rating*]
YN2............ Yeoman, Second Class [*Navy rating*]
YN3............ Yeoman, Third Class [*Navy rating*]
YNA........... Naiashquan [*Canada*] [*Airport symbol*]   (OAG)
YNB........... Yanbu [*Saudi Arabia*] [*Airport symbol*]   (OAG)
YNB........... Yeast Nitrogen Base
YNC........... Paint Hills [*Canada*] [*Airport symbol*]   (OAG)
YNC........... Yeoman, Chief [*Navy rating*]
YNC........... Yinchuan [*Republic of China*] [*Seismograph station code, US Geological Survey*]   (SEIS)
YNCM........ Yeoman, Master Chief [*Navy rating*]
YNCS .... Yeoman, Senior Chief [*Navy rating*]
YND........... Gatineau/Hull [*Canada*] [*Airport symbol*]   (OAG)
YNE .... Nor East Commuter Airlines [*East Boston, MA*] [*FAA designator*]   (FAAC)
YNE .... Norway House [*Canada*] [*Airport symbol*]   (OAG)
YNER........ Yale Near Eastern Researches [*New Haven/London*] [*A publication*]
YNG........... Gate Craft [*Non-self-propelled*] [*Navy symbol*]
YNG........... Youngstown [*Ohio*] [*Airport symbol*]   (OAG)
YNG........... Youngstown State University, Youngstown, OH [*OCLC symbol*]   (OCLC)
YNHA .... Yosemite Natural History Association   (EA)
YNHH .... Yale-New Haven Hospital
YNK........... Yankee Companies, Inc. [*American Stock Exchange symbol*]
YNM .... Matagami [*Canada*] [*Airport symbol*]   (OAG)
YNP .... Young National Party [*Australian*]   (ADA)
YNPS......... Yankee Nuclear Power Station   (NRCH)
YNR .... Yorkshire, North Riding [*County in England*]   (ROG)
YNSA .... Seaman Apprentice, Yeoman, Striker [*Navy rating*]
YNSN .... Seaman, Yeoman, Striker [*Navy rating*]
YNT .... Net Tender [*Tug Class*] [*Navy symbol*] [*Obsolete*]
YNT .... Yellowstone National Travelers   (EA)
YNTO .... Yugoslav National Tourist Office   (EA)
YNV .... Yanov [*USSR*] [*Later, LVV*] [*Geomagnetic observatory code*]
YO .... Airline ticket that can be used on any airline
YO .... Fuel Oil Barge [*Self-propelled*] [*Navy symbol*]
YO .... Yarn Over [*Knitting*]
YO .... Year-Old
YO .... Yes [*Citizens band radio slang*]
Yo.............. Yoma   (BJA)
Yo.............. Younge's English Exchequer Equity Reports   (DLA)
YOAN .... Youth of All Nations [*An association*] [*New York, NY*]   (EA)
YOB........... Year of Birth
YOB........... Youth Opportunities Board
YoB .... Yushodo Booksellers Ltd., Tokyo, Japan [*Library symbol*] [*Library of Congress*]   (LCLS)
YOC........... Old Crow [*Canada*] [*Airport symbol*]   (OAG)
YOC........... Youth Opportunity Campaign [*Civil Service Commission*]
YOC........... Youth Opportunity Centers
YOC........... Youth Opportunity Corps

YOCHINPROJ ... Younger Chemists International Project [*American Chemical Society*]
YOD........... Cold Lake [*Canada*] [*Airport symbol*]   (OAG)
YOD........... Year of Death
YOG........... Central Aviation, Inc. [*Chicago, IL*] [*FAA designator*]   (FAAC)
YOG........... Gasoline Barge [*Self-propelled*] [*Navy symbol*]
Yoga Jnl ... Yoga Journal [*A publication*]
YOGN........ Gasoline Barge [*Non-self-propelled*] [*Navy symbol*]
YOH........... Oxford House [*Canada*] [*Airport symbol*]   (OAG)
YOJ .... High Level [*Canada*] [*Airport symbol*]   (OAG)
YOJ .... Yonagunijima [*Ryukyu Islands*] [*Seismograph station code, US Geological Survey*]   (SEIS)
YOK........... Yokohama [*Japan*] [*Seismograph station code, US Geological Survey*]   (SEIS)
Yokogawa Tech Rep ... Yokogawa Technical Report [*Japan*] [*A publication*]
Yokohama Math J ... Yokohama Mathematical Journal [*A publication*]
Yokohama Med Bull ... Yokohama Medical Bulletin [*A publication*]
Yokohama Med J ... Yokohama Medical Journal [*Japan*] [*A publication*]
Yokufukai Geriatr J ... Yokufukai Geriatric Journal [*A publication*]
YOL........... Yola [*Nigeria*] [*Airport symbol*]   (OAG)
YOM .... State University of New York, College at Oswego, Oswego, NY [*OCLC symbol*]   (OCLC)
YOM .... Year of Marriage
Yom........... Yoma   (BJA)
YON........... Fuel Oil Barge [*Non-self-propelled*] [*Navy symbol*]
YON........... Yonago [*Japan*] [*Seismograph station code, US Geological Survey*]   (SEIS)
YON........... Yonkers School System, Yonkers, NY [*OCLC symbol*]   (OCLC)
Yon Act Med ... Yonago Acta Medica [*A publication*]
Yonago Acta Med ... Yonago Acta Medica [*A publication*]
Yonsei Eng Rev ... Yonsei Engineering Review [*South Korea*] [*A publication*]
Yonsei J Med Sci ... Yonsei Journal of Medical Science [*A publication*]
Yonsei Med J ... Yonsei Medical Journal [*A publication*]
Yonsei Rep Trop Med ... Yonsei Reports on Tropical Medicine [*A publication*]
Yool Waste ... Yool on Waste, Nuisance, and Trespass [*1863*]   (DLA)
YOP........... Rainbow Lake [*Canada*] [*Airport symbol*]   (OAG)
YOP........... Youth Opportunities Programme [*British*]
YOR........... Yale Oriental Research [*A publication*]   (BJA)
yor .... Yoruba [*MARC language code*] [*Library of Congress*]   (LCCP)
York .... York Legal Record [*Pennsylvania*]   (DLA)
YORK .... York Research [*NASDAQ symbol*]   (NQ)
York Ass ... Clayton's Reports, York Assizes   (DLA)
YorkCoHS ... York County Historical Society. Papers [*A publication*]
York Leg Rec ... York Legal Record [*Pennsylvania*]   (DLA)
York Leg Record ... York Legal Record [*Pennsylvania*]   (DLA)
York Leg Rec (PA) ... York Legal Record [*Pennsylvania*]   (DLA)
York Papers Ling ... York Papers in Linguistics [*A publication*]
YORKS....... Yorkshire [*County in England*]
Yorks Beekpr ... Yorkshire Beekeeper [*A publication*]
Yorks Geol Soc Occas Publ ... Yorkshire Geological Society. Occasional Publication [*A publication*]
Yorkshire Archaeol J ... Yorkshire Archaeological Journal [*A publication*]
Yorkshire Arch J ... Yorkshire Archaeological Journal [*A publication*]
Yorkshire Archt ... Yorkshire Architect [*A publication*]
Yorkshire Geol Soc Proc ... Yorkshire Geological Society. Proceedings [*A publication*]
Yorkshire G Polyt Soc Pr ... Yorkshire Geological and Polytechnic Society. Proceedings [*A publication*]
YOS........... Oil Storage Barge [*Non-self-propelled*] [*Navy symbol*]
YOS........... Yale Oriental Series [*A publication*]
YOS........... Years of Service [*Army*]   (INF)
YOS........... Yosiwara [*Japan*] [*Seismograph station code, US Geological Survey*] [*Closed*]   (SEIS)
YOSE .... Yosemite National Park
YoShiR....... Yokohama Shiritsu Daigaku Ronso [*Bulletin. Yokohama Municipal University Society*] [*A publication*]
YOSR .... Yale Oriental Series. Researches [*A publication*]
YOT........... Yale Oriental Texts [*A publication*]   (BJA)
YOU........... Young [*Australia*] [*Seismograph station code, US Geological Survey*]   (SEIS)
You............ Younge's English Exchequer Equity Reports [*1830-32*]   (DLA)
YOU........... Youngman Oil & Gas [*Vancouver Stock Exchange symbol*]
YOU........... Youth Opportunities Unlimited [*Project*]   (EA)
YOU........... Youth Organizations United
You & Coll Ch ... Younge and Collyer's English Chancery Reports [*1841-43*]   (DLA)
You & Coll Ex ... Younge and Collyer's English Exchequer Equity Reports [*1834-42*]   (DLA)
You & Jerv ... Younge and Jervis' English Exchequer Reports   (DLA)
Young .... Young's Reports [*21-47 Minnesota*]   (DLA)
Young Adm ... Young's Nova Scotia Admiralty Cases   (DLA)
Young Adm Dec ... Young's Nova Scotia Vice-Admiralty Decisions   (DLA)
Young Adm Dec (Nov Sc) ... Young's Nova Scotia Vice-Admiralty Decisions   (DLA)
Young Athl ... Young Athlete [*A publication*]
Young Child ... Young Children [*A publication*]
Young Cinema ... Young Cinema and Theatre/Jeune Cinema et Theatre [*A publication*]
Younge ...... Younge's English Exchequer Equity Reports [*159 English Reprint*]   (DLA)

Younge & C Ch ... Younge and Collyer's English Chancery Reports [*62-63 English Reprint*]　(DLA)

Younge & C Ch Cas (Eng) ... Younge and Collyer's English Chancery Cases [*62-63 English Reprint*]　(DLA)

Younge & C Exch ... Younge and Collyer's English Exchequer Equity Reports [*160 English Reprint*]　(DLA)

Younge & C Exch (Eng) ... Younge and Collyer's English Exchequer Equity Reports [*160 English Reprint*]　(DLA)

Younge & Ch Cas ... Younge and Collyer's English Chancery Cases [*62-63 English Reprint*] [*1841-43*]　(DLA)

Younge & Coll Ch ... Younge and Collyer's English Chancery Reports [*62-63 English Reprint*]　(DLA)

Younge & Coll Ex ... Younge and Collyer's English Exchequer Equity Reports [*160 English Reprint*]　(DLA)

Younge Exch ... Younge's English Exchequer Equity Reports [*159 English Reprint*] [*1830-32*]　(DLA)

Younge Exch (Eng) ... Younge's English Exchequer Equity Reports [*159 English Reprint*]　(DLA)

Younge & J ... Younge and Jervis' English Exchequer Reports [*148 English Reprint*]　(DLA)

Younge & Je ... Younge and Jervis' English Exchequer Reports [*148 English Reprint*]　(DLA)

Younge & J (Eng) ... Younge and Jervis' English Exchequer Reports [*148 English Reprint*]　(DLA)

Younge & Jerv ... Younge and Jervis' English Exchequer Reports [*148 English Reprint*]　(DLA)

Younge ML Cas ... Younge's English Maritime Law Cases　(DLA)

Young Lib ... Young Liberal [*A publication*]

Young ML Cas ... Young's English Maritime Law Cases　(DLA)

Young Naut Dict ... Young's Nautical Dictionary　(DLA)

Young VA Dec ... Young's Nova Scotia Vice-Admiralty Decisions　(DLA)

YOUR .... Your Own United Resources, Inc.　(OICC)

Your Mus Cue ... Your Musical Cue [*A publication*]

Your Okla Dent Assoc J ... Your Oklahoma Dental Association Journal [*A publication*]

Your Radiol ... Your Radiologist [*A publication*]

Youth Aid Bull ... Youth Aid Bulletin [*A publication*]

YOUTHS ..... Youth Order United Toward Highway Safety　(EA)

Youth and Soc ... Youth and Society [*A publication*]

Youth Soc ... Youth and Society [*A publication*]

YOW .... Ottawa [*Canada*] [*Airport symbol*]　(OAG)

YOYUA .... Yoyuen [*A publication*]

YP .... Patrol Craft [*Self-propelled*] [*Navy symbol*]

YP .... Robex Collection Center [*ICAO designator*]　(FAAC)

YP .... Yard Patrol

YP .... Yellow Pine

YP .... Yield Point [*Ordinarily expressed in PSI*]

YP .... Young People

3YP .... Three Year Plan [*From George Orwell's novel, "1984"*]

YPA .... Port Authority of New York and New Jersey Library, New York, NY [*OCLC symbol*]　(OCLC)

YPA .... Prince Albert [*Canada*] [*Airport symbol*]　(OAG)

YPA .... Yaw Precession Amplifier

YPA .... Yearbook Printers Association　(EA)

YPD .... Floating Pile Driver [*Non-self-propelled*] [*Navy symbol*]

YPD .... Parry Sound [*Canada*] [*Airport symbol*]　(OAG)

YPD .... Yaw Phase Detector

YPD .... Yellow Pages Datasystem [*National Planning Data Corp.*] [*Database*]

YPE .... Peace River [*Canada*] [*Airport symbol*]　(OAG)

YPE .... Yoho Pitch Extractor

YPEC .... Young Printing Executives Club of New York [*New York, NY*]　(EA)

YPG .... Yuma Proving Ground [*Arizona*] [*Army*]　(AABC)

YPH .... Port Harrison [*Canada*] [*Airport symbol*]　(OAG)

YPHJA .... Yo-Up Hoeji [*A publication*]

YPI .... Youth Policy Institute　(EA)

YPI .... Youth Pride, Incorporated　(EA)

YPK .... Pontoon Stowage Barge [*Navy symbol*] [*Obsolete*]

YPL .... Pickle Lake [*Canada*] [*Airport symbol*]　(OAG)

YPL .... White Plains Public Library, White Plains, NY [*OCLC symbol*]　(OCLC)

YPL .... York Papers in Linguistics [*A publication*]

YPL .... York Public Library [*UTLAS symbol*]

YPLA .... Young People's LOGO Association　(EA)

YPLA .... Your Public Lands. US Department of the Interior. Bureau of Land Mangement [*A publication*]

YPLL .... Years of Potential Life Lost [*Medicine*]

YPM .... Saint Pierre [*Saint Pierre and Miquelon*] [*Airport symbol*]　(OAG)

YPM .... State University of New York, College at Plattsburgh, Plattsburgh, NY [*OCLC symbol*]　(OCLC)

YPM .... Yale Peabody Museum

YPM .... Yokefellow Prison Ministry [*Formed by a merger of NYPM and Yokefellowship of Pennsylvania*] [*Sunbury, PA*]　(EA)

YPN .... Port Menier [*Canada*] [*Airport symbol*]　(OAG)

YPO .... Young Presidents' Organization [*New York, NY*]　(EA)

YPO .... Youth Programs Office [*Bureau of Indian Affairs*]

Y-POP .... Y-Body Axis Perpendicular to Orbit Plane [*Aerospace*]

YPQ .... Peterborough [*Canada*] [*Airport symbol*]　(OAG)

YPR .... Prince Rupert [*Canada*] [*Airport symbol*]　(OAG)

YPR .... Yale Poetry Review [*A publication*]

YPR .... Youth Population Ratio　(OICC)

YPR .... Youth Population Ration

YPS .... Yards per Second

YPS .... Yellow Pages Service [*Telecommunications*]　(TEL)

YPSCE .... Young People's Society of Christian Endeavor

YPSL .... Young Peoples Socialist League [*Later, YSD*]　(EA)

YPSSRB .... Yukon Public Service Staff Relations Board [*Canada*]

YPVS .... Yamaha Power Valve System

YPW .... Powell River [*Canada*] [*Airport symbol*]　(OAG)

YPW .... Putnam-Northern Westchester BOCES [*Boards of Cooperative Educational Services*], Yorktown Heights, NY [*OCLC symbol*]　(OCLC)

YPX .... Povungnituk [*Canada*] [*Airport symbol*]　(OAG)

YPY .... Fort Chipewyan [*Canada*] [*Airport symbol*]　(OAG)

YPZ .... Young Poalei Zion　(BJA)

YQB .... Quebec [*Canada*] [*Airport symbol*]　(OAG)

YQD .... [*The*] Pas [*Canada*] [*Airport symbol*]　(OAG)

YQF .... Red Deer [*Canada*] [*Airport symbol*] [*Obsolete*]　(OAG)

YQG .... Windsor [*Canada*] [*Airport symbol*]　(OAG)

YQH .... Watson Lake [*Canada*] [*Airport symbol*]　(OAG)

YQI .... Yarmouth [*Canada*] [*Airport symbol*]　(OAG)

YQK .... Kenora [*Canada*] [*Airport symbol*]　(OAG)

YQL .... Lethbridge [*Canada*] [*Airport symbol*]　(OAG)

YQM .... Moncton [*Canada*] [*Airport symbol*]　(OAG)

YQQ .... Comox [*Canada*] [*Airport symbol*]　(OAG)

YQR .... Regina [*Canada*] [*Airport symbol*]　(OAG)

YQR .... Rochester Public Library, Rochester, NY [*OCLC symbol*]　(OCLC)

YQT .... Thunder Bay [*Canada*] [*Airport symbol*]　(OAG)

YQU .... Grande Prairie [*Canada*] [*Airport symbol*]　(OAG)

YQV .... Yorkton [*Canada*] [*Airport symbol*]　(OAG)

YQX .... Gander [*Canada*] [*Airport symbol*]　(OAG)

YQY .... Sydney [*Canada*] [*Airport symbol*]　(OAG)

YQZ .... Quesnel [*Canada*] [*Airport symbol*]　(OAG)

YR .... Airline ticket that can be used only on airline issuing it

YR .... Floating Workshop [*Non-self-propelled*] [*Navy symbol*]

YR .... Romania [*Aircraft nationality and registration mark*]　(FAAC)

YR .... Yale Review [*A publication*]

YR .... Yaw Ring

Y-R .... Yaw-Roll　(AAG)

YR .... Year [*Online database field identifier*]

Yr. .... Yearbook　(BJA)

YR .... Yemeni Riyal　(BJA)

YR .... Young Republican

Y & R .... Young & Rubicam International [*Advertising agency*]

YR .... Younger

YR .... Your　(AAG)

YR .... Youth Resources [*An association*]　(EA)

YRA .... Yacht Racing Association [*British*]

YRAC .... Yacht Racing Associations Council　(EA)

YRAP .... Yellow Page Rate Base Analysis Plan [*Bell System*]

YRB .... Resolute [*Canada*] [*Airport symbol*]　(OAG)

YRB .... Submarine Repair and Berthing Barge [*Non-self-propelled*] [*Navy symbol*]

YRBK .... Yearbook

Yr Bk (Charleston SC) ... Year Book (Charleston, South Carolina) [*A publication*]

Yrbk Compar & Gen Lit ... Yearbook of Comparative and General Literature [*A publication*]

Yrbk Comp & Gen Lit ... Yearbook of Comparative and General Literature [*A publication*]

Yrbk Sch Law ... Yearbook of School Law [*A publication*]

Yrbk Sp Educ ... Yearbook of Special Education [*A publication*]

Yrbk World Aff ... Yearbook of World Affairs [*London*] [*A publication*]

YRBM .... Submarine Repair, Berthing, and Messing Barge [*Non-self-propelled*] [*Navy symbol*]

YRBM(L) .... Submarine Repair, Berthing, and Messing Barge (Large) [*Navy symbol*]

YRC .... Submarine Rescue Chamber [*Navy symbol*]

YRC .... Yaw Ratio Controller　(MCD)

YRDH .... Floating Dry Dock Workshop (Hull) [*Non-self-propelled*] [*Navy symbol*]

YRDM .... Floating Dry Dock Workshop (Machine) [*Non-self-propelled*] [*Navy symbol*]

YRDST .... Year-Round Daylight Saving Time

YRF .... Yoga Research Foundation　(EA)

YRFLN .... Year Flown　(MCD)

YRI .... Riviere-Du-Loup [*Canada*] [*Airport symbol*] [*Obsolete*]　(OAG)

YRI .... Yri-York Ltd. [*Toronto Stock Exchange symbol*]

YRINY .... Youth Research Institute of New York　(EA)

YRJ .... Roberval [*Canada*] [*Airport symbol*] [*Obsolete*]　(OAG)

YRK .... York International Corp. [*NYSE symbol*]

YRK .... York, KY [*Location identifier*] [*FAA*]　(FAAL)

YRK .... York University Library [*UTLAS symbol*]

YRL .... Covered Lighter (Repair) [*Navy symbol*] [*Obsolete*]

YRL .... Red Lake [*Canada*] [*Airport symbol*]　(OAG)

YRL .... York University Law Library [*UTLAS symbol*]

YRLY .... Yearly　(ROG)

YRM .... Rensselaer Polytechnic Institute, Troy, NY [*OCLC symbol*]　(OCLC)

YRNF.........	Young Republican National Federation　(EA)	YTB	Large Harbor Tug [*Self-propelled*] [*Navy symbol*]
YRR	Radiological Repair Barge [*Non-self-propelled*] [*Navy symbol*]	YTB	Yarn to Back [*Knitting*]　(ADA)
YRR	Scenic Airlines [*Las Vegas, NV*] [*FAA designator*]　(FAAC)	YTB	Yield to Broker [*Business and trade*]
YRS	Red Sucker Lake [*Canada*] [*Airport symbol*]　(OAG)	YTC	Yield to Call [*Business and trade*]
YRS	Yale Romanic Studies [*A publication*]	YTC	Yorkshire Trust Company [*Toronto Stock Exchange symbol*]
YRS	Yours		[*Vancouver Stock Exchange symbol*]
YRS	Yugoslav Relief Society	YTCA	Yorkshire Terrier Club of America　(EA)
YRST	Salvage Craft Tender [*Non-self-propelled*] [*Navy ship symbol*]	YTD	Year to Date　(MCD)
YRT	Rankin Inlet [*Canada*] [*Airport symbol*]　(OAG)	YTE	Cape Dorset [*Canada*] [*Airport symbol*]　(OAG)
YRT	Yearly Renewable Term [*Insurance*]	YTEC	Yarsley Technical Centre Ltd. [*Research center*] [*British*]　(IRC)
YRT	Yellowroot Tea [*Folk remedy, extract of buttercup root*]	YTELSA	Yearbook. Estonian Learned Society in America [*A publication*]
YRTMA.......	Yonsei Reports on Tropical Medicine [*A publication*]	YTEP	Youth Training and Employment Project
YS................	El Salvador [*Aircraft nationality and registration mark*]　(FAAC)	YTF.............	Yad Tikvah Foundation　(EA)
ys................	Southern Yemen (Aden) [*MARC country of publication code*]	YTF.............	Yarn to Front [*Knitting*]　(ADA)
	[*Library of Congress*]　(LCCP)	YTH	Thompson [*Canada*] [*Airport symbol*]　(OAG)
YS................	Stevedoring Barge [*Navy symbol*] [*Obsolete*]	YTHJ	Yeshivath Torah Hayim in Jerusalem　(EA)
YS................	Yard Superintendent	YTI	Yeshiba Toledot Isaac. Tetuan　(BJA)
YS................	Yellow Spot	YTJ.............	Terrace Bay [*Canada*] [*Airport symbol*]　(OAG)
YS................	Yidishe Shprakh [*A publication*]	YTL	Big Trout Lake [*Canada*] [*Airport symbol*]　(OAG)
YS................	Yield Strength [*Ordinarily expressed in PSI*]	YTL	Small Harbor Tug [*Self-propelled*] [*Navy symbol*]
YS................	Yield Stress	YTL	Youth Tennis League　(EA)
YS................	Yoshida Sarcoma [*Medicine*]	YTM............	Medium Harbor Tug [*Self-propelled*] [*Navy symbol*]
YS................	Young Socialists　(ADA)	YTM............	State University of New York, College at Utica-Rome, Utica, NY
YS................	Young Soldier		[*OCLC symbol*]　(OCLC)
YS................	Younger Son　(ROG)	YTM............	Yield to Maturity [*Finance*]
YS................	Youngstown & Southern Railway Co. [*AAR code*]	YTRES.......	Yankee Tractor Rocket Escape System　(MCD)
YSA	Young Socialist Alliance　(EA)	YTS	Timmins [*Canada*] [*Airport symbol*]　(OAG)
YSAF..........	Young Scientists of America Foundation　(EA)	YTS	Youth Training Scheme [*British*]
YSB	Salomon Brothers Library, New York, NY [*OCLC symbol*]　(OCLC)	YTS	Yuma Test Station [*Missiles*]
YSB	Sudbury [*Canada*] [*Airport symbol*]　(OAG)	YTT	Torpedo Testing Barge [*Navy symbol*] [*Obsolete*]
YSB	Yacht Safety Bureau　(EA)	YTTBT........	Yield Threshold Test Ban Treaty [*1976*]
YSB	Yield Stress Bonding	YTV	Yaw Thrust Vector
YSC............	South Central Research Library Council, Ithaca, NY [*OCLC symbol*]　(OCLC)	YTV	Yorkshire Television [*British*]
YSC............	Yearly Spares Cost　(MCD)	YTX	Planned District Craft [*Navy symbol*]
YSCECP Reports ...	Yugoslav-Serbo-Croatian-English Contrastive Project. Reports [*A publication*]	YTZ	Toronto [*Canada*] [*Airport symbol*]　(OAG)
YSCECP Studies ...	Yugoslav-Serbo-Croatian-English Contrastive Project. Studies [*A publication*]	YU	Yale Divinity School, New Haven, CT [*OCLC symbol*] [*Inactive*]　(OCLC)
YSD	Seaplane Wrecking Derrick [*Self-propelled*] [*Navy symbol*]	YU	Yale University
YSD	Young Social Democrats [*Formerly, YPSL*]　(EA)	YU	Yeshiva University [*New York*]
YSDB..........	Yield Stress Diffusion Bonding	yu	Yugoslavia [*MARC country of publication code*] [*Library of Congress*]　(LCCP)
YSE	Yale Studies in English [*A publication*]	YU	Yugoslavia [*Aircraft nationality and registration mark*]　(FAAC)
YSE	Yaw Steering Error	YU	Yugoslavia [*Two-letter standard code*]　(CNC)
YS/E............	Yield Strength to Elastic Modulus Ratio [*Dentistry*]	YU	Yukon News [*A publication*]
YSF	Stoney Rapids [*Canada*] [*Airport symbol*]　(OAG)	Yu.............	Yunost' [*Moscow*] [*A publication*]
YSF	Yield Safety Factor　(IEEE)	Yuasa Tech Inf ...	Yuasa Technical Information [*Japan*] [*A publication*]
YSh	Yidishe Shprakh [*A publication*]	YUB	Tuktoyaktuk [*Canada*] [*Airport symbol*]　(OAG)
YSI	Sans Souci [*Canada*] [*Airport symbol*]　(OAG)	YUBAA.......	Yuba Natural Resources, Inc. Cl A [*NASDAQ symbol*]　(NQ)
YSI	Yellow Springs Instrument Co.	Yubbie	Young Urban Baby [*Lifestyle classification*]
YSJ.............	Saint John [*Canada*] [*Airport symbol*]　(OAG)	Yubbie	Young Urban Breadwinner [*Lifestyle classification*]
YSK	Sanikiluaq [*Canada*] [*Airport symbol*]　(OAG)	YuBN..........	Narodna Biblioteka Socijalisticke Republike Srbije, Beograd, Yugoslavia [*Library symbol*] [*Library of Congress*]　(LCLS)
YSK	Yokosuka [*Japan*] [*Seismograph station code, US Geological Survey*] [*Closed*]　(SEIS)	YUBO	Yucca House National Monument
YSL	Saint Leonard [*Canada*] [*Airport symbol*]　(OAG)	YUC............	Yucana Resources, Inc. [*Vancouver Stock Exchange symbol*]
YSL	Yolk Syncytial Layer [*Embryology*]	YUC............	Yucatan
YSL	Yves Saint Laurent [*French couturier*]	YUCI...........	Yeshiva University Cumulative Index of Films of Jewish Interest [*A publication*]　(BJA)
Y-SLAV	Yugoslavia	Yuckie.......	Young, Ultimate, Creative Kitscher [*Lifestyle classification*] [*Advertising*]
YSLF...........	Yield Strength Load Factor　(IEEE)	Yuckie.......	Young Urban Catholic [*Lifestyle classification*]
YSM	Fort Smith [*Canada*] [*Airport symbol*]　(OAG)	YUF	Pelly Bay [*Canada*] [*Airport symbol*]　(OAG)
YSM	State University of New York at Stony Brook, Stony Brook, NY [*OCLC symbol*]　(OCLC)	Yuffie	Young Urban Failure [*Lifestyle classification*]
YSM	Yangtze Service Medal	YUG............	Yugoslavia [*Three-letter standard code*]　(CNC)
YSM	Young Socialist Movement	Yugoslav L ...	Yugoslav Law [*A publication*]
YSNC	Youth Suicide National Center [*Washington, DC*]　(EA)	Yugosl Chem Pap ...	Yugoslav Chemical Papers [*A publication*]
YSO............	Young Stellar Object	Yugosl Law ...	Yugoslav Law [*A publication*]
YSP	Pontoon Salvage Vessel [*Navy symbol*]	Yugosl Surv ...	Yugoslav Survey [*A publication*]
YSP	Years Service for Severance Pay Purposes [*Military*]	Yugosl Zavod Geol Geofiz Istrazivanja Raspr ...	Yugoslavia Zavod za Geoloska i Geofizicka Istrazivanja. Rasprave-Service Geologique et Geophysique. Memoires [*A publication*]
YSP	Yemen Socialist Party　(PD)	Yugosl Zavod Geol Geofiz Istrazivanja Vesn Geol ...	Yugoslavia Zavod za Geoloska i Geofizicka Istrazivanja-Institut de Recherches Geologiques et Geophysiques. Vesnik. Geologija. Serija A [*Belgrade*] [*A publication*]
YSR	Nanisivik [*Canada*] [*Airport symbol*]　(OAG)	
YSR	Sludge Removal Barge [*Non-self-propelled*] [*Navy symbol*]	
YSS	Yuzhno-Sakhalinsk [*USSR*] [*Seismograph station code, US Geological Survey*]　(SEIS)	Yug Soc Soil Sci Publ ...	Yugoslav Society of Soil Science. Publication [*A publication*]
YSS	Yuzhno-Sakhalinsk [*USSR*] [*Geomagnetic observatory code*]	YUIN...........	Yukon Indian News [*A publication*]
YST	Saint Therese Point [*Canada*] [*Airport symbol*]　(OAG)	YUK............	Youth Uncovering Krud [*Antipollution organization in Schenectady, New York*]
YST	Yolk Sac Tumor [*Oncology*]	YUK............	Yuzhno-Kurilsk [*USSR*] [*Seismograph station code, US Geological Survey*]　(SEIS)
YST	Youngest	
YSTC.........	Yorkshire Society of Textile Craftsmen [*A union*] [*British*]	Yuk Ord......	Yukon Ordinances [*Canada*]　(DLA)
YSY	Sachs Harbour [*Canada*] [*Airport symbol*]　(OAG)	Yuk Rev Ord ...	Yukon Revised Ordinances [*Canada*]　(DLA)
YT................	Harbor Tug [*Navy symbol*]	YUL	Montreal [*Canada*] [*Airport symbol*]　(OAG)
YT................	Yacht　(ROG)	YUL	Yale University Library
YT................	Yankee Team [*Phase of the Indochina bombing operation during US military involvement in Vietnam*]	YULG..........	Yale University. Library. Gazette [*A publication*]
		Yullie	Young Urban Laborer [*Lifestyle classification*]
YT................	Yaw Trim　(MCD)	YUM	Yale Medical School, New Haven, CT [*OCLC symbol*] [*Inactive*]　(OCLC)
YT................	Yom Tov　(BJA)	
Yt................	Yttrium [*See also Y*] [*Chemical element*]	YUM	Yuma [*Arizona*] [*Airport symbol*]　(OAG)
YT................	Yukon Territory [*Canada*] [*Postal code*]	
YTA.............	Pembroke [*Canada*] [*Airport symbol*]　(OAG)	
YTA.............	Yaw Trim Angle	
YTA.............	Yiddish Theatrical Alliance　(EA)	

YUM .... Yuma Gold Mines Ltd. [*Vancouver Stock Exchange symbol*]

YUM .... Yumen [*Republic of China*] [*Seismograph station code, US Geological Survey*] (SEIS)

Yummie ..... Young Upwardly Mobile Mountains [*Rocky Mountains*] [*Geological take-off on the abbreviation, Yuppie*] [*Canada*]

Yummie ..... Young Urban Minister [*Lifestyle classification*]

Yummy ...... Young Upwardly Mobile Mommy [*Lifestyle classification*]

Yumpie ...... Young Upwardly Mobile Professional [*Lifestyle classification*]

Yumpy .... Young Upwardly Mobile Papa [*Lifestyle classification*]

YUN .... Yearbook of the United Nations (DLA)

YUO .... Yuojima [*Bonin Islands*] [*Seismograph station code, US Geological Survey*] [*Closed*] (SEIS)

Yuppie .... Young Urban Professional [*Lifestyle classification*] [*In book title "The Yuppie Handbook"*]

YUS .... Yale University, New Haven, CT [*OCLC symbol*] (OCLC)

YUS .... Yushan [*Mount Morrison*] [*Republic of China*] [*Seismograph station code, US Geological Survey*] (SEIS)

YuSaN .... Narodne Biblioteka Bosne i Hercegovine [*National Library of Bosnia and Herzegovina*], Sarajevo, Yugoslavia [*Library symbol*] [*Library of Congress*] (LCLS)

YuSkN .... Nacionalna Biblioteka na Makedonija "Kliment Ohridaki", Skopje, Yugoslavia [*Library symbol*] [*Library of Congress*] (LCLS)

Yussie .... Young Unescorted Single [*Lifestyle classification*]

YUTR .... Yukon Teacher [*A publication*]

YUWM .... Yukon Water Management Bulletin. Westwater Research Centre [*A publication*]

YUX .... Hall Beach [*Canada*] [*Airport symbol*] (OAG)

YUY .... Rouyn-Noranda [*Canada*] [*Airport symbol*] (OAG)

YuZU .... Nacionalna i Sveucilisna Biblioteka [*National and University Library of Croatia*], Zagreb, Yugoslavia [*Library symbol*] [*Library of Congress*] (LCLS)

YV .... Drone Aircraft Catapult Control Craft [*Navy symbol*] [*Obsolete*]

YV .... Venezuela [*Aircraft nationality and registration mark*] (FAAC)

YV .... Yad Vashem (EA-IO)

YVA .... Moroni [*Comoro Islands*] [*Airport symbol*] (OAG)

YVA .... Yad Vashem Archives (BJA)

YVA .... Young Volunteers in ACTION

YVB .... Bonaventure [*Canada*] [*Airport symbol*] (OAG)

YVC .... Catapult Lighter [*Navy symbol*]

YVC .... Lac La Ronge [*Canada*] [*Airport symbol*] (OAG)

YVC .... Yellow Varnish Cambric

Y Viewers... Young Viewers [*A publication*]

YVM .... Broughton [*Canada*] [*Airport symbol*] (OAG)

YVO .... Onondaga Library System, Syracuse, NY [*OCLC symbol*] (OCLC)

YVO .... Val D'Or [*Canada*] [*Airport symbol*] (OAG)

YVP .... Fort Chimo [*Canada*] [*Airport symbol*] (OAG)

YVQ .... Norman Wells [*Canada*] [*Airport symbol*] (OAG)

YVR .... Vancouver [*Canada*] [*Airport symbol*] (OAG)

YVS .... Yad Vashem Studies [*A publication*]

YVT .... Buffalo Narrows [*Canada*] [*Airport symbol*] [*Obsolete*] (OAG)

YVT .... Yakima Valley Transportation Co. [*AAR code*]

YW .... Water Barge [*Self-propelled*] [*Navy symbol*]

YW .... Whitehorse Public Library, Yukon [*Library symbol*] [*National Library of Canada*] (NLC)

YW .... Year's Work in English Studies [*A publication*]

YW .... Yellow-White

YW .... Young Woman [*A publication*]

YW .... Young Women's [*Christian Association*]

YW .... Yreka Western Railroad Co. [*AAR code*]

YWA .... Year's Work in Archaeology [*A publication*]

YWA .... Yukon Archives, Whitehorse, Yukon [*Library symbol*] [*National Library of Canada*] (NLC)

YWAM .... Youth with a Mission [*Sunland, CA*] (EA)

YWC .... Year's Work in Classical Studies [*A publication*]

YWC .... Yukon College, Whitehorse, Yukon [*Library symbol*] [*National Library of Canada*] (NLC)

YWCA .... World Young Women's Christian Association (EA-IO)

YWCA .... Young Women Committed to Action [*Feminist group*]

YWCA-USA ... Young Women's Christian Association of the United States of America [*New York, NY*] (EA)

YWCJCLS ... Young Women of the Church of Jesus Christ of Latter-Day Saints (EA)

YWCS .... Year's Work in Classical Studies [*A publication*]

YWCTU ...... Young Women's Christian Temperance Union

YWDN .... Water Distilling Barge [*Non-self-propelled*] [*Navy symbol*]

YWE .... Year's Work in English Studies [*A publication*]

YWED .... Department of Economic Development: Mines and Small Business, Government of the Yukon, Whitehorse, Yukon [*Library symbol*] [*National Library of Canada*] (NLC)

YWEEP .... Environmental Protection Service, Environment Canada [*Service de la Protection de l'Environnement, Environnement Canada*] Whitehorse, Yukon [*Library symbol*] [*National Library of Canada*] (NLC)

YWES .... Year's Work in English Studies [*A publication*]

YWF .... Young World Federalists [*Later, World Federalist Youth*]

YWFD .... Young World Food and Development [*UN Food and Agriculture Organization*]

YWG .... Winnipeg [*Canada*] [*Airport symbol*] (OAG)

YWGASOYA ... You Won't Get Ahead Sitting on Your Afterdeck [*Slang*] [*Bowdlerized version*]

YWH .... Victoria [*Canada*] [*Airport symbol*] (OAG)

YWHA .... Young Women's Hebrew Association [*Later, YM-YWHA*]

YWHHR ...... Department of Health and Human Resources, Government of the Yukon, Whitehorse, Yukon [*Library symbol*] [*National Library of Canada*] (NLC)

YWHS .... Whitehorse Historical Society, Yukon [*Library symbol*] [*National Library of Canada*] (NLC)

YWHS .... Young Women's Help Society [*British*]

YWK .... Wabush [*Canada*] [*Airport symbol*] (OAG)

YWL .... Williams Lake [*Canada*] [*Airport symbol*] (OAG)

YWL .... Yawl

YWL .... Yukon Law Library, Whitehorse, Yukon [*Library symbol*] [*National Library of Canada*] (NLC)

YWLL .... Young Workers Liberation League

YWLS .... Library Services Branch, Government of the Yukon, Whitehorse, Yukon [*Library symbol*] [*National Library of Canada*] (NLC)

YWM .... United States Military Academy, West Point, NY [*OCLC symbol*] (OCLC)

YWML .... Year's Work in Modern Language Studies [*A publication*]

YWMLS ...... Year's Work in Modern Language Studies [*A publication*]

YWN .... Water Barge [*Non-self-propelled*] [*Navy symbol*]

YWN .... Winisk [*Canada*] [*Airport symbol*] (OAG)

YWOM .... [*The*] Old Log Church Museum, Whitehorse, Yukon [*Library symbol*] [*National Library of Canada*] (NLC)

YWP .... Sir Hugh Young's Working Party for Estimation of Civilian Relief Requirements [*World War II*]

YWPCN ...... National Historic Sites, Parks Canada [*Lieux Historiques Nationaux, Parcs Canada*] Whitehorse, Yukon [*Library symbol*] [*National Library of Canada*] (NLC)

YWPG .... Young World Promotion Group [*UN Food and Agriculture Organization*]

YWR .... Yorkshire, West Riding [*County in England*] (ROG)

YWRR .... Department of Renewable Resources, Government of the Yukon, Whitehorse, Yukon [*Library symbol*] [*National Library of Canada*] (NLC)

YWS .... Young Wales Society

YWT .... Yard-Walk-Throughs [*Navy*] (NG)

YWTA .... Department of Territorial Affairs, Government of the Yukon, Whitehorse, Yukon [*Library symbol*] [*National Library of Canada*] (NLC)

YWU .... Yiddish Writers Union (EA)

YWY .... Wrigley [*Canada*] [*Airport symbol*] (OAG)

YXC .... Cranbrook [*Canada*] [*Airport symbol*] (OAG)

YXD .... Edmonton [*Canada*] Municipal Airport [*Airport symbol*] (OAG)

YXE .... Saskatoon [*Canada*] [*Airport symbol*] (OAG)

YXF .... Four County Library System, Binghamton, NY [*OCLC symbol*] (OCLC)

YXH .... Medicine Hat [*Canada*] [*Airport symbol*] (OAG)

YXJ .... Fort St. John [*Canada*] [*Airport symbol*] (OAG)

YXK .... Rimouski [*Canada*] [*Airport symbol*] (OAG)

YXL .... Sioux Lookout [*Canada*] [*Airport symbol*] (OAG)

YXO .... Houghton College, Buffalo Campus, West Seneca, NY [*OCLC symbol*] (OCLC)

YXP .... Pangnirtung [*Canada*] [*Airport symbol*] (OAG)

YXR .... Earlton [*Canada*] [*Airport symbol*] (OAG)

YXS .... Prince George [*Canada*] [*Airport symbol*] (OAG)

YXT .... Terrace [*Canada*] [*Airport symbol*] (OAG)

YXU .... London [*Canada*] [*Airport symbol*] (OAG)

YXX .... Abbotsford [*Canada*] [*Airport symbol*] (OAG)

YXY .... Whitehorse [*Canada*] [*Airport symbol*] (OAG)

YXZ .... Wawa [*Canada*] [*Airport symbol*] (OAG)

YY .... Robert Lynd [*American author, 1892-1970*] [*Pseudonym*]

Y-Y .... Yaw Axis (AAG)

YY .... Yedi'ot Yanai (BJA)

YYB .... North Bay [*Canada*] [*Airport symbol*] (OAG)

YYC .... Calgary [*Canada*] [*Airport symbol*] (OAG)

YYCI .... Youth-to-Youth Committee International (EA)

YYD .... Smithers [*Canada*] [*Airport symbol*] (OAG)

YYE .... Fort Nelson [*Canada*] [*Airport symbol*] (OAG)

YYF .... Penticton [*Canada*] [*Airport symbol*] (OAG)

YYG .... Charlottetown [*Canada*] [*Airport symbol*] (OAG)

YYH .... Spence Bay [*Canada*] [*Airport symbol*] (OAG)

YYJ .... Victoria [*Canada*] [*Airport symbol*] (OAG)

YYL .... Lynn Lake [*Canada*] [*Airport symbol*] [*Obsolete*] (OAG)

YYP .... Yarns of Yesteryear Project [*University of Wisconsin*] [*Madison, WI*] (EA)

YYP .... Yeshiva University, New York, NY [*OCLC symbol*] (OCLC)

YYQ .... Churchill [*Canada*] [*Airport symbol*] (OAG)

YYR .... Goose Bay [*Canada*] [*Airport symbol*] (OAG)

YYT .... St. Johns [*Canada*] [*Airport symbol*] (OAG)

YYU .... Kapuskasing [*Canada*] [*Airport symbol*] (OAG)

YYY .... Mont Joli [*Canada*] [*Airport symbol*] (OAG)

YYY .... Yugntruf - Youth for Yiddish (EA)

YYYC .... Yu-Yen Yen-Chiu [*Linguistic Researches*] [*A publication*]

YYZ .... Toronto [*Canada*] [*Airport symbol*] (OAG)

YZA .... Albany Law School, Albany, NY [*OCLC symbol*] (OCLC)

YZF .... Yellowknife [*Canada*] [*Airport symbol*] (OAG)

YZG .... Sugluk [*Canada*] [*Airport symbol*] (OAG)

YZP .... Sandspit [*Canada*] [*Airport symbol*]   (OAG)
YZR .... Sarnia [*Canada*] [*Airport symbol*]   (OAG)
YZS .... Coral Harbour [*Canada*] [*Airport symbol*]   (OAG)
YZSZ .... Yarlung Zangbo Suture Zone [*Geophysics*]
YZT .... Port Hardy [*Canada*] [*Airport symbol*]   (OAG)
YZU .... Sept Iles [*Canada*] [*Airport symbol*]
YZV .... Sept-Iles [*Canada*] [*Airport symbol*]   (OAG)

Z

Z .... Administrative Aircraft [*When a suffix to Navy plane designation*]
Z .... Atomic Number [*Symbol*]
z .... Aza [*As substituent on nucleoside*] [*Biochemistry*]
z .... Azimuth Angle
z .... Charge Number of a Cell Reaction [*Symbol*] [*Electrochemistry*]
Z .... Collision Number [*Symbol*] [*IUPAC*]
Z .... Compression Factor [*Symbol*] [*Thermodynamics*]
z .... Contraction [*Medicine*]
Z .... Coriolis Correction
Z .... Figure of Merit [*Symbol*]   (DEN)
Z .... Glutamic Acid [*or Glutamine*] [*Also, Glx*] [*Symbol*] [*An amino acid*]
Z .... Greenwich Mean Time   (FAAC)
Z .... Impedance [*Symbol*] [*IUPAC*]
Z .... Jet Terminal Area [*Aviation symbol*]   (FAAC)
Z .... Normally Open [*Ship's fittings classification*]
z .... Partition Function, Particle [*Symbol*] [*IUPAC*]
Z .... Partition Function, System [*Symbol*] [*IUPAC*]
Z .... Planning [*Aircraft classification letter*]
Z .... Stadia [*Speedways, race tracks, etc.*] [*Public-performance tariff class*] [*British*]
Z .... Standard Score [*Psychology*]
Z .... Symbol for Magnetic Reluctance   (ROG)
Z .... Tower Control [*Aviation symbol*]   (FAAC)
Z .... [*The Third*] Unknown Quantity [*Mathematics*]   (ROG)
Z .... Vertical component of the earth's magnetic field
Z .... Woolworth [*F. W.*] Co. [*NYSE symbol*] [*Wall Street slang name: "Five & Dime"*]
Z .... Z-Axis
Z .... Zagreb [*A publication*]
Z .... Zaire [*Monetary unit in Zaire*]
Z .... Zambon [*Italy*] [*Research code symbol*]
Z .... Zebra [*Phonetic alphabet*] [*Royal Navy*] [*World War I*] [*Pre-World War II*] [*World War II*]   (DSUE)
Z .... Zenith
Z .... Zenith Distance [*Navigation*]
Z .... Zentrumspartei [*Center Party*] [*German*]   (PPE)
Z .... Zero
Z .... Zerubbabel [*Freemasonry*]   (ROG)
Z .... Zinc [*Chemical symbol is Zn*]
Z .... Zionist
Z .... Zircon [*CIPW classification*] [*Geology*]
Z .... Zirconium [*Chemical element*] [*Symbol is Zr*]   (ROG)
Z .... Zivot [*A publication*]
Z .... Zloty [*Monetary unit in Poland*]
Z .... Zone
Z .... Zone Marker
Z .... Zone Meridian [*Lower or upper branch*]
Z .... Zora [*A publication*]
Z .... Zuender [*Fuze*] [*German military*]
Z .... Zuercher Bibel   (BJA)
Z .... Zulu [*Phonetic alphabet*] [*International*]   (DSUE)
Z .... Zulu Time [*Greenwich Mean Time*]   (AFM)
(Z) .... Zusammen [*Together*] [*Chemistry*]
Z .... Zven'ya [*A publication*]
Z .... Zwingliana [*A publication*]
Z .... Zycie [*A publication*]
Z .... Zyma AG [*Switzerland*] [*Research code symbol*]
Z (Day) .... Zero Day [*The date fixed for any important military operation*] [*British*]
ZA .... South Africa [*Two-letter standard code*]   (CNC)
Za .... Zabriskie's Reports [*21-24 New Jersey*]   (DLA)
Z-A .... Zaire-Afrique [*A publication*]
za .... Zambia [*MARC country of publication code*] [*Library of Congress*]   (LCCP)
ZA .... Zeitschrift fuer Assyriologie und Verwandte Gebiete [*A publication*]
ZA .... Zeitschrift fuer Assyriologie und Vorderasiatische Archaeologie [*Berlin*] [*A publication*]

ZA .... Zenith Angle [*Geophysics*]
ZA .... Zentralarchiv fuer Empirische Sozialforschung [*Central Archives for Empirical Social Research*] [*University of Cologne*] [*Cologne, West Germany*] [*Information service*]   (EISS)
ZA .... Zero and Add
ZA .... Zero Adjuster   (MSA)
ZA .... Zionist Archives [*A publication*]
ZA .... Ziva Antika [*A publication*]
ZA .... Zone of Action
ZA .... Zunz Archive. Jewish National and University Library [*Jerusalem*] [*A publication*]
ZAA .... Alice Arm/Kitsault [*Canada*] [*Airport symbol*]   (OAG)
ZAA .... Zeeman-Effect Atomic Absorption [*Spectrometry*]
ZAA .... Zeitschrift fuer Anglistik und Amerikanistik [*A publication*]
ZAA .... Zero Angle of Attack
Z Aachener Geschichtsver ... Zeitschrift des Aachener Geschichtsvereins [*A publication*]
ZAAK .... Zeitschrift fuer Aesthetik und Allgemeine Kunstwissenschaft [*A publication*]
ZAAP .... Zero Antiaircraft Potential [*Missile*]
ZAB .... Albuquerque, NM [*Location identifier*] [*FAA*]   (FAAL)
Zab .... Zabim   (BJA)
ZAB .... Zabrze [*Poland*] [*Seismograph station code, US Geological Survey*]   (SEIS)
ZAB .... Zinc-Air Battery
ZABIA .... Zastita Bilja [*A publication*]
Zab (NJ) .... Zabriskie's Reports [*21-24 New Jersey*]   (DLA)
ZACH .... Zacharias [*Old Testament book*] [*Douay version*]
Z Acker-Pflanzenb ... Zeitschrift fuer Acker- und Pflanzenbau [*A publication*]
Z Acker Pflanzenbau ... Zeitschrift fuer Acker- und Pflanzenbau [*A publication*]
ZACMA ...... Zeitschrift fuer Anorganische Chemie [*A publication*]
ZAD .... Zadar [*Yugoslavia*] [*Airport symbol*]   (OAG)
ZAD .... Zenith Angle Distribution
ZADCC .... Zone Air Defense Control Center   (NATG)
ZADI .... Zentralstelle fuer Agrardokumentation und -Information [*Center for Agricultural Documentation and Information*] [*Databank originator*] [*Information service*] [*West Germany*]   (EISS)
ZADS .... Zeitschrift des Allgemeinen Deutschen Sprachvereins [*A publication*]
ZAED .... Zentralstelle fuer Atomkernenergie-Dokumentation beim Gmelin-Institut [*Central Agency for Atomic Energy Documentation of the Gmelin Institute*] [*Germany*] [*Database originator*] [*Also, AED*]
ZAED Phys Daten ... ZAED [*Zentralstelle fuer Atomkernenergie-Dokumentation*] Physik Daten [*A publication*]
ZAeg .... Zeitschrift fuer Aegyptische Sprache und Altertumskunde [*A publication*]
Z Aegypt Sprache ... Zeitschrift fuer Aegyptische Sprache und Altertumskunde [*A publication*]
Z Aegypt Sprache Altertumskd ... Zeitschrift fuer Aegyptische Sprache und Altertumskunde [*A publication*]
Za Ekon Topl ... Za Ekonomiyu Topliva [*A publication*]
Z Aerztl Fortbild ... Zeitschrift fuer Aerztliche Fortbildung [*A publication*]
Z Aerztl Fortbild (Jena) ... Zeitschrift fuer Aerztliche Fortbildung (Jena) [*A publication*]
ZAeS .... Zeitschrift fuer Aegyptische Sprache und Altertumskunde [*A publication*]
Z Aes Allg Kunst ... Zeitschrift fuer Aesthetik und Allgemeine Kunstwissenschaft [*A publication*]
ZAF .... South Africa [*Three-letter standard code*]   (CNC)
ZAF .... Zero Alignment Fixture
ZAFBA ...... Zeitschrift fuer Aerztliche Fortbildung [*A publication*]
ZAG .... Zagreb [*Yugoslavia*] [*Airport symbol*]   (OAG)
ZAG .... Zagreb [*Agram*] [*Yugoslavia*] [*Seismograph station code, US Geological Survey*]   (SEIS)
Zagad Ekon Roln ... Zagadnienia Ekonomiki Rolnej [*A publication*]
Zagadn Ekon Roln ... Zagadnienia Ekonomiki Rolnej [*A publication*]

Zagadn Eksploatacji Masz ... Zagadnienia Eksploatacji Maszyn [*Poland*] [*A publication*]
Zagadnienia Drgan Nieliniowych ... Zagadnienia Drgan Nieliniowych [*Nonlinear Vibration Problems*] [*A publication*]
Zagadnienie Dyn Rozwoju Czlowieka Zesz Probl Kosmosu ... Zagadnienie Dynamiki Rozwoju Czlowieka Zeszyty Problemowe Kosmosu [*A publication*]
Z Agrargesch Agrarsoziol ... Zeitschrift fuer Agrargeschichte und Agrarsoziologie [*A publication*]
Z Agrargesch u -Soziol ... Zeitschrift fuer Agrargeschichte und Agrarsoziologie [*A publication*]
ZAGV .... Zeitschrift des Aachener Geschichtsvereins [*A publication*]
ZAH .... Zahedan [*Iran*] [*Airport symbol*]   (OAG)
ZAHAL .... Z'va Hagana Le'Israel [*Israel Defense Forces*] [*Hebrew*]
Zahnaerztebl (Baden-Wuerttemb) ... Zahnaerzteblatt (Baden-Wuerttemberg) [*A publication*]
Zahnaerztl Gesundheitsdienst ... Zahnaerztlicher Gesundheitsdienst [*A publication*]
Zahnaerztl Mitt ... Zahnaerztliche Mitteilungen [*A publication*]
Zahnaerztl Praxisfuehr ... Zahnaerztliche Praxisfuehrung [*A publication*]
Zahnaerztl Rundsch ... Zahnaerztliche Rundschau [*A publication*]
Zahnaerztl Welt Zahnaerztl Reform ... Zahnaerztliche Welt und Zahnaerztliche Reform [*A publication*]
Zahn-Mund-Kieferheilkd ... Zahn-, Mund-, und Kieferheilkunde [*A publication*]
Zahn- Mund- Kieferheilkd Zentralbl ... Zahn-, Mund-, und Kieferheilkunde mit Zentralblatt [*German Democratic Republic*] [*A publication*]
ZAI .... Zeirei Agudath Israel [*An association*]   (EA)
ZAI .... Zero Address Instruction
Zaire-Afr ... Zaire-Afrique [*A publication*]
ZAK .... Zakamensk [*USSR*] [*Seismograph station code, US Geological Survey*]   (SEIS)
ZAK .... Zeitschrift fuer Aesthetik und Kunstwissenschaft [*A publication*]
Zakhist Rosl ... Zakhist Roslin [*A publication*]
Za Khlopk Nezavisimost ... Za Khlopkovuyu Nezavisimost [*A publication*]
Zakhyst Rosl Resp Mizhvid Temat Nauk Zb ... Zakhyst Roslyn Respublikans 'Kyi Mizhvidomchyi Tematychnyi Naukovyi Zbirnyk [*A publication*]
Zakupki Sel'skokhoz Prod ... Zakupki Sel'skokhozyaistvennykh Produktov [*A publication*]
ZAL .... State University of New York, Albany Library School, Albany, NY [*OCLC symbol*]   (OCLC)
ZAL .... Zionist Archives and Library   (BJA)
ZALIS .... Zinc and Lead International Service
Z Allgemeine Wissenschaftstheorie ... Zeitschrift fuer Allgemeine Wissenschaftstheorie [*A publication*]
Z Allgemeinmed ... Zeitschrift fuer Allgemeinmedizin [*A publication*]
Z Allg Mikr ... Zeitschrift fuer Allgemeine Mikrobiologie [*A publication*]
Z Allg Mikrobiol ... Zeitschrift fuer Allgemeine Mikrobiologie [*A publication*]
Z Allg Oesterr Apoth Ver ... Zeitschrift des Allgemeinen Oesterreichischen Apotheker-Vereines [*A publication*]
Z Allg Physiol ... Zeitschrift fuer Allgemeine Physiologie [*A publication*]
Z Allg Wiss ... Zeitschrift fuer Allgemeine Wissenschaftstheorie [*A publication*]
Z Allg Wissenschaftstheor ... Zeitschrift fuer Allgemeine Wissenschaftstheorie [*A publication*]
Z Alternsforsch ... Zeitschrift fuer Alternsforschung [*A publication*]
Z Altt W ...... Zeitschrift fuer die Alttestamentliche Wissenschaft [*A publication*]
Z Alt Wiss... Zeitschrift fuer die Alttestamentliche Wissenschaft [*A publication*]
ZAM .... State University of New York, Agricultural and Technical College at Alfred, Alfred, NY [*OCLC symbol*]   (OCLC)
ZAM .... Z-Axis Modulation
ZAM .... Zamboanga [*Philippines*] [*Airport symbol*]   (OAG)
ZAM .... Zeitschrift fuer Askese und Mystik [*A publication*]
Zambia Dep Game Fish Fish Res Bull ... Zambia. Department of Game and Fisheries. Fisheries Research Bulletin [*A publication*]
Zambia Dep Wildl Fish Natl Parks Annu Rep ... Zambia. Department of Wildlife, Fisheries, and National Parks. Annual Report [*A publication*]
Zambia Div For Res Annu Rep ... Zambia. Division of Forest Research. Annual Report [*A publication*]
Zambia For Res Bull ... Zambia Forest Research Bulletin [*A publication*]
Zambia Geogr Assoc Mag ... Zambia Geographical Association. Magazine [*A publication*]
Zambia Geol Surv Annu Rep ... Zambia. Geological Survey. Annual Report [*A publication*]
Zambia Geol Surv Dep Annu Rep ... Zambia. Geological Survey. Department Annual Report [*A publication*]
Zambia Geol Surv Dep Econ Rep ... Zambia. Ministry of Lands and Mines. Geological Survey Department. Economic Report [*A publication*]
Zambia Geol Surv Econ Rep ... Zambia. Geological Survey. Economic Report [*A publication*]
Zambia Geol Surv Rec ... Zambia. Geological Survey. Records [*A publication*]
Zambia Geol Surv Tech Rep ... Zambia. Geological Survey. Technical Report [*A publication*]

Zambia J Sci Technol ... Zambia Journal of Science and Technology [*A publication*]
Zambia LJ ... Zambia Law Journal   (DLA)
Zambia Minist Lands Nat Resour For Res Bull ... Zambia. Ministry of Lands and Natural Resources. Forest Research Bulletin [*A publication*]
Zambia Minist Rural Dev For Res Bull ... Zambia. Ministry of Rural Development. Forest Research Bulletin [*A publication*]
Zambia Nurse J ... Zambia Nurse Journal [*A publication*]
Zambia Rep Geol Surv ... Zambia. Ministry of Lands and Mines. Report of the Geological Survey [*A publication*]
ZAMM .... Zen and the Art of Motorcycle Maintenance [*A novel*]
ZAMNA .... ZFA (Zeitschrift fuer Allgemeinmedizin) [*A publication*]
ZAMP .... Zeitschrift fuer Angewandte Mathematik und Physik [*A publication*]
ZAMS .... Zero-Age Main Sequence
ZAN .... Anchorage, AK [*Location identifier*] [*FAA*]   (FAAL)
ZAN .... Zante [*Greece*] [*Seismograph station code, US Geological Survey*]   (SEIS)
ZAN .... Zantop International Airlines, Inc. [*Ypsilanti, MI*] [*FAA designator*]   (FAAC)
ZANA .... Zambia News Agency
Z Anal Chem ... Fresenius' Zeitschrift fuer Analytische Chemie [*A publication*]
Z Analyt Chem ... Zeitschrift fuer Analytische Chemie [*A publication*]
Z Anat Entwicklungsgesch ... Zeitschrift fuer Anatomie und Entwicklungsgeschichte [*A publication*]
ZANC .... Zambia National Congress - Southern Rhodesia
ZANCA .... Zeitschrift fuer Analytische Chemie [*A publication*]
Zane .... Zane's Reports [*4-9 Utah*]   (DLA)
ZANF .... Zeitschrift fuer Assyriologie und Vorderasiatische Altertumskunde. Neue Folge [*A publication*]
Z Ang & Amerik ... Zeitschrift fuer Anglistik und Amerikanistik [*A publication*]
Z Angew Baeder Klimaheilkd ... Zeitschrift fuer Angewandte Baeder und Klimaheilkunde [*A publication*]
Z Angew Chem ... Zeitschrift fuer Angewandte Chemie und Zentralblatt fuer Technische Chemie [*A publication*]
Z Angew Entomol ... Zeitschrift fuer Angewandte Entomologie [*A publication*]
Z Angew Geol ... Zeitschrift fuer Angewandte Geologie [*A publication*]
Z Angew Math und Mech ... Zeitschrift fuer Angewandte Mathematik und Mechanik [*A publication*]
Z Angew Math Mech ... Zeitschrift fuer Angewandte Mathematik und Mechanik [*A publication*]
Z Angew Math Phys ... Zeitschrift fuer Angewandte Mathematik und Physik [*A publication*]
Z Angew Met ... Zeitschrift fuer Angewandte Meteorologie [*A publication*]
Z Angew Mikrosk Klin Chem ... Zeitschrift fuer Angewandte Mikroskopic und Klinische Chemie [*A publication*]
Z Angew Phys ... Zeitschrift fuer Angewandte Physik [*A publication*]
Z Angew Psychol ... Zeitschrift fuer Angewandte Psychologie und Psychologische Forschung [*A publication*]
Z Angew Zool ... Zeitschrift fuer Angewandte Zoologie [*A publication*]
Z Ang Geol ... Zeitschrift fuer Angewandte Geologie [*A publication*]
Z Anglis Am ... Zeitschrift fuer Anglistik und Amerikanistik [*A publication*]
Z Ang Ma Me ... Zeitschrift fuer Angewandte Mathematik und Mechanik [*A publication*]
Z Ang Math ... Zeitschrift fuer Angewandte Mathematik und Physik [*A publication*]
ZANLA .... Zimbabwe African National Liberation Army   (PD)
Z Anorg A C ... Zeitschrift fuer Anorganische und Allgemeine Chemie [*A publication*]
Z Anorg Allg Chem ... Zeitschrift fuer Anorganische und Allgemeine Chemie [*A publication*]
Z Anorg Chem ... Zeitschrift fuer Anorganische und Allgemeine Chemie [*A publication*]
ZANPA .... Zeitschrift fuer Experimentelle und Angewandte Psychologie [*A publication*]
ZAnt .... Ziva Antika [*A publication*]
ZANU .... Zimbabwe African National Union   (PPW)
ZANU-PF.... Zimbabwe African National Union - Patriotic Front   (PD)
ZANZ......... Zanzibar
Zanzibar Protect Ann Rep Med Dept ... Zanzibar Protectorate. Annual Report on the Medical Department [*A publication*]
Zanzib Prot LR ... Zanzibar Protectorate Law Reports [*Africa*]   (DLA)
ZAO RV ...... Zeitschrift fuer Auslaendisches Oeffentliches Recht und Voelkerrecht [*A publication*]
zap .... Zapotec [*MARC language code*] [*Library of Congress*]   (LCCP)
ZAP .... Zero Ability to Pay [*Real estate*]
ZAP .... Zero and Add Packed
ZAP .... Zero Antiaircraft Potential [*Missile*]   (MCD)
ZAP .... Znamenity Amerikansky Pisatel [*Famous American Writer*] [*Russian*]
ZAP .... Zoological Action Program [*Defunct*]   (EA)
Zapadne Karpaty Ser Geol ... Zapadne Karpaty. Seria Geologia [*A publication*]
Zap Arm Otd Vses Mineral Ova ... Zapiski Armyanskogo Otdeleniya Vsesoyuznogo Mineralogicheskogo Obshchestva [*A publication*]
ZAPB.......... Zinc-Air Primary Battery

Zap Beloruss Gos Inst Sel'sk Lesn Khoz ... Zapiski Belorusskogo Gosudarstvennogo Instituta Sel'skogo i Lesnogo Khozyaistva [*A publication*]

Zap Cukotsk Kraeved Muz ... Zapiski Cukotskogo Kraevedceskogo Muzeja [*A publication*]

Zap Inst Khim Akad Nauk Ukr RSR ... Zapiski Institutu Khimii Akademiya Nauk Ukrains'koi RSR [*A publication*]

Zapisnici Srp Geol Drus ... Zapisnici Srpskog Geoloskog Drustva [*A publication*]

Zap Khar'k S-kh Inst ... Zapiski Khar'kovskogo Sel'skokhozyaistvennogo Instituta [*A publication*]

Zap Kiiv Tov Prirodozn ... Zapiski Kiivs'kogo Tovaristva Prirodoznavtsiv [*A publication*]

Zap Leningrad Sel'skokhoz Inst ... Zapiski Leningradskogo Sel'skokhozyaistvennogo Instituta [*A publication*]

Zap Leningr Gorn Inst ... Zapiski Leningradskogo Gornogo Instituta [*USSR*] [*A publication*]

Zap Leningr Sel'-khoz Inst ... Zapiski Leningradskogo Sel'skokhozyaistvennogo Instituta [*A publication*]

Zap Leningr S-kh Inst ... Zapiski Leningradskogo Sel'skokhozyaistvennogo Instituta [*A publication*]

Zap Nauchn Semin ... Zapiski Nauchnykh Seminarov [*A publication*]

Zap Nauchn Semin Leningr Otd Mat Inst Akad Nauk SSSR ... Zapiski Nauchnykh Seminarov Leningradskoe Otdelenie. Matematicheskii Institut. Akademia Nauka SSSR [*USSR*] [*A publication*]

Zap Naucn Sem Leningrad Otdel Mat Inst Steklov ... Zapiski Naucnyh Seminarov Leningradskogo Otdelenija Matematiceskogo Instituta Imeni V. A. Steklova Akademii Nauk SSSR [*A publication*]

Zap Odess Ark Obshch ... Zapiski. Odesskoe Arkheologicheskoe Obshchestvo [*Odessa, USSR*] [*A publication*]

Zap Ross Mineral Ova ... Zapiski Rossiiskogo Mineralogicheskogo Obshchestva [*A publication*]

Zap Sverdlov Otd Vsesoyuz Bot Obshch ... Zapiski Sverdlovskogo Otdeleniya Vsesoyuznogo Botanicheskogo Obshchestva [*A publication*]

Zap Tsentr Kavk Otd Vses Bot Ova ... Zapiski Tsentral'no-Kavkazskogo Otdeleniya Vsesoyuznogo Botanicheskogo Obshchestva [*A publication*]

ZAPU .... Zimbabwe African People's Union

Zap Uzb Otd Vses Mineral Ova ... Zapiski Uzbekistanskogo Otdeleniya Vsesoyuznogo Mineralogicheskogo Obshchestva [*A publication*]

Zap Voronezh Sel'-Khoz Inst ... Zapiski Voronezhskogo Sel'sko-Khozyaist-Vennogo Instituta [*A publication*]

Zap Voronezh S-kh Inst ... Zapiski Voronezhskogo Sel'skokhozyaistvennogo Instituta [*A publication*]

Zap Vost Sib Otd Vses Mineral Ova ... Zapiski Vostochno-Sibirskogo Otdeleniya Vsesoyuznogo Mineralogicheskogo Obshchestva [*A publication*]

Zap Vses Mineral Obshchest ... Zapiski Vsesoyuznogo Mineralogicheskogo Obshchestva [*A publication*]

Zap Vses Mineral O-va ... Zapiski Vsesoyuznogo Mineralogicheskogo Obshchestva [*A publication*]

Zap Zabaik Fil Geogr Ova SSSR ... Zapiski Zabaikal'skogo Filiala Geograficheskogo Obshchestva SSSR [*A publication*]

Zap Zabaik Otd Vses Geogr O-va ... Zapiski Zabaikal'skogo Otdela Vsesoyuznogo Geograficheskogo Obshchestva [*A publication*]

ZAR .... Zaire [*Three-letter standard code*] (CNC)

ZAR .... Zaria [*Nigeria*] [*Geomagnetic observatory code*]

ZAR .... Zeus Acquisition RADAR [*Missile defense*]

Z Arbeitsgem Oesterr Entomol ... Zeitschrift der Arbeitsgemeinschaft Oesterreichischer Entomologen [*A publication*]

Z Arbeitswiss N F ... Zeitschrift fuer Arbeitswissenschaft. Neue Folge [*A publication*]

Z Archaeol ... Zeitschrift fuer Archaeologie [*A publication*]

Za Rekonstr Tekst Promsti ... Za Rekonstruktsiyu Tekstil'noi Promyshlennosti [*A publication*]

ZARP .... Zuid Afrikaansche Republick Politie [*South African Republic Police*] (DSUE)

ZarSl .... Zaranie Slaskie [*A publication*]

ZAS .... Zeitschrift fuer Aegyptische Sprache und Altertumskunde [*A publication*]

ZAS .... Zero Access Storage

ZAS .... Zymosan-Activated Serum [*Immunology*]

ZASA .... Zeitschrift fuer Aegyptische Sprache und Altertumskunde [*A publication*]

Zashch Korroz Khim Promsti ... Zashchita ot Korrozii v Khimicheskoi Promyshlennosti [*A publication*]

Zashch Met ... Zashchita Metallov [*A publication*]

Zashch Pokrytiya Met ... Zashchitnye Pokrytiya na Metallakh [*A publication*]

Zashch Rast (Kiev) ... Zashchita Rastenii (Kiev) [*A publication*]

Zashch Rast (Leningrad) ... Zashchita Rastenii (Leningrad) [*A publication*]

Zashch Rast (Mosc) ... Zashchita Rastenii (Moscow) [*A publication*]

Zashch Rast (Moscow) ... Zashchita Rastenii (Moscow) [*A publication*]

Zashch Rast Vred Bolez ... Zashchita Rastenii ot Vreditelei i Boleznei [*A publication*]

Zashch Rast Vred Bolezn ... Zashchita Rastenii ot Vreditelei i Boleznei [*A publication*]

Zashch Rast Vredit Bolez ... Zashchita Rastenii ot Vreditelei i Boleznei [*A publication*]

Zashch Truboprovodov Korroz ... Zashchita Truboprovodov ot Korrozii [*A publication*]

Z Asiat Studien ... Zentralasiatische Studien [*Bonn*] [*A publication*]

Za Soc Zemed ... Za Socialisticke Zemedelstvi [*A publication*]

Za Sots Sel' -khoz Nauku ... Za Sotsialisticheskuyu Sel'skokhozyaistvennuyu Nauku [*A publication*]

Za Sots Sel'skokhoz Nauku Ser A ... Za Sotsialisticheskuyu Sel'skokhozyaistvennuyu Nauku. Seriya A [*A publication*]

Z Assyr .... Zeitschrift fuer Assyriologie [*A publication*]

Zast Bilja ... Zastita Bilja [*A publication*]

Z Asthet Al ... Zeitschrift fuer Asthetik und Allgemeine Kunstwissenschaft [*A publication*]

ZastMat ...... Zastosowania Matematyki [*A publication*]

Zast Mater ... Zastita Materijala [*A publication*]

Z Astrophys ... Zeitschrift fuer Astrophysik [*West Germany*] [*A publication*]

ZAT .... Zantop Airways, Inc.

ZAT .... Zhaotong [*China*] [*Airport symbol*] (OAG)

ZAT .... Zinc Atmospheric Tracer

ZAT .... Zydowska Agencja Telegraficzna (BJA)

ZATB .... Zeitschrift fuer die Alttestamentliche Wissenschaft. Beihefte [*A publication*]

Za Tekh Prog (Gorkly) ... Za Tekhnicheskii Progress (Gorkly) [*A publication*]

ZATPA .... Za Tekhnicheskii Progress [*A publication*]

ZATW .... Zeitschrift fuer die Alttestamentliche Wissenschaft [*A publication*]

ZAU .... Chicago, IL [*Location identifier*] [*FAA*] (FAAL)

Z Auslaend Landwirtsch ... Zeitschrift fuer Auslaendische Landwirtschaft [*A publication*]

Z Auslaend Oeff Voelkerrecht ... Zeitschrift fuer Auslaendisches Oeffentliches Recht und Voelkerrecht [*A publication*]

Z Ausland Landwirt ... Zeitschrift fuer Auslaendische Landwirtschaft [*A publication*]

Z Ausl Oeff Recht Voelkerrecht ... Zeitschrift fuer Auslaendisches Oeffentliches Recht und Voelkerrecht [*A publication*]

ZAV .... Zavalla [*Texas*] [*Seismograph station code, US Geological Survey*] [*Closed*] (SEIS)

Zav .... Zavim (BJA)

ZAVA .... Zeitschrift fuer Assyriologie und Vorderasiatische Archaeologie [*A publication*]

Zavod Lab ... Zavodskaya Laboratoriya [*A publication*]

ZAW .... Zeitschrift fuer die Alttestamentliche Wissenschaft [*A publication*]

ZAWEA ...... Zahnaerztliche Welt [*A publication*]

ZAZ .... Zaragoza [*Spain*] [*Airport symbol*] (OAG)

ZB .... Zeitschrift fuer Balkanologie [*A publication*]

ZB .... Zero Beat [*Radio*]

ZB .... Zinc Borate [*Trademark for a flame retardant compound*] [*Humphrey Chemical Co.*]

ZB .... Zuercherbibel (BJA)

ZB .... Zum Beispiel [*For Example*] [*German*]

ZBA .... Zero Bias Anomaly

ZBA .... Zero Bracket Amount [*IRS*]

ZBalk .... Zeitschrift fuer Balkanologie [*A publication*]

ZBAV .... Association of Byelorussian American Veterans in America (EA)

ZBB .... Zeitschrift fuer Bibliothekswesen und Bibliographie [*A publication*]

ZBB .... Zentralblatt fuer Bibliothekswesen [*A publication*]

ZBB .... Zero-Base Budgeting

Zb f Bibl ... Zentralblatt fuer Bibliothekswesen [*A publication*]

Zb Bioteh Fak Univ Ljubljani ... Zbornik Biotehniski Fakultete Univerze v Ljubljani [*A publication*]

Zb Bioteh Fak Univ Ljublj Kmetijstvo ... Zbornik Biotehniske Fakultete Univerze v Ljubljani. Kmetijstvo [*A publication*]

Zb Bioteh Fak Univ Ljublj Vet ... Zbornik Biotehniske Fakultete Univerze v Ljubljani. Veterinarstvo [*A publication*]

Zb Bioteh Fak Univ Ljublj Vet Supl ... Zbornik Biotehniske Fakultete Univerze v Ljubljani. Veterinarstvo. Suplement [*A publication*]

ZBDLG .... Zuercher Beitraege zur Deutschen Literatur und Geistesgeschichte [*A publication*]

ZBDSS .... Zuercher Beitraege zur Deutschen Sprach- und Stilgeschichte [*A publication*]

ZBE .... Zinc Battery Electrode

Z Beleuchtungswes Heizungs- Lueftungstech ... Zeitschrift fuer Beleuchtungswesen Heizungs- und Lueftungstechnik [*A publication*]

Z Berg Huetten Salinenwes Dtsch Reich ... Zeitschrift fuer das Berg-, Huetten-, und Salinenwesen im Deutschen Reich [*A publication*]

Z Bergrecht ... Zeitschrift fuer Bergrecht [*West Germany*] [*A publication*]

Z Betriebsw ... Zeitschrift fuer Betriebswirtschaft [*A publication*]

Z Betriebswirtsch ... Zeitschrift fuer Betriebswirtschaft [*A publication*]

Z Bewasserungswirtsch ... Zeitschrift fuer Bewasserungswirtschaft [*A publication*]

ZBF .... Zeitschrift fuer Buecherfreunde [*A publication*]

ZbFL .... Zbornik za Filologiju i Lingvistiku [*A publication*]

ZBG .... Zeitschrift des Bergischen Geschichtsvereins [*A publication*]

Zb Geol Vied Zapadne Karpaty ... Zbornik Geologichych Vied Zapadne Karpaty [*A publication*]
ZBGV......... Zeitschrift des Bergischen Geschichtsvereins [*A publication*]
Z Bibl und Bibliog ... Zeitschrift fuer Bibliothekswesen und Bibliographie [*A publication*]
Z Bibliot u Bibliog ... Zeitschrift fuer Bibliothekswesen und Bibliographie [*A publication*]
Z Bibliothekswes Bibliogr ... Zeitschrift fuer Bibliothekswesen und Bibliographie [*A publication*]
Z Bibliothekswesen und Bibl ... Zeitschrift fuer Bibliothekswesen und Bibliographie [*A publication*]
Z Bienenforsch ... Zeitschrift fuer Bienenforschung [*A publication*]
Z Binnenfisch DDR ... Zeitschrift fuer die Binnenfischerei der DDR [*A publication*]
Zb Inst Khim Tekhnol Akad Nauk Ukr RSR ... Zbirnik Institutu Khimichnoi Tekhnologii Akademiya Nauk Ukrains'koi RSR [*A publication*]
Z Biochem ... Zeitschrift fuer Biochemie [*A publication*]
Z Biol......... Zeitschrift fuer Biologie [*A publication*]
Zbirka Izbran Poglav Fiz ... Zbirka Izbranih Poglavij iz Fizike [*A publication*]
Zbirka Izbran Poglav Mat ... Zbirka Izbranih Poglavij iz Matematike [*A publication*]
ZbirP .... Zbirnyk Prac' Naukovoji Sevcenkivs'koji Konferenciji [*A publication*]
ZBK .... Zeitschrift fuer Bildende Kunst [*A publication*]
ZBK .... Zeitschrift fuer Buchkunde [*A publication*]
ZBK .... Zuercher Bibelkommentar [*A publication*]   (BJA)
ZBKG .... Zeitschrift fuer Bayerische Kirchengeschichte [*A publication*]
ZBL............ Brooklyn Law School, Brooklyn, NY [*OCLC symbol*]   (OCLC)
Zbl............. Zentralblatt fuer Mathematik und Ihre Grenzgebiete [*A publication*]
ZBL............ Zero-Based Linearity
Zbl Bakt A ... Zentralblatt fuer Bakteriologie. Reihe A [*A publication*]
Zbl Bakt B ... Zentralblatt fuer Bakteriologie. Reihe B [*A publication*]
Zbl f Bibl ... Zentralblatt fuer Bibliothekswesen [*A publication*]
Zbl DDR .... Zentralblatt der Deutschen Demokratischen Republik   (DLA)
ZBLG......... Zeitschrift fuer Bayerische Landesgeschichte [*A publication*]
Zbl Math..... Zentralblatt fuer Mathematik und Ihre Grenzgebiete [*A publication*]
Zbl Soz Vers ... Zentralblatt fuer Sozialversicherung und Versorgung [*German*]   (DLA)
Zbl Vet A .... Zentralblatt fuer Veterinaermedizin. Reihe A [*A publication*]
Zbl Vet B .... Zentralblatt fuer Veterinaermedizin. Reihe B [*A publication*]
ZBM........... State University of New York, College at Oneonta, Oneonta, NY [*OCLC symbol*]   (OCLC)
Zb Meteorol Hidrol Rad ... Zbornik Meteoroloskih i Hidroloskih Radova [*Yugoslavia*] [*A publication*]
ZBMP .... Zero-Base Media Planning
ZBN .... Brookhaven National Laboratory, Upton, NY [*OCLC symbol*]   (OCLC)
Zb Nauk Pr Aspir Kyyiv Univ Pryr Nauky ... Zbirnyk Naukovykh Prats' Aspirantiv Kyyivski Universytet Pryrodni Nauky [*A publication*]
Zb Nauk Pr L'viv Med Inst ... Zbirnyk Naukovykh Prats' L'viv'kyi Medychyni Instytut [*A publication*]
Zb Nauk Pr Umans'kyi Sil'skohospod Inst ... Zbirnyk Naukovykh Prats' Umans'kyi Sil'skohospodarskyi Instytut [*A publication*]
Zb Nauk Rob Khark Derzh Med Inst ... Zbirnik Naukovikh Robit Kharkivs'kogo Derzhavnogo Medichnogo Institutu [*A publication*]
ZbNPAF ..... Zbirnyk Naukovych Prac' Aspirantiv z Filolohiji [*A publication*]
ZBO........... Bowen [*Australia*] [*Airport symbol*] [*Obsolete*]   (OAG)
ZBO .... Zone of British Occupation [*Military*]
Zbor Arheol Muz ... Zbornik na Arheoloskiot Muzej [*A publication*]
Zbor Narod Muz Beogradu ... Zbornik Narodnog Muzeja u Beogradu [*A publication*]
Zbornik Rad Mat Inst (Beograd) ... Zbornik Radova. Matematicki Institut (Beograd) [*A publication*]
Zborn Rad ... Zbornik Radova [*A publication*]
Zborn Rad Poljopriv Fak Univ Beogr ... Zbornik Radova. Poljoprivrednog Fakulteta. Universitet u Beogradu [*A publication*]
Zborn Slov Nar Muz Prir Vedy ... Zbornik Slovenskeho Narodneho Muzea Prirodne Vedy [*A publication*]
Zbor Slov Narod Muz ... Zbornik Slovenskeho Narodneho Muzea [*A publication*]
Z Bot .... Zeitschrift fuer Botanik [*A publication*]
ZBP .... Zero-Base Programing [*Military*]
ZBPHA .... Zentralblatt fuer Bakteriologie, Parasitenkunde, Infektionskrankheiten, und Hygiene. Abteilung 1. Medizinisch-Hygienische Bakteriologie, Virusforschung, und Parasitologie. Originale [*A publication*]
Zb Prac Chem Fak SVST (Bratislava) ... Zbornik Prac Chemickotechnologickej Fakulty SVST (Bratislava) [*A publication*]
Zb Prav Fak Zagrebu ... Zbornik Pravnog Fakulteta u Zagrebu [*A publication*]
Zb Pr Chemickotechnol Fak SVST ... Zbornik Prac Chemickotechnologickij Fakulty SVST [*A publication*]
Zb Pr Chem-Technol Fak SVST ... Zbornik Prac Chemickotechnologickej Fakulty SVST [*A publication*]

Zb Pr Inst Teploenerg Akad Nauk Ukr RSR ... Zbirnik Prats' Institut Teploenergetiki. Akademiya Nauk Ukrains'koi RSR [*A publication*]
Zb Pr Nauk Inst Fiziol Kyyiv Univ ... Zbirnyk Prats' Naukovodoslidnyts'koho Instytuta Fiziolohiyi Kyyivs'koho Universytetu [*A publication*]
Zb Pr Naukovodosl Inst Fiziol Kyyiv Univ ... Zbirnyk Prats' Naukovodoslidnyts'koho Instytuta Fiziolokiyi Kyyivs'koho Universytetu [*A publication*]
Zb Pr Zool Muz Akad Nauk Ukr RSR ... Zbirnyk Prats' Zoolohichnoho Muzeyu Akademiyi Nauk Ukrayinskoyi RSR [*A publication*]
ZBR .... Chah-Bahar [*Iran*] [*Airport symbol*]   (OAG)
ZbR .... Zbirnyk Robit Aspirantiv Romano-Germans'koji i Klazycnoji Filolohiji [*A publication*]
ZBR .... Zero-Base Review
ZBR .... Zero Beat Reception [*Radio*]
ZBR .... Zero Bend Radius
Zb Rad Biol Inst (Beograd) ... Zbornik Radova. Bioloski Institut (Beograd) [*A publication*]
Zb Rad Biol Inst NR Srbye Beogr ... Zbornik Radova. Bioloski Institut NR Srbye Beograd [*A publication*]
Zb Rad Math Inst Beograd NS ... Beograd Matematicki Institut. Zbornik Radova. Nouvelle Serie [*A publication*]
Zb Rad Poljopr Inst Osijek ... Zbornik Radova. Poljoprivredni Institut Osijek [*A publication*]
Zb Rad Poljopriv Fak Univ Beogradu ... Zbornik Radova. Poljoprivrednog Fakulteta. Universitet u Beogradu [*A publication*]
Zb Rad Prir Mat Fak ... Zbornik Radova. Prirodno-Matematichkog Fakulteta [*Yugoslavia*] [*A publication*]
Zb Rad Prir-Mat Fak Ser Fiz ... Zbornik Radova. Prirodno-Matematickog Fakulteta. Serija za Fiziku [*A publication*]
Zb Rad Prir-Mat Fak Univ Novom Sadu ... Zbornik Radova. Prirodno-Matematichkog Fakulteta Univerzitet u Novom Sadu [*A publication*]
Zb Rad Srp Akad Nauka Geol Inst ... Zbornik Radova. Srpska Akademija Nauka Geoloski Institut [*A publication*]
Zb Rad Zavod Ratarstvo (Sarajevo) ... Zbornik Radova. Zavod za Ratarstvo (Sarajevo) [*A publication*]
Zbraslav Res Inst Land Reclam Improv Sci Monogr ... Zbraslav Research Institute for Land Reclamation and Improvement. Scientific Monograph [*A publication*]
ZbRFFZ ...... Zbornik Radova. Filozofskog Fakulteta. Svencilista u Zagrebu [*A publication*]
ZbRL .... Zbirnyk Robit Aspirantiv L'Vivskij Derzavnyj Universitet [*A publication*]
Zb Robit Aspir L'Viv Univ Pryr Nauk ... Zbirnyk Robit Aspirantiv L'Vivs'kyi Universytet Pryrodnykh Nauk [*A publication*]
ZBRS .... Z's Briefs. CPSU [*Cooperative Park Studies Unit, University of Alaska*] Newsletter [*A publication*]
ZbS .... Zbornik za Slavistiku [*A publication*]
ZBS .... Zeitschrift des Deutschen Vereins fuer Buchwesen und Schrifttum [*A publication*]
ZBS .... Zivena Beneficial Society   (EA)
ZbSAN .... Zbornik Radova. Srpske Akademije Nauke [*A publication*]
Zb Slov Nar Muz Prir Vedy ... Zbornik Slovenskeho Narodneho Muzea Prirodne Vedy [*A publication*]
ZBT .... Zeta Beta Tau [*Fraternity*]
ZBT .... Zion Bemishpat Tipadeh (Isaiah 1:27)   (BJA)
Zb Ved Prac Lesn Fak Vys Sk Lesn Drev Zvolene ... Zbornik Vedeckych Prac Lesnickej Fakulty Vysokej Skoly Lesnickej a Drevarskej vo Zvolene [*Czechoslovakia*] [*A publication*]
Zb Ved Pr Vys Sk Tech Kosiciach ... Zbornik Vedeckych Prac. Vysokej Skoly Technickej v Kosiciach [*A publication*]
Zb Vojnomed Akad ... Zbornik Vojnomedicinske Akademije [*A publication*]
Zb Vysk Pr Vysk Ustav Zvaracskeho Bratislave ... Zbornik Vyskumnych Prac Vyskumneho Ustavu Zvaracskeho v Bratislave [*A publication*]
ZBW .... Boston, MA [*Location identifier*] [*FAA*]   (FAAL)
ZBW .... Zentralblatt fuer Bibliothekswesen [*A publication*]
Zb Zgodovino Naravoslovja Tek ... Zbornik za Zgodovino Naravoslovja in Teknike [*A publication*]
Z-C .... Zapalote-Chico [*Race of maize*]
Zc .... Zechariah   (BJA)
ZC .... Ziegfeld Club   (EA)
ZC .... Zinfandel Club   (EA-IO)
ZC .... Zone Capacity
Z of C .... Zones of Communications [*Military*]
ZCA........... Z Club of America   (EA)
Z/CAL .... Zero Calibration   (MCD)
ZCB .... Chase Manhattan Bank, New York, NY [*OCLC symbol*]   (OCLC)
ZCB .... Zinc-Coated Bolt
ZCC .... Zeppelin Collectors Club   (EA)
ZCC........... Zirconia-Coated Crucible
ZCCI .... Zippy Collectors Club, Incorporated   (EA)
ZCCM........ Zambian Consolidated Copper Mines
ZCD........... Zero Crossing Detector
Z Chem ...... Zeitschrift fuer Chemie [*A publication*]
Z Chemie (Lpz) ... Zeitschrift fuer Chemie (Leipzig) [*A publication*]
Z Chemother Verw Geb Teil 1 ... Zeitschrift fuer Chemotherapie und Verwandte Gebiete. Teil 1. Originale [*A publication*]

Z Chemother Verw Geb Teil 2 ... Zeitschrift fuer Chemotherapie und Verwandte Gebiete. Teil 2. Referate [*A publication*]
ZChK......... Zeitschrift fuer Christliche Kunst [*A publication*]
ZChrK........ Zeitschrift fuer Christliche Kunst [*A publication*]
ZCIC.......... Zirconia-Coated Iridium Crucible
ZCK........... Zeitschrift fuer Christliche Kunst [*A publication*]
ZCL............ Zacatecas [*Mexico*] [*Airport symbol*]   (OAG)
ZCM .... State University of New York, Agricultural and Technical College at Canton, Canton, NY [*OCLC symbol*]   (OCLC)
ZCMI .... Zion's Cooperative Mercantile Institution [*Department store in Salt Lake City, UT*]
ZCN........... Zinc-Coated Nut
ZCP............ Zeitschrift fuer Celtische Philologie [*A publication*]
ZCP............ Zinc Chromate Primer
ZCPh.......... Zeitschrift fuer Celtische Philologie [*A publication*]
ZCR............ Zero Crossing Rate
ZCR............ Zero-Temperature Coefficient Resistor
ZCS............ Zinc-Coated Screw
ZCW........... Zinc-Coated Washer
ZCZ............ Cazenovia College, Witherill Learning Center, Cazenovia, NY [*OCLC symbol*]   (OCLC)
ZCzest .... Ziemia Czestochowska [*A publication*]
ZD............. Zeitschrift fuer Deutschkunde [*A publication*]
ZD............. Zener Diode
ZD............. Zenith Distance [*Navigation*]
ZD............. Zero Defects
ZD............. Zielsprache Deutsch [*A publication*]
ZD............. ZIP Code Distribution
ZD............. Zone Description
ZDA........... Zeitschrift fuer Deutsches Altertum und Deutsche Literatur [*A publication*]
ZDA........... Zinc Development Association   (EA-IO)
ZDADL ...... Zeitschrift fuer Deutsches Altertum und Deutsche Literatur [*A publication*]
ZDA/LDA/CA ... Zinc Development Association/Lead Development Association/Cadmium Association [*London, England*] [*Information service*]   (EISS)
Z f D Altert ... Zeitschrift fuer Deutsches Altertum und Deutsche Literatur [*A publication*]
Z Dampfkessel Maschinenbetr ... Zeitschrift fuer Dampfkessel und Maschinenbetrieb [*A publication*]
Z Dampfkesselunters Versicher Ges ... Zeitschrift der Dampfkesseluntersuchungs- und Versicherungs-Gesellschaft [*A publication*]
ZDB........... Zeitschrift fuer Deutsche Bildung [*A publication*]
ZDC........... Washington, DC [*Location identifier*] [*FAA*]   (FAAL)
ZDC........... Zero Defects Council
ZDC........... Zeus Defense Center [*Missile defense*]
ZDC........... Zinc Dibenzyldithiocarbamate [*Rubber accelerator*]
ZDC........... Zinc Die Casting
ZDCTBS..... Zeus Defense Center Tape and Buffer System [*Missiles*]   (IEEE)
ZDD........... Zero Delay Device
ZDDP......... Zinc Dialkyldithiophosphate [*Organic chemistry*]
ZDE .... Zagreb Dance Ensemble [*Yugoslav*]
ZDE .... Zentralstelle Dokumentation Elektrotechnik [*Electrical Engineering Documentation Center*] [*Offenbach, WG*] [*Originator and database*] [*Information service*]   (EISS)
ZDemogr.... Zeitschrift fuer Demographie und Statistik der Juden [*A publication*]
Z Desinfekt Gesundheitswes ... Zeitschrift fuer Desinfektions- und Gesundheitswesen [*A publication*]
Z Deut Alt... Zeitschrift fuer Deutsches Altertum und Deutsche Literatur [*A publication*]
Z Deut Geol Ges ... Zeitschrift der Deutschen Geologischen Gesellschaft [*A publication*]
Z Deuts Morgen G ... Zeitschrift der Deutschen Morgenlaendischen Gesellschaft [*Wiesbaden*] [*A publication*]
ZDF .... Zweites Deutsches Fernsehen [*Television network*] [*West Germany*]
ZDFALP ..... Z Dziejow Form Artystycznych Literaturze Polskiej [*A publication*]
ZDG........... Corning Community College, Corning, NY [*OCLC symbol*]   (OCLC)
ZDG........... Zeitschrift fuer Deutsche Geistesgeschichte [*A publication*]
ZDG........... Zeitschrift fuer Deutsche Geisteswissenschaft [*A publication*]
ZDG........... Zinc-Doped Germanium
ZDGG......... Zeitschrift fuer Deutsche Geistesgeschichte [*A publication*]
ZDK........... Zeitschrift fuer Deutschkunde [*A publication*]
ZDK........... Zen-Do Kai Martial Arts Association, International   (EA)
ZDKAA....... Zdravookhranenie Kazakhstana [*A publication*]
ZDKP......... Zeitschrift fuer Deutsche Kulturphilosophie [*A publication*]
ZDL .... Zeitschrift fuer Dialektologie und Linguistik [*A publication*]
ZDM........... Zeitschrift fuer Deutsche Mundarten [*A publication*]
ZDMG......... Zeitschrift der Deutschen Morgenlaendischen Gesellschaft [*A publication*]
Z DNA........ Deoxyribonucleic Acid, Zigzag [*DNA with left-handed helix*] [*Biochemistry, genetics*]
Zdorov'e Nauch Pop Gig Zhurnal ... Zdorov'e Nauchno Populiarnyi Gigienicheskii Zhurnal [*A publication*]
ZDP .... Zeitschrift fuer Deutsche Philologie [*A publication*]
ZDP .... Zero Defects Program

ZDP .... Zero Defects Proposal
ZDP .... Zero Delivery Pressure   (IEEE)
ZDP .... Zimbabwe Democratic Party   (PPW)
ZDPA......... Zero Defects Program Audit
ZDPG......... Zero Defects Program Guideline
ZDPh.......... Zeitschrift fuer Deutsche Philologie [*A publication*]
Z f D Phil .... Zeitschrift fuer Deutsche Philologie [*A publication*]
ZDPO......... Zero Defects Program Objective
ZDPR.......... Zero Defects Program Responsibility
ZDPV.......... Zeitschrift des Deutschen Palaestinavereins [*A publication*]
ZDR............ Zentraldeutsche Rundfunk [*Central German Radio*]
ZDR............ Zeus Discrimination RADAR [*Missile defense*]
Zdrav Aktual ... Zdravotnicke Aktuality [*A publication*]
Zdravookhr Beloruss ... Zdravookhranenie Belorussii [*A publication*]
Zdravookhr Belorussii ... Zdravookhranenie Belorussii [*A publication*]
Zdravookhr Kaz ... Zdravookhranenie Kazakhstana [*A publication*]
Zdravookhr Kirg ... Zdravookhranenie Kirgizii [*A publication*]
Zdravookhr Ross Fed ... Zdravookhranenie Rossiiskoi Federatsii [*A publication*]
Zdravookhr Sov Est Sb ... Zdravookhranenie Sovetskoi Estonii Sbornik [*A publication*]
Zdravookhr Tadzh ... Zdravookhranenie Tadzhikistana [*A publication*]
Zdravookhr Turkm ... Zdravookhranenie Turkmenistana [*A publication*]
Zdrav Prac ... Zdravotnicka Pracovnice [*A publication*]
Zdrav Tech Vzduchotech ... Zdravotni Technika a Vzduchotechnika [*A publication*]
Zdrav Vestn ... Zdravstveni Vestnik [*A publication*]
Zdrow Publiczne ... Zdrowie Publiczne [*A publication*]
ZDS .... Zeitschrift fuer Deutsche Sprache [*A publication*]
ZDS .... Zinc Detection System
ZDSJ .... Zeitschrift fuer Demographie und Statistik der Juden [*A publication*]
ZDStJ......... Zeitschrift fuer Demographie und Statistik der Juden [*A publication*]
Zdt............. Die Zoologie des Talmuds [*L. Lewysohn*] [*A publication*]   (BJA)
ZDT .... Zero-Ductility Transition   (IEEE)
Z Dtschen Morgenlaend Ges ... Zeitschrift der Deutschen Morgenlaendischen Gesellschaft [*A publication*]
Z Dtsch Geol Ges ... Zeitschrift der Deutschen Geologischen Gesellschaft [*A publication*]
Z Dtsch Morgenl Ges ... Zeitschrift der Deutschen Morganlaendischen Gesellschaft [*A publication*]
ZDV .... Denver, CO [*Location identifier*] [*FAA*]   (FAAL)
ZDV .... Zero Dead Volume [*Chromatography*]
ZDVGMS.... Zeitschrift des Deutschen Vereins fuer die Geschichte Maehrens und Schlesiens [*A publication*]
ZDW .... Zeitschrift fuer Deutsche Wortforschung [*A publication*]
ZDWDSU.... Zeitschrift fuer Deutschwissenschaft und Deutschunterricht [*A publication*]
ZE............. Zeitschrift fuer Ethnologie [*A publication*]
ZE............. Zenith Electronics Corp. [*NYSE symbol*]
ZE............. Zero Balance Entry [*Banking*]
ZE............. Zero Effusion
ZE............. Zollinger-Ellison [*Syndrome*] [*Medicine*]
ZE............. Zone Effect
ZE............. Zone Electrophoresis [*Analytical biochemistry*]
ZEA .... Zero Energy Assembly
ZEA .... Zero Entropy Automorphism
ZEASA ...... Zeitschrift fuer Astrophysik [*A publication*]
Zeb............ Zebahim   (BJA)
ZEB .... Zebra   (ROG)
ZEBED .... Zeitschrift fuer Bergrecht [*A publication*]
ZEBFA....... Zhurnal Evolyutsionnoi Biokhimii i Fiziologii [*A publication*]
ZEBLA....... Zeitschrift fuer Biologie [*A publication*]
ZEBRA ...... Zero Balance, Reimbursable Account [*Year-end reclassification of taxable income*]
ZEBRA ...... Zero Energy Breeder Reactor Assembly [*British*]
Zec............ Zechariah [*Old Testament book*]
ZEC .... Zero Energy Coefficient
ZEC .... Zinc-Electrochemical Cell
ZEC .... Zurich Energy Corporation [*Vancouver Stock Exchange symbol*]
ZECC .... Zinc-Electrochemical Cell
ZECC .... Zonal Electric Comfort Council   (EA)
Zech........... Zechariah [*Old Testament book*]
ZECM .... Zonal Elementary Circulative Mechanism
ZED .... Zero Energy Deuterium [*Type of nuclear reactor*]
ZED .... Zero Express Dialing
ZED .... Zimbabwe Environment and Design [*A publication*]
ZED .... Zur Erkenntnis der Dichtung [*A publication*]
ZEDRON.... Blimp Squadron [*Later separated into BLIMPRON and Blimp-HEDRON*] [*Navy*]
ZEE .... Zeitschrift fuer Evangelische Ethik [*A publication*]
Z EEG-EMG ... Zeitschrift fuer EEG-EMG [*Elektroenzephalographie, Elektromyographie, und Verwandte Gebiete*] [*German Federal Republic*] [*A publication*]
ZEELA....... Zeitschrift fuer Elektrochemie [*A publication*]
ZEEP.......... Zero End Expiratory Pressure [*Medicine*]
ZEEP.......... Zero Energy Experimental Pile [*Nuclear reactor*] [*Canada*]
ZEF............ Elkin, NC [*Location identifier*] [*FAA*]   (FAAL)
ZEG .... Senggo [*Indonesia*] [*Airport symbol*]   (OAG)

ZEG .... Zero Economic Growth
ZEG .... Zero Energy Growth
ZEGL .... Ziegler Co., Inc. [*NASDAQ symbol*] (NQ)
ZEI .... Zero Environmental Impact
ZEINA .... Zeitschrift fuer Instrumentenkunde [*A publication*]
Z Eisenbahnwes Verkehrstech Glasers Ann ... Zeitschrift fuer Eisenbahnwesen und Verkehrstechnik. Glasers. Annalen [*A publication*]
Z Eis Kaelte Ind ... Zeitschrift fuer Eis-und Kaelte-Industrie [*A publication*]
Zeiss Inf ..... Zeiss Information [*A publication*]
Zeiss Mitt ... Zeiss Mitteilungen [*A publication*]
Zeiss-Mitt Fortschr Tech Opt ... Zeiss-Mitteilungen ueber Fortschritte der Technischen Optik [*A publication*]
Zeiss-Mitt Fortsch Tech Optik ... Zeiss-Mitteilungen ueber Fortschritte der Technischen Optik [*A publication*]
Zeit f Deutk ... Zeitschrift fuer Deutschkunde [*A publication*]
Zeit f Deut Phil ... Zeitschrift fuer Deutsche Philologie [*A publication*]
Zeitgeschic ... Zeitgeschichte [*A publication*]
Zeit f Rom Phil ... Zeitschrift fuer Romanische Philologie [*A publication*]
Zeitschr Angew Geologie ... Zeitschrift fuer Angewandte Geologie [*A publication*]
Zeitschr Anorg u Allg Chemie ... Zeitschrift fuer Anorganische und Allgemeine Chemie [*A publication*]
Zeitschr Geomorphologie ... Zeitschrift fuer Geomorphologie [*A publication*]
Zeitschr Geomorphologie Neue Folge ... Zeitschrift fuer Geomorphologie. Neue Folge [*A publication*]
Zeitschr Geophysik ... Zeitschrift fuer Geophysik [*A publication*]
Zeitschr Gletscherkunde u Glazialgeologie ... Zeitschrift fuer Gletscherkunde und Glazialgeologie [*A publication*]
Zeitschr Kristallographie ... Zeitschrift fuer Kristallographie [*A publication*]
Zeitschr Physikal Chemie ... Zeitschrift fuer Physikalische Chemie [*A publication*]
Zeit f Volk ... Zeitschrift fuer Volkskunde [*A publication*]
Zeitwahr .... Zeitschrift fuer Wahrscheinlichkeitstheorie [*A publication*]
ZEIZA .... Zeitschrift fuer Elektrische Informations- und Energietechnik [*A publication*]
ZEKIA .... Zeitschrift fuer Kinderheilkunde [*A publication*]
Z Eksper Teoret Fiz ... Zurnal Eksperimental'noi i Teoreticeskoi Fiziki [*A publication*]
ZEL .... Bella Bella [*Canada*] [*Airport symbol*] (OAG)
ZEL .... Equitable Life Assurance Society of the United States, Medical Library, New York, NY [*OCLC symbol*] (OCLC)
ZEL .... Zelovo [*Enthusiastically*] [*Music*] (ROG)
ZEL .... Zero-Length Launch [*Missiles*]
Z Elek Informations- und Energietech ... Zeitschrift fuer Elektrische Informations- und Energietechnik [*A publication*]
Z Elektr Inf Energietech ... Zeitschrift fuer Elektrische Informations- und Energietechnik [*A publication*]
Z Elektr Inf & Energietech ... Zeitschrift fuer Elektrische Informations- und Energietechnik [*IET*] [*A publication*]
Z Elektr Informationstech Energietech ... Zeitschrift fuer Elektrische Informations- und Energietechnik [*IET*] [*A publication*]
Z Elektr Inform Energietech ... Zeitschrift fuer Elektrische Informations- und Energietechnik [*A publication*]
Z Elektrochem ... Zeitschrift fuer Elektrochemie [*A publication*]
Z Elektrochem Angew Phy Chem ... Zeitschrift fuer Elektrochemie und Angewandte Physikalische Chemie [*A publication*]
Z Elektrotech ... Zeitschrift fuer Elektrotechnik [*West Germany*] [*A publication*]
Zelezarski Zb ... Zelezarski Zbornik [*A publication*]
ZELL .... Zero-Length Launch [*Missiles*] (MCD)
Zell Papier ... Zellstoff und Papier [*A publication*]
Zellstoffchem Abh ... Zellstoffchemische Abhandlungen [*A publication*]
Zellst Pap (Berlin) ... Zellstoff und Papier (Berlin) [*A publication*]
Zellst Pap (Leipzig) ... Zellstoff und Papier (Leipzig) [*A publication*]
Zellwolle Dtsch Kunstseiden Ztg ... Zellwolle und Deutsche Kunstseiden-Zeitung [*A publication*]
ZELMAL ..... Zero-Length Launch and Mat Landing [*Missiles*] (MCD)
ZEM .... East Main [*Canada*] [*Airport symbol*] (OAG)
ZEM .... Hobart and William Smith Colleges, Geneva, NY [*OCLC symbol*] (OCLC)
ZEM .... Zero Electrophoretic Mobility [*Analytical chemistry*]
Zem Beton ... Zement und Beton [*A publication*]
Zemed Arch ... Zemedelsky Archiv [*A publication*]
Zemed Tech ... Zemedelska Technika [*Czechoslovakia*] [*A publication*]
Zemed Zahr ... Zemedeistvi v Zahranici [*A publication*]
ZEMHA .... Zeitschrift fuer Erzbergbau und Metallhuettenwesen [*A publication*]
Zem-Kalk-Gips ... Zement-Kalk-Gips [*A publication*]
Zemled .... Zemledelie [*A publication*]
Zemled Mekh ... Zemledel'cheskaya Mekhanika [*A publication*]
Zemled Zhivotnovod Mold ... Zemledelie i Zhivotnovodstvo Moldavii [*A publication*]
Zemlerob Resp Mizhvid Temat Nauk Zb ... Zemlerobstvo Respublikans'kyi Mizhvidomchyi Tematychnyi Naukovyi Zbirnyk [*A publication*]
Zemleustroistvo Plan Sel'sk Naselennykh Punktov Geod ... Zemleustroistvo. Planirovka Sel'skikh Naselennykh Punktov i Geodeziya [*A publication*]
Zemlj Biljka ... Zemljiste i Biljka [*A publication*]
ZEMTR .... Zeus Early Missile Test RADAR [*Missile defense*] (AABC)

zen .... Zenaga [*MARC language code*] [*Library of Congress*] (LCCP)
ZEN .... Zenith Laboratories, Inc. [*NYSE symbol*]
Z Energiewirtsch ... Zeitschrift fuer Energiewirtschaft [*German Federal Republic*] [*A publication*]
ZENI .... Zenith Laboratories, Incorporated [*NASDAQ symbol*] (NQ)
ZENITH ...... Zero Energy Nitrogen-Heated Thermal Reactor [*British*] (MCD)
ZENT .... Zentec Corp. [*NASDAQ symbol*] (NQ)
Zentbl Bakt ParasitKde ... Zentralblatt fuer Bakteriologie, Parasitenkunde, Infektionskrankheiten, und Hygiene [*A publication*]
Zentbl Bakt ParasitKed Abt I or II ... Zentralblatt fuer Bakteriologie, Parasitenkunde, Infektionskrankheiten, und Hygiene. Abteilung I or II [*A publication*]
Zentbl Biblioth ... Zentralblatt fuer Bibliothekswesen [*A publication*]
Zentbl Vet Med B ... Zentralblatt fuer Veterinaermedizin. B [*A publication*]
Zent Math ... Zentralblatt fuer Mathematik und Ihre Grenzgebiete [*A publication*]
Zentralbl Allg Pathol Pathol Anat ... Zentralblatt fuer Allgemeine Pathologie und Pathologische Anatomie [*A publication*]
Zentralbl Arbeitsmed ... Zentralblatt fuer Arbeitsmedizin und Arbeitsschutz [*A publication*]
Zentralbl Arbeitsmed Arbeitsschutz ... Zentralblatt fuer Arbeitsmedizin und Arbeitsschutz [*A publication*]
Zentralbl Arbeitsmed Arbeitsschutz Prophyl ... Zentralblatt fuer Arbeitsmedizin, Arbeitsschutz, und Prophylaxe [*West Germany*] [*A publication*]
Zentralbl Arbeitsmed Arbeitsschutz Prophylaxe ... Zentralblatt fuer Arbeitsmedizin, Arbeitsschutz, und Prophylaxe [*A publication*]
Zentralbl Arbeitsmed Arbeitsschutz Prophyl Ergon ... Zentralblatt fuer Arbeitsmedizin, Arbeitsschutz, Prophylaxe, und Ergonomie [*German Federal Republic*] [*A publication*]
Zentralbl Bakteriol (B) ... Zentralblatt fuer Bakteriologie, Parasitenkunde, Infektionskrankheiten, und Hygiene. Erste Abteilung Originale. Reihe B. Hygiene, Betriebshygiene, Praeventive Medizin [*A publication*]
Zentralbl Bakteriol Naturwiss ... Zentralblatt fuer Bakteriologie, Parasitenkunde, Infektionskrankheiten, und Hygiene. Zweite Naturwissenschaftliche Abteilung. Mikrobiologie der Landwirtschaft der Technologie und des Umweltschutzes [*A publication*]
Zentralbl Bakteriol Orig A ... Zentralblatt fuer Bakteriologie, Parasitenkunde, Infektionskrankheiten, und Hygiene. Erste Abteilung. Originale Reihe A. Medizinische, Mikrobiologie, und Parasitologie [*A publication*]
Zentralbl Bakteriol (Orig B) ... Zentralblatt fuer Bakteriologie, Parasitenkunde, Infektionskrankheiten, und Hygiene. Erste Abteilung Originale. Reihe B. Hygiene, Praeventive Medizin [*A publication*]
Zentralbl Bakteriol Parasitenkd Infektionskrankheiten Hyg II ... Zentralblatt fuer Bakteriologie, Parasitenkunde, Infektionskrankheiten, und Hygiene. Naturwissenschaftliche Abteilung [*A publication*]
Zentralbl Bakteriol Parasitenkd Infektionskr Hyg Abt 1 Ref ... Zentralblatt fuer Bakteriologie, Parasitenkunde, Infektionskrankheiten, und Hygiene. Abteilung 1. Medizinisch-Hygienische Bakteriologie, Virusforschung, und Parasitologie. Referate [*A publication*]
Zentralbl Bakteriol Parasitenkd Infektionskr Hyg Abt 2 ... Zentralblatt fuer Bakteriologie, Parasitenkunde, Infektionskrankheiten, und Hygiene. Abteilung 2. Allgemeine Landwirtschaftliche und Technische Mikrobiologie [*A publication*]
Zentralbl Bakteriol Parasitenkd Infektionskr Hyg Abt I Orig ... Zentralblatt fuer Bakteriologie, Parasitenkunde, Infektionskrankheiten, und Hygiene. Abteilung I Originale [*A publication*]
Zentralbl Bakteriol Parasitenk Infektionskr Hyg ... Zentralblatt fuer Bakteriologie, Parasitenkunde, Infektionskrankheiten, und Hygiene [*A publication*]
Zentralbl Bibliothekswesen ... Zentralblatt fuer Bibliothekswesen [*A publication*]
Zentralbl Biol Aerosol-Forsch ... Zentralblatt fuer Biologische Aerosol-Forschung [*A publication*]
Zentralbl Chir ... Zentralblatt fuer Chirurgie [*A publication*]
Zentralbl Chir Suppl ... Zentralblatt fuer Chirurgie. Supplement [*A publication*]
Zentralbl Exp Med ... Zentralblatt der Experimentellen Medizin [*A publication*]
Zentralbl Geol Palaeontol Teil 2 ... Zentralblatt fuer Geologie und Palaeontologie. Teil 2. Palaeontologie [*A publication*]
Zentralbl Geol Palaeontol Teil I ... Zentralblatt fuer Geologie und Palaeontologie. Teil I. Allgemeine, Angewandte, Regionale, und Historische Geologie [*A publication*]
Zentralbl Gesamte Forstwes ... Zentralblatt fuer das Gesamte Forstwesen [*A publication*]
Zentralbl Gesamte Hyg Einschluss Bakteriol Immunitaetsl ... Zentralblatt fuer die Gesamte Hygiene mit Einschluss der Bakteriologie und Immunitaetslehre [*A publication*]
Zentralbl Gesamte Hyg Ihre Grenzgeb ... Zentralblatt fuer die Gesamte Hygiene und Ihre Grenzgebiete [*A publication*]
Zentralbl Gesamte Physiol Pathol Stoffwechsels ... Zentralblatt fuer die Gesamte Physiologie und Pathologie des Stoffwechsels [*A publication*]

Zentralbl Gesamte Rechtsmed ... Zentralblatt fuer die Gesamte Rechtsmedizin und Ihre Grenzgebiete [*A publication*]

Zentralbl Ges Hyg ... Zentralblatt fuer die Gesamte Hygiene und Ihre Grenzgebiete [*A publication*]

Zentralbl Gewerbehyg Unfallverhuet ... Zentralblatt fuer Gewerbehygiene und Unfallverhuetung [*A publication*]

Zentralbl Gynaekol ... Zentralblatt fuer Gynaekologie [*A publication*]

Zentralbl Huetten Walzwerke ... Zentralblatt der Huetten- und Walzwerke [*A publication*]

Zentralbl Industriebau ... Zentralblatt fuer Industriebau [*A publication*]

Zentralbl Inn Med ... Zentralblatt fuer Innere Medizin [*A publication*]

Zentralbl Mineral Geol Palaeontol ... Zentralblatt fuer Mineralogie, Geologie, und Palaeontologie [*A publication*]

Zentralbl Mineral Geol Palaeontol Teil 1 ... Zentralblatt fuer Mineralogie, Geologie, und Palaeontologie. Teil 1. Kristallographie und Mineralogie [*A publication*]

Zentralbl Mineral Geol Palaeontol Teil 2 ... Zentralblatt fuer Mineralogie, Geologie, und Palaeontologie. Teil 2. Gesteinskunde, Lagerstaettenkunde, Allgemeine, und Angewandte Geologie [*A publication*]

Zentralbl Mineral Geol Palaeontol Teil 3 ... Zentralblatt fuer Mineralogie, Geologie, und Palaeontologie. Teil 3. Historische und Regionale Geologie, Palaeontologie [*A publication*]

Zentralbl Mineral Teil 1 ... Zentralblatt fuer Mineralogie. Teil 1. Kristallographie und Mineralogie [*A publication*]

Zentralbl Mineral Teil 2 ... Zentralblatt fuer Mineralogie. Teil 2. Petrographie, Technische Mineralogie, Geochemie, und Lagerstaettenkunde [*A publication*]

Zentralbl Neurochir ... Zentralblatt fuer Neurochirurgie [*A publication*]

Zentralbl Papierind ... Zentralblatt fuer die Papierindustrie [*A publication*]

Zentralbl Pharm ... Zentralblatt fuer Pharmazie [*A publication*]

Zentralbl Pharm Pharmakother Laboratoriumsdiagn ... Zentralblatt fuer Pharmazie, Pharmakotherapie, und Laboratoriumsdiagnostik [*A publication*]

Zentralbl Phlebol ... Zentralblatt fuer Phlebologie [*A publication*]

Zentralbl Physiol ... Zentralblatt fuer Physiologie [*A publication*]

Zentralbl Verkehrs-Med Verkehrs-Psychol Luft- Raumfahrt-Med ... Zentralblatt fuer Verkehrs-Medizin, Verkehrs-Psychologie Luft-, und Raumfahrt-Medizin [*A publication*]

Zentralbl Veterinaermed ... Zentralblatt fuer Veterinaermedizin [*A publication*]

Zentralbl Veterinaermed Beih ... Zentralblatt fuer Veterinaermedizin. Beiheft [*A publication*]

Zentralbl Veterinaermed Reihe A ... Zentralblatt fuer Veterinaermedizin. Reihe A [*A publication*]

Zentralbl Veterinaermed Reihe B ... Zentralblatt fuer Veterinaermedizin. Reihe B [*A publication*]

Zentralbl Veterinaermed Reihe C ... Zentralblatt fuer Veterinaermedizin. Reihe C [*A publication*]

Zentralinst Kernforsch Rossendorf Dresden (Ber) ... Zentralinstitut fuer Kernforschung Rossendorf bei Dresden (Bericht) [*A publication*]

Zentralinst Versuchstierzucht Annu Rep ... Zentralinstitut fuer Versuchstierzucht. Annual Report [*A publication*]

Zentr Bibl ... Zentralblatt fuer Bibliothekswesen [*A publication*]

Z Entwick P ... Zeitschrift fuer Entwicklungspsychologie und Paedagogische Psychologie [*A publication*]

Zent Ztg Opt Mech ... Zentral-Zeitung fuer Optik und Mechanik [*A publication*]

ZENXC .... Zenex Synthetic Lubricants, Inc. [*NASDAQ symbol*]   (NQ)

Zep .... Zephaniah [*Old Testament book*]

ZEP .... Zeppelin   (DSUE)

ZEPAD .... Zeitschrift fuer Parlamentsfragen [*A publication*]

Zeph .... Zephaniah [*Old Testament book*]

ZEPHYR ..... Zero Energy Plutonium-Fueled Fast Reactor [*British*]   (DEN)

ZEPL .... Zero Excess Propellants Line

ZER .... Pottsville, PA [*Location identifier*] [*FAA*]   (FAAL)

Zer .... Zera'im   (BJA)

ZER .... Zero Energy Reflection

ZERA .... Zero Energy Critical Assemblies Reactor [*British*]   (DEN)

ZERC .... Zero Energy Reflection Coefficient

Z Erdkundeunterricht ... Zeitschrift fuer Erdkundeunterricht [*A publication*]

ZERED .... Zeitschrift fuer Rechtspolitik [*A publication*]

Z Erkr Atmungsorgane ... Zeitschrift fuer Erkrankungen der Atmungsorgane [*A publication*]

ZERLINA .... Zero Energy Reactor for Lattice Investigation and New Assemblies [*India*]

Z Ernaehrung ... Zeitschrift fuer Ernaehrungswissenschaft [*A publication*]

Z Ernaehrungswiss ... Zeitschrift fuer Ernaehrungswissenschaft [*A publication*]

Z Ernaehrungswiss (Suppl) ... Zeitschrift fuer Ernaehrungswissenschaft. (Supplementa) [*A publication*]

Zernovye Maslichn Kul't ... Zernovye i Maslichnye Kul'tury [*A publication*]

Zero Popul Growth Natl Rep ... Zero Population Growth. National Reporter [*A publication*]

ZERT .... Zero Reaction Tool

Z Erzbergbau Metallhuettenwes ... Zeitschrift fuer Erzbergbau und Metallhuettenwesen [*German Federal Republic*] [*A publication*]

ZES .... Zeitschrift fuer Eingeborenen-Sprachen [*A publication*]

ZES .... Zero Energy System

ZES .... Zil Elwannyen Sesel [*Formerly, Zil Eliogne Sesel, then Zil Elwagne Sesel*]

ZES .... Zollinger-Ellison Syndrome [*Medicine*]

ZES .... Zone Electrophoresis System

ZESTA .... Zeitschrift fuer Schweisstechnik [*A publication*]

Zesz Muz Etnogr Wrocl ... Zeszyty Muzeum Etnograficznego Wroclawie [*A publication*]

Zesz Nauk Akad Ekon ... Zeszyty Naukowe Akademii Ekonomicznej w Katowicach [*A publication*]

Zesz Nauk Akad Ekon Krakow ... Zeszyty Naukowe Akademii Ekonomicznej w Krakowie [*A publication*]

Zesz Nauk Akad Ekon Poznan ... Zeszyty Naukowe Akademii Ekonomicznej w Poznaniu [*A publication*]

Zesz Nauk Akad Ekon Poznaniu Ser 2 ... Zeszyty Naukowe. Akademia Ekonomiczna w Poznaniu. Seria 2. Prace Habilitacyjne i Doktorskie [*A publication*]

Zesz Nauk Akad Ekon Wroclaw ... Zeszyty Naukowe Akademii Ekonomicznej w Wroclawiu [*A publication*]

Zesz Nauk Akad Gorn Hutn Cracow Geol ... Zeszyty Naukowe Akademii Gorniczo-Hutniczej Cracow Geologia [*A publication*]

Zesz Nauk Akad Gorn-Hutn (Cracow) Mat Fiz Chem ... Zeszyty Naukowe Akademii Gorniczo-Hutniczej (Cracow). Matematyka, Fizyka, Chemia [*A publication*]

Zesz Nauk Akad Gorn-Hutn (Cracow) Metal Odlew ... Zeszyty Naukowe Akademii Gorniczo-Hutniczej (Cracow). Metalurgia i Odlewnictwo [*A publication*]

Zesz Nauk Akad Gorn Hutn (Cracow) Rozpr ... Zeszyty Naukowe Akademii Gorniczo-Hutniczej (Cracow). Rozprawy [*A publication*]

Zesz Nauk Akad Gorn-Hutn Im Stanislawa Staszica Ceram ... Zeszyty Naukowe Akademii Gorniczo-Hutniczej Imienia Stanislawa Staszica. Ceramica [*A publication*]

Zesz Nauk Akad Gorn-Hutn Im Stanislawa Staszica Geol ... Zeszyty Naukowe Akademii Gorniczo-Hutniczej Imienia Stanislawa Staszica. Geologia [*A publication*]

Zesz Nauk Akad Gorn-Hutn Im Stanislawa Staszica Gorn ... Zeszyty Naukowe Akademii Gorniczo-Hutniczej Imienia Stanislawa Staszica. Gornictwo [*A publication*]

Zesz Nauk Akad Gorn-Hutn Im Stanislawa Staszica Mat Fiz Chem ... Zeszyty Naukowe Akademii Gorniczo-Hutniczej Imienia Stanislawa Staszica. Matematyka, Fizyka, Chemia [*A publication*]

Zesz Nauk Akad Gorn-Hutn Im Stanislawa Staszica Metal Odlew ... Zeszyty Naukowe Akademii Gorniczo-Hutniczej Imienia Stanislawa Staszica. Metalurgia i Odlewnictwo [*A publication*]

Zesz Nauk Akad Gorn-Hutn Im Stanislawa Staszica Ser Autom ... Zeszyty Naukowe Akademii Gorniczo-Hutniczej Imienia Stanislawa Staszica. Seria Automatyka [*Poland*] [*A publication*]

Zesz Nauk Akad Gorn-Hutn Im Stanislawa Staszica Zesz Spec ... Zeszyty Naukowe Akademii Gorniczo-Hutniczej Imienia Stanislawa Staszica. Zeszyt Specjalny [*A publication*]

Zesz Nauk Akad Gorn-Hutn Im Staszica Gorn ... Zeszyty Naukowe Akademii Gorniczo-Hutniczej Imienia Stanislawa Staszica. Gornictwo [*A publication*]

Zesz Nauk Akad Gorn-Hutn Im Staszica Mat Fiz Chem ... Zeszyty Naukowe Akademii Gorniczo-Hutniczej Imienia Stanislawa Staszica Matematyka, Fizyka, Chemia [*A publication*]

Zesz Nauk Akad Gorn-Hutn Im Staszica Zesz Spec ... Zeszyty Naukowe Akademii Gorniczo-Hutniczej Imienia Stanislawa Staszica Zeszyt Specjalny [*A publication*]

Zesz Nauk Akad Gorn-Hutn (Krakow) Ceram ... Zeszyty Naukowe Akademii Gorniczo-Hutniczej (Krakow). Ceramika [*A publication*]

Zesz Nauk Akad Gorn-Hutn (Krakow) Elektryf Mech Gorn Hutn ... Zeszyty Naukowe Akademii Gorniczo-Hutniczej (Krakow). Elektryfikacja i Mechanizacja Gornictwa i Hutnictwa [*A publication*]

Zesz Nauk Akad Gorn-Hutn (Krakow) Geol ... Zeszyty Naukowe Akademii Gorniczo-Hutniczej (Krakow). Geologia [*A publication*]

Zesz Nauk Akad Gorn-Hutn (Krakow) Gorn ... Zeszyty Naukowe Akademii Gorniczo-Hutniczej (Krakow). Gornictwo [*A publication*]

Zesz Nauk Akad Gorn-Hutn Krakowie Rozpr ... Zeszyty Naukowe Akademii Gorniczo-Hutniczej w Krakowie. Rozprawy [*Poland*] [*A publication*]

Zesz Nauk Akad Gorn-Hutn (Krakow) Mat Fiz Chem ... Zeszyty Naukowe Akademii Gorniczo-Hutniczej (Krakow). Matematyka, Fizyka, Chemia [*A publication*]

Zesz Nauk Akad Gorn-Hutn (Krakow) Metal Odlew ... Zeszyty Naukowe Akademii Gorniczo-Hutniczej (Krakow). Metalurgia i Odlewnictwo [*A publication*]

Zesz Nauk Akad Gorn-Hutn (Krakow) Ses Nauk ... Zeszyty Naukowe Akademii Gorniczo-Hutniczej (Krakow). Sesja Naukowa [*A publication*]

Zesz Nauk Akad Gorn-Hutn (Krakow) Sozologia Sozotechnika ... Zeszyty Naukowe Akademii Gorniczo-Hutniczej (Krakow). Sozologia i Sozotechnika [*Poland*] [*A publication*]

Zesz Nauk Akad Gorn-Hutn (Krakow) Zesz Spec ... Zeszyty Naukowe Akademii Gorniczo-Hutniczej (Krakow). Zeszyty Specjalny [*A publication*]

Zesz Nauk Akad Gorn-Hutn Stanislawa Staszica Geol ... Zeszyty Naukowe Akademii Gorniczo-Hutniczej Imienia Stanislawa Staszica. Geologia [*A publication*]

Zesz Nauk Akad Gorn-Hutn Stanisl Staszica ... Zeszyty Naukowe Akademii Gorniczo-Hutniczej Imienia Stanislawa Staszica. Metalurgia i Odlewnictwo [*A publication*]

Zesz Nauk Akad Gorn-Hutn Stanisl Staszica Autom ... Zeszyty Naukowe Akademii Gorniczo-Hutniczej Imienia Stanislawa Staszica. Automatyka [*A publication*]

Zesz Nauk Akad Gorn-Hutn Stanisl Staszica Geol ... Zeszyty Naukowe Akademii Gorniczo-Hutniczej Imienia Stanislawa Staszica. Geologia [*Poland*] [*A publication*]

Zesz Nauk Akad Gorn-Hutn Stanisl Staszica Mat Fiz Chem ... Zeszyty Naukowe Akademii Gorniczo-Hutniczej Imienia Stanislawa Staszica. Matematyka, Fizyka, Chemia [*A publication*]

Zesz Nauk Akad Roln Szczecinie ... Zeszyty Naukowe Akademia Rolnicza w Szczecinie [*Poland*] [*A publication*]

Zesz Nauk Akad Roln Szczecinie Ser Rybactwo Morsk ... Zeszyty Naukowe Akademii Rolniczej w Szczecinie. Seria Rybactwo Morskie [*Poland*] [*A publication*]

Zesz Nauk Akad Roln Tech Olsztynie ... Zeszyty Naukowe Akademii Rolniczo-Technicznej w Olsztynie [*A publication*]

Zesz Nauk Akad Roln Tech Olsztynie Technol Zywn ... Zeszyty Naukowe Akademii Rolniczo-Technicznej w Olsztynie. Technologie Zywnosci [*A publication*]

Zesz Nauk Akad Roln Warszawie Melior Rolne ... Zeszyty Naukowe Akademii Rolniczej w Warszawie. Melioracje Rolne [*A publication*]

Zesz Nauk Akad Roln Warszawie Ogrod ... Zeszyty Naukowe Akademii Rolniczej w Warszawie. Ogrodnictwo [*A publication*]

Zesz Nauk Akad Roln Warszawie Technol Drewna ... Zeszyty Naukowe Akademii Rolniczej w Warszawie. Technologia Drewna [*A publication*]

Zesz Nauk Akad Roln Warszawie Zootech ... Zeszyty Naukowe Akademii Rolniczej w Warszawie. Zootechnika [*A publication*]

Zesz Nauk Akad Roln Wroclawiu Melior ... Zeszyty Naukowe Akademii Rolniczej we Wroclawiu. Melioracja [*A publication*]

Zesz Nauk Akad Roln Wroclawiu Weter ... Zeszyty Naukowe Akademii Rolniczej we Wroclawiu. Weterynaria [*A publication*]

Zesz Nauk Akad Roln Wroclawiu Zootech ... Zeszyty Naukowe Akademii Rolniczej we Wroclawiu. Zootechnika [*A publication*]

Zesz Nauk Akad Roln Wrocl Wet ... Zeszyty Naukowe Akademii Rolniczej we Wroclawiu. Weterynaria [*A publication*]

Zesz Nauk Inst Ciezkiej Synt Org Blachowni Slask ... Zeszyty Naukowe Instytut Ciezkiej Syntezy Organicznej w Blachowni Slaskiej [*A publication*]

Zesz Nauk Mat Fiz Chem ... Zeszyty Naukowe. Matematyka, Fizyka, Chemia [*Poland*] [*A publication*]

Zesz Nauk Mechan Budownictwo Akad Roln-Tech Olsztyn ... Zeszyty Naukowe. Mechanika i Budownictwo-Akademia Rolniczo-Techniczna w Olsztynie [*A publication*]

Zesz Nauk Ochr Wod Rybactwo Srodladowe ... Zeszyty Naukowe. Ochrona Wod i Rybactwo Srodladowe [*A publication*]

Zesz Nauk Politech Czestochow ... Zeszyty Naukowe Politechniki Czestochowskiej [*A publication*]

Zesz Nauk Politech Czestochow Metal ... Zeszyty Naukowe Politechniki Czestochowskiej. Metalurgia [*A publication*]

Zesz Nauk Politech Czestochow Nauki Tech Hutn ... Zeszyty Naukowe Politechniki Czestochowskiej. Nauki Techniczne. Hutnictwo [*Poland*] [*A publication*]

Zesz Nauk Politech Gdansk Chem ... Zeszyty Naukowe Politechniki Gdanskiej. Chemia [*A publication*]

Zesz Nauk Politech Gdansk Elektr ... Zeszyty Naukowe Politechniki Gdanskiej. Elektryka [*A publication*]

Zesz Nauk Politech Gdansk Fiz ... Zeszyty Naukowe Politechniki Gdanskiej. Fizyka [*A publication*]

Zesz Nauk Politech Gdansk Mat ... Zeszyty Naukowe Politechniki Gdanskiej. Matematyka [*A publication*]

Zesz Nauk Politech Gdansk Mech ... Zeszyty Naukowe Politechniki Gdanskiej. Mechanika [*A publication*]

Zesz Nauk Politech Krakow Chem ... Zeszyty Naukowe Politechniki Krakowskiej. Chemia [*A publication*]

Zesz Nauk Politech Krakow Mech ... Zeszyty Naukowe Politechniki Krakowskiej. Mechanika [*A publication*]

Zesz Nauk Politech Lod Budow ... Zeszyty Naukowe Politechniki Lodzkiej. Budownictwo [*A publication*]

Zesz Nauk Politech Lodz Chem ... Zeszyty Naukowe Politechniki Lodzkiej. Chemia [*A publication*]

Zesz Nauk Politech Lodz Chem Spozyw ... Zeszyty Naukowe Politechniki Lodzkiej. Chemia Spozywcza [*A publication*]

Zesz Nauk Politech Lodz Elek ... Zeszyty Naukowe Politechniki Lodzkiej. Elektryka [*A publication*]

Zesz Nauk Politech Lodz Elektr ... Zeszyty Naukowe Politechniki Lodzkiej. Elektryka [*A publication*]

Zesz Nauk Politech Lodz Inz Chem ... Zeszyty Naukowe Politechniki Lodzkiej. Inzynieria Chemiczna [*A publication*]

Zesz Nauk Politech Lodz Mech ... Zeszyty Naukowe Politechniki Lodzkiej. Mechanika [*A publication*]

Zesz Nauk Politech Lodz Wlok ... Zeszyty Naukowe Politechniki Lodzkiej. Wlokiennictwo [*A publication*]

Zesz Nauk Politech Poznan Chem Inz Chem ... Zeszyty Naukowe Politechniki Poznanskiej. Chemia i Inzynieria Chemiczna [*A publication*]

Zesz Nauk Politech Poznan Elektr ... Zeszyty Naukowe Politechniki Poznanskiej. Elektryka [*A publication*]

Zesz Nauk Politech Slask ... Zeszyty Naukowe Politechniki Slaskiej [*A publication*]

Zesz Nauk Politech Slaska Energ ... Zeszyty Naukowe Politechnika Slaska. Energetyka [*A publication*]

Zesz Nauk Politech Slask Chem ... Zeszyty Naukowe Politechniki Slaskiej. Chemia [*A publication*]

Zesz Nauk Politech Slask Energ ... Zeszyty Naukowe Politechniki Slaskiej. Energetyka [*A publication*]

Zesz Nauk Politech Slask Gorn ... Zeszyty Naukowe Politechniki Slaskiej. Gornictwo [*A publication*]

Zesz Nauk Politech Slask Hutn ... Zeszyty Naukowe Politechniki Slaskiej. Hutnictwo [*A publication*]

Zesz Nauk Politech Slask Ser Elektr ... Zeszyty Naukowe Politechniki Slaskiej. Seria Elektryka [*A publication*]

Zesz Nauk Politech Slask Ser Mat-Fiz ... Zeszyty Naukowe Politechniki Slaskiej. Seria Matematyka-Fizyka [*A publication*]

Zesz Nauk Politech Swietokrz Probl Nauk Podst ... Zeszyty Naukowe Politechniki Swietokrzyska. Problemy Nauk Podstawowych [*A publication*]

Zesz Nauk Politech Wroclaw Chem ... Zeszyty Naukowe Politechniki Wroclawskiej. Chemia [*Poland*] [*A publication*]

Zesz Nauk Roln Akad Roln Warsz ... Zeszyty Naukowe. Rolnictwo Akademia Rolnicza w Warszawie [*A publication*]

Zesz Nauk Szk Gl Gospod Wiejsk Akad Roln Warszawie Ogrod ... Zeszyty Naukowe Szkoly Glownej Gospodarstwa Wiejskiego-Akademii Rolniczej w Warszawie. Ogrodnictwo [*A publication*]

Zesz Nauk Szk Gl Gospod Wiejsk Akad Roln Warszawie Wter ... Zeszyty Naukowe Szkoly Glownej Gospodarstwa Wiejskiego-Akademii Rolniczej w Warszawie. Weterynaria [*A publication*]

Zesz Nauk Szk Gl Gospod Wiejsk Warszawie Melior Rolne ... Zeszyty Naukowe Szkoly Glownej Gospodarstwa Wiejskiego w Warszawie. Melioracje Rolne [*A publication*]

Zesz Nauk Szk Gl Gospod Wiejsk Warszawie Ogrod ... Zeszyty Naukowe Szkoly Glownej Gospodarstwa Wiejskiego w Warszawie. Ogrodnictwo [*A publication*]

Zesz Nauk Szk Gl Gospod Wiejsk Warszawie Roln ... Zeszyty Naukowe Szkoly Glownej Gospodarstwa Wiejskiego w Warszawie. Rolnictwo [*Poland*] [*A publication*]

Zesz Nauk Szk Gl Gospod Wiejsk Warszawie Technol Drewna ... Zeszyty Naukowe Szkoly Glownej Gospodarstwa Wiejskiego w Warszawie. Technologia Drewna [*A publication*]

Zesz Nauk Szk Glow Gospod Wiejsk Warszawie ... Zeszyty Naukowe Szkoly Glownej Gospodarstwa Wiejskiego w Warszawie [*A publication*]

Zesz Nauk Szkol Gospod Wiejsk Warsz (Lesn) ... Zeszyty Naukowe Szkola Glowna Gospodarstwa Wiejskiego w Warszawie (Lesnictwo) [*A publication*]

Zesz Nauk Szkol Gospod Wiejsk Warsz Technol Drewna ... Zeszyty Naukowe Szkola Glowna Gospodarstwa Wiejskiego w Warszawie. Technologia Drewna [*A publication*]

Zesz Nauk Technol Drewna Akad Roln Warsz ... Zeszyty Naukowe. Technologia Drewna-Akademia Rolnicza w Warszawie [*A publication*]

Zesz Nauk Tech Wyzsza Szk Inz Lublinie ... Zeszyty Naukowo-Techniczny Wyzsza Szkola Inzynierska w Lublinie [*A publication*]

ZeszNauKUL ... Zeszyty Naukowe Katolickiego Uniwersytetu Lubelskiego [*Lublin*] [*A publication*]

Zesz Nauk Uniw Jagiellon Acta Cosmol ... Zeszyty Naukowe Uniwersytetu Jagiellonskiego. Acta Cosmologica [*A publication*]

Zesz Nauk Uniw Jagiellon Pr Biol Mol ... Zeszyty Naukowe Uniwersytetu Jagiellonskiego. Prace Biologii Molekularnej [*Poland*] [*A publication*]

Zesz Nauk Uniw Jagiellon Pr Chem ... Zeszyty Naukowe Uniwersytetu Jagiellonskiego. Prace Chemiczne [*Poland*] [*A publication*]

Zesz Nauk Uniw Jagiellon Pr Etnogr ... Zeszyty Naukowe Uniwersytetu Jagiellonskiego. Prace Etnograficzne [*A publication*]

Zesz Nauk Uniw Jagiellon Pr Fiz ... Zeszyty Naukowe Uniwersytetu Jagiellonskiego. Prace Fizyczne [*A publication*]

Zesz Nauk Uniw Jagiellon Ser Nauk Mat Przy ... Zeszyty Naukowe Uniwersytetu Jagiellonskiego. Seria Nauk Matematyczno-Prztrodniezych. Matematyka Fizyka Chemia [*A publication*]

Zesz Nauk Uniw Jagiellonsk Pr Bot ... Zeszyty Naukowe Uniwersytetu Jagiellonskiego. Prace Botaniczne [*A publication*]

Zesz Nauk Uniw Lodz ... Zeszyty Naukowe Uniwersytetu Lodzkiego [*A publication*]

Zesz Nauk Uniw Lodz Fiz ... Zeszyty Naukowe Uniwersytetu Lodzkiego. Fizyka [*A publication*]

Zesz Nauk Uniw Lodz Nauki Humanist-Spolecz ... Zeszyty Naukowe Uniwersytetu Lodzkiego. Nauki Humanistyczno-Spoleczne [*A publication*]

Zesz Nauk Uniw Lodz Nauki Mat Przyr ... Zeszyty Naukowe Uniwersytetu Lodzkiego. Nauki Matematyczno-Przyrodnicze [*A publication*]

Zesz Nauk Uniw Lodz Ser 2 ... Zeszyty Naukowe Uniwersytetu Lodzkiego. Seria 2. Nauki Matematyczno-Przyrodnicze [*Poland*] [*A publication*]

Zesz Nauk Uniw Lodz Ser II ... Zeszyty Naukowe Uniwersytetu Lodzkiego. Seria II [*A publication*]

Zesz Nauk Uniw Lodz Ser III ... Zeszyty Naukowe Uniwersytetu Lodzkiego. Seria III [*A publication*]

Zesz Nauk Uniw Poznaniu Mat Fiz Chem ... Zeszyty Naukowe Uniwersytetu Imienia Adama Mickiewicza w Poznaniu Matematyka, Fizyka, Chemia [*A publication*]

Zesz Nauk Uniw Slaski Katowicach Seke Chem ... Zeszyty Naukowe Uniwersytet Slaski w Katowicach Sekeja Chemii [*A publication*]

Zesz Nauk Wydz Mat Fiz Chem Uniw Gdanski Chem ... Zeszyty Naukowe Wydzialu Matematyki, Fizyki, Chemii. Uniwersytet Gdanski. Seria Chemia [*A publication*]

Zesz Nauk Wyzs Szk Ekon Poznaniu ... Zeszyty Naukowe Wyzszej Szkoly Ekonomicznej w Poznaniu [*A publication*]

Zesz Nauk Wyzs Szk Roln Krakowie ... Zeszyty Naukowe Wyzszej Szkoly Rolniczej w Krakowie [*A publication*]

Zesz Nauk Wyzs Szk Roln Krakowie Zootech ... Zeszyty Naukowe Wyzszej Szkoly Rolniczej w Krakowie. Zootechnika [*A publication*]

Zesz Nauk Wyzs Szk Roln Olsztynie ... Zeszyty Naukowe Wyzszej Szkoly Rolniczej w Olsztynie [*A publication*]

Zesz Nauk Wyzs Szk Roln Szczecinie ... Zeszyty Naukowe Wyzsza Szkola Rolnicza w Szczecinie [*A publication*]

Zesz Nauk Wyzs Szk Roln Wroclawiu ... Zeszyty Naukowe Wyzszej Szkoly Rolniczej we Wroclawiu [*A publication*]

Zesz Nauk Wyzs Szk Roln Wroclawiu Wet ... Zeszyty Naukowe Wyzszej Szkoly Rolniczej we Wroclawiu. Weterynaria [*A publication*]

Zesz Nauk Wyzsza Szk Ekon Poznaniu Ser 2 ... Zeszyty Naukowe Wyzsza Szkola Ekonomiczna w Poznaniu. Seria 2. Prace Habilitacyjne i Doktorskie [*A publication*]

Zesz Nauk Wyzsz Szk Inz Bialymstoku Mat Fiz Chem ... Zeszyty Naukowe Wyzszej Szkoly Inzynierskiej w Bialymstoku Matematyka, Fizyka, Chemia [*A publication*]

Zesz Nauk Wyzsz Szkoly Ekon Katowic ... Zeszyty Naukowe Wyzszej Szkoly Ekonomicznej w Katowicach [*A publication*]

Zesz Nauk Wyzsz Szkoly Ekon Poznan ... Zeszyty Naukowe Wyzszej Szkoly Ekonomicznej w Poznaniu [*A publication*]

Zesz Nauk Wyzsz Szk Pedagog Gdansku Mat Fiz Chem ... Zeszyty Naukowe Wyzszej Szkoly Pedagogicznej w Gdansku. Matematyka, Fizyka, Chemia [*A publication*]

Zesz Nauk Wyzsz Szk Pedagog Katowicach Sekc Fiz ... Zeszyty Naukowe Wyzszej Szkoly Pedagogicznej w Katowicach. Sekcja Fizyki [*A publication*]

Zesz Nauk Wyzsz Szk Roln Olsztynie ... Zeszyty Naukowe Wyzszej Szkoly Rolniczej w Olsztynie [*A publication*]

Zesz Nauk Wyzsz Szk Roln Szczecinie ... Zeszyty Naukowe Wyzszej Szkoly Rolniczej w Szczecinie [*A publication*]

Zesz Nauk Wyzsz Szk Roln Wroclawiu Melior ... Zeszyty Naukowe Wyzszej Szkoly Rolniczej we Wroclawiu. Melioracja [*A publication*]

Zesz Nauk Wyzsz Szk Roln Wroclawiu Roln ... Zeszyty Naukowe Wyzszej Szkoly Rolniczej we Wroclawiu. Rolnictwo [*A publication*]

Zesz Nauk Wyzsz Szk Roln Wroclawiu Weter ... Zeszyty Naukowe Wyzszej Szkoly Rolniczej we Wroclawiu. Weterynaria [*A publication*]

Zesz Nauk Wyzsz Szk Roln Wroclawiu Zootech ... Zeszyty Naukowe Wyzszej Szkoly Rolniczej we Wroclawiu. Zootechnika [*A publication*]

Zesz Nauk Wyzsz Szk Roln Wrocl Melior ... Zeszyty Naukowe Wyzszej Szkoly Rolniczej we Wroclawiu. Melioracja [*A publication*]

Zesz Nauk Wyzsz Szk Roln Wrocl Roln ... Zeszyty Naukowe Wyzszej Szkoly Rolniczej we Wroclawiu. Rolnictwo [*A publication*]

Zesz Probl Gorn ... Zeszyty Problemowe Gornictwa [*A publication*]

Zesz Probl Kosmosu ... Zeszyty Problemowe Kosmosu [*A publication*]

Zesz Probl Nauki Pol ... Zeszyty Problemowe Nauki Polskiej [*A publication*]

Zesz Probl Postep Nauk Roln ... Zeszyty Problemowe Postepow Nauk Rolniczych [*A publication*]

Zesz Probl Postepow Nauk Roln ... Zeszyty Problemowe Postepow Nauk Rolniczych [*A publication*]

Zesz Prob Postepow Nauk Roln ... Zeszyty Problemowe Postepow Nauk Rolniczych [*A publication*]

Zeszty Nauk Uniw Jagiellon Prace Mat ... Zeszyty Naukowe Uniwersytetu Jagiellonskiego. Prace Matematyczne [*A publication*]

Zeszyty Nauk Akad Gorn-Hutniczej Mat Fiz Chem ... Zeszyty Naukowe Akademii Gorniczo-Hutniczej Imienia Stanislawa Staszica. Matematyka-Fizyka-Chemia [*A publication*]

Zeszyty Nauk Politech Lodz Mat ... Zeszyty Naukowe Politechniki Lodzkiej. Matematyka [*A publication*]

Zeszyty Nauk Politech Slask Automat ... Zeszyty Naukowe Politechniki Slaskiej. Automatyka [*A publication*]

Zeszyty Nauk Politech Slask Mat-Fiz ... Zeszyty Naukowe Politechniki Slaskiej. Seria Matematyka-Fizyka [*A publication*]

Zeszyty Nauk Politech Szczecin ... Zeszyty Naukowe Politechniki Szczecinskiej [*A publication*]

Zeszyty Nauk Szkoly Glown Planowania i Statyst ... Zeszyty Naukowe Szkoly Glownej Planowania i Statystyki [*A publication*]

Zeszyty Nauk Uniw Jagiellon Prace Fiz ... Zeszyty Naukowe Uniwersytetu Jagiellonskiego. Prace Fizyczne [*A publication*]

Zeszyty Nauk Wyz Szkoly Ped w Opolu Fiz ... Zeszyty Naukowe Wyzszej Szkoly Pedagogicznej w Opolu. Fizyka [*A publication*]

Zeszyty Nauk Wyz Szkoly Ped w Opolu Mat ... Zeszyty Naukowe Wyzszej Szkoly Pedagogicznej w Opolu. Matematyka [*A publication*]

ZET .... Zero-Gravity Expulsion Technique

ZETA .... Zero Energy Thermonuclear Apparatus [*or Assembly*] [*AEC*]

ZETFA .... Zhurnal Eksperimentalnoi i Teoreticheskoi Fiziki [*A publication*]

ZEthn .... Zeitschrift fuer Ethnologie [*A publication*]

Z Ethnolog ... Zeitschrift fuer Ethnologie [*A publication*]

ZETR .... Zero Energy Thermal Reactor [*British*]

ZETUA .... Zeitschrift fuer Tuberkulose und Erkrankungen der Thoraxorgane [*A publication*]

ZEURA .... Zeitschrift fuer Urologie [*A publication*]

ZEUS .... Zero Energy Uranium System [*British*]

Zev .... Zevahim (BJA)

Z Evan Eth ... Zeitschrift fuer Evangelische Ethik [*A publication*]

ZEVBA .... Zeitschrift fuer Vererbungslehre [*A publication*]

ZevE .... Zeitschrift fuer Evangelische Ethik. Gutersloh [*A publication*] (BJA)

Z Ev Ethik ... Zeitschrift fuer Evangelische Ethik [*A publication*]

ZEV Glasers Ann ... ZEV [*Zeitschrift fuer Eisenbahnwesen und Verkehrstechnik*] Glasers Annalen [*A publication*]

ZEvR .... Zeitschrift fuer die Evangelischen Religionsunterricht [*A publication*] (BJA)

Z Exp A Psy ... Zeitschrift fuer Experimentelle und Angewandte Psychologie [*A publication*]

Z Exp Chir ... Zeitschrift fuer Experimentelle Chirurgie [*A publication*]

Z Exp Chir Chir Forsch ... Zeitschrift fuer Experimentelle Chirurgie und Chirurgische Forschung [*A publication*]

Z Exper & Angew Psychol ... Zeitschrift fuer Experimentelle und Angewandte Psychologie [*A publication*]

ZF .... Free Balloon [*Navy symbol*]

ZF .... Zahnradfabrik Friedrichshafen AG [*West Germany*]

ZF .... Zermelo-Fraenkel [*Set theory*] [*Mathematics*]

ZF .... Zero Frequency

ZF .... Ziegfeld Follies

ZF .... Zona Fasciculata [*Of adrenal cortex*] [*Anatomy*]

ZF .... Zona Franca [*A publication*]

ZF .... Zone of Fire [*Military*] (AAG)

ZF .... Zweig Fund [*NYSE symbol*]

ZfA .... Zeitschrift fuer Archaeologie [*A publication*]

ZFA (Dresden) ... Zeitschrift fuer Alternsforschung (Dresden) [*A publication*]

Z Farben Ind ... Zeitschrift fuer Farben Industrie [*A publication*]

Z Farben Text Chem ... Zeitschrift fuer Farben- und Textil-Chemie [*A publication*]

ZFA (Stuttgart) ... Zeitschrift fuer Allgemeinmedizin (Stuttgart) [*A publication*]

ZFA (Stuttgart) ... ZFA (Zeitschrift fuer Allgemeinmedizin) (Stuttgart) [*A publication*]

ZFB .... Signals Fading Badly

ZfB .... Zeitschrift fuer Buecherfreunde [*A publication*]

ZFC .... Zero Failure Criteria (IEEE)

ZFC .... Zipp-Forming Cells [*Immunology*]

ZFC .... Zirconia Fuel Cell

ZFDF .... Zeitschrift fuer Freie Deutsche Forschung [*A publication*]

ZFDG .... Zeitschrift fuer Deutsche Geistesgeschichte [*A publication*]

ZFDPh .... Zeitschrift fuer Deutsche Philologie [*A publication*]

ZfDSdJ .... Zeitschrift fuer Demographie und Statistik der Juden [*A publication*]

ZfE .... Zeitschrift fuer Ethnologie [*A publication*]

ZFE .... Zone of Flow Establishment

ZFEU .... Zeitschrift fuer Franzoesischen und Englischen Unterricht [*A publication*]

ZFFB .... Zbornik Filozofskog Fakulteta (Belgrade) [*A publication*]

ZfG .... Zeitschrift fuer Geschichtswissenschaft [*A publication*]

ZFGV .... Zeitschrift der Freiburger Geschichtsvereine [*A publication*]

ZfHb .... Zeitschrift fuer Hebraeische Bibliographie [*A publication*]

ZFI-Mitt ...... ZFI [*Zentralinstitut fuer Isotopen- und Strahlenforschung*]- Mitteilungen [*East Germany*]

Z Fisch Hilfswiss ... Zeitschrift fuer Fischerei und Deren Hilfswissenschaften [*A publication*]

ZfK .... Zeitschrift fuer Kunstgeschichte [*A publication*]

ZFKPhil ...... Zbornik Filozofickej Fakulty Univerzity Komenskeho- Philologica [*A publication*]

ZFL .... Zbornik za Filologiju i Lingvistiku [*A publication*]

ZFL .... Zeitschrift fuer Luftrecht- und Weltraumrechtsfragen [*German*] (DLA)

Z Fleisch Milchhyg ... Zeitschrift fuer Fleisch- und Milchhygiene [*A publication*]

Z Flugwiss ... Zeitschrift fuer Flugwissenschaften [*A publication*]

Z Flugwiss Weltraumforsch ... Zeitschrift fuer Flugwissenschaften und Weltraumforschung [*A publication*]

Z Flugwiss and Weltraumforsch ... Zeitschrift fuer Flugwissenschaften und Weltraumforschung [*A publication*]

ZFM .... Community College of the Finger Lakes, Canandaigua, NY [*OCLC symbol*] (OCLC)

ZFM .... Fort McPherson [*Canada*] [*Airport symbol*] (OAG)

ZFM .... Zeitschrift fuer Musik [*A publication*]

Zf Mus Theorie ... Zeitschrift fuer Musiktheorie [*A publication*]

ZfN .... Zeitschrift fuer Numismatik [*A publication*]

ZFNU .... Zeitschrift fuer Neusprachlichen Unterricht [*A publication*]

Z Forst Jagdwes ... Zeitschrift fuer Forst- und Jagdwesen [*A publication*]

ZFP............ Dokumentation Zerstorungsfreie Pruefung [*Nondestructive Testing Documentation*] [*Federal Institute for Materials Testing*] [*Berlin, West Germany*] [*Information service*]   (EISS)
ZFP............ Zyglo-Fluorescent Penetrant
ZfPhF........ Zeitschrift fuer Philosophische Forschung [*A publication*]
ZFPT .... Zyglo-Fluorescent Penetrant Testing
ZfRG.......... Zeitschrift fuer Religions- und Geistesgeschichte [*A publication*]
ZfRP .... Zeitschrift fuer Romanische Philologie [*A publication*]
ZFRPH....... Zeitschrift fuer Romanische Philologie [*A publication*]
ZFrSL .... Zeitschrift fuer Franzoesische Sprache und Literatur [*A publication*]
ZfRuGg....... Zeitschrift fuer Religions- und Geistesgeschichte [*A publication*]
ZfS .... Zeitschrift fuer Semitistik und Verwandte Gebiete [*Leipzig*] [*A publication*]
ZFS............ Zero Field Splitting
ZfSchKg..... Zeitschrift fuer Schweizerische Kirchengeschichte [*A publication*]
ZFSH .... Z & Z Fashions [*NASDAQ symbol*]   (NQ)
ZFSL .... Zeitschrift fuer Franzoesische Sprache und Literatur [*A publication*]
Zft f Celt Phil ... Zeitschrift fuer Celtische Philologie [*A publication*]
Zft f D Alt ... Zeitschrift fuer Deutsches Altertum und Deutsche Literatur [*A publication*]
Zft f Fr Sp u Lit ... Zeitschrift fuer Franzoesische Sprache und Literatur [*A publication*]
Zft f Rom Phil ... Zeitschrift fuer Romanische Philologie [*A publication*]
ZFV............ Fort Severn [*Canada*] [*Airport symbol*]   (OAG)
ZfV............ Zeitschrift fuer Versicherungswesen [*German*]   (DLA)
ZFV............ Zeitschrift fuer Volkskunde [*A publication*]
ZFW........... Fort Worth, TX [*Location identifier*] [*FAA*]   (FAAL)
ZFW........... Zero Fuel Weight [*Aviation*]
ZfZ............ Zeitschrift fuer Assyriologie [*Leipzig/Berlin*] [*A publication*]
ZG .... Zap Gun
Z-G .... Zapalote-Grande [*Race of maize*]
ZG .... Zeitschrift fuer Germanistik [*A publication*]
ZG .... Zero Gravity   (IEEE)
ZG .... Zerstoerergeschwader [*Twin-engine fighter wing*] [*German military - World War II*]
ZG .... Zinc Gluconate [*Organic chemistry*]
ZG .... Zollgesetz [*Tariff Law*] [*German*]
ZG .... Zona Glomerulosa [*Of adrenal cortex*] [*Anatomy*]
ZG .... Zoological Gardens
Z Gaerungsphysiol ... Zeitschrift fuer Gaerungsphysiologie [*A publication*]
ZGAKE....... Zeitschrift fuer Geschichte und Altertumskunde der Ermlands [*A publication*]
Z Gastroent ... Zeitschrift fuer Gastroenterologie [*A publication*]
Z Gastroenterol ... Zeitschrift fuer Gastroenterologie [*A publication*]
Z Gastroenterol Verh ... Zeitschrift fuer Gastroenterologie. Verhandlungsband [*A publication*]
ZGDJ......... Zeitschrift zur Geschichte des Deutschen Judentums [*A publication*]
ZGE .... Zero-Gravity Effect
ZGE .... Zero-Gravity Environment
ZGE .... Zero-Gravity Expulsion
Z Geburtshilfe Gynaekol ... Zeitschrift fuer Geburtshilfe und Gynaekologie [*Later, Zeitschrift fuer Geburtshilfe und Perinatologie*] [*A publication*]
Z Geburtshilfe Perinatol ... Zeitschrift fuer Geburtshilfe und Perinatologie [*A publication*]
ZGEIA .... Zhurnal Gigieny, Epidemiologii, Mikrobiologii i Immunologii [*A publication*]
ZGEMA ...... Zeitschrift fuer die Gesamte Experimentelle Medizin [*A publication*]
Z Geol Wiss ... Zeitschrift fuer Geologische Wissenschaften [*A publication*]
Z Geomorph ... Zeitschrift fuer Geomorphologie [*A publication*]
Z Geomorphol ... Zeitschrift fuer Geomorphologie [*A publication*]
Z Geomorphol Suppl ... Zeitschrift fuer Geomorphologie. Supplementband [*A publication*]
Z Geophys ... Zeitschrift fuer Geophysik [*German Federal Republic*] [*A publication*]
Z Gerontol ... Zeitschrift fuer Gerontologie [*A publication*]
Z Gesamte Brauwes ... Zeitschrift fuer das Gesamte Brauwesen [*A publication*]
Z Gesamte Exp Med ... Zeitschrift fuer die Gesamte Experimentelle Medizin [*A publication*]
Z Gesamte Exp Med Einschl Exp Chir ... Zeitschrift fuer die Gesamte Experimentelle Medizin Einschliesslich Experimenteller Chirurgie [*A publication*]
Z Gesamte Genossenschaftswes ... Zeitschrift fuer das Gesamte Genossenschaftswesen [*A publication*]
Z Gesamte Genossenschaftswesen ... Zeitschrift fuer das Gesamte Genossenschaftswesen [*A publication*]
Z Gesamte Hyg ... Zeitschrift fuer die Gesamte Hygiene und Ihre Grenzgebiete [*A publication*]
Z Gesamte Hyg Grenzgeb ... Zeitschrift fuer die Gesamte Hygiene und Ihre Grenzgebiete [*A publication*]
Z Gesamte Hyg Ihre Grenzgeb ... Zeitschrift fuer die Gesamte Hygiene und Ihre Grenzgebiete [*A publication*]

Z Gesamte Inn Med ... Zeitschrift fuer die Gesamte Innere Medizin und Ihre Grenzgebiete [*A publication*]
Z Gesamte Inn Med Grenzgeb ... Zeitschrift fuer die Gesamte Innere Medizin und Ihre Grenzgebiete [*A publication*]
Z Gesamte Inn Med Grenzgeb Klin Pathol Exp ... Zeitschrift fuer die Gesamte Innere Medizin und Ihre Grenzgebiete. Klinik, Pathologie, Experiment [*A publication*]
Z Gesamte Inn Med Ihre Grenzgeb Suppl ... Zeitschrift fuer die Gesamte Innere Medizin und Ihre Grenzgebiete. Supplementum [*East Germany*] [*A publication*]
Z Gesamte Kaelte Ind ... Zeitschrift fuer die Gesamte Kaelte-Industrie [*A publication*]
Z Gesamte Kaelte Ind Beih Ser 1 ... Zeitschrift fuer die Gesamte Kaelte-Industrie. Beihefte. Serie 1 [*A publication*]
Z Gesamte Kaelte Ind Beih Ser 2 ... Zeitschrift fuer die Gesamte Kaelte-Industrie. Beihefte. Serie 2 [*A publication*]
Z Gesamte Kaelte-Ind Beih Ser 3 ... Zeitschrift fuer die Gesamte Kaelte-Industrie. Beihefte. Serie 3 [*A publication*]
Z Gesamte Muehlenwes ... Zeitschrift fuer das Gesamte Muehlenwesen [*A publication*]
Z Gesamte Naturwiss ... Zeitschrift fuer die Gesamte Naturwissenschaft [*A publication*]
Z Gesamte Nervenheilkd Psychother ... Zeitschrift fuer die Gesamte Nervenheilkunde und Psychotherapie [*German Democratic Republic*] [*A publication*]
Z Gesamte Neurol Psychiatr ... Zeitschrift fuer die Gesamte Neurologie und Psychiatrie [*A publication*]
Z Gesamte Schiess-Sprengstoffw ... Zeitschrift fuer das Gesamte Schiess- und Sprengstoffwesen mit der Sonderabteilung Gasschutz [*West Germany*] [*A publication*]
Z Gesamte Textilind ... Zeitschrift fuer die Gesamte Textilindustrie [*A publication*]
Z Gesamte Text-Ind ... Zeitschrift fuer die Gesamte Textil-Industrie [*A publication*]
Z Gesamte Versicherungswiss ... Zeitschrift fuer die Gesamte Versicherungswissenschaft [*A publication*]
Z Gesch Erzieh u Unterr ... Zeitschrift fuer Geschichte der Erziehung und des Unterrichts [*A publication*]
Z Geschichtsw ... Zeitschrift fuer Geschichtswissenschaft [*A publication*]
ZGeschJud ... Zeitschrift fuer die Geschichte der Juden [*A publication*]
Z Gesch Oberrhein ... Zeitschrift fuer die Geschichte des Oberrheins [*A publication*]
Z Gesch Saar ... Zeitschrift fuer die Geschichte der Saargegend [*A publication*]
Z Geschv Muelheim ... Zeitschrift des Geschichtsvereins Muelheim an der Ruhr (Muelheim, West Germany) [*A publication*]
Z Gesch-Wiss ... Zeitschrift fuer Geschichtswissenschaft [*A publication*]
Z Ges Exp Med ... Zeitschrift fuer die Gesamte Experimentelle Medizin [*A publication*]
Z Ges Staatswiss ... Zeitschrift fuer die Gesamte Staatswissenschaft [*A publication*]
ZGET......... Zero-Gravity Expulsion Technique
ZGEU......... Zeitschrift fuer Geschichte der Erziehung und des Unterrichts [*A publication*]
ZGF .... Grand Forks [*Canada*] [*Airport symbol*] [*Obsolete*]   (OAG)
ZGF .... Zero Gravity Facility [*NASA*]
ZGG .... Zero-Gravity Generator
ZGGJT....... Zeitschrift der Gesellschaft fuer die Geschichte der Juden in der Tschechoslowakei [*A publication*]
ZGH .... Zonal Gravity Harmonic
ZGI .... Gods River [*Canada*] [*Airport symbol*]   (OAG)
ZGJ............ Zeitschrift fuer die Geschichte der Juden [*A publication*]
ZGJD......... Zeitschrift fuer die Geschichte der Juden in Deutschland [*Braunschwig/Berlin*] [*A publication*]
ZGJT .... Zeitschrift der Gesellschaft fuer die Geschichte der Juden in der Tschechoslowakei [*A publication*]
ZGL .... Zeitschrift fuer Germanistische Linguistik [*A publication*]
Z Gletscherk Glazialgeol ... Zeitschrift fuer Gletscherkunde und Glazialgeologie [*A publication*]
ZGM .... City University of New York, Graduate School, New York, NY [*OCLC symbol*]   (OCLC)
ZGM .... Zinc Glycinate Marker [*Immunochemistry*]
ZGMFA....... Zeszyty Naukowe Akademii Gorniczo-Hutniczej (Cracow). Matematyka, Fizyka, Chemia [*A publication*]
ZGMPA ...... Zeitschrift fuer Geomorphologie [*A publication*]
ZGMT .... Zu Gott Mein Trost [*In God My Comfort*] [*German*] [*Motto of Ernst, Duke of Braunschweig-Luneburg (1564-1611)*]
ZGN........... Zaghouan [*Tunisia*] [*Seismograph station code, US Geological Survey*]   (SEIS)
ZGO........... Zeitschrift fuer die Geschichte des Oberrheins [*A publication*]
Z Godschmiede Juwelerie Graveure ... Zeitschrift fuer Goldschmiede Juwelerie und Graveure [*A publication*]
ZGOR .... Zeitschrift fuer die Geschichte des Oberrheins [*A publication*]
ZGOrh .... Zeitschrift fuer die Geschichte des Oberrheins [*A publication*]
ZGR .... Little Grand Rapids [*Canada*] [*Airport symbol*]   (OAG)
ZGS .... Gethsemani [*Canada*] [*Airport symbol*]   (OAG)
ZGS .... Zero Gradient Synchrotron [*AEC*]
ZGS .... Zero-Gravity Shower
ZGS .... Zero-Gravity Simulator
ZGS .... Zirconia Grain Stabilized [*Metal alloys*]
ZGS .... Zone Gradient Synchrotron [*Nickname: Ziggy*]

ZGSHG....... Zeitschrift der Gesellschaft fuer Schleswig-Holsteinische Geschichte [*A publication*]
ZGSSA....... Zeitschrift fuer das Gesamte Schiess- und Sprengstoffwesen mit der Sonderabteilung Gasschutz [*A publication*]
ZGT .... Zero-Gravity Trainer [*NASA*]   (NASA)
ZGW .... Zeitschrift fuer Geschichtswissenschaft [*A publication*]
ZGWBS ...... Zero-Gravity Whole Body Shower
ZGWS........ Zane Grey's West Society [*Sullivan, IL*]   (EA)
ZH.............. Zinc Heads [*Freight*]
ZH.............. Zonal Harmonic
ZH.............. Zone Heater
ZHA............. Zhangjiang [*China*] [*Airport symbol*]   (OAG)
Zh Anal Khim ... Zhurnal Analiticheskoi Khimii [*A publication*]
Z Haut-Geschlechtskr ... Zeitschrift fuer Haut- und Geschlechtskrankheiten [*A publication*]
Z Hautkr..... Zeitschrift fuer Hautkrankheiten [*A publication*]
ZHB .... Zeitschrift fuer Hebraeische Bibliographie [*A publication*]
Zh Ehksp Teor Fiz Pis'ma Red ... Zhurnal Ehksperimental'noj i Teoreticheskoj Fiziki. Pis'ma - Redaktsiyu [*USSR*] [*A publication*]
Zh Eksp Biol Med ... Zhurnal Eksperimental'noi Biologii i Meditsiny [*A publication*]
Zh Eksp Klin Med ... Zhurnal Eksperimentalnoi i Klinicheskoi Meditsiny [*A publication*]
Zh Eksp Teo ... Zhurnal Eksperimentalnoi i Teoreticheskoi Fiziki [*A publication*]
Zh Eksp Teor Fiz ... Zhurnal Eksperimentalnoi i Teoreticheskoi Fiziki [*A publication*]
Zh Eksp i Teor Fiz ... Zhurnal Eksperimentalnoi i Teoreticheskoi Fiziki [*A publication*]
Zh Eksp Teor Fiz Pis ... Zhurnal Eksperimentalnoi i Teoreticheskoi Fiziki. Pis'ma [*A publication*]
Zh Eksp and Teor Fiz Pis'ma v Red ... Zhurnal Eksperimental'noi i Teoreticheskoi Fiziki. Pis'ma v Redaktsiyu [*A publication*]
Zheleznodorozhn Transp ... Zheleznodorozhnyi Transport [*USSR*] [*A publication*]
Zhelezn Splavy ... Zheleznye Splavy [*A publication*]
Zh Evol Biokhim Fiziol ... Zhurnal Evolyutsionnoi Biokhimii i Fiziologii [*A publication*]
ZHF .... Zone Heat Flux
Zh Fiz Khim ... Zhurnal Fizicheskoi Khimii [*A publication*]
Zh Geofiz ... Zhurnal Geofiziki [*A publication*]
Zh Gig Epidemiol Mikrobiol Immunol ... Zhurnal Gigieny, Epidemiologii, Mikrobiologii, i Immunologii [*A publication*]
Zhidkofazn Okislenie Nepredel'nykh Org Soedin ... Zhidkofaznoe Okislenie Nepredel'nykh Organicheskikh Soedinenii [*A publication*]
Zhilishchnoe Kommunal'n Khoz ... Zhilishchnoe i Kommunal'noe Khozyaistvo [*A publication*]
Z Hist Fors ... Zeitschrift fuer Historische Forschung [*A publication*]
Zhivot Nauki ... Zhivotnovudni Nauki [*A publication*]
Zhivotnov'd Nauki ... Zhivotnov'dni Nauki [*A publication*]
Zhivotnovod ... Zhivotnovodstvo [*A publication*]
Zhivotnovod Vet ... Zhivotnovodstvo i Veterinariya [*A publication*]
Zhivotnovud ... Zhivotnovodstvo [*A publication*]
Zhivotnovud Nauki ... Zhivotnovudni Nauki [*A publication*]
Zh Khim Promsti ... Zhurnal Khimicheskoi Promyshlennosti [*A publication*]
ZHKPA .... Zhurnal Khimicheskoi Promyshlennosti [*A publication*]
ZHL .... Hofstra University, Law School, Library, Hempstead, NY [*OCLC symbol*]   (OCLC)
ZHM .... Hunter College of the City University of New York, New York, NY [*OCLC symbol*]   (OCLC)
Zh Mikrob E ... Zhurnal Mikrobiologii, Epidemiologii, i Immunobiologi [*A publication*]
Zh Mikrobiol Epidemiol Immunobiol ... Zhurnal Mikrobiologii, Epidemiologii, i Immunobiologii [*A publication*]
Zh Mikrobiol Immunobiol ... Zhurnal Mikrobiologii i Immunobiologii [*A publication*]
ZHN .... Honolulu, HI [*Location identifier*] [*FAA*]   (FAAL)
Zh Nauchnoi i Prikl Fotogr i Kinematogr ... Zhurnal Nauchnoi i Prikladnoi Fotografii i Kinematografii [*A publication*]
Zh Nauchn Prikl Fotogr Kinematogr ... Zhurnal Nauchnoj i Prikladnoj Fotografii i Kinematografii [*A publication*]
Zh Neorg Kh ... Zhurnal Neorganicheskoi Khimii [*A publication*]
Zh Neorg Khim ... Zhurnal Neorganicheskoi Khimii [*A publication*]
Zh Nevropatol Psikhiatr ... Zhurnal Nevropatologii i Psikhiatrii Imeni S. S. Korsakova [*A publication*]
Zh Nevropatol Psikhiatr Im S S Korsakova ... Zhurnal Nevropatologii i Psikhiatrii Imeni S. S. Korsakova [*A publication*]
Zh NP Fotog ... Zhurnal Nauchnoi i Prikladnoi Fotografii i Kinematografii [*A publication*]
Zh Obs Biol ... Zhurnal Obshchei Biologii [*A publication*]
Zh Obshch Biol ... Zhurnal Obshchei Biologii [*A publication*]
Zh Obshch Khim ... Zhurnal Obshchei Khimii [*A publication*]
Zh Obshch Khim ... Zhurnal Obshchei Khimii [*A publication*]
Zh Obs Kh ... Zhurnal Obshchei Khimii [*A publication*]
Zh Opytn Agron ... Zhurnal Opytnoi Agronomii [*A publication*]
Zh Org Kh ... Zhurnal Organicheskoi Khimii [*A publication*]
Zh Org Khim ... Zhurnal Organicheskoj Khimii [*A publication*]

ZHPMA....... Zentralblatt fuer Bakteriologie, Parasitenkunde, Infektionskrankheiten, und Hygiene. Erste Abteilung. Originale Reihe B. Hygiene, Betriebshygiene, Praeventive Medizin [*A publication*]
Zh Priki Mekhan Tekh Fiz ... Zhurnal Prikladnoi Mekhaniki i Tekhnicheskoi Fiziki [*A publication*]
Zh Prikl Fiz ... Zhurnal Prikladnoi Fiziki [*A publication*]
Zh Prikl Khim ... Zhurnal Prikladnoi Khimii [*A publication*]
Zh Prikl Mekh Tekh Fiz ... Zhurnal Prikladnoi Mekhaniki i Tekhnicheskoi Fiziki [*A publication*]
Zh Prikl Spektrosk ... Zhurnal Prikladnoi Spektroskopii [*A publication*]
ZHR .... Zirconium Hydride Reactor
Zh Russ Fiz-Khim Ova ... Zhurnal Russkago Fiziko-Khimicheskago Obshchestva [*A publication*]
Zh Russ Fiz-Khim Ova Chast Fiz ... Zhurnal Russkogo Fiziko-Khimicheskogo Obshchestva Chast Fizicheskaya [*A publication*]
Zh Russ Fiz Khim Ova Chast Khim ... Zhurnal Russkogo Fiziko-Khimicheskogo Ovshchestva Chast Khimicheskaya [*A publication*]
Zh Russ Khim Ova ... Zhurnal Russkago Khimicheskago Obshchestva [*A publication*]
Zh Sakh Promsti ... Zhurnal Sakharnoi Promyshlennosti [*A publication*]
Zh Strukt Khim ... Zhurnal Strukturnoi Khimii [*A publication*]
ZHT .... Zeitschrift fuer Historische Theologie [*A publication*]
Zh Tekh Fiz ... Zhurnal Tekhnicheskoi Fiziki [*A publication*]
ZHU .... Houston, TX [*Location identifier*] [*FAA*]   (FAAL)
ZHUCA....... Zpravy Hornickeho Ustavu CSAV [*Ceskoslovenska Akademie Ved*] [*A publication*]
Zhurnal Mikrobiol ... Zhurnal Mikrobiologii [*A publication*]
Zh Ushn Nos Gorl Bolezn ... Zhurnal Ushnykh Nosovykh i Gorlovykh Boleznei [*A publication*]
Zh Ushn Nosov Gorlov Bolez ... Zhurnal Ushnykh Nosovykh i Gorlovykh Boleznei [*A publication*]
Zhu Us Nos i Gorl Bol ... Zhurnal Ushnykh Nosovykh i Gorlovykh Boleznei [*A publication*]
ZHVNS .... Zeitschrift des Historischen Vereins fuer Niedersachsen [*A publication*]
Zh Vopr Neirokhir ... Zhurnal Voprosy Neirokhirurgii Imeni N. N. Burdenko [*A publication*]
ZHVS .... Zeitschrift des Historischen Vereins fuer Steiermark [*A publication*]
Zh Vses Khi ... Zhurnal Vsesoyuznogo Khimicheskogo Obshchestva Imeni D. I. Mendeleeva [*A publication*]
Zh Vses Khim O-va Im D I Mendeleeva ... Zhurnal Vsesoyuznogo Khimicheskogo Obshchestva Imeni D. I. Mendeleeva [*A publication*]
Zh Vychisl Mat and Mat Fiz ... Zhurnal Vychislitel'noi Matematiki i Matematicheske Fiziki [*A publication*]
Zh Vychisl Mat Mat Fiz ... Zhurnal Vychislitelnoj Matematiki i Matematicheskoj Fiziki [*A publication*]
Zh Vyssh Nerv Deiatel ... Zhurnal Vysshei Nervnoi Deiatel'nosti [*A publication*]
Zh Vyssh Nervn Deyat Im I P Pavlova ... Zhurnal Vysshei Nervnoi Deyatel'nosti Imeni I. P. Pavlova [*A publication*]
Zh Vyss Ner ... Zhurnal Vysshei Nervnoi Deyatel'nosti Imeni I. P. Pavlova [*A publication*]
Z Hyg.......... Zeitschrift fuer Hygiene [*A publication*]
ZHYGA....... Zeitschrift fuer die Gesamte Hygiene und Ihre Grenzgebiete [*A publication*]
Z Hyg Infektionskr ... Zeitschrift fuer Hygiene und Infektionskrankheiten [*A publication*]
Z Hyg Infekt Kr ... Zeitschrift fuer Hygiene und Infektionskrankheiten [*A publication*]
Z Hyg InfektKrankh ... Zeitschrift fuer Hygiene und Infektionskrankheiten [*A publication*]
Z Hyg Zool Schaedlingsbekaempf ... Zeitschrift fuer Hygienische Zoologie und Schaedlingsbekaempfung [*A publication*]
Z I.............. Zeitschrift fuer Instrumentenbau [*A publication*]
ZI .... Zero Input
ZI .... Zinc Institute [*New York, NY*]   (EA)
ZI .... Zonal Index
Z of I.......... Zone of Interior [*Military*]
ZI .... Zone of Interior [*Military*]
ZI .... Zonta International [*An association*] [*Chicago, IL*]   (EA)
Z/I .... Zoom In [*Cinematography and Video*]
ZIA............. ZIA Airlines [*Las Cruces, NM*] [*FAA designator*]   (FAAC)
ZIA............. Zone of Interior Armies
ZIAD........... Ziyad, Inc. [*NASDAQ symbol*]   (NQ)
ZIALA........ Zeitschrift fuer Immunitaets- und Allergieforschung [*A publication*]
ZIAVA........ Zeitschrift fuer Induktive Abstammungs- und Vererbungslehre [*A publication*]
ZIAX .... Zantop International Airlines, Inc. [*Air carrier designation symbol*]
ZIC .... Zirconia-Iridium Crucible
ZICON .... Zone of the Interior Consumers Network   (MCD)
ZID .... Indianapolis, IN [*Location identifier*] [*FAA*]   (FAAL)
ZIF............. Zero Insertion Force [*Electronics*]
ZIG............. Ziguinchor [*Senegal*] [*Airport symbol*]   (OAG)
ZIG .... Zoster Immune Globulin [*Immunology*]

ZIGO............ Zygo Corp. [*NASDAQ symbol*]   (NQ)
ZIH............. Hofstra University, Hempstead, NY [*OCLC symbol*]   (OCLC)
ZIH............. Zihuatanejo [*Mexico*] [*Airport symbol*]   (OAG)
ZII.............. Zeitschrift fuer Indologie und Iranistik [*Leipzig*] [*A publication*]
ZIID .... Zentralinstitut fuer Information und Dokumentation [*Central Institute for Information and Documentation*] [*East Germany*] [*Information service*]   (EISS)
ZI Int........... ZI [*Ziegelindustrie*] International [*West Germany*] [*A publication*]
ZIK .... Zbornik Istorije Knijizevnosti [*A publication*]
ZIL............. Zork Interactive Language [*Computer science*]
Zilla CD ..... Zilla Court Decisions, Bengal, Madras, Northwest Provinces [*India*]   (DLA)
ZiM............. Ziemia i Morze [*A publication*]
ZIM............. Zimchurud [*USSR*] [*Seismograph station code, US Geological Survey*]   (SEIS)
ZIM............. Zimmer Corp. [*American Stock Exchange symbol*]
ZIM............. Zonal Interdiction Missile   (NVT)
Zimbabwe Agric J ... Zimbabwe Agricultural Journal [*A publication*]
Zimbabwe J Econ ... Zimbabwe Journal of Economics [*A publication*]
Zimb Agric J ... Zimbabwe Agricultural Journal [*A publication*]
Zimb J Agric Res ... Zimbabwe Journal of Agricultural Research [*A publication*]
Zimb Libr ... Zimbabwe Librarian [*A publication*]
ZIMG .... Zeitschrift der Internationalen Musik Gesellschaft [*A publication*]
Z Immun -Allergie-Forsch ... Zeitschrift fuer Immunitaets- und Allergieforschung [*A publication*]
Z Immun Exp ... Zeitschrift fuer Immunitaetsforschung. Experimentelle und Klinische Immunologie [*A publication*]
Z ImmunForsch Exp Ther ... Zeitschrift fuer Immunitaetsforschung und Experimentelle Therapie [*A publication*]
Z Immunitaets-Allergieforsch ... Zeitschrift fuer Immunitaets- und Allergieforschung [*A publication*]
Z Immunitaetsforsch ... Zeitschrift fuer Immunitaetsforschung [*A publication*]
Z Immunitaetsforsch Allerg Klin Immunol ... Zeitschrift fuer Immunitaetsforschung. Allergie und Klinische Immunologie [*A publication*]
Z Immunitaetsforsch Exp Klin Immunol ... Zeitschrift fuer Immunitaetsforschung. Experimentelle und Klinische Immunologie [*A publication*]
Z Immunitaetsforsch Exp Klin Immunol Suppl ... Zeitschrift fuer Immunitaetsforschung. Experimentelle und Klinische Immunologie. Supplemente [*A publication*]
Z Immunitaetsforsch Exp Ther ... Zeitschrift fuer Immunitaetsforschung und Experimentelle Therapie [*A publication*]
Z Immunitaetsforsch Exp Ther 1 ... Zeitschrift fuer Immunitaetsforschung und Experimentelle Therapie. 1. Originale [*A publication*]
Z Immunitaetsforsch Exp Ther 1 Abt Orig ... Zeitschrift fuer Immunitaetsforschung und Experimentelle Therapie. 1. Abteilung Originale [*A publication*]
Z Immunitaetsforsch Immunobiol ... Zeitschrift fuer Immunitaetsforschung. Immunobiology [*A publication*]
Z Immunitaetsforsch Immunobiol Suppl ... Zeitschrift fuer Immunitaetsforschung. Immunobiology. Supplemente [*A publication*]
ZIMordASSR ... Zapiski Naucno-Issledovatel'nogo Instituta pri Sovete Ministrov Mordovskoj ASSR [*A publication*]
ZIN .... Mount Zion Church [*South Carolina*] [*Seismograph station code, US Geological Survey*] [*Closed*]   (SEIS)
Zinc Res Dig ... Zinc Research Digest [*A publication*]
Z Indukt Abstammungs-Vererbungsl ... Zeitschrift fuer Induktive Abstammungs- und Vererbungslehre [*A publication*]
ZinEB .... Zinc Ethylenebis(dithiocarbamate) [*Agricultural fungicide*]
Zink........... Zero Income, No Kids [*Lifestyle classification*]
Zinn Ca Tr ... Zinn's Select Cases in the Law of Trusts   (DLA)
Zinn Verwend ... Zinn und Seine Verwendung [*A publication*]
Z Instrum ... Zeitschrift fuer Instrumentenkunde [*West Germany*] [*A publication*]
Z Instrumentenk ... Zeitschrift fuer Instrumentenkunde [*A publication*]
Z Instrumentenkd ... Zeitschrift fuer Instrumentenkunde [*A publication*]
Z Int Inst Zuckerruebenforsch ... Zeitschrift des Internationalen Instituts fuer Zuckerruebenforschung [*A publication*]
ZIO .... Zinc Iodide-Osmium [*Biological staining procedure*]
Zion........... Zionism   (BJA)
ZION.......... Zions Utah Bancorp [*NASDAQ symbol*]   (NQ)
ZiP............. Za i Przeciw [*A publication*]
ZIP............. Zero Interest Payment [*Banking*]
ZIP............. Zigzag In-Line Package [*Wells American*] [*Data processing*]
ZIP............. Zinc Impurity Photodetector
ZIP............. Zone Improvement Plan [*Postal Service code*]
ZIP............. Zoster Immune Plasma [*Immunology*]
ZIPA .... Zimbabwe People's Army
ZIPE .... Zentralinstitut Physik der Erde [*Potsdam*]
Zipp........... Zone of Inhibited Phage Plaques [*Immunology*]
ZIPRA .... Zimbabwe Independent People's Revolutionary Army   (PD)
ZIR............. Zero Internal Resistance
Ziraat Derg ... Ziraat Dergisi [*A publication*]
Ziraat Fak Derg Ege Univ ... Ziraat Fakultesi Dergisi Ege Universitesi [*A publication*]

Zisin (Seismol Soc Jap J) ... Zisin (Seismological Society of Japan. Journal) [*A publication*]
ZIS Mitt ...... ZIS [*Zentralinstitut fuer Schweisstechnik*] Mitteilungen [*A publication*]
ZISS .... Zebulun Israel Seafaring Society   (EA)
ZITL........... Zitel Corp. [*NASDAQ symbol*]   (NQ)
Ziv A .... Archiv fuer die Zivilistische Praxis [*German*] [*A publication*]
Ziva .... Ziva. Casopis pro Biologickou Praci [*A publication*]
ZIVAN........ Zapiski Instituta Vostokoveden'ia Akademii Nauk SSSR [*A publication*]
Zivocisna Vyroba Cesk Akad Zemed Ustav Vedeckotech Inf Zemed ... Zivocisna Vyroba-Ceskoslovenska Akademie Zemedelska. Ustav Vedeckotechnickych Informaci pro Zemedelstvi [*A publication*]
Zivoc Vyroba ... Zivocisna Vyroba [*A publication*]
ZIVP .... Zivotne Prostredie [*Czechoslovakia*] [*A publication*]
Ziz .... Zizit   (BJA)
ZJ .... Zeszyty Jezykoznawcze [*A publication*]
ZJ .... Zipper Jacket
ZJ .... Zivi Jezici [*A publication*]
Z Jagdwiss ... Zeitschrift fuer Jagdwissenschaft [*A publication*]
ZJC............ State University of New York, Central Administration, Albany, NY [*OCLC symbol*]   (OCLC)
ZJKF.......... Zpravy Jednoty Klasickych Filologu [*A publication*]
ZJSTD .... Zambia Journal of Science and Technology [*A publication*]
ZJX .... Jacksonville, FL [*Location identifier*] [*FAA*]   (FAAL)
ZK............. Barrage Balloon [*Navy symbol*]
ZK............. New Zealand [*Aircraft nationality and registration mark*]   (FAAC)
ZK............. Schering AG [*Germany*] [*Research code symbol*]
ZK............. Zeitschrift fuer Keilschriftforschung und Verwandte Gebiete [*A publication*]
ZK............. Zeitschrift fuer Kunstgeschichte [*A publication*]
ZK............. Zentralkommittee [*Central Committee*] [*of the Socialist Union Party of the German Democratic Republic*]
ZK............. Zera' Kodesh   (BJA)
ZKA........... Zeitschrift fuer Kulturaustausch [*A publication*]
Z Kardiol ... Zeitschrift fuer Kardiologie [*A publication*]
Z Kardiol Suppl ... Zeitschrift fuer Kardiologie. Supplementum [*A publication*]
ZKB .... Bomber [*Russian aircraft symbol*]
ZKB .... Kasaba Bay [*Zambia*] [*Airport symbol*]   (OAG)
ZKC........... Kansas City, MO [*Location identifier*] [*FAA*]   (FAAL)
ZKC........... Keuka College, Lightner Library, Keuka Park, NY [*OCLC symbol*]   (OCLC)
ZKE .... Kaschechewan [*Canada*] [*Airport symbol*]   (OAG)
ZKG .... Kegaska [*Canada*] [*Airport symbol*]   (OAG)
ZKG........... Zeitschrift fuer Kirchengeschichte [*A publication*]
Z Kindch G ... Zeitschrift fuer Kinderchirurgie und Grenzgebiete [*A publication*]
Z Kinderchir Grenzgeb ... Zeitschrift fuer Kinderchirurgie und Grenzgebiete [*A publication*]
Z Kinderheilkd ... Zeitschrift fuer Kinderheilkunde [*A publication*]
Z Kinder-Jugendpsychiatr ... Zeitschrift fuer Kinder- und Jugendpsychiatrie [*A publication*]
Z Kinderpsychiatr ... Zeitschrift fuer Kinderpsychiatrie [*A publication*]
Z Kind Jug ... Zeitschrift fuer Kinder- und Jugendpsychiatrie [*A publication*]
Z Kirch G ... Zeitschrift fuer Kirchengeschichte [*A publication*]
ZKJ............ Zbornik za Knjizevnost i Jezik [*A publication*]
ZKLCA .... Zeitschrift fuer Klinische Chemie [*A publication*]
Z Klin Chem ... Zeitschrift fuer Klinische Chemie und Klinische Biochemie [*A publication*]
Z Klin Chem Klin Biochem ... Zeitschrift fuer Klinische Chemie und Klinische Biochemie [*A publication*]
Z Klin Med ... Zeitschrift fuer Klinische Medizin [*A publication*]
Z Klin Psychol Psychother ... Zeitschrift fuer Klinische Psychologie und Psychotherapie [*A publication*]
ZKM .... Zeitschrift fuer die Kunde des Morgenlandes [*A publication*]
ZKN........... Training Balloon [*Navy symbol*]
ZKO........... Observation Balloon [*Navy symbol*]
Z Koeln Zoo ... Zeitschrift des Koelner Zoo [*A publication*]
Z Kompr Fluess Gase Pressluft-Ind ... Zeitschrift fuer Komprimierte und Fluessige Gase Sowie fuer die Pressluft-Industrie [*A publication*]
ZKPVF........ Zeitschrift fuer Keltische Philologie und Volksforschung [*A publication*]
ZKR .... Zeitschrift fuer Kirchenrecht [*A publication*]
Z Krankenpfl ... Zeitschrift fuer Krankenpflege [*A publication*]
Z Krebsf Kl ... Zeitschrift fuer Krebsforschung und Klinische Onkologie [*A publication*]
Z Krebsforsch ... Zeitschrift fuer Krebsforschung [*A publication*]
Z Krebsforsch Klin Onkol ... Zeitschrift fuer Krebsforschung und Klinische Onkologie [*A publication*]
Z Kreislaufforsch ... Zeitschrift fuer Kreislaufforschung [*A publication*]
Z Krist .... Zeitschrift fuer Kristallographie, Kristallgeometrie, Kristallphysik, Kristallchemie [*A publication*]
Z Kristall .... Zeitschrift fuer Kristallographie. Kristallgeometrie, Kristallphysik, Kristallchemie [*A publication*]
Z Kristallogr ... Zeitschrift fuer Kristallographie [*A publication*]

Z Kristallogr Kristallgeom Kristallphys Kristallchem ... Zeitschrift fuer Kristallographie, Kristallgeometrie, Kristallphysik, Kristallchemie [*A publication*]

Z Kristallogr Mineral ... Zeitschrift fuer Kristallographie und Mineralogie [*A publication*]

ZKRU............ Zeitschrift fuer Katholischen Religionsunterricht [*A publication*]

ZKT.............. Zeitschrift fuer Katholische Theologie [*A publication*]

ZKTh.......... Zeitschrift fuer Katholische Theologie [*A publication*]

ZKuG.......... Zeitschrift fuer Kunstgeschichte [*A publication*]

Z Kult-Tech Flurberein ... Zeitschrift fuer Kulturtechnik und Flurbereinigung [*A publication*]

Z Kulturaustausch ... Zeitschrift fuer Kulturaustausch [*A publication*]

Z Kulturtech ... Zeitschrift fuer Kulturtechnik [*A publication*]

Z Kulturtech Flurbereinig ... Zeitschrift fuer Kulturtechnik und Flurbereinigung [*A publication*]

ZKunstG .... Zeitschrift fuer Kunstgeschichte [*A publication*]

Z Kunstges ... Zeitschrift fuer Kunstgeschichte [*A publication*]

Z Kunstgesc ... Zeitschrift fuer Kunstgeschichte [*A publication*]

Z Kunstgesch ... Zeitschrift fuer Kunstgeschichte [*A publication*]

Z Kunstwis ... Zeitschrift fuer Kunstwissenschaft [*A publication*]

ZKW............ Zeitschrift fuer Kunstwissenschaft [*A publication*]

zkW............ Zero Kilowatt (IEEE)

ZKW.......... Zi-ka-wei [*Republic of China*] [*Seismograph station code, US Geological Survey*] (SEIS)

ZKWL........ Zeitschrift fuer Kirchliche Wissenschaft und Kirchliches Leben [*Leipzig*] [*A publication*]

ZL.............. Freezing Drizzle [*Meteorology*] (FAAC)

ZL.............. New Zealand [*Aircraft nationality and registration mark*] (FAAC)

ZL.............. Zero Lift

ZL.............. Zloty [*Monetary unit in Poland*]

ZL.............. Zycie Literackie [*A publication*]

ZLA .... Los Angeles, CA [*Location identifier*] [*FAA*] (FAAL)

Z Laboratoriumsdiagn ... Zeitschrift fuer Laboratoriumsdiagnostik [*A publication*]

Z Landeskult ... Zeitschrift fuer Landeskultur [*A publication*]

Z Landwirt Vers Untersuchungsw ... Zeitschrift fuer Landwirtschaftliches Versuchs- und Untersuchungswesen [*A publication*]

Z Landw Ver u Unters Wes ... Zeitschrift fuer Landwirtschaftliches Versuchs- und Untersuchungswesen [*A publication*]

Z Laryngol Rhinol Otol ... Zeitschrift fuer Laryngologie, Rhinologie, Otologie, und Ihre Grenzgebiete [*A publication*]

Z Laryngol Rhinol Otol Grenzgeb ... Zeitschrift fuer Laryngologie, Rhinologie, Otologie, und Ihre Grenzgebiete [*A publication*]

Z Laryngol Rhinol Otol Ihre Grenzgeb ... Zeitschrift fuer Laryngologie, Rhinologie, Otologie, und Ihre Grenzgebiete [*A publication*]

ZLB............. Balboa, CZ [*Location identifier*] [*FAA*] (FAAL)

ZLC .... Salt Lake City, UT [*Location identifier*] [*FAA*] (FAAL)

ZLC .... Zero Lift Cord

ZLD .... Zero Level Drift

ZLD .... Zero Lift Drag

ZLD .... Zodiacal Light Device

ZLDI .... Zentralstelle fuer Luft- Raumfahrtdokumentation und Information [*Center for Documentation and Information in Aeronautics and Astronautics*] [*Information service*] [*West Germany*]

Z Lebensmit ... Zeitschrift fuer Lebensmittel- Untersuchung und Forschung [*A publication*]

Z Lebensmittel Untersuch Forsch ... Zeitschrift fuer Lebensmittel- Untersuchung und Forschung [*A publication*]

Z Lebensm-Technol-Verfahrenstech ... Zeitschrift fuer Lebensmittel- Technologie und Verfahrenstechnik [*German Federal Republic*] [*A publication*]

Z Lebensm-Unters Forsch ... Zeitschrift fuer Lebensmittel- Untersuchung und Forschung [*A publication*]

ZLG .... Zero Line Gap

ZLGIA........ Zapiski Leningradskogo Gornogo Instituta [*A publication*]

ZLH .... Lincoln Hospital, Bronx, NY [*OCLC symbol*] (OCLC)

ZLH .... [*F.*] Zorell. Lexicon Hebraicum [*A publication*] (BJA)

ZLISP .... Zilog List Processor [*Programing language*] [*1979*] (CSR)

ZLit .... Zycie Literackie [*Krakow*] [*A publication*]

ZLJ.............. Zambia Law Journal (DLA)

ZLK .... Zaleski, OH [*Location identifier*] [*FAA*] (FAAL)

ZLL.............. Zero-Length Launch [*Missiles*]

ZLL.............. Zero Lot Line [*Real estate*]

ZLM............ State University of New York, College at New Paltz, New Paltz, NY [*OCLC symbol*] (OCLC)

ZLN .... Zwiazek Ludowo-Narodowy [*Populist-Nationalist Alliance*] [*Poland*] (PPE)

ZLO .... Manzanillo [*Mexico*] [*Airport symbol*] (OAG)

ZLP............. Zongo [*La Paz*] [*Bolivia*] [*Seismograph station code, US Geological Survey*] (SEIS)

ZLR............. Zanzibar Law Reports [*1919-50*] (DLA)

ZLR............. Zanzibar Protectorate Law Reports [*1868-1950*] (DLA)

ZLROA .... Zeitschrift fuer Laryngologie, Rhinologie, Otologie [*A publication*]

ZLSIA........ Zapiski Leningradskogo Sel'skokhozyaistvennogo Instituta [*A publication*]

ZLSM .... Zeiss Light Section Microscope

ZLT............. La Tabatiere [*Canada*] [*Airport symbol*] (OAG)

ZLThK .... Zeitschrift fuer die Gesamte Lutherische Theologie und Kirche [*Leipzig*] [*A publication*]

ZLTO .... Zero-Length Takeoff (MCD)

Z Luft-Weltraumrecht ... Zeitschrift fuer Luft- und Weltraumrecht [*A publication*]

Z-LV .... Z-Axis along Local Vertical (MCD)

ZLV............. Zero-Length Vector

Z Lymphol ... Zeitschrift fuer Lymphologie [*A publication*]

ZM.............. Impedance Measuring Devices [*JETDS nomenclature*] [*Military*] (CET)

ZM.............. New Zealand [*Aircraft nationality and registration mark*] (FAAC)

ZM.............. Zambia [*Two-letter standard code*] (CNC)

ZM.............. Zeitschrift fuer Missionskunde [*A publication*]

ZM.............. Zeitschrift fuer Mundartforschung [*A publication*]

ZM.............. Zeitschrift fuer Musik [*A publication*]

ZM.............. Zero Marker (MCD)

ZM.............. Zoom/MODEM [*ZOOM Telephonics, Inc.*]

Z-M............. Zuckerman-Moloff [*Sewage treatment method*]

ZM.............. Zycie i Mysl [*A publication*]

ZMA .... Miami, FL [*Location identifier*] [*FAA*] (FAAL)

ZMA .... Zinc Metaarsenite [*Insecticide, wood preservative*]

ZMaF .... Zeitschrift fuer Mundartforschung [*A publication*]

ZMag .... Z Magazine [*Zambia*] [*A publication*]

ZMAR .... Zeus Multifunction Array RADAR [*Missile defense*]

Z Math Log ... Zeitschrift fuer Mathematische Logik und Grundlagen der Mathematik [*A publication*]

Z Math Logik Grundlagen Math ... Zeitschrift fuer Mathematische Logik und Grundlagen der Mathematik [*A publication*]

Z Math Logik Grundlag Math ... Zeitschrift fuer Mathematische Logik und Grundlagen der Mathematik [*A publication*]

Z Mat Phys ... Zeitschrift fuer Mathematik und Physik [*East Germany*] [*A publication*]

ZMB............ Zambia [*Three-letter standard code*] (CNC)

ZMB............ Zero-Moisture Basis [*Analytical chemistry*]

ZMB............ Zinc Mercaptobenzimidazole [*Organic chemistry*]

ZMBT .... Zinc Mercaptobenzothiazole [*Organic chemistry*]

ZMBTA....... Zement und Beton [*A publication*]

ZMC............ Manhattan College, Library, Bronx, NY [*OCLC symbol*] (OCLC)

ZMD .... Zung Measurement of Depression [*Scale*]

ZME............ Memphis, TN [*Location identifier*] [*FAA*] (FAAL)

Z Med Chem ... Zeitschrift fuer Medizinische Chemie [*A publication*]

Z Med Lab Diagn ... Zeitschrift fuer Medizinische Laboratoriumsdiagnostik [*A publication*]

Z Med Laboratoriumsdiagn ... Zeitschrift fuer Medizinische Laboratoriumsdiagnostik [*A publication*]

Z Med Labortech ... Zeitschrift fuer Medizinische Labortechnik [*A publication*]

Z Med Mikrobiol Immunol ... Zeitschrift fuer Medizinische Mikrobiologie und Immunologie [*A publication*]

ZMEIA .... Zhurnal Mikrobiologii, Epidemiologii, i Immunobiologii [*A publication*]

Z Menschl Vererb-Konstitutionsl ... Zeitschrift fuer Menschliche Vererbungs- und Konstitutionslehre [*A publication*]

Z Metallk.... Zeitschrift fuer Metallkunde [*A publication*]

Z Metallkd ... Zeitschrift fuer Metallkunde [*A publication*]

Z Metallkun ... Zeitschrift fuer Metallkunde [*A publication*]

Z Meteorol ... Zeitschrift fuer Meteorologie [*A publication*]

Z Met Schmuckwaren Fabr Verchrom ... Zeitschrift fuer Metall- und Schmuckwaren. Fabrikation sowie Verchromung [*A publication*]

ZMF .... Zeitschrift fuer Mundartforschung [*A publication*]

ZMH .... Zeitschrift des Museums Hildesheim [*A publication*]

Z Mikrosk Anat Forsch ... Zeitschrift fuer Mikroskopische-Anatomische Forschung [*A publication*]

Z Mikrosk-Anat Forsch (Leipz) ... Zeitschrift fuer Mikroskopische-Anatomische Forschung (Leipzig) [*A publication*]

Z Militaermed ... Zeitschrift fuer Militaermedizin [*East Germany*] [*A publication*]

Z Miss-u Relig Wiss ... Zeitschrift fuer Missionswissenschaft und Religionswissenschaft [*A publication*]

Z Miss W .... Zeitschrift fuer Missionswissenschaft und Religionswissenschaft [*A publication*]

ZMK .... Zeitschrift fuer Missionskunde und Religionswissenschaft [*A publication*]

ZMK .... Zpravodaj Mistopisne Komise CSAV [*Ceskoslovenske Akademie Ved*] [*A publication*]

ZMKR .... Zone Marker

ZML............ Medical Library Center of New York, Standardized Cataloging Service, New York, NY [*OCLC symbol*] (OCLC)

ZMM........... State University of New York, Maritime College, Bronx, NY [*OCLC symbol*] (OCLC)

ZMM .... Zone Melting Model

ZMMAS ...... Zodiacal Microparticle Multiparameter Analysis System [*NASA*]

ZMMD .... Zurich, Mainz, Munich, Darmstadt [*A joint European university effort on ALGOL processors*]

ZMNP .... Zurnal Ministerstva Narodnogo Prosvescenija [*A publication*]

Z Morphol Anthropol ... Zeitschrift fuer Morphologie und Anthropologie [*A publication*]
Z Morphol Oekol Tiere ... Zeitschrift fuer Morphologie und Oekologie der Tiere [*A publication*]
Z Morphol Tiere ... Zeitschrift fuer Morphologie der Tiere [*A publication*]
Z Morph Tie ... Zeitschrift fuer Morphologie der Tiere [*A publication*]
ZMOS .... Zymos Corp. [*NASDAQ symbol*] (NQ)
ZMOTA ...... Zeitschrift fuer Morphologie und Oekologie der Tiere [*A publication*]
ZMP .... Minneapolis, MN [*Location identifier*] [*FAA*] (FAAL)
ZMP .... Zurnal Moskovskoi Patriarkhii [*Moscow*] [*A publication*]
ZMR .... Zeitschrift fuer Missionswissenschaft und Religionswissenschaft [*A publication*]
ZMRI .... Zinc Metals Research Institute
ZMRW .... Zeitschrift fuer Missionswissenschaft und Religionswissenschaft [*A publication*]
ZMS .... Zbornik Matrice Srpske [*A publication*]
ZMT .... Masset [*Canada*] [*Airport symbol*] (OAG)
ZMT .... ZIP [*Zone Improvement Plan*] Mail Translator [*Postal Service*]
ZMUC .... Zoologisk Museum, University of Copenhagen [*Denmark*]
ZMVKA .... Zeitschrift fuer Menschliche Vererbungs- und Konstitutionslehre [*A publication*]
ZMW .... Zeitschrift fuer Missionswissenschaft [*A publication*]
Z Mw .... Zeitschrift fuer Musikwissenschaft [*A publication*]
ZMX .... Zemex Corp. [*NYSE symbol*]
ZN .... Airship (Nonrigid) [*Navy symbol*]
Zn .... True Azimuth [*Symbol*] (MUGU)
ZN .... Zeitschrift fuer Nationaloekonomie [*A publication*]
ZN .... Zeitschrift fuer Numismatik [*A publication*]
ZN .... Zenith
ZN .... Zeszyty Naukowe [*A publication*]
ZN .... Ziehl-Neelsen [*A biological stain*]
Zn .... Zinc [*Chemical element*]
Zn .... Znamya [*Moscow*] [*A publication*]
ZN .... Zone
ZN .... Zycie Nauki [*A publication*]
ZNA .... Nanaimo [*Canada*] Harbour Airport [*Airport symbol*] (OAG)
ZNa .... Zycie Nauki [*A publication*]
ZNACD ...... Zeszyty Naukowe Akademii Gorniczo-Hutniczej Imienia Stanislawa Staszica. Matematyka, Fizyka, Chemia [*A publication*]
ZNAGB ...... Zeszyty Naukowe Akademii Gorniczo-Hutniczej (Krakow). Gornictwo [*A publication*]
Z Nahrungsm Unters Hyg Warenkd ... Zeitschrift fuer Nahrungsmittel-Untersuchung Hygiene und Warenkunde [*A publication*]
ZNAND .... Zootecnica e Nutrizione Animale [*A publication*]
ZNAT .... Zenith National Insurance Co. [*NASDAQ symbol*] (NQ)
Z Nationalo ... Zeitschrift fuer Nationaloekonomie [*A publication*]
Z Nationaloekonom ... Zeitschrift fuer Nationaloekonomie [*A publication*]
Z Nat-Oekon ... Zeitschrift fuer Nationaloekonomie [*A publication*]
Z Naturf B ... Zeitschrift fuer Naturforschung. Teil B [*A publication*]
Z Naturf C ... Zeitschrift fuer Naturforschung. Teil C. Biochemie, Biophysik, Biologie, Virologie [*A publication*]
Z Naturfo A ... Zeitschrift fuer Naturforschung. A [*A publication*]
Z Naturfo B ... Zeitschrift fuer Naturforschung. B [*A publication*]
Z Naturfo C ... Zeitschrift fuer Naturforschung. C [*A publication*]
Z Naturforsch ... Zeitschrift fuer Naturforschung [*A publication*]
Z Naturforsch A ... Zeitschrift fuer Naturforschung. Teil A. Astrophysik, Physik, und Physikalische Chemie [*A publication*]
Z Naturforsch B ... Zeitschrift fuer Naturforschung. Teil B [*A publication*]
Z Naturforsch B Anorg Chem Org Chem ... Zeitschrift fuer Naturforschung. Teil B. Anorganische Chemie, Organische Chemie [*A publication*]
Z Naturforsch B Anorg Chem Org Chem Biochem Biophys Biol ... Zeitschrift fuer Naturforschung. Teil B. Anorganische Chemie, Organische Chemie, Biochemie, Biophysik, Biologie [*West Germany*] [*A publication*]
Z Naturforsch C Biochem Biophys Biol Virol ... Zeitschrift fuer Naturforschung. Teil C. Biochemie, Biophysik, Biologie, Virologie [*West Germany*] [*A publication*]
Z Naturforsch C Biosci ... Zeitschrift fuer Naturforschung. Teil C. Biosciences [*West Germany*] [*A publication*]
Z Naturforsch Sect B ... Zeitschrift fuer Naturforschung. Section B. Inorganic Chemistry, Organic Chemistry [*A publication*]
Z Naturforsch Sect C Biosci ... Zeitschrift fuer Naturforschung. Section C. Biosciences [*A publication*]
Z Naturforsch Teil A ... Zeitschrift fuer Naturforschung. Teil A [*A publication*]
Z Naturforsch Teil C ... Zeitschrift fuer Naturforschung. Teil C. Biosciences [*A publication*]
Z Naturforsch Teil C Biochem Biophys Biol Virol ... Zeitschrift fuer Naturforschung. Teil C. Biochemie, Biophysik, Biologie, Virologie [*A publication*]
Z Naturheilk ... Zeitschrift fuer Naturheilkunde [*A publication*]
Z Naturwiss-Med Grundlagenforsch ... Zeitschrift fuer Naturwissenschaftlich-Medizinische Grundlagenforschung [*A publication*]
Z Naurforsch Teil B ... Zeitschrift fuer Naturforschung. Teil B. Anorganische Chemie, Organische Chemie [*A publication*]
ZNC .... New York City Technical College, Library, Brooklyn, NY [*OCLC symbol*] (OCLC)
ZNC .... Nyack, AK [*Location identifier*] [*FAA*] (FAAL)

ZNC .... Zone of Nonproliferating Cells [*Cytology*]
ZNCAV .... Zdenku Nejedlemu Ceskoslovenska Akademie Ved [*A publication*]
ZND .... Zinder [*Niger*] [*Airport symbol*] (OAG)
ZNE .... Newman [*Australia*] [*Airport symbol*] (OAG)
Z Neurol ..... Zeitschrift fuer Neurologie [*A publication*]
Z Neut W ... Zeitschrift fuer die Neutestamentliche Wissenschaft [*A publication*]
Z Neut Wiss ... Zeitschrift fuer die Neutestamentliche Wissenschaft und die Kunde der Alteren Kirche [*A publication*]
ZNF .... Zeitschrift fuer Namenforschung [*A publication*]
ZNG .... Negginan [*Canada*] [*Airport symbol*] (OAG)
ZNG .... Zeszyty Naukowe Wydzialu Humanistycznego, Wyzsza Szkola Pedagogiczna w Gdansku [*A publication*]
ZnG .... Zinc Gluconate [*Organic chemistry*]
ZNGGA .... Zeszyty Naukowe Akademii Gorniczo-Hutniczej (Krakow). Geologia [*A publication*]
ZNH .... Airship, Air-Sea Rescue [*Navy symbol*]
ZNIC .... Zonic Corp. [*NASDAQ symbol*] (NQ)
ZNIO .... Zaklad Narodowy Imeni Ossolinskich [*A publication*]
ZNJ .... Airship, Utility [*Navy symbol*]
ZNK .... Zeszyty Naukowe, Sekcja Jezykoznawcza, Wyzsza Szkola Pedagogiczna w Katowicach [*A publication*]
ZNKUL .... Zeszyty Naukowe Katolickiego Uniwersytetu Lubelskiego [*A publication*]
ZNLSA .... Zeszyty Naukowe Politechniki Lodzkiej. Chemia Spozywcza [*A publication*]
ZNM .... Nioga Library System, Niagara Falls, NY [*OCLC symbol*] (OCLC)
ZNN .... Nonrigid Training Airship [*Navy symbol*]
ZNO .... Nonrigid Observation Airship [*Navy symbol*]
ZNO .... North Country Community College, Saranac Lake, NY [*OCLC symbol*] (OCLC)
ZNO .... Zeitschrift fuer Nationaloekonomie [*A publication*]
ZNO .... Zenco Resources, Inc. [*Vancouver Stock Exchange symbol*]
ZNP .... Nonrigid Patrol Airship [*Navy symbol*]
ZNP .... Zanzibar Nationalist Party
ZNP .... Zinc Pyrithione [*Antibacterial*]
ZNP .... Zion Nuclear Plant (NRCH)
ZNPEA .... Zeszyty Naukowe Politechniki Lodzkiej. Elektryka [*A publication*]
ZNPIA .... Zhurnal Nevropatologii i Psikhiatrii Imeni S. S. Korsakova [*A publication*]
ZNR .... Zinc Resistor
ZNS .... Nonrigid Scouting Airship [*Navy symbol*]
ZNS .... Zeitschrift fuer Neuere Sprachen [*A publication*]
ZNSCA .... Zeszyty Naukowe Politechniki Slaskiej. Chemia [*A publication*]
ZNSGA .... Zeszyty Naukowe Politechniki Slaskiej. Gornictwo [*A publication*]
ZNSPK .... Zeszyty Naukowe Wyzszej Szkoly Pedagogicznej. Katowice [*A publication*]
ZNSPO .... Zeszyty Naukowe Wyzszej Szkoly Pedagogicznej. Opole [*A publication*]
ZNTFA .... Zeitschrift fuer Naturforschung [*A publication*]
ZNTHA .... Zeszyty Naukowe Politechniki Czestochowskiej. Nauki Techniczne - Hutnictwo [*A publication*]
ZNTS .... Zapysky Naukovoho Tovarystva Imeny Svecenka (Linguistic Series) [*A publication*]
ZNTSL .... Zapysky Naukovoho Tovarystva Imeny Svecenka (Literature Series) [*A publication*]
ZNTW .... Zeitschrift fuer die Neutestamentliche Wissenschaft [*A publication*]
ZNU .... Namu [*Canada*] [*Airport symbol*] [*Obsolete*] (OAG)
ZNU .... Zeitschrift fuer Neusprachlichen Unterricht [*A publication*]
ZNUFA .... Zeszyty Naukowe Uniwersytetu Jagiellonskiego. Prace Fizyczne [*A publication*]
ZNUG .... Zeszyty Naukowe Uniwersytetu Gdanskiego [*A publication*]
ZNUJ .... Zeszyty Naukowe Uniwersytetu Jagiellonskiego [*A publication*]
ZNUL .... Zeszyty Naukowe Uniwersytetu Lodzkiego [*A publication*]
ZNULHist ... Zeszyty Naukowe Uniwersytetu Lodzkiego. Nauki Humanistyczno-Spoleczne. Historia [*A publication*]
ZNum .... Zeitschrift fuer Numismatik [*A publication*]
ZNUMK ...... Zeszyty Naukowe Uniwersytetu M. Kopernika [*A publication*]
ZNUnWr ..... Zeszyty Naukowe Uniwersytetu Wroclawskiego [*A publication*]
ZNUP .... Zeszyty Naukowe Uniwersytetu Imienia Adama Mickiewicza w Poznaniu [*A publication*]
ZNUPHSzt ... Zeszyty Naukowe Uniwersytetu Imienia Adama Mickiewicza w Poznaniu. Historia Sztuki [*A publication*]
ZNUT .... Zeszyty Naukowe Uniwersytetu M. Kopernika w Toruniu. Nauki Humanistyczno-Spoleczne [*A publication*]
ZNUW .... Zeszyty Naukowe Uniwersytetu Wroclawskiego Imeni B. Bieruta [*A publication*]
ZNW .... Zeitschrift fuer die Neutestamentliche Wissenschaft [*A publication*]
ZNW .... Zeitschrift fuer die Neutestamentliche Wissenschaft und die Kunde des Urchristentums [*A publication*]
ZNWFA .... Zeszyty Naukowe Wyzszej Szkoly Pedagogicznej w Katowicach, Sekcja Fizyki [*A publication*]
ZNWKAK .... Zeitschrift fuer die Neutestamentliche Wissenschaft und die Kunde der Aelteren Kirche [*A publication*]

ZNWKU ...... Zeitschrift fuer die Neutestamentliche Wissenschaft und die Kunde des Urchristentums [*A publication*]

ZNWSPK .... Zeszyty Naukowe Wyzszej Szkoly Pedagogicznej. Katowice [*A publication*]

ZNWSPO .... Zeszyty Naukowe Wyzszej Szkoly Pedagogicznej. Opole [*A publication*]

ZNWSPOp ... Zeszyty Naukowe, Jezykoznawstwo, Wyzsza Szkola Pedagogiczna w Opolu [*A publication*]

ZNXPO .... Zeus-Nike X Program Office [*Missiles*]   (MCD)

ZNY .... New York, NY [*Location identifier*] [*FAA*]   (FAAL)

ZNZ .... Zanzibar [*Tanzania*] [*Airport symbol*]   (OAG)

ZO .... Zeitschrift fuer Ortsnamenforschung [*A publication*]

ZO .... Zeitschrift fuer Ostforschung [*A publication*]

ZO .... Zero Output

ZO .... Zoological Origin

Z/O .... Zoom Out [*Cinematography*]

ZOA .... Oakland, CA [*Location identifier*] [*FAA*]   (FAAL)

ZOA .... Zionist Organization of America   (EA)

ZOB .... Cleveland, OH [*Location identifier*] [*FAA*]   (FAAL)

ZOBO .... Zongo [*La Paz*] [*Bolivia*] [*Seismograph station code, US Geological Survey*]   (SEIS)

Zobozdrav Vestn ... Zobozdravstveni Vestnik [*A publication*]

ZOBW .... Zeitschrift fuer Oesterreichisches Bibliothekswesen [*A publication*]

ZOD .... Zero Order Detector   (MCD)

ZOD .... Zodiac   (ROG)

Zod .... Zodiac Records [*Record label*]

ZODIAC ...... Zone Defense Integrated Active Capability   (IEEE)

ZOE .... Zero Energy

ZOE .... Zinc Oxide-Eugenol [*Dental cement*]

ZOE .... Zone of Entry   (AABC)

ZOE .... Zone of Exclusion   (MCD)

Z Oeff Gem Wirtsch Unterneh ... Zeitschrift fuer Oeffentliche und Gemeinwirtschaftliche Unternehmen [*A publication*]

ZOEG .... Zeitschrift fuer die Oesterreichischen Gymnasien [*A publication*]

ZOEG .... Zeitschrift fuer Osteuropaeische Geschichte [*A publication*]

ZOEMS ...... Zeitschrift fuer die Oesterreichischen Mittelschulen [*A publication*]

ZOEP .... Zoe Products, Inc. [*NASDAQ symbol*]   (NQ)

ZOest G ...... Zeitschrift fuer die Oesterreichischen Gymnasien [*A publication*]

ZOF .... Ocean Falls [*Canada*] [*Airport symbol*] [*Obsolete*]   (OAG)

ZOf .... Zeitschrift fuer Ostforschung [*A publication*]

ZOF .... Zone of Fire [*Military*]

ZOfo .... Zeitschrift fuer Ostforschung [*A publication*]

ZOG .... Paramaribo [*Suriname*] [*Airport symbol*]

ZOG .... Zeitschrift fuer Osteuropaeische Geschichte [*A publication*]

ZOG .... Zionist Occupational Government

ZOH .... Zero Order Hold [*Telescope*]

ZOLD .... Zeroth Order Logarithmic Distribution

ZOLGA .... Zoologica [*A publication*]

Zolnierz Pol ... Zolnierz Polski [*Poland*] [*A publication*]

ZOMO .... Zmotoryzowane Oddzialy Milicji Obywatelskiej [*Motorized Units of People's Militia*] [*Poland's riot police*]

ZON .... Zeitschrift fuer Ortsnamenforschung [*A publication*]

ZON .... Zonda [*Argentina*] [*Seismograph station code, US Geological Survey*]   (SEIS)

ZON .... Zone Petroleum [*Vancouver Stock Exchange symbol*]

Zonar .... Zonaras [*Twelfth century AD*] [*Classical studies*]   (OCD)

ZOND .... Zondervan Corp. [*NASDAQ symbol*]   (NQ)

ZONEF .... Zone Petroleum Corp. [*NASDAQ symbol*]   (NQ)

ZOO .... Minnesota Zoological Garden, Apple Valley, MN [*OCLC symbol*]   (OCLC)

ZOOACT .... Zoological Action Committee   (EA)

ZOOCHEM ... Zoochemistry   (ROG)

ZOOGEOG ... Zoogeography   (ROG)

Zooiatr Rev Med Vet Prod Pecu ... Zooiatria Revista de Medicina Veterinaria y Produccion Pecuaria [*A publication*]

ZOOL .... Zoology

Zool Abh (Dres) ... Zoologische Abhandlungen (Dresden) [*A publication*]

Zool Afr ...... Zoologica Africana [*A publication*]

Zool Ann .... Zoologische Annalen [*A publication*]

Zool Anz .... Zoologischer Anzeiger [*A publication*]

Zool Anzeiger ... Zoologischer Anzeiger [*A publication*]

Zool Anz (Leipzig) ... Zoologischer Anzeiger (Leipzig) [*A publication*]

Zool Anz Suppl ... Zoologische Anzeiger. Supplement [*A publication*]

Zool B .... Zoological Bulletin [*A publication*]

Zool Beitr ... Zoologische Beitraege [*A publication*]

Zool Ber .... Zoologischer Bericht [*A publication*]

Zool Bidr Upps ... Zoologiska Bidrag fran Uppsala [*A publication*]

Zool Bidr Uppsala ... Zoologiska Bidrag fran Uppsala [*A publication*]

Zool Bijdr ... Zoologische Bijdragen [*A publication*]

Zool Biol Mar ... Zoologia e Biologia Marinha [*A publication*]

Zool Biol Mar (Sao Paulo) (Nova Ser) ... Zoologia e Biologia Marinha (Sao Paulo) (Nova Serie) [*A publication*]

Zool Entomol Listy ... Zoologicke a Entomologicke Listy [*A publication*]

Zool Gaert ... Zoologische Gaerten [*A publication*]

Zool Gart (Lpz) ... Zoologische Gaerten (Leipzig) [*A publication*]

Zool Inst Fac Sci Univ Tokyo Annu Rep ... Zoological Institute. Faculty of Science. University of Tokyo. Annual Report [*A publication*]

Zool Jahrb Abt Allg Zool Physiol Tiere ... Zoologische Jahrbuecher. Abteilung fuer Allgemeine Zoologie und Physiologie der Tiere [*A publication*]

Zool Jahrb Abt Anat Ontog Tiere ... Zoologische Jahrbuecher. Abteilung fuer Anatomie und Ontogenie der Tiere [*A publication*]

Zool Jahrb Abt Syst (Jena) ... Zoologische Jahrbuecher. Abteilung fuer Systematik Oekologie und Geographie der Tiere (Jena) [*A publication*]

Zool Jahrb Abt Syst Oekol Geogr Tiere ... Zoologische Jahrbuecher. Abteilung fuer Systematik Oekologie und Geographie der Tiere [*A publication*]

Zool Jb .... Zoologische Jahrbuecher [*A publication*]

Zool Jb Abt Allg Zool Physiol Tiere ... Zoologische Jahrbuecher. Abteilung fuer Allgemeine Zoologie und Physiologie der Tiere [*A publication*]

Zool Jb Abt Syst Okol Geog Tiere ... Zoologische Jahrbuecher. Abteilung fuer Systematik Oekologie und Geographie der Tiere [*A publication*]

Zool Jhrb Abt Allg Zool Physiol Tiere ... Zoologische Jahrbuecher. Abteilung fuer Allgemeine Zoologie und Physiologie der Tiere [*A publication*]

Zool J Linn ... Zoological Journal. Linnean Society [*A publication*]

Zool J Linn Soc ... Zoological Journal. Linnean Society [*A publication*]

Zool Listy ... Zoologicke Listy [*A publication*]

Zool Mag (Tokyo) ... Zoological Magazine (Tokyo) [*A publication*]

Zool Meded (Leiden) ... Zoologische Mededelingen (Leiden) [*A publication*]

Zool Meded Rijks Mus Nat Hist Leiden ... Zoologische Mededelingen. Rijks Museum van Natuurlijke Historie te Leiden [*A publication*]

Zool Muz Raksti Invertebrata ... Zoologijas Muzeja Raksti. Invertebrata [*A publication*]

Zoologica Pol ... Zoologica Poloniae [*A publication*]

Zoologica Scr ... Zoologica Scripta [*A publication*]

Zool Pol ...... Zoologica Poloniae [*A publication*]

Zool Publ Victoria Univ Wellington ... Zoology Publications. Victoria University of Wellington [*A publication*]

Zool Rec ..... Zoological Record [*A publication*]

Zool Revy ... Zoologisk Revy [*A publication*]

Zool Scr ..... Zoologica Scripta [*A publication*]

Zool Scr ..... Zoologien Scripta [*A publication*]

Zool Soc Egypt Bull ... Zoological Society of Egypt. Bulletin [*A publication*]

Zool Soc London Pr ... Zoological Society of London. Proceedings [*A publication*]

Zool Soc London Proc ... Zoological Society of London. Proceedings [*A publication*]

Zool Verh (Leiden) ... Zoologische Verhandelingen (Leiden) [*A publication*]

Zool Z .... Zoologiceskij Zhurnal [*A publication*]

Zool Zentralbl ... Zoologisches Zentralblatt [*A publication*]

Zool Zh .... Zoologicheskii Zhurnal [*A publication*]

Zoonoses Res ... Zoonoses Research [*A publication*]

Zoon Suppl ... Zoon. Supplement [*A publication*]

ZOOPH .... Zoophytology   (ROG)

Zoophysiol Ecol ... Zoophysiology and Ecology [*A publication*]

Zoo Rec ...... Zoological Record [*A publication*]

Zoo Rev Parque Zool Barc ... Zoo Revista del Parque Zoologico de Barcelona [*A publication*]

Zootech Experiment Stn Res Bull ... Zootechnical Experiment Station. Research Bulletin [*A publication*]

Zootec Nutr Anim ... Zootecnica e Nutrizione Animale [*A publication*]

Zootec Vet ... Zootecnica e Veterinaria [*A publication*]

Zootec Vet Agric ... Zootecnica. Veterinaria e Agricoltura [*A publication*]

ZOP .... Zero Order Predictor

ZOP .... Zinc Oxide Pigment

Z Operations Res Ser A-B ... Zeitschrift fuer Operations Research. Serie A. Serie B [*A publication*]

Z Oper Res B ... Zeitschrift fuer Operations Research. Serie B. Praxis [*A publication*]

Z Oper Res Ser A ... Zeitschrift fuer Operations Research. Serie A. Theorie [*A publication*]

Z Oper Res Ser B ... Zeitschrift fuer Operations Research. Serie B. Praxis [*A publication*]

ZOPI .... Zero Order Polynomial Interpolator

ZOPP .... Zero Order Polynomial Predictor

ZOR .... Zinc Oxide Resistor

ZOR .... Zone of Reconnaissance

ZOR .... Zorah Media Corp. [*Vancouver Stock Exchange symbol*]

Z Organ ...... Zeitschrift fuer Organisation [*A publication*]

ZORRO .... Zero Offset Rapid Reaction Ordnance

Z Orthop .... Zeitschrift fuer Orthopaedie und Ihre Grenzgebiete [*A publication*]

Z Orthop Grenzgeb ... Zeitschrift fuer Orthopaedie und Ihre Grenzgebiete [*A publication*]

Z Orthop Ihre Grenzgeb ... Zeitschrift fuer Orthopaedie und Ihre Grenzgebiete [*A publication*]

ZOS .... Zapata Corp. [*NYSE symbol*] [*Toronto Stock Exchange symbol*]

ZOS .... Zoom Optical System

ZOSC .... Zoologica Scripta [*A publication*]

Z Ostforsch ... Zeitschrift fuer Ostforschung [*A publication*]

Z fur die Ost Gym ... Zeitschrift fuer die Oesterreichischen Gymnasien [*A publication*]   (OCD)

ZOVBW ...... Zeitschrift des Oesterreichischen Vereins fuer Bibliothekswesen [*A publication*]

ZOW .... State University of New York, College at Old Westbury, Old Westbury, NY [*OCLC symbol*]   (OCLC)

ZOX .... Ground Zero [*Nevada*] [*Seismograph station code, US Geological Survey*] [*Closed*]   (SEIS)

ZP .... Paraguay [*Aircraft nationality and registration mark*]   (FAAC)

ZP .... Patrol and Escort Aircraft [*Lighter-than-Air*] [*Navy symbol*]   (MUGU)

ZP .... Revlon, Inc. [*Research code symbol*]

ZP .... Zeitschrift fuer Phonetik [*A publication*]

ZP .... Zeitschrift fuer Politik [*A publication*]

ZP .... Zep Energy [*Vancouver Stock Exchange symbol*]

Zp .... Zephaniah   (BJA)

ZP .... Zona Pellucida [*Embryology*]

ZPA .... Zero Period Acceleration [*Nuclear energy*]   (NRCH)

ZPA .... Zeus Program Analysis [*Missiles*]

ZPA .... Zone of Polarizing Activity [*Embryology, genetics*]

ZPAAD .... Zeitschrift fuer Physik. Sektion A. Atoms and Nuclei [*A publication*]

ZPalV .... Zeitschrift des Deutschen Palaestinavereins [*A publication*]

ZPapEpigr ... Zeitschrift fuer Papyrologie und Epigraphik [*A publication*]   (BJA)

Z Papyrologie Epigraphik ... Zeitschrift fuer Papyrologie und Epigraphik [*A publication*]

ZPAR .... Zeus Phased Array RADAR [*Missile defense*]

Z Parapsych ... Zeitschrift fuer Parapsychologie und Grenzgebiete der Psychologie [*A publication*]

Z Parasiten ... Zeitschrift fuer Parasitenkunde [*A publication*]

Z Parasitenkd ... Zeitschrift fuer Parasitenkunde [*A publication*]

Z ParasitKde ... Zeitschrift fuer Parasitenkunde [*A publication*]

Z Parlamentsfr ... Zeitschrift fuer Parlamentsfragen [*German Federal Republic*] [*A publication*]

Z Parlamentsfragen ... Zeitschrift fuer Parlamentsfragen [*A publication*]

ZPAS .... Zeitschrift fuer Phonetik und Allgemeine Sprachwissenschaft [*A publication*]

ZPB .... Zinc Primary Battery

ZPBBD .... Zeitschrift fuer Physik. Sektion B. Condensed Matter and Quanta [*A publication*]

ZPC .... Zinc-Phosphate Coating

ZPCA .... Zugzwang! Postal Chess Association   (EA)

ZPCAA .... Zeitschrift fuer Physikalische Chemie. Abteilung A [*A publication*]

ZPCBA ...... Zeitschrift fuer Physikalische Chemie. Abteilung B [*A publication*]

ZPCHA .... Zeitschrift fuer Physiologische Chemie [*A publication*]

ZPCLA .... Zeitschrift fuer Physikalische Chemie (Leipzig) [*A publication*]

ZPD .... Zero Path Difference

ZPDBA .... Zeitschrift fuer Pflanzenernaehrung Duengung Bodenkunde [*A publication*]

ZPE .... Zeitschrift fuer Papyrologie und Epigraphik [*A publication*]

ZPE .... Zero Point Energy

ZPE .... Zeta Phi Eta

ZPED .... Zeus Production Evaluation Program [*Missiles*]   (MCD)

ZPEN .... Zeus Project Engineer Network [*Missiles*]

ZPF .... Zeitschrift fuer Philosophische Forschung [*A publication*]

ZPFL .... Zanzibar and Pemba Federation of Labour

Z Pflanzenernaehr Bodenkd ... Zeitschrift fuer Pflanzenernaehrung und Bodenkunde [*A publication*]

Z Pflanzenernaehr Dueng Bodenkd ... Zeitschrift fuer Pflanzenernaehrung, Duengung, und Bodenkunde [*Later, Zeitschrift fuer Pflanzenernaehrung und Bodenkunde*] [*A publication*]

Z Pflanzenkr ... Zeitschrift fuer Pflanzenkrankheiten [*A publication*]

Z Pflanzenkr Gallenkd ... Zeitschrift fuer Pflanzenkrankheiten und Gallenkunde [*A publication*]

Z Pflanzenkr Pflanzenpathol Pflanzenschutz ... Zeitschrift fuer Pflanzenkrankheiten, Pflanzenpathologie, und Pflanzenschutz [*A publication*]

Z Pflanzenkr Pflanzenpathol Pflanzenschutz Sonderh ... Zeitschrift fuer Pflanzenkrankheiten, Pflanzenpathologie, und Pflanzenschutz. Sonderheft [*A publication*]

Z Pflanzenkr Pflanzenschutz ... Zeitschrift fuer Pflanzenkrankheiten und Pflanzenschutz [*A publication*]

Z Pflanzenp ... Zeitschrift fuer Pflanzenphysiologie [*A publication*]

Z Pflanzenphysiol ... Zeitschrift fuer Pflanzenphysiologie [*A publication*]

Z Pflanzenz ... Zeitschrift fuer Pflanzenzuechtung [*A publication*]

Z Pflanzenzuecht ... Zeitschrift fuer Pflanzenzuechtung [*A publication*]

Z PflErnahr Bodenk ... Zeitschrift fuer Pflanzenernaehrung und Bodenkunde [*A publication*]

Z PflErnahr Dung Bodenk ... Zeitschrift fuer Pflanzenernaehrung, Duengung, und Bodenkunde [*Later, Zeitschrift fuer Pflanzenernaehrung und Bodenkunde*] [*A publication*]

Z PflKrankh ... Zeitschrift fuer Pflanzenkrankheiten, Pflanzenpathologie, und Pflanzenschutz [*A publication*]

Z PflKrankh PflSchutz ... Zeitschrift fuer Pflanzenkrankheiten Pflanzenschutz [*A publication*]

Z PflPhysiol ... Zeitschrift fuer Pflanzenphysiologie [*A publication*]

ZPG .... Airship Group [*Navy symbol*]

ZPG .... Zero Population Growth [*An association*] [*Washington, DC*]   (EA)

ZPh .... Zeitschrift fuer Psychologie [*A publication*]

ZPH .... Zephyrhills, FL [*Location identifier*] [*FAA*]   (FAAL)

ZPhF .... Zeitschrift fuer Philosophische Forschung [*A publication*]

Z Phil Forsch ... Zeitschrift fuer Philosophische Forschung [*A publication*]

Z Philos Forsch ... Zeitschrift fuer Philosophische Forschung [*A publication*]

ZPhon .... Zeitschrift fuer Phonetik und Allgemeine Sprachwissenschaft [*A publication*]

Z Phonetik Sprachwiss Komm Forsch ... Zeitschrift fuer Phonetik, Sprachwissenschaft, und Kommunikationsforschung [*A publication*]

Z Phon Sprachwiss Kommunikationsforsch ... Zeitschrift fuer Phonetik, Sprachwissenschaft, und Kommunikationsforschung [*A publication*]

Z Phys .... Zeitschrift fuer Physik [*A publication*]

Z Phys A .... Zeitschrift fuer Physik. A. Atoms and Nuclei [*A publication*]

Z Phys B ..... Zeitschrift fuer Physik. B. Condensed Matter and Quanta [*A publication*]

Z Phys C ..... Zeitschrift fuer Physik. C. Particles and Fields [*German Federal Republic*] [*A publication*]

Z Phys Chem Abt A ... Zeitschrift fuer Physikalische Chemie. Abteilung A. Chemische Thermodynamik, Kinetik, Elektrochemie, Eigenschaftslehre [*A publication*]

Z Phys Chem Abt B ... Zeitschrift fuer Physikalische Chemie. Abteilung B. Chemie der Elementarprozesse, Aufbau der Materie [*A publication*]

Z Phys Chem Frankf Ausg Neue Folge ... Zeitschrift fuer Physikalische Chemie. Frankfurter Ausgabe. Neue Folge [*West Germany*] [*A publication*]

Z Phys Chem (Frankfurt/Main) ... Zeitschrift fuer Physikalische Chemie (Frankfurt/Main) [*A publication*]

Z Phys Chemie Stoechiom Verwandschaftsl ... Zeitschrift fuer Physikalische Chemie, Stoechiometrie, und Verwandschaftslehre [*A publication*]

Z Phys Chem (Leipzig) ... Zeitschrift fuer Physikalische Chemie (Leipzig) [*A publication*]

Z Phys Chem Materialforsch ... Zeitschrift fuer Physikalisch-Chemische Materialforschung [*A publication*]

Z Phys Chem Neue Folge ... Zeitschrift fuer Physikalische Chemie. Neue Folge [*A publication*]

Z Phys Chem Neue Fo (Wiesbaden) ... Zeitschrift fuer Physikalische Chemie. Neue Folge (Wiesbaden) [*A publication*]

Z Phys Chem (Wiesbaden) ... Zeitschrift fuer Physikalische Chemie (Wiesbaden) [*A publication*]

Z Phys Ch F ... Zeitschrift fuer Physikalische Chemie (Frankfurt) [*A publication*]

Z Phys Ch (L) ... Zeitschrift fuer Physikalische Chemie (Leipzig) [*A publication*]

Z Phys Diaet Ther ... Zeitschrift fuer Physikalische und Diaetetische Therapie [*A publication*]

Z Physik ..... Zeitschrift fuer Physik [*A publication*]

Z Physiol Chem ... Zeitschrift fuer Physiologische Chemie [*A publication*]

Z Physiol Chem Hoppe-Seylers ... Zeitschrift fuer Physiologische Chemie. Hoppe-Seylers [*German Federal Republic*] [*A publication*]

Z Physiother ... Zeitschrift fuer Physiotherapie [*A publication*]

ZPI .... New York State Psychiatric Institute, Medical Library Center of New York, New York, NY [*OCLC symbol*]   (OCLC)

ZPID .... Zentralstelle fuer Psychologische Information und Dokumentation [*Center for Psychological Information and Documentation*] [*Trier, West Germany*] [*Database operator*] [*Information service*]   (EISS)

Z Pilzkd ...... Zeitschrift fuer Pilzkunde [*A publication*]

ZPJIAK .... Zbirnyk Prat Jewrejskiej Istorychno-Arkheologichnoj Komisji [*Kiev*] [*A publication*]

Z Plast Chir ... Zeitschrift fuer Plastische Chirurgie [*A publication*]

ZPM .... State University of New York, College at Purchase, Purchase, NY [*OCLC symbol*]   (OCLC)

ZPMPA .... Zeitschrift fuer Psychotherapie und Medizinische Psychologie [*A publication*]

ZPN .... Impedance Pneumograph [*Apollo*] [*NASA*]

ZPO .... Zeus Project Office [*Missiles*]

ZPO .... Zinc Peroxide [*Pharmacology*]

ZPO .... Zivilprozessordnung [*German Code of Civil Procedure*]   (DLA)

Z Polit .... Zeitschrift fuer Politik [*A publication*]

Z Politik ...... Zeitschrift fuer Politik [*A publication*]

Z Pol N F .... Zeitschrift fuer Politik. Neue Folge [*A publication*]

ZPP .... Zimbabwe Progressive Party   (PPW)

ZPP .... Zinc Protophorphyrin [*Biochemistry*]

ZPPA .... Zeitschrift fuer Wissenschaftliche Photographie, Photophysik, und Photochemie [*A publication*]

ZPPP .... Zanzibar and Pemba People's Party

ZPPR .... Zero Power Plutonium Reactor

ZPR .... Zero Power Reactor

Z Praeklin Geriatr ... Zeitschrift fuer Praeklinische Geriatrie [*A publication*]

Z Praeklin Klin Geriatr ... Zeitschrift fuer Praeklinische und Klinische Geriatrie [*A publication*]

Z Praeventivmed ... Zeitschrift fuer Praeventivmedizin [*A publication*]

Z Prakt Anaesth ... Zeitschrift fuer Praktische Anaesthesie, Wiederbelebung, und- Intensivtherapie [*A publication*]

Z Prakt Geol ... Zeitschrift fuer Praktische Geologie [*A publication*]

Zpravy....... Zpravy pro Cestinare [*A publication*]

Zpr Cesk Keram Sklarske Spol ... Zpravy Ceskoslovenske Keramicke a Sklarske Spolecnosti [*A publication*]

ZPRF .... Zero Power Reactor Facility [*AEC*]

Z Prikl Meh i Tehn Fiz ... Zurnal Prikladnoi Mehaniki i Tehniceskoi Fiziki [*A publication*]

ZprMK....... Zpravodaj Mistopisne Komise CSAV [*Ceskoslovenske Akademie Ved*] [*A publication*]

ZPRON....... Patrol [*Lighter-than-Air*] Squadron [*Navy symbol*]

ZPRSN .... Zurich Provisional Relative Sunspot Number [*NASA*]

ZPs .... Zeitschrift fuer Psychologie [*A publication*]

ZPS .... [*William H.*] Zimmer Nuclear Power Station [*Also, WZNPS*] (NRCH)

ZPSEA....... Zeszyty Naukowe Politechnika Slaska. Energetyka [*A publication*]

ZPSK .... Zeitschrift fuer Phonetik, Sprachwissenschaft, und Kommunikationsforschung [*A publication*]

ZPSMA...... Zeitschrift fuer Psychosomatische Medizin [*A publication*]

ZPSS.......... Z Polskich Studiow Slawistycznych [*A publication*]

ZPSS.......... Zion Probabilistic Safety Study [*Nuclear energy*] (NRCH)

Z Psych Hyg ... Zeitschrift fuer Psychische Hygiene [*A publication*]

Z Psychol ... Zeitschrift fuer Psychologie [*A publication*]

Z Psycholog ... Zeitschrift fuer Psychologie [*A publication*]

Z Psychol Physiol Sinnesorg ... Zeitschrift fuer Psychologie und Physiologie der Sinnesorgane [*East Germany*] [*A publication*]

Z Psychol Z Angew Psychol ... Zeitschrift fuer Psychologie mit Zeitschrift fuer Angewandte Psychologie [*A publication*]

Z Psychol Z Angew Psychol Charakterkd ... Zeitschrift fuer Psychologie mit Zeitschrift fuer Angewandte Psychologie und Charakterkunde [*A publication*]

Z Psychos M ... Zeitschrift fuer Psychosomatische Medizin und Psychoanalyse [*A publication*]

Z Psychosom Med ... Zeitschrift fuer Psychosomatische Medizin [*Later, Zeitschrift fuer Psychosomatische Medizin und Psychoanalyse*] [*A publication*]

Z Psychosom Med Psychoanal ... Zeitschrift fuer Psychosomatische Medizin und Psychoanalyse [*A publication*]

Z Psychother Med Psychol ... Zeitschrift fuer Psychotherapie und Medizinische Psychologie [*A publication*]

Z Psychot M ... Zeitschrift fuer Psychotherapie und Medizinische Psychologie [*A publication*]

ZPT............ Zero Power Test

ZPT............ Zoxazolamine Paralysis Time [*In experimental animals*]

ZPWCA ...... Zeszyty Naukowe Politechniki Wroclawskiej. Chemia [*A publication*]

ZQC........... Queensborough Community College of the City University of New York, Library, Bayside, NY [*OCLC symbol*] (OCLC)

ZQM .... State University of New York, College at Potsdam, Potsdam, NY [*OCLC symbol*] (OCLC)

ZQN........... Queenstown [*New Zealand*] [*Airport symbol*] (OAG)

ZQT .... Zero Quantum Transition [*Physics*]

ZR............. Freezing Rain [*Meteorology*] (FAAC)

ZR............. Rigid Airship [*Navy symbol*]

ZR............. Zadarska Revija [*A publication*]

ZR............. Zaire [*Two-letter standard code*] (CNC)

ZR............. Zentralrat [*Central Board*] [*German*]

ZR............. Zero Coupon Issue (Security) [*In bond listings of newspapers*]

ZR............. Zionist Record [*A publication*]

ZR............. Zionist Review [*A publication*]

Zr............. Zirconium [*Chemical element*]

ZR............. Zona Reticularis [*Of adrenal cortex*] [*Anatomy*]

ZR............. Zone Refined

ZR............. Zone of Responsibility

ZR............. Zoological Record [*Bio Sciences Information Service*] [*Philadelphia, PA*] [*Information service*] (EISS)

ZRC .... Zenith Radio Corporation

ZRDI .... Zionic Research and Development Institute (EA)

ZRE .... Zero Rate Error (MCD)

Z Rechtsmed ... Zeitschrift fuer Rechtsmedizin [*Journal of Legal Medicine*] [*A publication*]

Z Rechtspolit ... Zeitschrift fuer Rechtspolitik [*A publication*]

Z Reich Geschmackstoffe ... Zeitschrift fuer Reich- und Geschmackstoffe [*A publication*]

Z Rel Geistesges ... Zeitschrift fuer Religions- und Geistesgeschichte [*Koeln*] [*A publication*]

Z Rel Gg ..... Zeitschrift fuer Religions- und Geistesgeschichte [*A publication*]

Z Relig- u Geistesgesch ... Zeitschrift fuer Religions- und Geistesgeschichte [*A publication*]

Z Reproduktionstech ... Zeitschrift fuer Reproduktionstechnik [*A publication*]

ZRG........... Zeitschrift fuer Religions- und Geistesgeschichte [*A publication*]

ZRG........... Zeitschrift der Savigny-Stiftung fuer Rechtsgeschichte [*A publication*]

ZRGA .... Zeitschrift der Savigny-Stiftung fuer Rechtsgeschichte. Germanistische Abteilung [*A publication*]

ZRGG .... Zeitschrift fuer Religions- und Geistesgeschichte [*A publication*]

ZRG (GA) ... Zeitschrift der Savigny-Stiftung fuer Rechtsgeschichte. Germanistische Abteilung [*A publication*]

ZRGGB....... Zeitschrift fuer Religions- und Geistesgeschichte. Beihefte [*A publication*]

ZRGGS....... Zeitschrift fuer Religions- und Geistesgeschichte. Sonderhefte [*A publication*]

ZRH........... Zurich [*Switzerland*] [*Airport symbol*] (OAG)

Z Rheumaforsch ... Zeitschrift fuer Rheumaforschung [*A publication*]

Z Rheumatol ... Zeitschrift fuer Rheumatologie [*A publication*]

Z Rheumatol Suppl ... Zeitschrift fuer Rheumatologie. Supplement [*A publication*]

ZRHMB...... Zeitschrift fuer Rheumatologie [*A publication*]

ZRI............ Serui [*Indonesia*] [*Airport symbol*] (OAG)

ZRI............ Zeischrift fuer die Religioesen Interessen des Judenthums [*Berlin*] [*A publication*]

ZRIO......... Zimbabwe Rhodesian Information Office [*An association*] (EA)

ZRL........... Zagadnienia Rodzajow Literackich [*A publication*]

ZRM.......... Sarmi [*Indonesia*] [*Airport symbol*] (OAG)

ZRN .... Rigid Training Airship [*Navy symbol*]

ZRN .... Zurn Industries, Inc. [*NYSE symbol*]

ZRNI .... Zapiski Russkogo Naucnogo Instituta [*A publication*]

ZRO.......... Zero Corp. [*NYSE symbol*]

Z Roman Ph ... Zeitschrift fuer Romanische Philologie [*A publication*]

Zroschuvane Zemlerob ... Zroshuvane Zemlerobstvo [*A publication*]

ZRP .... Rigid Patrol Airship [*Navy symbol*]

ZRP .... Zeitschrift fuer Romanische Philologie [*A publication*]

ZRP .... Zero Radial Play

ZRPBA ...... Zbornik Radova. Poljoprivrednog Fakulteta. Universitet u Beogradu [*A publication*]

ZRPH......... Zeitschrift fuer Romanische Philologie [*A publication*]

ZRS .... Rigid Scouting Airship [*Navy symbol*]

ZRS .... Russell Sage College, Troy, NY [*OCLC symbol*] (OCLC)

ZRSAN .... Zbornik Radova. Srpske Akademije Nauke [*A publication*]

ZRT .... Zero Reaction Tool

ZRTLS........ Zwolse Reeks van Taal-en Letterkundige Studies [*A publication*]

ZRU .... Zeitschrift fuer den Russisch-Unterricht [*A publication*]

ZRV .... Zero-Relative Velocity

ZRZ .... Zbornik Radova. Svenciliste u Zagrebu [*A publication*]

Z/S .... Operational Display System

ZS............. SARSAT Centre [*France*] [*ICAO designator*] (FAAC)

ZS............. Union of South Africa [*Aircraft nationality and registration mark*] (FAAC)

ZS............. Zeitschrift fuer die Gesamte Staatswissenschaft [*A publication*]

ZS............. Zeitschrift fuer Semitistik und Verwandte Gebiete [*Leipzig*] [*A publication*]

ZS............. Zeitschrift fuer Slawistik [*Berlin*] [*A publication*]

ZS............. Zero Shift

ZS............. Zero and Subtract

ZS............. Zero Suppress

ZS............. Zoological Society [*British*]

ZS............. Zoosporangia [*Botany*]

ZSA .... San Salvador [*Bahamas*] [*Airport symbol*] (OAG)

ZSA .... Southern Tier Library System, Corning, NY [*OCLC symbol*] (OCLC)

ZSA .... Zero-Set Amplifier (MSA)

Z Saeugetierkd ... Zeitschrift fuer Saeugetierkunde [*A publication*]

ZSAK........ Zeitschrift fuer Schweizerische Archaeologie und Kunstgeschichte [*A publication*]

ZSAKG....... Zeitschrift fuer Schweizerische Archaeologie und Kunstgeschichte [*A publication*]

Zs Allg Erdk ... Zeitschrift fuer Allgemeine Erdkunde [*A publication*]

Zs Anorg Chem ... Zeitschrift fuer Anorganische Chemie [*A publication*]

ZSAT .... Zinc Sulfide Atmospheric Tracer

ZSav.......... Zeitschrift der Savigny-Stiftung fuer Rechtsgeschichte. Romanistische Abteilung [*A publication*]

Z Savigny-Stift Rechtsgesch Kanon Abt ... Zeitschrift der Savigny-Stiftung fuer Rechts-Kanonistische Abteilung [*A publication*]

ZSavRG...... Zeitschrift der Savigny-Stiftung fuer Rechtsgeschichte Romanistische Abteilung [*Weimar*] [*A publication*]

ZSB .... Zinc Storage Battery

Zs Berg- Huetten- u Salinen-Wesen ... Zeitschrift fuer das Berg-, Huetten-, und Salinenwesen [*A publication*]

ZSC .... Stauffer Chemical Co., Information Services, Dobbs Ferry, NY [*OCLC symbol*] (OCLC)

ZSC .... Zero Subcarrier Chromaticity

ZSC .... Zinc Silicate Coat

ZSC .... Zose [*Republic of China*] [*Geomagnetic observatory code*]

ZSC .... Zose [*Shanghai Seh-Shan*] [*Republic of China*] [*Seismograph station code, US Geological Survey*] (SEIS)

Zschft f Ausl u Intl Privatr ... Zeitschrift fuer Auslaendisches und Internationales Privatrecht [*Berlin and Tubingen, Germany*] (DLA)

Zschft Luft- u Weltr-Recht ... Zeitschrift fuer Luftrecht- und Weltraumrechtsfragen (DLA)

Zschft Rechtsvergl ... Zeitschrift fuer Rechtsvergleichung [*Vienna, Austria*] (DLA)

Zschft Savigny-Germ ... Zeitschrift der Savigny-Stiftung fuer Rechtsgeschichte. Germanistische Abteilung [*A publication*]

Zschft Savigny-Kanon ... Zeitschrift der Savigny-Stiftung fuer Rechtsgeschichte. Kanonistische Abteilung [*A publication*]

Zschft Savigny-Rom ... Zeitschrift der Savigny-Stiftung fuer Rechtsgeschichte. Romanistische Abteilung

Zschft f Vergl Rechtswissenschaft ... Zeitschrift fuer Vergleichende Rechtswissenschaft [*A publication*]

Zschift f Ausl Offentl Recht ... Zeitschrift fuer Auslaendisches Oeffentliches Recht und Voelkerrecht [*A publication*]

Z Schles Holst Gesch ... Zeitschrift der Gesellschaft fuer Schleswig-Holsteinische Geschichte (Kiel, West Germany) [*A publication*]

Z Schw AKg ... Zeitschrift fuer Schweizerische Archaeologie und Kunstgeschichte [*A publication*]

Z Schweisstech ... Zeitschrift fuer Schweisstechnik [*A publication*]

Z Schweiz Archaeol Kunstgesch ... Zeitschrift fuer Schweizerische Archaeologie und Kunstgeschichte [*A publication*]

Z Schweiz Arch Kunstgesch ... Zeitschrift fuer Schweizerische Archaeologie und Kunstgeschichte [*A publication*]

Z f Schweiz Recht ... Zeitschrift fuer Schweizerisches Recht/Revue de Droit Suisse/Revista di Diritto Svizzero [*Basel, Switzerland*] (DLA)

ZSchwG ..... Zeitschrift fuer Schweizerische Geschichte [*A publication*]

ZSD .... Zebra Stripe Display

ZSD .... Zinc Sulfide Detector

ZSDG .... Zeitschrift fuer Sudetendeutsche Geschichte [*A publication*]

ZSDS .... Zinc Sulfide Detection System

ZSE .... Seattle, WA [*Location identifier*] [*FAA*] (FAAL)

ZSEM .... Zeitschrift fuer Semitistik und Verwandte Gebiete [*Leipzig*] [*A publication*]

ZSEV .... Z-Seven Fund, Inc. [*NASDAQ symbol*] (NQ)

ZSF .... Zeitschrift fuer Sozialforschung [*A publication*]

ZSG .... Zeitschrift fuer Schweizerische Geschichte [*A publication*]

ZSG .... Zero-Speed Generator

Zs Ges Naturw ... Zeitschrift fuer die Gesamten Naturwissenschaften [*A publication*]

Zs Gletscherk ... Zeitschrift fuer Gletscherkunde [*A publication*]

ZSI .... Z Solar Inertial (MCD)

ZSI .... Zero Size Image

Z Sinnephysiol ... Zeitschrift fuer Sinnephysiologie [*East Germany*] [*A publication*]

ZSISA .... Zeszyty Naukowe Politechniki Slaskiej. Inzynieria Sanitarna [*A publication*]

ZSJ .... St. John's University Library, Jamaica, NY [*OCLC symbol*] (OCLC)

ZSJ .... Zangri, S. J., Chicago IL [*STAC*]

ZSK .... Ze Skarbca Kultury [*A publication*]

ZSKG .... Zeitschrift fuer Schweizerische Kirchengeschichte [*A publication*]

ZSKHA .... Zeitschrift fuer Kinderheilkunde. Referate [*A publication*]

Zs Kryst ..... Zeitschrift fuer Krystallographie und Mineralogie [*A publication*]

ZSL .... Zeitschrift fuer Slawistik [*A publication*]

ZSL .... ZEROSLOTLAN [*Avatar Technologies, Inc.*] [*In Alliance ZSL, a PC network*]

ZSL .... Zjednoczone Stronnictwo Ludowe [*United Peasants' Party*] [*Poland*] (PPW)

Z Slav Philol ... Zeitschrift fuer Slavische Philologie [*A publication*]

Z Slawistik ... Zeitschrift fuer Slawistik [*A publication*]

ZSLPh .... Zeitschrift fuer Slavische Philologie [*A publication*]

Zs Miner (Leonhard) ... Zeitschrift fuer Mineralogie (Leonhard) [*A publication*]

ZSN .... Zoological Station of Naples

ZSN .... Zurich Sunspot Number [*Astrophysics*]

ZSNUA .... Zeitschrift fuer Neurologie [*A publication*]

ZSOB .... Zinc-Silver-Oxide Battery (RDA)

Z Soz .... Zeitschrift fuer Sozialpsychologie [*A publication*]

Z Sozialpsy ... Zeitschrift fuer Sozialpsychologie [*A publication*]

Z Sozialreform ... Zeitschrift fuer Sozialreform [*German Federal Republic*] [*A publication*]

Z Soziol ..... Zeitschrift fuer Soziologie [*A publication*]

Z Soziolog ... Zeitschrift fuer Soziologie [*A publication*]

Z Soz Psychol ... Zeitschrift fuer Sozialpsychologie [*A publication*]

ZSP .... Zeitschrift fuer Slavische Philologie [*A publication*]

ZSPG .... Zero-Speed Pulse Generator

Z Spiritusind ... Zeitschrift fuer Spiritusindustrie [*A publication*]

Zs Prak G ... Zeitschrift fuer Praktische Geologie [*A publication*]

ZS-RDS ...... Zung Self-Rating Depression Scale [*Psychology*]

ZSRK .... Zeitschrift der Savigny-Stiftung fuer Rechtsgeschichte. Kanonist [*A publication*]

ZSRS .... Zung Self-Rating Scale [*For depression*]

ZSS .... Sassandra [*Ivory Coast*] [*Airport symbol*] (OAG)

ZSS .... Zen Studies Society (EA)

ZSS .... Zinc Sulfide System

ZSSGerm ... Zeitschrift der Savigny-Stiftung fuer Rechtsgeschichte. Germanistische Abteilung [*A publication*]

ZSSKanon ... Zeitschrift der Savigny-Stiftung fuer Rechtsgeschichte. Kanonistische Abteilung [*Weimar*] [*A publication*]

ZSSRGGerm ... Zeitschrift der Savigny-Stiftung fuer Rechtsgeschichte. Germanistische Abteilung [*A publication*]

ZSSRGKan ... Zeitschrift der Savigny-Stiftung fuer Rechtsgeschichte. Kanonistische Abteilung [*A publication*]

ZSSRGRom ... Zeitschrift der Savigny-Stiftung fuer Rechtsgeschichte. Romanistische Abteilung [*A publication*]

ZSSRom ..... Zeitschrift der Savigny-Stiftung fuer Rechtsgeschichte. Romanistische Abteilung [*A publication*]

ZST .... Bratislava [*Czechoslovakia*] [*Seismograph station code, US Geological Survey*] (SEIS)

ZST .... Stewart [*Canada*] [*Airport symbol*] (OAG)

ZST .... Zeitschrift fuer Systematische Theologie [*A publication*]

ZST .... Zentralabteilung Strahlenschutz [*Central Department for Radiation Protection*] [*West Germany*]

ZST .... Zinc Sulfide Tracer

ZST .... Zone Standard Time

ZSTh .... Zeitschrift fuer Systematische Theologie [*Guetersloh/Berlin*] [*A publication*]

ZSU .... San Juan, PR [*Location identifier*] [*FAA*] (FAAL)

Zs Vulkan ... Zeitschrift fuer Vulkanologie [*A publication*]

ZSW .... Prince Rupert [*Canada*] [*Airport symbol*] [*Obsolete*] (OAG)

ZSW .... Zeitschrift fuer Sozialwissenschaft [*A publication*]

ZSysTh .... Zeitschrift fuer Systematische Theologie [*Guetersloh/Berlin*] [*A publication*]

ZT .... Training Aircraft [*Lighter-than-Air*] [*Navy symbol*] (MUGU)

ZT .... Union of South Africa [*Aircraft nationality and registration mark*] (FAAC)

ZT .... Zeitschrift fuer Tierpsychologie [*A publication*]

ZT .... Zipper Tubing

ZT .... Zone Time [*Navigation*]

ZTA .... Zeta Tau Alpha [*Sorority*]

ZTAT .... Zero Turn-Around Time [*Microcomputer*] [*Hitachi Ltd.*]

ZTB .... Tete A La Baleine [*Canada*] [*Airport symbol*] (OAG)

Ztbl .... Zentralblatt [*A publication*]

ZTC .... Zero-Temperature Coefficient (MSA)

Z Tech Biol ... Zeitschrift fuer Technische Biologie [*A publication*]

Z Tech Phys ... Zeitschrift fuer Technische Physik [*A publication*]

Z Tech Ueberwach ... Zeitschrift fuer die Technische Ueberwachung [*A publication*]

Z Tech Univ (Berlin) ... Zeitschrift der Technischen Universitaet (Berlin) [*A publication*]

Z Tech Univ (Hannover) ... Zeitschrift der Technischen Universitaet (Hannover) [*German Federal Republic*] [*A publication*]

ZTGAK .... Zeitschrift fuer Thueringische Geschichte und Altertumskunde [*A publication*]

Ztg Gesunde ... Zeitung fuer Gesunde [*A publication*]

ZTH .... Zakinthos [*Greece*] [*Airport symbol*] (OAG)

Z Theol Kir ... Zeitschrift fuer Theologie und Kirche [*A publication*]

Z Th K .... Zeitschrift fuer Theologie und Kirche [*A publication*]

Z Th Kirche ... Zeitschrift fuer Theologie und Kirche [*A publication*]

Z Tierernaehr Futtermittelkd ... Zeitschrift fuer Tierernaehrung und Futtermittelkunde [*A publication*]

Z Tierphysiol ... Zeitschrift fuer Tierphysiologie, Tierernaehrung, und Futtermittelkunde [*A publication*]

Z Tierphysiol Tierernaehr Futtermittelk ... Zeitschrift fuer Tierphysiologie, Tierernaehrung, und Futtermittelkunde [*A publication*]

Z Tierphysiol Tiernaehr Futtermittelkd ... Zeitschrift fuer Tierphysiologie, Tierernaehrung, und Futtermittelkunde [*A publication*]

Z Tierpsychol ... Zeitschrift fuer Tierpsychologie [*A publication*]

Z Tierpsychol Beih ... Zeitschrift fuer Tierpsychologie. Beiheft [*A publication*]

Z Tierz Zuechtungsbiol ... Zeitschrift fuer Tierzuechtung und Zuechtungsbiologie [*A publication*]

ZTJWG .... Zeus Target Joint Working Group [*Missiles*] (AAG)

ZTK .... Zeitschrift fuer Theologie und Kirche [*A publication*]

ZTL .... Atlanta, GA [*Location identifier*] [*FAA*] (FAAL)

ZTL .... Touro Law Library, New York, NY [*OCLC symbol*] (OCLC)

ZTM .... Mid-York Library System, Utica, NY [*OCLC symbol*] (OCLC)

ZTN .... Zinc Tannate of Naloxone [*Opiate antagonist*]

ZTO .... Zero Time Outage (NRCH)

ZTO .... Zone Transportation Officer [*Military*]

ZTOS .... Zydowskie Towarzystwo Ochrony Sierot [*A publication*]

ZTOS .... Zydowskie Towarzystwo Opieki Spolecznej [*A publication*]

ZTP .... Zero-Temperature Plasma

ZTP .... Zydowskie Towarzystwo Przeciwgruzliczego [*A publication*]

ZTPHA .... Zeitschrift fuer Technische Physik [*A publication*]

ZTPSA .... Zeitschrift fuer Psychologie [*A publication*]

Ztrbl .... Zentralblatt [*A publication*]

Z Tropenmed Parasitol ... Zeitschrift fuer Tropenmedizin und Parasitologie [*A publication*]

ZTRX .... Zytrex Corp. [*NASDAQ symbol*] (NQ)

Ztsch f Angew Psychol ... Zeitschrift fuer Angewandte Psychologie und Psychologische Forschung [*A publication*]

Ztsch f Angew Psychol Sammelforsch ... Zeitschrift fuer Angewandte Psychologie und Psychologische Sammelforschung [*A publication*]

Ztsch Gesch Erzieh u Unterr ... Zeitschrift fuer Geschichte der Erziehung und des Unterrichts [*A publication*]

Ztsch Mikr Fleischschau ... Zeitschrift fuer Mikroskopische Fleischschau und Populaere Mikroskopie [*A publication*]

Ztsch Militaeraerzte (Tokyo) ... Zeitschrift fuer Militaeraerzte (Tokyo) [*A publication*]

ZTSCHR ..... Zeitschrift [*Periodical*] [*German*]

Ztschr Aerztli Fortbild ... Zeitschrift fuer Aerztliche Fortbildung [*A publication*]

Ztschr Augenh ... Zeitschrift fuer Augenheilkunde [*A publication*]

Ztschr Fleisch u Milchhyg ... Zeitschrift fuer Fleisch- und Milchhygiene [*A publication*]

Ztschr Genossensch Tierversich ... Zeitschrift fuer Genossenschaftlichen Tierversicherung [*A publication*]

Ztschr Gewerbe Hyg ... Zeitschrift fuer Gewerbe Hygiene [*A publication*]

Ztschr Hyg ... Zeitschrift fuer Hygiene [*A publication*]

Ztschr Hyg u Infektionskr ... Zeitschrift fuer Hygiene und Infektionskrankheiten [*A publication*]

Ztschr Immunitaetsforsch u Exper Therap ... Zeitschrift fuer Immunitaetsforschung und Experimentelle Therapie [*A publication*]

Ztschr Infektionskr Haustiere ... Zeitschrift fuer Infektionskrankheiten, Parasitaere Krankheiten, und Hygiene der Haustiere [*A publication*]

Ztschr Klin Med (Berlin) ... Zeitschrift fuer Klinische Medizin (Berlin) [*A publication*]

Ztschr Krebsforsch ... Zeitschrift fuer Krebsforschung [*A publication*]

Ztschr Morphol u Oekol Tiere ... Zeitschrift fuer Morphologie und Oekologie der Tiere [*A publication*]

Ztschr Ophth ... Zeitschrift fuer die Ophthalmologie [*A publication*]

Ztschr Parasitenk (Berlin) ... Zeitschrift fuer Parasitenkunde (Berlin) [*A publication*]

Ztschr Parasitenk (Jena) ... Zeitschrift fuer Parasitenkunde (Jena) [*A publication*]

Ztschr Physiol Chem ... Zeitschrift fuer Physiologische Chemie [*A publication*]

Ztschr Tokio Med Gesellsch ... Zeitschrift der Tokio Medicinischen Gesellschaft [*A publication*]

Ztschr Vergleich Physiol ... Zeitschrift fuer Vergleichende Physiologie [*A publication*]

Ztschr Veterinaerk ... Zeitschrift fuer Veterinaerkunde [*A publication*]

Ztschr Wissensch Mikr ... Zeitschrift fuer Wissenschaftliche Mikroskopie [*A publication*]

Ztschr Wissensch Zool ... Zeitschrift fuer Wissenschaftliche Zoologie [*A publication*]

Z Tuberk .... Zeitschrift fuer Tuberkulose [*A publication*]

Z Tuberkulose Erkr Thoraxogane ... Zeitschrift fuer Tuberkulose und Erkrankungen der Thoraxorgane [*A publication*]

ZTUWA ...... Zeitschrift Technische Ueberwachung [*A publication*]

ZU .... Union of South Africa [*Aircraft nationality and registration mark*] (FAAC)

ZU .... Utility Aircraft [*Lighter-than-Air*] [*Navy symbol*] (MUGU)

ZU .... Zeitlich Untauglich [*Temporarily Unfit*] [*German military - World War II*]

ZUA .... Agana, GU [*Location identifier*] [*FAA*] (FAAL)

ZUA .... Central New York Union List of Serials, Syracuse, NY [*OCLC symbol*] (OCLC)

ZUB .... Allied Chemical Corp., Library, Solvay, NY [*OCLC symbol*] (OCLC)

ZuB .... Zuercher Bibelkommentare [*A publication*]

ZUC .... American Foundation for Management Research, Library, Hamilton, NY [*OCLC symbol*] (OCLC)

Zucker Beih ... Zucker Beihefte [*A publication*]

Zucker Frucht Gemueseverwert ... Zucker- Frucht- und Gemueseverwertung [*A publication*]

Zucker Suesswaren Wirtsch ... Zucker- und Suesswaren Wirtschaft [*A publication*]

Zuck u SuesswarWirt ... Zucker- und Suesswaren Wirtschaft [*A publication*]

ZUD .... Bristol Laboratories, Library, Syracuse, NY [*OCLC symbol*] (OCLC)

ZUE .... Carrier Corp., Library, Syracuse, NY [*OCLC symbol*] (OCLC)

ZUE .... Zuni Energy [*Vancouver Stock Exchange symbol*]

ZUG .... Community-General Hospital, Staff Library, Syracuse, NY [*OCLC symbol*] (OCLC)

ZUG .... Zugdidi [*USSR*] [*Seismograph station code, US Geological Survey*] [*Closed*] (SEIS)

ZugerNjb .... Zuger Neujahrsblatt [*A publication*]

ZUH .... Education Opportunity Center of the State University of New York, Syracuse, NY [*OCLC symbol*] (OCLC)

ZUI .... General Electric Co., Electronics Park Library, Syracuse, NY [*OCLC symbol*] (OCLC)

ZUJ .... General Electric Co., Information Resources Library, Utica, NY [*OCLC symbol*] (OCLC)

ZUJCA .... Zeszyty Naukowe Uniwersytetu Jagiellonskiego. Prace Chemiczne [*A publication*]

ZUK .... United States Veterans Administration, Hospital Library, Syracuse, NY [*OCLC symbol*] (OCLC)

ZUL .... Agway, Inc., Library, Syracuse, NY [*OCLC symbol*] (OCLC)

zul .... Zulu [*MARC language code*] [*Library of Congress*] (LCCP)

ZUL .... Zurich-Lageren [*Switzerland*] [*Seismograph station code, US Geological Survey*] (SEIS)

ZUM .... Churchill Falls [*Canada*] [*Airport symbol*] (OAG)

ZUM .... Supreme Court, Fifth Judicial District, Law Library, Utica, NY [*OCLC symbol*] (OCLC)

ZUM .... Zeitschrift fuer Urheber und Medienrecht [*NOMOS Datapool*] [*Database*]

Z Umweltpolit ... Zeitschrift fuer Umweltpolitik [*A publication*]

ZUN .... Saint Joseph's Hospital, Health Center Library, Syracuse, NY [*OCLC symbol*] (OCLC)

zun .... Zuni [*MARC language code*] [*Library of Congress*] (LCCP)

ZUN .... Zuni Pueblo, NM [*Location identifier*] [*FAA*] (FAAL)

ZUNBA .... Zhurnal Ushnykh Nosovykh i Gorlovykh Boleznei [*A publication*]

Z Unfallmed Berufskr ... Zeitschrift fuer Unfallmedizin und Berufskrankheiten [*A publication*]

Z Unter Lebensm ... Zeitschrift fuer Untersuchung der Lebensmittel [*A publication*]

Z Unters Nahr-u Genussmittel ... Zeitschrift fuer Untersuchung der Nahrungs- und Genussmittel [*A publication*]

ZUO .... Utica Mutual Insurance Co., Library, New Hartford, NY [*OCLC symbol*] (OCLC)

ZUP .... Utica/Marcy Psychiatric Center, Utica Campus Library, Utica, NY [*OCLC symbol*] (OCLC)

ZUP .... Zone a Urbaniser en Priorite [*Priority Urbanization Zone*] [*French*]

ZUPO .... Zimbabwe United People's Organization (PPW)

ZUQ .... Saint Luke's Memorial Hospital Center, Medical Library, Utica, NY [*OCLC symbol*] (OCLC)

ZUR .... Hancock Airbase Library, Hancock Field, NY [*OCLC symbol*] (OCLC)

ZUR .... Zurich [*Switzerland*] [*Seismograph station code, US Geological Survey*] (SEIS)

Zur Didak Phys Chem ... Zur Didaktik der Physik und Chemie [*A publication*]

ZURF .... Zeus Up-Range Facility [*Missiles*] (AAG)

Z Urol .... Zeitschrift fuer Urologie [*German Democratic Republic*] [*A publication*]

Z Urol Nephrol ... Zeitschrift fuer Urologie und Nephrologie [*A publication*]

ZUS .... Utica/Marcy Psychiatric Center, Marcy Campus Library, Utica, NY [*OCLC symbol*] (OCLC)

ZUS .... Zusammen [*Together*] [*Music*]

ZUT .... Maria Regina College, Library, Syracuse, NY [*OCLC symbol*] (OCLC)

ZUTRON ..... Airship Utility Squadron [*Navy symbol*]

ZUU .... Masonic Medical Research Laboratory, Library, Utica, NY [*OCLC symbol*] (OCLC)

ZUW .... Munson-Williams-Proctor Institute, Library, Utica, NY [*OCLC symbol*] (OCLC)

ZUX .... Mohawk Valley Learning Resource Center, Utica Library, Utica, NY [*OCLC symbol*] (OCLC)

ZUY .... Special Metals Corp., Library, New Hartford, NY [*OCLC symbol*] (OCLC)

ZUZ .... Crouse-Irving Hospital, School of Nursing, Library, Syracuse, NY [*OCLC symbol*] (OCLC)

ZUZZ .... Zug und Zerschneidezuender [*Pull-and-Cut Igniter*] [*German military - World War II*]

Z & V .... Zeiten und Voelker [*A publication*]

ZV .... Zeitschrift fuer Volkskunde [*A publication*]

ZV .... Zu Verfuegung [*At Disposal*] [*Business and trade*] [*German*]

Zv .... Zvezda [*A publication*]

ZVA .... Jervis Public Library, Rome, NY [*OCLC symbol*] (OCLC)

ZVA .... Miandrivazo [*Madagascar*] [*Airport symbol*] (OAG)

Zvaracsky Sb ... Zvaracsky Sbornik [*A publication*]

ZVB .... Syracuse Research Corp., Library, Syracuse, NY [*OCLC symbol*] (OCLC)

ZVC .... Utica Public Library, Utica, NY [*OCLC symbol*] (OCLC)

ZVD .... Supreme Court of New York, Library, Syracuse, NY [*OCLC symbol*] (OCLC)

ZVEI .... Zentralverband der Electro-technischen Industrie [*Central Union of the Electrical-Technical Industry*] [*West Germany*]

Z Verbungsl ... Zeitschrift fuer Vererbungslehre [*A publication*]

Z Ver Dtsch Ing ... Zeitschrift des Vereines Deutscher Ingenieure [*A publication*]

Z Ver Dtsch Zucker Ind ... Zeitschrift des Vereines der Deutschen Zucker-Industrie [*A publication*]

Z Ver Dtsch Zucker Ind Allg Teil ... Zeitschrift des Vereines der Deutschen Zucker-Industrie. Allgemeiner Teil [*A publication*]

Z Ver Dtsch Zucker Ind Tech Teil ... Zeitschrift des Vereines der Deutschen Zucker-Industrie. Technischer Teil [*A publication*]

Z Vererbungsl ... Zeitschrift fuer Vererbungslehre [*A publication*]

Z Vergl Physiol ... Zeitschrift fuer Vergleichende Physiologie [*A publication*]

Z Ver Hessische Gesch ... Zeitschrift des Vereins fuer Hessische Geschichte und Landeskunde [*A publication*]

Z Verkehrssicherheit ... Zeitschrift fuer Verkehrssicherheit [*A publication*]

Z Vermessungswes ... Zeitschrift fuer Vermessungswesen [*A publication*]

Zverolek Obz ... Zverolekarsky Obzor [*A publication*]

Z Vers Kund ... Zeitschrift fuer Versuchstierkunde [*A publication*]

Z Versuchstierkd ... Zeitschrift fuer Versuchstierkunde [*A publication*]

ZVGAK .... Zeitschrift fuer Vaterlaendische Geschichte und Altertumskunde [*A publication*]

Z Vgl Physiol ... Zeitschrift fuer Vergleichende Physiologie [*A publication*]

ZVGMS ...... Zeitschrift des Deutschen Vereins fuer die Geschichte Maehrens und Schlesiens [*A publication*]

ZVHFA .... Zeitschrift fuer Vitamin-, Hormon-, und Fermentforschung [*A publication*]

ZVHG .... Zeitschrift des Vereins fuer Hamburgische Geschichte [*A publication*]

ZVHGLK ..... Zeitschrift des Vereins fuer Hessische Geschichte und Landeskunde [*A publication*]

Z VitamForsch ... Zeitschrift fuer Vitaminforschung [*A publication*]

Z Vitam-Horm-Fermentforsch ... Zeitschrift fuer Vitamin-, Hormon-, und Fermentforschung [*A publication*]
Z Vitam-Horm- u Fermentforsch ... Zeitschrift fuer Vitamin-, Hormon-, und Fermentforschung [*A publication*]
Z Vitaminforsch ... Zeitschrift fuer Vitaminforschung [*A publication*]
ZVK .... Zeitschrift fuer Volkskunde [*A publication*]
ZVKOA .... Zhurnal Vsesoyuznogo Khimicheskogo Obshchestva Imeni D. I. Mendeleeva [*A publication*]
ZVKPS .... Zeitschrift des Vereins fuer Kirchengeschichte in der Provinz Sachsen und Anhalt [*A publication*]
ZVL .... Zeitschrift fuer Vergleichende Literaturgeschichte [*A publication*]
ZVM .... Mohawk Valley Community College, Utica, NY [*OCLC symbol*] (OCLC)
ZVNDA .... Zhurnal Vysshei Nervnoi Deyatel'nosti Imeni I. P. Pavlova [*A publication*]
ZVO .... Zapiski Vostochnovo Otdelenia [*A publication*]
Z Volksernaehr ... Zeitschrift fuer Volksernaehrung [*A publication*]
Z Volkskund ... Zeitschrift fuer Volkskunde [*A publication*]
ZVORAO .... Zapiski Vostochnovo Otdeleniia Imperatorskovo Ruskavo Arkheologicheskavo Obshchestva [*A publication*]
ZVR .... Zener Voltage Regulator
ZVRD .... Zener Voltage Regulator Diode
ZVRW .... Zeitschrift fuer Vergleichende Rechtswissenschaft [*A publication*]
ZVS .... Zeitschrift fuer Vergleichende Sprachforschung [*A publication*]
ZVS .... Zero Voltage Switch
ZVTGA ...... Zeitschrift des Vereins fuer Thueringische Geschichte und Altertumskunde [*A publication*]
ZVTGAK ..... Zeitschrift des Vereins fuer Thueringische Geschichte und Altertumskunde [*A publication*]
ZVV .... Zeitschrift des Vereins fuer Volkskunde [*A publication*]
ZvV .... Zvezda Vostoka [*A publication*]
Z Vycisl Mat i Mat Fiz ... Zurnal Vycislitel'noi Matematiki i Matematiceskoi Fiziki [*A publication*]
ZVZ .... Zavitx Technology, Inc. [*Toronto Stock Exchange symbol*]
ZW .... Air Wisconsin [*Airline code*]
ZW .... Zeitwende Monatsschrift [*A publication*]
ZW .... Zero Wear
Zw .... Zwischensatz [*Interpolation*] [*Music*]
ZWA .... Andapa [*Madagascar*] [*Airport symbol*] (OAG)
Z Wahrsch V ... Zeitschrift fuer Wahrscheinlichkeitstheorie und Verwandte Gebiete [*A publication*]
Z Wasser u Abwasserforsch ... Zeitschrift fuer Wasser und Abwasserforschung [*A publication*]
Z Wasser Abwasser Forsch ... Zeitschrift fuer Wasser- und Abwasserforschung [*A publication*]
Z Wasserrecht ... Zeitschrift fuer Wasserrecht [*A publication*]
ZWC .... Zero Word Count
ZWC .... Zone Wind Computer
Z Weltforstwirtsch ... Zeitschrift fuer Weltforstwirtschaft [*A publication*]
Z Werkstofftech ... Zeitschrift fuer Werkstofftechnik [*A publication*]
Z Werkstofftech J Mater Technol ... Zeitschrift fuer Werkstofftechnik/Journal of Materials Technology [*A publication*]
ZWG .... Sudhoffs Archiv. Zeitschrift fuer Wissenschaftsgeschichte [*A publication*]
Z Wien Ent Ges ... Zeitschrift der Wiener Entomologischen Gesellschaft [*A publication*]
Z Wien Entomol Ges ... Zeitschrift der Wiener Entomologischen Gesellschaft [*A publication*]
Zwierzeta Lab ... Zwierzeta Laboratoryjne [*A publication*]
Z Wirtschaftsgeographie ... Zeitschrift fuer Wirtschaftsgeographie [*West Germany*] [*A publication*]
Z Wirtschaftsgruppe Zuckerind ... Zeitschrift der Wirtschaftsgruppe Zuckerindustrie [*A publication*]
Z Wirtschaftsgruppe Zuckerind Allg Teil ... Zeitschrift der Wirtschaftsgruppe Zuckerindustrie. Allgemeiner Teil [*A publication*]
Z Wirtschaftsgruppe Zuckerind Tech Teil ... Zeitschrift der Wirtschaftsgruppe Zuckerindustrie. Technischer Teil [*A publication*]
Z Wirtschaftspol ... Zeitschrift fuer Wirtschaftspolitik [*A publication*]
Z Wirtsch Fertigung ... Zeitschrift fuer Wirtschaftliche Fertigung [*A publication*]
Z Wirtsch -u Soz -Wiss ... Zeitschrift fuer Wirtschafts- und Sozialwissenschaften [*A publication*]
Z Wiss Biol Abt A ... Zeitschrift fuer Wissenschaftliche Biologie. Abteilung A [*West Germany*] [*A publication*]
Z Wiss InsektBiol ... Zeitschrift fuer Wissenschaftliche Insektenbiologie [*A publication*]
Z Wiss Insektenbiol ... Zeitschrift fuer Wissenschaftliche Insektenbiologie [*West Germany*] [*A publication*]
Z Wiss Mikrosk ... Zeitschrift fuer Wissenschaftliche Mikroskopie und fuer Mikroskopische Technik [*A publication*]
Z Wiss Mikrosk Mikrosk Tech ... Zeitschrift fuer Wissenschaftliche Mikroskopie und Mikroskopische Technik [*A publication*]
Z Wiss Photogr Photophys Photchem ... Zeitschrift fuer Wissenschaftliche Photographie, Photophysik, und Photochemie [*A publication*]

Z Wiss Photogr Photophys Photochem ... Zeitschrift fuer Wissenschaftliche Photographie, Photophysik, und Photochemie [*East Germany*] [*A publication*]
Z Wiss Zool ... Zeitschrift fuer Wissenschaftliche Zoologie [*A publication*]
Z Wiss Zool Abt A ... Zeitschrift fuer Wissenschaftliche Zoologie. Abteilung A [*A publication*]
ZWL .... Wollaston Lake [*Canada*] [*Airport symbol*] (OAG)
ZWL .... Zeitschrift fuer Wuerttembergische Landesgeschichte [*A publication*]
ZWL .... Zero Wavelength
ZWLG .... Zeitschrift fuer Wuerttembergische Landesgeschichte [*A publication*]
ZWMIA .... Zeitschrift fuer Wissenschaftliche Mikroskopie und fuer Mikroskopische Technik [*A publication*]
ZWO .... Zuiver Wentenschappelijk Orderzock [*Netherlands*]
ZWOK .... Zirconium-Water Oxidation Kinetics (NRCH)
ZWP .... Zone Wind Plotter
ZWPGV ..... Zeitschrift des Westpreussischen Geschichtsvereins [*A publication*]
ZWR .... ZWR. Zahnaerztliche Welt, Zahnaerztliche Rundschau, Zahnaerztliche Reform [*A publication*]
ZWS .... Zentralwohlfahrtsstelle der Juden in Deutschland [*A publication*] (BJA)
ZWSt .... Zentralwohlfahrtsstelle der Juden in Deutschland [*A publication*] (BJA)
ZWT .... Zeitschrift fuer Wissenschaftliche Theologie [*A publication*]
ZWTh .... Zeitschrift fuer Wissenschaftliche Theologie [*A publication*]
ZWU .... Union College, Schenectady, NY [*OCLC symbol*] (OCLC)
ZWV .... Zero Wave Velocity
ZXC .... City College of New York, New York, NY [*OCLC symbol*] (OCLC)
ZXCFAR ..... Zero Crossing Constant False Alarm Rate (MSA)
ZXMP .... Zero Transmission Power
ZXX .... Exxon Corp., Information Center, Technical Service Coordinator, New York, NY [*OCLC symbol*] (OCLC)
ZY .... Aerodrome Security Services [*ICAO designator*] (FAAC)
ZY .... Zayre Corp. [*NYSE symbol*]
Zy .... Zygon [*A publication*]
ZYB .... Zionist Year Book [*A publication*] (BJA)
Zycie Weteryn ... Zycie Weterynaryjne [*A publication*]
ZYL .... Sylhet [*Bangladesh*] [*Airport symbol*] (OAG)
Zymol Chem Colloidi ... Zymologica e Chemica dei Colloidi [*A publication*]
ZYP .... Zefkrome Yarn Program [*Dow Chemical Co.*]
ZYT .... Zytec Computers [*Vancouver Stock Exchange symbol*]
ZYU .... New York University, New York, NY [*OCLC symbol*] (OCLC)
ZYWE .... Zeszyty Wroclawskie [*A publication*]
ZZ .... Datum Position [*Arbitrary*] [*Navy*] [*British*]
ZZ .... Lighter-than-Air [*Aircraft*] [*Navy symbol*] (MUGU)
Z-Z .... Roll Axis [*Aerospace*] (AAG)
ZZ .... Zeitschrift fuer die Wissenschaft des Judentums [*Leopold Zunz*] [*A publication*] (BJA)
ZZ .... Zig-Zag
ZZ .... Zinziber [*Ginger*] [*Pharmacology*] (ROG)
ZZ .... Zu [*or Zur*] Zeit [*At This Time*] [*German*]
ZZ .... Zugzuender [*Pull Igniter*] [*German military - World War II*]
ZZA .... Zamak Zinc Alloy
ZZACA .... Zeitschrift fuer Zellforschung und Mikroskopische Anatomie [*A publication*]
ZZC .... Zero-Zero Condition
ZZD .... Zig-Zag Diagram
Z Zellforsch Mikrosk Anat ... Zeitschrift fuer Zellforschung und Mikroskopische Anatomie [*A publication*]
Z Zellforsch Mikrosk Anat Abt Histochem ... Zeitschrift fuer Zellforschung und Mikroskopische Anatomie. Abteilung Histochemie [*A publication*]
Z Zool Syst Evolutionsforsch ... Zeitschrift fuer Zoologische Systematik und Evolutionsforschung [*A publication*]
ZZR .... Zig-Zag Rectifier
ZZR .... Zigzag Riveting (MSA)
ZZT .... Zu Zu [*Tennessee*] [*Seismograph station code, US Geological Survey*] [*Closed*] (SEIS)
Z Zuckerind Boehm ... Zeitschrift fuer die Zuckerindustrie in Boehmen [*A publication*]
Z Zuckerind Boehm Machren ... Zeitschrift fuer die Zuckerindustrie in Boehmen-Machren [*A publication*]
Z Zuckerind Cech Repub ... Zeitschrift fuer die Zuckerindustrie der Cechoslovakoschen Republik [*A publication*]
Z Zuckind ... Zeitschrift fuer die Zuckerindustrie [*A publication*]
ZZV .... Zanesville, OH [*Location identifier*] [*FAA*] (FAAL)
ZZV .... Zero-Zero Visibility
ZZW .... Zero-Zero Weather
ZZZZ .... Unknown Elements in Formatted Flight Plan [*Aviation code*] (FAAC)